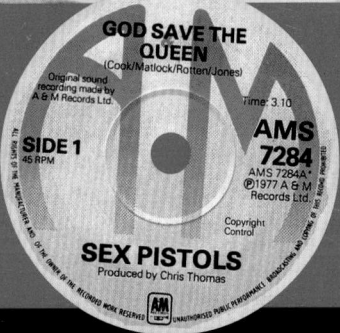

# RARE RECORD PRICE GUIDE 2018

Over 100,000 listings and values.
Available in softback, hardback,
online and as a download
on the iBookstore. 📖 Available on the iBookstore

See **www.rarerecordpriceguide.com** for details

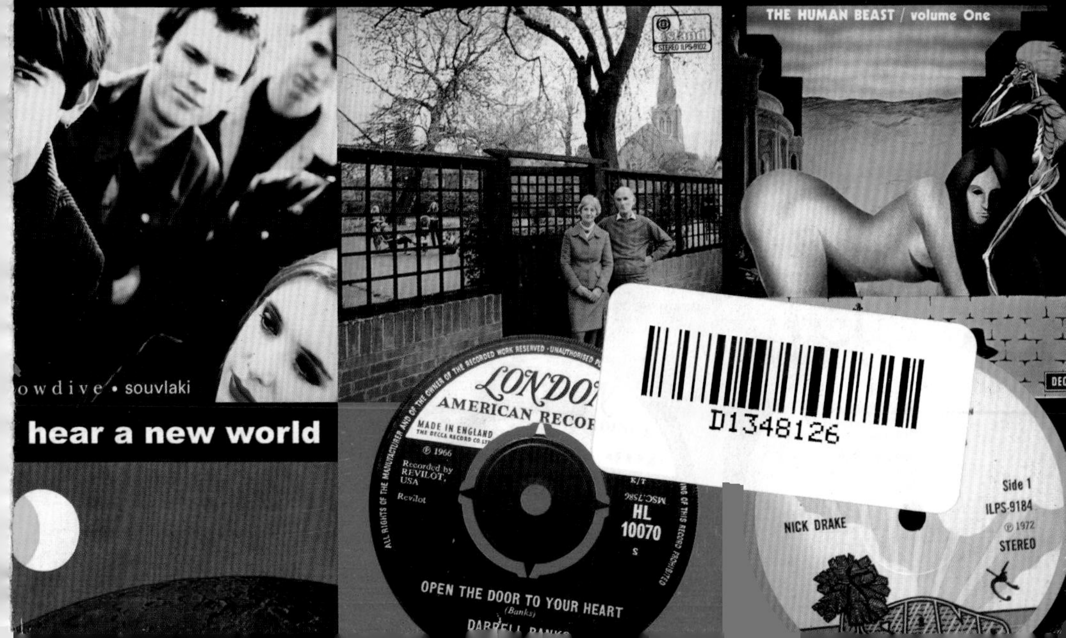

SOLD £7,200

SOLD £77,500

SOLD £61,000

SOLD £4,100

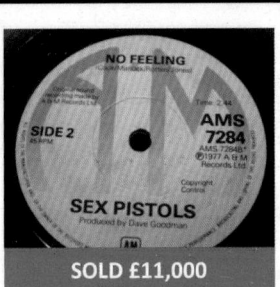

SOLD £11,000

SOLD £29,995

SOLD £23,000

SOLD £8,600

boom-jackie-
boom-chick

paul
gonsalves
quartet

SOLD £1,175

SOLD £1,995

SOLD £880

SOLD £59,000

# ENTERTAINMENT MEMORABILIA

Knightsbridge, London

**Entries now invited**

THE BEATLES:
An autographed copy of the album, 'With The Beatles', 1963,
**Sold for £11,250**

ENQUIRIES
+44 (0) 20 7393 3871
entertainment@bonhams.com

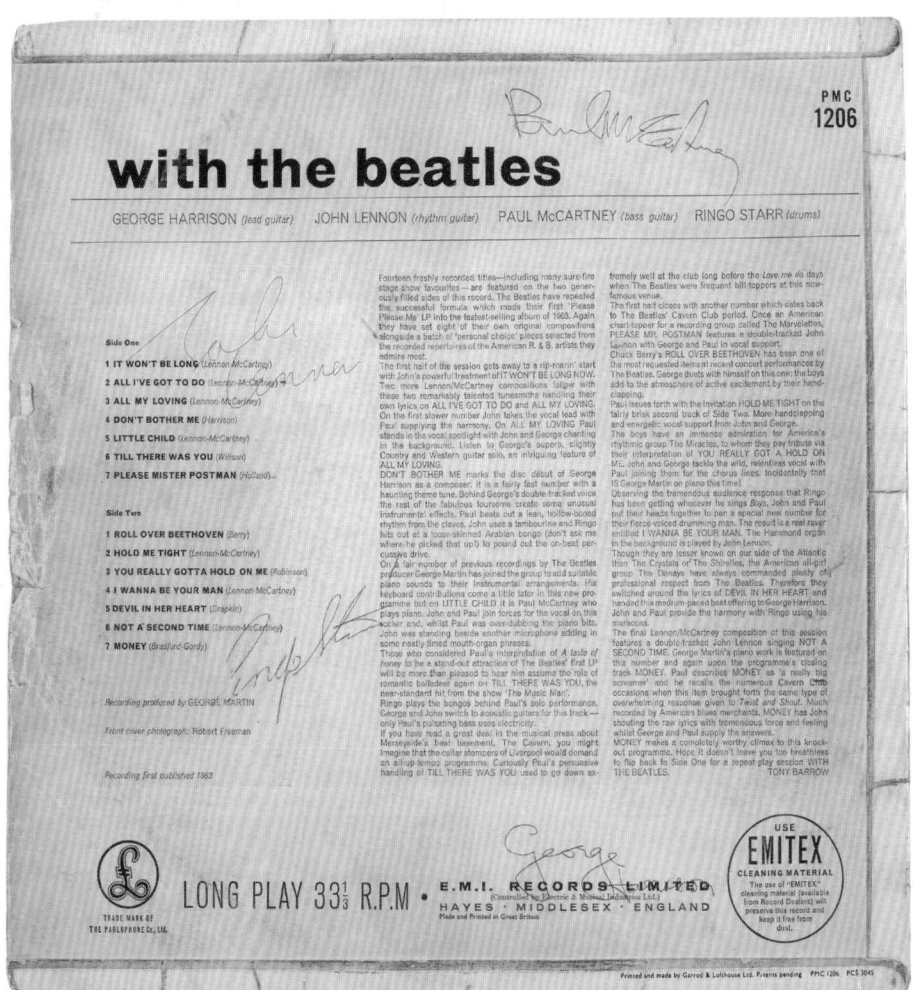

# Bonhams

bonhams.com/entertainment

Prices shown include buyer's premium. Details can be found at bonhams.com

# Established in 1988

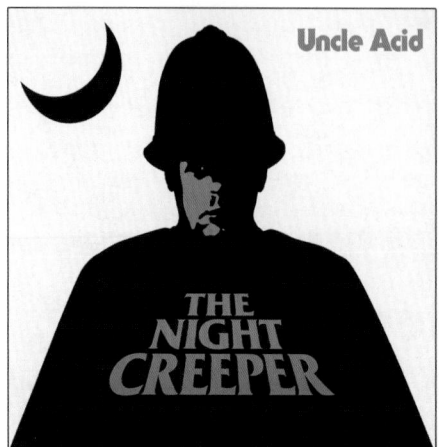

Uncle Acid - The Night Creeper

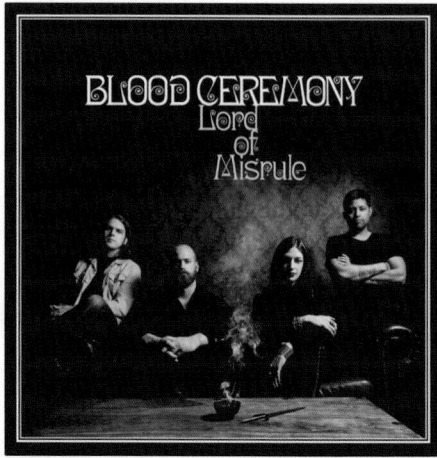

Blood Ceremony - Lord of Misrule

Ghost - Opus Eponymous

Church of Misery - And Then There Were..

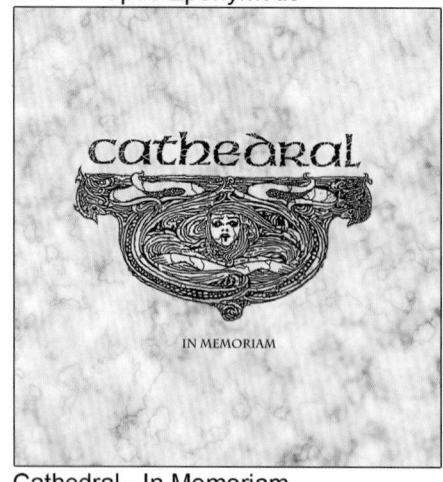

Cathedral - In Memoriam

With the Dead - With the Dead

# Rise Above Records & Relics

Galley Beggar - Silence & Tears

Beastmaker - Lusus Naturae

Rog & Pip - Our Revolution

Horse - For Twisted Minds Only

# All titles available on vinyl

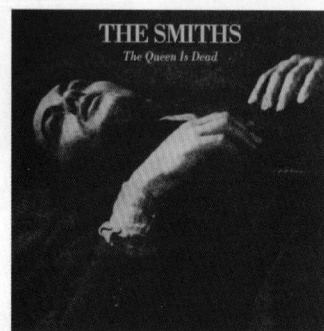
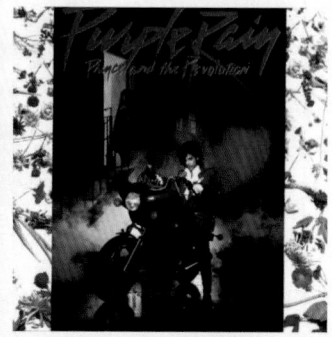

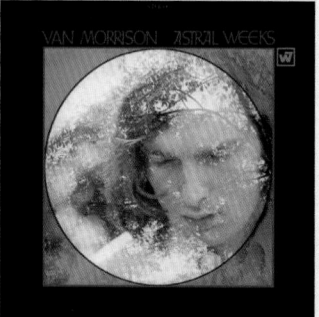

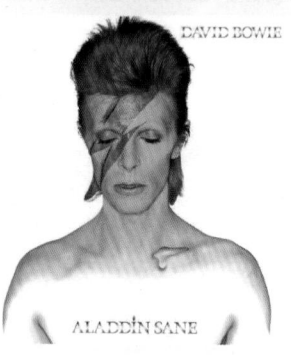

# Flashback Records is an independent record shop based in London, founded in 1997.

It started with one shop on Essex Road, buying in unwanted records for cash and selling them to music lovers who were looking for that same release to complete their collection.

With some of the rarest collectable vinyl in the world and over 10,000 titles available online and at three locations across London, much has changed since then, but our buying and selling policy remains the same.

A fair price for buying and selling vinyl records.

If you would like to sell your unwanted records or buy collectable vinyl, just come into one of our three locations or visit online.

## www.flashback.co.uk

50 Essex Road, Islington, N1 8LR          020 7354 9356
144 Crouch Hill, Crouch End, N8 9DX       020 8342 9633
131 Bethnal Green, Shoreditch, E2 7DG     020 3780 1900

# AUCTION YOUR RECORDS IN OUR SUCCESSFUL SPECIALISED SALES

**Thomas Plant**
**SAS Director & TV Expert**

We also sell all types of music related memorabilia, posters, programmes, tickets, autographs, flyers and instruments. We are very pleased to help by giving free expert advice.

**81 Greenham Business Park,**
**Newbury RG19 6HW**

# PlasticWax**Records**

*222 Cheltenham Rd, Bristol BS6 5QU*

## *Serving music lovers since 1978*

Plastic Wax Records is Bristol's longest established independent record shop with the largest range of used vinyl and CDs in the South West, including rare collector editions. We cover most genres: Rock, Reggae, Soul, Punk, Hip Hop, Prog, Indie, Electronica, Ska, Funk, African, Country, Jazz, Classical and Soundtracks.

We are the leading stockist for Bristol Archive Records, who showcase music from the diverse Bristol music scene and feature many artists and releases that are rare or have never before been released, and Reggae Archive Records, who feature music from British Reggae labels and artists.

We also offer special discounts for bulk purchases so please enquire for details.

**Looking to sell?** We are constantly looking to purchase good quality stock so if you are looking to sell your collection or even rare single records or CDs, please contact us.

**Tel: 0117 942 7368**

dkellard@plasticwaxrecords.com

plasticwaxrecords.com

Facebook: Plastic Wax Records

222 Cheltenham Rd, Bristol BS6 5QU

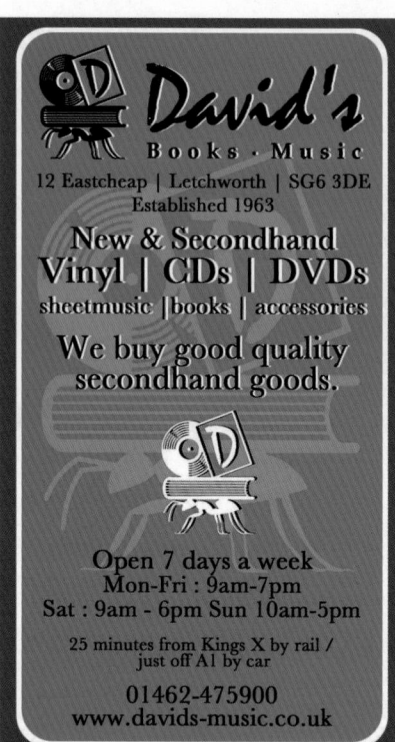

# C⦿VERS33

## RECORD, CD AND DVD ACCESSORIES

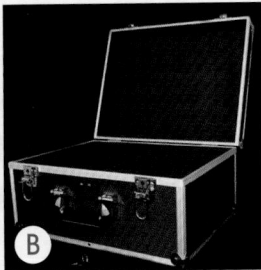

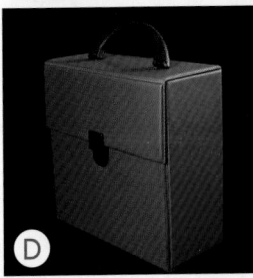

## DJ STORAGE CARRYING CASES

CARDBOARD STORAGE CASES (AVAILABLE FOR CD HOLDS APPROX. 70 CASES, 7" HOLDS APPROX. 200 SINGLES & 12" HOLDS APPROX. 50 LPS) A ........... 5 FOR £31.99

7" SINGLES CASE (HOLDS 100+) BLACK OR SILVER ................................................. £32.99

7" SINGLES CASE TWO LANE (HOLDS 200+) BLACK OR SILVER B .......................... £36.98

10" RECORD CASE (HOLDS 50 APPROX) SILVER ..................................................... £36.98

12" ALBUM RECORD CASE (HOLDS 50 APPROX) BLACK OR SILVER C .................. £36.98

CD 40 (HOLDS APPROX. 40 CDS) SILVER ............................................................. £19.99

CD CASE (HOLDS 100 CDS IN CASES) SILVER ....................................................... £36.98

DVD CASE (HOLDS APPROX. 60) SILVER ............................................................... £36.98

RETRO STYLE 7" RECORD CARRYING CASE (HOLDS APPROX. 30).
AVAILABLE IN GREY, BLACK, BURGUNDY OR BLUE D .............................................. £13.49

RETRO STYLE 12" RECORD CARRYING CASE (HOLDS APPROX. 50).
AVAILABLE IN BLACK OR RACING GREEN ONLY .................................................... £33.98

BLACK, RETRO STYLE RING BINDER FOR 7" SINGLES WITH PVC POCKETS.
10 X PVC POCKETS WITH EVERY RING BINDER. EXTERNAL DIMENSION FOR
RING BINDERS 25.5CM X 21CM X 5CM (EXTRA POCKETS £2.50/ PK OF 10) ........ £14.50

FULL RANGE OF CUSTOM MADE WOODEN STORAGE CASES AVAILABLE IN
BOTH 7" & 12" SIZE E ...................................................................................... £54.50

E-mail: covers33@covers33.co.uk
Website: www.covers33.co.uk Tel: 01422 822679
Commercial Mills, Oldham Rd, Ripponden West Yorks. HX6 4EH

    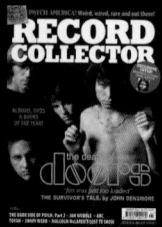

# RRPG 2018 ADVERTISING INDEX

| | | | | |
|---|---|---|---|---|
| IFC | 991.com | | 26 | RC Back Issues |
| 21 | Ace Records | | 32 | RC iPad |
| 20 | Audiogold | | 22 & 23 | RC Online |
| 20 | Awards UK | | 30 & 31 | RC Rare Vinyl Series |
| 20 | Ben's Collectors Records | | 28 & 29 | RC Subscribe |
| 15 | Black Barn Records | | IBC | Really Useful Products |
| 05 | Bonhams | | 14 | Record Shop (Amersham) |
| 19 | Collect & Protect | | 11 | Reckless Records |
| 21 | Collectors' Vinyl | | 19 | Repertoire Records |
| 25 | Covers 33 | | 06 & 07 | Rise Above Records |
| 18 | David's Music | | 10 | Rockaway Records |
| 18 | Disc-Covery Records | | 21 | Sam Hobden |
| 04 | Disk Union | | 24 | Soho Music |
| 09 | Flashback | | 18 | Sounds Original |
| 27 | Fruits De Mer | | 12 & 13 | Special Auction Services |
| 21 | Garden Recods | | 15 | Stacey's Auctioneers |
| 10 | Hakes | | 19 | Tracks |
| 20 | JP Records | | 14 & 18 | VVMO |
| 14 | Max Vinyl | | 21 | Vinyl Boutique/Sounds |
| 18 | Oldies Unlimited | | | That Swing |
| 02 & 03 | Omega Auctions | | 08 | Vinyl Collector |
| 16 & 17 | Plastic Wax Records | | 27 | Wanted Records |

# SER OUS ABOUT MUSIC?

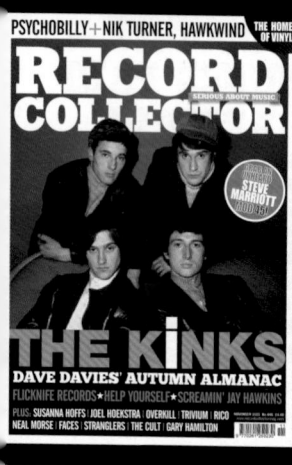

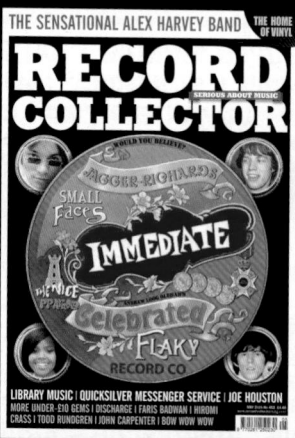
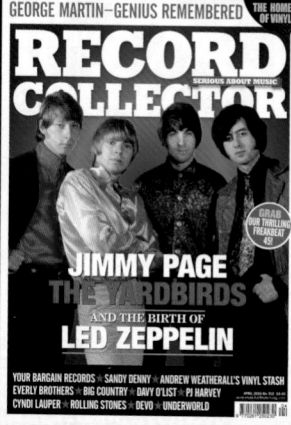

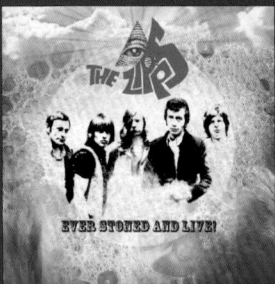

- All LPs strictly limited editions offered exclusively to *Record Collector* readers • Made as closely as possible to the original specifications, with care and attention to detail • Complete with numbered certificate of authenticity and notes by Ian Shirley, editor of the *Rare Record Price Guide* • On Beautiful 180G Vinyl

Deena Webster: Tuesday's Child

Ken Saul: Seashells

Motherlight: Bobak, Jons, Malone

Riot Squad: Making Up For Lost Time

Museum/Poppa Ben Hook

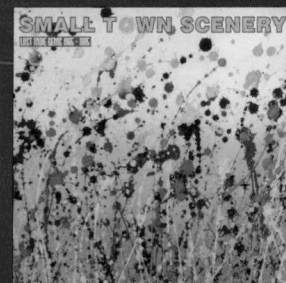

Small Town Scenery

Dane Hunter: The Drifter

Flare

Rise Above: Compilation

# CONTENTS

THE ULTIMATE COLLECTOR'S GUIDE .......................... 35

ACKNOWLEDGEMENTS ..................................... 36

HOW TO USE THE GUIDE .............................. 37

HISTORY OF THE GUIDE.................................... 41

STATE OF THE MARKET ................................. 43

USING THE GUIDE: A brief summary ............................ 46

ABBREVIATIONS used in this guide ........................ 47

IMPORTANT TERMS used in the guide............................ 48

## RARE RECORD PRICE GUIDE ........... 50

VARIOUS ARTISTS COMPILATIONS ......................... 1408

FILM & TV SOUNDTRACKS ........................................ 1431

ORIGINAL CAST RECORDINGS ................................. 1440

SPORTS RECORDINGS .................................... 1440

MUSIC LIBRARY LPs ...................................... 1441

TAX SCAM RECORDS .................................... 1448

BEATLES 7" COMPANY SLEEVES................................ 1450

RECORD COLLECTOR'S
    GRADING SYSTEM .................................... 1455

RECORD COLLECTOR'S
    GRADING READY RECKONER ............................. 1456

EDITOR
Ian Shirley

DESIGN & PRODUCTION MANAGEMENT
Val Cutts
Yura Surkov

ADVERTISING MANAGER
Bill Edwards

MARKETING MANAGER
Helen Bayram

PUBLISHER
David Harris

Published in the United Kingdom 2016 by
Diamond Publishing Ltd. Room 101, 140 Wales Farm Road, London W3 6UG

Copyright © 2016 Diamond Publishing Ltd.

Founded by Sean O'Mahony in 1987.

ISBN 978-0-9560639-9-1

# THE ULTIMATE COLLECTOR'S GUIDE

Welcome to the fourteenth edition of the *Rare Record Price Guide*, the largest and most comprehensive book of its kind. Like its predecessors, this volume has been compiled by the expert research team of *Record Collector*, the world's leading magazine in the field.

The goal of this book is simple: to list and value every collectable pop and rock record issued in the UK since 1950. As regular readers will already know, the *Rare Record Price Guide* doesn't just include vinyl singles, EPs and LPs, although they are still very heavily featured. It also provides information about every other way in which recorded music has been sold to the public over the last 60 years or more, from the brittle 78rpm shellac singles of the 1950s, to the latest permutations of digital sound on compact discs.

Musically, the coverage is equally diverse and thorough. Although the majority of items listed in this book could be at least vaguely described as 'rock' or 'pop', every aspect of music-making outside the specialist classical field is featured in these pages. For over 39 years, record collecting itself has expanded enormously, both in terms of the number of people taking part and the types of music that they are interested in.

Rest assured that no matter how obscure your tastes, you'll find the most sought-after items here whether your particular obsession is 60s MOR, freak-beat, 80s post-punk, psychedelia, hip-hop, reggae, NWOBHM, Northern Soul, British jazz, folk, progressive or today's indie bands. If it's collectable, and it was released in the UK, then you'll find it in the *Rare Record Price Guide*.

## WHO SAYS HOW MUCH IT'S WORTH?

The question we're always asked about the prices listed in this book is how we calculate them. The answer is a mix of our 39 years of experience in the field; our ongoing research into the latest prices at record fairs, shops, and sales both via mail order and online; and the invaluable help of a dedicated and extremely knowledgeable team of consultants and experts, who themselves regularly buy and sell items in their specialist areas.

As we always say, however, there is no *fixed* price for a second-hand record, no matter how rare it is. There are still bargains to be found out there, while in other situations like a feverishly competitive online auction particularly sought-after items can fetch prices way above their 'book' value. The price of a rare record is purely determined by what people are prepared to pay for it.

That said, our close scrutiny of the collecting market since the start of the 1980s allows us to make the best possible judgement about the records in this book. Prices may vary from one part of the country to another, or depending whether a disc is being sold in a shop, via an advert in *Record Collector*, at a major international fair, or on internet sites like 991.com, GEMM, Discogs, Raresoulman, Music Stack or eBay. But we believe that the guide values we list are the most accurate and realistic you'll find anywhere.

The other important point, which can't be repeated often enough, is that anyone selling records to a professional dealer can't expect to raise more than 50% of the prices listed here, except in very unusual cases. It doesn't matter whether you're selling rock'n'roll or jewellery, the same basic mark-up applies right across the collecting field, to cover the dealer's costs and profit margin. If you're selling directly to another collector, however, face-to-face or, as many collectors are now doing, over the internet, you can hope to obtain the prices we list or more, though please remember that all the values in this book are for records in absolutely perfect (or 'Mint') condition. To find out what you should be paying or charging, for a record in less than perfect condition, check the Ready Reckoner printed at the back of this book.

## ACROSS THE AGES

Although many of the most valuable items listed in the *Rare Record Price Guide* date back to the 1950s, 1960s, 1970s, 1980s and 1990s, record collecting is not all about the distant past. As you turn the pages, you'll find plenty of releases from the last two decades and collectables by major artists like Radiohead, for example, alongside limited edition albums by the Foals and Maccabees and new rarities which were on sale one day (especially Record Store Day!) and became fiendishly hard to track down even a few weeks later.

Check the details of those brand-new collectables, and you'll get some idea which of tomorrow's releases are likely to be sought-after in the future. But there are some things you can't predict, like the next 60s or 70s 7" that is worth £6 today but will be worth £60 in three months time. Or bands who were hot and collectable one year and saw their prices tumbling the next. Also, don't forget that virtually every record listed in this book, even the ones worth thousands of pounds, were once available for a few pounds, or even pence. For all those thousands of releases which have already become collector's items, however, the *Rare Record Price Guide* tells you what they are, what they look like, and how much they're going to cost.

# ACKNOWLEDGEMENTS

**CONSULTANTS** Billy Albert, Keith Ashford, Alan Barndale, John Barnjum, Rob Barrs, Mikael Billborn, Pete Bonner, Marco Bonacchi, Greg Brooks, Andy Brooksbank, Mark Burgess, Ian Clark, John Coleman, Nigel Cook, Augusto Croce, Peter Croxson, Brian Davis, Nick Farmer, Les Hare, Herve Denoyelle, Frank Deserto, John Esplen, Mark Evetts, Sean Forbes, Douglas Galloway, Joe Geesin, Roger Gobell, Kevin Goulding, Tim Greenhall, Steve Guntrip, Marco Henning, Rob Henson, Al Hine, Sam Hobden, John Hodgson, Dizzy Holmes, Justin Huntley, Max Hooley, Dudley Jaynes, Gordon Johnson, Michael Johnson, Sid Johnson, Damien Jones, Mark Jones, Tim Jones, Chris Knight, Freek Kinkelaar, Jake Kennedy, Graeme McLagen, John Manship, Haaken Eric Mathiesen, Ian McCann, Joel McIver, Lee Medhurst, Mike at Elista, Howie Moxon, Pol O' Maoleoin, Roscoe Patrol, Chas Pearson, Derek Penny, Ray Platt, Stephen Power, Andy Price, Jay Rathbone, Ian Roberts, Barry Smith, Phil Smith, Bob Solly, Bob Stoat, Torbjorn Stuhre, Brian Strong, Mitchell Thompson, Jonny Trunk, Rob Van Leeuwen, Peter Vickers, J Walton, Jamie Ward, Ben Watkins, Garry Warren, Martin Webb, Alan Whitaker, Eric White, Robin Wills, Alan Woodburn, Conrad Zimmer. Special thanks to all the many users of the online site and readers of Record Collector and those who took the RRPG survey who also submitted corrections, amendments or new additions too numerous to list here.
**FINALLY, SPECIAL THANKS** to previous editors, contributors and the vast numbers of fanzines, websites and fan clubs whose hard work and expertise has helped - and continues - to make the Guide what it is today.

# HOW TO USE THE GUIDE

## PRICING YOUR RECORDS

Although the *Rare Record Price Guide 2018* contains a comprehensive listing of collectable UK releases, it does NOT list all the recordings made by the artists we've included. More detailed discographies of important artists can be found every month in *Record Collector* magazine.

## MINIMUM VALUES FOR INCLUSION

ONLY THOSE RELEASES WHICH ARE CURRENTLY SOLD AT THE MINIMUM VALUES LISTED BELOW HAVE BEEN INCLUDED.
Any other releases sell for less than these prices.

> **7" SINGLES, MAXI-SINGLES, CASSETTE SINGLES,**
> **DOUBLE PACKS** ....................................................................**£5**
> **78s** ..........................................................................................**£20**
>
> **10" SINGLES & PICTURE DISCS** ...................................**£10**
> **EPs & 12" SINGLES** ..........................................................**£10**
> **LPs** ........................................................................................**£15**
> **DOUBLE-LPs** ......................................................................**£18**
> **CD SINGLES & CD ALBUMS** ..........................................**£25**

*NOTE: EPs from the 1950s and 1960s usually sold at around twice the retail price of a 7" single. But most so-called EPs released since 1976 actually retailed at the same price as 7" singles. These records have been included in the Guide if they are worth £5 or more.*

## CURRENT MINT VALUES

The prices listed in this book are for the original issues of records, cassettes and CDs in MINT condition. Bear in mind that most records which turn up from the 1950s, 60s, 70s, 80s 90s 00s and 10s are NOT in Mint condition and their value will be affected accordingly. To find out the value of any item which is in less than Mint condition, consult our Grading System and the Ready Reckoner located at the back of this Guide.

## ALPHABETICAL ORDER

The artists in this Guide are listed in alphabetical order, from A to Z. After the alphabetical listings, there is a section of Various Artists compilation releases, divided into several sections covering singles and 50s & 60s EPs, 70s, 80s & 90s EPs, LPs, film soundtrack LPs, original cast recordings from theatrical shows and library music.

The alphabetical order within the Guide has been determined by the first letter of a group name or an artist's surname. The word 'The' has not been taken into account when placing artists in alphabetical order; for instance, The Beatles' are listed under 'B', rather than 'T'.

The order follows the usual alphabetical principle of 'reading through' an artist's name or title, so that (for example) 'Peter Gabriel' is listed before 'Gabriel's Angels', and 'Generation X' is listed before 'Gen X'. Names and titles which include numbers appear as if the number was spelt out in full; e.g. the band '23 Skidoo' are listed as if their name was 'Twenty Three Skidoo'.

# CHRONOLOGICAL ORDER

Within each artist entry, records are listed in chronological order of release. Singles (including 7", 10", 12", CD, cassette, and double packs) are listed first; then EPs; and finally LPs (including cassette and CD albums).

In the case of long entries, different formats of releases have also been grouped together under separate headers to make them easier to find.

# PACKAGING AND INSERTS

All prices refer to records with all their original packaging and inserts (where applicable) intact. Wherever possible, we have provided details of inserts and special items of packaging for each entry – pointing out gatefold sleeves, lyric sheets and other bonus items like posters, for example.

Any record with some or all of these additional items missing will obviously be worth less than the values listed here. The level of depreciation depends on the missing items: in some cases, the value of an album can be dramatically reduced without its collectable insert (as in the case of the Who's *The Who Sell Out* LP, for example), while in others, it is the record itself that is desirable, and the insert is only of secondary importance (as with the Picadilly Line LP, *The Huge World Of Emily Small*).

# DOUBLE PRICES: PICTURE SLEEVES

Since 1978, all U.K. 7", 10" and 12" singles have usually been issued in picture sleeves. Before 1978, however, picture covers were the exception rather than the rule.

All those singles which originally appeared in a picture sleeve are listed with the abbreviation '(p/s)'. Where the picture sleeve was only available with the first batch of singles, there are two prices listed: the first refers to the record with its picture sleeve, the second without. If only one price is listed, then the single has to have its picture sleeve intact and in Mint condition to qualify for this value.

Most singles from the 1950s, 1960s and early 1970s were issued in 'company' sleeves, carrying the name and logo of the label which issued the record. Unless a picture sleeve is indicated, the prices listed in this guide are for singles with their company sleeves intact and, like the records themselves, in Mint condition. Many collectors are not too concerned about company sleeves - although in isolated cases (like the cult 60s label Planet), the company sleeves can be harder to find than the records themselves.

Company sleeves don't usually have much effect on a record's value. For example, an original Creation single from 1966, valued at £45, may only be worth £35 without its Planet company sleeve. At the other extreme, no 60s collector is going to be bothered if a copy of a rarity like Allen Pound's Get Rich's *Searchin' In The Wilderness*, valued at £1000 comes in a plain sleeve, or indeed, no sleeve at all - what matters here is that the record is in Mint condition.

# DOUBLE PRICES: FREEBIES & INSERTS

Two prices have been listed for those items which were available in more than one form. 'Freebie' singles given away with newspapers and magazines have two values: the first for the record with the publication, the second for the disc itself. Records which were issued only briefly with an insert, like a poster or lyric sheet, are often priced both with and without the extra packaging.

# DOUBLE PRICES: CHANGES IN DESIGN

Two or more prices have been given for records which were released more than once with the same catalogue number, but in slightly different form - with a change of label colour or sleeve design (for instance, the substitution of triangular centres by round centres on late 1950s singles), or the manufacture of more recent singles in a variety of different coloured vinyls.

These variations of packaging and presentation can make an enormous difference to the value of a record, which is why we have documented them here. They help collectors identify the first pressing or edition of each release, which is almost always more sought-after than later issues of the same record. One notable example is the first edition of the Beatles' *Please Please Me* LP, which featured the black-and-gold Parlophone label for a few weeks, before the introduction of the more modern-looking yellow-and-black label. Black-and-gold copies of the stereo version of this LP are worth up to £6000, whilst standard yellow and black label later pressings are worth between £3000 and £350.

Occasionally, second pressings can be worth more than the originals, as was the case with early Shadows and Cliff Richard singles. Green label copies of these 45s sold in their millions, while later re-pressings on black labels are much scarcer. So always check which pressing of any record you are buying before parting with your money.

## MONO AND STEREO

In the case of EPs and LPs from the 1950s and 1960s, mono and stereo releases often have different values – and different catalogue numbers. Both prices are listed, together with the separate catalogue numbers for the two versions of each release (mono first, then stereo). Where the mono and stereo editions are worth the same amount, only one price has been listed.

The last few years have seen a polarisation in the prices between mono and stereo pressings – increasingly so for those late mono releases from 1968 to 1970, when the single-channelled format was being phased out in favour of the twin-tracked stereo. Similarly, early stereo copies have proved to be sound investments.

## UK RELEASES AND EXPORT ISSUES

Only UK releases are included in the *Rare Record Price Guide*, not overseas issues. The exceptions to this rule are a handful of folk releases and U2 singles, all from the Irish Republic, which were heavily imported into Britain, but not officially issued here. The other exceptions are 'Export Releases'. These were manufactured in the UK in the 1950s and 1960s by companies like EMI and Decca for distribution to countries which didn't have their own pressing plants. Because they were pressed in very small quantities, and then distributed to the furthest corners of the globe, export records by artists like the Beatles and the Rolling Stones are often worth many times the values of similar items pressed for the UK.

## UK RELEASES PRESSED OVERSEAS

Although the great majority of the records we've listed were manufactured in the UK, not all UK releases were made in this country – or vice versa. For example, a large proportion of the Rolling Stones' US singles on the London label in the 1960s were actually manufactured in Britain. More recently, many British releases by major labels – notably Warners –

have been made in Europe, and sent in identical form to Britain and many other countries. In these cases, the record sleeves often carry many different catalogue numbers, to cater for every country where the records are being distributed.

The problem of identifying the country where a particular record has been issued has grown more difficult with the advent of CDs. In these cases, it is the packaging that helps you identify the origin of a particular CD, rather than the disc itself.

## 78 rpm RELEASES

The common misconception about 78s is that they are more valuable than 7" singles. In fact, the opposite is true in most cases, as far more 78s were sold in the 1950s than 45 rpm  7" singles.

The last batches of 78s issued from 1958 to 1960 are the main exception to this rule (see Eddie Cochran's entry, for example). As these were often only available in small quantities (as the public switched to 45s), or even by special order, they can prove to be much harder to find than their 45 rpm equivalents.

## COMMERCIAL RELEASES, NOT PROMOS

In general, this Guide only includes records which were manufactured for commercial release, or for distribution in some way to the public – as a freebie with a magazine, for example.

Promotional records, demos, acetates and test pressings have not usually been included, apart from exceptional cases where these items actually reached the public, or where (as with artists like the pre-Iron Maiden act, Urchin) one promo single has become so famous among collectors that it would have been misleading for it not to be mentioned. The major exceptions to this rule are artists like the Beatles, and modern artists like The Pet Shop Boys, Depeche Mode  and Madonna whose promos – often with extended and hard to find remixes – are sometimes more valuable than their commercial releases and highly sought after by their fans. Also, although we have included some CD-R promo releases in this Guide the value of these items usually fluctuate wildly upwards  before release and then fall alarmingly once the official album or single is in the shops. Some collectors do want them – especially completists – but we should state that the sale of watermarked and numbered CD-R's is illegal.

Full details of the values of non-commercial rarities like promos, demos, acetates and test pressings can be found in the articles and discographies in *Record Collector* every month.

# THE HISTORY OF THE RARE RECORD PRICE GUIDE

## RECORD COLLECTOR MAGAZINE

*Record Collector* was first published in 1979, and the magazine quickly established itself as the bible of pop and rock history. When the magazine was born, record collecting was a small, rather disorganised business, which wasn't making much effort to encourage new people to get involved.

From the start, *Record Collector* set out to provide the information that collectors needed, whether they'd been buying and selling records for years, or were just starting to build up a collection. There were two vital things they wanted to know: what records had been released by their favourite artists, and how much were they worth?

Every issue of *Record Collector* has provided complete discographies (lists of record releases, complete with full catalogue numbers, release dates and current Mint values) for an amazing variety of performers, from pre-rock stars like Frank Sinatra to the latest chart-bound arrivals and cult indie bands, via every imaginable style and genre along the way. Our in-depth features have provided the essential information to help readers get the most out of their music – by explaining the history of the artists and the records.

## THE CHANGING FACE OF THE RARE RECORD PRICE GUIDE

In 1987, we published our first price guide - a slim volume which was designed as a quick and easy reference source to records by around 2,000 important artists.

That was only the beginning, though. We soon began work on the first edition of the book you're holding. Published in late 1992, the first *Rare Record Price Guide* filled 960 pages and listed 60,000 rare and collectable records.

The response to that book was tremendous, but we quickly realised that the collecting market was changing so fast that we couldn't rest on our laurels. Every year, thousands of new records reach the shops, in a bewildering variety of formats - everything from 7" singles and cassettes to expensive multi-CD box sets.

A small but sizeable proportion of these new releases became instant collector's items. Over the last 20 years, it's been common for record companies to issue special limited editions – anything from a few hundred to a few thousand copies – which sell out in a few days. The most sought-after of these records can triple or quadruple their value within a few months.

At the same time, interest in vinyl from the past continues to grow. As collectors track down all the records they want in a particular genre, they start to broaden their horizons. As a result, obscure items from the 50s, 60s, 70s and 80s become much-wanted treasures on the collectors' market – and their prices rise to reflect the new demand.

That's why we published a second edition, a year later, which grew to 1152 pages, with 70,000 records listed. And this was expanded again for the 1995 edition (over 75,000 entries and 1252 pages) and 1997/98 edition (85,000 entries and 1440 pages), to take in all the latest collectable releases.

The Millennium Edition ran to 1504 pages; another two years on, the *Rare Record Price Guide 2002* was bigger than ever, the 2004 edition was 1536 pages the RRPG 2006 1504 pages, RRPG 2008 and 2010 1408 pages RRPG 2012 was 1440 pages, RRPG 2014 1432 pages and RRPG 2016 was 1440 pages. Now you're holding the latest edition covering more than 60 years of rare and collectable records.

## THE BIRTH OF COLLECTING

When the collecting scene was in its infancy in the 1970s, the market was focused on particular artists or genres. All the early attention was concentrated on 1950s rock'n'roll, and 1960s beat music. In addition, major artists like the Beatles, the Rolling Stones, Elvis Presley and David Bowie began to attract specialist collectors. But the whole collecting scene blossomed during the 1980s and it's now true to say that there aren't any musical styles which *aren't* collectable. Folk, jazz, techno, hip-hop, blues, heavy metal, punk, psychedelia, progressive rock, film soundtracks, soul, funk, reggae, disco, mainstream rock and pop, even easy listening - each genre boasts its share of in-demand rarities.

## LIMITED EDITIONS

In the late 1970s, the arrival of punk spawned scores of new, independent record labels, which had fresh views about the way to market their releases. It became common for singles to appear in picture sleeves, as they had done overseas since the 1960s.

Records also began to appear on coloured vinyl or as picture discs, in an attempt to attract more buyers. Never slow to cash in on a marketing trend, the major record companies soon joined in. By the early 1980s, they were issuing a bewildering variety of editions of the same record in slightly different formats.

This sudden change in marketing techniques helped to trigger an entirely new development on the collecting scene. For the first time, records were becoming instant collector's items. A limited-edition single could be released one week, and sell for twice its retail price a fortnight later.

That opened the floodgates. No longer were 1950s and 1960s records the only things you'd find in the collector's shops. Now, it was open season, for anything and everything from Tubby Hayes to U2.

## COMPACT DISCS

The arrival of CDs in the mid-1980s was greeted with doom and gloom in some quarters. But extensive remastering and reissue programs on CD have helped to increase the market for old vinyl releases.

If you grew up in the 1960s, you probably remember that it was difficult to find records that had been hits only a few years earlier. Now, you can go online and buy CD or download compilations and original albums with bonus tracks from every era of music history. For thousands of collectors, however, owning the music on CD or via download isn't enough – and they track down the original releases of music made and released before they were born.

The CD is now established as a collectable format – particularly for promotional items, limited edition singles, and some albums which have yet to be remastered on vinyl. Although more music is now sold through digital downloads or experienced through streaming, the CD remains the dominant physical format although vinyl sales are increasing by leaps and bounds.

# STATE OF THE MARKET

Since the last edition of the Rare Record Price Guide was published sales of new vinyl albums have continued to rise and last year over 2 million were sold in the U.K. alone which was the most sold since Oasis dropped their debut album *Definitely, Maybe* in 1994. This year, that figure is projected to shoot up to 3 million which is an increase of over 40 per cent. This does not include 12" and 7" singles so things are going very well indeed. But, what is driving such strong sales?

There are a number of factors. Crucially, LP sales are no longer pushed by the "hip/cool" factor as a broader demographic of people are buying albums. Whilst hardened collectors – like you and I – form an iron core there are a large number of teenagers and people in their 20s, 30s and even 40s – men and women – buying vinyl for the first time. They are playing these records as well, as the number of record players sold has also gone through the roof with reports stating that in the lead up to Christmas 2015 there was a record player being sold every second. The type of albums sold – in Rough Trade to Sainsbury's - range from mainstream artists like Adele, The 1975, Ed Sheeran to classic albums by Nirvana, Led Zeppelin, Fleetwood Mac, The Clash and The Beatles.

Record labels large and small have adapted their vinyl products to meet the times. Many albums now come with a free download card so that buyers can enjoy the album digitally as well as in its physical form. Pressings also range from audiophile quality on 180gm vinyl for £20 to a classic Sun Ra reissue for £9.99 pressed on thinner plastic. Amazon have also made a play to boost their own digital and streaming platform by offering a free download of some albums – even if it does not come with a download card. This is a crucial part of the equation as it allows the digital generation - which is all of us these days - to enjoy their music on phones or computers as well as actually owning and playing a physical product at home.

Another part of the appeal is the range of vinyl on offer. When Radiohead's *A Moon Shaped Pool* was flash-released in June 2016 those who wanted to buy the LP could choose from a variety of formats including a deluxe 2-LP, 2-CD set with a piece of master-tape (£60), a standard black vinyl 2-LP set (£20), CD (£10) and a no frills digital download (£9). There was also a special limited edition on opaque white vinyl limited to 3000 copies that soon cropped up on eBay as did the black vinyl edition! ABC's *Lexicon Of Love II* was also offered in a multi-faceted way ranging from £100 for a signed 2-LP, 3-DVD boxed set, to £30 for a signed LP and £80 for a test pressing. The trend here is basically for artists – and record labels – to maximise their financial return from fans by offering limited editions that collectors must have and will pay a premium for in addition to standard releases. Even the latest incarnation of New Order offered a limited signed edition of their comeback LP *Music Complete*. In many respects these special editions are a continuation of the trend of Record Store Day that has grown from something aimed at helping ailing record stores into a massive product avalanche that clogs up the arteries of record pressing plants and record shop racks with 'limited edition' releases still there months after the April festivities have ended.

Whilst I enjoy Record Store Day - vital financially for record shops in the U.K. - it does seems to have become engorged with too many releases. A better model is that run by Rough Trade who press up special editions of selected albums or 12" singles all year round to promote albums and drive customers to their website or through the doors of their record stores in London and Nottingham in the U.K.

The surge in sales has seen the BPI put together a vinyl LP and 7" chart. As you might imagine, the late David Bowie's *Blackstar* dominated LP sales for the first part of 2016 and the death of Prince saw Warner Brothers marketing his back catalogue on vinyl. However, some of the biggest selling albums in this chart were back catalogue LPs *like The Dark Side Of The Moon* and *The Stone Roses* which shows that a classic album whether it was recorded in 1973 or 1989 still has strong physical legs. Although not 'charting' re-pressed albums by artists like Joy Division, The Smiths, The Sex Pistols, Blur, Jeff Buckley, Lee Perry and Big Youth also sell to new fans and old.

Of course, vinyl LPs sales are a drop in the ocean with CDs still accounting for over 66 million units in the U.K. but the main market for music these days are streaming services like Spotify where you queue up tracks and even wrap your ears around a new album on its day of release. Such sites garner billions of plays although it has been widely reported that some established artists actually earn more money through vinyl sales due to favourable royalty rates than they do through streaming sites due to the small percentage that they earn for each play.

With regard to rare records the market remains buoyant. As many dealers will know, if you have the right records from the right genre in the right condition to sell then you can make a good living. Of course, finding those records is the hardest thing. Picking up a collection of mint ska records from the 60s or even a collection of obscure punk gems is no longer common. If a collector dies, their relatives (if they know what they have) are more likely to sell their rare records online or through auction sites like Hakes, Bonhams or Omega or a large company like 991.com. This is making it very hard for dealers across the country to source good collections and they also encounter the problem of sellers who think that the records they have for sale are worth a fortune when in fact they are hardly worth anything. Lest we forget, for every collectable record there are fifty records from the 50s to the 90s that are not sought after and only worth a few pounds. Lloyd Cole and The Commotions *Rattlesnakes* LP from 1984 might be a classic debut but can be picked up for as little as £5 in mint condition as can many early records by artists from The Associates to XTC. Ironically, those shops that managed to stay in business during the hard times - and those that have recently opened – seem to be getting good stock. People with collections to sell might see a shop in their area or find it online and make it their first port of call. True, in many cases the records brought in or offered are of low value or in poor condition but when the wheels of the fruit machine align with a choice collection of 60s singles, progressive albums or rare 90s LPs the dealer is in luck. Indeed, I know of one online dealer who opened a shop just to get more good collections offered to him.

As for what is selling, the market for rare psychedelic singles, progressive LPs, mod, punk, new wave obscure glam, freakbeat, ska, reggae, soul, jazz, hard rock, blues, northern soul and boogie remains strong – for the right records.

Hidden treasure is also surfacing with a stock copy of Darrell Banks *Open The Door To Your Heart/Our Love (Is In The Pocket)* on London from 1966 being sold by John Manship at auction for £14,000. Also the market for blue chip collectable artists like the Beatles, The Rolling Stones, The Small Faces, The Who, Pink Floyd, Deep Purple, Radiohead, Iron Maiden, The Velvet Underground, Captain Beefheart, The Sex Pistols, Black Sabbath, Queen and The Stooges remains strong - although in these instance condition is key.

There are, of course, areas that have cooled. The market, for many 50s and early 60s records are either falling in price or static with some exceptions. In many cases records might command our mint prices but if their condition is excellent or even very good they might only be worth a third or quarter of their mint value. This extends to Elvis Preseley and Cliff Richard as many collectors have all they need and there is not a sufficient number of new collectors coming online or walking into record shops who want to buy everything they ever recorded and released. As we always stress the price of a rare record is determined by what someone is prepared to pay for it and the market for singles by the Jones Boys is shrinking as collectors of that period are growing older or - sadly - moving on to that big record shop in the sky.

One area that is thriving is independent labels. As they have grown older 4AD, One Little Indian, Warp and Domino records have not only signed new artists but taken great care re-presenting the extensive tail of their back catalogue. Cherry Red has become a reissue empire to rival Ace and for many other independent record labels the key factor is finding the correct niche. With its commitment to quality and coloured vinyl Fruits De Mer goes from strength to strength generating a number of collectables whereas Rise Above continues to offer a great range of modern metal as well as some classic relics and unheard gems. Finders Keepers has a great ear for electronica and Trunk records remains one of the best vinyl boutiques in the U.K. Jazzman and Soul Jazz records continue to mine seams of great records on 7" LP and CD that – like Kent – have a willing market. Then there are small labels of love like Belter who series of *Bonehead Crunchers* and *Ultimate Bonehead* compilations LPs always sell out due to limited pressings and high quality music.

This latest edition of the Guide retains the starting price of £15 for a vinyl album introduced in the last edition although the entry price of £5 for vinyl singles and £10 for EPs and 12" singles remains the same. The entry point for 78rpm records is now £20 rather than £15. The entry level for CD's is £25. Of course, records valued below these prices remain in the online version of this Guide.

Finally, I am aware that collectors have a wide variety of online resources available to them to consult. These include *Popsike, Discogs, 45 Cat* and sites devoted to specific artists, labels and genres. The *Rare Record Price Guide* however, in its printed form, remains the benchmark that gives collectors new and old a quick and easy overview of the the price of rare records from the 50s until the present day - for the cost a couple of LPs. Well worth the money I think.

# USING THE GUIDE
## A BRIEF SUMMARY

## ALL PRICES REFER TO RECORDS AND PACKAGING IN MINT CONDITION
(See pages 1453-54 for Grading System and Ready Reckoner)

## ARTISTS AND GROUPS are listed in alphabetical order.
Numerical names (e.g. 2.3) are listed as if the numbers are spelt in full (i.e. Two.Three).

## ALL RECORDS LISTED ARE U.K. COMMERCIAL RELEASES
with the following exceptions:

> (1) Records pressed in the U.K. for export overseas.
>
> (2) Important demo or promo releases.
>
> (3) Records or flexidiscs included as freebies with magazines, books and other records.

**In general, promo and demo editions are not included, except when these records contain unique material and/or packaging, or are by major collectable artists.**

## EACH ENTRY includes:

SINGLES (7" 45s & cassettes) valued at £5 or more

78 rpm singles valued at £20 or more

10" singles & flexidiscs valued at £10 or more

EPs & 12" singles valued at £10 or more

LPs valued at £15 or more

DOUBLE-LPs valued at £18 or more

CD SINGLES AND ALBUMS valued at £25 or more

Records worth less than these prices have not been included.

## WITHIN EACH ENTRY, records are listed in chronological order of
release, within each of the following categories (where applicable):
78s, SINGLES, EPs, LPs, CDs, PROMOS. The exceptions are major artists like
the Beatles, the Rolling Stones and Elvis Presley, where the entry is further
divided into originals, reissues and label variations.

Where TWO PRICES are listed for a single item, they refer to

> (a) the record with and without a special insert or piece of packaging
>
> (b) mono and stereo editions of EPs and LPs
>
> (c) versions of the same record with different artwork, vinyl colour, etc.

# ABBREVIATIONS
## USED IN THIS GUIDE

| | | | |
|---|---|---|---|
| act | actually | mag. | magazine |
| alt | alternative | no. | number |
| b&w | black and white | no'd | numbered |
| cass. | cassette | p/s | picture sleeve |
| cat. no. | catalogue number | pic disc | picture disc |
| CD | compact disc | pt(s) | part(s) |
| co | company | sl. | sleeve |
| d/pack | double pack | st. | stereo |
| dble. | double | stkr | sticker |
| diff. | different | t/p | test pressing |
| edn | edition | vers. | version |
| EP | extended-play record | vol. | volume |
| ext. | extended | w/. | with |
| flexi. | flexidisc | w/l | white label |
| g/f(old) | gatefold sleeve | 2-CD or 2xCD | double CD |
| inst | instrumental | 2-LP or 2xLP | double LP |
| intl. | international | 2 x 45 | two 45rpm singles |
| LP | long-playing record | 3-LP | triple LP |
| m/s. | mono/stereo | 78. | 78rpm single |

## IMPORTANT RECORD COMPANY ABBREVIATIONS

| | |
|---|---|
| Amalgam | Amalgamated |
| B. Banquet | Beggars Banquet |
| B'full/Brains | Bucketfull Of Brains |
| Col. | Columbia |
| Elek | Elektra |
| Font | Fontana |
| L.T.T. Slaughter | Lambs To The Slaughter |
| M. For Nations | Music For Nations |
| MFP | Music For Pleasure |
| M. Minor | Major Minor |
| Parl. | Parlophone |
| PSI | Phil Spector International |
| Pye Intl | Pye International |
| R. Digest | Readers Digest |
| Regal Zono | Regal Zonophone |
| R. Stones | Rolling Stones |
| S'side | Stateside |
| St. Tones | Street Tones |
| Sweet Folk & C. | Sweet Folk And Country |
| T. Motown | Tamla Motown |
| UA | United Artists |
| W. Bros | Warner Brothers |
| WRC | World Record Club |

# IMPORTANT TERMS
## USED IN THIS GUIDE

| | |
|---|---|
| **acetate** | one-off disc cut by hand in a mastering studio, used for demonstration purposes |
| **adaptor** | plastic outer disc clipped onto 3" CDs to make them compatible with 5" CD players |
| **art sleeve** | pictorial cover using graphics rather than photographs or drawings |
| **artwork** | original design for sleeves or labels |
| **audiophile pressing** | high quality pressing for hi-fi enthusiasts |
| **blister pack** | shaped outer PVC packaging, usually for 3" CDs |
| **bonus disc** | disc given away free with another disc |
| **bootleg** | illegal pressing of material |
| **box set** | records or CDs in presentation case |
| **budget release** | pressing which retailed below full-price |
| **catalogue number** | manufacturer's reference number on record labels and sleeves |
| **CD-R** | one-off CD, digital equivalent of acetate |
| **CD-ROM** | audio/visual computer-compatible CD |
| **CD Video** | 5" CD containing several audio tracks and (usually) one video track; now obsolete |
| **company sleeve** | standard non-picture sleeve for singles, printed with name or logo of label |
| **counterfeit** | illegal reproduction of official release (a.k.a. pirates) |
| **DAT** | digital audio tape |
| **deleted** | no longer commercially available |
| **demo** | record issued for demonstration purposes; not commercially available |
| **die-cut sleeve** | sleeve with circular hole cut into the centre |
| **digipak** | gatefold CD sleeve with plastic inner tray |
| **DJ-only** | record issued for radio airplay only |
| **double groove** | record with two grooves pressed concentrically on same side |
| **double pack** | two singles issued together as one package |
| **DVDAC** | digital versatile disc Audio |
| **DVD** | digital versatile disc |
| **8-track cartridge** | 1970s tape format, popular for in-car entertainment; now obsolete |
| **EP** | extended play disc, with four or more tracks, usually in a picture sleeve |
| **EPK** | electronic press kit; i.e. short promo-only documentary available on video |
| **envelope p/s** | large mailing-type cover with envelope-style foldover flap |
| **etched disc** | one-sided vinyl record with laser-etched graphics (e.g. group's signatures) on other side |
| **export issue** | record or CD pressed in the UK for sale exclusively overseas |
| **factory custom pressing** | unofficial record pressed after hours (usually on coloured vinyl) at official pressing plant |
| **flexidisc** | thin, flexible record, usually issued free with magazine, etc. |
| **flipback sleeve** | LP or EP cover glued together with card flaps from the front folded over onto the back |
| **foldaround/foldout/ foldover sleeve** | sleeve which opens out as a poster, etc. |
| **freebie** | record given away free of charge |
| **gatefold sleeve** | double-size sleeve opening out like a book |
| **import** | record or CD pressed abroad but sold in the UK |
| **inlay** | printed paper booklet with CD packaging |
| **inner sleeve** | protective sleeve inside main cover |
| **insert** | loose item included as part of a record's packaging, e.g. postcard, poster, lyric sheet, etc. |
| **interview album** | spoken word record, often used as promo |

| | |
|---|---|
| jewel case | standard clear plastic case for cassettes and CDs |
| jukebox centre | plastic centre inserted into record with large centre hole |
| jukebox issue | record issued exclusively to jukebox franchise holders |
| laminated sleeve | cover with high-gloss plastic coating |
| large centre hole | 1.5 inch (3.8 cm) hole in singles |
| long box | tall, rectangular outer card packaging for CDs |
| LP | long playing vinyl record; standard album format superseded by CDs |
| matrix number | master tape number, scratched into the 'land' or run-off groove area; sometimes also found on the record label |
| maxi-single | early 70s term for an EP, featuring more than two tracks, often in a picture sleeve |
| megamix | medley of different tracks, often linked by dance beats |
| mid-price release | record which retails at a discount |
| mispressing | record or CD pressed with incorrect material |
| mono | one-channelled playback system |
| numbered (no'd) | individually numbered, limited edition release |
| obi | sealed paper strip wrapped around sleeve of disc; originated in Japan where obis were printed with Japanese translations of foreign titles |
| one-sided | vinyl record which plays on one side only |
| picture disc | novelty record made by sealing a picture within clear vinyl |
| picture sleeve | pictorial paper or card sleeve, used specifically for one particular record |
| plain sleeve | single sleeve without special printing or artwork |
| premium | record available via a special offer with another product e.g. food or drink |
| press kit | information pack with photos and biography, used by record companies to promote new releases |
| private pressing | record issued and distributed by private individuals rather than a company |
| promo | promotional record or item sent out to the media for publicity purposes |
| push-out centre | centre of a single connected to the rest of the disc at 3 or 4 points, so it can be pushed out for use on jukeboxes, etc. |
| quadrophonic | 1970s four-channelled playback system, now obsolete |
| reel-to-reel tape | 1960s tape format, superseded by cassette |
| reissue | re-release of a deleted disc |
| remix | different version of existing track created by rearranging its component parts |
| removeable/ replaceable centre | centre which can be removed from a record without damage and later replaced (not to be confused with jukebox or 'spider' centres) |
| re-pressing | a second run of a record or CD which hasn't been deleted |
| run-off groove | groove between end of playing surface and record label |
| sampler | compilation showcasing an artist or label |
| sealed/shrinkwrapped | machine-wrapped in cellophane |
| shaped disc | any non-circular record |
| shellac | brittle material used for 78s |
| slipcase | small card cover used for some CDs and cassette singles |
| solid centre | centre of record which cannot be removed, as on LPs |
| stickered sleeve | sleeve with sticker as an integral part of its packaging |
| stereo | two-channelled playback system |
| test pressing | manufacturer's sample record, pressed for quality control |
| tri-centre | push-out triangular centre on some 1950s singles/EPs |
| tri-fold | triple fold-out sleeve |
| uncut picture disc | shaped disc not yet trimmed to proper shape |
| unissued/unreleased | disc not made commercially available; may or may not have been pressed |
| vinyl | material from which records are made |
| warp | buckle in vinyl caused by heat |
| white label | usually blank, perhaps printed or handwritten labels, often for promo purposes; term also used for demo, promo or test pressing |
| withdrawn | record deliberately removed from sale by its manufacturer |

**AAAH!**
| | | | |
|---|---|---|---|
| 81 | Flesh Logic EJSP 9863 | Slip Away/Duty Calls (p/s) | 80 |
| 82 | Dangerous DRC 8401 | Input/Output (p/s) | 40 |

**AARDVARK**
| | | | |
|---|---|---|---|
| 70 | Deram Nova DN 17 | AARDVARK (LP, mono) | 325 |
| 70 | Deram Nova SDN 17 | AARDVARK (LP, stereo) | 250 |

*(see also Home)*

**AARDVARKS**
| | | | |
|---|---|---|---|
| 95 | Delerium DELEC LP 029 | BARGAIN (LP) | 15 |

**A-AUSTR**
| | | | |
|---|---|---|---|
| 70 | Holy Ground HG 113 | A-AUSTR - MUSICS FROM HOLY GROUND (LP, with booklet, 99 only) | 400 |
| 89 | Magic Mixture MM 1 | A-AUSTR (LP, reissue, 450 only) | 40 |
| 95 | Holy Ground 010101LP | A-AUSTR (LP, second reissue, foldover gatefold sleeve) | 20 |

**ABACUS**
| | | | |
|---|---|---|---|
| 74 | York YR 207 | Indian Dancer/Be That Way | 15 |
| 72 | Polydor 2371 215 | ABACUS (LP) | 50 |

**ABA SHANTI**
| | | | |
|---|---|---|---|
| 94 | Aba Shanti | Zulu Warrior/Verse II/Verse III/Verse IV (10") | 20 |
| 96 | Jalasha ABA LP 001 | THE WRATH OF JAH (LP) | 30 |
| 96 | Jalasha ABA LP 003 | JAH LIGHTNING & THUNDER VERSE II (LP) | 30 |
| 99 | Jalasha ABA LP 004 | JERICHO WALLS VERSE THREE HORNS OF JAH (LP) | 40 |

**ABBA**
| | | | |
|---|---|---|---|
| 73 | Epic EPC 1793 | Ring Ring/Rock'N'Roll Band (yellow label) | 70 |
| 74 | Epic EPC 2848 | So Long/I've Been Waiting For You (yellow label) | 15 |
| 79 | Epic EPC 7499 | Voulez Vous/Angel Eyes (red or yellow vinyl, p/s) | 300 |
| 82 | Epic EPCA 11-2971 | Under Attack/You Owe Me One (picture disc) | 10 |
| 83 | Epic A 3894 | Thank You For The Music/Our Last Summer (poster p/s) | 5 |
| 83 | Epic WA 3894 | Thank You For The Music/Our Last Summer (shaped picture disc) | 25 |
| 84 | Epic ABBA 26 | ANNIVERSARY BOXED SET (26 x blue vinyl 7", numbered, 2,000 only) | 300 |
| 84 | Epic ABBA 26 | ANNIVERSARY BOXED SET (26 x black vinyl 7") | 100 |
| 99 | Polydor 563 286-2 | ABBA Singles Collection 1974-1982 (29 CD singles in card sleeves & 1-track CD picture disc, with booklet, in silver tin, 20,000 only) | 50 |
| 04 | Polydor 982054-1 | Waterloo/Watch Out (picture disc, 2,000 only, numbered) | 25 |
| 79 | Epic EPC 11-86086 | VOULEZ VOUS (LP, picture disc) | 60 |
| 80 | Epic ABBOX 1 | SUPER TROUPER (LP, box set with book & poster) | 15 |
| 83 | Epic ABBOX 11-2/ ABBA-11-10 | THE SINGLES - THE FIRST TEN YEARS (2-LP, picture discs, with poster, ticket & booklet in box) | 40 |
| 92 | Polydor 517007 | GOLD (2-LP) | 20 |
| 99 | Simply Vinyl SVLP103 | ABBA (LP, 180 gram pressing) | 15 |
| 05 | Polar POLS 252 | COMPLETE STUDIO RECORDINGS (12-CD box set, 2 booklets) | 100 |

*(see also Hep Stars, Hootenanny Singers, Agnetha Faltskog, Frida, Northern Lights)*

**ABBASANI**
| | | | |
|---|---|---|---|
| 91 | Roots Rock RR 001 | Revelation Time/Version | 40 |
| 91 | Roots Rock RR 009 | REVELATION TIME (LP) | 30 |

**JOHN ABBEY BAND**
| | | | |
|---|---|---|---|
| 77 | Duck DUC 101 | Lady Mary/Let's Make Up | 10 |

**BILLY ABBOTT & JEWELS**
| | | | |
|---|---|---|---|
| 63 | Cameo Parkway P 874 | Groovy Baby/Come On And Dance With Me | 20 |

**ABERDEEN**
| | | | |
|---|---|---|---|
| 94 | Sarah SARAH 93 | Bryon/Toy Tambourine (p/s, insert) | 25 |
| 95 | Sarah SARAH 97 | Fireworks/When It Doesn't Matter/Sunny Summer (p/s, insert) | 25 |

**A BETTER MOUSETRAP**
| | | | |
|---|---|---|---|
| 87 | Cuddly SRT 7KS 1178/ CUD001 | The Road To Kingdom Come/We Are All Going To Die | 10 |

**A.B.H.**
| | | | |
|---|---|---|---|
| 78 | Music Bank BECK 694 | Geoffrey(Who Wants To Listen To Punk Rock)/Colt 45 Rock (no p/s) | 150 |

**SHIRLEY ABICAIR**
| | | | |
|---|---|---|---|
| 67 | Piccadilly 7N 35364 | I Will Be There/Am I Losing You | 7 |
| 58 | Fontana TFL 5029 | IT'S SHIRLEY! SHIRLEY ABICAIR SINGS SONGS FROM MANY LANDS (LP) | 15 |

**A BIGGER SPLASH**
| | | | |
|---|---|---|---|
| 82 | Mean BIGGER 1 | INNOCENT BYSTANDERS EP | 15 |

**ABRACADABRA**
| | | | |
|---|---|---|---|
| 72 | RCA 2252 | Maggie McGhee/Turn On To Me | 5 |

**MICK ABRAHAMS (BAND)**
| | | | |
|---|---|---|---|
| 71 | Chrysalis ILPS 9147 | (A MUSICAL EVENING WITH) THE MICK ABRAHAMS BAND (LP, g/fold sleeve) | 20 |
| 72 | Chrysalis CHR 1005 | AT LAST (LP, first pressing, circular foldout sleeve, Island logo and address in white on green label) | 75 |

*(see also Blodwyn Pig, Jethro Tull, Mighty Flyers)*

**ABRASIVE WHEELS**
| | | | |
|---|---|---|---|
| 81 | Riot City RIOT 4 | Vicious Circles/Attack/Voice Of Youth (p/s) | 6 |
| 81 | Abrasive ABW 1 | Army Song/Juvenile/So Low (p/s) | 12 |

| 82 | Riot City RIOT 9 | Army Song/Juvenile/So Slow (p/s, reissue, red vinyl) | 6 |
| 82 | Riot City RIOT 16 | Burn 'Em Down/Urban Rebels/Burn 'Em Down (p/s) | 6 |
| 82 | Riot City CITY 001 | WHEN THE PUNKS GO MARCHING IN (LP) | 20 |
| 84 | Clay CLAY 9 | BLACK LEATHER GIRL (LP) | 18 |
| 95 | Captain Oi! AHOY LP 025 | WHEN THE PUNKS GO MARCHING IN (LP, reissue, green vinyl) | 15 |

## ABS
| 87 | Shed 001 | GREASE YOUR RALPH (EP, fold-out p/s) | 12 |

## MIKE ABSALOM
| 60s | Sportsdisc ILP 1081 | THE MIGHTY ABSALOM SINGS BATHROOM BLUES (LP) | 20 |
| 69 | Saydisc SDL 162 | SAVE THE LAST GHERKIN FOR ME (LP) | 90 |
| 71 | Vertigo 6360 053 | MIKE ABSALOM (LP, swirl label, poster sleeve) | 400 |
| 72 | Philips 6308 131 | HECTOR AND OTHER PECCADILLOS (LP) | 60 |

## ABSENT FRIENDS
| 85 | Zebra 1 | Stand Up And Fight/Drift Apart (p/s) | 30 |

## ABSENTEES
| 83 | Awol AWOL 1 | If You Don't Want Me/AWOL (no p/s) | 25 |

## ABSOLUTE
| 85 | Reset 7 REST 5 | TV Glare/At The Third Stroke (p/s) | 10 |
| 85 | Reset 12 REST 5 | TV Glare/At The Third Stroke (12", p/s) | 20 |
| 87 | Reset 7 REST 8 | Can't You See/Love In My Heart (release cancelled) | 60 |

*(see also Erasure)*

## ABSOLUTE ALBERT
| 82 | Completely Different A MAD 1 | NOISES/In Flight (p/s) | 20 |

## ABSOLUTE BEGINNERS
| 84 | Roundabout RDA BS 1 | Dream In A Haze/Southern Beat (hand-made p/s) | 20 |

## ABSOLUTE ELSEWHERE
| 76 | Warner Bros K 16697 | Earthbound/Gold Of The Gods (p/s) | 5 |
| 76 | Warner Bros K 256192 | IN SEARCH OF ANCIENT GODS (LP, gatefold, die-cut, with booklet, quadrophonic) | 18 |

*(see also Bill Bruford)*

## ABSOLUTE ZERO
| 85 | Hotwirwe HWS 856 | You Will Fall/I Want To See Your Face (Irish pressing imported into U.K. p/s) | 7 |

## ABSTRAC & LADY PENELOPE
| 97 | Confetti Records COEP 12 | 10 TIMES A DAY E.P. (12", Promo) | 12 |

## ABYSSINIA
| 00 | Ital Lion IL 001 | Good Vibrations (Original Mix)/(Ecoshock Mix)/(Mental Steppas Mix) (12") | 12 |

## ABYSSINIANS
| 73 | Harry J. HJ 6652 | Yim Mas Gan/JOHN CROW GENERATION: Crank Shaft | 20 |
| 75 | Grounation GR 2029 | Love Comes And Goes/(Version) | 12 |
| 75 | Soundtracs SK1 | Tenayistillin Wandimae/Tenayistillin | 10 |
| 76 | Tropical S'tracks TST 109 | African Race/Satta A Massagana | 15 |
| 76 | Nationwide NW009 | Sweet Feelings/Version | 8 |
| 77 | Klik KL 631 | Forward On To Zion/Satta A Massagana | 10 |
| 78 | Different HAVED 7 | Satte A Massagana/I & I (12") | 30 |
| 79 | Different HAVE 18 | Declaration Of Rights/African Race | 8 |
| 78 | Different GETL 100 | FORWARD ON TO ZION (LP) | 40 |
| 78 | Virgin Front Line FL1019 | ARISE (LP, with lyric sheet) | 20 |

## ACADEMY
| 69 | Morgan Bluetown BTS 2 | Rachel's Dream/Munching The Candy (as Academy featuring Polly Perkins) | 25 |
| 69 | Morgan Bluetown BT 5001 | POP-LORE ACCORDING TO THE ACADEMY (LP) | 200 |

*(see also Polly Perkins)*

## ACCENT (1)
| 67 | Decca F 12679 | Red Sky At Night/Wind Of Change | 225 |

*(see also Rick Hayward)*

## ACCENT (2)
| 84 | Motion 1111 | We Are Lost/Blue And Royal Line (p/s with insert) | 8 |

## ACCENTS
| 59 | Coral Q 72351 | Wiggle, Wiggle/Dreamin' And Schemin' | 10 |

## ACCESS
| 81 | Ellie Jay EJSP 9674 STA001-7 | AUDACITY EP (EP, p/s) | 25 |

## ACCIDENT
| 84 | Flicknife SHARP 016 | A CLOCKWORK LEGION (LP) | 20 |
| 87 | Link LP 12 | CRAZY! (LP) | 20 |

*(see also Major Accident)*

## ACCIDENT ON THE EAST LANCS.
| 80 | Roach RR 1 | The Back End Of Nowhere/Rat Race (p/s) | 75 |
| 80 | Roach SPLIFF 001 | We Want It Legalised/Tell Me What Ya Mean (no p/s) | 50 |
| 14 | Ozit Dandelion | RAINY CITY PUNK VOLUME 2: ACCIDENT ON THE EAST LANCS (2-LP, purple vinyl, 500 only, numbered) | 20 |

## ACCIDENTS
| 80 | H. Line 'n' Sinker HOOK 1 | Blood Spattered With Guitars/Curtains For You (p/s) | 20 |
| 80 | Hook Line 'n' Sinker | KISS ME ON THE APOCALYPSE (LP, unreleased; test pressings only, White handwritten labels) | 150 |
| 90s | Detour DRLP04 | KISS ME ON THE APOCALYPSE (LP reissue of unissued album) | 15 |

## ACCOLADE
| 70 | Columbia DB 8688 | Natural Day/Prelude To A Dawn | 12 |
| 70 | Columbia SCX 6405 | ACCOLADE (LP) | 75 |
| 72 | Regal Zono. SLRZ 1024 | ACCOLADE 2 (LP) | 125 |

*(see also Gordon Giltrap, Wizz Jones, Pauline Filby, Don Partridge)*

## ACCURSED

| 80s | Wrek 'EM ACC 2 | Going Down (p/s) | 8 |
|---|---|---|---|
| 83 | Wrek 'EM ACC 1 | AGGRESSIVE PUNK (LP) | 20 |
| 83 | Wrek 'EM ACC 3 | UP WITH THE PUNKS (LP) | 15 |
| 84 | Wrek 'EM ACC 4 | LAUGHING AT YOU (LP) | 15 |

## AC/DC

### SINGLES

| 76 | Atlantic K 10745 | It's A Long Way To The Top (If You Wanna Rock'N'Roll)/Can I Sit Next To You, Girl? (no p/s) | 22 |
|---|---|---|---|
| 76 | Atlantic K 10805 | Jailbreak/Fling Thing (original issue with running times on label, dark label, heavy print, no p/s) | 22 |
| 76 | Atlantic K 10860 | High Voltage/Live Wire (in p/s) | 150 |
| 76 | Atlantic K 10860 | High Voltage/Live Wire (no p/s) | 15 |
| 77 | Atlantic K 10899 | Dirty Deeds Done Dirt Cheap/Big Balls/The Jack (maxi-single, 'schoolboy' p/s) | 120 |
| 77 | Atlantic K 11018 | Let There Be Rock (edit)/Problem Child (small label lettering & 3.06 timing, no p/s) | 12 |
| 77 | Atlantic K 11018 | Let There Be Rock (edit)/Problem Child (without small label lettering & 3.06 timing, no p/s) | 7 |
| 78 | Atlantic K 11142 | Rock'N'Roll Damnation/Sin City (initially with small label lettering & 3.05 timing, no p/s) | 6 |
| 78 | Atlantic K 11142T | Rock'N'Roll Damnation/Sin City (12", p/s) | 18 |
| 78 | Atlantic K 11207 | Whole Lotta Rosie (live)/Hell Ain't A Bad Place To Be (live) (dark labels; later reissued with lighter labels (worth less) no p/s) | 5 |
| 78 | Atlantic K 11207T | Whole Lotta Rosie (live)/Hell Ain't A Bad Place To Be (live) (12", no p/s) | 5 |
| 79 | Atlantic K 11321 | Highway To Hell/If You Want Blood (You've Got It) ('1979' on p/s) | 5 |
| 79 | Atlantic K 11406 | Girl's Got Rhythm/Get It Hot (p/s, initial pressing without 'Elephant Head' motif) | 6 |
| 79 | Atlantic K 11406E | Girl's Got Rhythm/If You Want Blood (You've Got It)/Hell Ain't A Bad Place To Be (live)/Rock'N'Roll Damnation (EP, gatefold envelope p/s) | 12 |
| 80 | Atlantic K 11435 | Touch Too Much/Live Wire (live)/Shot Down In Flames (live) (p/s) | 5 |
| 80 | Atlantic K 11435 | Touch Too Much/Live Wire (live)/Shot Down In Flames (live) (p/s, misprinted back-to-front) | 15 |
| 80 | Atlantic K 10805 | Jailbreak/Fling Thing (reissue, light label, fine print; first pressing initially without 'Elephant Head' motif on p/s) | 15 |
| 80 | Atlantic K 10805 | Jailbreak/Fling Thing (reissue, light label, fine print; with 'Elephant Head' motif on p/s) | 10 |
| 80 | Atlantic K 11142 | Rock'N'Roll Damnation/Sin City (reissue, without 'Elephant Head' motif on p/s) | 15 |
| 80 | Atlantic K 11321 | Rock'N'Roll Damnation/Sin City (reissue, with 'Elephant Head' motif on p/s) | 10 |
| 80 | Atlantic K 11321 | Highway To Hell/If You Want Blood (You've Got It) (reissue, '1980' on p/s) | 5 |
| 80 | Atlantic HM 1 | High Voltage/Live Wire (reissue, p/s) | 6 |
| 80 | Atlantic HM 2 | Dirty Deeds Done Dirt Cheap/Big Balls/The Jack (reissue, p/s) | 6 |
| 80 | Atlantic HM 3 | It's A Long Way To The Top (If You Wanna Rock'N'Roll)/ Can I Sit Next To You? (p/s, reissue) | 6 |
| 80 | Atlantic HM 4 | Whole Lotta Rosie (live)/Hell Ain't A Bad Place To Be (live) (p/s, reissue) | 6 |
| 80 | Atlantic K 11600 | You Shook Me All Night Long/Have A Drink With Me (p/s) | 5 |
| 80 | Atlantic K 11600 | You Shook Me All Night Long/Have A Drink With Me (p/s, mispressing, A-side plays "Shake A Leg") | 100 |
| 82 | Atlantic SAM 143 | For Those About To Rock (We Salute You)/C.O.D. (12", p/s, promo only) | 40 |
| 83 | Atlantic A 9774P | Guns For Hire/Landslide (logo-shaped picture disc) | 10 |
| 84 | Atlantic A 9651P | Nervous Shakedown/Rock'N'Roll Ain't Noise Pollution (live) (shaped picture disc) | 15 |
| 85 | Atlantic A 9532W | Danger/Back In Business (poster p/s) | 6 |
| 85 | Atlantic A 9532P | Danger/Back In Business (fly-shaped picture disc) | 20 |
| 86 | Atlantic A 9474P | Shake Your Foundations/Stand Up (Angus-shaped picture disc) | 20 |
| 86 | Atlantic A 9425P | Who Made Who/Guns For Hire (live) (shaped picture disc) | 20 |
| 86 | Atlantic A 9425TW | Who Made Who (remix)/Guns For Hire (live) (12", stickered p/s & poster) | 15 |
| 86 | Atlantic A 9377P | You Shook Me All Night Long/She's Got Balls (live) (shaped picture disc) | 20 |
| 88 | Atlantic A 9136TP | Heatseeker/Go Zone/Snake Eye (12", picture disc) | 15 |
| 90 | Atco B8907T | Thunderstruck/Fire Your Guns/DT/Chase The Ace (12" coloured test pressings, white, blue, red, clear, yellow, green & marbled swirl pattern) | 300 |
| 91 | Atco B8886T | Money Talks/Mistress For Christmas/Borrowed Time (12" poster p/s) | 20 |
| 91 | Atco 8830X | Are You Ready/Got You By The Balls (numbered p/s, with patch) | 5 |
| 91 | Atco 8830W | Are You Ready/Got You By The Balls (numbered 'satchel' p/s) | 8 |
| 93 | Atco B6073T | Dirty Deeds Done Cheap/Shoot To Thrill (live)/Dirty Deeds Done Cheap (live) (12") | 10 |
| 93 | Atco B8396T | Big Gun/Back To Black/For Those About To Rock (12", p/s) | 12 |
| 95 | East West A4368X | Hard As A Rock/Caught With Your Pants Down (p/s, yellow vinyl, numbered) | 8 |

### ALBUMS

| 76 | Atlantic K50257 | HIGH VOLTAGE (LP, cartoon sleeve) | 20 |
|---|---|---|---|
| 76 | Atlantic K50323 | DIRTY DEEDS DONE CHEAP (LP) | 15 |
| 77 | Atlantic K50483 | LET THERE BE ROCK (LP, etched matrix numbers K50366 A-1/B-2) | 18 |
| 77 | Atlantic K50366 | LET THERE BE ROCK (LP, mispressing, both sides play Side 1) | 200 |
| 78 | Atlantic K50483 | POWERAGE (LP) | 15 |
| 78 | Atlantic K50366 | IF YOU WANT BLOOD (LP) | 15 |
| 79 | Atlantic K50625 | HIGHWAY TO HELL (LP) | 20 |
| 79 | Atlantic K50628 | HIGHWAY TO HELL (LP, test pressing in alternative "live" proof sleeve) | 300 |
| 80 | Atlantic K50735 | BACK IN BLACK (LP, embossed sleeve, with inner, A1/B1 Matrixes) | 20 |
| 81 | Atlantic K50851 | FOR THOSE ABOUT TO ROCK (LP, gatefold) | 15 |
| 81 | Atlantic SAM 155 | JAPAN TOUR ' 81 (LP, picture disc, promo only, clear rim) | 150 |
| 81 | Atlantic SAM 155 | JAPAN TOUR ' 81 (LP, picture disc, promo only, black rim) | 120 |
| 81 | Atlantic 60149 | BOX SET (3-LP, including "High Voltage", "Dirty Deeds Done Cheap" & Powerage, promo 7" & poster; export issue) | 45 |
| 91 | Atco WX 364P | THE RAZOR'S EDGE (LP, picture disc with inlay card) | 15 |
| 95 | East West SAM 1693 | BALLBREAKERS (CD, promo only compilation, card sleeve) | 30 |
| 95 | East West 7559 61780-1 | BALLBREAKER (LP) | 25 |

| 97 | East West 7559 62162 2 | BONFIRE (CD boxed set) ............................................................... 30 |
| 03 | Epic 509298-7 | ACDCROCKS.com BOX (15 x CD box set) ...................................... 150 |
| 09 | Columbia 38377 | BLACK ICE (2-LP, gatefold, inner sleeves)................................... 18 |

*(see also Geordie, A II Z, Home)*

## ACE
| 71 | Decca F13216 | Speed Freak/Ace Of Spades ........................................................ 8 |

## C ACE & INSWINGS
| 74 | Tropical AL 026 | Hot Butter Dub/Pits And Pieces................................................. 30 |

## BUDDY ACE
| 68 | Action ACT 4504 | Got To Get Myself Together/Darling Depend On Me................. 30 |
| 64 | Vocalion VEP 1-70164 | BUDDY ACE (EP) ........................................................................ 100 |

## CHARLIE ACE
| 70 | High Note HS 051 | Creation (Version)/GAYTONES: Creation (Version Three) ........ 12 |
| 70 | Punch PH 49 | Silver And Gold/PHILL PRATT ALLSTARS: Bump And Bore......... 12 |
| 70 | Punch PH 53 | Book Of Books/WINSTON HARRIS: Musical Dove ..................... 10 |
| 70 | Punch PH 62 | Love I Madly/Especially For You (A-side by Charley & Lloyd) ..... 10 |
| 70 | Punch PH 67 | Do Something/MAYTONES: Run Babylon.................................. 10 |
| 71 | G.G. GG 4507 | Ontarius Version/G.G. ALL STARS: Ontarius Version 2 ............. 10 |
| 71 | G.G. GG 4518 | Do Something/MAYTONES: Groove Me ................................... 10 |
| 71 | Upsetter US 359 | The Creeper/UPSETTERS: The Creeper (Version) ..................... 20 |
| 71 | Smash SMA 2325 | Need No Whip/Grine Grine ....................................................... 10 |
| 72 | Camel CA 92 | The Commandments Of Joshua/GABY AND WILTON: Only Love ........ 10 |
| 73 | Ackee ACK 519 | Country Boy (as Charley Ace)/IMPACT ALL STARS: Country Boy Version ........ 8 |

*(see also Charles, Paulette & Gee, Gaytones, Phil Pratt Allstars, Maytones, G.G. Allstars, Upsetters, Gaby Wilton & Charlie Ace)*

## JOHNNY ACE
| 61 | Vogue V 9180 | Pledging My Love/Anymore ...................................................... 30 |
| 62 | Vogue VE 1-70150 | JOHNNY ACE (EP) ....................................................................... 60 |
| 61 | Vocalion VA 160177 | THE MEMORIAL ALBUM (LP) ..................................................... 150 |

## MARTIN ACE
| 81 | CJS CJS 1 | Eating/Sad Party (p/s) ................................................................ 10 |

## RICHARD ACE (& SOUND DIMENSIONS)
| 67 | Coxsone CS 7031 | Don't Let The Sun Catch You Crying/VICEROYS: Magadown ........ 50 |
| 67 | Studio One SO 2022 | I Need You/SOUL VENDORS: Cool Shade .................................. 120 |
| 69 | Studio One SO 2072 | More Reggae (with Sound Dimensions)/GLADIATORS: Hello Carol ........ 50 |
| 69 | Trojan TR 654 | Hang 'Em High/BLACK & GEORGE: Candy Lady ......................... 150 |
| 70 | Sugar SU 104 | Sound Of The Reggae/Got To Build A Wall ................................ 35 |

*(see also Viceroys, Soul Vendors, Gladiators, Ken Boothe)*

## ACE LANE
| 83 | Expulsion EXIT3 | SEE YOU IN HEAVEN (LP) ........................................................... 15 |

## ACEN
| 92 | Production House PNT 034 | Close Your Eyes (XXX mix)/Close Your Eyes (vitamin 'E' mix) (12") ............ 20 |
| 92 | Production House PNT 034 R | Close Your Eyes (Remix I: Optikonfusion!)/Close Your Eyes (Remix II: The Sequel) (12") ........ 20 |
| 93 | Production House PNT 034 R-A, PNT 051 A-2 | Close Your Eyes (Non Beatles Version Mispress) (12") ............... 90 |
| 92 | Production House PNT 042 | Trip II The Moon (Part 1)/Obsessed (12", die-cut p/s) ............. 25 |
| 92 | Production House PNT 042R | Trip II The Moon - Part 2 (12", Promo 100 copies) .................. 60 |
| 92 | Production House PNT 042 R | Trip II The Moon (Part 2, The Darkside)/The Life And Crimes Of A Ruffneck (12", die-cut p/s) ........ 25 |
| 92 | Production House PNT 042 RX | Trip II The Moon (Part 3, kaleidoscopiklimax)/Obsessed (Part 2, Pictures Of Silence) (12", die-cut p/s) ........ 25 |
| 93 | Production House PNT 051R | Window In The Sky (DMS Remix)/Window In The Sky (Nino's Night Remix) (white label 12") ........ 15 |
| 93 | Production House PNT 051 | Krystal Fairground (12", Promo, one-sided) ............................ 50 |

## A CERTAIN RATIO
| 79 | Factory FAC 5 | All Night Party/The Thin Boys (p/s, 5,000 only, 1,000 with sticker stating ltd. edition on poor quality vinyl) ........ 25 |
| 79 | Factory FAC 5 | All Night Party/The Thin Boys (p/s, 5,000 only, 4,000 without sticker stating ltd. edition on poor quality vinyl) ........ 20 |
| 80 | Factory FAC 22 | Blown Away/Flight/And Then Again (12", p/s, with inner sleeve)............... 12 |
| 81 | Factory FACT 42 | THE DOUBLE 12" ( 2x12", Flight/And Then Again (Version)/Blown Away//Do The Du/ The Fox/Shack Up/Son & Heir) ........ 10 |
| 82 | Factory FAC 62-7 | Knife Slits Water/Tumba Rumba (p/s) ...................................... 5 |
| 83 | Factory FAC 72-7 | I Need Someone Tonite (edit)/Don't You Worry 'Bout A Thing (edit) (promo) ........ 5 |
| 84 | Factory FAC 112P | Life's A Scream (edit)/There's Only This (edit) (promo pack including 7", photo & biography in custom ACR envelope) ........ 10 |
| 80 | Factory FACT 16C | THE GRAVEYARD & THE BALLROOM (cassette in plastic wallet, first 400 in orange, then later blue, green, brown, red and grey. 1000 only)........ 20 |
| 81 | Factory FACT 35 | TO EACH (LP) .............................................................................. 15 |
| 82 | Factory FACT 55 | SEXTET (LP, textured sleeve with insert) .................................. 15 |
| 85 | Factory FACT 16C | THE GRAVEYARD AND THE BALLROOM (reissue, cassette, in box with insert) ......... 25 |
| 86 | Factory FACT 135c | THE OLD AND THE NEW (cassette, in box with insert) .............. 25 |
| 86 | Factory FACT 166c | FORCE (cassette, in box with insert) ........................................ 25 |

*(see also Sir Horatio)*

## ACES (1)
| 63 | Parlophone R 5094 | Wait Till Tomorrow/The Last One ............................................. 7 |
| 64 | Parlophone R 5108 | I Count The Tears/But Say It Isn't So ........................................ 7 |

## ACES (2)
| 81 | Etc ETC 01 | One Way Street/Why Should It Be Mine (p/s) ......................... 18 |

*(see also Menace)*

## A CHOCOLATE MORNING
| | | | |
|---|---|---|---|
| 91 | Still CM 001 | WASTED EP (12" p/s) | 70 |

## ACHOR
| | | | |
|---|---|---|---|
| 76 | Cedar CEDAR 1 | END OF MY DAY (LP) | 15 |

*(see also Wine Of Lebanon, Valley Of Achor)*

## ACID ANGELS
| | | | |
|---|---|---|---|
| 88 | Fuel FUEL 1 | Speed Speed Ecstacy/Top Fuel Eliminator (no p/s) | 6 |

*(see also Jesus & Mary Chain)*

## ACID GALLERY
| | | | |
|---|---|---|---|
| 69 | CBS 4608 | Dance Around The Maypole/Right Toe Blues | 80 |

*(see also Christie, Epics, Carl Wayne & Vikings, Roy Wood)*

## ACID MOTHERS TEMPLE AND THE MELTING PARAISO UFO
| | | | |
|---|---|---|---|
| 01 | Staticresonance 2 | MONSTER OF THE UNIVERSE (Monster Of The Universe/Wholly Weary Flashback/Surfin' Paris-Texas/Midnight Mountain Dew (EP, 500 only, p/s 2 x 7" sold on tour, 500 only) | 15 |
| 01 | Staticresonance 5 | My Guitar Wants To Kiss Your Mother/NISHINIHON: Super Station (Hell In A Cell Version) (red vinyl, p/s) | 8 |
| 04 | Ochre OCH 057 | Hello Good Child/You're My Boy (300 on purple vinyl) | 6 |
| 01 | Staticresonance 1 | ABSOLUTELY FREAKOUT, (ZAP YOUR MIND) (LP, 1000 only) | 30 |

*(See also Cotton Casino)*

## ACKEE
| | | | |
|---|---|---|---|
| 86 | Heavyweight HW 003 | Call Me Rambo/Rambo Gun Salute (12", as Ackie) | 25 |
| 87 | Route One RO 004 | Ragamuffin Boogie Rock/Lick Them (Dance Hall Style) (12") | 100 |
| 87 | Route One RO 005 | Roughneck Time/Version (12") | 100 |

## DAVID ACKLES
| | | | |
|---|---|---|---|
| 68 | Elektra EKSN 45039 | La Route A Chicago/Down River | 5 |
| 69 | Elektra EKSN 45054 | Laissez Faire/Blue Ribbons | 5 |
| 70 | Elektra EKSN 45079 | Subway To The Country/That's No Reason To Cry | 5 |
| 68 | Elektra EKL 4022 | DAVID ACKLES (LP, orange label, mono) | 35 |
| 68 | Electra EKS 74022 | DAVID ACKLES (LP, orange label, stereo) | 25 |
| 70 | Elektra EKS 74060 | SUBWAY TO THE COUNTRY (LP, orange label) | 15 |
| 72 | Elektra K 42112 | AMERICAN GOTHIC (LP) | 15 |
| 73 | CBS 32466 | FIVE AND DIME (LP) | 15 |

## BARBARA ACKLIN
| | | | |
|---|---|---|---|
| 68 | MCA 1103 | Am I The Same Girl (Soulful Strut)/Be By My Side | 10 |
| 68 | MCA MU 1038 | Love Makes A Woman/Come And See Me Baby | 20 |
| 69 | MCA MU 1071 | Am I The Same Girl/Be By My Side (DJ Copy) | 50 |
| 69 | MCA MU 1071 | Am I The Same Girl/Be By My Side | 10 |
| 69 | MCA MU 1102 | Love Makes A Woman/Come And See Me Baby (reissue) | 10 |
| 69 | MCA MU 1103 | Am I The Same Girl/Be By My Side (reissue) | 6 |
| 73 | Brunswick BR 8 | I Call It Trouble/I'll Bake Me A Man | 10 |
| 69 | MCA MUP(S) 366 | LOVE MAKES A WOMAN (LP) | 25 |
| 71 | MCA MUPS 410 | SEVEN DAYS OF NIGHT (LP) | 20 |
| 71 | MCA MUPS 416 | SOMEONE ELSE'S ARMS (LP) | 20 |
| 75 | Capitol E-ST 11377 | A PLACE IN THE SUN (LP) | 15 |

*(see also Gene Chandler & Barbara Acklin)*

## ACME ATTRACTIONS
| | | | |
|---|---|---|---|
| 80 | A Trax KICK 007 | Anyway/Never Again (p/s) | 40 |
| 81 | Orchid OR1 | Eve Of Destruction/It's OK (p/s, with Bonnie Parker) | 20 |

## ACOUSTIC LADYLAND
| | | | |
|---|---|---|---|
| 06 | V2 VVR1043681 | SKINNY GRIN (LP) | 15 |

## A CRAZE
| | | | |
|---|---|---|---|
| 83 | Respond KOB 706 | Wearing Your Jumper/She Is So (p/s, produced by Paul Weller) | 7 |

## ACRYLIC TONES
| | | | |
|---|---|---|---|
| 90s | Detour DR010 | Girl/Theme From.../Rainbow Song (p/s) | 5 |

## ACT (1)
| | | | |
|---|---|---|---|
| 67 | Columbia DB 8179 | Cobbled Streets/One Heart | 25 |
| 67 | Columbia DB 8261 | Here Come Those Tears Again/Without You | 15 |
| 68 | Columbia DB 8331 | Just A Little Bit/The Remedies Of Doctor Brohnicoy | 70 |

## ACT (2)
| | | | |
|---|---|---|---|
| 81 | Act ACT 001 | Dance To Despair/Who Let The Flowers Fall? (p/s and lyric sheet) | 7 |

## ACT (3)
| | | | |
|---|---|---|---|
| 87 | ZTT 12ACT 28 | Snobbery And Decay (Naked Civil Remix)/Strong Poison/Theme From Snobbery And Decay (12", gatefold p/s, with poster) | 10 |
| 87 | ZTT CT 01 | Snobbery And Decay (Moonlighting Mix)/Instant 1/Instant 2 (12" promo, plain black die-cut sleeve) | 30 |
| 87 | ZTT VIMM 1 | Absolutely Immune 2/Bloodrush/States Of Logic (12", p/s) | 10 |
| 88 | ZTT BET 1 | Chance/Winner '88 (p/s, withdrawn) | 30 |
| 88 | ZTT BETT 1 | Chance (12 To 1 Mix)/Winner '88/Chance (We Give You Another Chance) (12", p/s, withdrawn) | 80 |
| 88 | ZTT BETCD 1 | Chance (12 To 1 Mix)/Winner '88/Chance (We Give You Another Chance) (CD, existence unconfirmed) | 0 |

*(see also Propaganda, Claudia Brucken, Glenn Gregory & Claudia Brucken, Thomas Leer)*

## ACTION
| | | | |
|---|---|---|---|
| 65 | Parlophone R 5354 | Land Of 1000 Dances/In My Lonely Room | 75 |
| 66 | Parlophone R 5410 | I'll Keep Holding On/Hey Sah-Lo-Ney | 75 |
| 66 | Parlophone R 5474 | Baby You've Got It/Since I Lost My Baby | 100 |
| 67 | Parlophone R 5572 | Never Ever/Twenty Fourth Hour | 100 |
| 67 | Parlophone R 5610 | Shadows And Reflections/Something Has Hit Me | 100 |

# FILM & TV SOUNDTRACK LPs
## (alphabetical by title, composers/artists in brackets)
## (Only the first issue of soundtracks by the Beatles and Elvis Presley are listed below: for later repressings see their entries)

## A

| | | | |
|---|---|---|---|
| 73 | United Artists UAS 29451 | ACROSS 110TH STREET (J.J. Johnson & Bobby Womack) | 15 |
| 62 | RCA RD 7512 | ADVISE AND CONSENT (Jerry Fielding) | 15 |
| 13 | Rook RFV 002 | A FIELD IN ENGLAND (2-LP, white vinyl, poster, blade of grass) | 100 |
| 64 | Parlophone PMC 1230 | A HARD DAY'S NIGHT (Beatles) (LP, mono, 1st pressing, with The Parlophone Co. Ltd label rim copy & "Sold In The UK..." text) | 80 |
| 64 | Parlophone PCS 3058 | A HARD DAY'S NIGHT (Beatles) (LP, stereo, 1st pressing, with "The Parlophone Co. Ltd" label rim copy & "Sold In The UK..." text; stereo, with mid-sized "stereo" | 200 |
| 67 | United Artists (S)ULP 1172 | AFRICA ADDIO (Riz Ortolani/Jimmy Roselli) | 20 |
| 66 | United Artists (S)ULP 1151 | AFTER THE FOX (Burt Bacharach/Hollies) | 25 |
| 56 | Nixa NPT 19010 | ALEXANDER THE GREAT (Mario Nascimbene) (10"; beware of counterfeits) | 40 |
| 69 | MGM CS 8112 | ALFRED THE GREAT (Ray Leppard) | 100 |
| 65 | Reprise R 6151 | AMERICANIZATION OF EMILY (Johnny Mandel) | 20 |
| 65 | RCA RD 7732 | THE AMOROUS ADVENTURES OF MOLL FLANDERS (John Addison) | 35 |
| 57 | Brunswick LAT 8175 | ANASTASIA (Alfred Newman) | 15 |
| 60 | Philips SBBL 514 | ANATOMY OF A MURDER (Duke Ellington) | 25 |
| 76 | BBC REB 236 | ANGELS AND 15 OTHER BBC TV THEMES (Alan Parker, et al.) | 15 |
| 72 | Polydor 2383 109 | ANTONY AND CLEOPATRA (John Scott) (foldout sleeve) | 20 |
| 60 | London HA-T 2287 | THE APARTMENT (Adolph Deutsch) | 18 |
| 79 | Elektra K 62025 | APOCALYPSE NOW (2-LP, music & dialogue) | 20 |
| 69 | CBS 70054 | APRIL FOOLS (Marvin Hamlisch) | 15 |
| 66 | RCA Victor RD 7817 | ARABESQUE (Henry Mancini) | 15 |
| 66 | Fontana FJL 135 | L'ASCENSEUR POUR L'ECHAFAUD/FEMME DISPARAISSANTE (Miles Davis/Art Blakey [1 side each]) | 30 |
| 54 | HMV DLPC 1 | AS LONG AS THEY'RE HAPPY (Jack Buchanan) (10") | 50 |
| 67 | Pye NPL 18198 | AT LAST THE 1948 SHOW (TV soundtrack) | 25 |
| 67 | Marble Arch MAL 695 | THE AVENGERS AND OTHER FAVOURITES (Laurie Johnson) | 35 |
| 61 | Fontana TFL 591 | ALL NIGHT LONG (LP, mono, Dave Brubeck, Tubby Hayes, Johnny Dankworth et al.) | 30 |
| 61 | Fontana STFL 591 | ALL NIGHT LONG (LP, stereo, Dave Brubeck, Tubby Hayes, Johnny Dankworth et al.) | 20 |

## B

| | | | |
|---|---|---|---|
| 66 | Fontana TL 5306 | BABY, THE RAIN MUST FALL (Elmer Bernstein) | 15 |
| 62 | Pye Intl. NPL 28020 | BARABBAS (Mario Nascimbene) | 15 |
| 68 | Stateside (S)SL 10260 | BARBARELLA (Bob Crewe/Charles Fox) | 75 |
| 67 | London HA-D 8337 | BAREFOOT IN THE PARK (Neal Hefti) | 15 |
| 13 | Silva SILLP 1316 | BATMAN BEGINS (2-LP, 500 only) | 25 |
| 66 | Stateside S(S)L 10179 | BATMAN (Nelson Riddle) (TV show music) | 50 |
| 66 | Warner Bros W 1617 | BATTLE OF THE BULGE (Benjamin Frankel) | 25 |
| 60 | Columbia 33SX 1225 | BEAT GIRL (John Barry/Adam Faith) | 50 |
| 57 | London HAP 2056 | BEAU JAMES (Joseph Lilley) | 25 |
| 64 | RCA Victor RD 7679 | BECKET (dialogue only) | 15 |
| 68 | Decca LK 4923 | BEDAZZLED (LP, mono, Peter Cook/Dudley Moore) | 120 |
| 70 | Island ILPS 9140 | BE GLAD FOR THE SONG HAS NO ENDING (Incredible String Band) | 15 |
| 15 | Finders Keepers FKR79L | BELLADONNA (leather sleeve) | 40 |
| 60 | Capitol W/SW 1435 | BELLS ARE RINGING (André Previn) (mono/stereo) | 15 |
| 60 | MGM MGM-C(S) 802 | BEN HUR (Miklos Rozsa) (box set with hardback book; mono/stereo) | 15 |
| 70 | Stateside SSL 10311 | BEYOND THE VALLEY OF THE DOLLS (Stu Phillips/Strawberry Alarm Clock) | 100 |
| 68 | MGM MGM-C(S) 8066 | BIGGEST BUNDLE OF THEM ALL (Riz Ortolani/Eric Burdon) | 20 |
| 69 | United Artists (S)ULP 1228 | THE BIG GUNDOWN (Ennio Morricone) | 15 |
| 67 | United Artists (S)ULP 1183 | BILLION DOLLAR BRAIN (Richard Rodney Bennett) | 30 |
| 73 | Polydor 2490 117 | BLACK CAESAR (James Brown) | 35 |
| 72 | Pye NSPL 18376 | BLOOMFIELD | 15 |
| 66 | MGM MGM-C(S) 8039 | BLOW-UP (Herbie Hancock/Yardbirds) | 80 |
| 68 | Dot (S)LPD 508 | BLUE (Manos Hadjidakis) | 30 |
| 61 | RCA RD 27238 | BLUE HAWAII (Elvis Presley) (black/silver label, mono) | 15 |
| 87 | Thats Entertainment TER 1127 | BLUE VELVET (Angelo Badalamenti) | 20 |
| 62 | RCA RD 7520 | BONANZA (L.Greene, M. Langdon) | 20 |
| 69 | MCA MUPS 360 | BOOM! (John Barry/Georgie Fame) | 60 |
| 68 | Warner Bros W 1742 | BONNIE AND CLYDE (Charles Strouse) | 20 |
| 70 | Paramount SPFL 263 | BORSALINO (Claude Bolling) | 15 |
| 58 | RCA RD 27054 | BOTH ENDS OF THE CANDLE (Gogi Grant) | 15 |
| 57 | Brunswick LAT 8193 | BOY ON A DOLPHIN (Hugo Friedhoffer) | 30 |
| 71 | Capitol E-SW 621 | THE BUGALOOS (LP) | 30 |
| 72 | Bell BELLS 209 | THE BURGLARS (Ennio Morricone) | 30 |
| 66 | RCA RD 7791 | BUNNY LAKE IS MISSING (Paul Glass/Zombies) | 65 |
| 65 | Liberty LBY 1246 | BURKE'S LAW (Herschel/Burke/Gilbert) (TV series music) | 15 |
| 61 | RCA SF 5115 | BLUE HAWAII (Elvis Presley) (black/silver label, stereo) | 20 |
| 63 | RCA Victor SF 7580 | BYE BYE BIRDIE (musical) (Charles Strouse; stereo) | 15 |
| 80 | Chrysalis CHR 1294 | BABYLON (blue/white label) | 20 |
| 05 | Trunk JBH 016LP/PD | BOD: WORDS & MUSIC (LP 1-sided picture disc) | 20 |
| 07 | Trunk JBH 023 LP | BLOOD ON SATAN'S CLAW (LP, 500 only) | 40 |

# C

| | | | |
|---|---|---|---|
| 66 | RCA Victor SF 7820 | CALIFORNIA HOLIDAY (Elvis Presley) (black/red dot labels, stereo) | 30 |
| 69 | Stateside (S)SL 10276 | CANDY (Dave Grusin/Steppenwolf, et al.) | 30 |
| 69 | MCA MUPS 380 | CAN HEIRONYMUS MERKIN EVER FORGET MERCY HUMPPE AND FIND TRUE HAPPINESS? (Anthony Newley) | 30 |
| 60 | Delyse DL 3057/DLS 6057 | CAPTAIN HORATIO HORNBLOWER (Robert Farnon) (mono) | 30 |
| 67 | RCA Victor RD/SF 7874 | CASINO ROYALE (Burt Bacharach/Herb Alpert/Dusty Springfield) (mono/stereo) | 30 |
| 66 | United Artists (S)ULP 1140 | CAST A GIANT SHADOW (Elmer Bernstein/Vince Hill) | 18 |
| 65 | Columbia SX 1756 | CATCH US IF YOU CAN (Dave Clark Five) | 45 |
| 62 | Warner Bros WS 8177 | THE CHAPMAN REPORT (Leonard Rosenman) | 15 |
| 63 | RCA SF 7620 | CHARADE (Henry Mancini) | 20 |
| 63 | MGM MGM-C 969 | THE CHARGE IS MURDER (John Green) | 20 |
| 68 | United Artists SULP 1189 | THE CHARGE OF THE LIGHT BRIGADE (John Addison/Manfred Mann) | 18 |
| 66 | CBS (S)BPG 62665 | THE CHASE (John Barry) (mono) (stereo copy is £30) | 20 |
| 69 | Polydor 583 736 | CHE! (Lalo Schifrin) | 15 |
| 67 | Fontana TL 5417 | CHIMES AT MIDNIGHT (Angelo Lavagnino) | 30 |
| 74 | ABC ABCL 5068 | CHINATOWN (Jerry Goldsmith) | 20 |
| 68 | RCA Victor RD/SF 7917 | CLAMBAKE (Elvis Presley) (black/red dot labels, mono/stereo) | 20 |
| 01 | Trunk SOUP 001LP | THE CLANGERS (Vernon Elliot) (TV soundtrack, with knitted sleeve, 26 only) | 125 |
| 63 | Stateside S(S)SL 10044 | CLEOPATRA (Alex North) | 15 |
| 65 | Fontana (S)TL 5259 | THE COLLECTOR (Maurice Jarre) | 25 |
| 67 | MGM MGM-C(S) 8058 | THE COMEDIANS (Laurence Rosenthal) | 15 |
| 72 | Pye NSPL 18389 | CONCERTO FOR HARRY - SOMETHING TO HIDE (Roy Budd) | 25 |
| 75 | Polydor 2383 350 | CONFESSIONS OF A POP PERFORMER (Three's A Crowd/Ed Welch) | 30 |
| 71 | Philips 6332 033 | CONTINENTAL CIRCUS (Gong) | 20 |
| 62 | Parlophone PMC 1194 | THE COOL MIKADO (John Barry Seven/Frankie Howerd, et al.) | 25 |
| 70 | United Artists UAS 29119 | COTTON COMES TO HARLEM (Galt McDermott) | 30 |
| 67 | Brunswick AXA 4544 | COUNTESS FROM HONG KONG (Charles Chaplin) (with booklet) | 15 |
| 70 | Capitol E-ST 640 | CROMWELL (Frank Cordell) | 15 |
| 70 | Word WST 5550 | THE CROSS & THE SWITCHBLADE (Ralph Carmichael) | 25 |
| 77 | EMI EMA 782 | CROSS OF IRON (Ernest Gold) (gatefold sleeve) | 15 |
| 80 | CBS 70182 | CRUISING (John Hiatt/Willy DeVille/Germs) | 25 |
| 73 | Buddah 2318 091 | CURTIS IN CHICAGO (Curtis Mayfield/Impressions/Jerry Butler, Gene Chandler, Leroy Hutson) (TV soundtrack, gatefold sleeve) | 15 |
| 68 | Stateside (S)SL 10222 | CUSTER OF THE WEST (Bernardo Segall) | 20 |
| 66 | RCA Victor RD 7820 | CALIFORNIA HOLIDAY (Elvis Presley) (black/red dot labels, mono) | 20 |
| 01 | Trunk SOUP 001LP | THE CLANGERS (Vernon Elliot) (TV soundtrack, without knitted sleeve) | 30 |

# D

| | | | |
|---|---|---|---|
| 81 | 2-Tone CHR TT 5004 | DANCE CRAZE (with poster) | 20 |
| 62 | Fontana TFL 5184 | DANGEROUS FRIENDSHIPS (Art Blakey, et. al.) | 25 |
| 63 | MGM MGM-C 952 | DAVID AND LISA (Mark Lawrence/Victor Feldman All Stars) | 15 |
| 67 | Stateside (S)SL 10217 | THE DAY THE FISH CAME OUT (Mikis Theodorakis) | 30 |
| 68 | Stateside (S)SL 10263 | DEADFALL (John Barry/Shirley Bassey) | 20 |
| 73 | Columbia SCX 6550 | DEAF SMITH AND JOHNNY EARS (Daniele Patucchi) | 35 |
| 74 | CBS 80546 | DEATH WISH (Herbie Hancock) | 15 |
| 68 | Stateside (S)SL 10259 | DECLINE AND FALL... OF A BIRDWATCHER (Ron Goodwin) | 100 |
| 55 | MGM MGM-C 754 | DEEP IN MY HEART (Howard Keel/Vic Damone, et al.) | 12 |
| 58 | London HA-D 2111 | DESIRE UNDER THE ELMS (Elmer Bernstein) | 20 |
| 63 | Colpix PXL 440 | DIAMOND HEAD (John Williams) | 15 |
| 76 | Pye Intl. NSPL 28219 | DIAMOND MERCENARIES (Georges Garvarentz) | 15 |
| 76 | Bradley BRADS 8002 | DIAMONDS (Roy Budd) | 50 |
| 71 | United Artists UAS 29216 | DIAMONDS ARE FOREVER (John Barry/Shirley Bassey) | 20 |
| 59 | Top Rank RX 3016 | THE DIARY OF ANNE FRANK (Alfred Newman) | 30 |
| 83 | Ripple (no cat. no.) | DIGITAL DREAMS (Bill Wyman) (promo only) | 50 |
| 68 | MGM MGM-C(S) 8048 | DIRTY DOZEN (Frank de Vol/Trini Lopez) (yellow label) | 18 |
| 65 | United Artists ULP 1097 | DOCTOR NO (Monty Norman) (mono) | 50 |
| 62 | Columbia 33SX 1446 | DON'T KNOCK THE TWIST (Chubby Checker/Gene Chandler, et al.) | 25 |
| 67 | RCA Victor SF 7892 | DOUBLE TROUBLE (Elvis Presley) (black/red dot labels, stereo) (Mono version RD7892 = £20) | 20 |
| 67 | CBS S 63189 | DR. FAUSTUS (Mario Nascimbene) | 75 |
| 65 | United Artists (S)ULP 1097 | DOCTOR NO (Monty Norman) (stereo) | 100 |
| 69 | Capitol EST 672 | THE DOUBLE DECKERS (TV soundtrack) | 30 |
| 87 | Crammed MTM 14 | DOWN BY LAW (John Lurie) | 20 |
| 70 | President PTLS 1068 | DRAKE'S DREAM (Paul Jones) | 20 |
| 59 | Parlophone PMCL 1101 | DRUMBEAT (Adam Faith/John Barry Seven, et al.) | 50 |
| 58 | Decca LF 1308 | THE DUKE WORE JEANS (Tommy Steele) (10") | 15 |
| 00 | Trunk/Bonk XXX 1 LP | DEEP THROAT (LP) | 20 |
| 04 | Trunk JBH 011 LP | DAWN OF THE DEAD (LP, 500 only) | 30 |

# E

| | | | |
|---|---|---|---|
| 58 | HMV DLP 1088 | EDDIE FOY AND THE SEVEN LITTLE FOYS (10", Bob Hope/James Cagney) | 30 |
| 54 | Brunswick LAT 8040 | THE EGYPTIAN (Alfred Newman) | 25 |
| 67 | Columbia S(C)X 6155 | EL DORADO (Nelson Riddle) | 25 |
| 63 | Colpix PXL 459 | ELIZABETH TAYLOR IN LONDON (John Barry) (stereo) (Mono = £30) | 35 |
| 69 | RCA Victor RD 8011 | ELVIS ("TV Special", mono) | 15 |
| 74 | Warner Bros K 56084 | EMMANUELLE (Pierre Bachelet) | 15 |
| 57 | Vogue Coral LVA 9063 | END AS A MAN (Kenyon Hopkins) | 30 |
| 74 | Warner Bros K 46275 | ENTER THE DRAGON (Lalo Schifrin) | 40 |

| 84 | Alt. Ten. VIRUS 30 | ERASERHEAD (Fats Waller/Peter Ivers/et al.) (with insert) | 40 |
|----|----|----|----|
| 12 | Death Waltz DW 0002 | ESCAPE FROM NEW YORK (poster, inner, orange/green vinyl, 100 only) | 40 |
| 76 | EMI EMC 3148 | ESCAPE FROM THE DARK (Ron Goodwin) | 15 |
| 63 | Parlophone PMC 1198 | THE ESTABLISHMENT (Peter Cook, et al.) | 20 |
| 83 | MCA MCA 70000 | E.T. - THE EXTRA TERRESTRIAL (John Williams) (box set, with booklet & poster) | 30 |
| 83 | MCA CAC 70000 | E.T. - THE EXTRA TERRESTRIAL (John Williams) (cassette, box set, with booklet & poster) | 15 |
| 67 | Brunswick LAT 8678 | AN EVENING WITH BORIS KARLOFF AND FRIENDS | 30 |
| 74 | Warner Bros K 56071 | THE EXORCIST (Jack Nitzsche, et al.) | 20 |
| 72 | Deram SML 1095 | EXTREMES (Tony Klinger & Michael Lyons) | 100 |

## F

| 57 | Capitol LCT 6139 | A FACE IN THE CROWD (Tom Glazer) (10") | 20 |
|----|----|----|----|
| 64 | CBS (S)BPG 62277 | FALL OF THE ROMAN EMPIRE (Dimitri Tiomkin) | 20 |
| 67 | Decca LK 4847 | THE FAMILY WAY (Paul McCartney/George Martin) (mono) | 70 |
| 67 | Decca SKL 4847 | THE FAMILY WAY (LP, stereo, soundtrack) | 90 |
| 60 | Top Rank 30/003/4/5 | FANTASIA (various classical pieces) (3-LP, with book) | 30 |
| 58 | Capitol LCT 6162 | A FAREWELL TO ARMS (Mario Nascimbene) | 15 |
| 67 | MGM MGM-C(S) 8053 | FAR FROM THE MADDING CROWD (Richard Rodney Bennett) | 20 |
| 68 | London HA-U/SH-U 8358 | THE FASTEST GUITAR ALIVE (Roy Orbison) | 20 |
| 67 | Stateside S(S)L 10213 | FATHOM (Johnny Dankworth) | 40 |
| 73 | Pye NSPL 18398 | FEAR IS THE KEY (Roy Budd) | 50 |
| 70 | United Artists UAS 29118 | FELLINI-SATYRICON (Nino Rota) | 20 |
| 65 | Columbia 33SX 1693 | FERRY CROSS THE MERSEY (Gerry & Pacemakers/Cilla Black/Fourmost) (also stereo SCX 3544 = £35) | 25 |
| 99 | Restless Records 74321716431 | FIGHT CLUB (2-LP) | 40 |
| 63 | CBS SBPG 62148 | 55 DAYS AT PEKING (Dimitri Tiomkin/Andy Williams) | 18 |
| 66 | Columbia SX 6079 | FINDERS KEEPERS (Cliff Richard) (with inner sleeve, mono) (stereo SCX 6079 = £15) | 15 |
| 57 | Brunswick LAT 8194 | FIRE DOWN BELOW (Arthur Benjamin) | 25 |
| 67 | RCA Victor RD/SF 7875 | A FISTFUL OF DOLLARS (Ennio Morricone) | 30 |
| 72 | United Artists UAS 29345 | A FISTFUL OF DYNAMITE (Ennio Morricone) | 40 |
| 65 | RCA Victor RD 7723 | FLAMING STAR AND SUMMER KISSES (Elvis Presley) (mono only, black labels) | 75 |
| 85 | Heavy Metal HMXD 29 | FLASHPOINT (Tangerine Dream) (CD, playable [most copies faulty]) | 50 |
| 61 | Golden Guinea GGL 0092 | THE FLINTSTONES (TV soundtrack) | 15 |
| 62 | Brunswick LAT 8392 | FLOWER DRUM SONG (Nancy Kwan, et al.) (also stereo STA 3054) | 15 |
| 64 | Ace Of Clubs ACL 1166 | FLYING CLIPPER (Riz Ortolani) | 15 |
| 13 | Death Waltz DW03.5 | THE FOG (black vinyl) | 40 |
| 13 | Death Waltz DW03.5 | THE FOG (splatter vinyl) | 30 |
| 73 | York BYK 715 | FOLLYFOOT (LP) | 20 |
| 65 | Ember NR 5029 | FOUR IN THE MORNING (John Barry) (mono) | 35 |
| 74 | T. Motown STML 11269 | FOXY BROWN (Willie Hutch) | 15 |
| 66 | RCA Victor RD 7793 | FRANKIE AND JOHNNY (Elvis Presley) (black/red dot labels, mono) (Stereo SF 7793 = £30) | 20 |
| 64 | Fontana TL 5208 | FREEDOM ROAD (Madeleine Bell, et al.) (TV production) | 15 |
| 63 | United Artists (S)ULP 1052 | FROM RUSSIA WITH LOVE (John Barry/Matt Monroe) (mono/stereo) | 25 |
| 60 | London HA-T 2257 | THE FUGITIVE KIND (Kenyon Hopkins) | 30 |
| 67 | RCA RD 7860 | FUNERAL IN BERLIN (Konrad Elfers/Puppets) | 20 |
| 63 | RCA Victor RD/SF 7609 | FUN IN ACAPULCO (Elvis Presley) (black/silver label, mono/stereo) | 20 |

## G

| 65 | Liberty (S)LBY 1261 | GENGHIS KHAN (Dusan Radic) (mono/stereo) | 20 |
|----|----|----|----|
| 56 | Vogue Coral LVA 9003 | GENTLEMEN MARRY BRUNETTES (Robert Farnon) | 30 |
| 53 | MGM MGM-D 116 | GENTLEMEN PREFER BLONDES (Marilyn Monroe, et al.) (10") | 75 |
| 65 | Mercury 20061 MCL | GENTLE RAIN (Luis Bonfa & Deodato) | 15 |
| 99 | Cinephile CINLP001 | GET CARTER (LP, gatefold) | 20 |
| 70 | RCA SF 8137 | GETTING STRAIGHT (Ronald Stein) | 20 |
| 57 | Capitol LCT 6122 | GIANT (Dimitri Tiomkin) | 15 |
| 60 | RCA RD 27192 | G.I. BLUES (Elvis Presley) (black/silver label, mono) (stereo SF 5078 = £25) | 15 |
| 66 | MGM MGM-C(S) 8034 | GIRL FROM U.N.C.L.E. (Jerry Goldsmith & Teddy Randazzo) | 40 |
| 65 | RCA Victor RD 7714 | GIRL HAPPY (Elvis Presley) (black/red dot labels, mono) (stereo SF 7714 = £30) | 20 |
| 68 | Polydor 583 714 | GIRL ON A MOTORCYCLE (Les Reed) | 15 |
| 63 | RCA Victor RD 7534 | GIRLS! GIRLS! GIRLS! (Elvis Presley) (black/silver labels, mono) (Stereo SF 7534 = £35) | 15 |
| 66 | United Artists SULP 1120 | THE GLORY GUYS (Riz Ortolani) | 30 |
| 72 | Paramount SPFA 7003 | THE GODFATHER (Nino Rota) (gatefold sleeve) | 15 |
| 75 | ABC ABCL 5128 | THE GODFATHER - PART 2 (Nino Rota) (gatefold sleeve) | 15 |
| 58 | London HA-T 2125 | GOD'S LITTLE ACRE (Elmer Bernstein) | 20 |
| 72 | Mother MO 4001 | GOLD (MC5/David McWilliams, et al.) | 35 |
| 73 | United Artists UAS 29576 | THE GOLDEN VOYAGE OF SINBAD (Miklos Rozsa) | 15 |
| 64 | United Artists ULP 1076 | GOLDFINGER (John Barry/Shirley Bassey) (mono) (Stereo, SULP 1076 = £30) | 15 |
| 64 | Decca LK 4673 | GONKS GO BEAT (Lulu/Nashville Teens/Graham Bond, et al.) | 100 |
| 68 | United Artists (S)ULP 1197 | THE GOOD, THE BAD AND THE UGLY (Ennio Morricone) | 15 |
| 69 | Warner Bros W(S) 1786 | GOODBYE COLUMBUS (Charles Fox/Association) | 18 |
| 70 | DJM DJLPS 408 | GOODBYE GEMINI (Christopher Gunning/Peddlers/Jackie Lee) | 50 |
| 63 | United Artists (S)ULP 1041 | THE GREAT ESCAPE (Elmer Bernstein) (mono/stereo) | 20 |
| 71 | Pye NSPL 18373 | GREAT SONGS AND THEMES FROM GREAT FILMS (Roy Budd) | 40 |
| 75 | MCA MCF 2707 | THE GREAT WALDO PEPPER (Henry Mancini) | 15 |
| 68 | United Artists SULP 1220 | GREAT WESTERN FILM THEMES (Various Artists) | 15 |
| 70 | Polydor 2384 021 | GROUPIE GIRL (Opal Butterfly/English Rose, et al.) | 40 |
| 67 | RCA RD/SF 7899 | GUNN (Henry Mancini) | 18 |

| 09 | Trunk JBH 032 LP | G SPOTS (LP) | 20 |

# H

| 65 | United Artists SULP 1106 | THE HALLELUJAH TRAIL (Elmer Bernstein) | 15 |
| 75 | Contour 2870 437 | THE HANGED MAN (Bullet) (TV soundtrack) | 40 |
| 68 | United Artists SULP 1204 | HANG 'EM HIGH (Dominic Frontiere) (stereo/mono) | 15 |
| 69 | United Artists SULP 1231 | HANNIBAL BROOKS (Francis Lai) | 30 |
| 70 | United Artists UAS 29084 | THE HAPPY ENDING (Michel Legrand) | 20 |
| 56 | Philips BBL 7100 | HAPPY HOLIDAY (Jo Stafford) | 15 |
| 65 | RCA Victor RD 7767 | HAREM HOLIDAY (Elvis Presley) (black/red dot labels, mono) (stereo SF 7767 = £25) | 20 |
| 65 | Warner Bros W 1599 | HARLOW (Neal Hefti) | 15 |
| 80s | PRT/Chips CHILP 1 | HAWK THE SLAYER (Harry Robertson) (gatefold sleeve) | 15 |
| 68 | RCA RD/SF 8051 | HEAD (Monkees) (mono/stereo) | 60 |
| 72 | Reprise K 44168 | THE HEIST (Quincy Jones/Little Richard) | 15 |
| 74 | Tamla Motown STML 11260 | HELL UP IN HARLEM (Edwin Starr) | 15 |
| 65 | Parlophone PMC 1255 | HELP! (Beatles) (1st pressing, with "The Gramophone Co. Ltd" & "Sold In The UK..." label text; mono, with "mono" in outline type on front cover) | 90 |
| 65 | Parlophone PCS 3071 | HELP! (Beatles) (1st pressing, with "The Gramophone Co. Ltd" & "Sold In The UK..." label text; stereo, with "stereo" in outline type on front cover) | 120 |
| 67 | United Artists ULP 1186 | HERE WE GO ROUND THE MULBERRY BUSH (Spencer Davis/Traffic/Andy Ellison) (mono) (stereo SULP 1186 = £35) | 40 |
| 59 | Capitol T 1160 | HEY BOY! HEY GIRL! (Louis Prima/Keely Smith, et al.) | 25 |
| 62 | Columbia 33SX 1421 | HEY, LET'S TWIST (Joey Dee, et al.) | 20 |
| 83 | A&R FILM 001 | HIGH ROAD TO CHINA (John Barry) | 15 |
| 70 | Columbia SCX 6443 | HIS LAND (Cliff Richard/Cliff Barrows) | 15 |
| 67 | United Artists ULP 1161 | THE HONEY POT (John Addison) | 15 |
| 59 | London HA-T 2197 | THE HORSE SOLDIERS (David Buttolph) | 15 |
| 59 | Philips BBL 7292 | HOUSEBOAT (George Duning) | 25 |
| 87 | Silva Screen FILM 041 | HOW TO GET AHEAD IN ADVERTISING/WITHNAIL & I | 20 |
| 65 | United Artists (S)ULP 1098 | HOW TO MURDER YOUR WIFE (Neal Hefti) | 15 |
| 72 | Atlantic K 40371 | HOW TO STEAL A DIAMOND IN FOUR UNEASY LESSONS (Quincy Jones) | 15 |
| 66 | Stateside S(S)L 10187 | HOW TO STEAL A MILLION (John Williams) | 25 |
| 67 | RCA Victor RD/SF 7877 | HURRY SUNDOWN (Hugo Montenegro) | 20 |

# I

| 70 | United Artists UAS 29044 | IF IT'S TUESDAY THIS MUST BE BELGIUM (Walter Scharf) | 15 |
| 67 | Brunswick LAT/STA 8689 | I'LL NEVER FORGET WHAT'S 'ISNAME (Francis Lai) | 50 |
| 65 | United Artists ULP 1105 | I'LL TAKE SWEDEN (Bob Hope/Frankie Avalon, et al.) | 15 |
| 68 | RCA Victor RD/SF 7931 | IN COLD BLOOD (Quincy Jones) | 20 |
| 65 | RCA RD 7707 | IN HARM'S WAY (Jerry Goldsmith) | 25 |
| 67 | Stateside S(S)L 10207 | IN LIKE FLINT (Jerry Goldsmith) | 50 |
| 68 | United Artists ULP 1201 | INSPECTOR CLOUSEAU (Ken Thorne) | 20 |
| 69 | RCA Victor RD/SF 7990 | INTERLUDE (Georges Delarue/Timi Yuro) | 15 |
| 62 | Colpix PXL 427 | THE INTERNS (Leith Stevens) | 18 |
| 67 | United Artists (S)ULP 1181 | IN THE HEAT OF THE NIGHT (Quincy Jones/Ray Charles) | 25 |
| 65 | CBS BPG 62530 | THE IPCRESS FILE (John Barry) (mono only) | 150 |
| 84 | Illuminated JAMS 35 | IN THE SHADOW OF THE SUN (Throbbing Gristle) | 20 |
| 66 | CBS (S)BPG 62843 | IS PARIS BURNING? (Maurice Jarre) | 18 |
| 69 | Paramount SPFL 256 | THE ITALIAN JOB (Quincy Jones/Matt Monro) | 75 |
| 63 | RCA Victor RD 7565 | IT HAPPENED AT THE WORLD'S FAIR (Elvis Presley) (black/silver label, mono) (stereo SF 7565 = £35) | 18 |
| 63 | Columbia 33SX 1533 | IT'S ALL HAPPENING (Tommy Steele/Shane Fenton, et al.) (also stereo SCX 3486) | 15 |
| 63 | United Artists (S)ULP 1053 | IT'S A MAD MAD MAD MAD WORLD (Ernest Gold) | 15 |
| 65 | Decca LK 4677 | I'VE GOTTA HORSE (Billy Fury/Bachelors, et al.) | 40 |
| 71 | CBS 70083 | I WALK THE LINE (Johnny Cash) | 15 |
| 07 | Trunk JBH 027 LP | IVOR THE ENGINE & POGLES WOOD (LP) | 15 |

# J

| 57 | Capitol LCT 6140 | THE JAMES DEAN STORY (Leith Stevens) | 25 |
| 54 | Brunswick LA 8671 | JAZZ THEMES FROM "THE WILD ONE" (Leith Stevens) (10") | 30 |
| 62 | HMV CLP 1582 | JESSICA (Mario Nascimbene) | 15 |
| 77 | Pye NSPH 28504 | JESUS OF NAZARETH (Maurice Jarre) (gatefold sleeve) | 15 |
| 73 | Reprise K 64017 | JIMI HENDRIX - SOUNDTRACK RECORDINGS FROM THE FILM (2-LP) | 18 |
| 71 | Mercury 6338 029 | JOE (Bobby Scott/Jenny Butler) | 20 |
| 64 | United Artists ULP 1060 | JOHNNY COOL (Billy May/Sammy Davis Jr.) | 25 |
| 72 | Reprise K 64015 | JOURNEY THROUGH THE PAST (Neil Young) (2-LP, fold-out cover with inner sleeves) | 25 |
| 77 | Polydor/EG 2302 079 | JUBILEE (Adam & Ants/Brian Eno, et al.) | 20 |
| 61 | HMV CLP 1545 | JUDGEMENT AT NUREMBURG (Ernest Gold) | 15 |
| 67 | Fontana (S)TL 5317 | JULIET OF THE SPIRITS (Nino Rota) | 30 |
| 63 | Decca LK 4524 | JUST FOR FUN (Tornados/Karl Denver, et al.) | 25 |
| 64 | Decca LK 4620 | JUST FOR YOU (Applejacks/Merseybeats, et al.) | 40 |
| 70 | Monument LMO/SMO 5031 | JUSTINE (Jerry Goldsmith) | 20 |

# K

| 71 | MGM 2315 019 | KELLY'S HEROES (Lalo Schifrin/Mike Curb) | 25 |
| 66 | United Artists (S)ULP 1139 | KHARTOUM (Frank Cordell) | 30 |
| 72 | Polydor 2383 102 | KIDNAPPED (Roy Budd/Mary Hopkin) | 25 |
| 58 | RCA RD 27088 | KING CREOLE (Elvis Presley) (black/silver labels) | 40 |
| 76 | Reprise K 54090 | KING KONG (John Barry) (with poster) | 15 |
| 61 | MGM MGM-CS 6043 | KING OF KINGS (Miklos Rozsa) | 20 |
| 58 | Capitol LCT 6165 | KINGS GO FORTH (Elmer Bernstein) | 15 |

| 66 | Fontana (S)TL 5302 | KING RAT (John Barry) | 18 |
| 64 | RCA Victor RD 7645 | KISSIN' COUSINS (Elvis Presley) (black/red dot labels, mono) (stereo SF 7645 = £30) | 18 |
| 54 | MGM MGM-C 753 | KISS ME KATE (Howard Keel, et al.) | 15 |
| 65 | United Artists ULP 1104 | THE KNACK (AND HOW TO GET IT) (John Barry) | 80 |
| 74 | Warner Bros K 46271 | KUNG FU (TV soundtrack) (with inner sleeve) (Jim Helms) | 20 |
| 01 | Trunk KES 001 LP | KES (LP - 1-sided) | 40 |

## L

| 61 | RCA RD 27202 | LA DOLCE VITA (Nino Rota) (gatefold sleeve) | 50 |
| 63 | Ace Of Hearts AH 70 | THE LADY AND THE TRAMP (Peggy Lee) | 20 |
| 69 | Stateside S(S)L 10267 | LADY IN CEMENT (Hugo Montenegro) | 40 |
| 71 | United Artists UAS 29120 | THE LANDLORD (Al Kooper) | 20 |
| 72 | MGM 2315 072 | THE LAST RUN (Jerry Goldsmith/Steve Lawrence) | 25 |
| 73 | United Artists UAS 29440 | LAST TANGO IN PARIS (Gato Barbieri) | 15 |
| 71 | Probe SPB 1027 | THE LAST VALLEY (John Barry) (mono, with insert) (stereo = £25) | 18 |
| 85 | United Artists 86002 | LEGEND (Jerry Goldsmith) | 25 |
| 74 | Warner Bros K 56085 | THE LEGEND OF THE 7 GOLDEN VAMPIRES (James Bernard/Peter Cushing) | 18 |
| 64 | Stateside S(S)L 10058 | THE LEOPARD (Nino Rota) | 30 |
| 70 | Apple PXS 1 | LET IT BE (Beatles) (LP box set, 1st pressing, dark green label, red Apple logo on LP rear sleeve & white inner, with Get Back book housed in black card tray ['PXS1'] not listed on package) | 800 |
| 70 | Apple PCS 7096 | LET IT BE (Beatles) (2nd pressing, green Apple logo on rear sleeve, plain white inner) | 40 |
| 60 | Philips BBL 7414/SBBL 592 | LET'S MAKE LOVE (Marilyn Monroe/Yves Montand/Frankie Vaughan) | 40 |
| 64 | Columbia SX 1626 | LILIES OF THE FIELD (Jerry Goldsmith) | 20 |
| 66 | MGM MGM-CS 8029 | THE LIQUIDATOR (Lalo Schifrin/Shirley Bassey) | 40 |
| 73 | United Artists UAS 29475 | LIVE AND LET DIE (George Martin/Wings) (gatefold sleeve) | 25 |
| 76 | MGM 2315 376 | LOGAN'S RUN (Jerry Goldsmith) | 20 |
| 62 | MGM MGM-C 896 | LOLITA (Nelson Riddle) | 25 |
| 67 | Polydor 583 014 | LONG DUEL (Patrick John Scott/Vince Hill) | 20 |
| 63 | Stateside S(S)L 10045 | THE LONGEST DAY (dialogue only) | 20 |
| 83 | CES CES 1001 | THE LONG GOOD FRIDAY (Francis Monkman) (numbered sleeve with insert, black label print, 2,000 only) | 50 |
| 83 | CES CES 1001 | THE LONG GOOD FRIDAY (Francis Monkman) (re-pressing, with insert, blue label print, 500 only) | 40 |
| 84 | CES CES 1001 | THE LONG GOOD FRIDAY (Francis Monkman) (3rd pressing, with insert, blue label print, 5,000 only) | 40 |
| 89 | Silva Screen FILM 020 | THE LONG GOOD FRIDAY (Francis Monkman) (reissue) | 20 |
| 89 | Silva Screen FILM 020 | THE LONG GOOD FRIDAY (Francis Monkman) (CD) | 25 |
| 70 | CBS 70073 | LOOT (Keith Mansfield/Steve Ellis) | 40 |
| 65 | Colpix PXL 521 | LORD JIM (Bronislau Kaper) | 15 |
| 69 | Uni UNLS 103 | LOST MAN (Quincy Jones) | 25 |
| 70 | CBS 70067 | LOVE CIRCLE (Ennio Morricone) | 50 |
| 57 | RCA RC 24001 | LOVING YOU (Elvis Presley) (10", silver spot label) | 90 |

## M

| 73 | Tamla Motown STMA 8003 | THE MACK (Willie Hutch) | 15 |
| 69 | Warner Bros WS 1805 | THE MADWOMAN OF CHAILLOT (Michael Lewis) | 15 |
| 70 | Pye Intl. NSPL 28133 | THE MAGIC CHRISTIAN (Ken Thorne/Badfinger, et al.) | 40 |
| 54 | Brunswick LAT 8045 | MAGNIFICENT OBSESSION (Frank Skinner) | 20 |
| 65 | MGM MGM-C 995 | THE MAGNIFICENT SHOWMAN (Dimitri Tiomkin) | 25 |
| 76 | Atlantic K 50308 | MAHONEY'S LAST STAND (Ronnie Lane & Ron Wood) | 15 |
| 63 | Ace Of Clubs ACL 1135 | MAIGRET (Ron Grainer) (TV series music) | 15 |
| 66 | CBS SBPG 62525 | MAJOR DUNDEE (Daniele Amfitheatrof/Mitch Miller) | 15 |
| 11 | Finders Keepers FKRO40LP | MALA MORSKA (ZDENEK LISKA) (foil/red wax edition) | 30 |
| 59 | Top Rank 35/043 | MAN FROM INTERPOL (Tony Crombie) (TV series music) | 25 |
| 66 | RCA Victor RD 7758 | THE MAN FROM U.N.C.L.E. (Hugo Montenegro) | 40 |
| 13 | Death Waltz DW 014 | MANIAC (flesh coloured vinyl) | 20 |
| 13 | Death Waltz DW 014 | MANIAC (silver vinyl) | 30 |
| 64 | Stateside S(S)L 10087 | MAN IN THE MIDDLE (Lionel Bart & John Barry) | 30 |
| 56 | Brunswick LAT 8101 | THE MAN WITH THE GOLDEN ARM (Elmer Bernstein) | 20 |
| 74 | United Artists UAS 29671 | THE MAN WITH THE GOLDEN GUN (John Barry/Lulu) | 15 |
| 63 | Stateside S(S)L 10048 | MARILYN (Marilyn Monroe) (mono/stereo) | 40 |
| 72 | MCA MUPS 441 | MARY QUEEN OF SCOTS (John Barry) | 20 |
| 70 | United Artists UAS 29122 | MASTER OF THE ISLANDS (Henry Mancini) | 15 |
| 69 | Philips SBL 7876 | MAYERLING (Francis Lai) | 20 |
| 64 | United Artists SULP 1059 | McLINTOCK (Frank De Vol) | 35 |
| 80 | Polydor POLD 5034 | McVICAR (Roger Daltrey) (some on clear vinyl) | 15 |
| 71 | Polydor 2383 043 | MELODY (Bee Gees, Richard Hewson, et al.) | 15 |
| 57 | London HA-P 2076 | MEN IN WAR (Elmer Bernstein) | 15 |
| 69 | Bell BELL 6053 | MERRY CHRISTMAS (David Frost/Billy Taylor) | 20 |
| 65 | MGM MGM-C 8001 | MICKEY ONE (Stan Getz & Eddie Sauter) (with booklet, mono) (stereo MGM-CS 8001 = £25) | 20 |
| 66 | Mercury 20072 (S)MCL | MIRAGE (Quincy Jones) | 25 |
| 61 | HMV CLP 1481 | THE MISFITS (Alex North) | 25 |
| 68 | Dot (S)LPD 503 | MISSION: IMPOSSIBLE - MUSIC FROM THE TV SERIES (Lalo Schifrin) | 40 |
| 54 | Mercury 25181 | MISS SADIE THOMPSON (George Duning) (10") | 30 |
| 66 | Fontana TL 5347 | MODESTY BLAISE (Johnny Dankworth) | 40 |
| 70 | Paramount SPFL 259 | THE MOLLY MAGUIRES (Henry Mancini) | 15 |
| 80 | BBC REB 384 | MONKEY (Godiego) (TV soundtrack) | 25 |
| 69 | Paramount SPFL 255 | MONTE CARLO OR BUST! (Ron Goodwin) | 25 |
| 79 | United Artists UAG 30247 | MOONRAKER (John Barry/Shirley Bassey) | 15 |

| | | | |
|---|---|---|---|
| 69 | Columbia SCX 6346 | MORE (Pink Floyd) (laminated flipback sleeve, 'couple facing west' photo on green-tinted rear sleeve) | 70 |
| 70s | Columbia SCX 6346 | MORE (Pink Floyd) (laminated non-flipback sleeve, 'couple facing west' photo on black-tinted rear sleeve) | 45 |
| 70s | Columbia SCX 6346 | MORE (Pink Floyd) (laminated non-flipback sleeve, 'couple facing east' photo on black-tinted rear sleeve) | 50 |
| 69 | Paramount SPFL 252 | MORE 'MISSION: IMPOSSIBLE' (Lalo Schifrin) | 40 |
| 60 | MGM MGM-C(S) 857 | MORE MUSIC FROM BEN-HUR (Miklos Rozsa) | 15 |
| 66 | RCA Victor RD 7832 | MORE MUSIC FROM 'THE MAN FROM U.N.C.L.E.' (Hugo Montenegro) | 45 |
| 62 | MGM | MORE MUSIC FROM 'MUTINY ON THE BOUNTY' (Bronislau Kaper) | 20 |
| 68 | MGM CS8063 | MORE THAN A MIRACLE (Piero Piccioni) | 15 |
| 67 | RCA RD 7847 | MURDERERS' ROW (Lalo Schifrin) | 50 |
| 80 | Unicorn Kachana KPM 7009 | MUSIC FROM THE AVENGERS, THE NEW AVENGERS AND THE PROFESSIONALS | 20 |
| 70 | Harvest SHSP 4008 | MUSIC FROM THE BODY (Ron Geesin & Roger Waters) (photos/green labels) | 50 |
| 62 | MGM MGM-CS 6060 | MUTINY ON THE BOUNTY (Bronislau Kaper) | 20 |
| 85 | Cloud Nine CN 4002 | MYSTERIOUS ISLAND (Bernard Herrman) | 15 |

## N

| | | | |
|---|---|---|---|
| 70 | United Artists UAS 29108 | NED KELLY (Shel Silverstein/Mick Jagger/Waylon Jennings) | 35 |
| 72 | Bell BELLS 202 | NICHOLAS AND ALEXANDRA (Richard Rodney Bennet) | 15 |
| 67 | RCA RD 7848 | NIGHT OF THE GENERALS (Maurice Jarre) | 30 |
| 65 | MGM MGM-C 994 | NIGHT OF THE IGUANA (Benjamin Frankel) | 15 |
| 69 | United Artists (S)ULP 1235 | THE NIGHT THEY RAIDED MINSKY'S (Charles Strouse) | 20 |
| 62 | Decca LK 4527 | NINE HOURS TO RAMA (Malcolm Arnold) | 50 |
| 68 | Dot (S)LPD 507 | NO WAY TO TREAT A LADY (American Breed) | 20 |

## O

| | | | |
|---|---|---|---|
| 72 | Harvest SHSP 4020 | OBSCURED BY CLOUDS (Pink Floyd) (rounded sleeve) | 50 |
| 76 | Phase 4 Stereo PF5 4381 | OBSESSION (Bernard Herrman) | 15 |
| 83 | A&M 394 967-2 | OCTOPUSSY (John Barry) (CD, withdrawn) | 75 |
| 68 | Dot (S)LPD 514 | THE ODD COUPLE (Neal Hefti) | 15 |
| 60 | London HA-T 2220 | ODDS AGAINST TOMORROW (John Lewis) | 20 |
| 57 | Brunswick LAT 8226 | OMAR KHAYYAM/THE MOUNTAIN (Victor Young/Daniele Amfitheatrof) | 30 |
| 75 | Fantasy FTA 3004 | ONE FLEW OVER THE CUCKOO'S NEST (Jack Nitzsche) (gatefold sleeve) | 15 |
| 69 | United Artists UAS 29020 | ON HER MAJESTY'S SECRET SERVICE (John Barry) (foldout sleeve) | 40 |
| 70 | Fontana SFJL 950 | ORFEU NEGRO (BLACK ORPHEUS) (Luis Bonfa/Antonio Carlos Jobim) | 15 |
| 69 | RCA SF 8014 | OTLEY (Stanley Myers/Don Partridge) | 25 |
| 66 | Stateside S(S)L 10174 | OUR MAN FLINT (Jerry Goldsmith) | 50 |
| 76 | Warner Bros K 56286 | THE OUTLAW JOSEY WALES (Jerry Fielding) | 25 |

## P

| | | | |
|---|---|---|---|
| 63 | Warner Bros WM 8141 | PALM SPRINGS WEEKEND (Frank Perkins) | 20 |
| 66 | RCA Victor SF 7810 | PARADISE, HAWAIIAN STYLE (Elvis Presley) (black/red dot labels, mono) (stereo SF 7810 = £30) | 20 |
| 61 | HMV CLP 1499 | PARIS BLUES (Duke Ellington) | 15 |
| 61 | Warner Bros WS 8044 | PARRISH (Max Steiner/George Creely) | 20 |
| 65 | Mercury 20063 SML | THE PAWNBROKER (Quincy Jones) | 30 |
| 66 | Philips (S)BL 7782 | THE PEKING MEDALLION (Georges Garvarentz/Dusty Springfield) | 20 |
| 67 | Ember NR 5040 | THE PENTHOUSE (John Hawksworth) | 40 |
| 71 | Pye NSPL 18365 | PERCY (Kinks) | 40 |
| 70 | Warner Bros WS 2554 | PERFORMANCE (First pressing, orange label, Mick Jagger/Jack Nitzsche/Randy Newman, et al. ) | 40 |
| 70 | Warner Bros WS 2554 | PERFORMANCE (Second pressing, green label, Mick Jagger/Jack Nitzsche/Randy Newman, et al. ) | 35 |
| 59 | RCA RD 27123/SF 5033 | PETER GUNN (Henry Mancini) | 15 |
| 79 | Gem GEM 102 | PHANTASM (Fred Myrow & Malcolm Seagrave) | 60 |
| 56 | Brunswick LAT 8120 | PICNIC (George Duning) | 20 |
| 68 | Philips SBL 7858 | PLAYTIME (Jacques Tati, Yan Tatore, Leo Petit) | 35 |
| 70 | Paramount SPFL 258 | POOKIE (Fred Karlin/Sandpipers) | 15 |
| 57 | Capitol LCT 6141 | THE PRIDE AND THE PASSION (Georges Antheil) | 15 |
| 86 | Bam Caruso WEBA 066 | THE PRISONER (Ron Grainer, et al.) (fan club issue, gatefold sleeve with inner sleeve, booklet, membership form, map & poster) | 40 |
| 67 | HMV CLP/CSD 3623 | PRIVILEGE (Paul Jones & Mike Leander) | 40 |
| 69 | RCA SF 8072 | THE PRODUCERS (John Morris) | 15 |
| 69 | United Artists UAS 29005 | A PROFESSIONAL GUN (Ennio Morricone) | 25 |
| 67 | RCA Victor RD/SF 7876 | THE PROFESSIONALS (Maurice Jarre) | 50 |
| 60 | Contemporary LAC 12293 | THE PROPER TIME (Shelly Manne) | 20 |
| 68 | Stateside S(S)L 10248 | PRUDENCE AND THE PILL (Bernard Ebbinghouse) | 25 |
| 75 | Unicorn RHS 336 | PSYCHO (Bernard Herrmann) | 20 |
| 03 | Trunk JBH002LP | PSYCHOMANIA | 60 |

## Q

| | | | |
|---|---|---|---|
| 71 | Sonet SNTF 622 | QUIET DAYS IN CLICHY (Country Joe McDonald) | 15 |
| 66 | CBS (S)BPG 62869 | THE QUILLER MEMORANDUM (John Barry/Matt Monro) (mono/stereo) | 25 |

## R

| | | | |
|---|---|---|---|
| 71 | Reprise K 44159 | RAINBOW BRIDGE (Jimi Hendrix) (matt gatefold sleeve, 'steamboat' label) | 20 |
| 75 | Dart ARTS 65376 | RANSOM (Jerry Goldsmith) | 40 |
| 60 | London HAD 2288 | THE RAT RACE (Sam Butera & The Witnesses) | 25 |
| 67 | United Artists (S)ULP 1184 | RED AND BLUE (Vanessa Redgrave) | 40 |
| 72 | Paramount SPFL 275 | THE RED TENT (Ennio Morricone) | 15 |

| Year | Label/Cat No | Title | Value £ |
|---|---|---|---|
| 75 | RCA Red Seal RS 1010 | THE RETURN OF THE PINK PANTHER (Henry Mancini) | 15 |
| 69 | United Artists ULP 29069 | REVOLUTION (Quicksilver Messenger Service/Steve Miller, et al.) | 20 |
| 70 | United Artists UAS 29137 | RIDER IN THE RAIN (Francis Lai) | 25 |
| 68 | MGM MGM-C(S) 8079 | THE RISE AND FALL OF THE THIRD REICH (Lalo Schifrin) | 20 |
| 53 | Brunswick LA 8578 | ROAD TO BALI (Bob Hope, Bing Crosby) (10") | 30 |
| 62 | Decca LKR 4427 | THE ROAD TO HONG KONG (Robert Farnon/Bob Hope & Bing Crosby) | 20 |
| 54 | Brunswick LAT 8031 | THE ROBE | 15 |
| 67 | Decca LK/SKL 4892 | ROBBERY (Johnny Keating/Jackie Lee) | 30 |
| 64 | Reprise R 2021 | ROBIN AND THE SEVEN HOODS (Nelson Riddle) | 20 |
| 61 | RCA RD 27233 | ROCCO AND HIS BROTHERS (Nino Rota) | 20 |
| 57 | Mercury MPT 7527 | ROCK ALL NIGHT (Platters, Norah Hayes, et al.) (10") | 175 |
| 67 | Polydor 583 013 | JULES VERNE'S ROCKET TO THE MOON (John Scott) | 100 |
| 57 | Brunswick LAT 8162 | ROCK, PRETTY BABY (Henry Mancini/Rod McKuen) | 80 |
| 87 | Ode RHVX 1 | ROCKY HORROR BOX SET (Richard O'Brien) (4-LP box, with inserts, numbered) | 20 |
| 87 | Ode RHBXLP 1 | ROCKY HORROR BOX SET (Richard O'Brien) (4-LP box, with different inserts to above) | 20 |
| 83 | Ode OSVP 78332 | THE ROCKY HORROR PICTURE SHOW ALBUM (picture disc) | 15 |
| 90 | Ode RHBXCD 1 | THE ROCKY HORROR PICTURE SHOW - 15TH ANNIVERSARY (Richard O'Brien, et al.) (4-CD box) | 40 |
| 68 | Dot (S)LPD 519 | ROSEMARY'S BABY (Kryzstophe Komeda) | 50 |
| 65 | Parlophone PMC 1262 | ROTTEN TO THE CORE (New Jazz Voices) | 20 |
| 64 | RCA Victor RD 7678 | ROUSTABOUT (Elvis Presley) (black/red dot labels, mono) (stereo SF 7678 = £25) | 15 |
| 64 | Capitol (S)T 1771 | ROUTE 66 AND OTHER GREAT T.V. THEMES (Nelson Riddle) (TV show) | 15 |
| 66 | United Artists ULP 1147 | THE RUSSIANS ARE COMING THE RUSSIANS ARE COMING (Johnny Mandel) | 15 |

## S

| Year | Label/Cat No | Title | Value £ |
|---|---|---|---|
| 72 | RCA SF 8211 | SACCO AND VANZETTI (Ennio Morricone/Joan Baez) | 20 |
| 53 | Brunswick LA 8604 | SALOMÉ (George Duning) (10") | 30 |
| 68 | United Artists SULP 1202 | SALT AND PEPPER (Johnny Dankworth/Sammy Davis Jr) | 15 |
| 65 | Mercury MCL 20065 | THE SANDPIPER (Johnny Mandel) | 15 |
| 78 | Polydor 2480 429 | SCOUSE THE MOUSE (Ringo Starr/Adam Faith, et al.) (some w/stickered sleeve & printed [not photocopied] competition insert) | 100 |
| 78 | Polydor 3194 429 | SCOUSE THE MOUSE (Ringo Starr/Adam Faith, et al.) (cassette) | 30 |
| 62 | Reprise R 2013 | SERGEANTS 3 (Billy May) | 20 |
| 73 | Paramount SPFL 296 | SERPICO (Mikis Theodorakis) | 26 |
| 64 | United Artists ULP 1072 | THE 7th DAWN (Riz Ortolani) | 15 |
| 74 | United Artists UAS 29763 | THE SEVENTH VOYAGE OF SINBAD (Bernard Hermann) | 20 |
| 72 | Probe SPB 1077 | SHAFT IN AFRICA (Johnny Pate/Four Tops) | 40 |
| 72 | MGM 2315 115 | SHAFT'S BIG SCORE! (Gordon Parks/O.C. Smith/Isaac Hayes) | 35 |
| 66 | CBS BPG 62755 | SHAKESPEARE WALLAH (Satyajit Ray) | 15 |
| 68 | Philips SBL 7867 | SHALAKO (Robert Farnon) | 15 |
| 80 | Warner Bros K 56827 | THE SHINING (Bela Bartok et al.) | 25 |
| 12 | Trunk RSD 001 | THE SHUTTERED ROOM (25 copies only, stamped white labels, inserts, stamped white sleeve) | 200 |
| 12 | Trunk RSD 001 | THE SHUTTERED ROOM (25 copies only, stamped white labels, inserts, screenprinted brown sleeve) | 300 |
| 70 | Stateside SSL 10307 | THE SICILIAN CLAN (Ennio Morricone) | 40 |
| 12 | Rook RFV 001 | SIGHTSEERS SESSIONS (45rpm red vinyl LP, poster, 150 only) | 100 |
| 72 | MCA MUPS 458 | SILENT RUNNING (Pete Schikele/Joan Baez) | 20 |
| 66 | RCA RD 7792 | THE SILENCERS (Elmer Bernstein/Vikki Carr) | 30 |
| 58 | Capitol T 929 | SING, BOY, SING (Tommy Sands) | 50 |
| 66 | MGM MGM-C(S) 8011 | THE SINGING NUN (Debbie Reynolds) | 15 |
| 78 | Charisma CAS 1139 | SIR HENRY AT RAWLINSON END (Vivian Stanshall) (with insert) | 20 |
| 64 | United Artists ULP 1071 | 633 SQUADRON (Ron Goodwin) | 20 |
| 69 | RCA SF 8010 | SKIDOO (Nilsson) | 20 |
| 73 | Polydor 2391 084 | SLAUGHTER'S BIG RIP-OFF (James Brown) | 30 |
| 66 | Mercury MCL 20080 | THE SLENDER THREAD (Quincy Jones) | 20 |
| 69 | NEMS 6-70059 | THE SMASHING BIRD I USED TO KNOW (Bobby Richards) | 20 |
| 68 | Stateside S(S)L 10224 | SMASHING TIME (John Addison) | 30 |
| 73 | PRT FBLP 8085 | SMIKE | 15 |
| 56 | Pye Disneyland DPL 39003 | SNOW WHITE AND THE SEVEN DWARFS (Disney Orchestra) | 30 |
| 70 | Pye NSPL 18348 | SOLDIER BLUE AND OTHER THEMES (Roy Budd) | 40 |
| 60 | London HA-T 2221 | SOLOMON AND SHEBA (Mario Nascimbene) | 75 |
| 59 | Capitol LCT 6180 | SOME CAME RUNNING (Elmer Bernstein) | 15 |
| 59 | London HA-T 2176 | SOME LIKE IT HOT (Marilyn Monroe) (also stereo SAH-T 6040 = £60) | 50 |
| 67 | RCA RD 7845 | SONGS FROM THE SWINGER (Marty Paich/Ann-Margret) | 30 |
| 74 | Rapple/RCA APL1-0220 | SON OF DRACULA (Ringo Starr/Harry Nilsson, fold-out sleeve) | 15 |
| 69 | RCA Victor SF 8024 | THE SOUTHERN STAR (Matt Monro/Georges Garvarentz) | 15 |
| 58 | London HA-D 2079 | SPANISH AFFAIR (Daniele Amfitheatrof) | 20 |
| 61 | Brunswick LAT 8363 | SPARTACUS (Alex North) (gatefold sleeve) | 20 |
| 68 | RCA Victor SF 7957 | SPEEDWAY (Elvis Presley/Nancy Sinatra) (black/red dot labels, mono) (stereo SF 7957 = £25) | 30 |
| 53 | Capitol CCL 7505 | SPELLBOUND/THE RED HOUSE (Miklos Rozsa) (10") | 25 |
| 66 | RCA RD 7787 | THE SPY WHO CAME IN FROM THE COLD (Sol Kaplan) | 20 |
| 68 | CBS 62919 | THE SPY WITH THE COLD NOSE (Riz Ortolani) | 35 |
| 66 | Fontana TL 5354 | STAGECOACH (Jerry Goldsmith) | 25 |
| 77 | 20th C. BTD 541 | STAR WARS (John Williams) (2-LP, with insert and poster) | 20 |
| 69 | CBS 70062 | STILETTO (Sid Ramin) | 30 |
| 52 | Capitol LC 6542 | A STREET CAR NAMED DESIRE (Alex North) (10") | 35 |
| 63 | Elstree Extra Range | SUMMER HOLIDAY (2-LP, full soundtrack recording, 80 copies only) | 250 |
| 63 | Columbia SCX 3462 | SUMMER HOLIDAY (Cliff Richard) (first pressing, stereo, with inner sleeve, with green labels) | 25 |

MINT VALUE £

| | | | |
|---|---|---|---|
| 57 | London HA-R 2077 | THE SUN ALSO RISES (Hugo Friedhofer) | 25 |
| 55 | HMV DLP 1104 | SUN VALLEY SERENADE (Glenn Miller) | 15 |
| 62 | Golden Guinea GGL 0106 | SUPERCAR - FLIGHT OF FANCY (Barry Gray/Edwin Astley) | 50 |
| 72 | Buddah 2318 065 | SUPERFLY (Curtis Mayfield) (gatefold sleeve) | 15 |
| 73 | Buddah 2318 087 | SUPER FLY T.N.T. (Osibisa) | 15 |
| 64 | Stateside SL 10089 | SURF PARTY (Astronauts, Routers, et al.) | 50 |
| 79 | EMI EMC 3222 | SUSPIRIA (Goblin) | 40 |
| 57 | Brunswick LAT 8195 | SWEET SMELL OF SUCCESS (Elmer Bernstein) | 20 |
| 68 | Stateside S(S)L 10250 | THE SWEET RIDE (Pete Rugolo/Dusty Springfield) | 15 |
| 68 | CBS 70043 | THE SWIMMER (Marvin Hamlisch) | 25 |
| 65 | MGM MGM-C 8012 | THE SWINGIN' SET (Dave Clark Five/Animals, et al.) | 30 |
| 66 | Mercury 20057 SMCL | SYLVIA (David Raksin) | 15 |

## T

| | | | |
|---|---|---|---|
| 70 | Pye NSPL 18353 | TAKE A GIRL LIKE YOU (Stanley Myers/Foundations) | 30 |
| 57 | Vogue Coral LVA 9070 | TAMMY/INTERLUDE (Frank Skinner/Debbie Reynolds) (1 film per side) | 30 |
| 63 | United Artists ULP 1025 | TARAS BULBA (Franz Waxman) | 25 |
| 76 | Arista ARTY 132 | TAXI DRIVER (Bernard Herrman) | 30 |
| 71 | RCA Victor SF 8162 | THAT'S THE WAY IT IS (Elvis Presley) (glossy or matt sleeve) | 15 |
| 63 | Parlophone PMC 1197 | THAT WAS THE WEEK THAT WAS (Millicent Martin, et al.) (also stereo PCS 3040) | 15 |
| 00 | Cinephile CINLP004 | THE BLACK WINDMILL (LP, gatefold) | 30 |
| 59 | Coral LVA 9102 | THEMES FROM HORROR MOVIES (Dick Jacobs) | 15 |
| 70 | United Artists UAS 29128 | THEY CALL ME MISTER TIBBS (Quincy Jones) | 60 |
| 69 | Philips SBL 7898 | THEY CAME TO ROB LAS VEGAS (Georges Gavarentz) | 40 |
| 70 | Stateside SSL 10305 | THEY SHOOT HORSES, DON'T THEY? (John Green) | 15 |
| 73 | Elektra K 46239 | THE THIEF WHO CAME TO DINNER (Henry Mancini) | 15 |
| 82 | MCA MCF 3148 | THE THING (Ennio Morricone) | 30 |
| 66 | Verve VLP 9147 | THIS PROPERTY IS CONDEMNED (Kenyon Hopkins) | 35 |
| 68 | United Artists SULP 1218 | THE THOMAS CROWN AFFAIR (Michel Legrand/Noel Harrison) | 35 |
| 70 | Sunset SLS 50519 | THE THOMAS CROWN AFFAIR (Michel Legrand, reissue) | 20 |
| 65 | Stateside SL 10136 | THOSE MAGNIFICENT MEN IN THEIR FLYING MACHINES (Ron Goodwin) | 20 |
| 54 | Capitol LC 6665 | THREE SAILORS AND A GIRL (Gordon MacRae, et al.) (10") | 30 |
| 61 | Golden Guinea GGL 0065 | THREE WORLDS OF GULLIVER (Bernard Herrmann) | 20 |
| 85 | Cloud Nine CN 4003 | THREE WORLDS OF GULLIVER (Bernard Herrmann) (reissue) | 15 |
| 65 | United Artists (S)ULP 1110 | THUNDERBALL (John Barry) (mono/stereo) | 15 |
| 67 | United Artists (S)ULP 1159 | THUNDERBIRDS ARE GO! (Barry Gray/Cliff Richard & Shadows) (mono) (stereo = £120) | 100 |
| 66 | NPL 18154 | TILL DEATH US DO PART (Warren Mitchell et al.) | 15 |
| 69 | Polydor 583 717 | TILL DEATH DO US PART (Wilfred Burns) | 15 |
| 63 | MGM MGM-C 934 | TO KILL A MOCKINGBIRD (Elmer Bernstein) | 20 |
| 59 | MGM MGM-C 772 | TOM THUMB (Russ Tamblyn) | 15 |
| 68 | Instant INLP 002 | TONITE LET'S ALL MAKE LOVE IN LONDON (Pink Floyd/Chris Farlowe, et al.) | 100 |
| 70 | RCA LSA 3008 | TOOMORROW (with insert) | 80 |
| 67 | Fontana (S)TL 5446 | TO SIR, WITH LOVE (Ron Grainer/ Lulu/Mindbenders) | 35 |
| 69 | Stateside S(S)L 10271 | THE TOUCHABLES (Ken Thorne/Nirvana/Wynder K. Frog, et al.) | 35 |
| 66 | Polydor 582 004 | THE TRAP (Ron Goodwin) | 40 |
| 96 | EMI EMC 3789 | TRAINSPOTTING (2-LP) | 80 |
| 67 | United Artists ULP 1176 | TRIPLE CROSS (Georges Garvarentz/Tony Allen) | 25 |
| 82 | CBS 70223 | TRON (Wendy Carlos/Journey) | 15 |
| 73 | T. Motown STML 11225 | TROUBLE MAN (Marvin Gaye) | 20 |
| 69 | Polydor 583 728 | TWISTED NERVE/LES BICYCLETTES DE BELSIZE (Les Reed/Barry Mason, Bernard Herman) | 80 |
| 69 | Columbia S(C)X 6330 | TWO CITIES (Jeff Wayne) | 30 |
| 67 | RCA RD/SF 7891 | TWO FOR THE ROAD (Henry Mancini) | 15 |
| 63 | United Artists ULP 1027 | TWO FOR THE SEESAW (André Previn) | 15 |
| 71 | United Artists UDF 50003 | 200 MOTELS (Frank Zappa) (2-LP, with booklet & poster) | 35 |
| 70 | MCA MKPS 2013 | TWO MULES FOR SISTER SARA (Ennio Morricone) | 30 |
| 62 | Columbia 33SX 1482 | TWO TICKETS TO PARIS (Joey Dee) | 20 |
| 06 | Trunk JBH 017 LP | THE TOMORROW PEOPLE (LP) | 40 |

## U

| | | | |
|---|---|---|---|
| 04 | Trunk JBHO10LP | UFO (500 black/500 clear vinyl) | 50 |
| 60 | London HA-T 2258 | THE UNFORGIVEN (Dimitri Tiomkin) | 18 |
| 68 | Fontana (S)TL 5460 | UP THE JUNCTION (Manfred Mann) | 50 |
| 70 | Fontana 6852 005 | UP THE JUNCTION (Manfred Mann) (reissue) | 25 |
| 69 | Stax (S)XATS 1005 | UPTIGHT (Booker T & MGs) | 15 |

## V

| | | | |
|---|---|---|---|
| 73 | Philips 6303 075 | THE VALACHI PAPERS (Riz Ortolani) | 25 |
| 11 | Finders Keepers FKRO48LP | VALERIE AND HER WEEK OF WONDERS (lubos Fiser) | 20 |
| 68 | Stateside (S)SL 10228 | VALLEY OF THE DOLLS (André Previn/John Williams) | 20 |
| 71 | London SH-U 8420 | VANISHING POINT (Delaney & Bonnie/Sam & Dave, et al.) | 20 |
| 82 | MGM 2315 437 | VICTOR, VICTORIA (Henry Mancini) | 15 |
| 63 | Colpix PXL 516 | THE VICTORS (Sol Kaplan/Frank Sinatra) | 15 |
| 58 | London HAT 2118 | THE VIKINGS (Mario Nascimbene) | 40 |
| 68 | Dot (S)LPD 515 | VILLA RIDES (Maurice Jarre) | 15 |
| 63 | MGM MGM-C 951/CS 6074 | THE VIPs (Miklos Rozsa) | 20 |
| 66 | United Artists (S)ULP 1126 | VIVA MARIA! (Georges Delerue) (mono/stereo) | 30 |

| | | |
|---|---|---|
| 60 | Mercury MMC 14033 | WAGON TRAIN (Stanley Wilson, et al.) ...... 25 |
| 62 | MGM MGM-C 891 | WALK ON THE WILD SIDE (Elmer Bernstein) ...... 15 |
| 66 | Brunswick STA 8636 | THE WAR LORD (Jerome Moross) ...... 35 |
| 78 | Satril SATL 4009 | THE WATER MARGIN (Godiego) (TV soundtrack) ...... 20 |
| 67 | Virtuoso TPLS 13010 | WELLES RAISES KANE (Bernard Herrman) ...... 30 |
| 64 | Piccadilly N(S)PL 38011 | WHAT A CRAZY WORLD (Joe Brown/Susan Maughan/Marty Wilde; mono/stereo)...... 22 |
| 66 | RCA SF 7818 | WHAT DID YOU DO IN THE WAR, DADDY? (Henry Mancini) ...... 15 |
| 65 | United Artists ULP 1096 | WHAT'S NEW PUSSYCAT? (Burt Bacharach/Tom Jones/Manfred Mann, et al.) ...... 20 |
| 66 | MGM MGM-C(S) 8006 | WHEN THE BOYS MEET THE GIRLS (Connie Francis/Herman's Hermits) (mono/stereo) . 15 |
| 69 | MGM MGM-C(S) 8102 | WHERE EAGLES DARE (Ron Goodwin)...... 20 |
| 66 | United Artists (S)ULP 1166 | WHIPLASH WILLIE (André Previn) ...... 15 |
| 67 | United Artists (S)ULP 1168 | THE WHISPERERS (John Barry) ...... 40 |
| 67 | Warner Bros W 1656 | WHO'S AFRAID OF VIRGINIA WOOLF? (Alex North) ...... 25 |
| 98 | Trunk BARKED 4 | THE WICKER MAN (Giovanni) (2nd pressing, red vinyl with inserts)...... 60 |
| 90 | London 845128 | WILD AT HEART ...... 20 |
| 57 | London HA-N 2023 | WILD BILL HICKOCK AND JINGLES ON THE SANTA FE TRAIL (TV s/track) ...... 18 |
| 69 | Warner Bros WS 1814 | THE WILD BUNCH (Jerry Fielding) (orange label original) ...... 25 |
| 71 | Warner Bros K 46035 | THE WILD BUNCH (Jerry Fielding) (reissue) ...... 15 |
| 78 | A&M AMLH 64730 | THE WILD GEESE (Roy Budd/Joan Armatrading) ...... 15 |
| 68 | Capitol (S)T 5099 | WILD IN THE STREETS (Les Baxter/Gurus) (original issue, black label, rainbow rim) ...... 25 |
| 71 | MGM 2315 062 | WILD ROVERS (Jerry Goldsmith) ...... 20 |
| 83 | Chrysalis CHR 1453 | WILD STYLE (various artists) ...... 20 |
| 71 | Paramount SPFL 274 | WILLY WONKA AND THE CHOCOLATE FACTORY (Leslie Bricusse) ...... 25 |
| 75 | Arista ARTY 111 | THE WIND AND THE LION (Jerry Goldsmith) ...... 15 |
| 87 | Filmtrax MOMENT 110 | WITHNAIL AND I (David Dundas) ...... 30 |
| 57 | MGM MGM-C 757 | THE WIZARD OF OZ (Judy Garland, et al.) ...... 40 |
| 67 | Capitol (S)T 2800 | WOMAN TIMES SEVEN (Riz Ortolani) ...... 18 |
| 64 | Elstree Extra Range | WONDERFUL LIFE (2-LP, full soundtrack recording, 150 copies only) ...... 150 |
| 68 | Apple (S)APCOR 1 | WONDERWALL MUSIC (George Harrison) (with insert & black inner sleeve, mono/stereo) ...... 250 |
| 70 | Atlantic 2663 001 | WOODSTOCK (Jimi Hendrix/Who/Joe Cocker, et al.) (3-LP in foldout sleeve with inners) ...... 18 |
| 60 | RCA RD 27198 | THE WORLD OF SUZIE WONG (George Duning) ...... 15 |
| 57 | Brunswick LAT 8174 | WRITTEN ON THE WIND/FOUR GIRLS IN TOWN (Frank Skinner) ...... 25 |
| 98 | Trunk BARKED 4 | THE WICKER MAN (Giovanni) (1 st pressing, black vinyl)...... 60 |

# Y

| | | |
|---|---|---|
| 69 | Apple PMC 7070 | YELLOW SUBMARINE (Beatles) (1st pressing, laminated flipback sleeve with red lines above & below rear liner note & black inner; with "Sold In The UK..." label text, mono) ...... 225 |
| 69 | Apple PCS 7070 | YELLOW SUBMARINE (Beatles) (1st pressing, laminated flipback sleeve with red lines above & below rear liner note & black inner; with "Sold In The UK..." label text, stereo) ...... 80 |
| 69 | CBS (S) 70045 | YOU ARE WHAT YOU EAT (Tiny Tim/Electric Flag, et al.)...... 18 |
| 79 | MCA MCF 2804 | YOUNGBLOOD (War) ...... 15 |
| 66 | Philips (S)BL 7792 | YOUNG GIRLS OF ROCHEFORT (Michel Legrand) ...... 25 |
| 57 | Brunswick LAT 8252 | THE YOUNG LIONS (Hugo Friedhofer) ...... 35 |
| 61 | Columbia 33SX 1384 | THE YOUNG ONES (Cliff Richard) (with inner sleeve, also stereo SCX 3397 = £30)...... 15 |
| 67 | United Artists (S)ULP 1171 | YOU ONLY LIVE TWICE (John Barry/Nancy Sinatra) ...... 15 |
| 65 | MGM MGM-CS 6081 | YOUR CHEATIN' HEART (Hank Williams Jr.) ...... 15 |
| 67 | Kama Sutra KLP 402 | YOU'RE A BIG BOY NOW (Lovin' Spoonful)...... 18 |

# Z

| | | |
|---|---|---|
| 70 | MGM MGM CS 8120 | ZABRISKIE POINT (Pink Floyd/Jerry Garcia/Kaleidoscope, et al.)...... 30 |
| 69 | Philips 600-287 | ZITA...... 40 |
| 12 | Death Waltz DW001 | ZOMBIE 2 (clear splatter vinyl) ...... 25 |
| 12 | Death Waltz DW001 | ZOMBIE 2 (red vinyl) ...... 15 |
| 64 | Ember NR 5012 | ZULU (John Barry) (yellow/orange label, flipback sleeve) ...... 20 |

MINT VALUE £

## ORIGINAL STAGE SHOW & RADIO CAST RECORDING LPs
### A-Z

| | | | |
|---|---|---|---:|
| 59 | Decca SKL 4136 | BELLE - OR THE BALLAD OF DOCTOR CRIPPEN | 15 |
| 65 | Parlophone PMC 1238 | BEYOND OUR KEN | 15 |
| 56 | HMV CLP 1064 | BUCCANEER (Kenneth Williams) | 30 |
| 61 | HMV CSD 1366 | BYE BYE BIRDIE (Studio cast including Sid James) | 35 |
| 60s | Encore | CAN CAN | 30 |
| 65 | Pye N(S)PL 18408 | THE CARD | 30 |
| 67 | Columbia S(C)X 6103 | CINDERELLA (Cliff Richard/Shadows) | 20 |
| 66 | Decca LK/SKL 4810 | COME SPY WITH ME (Barbara Windsor) | 20 |
| 56 | HMV CLP 1082 | CRANKS (Anthony Newley) | 20 |
| 60 | HMV CLP 1375 | NEW CRANKS (Bernard Cribbins) | 20 |
| 70 | CBS 70063 | DAMES AT SEA | 18 |
| 58 | Pye NPL 18016 | EXPRESSO BONGO (Millicent Martin) | 20 |
| 63 | HMV CLP 1685 | A FUNNY THING HAPPENED ON THE WAY TO THE FORUM (Frankie Howerd) | 18 |
| 57 | Oriole MG 20014 | HARMONY CLOSE (Bernard Cribbins) | 18 |
| 64 | Pye NPL 18100/NSPL 83022 | HIGH SPIRITS | 15 |
| 64 | Oriole PS 40062 | INSTANT MARRIAGE | 25 |
| 75 | MCA MCF 2726 | JEEVES | 40 |
| 74 | RSO 2394 141 | JOHN, PAUL, GEORGE, RINGO AND BERT (with London cast) | 20 |
| 58 | Decca LK 4352 | JOHNNY THE PRIEST | 30 |
| 61 | HMV CLP 1459/CSD 1370 | OLIVER! (mono/stereo) (Alma Cogan) | 40 |
| 61 | Decca LK 4393/SKL 4133 | ONE OVER THE EIGHT (mono/stereo) (Kenneth Williams) | 20 |
| 63 | CBS 60005 | ON THE TOWN | 15 |
| 63 | Parlophone PMC 1198 | PETER COOK PRESENTS THE ESTABLISHMENT | 15 |
| 69 | Philips SBL 7916 | PHIL THE FLUTER | 15 |
| 59 | Decca LK 4337 | PIECES OF EIGHT (Kenneth Williams) | 15 |
| 59 | Decca SKL 4084 | PIECES OF EIGHT (stereo) (Kenneth Williams) | 20 |
| 60s | Philips 632 303 BL | SPACE IS SO STARTLING | 15 |
| 66 | United Artists (S)ULP 1116 | TWANG! (Lionel Bart) | 25 |
| 65 | HMV CLP 1834/CSD 1587 | THE WAYWARD WAY | 20 |

### SPORT RECORDINGS

| | | | |
|---|---|---|---:|
| 73 | Quality QP 12/73 | EUROPEAN CUP: THE MATCH 1968 - MANCHESTER UNITED V BENFICA | 15 |
| 66 | Centaur CPC 1234 | WORLD CUP '66 | 30 |

## MUSIC LIBRARY LPs

*At one point in time little was known about the mysterious and often forgotten sub genre of music known as library, or rather non-commercial music pressed just for use in film, TV and radio. Thankfully, the internet has allowed light to be shined into the darkest nooks and crannies of this genre and labels like Trunk have reissued many wonderful examples of this music. Since the mid 1990s collecting interest has peaked, dropped away and is now well on the rise again, as are prices for some of the rarer and more important pieces. Collectors either favour early recordings by famous artists such as Jimmy Page or Tubby Hayes or those of a more funky persuasion that can be mined for breakbeats. Original pressing numbers and distribution still remain mysterious, although most people guestimate that 500 to 1,000 copies for each library pressing is about the average, especially as we move towards the mid 1970s. Older and larger music companies such as De Wolfe originally issued recordings on ten inch (throughout the late 1960s) in incredibly short runs - maybe only 200 - 300 copies, and if these recordings proved commercially successful they were repressed later on twelve inch. Obviously the original smaller pressings are more desirable. But still pressing numbers and habits remain shrouded in mystery. It has to be noted that many international and desirable labels distributed their library recordings over here and these do turn up from time to time, however we only list original UK pressings in this price guide. Also, it is worth noting that for libraries such as Chappell and Conroy, not all LPs have titles, they simply list the artist names and track titles. In these cases we have just put own the LP catalogue numbers. One final note, all library records are still the property of the libraries companies that issued them and they can, at any time, ask for them back. Like promos for pop and rock artists this is all a little unlikely, but you have been warned.*

### AMPHONIC
| | | | |
|---|---|---|---|
| 73 | AMPSLP1001 | Moodsetter/Pacesetter | 20 |
| 73 | AMPS 1001 | Small Group & Synthesiser | 20 |
| 73 | AMPS1002 | Scene Setter | 20 |
| 73 | AMPS1005 | Action! | 30 |
| 73 | AMPS 111 | The London Life | 30 |
| 74 | AMPS108 | Super Sounds Unlimited | 40 |
| 75 | AMPS 112 | Special Assignments | 40 |
| 76 | AMPS 118 | Pictures In Sound | 40 |
| 75 | AMPS114 | Sounds 80 | 20 |
| 76 | AMPS117 | It's All In The Beat | 20 |
| 79 | AMPS123 | Night Bird | 40 |

### APOLLO SOUND
| | | | |
|---|---|---|---|
| 73 | APP5021 | Colours In Rhythm 2 | 30 |
| 71 | APP5010 | Melody And Rhythm 4 | 40 |
| 71 | APP5011 | Melody And Rhythm 5 | 20 |
| 71 | APP 5012 | Robin Jones - DENGA (blue label) | 40 |
| 71 | APP5013 | Colours In Rhythm 1 | 30 |
| 71 | APP5015 | Jazz In Landscape | 20 |
| 71 | APP 5016 | Robin Jones - EL MAJA (blue label) | 125 |
| 73 | APP5023 | Melody And Rhythm 7 | 40 |
| 74 | APP5024 | Colours In Rhythm 4 | 60 |
| 75 | APP5026 | Colours In Rhythm 5 | 60 |
| 75 | APP5027 | Melody And Rhythm 9 | 30 |
| 75 | APP5028 | Colours In Rhythm 6 | 50 |
| 76 | APP5030 | Melody And Rhythm 10 | 40 |
| 77 | APP5031 | Colours In Rhythm 7 | 40 |
| 77 | APP5033 | Melody And Rhythm 12 | 30 |
| 78 | APP5035 | Melody And Rhythm 14 | 30 |
| 78 | APP5036 | Colours In Rhythm 8 | 30 |
| 80 | APP5037 | Melody And Rhythm 15 | 15 |

### BOSWORTH
| | | | |
|---|---|---|---|
| 66 | BLP 102 | ELECTRONIC MUSIC (10") | 40 |
| 67 | BLP 104 | ATONAL JAZZ STRUCTURES (10") | 25 |
| 68 | BLP 108 | JAZZ DRAMATICS (10") | 20 |
| 69 | BLP 109 | MODERN RHYTHM (10") | 20 |
| 69 | BLP 110 | Modern Industrials | 20 |
| 70 | BLP 116 | INDUSTRIAL ROCK (10") | 15 |
| 69 | BLP 117 | Orchestral Potpourri | 30 |
| 70 | BLP 118 | MODERN DRAMATICS (10") | 25 |
| 70 | BLP 120 | HARD AND FAST (10") | 25 |
| 71 | BLP 121 | MISCELLANEA (10") | 25 |
| 72 | BLP 126 | RHYTHMIC MOODS (10") | 15 |
| 73 | BLP 130 | KEYBOARD PLUS | 20 |
| 73 | BLP 133 | Dramatic Electonics | 30 |
| 73 | BLP 134 | Dramatic Diversions | 30 |
| 74 | BLP 135 | RHYTHM AT RANDOM | 40 |
| 75 | BLP 141 | AMERICA '76 | 75 |
| 75 | BLP 142 | LET'S GO SOLO | 25 |
| 75 | BLP 143 | MUSICAL COCKTAIL | 75 |
| 76 | BLP 145 | Hard And Fast | 20 |
| 76 | BLP 146 | Romantic Strings/Dramatic Sounds | 30 |
| 77 | BLP 148 | Soft, Sweet Swing | 40 |

MINT VALUE £

| | | | |
|---|---|---|---|
| 77 | BLP 149 | The '77 Sound | 25 |
| 77 | BLP 150 | Musical Conceptions | 40 |
| 77 | BLP 151 | Musical Cocktail (No. 4) | 30 |

## BRUTON

| | | | |
|---|---|---|---|
| 78 | Bruton BRL 1 | Auturbine | 20 |
| 78 | BRI 1 | Terrestrial Journey | 30 |
| 79 | BRI 6 | Frontiers Of Science | 40 |
| 79 | BRJ 4 | Thriller | 25 |
| 78 | Bruton BRH2 | Heavy Rock | 30 |
| 78 | Bruton BRI 2 | Tempus Fugit | 30 |
| 78 | Bruton BRJ 2 | Drama Montage | 75 |
| 78 | Bruton BRJ 8 | Drama Montage Volume 2 | 75 |
| 78 | Bruton BRN 8 | Expanding Horizons | 15 |
| 80 | BRI 9 | Suspensions/Galaxy | 20 |
| 78 | Bruton BRI 10 | Fantasia | 15 |
| 80 | BRI 11 | The Video Age | 20 |
| 80 | BRI 21 | Tomorrow's World | 50 |
| 78 | Bruton BRJ 12 | Wildlife | 30 |
| 78 | Bruton BRJ 22 | Interpol | 30 |
| 78 | Bruton BRJ 24 | Earth | 15 |
| 78 | Bruton BRI 23 | Forecefield | 15 |
| 78 | Bruton BRK 9 | High Tension | 20 |
| 78 | Bruton BRJ 9 | Web Of Intrigue | 20 |
| 78 | BRD 8 | Tone Poems | 20 |
| 78 | BRG 6 | Sunny Sides | 40 |
| 80 | BRD 13 | Serenity | 20 |
| 79 | Bruton BRM 1 | Menace | 20 |
| 78 | BRD 10 | Relax | 15 |
| 79 | BRJ 9 | Web Of Intrigue | 20 |
| 79 | BRJ 9 | High Adventure | 20 |
| 79 | BRK 5 | Contemporary Action | 20 |
| 79 | BRS 3 | Small Band Jazz | 15 |
| 79 | Bruton BRM 3 | Darkside | 30 |
| 79 | Bruton BRK 5 | Contemporary Motion | 20 |
| 79 | Bruton BRL 4 | Futurama | 20 |
| 79 | Bruton BRG 7 | Spread Your Wings | 20 |
| 79 | Bruton BHR 5 | Light My Fire | 15 |
| 79 | Bruton BRJ 25 | Espionage | 15 |
| 79 | BRE 3 | Kids And Cartoons | 20 |
| 80 | Bruton BRK 1 | Driving Force | 15 |
| 80 | Bruton BRK 3 | Speed Fever | 20 |
| 80 | Bruton BRK 4 | Dramatic Action | 15 |
| 80 | Bruton BRL 6 | Undergroove | 30 |
| 80 | BRL 7 | Music Machine | 20 |
| 80 | Bruton BRM 13 | String Tension | 15 |
| 80 | Bruton BRI 12 | Gyroscope | 50 |
| 81 | BRM 4 | Fear | 20 |
| 81 | BRM 5 | House Of Horror | 15 |
| 81 | BRM 6 | Building Tension | 20 |
| 81 | BRM 8 | Watchful Eye | 30 |
| 81 | BRM 9 | Survival | 40 |
| 83 | BRM 11 | Strange | 20 |
| 81 | BRM 13 | String Tension | 15 |
| 84 | BRR 18 | East Meets West | 30 |

*(These LPs are listed by catalogue number first, then year)*

## CHAPPELL

| | | | |
|---|---|---|---|
| 66 | LPC 961-866 | 861-866 | 30 |
| 66 | LPC 781-885 | 781-785 | 20 |
| 66 | LPC 712-717 | 712-717 | 25 |
| 66 | LPC 377-381 | 377-381 | 20 |
| 68 | LPC 1005-1009 | 1005-1009 | 20 |
| 70 | CIS 5003 | INDUSTRIAL SOUNDS VOL 2 | 25 |
| 70 | CIS 5007 | LIGHT ATMOSPHERE VOL 2 | 40 |
| 70 | CIS 5008 | MUSIC FOR DRAMA VOL 1 (John Barry etc) | 30 |
| 70 | CIS 5009 | MUSIC FOR DRAMA VOL 2 | 25 |
| 70 | CIS 5013 | DANCE MUSIC VOLUME 1 (Night Club) | 25 |
| 70 | CIS 5023 | JAZZ (SMALL GROUP) (John Barry etc) | 30 |
| 70 | CIS 5024 | MUSIC FOR DRAMA VOL 3 (Robert Farnon) | 30 |
| 75 | CIS 5047 | POP SOUNDS | 40 |
| 70 | 672-677 | 672-677 | 25 |
| 70 | 678-682 | 678-682 | 20 |
| 70 | LPC 1032 | 1032 | 30 |
| 70 | LPC 1034 | 1034 | 30 |
| 70 | LPC 1036 | 1036 | 30 |
| 70 | LPC 1039 | 1039 | 30 |
| 71 | 1040 | 1040 | 15 |
| 70 | LPC 1042 | 1042 | 20 |
| 70 | LPC 1043 | 1043 | 20 |
| 70 | LPC 1044 | 1044 | 20 |

| 72 | LPC 1045 | Lee Mason | 200 |
|----|----------|-----------|-----|
| 70 | LPC 1047 | 1047 | 30 |
| 70 | LPC 1049 | 1049 | 20 |
| 72 | LPC 1051 | Lee Mason | 75 |
| 72 | LPC 1052 | Mark Duval | 50 |
| 72 | LPC 1053 | Pop Sounds | 30 |
| 73 | LPC 1055 | Electronic Music | 35 |
| 73 | LPC 1056 | Cacavas / Hawksworth - Mark Duval | 50 |
| 73 | LPC 1058 | Mark Duval | 50 |
| 73 | LPC 1059 | Lee Mason | 75 |
| 73 | LPC 1060 | Robert Farnon | 20 |
| 73 | LPC 1063 | Roger Webb | 30 |
| 73 | LPC 1065 | Rhythm'n'Brass - Mark Duval | 80 |
| 73 | LPC 1068 | Dave Holland | 30 |
| 73 | LPC 1069 | Light And Bright - Mark Duval | 40 |
| 74 | LPC 1070 | Mark Duval | 100 |
| 74 | LPC 1711 | Mark Duval | 30 |
| 74 | LPC 1075 | Mark Duval | 20 |
| 74 | LPC 1076 | Mark Duval | 100 |
| 74 | LPC 1077 | Mark Duval | 30 |

## CHAPPELL INTERNATIONAL

| 73 | CAL 4002 | Moog Synthesiser Music | 30 |
|----|----------|------------------------|-----|
| 73 | CAL 4004 | Sounds Electronic | 30 |
| 73 | CAL 4007 | Small Group Sounds | 15 |
| 73 | CAL 4009 | The Sound Of Strings | 40 |
| 74 | CAL 4013 | Small Group sounds | 120 |

## CONROY

| 70 | BMLP070 | BMLP070 | 15 |
|----|---------|---------|-----|
| 70 | BMLP071 | BMLP071 | 20 |
| 70 | BMLP074 | Theme Sets | 70 |
| 70 | BMLP078 | Double Cross | 20 |
| 70 | BMLP079 | Capital Cities | 30 |
| 70 | BMLP072 | Electronic Percussion Points | 30 |
| 70 | BMLP074 | Theme Sets | 70 |
| 70 | BMLP074 | Theme And Variation | 20 |
| 70 | BMLP080 | Electroscope | 20 |
| 70 | BMLP 080 | Background Action | 100 |
| 71 | BMLP089 | BMLP089 | 20 |
| 72 | BMLP090 | BMLP090 | 25 |
| 71 | BMLP085 | BMLP085 (No Title) | 20 |
| 72 | BMLP090 | Larry Robbins Percussion | 50 |
| 72 | BMLP092 | London's Underground | 75 |
| 72 | BMLP093 | Larry Robbins Sportstudio Band | 50 |
| 73 | BMLP093 | BMLP093 | 80 |
| 73 | BMLP097 | Mood Movement, Afro Patterns | 80 |
| 73 | BMLPP098 | Modern Movement | 30 |
| 74 | BMLP101 | Happy Moog | 15 |
| 73 | BMLP102 | Larry Robbins Dynamic Drums Plus | 50 |
| 74 | BMLP103 | Clap Trap | 50 |
| 75 | BMLP107 | Background Action - Action Tracks | 200 |
| 75 | BMLP107 | Modern Movement - Action Tracks | 30 |
| 74 | BMLP104 | Moderate Beat Movements | 30 |
| 73 | BMLP107 | Klaus Weiss Sounds And Percussion | 100 |
| 74 | BMLP114 | Soft Sounds | 30 |
| 75 | BMLP115 | Londons Underground 2 | 20 |
| 75 | BMLP117 | Sounds And Percussion | 20 |
| 75 | BMLP123 | Electronic Sounds | 30 |
| 75 | BMLP124 | Dramatic Tempi | 100 |
| 75 | BMLP128 | Chromozones | 35 |
| 75 | BMLP131 | On The Road | 40 |
| 75 | BMLP132 | Sounds Funky | 20 |
| 75 | BMLP143 | Feelings | 400 |
| 75 | BMLP145 | New Dimension | 50 |
| 75 | BMLP150 | Drama Tension | 40 |
| 76 | BMLP162 | Action Activity | 30 |
| 76 | BMLP163 | Space Age | 30 |
| 76 | BMLP167 | Brassbound Background | 30 |

## CONROY EUROBEATS SERIES

| 73 | EURO 1 | Silly Synthesisers | 15 |
|----|--------|--------------------|-----|
| 73 | EURO 2 | Ethnic/India | 50 |
| 73 | EURO 3 | Modern baroque | 20 |
| 73 | EURO 4 | Romantic backgrounds | 50 |
| 73 | EURO 5 | Dramatic backgrounds | 100 |
| 73 | EURO 7 | Going West - Two Guitars | 20 |
| 73 | EURO 9 | Themes And Backgrounds/Two Moods | 20 |
| 73 | EURO 10 | World At Work | 150 |
| 73 | EURO 11 | Colla Voce | 100 |

## DE WOLFE

| 64 | DW/LP 2824 | Young World | 30 |
|----|------------|-------------|-----|

MINT VALUE £

| | | | |
|---|---|---|---|
| 64 | DW/LP2853 | Guitars In Motion | 15 |
| 64 | DW/LP2969 | An Eye For An Eye | 30 |
| 65 | DW LP2949 | Band 8 (10") | 60 |
| 65 | DW LP2950 | High Speed Jazz (10") | 30 |
| 65 | DW/LP2966 | Mind On The Run (10") | 100 |
| 66 | DW/LP2981 | On The Town | 20 |
| 66 | DW/LP2987 | Continent 7 | 20 |
| 66 | DW/LP2968 | Journey Into Sound (10") | 40 |
| 66 | DW LP2973 | Abstractions Of The Industrial North (10") | 150 |
| 66 | DW LP2974 | The Wild One (10") - (features Jimmy Page) | 120 |
| 67 | DW/LP2975 | Town Beat (10") | 60 |
| 67 | DW/LP3022 | Checkpoint (10") | 20 |
| 67 | DW/LP3023 | Swinging City | 20 |
| 67 | DW/LP3029 | Polaris | 30 |
| 67 | DW/LP3030 | Lunar Probe | 60 |
| 67 | DWL/LP 3033 | Chapter 2 - Beat Groups (10" LP) | 25 |
| 67 | DW/LP3040 | Electric Banana (10") | 100 |
| 67 | DW/LP 3046 | Young Friends (10" LP) | 20 |
| 67 | DW/LP3049 | Z Patrol | 20 |
| 67 | DW/LP3063 | Assignment London | 30 |
| 67 | DW/LP3066 | Don't Lose Your Cool (10") | 150 |
| 68 | DW/LP3069 | More Electric Banana (10") | 150 |
| 68 | DWL/LP 3084 | Electroshake (10" LP) | 30 |
| 68 | DW/LP 3097 | On The Button (10" LP) | 20 |
| 68 | DW/LP3088 | Quietly With Johann (10") | 20 |
| 69 | DW/LP3114 | Who's Gonna Buy? (The Lemon Dips) (10") | 75 |
| 66 | DW LP3115 | Caribbean Sound (10") | 20 |
| 69 | DW/LP3123 | Even More Electric Banana (10") | 60 |
| 69 | DW/LP3135 | Electroshake Vol 2 (10") | 25 |
| 69 | DW/LP3136 | Pop Sounds by The Cool (10") | 40 |
| 70 | DW/LP3154 | Heavy Gravy (10") | 25 |
| 71 | DW/LP3182 | Vocal Patterns | 40 |
| 71 | DW/LP3199 | Atomic Butterfly | 30 |
| 71 | CW/LP3200 | Sing Me A Song | 30 |
| 71 | DW/LP3212 | Moonshade | 30 |
| 71 | DW LP3214 | Anglo Amercan Jazz | 100 |
| 71 | DW/LP3220 | Afro-Rock | 70 |
| 71 | DW/LP3224 | Little Bossa | 30 |
| 71 | DW/LP3227 | Vocal Shades And Tones | 125 |
| 72 | DW/LP3243 | Hogan, The Hawk And Dirty John Crown | 40 |
| 72 | CW/LP3262 | Black Pearl | 40 |
| 73 | DW/LP3285 | Big Beat | 150 |
| 74 | DW/LP3318 | Hard Hitter | 100 |
| 75 | CW/DW3315 | Dangerous Connection | 20 |
| 75 | CW/LP3319 | Metal Sunrise | 20 |
| 75 | DW/LP3324 | Bite Hard | 40 |
| 75 | CW 3328 | Rythmes | 150 |
| 76 | CW/LP3331 | Rubber Riff | 40 |
| 76 | CW/LP3346 | Feeling High | 40 |
| 76 | DW/LP3347 | A Rose For Dracula | 25 |
| 76 | CW/LP3366 | Sun High | 50 |
| 78 | CW/LP3385 | Forest Of Evil | 50 |
| 78 | CW/LP3392 | Mean And Dirty | 60 |
| 81 | CW/LP3469 | Forest Of Evil Part II | 60 |

## DE WOLFE "IN EDITIONS" SERIES

| | | | |
|---|---|---|---|
| 76 | Timing 12 | Conversations Between East And West | 60 |
| 76 | Timing 14 | Cradle Of Time | 30 |

## FRANCIS, DAY & HUNTER

| | | | |
|---|---|---|---|
| 68 | FDH1011 | Spectrum Of Colour | 20 |
| 68 | FDH 1018 | Diplomatic Immunity | 70 |
| 68 | FDH1020 | Progressions | 20 |
| 68 | FDH1023 | Projections/Diametrics | 20 |

## HARMONIC

| | | | |
|---|---|---|---|
| 68 | CBD609 | Beat! | 20 |
| 68 | CBL618 | Fonteyns Folk Jazz (10") | 30 |
| 69 | CBL621 | More Beat (10") | 20 |
| 69 | CNW 598 | Ronnie Ross Plays (no 1) | 200 |
| 76 | CBD671 | A Good Mixture | 20 |
| 76 | CBG672 | Modern Dramatic Action | 40 |
| 76 | CBG674 | Underscores | 40 |
| 72 | CBJ670 | Synthtronics | 40 |
| 72 | CBJ674 | Synthetics | 40 |
| 67 | CBO613 | Industrial Espionage Suite | 150 |
| 71 | CBO640 | Studies In Drama | 20 |
| 72 | CBO654 | City Visit | 40 |
| 72 | CBO665 | Weighty And Solid | 40 |
| 68 | CBW616 | Shakin And Soulin | 40 |
| 68 | CBW617 | Novelty Beat | 30 |
| 69 | CBW622 | Suite In Beat | 20 |

| 70 | CBW628 | Beat Drama | 20 |
|----|--------|------------|-----|
| 71 | CBW637 | Drama In Rhythm | 50 |
| 71 | CBW639 | Psycho Soul | 50 |
| 72 | CBW660 | Theme In Beat | 75 |
| 72 | CBW659 | Studies For Guitar And Drama Beat | 40 |

*(listed by catalogue number rather than year)*

## HUDSON

| 72 | HMC 506 | Mindbender (Peter Merrick) | 20 |
|----|---------|---------------------------|-----|
| 72 | HMC 507 | Dramaturgy - Cosmogony | 20 |
| 74 | HMC 509 | Empty Horizons | 20 |
| 74 | HMC 511 | Hot Breath | 20 |
| 75 | HMC 513 | Blood On The Flowers | 30 |

## KPM

| 66 | KPM 001 | The Mood Modern | 20 |
|----|---------|-----------------|-----|
| 66 | KPM 1002 | The Sounds of Syd Dale | 40 |
| 66 | KPM 1009 | Accent On Percussion | 15 |
| 66 | KPM 1017 | Impact And Action | 30 |
| 66 | KPM/ACW1 | Music For Your Movies | 20 |
| 67 | KPM1014 | All That Jazz | 20 |
| 67 | KPM1015 | The Sound Of Pop | 30 |
| 68 | KPM INT 001 | Jazz Convention Volume 1 | 60 |
| 68 | KPM INT 002 | Jazz Convention Volume II | 80 |
| 68 | KPM INT 004 | Jazz Convention III | 100 |
| 68 | KPM1035 | Underscore | 30 |
| 69 | KPM1021 | Light Jazz Feeling | 30 |
| 69 | KPM1027 | Soul Organ Showcase (Alan Hawkshaw) | 50 |
| 69 | KPM1029 | Colours In Rhythm | 30 |
| 69 | KPM1037 | Flamboyant Themes | 20 |
| 69 | KPM1038 | Flamboyant Themes 2 | 25 |
| 69 | KPM1042 | Jazz Graphics/Spy Set | 25 |
| 69 | KPM1043 | Beat Incidental (Alan Hawkshaw/Keith Mansfield) | 50 |
| 69 | KPM1043 | Beat Incidental | 40 |
| 69 | KPM1044 | The Big Beat (Mohawks & Alan Hawkshaw) | 80 |
| 69 | KPM1046 | Sounds In Percussion | 20 |
| 69 | KPM1043 | Single Instruments Volume 1 Percussion | 40 |
| 69 | KPM1049 | Chorus And Orchestra (Syd Dale) | 60 |
| 69 | KPM1054 | Native Africa | 25 |
| 70 | KPM1055 | Dramatic Background | 40 |
| 69 | KPM1061 | Impact And Action | 20 |
| 69 | KPM1063 | Contemporary Colour (Syd Dale) | 20 |
| 70 | KPM1067 | The Big Beat - Volume 2 (Alan Moorhouse) | 80 |
| 70 | KPM1070 | Bugaloo In Brazil (Les Baxter) | 80 |
| 70 | KPM1071 | The Brazillian Suite (Roger Duprat) | 80 |
| 70 | KPM1077 | Progressive Pop | 30 |
| 71 | KPM1076 | Speed And Excitement (Mansfield, Hawkshaw, Pearson) | 35 |
| 72 | KPM1079 | Beat Industrial | 40 |
| 72 | KPM1080 | Beat Incidental (Alan Hawkshaw) | 50 |
| 72 | KPM 1080 | Flute For Moderns (with Alan Hawkshaw, Alan Parker and Joe Hailer) | 35 |
| 72 | KPM1084 | Mediterranean Intrigue (Neil Ardley) | 60 |
| 71 | KPM1085 | Electronic Music | 50 |
| 71 | KPM1086 | Music For A Young Generation (Alan Hawkshaw) | 50 |
| 71 | KPM1087 | Technical Viewpoint | 50 |
| 71 | KPM1088 | Bass Guitar And Percussion - Volume 1 | 50 |
| 71 | KPM1089 | Bass Guitar And Percussion - Volume 2 (Herbie Flowers) | 30 |
| 71 | KPM1090 | Bass Guitar And Percussion - Volume 3 | 20 |
| 71 | KPM1091 | Vibraphone Jazz Quartet | 20 |
| 71 | KPM1094 | Accent on Percussion/Construction In Jazz | 40 |
| 71 | KPM1095 | Theme Suites / Mustang (John Cameron/Keith Mansfield) | 60 |
| 71 | KPM1097 | Jazzrock (John Cameron) | 45 |
| 71 | KPM1100 | The Big Screen (Johnny Pearson) | 20 |
| 72 | KPM1102 | Electrosound (Ron Geesin) | 60 |
| 72 | KPM1103 | Electromusic | 30 |
| 72 | KPM1104 | Electrosonic (Delia Derbyshire) | 60 |
| 72 | KPM1111 | Brass Plus Moog | 50 |
| 72 | KPM1122 | Move With The Times | 25 |
| 72 | KPM1124 | Big Business (Keith Mansfield) | 35 |
| 72 | KPM1125 | Voices In Harmony (John Cameron/Keith Mansfield) | 40 |
| 73 | KPM1126 | Summer Songbirds | 40 |
| 73 | KPM1128 | Counterpoint In Rhythm | 40 |
| 73 | KPM1130 | Afro Rock (John Cameron/Alan Parker) | 100 |
| 73 | KPM1131 | Trendsetters | 25 |
| 74 | KPM1136 | Industrial Panorama (Johnny Pearson/Keith Mansfield) | 35 |
| 75 | KPM1160 | Friends anf Lovers (Brian Bennett, David Lindup, Duncan Lamont etc) | 30 |
| 74 | KPM1161 | Industry Volume 1 | 40 |
| 74 | KPM1163 | Rock Spectrum | 50 |
| 74 | KPM1165 | Jazz Inclination | 25 |
| 74 | KPM1166 | Piano Vibrations | 30 |
| 74 | KPM1168 | Drama | 40 |
| 74 | KPM1170 | Sounds Of The Time | 20 |

MINT VALUE £

| 74 | KPM1171 | Impact (Keith Mansfield/Brian Bennett) | 30 |
| 74 | KPM1177 | Hot Wax (Alan Hawkshaw/Brian Bennett) | 30 |
| 77 | KPM1183 | Middle East Suite | 40 |
| 77 | KPM1191 | Landscapes | 15 |
| 77 | KPM1196 | Rock On | 30 |
| 77 | KPM1214 | Pulse Of The City | 15 |

## PEER INTERNATIONAL

| 70 | PIL9004 | Soul Of A City | 20 |
| 70 | PIL9006 | My Thing | 150 |
| 71 | PIL9009 | BIG HAMMER | 60 |
| 72 | PIL9013 | Mindbender | 350 |
| 73 | PIL9021 | Flip Top | 20 |
| 73 | PIL9023 | Reggae For Real | 150 |
| 74 | PIL9026 | Solar Flares | 80 |
| 74 | PIL9027 | Electric Bazaar | 80 |
| 75 | PIL9028 | Scoop! | 50 |
| 76 | PIL9029 | 5+4 | 150 |
| 75 | PIL9034 | Earth Shaker | 50 |
| 77 | PIL9037 | Hit Man | 50 |
| 77 | PIL9038 | Hangover | 40 |
| 78 | PIL9039 | Lost Star | 150 |
| 79 | PIL9040 | Point Blank | 40 |
| 80 | PIL9043 | Workforce | 50 |

## PROGRAMME MUSIC

| 73 | PM 002 | Contrasts | 30 |
| 75 | PM8 | On The Side Of Angels | 35 |
| 75 | PM11 | Music To Varnish Owls By | 60 |
| 79 | PM 025 | Hey Disco! | 20 |

## REGENCY LINE

| 75 | RL1001 | Light Background Vol. 1 | 15 |
| 75 | RL1002 | Themes | 15 |
| 75 | RL1003 | Rock | 15 |
| 75 | RL1004 | Rock | 15 |
| 75 | RL1008 | Synthesiser Spots | 15 |
| 75 | RL1010 | Heavy Rock | 50 |
| 76 | RL1013 | Dramatic Moods | 20 |
| 76 | RL1019 | The Detectives | 25 |

## ROUGE MUSIC

| 75 | RMS 101 | Skyboat | 35 |
| 75 | RMS 102 | Sweet Soul | 30 |
| 75 | RMS 103 | Interlace | 35 |
| 75 | RMS 104 | The King And The Clown | 40 |
| 75 | RMS 105 | Hi-Fly | 40 |
| 75 | RMS 106 | Blackout | 70 |
| 76 | RMS 107 | Return To Base | 15 |
| 76 | RMS 108 | Cobra | 40 |
| 77 | RMS 109 | Meal Ticket | 25 |
| 77 | RMS 110 | Music Report | 20 |
| 77 | RMS 111 | Kites "Electronic Music" | 20 |
| 77 | RMS 112 | Let The Music Play | 20 |
| 78 | RMS 113 | Hard As A Rock | 20 |
| 78 | RMS 114 | Soft And Tender | 20 |
| 78 | RMS 115 | Do It (Wally Waller Band - ex Pretty Things) | 25 |
| 78 | RMS 116 | Faded Jeans | 20 |
| 78 | RMS 117 | All About The Sea | 15 |
| 78 | RMS 118 | Discos Like This | 40 |
| 79 | RMS 119 | Pulses "Electronic Music" | 25 |
| 79 | RMS 120 | Candover | 25 |
| 79 | RMS 121 | Friday Girl | 30 |
| 79 | RMS 122 | Robot Dancer | 20 |
| 81 | RMS 124 | Country Grass | 20 |
| 81 | RMS 125 | Making Tracks | 20 |
| 81 | RMS 126 | Patterns | 20 |
| 81 | RMS 127 | Dancing Grass | 15 |
| 81 | RMS 128 | Impetus | 15 |
| 81 | RMS 129 | Play On (by Patchwork) | 20 |
| 81 | RMS 130 | Glass-Head | 25 |
| 81 | RMS 131 | Superdoup | 20 |
| 81 | RMS 132 | Sliced Apple | 20 |
| 81 | RMS 133 | Pipsqueek | 15 |
| 81 | RMS 134 | Whisper To The Moon | 20 |
| 81 | RMS 135 | History Of Jazz | 15 |
| 82 | RMS 136 | Telletext "Electronic" Music | 30 |
| 82 | RMS 137 | Voyage Of Discovery | 20 |
| 82 | RMS 138 | Movement | 30 |
| 82 | RMS 140 | Instant Reggae (by Roots) | 15 |
| 82 | RMS 142 | Red Kite | 20 |
| 82 | RMS 143 | New-Age | 15 |
| 82 | RMS 144 | Remember | 25 |

| 82 | RMS 145 | Drumatics | 20 |
|----|---------|-----------|----|
| 82 | RMS 146 | Eight Orchestral Sketches | 15 |
| 83 | RMS 147 | Cutaway | 20 |
| 83 | RMS 148 | Solarium | 20 |
| 83 | RMS 149 | Some Shufflin' | 15 |
| 83 | RMS 150 | Bass Moods Vol 1 | 15 |
| 83 | RMS 151 | Bass Moods Vol 2 | 15 |
| 83 | RMS 152 | Undercover | 30 |
| 84 | RMS 156 | Frontrunner | 15 |
| 84 | RMS 157 | Breakdance | 15 |
| 84 | RMS 158 | Topsy Turvy | 15 |
| 85 | RMS 160 | New-Outlook | 15 |
| 85 | RMS 165 | Sound On Sound | 15 |
| 86 | RMS 166 | Music Break | 15 |
| 86 | RMS 168 | Audiotronics | 15 |
| 86 | RMS 169 | Highlights (by Darryl Way) | 15 |
| 87 | RMS 173 | Pace-Age | 15 |
| 87 | RMS 174 | Breaking Ground | 15 |
| 87 | RMS 175 | Changing Seasons | 25 |
| 87 | RMS 178 | Kinetics (Alan Parker) | 20 |

## SOUNDS OF NOW

| 71 | Sounds of Now 1 | Sounds Of Now 1 (LP) | 50 |
|----|-----------------|----------------------|----|
| 71 | Sounds Of Now 2 | Sounds Of Now 2 (LP) | 75 |
| 72 | Sounds Of Now 3 | Sounds Of Now 3 (LP) | 100 |

## SOUND STAGE

| 81 | AVF1 | Sound Stage 1 Thematic Scenarios | 20 |
|----|------|----------------------------------|----|
| 81 | AVF3 | Sound Stage 3 Thematic Scenarios | 20 |
| 82 | AVF7 | Sound Stage 7 Powerful, Agressive, Thematic | 20 |

## SOUTHERN MUSIC

| 66 | MQLP 19 | Electronic Music | 20 |
|----|---------|------------------|----|
| 68 | MQLP 27 | The Scottmen | 20 |
| 70 | MQ/LP47 | Jazz Beat/Jazz Beat Bossa Nova | 30 |
| 71 | MQLP 32 | Jazz Dramatic | 30 |
| 72 | MQLP 38 | Electronic Music | 75 |
| 72 | MQLP 29 | Afro Spooky | 200 |
| 73 | MQLP 40 | Electronic Music | 30 |
| 78 | MQLP 48 | Electronic Music | 75 |
| 78 | MQLP 51 | Exotica | 30 |

## STANDARD

| 70 | ESL 196 | National Balkan Ensemble | 20 |
|----|---------|--------------------------|----|
| 74 | ESL 127 | Electronic Music | 40 |
| 75 | Standard ESL 133 | Encore Electronic | 40 |
| 69 | ESL 103 | Solo Guitar (Michael Chapman) | 60 |
| 00 | ESL 104 | Electronic Music | 100 |

## STUDIO G

| 70 | LPSG1001 | Beat Group | 50 |
|----|----------|------------|----|
| 70 | LPSG1002 | Big Jazz & Big Beat | 20 |
| 70 | LPSG1008 | Dramatic And Horror | 20 |
| 70 | LPSG1009 | Electronic Age | 50 |
| 74 | LPSG 2001 | Disco Beat | 40 |
| 74 | LPSG2002 | Cool Beat | 30 |
| 74 | LPSG2009 | Abstract | 50 |
| 76 | LPSG3001 | Pop | 40 |
| 76 | LPSG3002 | Beat Underscore | 80 |
| 76 | LPSG3007 | Rhythm | 125 |
| 78 | LPSG3009 | Music For Synthesizers | 30 |
| 80 | LPSG4004 | Abstract | 30 |
| 09 | JBH032LP | G Spots | 30 |

## STUDIO ONE

| 71 | SO7 | MAURICE POP | 15 |
|----|-----|-------------|----|
| 73 | SO14 | PIERRE LAVIN POP BAND | 30 |

## SYLVESTER MUSIC

| 67 | SMC/LP501 | Jazz Waves (10") | 15 |
|----|-----------|------------------|----|
| 67 | SMC/LP502 | Voices In The Wind (10") | 20 |
| 67 | SMC/LP503 | Striptease (10") | 15 |
| 67 | SMC/LP504 | Aquaplane (10") | 15 |
| 67 | SMC/LP505 | And So On (10") | 15 |
| 67 | SMC/LP506 | Tutti Flutti (10") | 15 |
| 67 | SMX/LP507 | Go (10") | 15 |
| 68 | SMX/LP511 | Rhythm For Ursula (10") | 20 |
| 68 | SMX/LP512 | Exchanges (10") | 20 |
| 68 | SMX/LP516 | Racing Tempo (10") | 15 |
| 69 | SMX/LP520 | Plaques Tourantes | 50 |
| 70 | SMC/LP525 | Jazz For Action | 25 |
| 71 | SMC/LP526 | Post Combustion | 15 |
| 71 | SMC/LP527 | Blue Cylinder | 30 |
| 71 | SMC/LP528 | Chronoradial | 20 |
| 71 | SMC/LP529 | Ultra Pop-Op | 60 |

MINT VALUE £

| | | | |
|---|---|---|---|
| 72 | SMCS/LP557 | Bright And Shining | 30 |

## THEMES INTERNATIONAL

| | | | |
|---|---|---|---|
| 70 | TIM1002 | New Blood | 40 |
| 70 | TIM1003 | Main Theme And Sig Tunes | 30 |
| 73 | TIM1011 | The Rock Machine | 20 |
| 74 | TIM1012 | Synthesizer And Percussion | 60 |
| 74 | TIM1013 | Breath Of Danger | 50 |
| 74 | TIM1014 | Freedom Road | 20 |
| 74 | TIM1015 | Mystery Movie | 50 |
| 75 | TIM1018 | The All American Powerhouse | 60 |
| 76 | TIM1021 | The Voice Of Soul | 120 |
| 76 | TIM1022 | The Sound Of Soul | 100 |
| 76 | TIM1024 | Drama Suite - Part 1 | 100 |
| 76 | TIM1025 | The Drama Suite - Part II (Alan Tew) | 175 |

## TIMING

| | | | |
|---|---|---|---|
| 76 | Timing No 14 | Cradle Of Time | 50 |

# TAX SCAM RECORDS

*Back in the late 70s there was a legal loophole that was exploited in America where the potential sales of a record could be legally offset against costs. This led to the formation of a number of 'tax scam' labels where albums were recorded and pressed up in small numbers with the sole intention of avoiding tax. There was, as you might imagine, much more to the process than that but the key thing was to make it look as if the record had been released in order to generate the tax loss that could lead to a profit for the company or investors concerned. As far as we know most of these labels were confined to America but it appears that Ebonite Records was a label that licensed material to the U.K.. This label then pressed records up with a view to selling them in the normal legal fashion. These records were, however, all released at once as an advert in Melody Maker in 1978 suggests. There were over 80 titles. The advert stated "the most extensive collection of hit product to hit the world." This was somewhat far from the truth as many of the records - that ranged from jazz standards to pop covers - were very poor as the musicians involved (all working under a number of made-up names) recorded, in some instances, some awful cover versions that - for some reason - went on for several minutes or more in order that the record could be classed as an LP - even though they were marketed as 12" singles. indeed. It is probably true to suggest that it was quantity rather than quality that was the order of the day as some records have different artist titles but it is obvious from the playing - and in some cases awful singing - that they were recorded by the same people at the same session and then spread over different releases. Of course, some of the musicians involved were very good and turned out slabs of funk/disco/soul that is now sought after and collectable. There are some absolute killers out there and some of the excellent records put out by Ebonite in the U.K. testify to this. The Returners 12" is a case in point whereas others are so bad that is is not even funny. This list is not exhaustive as some records were named in that 1978 advert that have, as far as we know, not surfaced - as yet. These artists have mouth watering names like Blind Faith, Midshipmen, The Bodybuilders, Cabaret, The Short People, The Astronomers, Wrecking Havok and The Earth City Rockers etc.. If you find any of them or know of any other examples of tax related records pressed for the U.K. please let us know. Finally, although the ultra collectable DISCO FOX LP was listed in that Melody Maker advert we have yet to see a UK pressing. Those that have surfaced so far have been US pressings.*

| | | | |
|---|---|---|---|
| 78 | Ebonite EE001 | VOYAGE: Watermelon Man/Maiden Voyage (33rpm 12") | 15 |
| 78 | Ebonite EE004 | AFTER TIME: Itchy Fingers/When Your Lovers Gone/Time After Time/Love For Sale (33rpm 12") | 12 |
| 78 | Ebonite EE005 | BLUESERS: All Blues/Blues In G (33rpm 12") | 15 |
| 78 | Ebonite EE007 | MISTY TIME: Laura/Now's The Time//Misty (33rpm 12") | 12 |
| 78 | Ebonite EE009 | ANYTIME: Do It Any Way You Want To Do It/The World Is A Ghetto (33rpm 12") | 15 |
| 78 | Ebonite EE010 | JOGGERS: Killer Joe/Milestones/The Nearness Of You (33rpm 12") | 12 |
| 78 | Ebonite EE011 | RELATIVITY: Bad Luck/Peace Song/Low Down (33rpm 12") | 25 |
| 78 | Ebonite EE019 | SOMEBODY: Meditations/There Will Never Be Another You/Everybody Loves Somebody (33rpm 12") | 12 |
| 78 | Ebonite EE027 | CLASS ACT: When The Lights Are Low/The Strut/Stairway To The Stars (33rpn 12") | 12 |
| 78 | Ebonite EE030 | SECRET SERVICE: Maiden Voyage/Secret Love/Bongo Bop (33rpm 12") | 15 |
| 78 | Ebonite EE034 | RINGS AND THINGS: My Favourite Things/Rhythm-A-Ning (33rpm 12") | 10 |
| 78 | Ebonite EE033 | ENGINEERS: Long Train Running/Silly Love Songs/ Donna Lee (33rpm 12") | 12 |
| 78 | Ebonite EE038 | LADY MAKERS: Ain't No Sunshine When She's Gone/East Of The Sun/Mr Luckt (33rpm 12") | 12 |
| 78 | Ebonite EE037 | QUIZMASTERS: If You Want Me To Stay/Fever (33rpm 12") | 12 |
| 78 | Ebonite EE055 | PEPPER SHAKERS: Fever/Shake Your Booty (33rpm 12") | 12 |
| 78 | Ebonite EE043 | BARTENDERS: I Love Everything About You/Love Hangover (33rpm 12") | 12 |
| 78 | Ebonite EE056 | SENTIMENTALISTS: Getting Sentimental Over You/Poincianna/Love Walked In (33rpm 12") | 12 |
| 78 | Ebonite EE069 | AMOURIZERS: Our Love Is Here To Stay/Naima (33rpm 12") | 15 |
| 78 | Ebonite EE067 | G MEN: Somewhere In The Night/You'd Be So Nice To Come Home To/Godfathers Theme/Blues In G (33rpm 12") | 12 |
| 78 | Ebonite EE080 | CITY OF ANGELS: Angel Eyes/Au Preavauve/Living For The City (33rpm 12") | 12 |
| 78 | Ebonite EE088 | LITTLE SUNFLOWER: Little Sunflower/Hang Up Your Hangups (33rpm 12") | 30 |
| 78 | Ebonite EE089 | WARLOCKS: Witchcraft/Impressions (33rpm 12") | 10 |
| 78 | Ebonite EE104 | PERSUASIVE JAZZ: Nicole/Polynesian/Pretty Elizabeth Jane (33rpm 12" in Persuasive Jazz sleeve) | 20 |
| 78 | Ebonite EE173 | SONGSTERS: I'm Gonna Love You A Little Bit More/Sing A Song (33rpm 12") | 25 |
| 78 | Ebonite EE178 | CYMBALISM: Mercury 49/Mr Tambourine Man/Feel Like Making Love (33rpm 12") | 10 |

| | | | |
|---|---|---|---|
| 78 | Ebonite EE142 | TRAILBLAZER: Don't Want To Be The Lone Ranger/Sing A Song/Walk On By (33rpm 12").......................................................................................................... | 10 |
| 78 | Ebonite EE074 | STOMPERS: Killing Me Softly/Stomping at The Savoy (33rpm 12") .............................. | 10 |
| 78 | Ebonite EE092 | UMBRELLISTICS: Ease On Down The Road/Here's That Rainy Day/Sunny (33rpm 12") .. | 10 |
| 78 | Ebonite EE096 | MARKSMEN: Watermelon Man/Disco Queen (33rpm 12") ........................................... | 20 |
| 78 | Ebonite EE169 | SKY LAW: That's The Way Of The World/Kalimba (33rpm 12")..................................... | 15 |
| 78 | Ebonite EE172 | MOUNTAIN WOMAN: Ain't No Mountain High Enough/Super Woman (33rpm 12") ..... | 10 |
| 78 | Ebonite EE 077 | THE RETURNERS: It Seems That Way/Long Road Back/Here We Go (33rpm 12") .......... | 50 |
| 78 | Ebonite EE142 | FLOORWARD: Let's Groove/Dance To The Music (33rpm 12")....................................... | 10 |
| 78 | Ebonite EE171 | FORAGERS: What's Going On/Grapevine/You're All I Need (33rpm 12") ...................... | 12 |
| 78 | Ebonite EE148 | CHAMELEONS: Chameleon/Sure Is unky/Foot Stompin Music (33rpm 12") ................. | 20 |
| 78 | Ebonite EE 177 | SECRET RAINBOW: April In Paris/Secret Love/Somewhere Over The Rainbow (33rpm 12")................................................................................................................. | 10 |
| 78 | Ebonite EE179 | PSYCHOSIS: Amalgamation/I Mean You/Tenor Madness (33rpm 12").......................... | 10 |
| 78 | Ebonite EE181 | SEVEN COLOURS: Summertime/Canadian Sunset/Girl Talk (33rpm 12") ..................... | 10 |
| 78 | Ebonite EE524 | INVERTERS: Colours/Nobody Loves You When You're Down And Out (33rpm 12") ....... | 10 |
| 78 | Ebonite EE 520 | CALENDARS: Like A Rolling Stone/Taxman/Last TIme (33rpm 12")............................... | 12 |
| 78 | Ebonite EE544 | MEASURING STICK: I Love Music/How Long Has This Been Going On (33rpm 12")........ | 25 |
| 78 | Ebonite EE595 | JOG WALKERS: Walking To New Orleans/Life In The Jungle Boogie/California Dreaming (33rpm 12") ......................................................................................... | 10 |
| 78 | Ebonite EE605 | SANDSTORM: Season Of The Witch/All Along The Watch Tower/Take FIve (33rpm 12")................................................................................................................. | 10 |
| 78 | Ebonite EE 1009 | THE WORKING MAN: Coming Home/Georgia (33rpm 12") .......................................... | 10 |
| 78 | Ebonite EE 5017 | INSPECTOR GENERALS: (33rpm 12")........................................................................ | 15 |
| 78 | Ebonite EE 5021 | POLARIZATION: (LP, die cut sleeve)......................................................................... | 15 |
| 78 | Ebonite EE 7010 | THE INVISIBLE CHASE: Red House Blues/Catch The Wind/I Want You (33rpm 12")........ | 12 |

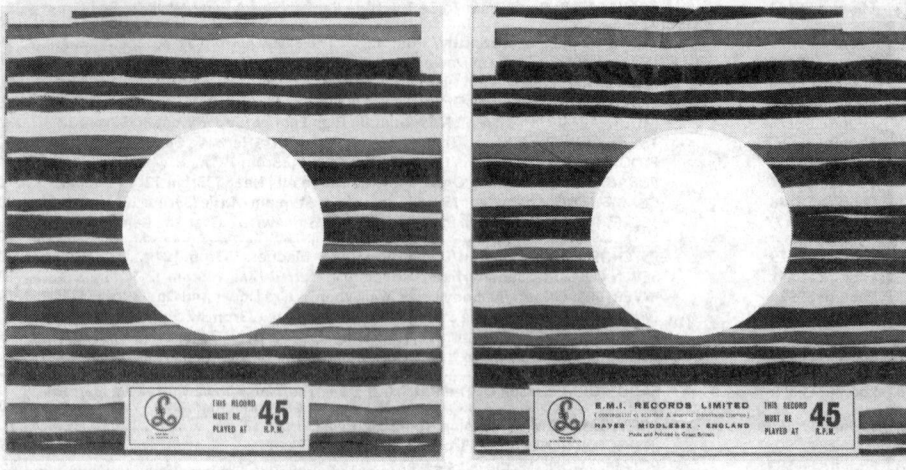

Sleeve Type A: coloured wavy lines with small box on front (left), large box on reverse (right).

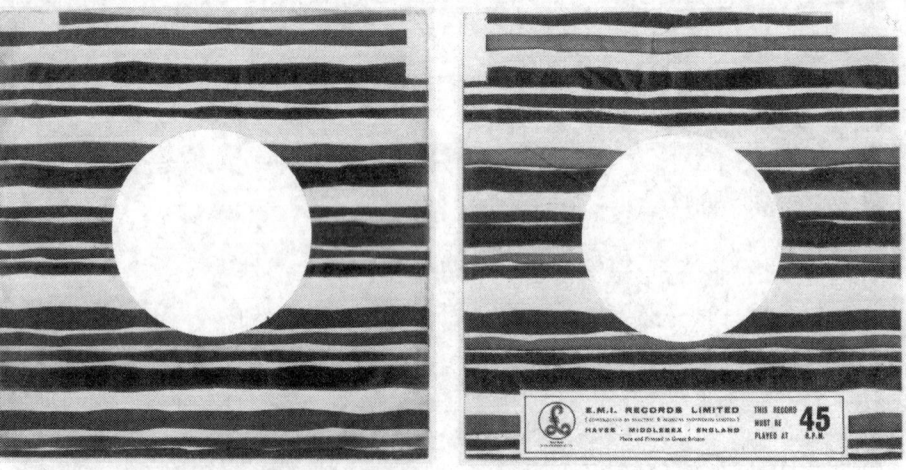

Sleeve Type B: coloured wavy lines without box on front (left), with large box on reverse (right).

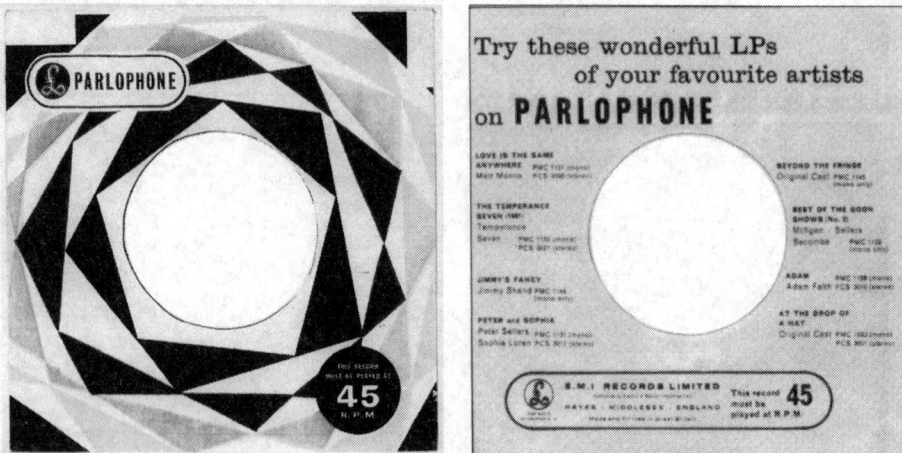

Sleeve Type C: multicoloured shapes on front (left) and LP details on reverse (right).

Green sleeve Type 1: straight cut at top (left) and '6/- to 50/- record tokens' on reverse (right).

Green sleeve Type 1B: wavy cut at top (left) and '6/- to 50/- record tokens' on reverse (right).

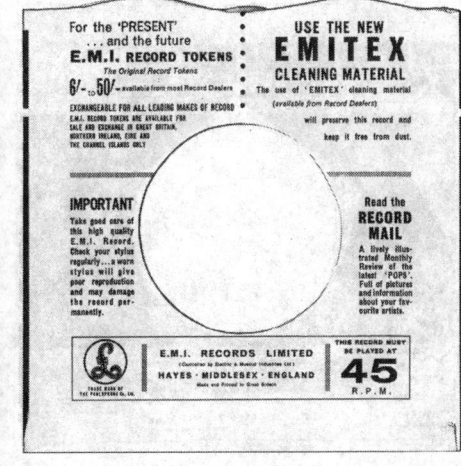

Green sleeve Type 2: rectangular box on front (left),'6/- to 50/- record tokens' on reverse (right).

Green sleeve Type 3: wavy cut at top (left) and 'Fran The Fan' advert on reverse (right).

Green sleeve Type 4: wavy cut at top (left) and 'Morphy-Richards offer' advert on reverse (right).

Green sleeve Type 5: straight cut at top (left), 'Fran The Fan, Dear Miss Brown' ad. on reverse (right).

Green sleeve Type 6: top wavy cut, front rectangular box (left), '6/- to 50/-' on reverse (right).

Green sleeve Type 7: wavy cut at top (left) and 'Big M' advert on reverse (right).

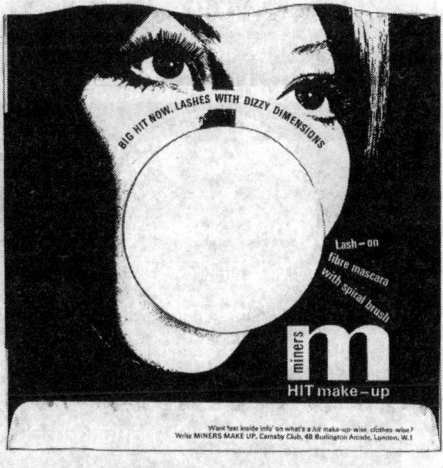

Green sleeve Type 8: wavy cut at top (left) and 'Hit make-up' advert on revesre (right).

# RECORD COLLECTOR
# BACK ISSUES

Full details of the content for each issue, and up-to-date availability are on our website – **www.recordcollectormag.com** You can order and pay by credit card on our site.

Alternatively you can order back issues in a number of ways:

* **By post:** enclosing a cheque payable to Diamond Publishing Limited, and sent to Record Collector Back Issues, Metropolis, 140 Wales Farm Road, London W3 6UG
* **By phone:** telephone Sue on +44 (0)20 8752 8193 paying by credit or debit card
* **By email:** sue.maritz@metropolis.co.uk

# RECORD COLLECTOR'S
# GRADING SYSTEM

In order to assist everyone who buys and sells rare discs, *Record Collector* magazine has originated a set of standards for the condition of second-hand records, cassettes and CDs. Anyone buying or selling records through the magazine must use our conditions to state what amount of wear and tear the disc, its sleeve and/or contents have been subject to. The seven standard condition categories, and a description of what each one means, are listed below:

**MINT:** The record itself is in brand new condition with no surface marks or deterioration in sound quality. The cover and any extra items such as the lyric sheet, booklet or poster are in perfect condition. Records advertised as Sealed or Unplayed should be Mint.

**EXCELLENT:** The record shows some signs of having been played, but there is very little lessening in sound quality. The cover and packaging might have slight wear and/or creasing.

**VERY GOOD:** The record has obviously been played many times, but displays no major deterioration in sound quality, despite noticeable surface marks and the occasional light scratch. Normal wear and tear on the cover or extra items, without any major defects, is acceptable.

**GOOD:** The record has been played so much that the sound quality has noticeably deteriorated, perhaps with some distortion and mild scratches. The cover and contents suffer from folding, scuffing of edges, spine splits, discoloration, etc.

**FAIR:** The record is still just playable but has not been cared for properly and displays considerable surface noise; it may even jump. The cover and contents will be torn, stained and/or defaced.

**POOR:** The record will not play properly due to scratches, bad surface noise, etc. The cover and contents will be badly damaged or partly missing.

**BAD:** The record is unplayable or might even be broken, and is only of use as a collection-filler.

**CDs & CASSETTES:** As a general rule, CDs and cassettes either play perfectly — in which case they are in Mint condition — or they don't, in which case their value is minimal. Cassette tape is liable to deteriorate with age, even if it remains unplayed, so care should be taken when buying old tapes. CDs are difficult to grade visually: they can look perfect but actually be faulty, while in other cases they may appear damaged but still play perfectly. Cassette and CD inlays and booklets should be graded in the same way as record covers and sleeves. In general, the plastic containers for cassettes and CDs can easily be replaced if they are broken or scratched, but card covers and digipaks are subject to the same wear as record sleeves.

# RECORD COLLECTOR'S
# GRADING READY RECKONER

This Ready Reckoner will help you work out the value of a record in any condition. For example, if you see a disc which is valued at £10 in Mint condition, but which you consider to be in only Very Good condition, then you can consult the Ready Reckoner and find out the appropriate price for the record — in this case, £5. As very few collectors are interested in records in Poor or Bad condition, we consider that any disc worth less than £10 in Mint condition is effectively worthless in Poor or Bad condition.

| MINT | EX | VG | Good | Fair | Poor | Bad |
|------|------|------|------|------|------|------|
| 1,000 | 800 | 500 | 300 | 150 | 80 | 25 |
| 500 | 400 | 250 | 150 | 75 | 40 | 12 |
| 300 | 240 | 150 | 90 | 45 | 25 | 8 |
| 250 | 200 | 125 | 75 | 38 | 20 | 6 |
| 200 | 160 | 100 | 60 | 30 | 15 | 5 |
| 150 | 120 | 75 | 45 | 25 | 13 | 4 |
| 125 | 100 | 60 | 38 | 18 | 12 | 3 |
| 100 | 80 | 50 | 30 | 15 | 8 | 2.50 |
| 75 | 60 | 35 | 22 | 10 | 6 | 2 |
| 50 | 40 | 25 | 15 | 8 | 4 | 1.50 |
| 40 | 32 | 20 | 12 | 6 | 3 | 1 |
| 30 | 25 | 15 | 9 | 4.50 | 2.50 | — |
| 25 | 20 | 12 | 7.50 | 3.50 | 2 | — |
| 22 | 18 | 11 | 6.50 | 3 | 1.75 | — |
| 20 | 16 | 10 | 6 | 2.50 | 1.50 | — |
| 15 | 12 | 8 | 4.50 | 2 | 1 | — |
| 12 | 10 | 6 | 3.50 | 1.75 | 0.75 | — |
| 10 | 8 | 5 | 3 | 1.50 | — | — |
| 8 | 6 | 4 | 2.50 | 1 | — | — |
| 7 | 5 | 3.50 | 2 | 0.75 | — | — |
| 6 | 4.50 | 3 | 1.75 | — | — | — |
| 5 | 4 | 2.50 | 1.50 | — | — | — |
| 4 | 3.25 | 2 | 1.25 | — | — | — |
| 3 | 2.50 | 1.50 | 1 | — | — | — |
| 2 | 1.75 | 1 | — | — | — | — |

| | | | |
|---|---|---|---|
| 67 | Parlophone R 5410 | Shadows And Reflections/Something Has Hit Me (p/s for export to Holland) | 150 |
| 81 | Edsel E 5001 | I'll Keep Holding On/Wasn't It You? (p/s) | 10 |
| 81 | Edsel E 5002 | Since I Lost My Baby/Never Ever/Wasn't It You (p/s) | 10 |
| 82 | Edsel E 5003 | Shadows And Reflections/Something Has Hit Me (p/s) | 10 |
| 84 | Edsel E 5008 | Hey Sah-Lo-Ney/Come On, Come With Me (p/s) | 10 |
| 80 | Edsel ED 101 | THE ULTIMATE ACTION (LP, with inner sleeve, first pressing with extra tracks) | 25 |
| 85 | Castle DOJO LP 3 | ACTION SPEAK LOUDER THAN... (mini-LP) | 15 |
| 95 | Dig The Fuzz DIG 005 | BRAIN - THE LOST RECORDINGS (LP, insert, booklet) | 20 |
| 98 | Dig The Fuzz DIG 025 | ROLLED GOLD (LP) | 15 |

*(see also Boys, Sandra Barry & Boys, Mighty Baby, Reg King, Stone's Masonry)*

**ACTION PACT**

| | | | |
|---|---|---|---|
| 81 | Subversive ANARCHO 1 | HEATHROW TOUCHDOWN (EP, 1 side by Dead Man's Shadow) | 20 |
| 82 | Fallout FALL 003 | Suicide Bag/Stanwell/Blue Blood (p/s) | 10 |
| 83 | Fallout FALL 010 | People/Times Must Change/Sixties Flix (p/s) | 10 |
| 83 | Fallout FALL 019 | Question Of Choice/Hook Line & Sinker (p/s) | 10 |

**ACTION PAINTING!**

| | | | |
|---|---|---|---|
| 90 | Sarah SARAH 028 | These Things Happen/Boy Meets World (wraparound p/s, with insert) | 10 |
| 93 | Sarah SARAH 73 | Classical Music/Sensation No. 5/Hip To Hate (p/s, insert) | 12 |
| 93 | Sarah SARAH 87 | Mustard Gas/Art Student/Collapsing Cloud (p/s, insert) | 15 |

**ACTION REPLAY**

| | | | |
|---|---|---|---|
| 79 | Rok ROK XV/XVI | Decisions/ZEROS: What's Wrong With Pop Group (die-cut company sleeve) | 15 |

**ACTION TRANSFERS**

| | | | |
|---|---|---|---|
| 82 | SRTS 82 CUS 1635 | Into The House/I Sing You Cry (hand-made fold-out sleeve) | 10 |
| 84 | Rewind REW 17 | The Light (Oh Baby)/The Right To Remain Silent (p/s) | 6 |
| 84 | Rewind REW 20 | If I Loose It/Colours (p/s) | 6 |

**ACTIVE RESTRAINT**

| | | | |
|---|---|---|---|
| 82 | Sticky PEEL OFF 3 | Terror In My Home/Turns Out Roses | 25 |

**ACTIVES**

| | | | |
|---|---|---|---|
| 83 | Quiet Records QS 001 | RIOT (EP) | 40 |
| 84 | Quiet Records QS 004 | WAIT & SEE (EP" 12") | 30 |
| 83 | Quiet Records QLP 4 | KICK IT DOWN (LP, with insert) | 70 |

**ACTRESS**

| | | | |
|---|---|---|---|
| 69 | CBS 4016 | It's What You Give/Good Job With Prospects | 150 |

**ROY ACUFF & SMOKY MOUNTAIN BOYS**

| | | | |
|---|---|---|---|
| 57 | Brunswick 05635 | I Like Mountain Music/It's Hard To Love (And Not To Be In Love) | 6 |

**ACUTE LOGIC**

| | | | |
|---|---|---|---|
| 81 | Illogical EJSP 9589 | Morrocan Nights/The Obsession/The Balcony (p/s, insert) | 30 |

**ADAM & THE ANTS**

| | | | |
|---|---|---|---|
| 78 | Decca F 13803 | Young Parisians/Lady (in p/s, original with paper labels) | 12 |
| 78 | Decca F 13803 | Young Parisians/Lady (company sleeve) | 6 |
| 79 | Do It DUN 8 | Zerox/Whip In My Valise (mispressing with 'Physical' on B-side but 'Whip In My Valise' on label. Matrix DUN 8 B1 or W-1KD DUN 8 B1) | 8 |
| 79 | Do It DUN8 | Zerox/Whip In My Valise | 5 |
| 79 | Want 1 | Cartrouble Part 1/Cartrouble Part 2/Kick (1-sided promo) | 15 |
| 80 | Do It DUN 10 | Cartrouble/Kick (p/s) | 5 |
| 88 | Damaged Goods FNARR 7 | Young Parisians/Lady/Interviews (12" reissue with fanzine) | 20 |
| 79 | Do It RIDE 3 | DIRK WEARS WHITE SOX (LP, 1st pressing with 'Do It' labels) | 15 |
| 80 | CBS 4025361 | DIRK WEARS WHITE SOX (cassette reissue) | 20 |
| 90 | Strange Fruit SFRLP 115 | PEEL SESSIONS (LP) | 15 |
| 00 | Sony ANTBOX 5007822 | ANTBOX (3-CD with book in 7" sized box) | 35 |
| 06 | Sony 88697009032 | ADAM & THE ANTS - REMASTERED (7-CD, box set) | 40 |

*(see also Adam Ant, Maneaters, Models, Danny & Nogoodniks)*

**ADAM AND DEE**

| | | | |
|---|---|---|---|
| 69 | Tangerine DP 0002 | Question Of Childhood/Run To Her | 120 |

**ALICIA ADAMS**

| | | | |
|---|---|---|---|
| 61 | Capitol CL 15195 | Love Bandit/Oom Dooby Doom Lovey Dovey Sh' Boom | 5 |

**ARTHUR ADAMS**

| | | | |
|---|---|---|---|
| 81 | RCA RCAT 146 | You Got The Floor/Stay With Me Tonight (12") | 10 |

**ARTHUR K. ADAMS**

| | | | |
|---|---|---|---|
| 68 | Blue Horizon 57-3136 | She Drives Me Out Of My Mind/Gimme Some Of Your Lovin' | 25 |

**BILLY ADAMS (1)**

| | | | |
|---|---|---|---|
| 60 | Capitol CL 15107 | Count Every Star/Peggy's Party | 15 |

**BILLY ADAMS (2)**

| | | | |
|---|---|---|---|
| 69 | London 10258 | I Need Your Love/Why Don't You Believe Me (DJ Copy) | 20 |
| 69 | London HL 10258 | I Need Your Love/Why Don't You Believe Me | 10 |

**ADAMS (CHRIS AND PAULINE)**

| | | | |
|---|---|---|---|
| 75 | Charisma CB 244 | If Only The Good Die Young/The City At Night | 8 |

**DERROLL ADAMS**

| | | | |
|---|---|---|---|
| 67 | Ace Of Clubs ACL 1227 | PORTLAND TOWN (LP) | 60 |
| 72 | Village Thing VTS 17 | FEELIN' FINE (LP, with inner sleeve) | 70 |
| 72 | Village Thing VTS 17 | FEELIN' FINE (LP, without inner sleeve) | 40 |

*(see also Ramblin' Jack Elliott)*

**FAYE ADAMS**

| | | | |
|---|---|---|---|
| 56 | London HLU 8339 | I'll Be True/Happiness To My Soul (Gold Tri label) | 500 |
| 56 | London HLU 8339 | I'll Be True/Happiness To My Soul (78) | 25 |

**GAYLE ADAMS**

| | | | |
|---|---|---|---|
| 82 | Epic A 2167 | Baby I Need Your Loving/Don't Jump To Conclusions | 12 |

MINT VALUE £

| | | | |
|---|---|---|---|
| 82 | Epic A13 2167 | Baby I Need Your Loving/Don't Jump To Conclusions (12") | 15 |

## GLADSTON ADAMS
| | | | |
|---|---|---|---|
| 69 | Trojan TR 659 | Dollars And Cents/TOMMY McCOOK: Popcorn Reggay | 20 |

*(see also Gladstone Anderson)*

## GLEN ADAMS
| | | | |
|---|---|---|---|
| 67 | Island WI 3072 | Silent Lover/I Remember | 60 |
| 67 | Island WI 3083 | She (actually titled "I'm Shocking")/SONNY BURKE: Some Other Time | 60 |
| 67 | Island WI 3099 | Grab A Girl/DELROY WILSON: This Heart Of Mine | 50 |
| 67 | Island WI 3100 | Hold Down Miss Winey/VINCENT GORDON: Sounds And Soul | 70 |
| 67 | Island WI 3120 | She's So Fine/ROY SHIRLEY: Girlie | 50 |
| 68 | Blue Cat BS 126 | She Is Leaving/UNIQUES: Girls Like Dirt | 30 |
| 68 | Trojan TR 621 | Rent Too High/Every Time | 25 |
| 68 | Duke DU 58 | My Girl/GLADIATORS: You Were To Be | 20 |
| 68 | Bullet BU 414 | Cat Woman/PETER TOUCH: Selassie Serenade (B-side actually by Peter Tosh) | 20 |
| 68 | Collins Downbeat CR 010 | King Sized/I'm Gonna Take You Back (B-side actually by Owen Gray) | 90 |
| 68 | Collins Downbeat CR 006 | Cool Cool Rock Steady (as Glen Addams & Collins Band)/OWEN GRAY & COLLINS BAND: Girl I Will Be Leaving | 125 |
| 68 | Giant GN 33 | Lonely Girl/ROY SHIRLEY: Warming Up The Scene | 175 |
| 69 | Amalgamated AMG 837 | She's So Fine/ERNEST WILSON: Private Number | 50 |
| 69 | Crab CRAB 21 | Mighty Organ/ERNEST WILSON: Just Once | 25 |
| 69 | Sound Systems SS 105 | Down To Earth Reggae/Reggae From Mankind | 20 |
| 70 | Gas GAS 141 | Leaving On A Jet Plane/REGGAE BOYS: Phrases | 35 |
| 70 | Junior JR 110 | Sound In/Sound & Pleasure | 20 |
| 71 | Big BG 321 | Weary Version 3/TONY BREVETT: Hills And Valleys | 18 |
| 71 | Explosion EX 2048 | Never Fall In Love/JET SCENE: Jet 747 | 12 |
| 71 | Upsetter US 367 | Never Had A Dream/UPSETTERS: Version | 45 |

*(see also Glen Adams, Reggae Boys, Roy Shirley, Maxie & Glen, Delroy Wilson, Derrick Morgan, Ernest Wilson, Owen Gray)*

## JUNE ADAMS
| | | | |
|---|---|---|---|
| 66 | King KG 1038 | River Keep Movin'/Heavenly Father | 12 |

## LLOYD ADAMS
| | | | |
|---|---|---|---|
| 62 | Wasp W001 | I Wish Your Picture Was You/Pleading For Love (Possibly unreleased) | 35 |
| 62 | Wasp W009 | I Wish Your Picture Was You/Pleading For Love | 20 |

## MARIE ADAMS
| | | | |
|---|---|---|---|
| 59 | Capitol CL 14963 | A Fool In Love/What Do You Want To Make Those Eyes At Me For | 40 |
| 59 | Capitol CL 14964 | A Fool In Love/What Do You Want To Make Those Eyes At Me For (promo copy in picture sleeve) | 60 |

*(see also Johnny Otis)*

## PAUL & LINDA ADAMS
| | | | |
|---|---|---|---|
| 75 | Sweet Folk & Country SFA 27 | FAR OVER THE FELL (LP) | 15 |

## PEPPER ADAMS
| | | | |
|---|---|---|---|
| 58 | Vogue LAE 12134 | CRITICS CHOICE (LP) | 25 |
| 59 | Pye NLP 28007 | COOL SOUND (LP) | 20 |

## RITCHIE ADAMS
| | | | |
|---|---|---|---|
| 60 | London HLU 9200 | Back To School/Don't Go My Love, Don't Go | 30 |

## RYAN ADAMS
| | | | |
|---|---|---|---|
| 03 | Lost Highway 9861613 | So Alive/Luxury (p/s, numbered edition) | 12 |
| 04 | Lost Highway 602498630990 | Wonderwall/One By One (p/s) | 20 |
| 00 | Cooking Vinyl COOK 205 | HEARTBREAKER (LP, with inner) | 35 |
| 03 | Lost Highway 986 100 1 | ROCK N ROLL (LP) | 35 |
| 03 | Lost Highway 986 100-1 | ROCK N ROLL (LP, 'blood' cover) | 50 |
| 03 | Lost Highway 986 136-1 | LOVE IS HELL PARTS 1 & 2 (LP, as 2x10") | 25 |
| 05 | Lost Highway B0004707-01 | JACKSONVILLE CITY NIGHTS (2-LP as Ryan Adams & The Cardinals) | 20 |
| 08 | Lost Highway 02517872608 | CARDINOLOGY (2-LP) | 25 |
| 05 | Lost Highway B0004343-01 | COLD ROSES (2-LP, embossed cover, as Ryan Adams And The Cardinals) | 50 |
| 11 | Columbia 88697973101 | ASHES AND FIRE (LP) | 18 |

## STEVE ADAMS
| | | | |
|---|---|---|---|
| 77 | Mind's Ear MER 2010 | STEVE ADAMS (LP) | 15 |

## SUZIE ADAMS
| | | | |
|---|---|---|---|
| 80 | Waterfront WFS1 | Casey's Last Ride/Nostradamus (p/s) | 5 |

## WOODROW ADAMS
| | | | |
|---|---|---|---|
| 65 | Blue Horizon BH 1001 | Baby You Just Don't Know/Wine Head Woman (99 copies only) | 250 |

## ZAYNE ADAMS
| | | | |
|---|---|---|---|
| 69 | NEMS 56 4473 | Can't You See Me/If You Were My Woman | 15 |

## ADAM'S APPLES
| | | | |
|---|---|---|---|
| 77 | Brunswick BR 42 | Don't Take It Out On This World/Don't You Want To Take Me Home | 18 |
| 85 | Kent Town 101 | Don't Take It Out On This World/JACKIE WILSON: I Don't Want To Lose You | 12 |

## ADAMS FAMILY
| | | | |
|---|---|---|---|
| 93 | Loose LOOSE 02 | Frustration/Timewaster (p/s) | 6 |

## BARRY ADAMSON
| | | | |
|---|---|---|---|
| 89 | Mute STUMM 53 | MOSS SIDE STORY (LP) | 15 |
| 96 | Mute STUMM 134 | OEDIPUS SCHMOEDIPUS (LP) | 15 |
| 98 | Mute STUMM 161 | AS ABOVE SO BELOW (LP) | 15 |
| 02 | Mute STUMM 176 | THE KING OF NOTTING HILL (2-LP) | 18 |

## A DANCING MIRAGE
| | | | |
|---|---|---|---|
| 82 | Wide WIDE 001 | BOYS IN COLOUR EP | 25 |

## AD ASTRA
| | | | |
|---|---|---|---|
| 83 | Sane 45001 | Give Me The Girl/Find The Time | 25 |

### AD CONSPIRACY
| | | | |
|---|---|---|---|
| 79 | Diamond Age AD 22957 | AD CONSPIRACY (LP) | 70 |

### CANNONBALL ADDERLEY
| | | | |
|---|---|---|---|
| 61 | Riverside RIV 33457 | African Waltz/Kelly Blue | 5 |
| 67 | Capitol CL 15489 | Mercy Mercy Mercy/Games | 10 |
| 59 | Riverside 12-30333 | CANNONBALL TAKES CHARGE (LP) | 20 |
| 61 | Riverside RLP 377 | AFRICAN WALTZ (LP) | 25 |
| 62 | Riverside RLP 12-311 | THE CANNONBALL ADDERLEY QUINTET IN SAN FRANCISCO (LP) | 20 |
| 63 | Riverside RLP 433 | KNOW WHAT I MEAN (LP, with BILL EVANS) | 25 |
| 64 | Riverside RLP 477 | NIPPON SOUL (LP) | 20 |
| 67 | Capitol ST 2663 | MERCY! MERCY! MERCY! (LP) | 20 |
| 67 | Capitol T2617 | WHY AM I TREATED SO BAD? (LP) | 20 |
| 68 | Mercury LML/SLML 4022 | THEM ADDERLEYS (LP, mono/stereo) | 20 |
| 73 | Fantasy FT 517 | INSIDE STRAIGHT (LP) | 15 |
| 84 | Blue Note BST 81595 | SOMETHIN' ELSE (LP, reissue) | 15 |

*(see also Nancy Wilson, Miles Davis, John Coltrane)*

### NAT ADDERLEY
| | | | |
|---|---|---|---|
| 62 | Riverside RLP 12-330 | THAT'S RIGHT! (LP, as Nat Adderley and the Big Sax Section) | 20 |
| 56 | London LTZC 15018 | THAT'S NAT (LP) | 20 |
| 62 | Riverside RLP 12-318 | WORK SONG (LP) | 25 |
| 65 | Fontana FJL 118 | NATURALLY (LP) | 20 |
| 65 | Atlantic ATL 5032 | AUTOBIOGRAPHY (LP) | 20 |
| 66 | Atlantic 587 023/588 023 | SAYIN' SOMETHIN' (LP, Mono/Stereo) | 20 |
| 68 | Mercury LML/SLML 4022 | THEM ADDERLEYS (LP, mono/stereo) | 20 |
| 69 | A&M AMLS 947 | CALLING OUT LOUD (LP) | 18 |

### ADDICTION
| | | | |
|---|---|---|---|
| 92 | Vicious Pumpin' OBS 002 | ADDICTION EP (12", stamped white label) | 20 |
| 92 | Vicious Pumpin' VIC 003 | MIND PENETRATION EP (12", stamped white label) | 25 |
| 92 | Vicious Pumpin' VIC 003R | MIND PENETRATION (THE REMIXES) EP (12", stamped white label) | 40 |
| 92 | Vicious Vinyl VIC 001 | THE CREATIVE DUB EP (12") | 15 |
| 93 | Vicious Pumpin' VIC 013 | Wildstyle/Untitled (12") | 10 |

### ADDICTS
| | | | |
|---|---|---|---|
| 64 | Decca F 11902 | That's My Girl/Here She Comes | 20 |

### ADDIS ROCKERS
| | | | |
|---|---|---|---|
| 85 | Warrior WAR 2 | ENTER ADDIS ABABA (LP) | 20 |

### ADDIX
| | | | |
|---|---|---|---|
| 79 | Zig Zag ZZ 22002 | Too Blind To See/(No Such Thing As A) Bad Boy (p/s) | 15 |

### ADD N TO X
| | | | |
|---|---|---|---|
| 99 | Mute STUMM 170 | AVANT HARD (2-LP, gatefold) | 18 |

### ADDRISSI BROTHERS
| | | | |
|---|---|---|---|
| 59 | Columbia DB 4370 | Back To The Old Salt Mine/It's Love | 30 |

### JEAN ADEBAMBO
| | | | |
|---|---|---|---|
| 79 | Ade J AJ 101 | Say That You Love Me/Dance Of Love (12") | 20 |
| 83 | Ade J AJ 0123 | FEELINGS (LP) | 25 |
| 85 | Ade J AJ 0124 | OFF KEY LOVING (LP) | 15 |

### ADELE
| | | | |
|---|---|---|---|
| 07 | Pacemaker 1 | Hometown Glory/Best For Last (7", 500 only) | 15 |
| 08 | XL S321 | Chasing Pavements/That's It I Quit | 30 |
| 08 | XL XLT 374 | Hometown Glory - Remixes (12". stickered company sleeve) | 12 |
| 08 | XL XLS 393 | Make You Feel My Love/Painting Pictures (p/s, 500 only) | 15 |
| 08 | XL XLLP 313 | 19 (LP, inner) | 15 |

### BOBBY ADENO
| | | | |
|---|---|---|---|
| 66 | Vocalion V 9279 | The Hands Of Time/It's A Sad World (DJ copy) | 40 |
| 66 | Vocalion V 9279 | The Hands Of Time/It's A Sad World | 25 |

### SEGUN ADEWALE
| | | | |
|---|---|---|---|
| 85 | Stern's Africa STERNS1009 | OJO JE (LP) | 15 |

### ADICTS
| | | | |
|---|---|---|---|
| 81 | Dining Out TUX 1 | LUNCH WITH THE ADICTS (EP, with insert & screen-printed p/s) | 50 |
| 82 | Fall Out FALL 002 | Viva La Revolution/Steamroller (p/s) | 20 |
| 82 | Razor RZS 101 | Chinese Takeaway/You'll Never Walk Alone (p/s) | 10 |
| 83 | Razor RZS 104 | Bad Boy/Shake, Rattle, Bang Your Head (p/s) | 10 |
| 83 | Razor RZLP 104 | Bad Boy/Shake, Rattle, Bang Your Head (shaped picture disc) | 12 |
| 81 | Dwed SMT 008 | SONGS OF PRAISE (LP) | 50 |
| 81 | Fall Out FALL LP 006 | SONGS OF PRAISE (LP, reissue, yellow vinyl, 2,000 only) | 20 |
| 81 | Fall Out FALL LP 006P | SONGS OF PRAISE (LP, reissue, picture disc) | 20 |
| 82 | Razor RAZ 2 | SOUND OF MUSIC (LP) | 20 |
| 85 | Razor RAZ15 | SMART ALEX (LP) | 15 |
| 87 | Fall Out FALL LP021 | THIS IS YOUR LIFE (LP) | 18 |
| 87 | Fall Out FALL LP 042 | FIFTH OVERTURE (LP) | 20 |
| 90 | Fall Out FALL LP 046 | ROCKERS INTO ORBIT (LP, green vinyl, stickered sleeve) | 18 |

*(see also ADX)*

### BETH ADLAM WITH BUZZ & BOYS
| | | | |
|---|---|---|---|
| 60 | Starlite ST45 024 | Seventeen/I'll Walk Into The Sea | 10 |

### ADLIBS (U.K.)
| | | | |
|---|---|---|---|
| 65 | Fontana TF 584 | Neighbour Neighbour/Lovely Ladies | 50 |

### AD-LIBS (U.S.)
| | | | |
|---|---|---|---|
| 66 | Red Bird RB 10-102 | The Boy From New York City/Kicked Around (DJ Copy) | 50 |

# ADMIRAL SIR CLOUDESLEY SHOVELL

| | | | |
|---|---|---|---|
| 66 | Red Bird RB 10-102 | The Boy From New York City/Kicked Around | 35 |
| 69 | Deep Soul DS 9102 | Giving Up/Appreciation | 35 |
| 75 | Contempo CS 9029 | The Boy From New York City/Johnny My Boy | 10 |
| 79 | Inferno HEAT 1 | New York In The Dark/The Boy From New York City (p/s, coloured vinyl) | 7 |
| 04 | Soul City 142 | I Don't Need No Fortune (Teller)/New York In The Dark (reissue) | 5 |

## ADMIRAL SIR CLOUDESLEY SHOVELL
| | | | |
|---|---|---|---|
| 10 | Rise Above RISE 7 123 | Return To Zero/Day After (p/s, 300 only) | 10 |

## ADMIRALS (1)
| | | | |
|---|---|---|---|
| 65 | Fontana TF 597 | Promised Land/Palisades Park | 30 |

## ADMIRALS (2)
| | | | |
|---|---|---|---|
| 75 | Angen ANG 102 | Natty Should Be Free/ANSEL COLLINS: Far East Special | 10 |

## ADMIRAL TIBET
| | | | |
|---|---|---|---|
| 86 | Redman Intl. RED 4 | New Tactics/RED DRAGON: Ease Off (12") | 20 |
| 86 | Rix RIZ 006 | Permission/Sixth Commandment Dub/Version (12") | 30 |
| 80s | Live & Love LLD301 | Victim of Babylon/GREGORY PECK: Wah Do You (12") | 15 |

*(see also Red Dragon)*

## ADMIRATIONS
| | | | |
|---|---|---|---|
| 02 | Soul City 135 | You Left Me/I Want To Be Free (reissue) | 12 |

## ADMIT YOU'RE SHIT
| | | | |
|---|---|---|---|
| 81 | Mortarhate MORT 17 | EXPECT NO MERCY (EP) | 25 |
| 86 | Mortarhate MORT 27 | 12 INCHES OF AYS (12" EP) | 10 |

## AD NAUSEUM
| | | | |
|---|---|---|---|
| 83 | Flicknife FLS 12 | BRAINSTORM (EP, p/s) | 10 |
| 87 | | THE GREATEST SHOW ON EARTH (Mini-LP) | 20 |

## A.D. 1984
| | | | |
|---|---|---|---|
| 79 | Voyage International VOY 005 | The Russians Are Coming/New Moon Falling (p/s) | 20 |
| 80 | Grand Prix 001/002 | Race To Nowhere/Leisure Crime (with lyric sheet) | 15 |
| 81 | Grand Prix GP 003 | The Clockwork Generation/Melody In The Key Of Time (p/s) | 10 |
| 83 | Grand Prix GP 011 | Mushroom Music (& Mayhem)/1984 | 15 |
| 83 | Grand Prix GP 014 | 1984/Mushroom Music | 12 |

## ADOLESCENTS
| | | | |
|---|---|---|---|
| 90 | Overground OVER 07 | ADOLESCENTS (LP, reissue of original US pressing) | 15 |

## ADRENALIN
| | | | |
|---|---|---|---|
| 79 | Hithouse 12 HIT 2 | Feel The Real/Feel The Real (Instrumental) (12" stamped white label) | 30 |

## AD VANCE VS GESCOM
| | | | |
|---|---|---|---|
| 98 | Fat Cat 12FAT 009 | Viral/FOEHN: Shrouded/Funeral In Space (12", p/s) | 10 |

## ADVENTURERS
| | | | |
|---|---|---|---|
| 60 | Capitol CL 15108 | Trail Blazer/Rip Van Winkle | 10 |

## ADVENTURES
| | | | |
|---|---|---|---|
| 61 | Philips BBL 7548 | CAN'T STOP TWISTIN' (LP) | 30 |

## ANTHONY ADVERSE
| | | | |
|---|---|---|---|
| 86 | él GPO 13 | Our Fairy Tale/Eine Symphonie Des Grauens (p/s) | 5 |
| 87 | él GPO 29 | Imperial Violets/Fountain (p/s) | 5 |
| 85 | El ACME 11 | RED SHOES (LP) | 20 |

## ADVERTISING
| | | | |
|---|---|---|---|
| 77 | EMI EMI 2710 | Lipstick/Lonely Guys (p/s) | 5 |
| 77 | EMI EMI 2754 | Stolen Love/Suspender Fun (p/s) | 5 |
| 78 | EMI EMC 3253 | ADVERTISING JINGLES (LP) | 18 |

*(see also Secret Affair, Innocents, Simon Boswell)*

## ADVERTS
| | | | |
|---|---|---|---|
| 77 | Stiff BUY 13 | One Chord Wonders/Quickstep (p/s, 1st pressing with push-out centre) | 25 |
| 77 | Stiff BUY 13 | One Chord Wonders/Quickstep (p/s, re-pressing with solid centre) | 10 |
| 77 | Anchor ANC 1043 | Gary Gilmore's Eyes/Bored Teenagers (p/s) | 8 |
| 77 | Anchor ANC 1047 | Safety In Numbers/We Who Wait (p/s) | 8 |
| 78 | Bright BR 1 | No Time To Be 21/New Day Dawning (p/s) | 7 |
| 78 | RCA PB 5128 | Television's Over/Back From The Dead (p/s) | 6 |
| 79 | RCA 5160 | My Place/New Church (p/s) | 6 |
| 83 | Bright BULB 1 | Gary Gilmore's Eyes/We Who Wait/New Day Dawning (p/s) | 10 |
| 87 | Strange Fruit SFPS 034 | PEEL SESSIONS (12", metallic finish) | 10 |
| 78 | Bright BRL 201 | CROSSING THE RED SEA WITH THE ADVERTS (LP, red vinyl, 5,000 only) | 25 |
| 78 | Bright BULB 1 | CROSSING THE RED SEA WITH THE ADVERTS (LP, black vinyl second pressing) | 15 |
| 79 | RCA PL 25246 | CAST OF THOUSANDS (LP) | 20 |
| 81 | Butt/Bright ALSO 002 | CROSSING THE RED SEA WITH THE ADVERTS (LP, reissue, red vinyl) | 15 |

## ADVOCATES
| | | | |
|---|---|---|---|
| 73 | Dovetail DOVE 1 | ADVOCATES (LP) | 30 |
| 75 | Dovetail DOVE 7 | HERE I REST MY CASE (LP) | 30 |

## ADX
| | | | |
|---|---|---|---|
| 85 | Sire U 9070 | Falling In Love Again/Come Along (p/s) | 5 |

*(see also Adicts)*

## AERIAL FX
| | | | |
|---|---|---|---|
| 80 | Square SQS 3 | So Hard/It's About Time | 8 |
| 81 | Island WIP 6698 | Take It From Here/Somewhere (p/s) | 10 |
| 82 | Kamera ERA 012 | Instant Feelings/5:15 (p/s, pressed in France but issued in U.K.) | 15 |
| 82 | Kamera KAM 008 | WATCHING THE DANCE (LP, pressed in France but issued in U.K.) | 30 |

## AEROPHONE
| | | | |
|---|---|---|---|
| 71 | RPM 357 | Sweet Sweet Suzie/Of Tomorrow | 15 |

## AEROSMITH

| | | | |
|---|---|---|---|
| 73 | CBS 1898 | Dream On/Somebody | 10 |
| 76 | CBS 4000 | Dream On/Somebody (reissue) | 5 |
| 76 | CBS 4452 | Last Child/Combination | 5 |
| 77 | CBS 4878 | Walk This Way/Uncle Salty | 5 |
| 77 | CBS S AR 2 | Draw The Line/Bright, Light, Fright (p/s) | 5 |
| 78 | CBS 6584 | Come Together/Kings And Queens | 5 |
| 80 | CBS 8220 | Remember (Walking In The Sand)/Bone To Bone (p/s) | 5 |
| 87 | Geffen GEF 29TP | Dude (Looks Like A Lady)/Simoriah/Once Is Enough (12", picture disc) | 10 |
| 89 | Geffen GEF 68P | Janie's Got A Gun/Voodoo Medicine Man (shaped picture disc) | 10 |
| 98 | Columbia 6664087 | I Don't Want To Miss A Thing/Taste Of India (picture disc) | 10 |
| 73 | CBS 32005 | AEROSMITH (LP) | 20 |
| 74 | CBS 80015 | GET YOUR WINGS (LP) | 15 |
| 93 | Geffen GEF 24444 | GET A GRIP (2-LP, inners) | 40 |

*(see also Run DMC)*

## AEROVONS

| | | | |
|---|---|---|---|
| 69 | Parlophone R 5790 | The Train/A Song For Jane | 40 |
| 69 | Parlophone R 5804 | World Of You/Say Georgia | 120 |

## A FAIR SET

| | | | |
|---|---|---|---|
| 65 | Decca F 12168 | Honey And Wine/Run Around | 20 |

## PETER AFENDOULIS

| | | | |
|---|---|---|---|
| 78 | Folkland FL 1018 | THERE'S ONLY ONE F IN AFENDOULIS (LP, mail-order only) | 40 |

## AFEX

| | | | |
|---|---|---|---|
| 67 | King KG 1058 | She Got The Time/I Never Knew Love Was Like This | 140 |

## AFFAIRS OF THE HEART

| | | | |
|---|---|---|---|
| 83 | Heartbeat PULSE 100 | Waterloo Sunset/Waterloo Version (p/s) | 10 |

## AFFINITY

| | | | |
|---|---|---|---|
| 70 | Vertigo 6059 007 | I Wonder If I Care As Much/Three Sisters | 35 |
| 70 | Vertigo 6360 004 | AFFINITY (LP, gatefold sleeve, large swirl label) | 400 |

*(see also Linda Hoyle, Jeff Beck Group, Queen, Ice)*

## AFFLICTED (1)

| | | | |
|---|---|---|---|
| 71 | Scott SC 02 | Miranda/Stolen Dreams | 100 |

## AFFLICTED (2)

| | | | |
|---|---|---|---|
| 81 | Bonk AFF 1 | I'm Afflicted/Be Aware (rubber-stamped white labels, p/s, with insert) | 70 |
| 81 | Bonk AFF 1 | I'm Afflicted/Be Aware (rubber-stamped white labels, p/s, without insert) | 30 |
| 82 | Bonk AFF 2 | All Right Boy/Who Can Tell (with p/s, stamped white labels) | 60 |
| 82 | Bonk AFF 2 | All Right Boy/Who Can Tell (without p/s, stamped white labels) | 10 |
| 82 | Bonk AFF 4 | One Forty Two/Senseless Whale Stalker (untitled single in stamped striped bag) | 20 |
| 82 | Bonk AFF 3 | THE AFFLICTED MAN'S MUSICAL BAG (LP, stamped white label in stamped bag sleeve) | 25 |

## AFFLICTED MAN

| | | | |
|---|---|---|---|
| 80 | Human HUM1 | I'M OFF MI HEAD (LP) | 20 |

## AFGHAN WHIGS

| | | | |
|---|---|---|---|
| 93 | Blast First BFFP 90 | GENTLEMEN (LP) | 20 |
| 96 | Mute STUMM 143 | BLACK LOVE (LP) | 40 |
| 10 | Music On Vinyl MOVLP 149 | 1965 (2-LP, reissue) | 20 |
| 14 | Music On VInyl MOVLP 821 | BLACK LOVE (LP, reissue) | 18 |

## AFI

| | | | |
|---|---|---|---|
| 99 | Nitro ADELINE 002 | A FIRE INSIDE EP (ps, insert) | 10 |
| 01 | Nitro 15843-2 | The Days Of The Phoenix/A Winter's Tale/Wester (CD, 500 only) | 25 |
| 03 | Nitro 450 460-2 | Girl's Not Grey/The Hanging Garden (p/s, grey vinyl) | 10 |
| 03 | Nitro 450 462-6 | The Leaving Song Pt. II/The Great Disappointment (Demo) (p/s, green vinyl) | 8 |
| 09 | DGC/Interscope 2721645/7 | Medicate/Carcinogen Crush//Medicate/Ether (2 x 7", stickered sleeves, 1000 only, numbered) | 7 |
| 10 | Polydor 2736938 | Beautiful Thieves (1-sided 7", etched B-side, p/s, 500 only) | 8 |
| 03 | Nitro 65522300261 | SING THE SORROW (2-LP, red vinyl, inner sleeves) | 50 |
| 03 | Universal | SING THE SORROW (CD, with DVD in black hardback book 500 only, sold on tour) | 40 |

## A FINAL DISCIPLINE

| | | | |
|---|---|---|---|
| 82 | Clock House CH 0504 | Empty Pictures/And Still I Miss You | 20 |

## A FLEETING GLANCE

| | | | |
|---|---|---|---|
| 70 | Private Pressing AS 2324 | A FLEETING GLANCE (LP) | 2000 |

## AFRICAN

| | | | |
|---|---|---|---|
| 72 | Sioux SI 006 | Cock Mouth Kill Cock/ERROL T: I Need To Know | 20 |

## AFRICAN BEAVERS

| | | | |
|---|---|---|---|
| 65 | RCA RCA 1447 | Find My Baby/Jungle Fever | 20 |

## AFRICAN BROTHER (ACTUALLY MATUMBI)

| | | | |
|---|---|---|---|
| 77 | Mainline ML 1 | Gimme Gimmie African Love/PURE ROOTS: African Love Dub | 15 |
| 79 | Greensleeves GRED 14 | A Di System/Gimme Gimme African Love (12") | 12 |

## AFRICAN BROTHERS BAND

| | | | |
|---|---|---|---|
| 73 | Afribros PAB 003 | HIGHLIFE TIME (LP) | 40 |
| 73 | Leo Mensah PN 06 | HIGHLIFE TIME (LP) | 35 |
| 74 | Afribros PAB 003 | HIGHLIFE TIME (LP, reissue, different cover) | 35 |

## AFRICAN HEAD CHARGE

| | | | |
|---|---|---|---|
| 81 | ON-U LP 13 | MY LIFE IN A HOLE IN THE GROUND (LP) | 20 |
| 82 | ON-U LP 19 | ENVIRONMENTAL STUDIES (LP) | 20 |
| 83 | ON-U LP 27 | DRASTIC SEASON (LP) | 20 |
| 86 | ON-U LP 40 | OFF THE BEATEN TRACK (LP) | 15 |

MINT VALUE £

| | | |
|---|---|---|
| 93 | On-U LP 65 | IN PURSUIT OF SHASHAMANE LAND (LP, with free 7") ........................................ 20 |

**AFRICAN MESSENGERS**
| | | |
|---|---|---|
| 64 | Page One P04043 | Highlife Picadilly/Blues For The Messengers ............................................. 12 |

**AFRICAN MUSIC MACHINE**
| | | |
|---|---|---|
| 72 | Mojo 2092 046 | Black Water Gold (Pearl)/Making Nassau Fruit Drink .................................. 15 |
| 73 | Contempo CR 13 | Tropical/The Girl In France ....................................................... 10 |
| 73 | Contempo CR 25 | Never Name A Baby/Dapp ......................................................... 10 |
| 74 | Contempo CS 2025 | Mr Brown/Camel Time ............................................................ 8 |

**AFRICAN PRINCESS**
| | | |
|---|---|---|
| 81 | Jah Shaka SHAKA 809 | Jah Jah Children Cry/Jah Jah Dub (12") ............................................ 40 |

**AFRICAN STONE**
| | | |
|---|---|---|
| 76 | Concrete Jungle CJ 600 | How Long Must I Wait/4TH STREET ORCHESTRA: Long Wait ..................... 20 |
| 76 | Concrete Jungle CJ 604 | Singer Man/Song (as African Stones) ............................................ 15 |
| 78 | Tempus TEM 1260 | Choose Me/Right Choice ......................................................... 10 |
| 76 | K & B | Run Rasta Run/Run Rasta Run .................................................... 25 |

**AFRICANS**
| | | |
|---|---|---|
| 81 | Lord Koos KLP 2 | HAVE A GRAND TIME (LP, compilation) ........................................... 40 |

**AFRIKA**
| | | |
|---|---|---|
| 82 | L 100 | I Want You Tonight/I Want You Tonight (Remix) (12", p/s) ...................... 150 |

**AFRIQUE**
| | | |
|---|---|---|
| 73 | Pye International 7N 25616 | Soul Makossa/Hot Mud ......................................................... 8 |
| 74 | Mainstream MSL 1018 | SOUL MAKOSSA (LP) ............................................................ 20 |

**AFRO**
| | | |
|---|---|---|
| 71 | Punch PH 89 | Lonely World/ALTON ELLIS ALL STARS: Put It On ................................. 15 |

**AFRO AKINO**
| | | |
|---|---|---|
| 74 | Afrodesia 1001 | Hwe Anna/Maria ............................................................... 10 |

**AFRO DIMENSIONS**
| | | |
|---|---|---|
| 72 | Ackee 535 | Dance With Me/Lonely Nights ................................................... 15 |
| 72 | Jay Boy BOY 84 | If You Don't Want My Love/Just Because ......................................... 20 |

**AFRO ENCHANTERS**
| | | |
|---|---|---|
| 63 | Island WI 071 | Peace And Love/Wayward African ................................................ 25 |

**AFRO FUNK**
| | | |
|---|---|---|
| 75 | Kabana KAB 1 | Obanya Special/Try And Try ..................................................... 15 |
| 75 | Kabana BSC 01 | BODY MUSIC (LP) ............................................................... 50 |

**AFROTONES**
| | | |
|---|---|---|
| 69 | Trojan TR 655 | Things I Love/ERIC FATTER: Since You've Been Gone ............................. 20 |
| 69 | Duke DU 19 | Freedom Sound/BOYS: Easy Sound .............................................. 20 |
| 69 | High Note HS 023 | All For One/BELTONES: Broken Heart ............................................ 15 |

*(see also Delroy Wilson)*

**AFTER DARK**
| | | |
|---|---|---|
| 81 | After Dark AD 001 | Evil Woman/Johnny/Lucy (p/s) .................................................. 35 |
| 83 | Lazer PROMO 1 | Deathbringer/Call Of The Wild (picture disc, promo only) ...................... 30 |
| 83 | Lazer PROMO 1 | Deathbringer/Call Of The Wild (white label test pressing) ..................... 60 |

**AFTERMATH (U.K.)**
| | | |
|---|---|---|
| 81 | Red Star AFTERMATH 0001 | The Freedom Fighter/All The Others/1980 (p/s) ................................. 15 |

**AFTERSHAVE**
| | | |
|---|---|---|
| 73 | Splendid SPS 401 | Warmaker/One Of The Best ..................................................... 175 |

**AFTER TEA**
| | | |
|---|---|---|
| 68 | Ace Of Clubs SCL-R 1251 | AFTER TEA (LP) ................................................................ 50 |

*(see also Ray Fenwick)*

**AFTER THE FIRE**
| | | |
|---|---|---|
| 80 | Epic EPC 8394 | Love Will Always Make You Cry/Every Mother's Son (p/s, withdrawn) ............ 5 |
| 75 | Rapid RR 001 | SIGNS OF CHANGE (LP, with insert) .............................................. 25 |

*(see also Narnia, Waiting For The Sun)*

**A FURTHER ROOM**
| | | |
|---|---|---|
| 80 | Test Pressing Records TP2 | Would You Wanna Die For England/Animals ...................................... 12 |

**AGATHOCLES**
| | | |
|---|---|---|
| 90 | Deaf DEAF 01 | SUPPOSE IT WAS YOU (split LP with DRUDGE) ................................... 20 |

**YASUKO AGAWA**
| | | |
|---|---|---|
| 86 | Blue Bird BRT 26 | L.A. Nights/New York Afternoon (12") ........................................... 15 |

**AGENT ORANGE**
| | | |
|---|---|---|
| 92 | Dog Tag AO 001 | Sounds Flakey To Me (Jungle Mix)/Only You Have The Bass/Sounds Flakey To Me (Original Mix) (12") ........................................................ 18 |
| 93 | Dog Tag AO 002 | TECNOSKA EP: The Nuttiest Ska/Gettin' Rougher (Ska Mix)/Gettin' Rougher (Kaos Remix) (12") ............................................................. 15 |

**AGENT FINCH & SPECIFIK**
| | | |
|---|---|---|
| 12 | B-Line 104740H1 | I Remember When/Still Der Defiance .............................................. 6 |

**AGENTS**
| | | |
|---|---|---|
| 79 | Grapevine GRP 142 | Trouble/The Love I Hold .......................................................... 15 |

**AGGRESSORS**
| | | |
|---|---|---|
| 70 | Pye 7N 17889 | Whisky And Soda/Soul Of The Jungle ............................................ 15 |
| 70 | Marble Arch 1260 | REGGAE STEADAE GO (LP) ....................................................... 15 |

**AGGROVATORS**
| | | |
|---|---|---|
| 70 | Jackpot JP 751 | Sex Machine/You Left Me And Gone (both act. by Dave Barker & Aggrovators) ........... 20 |
| 70 | Smash SMA 2302 | Big Red Ball Parts 1 & 2 (A-side actually "Big Red Bumble" by Lloyd Tyrell; B-side actually "Big Bumble Version" by Lloyd & Devon) ............................... 20 |
| 71 | Smash SMA 2312 | One More Bottle Of Beer/Beer Version ........................................... 10 |

| | | | |
|---|---|---|---|
| 73 | Smash SMA 2339 | Straight To Jackson Head/You Are My Angel | 12 |
| 73 | Downtown DT 500 | Dreadlocks Man/Rasta Want Peace (both actually by Rasta Twins) | 12 |
| 76 | Grounation GROL 507 | RASTA DUB '76 (LP) | 40 |
| 78 | Live & Love LAP 04 | JAMMIES IN A LION STYLE DUB (LP) | 35 |
| 78 | Third World TWS 939 | KAYA DUB (LP) | 45 |
| 78 | Conflict COLP 2006 | RASTA DUB 2000 (LP) | 30 |

*(see also Dave Barker, Dennis Alcapone, Jerry Lewis [Jamaica], Delroy Wilson, John Holt, Alton Ellis, Cornell Campbell)*

## AGGROVATORS AND THE REVOLUTIONARIES

| | | | |
|---|---|---|---|
| 77 | Third World TWS 900 | THE AGGROVATORS MEET THE REVOLUTIONARIES AT CHANNEL ONE (LP) | 30 |
| 78 | Burning Sounds BS 1028 | GUERILLA DUB (LP) | 35 |

## AGINCOURT

| | | | |
|---|---|---|---|
| 70 | Merlin HF 3 | FLY AWAY (LP, with insert) | 1000 |

*(see also Friends, Ithaca, Alice Through The Looking Glass, Tomorrow Come Someday)*

## AGNES STRANGE

| | | | |
|---|---|---|---|
| 75 | Birdsnest BN 1 | Give Yourself A Chance/Clever Fool | 12 |
| 77 | Baal BDN 38048 | Can't Make Up My Mind/Johnny B. Goode | 10 |
| 75 | Birdsnest BRL 9000 | STRANGE FLAVOUR (LP) | 150 |

## AGNOSTIC FRONT

| | | | |
|---|---|---|---|
| 85 | Rough Justice JUST 3 | CAUSE FOR ALARM (LP) | 15 |

## AGONY BAG

| | | | |
|---|---|---|---|
| 80 | Monza MON 2 | Rabies Is A Killer/Never Never Never (p/s) | 10 |

*(see also Pesky Gee, Black Widow)*

## AGONY COLUMN

| | | | |
|---|---|---|---|
| 79 | Tyger TYG 2 | (I Had It) All Worked Out/Good Grief (p/s) | 10 |
| 80 | Back Door DOOR 8 | Love In The Head/Free Of Love (p/s) | 8 |
| 82 | Lightbeat LIGHT 003 | Love Is A blanket Expression/Only U/Missing Person (p/s) | 6 |

## AGORA

| | | | |
|---|---|---|---|
| 94 | Z Records ZEDD 010 | LATIN CONNECTION EP (12") | 10 |

## AGROS

| | | | |
|---|---|---|---|
| 71 | Punch PH 56 | What Do You Fall In Love For/SLICKERS: Too Much | 20 |
| 70 | Pye 17889 | Whisky & Soda/Soul Of The Jungle | 15 |

## CHRISTINA AGUILERA

| | | | |
|---|---|---|---|
| 06 | RCA 82876 82639 | BACK TO BASICS (3-LP, numbered) | 75 |

## A GUY CALLED GERALD

| | | | |
|---|---|---|---|
| 88 | Rham RS8804 | Voodoo Ray/Escape/Rhapsody In Acid/Blow Your House Down (12", p/s) | 25 |
| 90 | Columbia XPR 1535 | Emotions Electric (Frankie Foncett Remix 1)/Emotions Electric (Frankie Foncett Remix 2)(12", promo in stickered plain sleeve) | 15 |
| 92 | Juice Box JBOX 001 | Digital Bad Boy/Let It Move You/A Storm Is Coming/Could You Understand? (12", tracks 1 and 4 vocals by MC Tunes) | 12 |
| 92 | Juice Box JBOX 003 | Cops/The Trak/28 Gun Bad Boy/Paranoia (12") | 40 |
| 92 | Juice Box JBOX 004 | Ses Makes You Wise/Sunshine/King Of The Jungle/Boase up (12") | 15 |
| 92 | Juice Box JBOX 005 | The Musical Magical Midi Machine/Let It Go/Like A Drug/Free Africa (12") | 15 |
| 92 | Columbia XPR 1684 | Cops/The Track/Paranoia/28 Gun Bad Boy (12" white label promo) | 40 |
| 93 | Juice Box JBOX 009 | Too Fucked To Dance/Darker Than I Should Be/Anything v2.1/Is The Right Time (12") | 12 |
| 93 | Juice Box JBOX 014 | The Glok Track/Gerald's Bassline/Ease The Pressure/Take Me (12") | 12 |
| 94 | Juice Box JBOX 019 | Darker Than I Should Be (Ladies Mix)/Gloc (Remix) (12") | 12 |

## A-HA

| | | | |
|---|---|---|---|
| 84 | Warner Bros W 9146 | Take On Me/And You Tell Me (silver/blue p/s) | 40 |
| 84 | Warner Bros W 9146T | Take On Me (Extended)/And You Tell Me/Stop And Make Your Mind Up (12", silver/blue p/s, with poster & stickers) | 100 |
| 84 | Warner Bros W 9146T | Take On Me (Extended)/And You Tell Me/Stop And Make Your Mind Up (12", silver/blue p/s, without poster & stickers) | 50 |
| 85 | Warner Bros W 9006T | Take On Me/Love Is The Reason (12", black & white p/s) | 10 |
| 85 | Warner Bros W 9006 | Take On Me/Love Is The Reason (reissue, colour p/s with gatefold booklet) | 5 |
| 86 | Warner Bros W 8663TP | Hunting High And Low (Extended)/Hunting High And Low (Remix)/ The Blue Sky (Demo) (12", picture disc) | 10 |
| 86 | Warner Bros W 8500TP | Cry Wolf (Extended)/Cry Wolf (7" Version)/Maybe Maybe (12", picture disc) | 10 |
| 87 | Warner Bros W 8305TP | The Living Daylights (Extended)/(7" Remix)/(Instrumental) (12", picture disc) | 10 |
| 88 | Warner Bros W 7840TP | The Blood That Moves The Body (Extended)/The Blood That Moves The Body (LP Version)/There's Never A Forever Thing (12", picture disc) | 10 |
| 88 | Warner Bros. W7749W | Touchy!/Hurry Home ('felt' p/s) | 20 |
| 91 | Warner Bros. W001213 | Early Morning/East Of The Sun (7" box set with 3 postcards) | 8 |

*(see also Phenomena)*

## AHAB

| | | | |
|---|---|---|---|
| 82 | Chicken Jazz JAZZ 5 | Party Girl/Don't Give Up On Us (p/s) | 5 |

*(see also Another Pretty Face)*

## A HEADS

| | | | |
|---|---|---|---|
| 82 | TW Records HIT 107 | Dying Man/Hell Cell/Changing Places (p/s) | 18 |
| 83 | Bluurg FISH 3 | Forgotten Hero/Isolated/Love Or Pain (p/s) | 10 |

## AIKEN'S DRUM

| | | | |
|---|---|---|---|
| 81 | Private Pressing SRTX/CUS 1134 | AIKEN'S DRUM (LP) | 40 |

## AIL SYMUDIAD

| | | | |
|---|---|---|---|
| 80 | Sain 765 | Ad Drefnu/Whisgi A Soda (p/s) | 10 |
| 81 | Fflach RF 001 | Twristiaid Yn Y Dre/Modur Sanctaiddy/Hyfyed Bingo (500 only, first 100 in dayglo sleeve) | 10 |
| 81 | Fflach RF AS 002 | Geiriau/Annwyl Rhywun/Cura Dy Law (p/s) | 10 |
| 81 | Fflach RF AS 003 | Garej Paradwys/Ffarwel L'e Fyddin (p/s) | 10 |
| 82 | Fflach FR AS 004 | Lleisau O'r Gorffennol/Dilyn Y Sebon (p/s) | 10 |
| 82 | Fflach RF AS 005 | Edrych Trwy Y Camerau/ANGYLION STANLI: Emyn Roc A Roi (split single, p/s) | 10 |

## AIM (1)
| 94 | Detour DR 018 | Call Your Name/Out On The Streets (p/s,1,000 only, 100 on blue vinyl) .......................... 8 |
| 94 | Detour DR 018 | Call Your Name/Out On The Streets (p/s,1,000 only, black vinyl) ............................ 6 |

## AIM (2)
| 99 | Grand Central GCLP 105 | COLD WATER MUSIC (2-LP) ................................................. 20 |

## AIR (1)
| 71 | Atlantic 2400 148 | AIR (LP) .................................................... 20 |

## AIR (2)
| 98 | Source V 2848 | MOON SAFARI (LP, with inner) ......................................... 20 |
| 00 | Record Makers V2910 | VIRGIN SUICIDES (LP) ............................................. 50 |
| 05 | Virgin 72435 966322 7 | TALKIE WALKIE (LP) ........................................... 20 |
| 07 | EMI V 3032 | POCKET SYMPHONY (LP, white vinyl) ..................................... 15 |
| 12 | Vinyl Factory VF043 | LA VOYAGE DANS LA LUNE (4-LP, art print, DVD, cloth box) ..................... 80 |
| 14 | Vinyl Factory VF112 | MUSIC FOR MUSEUM (2-LP, clear vinyl, poster) ........................ 50 |

## AIRBORNE
| 83 | Clubland SJP 844 | Burn In Hell/Lord Satan/Temple Of Metal (p/s) ...................... 12 |

## AIRBRIDGE
| 83 | Rattees RATT 001 | Words And Pictures/Zero Minus One ................................ 15 |

## JANE AIRE & THE BELVEDERES
| 78 | Stiff BUY 26 | Yankee Wheels/Nasty Nice (p/s) .................................... 5 |

## DEBRAH AIRE
| 67 | Polydor 56180 | This Land Is Mine/What The World Needs Now Is Love ........................ 10 |

*(see also Sharon Tandy)*

## AIRHEAD
| 92 | Korova 9030 74679 2 | BOING! (LP) ................................................. 20 |

## AIRKRAFT
| 79 | Lathe TSR1 | Here Comes That Sound/Video Romance/White Boys ...................... 25 |
| 80 | Square SQS 5 | Move In Rhythm/Pumping Iron .................................... 12 |

## AIRMAIL
| 79 | Graffiti GIT 001 | No Human Feeling/In A Moment ................................... 8 |

## AIRSHIP
| 79 | Decca FR 13856 | Get Out, Take Your Mother With You/Gimme A Can Of Spray Paint ............. 40 |

## AIRTO
| 71 | Buddah 2318 040 | SEEDS ON THE GROUND - THE NATURAL SOUNDS OF AIRTO (LP, gatefold) .......... 20 |
| 73 | CTI CTL 18 | FINGERS (LP) .................................................. 15 |
| 74 | CTI CTL 21 | IN CONCERT (LP, with Deodato) ................................... 15 |
| 74 | CTI CTL 23 | VIRGIN LAND (LP) .............................................. 15 |

## AIR TRAFFIC CONTROL
| 77 | Epic S EPC 5665 | Gotta Get A Message Back To You/Move On Up ........................ 8 |

## AISHA
| 86 | Ariwa ARI 48 | Dancing Time/The Creator (12") ................................... 18 |
| 86 | Ariwa ARI 060 | Prophecy/Dub (12") ............................................ 20 |
| 94 | Ariwa ARI 153 | Only Jah Works/Crisis (12") ...................................... 18 |

## AITCH
| 71 | Decca F13150 | Let It Be Me/Let Me Say This ..................................... 6 |

## BOBBY AITKEN (& CARIBBEATS)
| 62 | Island WI 028 | Baby Baby (actually with Patsy)/Lonely Boy ............................ 18 |
| 62 | Blue Beat BB 93 | Never Never (South Virginia)/Isabella (as Bobby Aitken & Buster's Group) .......... 18 |
| 63 | Blue Beat BB 146 | Don't Leave Me/Mom And Dad (as Bobby Aitken & Tinse) ................... 18 |
| 63 | Rio R 14 | I've Told You/Please Go Back ...................................... 18 |
| 63 | Rio R 15 | It Takes A Friend/LAUREL AITKEN: Sunshine ............................ 18 |
| 64 | Rio R 34 | Rolling Stone/LESTER STERLING'S GROUP: Man About Town ................... 40 |
| 64 | Rio R 40 | Garden Of Eden/Whiplash ........................................ 20 |
| 64 | Rio R 50 | Little Girl/Together ............................................. 20 |
| 65 | Rio R 52 | Rain Came Tumbling Down/SHENLEY & LUNAN: Something Is On Your Mind ........ 15 |
| 65 | Rio R 64 | Mr Judge/BINZ: Times Have Changed ................................ 18 |
| 65 | Black Swan WI 441 | Jerico/LESTER STERLING: Lunch Time ................................ 25 |
| 66 | Ska Beat JB 252 | Thunderball/ORIGINATORS: Chelip Chelip .............................. 200 |
| 67 | Doctor Bird DB 1071 | Keep On Pushing/You Won't Regret It ................................ 60 |
| 67 | Doctor Bird DB 1072 | Let Them Have A Home/Temptation (with Caribbeats) ...................... 30 |
| 67 | Doctor Bird DB 1077 | Sweets For My Sweet/How Sweet It Is (with Caribbeats) .................... 50 |
| 67 | Island WI 3028 | Kiss Bam Bam/CYNTHIA RICHARDS: How Could I ......................... 70 |
| 67 | Giant GN 11 | What A Fool/Curfew (with Caribbeats) ............................... 45 |

*(see also Caribbeats, Laurel Aitken, Frank Cosmo, Lloyd & Glen)*

## LAUREL AITKEN (& BLUE BEATS)
| 59 | Kalypso XX 15 | Sweet Chariot/Nebuchnezer ...................................... 30 |
| 59 | ~~Kalypso XX 16~~ | Aitken's Boogie/Cherrie ......................................... 30 |
| 60 | Kalypso XX 19 | Baba Kill Me Goat/Tribute To Collie Smith ............................ 20 |
| 60 | Starlite ST45 011 | Boogie In My Bones/Little Sheila .................................... 40 |
| 60 | Starlite ST45 014 | Honey Girl (with Caribs)/Drinkin' Whisky (with Bluebeats) ................... 40 |
| 60 | Melodisc M 1570 | Mary Lee/Lonesome Lover (with Bluebeats) ........................... 30 |
| 60 | Blue Beat B 1 | Boogie Rock/Heavenly Angel (with the BOOGIE CATS) (white label) ............ 50 |
| 60 | Blue Beat BB 1 | Boogie Rock/Heavenly Angel (with the BOOGIE CATS) (blue label) ............. 30 |
| 60 | Blue Beat BB 10 | Jeannie Is Back/If It's Money You Need .............................. 30 |
| 60 | Blue Beat BB 14 | Judgment Day/Yea Yea Baby ..................................... 15 |
| 60 | Blue Beat BB 22 | Railroad Track/Tell Me Darling (with the Blue Beats) .................... 20 |
| 60 | Blue Beat BB 25 | More Whisky/LLOYD CLARKE: Parapinto Boogie ......................... 20 |

| 61 | Starlite ST45 034 | Love Me Baby/Stars Were Made ........................................................ | 30 |
|----|-------------------|------------------------------------------------------------------------|----|
| 61 | Blue Beat BB 40 | Bartender/Mash Potato Boogie........................................................ | 20 |
| 61 | Blue Beat BB 52 | Bouncing Woman/Nursery Rhyme Boogie (with Blue Beats) ................. | 30 |
| 61 | Blue Beat BB 70 | Mighty Redeemer/Please Don't Leave Me............................................ | 15 |
| 62 | Blue Beat BB 84 | Brother David/Back To New Orleans (with Blue Beats) ....................... | 15 |
| 62 | Blue Beat BB 109 | Lucille/I Love You More Everyday ..................................................... | 15 |
| 62 | Blue Beat BB 120 | Sixty Days And Sixty Nights/Going To Kansas City (with Les Dawson Trio)...... | 40 |
| 62 | Blue Beat BB 142 | Jenny Jenny/Weary Wanderer (with Bandits and Ruddy & Sketto)......... | 20 |
| 62 | Dice CC 1 | Mabel/You Got Me Rocking (with Hyacinth) ....................................... | 20 |
| 63 | Dice CC 13 | Sweet Jamaica/Bossa Nova Hop ...................................................... | 20 |
| 63 | Blue Beat BB 164 | Zion/Swing Low Sweet Chariot ........................................................ | 20 |
| 63 | Blue Beat BB 194 | Little Girl/Daniel Saw The Stone (with Ruddy and Sketto) ................. | 20 |
| 63 | Duke DK 1002 | Low Down Dirty Girl/Pink Lane Shuffle.............................................. | 30 |
| 63 | Island WI 092 | I Shall Remove/We Got To Move ..................................................... | 40 |
| 63 | Island WI 095 | What A Weeping/Zion City Wall ....................................................... | 25 |
| 63 | Island WI 099 | In My Soul/One More River To Cross................................................ | 40 |
| 63 | Rio R 11 | Adam & Eve/BOBBY AITKEN: Devil Woman ...................................... | 20 |
| 63 | Rio R 12 | Mary/Hometown ........................................................................... | 20 |
| 63 | Rio R 13 | Bad Minded Woman/Life ............................................................... | 20 |
| 63 | Rio R 17 | Devil Or Angel/Fire....................................................................... | 20 |
| 63 | Rio R 18 | Freedom Train/Peace Perfect Peace ................................................ | 20 |
| 64 | Rio R 35 | Rock Of Ages/The Mule.................................................................. | 18 |
| 64 | Rio R 36 | Leave Me Standing/Bagaboo (Bug-A-Boo) ........................................ | 18 |
| 64 | Rio R 37 | John Saw Them Coming/Jericho....................................................... | 20 |
| 64 | R&B JB 167 | Yes Indeed/You Can't Stop Me From Loving You ............................... | 20 |
| 64 | R&B JB 170 | Pick Up Your Bundle And Go/Let My People Go .................................. | 20 |
| 64 | R&B JB 171 | Bachelor Life/You Was Up .............................................................. | 20 |
| 64 | Columbia DB 7280 | Be Mine/Don't Stay Out Late.......................................................... | 15 |
| 64 | Blue Beat BB 249 | This Great Day/I May Never See My Baby ......................................... | 25 |
| 64 | J.N.A.C. 1 | West Indian Cricket Test/3 Cheers For Worrell .................................. | 25 |
| 64 | Black Swan WI 401 | Lion Of Judah/Remember My Darling (B-side with Cynthia Richards) ...... | 40 |
| 64 | Black Swan WI 411 | The Saint/Go Gal Go...................................................................... | 40 |
| 64 | Dice CC 28 | Jamaica/I Don't Want No More ....................................................... | 25 |
| 65 | Dice CC 31 | We Shall Overcome/You Left Me Standing......................................... | 25 |
| 65 | Rio R 53 | Mary Don't You Weep/I Believe ...................................................... | 20 |
| 65 | Rio R 54 | Mary Lou/Jump And Shout ............................................................. | 20 |
| 65 | Rio R 56 | One More Time/Ring Don't Mean A Thing.......................................... | 20 |
| 65 | Rio R 60 | Come And Let Us Go/Lonely Nights ................................................. | 25 |
| 65 | Rio R 65 | Let's Be Lovers/I Need You ............................................................. | 25 |
| 65 | Venus VE 4 | How Can I Forget You?/Weeping And Crying ...................................... | 10 |
| 65 | Island WI 198 | Boogie In My Bones/Little Sheila..................................................... | 25 |
| 65 | Island WI 252 | How Can I Forget You/Weeping And Crying (white label, existence unconfirmed)........... | 0 |
| 66 | Blue Beat BB 340 | Clementine/Bongo Jerk .................................................................. | 30 |
| 66 | Blue Beat BB 369 | Shame And Scandal/Coconut Woman ............................................... | 40 |
| 66 | Ska Beat JB 232 | Jamboree/Looking For My Baby ...................................................... | 40 |
| 66 | Ska Beat JB 236 | Propaganda/Shake ....................................................................... | 35 |
| 66 | Ska Beat JB 239 | Green Banana/Darling.................................................................... | 35 |
| 66 | Rio R 91 | How Can I Forget You/I've Been Weeping And Crying ......................... | 15 |
| 66 | Rio R 92 | Baby Don't Do It/That Girl.............................................................. | 15 |
| 66 | Rio R 97 | We Shall Overcome/Street Of Glory ................................................. | 15 |
| 66 | Rio R 99 | Clap Your Hands/Revival ................................................................ | 15 |
| 66 | Rainbow RAI 101 | Don't Break Your Promises/Last Night (with Soulmen) ....................... | 40 |
| 66 | Rainbow RAI 106 | Voodoo Woman/Bewildered And Blue (B-side with Carols) ................. | 40 |
| 67 | Rainbow RAI 111 | Sweet Precious Love/I Want To Love You Forever (with Carols)............ | 40 |
| 67 | Columbia Blue Beat DB 102 | Rock Steady/Blowin' In The Wind.................................................... | 30 |
| 67 | Columbia Blue Beat DB 106 | I'm Still In Love With You Girl/Blue Rhythm...................................... | 30 |
| 67 | Fab FAB 5 | Never You Hurt/I Need You (as Laurel Aitken & Soulmen).................... | 50 |
| 68 | Fab FAB 45 | For Sentimental Reasons/Last Waltz (as Laurel Aitken & Rainbows) ...... | 30 |
| 68 | Doctor Bird DB 1160 | Mr Lee/Birmingham Girl .................................................................. | 30 |
| 68 | Doctor Bird DB 1161 | La La La (Means I Love You)/DETOURS: Sunnyside ............................. | 25 |
| 69 | Ackee ACK 105 | Skinheads Are Wrecking The Town (white label only, unissued) ........... | 250 |
| 69 | Doctor Bird DB 1187 | Fire In Your Wire/Quando Quando ................................................... | 30 |
| 69 | Doctor Bird DB 1190 | Rice And Peas/CLASSICS: Worried Over Me....................................... | 40 |
| 69 | Doctor Bird DB 1196 | Reggae Prayer/Deliverance Will Come.............................................. | 40 |
| 69 | Doctor Bird/J.J. DB 1197 | The Rise And Fall (Of Laurel)/If You're Not Black............................... | 40 |
| 69 | Doctor Bird DB 1202 | Haile Haile (The Lion)/SEVEN LETTERS: Call Collect .......................... | 50 |
| 69 | Doctor Bird DB 1203 | Carolina/Kingston Town ................................................................. | 40 |
| 69 | Junior JR 105 | Think Me No Know/RECO: Trombone Man ......................................... | 30 |
| 69 | Nu Beat NB 024 | Woppi King/Mr Soul ...................................................................... | 25 |
| 69 | Nu Beat NB 025 | Suffering Still (with Girlie)/Reggae '69............................................. | 25 |
| 69 | Nu Beat NB 032 | Haile Selassie/Blues Dance ............................................................ | 25 |
| 69 | Nu Beat NB 033 | Lawd Doctor (with Girlie)/Big Fight In Hell Stadium............................ | 25 |
| 69 | Nu Beat NB 035 | Run Powell Run/RICO RODRIGUEZ: A Message To You......................... | 30 |
| 69 | Nu Beat NB 039 | Save The Last Dance/Walk Right Back .............................................. | 20 |
| 69 | Nu Beat NB 040 | Don't Be Cruel/John B. .................................................................. | 20 |
| 69 | Nu Beat NB 043 | Shoo Be Doo/Babylon Gone ........................................................... | 20 |
| 69 | Nu Beat NB 044 | Landlords And Tenants/Everybody Sufferin' ...................................... | 20 |
| 69 | Nu Beat NB 045 | Jesse James/Freedom .................................................................... | 30 |
| 69 | Nu Beat NB 046 | Pussy Price Gone Up/Gimme Back Me Dollar ..................................... | 20 |

MINT VALUE £

| 69 | Junior JR 106 | River Nile (existence unconfirmed, white labels only) | 40 |
|---|---|---|---|
| 69 | Nu Beat NB 047 | Skinhead Train/GRUVY BEATS: Kent People | 65 |
| 70 | Nu Beat NB 048 | Skinhead Invasion/Benwood Dick (unissued, blank white label demos only) | 125 |
| 70 | Nu Beat NB 048 | Mr Popcorn/GRUVY BEATS: Share Your Popcorn | 18 |
| 70 | Nu Beat NB 049 | I've Got Your Love/GRUVY BEATS: Blue Mink | 15 |
| 70 | Nu Beat NB 050 | Scandal In Brixton Market/Soul Grinder (both sides with Girlie) | 20 |
| 70 | New Beat NB 054 | Nobody But Me/Baby Please Don't Go | 12 |
| 70 | New Beat NB 056 | I'll Never Love Any Girl/The Best I Can | 12 |
| 70 | New Beat NB 057 | Reggae Popcorn/Take Me Back | 20 |
| 70 | New Beat NB 063 | Baby I Need Your Loving/Think It Over | 20 |
| 70 | New Beat NB 065 | Sex Machine/Since You Left | 20 |
| 70 | New Beat NB 072 | Pachanga/Version | 20 |
| 70 | Ackee ACK 104 | Pussy Got Thirteen Life/Single Man | 25 |
| 70 | Ackee ACK 106 | Sin Pon You/Everynight | 80 |
| 70 | Bamboo BAM 16 | Moon Rock/Cut Up Munno (apparently, white labels only) | 80 |
| 70 | Pama PM 818 | Mary's Boy Child/RUPIE EDWARDS ALLSTARS: Version | 12 |
| 70 | Pama Supreme PS 300 | Why Can't I Touch You/Can't Turn Your Back On Me | 12 |
| 71 | Trojan TR 7826 | It's Too Late/AITKEN'S BAND: Slow Rock | 10 |
| 71 | New Beat NB 078 | True Love/The Best I Can | 6 |
| 71 | New Beat NB 089 | I Can't Stop Loving You/El Paso | 6 |
| 71 | Black Swan BW 1408 | If It's Hell Below/Just A Little Bit Of Love | 40 |
| 71 | Big Shot BI 595 | Dancing With My Baby/Do The Boogaloo | 20 |
| 72 | Big Shot BI 605 | Take Me In Your Arms/Two-Timing Woman | 8 |
| 72 | Camel CA 90 | Africa Arise/GI GINGRI: Holy Mount Zion | 12 |
| 72 | Columbia DB 8914 | Pretty Face In The Market Place/Come Back To My Lonely World | 6 |
| 75 | Camel CA 2007 | La Vien En Rose/Spanish Eyes | 8 |
| 75 | Punch PU 121 | Fattie Bum Bum/Fattie Bum Bum | 5 |
| 80 | I-Spy SEE 4 | Big Fat Man/It's Too Late (as Laurel Aitken & Unitone) | 5 |
| 80 | I-Spy SEE 6 | Rudi Got Married/Honey Come Back To Me | 5 |
| 66 | Rio LR 1 | SKA WITH LAUREL (LP) | 250 |
| 67 | Doctor Bird DLM 5012 | SAYS FIRE (LP) | 150 |
| 69 | Pama PSP 1012 | THE HIGH PRIEST OF REGGAE (LP) | 100 |
| 69 | Pama ECO 8 | SCANDAL IN BRIXTON MARKET (LP, with Girlie) | 100 |
| 69 | J.J. | RISE AND FALL (LP) | 120 |
| 73 | Count Shelly CSLP1 | SOPHIA (LP) | 45 |
| 93 | GAZ 009 | GODFATHER OF SKA (LP) | 18 |

(see also Laurel & Owen, Girlie, King Horror, Lorenzo, Ruts, Bobby Aitken, Classics, Beresford Ricketts, Duke Reid, Tommy McCook)

## A-JAES
| 64 | Oak RGJ 132 | I'm Leaving You/Kansas City | 700 |
|---|---|---|---|

## AJL BAND
| 76 | Baal BDN 38033 | Sweet Sticky Thing/Classical Salsa | 8 |
|---|---|---|---|

## AKA & CHARLATANS
| 78 | Vanity VANE 1 | Heroes Are Losers/Lady Of The Night/Perhaps One Day (12", various screen-printed die-cut p/s) | 12 |
|---|---|---|---|

## AKAPEL
| 92 | Phlange AK001 | Pick It Up (vocal)/(Instrumental)/Stick Your Big Dinky In/Background Beats/Let Me Hear You Say/Keep On/They Won't Believe Me (12") | 12 |
|---|---|---|---|

## AKERCOCKE
| 05 | Earache 7MOSH 322 | Eyes Of The Dawn (Demo)/The Fulcrum (transluscent red vinyl, no p/s) | 15 |
|---|---|---|---|

## AK 47
| 81 | Output ORR 202 | Stop! Dance!/Autobiography/Hilversum-Ao (p/s) | 10 |
|---|---|---|---|
| 91 | Rugger Bugger SEEP 004 | DON'T CALL ME VANILLA (LP, with lyric sheet) | 30 |

(see also AK Process, File Under Pop)

## TOSHIKO AKIYOSHI
| 58 | Columbia 33CX 101101 | NEWPORT JAZZ FESTIVAL 1957 (LP) | 15 |
|---|---|---|---|

## JAN AKKERMAN
| 73 | Harvest HAR 5069 | Blue Boy/Minstrel-Farmers Dance | 6 |
|---|---|---|---|
| 72 | Harvest SHSP 4026 | PROFILE (LP) | 20 |
| 73 | Atlantic K40522 | TABERNAKEL (LP, gatefold) | 15 |

(see also Hunters [Holland], Brainbox, Focus)

## AK PROCESS
| 79 | Output OPR 101 | Electronic Music: After All Love/Post Town (p/s, white labels) | 6 |
|---|---|---|---|

(see also AK 47)

## AKRYLYKZ
| 80 | Double R RED 2 | Spyderman/Smart Boy (p/s) | 6 |
|---|---|---|---|
| 80 | Polydor POSP 128 | Smart Boy/Spyderman (reissue, p/s) | 5 |
| 80 | Polydor 2059 253 | J.D./Ska'd For Life (p/s) | 5 |

## AL ET ALL
| 80 | Arny's Shack As 047 | STRANGE AFFAIR (LP) | 200 |
|---|---|---|---|

## AL & VIBRATORS
| 67 | Doctor Bird DB 1085 | Move Up/Lonesome Lover | 40 |
|---|---|---|---|
| 69 | High Note HS 005 | Check Up/I'll Come Back (featuring Byron Lee & The Dragonaires) | 20 |
| 69 | High Note HS 007 | Move Up Calypso/PATSY: Fire In Your Wire | 20 |

(see also Vibrators, Patsy Todd, Lord Power)

## STEVE ALAIMO
| 63 | Pye International 7N 25174 | Every Day I Have To Cry/(Please Take A Chance On Me) Little Girl (DJ Copy) | 50 |
|---|---|---|---|
| 63 | Pye International 7N 25174 | Every Day I Have To Cry/(Please Take A Chance On Me) Little Girl | 30 |
| 63 | Pye International 7N 25199 | It's A Long Long Way To Happiness/A Lifetime Of Loneliness | 10 |

| | | | |
|---|---|---|---|
| 66 | HMV POP 1531 | So Much Love/Truer Than True (DJ Copy) | 30 |
| 66 | HMV POP 1531 | So Much Love/Truer Than True | 20 |
| 68 | Atlantic 588 227 | Watching The Trains Go By/Thank You For The Sunshine Days | 10 |

## ALARM

| | | | |
|---|---|---|---|
| 81 | White Cross W 3/4 | Unsafe Buildings/Up For Murder (gatefold p/s) | 25 |
| 82 | Illegal ILS 0032 | Marching On/Across The Border/Lie Of The Land (p/s) | 5 |
| 83 | I.R.S. PFPC 1023 | 68 Guns Parts 1 & 2 (p/s, with free cassette: The Stand/Across The Border/ Marching On/Lie Of The Land/For Freedom" (all live) [CS 70504]) | 5 |
| 84 | I.R.S. IRS 103 | The Deceiver/Reason 41 (p/s, clear vinyl) | 5 |
| 84 | I.R.S. IRS 103 | The Deceiver/Reason 41 (p/s, mispress on mustard vinyl) | 45 |
| 84 | I.R.S. IRSD 103/103A | The Deceiver/Reason 41/Lie Of The Land/Legal Matter (double pack, g/fold p/s) | 5 |
| 02 | Vinyl Japan ASK LP 135 | A FLASHING BLUR OF STRIPPED DOWN EXCITEMENT (LP) | 20 |
| 02 | Vinyl Japan ASK CD 135 | A FLASHING BLUR OF STRIPPED DOWN EXCITEMENT (CD) | 30 |

*(see also Seventeen)*

## ALARM CLOX

| | | | |
|---|---|---|---|
| 80 | Ring RING 1 | Protector/Restaurant (no p/s) | 7 |

## ALASKA

| | | | |
|---|---|---|---|
| 82 | Kingdom KV 8025 | Bailando/Red Rum | 5 |

## DAMON ALBARN

| | | | |
|---|---|---|---|
| 08 | Vinyl Factory VF 001 | MONKEY: JOURNEY TO THE WEST (2-LP, signed print, progamme, tone generator, 500 only) | 60 |

*(see also Blur, Gorillaz, Monkey, GB & TQ)*

## ALBATROSS

| | | | |
|---|---|---|---|
| 74 | Mooncrest Moon 29 | Rock 'N' Roll Boogie Man/Witchy Witchy Lady | 5 |
| 74 | Mooncrest Moon 36 | Anything I Want To/Bournemouth Rock | 6 |
| 75 | Mooncrest Moon 42 | Darlin/The Band Played On | 5 |
| 75 | Gull GULS. 16 | Tobacco Road/Let It Roll | 5 |

*Prices fine*

## ALBERT EMBANKMENT

| | | | |
|---|---|---|---|
| 71 | Decca F23152 | As Tears Go By/Cover Me | 5 |

## ALBERTO Y LOST TRIOS PARANOIAS

| | | | |
|---|---|---|---|
| 76 | Big T BIG 541 | Dread Jaws/De Version | 6 |
| 77 | Stiff LAST 2 | SNUFF ROCK EP (12" promo, only 50 pressed) | 200 |
| 78 | Logo GO(D) 323 | Heads Down No Nonsense Mindless Boogie/Thank You/Fuck You/Dead Meat (double pack, gatefold p/s) | 5 |
| 78 | Logo GO 340 | Juan Lopez (The Lonely Goatherd)/Teenage Paradise/Dead Meat Part III | 6 |
| 76 | Transatlantic TRA 316 | ALBERTO Y LOST TRIOS PARANOIAS (LP, with insert) | 15 |
| 77 | Transatlantic TRA 349 | ITALIANS FROM OUTER SPACE (LP) | 15 |
| 78 | Logo LOGO 1009 | SKITE (LP) | 15 |

*(see also Mothmen, Charlie Parkas)*

## ALBIANS

| | | | |
|---|---|---|---|
| 79 | K & K 003 | Princess/Princess Dub (12", with Ranking Neville) | 12 |
| 80 | K & K KK 0012 | Who Is Going To Love Me/VIN GORDON: Who Is Going To Rock Me Tonight (12") | 20 |

*(See also N. McCoy & Albians)*

## ALBINO GORILLA

| | | | |
|---|---|---|---|
| 72 | Ember EMBS321 | Shake Me, Wake Me/Going To A Go Go | 6 |

## ALBION BAND

| | | | |
|---|---|---|---|
| 76 | Harvest HAR 5113 | Hopping Down In Kent/Merry Sherwood Rangers (as Albion Dance Band) | 5 |
| 77 | Harvest HAR 5128 | The Postman's Knock/La Sexte Estample Real (as Albion Dance Band) | 5 |
| 78 | Harvest HAR 5156 | Poor Old Horse/Ragged Heroes (p/s) | 5 |
| 79 | Harvest HAR 5175 | Pain And Paradise/Lay Me Low (p/s) | 5 |
| 73 | Island HELP 25 | BATTLE OF THE FIELD (LP, as Albion Country Band) | 20 |

*(see also Shirley Collins, Fairport Convention)*

## MICHAEL ALBUQUERQUE

| | | | |
|---|---|---|---|
| 69 | United Artists UP 35037 | Better Men Than Me/Burn Burn Burn | 10 |
| 70 | United Artists UP 35098 | Roll Him Over/Blind Man | 8 |

*(see also Michael D'Albuquerque, E.L.O.)*

## DENNIS ALCAPONE

| | | | |
|---|---|---|---|
| 70 | Explosion EX 2039 | Revelation Version/Marka Version | 15 |
| 70 | Supreme SUP 214 | You Must Believe Me (with Niney)/RUPIE EDWARDS ALLSTARS: Funk The Funk | 12 |
| 70 | Big Shot BI 565 | Shades Of Hudson/Spanish Amigo | 30 |
| 71 | Treasure Isle TI 7069 | The Great Woggie/TOMMY McCOOK & SUPERSONICS: Buttercup Version | 20 |
| 71 | Banana BA 328 | Duppy Serenade (as Innkeeper)/Sunshine Version | 20 |
| 71 | Banana BA 341 | (Love Me) Forever Version/I Don't Want To See You Cry | 25 |
| 71 | Upsetter US 373 | Well Dread/UPSETTERS: Dread Version | 12 |
| 71 | Upsetter US 377 | Alpha And Omega/JUNIOR BYLES: Beat Down Babylon | 15 |
| 71 | Duke DU 125 | Medley Version/Version Two | 8 |
| 71 | Prince Buster PB 8 | Sons Of Zion/ANSELL COLLINS: Short Circuit | 12 |
| 71 | Prince Buster PB 12 | Let It Roll (with Max Romeo)/ANSELL COLLINS: Clear Blue | 15 |
| 71 | Jackpot JP 773 | Jumping Jack (with John Holt)/AGGROVATORS: King Of The Track | 8 |
| 71 | Jackpot JP 775 | Togetherness (Black & White) (with John Holt)/DELROY WILSON: Live Good | 8 |
| 71 | Jackpot JP 776 | Tell It Like It Is/DELROY WILSON : Come Along | 8 |
| 71 | Dynamic DYN 421 | Horse And Buggy/ROLAND ALPHONSO & DENZIL LAING: Buggy And Horse | 12 |
| 71 | Dynamic DYN 422 | Ripe Cherry/INNER CIRCLE: Red Cherry | 10 |
| 71 | Dynamic DYN 427 | Alcapones Guns Don't Bark/Alcapones Guns Don't Bark Version | 15 |
| 71 | Camel CA 74 | This A Butter/PHIL PRATT ALLSTARS: Version | 12 |
| 71 | Tropical AL 003 | False Prophet/MAX ROMEO: Rude Medley | 12 |
| 72 | Downtown DT 496 | Swinging along/DELROY WILSON: My Baby Is Gone | 20 |
| 72 | Tropical AL 019 | Worldwide Love (with Twinkle Brothers)/CARL MASTERS: Gable Up | 12 |

MINT VALUE £

| 72 | Ackee ACK 146 | Power Version/BLUESBLASTERS: Martie (B-side actually titled "Margie") | 18 |
| 72 | Prince Buster PB 24 | Giant/PRINCE BUSTER: Science | 20 |
| 72 | Upsetter US 381 | Wonderman (with Dave Barker, actually by Dave Barker)/ Place Called Africa (with Dave Barker & Junior Byles) | 20 |
| 72 | Upsetter US 388 | Master Key/UPSETTERS: Keyhole | 20 |
| 72 | Grape GR 3035 | Rasta Dub/UPSETTERS: Rasta Version | 20 |
| 72 | Attack ATT 8027 | Fine Style/WINSTON SCOTLAND: On The Track | 15 |
| 72 | Duke DU 131 | The Sky's The Limit/HUDSON'S ALLSTARS: Limit Version | 12 |
| 72 | Duke DU 147 | Get In The Groove (with Dennis Brown)/DYNAMITES: Version | 12 |
| 72 | Techniques TE 918 | Look Into Yourself/TECHNIQUES ALLSTARS: Yourself Version | 15 |
| 72 | Green Door GD 4041 | Rub Up A Daughter/TONY'S ALLSTARS: Daughter Version | 15 |
| 72 | Bullet BU 509 | Dub Up A Daughter/PRINCE TONY ALL STARS: Version | 15 |
| 72 | Treasure Isle TI 7069 | Great Woogie/Buttercup | 25 |
| 73 | Prince Buster PB51 | Kings And Castles/Version | 10 |
| 73 | Downtown DT 508 | You Don't Say/TONY'S ALLSTARS: Version | 10 |
| 73 | Treasure Isle TI 7074 | Wake Up Jamaica/Version (with Tommy McCook) | 25 |
| 73 | Jackpot JP 808 | Cassius Clay/SLIM SMITH: Love And Affection | 18 |
| 73 | Bread BR 1121 | Musical Liquidator/Lorna Banana (B-side with Prince Jazzbo) | 15 |
| 73 | G.G. GG 4538 | Musical Alphabet/BUCKLEY ALLSTARS: Things Gonna Change (B-side actually by Maytones) | 12 |
| 73 | Pyramid PYR 7008 | Belch It Off/Jack Horner | 8 |
| 74 | Harry J HJ 6666 | Sorry Harry/Party Time | 8 |
| 76 | Ethnic Fight EF 001 | Pressure In A Babylon/ETHNIC FIGHT BAND: Pressure Dub | 6 |
| 71 | Trojan TBL 187 | GUNS DON'T ARGUE (LP) | 40 |
| 73 | Magnet MGT 001 | KING OF THE TRACK (LP) | 30 |
| 74 | Attack ATLP 1005 | BELCH IT OFF (LP) | 20 |
| 75 | Live And Love LALP 104 | DREAD CAPONE (LP) | 30 |
| 77 | Third World TWS 801 | SIX MILLION DOLLAR MAN (LP) | 15 |
| 77 | Third World TWS 911 | INVESTIGATOR ROCK (LP) | 15 |

*(see also El Paso, Dennis & Lizzy, Mad Roy, D. Smith, Wailing Souls, Innkeepers, GG Allstars, Stranger Cole, Lizzy & Dennis, Lee)*

## CRAIG ALDEN
| 60 | London HLW 9224 | Crazy Little Horn/Goggle-Eye'd | 25 |

## STEVE ALDO (& CHALLENGERS)
| 64 | Decca F 12041 | Can I Get A Witness/Baby What You Want Me To Do (with Challengers) | 50 |
| 66 | Parlophone R 5432 | Everybody Has To Cry/You're Absolutely Right (solo) | 200 |
| 66 | Parlophone R 5432 | Everybody Has To Cry/You're Absolutely Right (solo) (DJ Copy) | 150 |

## URIE ALDRIDGE
| 71 | Harry J. HJ 6634 | Set Me Free/LLOYD WILLIS: Free Version | 8 |

*(see also John Holt)*

## ALEANNA
| 78 | Inchecronin INC 7421 | ALEANNA (LP) | 40 |

## ALEEM
| 84 | Streetwave MKHAN 26 | Release Yourself/Dub (12") | 20 |
| 84 | Streetwave MKHAN 61 | Get Loose/Release Yourself (12") | 15 |

## AKI ALEONG (& HIS LICORICE TWISTERS)
| 61 | Reprise R 20021 | Trade Winds, Trade Winds/Without Your Love | 5 |
| 61 | Reprise R 20042 | Moon River (Twist)/Tonight (Twist) | 6 |

## ALETHIANS
| 72 | Myrrh MST 6506 | ONE WAY (LP, David Pope and the Right Angle on side 2) | 30 |
| 73 | Myrrh Gold MYR 1002 | R.S.V.P. (LP) | 40 |

## ARTHUR ALEXANDER
| 62 | London HLD 9523 | You Better Move On/A Shot Of Rhythm And Blues | 40 |
| 63 | London HLD 9566 | Where Have You Been/Soldier Of Love | 30 |
| 63 | London HLD 9641 | Anna/I Hang My Head And Cry | 35 |
| 63 | London HLD 9667 | Go Home Girl/You're The Reason | 20 |
| 64 | London HLD 9899 | Black Night/Ole John Amos | 20 |
| 66 | London HLU 10023 | (Baby) For You/The Other Woman | 20 |
| 76 | Buddah BDS 439 | Everyday I Have To Cry/Everybody Needs Somebody To Love | 10 |
| 63 | London RE-D 1364 | ALEXANDER THE GREAT (EP) | 40 |
| 63 | London RE-D 1401 | ARTHUR ALEXANDER (EP) | 40 |
| 62 | London HA-D 2457 | YOU BETTER MOVE ON (LP) | 80 |

## DAVID ALEXANDER
| 74 | Rare Earth RES112 | Love, Love, Love/Missy | 6 |

## GOLDIE ALEXANDER
| 81 | Project PRJ 1 | Show You My Love/Get Back | 7 |

## JEFF ALEXANDER & HIS ORCHESTRA
| 58 | London HA-P 2130 | ALFRED HITCHCOCK PRESENTS - MUSIC TO BE MURDERED BY (LP, mono) | 20 |
| 58 | London SH-P 6012 | ALFRED HITCHCOCK PRESENTS - MUSIC TO BE MURDERED BY (LP, stereo) | 20 |

## LLOYD ALEXANDER REAL ESTATE
| 68 | President PT 157 | Gonna Live Again/Watcha Gonna Do | 80 |

## LUCIEN ALEXANDER
| 67 | Polydor 56205 | Baby, You've Been On My Mind/Play Along (Miss R) | 20 |

## ALEXISONFIRE
| 04 | Sorepoint | Counterparts And Number Them/THE BLED: Ruth Buzzi Better Watch Her Back (die-cut sleeve, purple vinyl) | 10 |
| 05 | Sorepoint SORE 0398 | Accidents/No Transitory (p/s, green vinyl) | 8 |
| 06 | Hassle HOFF016LP | CRISIS (LP, die-cut sleeve, 500 only) | 60 |

**ALFALPHA**
75   EMI 2650                    If I Can Just Get Through Tonight/Railroad ................................................ 8

**ALFI & HARRY**
56   London HLU 8242          Trouble With Harry/A Little Beauty (triangular centre, gold lettering on label) ............ 10
*(see also David Seville)*

**ALFIE**
01   Regal (no cat. no.)        Zoom (p/s, 1-track square, 300 only) ...................................................... 8

**CLEM ALFORD**
74   Columbia SCX 6571        MIRROR IMAGE - THE ELECTRONIC SITAR OF CLEM ALFORD (LP) ................ 40
75   KPM KPM 1183            INDIA (LP, music library issue, side 2 only) ............................................ 30
*(see also Magic Carpet)*

**ALFRED & MELMOTH**
68   Island WI 3130            I Want Someone/ALFRED BROWN: One Scotch One Bourbon One Beer ............... 20

**SANDRA ALFRED**
58   Oriole CB 1408           Rocket And Roll/Six Day Rock............................................................... 40
*(see also Sandra Barry, Slack Alice)*

**LYNN ALICE**
76   K&B KB 5520              (You Keep Me) Hanging On/(You Keep Me) Hanging On ............................. 7

**ALICE THROUGH THE LOOKING GLASS**
69   H&F Recording/SNP (no cat.  ALICE THROUGH THE LOOKING GLASS (LP, private pressing, handmade sleeve,
no.)                         actually by Peter Howell & John Ferdinando) ......................................... 1000
97   Tenth Planet TP 032       ALICE THROUGH THE LOOKING GLASS (LP, reissue, no'd, 1,000 only) ............ 20
*(see also Ithaca, Friends, Agincourt, Tomorrow Come Someday, BBC Radiophonic Workshop/Peter Howell)*

**ALICE IN CHAINS**
92   Columbia 658 888-7       Would?/Man In The Box (picture disc, numbered, PVC sleeve) ...................... 10
93   Columbia 659 090-6       Them Bones/We Die Young/Got Me Wrong/Am I Inside (12", no'd, blue vinyl) ........... 10
93   Columbia 659 090-0       Them Bones/We Die Young (p/s, numbered poster) ............................... 10
93   Columbia 659 365-7       Angry Chair/I Know Somethin' About You (snakeskin wallet sleeve) ................ 10
93   Columbia 659 751-7       Down In A Hole/Rooster (picture disc) ............................................... 10
95   Columbia 662 623-7       Grind/Nutshell (green vinyl, numbered card) ......................................... 8
96   Columbia 662 893-7       Heaven Beside You/Would? (live) (white vinyl, foldover p/s in stickered PVC sleeve)...... 5
91   Columbia 467201-1        FACELIFT (LP)............................................................................... 60
92   Columbia 472330-1        DIRT (LP).................................................................................... 40
94   Columbia 475713-1        JAR OF FLIES/SAP (LP, yellow vinyl with blue vinyl, 1-sided, etched 12" EP) ......... 40
95   Columbia 481114-1        ALICE IN CHAINS (double LP, gatefold sleeve, inners) ............................... 50
01   Simply Vinyl SVLP 0025   DIRT (LP, reissue 180gm vinyl) ....................................................... 20
10   Virgin 50999 9 67159 1 8  BLACK GIVES WAY TO BLUE (2-LP)................................................... 18
10   Music On Vinyl MOVLP 138  MTV UNPLUGGED (2-LP, reissue, 180gm).......................................... 18
10   Music On Vinyl MOVLP 086  JAR OF FLIES/SAP (2-LP, reissue, gatefold, orange and blue vinyl) ............... 25

**ALICE ISLAND BAND**
74   Warren WAR 341           SPLENDID ISOLATION (LP, with insert, allegedly 50 only) ........................ 400

**ALIEN**
92   Alien And Monster MDF15  How'd Ya Feel/Ruff House (12") ...................................................... 20

**ALIEN KULTURE**
81   RAR LRAR 1               Asian Youth/Culture Crossover (p/s) ................................................ 40

**ALIEN SEX FIEND**
84   Anagram 11 ANA 25        E.S.T. (Trip To The Moon)/Boneshaker Baby/I Am A Product (live) (11", PVC sleeve
                             with insert) ............................................................................... 10
90   Windsong 02              ASF BOX (box set, export issue, 4,000 only, with 3 coloured vinyl singles [12", 11" &
                             10"], poster, T-shirt & imitation dog turd)........................................... 35
93   Anagram GRAM 69          LEGENDARY BATCAVE TAPES (LP) .................................................. 15
*(see also Demon Preacher, Demons)*

**ALIENS (1)**
78   Alien ALI 001            When The River Runs Dry/Winds Of Time (no p/s) ............................... 40

**ALIENS (2)**
07   EMI 9463868181           ASTRONOMY FOR DOGS (2-LP)...................................................... 20
08   Petrock LP 002           LUNA (2-LP)................................................................................ 20
*(see also Beta Band)*

**ALIMANTADO (DR.)**
73   Atra ATRA 007            Return Of Muhummad Ali/Black Love ............................................... 12
75   Sun & Star ST 003        Best Dress Chicken/She Wreng-Ep .................................................. 15
77   Greensleeves GRE 002     Born For A Purpose/Reason For Living (with the Rebels) ......................... 10
78   Virgin VOLE 1            Slavery Let I Go/Find The One (12")................................................. 10
78   Greensleeves GRE 5       Still Alive/Life All Over (with the Rebels) .......................................... 6
78   Greensleeves GRE 13      Best Dressed Chicken In Town/Can't Conquer Natty Dreadlocks (yellow vinyl)..... 15
79   Greensleeves GRED 10     Born For A Purpose/Reason For Living/Still Alive/Life All Over (12", with the Rebels) ..25
79   Greensleeves GRED 17     Sitting In The Park/Skanking In The Park (12", with the Rebels)................. 10
80   Isda SUS 11              It Cold In A Babylon/Version (12")................................................... 10
78   Greensleeves GREL 1      BEST DRESSED CHICKEN IN TOWN (LP) ........................................... 30
79   Ital ISA 5000            KINGS BREAD (LP) ................................................................... 20
81   Greensleeves GREL 22     SONS OF THUNDER (LP).............................................................. 20

**ALISON, ANN, KEN, BLUE & TAF**
72   TEB SLE 50               SONGS FROM AN OLD BARN (EP) .................................................. 25

**ALKALINE TRIO**
05   Vagrant VRUK 012LP       CRIMSON (LP, red vinyl, stickered sleeve, inner) ................................ 15

**ALKATRAZ**
76   Rockfield UAS 30001      DOING A MOONLIGHT (LP)........................................................... 20
*(see also Man, Quicksand)*

MINT VALUE £

## ALL ABOUT EVE
85 Eden EDEN 1    D For Desire/Don't Follow Me (12", p/s) ...................................................... 12
*(see also Ghost Dance, Gene Loves Jezebel)*

## ALL BECAUSE THE LADY LOVES
80 Sweet    IF YOU RISK EVERYTHING (EP, with insert) ............................................ 25

## ALL SORTS OF FOLK
72 Private Pressing CH 101  ALL SORTS OF FOLK (LP) ........................................................ 175

## ALL SOUNDBWOY OUT
07 ASBO 001    ASBO (1-sided white label 12") ................................................ 30
*(see also Loefa)*

## ALLAH & MR. LONELY
73 Fab FAB 190    Hide & Seek/CANCER ALL STARS : Version (actually by Allen & Mr. Lonely) .................. 8

## JOHNNIE ALLAN
74 Oval 1001    Promised Land/SHELTON DUNAWAY: Betty And Dupree .......................... 5
78 Oval Stiff LOT 1   Promised Land/PETE FOWLER: One Heart, One Song (p/s) ...................... 5

## ALL DAY
73 private pressing   YORK POP MUSIC PROJECT (LP) ................................................ 150

## ANNISTEEN ALLEN
55 Capitol CL 14264   Fujiyama Mama/Wheels Of Love ............................................ 200
57 Brunswick 05639   Don't Nobody Move/The Money Tree ...................................... 40

## DAEVID ALLEN
75 Virgin VS 123    Fred The Fish/It's The Time Of Your Life (p/s, promo only) ...................... 8
79 Charly CY 51056   Much Too Old/I Am A Freud (with New York Gong, p/s with insert).............. 6
75 Caroline C 1512   BANANA MOON (LP, black and white 'Twins' label, ends in a continuous loop) ............ 20
76 Virgin V 5024    GOOD MORNING! (LP, by Daevid Allen & Euterpe) .............................. 20
*(see also Gong, Planet Gong, Soft Machine)*

## DEAN ALLEN
58 London HLM 8698   Rock Me To Sleep/Ooh-Ooh Baby Baby .................................... 18

## JEFF ALLEN
57 HMV JO 477    That'll Be The Day/Guilty Mind (export issue) ................................ 25

## LEE ALLEN (& HiS BAND)
58 HMV POP 452    Walkin' With Mr. Lee/Promenade ........................................ 20
59 Top Rank JAR 265   Cat Walk/Creole Alley .................................................. 10
59 Top Rank JKR 8020   WALKIN' WITH MR LEE (EP) .............................................. 15
62 Ember ELR 3312   MOOD MUSIC LIBRARY (LP, uncredited library issue, generic sleeve) ........ 30
*(see also Huey 'Piano' Smith & Clowns)*

## LILY ALLEN
06 No Label LILY 001   LDN/Knock Em Down (500 only, jukebox centre) ............................ 6
06 Regal 7REG 135   Smile/Smile (Gutter Mix) (stickered, black, die-cut sleeve) .................. 5
06 Regal 3694931   ALRIGHT, STILL (LP, approx 200 pressed) .................................. 35
09 Regal REG 151LP,   IT'S NOT ME IT'S YOU (LP) .............................................. 18

## MAURICE ALLEN
58 Pye Nixa 7N 15128   Ooh Baby/Rockhearted .................................................. 10

## PATRICK ALLEN
77 Kab KB 5540    Groovy Feeling/Instrumental ............................................ 20

## REX ALLEN
54 Brunswick 05341   This Ole House/They Were Doin' The Mambo (with Tex Williams) ............ 15
*(see also Tex Williams)*

## RODNEY ALLEN
88 Subway 18T    CIRCLE LINE EP (12" p/s) .............................................. 15
87 Subway SUBORG 2   HAPPYSAD (LP) ........................................................ 15
*(Blue Aeroplanes)*

## STEVE ALLEN
72 M&M FFMS 10021   Life On Mars/Baby I'm A Want You/Everything I Own/Diary (Medley) ............ 20

## TONY ALLEN (1)
00 Strut STRUTAALP001   JEALOUSY (LP, reissue with Africa 70) .................................... 15
00 Strut STRUTAALP002   NO DISCRIMINATION (LP, reissue with Afro Messengers).................... 15
00 Strut STRUTAALP003   NO ACCOMODATION FOR LAGOS (LP, reissue with Africa 70) ................ 15

## TONY ALLEN (2)
84 Earthworks MWKS 3001  NEPA (LP) ............................................................ 30

## VERNON ALLEN
64 R&B JB 169    Far I Come/Babylon .................................................... 600

## (VERNON) ALLEN & (MILTON) HAMILTON
66 Blue Beat BB 348   It Is I/Baby What's More .............................................. 15
66 Blue Beat BB 353   You're The Angel/Someone Like You...................................... 15

## ALLENS
75 Mowest MW 3029   High Tide/California Music .............................................. 6

## ALLEY
74 Jay Boy BOY 82   Singing In Poverty/Tip Toe ............................................ 6

## ALLEY CATS
59 Vogue V 9155    Last Night/Snap-Crackle And Pop ........................................ 10

## ALLIES
79 Harp HSP 1025   Plush Living/Computer (p/s, 500 only despite numbering) .................. 8

## ALLISON
94 Twinkle NG 544   WAILING (LP) .......................................................... 15

### BOBBY ALLISON
64    Solar SRP 103      You've Got Everything/Change Your Mind ...................................................... 5

### GENE ALLISON
58    London HLU 8605      Hey, Hey, I Love You/You Can Make It If You Try ..................................... 125

### GEORGE ALLISON
80    Cartridge CR-D 107      Ten To One/Hard Times (12") ......................................................... 75

### JERRY ALLISON & CRICKETS
65    Liberty LIB 10196      Now Hear This/Everybody's Got A Little Problem ................................. 20

*(see also Crickets, Ivan)*

### LUTHER ALLISON
71    Delmark DS 625      LOVE ME MAMA (LP, blue label) .................................................. 15

### LYNN ALLISON
57    Columbia DB 3867      Mama From The Train (A Kiss, A Kiss)/Song Of The Sparrow ................. 5

### MOSE ALLISON
61    Fontana H 292      Baby Please Don't Go/Deed I Do ................................................... 20
64    Columbia DB 7330      I Love The Life I Live/Life Is Suicide .............................................. 8
59    Esquire EP 214      PARCHMAN FARM (EP) ............................................................ 15
64    Columbia SEG 8353      ALLISON SINGS THE BLUES (EP) ................................................. 20
59    Esquire 32-051      BACK COUNTRY SUITE (LP) ........................................................ 25
59    Esquire 32-071      LOCAL COLOUR (LP) ................................................................ 25
59    Esquire 32-083      YOUNG MAN MOSE (LP) ............................................................ 25
60    Esquire 32-094      CREEK BANK (LP) .................................................................. 20
61    Esquire 32-131      AUTUMN SONG (LP) ............................................................... 20
62    Esquire 32-171      RAMBLIN' WITH MOSE (LP) ...................................................... 15
63    London HA-K 8083      SWINGIN' MACHINE (LP, as Mose Allison Jazz Group) .......................... 15
64    Columbia SX 6058      V-8 FORD (LP) ..................................................................... 15

### ALLISONS (U.K.)
61    Fontana H 304      Words/Blue Tears ................................................................... 5
61    Fontana H 336      What A Mess!/Lorraine (p/s) ...................................................... 10
61    Fontana TFE 17339      THE ALLISONS (EP) ................................................................ 10

### ALLISONS (U.S.)
64    Stateside SS 289      Surfer Street/Money (vocal: Darlene Love) ...................................... 35

*(see also Blossoms, Darlene Love)*

### ALLMAN BROTHERS BAND
69    Atco 228 033      THE ALLMAN BROTHERS BAND (LP, gatefold sleeve) ........................ 100
71    Atco 2400 032      IDLEWILD SOUTH (LP) ............................................................ 80
71    Atlantic 2402 035      AT FILLMORE EAST (2-LP, 1st pressing, Plum/orange labels, gatefold sleeve) ........ 50
71    Atlantic K60011      AT FILLMORE EAST (2-LP, 2nd pressing, green/orange labels, gatefold sleeve) ........ 20
72    Capricorn K67501      EAT A PEACH (2-LP, gatefold sleeve with insert) ............................... 30
73    Capricorn K47507      BROTHERS AND SISTERS (LP, gatefold sleeve with insert) ..................... 15
75    Warner Bros. 2659 034      EAT A PEACH (LP, reissue, gatefold) ............................................ 15

*(see also Gregg Allman, Duane & Gregg Allman, Allman Joys, Hour Glass)*

### DUANE & GREGG ALLMAN
73    Polydor 2310 235      DUANE & GREGG ALLMAN (LP, laminated sleeve) ............................ 15

*(see also Allman Brothers, Gregg Allman)*

### GREGG ALLMAN
73    Capricorn K 47508/CP0116      LAID BACK (LP) ................................................................. 15

*(see also Allman Brothers, Duane & Gregg Allman)*

### ALLMAN JOYS
73    Mercury 6398 005      ALLMAN JOYS (LP) ................................................................ 20

### ALL NIGHT BAND
79    Contact CON 5      Lovely Ladies/It's My Life ......................................................... 15

### ALL THE RAGE
82    Rage RR 001      Concrete City/Emergency (p/s) .................................................. 150

### JOHNNY ALMOND MUSIC MACHINE
69    Deram DM 266      Solar Level/To R.K. ................................................................ 35
69    Deram DML/SML 1043      PATENT PENDING (LP) ............................................................ 70
70    Deram SML 1057      HOLLYWOOD BLUES (LP) ......................................................... 60

*(see also Alan Price Set, Zoot Money, Paul Williams Set, John Mayall & Bluesbreakers, Mark-Almond, Jon Mark)*

### ALMOND LETTUCE
68    Columbia DB 8442      The Tree Dog Song/To Henry With Hope ........................................ 6
69    Philips BF 1764      Magic Circle/Twenty Weary Miles ............................................... 10

### MARC ALMOND
82    Lyntone LYN 12505      Discipline (as 'Marc Almond & Friends', pink flexidisc with Flexipop issue 23. Friends are Throbbing Gristle) ............................................... 20
84    Gutter Hearts GH 1      BITE BACK + BLUES (fan club-only LP, credited to "Raoul & The Ruined") ........ 30
88    Parlophone PSR 500      Kept Boy (1-sided 7" with etched reverse - intended to be free with THE STARS WE ARE LP - but plans scrapped) ............................................. 20

*(see also Soft Cell, Marc & Mambas, Burmoe Brothers, Vicious Pink Phenomena, Flesh Volcano, Annie Hogan, Sally Timms, Gene Pitney)*

### ALMOND MARZIPAN
70    Trend TNT 53      Open Up Your Heart/Summer Love ............................................. 15
70    Trend TNT 55      Marie Take A Chance/I'll Forget You ............................................. 6

### ALMOST A DREAM
73    Box BX1      Something's Moving/The Undead ............................................... 30

### ALMOST ALONE
84    Family FAM 001      Blue City/It's So Sad (p/s) ......................................................... 20

## ALONE AGAIN OR
| | | | |
|---|---|---|---|
| 84 | All One ALG 1 | Drum The Beat (In My Soul)/Smartie Edit (p/s) | 5 |

*(see also Shamen)*

## ALPHA & OMEGA
| | | | |
|---|---|---|---|
| 96 | A&O 1201 | Ancient African Civilisation/DISCIPLES & ALPHA & OMEGA: Eternal Dub (12") | 25 |
| 90 | A&O 001 | DANIEL IN THE LIONS DEN (LP) | 50 |
| 92 | A&O 009 | KING & QUEEN (LP) | 45 |
| 92 | A&O 077 | ALMIGHTY JAH (LP, listed as Alpha & Omega Meets Dub Judah) | 40 |
| 92 | A&O 027 | WATCH AND PRAY (LP) | 45 |
| 93 | A&O 093 | EVERYDAY LIFE (LP) | 50 |
| 94 | A&O 094 | SAFE IN THE ARK (LP) | 40 |
| 96 | A&O 096 | TREE OF LIFE (LP) | 30 |
| 96 | A&O 097 | VOICE IN THE WILDERNESS (LP) | 35 |

## ALPHABET
| | | | |
|---|---|---|---|
| 81 | No Label or Cat. No | This Strange Love/The Handsome Beast (p/s) | 15 |

## ALPHA BETA
| | | | |
|---|---|---|---|
| 79 | Magnet MAG 158 | Space Invaders/Innocent (p/s) | 10 |

## ORVILLE ALPHANSO
| | | | |
|---|---|---|---|
| 65 | Caribou CRC 1 | Bellylick/Inspiration | 40 |

## ALPHASTONE
| | | | |
|---|---|---|---|
| 90s | Enraptured RAPTLP 33 | LIFE IS A MOTORWAY EP (2 x 12", gatefold sleeve, limited issue) | 10 |
| 90s | Enraptured RAPTLP 18 | ELASTICATED WAVEBAND (LP, clear vinyl, 100 only) | 15 |

## CARLTON ALPHONSO
| | | | |
|---|---|---|---|
| 67 | Pama PM 700 | Where In This World/Peace Makers | 50 |
| 69 | Grape GR 3000 | Belittle Me/Keep Your Love | 30 |

## CLYDE ALPHONSO
| | | | |
|---|---|---|---|
| 69 | Studio One SO 2076 | Good Enough/Let The Music Play | 130 |

## PANCHO ALPHONSO AND THE REVOLUTIONARIES
| | | | |
|---|---|---|---|
| 79 | Attack ATT TACK 8 | Never Give Up In A Babylon/Love Is A Pleasure (12") | 20 |
| 78 | Trojan TRLS 165 | NEVER GET TO ZION (LP) | 18 |

*(see also Alphonso Pancho)*

## ROLAND ALPHONSO (ALIAS ROLAND AL)
| | | | |
|---|---|---|---|
| 61 | Blue Beat BB 58 | Blackberry Brandy/ALVIN & CECIL: Marjorie | 25 |
| 62 | Blue Beat BB 112 | Four Corners Of The World (with Alley Cats)/SHINERS: Romantic Shuffle | 30 |
| 64 | R&B JB 161 | Mr President/The MAYTALS: A Man Who Knows | 25 |
| 64 | R&B JB 164 | Crime Wave/MAYTALS: Hello Honey | 45 |
| 65 | Island WI 217 | El Pussy Cat/LORD BRYNNER: Tiger In Your Tank | 25 |
| 65 | Ska Beat JB 210 | Nimble Foot/ANDY & JOEY: Love Is Stronger | 60 |
| 65 | Ska Beat JB 216 | Nuclear Weapon (with Baba Brooks)/STRANGER COLE: Love Thy Neighbour | 50 |
| 65 | Rio R 5804 | Jazz Ska/HYACINTH: Oh Gee | 50 |
| 66 | Blue Beat BB 356 | Just A Closer Walk/Jericho Train | 250 |
| 66 | Island WI 259 | James Bond/LEE PERRY: Just Keep It Up | 175 |
| 66 | Doctor Bird DB 1010 | From Russia With Love/Cleopatra (with Soul Brothers) | 80 |
| 66 | Doctor Bird DB 1011 | Sufferer's Choice (with Soul Brothers)/SOULETTES: I Want To Be | 50 |
| 66 | Doctor Bird DB 1013 | WAILERS: Rude Boy/ROLANDO AL & SOUL BROTHERS: Ringo's Theme (This Boy) | 90 |
| 66 | Doctor Bird DB 1017 | Sugar And Spice/Get Out Of My Life (with Soul Brothers) | 50 |
| 66 | Doctor Bird DB 1020 | Phoenix City (with Soul Brothers)/DEACONS: Men Alone | 30 |
| 66 | Doctor Bird DB 1023 | Doctor Ring-A-Ding/FREDDIE & HEARTACHES: Here Is My Heart | 80 |
| 66 | Doctor Bird DB 1039 | I Love You/Song Of Love | 25 |
| 66 | Doctor Bird DB 1039 | WAILERS: Rasta Put It On/ROLAND AL & SOUL BROTHERS: Ska With Ringo | 150 |
| 66 | Ska Beat JB 231 | Rinky Dink (So Good) (with Studio One Orchestra)/ SCRATCH & DYNAMITES: Deacon Johnson | 45 |
| 67 | Pyramid PYR 6003 | Middle East/Wise Man | 30 |
| 67 | Pyramid PYR 6005 | Women Of The World (& Beverley's Allstars)/SPANISHTONIANS: Kisses | 30 |
| 67 | Pyramid PYR 6006 | On The Move (& Beverley's Allstars)/DESMOND DEKKER & ACES: It's A Shame | 25 |
| 67 | Pyramid PYR 6007 | Jungle Bit (& Beverley's Allstars)/NORMAN GRANT: Somebody Please Help Me | 25 |
| 67 | Pyramid PYR 6008 | The Cat/DESMOND DEKKER & ACES: Rudy Got Soul | 30 |
| 67 | Pyramid PYR 6009 | Guantanamera Ska (& Beverley's Allstars)/SPANISHTONIANS: Suffer Me Not | 30 |
| 67 | Pyramid PYR 6011 | Nothing For Nothing/DESMOND DEKKER & ACES: Rude Boy Train | 25 |
| 67 | Pyramid PYR 6018 | Sock It To Me (& Beverley's Allstars)/SPANISHTONIANS: Rudie Gets Plenty | 100 |
| 68 | Pyramid PYR 6022 | Whiter Shade Of Pale/On The Move | 80 |
| 68 | Pyramid PYR 6030 | Dreamland/MAYTALS: 54-46, That's My Number | 30 |
| 68 | Pyramid PYR 6043 | Stream Of Life/MAYTALS: Struggle | 45 |
| 68 | Coxsone CS 7077 | Reggae In The Grass/ROY RICHARDS: Get Smart | 45 |
| 69 | Gas GAS 112 | A Thousand Tons Of Megaton (actually by Derrick Morgan)/Musical Resurrection | 40 |
| 70 | Punch PH 39 | Roll On (& Upsetters)/CARL DAWKINS: True Love | 45 |
| 71 | Banana BA 340 | Mellow Mood (Way To My Heart)/MAYTALS: Marching On | 20 |
| 12 | Duke Reid's THB 7017 | Easter Bonnet/STRANGER AND KEN: Feeling Of Love | 8 |
| 68 | Hi Note BSLP 5001 | ABC ROCK STEADY (with the Originals Orchestra) | 150 |

## ALPHORAS
| | | | |
|---|---|---|---|
| 78 | Junior JR 107 | Running Out Of Love/It Pains Me (actually by LEROY SMART) | 15 |

## ALPINES
| | | | |
|---|---|---|---|
| 68 | Double D DD 110 | Get Ready/CARIBBEATS: Come Back Charlie | 25 |

## ALQUIN
| | | | |
|---|---|---|---|
| 73 | Polydor 2480 152 | MARKS (LP) | 15 |

## ALSATIANS
| | | | |
|---|---|---|---|
| 80 | SRT SRTS/80/CUS-629 | Teen Romance/Our Man In Marrakesh (no p/s, 1000 only) | 40 |

**RITA ALSTON**
| | | | |
|---|---|---|---|
| 70 | Trojan TR 7751 | Popcorn Funky Reggae/NAT COLE: My Love | 20 |
| 70 | Trojan TR 7752 | All Kinds Of Everything/CARL LEVEY: Instrumental Version | 6 |

*(see also Rita, Nat Cole)*

**SHIRLEY ALSTON**
| | | | |
|---|---|---|---|
| 75 | London HLA 10506 | I'd Rather Not Be Loving You/Can't Stop Singin' 'Bout The Boy I Love) | 25 |
| 75 | London SHA 8491 | WITH A LITTLE HELP FROM MY FRIENDS (LP) | 25 |

*(see also Shirelles)*

**ALTECS**
| | | | |
|---|---|---|---|
| 61 | London HLU 9387 | Easy/Recess | 15 |

*(see also The Black Dog)*

**ALTERATIONS**
| | | | |
|---|---|---|---|
| 78 | Bead Records BEAD 9 | CUSACK/BERESFORD/DAY/TOOP (LP) | 30 |

**ALTERED STATES**
| | | | |
|---|---|---|---|
| 88 | Red Rhino CALC 31 | IS ANYONE OUT THERE? (LP) | 60 |

**ALTERN 8**
| | | | |
|---|---|---|---|
| 92 | Network Records A8 PIC 1 | FULL ON...MASK HYSTERIA (LP) | 15 |
| 92 | Network TOP LP1 | FULL ON...MASK HYSTERIA (LP & 12") | 20 |

**ALTERNATIVE**
| | | | |
|---|---|---|---|
| 82 | Crass Records 221984/8 | IN NOMINE PATRI (EP) | 10 |
| 83 | Corpus Christi CHRIST 13 | IF THEY TREAT YOU LIKE SHIT - ACT LIKE MANURE (LP, insert) | 50 |

**ALTERNATIVE BRITISH ARMY**
| | | | |
|---|---|---|---|
| 80 | Hit HIT 1 | Angry - The Killer Was A Cop/Bleak Streets (p/s) | 10 |

**ALTERNATIVE TV**
| | | | |
|---|---|---|---|
| 77 | Sniffing Glue SG 75 RPS | Love Lies Limp (1-sided flexidisc with Sniffing Glue fanzine issue 12) | 20 |
| 77 | Deptford Fun City DFC 02 | How Much Longer/You Bastard (p/s) | 7 |
| 77 | Deptford Fun City DFC 02 | How Much Longer/You Bastard (p/s, labelled 'alternate versions') | 7 |
| 78 | Deptford Fun City DFC 04 | Life After Life/Life After Dub (p/s) | 6 |
| 78 | Deptford Fun City DFC 05 | Life/Love Lies Limp (p/s) | 7 |
| 78 | Deptford Fun City DFC 07 | Action Time Vision/Another Coke (live p/s) | 10 |
| 79 | Deptford Fun City DFC 10 | The Force Is Blind/Lost In Room (Vibing Up The Senile Man) (p/s, last track uncredited) | 5 |
| 78 | Deptford Fun City DLP 01 | THE IMAGE HAS CRACKED (LP) | 20 |
| 79 | Crystal CLP 01 | LIVE AT THE RAT CLUB (LP) | 15 |
| 80 | Deptford Fun City DLP 05 | ACTION TIME VISION (LP, with inner sleeve) | 15 |

*(see also Mark Perry, Good Missionaries, The Door & The Window, Reflections, Jools Holland, Alex Fergusson, Rat & Whale)*

**ALTERNATORS**
| | | | |
|---|---|---|---|
| 78 | Energy NRG 001 | No Answers/The Kid Don't Know (no p/s) | 60 |

**ALTERNOMEN UNLIMITED**
| | | | |
|---|---|---|---|
| 79 | Object OM 06 | Facade/Connections (p/s) | 6 |

*(see also Spherical Objects, Steve Miro & Eyes)*

**ALTHEA & DONNA**
| | | | |
|---|---|---|---|
| 78 | Virgin Frontline FL1012 | UPTOWN TOP RANKING (LP) | 15 |

**ALTON (ELLIS) & EDDY**
| | | | |
|---|---|---|---|
| 60 | Blue Beat BB 17 | Muriel/CLUE J. & HIS BLUES BLASTERS: Silky | 15 |
| 62 | Island WI 009 | My Love Divine/Let Me Dream | 20 |

*(see also Alton Ellis)*

**ALVARO**
| | | | |
|---|---|---|---|
| 77 | Squeaky Shoes SSRM 1 | DRINKING MY OWN SPERM (LP) | 20 |
| 79 | Squeaky Shoes SSRM 2 | MUMS MILK NOT POWDER (LP) | 15 |

*(see also 101'ers)*

**ALVIN'S HEARTBEATS**
| | | | |
|---|---|---|---|
| 74 | Magnet MAG 24 | Chilli Willi/Chilli Willi (Part 2) | 5 |

**ALVYN**
| | | | |
|---|---|---|---|
| 69 | Morgan Bluetown MR 18S | You've Gotta Have An Image/Mind The Gap | 15 |

**AMALGAM (1)**
| | | | |
|---|---|---|---|
| 69 | Transatlantic TRA 196 | A PRAYER FOR PEACE (LP) | 70 |
| 73 | A Records A 002 | PLAY BLACKWELL & HIGGINS (LP) | 50 |
| 74 | Goodwill WS 1 | JUST OTHERS (LP, with insert, 250 only) | 1000 |

**AMALGAM (2)**
| | | | |
|---|---|---|---|
| 80 | Impetus IMPLP 47901 | WIPE OUT (4-LP box set with booklet) | 50 |

**GLEN AMAMS**
| | | | |
|---|---|---|---|
| 69 | Escort ES 804 | Rich In Love/WOODPECKERS: Zumbelly | 20 |

*(see also Glen Adams)*

**AMANDA**
| | | | |
|---|---|---|---|
| 76 | DJM DJS 10730 | I'm Gonna Enjoy Christmas/Catch That Boy | 7 |

**AMAZIAH**
| | | | |
|---|---|---|---|
| 74 | Sunrise SR 001 | STRAIGHT TALKER (LP, private pressing with insert) | 75 |

**AMAZING BLONDEL**
| | | | |
|---|---|---|---|
| 72 | Island WIP 6153 | Alleluia (Cantus Firmus To Counterpoint)/Safety In God Alone | 5 |
| 70 | Bell SBLL 131 | THE AMAZING BLONDEL AND A FEW FACES (LP, blue/silver label) | 300 |
| 70 | Island ILPS 9136 | EVENSONG (LP, gatefold sleeve) | 25 |
| 71 | Island ILPS 9156 | FANTASIA LINDUM (LP, with inner lyric sleeve) | 30 |
| 71 | Island ILPS 9156 | FANTASIA LINDUM (LP, without inner lyric sleeve) | 15 |
| 72 | Island ILPS 9205 | ENGLAND (LP, gatefold) | 25 |
| 73 | Island ILPS 9257 | BLONDEL (LP, gatefold sleeve) | 20 |
| 74 | DJM DJF 20442 | MULGRAVE STREET (LP) | 15 |
| 75 | DJM DJF 20446 | INSPIRATION (LP) | 15 |

## AMAZING DANCING BAND
*(see also Dimples, Gospel Garden, Methusilah)*

### AMAZING DANCING BAND
| 68 | Verve VS 567 | Deep Blue Train/Simon Smith & His Amazing Dancing Bear | 10 |
| 67 | Verve VLP/SVLP 9214 | AMAZING DANCING BAND (LP, mono/stereo) | 20 |
| 68 | Verve VLP 9234 | VOLUME TWO - THESE BOOTS ARE MADE FOR DANCIN' (LP, mono) | 18 |
| 68 | Verve SVLP 9234 | VOLUME TWO - THESE BOOTS ARE MADE FOR DANCIN' (LP, stereo) | 15 |

### AMAZING FRIENDLY APPLE
| 69 | Decca F 12887 | Water Woman/Magician | 100 |

### AMAZING SPACE FROGS
| 79 | Ribbett RIB 1 | THE DIRTY HABITS EP | 300 |

*(see also Basczax, Blitzkrieg Bop, No Way)*

### AMAZON
| 81 | Megamusic MEGA 1 | Fallen Angel/Hypnotising You (p/s) | 20 |

### AMAZON TRUST
| 70 | Polydor 2058065 | Run Baby Run/Sheila Lee | 50 |
| 71 | Jade JD 03 | Seeing What I See/Night Of Fear | 100 |

### AMAZORBLADES
| 77 | NS 20 | Common Truth/Mess Around (p/s) | 7 |

### AMBASSADOR 277
| 88 | El GPUT37 | Pop Up Man/Malediction (10" p/s) | 10 |

### AMBASSADORS OF SWING
| 92 | Kold Sweat KSEP 204 | RAP GAME EP | 5 |

### AMBER ASYLUM
| 96 | Elfenblut SAG 1 | FROZEN IN AMBER (LP, inner) | 15 |

### AMBERGRIS
| 70 | Paramount SPFL 262 | AMBERGRIS (LP) | 15 |

### AMBER SQUAD
| 80 | Sound Of Leicester ST 1 | (I Can't) Put My Finger On You/Tell You A Lie (p/s) | 25 |
| 80 | Dead Good DEAD 17 | Can We Go Dancing?/You Should See (What I Do To You In My Dreams) (p/s) | 20 |

### AMBOY DUKES (U.K.)
| 68 | Polydor 56228 | Judy In Disguise/Who's Foolin' Who | 10 |
| 68 | Polydor 56243 | Simon Says/The Marquis | 10 |

### (AMERICAN) AMBOY DUKES
| 68 | Fontana TF 971 | Let's Go Get Stoned/It's Not True | 20 |
| 67 | Fontana (S)TL 5468 | THE AMBOY DUKES (LP) | 75 |
| 69 | London HA-T/SH-T 8378 | JOURNEY TO THE CENTER OF THE MIND (LP, as American Amboy Dukes) | 80 |
| 69 | London HA-T/SH-T 8392 | MIGRATION (LP, as American Amboy Dukes) | 45 |
| 74 | Discreet DS 2203 | TOOTH, FANG AND CLAW (LP) | 15 |

*(see also Ted Nugent)*

### SAMMY AMBROSE
| 65 | Stateside SS 385 | This Diamond Ring/Bad Night | 100 |
| 65 | Stateside SS 399 | Monkey See Monkey Do/Welcome To Dreamsville (DJ Copy) | 400 |
| 65 | Stateside SS 399 | Monkey See Monkey Do/Welcome To Dreamsville | 250 |
| 87 | Kent 6T3 | Welcome To Dreamsville/PLATTERS: Not My Girl | 25 |

### AMBROSE SLADE
| 69 | Fontana TF 1015 | Genesis/Roach Daddy | 300 |
| 69 | Fontana STL 5492 | BEGINNINGS (LP, laminated sleeve, black label with silver print; beware of counterfeits with matt sleeve & black & white label) | 900 |
| 75 | Contour 6870 678 | BEGINNINGS OF SLADE (LP, reissue, different cover & running order, withdrawn) | 70 |
| 10 | Morgan Blue Town BT5006 | BEGINNINGS (LP, reissue, 750 only with insert & signed certificate) | 20 |

*(see also Slade, 'N Betweens)*

### AMBROSETTI QUARTET
| 55 | Columbia SEG 7595 | AMBROSETTI QUARTET (EP, company sleeve, no p/s) | 6 |

### AMEBIX
| 82 | Spiderleg SDL 6 | Who's The Enemy/Carnage/No Gods No Masters/Enemies (p/s) | 30 |
| 83 | Spiderleg SDL 10 | Winter/Beginning Of The End (p/s) | 25 |
| 82 | Spiderleg SDLP 14 | NO SANCTUARY (LP) | 30 |
| 85 | Alternative Tentacles VIRUS46 | ARISE (LP) | 20 |
| 87 | Heavy Metal HMRLP 99 | MONOLITH (LP) | 25 |
| 10 | Back On Black BOBV217LP | MONOLITH (LP, clear vinyl reissue) | 18 |

### AMEN CORNER
| 67 | Deram DM 136 | Gin House Blues/I Know (early copies entitled "Gin House" on label) | 6 |
| 67 | Deram DM 151 | The World Of Broken Hearts/Nema | 7 |
| 68 | Deram DM 172 | Bend Me, Shape Me/Satisnek The Jobsworth | 5 |
| 68 | Deram DM 197 | High In The Sky/Run Run Run | 6 |
| 69 | Deram 228 | The World Of Broken Hearts/Gin House Blues | 5 |
| 69 | Immediate IM 073 | (If Paradise Is) Half As Nice/Hey Hey Girl | 5 |
| 69 | Immediate IM 081 | Hello Susie/Evil Man's Gonna Win | 5 |
| 69 | Immediate IM 084 | Get Back/Farewell To The Real Magnificent Seven | 5 |
| 69 | Immediate AS 3 | So Fine (promo only 'single sampler' for IMSP 023) | 20 |
| 68 | Deram DML/SML 1021 | ROUND AMEN CORNER (LP) | 30 |
| 69 | Immediate IMSP 023 | THE NATIONAL WELSH COAST LIVE EXPLOSION COMPANY (LP, g/fold sleeve, pink label) | 30 |
| 69 | Immediate IMSP 028 | FAREWELL TO THE REAL MAGNIFICENT SEVEN (LP, gatefold sleeve) | 30 |

*(see also Andy Fairweather-Low, Fairweather, Mayfield's Mule, Judas Jump)*

### AMERICAN BREED
| 67 | CBS 2888 | Step Out Of Your Mind/The Same Old Thing | 10 |

| | | | |
|---|---|---|---|
| 67 | CBS 2972 | Step Out Of Your Mind/The Same Old Thing (reissue) | 5 |
| 68 | Stateside SS 2078 | Bend Me Shape Me/Mindrocker | 10 |
| 68 | Dot DOT 101 | Green Light/Don't It Make You Cry | 15 |
| 68 | Dot DOT 106 | Ready, Willing And Able/Take Me If You Want Me | 8 |
| 67 | Dot DOLP 255 | AMERICAN BREED (LP) | 15 |
| 68 | Dot (S)LPD 502 | BEND ME, SHAPE ME (LP) | 15 |
| 68 | Dot (S)LPD 507 | NO WAY TO TREAT A LADY (LP, soundtrack) | 20 |
| 68 | Dot (S)LPD 518 | PUMPKIN, POWDER, SCARLET AND GREEN (LP) | 20 |

### AMERICAN GYPSY
| | | | |
|---|---|---|---|
| 71 | CBS 7027 | Gypsy Queen Pt 1/Dead & Gone | 12 |
| 75 | BTM SBT 101 | Angel Eyes/Lady Eleanor | 15 |
| 70 | CBS 64276 | AMERICAN GYPSY (2-LP) | 30 |
| 75 | BTM BTM 1001 | AMERICAN GYPSY (LP) | 20 |

### AMERICAN JAM (BAND)
| | | | |
|---|---|---|---|
| 72 | Parlophone R5971 | American Jam/Natures Child | 20 |
| 74 | Young Blood YB 1056 | Jam Jam/Back On The Road | 18 |

*(see also Kansas Hook)*

### AMERICAN MUSIC CLUB
| | | | |
|---|---|---|---|
| 87 | Zippo ZONG 0202 | ENGINE (LP, with inner sleeve) | 15 |
| 93 | Virgin V2708 | MERCURY (LP) | 15 |

### AMERICAN POETS
| | | | |
|---|---|---|---|
| 66 | London HLC 10037 | She Blew A Good Thing/Out To Lunch (as American Poets) (DJ copy) | 200 |
| 66 | London HLC 10037 | She Blew A Good Thing/Out To Lunch (as American Poets) | 100 |
| 71 | United Artists UP 35308 | She Blew A Good Thing/Out To Lunch (reissue, as Poets) | 20 |

### AMERICAN SPRING
| | | | |
|---|---|---|---|
| 72 | United Artists UP 35376 | Good Time/Sweet Mountain | 15 |
| 72 | United Artists UP 35421 | Mama Said/Tennessee Waltz | 15 |
| 73 | CBS CBS 1590 | Shyin' Away/Falling In Love | 20 |
| 72 | United Artists UAG 29363 | AMERICAN SPRING (LP, "Tree" cover) | 50 |
| 72 | United Artists UAG 29363 | AMERICAN SPRING (LP, "Tree" gatefold cover with picture of group) | 60 |

*(see also Beach Boys, Honeys)*

### AMERICAN YOUTH CHOIR
| | | | |
|---|---|---|---|
| 71 | Polydor 2066 013 | Together We Can Make It/Keep Your Fine Self Near Me | 30 |

### AMES BROTHERS
| | | | |
|---|---|---|---|
| 54 | HMV 7M 179 | I Can't Believe That You're In Love/Boogie Woogie Maxine | 20 |

### NANCY AMES
| | | | |
|---|---|---|---|
| 66 | Columbia DB 7809 | Friends And Lovers Forever/I've Got A Lot Of Love (Left In Me) | 20 |
| 66 | Columbia DB 8039 | Cry Softly/I Don't Want To Talk About It (DJ copy) | 200 |
| 66 | Columbia DB 8039 | Cry Softly/I Don't Want To Talk About It | 100 |

### AMIGO
| | | | |
|---|---|---|---|
| 76 | Lucky LY 6015 | Judas A No Rasta/Version | 70 |

### AMIN-PECK
| | | | |
|---|---|---|---|
| 82 | Connection CON 8201 | Love Disgrace/Singing In The Wind (p/s) | 40 |
| 82 | Connection CONT 8204 | Girls On Me/Anxiety/Coda (12") | 15 |

### AMITY
| | | | |
|---|---|---|---|
| 76 | Red Rag RRR 001 | AMITY (LP) | 150 |

### AMM
| | | | |
|---|---|---|---|
| 66 | Incus EP 1 | AT THE ROUNDHOUSE (EP) | 80 |
| 67 | Elektra EUKS 7256 | AMM MUSIC (LP) | 140 |
| 87 | Matchless MR13 | INEXHAUSTABLE DOCUMENT (LP) | 20 |

*(see also Eddie Provost Band)*

### ALBERT AMMONS
| | | | |
|---|---|---|---|
| 54 | Mercury MG 25012 | ALBERT AMMONS (10" LP) | 20 |

*(see also [Big] Joe Turner)*

### ALBERT AMMONS, PETE JOHNSON & MEADE 'LUX' LEWIS
| | | | |
|---|---|---|---|
| 55 | Columbia SEG 7528 | SHOUT FOR JOY (EP) | 10 |

*(see also Pete Johnson, Meade 'Lux' Lewis)*

### GENE AMMONS (BAND)
| | | | |
|---|---|---|---|
| 60 | Starlite ST45 017 | Echo Chamber Blues/Ammons' Boogie | 40 |
| 63 | Starlite ST45 097 | Anna/Cae' Cae' | 10 |
| 58 | Esquire 32-047 | HI FI JAM SESSION (LP) | 20 |
| 59 | Esquire 32-077 | FUNKY (LP) | 30 |
| 60 | Esquire 32-097 | JAMMIN' WITH GENE (LP) | 25 |
| 62 | Esquire 32-147 | BLUE GENE (LP) | 20 |
| 63 | Esquire 32-177 | BOSS TENOR (LP) | 25 |
| 63 | Esquire 32-178 | BAD! BOSSA NOVA (LP) | 25 |
| 72 | Prestige PR 24021 | JUG & DODO (LP, with Dodo Marmarosa) | 15 |
| 73 | Prestige PR 10019 | YOU TALK THAT TALK (LP) | 15 |
| 73 | Prestige PR 10021 | BROTHER JUG (LP) | 20 |

### AMON DÜÜL
| | | | |
|---|---|---|---|
| 81 | Illuminated JAMS 24 | HAWK MEETS PENGUIN (LP) | 20 |

### AMON DÜÜL II
| | | | |
|---|---|---|---|
| 70 | Liberty LBF 15355 | Archangel's Thunderbird/Burning Sister | 25 |
| 69 | Liberty LBS 83279 | PHALLUS DEI (LP) | 250 |
| 70 | Liberty LSP 101/LBS 83359 | YETI (2-LP, gatefold sleeve) | 125 |
| 71 | United Artists UAD 60003/4 | DANCE OF THE LEMMINGS (2-LP, laminated gatefold sleeve) | 70 |
| 72 | Sunset SLS 50257 | PHALLUS DEI (LP, reissue) | 20 |

MINT VALUE £

| | | | |
|---|---|---|---|
| 72 | United Artists UAG 23937 | CARNIVAL IN BABYLON (LP, gatefold sleeve) | 35 |
| 72 | United Artists UAG 29406 | WOLF CITY (LP, gatefold sleeve) | 30 |
| 73 | United Artists USP 102 | LIVE IN LONDON (LP) | 20 |
| 73 | United Artists UAS 29504 | VIVE LA TRANCE (LP, with inner sleeve) | 20 |
| 75 | United Artists UA 29723 G | LEMMINGMANIA (LP) | 20 |
| 74 | Atlantic K 50136 | HIJACK (LP) | 20 |

*(see also Utopia)*

**GLADYS AMONI**

| | | | |
|---|---|---|---|
| 76 | Untouchable UT 002 | Your Best Friend/Your Best Dub | 8 |

**AMORPHOUS ANDROGYNOUS**

| | | | |
|---|---|---|---|
| 93 | Quigley LPEBV 1 | TALES OF EPHIDRINA (LP) | 15 |

*(see also Future Sound Of London)*

**TORI AMOS**

| | | | |
|---|---|---|---|
| 92 | East West A7504DJ | Winter (radio edit)/The Pool (promo 7" in p/s) | 15 |
| 92 | East West 7567 82358-1 | LITTLE EARTHQUAKES (LP) | 40 |
| 92 | East West 7567-82358-2 | LITTLE EARTHQUAKES ('Wooden box' CD set) | 35 |
| 94 | East West 7567-82567-1 | UNDER THE PINK (LP) | 25 |
| 96 | East West 7567 82862-1 | BOYS FOR PELE (2-LP, clear vinyl) | 40 |
| 98 | East West 7567 83095-1 | FROM THE CHOIRGIRL HOTEL (LP) | 40 |
| 06 | Epic (No cat no) | THE ORIGINAL BOOTLEGS (12 CD box set, 6 stickers) | 50 |
| 07 | Epic 86140 | AMERICAN DOLL POSSE (2-LP) | 20 |

**AMPHETAMEANIES**

| | | | |
|---|---|---|---|
| 99 | F&J Records SHAG024 | Last Night/Suzie The Muppet Ltd (7" p/s 600 pressed) | 8 |

*(see also Belle and Sebastian, Franz Ferdinand)*

**CURTIS AMY**

| | | | |
|---|---|---|---|
| 60 | Vogue LAE 12277 | THE BLUES MESSAGE (LP, with Paul Bryant) | 15 |
| 61 | Vogue LA 12287 | GROOVIN' BLUE (LP, with Frank Butler) | 30 |
| 62 | Vogue LAE 12298 | MEETIN' HERE (LP, with Paul Bryant) | 15 |
| 63 | Fontana 688136ZL | KATANGA (LP) | 25 |

**ANABAS**

| | | | |
|---|---|---|---|
| 83 | Flame On FLAME 003 | Barricades/Dream Dance (p/s) | 15 |

**ANACOSTIA**

| | | | |
|---|---|---|---|
| 75 | CBS 3742 | All I Need/One Less Morning | 6 |

**ANACRUSIS**

| | | | |
|---|---|---|---|
| 91 | Metal Blade ZORRO 23 | MANIC IMPRESSIONS (LP) | 18 |

**ANA HAUSEN**

| | | | |
|---|---|---|---|
| 81 | Human HUM 12 | Professionals/Tunnel Vision | 8 |

**ANAL FLEAS**

| | | | |
|---|---|---|---|
| 82 | Rectal FLEA 45 | Psych/Over the Edge/Landlord/Go Down (p/s, with insert) | 100 |

**ANALYSIS**

| | | | |
|---|---|---|---|
| 81 | Survival SUR 003 | Surface Tension/Connections (p/s) | 30 |

**ANAN**

| | | | |
|---|---|---|---|
| 68 | Pye 7N 17571 | Haze Woman/I Wonder Where My Sister's Gone | 50 |
| 68 | Pye 7N 17642 | Madena/Standing Still | 20 |

**PETER ANATHAN**

| | | | |
|---|---|---|---|
| 66 | Fontana TF 705 | You Can't Stop Me Loving You/Feel I'm Falling | 10 |

**ANATHEMA**

| | | | |
|---|---|---|---|
| 90 | Private Pressing | AN ILLIAD OF WOES EP (4 track demo cassette) | 30 |
| 91 | Private Pressing | ALL FAITH IS LOST EP (4 track demo cassette) | 30 |
| 92 | Peaceville VILE 36T | THE CRESTFALLEN EP (12", p/s) | 30 |
| 94 | Peaceville CC 6 | WE ARE THE BIBLE EP (purple vinyl, p/s) | 25 |
| 93 | Peaceville VILE 34 | SERENADES (LP) | 30 |
| 95 | Peaceville VILE 52 | THE SILENT ENIGMA (LP) | 25 |
| 96 | Peaceville VILE 64 | ETERNITY (LP) | 25 |
| 99 | Music For Nations MFN 250 | JUDGEMENT (LP) | 35 |
| 01 | Music For Nations MFN 260 | A FINE DAY TO EXIT (LP) | 25 |
| 02 | Peaceville VILELP 73 | ALTERNATIVE 4 (LP, first issued on CD in 1998) | 30 |
| 10 | Peaceville VILELP 305 | A NATURAL DISASTER (2-LP, first issued on CD in 2003) | 20 |
| 10 | Kscope 812 | WE'RE HERE BECAUSE WE'RE HERE (2-LP, 2000 only) | 20 |

**ANCIENT GREASE**

| | | | |
|---|---|---|---|
| 71 | Mercury 6338 033 | WOMAN AND CHILDREN FIRST (LP, black/silver labels) | 250 |

*(see also Eyes Of Blue, Big Sleep, Man, Gary Pickford-Hopkins, Gentle Giant)*

**AND ALSO THE TREES**

| | | | |
|---|---|---|---|
| 84 | Reflex RE 3 | The Secret Sea/Secrecy (p/s) | 8 |
| 84 | Reflex 12 RE 6 | The Secret Sea/Secrecy/There Were No Bounds/The Tease The Tear/ Midnight Garden/Wallpaper Dying (12", p/s) | 10 |
| 84 | Reflex FS 9 | Shantell/Wallpaper Dying (p/s) | 5 |
| 84 | Reflex LEX 1 | AND ALSO THE TREES (LP) | 18 |

**ERIC ANDERSEN**

| | | | |
|---|---|---|---|
| 65 | Fontana TFL 6061 | TODAY IS THE HIGHWAY (LP) | 60 |
| 68 | Fontana TFL/STFL 6068 | 'BOUT CHANGES AND THINGS TAKE 2 (LP, black/silver label, mono/stereo) | 40 |
| 68 | Vanguard SVRL 19003 | MORE HITS FROM TIN CAN ALLEY (LP) | 20 |
| 72 | CBS 65145 | BLUE RIVER (LP) | 15 |

**CAROL ANDERSON**

| | | | |
|---|---|---|---|
| 79 | Grapevine GRP 133 | Sad Girl/I'll Get Off At The Next Stop | 15 |
| 03 | Grapevine 2000 141 | Taking My Mind Off Love/Sad Girl (reissue) | 10 |

## CHRISTIAN ANDERSON
| | | | |
|---|---|---|---|
| 74 | DJM DJS 330 | Supergirl/My Imagination (DJ Copy) | 15 |
| 74 | DJM DJS 330 | Supergirl/My Imagination | 6 |

## ERNESTINE ANDERSON
| | | | |
|---|---|---|---|
| 61 | Mercury AMT 1137 | A Lover's Question/That's All I Want From You | 15 |
| 64 | Sue WI 309 | Keep An Eye On Love/Continental Mind | 70 |
| 65 | Stateside SS 455 | Somebody Told You/How Many Times | 10 |
| 65 | Mercury MF 912 | Jerk & Twine/You Can't Buy Love | 20 |
| 64 | Sue ILP 911 | THE NEW SOUND OF ERNESTINE ANDERSON (LP, unissued) | 150 |

## GLADSTONE ANDERSON (& FOLLOWERS)
| | | | |
|---|---|---|---|
| 69 | Blue Cat BS 172 | Judas/The World Come To An End (with Followers) | 40 |
| 74 | Ashanti ASH 413 | It May Sound Silly/Gladdy's Workshop | 15 |
| 73 | Ashanti SHAN 103 | IT MAY SOUND SILLY (LP) | 20 |
| 94 | Roots RRLP 009 | FOREVER DUB (LP) | 18 |

*(see also Stranger & Gladdy, Tommy McCook)*

## HALEY ANDERSON
| | | | |
|---|---|---|---|
| 83 | Magnet 12 MID 5 | All To Myself (Dance Mix)/(7" Version)/(Instrumental) (12") | 30 |

## IAN (A.) ANDERSON
| | | | |
|---|---|---|---|
| 71 | Village Thing VTSX 1002 | One More Chance/Policeman's Ball | 18 |
| 69 | Saydisc EP SD 134 | ALMOST THE COUNTRY BLUES (EP, with Elliot Jackson) | 50 |
| 68 | Saydisc Matchbox SDM 159 | THE INVERTED WORLD (LP, with Mike Cooper) | 70 |
| 69 | Liberty LBS 83242E | STEREO DEATH BREAKDOWN (LP, blue label, as Ian Anderson Country Blues Band) | 60 |
| 70 | Fontana STL 5542 | BOOK OF CHANGES (LP, black/silver labels) | 120 |
| 70 | Village Thing VTS 3 | ROYAL YORK CRESCENT (LP, with lyric insert) | 35 |
| 72 | Village Thing VTS 9 | A VULTURE IS NOT A BIRD YOU CAN TRUST (LP, laminated front cover) | 40 |
| 72 | Village Thing VTS 18 | SINGER SLEEPS ON AS BLAZE RAGES (LP) | 60 |

*(see also Mike Cooper, Anderson Jones Jackson)*

## JAMES ANDERSON
| | | | |
|---|---|---|---|
| 71 | Atlantic 2091-055 | Mama Mama/Muskatel Muskatel | 20 |

## JON ANDERSON
| | | | |
|---|---|---|---|
| 76 | Atlantic K 10840 | Flight Of The Moorglade/To The Runner | 5 |
| 76 | Atlantic K50261 | OLIAS OF SUNHILLOW (LP, gatefold) | 30 |

*(see also Hans Christian, Warriors, Yes, Mike Oldfield)*

## KIP ANDERSON
| | | | |
|---|---|---|---|
| 67 | President PT 163 | You'll Lose A Good Thing/I'm Out Of Love | 15 |

## MILLER ANDERSON
| | | | |
|---|---|---|---|
| 71 | Deram DM 337 | Bright City/Another Time, Another Place | 15 |
| 71 | Deram SDL 3 | BRIGHT CITY (LP, gatefold sleeve) | 175 |

*(see also Voice, At Last The 1958 Rock'n'Roll Show, Keef Hartley Band, Hemlock, Dog Soldier, Lyn Dobson)*

## REUBEN ANDERSON
| | | | |
|---|---|---|---|
| 66 | Doctor Bird DB 1045 | Christmas Time Again/DESMOND TUCKER: Oh Holy Night | 25 |

## SONNY ANDERSON
| | | | |
|---|---|---|---|
| 60 | London HLP 9036 | Lonely Lonely Train/Yes, I'm Gonna Love You | 40 |

## UDELL T. ANDERSON
| | | | |
|---|---|---|---|
| 69 | Direction 58-4212 | Love Ain't Love/Funky Walk | 15 |
| 69 | Direction 58-4459 | Keep On Loving Me/Rainmaker | 15 |
| 69 | Direction 58-4645 | Don't Go Away/Thank You Darling | 8 |

## VICKI ANDERSON
| | | | |
|---|---|---|---|
| 71 | Mojo 2001 150 | Super Good Part 1/Super Good Part 2 | 10 |
| 73 | Mojo 2093 005 | I'm Too Tough For Mr Big Stuff (Hot Pants)/Sound Funky | 20 |
| 74 | Mojo 2093 028 | Don't Throw Your Love In The Garbage Can/Land Of Milk And Honey/BOBBY BYRD: Sayin' It And Doin' It Are Two Different Things | 10 |

*(see also Bobby Byrd, James Brown)*

## ANDERSON, JONES, JACKSON
| | | | |
|---|---|---|---|
| 68 | Saydisc 33 SD 125 | ANDERSON, JONES, JACKSON (EP) | 35 |

*(see also Ian A. Anderson)*

## ANDERSON'S ALLSTARS
| | | | |
|---|---|---|---|
| 68 | Blue Cat BS 133 | Intensified Girls/Jump And Shout | 150 |

## PETER ANDREOLII
| | | | |
|---|---|---|---|
| 77 | 20th Century BTC 2342 | Mind Excursion/When I Open Up My Eyes | 5 |

## BARBARA ANDREWS
| | | | |
|---|---|---|---|
| 70 | Escort ERT 838 | Lonesome Feeling/RAINY BOP: Hop Scotch | 20 |

## BARRY ANDREWS
| | | | |
|---|---|---|---|
| 80 | Virgin VS 378 | Rossmore Road (NW1)/Win A Night Out With A Well Known Paranoiac (p/s) | 6 |

*(see also XTC, Shriekback, Robert Fripp)*

## CATHERINE ANDREWS
| | | | |
|---|---|---|---|
| 80 | Cat Tracks PURR LP 2 | FRUITS (LP, with lyric sheet & poster sleeve) | 50 |

*(see also Gordon Giltrap, Inner City Unit)*

## CHRIS ANDREWS
| | | | |
|---|---|---|---|
| 67 | Decca F 22668 | Hold On/Easy | 25 |

*(see also Chris Ravel & Ravers)*

## DAVE ANDREWS & SUGAR
| | | | |
|---|---|---|---|
| 68 | Jewel JL 04 | I'm On My Way/Beatin' Of My Heart | 60 |

*(see also Heinz)*

## ERNIE ANDREWS
| | | | |
|---|---|---|---|
| 60 | Vogue V 9166 | 'Round Midnight/Lover Come Back To Me | 5 |
| 65 | Capitol CL 15407 | Where Were You/What Do I See In The Girl | 25 |

MINT VALUE £

| | | | |
|---|---|---|---|
| 76 | Capitol CL 15873 | Fine Young Girl/Then I'll Know | 5 |

## HARVEY ANDREWS
| | | | |
|---|---|---|---|
| 72 | Cube BUG 20 | Soldier/In The Darkness | 5 |
| 72 | Cube BUG 26 | Learning The Game/Don't Know The Time | 5 |
| 65 | Transatlantic TRAEP 133 | HARVEY ANDREWS (EP) | 35 |
| 75 | Transatlantic BIG 525 | (I'm Resigning) From Today/Darby And Joan (with Graham Cooper) | 6 |
| 70 | Decca Nova SDN 9 | PLACES AND FACES (LP) | 50 |
| 73 | Fly HIFLY 15 | FRIENDS OF MINE (LP, gatefold sleeve) | 15 |

## INEZ ANDREWS & ANDREWETTES
| | | | |
|---|---|---|---|
| 65 | Vogue EDVP 1283 | INEZ ANDREWS & ANDREWETTES (EP) | 40 |

## JOHN ANDREWS & LONELY ONES
| | | | |
|---|---|---|---|
| 66 | Parlophone R 5455 | A Rose Growing In The Ruins/It's Just Love (DJ copy) | 300 |
| 66 | Parlophone R 5455 | A Rose Growing In The Ruins/It's Just Love | 175 |

## LEE ANDREWS (& HEARTS)
| | | | |
|---|---|---|---|
| 57 | London HL 7031 | Teardrops/Girl Around The Corner (solo, export issue) | 100 |
| 58 | London HLM 8546 | Teardrops/Girl Around The Corner (solo) | 100 |
| 58 | London HLU 8661 | Try The Impossible/Nobody's Home (as Lee Andrews & Hearts) | 150 |

## RUBY ANDREWS
| | | | |
|---|---|---|---|
| 76 | ABC 4156 | I Got A Bone To Pick With You/I Don't Know How To Love You | 20 |

## ANDREWS SISTERS
| | | | |
|---|---|---|---|
| 57 | Capitol CL 14705 | Rum And Coca-Cola/No, Baby | 5 |

## TIM ANDREWS
| | | | |
|---|---|---|---|
| 67 | Parlophone R 5656 | Sad Simon Lives Again/You Won't Be Seeing Me Anymore | 20 |
| 68 | Parlophone R 5695 | (Something About) Suburbia/Your Tea Is Strong | 20 |
| 70 | Parlophone R 5824 | Tiny Goddess/Josephine | 40 |

*(see also Fleur De Lys, Rupert's People)*

## TIM ANDREWS & PAUL KORDA
| | | | |
|---|---|---|---|
| 68 | Parlophone R 5714 | Smile If You Want To/Makin' Love To Him | 10 |
| 68 | Parlophone R5046 | Angel Face/Waiter Get Me A Drink Of Water | 10 |

*(see also Paul Korda)*

## ANDROIDS
| | | | |
|---|---|---|---|
| 79 | Android AND 001 | Robot Riot/Andwellas Dream (p/s) | 15 |

## ANDROIDS OF MU
| | | | |
|---|---|---|---|
| 80 | Fuck Off FLP 01 | BLOOD ROBOTS (LP) | 45 |

## ANDROMEDA
| | | | |
|---|---|---|---|
| 69 | RCA RCA 1854 | Go Your Way/Keep Out 'Cos I'm Dying | 30 |
| 69 | RCA SF 8031 | ANDROMEDA (LP) | 1000 |
| 90 | Reflection MM 06 | SEVEN, LONELY STREET (LP, with numbered & signed booklet, 500 only) | 25 |
| 95 | Kissing Spell KSLP 9497 | LIVE 1967 (LP) | 15 |

*(see Attack, Five Day Week Straw People, Hard Stuff, Atomic Rooster, John Du Cann, Fuzzy Duck)*

## AND SO TO BED
| | | | |
|---|---|---|---|
| 78 | Stonehouse SH004 | THE EP | 12 |

## AND THE INDIAN LOGIC
| | | | |
|---|---|---|---|
| 00s | Logic KJR 01 | Beggar Man/The Change (p/s) | 10 |

## AND THE NATIVE HIPSTERS
| | | | |
|---|---|---|---|
| 79 | Heater Volume HVR 003 | There Goes Concorde Again.../Stands, Still The Building.../ I Wanna Be Around (several different coloured photocopied foldaround sleeves with insert in ploythene bag) | 30 |
| 82 | Illuminated/Glass HIP 1 | TENDERLY HURT ME (Poor Prince/Hang Ten/Tenderly Hurt Me/Stuck) (12" EP, p/s) | 15 |

## ANDWELLA('S DREAM)
| | | | |
|---|---|---|---|
| 69 | CBS 4301 | Sunday/Midday Sun (as Andwella's Dream) | 35 |
| 69 | CBS 4469 | Mrs. Man/Felix (as Andwella's Dream) | 80 |
| 69 | CBS 4634 | Mr. Sunshine/Shades Of Grey (as Andwella's Dream) | 50 |
| 70 | Reflection RS 1 | Every Little Minute/Michael Fitzhenry (as Andwellas Dream) | 15 |
| 70 | Reflection RS 3 | Hold Onto Your Mind/Shadow Of The Night (as Andwella) | 30 |
| 71 | Reflection RS 6 | People's People/Are You Ready (as Andwella) | 10 |
| 69 | CBS 63673 | LOVE AND POETRY (LP, as Andwella's Dream) | 1000 |
| 70 | Reflection REFL 10 | WORLD'S END (LP, as Andwella, stickered sleeve with poster) | 150 |
| 70 | Reflection REFL 10 | WORLD'S END (LP, without poster) | 80 |
| 71 | Reflection REF 1010 | PEOPLE'S PEOPLE (LP, as Andwella) | 100 |
| 09 | Sunbeam SDR2LP 5063 | LOVE & POETRY (2-LP, reissue) | 20 |

*(see also David Lewis, David Baxter)*

## BOB ANDY
| | | | |
|---|---|---|---|
| 67 | Island WI 3040 | I've Got To Get Back Home/SONNY BURKE: Rudy Girl | 70 |
| 68 | Studio One SO 2063 | Too Experienced/Let Them Stay | 50 |
| 68 | Coxsone CS 7074 | Born A Man(miscredited to Alton Ellis)/MARCIA GRIFFITHS: Mark My Word | 75 |
| 69 | Doctor Bird DB 1183 | The Way I Feel/ETHIOPIANS: Long Time Now | 100 |
| 69 | Doctor Bird DB 1191 | Games People Play/The Sun Shines For Me | 25 |
| 69 | Studio One SO 2075 | I'm Going Home/SOUND DIMENSION: Straight Flush | 40 |
| 70 | Harry J. HJ 6612 | Peace Of Mine/Weep | 8 |
| 71 | Trojan TR 7809 | Green Green Valley/Peace Of Mind | 6 |
| 71 | Trojan TR 7821 | One Woman/You Don't Know (B-side actually "Save Me Version" by Bob Andy Band) | 6 |
| 71 | Trojan TR 7840 | One Woman/You Don't Know | 6 |
| 71 | London HLJ 7127 | Games People Play/GAYLETTES: Son Of A Preacher Man (export issue) | 10 |
| 72 | Sioux SI 019 | Baby I Need Your Loving/CIRCLES: Mammy Blue | 10 |
| 72 | Sioux SI 020 | Everyday People/HONG GANG: Smoking Wild | 10 |
| 72 | Green Door GD 4047 | Life/HARRY J. ALL STARS: Version | 15 |
| 73 | Green Door GD 4059 | You Don't Know/The Border Song | 90 |

| 73 | Horse HOSS 31 | One Woman/Second Hand Love | 6 |
| 75 | Fab FAB 241 | Feeling Soul/SOUND DIMENSION: Part 2 | 15 |
| 75 | Sound Tracs SK2 8 | Nyah/Nyah Dub | 8 |
| 76 | Tropical TST 110 | Feeling Soul/Rock It Down | 10 |
| 76 | DEB | War In The City/Version | 30 |
| 70s | Sky Note SKY 1011 | The Ghetto Stay In The Mind/Ghetto Dub | 15 |
| 78 | Skynote SJYLP 15 | LOTS OF LOVE AND I (LP) | 15 |

*(see also Bob & Marcia, Larry & Alvin)*

## HORACE ANDY
| 72 | Count Shelley 2 | Cha Cha Children/Version | 8 |
| 72 | Attack ATT 8026 | Feel Good All Over/PHIL PRATT ALLSTARS: Feel Good (Version) | 6 |
| 72 | Song Bird SB 1085 | Lonely Woman/Lonely Version | 20 |
| 73 | Bread BR 1170 | Don't Try To Use Me/Goddess Of Love | 12 |
| 73 | Randy's RAN 533 | Don't Think About Me (with Earl Flute)/DINO PERKINS: Skin Him Alive | 20 |
| 73 | Atra ATRA 008 | Children Of Israel/Part 2 | 8 |
| 73 | RCA TCA 2401 | I Stand Before You/Unity Strength And Love | 70 |
| 74 | Ackee ACK 530 | Til/IMPACT ALLSTARS: Version | 6 |
| 75 | Attack ATT 8117 | Nice And Easy/Version | 10 |
| 75 | Fab FAB 260 | Oh Lord Why Lord/SOUND DIMENSION: Part 2 | 10 |
| 75 | Morpheus MOR 1010 | Got To Get You | 6 |
| 76 | Venture VEN 7706 | Skylarking/Version | 10 |
| 76 | Terminal TM 105 | Thank The Lord/Part Two (actually the SUNSHOT BAND) | 10 |
| 77 | Serious Business SB 02 | Rock To Sleep/Version | 35 |
| 78 | Carib Gems CGDD110 | Guiding Star (with Tapper Zukie)/Zion Gate (12") | 20 |
| 79 | Sufferer's Height SUFF 005 | Pure Ranking/The Return Of Jammy's Hi-Fi (Round One)/TREVOR RANKING: Whip Them Jah Jah (12") | 30 |
| 79 | Star PTP 1024 | Tonight/Don't Let Problems Get You Down (12") | 30 |
| 70s | Terminal TM 101 | Roots Of All Evil/I Will Forgive You | 15 |
| 80 | Unity UN 002 | This Must Be Hell/If I Wasn't A Man (12", with DEADLY HEADLEY) | 15 |
| 84 | Music Hawk MHD 13 | Confusion/Version (12") | 40 |
| 84 | Blacker Dread BD 009 | Cus-Cus/S.C.O.M RHYTHM SECTION: Watch Your Step | 15 |
| 84 | Blacker Dread BD 012 | Money Money Money/Evil Money (no centre) | 15 |
| 85 | Rough Trade RTT 172 | Get Down/RHYTHM POSSE : Get Down Deeper (12") | 50 |
| 80s | Solid Groove SGL 014 | Serious Thing/Love Hangover (12") | 10 |
| 95 | Blood & Fire BAFT 01 | Problems/Problems Dub (12" reissue) | 15 |
| 02 | Glimmer GLM 1008 | Mr. Bassie/Don't Let Problems Get You Down (10", reissue) | 12 |
| 72 | Trojan TBL 197 | YOU ARE MY ANGEL (LP) | 25 |
| 78 | Solid Groove SGL 107 | EXCLUSIVELY (LP) | 40 |
| 84 | Music Hawk MHLP001 | CONFUSION (LP) | 20 |
| 95 | Blood & Fire BAFLP 007 | IN THE LIGHT DUB (LP, reissue) | 20 |
| 99 | Virgin SADLP 9 | LIVING IN THE FLOOD (LP) | 15 |

*(see also Jon Cuno, Big Youth)*

## HORACE ANDY & FREDDIE MCKAY
| 75 | Treble 7 | Talking Love/Dub | 8 |

## PATRICK ANDY
| 78 | Grove Music GMDM 3 | Woman, Woman, Woman/TOMMY MCCOOK: Lamb's Bread (12") | 35 |

## ANDY & CLYDE
| 65 | Rio R 62 | Never Be A Slave/Magic Is Love | 12 |
| 65 | Rio R 69 | I'm So Lonesome/WINSTON STEWART: Day After Day | 12 |
| 65 | Rio R 71 | We All Have To Part/UPSETTERS: Scandalizing | 80 |

## ANDY & JOEY
| 62 | Island WI 056 | Have You Ever/Cross My Heart | 25 |
| 64 | Port-O-Jam PJ 4009 | I Want To Know/My Love Has Gone | 40 |
| 64 | Ska Beat JB 162 | You're Wondering Now/You'll Never (copies also exist on R&B label) | 30 |

*(see also Roland Alphonso)*

## JOHNNY ANGEL
| 60 | Parlophone R 4642 | Chinese Butterfly/My Very Good Friend The Milkman | 5 |
| 60 | Parlophone R 4679 | Too Young To Go Steady/You're Thrilling | 5 |
| 61 | Parlophone R 4750 | What Happens To Love/Luna Luna Luna Lu | 5 |
| 61 | Parlophone R 4795 | Web Of Love/Trocadero-Double-Nine-One-O | 5 |
| 62 | Parlophone R 4874 | Look, Look Little Angel/Jenny From Missouri | 8 |
| 62 | Parlophone R 4948 | Better Luck Next Time/The Power Of You | 5 |
| 63 | Parlophone R 5026 | A Touch Of Venus/The Two Together | 5 |

## MARIAN ANGEL
| 65 | Columbia DB 7537 | It's Gonna Be Alright/Tomorrow's Fool | 30 |
| 65 | Columbia DB 7705 | You Can't Buy My Love/One Way Only | 25 |
| 66 | CBS 202391 | A Little Bit Of Sunshine/All The Time In The World | 20 |

## ANGEL PAVEMENT
| 69 | Fontana TF 1059 | Baby You've Gotta Stay/Green Mello Hill | 20 |
| 70 | Fontana TF 1072 | Tell Me What I've Got To Do/When Will I See June Again | 25 |

*(see also Fortes Mentum, Pussy)*

## ANGEL STREET
| 79 | Ellie Jay EJSP 9290 | Done It Again/Song For You (500 only) | 200 |

## ANGEL WITCH
| 80 | EMI EMI 5064 | Sweet Danger/Flight Nineteen (p/s, credits Angelwitch) | 10 |
| 80 | EMI 12EMI 5064 | Sweet Danger/Hades Paradise/Flight Nineteen (12", p/s) | 20 |
| 80 | Bronze BRO 108 | Angel Witch/Gorgon (p/s) | 8 |
| 81 | Bronze BRO 121 | Loser/Suffer/Dr Phibes (p/s) | 10 |

## ANGEL (1)

| | | | |
|---|---|---|---|
| 85 | Killerwatt KIL 3001 | Goodbye/Reawakening (no p/s) | 15 |
| 80 | Bronze BRON 532 | ANGELWITCH (LP) | 20 |
| 86 | Killerwatt KILP 4003 | FRONTAL ASSAULT (LP) | 18 |
| 85 | Killerwatt KILP 4001 | SCREAMIN' N' BLEEDIN' (LP) | 15 |
| 12 | Rise Above RISELP145 | AS ABOVE, SO BELOW (2-LP, clear vinyl, 1-sided 7" (Devil's Tower), A2 poster, 100 only) | 70 |
| 12 | Rise Above RISELP145 | AS ABOVE, SO BELOW (LP, 2 x white vinyl 12" 45rpm, inners, insert) | 30 |

(see also Tytan)

## ANGEL (1)

| | | | |
|---|---|---|---|
| 74 | Cube BUG 41 | Little Boy Blue/Tragedy Queen | 7 |
| 74 | Cube BUG 51 | Good Time Fanny/Who D'Ya Think Your Fooling | 7 |

## ANGEL (2)

| | | | |
|---|---|---|---|
| 77 | Casablanca CBC 104 | Magic Touch/Big Boy | 5 |
| 76 | Casablanca CBC 4007 | ANGEL (LP, with insert) | 15 |

## ANGELA & HER FANS

| | | | |
|---|---|---|---|
| 66 | Pye 7N 17108 | Love Ya Illya/I Know You | 10 |

(see also Alma Cogan)

## ANGELIC UPSTARTS

| | | | |
|---|---|---|---|
| 78 | Dead IS/AU/1024 | Murder Of Liddle Towers/Police Oppression (p/s, 1,000 only) | 60 |
| 78 | Rough Trade RT/SW 001 | Murder Of Liddle Towers/Police Oppression (reissue, p/s) | 12 |
| 79 | Warner Bros K 17354 | I'm An Upstart/Leave Me Alone (green vinyl, no p/s) | 5 |
| 79 | Warner Bros K 17426C | Teenage Warning/The Young Ones (red vinyl, no p/s) | 5 |
| 80 | Zonophone Z 7 | Last Night Another Soldier/The Man Who Came In From The Beano (p/s) | 5 |
| 81 | Zonophone Z 12 | England/Stick's Diary (p/s) | 12 |
| 83 | Anagram ANA 12 | The Burglar (p/s, unissued) | 0 |
| 85 | Gas GM 3010 | Brighton Bomb/Thin Red Line/Soldier (12", banned 'Maggie Thatcher' p/s) | 15 |
| 79 | Warner Bros K 56717 | TEENAGE WARNING (LP) | 15 |
| 81 | Zonophone ZEM 102 | LIVE (LP, with free live flexidisc: "We're Gonna Take The World"/Leave Me Alone/ "The Young Ones"/"White Riot" [no cat. no.]) | 15 |
| 85 | Razor RAZM 32 | LIVE IN YUGOSLAVIA (LP) | 15 |
| 90 | Link LP 140 | LOST & FOUND (LP) | 15 |

## ANGELIQUE

| | | | |
|---|---|---|---|
| 77 | Tempus TEM 102 | Cry/Crying | 5 |

## BOBBY ANGELO & TUXEDOS

| | | | |
|---|---|---|---|
| 61 | HMV POP 892 | Baby Sitting/Skinny Lizzie | 25 |
| 61 | HMV POP 982 | I Gotta Have You/Don't Stop | 30 |

(see also Innocents [UK], End)

## JERRY ANGELO

| | | | |
|---|---|---|---|
| 59 | Parlophone R 4548 | Crush Me/Mary Lou | 5 |
| 59 | Parlophone R 4561 | If You Change Your Mind/I Love You My Love | 5 |
| 60 | Parlophone R 4656 | Maria Elena/Old Man River | 5 |
| 62 | Palette PG 9031 | Lonely Hill/Make Her Mine | 5 |
| 62 | Palette PG 9034 | Innocent Angel/The Boy Who Walks Alone | 5 |

## MICHAEL ANGELO & HIS ORCHESTRA

| | | | |
|---|---|---|---|
| 61 | Columbia DB 4705 | Rocco's Theme/Spinneree | 5 |

(see also John Barry)

## ANGELS

| | | | |
|---|---|---|---|
| 62 | Pye International 7N 25150 | Everybody Loves A Lover/Blow Joe | 10 |
| 63 | Mercury AMT 1211 | My Boyfriend's Back/(Love Me) Now | 10 |
| 63 | Mercury AMT 1215 | I Adore Him/Thank You And Goodnight | 10 |
| 64 | Philips BF 1312 | Wow Wee Wee/Snowflakes And Teardrops | 10 |

(see also Beach-Nuts)

## ANGELS & AIRWAVES

| | | | |
|---|---|---|---|
| 06 | Geffen 1702866 | It Hurts/The Gift (live) (Picture disc in stickered PVC sleeve) | 12 |
| 06 | Geffen MCS 40461 | The Adventure (1-sided picture disc in stickered PVC sleeve) | 12 |
| 07 | Geffen 1751195 | Everything's Magic/Do It For Me Now (Acoustic) (picture disc in stickered PVC sleeve) | 10 |

(see also Blink 182, Box Car Racer)

## ANGELS AND EIGHTEEN

| | | | |
|---|---|---|---|
| 72 | RAK 137 | Midnight Flight/Flight 2 | 80 |

## ANGELS ONE 5

| | | | |
|---|---|---|---|
| 82 | Galaxy GAL 005 | Cut And Dried/Countdown | 8 |

## ANGIE

| | | | |
|---|---|---|---|
| 79 | Stiff BUY 51 | Peppermint Lump/Breakfast In Naples (p/s) | 10 |

## GUY ANGIER

| | | | |
|---|---|---|---|
| 70 | (No label or cat no) | GUITAR AND BANANAS (LP, with insert) | 80 |

## ANGLIANS

| | | | |
|---|---|---|---|
| 67 | CBS 202489 | A Friend Of Mine/Daytime Lover | 15 |

(see also Moving Finger)

## ANGLOS

| | | | |
|---|---|---|---|
| 65 | Brit WI 004 | Incense/You're Fooling Me | 60 |
| 65 | Fontana 561 | Incense/You're Fooling Me (unissued) | 200 |
| 65 | Fontana TF 589 | Incense/You're Fooling Me (reissue) | 25 |
| 67 | Sue WI 4033 | Incense/You're Fooling Me (unissued) | 200 |
| 69 | Island WIP 6061 | Incense/You're Fooling Me (2nd reissue) | 10 |

(see also Spencer Davis Group, Stevie Winwood)

## ANGOR WAT

| | | | |
|---|---|---|---|
| 85 | Children Of The Revolution GURT8 | GENERAL STRIKE (LP) | 15 |

## ANIKA
| | | | |
|---|---|---|---|
| 10 | Invada INV099LP | ANIKA (LP) | 15 |

## ANIMAL COLLECTIVE
| | | | |
|---|---|---|---|
| 04 | Paw Tracks PAW 003 | Wastered/Wastered (12" one side BLACK DICE, 1,000 only) | 12 |
| 04 | Fat Cat 7FAT 15 | Who Could Win A Rabbit/Baby Day (p/s) | 8 |
| 05 | Fat Cat 7FAT 19 | Grass/Must Be Treeman/Ficle Cycle (p/s) | 10 |
| 06 | No label or Cat. No.) | Purple Bottle/Polly (tour 7", white label, plain white die-cut sleeve. Later pressings have track info on sleeve) | 15 |
| 06 | Fat Cat 12FAT 060 | People/Tikwid/My Favourite Colours/People (live) (12") | 10 |
| 07 | Domino RUG 270T | Fireworks (1-sided pink vinyl other side etched 10", stickered, die-cut pink sleeve) | 15 |
| 04 | Fat Cat FATSPLP 08 | SUNG TONGS (2-LP) | 20 |
| 05 | Fat Cat FATSLP 11 | FEELS (2-LP) | 18 |
| 06 | Domino WIGLP199 | STRAWBERRY JAM (2-LP, gatefold with inners) | 18 |
| 09 | Domino WIGLP216 | MERRIWEATHER POST PAVILION (2-LP, gatefold) | 18 |
| 15 | Domino WIGLP 364 | LIVE AT 9.30 (3-LP boxset, poster, hand numbered with screenprint) | 35 |
| 15 | Domino WIGLP 364 | LIVE AT 9.30 (3-LP boxset, poster, hand numbered without screenprint) | 25 |

*(see also Panda Bear, Avey Tare)*

## ANIMAL FARM
| | | | |
|---|---|---|---|
| 84 | Rot Records ASS 7 | Model Soldier/John And Julie (p/s) | 15 |

## ANIMALS
| | | | |
|---|---|---|---|
| 64 | Columbia DB 7247 | Baby Let Me Take You Home/Gonna Send You Back To Walker | 10 |
| 64 | Columbia DB 7301 | The House Of The Rising Sun/Talkin' 'Bout You | 5 |
| 64 | Columbia DB 7354 | I'm Crying/Take It Easy | 5 |
| 65 | Columbia DB 7445 | Don't Let Me Be Misunderstood/Club-A-Go Go (standard issue, matrix: '2N') | 5 |
| 65 | Columbia DB 7445 | Don't Let Me Be Misunderstood/Club-A-Go Go (mispressing, with 'demo' version of A-side, matrix: '1N') | 10 |
| 65 | Columbia DB 7539 | Bring It On Home To Me/For Miss Caulker | 5 |
| 65 | Columbia DB 7639 | We've Gotta Get Out Of This Place/I Can't Believe It | 5 |
| 65 | Columbia DB 7741 | It's My Life/I'm Going To Change The World | 5 |
| 66 | Decca F 12332 | Inside Looking Out/Outcast | 10 |
| 66 | Decca F 12407 | Don't Bring Me Down/Cheating | 10 |
| 63 | Graphic Sound ALO 10867 | I JUST WANNA MAKE LOVE TO YOU (12" EP, 1-sided, 99 only, as Alan Price Rhythm & Blues Group or as Animals, private pressing, blank white cover, typed label) | 500 |
| 64 | Columbia SEG 8374 | THE ANIMALS IS HERE (EP) | 20 |
| 65 | Columbia SEG 8400 | THE ANIMALS (EP) | 20 |
| 65 | Columbia SEG 8439 | THE ANIMALS NO. 2 (EP) | 20 |
| 65 | Columbia SEG 8452 | THE ANIMALS ARE BACK (EP) | 35 |
| 65 | Decca DFE 8643 | IN THE BEGINNING THERE WAS EARLY ANIMALS (EP, reissue of Graphic Sound EP) | 30 |
| 66 | Columbia SEG 8499 | ANIMAL TRACKS (EP) | 45 |
| 64 | Columbia 33SX 1669 | THE ANIMALS (LP, blue/black label with "sold in the U.K..." label text) | 100 |
| 64 | EMI Regal SREG 1104 | THE ANIMALS (LP, export issue) | 80 |
| 65 | Columbia 33SX 1708 | ANIMAL TRACKS (LP, first pressing with 33SX on label) | 120 |
| 66 | Columbia SX 1708 | ANIMAL TRACKS (LP, second pressing, SX 1708 on labels) | 75 |
| 66 | Columbia SX 6035 | THE MOST OF THE ANIMALS (LP) | 25 |
| 66 | Decca LK 4797 | ANIMALISMS (LP) | 60 |

*(see also Eric Burdon & Animals, Alan Price, Danny McCullough)*

## ANIMALS & MEN
| | | | |
|---|---|---|---|
| 80 | Strange Days DAYS 1 | The Terraplane Fixation/Shell Shock (p/s) | 7 |
| 80 | TW HIT 101 | Don't Misbehave In The New Age/Machines (p/s) | 5 |

## ANIMATED EGG
| | | | |
|---|---|---|---|
| 69 | Marble Arch MAL 890 | ANIMATED EGG (LP) | 25 |

## ANIMATION
| | | | |
|---|---|---|---|
| 82 | Dance Fools Dance DF 2 2 | FRAME ON EP | 20 |

## PAUL ANKA
### SINGLES
| | | | |
|---|---|---|---|
| 57 | Columbia DB 3980 | Diana/Don't Gamble With Love (mauve label) | 5 |
| 68 | RCA RCA 1676 | Can't Get You Out Of My Mind/When We Get There | 40 |
| 68 | RCA RCA 1676 | Can't Get You Out Of My Mind/When We Get There (DJ copy) | 60 |

### ALBUMS
| | | | |
|---|---|---|---|
| 58 | Columbia 33SX 1092 | PAUL ANKA (LP, green label) | 20 |

*(see also Micki Marlo & Paul Anka, Neil Sedaka)*

## ANNABEL DREAM
| | | | |
|---|---|---|---|
| 60s | Oak (no cat no) | My Last Date With You/Gary, Won't You Marry Me (Unreleased - acetate only) | 50 |

## ANNALISE
| | | | |
|---|---|---|---|
| 99 | Boss Tunage BOSTAGE 701 | Signposts And Alleyways/Empire Builder (p/s, 1-sided green vinyl with free CD, numbered, 250 copies only) | 10 |

## ANNETTE (& AFTERBEATS)
| | | | |
|---|---|---|---|
| 64 | HMV POP 1270 | Muscle Beach Party/I Dream About Frankie | 20 |
| 64 | HMV POP 1322 | Scrambled Egghead/Merlin Jones | 10 |
| 65 | HMV POP 1447 | The Monkey's Uncle (with The Beach Boys)/How Will I Know My Love | 25 |
| 59 | Gala 45XP 1046 | TALL PAUL (EP) | 10 |
| 61 | Buena Vista BV 3305 | DANCE ANNETTE (LP) | 20 |
| 64 | HMV CLP 1782 | ANNETTE'S BEACH PARTY (LP) | 20 |
| 64 | Buena Vista BV 3325 | PAJAMA PARTY (LP) | 20 |

## ANNETTE & KEYMEN
| | | | |
|---|---|---|---|
| 64 | King KG 1006 | Look Who's Blue/How Can I Tell Him | 5 |

## ANNIS
| | | | |
|---|---|---|---|
| 79 | GTO GT 266 | Don't Play Your Games/After Me | 15 |

## ANNIVERSARY
78   Aerco AERE 102     GIVE ME A SMILE (EP) ........................................................................... 25

## ANN-MARGRET
61   RCA RCA 1245     I Just Don't Understand/I Don't Hurt Anymore .................................... 10
64   RCA RCX 7148     THE VIVACIOUS ONE (EP) ........................................................... 15
62   RCA RD 27239/SF 5116     AND HERE SHE IS (LP, mono/stereo) .............................................. 15

## ANNO DOMINI
71   Deram SML-R 1085     ON THIS NEW DAY (LP) ............................................................ 400

## ANONYMOUSLY YOURS
69   Trojan TR 680     Get Back/ERNIE SMITH : Not For Sale ........................................... 15
69   Trojan TR 681     It's Your Thing/69 (B-side actually by Wallace Wilson) ....................... 15
69   Duke DU 38     Dream Baby/Staggerlee .............................................................. 15
69   Duke DU 40     Organism/Itch ........................................................................... 15

## ANOREXIA
80   Slim SJP 812     Rapist In The Park/I'm A Square/Pets ........................................... 35
82   Slim BRS 011     Softly Quietly Or Shout/Steven/Inanimate Objects/Marching Song (p/s) ...... 8

## ANOTHER MAN'S POISON
92   Tick Tock TT 1     Alf Garnet's Heart Attack/Now That's What I Call (hand stamped die cut paper
     sleeve) ................................................................................... 10
92   Tick Tock TT 2     I Spit On My Fist/Wallop (p/s) ...................................................... 7

## ANOTHER PRETTY FACE
79   New Pleasure Z1     All The Boys Love Carrie/That's Not Enough (green and white foldout p/s) .... 18
79   New Pleasure Z2     All The Boys Love Carrie/That's Not Enough (red and white p/s) ............. 10
80   Chicken Jazz JAZZ 1     Heaven Gets Closer Every Day/Only Heroes Live Forever (p/s) ............... 7
80   Virgin VS 320     Whatever Happened To The West?/Goodbye 1970's (p/s) ................... 10
80   Chicken Jazz JAZZ 2     I'M SORRY THAT I BEAT YOU, I'M SORRY THAT I SCREAMED, FOR A MOMENT THERE I
     REALLY LOST CONTROL (8-track cassette with fanzine and badge. Some copies exist
     with tracks of DNV single taped onto the end) ................................. 30
81   Chicken Jazz JAZZ 3     Soul To Soul/A Woman's Place/God On The Screen (foldout p/s) ........... 15

## ANOTHER SUNNY DAY
88   Sarah SARAH 003     Anorak City (flexidisc free with Are You Scared To Get Happy fanzine (SARAH 004,
     1,500 only – must be together) ................................................. 45
88   Sarah SARAH 007     I'm In Love With A Girl Who Doesn't Know I Exist/Things Will Be Nice/ The Centre Of
     My Little World (14" x 10" foldout poster p/s) .............................. 25
89   Caff CAFF 7     Genetic Engineering/Kilburn Towers (p/s, with inner) ....................... 30
89   Sarah SARAH 016     What's happened?/Can't You Tell It's True?/Impossible (foldover p/s in poly bag,
     insert) ................................................................................... 10
89   Sarah SARAH 022     You Should All Be Murdered/Horseriding/Green (foldover p/s in poly bag, insert) ...... 15
90   Sarah SARAH 035     Rio/The Very Beginning (p/s, insert) ........................................... 10
92   Sarah SARAH 060     New Year's Honours/I Don't Suppose I'll Get A Second Chance (p/s, insert) ...... 10
92   Sarah SARAH 613     LONDON WEEKEND (LP) ........................................................ 30

## ANSEL SCANDAL
76   Dynamic DYN 105     Roots Food/Roots Food - Dub .................................................... 6

## BRETT ANSELL
62   Oriole CB 1701     That's Where Lonesome Lives/The Door Is Open .............................. 30
62   Oriole CB 1725     Rosalita/The Outsider ................................................................ 10

## ANSELL (COLLINS) & ELAINE
72   Camel CA 98     Presenting Cheater/RON WILSON: Official Trombone ....................... 15

## MARK ANSLEY
70   Mother MOT 2     909/Venus ............................................................................. 50

## ANSWER
05   Albert JAS UK 015     Keep On Believin'/New Day Rising ............................................... 8
05   Albert JAS UK 017     Never Too Late/Some Unity (stickered p/s) ..................................... 7

## ANSWERS (1)
66   Columbia DB 7847     It's Just A Fear/You've Gotta Believe Me ..................................... 200
66   Columbia DB 7953     That's What You're Doing To Me/Got A Letter From My Baby ............... 70
*(see also Misunderstood, High Tide)*

## ANSWERS (2)
71   Spark SRL 1058     Give Me All That I Need/Tawny Wood ......................................... 20

## ANT
74   Pye 7N 45332     Banana Pie/No Road Goes Your Way .......................................... 15

## ADAM ANT
95   EMI CDEMS370     Beautiful Dream (single version)/Let's Have A Fight/Billy Boy/Wonderful (acoustic)
     (CD withdrawn, 7 known copies) .............................................. 100
95   EMI CDEM370     Beautiful Dream (single version)/Shake Your Hips/Antmusic (Acoustic)/Beautiful
     Dream (Lucas Full Length Mix) (CD, withdrawn, 2 known copies) ........... 150
*(see also Adam & The Ants, Maneaters)*

## ANT & DDR
05   Stay Up Forever SUF 79:000mg     Acid Techno...All The Time (12") ................................................ 12
*(see also DDR)*

## ANTEEEKS
66   Philips BF 1471     I Don't Want You/Ball And Chain .............................................. 200

## ANTENA
82   Operation Twilight OPT 02     The Boy From Ipamema/Spiral Staircase (p/s) ................................. 5

## ANTHEM (1)
71   Buddah 2359017     ANTHEM (LP) ......................................................................... 40

## ANTHEM (2)
81   EJSP9576     England/Some Like It Hot/Do You Mind (EP, p/s, 500 only) ............... 140

## ANTHILL MOB (1)

| | | | |
|---|---|---|---|
| 92 | Anthill ANT 1T | Penelope's Theme (12" white label) | 35 |
| 93 | Anthill ANT 2T | Antology/Black Rushin'/The Hooded Claw (Tango Mix) (12") | 30 |
| 93 | Anthill ANT 3T | Antology (The Top Buzz Stonehenge Remix)/Black Rushin' (Anthill Remix) (12") | 20 |

## ANTHILL MOB (2)

| | | | |
|---|---|---|---|
| 95 | Confetti MK 01 | Feel It/Deep Down/Untitled/Untitled (white label 12") | 30 |
| 95 | Confetti MK001 | MAKESHIFT EP (12") | 90 |
| 96 | Confetti COEP 01 | Promise Of... /Was She Ever Mine?/So In Love/Got To Do It (12") | 35 |
| 96 | Confetti COEP 02 | Feel The Groove/ANTHILL MOB FEATURING P. PITSTOP - Do You Know?/P. PITSTOP - I Know How To Love! (12") | 25 |
| 97 | Confetti COEP 05 | Why (Inside The Rise)/Things Just Started (12") | 25 |
| 97 | Confetti COEP 06 | Cloudy Day/Agitator (12") | 15 |
| 97 | Confetti COEP 01 | Missing/Player/X2C/Flava/Sound/Cuts (2 x 12") | 70 |
| 97 | Confetti COEP 08 | Higher/How Ya Feeling (12") | 15 |
| 97 | Love Peace & Unity LOVE 03 | Burning (The Original Mix) (10" picture disc, 500 only, same track both sides) | 35 |
| 97 | Makeshift MR 001 | Set You Free/In The Name/Shake The House/Heaven Knows (12") | 15 |
| 98 | Makeshift MR 002 | Never Ever Time/Time To Move/Don't Know/Give Me (12") | 20 |
| 98 | Quench QUE 14 | Don't Leave Me/Listen (12") | 30 |
| 00 | Confetti COEP 19 | ANTHILL MOB EP (12") | 25 |
| 97 | Love Peace & Unity LOVE 04 | A SPECIAL COLLECTION OF ENCHANTED RHYTHMS (2 x LP) | 40 |

*(see also Mystic matt And The Anthill Mob)*

## BILLIE ANTHONY

| | | | |
|---|---|---|---|
| 54 | Columbia SCM 5143 | This Ole House/Oh, What A Dream | 6 |
| 55 | Columbia SCM 5164 | Butterscotch Hop/No More | 5 |
| 55 | Columbia SCM 5174 | Tweedlee Dee/Shake The Hand Of A Stranger | 5 |
| 57 | Columbia DB 3935 | Rock-A-Billy/A Needle And Thread | 5 |

*(see also Big Ben Banjo Band)*

## DAVID ANTHONY

| | | | |
|---|---|---|---|
| 68 | Island WI 3148 | All Night/Get Out Of My Mind | 40 |

*(see also Dave Anthony's Moods)*

## JIM ANTHONY

| | | | |
|---|---|---|---|
| 72 | Satril SAT 4 | Sasha/White Rose | 5 |

## LITTLE WAYNE ANTHONY

| | | | |
|---|---|---|---|
| 73 | Jay Boy BOY 79 | Hey Naw/Freedom To Love (reissue) | 10 |

## MALCOLM ANTHONY

| | | | |
|---|---|---|---|
| 70 | Nashville 6076 004 | Memories/Traces Of Tomorrow (demo) | 15 |
| 70 | Vertigo 6076 004 | Memories/Traces Of Tomorrow | 50 |

## MARK ANTHONY & JETS

| | | | |
|---|---|---|---|
| 70 | Unity UN 565 | More Balls/TONY KING: Bum Ball (Chapter II) | 5 |

## RAY ANTHONY (1)

| | | | |
|---|---|---|---|
| 55 | Capitol CL 14243 | Juke Box Special/Heat Wave | 10 |
| 55 | Capitol CL 14345 | Pete Kelly's Blues/DC-7 | 5 |
| 55 | Capitol CL 14354 | Hernando's Hideaway/The Bunny Hop | 5 |
| 56 | Capitol CL 14525 | Flip-Flop/Hurricane Anthony | 10 |
| 57 | Capitol CL 14689 | Rock Around The Rock Pile/The Girl Can't Help It | 20 |
| 57 | Capitol CL 14703 | Plymouth Rock/Calypso Dance | 5 |
| 57 | Capitol CL 14769 | The Bunny Hop/The Hokey Pokey | 5 |
| 58 | Capitol CL 14929 | Peter Gunn/Tango For Two (Mmm Shall We Dance?) | 5 |
| 59 | Capitol CL 15019 | The Bunny Hop Rock/Walkin' To Mother's | 5 |
| 57 | Capitol EAP 1-823 | THE GIRL CAN'T HELP IT (EP) | 25 |
| 57 | Capitol EAP 1-958 | ROCK AND ROLL WITH RAY ANTHONY (EP) | 25 |

*(see also Gordon MacRae & Ray Anthony)*

## RAY ANTHONY (2)

| | | | |
|---|---|---|---|
| 79 | Mango Media 23 | The Arabian Funk/Time | 25 |

## RAYBURN ANTHONY

| | | | |
|---|---|---|---|
| 60 | London HLS 9167 | Who's Gonna Shoe Your Pretty Little Feet/There's No Tomorrow | 15 |

## DAVE ANTHONY'S MOODS

| | | | |
|---|---|---|---|
| 66 | Parlophone R 5438 | New Directions/Give It A Chance | 60 |

*(see also David Anthony)*

## ANTHRAX (U.K.)

| | | | |
|---|---|---|---|
| 83 | Small Wonder SMALL 27 | THEY'VE GOT IT ALL WRONG (EP, p/s) | 10 |
| 83 | Crass 221984/9 | CAPITALISM IS CANNIBALISM (EP, foldout p/s) | 20 |

## ANTHRAX (U.S.)

| | | | |
|---|---|---|---|
| 86 | Island 12ISP 285 | Madhouse/Air/God Save The Queen (12", picture disc) | 20 |
| 86 | Island 12IS 285 | Madhouse/Air/God Save The Queen (12", p/s with patch) | 15 |
| 87 | Island ISP 338 | I'm The Man/Caught In The Mosh (Live) (Anthrax logo shaped picture disc) | 10 |
| 87 | Island ISX 316 | I Am The Law (live)/Bud E. Luvbomm And Satan's Lougne Band/Madhouse (live) (red vinyl, p/s) | 20 |
| 86 | Island ISP 325 | Indians/Sabbath Bloody Sabbath (orange vinyl, mispressing, B-side plays Imitation Of Life) | 10 |
| 87 | Island ISP 325 | Indians/Sabbath Bloody Sabbath (picture disc with sticker) | 10 |
| 89 | Island IS 409 | Anti Social/Parasite (p/s) | 10 |
| 86 | Music For Nations MFN62 | SPREADING THE DISEASE (LP) | 20 |
| 86 | Music For Nations MFN62P | SPREADING THE DISEASE (LP, picture disc) | 20 |
| 87 | Music For Nations MFN14 | FISTFUL OF METAL (LP) | 15 |
| 87 | Music For Nations MFN14P | FISTFUL OF METAL (LP, picture disc) | 20 |
| 87 | Island PILPS 9865 | AMONG THE LIVING (LP, picture disc) | 20 |
| 90 | Island ILPSP 9967 | PERSISTENCE OF TIME (LP, picture disc) | 15 |

MINT VALUE £

| 94 | BMG 74321 19059 1 | LIVE - THE ISLAND YEARS (LP) | 20 |

## ANTI ESTABLISHMENT
| 80 | Charnel House CADAV 1 | 1980/Mechanical Man (p/s) | 10 |
| 82 | Glass GLASS 022 | Future Girl/No Trust (p/s) | 5 |
| 83 | Glass GLASS 023 | Anti Men/Misunderstood (p/s) | 5 |

## ANTILLES
| 83 | Creole CR 12-51 | I've Got To Have You/Latin Dream (12") | 30 |

## ANTI NOWHERE LEAGUE
| 81 | WXYZ ABCD 1 | Streets Of London (1-sided test pressing) | 35 |
| 82 | WXYZ ABCD 1 | So What/Streets Of London (p/s, withdrawn) | 8 |
| 82 | WXYZ ABCD 2 | I Hate ... People/Let's Break The Law (p/s) | 6 |
| 87 | GWR A1 | Crime/Working For The Company (Unreleased Test Pressing) | 20 |
| 82 | WXYZ LMNOP1 | WE ARE...THE LEAGUE (LP) | 15 |

## ANTI PASTI
| 80 | Dose DOSE1 | FORE SORE POINTS (EP, 500 only, clear and black vinyl) | 18 |

## ANTI SECT
| 84 | Endangered Music EDR 4 | Out From The Void/Hope Future Poisoned By Fear | 25 |
| 11 | Anti Sect ANTI 010 | 4 Minutes Past Midnight/Out From The Void (Part 2) (10", gig only, limited edition of 300) | 10 |
| 83 | Spiderleg SDL 16 | IN DARKNESS THERE IS NO CHOICE (LP) | 30 |
| 84 | Clown Disc Big Top 1/2 | LIVE IN THE DARKNESS (LP, splattered grey vinyl with insert, 1,000 only) | 20 |
| 94 | Discipline DISCLP 03 | PEACE IS BETTER THAN A PLACE IN HISTORY (LP) | 20 |

## ANTI-SOCIAL WORKERS & MAD PROFESSOR
| 83 | Ariwa ARI008LP | POSITIVE STYLE PUNKY REGGAE PARTY (LP) | 20 |

## ANTI SOCIAL (1)
| 77 | Dynamite DRO 1 | Traffic Lights/Teacher Teacher (no p/s) | 500 |
| 82 | Beat The System BTS 2 | Battle Scarred Skinheads/Sewer Rat/Official Hooligan (p/s) | 18 |
| 82 | Beat The System FIT 2 | Too Many People/Let's Have Some (p/s) | 10 |

## ANTI SOCIAL (2)
| 82 | Lightbeat SOCIAL 1 | MADE IN ENGLAND (EP) | 20 |

## ANTI STATE CONTROL
| 83 | Asc Records ASC1 | Glue Sniffing Blues/M.U.S.E/Third World Bomb | 200 |

## ANTI SYSTEM
| 83 | Reconcilliation RECONCILE 3 | Strangelove/So Long As/MORBID HUMOUR: Oh My God (Parts 1 and 2) | 30 |
| 83 | Paragon/Pax PAX 11 | DEFENCE OF THE REALM (EP) | 25 |
| 86 | Reconcilliation RECONCILE 4 | A LOOK AT LIFE (12" EP) | 20 |
| 85 | Reconcilliation RECONCILE 1 | NO LAUGHING MATTER (LP) | 30 |

## ANTOINE
| 66 | Vogue VRL 3024 | ANTOINE (LP) | 20 |
| 67 | Vogue VRL 3032 | ANTOINE (LP) | 15 |

## ANTOINETTE
| 64 | Decca F 11820 | Jenny Let Him Go/Please Don't Hurt Me Anymore | 10 |
| 64 | Piccadilly 7N 35201 | There He Goes (The Boy I Love)/Little Things Mean A Lot | 5 |
| 66 | Piccadilly 7N 35293 | Why Don't I Run Away From You/There's No-One In The Whole Wide World | 20 |
| 66 | Piccadilly 7N 35310 | Lullaby Of Love/I'm For You | 5 |

*(see also Toni Daly)*

## ANTON
| 75 | Spark 1120 | Shot Down In Action/Mine All Mine | 8 |

## REY ANTON
| 62 | Oriole CB 1722 | As If I Care/After The Laughter | 5 |
| 62 | Oriole CB 1771 | Hey Good Looking/Mary Lou | 10 |
| 63 | Oriole CB 1811 | Peppermint Man/Can't Say More Than That (with Batons) | 10 |
| 63 | Oriole CB 1843 | How Long Can This Last/If You Don't Want Me Now | 10 |
| 64 | Parlophone R 5132 | You Can't Judge A Book By The Cover/It's Cold Outside (with Peppermint Men) | 10 |
| 64 | Parlophone R 5172 | Heard It All Before/I Want You (with Peppermint Men) | 15 |
| 65 | Parlophone R 5245 | Wishbone/Kingsway (with Peppermint Men) | 10 |
| 65 | Parlophone R 5274 | Girl You Don't Know Me/Don't Treat Me Bad (with Peppermint Men) | 20 |
| 65 | Parlophone R 5310 | Nothing Comes Easy/Breakout (with Peppermint Men) | 10 |
| 65 | Parlophone R 5358 | Premeditation/Now That It's Over (with Pro Form) | 30 |
| 66 | Parlophone R 5410 | Don't You Worry Boy/Hold It Babe (with Pro Formula) | 10 |
| 66 | Parlophone R 5487 | Things Get Better/Newsboy (with Pro Form) | 10 |

## TONY ANTONIU
| 84 | Spartan 12 SP 12 | Send In The Night/(Extended Version) (12") | 30 |

## ANTONY
| 67 | Westleigh WSC 1 | No Ones Caring/Be Aware Of The Dark | 30 |

## DAVE ANTONY
| 68 | Mercury MF 1031 | Race With The Wind/Playin' Hide And Seek | 20 |

*(see also Dave Anthony['s Moods])*

## MARK ANTONY & AVENGERS
| 60s | Malconi MCD LP 17 | MARK ANTONY & THE AVENGERS (LP, private pressing, plain sleeve) | 100 |

## MIKI ANTONY
| 70 | RCA 1906 | Cinnamon/Easy Rider | 7 |
| 71 | Columbia DB 8759 | Sally Sunshine/It's Good To See You | 8 |
| 71 | Bell BLL 1179 | Simon's Doorstep/Eldorado Gold | 7 |
| 72 | Bell BELL 1243 | Funny Sorta Day/Home To Kinoki | 6 |
| 74 | Bradley's BRAD 7414 | We Made It Last Summertime/Hey Suzanne | 6 |
| 75 | Bradley's BRAD 7503 | Get Your Dancin Shoes On/Schoolgirl | 5 |

| | | | |
|---|---|---|---|
| 75 | Bradley's BRAD 7514 | True Love Ways/I Think I'll Write A Love Song | 5 |
| 76 | Bradley's BRAD 7613 | You Give Me Good Love/Hey Suzanne | 5 |
| 77 | EMI EMI 2683 | Can't Get You (Out Of My Mind)/Hey Friend (p/s) | 6 |
| 78 | EMI EMI 2826 | If You Never Had The Chance To Fall In Love/Camouflage | 6 |
| 78 | EMI EMC 3259 | CITY OF THE ANGELS (LP) | 15 |

*(see also Miki)*

## ANTS
| | | | |
|---|---|---|---|
| 63 | Parlophone R 5082 | Christmas Star/Wandering | 5 |

## ANNIE ANXIETY
| | | | |
|---|---|---|---|
| 81 | Crass Records 32984/3 | BARBED WIRE HALO: Cyanide Tears/Hello Horror (gatefold sleeve) | 10 |

*(see also Crass)*

## ANY TROUBLE
| | | | |
|---|---|---|---|
| 79 | Pennine PSS 7165 | Yesterdays Love/Nice Girls, (1000 only, 100 with 'sewn' p/s) | 20 |
| 79 | Pennine PSS 7165 | Yesterdays Love/Nice Girls, (1000 only, p/s) | 15 |

## ANYWAYS/SHAKE APPEAL
| | | | |
|---|---|---|---|
| 88 | Jericho JR 001 | Wall of Hurt/Amphetamine (no sleeve) | 15 |

## AOA
| | | | |
|---|---|---|---|
| 85 | COR COR 4 | WHO ARE THEY TRYING TO CON (EP, 12", comes with 7" sleeve with lyrics) | 20 |
| 86 | COR GURT 12 | UNLIMITED GENOCIDE (Split LP with OI POLLOI, insert) | 20 |
| 88 | ENDANGERED EDR LP 2 | SATISFACTORY ARRANGEMENT (LP) | 30 |

## AOS3
| | | | |
|---|---|---|---|
| 94 | Words Of Warning WOWLP28 | GODS SECRET AGENT (LP) | 20 |
| 95 | Inna State ANOKLP001 | DIVERSIONARY TACTICS (LP) | 15 |

## APARTMENT
| | | | |
|---|---|---|---|
| 80 | Heartbeat PULSE 7 | The Car/Winter (p/s) | 20 |

## APATCHI BAND
| | | | |
|---|---|---|---|
| 73 | President PT 392 | Issmak/Crashpad | 30 |

## APES
| | | | |
|---|---|---|---|
| 72 | Leicester Recording Co LRS LS 1 | APES (LP) | 50 |

## APEX RHYTHM & BLUES ALLSTARS
| | | | |
|---|---|---|---|
| 59 | John Lever AP 100 | Yorkshire Relish/Caravan | 40 |
| 60s | John Lever JLEP 1 | APEX RHYTHM & BLUES ALLSTARS (EP, no p/s) | 350 |

*(see also Ian Hunter)*

## APHEX TWIN
| | | | |
|---|---|---|---|
| 91 | Mighty Force 01 | ANALOGUE BUBBLEBATH VOL. 1 (12" EP, label on 1 side only, other side has white label, some stamped) | 25 |
| 91 | Rabbit City CUT 002 | ANALOGUE BUBBLEBATH VOL. 2 (12" EP, stamped white label) | 30 |
| 92 | R&S RSUK 12 | Didgeridoo/Analogue Bubblebath 1/Flaphead/Isoprophlex (12", stickered R&S sleeve, 'Isoprophlex' is actually 'Phloam') | 20 |
| 93 | Rephlex CAT 008 | ANALOGUE BUBBLEBATH VOL. 3 (12" EP, paper bag sleeve) | 18 |
| 93 | Warp WAP 39 | ON EP (2x12" in special sleeve) | 25 |
| 93 | Warp WAP 39R | On (D-Scape Mix)/On (Reload Mix)/On (µ-Ziq Mix)/On (28 Mix) (12", p/s) | 15 |
| 93 | Warp WAP 60 | VENTOLIN EP (12", p/s) | 15 |
| 93 | Warp WAP 60R | VENTOLIN EP (THE REMIXES) (12", p/s) | 15 |
| 93 | Warp WAP 60/WAP 60R | VENTOLIN EP (2 x 12", includes both above 12"s, stickered gatefold p/s) | 25 |
| 94 | Rephlex CAT 019 EP | ANALOGUE BUBBLEBATH VOL. 4 (12" EP, p/s with insert, as AFX) | 15 |
| 95 | Rephlex CAT 034 | ANALOGUE BUBBLEBATH VOL. 5 (as AFX, 12" white label only) | 400 |
| 95 | Warp WAP 63 | Donkey Rhubarb/Vaz Deferenz/Icct Hedral (Philip Glass Orchestration)/ Pancake Lizard (12", p/s) | 12 |
| 95 | Warp WAP 67 | HANGABLE AUTO BULB EP (12",as AFX) | 40 |
| 95 | Warp WAP 69 | HANGABLE AUTO BULB 2 EP (12", as AFX) | 40 |
| 96 | Warp WAP 78 | Boy/Girl | 20 |
| 97 | Warp WAP 94P/WAP 94RP | Come To Daddy(Pappy Mix)/Flim/Come To Daddy (Little Lord Faulteroy Mix)/ Bucephalus Bouncing Ball/To Cure A Weakling Child (Contour Regard)/Funny Little Man/Come To Daddy (Mummy Mix)/IZ-US (2 x promo 12", 500 only) | 40 |
| 99 | Warp WAP105 | Windowlicker/(Impossible to title)/Nanno (12", inner) | 12 |
| 01 | Warp DRUKQS 01 54 | Cymru Beats (Argonaut Mix)/Cock 10 (Delco Freedom Mix) (12", stickered black sleeve) | 12 |
| 05 | Rephlex ANALORD 10 | Fenix Funk 5/XMD 5a (12" in PVC binder with 12 sleeves for the Analord series) | 200 |
| 05 | Warp WAP 195 | 46 Analord-Masplid/Naks 11 (Mono) (as AFX)/LFO: Flue Shot (Kringlan)/Pathfinder (12") | 20 |
| 05 | Rephlex ANALORD 01 | ANALORD 01 (12" EP, stickered plastic sleeve as AFX) | 20 |
| 05 | Rephlex ANALORD 02 | ANALORD 02 (12" EP as AFX) | 20 |
| 05 | Rephlex ANALORD 03 | ANALORD 03 (12" EP as AFX) | 20 |
| 05 | Rephlex ANALORD 04 | ANALORD 04 (12" EP as AFX) | 20 |
| 05 | Rephlex ANALORD 05 | ANALORD 05 (12" as AFX) | 18 |
| 05 | Rephlex ANALORD 06 | ANALORD 06 (12" EP as AFX) | 15 |
| 05 | Rephlex ANALORD 07 | ANALORD 07 (12" EP as AFX) | 15 |
| 06 | Rephlex ANALORD 08 | ANALORD 08 (12" EP as AFX) | 15 |
| 05 | Rephlex ANALORD 09 | ANALORD 09 (12" EP as AFX) | 15 |
| 05 | Rephlex ANALORD 10 | ANALORD 10 (12" EP as AFX) | 20 |
| 05 | Rephlex ANALORD10PIC | ANALORD 10 (12" EP as AFX, picture disc) | 25 |
| 05 | Rephlex ANALORD 11 | ANALORD 11 (12" EP as AFX) | 20 |
| 92 | R&S/Apollo AMBLP 3922 | SELECTED AMBIENT WORKS 85-92 (2-LP, 1st issue with no barcode) | 40 |
| 94 | Warp WARPLP 21 | SELECTED AMBIENT WORKS VOL. 2 (3-LP, brown vinyl, black and white sleeve with numbered sticker) | 60 |
| 94 | Warp WARPLP 21 | SELECTED AMBIENT WORKS VOL. 2 (3-LP, black vinyl, stickered colour sleeve) | 45 |
| 95 | Warp WARPLP 30 | I CARE BECAUSE YOU DO (2-LP, stickered sleeve) | 40 |
| 96 | Warp WARPLP 43 | RICHARD D. JAMES (LP) | 25 |

Rare Record Price Guide 2018

| | | | MINT VALUE £ |
|---|---|---|---|
| 02 | Warp WARPLP 92 | DRUKQS (4-LP) | 50 |
| 02 | Warp WARPLP 92 | DRUKQS (4-LP, 1st pressing with mispressed side B containing 2 tracks by unknown artist) | 80 |
| 02 | Warp WARPLP 92X | DRUKQS (4-LP in 12" x 17" numbered box, 1,000 only) | 80 |
| 14 | Warp WARPLP 247X | SYRO (3-LP special 'ballot' edition of 200 copies in box with additional track on playable print) | 300 |

*(see also Caustic Window, Polygon Window, Q-Chastic, Kosmic Kommando, Tuss)*

## APHRODITE'S CHILD

| | | | |
|---|---|---|---|
| 68 | Mercury MF 1039 | Rain & Tears/Don't Try To Catch A River | 15 |
| 69 | Mercury MF 1079 | End Of The World/You Always Stand In My Way | 15 |
| 69 | Polydor 56769 | I Want To Live/Magic Mirror | 20 |
| 69 | Polydor 56785 | Let Me Love, Let Me Live/Marie Jolie | 5 |
| 70 | Polydor 56791 | It's Five O'Clock/Funky Mary | 5 |
| 72 | Vertigo 6032 900 | Break/Babylon | 15 |
| 68 | Mercury SMCL 20140 | END OF THE WORLD/RAIN AND TEARS (LP, black/silver label, laminated sleeve) | 35 |
| 69 | Polydor 2384 005 | IT'S FIVE O'CLOCK (LP, gatefold sleeve) | 40 |
| 72 | Vertigo 6673 001 | 666 - THE APOCALYPSE OF JOHN (2-LP, swirl labels, gatefold, red laminated sleeve. NB. Sleeve has catalogue number 6673 001 whilst albums have 6333500/6333501 on labels) | 1000 |
| 75 | Philips 6483025 | RAIN & TEARS (LP) | 15 |
| 77 | Vertigo 6641 581 | 666 (2-LP, reissue, as Aphrodite's Child with Demis Roussos & Vangelis, different sleeve, 'spaceship' labels) | 60 |

*(see also Vangelis, Forminx)*

## APOCALYPSE

| | | | |
|---|---|---|---|
| 82 | Gate GATE 2 | Storm Child/Chosen Few (p/s) | 125 |

## APOLLO XI

| | | | |
|---|---|---|---|
| 91 | Wau! Mr. Modo APOLLO 11 | Peace (In The Middle East) (7" Mix 2)/Peace (Sea Of Tranquility Mix)/Peace (Is This Really The Orb? Mix) (12") | 10 |

*(see also Orb)*

## APOLLOS

| | | | |
|---|---|---|---|
| 60 | Mercury AMT 1096 | Rockin' Horses/Just Dreaming | 10 |

## A POPULAR HISTORY OF SIGNS

| | | | |
|---|---|---|---|
| 80 | Melodia M1 | Justice Not Vengeance/Possession (p/s) | 12 |
| 81 | Melodia M2 | Crowds/Crossing The Border (p/s, insert) | 10 |
| 82 | Melodia M4 | Dancing with Ideas/The Traveller (p/s) | 15 |

## APOSTLES

| | | | |
|---|---|---|---|
| 82 | No Label | BLOW IT UP BURN IT DOWN KICK IT TILL IT BREAKS EP (fold out p/s) | 15 |
| 83 | Scum SCUM 3 | THE CURSE OF THE CREATURE EP | 10 |
| 84 | Scum SCUM 2 | RISING FROM THE ASHES EP | 10 |
| 84 | Scum SCUM 4 | THE GIVING OF LOVE COSTS NOTHING EP | 10 |
| 86 | Fight Back FIGHT 9 | DEATH TO WACKY POP (Split EP with THE JOY OF LIVING) | 8 |
| 85 | Mortarhate MORT 9 | SMASH THE SPECTACLE! EP | 10 |
| 89 | Active Sounds ASP 10 | NO FAITH NO FEAR? (EP, 3 A side tracks by STATEMENT, 2 b side tracks by APOSTLES) | 10 |
| 83 | Cause For Concern CFC 2 | LIVE AT THE LMC (LP, one side by THE MOB) | 25 |
| 86 | Acid Strings 001 | HOW MUCH LONGER? (LP, with inserts) | 20 |
| 86 | Children Of The Revolution GURT 11 | THE LIVES AND TIMES OF THE APOSTLES (LP, inserts) | 20 |
| 87 | Active Sounds AB 001 | EQUINOX SCREAMS (LP) | 18 |
| 86 | Mortarhate MORT 23 | PUNK OBITUARY (LP, gatefold, insert, lyric sheet) | 15 |
| 88 | Acid Strings ASR 002 | THE ACTS OF THE APOSTLES IN THE THEATRE OF FEAR (LP) | 25 |
| 88 | Active Sounds ASP 20 | SPLIT (LP, with booklet/inserts, one side by STATEMENT) | 30 |

## APOSTOLIC INTERVENTION

| | | | |
|---|---|---|---|
| 67 | Immediate IM 043 | (Tell Me) Have You Ever Seen Me/Madame Garcia | 250 |

*(see also Small Faces, Humble Pie)*

## APPALACHIANS

| | | | |
|---|---|---|---|
| 63 | HMV POP 1158 | Bony Moronie/It Takes A Man | 5 |

## APPALOOSA

| | | | |
|---|---|---|---|
| 94 | Recoil RCL 003 | UNPLUGGED EP (12", 3-track, die-cut sleeve) | 15 |

*(see also Global Communications)*

## APPLE

| | | | |
|---|---|---|---|
| 68 | Page One POF 101 | Let's Take A Trip Down The Rhine/Buffalo Billy Can | 100 |
| 68 | Page One POF 110 | Doctor Rock/The Other Side | 90 |
| 69 | Page One POLS 016 | AN APPLE A DAY (LP, textured sleeve, blue/silver labels with 'apple' insert) | 1500 |
| 69 | Page One POLS 016 | AN APPLE A DAY (LP, without 'apple' insert) | 1000 |

## APPLE PIE AND CUSTARD

| | | | |
|---|---|---|---|
| 74 | Philips 6006439 | Five Sisters/Doctor Fantastic | 8 |

## APPLE BOUTIQUE

| | | | |
|---|---|---|---|
| 87 | Creation CRE052T | Love Resistance/ Don't Even Believe In You/The Ballad Of Jet Harris (12") | 20 |

## GEOFF APPLEBY

| | | | |
|---|---|---|---|
| 76 | Virgin VS157 | Hey Sadie/Move On Down The Road | 6 |

## APPLEJACKS (U.K.)

| | | | |
|---|---|---|---|
| 64 | Decca F 11833 | Tell Me When/Baby Jane | 5 |
| 64 | Decca F 11916 | Like Dreamers Do/Everybody Fall Down | 5 |
| 64 | Decca F 11981 | Three Little Words/You're The One For Me | 5 |
| 65 | Decca F 12050 | Chim Chim Chiree/It's Not A Game Anymore (export, unissued) | 25 |
| 65 | Decca F 12106 | It's Not A Game Anymore/Bye Bye Girl | 10 |
| 65 | Decca F 12216 | I Go To Sleep/Make Up Or Break Up | 20 |
| 65 | Decca F 12301 | I'm Through/We Gotta Get Together | 5 |
| 67 | CBS 202615 | You've Been Cheating/Love Was In My Eyes | 40 |

| 64 | Decca LK 4635 | THE APPLEJACKS (LP) | 100 |

## APPLEJACKS (U.S.)
| 58 | London HLU 8753 | Mexican Hat Rock/Stop, Stop Red Light | 5 |

*(see also Dave Appell)*

## APPLETREE THEATRE
| 68 | Verve (S)VLP 6018 | PLAYBACK (LP) | 70 |

## CHARLIE APPLEWHITE
| 54 | Brunswick 05358 | No One But You/Parade | 5 |
| 55 | Brunswick 05411 | Prize Of Gold/Mister Publisher (Have I Got A Song For You) | 5 |
| 55 | Brunswick 05416 | Blue Star - The Medic Theme/A Prayer Was Born | 5 |

## APPOLINAIRES
| 82 | Two Tone 20 TT | The Feelings Gone/Feelings Back (paper labels, p/s) | 12 |
| 82 | Two Tone CHS TT 12 20 | The Feelings Gone (Dance Mix)/The Feelings Back/The Bongo Medley (Extremely Long Version) (12", p/s) | 15 |
| 82 | Two Tone CHS TT 22 | Envy The Love/Give It Up (p/s) | 12 |
| 82 | Two Tone CHS TT 12 22 | Envy The Love/Give It Up (12", p/s) | 25 |

## APPRECIATIONS
| 77 | Destiny 1016 | I Can't Hide It/Instrumental Version (2 acetates only) | 175 |
| 80s | Soul City 157 | I Can't Hide It/No No No (reissue) | 15 |

## APPROACHING FOOTSTEPS
| 82 | Sanctuary HEH 001 | Autumn/Fire And Ashes | 25 |

## APRIL LOVE
| 79 | Ariola ARO 177 | Switchboard/Jerry Hall (p/s) | 5 |

## APRIL SHOWERS (1)
| 73 | Ritual RT2 | Nowhere To Hide/Suzy Q | 15 |

## APRIL SHOWERS (2)
| 84 | Chrysalis CHS 2787 | Abandon Ship/Everytime We Say Goodbye | 50 |
| 84 | Chrysalis CHS 122787 | Abandon Ship/Everytime We Say Goodbye (12", p/s) | 90 |

## APRIL WINE
| 72 | Pye 7N 45145 | You Could Have Been A Lady/Teacher | 25 |
| 72 | Pye 7N 45163 | Bad Side Of The Moon/Believe In Me | 10 |
| 73 | Pye 7N 45624 | Weeping Widow/Just Like That | 6 |
| 76 | London HLU 10549 | You Won't Dance With Me/Shot Down | 6 |
| 81 | Capitol CL 16184 | Just Between You And Me/Big City Girls (p/s) | 5 |

## AQUA LEVI & THE ROOTS IMENSION
| 91 | Roots RI 001 | His Foundation/His Dub (12") | 60 |
| 92 | Roots RI 003 | Gather My Children/Gather My Dub (12") | 40 |
| 92 | Roots RI 7002 | Babylon Must Set Me Free/Freedom Dub | 35 |

## AQUARIAN AGE
| 68 | Parlophone R 5700 | 10,000 Words In A Cardboard Box/Good Wizard Meets Naughty Wizard | 500 |

*(see also Twink, Tomorrow, Clem Cattini Ork, Nicky Hopkins)*

## AQUARIAN DREAM
| 76 | Buddah BDS 455 | Phoenix/Once Again | 6 |
| 79 | Elektra LV 7 | You're A Star/Play It For Me (One More Time) | 8 |
| 79 | Buddah BDS 488 | Phoenix/East 6th Street | 5 |
| 79 | Buddah BDSL 488 | Phoenix/East 6th Street (12") | 20 |
| 76 | Buddah DISC 008 | NORMAN CONNORS PRESENTS AQUARIAN DREAM (LP) | 50 |
| 78 | Elektra K 52109 | FANTASY (LP) | 15 |

*(see also Norman Connors)*

## AQUARIANS
| 71 | Ackee ACK 135 | Circy Cap/Circy Version | 12 |
| 71 | Ackee ACK 137 | Rebel/Invasion Version | 35 |

*(see also Augustus Pablo, Herman)*

## AQUATONES
| 58 | London HLO 8631 | You/She's The One For Me | 25 |

## AQUILA (1)
| 70 | RCA SF 8126 | THE AQUILA SUITE (LP, gatefold sleeve, orange labels) | 150 |

*(see also Patrick Campbell-Lyons)*

## AQUILA (2)
| 83 | Graphic S82 CUS 1486 1982 | Fall/Threatened (p/s) | 20 |

*(see also 101ers)*

## ARABESQUE
| 72 | Polydor 2058-237 | Fairytale/Solace And Jamboree | 8 |

## ARABIS
| 69 | Doctor Bird DB 1204 | Jump High Jump Low/TONY SHABAZZ: Stool Pigeon | 18 |

## ARABS
| 78 | Hit Run APLP 9002 | CRY TUFF - DUB ENCOUNTER CHAPTER 1 | 55 |

*(see also Prince Far I)*

## ARAB STRAP
| 96 | Chemikal U'nd CHEM 007 | The First Big Weekend/Gilded (700 only) | 20 |
| 97 | Chemikal U'nd CHEM 017 | Hey! Fever/Girls Of Summer (p/s) | 8 |
| 98 | Too Many Cooks BROTH 001 | Live: Packs Of Three/Blood | 5 |
| 03 | Chemikal U'nd CHEM 0677 | THE SHY RETIRER EP : Radio Edit, Dirty Hospital Remix, Why Can't This Be Love, Good Part, New Saturday (12") | 10 |
| 96 | Chemikal U'nd CHEM 010 | THE WEEK NEVER STARTS AROUND HERE (LP) | 25 |
| 98 | Chemikal U'nd CHEM 021 | PHILOPHOBIA (2-LP) | 25 |
| 99 | Go! Beat 547387 | MAD FOR SADNESS (LP, 1000 only) | 30 |

| | | | |
|---|---|---|---|
| 99 | Go! Beat 5478051 | ELEPHANT SHOE (LP) | 30 |
| 01 | Chemikal Underground CHEM 050 | THE RED THREAD (LP) | 25 |
| 05 | Chemikal Underground CHEM 082 | THE LAST ROMANCE (LP) | 25 |
| 08 | Chemikal Underground CHEM 065 | MONDAY AT THE HUG & PINT (LP) | 15 |
| 10 | Chemikal Underground CHEM 135 | SCENES OF A SEXUAL NATURE (3-CD, CD Rom, 4-LP & cassette, 1000 only, numbered with certificate) | 100 |

## ARAGORN
| | | | |
|---|---|---|---|
| 81 | Neat NEAT 07 | Black Ice/Noonday (p/s) | 15 |

## A RAINCOAT
| | | | |
|---|---|---|---|
| 75 | EMI EMI 2289 | I Love You For Your Mind (Not Your Body)/Vote For Me | 8 |
| 75 | EMI WMI 2331 | Nostalgia 75/ Sneak Preview From 'Macs By Graves' You Can Heavy Breathe On Me/Morocco/Still Waters (Demo Only) | 12 |
| 75 | EMI EMI 2331 | Nostalgia 75/Not Waving But Drowning | 10 |
| 76 | EMI EMI 2393 | It Came In The Night/Morocco | 10 |
| 75 | EMI EMC 3090 | DIGALONGAMACS (LP) | 15 |

## ARANBEE POP SYMPHONY ORCHESTRA
| | | | |
|---|---|---|---|
| 66 | Immediate IMLP/IMSP 003 | TODAY'S POP SYMPHONY (LP, lilac labels) | 125 |

*(see also Andrew Oldham Orchestra, Keith Richard[s])*

## ARBITRATER
| | | | |
|---|---|---|---|
| 93 | Cyclone CYCLONE 2 | DARKENED REALITY (CD) | 100 |

## ARBORS
| | | | |
|---|---|---|---|
| 69 | CBS 4137 | The Letter/Most Of It | 7 |
| 69 | CBS 4640 | Motel Overture/Touch Me | 7 |

## ARBRE
| | | | |
|---|---|---|---|
| 75 | DJM DJS 397 | Fallin'/Doin' Alright | 10 |
| 76 | DJM DJS 10716 | Senorita/Zero To Four (with promo p/s) | 12 |

## A.R.C. ROCKBAND
| | | | |
|---|---|---|---|
| 79 | Rock Records | Homemade Wine/The Chase (p/s) | 80 |

## ARC (1)
| | | | |
|---|---|---|---|
| 71 | Decca SKL-R 5077 | ARC . . . AT THIS (LP, blue/silver "boxed" Decca labels) | 200 |

*(see also Heavy Jelly, Skip Bifferty, Bell & Arc, Blockheads)*

## ARC (2)
| | | | |
|---|---|---|---|
| 80 | Orchrist ORC 1 | Tribute To Mike Hailwood/For My Next Kick (p/s) | 50 |
| 81 | Slipped Disc SD001 | War Of The Ring/Ice Cream Theme (p/s) | 100 |

## ARCADE FIRE
| | | | |
|---|---|---|---|
| 05 | Rough Trade RTRADS225 | Neighbourhood #2/My Buddy (p/s) | 5 |
| 05 | Rough Trade RTRADS232 | Neighbourhood #2/My Buddy (luminous vinyl, p/s) | 5 |
| 05 | Rough Trade RTRADSX 232 | Neighbourhood #3 (live)/Power Out (Live)/This Must Be The Place (Live, featuring David Byrne) (p/s) | 5 |
| 05 | Rough Trade RTRADS 254 | Cold Wind/Brazil (clear vinyl, poly sleeve, stickered, PVC insert) | 5 |
| 07 | Sonovox 1736028 | No Cars Go/Surf City Easter Bloc (p/s) | 5 |
| 10 | Rough Trade | We Used To Wait (1-sided promo, white label 1000 only) | 10 |
| 13 | Sonovox 3752123 | Reflektor/Reflektor Instrumental (12", as The Reflektors, p/s) | 10 |
| 14 | Transgressive TRANS 183 | Afterlife (Flume remix) (12", stamped sleeve, white label) | 12 |
| 15 | Virgin EMI 4750774 | Get Right/Crucified Again | 5 |
| 05 | Rough Trade RTRADLP 219 | FUNERAL (LP) | 20 |
| 06 | Universal 1724447 | NEON BIBLE (2-LP, 4th side etched, stickered sleeve) | 18 |

## ARCADIA
| | | | |
|---|---|---|---|
| 85 | EMI 12 NSRX 1 | Election Day (The Fact And Story Mix) (12", 1-sided, white label, plain black black sleeve, promo only) | 20 |
| 85 | EMI 12 NSR 2 | The Promise (Extended Remix)/Rose Arcana/The Promise 7" version (12" gold cover with sticker and poster insert) | 12 |

*(see also Duran Duran)*

## ARCADIUM
| | | | |
|---|---|---|---|
| 69 | Middle Earth MDS 102 | Sing My Song/Riding Alone | 200 |
| 69 | Middle Earth MDLS 302 | BREATHE AWHILE (LP, laminated sleeve) | 1000 |

*(see also Kingdom Come, 'Middle Earth Sampler' in Various Artists)*

## ARCH CRIMINALS
| | | | |
|---|---|---|---|
| 86 | Fight Back FIGHT 8 | HANG (12" EP, with insert) | 10 |

## ELIZABETH ARCHER & THE EQUATORS
| | | | |
|---|---|---|---|
| 77 | Lightning TRO 9011 | Feel Like Making Love/Version | 30 |

## ARCHIE WHITEWATER
| | | | |
|---|---|---|---|
| 70 | Pye Intl. NSPL 28143 | ARCHIE WHITEWATER (LP) | 100 |

## ARCTIC MONKEYS
| | | | |
|---|---|---|---|
| 05 | Bang Bang (No Cat no) | FIVE MINUTES WITH EP (7" white label with stickered die-cut sleeve) | 60 |
| 05 | Bang Bang BANGB 71 | FIVE MINUTES WITH EP (500 only, p/s) | 80 |
| 05 | Bang Bang BANGBCD | FIVE MINUTES WITH EP (CD, 1000 only) | 70 |
| 05 | Domino RUG 212 | I Bet You Look Good On The Dancefloor/Bigger Boys And Stolen Sweethearts (p/s) | 8 |
| 06 | Domino RUG 216 | When The Sun Goes Down/Settle For A Draw (p/s) | 5 |
| 06 | Domino RUG 236 | Leave Before The Lights Come On/Baby I'm Yours (p/s) | 6 |
| 07 | Domino (No Cat No) | RADIO SESSION (7-track CD-R) | 25 |
| 07 | Domino RUG 258 | Matador/Deframe2r (die-cut p/s, white vinyl, 1000 only) | 8 |
| 07 | Domino RUF 279 | Death Ramps/Nettles (As DEATH RAMPS, 250 only, stamped labels) | 25 |
| 09 | Domino RUG 349 | Cornerstone/Catapult | 8 |
| 09 | Domino RUG 338 | Crying Lightning/Red Right Hand (signed 7", 55 only for Oxfam Charity) | 20 |
| 09 | Domino RUG 349T | Cornerstone/Catapult/Sketchhead/Fright Lined Dining Rooms (10") | 30 |

| 11 | Domino RUG 422 | The Hellcat Spangled Shalala/Little Illusion Machine (Wirrel Riddler) (p/s, with download card, heavyweight vinyl, most destroyed in PIAS distribution fire, 500 later repressed on thinner vinyl) ........ 7 |
|----|----------------|---|
| 11 | Domino RUG 406T | Don't Sit Down Cause I've Moved Your Chair/The Blond-O-Sonic Shimmer Trap/I.D.S.T. (10") ........ 10 |
| 11 | Domino RUG 438 | Suck It And See/Evil Twin ........ 8 |
| 12 | Domino RUG 449 | Black Treacle/RICHARD HAWLEY AND THE DEATH RAMPS: You & I ........ 8 |
| 12 | Domino RUG 468 | R U MINE/Electricity (7" purple vinyl white label with stickered die-cut sleeve, 1750 only) ........ 50 |
| 13 | Domino RUG 542 | Do I Wanna Know/2013 ........ 7 |
| 13 | Domino RUG 547 | Why'd You Only Call Me When You're High?/Stop The World I Wanna Get Off With You 5 |
| 06 | Domino WIG 162 | WHATEVER PEOPLE SAY I AM THATS WHAT I'M NOT (LP) ........ 15 |
| 08 | Domino DOMDVD005X | AT THE APOLLO (LP, box set DVD & stickered sleeve) ........ 40 |
| 07 | Domino WIGLP 188 | FAVOURITE WORST NIGHTMARE (LP) ........ 18 |
| 13 | Domino WIGLP 317 | AM (LP, with free 7") ........ 25 |

## ARCTIC STRINGS
| 75 | Black Magic DEMO 2 | Turn Me On/Non Stop ........ 20 |
|----|----|----|

## ARCTURUS
| 97 | Music For Nations MFN 230 | LA MASQUERADE INFENALE (LP, 1000 only) ........ 60 |
|----|----|----|
| 96 | Ancient Lore Creations ALC 002 PLP | ASPERA HIEMS SYMFONIA (LP, picture disc, 1000 only) ........ 40 |

## ARCWELDER
| 92 | Duophonic DS 45 03 | Favor/Plastic (orange vinyl, p/s, 300 only) ........ 12 |
|----|----|----|
| 92 | Duophonic DS 45 03 | Favor/Plastic (p/s, 1000 only) ........ 8 |

## TONI ARDEN
| 57 | Brunswick 05645 | Little By Little/Without Love (There Is Nothing) ........ 5 |
|----|----|----|
| 57 | Brunswick 05679 | My Empty Heart/Like A Baby ........ 5 |

## NEIL ARDLEY
| 79 | Decca FR 13847 | Leap In The Dark/Summer Ice ........ 5 |
|----|----|----|
| 65 | Decca SKL 4690 | WESTERN UNION (LP) ........ 150 |
| 70 | Columbia SCX 6414 | GREEK VARIATIONS (LP, with Ian Carr & Don Rendell) ........ 250 |
| 72 | Regal Zono. SLRZ 1028 | A SYMPHONY OF AMARANTHS (LP, red/silver labels) ........ 200 |
| 74 | Argo ZDA 164/5 | WILL POWER (2-LP, with Ian Carr, Stan Tracey & Mike Gibbs) ........ 125 |
| 75 | Gull GULP 1018 | KALEIDOSCOPE OF RAINBOWS (LP) ........ 18 |
| 78 | Decca TXS-R 133 | HARMONY OF THE SPHERES (LP, featuring John Martyn) ........ 20 |
| 09 | Gull/Pure Pleasure GULP 1018 | KALEIDOSCOPE OF RAINBOWS (2-LP, reissue) ........ 18 |

*(see also Don Rendell, New Jazz Orchestra, Michael Gibbs)*

## AREA CODE 615
| 70 | Polydor 2066 249 | Stone Fox Chase/Always The Same (first issue on paper labels, later moulded labels are second pressing) ........ 6 |
|----|----|----|

## COLIN AREETY
| 72 | Deram DM 370 | Holy Cow/Can't Do It For You ........ 8 |
|----|----|----|
| 73 | Deram 383 | (If Loving You Is Wrong) I Don't Want To Be Right/One Night Affair ........ 20 |

## ARENA TWINS
| 59 | London HL 7071 | Mama, Care Mama/Little Pig (export issue) ........ 10 |
|----|----|----|

## ARGENT
| 71 | Epic EPC 5423 | Celebration/Kingdom ........ 10 |
|----|----|----|
| 71 | Epic EPC 9135 | Hold Your Head Up/Closer To Heaven/Keep On Rollin' (33rpm EP, p/s) ........ 12 |
| 72 | Epic S EPC 7786 | Hold Your Head Up/Keep On Rollin' ........ 5 |
| 72 | Epic EPC 8115 | Tragedy/Rejoice ........ 7 |
| 73 | Epic EPC 1243 | God Gave Rock And Roll To You/Christmas For The Free ........ 5 |
| 73 | Epic EPC 1628 | It's Only Money Part 2/Candles On The River ........ 5 |
| 74 | Epic EPC 2147 | Thunder And Lightning/Keeper Of The Flame ........ 8 |
| 74 | Epic EPC 2448 | Man For All Reasons/Music From The Spheres ........ 8 |
| 75 | Epic EPC 80691 | Highwire/Circus ........ 5 |
| 74 | Epic SEPC 2849 | Keep On Rollin'/I Am The Dance Of Ages ........ 10 |
| 70 | CBS 63781 | ARGENT (LP, gatefold sleeve) ........ 60 |
| 71 | Epic EPC 64190 | RING OF HANDS (LP, gatefold sleeve) ........ 30 |
| 72 | Epic EPC 64962 | ALL TOGETHER NOW (LP, gatefold sleeve, with booklet) ........ 25 |
| 74 | Epic EQ 32195/Q 65475 | IN DEEP (LP, quadrophonic) ........ 25 |
| 75 | RCA RS 1020 | COUNTERPOINTS (LP) ........ 15 |

*(see also Zombies, Unit 4 + 2, Roulettes, John Verity Band)*

## ARGONAUTS
| 85 | Lyntone LYN 18249/50 | Apeman/Under My Thumb (signed white label, no p/s) ........ 60 |
|----|----|----|

*(see also Madness)*

## ARGOSY
| 69 | DJM DJS 214 | Mr. Boyd/Imagine ........ 120 |
|----|----|----|

*(see also Elton John, Supertramp)*

## ARGUS
| 84 | ABS SRT 4KS258 | Holocaust/The Widow (title sleeve) ........ 100 |
|----|----|----|

*(see also People Like Us)*

## ARIEL
| 74 | Harvest HAR 5085 | Jamaican Farewel/And I'm Blue ........ 7 |
|----|----|----|
| 74 | Harvest HAR 5088 | Yeah Tonite/Laughing Man ........ 10 |
| 75 | Harvest HAR 5093 | I'll Be Gone/Rock And Roll Scars ........ 10 |
| 73 | Harvest SHSP 4028 | A STRANGE FANTASTIC DREAM (LP, textured sleeve) ........ 20 |
| 75 | Harvest SHSP 4039 | ROCK AND ROLL SCARS (LP) ........ 15 |

## ARIEL M
97   Domino WIGLP 37               ARIEL M (LP) ........................................................................................... 18

## ARIEL PINK'S HAUNTED GRAFFITI
10   4AD AD3X24                Round And Round/Mistaken Wedding (p/s) ......................................... 6

## ARIZONA SWAMP COMPANY
70   Parlophone R 5841         Train Keeps Rollin'/Tennessee Woman ............................................... 50

*(see also Nashville Teens)*

## ARKITEX
79   Arkitex AKX 1              Only One/Drivin All Night/Big Brother (no p/s) ................................. 125

## DEE ARLEN
59   Philips PB 950             Stay/Why Should We Wait Any Longer ................................................. 5

## STEVE ARLEN
58   Melodisc M 1458          That's Love/Easy 'N' Free .................................................................... 5
62   HMV POP 1021           They Took John Away/Down In The Valley ........................................... 5

## WANDA ARLETTY
72   Columbia 8954            Counting Each Minute/Motor Car ...................................................... 6

## DEKE ARLON (& OFFBEATS)
64   HMV POP 1340           I Need You/I Must Go And Tell Her ..................................................... 5
64   Columbia DB 7194       I'm Just A Boy/Can't Make Up My Mind ............................................. 5
65   Columbia DB 7487       If I Didn't Have A Dime/Gotta Little Girl ............................................ 5
65   Columbia DB 7753       Little Piece Of Paper/I've Been Away (solo) ....................................... 5
66   Columbia DB 7841       Hard Times For Young Lovers/Little Boy (solo) ................................... 5

## ARMADA ORCHESTRA/ULTRAFUNK
75   Contempo 2089          The Love I Lost (Part 1)/The Love I Lost (Part 2) ............................... 7

## ARMAGEDDON
75   A&M AMLH 64513       ARMAGEDDON (LP, with lyric inner sleeve, silver labels) .................. 60

*(see also Keith Relf, Steammhammer, Captain Beyond)*

## JOAN ARMATRADING
85   A&M AMLH 64588       JOAN ARMATRADING (LP, 'Nimbus' supercuts repressing) .............. 25

## ARMED FORCE
80   Armed Forces AF1       Popstar/Attack (p/s, 500 only) .......................................................... 20

## ARMENIAN JAZZ QUARTET
57   London HLR 8454        Pretty Girl/Harem Dance .................................................................... 5

## ARMENTA
83   Savoir Faire FAIT 005     I Wanna Be With You/Part 2/Part 3 (12") ......................................... 15

## ARMS & LEGS
76   MAM MAM 140          Janice/She'll Surprise You ................................................................... 6
76   MAM MAM 147          Heat Of The Night/Good Times ........................................................... 6
77   MAM MAM 156          Is There Any More Wine/She'll Surprise You ...................................... 6

## RUSSELL ARMS
57   London HLB 8406        Cinco Robles (Five Oaks)/The World Is Made Of Lisa (gold label) ..... 20

## CHUCK ARMSTRONG
73   Action ACT 4620        God Bless The Children/Black Foxy Woman ....................................... 15

## FRANKIE ARMSTRONG (& FRIENDS)
79   Action Against Corrie RRFA   We Must Choose/RED RINSE: A Woman's Right To Choose (private pressing) .............. 30
     001
83   Plant Life TPLS 03        Message From Mother Earth/Shall There Be Womanly Times Or Shall We Die? ........... 10
72   Topic 12TS 216          LOVELY ON THE WATER (LP) ............................................................. 30
75   Topic 12TS 273          SONGS AND BALLADS (LP) ................................................................ 18

*(see also A.L. Lloyd)*

## JACK ARMSTRONG
74   Saydisc SDL 252         CELEBRATED MINSTREL (LP) .............................................................. 15

## LORNA ARMSTRONG
74   Ackee 535               Dance With Me/Lonely Nights ........................................................... 15

## HERBIE ARMSTRONG
80   Avatar 108              Real Real Gone/Blackout ................................................................... 10

## B.J. ARNAU
71   Mojo 2092 028          I Want To Go Back There Again/I Love You .......................................... 5
72   Polydor 2058238        The Big Hurt/Hey Brenda! ................................................................... 8
72   RCA 2284               Every Girl Becomes A Woman/Jubilation ........................................... 8

*(see also Brenda Arnau)*

## BRENDA ARNAU
68   United Artists UP 2244    Gonna Spread Love/Christian .............................................................. 5
68   United Artists UP 2265    Yesterday I Heard The Rain/Where Do You Go/Until You've Been There .......... 5
74   Bell 1351               A Step In The Right Direction/Superman ............................................ 7

## GINNY ARNELL
63   MGM MGM 1217         Dumb Head/How Many Times Can One Heart Break ........................ 20
63   MGM MGM 1243         I Wish I Knew What Dress To Wear/He's My Little Devil ................... 20
65   MGM MGM 1270         Just Like A Boy/Portrait Of A Fool ..................................................... 18
65   MGM MGM 1283         A Little Bit Of Love Can Hurt/B-I-I-I-Why ......................................... 20

## CHICO ARNEZ (& HIS LATIN AMERICAN ORCHESTRA)
59   Pye Nixa NPL 18035      THIS IS CHICO (LP) ............................................................................. 20

## CALVIN ARNOLD
68   MGM MGM 1378         Funky Way/Snatchin' Back ................................................................. 20
68   MGM MGM 1449         Mama In Law/Mini Skirt .................................................................... 20

## EDDY ARNOLD
| 54 | HMV 7MC 22 | Hep Cat Baby/This Is The Thanks I Get (For Loving You) (export issue) | 10 |
| 59 | RCA RCA 1138 | Tennessee Stud/What's The Good (Of All This Love) | 10 |
| 54 | HMV 7EG 8020 | EDDY ARNOLD (EP) | 10 |

## KOKOMO ARNOLD
| 69 | Saydisc Matchbox SDR 163 | KOKOMO ARNOLD (LP) | 30 |

## P.P. ARNOLD
| 66 | Immediate IM 040 | Everything's Gonna Be Alright/Life Is But Nothin' | 200 |
| 66 | Immediate IM 040 | Everything's Gonna Be Alright/Life Is But Nothin' (DJ copy) | 300 |
| 67 | Immediate IM 047 | The First Cut Is The Deepest/Speak To Me | 25 |
| 67 | Immediate IM 055 | The Time Has Come/If You See What I Mean | 20 |
| 68 | Immediate IM 061 | (If You Think You're) Groovy/Though It Hurts Me Badly | 20 |
| 68 | Immediate IM 067 | Angel Of The Morning/Life Is But Nothin' | 5 |
| 69 | Immediate IM 079 | The First Cut Is The Deepest/The Time Has Come | 5 |
| 69 | Polydor 56350 | Bury Me Down The River/Give A Hand, Take A Hand | 7 |
| 70 | Polydor 2058 061 | Likely Piece Of Work/May The Winds Blow | 7 |
| 80 | Virgin/NEMS SV 103 | Angel Of The Morning/Everything's Gonna Be Alright/The First Cut Is The Deepest/Groovy/The Time Has Come (doublepack, gatefold p/s) | 10 |
| 75 | Immediate IM 109 | First Cut Is The Deepest/King Of Kings (re-issue) | 5 |
| 67 | Immediate IMLP/IMSP 011 | THE FIRST LADY OF IMMEDIATE (LP, withdrawn) | 400 |
| 68 | Immediate IMSP 017 | KAFUNTA (LP, gatefold sleeve) | 100 |
| 83 | See For Miles SEE 235 | KAFUNTA - THE BEST OF (LP) | 20 |

*(see also Ikettes, Nice, Small Faces, Spectrum, P.P. & Primes)*

## P.P. ARNOLD & THE JEFF WAYNE SINGERS
| 60s | Pepsi Lyntone 2498 | We've Got Pepsi (1-sided with Pepsi Company sleeve) | 15 |

## ARPADYS
| 77 | Polydor 2933802 | ARPADYS (LP) | 25 |

## ARRIVAL
| 69 | Decca F 12986 | Friends/Don't Turn His Love Away | 6 |
| 70 | Decca F 13026 | I Will Survive/See The Lord | 6 |
| 71 | CBS S 7617 | Family Tree/Part Of My Dream | 10 |
| 70 | Decca SKL 5055 | ARRIVAL (LP, blue/silver with 'boxed' Decca logo) | 20 |

## ARRIVALS
| 69 | Pye 7N 17761 | Scooby Doo/She's About A Mover | 12 |

## ARROGANT
| 80 | Rocket XPRES 43 | Ego/So Near So Far (p/s) | 12 |

## ARROWS (U.S.)
| 65 | Capitol CL 15386 | Apache '65/Blue Guitar | 5 |

## ARROWS (1) (U.K.)
| 69 | Pye 7N 17756 | Mercy/See Saw | 5 |

## ARROWS (2) (U.K.)
| 75 | RAK RAK 205 | I Love Rock 'n' Roll/Broken Down Heart | 6 |

## CLIVE ARROWSMITH
| 74 | Scratchy CHS 2027 | Desire/Almost Gone | 8 |

## ARSENAL 1ST TEAM SQUAD
| 71 | Pye 7N 46067 | Good Old Arsenal/The Boys From Highbury (in p/s) | 7 |

## ARS NOVA
| 68 | Elektra EKSN 45029 | Zoroaster/Pavan For My Lady | 12 |
| 68 | Elektra EKSN 45034 | Fields Of People/Song To The City | 12 |
| 68 | Elektra EKS 74020 | ARS NOVA (LP, orange label, gatefold sleeve) | 40 |
| 69 | Atlantic 588 196 | SUNSHINE AND SHADOWS (LP) | 40 |

## ART
| 67 | Island WIP 6019 | What's That Sound (For What It's Worth)/Rome Take Away Three | 20 |
| 69 | Island WIP 6048 | Room With A View/SPOOKY TOOTH: Nobody There At All (promo only) | 50 |
| 75 | Island WIP 6048 | What's That Sound (For What It's Worth)/Flying Anchors (with promo Art sleeve) | 30 |
| 75 | Island WIP 6224 | What's That Sound (For What It's Worth)/Flying Anchors | 7 |
| 67 | Island ILP 967 | SUPERNATURAL FAIRY TALES (LP, first pressing, pink label with black/orange circle logo, laminated sleeve) | 400 |
| 70 | Island ILP 967 | SUPERNATURAL FAIRY TALES (LP, second pressing, pink label with 'i' logo and factory stamped matrix numbers, those with hand written matrixes are bootlegs, laminated sleeve) | 300 |
| 75 | Island ILP 967 | SUPERNATURAL FAIRY TALES (LP, reissue, matt sleeve, 'palm tree' label) | 35 |

*(see also V.I.P.'s, Baron With His Pounding Piano, Spooky Tooth, Luther Grosvenor, Hapshash & Coloured Coat)*

## ART ZOYD
| 82 | Recommended RR 14.15 | Menáge (12.59) (1-sided, other side printed, foldout sleeve in PVC sleeve, existence unconfirmed) | 10 |
| 82 | Recommended RR 14/15 | PHASE V (2-LP with booklet, inserts and free 1-sided 7" Maege (RR 14.5)) | 20 |

## ART ATTACKS
| 78 | Albatross TIT 1 | I'm A Dalek/Neutron Bomb (p/s) | 20 |
| 79 | Fresh FRESH 3 | First And Last: Punk Rock Stars/Rat City/First And Last (p/s) | 20 |
| 96 | Overground OVER 58 | OUTRAGE AND HORROR (LP, 600 only, pressed in U.K. for export to Japan) | 25 |

*(see also Monochrome Set, Tagmemics, Kray Cherubs)*

## ART BEARS
| 79 | Recommended RR 7904 | Rats & Monkeys/Collapse | 5 |
| 81 | Recommended RE 6622 | CODA to "MAN AND BOY" (EP, live, 1-sided clear vinyl, silk-screened p/s, 1,750 only, this price for 500 signed & numbered for subscribers) | 12 |
| 78 | Recommended REC 2188 | HOPES AND FEARS (LP, gatefold sleeve with poster & booklet) | 20 |
| 79 | Recommended REC 0618 | WINTER SONGS (LP, with booklet) | 20 |

*(see also Henry Cow, Slapp Happy)*

## ARTERY

| | | | |
|---|---|---|---|
| 79 | Limited Edition TAKE 1 | Mother Moon/Pretends/Heinz (p/s) | 10 |
| 81 | Aardvark AARD 5 | Cars In Motion/Life And Death (p/s) | 6 |
| 81 | Armageddon AS 026 | Afterwards/Into The Garden (p/s) | 6 |
| 83 | Red Flame RFB25 | Alabama Song/A Song For Lena (p/s) | 7 |
| 83 | Red Flame RF 18 | ONE AFTERNOON IN A HOT AIR BALOON (LP) | 18 |
| 84 | Golden Dawn GDLP 01 | SECOND COMING (LP) | 15 |
| 85 | Golden Dawn GDLP 02 | NUMBER FOUR (LP) | 15 |

(see also Mission)

## ART FAILURE

| | | | |
|---|---|---|---|
| 79 | Vague VOG 1 | Scream In Pain/In Vogue (p/s) | 6 |

## DAVE & TONI ARTHUR

| | | | |
|---|---|---|---|
| 70 | Trailer LER 1 | Bushes And Briars/Lazio Feher | 8 |
| 67 | Transatlantic TRA 154 | MORNING STANDS ON TIPTOE (LP) | 60 |
| 69 | Topic 12T 190 | THE LARK IN THE MORNING (LP, blue label) | 30 |
| 71 | Trailer LER 2017 | HEARKEN TO THE WITCHES' RUNE (LP, red label) | 20 |

## ARTHUR'S MOTHER

| | | | |
|---|---|---|---|
| 71 | Polydor 2058093 | On The Dole/Butterfly | 8 |

## ANDY ARTHURS

| | | | |
|---|---|---|---|
| 77 | EMI 2618 | Listen To My Brain (Kapounding)/Come To The Party (p/s) | 5 |
| 78 | Radar ADA 7 | I Can Detect You (For 1000 Miles)/I Am A Machine (p/s, withdrawn) | 10 |
| 78 | TDS TDS 3 | I Can Detect You (For 1000 Miles)/I Am A Machine (p/s, reissue) | 5 |
| 79 | TDS TDS 6 | I Feel Flat/Play The Music (p/s) | 7 |

## ARTICLE 58

| | | | |
|---|---|---|---|
| 81 | Rational RATE 4 | Event To Come/Echoes/Lost And Found (p/s) | 8 |

## ART INTERFACE

| | | | |
|---|---|---|---|
| 83 | ART ART 2 | Secretaries From Heaven (Radio Version)/Secretaries From Heaven (Real Version) (p/s) | 10 |

## ARTISTICS

| | | | |
|---|---|---|---|
| 66 | Coral Q 72488 | I'm Gonna Miss You/Hope We Have | 80 |
| 66 | Coral Q 72488 | I'm Gonna Miss You/Hope We Have (DJ Copy) | 150 |
| 67 | Coral Q 72492 | Girl I Need You/I'm Glad I Met You | 60 |
| 67 | Coral Q 72492 | Girl I Need You/I'm Glad I Met You (DJ Copy) | 150 |
| 70 | MCA MU 1117 | I'm Gonna Miss You/Hope We Have (reissue) | 10 |
| 76 | Brunswick BR 39 | I'm Gonna Miss You/GENE CHANDLER: There Was A Time | 8 |
| 66 | Columbia | GET MY HANDS ON SOME LOVIN' (LP, unconfirmed existence) | 250 |

## ART MOVEMENT

| | | | |
|---|---|---|---|
| 67 | Livingston LRL/PR 141 | Bitter Suite/Here Today/Blame Yourself/She Was Really Saying Something | 30 |
| 68 | Decca F 12768 | I Love Being In Love With You/The Game Of Love | 20 |
| 68 | Decca F 12836 | Loving Touch/Happy Song | 10 |
| 69 | Columbia DB 8602 | Yes Sir . . . No Sir/Sally Goes Round The Moon | 15 |
| 70 | Columbia DB 8651 | For As Long As You Need Me/Nice 'n' Easy | 12 |
| 70 | Columbia DB 8697 | The Sooner I Get To You/Morning Girl | 15 |

## ART NOUVEAU

| | | | |
|---|---|---|---|
| 79 | Gimpy Dak DAK 1 | Fear Machine/Animal Instincts (p/s) | 50 |

## ART NOUVEAUX

| | | | |
|---|---|---|---|
| 64 | Fontana TF 483 | Extra Terrestrial Visitations/The Way To Play It | 35 |

## ART OBJECTS

| | | | |
|---|---|---|---|
| 80 | Heartbeat PULSE 10 | Showing Off To Impress The Girls/Our Silver Sister (live) (p/s) | 12 |
| 81 | Fried Egg EGG 007 | Hard Objects/Bibliotheque/Fit Of Pique (p/s) | 10 |
| 81 | Heartbeat HB 5 | BAGPIPE MUSIC (LP) | 18 |

## ART OF NOISE

| | | | |
|---|---|---|---|
| 85 | ZTT 12 ZTPS 1 | CLOSE TO THE EDIT (12", stamped green label, unreleased) | 10 |
| 86 | China WOKP 9 | Paranoimia/Why Me (shaped picture disc) | 15 |
| 91 | China CHINX 23 | Art Of Love/(Ambience Of Love Mix) (12", p/s) | 10 |

## ART SCIENCE TECHNOLOGY

| | | | |
|---|---|---|---|
| 90 | Debut DEBTX 3100 | A.S.T./Esus Flow (2 mixes) (12", p/s) | 12 |

(see also Future Sound Of London)

## ARTWOODS

| | | | |
|---|---|---|---|
| 64 | Decca F 12015 | Sweet Mary/If I Ever Get My Hands On You | 70 |
| 65 | Decca F 12091 | Oh My Love/Big City | 60 |
| 65 | Decca F 12206 | Goodbye Sisters/She Knows What To Do | 60 |
| 66 | Decca F 12384 | I Take What I Want/I'm Looking For A Saxophonist Doubling French Horn Wearing Size 37 Boots | 80 |
| 66 | Decca F 12465 | I Feel Good/Molly Anderson's Cookery Book | 90 |
| 67 | Parlophone R 5590 | What Shall I Do/In The Deep End | 100 |
| 66 | Decca DFE 8654 | JAZZ IN JEANS (EP) | 500 |
| 66 | Decca LK 4830 | ART GALLERY (LP, red/silver label with 'unboxed' Decca logo and 'FFrr" laminated front sleeve) | 700 |
| 70 | Decca Eclipse ECM 2025 | ART GALLERY (LP, reissue in different sleeve, also stereo [ECS 2025]) | 125 |
| 73 | Spark SRLM 2006 | THE ARTWOODS (LP) | 60 |

(see also St. Valentine's Day Massacre, Keef Hartley Band, Jon Lord, Dog Soldier, Lucas & Mike Cotton Sound)

## ARTWORK

| | | | |
|---|---|---|---|
| 02 | Big Apple BAM 001 | RED EP (12") | 15 |
| 02 | Big Apple BAM 001 | RED EP (12", red vinyl) | 20 |

## ARZACHEL

| | | | |
|---|---|---|---|
| 69 | Evolution Z 1003 | ARZACHEL (LP, blue label, laminated front sleeve) | 1000 |

(see also Egg, Steve Hillage, Khan, Hatfield & the North, National Health, Gong)

## ARZENBOYS
| | | | |
|---|---|---|---|
| 75 | DJM DJS 370 | Bump On My Head/Instrumental Version | 6 |

## ASGARD
| | | | |
|---|---|---|---|
| 72 | Threshold TH 10 | Friends/Children Of A New Born Age | 6 |
| 73 | Threshold TH 15 | In The Realm Of Asgard/Town Cryer | 6 |
| 72 | Threshold THS 6 | IN THE REALM OF ASGARD (LP, white/blue label, gatefold sleeve) | 175 |

## VIC ASH QUARTET
| | | | |
|---|---|---|---|
| 56 | Tempo A 135 | Blue Lou/Doxy | 6 |
| 56 | Tempo A 137 | Early Morning/Just One Of Those Things | 6 |
| 56 | Nixa NJE 1032 | VIC ASH & FOUR (EP) | 15 |
| 56 | Columbia SEG 7634 | CLARINET VIRTUOSO (EP) | 15 |
| 56 | Tempo EXA 44 | MODERN JAZZ SCENE (EP) | 50 |

*(see also Maxine Sullivan, Jazz Five)*

## ASH (1)
| | | | |
|---|---|---|---|
| 83 | Criminal CRI MLP 137 | Chase The Spotlight/Evermore (no p/s) | 15 |

## ASH (2)
| | | | |
|---|---|---|---|
| 94 | La La Land LA LA 001 | Jack Names The Planets/Don't Know (wraparound p/s in poly bag, 5,000 only) | 10 |
| 94 | Infectious INFECT 13S | Petrol/The Little Pond/A Message From Oscar Wilde And Patrick The Brewer (p/s, 500 only) | 15 |
| 94 | Infectious INFECT 16S | Uncle Pat/Different Today (p/s, 1,000 only) | 10 |
| 95 | Infectious INFECT 21J | Kung Fu/Day Of The Triffids (p/s, 'Japanese' wraparound no'd p/s in poly bag) | 8 |
| 95 | Fantastic Plastic FP 004 | Get Ready/Zero Zero Zero (red vinyl, 1,000 only, mail order only) | 12 |
| 95 | Infectious INFECT 24S | Girl From Mars/Astral (Conversations With Toulouse Lautrec)/Cantina Band (p/s) | 8 |
| 97 | Barbie Records KEN 1 | I Only Want To Be With You/Kung Fu (Live) (silver speckled vinyl p/s, fan club 7") | 40 |
| 12 | Noyes NR 031 | LITTLE INFINITY EP (12", hand-numbered) | 15 |
| 94 | Infectious INFECT 14LP | TRAILER (LP, with yellow vinyl 7", "Silver Surfer"/"Jazz '59" [INFECT 14S]) | 20 |
| 96 | Infectious INFECT 40LP | 1977 (LP, gatefold) | 30 |
| 98 | Infectious INFECT 60LP | NU-CLEAR SOUNDS (LP, gatefold, clear vinyl) | 20 |
| 01 | Infectious INFECT 100LP | FREE ALL ANGELS (LP, gatefold) | 20 |
| 04 | Infectious 5050467319714 | MELTDOWN (LP, laminated sleeve) | 18 |

## HAROLD ASHBY
| | | | |
|---|---|---|---|
| 61 | Columbia 33SX 1379 | TENOR STUFF (LP, with Paul Gonsalves) | 50 |

## IRVING ASHBY & HIS COMBO
| | | | |
|---|---|---|---|
| 58 | London HLP 8578 | Big Guitar/Motatin' | 10 |

## ASH CAN SCHOOL
| | | | |
|---|---|---|---|
| 86 | Unit Two TWO 01 | She's Only Sleeping/A Day Out Of Paris (p/s) | 30 |

## PEGGY ASHCROFT & MARTIN BEST
| | | | |
|---|---|---|---|
| 72 | Argo ZSW 532 | SENSE AND NONSENSE (LP) | 20 |

## RICHARD ASHCROFT
| | | | |
|---|---|---|---|
| 00 | Hut HUTDLP 63 | ALONE WITH EVERYBODY (2-LP) | 25 |
| 02 | Hut HUTDLP 77 | HUMAN CONDITIONS (2-LP) | 20 |

## DOUG ASHDOWN
| | | | |
|---|---|---|---|
| 66 | CBS 202083 | Guess I'm Doing Fine/I Sure Ain't Standing Still | 8 |

## RAFMRA ASHER
| | | | |
|---|---|---|---|
| 78 | Maccabees FG1 | Fourth Generation/Version | 20 |

## ASHFORD & SIMPSON
| | | | |
|---|---|---|---|
| 74 | Warner Bros. K16373 | Have You Ever Tried It/Time | 7 |
| 77 | Warner Bros. K17679 (T) | Love Don't Make It Right/Bourgie Bourgie (with incorrect mastering) (12") | 20 |
| 77 | Warner Bros. K17679 (T) | Love Don't Make It Right/Bourgie Bourgie (with correct mastering) (12") | 50 |
| 78 | Warner Bros. 12K 17096 | Don't Cost You Nothing/Let Love Use Me (12") | 15 |

## ASHKAN
| | | | |
|---|---|---|---|
| 70 | Decca Nova DN-R 1 | IN FROM THE COLD (LP, mono) | 250 |
| 70 | Decca Nova SDN-R 1 | IN FROM THE COLD (LP, stereo) | 175 |

*(see also Fleetwood Mac)*

## STEVE ASHLEY
| | | | |
|---|---|---|---|
| 74 | Gull GULP 1003 | STROLL ON (LP, with lyric inner) | 20 |

## TYRONE ASHLEY
| | | | |
|---|---|---|---|
| 76 | Tomorrow 004 | Feet Start Moving/Movin On (promo only) | 8 |
| 76 | Tomorrow 010 | Nothing Short Of A Miracle/Instrumental Version (promo only) | 8 |

## MICKEY ASHMAN
| | | | |
|---|---|---|---|
| 60 | Pye Jazz NJL 25 | TAKING THE MICKEY (LP) | 20 |
| 61 | Pye Jazz NJL 29 | THROUGH DARKEST ASHMAN (LP) | 50 |

## ASHRA
| | | | |
|---|---|---|---|
| 77 | Virgin V 2080 | NEW AGE OF EARTH (LP) | 15 |

## ASHTON, GARDNER & DYKE
| | | | |
|---|---|---|---|
| 69 | Polydor 56306 | Maiden Voyage/See The Sun In My Eyes | 80 |
| 70 | Capitol CL 15665 | The Resurrection Shuffle/Hymn To Everyone | 5 |
| 69 | Polydor 583 081 | ASHTON, GARDNER & DYKE (LP) | 25 |
| 70 | Capitol E-ST 563 | THE WORST OF ASHTON, GARDNER AND DYKE (LP) | 18 |
| 72 | Capitol EA-ST 22862 | WHAT A BLOODY LONG DAY IT'S BEEN (LP, gatefold sleeve) | 20 |

*(see also Ashton & Lord, Remo Four, Creation, Birds, Mike Hurst & Method, Badger, Medicine Head)*

## MARK ASHTON
| | | | |
|---|---|---|---|
| 72 | United Artists UP 353390 | Get Up And Groove/Barking Dogs | 15 |

## ASHTON ON RIBBLE HIGH SCHOOL MUSIC SOCIETY
| | | | |
|---|---|---|---|
| 74 | (No label or cat no) | ASHTON SOUND 74 (LP, with inserts) | 100 |

## (TONY) ASHTON & (JON) LORD
| | | | |
|---|---|---|---|
| 72 | Purple PUR 109 | Celebration/Sloeback | 7 |

MINT VALUE £

| 74 | Purple PUR 121 | We're Gonna Make It/Band Of The Salvation Army Band | 7 |
| 74 | Oyster OYR 101 | TONY ASHTON: The Resurrection Shuffle/Ballad Of Mr Giver | 6 |
| 74 | Purple TPS 3507 | FIRST OF THE BIG BANDS (LP) | 25 |

*(see also Ashton Gardner & Dyke, Paice Ashton & Lord, Jon Lord, Deep Purple, Green Bullfrog, Cozy Powell)*

## ASIA
| 82 | Geffen WA 3580 | Don't Cry/True Colours (blue or green logo-shaped picture disc) | 10 |
| 92 | IRS 951.959 | AQUA (LP, gatefold sleeve) | 18 |

*(see also Yes, Emerson Lake & Palmer, Steve Howe)o*

## ASIA FIELDS
| 90 | Frank FRANK 2 | Friction/Jack-knifed (12", test pressing only, plain white die-cut sleeve) | 25 |

## ASIAN DUB FOUNDATION
| 98 | LONDON FFRR 556 066 | RAFI'S REVENGE (2-LP) | 20 |
| 95 | Nation NAT 58 LP | FACTS AND FICTIONS (2-LP) | 18 |
| 00 | FFRR 8573 820421 | COMMUNITY MUSIC (2-LP) | 18 |

## ED ASKEW
| 69 | Fontana STL 5519 | ED ASKEW (LP) | 60 |

## ASLAN
| 76 | Profile GMOR 006 | PAWS FOR THOUGHT (LP) | 70 |
| 77 | Profile GMOR 144 | SECOND HELPINGS (LP) | 70 |

## AS ONE
| 95 | New Electronica Elec 23LP | REFLECTIONS ON REFLECTIONS (2xLP) | 25 |
| 95 | New Electronica Elec 26LP | CELESTIAL SOUL (2xLP) | 20 |

## ASPECTS
| 98 | Hombre MEX007 | 2012 (EP) | 10 |
| 13 | Psycho Boogie BOOGS 002 | LEFT HAND PATH (LP) | 15 |

## MONICA ASPELUND
| 77 | RCA PB 9044 | Lapponia/La-La, Sing A Song | 8 |

## RON ASPERY
| 72 | Blakey BLP5989 | BACK DOOR (LP) | 40 |

## GARY & VERA ASPEY
| 76 | Topic 12TS 299 | A TASTE OF HOT POT (LP) | 25 |

## ASPHALT RIBBONS
| 88 | Tigerlily LILY 002 | DOWNSIDE EP (12", p/s) | 25 |
| 89 | In Tape IT 063 | THE ORCHARD EP (p/s) | 30 |
| 89 | In Tape ITTI 063 | THE ORCHARD EP (12", p/s) | 35 |
| 89 | In Tape ITTI 063 | THE ORCHARD EP (12", p/s + T-Shirt inset) | 50 |
| 89 | In Tape ITTI 063 | THE ORCHARD EP (12", 200 pressed at 48rpm and withdrawn) | 40 |
| 89 | In Tape IT 068 | Good Love/Long Lost Uncle/The Day I Turned Bad (p/s) | 35 |
| 89 | In Tape ITTI 068 | Good Love/Long Lost Uncle/The Day I Turned Bad (12", p/s) | 25 |
| 89 | In Tape IT 6545 1 | Over Again/EVA: Unquenchable (p/s, promo only) | 25 |
| 91 | Tiger Lily LILY 001 | A Time To Go/LIFE WITH PATRICK: Wrong (7" sampler) | 10 |
| 91 | Tiger Lily LILY 002 | PASSION, COOLNESS, INDIFFERENCE, BOREDOM, MOCKERY, CONTEMPT, DISGUST EP (12") | 25 |
| 91 | ETT 101-1 | OLD HORSE (LP) | 25 |

*(see also Tindersticks, Stuart A. Staples)*

## MARY ASQUITH
| 78 | Mother Earth MUM 1204 | CLOSING TIME (LP) | 30 |

## ASSAGAI
| 71 | Vertigo 6059 034 | Telephone Girl/I'll Wait For You | 40 |
| 71 | Vertigo 6360 030 | ASSAGAI (LP, gatefold sleeve, large swirl label) | 250 |
| 72 | Philips 6308 079 | ZIMBABWE (LP, black/silver labels) | 120 |
| 74 | Contour 2870 394 | ASSAGAI (LP, reissue of Philips 6308 079) | 15 |

## ASSEMBLED MULTITUDE
| 70 | Atlantic 2091 022 | Overture For Tommy/Mud | 7 |
| 71 | Atlantic 2091 052 | Medley From Jesus Christ Superstar/Woodstock | 5 |
| 70 | Atlantic 2466 004 | THE ASSEMBLED MULTITUDE (LP) | 20 |

## ASSOCIATES
| 79 | Double Hip DHR 1 | Boys Keep Swinging/Mona Property Girl (no p/s, 500 only) | 80 |
| 79 | MCA MCA 537 | Boys Keep Swinging/Mona Property Girl (no p/s, demos more common, £15) | 25 |
| 80 | Fiction FICS 11 | The Affectionate Punch/You Were Young (p/s) | 5 |
| 81 | Fiction FICSX 13 | A/Would I ... Bounce Back (p/s) | 5 |
| 81 | RSO RSO 78 | Kites/A Girl Named Property (p/s, band on A-side credited as "39 Lyon St.") | 5 |
| 82 | Beggars Banquet BEG 86 | Tell Me Easter's On Friday/Straw Towels (unreleased, white labels only) | 15 |
| 88 | WEA YZ 329T | Country Boy/Heart Of Glass (Dub Mix)/Just Can't Say Goodbye (12" Mix) (12", p/s, unissued, white labels only) | 20 |
| 80 | Fiction FIX 05 | THE AFFECTIONATE PUNCH (LP) | 20 |
| 82 | Beggars Banquet BEGA 43 | FOURTH DRAWER DOWN (LP, gatefold sleeve with poster, label credits SITU 2) | 15 |
| 88 | WEA WX 222C | THE GLAMOUR CHASE (unreleased advance cassette only: with extra track Take Me To The Girl) | 30 |

*(see also Jih)*

## ASSOCIATION
| 66 | London HLT 10054 | Along Comes Mary/Your Own Love | 10 |
| 66 | London HLT 10074 | Cherish/Don't Blame It On Me | 10 |
| 66 | London HLT 10098 | Pandora's Golden Heebie Jeebies/Standing Still | 10 |
| 67 | London HLT 10118 | No Fair At All/Looking Glass | 10 |
| 67 | London HLT 10140 | Windy/Sometime | 10 |
| 67 | London HLT 10157 | Never My Love/Requiem For The Masses | 8 |
| 68 | Warner Bros WB 6113 | Everything That Touches You/Requiem For The Masses | 6 |

| | | | |
|---|---|---|---|
| 68 | Warner Bros WB 7163 | Everything That Touches You/We Love Us | 5 |
| 68 | Warner Bros WB 7195 | Time For Livin'/Birthday Morning | 5 |
| 68 | Warner Bros WB 7229 | Six Man Band/Like Always | 5 |
| 69 | Warner Bros WB 7267 | Goodbye Columbus/The Time It Is Today | 8 |
| 69 | Warner Bros WB 7119 | Windy/Never My Love | 7 |
| 70 | Warner Bros WB 7372 | Just About The Same/Look At Me, Look At You | 6 |
| 72 | CBS S 8062 | Darling Be Home Soon/Indian Wells Woman | 6 |
| 67 | London HA-T 8305 | AND THEN . . . ALONG COMES THE ASSOCIATION (LP) | 40 |
| 67 | London HA-T 8313 | RENAISSANCE (LP) | 35 |
| 67 | London HA-T/SH-T 8342 | INSIGHT OUT (LP) | 35 |
| 68 | Warner Bros W(S) 1733 | BIRTHDAY (LP) | 30 |
| 69 | Warner Bros W(S) 1767 | GREATEST HITS (LP) | 20 |
| 69 | Warner Bros W(S) 1786 | GOODBYE COLUMBUS (LP, soundtrack) | 18 |
| 69 | Warner Bros W(S) 1800 | THE ASSOCIATION (LP) | 20 |
| 72 | CBS S 65009 | WATERBEDS IN TRINIDAD! (LP) | 15 |

**A STATE OF MIND**

| | | | |
|---|---|---|---|
| 85 | Mind Matters NO THOUGHT 4 | What's The Difference?/Animal Human Exploitation (fold out p/s) | 15 |

**ASTERIX**

| | | | |
|---|---|---|---|
| 70 | Decca F 13075 | Everybody/If I Could Fly | 20 |

**EDWIN/TED ASTLEY (ORCHESTRA)**

| | | | |
|---|---|---|---|
| 63 | Oriole CB 1880 | The World Ten Times Over/Soho | 5 |
| 65 | RCA RCA 1492 | Danger Man/The Saint | 40 |
| 66 | Decca F 12389 | The Baron/Drop Head (as Ted Astley) | 10 |

**VIRGINIA ASTLEY**

| | | | |
|---|---|---|---|
| 82 | Why Fi WFI 001 | Love's A Lonely Place To Be/Soaring (p/s with lyric insert) | 5 |
| 82 | Why Fi WHY 08 | A BAO A QU (10" EP) | 10 |
| 87 | Warner Bros. WEA YZ 107 | Some Small Hope/A Summer Long Since Passed (P/s, featuring David Sylvian) | 6 |

*(see also David Sylvian)*

**ASTON HALL**

| | | | |
|---|---|---|---|
| 80 | Tamebeat TAME 001 | The Daily Sun/Popular People (p/s) | 15 |

**ASTON & YEN**

| | | | |
|---|---|---|---|
| 66 | Doctor Bird DB 1064 | Skillamy/BABA BROOKS & BAND: Party Time | 30 |

**ASTORS**

| | | | |
|---|---|---|---|
| 65 | Atlantic AT 4037 | Candy/I Found Out | 80 |
| 65 | Atlantic AT 4037 | Candy/I Found Out (DJ Copy) | 120 |
| 69 | Atlantic 584 245 | Candy/I Found Out (reissue) | 15 |

**ASTRA**

| | | | |
|---|---|---|---|
| 10 | Rise Above RISE 127 FREE | Empty Spaces/DIAGONAL: Stop (300 only, gig freebie) | 12 |

**ASTRA NOVA ORCHESTRA**

| | | | |
|---|---|---|---|
| 74 | Alaska ALA 26 | Ev'ry Little Beat Of Your Heart/Soul Sleeper | 30 |

**ASTRAL NAVIGATIONS**

| | | | |
|---|---|---|---|
| 71 | Holyground HG 114/ NSR 172 | ASTRAL NAVIGATIONS (LP, actually by Lightyears Away & Thundermother, poster cover & booklet, 250 copies only, some numbered) | 500 |
| 89 | Magic Mixture MM 2 | ASTRAL NAVIGATIONS (LP, reissue with booklet, 425 copies only) | 35 |

*(see also David John & Mood)*

**A STREAM**

| | | | |
|---|---|---|---|
| 82 | SRTS 82 CUS 1294 | Hero/Space Invaders | 20 |

**ASTRONAUTS (U.K.)**

| | | | |
|---|---|---|---|
| 79 | Bugle BLAST 1 | THE ASTRONAUTS EP (All Night Party/Back Soon/Everything Stops The Baby/ Survivors) (p/s) | 15 |
| 82 | Stiff BUY DJ 145 | I'm Your Astronaut (Promo only, p/s) | 10 |
| 80 | Bugle BLAST 5 | PRANKSTERS IN REVOLT (EP) | 20 |
| 81 | Bugle GENIUS 001 | PETER PAN HITS THE SUBURBS (LP) | 50 |
| 86 | All The Madmen MAD 5 | IT'S ALL DONE BY MIRRORS (LP) | 15 |
| 87 | All The Madmen MADLP005 | THE SEEDY SIDE OF (LP) | 15 |

*(see also Restricted Hours, Syndicate)*

**ASTRONAUTS (1)**

| | | | |
|---|---|---|---|
| 63 | RCA Victor RCA 1349 | Baja/Kuk | 5 |
| 63 | RCA Victor RD 7662 | ORBIT KAMPUS (LP) | 20 |

**ASWAD**

| | | | |
|---|---|---|---|
| 76 | Island WIP 6312 | Back to Africa/Africa | 12 |
| 76 | Island WIP 6338 | Three Babylon/Ire Woman | 8 |
| 78 | Grove Music GMDM 9 | It's Not Our Wish (That We Should Fight)/Stranger (green vinyl) | 20 |
| 80 | Grove Music 12WIP 6575 | Rainbow Culture/Covenant (dub) (12") | 18 |
| 80 | Island WIP 6646 | Warrior Charge/Dub Charge | 8 |
| 80 | Island 12WIP 6646 | Warrior Charge/Dub Charge (12") | 15 |
| 80 | Island IPR 2037 | Warrior Charge/Dub Charge (12", limited edition) | 18 |
| 81 | Grove Music 12WIP 6693 | Babylon/Behold (12") | 20 |
| 81 | Grove Music IPR 2037 | Warrior Charge/Dub Charge (12") | 35 |
| 82 | CBS XPS 148 | Unsatisfied/Oh Jah (Dub) (10") | 12 |
| 84 | Simba SIM 014 | Hooked On You/Version | 8 |
| 76 | Island ILPS 9399 | ASWAD (LP, inner) | 15 |
| 79 | Grove Music GMLP 6 | HULET (LP) | 15 |
| 82 | Island ILPS 9711 | NEW CHAPTER OF DUB (LP) | 20 |

**ASYLUM CHOIR**

| | | | |
|---|---|---|---|
| 68 | Mercury SMCL 21041 | A LOOK INSIDE THE ASYLUM CHOIR (LP) | 30 |

*(see also Leon Russell)*

## ASYLUM (1)
| | | | |
|---|---|---|---|
| 74 | Wax SR 2073 | It's My Destiny - Lazy Love/Suzy's Back (p/s) | 100 |

## ASYLUM (2)
| 79 | Peeping Tom HRSL 291/EJSP 9280 | COMMERCIAL QUEEN EP (p/s) | 40 |

## ATACAMA
| 71 | Charisma CAS 1039 | ATACAMA (LP, pink/white 'scroll' label) | 35 |
| 72 | Charisma CAS 1060 | THE SUN BURNS UP ABOVE (LP, large 'mad hatter' label) | 30 |

## ATAVISTIC
| 87 | Peaceville WARP 3 | LIFE DURING WARTIME EP (p/s) | 10 |
| 90 | Deaf DEAF 3 | VANISHING POINT (LP) | 15 |

## ATGYFODIAD
| 74 | Sain SAIN 41 | DISGYN MAE'R GLAW (EP) | 12 |

## ATHENIANS
| 64 | ESC ESC 1 | You Tell Me/Little Queenie (custom sleeve) | 50 |
| 64 | Waverley SLP 532 | I've Got Love If You Want It/I'm A Lover Not A Fighter (p/s) | 120 |
| 64 | Waverley SLP 532 | I've Got Love If You Want It/I'm A Lover Not A Fighter | 60 |
| 65 | Waverley SLP 533 | Thinking Of Your Love/Mercy Mercy (in custom sleeve) | 60 |
| 65 | Waverley SLP 533 | Thinking Of Your Love/Mercy Mercy (not in custom sleeve) | 30 |

## GLENN ATHENS & TROJANS
| 65 | Spot 7E 1018 | GLENN ATHENS & TROJANS (EP) | 200 |

## ATHLETE
| 02 | Parlophone 5822 991 | VEHICLES AND ANIMALS (LP, stickered sleeve) | 20 |

## JUAN ATKINS
| 91 | ULR ULRT 3001 | THE FUTURE SOUND EP (12") | 20 |

## PETE ATKIN
| 70 | Philips 6006 050 | Be Careful When They Offer You The Moon/Master Of The Revels | 5 |
| 67 | Private pressing | WHILE THE MUSIC LASTS (LP, 99 copies, with Julie Covington) | 125 |
| 67 | Private pressing | THE PARTY'S MOVING ON (LP, 160 copies, with Julie Covington) | 175 |
| 70 | Fontana 6309 011 | BEWARE THE BEAUTIFUL STRANGER (LP, black/silver labels) | 30 |
| 71 | Philips 6308 070 | DRIVING THROUGH MYTHICAL AMERICA (LP) | 30 |

## BENNY ATKINS
| 60 | Mercury AMT 1113 | Lipstick On Your Lips/I'm Following You | 10 |

## CHET ATKINS
| 60 | RCA Victor RD 27168 | TEENSVILLE (LP) | 20 |

*(see also Country Hams, Hank Snow, Mark Knopfler, Jerry Reid)*

## DAVE ATKINSON
| 76 | (No label or cat no) | THE BEGGAR & THE SAND (LP) | 50 |

## ATLANTIC BRIDGE
| 71 | Dawn DNX 2507 | I Can't Lie To You/Hilary Dickson/Childhood Room (p/s) | 10 |
| 70 | Dawn DNLS 3014 | ATLANTIC BRIDGE (LP, gatefold sleeve, red/black labels) | 70 |

## ATLANTICS (1)
| 64 | Windsor WPS 129 | Don't Say No/Send Him To Me | 20 |

## ATLANTIS
| 72 | Fury FY 302 | I Ain't Got Time/Teddy Boyd's Rock 'N' Roll Show | 100 |
| 73 | Vertigo 6360 609 | ATLANTIS (LP, small swirl label, sleeve printed in Germany) | 40 |

*(see also Rocking Horse)*

## ATLANTIS RISING
| 83 | CMI CMI700 | Tightrope/Reverie: A Vision | 20 |

## ATLAS
| 78 | Emerging WIL 001 | AGAINST ALL THE ODDS (LP, private pressing) | 25 |

## AT LAST THE 1958 ROCK & ROLL SHOW
| 68 | CBS 3349 | I Can't Drive/Working On The Railroad | 25 |

*(see also Ian Hunter, Mott The Hoople, Freddie 'Fingers' Lee, Miller Anderson, Charles Woolfe)*

## ATMOSFEAR
| 79 | Elite DAZZ 1 | Dancing In Outer Space/Outer Space (Version) (12") | 15 |
| 79 | MCA 12 MCA 543 | Dancing In Outer Space/Outer Space (Version) (12", co. sleeve) | 10 |
| 82 | Elite/City Sounds LDAZZ 12 | Xtra Special (Dry Mix)/(Wet Mix) (12") | 15 |
| 81 | MCA MCF 3110 | EN TRANCE (LP) | 15 |
| 84 | Elite ATM 33-1 | FIRST/FOURMOST (mini-LP) | 15 |

*(see also Norma Lewis)*

## ATMOSPHERES
| 59 | London HLW 8977 | Kabalo/The Fickle Chicken | 10 |
| 60 | London HLW 9091 | Telegraph/Caravan | 10 |

## ATOM SPIES
| 87 | Cake 12 SLICE 3 | AND THEIR TRECHEROUS POP ON MICRODOT (12", EP) | 12 |

## ATOMIC ROOSTER
| 70 | B&C CB 121 | Friday The 13th/Banstead (initial copies in p/s) | 15 |
| 70 | B&C CB 121 | Friday The 13th/Banstead | 8 |
| 72 | Dawn DNS 1027 | Stand By Me/Never To Lose | 6 |
| 72 | Dawn DNS 1029 | Save Me/Close Your Eyes | 8 |
| 74 | Decca FR 13503 | Tell Your Story (Sing Your Song)/O.D. (as Vincent Crane's Atomic Rooster) | 8 |
| 80 | EMI EMI 5084 | Do You Know Who's Looking For You/Throw Your Life Away (p/s) | 6 |
| 80 | EMI 12EMI 5084 | Do You Know Who's Looking For You (Ext.)/Throw Your Life Away (12", p/s) | 10 |
| 81 | Polydor POSP 334 | Play It Again/Start To Live (p/s) | 5 |
| 82 | Polydor POSP 408 | End Of The Day/Living Underground (p/s) | 5 |
| 70 | B&C CAS 1010 | ATOMIC ROOSTER (LP, Matrix CAS +1010 + A/CAS + 1010 + B (Flute Mix)) | 200 |

| 70 | B&C CAS 1010 | ATOMIC ROOSTER (LP, Matrix CAS +1010 + A2/CAS + 1010 + B2 (Flute Mix)) | 150 |
|---|---|---|---|
| 70 | B&C CAS 1010 | ATOMIC ROOSTER (LP, Matrix CAS +1010 + A1U/CAS + 1010 + B1U (Guitar mix)) | 70 |
| 70 | B&C CAS 1026 | DEATH WALKS BEHIND YOU (LP, gatefold sleeve) | 70 |
| 71 | Pegasus PEG 1 | IN HEARING OF ATOMIC ROOSTER (LP, gatefold sleeve) | 50 |
| 72 | Dawn DNLS 3038 | MADE IN ENGLAND (LP, limited 'denim' cover, gatefold, with poster, lilac label) | 100 |
| 73 | Dawn DNLS 3038 | MADE IN ENGLAND (LP, re-pressing, standard cover, gatefold insert, lilac label) | 30 |
| 73 | Dawn DNLS 3049 | NICE'N'GREASY (LP, lilac label) | 40 |
| 80 | EMI EMC3341 | ATOMIC ROOSTER (LP) | 15 |
| 83 | Towerbell TOW LP 4 | HEADLINE NEWS (LP) | 15 |

(see also Cactus, Crane/Farlowe, Chris Farlowe, Crazy World Of Arthur Brown, Hard Stuff, Leaf Hound, Andromeda, John Du Cann, Bullet. Bernie Torme, David Gilmore)

## ATOMS
| 79 | Rinka R 23 | Max Bygraves Killed My Mother/Beatles Jacket (colour silk-screened p/s in poly bag with inserts) | 12 |
|---|---|---|---|

## ATOMS FOR PEACE
| 13 | XL XLT 605 | Judge, Jury & Executioner/S.A.D. (12" hand-printed sleeve, 100 only) | 20 |
|---|---|---|---|
| 13 | XL XLT 605 | Before Your Very Eyes/Magic Beanz (12" hand-printed sleeve, 100 only) | 20 |
| 13 | XL XLLP 583X | AMOK (2-LP, hand-printed cover, 50 only) | 100 |
| 13 | XL (No Cat. No.) | AMOK (9 x 1-sided 12" with hand printed sleeves, box set) | 70 |

(see also Radiohead, Red Hot Chilli Pewppers)

## ATORIE
| 89 | Conscious CON001 | It's My Time/Peace Of Mind (12") | 35 |
|---|---|---|---|

## A II Z
| 81 | Polydor POSP 243 | No Fun After Midnight/Treason (no p/s) | 10 |
|---|---|---|---|
| 81 | Polydor POSPX 243 | No Fun After Midnight/Treason/Valhalla's Force (12", p/s, red vinyl) | 15 |
| 81 | Polydor POSP 314 | I'm The One Who Loves You/Ringside Seat (p/s) | 12 |
| 80 | Polydor 2383 587 | THE WITCH OF BERKELEY - LIVE (LP, initially sealed with sew-on patch) | 20 |
| 80 | Polydor 2383 587 | THE WITCH OF BERKELEY - LIVE (LP) | 15 |

(see also AC/DC)

## ATRIX
| 80 | Double D D DEE 8 | Treasure On The Wasteland/Graphite Pile (p/s) | 8 |
|---|---|---|---|

## ATTACK (U.K.)
| 67 | Decca F 12550 | Try It/We Don't Know | 150 |
|---|---|---|---|
| 67 | Decca F 12578 | Any More Than I Do/Hi-Ho Silver Lining | 45 |
| 67 | Decca F 12631 | Created By Clive/Colour Of My Mind | 100 |
| 67 | Decca F 12631 | Created By Clive/Colour Of My Mind (p/s for export to Holland) | 200 |
| 68 | Decca F 12725 | Neville Thumbcatch/Lady Orange Peel | 175 |
| 72 | Decca F 13353 | Hi-Ho Silver Lining/Any More Than I Do (reissue, unissued) | 0 |
| 90 | Reflection MM 08 | MAGIC IN THE AIR (LP) | 25 |

(see also Andromeda, Five Day Week Straw People, Nice)

## ATTACK (U.S.)
| 67 | Philips BF 1585 | Washington Square/Please Phil Spector | 18 |
|---|---|---|---|

## ATTACK WAVE PESTREPELLER
| 98 | Prescription DRUG 4 | NUG YAR (LP, hand-made sleeve, label, with insert 99 copies only) | 18 |
|---|---|---|---|

## ATTAK
| 82 | Oi Oi 7 | Today's Generation/Hell/No Escape (p/s) | 10 |
|---|---|---|---|
| 82 | No Future Oi 17 | Murder In The Subway/Future Dreams (p/s) | 8 |
| 83 | No Future PUNK 6 | THEY WILL EAT YOU WHEN THEY MEAT YOU (LP) | 15 |

## ATTEMPTED MOUSTACHE
| 78 | Skeleton SKL 003 | Superman/No Way Out (folded p/s) | 8 |
|---|---|---|---|

## ATTENDANTS
| 80 | Black & White BW 2 | Happy Families/Deadbeats & Knowones (p/s) | 20 |
|---|---|---|---|

## AT THE DRIVE IN
| 00 | Virgin VUS 189 | Rolodex Propaganda (Album Version)/Extracurricular/One Armed Scissor (Lamacq Version) (p/s) | 6 |
|---|---|---|---|
| 00 | Virgin VUS 193 | Invalid Litter Dept/Initiation (Lamacq Version) (p/s, yellow vinyl) | 8 |
| 13 | Transgressive TRANS 154X | ACROBAT TENEMENT (LP, red vinyl reissue) | 18 |
| 13 | Transgressive TRANS 155X | RELATIONSHIP OF COMMAND (2-LP, 4000 copies, orange vinyl reissue) | 25 |

## AT THE GATES
| 94 | Peaceville CC7 | Gardens Of Grief (yellow vinyl, members only release) | 20 |
|---|---|---|---|
| 94 | Peaceville CC 7 | Souls Of The Evil Departed/All Life Ends (yellow vinyl, p/s) | 30 |
| 92 | Deaf DEAF 10 | THE RED IN THE SKY IS OURS (LP) | 25 |
| 93 | Deaf DEAF 14 | WITH FEAR I KISS THE BURNING DARKNESS (LP) | 25 |
| 94 | Peaceville VILE 47 | TERMINAL SPIRIT DISEASE (LP, inner) | 50 |
| 95 | Earache MOSH 143 | SLAUGHTER OF THE SOUL (LP, inner) | 40 |
| 02 | Earache MOSH 143 | SLAUGHTER OF THE SOUL (LP, reissue, inner) | 25 |
| 02 | Earache MOSH 143 | SLAUGHTER OF THE SOUL (LP, orange vinyl reissue) | 25 |
| 06 | Earache MOSH 143 PD | SLAUGHTER OF THE SOUL (LP, 2nd reissue, picture disc) | 20 |

## AT THE SIGNE OF THE BULL
| 72 | Guildhall/Boston Sound GHS 7 | AT THE SIGNE OF THE BULL (LP) | 25 |
|---|---|---|---|

## ATTITUDES
| 75 | Dark Horse AMS 5504 | Ain't Love Enough/The Whole World's Crazy | 10 |
|---|---|---|---|
| 76 | Dark Horse AMS 5508 | Sweet Summer Music/If We Want To | 10 |

## ATTRACTION
| 66 | Columbia DB 7936 | Stupid Girl/Please Tell Me | 40 |
|---|---|---|---|
| 66 | Columbia DB 8010 | Party Line/She's A Girl | 125 |

MINT VALUE £

## ATTRITION
| | | | |
|---|---|---|---:|
| 85 | Third Mind TMS 04 | Shrinkwrap/Pendulum Turns (12", p/s with insert) | 10 |
| 82 | Private AC 001 | DEATH HOUSE (cassette) | 25 |
| 84 | Third Mind TMLP 06 | THE ATTRITION OF REASON (LP) | 15 |

## ATTRIX
| | | | |
|---|---|---|---:|
| 78 | Attrix RB 01 | Lost Lenore/Hard Times (p/s, stamped white labels) | 15 |
| 81 | Scoff DT 011 | Procession/11th Hour (p/s) | 10 |

## AU GO-GO SINGERS
| | | | |
|---|---|---|---:|
| 65 | Columbia DB 7493 | San Francisco Bay Blues/Pink Polemoniums | 5 |
| 64 | Columbia 33SX 1696 | THEY CALL US AU GO-GO SINGERS (LP) | 25 |

*(see also Buffalo Springfield, Stephen Stills)*

## (THE) AU PAIR
| | | | |
|---|---|---|---:|
| 69 | Mercury MF 1126 | Casatschok/Don't Boy | 6 |

## AU PAIRS
| | | | |
|---|---|---|---:|
| 79 | 021 OTO 2 | You/Domestic Departures/Kerb Crawler (rubber stamped labels) | 20 |
| 80 | Human OTO 2 | You/Domestic Departure/Kerb Crawler | 8 |
| 80 | Human OTO 4 | It's Obvious/Diet | 8 |
| 81 | Human HUM 8 | Inconvenience/Pretty Boys (p/s) | 8 |
| 81 | Human HUM 8-12 | Inconvenience/Pretty Boys/Headache (For Michelle) (12") | 10 |
| 81 | Human HUMAN 1 | PLAYING WITH A DIFFERENT SEX (LP, with iron-on transfer) | 20 |
| 81 | Human HUMAN 1 | PLAYING WITH A DIFFERENT SEX (LP, without iron-on transfer) | 15 |
| 82 | Kamera KAM 010 | SENSE AND SENSUALITY (LP, with insert) | 15 |

## AUBREY SMALL
| | | | |
|---|---|---|---:|
| 72 | Polydor 2058 204 | Loser/Oh What A Day It's Been | 15 |
| 71 | Polydor 2383 048 | AUBREY SMALL (LP, with gatefold insert) | 125 |

*(see also Sons Of Man)*

## AUDIENCE
| | | | |
|---|---|---|---:|
| 71 | Charisma CB 126 | Belladonna Moonshine/The Big Spell | 6 |
| 71 | Charisma CB 141 | Indian Summer/It Brings A Tear/Priestess (p/s) | 12 |
| 71 | Charisma CB 156 | You're Not Smiling/Eye To Eye | 10 |
| 71 | Charisma CB 156 | Eye To Eye/Eye To Eye (double B side mispressing) | 25 |
| 72 | Charisma CB 185 | Stand By The Door/Thunder And Lightnin' | 5 |
| 72 | Charisma CB 196 | Raviole/Hard Cruel World | 5 |
| 69 | Polydor 583 065 | AUDIENCE (LP) | 300 |
| 70 | Charisma CAS 1012 | FRIEND'S FRIEND'S FRIEND (LP, pink label with 'scroll' logo) | 100 |
| 71 | Charisma CAS 1032 | THE HOUSE ON THE HILL (LP, pink scroll label, gatefold sleeve with lyric inner sleeve) | 50 |
| 72 | Charisma CAS 1054 | LUNCH (LP, gatefold sleeve, with lyric inner sleeve) | 50 |

*(see also Howard Werth & Moonbeams, Stackridge, Hot Chocolate)*

## AUDIO ARTS
| | | | |
|---|---|---|---:|
| 87 | New Media NMW 004 | ACCENT FOR A START (LP) | 40 |

## AUDIO ACTIVE
| | | | |
|---|---|---|---:|
| 94 | On U Sound ONULP 73 | WE ARE AUDIO ACTIVE (TOKYO SPACE COWBOYS) (LP) | 18 |

## AUDREY
| | | | |
|---|---|---|---:|
| 69 | Downtown DT 414 | Love Me Tonight/BROTHER DAN ALLSTARS: Show Them Amigo | 20 |
| 69 | Downtown DT 418 | Lover's Concerto/HERBIE GREY & RUDIES Along Came Roy | 25 |
| 69 | Downtown DT 436 | You'll Lose A Good Thing/DESMOND RILEY: If I Had Wings | 100 |
| 69 | Downtown DT 449 | Pop Your Corn/Pledging My Love | 20 |
| 70 | Downtown DT 452 | Sweeter Than Sugar/The Way You Move | 35 |
| 70 | Downtown DT 454 | Oh I Was Wrong/Let's Try It Again (B-side with Dandy) | 20 |
| 70 | Downtown DT 457 | Someday We'll Be Together/MUSIC DOCTORS: Sunset Rock | 15 |
| 70 | Downtown DT 463 | How Glad I Am/DANDY & AUDREY: I'm So Glad | 8 |
| 70 | Trend 6099 006 | Getting Ready For A Heartache/M Y O B: Leave Me Alone | 10 |
| 81 | Jah Shaka 826 | English Girl/African Queen (12") | 25 |
| 84 | Ariwa ARI 122 | English Girl/English Girl (Dub)/English Girl (Riddim) (12", as Sister Audrey) | 15 |

*(see also Dandy)*

## AUDREY & THE DREAMERS
| | | | |
|---|---|---|---:|
| 68 | Downtown DT408 | I Second That Emotion/THE DREAMERS: Dear Love | 20 |

## MIKE AUDSLEY
| | | | |
|---|---|---|---:|
| 72 | Sonet SNTF 641 | DARK AND DEVIL WATERS (LP, with insert) | 18 |

## LOREN AUERBACH
| | | | |
|---|---|---|---:|
| 84 | Christabel CRL 001 | AFTER THE LONG NIGHT (LP) | 40 |
| 85 | Christabel CRL 002 | PLAYING THE GAME (LP) | 40 |

## BRIAN AUGER (&) TRINITY
| | | | |
|---|---|---|---:|
| 65 | Columbia DB 7590 | Fool Killer/Let's Do It Tonight (as Brian Auger Trinity) | 60 |
| 65 | Columbia DB 7715 | Green Onions '65/Kiko (as Brian Auger Trinity) | 75 |
| 67 | Columbia DB 8163 | Tiger/Oh Baby, Won't You Come Back Home To Croydon, Where Everybody Beedle's And Bo's (solo) | 60 |
| 67 | Marmalade 598 003 | Red Beans And Rice Pts 1 & 2 | 45 |
| 68 | Marmalade 598 006 | I Don't Know Where You Are/A Kind Of Love In (with Julie Driscoll, unissued in favour of "This Wheel's On Fire") | 0 |
| 69 | Marmalade 598 015 | What You Gonna Do/Bumpin' On Sunset | 18 |
| 70 | RCA RCA 1947 | I Want To Take You Higher/Just Me Just You | 10 |
| 71 | Polydor 2058 119 | This Wheel's On Fire/Road To Cairo (as Brian Auger & Julie Driscoll) | 8 |
| 71 | Polydor 2058 133 | Marie's Wedding/Tomorrow City (as Brian Auger's Oblivion Express) | 6 |
| 73 | CBS 1444 | Inner City Blues/Light Of The Path (as Brian Auger's Oblivion Express) | 10 |
| 74 | CBS 2309 | Straight Ahead/Change | 8 |
| 68 | Marmalade 608 004 | DON'T SEND ME NO FLOWERS (LP, with Jimmy Page & Sonny Boy Williamson) | 120 |
| 69 | Marmalade 607/608 003 | DEFINITELY WHAT! (LP) | 100 |

| 69 | Polydor 2334 004 | THE BEST OF BRIAN AUGER, JULIE DRISCOLL & THE TRINITY (LP) | 20 |
|----|------------------|-----|----|
| 70 | RCA SF 8101 | BEFOUR (LP) | 35 |
| 71 | RCA SF 8170 | OBLIVION EXPRESS (LP) | 25 |
| 71 | Polydor 2383 062 | BETTER LAND (LP, as Brian Auger's Oblivion Express) | 30 |
| 72 | Polydor 2383 104 | SECOND WIND (LP, as Brian Auger's Oblivion Express) | 30 |
| 73 | CBS 65625 | CLOSER TO IT (LP) | 15 |
| 74 | CBS 80058 | STRAIGHT AHEAD (LP) | 20 |

*(see also Julie Driscoll Brian Auger & Trinity, Shotgun Express, Jimmy Page, Sonny Boy Williamson)*

## NAT AUGUSTIN
| 83 | Debut DEBT 12 6 | All Of My Love/Summer Is Here Again (12") | 60 |
|----|----|----|----|

## AUM
| 69 | London HA-K/SH-K 8401 | BLUESVIBES (LP) | 45 |
|----|----|----|----|

## CLIFF AUNGIER
| 68 | Polydor 56250 | Time/Fisherboy | 30 |
|----|----|----|----|
| 68 | RCA RCA 1730 | My Love And I/Abigail | 10 |
| 69 | Pye 7N 17753 | Lady From Baltimore/Back On The Road Again | 10 |
| 69 | Pye NSPL 18294 | THE LADY FROM BALTIMORE (LP) | 20 |

*(see also Royd Rivers & Cliff Aungier)*

## AUNTIEPUS
| 79 | Septic AUNT 1 | Half-Way To Venezuela/Marmalade Freak (p/s) | 6 |
|----|----|----|----|

*(see also Damned)*

## AUNTIE SOCIAL
| 83 | SRT S83-CUS-2014 | Preacher/I Want You Back (p/s) | 80 |
|----|----|----|----|

## AURORA
| 83 | Aurora RAM 9 | I'll Be Your Fantasy/If I Really Knew Her (no p/s) | 40 |
|----|----|----|----|

*(see also AC/DC)*

## AURRA
| 82 | Battersea BATTL 1 | A Little Love/Make Up Your Mind (12") | 10 |
|----|----|----|----|

## AUSGANG
| 85 | FM WKFM LP 52 | MANIPULATE (LP, with booklet) | 15 |
|----|----|----|----|

## AUSTIN
| 93 | Suburban Base SUBBASE 18 | THE AUSTIN EP (12", stamped white label) | 30 |
|----|----|----|----|

## PATTI AUSTIN
| 69 | United Artists UP 35018 | The Family Tree/Magical Boy | 7 |
|----|----|----|----|
| 70 | United Artists UP 35097 | Your Love Made The Difference In Me/It's Easier To Laugh Than Cry | 6 |
| 71 | CBS 7180 | Are We Ready For Love/Now That I Know What Loneliness Is | 30 |
| 74 | Probe PRO 608 | Music To My Heart/Love 'Em And Leave 'Em Kind Of Love | 15 |

## PETER AUSTIN
| 68 | Caltone TONE 125 | Your Love/Time Is Getting Harder | 120 |
|----|----|----|----|
| 75 | Terminal 108 | When You Are Near/Dub | 7 |

*(see also Little Freddy, Mr. Foundation)*

## REG AUSTIN
| 65 | Pye 7N 15885 | My Saddest Day/I'll Find Her | 40 |
|----|----|----|----|

## SIL AUSTIN
| 58 | Mercury 7MT 220 | Don't You Just Know It/Rainstorm | 10 |
|----|----|----|----|
| 58 | Mercury 7MT 225 | Hey, Eula/The Last Time | 10 |
| 58 | Mercury MEP 9540 | THE BAND WITH THE BEAT (EP) | 15 |
| 58 | Mercury MEP 9541 | GO SIL GO (EP) | 15 |
| 58 | Mercury MPL 6534 | SLOW WALK ROCK (LP) | 15 |

## AUSTRALIAN CRICKET TEAM
| 72 | Penny Farthing PEN 739 | Bowl, Ball, Swing, Bat/Here Come The Aussies | 7 |
|----|----|----|----|

## AUSTRALIAN PLAYBOYS
| 67 | Immediate IM 054 | Black Sheep R.I.P./Sad | 800 |
|----|----|----|----|

*(see also Procession, Manfred Mann Earth Band)*

## AUTECHRE
| 91 | Hardcore HARD 003 | Cavity Job/Accelera 1 + 2 (12", 1,000 only) | 40 |
|----|----|----|----|
| 94 | Warp WAP 54 | ANTI EP (12", p/s sealed with sticker) | 15 |
| 94 | Warp 10WAP 44 | BASSCADET EP (3 x 10" p/s in box) | 18 |
| 95 | Warp WAP64r | ANVIL VAPRE EP (12") | 12 |
| 95 | Warp WAP 58 | GARBAGE EP (12") | 15 |
| 96 | Warp WAP 72 | We R Are Why/Are Y Are We (12, p/s, mail order only) | 25 |
| 97 | Warp WAP96r | CICHLISUITE EP (12") | 12 |
| 97 | Warp WAP 89X | EVANE: Laughing Quarter/Draun Quarter (12") | 10 |
| 99 | Warp WAP 124 | SPLTRMX: Weissensee Against Im Gluck/At Drowning In A Sea Of Independence (12", 3000 only) | 18 |
| 99 | Warp WAPEP7.1 | EP 7.1 (12") | 10 |
| 99 | Warp WAPE7.2 | EP 7.2 (12") | 10 |
| 99 | Warp WAP 112 | PEEL SESSION (12") | 12 |
| 93 | Warp LP 17LTD | INCUBABULA (2-LP set, silver vinyl) | 35 |
| 94 | Warp WARPL 25 | AMBER (2-LP) | 35 |
| 95 | Warp WARPLP 38 | TRI REPETAE (2-LP) | 30 |
| 08 | Warp WARPCD 333X | QUARISTICE (2-CD metal sleeve) | 70 |

*(see also Gescom)*

## AUTEURS
| 91 | No Label or cat no | THE DEMO EP (cassette, hand-drawn labels, 6 tracks) | 50 |
|----|----|----|----|
| 92 | Hut HUTL 2 | She Might Take A Train/Untitled | 8 |
| 93 | Hut HUTFS | ACOUSTIC EP (live 7", not sold but given away) | 10 |
| 92 | Hut PM 264 | NEW WAVE (LP with free 7") | 20 |

MINT VALUE £

| 94 | Hut Recordings HUTLPX 16 | NOW I'M A COWBOY (LP, with free 1-sided 7")................................... | 20 |
| 96 | Hut HUT LP33 | AFTER MURDER PARK (LP)........................................................................ | 20 |
| 99 | Hut HUT LP53 | HOW I LEARNED TO LOVE THE BOOTBOYS (LP)......................................... | 20 |

## AUTO DA FÉ (IRELAND)
| 82 | Auto Dafé A.D.F. 003 | November November/For Rich People (p/s)........................................ | 10 |
| 82 | Auto Dafé A.D.F. 004 | Bad Experience/Lot 3 (Live Instrumental)........................................ | 10 |
| 82 | Rewind REWIND 13 | November November/For Rich People ................................................ | 8 |

## AUTOGRAPHS
| 78 | RAK RAK 281 | While I'm Still Young/Fabulous (p/s)............................................. | 15 |
| 78 | Strawberry Mastering | While I'm Still Young (different version, acetate only)................... | 30 |

## AUTOMATIC DLAMINI
| 87 | D For Drum DLAM 2 | I Don't Know You But... /I've Never Seen That Colour Anywhere Before (p/s, with insert)......... | 5 |
| 87 | Idea IDEA 009 | Me And My Conscience (p/s)...................................................... | 5 |
| 92 | Big Intl. BOT 04 | FROM A DIVA TO A DIVER (LP)..................................................... | 20 |

## AUTOMATIC FINE TUNING
| 76 | Charisma CAS 1122 | A.F.T (LP) ........................................................................ | 25 |

## AUTOMATICS
| 78 | Island WIP 6433 | Wakin' With The Radio On/Watch Her Now (unissued) ........................ | 0 |
| 78 | Island WIP 6439 | When Tanks Roll Over Poland Again/Watch Her Now (p/s)................ | 15 |

## AUTOPILOT
| 79 | Merimusic/Ze-La Records JHEPS 2244 | LOVE IS A PROCESS EP (oversize card p/s)................................. | 40 |

## AUTOPSY
| 89 | Peaceville VILE 12 | SEVERED SURVIVAL (LP, with inner)............................................ | 25 |
| 89 | Peaceville VILE 12 | SEVERED SURVIVAL (LP, picture disc)......................................... | 30 |
| 91 | Peaceville VILE 25 | MENTAL FUNERAL (LP, green vinyl, inner).................................... | 40 |
| 91 | Peaceville VILE 25 | MENTAL FUNERAL (LP, picture disc)........................................... | 30 |
| 92 | Peaceville VILE 33 | ACTS OF THE UNSPEAKABLE (LP) ................................................ | 15 |
| 11 | Peaceville VILELP 317 | MACABRE ETERNAL (2-LP, blue vinyl with poster)....................... | 20 |

## AUTOSALVAGE
| 88 | Edsel ED 286 | AUTOSALVAGE (LP, reissue) .................................................... | 25 |

## AUTUMN
| 71 | Pye 7N 45090 | My Little Girl/Sun Sunshine................................................... | 7 |
| 72 | Pye 7N45144 | Stood Up/Not The Way She Looks............................................. | 20 |
| 73 | Pye 7N 45249 | Down Down Down/October..................................................... | 15 |

## AUTUMN VINE
| 70 | Evolution E 2447 | He Ain't No Superman/Maxi Baby............................................. | 15 |

## AVALANCHE (1)
| 71 | Parlophone R 5890 | Finding My Way Home/Rabbits................................................. | 40 |

*(see also Norman Haines Band)*

## AVALANCHE (2)
| 80 | Childers AVA 1 | The Preacher/Mean Lady (no p/s).............................................. | 90 |

## AVALANCHES
| 99 | Rex REKD 01T | Undersea Community/Yamaha Superstar/Slow Walking/Thank You Caroline............... | 15 |
| 99 | Rex REKD 05 | Electricity/Information............................................................ | 8 |
| 01 | XL XLS 128 | Since I Left You/Thank You Caroline (Andy Votel Mix) (with tattoo) ............ | 15 |
| 01 | XL XLT 134 | Frontier Psychiatrist/Frontier Psychiatrist (Mario Caldato's 85% Mix)/Frontier Psychiatrist (85% instrumental) (12") ............ | 10 |
| 01 | XL Recordings XLLP 138 | SINCE I LEFT YOU (2-LP) ............................................................ | 60 |

## AVALON
| 82 | SRTS 82/CUS/1296 | Going Thru'/Gypsy Secret (not released in p/s)........................... | 130 |

## FRANKIE AVALON
| 58 | HMV POP 453 | Dede Dinah/Ooh-La-La............................................................ | 10 |
| 58 | London HL 8636 | You Excite Me/Darlin'............................................................ | 15 |
| 58 | HMV POP 517 | Ginger Bread/Blue Betty........................................................ | 15 |
| 59 | HMV POP 569 | I'll Wait For You/What Little Girl?.............................................. | 5 |
| 59 | HMV POP 603 | Venus/I'm Broke ................................................................... | 5 |
| 59 | HMV POP 636 | Bobby Sox To Stockings/A Boy Without A Girl ......................... | 5 |
| 59 | HMV POP 658 | Just Ask Your Heart/Two Fools................................................. | 5 |
| 60 | HMV POP 742 | The Faithful Kind/Gee Whizz - Whilikins - Golly Gee ................... | 5 |
| 60 | HMV POP 766 | Where Are You/Tuxedo Junction............................................. | 5 |
| 61 | HMV POP 879 | Gotta Get A Girl/Who Else But You.......................................... | 5 |
| 62 | Pye Int. 7N 25171 | Dance The Bossa Nova/Welcome Home Baby............................ | 5 |
| 63 | Pye Int. 7N 25183 | My Ex-Best Friend/First Love Never Dies.................................. | 5 |
| 63 | Pye Int. 7N 25203 | Cleopatra/Heartbeats.......................................................... | 5 |
| 58 | HMV 7EG 8471 | FRANKIE AVALON (EP)............................................................ | 10 |
| 58 | HMV 7EG 8482 | FRANKIE AVALON NO. 2 (EP)................................................... | 10 |
| 58 | HMV 7EG 8507 | FRANKIE AVALON NO. 3 (EP)................................................... | 10 |
| 64 | United Artists ULP 1078 | MUSCLE BEACH PARTY (LP)...................................................... | 20 |

## AVALONS
| 66 | Island WI 263 | Everyday/I Love You ............................................................. | 15 |

## AVANT-GARDE
| 68 | CBS 3704 | Naturally Stoned/Honey And Gall ............................................ | 15 |

## AVENGER
| 83 | Neat NEAT 31 | Too Wild To Tame/On The Rocks (p/s, with insert)..................... | 10 |
| 84 | Neat NEAT 1018 | BLOOD SPORTS (LP)............................................................... | 15 |
| 85 | Neat NEAT 1026 | KILLER ELITE (LP, with lyric insert) ......................................... | 15 |

## AVENGERS (1)
68    Parlophone R 5661      Everyone's Gonna Wonder/Take My Hand ....................................... 15

*(see also Vanity Fair)*

## AVENGERS (2)
72    Bullet BU 521      Highjack Plane/Shower Of Rain ....................................... 5

## AVERAGE WHITE BAND
74    MCA 102      How Can You Go Home/Twilight Zone ....................................... 5
74    Atlantic 10498      Nothing You Can Do/I Just Can't Give You Up ....................................... 5
73    MCA MUPS 486      SHOW YOUR HAND (LP, black/silver labels) ....................................... 25

## AVIATOR
80    Harvest SHSP 4107      TURBULENCE (LP) ....................................... 15

## AVO-8
80    Stroppo STROP 1      Gone Wrong/Target One/No Hesitation (p/s) ....................................... 10

## AVOCADOS
81    Choo Choo Train CHUG 3      I Neve Knew/Television Brought Me Up ....................................... 35

## ALAN AVON & TOY SHOP
70    Concord CON 005      These Are The Reasons/Night To Remember ....................................... 150

*(see also Hedgehoppers Anonymous)*

## AVON CITIES
70    UPC 1004      BRISTOL FASHION (LP) ....................................... 15

*(see also Avon Cities Jazz Band)*

## VALERIE AVON
67    Columbia DB 8201      He Knows I Love Him Too Much/To Be Let ....................................... 5

*(see also Avons)*

## AVONS
59    Columbia DB 4363      Seven Little Girls Sitting In The Back Seat/Alone At Eight ....................................... 5
61    Columbia DB 4700      Skin Divin'/Little Bo Peep ....................................... 5
62    Columbia DB 4899      A Wonderful Dream/Tonight You Belong To Me ....................................... 5
63    Decca F 11588      Hey Paula/I Wanna Do It ....................................... 5
63    Decca F 11641      Love Should Be True/All About You ....................................... 5
64    Fontana TF 442      I Am The Girl/Once Upon A Summer's Day ....................................... 5

*(see also Valerie Avon, Avon Sisters)*

## AVON SISTERS
59    Columbia DB 4236      Jerri-Lee (I Love Him So)/Baby-O ....................................... 5

## AWAY FROM THE SAND
73    Beaujangle DV 003      AWAY FROM THE SAND (LP, allegedly only 50 copies) ....................................... 100

## AXEGRINDER
89    Peaceville VILE 7      RISE OF THE SERPENT MEN (LP) ....................................... 30

## DAVID AXELROD
68    Capitol ST 2982      SONG OF INNOCENCE (LP, 'Sold in the U.K...' on label) ....................................... 45
71    RCA LSP 4636      MESSIAH (LP) ....................................... 40
73    MCA MUPS 472      THE AUCTION (LP, black/blue hexagon label) ....................................... 40

*(see also Electric Prunes)*

## AXIS
80    Metal Minded ISAX 1047      Lady/Messiah (p/s) ....................................... 8
81    Axis AM 001      When You Hold Me/Galaxy Of Love (p/s) ....................................... 8
81    Neat NEAT 13      You Got It/One Step Ahead (p/s) ....................................... 5

## HOYT AXTON
63    Saga SS503      Greenback Dollar/The Crawdad Song ....................................... 6
69    CBS 4316      It's All Right Now/Way Before The Time Of Towns ....................................... 10
79    Young Blood YB 32      Della And The Dealer/Gotta Keep Rollin' ....................................... 5
64    Stateside SL 10082      GREENBACK DOLLAR (LP) ....................................... 20
64    Stateside SL 10096      THUNDER 'N' LIGHTNIN' (LP) ....................................... 20
66    London HA-F/SH-F 8276      THE BEST OF HOYT AXTON (LP) ....................................... 20

## AXXESS
83    Lamborghini LMGLP 100      NOVELS FOR THE MOONS (LP) ....................................... 30

## AYERS, CALE, NICO & ENO
74    Island ILPS 9291      JUNE 1ST, 1974 (LP) ....................................... 18

*(see also Kevin Ayers, John Cale, Nico, Brian Eno)*

## KEVIN AYERS (& WHOLE WORLD)
70    Harvest HAR 5011      Singing A Song In The Morning/Eleanor's Cake Which Ate Her ....................................... 20
70    Harvest HAR 5027      Butterfly Dance/Puis-Je? (with Whole World) ....................................... 25
71    Harvest HAR 5042      Stranger In Blue Suede Shoes/Stars (with Whole World) ....................................... 10
72    Harvest HAR 5064      Oh! Wot A Dream/Connie On A Rubber Band ....................................... 10
73    Harvest HAR 5071      Caribbean Moon/Take Me To Tahiti (p/s) ....................................... 20
74    Island WIP 6194      The Up Song/Everybody's Sometimes & Some People's All The Time Blues ....................................... 6
74    Island WIP 6201      After The Show/Thank You Very Much ....................................... 6
75    Harvest HAR 5100      Caribbean Moon/Take Me To Tahiti ....................................... 6
76    Island WIP 6271      Falling In Love Again/Everyone Knows The Song ....................................... 6
76    Harvest HAR 5107      Stranger In Blue Suede Shoes/Fake Mexican Tourist Blues (possibly in p/s) ....................................... 20
76    Harvest HAR 5107      Stranger In Blue Suede Shoes/Fake Mexican Tourist Blues ....................................... 5
76    Harvest HAR 5109      Caribbean Moon/Take Me To Tahiti (reissue) ....................................... 5
76    Harvest HAR 5109      Caribbean Moon/Take Me To Tahiti (reissue, in different p/s) ....................................... 20
77    Harvest HAR 5124      Star/The Owl ....................................... 6
80    Harvest HAR 5198      Money, Money, Money/Stranger In Blue Suede Shoes (p/s) ....................................... 6
83    Charly/Celluloid CYZ 7107      My Speeding Heart/Champagne & Valium (p/s) ....................................... 10
86    Illuminated LEV 71      Stepping Out/Only Heaven Knows (no p/s) ....................................... 10

| | | | MINT VALUE £ |
|---|---|---|---|
| 70 | Harvest SHVL 763 | JOY OF A TOY (LP, gatefold sleeve, 1st pressing with no EMI box) | 150 |
| 70 | Harvest SHSP 4005 | SHOOTING AT THE MOON (LP, with Whole World) | 80 |
| 72 | Harvest SHVL 800 | WHATEVERSHEBRINGSWESING (LP, gatefold sleeve) | 60 |
| 73 | Harvest SHVL 807 | BANANAMOUR (LP, gatefold sleeve, with booklet) | 200 |
| 73 | Harvest SHVL 807 | BANANAMOUR (LP, gatefold sleeve, without booklet) | 30 |
| 74 | Island ILPS 9263 | THE CONFESSIONS OF DR. DREAM AND OTHER STORIES (LP, with inner) | 30 |
| 75 | Island ILPS 9322 | SWEET DECEIVER (LP, with inner sleeve) | 15 |
| 75 | Harvest SHDW 407 | JOY OF A TOY/SHOOTING AT THE MOON (2-LP, reissue, gatefold sleeve) | 25 |
| 76 | Harvest SHSP 2005 | ODD DITTIES (LP) | 18 |
| 76 | Harvest SHSP 4057 | YES WE HAVE NO MAÑANAS (LP, textured sleeve, with inner sleeve) | 20 |
| 78 | Harvest SHSP 4085 | RAINBOW TAKEAWAY (LP) | 15 |
| 80 | Harvest SHSP 4106 | THAT'S WHAT YOU GET BABE (LP) | 15 |
| 86 | Illuminated AMA 25 | AS CLOSE AS YOU THINK (LP) | 25 |
| 86 | Harvest Black EMS 1124 | BANANAMOUR (LP, reissue) | 15 |
| 92 | Permanent PERM LP 5 | STILL LIFE WITH GUITAR (LP) | 15 |

*(see also Soft Machine, Lady June, Lol Coxhill, David Bedford, Mike Oldfield, Bridget St. John)*

## ROY AYERS (UBIQUITY)

| | | | |
|---|---|---|---|
| 75 | Polydor 2066 671 | Evolution/Mystic Voyage (as Roy Ayers Ubiquity) | 7 |
| 77 | Polydor 2066 842 | Running Away/Cincinnati Growl (as Roy Ayers' Ubiquity) | 5 |
| 80 | Polydor POSP 135 | Running Away/Can't You See Me | 5 |
| 80 | Polydor POSPX 135 | Running Away/Can't You See Me (12") | 10 |
| 87 | Urban URBX 6 | Can't You See Me/Love Will Bring Us Back Together/Sweet Tears (12", p/s) | 15 |
| 72 | Polydor PD 5022 | HE'S COMING (LP, as Roy Ayers Ubiquity) | 40 |
| 75 | Polydor PD 6057 | MYSTIC VOYAGE (LP) | 20 |
| 77 | Polydor 2391 246 | VIBRATIONS (LP, as Roy Ayers Ubiquity) | 15 |
| 81 | Polydor 2391 517 | AFRICA, CENTRE OF THE WORLD (LP) | 15 |
| 83 | Uno Melodic UMLP 1 | SILVER VIBRATIONS (LP) | 50 |
| 83 | Uno Melodic UMLP 2 | DRIVIN' ON UP (LP) | 20 |
| 88 | Urban UMID 1 | EVERYBODY LOVES THE SUNSHINE (LP, as Roy Ayers Ubiquity) | 15 |

*(see also Jack Wilson Quartet)*

## ALBERT AYLER

| | | | |
|---|---|---|---|
| 64 | Transatlantic TRA 130 | SPIRITS (LP) | 40 |
| 64 | Fontana Jazz SFJL 925 | GHOSTS (LP) | 40 |
| 64 | Fontana Jazz STJL 927 | MY NAME IS (LP) | 45 |
| 65 | Fontana 933 SFJL | SPIRITUAL UNITY (LP) | 50 |
| 65 | Fontana SFJL 925 | GHOSTS (LP, reissue) | 30 |
| 65 | Fontana Jazz SFJL 927 | MY NAME IS (LP, reissue) | 30 |
| 67 | Polydor 2383089 | WITCHES & DEVILS (LP) | 40 |
| 68 | Impulse IMPL 8022 | NEW GRASS (LP, gatefold sleeve) | 30 |
| 69 | Impulse SIPL 519 | NEW GRASS (LP, reissue, single sleeve) | 20 |
| 69 | Sonet SNTF 604 | FIRST RECORDINGS (LP) | 20 |
| 70s | Freedom 41000 FLP | VIBRATIONS (LP) | 15 |

## J AYRES

| | | | |
|---|---|---|---|
| 77 | Hawkeye HE 004 | Pretty Looks/THE REVOLUTIONARIES - Ugly | 6 |

## AYRSHIRE FOLK

| | | | |
|---|---|---|---|
| 74 | Deroy DER 1052 | AYRSHIRE FOLK (LP, private pressing) | 70 |

## AYSHEA

| | | | |
|---|---|---|---|
| 65 | Fontana TF 627 | Eeny Meeny/Peep My Love | 20 |
| 68 | Polydor 56276 | Celebration Of The Year/Only Love Can Save Me Now | 30 |
| 69 | Polydor 56302 | Another Night/Taking The Sun From My Eyes | 12 |
| 70 | Polydor 2001 029 | Mr White's White Flying Machine/Ship Of The Line | 30 |
| 70 | Polydor 2058 074 | Who's Gonna Rescue Jesus/The Flowers Are Mine | 5 |
| 71 | MAM MAM 59 | Old Fashioned Love Song/Family Of A Man | 5 |
| 73 | Harvest HAR 5073 | Farewell/The Best Years Of My Life | 8 |
| 74 | DJM DJS 339 | Another Without You Day/Moonbeam | 6 |
| 70 | Polydor 2384 026 | AYSHEA (LP) | 30 |

*(see also Ayshea Brough, Roy Wood)*

## AZTEC CAMERA

| | | | |
|---|---|---|---|
| 81 | Postcard 81-3 | Just Like Gold/We Could Send Letters (die-cut sleeve, with card) | 50 |
| 81 | Postcard 81-3 | Just Like Gold/We Could Send Letters (die-cut sleeve, without card) | 20 |
| 81 | Postcard 81-8 | Mattress Of Wire/Lost Outside The Tunnel (p/s) | 30 |
| 82 | Rough Trade RT 112 | Pillar To Post/Queen's Tattoos (p/s) | 5 |
| 83 | Rainhill ACFC 1 | Oblivious (Langer/Winstanley Remix)/Oblivious (Colin Fairley Remix) (fan club issue, no p/s) | 20 |

*(see also French Impressionists)*

## AZUL

| | | | |
|---|---|---|---|
| 77 | Venture VEN7778 | Babylon Special/Version | 10 |

## AZYMUTH

| | | | |
|---|---|---|---|
| 79 | Milestone MRC 101 | Jazz Carnival/Fly Over The Horizon (12") | 10 |
| 80 | Milestone MRC 102 | Dear Limmertz/Papasong (12") | 15 |

### FRANKIE 'ALROUNDER' B
| | | | |
|---|---|---|---|
| 86 | Ital Stuff IS 001 | Scratch Mi Back/Version (12") | 100 |

### IKE B & CRYSTALITES
| | | | |
|---|---|---|---|
| 68 | Island WI 3151 | Try A Little Merriness/Patricia | 25 |

### JOHN B
| | | | |
|---|---|---|---|
| 72 | Decca F 13362 | Take A Look Around/Run Run Run | 6 |

### B TROOP
| | | | |
|---|---|---|---|
| 81 | Illuminated JAMS 6 | EUROPEANS (LP) | 15 |

### MEHER BABA
| | | | |
|---|---|---|---|
| 70 | Univ. Spiritual League 1 | HAPPY BIRTHDAY (LP, with booklet and lyric sheet 6 Pete Townshend tracks, 100 only) | 200 |
| 70 | Univ. Spiritual League 2 | I AM (LP, with inserts, features 5 Pete Townshend tracks) | 100 |
| 76 | Univ. Spiritual League 3 | WITH LOVE (LP, features 3 Pete Townshend tracks) | 100 |
| 70s | MBO MBO 1 | STAR OF THE SILENT SCREEN . . . MEHER BABA (LP, reissue of "Happy Birthday" without inserts) | 20 |
| 70s | MBO MBO 2 | I AM (LP, reissue, without inserts) | 20 |

*(see also Pete Townshend)*

### BABE RUTH
| | | | |
|---|---|---|---|
| 71 | Decca F13234 | Rupert's Magic Feather/Flood | 6 |
| 71 | Capitol CL 15869 | Elusive/Say No More | 5 |
| 71 | Capitol CL 15869 | Elusive/Say No More (DJ Copy) | 12 |
| 72 | Harvest HAR 5087 | Wells Fargo/Theme From A Few Dollars More | 5 |
| 75 | Harvest HAR 5090 | Private Number/Somebody's Nobody | 5 |
| 72 | Harvest SHSP 4022 | FIRST BASE (LP, 1st pressing with 'Sympathy Music Ltd' credit for 'Wells Fargo' with lyric insert) | 40 |
| 72 | Harvest SHSP 4022 | FIRST BASE (LP, 2nd pressing with 'Tone Music' credit for 'Wells Fargo' with lyric insert) | 20 |
| 74 | Harvest SHVL 812 | AMAR CABALLERO (LP, gatefold sleeve) | 20 |
| 75 | Harvest SHSP 4038 | BABE RUTH (LP, inner lyric sleeve) | 20 |

*(see also Wild Turkey, Elias Hulk, Liquid Gold, Whitesnake)*

### BABLA AND HIS ORCHESTRA
| | | | |
|---|---|---|---|
| 79 | Savera SAV 1001 | YESTERDAY ONCE MORE (LP) | 18 |

### MONTY BABSON
| | | | |
|---|---|---|---|
| 59 | London HLJ 8877 | All Night Long/The Things Money Cannot Buy (silver top tri) | 5 |
| 67 | CBS 2996 | If My Friends Could See Me Now/Here Today Gone Tomorrow | 5 |
| 68 | CBS 3313 | Get Out Of My Heart/I Smoke Too Much I Drink Too Much And I Cry | 5 |

### BABY
| | | | |
|---|---|---|---|
| 69 | Spark SRL 1030 | Heartbreaker/Michael Blues | 20 |

### BABY LAUREL
| | | | |
|---|---|---|---|
| 82 | Badger SRTS 82 CUS 1483 | Trouble In The Air/Leavin Home | 50 |

### BABY D
| | | | |
|---|---|---|---|
| 92 | Production House PNT 043RX | Let Me Be Your Fantasy (Acen In Wonderland)/Fantasy (Ray Keith Remix)(12") | 15 |
| 96 | Systematic 828683 1 | DELIVERANCE (3-LP) | 20 |

### BABY GRUNTING
| | | | |
|---|---|---|---|
| 71 | United Artists UP 35258 | Keep The Circle Turning/Way Down The Line | 6 |

### BABY HUEY
| | | | |
|---|---|---|---|
| 71 | Buddah 2365 001 | LIVING LEGEND - THE BABY HUEY STORY (LP) | 40 |

### BABY JANE & ROCKABYES
| | | | |
|---|---|---|---|
| 63 | United Artists UP 1010 | How Much Is That Doggie In The Window/My Boy John | 15 |

### BABY LEMONADE
| | | | |
|---|---|---|---|
| 87 | Narodnik NRK 004 | The Secret Goldfish/Real World (p/s) | 8 |

### BABYLON
| | | | |
|---|---|---|---|
| 69 | Polydor 56356 | Into The Promised Land/Nobody's Fault But Mine (p/s) | 40 |
| 69 | Polydor 56356 | Into The Promised Land/Nobody's Fault But Mine (no p/s) | 25 |

*(see also Carole Grimes)*

### BABYLON TIMEWARP
| | | | |
|---|---|---|---|
| 93 | Subliminal TENSE 001 | Durban Poison/Durban Poison (-32Hz And Dropping Mix)/ Durban Poison (The Kashmir Mix)(12") | 40 |

### BABYSHAMBLES
| | | | |
|---|---|---|---|
| 04 | High Society (no cat no) | What Katie Did (Demo) (1,000 numbered copies of clear flexi, with Annelise's Magazine. With magazine) | 20 |
| 04 | High Society (no cat no) | What Katie Did (Demo) (1,000 numbered copies of clear flexi, with Annelise's Magazine. Without magazine) | 18 |
| 04 | High Society HS7IN011 | Babyshambles/At The Flophouse (p/s, 1000 only) | 18 |
| 06 | Regal 379 9021 | BLINDING EP (12") | 25 |
| 05 | Rough Trade RTRADLP240 | DOWN IN ALBION (2xLP with side 4 etched) | 40 |
| 07 | Parlophone 508 6201 | SHOTTER'S NATION (LP) | 30 |

*(see also Libertines, Wolfman)*

### BABY SUNSHINE
| | | | |
|---|---|---|---|
| 75 | Deroy DER 1301 | BABY SUNSHINE (LP, with insert) | 80 |

*(see also Fairy's Moke)*

## BACCA
| | | | |
|---|---|---|---|
| 73 | Grape GR 3048 | George Foreman/Version | 10 |

## BURT BACHARACH
| | | | |
|---|---|---|---|
| 65 | London HLR 9968 | Trains And Boats And Planes/Wives And Lovers | 5 |
| 65 | London HLR 9983 | What's New Pussycat/My Little Red Book (B-side with Tony Middleton) | 20 |
| 69 | A&M AMS 702 | Bond Street/Alfie | 5 |
| 67 | RCA Victor RD 7874 | CASINO ROYALE (LP, soundtrack, mono) | 40 |
| 67 | RCA Victor SF 7874 | CASINO ROYALE (LP, soundtrack, stereo) | 30 |

*(see also Tony Middleton, Breakaways)*

## BACHDENKEL
| | | | |
|---|---|---|---|
| 77 | Initial IRL 001 | LEMMINGS (LP, stickered gatefold sleeve, with bonus EP) | 50 |
| 77 | Initial IRL 001 | LEMMINGS (LP) | 15 |
| 77 | Initial IRL 002 | STALINGRAD (LP, numbered with lyric insert) | 40 |

## JOHNNY BACHELOR
| | | | |
|---|---|---|---|
| 60 | London HLN 9074 | Mumbles/Arabella Jean | 50 |

## BACHELOR PAD
| | | | |
|---|---|---|---|
| 87 | Sha La La Ba Ba Ba Ba 003 | Girl Of Your Dreams/BABY LEMONADE: Jiffy Neckware Creation (p/s, flexi with Are You Scared To Get Happy or Simply Thrilled 3 fanzines) | 10 |

## BACHELORS (U.K.)
| | | | |
|---|---|---|---|
| 58 | Parlophone R 4454 | Platter Party/Love Is A Two Way Street | 20 |
| 59 | Parlophone R 4547 | Please Don't Touch/Ding Dong | 15 |
| 60 | Decca F 11300 | Lovin' Babe/Why Can't It Be Me | 5 |

## BACH TWO BACH
| | | | |
|---|---|---|---|
| 71 | Mushroom 100 MR 10 | BACH TWO BACH (LP) | 20 |

## BACK O TOWN SYNCOPATORS
| | | | |
|---|---|---|---|
| 64 | Columbia DB 7358 | Manhattan Spiritual/Colonel Bogey | 6 |

## BACK TO ZERO
| | | | |
|---|---|---|---|
| 79 | Fiction FICS 004 | Your Side Of Heaven/Back To Back | 10 |

## BACK ALLEY CHOIR
| | | | |
|---|---|---|---|
| 72 | York SYK 517 | Smile Born Of Courtesy/Why Are You Here | 40 |
| 73 | York FYK 406 | BACK ALLEY CHOIR (LP, 500 only) | 600 |

## BACK DOOR
| | | | |
|---|---|---|---|
| 72 | Blakey BLP 5989 | BACK DOOR (LP, sold at gigs) | 70 |
| 73 | Warner Bros. K46231 | BACK DOOR (LP) | 20 |
| 76 | Warner Bros. K56243 | ACTIVATE (LP) | 15 |

*(see also Whitesnake)*

## BACKHOUSE JAMES BLUES BAND
| | | | |
|---|---|---|---|
| 68 | private pressing | BACKHOUSE JAMES BLUES BAND (LP, 30 copies only, white labels in sleeve) | 800 |
| 13 | RCLP 007 | BACKHOUSE JAMES BLUES BAND (LP, reissue with signed and numbered certificate) | 20 |

## MIRIAM BACKHOUSE
| | | | |
|---|---|---|---|
| 77 | Mother Earth MUM 1203 | GYPSY WITHOUT A ROAD (LP) | 120 |

## BACKLASH
| | | | |
|---|---|---|---|
| 80 | Gargoyle GRGL 777 | OFF WITH HIS HEAD (EP) | 50 |

## BACK PORCH MAJORITY
| | | | |
|---|---|---|---|
| 65 | Columbia DB 7627 | Ramblin' Man/Good Time Joe | 8 |

## BACKSEAT ROMEOS
| | | | |
|---|---|---|---|
| 80 | Future Earth FER 007 | Zero Ambition/In The Night (p/s) | 35 |

## BACK STREET BAND
| | | | |
|---|---|---|---|
| 69 | Ember EMBS 277 | This Ain't The Road/Daybreak (p/s) | 8 |

## BACKTRAX
| | | | |
|---|---|---|---|
| 80 | S 80 CUS 842 | It's Never Too Late/Be Mine | 25 |

## BACKYARD BABIES
| | | | |
|---|---|---|---|
| 98 | Bad Afro FROO 12 | (Is It) Still Alright To Smile/B. Babylon (featuring Ginger from Wildhearts) (p/s, yellow vinyl) | 10 |
| 09 | Spinefarm 2701938 | Degenerated/SUPERSHIT 666: Star War Jr. (hand-numbered p/s, blue vinyl, 500 only) | 7 |
| 98 | Coalition COLA 046 | Look At You/Powderhead/Can't Find The Door/Wireless Mind (gatefold p/s) | 8 |
| 98 | Coalition COLA 051 | Bombed (Out Of My Mind)/Rocker (featuring Michael Monroe) (yellow vinyl, fully-autographed numbered (apart from promos) gatefold p/s, 2000 only) | 10 |
| 99 | Coalition COLA 073 | Babylon (featuring "Wildhearted Ginger")/Stars (red vinyl, foldover p/s & insert in poly bag, 1000 copies sold at gigs only) | 10 |

*(see also Super$hit666, Wildhearts)*

## BACKYARD HEAVIES
| | | | |
|---|---|---|---|
| 73 | Action ACT 4616 | Just Keep On Truckin'/Never Can Say Goodbye | 30 |

## BACON FAT
| | | | |
|---|---|---|---|
| 70 | Blue Horizon 57-3171 | Nobody But You/Small's On 53rd | 18 |
| 70 | Blue Horizon 57-3181 | Evil/Blues Feeling | 25 |
| 70 | Blue Horizon 7-63858 | GREASE ONE FOR ME (LP) | 100 |
| 71 | Blue Horizon 2431 001 | TOUGH DUDE (LP) | 100 |

*(see also Dirty Blues Band, George 'Harmonica' Smith)*

## GAR BACON
| | | | |
|---|---|---|---|
| 58 | Felsted AF 107 | Mary Jane/Chains Of Love | 20 |
| 59 | Fontana H 196 | Marshal, Marshal/Too Young To Love | 30 |

## BAD LUCK
| | | | |
|---|---|---|---|
| 81 | Bad Luck IS/BL/1054 | Mutton Dressed As Lamb/Bad Luck (p/s) | 8 |

## BAD ACTORS
| | | | |
|---|---|---|---|
| 80 | Sophist. Noise SONO 1 | Strange Love/Energy Society (p/s) | 10 |
| 80 | Plastic Speech PLAS 1 | Love Song/Are They Hostile (p/s) | 12 |

**BAD BOYS**
64 Piccadilly 7N 35208 The Owl And The Pussycat/That's What I'll Do ................................................5

**BAD BRAINS**
82 Alt. Tentacles VIRUS 13 I Luv Jah/Sailin' On/Big Takeover (12", p/s) ....................................18
83 Food For Thought YUMT101 I And I Survive (An' T'ing)/Destroy Babylon (12", insert, p/s) ...........20
83 Abstract ABT 007 ROCK FOR LIGHT (LP) ...................................................................20
91 Caroline CARLP 8 ROCK FOR LIGHT (LP, reissue, stickered sleeve with 3 bonus tracks).........15

**BAD COMPANY (1)**
74 Island ILPS 9279 BAD COMPANY (LP, first pressing, A-1U TG 2/B-1U HR 2, Robor limited gatefold sleeve, no "Published by Island Music Ltd") ......40
75 Island ILPS 9304 STRAIGHT SHOOTER (LP) ...............................................................20
76 Island ILSP 9346 RUN WITH THE PACK (LP) ...............................................................20
77 Island ILPS 9279 BAD COMPANY (LP, later EMI pressing with "Published by Island Music Ltd" label credit) ................15

**BAD COMPANY (2)**
98 BC Recordings BCR 001 The Nine/The Bridge (company p/s) ................................................20
99 Prototype PROUK 001 The Pulse/China Cup (12", die-cut p/s) ...........................................10
00 BC R'dings BCRUKLPS 001 DIGITAL NATION ALBUM SAMPLER: Flashback (Tumpa)/Spacewalk (promo 12", stickered black die-cut sleeve, A-side with Trace) ......12
01 BC R'dings BCRUKEP 001 BOOK OF THE BAD VOL. 1 EP: The Voice/Numbers/Spider/Believe (2 x 12", p/s) .........10
01 BC R'dings BCRUKEP 002 BOOK OF THE BAD VOL. 2 EP: Dogs On The Moon/Grunge/Ladies of Spain/ The Running Man (2 x 12", p/s) ......10
01 BC R'dings BCRUKEP 003 BOOK OF TH BAD VOL. 3 EP: Mindgames/Rodeo/Miami flashback/ Storyteller (2 x 12", p/s) ......10
01 Prototype PROUK 003 Planet Dust/Speedball (12", p/s) .................................................10
00 BC R'dings BCRLP 001 INSIDE THE MACHINE (5 x 12") ....................................................35
00 BC R'dings BCRUKLP 001 DIGITAL NATION (5 x 12") .......................................................25

**BAD DREAM FANCY DRESS**
88 El GPO 41 The Supremes/Choirboy Gas (p/s) ...........................................8
89 El GPO 42 Flair/You Wind Me Up (p/s) .................................................5
88 El ACME 18 CHOIRBOY GAS (LP) .........................................................20

**BADFINGER**
70 Apple APPLE 20 Come And Get It/Rock Of All Ages (p/s) ....................................10
70 Apple APPLE 31 No Matter What/Better Days (p/s) ...........................................15
71 Apple APPLE 35 Name Of The Game/Suitcase (unreleased) ....................................0
72 Apple APPLE 40 Day After Day/Sweet Tuesday Morning (p/s) ..................................15
72 Apple APPLE 42 Baby Blue/Flying (unreleased in U.K.) .......................................0
74 Apple APPLE 49 Apple Of My Eye/Blind Owl (Demo) ..........................................80
74 Apple APPLE 49 Apple Of My Eye/Blind Owl .................................................40
70 Apple SAPCOR 12 MAGIC CHRISTIAN MUSIC (LP) ................................................70
70 Apple SAPCOR 16 NO DICE (LP, gatefold sleeve) .............................................70
72 Apple SAPCOR 19 STRAIGHT UP (LP) ..........................................................100
73 Warner Bros K 56023 BADFINGER (LP, with insert) ...............................................50
74 Apple SAPCOR 27 ASS (LP, with inner sleeve) ................................................80
74 Warner Bros K 56076 WISH YOU WERE HERE (LP, withdrawn) ........................................150
79 Elektra K52129 AIRWAVES (LP, with lyric inner sleeve) .....................................20
91 Apple SAPCOR 12 MAGIC CHRISTIAN MUSIC (LP, reissue, gatefold sleeve with bonus 12" [Sapcor 121]) ...30
92 Apple SAPCOR 16 NO DICE (LP, reissue, gatefold sleeve with bonus 12" [SAPCOR 161]) ...........30
93 Apple SAPCOR 19 STRAIGHT UP (LP, reissue, gatefold sleeve with bonus 12" [SAPCOR 191]) ........30
95 Apple SAPCOR 28 COME AND GET IT - THE BEST OF BADFINGER (2-LP, gatefold sleeve) .............30

*(see also Iveys, Masterminds, Gary Walker & Rain, Natural Gas, Blue Goose)*

**BADGE**
81 Metal Minded MM 2 Silver Woman/Something I've Lost (p/s) ......................................25

**BADGER BELL BAND**
85 Noize Gate SETT 001 Nothing Left/Rock The Vicar (no p/s) .......................................40

*(see also Badger (2))*

**BADGER (1)**
74 Epic EPC 2326 White Lady/Don't Pull The Trigger .........................................5
73 Atlantic K 40473 ONE LIVE BADGER (LP, gatefold pop-up sleeve) ..............................40
74 Epic EPC 80009 WHITE LADY (LP) ...........................................................15

*(see also Ashton Gardner & Dyke, Jackie Lomax, Yes, Flash, Jeff Beck)*

**BADGER (2)**
81 Noize Gate NG 02 Over The Wall/Faceless Gang (p/s) ..........................................40

**BADGEWEARER**
90 Grugg GRUGG 002 THIS BAG IS NOT A TOY (EP) ................................................5
95 Amanita AMA LP 05 A TOY GUN IN SAFE HANDS (LP) ..............................................15

**HENK BADINGS**
60 Philips SABL 206 ELECTRONIC MUSIC (LP, gatefold) ...........................................30

**BADLY DRAWN BOY**
97 Mo Wax (no cat no) Nursery Rhyme (with UNKLE, 5" promo 150 only) ............................40
98 Twisted Nerve TNXL001 Roadmovie/My Friend Cubilas (feat. Doves) (die-cut sleeve, with insert) .........6
90s Twisted Nerve (no cat. no.) I Love You All (one-track musical box, 150 only) .......................100
98 Twisted Nerve TNXMS1 Donna And Blitzen (1 track on 5 track one-sided red vinyl 7", 195 copies, p/s).........50
97 Twisted Nerve TN 001 EP1 (EP, 500 only) ........................................................50
98 Twisted Nerve TN 002 EP2: I Love You All/The Treeclimber/I Love You All (I Loop You All Andy Votel Mix)/ Thinking Of You (EP, 1,000 only) ......30
06 EMI (no cat no) BORN IN THE UK (3 x 7" 200 of each red, blue, green in "chip bag" with Wooden fork, stickered, price is same for each) ......5
11 One Last Fruit BDBX10 LOST FOR WORDS (EP, signed photo insert) ..................................10

**Rare Record Price Guide 2018**

# BADOO

| | | | |
|---|---|---|---|
| 00 | Twisted Nerve TNXLCD 133 | THE HOUR OF THE BEWILDERBEAST (LP, 1st pressing, withdrawn, with version of 'Magic In The Air' with the line "Love Is Contagious", and Woody Allen on sleeve) | 20 |
| 10 | One Last Fruit OLFCDXX 01 | IT'S WHAT I'M THINKING (PART 1 PHOTOGRAPHING SNOWFLAKES) (box set, LP, 2-CD, 4 badges, signed) | 60 |

(see also Doves)

**BADOO**
| 80 | KG Imperial KG 001 | Rocking Of The Five Thousand/BADOO & TOYAN: Reaching To Be Free (12") | 20 |

**HENRY BADOWSKI**
| 79 | Deptford Fun City Records DFC 11 | Making Love With My Wife/Baby Sign Here With Me (p/s) | 6 |
| 79 | A&M AMS 7478 | Making Love With My Wife/Baby Sign Here With Me (reissue p/s) | 5 |

**BAD TASTE**
| 88 | Newgate SRT8KS 1554 | Rockin' Girl (p/s, with insert) | 30 |
| 88 | Newgate SRT8KS 1554 | Rockin' Girl (p/s, without insert) | 10 |

**BAD WEATHER INC.**
| 02 | Soul City 132 | You Really Got A Hold On Me/I Never Never Knew (reissue) | 10 |

**BAGGA**
| 77 | Matumbi MAT 002 | Daughter Of Zion/Version | 50 |

**DON BAGLEY**
| 58 | Pye NPL 28008 | JAZZ ON THE ROCKS (LP) | 20 |

**BAG-O-WIRE**
| 75 | Klik KLP 9007 | BAG-O-WIRE (LP) | 40 |
| 77 | Epic 82133 | BAG-O-WIRE (LP) | 30 |

**BURR BAILEY (& SIX SHOOTERS)**
| 63 | Decca F 11686 | San Francisco Bay/Like A Bird Without Feathers (with Six Shooters) | 20 |
| 64 | Decca F 11846 | Chahawki/You Made Me Cry | 50 |

**CLIVE BAILEY & RICO'S GROUP**
| 62 | Blue Beat BB 92 | Evening Train/Take Me Home (as Recko and his Blues Group) | 20 |
| 68 | Double D DD104 | Drink & Drive/Oh Oh Sugar (with Double D band) | 35 |

**DEREK BAILEY**
| 70 | Incus INCUS 2 | SOLO GUITAR (LP) | 70 |
| 71 | Incus INCUS 2R | SOLO GUITAR (LP) | 70 |
| 74 | Incus INCUS 12 | LOT 74 (LP) | 60 |
| 80 | Incus INCUS 40 | AIDA (LP) | 70 |
| 85 | Incus INCUS 48 | NOTES (LP) | 25 |
| 04 | Organ Of Corti 10 | TAPS (LP, 220gm vinyl, limited issue) | 15 |

(see also Tony Oxley, Springbeach, Steve Lacy & Derek Bailey, Anthony Braxton & Derek Bailey, Jamie Muir & Derek Bailey)

**DEREK BAILEY, BARRY GUY & PAUL RUTHERFORD**
| 70 | Incus INCUS 3/4 | ISKRA 1903 (LP) | 50 |

(see also Barry Guy)

**DEREK BAILEY & HAN BENNINK**
| 72 | Incus INCUS 9 | SELECTIONS FROM LIVE PERFORMANCES AT VERITY'S PLACE (LP) | 50 |
| 76 | Incus INCUS 25 | COMPANY 3 (LP) | 50 |

**DEREK BAILEY, ANTHONY BRAXTON & EVAN PARKER**
| 76 | Incus INCUS 23 | COMPANY 2 (LP) | 50 |

**DEREK BAILEY & TONY COE**
| 79 | Incus INCUS 34 | TIME (LP) | 50 |

**DEREK BAILEY, HUGH DAVIES, JAMIE MUIR, EVAN PARKER**
| 75 | Incus INCUS 17 | THE MUSIC IMPROVISATION COMPANY 1968-1971 (LP) | 40 |

**DEREK BAILEY & TRISTAN HONSINGER**
| 76 | Incus INCUS 20 | DUO (LP) | 50 |

**DEREK BAILEY & EVAN PARKER**
| 75 | Incus INCUS 16 | THE LONDON CONCERT (LP) | 50 |
| 85 | Incus INCUS 50 | COMPATIBLES (LP) | 50 |

(see also Evan Parker)

**DEREK BAILEY, EVAN PARKER & HAN BENNINK**
| 70 | Incus INCUS 1 | THE TOPOGRAPHY OF THE LUNGS (LP) | 150 |

**ROY BAILEY (U.K.)**
| 82 | Fuse CF 382 | HARD TIMES (LP, with insert) | 15 |

(see also Leon Rosselson)

**ROY BAILEY (JAMAICA)**
| 72 | Duke DU 146 | Run Away Child/Wedding March | 7 |

**ZEDDIE BAILEY**
| 73 | Grape GR 3037 | Babylon Gone/TONY KING: Speak No Evil | 12 |

**ELROY BAILY**
| 80 | Arawak ARK DD 027 | 24 Hour Love/Wabadab (12") | 30 |

(see also Ras Elroy)

**ALY BAIN & MIKE WHELLANS**
| 70s | Trailer LER 2022 | ALY BAIN & MIKE WHELLANS (LP) | 15 |

**BOB BAIN & HIS MUSIC**
| 58 | Capitol T965 | ROCKIN' ROLLIN' AND STROLLIN' (LP) | 30 |

**ARTHUR BAIRD SKIFFLE GROUP**
| 56 | Beltona BL 2669 | Union Train/Union Maid | 15 |

**BINKY BAKER**
| 78 | Stiff BUY 41 | Toe Knee Black Burn/Rainy Day In Brighton (p/s) | 7 |

**CARROLL BAKER**
| 76 | RCA PB 9056 | It's My Party/Loves Golden Rule | 6 |

| | | | |
|---|---|---|---|
| 78 | RCA PB 9370 | I'm Getting High Remembering/If It Wasn't For You ........................................... | 6 |

## CHET BAKER (QUARTET)

| | | | |
|---|---|---|---|
| 54 | Vogue LDE 045 | CHET BAKER QUARTET (10" LP) ............................................................. | 30 |
| 55 | Philips BBL 7022 | CHET BAKER AND STRINGS (LP) ............................................................ | 20 |
| 55 | Vogue LDE 116 | CHET BAKER QUARTET (10" LP) ............................................................. | 20 |
| 56 | Vogue LAE 12018 | CHET BAKER SINGS (LP) ..................................................................... | 20 |
| 56 | Vogue LDE 159 | CHET BAKER SEXTET (10" LP) .............................................................. | 25 |
| 56 | Vogue LDE 163 | CHET BAKER ENSEMBLE (10" LP) .......................................................... | 25 |
| 56 | Vogue LDE 182 | CHET BAKER SINGS (10" LP) ................................................................ | 20 |
| 56 | Felsted PDL 85008 | CHET BAKER QUARTET VOL. 1 (LP) ....................................................... | 25 |
| 56 | Felsted PDL 85013 | CHET BAKER QUARTET VOL. 2 (LP) ....................................................... | 20 |
| 57 | Felsted PDL 85036 | I GET CHET (LP, with Bobby Jaspar) ...................................................... | 20 |
| 57 | Vogue LAE 12044 | CHET BAKER QUARTET AT ANN ARBOR (LP) ............................................ | 20 |
| 57 | Vogue LAE 12076 | CHET BAKER AND HIS CREW (LP, mono) ................................................. | 25 |
| 58 | Vogue LAE 12109 | CHET BAKER - PHIL'S BLUES (LP) .......................................................... | 20 |
| 59 | Vogue SEA 5005 | CHET BAKER AND HIS CREW (LP, stereo) ............................................... | 20 |
| 59 | Vogue LAE 12164 | CHET BAKER SINGS (LP) ..................................................................... | 20 |
| 59 | Vogue LAE 12183 | CHET BAKER AND ART PEPPER SEXTET - PLAYBOYS! (LP) .......................... | 30 |

*(see also Art Pepper, Russ Freeman & Chet Baker Quartet, Gerry Mulligan)*

## DESMOND BAKER & CLAREDONIANS

| | | | |
|---|---|---|---|
| 66 | Island WI 295 | Rude Boy Gone Jail/SHARKS: Don't Fool Me .......................................... | 25 |

*(see also Claredonians)*

## DOROTHY BAKER

| | | | |
|---|---|---|---|
| 63 | Parlophone R5040 | A Little Like Lovin'/Try Being Nice To Me ............................................. | 5 |

## ERNEST BAKER

| | | | |
|---|---|---|---|
| 00 | Grapevine 2000 110 | Alone Again/Do It With Feeling ........................................................... | 15 |

## GEORGE BAKER SELECTION

| | | | |
|---|---|---|---|
| 70 | Penny Farthing 717 | Little Green Bag/Pretty Little Dreamer ................................................. | 15 |

## GINGER BAKER('S AIRFORCE)

| | | | |
|---|---|---|---|
| 70 | Polydor 56380 | Man Of Constant Sorrow/Doin' It ......................................................... | 5 |
| 71 | Polydor 2058 107 | Atunde! (We Are Here)/Part 2 (as Ginger Baker Drum Choir) .................... | 5 |
| 70 | Polydor 2662 001 | GINGER BAKER'S AIRFORCE (2-LP, gatefold sleeve) ............................... | 50 |
| 70 | Polydor 2383 029 | AIRFORCE II (LP, gatefold sleeve, with insert) .................................... | 30 |
| 72 | Polydor 2383 133 | STRATAVARIOUS (LP) ........................................................................ | 20 |

*(see also Graham Bond Organisation, Cream, Blind Faith, Fela Ransome-Kuti [& Africa '70], Harold McNair, Griffin, Baker-Gurvitz Army)*

## GLEN BAKER

| | | | |
|---|---|---|---|
| 85 | The Stand THE STAND 3 | BRIEF ENCOUNTER (LP) ................................................................... | 20 |

*(see also Enid)*

## JEANETTE BAKER

| | | | |
|---|---|---|---|
| 59 | Vogue Pop V 9143 | Everything Reminds Me Of You/JEANETTE & DECKY: Crazy With You ......... | 150 |

## JOHN BAKER

| | | | |
|---|---|---|---|
| 08 | Trunk JBH 030 LP | THE JOHN BAKER TAPES (LP, 500 only) ............................................. | 20 |

## KENNY BAKER

| | | | |
|---|---|---|---|
| 55 | Jazz Today JTL 1 | OPERATION JAM SESSION (10" LP, with The Jazz Today Unit) ................. | 60 |
| 55 | Jazz Today JTL 4 | KENNY BAKER QUARTET/AFTER HOURS GROUP (10" LP) ....................... | 30 |
| 55 | Jazz Today JTL 5 | TRIBUTE TO BENNY CARTER (10" LP, with The Jazz Today Unit, one side by Bertie King Jazz Group) ........... | 20 |
| 59 | Columbia 33S1140 | BLOWIN' UP A STORM (10" LP) ........................................................ | 20 |
| 78 | 77 77S 56 | BAKER'S JAM (LP) ......................................................................... | 20 |

## LAVERN BAKER (& GLIDERS)

| | | | |
|---|---|---|---|
| 55 | Columbia SCM 5172 | Tweedle Dee/Tomorrow Night (with Gliders) ....................................... | 300 |
| 55 | London HLA 8199 | Play It Fair/That Old Lucky Sun (with Gliders) ................................... | 150 |
| 56 | London HLE 8260 | My Happiness Forever (with Gliders)/Get Up! Get Up! (You Sleepy Head) .. | 100 |
| 57 | Columbia DB 3879 | Jim Dandy/Tra La La (with Gliders) ................................................... | 150 |
| 57 | London HLE 8396 | I Can't Love You Enough/Still .......................................................... | 100 |
| 57 | London HLE 8442 | Game Of Love/Jim Dandy Got Married ............................................... | 100 |
| 57 | London HLE 8524 | Humpty Dumpty Heart/Love Me Right ............................................... | 50 |
| 58 | London HLE 8638 | Learning To Love/Substitute ........................................................... | 50 |
| 58 | London HLE 8672 | Whipper Snapper/Harbour Lights ..................................................... | 50 |
| 59 | London HLE 8790 | I Cried A Tear/St. Louis Blues .......................................................... | 20 |
| 59 | London HLE 8871 | I Waited Too Long/You're Teasing Me ................................................ | 20 |
| 59 | London HLE 8945 | So High So Low/If You Love Me (I Won't Care) .................................... | 20 |
| 60 | London HLE 9023 | Tiny Tim/For Love Of You ............................................................... | 20 |
| 60 | London HLE 9252 | Bumble Bee/My Turn Will Come ....................................................... | 20 |
| 61 | London HLE 9300 | You're The Boss/I'll Never Be Free (with Jimmy Ricks) ......................... | 20 |
| 61 | London HLK 9343 | Saved/Don Juan .......................................................................... | 30 |
| 61 | London HLK 9468 | Hey, Memphis/Voodoo Voodoo ...................................................... | 50 |
| 63 | London HLK 9649 | See See Rider/The Story Of My Love (I Had A Dream) .......................... | 15 |
| 65 | Atlantic AET 6009 | THE BEST OF LAVERN BAKER (EP) .................................................. | 60 |
| 58 | London HA-E 2107 | ROCK 'N' ROLL WITH LAVERN BAKER (LP, with thin card cover) ............ | 200 |
| 58 | London Jazz LTZK 15139 | SINGS BESSIE SMITH (LP) ............................................................ | 50 |
| 61 | London HA-K 2422 | SAVED (LP) ................................................................................ | 30 |
| 63 | London HA-K 8074 | SEE SEE RIDER (LP) ..................................................................... | 20 |
| 64 | Atlantic ATL 5002 | THE BEST OF LAVERN BAKER (LP, plum label) ................................... | 20 |

## MICKEY BAKER

| | | | |
|---|---|---|---|
| 70 | Major Minor SMLP 67 | IN BLUNDERLAND (LP) .................................................................. | 50 |

*(see also Mighty Flea, Champion Jack Dupree, MIckey & Sylvia)*

MINT VALUE £

**SALLY BAKER**
70s   Old Dog PUP 1           IN THE SPOTLIGHT (LP) .................................................................. 50

**SAM BAKER**
68   Monument MON 1009      I Believe In You/I'm Number One ................................................. 30

**TOM BAKER**
79   Argo ZDSW 722/3         THE STRANGE CASE OF DR. JEKYLL & MR. HYDE (2-LP) ...................... 20

**TWO-TON BAKER**
55   London HL 8121          Clink, Clank (In My Piggy Bank)/Mr. Froggie (Went A Courtin') ........... 15

**VICKY BAKER**
64   London HLU 9856         No More Foolish Stories/Darling Say The Word ............................ 15

**YVONNE BAKER**
77   London HLU 10553        You Didn't Say A Word/BOBBY PARIS: Night Owl ........................ 10
   *(see also Sensations, Bobby Paris)*

**DAVE BAKER**
80   Black Jack BJD 4507     Glow Of Love/Version (12") ................................................... 20

**BAKER-GURVITZ ARMY**
75   Mountain TOP 4          The Gambler/Time ............................................................... 5
74   Vertigo 9103 201        BAKER-GURVITZ ARMY (LP, with lyric insert) .............................. 25
   *(see also Ginger Baker('s Airforce), Three Man Army, Parrish & Gurvitz, Gun, Sharks)*

**BAKERLOO**
69   Harvest HAR 5004        Driving Backwards/Once Upon A Time ....................................... 25
69   Harvest SHVL 762        BAKERLOO (LP, gatefold sleeve, no EMI on label) ........................ 300
   *(see also Colosseum, Uriah Heep, Humble Pie)*

**BAKER STREET PHILHARMONIC**
71   Pye International 7N 25540   The Last One/Theme From 'Love Story' .............................. 5
   *(see also Mike Vickers)*

**BAKER TWINS**
64   Pye 7N 15628            He's No Good/Words Written On Water ..................................... 15

**BALANCE**
81   Portrait PRTA 1477      Breaking Away/It's So Strange ............................................... 8
73   Incus INCUS 11          BALANCE (LP) ................................................................. 100
73   private pressing        IN FOR THE COUNT (LP) ...................................................... 30

**BALDHEAD GROWLER**
67   Jump Up JU 531          Sausage/Bingo Woman ......................................................... 8

**CHRIS BALDO**
68   Vogue VRS 7029          Living For Your Love/Arretez - Vous A Saint Michel ..................... 15

**LONG JOHN BALDRY**
64   United Artists UP 1056     You'll Be Mine (with Rod Stewart)/Up Above My Head (I Hear Music In The Air) ...... 50
65   United Artists UP 1078     I'm On To You Baby/Goodbye Baby ...................................... 20
65   United Artists UP 1107     How Long Will It Last/House Next Door ................................ 30
66   United Artists UP 1124     Unseen Hands/Turn On Your Lovelight ................................. 10
66   United Artists UP 1136     The Drifter/Only A Fool Breaks His Own Heart ....................... 50
66   United Artists UP 1158     Cuckoo/Bring My Baby Back To Me ..................................... 30
67   United Artists UP 1204     Only A Fool Breaks His Own Heart/Let Him Go (And Let Me Love You) ... 20
65   United Artists UEP 1013    LONG JOHN'S BLUES (EP, with Hoochie Coochie Men) ................... 100
64   United Artists ULP 1081    LONG JOHN'S BLUES (LP, with Hoochie Coochie Men) .................. 50
66   United Artists (S)ULP 1146  LOOKING AT LONG JOHN (LP) ........................................ 40
68   Pye N(S)PL 18228        LET THERE BE LONG JOHN (LP, unissued) .................................. 0
69   Pye N(S)PL 18306        WAIT FOR ME (LP) ............................................................ 15
   *(see also Rod Stewart, Alexis Korner, Bluesology)*

**BALDWIN**
67   Decca F22624            The Land At Rainbows End/Beautiful Butterfly ........................... 30

**KEITH BALFOUR**
69   Studio One SO 2079      Dreaming/Tired Of Waiting .................................................. 20

**BALIL**
93   Rising High RSN 72      Parasight/Island/Rosary Pilots/Avidya (12") ............................ 20

**CANNON BALL (CARL BRYAN) & JOHNNY MELODY (MOORE)**
69   Big Shot BI 518         Parapinto/Cool Hand Luke ................................................... 100

**DAVE BALL**
83   Some Bizarrre BIZL5     IN STRICT TEMPO (LP) ......................................................... 15
   *(see also Soft Cell)*

**DAVE BALLANTYNE**
66   Columbia DB 7807        I Can't Express It/Ginger Eyes ............................................... 5
66   Columbia DB 7896        Love Around The World/World Full Of Women ............................... 5
   *(see also Just Plain Jones, Esprit De Corps)*

**FLORENCE BALLARD**
68   Stateside SS 2113       It Doesn't Matter How I Say It (It's What I Say That Matters)/ Goin' Out Of My Head .... 75
68   Stateside SS 2113       It Doesn't Matter How I Say It (It's What I Say That Matters)/ Goin' Out Of My Head
                             (DJ Copy) ...................................................................... 100
   *(see also Supremes)*

**HANK BALLARD (& MIDNIGHTERS)**
59   Parlophone R 4558       The Twist/Kansas City ......................................................... 20
60   Parlophone R 4682       Finger Poppin' Time/I Love You, I Love You So-o-o ...................... 20
60   Parlophone R 4688       The Twist/Teardrops On Your Letter ....................................... 20
60   Parlophone R 4707       Let's Go, Let's Go, Let's Go/If You'd Forgive Me ....................... 20
61   Parlophone R 4728       The Hoochie Coochie Coo/LITTLE WILLIE JOHN: Walk Slow ............... 20
61   Parlophone R 4762       Let's Go Again/Deep Blue Sea ............................................... 50

| | | | |
|---|---|---|---|
| 61 | Parlophone R 4771 | The Continental Walk/What Is This I See | 20 |
| 72 | Mojo 2093 010 | Annie Had A Baby/Teardrops On Your Letter | 10 |
| 80s | Urban | From The Loveside/FOSTER SYLVERS: Misdemeanor | 10 |
| 61 | Parlophone PMC 1158 | SPOTLIGHT ON HANK BALLARD (LP) | 100 |
| 63 | London HA 8101 | THE JUMPIN' HANK BALLARD (LP) | 50 |

*(see also Midnighters)*

### RUSS BALLARD
| | | | |
|---|---|---|---|
| 74 | Epic EPC 2670 | Fly Away/Danger Zone Part 2 | 5 |
| 74 | Epic EPC 3122 | Loose Women/Danger Zone Part 1 | 5 |
| 74 | Epic SEPC 4995 | Some Kinda Hurricane/You Can Do Voodoo | 6 |
| 75 | Epic EPC 3925 | Since You've Been GOne/Venus (Shine Your Light) | 5 |

### BALLOON BUSTERS
| | | | |
|---|---|---|---|
| 69 | Pye 7N 17748 | Alcock And Brown/Bluer Than Blue (p/s) | 10 |
| 69 | Pye 7N 17748 | Alcock And Brown/Bluer Than Blue | 5 |

### BALLOON CORPS
| | | | |
|---|---|---|---|
| 69 | Stateside SS8034 | Make It Right/Muddy Water | 20 |

### BALLOON FARM
| | | | |
|---|---|---|---|
| 68 | London HLP 10185 | A Question Of Temperature/Hurtin' For Your Love | 120 |

### BALLOONS
| | | | |
|---|---|---|---|
| 78 | Earwacks WAK 001 | Calling All Human Beings/(Love Runs) Through Your Elbow | 20 |
| 80 | Earwacks WAK 002 | Jean Paul's Wife/The Slope | 8 |

### BALLS
| | | | |
|---|---|---|---|
| 71 | Wizard WIZ 101 | Fight For My Country/Janie Slow Down | 30 |

*(see also Denny Laine, Lemon Tree, Trevor Burton, Uglys, Wizzard)*

### LORI BALMER
| | | | |
|---|---|---|---|
| 68 | Polydor 56293 | Treacle Brown/Four Faces West | 40 |

### BALTIMORE & OHIO MARCHING BAND
| | | | |
|---|---|---|---|
| 67 | Stateside SS 2065 | Lapland/Condition Red | 60 |
| 67 | Stateside SS 2065 | Lapland/Condition Red (DJ copy) | 200 |
| 68 | Stateside (S)SL 10231 | LAPLAND (LP) | 20 |

### BAMA WINDS
| | | | |
|---|---|---|---|
| 69 | Island ILPS 9096 | WINDY (LP) | 30 |

### BAM BAM (1)
| | | | |
|---|---|---|---|
| 81 | Vox Populi VOP 001 | Polka Dot!/Crocodile Tears (p/s) | 20 |

### BAM BAM (2)
| | | | |
|---|---|---|---|
| 88 | Desire Records WANTX 7 | Where's Your Child/Spend The Night (12") | 10 |

### BAMBI
| | | | |
|---|---|---|---|
| 76 | Sol-Doon SDR 019 | Lady Of Lies/Somebody Told Me | 15 |

### BAMBIS
| | | | |
|---|---|---|---|
| 64 | Oriole CB 1965 | Not Wrong/Handle With Care | 40 |
| 65 | CBS 201778 | Baby Blue/If This Is Love | 40 |

### BAMBOO FRINGE
| | | | |
|---|---|---|---|
| 82 | Probe Plus PP 4 | Dorian Grey/How Do I Dance To This Music (p/s) | 8 |

### BAMBOO SHOOT
| | | | |
|---|---|---|---|
| 68 | Columbia DB 8370 | The Fox Has Gone To Ground/There And Back Again Lane | 200 |

### BAMBOO ZOO
| | | | |
|---|---|---|---|
| 81 | Phoney Gram PH 45 01 | Ghost Party/Binding Wire (p/s) | 12 |
| 81 | Phoney Gram PHOG 8101 | LOOK! LISTEN! CONSUME! (LP) | 18 |

### BAMBOOS
| | | | |
|---|---|---|---|
| 07 | Tru Thoughts TRULP125 | RAWVILLE (LP) | 20 |

### BAMBOOS OF JAMAICA
| | | | |
|---|---|---|---|
| 70 | Pye Intl. 7N 25515 | Reggae Man/Candy | 8 |

### BANANA BUNCH
| | | | |
|---|---|---|---|
| 70 | Page One POF 183 | Tra-La-La Song/Funky Hoe | 15 |
| 71 | DJM DJS 252 | Tra-La-La Song/Season Of The Rain | 10 |

*(see also Nite People)*

### BANANAMEN
| | | | |
|---|---|---|---|
| 83 | Big Beat NS 88 | The Crusher/Love Me/Surfin' Bird (p/s) | 5 |

### BANBARRA
| | | | |
|---|---|---|---|
| 76 | United Artists UP 36113 | Shack Up Parts 1 & 2 | 10 |
| 85 | Stateside 12STATES 1 | Shack Up (Extended )/Shack Up (Part 1)/Shack Up (Part II) (12" p/s) | 10 |

### BANCO DE GAIA
| | | | |
|---|---|---|---|
| 95 | Bark L 011 S | LAST TRAIN TO LHASA (4-LP, limited edition) | 18 |

### THE BAND
| | | | |
|---|---|---|---|
| 68 | Capitol CL 15559 | The Weight/I Shall Be Released | 8 |
| 69 | Capitol CL 15613 | Up On Cripple Creek/The Night They Drove Old Dixie Down | 8 |
| 69 | Capitol CL 15629 | Rag Mama Rag/The Unfaithful Servant | 5 |
| 73 | Capitol CL 15767 | Ain't Got No Home/Get Up Jake | 5 |
| 78 | Warner Bros K 17187 | Theme From The Last Waltz/Out Of The Blue | 5 |
| 68 | Capitol T 2955 | MUSIC FROM BIG PINK (LP, black/rainbow label, mono) | 70 |
| 68 | Capitol ST 2955 | MUSIC FROM BIG PINK (LP, black/rainbow label, stereo) | 40 |
| 69 | Capitol EST 132 | THE BAND (LP) | 20 |
| 97 | EMI LPCENT 23 | THE BAND (LP, reissue, EMI 100 Centenary, stickered sleeve) | 15 |

*(see also Levon & The Hawks, Bob Dylan, Ronnie Hawkins, Robbie Robertson)*

### BANDITS
| | | | |
|---|---|---|---|
| 85 | Hosspig HPG1 | Treasure Trove/Right In The Head (p/s) | 25 |

MINT VALUE £

## BANDITZ
| | | | |
|---|---|---|---|
| 80 | Phaeton SPIN 2 | JCB/Damage Your Health (p/s) | 15 |

## BAND OF ANGELS
| | | | |
|---|---|---|---|
| 64 | United Artists UP 1049 | Not True As Yet/Me | 15 |
| 64 | United Artists UP 1066 | She'll Never Be You/Gonna Make A Woman Of You | 15 |
| 66 | Piccadilly 7N 35279 | Leave It To Me/Too Late My Love | 15 |
| 66 | Piccadilly 7N 35292 | Invitation/Cheat And Lie | 100 |

*(see also Mike D'Abo, Manfred Mann)*

## BAND OF HORSES
| | | | |
|---|---|---|---|
| 07 | Kids KIDS 014 | Funeral/The Ends Not Near (p/s, 750 only, no'd, with download card) | 12 |

## BAND OF JOY
| | | | |
|---|---|---|---|
| 78 | Poydor 2310588 | BAND OF JOY (LP, with lyric insert) | 25 |

## BAND OF MERCY & SALVATION
| | | | |
|---|---|---|---|
| 69 | Duke DU 20 | Suffering Stink/BOB MELODY: The Break (B-side actually by Winston Francis) | 175 |

## BANDOGGS
| | | | |
|---|---|---|---|
| 78 | Transatlantic LTRA 504 | BANDOGGS (LP, cream label) | 18 |

*(see also Peter & Chris Coe)*

## BANDY LEGS
| | | | |
|---|---|---|---|
| 74 | WWW WWS 01 | Ride Ride/Don't Play Games | 20 |
| 76 | Jet JET 783 | Bet You Can't Dance/Circles | 20 |

*(see also Quartz)*

## HONEY BANE
| | | | |
|---|---|---|---|
| 79 | Crass 521984/1 | YOU CAN BE YOU EP | 10 |

*(see also Crass)*

## BANG (1)
| | | | |
|---|---|---|---|
| 72 | EST 11015 | BANG (LP) | 60 |

*(see also Quartz)*

## BANG (2)
| | | | |
|---|---|---|---|
| 72 | Capitol CL15722 | Questions/Future Shock | 20 |

## ED BANGER
| | | | |
|---|---|---|---|
| 78 | Rabid TOSH 106 | Kinnel Tommy/Baby Was A Baby (p/s) | 7 |
| 78 | EMI International INT 571 | Kinnel Tommy/Baby Was A Baby (reissue, numbered p/s) | 7 |
| 81 | Spiv DIV 1 | I've Just Had My Car Nicked/P.C. Plod/Sponge (p/s, with photo insert) | 8 |
| 83 | Cloud Nine CNS 01 | Poor People/Vicars In The Dark (p/s) | 7 |

*(see also Nosebleeds, Slaughter & The Dogs, Eddie Fiction)*

## BANGOR FLYING CIRCUS
| | | | |
|---|---|---|---|
| 70 | Stateside-Dunhill SSL 5022 | BANGOR FLYING CIRCUS (LP) | 40 |

## DEVENDRA BANHART
| | | | |
|---|---|---|---|
| 05 | XL XLLP 185 | REJOICING IN THE HANDS/NINO ROJO (2-LP) | 20 |
| 13 | Nonesuch 534455-1 | MALA (2-LP with poster, CD and 7") | 15 |

## BANISHED
| | | | |
|---|---|---|---|
| 93 | Peaceville CC 3 | Altered Minds/Cast Out THe Flesh (blue vinyl, p/s) | 15 |
| 93 | Deaf DEAF 13 | DELIVER ME UNTO PAIN (LP) | 25 |

*(see also Baphomet)*

## BESSIE BANKS
| | | | |
|---|---|---|---|
| 64 | Red Bird BC 106 | Go Now/Sounds Like My Baby | 100 |
| 64 | Red Bird BC 106 | Go Now/Sounds Like My Baby(DJ Copy) | 150 |
| 67 | Verve VS 563 | I Can't Make It (Without You Baby)/Need You | 120 |
| 67 | Verve VS 563 | I Can't Make It (Without You Baby)/Need You (DJ Copy) | 100 |
| 68 | Soul City SC 105 | Go Now/Sounds Like My Baby (reissue) | 25 |
| 75 | Contempo CS 2070 | Baby You Sure Know How To Get To Me/Try To Leave Me If You Can | 35 |

## DARRELL BANKS
| | | | |
|---|---|---|---|
| 66 | London HL 10070 | Open The Door To Your Heart/Our Love (Is In The Pocket) (demo only) | 900 |
| 66 | London HL 10070 | Open The Door To Your Heart/Our Love (Is In The Pocket) (1 known stock copy) | 12000 |
| 66 | Stateside SS 536 | Open The Door To Your Heart/Our Love (Is In The Pocket) (1st pressing demo with white/red label) | 200 |
| 66 | Stateside SS 536 | Open The Door To Your Heart/Our Love (Is In The Pocket) (1st pressing) | 40 |
| 66 | Stateside SS 536 | Open The Door To Your Heart/Our Love (Is In The Pocket) (2st pressing demo with green/white label) | 100 |
| 66 | Stateside SS 536 | Open The Door To Your Heart/Our Love (Is In The Pocket) (2nd pressing) | 20 |
| 67 | Atlantic 584 120 | Angel Baby (Don't You Ever Leave Me)/Look Into The Eyes Of A Fool | 70 |
| 69 | Stax STAX 124 | Just Because Your Love Is Gone/I'm The One Who Loves You | 100 |
| 77 | Atlantic K 10879 | Angel Baby (Don't You Ever Leave Me)/Look Into The Eyes Of A Fool (reissue) | 20 |
| 78 | Contempo 8005 | Open The Door To Your Heart/Angel Baby (reissue) | 8 |
| 10 | Outta Sight OSV 001 | I'm The One Who Loves You/I'm Knocking At Your Heart (reissue) | 6 |
| 69 | Stax SXATS 1011 | HERE TO STAY (LP) | 50 |

## HOMER BANKS
| | | | |
|---|---|---|---|
| 66 | Liberty LIB 12028 | A Lot Of Love/Fighting To Win | 30 |
| 66 | Liberty LIB 12028 | A Lot Of Love/Fighting To Win (DJ Copy) | 60 |
| 67 | Liberty LIB 12047 | 60 Minutes Of Your Love/Do You Know What | 30 |
| 67 | Liberty LIB 12047 | 60 Minutes Of Your Love/Do You Know What (DJ Copy) | 60 |
| 67 | Liberty LIB 12060 | Hooked By Love/Lady Of Stone | 40 |
| 67 | Liberty LIB 12060 | Hooked By Love/Lady Of Stone (DJ Copy) | 75 |
| 68 | Minit MLF 11004 | Round The Clock Lover Man/Foolish Hearts Break Fast | 15 |
| 68 | Minit MLF 11007 | 60 Minutes Of Your Love/A Lot Of Love | 15 |
| 69 | Minit MLF 11015 | Me Or Your Mama/I Know You Know I Know You Know | 10 |
| 70 | Liberty LBF 15392 | 60 Minutes Of Your Love/I Know You Know I Know You Know | 15 |
| 72 | United Artists UP 35360 | Hooked By Love/Lady Of Stone (reissue) | 5 |

**LARRY BANKS**
| | | | |
|---|---|---|---|
| 67 | Stateside SS 579 | I Don't Wanna Do It/I'm Coming Home | 60 |
| 67 | Stateside SS 579 | I Don't Wanna Do It/I'm Coming Home (DJ Copy) | 75 |
| 09 | Kent 6T 25 | My Life Is No Better/JACKIE DAY: Get To Steppin | 20 |
| 10 | Kent Select City 019 | Ooh It Hurts Me/BOBBY PENN: Without Your Love | 8 |

**LLOYD BANKS**
| | | | |
|---|---|---|---|
| 66 | Reaction 591 008 | We'll Meet Again/Look Out Girl | 20 |

**PETER BANKS**
| | | | |
|---|---|---|---|
| 73 | Sovereign SVNA 7256 | PETER BANKS (LP, gatefold sleeve) | 40 |

*(see also Syndicats, Syn, Neat Change, Yes, Flash, Jan Akkerman, Phil Collins, Steve Hackett)o*

**BANNED**
| | | | |
|---|---|---|---|
| 77 | Can't Eat EAT 1 UP | Little Girl/CPGJ's (stamped white labels, in handmade p/s) | 60 |
| 77 | Can't Eat EAT 1 UP | Little Girl/CPGJ's (stamped white labels) | 25 |
| 78 | Harvest HAR 5149 | Him Or Me/You Dirty Rat | 5 |

*(see also Gryphon)*

**BANSHEES**
| | | | |
|---|---|---|---|
| 64 | Columbia DB 7361 | I Got A Woman/Don't Say Goodnight And Mean Goodbye | 25 |
| 65 | Columbia DB 7530 | Big Buildin'/Mockingbird | 20 |
| 65 | Columbia DB 7752 | I'm Gonna Keep On Loving You/Yes Indeed | 15 |

**BANTAM**
| | | | |
|---|---|---|---|
| 70 | COUN 248 | BANTAM (LP, private pressing, white label, hand-made wraparound sleeve) | 175 |

**PATO BANTON**
| | | | |
|---|---|---|---|
| 85 | Ariwa ARI LP 023 | MAD PROFESSOR CAPTURES PATO BANTON (LP) | 15 |

**STARKY BANTON**
| | | | |
|---|---|---|---|
| 97 | Dub Organiser DOT 101 | I And I Saw Dem Coming/I And I Dub/The Herb/Herbal Dub (10") | 15 |

**BAPHOMET**
| | | | |
|---|---|---|---|
| 92 | Peaceville VILE 31 | THE DEAD SHALL INHERIT (LP) | 25 |

*(see also Banished)*

**SELWYN BAPTISTE**
| | | | |
|---|---|---|---|
| 70 | Black Swan BW 1402 | Mo' Bay/RECO'S ALL STARS: Going West | 20 |

**BARBARA & ERNIE**
| | | | |
|---|---|---|---|
| 71 | Atlantic 2466 015 | PRELUDE TO (LP) | 50 |

**BARBARA AND THE BROWNS**
| | | | |
|---|---|---|---|
| 08 | Kent Select CITY 008 | I'm Gonna Start A War/OTIS REDDING: Love By The Pound | 10 |

**BARBARA & BRENDA**
| | | | |
|---|---|---|---|
| 68 | Direction 58-3799 | Never Love A Robin/Sally's Party | 15 |

**BARBARA & WINSTON**
| | | | |
|---|---|---|---|
| 64 | Island WI 418 | The Dream/I Love You | 18 |

**BARBARA ANN**
| | | | |
|---|---|---|---|
| 65 | Piccadilly 7N 35221 | You've Lost That Loving Feeling/Till The Summer Time | 10 |

**BARBARIANS**
| | | | |
|---|---|---|---|
| 65 | Stateside SS 449 | Are You A Boy Or Are You A Girl/Take It Or Leave It | 25 |
| 66 | Stateside SS 497 | Moulty/I'll Keep On Seeing You | 30 |

**BARBECUE BOB**
| | | | |
|---|---|---|---|
| 67 | Kokomo K 1002 | GEORGIA BLUES NO. 1 (LP, 99 copies only) | 100 |

**BARBED WIRE**
| | | | |
|---|---|---|---|
| 86 | Oi Records OIR 006 | THE AGE THAT DIDN'T CARE (LP) | 20 |

**JOHN HENRY BARBEE**
| | | | |
|---|---|---|---|
| 65 | Storyville 616 013 | I AIN'T GONNA PICK NO MORE COTTON (LP) | 20 |
| 65 | Storyville 670 171 | PORTRAITS IN BLUES VOLUME 9 (LP) | 25 |

**CHRIS BARBER AND HIS BAND**
| | | | |
|---|---|---|---|
| 67 | Marmalade 598 005 | Catcall/Mercy Mercy Mercy | 75 |
| 69 | Marmalade 558 013 | Battersea Rain Dance/Sleepy Joe | 25 |
| 69 | Marmalade 608 009 | BATTERSEA RAIN DANCE (LP, as Chris Barber & His Band) | 50 |
| 69 | Polydor 2384 020 | BATTERSEA RAIN DANCE (LP) (2nd Pressing) | 25 |

**CHRIS BARBER SOUL BAND**
| | | | |
|---|---|---|---|
| 65 | Columbia DB 7461 | Finishing Straight/Morning Train | 30 |

*(see also Louis Jordan & Chris Barber)*

**KEITH BARBOUR**
| | | | |
|---|---|---|---|
| 69 | CBS 4606 | Echo Park/Here I Am Losing You | 6 |

**EDDIE BARCLAY & HIS ORCHESTRA**
| | | | |
|---|---|---|---|
| 57 | Felsted ESD 3041 | JAMES DEAN - MUSIC FROM HIS FILMS (EP) | 10 |

**EDDIE BARCLAY & QUINCY JONES**
| | | | |
|---|---|---|---|
| 58 | Felsted PDL 85056 | EDDIE AND QUINCY (LP) | 15 |

**RUE BARCLAY & PEGGY DUNCAN**
| | | | |
|---|---|---|---|
| 54 | London HL 8033 | Tongue Tied Boy/River Of Tears | 15 |

**TIMOTHY BARCLAY**
| | | | |
|---|---|---|---|
| 70 | Penny Farthing PEN 740 | Catch The Wind/The Girl From Indiana | 12 |

**BARCLAY JAMES HARVEST**
| | | | |
|---|---|---|---|
| 68 | Parlophone R 5693 | Early Morning/Mr. Sunshine | 35 |
| 69 | Harvest HAR 5003 | Brother Thrush/Poor Wages | 15 |
| 70 | Harvest HAR 5025 | Taking Some Time On/The Iron Maiden | 15 |
| 71 | Harvest HAR 5034 | Mocking Bird/Vanessa Simmons | 10 |
| 72 | Harvest HAR 5051 | I'm Over You/Child Of Man | 10 |
| 72 | Harvest HAR 5058 | Thank You/Medicine Man | 10 |
| 73 | Harvest HAR 5068 | Rock And Roll Woman/The Joker (BJH logo p/s) | 12 |

MINT VALUE £

| 74 | Polydor 2058 474 | Poor Boy Blues/Crazy City | 7 |
| 74 | Polydor (matrix: SH 1041/2) | Negative Earth/RARE BIRD: Diamonds (33rpm flexidisc free with Sounds magazine) | 10 |
| 75 | Harvest HAR 5094 | Mocking Bird/Galadriel | 5 |
| 70 | Harvest SHVL 770 | BARCLAY JAMES HARVEST (LP, gatefold sleeve, no EMI box on label) | 50 |
| 71 | Harvest SHVL 788 | ONCE AGAIN (LP, gatefold sleeve, no EMI box on label) | 30 |
| 71 | Harvest SHVL 794 | BARCLAY JAMES HARVEST AND OTHER SHORT STORIES (LP, gatefold sleeve) | 25 |
| 72 | Harvest Q4SHVL 788 | ONCE AGAIN (LP, quadrophonic) | 40 |
| 73 | Harvest SHSP 4023 | BABY JAMES HARVEST (LP, inner) | 20 |
| 76 | Harvest SHVL 770 | BARCLAY JAMES HARVEST (LP, gatefold sleeve, repressing EMI box on label) | 15 |

*(see also Bombadil, John Lees)*

## PETER BARDENS

| 70 | Transatlantic TRA 222 | THE ANSWER (LP, white/lilac label with 't' logo) | 100 |
| 71 | Transatlantic TRA 243 | PETER BARDENS (LP, gatefold sleeve, side one label is multi-coloured) | 50 |
| 76 | Transatlantic TRASAM 36 | VINTAGE '69 (LP, featuring Peter Green, clear vinyl) | 20 |
| 76 | Transatlantic TRASAM 36 | VINTAGE '69 (LP, featuring Peter Green) | 15 |

*(see also Cheynes, Peter B's, Shotgun Express, Them, Village, Camel, Steve Tilston)*

## BARDO POND

| 11 | Agitated AGIT 009 | Fallen/CARLTON MELTON: Slow Growth (12", clear vinyl, 100 only) | 15 |
| 11 | Agitated AGIT 009 | Fallen/CARLTON MELTON: Slow Growth (12", black vinyl, 100 only) | 10 |
| 01 | Matador Ole 459-1 | DILATE (2-LP) | 20 |
| 03 | ATP ATPRLP6 | ON THE ELLIPSE (2-LP, gatefold) | 25 |

## BRIGITTE BARDOT

| 66 | Vogue VRS 7018 | Mister Sun/Gang Gang (p/s) | 100 |
| 66 | Vogue VRS 7018 | Mister Sun/Gang Gang | 30 |
| 68 | Pye International 7N 25450 | Harley-Davidson/Contact (p/s) | 100 |
| 68 | Pye International 7N 25450 | Harley-Davidson/Contact | 20 |
| 63 | Philips BL 7561 | BRIGITTE BARDOT (LP) | 120 |
| 64 | Philips B 77 984 | 'BB' | 100 |

## BARDS (1)

| 68 | Capitol CL 15536 | The Owl And The Pussycat/Light Of Love | 15 |

## BARDS (2)

| 71 | Folk Heritage FHR 019M | TIME FOR THE BARDS (LP) | 120 |

## BARDS OF BARLEYCORN

| 77 | Beet Music BMR 101 | WHEN GRANDMA USED TO CALL (LP) | 20 |

## BARE FOOT

| 71 | Pye 7N 45110 | Frightened/Girl Are You A Woman Now (Promo copies say "Bear Foot") | 20 |

## BAREFOOT BLUES BAND

| 70 | Beacon BEA 163 | Can't You See/Sunday Morning Barefoot Blues | 25 |
| 72 | Deram DM 353 | The Spirit Of Joe Hill/I Believe In Music | 8 |
| 73 | Deram DM 372 | Getting Better All The Time/Half Of Me | 6 |

## JOHN BARHAM & ASHISH KHAN

| 73 | Elektra K 42129 | JUGALBANDI (LP) | 15 |

## MARK BARKAN

| 66 | Stateside SS 2064 | A Great Day For The Clown/Pity The Woman | 10 |
| 67 | Stateside SS 2064 | A Great Day For The Clown/Pity The Woman (DJ copy) | 40 |

## BAR-KAYS

| 67 | Stax 601 014 | Soul Finger/Knucklehead | 6 |
| 68 | Stax 601 036 | A Hard Day's Night/I Want Someone | 6 |
| 69 | Atlantic 584 244 | Soul Finger/Knucklehead (reissue) | 8 |
| 69 | Stax STAX 135 | Midnight Cowboy/A.J. The House Fly | 5 |
| 70 | Stax STAX 146 | Sing And Dance/I Thank You | 5 |
| 78 | Stax 12 STAX 505 | Holy Ghost/Monster (12") | 15 |
| 69 | Atco 228 030 | SOUL FINGER (LP) | 20 |
| 69 | Stax SXATS 1009 | GOTTA GROOVE (LP) | 20 |
| 71 | Stax 2362 003 | BLACK ROCK (LP) | 20 |
| 73 | Stax 2325 087 | DO YOU SEE WHAT I SEE? (LP) | 20 |
| 76 | Stax STX 1033 | COLD BLOODED (LP) | 15 |

*(see also Otis Redding)*

## DAVE BARKER

| 70 | Duke DU 74 | Funkey Reggae/TOMMY McCOOK & SUPERSONICS: I Love You My Baby (B-side actually by Versatiles) | 40 |
| 70 | Punch PH 20 | Prisoner Of Love/BUSTY & UPSETTERS: Soul Juice | 25 |
| 70 | Punch PH 22 | You Betray Me/Will You Still Love Me Tomorrow? | 25 |
| 70 | Punch PH 25 | Shocks Of Mighty Parts 1 & 2 | 15 |
| 70 | Punch PH 42 | Reggae Meeting/MARTIN ALL STARS: Soul Bone | 20 |
| 70 | Jackpot JP 736 | The Fastest Man Alive/NORMAN GRANT: Bloodshot Eyes | 15 |
| 70 | Jackpot JP 742 | Wet Version/I Got To Get Away | 15 |
| 70 | Jackpot JP 745 | Girl Of My Dreams/On Broadway | 20 |
| 70 | High Note HS 049 | She Want It/FIRST GENERATION: Give Him Up | 30 |
| 70 | Randy's RAN 503 | October/RANDY'S ALLSTARS: Time Out | 70 |
| 70 | Unity UN 567 | Blessed Are The Meek (with Slim Smith)/JEFF BARNES & UNIQUES: The People's Voice | 20 |
| 70 | Techniques TE915 | Karatae/Version | 12 |
| 70 | Upsetter US 331 | Shocks Of Mighty/Set Me Free (with Upsetters) | 25 |
| 70 | Upsetter US 344 | Some Sympathy/UNTOUCHABLES: Tender Love | 30 |
| 70 | Upsetter US 347 | Sound Underground/Don't Let The Sun Catch You Crying (features the Wailers) | 50 |
| 71 | Upsetter US 358 | Shocks '71/HURRICANES: You've Got To Be Mine | 20 |
| 71 | Upsetter US 362 | Groove Me/UPSETTERS: Screwdriver | 30 |

| 71 | Upsetter US 364 | What A Confusion/UPSETTERS: Confusion - Version 2 | 30 |
| 71 | Ackee ACK 113 | Johnny Dollar/Version | 30 |
| 71 | Ackee ACK 119 | Life Of A Millionaire/Version | 15 |
| 71 | Trojan TR 7851 | Sex Machine/You Left Me And Gone (both sides with Aggrovators) | 20 |
| 71 | Punch PH 69 | What A Confusion/BOB MARLEY: Small Axe | 45 |
| 71 | Supreme SUP 228 | Double Heavy/Johnny Dollar | 30 |
| 71 | Downtown DT 482 | Only The Strong Survive/Only The Strong - Version | 15 |
| 72 | Jackpot JP 803 | You'll Be Sorry/Green Grow The Lilacs | 10 |
| 72 | Big Shot BI 614 | Are You Sure/I Don't Know Why (B-side actually by Sensations) | 10 |
| 72 | Fab FAB 25 | Green Grow The Lilacs/JIMMY RILEY: Keep An Eye (On Your Closest Friend) (white label) | 15 |
| 76 | Trojan TRL 127 | PRISONER OF LOVE (LP) | 60 |

*(see also Glen & Dave, Bobby & Dave, Aggrovators, David Crooks, Dennis Alcapone, Don Drummond, Owen Gary, Lizzy & Dennis, Bob Marley, Lester Sterling, Busty Brown)*

**STAN BARKER**

| 79 | Nelson N1001 | VOLUME 1 (LP) | 40 |

**BARKING MAD**

| 90 | Ham West 001 | My Cat Is Better Than Your Cat/I Wanna Sleep WIth A Troll | 8 |

**BARK PSYCHOSIS**

| 92 | 3rd Stone STONE 006T | Scum (1-sided etched 12", p/s) | 12 |
| 94 | Circa CIRCA 29 | HEX (LP) | 50 |
| 04 | Fire FIRELP 90 | CODENAME: DUSTSUCKER (LP, inner) | 30 |

**BARLASTON DOWN**

| 73 | Decca F13321 | Always/Mean Woman Mambo | 15 |

**BARLEY BREE**

| 67 | Piccadilly 7N 35393 | Sometime In The Morning/Save Your Love | 15 |

**BARNABY RUDGE**

| 68 | CBS 3262 | Joe, Organ & Co./Railway Jim | 10 |

*(see also Will Malone)*

**BARNES/ADAMS**

| 60s | Lyntone LYN 1021 | When It Comes To The Crunch (It's Smiths Time)/Rhythm And Crunch (flexi, p/s) | 15 |

**BARNEY J. BARNES & INTRO.**

| 67 | Decca F 12662 | It Must Be Love/Can't Stand The Pain | 100 |

**BENNY BARNES**

| 60 | Mercury AMT 1094 | Token Of Love/That-A-Boy Willie | 10 |

**DENA BARNES**

| 80 | Grapevine GRP 141 | If You Ever Walked Out Of My Life/Who Am I | 20 |

**JEFF BARNES**

| 70 | Jackpot JP 735 | Get In The Groove/JOHN HOLT: A Little Tear | 8 |
| 70 | Unity UN 568 | 1,000 Tons Of Version/Wake The Nation (B-side with Hugh Roy) | 50 |
| 70 | Pama PM 802 | Jeff Barnes Thing/LENNOX BROWN: Lover's Mood | 20 |
| 71 | Smash SMA 2313 | Wake The Nation (with Hugh Roy)/1,000 Tons Of Version | 35 |
| 71 | Gas 163 | Peoples Version (work Out) (with PAT KELLY)/TONY LEE & PAT KELLY: Too Late | 30 |

*(see also Hugh Roy, Dave Barker, Darker Shade Of Blue, Delroy Wilson)*

**J.J. BARNES**

| 67 | Polydor 56722 | Day Tripper/Deeper In Love | 35 |
| 69 | Stax STAX 130 | Baby Please Come Back Home/Easy Living | 35 |
| 73 | Tamla Motown TMG 870 | Real Humdinger/Please Let Me In/I Ain't Gonna Do It | 12 |
| 74 | Contempo CLS 2009 | To An Early Grave/To An Early Grave (Instrumental Version) | 5 |
| 74 | Contempo CLS 2048 | Sweet Sherry/Chains On Love | 5 |
| 75 | Contempo CLS 2063 | Baby Please Come Home/Cloudy Days (reissue) | 6 |
| 76 | Contempo CLS 2111 | Sara Smile/Let Me Feel The Funk | 6 |
| 78 | Contempo 2105 | She's Mine/Erroll Flynn | 20 |
| 00 | Achievement 10011 | Talk Of The Grapevine/On Top Of The World | 5 |
| 04 | Hayley HR006 | Love At First Sight/I Think I Got A Good Chance | 6 |
| 75 | Contempo CLP 520 | THE GROOVESVILLE MASTERS (LP) | 15 |
| 77 | Contempo CLP 604 | SARA SMILE (LP) | 20 |

**J.J. BARNES/STEVE MANCHA**

| 69 | Stax SXATS 1012 | RARE STAMPS (LP) | 60 |

**LLOYD BARNES**

| 64 | Blue Beat BB 235 | Time Is Hard/BUSTER'S ALLSTARS: Reincarnation | 30 |

**ORTHEIA BARNES**

| 12 | Kent Select CITY 026 | Never Ever Leave Me/DAVID HAMILTON ORCHESTRA: What Should I Do (inst.) | 7 |

**RICHARD BARNES**

| 70 | Philips BF 1840 | Take To The Mountains/But It's Now I Need Your Love | 8 |
| 70 | Philips 630 8027 | RICHARD BARNES (LP, black/silver label) | 40 |

*(see also Quiet Five, Tony Hazzard)*

**SIDNEY BARNES**

| 76 | Charly CYS 1007 | I Hurt On The Other Side/Good Lovin' (as Sid Barnes) | 18 |

**BARRY BARNETT**

| 58 | HMV POP 487 | The Book Of Love/All I Have To Do Is Dream | 5 |

**ERIC BARNET(T)**

| 68 | Gas GAS 100 | The Horse (actually by Theo Beckford & Group)/Action Line (actually by Versatiles) | 30 |
| 69 | Gas GAS 106 | Te Ta Toe (act. by Theo Beckford & Group)/MILTON BOOTHE: Lonely And Blue | 20 |
| 69 | Crab CRAB 37 | Quaker City/Double Up (both actually by Theo Beckford & Group) | 50 |
| 70 | Gas GAS 130 | Pink Shark/Swing Free (both actually by Theo Beckford & Group, white labels only) | 30 |
| 70 | Gas GAS 147 | Bumper To Bumper/Fat Turkey (both actually by Theo Beckford & Group) | 20 |

*(see also Theo[philus] Beckford)*

## BARNFATHER
73  Bell BLL 1341 — Clock On The Wall/Hollywood Girls ..............................................5

## H.B. BARNUM
61  Fontana H 299 — Lost Love/Hallelujah ..............................................15
65  Capitol CL 15391 — The Record (Baby I Love You)/I'm A Man ..............................................40
65  Capitol CL 15391 — The Record (Baby I Love You)/I'm A Man (DJ Copy)..............................................80
76  Capitol CL 15851 — Heartbreaker/Searchin' For My Soul ..............................................10
79  Capitol CL 16067 — Heartbreaker/BOBBY PARIS: I Walked Away ..............................................15
64  RCA Victor RCX 7147 — THE GREAT H.B. BARNUM (EP) ..............................................150
62  RCA Victor RD/SF 7500 — THE BIG VOICE OF BARNUM . . . H.B., THAT IS (LP, mono/stereo) ..............................................15
63  RCA Victor RD/SF 7543 — EVERYBODY LOVES H.B. (LP, mono/stereo)..............................................15

*(see also Robins)*

## CARL BARON & CHEETAHS
63  Columbia DB 7162 — This Is Only The Beginning/Beg Borrow Or Steal..............................................15

## RIKKY BARON
60  Parlophone R 4706 — Angry Young Man/My Lonely Heart ..............................................10

## BARON WITH HIS POUNDING PIANO
65  Sue WI 398 — Is A Blue Bird Blue/In The Mood..............................................50

*(see also V.I.P.'s)*

## BARONS (U.K.)
61  Oriole CB 1608 — Cossack/Summertime ..............................................5
61  Oriole CB 1620 — Samurai/Whirlwind..............................................5

## BARONS (U.S.)
57  London HLP 8391 — Don't Walk Out/Once In A Lifetime ..............................................1500
57  London HLP 8391 — Don't Walk Out/Once In A Lifetime (78) ..............................................60
71  Jay Boy BOY 45 — No More Baby Love/Society Don't Let Us Down ..............................................10

## BARONS OF SOUL
05  Grapevine 2000 151 — You Need Love/You Need Love (unissued, demo copies only)..............................................40

## BARRABAS
73  RCA RCA 2339 — Wild Safari/Woman ..............................................12

## BARRACUDA
73  EMI EMI 2027 — Summer Girls/I Feel So Down..............................................8

## BARRACUDAS
79  Cells CELLOUT 1 — I Want My Woody Back/Subway Surfin' (p/s) ..............................................20
80  Zonophone Z 5 — Summer Fun/Chevy Baby (p/s, with stickers) ..............................................15
80  Zonophone Z 5 — Summer Fun/Chevy Baby (p/s, without stickers) ..............................................6
80  Zonophone Z 8 — His Last Summer/Barracuda Waver/Surfers Are Back (p/s) ..............................................8
80  Zonophone Z 11 — (I Wish It Could Be) 1965 Again/Rendezvous (p/s) ..............................................8
81  Zonophone Z 17 — I Can't Pretend/The KGB (Made A Man Out Of Me) (p/s)..............................................8

## MARTIN BARRE
93  Presshouse MBSBCD 92 — A SUMMER BAND (LP, 500 only) ..............................................30

*(see also Jethro Tull)*

## DICKIE BARRETT
58  MGM MGM 976 — Smoke Gets In Your Eyes/Remember Me..............................................30

## RICHARD BARRETT & CHANTELS
59  HMV POP 609 — Come Softly To Me/Walking Through Dreamland ..............................................20

*(see also Chantels)*

## RICHIE BARRETT
62  London HLK 9552 — Some Other Guy/Tricky Dicky..............................................40

## SYD BARRETT
69  Harvest HAR 5009 — Octopus/Golden Hair ..............................................250
69  Harvest HAR 5009 — Octopus/Golden Hair (Promo with mispelt 'Barratt' and release date 14.11.69) ..............350
88  Strange Fruit SFPS 043 — THE PEEL SESSIONS (12", EP, initial pressing with metallic sleeve) ..............................................15
88  Strange Fruit SFPS 043 — THE PEEL SESSIONS (12", EP) ..............................................15
70  Harvest SHVL 765 — THE MADCAP LAUGHS (LP, laminated sleeve, no EMI box on label) ..............................................200
70  Harvest SHVL 765 — THE MADCAP LAUGHS (LP, matt gatefold sleeve, no EMI box on label) ..............................................100
70  Harvest SHSP 4007 — BARRETT (LP, laminated sleeve, first pressing with no EMI boxed label) ..............................................300
70  Harvest SHSP 4007 — BARRETT (LP, textured flipback sleeve, no EMI logo) ..............................................80
72  Harvest SHSP 4007 — BARRETT (LP, textured non-flipback sleeve, second pressing with EMI boxed logo)..............................................20
74  Harvest SHDW 404 — SYD BARRETT (2-LP, reissue of "Madcap" & "Barrett", gatefold sleeve) ..............................................40
88  Harvest SHVL 765 — BARRETT (LP, reissue with black 'Harvest' label) ..............................................30
88  Harvest SHSP 4126 — OPEL (LP, gatefold sleeve, black label) ..............................................20
93  EMI SYD BOX 1 — CRAZY DIAMOND (3-CD box set, with booklet)..............................................25
97  Harvest 7423 855663 18 — THE MADCAP LAUGHS (LP, 180gm reissue, heavy quality sleeve) ..............................................20
97  Harvest 7423 821450 11 — BARRETT (LP, 180gm reissue, heavy quality sleeve) ..............................................20
99  Simply Vinyl SVLP 153 — OPEL (LP 180gm reissue, heavy quality gatefold sleeve) ..............................................25
00  Simply Vinyl SVLP 281 — BARRETT (LP, 180gm reissue, heavy quality gatefold sleeve)..............................................22
00  Simply Vinyl SVLP 289 — THE MADCAP LAUGHS (LP, 180gm reissue, heavy quality gatefold sleeve) ..............................................20
10  Harvest 985031 — AN INTRODUCTION TO (2-LP) ..............................................20

*(see also Pink Floyd)*

## WILD WILLY BARRETT
86  Galvanised DIP 1 — ORGANIC BONDAGE (LP, with Stephen Two Names; in wooden sleeve) ..............................................15

*(see also John Otway/Wild Willy Barrett)*

## RAY BARRETTO
63  Columbia DB 7051 — El Watusi/Ritmo Sabroso ..............................................10
65  Columbia DB 7684 — El Watusi/Swingin' Shepherd Blues ..............................................10

| 69 | London HL 10262 | Acid/Mercy Mercy Baby (withdrawn) | 100 |
| 67 | Island ILP 946 | EL WATUSI (LP) | 40 |
| 69 | London HA/SH 8383 | ACID (LP) | 50 |

## BARRIER
| 68 | Eyemark EMS 1013 | Georgie Brown/Dawn Breaks Through (in handmade p/s) | 450 |
| 68 | Eyemark EMS 1013 | Georgie Brown/Dawn Breaks Through | 250 |
| 68 | Philips BF 1692 | The Tide Is Turning/Place In Your Heart | 15 |
| 68 | Philips BF 1731 | Spot The Lights/Uh | 70 |

## BARRINO BROTHERS
| 72 | Invictus INV 523 | I Shall Not Be Moved/When Love Was A Child | 15 |

## BARRON KNIGHTS
| 64 | Columbia DB 7188 | Comin' Home Baby/Peanut Butter | 30 |
| 67 | Columbia DB 8161 | Lazy Fat People/In The Night | 15 |
| 72 | Penny Farthing PEN 786 | You're All I Need/Nothin' Doin' | 15 |

## BARROW POETS
| 67 | Barrow BR 1 | AT THE PRINTER'S DEVIL (EP, private pressing) | 10 |

## AL BARRY
| 70 | Duke DU 81 | Ooh Wee/Hold It Baby | 5 |
| 70 | Doctor Bird DB 1502 | Morning Sun/MARKONIANS: Over And Over | 400 |
| 71 | Creole 1005 | Down We Go/It Pays To Do Good | 30 |
| 11 | Creole THB 7006 | Treat Me Good/Down We Go | 10 |
| 12 | Doctor Bird DB 1502 | Morning Sun/MARKONIANS: Over And Over (reissue, jukebox centre) | 25 |

*(see also Desmond Dekker & Aces)*

## DAVE BARRY & SARA BERNER
| 56 | London HLU 8324 | Out Of This World With Flying Saucers Parts 1 & 2 (Tri Gold) | 40 |

## DAWN BARRY
| 71 | Phoenix NIX 118 | My World Keeps Getting Smaller Evry Day/No Love At All | 6 |

## JOE BARRY
| 61 | Mercury AMT 1149 | I'm A Fool To Care/I Got A Feeling | 5 |
| 68 | Stateside SS 2127 | I Started Loving You Again/California Bound | 5 |
| 62 | Mercury ZEP 10130 | A FOOL TO CARE (EP) | 40 |

## JOHN BARRY (SEVEN)
### SINGLES
| 57 | Parlophone R 4363 | Zip Zip/Three Little Fishes (as John Barry & The Seven) | 40 |
| 58 | Parlophone R 4394 | Every Which Way/You've Gotta Way (as John Barry Seven) | 15 |
| 58 | Parlophone R 4418 | Big Guitar/Rodeo (as John Barry Seven) | 10 |
| 58 | Parlophone R 4453 | Pancho/Hideaway (as John Barry Seven) | 5 |
| 58 | Parlophone R 4488 | Farrago/Bee's Knees (as John Barry Seven) | 5 |
| 59 | Parlophone R 4530 | Long John/Snap 'n' Whistle (as John Barry Seven) | 5 |
| 59 | Parlophone R 4560 | Little John/For Pete's Sake (as John Barry Seven) | 5 |
| 59 | Parlophone R 4582 | Twelfth Street Rag/Christella (as John Barry Seven) | 5 |
| 60 | Columbia DB 4414 | Hit And Miss/Rockin' Already (as John Barry Seven) | 5 |
| 60 | Columbia DB 4446 | Beat For Beatniks/Big Fella (as John Barry Orchestra) | 5 |
| 60 | Columbia DB 4480 | Blueberry Hill/Never Let Go (as John Barry Orchestra) | 5 |
| 60 | Columbia DB 4505 | Walk Don't Run/I'm Movin' On (as John Barry Seven) | 5 |
| 60 | Columbia DB 4554 | Black Stockings/Get Lost Jack Frost (as John Barry Seven) | 5 |
| 61 | Columbia DB 4598 | The Magnificent Seven/Skid Row (as John Barry Seven) | 5 |
| 61 | Columbia DB 4659 | The Menace/Rodeo (as John Barry Orchestra) | 5 |
| 61 | Columbia DB 4699 | Starfire/A Matter Of Who (as John Barry Seven) | 5 |
| 61 | Columbia DB 4746 | Watch Your Step/Twist It (as John Barry Seven) | 5 |
| 62 | Columbia DB 4806 | Cutty Sark/Lost Patrol (as John Barry Seven & Orchestra) | 5 |
| 62 | Columbia DB 4898 | The James Bond Theme/The Blacksmith Blues (with Orchestra) (green or black labels) | 10 |
| 62 | Columbia DB 4941 | The Lolly Theme/March Of The Mandarins (as John Barry Seven & Orchestra) | 5 |
| 63 | Columbia DB 7003 | The Human Jungle/Onward, Christian Spacemen (in p/s) | 10 |
| 64 | Columbia DB 7414 | Twenty-Four Hours Ago/Seven Faces | 20 |
| 63 | Ember EMB S 178 | Kinky/Fancy Dance | 5 |
| 63 | Ember EMB S 181 | 007/From Russia With Love (in p/s) | 15 |
| 63 | Ember EMB S 183 | Elizabeth/The London Theme | 5 |
| 63 | Ember EMB S 185 | Zulu Stamp/Monkey Feathers (mauve/grey or red/yellow label; in p/s) | 10 |
| 63 | Lyntone LYN 378 | Theme Music From The Ingersoll Trendsetters T.V. Commercial flexidisc with 8-page A4 promo booklet) | 10 |
| 64 | United Artists UP 1060 | Seance On A Wet Afternoon/Oublie Ça | 5 |
| 64 | United Artists UP 1068 | Goldfinger/Troubador | 5 |
| 64 | Stateside SS 296 | Barney's Blues/Theme From The Film "Man In The Middle" (No More) | 5 |
| 65 | CBS 201747 | A Man Alone (Ipcress File Theme)/Barbara's Theme | 5 |
| 65 | CBS 201822 | The Syndicate/What A Question | 5 |
| 66 | CBS 202390 | Vendetta/The Danny Scipio Theme | 5 |
| 67 | CBS 202451 | Wednesday's Child (Quiller Memorandum)/Sleep Well My Darling | 5 |
| 67 | CBS 2825 | You Only Live Twice/The Girl With The Sun In Her Hair | 5 |
| 67 | Ember EMB S 243 | 007/The Loneliness Of Autumn (in p/s) | 10 |
| 69 | CBS 3935 | The Lion In Winter Parts 1 & 2 | 5 |
| 69 | CBS 4468 | Midnight Cowboy/Fun City | 5 |
| 69 | CBS 4680 | On Her Majesty's Secret Service/We Have All The Time In The World | 5 |
| 70 | Probe PRO 518 | The Last Valley/Main Title Theme | 5 |
| 71 | CBS 7469 | Theme From "The Persuaders"/The Girl With The Sun In Her Hair | 5 |

### EPs
| 58 | Parlophone GEP 8737 | THE BIG BEAT (as John Barry Seven) | 40 |

# Len BARRY

| | | | |
|---|---|---|---|
| 62 | Columbia SEG 8138 | BEAT GIRL (as John Barry Seven, with Adam Faith) | 20 |
| 63 | Columbia SEG 8255 | JOHN BARRY THEME SUCCESSES | 10 |
| 63 | United Artists UEP 1011 | FROM RUSSIA WITH LOVE (soundtrack) | 10 |
| 64 | Ember EMB EP 4544 | LONELINESS OF AUTUMN | 10 |
| 64 | United Artists UEP 1012 | GOLDFINGER (soundtrack) | 10 |
| 65 | Ember EMB EP 4551 | JAMES BOND IS BACK | 25 |
| 65 | United Artists UEP 1015 | THUNDERBALL: Thunderball/Death Of Fiona/Bond Below Disco Volante/ Mr Kiss Kiss Bang Bang (soundtrack) | 10 |
| 67 | CBS WEP 1126 | THEMES FROM JAMES BOND FILMS (mail order via Carr's Sport biscuits) | 10 |
| 67 | CBS WEP 1129 | BIG THEMES FROM THE BIG SCREEN (mail order via Wall's) | 10 |
| 67 | CBS WEP 1131 | GREAT SCREEN THEMES (mail order via Lyon's Bakery) | 10 |

## ALBUMS

| | | | |
|---|---|---|---|
| 60 | Columbia 33SX 1225 | BEAT GIRL (soundtrack, with Adam Faith) | 40 |
| 61 | Columbia 33SX 1358 | STRINGBEAT (mono) | 30 |
| 61 | Columbia SCX 3401 | STRINGBEAT (stereo) | 35 |
| 63 | United Artists (S)ULP 1052 | FROM RUSSIA WITH LOVE (soundtrack, mono) | 25 |
| 63 | United Artists (S)ULP 1052 | FROM RUSSIA WITH LOVE (soundtrack, stereo) | 25 |
| 63 | Colpix PXL 459 | ELIZABETH TAYLOR IN LONDON (mono) | 20 |
| 63 | Colpix PXL 459 | ELIZABETH TAYLOR IN LONDON (stereo) | 20 |
| 64 | Ember NR 5012 | ZULU (soundtrack, yellow/orange label, flipback sleeve) | 20 |
| 64 | Stateside S(S)L 10087 | MAN IN THE MIDDLE (soundtrack, with Lionel Bart) | 15 |
| 64 | United Artists (S)ULP 1076 | GOLDFINGER (soundtrack, mono) | 15 |
| 64 | United Artists (S)ULP 1076 | GOLDFINGER (soundtrack, stereo) | 15 |
| 65 | Ember NR 5025 | JOHN BARRY PLAYS 007 | 20 |
| 65 | CBS BPG 62530 | THE IPCRESS FILE (soundtrack, mono only) | 150 |
| 65 | United Artists ULP 1104 | THE KNACK (AND HOW TO GET IT) (soundtrack) | 80 |
| 65 | United Artists (S)ULP 1110 | THUNDERBALL (soundtrack, mono) | 15 |
| 65 | United Artists (S)ULP 1110 | THUNDERBALL (soundtrack, stereo) | 15 |
| 66 | Fontana STL 5387 | THE WRONG BOX (soundtrack, release cancelled) | 0 |
| 66 | CBS (S)BPG 62869 | THE QUILLER MEMORANDUM (soundtrack, mono) | 25 |
| 66 | CBS (S)BPG 62869 | THE QUILLER MEMORANDUM (soundtrack, stereo) | 25 |
| 67 | United Artists (S)ULP 1168 | THE WHISPERERS (soundtrack) | 40 |
| 67 | United Artists (S)ULP 1171 | YOU ONLY LIVE TWICE (soundtrack) | 15 |
| 68 | Stateside S(S)L 10263 | DEADFALL (soundtrack, Shirley Bassey on 1 track) | 20 |
| 69 | United Artists UAS 29020 | ON HER MAJESTY'S SECRET SERVICE (soundtrack, foldout sleeve) | 25 |
| 69 | MCA MUPS 360 | BOOM! (soundtrack, with Georgie Fame) | 30 |
| 71 | United Artists UAS 29216 | DIAMONDS ARE FOREVER (soundtrack) | 20 |
| 71 | Probe SPB 1027 | THE LAST VALLEY (soundtrack, with insert) | 15 |
| 72 | Ember SE 8008 | JOHN BARRY REVISITED (foldout sleeve, initial pressing in 'nude' gatefold sleeve) | 30 |

*(see also Alan Bown, Chad & Jeremy, Adam Faith, Elizabeth Taylor, Desmond Lane, Johnny Pearson, Jim Lowe, Lyn Paul, Lance Fortune, Alan Haven, Countdowns, Johnny De Little, Marion Ryan, Dick Kallman)*

## LEN BARRY

| | | | |
|---|---|---|---|
| 65 | Cameo Parkway P 969 | Hearts Are Trump/Little White House | 30 |
| 65 | Brunswick 05942 | 1-2-3/Bullseye | 10 |
| 65 | Brunswick 05942 | 1-2-3/Bullseye (DJ Copy) | 30 |
| 66 | Brunswick 05949 | Like A Baby/Happiness (Is A Girl Like You) | 10 |
| 66 | Brunswick 05949 | Like A Baby/Happiness (DJ Copy) | 30 |
| 66 | Brunswick 05955 | Somewhere/It's A Crying Shame | 10 |
| 66 | Brunswick 05955 | Somewhere/It's A Crying Shame (DJ Copy) | 30 |
| 66 | Brunswick 05962 | It's That Time Of The Year/Happily Ever After | 10 |
| 66 | Brunswick 05962 | It's That Time Of The Year/Happily Ever After (DJ Copy) | 30 |
| 66 | Brunswick 05966 | I Struck It Rich/Love Is | 20 |
| 66 | Brunswick 05966 | I Struck It Rich/Love Is (DJ Copy) | 40 |
| 67 | RCA RCA 1588 | The Moving Finger Writes/Our Love | 20 |
| 67 | RCA RCA 1588 | The Moving Finger Writes/Our Love (DJ Copy) | 30 |
| 68 | Bell BLL 1022 | 4-5-6 Now I'm Alone/Funky Night | 10 |
| 71 | Now! NOW 1003 | Now I'm Alone/Funky Night | 6 |
| 72 | MCA MU 1172 | 1-2-3/You Baby | 5 |
| 73 | Paramount PARA 3031 | Heaven And Earth/I'm Marching To The Music | 15 |
| 73 | Paramount PARA 3039 | It's Time To Fall In Love/Touching, Holding, Feeling | 5 |
| 66 | Cameo Parkway CPE 556 | HAVIN' A GOOD TIME (EP) | 30 |
| 65 | Brunswick LAT 8637 | 1-2-3 (LP) | 25 |
| 66 | Brunswick LAT 8656 | IT'S THAT TIME OF YEAR (LP, unreleased, sleeve may not exist) | 900 |
| 66 | Cameo Parkway C 1082 | LEN BARRY AND THE DOVELLS (LP) | 30 |
| 69 | Bulldog BDL 1013 | MORE FROM THE 1-2-3 MAN (LP) | 20 |

*(see also Dovells, Electric Indian)*

## MARGARET BARRY (& MICHAEL GORMAN)

| | | | |
|---|---|---|---|
| 58 | Topic 10T 6 | STREET SONGS AND FIDDLE TUNES OF IRELAND (10" LP, mid-blue label, later buff/ black or dark blue/silver labels) | 15 |

## SANDRA BARRY (& THE BOYS)

| | | | |
|---|---|---|---|
| 64 | Decca F 11851 | Really Gonna Shake/When We Get Married (as Sandra Barry & Boys) | 100 |
| 65 | Pye 7N 15753 | The End Of The Line/We Were Lovers | 15 |
| 65 | Pye 7N 15840 | Question/You Can Take It From Me | 10 |
| 66 | Pye 7N 17102 | Stop! Thief/I Won't Try To Change Your Mind | 10 |

*(see also Boys, Sandra Alfred, Slack Alice)*

## BARRY & THE TAMERLANES

| | | | |
|---|---|---|---|
| 63 | Warner Bros WB 116 | I Wonder What She's Doing Tonight/Don't Go | 10 |
| 64 | Warner Bros WB 124 | Roberta/Butterfly | 5 |
| 64 | Warner Bros WM 8145 | I WONDER WHAT SHE'S DOING TONIGHT (LP) | 20 |

*(see also Barry De Vorzon)*

## BARRY SISTERS (U.S.)
| | | | |
|---|---|---|---|
| 56 | London HLA 8248 | Cha Cha Joe/Baby Come A Little Closer | 20 |
| 56 | London HLA 8304 | Till You Come Back To Me/Intrigue | 70 |
| 60 | Columbia 33SX 1309 | SIDE BY SIDE (LP) | 15 |

*(see also Three Barry Sisters)*

## LIONEL BART
| | | | |
|---|---|---|---|
| 68 | Deram SML 1028 | ISN'T THIS WHERE WE CAME IN (LP, stereo, gatefold sleeve) | 40 |

## CHRIS BARTLEY
| | | | |
|---|---|---|---|
| 67 | Cameo Parkway P 101 | The Sweetest Thing This Side Of Heaven/Love Me Baby | 70 |
| 67 | Cameo Parkway P 101 | The Sweetest Thing This Side Of Heaven/Love Me Baby (DJ Copy) | 125 |
| 68 | Bell BLL 1031 | I Found A Goodie/Be Mine Forever | 30 |
| 75 | Right On RO 105 | I See Your Name/I See Your Name (Instrumental) | 12 |
| 86 | Move MIS 4 | Baby I'm For Real/I've Found A Goodie/Truer Words Were Never Spoken/The Sweetest Thing This Side Of Heaven (12", p/s) | 15 |

## BARTOK
| | | | |
|---|---|---|---|
| 82 | On ON 1 | Insanity/I Am The Bomb (p/s) | 12 |

*(see also Jah Wobble, Damned)*

## RIA BARTOK
| | | | |
|---|---|---|---|
| 64 | Columbia DB 7362 | See If I Care/I Don't Wanna Leave You | 6 |

## EILEEN BARTON
| | | | |
|---|---|---|---|
| 55 | Vogue Coral Q 72060 | The Year We Fell In Love/I Don't Want To Mambo Polka | 5 |
| 55 | Vogue Coral Q 72075 | Fujiyama Mama/I'd've Baked A Cake | 100 |
| 56 | Vogue Coral Q 72122 | Cry Me A River/Come Home | 10 |
| 56 | Vogue Coral Q 72148 | Teenage Heart/My Social Hot Dog | 10 |
| 57 | Vogue Coral Q 72250 | Too Close For Comfort/Here I Am In Love Again | 5 |
| 57 | Vogue Coral Q 72270 | Without Love/The Scene Of The Crime | 5 |

## MARIA BARTON
| | | | |
|---|---|---|---|
| 80 | Airship AP 56 | RAINFUL DAYS (LP) | 100 |

## ROD BARTON (& THE LINCOLNAIRES)
| | | | |
|---|---|---|---|
| 62 | Salvo SLO 1812 | Dear Old San Francisco/NERVOUS NORVOUS: Does A Chinese Chicken Have A Pigtail | 10 |

## DAVE BARTRAM
| | | | |
|---|---|---|---|
| 83 | Utopia UTO 2 | Black Ice/Excitement (p/s) | 5 |

## BASCZAX
| | | | |
|---|---|---|---|
| 79 | Pipeline ICI ONE | Madison Fallout/Auto Mekanik Destruktor (4 single sided 7" pages as sleeve) | 25 |

*(see also The Amazing Space Frogs, Blitzkrieg Bop, The Gynaecologists)*

## BASE
| | | | |
|---|---|---|---|
| 80 | Base BASE001 | Violent Death/Frenchmen/One-Way Girl (hand-made p/s) | 25 |

## BASELINE
| | | | |
|---|---|---|---|
| 81 | Extrabit EX 1 | Suspended Animation/Truth About The Lies (with p/s) | 125 |
| 81 | Extrabit EX 1 | Suspended Animation/Truth About The Lies (without p/s) | 50 |

## BASEMENT 5
| | | | |
|---|---|---|---|
| 80 | Island ILPS9641 | 1965-80 (LP, with inner, poster and embossed sleeve) | 15 |

## BASEMENT PHIL
| | | | |
|---|---|---|---|
| 91 | Basement BRSS 001 | Take Me Up (Part 1)/(Part 2)/(Part 3) (12" promo) | 25 |
| 92 | Basement BRSS 002 | Bachbeat (Part 1)/I Love You/Bachbeat (Part 2) (12" promo) | 12 |
| 92 | Basement BRSS 009 | WE CAN ROCK IT EP (12", as Basement Phil And The Engineers) | 10 |

## BASES
| | | | |
|---|---|---|---|
| 67 | Coxsone CS 7030 | River Jordan/SOUL VENDORS: Swing Easy | 150 |

## BASH STREET KIDS
| | | | |
|---|---|---|---|
| 79 | Agenda GM 480 | C'mon Kids/Travelling Man (p/s) | 40 |

## BASHERS
| | | | |
|---|---|---|---|
| 76 | Virgin VS 154 | The Womble Bashers/Womble Bashers Wock | 20 |

*(see also Mike McGear)*

## BASHFUL ALLEY
| | | | |
|---|---|---|---|
| 82 | Ellie Jay BA 001 | Running Blind/My, My, My (p/s, black-and-white or black-and-yellow sleeve) | 50 |
| 82 | Graffiti BA 001 | Running Blind/My, My, My (p/s, reissue) | 35 |

## ROBBIE BASHO
| | | | |
|---|---|---|---|
| 69 | Sonet SNTF 612 | THe FALCONERS ARM VOL 1. (LP) | 20 |

## BASIC BLACK AND PEARL
| | | | |
|---|---|---|---|
| 75 | Bus Stop BUS 1030 | There'll Come A Time, There'll Come A Day/Right On Baby | 30 |

## COUNT BASIE & HIS ORCHESTRA
| | | | |
|---|---|---|---|
| 67 | Coral Q 72497 | Green Onions/Hang On Sloopy | 15 |

*(see also Joe Williams, Jackie Wilson, Lester Young, Ella Fitzgerald)*

## BASIL
| | | | |
|---|---|---|---|
| 87 | Serpent Sounds CBH 1561 | Come Dance With Me/Instrumental Version (12") | 20 |

## BASKIN & COPPERFIELD
| | | | |
|---|---|---|---|
| 70 | Decca F 13053 | The Long And Winding Road/Beautiful Blue Eyes | 7 |
| 70 | Decca F 23079 | I Never See The Sun/Stranger On The Ground | 7 |

## BASKING SHARKS
| | | | |
|---|---|---|---|
| 83 | Fin FON 01 | Diamond Age/New Industry (p/s, insert) | 15 |
| 83 | SRR SRR 0013 | THRILL OF THE GAME EP | 20 |
| 83 | RS 001 | SHARK ISLAND (LP) | 35 |

## BILLY BASS
| | | | |
|---|---|---|---|
| 69 | Pama PM 761 | I Need Your Love So Bad/I'm Coming To | 50 |

MINT VALUE £

## FONTELLA BASS

| Year | Label/Cat No | Title | Value |
|---|---|---|---|
| 65 | Chess CRS 8007 | Don't Mess Up A Good Thing (with Bobby McClure)/OLIVER SAIN: Jerk Loose | 30 |
| 65 | Chess CRS 8007 | Don't Mess Up A Good Thing/Baby What You Want Me To Do (different B-side, existence unconfirmed) | 0 |
| 65 | Chess CRS 8023 | Rescue Me/Soul Of The Man | 15 |
| 65 | Chess CRS 8023 | Rescue Me/Soul Of The Man (DJ Copy) | 70 |
| 66 | Chess CRS 8027 | Recovery/Leave It In The Hands Of Love | 20 |
| 66 | Chess CRS 8027 | Recovery/Leave It In The Hands Of Love (DJ Copy) | 35 |
| 66 | Chess CRS 8032 | I Can't Rest/Surrender | 30 |
| 66 | Chess CRS 8032 | I Can't Rest/Surrender (DJ Copy) | 80 |
| 66 | Chess CRS 8042 | Safe And Sound/You'll Never Know | 10 |
| 66 | Chess CRS 8042 | Safe And Sound/You'll Never Know (DJ Copy) | 40 |
| 69 | Chess CRS 8090 | Rescue Me/I Can't Rest | 10 |
| 69 | Chess CRS 8090 | Rescue Me/I Can't Rest (DJ Copy) | 25 |
| 71 | Chess CRS 8023 | Rescue Me/Soul Of The Man (reissue) | 5 |
| 72 | Mojo 2092 032 | Who You Gonna Blame/Hold On This Time | 5 |
| 72 | Mojo 2092 045 | I Want Everyone To Know/I Need To Be Loved | 5 |
| 66 | Chess CRE 6015 | FONTELLA'S HITS (EP) | 25 |
| 66 | Chess CRE 6020 | I CAN'T REST (EP) | 50 |
| 66 | Chess CRE 6025 | FONTELLA BASS AND BOBBY McCLURE (EP) | 40 |
| 66 | Chess CRL 4517 | THE NEW LOOK (LP) | 60 |

## JEWEL BASS

| Year | Label/Cat No | Title | Value |
|---|---|---|---|
| 76 | Special Agent 9001 | Overflowing (for You)/I Don't Trust Myself | 8 |

## BAS-SHEVA

| Year | Label/Cat No | Title | Value |
|---|---|---|---|
| 55 | Capitol CL 14218 | Flame Of Love/I Just Wanna Be Your Loving Baby | 10 |

## BASTILLE

| Year | Label/Cat No | Title | Value |
|---|---|---|---|
| 11 | Young & Lost Club | Flaws/Icarus | 10 |
| 12 | Virgin VS 2037 | Overjoyed/Sleepsong | 8 |
| 12 | Virgin VS 2041 | Bad Blood/Hunt (Demo) | 8 |

## JOE BATAAN

| Year | Label/Cat No | Title | Value |
|---|---|---|---|
| 75 | RCA RCA 2457 | Latin Strut/Peace, Friendship And Solidarity | 12 |
| 75 | RCA RCA 2553 | The Bottle/When You're Down | 12 |
| 69 | London HA/SH 8386 | RIOT! (LP) | 40 |

## JUNE BATEMAN

| Year | Label/Cat No | Title | Value |
|---|---|---|---|
| 64 | Sue WI 347 | I Don't Wanna/NOBLE 'THIN MAN' WATTS & HIS BAND: Noble's Theme | 75 |

## COLLIN BATES TRIO

| Year | Label/Cat No | Title | Value |
|---|---|---|---|
| 68 | Fontana SFJL 913 | BREW (LP) | 200 |

## MARTYN BATES

| Year | Label/Cat No | Title | Value |
|---|---|---|---|
| 82 | Cherry Red TRED 38 | LETTERS WRITTEN (10" EP) | 10 |

*(see also Eyeless In Gaza)*

## BAT FOR LASHES

| Year | Label/Cat No | Title | Value |
|---|---|---|---|
| 04 | No label or Cat. No. | WHO STOLE PETRETSKI'S THUNDER? (CD-R tour only EP, hand-drawn cover) | 35 |
| 06 | Echo ECS 185 | The Wizard/I Saw A Light (demo) | 12 |
| 06 | Echo ECS 188 | Trophy/How! (p/s) | 5 |
| 11 | Parlophone R6836 | Let's Get Lost (with Beck)/Dark Time (demo) | 10 |
| 09 | Echo 6930191 | TWO SUNS (LP, gatefold, inner) | 20 |
| 12 | Echo/Parlophone P915 5402 | THE HAUNTED MAN (2-LP, with CD) | 20 |
| 12 | Echo/Parlophone P915 5402 | THE HAUNTED MAN (2-LP, white vinyl with CD) | 25 |

*(see also Sexwitch)*

## BATHORY

| Year | Label/Cat No | Title | Value |
|---|---|---|---|
| 84 | Under One Flag FLAG 8 | BATHORY (LP) | 20 |
| 85 | Under One Flag FLAG 9 | THE RETURN... (LP, inner) | 40 |
| 87 | Under One Flag FLAG 11 | UNDER THE SIGN OF THE BLACK MARK (LP) | 20 |
| 88 | Under One Flag FLAG 26 | BLOOD FIRE DEATH (LP, gatefold sleeve, insert) | 30 |
| 88 | Under One Flag FLAG 26 P | BLOOD FIRE DEATH (LP, picture disc) | 35 |

## BATMAN THEME

| Year | Label/Cat No | Title | Value |
|---|---|---|---|
| 88 | Bam Caruso NRIC 107 | Batman Theme/Batman Theme (Instrumental Mix) (p/s) | 15 |

*(see also Jan & Dean)*

## STIV BATORS

| Year | Label/Cat No | Title | Value |
|---|---|---|---|
| 79 | London/Bomp HLZ 10575 | It's Cold Outside/The Last Year (p/s) | 15 |
| 03 | TRY 001 | King Of The Brats/Young Don't Cry (p/s) | 5 |

*(see also Dead Boys, Lords Of The New Church, Wanderers)*

## BATS

| Year | Label/Cat No | Title | Value |
|---|---|---|---|
| 64 | Columbia DB 7429 | Accept It/Lovers Lie Sleeping | 10 |
| 66 | Decca F 22534 | Listen To My Heart/Stop Don't Do It | 25 |
| 67 | Decca F 22568 | You Will Now, Won't You?/You Look Good Together | 25 |
| 67 | Decca F 22616 | Hard To Get Up In The Morning/Take Me As I Am | 10 |

## MIKE BATT

| Year | Label/Cat No | Title | Value |
|---|---|---|---|
| 68 | Liberty LBF 15093 | Mister Poem/Fading Yellow | 25 |
| 68 | Liberty LBF 15122 | I See Wonderful Things In You/Mary Goes Round | 25 |
| 69 | Liberty LBF 15210 | Your Mother Should Know/Suddenly | 20 |
| 75 | Epic EPC 3460 | Summertime City/Children Of The Storm | 5 |
| 70 | Midland Counties Ice Cream RMS1 | Liberate A Lolly | 10 |
| 77 | Epic A 3957 | Railway Hotel/The Ride To Agadir | 8 |
| 70 | Penny Farthing PAGS 534 | BATT TRACKS (LP) | 15 |

*(see also Hapshash & Coloured Coat, Anderson Harley & Batt, Mad Hatters)*

## BATTERED ORNAMENTS
| | | | |
|---|---|---|---|
| 70 | Harvest HAR 5013 | Goodbye We Loved You (Madly)/CHRIS SPEDDING: Rock'n'Roll Band | 25 |
| 69 | Harvest SHVL 758 | MANTLE-PIECE (LP, gatefold sleeve, no EMI box on label) | 500 |
| 82 | GI WAX 3 | MANTLE-PIECE (LP, reissue) | 20 |

*(see also Pete Brown & His Battered Ornaments, Chris Spedding, People Band)*

## BATTERSEA
| | | | |
|---|---|---|---|
| 78 | Rak RK 1013 | Born And Bred/Summer Rain (no p/s) | 15 |

## SKIP BATTIN
| | | | |
|---|---|---|---|
| 72 | Signpost SGP 756 | Central Park/St. Louis Browns | 6 |
| 72 | Signpost SG 4255 | SKIP (LP) | 18 |

*(see also Skip & Flip, Byrds, Flying Burrito Brothers, Evergreen Blueshoes)*

## LUCIO BATTISTI
| | | | |
|---|---|---|---|
| 77 | RCA PB 6129 | To Feel In Love/Only (demo) | 30 |
| 79 | RCA PB 9439 | Baby It's You/Lady (demo) | 50 |

## BATTLEAXE
| | | | |
|---|---|---|---|
| 82 | Guardian GRC 132 | Burn This Town/Battleaxe (no p/s) | 40 |
| 83 | Music For Nations MFN8 | BURN THIS TOWN (LP) | 15 |

## BATWING CHAPS
| | | | |
|---|---|---|---|
| 84 | Full Moon FM 01 | I Won't Change/Crave (p/s) | 6 |

## BAUHAUS
| | | | |
|---|---|---|---|
| 79 | Small Wonder TEENY 2 | Bela Lugosi's Dead/Boys/Dark Entries (not listed on sleeve) (12") | 10 |
| 79 | Small Wonder TEENY 2 | Bela Lugosi's Dead/Boys/Dark Entries (12", p/s, white vinyl, 5000 only) | 25 |
| 80 | Axis AXIS 3 | Dark Entries/Untitled (brown label, p/s) | 18 |
| 80 | Axis AD 3 | Dark Entries/Untitled (blue label, p/s) | 8 |
| 80 | 4AD BEG 37 | Dark Entries/Untitled (p/s, blue 4AD labels, lists BEG 37 on sleeve) | 10 |
| 80 | Beggars Banquet BEG 37 | Dark Entries/Untitled (p/s, red Beggars Banquet labels) | 10 |
| 80 | 4AD AD 7 | Terror Couple Kill Colonel/Scopes/Terror Couple Kill Colonel II (version) (mispressed with 'rejected' version of third track, p/s) | 15 |
| 81 | Beggars Banquet BEG 54T | Kick In The Eye/Satori (12", white label in stamped plain sleeve) | 15 |
| 81 | Beggars Banquet BEG 59 | The Passion Of Lovers/1.2.3.4 (card sleeve with lyric insert) | 6 |
| 81 | Beggars Banquet BEG 59 | The Passion Of Lovers/1.2.3.4 (paper sleeve, mispressing with A side label on both sides) | 8 |
| 82 | Beggars Banquet BEG 79 | Spirit/Terror Couple Kill Colonel (live in Paris) (Beggars logo labels and sleeve titles) | 5 |
| 82 | Beggars Banquet AD 3 | Dark Entries/Untitled (reissue, 'nudes wrestling' label, no contact address on p/s) | 8 |
| 82 | Beggars Banquet BEG 79 | Spirit/Terror Couple Kill Colonel (live in Paris) (Beggars logo labels and no sleeve titles) | 7 |
| 82 | Beggars Banquet BEG 74T | Kick In The Eye/Poison Pen/Harry/Earwax (12" mispressing, p/s, matrix: A1) | 25 |
| 82 | Beggars Banquet BEG 79 | Spirit/Terror Couple Kill Colonel (live) (p/s, mispressed, A-side plays Gary Numan's "We Take Mystery [To Bed]") | 25 |
| 82 | Lyntone LYN 12106 | A God In An Alcove (Early Version) (hard vinyl test pressing) | 15 |
| 82 | Beggars Banquet BEG 83 | Ziggy Stardust/Third Uncle (original glossy card sleeve) | 5 |
| 82 | Beggars Banquet BEG 83 | Ziggy Stardust/Third Uncle (original glossy card sleeve, signed by band for record company staff) | 30 |
| 82 | Beggars Banquet BEG 83 | Ziggy Stardust/Third Uncle (Beggars Banquet labels no picture sleeve) | 8 |
| 82 | Beggars Banquet BEG 83T | Ziggy Stardust/Party Of The First Part/Third Uncle/Waiting For The Man, 12" p/s, with stickered poster p/s) | 8 |
| 82 | Beggars Banquet BEG 83T | Ziggy Stardust/Party Of The First Part/Third Uncle/Waiting For The Man, (12", repressing in thin spineless sleeve with reversed artwork) | 10 |
| 82 | Beggars Banquet BEG 83T | Ziggy Stardust/Party Of The First Part/Third Uncle/Waiting For The Man, 12" glossy card p/s, no poster, signed for record company staff) | 30 |
| 82 | Beggars Banquet BH 1 | SATORI IN PARIS : Hair Of The Dog (live in Paris)/Double Dare (live in Paris) | 5 |
| 83 | Lyntone LYN 13777/8 | The Sanity Assassin/Spirit In The Sky (fan club freebie, 320 only) | 300 |
| 88 | Small Wonder TEENY 2P | Bela Lugosi's Dead/Boys/Dark Entries (12", reissue, luminous picture disc in PVC sleeve) | 25 |
| 89 | Small Wonder TEENY 2 | Bela Lugosi's Dead/Boys/Dark Entries (12", reissue, green vinyl, p/s) | 25 |
| 89 | Small Wonder TEENY 2 | Bela Lugosi's Dead/Boys/Dark Entries (12", reissue, blue vinyl, p/s) | 25 |
| 90 | Beggars Banquet BEG 74T | Kick In The Eye/In Fear Of Dub/Harry/Earwax (Searching For Satori EP) (12", reissue, black sleeve lettering, green/gold labels) | 15 |
| 91 | Small Wonder TEENY 2 | Bela Lugosi's Dead/Boys/Dark Entries (12", reissue, pink, clear or purple vinyl, in corresponding coloured p/s) | 25 |
| 80 | 4AD CAD 13 | IN THE FLAT FIELD (LP, 8 Hogarth Road address on rear sleeve) | 20 |
| 81 | Beggars Banquet BEGA 29 | MASK (LP, gatefold, group photo inside, Beggars Banquet labels) | 15 |
| 82 | Beggars Banquet BEGA 38 | PRESS THE EJECT AND GIVE ME THE TAPE (LP, with bonus 45 "Satori In Paris" [BH 1] & poster) | 20 |
| 82 | Beggars Banquet BEGA 42 | THE SKY'S GONE OUT (LP, with bonus LP "Press The Eject And Give Me The Tape" [BEGA 38] inner sleeves & stickered sleeve) | 18 |
| 83 | Beggars Banquet BEGA 45P | BURNING FROM THE INSIDE (LP, picture disc) | 20 |
| 83 | Beggars Banquet BEGA 45P | BURNING FROM THE INSIDE (LP, with 5" die cut and BEGA 45P cat number on sleeve) | 15 |
| 85 | Beggars Banquet BEGA 64 | 1979-1983 (2-LP, with inserts, 50,000 copies, numbered) | 25 |

*(see also Sinister Ducks, Tones On Tail, David J, Bubblemen)*

## ART BAXTER
| | | | |
|---|---|---|---|
| 57 | Philips BBR 8107 | ROCK YOU SINNERS (10" LP) | 125 |

## DAVID BAXTER
| | | | |
|---|---|---|---|
| 70 | Reflection REFL 9 | GOODBYE DAVE (LP, white/brown label) | 100 |

*(see also David Lewis)*

## LES BAXTER & HIS ORCHESTRA
| | | | |
|---|---|---|---|
| 55 | Capitol CL 14239 | Earth Angel/Happy Baby (as Les Baxter & Bombers) | 30 |
| 55 | Capitol CL 14249 | I Ain't Mad At You (with Bombers)/Blue Mirage | 5 |
| 55 | Capitol CL 14257 | Unchained Melody/Blue Star (The Medic Theme) | 5 |

*(see also Leonard Pennario)*

## B.B. BLUNDER
| | | | |
|---|---|---|---|
| 71 | United Artists UP 35203 | Sticky Living/Rocky Yagbatee Yagbag | 10 |

# BBC RADIOPHONIC WORKSHOP/PETER HOWELL

MINT VALUE £

| 71 | United Artists UP 35204 | Little Boy/10,000 Miles | 20 |
| 71 | United Artists UAG 29156 | WORKERS' PLAYTIME (LP, gatefold sleeve) | 60 |

*(see also Reg King & B.B. Blunder, Action, Julie Driscoll Brian Auger & Trinity, Kevin Westlake, Mark Charig, Blossom Toes)*

## BBC RADIOPHONIC WORKSHOP/PETER HOWELL

| 64 | Decca F 11837 | Doctor Who/BRENDA & JOHNNY: This Can't Be Love (unboxed Decca logo) | 30 |
| 72 | Decca F 11837 | Doctor Who/BRENDA & JOHNNY: This Can't Be Love (reissue, boxed logo) | 10 |
| 73 | BBC RESL 11 | Doctor Who/Reg (blue label, credits 'Delia Derbyshire', 'TARDIS' p/s) | 10 |
| 73 | BBC RESL 11 | Doctor Who/Reg (white label, credits 'Delia Derbyshire', 'TARDIS' p/s) | 6 |
| 76 | BBC RESL 11 | Doctor Who/Reg (reissue, no p/s, silver label) | 6 |
| 78 | BBC RESL 11 | Doctor Who/Reg (2nd reissue, in 'TARDIS' p/s, blue label, white rim) | 6 |
| 80 | PRT RESL 80 | Doctor Who/The Astronauts ('Tom Baker' p/s, as 'Peter Howell & BBC Radiophonic Workshop') | 8 |
| 82 | PRT RESL 80 | Doctor Who/The Astronauts (reissue, 'Peter Davison' p/s) | 8 |
| 84 | PRT RESL 80 | Doctor Who/The Astronauts (2nd reissue, 'Colin Baker' p/s) | 5 |
| 68 | BBC Enterprises REC 25M | BBC RADIOPHONIC WORKSHOP (LP) | 45 |
| 72 | BBC REC 93S | TEST CARD MUSIC (LP) | 25 |
| 73 | BBC RED 93 S | FOURTH DIMENSION (LP) | 15 |
| 76 | BBC REC 225 | OUT OF THIS WORLD (LP) | 15 |
| 70 | BBC REC 25 M | BBC RADIOPHONIC MUSIC - WORK BY DELIA DERBYSHIRE (LP) | 30 |
| 78 | BBC REC 307 | THROUGH A GLASS DARKLY (LP) | 30 |
| 78 | BBC REC 316 | DOCTOR WHO SOUND EFFECTS No. 19 (LP) | 18 |
| 83 | BBC REH 462 | DR. WHO - THE MUSIC (LP) | 15 |
| 04 | Rephlex 147 LP | MUSIC FROM THE BBC RADIOPHONIC WORKSHOP (4 x 10") | 30 |

*(see also Dr. Who, Jon Pertwee, Ray Cathode, Radiophonic Workshop, Ithaca, Alice Through The Looking Glass, Agincourt, Blossom Toes, Dudley Simpson & Brian Hodgson)*

## BEACH BOYS

### SINGLES

| 62 | Capitol CL 15273 | Surfin' Safari/409 | 50 |
| 63 | Capitol CL 15285 | Ten Little Indians/County Fair | 100 |
| 63 | Capitol CL 15305 | Surfin' USA/Shut Down | 20 |
| 64 | Capitol CL 15339 | Fun, Fun, Fun/Why Do Fools Fall In Love | 25 |
| 64 | Capitol CL 15350 | I Get Around/Don't Worry Baby (First pressing with purple labels) | 8 |
| 64 | Capitol CL 15361 | When I Grow Up (To Be A Man)/She Knows Me Too Well | 8 |
| 65 | Capitol CL 15370 | Dance, Dance, Dance/The Warmth Of The Sun | 10 |
| 65 | Capitol CL 15384 | All Summer Long/Do You Wanna Dance | 10 |
| 65 | Capitol CL 15392 | Help Me Rhonda/Kiss Me Baby | 10 |
| 65 | Capitol CL 15409 | California Girls/Let Him Run Wild | 10 |
| 65 | Capitol CL 15425 | The Little Girl I Once Knew/There's No Other (Like My Baby) | 15 |
| 66 | Capitol CL 15432 | Barbara Ann/Girl Don't Tell Me | 7 |
| 66 | Capitol CL 15441 | Sloop John B/You're So Good To Me | 8 |
| 66 | Capitol CL 15459 | God Only Knows/Wouldn't It Be Nice | 7 |
| 66 | Capitol CL 15475 | Good Vibrations/Wendy | 6 |
| 67 | Capitol CL 15502 | Then I Kissed Her/Mountain Of Love | 7 |
| 67 | Capitol CL 15510 | Heroes And Villains/You're Welcome | 7 |
| 67 | Capitol CL 15521 | Wild Honey/Wind Chimes | 8 |
| 68 | Capitol CL 15527 | Darlin'/Country Air | 6 |
| 68 | Capitol CL 15545 | Friends/Little Bird | 6 |
| 68 | Capitol CL 15554 | Do It Again/Wake The World | 6 |
| 68 | Capitol CL 15572 | Bluebirds Over The Mountain/Never Learn Not To Love | 6 |
| 69 | Capitol CL 15598 | Break Away/Celebrate The News | 5 |
| 70 | Capitol CL 15640 | Cottonfields/The Nearest Faraway Place (black label) | 5 |
| 70 | Stateside SS 2181 | Tears In The Morning/It's About Time | 5 |
| 71 | Stateside SS 2190 | Long Promised Road/Deirdre | 6 |
| 71 | Stateside SS 2194 | Don't Go Near The Water/Student Demonstration Time (demos in p/s £20) | 6 |
| 72 | Reprise K 14173 | You Need A Mess Of Help To Stand Alone/Cuddle Up (p/s) | 10 |
| 72 | Capitol CMS 1 | Wouldn't It Be Nice/Fun Fun Fun/California Girls (printed sleeve) | 6 |
| 72 | Capitol CMS 2 | Barbara Ann/Dance Dance Dance/You're So Good To Me (printed sleeve) | 6 |
| 74 | Reprise K 14346 | California Saga: California/Sail On Sailor/Marcella/I'm The Pied Piper (printed sleeve) | 5 |
| 76 | Reprise K 14411 | Child Of Winter/Susie Cincinnati (withdrawn) | 125 |
| 76 | Reprise K 14440 | Rock And Roll Music/The T.M. Song (p/s) | 5 |
| 76 | EMI PSR 402 | Commercial for "20 Golden Greats"/Good Vibrations/Carl Wilson Interview (promo) | 10 |
| 77 | Reprise K 14481 | Mona/Rock And Roll Music/Sail On Sailor/Marcella (p/s) | 5 |
| 77 | Capitol CL 15954 | Little Saint Nick/Little Saint Nick (Instr.)/Santa Claus Is Coming To Town | 7 |
| 78 | Capitol CL 15969 | Little Deuce Coupe/SUNRAYS: I Live For The Sun/SUPERSTOCKS: Hot Rod High (p/s) | 5 |
| 79 | Caribou 12-7204 | Here Comes The Night/(Disco Version)/Baby Blue (12", p/s, blue vinyl) | 10 |
| 79 | Capitol BBP 26 | SINGLES COLLECTION (26 x 7" box set) | 50 |

### EPs

| 63 | Capitol EAP 1-20540 | SURFIN' USA | 30 |
| 64 | Capitol EAP 1-20603 | FUN, FUN, FUN | 30 |
| 64 | Capitol EAP 5267 | FOUR BY THE BEACH BOYS | 25 |
| 64 | Capitol EAP 4-2198 | BEACH BOYS CONCERT | 25 |
| 64 | Capitol EAP 1-20781 | THE BEACH BOYS HITS | 15 |
| 67 | Capitol EAP 6-2458 | GOD ONLY KNOWS | 30 |

### ALBUMS

| 62 | Capitol T 1808 | SURFIN' SAFARI (mono only) | 50 |
| 63 | Capitol T 1890 | SURFIN' USA (mono) | 35 |
| 63 | Capitol (S)T 1890 | SURFIN' USA (stereo) | 50 |
| 63 | Capitol ST 1981 | SURFER GIRL (mono) | 35 |

| | | | |
|---|---|---|---|
| 63 | Capitol ST 1981 | SURFER GIRL (stereo) | 50 |
| 63 | Capitol ST 1998 | LITTLE DEUCE COUPE (mono) | 30 |
| 63 | Capitol ST 1998 | LITTLE DEUCE COUPE (stereo) | 50 |
| 63 | Capitol T 2027 | SHUT DOWN VOLUME 2 (mono) | 30 |
| 63 | Capitol ST 2027 | SHUT DOWN VOLUME 2 (stereo) | 50 |
| 64 | Capitol T 2164 | THE BEACH BOYS' CHRISTMAS ALBUM (mono) | 35 |
| 64 | Capitol ST 2164 | THE BEACH BOYS' CHRISTMAS ALBUM (stereo) | 40 |
| 64 | Capitol T 2198 | BEACH BOYS CONCERT (mono) | 20 |
| 64 | Capitol ST 2198 | BEACH BOYS CONCERT (stereo) | 25 |
| 64 | Capitol T 2110 | ALL SUMMER LONG (mono) | 30 |
| 64 | Capitol ST 2110 | ALL SUMMER LONG (stereo) | 40 |
| 65 | Capitol T 2269 | BEACH BOYS TODAY! (mono) | 25 |
| 65 | Capitol ST 2269 | BEACH BOYS TODAY! (stereo) | 30 |
| 65 | Capitol ST 2354 | SUMMER DAYS (AND SUMMER NIGHTS!!) (mono) | 25 |
| 65 | Capitol ST 2354 | SUMMER DAYS (AND SUMMER NIGHTS!!) (stereo) | 30 |
| 65 | Capitol (S)T 2398 | BEACH BOYS' PARTY! (mono) | 20 |
| 65 | Capitol (S)T 2398 | BEACH BOYS' PARTY! (stereo) | 25 |
| 66 | Capitol T 2458 | PET SOUNDS (mono) | 50 |
| 66 | Capitol ST 2458 | PET SOUNDS (stereo) | 70 |
| 66 | Capitol T 20856 | THE BEST OF THE BEACH BOYS (mono) | 15 |
| 66 | Capitol ST 20856 | THE BEST OF THE BEACH BOYS (sterero) | 18 |
| 67 | Capitol ST 20956/T 20956 | THE BEST OF THE BEACH BOYS VOL. 2 (stereo or mono) | 15 |
| 67 | Capitol T 9001 | SMILEY SMILE (mono) | 45 |
| 67 | Capitol ST 9001 | SMILEY SMILE (stereo) | 35 |
| 68 | Capitol ST 2859 | WILD HONEY (mono) | 45 |
| 68 | Capitol ST 2859 | WILD HONEY (stereo) | 25 |
| 68 | Capitol T 2895 | FRIENDS (mono) | 30 |
| 68 | Capitol (S)T 2895 | FRIENDS (stereo) | 20 |
| 69 | Capitol T 21142 | THE BEST OF THE BEACH BOYS VOL. 3 (mono) | 15 |
| 69 | Capitol E-T 133 | 20/20 (mono, gatefold sleeve) | 20 |
| 69 | Capitol E-ST 133 | 20/20 (stereo, gatefold sleeve) | 18 |

*(The above LPs were originally issued with flipback sleeves & rainbow-rim black labels; later yellow label copies from 1969 and 70s orange label pressings - in stereo - are worth up to half the value.)*

| | | | |
|---|---|---|---|
| 70 | Stateside SSLA 8251 | SUNFLOWER (gatefold sleeve) | 22 |
| 71 | Stateside SSL 10313 | SURF'S UP (textured sleeve, with gatefold insert) | 20 |
| 71 | Stateside SSL 10313 | SURF'S UP (textured sleeve, without gatefold insert) | 15 |
| 73 | Reprise/Brother K 54008 | HOLLAND (with insert & bonus EP "Mount Vernon And Fairway" [K 54008/7] in p/s) | 30 |
| 75 | Capitols ST 2458 | PET SOUNDS (LP, reissue, orange label, stereo) | 15 |
| 81 | WRC SM 651-657 | THE CAPITOL YEARS (7-LP box set) | 25 |
| 97 | EMI LPCENT2 | PET SOUNDS (LP, reissue, EMI 100 Centenary, stickered sleeve) | 30 |
| 99 | Simply Vinyl SVLP 149 | PET SOUNDS (LP, reissue, 180gm vinyl) | 20 |
| 00 | Simply Vinyl SVLP 219 | SMILEY SMILE (LP, reissue 180gm vinyl) | 15 |

*(see also Brian Wilson, Dennis Wilson, Bruce Johnston, Legendary Masked Surfers, American Spring, Annette,s, California Music, Rutles, Moon, Murry Wilson, Mike Love, Survivors)*

## BEACH HOUSE

| | | | |
|---|---|---|---|
| 10 | Bella Union Bellav 229 | Norway/Baby (red vinyl, p/s) | 12 |
| 12 | Bella Union Bellav 338 | Lazuli/Equal Mind (blue/purple vinyl) | 6 |
| 10 | Bella Union BELLAV 225 | TEEN DREAM (2-LP, DVD, CD) | 20 |
| 12 | Bella Union BELLAV 144 | BEACH HOUSE (LP, white vinyl, with CD) | 15 |
| 12 | Bella Union BELLAV 160 | DEVOTION (LP, blue vinyl with CD) | 15 |
| 12 | Bella Union BELLAV 334 | BLOOM (2-LP with CD) | 20 |
| 15 | Bella Union BELLA 500VX | DEPRESSION CHERRY (LP, white vinyl, CD, felt cover) | 20 |
| 15 | Bella Union BELLA 500V | DEPRESSION CHERRY (LP, clear vinyl, 200 only) | 30 |

## BEACHCOMBER

| | | | |
|---|---|---|---|
| 70 | Parlophone R 5850 | Surfin' Soul/Nothing To Say | 10 |

## BEACHCOMBERS

| | | | |
|---|---|---|---|
| 63 | Columbia DB 7124 | Mad Goose/You Can't Sit Down | 20 |
| 64 | Columbia DB 7200 | Night Train/The Keel Row | 20 |

*(see also Pat Wayne)*

## BEACH-NUTS

| | | | |
|---|---|---|---|
| 65 | London HL 9988 | Out In The Sun (Hey-O)/Someday Soon | 30 |

*(see also Angels, Strangeloves)*

## BEACON STREET UNION

| | | | |
|---|---|---|---|
| 68 | MGM MGM 1416 | Blue Suede Shoes/Four Hundred And Five | 25 |
| 68 | MGM MGM-C(S) 8069 | THE EYES OF THE BEACON STREET UNION (LP) | 100 |

## BEADS

| | | | |
|---|---|---|---|
| 71 | Decca F13244 | Eeo Eio/Sweetie Peetie | 8 |

## BEADY EYE

| | | | |
|---|---|---|---|
| 10 | Beady Eye EYE 1 | Bring The Light/Sons Of The Stage (4,000 only) | 15 |
| 10 | Beady Eye EYE 3 | Four Letter Word/World Outside My Room (4,000 only) | 18 |
| 11 | Beady Eye EYE 4 | The Roller/Two Of A Kind (heavyweight vinyl sold via website, numbered) | 8 |
| 11 | Columbia BOX 1 | SINGLES BOX SET (5 x 7" in special box) | 40 |
| 11 | Columbia 88883721371 | BE (2-LP, pre-order version with poster, signed) | 50 |
| 11 | Columbia 88883721371 | BE (CD, pre-order version, signed) | 40 |

## BEAK>

| | | | |
|---|---|---|---|
| 10 | Wulfstan Wulfstan 01 | Wulfstan/Ham Green (live)/Wulfstan (live)/Blagdon Lake (live) (12") | 10 |
| 12 | Invada INV 112 | Mono/Kenn (red vinyl, 300 only) | 8 |
| 15 | Invada INV 149 | BEAK> V KAEB EP (12" blue vinyl) | 12 |
| 09 | Invada INV 100LP | BEAK> (2-LP, white vinyl) | 25 |

MINT VALUE £

| 10 | Invada INV 100LP | BEAK> (2-LP, blue vinyl repressing) | 20 |
| 10 | Invada (No cat no) | BEAK> (2-CD in 12" pizza box, 250 copies) | 40 |
| 12 | Invada INV 107LP | >> (2-LP, white signed cover, tour edition, 100 only) | 40 |
| 12 | Invada INV 107LP | >> (2-LP, orange vinyl repressing) | 20 |
| 12 | Invada INV 100LP | BEAK> (2-LP, red vinyl repressing) | 20 |
| 12 | Invada INV 107LP | >> (2-LP) | 20 |
| 14 | Invada INV 137LPCOL | + (LP, orange and white swirl vinyl or black and white swirl vinyl) | 18 |

*(see also Portishead)*

## BEAKS
| 79 | Alien ALIX 004 | Doktor X/Intellectual (p/s) | 12 |

## CARL BEAN
| 78 | Motown TMG 1108 | I Was Born This Way/Instrumental | 6 |
| 78 | Tamla Motown TMG 1108-12 | I Was Born This Way (Remix)/Instrumental (12") | 12 |

## GEORGE BEAN
| 63 | Decca F 11762 | Secret Love/Lonely Weekends | 25 |
| 65 | Decca F 12228 | She Belongs To Me/Why Must They Criticise? (as George Bean & Runners) | 15 |
| 67 | CBS 2801 | The Candy Shop Is Closed/Smile From Sequin | 25 |
| 68 | CBS 3374 | Bring Back Lovin'/Floatin' | 35 |

*(see also Trifle, Bean & Loopy's Lot)*

## BEAN & LOOPY'S LOT
| 66 | Parlophone R 5458 | A Stitch In Time/Haywire | 50 |

*(see also Alan Bown Set)*

## BEANO
| 75 | Deram DM 427 | Little Cinderalla/Bye And Bye | 7 |
| 77 | Decca F 13690 | Everybody Knows/Clowns Painted Smile (p/s) | 6 |

## BEAR
| 68 | Verve FTS 3059 | GREETINGS CHILDREN OF PARADISE (LP) | 35 |

## DEAN BEARD & CREW CATS
| 57 | London HLE 8463 | Rakin' And Scrapin'/On My Mind Again | 300 |
| 57 | London HLE 8463 | Rakin' And Scrapin'/On My Mind Again (78) | 20 |

## BEARDED LADY
| 74 | Young Blood YB 1018 | Rock Star/Country Lady | 15 |

## BEARS
| 79 | Good Vibrations Intl. GVI 1 | Insane/Decisions (p/s) | 15 |
| 79 | Waldo's JS 001 | On Me/Wot's Up Mate (p/s, various designs, with insert) | 15 |
| 86 | Tigerbeat GROWL 001 | INSANE!! (LP) | 20 |

## BEARZ
| 80 | Axis AXIS 2 | She's My Girl/Girls Will Do (p/s) | 20 |
| 84 | Occult OCC 1 | Darwin/Julie (p/s) | 12 |

## BEAS
| 68 | Pama PM 744 | Dr. Goldfoot And His Bikini Machine/Where Do I Go From You | 50 |

## BEAST
| 83 | I.D. EYE 3 | New Moone/Guardian (p/s, insert) | 5 |
| 83 | I.D. EYE T3 | New Moone/Guardian (12". p/s) | 10 |

*(see also the Cramps)*

## BEASTIE BOYS
| 86 | Def Jam A 7055 | Hold It, Now Hit It/Acapulco (p/s) | 5 |
| 86 | Def Jam TA 7055 | Hold It, Now Hit It/Acapulco (12", p/s) | 10 |
| 86 | Def Jam 650 114 7 | She's On It/Slow'n'Low (p/s with 3 badges) | 12 |
| 86 | Def Jam 650 114 6 | She's On It/Slow'n'Low/Hold On, Now Hit It (12", p/s) | 10 |
| 87 | Def Jam 650 169 7 | It's The New Style/Paul Revere (p/s) | 5 |
| 87 | Def Jam 650 169 6 | It's The New Style/It's The New Style (Instrumental)/Paul Revere/ Paul Revere (Instrumental) (12", p/s) | 10 |
| 87 | Def Jam 650 418 6 | (You Gotta) Fight For Your Right (To Party)/Time To Get Ill (12", p/s) | 10 |
| 87 | Def Jam BEASTP 1 | No Sleep Till Brooklyn/Posse In Effect (plane-shaped picture disc) | 25 |
| 87 | Def Jam BEASTT 1 | No Sleep Till Brooklyn/Posse In Effect (12", p/s) | 10 |
| 89 | Capitol 12CL 540 | HEY LADIES (LOVE AMERICAN STYLE EP) (12", p/s) | 15 |
| 94 | Capitol CL 716 | Get It Together/Sabotage/Dope Little Song (green vinyl, p/s) | 6 |
| 94 | Capitol 10CL716 | Get It Together/(Buck Wild Remix)/(Intrumental)/Sabotage (10" p/s) | 8 |
| 94 | Capitol 7243 8 8173476 | Sure Shot/Mullet Head/Sure Shot (Caldato Mix) (red vinyl, p/s) | 6 |
| 94 | Capitol 10CL726 | Sure Shot/Mullet Head/Sure Shot (Caldato Mix) (10" p/s) | 10 |
| 87 | Def Jam 450 062 1 | LICENSED TO ILL (LP, with poster) | 22 |
| 89 | Capitol EST2102 | PAUL'S BOUTIQUE (LP) | 20 |
| 92 | Grand Royal EST 2171 | CHECK YOUR HEAD (2-LP) | 25 |
| 94 | Grand Royal GR006 | ILL COMMUNICATION (2-LP) | 20 |
| 98 | Grand Royal GR062 | HELLO NASTY (2-LP, orange vinyl) | 35 |
| 04 | Capitol 7243 4 73397 | TO THE 5 BOROUGHS (2-LP) | 20 |

## BEASTS IN CAGES
| 81 | Fresh 34 | My Coo Ca Choo/Sandcastles (p/s) | 8 |

*(see also Craze)*

## BEAT
| 79 | 2-Tone CHS TT 6 | Tears Of A Clown/Ranking Full Stop (paper label, company sleeve) | 8 |
| 79 | 2-Tone TT 6 | Tears Of A Clown/Ranking Full Stop (later pressing, moulded label, company sleeve) | 5 |
| 80 | Go-Feet BEAT 001 | JUST CAN'T STOP IT (LP, with inner) | 15 |

*(see also Fine Young Cannibals)* .

## NICKY BEAT & THE BEATNICKS
| 78 | Rigid IS BEAT 1033 | I Can Hear Voices/Split Second Love/Starstruck (oversized p/s, poster insert) | 150 |

## BEAT BOYS
63   Decca F 11730     That's My Plan/Third Time Lucky..................................................................... 25

## BEAT BROTHERS
63   Polydor NH 52185     Nick Nack Hully Gully/Lantern Hully Gully ..................................................... 25

*(see also Tony Sheridan & Beat Brothers, Bobby Patrick Big Six)*

## BEAT CHICS
64   Decca F 12016     Skinny Minnie/Now I Know............................................................................. 25

## BEATHOVEN
88   CBS 651 626-7     Socrates/Socrates (withdrawn) ..................................................................... 30

## THE BEATLES

### SINGLES : 1962

*(Original Parlophone Beatles singles came in a variety of company sleeves which are referred to here as "Type A, B" etc. and are depicted in the illustrations at the back of this Guide. Dealers and collectors need to be aware of very specific label information for different pressings of Beatles singles and this is given either at the top of each year or in the body of the entry itself. Thus when it comes to these two pressings of their debut single issued in 1962 labels will have "The Parlophone Co. Ltd." in upper or lower case & "Recording first published 1962," label text, without "Sold in UK ...". Also, please note that all Beatles 7" singles issued before 1967 have a push-out centre: unless otherwise stated)*

62   Parlophone 45-R 4949     Love Me Do/P.S. I Love You (First pressing, red label, 'Ringo on drums & no tambourine' version; with or without "Made In Great Britain" credit, Matrix 7XCE 17144-1N/7XCE 17145-1N, in sleeve Type A, B or C) ...................................... 150

62   Parlophone 45-R 4949     Love Me Do/P.S. I Love You (First pressing, red label, 'Ringo on drums & no tambourine' version; label variation with "Made In Great Britain" credit on only one side, Matrix 7XCE 17144-1N/7XCE 17145-1N, in sleeve Type A, B, or C) ..................... 130

### SINGLES : 1963

*(with "The Parlophone Co. Ltd." in either upper or lower case & "Recording first published 1963" label text without "Sold in the UK..." unless otherwise stated)*

63   Parlophone 45-R 4983     Please Please Me/Ask Me Why (First pressing, red label; with or without "Made In Great Britain" credit, Matrix 7XCE 17217-1N/&XCE 17218-1N, in sleeve Type A, B or C) ......................................................................................................... 200

63   Parlophone R 5015     From Me To You/Thank You Girl (First pressing, Matrixes: 7XCE 17329 - 1N/7XCE 17330 - 1N, in Type 1 sleeve) ......................................................................... 15

63   Parlophone R 5055     She Loves You/I'll Get You (First pressing, Matrix numbers: 7XCE 17395-1N/7XCE 17396-1N in Type 1 sleeve) ......................................................................... 15

63   Parlophone R 5055     She Loves You/I'll Get You (First pressing, label variation with elongated "Northern Songs Ltd" and different typography for "7XCEE. 17395" and "Recording First Published 1963" Matrix numbers: 7XCE 17395-1N/7XCE 17396-1N, in Type 1 sleeve) ... 15

63   Parlophone R 5055     She Loves You/I'll Get You (First pressing, second label variation, smaller "She Love You" typography and "Northern Songs Ltd" on three lines; Matrix numbers: 7XCE 17395-1N/7XCE 17396-1N, in Type 1 sleeve).................................................... 15

63   Parlophone R 5084     I Want To Hold Your Hand/This Boy (First pressing, with "The Parlophone Co. Ltd" in upper-case only, Matrixes: 7XCE 17559-1N/7XCE 17560-1N, in Type 1 sleeve) ... 15

63   Parlophone R 5084     I Want To Hold Your Hand/This Boy (First pressing, label variation with "N.C.B." after "Northern Songs Mus Ltd" with "The Parlophone Co. Ltd" in upper-case only, Matrixes: 7XCE 17559-1N/7XCE 17560-1N) ................................................ 15

63   Parlophone R 4949     Love Me Do/P.S. I Love You (Second pressing, black label, with The Parlophone Co. Ltd in upper-lower case, matrix suffixed with '1N' indicating 'Ringo on drums & no tambourine' version)................................................................................ 150

63   Parlophone 45-R 4983     Please Please Me/Ask Me Why (Second pressing, black label, with "The Parlophone Co. Ltd" in upper-lower case, with "45" prefix, Matrixes: 7XCE 17217-1N/7XCE 17218-1N) ................................................................................. 20

63   Parlophone R 4983     Please Please Me/Ask Me Why (Third pressing, black label, with "The Parlophone Co. Ltd" in upper-lower case, without "45" prefix) ............................................. 20

### SINGLES : 1964

*(with "The Parlophone Co. Ltd." in either upper or lower case & "Recording first published 1964" label text with "Sold in the UK..." unless otherwise stated)*

64   Parlophone R 5114     Can't Buy Me Love/You Can't Do That (First pressing, with "The Parlophone Co. Ltd" in upper case, in Type 1 sleeve) ........................................................... 20

64   Parlophone R 5114     Can't Buy Me Love/You Can't Do That (First pressing with label variation, with "The Parlophone Co. Ltd" in upper case but "NCB" added after "Northern Songs") ............. 20

64   Parlophone R 5160     A Hard Day's Night/Things We Said Today (First pressing in Type 1B sleeve) ................ 20

64   Parlophone R 5200     I Feel Fine/She's A Woman (First pressing, with "The Parlophone Co. Ltd" in upper case, in Type 1B sleeve)......................................................................... 20

64   Parlophone R 5200     I Feel Fine/She's A Woman (First pressing, label variation, different "Northern Songs NCB" layout and "Recording First Published 1964" below Maxtrix number) ................ 20

64   Parlophone R 5084     I Want To Hold Your Hand/This Boy (Second pressing)............................................. 60

64   Parlophone R 4949     Love Me Do/P.S. I Love You (Third pressing, black label, with "The Parlophone Co. Ltd' in upper case, matrix suffixed with 1N' indicating 'Ringo on drums & no tambourine' version)........................................................................................... 80

*(with "The Parlophone Co. Ltd.", "Recording first published 1962" & Sold in UK ... label text)*

64   Parlophone R 4983     Please Please Me/Ask Me Why (Fourth pressing, with "The Parlophone Co. Ltd" in upper/lower case and "Sold in the U.K." label text)........................................... 80

### SINGLES : 1965

*(with "The Parlophone Co. Ltd." in upper case & "Sold in the UK...". 2nd and other pressings from 1965 have "The Gramophone Co. Ltd" unless otherwise stated)*

65   Parlophone DP 562     If I Fell/Tell Me Why (First U.K. pressing of 1964 export single, Matrixes: &XCE 17756-1N/7XCE 17757-1N, in Type 1B sleeve) .................................................. 100

65   Parlophone R 5265     Ticket To Ride/Yes It Is (First pressing, in Type 2 sleeve)....................................... 15

65   Parlophone R 5265     Ticket To Ride/Yes It Is (First pressing, label variation, smaller "Sold in U.K..." text, larger "Northern Songs NCB" type and (Lennon-McCartney) credit longer than "Ticket To Ride" song title)................................................................................. 15

65   Parlophone R 5265     Ticket To Ride/Yes It Is (First pressing, label variation, smaller "Northern Songs NCB" type, brackets around matrix number, larger "Trade Mark" and "Parlophone" logos and "T" in "Gt Britain" is in upper (T), not lower case (t)) ............................................. 15

65   Parlophone R 5305     Help!/I'm Down (First pressing, in Type 2 sleeve) ................................................. 20

65   Parlophone R 5305     Help!/I'm Down (Second pressing, with "The Gramophone Co Ltd" label text) ............. 15

65   Parlophone R 5389     We Can Work It Out/Day Tripper (First pressing, in Type 3 sleeve)............................. 20

65   Parlophone R 5389     We Can Work It Out/Day Tripper (Second pressing, with "The Gramophone Co Ltd" label text)........................................................................................... 15

| 65 | Parlophone R 5389 | We Can Work It Out/Day Tripper (Second pressing, label variation with different type for "Sold In U.K...", "Northern Songs NCB", matrix number and date. Comma "," separates "Lennon, McCartney" rather than a dash "-") | 15 |
| 65 | Parlophone R 4949 | Love Me Do/P.S. I Love You (Fourth pressing, black label, with "The Parlophone Co. Ltd" in upper case, "T" in "Gt Britain" now upper case to read "GT. Britain" "Recorded first published" also now in lower case: matrix suffixed with 1N' indicating 'Ringo on drums & no tambourine' version) | 100 |

## SINGLES : 1966

*(with "The Gramophone Co. Ltd." in upper case & "Sold in the UK...". label text, unless otherwise stated)*

| 66 | Parlophone R 5452 | Paperback Writer/Rain (First pressing, in Type 4 or 5 sleeve) | 15 |
| 66 | Parlophone R 5452 | Paperback Writer/Rain (First pressing, label variation, with larger "Northern Songs, NCB" credit and larger "P" before "1966") | 15 |
| 66 | Parlophone R 5493 | Yellow Submarine/Eleanor Rigby (First pressing, in Type 5 or 6 sleeve) | 15 |
| 66 | Parlophone R 5493 | Yellow Submarine/Eleanor Rigby (First pressing, label variation with larger "Northern Songs, NCB", no brackets on Matrix number, larger circled "P" and larger typeface for "Eleanor Rigby") | 15 |
| 66 | Parlophone R 5493 | Yellow Submarine/Eleanor Rigby (First pressing, label variation with mid-size "Northern Songs, NCB", no brackets on Matrix number, "," separating "Lennon, McCartney" rather than a "-" "Lennon-McCartney", larger typeface for "Eleanor Rigby" and "Sold In U.K...") | 15 |
| 66 | Parlophone R5493 | Yellow Submarine/Eleanor Rigby (Second pressing, solid centre, label variation, larger "Northern Songs, NCB" text, smaller "Lennon-McCartney" credit and larger circled "P") | 20 |
| 66 | Parlophone R 5493 | Yellow Submarine/Eleanor Rigby (Second pressing, solid centre label variation, larger "Northern Songs, NCB" text, no brackets on Matrix number and larger typeface on "Eleanor Rigby") | 15 |
| 66 | Parlophone R 5084 | I Want To Hold Your Hand/This Boy (Third pressing, solid centre, "The Parlophone Co" rim text) | 250 |
| 66 | Parlophone R 5114 | Can't Buy Me Love/You Can't Do That (Second pressing, solid centre, with "The Parlophone Co. Ltd" label text) | 150 |
| 66 | Parlophone R 5200 | I Feel Fine/She's A Woman (Second pressing, solid centre) | 150 |

## SINGLES : 1967

*(All pressings after 1967 have push-out or solid centres with "The Gramophone Co. Ltd." in upper case & "Sold in the UK..." label text, unless otherwise stated)*

| 67 | Parlophone R 5570 | Strawberry Fields Forever/Penny Lane (First pressing, 250,000 only in p/s) | 75 |
| 67 | Parlophone R 5570 | Strawberry Fields Forever/Penny Lane (Second pressing, in Type 5,6 or 7 sleeve) | 15 |
| 67 | Parlophone R 5655 | Hello, Goodbye/I Am The Walrus (First pressing, company sleeve, with "7/- to 50/- " on reverse) | 12 |
| 67 | Parlophone R 5655 | Hello Goodbye/I Am The Walrus (First pressing, label variation with "Northern Songs NCB" on three lines not two, different typeface and matrix number appearing beneath date of "1967", smaller typeface for "Hello, Goodbye" and ""Lennon, McCartney" separated by a "," rather than a "-", "Lennon-McCartney") | 15 |
| 67 | Parlophone R 5620 | All You Need Is Love/Baby You're A Rich Man (First pressing, solid or pushout centre, with no reference to "Live World Television Transmission") | 70 |
| 67 | Parlophone R 5620 | All You Need Is Love/Baby You're A Rich Man (Second pressing, with reference to "Live World Television Transmission") | 15 |
| 67 | Parlophone R 5620 | All You Need Is Love/Baby You're A Rich Man (Second pressing, label variation, push-out/solid centre with reference to "Live World Television Transmission" and "Northern Songs NCB" on three lines rather than two, brackets around matrix number, "1967" above Matrix number and "Recorded during 'Live;..." text starts after Lennon-McCartney credit rather than beneath it) | 25 |
| 67 | Parlophone R 5452 | Paperback Writer/Rain (Second pressing, solid centre only) | 80 |
| 67 | Parlophone R 5493 | Yellow Submarine/Eleanor Rigby (Second pressing, solid centre only) | 15 |
| 67 | Parlophone R5305 | Help/I'm Down (Third pressing, solid centre, "The Gramophone Co. Ltd" and "Sold in U.K..." label text) | 100 |
| 67 | Parlophone R5305 | Help/I'm Down (Third pressing, solid centre, "The Parlophone Co. Ltd" and "Sold in U.K..." label text) | 90 |

## SINGLES : 1968

*(All Apple pressings except for early issues of "Let It Be" come in black glossy 'Apple' sleeves)*

| 68 | Parlophone R 5675 | Lady Madonna/The Inner Light (First pressing, with Fan Club insert; sleeve with 7/- to 50/- on reverse) | 60 |
| 68 | Apple R 5722 | Hey Jude/Revolution (First pressing, push-out or solid centre) | 20 |
| 68 | Parlophone R 5675 | Lady Madonna/The Inner Light (Second pressing, no insert) | 15 |
| 68 | Parlophone R 5084 | I Want To Hold Your Hand/This Boy (Fourth pressing, solid centre, with "The Gramophone Co" rim text) | 300 |

## SINGLES : 1969

*(All Apple pressings except for early issues of "Let It Be" come in black gloss "Apple" sleeves)*

| 69 | Apple R 5777 | Get Back/Don't Let Me Down (First pressing, push-out or solid centre, as "The Beatles with Billy Preston") | 20 |
| 69 | Apple R 5777 | Get Back/Don't Let Me Down (First pressing, label variation with "Northern Songs/ NCB" rather than "Northern Songs" solid centre or push-out centre, as "The Beatles with Billy Preston") | 20 |
| 69 | Apple R 5777 | Get Back/Don't Let Me Down (Second pressing, solid centre or push-out centre as "The Beatles with Billy Preston", without "Sold in UK..." label text)) | 20 |
| 69 | Apple R 5786 | Ballad Of John And Yoko/Old Brown Shoe (First pressing, solid or push-out centre) | 20 |
| 69 | Apple R 5786 | Ballad Of John And Yoko/Old Brown Shoe (Second pressing, solid centre or push-out centre without "Sold in UK..." label text) | 18 |
| 69 | Apple R 5814 | Something/Come Together (First pressing, solid centre or push-out centre without "Sold in UK..." label text) | 45 |
| 69 | Apple R 5722 | Hey Jude/Revolution (Second pressing, without "Sold in UK..." label text) | 15 |
| 69 | Parlophone R 5305 | Help!/I'm Down (Fourth pressing, with "The Parlophone Co. Ltd" but no "Sold In U.K..." label text) | 40 |
| 69 | Parlophone R 5389 | We Can Work It Out/Day Tripper (Third pressing, solid centre, no "sold in U.K..." label text) | 80 |
| 69 | Parlophone R 5452 | Paperback Writer/Rain (Third pressing, no "Sold in U.K...." label text) | 40 |
| 69 | Parlophone R 5570 | Strawberry Fields Forever/Penny Lane (Third pressing, no "Sold In U.K..." label text) | 35 |
| 69 | Parlophone R 5493 | Yellow Submarine/Eleanor Rigby (Third pressing, no "Sold in U.K...." label text) | 40 |
| 69 | Parlophone R 5620 | All You Need Is Love/Baby You're A Rich Man (Third pressing, no "Sold in U.K..." label text, push-out centre) | 40 |

| | | | |
|---|---|---|---|
| 69 | Parlophone R5675 | Lady Madonna/The inner Burning Light (Third pressing, with "pip" in centre of label, no "Sold UN U.K..." label text) | 35 |
| 69 | Parlophone R 5675 | Lady Madonna/The Inner Burning Light (Fourth pressing, with no "Sold In U.K..." label text) | 35 |

## SINGLES : 1970

| | | | |
|---|---|---|---|
| 70 | Apple R 5833 | Let It Be/You Know My Name (Look Up The Number) (First pressing, scratched-out B-side matrix: APPLES 1002, p/s) | 30 |
| 70 | Apple R 5833 | Let It Be/You Know My Name (Look Up The Number) (Second pressing, scratched-out B-side matrix: APPLES 1002, no p/s) | 15 |
| 70 | Apple R 5833 | Let It Be/You Know My Name (Look Up The Number) (Third pressing, B-side matrix: 7YCE 21408, no p/s) | 15 |

## SINGLES : 70S, 80S, 90S & 00S SINGLES: REISSUES AND PICTURE DISCS

*(Please note that 1970s Parlophone copies of Beatles singles with EMI boxed logos are of nominal value. Add £10 to the value for any single with a red & white 'Factory Sample Not For Sale' sticker.)*

| | | | |
|---|---|---|---|
| 78 | Parlophone R 6022 | Sgt. Pepper's Lonely Hearts Club Band/With A Little Help From My Friends/A Day In The Life | 8 |
| 82 | Parlophone R 4949 | Love Me Do/P.S. I Love You (p/s, red label reissue, with "mono" notice &publishing miscredited to "Ardmore & Beechwood" -4 Matrix, Andy White version) | 10 |
| 82 | Parlophone RP 4949 | Love Me Do/P.S. I Love You (7" picture disc, with/without publishing miscredit) | 10 |
| 82 | Parlophone 12R 4949 | Love Me Do/P.S. I Love You/Love Me Do (Original Single Version) (12", p/s) | 10 |
| 83 | Parlophone RP 5015 | From Me To You/Thank You Girl (picture disc, some with Souvenir From Abbey Road Studios sticker on sleeve) | 10 |
| 83 | Parlophone RP 5055 | She Loves You/I'll Get You (picture disc) | 12 |
| *(Issued in PVC sleeve)* | | | |
| 83 | Parlophone R 5570 | Penny Lane/Strawberry Fields Forever | 8 |
| 84 | Parlophone RP 5160 | A Hard Day's Night/Things We Said Today (picture disc) | 15 |
| 86 | Parlophone RP 5452 | Paperback Writer/Rain (picture disc) | 15 |
| 87 | Parlophone 12R 5620 | All You Need Is Love/Baby You're A Rich Man (12", p/s) | 10 |
| *(Issued in PVC sleeve)* | | | |
| 88 | Apple 12R 5722 | Hey Jude/Revolution (12", p/s) | 30 |
| 88 | Apple 12RP 5722 | Hey Jude/Revolution (12", picture disc with "Apple" insert) | 12 |
| 95 | Apple R 6422 | Free As A Bird/Christmastime Is Here Again (7", p/s) | 8 |
| 96 | Apple R 6425 | Real Love/Baby's In Black (7", p/s) | 8 |
| 10 | Parlophone 5099964163970 | Paperback Writer/Rain (jukebox centre) | 40 |
| 12 | Parlophone 45-R 4949 | Love Me Do/PS I Love You (reissue, withdrawn as A side has album version with Andy White on drums and Ringo on tambourine, Matrixes: BC88258-01A1 01740174/ BC88258-01B1 0174017 J G i i and incorrect catalogue number R 47414 on B-side) | 20 |

## SINGLES : CONTRACT PRESSINGS: SINGLES

*Records were often pressed by rival companies on behalf of one another under contract to meet spikes in demand. Non-EMI companies frequently pressed batches of Beatles' records for Parlophone. Occasionally demand for a record was so strong that more than one company was contracted to press batches simultaneously. Subtle differences indicating the origin of a contract pressing can be identified. Many collectors like to include examples in their collections. EMI Pressings: Pre-1966 EMI pressings have flat push-out centres. Thereafter many records were produced with a mix of push-out and solid centres. EMI always pressed Stamper Letters into the vinyl's run-out area positioned at 3 o'clock to the Matrix Number. Up to three letters from the code 'GRAMOPHLTD' were used, each representing a number from 1 to 0. Mother Plate Numbers using a conventional numbering sequence starting with 1 were pressed into the vinyl at 9 o'clock to the Matrix Number. The edges of EMI pressings are all straight-cut. Non-EMI Pressings: Philips' contract pressings (the 'Hey Jude' single) are the easiest to spot as they alone have three-pronged centres. All the others had four prongs except some ORIOLE pressings of "Can't Buy Me Love" which have solid centres. The centres of Decca and PYE pressings have similar raised sections containing the spindle hole, though PYE's are much less prominent. The outermost edges of records made by CBS, PHILIPS, ORIOLE and PYE are not straight-cut but are slightly tapered-off. The edges of Decca pressings are all straight-cut. EMI Stamper Letters are seldom seen on contract pressings though Mother Plate Numbers almost always appear. Controversy long surrounded one style of Beatles' contract pressing. Previously thought to have been pressed by PYE they are now considered to have been made by ORIOLE before its acquisition by CBS in September 1964. The labels on the essentially flat centres of these pressings are often rough-textured with rough edges. The vinyl is thicker and heavier than other pressings. Some November 1964 pressings of 'I Feel Fine' also have these characteristics and are assumed to have come from this source, CBS by then using the old ORIOLE presses. Some 1968 copies of 'Hey Jude' are identical in appearance but are less heavy. Both are now considered to be CBS contract pressings. PYE is believed to have pressed copies of one Beatles' 45 ('Hey Jude') and one EP ('Million Sellers'). The centres of these two pressings look very similar to those made by Decca but they have a less prominent ridge and the edges of the records are slightly tapered. Beatles fans and collectors worldwide continue to scrutinise the magical mystery tour of Beatles' contract pressings and new information continues to be unearthed. The following details are where we at Record Collector stand at the present time*

| | | | |
|---|---|---|---|
| 63 | Parlophone R 5055 | She Loves You/I'll Get You (Decca pressing) | 30 |
| 63 | Parlophone R 5055 | She Loves You/I'll Get You (Decca pressing, variation, "Parlophone Co.Ltd" in upper case, different typography for "Northern Songs" Matrix number and "Recording First Published 1963") | 25 |
| 63 | Parlophone R 5084 | I Want To Hold Your Hand/This Boy (Decca pressing) | 25 |
| 63 | Parlophone R 5084 | I Want To Hold Your Hand/This Boy (Decca pressing, label variation with "N.C.B." after "Northern Songs Mus. Ltd.") | 25 |
| 63 | Parlophone R 5084 | I Want To Hold Your Hand/This Boy (Oriole pressing) | 30 |
| 63 | Parlohone R 5084 | I Want To Hold Your Hand/This Boy (Pye pressing, label variant with differnt typography and "N.C.B." after "Northern Songs Mus Ltd.") | 25 |
| 64 | Parlophone R 5114 | Can't Buy Me Love/You Can't Do That (Oriole pressing) | 25 |
| 64 | Parlophone R 5114 | Can't Buy Me Love/You Can't Do That (Oriole pressing with solid centre) | 45 |
| 64 | Parlophone R5114 | Can't Buy Me Love/You Can't Do That (Pye contract pressing with solid centre, side 1, matrix 7XCE 17657-1N) | 40 |
| 64 | Parlophone R 5114 | Can't Buy Me Love/You Can't Do That (Pye pressing label variation with "NCB" out of alignment with the "N" and "S" of "Northern Songs") | 25 |
| 64 | Parlophone R 5200 | I Feel Fine/She's A Woman (Pye pressing) | 25 |
| 64 | Parlophone R 5200 | I Feel Fine/She's A Woman (CBS pressing) | 25 |
| 64 | Parlophone R 5200 | I Feel Fine/She's A Woman (Decca pressing) | 25 |
| 65 | Parlophone R 5305 | Help!/I'm Down (Decca contract pressing) | 25 |
| 67 | Parlophone R 5655 | Hello Goodbye/I Am The Walrus (Decca pressing) | 25 |
| 67 | Parlophone R 5655 | Hello Goodbye/I Am The Walrus (Decca contract pressing, label variation, "Northern Songs NCB" on three lines not two, "1967" above not below matrix number and "Lennon, McCartney" separated by a comma "," rather than a "-", "Lennon-McCartney") | 25 |
| 68 | Apple R 5722 | Hey Jude/Revolution (Decca contract pressing) | 40 |

| | | | MINT VALUE £ |
|---|---|---|---|
| 68 | Apple R 5722 | Hey Jude/Revolution (Pye contract pressing) | 40 |
| 68 | Apple R 5722 | Hey Jude/Revolution (CBS contract pressing) | 40 |
| 68 | Apple R 5722 | Hey Jude/Revolution (Philips contract pressing, three-pronged push-out centre) | 70 |

### SINGLES : DEMO SINGLES

*(Beatles demo singles between 1962 and 1966 have a red "A" on the A side unless otherwise stated. Demos from All You Need Is Love (1967) to Something (1969) have a white "A" on a green label. Finally, demos with the centre's missing are worth half these values)*

| | | | |
|---|---|---|---|
| 62 | Parlophone 45-R 4949 | Love Me Do/P.S. I Love You (Demo copy, McCartney misspelt "McArtney", 250 only) | 5000 |
| 63 | Parlophone 45-R 4983 | Please Please Me/Ask Me Why (demo copy) | 2000 |
| 63 | Parlophone (45-)R 5015 | From Me To You/Thank You Girl (Demo copy, with or without '45-' prefix) | 1000 |
| 63 | Parlophone R 5055 | She Loves You/I'll Get You (Demo copy) | 800 |
| 63 | Parlophone R 5084 | I Want To Hold Your Hand/This Boy (Demo copy) | 800 |
| 64 | Parlophone R 5114 | Can't Buy Me Love/You Can't Do That (Demo copy) | 800 |
| 64 | Parlophone R 5160 | A Hard Day's Night/Things We Said Today (Demo copy, red "A" on both sides) | 800 |
| 64 | Parlophone R 5200 | I Feel Fine/She's A Woman (Demo single, existence unconfirmed) | 0 |
| 65 | Parlophone R 5265 | Ticket To Ride/Yes It Is (Demo copy) | 700 |
| 65 | Parlophone R 5305 | Help!/I'm Down (Demo copy, existence unconfirmed) | 0 |
| 65 | Parlophone R 5389 | We Can Work It Out/Day Tripper (Demo copy, red "A" on both sides) | 600 |
| 66 | Parlophone R 5452 | Paperback Writer/Rain (Demo copy) | 600 |
| 66 | Parlophone R 5493 | Yellow Submarine/Eleanor Rigby (Demo copy, existence unconfirmed) | 0 |
| 67 | Parlophone R 5570 | Strawberry Fields Forever/Penny Lane (existence unconfirmed) | 0 |
| 67 | Parlophone R 5655 | Hello, Goodbye/I Am The Walrus | 500 |
| 67 | Parlophone R 5620 | All You Need Is Love/Baby You're A Rich Man (Demo copy) | 450 |
| 68 | Apple (no cat. no.) | Hey Jude/Revolution (Demo copy, green & white Apple 'custom' label, handwritten details) | 450 |
| 69 | Apple R 5777 | Get Back/Don't Let Me Down (Demo copy, green and white Apple 'custom' label test pressing, typed details) | 400 |
| 69 | Parlophone R 5786 | Ballad Of John And Yoko/Old Brown Shoe (Demo copy, existence unconfirmed) | 0 |
| 68 | Parlophone R 5675 | Lady Madonna/The Inner Light (Demo copy) | 500 |
| 69 | Parlophone R 5814 | Something/Come Together (Demo copy) | 600 |
| 70 | Parlophone R 5833 | Let It Be/You Know My Name (Look Up The Number) (existence unconfirmed) | 0 |
| 76 | Parlophone R 6013 | Yesterday/I Should Have Known Better (Demo, silver/black paer label with a silver "A", green generic p/s) | 25 |
| 76 | Parlophone R 6016 | Back In The U.S.S.R./Twist And Shout (silver/black paper label with a silver "A", green generic p/s) | 25 |
| 78 | Parlophone R 6022 | Sgt. Pepper's Lonely Hearts Club Band/With A Little Help From My Friends/A Day In The Life (silver/black paper label with a silver "A", p/s) | 25 |

### SINGLES : FRENCH PRESSINGS - SINGLES

| | | | |
|---|---|---|---|
| 67 | Parlophone R 5655 | Hello Goodbye/I Am The Walrus (Pathé Marconi pressing, alleged push-out centre version) | 100 |
| 67 | Parlophone R 5655 | Hello Goodbye/I Am The Walrus (Pathé Marconi pressing) | 25 |

### SINGLES : POLYDOR RECORDINGS

*(With push-out centres & orange labels)*

| | | | |
|---|---|---|---|
| 62 | Polydor NH 66833 | My Bonnie/The Saints (When The Saints Go Marching In) (as Tony Sheridan & The Beatles; 1st pressing, 'broad' title & "Made In England" label text) | 100 |
| 63 | Polydor NH 66833 | My Bonnie/The Saints (When The Saints Go Marching In) (as Tony Sheridan & The Beatles; 2nd pressing, push-out or solid centre, 'narrow' title & "Made In England" label text) | 70 |
| 64 | Polydor NH 52275 | Cry For A Shadow (A-side credited to 'Beatles')/TONY SHERIDAN & THE BEATLES: Why (Can't You Love Me Again) ('scroll' label, with "Made In England" text) | 50 |
| 64 | Polydor NH 52317 | Ain't She Sweet (A-side as 'The Beatles, vocal: John Lennon')/If You Love Me, Baby (B-side credited to 'The Beatles with Tony Sheridan, vocal: John Lennon'); 1st pressing, 'scroll' label with "Made In England" text) | 45 |
| 64 | Polydor NH 52317 | Ain't She Sweet/If You Love Me, Baby (2nd pressing, red label, with "Made In England" text) | 20 |
| 64 | Polydor NH 52906 | Sweet Georgia Brown/Nobody's Child (German import only, unissued in U.K.) | 40 |

### SINGLES : SINGLES BOX SETS

| | | | |
|---|---|---|---|
| 76 | Parlophone/Apple BS 24 | THE BEATLES' SINGLES COLLECTION 1962-1970 (24 x 7", each in green p/s, green & white stickered box set) | 45 |
| 76 | Parlophone/Apple/ World Record Club | THE BEATLES' COLLECTION (24 x 7", mail-order black box set; later copies with "Sgt. Pepper's Lonely Hearts Club Band" [R 6022] | 45 |
| 78 | Parlophone/Apple BSC 1 | THE BEATLES' SINGLES COLLECTION (26 x 7" blue box set, with insert; some copies include mispressing of "Get Back" [Apple R 5777] | 40 |
| 82 | Parlophone/Apple BSCP 1 | THE BEATLES' SINGLES COLLECTION (27 x 7" blue box set, with bonus picture disc "Love Me Do"/"Love Me Do" [RP 4949], export issue) | 45 |
| 82 | Parlophone/Apple BSCP 1 | THE BEATLES' SINGLES COLLECTION (27 x 7" blue box set, with mispressed picture disc Love Me Do/"Love Me Do" [RP 4949], export issue) | 50 |
| 89 | Parlophone/Apple CDBSC 1 | THE BEATLES' SINGLES COLLECTION (22 x 3" CD single box set) | 75 |
| 89 | Parlophone/Apple CDBSCP 1 | THE BEATLES' SINGLES COLLECTION (22 x 5" CD single box set) | 65 |
| 12 | Apple 5099968 | SINGLES BOX SET (4x7", poster) | 25 |

### SINGLES : UNIQUE PROMO SINGLES

| | | | |
|---|---|---|---|
| 68 | Apple (no cat. no.) | OUR FIRST FOUR (4 x 7" in presentation pack, including "Hey Jude" [R 5722] & "Those Were The Days" by Mary Hopkin [APPLE 2], "Sour Milk Sea" by Jackie Lomax [APPLE 3] & "Thingumybob" by Black Dyke Mills Band [APPLE 4]; each mounted in PVC pocket on printe | 2500 |
| 68 | Apple (no cat. no.) | OUR FIRST FOUR (4 x 7" in presentation pack, including "Hey Jude" [R 5722] & "Those Were The Days" by Mary Hopkin [APPLE 2], "Sour Milk Sea" by Jackie Lomax [APPLE 3] & "Thingumybob" by Black Dyke Mills Band [APPLE 4]; each mounted in PVC pocket on printe | 1000 |
| 76 | EMI SPSR 401 | Medley Of Songs For "Rock'n'Roll Music" (excerpts) | 600 |

### EXPORT SINGLES

| | | | |
|---|---|---|---|
| 64 | Parlophone DP 562 | If I Fell/Tell Me Why (First pressing, export single without "Sold in UK..." label text) | 100 |
| 65 | Parlophone DP 563 | Yesterday/Dizzy Miss Lizzy (export single) | 100 |
| 66 | Parlophone DP 564 | Michelle/Drive My Car (export single) | 175 |

| 68 | Parlophone DP 570 | Hey Jude/Revolution (Export copy with Swedish p/s) | 60 |
| 68 | Parlophone DP 570 | Hey Jude/Revolution (Export copy without Swedish p/s) | 45 |
| 70 | Parlophone P-R 5833 | Let It Be/You Know My Name (Look Up The Number) (Export copy, no p/s) | 60 |

*("Let It Be" was pressed with "Parlophone" label text on one side & "Gramophone" on the other)*

| 70 | Apple P-R 5833 | Let It Be/You Know My Name (Look Up The Number) (Export copy, no p/s) | 300 |

## EPS : 1963

*(With "The Parlophone Co. Ltd" and "Recording first published 1963" label text. Unless otherwise stated, all 60s EPs have push-out centres and laminated flipback sleeves.)*

| 63 | Parlophone GEP 8882 | TWIST AND SHOUT (EP, First pressing) | 30 |
| 63 | Parlophone GEP 8880 | THE BEATLES' HITS (EP, First pressing, without "Recording first published 1963" label text) | 20 |
| 63 | Parlophone GEP 8883 | THE BEATLES (No. 1) (EP, first pressing, without "Recording first published 1963" label text) | 25 |
| 63 | Parlophone GEP 8880 | THE BEATLES' HITS (EP, Second pressing) | 20 |

## EPS : 1964

*(With "The Parlophone Co. Ltd." & "Recording first published 1964" label text & "Sold in the UK..." unless otherwise stated.)*

| 64 | Parlophone GEP 8891 | ALL MY LOVING (EP, First pressing without "Sold in UK" label text) | 35 |
| 64 | Parlophone GEP 8891 | ALL MY LOVING (EP, Second pressing, with "Sold in U.K...." label text) | 20 |
| 64 | Parlophone GEP 8899 | GOLDEN DISCS (unreleased, 2 x 1-sided test pressings [matrices: 7TCE-1N & 7TCE-1N] & 1 set of label proofs only; price does not include labels) | 2500 |
| 64 | Parlophone GEP 8913 | LONG TALL SALLY (EP, First pressing) | 25 |
| 64 | Parlophone GEP 8920 | EXTRACTS FROM THE FILM "A HARD DAY'S NIGHT" (EP) | 30 |
| 64 | Parlophone GEP 8924 | EXTRACTS FROM THE ALBUM "A HARD DAY'S NIGHT" (EP) | 40 |
| 64 | Parlophone GEP 8882 | TWIST AND SHOUT (EP, Second pressing) | 12 |

## EPS : 1965

*(With "The Parlophone Co. Ltd", & "Sold in UK.." label text, unless otherwise stated.)*

| 65 | Parlophone GEP 8931 | BEATLES FOR SALE (EP, First pressing) | 35 |
| 65 | Parlophone GEP 8938 | BEATLES FOR SALE (No. 2) (EP, first pressing) | 40 |
| 65 | Parlophone GEP 8946 | THE BEATLES MILLION SELLERS (EP, with 'Golden Discs' text on labels) | 20 |
| 65 | Parlophone GEP 8883 | THE BEATLES (No. 1) (EP, Second pressing, with "The Gramophone Co Ltd" & "Sold in UK..." label text) | 10 |
| 65 | Parlophone GEP 8880 | THE BEATLES' HITS (EP, Third pressing, with "The Gramophone Co Ltd" & "Sold in UK..." label text) | 10 |
| 65 | Parlophone GEP 8882 | TWIST AND SHOUT (Third pressing, with "The Gramophone Co Ltd" & "Sold in UK..." label text) | 10 |

## EPS : 1966

*(With "The Gramophone Co. Ltd" & "Sold in UK..." label text unless otherwise stated.)*

| 66 | Parlophone GEP 8948 | YESTERDAY (EP, First pressing) | 80 |
| 66 | Parlophone GEP 8952 | NOWHERE MAN (EP, first pressing) | 120 |
| 66 | Parlophone GEP 8946 | THE BEATLES' MILLION SELLERS (EP, Second pressing, with "Million Sellers" label text) | 15 |

## EPS : 1967 (EPS)

*(With "The Gramophone Co. Ltd" & "Sold in UK..." label text unless otherwise stated. Please note that any EP titles with "The Gramophone Co Ltd" but without "Sold in UK..." are 70s re-pressing with EMI label text & varnished sleeves).*

| 67 | Parlophone MMT-1 | MAGICAL MYSTERY TOUR (2-EP, gatefold sleeve, first pressing with booklet & blue lyric sheet; push-out or solid centre; mono) | 65 |
| 67 | Parlophone SMMT-1 | MAGICAL MYSTERY TOUR (2-EP, gatefold sleeve, first pressing with booklet & blue lyric sheet; stereo) | 75 |
| 67 | Parlophone GEP 8931 | BEATLES FOR SALE (EP, Second pressing with "The Parlophone Co. Ltd" label text; solid centre) | 25 |
| 67 | Parlophone GEP 8952 | NOWHERE MAN (EP, Second pressing solid centre) | 35 |

## EPS : CONTRACT PRESSINGS : EPS

| 66 | GEP 8946 | THE BEATLES MILLION SELLERS (EP, Pye contract pressing, with 'Golden Discs' text on labels) | 50 |

## EPS : EPS REISSUES AND BOXED SETS

*(EPs reissued in the 70s have EMI label text and come in varnished sleeves with flipbacks. Later 80s reissues are housed in cheaper varnished sleeves without flipbacks are are generally worth £8-£10).*

| 73 | Parlophone SMMT-1 | MAGICAL MYSTERY TOUR (2-EP, gatefold sleeve, stereo only, with booklet & yellow lyric sheet) | 15 |
| 81 | Parlophone BEP 14 | THE BEATLES EP COLLECTION (14-EP box set, with bonus stereo EP [SGE 1]) | 120 |
| 70s | Parlophone GEP 8882 | TWIST AND SHOUT (reissue, 'EMI' text on label) | 12 |
| 70s | Parlophone GEP 8880 | THE BEATLES HITS (reissue with 'EMI' text) | 12 |
| 70s | Parlophone GEP 8883 | THE BEATLES NO. 1 (reissue, with 'EMI' text) | 12 |
| 70s | Parlophone GEP 8891 | ALL MY LOVING (reissue with 'EMI' text) | 12 |
| 70s | Parlophone GEP 8913 | LONG TALL SALLY (reissue with 'EMI' text) | 12 |
| 70s | Parlophone GEP 8920 | EXTRACTS FROM THE FILM "A HARD DAY'S NIGHT" (reissue with 'EMI' text) | 15 |
| 70s | Parlophone GEP 8924 | EXTRACTS FROM THE ALBUM "A HARD DAY'S NIGHT" (reissue with 'EMI' text) | 15 |
| 70s | Parlophone GEP 8931 | BEATLES FOR SALE (reissue with 'EMI' text) | 15 |
| 70s | Parlophone GEP 8938 | BEATLES FOR SALE (No. 2) (reissue with 'EMI' text) | 15 |
| 70s | Parlophone GEP 8946 | THE BEATLES MILLION SELLERS (reissue with 'EMI' text) | 12 |
| 70s | Parlophone GEP 8948 | YESTERDAY (reissue with 'EMI' text) | 18 |
| 70s | Parlophone GEP 8952 | NOWHERE MAN (reissue with 'EMI' text) | 25 |
| 70s | Parlophone SMMT-1 | MAGICAL MYSTERY TOUR (reissue with 'EMI' text) | 25 |
| 95 | Apple R 6406 | BABY IT'S YOU (7" EP) | 15 |

## EPS : POLYDOR RECORDINGS : EPS

| 64 | Polydor EPH 21 610 | TONY SHERIDAN WITH THE BEATLES (1st pressing, German import in U.K. p/s, orange 'scroll' label; Why songwriting credit as 'Sheridan' or 'Sheridan-Crompton') | 125 |
| 64 | Polydor EPH 21 610 | TONY SHERIDAN WITH THE BEATLES (2nd pressing, German import in U.K. p/s, red label;Why songwriting credit as 'Sheridan' or 'Sheridan-Crompton') | 50 |

## ALBUMS : PLEASE PLEASE ME

*(First pressings from 1963 have 'The Parlophone Co Ltd' label text but no 'Sold in UK...' label text unless otherwise stated. 1963 pressings come in polythene-lined 'Use Emitex' die-cut inners with flipback sleeves. All later label and sleeve variations are clearly stated in the entry for each repressing)*

| 63 | Parlophone PMC 1202 | PLEASE PLEASE ME (First pressing, black & gold label, with "Dick James Mus. Co." publishing credit for "I Saw Her Standing There", "Misery", Do You Want To Know A Secret & "There's A Place"; "Made by Ernest J Day Ltd" sleeve with printers credit on right hand side rear of sleeve; Front photo credited to "Angus McBean" at bottom far right of front cover of sleeve less than 5mm from edge. "A" of Angus starting under second letter "S" in the word "songs" in the album title: large mono in top right corner. Research estimates that around 25,000 pressed) ...... 1200 |
|---|---|---|
| 63 | Parlophone PCS 3042 | PLEASE PLEASE ME (First pressing, black & gold label, with "Dick James Mus. Co."publishing credit for "Please Please Me", "I Saw Her Standing There", "Misery", Do You Want To Know A Secret & "There's A Place"; E. J. Day sleeve; stereo) ...... 6000 |
| 63 | Parlophone PMC 1202 | PLEASE PLEASE ME (Second pressing, black & gold label, with "Northern Songs" publishing credit for "I Saw Her Standing There", "Misery", Do You Want To Know A Secret & "There's A Place"; Made by Ernest J Day Ltd" sleeve with printers credit on right hand side rear of sleeve; Front photo credited to "Angus McBean" at bottom far right of front cover of sleeve less than 5mm from edge. "A" of Angus starting under second letter "S" in the word "songs" in the album title: large mono in top right corner. Research estimates that around 12,000 pressed) ...... 1200 |
| 63 | Parlophone PCS 3042 | PLEASE PLEASE ME (Second pressing, black & gold label, with "Northern Songs" publishing credit for "Please Please Me", "I Saw Her Standing There", "Misery", Do You Want To Know A Secret & "There's A Place"; E. J. Day sleeve; stereo) ...... 5000 |
| 63 | Parlophone PMC 1202 | PLEASE PLEASE ME (Third pressing, black & gold label with 33 1/3 RPM on label next to matrix number. Many of these records have LOWER stamper numbers than some black and gold second pressings (with Northern Songs credit) suggesting that these records were being pressed at the same time. Made by Ernest J Day Ltd sleeve with printers credit on right hand side rear of sleeve; Front photo credited to "Angus McBean" at bottom far right of front cover of sleeve less than 5mm from edge. "A" of Angus starting under second letter "S" in the word "songs" in the album title: large mono in top right corner. Research estimates that around 5,000 pressed) ...... 500 |
| 63 | Parlophone PCS 3042 | PLEASE PLEASE ME (Third pressing, black & yellow label with 33 1/3 on label, stereo) ...... 3000 |
| 63 | Parlophone PMC 1202 | PLEASE PLEASE ME (Fourth pressing, black/yellow label Made by Ernest J Day Ltd" sleeve with printers credit on right hand side rear of sleeve; Front photo credited to "Angus McBean" at bottom far right of front cover of sleeve less than 5mm from edge. "A" of Angus starting under second letter "S" in the word "songs" in the album title: large mono in top right corner. Research estimates that around 25,000 pressed. Please note that there are some in sleeves with the Angus McBean credit around 20mm from the edge with the "A" of Angus starting under the letter "G" in "songs".) ...... 150 |
| 63 | Parlophone PCS 3042 | PLEASE PLEASE ME (Fourth pressing, with large "stereo" on front cover; E. J. Day sleeve; stereo) ...... 250 |
| 63 | Parlophone PMC 1202 | PLEASE PLEASE ME (Fifth pressing, "Recording first published 1963" added below matrix number. Research estimates around 184,000 pressed. E. J. Day sleeve with medium mono and"A" of "Angus" starting under the letter "G" in "Songs" or Garrod & Lofthouse Ltd sleeve with large mono and McBean credit around 20mm from edge with "A" of "Angus" starting under letter "G" in "Songs." Large "mono"on front cover; mono) ...... 100 |
| 63 | Parlophone PCS 3042 | PLEASE PLEASE ME (Fifth pressing, G & L or E. J. Day sleeve, with large "stereo"on front cover; stereo) ...... 150 |
| 64 | Parlophone PCS 3042 | PLEASE PLEASE ME (sixth pressing, with 'The Parlophone Co. Ltd', 'Recording first published 1963' & 'Sold in UK...' label text. G & L sleeve, with large "stereo" on front cover; stereo) ...... 80 |
| 65 | Parlophone PMC 1202 | PLEASE PLEASE ME (sixth pressing, from July 1965 until August 1969 "Sold in U.K. subject to resale price conditions, see price lists." printed on centre of all labels. In February 1965 "Recording first published" replaced with (P) in a circle 1963. Records with (P) 1963 start with side 2 matrix XEX 422 - 2N: Research suggests that 250,000 copies pressed. G & L sleeve, with large or small "mono" with McBean credit around 20mm from edge with "A" of "Angus" starting under letter "G" in "Songs; mono) ...... 70 |
| 65 | Parlophone PCS 3042 | PLEASE PLEASE ME (Seventh pressing, with 'The Gramophone Co Ltd' & 'Sold in UK...' label text, stereo, with small "stereo" on front cover) ...... 60 |
| 69 | Parlophone PMC 1202 | PLEASE PLEASE ME (Seventh pressing, pressed between August to December 1969, "Sold in U.K. .." text removed mono, with small "mono" on front cover made by Garrod & Lofthouse Ltd. Angus McBean credit 20mm from the edge with the "A" of "Angus" starting under the letter "G" in "Songs". Research estimates than only 1000 copies pressed) ...... 400 |
| 69 | Parlophone PCS 3042 | PLEASE PLEASE ME (Eigth pressing, 'The Gramophone Co Ltd' label text, small "stereo" on front cover; stereo) ...... 60 |
| 69 | Parlophone PMC 1202 | PLEASE PLEASE ME (Re-pressing 1969, mono) ...... 50 |
| 69 | Parlophone PCS 3042 | PLEASE PLEASE ME (1969 re-pressing, stereo, with one boxed EMI logo on label) ...... 100 |

*(with laminated flipback sleeves & silver/black labels with one boxed EMI logo)*

| 70 | Parlophone PMC 1202 | PLEASE PLEASE ME (Eigth pressing, black and silver label, single boxed EMI logo at 6 'o' clock, with G & L sleeve & sepia "LP advertising" inner. Label has "The Gramophone Co. Ltd." but no "Sold in UK ..."small "mono" on front cover made by Garrod & Lofthouse Ltd. Angus McBean credit 20mm from the edge with the "A" of "Angus" starting under the letter "G" in "Songs". Research suggests that around 1000 copies pressed; mono) ...... 350 |
|---|---|---|
| 73 | Parlophone PCS 3042 | PLEASE PLEASE ME (French pressing) ...... 15 |
| 82 | Parlophone PMC 1202 | PLEASE PLEASE ME (mono) ...... 15 |

*(lightweight vinyl with yellow/black labels listing "mono")*

| 95 | Parlophone PMC 1202 | PLEASE PLEASE ME (LP, mono) ...... 20 |
|---|---|---|

## ALBUMS : WITH THE BEATLES

*(First pressings from 1963 have 'The Parlophone Co Ltd' label text but no 'Sold in UK...' label text unless otherwise stated. 1963 pressings come in polythene-lined 'Use Emitex' die-cut inners with flipback sleeves. All later label and sleeve variations are clearly stated in the entry for each repressing)*

| 63 | Parlophone PMC 1206 | WITH THE BEATLES (First pressing, black & yellow label, with "Recording first published", & "Jobete" publishing credit for "Money"; G&L or E.J. Day sleeve, with large "Mono" on front cover, mono) ...... 200 |
|---|---|---|
| 63 | Parlophone PCS 3045 | WITH THE BEATLES (First pressing black & yellow label, with "Recording first published", & "Jobete" publishing credit for "Money"; G & L or E. J. Day sleeve, with large "stereo" on front cover; stereo) ...... 250 |

| 63 | Parlophone PMC 1206 | WITH THE BEATLES (Second pressing, black & yellow label, with "Recording first published",& "Dominion, Belinda" publishing credit for "Money"; G & L or E. J. Day sleeve, with large "mono" on front cover; mono) ............ 125 |
| 63 | Parlophone PCS 3045 | WITH THE BEATLES (Second pressing, black & yellow label, with "Recording first published",& "Dominion, Belinda" publishing credit for "Money"; G & L or E. J. Day sleeve,with large "stereo" on front cover; stereo) ............ 200 |
| 65 | Parlophone PCS 3045 | WITH THE BEATLES (Third pressing, 'The Gramophone Co Ltd' & 'Sold in UK...' label text, small "stereo" on front cover; stereo) ............ 60 |
| 69 | Parlophone PCS 3045 | WITH THE BEATLES (Fourth pressing, with 'The Gramphone Co Ltd' label text but no 'Sold in UK...' label text, G&L sleeve with either plain white or sepia 'LP advertising' inner, small "stereo" on front cover; stereo) ............ 60 |
| 69 | Parlophone PCS 3045 | WITH THE BEATLES ( silver/black labels with one boxed EMI logo, stereo only) ............ 30 |
| 73 | Parlophone PCS 3045 | WITH THE BEATLES (French pressing, with 'Made In France' on EMI rim copy) ............ 15 |
| 82 | Parlophone PMC 1206 | WITH THE BEATLES (repressing with yellow/black labels on lightweight vinyl, mono) ... 15 |

## ALBUMS : A HARD DAY'S NIGHT

*(First pressings from 1964 have 'The Parlophone Co Ltd' & 'Sold in UK...' label text. All later label and sleeve variations are clearly stated in the entry for each repressing)*

| 64 | Parlophone PMC 1230 | A HARD DAY'S NIGHT (First pressing, G & L or E. J. Day sleeve, mid-sized "mono" on front cover; mono) ............ 100 |
| 64 | Parlophone PCS 3058 | A HARD DAY'S NIGHT (First pressing, G & L or E. J. Day sleeve, mid-sized "stereo"on front cover; stereo) ............ 250 |
| 65 | Parlophone PMC 1230 | A HARD DAY'S NIGHT (Second pressing, small "mono" on front cover; mono) ............ 60 |
| 65 | Parlophone PCS 3058 | A HARD DAY'S NIGHT (Second pressing, small "stereo" on front cover; stereo) ............ 75 |
| 65 | Parlophone PCS 3058 | A HARD DAY'S NIGHT (Second pressing, outline "stereo" on front cover; stereo) ........ 200 |
| 69 | Parlophone PMC 1230 | A HARD DAY'S NIGHT (Third pressing, with 'The Gramophone Co Ltd' label text but no 'Sold in UK...' label text, G&L sleeve with plain white or sepia 'LP advertising' inners.Small "mono" on front cover; mono) ............ 60 |
| 69 | Parlophone PCS 3058 | A HARD DAY'S NIGHT (Third pressing, with 'The Gramophone Co Ltd' label text but no 'Sold in UK...' label text, G&L sleeve with plain white or sepia 'LP advertising' inners.Small "stereo" on front cover; stereo) ............ 60 |
| 69 | Parlophone PCS 3058 | A HARD DAY'S NIGHT (stereo only, with laminated flipback sleeves & silver/black labels with one boxed EMI logo) ............ 30 |
| 73 | Parlophone PCS 3058 | A HARD DAY'S NIGHT (French pressing, 'Made in France' on EMI rim copy) ............ 15 |
| 82 | Parlophone PMC 1230 | A HARD DAY'S NIGHT (lightweight vinyl with yellow/black labels listing "mono") ........ 15 |

## ALBUMS : BEATLES FOR SALE

*(First pressings from 1964 have 'The Parlophone Co Ltd' & 'Sold in UK...' rim text with flipback sleeves)*

| 64 | Parlophone PMC 1240 | BEATLES FOR SALE (First pressing, G & L gatefold sleeve with visible flaps inside gatefold sleeve, with outline "mono" on front cover; mono) ............ 100 |
| 64 | Parlophone PCS 3062 | BEATLES FOR SALE (First pressing, G & L gatefold sleeve with visible flaps inside gatefold, with outline "stereo" on front cover; stereo) ............ 200 |
| 65 | Parlophone PCS 3062 | BEATLES FOR SALE (Second pressing, with 'The Gramophone Co Ltd' & 'Sold in UK...' label rim text, outline "stereo" on front gatefold sleeve; stereo) ............ 75 |
| 69 | Parlophone PCS 3062 | BEATLES FOR SALE (Third pressing with The Gramophone Co Ltd' label rim text but no 'Sold in UK...' text, gatefold sleeve; stereo) ............ 60 |
| 69 | Parlophone PCS 3062 | BEATLES FOR SALE (1969 repressing - gatefold sleeve, stereo only, with laminated flipback sleeve & silver/black labels with one boxed EMI logo) ............ 30 |
| 73 | Parlophone PCS 3062 | BEATLES FOR SALE (French pressing with 'Made in France' on EMI rim copy, gatefold sleeve) ............ 15 |
| 98 | Parlophone PMC 1240 | BEATLES FOR SALE (LP, gatefold, mono) ............ 20 |

## ALBUMS : HELP!

| 65 | Parlophone PMC 1255 | HELP! (LP, first pressing, G & L sleeve, with outline "mono" on front cover; mono)..... 100 |
| 65 | Parlophone PCS 3071 | HELP! (LP, first pressing, G & L sleeve, with outline "stereo" on front cover; stereo) ... 150 |
| 66 | Parlophone PMC 1255 | HELP! (LP, second pressing, G & L sleeve, plain white or sepia "LP advertising" inner sleeves; mono, with small solid black "mono" on front cover) ............ 70 |
| 66 | Parlophone PCS 3071 | HELP! (LP, second pressing, G & L sleeve, plain white or sepia "LP advertising" inner sleeves; stereo, with small solid black "stereo" on front cover) ............ 80 |
| 69 | Parlophone PMC 1255 | HELP! (LP, third pressing, small solid black "mono" on front cover; mono) ............ 60 |
| 69 | Parlophone PCS 3071 | HELP! (LP, third pressing, small solid black "stereo" on front cover; stereo) ............ 60 |
| 69 | Parlophone PMC 1255 | HELP! (LP, 1969 repressing, mono, one EMI boxed logo, with laminated flipback sleeve & silver/black labels with one boxed EMI logo) ............ 400 |
| 69 | Parlophone PCS 3071 | HELP! (LP, 1969 repressing, stereo, with laminated flipback sleeve & silver/black labels with one boxed EMI logo) ............ 30 |
| 73 | Parlophone PCS 3071 | HELP! (French pressing, with 'Made in France' on EMI label rim) ............ 15 |

## ALBUMS : RUBBER SOUL

*(First pressings from 1965 have 'The Gramophone Co Ltd' & 'Sold in UK...' label text.)*

| 65 | Parlophone PMC 1267 | RUBBER SOUL (First pressing, G & L or E. J. Day sleeve; mono, "loud cut" with XEX 579-1 and EXE 580-1 matrixes) ............ 250 |
| 65 | Parlophone PCS 3075 | RUBBER SOUL (First pressing, G & L or E. J. Day sleeve; stereo) ............ 225 |
| 65 | Parlophone PMC 1267 | RUBBER SOUL (Second pressing, matrix: [XEX 579-4 or 5]; mono) ............ 90 |
| 69 | Parlophone PCS 3075 | RUBBER SOUL (Second pressing, with 'The Gramophone Co Ltd' label text but no 'Sold In UK...' label text, some with E. J. Day sleeve; stereo) ............ 60 |
| 69 | Parlophone PMC 1267 | RUBBER SOUL (Third pressing, mono) ............ 60 |
| 69 | Parlophone PCS 3075 | RUBBER SOUL (1969 repressing, with laminated flipback sleeves & silver/black labels with one boxed EMI logo, stereo only) ............ 60 |
| 73 | Parlophone PCS 3075 | RUBBER SOUL (French pressing, with 'Made in France' on EMI rim copy) ............ 15 |

## ALBUMS : REVOLVER

*(First pressings from 1966 have 'The Gramophone Co Ltd' & 'Sold in UK...' label text)*

| 66 | Parlophone PMC 7009 | REVOLVER (First pressing, Side Two matrix [XEX 606-1], (G & L or E. J. Day sleeve; mono) ............ 400 |
| 66 | Parlophone PMC 7009 | REVOLVER (First pressing, G & L or E. J. Day sleeve; mono) ............ 100 |
| 66 | Parlophone PCS 7009 | REVOLVER (First pressing, G & L or E. J. Day sleeve; stereo) ............ 150 |
| 66 | Parlophone PMC 7009 | REVOLVER (Second pressing, G & L or E. J. Day sleeve, plain white or sepia "LP advertising" inner sleeves mono) ............ 100 |
| 69 | Parlophone PMC 7009 | REVOLVER (Third pressing, with 'The Gramophone Co Ltd' label text but no 'Sold in UK...' label text, plain white or sepia 'LP advertising' inners, mono) ............ 75 |

MINT VALUE £

| 69 | Parlophone PCS 7009 | REVOLVER (Second pressing, with 'The Gramophone Co Ltd' label text but no 'Sold in UK...' label text, plain white or sepia 'LP advertising' inners stereo) | 50 |
| 69 | Parlophone PCS 7009 | REVOLVER (1969 repressing, with laminated flipback sleeves & silver/black labels with one boxed EMI logo, stereo only) | 50 |
| 73 | Parlophone PCS 7009 | REVOLVER (French pressing with 'Made in France' on EMI rim copy) | 15 |
| 80 | Parlophone PMC 7009 | REVOLVER (mono, pressed between 1980 and 1982, Black label with two white-black EMI logos and silver print. Matrix numbers: Side 1: YEX 605-3; Side 2: YEX 606-4) | 15 |

## ALBUMS : A COLLECTION OF BEATLES OLDIES

*(First pressing from 1966 has 'The Gramophone Co Ltd' & 'Sold in UK...' label text.)*

| 66 | Parlophone PMC 7016 | A COLLECTION OF BEATLES OLDIES (First pressing, G & L or E. J. Day sleeve; mono) | 100 |
| 66 | Parlophone PCS 7016 | A COLLECTION OF BEATLES OLDIES (First pressing, G & L or E. J. Day sleeve; stereo) | 100 |
| 69 | Parlophone PMC 7016 | A COLLECTION OF BEATLES OLDIES (Second pressing, with 'The Gramophone Co Ltd' label text but no 'Sold in UK...' label text, plain white or sepia 'LP advertising' inners mono) | 40 |
| 69 | Parlophone PCS 7016 | A COLLECTION OF BEATLES OLDIES (Second pressing, with 'The Gramophone Co Ltd' label text but no 'Sold in UK...' label text, plain white or sepia 'LP advertising' inners stereo) | 35 |
| 69 | Parlophone PCS 7016 | A COLLECTION OF BEATLES OLDIES (stereo only, with laminated flipback sleeves & silver/black labels with one boxed EMI logo) | 25 |
| 73 | Parlophone PCS 7016 | A COLLECTION OF BEATLES OLDIES (LP, French pressing, with 'Made in France' on EMI rim copy) | 15 |

## ALBUMS : SGT. PEPPER'S LONELY HEARTS CLUB BAND

*(First pressing from 1967 has 'The Gramophone Co Ltd' & 'Sold in UK...' label text)*

| 67 | Parlophone PMC 7027 | SGT. PEPPER'S LONELY HEARTS CLUB BAND (First pressing, G & L laminated gatefold sleeve, visible flaps inside gatefold sleeve, with red & white inner & cut-out insert; mono) | 150 |
| 67 | Parlophone PCS 7027 | SGT. PEPPER'S LONELY HEARTS CLUB BAND (First pressing, G & L laminated gatefold sleeve, visible flaps inside gatefold sleeve, with red & white inner & cut-out insert; stereo) | 175 |
| 69 | Parlophone PCS 7027 | SGT. PEPPER'S LONELY HEARTS CLUB BAND (Second pressing, with 'The Gramophone Co Ltd' label text but no 'Sold in UK...' label text, plain white or sepia 'LP advertising' inners gatefold sleeve, with white inner and cut-out insert; stereo) | 35 |
| 69 | Parlophone PMC 7027 | SGT. PEPPER'S LONELY HEARTS CLUB BAND (Third pressing, with 'The Gramophone Co Ltd' label text but no 'Sold in UK...' label text, plain white or sepia 'LP advertising' inners laminated gatefold sleeve,& cut-out insert; mono) | 60 |
| 69 | Parlophone PMC 7027 | SGT. PEPPER'S LONELY HEARTS CLUB BAND (1969 repressing, laminated gatefold sleeve, with cut-out insert, mono, with laminated flipback sleeves & silver/black labels with one boxed EMI logo) | 60 |
| 69 | Parlophone PCS 7027 | SGT. PEPPER'S LONELY HEARTS CLUB BAND (1969 repressing, laminated gatefold sleeve, with cut-out insert, stereo, with laminated flipback sleeves & silver/black labels with one boxed EMI logo) | 30 |
| 73 | Parlophone PCS 7027 | SGT. PEPPER'S LONELY HEARTS CLUB BAND (French pressing, gatefold sleeve with cut-out insert, some copies with banded vinyl, with 'Made In France' on EMI rim) | 18 |
| 84 | Parlophone/Nimbus PCS 7027 | SGT. PEPPER'S LONELY HEARTS CLUB BAND (mail-order only, from Practical Hi-Fi Magazine, Nimbus pressing) | 600 |

## ALBUMS : THE BEATLES (THE WHITE ALBUM)

| 68 | Apple PMC/PCS 7067/8 | THE BEATLES (WHITE ALBUM) (First pressing, mono or stereo, numbered below 0000010) | 10000 |
| 68 | Apple PMC/PCS 7067/8 | THE BEATLES (WHITE ALBUM) (First pressing, 2-LP, mono or stereo, numbered between 0000011 & 0001000) | 3000 |
| 68 | Apple PMC/PCS 7067/8 | THE BEATLES (WHITE ALBUM) (First pressing, 2-LP, mono or stereo, numbered between 0001001 & 0010000) | 1000 |
| 68 | Apple PMC 7067/8 | THE BEATLES (WHITE ALBUM) (First pressing, 2-LP, mono, numbered above 0010000) | 300 |
| 68 | Apple PCS 7067/8 | THE BEATLES (WHITE ALBUM) (First pressing, 2-LP, stereo, numbered above 0010000) | 250 |
| 69 | Apple PCS 7067/8 | THE BEATLES (WHITE ALBUM) (Second pressing, 2-LP, side opening, numbered g/fold sl., poster & 4 colour prints; stereo) | 100 |
| 73 | Apple PCS 7067/8 | THE BEATLES (WHITE ALBUM) (2-LP, French pressing, un-numbered, laminated, side-opening gatefold sleeve, with four colour prints & poster, 'Made in France by Pathe Marconi EMI' rim copy) | 25 |
| 73 | Apple PCS 7067/8 | THE BEATLES (WHITE ALBUM) (2-LP, un-numbered, laminated, side-opening gatefold sleeve, with poster & 4 soft card colour prints, stereo only) | 35 |
| 82 | Apple PMC 7067/8 | THE BEATLES (WHITE ALBUM) (2-LP, un-numbered, side-opening gatefold sleeve, with poster & 4 prints, light green Apple label; mono) | 30 |
| 95 | Apple PCS 7067/8 | THE BEATLES (WHITE ALBUM) (2-LP) | 20 |

## ALBUMS : YELLOW SUBMARINE

| 69 | Apple PMC 7070 | YELLOW SUBMARINE (LP, first pressing with red lines above & below rear sleevenote; mono) | 300 |
| 69 | Apple PCS 7070 | YELLOW SUBMARINE (LP, first pressing with red lines above & below rear sleevenote; stereo) | 125 |
| 73 | Apple PCS 7070 | YELLOW SUBMARINE (LP, second pressing with red lines above & below rear sleevenote; stereo) | 50 |
| 73 | Apple PCS 7070 | YELLOW SUBMARINE (LP, French pressing, with 'Made in France by Pathe Marconi EMI' on rim) | 15 |
| 99 | Apple 521 4811 | YELLOW SUBMARINE SONGTRACK (yellow vinyl, gatefold stickered sleeve) | 35 |
| 99 | Apple 521 4811 | YELLOW SUBMARINE SONGTRACK (LP, gatefold stickered sleeve) | 30 |

## ALBUMS : ABBEY ROAD

| 69 | Apple PCS 7088 | ABBEY ROAD (LP, first pressing, black or plain white inner sleeve, with Apple logo aligned to Side 1 track listing on rear sleeve; with "Her Majesty" credit on label) | 80 |
| 69 | Apple PCS 7088 | ABBEY ROAD (LP, first pressing Apple logo misaligned to Side 1 track listing on rear sleeve; with or without "Her Majesty" credit on label; black or plain white inner sleeve) | 100 |
| 73 | | ABBEY ROAD (some copies with banded vinyl, French Pressing, with 'Made in France by Pathe Marconi EMI' rim copy) | 15 |

## ALBUMS : LET IT BE

| 70 | Apple PXS 1 | LET IT BE (LP box set, first pressing dark green label red Apple logo on rear sleeve & white inner, with Get Back book housed in black card tray ['PXS 1' not listed on package], with rare Apple mini poster) | 1000 |

| | | | |
|---|---|---|---|
| 70 | Apple PXS 1 | LET IT BE (LP box set, first pressing dark green label red Apple logo on rear sleeve & white inner, with Get Back book housed in black card tray ['PXS 1' not listed on package], without rare Apple mini poster) | 800 |
| 73 | Apple PCS 7096 | LET IT BE (French pressing with 'Made in France by Pathe Marconi EMI' rim text) | 15 |

## ALBUMS : 1969

*(Apple LPs have G&L sleeves & black inners. Dark green labels with "Sold in UK..." text unless otherwise stated. Parlophone repressings are in G&L sleeves with "The Gramophone Co. Ltd." but without "Sold in UK..." label text unless otherwise stated. These pressings also have plain white or sepia "LP advertising" inners.)*

| | | | |
|---|---|---|---|
| 69 | Apple PCS 7080 | GET BACK (LP, unreleased, acetates only) | 0 |

## ALBUMS : 1970

*(With G&L sleeves and dark green labels, unless otherwise stated.)*

| | | | |
|---|---|---|---|
| 70 | Apple/Lyntone LYN 2154 | FROM THEN TO YOU (The Beatles' Christmas Album) | 500 |

## ALBUMS : ALBUM BOX SETS

| | | | |
|---|---|---|---|
| 78 | Parlophone BC 13 | THE BEATLES COLLECTION (13 x LP, stereo, some with poster) | 150 |
| 80 | World Record Club SM 701/ 708 | THE BEATLES BOX (8-LP, mail order only) | 80 |
| 82 | Parlophone BMC 10 | THE BEATLES MONO COLLECTION (10 x LP, red box) | 350 |

## ALBUMS : CD ALBUMS AND BOX SETS

| | | | |
|---|---|---|---|
| 87 | HMV BEACD 25/1 | PLEASE PLEASE ME/WITH THE BEATLES/A HARD DAY'S NIGHT/BEATLES FOR SALE (4 x CD, numbered 12" black box set withBook Of Beatles Lists paperback book) | 100 |
| 87 | HMV BEACD 25/2 | HELP!/RUBBER SOUL/REVOLVER (3 x CD, numbered 12" red box set with insert & reprint of Beatles Book Monthly, issue 12) | 50 |
| 87 | HMV BEACD 25/4 | THE BEATLES (2-CD, numbered 12" box set with booklet & badge) | 30 |
| 87 | HMV BEACD 25/5 | YELLOW SUBMARINE (CD, numbered 12" box set with insert, cut-outs & badge) | 50 |
| 87 | HMV BEACD 25/3 | SGT. PEPPER'S LONELY HEARTS CLUB BAND (CD, numbered 12" box set with booklet, cut-outs & badge) | 18 |

## ALBUMS : CONTRACT PRESSINGS : LPS

*(Records were often pressed by non-EMI companies under contract, owing to overwhelming demand for Beatles records. Subtle differences indicating their origin can be detected. Philips pressings (the 'Hey Jude' single only) are the easiest to spot as they alone have three-pronged centres. All the others had four except for the French Pathe-Marconi pressings of 'Hello Goodbye' which have solid centres and 'Made In France' at the foot of the label. The centre of a Decca contract pressing has a circular ridge 3mm from the perimeter. Pre-1966 EMI pressings have flat push-out centres. Thereafter many records were produced with a mix of push-out and solid centres. EMI always pressed stamper letters into the vinyl, positioned at 3 o' clock to the matrix number. Up to three letters from the code 'GRAMOPHLTD' were used each representing a number. EMI stamper letters are seldom seen on contract pressings. Great controversy has surrounded the origin of the only other known style of pre-1965 Beatles' contract pressings. Previously thought to have been made by Pye they are now believed to have been pressed at the ORIOLE pressing plant before their September 1964 aquisition by CBS. The centres of these pressings have no ridge and are finished with rough edges. They are also thicker and heavier than any of the other pressings. Although released in November 1964 'I Feel Fine' also has these characteristics and is assumed to have come from this source. CBS using the old ORIOLE presses. However, it is thought that PYE actually pressed one Beatles 45 and one EP after 1964. The centres of these two pressings look very similar to those made by DECCA but have a less prominent ridge. The edges of records made by PHILIPS, ORIOLE and PYE are not straight-cut but are tapered off. The edges of EMI, DECCA and Pathe-Marconi pressings are all straight-cut. (Decca contract pressings have no stamper letters (G or D) positioned at 3 o'clock to the matrix number; the label has a circularimpression 15mm from the outer edge. Pye pressings between 1973 and 1979 are a dark, translucent red when held up to a strong light.) Let us hope that the online community of Beatles fans and collectors worldwide will one day solve the magical mystery tour of Beatles contract pressings. Until that day, the following is where we at Record Collector are at the present time)*

| | | | |
|---|---|---|---|
| 63 | Parlophone PMC 1202 | PLEASE PLEASE ME (Decca contract pressing) | 200 |
| 63 | Parlophone PMC 1206 | WITH THE BEATLES (Pye contract pressing) | 150 |
| 63 | Parlophone PMC 1206 | WITH THE BEATLES (Decca contract pressing) | 150 |
| 68 | Parlophone P-PCS 7067/8 | THE BEATLES (WHITE ALBUM) (2-LP, Decca contract pressing, yellow & black labels) | 3000 |

*(Decca contract pressings have no stamper letters (G or D) positioned at 3 o'clock to the matrix number; the label has a circularimpression 15mm from the outer edge. Pye pressings are a dark, translucent red when held up to a strong light.)*

| | | | |
|---|---|---|---|
| 69 | Parlophone P-PCS 7088 | ABBEY ROAD (LP, contract pressing export issue, yellow & black labels, Decca pressing) | 1000 |
| 69 | Parlophone P-PCS 7099 | ABBEY ROAD (LP, contract pressing, export issue, silver & black labels, Decca pressing) | 500 |
| 70s | Apple PCSP 717 | THE BEATLES 1962-1966 (2-LP, gatefold sleeve with lyric inners, Pye pressing) | 50 |

## ALBUMS : EXPORT LPS : ORIGINALS

*(with black/yellow labels unless otherwise stated)*

| | | | |
|---|---|---|---|
| 68 | Parlophone PCS 3075 | RUBBER SOUL (LP, with "Sold in U.K." label text, but silver 'Stereo' on top right hand corner, small batch pressed for export) | 400 |
| 68 | Parlophone PCS 3075 | RUBBER SOUL (LP, with "Sold in U.K." label text, but black 'Stereo' on top right hand corner, small batch pressed for export) | 150 |
| 65 | Parlophone CPCS 101 | SOMETHING NEW (LP, export 2nd pressing, with "Parlophone Co. Ltd." label text, no "sold in the U.K." label text) | 500 |
| 65 | Parlophone CPCS 101 | SOMETHING NEW (LP, export 2nd pressing, with "Gramophone Co. Ltd." label text) | 350 |
| 66 | Parlophone CPCS 103 | THE BEATLES' SECOND ALBUM (LP, export, first pressing with yellow/black labels) | 450 |
| 66 | Parlophone CPCS 104 | BEATLES VI (LP, first export pressing with yellow/black labels) | 500 |
| 68 | Parlophone P-PCS 7067/8 | THE BEATLES (WHITE ALBUM) (2-LP, export pressing, yellow/black labels, numbered, top opening 'mono' gatefold sleeve with "stereo" sticker & black inners, poster & 4 colour prints) | 800 |
| 69 | Odeon PPCS 7070 | YELLOW SUBMARINE (LP, export pressing Odeon sticker on rear of Apple sleeve) | 2000 |

*(with yellow/black labels)*

| | | | |
|---|---|---|---|
| 69 | Parlophone P-PCS 7088 | ABBEY ROAD (LP, export pressing, Parlophone sticker on rear of Apple sleeve, Apple logo on label) | 800 |
| 70 | Parlophone P-PCS 7096 | LET IT BE (LP, First export pressing with silver/black labels, one EMI boxed logo) | 750 |

*(with silver/black labels)*

| | | | |
|---|---|---|---|
| 70 | Parlophone CPCS 106 | HEY JUDE (silver/black label, large boxed Parlophone label at top and small EMI boxed logo at bottom, laminated sleeve) | 600 |

## ALBUMS : EXPORT LPS : REISSUES

| | | | |
|---|---|---|---|
| 69 | Parlophone P-PCS 7088 | ABBEY ROAD (LP, export copy reissue, Parlophone sticker on rear of Apple sleeve; one EMI boxed logo) | 125 |
| 69 | Apple CPCS 106 | HEY JUDE (2nd reissue, dark green label) | 75 |
| 69 | Parlophone CPCS 101 | SOMETHING NEW (one EMI boxed logo) | 150 |

MINT VALUE £

| 69 | Parlophone CPCS 103 | THE BEATLES' SECOND ALBUM (LP, export, second pressing with sliver/black labels, one EMI boxed logo) | 150 |
|---|---|---|---|
| 69 | Parlophone CPCS 104 | BEATLES VI (LP, second export pressing with silver/black labels, one EMI boxed logo) | 250 |
| 70 | Parl./Apple (P-)PCS 7096 | LET IT BE (LP, export pressing second reissue, Apple label [PCS 7096] in Parlophone sleeve) | 35 |
| | *(with silver/black labels)* | | |
| 70 | Parlophone CPCS 103 | THE BEATLES' SECOND ALBUM (LP, export, 2nd reissue, silver/black labels two EMI boxed logos) | 100 |
| 73 | Apple CPCS 106 | HEY JUDE (3rd reissue, light green label) | 25 |
| 78 | Apple PCS 7067/8 | THE BEATLES (WHITE ALBUM) (2-LP, export pressing, white vinyl, gatefold sleeve) | 40 |
| 78 | Parlophone PCTC 255 | MAGICAL MYSTERY TOUR (LP, transparent yellow vinyl) | 50 |
| | *(with silver/black labels)* | | |
| 78 | Apple PCS 7088 | ABBEY ROAD (LP, green vinyl) | 50 |
| 78 | Apple PCS 7096 | LET IT BE (LP white vinyl) | 50 |
| 70s | Parl./Apple (P-)CPCS 106 | HEY JUDE (Apple label [CPCS 106] in Parlophone sleeve [P-CPSC 106]) | 35 |

## ALBUMS : LPS : 1970S RE-PRESSINGS

*(Black and silver labels with 'EMI Records Ltd' on label and 2 EMI boxes. Unless otherwise specified all have front laminated and non-flipback sleeves. Those albums with Apple labels are slightly lighter than those on 60s original pressings)*

| 70s | Parlophone PCS 3042 | PLEASE PLEASE ME (LP) | 25 |
|---|---|---|---|
| 70s | Parlophone PCS 3045 | WITH THE BEATLES (LP) | 20 |
| 70s | Parlophone PCS 3058 | A HARD DAYS NIGHT (LP) | 25 |
| 70s | Parlophone PCS 3062 | BEATLES FOR SALE (LP) | 20 |
| 70s | Parlophone PCS 3071 | HELP! (LP) | 20 |
| 70s | Parlophone PCS 3075 | RUBBER SOUL (LP) | 30 |
| 70s | Parlophone PCS 7009 | REVOLVER (LP) | 30 |
| 70s | Parlophone PCS 7016 | A COLLECTION OF BEATLES OLDIES (LP) | 20 |
| 70s | Parlophone PCS 7027 | SGT. PEPPER'S LONELY HEARTS CLUB BAND (LP, fully laminated sleeve) | 30 |
| 70s | Apple PCS 7067/68 | THE BEATLES (WHITE ALBUM) (2-LP, fully laminated sleeve) | 40 |
| 76 | Parlophone PCTC 255 | MAGICAL MYSTERY TOUR (LP, with booklet) | 40 |
| 70s | Apple PCS 7070 | YELLOW SUBMARINE (LP) | 25 |
| 70s | Apple PCS 7088 | ABBEY ROAD (LP, fully laminated sleeve) | 25 |
| 70s | Apple PCS 7096 | LET IT BE (LP, fully laminated sleeve) | 25 |

## ALBUMS : LPS : 1980S RE-PRESSINGS

*(These repressings come in non-laminated 'varnished' sleeves and have black and silver labels. Most sleeves have barcodes)*

| 88 | Parlophone PCTC 255 | MAGICAL MYSTERY TOUR (gatefold, with booklet) | 18 |
|---|---|---|---|
| 80s | Parlophone PMC 1202 | PLEASE PLEASE ME (LP, mono) | 18 |
| 80s | Parlophone PMC 1206 | WITH THE BEATLES (LP, mono) | 15 |
| 80s | Parlophone PMC 1230 | A HARD DAYS NIGHT (LP, mono) | 15 |
| 80s | Parlophone PMC 1240 | BEATLES FOR SALE (LP, mono) | 15 |
| 80s | Parlophone PCS 3071 | HELP! (LP, stereo) | 15 |
| 80s | Parlophone PCS 3075 | RUBBER SOUL (LP, stereo) | 15 |
| 80s | Parlophone PCS 7009 | REVOLVER (LP, stereo) | 20 |
| 80s | Parlophone PCS 7016 | A COLLECTION OF BEATLES OLDIES (LP, stereo) | 20 |
| 80s | Parlophone PCS 7027 | SGT. PEPPER'S LONELY HEARTS CLUB BAND (LP, stereo) | 20 |
| 80s | Apple PCS 7067/68 | THE BEATLES (WHITE ALBUM) (2-LP, stereo) | 25 |
| 80s | Apple PCS 7070 | YELLOW SUBMARINE (LP, stereo) | 18 |
| 80s | Apple PCS 7088 | ABBEY ROAD (LP, stereo) | 18 |
| 80s | Apple PCS 7096 | LET IT BE (LP, stereo) | 18 |

## ALBUMS : LPS : RETROSPECTIVES

| 73 | Apple PCSP 717 | THE BEATLES 1962-1966 (2-LP, labels state PCS 7171 and PCS 7172) | 40 |
|---|---|---|---|
| 73 | Apple PCSP 718 | THE BEATLES 1967-1970 (2-LP, labels state 7181 and 7182) | 40 |
| 76 | Parlophone PCSP 719 | ROCK N ROLL MUSIC (2-LP, gatefold) | 30 |
| 76 | Polydor 2683 068 | THE BEATLES TAPES (2-LP) | 30 |
| 77 | EMI EMTV 4 | THE BEATLES AT THE HOLLYWOOD BOWL (gatefold sleeve, with inner) | 15 |
| 77 | Lingasong LNS 1 | LIVE AT THE STAR CLUB 1962 (2-LP) | 30 |
| 77 | Parlophone PCSP 721 | LOVE SONGS (2-LP, gatefold) | 30 |
| 77 | EMI HRL 026 | HISTORY OF ROCK VOL.26 THE BEATLES (2-LP gatefold sleeve) | 30 |
| 78 | Apple PCSPR 717 | THE BEATLES 1962-1966 (2-LP, red vinyl, gatefold stickered sleeve with lyric inners) | 20 |
| 78 | Apple PCSPB 718 | THE BEATLES 1967-1970 (2-LP, blue vinyl, gatefold stickered sleeve with lyric inners) | 20 |
| 79 | Parlophone PCM 1001 | RARITIES (LP) | 30 |
| 82 | Parlophone EMTVS 34 | THE BEATLES' GREATEST HITS (2-LP, unreleased) | 0 |
| 88 | HMV BPM 1 | PAST MASTERS VOLUME 1 & 2 (2-LP, gatefold sleeve) | 45 |
| 94 | Apple PCSP 726 | LIVE AT THE BBC (2-LP, gatefold sleeve, with inners) | 40 |
| 95 | Apple PCSP 727 | ANTHOLOGY 1 (3-LP, gatefold sleeve, with inners) | 50 |
| 96 | Apple PCSP 728 | ANTHOLOGY 2 (3-LP, gatefold sleeve, with inners) | 50 |
| 96 | Apple PCSP 729 | ANTHOLOGY 3 (3-LP, gatefold sleeve, with inners) | 50 |
| 00 | Apple 529 3251 | THE BEATLES 1 (2-LP, gatefold sleeve, with poster & 4 prints) | 40 |
| 03 | Apple 595 4380 | LET IT BE...NAKED (LP, gatefold sleeve PLUS "Fly On The Wall" 7" EP) | 40 |
| 07 | Apple 379 8081 | LOVE (2-LP, gatefold sleeve, with inners) | 30 |

## ALBUMS : POLYDOR RECORDINGS : LPS

| 64 | Polydor Hi-Fi 46 432 | THE BEATLES' FIRST (purple/black sleeve, Germany only, unissued in U.K.) | 100 |
|---|---|---|---|
| 67 | Polydor Special 236 201 | THE BEATLES' FIRST (as Tony Sheridan & The Beatles, 1st pressing, without 'stereo' on label or sleeve, 'pop art' sleeve) | 50 |
| 67 | Polydor Special 236 201 | THE BEATLES' FIRST (later pressings with 'stereo' on label & sleeve, minor label variations, 'pop art' sleeve) | 30 |

## ALBUMS : REEL-TO-REEL TAPES: ORIGINALS

*(All Beatles Reel-to-Reel tapes up to 1967 (from PLEASE PLEASE ME to SGT. PEPPERS LONELY HEARTS CLUB BAND were issued on 4 inch spools with printed leaders and were housed in card trays in card boxes. From THE BEATLES (WHITE ALBUM) to LET IT BE albums were still 4 inch spools but housed in jewel cases with card inlays)*

| | | | |
|---|---|---|---|
| 65 | Parlophone TA-PMC 1240 | BEATLES FOR SALE (Mono only) | 20 |
| 65 | Parlophone TA-PMC 1255 | HELP! (Mono-only) | 20 |
| 65 | Parlophone TA-PMC 1267 | RUBBER SOUL (Mono only, reel-to-reel tape) | 20 |
| 66 | Parlophone TA-PMC 7009 | REVOLVER (Mono only) | 25 |
| 70 | Apple TD-PCS 7088 | ABBEY ROAD (Stereo, jewel case) | 70 |
| 70 | Apple TA-PMC 7088 | ABBEY ROAD (Mono, jewel case) | 100 |
| 69 | Apple DTD-PCS 7067/8 | THE BEATLES (WHITE ALBUM) (5 inch spool, Stereo, jewel case) | 100 |
| 69 | Apple DTA-PMC 7067/8 | THE BEATLES (WHITE ALBUM) (5 inch spool, Mono, jewel case) | 100 |
| 67 | Parlophone TA-PMC 7027 | SGT. PEPPER'S LONELY HEARTS CLUB BAND (Mono only) | 30 |

*(All Beatles Reel-to-Reel tapes up to 1967 (from PLEASE PLEASE ME to SGT. PEPPERS LONELY HEARTS CLUB BAND) were issued on 4 inch spools with printed leaders and were housed in card trays in card boxes)*

| | | | |
|---|---|---|---|
| 67 | Parlophone TA-PMC 7016 | A COLLECTION OF BEATLES OLDIES (Mono only) | 20 |
| 63 | Parlophone TA-PMC 1202 | PLEASE PLEASE ME (Mono only) | 25 |
| 64 | Parlophone TA-PMC 1206 | WITH THE BEATLES (Mono only) | 25 |
| 64 | Parlophone TA-PMC 1230 | A HARD DAYS NIGHT (Mono only) | 20 |
| 70 | Apple TA-PMC 7096 | LET IT BE (Mono, jewel case) | 100 |
| 70 | Apple TD-PCS 7096 | LET IT BE (Stereo, jewel case) | 80 |

## ALBUMS : REEL-TO-REEL TAPES: REISSUES

*(These albums were all reissued on reel-to-reel tape in 1968 and are all on 4 inch tape inside jewel cases with card inserts)*

| | | | |
|---|---|---|---|
| 68 | Parlophone TA-PMC 1202 | PLEASE PLEASE ME (Reissue, Mono, jewel case) | 25 |
| 68 | Parlophone TD-PCS 3042 | PLEASE PLEASE ME (Reissue, Stereo, jewel case) | 25 |
| 68 | Parlophone TA-PMC 1206 | WITH THE BEATLES (Reissue, Mono, jewel case) | 30 |
| 68 | Parlophone TD-PCS 3045 | WITH THE BEATLES (Reissue, Stereo, jewel case) | 25 |
| 68 | Parlophone TA-PMC 1230 | A HARD DAY'S NIGHT (Reissue, Mono, jewel case) | 25 |
| 68 | Parlophone TD-PCS 3058 | A HARD DAY'S NIGHT (Reissue, Stereo, jewel case) | 25 |
| 68 | Parlophone TA-PMC 1240 | BEATLES FOR SALE (Reissue, Mono, jewel case) | 30 |
| 68 | Parlophone TD-PCS 3062 | BEATLES FOR SALE (Reissue, Stereo, jewel case) | 25 |
| 68 | Parlophone TA-PCM 1255 | HELP! (Reissue, Mono, jewel case) | 25 |
| 68 | Parlophone TD-PCS 3071 | HELP! (Reissue, Stereo, jewel case) | 25 |
| 68 | Parlophone TA-PMC 1267 | RUBBER SOUL (Reissue, Mono, jewel case) | 30 |
| 68 | Parlophone TD-PCS 3075 | RUBBER SOUL (Reissue, Stereo, jewel case) | 25 |
| 68 | Parlophone TA-PMC 7009 | REVOLVER (Reissue, Mono, jewel case) | 30 |
| 68 | Parlophone TD-PCS 7009 | REVOLVER (Reissue, Stereo, jewel case) | 25 |
| 68 | Parlophone TA-PMC 7016 | A COLLECTION OF BEATLES OLDIES (Reissue, Mono, jewel case) | 30 |
| 68 | Parlophone TD-PCS 7016 | A COLLECTION OF BEATLES OLDIES (Reissue, Stereo, jewel case) | 25 |
| 68 | Parlophone TA-PMC 7027 | SGT. PEPPER'S LONELY HEARTS CLUB BAND (Reissue, Mono, jewel case) | 40 |
| 68 | Parlophone TD-PCS 7027 | SGT. PEPPER'S LONELY HEARTS CLUB BAND (Reissue, Stereo, jewel case) | 35 |

## MISPRESSINGS

| | | | |
|---|---|---|---|
| 63 | Parlophone R 4983 | Please Please Me/Ask Me Why (Mispressing, A-side actually plays 'Quiet Morning' by the Brian Fahey Orchestra) | 50 |
| 64 | Parlophone GEP 8882 | TWIST AND SHOUT (label error: "Do You Want A Know A Secret") | 20 |
| 64 | Parlophone PCS 3062 | BEATLES FOR SALE (label error: "I'm A Losser") | 250 |
| 65 | Parlophone GEP 8946 | THE BEATLES' MILLION SELLERS (label error: "Beatles Golden Discs") | 400 |
| 65 | Parlophone PCS 3075 | RUBBER SOUL (label error: "Norweigian Wood") | 400 |
| 65 | Parlophone CPCS 101 | SOMETHING NEW (LP, 1st pressing, 1G/1G mother stampers, export issue, label misprint: "Sold in UK") | 500 |
| 66 | Parlophone PMC 7009 | REVOLVER (copies with side 2 matrix no.: XEX 606-1 have 'Remix 11' of Tomorrow Never Knows, G & L or E. J. Day sleeve; mono only) | 500 |
| 66 | Parlophone CPCS 106 | BEATLES VI (LP, export issue, label error: "Sold in UK") | 500 |
| 67 | Parlophone PMC 7027 | SGT. PEPPER'S LONELY HEARTS CLUB BAND (First pressing with label misprint omits "A Day In The Life" credit; G & L laminated gatefold sleeve, with plain white inner & insert;; mono only) | 200 |

*With "The Gramophone Co Ltd" & "Sold in the UK..." label text*

| | | | |
|---|---|---|---|
| 68 | Apple PCS 7067/8 | THE BEATLES (WHITE ALBUM) (2-LP label misprinting error: "Rocky Racoon") | 200 |
| 69 | Apple PCS 7088 | ABBEY ROAD (label omits "Her Majesty") | 35 |
| 69 | Apple CPCS 106 | HEY JUDE (label misprint error: "Revolutions") | 300 |
| 69 | Parlophone PCS 7009 | REVOLVER (1969 repressing, stereo only with misprint "I Got To Get You Into My Life" on side 2) | 70 |

*(with laminated flipback sleeves & silver/black labels with one boxed EMI logo)*

| | | | |
|---|---|---|---|
| 69 | Parlophone PMC 7027 | SGT. PEPPER'S LONELY HEARTS CLUB BAND (1969 Mispressing, mono; matrix YEX 637/8; plays stereo) | 200 |
| 99 | Parlophone PCS 3075 | RUBBER SOUL (label error: pressed on Apple) | 100 |
| 12 | Parlophone 45-R 4949 | Love Me Do/PS I Love You (reissue, withdrawn as A side has album version with Andy White on drums and Ringo on tambourine, Matrixes: BC88258-01A1 01740174/ BC88258-01B1 0174017 J G i i and incorrect catalogue number R 47414 on B-side ) | 20 |

## FLEXIDISCS

*(Fan club flexidiscs are worth around £20 less without newsletters and half the listed values without picture sleeves.)*

| | | | |
|---|---|---|---|
| 63 | Lyntone LYN 492 | The Beatles' Christmas Record (Flexidisc, gatefold p/s) | 120 |
| 64 | Lyntone LYN 757 | Another Beatles Christmas Record (Flexidisc, p/s, with gatefold newsletter insert) | 100 |
| 65 | Lyntone LYN 948 | The Beatles' Third Christmas Record (Flexidisc, p/s, with gatefold newsletter insert) | 100 |
| 66 | Lyntone LYN 1145 | Pantomime: Everywhere It's Christmas (Flexidisc, p/s, with 7" x 7" newsletter insert) | 100 |
| 67 | Lyntone LYN 1360 | Christmas Time (Is Here Again) (Flexidisc, p/s, with 7" x 7" newsletter insert) | 100 |
| 68 | Lyntone LYN 1743/4 | The Beatles' Sixth Christmas Record (Flexidisc, p/s, with 'Superpix' sales insert) | 100 |
| 68 | Lyntone LYN 1743/4 | The Beatles' Sixth Christmas Record (Flexidisc, p/s, without "Superpix" sales insert) | 100 |
| 69 | Lyntone LYN 1970/1-IL | The Beatles' Seventh Christmas Record (Flexidisc, p/s, with 2 x foolscap fan club newsletters) | 100 |
| 69 | Lyntone LYN 1970/1-IL | The Beatles' Seventh Christmas Record (p/s) | 75 |

*(see also John Lennon, Paul McCartney/Wings, George Harrison, Ringo Starr, Pete Best Four, Quarry Men, Tony Sheridan, George Martin, Billy Preston, Yoko Ono)*

## BEATMEN

| | | | |
|---|---|---|---|
| 64 | Pye 7N 15659 | You Can't Sit Down/Come On Pretty Babe | 20 |

MINT VALUE £

| 65 | Pye 7N 15792 | Now The Sun Has Gone/Please Believe | 40 |

## BEAT MERCHANTS
| 64 | Columbia DB 7367 | Pretty Face/Messin' With The Man | 80 |
| 65 | Columbia DB 7492 | So Fine/She Said Yeah | 70 |

## BEAT NECESSITY
| 81 | Newtown NTP 2 | Pleasure Pain/VELDT: Ghost Child | 15 |
| 82 | Newtown NTP 3 | When You're Down On Your Luck/Telephone/Don't Know | 15 |

## BEATPUMP
| 80 | Slow Lorries SLOW 1 | THE FIVE MONTH PLAN EP (p/s) | 25 |

## BEAT SIX
| 64 | Decca F 12011 | Bernadine/The River And I | 5 |

*(see also Guys)*

## BEATSTALKERS
| 65 | Decca F 12259 | Ev'rybody's Talking 'Bout My Baby/Mr. Disappointed | 80 |
| 66 | Decca F 12352 | Left Right Left/You'd Better Get A Better Hold On | 60 |
| 66 | Decca F 12460 | A Love Like Yours/Base Line | 60 |
| 67 | CBS 2732 | My One Chance To Make It/Ain't No Soul (Left In These Ole Shoes) | 80 |
| 67 | CBS 3105 | Silver Treetop School For Boys/Sugar Coated Man | 75 |
| 68 | CBS 3557 | Rain Coloured Roses/Everything Is For You | 60 |
| 69 | CBS 3936 | Little Boy/When I'm Five | 70 |

## PAUL BEATTIE
| 57 | Parlophone R 4385 | I'm Comin' Home/Nothing So Strange | 30 |
| 58 | Parlophone R 4429 | Me, Please Me/Wanderlust | 5 |
| 58 | Parlophone R 4468 | A House, A Car, And A Wedding Ring/Banana | 10 |
| 68 | Parlophone R 4664 | Slick Chick/The Big Bounce | 30 |

## E.C. BEATTY
| 59 | Felsted AF 127 | Ski King/I'm A Lucky Man | 10 |

## BEAU
| 69 | Dandelion S 4403 | 1917 Revolution/Sleeping Town | 10 |
| 69 | Dandelion S 63751 | BEAU (LP, black/red/silver label) | 50 |
| 71 | Dandelion DAN 8006 | CREATION (LP, with The Way We Live) | 40 |

*(see also Way We Live)*

## BEAU BRUMMEL
| 82 | Moonlight MNS 004 | Hot George/Oscar | 15 |

*(see also Paul Roland, Andy Ellison, Knox)*

## BEAU BRUMMELS
| 65 | Pye International 7N 25293 | Laugh, Laugh/Still In Love With You Baby | 5 |
| 65 | Pye International 7N 25306 | Just A Little/They'll Make You Cry | 5 |
| 65 | Pye International 7N 25318 | You Tell Me Why/I Want You | 5 |
| 65 | Pye International 7N 25333 | Don't Talk To Strangers/In Good Time | 5 |
| 66 | Pye International 7N 25342 | Good Time Music/Sad Little Girl (unissued) | 0 |
| 65 | Pye International NPL 28062 | INTRODUCING THE BEAU BRUMMELS (LP, mono only) | 20 |

## BEAU-MARKS
| 60 | Top Rank JAR 377 | Clap Your Hands/Daddy Said | 20 |

*(see also Del-Tones, Milton De Lugg Orchestra)*

## JIMMY BEAUMONT
| 66 | London HLZ 10059 | You Got Too Much Going For You/I Never Loved Her Anyway | 100 |
| 66 | London HLZ 10059 | You Got Too Much Going For You/I Never Loved Her Anyway (DJ Copy) | 200 |

## BEAUTIFUL SOUTH
| 94 | Go! Discs 828 507-1 | MIAOW (LP, withdrawn HMV-style 'dog' sleeve with lyric inner) | 20 |
| 96 | Go! Discs 828 845-1 | BLUE IS THE COLOUR (LP, with lyric inner) | 15 |
| 98 | Go Discs 538166 | QUENCH (LP, inner) | 30 |
| 07 | Mercury 175 252-3 | SOUP ('deluxe Fan Edition', in sealed/stickered tin: CD, DVD, T-shirt and mug) | 60 |

## BEAVERS
| 58 | Capitol CL 14909 | Road To Happiness/Low As I Can Be | 5 |

## JACKIE BEAVERS
| 75 | Buddah BDS 423 | Mr Bump Man (Give A Hand) Part II/Somebody Help The Beggar | 5 |
| 76 | Jay Boy BOY 102 | Trying To Get Back To You Girl/Trying To Get Back To You Girl (Version) | 12 |
| 98 | Wigan Casino 202 | I Need My Baby/JOE MATTHEWS: She's My Beauty Queen (p/s reissue) | 8 |

## BEAZERS
| 64 | Decca F 11827 | Blue Beat/I Wanna Shout | 45 |

*(see also Chris Farlowe, Little Joe Cook)*

## BE-BOP DELUXE
| 73 | Smile LAFS 001 | Teenage Archangel/Jets At Dawn (mono, 1,000 only) | 25 |
| 74 | Harvest HAR 5081 | Jet Silver (And The Dolls Of Venus)/Third Floor Heaven | 6 |
| 75 | Harvest HAR 5091 | Between The Worlds/Lights (withdrawn) | 50 |
| 75 | Harvest HAR 5098 | Maid In Heaven/Lights | 5 |
| 76 | Harvest HAR 5110 | Kiss Of The Light/FUNKY PHASER & HIS UNEARTHLY MERCHANDISE: Shine | 5 |
| 74 | Harvest SHVL 813 | AXE VICTIM (LP, gatefold sleeve) | 18 |
| 77 | Harvest SHVL 816 | LIVE! IN THE AIR AGE (LP, with bonus EP "Live! In The Air Age" [PSR 412]) | 20 |
| 78 | Harvest SHDW 410 | THE BEST AND THE REST OF BE BOP DELUXE (2-LP) | 15 |

*(see also A-Austr, Axe Victim)*

## BE-BOP PRESERVATION SOCIETY
| 71 | Dawn DNLS 3027 | THE BE-BOP PRESERVATION SOCIETY (LP, gatefold sleeve, orange label with insert) | 30 |

## BECK
| 94 | Geffen GFS 67 | Loser/Alcohol/Fume (p/s) | 10 |
| 94 | Geffen GFSJB 67 | Loser/Loser (jukebox issue, no p/s) | 8 |

| 94 | Geffen GFS 73 | Pay No Mind (Snoozer)/Special People (withdrawn)..........................................................40 |
|----|---------------|---------------------------------------------------------------------------------------------------|
| 94 | Geffen GFST 73 | Pay No Mind (Snoozer)/Special People/Trouble All My Days/Super Golden (Sunchild) (12", p/s, withdrawn - at least 100 pressed up) ................................................50 |
| 94 | Geffen GFS 19235 | Beercan/Spanking Room (p/s, 1500 copies) ................................................................20 |
| 96 | Geffen GFS 22183 | Devil's Haircut/Lloyd Price Express (Remix By John King) (p/s) ...................................5 |
| 96 | Geffen GFS 22205 | The New Pollution/Electric Music And The Summer People (p/s) ...............................5 |
| 97 | Geffen GFS 22253 | Sissyneck/Feather In Your Cap (p/s) ........................................................................5 |
| 97 | Select SELECT 12 | Clock/The Little Drum Machine Boy/Totally Confused (with Select mag) .................5 |
| 97 | Geffen GFS 22276 | Jack-Ass (Butch Vig Mix)/Strange Invitation/Devil Got My Woman/Jack-Ass(Lowrider Mix By Butch Vig) Burro Brother (Double 7" gatefold some have Butch Vig Mix with no Lowrider Mix) ..............................................................................................................6 |
| 00 | Geffen 497312-7 | Mixed Bizness/(Dirty Bixin Mizness Remix) (gatefold p/s - 1,500 copies) ...............5 |
| 06 | Interscope 1709487 | Cellphone's Dead/O Menina (stickered p/s with stickers insert) .............................5 |
| 09 | Parlophone 50999 244075 7 1 | Leopard-Skin Pill-Box Hat/BOB DYLAN: Leopard-Skin Pill-Box Hat (die-cut sleeve)..........5 |
| 09 | Matador OLE 865-7 | Green Light/SONIC YOUTH: Pay No Mind (green vinyl, very few sold in UK for Record Store Day) ..........................................................................................................60 |
| 11 | Parlophone R 6841 | Let's Get Lost (with BAT FOR LASHE/BAT FOR LASHES: Dark Time (demo) ...............5 |
| 94 | Geffen GEF 24634 | MELLOW GOLD (LP, inner) ....................................................................................30 |
| 05 | Interscope 9864087 | GUERO (2-LP) ......................................................................................................18 |

### BECK, BOGERT & APPICE
| 75 | CBS EQ 32140/Q 65455 | BECK, BOGERT & APPICE (LP, quadrophonic) ...........................................................18 |

*(see also Jeff Beck, Vanilla Fudge, Cactus)*

### GORDON BECK (QUARTET)
| 68 | Morgan MJ 1 | GYROSCOPE (LP) ..................................................................................................250 |
|----|-------------|----------------------------------------------------------------------------------------------------|
| 69 | M. Minor MMLP/SMLP 21 | EXPERIMENTS WITH POPS (LP, as Gordon Beck Quartet) ........................................125 |
| 69 | M. Minor MMLP/SMLP 22 | HALF A JAZZ SIXPENCE (LP) ...................................................................................100 |
| 69 | Major Minor SMLP 88 | DR. DOOLITTLE LOVES JAZZ (LP) .............................................................................50 |
| 72 | Dire FO 341 | BECK-MATTHEWSON-HUMAIR TRIO (LP) ................................................................30 |

*(see also Seven Ages Of Man)*

### JEFF BECK
| 67 | Columbia DB 8151 | Hi-Ho Silver Lining/Beck's Bolero ........................................................................10 |
|----|------------------|---------------------------------------------------------------------------------------------------|
| 67 | Columbia DB 8227 | Tallyman/Rock My Plimsoul ..................................................................................10 |
| 68 | Columbia DB 8359 | Love Is Blue (L'Amour Est Bleu)/I've Been Drinking ...............................................10 |
| 69 | Columbia DB 8590 | Plinth (Water Down The Drain)/Hangman's Knee (unissued) ....................................0 |
| 72 | Epic EPC 7720 | Got The Feeling/Situation ........................................................................................5 |
| 68 | Columbia S(C)X 6293 | TRUTH (LP, 1st pressing, blue/black labels, stereo with "sold in U.K." label text) ..........150 |
| 68 | Columbia SX 6293 | TRUTH (LP, 1st pressing, blue/black labels, mono with "sold in U.K." label text) ........200 |
| 68 | Columbia SX 6293 | TRUTH (LP, 2nd pressing, silver/black labels, boxed Columbia logo, with "sold in U.K." label text mono) ..................................................................................................70 |
| 69 | Columbia SX 6351 | BECK-OLA (LP, 1st pressing, blue/black labels, mono, existence unconfirmed) ...........70 |
| 69 | Columbia S(C)X 6351 | BECK-OLA (LP, 1st pressing, blue/black labels, stereo) ..........................................50 |
| 69 | Columbia SCX 6293 | TRUTH (LP, 3rd pressing, silver/black labels, stereo) ..............................................15 |
| 69 | Columbia SX 6351 | BECK-OLA (LP, 2nd pressing, silver/black labels, mono) ........................................20 |
| 69 | Columbia SCX 6351 | BECK-OLA (LP, 2nd pressing, silver/black labels, stereo)........................................15 |
| 72 | Epic EPC 64619 | ROUGH AND READY (LP, yellow label) ...................................................................30 |
| 72 | Epic EPC 64899 | JEFF BECK GROUP (LP, yellow label) ......................................................................20 |
| 72 | Epic EQ 30973 | ROUGH AND READY (LP, quadrophonic) .................................................................40 |
| 74 | CBS EQ 31331 | JEFF BECK GROUP (LP, quadrophonic) ...................................................................20 |
| 97 | EMI LPCENT 3 | BECK-OLA (LP, reissue, EMI centenary issue, stickered sleeve) ...............................20 |

*(see also Yardbirds, Beck Bogert Appice, Donovan, Rod Stewart, Cozy Powell, Honeydrippers, Buddy Guy)*

### ROBIN BECK
| 79 | Mercury BECK !2 | Sweet Talk/Shake It Through The Night (12") ........................................................12 |

### BECKETT
| 73 | Raft RA 18506 | Little Girl/My Lady .................................................................................................5 |
|----|---------------|---------------------------------------------------------------------------------------------------|
| 74 | Raft RA 48502 | BECKETT (LP, with lyric insert) ..............................................................................20 |

### HAROLD BECKETT
| 71 | Philips 6308 026 | FLARE UP (LP) ....................................................................................................120 |
|----|------------------|---------------------------------------------------------------------------------------------------|
| 72 | RCA SF 8225 | WARM SMILES (LP)..............................................................................................100 |
| 73 | RCA SF 8264 | THEME FOR FEGA (LP) ..........................................................................................60 |
| 75 | Cadillac SGC 1004 | JOY UNLIMITED (LP) .............................................................................................30 |
| 76 | Ogun OG 800 | MEMORIES OF BACARES (LP, as Harry Beckett's Joy Unlimited).............................15 |

*(see also Graham Collier, Galliard, Ninesense)*

### STUART BECKETT
| 60s | Sherwood SRS 1001 | Kariline/Breakthrough .........................................................................................15 |

### (KEE) LYN BECKFORD
| 68 | Island WI 3144 | Combination/Hey Little Girl ..................................................................................40 |
|----|----------------|---------------------------------------------------------------------------------------------------|
| 69 | Jackpot JP 707 | Kiss Me Quick/MRS. MILLER: Feel It .......................................................................20 |
| 69 | Big Shot BI 521 | Suzie Wong (as K. Beckford)/SWINGING KINGS: Deebo .........................................50 |
| 71 | G.G. GG 4514 | Groove Me/Groove Version (as Keeling Beckford) ..................................................35 |

### THEO(PHILUS) BECKFORD
| 61 | Blue Beat BB 33 | Jack And Jill Shuffle/Little Lady (as Theophilus Beckford & Clue J. & His Blues Blasters)..........................................................................................................20 |
|----|-----------------|---------------------------------------------------------------------------------------------------|
| 61 | Blue Beat BB 50 | Georgie And The Old Shoe/That's Me (as Theo Beckford & City Slickers) ...............20 |
| 62 | Blue Beat BB 87 | Walking Down King Street/The Clock (B-side actually by Sir D's Group) .................20 |
| 62 | Blue Beat BB 132 | Bringing In The Sheep (song actually "Bringing In The Sheaves")/Run Away ...........20 |
| 62 | Island WI 026 | I Don't Want You (actually by King Edward's All Stars)/Seven Long Years ...............15 |
| 63 | Island WI 106 | Daphney/Boller Man.............................................................................................12 |
| 63 | R & B JB 136 | Bullo Man/Daphney .............................................................................................25 |
| 64 | Blue Beat BB 250 | She's Gone/Old Flame (as Cotheo Beckford, B-side act. by Frederick Hibbert) ..........15 |

MINT VALUE £

| | | | |
|---|---|---|---|
| 64 | Blue Beat BB 257 | Don't Worry To Cry/Love Me Or Leave Me (as Theophilus Beckford, B-side actually by Lloyd Clarke) | 20 |
| 64 | Blue Beat BB 256 | Glamour Girl/BUSTER'S ALLSTARS: Down Beat Burial | 25 |
| 64 | Blue Beat BB 287 | On Your Knees/Now You're Gone (with Yvonne Harrison) | 15 |
| 65 | Blue Beat BB 303 | Dig The Dig (as Basil Gabbidon)/Don't Let Me Cry No More | 15 |
| 65 | Black Swan WI 452 | Take Your Time/STRANGER COLE: Happy-Go-Lucky | 20 |
| 65 | Island WI 238 | Trench Town People/PIONEERS: Sometime | 25 |
| 65 | Island WI 243 | You Are The One Girl/Grudgeful People | 20 |
| 65 | Island WI 246 | If Life Was A Thing/L. CLARKE: Parro Saw The Light (B-side actually "Pharaoh Saw The Light" by Lloyd Clarke) | 18 |
| 65 | Island WI 248 | What A Whoe/Bajan Girl | 20 |
| 68 | Nu Beat NB 009 | Easy Snappin'/ERIC MORRIS: My Lonely Days | 30 |
| 69 | Crab CRAB 25 | Brother Ram Goat (as T. Beckford)/STARLIGHTS: What A Condition | 20 |

*(see also Eric Barnet[t], Maytals, Clue J & His Bluesblasters)*

## BED BUGS
| | | | |
|---|---|---|---|
| 90 | Snake Rattle 01 | Haywire/No Safe Haven | 15 |

## CHUCK BEDFORD
| | | | |
|---|---|---|---|
| 74 | Bell 1378 | When I See You Smile/Don't Make Me History | 15 |

## DAVID BEDFORD
| | | | |
|---|---|---|---|
| 75 | Virgin VDJ 10 | An Extract From THE RIME OF THE ANCIENT MARINER - Part Two/An Extract From THE RIME OF THE ANCIENT MARINER - Part 2 (B&W girl and dragon logo) | 25 |
| 70 | Argo ZRG 638 | MUSIC FOR ALBION MOONLIGHT (LP, 1 side by Elizabeth Lutyens) | 25 |
| 72 | Dandelion 2310 165 | NURSE'S SONG WITH ELEPHANTS (LP, gatefold sleeve) | 30 |
| 75 | Virgin V2020 | STAR'S END (LP, stickered) | 15 |

*(see also Coxhill/Bedford Trio, Kevin Ayers & Whole World, Mike Oldfield, Roy Harper, Edgar Broughton Band)*

## BEDLAM
| | | | |
|---|---|---|---|
| 73 | Chrysalis CFB 1 | I Believe In You/Whiskey And Wine | 8 |
| 73 | Chrysalis CHR 1048 | BEDLAM (LP) | 20 |

*(see also Cozy Powell, Ace Kefford Stand, Big Bertha, Youngblood)*

## BEDROCKS
| | | | |
|---|---|---|---|
| 68 | Columbia DB 8516 | Ob-La-Di-Ob-La-Da/Lucy | 7 |

## EDWIN BEE
| | | | |
|---|---|---|---|
| 68 | Decca F 12781 | I've Been Loving You/Call For My Baby | 12 |

## MOLLY BEE
| | | | |
|---|---|---|---|
| 57 | London HLD 8400 | Since I Met You, Baby/I'll Be Waiting For You | 10 |
| 58 | Capitol CL 14849 | Going Steady (With A Dream)/Magic Mirror | 5 |
| 58 | Capitol CL 14880 | Don't Look Back/Please Don't Talk About Me When I'm Gone | 5 |
| 58 | Capitol CL 14949 | After You've Gone/Five Points Of A Star | 5 |
| 64 | Liberty LIB 55691 | He Doesn't Want You/Our Secret | 5 |
| 65 | MGM MGM 1280 | Single Girl Again/Keep It A Secret | 5 |

## BEE BEE CEE
| | | | |
|---|---|---|---|
| 77 | Rel RE 48-S | You Gotta Know Girl/We Ain't Listening (p/s, 2,000 only) | 70 |

## BEECH NUT
| | | | |
|---|---|---|---|
| 70 | Pastel PT 1 | Send For The Magician/Shot In The Dark | 30 |

## JOHNNY BEECHER
| | | | |
|---|---|---|---|
| 63 | Warner Bros WB89 | Sax Fifth Avenue/Jack Sax The City | 5 |

## BEEFEATERS
| | | | |
|---|---|---|---|
| 64 | Pye International 7N 25277 | Please Let Me Love You/Don't Be Long | 100 |
| 70 | Elektra 2101 007 | Please Let Me Love You/Don't Be Long (reissue) | 15 |

*(see also Byrds)*

## BEE GEES
| | | | |
|---|---|---|---|
| 67 | Polydor 56727 | Spicks And Specks/I Am The World | 8 |
| 67 | Polydor 56161 | New York Mining Disaster 1941/I Can't See Nobody | 6 |
| 67 | Polydor 56178 | To Love Somebody/Close Another Door | 5 |
| 67 | Polydor 56192 | Massachusetts/Barker Of The U.F.O. | 5 |
| 67 | Polydor 56220 | World/Sir Geoffrey Saved The World | 5 |
| 68 | Polydor 56229 | Words/Sinking Ships | 5 |
| 68 | Polydor 56242 | Jumbo/The Singer Sang His Song | 5 |
| 68 | Polydor 56273 | I've Gotta Get A Message To You/Kitty Can | 5 |
| 69 | Polydor 56304 | Odessa Parts 1 & 2 (unissued) | 0 |
| 69 | Polydor 56304 | First Of May/Lamplight | 5 |
| 69 | Polydor 56331 | Tomorrow Tomorrow/Sun In My Morning | 5 |
| 69 | Polydor 56343 | Don't Forget To Remember/The Lord | 5 |
| 70 | Polydor 56377 | I.O.I.O./Sweetheart | 8 |
| 70 | Polydor 2001 104 | Lonely Days/Man For All Seasons | 5 |
| 71 | Polydor 2058 115 | How Can You Mend A Broken Heart/Country Woman | 5 |
| 81 | RSO SNF 1 | Night Fever (promo only 7" with p/s to coincide with ITV showing 'Saturday Night Fever' on Royal Wedding Day) | 20 |
| 67 | Polydor 582/583 012 | BEE GEES 1ST (LP) | 25 |
| 68 | Polydor 582/583 020 | HORIZONTAL (LP) | 25 |
| 68 | Polydor 236 221 | RARE PRECIOUS AND BEAUTIFUL (LP) | 15 |
| 68 | Polydor 236 513 | RARE PRECIOUS AND BEAUTIFUL VOL. 2 (LP) | 15 |
| 68 | Polydor 582/583 036 | IDEA (LP) | 15 |
| 69 | Polydor 236 556 | RARE PRECIOUS AND BEAUTIFUL VOL. 3 (LP) | 15 |
| 69 | Polydor 582 049/050 | ODESSA (2-LP, felt cover, gatefold sleeve) | 50 |
| 70 | Polydor 2383 010 | CUCUMBER CASTLE (LP) | 20 |
| 70 | Polydor 2310 069 | TWO YEARS ON (LP) | 15 |
| 71 | Polydor 2383 052 | TRAFALGAR (LP) | 20 |
| 72 | Polydor 2383 139 | TO WHOM IT MAY CONCERN (LP) | 15 |

*(see also Barry Gibb, Robin Gibb, Maurice Gibb, Humpy Bong, Fut)*

## BEEKEEPERS
| | | | |
|---|---|---|---|
| 81 | Rundown ACE 40 | PLATFORM FIVE EP | 10 |

## MARK BEER
| | | | |
|---|---|---|---|
| 78 | Waste WAS 001 | ISOLATIONS EP | 10 |
| 81 | Rough Trade RT 070 | Pretty/Per(version) (p/s) | 5 |
| 81 | My China TAO 001 | DUST ON THE ROAD (LP) | 15 |

## BEES MAKE HONEY
| | | | |
|---|---|---|---|
| 73 | EMI EMI 2078 | Knee Trembler/Caldonia | 5 |
| 73 | EMI EMC 3013 | MUSIC EVERY NIGHT (LP) | 20 |

## BEES (UK) (1)
| | | | |
|---|---|---|---|
| 67 | Columbia Blue Beat DB 101 | Jesse James Rides Again/The Girl In My Dreams | 15 |
| 68 | Columbia Blue Beat DB 111 | The Prisoner From Alcatraz/The Ska's The Limit | 15 |

## BEES (UK) (2)
| | | | |
|---|---|---|---|
| 80 | Paw THF 003 | Leave Willie Alone/Mr Gaynor | 20 |

## BEES (UK) (3)
| | | | |
|---|---|---|---|
| 00 | We Love You AMOUR8S | No Trophy/Version | 5 |
| 01 | We Love You AMOUR10S | Punchbag/A Minha Menina | 5 |
| 02 | We Love You AMOUR14S | a Minha Menina/Out For The Count | 5 |
| 04 | Virgin VS 1884 | Chicken Payback/These Are The Ghosts (Undead Version) | 6 |
| 01 | We Love You AMOUR 6LP | SUNSHINE HIT ME (LP, inner sleeve) | 30 |
| 04 | Virgin V 2983 | FREE THE BEES (2-LP, gatefold, with transfer) | 30 |
| 07 | Virgin V 3024 | OCTOPUS (LP, with inner sleeve) | 18 |

## BILLY BEETHOVEN
| | | | |
|---|---|---|---|
| 75 | DJM DJS 10377 | Dreams (Out In The Forest)/We're Free | 80 |

*(see also Graham Bonnet)*

## BEEZ
| | | | |
|---|---|---|---|
| 78 | Edible SNACK 002 | THE BEEZ EP: Do The Suicide (no p/s, stickered sleeve) | 200 |
| 79 | Edible SNACK 001 | Easy/Vagrant (gatefold p/s) | 200 |

## B.E.F. (BRITISH ELECTRIC FOUNDATION)
| | | | |
|---|---|---|---|
| 91 | Ten TEN 386 | Free (Edit)/Secret Life Of Arabia (stickered/unstickered p/s, as B.E.F. Featuring Billy MacKenzie, unissued 200 copies only) | 40 |

*(see also Heaven 17)*

## SI BEGG MEETS NEIL LANDSTRUMM
| | | | |
|---|---|---|---|
| 01 | Mosquito MSQ 017 | TOKYO ASSASSIN (12" EP) | 10 |

## BEGGARS FARM
| | | | |
|---|---|---|---|
| 84 | White Rabbit WR 1001 | THE DEPTH OF A DREAM (LP) | 25 |

## BEGGARS HILL
| | | | |
|---|---|---|---|
| 76 | Moonshine MS 60 | BEGGARS HILL (LP, private pressing) | 175 |

## BEGGARS OPERA
| | | | |
|---|---|---|---|
| 70 | Vertigo 6059 026 | Sarabande/Think | 20 |
| 72 | Vertigo 6059 060 | Hobo/Pathfinder | 20 |
| 73 | Vertigo 6059 088 | Two Timing Woman/Lady Of Hell Fire | 8 |
| 74 | Vertigo 6059 105 | Classical Gas/Sweet Blossom Woman | 6 |
| 70 | Vertigo 6360 018 | ACT ONE (LP, large swirl label, gatefold sleeve) | 125 |
| 71 | Vertigo 6360 054 | WATERS OF CHANGE (LP, small swirl label, gatefold sleeve) | 200 |
| 72 | Vertigo 6360 073 | PATHFINDER (LP, small swirl label, foldout poster cover) | 200 |
| 73 | Vertigo 6360 090 | GET YOUR DOG OFF ME! (LP, 'spaceship' label) | 30 |

## BEGINNING OF THE END
| | | | |
|---|---|---|---|
| 71 | Atlantic 2091 097 | Funky Nassau Parts 1 & 2 (initial pressing on red label) | 15 |
| 71 | Atlantic 2091 097 | Funky Nassau Parts 1 & 2 | 5 |
| 72 | Atlantic 2091 166 | Monkey Tamarind/Hey Pretty Girl | 15 |
| 76 | Warner Bros. WEA K10021 | Funky Nassau (Full Length Version)/Funky Nassau Parts 1 & 2 (12") | 40 |
| 71 | Atlantic K 40304 | FUNKY NASSAU (LP) | 30 |

## BEIL TEECS
| | | | |
|---|---|---|---|
| 71 | Bullet BU 491 | So Far Away/BRUTE FORCE & IGNORANCE: So Far (Version) | 8 |

## SVEINBJORN BEINTEINSSON
| | | | |
|---|---|---|---|
| 90 | Durtro 005 | EDDA (LP, with booklet) | 20 |

## BEL CANTOS
| | | | |
|---|---|---|---|
| 65 | R&B MRB 5003 | Feel Aw Right Parts 1 & 2 | 20 |

## ADRIAN BELEW
| | | | |
|---|---|---|---|
| 90 | Atlantic A7904 | Pretty Pink Rose (featuring David Bowie)/Heartbeat (p/s) | 5 |

*(see also King Crimson)*

## BELFAST GYPSIES
| | | | |
|---|---|---|---|
| 66 | Island WI 3007 | Gloria's Dream/Secret Police | 80 |
| 77 | Sonet SNTF 738 | LEGENDARY MASTER RECORDINGS (LP) | 25 |

*(see also Them, Jackie McAuley, Freaks Of Nature)*

## ALEXANDER BELL
| | | | |
|---|---|---|---|
| 67 | CBS 2977 | Alexander Bell Believes/Hymn ... With Love | 30 |

## ARCHIE BELL & THE DRELLS
| | | | |
|---|---|---|---|
| 68 | Atlantic 584 185 | Tighten Up/Dog Eat Dog | 15 |
| 68 | Atlantic 584 217 | I Can't Stop Dancing/You're Such A Beautiful Child | 15 |
| 71 | Atlantic 2091 156 | Tighten Up/I Can't Stop Dancing/(There's Gonna Be A) Showdown | 8 |
| 72 | Atlantic K 10210 | Here I Go Again/A World Without Music | 10 |
| 73 | Atlantic K 10263 | There's Gonna Be A Showdown/Tighten Up | 6 |
| 76 | Philly Int. 4803 | Where Will You Go When The Party's Over?/I Swear You're Beautiful | 15 |
| 86 | Nightmare MARE 16 | Look Back Over Your Shoulder/Look Back Over Your Shoulder (Dub Mix) (12") | 25 |

MINT VALUE £

| | | | |
|---|---|---|---|
| 73 | President PT 418 | Girls Grow Up Faster Than Boys/Love's Gonna Rain On You | 10 |
| 86 | Portrait 7254 | Don't Let Love Get You Down/Where Will You Go When The Party's Over/The Soul City Walk | 10 |
| 99 | Achievement 10006 | Look Back Over Your Shoulder/(Instrumental) | 8 |
| 04 | UK Atlantic 504676251 | A Thousand Wonders/Here I Go Again (promo only) | 15 |
| 68 | Atlantic | TIGHTEN UP (LP) | 20 |
| 72 | Atlantic K 40454 | HERE I GO AGAIN (LP) | 20 |

**BELINDA BELL**

| | | | |
|---|---|---|---|
| 73 | Columbia DB 8995 | If Only You Believe/Stone Valley | 5 |
| 73 | Columbia SCXA 9255 | STONE VALLEY (LP, gatefold sleeve) | 15 |

**BENNY BELL & BLOCK BUSTERS**

| | | | |
|---|---|---|---|
| 57 | Parlophone R 4372 | The Sack Dress/Dr. Jazz | 5 |

**CHARLES BELL & CONTEMPORARY JAZZ QUARTET**

| | | | |
|---|---|---|---|
| 63 | London HA-K/SH-K 8095 | ANOTHER DIMENSION (LP) | 30 |

**EDDIE BELL**

| | | | |
|---|---|---|---|
| 72 | Injun 109 | Johnny B. Goode In Hollywood/ROYCE PORTER: A Woman Can Make You Blue | 10 |

**ERIC BELL BAND**

| | | | |
|---|---|---|---|
| 81 | Hobo HOS 016 | Lonely Man/Anyone Seen My Baby (p/s) | 30 |

*(see also Thin Lizzy)*

**FREDDIE BELL & BELLBOYS**

| | | | |
|---|---|---|---|
| 56 | Mercury MEP 9508 | ROCK WITH THE BELL BOYS (EP) | 20 |
| 57 | Mercury MEP 9512 | ROCK WITH THE BELL BOYS VOL. 2 (EP) | 20 |

**FREDRICK BELL**

| | | | |
|---|---|---|---|
| 68 | Nu Beat NB 004 | Rocksteady Cool/CARLTON ALPHONSO: I Have Changed | 35 |

**GARY BELL**

| | | | |
|---|---|---|---|
| 67 | CBS 202234 | Is This What I Get For Loving You?/To Keep You | 15 |
| 67 | CBS 2646 | Anyway That You Want Me/Leave It To Me | 10 |

**GRAHAM BELL**

| | | | |
|---|---|---|---|
| 66 | Polydor 56067 | How Can I Say I Don't Love You/If You're Gonna Go | 10 |
| 72 | Charisma CAS 1061 | GRAHAM BELL (LP, large 'mad hatter' label) | 20 |

*(see also Heavy Jelly, Griffin, Every Which Way, Skip Bifferty, Bell & Arc)*

**MADELINE BELL**

| | | | |
|---|---|---|---|
| 63 | HMV POP 1215 | I Long For Your Love/Because You Didn't Care | 20 |
| 64 | Columbia DB 7257 | You Don't Love Me No More/Don't Cross Over To My Side Of The Street | 20 |
| 65 | Columbia DB 7512 | Daytime/Don't Cry My Heart | 12 |
| 65 | Philips BF 1448 | What The World Needs Now Is Love/I Can't Wait To See My Baby's Face | 20 |
| 66 | Philips BF 1501 | Don't Come Running To Me/I Got Carried Away | 25 |
| 67 | Philips BF 1611 | Picture Me Gone/Go Ahead On | 30 |
| 66 | Philips BF 1526 | One Step At A Time/You Won't See Me | 15 |
| 68 | Philips BF 1656 | I'm Gonna Make You Love Me/I'm Gonna Leave You | 15 |
| 68 | Philips BF 1688 | Thinkin'/Don't Give Your Love Away | 10 |
| 68 | Philips BF 1726 | Hold It/What Am I Supposed To Do? | 6 |
| 69 | Philips BF 1799 | We're So Much In Love/How Much Do I Love You | 5 |
| 71 | Philips 6006 082 | If You Didn't Hear Me The First Time/You Walked Away | 5 |
| 67 | Philips (S)BL 7818 | BELLS A POPPIN' (LP) | 60 |
| 68 | Philips SBL 7865 | DOIN' THINGS (LP) | 35 |
| 76 | Pye NSPL 18483 | THIS IS ONE GIRL (LP) | 18 |

*(see also Seven Ages Of Man, Underground, Ian Green [Revelation])*

**SIMON BELL**

| | | | |
|---|---|---|---|
| 78 | Pye 7N 46050 | Givin' It Plenty/Love Like Lightning | 5 |

**WILLIAM BELL**

| | | | |
|---|---|---|---|
| 67 | Atlantic 584 076 | Never Like This Before/Soldier's Goodbye | 12 |
| 69 | Atlantic 584 259 | Everyday Will Be Like A Holiday/Ain't Got No Girl | 10 |
| 67 | Stax 601 019 | Eloise (Hang On In There)/One Plus One | 5 |
| 68 | Stax 601 038 | A Tribute To A King/Every Man Oughta Have A Woman | 5 |
| 69 | Stax STAX 110 | I Forgot To Be Your Lover/Bring The Curtain Down | 8 |
| 69 | Stax STAX 121 | My Whole World Is Falling Down/All God's Children Got Soul | 8 |
| 69 | Stax STAX 128 | Happy/Johnny I Love You | 40 |
| 86 | Absolute ABSOLUTE 1 | Headline News/That's What You Get | 10 |
| 69 | Atco 228 003 | A TRIBUTE TO A KING (LP) | 30 |
| 69 | Stax SXATS 1016 | BOUND TO HAPPEN (LP) | 30 |
| 71 | Stax 2362 009 | WOW . . . WILLIAM BELL (LP) | 20 |
| 72 | Stax 2362 027 | PHASES OF REALITY (LP) | 25 |

*(see also Judy Clay & William Bell)*

**BELLA & ME**

| | | | |
|---|---|---|---|
| 67 | Columbia DB 8243 | Whatever Happened To The Seven Day Week/Help Me Break This Habit | 8 |

**GEORGE BELLAMY**

| | | | |
|---|---|---|---|
| 65 | Parlophone R 5282 | Where I'm Bound/How Could I Ever | 20 |
| 72 | Chapter One CH 167 | Maman/Come To The Party | 5 |

*(see also Tornados)*

**PETER BELLAMY**

| | | | |
|---|---|---|---|
| 68 | Xtra XTRA 1010 | PETER BELLAMY (LP) | 25 |
| 68 | Argo | MAINLY NORFOLK (LP) | 40 |
| 69 | Xtra XTRA 1075 | FAIR ENGLAND'S SHORE (LP) | 40 |
| 69 | Topic 12T 200 | THE FOX JUMPS OVER THE PARSON'S GATE (LP, blue label) | 20 |
| 70 | Argo ZFB 11 | OAK, ASH AND THORN (LP) | 20 |
| 72 | Argo ZFB 37 | WON'T YOU GO MY WAY (LP) | 20 |
| 72 | Argo ZFB 81 | MERLIN'S ISLE OF GRAMARYE (LP) | 20 |

| 74 | Trailer LER 2089 | TELL IT LIKE IT IS (LP) | 15 |
| 77 | Free Reed 21/22 | TRANSPORTS (2-LP, gatefold, booklet) | 20 |
| 79 | Topic 12TS 400 | BOTH SIDES THEN (LP) | 15 |

*(see also Young Tradition)*

## BELL & ARC
| 71 | Charisma CB 170 | She Belongs To Me/Dawn | 6 |
| 71 | Charisma CAS 1053 | BELL & ARC (LP, gatefold sleeve, pink scroll label) | 30 |

*(see also Skip Bifferty, Arc, Every Which Way, Graham Bell)*

## BELL BROTHERS
| 68 | Action ACT 4510 | Tell Him No/Throw Away The Key | 30 |

## BELLE & SEBASTIAN
| 97 | Jeepster JPR 7001 | Dog On Wheels/The State I Am In (p/s, 1,000 only) | 6 |
| 97 | Jeepster JPR 12 001 | Dog On Wheels/The State I Am In/String Bean Jim/Belle & Sebastian) (12") | 15 |
| 97 | Jeepster JPR 7002 | Lazy Line Painter Jane/You Made Me Forget My Dreams (p/s, 1,000 only) | 6 |
| 97 | Jeepster JPR 12 002 | Lazy Line Painter Jane/You Made Me Forget My Dreams/Photo Jenny/A Century Of Elvis (12") | 15 |
| 10 | Rough Trade RTRADS 574 | God Help The Girl: Baby You're Blind/A Down And Dusky Blond | 7 |
| 96 | Elektric Honey EHRLP 5 | TIGERMILK (LP, 1,000 only) | 230 |
| 96 | Jeepster JPRLP001 | IF YOU'RE FEELING SINISTER (LP, gatefold) | 20 |
| 96 | Jeepster JPRLP007 | TIGERMILK (LP, reissue) | 15 |
| 98 | Jeepster JPRLP003 | THE BOY WITH THE ARAB STRAP (LP, gatefold) | 20 |
| 00 | Jeepster JPRLP010 | FOLD YOUR HANDS CHILD, YOU WALK LIKE A PEASANT (LP, gatefold) | 15 |
| 02 | Jeepster JPRLP014 | STORYTELLING (LP, gatefold) | 15 |
| 05 | Jeepster JRPLP 015 | PUSH BARMAN TO OPEN OLD WOUNDS (3-LP) | 50 |
| 06 | Rough Trade RTRADELP 280 | THE LIFE PURSUIT (2-LP) | 20 |
| 10 | Rough Trade RTRADELP 480 | WRITE ABOUT LOVE (LP, with free 7") | 15 |
| 15 | Concert Live CLCD 473 | LIVE 2015 (3-CD, signed) | 30 |

*(see also Amphetameanies)*

## BELLES
| 70 | President PT 311 | Don't Pretend/Words Can't Explain | 15 |
| 70 | Contempo Rarities CS 9027 | Don't Pretend/Words Can't Explain | 8 |
| 98 | Wigan Casino 210 | Don't Pretend/BETTY BOO: Say It Isn't So (p/s) | 10 |

## BELLFIELD
| 73 | Downtown DT 514 | Sugar Plum/Sugar Plum Dub | 6 |

## BELLINO
| 63 | Fontana 267259 | Boss Bossa Nova/Bossa Rock | 12 |

## BELL NOTES
| 59 | Top Rank JAR 102 | I've Had It/Be Mine | 5 |
| 59 | Top Rank JAR 147 | Old Spanish Town/She Went That-A-Way | 5 |
| 59 | Top Rank JAR 201 | That's Right/Betty Dear | 15 |

## ERROL BELLOT
| 82 | Jet Sounds JS 001 | Don't Joke With Love/Wicked Them (with Militant Mikey, 12") | 40 |
| 85 | Jah Tubbys JT 012 | New Kind Of Sound/Version (12", with the Offbeat Posse) | 40 |
| 86 | Jah Tubbys JT 019 | Sound In Fury/Trouble Maker (12", with the Offbeat Posse) | 40 |
| 00 | Jah Tubbys JT 7002 | Glory Hallalujah/DUB TEACHER: Glory Dub | 15 |
| 00 | Jah Tubbys JT 7004 | Jah Creation/DISCIPLES RIDDIM SECTION: Creation Style | 15 |
| 01 | Jah Tubbys JT 7007 | Roots Gone International/OFFBEAT POSSE: International Ridim | 15 |
| 03 | Jah Tubbys JT 014 | It's War/Don't Judge (10", with the Offbeat Posse) | 30 |
| 03 | Jah Tubbys JT 10016 | Praise H.I.M/New Life (10", with the Offbeat Posse) | 30 |

## ERROL BELLOT & DIXIE PEACH
| 03 | Jah Tubbys JT 10011 | The Warning/THE OFFBEAT POSSE: Dub Warning (10") | 30 |

*(see also Dixie Peach)*

## BELLS
| 70 | Polydor 2058 099 | Fly Little White Dove Fly/Follow The Sun | 8 |
| 71 | Philips 6006116 | Stay Awhile/Simple Song Of Freedom | 6 |
| 72 | Polydor 2121-109 | Oh My Love/You, You. You | 8 |

## BELL SOUNDS
| 59 | HMV POP 685 | Marching Guitars/Chloe | 5 |

## TONY BELLUS
| 59 | London HL 8933 | Robbin' The Cradle/Valentine Girl | 40 |

## BELLY
| 93 | 4AD CAD 3002 | STAR (LP) | 15 |
| 95 | 4AD CAD 5044 | KING (LP) | 15 |

## BELMONTS
| 61 | Pye International 7N 25094 | Tell Me Why/Smoke From Your Cigarette | 30 |
| 62 | Stateside SS 128 | Come On Little Angel/How About Me? | 35 |

*(see also Dion & Belmonts)*

## BELOVED
| 86 | Flim Flam HARP 2 | A Hundred Words (Radio Mix)/Slow Drowning (freebie) | 5 |
| 86 | Flim Flam HARP 3 | This Means War/If Only (p/s) | 5 |
| 87 | Flim Flam HARP 7 | Forever Dancing/Surprise Me (p/s) | 5 |

## BELOVED ONES
| 68 | CBS 3303 | My Year Is A Day/She And I | 15 |

## BELT & BRACES ROADSHOW BAND
| 75 | Belt & Braces Roadshow | BELT & BRACES ROADSHOW BAND (LP, with lyric sheet) | 15 |

## BELTANE FIRE
| 85 | CBS A6285 | Fortune Favours The Brave/(radio edit) (promo) | 5 |

MINT VALUE £

## BELTONES
| | | | |
|---|---|---|---|
| 68 | Trojan TR 628 | No More Heartaches/I'll Follow You | 25 |
| 69 | Duke DU 17 | Home Without You/Why Pretend | 50 |
| 69 | High Note HS 017 | Mary Mary/Going Away | 25 |
| 69 | High Note HS 023 | A Broken Heart/AFROTONES: All For One | 20 |
| 72 | Ackee ACK 150 | Wrapped Up In Love/SOUND DIMENSION: Pasero | 20 |

*(see Bop & Beltones, Trevor Shield)*

## JOHN BELTRAN
| | | | |
|---|---|---|---|
| 96 | Peacefrog PF 049 | TEN DAYS OF BLUE (2-LP) | 18 |

## JESSE BELVIN
| | | | |
|---|---|---|---|
| 59 | RCA RCA 1119 | Guess Who/Funny | 10 |

## BEN
| | | | |
|---|---|---|---|
| 71 | Vertigo 6360 052 | BEN (LP, gatefold sleeve, small swirl label) | 1500 |

*(see also Jonathan Kelly)*

## BENDY DOG
| | | | |
|---|---|---|---|
| 72 | Jam JAM 20 | I Wanna Hear (Rock 'N' Roll Music)/Carry My Mind | 10 |

## BENGA
| | | | |
|---|---|---|---|
| 02 | Big Apple BAM 002 | Skank/Dose (12") | 10 |
| 02 | Big Apple BAM 002 | Skank/Dose (12", blue vinyl) | 25 |
| 03 | Big Apple BAM 003 | The Judgement (with Skream)/SKREAM: The Bug/BENGA: Amber (12") | 30 |
| 03 | Big Apple BAM 003 | The Judgement (with Skream)/SKREAM: The Bug/BENGA: Amber (12", green vinyl) | 30 |
| 04 | Benga Beats BBV 01 | BENGA BEATS VOLUME 1 EP (12") | 20 |
| 04 | Big Apple BAM 005 | Hydro/Walkin' Bass/SKREAM: Elektro/Afrika (12") | 20 |

## BENNY BENGIMAN
| | | | |
|---|---|---|---|
| 81 | Negus Roots NERT 010 | Health And Sorrow/Love A Dub Song | 25 |

## JOE BENJAMIN
| | | | |
|---|---|---|---|
| 69 | UPC 106 | Good Morning Baby/Tell Me Why | 30 |
| 70 | UPC 111 | Same Old Song/Let Us Break Bread | 25 |

## TONY BENJAMIN & THE SANE INMATES
| | | | |
|---|---|---|---|
| 82 | Ariwa ARI 008 | Treasures In The World/Psychological Pen (12") | 40 |
| 83 | Ariwa ARILP 009 | AFRICAN REBEL (LP) | 70 |

## BOBBY BENNETT (U.K.)
| | | | |
|---|---|---|---|
| 67 | CBS 202511 | Just Say Goodbye/She Believes In Me | 7 |
| 68 | Columbia DB 8435 | All My Life Is You/To Give (The Reason I Live) | 7 |
| 69 | Columbia DB 8532 | Music Mother Made/You're Ready Now | 50 |

## BOBBY BENNETT (U.S.)
| | | | |
|---|---|---|---|
| 69 | London HL 10274 | Big New York/Baby, Try Me | 10 |

## BOYD BENNETT & HIS ROCKETS (WITH BIG MOE)
| | | | |
|---|---|---|---|
| 55 | Parlophone MSP 6161 | Everlovin'/Boogie At Midnight (with Big Moe) | 100 |
| 55 | Parlophone MSP 6180 | Seventeen/Little Ole You-All (as Boyd Bennett & His Rockets) | 50 |
| 56 | Parlophone MSP 6203 | My Boy - Flat Top/Banjo Rock And Roll (with Big Moe) | 100 |
| 56 | Parlophone MSP 6233 | Blue Suede Shoes/Oo-Oo-Oo (with Big Moe) | 100 |
| 56 | Parlophone R 4214 | The Groovy Age/Hit That Jive, Jack (as Big Moe with Boyd Bennett & His Rockets) | 100 |
| 56 | Parlophone R 4252 | The Most/Rockin' Up A Storm (as Big Moe with Boyd Bennett & His Rockets) | 100 |
| 58 | Parlophone R 4423 | Click Clack/Move (as Boyd Bennett & His Rockets) | 100 |
| 59 | Mercury AMT 1031 | Tear It Up/Tight Tights (as Big Moe & His Orchestra) | 30 |

*(see also Moon Mullican)*

## BRIAN BENNETT
| | | | |
|---|---|---|---|
| 67 | Columbia DB 8294 | Canvas/Slippery Jim De Grize | 20 |
| 74 | Fontana 6007 040 | Chase Side Shoot-Up/Pegasus | 20 |
| 76 | DJM DJS 10714 | Thunderbolt/Clearing Skies (promo in p/s) | 10 |
| 77 | DJM DJS 10756 | Saturday Night Special/Farewell To A Friend (promo in p/s) | 10 |
| 77 | DJM DJS 10791 | The Girls Back Home/Jonty Jump (as the Brian Bennett Band) | 10 |
| 67 | Columbia S(C)X 6144 | CHANGE OF DIRECTION (LP) | 50 |
| 69 | Col. Studio Two TWO 268 | THE ILLUSTRATED LONDON NOISE (LP) | 60 |
| 77 | DJM DJF 20499 | ROCK DREAMS (LP, with insert, as the Brian Bennett Band) | 20 |
| 78 | DJM DJF 20532 | VOYAGE (LP) | 20 |

*(see also Shadows, Thunder Company, Wasp, Marty Wilde, Krewcats, Collage, Alan Skidmore, Big Jim Sullivan, Heat Exchange, Julian [Scott], Mean Machine)*

## BRUCE BENNETT
| | | | |
|---|---|---|---|
| 71 | Big BG 311 | If You Don't Mind/Lenore (both actually by Dobby Dobson) | 7 |

## CAROLE BENNETT
| | | | |
|---|---|---|---|
| 57 | Capitol CL 14692 | Play The Music/Miser's Gold | 10 |
| 57 | Capitol CL 14725 | Haunted Lover/Let The Chips Fall (Where They May) | 20 |

## CLIFF BENNETT & REBEL ROUSERS
| | | | |
|---|---|---|---|
| 61 | Parlophone R 4793 | You've Got What I Like/I'm In Love With You | 30 |
| 61 | Parlophone R 4836 | That's What I Said/When I Get Paid | 25 |
| 62 | Parlophone R 4895 | Poor Joe/Hurtin' Inside (Twist) | 15 |
| 63 | Parlophone R 5046 | Everybody Loves A Lover/My Old Stand-By | 10 |
| 63 | Parlophone R 5080 | You Really Got A Hold On Me/Alright | 20 |
| 63 | Parlophone DP 560 | Poor Joe/Hurtin' Inside (Twist) (export issue, black label) | 10 |
| 63 | Parlophone DP 561 | When I Get Paid/That's What I Said (export issue, black label) | 15 |
| 64 | Parlophone R 5119 | Got My Mojo Working/Beautiful Dreamer | 10 |
| 64 | Parlophone R 5173 | One Way Love/Slow Down | 5 |
| 65 | Parlophone R 5229 | I'll Take You Home/Do You Love Him? | 5 |
| 65 | Parlophone R 5259 | Three Rooms Of Running Water/If Only You'd Reply | 5 |
| 65 | Parlophone R 5317 | I Have Cried My Last Tear/As Long As She Looks Like You | 5 |

| 66 | Parlophone R 5406 | You Can't Love 'Em All/Need Your Loving Tonight | 5 |
|----|-------------------|------------------------------------------------|---|
| 66 | Parlophone R 5466 | Eyes For You/Hold On I'm Coming | 5 |
| 66 | Parlophone R 5489 | Got To Get You Into My Life/Baby Each Day | 5 |
| 66 | Parlophone R 5534 | Never Knew Lovin' Could Be So Doggone Good/Don't Help Me Out | 5 |
| 67 | Parlophone R 5565 | I'm Sorry/I'll Take Good Care Of You | 5 |
| 67 | Parlophone R 5598 | I'll Be There/Use Me | 5 |
| 69 | Parlophone R 5792 | Memphis Streets/But I'm Wrong | 5 |
| 65 | Parlophone GEP 8923 | CLIFF BENNETT AND THE REBEL ROUSERS (EP) | 20 |
| 65 | Parlophone GEP 8936 | TRY IT BABY (EP) | 20 |
| 66 | Parlophone GEP 8955 | WE'RE GONNA MAKE IT (EP) | 20 |
| 64 | Parlophone PMC 1242 | CLIFF BENNETT AND THE REBEL ROUSERS (LP, yellow/black label) | 50 |
| 66 | EMI Regal REG 1039 | CLIFF BENNETT (LP, export issue) | 20 |
| 67 | Parlophone PMC/PCS 7017 | GOT TO GET YOU INTO OUR LIFE (LP, yellow/black label) | 40 |

## CLIFF BENNETT BAND

| 68 | Parlophone R 5666 | Take Your Time/House Of A Thousand Dolls | 5 |
|----|-------------------|------------------------------------------|---|
| 68 | Parlophone R 5691 | You're Breaking Me Up (And I'm Wasting Away)/I Hear Her Voice | 10 |
| 68 | Parlophone R 5711 | Lonely Weekends/Good Times | 10 |
| 68 | Parlophone R 5728 | One More Heartache/Nobody Runs Forever | 10 |
| 68 | Parlophone R 5749 | Back In The USSR/This Man | 10 |
| 68 | Parlophone PMC/PCS 7054 | BRANCHES OUT (LP, yellow/black label, with "sold in the U.K." label text) | 40 |

## CLIFF BENNETT'S REBELLION

| 71 | CBS 7231 | Amos Moses/Movin' And Travelin' On | 10 |
|----|----------|------------------------------------|----|
| 71 | CBS 64487 | CLIFF BENNETT'S REBELLION (LP) | 20 |

*(see also Charles Hodges, Rebel Rousers, Toefat, Screaming Lord Sutch & Savages)*

## DICKIE BENNETT

| 55 | Decca F 10595 | There, But For The Grace Of God Go I/Stars Shine In Your Eyes | 5 |
|----|---------------|--------------------------------------------------------------|---|
| 56 | Decca F 10697 | Dungaree Doll/Can't We Be Partners (After The Dance) | 5 |
| 56 | Decca F 10782 | You Don't Know Me/Cry Upon My Shoulder | 5 |

## DUSTER BENNETT

| 68 | Blue Horizon 57-3141 | It's A Man Down There/Things Are Changing | 25 |
|----|----------------------|-------------------------------------------|----|
| 69 | Blue Horizon 57-3148 | Raining In My Heart/Jumpin' For Joy | 20 |
| 69 | Blue Horizon 57-3154 | Bright Lights, Big City/Fresh Country Jam (with His House Band) | 25 |
| 69 | Blue Horizon 57-3164 | I'm Gonna Wind Up Endin' Up Or I'm Gonna End Up Windin' Up With You/ Rock Of Ages, Cleft For Me | 25 |
| 70 | Blue Horizon 57-3173 | I Chose To Sing The Blues/If You Could Hang Your Washing Like You Hang Your Lines | 15 |
| 70 | Blue Horizon 57-3179 | Act Nice And Gentle/I Want You To Love Me | 12 |
| 74 | Rak RAK 177 | Comin' Home/Pretty Little Thing | 10 |
| 68 | Blue Horizon 7-63208 | SMILING LIKE I'M HAPPY (LP, mono with His House Band, i.e. Fleetwood Mac) | 70 |
| 68 | Blue Horizon S 7-63208 | SMILING LIKE I'M HAPPY (LP, stereo with His House Band, i.e. Fleetwood Mac) | 50 |
| 69 | Blue Horizon S 7-63221 | BRIGHT LIGHTS... (LP, gatefold sleeve) | 100 |
| 70 | Blue Horizon 7-63868 | 12 DB's (LP, with lyric sheet) | 50 |

*(see also Fleetwood Mac)*

## JO JO BENNETT

| 67 | Doctor Bird DB 1097 | The Lecture/Cantelope Rock (with Fugitives) | 50 |
|----|---------------------|---------------------------------------------|----|
| 67 | Doctor Bird DB 1116 | Rocksteady/Real Gone Loser (with Fugitives) | 50 |
| 70 | Explosion EX 2029 | Groovy Jo Jo/Ten Steps To Soul (both actually with Mudie's All Stars) | 30 |
| 70 | Trojan TR 7774 | Leaving Rome/In The Nude (both with Mudie's All Stars) | 15 |
| 71 | Moodisc MU 3514 | Snowbird/MUDIE'S ALLSTARS: Change The Tide | 12 |
| 71 | Moodisc HME 108 | Poison Ivy/MUDIE'S ALLSTARS: Ivy Poison | 12 |
| 70 | Trojan TBL 133 | GROOVY JO JO (LP, with Mudie's Allstars) | 50 |

*(see also Fugitives, I Roy)*

## JOE BENNETT & SPARKLETONES

| 57 | HMV POP 399 | Black Slacks/Boppin' Rock Boogie | 150 |
|----|-------------|----------------------------------|-----|
| 58 | HMV POP 445 | Rocket/Penny Loafers And Bobby Socks | 150 |

## LEE BENNETT & SUNLINERS

| 64 | Decca F 12024 | Poor Bachelor Boy/Fool, Fool, Fool | 5 |
|----|---------------|------------------------------------|---|

## LORNA BENNETT

| 72 | Blue Mountain BM 1013 | Breakfast In Bed/Skank In Bed | 10 |
|----|-----------------------|------------------------------|----|
| 75 | Island WIP 6237 | Breakfast In Bed/Skank In Bed (reissue) | 6 |

## PETER E, BENNETT

| 71 | RCA SF 8190 | THE BALLAD OF GALDWAIN (LP, lyric insert, orange/white label) | 15 |
|----|-------------|---------------------------------------------------------------|----|

## RAY BENNETT

| 62 | Decca F 11550 | Go Away Little Girl/Twistin' To The Blues | 5 |
|----|---------------|-------------------------------------------|---|
| 62 | Decca DFE 8516 | INTRODUCING RAY BENNETT (EP) | 30 |

## ROY BENNETT

| 68 | Blue Cat BS 146 | I Dangerous/DEE SET: I Know A Place | 50 |
|----|-----------------|-------------------------------------|----|

## RUDI BENNETT

| 68 | Decca F 12741 | I'm So Proud/WHISTLING JACK SMITH: Havah Nagilah | 5 |
|----|---------------|--------------------------------------------------|---|
| 68 | Decca F12729 | I'm So Proud/You're My Adee | 20 |

## VAL BENNETT

| 68 | Island WI 3113 | Jumping With Mr. Lee/ROY SHIRLEY: Keep Your Eyes On The Road | 50 |
|----|----------------|-------------------------------------------------------------|----|
| 68 | Island WI 3146 | The Russians Are Coming (Take Five)/LESTER STERLING: Sir Lee's Whip | 80 |
| 68 | Trojan TR 611 | Spanish Harlem/ROY SHIRLEY: If I Did Know | 20 |
| 69 | Trojan TR 640 | Baby Baby/Barbara | 30 |
| 69 | Crab CRAB 6 | Reggae City/CANNON KING: Mellow Trumpet (B-side actually by Carl 'King Cannon Ball' Bryan) | 80 |
| 69 | Camel CA 24 | Midnight Spin/SOUL CATS: Money Money | 60 |

*(see also Roy Shirley, Max Romeo, Derrick Morgan, Clancy Eccles, Harry J Allstars, George A Penny, Lloyd Terrell,*

MINT VALUE £

**MARC BENNO**
71   A & M AMS850                                Good Year/Second Story Window ......................................................................... 8

**JON BENNS**
80   Aveda AVA 106                               BENNS MEANS LAFFS (LP)................................................................................. 15
*(see also The Enid)*

**BENNY & TINA**
69   Mercury MF 1133                             This Love Is Real/Over My Dead Body ................................................................ 10

**BARRY BENSON**
66   Parlophone R 5446                           Stay A Little While/That's For Sure ................................................................... 35
66   Parlophone R 5446                           Stay A Little While/That's For Sure (DJ Copy) ................................................... 50
66   Parlophone R 5484                           Not A One Girl Guy/Sunshine Child .................................................................. 25
66   Parlophone R 5544                           Always Waitin'/My Friend And I ......................................................................... 8
67   Parlophone R 5578                           Cousin Jane/Meet Jacqueline ........................................................................... 20
67   Page One POF 034                            I Can't Wait/Oh No ............................................................................................ 10

**GARY BENSON**
73   Birth RAB 1002                              The Concert/To Kill Another Day ...................................................................... 10
70   Penny Farthing PELS 506                     THE REUNION (LP) ............................................................................................ 50
73   Birth RAB 5                                 THE CONCERT (LP, gatefold sleeve) ................................................................. 30

**GEORGE BENSON (QUARTET)**
66   CBS (S)BPG 62817                            IT'S UPTOWN (LP, flipback sleeve, as George Benson Quartet).................... 25
67   CBS (S)BPG 62971                            THE GEORGE BENSON COOKBOOK (LP) ......................................................... 15

**MARIE BENSON & THE LONDONAIRES**
55   Decca F 10452                               Mambo Italiano/Mobile....................................................................................... 10

**BRIAN BENTLEY & THE BACHELORS**
60   Philips PB 1085                             Wishing Well/Please Make Up Your Mind ......................................................... 25
60   Philips PB 1086                             First Flight East/Sunday Break .......................................................................... 5
62   Salvo SLO 1813                              Caramba/Nellie Dean (99 copies only).............................................................. 10

**JAY BENTLEY & THE JET SET**
64   Vocalion VN 9230                            Watusi '64/I'll Get You........................................................................................ 5

**ACE BENTLEY**
81   Traffic Light TL 181                        Beat Boys/Sometimes In The Night (p/s) .......................................................... 15

**BROOK BENTON**
58   RCA RCA 1044                                A Million Miles From Nowhere/Devoted ........................................................... 10
58   RCA RCX 169                                 BROOK BENTON (EP, tri centre) ....................................................................... 15

**BROOK BENTON & DINAH WASHINGTON**
60   Mercury AMT 1083                            Baby (You've Got What It Takes)/I Do .............................................................. 12
60   Mercury AMT 1099                            A Rockin' Good Way/I Believe .......................................................................... 12
61   Mercury ZEP 10120                           A ROCKING GOOD WAY (EP, mono) ................................................................ 12
61   Mercury SEZ 19022                           A ROCKING GOOD WAY (EP, stereo) ............................................................... 15
64   Mercury 20069 MCL                           THE TWO OF US (LP)......................................................................................... 15

**STEVE BERESFORD**
75   Incus INCUS 15                              TEATIME (LP) ..................................................................................................... 40

**BERETS**
70   Avant Garde AVS 116                         THE MASS FOR PEACE (LP, with insert) .......................................................... 20

**BERKELEY KITES**
68   Polydor 56742                               Hang Up City/Mary-Go-Round ......................................................................... 10
69   Polydor 56770                               Alice In Wonderland/What Goes Up Must Come Down ................................. 10

**BERLIN RITZ**
80   Big Muff BM 001                             Crazy Nights/You're Where I Belong (no p/s) .................................................. 10

**BERMUDAS**
64   London HLN 9894                             Donnie/Chu Sen Ling......................................................................................... 10

**BERNADETTE**
67   Rim RIM 2                                   Come Kiss Me Love/Let Me Do The Talking..................................................... 20
68   Philips 1725                                Toys, Toys, Toys/Kiss And Run Away ................................................................ 10

**JACKIE BERNARD**
78   One Stop OSM 001                            Keep Rowing/Version (12") ............................................................................... 50

**KENNY BERNARD (& WRANGLERS)**
65   Pye 7N 15920                                The Tracker/You Gotta Give (with Wranglers) ................................................ 20
65   Pye 7N 15920                                The Tracker/You Gotta Give (with Wranglers) (DJ Copy) .............................. 125
66   Pye 7N 17131                                Nothing Can Change This Love/What Love Brings .......................................... 70
66   Pye 7N 17131                                Nothing Can Change This Love/What Love Brings (DJ Copy)........................ 100
67   Pye 7N 17233                                Ain't No Soul (Left In These Old Shoes)/Hey Woman ................................... 40
67   Pye 7N 17284                                I Do/Isn't That A Good Idea ............................................................................. 15
67   CBS 2936                                    Somebody/Pity My Feet ................................................................................... 100
67   CBS 2936                                    Somebody/Pity My Feet (DJ copy).................................................................. 150
68   CBS 3860                                    Victim Of Perfume And Lace/A Change Is Gonna Come ................................. 25
*(see also Kenny & Wranglers, Wranglers, Cat's Pyjamas)*

**ROD BERNARD**
59   London HLM 8849                             This Should Go On Forever/Pardon, Mr. Gordon.............................................. 20
59   Mercury AMT 1070                            One More Chance/Shedding Teardrops Over You .......................................... 10

**AGNES BERNELL**
63   HMV 7EG 8696                                THE LOST NOISES OFFICE (EP) ........................................................................ 10

**BERNHARDTS**
84   Parlophone 12R 6078                         I Hear You Calling (Extended)/Send Your Heart To Me (Extended) (12" p/s) ............... 20
84   Parlophone R6078                            I Hear You Calling/Send Your Heart To Me ...................................................... 7

## BERNIE & BUZZ BAND

| 68 | Decca F 22829 | The House That Jack Built/PETE KELLY'S SOULUTION: Midnight Confessions (export issue) .......18 |
| 68 | Deram DM 181 | When Something's Wrong With My Baby/Don't Knock It ....... 35 |

*(see also Pete Kelly's Soulution)*

## BERNIE & MYSTERIONS

| 81 | Chipping Norton CHIP 5 | Another Night/Front Seat Love (no p/s) ....... 8 |

## ELMER BERNSTEIN

| 56 | Brunswick 05544 | Clark Street Parts 1 & 2 (gold print on label) ....... 5 |
| 59 | Capitol CL 15101 | Staccato's Theme/The Jazz At Waldo's ....... 5 |
| 63 | MGM MGM 1238 | Rat Race/Saints & Sinners ....... 20 |
| 63 | MGM MGM 1238 | Rat Race/Saints & Sinners (DJ Copy) ....... 40 |
| 66 | United Artists UP 1163 | The Magnificent Seven/Return Of The Seven ....... 5 |
| 60 | Capitol EAP1 1287 | STACCATO (EP) ....... 10 |
| 56 | Brunswick LAT 8101 | THE MAN WITH THE GOLDEN ARM (LP, soundtrack) ....... 20 |
| 57 | Brunswick LAT 8195 | SWEET SMELL OF SUCCESS (LP, soundtrack) ....... 20 |
| 62 | MGM MGM-C 891 | WALK ON THE WILD SIDE (LP, soundtrack) ....... 15 |
| 63 | MGM MGM-C 934 | TO KILL A MOCKINGBIRD (LP, soundtrack) ....... 15 |
| 63 | United Artists ULP 1041 | THE GREAT ESCAPE (LP, soundtrack, mono/stereo) ....... 15 |
| 67 | RCA Victor RD 7792 | THE SILENCERS (LP, soundtrack, feat. Vikki Carr) ....... 30 |

## ROCK BERNTSEN

| 84 | Forest Tracks FT 3017 | KELPERS AFTER ALL (LP, with insert) ....... 18 |

## CHUCK BERRY

### 78s

| 56 | London HLU 8275 | Down Bound Train/No Money Down ....... 50 |
| 57 | London HLN 8375 | You Can't Catch Me/Havana Moon ....... 35 |
| 57 | London HLU 8428 | Roll Over Beethoven/Drifting Heart ....... 25 |
| 58 | London HL 8677 | Beautiful Delilah/Vacation Time ....... 20 |
| 58 | London HL 7055 | Carol/Hey Pedro (export single) ....... 30 |
| 58 | London HL 8712 | Carol/Hey Pedro ....... 25 |
| 58 | London HLM 8767 | Sweet Little Rock And Roller/Jo Jo Gun ....... 35 |
| 59 | London HLM 8853 | Almost Grown/Little Queenie ....... 50 |
| 59 | London HLM 8921 | Back In The U.S.A./Memphis, Tennessee ....... 50 |

### SINGLES

| 56 | London HLU 8275 | No Money Down/Down Bound Train (silver lettering on label, triangular centre) ....... 400 |
| 56 | London HLU 8275 | No Money Down/Down Bound Train (silver lettering on label, round centre) ....... 150 |
| 57 | London HLN 8375 | You Can't Catch Me/Havana Moon (gold lettering on label) ....... 350 |
| 57 | London HLN 8375 | You Can't Catch Me/Havana Moon (silver lettering on label) ....... 100 |
| 57 | London HLU 8428 | Roll Over Beethoven/Drifting Heart ....... 50 |
| 57 | Columbia DB 3951 | School Day (Ring! Ring! Goes The Bell)/Blue Feeling ....... 50 |
| 57 | London HLM 8531 | Rock And Roll Music/Blue Feeling ....... 30 |
| 58 | London HLM 8585 | Sweet Little Sixteen/Reelin' And Rockin' ....... 30 |
| 58 | London HLM 8629 | Johnny B. Goode/Around And Around ....... 25 |
| 58 | London HL 8677 | Beautiful Delilah/Vacation Time ....... 25 |
| 58 | London HL 8712 | Carol/Hey Pedro ....... 25 |
| 58 | London HL 7055 | Carol/Hey Pedro (export issue) ....... 25 |
| 58 | London HLM 8767 | Sweet Little Rock And Roller/Jo Jo Gun ....... 25 |
| 59 | London HLM 8853 | Almost Grown/Little Queenie ....... 25 |
| 59 | London HLM 8921 | Back In The U.S.A./Memphis, Tennessee ....... 25 |

*(Originally issued with triangular centres; later silver top label/round centre pressings are worth half to two-thirds these values.)*

| 60 | London HLM 9069 | Let It Rock/Too Pooped To Pop ....... 25 |
| 60 | London HLM 9159 | Bye Bye Johnny/Mad Lad ....... 25 |
| 61 | Pye International 7N 25100 | I'm Talkin' 'Bout You/Little Star (blue label) ....... 25 |
| 61 | Pye International 7N 25100 | I'm Talkin' 'Bout You/Little Star (later red/yellow label) ....... 10 |
| 63 | Pye International 7N 25209 | Go Go Go/Come On ....... 10 |
| 63 | Pye International 7N 25218 | Memphis, Tennessee/Let It Rock ....... 5 |
| 63 | Pye International 7N 25228 | Run Rudolph Run/Johnny B. Goode ....... 10 |
| 64 | Pye International 7N 25236 | Nadine (Is It You?)/O Rangutang ....... 10 |
| 64 | Pye International 7N 25242 | No Particular Place To Go/Liverpool Drive ....... 5 |
| 64 | Pye International 7N 25257 | You Never Can Tell/Brenda Lee ....... 5 |
| 64 | Pye International 7N 25271 | Little Marie/Go Bobby Soxer ....... 10 |
| 65 | Pye International 7N 25285 | The Promised Land/The Things I Used To Do ....... 10 |
| 65 | Chess CRS 8006 | I Got A Booking/Lonely School Days ....... 10 |
| 65 | Chess CRS 8012 | Dear Dad/My Little Lovelight ....... 5 |
| 65 | Chess CRS 8022 | It Wasn't Me/It's My Own Business ....... 5 |
| 66 | Chess CRS 8037 | Ramona Say Yes/Lonely School Days ....... 5 |
| 66 | Mercury MF 958 | Club Nitty Gritty/Laugh And Cry ....... 5 |
| 67 | Mercury MF 994 | Back To Memphis/I Do Really Love You ....... 5 |
| 68 | Mercury MF 1057 | St. Louis To Frisco/Ma Dear ....... 5 |
| 69 | Mercury MF 1102 | Back To Memphis/Roll Over Beethoven ....... 5 |
| 68 | Chess CRS 8075 | Johnny B. Goode/Sweet Little Sixteen ....... 5 |
| 69 | Chess CRS 8089 | No Particular Place To Go/It Wasn't Me ....... 5 |
| 72 | Chess 6145 007 | Rock And Roll Music/Johnny B. Goode/School Days ....... 5 |
| 73 | Chess 6145 020 | Reelin' And Rockin' (Live)/I Will Not Let You Go ....... 5 |
| 73 | Chess 6145 027 | South Of The Border (Live)/Bio ....... 5 |
| 75 | Chess 6145 038 | Shake Rattle And Roll/I'm Just A Name ....... 5 |
| 79 | Atlantic K 11354 | Oh What A Thrill/California ....... 5 |

## EPs

| | | | |
|---|---|---|---|
| 56 | London REU 1053 | RHYTHM AND BLUES WITH CHUCK BERRY (maroon/gold label, tri-centre) | 150 |
| 56 | London REU 1053 | RHYTHM AND BLUES WITH CHUCK BERRY (later pressing, maroon/silver label, round centre) | 40 |
| 60 | London REM 1188 | REELIN' AND ROCKIN' (maroon and gold label, tri centre) | 250 |
| 60 | London REM 1188 | REELIN' AND ROCKIN' (round centre) | 100 |
| 63 | Pye Intl. NEP 44011 | CHUCK BERRY | 15 |
| 63 | Pye Intl. NEP 44013 | THIS IS CHUCK BERRY | 15 |
| 64 | Pye Intl. NEP 44018 | THE BEST OF CHUCK BERRY | 15 |
| 64 | Pye Intl. NEP 44028 | CHUCK BERRY HITS | 15 |
| 64 | Pye Intl. NEP 44033 | BLUE MOOD | 15 |
| 65 | Chess CRE 6002 | THE PROMISED LAND | 15 |
| 65 | Chess CRE 6005 | COME ON | 15 |
| 66 | Chess CRE 6012 | I GOT A BOOKING | 15 |
| 66 | Chess CRE 6016 | YOU CAME A LONG WAY FROM ST. LOUIS | 25 |

## ALBUMS

| | | | |
|---|---|---|---|
| 58 | London HA-M 2132 | ONE DOZEN BERRYS | 150 |
| 62 | Pye Intl. NPL 28019 | NEW JUKE BOX HITS | 30 |
| 63 | Pye Intl. NPL 28024 | CHUCK BERRY | 20 |
| 63 | Pye Intl. NPL 28027 | CHUCK BERRY ON STAGE | 20 |
| 63 | Pye Intl. NPL 28028 | MORE CHUCK BERRY | 20 |
| 64 | Pye Intl. NPL 28031 | THE LATEST AND THE GREATEST | 20 |
| 64 | Pye Intl. NPL 28039 | YOU NEVER CAN TELL | 20 |
| 65 | Chess CRL 4005 | CHUCK BERRY IN LONDON | 30 |
| 65 | Chess CRL 4506 | FRESH BERRYS | 30 |
| 66 | Chess CRL 4548 | CHUCK BERRY'S GREATEST HITS | 15 |
| 67 | Mercury 20110 (S)MCL | CHUCK BERRY IN MEMPHIS | 20 |
| 67 | Mercury 20112 (S)MCL | LIVE AT THE FILLMORE AUDITORIUM - SAN FRANCISCO | 15 |
| 69 | Mercury 20162 (S)MCL | CONCERTO IN B. GOODE | 15 |
| 72 | Chess 6310 113 | BACK HOME | 15 |
| 72 | Chess 6310 115 | SAN FRANCISCO DUES | 15 |

## CHUCK BERRY/BO DIDDLEY

| | | | |
|---|---|---|---|
| 63 | Pye Intl. NEP 44009 | CHUCK AND BO (EP) | 10 |
| 63 | Pye Intl. NEP 44012 | CHUCK AND BO, VOL. 2 (EP) | 10 |
| 64 | Pye Intl. NEP 44017 | CHUCK AND BO, VOL. 3 (EP) | 10 |

*(see also Bo Diddley)*

## DAVE BERRY (& CRUISERS)

| | | | |
|---|---|---|---|
| 63 | Decca F 11734 | Memphis Tennessee/Tossin' & Turnin' (with Cruisers) | 5 |
| 63 | Decca F 11803 | My Baby Left Me/Hoochie Coochie Man (B-side with Cruisers) | 5 |
| 64 | Decca F 11876 | Baby It's You/Sweet And Lovely | 5 |
| 64 | Decca F 11937 | The Crying Game/Don't Gimme No Lip Child | 5 |
| 64 | Decca F 12020 | One Heart Between Two/You're Gonna Need Somebody | 10 |
| 65 | Decca F 12103 | Little Things/I've Got A Tiger By The Tail | 5 |
| 65 | Decca F 12188 | This Strange Effect/Now | 5 |
| 65 | Decca F 12258 | I'm Gonna Take You There/Just Don't Know | 5 |
| 66 | Decca F 12337 | If You Wait For Love/Hidden | 5 |
| 66 | Decca F 12435 | Mama/Walk, Walk, Talk, Talk | 5 |
| 66 | Decca F 12513 | Picture Me Gone/Ann | 10 |
| 67 | Decca F 12579 | Stranger/Stick By The Book | 5 |
| 67 | Decca F 12651 | Forever/And I Have Learned To Dream | 5 |
| 68 | Decca F 12739 | Just As Much As Ever/I Got A Feeling | 5 |
| 68 | Decca F 12771 | (Do I Figure) In Your Life/Latisha | 5 |
| 69 | Decca F 12905 | Huma Lama Oh What A Life (by Dave Berry & Sponge) | 5 |
| 70 | Decca F 12999 | Change Our Minds/Long Walk To D.C. | 5 |
| 70 | Decca F 13080 | Chaplin House/Trees | 5 |
| 72 | CBS 7780 | Movin' On (Turn Around)/Don't Bring Me Down | 5 |
| 88 | Flagstaff 002 | Out Of Time/Serenade To Alice (p/s, 200 only) | 5 |
| 64 | Decca DFE 8601 | DAVE BERRY (EP) | 10 |
| 65 | Decca DFE 8625 | CAN I GET IT FROM YOU (EP) | 10 |
| 64 | Decca LK 4653 | DAVE BERRY (LP) | 15 |
| 66 | Ace Of Clubs ACL 1218 | ONE DOZEN BERRIES (LP, also stereo SCL 1218) | 15 |
| 66 | Decca LK 4823 | THE SPECIAL SOUND OF DAVE BERRY (LP) | 15 |
| 68 | Decca LK/SKL 4932 | DAVE BERRY '68 (LP) | 15 |

*(see also Cruisers)*

## LEN & BARBARA BERRY

| | | | |
|---|---|---|---|
| 60s | Greenwich Village GVR 229 | THE PORTWAY PEDDLERS (LP) | 50 |

## MIKE BERRY (& THE OUTLAWS)

| | | | |
|---|---|---|---|
| 61 | Decca F 11314 | Will You Love Me Tomorrow/My Baby Doll (with The Outlaws) | 10 |
| 61 | HMV POP 912 | Tribute To Buddy Holly/What's The Matter (with The Outlaws) | 5 |
| 62 | HMV POP 979 | It's Just A Matter Of Time/Little Boy Blue (backing group miscredited as Admirals, actually The Outlaws) | 5 |
| 62 | HMV POP 1042 | Every Little Kiss/How Many Times | 5 |
| 62 | HMV POP 1105 | Don't You Think It's Time/Loneliness (with The Outlaws) (blue label) | 5 |
| 63 | HMV POP 1142 | My Little Baby/You'll Do It, You'll Fall In Love | 5 |
| 63 | HMV POP 1194 | It Really Doesn't Matter/Try A Little Bit Harder | 5 |
| 64 | HMV POP 1257 | This Little Girl On My Mind | 10 |
| 64 | HMV POP 1284 | Lovesick/Letter Of Love | 5 |
| 64 | HMV POP 1314 | Who Will It Be/Talk (with Innocents) | 5 |
| 64 | HMV POP 1362 | Two Lovers/Don't Try To Stand In My Way | 5 |

| 65 | HMV POP 1449 | That's All I Ever Wanted From You/She Didn't Care | 5 |
| 65 | HMV POP 1494 | It Comes And Goes/Gonna Fall In Love | 5 |
| 66 | HMV POP 1530 | Warm Baby/Just Thought I'd 'Phone | 5 |
| 67 | Polydor 56182 | Raining In My Heart/Eyes | 5 |
| 72 | York SYK 516 | Going Down To Virginia/Love Her | 5 |
| 72 | York SYK 530 | Drift Away/Keep Your Eyes On The Road | 5 |
| 76 | Polydor 2058 700 | Tribute To Buddy Holly/Dial My Number | 10 |
| 63 | HMV 7EG 8793 | IT'S TIME FOR MIKE BERRY (EP, with Outlaws) | 15 |
| 63 | HMV 7EG 8808 | A TRIBUTE TO BUDDY HOLLY (EP) | 15 |

*(see also Outlaws, Le Roys, Shepperton Flames, Innocents [U.K], UK Jones)*

## RICHARD BERRY & PHARAOHS
| 64 | Ember EMB EP 4527 | RHYTHM AND BLUES VOL. 3 (EP) | 100 |

## CINDY LEE BERRYHILL
| 89 | Awareness AWP 001 | Me, Steve, Kirk And Keith/Baby (Should I Have The Baby) (p/s) | 6 |

## BERRY STREET STATION
| 75 | Crystal CR 7024 | Chocolate Sugar/All I Want Is You | 15 |

## BERTY B AND DILLINJA
| 95 | Lionheart BERT1 | Lionheart/Art Of Control (12") | 15 |

*(see also Dillinja, Cybotron Featuring Dillinja)*

## BESHARA
| 82 | Home Spun HS 002 | Glory Glory/Version (12") | 80 |
| 84 | Mass Media Music MM121004 | Men Cry Too/Version (12", purple vinyl) | 20 |

## ADAM BEST
| 70 | Fontana SFL 13209 | WALL OF SOUND (LP) | 20 |

## JON BEST
| 65 | Decca F 12077 | Young Boy Blues/Living Without Love | 5 |

## PETE BEST FOUR
| 64 | Decca F 11929 | I'm Gonna Knock On Your Door/Why Did I Fall In Love With You? | 50 |

*(see also Beatles, Lee Curtis & All Stars)*

## BEST EVER
| 75 | Polydor 2001594 | Rope A Dope/People's Choice (with Muhammad Ali) | 20 |

## RICHARD BESWICK & PHILIPP WACHSMANN
| 81 | Bead Records BEAD 18 | HELLO BRENDA! (LP) | 25 |

## BETA BAND
| 97 | Regal REG 16 | CHAMPION VERSIONS EP: Dry The Rain/I Know/B+A/Dog's Got A Bone (12", p/s, 1,000 only) | 60 |
| 98 | Regal REG 18 | THE PATTY PATTY SOUND EP: Inner Meet Me/The House/The Monolith/ She's The One (2 x 12", p/s, 1,000 only) | 30 |
| 98 | Regal REG 20 | LOS AMIGOS DEL BETA BANDITOS EP: Push It Out/It's Over/Dr Baker/Needles In My Eyes (12", p/s) | 20 |
| 13 | Regal REGS 16 | CHAMPION VERSIONS (12", reissue 750 only) | 18 |
| 13 | Regal REGS 18 | THE PATTY PATTY SOUND (12", reissue, 750 only) | 12 |
| 13 | Regal REGS 20 | LOS AMIGOS DEL BETA BANDITOS (12", reissue, 750 only) | 10 |
| 99 | Regal REG 30 | THE BETA BAND (2-LP) | 20 |
| 01 | Regal REG 59 | HOT SHOTS II (2-LP) | 20 |
| 04 | Regal REG 101 | HEROS TO ZEROS (2-LP, gatefold sleeve) | 20 |

*(see also Aliens)*

## BETTERDAYS
| 65 | Polydor BM 56024 | Don't Want That/Here 'Tis | 175 |
| 96 | Dig The Fuzz DIG 008 | HOWLIN' (LP, with booklet) | 15 |

## HAROLD BETTERS
| 65 | Sue WI 378 | Do Anything You Wanna (Parts 1 & 2) | 60 |

## AL BETTS
| 73 | Peer Int. PIL 9018 | CONTRASTS IN JAZZ VOLUME 2 (LP) | 15 |

## BETWEEN PICTURES
| 81 | A Side AS 002 | Treat Me Like An Equal/Life On Your Own | 15 |
| 81 | Applause CLAP 3 | Birthday Card/Down At The Factory (p/s) | 6 |

## JOHNNY BEV
| 63 | Pye 7N 15523 | Treat Her Right/For Always | 5 |
| 63 | Pye 7N 15576 | What Am I To Do/Save All Your Kisses For Me | 5 |
| 65 | Columbia DB 7579 | You Pass Me By/Leaving My Teardrops Behind | 5 |
| 65 | Columbia DB 7767 | The World Goes Away/The House | 5 |
| 67 | CBS 3031 | Soft As A Kiss/Welcome Stranger | 5 |

## BEVERLEY
| 66 | Deram DM 101 | Happy New Year/Where The Good Times Are | 50 |
| 67 | Deram DM 137 | Museum/DENNY CORDELL TEA TIME ENSEMBLE: A Quick One For Sanity | 35 |

*(see also John & Beverley Martyn, Levee Breakers)*

## BEVERLEY SISTERS
| 56 | Decca F 10705 | Willie Can/I've Started Courtin' | 5 |
| 56 | Decca F 10729 | Rickshaw Boy/You Ought To Have A Wife | 5 |
| 56 | Decca F 10770 | Born To Be With You/It's Easy | 5 |
| 56 | Decca F 10813 | Come Home To My Arms/Doodle-Doo-Doo | 5 |
| 57 | Decca F 10832 | I Dreamed/Mama From The Train (A Kiss, A Kiss) | 5 |
| 57 | Decca F 10909 | Bye, Bye Love/It's Illegal, It's Immoral, Or It Makes You Fat | 5 |
| 57 | Decca F 10943 | Riding Down From Bangor/The Young Cavaliero | 5 |
| 58 | Decca F 10971 | Long Black Nylons/Without You | 10 |

### BEVERLEY'S ALLSTARS
| | | | |
|---|---|---|---|
| 65 | Black Swan WI 449 | Go Home/THEO BECKFORD: Ungrateful People | 25 |
| 69 | Trojan TR 683 | Double Shot/Gimme Gimme Gal (B-side act. "Banana Water" by Mellotones) | 35 |
| 70 | Trojan TR 7729 | Moon Dust/Fat Cat (both sides actually by Ansell Collins) | 30 |

*(see also Clarendoinians, Gaylads, Ken Boothe, Glen Brown, Desmond Dekker, Bob Marley, Maytals, Melodians, Derrick Morgan, Pioneers, Rockstones, Bruce Ruffin, Delroy Wilson)*

### FRANK BEVERLY & BUTLERS
| | | | |
|---|---|---|---|
| 79 | Inferno HEAT 4 | If That's What You Wanted/Love (Your Pain Goes Deep) (with p/s) | 10 |
| 79 | Inferno HEAT 4 | If That's What You Wanted/Love (Your Pain Goes Deep) (without p/s) | 5 |

### BEVERLY HILLS BLUES BAND
| | | | |
|---|---|---|---|
| 76 | Warner Bros K 16752 | Just Because/If I Can Just Get Through Tonight | 15 |

*(see also Four Seasons)*

### BEVIS FROND
| | | | |
|---|---|---|---|
| 88 | Bucketfull/Brains BOB 21 | High In A Flat/DREAM SYNDICATE: Blind Willie McTell (free with Bucketfull Of Brains issue 27, 33rpm, yellow die-cut sleeve) | 12 |
| 88 | Bucketfull/Brains BOB 21 | High In A Flat/DREAM SYNDICATE: Blind Willie McTell (without Bucketfull Of Brains issue 27) | 7 |
| 90 | Clawfist PIS 1 | Sexorcist/WALKINGSEEDS: Reflection In A Tall Mirror (p/s, mail-order only) | 5 |
| 87 | Woronzow WOO 3 | MIASMA (LP, laminated cover, 500 copies only) | 15 |
| 87 | Woronzow WOO 5 1/2 | BEVIS THROUGH THE LOOKING GLASS - THE GREAT MAGNET DISASTER (2-LP, 500 only, originals all signed, with booklet; counterfeits unsigned) | 40 |
| 88 | Woronzow WOO 8 | TRIPTYCH (LP) | 20 |
| 80s | Reckless RECKLP 15 | TRIPTYCH (LP, reissue) | 15 |
| 91 | Woronzow WOO 16 | NEW RIVER HEAD (2-LP, 1st 500 with EP & insert) | 18 |
| 92 | Woronzow WOO 26 | SUPERSEEDER (2-LP) | 25 |
| 96 | Woronzow WOO28 | SON OF WALTER (2-LP) | 18 |
| 97 | Woronzow WOO 406 | NORTH CIRCULAR (3-LP, with insert, 750 only, signed & numbered) | 25 |

*(see also Von Trap Family, Room 13)*

### RODNEY BEWES
| | | | |
|---|---|---|---|
| 69 | Revolution REV 1003 | Remember When/Dear Mother Love Albert | 10 |
| 70 | Revolution Pop REVP 1001 | Dear Mother Love Albert/Meter Maid | 10 |

*(see also Highly Likely)*

### BEYOND THE IMPLODE
| | | | |
|---|---|---|---|
| 79 | Diverse DIVE 101 | LAST THOUGHTS EP (EP, 250 copies with hand-written labels, numbered, with 'Look Back' Fanzine) | 150 |
| 80 | Diverse DIVE 102 | 11th HOUR BREAKDOWN EP | 75 |

### BEYOND THE WIZARD'S SLEEVE
| | | | |
|---|---|---|---|
| 05 | 3rd Mynd 02 | BEYOND THE WIZARD'S SLEEVE (LP) | 15 |
| 06 | 3rd Mynd 03 | SPRING (LP) | 18 |
| 07 | 3rd Mynd 04 | GEORGE (LP, red vinyl) | 15 |
| 07 | 3rd Mynd 05 | WEST (LP, clear vinyl) | 15 |

### BEYOND THE QUARRY
| | | | |
|---|---|---|---|
| 92 | Flair (No Cat. No) | Comedown/Disappointment/One Way/Relegate (12", purple vinyl) | 70 |

### B-52'S
| | | | |
|---|---|---|---|
| 79 | Island WIP 6527 | 6060-842/Hero Worship (p/s) | 5 |
| 79 | Island ILPS 9580 | THE B-52's (LP, with bonus single "Rock Lobster"/"52 Girls" [PSR 438]) | 15 |

### B FILM
| | | | |
|---|---|---|---|
| 80 | Plastic Records BEE 001 | Night Running/Danger Man | 20 |

### BG AND THE MOUSE
| | | | |
|---|---|---|---|
| 82 | Maestro MR 003 | Da Doo Ron Ron/Clever Boy (no p/s) | 10 |

### BG FROM BASS INC
| | | | |
|---|---|---|---|
| 88 | Black Steel BS002 | Rock The Boat (12") | 10 |

### MAURICIO BIANCHI
| | | | |
|---|---|---|---|
| 81 | Sterile SR 2 | SYMPATHY FOR A GENOCIDE (LP, 200 only) | 200 |
| 83 | Broken BV 3 | THE PLAIN TRUTH (LP) | 70 |

### GENE BIANCO GROUP
| | | | |
|---|---|---|---|
| 60 | Vogue V 9167 | Alarm Clock Rock/Harp Rock Boogie | 30 |

### BIBBY
| | | | |
|---|---|---|---|
| 65 | Blue Beat BB 289 | Rub It Down/Wicked Man (actually by Harris Seaton) | 30 |

*(see also B.B. Seaton, Horace Seaton)*

### BIBIO
| | | | |
|---|---|---|---|
| 09 | Warp WARPLP177 | AMBIVALANCE AVENUE (2-LP) | 30 |
| 09 | Warp WARLP 190 | THE APPLE AND THE TOOTH (LP) | 25 |

### BIDDU
| | | | |
|---|---|---|---|
| 67 | Regal Zonophone RZ 3002 | Look Out Here I Come/Daughter Of Love | 15 |
| 77 | Epic EPC 5416 | Soul Coaxing/Nirvana (12", p/s) | 15 |
| 78 | Epic EPCS 6230 | Blacker Than Berry/James Bond Disco Theme (12", white label promo only) | 15 |

### BIFF BANG POW!
| | | | |
|---|---|---|---|
| 84 | Creation CRE 003 | Fifty Years Of Fun/Then When I Scream (foldaround sprayed p/s in poly bag) | 30 |
| 84 | Creation CRE 007 | There Must Be A Better Life/The Chocolate Elephant Man (foldaway p/s in poly bag) | 30 |
| 90 | Caff CAFF 13 | Sleep/TIMES: Extase (p/s, with insert) | 20 |
| 90 | Creation CRELP 058 | SONGS FOR THE SAD EYED GIRL (LP) | 15 |
| 91 | Creation CRELP 099 | L'AMOUR, DEMURE, STENHOUSEMUIR (LP) | 20 |

*(see also Laughing Apple, Times)*

### BIFFY CLYRO
| | | | |
|---|---|---|---|
| 99 | Babi Yaga YAGA 001 | Iname/All The Way Down (Chapter 2)/Travis Perkins (CD) | 100 |
| 00 | Electric Honey HER 013 CD | Thekidswhopoptodaywillrocktomorrow (CD, 1000 only) | 80 |
| 01 | Beggars Banquet BBQ 335 | Justboy/Unsubtle/Being Gabriel (p/s) | 20 |

| 01 | Beggars Banquet BBQ 352 | 27/Breatheher/Instructio4 (p/s) | 20 |
|---|---|---|---|
| 02 | Beggars Banquet BBQ 358 | 57/Kill The Old, Torture Their Young (Evening Session Version) (p/s) | 20 |
| 02 | Beggars Banquet BBQ 361 | Joy. Discovery. Invention/Toys Toys Toys Choke/Toys Toys Toys/ All The Way Down Chapter 2 (p/s) | 12 |
| 03 | Beggars Banquet BBQ 365 | The Ideal Height/...And With The Scissorkick Is Victorious (p/s) | 10 |
| 03 | Beggars Banquet BBQ 374 | Eradicate The Doubt/The Ideal Height (Live)/Justboy (Live) (p/s, numbered) | 10 |
| 04 | Beggars Banquet BBQ 377 | Glitter And Trauma/There's No Such Thing As A Jaggy Snake (Peel Session) (p/s) | 8 |
| 04 | Beggars Banquet BBQ 379 | My Recovery Injection/Diary Of Always (acoustic) (p/s) | 5 |
| 07 | 14th Floor 14FLR21V1 | Living Is A Problem Because Everything Dies/Loneliness (p/s, blue vinyl, poster) | 5 |
| 07 | 14th Floor 14FLR21V2 | Living Is A Problem Because Everything Dies/Kittens Cakes And Cuddles (p/s, red vinyl, poster) | 5 |
| 07 | 14th Floor 14FR24V1 | Folding Stars/Coward (stickered p/s, with poster, blue vinyl) | 5 |
| 07 | 14th Floor 14FR24V2 | Folding Stars/A Headline (stickered p/s, with poster, white vinyl) | 5 |
| 07 | 14th Floor 14FLR27V1 | Machines (Alternative Version)/Classical Machines (gatefold p/s, sky blue vinyl, poster, numbered) | 8 |
| 02 | Beggars Banquet BBQLP226 | BLACKENED SKY (LP) | 25 |
| 03 | Beggars Banquet BBQLP233 | THE VERTIGO OF BLISS (LP) | 18 |
| 04 | Beggars Banquet BBQLP238 | INFINITY LAND (LP) | 18 |
| 09 | 14th Floor 5051865629702 | ONLY REVOLUTIONS (LP, 2-CD, DVD box set) | 35 |

## BIG AMONGST SHEEP
| 83 | Rock Solid RSS 01 | ASTROPOP (12" EP, p/s) | 12 |
|---|---|---|---|
| 82 | Rock Solid RSR 2001 | TERMINAL VELOCITY (LP) | 60 |

*(see also Inner City Unit, Silverwing)*

## BIG BARON
| 60 | Top Rank JAR 404 | Swinging Bells (Oberon Jump)/Romance | 5 |
|---|---|---|---|

## BIG BERTHA FEATURING ACE KEFFORD
| 69 | Atlantic 584 298 | This World's An Apple/Gravy Booby Jamm | 35 |
|---|---|---|---|

*(see also Cozy Powell, Ace Kefford Stand, Bedlam, Youngblood)*

## BIG BLACK
| 85 | Homestead HMS 007 | RACER-X (12" EP, with insert) | 12 |
|---|---|---|---|
| 87 | Blast First BFFP 14T | HEADACHE (12" p/s, 1,000 only, free 45, Heartbeat/"Things To Do Today"/"I Can't Believe") | 12 |
| 87 | Blast First BFFP 24 | He's A Whore/The Model (p/s) | 5 |
| 86 | Homestead HMS 044 | HAMMER PARTY (LP) | 15 |
| 86 | Blast First BFFP 11 | ATOMIZER (LP) | 18 |
| 87 | Blast First BFFP 19 | SONGS ABOUT FUCKING (LP, usually with sticker over 'Fucking') | 20 |
| 87 | Blast First CHAT 2 | TALK ABOUT FUCKING (LP, promo interview disc with question sheet insert) | 15 |
| 87 | NOT 2 (BUT 1) | SOUND OF IMPACT (LP, matt sleeve, numbered up to 1,000, with 8-page booklet) | 30 |
| 87 | NOT 2 (BUT 1) | SOUND OF IMPACT (LP, laminated sleeve, numbered from 1,001-1,500, with 8-page booklet) | 20 |
| 92 | Touch & Go TG24 | SONGS ABOUT FUCKING (LP, reissue) | 15 |
| 92 | Touch & Go TG 81 | PIGPILE (LP, boxed set with video & T-shirt with insert) | 30 |

*(see also Rapeman)*

## BIG BOB
| 59 | Top Rank JAR 185 | Your Line Was Busy/What Am I | 20 |
|---|---|---|---|

## BIG BOPPER
| 58 | Mercury AMT 1002 | Chantilly Lace/The Purple People Eater Meets The Witchdoctor | 20 |
|---|---|---|---|
| 59 | Mercury AMT 1017 | Big Bopper's Wedding/Little Red Riding Hood | 25 |
| 59 | Mercury AMT 1046 | It's The Truth, Ruth/That's What I Am Talking About | 25 |
| 59 | Mercury ZEP 10004 | THE BIG BOPPER (EP) | 100 |
| 59 | Mercury ZEP 10027 | PINK PETTICOATS (EP) | 100 |
| 58 | Mercury MMC 14008 | CHANTILLY LACE (LP) | 150 |

## BIG BOSS MAN
| 01 | Blow Up BU017 | Sea Groove/Sea Groove (Version) | 10 |
|---|---|---|---|

## BIG BOY PETE
| 68 | Camp 602 005 | Cold Turkey/My Love Is Like A Spaceship | 80 |
|---|---|---|---|
| 96 | Tenth Planet TP 026 | HOMAGE TO CATATONIA (LP) | 18 |

*(see also Miller, Pete Miller)*

## BIG BROTHER & HOLDING COMPANY
| 67 | Fontana TF 881 | Bye Bye Baby/All Is Loneliness | 25 |
|---|---|---|---|
| 68 | CBS 3683 | Piece Of My Heart/Turtle Blues (p/s) | 20 |
| 68 | CBS 3683 | Piece Of My Heart/Turtle Blues (without p/s) | 7 |
| 68 | London HLT 10226 | Down On Me/Call On Me | 10 |
| 67 | Fontana TL 5457 | BIG BROTHER & THE HOLDING COMPANY (LP, with Janis Joplin, mono) | 50 |
| 67 | Fontana (S)TL 5457 | BIG BROTHER & THE HOLDING COMPANY (LP, with Janis Joplin, stereo) | 35 |
| 68 | CBS 63392 | CHEAP THRILLS (LP, with Janis Joplin, laminated single sleeve, mono) | 45 |
| 68 | CBS (S)63392 | CHEAP THRILLS (LP, with Janis Joplin, laminated single sleeve, stereo) | 30 |
| 69 | London HA-T/SH-T 8377 | BIG BROTHER & THE HOLDING COMPANY (LP, reissue, mono/stereo) | 20 |
| 71 | CBS S 64118 | BE A BROTHER (LP) | 25 |

*(see also Janis Joplin, Nick Gravenites)*

## BIG CARROT
| 73 | EMI EMI 2047 | Blackjack/Squint Eye Mangle | 50 |
|---|---|---|---|
| 73 | EMI EMI 2047 | Blackjack/Squint Eye Mangle (Demo copy) | 50 |

*(see also Marc Bolan/T. Rex)*

## BIG CHARLIE
| 64 | Blue Beat BB 241 | Red Sea/You May Not Believe | 40 |
|---|---|---|---|

## BIG COUNTRY
| 84 | Mercury COUNT 5-5 | Wonderland/Giant//Lost Patrol (Live - parts 1 & 2) (2 x 7") | 10 |
|---|---|---|---|

# BIG DADDY KANE

| 84 | Mercury MERD 185 | Where The Rose Is Sown/Belief In The Small Man//Wonderland (Live)/In A Big Country (Live)/Auld Lang Syne (Live) (2 x 7")................................................ 10 |
|---|---|---|
| 91 | Vertigo 510230-1 | NO PLACE LIKE HOME (LP) .................................................................................. 15 |

*(see also Skids)*

## BIG DADDY KANE
| 88 | Cold Chillin' W7676 | Set It Off/Get Into It (p/s) ..................................................................................... 40 |
|---|---|---|
| 88 | Cold Chillin' W7676 | Set It Off (Extended Mix)/Get Into It, Set It Off (12", p/s) ................................ 40 |
| 88 | Cold Chillin' W7953 | Word To The Mother (Land)/Raw (p/s, original US issue released in 1987) ......... 40 |

## BIG DAISY
| 80 | Ellie Jay 9428 | Fever/Footprints (p/s) ....................................................................................... 250 |
|---|---|---|

*(see also Wishbone Ash)*

## BIG DAVE (CAVANAUGH) & HIS ORCHESTRA
| 54 | Capitol CL 14195 | Loosely With Feeling/The Cat From Coos Bay (triangular centre).................... 10 |
|---|---|---|
| 55 | Capitol CL 14245 | Rock And Roll Party/Your Kind Of Love (triangular centre)............................. 30 |

## BIG DREAD
| 76 | Nice One N002 | I Got To Go Girl/Blood & Fire ............................................................................ 12 |
|---|---|---|

## BIG FLAME
| 84 | Laughing Gun PLAQUE 001 | Sink/The Illness/Sometimes (p/s, with insert) ................................................ 10 |
|---|---|---|
| 86 | Ron Johnson ZRON 7 | Why Popstars Can't Dance/Chanel Samba/Breath Of A Nation (p/s)............... 8 |

## BIG GEE
| 71 | Horse HOSS 4 | Chick-A-Boom/Sunflower Wine ........................................................................... 5 |
|---|---|---|

## BIG IN JAPAN
| 77 | Eric's ERICS 0001 | Big In Japan/CHUDDIE NUDDIES: Do The Chud (p/s) ..................................... 15 |
|---|---|---|
| 78 | Zoo CAGE 1 | FROM Y TO Z AND NEVER AGAIN (EP, foldout p/s)........................................ 15 |

*(see also Pink Industry/Military, Holly, Holly Johnson, Yachts, Bill Drummond, Siouxsie & Banshees, Lightning Raiders)*

## BIG JOE (JOSEPH SPALDING)
| 73 | Chanan Jah 1003 | Natty Love/Musical Air Raid .............................................................................. 10 |
|---|---|---|
| 73 | Atra ATRA 005 | Jah Guide/SWEET HARMONY: Student Dub ...................................................... 12 |
| 73 | Atra ATRA 010 | Down Santic Way/Santic Dub ............................................................................ 15 |
| 74 | Dip DL 5007 | Selassie Skank/Version ....................................................................................... 15 |
| 74 | Dip DL 5008 | Weed Specialist/CHERRY & DUB MASTER: Rub A Daughter ........................... 15 |
| 74 | Dip DL 5027 | Hog In A Me Minty/Sweet Melody ..................................................................... 30 |
| 75 | Fab FAB 243 | American Pum Pum/Tape White Wash ............................................................. 10 |
| 76 | Bimbo Music BM 4 | Zion Dread/D. MORGAN: What A Disturbance ................................................ 15 |
| 76 | Burning Sounds BS 008 | Natty Dread Don't Bow/CHANNEL ONE: Natty Dubbing................................ 15 |
| 77 | ATA ATA 1001 | Set Your Face At Ease/Version ........................................................................... 20 |
| 77 | Venture VEN7770 | Natty Don't Make War/CHANNEL ONE FLYERS: War Dubbing...................... 15 |
| 78 | Attack ATT 8136 | Tubby At The Controls/Dignity And Principle .................................................. 10 |
| 79 | Tribesman TM 013 | Respect Jah Word (with Rodney)/The Profit Says (12")................................... 20 |
| 77 | Live & Love LAP001 | KEEP ROCKING AND SWINGING (LP) ................................................................ 45 |
| 78 | Trojan TRLS 152 | AFRICAN PRINCESS (LP) ..................................................................................... 30 |

## BIG JUMP BAND
| 73 | Decca F 13411 | All I Want/Utopia ................................................................................................. 7 |
|---|---|---|

## BIG LUCKY, BIG AMOS & DONALD HINES
| 72 | London SHU 8425 | RIVER TOWN BLUES (LP) ..................................................................................... 25 |
|---|---|---|

## BIG MAYBELLE
| 57 | London HLC 8447 | I Don't Want To Cry/All Of Me ........................................................................... 50 |
|---|---|---|
| 59 | London HLC 8854 | Baby, Won't You Please Come Home/Say It Isn't So ........................................ 20 |
| 65 | London HL 9941 | Careless Love/My Mother's Eyes ....................................................................... 10 |
| 67 | CBS 2735 | Turn The World Around The Other Way/I Can't Wait Any Longer ................... 20 |
| 67 | CBS 2926 | Mama (He Treats Your Daughter Mean)/Keep That Man ................................. 50 |
| 68 | Direction 58-3312 | Quittin' Time/I Can't Wait Any Longer ............................................................. 30 |
| 68 | Direction 58-3312 | Quittin' Time/I Can't Wait Any Longer (DJ Copy)............................................ 40 |
| 67 | CBS 62999 | THE PURE SOUL OF BIG MAYBELLE (LP)........................................................... 30 |

## BIG MOOSE (WALKER)
| 68 | Python PKM 01 | Ramblin' Woman/Puppy Howl Blues ................................................................. 50 |
|---|---|---|

## BIG PINK
| 08 | House Anxiety HA 001 | Too Young To Love/Crystal Visions ................................................................... 12 |
|---|---|---|

## BIG ROY
| 76 | Rockers 6 | In The Desert/Natty Judge ................................................................................... 6 |
|---|---|---|

## BIG SLEEP
| 71 | Pegasus PEG 4 | BLUEBELL WOOD (LP, gatefold sleeve) ........................................................... 150 |
|---|---|---|

*(see also Eyes Of Blue, Ancient Grease, Gentle Giant, Man, Ritchie Francis, Gary Pickford-Hopkins)*

## BIG SPENDERS
| 70 | Gemini GMS 008 | If It Feels Good, Do It/Why Don't Ya Tend To Your Business ......................... 12 |
|---|---|---|
| 70 | Gemini GMS 010 | Who's Making Love/Cum Ba Ye ........................................................................ 15 |

## BIG STAR
| 78 | Stax STAX 504 | September Gurls/Mod Lang ............................................................................... 20 |
|---|---|---|
| 78 | Aura AUS 103 | Kizza Me/Dream Lover (p/s) ............................................................................... 20 |
| 78 | Aura AUS 107 | Jesus Christ/Big Black Car ................................................................................. 20 |
| 78 | Stax SXSP 302 | RADIO CITY/BIG STAR (2-LP) ............................................................................ 30 |
| 78 | Aura AUL 703 | THIRD ALBUM (LP) ............................................................................................. 20 |
| 90 | Big Beat WIK 53 | NO. 1 RECORD (LP, reissue)................................................................................ 15 |
| 90 | Big Beat WIK 54 | RADIO CITY (LP, reissue) ................................................................................... 15 |
| 09 | Rhino 8122 73858-7 | KEEP AN EYE ON THE SKY (4-CD box set)......................................................... 40 |
| 11 | Omnivore | BIG STAR III (replica test pressing in box, inserts, 2000 only)......................... 35 |

*(see also Alex Chilton, Box Tops)*

**BIG T**
| 73 | Avalanche AV 67324 | Tea For Two/I Know A Place | 25 |

**BIG THREE (U.K.)**
| 63 | Decca F 11614 | Some Other Guy/Let True Love Begin | 10 |
| 63 | Decca F 11689 | By The Way/Cavern Stomp | 10 |
| 63 | Decca F 11752 | I'm With You/Peanut Butter | 10 |
| 64 | Decca F 11927 | If You Ever Change Your Mind/You've Got To Keep Her Under Hand | 10 |
| 73 | Polydor 2058 343 | Some Other Guy/Let It Rock/If You Gotta Make A Fool Of Somebody | 5 |
| 63 | Decca DFE 8552 | AT THE CAVERN (EP) | 15 |
| 73 | Polydor 2383 199 | RESURRECTION (LP) | 15 |

*(see also Escorts, Paddy Klaus & Gibson, Johnny Gustafson, Faron's Flamingos, Johnny & John)*

**BIG THREE (U.S.)**
| 68 | Roulette RCP 5002 | THE BIG THREE FEATURING MAMA CASS (LP) | 30 |

*(see also Mama Cass [Elliot], Mamas & Papas)*

**BIG TROUBLE**
| 72 | Pye 7N45292 | Cyclone Blues/You Said A Bad Word | 15 |

**BIG VERN & CHATTERBOX**
| 93 | Straight From The Bedroom | Volume 3 (12") | 35 |

**BIG WHEEL**
| 73 | Bell Bell 1310 | Shake-A-Tail Part 1/Shake-A-Tail Part 2 | 8 |

**BIG YOUTH**
| 72 | Blue Beat BB 424 | Chi Chi Run/JOHN HOLT: OK Fred | 25 |
| 73 | Downtown DT 497 | Dock Of The Bay/CRYSTALITES: Bass And Drums (Version) | 20 |
| 73 | Gayfeet CS 206 | Medicine Doctor/Facts Of Life | 20 |
| 73 | Prince Buster PB 46 | Chi Chi Run/Drums And Bass (Version) | 12 |
| 73 | Prince Buster PB 48 | Leggo Beast/Leave Your Skeng | 12 |
| 73 | Prince Buster PB 50 | Cain And Abel/Cain And Abel (Version) | 20 |
| 73 | Grape GR 3040 | Foreman Versus Frazier/Foreman Versus Frazier Round Two | 20 |
| 73 | Grape GR 3044 | JA To UK/JA To UK (Version) | 12 |
| 73 | Grape GR 3051 | Opportunity Rock/Double Attack | 20 |
| 73 | Grape GR 3061 | Concrete Jungle/Screaming Tonight | 15 |
| 73 | Green Door GD 4051 | Cool Breeze/CRYSTALITES: Windstorm | 25 |
| 73 | Summit SUM 8542 | A So We Say (with Dennis Brown)/WINSTON SCOTLAND: Scarface | 8 |
| 74 | Harry J. HJ 6682 | Ride On Ride On/Wild Goose Chase (both with Dennis Brown) | 8 |
| 75 | Action ACT 101 | Notty No Jester/Instrumental | 8 |
| 75 | Angem ANG 103 | All Nations/ANSEL COLLINS : Stalag 17 | 12 |
| 75 | Attack ATT 8096 | House Of Dread Locks/GROOVEMASTER: Tangle Locks | 8 |
| 75 | Attack ATT 8104 | Mammy Hot And Daddy Cold/GROOVEMASTERS: Some Like It Dread | 8 |
| 75 | Dip DL 5097 | Big Youth Dread/Another Version | 10 |
| 75 | Lucky DL 5103 | Natty Warning/Version | 8 |
| 75 | Klik KLP 9001 | Dread Locks Dread | 15 |
| 76 | Lucky LY 6001 | Get Up Stand Up/Version (with Dennis Brown) | 8 |
| 77 | Eji E 011 | Strictly Rockers/AUGUSTUS PABLO : No Entry (12") | 40 |
| 78 | Wildflower WF 538 | Jah Jah Love Them/Oven Baking | 8 |
| 72 | Fab MS 8 | CHI CHI RUN (LP) | 45 |
| 73 | Trojan TRLS 61 | SCREAMING TARGET (LP, orange & white label) | 35 |
| 75 | Klik KLP9001 | DREAD LOCKS DREAD (LP) | 15 |
| 78 | Virgin Front Line FL 1011 | ISIAH, FIRST PROPHET OF OLD (LP) | 18 |
| 78 | Virgin Front Line FL 1014 | DREAD LOCKS DREAD (LP) | 15 |
| 77 | Trojan BYD 1 | REGGAE PHENOMENON (2-LP) | 18 |
| 80 | Trojan TRLS 189 | EVERYDAY SKANK (LP) | 15 |

*(see also Upsetters)*

**BIG YOUTH & KEITH HUDSON**
| 73 | Pyramid PYR 7055 | Can You Keep A Secret/HORACE ANDY & EARL FLUTE: Peter And Judas | 25 |

**BIGGA DREAD**
| 02 | Chariot Cha 001 | Batty Dread/Closet Bwoy/Truck Inna Garage/Special Request (10") | 30 |

**EDWINA BIGLET AND THE MIDGETS**
| 72 | RCA RCA 2193 | Thing/Vanessa's Luminous Coat | 10 |

**BIG OUTDOOR TYPE**
| 84 | Havasac SAC 01 | Call You On Sundays/Seventeen (p/s) | 50 |

**BIJOUX TOO**
| 86 | Apex APE 002 | Shadows In My Heart/Come On Back (oversized p/s, Welsh-only release) | 30 |

**THEO BIKEL**
| 69 | Reprise RS 2344 | I Love My Dog/The Great Mandela (The Wheel Of Life) | 15 |

**BIKINIS**
| 58 | Columbia DB 4149 | Bikini/Boogie Rock And Roll | 15 |

**BILBO BAGGINS**
| 74 | Polydor 2058 479 | Saturday Night/Monday Morning Blues | 15 |

**BILL THE MURDERER**
| 78 | SRT | I'd Find You/Spring Rain (no p/s) | 100 |

**BILLIE & EDDIE**
| 59 | Top Rank JAR 249 | The King Is Coming Back/Come Back, Baby | 15 |

**TREVOR BILLMUSS**
| 70 | Charisma CB 130 | Whoops Amour/Sunday Afternoon In Belgrave Square | 15 |
| 71 | B & C CB 158 | English Pastures/Fishing Song | 8 |
| 70 | Charisma CAS 1017 | FAMILY APOLOGY (LP) | 30 |

MINT VALUE £

## EDDIE BILLUPS
| 02 | Grapevine 2000 126 | Ask My Heart/A Soldier's Prayer | 10 |

## BONNIE 'PRINCE' BILLY
| 07 | No label or Cat. No. | BONNY (7" tour EP) | 15 |
| 12 | Spiritual Pyjamas SPIRITUAL 004 | Hummingbird/Tribulations/Because Of Your Eyes (10") | 20 |
| 99 | Domino WIGLP 59 | I SEE A DARKNESS (LP) | 18 |
| 01 | Domino WIGLP 89 | EASE DOWN THE ROAD (LP) | 15 |
| 03 | Palace/Domino WIGLP121 | MASTER & EVERYONE (LP, insert) | 15 |
| 04 | Domino WIGLP 140 | SINGS GREATEST PALACE MUSIC (LP, 1-sided) | 15 |
| 09 | Domino WIGLP 233 | BEWARE (LP) | 15 |
| 12 | Faber And Faber FAB 02EP | WILL OLDHAM ON BONNIE PRINCE BILLY (2 x 10" in box with book, 300 only) | 200 |

## BILLY & ESSENTIALS
| 63 | London HLW 9657 | Over The Weekend/Maybe You'll Be There | 30 |

## BILLY & LILLIE (& BILLY FORD & THUNDERBIRDS)
| 58 | London HLU 8564 | La Dee Dah/BILLY FORD'S THUNDERBIRDS: The Monster | 20 |
| 58 | London HLU 8630 | Creepin', Crawlin', Cryin'/Happiness (with Billy Ford & Thunderbirds) | 30 |
| 59 | London HLU 8795 | I Promise You/Lucky Ladybug | 20 |
| 59 | Top Rank JAR 157 | Bells, Bells, Bells/Honeymoonin' (as Billie & Lillie) | 10 |

## BILLY & BARRY BELLY
| 87 | Sidetrack SIDE 001 | Do They Know/Conversations With... (p/s) | 25 |

*(see also Chris Sievey, Frank Sidebottom)*

## BIM & BAM
| 70 | Crab CRAB 48 | The Pill (with Clover)/TOMMY McCOOK: Spring Fever | 15 |
| 70 | Crab CRAB 49 | Immigrant Plight (w/ Clover)/PETER AUSTIN & HORTENSE: Bang Shangalang | 15 |
| 73 | Gayfeet GS 201 | Fatty/Landlord | 10 |

## BIM, BAM & CLOVER
| 70 | Trojan TR 7754 | Party Time Parts 1 & 2 | 8 |

## BINGO
| 79 | Polydor 2066365 | We Can't Get Enough/Mumblin' Man | 20 |

## SONNY BINNS (& RUDIES)
| 69 | Downtown DT 420 | The Untouchables/Lazy Boy | 20 |
| 69 | Downtown DT 424 | Wheels/Night Train | 25 |
| 70 | Escort ES 818 | Boss A Moon (as S. Binns)/BUNNY LEE ALLSTARS: Brotherly Love | 40 |

*(see also Rudies)*

## TONY BINNS
| 71 | Explosion EX 2044 | Love I Madly/Musical Shower | 10 |
| 71 | Explosion EX 2046 | Humpty Dumpty/Got To Get A Message | 8 |

## BINO
| 81 | Upper Class CPS 1 | Dream (For My Sake)/Tonight (p/s) | 15 |

## BINTANGS
| 70 | Decca F22995 | Ridin' On The L And N/Down South Blues | 18 |

## BIONIC ECHO
| 86 | Josiah KJ 003 | Digital/Chatty Chatty Mouth (12") | 80 |

## BIOTA
| 85 | Recommended DYS 12 & 13 | RACKABONES (LP, with inserts) | 30 |

## KEV BIRD
| 91 | Basement BRSS 003 | Inside Your Mind (Full Length Mix)/En Bass (Original Mix)/En Bass (Crash Mix) (12", promo) | 20 |
| 92 | Basement BRSS 006 | THE VISIT TO 14B EP (12", with The Wax Doctor) | 15 |
| 92 | Basement BRSS 012 | This Is A Trip/Let's Turn It out/Eloquence (12") | 10 |
| 94 | Basement BRSS 031 | Kano/Sub Zero (12") | 10 |

## BIRD LEGS & PAULINE
| 66 | Sue WI 4014 | Spring/In So Many Ways | 40 |

## STANLEY & JEFFREY BIRD
| 60 | HMV POP 702 | Johnny At The Crossheads/Betty, Betty (Go Steady With Me) | 10 |

## BIRD TWINS
| 61 | HMV POP 864 | Momma - Poppa/Banned In Boston | 5 |

## BIRD CURTIS
| 67 | Tony Pike TPMLP 144 | BIRD CURTIS QUINTET (LP) | 350 |

## BIRDS
| 64 | Decca F 12031 | You're On My Mind/You Don't Love Me (You Don't Care) | 100 |
| 65 | Decca F 12140 | Leaving Here/Next In Line | 100 |
| 65 | Decca F 12257 | No Good Without You Baby/How Can It Be | 90 |
| 85 | Demon WEST 901 | THESE BIRDS ARE DANGEROUS (LP) | 15 |

*(see also Birds Birds, Ron Wood, Faces, Creation, Ashton Gardner & Dyke)*

## BIRDS BIRDS
| 66 | Reaction 591 005 | Say Those Magic Words/Daddy Daddy | 500 |

*(see also Birds, Gods)*

## BIRDS OF A FEATHER
| 69 | Page One POF 156 | Blacksmith Blues/Sing My Song And Pray | 10 |
| 70 | Page One POF 179 | All God's Children Got Soul/Get It Together | 6 |
| 72 | Jam JAM 23 | You Know Me Better/Summer Has Gone | 5 |
| 72 | DJM DJS 243 | Thank You/Baby Don't You Bring Me Down | 5 |
| 70 | Page One POLS 027 | BIRDS OF A FEATHER (LP) | 100 |

*(see also Chanters)*

## BIRDS & BRASS
| | | | |
|---|---|---|---:|
| 70 | Rediffusion ZS 57 | SOUNDSATIONAL (LP) | 15 |
| 74 | Rediffusion 0100 171 | ... ARE BACK (LP) | 15 |

## JANE BIRKIN & SERGE GAINSBOURG
| | | | |
|---|---|---|---:|
| 74 | Antic K 11511 | Je T'Aime, Moi Non Plus/Jane B (3rd reissue, 'nude' p/s) | 5 |
| 69 | Fontana STL 5493 | JANE BIRKIN AND SERGE GAINSBOURG (LP) | 15 |

## BIRMINGHAM
| | | | |
|---|---|---|---:|
| 71 | Grosvenor GRS 1011 | BIRMINGHAM (LP) | 80 |

*(see also Dave Peace Quartet)*

## BIRTH CONTROL
| | | | |
|---|---|---|---:|
| 71 | Charisma CAS 1036 | BIRTH CONTROL (LP, pink/white 'scroll' label) | 150 |

## BIRTHDAY PARTY
| | | | |
|---|---|---|---:|
| 80 | 4AD AD 12 | The Friend Catcher/Waving My Arms/Cat Man (p/s) | 12 |
| 80 | Missing Link ML-18 | Mr. Clarinet/Happy Birthday | 50 |
| 81 | 4AD AD 111 | Release The Bats/Blast Off (p/s) | 10 |
| 81 | 4AD AD 114 | Mr. Clarinet/Happy Birthday (p/s) | 12 |
| 81 | (no cat. no.) | Mr. Clarinet/Missing Link (sold at gigs only) | 50 |
| 82 | 4AD BAD 301 | THE BAD SEED EP | 15 |
| 82 | 4AD JAD 202 | DRUNK ON THE POPE'S BLOOD/THE AGONY IS THE ECSTACY (12" EP, with Lydia Lunch) | 15 |
| 87 | Strange Fruit SFSP 020 | PEEL SESSIONS 1 (12") | 10 |
| 88 | Strange Fruit SFSP 058 | PEEL SESSIONS 2 (12") | 10 |
| 81 | 4AD CAD 104 | PRAYERS ON FIRE (LP, inner) | 20 |
| 82 | 4AD CAD 207 | JUNK YARD (LP, with inner) | 20 |
| 83 | Mute MUTE 29 | MUTINY (LP, insert) | 15 |
| 92 | 4AD DAD 2016 | HITS (2-LP) | 30 |

*(see also Nick Cave & Bad Seeds, Roland S. Howard & Lydia Lunch, These Immortal Souls)*

## BISH
| | | | |
|---|---|---|---:|
| 80 | Rainbow RS 2 | Modern Women/He's So Foggy (p/s) | 10 |

## DAVE BISHOP
| | | | |
|---|---|---|---:|
| 78 | Bible COM L | FIRST EP (with The Apostles, fold-out p/s) | 15 |

## DICKIE BISHOP & SIDEKICKS
| | | | |
|---|---|---|---:|
| 57 | Decca F 10869 | Cumberland Gap/No Other Baby | 5 |
| 57 | Decca F 10959 | The Prisoner's Song/Please Remember Me | 5 |
| 58 | Decca F 10981 | Skip To My Lou/No Other Baby | 5 |
| 58 | Decca F 11028 | They Can't Take That Away From Me/Jumpin' Judy | 5 |

## TOMMY BISHOP'S RICOCHETS
| | | | |
|---|---|---|---:|
| 65 | Decca F 12238 | I Should Have Known/On The Other Hand | 5 |

*(see also Rock 'n' Roll Revival Show, Rush, Tinkerbell's Fairydust)*

## BITCH (1)
| | | | |
|---|---|---|---:|
| 71 | B & C CB 151 | Laughing/House Where I Live | 8 |
| 72 | Warners K16235 | Good Time Coming/At The Party | 6 |

## BITCH (2)
| | | | |
|---|---|---|---:|
| 79 | Hurricane FIRE 5 | Big City/Wild Kids (p/s) | 20 |

## BITCH (3)
| | | | |
|---|---|---|---:|
| 81 | Rutland RX 101 | First Bite/Maggie (with p/s & promo insert) | 20 |
| 81 | Rutland RX 101 | First Bite/Maggie | 15 |

## BITCHES SIN
| | | | |
|---|---|---|---:|
| 81 | Neat NEAT 09 | Always Ready For Love/Sign Of The Times (p/s) | 8 |
| 83 | Quiet QT 001 | No More Chances/Overnight/Ice Angels (12", p/s) | 25 |
| 82 | Heavy Metal HMRLP 4 | PREDATOR (LP, textured sleeve) | 20 |

## BITCH MAGNET
| | | | |
|---|---|---|---:|
| 91 | Caff CAFF 14 | Sadie/Ducks And Drakes (p/s, with insert) | 12 |

## BITCH SLAPS BITCH
| | | | |
|---|---|---|---:|
| 98 | Brighton Rock ROK 1 | Ladyboy/Locked In a Limo (p/s, 200 only) | 5 |

## BITING TONGUES
| | | | |
|---|---|---|---:|
| 81 | Situation 2 SITU 1 | DON'T HEAL (LP) | 15 |

## BITTER ALMOND
| | | | |
|---|---|---|---:|
| 70 | Warner Bros WB 8008 | In The Morning/Silver | 10 |
| 71 | United Artists UP35197 | Loving Each Other/We Need Someone | 12 |

## BITTER SUITE
| | | | |
|---|---|---|---:|
| 73 | Jam 43 | Six O' Clock News/Here's Hoping | 8 |
| 75 | Bus Stop BUS 1028 | How Married Are You Marianne/Love Is A Friend Of Mine | 5 |

## BITTER END SINGERS
| | | | |
|---|---|---|---:|
| 67 | Atlantic 584 075 | A Taste Of Your Love/Everybody Knows My Name | 10 |

## BITTERNESS
| | | | |
|---|---|---|---:|
| 74 | Brent BR 1 | She Flies/Have We Seen Tomorrow | 20 |

## BIZ
| | | | |
|---|---|---|---:|
| 93 | Warp WARP LP 9 | ELECTRO SOMA (LP, orange vinyl) | 15 |

## BIZARRE
| | | | |
|---|---|---|---:|
| 79 | Polydor 2383 553 | BIZARRE (LP) | 20 |

*(see also Alan Hawkshaw)*

## BIZARRE INC
| | | | |
|---|---|---|---:|
| 91 | Vinyl Solution STORM 25 | Playing With Knives (12") | 10 |
| 91 | Vinyl Solution STORM 25 RT | Playing With Knives (The Climax) (12") | 10 |
| 89 | Blue Chip BLUE TEC. 1 | TECHNOLOGICAL (LP) | 15 |

| | | MINT VALUE £ |
|---|---|---|

**BIZARRE UNIT**

| 81 | MRS MRS 004 | Dancing/Away From The Screaming Car | 20 |
|---|---|---|---|

*(see also Paul Nova)*

**BIZ MARKIE**

| 88 | Cold Chillin' W7890 | Vapors/The Do Do (p/s) | 25 |
|---|---|---|---|
| 88 | Cold Chillin' W7930 | Biz Is Goin' Off/The Doo Doo (p/s) | 20 |
| 90 | Warners W9823 | Just A Friend ('Ard Done By Mix)/Just A Friend (LP version) (p/s) | 8 |

**BJÖRK**

| 93 | One Little Indian 112TP12 | Human Behavior : Underworld Mix/Close To Human Mix/Dom T Mix (12" p/s) | 10 |
|---|---|---|---|
| 93 | O. L. Indian 122TP7 | Venus As A Boy : Edit/7" Dream Mix | 6 |
| 96 | O. L. Indian 193TP712TD | Possibly Maybe (Calcutta Cyber Café Mix)/I Miss You (Dobie's Rub Part One (12", 1,000 only) | 12 |
| 96 | O.L. Indian 193TP12DM | Enjoy (Beats Mix)/Possibly Maybe (Lucy Mix) (p/s, 1,000 only, numbered) | 15 |
| 96 | O. L. Indian 193TP12DM | Enjoy/Possibly Maybe (12", 1,000 only, numbered p/s) | 18 |
| 96 | O. L. Indian 193TP12TD | POSSIBLY MAYBE (12" EP, 1,000 only, numbered p/s) | 12 |
| 97 | O. L. Indian TPLP 81 | JOGA (12" triple-pack, inner sleeves, p/s) | 12 |
| 97 | O. L. Indian 20 TP7 BOX | JOGA (CD box set, 3 x CD singles & 1-track video, 3,000 only) | 30 |
| 98 | Fat Cat 12FAT 022 | All Is Full Of Love (FunkstÖrung Remix)/The Shit (12", custom stamped sleeve) | 12 |
| 98 | One L. Indian 222TP7BOX | HUNTER (3 x CD singles & 1-track video) | 25 |
| 08 | One L. Indian 805TP12 | EARTH INTRUDERS (CD, DVD & 2 x 12") | 20 |
| 08 | One L. Indian 837TP12 | DECLARE INDEPENDENCE (CD, DVD & 2 x 12") | 20 |
| 08 | One L. Indian 838TP12 | INNOCENCE (CD, DVD & 2 x 12") | 20 |
| 08 | One L. Indian 853TP12 | WANDERLUST (CD, DVD & 2 x 12") | 20 |
| 93 | O. L. Indian TPLP 31L | DEBUT (LP, 5,000 with 16-page lyric booklet) | 25 |
| 93 | O. L. Indian TPLP 31L | DEBUT (LP) | 15 |
| 94 | O. L. Indian 152TP 12 | THE BEST MIXES FROM THE ALBUM "DEBUT" FOR THOSE PEOPLE WHO DON'T BUY WHITE LABELS (mini-LP) | 20 |
| 95 | One L. Indian TPLP 51L | POST (LP, pink vinyl, with inner sleeve) | 30 |
| 97 | One L. Indian TPLP71 | HOMOGENIC (LP) | 25 |
| 00 | One L. Indian TPLP151 | SELMA SONGS (LP) | 25 |
| 01 | One L. Indian TPLP101 | VESPERTINE (2 x LP, gatefold) | 25 |
| 02 | One L. Indian TPLP359 | GREATEST HITS (2 x LP, gatefold) | 20 |
| 02 | One L. Indian TPLP365CD | GREATEST HITS & FAMILY TREE (CD x 6 boxed set) | 25 |
| 04 | One L. Indian TPLP358 | MEDULLA (2 x LP) | 25 |
| 06 | One L. Indian TPLP101SACD | SURROUNDED (7 dualdisc box-set of all albums) | 60 |
| 07 | One L. Indian TPLP460H | VOLTA (2 x LP fold-out cover) | 20 |
| 09 | One L. Indian TPLP916 | VOLTAIC (2-LP, 2-CD and 2-DVD) | 30 |
| 11 | One L. Indian TPLP1016 | BIOPHILIA (LP, 2x12") | 18 |

*(see also Sugarcubes, Kukl)*

**BLACK**

| 81 | Rox ROX 17 | Human Features/Electric Church (p/s) | 20 |
|---|---|---|---|
| 82 | Wonderful World WWW3 | More Than The Sun/Jump (no p/s) | 20 |

**BILL BLACK'S COMBO**

| 59 | Felsted AF 129 | Smokie Parts 1 & 2 | 10 |
|---|---|---|---|
| 64 | London HLU 9925 | Little Queenie/Boo-Ray | 30 |
| 64 | London HLU 9925 | Little Queenie/Boo-Ray (DJ Copy) | 100 |
| 60 | London REU 1277 | BILL BLACK'S COMBO (EP) | 10 |
| 63 | London REU 1369 | THE UNTOUCHABLE SOUND OF BILL BLACK (EP) | 10 |
| 62 | London HA-U 2310 | SOLID AND RAUNCHY (LP) | 15 |
| 62 | London HA-U 2433 | MOVIN' (LP) | 15 |
| 63 | London HA-U 8080 | THE UNTOUCHABLE SOUND OF BILL BLACK (LP) | 15 |
| 63 | London HA-U 8113 | GREATEST HITS (LP) | 15 |
| 64 | London HA-U 8187 | PLAYS CHUCK BERRY (LP) | 15 |
| 68 | London HA-U/SH-U 8367 | BILL BLACK'S BEAT GOES ON (LP) | 15 |
| 69 | London HA-U/SH-U 8373 | TURN ON YOUR LOVE LIGHT (LP) | 15 |
| 69 | London HA-U/SH-U 8389 | SOULIN' THE BLUES (LP) | 15 |

*(see also Elvis Presley)*

**BLACK CAT**

| 81 | Gate MS02 | Queen Of The Hop/Let's Rock/Rockin Chair/Black Cat Boogle (p/s) | 15 |
|---|---|---|---|
| 81 | Cheapskate CHEAP 32 | Gonna Type A Letter/Race With The Devil (p/s) | 10 |
| 83 | Underworld BBUW 09 | Dance With The Dolly/She's A Rocker (p/s) | 40 |
| 83 | Hot Wax HOT WAX 4501 | STROLLING AFTER DARK EP | 10 |

**CILLA BLACK**

| 63 | Parlophone R 5065 | Love Of The Loved/Shy Of Love | 6 |
|---|---|---|---|

**BLACK FANTASY**

| 84 | Dingle TIG 001 | Evil Places/Fade Away From Me (p/s) | 100 |
|---|---|---|---|

**FRANK BLACK**

| 93 | 4AD CADD 3004 | FRANK BLACK (LP, die-cut screen-printed sleeve, with lyric inner) | 20 |
|---|---|---|---|
| 96 | EPC 481647 | THE CULT OF RAY (LP) | 25 |
| 99 | 4AD DAD 4009 | TEENAGER OF THE YEAR (2-LP) | 25 |

*(see also Pixies)*

**BLACK HEAT**

| 72 | Atlantic 10270 | Streets Of Tears/Chips Funk | 10 |
|---|---|---|---|

**IKA BLACK & THE NATIONS CRK**

| 81 | I One I IONE 001 | Human Life/Better Life (12") | 25 |
|---|---|---|---|

**JEANNE BLACK**

| 60 | Capitol CL 15146 | Lisa/JEANNE & JANIE - Journey Of Love | 5 |
|---|---|---|---|

*(see also Jeanne &)*

## LINCOLN BLACK
| | | | |
|---|---|---|---|
| 70 | Penny Farthing PEN 712 | Famous Last Words/You Built Me Up So High | 12 |

## MARY BLACK
| | | | |
|---|---|---|---|
| 92 | Grapevine GRALP 009 | NO FRONTIERS (LP, with lyric inner sleeve) | 25 |
| 92 | Grapevine GRALP 009 | NO FRONTIERS (LP, audiophile pressing, white sleeve) | 30 |
| 92 | Grapevine GRALP 009 | NO FRONTIERS (LP, audiophile pressing, red sleeve with different design and inner sleeve) | 30 |
| 95 | Grapevine GRALP 011 | THE HOLY GROUND (LP, audiophile pressing) | 20 |
| 95 | Grapevine GRALP 014 | CIRCUS (LP, audiophile pressing with lyric inner) | 20 |

## MATT BLACK & THE DOODLEBUGS
| | | | |
|---|---|---|---|
| 76 | Punk BCS 0005 | Punky Xmas/Nightmare (no p/s) | 8 |

## BLACK ROD
| | | | |
|---|---|---|---|
| 73 | Phoenix NIX 133 | See What You Get Out Of Me/Mad Donkey | 15 |

## SAM BLACK
| | | | |
|---|---|---|---|
| 74 | DJM DJS 334 | I'm Goin' Left/Take Me With You | 50 |

## BLACK ABBOTTS
| | | | |
|---|---|---|---|
| 70 | Chapter One CH 123 | She Looked Away/I Don't Mind | 7 |
| 71 | Evolution E 3001 | How About Me/Everybody Needs A Little Sunshine | 7 |
| 71 | Evolution E 3004 | Love Is Alive/The Painter | 25 |

## BLACK ACE
| | | | |
|---|---|---|---|
| 61 | XX MIN 701 | BLACK ACE (EP) | 30 |
| 62 | Heritage HLP 1006 | BLACK ACE (LP, 99 copies only) | 120 |

## BLACK AND WHITE LOVERS
| | | | |
|---|---|---|---|
| 86 | Guillotine GR 001 | Best Years Of Our Lives/Boulevard Of Broken Dreams (p/s) | 8 |

## BLACK ARK PLAYERS
| | | | |
|---|---|---|---|
| 80 | Black Ark Intl. BALP 4000 | BLACK ARK IN DUB (LP) | 30 |

## BLACK AXE
| | | | |
|---|---|---|---|
| 80 | Metal MELT 1 | Highway Rider/Red Lights (in p/s) | 20 |
| 80 | Metal MELT 1 | Highway Rider/Red Lights | 6 |

## BLACKBEARD
| | | | |
|---|---|---|---|
| 78 | Ballistic LBR 1013 | STRICTLY DUB WISE (LP) | 20 |
| 80 | More Cut RDC 2002 | I WAH DUB (LP) | 25 |

## BLACK BEATLES
| | | | |
|---|---|---|---|
| 70 | Pama PM 804 | Reggae And Shout/LENOX BROWN: The Green Hornet | 30 |

## BLACKBIRDS
| | | | |
|---|---|---|---|
| 68 | Saga OPP 3 | No Destination/Space (either p/s or company sleeve, possibly promo only) | 30 |
| 68 | Saga FID 2113 | NO DESTINATION (LP, black/silver label) | 40 |

## BLACK BLOOD
| | | | |
|---|---|---|---|
| 76 | Bradleys 1002 | Rasteferai/Ewohe Dance | 6 |

## TONY BLACKBURN
| | | | |
|---|---|---|---|
| 65 | Fontana TF 562 | Don't Get Off That Train/Just To Be With You Again | 5 |
| 68 | MGM 1375 | So Much Love/In The Night | 5 |
| 69 | MGM 1467 | It's Only Love/Janie | 8 |

## BLACKBYRDS
| | | | |
|---|---|---|---|
| 75 | Fantasy FTC 114 | Walking In Rhythm/The Baby | 5 |
| 76 | Fantasy FTC 122 | Rock Creek Park/Flying High | 5 |
| 78 | Fantasy FTCT 194 | Rock Creek Park/Don't Know What To Say (12") | 20 |
| 85 | Streetwave SWAVE 3 | Rock Creek Park/Walking In Rhythm (12") | 15 |
| 75 | Fantasy FT 9444 | BLACKBYRDS (LP) | 20 |
| 75 | Fantasy FT 522 | FLYING START (LP) | 15 |
| 77 | Fantasy FT 534 | ACTION (LP) | 15 |
| 79 | Fantasy FT 555 | NIGHT GROOVES - THE BEST OF THE BLACKBYRDS (LP) | 15 |

*(see also Donald Byrd)*

## BLACK CAT BONES
| | | | |
|---|---|---|---|
| 68 | Sceptre SALR 1216 | COME ABOARD QE2 (LP, sold on liner, one track by Black Cat Bones) | 25 |
| 70 | Decca Nova DN 15 | BARBED WIRE SANDWICH (LP, mono, blue/silver label) | 500 |
| 70 | Decca Nova SDN 15 | BARBED WIRE SANDWICH (LP, stereo, blue/silver label) | 600 |

*(see also Leaf Hound, Brian Short, Free, Foghat)*

## BLACK CLAW
| | | | |
|---|---|---|---|
| 69 | Bell BLL 1089 | Across The Great Divide/Sally | 8 |

## BLACK COUNTRY THREE
| | | | |
|---|---|---|---|
| 66 | W.F.C. WS 100 | BLACK COUNTRY SONGS (EP) | 250 |
| 66 | Transatlantic TRA 140 | BLACK COUNTRY THREE (LP) | 50 |

*(see also Jon Raven)*

## BLACK CROWES
| | | | |
|---|---|---|---|
| 91 | Def American 7-17580 | HARD TO HANDLE (7 x 7" box set, with 2 bonus tracks) | 20 |
| 90 | Def American 842515 | SHAKE YOUR MONEY MAKER (LP) | 30 |
| 92 | Def American 512263 | SOUTHERN HARMONY AND MUSICAL COMPANION (LP) | 30 |
| 94 | American 74321 23682 1 | AMORICA (LP, white vinyl) | 60 |
| 99 | American 491699 1 | BY YOUR SIDE (LP) | 60 |

## BLACK DOG
| | | | |
|---|---|---|---|
| 91 | GPR GENP(X) 2 | PARALLEL EP (12", p/s) | 30 |
| 92 | Black Dog Prods BDP 001 | VIRTUAL (12", p/s) | 80 |
| 92 | Black Dog Prods BDP 002 | AGE OF SLACK (12", p/s) | 100 |
| 92 | Black Dog Prods BDP 003 | BLACK DOG EP (12", p/s, 500 only) | 125 |
| 92 | GPR GENP(X) 3 | VIR 2 L (12", custom sleeve) | 100 |
| 92 | GPR GENP(R) 03 | VIR 2 L/Shout (12" remix with SHIVA) | 70 |

# BLACK DYKE MILLS BAND

| | | | |
|---|---|---|---:|
| 92 | GPR GENP(X) 9 | VANTOOL EP (12", custom sleeve) | 100 |
| 93 | GPR GENP(X) 17 | COST II (12", custom sleeve) | 15 |
| 93 | Rising High RSN 046 | BLACK DOG PRODUCTIONS (12", 4-track, p/s) | 20 |
| 99 | Warp WAP 115 | PEEL SESSION (12") | 10 |
| 91 | GPR GPR 004 | PARALLEL SQUELCH (LP) | 30 |
| 92 | GPR GPRLP 1 | TEMPLE OF TRANSPARENT BALLS (2-LP, with poster) | 45 |
| 92 | GPR GPRLP 1 | TEMPLE OF TRANSPARENT BALLS (2-LP, without poster) | 30 |
| 95 | GPR GPRLP 15 | PARALLEL (2-LP) | 35 |
| 95 | GPR GPRCD 15 | PARALLEL (CD) | 30 |
| 95 | Warp PUPLP 1 | SPANNERS (2-LP) | 40 |
| 95 | Warp WAP LP 8LTD | BYTES (LP, bronze vinyl) | 40 |

*(see also Alter Ego, Plaid, Repeat, Unexplored Beats, Shiva)*

## BLACK DYKE MILLS BAND
| | | | |
|---|---|---|---:|
| 68 | Apple APPLE 4 | Thingumybob/Yellow Submarine | 40 |

## BLACK DYNAMITES
| | | | |
|---|---|---|---:|
| 60 | Top Rank JAR 319 | Brush Those Tears/Lonely Cissy | 5 |

## BLACK EASTER
| | | | |
|---|---|---|---:|
| 82 | Illuminated KILL 13 | READY TO ROT (EP, p/s) | 10 |

## BLACK-EDS
| | | | |
|---|---|---|---:|
| 80 | Acne ACNE 1 | Isn't It Strange/Living Doll/Jimmy 2 Stroke (p/s) | 20 |

## BLACK FAITH
| | | | |
|---|---|---|---:|
| 70 | Phillips 6006065 | Woman In My Life | 12 |
| 70 | Phillips 6007018 | Song For A Dollar/Peace In The Family | 10 |
| 74 | Fresh Air 6121107 | The Vow/Stop The World | 20 |

## BLACK FLAG
| | | | |
|---|---|---|---:|
| 81 | Alt. Tentacles VIRUS 9 | Six Pack/I've Heard It All Before/American Waste (p/s) | 12 |
| 84 | SST SST 12001 | Family Man/I Won't Stick Any Of You Unless And Until I Can Stick All Of You (12", p/s) | 10 |

## 'FLIP' BLACK & BOYS UPSTAIRS
| | | | |
|---|---|---|---:|
| 59 | Capitol CL 15037 | For You My Lover/Tell Her Mister Moon | 5 |

## J.D. BLACKFOOT
| | | | |
|---|---|---|---:|
| 71 | Mercury 6338 031 | THE ULTIMATE PROPHECY (LP) | 70 |

## BLACKFOOT SUE
| | | | |
|---|---|---|---:|
| 73 | DJM DJS 296 | Bye Bye Birmingham/Messiah | 10 |
| 74 | DJM DJS 326 | You Need Love/Tobago Rose | 12 |
| 73 | Jam JAL 104 | NOTHING TO HIDE (LP, gatefold sleeve with poster) | 50 |
| 73 | Jam JAL 104 | NOTHING TO HIDE (LP, gatefold sleeve without poster) | 20 |
| 75 | DJM DJLPS 455 | GUN RUNNING (LP, withdrawn) | 65 |

## BLACK FOUNDATION
| | | | |
|---|---|---|---:|
| 77 | Burning Sounds BS 1023 | BLACK FOUNDATION DUB (LP) | 30 |

*(see also Augustus 'Gussie' Clarke)*

## BLACK GORILLA
| | | | |
|---|---|---|---:|
| 77 | Response (PYE) SR 502 | Gimme Dat Banana/Funky Jungle | 6 |

## BLACK GRAPE
| | | | |
|---|---|---|---:|
| 95 | Radioactive RAR 11224 | IT'S GREAT WHEN YOU'RE STRAIGHT YEAH (LP) | 20 |
| 97 | Radioactive RAR 11716 | STUPID STUPID STUPID (LP) | 15 |

*(see also Happy Mondays)*

## BLACK HARMONY
| | | | |
|---|---|---|---:|
| 79 | Burning Sounds BS 14 | I'm Still Waiting/Love Marcus | 8 |
| 79 | Laser LAS 9 | Don't Let It Go To Your Head/DEB PLAYERS : Don't Let It Go To Your Brain (12") | 18 |

## BLACK IVORY
| | | | |
|---|---|---|---:|
| 74 | Kwanza K19500 | What Goes Around/No One Else Will Do | 8 |

## BLACKJACK
| | | | |
|---|---|---|---:|
| 80 | Polydor POSP 76 | Without Your Love/Heart Of Mine (p/s) | 18 |
| 79 | Polydor 2391 411 | BLACKJACK (LP) | 18 |

*(see also Michael Bolton)*

## BLACKJACKS
| | | | |
|---|---|---|---:|
| 63 | Pye 7N 15586 | Woo Hoo/Red Dragon | 10 |

*(see also Pat Harris & Blackjacks)*

## BLACK KEYS
| | | | |
|---|---|---|---:|
| 03 | Fat Possum 111-7 | Hard Row/Evil (p/s) | 15 |
| 03 | Fat Possum 1130-7 | Have Love WIll Travel/No Trust (live)/The Moan (live) (p/s, yellow vinyl) | 10 |
| 04 | Fat Possum 11747 | 10AM Automatic/Summertime Blues (p/s) | 6 |
| 06 | V2 VVR5043087 | Your Touch/The Breaks | 12 |
| 07 | V2 VVR5048347 | Just Got To Be/Black Door (p/s, no'd) | 6 |
| 08 | V2 VVR5051097 | I Got Mine/Here I Am I Always Am | 12 |
| 13 | Warner Bros. 7559-79592-4 | No Fun/THE STOOGES: No Fun (orange vinyl) | 8 |
| 06 | V2 VVR1042541 | MAGIC POTION (LP) | 20 |
| 09 | VVR737199 | BROTHERS (2-LP) | 18 |
| 12 | Fat Possum FP803713 | THICKFREAKNESS (LP, picture disc, 300 only) | 15 |
| 12 | Fat Possum 80379-3 | RUBBER FACTORY (LP, picture disc) | 15 |
| 12 | Nonesuch 530454-1 | EL CAMINO (2-LP, CD, numbered) | 20 |

## BLACK KNIGHTS
| | | | |
|---|---|---|---:|
| 65 | Columbia DB 7443 | I Gotta Woman/Angel Of Love | 25 |

## BLACK LIPS
| | | | |
|---|---|---|---:|
| 07 | Vice VICE 004LP | GOOD BAD NOT EVIL (LP, gatefold) | 15 |

## DON BLACKMAN
| | | | |
|---|---|---|---:|
| 82 | Arista RIST 30 | Hearts Desire/Let Your Conscience Be Your Guide (12", EP) | 15 |

## HONOR BLACKMAN
| | | | |
|---|---|---|---|
| 68 | CBS 3896 | Before Today/I'll Always Be Loving You (in p/s) | 30 |
| 68 | CBS 3896 | Before Today/I'll Always Be Loving You | 10 |
| 64 | Decca LK/SKL 4642 | EVERYTHING I'VE GOT (LP, mono/stereo) | 20 |
| 80 | Deram 844057-1 | KINKY BOOTS (LP) | 20 |

*(see also Patrick MacNee & Honor Blackman)*

## PAUL BLACKMAN
| | | | |
|---|---|---|---|
| 79 | Daddy Kool DKR 123 | Earth, Wind & Fire/A. Pablo: Ras-Menlik Congo (12") | 50 |

## RITCHIE BLACKMORE (ORCHESTRA)
| | | | |
|---|---|---|---|
| 65 | Oriole CB 314 | Getaway/Little Brown Jug (Spelt "Richie" on label) | 600 |

*(see also Outlaws, Neil Christian & Crusaders, Deep Purple, [Ritchie Blackmore's] Rainbow, Rally Rounders, Green Bullfrog)*

## BLACK NASTY
| | | | |
|---|---|---|---|
| 79 | Grapevine 140 | Cut Your Motor Off/Keep On Stepping (reissue) | 10 |

## BLACK OAK ARKANSAS
| | | | |
|---|---|---|---|
| 75 | Atlantic K 10621 | Fancy Nancy/Keep On | 7 |
| 71 | Atlantic 2400 180 | BLACK OAK ARKANSAS (LP) | 15 |

## BLACK PROPHETZ
| | | | |
|---|---|---|---|
| 91 | GTI KICK8 | Fax On Wax (EP) | 12 |

## BLACK RADICAL MK II
| | | | |
|---|---|---|---|
| 91 | Mango 12 MNG 782DJ | Sign Of The Beast (12" - Grey Vinyl/Promo only) | 12 |

## BLACK RADICAL/SIR NOVA
| | | | |
|---|---|---|---|
| 88 | Bass Inc B1001 500 | B Boys Be Wise/We Outta Here (12") | 30 |

## BLACK REBEL MOTORCYCLE CLUB
| | | | |
|---|---|---|---|
| 02 | Virgin VUSLP 224 | BLACK REBEL MOTORCYCLE CLUB (LP) | 30 |
| 03 | Virgin VUSLP 245 | TAKE THEM ON YOUR OWN (2-LP, gatefold, with inner sleeves) | 30 |
| 05 | Echo ECHLP 67 | HOWL (2-LP, with inner sleeves) | 50 |
| 10 | Cobraside CSDLP 1142 | BEAT THE DEVIL'S TATTOO (2-LP, white vinyl 400 copies, tour only) | 30 |
| 10 | Cobraside CSDLP 1142 | BEAT THE DEVIL'S TATTOO (2-LP, grey vinyl) | 20 |

## BLACK RIDERS
| | | | |
|---|---|---|---|
| 85 | Plastic Head GILP 555 | CHOSEN FEW (LP) | 15 |

## BLACK ROOTS
| | | | |
|---|---|---|---|
| 81 | Nubian NR 0021D | Chanting For Freedom/Confusion/What Them A Do (12") | 15 |
| 83 | Silvertown STST 002 | Move On/What Them A Do (12") | 12 |
| 84 | Bullet BOL 9 | Boys Will Be Boys/Liar (p/s, some with patch) | 35 |
| 84 | Nubian NR 001 | Bristol Rock/Tribal War/The Father/The System (12") | 25 |
| 84 | BBC REC 555 | THE FRONT LINE (LP) | 20 |
| 83 | Kick KIC LP 02 | BLACK ROOTS (LP) | 25 |
| 84 | BBC REC 5570 | IN SESSION (LP) | 20 |
| 11 | Bristol Archive ARC219V | REGGAE SINGLES ANTHOLOGY (2-LP) | 18 |

## BLACK ROSE
| | | | |
|---|---|---|---|
| 82 | Teesbeat TB 5 | Sucker For Your Love/No Point Runnin' (in p/s) | 125 |
| 82 | Teesbeat TB 5 | Sucker For Your Love/No Point Runnin' | 35 |

## BLACK SABBATH
### SINGLES
| | | | |
|---|---|---|---|
| 70 | Fontana TF 1067 | Evil Woman/Wicked World | 125 |
| 70 | Vertigo V2 | Evil Woman/Wicked World (reissue, Vertigo 'swirl' sleeve) | 35 |
| 70 | Vertigo V2 | Evil Woman/Wicked World (reissue, later silver label) | 15 |
| 70 | Vertigo 6059 010 | Paranoid/The Wizard (Vertigo 'swirl' sleeve) | 15 |
| 72 | Vertigo 6059 061 | Tomorrow's Dream/Laguna Sunrise (Vertigo 'swirl' sleeve) | 25 |
| 72 | Phonogram DJ 005 | Children Of The Grave/STATUS QUO: Roadhouse Blues (100 promo copies only) | 400 |
| 73 | WWA WWS 002 | Sabbath Bloody Sabbath/Changes (company sleeve) | 8 |
| 75 | NEMS 6165 300 | Am I Going Insane? (Radio)/Hole In The Sky (no p/s) | 10 |
| 77 | NEMS NES 112 | Paranoid/Sabbath Bloody Sabbath (p/s) | 10 |
| 78 | Vertigo SAB 001 | Never Say Die/She's Gone (p/s) | 8 |
| 78 | Vertigo SAB 002 | Hard Road/Symptom Of The Universe (purple or black vinyl) | 6 |
| 80 | Vertigo SAB 3 | Neon Knights/Children Of The Sea (live) (p/s) | 6 |
| 81 | Vertigo SAB 512 | Mob Rules/Die Young (live) (12", p/s) | 10 |
| 86 | Vertigo SABDJ 12 | In For The Kill/Turn To Stone/Heart Like A Wheel (12", promo only) | 15 |
| 87 | Vertigo SABAF 1 | 4 SONGS FROM THE ETERNAL IDOL (12", p/s, promo only) | 15 |
| 89 | I.R.S. EIRS CB 107 | Headless Cross (Edit)/Cloak And Dagger (signed label, insert & 2 postcards) | 6 |
| 89 | I.R.S. EIRSB 115 | Devil And Daughter (box set, 1-sided disc with stencil, insert & 2 postcards) | 8 |
| 10 | Vertigo 00602527391199 | Paranoid (Alternative Lyric Version)/METALLICA: Frantic (UNKLE Remix) (12", 1000 only) | 20 |

### ALBUMS
| | | | |
|---|---|---|---|
| 70 | Vertigo VO 6 | BLACK SABBATH (LP, 1st pressing, with black gatefold inner sleeve, no composers/publishers credits on cross; large swirl label with "A Philips record product" text on label) | 400 |
| 70 | Vertigo VO 6 | BLACK SABBATH (LP, 2nd pressing, with white gatefold sleeve and Dunbar credit for 'Warning'; swirl label, with – allegedly – laminated sleeve) | 200 |
| 70 | Vertigo VO 6 | BLACK SABBATH (LP, 2nd pressing, with white gatefold sleeve and Dunbar credit for 'Warning'; swirl label) | 100 |
| 70 | Vertigo 6360 011 | PARANOID (LP, gatefold sleeve with 'Jim Simpson' credit, 1st press large swirl label) | 250 |
| 70 | Vertigo 6360 011 | PARANOID (LP, gatefold sleeve, 2nd press, small swirl label, laminated sleeve) | 60 |
| 70 | Vertigo 6360 011 | PARANOID (LP, gatefold sleeve, 2nd press, small swirl label) | 50 |
| 70 | Vertigo 6360 011 | PARANOID (LP, gatefold sleeve, later spaceship label) | 70 |
| 71 | Vertigo 6360 050 | MASTER OF REALITY (LP in box cover, swirl label, with poster) | 400 |
| 71 | Vertigo 6360 050 | MASTER OF REALITY (LP in box cover, swirl label, without poster) | 70 |
| 71 | Vertigo VO 6 | BLACK SABBATH (LP, 3rd pressing, 'Vertigo' lettering beneath small swirl above centre hole) | 40 |

# BLACK SLATE

| | | | |
|---|---|---|---|
| 72 | Vertigo 6360 071 | BLACK SABBATH VOL. 4 (LP, 1st pressing, no "Made in England" beneath 1972 on top right hand side" gatefold sleeve with booklet attached, small swirl label) | 100 |
| 72 | Vertigo 6360 071 | BLACK SABBATH VOL. 4 (LP, gatefold sleeve with booklet attached, 'spaceship' label) | 150 |
| 73 | Vertigo VO6 | BLACK SABBBATH (LP, 4th pressing, 'spaceship' label) | 20 |
| 73 | Vertigo 6360 071 | BLACK SABBATH VOL. 4 (LP, 2nd pressing, with "Made in England" beneath 1972 on top right hand side" gatefold sleeve with booklet attached, small swirl label) | 40 |
| 73 | WWA WWA 05 | SABBATH BLOODY SABBATH (LP, 1st pressing, no ridge around rim, 1 Y 1/ 2 Y 1 matrix numbers, silver WWA logo, gatefold with "Manufactured and printed in England" (no "Howard's Printers" reference), inside image extends to edge of sleeve with no border, textured lyric inner) | 60 |
| 73 | WWA 006 | BLACK SABBATH (LP, reissue) | 20 |
| 73 | WWA 007 | PARANOID (LP, reissue) | 25 |
| 73 | Vertigo 6360 050 | MASTER OF REALITY (LP, ' spaceship' label, with poster, reissue) | 50 |
| 73 | WWA 008 | MASTER OF REALITY (LP, label, with poster, reissue) | 30 |
| 75 | NEMS 9119001 | SABOTAGE (LP, 1st pressing with matrix numbers 1//Y2 S 1 3 5 & 2 Y2 S 1 1 4 with 'Sterling' stamped into dead wax on both sides, textured sleeve made by 'Robert Stace') | 30 |
| 75 | NEMS 6641 335 | WE SOLD OUT SOUL FOR ROCK N ROLL (2-LP) | 18 |
| 76 | Vertigo 9102 750 | TECHNICAL ECSTACY (LP, insert) | 25 |
| 76 | NEMS NEL 6003 | PARANOID (LP, reissue) | 15 |
| 76 | NEMS NEL 6005 | BLACK SABBATH VOL 4 (LP, reissue, gatefold) | 15 |
| 78 | Vertigo 9102 751 | NEVER SAY DIE (LP, laminated sleeve, inner) | 15 |
| 80 | Vertigo 9102 752 | HEAVEN AND HELL (LP, A1/B2 matrixes) | 20 |
| 81 | Vertigo 6302 119 | MOB RULES (LP) | 15 |
| 83 | Vertigo SAB 10 | LIVE EVIL (2-LP, gatefold, inners orange Vertigo label) | 18 |
| 83 | Vertigo VER 8 | BORN AGAIN (LP) | 18 |
| 85 | Nems BSBLP 001 | THE SABBATH COLLECTION (7-LP box set) | 15 |
| 86 | Vertigo VERH 29 | SEVENTH STAR (LP, as Black Sabbath featuring Tony Iommi) | 50 |
| 88 | Castle BSBCD 001 | THE BLACK SABBATH CD COLLECTION (6-CD box set with badge & book, numbered, 3,000 only) | 40 |
| 89 | IRS METAL 24 1005 | HEADLESS CROSS (LP, poster) | 20 |
| 89 | IRS EIRSAPD 1002 | HEADLESS CROSS (LP, picture disc with extra track) | 15 |
| 89 | Vertigo 8388181 | BLACKEST SABBATH (2-LP) | 18 |
| 90 | IRS EIRSA 1038 | TYR (LP, inner) | 35 |
| 90 | IRS EIRSAPD 1038 | TYR (LP, picture disc with 2 extra tracks) | 18 |
| 91 | Essential ESBLP 142 | THE OZZY OSBOURNE YEARS (5-LP box set) | 30 |
| 92 | IRS 713155 1 | DEHUMANIZER (LP) | 25 |
| 94 | IRS 07777132221 1 | CROSS PURPOSES (LP, with inner) | 35 |
| 97 | Castle ORRLP 004 | BLACK SABBATH (LP, reissue, 5000 only with free 7") | 20 |
| 00 | Raw Power RAWLP 145 | THE BEST OF BLACK SABBATH (4-LP, gatefold sleeve, numbered and stickered) | 30 |
| 02 | Earmark 41045 | PAST LIVES (2-LP) | 40 |
| 13 | Vertigo 602537349593 | 13 (2-LP, 2-CD, DVD, box set) | 40 |

*(see also Ozzy Osborne, Dio, Elf, Cozy Powell, Quartz, Phenomena, Brian May)*

## BLACK SLATE

| | | | |
|---|---|---|---|
| 76 | King George KG 001 | Mixed Up Man/Put Your Head On My Shoulder | 8 |
| 78 | Ted TCDD 006 | Mind Your Motion/Version | 35 |
| 78 | Ted TCDD 008 | Sticks Man/Version(12") | 25 |
| 78 | Slate KG 008 | Live Up To Love/Jah In The Ghetto (12") | 12 |
| 81 | TCD TCDLP 02 | OGIMA (DUB SLATE) (LP) | 40 |

## BLACK STASH

| | | | |
|---|---|---|---|
| 76 | Seville 1004 | Mighty Love Man/Mighty Love Man Part 2 | 15 |

## BLACK STONES

| | | | |
|---|---|---|---|
| 76 | Daddy Kool DK 003 | We Nah Go Suffer/Unity Dub | 10 |
| 78 | Chanah Jah CJ3026 | Punk Rockers/Open The Gates (12" p/s) | 15 |
| 81 | KG Imperial KG 005 | Created By One Power/Satisfy Her Soul (12") | 12 |

## BLACKSTONES

| | | | |
|---|---|---|---|
| 81 | Jah Liion JLDC610 | Sweet Feeling/Riding High (12") | 12 |

## BLACK SWAN

| | | | |
|---|---|---|---|
| 71 | Ember EMBS 303 | Echoes And Rainbows/Belong Belong (with p/s) | 15 |
| 71 | Ember EMBS 303 | Echoes And Rainbows/Belong Belong (without p/s) | 8 |

## BLACK SYMBOL

| | | | |
|---|---|---|---|
| 79 | Black Symbol BS 001 | Non A Jah Jah Children Passing/Version (12") | 50 |
| 80 | Black Symbol BS 003 | Loving Jah/Everything Has Time (12") | 70 |
| 80 | Black Symbol BS 006 | My Heart Reveal Dancer/Dub Piano | 25 |
| 82 | Black Symbol BS 008 | Solidarity/Tension (12") | 30 |

## BLACKTHORN

| | | | |
|---|---|---|---|
| 77 | WHM 1921 | BLACKTHORN (LP) | 60 |
| 78 | WHM 1923 | BLACKTHORN II (LP) | 100 |

## BLACK UHURU

| | | | |
|---|---|---|---|
| 77 | Carib Gems CG 015 | Sun Is Shining/REVOLUTIONARIES : Version | 15 |
| 77 | Third World TWDIS 009 | Natural Mystic/Sorry For The Man (12") | 20 |
| 79 | Warrior WAR 140 | Bad Girl/African Love/PRINCE HAMMER - Yogi Bear (12") | 25 |
| 79 | DEB DEB 034 | Rent Man/Rent Board/ALTON ELLIS - La La Means I Love You/Version (12") | 18 |
| 79 | DEB DEB 036 | Wood For My Fire/EARL CUNNINGHAM/JAH THOMAS - Words Of The Father (12") | 15 |
| 79 | D Roy DDR 09 | Plastic Smile/Guess Who's Coming To Dinner (12") | 25 |
| 79 | D Roy DRDD 15 | Shine Eye (featuring Keith Richards)/D-ROY BAND: Licking Stick (12") | 25 |
| 80 | Island 12WIP 6626 | Sinsemilla (Discomix)/Guess Who's Coming To Dinner (Discomix) (12") | 10 |
| 85 | Taxi BUT 1 | Fit You Haffe Fit/Fitness (12") | 25 |
| 77 | Third World TWS 925 | LOVE CRISIS (LP, as Black Sounds Uhro) | 40 |
| 79 | D-Roy DRLP 1003 | SHOWCASE (LP) | 25 |

| | | | |
|---|---|---|---|
| 81 | Greensleeves GREL 23 | BLACK SOUNDS OF FREEDOM (LP) | 15 |

*(See also Don Carlos)*

## BLACK VELVET

| | | | |
|---|---|---|---|
| 69 | Beacon BEA 129 | African Velvet/Whatcha' Gonna Do 'Bout It | 8 |
| 69 | Beacon BEA 137 | Peace And Love Is The message/Clown | 8 |
| 70 | Beacon BEA 151 | Please Let Me In/Clown | 20 |
| 70 | Beacon BEA 162 | What Am I To Do/Coal Mine | 12 |
| 70 | Beacon BEA 170 | Thought I Had Me A Good Thing/Love Makes The World Go Round | 10 |
| 71 | Mams MAM 47 | Make It Better/Tropicana | 15 |
| 73 | Pye 7N 45338 | There Must Be A Way/Domestic Man | 12 |
| 70 | Beacon BEAS 16 | THIS IS BLACK VELVET (LP) | 25 |
| 72 | Pye NSPL 18392 | PEOPLE OF THE WORLD (LP) | 25 |
| 73 | Seven Sun SUNLP1 | CAN YOU FEEL IT? (LP) | 80 |

## CHARLES BLACKWELL ORCHESTRA

| | | | |
|---|---|---|---|
| 61 | HMV POP 977 | Taboo/Midnight In Luxembourg | 10 |
| 62 | Columbia DB 4839 | Supercar/Persian Theme | 5 |
| 62 | Columbia DB 4919 | Freight Train/Death Valley | 5 |
| 63 | Columbia DB 4994 | High Noon/For Me And My Gal | 5 |
| 65 | Columbia BD 7501 | Meditation/La Bamba | 5 |
| 67 | United Artists UP 1157 | Sailor From Gibraltar/Hoi | 5 |
| 60 | Triumph TRY 4000 | THOSE PLUCKING STRINGS (LP, unreleased, test pressings only) | 500 |

## OTIS BLACKWELL

| | | | |
|---|---|---|---|
| 58 | London HLE 8616 | Make Ready For Love/When You're Around | 40 |

## RORY BLACKWELL & HIS BLACKJACKS

| | | | |
|---|---|---|---|
| 57 | Parlophone R 4326 | Bye Bye Love/Such A Shame | 20 |

## SCRAPPER BLACKWELL

| | | | |
|---|---|---|---|
| 67 | Collector JEN 7 | SCRAPPER BLACKWELL (EP) | 10 |
| 63 | '77' LA 12/4 | BLUES BEFORE SUNRISE (LP) | 40 |
| 60s | Xtra XTRA 5011 | MR SCRAPPER'S BLUES (LP) | 25 |

## BLACKWELLS (U.K.)

| | | | |
|---|---|---|---|
| 65 | Columbia DB 7442 | Why Don't You Love Me/All I Want Is Your Love | 15 |

## BLACKWELLS (U.S.)

| | | | |
|---|---|---|---|
| 60 | London HLW 9135 | Unchained Melody/Mansion On The Hill | 5 |
| 61 | London HLW 9334 | Love Or Money/Big Daddy And The Cat | 5 |

## BLACK WIDOW

| | | | |
|---|---|---|---|
| 70 | CBS 5031 | Come To The Sabbat/Way To Power | 20 |
| 71 | CBS 7596 | Wish You Would/Accident | 20 |
| 70 | CBS 63948 | SACRIFICE (LP, gatefold sleeve) | 100 |
| 70 | CBS 64133 | BLACK WIDOW II (LP, gatefold sleeve) | 100 |
| 72 | CBS 64562 | BLACK WIDOW III (LP, with inner) | 100 |

*(see also Pesky Gee, Agony Bag)*

## BLADE

| | | | |
|---|---|---|---|
| 88 | Chart Moves 732-1532 | Chart Moves (12", not officially released. Intended to be instructions to game of same name but never used in final version of game) | 40 |
| 89 | Raw Bass 1202 | Lyrical Maniac/The Comin' Is Near/We're Going Independent (12") | 15 |
| 89 | 691 Influential 1203 | Mind Of An OrdinaryCitizen/Forward (12") | 12 |
| 91 | 691 Influential 1204 | Rough It Up/Whatcha Waitin' For?/You Better Get Yours (12") | 12 |
| 93 | 691 Influential 1206 | Clear The Way/They Ain't Shit To Me (12", white vinyl, Blade gave this to fans who paid in advance for his THE LION GOES FROM STRENTH TO STRENGTH LP) | 18 |
| 96 | 691 Influential SURV 1 | Survival Of The Hardest Working (12") | 18 |
| 97 | Bomb 2006 | Rhyme Bomb/The Way It Has To Be (12") | 10 |
| 92 | 691 Influential 1205 | SURVIVAL OF THE HARDEST WORKING (LP) | 20 |
| 93 | 691 Influential 1202 | THE LION GOES FROM STRENGTH TO STRENGTH (LP) | 20 |
| 95 | 691 Influential 1208 | PLANNED AND EXECUTED (LP, limited edition on red vinyl) | 25 |

## ANDY BLADE

| | | | |
|---|---|---|---|
| 80 | SMS SMS 001 | Break The News/Girl With The Goods (p/s) | 18 |

*(see also Eater)*

## BLADE RUNNER

| | | | |
|---|---|---|---|
| 84 | Ebony EBON 26 | Back Street Lady/Too Far Too Late | 6 |
| 84 | Ebony EBON 21 | HUNTED (LP) | 15 |

## BLADES

| | | | |
|---|---|---|---|
| 81 | Reekus RKS005 | The Bride Wore White/Animation (p/s) | 25 |
| 80 | Energy NRG 3 | Hot For You/The Reunion (p/s; Irish with paper labels) | 20 |
| 80 | Energy NRG 3 | Hot For You/The Reunion (p/s; later UK pressing with plastic labels, in plastic sleeve) | 15 |
| 81 | Energy NRG 5 | Ghost Of A Chance/Real Emotion (p/s; Irish with paper labels) | 20 |
| 81 | Energy NRG 5 | Ghost Of A Chance/Real Emotion (p/s; later UK pressing with plastic labels, in plastic sleeve) | 12 |
| 84 | Reekus RKS 013 | The Last Man In Europe/Sadlands (p/s) | 12 |
| 85 | Reekus RKS 15 | Those Were The Days (p/s) | 10 |
| 85 | Reekus RKSY 15 | Those Were The Days/Stand By Me Now (picture disc) | 12 |
| 86 | Reekus RKS 017 | Downmarket/Truth Don't Hurt (as Blades with Paul Cleary) | 10 |
| 84 | Reekus RKLP 1 | THE LAST MAN IN EUROPE (LP) | 20 |
| 86 | Reekus RKLP 3 | RAY TOWN REVISITED (LP) | 20 |

*(see also Partisans)*

## BLADES OF GRASS

| | | | |
|---|---|---|---|
| 67 | Stateside SS 2040 | Happy/That's What A Boy Likes | 15 |
| 68 | Stateside SS 2101 | Charlie And Fred/You Won't Find That Girl | 10 |

## BLAGGER
70  Mount Clifton MCL 002      Day After Day/The Hunt Is On ................................................................ 30

## BLAH BLAH BLAH
79  Absurd ABSURD 1            In The Army/Why Diddle? (p/s) ................................................................ 5
81  Some Bizzare               BLAH BLAH BLAH (LP, unreleased, stickered sleeve, white label test pressings only) ..... 40

## HAL BLAINE (& YOUNG COUGARS)
64  RCA RCA 1379               Gear Stripper/Challenger II (with Young Cougars) ................................ 10
64  RCA RD 7624                DEUCES, T'S, ROADSTERS AND DRUMS (LP, mono) .......................... 15
64  RCA SF 7624                DEUCES, T'S, ROADSTERS AND DRUMS (LP, stereo) ......................... 15

## VIVIAN BLAINE
54  Parlophone MSP 6070        Changing Partners/Lonely .......................................................... 5

## BLAIR
79  Miracle M4                 Night Life/Virgo Princess ........................................................... 8
79  Miracle M4-12              Night Life/Virgo Princess (12") ................................................. 40

## ARNOLD BLAIR
76  Curtom NEET 1024           Trying To Get Next To You/I Won The Big Deal/House Party (12" with Fred Wesley) ..... 15

## BEVERLEY BLAIR
58  Mercury 7MT 209            With Love We Live/Tony ............................................................ 10

## BARDI BLAISE
80  Din Disc DIN 8             Trans Siberian Express/Competition Side (p/s) ........................... 6

## COREY BLAKE
04  Grapevine 2000 G2K 45-144  How Can I Go On Without You/Your Love Is Like A Boomerang ......... 8

## DAVID BLAKE
69  SNB 55-4178                We'll Meet Again/Now is The Time ........................................... 7

## ERIC BLAKE
80  Carrere CAR 141            Sin City/Zero 6 (p/s) ............................................................... 10
81  Carrere CAR 179            Born To Be Special/80s Girl/Give Generously (p/s) ...................... 10

## GARRY BLAKE
66  Columbia DB 7885           Strawberries And Cream/Look Out Now! .................................. 8
66  Columbia DB 7977           Wait Until Dark/Jungle Juice ................................................... 8
66  Columbia DB 8074           The Danny Scipio Theme/Celebration Day ............................... 10

## KARL BLAKE
83  Glass GLASS 013            THE PREHENSILE TAPES (LP) .................................................. 20
*(see also Lemon Kittens, Shock Headed Peters, Gland Shrouds, Fur Fur, Sol Invictus)*

## KEITH BLAKE
68  Blue Cat BS 102            Musically/I'm Moving On ...................................................... 175
*(see also Overtakers, Uniques)*

## TIM BLAKE
78  Barclay Towers BAR 711     Generator Laserbeam/Woodland Voice (p/s) ............................ 8
*(see also Gong, Hawkwind)*

## WINSTON BLAKE & M-SQUAD
69  Crab 40                    Big Thing/RUPIE EDWARDS : Exclusively Yours ......................... 20
71  Green Door GD 4003         Carrol Street/ANSELL COLLINS & M-SQUAD: Carol St. Version ..... 12

## ART BLAKEY JAZZ MESSENGERS
57  Parlophone PMC 1084        HARD DRIVE (LP) .................................................................. 25
58  Parlophone PMC 1099        BIG BAND (LP) ..................................................................... 25
59  Vogue LAE 12096            RITUAL (LP) ......................................................................... 25
59  London 15157               ART BLAKEY'S JAZZ MESSENGERS WITH THELONIOUS MONK (LP) ... 20
61  Fontana TFL 5116           OLYMPIA CONCERT (LP) ....................................................... 25
62  HMV CLP 1532               ART BLAKEY JAZZ MESSENGERS (LP, also stereo CSD 1423) .......... 30
62  Fontana TFL 5184           DANGEROUS FRIENDSHIPS (LP, soundtrack) ........................... 25
63  RCA Victor RD 7555         A NIGHT IN TUNISIA (LP) ...................................................... 25
63  United Artists (S)ULP 1017 THREE BLIND MICE (LP, mono/stereo) ................................... 20
64  Riverside RLP 438          CARAVAN (LP) ..................................................................... 20
64  HMV CLP 1760               A JAZZ MESSAGE (LP) ........................................................... 30
64  Riverside RLP 464          UGETSU (LP) ........................................................................ 30
65  Limelight (S)LML 4000      'S MAKE IT (LP) .................................................................... 20
66  Limelight (S)LML 4012      SOUL FINGER (LP) ............................................................... 20
66  Limelight (S)LML 4021      BUTTERCORN LADY (LP) ...................................................... 20
66  Fontana FJL 111            SOUL! (LP) .......................................................................... 20
67  Limelight (S)LML 4023      HOLD ON, I'M COMIN' (LP) .................................................. 20
67  Atlantic 590 009           BLUE MONK (LP, with Thelonious Monk) ............................... 20
68  Riverside 673013           KYOTO (LP) ........................................................................ 20
69  Polydor 545101             DRUM THUNDER (LP) .......................................................... 15
*(see also Annie Ross)*

## ART BLAKEY/MILES DAVIS
66  Fontana FJL 135            L'ASCENSEUR POUR L'ECHAFAUD/FEMME DISPARAISSANTE (LP, soundtrack, 1 side each) ... 30
*(see also Thelonious Monk, Miles Davis)*

## ALAN BLAKLEY
75  DJM DJS 367                Sorry (Lyn's Song)/Windows Are Nice ................................... 8

## BLAK TWANG
95  Sound Of Money SNM 005     Queen's Head/Mr Jam Promota (12" with Roots Manuva) .......... 12
96  Sound Of Money SNM 008     DETTWORK SOUTH EAST (LP - unissued) ................................ 75

## MEL BLANC
58  Capitol CL 14950           I Taut I Taw A Puddy Cat/K-K-K-Katy .................................... 5
60  Warner Bros WB 26          Tweety's Twistmas Twouble/I Keep Hearing Those Bells ........... 5

## BURT BLANCA
| | | | |
|---|---|---|---|
| 60 | Zodiac ZR 004 | Texas Rider/Shamash | 5 |

## BLANCK MASS
| | | | |
|---|---|---|---|
| 11 | Rock Action ROCKACT 58LP | BLANCK MASS (2-LP) | 20 |

## BLANCMANGE
| | | | |
|---|---|---|---|
| 80 | Blaah Music MFT-1 | IRENE AND MAVIS (EP, gatefold p/s) | 40 |
| 82 | London SHPD 8552 | HAPPY FAMILIES (LP, picture disc) | 12 |
| 84 | London SHPD 8554 | MANGE TOUT (LP, picture disc) | 12 |

## BILLY BLAND
| | | | |
|---|---|---|---|
| 60 | London HL 9096 | Let The Little Girl Dance/Sweet Thing | 10 |
| 71 | Atlantic 2091 130 | Let The Little Girl Dance/Chicken Hop | 5 |

## BOBBY BLAND
| | | | |
|---|---|---|---|
| 61 | Vogue V 9178 | Cry Cry Cry/I've Been Wrong So Long | 30 |
| 61 | Vogue V 9182 | Lead Me On/Hold Me Tenderly | 30 |
| 61 | Vogue V 9188 | Don't Cry No More/St. James Infirmary | 30 |
| 62 | Vogue V 9190 | You're The One (That I Need)/Turn On Your Love Light | 30 |
| 62 | Vogue V 9192 | Blue Moon/Who Will The Next Fool Be? | 30 |
| 64 | Vocalion VP 9222 | Ain't Nothing You Can Do/Honey Child | 30 |
| 64 | Vocalion VP 9229 | After It's Too Late/Share Your Love With Me | 30 |
| 65 | Vocalion VP 9232 | Yield Not To Temptation/How Does A Cheating Woman Feel? | 30 |
| 65 | Vocalion VP 9251 | These Hands (Small But Mighty)/Today | 30 |
| 66 | Vocalion VP 9262 | I'm Too Far Gone (To Turn Around)/ If You Could Read My Mind | 25 |
| 66 | Vocalion VP 9273 | Good Time Charlie/Good Time Charlie (Working His Groove Bag) | 35 |
| 68 | Sue WI 4044 | That Did It/A Touch Of The Blues | 50 |
| 69 | Action ACT 4524 | Rockin' In The Same Old Boat/Wouldn't You Rather Have Me? | 30 |
| 69 | Action ACT 4538 | Gotta Get To Know You/Baby I'm On My Way | 30 |
| 69 | Action ACT 4548 | Share Your Love With Me/Honey Child | 40 |
| 69 | Action ACT 4553 | Chains Of Love/Ask Me 'Bout Nothing But The Blues | 30 |
| 74 | ABC ABC 4014 | Ain't No Love In The Heart Of The City/Twenty Four Blues | 10 |
| 75 | ABC ABC 4030 | I Wouldn't Treat A Dog (The Way You Treat Me)/I Ain't Gonna Be The First To Cry | 5 |
| 77 | ABC ABC 4186 | The Soul Of A Man/If I Weren't A Gambler | 5 |
| 85 | Kent Town 108 | Shoes/Call On Me/Getting Used To The Blues/Good Time Charlie (EP, p/s) | 10 |
| 63 | Vocalion VEP 170153 | YIELD NOT INTO TEMPTATION (EP) | 80 |
| 64 | Vocalion VEP 170157 | BOBBY BLAND (EP) | 80 |
| 60 | Vogue VA 160183 | TWO STEPS FROM THE BLUES (LP) | 150 |
| 61 | Vocalion VA 160183 | TWO STEPS FROM THE BLUES (LP) | 70 |
| 61 | Vogue VAP 8027 | AIN'T NOTHING YOU CAN DO (LP) | 75 |
| 64 | Vocalion VAP 8027 | AIN'T NOTHING YOU CAN DO (LP) | 40 |
| 63 | Vogue VAP 8034 | CALL ON ME/ THAT'S THE WAY LOVE IS (LP) | 75 |
| 64 | Vocalion VAP 8034 | CALL ON ME/ THAT'S THE WAY LOVE IS (LP) | 40 |
| 66 | Vocalion VAP 8041 | HERE'S THE MAN (LP) | 50 |
| 68 | Island ILP 974 | A TOUCH OF THE BLUES (LP) | 70 |
| 69 | Action ACLP 6006 | A PIECE OF GOLD (LP) | 40 |
| 74 | Polydor 2383 257 | BLUES FOR MR. CRUMP (LP, with tracks by Junior Parker & Howlin' Wolf) | 20 |
| 85 | Kent 044 | THE SOULFUL SIDE OF BOBBY BLAND (LP) | 15 |

## MARCIE BLANE
| | | | |
|---|---|---|---|
| 62 | London HLU 9599 | Bobby's Girl/A Time To Dream | 15 |
| 63 | London HLU 9673 | What Does A Girl Do/How Can I Tell Him | 15 |
| 63 | London HLU 9744 | Little Miss Fool/Ragtime Sound | 15 |
| 63 | London HLU 9787 | You Gave My Number To Billy/Told You So | 15 |
| 63 | London REU 1393 | MARCIE BLANE (EP) | 150 |

## BLANKS
| | | | |
|---|---|---|---|
| 79 | Void SRTS/79/CUS/560 | The Northern Ripper/Understand (p/s) | 70 |

*(see also Destructors)*

## BLANK STUDENTS
| | | | |
|---|---|---|---|
| 80 | Dexter Discs | We Are Natives/I Want To Be Happy (500 only) | 25 |

## BLARNEY SISTERS
| | | | |
|---|---|---|---|
| 67 | GO AJ11407 | The Greatest Blessing/Golden Band | 15 |

## BLAST FURNACE AND THE HEATWAVES
| | | | |
|---|---|---|---|
| 78 | HOT 1 | BLUE WAVE (EP) | 8 |

## BLAZE
| | | | |
|---|---|---|---|
| 99 | Slip And Slide SLIP 99 | Wishing You Were Here/(mixes) (2x12") | 10 |

## BLAZE X
| | | | |
|---|---|---|---|
| 80 | Fixed Wheel FX 1 | Some Hope/Rippy (Irish pressing, gatefold p/s) | 150 |

## BLAZER, BLAZER
| | | | |
|---|---|---|---|
| 78 | Logo GO 362 | Cecil B. Devine/Warsaw/Six O'Clock In The Morning (p/s) | 10 |

## BLAZERS
| | | | |
|---|---|---|---|
| 58 | Fontana TFR 6010 | ROCK AND ROLL (10" LP) | 50 |

## BLAZING SONS
| | | | |
|---|---|---|---|
| 83 | Cool Ghoul COOL 002 | Chant Down The National Front/N.F. Dub (no p/s) | 10 |

*(see also Phantom)*

## BLEACH BOYS
| | | | |
|---|---|---|---|
| 78 | Tramp THF 002 | Chloroform/You've Got Nothing (no p/s, 1,000 only) | 60 |
| 85 | Zombie International ZOMBO 103010 | Stocking-Clad Nazi Death Squad Bitches/Death Before Disco/Gimme That Neutron Taste (12", p/s) | 25 |

## BLEAK HOUSE
| | | | |
|---|---|---|---|
| 80s | Buzzard BUZZ 1 | Rainbow Warrior/Isandlhwana/Inquisition (in p/s) | 100 |

# BLEECHERS

| 80s | Buzzard BUZZ 1 | Rainbow Warrior/Isandlhwana/Inquisition | 30 |
| 82 | Buzzard BUZZ 2 | LIONS IN WINTER (Chase The Wind/No Reply/Down To Zero/ Flight Of The Salamander) (EP, p/s with insert) | 90 |

## BLEECHERS
| 69 | Trojan TR 679 | Ease Up/You're Gonna Feel It | 15 |
| 69 | Upsetter US 314 | Come Into My Parlour/MELOTONES: Dry Up Your Tears | 15 |
| 70 | Col. Blue Beat DB 118 | Send Me The Pillow (That You Dream On)/Adam And Eve | 20 |
| 71 | Duke DU 118 | Put It Good/J.J. ALLSTARS: Good Good Version | 20 |

*(see also Busty Brown, Upsetters)*

## BLEEDING HEARTS
| 80 | Crazy Plane SP 003 | This Is The Way/OK | 30 |

## PETER BLEGVAD
| 77 | Virgin V 2082 | KEW RHONE (LP, with John Greaves) | 15 |

*(see also Slapp Happy)*

## BLENDELLS
| 64 | Reprise RS 20291 | La La La La La La/Huggies Bunnies | 10 |
| 64 | Reprise RS 20291 | La La La La La La/Huggies Bunnies (DJ Copy) | 20 |
| 64 | Reprise RS 20340 | Dance With Me/Get Your Baby | 50 |
| 64 | Reprise RS 20340 | Dance With Me/Get Your Baby (DJ Copy) | 60 |

## CARLA BLEY
| 72 | JCOA JT 4001 | ESCALATOR OVER THE HILL (3xLP, gatefold with Paul Haines & Jack Bruce) | 25 |
| 74 | Watt WATT 1 | TROPIC APPETITES (LP, gatefold sleeve) | 15 |

*(see also Jazz Composers Orchestra, Michael Mantler, Jack Bruce)*

## PAUL BLEY TRIO
| 69 | Fontana SFJL 929 | TOUCHING (LP) | 100 |

*(see also Bley-Peacock Synthesizer Show, Annette Peacock)*

## BLEY-PEACOCK SYNTHESIZER SHOW
| 72 | Polydor 2425 043 | REVENGE (LP) | 250 |

*(see also Annette Peacock, Paul Bley)*

## ARCHIE BLEYER & HIS ORCHESTRA
| 54 | London HL 8035 | Amber/Julie's Jump | 8 |
| 54 | London HL 8111 | The Naughty Lady Of Shady Lane/While The Vesper Bells Were Ringing | 8 |
| 55 | London HLA 8176 | Hernando's Hideaway/S'il Vous Plait | 8 |
| 56 | London HLA 8243 | Nothin' To Do/JANET BLEYER: 'Cause You're My Lover | 10 |
| 56 | London HLA 8263 | Bridge Of Happiness/You Tell Me Your Dream, I'll Tell You Mine (Gold Tri) | 10 |

## B,L&G
| 71 | Birds Nest BN 3 | Live In The Mountains/Janie Slow Down | 7 |

*(see also Trevor Burton, Denny Laine, Steve Gibbons)*

## BLIND BLAKE
| 58 | Ristic LP 18 | THE LEGENDARY BLIND BLAKE (10" LP) | 50 |
| 59 | Jazz Collector JLP 2001 | THE LEGENDARY BLIND BLAKE (10" LP, reissue) | 12 |

*(see also Paramount Allstars)*

## BLIND BLAKE/CHARLIE JACKSON
| 50s | Heritage HLP 1011 | BLIND BLAKE AND CHARLIE JACKSON (LP, 99 only) | 70 |

## BLIND FAITH
| 69 | Island (no cat. no.) | Change Of Address From June 23rd 1969 (promo issue, 500 only) | 400 |
| 69 | Polydor 583 059 | BLIND FAITH (LP, gatefold sleeve, first pressing with single paper on left gatefold stating distribution by Polydor and Island) | 100 |
| 69 | Polydor 583 059 | BLIND FAITH (LP, gatefold sleeve, later issue without Polydor and Island distribution credit) | 40 |
| 77 | RSO 2394142 | BLIND FAITH (LP, reissue) | 15 |
| 08 | RSO 53167 | BLIND FAITH (LP, reissue 180gm vinyl) | 15 |

*(see also Stevie Winwood, Ginger Baker, Eric Clapton)*

## BLIND LEMON CLEGG
| 80 | Pollen PBM 029 | RUN FOR YOUR MONEY EP | 50 |

## BLINK 182
| 04 | Geffen MCS 40400 | Always/I Miss You (Live In Minneapolis) (Picture disc) | 5 |
| 05 | MCA B000C5E791 | Not Now/All The Small Things (live) (p/s, stickered) | 5 |
| 05 | MCA B000C5E78X | Not Now/Dammit (Live) (p/s. stickered) | 5 |

## BLINKERS
| 69 | Pye 7N 17752 | Original Sin/Dreams Secondhand | 60 |

## BLINKY & EDWIN STARR
| 69 | Tamla Motown TMG 720 | Oh How Happy/Ooo Baby Baby (unissued, demos only) | 375 |
| 70 | Tamla Motown TMG 748 | Oh How Happy/Ooo Baby Baby | 10 |
| 70 | T. Motown (S)TML 11131 | JUST WE TWO (LP, as Edwin Starr & Blinky) | 25 |

*(see also Edwin Starr)*

## BLISS
| 69 | Chapter One CH 107 | Courtyards In Castile/Lifetime | 15 |

## MELVIN BLISS
| 77 | Contempo CS 2013 | Reward/Synthetic Substitution | 30 |

## BLITZ
| 81 | No Future OI 1 | ALL OUT ATTACK (EP, rubber-stamped labels, 500 only, fold-out sleeve) | 30 |
| 81 | No Future OI 1 | ALL OUT ATTACK (EP, reissue, initially with white labels, fold-out sleeve) | 15 |
| 81 | No Future OI 1 | ALL OUT ATTACK (EP, reissue, later printed labels) | 10 |
| 82 | No Future OI 6 | Never Surrender/Razor In The Night (p/s) | 12 |
| 82 | No Future OI 16 | Warriors/Youth (p/s) | 12 |
| 82 | No Future PUNK 1 | VOICE OF A GENERATION (LP, with inner sleeve) | 30 |

*(see also Rose Of Victory)*

## BLITZ BOYS
| 80 | Told You So TYS 001 | Eddy's New Shoes/Eddie's Friend/She Told My Friends (foldover p/s) .................... 125 |

## BLITZKREIG (1)
| 79 | Ellie Jay/BRP EJSP 9257 | SURVIVAL (LP) .................................................................................................. 100 |

## BLITZKRIEG (2)
| 81 | Neat NEAT 10 | Buried Alive/Blitzkrieg (p/s) ............................................................................. 60 |
| 91 | Roadrunner R 09302 | 10 YEARS OF BLITZKRIEG (EP) ......................................................................... 10 |
| 85 | Neat NEAT 1023 | A TIME OF CHANGES (LP) .................................................................................. 40 |

## BLITZKRIEG (3)
| 82 | No future OI 8 | LEST WE FORGET (EP) ...................................................................................... 10 |
| 83 | Sexual Phonograph SPH2 | Animals In Lipstick/Land Of Failure/No Compromise (p/s, SPH2 on cover but SPH3 on label) .............................................................................................................. 15 |

## BLITZKRIEG BOP
| 77 | Mortonsound MTN 3172/3 | Let's Go/Nine Till Five/Bugger Off (p/s, 500 only) .......................................... 100 |
| 77 | Lightning GIL 504 | Let's Go (re-recorded)/Life Is Just A So-So/Mental Case (p/s) ......................... 20 |
| 78 | Lightning GIL 543 | U.F.O./Bobby Joe (p/s) ................................................................................... 20 |

*(see also Basczax, The Gynaecologists, Nicky Beat)*

## BLIZZARD
| 71 | CBS CBS 7238 | Baby Blue/Mama, The Sparrow And The Tree ............................................... 8 |

## BLO
| 75 | Afrodisia DWAPS 2009 | PHASE IV (LP) .................................................................................................... 40 |
| 01 | Strut STRUTALP 004 | PHASES 1972-1982 (2-LP) ................................................................................. 25 |

## BLOATED TOADS
| 79 | Shattered SHAT 4 | Why/Essential In Some Form/Happy Home/Yankee TV Victim (p/s, with insert)............ 5 |

## BLOC PARTY
| 04 | Wichita WEBB 070S | Helicoper/Skeleton (green vinyl) ................................................................... 8 |
| 04 | Trash Aesthetics TA701 | She's Hearing Voices/The Marshals Are Dead/The Answer (p/s clear vinyl, 500 only) ... 50 |
| 04 | Moshi Moshi MOSHI10 | Banquet/Staying Fat (p/s, 500 only) ............................................................. 15 |
| 04 | Wichita WEBB067S | Little Thoughts/Storm And Stress (Blue vinyl, p/s) ...................................... 6 |
| 05 | Wichita WEBB088S | The Pioneers/The Pioneers (Bloc Party vs Mystery Jets) (numbered pic disc)............... 10 |
| 07 | Wichita WEBB 118S | The Prayer/England (1st 7" of 2 and comes in box) ....................................... 15 |
| 08 | Wichita WEBB 180T | MERCURY EP (2 x 7", CD in box) .................................................................... 15 |
| 12 | Transgressive TRANS 137 | She's Hearing Voices/The Marshals Are Dead/The Answer (red vinyl, 500 only) ......... 15 |
| 12 | Frenchkiss FKR06-1A | Octopus/Straight Thru Cru (red vinyl) ........................................................... 5 |
| 05 | Wichita WEBB075LP | SILENT ALARM (LP) ........................................................................................ 30 |
| 05 | Wichita WEBB075PD | SILENT ALARM (LP, picture disc) ..................................................................... 40 |
| 05 | Wichita WEBB090LP | SILENT ALARM REMIXED (2-LP) ....................................................................... 25 |
| 07 | Wichita WEBB 120 LP | A WEEKEND IN THE CITY (LP) ......................................................................... 15 |
| 07 | Wichita WEBB 120 PD | A WEEKEND IN THE CITY (LP, picture disc) .................................................... 30 |
| 08 | Wichita WEBB 185PD | INTIMACY (LP, picture disc, 500 only) ............................................................ 15 |
| 09 | Wichita WEBB 210LP | INTIMACY REMIXED (3-LP) .............................................................................. 18 |

## BLOCKHEAD
| 04 | Ninja Tune ZEN 88 | MUSIC BY CAVELIGHT (2xLP) ........................................................................... 25 |

## BLODWYN PIG
| 69 | Island WIP 6059 | Dear Jill/Sweet Caroline ................................................................................ 15 |
| 69 | Island WIP 6069 | Walk On The Water/Summer Day .................................................................. 15 |
| 70 | Chrysalis WIP 6078 | Same Old Story/Slow Down ........................................................................... 10 |
| 69 | Island ILPS 9101 | AHEAD RINGS OUT (LP, 1st pressing, gatefold sleeve, pink label with black/orange circle logo) ................................................................................................... 100 |
| 69 | Island ILPS 9101 | AHEAD RINGS OUT (LP, 2nd pressing, gatefold sleeve, with block logo) ....................... 50 |
| 70 | Island ILPS 9101 | AHEAD RINGS OUT (LP, gatefold sleeve, 3rd pressing with white i' logo) ..................... 40 |
| 70 | Chrysalis ILPS 9122 | GETTING TO THIS (LP, gatefold sleeve, island logo and address in white on green label) ............................................................................................................. 70 |
| 70s | Island ILPS 9101 | AHEAD RINGS OUT (LP, gatefold sleeve, reissue 'pink rim palm tree' label) ............... 15 |

*(see also Mick Abrahams, Jethro Tull)*

## BLOND
| 69 | Fontana TF 1040 | (I Will Bring You) Flowers In The Morning/I Wake Up And Call................................ 12 |
| 69 | Fontana STL 5515 | THE LILAC YEARS (LP, gatefold sleeve) ........................................................... 125 |

*(see also Tages)*

## BLONDE ON BLONDE
| 69 | Pye 7N 17637 | All Day All Night/Country Life...................................................................... 40 |
| 70 | Ember EMB S 279 | Castles In The Sky/Circles (in p/s) ................................................................. 20 |
| 70 | Ember EMB S 279 | Castles In The Sky/Circles (no p/s) ................................................................ 12 |
| 72 | Ember EMB S 316 | Sad Song For An Easy Lady/Happy Families (p/s) .......................................... 15 |
| 69 | Pye NSPL 18288 | CONTRASTS (LP, gatefold sleeve, blue/black label with logo/banner on top) ............. 175 |
| 70 | Ember NR 5049 | RE-BIRTH (LP, gatefold sleeve) ..................................................................... 100 |
| 71 | Ember NR 5058 | REFLECTIONS ON A LIFE (LP, gatefold sleeve) ............................................... 100 |
| 70s | Ember LP 7005 | BLONDE ON BLONDE (LP, unissued, test pressings only) .............................. 300 |

## BLONDIE
| 77 | Private Stock PVT 90 | X Offender/In The Sun (unissued, promos or stock copies, no p/s) ................. 2000 |
| 76 | Private Stock PVT 105 | In The Flesh/X Offender (demo in promo p/s) ............................................... 50 |
| 76 | Private Stock PVT 105 | In The Flesh/X Offender (no p/s) ................................................................... 20 |
| 77 | Chrysalis CHS 2180 | Rip Her To Shreds/In The Flesh/X Offender (p/s) ........................................... 5 |
| 78 | Chrysalis CHS 2204 | Denis (Denee)/Contact In Red Square (red/blue p/s)..................................... 5 |
| 78 | Chrysalis CHS 2242 | Picture This/Fade Away (And Radiate) (p/s, yellow vinyl) ............................. 8 |
| 78 | Chrysalis CHE 2266 | Hanging On The Telephone/Will Anything Happen (p/s, export issue) ............. 6 |
| 78 | Chrysalis CHE 2275 | Heart Of Glass/Rifle Range (p/s, export issue with "pain in the ass" lyrics)............ 8 |
| 98 | EMI 12 ATOM 150 | ATOMIC 98 (Remixes) (12", p/s, withdrawn) ................................................ 15 |

MINT VALUE £

| | | | |
|---|---|---|---|
| 76 | Private Stock PVLP 1017 | BLONDIE (LP) | 20 |
| 77 | Chrysalis CHR 1166 | PLASTIC LETTERS (LP) | 15 |
| 78 | Chrysalis CHR 1166-P | PLASTIC LETTERS (LP, picture disc) | 20 |
| 82 | Chrysalis PCDL 1384 | THE HUNTER (LP, picture disc) | 15 |
| 97 | Chrysalis 7243821459 1 2 | PARALLEL LINES (LP, reissue, part of EMI 100 series, stickered sleeve) | 20 |

*(see also Debbie Harry, Wind In The Willows, Rodney & Brunettes)*

**BLOOBLO**
| | | | |
|---|---|---|---|
| 76 | Feelgood FLG 104 | Please Mister Please/Chaka | 12 |
| 78 | Mother & Son | IS THAT YOU (LP) | 25 |

**BLOOD**
| | | | |
|---|---|---|---|
| 83 | No Future OI 22 | Megalomania/Calling The Shots/Parasite In Paradise (p/s) | 20 |
| 83 | Noise NOY 1 | Stark Raving Normal/Mesrine (p/s) | 18 |
| 82 | Noise NOYZLP 1 | FALSE GESTURES FOR A DEVIOUS PUBLIC (LP, inner) | 25 |
| 85 | Conquest QUEST 3 | SE PARARE NEX (LP) | 15 |
| 89 | Link Classics CLINK 5 | FALSE GESTURES FOR A DEVIOUS PUBLIC (LP, reissue, red vinyl) | 15 |

**BARRY BLOOD**
| | | | |
|---|---|---|---|
| 75 | Alaska ALA 24 | Poor Annie/On The Run | 40 |
| 82 | Wretchord WOO 1 | She's The Queen Of My Rock And Roll/What D'Ya Say? | 40 |

**BLOOD DIVINE**
| | | | |
|---|---|---|---|
| 96 | Peaceville VILE 62 | AWAKEN (LP) | 18 |

*(see also Cradle Of filth, Anathema)*

**BLOOD & ROSES**
| | | | |
|---|---|---|---|
| 85 | Audiodrome ASSAULT | (Some) Like It Hot/Paradise | 5 |

**BLOOD DONOR**
| | | | |
|---|---|---|---|
| 79 | Arista ARIRV 262 | Rubber Revolution/Chemical Babies (p/s red vinyl) | 8 |
| 79 | Arista ARIST 269 | Rice Harvest/Something Happened (p/s) | 10 |
| 81 | Safari SAFE 29 | Doctor/Soap Box Blues (p/s) | 10 |

**BLOOD RED SHOES**
| | | | |
|---|---|---|---|
| 06 | Jonson Family | Bless His Heart/Don't Always Say Yes/Victory For The Magpie (p/s, insert, 500 only) | 25 |
| 06 | Try Harder | Stitch Me Back/Meet Me At Eight (500 only) | 30 |
| 07 | V2 B000PHX186 | It's Getting Boring By The Sea/Box Of Secrets (p/s) | 8 |
| 08 | V2 1763548 | BOX OF SECRETS (LP) | 25 |
| 10 | V2 VVR736628 | FIRE LIKE THIS (LP, silkscreened sleeve) | 15 |
| 12 | V2 VVR795935 | IN TIME TO VOICES (LP, silkscreened cover with CD) | 20 |

**BLOODROCK**
| | | | |
|---|---|---|---|
| 71 | Capitol CL 15670 | D.O.A./Children's Heritage | 8 |
| 71 | Capitol E-ST 491 | BLOODROCK 2 (LP) | 15 |
| 71 | Capitol E-ST 765 | BLOODROCK 3 (LP) | 15 |

**BLOOD SHANTI**
| | | | |
|---|---|---|---|
| 96 | Aba Shanti ABA 12003 | Tear Down Babylon/Verse 1/Verse 2/Verse 3 (12") | 20 |
| 00 | Flasha AB12003 | What A Gwan/Dub/Banks Of The Nile/Dub (12") | 10 |
| 00 | Flasha AB12004 | Jah Liveth (One Love)/Dub/Hail Jah/Dub (12") | 30 |
| 02 | Aba Shanti ABALP 002 | PURE SPIRIT (LP) | 25 |
| 02 | Aba Shanti ABALP 005 | UNDILUTED (LP) | 20 |

**BLOOD SISTERS**
| | | | |
|---|---|---|---|
| 79 | Sound City SCD 002 | Ring My Bell/Dub (12") | 20 |
| 79 | Sound City SCD 004 | What About Me/I'd Rather Go Blind (12") | 15 |

**BLOOD, SWEAT & TEARS**
| | | | |
|---|---|---|---|
| 68 | CBS 3563 | I Can't Quit Her/House In The Country | 20 |
| 69 | CBS 4116 | You've Made Me So Very Happy/The Blues, Part 2 | 5 |
| 69 | CBS 4220 | Spinning Wheel/More And More | 5 |
| 74 | CBS 2462 | Tell Me That I'm Wrong/Rock Reprise | 20 |
| 68 | CBS 63296 | CHILD IS THE FATHER TO THE MAN (LP) | 20 |

*(see also Al Kooper)*

**ROGER BLOOM'S HAMMER**
| | | | |
|---|---|---|---|
| 67 | CBS 202654 | Out Of The Blue/Life's A Gamble | 12 |
| 67 | CBS 2848 | Polly Pan/Fifteen Degree Temperature Rise | 8 |

**MIKE BLOOMFIELD**
| | | | |
|---|---|---|---|
| 69 | CBS 63652 | IT'S NOT KILLING ME (LP) | 20 |

*(see also Barry Goldberg Reunion, Stephen Stills, K.G.B.)*

**MIKE BLOOMFIELD & AL KOOPER**
| | | | |
|---|---|---|---|
| 69 | CBS 4094 | The Weight/59th Street Bridge Song | 10 |
| 69 | CBS 66216 | THE LIVE ADVENTURES OF MIKE BLOOMFIELD AND AL KOOPER (2-LP, mono) | 60 |
| 69 | CBS 66216 | THE LIVE ADVENTURES OF MIKE BLOOMFIELD AND AL KOOPER (2-LP, stereo) | 25 |

*(see also Al Kooper, Paul Butterfield Blues Band, Electric Flag)*

**BLOOMFIELDS**
| | | | |
|---|---|---|---|
| 72 | Pye 7N 45114 | The Loner/Homing In On The Next Trade Wind | 15 |

**BLOSSOM TOES**
| | | | |
|---|---|---|---|
| 67 | Marmalade 598 002 | What On Earth/Mrs Murphy's Budgerigar/Look At Me I'm You (in p/s) | 70 |
| 67 | Marmalade 598 002 | What On Earth/Mrs Murphy's Budgerigar/Look At Me I'm You | 30 |
| 68 | Marmalade 598 009 | I'll Be Your Baby Tonight/Love Is | 30 |
| 68 | Marmalade 598 012 | Postcard/Everyone's Leaving Me Now | 30 |
| 69 | Marmalade 598 014 | Peace Loving Man/Up Above My Hobby Horse's Head | 30 |
| 69 | Marmalade 598 022 | New Day/Love Bomb (unissued, existence unconfirmed) | 0 |
| 67 | Marmalade 607 001 | WE ARE EVER SO CLEAN (LP, mono) | 700 |
| 67 | Marmalade 608 001 | WE ARE EVER SO CLEAN (LP, stereo) | 800 |
| 69 | Marmalade 608 010 | IF ONLY FOR A MOMENT (LP) | 800 |

| 07 | Sunbeam SBR2LP5035 | WE ARE EVER SO CLEAN (2-LP, reissue) .................................................. 20 |
|----|--------------------|------------------------------------------------|
| 07 | Sunbeam SBR2LP5036 | IF ONLY FOR A MOMENT (2-LP, reissue) .................................................. 20 |

*(see also B.B. Blunder, Stud, Kevin Westlake, Solid Gold Cadillac)*

## BLOSSOMS
| 58 | Capitol CL 14833 | Move On/He Promised Me ........................................................ 50 |
|----|------------------|------------------------|
| 58 | Capitol CL 14856 | Little Louie/Have Faith In Me ........................................ 40 |
| 58 | Capitol CL 14947 | No Other Love/Baby Daddy-O ...................................... 40 |
| 68 | MGM MGM 1435 | Tweedle Dee/You Got Me Hummin' .......................... 20 |
| 71 | Pama PM 814 | Stand By/Soul And Inspiration .................................. 30 |

*(see also Darlene Love, Allisons [U.S.])*

## MICHAEL BLOUNT
| 70 | CBS 5248 | Ryba Jyba/Acorn Street .................................................. 15 |
|----|----------|----------------------|
| 70 | CBS 7022 | Sometimes/Angelina Baby ............................................ 5 |
| 72 | York SYK 519 | Beautiful Morning/Feathered Cloud ...................... 5 |
| 72 | York SYK 528 | Tackle And Sack/Pretty Face .................................... 5 |
| 72 | York SKY 535 | Rosie/Trombone Man ...................................................... 5 |
| 71 | CBS 64230 | PATCHWORK (LP) ................................................................ 20 |
| 72 | York FYK 401 | SOUVENIRS (LP) .................................................................. 20 |
| 73 | York FYK 414 | FANTASIES (LP) .................................................................... 20 |

## BLOWZABELLA
| 70s | Plant Life PLR 051 | IN COLOUR (LP) .................................................................... 30 |
|-----|--------------------|------------------------|
| 90 | Special Delivery SPD 1028 | VANILLA (LP) ........................................................................ 40 |

## BLUE
| 73 | RSO 2090 109 | Red Light Song/Look Around .................................... 6 |
|----|--------------|----------------------|
| 73 | RSO 2090 114 | Little Jody/The Way Things Are ................................ 6 |
| 73 | RSO 2394 105 | BLUE (LP) ................................................................................ 15 |

*(see also Poets, Thunderclap Newman)*

## BABBITY BLUE
| 65 | Decca F 12053 | Don't Make Me (Fall In Love With You)/I Remembered How To Cry ............... 5 |
|----|---------------|----------------------|
| 65 | Decca F 12149 | Don't Hurt Me/Question ................................................ 5 |

## BOBBY BLUE
| 70 | Duke DU 86 | Going In Circles (actually by Lloyd Charmers)/Doggone Right (actually by Winston Francis) ................................................................................ 15 |
|----|------------|----------------------|

## DAVID BLUE
| 69 | Reprise RS20830 | Beautiful Susan/You Don't Need A Thing ............ 8 |
|----|-----------------|----------------------|
| 67 | Elektra EKL 4003 | DAVID BLUE (LP, red label) ........................................ 50 |
| 72 | Asylum SYL 9001 | STORIES (LP) ........................................................................ 20 |
| 73 | Asylum SYL 9009 | NICE BABY AND THE ANGEL (LP) ............................ 20 |
| 75 | Asylum SYL 9025 | COMIN' BACK FOR MORE (LP) .................................. 20 |
| 76 | Asylum K 53056 | CUPID'S ARROW (LP) ...................................................... 20 |

## PAMELA BLUE
| 63 | Decca F 11761 | My Friend Bobby/Hey There Stranger .................. 70 |
|----|---------------|----------------------|

## BLUE RONDOS
| 64 | Pye 7N 15734 | Little Baby/Baby I Go For You .................................. 30 |
|----|--------------|----------------------|
| 65 | Pye 7N 15833 | Don't Want Your Lovin' No More/What Can I Do ............ 40 |

## BLUE SAND
| 67 | Saturn HEY 006 | Florida Bound/Blue Mama/The Dream/Name Of The Game ............ 35 |
|----|----------------|----------------------|

## TIMOTHY BLUE
| 68 | Spark SRL 1014 | The Room At The Top Of The Stairs/She Won't See The Light ............ 20 |
|----|----------------|----------------------|

## BLUE ACES
| 64 | Pye 7N 15672 | Land Of Love/Love Song Of The Waterfall .................. 15 |
|----|--------------|----------------------|
| 64 | Pye 7N 15713 | I Beat You To It/I Just Can't Help Loving You .......... 15 |
| 65 | Pye 7N 15821 | Ain't What You Say/You Don't Care ........................ 15 |
| 65 | Columbia DB 7755 | Tell Me What You're Gonna Do/All I Want .......... 100 |
| 66 | Columbia DB 7954 | That's All Right/Talk About My Baby .................... 100 |

*(see also Riot Squad)*

## BLUE ANCHOR
| 79 | Workhouse WHR 6 | PLENTY LOVE & BACON (LP) ...................................... 15 |
|----|-----------------|----------------------|

## BLUE & FERRIS
| 68 | Blue Cat BS 147 | You Stole My Money/Tell Me The Reason ............ 40 |
|----|-----------------|----------------------|

## BLUE ANGEL
| 80 | Polydor POSP 212 | I'm Gonna Be Strong/Anna Blue (no p/s) ............ 6 |
|----|------------------|----------------------|
| 81 | Polydor POSP 241 | I Had A Love/Can't Blame Me .................................. 8 |
| 84 | Polydor POSP 212 | I'm Gonna Be Strong/Anna Blue (p/s, reissue) ............ 8 |
| 80 | Polydor 2391 486 | BLUE ANGEL (LP) .............................................................. 25 |

## BLUE AQUARIUS
| 73 | Akashic 998 | The Ultimate Train/At The Feet Of The Master .................. 30 |
|----|-------------|----------------------|

## BLUE ARSED FLY
| 95 | Ferox FER 012 | IN THE BAG EP (12") ........................................................ 15 |
|----|---------------|----------------------|
| 96 | Mosquito MSQ 04 | BLUE ARSED FLY EP (12") ............................................ 20 |

*(see also Christian Vogel, Neil Landstrumm)*

## BLUE BEARD
| 71 | Ember EMB S 302 | Country Man/Sly Willy (in p/s) ................................ 30 |
|----|-----------------|----------------------|
| 71 | Ember EMB S 302 | Country Man/Sly Willy (no p/s) .............................. 20 |
| 71 | Ember LT 7004 | BLUE BEARD (LP, unreleased, test pressings only) ............ 200 |

## BLUEBEATERS
| 64 | Piccadilly 7N 35181 | Little David/Ain't Got A Care .................................... 5 |
|----|---------------------|----------------------|

| | | | |
|---|---|---|---|
| 64 | Piccadilly 7N 35191 | Early In The Morning/There I Go ........................................... | 5 |

**BLUEBEATS**

| | | | |
|---|---|---|---|
| 64 | Ember EMB EP 4525 | THE FABULOUS BLUEBEATS VOL. 1 (EP) ................................. | 25 |
| 64 | Ember EMB EP 4526 | THE FABULOUS BLUEBEATS VOL. 2 (EP) ................................. | 25 |

**BLUE BEATS**

| | | | |
|---|---|---|---|
| 60 | Blue Beat 45/BB 20 | Baby What You Done Me Wrong/Go Pretty Baby Go .................. | 20 |

**BLUE-BELLES**

| | | | |
|---|---|---|---|
| 62 | HMV POP 1029 | I Sold My Heart To The Junkman/Itty Bitty Twist .................. | 25 |

*(see also Patti Labelle)*

**BLUE BELLS & JAH BERRY**

| | | | |
|---|---|---|---|
| 78 | Burning Rockers BRD 001 | Teacher Teach, Teach The Youth/Golden Rule (12") ............... | 30 |

**BLUEBERRIES**

| | | | |
|---|---|---|---|
| 66 | Mercury MF 894 | It's Gonna Work Out Fine/Please Don't Let Me Know .............. | 75 |

**BLUE BLOOD**

| | | | |
|---|---|---|---|
| 70 | Sonet SNTF 615 | BLUE BLOOD (LP) ............................................................. | 25 |

**BLUE BLUDD**

| | | | |
|---|---|---|---|
| 87 | Blud Donor no cat. No. | LIQUOR 'N' POKER (EP) ..................................................... | 20 |

**BLUEBOY**

| | | | |
|---|---|---|---|
| 91 | Sarah SARAH 55 | Clearer/Alison (p/s, insert) ............................................... | 20 |
| 93 | Sarah SARAH 70 | Cloud Babies (6" one-sided flexi with fanzine) .................... | 15 |
| 92 | Sarah SARAH 65 | Popkiss/Chelsea Guitar/Fearon (p/s, insert) ....................... | 20 |
| 93 | Sarah SARAH 74 | Meet Johnny Rave/Elle/Air France (p/s) .............................. | 15 |
| 93 | Sarah SARAH 80 | SOME GORGEOUS ACCIDENT EP (wraparound p/s in ply bay, insert) ...... | 15 |
| 94 | Sarah SARAH 88 | River/Nimbus/Hit ............................................................ | 15 |
| 95 | Sarah SARAH 99 | Dirty Mags/Loony Tunes/Toulouse (p/s) .............................. | 20 |
| 96 | Shinkansen SHINKANSEN 4 | Love Yourself/Melancholia (p/s) .................................... | 5 |
| 92 | Sarah SARAH 612 | IF WISHES WERE HORSES (LP) ........................................... | 40 |
| 94 | Sarah SARAH 620 | UNISEX (LP) .................................................................. | 40 |

**BLUE CATS**

| | | | |
|---|---|---|---|
| 80 | Charly CYS 1072 | I'm Gonna Die/I'm Going Home (p/s) ................................... | 5 |
| 81 | Charly CYS 1075 | Wild Night/Jump Cat Jump (p/s) ......................................... | 5 |

*(see also G men, Beltane Fire)*

**BLUE CHEER**

| | | | |
|---|---|---|---|
| 68 | Philips BF 1646 | Summertime Blues/Out Of Focus ........................................ | 25 |
| 68 | Philips BF 1684 | Just A Little Bit/Gypsy Ball ............................................. | 12 |
| 68 | Philips BF 1711 | Feathers From Your Tree/Sun Cycle ................................... | 12 |
| 69 | Philips BF 1778 | West Coast Child Of Sunshine/When It All Gets Old .............. | 15 |
| 71 | Philips 6051 010 | Pilot/Babaji (Twilight Raga) ............................................ | 15 |
| 68 | Philips BL 7839 | VINCEBUS ERUPTUM (LP, mono) ...................................... | 75 |
| 68 | Philips (S)BL 7839 | VINCEBUS ERUPTUM (LP, stereo) .................................. | 50 |
| 68 | Philips SBL 7860 | OUTSIDEINSIDE (LP, gatefold sleeve) ................................ | 60 |
| 69 | Philips SBL 7896 | NEW! IMPROVED! (LP) ..................................................... | 60 |
| 69 | Philips 6336 001 | BLUE CHEER (LP) ........................................................... | 60 |
| 71 | Philips 6336 004 | B.C. #5 THE ORIGINAL HUMAN BEING (LP) ....................... | 60 |

*(see also Leigh Stephens, Group B)*

**BLUE CHIPS**

| | | | |
|---|---|---|---|
| 65 | Pye 7N 15970 | I'm On The Right Side/You're Good To Me ............................ | 30 |
| 66 | Pye 7N 17111 | Some Kind Of Lovin'/I Know A Boy ..................................... | 20 |
| 66 | Pye 7N 17155 | Tell Her/Good Lovin' Never Hurt ....................................... | 20 |

**BLUE DANUBE**

| | | | |
|---|---|---|---|
| 80 | EMI EMI 5070 | You Are A Song (Du Bist Musik)/Let Me Hear That Song Again/Du Bist Musik .......... | 8 |

**BLUE EPITAPH**

| | | | |
|---|---|---|---|
| 74 | Holyground HG 117 | ODE (LP, 99 copies only) ............................................... | 400 |
| 91 | Holyground HG 117 | ODE (LP, reissue, folded gatefold sleeve) ......................... | 25 |

*(see also Magus)*

**BLUE EYES**

| | | | |
|---|---|---|---|
| 91 | Union Hall 001 | Pick Up The Mic On A Soul Tip/The Law (12") ...................... | 15 |

**BLUE FLAMES**

| | | | |
|---|---|---|---|
| 63 | R&B JB 114 | J.A. Blues/Orange Street ................................................. | 60 |
| 63 | R&B JB 126 | Stop Right Here/Rik's Tune .............................................. | 60 |

*(see also Georgie Fame & Blue Flames)*

**BLUE GOOSE**

| | | | |
|---|---|---|---|
| 75 | Anchor ANC 1015 | Loretta/Call On Me ........................................................ | 5 |
| 75 | Anchor ANCL 2005 | BLUE GOOSE (LP) ........................................................... | 15 |

*(see also Badfinger, Curtis Knight & Zeus, Motorhead)*

**BLUE HORIZON**

| | | | |
|---|---|---|---|
| 71 | Folk Heritage FHR 022S | BLUE HORIZON (LP) ..................................................... | 350 |

**BLUE ICE**

| | | | |
|---|---|---|---|
| 82 | Vulcan | Falling Tears/The Rocker/That Place/A Dream Come True ....... | 8 |

**BLUE JEANS**

| | | | |
|---|---|---|---|
| 69 | Columbia DB 8555 | Hey Mrs. Housewife/Sandfly ............................................ | 50 |

*(see also Swinging Blue Jeans, Ray Ennis & Blue Jeans)*

**BLUES MASTERS**

| | | | |
|---|---|---|---|
| 63 | Island WI 078 | 5 O'Clock Whistle/African Blood (both sides actually by Baba Brooks) .......... | 40 |

**BLUE MAXI**

| | | | |
|---|---|---|---|
| 70 | Major Minor MM 705 | Here Comes Summer/Famous Last Words ........................... | 8 |

*(see also Jean-Jacques Burnel & Dave Greenfield)*

## BLUE MEN
| | | | |
|---|---|---|---|
| 60 | Triumph RGXST 5000 | I HEAR A NEW WORLD (PART ONE) (EP) | 300 |
| 60 | Triumph RGXST 5001 | I HEAR A NEW WORLD (PART TWO) (EP, only sleeves exist, this price is for sleeve) | 25 |
| 60 | Triumph TRX ST 9000 | I HEAR A NEW WORLD (LP, unreleased, white label demos only) | 800 |

*(see also Joe Meek, Peter Jay & Blue Men, Rodd-Ken & Cavaliers)*

## BLUE MINK
| | | | |
|---|---|---|---|
| 74 | EMI EMC3021 | FRUITY (LP) | 15 |

## BLUE MOVIES
| | | | |
|---|---|---|---|
| 79 | ROK ROK 9 | Mary Jane/THE NOISE: Criminal (company sleeve) | 15 |

## BLUE NILE
| | | | |
|---|---|---|---|
| 81 | RSO RSO 84 | I Love This Life/The Second Act (p/s) | 20 |
| 84 | Linn LKS 1 | Stay/Saddle The Horses (white p/s) | 8 |
| 84 | Linn LKS 1 | Stay (Remix)/Saddle The Horses (p/s) | 5 |
| 84 | Linn LKSD 1 | Stay (Remix)/Saddle The Horses/Tinsel Town In The Rain/Heatwave (Instrumental) (p/s, double pack) | 8 |
| 84 | Linn LKS 2 | Tinsel Town In The Rain/Heatwave (Instrumental) (p/s) | 5 |

## BLUE NOTES
| | | | |
|---|---|---|---|
| 87 | OGUN OG 532 | BLUE NOTES FOR JOHNNY (LP) | 20 |

## BLUENOTES
| | | | |
|---|---|---|---|
| 60 | Top Rank JAR 291 | I Don't Know What It Is/You Can't Get Away From Love | 10 |

## BLUE ORCHIDS
| | | | |
|---|---|---|---|
| 81 | Rough Trade RT 065 | Disney Boys/The Flood (p/s) | 5 |
| 81 | Rough Trade RT 067 | Work/The House That Faded Out (p/s) | 5 |
| 84 | Rough Trade ROUGH 36 | GREATEST HITS (LP) | 15 |

*(see also Nosebleeds, Fall, Fates)*

## BLUE OX BABES
| | | | |
|---|---|---|---|
| 88 | Go! Discs GOLP 14 | APPLES AND ORANGES (LP, unissued, test pressings only) | 50 |
| 88 | Go! Discs ZGOLP 14 | APPLES AND ORANGES (cassette, printed inlay, unreleased) | 20 |

## BLUE ÖYSTER CULT
| | | | |
|---|---|---|---|
| 76 | CBS 4483 | (Don't Fear) The Reaper/R U Ready 2 Rock | 5 |
| 76 | CBS 4483 | (Don't Fear) The Reaper/Tattoo Vampire (promo with different B-side) | 10 |
| 78 | CBS 5689 | Going Through The Motions/Searching For The Celine | 5 |
| 79 | CBS 7763 | Mirrors/Lonely Teardrops (clear vinyl, foil p/s) | 5 |
| 81 | CBS A 1453 | Burnin' For You/Heavy Metal (p/s) | 5 |
| 73 | CBS 64904 | BLUE ÖYSTER CULT (LP) | 15 |

## BLUE PHANTOM
| | | | |
|---|---|---|---|
| 72 | Kaleidoscope KAL 101 | DISTORTIONS (LP, laminated front cover, yellow label) | 150 |

## BLUE RIDGE RANGERS
| | | | |
|---|---|---|---|
| 73 | Fantasy FTC 105 | Hearts Of Stone/Somewhere Listening For My Name | 6 |
| 73 | Fantasy FTC 110 | You Don't Own Me/Back In The Hills | 6 |
| 73 | Fantasy FT 511 | BLUE RIDGE RANGERS (LP) | 18 |

*(see also John Fogerty, Creedence Clearwater Revival)*

## BLUES
| | | | |
|---|---|---|---|
| 81 | Precious PRE 1 | Aim For The Eyes/Out Of Town | 20 |

## BLUES EXPLOSION
| | | | |
|---|---|---|---|
| 04 | Mute STUMM 236 | DAMAGE (LP, gatefold with booklet) | 18 |

## BLUES BAND
| | | | |
|---|---|---|---|
| 80 | Blues Band BBBP 101 | OFFICIAL BOOTLEG ALBUM (LP, numbered, with autographs, 3000 only) | 18 |

*(see also Paul Jones, McGuinness-Flint, Manfred Mann)*

## BLUES BENDERS
| | | | |
|---|---|---|---|
| 66 | Rio R93 | Girl Next Door/Leave Me Out | 20 |

## BLUES BUSTERS
| | | | |
|---|---|---|---|
| 59 | Limbo XL101 | Little Vilma/ Early One Morning | 20 |
| 61 | Starlite ST45 031 | The Spiritual/ Lost My Baby | 40 |
| 61 | Blue Beat BB55 | Donna/You're Driving Me Crazy | 15 |
| 62 | Blue Beat BB73 | There's Always Sunshine/ You Had It Wrong | 15 |
| 62 | Starlite ST45 072 | Your Love/You Send Me Crazy | 25 |
| 62 | Island WI-023 | Behold/ Oh Baby | 20 |
| 62 | Blue Beat BB102 | Tell Me Why/ I've Done You Wrong | 20 |
| 65 | Island WI-214 | How Sweet It Is/ I Had A Dream | 40 |
| 65 | Island WI-219 | Wide Awake In A Dream (actually by Philip James solo)/ MAYTALS: Tell Me The Reason | 75 |
| 65 | Island WI-222 | Wings Of A Dove/ BYRON LEE & DRAGONAIRES: Dan Is The Man | 25 |
| 66 | Doctor Bird DB1030 | I've Been Trying/ Pretty Girls | 50 |
| 67 | Doctor Bird DB 1078 | There's Always Sunshine/ Lovers' Reward | 30 |
| 71 | Dynamic DYN408 | Each One Teach One/ Thinking Of You | 10 |
| 71 | Jay Boy BOY 44 | I Can't Stop/Inspired To Love You | 10 |
| 71 | Trojan TR7819 | Thinking Of You/ Version | 10 |
| 70s | Spank SP 20 | The Closer I Get To You/WILLIE LINDO: Midnight (12") | 30 |
| 65 | Island ILP-923 | BEHOLD! (LP) | 60 |
| 67 | Doctor Bird DLM5008 | BEST OF THE BLUES BUSTERS (LP) | 100 |
| 76 | Dynamic DYLP 3007 | PHILLIP & LLOYD (LP) | 20 |

## BLUES BY FIVE
| | | | |
|---|---|---|---|
| 64 | Decca F 12029 | Boom Boom/I Cried | 120 |

## BLUES COUNCIL
| | | | |
|---|---|---|---|
| 65 | Parlophone R 5264 | Baby Don't Look Down/What Will I Do | 100 |

## BLUE SCREAMING
| | | | |
|---|---|---|---|
| 78 | Albatross TIT 2 | Bland Hotel/Thin X Cinema (p/s) | 10 |

MINT VALUE £

## BLUES 5
| | | | |
|---|---|---|---|
| 64 | Studio 36 (no cat. no.) | Hey Baby/When You're In Love | 150 |

## BLUE SKIES
| | | | |
|---|---|---|---|
| 70 | Pendant PN 004 | Nightmares/Marigold | 50 |
| 70 | Fontana 6007026 | Happy/Nightingale | 12 |

## BLUES MAGOOS
| | | | |
|---|---|---|---|
| 66 | Mercury MF 954 | (We Ain't Got) Nothin' Yet/Gotta Get Away | 30 |
| 67 | Fontana TF 848 | One By One/Love Seems Doomed | 15 |
| 71 | Probe PRO 522 | Can't Get Enough Of You/Sea Breeze Express | 5 |
| 66 | Fontana TL 5402 | BLUES MAGOOS (LP, mono) | 50 |
| 66 | Fontana (S)TL 5402 | BLUES MAGOOS (LP, stereo) | 30 |
| 71 | Probe SPB 1024 | GULF COAST BOUND (LP) | 20 |

## BLUESOLOGY
| | | | |
|---|---|---|---|
| 65 | Fontana TF 594 | Come Back Baby/Time's Getting Tougher Than Tough | 275 |
| 66 | Fontana TF 668 | Mister Frantic/Everyday (I Have The Blues) | 300 |

*(see also Stu Brown & Bluesology, Elton John, Long John Baldry, Elton Dean, Mark Charig)*

## BLUES PROJECT
| | | | |
|---|---|---|---|
| 67 | Verve Forecast VS 1505 | I Can't Keep From Crying/The Way My Baby Walks | 35 |
| 67 | Verve (S)VLP 6004 | PROJECTIONS (LP) | 75 |

*(see also Al Kooper, Tommy Flanders, Seatrain)*

## BLUE STARS
| | | | |
|---|---|---|---|
| 65 | Decca F 12303 | Please Be A Little Kind/I Can Take It | 200 |
| 94 | Dig The Fuzz DIG 020 | THE BLUE STARS (LP) | 20 |

## BLUE STEAM
| | | | |
|---|---|---|---|
| 78 | Rip Off RIP 5 | Lizard King/Cortina Cowboys (p/s) | 10 |

## BLUETONES
| | | | |
|---|---|---|---|
| 95 | Superior Quality TONE 001 | Slight Return/The Fountainhead (blue vinyl, plain white sleeve in stickered polythene bag, 2,000 only sold by mail-order or at gigs, some numbered) | 6 |
| 95 | Superior Quality TONE 001 | Slight Return/The Fountainhead (red vinyl, foldover p/s in poly bag, 1,000 only, export issue to Japan) | 12 |
| 96 | Superior Quality BLUE 003X | Slight Return/Don't Stand Me Down (red vinyl, export issue to Japan with Japanese text on rear of p/s) | 12 |
| 96 | Superior Quality BLUELP 004 | EXPECTING TO FLY (LP, booklet, numbered) | 25 |
| 98 | Superior Quality BLUE V008 | RETURN TO THE LAST CHANCE SALOON (LP, white vinyl) | 15 |

## BLUE TRAIN
| | | | |
|---|---|---|---|
| 87 | Dreamworld DREAM 007T | LAND OF GOLD (12" EP) | 40 |

## BLUE U
| | | | |
|---|---|---|---|
| 72 | York SYK 524 | I've Been Lonely For So Long/BLUE ME: Melinda Marie | 10 |

## BLUE VELVET BAND
| | | | |
|---|---|---|---|
| 69 | Warner Bros WS 1802 | SWEET MOMENTS WITH THE BLUE VELVET BAND (LP, gatefold sleeve) | 20 |

## BLUEWATER FOLK
| | | | |
|---|---|---|---|
| 70 | Folk Heritage FHJR 013S | BLUEWATER FOLK (LP) | 50 |

## BLUE YOGURT
| | | | |
|---|---|---|---|
| 70 | Penny Farthing PEN 732 | Lydia/Umbrella Man | 40 |

## BLUNDERBUSS
| | | | |
|---|---|---|---|
| 71 | Penny Farthing PEN 762 | New Day/Emma | 12 |

## COLIN BLUNSTONE
| | | | |
|---|---|---|---|
| 71 | Epic EPC 64557 | ONE YEAR (LP, textured sleeve) | 15 |
| 72 | Epic EPC 65278 | ENNISMORE (LP, textured sleeve) | 15 |

*(see also Zombies, Neil MacArthur, Mitchell-Coe Mysteries)*

## BLUNT INSTRUMENT
| | | | |
|---|---|---|---|
| 78 | Diesel DCL 01 | No Excuse/Interrogation (p/s) | 15 |

## JAMES BLUNT
| | | | |
|---|---|---|---|
| 05 | Atlantic ATO 207 | You're Beautiful (Edit)/So Long Jimmy (Acoustic) | 10 |
| 05 | Atlantic ATO 230 | Goodbye My Lover/Where Is My Mind? (Live In Manchester) | 6 |
| 07 | Atlantic ATO 285 | 1973/So Happy (pink vinyl, stickered, p/s) | 6 |

## BLUR
### SINGLES
| | | | |
|---|---|---|---|
| 90 | Food FOOD 26 | She's So High (Edit)/I Know (7", p/s) | 8 |
| 90 | Food 12FOOD 26 | She's So High (Definitive)/Sing/I Know (Extended) (12", p/s) | 12 |
| 91 | Food FOOD 29 | There's No Other Way/Inertia (p/s) | 5 |
| 91 | Food 12 FOODX 29 | There's No Other Way (The Blur Remix)/Won't Do It/ Day Upon Day (live) (12", p/s lists '12 FOODDX 29') | 20 |
| 91 | Food 12FOOD 29 | There's No Other Way (Extended)/Inertia/Mr. Briggs/I'm All Over (12", p/s) | 10 |
| 92 | Food FOOD 37 | Popscene/Mace (p/s) | 15 |
| 92 | Food 12FOOD 37 | Popscene/I'm Fine/Mace/Garden Central (12", p/s) | 18 |
| 93 | Food FOODS 45 | Chemical World/Maggie May (7" red vinyl, paper labels, p/s) | 8 |
| 92 | Food BLUR 6 | The Wassailing Song (1-sided 7" gig freebie, as "Gold, Frankinscence and Blur" no p/s, 500 only) | 150 |
| 93 | Food FOODS 46 | Sunday Sunday/Tell Me, Tell Me (B-side as "Blur featuring Seymour") (yellow vinyl 7", p/s) | 8 |
| 94 | Food FOODS 47 | Girls And Boys/Magpie/People In Europe (7" p/s, numbered) | 8 |
| 94 | Food FOOD 56 | End Of A Century/Red Necks (p/s, numbered) | 6 |
| 97 | Food FOOD 93 | Song 2/Get Out Of Cities (p/s. purple vinyl) | 12 |
| 97 | Food FOOD 98 | On Your Own/Pop Scene (Live)/Song 2 (Live) (p/s, white vinyl) | 7 |
| 99 | Food FOOD 117 | Tender/All We Want (p/s, blue vinyl, numbered) | 6 |
| 99 | Food BLURBOX 10 | THE 10 YEAR ANNIVERSARY BOX SET (22xCD singles) | 59 |
| 03 | EMI R 6619 | Good Song/Morricone (p/s, red vinyl) | 7 |

| | | | |
|---|---|---|---|
| 05 | Fan Club SGLAD 01 | Some Glad Morning (CD, card wallet, fan club issue) | 30 |
| 10 | Parlophone LCO 3098 | Fools Day (1-sided 7", jukebox centre, blue Parlophone sleeve, 1000 only) | 30 |
| 15 | Parlophone 08256117833 | Y'All Doomed (red vinyl, numbered) | 12 |

### ALBUMS : LPS

| | | | |
|---|---|---|---|
| 91 | Food FOODLP 6 | LEISURE (LP) | 25 |
| 93 | Food FOODLP 9 | MODERN LIFE IS RUBBISH (LP, with inner) | 30 |
| 94 | Food FOODLP 10 | PARKLIFE (LP, with inner) | 30 |
| 95 | Food FOODLP 14 | THE GREAT ESCAPE (LP, with inner) | 25 |
| 95 | Food FOODLP 14 | THE GREAT ESCAPE (LP, in 12" box with book and print. Produced by Vinyl Experience, 2000 only) | 70 |
| 97 | Food CFOODLP19 | BLUR (2-LP) | 40 |
| 97 | Food FOODLP19 | BLUR (1-LP version) | 20 |
| 99 | Food FOODLP29 | 13 (2-LP, stickered, gategold, with inner sleeves) | 40 |
| 00 | Food FOODLPD 33 | THE BEST OF (2-LP) | 40 |
| 03 | Parlophone 07243-582887-1-7 | THINK TANK (2-LP) | 25 |
| 12 | EMI BLURBOXLP 1 | BLUR 21 (6 x 2-LP box set) | 150 |
| 12 | EMI BLURBOX21 | BLUR 21 (18 CD, 3 DVD & 7" box set) | 70 |
| 12 | Food 509997942320 | PARKLIVE (3-LP, bonus disc version) | 20 |

### PROMOS

| | | | |
|---|---|---|---|
| 90 | no cat. no. | Bad Day/Bad Day (version) (white label) | 20 |
| 92 | Food 12BLUR5 | Popscene (1-sided promo 12" in die cut company sleeve. 1000 only) | 10 |
| 94 | Food FOODLP19 | PARKLIFE (LP, blue vinyl promo) | 40 |
| 93 | Food 12FOODDJ 40 | For Tomorrow (Visit to Primrose Hill extended version/Into Another/Hanging Over (12" in company die cut sleeve) | 10 |
| 93 | Food BBLUR1 | BASICALLY BLUR (CD, interview disc with 3 tracks from Modern Life Is Rubbish) | 80 |
| 94 | Food CD5 BET BET BET | Girls and Boys/Jubilee/Trouble In The Message Centre/Lot 105 (Live CD promo produced for Mark Radcliffe show) | 30 |
| 97 | Food 12BLURDJ 7 | On Your Own (Crouch End Broadway Mix) (12", 1-sided, promo only) | 10 |
| 91 | Food 12BLUR 4 | High Cool (Easy Listening Mix)/Bad Day (Leisurely Mix) (12", blue & gold company sleeve, promo, 1,000 only) | 25 |
| 00 | Food 10FOODDJ 135 | Music Is My Radar (12" one-sided w/10" cat. No., white die cut sleeve, stamped label) | 10 |
| 98 | Food FOODLH 117 | Tender (Radio Edit)/Song 2 (jukebox copy, no centre) | 10 |
| 99 | Food FOOD CDJX 29 | 13 (CD in duffelbag with folder, photos, ski-hat and biography, promo only) | 80 |
| 99 | Food 10FOODDJ 117 | Tender (10" promo record plays inside to out, foil sealed) | 20 |
| 02 | The Bombo! | (red label, bearing Arabic writing which translates as "Don't bomb when you are the bomb"; large centre hole; 1,000 7" were pressed, but many were blown up) | 35 |

*(see also Graham Coxon, Gorillaz, Damon Albarn)*

## BLURT

| | | | |
|---|---|---|---|
| 80 | Test Pressing TP 1 | My Mother Was A Friend Of An Enemy Of The People/Get (p/s) | 5 |
| 81 | Armageddon AS 013 | The Fish Needs A Bike/This Is My Royal Wedding Souvenir (p/s) | 5 |

## BLUSH

| | | | |
|---|---|---|---|
| 79 | Venal Vinyl PMB 117 | Everyday/Before We Came Together (no p/s, 200 only) | 150 |

## B-MOVIE

| | | | |
|---|---|---|---|
| 80 | Dead Good DEAD 9 | TAKE THREE (EP) | 20 |
| 80 | Dead Good BIG DEAD 12 | NOWHERE GIRL (12" EP, with insert, 800 only) | 20 |
| 81 | Deram DM 443 | Marilyn Dreams/Film Music (Part 1) (p/s) | 5 |
| 88 | Wax 12 WAX 3 | Nowhere Girl/Remembrance Day (12", p/s, 250 on orange vinyl, numbered) | 15 |
| 88 | Wax 12 WAX 3 | Nowhere Girl/Remembrance Day (12", p/s, pink vinyl, numbered) | 15 |
| 88 | Wax WAXLP 1P | THE DEAD GOOD TAPES (LP, picture disc) | 12 |

## BMX BANDITS

| | | | |
|---|---|---|---|
| 86 | 53rd & 3rd AGARR 3 | Sad?/E102 (p/s, with comic) | 10 |
| 87 | 53rd & 3rd AGARR 6 | What A Wonderful World/The Day Before Tomorrow (p/s) | 6 |

*(see also Soup Dragons, Boy Hairdressers, Teenage Fanclub, Vaselines)*

## EDDIE BO

| | | | |
|---|---|---|---|
| 73 | Action ACT 4609 | Check Your Bucket Parts 1 & 2 | 30 |

## BO & PEEP

| | | | |
|---|---|---|---|
| 64 | Decca F 11968 | Young Love/The Rise Of The Brighton Surf | 40 |

*(see also Andrew Oldham Orchestra)*

## HARRY BOARDMAN & DAVE HILLERY

| | | | |
|---|---|---|---|
| 71 | Topic 12TS 215 | TRANS PENNINE (LP) | 15 |

## BOARDS OF CANADA

| | | | |
|---|---|---|---|
| 94 | Music 70 AOMC43 | PLAY BY NUMBERS EP (Cassette) | 50 |
| 94 | Music 70 AOCS43 | PLAY BY NUMBERS EP (CD) | 60 |
| 94 | Music 70 THS 012 | HOOPER'S BAY (12" EP) | 100 |
| 94 | Music 70 THS 012 | HOOPER'S BAY (cassette EP) | 30 |
| 96 | Skam SKA 008 | Hi Scores/Turquoise Hexagon Sun/Nlagon/June 9th/ See Ya Later/Everything You Do Is A Balloon (12", p/s) | 60 |
| 98 | Skam KMAS 1 | Aquarius/Chinook (p/s, with insert, 500 only) | 60 |
| 98 | Warp 10WARP LP 55P | Telephasic Workshop/Roygbiv (10" promo, 2000 only) | 25 |
| 00 | Warp Records WAP 144 | In A Beautiful Place Out In The Country (12", EP) | 40 |
| 99 | Warp WAP 114 | THE PEEL SESSIONS (12", p/s) | 15 |
| 06 | Warp WAP 200 | TRANS CANADA HIGHWAY EP (12", white vinyl) | 20 |
| 13 | Warp 37367 | ------ / ------ / ------ / XXXXXX / ------ / ------ (12" p/s. 6 known copies) | 1000 |
| 95 | Music 70 BOARD 1 | TWOISM (LP, 100 copies only) | 400 |
| 95 | Music 70 BOARD 1 | TWOISM (Cassette, 100 copies only) | 100 |
| 98 | Warp Records 10 WARP LP 55 P | MUSIC HAS THE RIGHT TO CHILDREN (10", Promo) | 40 |

# BOARDWALKERS

| | | | |
|---|---|---|---|
| 98 | Warp Records, Skam WARP LP 55, SKALP001 | MUSIC HAS THE RIGHT TO CHILDREN (2-LP) | 65 |
| 02 | Warp | GEOGADDI (LP, blue vinly test pressing - etched - 10 only) | 200 |
| 02 | Warp/Music 70 | GEOGADDI (3-LP) | 60 |
| 02 | Warp WARPLP 70 | TWOISM (LP, reissue, die-cut sleeve) | 20 |
| 05 | Warp WARPLP 123 | CAMPFIRE HEADPHASE (2-LP) | 30 |
| 13 | Warp WARPLP 257 | TOMORROW'S HARVEST (2-LP) | 20 |

## BOARDWALKERS
| | | | |
|---|---|---|---|
| 60s | own label J.C. 1 | A Miracle/Any Man's Girl | 200 |

*(see also Warren Davis)*

## TOOTER BOATMAN
| | | | |
|---|---|---|---|
| 72 | Injun 108 | Thunder & Lightning/The Will Of Love | 10 |

## BOATMEN
| | | | |
|---|---|---|---|
| 70s | Sweet Folk SFA 018 | STRAIGHT FROM THE TUNNEL'S MOUTH (LP) | 40 |

## BOBALOUIS
| | | | |
|---|---|---|---|
| 81 | WEA K18441 | Not A Second Chance/City Boys | 20 |

## BOB & CAROL
| | | | |
|---|---|---|---|
| 67 | CBS 2738 | On My Life/Mary Jane | 8 |

## BOB (RELF) & EARL (NELSON)
| | | | |
|---|---|---|---|
| 65 | Sue WI 374 | Harlem Shuffle/I'll Keep Running Back | 20 |
| 65 | Sue WI 393 | Baby I'm Satisfied/The Sissy | 40 |
| 67 | Sue WI 4030 | Don't Ever Leave Me/Fancy Free | 75 |
| 69 | B&C CB 102 | Dancin' Everywhere/Baby It's Over | 5 |
| 69 | Warner Bros WB 6059 | Everybody Jerk/He's A Playbrother | 40 |
| 70 | Uni UN 519 | Pickin' Up Love's Vibrations/Uh, Uh, Naw Naw Naw | 5 |
| 72 | Jay Boy BOY 72 | I Can't Get Away/I'll Keep Running Back | 10 |
| 72 | Jay Boy BOY 73 | My Little Girl/His & Her Shuffle (as Bob & Earl Band) | 10 |
| 73 | Contempo C 4 | Harlem Shuffle/Harlem Shuffle (Instrumental Version) | 5 |
| 67 | Sue ILP 951 | HARLEM SHUFFLE (LP) | 100 |
| 69 | B & C BCB 1 | BOB & EARL (LP) | 15 |
| 69 | Joy JOYS 199 | TOGETHER (LP) | 15 |

*(see also Bob Relf, Jackie Lee, Earl Nelson, Hollywood Flames)*

## BOB & JERRY
| | | | |
|---|---|---|---|
| 58 | Pye International 7N 25003 | Ghost Satellite/Nothin' | 15 |
| 61 | Philips PB 1205 | Dreamy Eyes/We're The Guys (Who Drive Your Baby Wild) | 5 |

## BOB (ANDY) & MARCIA (GRIFFITHS)
| | | | |
|---|---|---|---|
| 70 | Bamboo BAM 40 | Always Together/BOB ANDY: Desperate Lover | 22 |
| 70 | Harry J. HJ 6605 | Young, Gifted And Black/JAY BOYS: Young, Gifted & Black (Instrumental) | 6 |
| 70 | Escort ES 824 | Young, Gifted And Black/BARRINGTON BIGGS: My Cheri Amour (Different version: no strings) | 15 |
| 71 | Trojan TR 7818 | Pied Piper/Save Me | 5 |
| 72 | Trojan TR 7854 | But I Do/I Don't Care | 5 |
| 70 | Trojan TBL 122 | YOUNG, GIFTED & BLACK (LP) | 30 |
| 72 | Trojan TRLS 26 | PIED PIPER (LP) | 15 |

*(see also Bob Andy, Marcia Griffiths)*

## BOB (ANDY) & TIE (TYRONE EVANS)
| | | | |
|---|---|---|---|
| 69 | Coxsone CS 7086 | I Don't Care/LASCELLES PERKINS: Little Green Apples | 60 |

## BOB(B)ETTES
| | | | |
|---|---|---|---|
| 57 | London HLE 8477 | Mr. Lee/Look At The Stars | 40 |
| 58 | London HLE 8597 | Come-A Come-A/Speedy | 40 |
| 58 | London HLE 8597 | Come-A Come-A/Speedy (78) | 20 |
| 60 | London HLE 9173 | I Shot Mr. Lee/Untrue Love | 60 |
| 60 | London HLE 9248 | Have Mercy Baby/Dance With Me Georgie | 40 |
| 60 | Pye International 7N 25060 | I Shot Mr. Lee/Billy (as Bobettes) | 40 |
| 72 | Action ACT 4603 | That's A Bad Thing To Know/All In Your Mind | 18 |

## BOBBSEY TWINS
| | | | |
|---|---|---|---|
| 57 | London HLA 8474 | A Change Of Heart/Part-Time Gal | 15 |

## BOBBY & DAVE
| | | | |
|---|---|---|---|
| 71 | Ackee ACK 116 | Build My World Around You/LIZZY & TONY BOP: Sammy Version | 15 |

*(see also Dave Barker, Lizzy & Dennis)*

## BOBBY & JIM
| | | | |
|---|---|---|---|
| 58 | Capitol CL 14877 | Carry My Books/A Lover Can Tell | 6 |

## BOBBY & LAURIE
| | | | |
|---|---|---|---|
| 66 | Parlophone R 5480 | Hitch Hiker/You'll Come 'Round | 15 |

## BOBBY & MIDNITES
| | | | |
|---|---|---|---|
| 84 | CBS 26046 | WHERE THE BEAT MEETS THE STREET (LP) | 25 |

*(see also Bob Weir, Grateful Dead)*

## BOBBY (ELLIS) & TOMMY (MCCOOK)
| | | | |
|---|---|---|---|
| 74 | Attack ATLP 1004 | GREEN MANGO (LP) | 35 |

## BOBCATS
| | | | |
|---|---|---|---|
| 67 | Pye 7N 17242 | Can't See For Looking/Let Me Get By | 25 |

## WILLIE BOBO
| | | | |
|---|---|---|---|
| 66 | Verve VS 548 | Sunshine Super Man/Sockit To Me | 12 |
| 66 | Verve SVLP9134 | ELATION (LP) | 20 |
| 71 | A&M AMLS 68034 | DO WHAT YOU WANT TO DO (LP) | 25 |

## FRIDA BOCCARA
| | | | |
|---|---|---|---|
| 69 | Philips BF 1765 | Through The Eyes Of A Child/So Fair | 10 |

**BOCKY & VISIONS**
65   Atlantic AT 4049 — I Go Crazy/Good Good Lovin' ........................................................ 40

**J.P. BODDY**
73   Columbia DB 89789 — Stop Me Spinning (Like A Spinning Top)/Song Without A Word ................ 8

**BODEAN**
76   DJM DJS 10697 — Saturday Woman/Flying High (promo, p/s) ...................................... 7

**BODGERS**
82   SRTS/82/CUS/1484 — Stutter/I Hate Phoning Girls (no p/s) ..................................... 100

**BODGER'S MATE**
78   Cottage COT 521 — BRIGHTER THAN USUAL (LP) ................................................... 20

**BODIES**
79   Waldo's HS 007 — Art Nouveau/Machinery (poster p/s, 5 different colours) ...................... 5

**BODKIN**
72   West CSA 104 — BODKIN (LP, private pressing, red label 10-20 in silk screened cover) .......... 1200
72   West CSA 104 — BODKIN (LP, private pressing, red label, in posthumously designed sleeve) ...... 800
12   Acme ADLP 1085 — BODKIN (LP, reissue) ....................................................... 15

**BODY**
81   Recession — THE BODY ALBUM (LP, private pressing with booklet) ............................... 50

**BODY AND SOUL**
70   Penny Farthing PEN 720 — Here Comes That Feeling/Go Back To School ........................... 7

**BODYSNATCHERS (1)**
80   2-Tone CHS TT 9 — Let's Do Rocksteady/Ruder Than You (paper label, company sleeve) ........... 15
80   2-Tone CHS TT 9 — Let's Do Rocksteady/Ruder Than You (injection moulded labels) .............. 7
80   2-Tone CHS TT 12 — Easy Life/Too Experienced (paper label, company sleeve) ................... 12
80   2-Tone CHS TT 12 — Easy Life/Too Experienced (injection moulded labels) ...................... 7

**BODYSNATCHERS (2)**
97   Backbone (No Cat. No) — GENOCIDE (EP, 30 test copies) ........................................ 75

*(see also Icepick)*

**BOEING DUVEEN & BEAUTIFUL SOUP**
68   Parlophone R 5696 — Jabberwock/Which Dreamed It (demos without p/s) ......................... 100
68   Parlophone R 5696 — Jabberwock/Which Dreamed It (demos with p/s) ............................ 250
68   Parlophone R 5696 — Jabberwock/Which Dreamed It ............................................. 150

**BOFFALONGO**
70   United Artists UP 35144 — Dancing In The Moonlight/Endless Questions ......................... 6
71   United Artists UAG 29130 — BEYOND YOUR HEAD (LP) ............................................ 15

**BOG UGLY AND THE WOOFTERS**
78   Toadstool GOOD 2 — Disco Veteran/I've Seen It Vomit (p/s) .................................... 25

**BOGAZ**
83   AGR 12 AGR 2 — I've Got Love/I've Got Love (Instrumental) (12") ............................. 25

**BOGDAN**
81   Black Label GB 3 — Oh Eddie/Reet Petite (p/s) .............................................. 10
81   Brilliant HIT 1 — Who Do You Think You Are?/Take Me Back (p/s) .............................. 10

*(see also Whitesnake)*

**BOGIES**
64   private press (no cat. no.) — THE BOGIES ON CAMPUS (LP) ..................................... 150
64   private press (no cat. no.) — BYE BYE BOGIES (LP) .......................................... 150

**ERIC BOGLE**
77   Autogram ALLP 211 — LIVE IN PERSON (LP) .................................................... 35
81   Plant Life PLR 033 — PLAIN AND SIMPLE (LP) ................................................. 15
83   Plant Life PLR 046 — SCRAPS OF PAPER (LP) .................................................. 15
85   Topic 12TS 437 — WHEN THE WIND BLOWS (LP) .................................................. 15
88   Plant Life PLR 042 — NOW I'M EASY (LP) ..................................................... 15

**LEE BOGLE**
71   Black Swan BW 1406 — Tomorrow's Dreams/SWANS: Hot Pants Reggae ............................. 15

**BOGUS ORDER**
90   Ninja Tune ZEN 01 — ZEB BRAKES (LP) ........................................................ 25

**BUDDY BOHN**
71   Regal Zonophone RX 3040 — Piccalilli Lady/Summer Song ....................................... 8
71   Purple TPSA 7503 — A DROP IN THE OCEAN (LP, gatefold sleeve) ............................... 30

**BOILER SHOP**
72   Music Box MB 03 — Seeing Things In Colour/Darkness ......................................... 40

**HOUSTON BOINES**
66   Blue Horizon 45 BH 1006 — Superintendent Blues/Monkey Motion (99 copies only, Ike Turner on piano) .......... 200

**BOISTEROUS**
95   Hammer HR 5 — SKIP RAIDERS (LP) ............................................................ 15

**BOK BOK**
80   Bok Bok BOK 2 — Come Back To Me/Misfit (p/s) ............................................... 10

**BOLA**
95   Skam SKA 5 — Forcasa 3/Krak Jakomo/Metalurg 2/Ballom (12", custom sleeve) ................... 50
98   Skam KMAS002 — KS (500 pressed) ............................................................ 30
01   Skam KMAS 007 — Pae Paoe (1,000 pressed) ................................................... 5
00   33 33Shapes — SHAPES (LP, 3x12") ........................................................... 35

**MARC BOLAN**
65   Decca F 12288 — The Wizard/Beyond The Rising Sun (some as Marc Bölan) ....................... 500
65   Decca F 12288 — The Wizard/Beyond The Rising Sun (demo copy) ............................... 350
66   Decca F 12413 — The Third Degree/San Francisco Poet ........................................ 500

MINT VALUE £

| | | | |
|---|---|---|---|
| 66 | Decca F 12413 | The Third Degree/San Francisco Poet (demo copy) | 350 |
| 66 | Parlophone R 5539 | Hippy Gumbo/Misfit | 650 |
| 66 | Parlophone R 5539 | Hippy Gumbo/Misfit (demo copy) | 500 |
| 72 | Track 2094 013 | Jasper C. Debussy/Hippy Gumbo/The Perfumed Garden Of Gulliver Smith (p/s, withdrawn) | 50 |
| 72 | Track 2094 013 | Jasper C. Debussy/Hippy Gumbo/The Perfumed Garden Of Gulliver Smith (white label demo) | 70 |
| 81 | Rarn MBFS 001C | Sing Me A Song/Endless Sleep (Extended Version)/The Lilac Hand Of Menthol Dan (12", no p/s, clear vinyl, handwritten labels) | 10 |
| 81 | Rarn MBFS 001P | Sing Me A Song/Endless Sleep (Extended Version)/The Lilac Hand Of Menthol Dan (12" picture disc, misprinted with black rim) | 15 |
| 81 | Rarn MBFS 001P | Sing Me A Song/Endless Sleep (Extended Version)/The Lilac Hand Of Menthol Dan (12", picture disc misprinted back-to-front) | 15 |
| 81 | Cherry Red CHERRY 29 | You Scare Me To Death/The Perfumed Garden Of Gulliver Smith (initial copies with bronze label, glossy p/s & free flexidisc [Lyntone LYN 10086]) | 10 |
| 81 | Cherry Red CHERRY 29 | You Scare Me To Death/The Perfumed Garden Of Gulliver Smith (later pressing with silver label/matt p/s) | 5 |
| 81 | Cherry Red CHERRY 32 | Cat Black/Jasper C. Debussy (p/s) | 5 |
| 82 | Cherry Red CHERRY 39 | The Wizard/Beyond The Rising Sun/Rings Of Fortune (p/s) | 5 |
| 72 | Track 2406 101 | HARD ON LOVE (LP, unreleased, white label test pressing, 3 known copies) | 1000 |
| 72 | Track 2406 009 | HARD ON LOVE (LP, unreleased, 2-sided EMIdisc acetate with "swearing intro") | 2250 |
| 74 | Track 2410 201 | THE BEGINNING OF DOVES (LP, laminated sleeve, black/silver label) | 35 |
| 81 | Cherry Red PERED 20 | YOU SCARE ME TO DEATH (LP, picture disc) | 15 |
| 89 | Media Motion MEDIA 2 | THE BEGINNING OF DOVES (LP, reissue, 750 only, withdrawn) | 25 |

*(see also Marc Bolan/T. Rex, Marc Bolan & Gloria Jones, Toby Tyler, John's Children, Big Carrot, Dib Cochran & The Earwigs)*

## MARC BOLAN & GLORIA JONES

| | | | |
|---|---|---|---|
| 77 | EMI EMI 2572 | To Know Him Is To Love Him/City Port | 15 |

*(see also Gloria Jones)*

## MARC BOLAN/T. REX
### SINGLES

| | | | |
|---|---|---|---|
| 70 | Octopus OCTO 1 | Ride A White Swan/Summertime Blues/Jewel (unreleased, handwritten white label, 2/3 test pressings only) | 2500 |
| 70 | Fly BUG 1 | Ride A White Swan/Is It Love/Summertime Blues (p/s, purple labels) | 20 |
| 70 | Fly BUG 1 | Ride A White Swan/Is It Love/Summertime Blues (p/s, later pressing with mustard labels) | 7 |
| 71 | Fly | Hot Love/Woodland Rock/King Of The Mountain Cometh (IBC Sound Recordings Studios acetate) | 280 |
| 71 | Fly BUG 6 | Hot Love/Woodland Rock/King Of The Mountain Cometh (mustard labels) | 10 |
| 71 | Fly BUG 6 | Hot Love/Woodland Rock/King Of The Mountain Cometh (mustard labels, later pressing with 'fly' design) | 5 |
| 71 | Fly BUG 10 | Get It On/There Was A Time/Raw Ramp (p/s, black label with silver 'fly' logo) | 15 |
| 71 | Fly BUG 10 | Get It On/There Was A Time/Raw Ramp (p/s, 1st pressing, black label with silver fly) | 6 |
| 71 | Fly BUG 10 | Get It On/There Was A Time/Raw Ramp (p/s, 2nd pressing, black label with white fly, many not in p/s) | 5 |
| 71 | Fly GRUB 1 | Electric Warrior Preview Single: Jeepster/Life's A Gas (gig freebie, in pink envelope sleeve) | 200 |
| 71 | Fly GRUB 1 | Electric Warrior Preview Single: Jeepster/Life's A Gas (gig freebie, originally in pink envelope sleeve, this price is for later standard paper sleeve) | 145 |
| 71 | Fly BUG 16 | Jeepster/Life's A Gas (white 'fly' label) | 5 |
| 71 | Fly BUG 16 | Jeepster/Life's A Gas (scarce issue w/out 'GRUB 1A' ref.) | 6 |
| 72 | EMI T REX 101 | Telegram Sam/Cadillac/Baby Strange | 6 |
| 72 | Magni Fly ECHO 102 | One Inch Rock/The Woodland Bop/The Throat Of Winter (unreleased, rejected 1-sided test pressing for B-side of "Deborah"/"One Inch Rock", stamped white label) | 150 |
| 72 | Magni Fly ECHO 102 | Debora/One Inch Rock/The Woodland Bop/Seal Of Seasons (p/s) | 6 |
| 72 | EMI MARC X | Metal Guru (rejected 1-sided test pressing with Marc's annotation 'bad cut') | 300 |
| 72 | EMI MARC 1 | Metal Guru/Thunderwing/Lady | 8 |
| 72 | EMI MARC 2 | Children Of The Revolution/Jitterbug Love/Sunken Rags | 6 |
| 72 | EMI MARC 3 | Solid Gold Easy Action/(5th Dimension track) (mispressing) | 15 |
| 72 | EMI MARC 3 | Solid Gold Easy Action/(Partridge Family track) (mispressing) | 15 |
| 72 | EMI SPRS 346 | Chariot Choogle/The Slider (promo only, 'T. Rex' picture label) | 425 |
| 72 | EMI SPRS 346 | Chariot Choogle/The Slider (promo only, white label) | 375 |
| 72 | Lyntone | Christmas Time/Wanna Spend My Christmas With You/ Christmas/Everybody Knows It's Christmas (fan club flexi, with letter in brown envelope) | 45 |
| 72 | Lyntone | Christmas Time/Wanna Spend My Christmas With You/ Christmas/Everybody Knows It's Christmas (fan club flexi, without letter in brown envelope) | 30 |
| 73 | EMI MARC 4 | 20th Century Boy/Free Angel | 6 |
| 73 | EMI MARC 5 | The Groover/Midnight | 6 |
| 73 | EMI MARC 6 | Truck On (Tyke)/Sitting Here | 6 |
| 74 | EMI MARC 7 | Teenage Dream/Satisfaction Pony (credited to 'Marc Bolan & T. Rex') | 6 |
| 74 | EMI MARC 7 | Teenage Dream/Satisfaction Pony (credited to 'Marc Bolan') | 8 |
| 74 | EMI MARC 8 | Light Of Love/Explosive Mouth | 6 |
| 74 | EMI MARC 9 | Zip Gun Boogie/Space Boss | 6 |
| 75 | EMI MARC 10 | New York City/Chrome Sitar | 6 |
| 75 | EMI MARC 11 | Dreamy Lady/Do You Wanna Dance?/Dock Of The Bay (as T. Rex Disco Party) | 6 |
| 75 | EMI MARC 12 | Christmas Bop/Telegram Sam/Metal Guru (unreleased, A- & B-side paper labels exist, 2 sets only this price is for the labels) | 1250 |
| 76 | EMI MARC 13 | London Boys/Solid Baby | 6 |
| 76 | Cube BUG 66 | Hot Love/Get It On | 6 |
| 76 | EMI MARC 14 | I Love To Boogie/Baby Boomerang | 6 |
| 76 | EMI MARC 15 | Laser Love/Life's An Elevator | 6 |
| 77 | EMI MARC 16 | The Soul Of My Suit/All Alone | 8 |
| 77 | EMI MARC 17 | Dandy In The Underworld/Groove A Little/Tame My Tiger (p/s) | 10 |
| 77 | EMI MARC 18 | Celebrate Summer/Ride My Wheels (p/s) | 10 |

| | | | |
|---|---|---|---|
| 78 | EMI MARC 19 | Crimson Moon/Jason B. Sad (p/s) | 10 |
| 78 | Cube ANT 2 | Hot Love/Raw Ramp/Lean Woman Blues (p/s, misprinted Raw Amp, sleeve credits 'Bolan', label credits 'T.Rex') | 8 |
| 79 | Cube ANTS 001 | Life's A Gas/Find A Little Wood/Once Upon The Seas Of Abyssinia/ Blessed Wild Apple Girl (12", p/s) | 12 |
| 82 | Marc ABOLAN 2 | THE CHILDREN OF RARN (10" EP, p/s, 33rpm, gatefold sleeve with 12-page lyric book) | 25 |
| 82 | Marc SBOLAN 13 | Mellow Love/Foxy Box/Lunacy's Back (p/s, blue vinyl, as Marc Bolan) | 8 |
| 82 | Rarn MBFS RAP 2 | Deep Summer/Oh Baby/One Inch Rock (unreleased version) (12", p/s, blue vinyl) | 10 |
| 83 | Marc SBOLAN 12EP | CHRISTMAS BOP EP (12", p/s, OMBFS only, extra tracks: acoustic versions of "King Of The Rumbling Spires" & "Savage Beethoven") | 10 |
| 84 | Marc On Wax SPS 1 | Mister Motion (1-sided, from "Child Of The Revolution - 14 Greats" LP, p/s) | 8 |
| 84 | Cube BUG 99 | Sailor Of The Highway/Do You Remember (7" in plain black sleeve) | 15 |
| 84 | Cube HBUG 99 | RARE MAGIC (12" EP) | 15 |
| 87 | Strange Fruit SFPS 031 | PEEL SESSIONS (12") | 15 |
| 94 | Edsel MBPROMO 1 | T. REX (CD, picture disc, 4-track sampler, tri-fold digipak, promo only) | 15 |
| 07 | Edsel BOLAN 1 | Metal Guru/The Slider (Acoustic Demo) (Blue vinyl, numbered, 1,000 only) | 15 |
| 07 | Edsel BOLAN 2 | Children Of The Revolution/The Leopards (Electric Demo) (Red vinyl, numbered, 1,000 only) | 15 |
| 07 | Edsel BOLAN 3 | 20th Century Boy/Teenager In Love (Marc & Gloria acoustic duet) (White vinyl, numbered, 1,000 only) | 12 |
| 07 | Edsel TREXMAS 1 | Christmas Bop/The Xmas Riff/Xmas Flexi message (7", promo) | 60 |
| 12 | Universal 533812-3 | ELECTRIC SEVENS (4 x 7" box set) | 20 |

**ALBUMS**

| | | | |
|---|---|---|---|
| 70 | Fly HIFLY 2 | T. REX (semi-gatefold sleeve, white label with 'Fly' logo) | 50 |
| 71 | Fly HIFLY 6 | ELECTRIC WARRIOR (unreleased version with "Jeepster" on side 2, 1 test pressing copy only, with Marc's annotations on white sleeve) | 700 |
| 71 | Fly HIFLY 6 | ELECTRIC WARRIOR (with poster & inner sleeve, stickered sleeve, white label with 'Fly' logo) | 100 |
| 71 | Fly HIFLY 6 | ELECTRIC WARRIOR (with poster & inner sleeve, non-stickered sleeve, white label with 'Fly' logo) | 50 |
| 72 | Fly HIFLY 8 | BOLAN BOOGIE (1-sided test pressing with "The Visit" instead of "Jewel") | 375 |
| 72 | Fly HIFLY 8 | BOLAN BOOGIE | 15 |
| 72 | EMI BLN 5001 | THE SLIDER (with lyric inner sleeve, sleeve with 'sniped' spine edges, flicpbacks, blue/red T-Rex label) | 40 |
| 73 | EMI BLN 5002 | TANX (with poster & inner sleeve) | 30 |
| 73 | EMI BLN 5003 | GREAT HITS (with poster) | 15 |
| 74 | EMI BNLA 7751 | ZINC ALLOY AND THE HIDDEN RIDERS OF TOMORROW (with 3-way numbered promo fold-out sleeve & inner, given as competition prize with letter from Pink or Mirabelle magazines, 1,000 only) | 300 |
| 74 | EMI BNLA 7751 | ZINC ALLOY AND THE HIDDEN RIDERS OF TOMORROW (with 3-way promo fold-out sleeve & inner, without letter; numbered) | 300 |
| 74 | EMI BNLA 7751 | ZINC ALLOY AND THE HIDDEN RIDERS OF TOMORROW (with 3-way promo fold-out sleeve & inner, without letter; unnumbered) | 250 |
| 74 | EMI BLNA 7751 | ZINC ALLOY AND THE HIDDEN RIDERS OF TOMORROW (commercial gatefold sleeve with lyric inner sleeve) | 20 |
| 75 | EMI BNLA 7752 | BOLAN'S ZIP GUN (diamond-cut laminated sleeve & inner sleeve, blue/red T-Rex label) | 25 |
| 76 | EMI BLNA 5004 | FUTURISTIC DRAGON (with lyric inner sleeve) | 25 |
| 77 | EMI BLNA 5005 | DANDY IN THE UNDERWORLD (with round-cut sleeve & lyric inner sleeve) | 25 |
| 78 | Cube HIFLD 1 | MARC: THE WORDS AND MUSIC OF MARC BOLAN 1947-1977 (2-LP, gatefold sleeve, with free single [BINT 1]) | 20 |
| 81 | Marc ABOLAN 1P | T. REX IN CONCERT (picture disc, 2 designs) | 20 |
| 82 | Cube/Dakota ICSX 1004 | ACROSS THE AIRWAVES (picture disc) | 20 |
| 82 | Marc ABOLAN 3P | ELECTRIC WARRIOR (picture disc) | 20 |
| 84 | Marc ABOLAN 5 | T. REXTASY (with 12" "Jam (live)"/Elemental Child (live) [ABOLAN 5F], Official Fanclub only) | 18 |
| 80 | EMI NUT 28 | THE UNOBTAINABLE T-REX (LP, initial batch with rejected rear sleeve photo of Bolan with tongue out) | 200 |
| 86 | Marc On Wax WARRIOR 1/4 | HISTORY OF T. REX (4-LP, numbered picture disc set, with free fanclub T-shirt) | 45 |
| 86 | Marc On Wax WARRIOR 1/4 | HISTORY OF T. REX (4-LP, numbered picture disc set, without free fanclub T-shirt) | 35 |

*(see also Marc Bolan, Tyrannosaurus Rex, Dib Cochran & the Earwigs, John's Children, Big Carrot)*

**FRANCY BOLAND**

| | | | |
|---|---|---|---|
| 75 | Freedom FLP40176 | PAPILLON NOIR (LP) | 18 |

*(see also Kenny Clarke with Francy Boland)*

**TOMMY BOLIN**

| | | | |
|---|---|---|---|
| 76 | Nemperor K 10730/NE 4 | The Grind/Homeward Strut | 10 |
| 75 | Atlantic K 50208 | TEASER (LP, stickered) | 25 |
| 75 | Atlantic K 50208 | TEASER (LP, unstickered) | 15 |
| 76 | CBS S 81612 | PRIVATE EYES (LP) | 15 |

*(see also James Gang, Deep Purple)*

**BOLLARD**

| | | | |
|---|---|---|---|
| 72 | Satril SAT 1 | I Need Your Love/Sunshine In The Morning | 6 |

**BOLLARDS**

| | | | |
|---|---|---|---|
| 70s | Bumkin Records | BOLLARDS (LP) | 15 |

**BOLLWEEVIL**

| | | | |
|---|---|---|---|
| 81 | Ellie Jay EJSP 9715 | Rock Solid/Sands Of Time (p/s) | 90 |

**BOLT THROWER**

| | | | |
|---|---|---|---|
| 88 | Strange Fruit SFPS 056 | PEEL SESSIONS (12") | 20 |
| 91 | Strange Fruit SFRLP 116 | PEEL SESSIONS 19880-90 (LP) | 20 |
| 88 | Vinyl Solution SOL 11 | IN BATTLE THERE IS NO LAW (LP, with insert) | 20 |
| 89 | Earache MOSH 13 | REALM OF CHAOS (LP, picture disc) | 15 |
| 89 | Earache MOSH 12 | REALM OF CHAOS (LP, with booklet) | 20 |
| 91 | Earache MOSH 29 | WAR MASTER (LP, booklet) | 25 |

## BOMAR
68  Flesh FH 01  Suddenly A Dream/Terry O McDonald's Son ......................................................................... 18

## BOMB AND DAGGER
86  SSR BDSS01  Wake Up/No Real Place (p/s) ........................................................................................ 10

## BOMBADIL
72  Harvest HAR 5056  Breathless/When The City Sleeps (p/s) ................................................................... 8
75  Harvest HAR 5095  Breathless/When The City Sleeps (p/s, reissue) ...................................................... 8
*(see also Barclay James Harvest)*

## BOMBAY DUCKS
80  Complete Control CON 1  Sympathy For The Devil/1-0-6-9 (p/s) ........................................................... 10
80s  United Dairies UD 05  DANCE MUSIC (LP) .................................................................................. 15

## BON JOVI
84  Vertigo VER 11  She Don't Know Me/Breakout (p/s) ........................................................................... 10
84  Vertigo VERX 11  She Don't Know Me/Breakout (12", p/s) ................................................................... 15
84  Vertigo VER 14  Runaway/Breakout (live) (p/s) ................................................................................. 12
84  Vertigo VERX 14  Runaway/Breakout (live)/Runaway (live) (12", p/s) ................................................. 20
85  Vertigo VER 19  In And Out Of Love/Roulette (live) (p/s) .................................................................. 10
85  Vertigo VERP 19  In And Out Of Love/Roulette (live) (picture disc) ................................................... 35
85  Vertigo VERDP 22  The Hardest Part Is The Night/Always Run To You//Tokyo Road (live)/ Shot Through The Heart (live) (double pack, gatefold p/s) ........................................................... 8
85  Vertigo VERXR 22  Red Hot And Two Parts Live: The Hardest Part Is The Night/ Tokyo Road (live)/In And Out Of Love (live) (12", p/s, red vinyl) ...................................................................... 20
86  Vertigo VERP 26  You Give Love A Bad Name/Let It Rock (10", shaped picture disc) ............................. 15
86  Vertigo VERPA 28  Livin' On A Prayer/Wild In The Streets (p/s, with patch, sealed) ............................. 15
89  Vertigo JOVS 661-663  Lay Your Hands On Me/Bad Medicine (live) (3 x 7", red, blue or white vinyl, paper box set) ................................................................................................................................ 5
88  Vertigo VERHP 38  SLIPPERY WHEN WET (LP, picture disc with poster) .......................................... 15
88  Vertigo VERHP 62  NEW JERSEY (LP, picture disc, stickered PVC sleeve) ........................................ 15
95  Mercury 528 248-1  THESE DAYS (2-LP) ..................................................................................... 30

## JON BON JOVI
90  Vertigo JBJP 212  Miracle/Dyin' Ain't Much Of A Livin'/Going Back (live) (12", picture disc with insert) ... 10

## BONA DISH
82  In Phaze  BONA DISH ON C30 (cassette) ................................................................................... 70
82  In Phase IP 010  EP (cassette) ............................................................................................................ 40
82  In Phaze  CARDBOARD TUBE (cassette in cardboard tube packaging) ........................................ 50

## JOE BONAMASSA
06  Provogue PRD71851  YOU AND ME (LP, pressed in Netherlands) ........................................................ 15

## BON-BONS
55  London HL 8139  That's The Way Love Goes/Make My Dreams Come True ........................................ 20
56  London HLU 8262  Circle/Frog On A Log ............................................................................................. 20

## BOBBY BOND
61  Pye International 7N 25081  You're A Livin' Doll/Sweet Love ............................................................... 5
69  Warner Bros WB 7292  One More Mile, One More Town/If You're Leaving Me ................................. 5

## BRIGITTE BOND
64  Blue Beat BB 212  Oh Yeah Baby/Blue Beat Baby ............................................................................... 45

## GRAHAM BOND (ORGANISATION)
64  Decca F 11909  Long Tall Shorty/Long Legged Baby (as Graham Bond Organization) ........................ 50
65  Columbia DB 7471  Wade In The Water/Tammy (as Graham Bond Organisation) ............................... 50
65  Columbia DB 7528  Tell Me (I'm Gonna Love Again)/Love Come Shining Through (as Graham Bond Organisation) ................................................................................................................... 50
65  Columbia DB 7647  Lease On Love/My Heart's In Little Pieces (as Graham Bond Organisation) ...... 35
66  Columbia DB 7838  St James Infirmary/Soul Tango (as Graham Bond Organisation) ........................ 40
67  Page One POF 014  You've Gotta Have Love Babe/I Love You ....................................................... 50
70  Warner Bros WB 8004  Walking In The Park/Springtime In The City (solo) .............................. 15
71  Vertigo 6059 042  Twelve Gates To The City/Water Water (as Graham Bond with Magick) ............. 30
65  Columbia 33SX 1711  THE SOUND OF '65 (LP, 1st pressing, with '33SX' on blue/black label and "sold in the U.K." label text) ................................................................................................. 400
*(N.B, LP has '33SX' on the sleeve, but only the 1st pressings have '33SX' on the label)*
65  Columbia 33SX 1750  THERE'S A BOND BETWEEN US (LP, 1st pressing, with '33SX' on blue/black label and "sold in the UK" label text) ......................................................................... 400
66  Columbia SX 1711  THE SOUND OF '65 (LP, 2nd pressing, with 'SX' on blue/black label) ............ 200
66  Columbia SX 1750  THERE'S A BOND BETWEEN US (LP, 2nd pressing, with 'SX' on blue/black label) ......... 150
69  Columbia SX 1750  THERE'S A BOND BETWEEN US (LP, 3rd Pressing, black/silver with boxed EMI logol) .... 60
69  Columbia SX 1711  THE SOUND OF '65 (LP, 3rd pressing, with boxed logo on silver/black label) ................. 60
71  Warner Bros WS 3001  SOLID BOND (2-LP, gatefold sleeve, orange label) ............................... 50
71  Vertigo 6360 021  HOLY MAGICK (LP, gatefold sleeve, large swirl label, as Graham Bond & Magick) ........ 150
71  Vertigo 6360 042  WE PUT OUR MAGICK ON YOU (LP, gatefold sleeve, swirl label, ............... 150
72  Philips 6382 010  BOND IN AMERICA (2-LP, solo [individual discs: 6499 200/1], unreleased) ................... 35
72  Philips 6382 010  THIS IS GRAHAM BOND (LP, solo) ......................................................... 20
88  Edsel DED 254  THE SOUND OF '65/THERE'S A BOND BETWEEN US (2-LP, reissue) ........................ 30
*(see also Jack Bruce, Dick Heckstall-Smith, Ginger Baker, Duffy Power, Who, Don Rendell, Steve York's Camelo Pardalis)*

## GRAHAM BOND & PETE BROWN
71  Greenwich GSS 104  Lost Tribe/Macumbe/Milk Is Turning Sour In My Shoes (maxi-single) ............... 25
72  Chapter One CHS-R 813  TWO HEADS ARE BETTER THAN ONE (LP) ..................................... 250
*(see also Pete Brown)*

## ISABEL BOND
68  Major Minor MM 565  Cry/When A Woman Loves A Man (in p/s) ......................................... 20
68  Major Minor MM 565  Cry/When A Woman Loves A Man ...................................................... 10
69  Major Minor MM 627  Don't Forget About Me/You'll Never Get The Chance Again ..................... 10

| | | | |
|---|---|---|---|
| 68 | Major Minor MMLP 28 | THE HEART AND SOUL OF ISABEL BOND (LP) | 50 |

## JACKI BOND
| | | | |
|---|---|---|---|
| 65 | Columbia DB 7719 | My Sister's Boy/Now I Know | 20 |
| 66 | Strike JH 302 | Tell Him To Go Away/Don't You Worry | 25 |
| 66 | Strike JH 320 | He Say/Why Can't I Love Him | 50 |

## JOHNNY BOND
| | | | |
|---|---|---|---|
| 60 | London HLU 9189 | Hot Rod Jalopy/Five-Minute Love Affair | 15 |
| 60 | London HL 7100 | Hot Rod Lincoln/Five-Minute Love Affair (export issue) | 15 |

## JOYCE BOND
| | | | |
|---|---|---|---|
| 66 | Island WI 3019 | Tell Me What It's All About/Tell Me Right Now | 50 |
| 67 | Airborne NBP 0011 | It's Alright/Mrs. Soul | 125 |
| 67 | Island WIP 6010 | Do The Teasy/Sugar | 20 |
| 67 | Island WIP 6018 | This Train/Not So With Me | 20 |
| 68 | Island WIP 6051 | Ob-La-Di, Ob-La-Da/Robin Hood Rides Again (as Joyce Bond Review) | 20 |
| 68 | Pama PM 718 | Back To School/They Wish | 18 |
| 69 | Pama PM 771 | Mr. Pitiful/Let's Get Married (as Joyce Bond & Little John) | 18 |
| 70 | Upfront UPF 5 | Wind Of Change/First In Line | 10 |
| 71 | Trojan TR 7837 | Help Me Make It Through The Night/Reconsider Our Love | 10 |
| 68 | Island ILP 968 | SOUL AND SKA (LP, mono only) | 175 |
| 72 | Windmill WMD 121 | SOUL OF CHANGE (LP) | 35 |

## LOUIS BOND
| | | | |
|---|---|---|---|
| 74 | Cooltempo 2005 | Tell Me When/Instrumental | 8 |

## OLIVER BOND
| | | | |
|---|---|---|---|
| 66 | Parlophone R 5476 | I Saw You All Alone/Let Me Love You | 20 |

*(see also Oliver Bone)*

## PETER BOND
| | | | |
|---|---|---|---|
| 77 | Trailer LER 2108 | IT'S ALL RIGHT FOR SOME (LP, yellow label) | 15 |

## RONNIE BOND (1)
| | | | |
|---|---|---|---|
| 69 | Page One POF 123 | Anything For You/Carolyn | 20 |

*(see also Troggs)*

## RONNIE BOND (2)
| | | | |
|---|---|---|---|
| 80 | Clap CLAP 1 | Fly On The Wall/You Can't Expect Miracles To Happen Tonight (p/s) | 10 |

## TONY BOND
| | | | |
|---|---|---|---|
| 66 | Decca SKL 4776 | PRESENTING TONY BOND (LP) | 20 |

*(see also Kestrels)*

## GARY (U.S.) BONDS
| | | | |
|---|---|---|---|
| 60 | Top Rank JAR 527 | New Orleans/Please Forgive Me (as U.S. Bonds) | 10 |
| 61 | Top Rank JAR 566 | Not Me/Give Me One More Chance (as U.S. Bonds) | 5 |
| 61 | Top Rank JAR 575 | Quarter To Three/Time Ole Story (as U.S. Bonds) | 5 |
| 61 | Top Rank JAR 581 | School Is Out/One Million Tears | 5 |
| 61 | Top Rank JAR 595 | School Is In/Trip To The Moon | 5 |
| 62 | Top Rank JAR 602 | Dear Lady Twist/Havin' So Much Fun | 5 |
| 62 | Top Rank JAR 615 | Twist Twist Senora/Food Of Love | 5 |
| 62 | Stateside SS 111 | Seven Day Weekend/Gettin' A Groove | 5 |
| 62 | Stateside SS 125 | Copy Cat/I'll Change That Too | 6 |
| 63 | Stateside SS 144 | Mixed Up Faculty/I Dig This Station | 6 |
| 63 | Stateside SS 179 | Where Did That Naughty Little Girl Go?/Do The Limbo With Me | 6 |
| 63 | Stateside SS 219 | What A Dream/I Don't Wanta Wait | 6 |
| 64 | Stateside SS 271 | New Orleans/Quarter To Three | 6 |
| 64 | Stateside SS 308 | My Sweet Baby Rose/Ella Is Yella | 6 |
| 67 | Stateside SS 2025 | Send Her To Me/Workin' For My Baby | 10 |
| 75 | London HLA 10485 | Grandma's Washboard Band/Believing You | 5 |
| 61 | Top Rank 35/114 | DANCE 'TIL QUARTER TO THREE WITH U.S. BONDS (LP) | 20 |
| 62 | Stateside SL 10001 | TWIST UP CALYPSO (LP) | 15 |

## OLIVER BONE & SOUNDS MAXIMUM
| | | | |
|---|---|---|---|
| 66 | Parlophone R 5527 | Knock On Wood/Jugger Tea | 30 |

*(see also Oliver Bond)*

## MATTHEW BONES
| | | | |
|---|---|---|---|
| 71 | Pye 7N 45100 | I Am The Pixi/Two Sugars | 15 |

## BONESCHI ELECTRONIC COMBO
| | | | |
|---|---|---|---|
| 73 | Chappell International CAL 4004 | SOUNDS ELECTRONIC (LP) | 30 |

## BONESHAKER
| | | | |
|---|---|---|---|
| 71 | London HLU 10332 | Sweetness/Badman Strikes Again | 60 |

## BONGO HERMAN (DAVIS)
| | | | |
|---|---|---|---|
| 70 | Songbird SB 1018 | True Grit/True Grit Version 2 (both credited with Les Crystalites but actually with Les & Crystalites) | 20 |
| 71 | Songbird SB 1060 | BONGO HERMAN & LES BUNNY: Know For I/CRYSTALITES: Version (B-side actually titled 'Know Fari') | 20 |
| 71 | Songbird SB 1066 | BONGO HERMAN & LES & BUNNY: Salaam (Peace)/CRYSTALITES: Scraper | 20 |
| 72 | Big BG 332 | Eternal Drums/ERROL DUNKLEY: Darling Ooh Wee (both actually by Hugh Roy Junior). | 20 |
| 72 | Green Door GD 4049 | African Breakfast/BONGO HERMAN & LES AND BUNNY: Chairman Of The Board | 20 |
| 72 | Songbird SB 1069 | We Are Praying/CRYSTALITES: Version | 15 |

## BONGO LES & HERMAN
| | | | |
|---|---|---|---|
| 69 | Explosion EX 2002 | Dr. Who Part 1/Dr. Who Part II | 20 |
| 71 | Songbird SB 1050 | Home Sweet Home/Hail I | 30 |

*(see also Heptones, Meditators)*

## JUKE BOY BONNER
| | | | |
|---|---|---|---|
| 69 | Blue Horizon 57-3163 | Runnin' Shoes/Jackin' In My Plans | 40 |
| 60s | Jan & Dil JR 451 | MORE DOWN HOME BLUES (EP) | 50 |
| 68 | Flyright LP 3501 | THE ONE MAN TRIO (LP) | 25 |
| 69 | Liberty LBS 83319 | THINGS AIN'T RIGHT (LP) | 25 |

## GRAHAM BONNET
| | | | |
|---|---|---|---|
| 72 | RCA RCA 2230 | Rare Specimen/Whisper In The Night | 25 |
| 73 | RCA RCA 2380 | Trying To Say Goodbye/Castles In The Air | 15 |
| 74 | DJM DJS 328 | Back Row In The Stalls/Ghost Writer In My Eye | 10 |
| 77 | Ring O' 2017 105 | It's All Over Now, Baby Blue/Heroes On My Picture Wall (company sleeve) | 8 |
| 77 | Ring O' 2017 106 | Danny/Rock Island Line (promo p/s) | 18 |
| 77 | Ring O' 2017 106 | Danny/Rock Island Line (company sleeve) | 6 |
| 77 | Ring O' 2017 110 | Goodnight And Goodmorning/Wino Song (company sleeve) | 6 |
| 78 | Ring O' 2017 114/POSP 2 | Warm Ride/10/12 Observation (company sleeve) | 6 |
| 78 | Ring O' POSP 002 | Warm Ride/10/12 Observation (12", company sleeve) | 10 |
| 81 | Vertigo VER 4 | That's The Way That It Is/Don't Tell Me To Go (p/s) | 6 |
| 81 | Vertigo VER 1 | Night Games/Out On The Water (p/s) | 5 |
| 81 | Vertigo VER 2 | Liar/Bad Days Are Gone (p/s) | 6 |
| 77 | Ring O' 2320 103 | GRAHAM BONNET (LP, with inner sleeve) | 18 |

*(see also Marbles, Rainbow, Cozy Powell, Forcefield, Fut, Michael Schenker Group, Jon Lord)*

## GRAHAM BONNEY
| | | | |
|---|---|---|---|
| 65 | Columbia DB 7773 | My Little World Is All Blue/Why Can't We Be Friends | 10 |
| 66 | Columbia DB 7843 | Super Girl/Hill Of Lovin' | 10 |
| 66 | Columbia DB 7934 | Baby's Gone/Later Tonight | 10 |
| 66 | Columbia DB 8005 | No One Knows/Mixed Up Baby Girl | 10 |
| 67 | Columbia DB 8111 | Thank You Baby/Briony | 5 |
| 67 | Columbia DB 8142 | Happy Together/That Bad Day | 5 |
| 67 | Columbia DB 8283 | Papa Joe/My Jenny | 5 |
| 68 | Columbia DB 8338 | By The Way I Love You/Devil's Child | 5 |
| 68 | Columbia DB 8382 | I'll Be Your Baby Tonight/Back From Baltimore | 5 |
| 68 | Columbia DB 8464 | Frenzy/Something I've Got To Tell You | 5 |
| 69 | Columbia DB 8531 | Get Ready/Fly Me High Lorelei | 10 |
| 69 | Columbia DB 8592 | Leanda Angeline/Mixing The Wine | 5 |
| 70 | Columbia DB 8648 | Sign On The Dotted Line/Words We Said | 25 |
| 70 | Columbia DB 8687 | When Evelyn Was Mine/Sunny Has Gone | 20 |
| 66 | Columbia SX/SCX 6052 | SUPER GIRL (LP, mono/stereo) | 20 |

*(see also Riot Squad)*

## BONNIE
| | | | |
|---|---|---|---|
| 67 | Ska Beat JB 270 | Do You Get The Message/A Man Called Dan | 20 |
| 69 | Jolly JY 014 | Loving You/Shoo Be Doo | 15 |

## BONNIE & SKITTO
| | | | |
|---|---|---|---|
| 63 | Island WI 122 | Get Ready (actually by Vikings [alias Maytals])/ DON DRUMMOND: The Rocket | 30 |

## BONNIE & TREASURES
| | | | |
|---|---|---|---|
| 65 | London HLU 9998 | Home Of The Brave/Our Song | 35 |

## BONO & GAVIN FRIDAY
| | | | |
|---|---|---|---|
| 94 | Island 12IS593 | In The Name Of The Father (7" Edit)/(12" Remix)/(12" Beats Mix)/ (LP Instrumental) (12" single) | 10 |

*(see also U2, Clannad & Bono, The Passengers, Virgin Prunes)*

## BONOBO
| | | | |
|---|---|---|---|
| 00 | Tru Thoughts TRU 004 | Terrapin (12") | 15 |
| 00 | Tru Thoughts TRU LP 007 | ANIMAL MAGIC (2xLP) | 30 |
| 01 | Ninja Tune ZEN 63 | ANIMAL MAGIC (2xLP) | 30 |
| 02 | Tru Thoughts TRU LP 031 | ONE OFFS...REMIXES & B SIDES (2xLP) | 30 |
| 03 | Ninja Tune ZEN 80 | DIAL M FOR MONKEY (2xLP) | 30 |
| 06 | Ninja Tune ZEN 119 | DAYS TO COME (2xLP) | 30 |

## BONZO DOG (DOO-DAH) BAND
| | | | |
|---|---|---|---|
| 66 | Parlophone R 5430 | My Brother Makes The Noises For The Talkies/I'm Gonna Bring A Watermelon To My Gal Tonight | 20 |
| 66 | Parlophone R 5499 | Alley Oop/Button Up Your Overcoat | 20 |
| 67 | Liberty LBF 15040 | Equestrian Statue/The Intro And The Outro | 10 |
| 68 | Liberty LBF 15144 | Urban Spaceman/Canyons Of Your Mind (initially pressing with spoken intro to B-side) | 10 |
| 68 | Liberty LBF 15144 | Urban Spaceman/Canyons Of Your Mind (later pressing without spoken intro to A-side) | 5 |
| 69 | Liberty LBF 15201 | Mr. Apollo/Ready Mades | 7 |
| 69 | Liberty LBF 15273 | I Want To Be With You/We Were Wrong | 7 |
| 70 | Liberty LBF 15314 | You Done My Brain In/Mr. Slater's Parrot | 7 |
| 73 | United Artists UP 35602 | The Intro And The Outro/Hello Mabel | 7 |
| 74 | United Artists UP 35662 | Mr. Slater's Parrot/Noises For The Leg | 7 |
| 92 | China WOK 2021 | No Matter Who You Vote For The Government Always Gets In/ NEIL INNES: Them (promo only) | 15 |
| 67 | Liberty LBL 83056 | GORILLA (LP, mono with booklet) | 80 |
| 67 | Liberty LBS 83056 | GORILLA (LP, stereo with booklet) | 40 |
| 67 | Liberty LBL/LBS 83056 | GORILLA (LP, without booklet, blue label) | 20 |
| 71 | Liberty LBL/LBS 83158E | THE DOUGHNUT IN GRANNY'S GREENHOUSE (LP, gatefold sleeve, with booklet, blue label) | 70 |
| 71 | Liberty LBS 83158E | THE DOUGHNUT IN GRANNY'S GREENHOUSE (LP, gatefold sleeve, without booklet, blue label) | 25 |
| 69 | Liberty LBS 83257 | TADPOLES (LP, die-cut sleeve, with insert, blue label) | 50 |
| 69 | Liberty LBS 83257 | TADPOLES (LP, die-cut sleeve, without insert, blue label) | 25 |

| | | | |
|---|---|---|---|
| 69 | Liberty LBS 83290 | KEYNSHAM (LP, gatefold sleeve, blue label) | 35 |
| 72 | United Artists UAS 29288 | LET'S MAKE UP AND BE FRIENDLY (LP) | 22 |
| 74 | United Artists UAD 60071/2 | THE HISTORY OF THE BONZOS (2-LP, gatefold sleeve with booklet) | 25 |

*(see also Vivian Stanshall, Neil Innes, Grimms, Roger Ruskin Spear, Topo D. Bill)*

## BETTY BOO
| | | | |
|---|---|---|---|
| 79 | Grapevine GRP 125 | Say It Isn't So/Say It Isn't So (Instrumental) | 20 |
| 98 | Wigan Casino 210 | Say It Isn't So/BELLES: Don't Pretend (p/s) | 10 |

## BOOGALOOS
| | | | |
|---|---|---|---|
| 69 | President PT 253 | Rule Britannia/Love Is Blind | 12 |

## BOOK EM DANNO
| | | | |
|---|---|---|---|
| 89 | Splinter SG 1 | Brand New Disease/Eighties Hero/Top Of The Agenda/You'd Better Believe It (12") | 80 |

## JAMES BOOKER
| | | | |
|---|---|---|---|
| 61 | Vogue V 9177 | Cool Turkey/Gonzo | 30 |
| 63 | Vocalion VEP 170154 | GONZO (EP) | 60 |

## BOOKER T (JAMAICA)
| | | | |
|---|---|---|---|
| 75 | Ethnic Fight EF 016 | Down Pressure/Pressure Dub | 25 |
| 76 | Ethnic Fight 2 | Eleanor/Version | 5 |

## BOOKER T. & THE M.G.S
| | | | |
|---|---|---|---|
| 62 | London HLK 9595 | Green Onions/Behave Yourself | 20 |
| 63 | London HLK 9670 | Jelly Bread/Aw' Mercy | 10 |
| 63 | London HLK 9784 | Chinese Checkers/Plum Nellie | 10 |
| 65 | Atlantic AT 4033 | Boot-Leg/Outrage | 10 |
| 66 | Atlantic AT 4063 | Be My Lady/Red Beans And Rice | 10 |
| 66 | Atlantic 584 044 | My Sweet Potato/Booker Loo | 10 |
| 66 | Atlantic 584 060 | Jingle Bells/Winter Wonderland | 5 |
| 67 | Atlantic 584 088 | Green Onions/Boot-Leg | 6 |
| 67 | Stax 601 009 | Hip Hug Her/Summertime (initially dark blue label) | 10 |
| 67 | Stax 601 009 | Hip Hug Her/Summertime (later pressing with light blue label) | 5 |
| 67 | Stax 601 018 | Groovin'/Slim Jenkins' Place | 5 |
| 67 | Stax 601 026 | Chinese Checkers/Plum Nellie (reissue) | 5 |
| 68 | Stax STAX 102 | Soul Limbo/Heads Or Tails | 5 |
| 69 | Stax STAX 119 | Time Is Tight/Hang 'Em High | 10 |
| 69 | Stax STAX 127 | Soul Clap '69/Mrs. Robinson | 10 |
| 69 | Stax STAX 136 | The Horse/Slum Baby | 5 |
| 71 | Stax 2025 026 | Melting Pot/Kinda Easy Like | 5 |
| 72 | Stax 2025 074 | Jamaica This Morning (as the MGs)/Fuquawi | 5 |
| 63 | London REK 1367 | R&B WITH BOOKER T (EP) | 20 |
| 64 | Atlantic AET 6002 | R&B WITH BOOKER T VOL. 2 (EP) | 20 |
| 64 | London HA-K 8182 | GREEN ONIONS (LP, plum label) | 30 |
| 65 | Atlantic ATL 5027 | SOUL DRESSING (LP, plum label, 1st pressing with green & white sleeve) | 30 |
| 66 | Atlantic 587/588 033 | GREEN ONIONS (LP, reissue, mono/stereo) | 15 |
| 67 | Stax 589 002 | AND NOW! (LP) | 30 |
| 68 | Stax 589 013 | SOUL CHRISTMAS (LP) | 15 |
| 68 | Stax 230 002/231 002 | DOIN' OUR THING (LP) | 15 |
| 68 | Stax (S)XATS 1001 | SOUL LIMBO (LP) | 15 |
| 69 | Atco 228 004 | GET READY (LP) | 15 |
| 69 | Stax (S)XATS 1005 | UPTIGHT (LP, soundtrack, with Judy Clay) | 15 |
| 69 | Stax (S)XATS 1015 | THE BOOKER T. SET (LP) | 15 |
| 69 | Atco 228 015 | THE BEST OF BOOKER T. AND THE M.G.s (LP) | 15 |
| 70 | Stax SXATS 1031 | McLEMORE AVENUE (LP) | 15 |
| 71 | Stax 2325 030 | MELTING POT (LP) | 15 |

*(see also Mar-Keys, Steve Cropper, Albert King, Judy Clay)*

## BOOMBACK
| | | | |
|---|---|---|---|
| 85 | Headphone HP/DC/003 | Ghetto Life/Roadblock (12") | 125 |

## BOOMERANGS
| | | | |
|---|---|---|---|
| 64 | Fontana TF 507 | Rockin' Robin/Don't Let Her Be Your Baby | 10 |
| 66 | Pye 7N 17049 | Dream World/Upgraded | 5 |
| 65 | Fontana TF 555 | Another Tear Falls/Fun Fun Fun | 5 |

## PAT BOONE
### SINGLES
| | | | |
|---|---|---|---|
| 55 | London HLD 8172 | Ain't That A Shame/Tennessee Saturday Night ()gold label) | 35 |
| 55 | London HLD 8197 | At My Front Door/No Arms Can Ever Hold You | 10 |
| 56 | London HLD 8233 | Gee Whittakers/Take The Time | 10 |
| 56 | London HLD 8253 | I'll Be Home/Tutti Frutti | 10 |
| 56 | London HLD 8291 | Long Tall Sally/Just As Long As I'm With You | 10 |
| 56 | London HLD 8303 | I Almost Lost My Mind/I'm In Love With You | 10 |
| 56 | London HLD 8316 | Two Hearts, Two Kisses/Rich In Love | 5 |
| 56 | London HLD 8346 | Friendly Persuasion (Thee I Love)/Chains Of Love | 5 |

*(The above 45s were originally issued with gold lettering labels; later silver lettering copies are worth half these values.)*

| | | | |
|---|---|---|---|
| 59 | London HLD 8824 | There's Good Rockin' Tonight/With The Wind And The Rain In Your Hair | 10 |

### EXPORT SINGLES
| | | | |
|---|---|---|---|
| 56 | London HL 7007 | I'll Be Home/Tutti Frutti | 10 |
| 56 | London HL 7010 | Long Tall Sally/Just As Long As I'm With You | 10 |

### ALBUMS
| | | | |
|---|---|---|---|
| 63 | London HA-D 8109 | SINGS ... GUESS WHO? (LP, mono) | 20 |
| 63 | London SH-D 8109 | SINGS ... GUESS WHO? (LP, stereo) | 30 |

*(see also Fontane Sisters)*

## BOONE FAMILY
| | | | |
|---|---|---|---|
| 74 | Mowest MW 3022 | Please Mr Postman/Friends | 5 |

## BOONES FARM
| | | | |
|---|---|---|---|
| 72 | CBS 8212 | If You Can't Be My Woman/Start Today | 20 |

## BOO RADLEYS
| | | | |
|---|---|---|---|
| 92 | Creation CRELP 120 | EVERYTHING'S ALRIGHT FOREVER (LP, first 1000 with free Sunfly 7") | 15 |
| 93 | Creation CRELP 149 | GIANT STEPS (2-LP) | 25 |
| 95 | Creation CRELP 179 | WAKE UP! (LP, gatefold sleeve) | 15 |

## ANTHONY BOOTH
| | | | |
|---|---|---|---|
| 69 | Tangerine DP 0008 | Till Death Do Us Part/September Days | 7 |

## BILL BOOTH REVIVAL MACHINE
| | | | |
|---|---|---|---|
| 75 | Private Press HEADSRTM/ CUS038 | FACE TO FACE (LP) | 18 |

## KEN BOOTHE
| | | | |
|---|---|---|---|
| 66 | Island WI 3020 | The Train Is Coming/This Is Me | 50 |
| 66 | Island WI 3035 | I Don't Want To See You Cry/Baby I Need You (B-side actually by Wailers) | 100 |
| 66 | Ska Beat JB 248 | You're No Good/SOULETTES: Don't Care What The People Say | 80 |
| 67 | Doctor Bird DB 1110 | Say You/LYN TAITT & JETS: Smokey Places | 50 |
| 67 | Coxsone CS 7006 | Lonely Teardrops/Oowee Baby | 70 |
| 67 | Coxsone CS 7020 | Home Home Home/SOUL BROTHERS: Windell | 40 |
| 67 | Caltone TONE 107 | The One I Love/You Left The Water Running | 75 |
| 67 | Studio One SO 2000 | Feel Good/Mustang Sally | 35 |
| 67 | Studio One SO 2012 | Puppet On A String/ROLAND ALPHONSO: Look Away | 18 |
| 67 | Studio One SO 2014 | Fatty Fatty (actually Heptones)/Mother Word (actually by Delroy Wilson) | 20 |
| 67 | Studio One SO 2026 | Why Did You Leave (actually by Leroy Sibbles)/Don't Try To Reach Me (actually by Gaylads) | 30 |
| 68 | Studio One SO 2039 | When I Fall In Love/HEPTONES: Christmas Time | 35 |
| 68 | Studio One SO 2041 | The Girl I Left Behind/TERMITES: My Last Love | 90 |
| 68 | Studio One SO 2053 | Tomorrow/Movin' Away | 70 |
| 68 | Fab FAB 63 | I Remember Someone/Can't You See? | 150 |
| 68 | Coxsone CS 7041 | Everybody Knows/GAYLADS: I'm Free | 60 |
| 69 | Coxsone CS 7094 | Sherry/I've Got You | 40 |
| 69 | Studio One SO 2073 | You're On My Mind/RICHARD ACE & SOUND DIMENSIONS: Love To Cherish | 40 |
| 69 | High Note HS 003 | Lady With The Starlight/LESLIE BUTLER & COUNT OSSIE: Gay Drums | 25 |
| 69 | Bamboo BAM 4 | Pleading/COUNT MATCHUKI & SOUND DIMENSION: Call 1143 | 70 |
| 69 | Bamboo BAM 8 | Be Yourself/SOUND DIMENSION: Rathid | 70 |
| 70 | Trojan TR 7716 | Why, Baby Why/Keep My Love From Fading | 15 |
| 70 | Trojan TR 7756 | Freedom Street/BEVERLEY'S ALLSTARS: Freedom Version | 15 |
| 70 | Trojan TR 7772 | It's Gonna Take A Miracle/Now I Know | 25 |
| 70 | Trojan TR 7780 | Drums Of Freedom/BEVERLEY'S ALLSTARS: Version | 15 |
| 70 | Gas GAS 169 | Give To Me/Why | 8 |
| 70 | Jackpot JP 748 | You Left The Water Running/PHIL PRATT ALL STARS: Cut Throat | 30 |
| 70 | Punch PH 30 | Artibella/PRATT ALLSTARS: Version Of Artibella | 30 |
| 70 | Punch PH 33 | Morning/Morning (Version) | 8 |
| 71 | Punch PH 70 | Stop Your Crying/CONSCIOUS MINDS: Suffering Through The Nation | 10 |
| 71 | Banana BA 352 | Original Six (Parts 1 & 2) | 12 |
| 71 | Summit SUM 8518 | I Wish It Could Be Peaceful Again/BEVERLEY'S ALLSTARS: Peaceful Version | 15 |
| 71 | Summit SUM 8519 | Your Feeling And Mine/BEVERLEY'S ALLSTARS: Your Feeling Version | 15 |
| 71 | Big Shot BI 590 | So Nice/So Nice Version | 20 |
| 71 | Green Door GD 4002 | Medley Version/Medley Version 2 | 10 |
| 71 | Dynamic DYN 411 | Hallelujah/Trying To Reach | 10 |
| 72 | Camel CA 91 | Ain't No Sunshine/LLOYD & HORTENSE: You Are Everything | 25 |
| 72 | Dynamic DYN 453 | Tears From My Eyes/CONSCIOUS MINDS: Tears From My Eyes Version | 5 |
| 72 | Pama Supreme PS 369 | Look What You've Done/LLOYD CHARMERS: Look What You've Done Version | 10 |
| 72 | Ashanti ASH 403 | Make Me Feel Alright (with The Incrowd)/INCROWD: Down On The Corner | 8 |
| 73 | Trojan TR 7893 | Is It Because I'm Black/Black, Gold And Green | 12 |
| 73 | Green Door GD 4053 | Silver Words/Rasta God Version | 8 |
| 73 | Mirto 100 | Is It Because I'm Black?/Just Like A Shelter (as The Messengers) | 5 |
| 74 | Trojan TR 7920 | Everything I Own/Drum Song | 5 |
| 74 | Trojan TR 7944 | Crying Over You/Now You Can See Me Again | 5 |
| 75 | Fab FAB 270 | Thinking/Moving Away | 20 |
| 75 | Torpedo TOR 35 | Lady With The Starlight/Light Version | 15 |
| 75 | Torpedo TOR 54 | Say You/You Version | 8 |
| 78 | Trojan TR 9036 | Freedom Day/Love Don't Love Nobody | 10 |
| 79 | Attack TACK 6 | You're No Good/PRINCE JAMMY: Out Of Order Dub (12") | 12 |
| 67 | Studio One SOL 9001 | MR. ROCK STEADY (LP) | 200 |
| 73 | Trojan TRLS 58 | BLACK, GOLD AND GREEN (LP) | 40 |
| 74 | Trojan TRLS 83 | LETS GET IT ON (LP) | 20 |
| 74 | Trojan TRLS 95 | EVERYTHING I OWN (LP) | 15 |
| 75 | Trojan TRLS 120 | FREEDOM STREET (LP) | 15 |
| 79 | Phil Pratt PP01LP | GOT TO GET AWAY (LP) | 40 |
| 87 | Trojan TRLS 249 | EIGHTEEN CLASSIC SONGS (LP) | 15 |

*(see also Stranger & Ken, Gaylads, Richard Ace, Lloyd & Ken)*

## BOOTLES
| | | | |
|---|---|---|---|
| 64 | Vocalion VN 9216 | I'll Let You Hold My Hand/Never Till Now | 25 |

## BOOTS
| | | | |
|---|---|---|---|
| 68 | CBS 3550 | Even The Bad Times Are Good/The Animal In Me | 20 |
| 68 | CBS 3833 | Keep Your Lovelight Burning/Give Me One More Chance | 25 |
| 70 | Youngblood YB 1018 | You Better Run/A To D | 60 |

## DAVE BOOTS
| | | | |
|---|---|---|---|
| 60s | Solent SM 013 | GREEN SATIN AND GOLD (LP) | 100 |

## BOOTS FOR DANCING
| | | | |
|---|---|---|---|
| 80 | Pop Aural POP 002 | BOOTS FOR DANCING EP (12") | 15 |
| 80 | Pop Aural POP 006 | Hesitate/Rain Song (p/s) | 10 |
| 82 | Repop X WAY 100 | Ooh Bop Sh'bam/Money (p/s) | 8 |

## BOOTSY'S RUBBER BAND
| | | | |
|---|---|---|---|
| 76 | Warner Bros K 56200 | STRETCHIN' OUT IN BOOTSY'S RUBBER BAND (LP) | 18 |
| 77 | Warner Bros K 56302 | AHH... THE NAME IS BOOTSY, BABY! (LP, gatefold sleeve) | 18 |
| 78 | Warner Bros K 56424 | BOOTSY? PLAYER OF THE YEAR (LP, gatefold sleeve) | 15 |
| 79 | Warner Bros K 56615 | THE BOOT IS MADE FOR FONK-N (LP, with inner sleeve) | 15 |
| 81 | Warner Bros K 56998 | THE ONE GIVETH, THE COUNT TAKETH AWAY (LP) | 15 |

*(see also Parliament, Funkadelic)*

## BOOVER BOYS
| | | | |
|---|---|---|---|
| 70 | Torpedo TOR 22 | A.G.G.R.O/Sha La La La Lee | 100 |

## BOP & BELTONES
| | | | |
|---|---|---|---|
| 67 | Coxsone CS 7012 | Treat Me Good/PETER TOUCH & WAILERS: Dancing Time (B-side actually by Bop & Beltones) | 50 |

*(see also Beltones, Soul Vendors, Jackie Mittoo)*

## RANNY BOP
| | | | |
|---|---|---|---|
| 70 | Escort ERT 837 | Crock Iron/Memphis Bop | 20 |
| 70 | Gas GAS 155 | Pipe Dream/Suck Suck | 20 |

## BORDER
| | | | |
|---|---|---|---|
| 78 | Pear PEAR 1 | Song For J/Easy/Going Away (p/s, 500 only) | 40 |

## BORE-TOWN BOP
| | | | |
|---|---|---|---|
| 81 | Vital VIS001 | Try/Surf's Up (p/s) | 15 |

## RICHARD BORIE & PDF
| | | | |
|---|---|---|---|
| 80 | Don't Panic PDF 1 | On and On/Sorry (p/s) | 8 |

## BORZOI
| | | | |
|---|---|---|---|
| 87 | CS 2509 | It's Called Rincarnation/I'm At War (p/s) | 20 |

## BOSCH
| | | | |
|---|---|---|---|
| 80 | Trific TRIF 1 | The Two Tree/Packing Jean (p/s) | 25 |

## BOSS
| | | | |
|---|---|---|---|
| 86 | Power House (no cat. no.) | One Good Reason/Wake Up Children (p/s, with lyric sheet) | 6 |

## BOSS ATTACK
| | | | |
|---|---|---|---|
| 71 | Fab FAB 187 | Hell-El/TEARDROPS: Let Me Be Free | 15 |

## BOSS COMBO
| | | | |
|---|---|---|---|
| 62 | Coral LVA 9205 | GOLDEN ROCK AND ROLL INSTRUMENTALS (LP) | 20 |

## BOSS GUITARS
| | | | |
|---|---|---|---|
| 65 | London HA-R/SH-R 8237 | PLAY THE WINNERS (LP) | 20 |

## EARL BOSTIC (ORCHESTRA)
### SINGLES
| | | | |
|---|---|---|---|
| 54 | Parlophone MSP 6075 | Off Shore/What! No Pearls | 10 |
| 54 | Parlophone MSP 6089 | Deep Purple/Smoke Rings | 10 |
| 54 | Parlophone MSP 6105 | Melancholy Serenade/Don't You Do It | 10 |
| 54 | Parlophone MSP 6110 | Jungle Drums/Danube Waves | 10 |
| 54 | Parlophone MSP 6119 | Mambolino/Blue Skies | 10 |
| 54 | Parlophone MSP 6131 | These Foolish Things/Mambostic | 10 |
| 54 | Parlophone CMSP 8 | Cherokee/The Song Is Ended (export issue) | 10 |
| 55 | Parlophone MSP 6162 | Melody Of Love/Sweet Lorraine | 10 |
| 56 | Vogue V 2145 | Flamingo/Sleep | 10 |
| 56 | Vogue V 2148 | Moonglow/Ain't Misbehaving | 10 |
| 56 | Parlophone R 4208 | The Bo-Do Rock (with Bill Doggett)/Mean To Me | 10 |
| 56 | Parlophone R 4232 | For All We Know/Beyond The Blue Horizon | 10 |
| 57 | Parlophone R 4263 | I Hear A Rhapsody/Harlem Nocturne | 8 |
| 57 | Parlophone R 4278 | Bubbins Rock/Indiana (with Bill Doggett) | 8 |
| 57 | Parlophone R 4305 | Avalon/Too Fine For Crying (B-side with Bill Jones) | 8 |
| 57 | Parlophone R 4370 | Temptation/September Song | 8 |
| 58 | Parlophone R 4460 | Over The Waves Rock/Twilight Time | 8 |
| 59 | Parlophone DP 553 | Barcarolle/My Reverie (export single) | 8 |
| 62 | Ember JBS 708 | Tuxedo Junction/Air Mail Special | 8 |
| 66 | Island WI 271 | Honeymoon Night/PATSY COLE: Disappointed Bride | 15 |

### EPs
| | | | |
|---|---|---|---|
| 54 | Parlophone GEP 8506 | FLAMINGO | 10 |
| 55 | Parlophone GEP 8513 | LINGER AWHILE | 10 |
| 55 | Parlophone GEP 8520 | EARL BOSTIC AND HIS ALTO SAX | 15 |
| 55 | Vogue EPV 1010 | EARL BOSTIC | 15 |
| 56 | Vogue EPV 1111 | VELVET SUNSET | 10 |
| 56 | Parlophone GEP 8539 | WRAP IT UP | 10 |
| 58 | Parlophone GEP 8701 | BOSTIC BEAT | 20 |
| 58 | Parlophone GEP 8741 | ROCKING WITH BOSTIC | 20 |

### ALBUMS
| | | | |
|---|---|---|---|
| 54 | Vogue LDE 100 | EARL BOSTIC AND HIS ORCHESTRA (10") | 30 |
| 54 | Parlophone PMD 1016 | EARL BOSTIC AND HIS ALTO SAX (10" LP) | 25 |
| 56 | Parlophone PMD 1040 | EARL BOSTIC AND HIS ALTO SAX NO. 2 | 25 |
| 58 | Parlophone PMD 1054 | BOSTIC MEETS DOGGETT (10" LP, with Bill Doggett) | 30 |
| 58 | Parlophone PMD 1068 | BOSTIC ROCKS (10" LP) | 30 |

MINT VALUE £

| | | | |
|---|---|---|---|
| 59 | Parlophone PMD 1071 | BOSTIC SHOWCASE OF SWINGING DANCE HITS (10" LP) | 20 |
| 59 | Parlophone PMD 1074 | SWEET TUNES OF THE FANTASTIC FIFTIES | 20 |
| 59 | Parlophone PMD 1115 | SWEET TUNES OF THE ROARIN' TWENTIES (10" LP) | 15 |
| 59 | Parlophone PMD 1117 | SWEET TUNES OF THE SWINGIN' THIRTIES (10" LP) | 15 |
| 59 | Parlophone PMD 1119 | SWEET TUNES OF THE SENTIMENTAL FORTIES (10" LP) | 15 |
| 60 | Parlophone PMC 1125 | PLAYS THE HIT TUNES OF THE BIG BROADWAY SHOWS (12" LP) | 15 |

*(see also Bill Doggett, Sonny Carter)*

## BOSTON
| | | | |
|---|---|---|---|
| 76 | Epic EPCH 81611 | BOSTON (LP, audiophile pressing) | 20 |
| 76 | Epic EPC 81611 | BOSTON (LP, picture disc) | 12 |
| 78 | Epic E 9945050 | DON'T LOOK BACK (LP, picture disc) | 12 |
| 86 | MCA MCGP 6017 | THIRD STAGE (LP, picture disc) | 15 |
| 94 | MCA MCGP 6017 | WALK ON (LP, picture disc) | 15 |

## BOSTON BOPPERS
| | | | |
|---|---|---|---|
| 74 | Penny Farthing PEN 828 | Did You Get What You Wanted/Whirlwind Girl | 25 |

## BOSTON CRABS
| | | | |
|---|---|---|---|
| 65 | Columbia DB 7586 | Down In Mexico/Who? | 20 |
| 65 | Columbia DB 7679 | As Long As I Have You/Alley Oop | 20 |
| 66 | Columbia DB 7830 | Gin House/You Didn't Have To Be So Nice | 20 |

## BOSTON DEXTERS
| | | | |
|---|---|---|---|
| 64 | Contemporary CR 101 | Matchbox/La Bamba | 200 |
| 64 | Contemporary CR 102 | You've Been Talking About Me/Nothing's Gonna Change Me | 150 |
| 64 | Contemporary CR 103 | What Kind Of Girl Are You/I've Got Troubles Of My Own | 150 |
| 65 | Columbia DB 7498 | I Believe To My Soul/I've Got Something To Tell You | 50 |
| 65 | Columbia DB 7641 | Try Hard/No More Tears | 45 |

*(see also Tam White)*

## JACK ANGLIN BOSTON AND THE SOULITES
| | | | |
|---|---|---|---|
| 69 | Ackee ACK 103 | Starvation/Slave | 15 |

## BO STREET RUNNERS
| | | | |
|---|---|---|---|
| 64 | Decca F 11986 | Bo Street Runner/Tell Me | 50 |
| 65 | Columbia DB 7488 | Tell Me What You're Gonna Do/And I Do Just What I Want | 60 |
| 65 | Columbia DB 7640 | Baby Never Say Goodbye/Get Out Of My Way | 60 |
| 66 | Columbia DB 7901 | Drive My Car/So Very Woman (featuring Mike [Too Much] Patto) | 70 |
| 64 | Oak RGJ 131 | BO STREET RUNNERS (EP, 49 copies only) | 1000 |

*(see also [Mike] Patto, Timebox, Chicago Line, Cheynes, Fleetwood Mac)*

## CONNIE BOSWELL
| | | | |
|---|---|---|---|
| 54 | Brunswick 05319 | T-E-N-N-E-S-S-E-E (Spells ...)/If I Give My Heart To You | 7 |
| 55 | Brunswick 05397 | How Important Can It Be?/Fill My Heart With Happiness | 7 |

## EVE BOSWELL
| | | | |
|---|---|---|---|
| 53 | Parlophone MSP 6006 | Sugar Bush/Moon Above Malaya (China Nights) | 10 |
| 55 | Parlophone MSP 6158 | Ready, Willing And Able/Pam-Poo-Dey | 10 |
| 55 | Parlophone MSP 6160 | The Heart You Break (May Be Your Own)/Tika Tika Tok | 10 |
| 56 | Parlophone MSP 6208 | Young And Foolish/Where You Are | 10 |
| 56 | Parlophone MSP 6220 | It's Almost Tomorrow/Cookie | 10 |
| 56 | Parlophone MSP 6250 | Saries Marias/Come Back My Love | 10 |
| 56 | Parlophone R 4230 | True Love/Where In The World Is Billy? | 10 |
| 57 | Parlophone R 4275 | Rock Bobbin' Boats/Tra La La | 10 |
| 57 | Parlophone R 4299 | Chantez, Chantez/She Said (Aunt Magnolia) | 5 |
| 57 | Parlophone R 4328 | With All My Heart/Sugar Candy | 5 |
| 57 | Parlophone R 4341 | The Gypsy In My Soul/Stop Whistlin' Wolf | 5 |
| 57 | Parlophone R 4362 | Swedish Polka (Chickadee)/Tell My Love | 5 |
| 57 | Parlophone GEP 8601 | THE ENCHANTING EVE (EP) | 10 |
| 56 | Parlophone PMD 1039 | SUGAR AND SPICE (10" LP) | 75 |
| 57 | Parlophone PMC 1038 | SENTIMENTAL EVE (LP) | 200 |
| 59 | Parlophone PMC 1105 | FOLLOWING THE SUN AROUND (LP) | 100 |

## SIMON BOSWELL
| | | | |
|---|---|---|---|
| 75 | Transatlantic TRA 307 | MIND PARASITES (LP) | 18 |

*(see also Advertising)*

## BOTHY BAND
| | | | |
|---|---|---|---|
| 75 | Polydor 2383379 | THE BOTHY BAND (LP) | 18 |

## RAMON BOUCHE
| | | | |
|---|---|---|---|
| 67 | Columbia 8257 | I Gotta Be With You/The Real Thing (DJ Copy) | 200 |

## BOULEVARD
| | | | |
|---|---|---|---|
| 79 | Chopper CHOP 5D | MAGIC MAN (12", red vinyl, no p/s) | 15 |
| 81 | Boulevard VARD 1 | Dawn Raid/Take It Or Leave It (p/s) | 40 |

## BOUNCING FLOWERS
| | | | |
|---|---|---|---|
| 81 | Rewind REWIND 8 | Fire/Expanding Cases (p/s) | 10 |

## BOURBON STREET MISSION
| | | | |
|---|---|---|---|
| 71 | Horse HOSS 5 | Jesus Is Just Alright/You Knew How To Hurt A Man | 5 |

## DENNIS BOVELL
| | | | |
|---|---|---|---|
| 78 | Tempus TEMLP 001 | STRICTLY DUBWISE (LP) | 25 |

*(see also Matumbi, Rama)*

## BOW BELLS
| | | | |
|---|---|---|---|
| 65 | Polydor 56030 | Not To Be Taken/I'll Try Not To Hold It Against You | 6 |
| 66 | Parlophone R 5520 | Belinda/When You're In | 6 |

*(see also Nola York)*

## RICKY BOWDEN
| 63 | HMV POP 1162 | Alone To Cry/I'd Be Ashamed ............................................................. 10 |

## JIMMY BOWEN
| 57 | Columbia DB 3915 | I'm Stickin' With You/Ever Lovin' Fingers ........................................ 30 |
| 57 | Columbia DB 3984 | Warm Up To Me, Baby/I Trusted You ............................................. 30 |
| 57 | Columbia DB 4027 | Cross Over/It's Shameful ................................................................ 15 |
| 58 | Columbia DB 4184 | The Two Step/By The Light Of The Silvery Moon ........................... 15 |
| 65 | Reprise RS 23043 | The Eagle (demos & some issues list "The Golden Eagle")/Spanish Cricket ................ 15 |
| 58 | Columbia SEG 7757 | MEET JIMMY BOWEN (EP) ............................................................. 30 |
| 58 | Columbia SEG 7793 | MEET JIMMY BOWEN NO. 2 (EP) ................................................... 30 |

## BEN BOWERS
| 55 | Columbia SCM 5192 | The Kentuckian Song/The Man From Laramie ................................. 5 |

## DAVID BOWIE
### SINGLES : DEMO SINGLES
| 66 | Pye 7N 17020 | Can't Help Thinking About Me/And I Say To Myself (Demo copy, push-out centre) ... 1000 |
| 66 | Pye 7N 17020 | Can't Help Thinking About Me/And I Say To Myself (demo copy, solid centre) ............ 500 |
| 66 | Pye 7N 17079 | Do Anything You Say/Good Morning Girl (Demo copy, push-out centre) .................... 1000 |
| 66 | Pye 7N 17079 | Do Anything You Say/Good Morning Girl (Demo copy, solid centre) ...................... 500 |
| 66 | Pye 7N 17157 | I Dig Everything/I'm Not Losing Sleep (Demo copy, push-out centre) ....................... 1000 |
| 66 | Pye 7N 17157 | I Dig Everything/I'm Not Losing sleep (Demo copy, solid centre) ....................... 500 |
| 66 | Deram DM 107 | Rubber Band/The London Boys (Demo copy) ............................................. 300 |
| 67 | Deram DM 123 | The Laughing Gnome/The Gospel According To Tony Day (Demo copy) ............ 200 |
| 67 | Deram DM 135 | Love You Till Tuesday/Did You Ever Have A Dream (Demo copy) ............... 200 |
| 70 | Mercury MF 1135 | The Prettiest Star/Conversation Piece (Demo copy) ............................. 300 |
| 70 | Mercury 6052 026 | Memory Of A Free Festival Parts 1 & 2 (Demo copy, large centre) ............ 300 |
| 70 | Mercury 6052 026 | Memory Of A Free Festival Parts 1 & 2 (Demo copy, push-out centre) ......... 175 |
| 71 | Mercury 6052 049 | Holy Holy/Black Country Rock (Demo copy) ......................................... 175 |
| 72 | RCA 2160 | Changes/Andy Warhol (Demo copy) ..................................................... 45 |
| 72 | RCA 2160 | Starman/Suffragette City (Demo copy in p/s) ...................................... 75 |
| 72 | RCA 2199 | Starman/Suffragette City (Demo copy, not in p/s) ............................... 25 |
| 72 | RCA 2302 | The Jean Genie/Ziggy Stardust (Demo copy) ....................................... 20 |
| 72 | RCA 2263 | John, I'm Only Dancing/Hang Onto Yourself (Demo copy) ................... 25 |
| 73 | RCA 2316 | Life On Mars?/The Man Who Sold The World (Demo copy in p/s) ............ 40 |
| 73 | RCA 2316 | Life On Mars?/The Man Who Sold The World (Demo copy without p/s) ...... 15 |
| 73 | RCA 2352 | Drive-In Saturday/Round And Round (Demo copy) ............................... 30 |
| 73 | RCA 2424 | Sorrow/Amsterdam (Demo copy) ........................................................ 15 |
| 74 | RCA LPBO 5009 | Rebel Rebel/Queen Bitch (Demo copy, label states "Bowie" not "David Bowie") ........ 25 |
| 74 | RCA LPBO 5009 | Rock'N'Roll Suicide/Quicksand (Demo copy) ....................................... 20 |
| 74 | RCA APBO 0293 | Diamond Dogs/Holy Holy (Demo copy, as "Bowie" not "David Bowie", push-out centre) ..... 25 |
| 74 | RCA APBO 0293 | Diamond Dogs/Holy Holy (as "Bowie" not "David Bowie", solid centre) ........... 35 |
| 74 | RCA 2466 | Knock On Wood/Panic In Detroit (Demo copy) .................................... 15 |
| 75 | RCA 2523 | Young Americans (short version)/Young Americans (long version) (Demo copy) ........... 25 |
| 75 | RCA 2640 | Golden Years/Can You Hear Me (Demo copy, solid centre, as "Bowie" not "David Bowie") ..... 60 |
| 75 | RCA 2640 | Golden Years/Can You Hear Me (Demo copy, push-out centre, as "Bowie" not "David Bowie") ..... 15 |
| 75 | Decca F 13579 | The London Boys/Love You Till Tuesday (Demo) ................................ 40 |
| 75 | RCA 2579 | Fame/Right (Demo copy) ................................................................... 15 |
| 75 | RCA 2593 | Space Oddity/Velvet Goldmine (Demo copy in p/s) ............................. 30 |
| 75 | RCA 2593 | Space Oddity/Velvet Goldmine (Demo copy, no p/s) ........................... 15 |
| 76 | RCA 2682 | TVC15/We Are The Dead (Demo copy) ............................................... 15 |
| 76 | RCA 2726 | Suffragette City/Stay (Demo copy in p/s) ........................................... 25 |
| 76 | RCA 2726 | Suffragette City/Stay (Demo copy, no p/s) ......................................... 15 |
| 77 | RCA PB 0905 | Sound And Vision/A New Career In A New Town (Demo copy) .............. 15 |
| 77 | RCA PB 1017 | Be My Wife/Speed Of Life (Demo copy in promo sleeve with titles on front) ......... 500 |
| 77 | RCA PB 1017 | Be My Wife/Speed Of Life (Demo copy not in sleeve) ......................... 15 |
| 77 | RCA PB 1121 | Heroes/V-2 Schneider (Demo copy) ................................................... 20 |
| 78 | RCA BOW 1 | Breaking Glass/Art Decade/Ziggy Stardust (Demo copy with p/s) ......... 20 |
| 77 | RCA PB 1190 | Beauty And The Beast/Sense Of Doubt (Demo copy with p/s) ............... 20 |
| 79 | RCA BOW 2 | Boys Keep Swinging/Fantastic Voyage (Demo copy) ........................... 15 |
| 79 | RCA BOW 3 | DJ/Repetition (Demo copy) ................................................................ 15 |
| 79 | RCA BOW 4 | John, I'm Only Dancing (Again)(1975)/John, I'm Only Dancing (1972) (Demo copy p/s). 15 |
| 80 | RCA BOW 5 | Alabama Song/Space Oddity (Demo copy, poster p/s) ........................ 20 |

### SINGLES : IRISH PRESSINGS
| 70 | Mercury EMF 1135 | The Prettiest Star/Conversation Piece (Irish pressing) .......................... 2000 |
| 73 | RCA 2352 | Drive-In Saturday/Round And Round (Irish pressing) ........................... 100 |
| 73 | RCA 2424 | Sorrow/Amsterdam (Irish pressing) ................................................... 30 |
| 73 | Deram DM(1) 123 | The Laughing Gnome/The Gospel According To Tony Day (Irish pressing) ........... 120 |
| 73 | Deram DM(1) 123 | The Laughing Gnome/The Gospel According To Tony Day (Irish pressing) ............ 120 |
| 74 | RCA LPBO 5009 | Rebel Rebel/Queen Bitch (Irish pressing) ........................................... 100 |
| 74 | RCA LPBO 5021 | Rock'N'Roll Suicide/Quicksand (Irish pressing) .................................. 100 |
| 75 | RCA 2523 | Young Americans/Sufragette City (Irish pressing) ............................... 100 |
| 79 | RCA 2316 | Life On Mars?/The Man Who Sold The World (Irish pressing) .............. 100 |
| 82 | RCA BOW 11 | Wild Is The WInd/Golden Years (Irish pressing, p/s) ............................ 15 |
| 83 | RCA BOW 503 | Rock 'n' Roll Suicide/Quicksand (Irish pressing) ................................ 10 |
| 83 | RCA BOW 502 | Life On Mars?/The Man Who Sold The World (Irish pressing) .............. 10 |
| 83 | RCA BOW 504 | Diamond Dogs/Holy Holy (Irish issue) ............................................... 10 |
| 83 | RCA BOW 501 | Drive-In Saturday/Round And Round (Irish pressing, p/s) .................... 10 |

# David BOWIE

## SINGLES

| | | | |
|---|---|---|---|
| 66 | Pye 7N 17020 | Can't Help Thinking About Me/And I Say To Myself (with Lower Third) | 300 |
| 66 | Pye 7N 17079 | Do Anything You Say/Good Morning Girl | 400 |
| 66 | Pye 7N 17157 | I Dig Everything/I'm Not Losing Sleep | 400 |
| 66 | Deram DM 107 | Rubber Band/The London Boys | 450 |
| 67 | Deram DM 123 | The Laughing Gnome/The Gospel According To Tony Day (with inverted matrix number on label) | 60 |
| 67 | Deram DM 135 | Love You Till Tuesday/Did You Ever Have A Dream | 200 |
| 69 | Philips BF 1801 | Space Oddity/Wild Eyed Boy From Freecloud (mono, solid centre) | 150 |
| 69 | Philips BF 1801 | Space Oddity/Wild Eyed Boy From Freecloud (mono, push-out centre) | 20 |
| 69 | Philips BF 1801 | Space Oddity/Wild Eyed Boy From Freecloud (unreleased p/s, only 2 or 3 copies known to exist) | 3000 |
| 69 | Philips BF 1801 | Space Oddity/Wild Eyed Boy From Freecloud (UK pressed stereo 45: unconfirmed) | 0 |
| | | *(is this really a UK pressing or a Dutch pressing as is generally acknowledged?)* | |
| 69 | Philips BF 1801 | Space Oddity/Wild Eyed Boy From Freecloud (mono, large centre) | 15 |
| 70 | Mercury MF 1135 | The Prettiest Star/Conversation Piece | 200 |
| 70 | Mercury 6052 026 | Memory Of A Free Festival Parts 1 & 2 (large centre) | 200 |
| 70 | Mercury 6052 026 | Memory Of A Free Festival Parts 1 & 2 (push-out centre) | 175 |
| 71 | Mercury 6052 049 | Holy Holy/Black Country Rock | 150 |
| 72 | RCA RCA 2160 | Changes/Andy Warhol | 25 |
| 72 | RCA RCA 2199 | Starman/Suffragette City (in p/s) | 60 |
| 72 | RCA 2199 | Starman/Suffragette City (orange label) | 5 |
| 72 | RCA RCA 2302 | The Jean Genie/Ziggy Stardust (re-issue, black label) | 5 |
| 72 | RCA 2302 | The Jean Genie/Ziggy Stardust (re-issue, black label) | 5 |
| 72 | Pye 7NX 8002 | FOR THE COLLECTOR EP (Do Anything You Say/I Dig Everything//I Can't Help Thinking About Me/I'm Not Losing Sleep (re-issue, blue label with art sleeve) | 20 |
| 72 | Pye 7NX 8002 | FOR THE COLLECTOR EP (Do Anything You Say/I Dig Everything//I Can't Help Thinking About Me/I'm Not Losing Sleep (re-issue, pink label with push-out centre) | 20 |
| 72 | Pye PRT 7NX 8002 | FOR THE COLLECTOR EP (Do Anything You Say/I Dig Everything//I Can't Help Thinking About Me/I'm Not Losing Sleep (re-issue) | 10 |
| 72 | Pye 7NX 8002 | FOR THE COLLECTOR EP (Do Anything You Say/I Dig Everything//I Can't Help Thinking About Me/I'm Not Losing Sleep (re-issue, pink label, solid centre) | 6 |
| 72 | Pye 7NX 8002 | FOR THE COLLECTOR EP (Do Anything You Say/I Dig Everything//I Can't Help Thinking About Me/I'm Not Losing Sleep (re-issue, grey label) | 6 |
| 72 | RCA RCA 2263 | John, I'm Only Dancing/Hang Onto Yourself (original pressing with slow 'acoustic guitar' version) | 6 |
| 73 | RCA RCA 2316 | Life On Mars?/The Man Who Sold The World (in p/s) | 20 |
| 73 | RCA RCA 2316 | Life On Mars?/The Man Who Sold The World | 5 |
| 73 | RCA RCA 2352 | Drive-In Saturday/Round And Round | 5 |
| 73 | RCA 2263 | John, I'm Only Dancing/Hang Onto Yourself (2nd issue, sax version, orange label, MATRIX BGBS 1056 2E) | 7 |
| 73 | Deram DM 123 | The Laughing Gnome/The Gospel According To Tony Day (reissue, matrix number correct way up on label) | 5 |
| 74 | RCA RCA 2424 | Sorrow/Amsterdam | 5 |
| 74 | RCA LPBO 5009 | Rebel Rebel/Queen Bitch (label states "Bowie" not "David Bowie") | 15 |
| 74 | RCA LPBO 5009 | Rebel Rebel/Queen Bitch (US import for UK market, as "David Bowie") | 5 |
| 74 | RCA LPBO 5021 | Rock'N'Roll Suicide/Quicksand | 7 |
| 74 | RCA APBO 0293 | Diamond Dogs/Holy Holy ("Bowie" not "David Bowie", solid centre) | 25 |
| 74 | RCA APBO 0293 | Diamond Dogs/Holy Holy (as "Bowie" not "David Bowie", push-out centre) | 10 |
| 74 | RCA/Mainman | Bowie's Greatest Hits (excerpts from Knock On Wood/ Lyntone LYN 2929 Space Oddity/The Man Who Sold The World/Life On Mars?/Starman/Jean Genie/Sorrow/Diamond dogs) 33rpm 1-sided flexidisc with Record Mirror/Popswop magazines) | 35 |
| 74 | RCA RCA 2466 | Knock On Wood/Panic In Detroit | 5 |
| 75 | RCA RCA 2523 | Young Americans/Suffragette City | 5 |
| 75 | RCA RCA 2640 | Golden Years/Can You Hear Me (as "Bowie" not "David Bowie") | 5 |
| 75 | Decca F 13579 | The London Boys/Love You Till Tuesday (paper labels) | 5 |
| 75 | Decca F 13579 | London Boys/Love You Till Tuesday (plastic moulded label) | 8 |
| 75 | RCA RCA 2579 | Fame/Right | 5 |
| 75 | RCA RCA 2593 | Space Oddity/Changes/Velvet Goldmine (p/s) | 10 |
| 76 | RCA RCA 2682 | TVC15/We Are The Dead | 5 |
| 76 | RCA RCA 2726 | Suffragette City/Stay (p/s) | 15 |
| 76 | RCA RCA 2726 | Suffragette City/Stay (no p/s) | 5 |
| 77 | RCA PB 0905 | Sound And Vision/A New Career In A New Town | 5 |
| 77 | RCA PB 0905 | Sound And Vision/A New Career In A New Town (re-issue, black label) | 7 |
| 77 | RCA PB 1017 | Be My Wife/Speed Of Life (solid centre) | 20 |
| 77 | RCA PB 1017 | Be My Wife/Speed Of Life (push-out centre) | 5 |
| 77 | RCA PB 1121 | Heroes/V-2 Schneider (Orange label, solid centre) | 10 |
| 77 | RCA PB 1121 | Heroes/V-2 Schneider (Orange label, push-out centre) | 5 |
| 77 | RCA PB 1121 | Heroes/V-2 Schneider (plastic moulded label in white sleve) | 10 |
| 77 | RCA PB 1121 | Heroes/V-2 Schneider (plastic moulded label, no sleeve) | 5 |
| 78 | RCA BOW 1 | Breaking Glass/Art Decade/Ziggy Stardust (p/s) | 8 |
| 77 | RCA PB 1190 | Beauty And The Beast/Sense Of Doubt (sold centre centre with p/s) | 20 |
| 78 | RCA PB 1190 | Beauty And The Beast/Sense Of Doubt (push-out centre with p/s) | 8 |
| 79 | RCA BOW 2 | Boys Keep Swinging/Fantastic Voyage (p/s) | 7 |
| 79 | RCA BOW 3 | DJ/Repetition (p/s) | 7 |
| 79 | RCA BOW 3 | DJ/Repetition (p/s, green vinyl) | 50 |
| 79 | RCA LPBO 5009 | Rebel Rebel/Queen Bitch (re-issue, black label) | 7 |
| 79 | RCA 2424 | Sorrow/Amsterdam (re-issue) | 7 |
| 79 | RCA 2199 | Starman/Suffragette City (re-issue, black label solid centre) | 7 |
| 79 | RCA 2199 | Starman/Suffragette City (re-issue, black label/push-out centre) | 5 |
| 79 | RCA BOW 4 | John, I'm Only Dancing (Again)(1975)/John, I'm Only Dancing (1972) (p/s) | 7 |
| 79 | RCA 2263 | John, I'm Only Dancing/Hang Onto Yourself (re-issue, sax version, black label) | 7 |

| Year | Catalogue | Description | Value |
|---|---|---|---|
| 79 | RCA 2316 | Life On Mars?/The Man Who Sold The World (re-issue, black label, solid centre) | 15 |
| 79 | RCA 2316 | Life On Mars?/The Man Who Sold The World (re-issue, black label, push-out centre) | 7 |
| 80 | RCA 2263 | John, I'm only Dancing/Hang Onto Yourself (re-issue, original version, black label) | 7 |
| 80 | RCA LPBO 5009 | Rebel Rebel/Queen Bitch (re-issue, black label, B-side plays "Song For Bob Dylan") | 10 |
| 80 | RCA BOW 5 | Alabama Song/Space Oddity (pink vinyl, custom factory pressing, poster p/s) | 500 |
| 80 | RCA BOW 5 | Alabama Song/Space Oddity (poster p/s) | 10 |
| 80 | RCA BOW 6 | Ashes To Ashes/Move On (with 3 different p/s & 4 different sheets of 9 stamps) | 12 |
| 80 | RCA BOW 7 | Fashion/Scream Like A Baby (p/s) | 5 |
| 80 | RCA BOW 8 | Scary Monsters/Because You're Young (p/s) | 5 |
| 80 | RCA BOW 9 | Up The Hill Backwards/Crystal Japan (orange label, solid centre, p/s) | 8 |
| 80 | RCA BOW 9 | Up The Hill Backwards/Crystal Japan (black label, push-out centre, p/s) | 5 |
| 81 | RCA BOW 9 | Up The Hill Backwards/Crystal Japan (orange label, push-out centre, p/s) | 6 |
| 81 | RCA BOW 10 | Wild Is The Wind/Golden Years (push-out centre. with p/s) | 7 |
| 81 | RCA BOW 10 | Wild Is The WInd/Golden Years (solid centre, p/s) | 8 |
| 82 | RCA BOW 11 | IN BERTHOLT BRECHT'S "BAAL" (Baal's Hymn/Remembering Marie A//Ballad Of The Adventureres/The Drowned Girl/Dirty Song, EP, foldout p/s) | 10 |
| 83 | RCA BOW 511 | Be My WIfe/Speed Of Life (Reissue, p/s) | 5 |
| 82 | RCA BOW 100 | FASHIONS (10 x 7" picture discs in plastic wallet [BOWP 101-110), each £4) | 60 |
| 83 | RCA BOW 501 | Drive-In Saturday/Round And Round (reissue, p/s) | 5 |
| 83 | RCA BOW 503 | Rock 'n' Roll Suicide/Quicksand (reissue, p/s) | 5 |
| 83 | RCA BOW 502 | Life On Mars?/The Man Who Sold The World (reissue, p/s) | 5 |
| 83 | RCA BOW 504 | Diamond Dogs/Holy Holy (reissue, p/s) | 5 |
| 83 | RCA BOW 505 | Knock On Wood/Panic In Detroit (Reissue) | 5 |
| 83 | RCA BOW 506 | Young Americans/Suffragette City (Reissue) | 5 |
| 83 | RCA BOW 507 | Fame/Right (Reissue, p/s) | 5 |
| 83 | RCA BOW 508 | Golden Years/Can You Hear Me (Reissue) | 5 |
| 83 | RCA BOW 509 | TVC15/We Are The Dead (Reissue, p/s) | 5 |
| 83 | RCA BOW 510 | Sound And Vision/A New Career In A New Town (Reissue, p/s) | 5 |
| 83 | RCA BOW 512 | Beauty And The Beast/Sense Of Doubt (Reissue, p/s) | 5 |
| 83 | RCA BOW 513 | Heroes/V-2 Schneider (Reissue, p/s) | 5 |
| 83 | RCA BOW 514 | Rebel Rebel/Queen Bitch (Reissue, p/s) | 7 |
| 83 | RCA BOW 514 | Rebel Rebel/Queen Bitch (plays Song For Bob Dylan) (Reissue, p/s) | 7 |
| 83 | RCA BOW 515 | The Jean Genie/Ziggy Stardust (Reissue, p/s) | 5 |
| 83 | RCA BOW 516 | DJ/Repetition (Reissue, p/s) | 5 |
| 83 | RCA BOW 517 | John I'm Only Dancing/Hang Onto Yourself (Reissue, p/s) | 5 |
| 83 | RCA BOW 518 | Space Oddity/Changes/Velvet Goldmine (Reissue, p/s) | 5 |
| 83 | RCA BOW 519 | Sorrow/Amsterdam (Reissue. p/s) | 5 |
| 83 | RCA BOW 520 | Breaking Glass/Art Decade/Ziggy Stardust (Reissue, p/s) | 5 |
| 84 | EMI America EA 187 | Tonight/Tumble And Twirl (poster p/s) | 6 |
| 85 | EMI America EAP 195 | Loving The Alien (Remixed Version)/Don't Look Down (Remixed Version) (shaped picture disc) | 10 |
| 85 | EMI America 12EAP 195 | Loving The Alien (Extended Dance Mix)/Don't Look Down (Extended Dance Mix)/ Loving The Alien (Extended Dub Mix) (12" picture disc) | 10 |
| 86 | Virgin VSS 906 | When The Wind Blows/When The Wind Blows (Instrumental) (shaped pic disc) | 8 |
| 87 | EMI America EAP 237 | Time Will Crawl (Single Version)/Girls (Single Edit) (poster p/s) | 8 |
| 87 | EMI America EAP 239 | Never Let Me Down/'87 And Cry (picture disc) | 12 |
| 92 | Warner Bros W 0127 | Real Cool World/Real Cool World (Instrumental) (White label with "Made in the UK", art sleeve) | 10 |
| 92 | Warner Bros W 0127 | Real Cool World/Real Cool World (Instrumental) (silver label, art sleeve) | 10 |
| 93 | BMG Arista 136977 | Jump They Say (Radio Edit)/Pallas Athena (Don't Stop Praying Mix) (jukebox issue, no p/s) | 6 |
| 93 | Arista 74321 162267 | Miracle Tonight/Looking For Lester (p/s) | 7 |
| 93 | Arista 74321 177057 | The Buddah Of Suburbia/Dead Against It (p/s) | 7 |
| 93 | BMG Arista 74321 148687 | Black Tie White Noise/You've Been Around (black moulded label, large centre) | 15 |
| 93 | BMG Arista 74321 148687 | Black Tie White Noise/You've Been Around (silver moulded label, p/s) | 7 |
| 95 | RCA 329407 | Strangers When We Meet (Edit)/The Man Who Sold The World (live) (green vinyl, stickered card p/s) | 8 |
| 95 | RCA 353847 | Hallo Spaceboy (Remix)/The Heart's Filthy Lesson (Radio Edit) (pink vinyl, stickered card p/s) | 10 |
| 95 | RCA 74321 353847JB | Hallo Spaceboy (Remix)/The Heart's Filthy Lesson (Radio Edit) (juke box issue, moulded label) | 50 |
| 97 | RCA 7432 1475841 | Dead Man Walking/Hous/Vigor Mortis/Paradox (plain sleeve, stickered) | 6 |
| 97 | RCA 512347 | Seven Years In Tibet (Edit)/Seven Years In Tibet (Mandarin Version) (p/s, clear vinyl) | 8 |
| 99 | Castle ESBO7 765 | I DIG EVERYTHING: THE 1966 PYE SINGLES (box set) | 20 |
| 02 | Columbia COL 672744 7/6727447000 | Slow Burn/Wood Jackson (orange vinyl, p/s) | 15 |
| 09 | Parlophone LCO 299 | DAVID BOWIE : Heroes/TV ON THE RADIO : Heroes | 40 |
| 13 | EMI DBSTAR40 | Starman (original version)/Top Of The Pops Version (picture disc, stickered PVC sleeve) | 50 |
| 13 | EMI DBDRIVE 40 | Drive In Saturday/(Russell Harty Plus Pop Version) (picture disc in PVC stickered sleeve) | 20 |
| 13 | Sony 88883705557 | The Stars (Are Out Tonight)/Where Are We Now (white vinyl, p/s) | 10 |

## ALBUMS

| Year | Catalogue | Description | Value |
|---|---|---|---|
| 67 | Deram DML 1007 | DAVID BOWIE (mono) | 900 |
| 67 | Deram SML 1007 | DAVID BOWIE (stereo) | 900 |
| 69 | Philips SBL 7912 | DAVID BOWIE (gatefold sleeve, black/silver label) | 600 |
| 70 | Decca PA 58 | THE WORLD OF DAVID BOWIE (mono) | 30 |
| 71 | Mercury 6338 041 | THE MAN WHO SOLD THE WORLD (LP, black/silver labels with 'dress' cover) | 1000 |
| 71 | Mercury 6338 041 | THE MAN WHO SOLD THE WORLD (cassette, with 'dress' cover) | 50 |
| 71 | RCA SF 8244 | HUNKY DORY (orange label with lyric sheet, 1st pressing with laminated sleeve, no GEM logo on right hand top corner of rear cover and no Mainman reference on sleeve or labels) | 350 |

| | | | |
|---|---|---|---|
| 71 | RCA SF 8244 | HUNKY DORY (orange label with lyric sheet) | 25 |
| 72 | RCA SF 8287 | THE RISE AND FALL OF ZIGGY STARDUST AND THE SPIDERS FROM MARS (1st pressing, Stamped matrixes: BGBS 0864 1E/0865 1E (with A4S etched into dead wax on side 1, B2K etched into dead wax on side 2) with with 'Gem Productions' and no 'Mainman' logo on rear sleeve, "Victor" under RCA label not "International", glossy orange label with "Titanic/Chrysalis" credits on labels, lyric inner sleeve) | 200 |
| 72 | RCA SF 8287 | THE RISE AND FALL OF ZIGGY STARDUST AND THE SPIDERS FROM MARS (2nd pressing, Gem Production and Mainman on rear of sleeve) | 30 |
| 72 | RCA LSP 4813 | SPACE ODDITY (reissue of SBL 7912 in different sleeve, orange label with lyric inner sleeve & poster) | 25 |
| 72 | RCA LSP 4816 | THE MAN WHO SOLD THE WORLD (orange label with inner sleeve & poster) | 15 |
| 73 | RCA RS 1001 | ALADDIN SANE (gloss orange label with 'Victor' on right side, 'Shorewood' gatefold sleeve & lyric inner sieeve, with fan club membership folder. Matrix numbers: CPRY 4543-3T/4544-3T) | 70 |
| 73 | RCA RS 1001 | ALADDIN SANE (orange label, gatefold sleeve & lyric inner sleeve) | 25 |
| 73 | RCA RS 1003 | PIN UPS (LP, insert, orange label) | 20 |
| 74 | RCA APL1 0576 | DIAMOND DOGS (LP, gatefold sleeve, orange label) | 30 |
| 74 | RCA APL 2-0771 | DAVID LIVE (2-LP, 1st pressing, gatefold sleeve, orange label, photos on inners. 1st pressing has July 14th and 15th dates on inside cover, later pressings from 1974 have corrected dates of July 12nd and 13th) | 30 |
| 75 | RCA Victor RS 1006 | YOUNG AMERICANS | 30 |
| 76 | RCA APL 1 1327 | STATION TO STATION (LP, 1st pressing, 'Garrodprint Ltd' on sleeve with 'ZZ' in top rear right corner, matt orange label, lyric inner with cat no, Matrix numbers: two sets crossed out before APLI-1327-A-1E/B-1E) | 40 |
| 76 | RCA RS 1055 | CHANGESONEBOWIE (with 'sax' version of "John I'm Only Dancing") | 25 |
| 76 | RCA APLI 1327 | STATION TO STATION (with original colour proof sleeve) | 500 |
| 77 | RCA INTS 5065 | LOW (red vinyl, semi-official 'factory custom pressing') | 500 |
| 77 | RCA PL12030 | LOW (LP, insert, fan club flyer, stickered sleeve) | 50 |
| 77 | RCA PL12030 | LOW (LP, insert, stickered sleeve) | 20 |
| 77 | RCA PL 12522 | HEROES (LP, with insert, laminated sleeve, orange label) | 20 |
| 78 | RCA PL 02913 | STAGE (2-LP, gatefold sleeve, yellow vinyl) | 30 |
| 78 | RCA PL 02913 | STAGE (2-LP, gatefold sleeve) | 25 |
| 78 | RCA Red Seal RL 12743 | DAVID BOWIE NARRATES PROKOFIEV'S PETER AND THE WOLF | 20 |
| 79 | RCA BOW 1 | LODGER (gatefold sleeve) | 30 |
| 80 | RCA BOW LP 2 | SCARY MONSTERS (AND SUPER CREEPS) (purple vinyl, semi-official 'factory custom pressing') | 600 |
| 80 | RCA BOWLP2 | SCARY MONSTERS AND SUPER CREEPS | 20 |
| 80 | RCA International INTS 5066 | HEROES (LP, repressing, insert, green label) | 15 |
| 80s | RCA Int. RCAPL 12030 | LOW (LP, repressing, green label) | 18 |
| 80 | RCA International INS 5063 | THE RISE AND FALL OF ZIGGY STARDUST AND THE SPIDERS FROM MARS (LP, reissue, green label) | 25 |
| 81 | RCA International INTS 5067 | ALADDIN SANE (LP, reissue, single sleeve, green label) | 18 |
| 83 | EMI America AMLP 3029 | LET'S DANCE (picture disc) | 12 |
| 83 | RCA International NL 83843 | THE RISE AND FALL OF ZIGGY STARDUST AND THE SPIDERS FROM MARS (LP, reissue, black label) | 15 |
| 83 | RCA PL 84862(2) | ZIGGY STARDUST - THE MOTION PICTURE (2-LP) | 25 |
| 84 | RCA BOPIC 3 | ZIGGY STARDUST (picture disc with numbered insert) | 18 |
| 84 | RCA BOPIC 5 | DIAMOND DOGS (picture disc with numbered insert) | 18 |
| 84 | RCA BOPIC 4 | PIN-UPS (picture disc with numbered insert) | 18 |
| 84 | RCA BOPIC 2 | HUNKY DORY (picture disc with numbered insert) | 18 |
| 84 | Deram 800 087-1 | DAVID BOWIE (reissue) | 20 |
| 84 | RCA BOPIC 1 | ALADDIN SANE (picture disc with numbered insert) | 18 |
| 90 | EMI EMC 3571 | SPACE ODDITY (LP, 1990 reissue, gatefold with extra tracks) | 25 |
| 90 | EMI EMC 3577 | ZIGGY STARDUST (LP, 1990 reissue, gatefold with unreleased tracks) | 20 |
| 90 | EMI WMC 3572 | HUNKY DORY (LP, reissue, gatefold with bonus tracks) | 20 |
| 91 | EMI EMD 1021 | YOUNG AMERICANS (remastered with 3 bonus tracks) | 25 |
| 91 | EMI EMD 1020 | STATION TO STATION (remastered with 2 bonus tracks, gatefold sleeve) | 30 |
| 90 | EMI DBTV1 | CHANGESBOWIE (2-LP, gatefold) | 18 |
| 93 | BMG 74321 13697 1 | BLACK TIE WHITE NOISE (LP) | 45 |
| 93 | EMI EM 1512 | THE SINGLES COLLECTION (3-LP) | 50 |
| 94 | MAINMAN GYLP 002 | SANTA MONICA LIVE '72 (2xLP, clear vinyl) | 40 |
| 95 | RCA 307021 | EXCERPTS FROM OUTSIDE (with 12" booklet & lyric sheet) | 50 |
| 97 | RCA 44949 | EARTHLING (gatefold sleeve) | 50 |
| 97 | EMI LPCENT 4 | THE RISE AND FALL OF ZIGGY STARDUST AND THE SPIDERS FROM MARS (LP, reissue, EMI 100 Centenary, stickered lseeve) | 30 |
| 97 | EMI LPCENT 21 | HUNKY DORY (LP, reissue, EMI 100 Centenary edition, stickered sleeve) | 30 |
| 99 | EMI 7243 4 99463 1 6 | ALADDIN SANE (LP, reissue, gatefold) | 20 |
| 02 | Columbia 508222 1 | HEATHEN (LP) | 40 |
| 03 | EMI 0724359451121 | SOUND AND VISION (4-CD box set with booklet) | 30 |
| 09 | EMI DBSOLP 40 | DAVID BOWIE (LP, reissue, gatefold with poster) | 20 |
| 11 | Deram 532760-1 | DAVID BOWIE (2-LP, reissue, gatefold) | 20 |
| 11 | Music On Vinyl MOVLP 470 | HEATHEN (LP, reissue, standard black vinyl, 180gm) | 20 |
| 12 | EMI DBZSX 40 | ZIGGY STARDUST AND THE SPIDERS FROM MARS (LP, with DVD) | 20 |
| 13 | Music On Vinyl MOVLP 470 | HEATHEN (LP, orange vinyl, 500 only, V&A Exhibition exclusive, numbered stickered sleeve) | 100 |
| 13 | Music On vinyl MOVLP500 | OUTSIDE (LP, reissue, green vinyl 500 only, V&A Exhibition exclusive, numbered stickered sleeve) | 100 |
| 13 | Sony Music 88765 461861 | THE NEXT DAY (2-LP, CD, 180gram vinyl) | 35 |
| 14 | Music On Vinyl MOVLP875 | REALITY (LP, reissue, 180gm vinyl) | 25 |
| 16 | Sony Music 88875173871 | * (BLACK STAR) (Clear vinyl, die-cut sleeve, booklet, download, 5000 pressed) | 100 |
| 16 | Sony Music 88875173871 S1 | * (BLACK STAR) (black vinyl, die-cut sleeve, booklet, download, 1st pressing with '(c) & (p) 2015 ISO Records' on back cover and not 2015, 2016 which is repressing) | 30 |

**ALBUMS : CDS**

| | | | |
|---|---|---|---|
| 84 | Deram 800 087-2 | DAVID BOWIE (withdrawn with white title) | 80 |

| 84 | RCA PD 84202 | CHANGESTWOBOWIE (withdrawn) | 30 |
|---|---|---|---|
| 84 | RCA PD 89002 | STAGE (2-CD, withdrawn) | 40 |
| 84 | RCA PD 94792 | GOLDEN YEARS (withdrawn) | 30 |
| 84 | RCA PD 84919 | FAME AND FASHION (ALL TIME GREATEST HITS) (withdrawn) | 50 |
| 85 | RCA PD 84813 | SPACE ODDITY (withdrawn) | 25 |
| 85 | RCA PD 84654 | THE MAN WHO SOLD THE WORLD (withdrawn) | 25 |
| 85 | RCA PD 83889 | DIAMOND DOGS (withdrawn) | 25 |
| 85 | RCA PD 81732 | CHANGESONEBOWIE (withdrawn) | 35 |
| 85 | RCA PD 81327 | STATION TO STATION (withdrawn) | 25 |
| 85 | RCA PD 83647 | SCARY MONSTERS (AND SUPER CREEPS) (withdrawn) | 25 |

## PROMOS

| 71 | None | HUNKY DORY (LP, preview pressing. Green labels with large red G and track listing, Matrixes Side 1: APRS-5947-35-A1A R Side 2: APRS-5948-35-A1A R, white sleeve with typed track listing and handwritten details "David Bowie Hunky Dory Preview Pressing 19 October 1971") | 1500 |
| 71 | Gem BOWPROMO 1 | BOWPROMO (LP, white label only, also known as HUNKY DORY SAMPLER Some with handwritten sleeve or Gem sticker on A-side, B-side features DANA GILLESPIE, 500 only) | 1500 |
| 77 | RCA BOW-1E | From The New Album 'Low" (1-sided promo, excerpts from Speed Of Life, Breaking Glass, What In The World, Sound And Vision) | 1500 |
| 83 | RCA LIFETIMES 1 | LIFETIMES (LP, promo, numbered, with insert) | 50 |
| 90 | BMG BOW 908 | SO FAR (CD, 8-track sampler for "Sound & Vision" box set) | 40 |
| 91 | Rykodisc VRCD 0142 | BOWIE/ENO: IT'S TIME TO LISTEN (CD, 9-track sampler from Ryko reissues; includes "Sound + Vision", "Be My Wife", "Some Are", "Heroes", "Joe The Lion", Abdulmajid, DJ, Boys Keep Swinging, Look Back in Anger) | 25 |
| 93 | EMI BOWIE 1 | SELECTIONS FROM THE SINGLES COLLECTION 10-track sampler,card p/s, promo only) | 18 |
| 93 | BMG MEAT 1 | Pallas Athena (12", white label, no p/s, includes two exclusive Meat Beat Manifesto remixes) | 40 |
| 93 | Back To Basics HOME 1 | Night Flights//(B-side by Moodswings) (12") | 18 |
| 93 | BBC MMCD 0072 | BBC SESSIONS 1969-1972 (CD, picture disc, promo-only, withdrawn) | 75 |
| 95 | RCA HALLO 2 | Hallo Spaceboy (12" Remix) (12", 1-sided, no p/s) | 18 |
| 95 | BMG SOLO 1 | EXCLUSIVE TOUR CD: Strangers When We Meet/MORRISSEY: The Boy Racer (Outside Tour CD) | 90 |
| 95 | RCA OUT 1 | The Heart's Filthy Lesson (12", 1-sided promo) | 10 |
| 96 | RCA SPACE 2 | Hallo Spaceboy (12" Remix) (1-sided 12", some copies listed as RCA HALLO 2, no p/s) | 25 |
| 96 | RCA SPACE 3 | Hallo Spaceboy (Double Click Mix)/Hallo Spaceboy (Instrumental)/ Hallo Spaceboy (Lost In Space Mix) (12", no p/s) | 50 |
| 99 | EMI QUEENWL 28 | Under Pressure (Remixes) (with Queen) (12", white label, unreleased mix, promo only) | 30 |

*(see also Davie Jones & King Bees, Davy Jones & Lower Third, Manish Boys, Arnold Corns, Spiders From Mars, Mick Ronson, Queen, Tao Jones Index, Bing Crosby)*

## DAVID BOWIE AND BING CROSBY

| 82 | RCA BOW 12 (PRO) | Peace On Earth/Little Drummer Boy//Dialogue/Peace On Earth/LDB (Demo copy, p/s) | 20 |
| 82 | RCA BOW 12 | Peace On Earth/Little Drummer Boy/Fantastic Voyage (push-out centre, p/s) | 5 |
| 82 | RCA BOW 12 | Peace On Earth/Little Drummer Boy/Fantastic Voyage (solid centre, p/s) | 5 |
| 82 | RCA BOW 12 | Peace On Earth/Little Drummer Boy/Fantastic Voyage (Irish pressing, p/s) | 15 |

*(see also David Bowie, Bing Crosby)*

## CANDY BOWMAN

| 81 | RCA RCAT 148 | Since I Found You/I Wanna Feel Your Love (12") | 15 |

## BOWMAN-HYDE PLAYERS

| 61 | Ember EMB S 141 | I Like A Little Honey/Teenage Kiss | 8 |
| 61 | Parlophone PMC 1155 | SING ME A SOUVENIR (LP) | 20 |

## ALAN BOWN (SET)

| 65 | Pye 7N 15934 | Can't Let Her Go/I'm The One | 30 |
| 66 | Pye 7N 17084 | Baby Don't Push Me/Everything's Gonna Be Alright | 30 |
| 66 | Pye 7N 17148 | Headline News/Mister Pleasure | 50 |
| 66 | Pye 7N 17192 | Emergency 999/Settle Down | 60 |
| 67 | Pye 7N 17256 | Gonna Fix You Good (Everytime You're Bad)/I Really Really Care | 50 |
| 67 | Music Factory CUB 1 | We Can Help You/Magic Handkerchief (as the Alan Bown!) | 12 |
| 67 | MGM MGM 1355 | Toyland/Technicolour Dream | 10 |
| 68 | MGM MGM 1387 | Story Book/Little Lesley | 25 |
| 69 | Deram DM 259 | Still As Stone/Wrong Idea (as The Alan Bown) | 10 |
| 69 | Deram DM 278 | Gypsy Girl/All I Can | 6 |
| 70 | Island WIP 6091 | Pyramid/Crash Landing | 5 |
| 75 | CBS 3721 | Rockford Files/I Don't Know | 6 |
| 75 | CBS 3366 | Moanin'/Time To Change | 6 |
| 68 | Music Factory CUB LM/LS 1 | OUTWARD BOWN (LP) | 100 |
| 69 | Deram DML/SML 1049 | THE ALAN BOWN! (LP) | 70 |
| 70 | Island ILPS 9131 | LISTEN (LP, with inner sleeve) | 30 |
| 71 | Island ILPS 9163 | STRETCHING OUT (LP, gatefold sleeve) | 30 |

*(see also John Barry Seven, Bronco, Jonesy)*

## ALAN BOWN SET/JIMMY JAMES & VAGABONDS

| 68 | Pye N(S)PL 18156 | LONDON SWINGS - LIVE AT THE MARQUEE CLUB (LP, 1 side each) | 30 |

*(see also Jimmy James & Vagabonds)*

## ANDREW BOWN

| 70 | Parlophone R 5856 | Tarot (Theme From 'Ace Of Wands')/Lulli Rides Again | 75 |

*(see also Andy Bown)*

## ANDY BOWN

| 75 | GM GMS 9039 | Supersonic/Feeling Better | 10 |
| 79 | EMI EMI 2906 | Another Shipwreck/Another Night With You | 6 |
| 79 | EMI EMI 2943 | Good Advice/One More Chance | 5 |

# BENDALLS BOX

| | | | |
|---|---|---|---|
| 81 | EMI EMI 5245 | Say It Was Magic/One Forward Two Back Again (in p/s) | 10 |
| 82 | EMI EMI 5312 | Marianne/One Forward Two Back Again | 5 |
| 82 | EMI EMI 5372 | Help Me/Marianne (p/s) | 5 |
| 72 | Mercury 6310 002 | GONE TO MY HEAD (LP) | 20 |
| 73 | GM GML 1001 | SWEET WILLIAM (LP) | 20 |

*(see also Andrew Bown, Herd, Judas Jump, Status Quo, Rossi & Frost, Storyteller)*

## BENDALLS BOX
| | | | |
|---|---|---|---|
| 81 | Circus CIRC 004 | Nightmares/Games Today (p/s) | 25 |

## BOX CAR RACER
| | | | |
|---|---|---|---|
| 02 | MCA MCS 40290 | I Feel So/Cat Like Thief (picture disc) | 12 |

*(see also Blink 182)*

## DAVID BOX
| | | | |
|---|---|---|---|
| 64 | London HLU 9874 | If You Can't Say Something Nice/Sweet Sweet Day | 10 |
| 64 | London HLU 9924 | Little Lonely Summer Girl/No One Will Ever Know | 12 |

*(see also Crickets)*

## BOXER
| | | | |
|---|---|---|---|
| 75 | Virgin VDJ 12 | All The Time In The World/Don't Wait (12", promo only) | 15 |
| 75 | Virgin V 2049 | BELOW THE BELT (LP, gatefold sleeve with uncensored full-frontal back cover) | 30 |
| 76 | Virgin V 2049 | BELOW THE BELT (LP, censored sleeve) | 15 |
| 76 | Virgin V 2073 | BLOODLETTING (LP, withdrawn) | 100 |

*(see also Patto, Timebox, Koobas, May Blitz)*

## BOX TOPS
| | | | |
|---|---|---|---|
| 67 | Stateside SS 2044 | The Letter/Happy Times | 10 |
| 67 | Stateside SS 2070 | Neon Rainbow/She Knows How | 5 |
| 68 | Bell BLL 1001 | Cry Like A Baby/The Door You Closed To Me | 5 |
| 68 | Bell BLL 1017 | Choo Choo Train/Fields Of Clover | 5 |
| 68 | Bell BLL 1035 | I Met Her In Church/People Gonna Talk | 5 |
| 69 | Bell BLL 1045 | Sandman/Sweet Cream Ladies, Forward March | 5 |
| 69 | Bell BLL 1063 | I Shall Be Released/I Must Be The Devil | 5 |
| 69 | Bell BLL 1068 | Soul Deep/The Happy Song | 5 |
| 69 | Bell BLL 1084 | Turn On A Dream/Together | 5 |
| 70 | Bell BLL 1097 | You Keep Tightening Up On Me/Come On Honey | 5 |
| 68 | Stateside (S)SL 10218 | THE LETTER/NEON RAINBOW (LP) | 15 |
| 68 | Bell MBLL/SBLL 105 | CRY LIKE A BABY (LP) | 15 |
| 69 | Bell MBLL/SBLL 108 | NON-STOP (LP) | 15 |
| 69 | Bell SBLL 120 | DIMENSIONS (LP) | 15 |

*(see also Big Star, Alex Chilton)*

## JUNIOR BOYCE (ACTUALLY JR. BYLES)
| | | | |
|---|---|---|---|
| 77 | Observer OB 004 | Natty Dreadlocks/Sick-More Tree/What Kind Of World/Sic Easy Stepping (12", with Ranking Buckers) | 30 |

*(see also Junior Byles)*

## TOMMY BOYCE
| | | | |
|---|---|---|---|
| 65 | MGM MGM 1287 | Pretty Thing/I Don't Have To Worry 'Bout You | 10 |

## TOMMY BOYCE & BOBBY HART
| | | | |
|---|---|---|---|
| 67 | A&M AMS 705 | Out And About/My Little Chickadee | 5 |
| 67 | A&M AMS 710 | Sometimes She's A Little Girl/Love Every Day | 5 |
| 68 | A&M AMS 714 | I Wonder What She's Doing Tonight?/Ambushers | 5 |
| 68 | A&M AMS 722 | Goodbye Baby/Where Angels Go Trouble Follows | 5 |
| 68 | A&M AMS 729 | Alice Long (You're Still My Favourite Girlfriend)/P.O. Box 9847 | 5 |
| 67 | A&M AML 907 | TEST PATTERNS (LP) | 25 |

*(see also Monkees, Tommy Boyce)*

## EDDIE BOYD
| | | | |
|---|---|---|---|
| 66 | Blue Horizon 45 BH 1009 | It's So Miserable To Be Alone/Empty Arms | 150 |
| 67 | Blue Horizon 57-3137 | The Big Boat/Sent For You Yesterday (with Fleetwood Mac) | 40 |
| 62 | Esquire EP 247 | BOYD'S BLUES (EP, as Eddie Boyd Blues Combo) | 70 |
| 65 | Fontana SFJL 905 | FIVE LONG YEARS (LP) | 60 |
| 67 | Decca LK/SKL 4872 | EDDIE BOYD AND HIS BLUES BAND FEATURING PETER GREEN (LP) | 120 |
| 68 | Blue Horizon 7-63202 | 7936 SOUTH RHODES (LP, with Fleetwood Mac) | 100 |
| 68 | Storyville SLP 4054 | IN CONCERT (LP) | 25 |

*(see also Fleetwood Mac)*

## EDDIE BOYD/BUDDY GUY
| | | | |
|---|---|---|---|
| 66 | Chess CRE 6009 | WITH THE BLUES (EP, 2 tracks each) | 25 |

*(see also Buddy Guy)*

## JIMMY BOYD
| | | | |
|---|---|---|---|
| 53 | Columbia SCM 5072 | I Saw Mommy Kissing Santa Claus/Little Train A-Chuggin' In My Heart | 5 |

## BOY FRIDAY (& GROOVERS)
| | | | |
|---|---|---|---|
| 70 | Downtown DT 470 | Version Girl/Grumble Man | 15 |
| 71 | Downtown DT 471 | Music So Good/Right Track (both with Groovers) | 35 |
| 71 | Downtown DT 472 | Sounds I Remember/JOAN LONG: Reconsider Our Love | 18 |
| 71 | Downtown DT 473 | Take A Message Ruby/Second Note | 25 |
| 71 | Downtown DT 476 | There'll Always Be Sunshine/Sunshine Track | 20 |
| 71 | Downtown DT 477 | Hot Pants Girl/Raunchy | 15 |
| 71 | Downtown DT 481 | El Raunchy/Conversation (as Boy Friday & Collins) | 15 |
| 71 | J-Dan JDN 4416 | I Don't Want No War/Third Note Swing | 7 |
| 71 | J-Dan JDN 4418 | Situation Version/OUR BAND: Keep Tracking | 7 |

*(see also Dandy & Superboys)*

## BOYFRIENDS
| | | | |
|---|---|---|---|
| 78 | United Artists UP 36424 | I'm In Love Today/Saturday Night (p/s) | 10 |

| 78 | United Artists UP 36442 | Jenny/Don't Ask Me To Explain (p/s) | 10 |
| 78 | United Artists UP 36478 | Last Bus Home/Romance (p/s) | 10 |

*(see also Vibrators)*

## BOYFRIENDS
| 82 | Plastic PRES 001 | Boyfriend/Give A Little, Take A Little (p/s) | 40 |

## BOY HAIRDRESSERS
| 88 | 53rd & 3rd AGARR T12 | Golden Showers/Tidalwave/The Assumption As An Elevator (12", p/s) | 30 |

*(see also Teenage Fanclub, BMX Bandits, Clouds)*

## BILLY BOYLE
| 62 | Decca F 11503 | My Baby's Crazy 'Bout Elvis/Held For Questioning | 15 |
| 70 | UPC UPC112 | Lookin' For Love/Pisces Man | 20 |

*(see also Le Roys)*

## A. BOYNE
| 70 | Punch PH 36 | Oh My Darling (actually Audley Rollins)/DENNIS SMITH: Ball Of Confusion | 10 |

## BILLY BOYO
| 82 | Greensleeves GRELD 89 | Righteousness/Itie Title Girl (12") | 15 |

## BOYRACER
| 92 | Fluff HONEY 2 | Railway/Reverse (p/s) | 10 |
| 93 | Sarah SARAH 76 | B IS FOR BOYRACER EP (p/s, insert) | 15 |
| 93 | Sarah SARAH 85 | FROM PURITY TO PURGATORY EP (p/s, insert) | 15 |
| 94 | Sarah SARAH 96 | PURE HATED EP (p/s, insert) | 12 |

## BOYS IN DARKNESS
| 81 | Bid For Freedom BID 1 | Back To France/A Man An Island (no p/s) | 15 |
| 81 | Champagne BUBL-702 | Back To France/A Man An Island (p/s) | 10 |
| 81 | Champagne BUBLY-702 | Back To France/A Man An Island (12" p/s) | 12 |

## BOYS (JAMAICA)
| 69 | Duke DU 19 | Easy Sound/AFROTONES: Freedom Sound | 20 |

*(see also Harry J. Allstars)*

## BOYS BLUE
| 65 | HMV POP 1427 | You Got What I Want/Take A Heart | 50 |

*(see also Jeff Elroy & Boys Blue)*

## BOYS (U.K.) (1)
| 63 | Parlophone R 5027 | Polaris/Jumpin' | 20 |
| 64 | Pye 7N 15726 | It Ain't Fair/I Want You | 100 |

## BOYS (U.K.) (2)
| 77 | NEMS NES 102 | I Don't Care/Soda Pressing (p/s) | 15 |
| 77 | NEMS NES 111 | First Time/Whatcha Gonna Do/Turning Grey (p/s) | 15 |
| 78 | NEMS NES 116 | Brickfield Nights/Teacher's Pet (p/s) | 10 |
| 79 | Safari SAFE 21 | Kamikaze/Bad Days (p/s, with booklet) | 6 |
| 80 | Safari SAFE 23 | Terminal Love/I Love Me (p/s) | 5 |
| 80 | Safari SAFE 27 | You Better Move On/Schoolgirls (p/s) | 5 |
| 80 | Safari SAFE 31 | Weekend/Cool (p/s) | 5 |
| 80 | Safari SAFE 33 | Let It Rain/Lucy (p/s) | 6 |
| 77 | NEMS NES 6001 | THE BOYS (LP) | 15 |
| 78 | NEMS NEL 6015 | ALTERNATIVE CHARTBUSTERS (LP, with inner sleeve) | 15 |
| 79 | Safari 1-2 BOYS | TO HELL WITH THE BOYS (LP, with songbook & stickered sleeve) | 25 |
| 80 | Safari BOYS 4 | BOYS ONLY (LP) | 15 |

*(see also Yobs, Rowdies, Hollywood Brats)*

## BOYS (U.K.) (3)
| 88 | Cleversounds BOYS 1 | Happy Days/Standard Avenue/Learn How To Dance (p/s) | 8 |

*(see also Ocean Colour Scene)*

## BOZ
| 66 | Columbia DB 7832 | You're Just The Kind Of Girl I Want/Isn't That So | 30 |
| 66 | Columbia DB 7889 | Meeting Time/No (Ah) Body Knows The Blues | 30 |
| 66 | Columbia DB 7941 | Pinocchio/Stay As You Are | 10 |
| 66 | Columbia DB 7972 | The Baby Song/Carry On Screaming | 20 |
| 68 | Columbia DB 8406 | I Shall Be Released/Down In The Flood | 30 |
| 68 | Columbia DB 8468 | Light My Fire/Back Against The Wall | 15 |

*(see also King Crimson, Bad Company, Alexis Korner)*

## BOZOS
| 78 | Other BOZ 101 | Weekend Girl/Fool Out Of Me | 25 |

## JANET BRACE
| 55 | Brunswick 05272 | Teach Me Tonight/My Old Familiar Heartache | 6 |

## BRACKEN
| 79 | Look LKLP 6438 | PRINCE OF THE NORTHLANDS (LP, private pressing, with insert) | 60 |

## WILLIE BRACKENRIDGE
| 79 | Burning Vibrations BVD 005 | Blood Money/You Are On My Mind (12") | 20 |

## KIM & KELLY BRADEN
| 67 | Columbia DB 8312 | Didn't I/You're Leaving, She's Crying, I'm Laughing | 5 |
| 68 | Columbia DB 8421 | Happiness Is/Sing A Rainbow | 5 |

## BOBBY BRADFORD
| 73 | Emanem 302 | LOVE'S DREAM (LP) | 25 |

## GEORGE BRADLEY & HIS BAND
| 65 | HMV POP 1459 | Breakout/Vendetta | 5 |

## JAN BRADLEY
| 63 | Pye International 7N 25182 | Mama Didn't Lie/Lovers Like Me | 35 |

**MARTIN BRADLEY**
80    Greenwich Village GVR 205    TIME CAN'T STAND STILL (LP) ............................................................................ 15

**OWEN BRADLEY (ORCHESTRA/QUINTET)**
58    Brunswick 05736    Big Guitar/Sentimental Dream (as Owen Bradley Quintet) ...................... 10
60    Brunswick LAT 8327    THE BIG GUITAR (LP) ....................................................................................... 20

**BRADLEY STRYDER**
92    Rephlex CAT 001    BRADLEY'S BEAT (12" EP, logo sleeve) ....................................................... 20
96    Rephlex CAT 020    BRADLEY'S ROBOT (12" EP, poster p/s) ..................................................... 10

**BUDDY BRADSHAW**
59    Capitol CL 15036    Nothing You Can Say/Tonight I Walk Alone ............................................... 10
*(see also Owen Gray)*

**SONNY BRADSHAW QUINTET**
62    Top TD 106    This Is Happiness/Island In The Sun .................................................................. 15

**SONNY BRADSHAW (& YOUNG JAMAICA)**
61    Duke DK 1003    Yellow Birds/Festival Jump Up ............................................................................ 10
71    Big Shot BI 576    Wig Wam/Peace And Love (as Sonny Bradshaw & Young Jamaica) ...................... 10

**TINY BRADSHAW & HIS ORCHESTRA**
54    Parlophone GEP 8507    TRAIN KEPT A ROLLING (EP) ..................................................................... 35
56    Parlophone GEP 8552    POMPTON TURNPIKE (EP) ........................................................................ 15
50s    Parlophone CGEP 2    TINY BRADSHAW (export EP) ...................................................................... 12

**TINY BRADSHAW ORCHESTRA/WYNONIE HARRIS**
70    Polydor 623 273    KINGS OF RHYTHM AND BLUES (LP, 1 side each) ........................................ 15
*(see also Wynonie Harris)*

**DON BRADSHAW-LEATHER**
72    Distance DIST 101    DISTANCE BETWEEN US (2-LP, gatefold sleeve, private pressing) .................. 80

**BOB BRADY & CONCHORDS**
68    Bell BLL 1025    Everybody's Goin' To The Love-In/It's Been A Long Time Between Kisses ..................... 15
70    Bell BLL 1114    Everybody's Goin' To The Love-In/It's Been A Long Time Between Kisses (reissue) ......... 5

**JOE BRADY**
63    Pye 7N 15569    The Great Train Robbery/Is This Where We Say Goodbye? ................................ 5

**MAJELLA BRADY**
65    Rex R11015    Light In My Window/Girl ......................................................................................... 8

**PHIL BRADY & THE RANCH SET**
67    Go AJ 11406    Lonesome For You/Please Come Back ............................................................... 18

**VICTOR BRADY**
70    Polydor    BROWN RAIN (LP) ...................................................................................................... 20

**BRADY BUNCH**
73    Paramount SPFL 284    MEET THE BRADY BUNCH (LP) .................................................................. 15

**JOHNNY BRAGG**
79    Inferno 2    They're Talking About Me/Is It True (p/s, orange vinyl) .................................... 8

**AL 'TNT' BRAGGS**
66    Vocalion VP 9278    Earthquake/How Long (Do You Hold On) ............................................... 20
66    Vocalion VP 9278    Earthquake/How Long (Do You Hold On) (DJ Copy) ............................. 60
68    Action ACT 4506    Earthquake/How Long (Do You Hold On) (reissue) .................................. 20
69    Action ACT 4526    I'm A Good Man/I Like What You Do To Me ............................................ 15
65    Vocalion VEP 170163    AL 'TNT' BRAGGS (EP) ................................................................................ 125

**ERNEL BRAHAM**
66    Rio R 79    Musical Fight/EDWARDS ALLSTARS: Pipeline ..................................................... 35
*(see also Kent Walker)*

**ROY BRAHAM**
64    R&B 166    Believe Me/Red Sea ................................................................................................. 30

**BRAIN**
67    Parlophone R 5595    Nightmares In Red/Kick The Donkey ....................................................... 160
87    Bam Caruso OPRA 63    Nightmares In Red/SRC: Black Sheep (jukebox edition, die-cut company sleeve) .......... 10
*(see also Giles Giles & Fripp, Trendsetters Ltd, League Of Gentlemen)*

**BRAIN DONOR**
06    Invada INV031LP    DRAIN'D BONER (12" gatefold, picture disc) ........................................... 10

**BRAINBOX**
69    Parlophone R 5775    Woman's Gone/Down Man ...................................................................... 20
70    Parlophone R 5842    So Helpless/To You ................................................................................... 15
70    Parlophone PCS 7094    BRAINBOX (LP, black/silver/white boxed Parlophone label) ............... 200
*(see also Jan Akkerman, Hunters, Focus)*

**BRAINCHILD**
70    A&M AMS 805    Cage/Autobiography ............................................................................................ 10
70    A&M AMLS 979    HEALING OF THE LUNATIC OWL (LP, brown label) ..................................... 120

**BRAINIAC 5**
80    Roach RR 5002    Working/Feel (p/s) .................................................................................................. 10
78    Roach RREP 5001    MUSHY DOUBT (EP, 33rpm, p/s) ............................................................. 10

**BRAINKILLERS**
93    Vibe Alive VALV 36    Crackhead/Dark Moon/Stupid/This Is Where It Takes Us (12", with Lewi Cifer) ........... 25
93    Vibe Alive VALV 76    On A Different Mission/One Stype/Hurt Me/Girl U Look Good (12", stickered die-cut
paper sleeve, with Lewi Cifer) ........................................................................................................................................ 20
94    3rd Party, Kemet KM3RD#1    BORDER LINE EP (with FAMILY OF INTELLIGENCE) (12") ............... 20

**BRAINSTORM**
79    Miracle M5    Lovin' Is Really My Game/Stormin' (12", red or black vinyl no p/s) ...................... 20

## BRAINTAX
| | | | |
|---|---|---|---|
| 92 | Low Life Low 2 | FAT HEAD (EP 12" - 500 pressed) | 40 |
| 97 | Low Life Low 4 | FUTURE YEARS (EP, 12") | 25 |
| 06 | Low Life Low 44 | D90 Rules (Vocal)/D90 Rules (Instrumental) | 5 |
| 01 | Low Life LOW 15 | BIRO FUNK (2-LP) | 40 |
| 06 | Low Life LOW 50 | PANORAMA (LP) | 25 |
| 08 | Low Life LOW 50 | MY LAST AND BEST ALBUM (LP) | 25 |

## BRAKES
| | | | |
|---|---|---|---|
| 80 | Magnet MAGL | FOR WHY YOU KICKA MY DONKEY? (LP) | 15 |

## DELANEY BRAMLETT
| | | | |
|---|---|---|---|
| 64 | Vocalion VP 9227 | Heartbreak Hotel/You Never Looked Sweeter | 15 |
| 65 | Vocalion VP 9237 | Liverpool Lou/You Have No Choice | 30 |
| 65 | Vocalion VP 9237 | Liverpool Lou/You Have No Choice (DJ Copy) | 50 |

*(see also Delaney & Bonnie, King Curtis with Delaney & Friends)*

## BRAM STOKER
| | | | |
|---|---|---|---|
| 72 | Windmill WMD 117 | HEAVY ROCK SPECTACULAR (LP) | 15 |

## BRAN
| | | | |
|---|---|---|---|
| 74 | Gwawr GWA 104 | BRAN EP | 50 |
| 75 | Sain 1038M | AIL-DDECHRA (LP) | 300 |
| 76 | Sain 1070M | HEDFAN (LP) | 100 |
| 78 | Sain 1120M | GWRACH Y NOS (LP) | 40 |

## BRAND
| | | | |
|---|---|---|---|
| 64 | Piccadilly 7N 35216 | I'm A Lover Not A Fighter/Zulu Stomp | 100 |

## BRAND NEW
| | | | |
|---|---|---|---|
| 03 | Eat Sleep | Jude Law And A Semester Abroad/Am I Wrong (p/s) | 30 |
| 03 | Sore Point SORE 004S | The Quiet Things That No One Ever Knows/Jude Law And A Session Abroad (live in session) (die-cut sleeve, red vinyl) | 15 |
| 04 | Sore Point SORE 0145 | The Quiet Things That No One Ever Knows/The No Seatbelt Song (live) (p/s, green vinyl) | 8 |
| 04 | Sore Point SORE 011S | Sic Transit Gloria...Glory Fades/Jaws Theme Swimming (Demo) (pink vinyl) | 15 |

## BRAND NEW HEAVIES
| | | | |
|---|---|---|---|
| 91 | Acid Jazz JAZID 39P | Never Stop (12", company sleeve, withdrawn) | 20 |

## BILL BRANDON
| | | | |
|---|---|---|---|
| 73 | Mercury 6052 186 | I Am Free Of Your Love/(Take Another Little) Piece Of My Heart | 8 |

## JOHNNY BRANDON
| | | | |
|---|---|---|---|
| 56 | Parlophone MSP 6238 | Rock-A-Bye Baby/Lonely Lips | 60 |
| 56 | Parlophone R 4207 | Shim Sham Shuffle/I Didn't Know | 60 |
| 56 | Decca F 10778 | Glendora/Song For A Summer Night | 20 |
| 57 | Decca F 10858 | Nothing Is Too Good For You/A Sort-Of-A-Feeling | 10 |
| 59 | Top Rank JAR 241 | Santa Claus Jnr./I Heard A Bluebird Sing | 5 |
| 55 | Pye NEP 24003 | JOHNNY BRANDON HITS (EP) | 15 |

## KIRK BRANDON & PACK OF LIES
| | | | |
|---|---|---|---|
| 87 | SS SS1N2/SS2N1 | KIRK BRANDON AND THE PACK OF LIES (EP) | 10 |

*(see also Theatre Of Hate, Spear Of Destiny, Senate, Pack)*

## VERN BRANDON
| | | | |
|---|---|---|---|
| 62 | Decca F 11472 | Let Me Be The One/Gotta Know The Reason | 20 |

## BRANDY BOYS
| | | | |
|---|---|---|---|
| 65 | Columbia DB 7507 | Gale Winds/Don't Come Knocking At My Door | 10 |

## BRANDY WINE BRIDGE
| | | | |
|---|---|---|---|
| 77 | Cottage COT 311 | THE GREY LADY (LP, as Brandywinebridge) | 25 |
| 78 | Cottage COT 321 | AN ENGLISH MEADOW (LP, hand-drawn sleeve with insert) | 25 |

## BRANDY WINE SINGERS
| | | | |
|---|---|---|---|
| 68 | President PT 204 | Mandy/Two Little Boys | 6 |

## LINDA BRANNON
| | | | |
|---|---|---|---|
| 63 | Columbia DB 7156 | Funny Face/Will It Last | 15 |

## JOHNNY BRANTLEY'S ALL STARS
| | | | |
|---|---|---|---|
| 58 | London HLU 8606 | The Place/Pot Luck | 20 |

## BRASS BIRD
| | | | |
|---|---|---|---|
| 68 | TP TO 024 | Simple Life/A Place To Die | 60 |

## BRASS ALLEY
| | | | |
|---|---|---|---|
| 73 | Alaska ALA 11 | You Better Run/Be My Friend | 20 |

*(see under Various Artists Eps)*

## BRASS CONSTRUCTION
| | | | |
|---|---|---|---|
| 75 | United Artists UP 617 | Movin'/Changin' (12") | 10 |
| 82 | United Artists UAS 29923 | BRASS CONSTRUCTION (LP) | 15 |

## ANDRÉ BRASSEUR
| | | | |
|---|---|---|---|
| 65 | Pye International 7N 25332 | Early Bird Satellite/Special 230 | 10 |
| 67 | CBS 202557 | The Kid/Holiday | 20 |
| 67 | CBS 202557 | The Kid/Holiday (DJ Copy) | 50 |
| 71 | CBS 2557 | The Kid/Holiday (reissue) | 8 |
| 66 | CBS 62858 | TASTY (LP) | 15 |

## BRASS INCORPORATED
| | | | |
|---|---|---|---|
| 70 | Pye International 7N 25520 | At The Sign Of The Swinging Cymbal/Just Like That | 25 |

## BRASS MONKEY
| | | | |
|---|---|---|---|
| 71 | Philips 6303 025 | BRASS MONKEY (LP) | 30 |
| 71 | Philips 6303 027 | NO VISIBLE MEANS OF SUPPORT (LP) | 30 |

MINT VALUE £

### BRASS TACKS
| | | | |
|---|---|---|---|
| 68 | Big T BIG 110 | I'll Keep On Holding On/Let The Sunshine In | 35 |
| 68 | Big T BIG 114 | Maxwell Ferguson/Sunshine After The Rain | 100 |

### BRASS WYNDS
| | | | |
|---|---|---|---|
| 67 | Pye 7N 17255 | Music To Watch Girls By/Sugar's Sweet | 5 |

### BRATZ
| | | | |
|---|---|---|---|
| 80 | A Famous Record AFR 1 | The Bratz Are Coming/Coast To Coast/Everyone Wants To Be Elvis (p/s) | 6 |

### RICHARD BRAUTIGAN
| | | | |
|---|---|---|---|
| 69 | Zapple ZAPPLE 03 | LISTENING TO RICHARD BRAUTIGAN (LP, unreleased, acetates exist) | 1500 |

### CEDRIC BRAVO
| | | | |
|---|---|---|---|
| 65 | Ska Beat JB 229 | Merry Christmas/Sugar Baby | 15 |

### LOS BRAVOS
| | | | |
|---|---|---|---|
| 66 | Decca F 22529 | Going Nowhere/Brand New Baby | 20 |
| 68 | Decca F 22765 | Bring A Little Lovin'/Make It Last | 8 |

*(see also Mike Kennedy)*

### ANTHONY BRAXTON
| | | | |
|---|---|---|---|
| 85 | Leo 414/415/416 | QUARTET (2-LP box set with insert) | 35 |

### ANTHONY BRAXTON & DEREK BAILEY
| | | | |
|---|---|---|---|
| 73 | Emanem 601 | DUO (2-LP) | 30 |
| 84 | Incus INCUS 43 | ROYAL VOLUME 1 (LP) | 20 |

*(see also Derek Bailey)*

### PRISCILLA BRAZIER
| | | | |
|---|---|---|---|
| 74 | Dovetail DOVE 9 | PRISCILLA BRAZIER (LP) | 25 |
| 76 | Key KL 038 | SOMETHING BEAUTIFUL (LP) | 35 |

### BREAD
| | | | |
|---|---|---|---|
| 69 | Elektra EKS 74044 | BREAD (LP) | 25 |

*(see also David Gates, Pleasure Fair)*

### BREAD & BEER BAND
| | | | |
|---|---|---|---|
| 69 | Decca F 12891 | Dick Barton Theme (The Devil's Gallop)/Breakdown Blues | 75 |
| 72 | Decca F 13354 | Dick Barton Theme (The Devil's Gallop)/Breakdown Blues (reissue) | 40 |
| 69 | Rubbish (no cat. no.) | THE BREAD AND BEER BAND (LP, 1 copy known to exist) | 2000 |

*(see also Elton John, Caleb)*

### BREAD, LOVE & DREAMS
| | | | |
|---|---|---|---|
| 69 | Decca F 12958 | Virgin Kiss/Switch Out The Sun | 22 |
| 69 | Decca LK/SKL 5008 | BREAD, LOVE AND DREAMS (LP, unboxed large Decca on label) | 250 |
| 70 | Decca LK/SKL 5048 | THE STRANGE TALE OF CAPTAIN SHANNON AND THE HUNCHBACK FROM GIGHA (LP, small boxed Decca label) | 250 |
| 71 | Decca SKL 5081 | AMARYLLIS (LP, small boxed Decca label) | 800 |
| 07 | Sunbeam SBRLP 5027 | AMARYLLIS (LP, reissue) | 15 |
| 08 | Sunbeam SBRLP 5042 | THE STRANGE TALE OF CAPTAIN SHANNON AND THE HUNCHBACK FROM GIGHA (LP, reissue) | 20 |

*(see also Human Beast)*

### BREAKAWAYS
| | | | |
|---|---|---|---|
| 62 | Pye 7N 15471 | He's A Rebel/Wishing Star | 15 |
| 63 | Pye 7N 15585 | That Boy Of Mine/Here She Comes | 10 |
| 64 | Pye 7N 15618 | That's How It Goes/He Doesn't Love Me | 10 |
| 65 | Pye 7N 15973 | Danny Boy/Your Kind Of Love | 10 |
| 67 | CBS 2833 | Sacred Love/Don't Be A Baby | 10 |
| 68 | MCA MU 1018 | Santo Domingo/So In Love Are We | 5 |

*(see also Vernons Girls, Burt Bacharach Orchestra, Mike Patto, Ken Cope, Sharades, De Laine Sisters)*

### BREAKDOWN
| | | | |
|---|---|---|---|
| 77 | MCP 001 | MEET ME ON THE HIGHWAY (LP, private pressing with insert) | 30 |

### BREAKERS
| | | | |
|---|---|---|---|
| 81 | Riot RS 1001 | Radio Love/My Momma Told Me (p/s) | 20 |

### BREAKING THE ILLUSION
| | | | |
|---|---|---|---|
| 92 | Lowlife LOW 1 | WHERE WILL IT END? (EP, 12" p/s, 1000 pressed) | 15 |
| 93 | Lowlife LOW 3 | LOSE YOUR ILLUSION (EP) | 12 |

### BREAKOUT
| | | | |
|---|---|---|---|
| 81 | Guardian GRC 101 | Wall Of Solitude/Get Out Fight Back | 80 |

### BREAKTHRU'
| | | | |
|---|---|---|---|
| 68 | Mercury MF 1066 | Ice Cream Tree/Julius Caesar | 25 |

### BREAKWATER
| | | | |
|---|---|---|---|
| 86 | Arista ARIST 12674 | Say You Love Me Girl/Work It Out (12", p/s) | 15 |

### BREATHERS
| | | | |
|---|---|---|---|
| 80 | Diversion DIV 1 | Living In The Age Age/Counting On Counting | 15 |

### BREATHING AGE
| | | | |
|---|---|---|---|
| 81 | Edge EDGE 13 | Here We Go/Camera Room (p/s) | 10 |

### BREATHLESS
| | | | |
|---|---|---|---|
| 81 | Magnum Force MFEP 005 | SOCK HOP BOPPIN' (EP) | 20 |

### BREEDERS
| | | | |
|---|---|---|---|
| 90 | 4AD CAD 0006 | POD (LP) | 25 |
| 93 | 4AD CAD 3014 | LAST SPLASH (LP, with free 7") | 25 |
| 02 | 4AD CAD 2205 | TITLE TK (LP, inner) | 20 |
| 08 | 4AD CAD 2803 | MOUNTAIN BATTLES (LP, inner sleeve and booklet) | 15 |
| 13 | 4AD DAD 3308 | LSXX (3-LP, 4 x 10" box set) | 50 |

### JIMMY BREEDLOVE
| | | | |
|---|---|---|---|
| 57 | London HLE 8490 | Over Somebody Else's Shoulder/That's My Baby | 100 |

| | | | |
|---|---|---|---|
| 62 | Pye International 7N 25121 | You're Following Me/Fabulous | 30 |
| 75 | Pye Disco Demand DDS 110 | I Can't Help Loving You/I Saw You | 5 |

*(see also Cues)*

## BOBBY BREEN
| | | | |
|---|---|---|---|
| 62 | Fontana 373 | When The Lights Go Out/Everybody Twist | 10 |

## BRELLO CABAL
| | | | |
|---|---|---|---|
| 67 | CBS 3214 | Margarine Flavoured Pineapple Chunk/Follow That (as The Brello Cabal) | 10 |

*(see also Anita Harris)*

## BEVERLEY BREMERS
| | | | |
|---|---|---|---|
| 72 | Wand WN 18 | Get Smart Girl/Don't Say You Don't Remember | 15 |
| 72 | Wand WN 28 | We're Free/Colours Of Love | 5 |
| 72 | Wand WN 34 | I'll Make You Music/I Made A Man Out Of You Jimmy | 5 |

## BRENDA & TABULATIONS
| | | | |
|---|---|---|---|
| 67 | London HL 10127 | Dry Your Eyes/The Wash | 30 |
| 67 | London HL 10174 | When You're Gone/Hey Boy | 25 |
| 68 | Direction 58-3678 | Baby You're So Right For Me/To The One I Love | 15 |
| 69 | Action ACT 4541 | That's In The Past/I Can't Get Over Her | 30 |
| 70 | London HL 10325 | A Child No One Wanted/'Scuse Uz Y'all | 15 |
| 71 | CBS 7279 | Right On The Tip of My Tongue/Always And Forever | 15 |
| 73 | Epic EPC 1361 | One Girl Too Late/The Magic Of Your Love | 10 |
| 69 | Action ACLP 6003 | DRY YOUR EYES (LP) | 50 |

## BUDDY BRENNAN QUARTET
| | | | |
|---|---|---|---|
| 60 | London HLU 9049 | Big River/The Chase | 5 |

## ROSE BRENNAN
| | | | |
|---|---|---|---|
| 55 | HMV 7M 299 | Ding Dong/Sincerely | 15 |
| 55 | HMV 7M 328 | Wake The Town And Tell The People/Ten Little Kisses | 7 |

## BRENT FORD & NYLONS
| | | | |
|---|---|---|---|
| 78 | Brumbeat | 19th Nervous Breakdown/Big Rock Candy Mountain (handmade foldout p/s) | 50 |

## TONY BRENT
| | | | |
|---|---|---|---|
| 58 | Columbia SEG 7824 | TONY CALLS THE TUNE (EP) | 10 |
| 58 | Columbia SEG 7869 | TIME FOR TONY (EP) | 10 |
| 59 | Columbia SEG 8019 | OFF STAGE (EP) | 10 |
| 59 | Columbia SEG 8040 | OFF STAGE NO. 2 (EP) | 10 |

*(see also Coronets)*

## TONY BRENT & JULIE DAWN
| | | | |
|---|---|---|---|
| 53 | Columbia SCM 5029 | Ding Dong Boogie/When Are We Gonna Get Married? | 15 |

*(see also Julie Dawn)*

## BRENTWOOD ROAD ALLSTARS
| | | | |
|---|---|---|---|
| 70 | Bamboo BAM 23 | Love At First Sight/MAYTALS: Life Could Be A Dream | 30 |
| 70 | Bamboo BAM 25 | Soul Shake/Moon Ride | 30 |

## PAUL BRETT('S SAGE)
| | | | |
|---|---|---|---|
| 70 | Pye 7N 17974 | Three D Mona Lisa/Mediterranean Lazy Heat Wave | 15 |
| 71 | Dawn DNX 2508 | Reason For Your Askin'/Everlasting Butterfly/Savannah Ladies/ To Everyman (Freedom) (p/s) | 10 |
| 71 | Dawn DNS 1010 | Goodbye Forever/Good Old Fashioned Funky Kind Of Music | 6 |
| 72 | Dawn DNS 1021 | Dahlia/Cottage Made For Two | 6 |
| 73 | Bradley's BRAD 301 | Mr. Custer/Good Times, Hard Times | 6 |
| 73 | Bradley's BRAD 305 | Summer Driftin'/Clocks (p/s) | 7 |
| 70 | Pye NSPL 18347 | PAUL BRETT SAGE (LP, blue/black label with logo banner on top) | 75 |
| 71 | Dawn DNLS 3021 | JUBILATION FOUNDRY (LP, gatefold sleeve, as Paul Brett's Sage, orange label) | 50 |
| 72 | Dawn DNLS 3032 | SCHIZOPHRENIA (LP, foldout sleeve, as Paul Brett's Sage, lilac label) | 50 |
| 73 | Bradley's BRADL 1001 | PAUL BRETT (LP, fully laminate envelope sleeve with inner) | 30 |
| 73 | Bradley's BRADL 1004 | CLOCKS (LP) | 15 |
| 75 | PF private pressing PF 001 | PHOENIX FUTURE (LP, 500 only, numbered on rear sleeve) | 30 |
| 70s | Private pressing | MUSIC MANIFOLD (LP, library issue) | 25 |

*(see also Elmer Gantry's Velvet Opera, Fire)*

## STEVE BRETT & MAVERICKS
| | | | |
|---|---|---|---|
| 65 | Columbia DB 7470 | Wishing/Anything That's Part Of You | 85 |
| 65 | Columbia DB 7581 | Sad, Lonely And Blue/Candy | 125 |
| 65 | Columbia DB 7794 | Sugar Shack/Chains On My Heart | 100 |

*(see also 'N Betweens, Slade)*

## TONY BREVETT
| | | | |
|---|---|---|---|
| 71 | Supreme SUP 224 | Don't Get Weary/BREVETT ALLSTARS: Version | 20 |
| 71 | Bullet BU 497 | So Ashamed/GREGORY ISAACS: My Only Lover | 20 |
| 74 | Dip DL 5019 | From Dusk To Dawn/JAH ALI: Black Snowfall | 20 |
| 74 | Dip DL 5028 | You Don't Love Me/Version | 20 |
| 76 | Stop Points SPR 001 | Words Of Prophecy/Version | 10 |

*(see also Melodians, Glen Adams)*

## BREW
| | | | |
|---|---|---|---|
| 60s | Oak LONDON | Crossroads/Play Your Tune (acetate, unreleased, handwritten labels) | 150 |

*(see also Camel)*

## TERESA BREWER
### SINGLES
| | | | |
|---|---|---|---|
| 54 | Vogue Coral Q 2011 | Skinny Minnie (Fishtail)/I Had Someone Else Before I Had You | 10 |
| 54 | Vogue Coral Q 2029 | Au Revoir/Danger Signs | 12 |
| 55 | Vogue Coral Q 72043 | Let Me Go, Lover (with Lancers)/Baby, Baby, Baby | 10 |
| 55 | Vogue Coral Q 72065 | How Important Can It Be?/What More Is There To Say? | 10 |
| 55 | Vogue Coral Q 72066 | Tweedlee Dee/Rock Love | 20 |

MINT VALUE £

| 55 | Vogue Coral Q 72077 | Pledging My Love/I Gotta Go Get My Baby | 10 |
| 55 | Vogue Coral Q 72083 | You're Telling Our Secret/Time | 8 |

**EPs**

| 50s | London BEP 6039 | TERESA BREWER WITH THE ALL STARS (export issue) | 10 |
| 50s | London BEP 6041 | TERESA BREWER WITH JACK PLEIS AND THE ALL STARS (export issue) | 10 |
| 59 | Coral FEP 2013 | HULA HOOP TIME WITH TERESA BREWER | 10 |

**ALBUMS**

| 51 | London H-APB 1006 | SHOWCASE (10") | 15 |
| 57 | Vogue Coral LVA 9020 | MUSIC! MUSIC! MUSIC! | 30 |
| 58 | Coral LVA 9075 | FOR TEENAGERS IN LOVE | 15 |
| 59 | Coral LVA 9095 | TIME FOR TERESA BREWER | 15 |
| 59 | Coral LVA 9100 | WHEN YOUR LOVER HAS GONE (also stereo SVL 3003) | 15 |
| 60 | Coral LVA 9129 | RIDIN' HIGH | 15 |

*(see also Snooky Lanson)*

## BREWER'S DROOP

| 72 | RCA RCA 2216 | Sweet Thing/Heart Of Stone/It Ain't The Meat - It's The Motion (p/s) | 6 |
| 72 | RCA SF 8301 | OPENING TIME (LP, gatefold sleeve, orange label) | 25 |

*(see also McGuinness Flint)*

## BRIAR

| 82 | Happy Face MM 142 | Rainbow (To The Skies)/Crying In The Rain (p/s) | 12 |
| 87 | PRT BRIART 1 | Edge Of A Broken Heart/Don't Forget Me When You're On Your Own (shaped picture disc, with headband) | 12 |
| 87 | UK UKALP 002 | CROWN OF THORNS (LP) | 15 |

## DICK BRICE

| 80s | Sylvan SYL 101R | A FEW ON 'IMS OWN (LP) | 50 |

## BRICKS

| 79 | Trans Galactic TGR 801 | Startrekker/Smash And Grab | 10 |

## BRIDGE

| 85 | Atlantic 9565(T) | Baby, Don't Hold Your Love Back/(Instrumental Version) (12") | 20 |

## BOBBY BRIDGER

| 70 | Beacon BEA 149 | The World Is Turning On/Why Do I Love You | 10 |
| 70 | Beacon BEA 159 | Sugar Shaker/You're In Love | 15 |

*(see also Errol Sobers)*

## SLIM BRIDGES & THE WILD FLOWERS

| 81 | Cricus CIRC 0006 | Rocking Goose/Mole At The Circus (p/s) | 20 |

## MARC BRIERLEY

| 68 | CBS 3857 | Hold On, Hold On, The Garden Sure Looks Good Spread On The Floor/Autograph Of Time | 15 |
| 69 | CBS 4191 | Stay A Little Longer Merry Ann/Flaxen Hair | 10 |
| 69 | CBS 4632 | Lady Of The Light/Sunny Weather | 10 |
| 70 | CBS 5266 | Be My Brother/If You Took The Bandage Off | 8 |
| 60s | Transatlantic TRAEP 147 | MARC BRIERLEY (EP) | 50 |
| 68 | CBS 63478 | WELCOME TO THE CITADEL (LP, orange label with textured surface) | 400 |
| 69 | CBS 63835 | HELLO (LP, gatefold sleeve, stickered sleeve, orange label) | 100 |
| 69 | CBS 63835 | HELLO (LP, gatefold sleeve, no sticker, orange label) | 90 |

*(see also Tractor)*

## ANNE BRIGGS

| 63 | Topic TOP 94 | THE HAZARDS OF LOVE (EP, with leaflet) | 150 |
| 14 | Topic TOP 94 | THE HAZARDS OF LOVE (EP, reissue, insert) | 10 |
| 71 | Topic 12TS 207 | ANNE BRIGGS (LP) | 300 |
| 71 | CBS 64612 | THE TIME HAS COME (LP) | 500 |
| 15 | Topic 12T2207 | ANNE BRIGGS (LP, reissue) | 18 |

*(see also A.L. Lloyd)*

## DUGGIE BRIGGS

| 78 | It IT 3 | Punk Rockin' Granny/I'm A Flasher (p/s) | 12 |
| 78 | It ITEP 5 | THE DUGGIE BRIGGS FLASHES ON IT AGAIN (EP) | 18 |

## LILLIAN BRIGGS

| 60 | Coral Q 72408 | Not A Soul (Blanket Roll Blues)/Smile For The People | 5 |

## ANNIE BRIGHT

| 70 | Columbia DB 8717 | Peaceful Mountain/Heartbreak House | 12 |
| 69 | Columbia DB 8587 | Concerning Love/Sneakin' Up On You | 15 |

## GREGORY BRIGHT

| 69 | Private Pressing | ROOM BY GREG (LP) | 400 |

## LEN BRIGHT COMBO

| 86 | Empire LEN 1 | Someone Must've Nailed Us Together/Mona (p/s) | 18 |
| 86 | Empire NICE 1 | THE LEN BRIGHT COMBO (LP) | 20 |
| 86 | Ambassador AMBAS 1 | COMBO TIME! (LP) | 20 |

*(see also Wreckless Eric, Milkshakes)*

## BRIGHTER

| 89 | Sarah SARAH 019 | Around The World In 80 Days (p/s, with inserts) | 10 |
| 90 | Sarah SARAH 27 | Noah's Ark/I Don't Think It Matters/Does Love Last Forever? (foldover p/s, postcard insert) | 12 |
| 91 | Sarah SARAH 56 | Poppy Day/Half-Hearted/So You said (p/s, insert) | 10 |
| 92 | Sarah SARAH 69 | DISNEY EP (10", p/s) | 15 |
| 91 | Sarah SARAH 404 | LAUREL (LP, 10") | 20 |

## BRIGHT EYES (1)

| 77 | Wild Dog DOG 14 | Miss In Betweener/Way of The Bow (500 only, no p/s) | 10 |

## BRIGHT EYES (2)
| | | | |
|---|---|---|---|
| 00 | Wichita WEBB 005S | The Calendar Hung Itself/HER SPACE HOLIDAY :The Doctor And The DJ | 6 |
| 04 | Saddle Creek SCE 68 | Lua/I Woke Up With This Song In My Head This Morning (p/s) | 8 |
| 05 | Saddle Creek SCE 79V | First Day Of My Life/When The President Talks To God (p/s) | 20 |
| 02 | Wichita WEBB 034 | LIFTED OR THE STORY IS IN THE SOIL, KEEP YOUR EAR TO THE GROUND (LP) | 15 |
| 05 | Saddle Creek SCE 72 | I'M WIDE AWAKE IT'S MORNING (LP) | 15 |
| 10 | Wichita WEBB 001 LPTEN | FEVERS AND MIRRORS (LP, reissue) | 15 |

## SARAH BRIGHTMAN
| | | | |
|---|---|---|---|
| 79 | Ariola Hansa AHA 585 | Love In a UFO/Illusions Of Love | 6 |
| 81 | Whisper WSP 104 | Not Having That/Echo 4 | 12 |
| 81 | Whisper WSP 102 | My Boyfriend's Back/Sleeping Beauty | 5 |
| 83 | Polydor POSP 659 | Rhythm Of The Rain/Action Man (p/s) | 20 |
| 87 | Polydor POSP 862 | Theme From 'A Room With A View'/O Mio Babbino Caro (p/s) | 10 |
| 90 | Polydor PZCD 74 | Something To Believe In/Brown Eyes/Love Changes Everything (CD single) | 30 |

## IAN BRIGHTON
| | | | |
|---|---|---|---|
| 77 | Bead Records BEAD 3 | MARSH GAS (LP) | 50 |

## BRIGHTON HORNS
| | | | |
|---|---|---|---|
| 66 | Stateside SS 526 | Surf Dell'amore/High Midnight | 8 |

## BRIGHTWINTER
| | | | |
|---|---|---|---|
| 70s | Myrrh MYR 1030 | A BAND FOR ALL SEASONS (LP) | 25 |

## BRILLIANT CORNERS
| | | | |
|---|---|---|---|
| 84 | SS20 SS21 | She's Got Fever/Black Water (red p/s) | 15 |
| 84 | SS20 SS21 | She's Got Fever/Black Water (pink p/s) | 30 |
| 84 | SS20 SS22 | Big Hip/Tangled Up In Blue (p/s) | 10 |
| 88 | McQueen MCQ2T | Why Do You Have To Go Out With Him?/Shangri La (12" p/s) | 10 |
| 86 | McQueen McQLP2 | WHAT'S IN A WORD (LP) | 18 |
| 88 | McQueen MCQLP | SOMEBODY UP THERE LIKES ME (LP, with inner) | 15 |
| 00 | Vinyl Japan ASKLP 117 | THE BBC SESSIONS (LP) | 15 |

## JOHN BRIMACOMBE
| | | | |
|---|---|---|---|
| 72 | Pye 7N 45159 | Try A Little Harder/Four Sad Men | 8 |

## CHARLES BRIMMER
| | | | |
|---|---|---|---|
| 80 | Special Agent 9005 | I Stand Accused/God Bless Our Love | 10 |

## BRIMSTONE
| | | | |
|---|---|---|---|
| 71 | Deram DM 322 | Keyhole Jake/The Monkey Song | 6 |
| 71 | Decca DF 13222 | If Ever You See Me/Work Out | 5 |

## LOS BRINCOS
| | | | |
|---|---|---|---|
| 67 | Page One POF 023 | Lola/Passport (1st 5,000 in p/s) | 35 |
| 67 | Page One POF 023 | Lola/Passport (no p/s) | 10 |
| 67 | Page One POF 031 | Nobody Wants You Now/Train (as Brincos) | 60 |

## BRINDLEY BRAE
| | | | |
|---|---|---|---|
| 73 | Harmony DB 0002 | VILLAGE MUSIC (LP, 50 copies only, private pressing with insert) | 150 |

*(see also Bev Pegg, Away From The Sand)*

## BRINSLEY SCHWARZ
| | | | |
|---|---|---|---|
| 70 | United Artists UP 35118 | Shining Brightly/What Do You Suggest | 10 |
| 71 | Liberty LBY 15419 | Country Girl/Funk Angel | 15 |
| 72 | United Artists UP 35312 | Country Girl/Funk Angel (reissue) | 6 |
| 73 | United Artists UP 35588 | Speedo/I Worry | 5 |
| 74 | United Artists UP 35642 | I've Cried My Last Tear/Bringdown | 5 |
| 74 | United Artists UP 35700 | (What's So Funny 'Bout) Peace, Love And Understanding/ Ever Since You're Gone | 6 |
| 75 | United Artists UP 35768 | Everybody/I Like You, I Don't Love You | 6 |
| 75 | United Artists UP 35812 | There's A Cloud In My Heart/I Got The Real Thing | 6 |
| 70 | United Artists UAS 29111 | BRINSLEY SCHWARZ (LP, gatefold sleeve, orange/pink label) | 50 |
| 70 | Liberty LBG 83427 | DESPITE IT ALL (LP, gatefold sleeve) | 35 |
| 72 | United Artists UAS 29217 | SILVER PISTOL (LP, with poster) | 35 |
| 72 | United Artists UAS 29374 | NERVOUS ON THE ROAD (LP) | 15 |
| 73 | United Artists UAS 29489 | PLEASE DON'T EVER CHANGE (LP) | 20 |
| 78 | United Artists UAK 30177 | FIFTEEN THOUGHTS OF BRINSLEY SCHWARTZ (LP, poster) | 20 |

*(see also Kippington Lodge, Hitters, Knees, Limelight, Nick Lowe, Ernie Graham, Rumour, Chilli Willi & Red Hot Peppers, Ducks Deluxe)*

## LLOYD BRISCO
| | | | |
|---|---|---|---|
| 64 | Rio R42 | Fabulous Eyes/What You See | 20 |
| 64 | Island WI 187 | Jonah The Master/Mr. Cleveland | 20 |

## JOHNNY BRISTOL
| | | | |
|---|---|---|---|
| 80 | Ariola AHA 567 | Love No Longer Has A Hold On Me/Till I See You Again | 10 |

## BRITANIA
| | | | |
|---|---|---|---|
| 73 | EMI EMI 2038 | Right Down The Line/Judy Brings Me Down | 5 |

## BRITISH LIONS
| | | | |
|---|---|---|---|
| 78 | Vertigo 6059 192 | One More Chance To Run/Booster (p/s) | 5 |
| 78 | Vertigo 6059 201 | International Heroes/Eat The Rich | 5 |
| 78 | Vertigo 9102 019 | BRITISH LIONS (LP, with inner sleeve) | 15 |
| 80 | Cherry Red ARED 7 | TROUBLE WITH WOMEN (LP) | 15 |

*(see also Mott The Hoople, Medicine Head)*

## BRITISH SEA POWER
| | | | |
|---|---|---|---|
| 01 | Rough Trade RTRADE S032 | Remember Me/A Lovely Day Tomorrow (p/s, 1264 only) | 6 |
| 02 | Rough Trade RTRADE 048 | The Lonely/Spirit Of St. Louis | 6 |
| 02 | Rough Trade RTRADES 069 | Childhood Memories/Favours In The Beetroot Fields (p/s, 1000 only) | 6 |
| 03 | Rough Trade RTRADE S092 | Carrion/Apologies To Insect Life (handdrawn, textured sleeve, 2003 only) | 12 |
| 03 | Rough Trade RTRADES 125 | Remember Me/The Scottish Wildlife Experience (hand-drawn name on 2003 copies) | 8 |

| 05 | None | Thirteen Ways To Disappear (CD-R sent to first 13 buyers from BSP web shop) | 20 |
| 05 | Rough Trade RTRADS302 | Remember Me/I Am A Cider Drinker (7" limited edition. 1,966 copies) | 10 |
| 12 | Golden Chariot GOLDEN CHARIOT 006-011 | BSP EP BOX SET (6 x CD box set) | 120 |
| 02 | Rough Trade RTRADELP 090 | THE DECLINE OF BRITISH SEA POWER (2-LP, insert) | 18 |
| 05 | Rough Trade RTRADLP 200 | OPEN SEASON (LP) | 15 |
| 08 | Rough Trade RTRADLP 300 | DO YOU LIKE ROCK MUSIC? (LP) | 18 |

*(see also The Wurzels)*

## BRITISH SHOES
| 79 | NWJ SRTS/79/CUS 542 | Running From Mummy/Where Would We Be Without Shoes (p/s) | 100 |
| 79 | NWJ SRTS/79/CUS 542 | Running From Mummy/Where Would We Be Without Shoes (no p/s) | 50 |

## BRITISH WALKERS
| 65 | Pye International 7N 25298 | I Found You/Diddley Daddy | 25 |

## BRITT
| 66 | Piccadilly 7N 35273 | You Really Have Started Something/Leave My Baby Alone | 30 |

## TINA BRITT
| 65 | London HLC 9974 | The Real Thing/Teardrops Fell | 70 |
| 65 | London HLC 9974 | The Real Thing/Teardrops Fell (DJ Copy) | 100 |

## BUDDY BRITTEN & REGENTS
| 62 | Piccadilly 7N 35075 | My Pride, My Joy/Long Gone Baby | 15 |
| 62 | Decca F 11435 | Don't Spread It Around/The Beat Of My Heart | 15 |
| 63 | Oriole CB 1827 | If You Gotta Make A Fool Of Somebody/Money | 15 |
| 63 | Oriole CB 1839 | Hey There/I'll Cry No More | 15 |
| 63 | Oriole CB 1859 | My Resistance Is Low/When I See You Smile | 12 |
| 63 | Oriole CB 1889 | Money/Sorrow Tomorrow | 20 |
| 64 | Oriole CB 1911 | I Guess I'm In The Way/Zip-A-Dee-Doo-Dah | 15 |
| 65 | Piccadilly 7N 35241 | She's About A Mover/Since You've Gone | 15 |
| 65 | Piccadilly 7N 35257 | Right Now/Jailer Bring Me Water | 5 |

*(see also Regents)*

## TERRY BRITTEN
| 69 | Columbia DB8580 | 2000 Weeks/Bargain Day | 100 |

## CHRIS BRITTON
| 69 | Page One POLS 022 | AS I AM (LP, gatefold sleeve, blue/silver label) | 400 |

*(see also Troggs)*

## JEFF BRITTON & THE SPITFIRES
| 76 | Decca F13643 | Rub Out/Breakwood | 20 |

## MAGGIE BRITTON
| 80 | Piccadilly 7P191 | Goodship Earth/No Secrets | 6 |

## BRIXTON MARKET
| 69 | Beacon BEA 138 | Children Get Ready/Bangarang | 15 |
| 69 | Beacon SBEAB 8 | BLACK FUNK (LP) | 15 |

## JO BROADBERY & THE STANDOUTS
| 80 | Revenge REV-S-1 | Out Of The Real/Breaking Down (no p/s) | 10 |
| 80 | Revenge REVLP-1 | JO BROADBERRY AND THE STANDOUTS (LP) | 20 |

## BROADCAST
| 96 | Wurlitzer Jukebox WJ 6 | Accidentals/We've Got Time (p/s, with sticker) | 40 |
| 96 | Wurlitzer Jukebox WJ 6 | Accidentals/We've Got Time (p/s, without sticker) | 10 |
| 96 | Duophonic DS 45-14 | Living Room/Phantom (wraparound p/s, 1,500 only) | 12 |
| 96 | Duophonic DS 45-16 | THE BOOK LOVERS EP (12", p/s, 2,000) | 25 |
| 99 | Warp 7WAP 125 | Echo's Answer/Test Area | 15 |
| 00 | Warp 7WAP 132 | Come On Let's Go/Distant Call (p/s) | 8 |
| 00 | Warp WAP 129 | EXTENDED PLAY (12" EP) | 10 |
| 00 | Warp WAP 141 | EXTENDED PLAY TWO EP (12", p/s) | 15 |
| 03 | Warp WAP 162 | Pendulum/Small Song IV/One Hour Empore/Still Feel Like Tears/Violent Playground/Minus Two (12" p/s) | 15 |
| 05 | Warp 7WAP 193 | America's Boy/Tender Buttons (p/s) | 8 |
| 97 | Warp WARPLP 52 | WORK & NON WORK (LP) | 40 |
| 00 | Warp WARPLP 65 | THE NOISE MADE BY PEOPLE (LP, gatefold sleeve, insert) | 40 |
| 03 | Warp WARPLP 106 | HAHA SOUND (LP) | 30 |
| 05 | Warp WARPLP 136 | TENDER BUTTONS (LP) | 30 |
| 06 | Warp WARPLP 146 | THE FUTURE CRAYON (2-LP) | 40 |
| 09 | Warp WARPLP 189 | INVESTIGATES WITCH CULTS OF THE RADIO AGE (LP, with the Focus Group) | 30 |

## BROADSIDE
| 71 | Lincolnshire Ass. LA 4 | THE GIPSY'S WEDDING DAY (10" LP) | 50 |
| 73 | Topic 12TS 228 | THE MOON SHONE BRIGHT (As The Broadside From Grimsby) (LP, blue label) | 40 |
| 75 | Guildhall GHS 5 | SONGS FROM THE STOCKS (LP) | 80 |
| 75 | Guildhall GHS 12 | DRIVE THE DARK AWAY (LP) | 50 |

## BROADSIDE OUTCASTS
| 78 | Profile GMOR 154 | ABO EP | 20 |

## DAVE BROCK
| 83 | Flicknife FLS 024 | Social Alliance/Raping Robots In The Street (p/s) | 5 |

*(see also Dr. Technical & Machines, Hawkwind)*

## NORAH BROCKSTEDT
| 60 | Top Rank JAR 353 | Big Boy/Tell Me No Lies | 5 |

## PETER BROGGS
| 79 | Hit Run HITDD 13 | Higher Field Marshall (Feat. Prince Far I)/I And I A The Chosen One/PRINCE FAR I & BRIGADIER JAM DOWN : Loved By Everyone (12") | 40 |
| 80 | Cha Cha CHAD 25 | Never Forget Jah/CORNWALL CAMPBELL : Rainbow (12") | 30 |

| | | |
|---|---|---|
| 80 | Selena SO 006 | Jah Golden Throne/DEXTER MCKINTYRE : 144.00 Saints............................................50 |
| 79 | Shashamani IMF 004 | PROGRESSIVE YOUTH (LP) ..........................................................................50 |

## BROKEN BONES
| | | |
|---|---|---|
| 84 | Fall Out FALL 020 | Decapitated/Problem/Liquidated Brains (p/s) ...............................................5 |
| 84 | Fall Out FALL 025 | Crucifix/Fight The Good Fight ...................................................................10 |
| 85 | Fall Out FALL 10034 | Seeing Through My Eyes/The Point Of Agony/It's Like/Decapitated/Part 2/Death Is Imminent (10", p/s)........................................................................8 |
| 83 | Fall Out FALL LP 028 | BROKEN BONES (LP) .................................................................................15 |
| 84 | Stoned Spliff 1 | LIVE AT THE 100 CLUB (LP) .......................................................................20 |

*(see also Discharge)*

## BROKEN BOW
| | | |
|---|---|---|
| 87 | Sodium | Vagrant/Bite Back .....................................................................................25 |

## BROKEN GLASS (1)
| | | |
|---|---|---|
| 75 | Capitol E-ST 11510 | BROKEN GLASS (LP, with insert)................................................................18 |

*(see also Chicken Shack, Warhorse, Miller Anderson, Bronco)*

## BROKEN GLASS (2)
| | | |
|---|---|---|
| 84 | Streetwave MKHAN 17 | Style Of The Street (12")..........................................................................15 |

## BROKEN ROSE
| | | |
|---|---|---|
| 86 | Exhibit 1 EXL 006 | WAR TEARS (LP) .....................................................................................100 |

*(see also Bizarre Unit, Paul Nova)*

## JOHN BROMLEY
| | | |
|---|---|---|
| 68 | Polydor 56224 | What A Woman Does/My My .....................................................................30 |
| 68 | Polydor 56287 | And The Feeling Goes/Sweet Little Princess ...............................................20 |
| 69 | Polydor 56305 | Melody Fayre/Sugar Love .........................................................................40 |
| 69 | Polydor 56340 | Hold Me Woman/Weather Man .................................................................30 |
| 69 | Atlantic 584 289 | Kick A Tin Can/Wonderland Avenue U.S.A..................................................30 |
| 69 | Polydor 583 048 | SING (LP) ...............................................................................................100 |

*(see also Fleur De Lys, Three People)*

## BILLY BRIMSTONE
| | | |
|---|---|---|
| 05 | YNR YNR 021 | Keep It Live (Vocal)/Keep It Live (Instrumental) .........................................8 |

*(see also Jehst)*

## BRONCO
| | | |
|---|---|---|
| 70 | Island WIP 6096 | Lazy Now/A Matter Of Perspective ...........................................................20 |
| 73 | Polydor 2058 395 | The Traveller/Steal That Gold ....................................................................6 |
| 70 | Island ILPS 9124 | COUNTRY HOME (LP, gatefold sleeve, pink 'i' label) ...................................40 |
| 70 | Island ILPS 9124 | COUNTRY HOME (LP, gatefold sleeve, 'pink rim palm tree' label) .................20 |
| 71 | Island ILPS 9161 | ACE OF SUNLIGHT (LP, gatefold sleeve, 'pink rim palm tree' label) .............25 |
| 73 | Polydor 2383 215 | SMOKIN' MIXTURE (LP, gatefold sleeve) ....................................................15 |

*(see also Alan Bown Set)*

## BRONNT INDUSTRIES
| | | |
|---|---|---|
| 05 | Static Caravan | KAPITAL BROCKEN (EP) (8" lathe cut, clear vinyl, hand-stamped bag, 100 only) ...........25 |

## BRONX CHEER
| | | |
|---|---|---|
| 70 | Parlophone R 5865 | Drive My Car/Foxtrot ................................................................................8 |
| 71 | Dawn DNX 2512 | Barrelhouse Player/Surprising Find/Whether Or Not/Party For One (p/s) .......8 |
| 72 | Dawn DNS 1019 | Hold On To Me/Late Date ..........................................................................6 |
| 72 | Dawn DNLS 3004 | GREATEST HITS VOLUME 3 (LP, gatefold sleeve with insert, lilac label) .........20 |

## BRONZ
| | | |
|---|---|---|
| 84 | Bronze BRO 178 | Send Down An Angel/Tiger (p/s) ................................................................5 |

## DAVID BROOK
| | | |
|---|---|---|
| 68 | President PT 196 | Witchfinder General/Janie ........................................................................10 |

## MICHAEL BROOK
| | | |
|---|---|---|
| 92 | 4AD CAD 2007 | COBALT BLUE (LP, featuring Brian Eno) ......................................................20 |

## PATTI BROOK (& DIAMONDS)
| | | |
|---|---|---|
| 60 | Pye 7N 15300 | Since You've Been Gone/That's The Way It's Gonna Be (as Patti Brook & Diamonds) ......5 |
| 61 | Pye 7N 15339 | When The Red Red Robin/Look What You've Done To Me ...............................5 |
| 61 | Pye 7N 15378 | Heaven Is Being With You/Your Love Came Into My Heart...............................5 |
| 62 | Pye 7N 15422 | I Love You, I Need You/Unloved, Unwanted..................................................5 |

## TONY BROOK & BREAKERS
| | | |
|---|---|---|
| 64 | Columbia DB 7279 | Meanie Genie/Ooh Poo Pah Doo (in p/s)..................................................200 |
| 64 | Columbia DB 7279 | Meanie Genie/Ooh Poo Pah Doo..............................................................80 |
| 65 | Columbia DB 7444 | Love Dances On/I Won't Hurt You .............................................................15 |

## GARY BROOKER
| | | |
|---|---|---|
| 81 | Chrysalis CHS 2396 | Leave The Candle/Chasing The Chop (Eric Clapton guest appearance) .........100 |

## HOWARD S BROOKING
| | | |
|---|---|---|
| 82 | H.S.B. S82/CUS/1596 | In The Autumn Gold/Checkmate (no p/s) ..................................................15 |

## BROOKLYN
| | | |
|---|---|---|
| 80 | Rondelet ROUND 3 | I Wanna Be A Detective (p/s)....................................................................30 |
| 81 | Rondelet ROUND 6 | Hollywood/Late Again (p/s) ......................................................................20 |
| 80 | Rondelet ABOUT 3 | YOU NEVER KNOW WHAT YOU'LL FIND (LP)...............................................30 |

## BROOKLYN BRIDGE
| | | |
|---|---|---|
| 68 | Pye International 7N 25473 | From My Window I Can See/Little Red Boat By The River ...............................8 |
| 69 | Buddah 201 029 | The Worst That Could Happen/Your Kite, My Kite .......................................10 |
| 70 | Buddah 2011 010 | Free As The Wind/He's Not A Happy Man ....................................................6 |
| 70 | Buddah 2011 034 | Down By The River/Look Again ...................................................................6 |

*(see also Johnny Maestro, Crests)*

## BABA BROOKS
| | | |
|---|---|---|
| 63 | Island WI 078 | 5 O'Clock Whistle/African Blood (by Blues Masters).....................................50 |

MINT VALUE £

| 63 | Island WI 096 | Bank To Bank (Parts 1 & 2) | 35 |
| 63 | Island WI 127 | Three Blind Mice/BILLY & BOBBY: We Ain't Got Nothing | 30 |
| 63 | R&B JB 125 | Water Melon Man/STRANGER COLE: Things Come To Those Who Wait | 40 |
| 64 | Black Swan WI 137 | Portrait Of My Love/STRANGER COLE: Goodbye Peggy | 20 |
| 64 | Black Swan WI 412 | Jelly Beans/ERIC MORRIS: Sampson | 30 |
| 64 | Black Swan WI 414 | Key To The City/ERIC MORRIS: Solomon Grundie | 40 |
| 64 | Black Swan WI 434 | Spider/Melody Jamboree | 30 |
| 64 | Black Swan WI 438 | Cork Foot/HERSANG COMBO: B.B.C. Channel 2 | 30 |
| 65 | Black Swan WI 442 | Musical Workshop/DUKE WHITE: Be Wise | 35 |
| 65 | Black Swan WI 444 | Bus Strike/DUKE WHITE: Sow Good Seeds | 35 |
| 65 | Black Swan WI 451 | Ethiopia/ARCHIBALD TROTT: Promised Land | 30 |
| 65 | Black Swan WI 466 | Baby Elephant Walk/DON DRUMMOND: Don's Special | 30 |
| 65 | Ska Beat JB 189 | Dr. Decker/OWEN & LEON SILVERA : Woman | 15 |
| 65 | Ska Beat JB 220 | One Eyed Giant (with His Band)/DYNAMITES: Walk Out On Me | 40 |
| 65 | Island WI 229 | Guns Fever/DOTTY & BONNIE: Don't Do It | 35 |
| 65 | Island WI 233 | Independent Ska/STRANGER & CLAUDETTE: Seven Days | 30 |
| 65 | Island WI 235 | Duck Soup/ZODIACS: Renegade | 150 |
| 65 | Island WI 239 | Vitamin A/ALTON ELLIS: Dance Crasher | 50 |
| 65 | Island WI 241 | Teenage Ska/ALTON ELLIS: You Are Not To Blame | 70 |
| 65 | Rio R 061 | Shenk I Sheck (& Band)/SHENLEY & HIACYNTH: Set Me Free | 50 |
| 66 | Doctor Bird DB 1042 | The Clock (& Band)/LYN TAITT & COMETS & SILVERTONES: Raindrops | 40 |
| 66 | Doctor Bird DB 1046 | Jam Session (with His Band)/CONQUERORS: What A Agony | 40 |
| 67 | Ska Beat JB 268 | One Eyed Giant (with His Band)/DYNAMITES: Walk Out On Me (reissue) | 20 |

*(see also Blues Masters, Eric Brooks, Stranger & Patsy, Riots, Joey Smith, Saints, Richard Brothers, Derrick Morgan, Lord Tanamo, Lord Brisco, Hippy Boys, Roy Panton, Higgs & Wilson, Vinley Gayle, Joe White, Stranger & Patsy)*

## CEDRIC 'IM' BROOKS
| 73 | Tropical AL046 | South African Reggae/Part 2 | 10 |
| 78 | Water Lily ARCO LP 009 | UNITED AFRICA (LP) | 25 |

## CHUCK BROOKS
| 69 | Soul City SC 116 | Black Sheep/I've Got To Get Myself Together | 20 |
| 69 | Soul City SC 116 | Black Sheep/I've Got To Get Myself Together (DJ Copy) | 75 |

## D. BROOKS
| 70 | Big BG 304 | Oh Me Oh My (actually "Every Time" by Hi-Tals)/ANSEL COLLINS: Staccato (actually "Every Time Version" by Rupie Edwards Allstars) | 12 |

## DALE BROOKS
| 65 | King KG 1025 | Army Green/Reminds Me Of You | 10 |
| 66 | Stateside SS 553 | I Wanna Be Your Girl/Like Other Girls Do | 30 |

## DONNIE BROOKS
| 61 | London HA-N 2391 | THE HAPPIEST DONNIE BROOKS (LP) | 15 |

## ELKIE BROOKS
| 64 | Decca F 11928 | Something's Got A Hold On Me/Hello Stranger | 40 |
| 64 | Decca F 11983 | Nothing Left To Do But Cry/Strange Though It Seems | 40 |
| 65 | Decca F 12061 | The Way You Do The Things You Do/Blue Tonight | 40 |
| 65 | HMV POP 1431 | He's Gotta Love Me/When You Appear | 40 |
| 65 | HMV POP 1431 | He's Gotta Love Me/When You Appear (DJ Copy) | 80 |
| 65 | HMV POP 1480 | All My Life/Can't Stop Thinking Of You | 20 |
| 66 | HMV POP 1512 | Baby Let Me Love You/Stop The Music | 30 |
| 66 | HMV POP 1512 | Baby Let Me Love You/Stop The Music (DJ Copy) | 80 |
| 69 | NEMS 56-4136 | Come September/If You Should Go | 7 |
| 74 | Chrysalis CHS 2069 | Sacrifice/ALICE COOPER: I'm Flash (p/s, unissued, promo only) | 35 |
| 84 | A & M SCREEN 1 | SCREEN GEMS (CD, beware of copies!) | 50 |

*(see also Dada, Vinegar Joe, Steve York's Camelo Pardalis, Elki & Owen)*

## BROOKS & JERRY
| 68 | Direction 58-3267 | I Got What It Takes Parts 1 & 2 | 15 |
| 68 | Direction 58-3267 | I Got What It Takes Parts 1 & 2 (DJ Copy) | 30 |

## JOE BROOKS COLLECTIVE
| 71 | CBS 7234 | Messing Up The Mind Of A Young Girl/Before The Sand Has Run Out Of The Hour Glass | 12 |

## JULIAN BROOKS
| 70 | Pye 7N17996 | Justine/Lazy Guy | 25 |

## MIKE BROOKS
| 79 | Hit Run HIT DD 9 | Love Is Like A Password/Feeling Of Reggae (12") | 25 |
| 79 | Hit Run HIT DD 23 | Long Long Time/Dub In Time | 30 |
| 76 | Burning Sounds BSLP 1026 | WHAT A GATHERING (LP) | 15 |

## NORMAN BROOKS & G-BOYS
| 54 | London L 1166 | Hello Sunshine/You're My Baby | 15 |
| 54 | London L 1202 | Somebody Wonderful/You Shouldn't Have Kissed Me The First Time | 15 |
| 54 | London L 1228 | A Sky-Blue Shirt And A Rainbow Tie/This Waltz With You | 15 |
| 54 | London HL 8015 | I'm Kinda Crazy/I'd Like To Be In Your Shoes, Baby | 15 |
| 54 | London HL 8041 | I Can't Give You Anything But Love (solo)/GO-BOYS: Johnny's Tune | 15 |
| 54 | London HL 8051 | Candy Moon/My 3-D Sweetie | 10 |
| 55 | London HL 8115 | Back In Circulation/Lou Lou Louisiana | 10 |
| 54 | London RE-P 1004 | PRESENTING NORMAN BROOKS VOLUME 1 (EP) | 10 |
| 55 | London RE-P 1021 | BABY MINE (EP) | 10 |

## PAM BROOKS
| 70 | Big BG 307 | Oh Me Oh My/ANSELL COLLINS: Staccato | 18 |

## RAY BROOKS
| 72 | Polydor 2001334 | Pictures/On My Own | 10 |

## WES BROOKS
| | | | |
|---|---|---|---|
| 77 | ATA ATA 1003 | Lay Down Your Arms/Version | 70 |

## BIG BILL BROONZY/CHICAGO BILL
| | | | |
|---|---|---|---|
| 52 | Melodisc 1203 | Five Foot Seven/Plough Hand Blues (78, as Chicago Bill) | 10 |
| 58 | Vogue V 2351 | Guitar Shuffle/When Did You Leave Heaven | 30 |
| 61 | Storyville A 44053 | Midnight Special/Black Brown And White | 10 |
| 55 | Vogue EPV 1024 | HEY BUD BLUES (EP) | 20 |
| 56 | Vogue EPV 1074 | SINGS THE BLUES (EP) | 20 |
| 56 | Vogue EPV 1107 | GUITAR SHUFFLE (EP) | 20 |
| 56 | Pye Jazz NJE 1005 | MISSISSIPPI BLUES VOLUME 1 (EP) | 20 |
| 56 | Pye Jazz NJE 1015 | MISSISSIPPI BLUES VOLUME 2 (EP) | 20 |
| 56 | Melodisc EPM7 65 | KEEP YOUR HANDS OFF (EP) | 20 |
| 57 | Pye Jazz NJE 1047 | SOUTHERN SAGA (EP) | 20 |
| 57 | Columbia SEG 7674 | BIG BILL BROONZY SINGS THE BLUES (EP) | 15 |
| 57 | Tempo EXA 61 | BILL BAILEY WON'T YOU PLEASE COME HOME (EP) | 15 |
| 58 | Columbia SEG 7790 | BIG BILL BROONZY SINGS THE BLUES NO. 2 (EP) | 15 |
| 60 | Mercury ZEP 10065 | WALKIN' DOWN A LONESOME ROAD (EP) | 15 |
| 60 | Mercury ZEP 10093 | HOLLERIN' BLUES (EP) | 22 |
| 60s | Mercury/Emearcy MMB 12003 | THE BLUES (LP) | 20 |
| 62 | Storyville SEP 383 | BLUES ANTHOLOGY VOLUME 3 (EP) | 12 |
| 64 | Mercury 10003 MCE | BLUES-GOSPEL-SPIRITUAL (EP) | 15 |
| 57 | Vogue LAE 12009 | BIG BILL BLUES (LP) | 35 |
| 57 | Philips BBL 7113 | BIG BILL BROONZY (LP) | 35 |
| 58 | Vogue LAE 12063 | THE BLUES (LP) | 35 |
| 58 | Pye Nixa Jazz NJL 16 | TRIBUTE TO BIG BILL (LP) | 35 |
| 59 | Tempo TAP 23 | AN EVENING WITH BIG BILL BROONZY (LP) | 40 |
| 61 | HMV CLP 1544 | LAST SESSION PART 1 (LP) | 20 |
| 62 | HMV CLP 1551 | LAST SESSION PART 2 (LP) | 20 |
| 62 | HMV CLP 1562 | LAST SESSION PART 3 (LP) | 20 |
| 65 | Storyville SLP 143 | AN EVENING WITH BROONZY (LP) | 15 |
| 65 | Fontana 688 206ZL | TROUBLE IN MIND (LP) | 15 |

## BIG BILL BROONZY & PETE SEEGER
| | | | |
|---|---|---|---|
| 64 | Xtra XTRA 1006 | IN CONCERT (LP) | 20 |
| 66 | Verve Folkways VLP 5006 | IN CONCERT (LP, reissue, also stereo SVLP 506) | 15 |

(see also Pete Seeger)

## BIG BILL BROONZY/SONNY BOY WILLIAMSON [I]
| | | | |
|---|---|---|---|
| 65 | RCA Victor RD 7685 | BIG BILL AND SONNY BOY (LP) | 30 |

(see also Sonny Boy Williamson [I])

## BIG BILL BROONZY, SONNY TERRY & BROWNIE MCGHEE
| | | | |
|---|---|---|---|
| 64 | Xtra XTRA 1004 | BIG BILL BROONZY/SONNY TERRY/BROWNIE McGHEE (LP) | 30 |

(see also Sonny Terry & Brownie McGhee, Washboard Sam)

## BROTH
| | | | |
|---|---|---|---|
| 71 | Mercury 6338 032 | BROTH (LP) | 60 |

## BROTHER BARON
| | | | |
|---|---|---|---|
| 70s | Fab FAB 281 | Your Love/Your Love Version | 6 |

## BROTHER BUNG
| | | | |
|---|---|---|---|
| 68 | Avenue BEV 1054 | BLUES CRUSADE (EP) | 15 |

(see also Bob Pearce)

## BROTHER D & THE COLLECTIVE EFFORT
| | | | |
|---|---|---|---|
| 80 | Island IPR 2005 | How We Gonna Make The Black Nation Rise (12") | 10 |

## BROTHER DAN ALLSTARS
| | | | |
|---|---|---|---|
| 68 | Trojan TR 601 | Donkey Returns/Tribute To Sir K.B. | 20 |
| 68 | Trojan TR 602 | Eastern Organ/JIVERS: Our Love Will Last | 40 |
| 68 | Trojan TR 603 | Hold Pon Them/OWEN GRAY: Answer Me | 18 |
| 68 | Trojan TR 607 | Read Up/Gallop | 15 |
| 68 | Trojan TR 608 | Another Saturday Night/Bee's Knees | 10 |
| 68 | Trojan TBL 101 | LET'S CATCH THE BEAT (LP) | 100 |
| 69 | Trojan TRL 1 | FOLLOW THAT DONKEY (LP) | 100 |

(see also Pooch Jackson)

## BROTHER SUSAN
| | | | |
|---|---|---|---|
| 74 | EMI EMI 2117 | See My Fingers Fly/Full Blooded Natural Man | 18 |
| 74 | EMI EMI 2174 | Ride Ride Ride/Flash | 18 |

## BROTHER TREVOR & U BROWN
| | | | |
|---|---|---|---|
| 78 | Matumbi Music MM005 | Skip Away/Selassi I (12") | 25 |

(see also Matumbi)

## BROTHER (1)
| | | | |
|---|---|---|---|
| 92 | Tribal Bass TRIBE 10 | Ghettogedden | 7 |

## BROTHER (2)
| | | | |
|---|---|---|---|
| 11 | Chess Club CC 035 | Darling Buds Of May/Homesick (Demo) (p/s, 500 only) | 7 |

## BROTHERHOOD (1)
| | | | |
|---|---|---|---|
| 69 | Philips BF 1756 | Paper Man/Give It To Me Now | 15 |

## BROTHERHOOD (2)
| | | | |
|---|---|---|---|
| 91 | Bite It BITE 1 | DESCENDANTS OF THE HOLOCAUST (EP) | 30 |
| 91 | Bite It BITE 2 | DESCENDANTS OF THE HOLOCAUST (remix 12") | 15 |

## BROTHERHOOD OF BREATH
| | | | |
|---|---|---|---|
| 74 | Ogun OG 100 | LIVE AT WILLISAU (LP, with Chris McGregor) | 20 |

(see also Chris McGregor's Brotherhood Of Breath, Mark Charig)

## BROTHERHOOD OF LIZARDS
| | | | |
|---|---|---|---|
| 89 | Deltic DELT LP5 | LIZARDLAND (LP) | 20 |

*(see also Gypp, Martin Newell, Cleaners From Venus)*

## BROTHERHOOD OF MAN
| | | | |
|---|---|---|---|
| 69 | Deram DM 276 | Love One Another/A Little Bit Of Heaven | 6 |
| 70 | Deram DM 317 | This Boy/You Can Depend On Me | 6 |
| 71 | Deram DM 327 | Reach Out Your Hand/Better Tomorrow | 15 |
| 74 | Dawn DNS 1055 | When Love Catches Up With You/How Can You Love (p/s) | 6 |

*(see also Sue & Sunny, Sue & Sunshine, Stockingtops)*

## BROTHERLY LOVE
| | | | |
|---|---|---|---|
| 67 | CBS 2978 | Ocean Of Tears/Mr Average Man | 15 |
| 73 | CBS S CBS 1737 | Public Enemy No.1/Here Stands A Better Man | 5 |

## BROTHERS
| | | | |
|---|---|---|---|
| 67 | London HLU 10158 | Love Story/The Girl's Alright | 7 |

## BROTHERS & SISTERS (U.K.)
| | | | |
|---|---|---|---|
| 68 | private pressing | ARE WATCHING YOU (LP) | 90 |

## BROTHERS & SISTERS (U.S.)
| | | | |
|---|---|---|---|
| 69 | CBS 4583 | Mighty Quinn/Chimes Of Freedom | 5 |
| 69 | CBS 63746 | DYLAN'S GOSPEL (LP) | 15 |

## BROTHERS GRIMM
| | | | |
|---|---|---|---|
| 65 | Decca F 12224 | Lost Love/Make It Or Break It | 10 |
| 66 | Ember EMB 222 | A Man Needs Love/Looky Looky | 50 |

## BROTHERS KANE
| | | | |
|---|---|---|---|
| 66 | Decca F 12448 | Walking In The Sand/Won't You Stay Long | 25 |

*(see also Sarstedt Brothers, Peter Lincoln, Peter Sarstedt, Clive Sands, Wes Sands, Eden Kane)*

## BROTHERS TWO
| | | | |
|---|---|---|---|
| 68 | Action ACT 4513 | Here I Am, In Love Again/I'm Tired Of You Baby | 30 |

## BROTHERS WILLIAM
| | | | |
|---|---|---|---|
| 65 | Parlophone R 5293 | Linda Jane Blues/Honey Love | 8 |

## BROTHERS (U.S.)
| | | | |
|---|---|---|---|
| 75 | RCA 2618 | Are You Ready For This/Everybody Loves A WInner | 6 |

## AYSHEA BROUGH
| | | | |
|---|---|---|---|
| 71 | RCA RCA 2105 | Master Jack/Both Sides Now | 7 |

*(see also Ayshea)*

## EDGAR BROUGHTON BAND
| | | | |
|---|---|---|---|
| 69 | Harvest HAR 5001 | Evil/Death Of An Electric Citizen | 15 |
| 70 | Harvest HAR 5015 | Out Demons Out/Momma's Reward | 7 |
| 70 | Harvest HAR 5021 | Up Yours!/Officer Dan | 8 |
| 70 | Harvest HAR 5032 | Apache Drop Out/Freedom | 7 |
| 71 | Harvest HAR 5040 | Hotel Room/Call Me A Liar | 10 |
| 72 | Harvest HAR 5049 | Gone Blue/Someone/Mr. Crosby | 8 |
| 69 | Harvest SHVL 757 | WASA WASA (LP, 1st pressing, gatefold sleeve, no EMI box on label with"the Gramophone Co" and "sold in U.K." label text) | 170 |
| 69 | Harvest SHVL 757 | WASA WASA (LP, 2nd pressing, gatefold sleeve, later issue with EMI box on label) | 50 |
| 69 | Harvest SHVL 757 | WASA WASA (LP, 2nd pressing variation, gatefold sleeve, no EMI box on label or "the Gramophone Co" and "sold in U.K." label text) | 40 |
| 70 | Harvest SHVL 772 | SING BROTHER SING (LP, gatefold sleeve, with lyric insert, no EMI on label) | 100 |
| 71 | Harvest SHVL 791 | THE EDGAR BROUGHTON BAND (LP, 1st pressing, textured gatefold) | 90 |
| 71 | Harvest SHVL 791 | THE EDGAR BROUGHTON BAND (LP, 2nd pressing with EMI boxed logo on side 1 only, textured gatefold) | 30 |
| 72 | Harvest SHTC 252 | IN SIDE OUT (LP, multifold gatefold sleeve with lyric sheet, some copies come with Harvest "Letter of introduction".) | 80 |
| 73 | Harvest SHVL 810 | OORA (LP, wraparound card sleeve in clear artwork plastic bag, inner sleeve) | 80 |
| 75 | Harvest SHSM 2001 | A BUNCH of 45s (LP) | 18 |
| 76 | Nems NEL 6006 | BANDAGES (LP with lyric inner sleeve) | 20 |

## AL BROWN (JAMAICA)
| | | | |
|---|---|---|---|
| 71 | Banana BA 360 | No Soul Today/RUFFIANS: Where Did I Go Wrong (B-side actually "Bang Shang Alang" by Peter Austin & Hortense Ellis) | 25 |
| 71 | Fab FAB 186 | Ain't Got No Soul/TEARDROPS: I Got A Feeling | 20 |
| 76 | Burning Sounds BS 001 | Revival Festival/Version | 5 |

## AL BROWN'S TUNETOPPERS (U.S.)
| | | | |
|---|---|---|---|
| 60 | Top Rank JAR 374 | The Madison/Mo' Madison | 6 |

## ARTHUR BROWN (CRAZY WORLD OF)
| | | | |
|---|---|---|---|
| 65 | Lyntone LYN 770/1 | You Don't Know (as Arthur Brown & Diamonds)/DIAMONDS: You'll Be Mine (Reading University Rag Week flexidisc) | 60 |
| 67 | Track 604 008 | Devil's Grip/Give Him A Flower | 12 |
| 68 | Track 604 022 | Fire!/Rest Cure (push-out centre) | 6 |
| 68 | Track 604 022 | Fire!/Rest Cure (large centre) | 5 |
| 68 | Track 604 026 | Nightmare/What's Happening (some copies list "Music Man" as B-side) | 6 |
| 74 | Gull GULS 4 | Gypsies/Dance | 5 |
| 75 | Gull GULS 13 | We Gotta Get Out Of This Place/Here I Am | 5 |
| 68 | Track 612 005 | THE CRAZY WORLD OF ARTHUR BROWN (LP, mono, black/silver label) | 120 |
| 68 | Track 613 005 | THE CRAZY WORLD OF ARTHUR BROWN (LP, stereo, black/silver labels) | 80 |
| 74 | Gull GULP 1008 | DANCE (LP) | 15 |
| 77 | Gull GUD 2003/4 | THE LOST EARS (2-LP, gatefold sleeve, as Arthur Brown's Kingdom Come) | 22 |
| 88 | Reckless 2 RECK | STRANGELANDS (LP, unreleased) | 0 |

*(see also Kingdom Come, Nick Greenwood, Atomic Rooster, Crane/Farlowe)*

## BARRY BROWN
| | | | |
|---|---|---|---|
| 78 | Justice JUDIS 104 | Step It Up/Youthman Version (12", with SHORTY THE PRESIDENT) | 20 |

| 78 | Tribesman TM 008 | Unity Is Strength/DRUMMIE BENJI: Higher Region (12")................................ | 35 |
| 79 | D Roy DRDD 12 | Conscious Girl/School Days (12")....................................................... | 10 |
| 79 | Justice JUDIS 126 | Big Big Politician/No Wicked Shall Enter (12")......................................... | 30 |
| 79 | Justice JUDIS 135 | We Can't Live Like This/From Creation I Man There (12")............................... | 30 |
| 79 | Sufferer's Heights SUFF 003 | I Love Sweet Jah Jah/RANKING JOE : Youthman Promotion (12")........................... | 40 |
| 80 | Daddy Kool DKR 124 | Peace And Love (with Ranking Toyan) JAH THOMAS & ROOTS RADICS: Adapter Chapter (12").... | 50 |
| 80 | Strong Like Sampson SLSD 07 | Natty Dread Nah Run/ANTHONY JOHNSON: Life Is Not Easy (12")........................... | 40 |
| 80 | Strong Like... SLSD 010 | Don't You Try/ANTHONY JOHNSON: Hey Mr Rich Man (12").................................. | 40 |
| 80 | Attack TACK 17 | Mr. CID/SCIENTIST AND ROOTS RADICAL BAND: King Tubby's Rockers (12").................. | 35 |
| 80 | Black Roots BR 009 | Things And Time/Time Dub (12")........................................................ | 10 |
| 80 | Attack TACK 21 | Separation/Scientist In A Fine Style (12")............................................ | 50 |
| 80 | JB JBD 022 | Jealous Lover/Seven To One (12" with Jah Thomas)...................................... | 12 |
| 80 | Attack TACK 23 | Living As A Brother/SCIENTIST: Second Hand Girl (12").................................. | 30 |
| 80 | Justice JUDIS 135 | We Can't Live Like This/From Creation I Man Free (12")................................ | 40 |
| 81 | City Sounds CSD 003 | Warmonger/ROOTS RADICS BAND: Radical Style (12", green vinyl)......................... | 50 |
| 81 | Greensleeves GRED 68 | Give Israel Another Try/Sweet Sixteen (12")........................................... | 30 |
| 82 | Selena SD004 | Them Ha Fi Get A Beatin'/ROOTS RADICS BAND : Stop The Fighting (12")................. | 40 |
| 82 | Selena SD008 | Physical Fitness/HEPTONES : Lovers Feeling (12", blue vinyl).......................... | 35 |
| 83 | Downbeat DBD 004 | Belly Full (with General Saint)/WAYNE WADE: Little Suzie (12")........................ | 40 |
| 84 | Greensleeves GRED 150 | Belly Move/Why The World Stay So (12")................................................ | 20 |
| 03 | Trojan TACK 23 | Living As A Brother/Caring For My Sister (12")........................................ | 15 |
| 79 | Paradise PDL 006 | STEP IT UP YOUTHMAN (LP)............................................................... | 20 |
| 80 | Trojan TRLS 191 | COOL PON YOUR CORNER (LP).............................................................. | 40 |
| 80 | Third World TWS 937 | SHOWCASE (LP).......................................................................... | 40 |
| 84 | Uptempo UT 003 | ROOTS & CULTURE (LP)................................................................... | 25 |

## BEN BROWN
| 67 | Polydor 56198 | Ask The Lonely/Sidewinder............................................................. | 50 |

## BUSTER BROWN
| 60 | Melodisc 1559 | Fannie Mae/Lost In A Dream............................................................ | 70 |
| 65 | Sue WI 368 | Fannie Mae/Lost In A Dream (reissue).................................................. | 40 |
| 67 | Island WI 3031 | My Blue Heaven/Two Women.............................................................. | 20 |
| 69 | Blue Horizon 57-3147 | Sugar Babe/I'm Going, But I'll Be Back................................................ | 45 |
| 60s | No Cat No | B. AND BUSTER BROWN (EP, with B. Brown).............................................. | 20 |

## BUSTY BROWN
| 68 | Doctor Bird DB 1158 | Here Comes The Night/Don't Look Back.................................................. | 30 |
| 69 | Upsetter US 304 | What A Price/How Can I Forget?........................................................ | 12 |
| 69 | Upsetter US 308 | To Love Somebody/BLEECHERS: Farmer's In The Den...................................... | 20 |
| 69 | Punch PH 10 | Broken Heart/Tribute To A King........................................................ | 40 |
| 70 | Punch PH 38 | Greatest Love/I Love You Madly........................................................ | 15 |
| 70 | Escort ES 822 | Fight For Your Right/MEDITATORS: Soul Fight (Busty Top A Pop) (B-side actually "Soul Fight" by Busty Brown)... | 25 |
| 70 | Escort ES 845 | Man Short (with Gaytones)/DAVE BARKER: She Want It.................................... | 12 |
| 70 | Gas GAS 154 | I Love You Madly/Greatest Love........................................................ | 10 |
| 70 | High Note HS 048 | Man Short (with Gaytones)/GAYTONES: Another Version.................................. | 12 |
| 71 | Bullet BU 476 | Never Love Another/Version............................................................ | 6 |
| 71 | Punch PH 72 | You Inspire Me/UPSETTERS: Version..................................................... | 12 |
| 71 | Pama Supreme PS 356 | Throw Away Your Gun/TWINKLE BROTHERS: Sad Song........................................ | 20 |

## CHARLES BROWN (BAND)
| 56 | Vogue V 9061 | I'll Always Be In Love With You/Soothe Me............................................. | 400 |
| 57 | Vogue V 9065 | Confidential/Trouble Blues............................................................ | 300 |
| 61 | Parlophone R 4848 | It's Christmas All Year Round/Christmas Question...................................... | 7 |

*(see also Brown Brothers)*

## CLARENCE 'GATEMOUTH' BROWN
| 65 | Vocalion VE 170161 | CLARENCE 'GATEMOUTH' BROWN (EP)....................................................... | 90 |
| 72 | Python PLP 26 | CLARENCE 'GATEMOUTH' BROWN VOL. 1: 1948-1953 (LP)..................................... | 25 |
| 72 | Python PLP 27 | CLARENCE 'GATEMOUTH' BROWN VOL. 2: 1956-1965 (LP)..................................... | 25 |

## CLIFFORD BROWN (& HIS GROUP)
| 55 | Vogue EPV 1027 | GIGI GRYCE - CLIFFORD BROWN ORCHESTRA (EP)............................................ | 10 |
| 55 | Vogue EPV 1041 | CONCEPTION (EP)....................................................................... | 10 |
| 56 | Vogue EPV 1119 | CLIFFORD BROWN ENSEMBLE (EP).......................................................... | 10 |
| 54 | Vogue LDE 042 | CLIFFORD "BROWNIE" BROWN QUARTET (10" LP)............................................. | 30 |
| 55 | Vogue LDE 121 | THE CLIFFORD BROWN SEXTET (10" LP).................................................... | 30 |
| 58 | Emarcy EJL 1278 | STUDY IN BROWN (LP)................................................................... | 25 |

*(see also Art Farmer, Sonny Rollins, Max Roach)*

## CLYDE BROWN
| 73 | Atlantic 10362 | Ghetto Cowboy/You've Gone Too Far..................................................... | 6 |

## DENNIS BROWN
| 70 | Bamboo BAM 56 | Love Grows/SOUND DIMENSION: Less Problem.............................................. | 35 |
| 70 | Banana BA 309 | No Man Is An Island/SOUL SISTERS: Another Night....................................... | 30 |
| 71 | Banana BA 336 | Never Fall In Love/Make It With You................................................... | 25 |
| 71 | Ocean OC 001 | Little Green Apples/SOUND DIMENSION: Version.......................................... | 10 |
| 72 | Duke DU 139 | What About The Half/What About The Half Version....................................... | 30 |
| 72 | Explosion EX 2068 | Black Magic Woman/PHILL PRATT ALL STARS: Black Magic Woman Pt 2........................ | 15 |
| 72 | Pressure Beat PR 5513 | Money In My Pocket/JOE GIBBS ALLSTARS: Money Love..................................... | 15 |
| 72 | Randy's RAN 526 | Cheater/TOMMY McCOOK & IMPACT ALLSTARS: Harvest In The East........................... | 20 |
| 72 | Randy's RAN 528 | Meet Me On The Corner (actually unknown instrumental)/IMPACT ALLSTARS: Version......... | 10 |

MINT VALUE £

| | | | |
|---|---|---|---|
| 72 | Songbird SB 1074 | Silhouettes/CRYSTALITES: Version | 12 |
| 73 | Ashanti ASH 402 | It's Too Late/Song My Mother Used To Sing | 12 |
| 73 | Jackpot JP 813 | He Can't Spell/CRYSTALITES: Acid Version | 10 |
| 73 | Smash SMA 2327 | Concentration/Version | 12 |
| 74 | Sydna SYD 5027 | No More Shall I Roam/Coming Home | 10 |
| 76 | Doctor DR 03 | Out In The Rain/Version | 8 |
| 76 | Hawkeye HE 01 | Whip Them Jah/Version | 12 |
| 77 | Observer OBS 999 | Jah Is Watching/Hustling/Rock On/Murder Observer Style (12" with DILLINGER) | 40 |
| 77 | Observer OB 003 | Tenement Yard/Kill Landlord/HORACE ANDY: Them Never Tell I/Teacher Gal (12", with Ranking Buckers) | 25 |
| 77 | DEB 0002 | Half/Troubled World (12") | 20 |
| 77 | Deb DBR102 | Emanuel/Wolfs And Leopards | 10 |
| 78 | DEB DDDEB 010 | Oh What A Day/Man Next Door (12") | 20 |
| 78 | Diamond DM DC 702 | Children Of Israel/Version (12", p/s) | 20 |
| 79 | Laser LAS 20 | Slave Driver/Version | 20 |
| 79 | Laser LAS 20(T) | Slave Driver/Dub Driver (12") | 15 |
| 79 | Observer OBS 902 | Blessed Are The Men (The Pill)/JUNIOR DELGADO : Cry Cry (12") | 20 |
| 79 | 3 in 1 SKLP 001 | Tribulation (with Jah Bop)/JUNIOR BYLES: Can You Feel It (12") | 20 |
| 80 | High Times HT 001 | Blood City/FREDDIE McGREGOR : Natural Collie (12") | 35 |
| 80 | Pratt PP 30 | Black Magic Woman/Version (12") | 40 |
| 80 | DEB DEB 039 | I Don't Want To Be No General/General (Version) (12" with Ranking Dread) | 25 |
| 83 | Tad's TRD 21483 | Easy Take It Easy/Easy Version (12") | 25 |
| 83 | Natty Congo NCDM 020 | Breaking Down The Barriers/Dubbing The Barriers (12") | 40 |
| 83 | Taxi IPR 2059 | Revolution/Dub Revolution (12") | 15 |
| 84 | Tad TRD 111585 | Here I Come/Version | 10 |
| 84 | Blue Moon BMS 1002 | Slave Driver/Version (12") | 15 |
| 84 | Greensleeves GRED 167 | It's Magic/PAD ANTHONY: Crazy Love (12") | 25 |
| 85 | Greensleeves GRED 175 | Slow Down Woman/Lord Is My Shepherd (12") | 12 |
| 86 | Jakki JM 468 | Rebel With A Cause/JACKIE MITTOO: Trade Mark (12") | 25 |
| 80s | Live & Love LLD 117 | Little Village/Version (12") | 15 |
| 73 | Trojan TRLS 57 | SUPER REGGAE & SOUL HITS (LP) | 22 |
| 75 | Trojan TRLS 107 | JUST DENNIS (LP) | 15 |
| 77 | DEB DEBLP 01 | WOLF AND LEOPARDS (LP) | 25 |
| 77 | Pioneer PIO LP2 | MEETS HARRY HIPPY (LP) | 80 |
| 78 | Lightning LIP 7 | VISIONS OF (LP) | 18 |
| 78 | Laser LASL 1 | WORDS OF WISDOM (LP, stickered sleeve with free 12" Money In My Pocket) | 25 |
| 78 | Laser LASL 1 | WORDS OF WISDOM (LP) | 20 |
| 80 | Laser LASL 6 | JOSEPH'S COAT OF MANY COLOURS (LP) | 18 |
| 86 | Trojan TRSL 238 | THE EXIT (LP) | 15 |

*(see also Big Youth & Dennis Brown, Hugh Roy, Big Youth, Sound Dimension)*

## DENNIS BROWN & ASWAD
| 80 | Simba SM003 | Promised Land/More Dub (12") | 20 |
|---|---|---|---|

## DUSTY BROWN
| 61 | Starlite ST45 058 | Please Don't Go/Well You Know | 15 |
|---|---|---|---|

## ERROL BROWN & CHOSEN FEW
| 72 | Songbird SB 1082 | People Make The World Go Round/People Make The World Go Round (Version) | 8 |
|---|---|---|---|

*(see also Hot Chocolate)*

## ERROL BROWN
| 73 | Count Shelly CS 008 | Time Is My Love/SOUL REBEL: I Don't Want To Lose You | 6 |
|---|---|---|---|

## FAITH BROWN
| 70 | CBS 4728 | Lock Me In/The Game Of Love | 5 |
|---|---|---|---|
| 71 | Penny Farthing PEN 766 | Any Way That You Want Me/City Wine | 5 |
| 72 | Regal Zonophone RZ 3063 | Take Me With You/If We Only Have Love | 5 |

*(see also Carrolls)*

## FAY BROWN
| 55 | Columbia SCM 5185 | Unchained Melody/I Was Wrong | 15 |
|---|---|---|---|

## FUNKY BROWN
| 72 | Sioux SI 018 | African (Indian Reservation)/JUMBO STERLING: Elizabethan Reggae | 6 |
|---|---|---|---|

## GABRIEL BROWN
| 77 | Policy Wheel PW 4592 | GABRIEL BROWN AND HIS GUITAR (LP, withdrawn) | 15 |
|---|---|---|---|

## GEORGIA BROWN
| 72 | Bug 18 | Turn Out The Light/I Scare Myself | 10 |
|---|---|---|---|

## GLEN BROWN
| 68 | Blue Cat BS 131 | Way Of Life (with Joe White & Trevor)/ KARL BRYAN & LYN TAITT: I'm So Proud | 150 |
|---|---|---|---|
| 70 | Summit SUM 8502 | Collie And Wine/BEVERLEY'S ALLSTARS: Version | 10 |
| 70 | Songbird SB 1021 | Love I/CRYSTALITES: Heavy Load | 12 |
| 72 | Songbird SB 1081 | Smokey Eyes (with Crystalites)/Smokey Eyes (Version) | 20 |
| 79 | Kingley REX 4 | Marcus Garvey Words/SLYFORD WALKER: Africa (12") | 20 |
| 96 | Blood & Fire BAFLP 015 | TERMINATION DUB (LP, as Glen Brown & King Tubby) | 20 |

## GLENMORE BROWN & HOPETON LEWIS
| 68 | Fab FAB 42 | Girl You're Cold/Soul Man | 100 |
|---|---|---|---|

*(see also Hopeton Lewis & Glenmore Brown)*

## HENRY BROWN
| 61 | '77' LA 12-5 | HENRY BROWN BLUES (LP) | 30 |
|---|---|---|---|

## HUX BROWN & SCOTTY
| 71 | High Note HS 056 | Unbelievable Sounds/GAYTONES: Unbelievable Sounds Version | 25 |
|---|---|---|---|

## HYLO BROWN (& TIMBERLINERS)
| 59 | Capitol CL 15075 | You Can't Relive The Past/Thunder Clouds Of Love | 5 |
|---|---|---|---|

| 60 | Capitol CL 15139 | I've Waited As Long As I Can/Just Any Old Love ......................................................... 5 |

## IAN BROWN

| 98 | Polydor 571 986-7 | My Star/See The Dawn (7", gatefold p/s) .................................................................. 5 |
| 00 | Polydor 561 908-1 | Thriller/Billie Jean (12", p/s) .................................................................................. 10 |
| 01 | Polydor 5872847 | F.E.A.R/F.E.A.R. (Instrumental) (stickered p/s) ........................................................ 8 |
| 09 | Fiction 2717752 | Stellify/Crowning Of The Poor (red vinyl, 1000 only, numbered)............................. 10 |
| 98 | Polydor 539 916-1 | UNFINISHED MONKEY BUSINESS (LP, gatefold, booklet) ........................................ 30 |
| 99 | Polydor 543 141-1 | GOLDEN GREATS (LP, yellow vinyl, p/s) ................................................................... 30 |
| 01 | Polydor 589 126-1 | MUSIC OF THE SPHERES (LP) .................................................................................... 25 |
| 02 | Polydor SPHERE2 | REMIXES OF THE SPHERES (2x12" Promo Sampler) ................................................. 20 |
| 02 | Polydor 065 927-1 | REMIXES OF THE SPHERES (2-LP) ............................................................................. 20 |
| 05 | Fiction 987289 | GREATEST (2-LP) ..................................................................................................... 25 |
| 07 | Polydor 174 341-4 | THE WORLD IS YOURS (2-LP) ................................................................................... 30 |
| 09 | Fiction 2717470 | MY WAY (LP) ............................................................................................................ 25 |
| 12 | Fiction (No Cat No) | COLLECTED (10-CD, LP, DVD boxed set, 1000 only) ................................................. 80 |

*(see also Stone Roses)*

## IRVING BROWN

| 70 | Bamboo BAM 36 | Today/SOUND DIMENSION: Young Gifted And Black Version .................................... 15 |
| 70 | Bamboo BAM 58 | I'm Still Around/Run Come .................................................................................... 18 |
| 70 | Bamboo BAM 61 | Let's Make It Up (actually by Larry Marshall)/BURNING SPEAR: Free .................... 35 |
| 71 | Bamboo Now BN 1003 | Now I'm Alone/Funky Night ................................................................................... 18 |

*(see also Larry Marshall)*

## JACKIE BROWN

| 72 | High Note HS 057 | One Night/GAYTONES: One Night Version ................................................................. 8 |
| 72 | High Note HS 060 | Last Dance/GAYTONES: Last Dance Version ............................................................. 8 |
| 75 | Black Wax 10 | Send Me The Pillow/MIGHTY TWO: Pillow With Strings ........................................... 6 |

## JAMES BROWN (& FAMOUS FLAMES)
### SINGLES

| 60 | Parlophone R 4667 | Think/You've Got The Power (with Famous Flames) ................................................. 50 |
| 60 | Fontana H 273 | This Old Heart/Wonder When You're Coming Home ................................................ 35 |
| 62 | Parlophone R 4922 | Night Train/Why Does Everything Happen To Me (with Famous Flames) ................. 40 |
| 62 | Parlophone R 4952 | Shout And Shimmy/Come Over Here (with Famous Flames)..................................... 30 |
| 63 | London HL 9730 | Prisoner Of Love/Choo-Choo (Locomotion) (with Famous Flames) ......................... 20 |
| 63 | London HL 9775 | These Foolish Things/(Can You) Feel It (Part 1) (with Famous Flames) .................... 20 |
| 64 | Philips BF 1368 | Out Of Sight/Maybe The Last Time (& His Orchestra) .............................................. 25 |
| 64 | Sue WI 360 | Night Train/Why Does Everything Happen To Me (with Famous Flames) ................. 35 |
| 65 | London HL 9945 | Have Mercy Baby/Just Won't Do Right (with Famous Flames) ................................. 18 |
| 65 | London HL 9990 | Papa's Got A Brand New Bag Parts 1 & 2 (with Famous Flames) ............................. 20 |
| 65 | Ember EMB S 216 | Tell Me What You're Gonna Do/Lost Someone (p/s) ............................................... 40 |
| 65 | Ember EMB S 216 | Tell Me What You're Gonna Do/Lost Someone ....................................................... 20 |
| 65 | Philips BF 1458 | Try Me/Papa's Got A Brand New Bag ...................................................................... 20 |
| 66 | Philips BF 1481 | New Breed Parts 1 & 2 ............................................................................................ 20 |
| 66 | Pye International 7N 25350 | I Got You (I Feel Good)/I Can't Help It (I Just Do-Do-Do) (with Famous Flames)............ 15 |
| 66 | Pye International 7N 25367 | Ain't That A Groove Parts 1 & 2 (with Famous Flames) .......................................... 10 |
| 66 | Pye International 7N 25371 | It's A Man's Man's Man's World/Is It Yes Or Is It No? (with Famous Flames)........... 8 |
| 66 | Pye International 7N 25379 | Money Won't Change You Parts 1 & 2 (with Famous Flames).................................. 15 |
| 66 | Pye International 7N 25394 | Don't Be A Drop-Out/Tell Me That You Love Me (with Famous Flames) ................. 10 |
| 67 | Pye International 7N 25411 | Bring It Up/Nobody Knows (with Famous Flames)................................................... 10 |
| 67 | Pye International 7N 25418 | Kansas City/Stone Fox (with Famous Flames) ......................................................... 10 |
| 67 | Pye International 7N 25423 | Let Yourself Go/Good Rockin' Tonight (with Famous Flames).................................. 10 |
| 67 | Pye International 7N 25430 | Cold Sweat Parts 1 & 2 (with Famous Flames) ........................................................ 10 |
| 67 | Pye International 7N 25441 | Get It Together Parts 1 & 2 (with Famous Flames) .................................................. 15 |
| 68 | Polydor 56740 | I Can't Stand Myself/There Was A Time................................................................. 15 |
| 68 | Polydor 56743 | I Got The Feelin'/If I Ruled The World..................................................................... 5 |
| 68 | Polydor 56744 | Licking Stick, Licking Stick Parts 1 & 2 ................................................................... 5 |
| 68 | Polydor 56752 | Say It Loud, I'm Black And I'm Proud Parts 1 & 2.................................................... 8 |
| 68 | Polydor 56540 | That's Life/Please, Please, Please (with Famous Flames) ........................................ 15 |
| 69 | Polydor 56776 | Mother Popcorn Parts 1 & 2 .................................................................................. 6 |
| 69 | Polydor 56780 | The World Parts 1 & 2 ............................................................................................ 6 |
| 69 | Polydor 56783 | Let A Man Come In And Do The Popcorn/Sometimes .............................................. 10 |
| 69 | Polydor 56787 | There Was A Time/I Can't Stand Myself (When You Touch Me)................................ 12 |
| 70 | Polydor 56793 | Ain't It Funky Now Parts 1 & 2 ............................................................................... 6 |
| 70 | Polydor 2001 018 | It's A New Day/Georgia On My Mind....................................................................... 6 |
| 70 | Polydor 2001 071 | Get Up, I Feel Like Being A Sex Machine Parts 1 & 2 (paper label) ......................... 6 |
| 70 | Polydor 2001 071 | Get Up, I Feel Like Being A Sex Machine Parts 1 & 2 (plastic label) ........................ 5 |
| 70 | Polydor 2001 097 | Call Me Super Bad Parts 1, 2 & 3 ........................................................................... 6 |
| 71 | Polydor 2001 163 | Soul Power Parts 1, 2 & 3 ...................................................................................... 6 |
| 71 | Polydor 2001 190 | I Cried/Get Up, Get Into It, Get Involved ................................................................ 6 |
| 71 | Polydor 2001 213 | Hot Pants (She Got To Use What She Got To Get What She Wants) Parts 1, 2 & 3 .......... 6 |
| 71 | Polydor 2001 223 | Make It Funky Parts 1 & 2 ...................................................................................... 6 |
| 71 | Mojo 2093 006 | Hey America!/Brother Rapp (Part 1)....................................................................... 6 |
| 71 | Polydor 2066 153 | I'm A Greedy Man Parts 1 & 2 ................................................................................ 6 |
| 72 | Polydor 2066 185 | King Heroin/Theme From King Heroin .................................................................... 20 |
| 72 | Polydor 2066 210 | There It Is Parts 1 & 2 ............................................................................................ 7 |
| 72 | Polydor 2066 216 | Honky Tonk Parts 1 & 2 .......................................................................................... 10 |
| 72 | Polydor 2066 231 | Get On The Good Foot Parts 1 & 2 ......................................................................... 10 |
| 72 | Polydor 2066 283 | What My Baby Needs Now Is A Little More Lovin'/ This Guy's In Love With You (with Lyn Collins)................................................................................................... 15 |
| 73 | Polydor 2066 285 | I've Got A Bag Of My Own/I Know It's True ............................................................ 7 |

MINT VALUE £

| 73 | Polydor 2141 008 | Papa's Got A Brand New Bag/Out Of Sight/It's A Man's Man's Man's World (p/s) ..........5 |
| 73 | Polydor 2066 296 | I Got Ants In My Pants Parts 1, 15 & 16 ...................................................................5 |
| 73 | Polydor 2066 329 | Think/Something ................................................................................................5 |
| 73 | Polydor 2066 370 | Woman Parts 1 & 2 .............................................................................................5 |
| 74 | Polydor 2066 411 | Stone To The Bone/Sexy, Sexy, Sexy ....................................................................6 |
| 74 | Polydor 2066 485 | My Thang/The Payback ......................................................................................6 |
| 74 | Polydor 2066 513 | It's Hell/Papa Don't Take No Mess ......................................................................5 |
| 75 | Polydor 2066 520 | Funky President (People It's Bad)/Cold Blooded ..................................................5 |
| 76 | Polydor 2066 642 | Hot (I Need To Be Loved, Loved, Loved)/Superbad, Superslick (Part 1)................5 |
| 76 | Polydor 2066 687 | Get Up Offa That Thing/Release The Pressure ....................................................5 |
| 77 | Polydor 2066 763 | Bodyheat Part 1/Bodyheat Part 2 .......................................................................5 |
| 77 | Polydor 2066 834 | Honky Tonk/Brother Rapp ..................................................................................5 |
| 78 | Polydor 2066 915 | Eyesight/I Never, Never, Never Will Forget .........................................................5 |
| 78 | Polydor 2066 984 | Nature Parts 1 & 2 .............................................................................................5 |
| 79 | Polydor POSP 24 | For Goodness Sakes, Look At Those Cakes/ Get Up, I Feel Like Being A Sex Machine (red label) ................................................................................................................8 |
| 79 | Polydor POSP 24 | For Goodness Sakes, Look At Those Cakes/ Get Up, I Feel Like Being A Sex Machine (silver label) ......................................................................................................5 |
| 79 | Polydor POSPX 24 | Get Up, I Feel Like Being A Sex Machine/For Goodness Sakes, Look At Those Cakes (12") ...............................................................................................................10 |
| 79 | Polydor POSPX 68 | It's Too Funky In Here/Are We Really Dancing? (12") .........................................10 |
| 79 | Polydor STEP 2 | Star Generation/Let The Boogie Do The Rest .....................................................5 |
| 80 | Polydor POSP 121 | Regrets/Stone Cold Drag ....................................................................................5 |

### EPs

| 64 | London RE 1410 | JAMES BROWN AND THE FAMOUS FLAMES .......................................................90 |
| 64 | Ember EMB EP 4549 | I DO JUST WHAT I WANT ..................................................................................40 |
| 66 | Pye Intl. NEP 44059 | I GOT YOU .......................................................................................................40 |
| 66 | Pye Intl. NEP 44068 | I'LL GO CRAZY ..................................................................................................40 |
| 67 | Pye Intl. NEP 44072 | PRISONER OF LOVE ..........................................................................................40 |
| 67 | Pye Intl. NEP 44076 | HOW LONG DARLING .......................................................................................40 |
| 67 | Pye Intl. NEP 44088 | BRING IT UP ......................................................................................................45 |
| 70 | Polydor 580 701 | TURN IT LOOSE..................................................................................................30 |

### ALBUMS

| 64 | London HA 8177 | PURE DYNAMITE! (as James Brown & Famous Flames) ......................................80 |
| 64 | London HA 8184 | LIVE AT THE APOLLO (as James Brown & Famous Flames) .................................60 |
| 64 | Ember EMB 3357 | TELL ME WHAT YOU'RE GONNA DO ................................................................45 |
| 64 | Philips BL 7630 | SHOWTIME .......................................................................................................30 |
| 65 | London HA 8203 | UNBEATABLE 16 HITS........................................................................................45 |
| 65 | London HA 8231 | PLEASE, PLEASE, PLEASE (as James Brown & Famous Flames) ..........................80 |
| 65 | Philips BL 7664 | GRITS AND SOUL ..............................................................................................60 |
| 65 | London HA 8240 | JAMES BROWN TOURS THE U.S.A. (with Famous Flames) .................................50 |
| 66 | London HA 8262 | PAPA'S GOT A BRAND NEW BAG (as James Brown & Famous Flames)................50 |
| 66 | Philips BL 7697 | JAMES BROWN PLAYS JAMES BROWN TODAY AND YESTERDAY .......................40 |
| 66 | Pye Intl. NPL 28074 | I GOT YOU (I FEEL GOOD) .................................................................................50 |
| 66 | Philips BL 7718 | JAMES BROWN PLAYS NEW BREED ..................................................................20 |
| 66 | Pye Intl. NPL 28079 | IT'S A MAN'S MAN'S MAN'S WORLD .................................................................30 |
| 66 | Pye Intl. NPL 28097 | THE JAMES BROWN CHRISTMAS ALBUM ..........................................................40 |
| 67 | Pye Intl. NPL 28093 | MIGHTY INSTRUMENTALS ................................................................................40 |
| 67 | Philips (S)BL 7761 | HANDFUL OF SOUL ..........................................................................................25 |
| 67 | Pye Intl. NPL 28099 | PAPA'S GOT A BRAND NEW BAG (reissue).........................................................20 |
| 67 | Pye Intl. NPL 28100 | MR. EXCITEMENT ..............................................................................................30 |
| 67 | Polydor 582 703 | THE JAMES BROWN SHOW (live) ......................................................................20 |
| 67 | Pye Intl. NPL 28103 | SINGS RAW SOUL .............................................................................................30 |
| 67 | Pye Intl. NPL 28104 | LIVE AT THE GARDEN .......................................................................................35 |
| 68 | Philips (S)BL 7823 | JAMES BROWN PLAYS THE REAL THING ............................................................25 |
| 68 | Polydor 184 136 | I CAN'T STAND MYSELF......................................................................................20 |
| 69 | Polydor 184 148 | SOUL FIRE .........................................................................................................15 |
| 69 | Mercury 20133 SMCL | JAMES BROWN SINGS OUT OF SIGHT ...............................................................25 |
| 69 | Polydor 583 729/30 | LIVE AT THE APOLLO VOLUME TWO (2-LP) .......................................................18 |
| 69 | Polydor 583 741 | SAY IT LOUD - I'M BLACK AND I'M PROUD .......................................................20 |
| 69 | Polydor 583 768 | IT'S A MOTHER...................................................................................................20 |
| 69 | Polydor 643 317 | THIS IS ... JAMES BROWN .................................................................................15 |
| 70 | Polydor 583 742 | GETTIN' DOWN TO IT ........................................................................................20 |
| 70 | Polydor 184 319 | THE POPCORN...................................................................................................20 |
| 70 | Polydor 2343 010 | AIN'T IT FUNKY..................................................................................................25 |
| 71 | Polydor 2625 004 | SEX MACHINE (2-LP)..........................................................................................20 |
| 71 | Polydor 2310 022 | SOUL ON TOP ...................................................................................................20 |
| 71 | Polydor 2310 029 | IT'S A NEW DAY ................................................................................................20 |
| 71 | Polydor 2310 089 | SUPER BAD .......................................................................................................20 |
| 72 | Polydor 2659 011 | REVOLUTION OF THE MIND: RECORDED LIVE AT THE APOLLO VOL. III (2-LP)..............20 |
| 72 | Polydor 2391 033 | THERE IT IS........................................................................................................20 |
| 73 | Polydor 2659 018 | GET ON THE GOOD FOOT (2-LP) .......................................................................25 |
| 73 | Polydor 2490 117 | BLACK CAESAR (soundtrack) .............................................................................35 |
| 73 | Polydor 2391 084 | SLAUGHTER'S BIG RIP-OFF (soundtrack) ...........................................................30 |
| 74 | Polydor 2659 030 | THE PAYBACK (2-LP)...........................................................................................25 |
| 74 | Polydor 2659 036 | IT'S HELL (2-LP)..................................................................................................25 |
| 75 | Polydor 2391 175 | SEX MACHINE TODAY .......................................................................................15 |
| 75 | Polydor 2391 197 | EVERYBODY'S DOIN' THE HUSTLE AND DEAD ON THE DOUBLE BUMP..................15 |
| 77 | Polydor 2391 300 | MUTHA'S NATURE (by James Brown & the New J.B,'s) .......................................15 |

*(see also Lyn Collins, JBs, Maceo & All King's Men, Nat Kendrick & Swans)*

## JAMES BROWN (JAMAICA)
| | | | |
|---|---|---|---|
| 71 | Punch PH 76 | Don't Say/TRANS AM ALLSTARS: Don't Say Version | 8 |
| 72 | Ashanti ASH 408 | Mama Don't Want To See You/Mama Don't Want To See You Version | 7 |
| 75 | Mango MAN 1001 | Stop The War In Babylon/Dub In Peace | 15 |

## JIM EDWARD (BROWN) & MAXINE BROWN
| | | | |
|---|---|---|---|
| 55 | London HL 8123 | Itsy Witsy Bitsy Me/Why Am I Falling? | 30 |
| 55 | London HLU 8166 | Your Love Is Wild As The West Wind/Draggin' Mainstreet | 30 |
| 55 | London HLU 8200 | You Thought I Thought/Here Today And Gone Tomorrow (B-side with Bonnie) | 30 |
| 55 | London R-EP 1024 | COUNTRY SONGS (EP) | 10 |
| 55 | London R-EU 1044 | COUNTRY SONGS VOLUME 3 (EP) | 10 |

## JOE BROWN (& BRUVVERS)
| | | | |
|---|---|---|---|
| 59 | Decca F 11185 | People Gotta Talk/Comes The Day (solo, triangular centre) | 15 |
| 60 | Decca F 11207 | Darktown Strutter's Ball/Swagger (solo) | 5 |
| 62 | Decca DFE8500 | A PICTURE OF JOE BROWN (EP) | 10 |
| 62 | Picadilly NEP 34025 | JOE BROWN HIT PARADE (EP) | 10 |

*(see also Vicki Brown, Browns Homebrew)*

## JOHNNY BROWN
| | | | |
|---|---|---|---|
| 61 | Philips PB 1119 | Walkin' Talkin' Kissin' Doll/Sundown | 10 |

## KENT BROWN & RAINBOWS
| | | | |
|---|---|---|---|
| 68 | Fab FAB 53 | When You Going To Show Me How/Come Ya Come Ya | 10 |

*(see also Kent & Jeannie, Sir D's Group)*

## LENNOX BROWN
| | | | |
|---|---|---|---|
| 72 | Green Door GD 4023 | High School Serenade/WINSTON SCOTLAND: On The Track (1st issue) | 7 |
| 72 | Bullet BU 501 | High School Serenade/WINSTON SCOTLAND: On The Track (2nd issue) | 7 |

*(see also Jeff Barnes, Peter Tosh)*

## LEROY BROWN
| | | | |
|---|---|---|---|
| 78 | Revue REVD 10 | Blood A Go Run/Taxi (12") | 40 |

## LES BROWN & HIS BAND OF RENOWN
| | | | |
|---|---|---|---|
| 54 | Vogue Coral Q 2034 | Ramona/Hot Point | 5 |
| 54 | Vogue Coral Q 2042 | St. Louis Blues Mambo/Moon Song | 5 |
| 55 | Vogue Coral Q 72049 | The Man That Got Away/Doodle-Doo-Doo | 5 |
| 55 | Capitol CL 14331 | Frenesi/Perfidia | 5 |
| 55 | Capitol CL 14350 | He Needs Me/Simplicity | 5 |
| 55 | Vogue Coral Q 72107 | Lullaby Of Birdland/Bernie's Tune | 5 |
| 56 | Vogue Coral Q 72123 | Hong Kong Blues (with Hoagy Carmichael & Band Of Renown)/ It's All Right With Me | 8 |

## LES BROWN (JR)
| | | | |
|---|---|---|---|
| 60s | Vocalion VA 8011 | WILDEST DRUMS YET (LP) | 15 |

## MARION BROWN
| | | | |
|---|---|---|---|
| 69 | Polydor 583724 | PORTO NOVO (LP) | 60 |

## MATT BROWN
| | | | |
|---|---|---|---|
| 01 | Grapevine 2000 G2K 45-107 | Thank You Baby/Sweet Thing | 8 |
| 03 | Grapevine G2K 45-133 | Everyday (I Love You Just A Little Bit More)/Baby I'm A Want You | 8 |

## MAXINE BROWN
| | | | |
|---|---|---|---|
| 61 | London HLU 9286 | All In My Mind/Harry, Let's Marry | 40 |
| 62 | HMV POP 1102 | Am I Falling In Love/Promise Me Anything | 100 |
| 63 | Stateside SS 188 | Ask Me/Yesterday's Kisses | 40 |
| 64 | Pye International 7N 25272 | Oh No Not My Baby/You Upset My Soul | 30 |
| 65 | Pye International 7N 25299 | It's Gonna Be Alright/You Do Something To Me | 30 |
| 65 | Pye International 7N 25317 | One Step At A Time/Anything For A Laugh | 40 |
| 67 | Pye International 7N 25410 | I've Got A Lot Of Love Left In Me/Hold On (I'm Comin') (B-side with Chuck Jackson) | 30 |
| 67 | Pye International 7N 25434 | Since I Found You/Gotta Find A Way | 25 |
| 70 | Major Minor MM 709 | Reason To Believe/I Can't Get Along Without You | 25 |
| 73 | Avco 6105 022 | Picked Up, Packed Up And Put Away/Bella Mia | 10 |
| 75 | Pye Disco Demand DDS 117 | One In A Million/Let Me Give You My Lovin' | 10 |
| 90s | Kent TOWN 110 | It's Torture/I Got Love | 12 |
| 85 | Kent 047 | LIKE NEVER BEFORE (LP) | 15 |

*(see also Chuck Jackson & Maxine Brown)*

## NAPPY BROWN (& HIS BAND)
| | | | |
|---|---|---|---|
| 55 | London HL 8145 | Don't Be Angry/It's Really You | 300 |
| 55 | London HLC 8182 | Pitter Patter/There'll Come A Day | 250 |
| 57 | London HLC 8384 | Little By Little/I'm Getting Lonesome (& His Band) (gold lettering on label) | 250 |
| 57 | London HLC 8384 | Little By Little/I'm Getting Lonesome (& His Band) (silver lettering on label) | 100 |
| 58 | London HLC 8760 | It Don't Hurt No More/My Baby | 50 |

## NOEL BROWN
| | | | |
|---|---|---|---|
| 50s | Parlophone MP 134 | Take Me Back To Africa/Virgin Islands (Get Happy In A Hurry) (78, export) | 5 |
| 68 | Island WI 3149 | Man's Temptation/Heartbreak Girl | 60 |
| 69 | Songbird SB 1012 | By The Time I Get To Phoenix/Heartbreak Girl | 20 |
| 70 | Bullet BU 423 | Phoenix (actually by "By The Time I Get To Phoenix")/Heartbreak Girl | 20 |

*(see also Bunny Brown)*

## PAMELA BROWN
| | | | |
|---|---|---|---|
| 70 | Joe JRS 8 | People Are Running/CRITICS: School Days | 15 |

## PATRICK BROWN
| | | | |
|---|---|---|---|
| 82 | Kufe EB 003 | Fantasy/On The Right Track (12") | 40 |

## PETE BROWN(& PIBLOKTO)
| | | | |
|---|---|---|---|
| 69 | Parlophone R 5767 | The Week Looked Good On Paper/Morning Call (as Pete Brown & His Battered Ornaments, promo p/s) | 65 |

# Polly BROWN

| 69 | Parlophone R 5767 | The Week Looked Good On Paper/Morning Call (as Pete Brown & His Battered Ornaments)........................................................................................22 |
| 69 | Harvest HAR 5008 | Living Life Backwards/High Flying Electric Bird (as Pete Brown & Piblokto!)...............20 |
| 70 | Harvest HAR 5023 | Can't Get Off The Planet/Broken Magic (with His Battered Ornaments).......................15 |
| 70 | Harvest HAR 5028 | Flying Hero Sandwich/My Last Band (as Pete Brown & Piblokto!).............................25 |
| 69 | Harvest SHVL 752 | A MEAL YOU CAN SHAKE HANDS WITH IN THE DARK (LP, as Pete Brown & His Battered Ornaments, with "Sold in U.K" label text on 4 lines, stereo) ..........................350 |
| 70 | Harvest SHVL 768 | THE ART SCHOOL DANCE GOES ON FOREVER (LP, as Pete Brown & Piblokto!, gatefold sleeve, no EMI on label) ...........................................................................350 |
| 70 | Harvest SHVL 782 | THOUSANDS ON A RAFT (LP, as Pete Brown & Piblokto!, gatefold sleeve, no EMI on label) .............................................................................................................300 |
| 73 | Deram SML 1103 | THE NOT FORGOTTEN ASSOCIATION (LP, with Graham Bond) ........................100 |
| 77 | Harvest SHSM 2017 | MY LAST BAND (LP, as Pete Brown & Piblokto) ...........................................20 |
| 82 | Discs Intl. INTLP 1 | PARTY IN THE RAIN (LP, with Ian Lynn, private pressing) .............................15 |
| 12 | Pure Pleasure PPAN SHVL 752 | A MEAL YOU CAN SHAKE HANDS WITH IN THE DARK (2-LP, reissue) ...............20 |

*(see also Battered Ornaments, Graham Bond & Pete Brown, Deke Leonard, Cream)*

## POLLY BROWN

| 72 | Pye 7N 45197 | I'll Cry My Heart Out For You/Teardrops WIll Fall .......................................10 |
| 72 | Pye 7N 45148 | The Feeling's Right/I Can't Do Without You .............................................10 |
| 75 | GTO GT 14 | Dial L For Love/Love Lovin' You .........................................................6 |
| 76 | GTO GT 61 | Love Bug/Love Bug Buzzin' ..............................................................6 |
| 77 | GTO GT 88 | Beautiful Things For You/MY Heart Keeps Breaking Over You ...........................6 |
| 73 | Pye NSPL 18396 | POLLY BROWN (LP).....................................................................20 |

## ROY BROWN

| 57 | London HLP 8398 | I'm Sticking With You/Party Doll (gold label print) .................................400 |
| 57 | London HLP 8398 | I'm Sticking With You/Party Doll (later silver print pressing) ......................150 |
| 57 | London HLP 8448 | Saturday Night/Everybody ..............................................................500 |

## RUTH BROWN (& HER RHYTHMAKERS)

| 55 | London HL 8153 | Mambo Baby/Mama (He Treats Your Daughter Mean) (with Rhythmakers)...............300 |
| 55 | London HLE 8210 | As Long As I'm Moving/R.B. Blues (with Her Rhythmakers) .........................300 |
| 56 | London HLE 8310 | I Want To Do More/Sweet Baby Of Mine ...............................................200 |
| 57 | London HLE 8401 | Mom Oh Mom/I Want To Be Loved (But Only By You) .................................200 |
| 57 | Columbia DB 3913 | Lucky Lips/My Heart Is Breaking Over You ...........................................350 |
| 57 | London HLE 8483 | When I Get You Baby/One More Time ...................................................100 |
| 58 | London HLE 8552 | A New Love/Look Me Up ..................................................................100 |
| 58 | London HLE 8645 | Just Too Much/Book Of Lies ...........................................................100 |
| 58 | London HLE 8757 | This Little Girl's Gone Rockin'/Why Me ................................................80 |
| 58 | London HL 7061 | This Little Girl's Gone Rockin'/Why Me (export issue) .................................75 |
| 59 | London HLE 8887 | Jack O' Diamonds/I Can't Hear A Word You Say ........................................25 |
| 59 | London HLE 8946 | I Don't Know/Papa Daddy ..............................................................25 |
| 59 | London HLE 8946 | I Don't Know/Papa Daddy (78) ..........................................................35 |
| 60 | London HLE 9093 | Don't Deceive Me/I Burned Your Letter ................................................25 |
| 61 | London HLK 9304 | Sure 'Nuff/Here He Comes ..............................................................25 |
| 64 | Brunswick 05904 | Yes Sir That's My Baby/What Happened To You .........................................10 |
| 76 | President PT 457 | Sugar Babe/Stop Knocking .............................................................10 |
| 55 | London REE 1038 | THE QUEEN OF R&B (EP) ...............................................................150 |
| 63 | Philips BE 12537 | GOSPEL TIME (EP) ......................................................................50 |
| 60 | London Jazz LTZ-K 15187 | LAST DATE WITH RUTH BROWN (LP) ....................................................60 |
| 62 | Philips 652 012 BL | ALONG COMES RUTH (LP) ..............................................................50 |
| 63 | Philips 652 020 BL | GOSPEL TIME (LP) ......................................................................40 |
| 64 | Atlantic ATL 5007 | THE BEST OF RUTH BROWN (LP, plum label) ...........................................100 |
| 76 | President PTLS 1067 | SUGAR BABE (LP) ......................................................................20 |
| 84 | Charly CRB 1069 | ROCKIN' WITH RUTH (LP) ...............................................................15 |

## RUTH BROWN/JOE TURNER

| 56 | London REE 1047 | THE KING AND QUEEN OF R&B (EP, 2 tracks each) ....................................200 |

## SAMMI BROWN

| 68 | Fontana TF 947 | Daydream/Stop The Music ...............................................................7 |

## SANDY BROWN('S JAZZ BAND)

| 58 | Tempo A 124 | African Queen/Special Delivery (as Sandy Brown's Jazz Band)...........................5 |
| 53 | Esquire EP 28 | SANDY BROWN'S JAZZ BAND (EP)........................................................10 |
| 55 | Tempo EXA 13 | SANDY BROWN'S JAZZ BAND (EP)........................................................10 |
| 55 | Tempo EXA 33 | SANDY BROWN'S JAZZ BAND (EP)........................................................10 |
| 56 | Tempo EXA 49 | TRADITIONAL JAZZ SCENE '56 (EP)......................................................10 |
| 57 | Nixa NJE 1054 | BLUE McJAZZ (EP)......................................................................10 |
| 57 | Nixa NJE 1056 | AFRO McJAZZ (EP)......................................................................10 |
| 53 | Esquire 20-022 | SANDY BROWN (10" LP, with Bobby Mickleburgh) .....................................20 |
| 56 | Tempo TAP 3 | SANDY'S SIDEMEN PLAYING COMPOSITIONS BY AL FAIRWEATHER (LP) ................25 |
| 57 | Nixa Jazz Today NJL 9 | McJAZZ (LP) ..........................................................................15 |
| 66 | Fontana TE1 7473 | SANDY BROWN ALL STARS (LP) .........................................................15 |
| 69 | Fontana SFJL 921 | HAIR AT ITS HAIRIEST (LP, as Sandy Brown & His Gentlemen Friends) ................15 |

*(see also Wally Fawkes, Sandy & Teachers)*

## SHIRLEY BROWN

| 75 | Stax STXS 2019 | Woman To Woman/Yes Sir, Brother.......................................................6 |
| 75 | Stax STXS 2032 | I Can't Give You Up/It Ain't No Fun ..................................................20 |
| 77 | Arista 102 | Blessed Is The Woman (With A Man Like Mine)/Lowdown Dirty Good Lover .............8 |
| 75 | Stax STX 1031 | WOMAN TO WOMAN (LP) ................................................................20 |

*(see also Oliver Sain)*

## STU BROWN & BLUESOLOGY

| 67 | Polydor 56195 | Since I Found You Baby/Just A Little Bit ...............................................300 |

*(see also Bluesology, Elton John)*

## TEDDY BROWN
| | | | |
|---|---|---|---|
| 70 | Trojan TR 7793 | What Greater Love/Lady Love | 6 |
| 71 | Trojan TR 7827 | Walk The World Away/Senorita Rita | 6 |

## U BROWN
| | | | |
|---|---|---|---|
| 75 | Fay FM 606 | Jah Jah Whip Them/Skanking in Dub | 40 |
| 76 | Fay Music FM 608 | Wet Up Your Pant/Ringo Don't Take Your Gun To Town (with Little Youth) | 20 |
| 78 | Cancer CAN 702 | Starsky And Hutch/Version | 6 |
| 77 | Klik KLP 9018 | SATTA DREAD (LP) | 60 |
| 78 | Virgin Frontline FL 1003 | MR. BROWN SOMETHING (LP) | 18 |
| 79 | Virgin Frontline FL 1030 | CAN'T KEEP A GOOD MAN DOWN (LP) | 15 |
| 84 | VSLP 5005 | SUPERSTAR (LP) | 15 |

## VIC BROWN COMBO
| | | | |
|---|---|---|---|
| 63 | Rio R 7 | Swanee River/Robert E. Lee | 5 |

## VICKI BROWN
| | | | |
|---|---|---|---|
| 77 | Power Exchange PXL 012 | FROM THE INSIDE (LP) | 15 |

## VINCENT BROWN
| | | | |
|---|---|---|---|
| 70 | Gas GAS 128 | Look What You're Going To Do/Hold On To What You Have Got | 8 |

## WATSON T. BROWN (& EXPLOSIVE)
| | | | |
|---|---|---|---|
| 68 | President PT 207 | Some Lovin'/Home Is Where Your Heart Lies | 6 |
| 68 | President PT 221 | Crying All Night/I Close My Eyes | 10 |
| 70 | Bell BLL 1109 | Will You Still Love Me Tomorrow/Save The Last Dance For Me (solo) | 6 |
| 71 | MAM MAM 16 | I'm On The Road Again/Feeling Bad | 6 |

*(see also Explosive)*

## WILLIAM BROWN
| | | | |
|---|---|---|---|
| 71 | Ackee ACK 128 | I'm Alone/BELTONES: Soul People | 10 |

## BROWN BROTHERS
| | | | |
|---|---|---|---|
| 59 | Vogue V 9131 | Let The Good Times Roll/You're Right, I'm Left | 150 |

*(see also Charles Brown)*

## CHARLEY BROWNE
| | | | |
|---|---|---|---|
| 78 | Hurry! LT1113 | Feeling Under The Weather/Sez Lez (no p/s) | 15 |

## DUNCAN BROWNE
| | | | |
|---|---|---|---|
| 68 | Immediate IM 070 | On The Bombsite/Alfred Bell | 25 |
| 70 | Bell BLL 1119 | Resurrection Joe/Final Asylum | 12 |
| 73 | Rak RAK 162 | Send Me The Bill/My Only Son | 6 |
| 78 | Logo GO 329 | Wild Places/Camino Real | 6 |
| 68 | Immediate IMSP 018 | GIVE ME, TAKE YOU (LP, with insert, lilac label with "sold in U.K." label text) | 600 |
| 73 | RAK SRKA 6754 | DUNCAN BROWNE (LP, gatefold sleeve) | 50 |

## FRIDAY BROWN(E)
| | | | |
|---|---|---|---|
| 66 | Parlophone R 5396 | Getting Nowhere/And (To Me He Meant Everything) (as Friday Browne) | 25 |
| 66 | Fontana TF 736 | 32nd Love Affair/Born A Woman | 150 |
| 67 | Fontana TF 851 | Ask Any Woman/Outdoor Seminar | 5 |
| 69 | Fontana TF 996 | Stand By Your Man/I Want To Rain | 6 |
| 72 | Philips 6006 239 | Shake A Hand/Everything's Alright | 5 |
| 73 | Philips 6006 324 | Groovy Kind Of Love/Salford | 5 |
| 71 | Philips 6308 074 | FRIDAY BROWN (LP) | 40 |

*(see also Marianne & Mike, High Society, Manchester Mob, Graham Gouldman)*

## GEORGE BROWNE
| | | | |
|---|---|---|---|
| 54 | Parlophone CMSP 6 | Calypso Mambo/The Peanut Vendor (export issue) | 10 |
| 54 | Parlophone CMSP 17 | Somebody Bad Stole De Wedding Bell (Who's Got De Ding Dong?)/ Matilda, Matilda! (export issue) | 7 |
| 57 | Columbia DB 3940 | Sound Barrier/Te-Le-Le | 5 |

*(see also Humphrey Lyttleton)*

## JACKSON BROWNE
| | | | |
|---|---|---|---|
| 74 | Asylum K2 43007 | LATE FOR THE SKY (LP, quadrophonic) | 15 |
| 85 | Asylum K53070 | RUNNING ON EMPTY (LP, Nimbus Supercut, mail order only via through Hi Fi Today) | 50 |

## SANDRA BROWNE (& BOYFRIENDS)
| | | | |
|---|---|---|---|
| 63 | Columbia DB 4998 | By Hook Or By Crook/Johnny Boy (as Sandra Browne & Boyfriends) | 15 |
| 63 | Columbia DB 7109 | You'd Think He Didn't Know Me/Mama Never Told Me | 15 |
| 65 | Columbia DB 7465 | Knock On Any Door/I Want Love | 15 |

## TEDDY BROWN(E)
| | | | |
|---|---|---|---|
| 59 | Capitol CL 15059 | A Corner In Paradise/The Everglades | 5 |
| 61 | Starlite ST45 033 | Pretty Little Baby/Genevieve (as Teddy Brown) | 5 |

## THOMAS F. BROWNE
| | | | |
|---|---|---|---|
| 71 | Vertigo 6325 250 | WEDNESDAY'S CHILD (LP, gatefold sleeve, small swirl label) | 400 |

*(see also Gary Wright, The Gladiators)*

## TOBY BROWNE
| | | | |
|---|---|---|---|
| 64 | Parlophone 5192 | Play The Music, Keep On Dancing/Child | 15 |

## TOM BROWNE
| | | | |
|---|---|---|---|
| 80 | Arista ARIST 12357 | Funkin' For Jamaica (N.Y.)/Her Silent Smile (12") | 10 |

## DUKE BROWNER
| | | | |
|---|---|---|---|
| 79 | Grapevine GRP 145 | Crying Over You/Crying Over You (Instrumental) | 20 |

*(see also Kaddo Strings)*

## BROWNHILL'S STAMP DUTY
| | | | |
|---|---|---|---|
| 69 | Columbia DB 8625 | Maxwell's Silver Hammer/My Woman's Back | 10 |

## BILL BROWNING
| | | | |
|---|---|---|---|
| 80s | Roller Coaster RRC 2003 | Wash Machine Boogie/Ramblin' Man (p/s) | 8 |

MINT VALUE £

## BROWNS
| | | | |
|---|---|---|---|
| 59 | RCA RCA 1140 | The Three Bells/Heaven Fell Last Night (tri centre) | 5 |

*(see also Jim Edward & Maxine Brown)*

## BROWN'S FERRY FOUR
| | | | |
|---|---|---|---|
| 54 | Parlophone CMSP 11 | I Need The Prayers/Through The Pearly Gates (with Clyde Moody, export issue) | 15 |

*(see also Merle Travis)*

## BROWNS HOME BREW
| | | | |
|---|---|---|---|
| 72 | Bell BELL 1211 | Billy Come Down/Hit Me Across The Head With A Spoon | 5 |

*(see also Joe Brown)*

## BROWN SUGAR (1)
| | | | |
|---|---|---|---|
| 77 | Lovers Rock CJ 613 | I'm In Love With A Dreadlocks/Version | 30 |
| 77 | Lovers Rock CJ 614 | Hello Stranger/Version | 20 |
| 77 | Lovers Rock CJ 619 | Black Pride/Version | 20 |
| 77 | Lovers Rock CJ 624 | Do You Really Love Me/Version | 20 |
| 79 | Studio 16 WE 014 | You And Your Smiling Face/Version (12") | 20 |
| 79 | Studio 16 WE 017 | Our Reggae Music/Dub (12") | 12 |
| 80 | African Drums AF 002 | Hello Stranger/Black Is The Colour (12") | 12 |
| 80 | Studio 16 WE 092 | Dreaming Of Zion/Version (12") | 40 |
| 80 | Studio 16 WE 106 | Confession Hurts/Version (12") | 30 |
| 80 | Studio 16 WE 113 | Runaway Love/Version (12") | 30 |
| 80 | Black Roots BRLP 1000 | NOT SO LUCKY (LP) | 15 |

## ANNETTE (REIS) & VICTOR BROX
| | | | |
|---|---|---|---|
| 65 | Fontana TF 536 | I've Got The World In A Jug/Wake Me And Shake Me | 10 |
| 74 | Sonet SNTF 663 | ROLLIN' BACK (LP) | 15 |

*(see also Aynsley Dunbar Retaliation)*

## DAVE BRUBECK (QUARTET)
| | | | |
|---|---|---|---|
| 54 | Vogue LDE 090 | DAVE BRUBECK TRIO (10" LP) | 15 |
| 54 | Vogue LDE 095 | DAVE BRUBECK QUARTET (10" LP) | 15 |
| 54 | Vogue LDE 104 | DAVE BRUBECK QUARTET VOL. 2 (10" LP) | 15 |
| 55 | Vogue LDE 114 | DAVE BRUBECK QUARTET VOL. 3 (10" LP) | 15 |

*(see also Jimmy Rushing, Carmen McRae)*

## JACK BRUCE
| | | | |
|---|---|---|---|
| 65 | Polydor BM 56036 | I'm Getting Tired (Of Drinking And Gambling)/Rootin' Tootin' | 100 |
| 71 | Polydor 2058 153 | The Consul At Sunset/Letter Of Thanks | 15 |
| 74 | RSO 2090 141 | Keep It Down/Golden Days | 5 |
| 69 | Polydor 583 058 | SONGS FOR A TAILOR (LP, laminated gatefold sleeve) | 18 |
| 70 | Polydor 2343 033 | THINGS WE LIKE (LP) | 18 |
| 71 | Polydor 2310 070 | THINGS WE LIKE (LP, reissue) | 15 |
| 71 | Polydor 2310 107 | HARMONY ROW (LP, gatefold sleeve) | 20 |

*(see also Alexis Korner's Blues Incorporated, Cream, Manfred Mann, Graham Bond Organisation, John Mayall, West Bruce & Laing, Lifetime, Rocket 88, Carla Bley, Duffy Power, Cozy Powell)*

## TOMMY BRUCE (& BRUISERS)
| | | | |
|---|---|---|---|
| 60 | Columbia DB 4453 | Ain't Misbehavin'/Got The Water Boilin' (with Bruisers) | 5 |
| 60 | Columbia DB 4498 | Broken Doll/I'm On Fire (with Bruisers) | 5 |
| 60 | Columbia DB 4532 | On The Sunny Side Of The Street/My Little Girl (with Bruisers) | 5 |
| 61 | Columbia DB 4581 | You Make Love So Well/I'm Crazy 'Bout My Baby (with Bruisers) | 5 |
| 61 | Columbia DB 4682 | Love, Honour And Oh! Baby/I'm Gonna Sit Right Down And Write | 5 |
| 62 | Columbia DB 4776 | Babette/Honey Girl, You're Lonely | 5 |
| 62 | Columbia DB 4850 | Horror Movies/It's You | 7 |
| 62 | Columbia DB 4927 | Buttons And Bows/London Boys | 5 |
| 64 | Columbia DB 7387 | Over Suzanne/It's Drivin' Me Wild | 20 |
| 65 | Polydor BM 56006 | Boom Boom/Can Your Monkey Do The Dog (with Bruisers) | 30 |
| 66 | RCA RCA 1535 | Monster Gonzales/I Hate Getting Up In The Morning | 25 |
| 61 | Columbia SEG 8077 | KNOCKOUT (EP) | 30 |

## HEIDI BRÜHL
| | | | |
|---|---|---|---|
| 60 | Philips PB 1095 | Ring Of Gold/I'll Belong To You Forever (in p/s) | 10 |
| 60 | Philips PB 1095 | Ring Of Gold/I'll Belong To You Forever | 5 |
| 63 | Philips 345 579 BF | Marcel/Talk It Over With Someone | 5 |
| 69 | Philips BF 1768 | The Drifter/Berlin | 200 |
| 69 | Philips BF 1768 | The Drifter/Berlin (DJ Copy) | 250 |

## BRUISERS
| | | | |
|---|---|---|---|
| 63 | Parlophone R 5042 | Blue Girl/Don't Cry | 10 |
| 63 | Parlophone R 5092 | Your Turn To Cry/Give It To Me | 10 |

*(see also [Peter] Lee Stirling & Bruisers)*

## BRUMBEATS
| | | | |
|---|---|---|---|
| 64 | Decca F 11834 | Cry Little Girl, Cry/I Don't Understand | 15 |

## BEAU BRUMMEL ESQUIRE
| | | | |
|---|---|---|---|
| 65 | Columbia DB 7447 | I Know Know Know/Shoppin' Around | 6 |
| 65 | Columbia DB 7538 | The Next Kiss/Come And Get Me | 6 |
| 65 | Columbia DB 7675 | A Better Man Than I/Teardrops | 6 |
| 66 | Columbia DB 7878 | You Don't Know What You've Got/Take Me Like I Am | 6 |

## BRUNNING (HALL) SUNFLOWER BLUES BAND
| | | | |
|---|---|---|---|
| 68 | Saga FID 2118 | BULLEN STREET BLUES (LP, as Brunning Sunflower Blues Band, with black/silver label) | 30 |
| 69 | Saga EROS 8132 | TRACKSIDE BLUES (LP, black/silver labels) | 45 |
| 70 | Saga EROS 8150 | I WISH YOU WOULD (LP, as Brunning Sunflower Blues Band, with black/silver labels) | 75 |
| 71 | Gemini GM 2010 | THE BRUNNING/HALL SUNFLOWER BLUES BAND (LP, with white/red labels) | 120 |

*(see also Five's Company, Fleetwood Mac, Leaf Hound)*

## BRUNO
| | | | |
|---|---|---|---|
| 66 | Parlophone R5450 | Wonderboy/Window In My Room | 20 |
| 66 | Parlophone R5507 | The English Girl/The Driver | 20 |

## TONY BRUNO
| | | | |
|---|---|---|---|
| 68 | Capitol CL 15534 | What's Yesterday/Small Town, Bring Down | 50 |

## BRUTE FORCE
| | | | |
|---|---|---|---|
| 69 | Apple APPLE 8 | King Of Fuh/Nobody Knows (unissued) | 2000 |

## BRUTUS
| | | | |
|---|---|---|---|
| 75 | Purple PUR 126 | Payroll/New Deal Princess | 7 |

## TONY BRUTUS
| | | | |
|---|---|---|---|
| 83 | Intense INT 013 | Water Pistol/Shooting Water (12") | 100 |

## CARL BRYAN
| | | | |
|---|---|---|---|
| 69 | Trojan TR 673 | Red Ash/SILVERTONES: Bluebirds Flying Over | 30 |
| 69 | Duke DU 13 | Soul Pipe/Overproof | 30 |
| 69 | Camel CA 22 | Run For Your Life/TWO SPARKS: When We Were Young | 25 |
| 69 | Gas GAS 133 | Stagger Back/The Creeper | 45 |
| 69 | Gas GAS 134 | Walking The Dead/TREVOR & KEITH: Got What You Want | 30 |

*(see also Cannon Ball & Johnny Melody, King Cannon, Vincent Foster, Hugh Malcolm, King Cannonball, Glen Brown, Shenley Duffas, Alton Ellis, Kid Gungo, Jackie Mittoo, Johnny Moore, Joe White, Royals)*

## RAD BRYAN
| | | | |
|---|---|---|---|
| 71 | Techniques TE 909 | Jumping Jack/ANSELL COLLINS: Point Blank | 30 |
| 71 | Bullet BU 463 | Shock Attack/Cuban Waltz | 30 |
| 71 | Big Shot BI 559 | Just Do The Right Things/Corporal Jones | 20 |
| 71 | Big Shot BI 591 | I'll Be Right There (actually by Techniques)/PLAYBOYS: Hot Pants Rock | 20 |
| 71 | Big Shot BI 592 | My Best Girl/My Best Girl Version | 20 |
| 71 | Black Swan BW 1410 | Girl You Rock My Soul/Version | 35 |
| 72 | Attack ATT 8040 | Standing In The Rain (actually by Neville Grant)/Standing In The Rain Version | 10 |
| 75 | Love 1 | Rock Children/Version | 7 |

## TIM BRYAN
| | | | |
|---|---|---|---|
| 71 | Phillips 6006026 | Mary Anne/It's So Easy | 8 |

## WES BRYAN
| | | | |
|---|---|---|---|
| 58 | London HLU 8607 | Lonesome Love/Tiny Spaceman | 40 |
| 59 | London HLU 8978 | Honey Baby/So Blue Over You | 50 |

## BRYAN & BRUNELLES
| | | | |
|---|---|---|---|
| 65 | HMV POP 1394 | Jacqueline/Louie Louie | 45 |

## ANITA BRYANT
| | | | |
|---|---|---|---|
| 66 | CBS 202026 | Another Year, Another Love/My Mind's Playing Tricks On Me Again | 50 |

## BOUDLEAUX BRYANT
| | | | |
|---|---|---|---|
| 60 | Polydor NH 66952 | Hot Spot/Touché (with Sparks) | 6 |

*(see also Bood & Fileece Bryant)*

## DON BRYANT
| | | | |
|---|---|---|---|
| 70 | London HA-U/SH-U 8409 | PRECIOUS SOUL (LP) | 40 |

## JAY DEE BRYANT
| | | | |
|---|---|---|---|
| 76 | Island WIP 6273 | Standing Ovation For Love/I Want To Thank You Baby | 10 |

## JOHN BRYANT (1)
| | | | |
|---|---|---|---|
| 65 | Fontana H 625 | Tell Me What You See/Poor Unfortunate Me | 15 |
| 71 | Polydor 2383069 | JOHN BRYANT (LP, gatefold sleeve) | 20 |

## JOHN BRYANT (2)
| | | | |
|---|---|---|---|
| 69 | Decca 12894 | She's In Need Of Love | 25 |
| 68 | MCA MU 1020 | Columbine/I Bring The Sun | 20 |
| 71 | Polydor 2058-145 | Back On The Road/I Won't Sleep Tonight/Ain't Got No Woman | 6 |

## LAURA K. BRYANT
| | | | |
|---|---|---|---|
| 58 | London HLU 8551 | Bobby/Angel Tears | 20 |

## MARIE/MARGARET BRYANT
| | | | |
|---|---|---|---|
| 61 | Kalypso XX 27 | Water Melon/Tomato | 6 |
| 61 | Kalypso XX 28 | Don't Touch Me Nylons/Little Boy | 6 |
| 60s | Melodisc MLP 12 132 | DON'T TOUCH ME NYLONS (LP, with sleeve) | 25 |

## RAY BRYANT TRIO/COMBO
| | | | |
|---|---|---|---|
| 60 | Pye International 7N 25052 | Little Susie Parts 2 & 4 | 5 |
| 60 | Philips PB 1003 | Little Susie Parts 1 & 3 | 5 |
| 60 | Philips PB 1014 | The Madison Time Parts 1 & 2 | 5 |

## RUSTY BRYANT
| | | | |
|---|---|---|---|
| 57 | London HB-D 1066 | RUSTY BRYANT (10" LP) | 30 |

## SANDRA BRYANT
| | | | |
|---|---|---|---|
| 67 | Major Minor MM 523 | Girl With Money/Golden Hours | 10 |
| 68 | Major Minor MM 553 | Out To Get You/There's No Lock Upon My Door | 30 |

## GAVIN BRYARS
| | | | |
|---|---|---|---|
| 75 | Obscure OBS 1 | THE SINKING OF THE TITANIC (LP) | 70 |
| 78 | Obscure OBS 8 | MACHINE MUSIC (split LP with John White) | 20 |
| 87 | EG EGED 21 | THE SINKING OF THE TITANIC (LP, reissue) | 20 |

*(see also Brian Eno)*

## CALUM BRYCE
| | | | |
|---|---|---|---|
| 68 | Condor PS 1001 | Lovemaker/I'm Glad | 475 |

## BERYL BRYDEN('S BACK-ROOM SKIFFLE)
| | | | |
|---|---|---|---|
| 56 | Decca F 10823 | Casey Jones/Kansas City Blues | 20 |
| 57 | Decca (no cat. no.) | Rock Me/This Train (test pressing, with Alexis Korner & Cyril Davies) | 60 |

MINT VALUE £

| 63 | Columbia DB 4860 | I'm Movin' On/Moanin' | 10 |
| 63 | Columbia DB 7010 | I'm Living With The Blues/Big Daddy | 10 |
| 56 | Melodisc EPM 7-69 | BERYL BRYDEN WITH FATTY GEORGE'S JAZZ BAND (EP) | 10 |

*(see also Alexis Korner, Cyril Davies)*

## BETSY BRYE
| 59 | Columbia DB 4350 | Sleep Walk/Daddy Daddy (Gotta Get A Phone In My Room) | 25 |

## BRYGADA KRYZYS
| 82 | Fresh Records FRESH 13 | BRYGADA KRYZYS (LP) | 25 |

## B'S
| 70s | private pressing | IN YOUR BONNET (LP) | 35 |

## B SIDE
| 93 | B Promo B Side | Rip Piece Off/Can't Slow Me Down (12") | 40 |

## B.T.B.
| 68 | Liberty LBF 15067 | Do It To 'Em/Sparrows And Daisies | 15 |

## B.T.P. FOLDERS
| 80 | Future Earth FER 005 | Radio/All Of A Sudden (p/s) | 50 |

## B12
| 93 | Warp WAPLP 9LTD | ELECTRO - SOMA (2-LP, orange vinyl) | 40 |
| 94 | B12 15 | B12 (12", 4-track promo only, 10 copies pressed) | 40 |
| 96 | Warp WARPLP 37 | TIME TOURISTS (2-LP) | 20 |
| 07 | B12 B1215 | Practopia (12") | 20 |

*(see also Redcell, Musicology)*

## BUBA & SHOP ASSISTANTS
| 85 | Villa 21 002 | Something To Do/Dreaming Backwards (p/s, with insert in poly bag) | 75 |

*(see also Shop Assistants, Pastels)*

## BUBBLEGUM
| 68 | Philips BF1677 | Little Red Bucket/With The Sun In Your Hair | 45 |

## BUBBLEGUM SPLASH
| 87 | Bonk On 001 | If Only/THE DARLING BUDS: Spin (flexidisc free with So Naive fanzine) | 10 |
| 88 | Subway 13 | SPLASHDOWN EP | 10 |

## BUBBLEMEN
| 88 | Beggars Banquet BUB1 | The Bubblemen Are Coming/B Side (p/s, comic included) | 8 |

*(see also Bauhaus)*

## BUBBLES & CO
| 65 | Pye 7N 15875 | Underneath My Pillow/Just One Girl | 8 |

## BUBBLES (1)
| 63 | Duke DK 1001 | The Wasp/Bopping In The Barnyard (matrix: DK 1001A-1, plays Rocking Crickets by Hot Toddy's) | 18 |

## BUBBLES (2)
| 72 | Bumble GE 117 | Hazy Hazy Crazy Crazy/Audrey | 8 |
| 75 | Decca F 13583 | This Is Where The Hurdie Gurdie Heebie Geebie Greenie Meenie Man Came In/Zap N' Cat | 35 |
| 78 | Rainbow RS 611 | Jamais/Night Life | 8 |

## BUCCA
| 82 | Plant Life PLR 039 | THE HOLE IN THE HARPERS HEAD (LP) | 20 |

## BUCHANAN BROTHERS
| 69 | Page One POF 139 | Medicine Man Part 1/Part 2 | 8 |
| 69 | Page One POF 154 | Son Of A Lovin' Man/I'll Never Get Enough | 5 |
| 70 | Penny Farthing PEN 725 | Rosianna/The Feeling That I Get When Your Near | 6 |

## GILLY BUCHANAN
| 80 | Toe TOE 002 | Me No Mix/PATRICK ANDY: Ain't No Me (12") | 80 |

## BUCKINGHAM-NICKS
| 74 | Polydor 2066 398 | Don't Let Me Down Again/Races Are Run | 15 |
| 76 | Polydor 2066 700 | Don't Let Me Down Again/Crystal | 10 |
| 73 | Polydor 2391 013 | BUCKINGHAM-NICKS (LP, with insert, with stickered sleeve) | 40 |
| 73 | Polydor 2391 093 | BUCKINGHAM-NICKS (LP, with insert, without stickered sleeve) | 35 |
| 81 | Polydor 2482 378 | BUCKINGHAM-NICKS (LP, reissue with insert) | 25 |

*(see also Lindsay Buckingham, Fleetwood Mac)*

## BUCKINGHAMS (U.K.)
| 65 | Pye 7N 15848 | I'll Never Hurt You No More/She Lied | 5 |
| 65 | Pye 7N 15921 | To Be Or Not To Be/I Was Your First Guy | 5 |

## BUCKINGHAMS (U.S.)
| 67 | Stateside SS 588 | Kind Of A Drag/You Make Me Feel So Good | 12 |
| 67 | CBS 2859 | Mercy Mercy Mercy/You Are Gone | 12 |
| 67 | CBS 2995 | Hey Baby/And Our Love | 15 |
| 68 | CBS 2640 | Don't You Care/Why Don't You Love Me | 25 |
| 68 | CBS 3559 | Back In Love Again/You Misunderstand Me | 6 |
| 69 | CBS 3195 | Susan/Foreign Policy | 10 |

## BOB BUCKLE
| 73 | Ash ALP 107 S | COME LISTEN TO (LP) | 50 |

## BUCKLEY
| 72 | CBS 58303 | My My My/Goodbye Wurzel Gummage | 12 |

## JEFF BUCKLEY
| 93 | Big Cat ABB 61XCD | LIVE AT SIN-E EP (Mojo Pin/Eternal Life/Je N'en Connais Pas La Fin/The Way Young Lovers Do (CD) | 30 |
| 95 | Columbia 662042 1 | Last Goodbye (Edit)/Lover, You Should've Come Over (Live And Acoustic In Japan)/ Tongue (Live) (10", p/s, 5000 only) | 30 |
| 95 | Columbia 661498 | Last Goodbye/Last Goodbye (Full)/So Real (Live)/Dream Brother (Live) (12") | 30 |

| | | | |
|---|---|---|---|
| 95 | Columbia 88697098847 | Hallelujah/I Know It's Over (Live 1995) (p/s, numbered sleeve, 2,700 only, blue/black vinyl) | 20 |
| 13 | Music On Vinyl MOV 7017 | Hallelujah/LEONARD COHEN: Hallelujah (numbered 7") | 6 |
| 94 | Columbia 475928 | GRACE (LP, with insert) | 50 |
| 98 | Columbia 3C 67229 | SKETCHES FOR MY SWEETHEART THE DRUNK (3-LP) | 30 |
| 01 | Simply Vinyl SVLP 077 | GRACE (LP, reissue, insert) | 18 |
| 07 | Columbia 4979721 | MYSTERY WHITE BOY LIVE 95-96 (LP) | 20 |

## SEAN BUCKLEY & BREADCRUMBS
| | | | |
|---|---|---|---|
| 65 | Stateside SS 421 | It Hurts Me When I Cry/Everybody Knows | 70 |

## TIM BUCKLEY
| | | | |
|---|---|---|---|
| 67 | Elektra EKSN 45008 | Aren't You The Girl/Strange Street Affair Under Blue | 15 |
| 67 | Elektra EKSN 45018 | Morning Glory/Knight-Errant | 10 |
| 68 | Elektra EKSN 45023 | Once I Was/Phantasmagoria In Two | 7 |
| 68 | Elektra EKSN 45031 | Wings/I Can't See You | 7 |
| 68 | Elektra EKSN 45041 | Pleasant Street/Carnival Song | 10 |
| 70 | Straight S 4799 | Happy Time/So Lonely | 20 |
| 91 | Strange Fruit SFPS082 | THE PEEL SESSIONS: Morning Glory/Coming Home To You/ Sing A Song For You/ Hallucinations/Troubadour/Once I Was (12", p/s ) | 10 |
| 66 | Elektra EKL/EKS 4004 | TIM BUCKLEY (LP, orange label) | 75 |
| 67 | Elektra EKL/EKS 318 | GOODBYE AND HELLO (LP, orange label, gatefold sleeve) | 70 |
| 68 | Elektra EKS 74045 | HAPPY SAD (LP, orange label) | 70 |
| 69 | Straight STS 1060 | BLUE AFTERNOON (LP) | 80 |
| 70 | Elektra 2410 005 | LORCA (LP) | 50 |
| 71 | Straight STS 1064 | STARSAILOR (LP) | 100 |
| 74 | Warner Bros K 46176 | GREETINGS FROM L.A. (LP, gatefold sleeve, postcard) | 25 |
| 74 | Elektra K42072 | HAPPY SAD (LP, reissue, butterfly label) | 20 |
| 74 | Discreet K 49201 | SEFRONIA (LP) | 25 |
| 74 | Discreet K 59204 | LOOK AT THE FOOL (LP) | 25 |
| 76 | Elektra K42079 | GOODBYE AND HELLO (LP, reissue, inside loading gatefold sleeve, Butterfly label) | 20 |
| 84 | Elektra ELK 42079 | GOODBYE AND HELLO (LP, reissue, red label) | 15 |
| 90 | Demon DFIEND 200 | DREAM LETTER - LIVE IN LONDON 1968 (2-LP) | 25 |

## VERNON BUCKLEY
| | | | |
|---|---|---|---|
| 73 | Grape GR 3057 | Mr Softhand/G.G. ALLSTARS: Dub | 10 |
| 73 | Grape GR 3058 | Ital Queen/G.G. ALLSTARS: Dub | 10 |

## SID BUCKNER PRODUCTIONS
| | | | |
|---|---|---|---|
| 76 | Lyntone/Tropical Sounds DSR SB1008/1009 | DUB SENSATION (LP, 50 copies, promo only in stamped white card sleeve) | 250 |

## BUCKY & STRINGS
| | | | |
|---|---|---|---|
| 62 | Salvo SLO 1807 | Lolita's On The Loose/Lonely Island (99 copies only) | 20 |

## BUD & HIS BUDDIES
| | | | |
|---|---|---|---|
| 58 | Starlite ST45 006 | June, July And August/Sing A Little Sweeter | 5 |

## BUD & TRAVIS
| | | | |
|---|---|---|---|
| 59 | London HLU 8965 | Bonsoir Dame/Truly Do | 5 |
| 60 | London HLG 9211 | The Ballad Of The Alamo/The Green Leaves Of Summer | 5 |

## BILLY BUDD
| | | | |
|---|---|---|---|
| 69 | Page One POF 138 | Alice Long (You're Still My Favourite Girlfriend)/The Straight Life | 20 |
| 70 | Pye 7N 45010 | You're Sailing Away/I'm Gonna Change It | 12 |

## HAROLD BUDD
| | | | |
|---|---|---|---|
| 78 | Obscure OBS 10 | PAVILLION OF DREAMS (LP) | 20 |

## HAROLD BUDD & BRIAN ENO
| | | | |
|---|---|---|---|
| 80 | Editions EG EGAMB 002 | AMBIENT 2 (THE PLATEAUX OF MIRRORS) (LP) | 20 |
| 87 | Editions EG EGED 18 | AMBIENT 2 (THE PLATEAUX OF MIRRORS) (LP, reissue) | 15 |

## ROY BUDD
| | | | |
|---|---|---|---|
| 65 | Pye 7N 15807 | Birth Of The Budd/M'Ghee M'Ghee | 15 |
| 66 | Parlophone R 5514 | Summer Samba/Bahama Sound | 5 |
| 67 | Pye 7N 17279 | Mr Rose/Summer Rain | 10 |
| 68 | Pye 7N 17652 | Pavanne/Whizz Ball | 5 |
| 69 | Pye 7N 17773 | Tijuana Piano/Lead On | 5 |
| 70 | Pye 7N 17987 | Borsalino (Theme)/It Only Goes To Show | 5 |
| 70 | Pye 7N 45051 | Carter (Theme)/Plaything (in p/s) | 70 |
| 70 | Pye 7N 45051 | Carter (Theme)/Plaything | 50 |
| 68 | Pye NPL 18212 | AT NEWPORT (LP) | 18 |
| 71 | Pye NSPL 18348 | PLAYS SOLDIER BLUE AND OTHER THEMES (LP) | 20 |
| 72 | Polydor 2383 102 | KIDNAPPED (Roy Budd/Mary Hopkin) | 25 |
| 72 | Pye NSPL 18389 | CONCERTO FOR HARRY - SOMETHING TO HIDE (Roy Budd) | 25 |
| 73 | Pye NSPL 18398 | FEAR IS THE KEY (LP, soundtrack) | 25 |
| 76 | Bradley's BRADS 8002 | DIAMONDS (LP, soundtrack) | 50 |
| 70s | Pye NSPL 19494 | EVERYTHING'S COMING UP (LP) | 15 |
| 99 | Cinephile CINLP001 | GET CARTER (LP, gatefold) | 25 |
| 00 | Cinephile CINLP004 | THE BLACK WINDMILL (LP, gatefold) | 30 |

## BUDDY & SKETTO
| | | | |
|---|---|---|---|
| 62 | Dice 45/CC 7 | Little Schoolgirl/Hush Baby | 25 |

*(see also Father Sketto, Ruddy & Sketto, Sketto Rich)*

## BUDGIE
| | | | |
|---|---|---|---|
| 71 | MCA MK 5072 | Crash Course In Brain Surgery/Nude Disintegrating Parachutist Woman | 18 |
| 72 | MCA MK 5085 | Whisky River/Guts | 8 |
| 74 | MCA MCA 133 | Zoom Club (Edited Version)/Wondering What Everyone Knows | 6 |
| 75 | MCA MCA 175 | I Ain't No Mountain/Honey | 6 |

MINT VALUE £

| 78 | A&M AMS 7342 | Smile Boy Smile/All At Sea | 6 |
| 80 | Active BUDGE | Wildfire/Wildfire (promo only) | 10 |
| 80 | Active BUDGE 1 | IF SWALLOWED DO NOT INDUCE VOMITING (12" EP) | 10 |
| 80 | Active BUDGE 2 | Crime Against The World/Hellbender (p/s) | 8 |
| 81 | RCA BUDGE 3 | Keeping A Rendezvous/Apparatus (p/s) | 5 |
| 81 | RCA BUDGE 4 | I Turned To Stone (Part 1)/I Turned To Stone (Part 2) (orange vinyl) | 5 |
| 82 | RCA RCA 271 | Bored With Russia/Don't Cry (poster p/s) | 5 |
| 71 | MCA MKPS 2018 | BUDGIE (LP, pink/red label, initial pressing with laminated sleeve and poster) | 120 |
| 71 | MCA MKPS 2018 | BUDGIE (LP, pink/red label, with no poster) | 50 |
| 71 | MCA MKPS 2018 | BUDGIE (LP, later pressing with blue/black label) | 15 |
| 72 | MCA MKPS 2023 | SQUAWK (LP, 1st pressing, Matrix numbers: 7-LNMG-216-1l/262-1L, blue/black hexagon label, matt sleeve) | 30 |
| 73 | MCA MDKS 8010 | NEVER TURN YOUR BACK ON A FRIEND (LP, blue/black label, g/fold sleeve) | 25 |
| 74 | MCA MCF 2546 | IN FOR THE KILL (LP, rainbow label) | 15 |
| 76 | A&M AMLH 68377 | IF I WAS BRITANNIA I'D WAIVE THE RULES (LP, silver/green label) | 15 |
| 80 | RCA RCALP 3046 | POWER SUPPLY (LP, reissue, with different back sleeve) | 20 |

*(see also Tredegar, Phenomena, George Hatcher Band)*

## DENNIS BUDLIMAR
| 67 | Fontana TL 5307 | THE CREEPER (LP) | 20 |

## BUENA VISTAS
| 66 | Stateside SS 525 | Hot Shot/T.N.T. | 25 |

## BUFFALO
| 81 | Heavy Metal HEAVY 3 | Battle Torn Heroes/Women Of The Night (p/s) | 30 |
| 82 | Heavy Metal HEAVY 15 | Mean Machine/The Rumour (p/s) | 25 |

## BUFFALO SPRINGFIELD
| 67 | Atlantic 584 077 | For What It's Worth (Stop Hey What's That Sound)/Do I Have To Come Right Out And Say It | 25 |
| 67 | Atlantic 584 145 | Rock'n'Roll Woman/A Child's Claim To Fame | 15 |
| 68 | Atlantic 584 165 | Expecting To Fly/Everydays | 15 |
| 68 | Atlantic 584 189 | Uno-Mundo/Merry-Go-Round | 15 |
| 69 | Atco 226 006 | Pretty Girl Why/Questions | 10 |
| 72 | Atlantic K 10237 | Bluebird/Mr Soul/Rock'n'Roll Woman/Expecting To Fly (p/s) | 6 |
| 67 | Atlantic 587 070 | BUFFALO SPRINGFIELD (LP, plum label, mispressing, lists "For What It's Worth" but plays "Baby Don't Scold Me"; matrix no. ends '1' mono) | 120 |
| 67 | Atlantic 588 070 | BUFFALO SPRINGFIELD ((LP, plum label, mispressing, lists "For What It's Worth" but plays "Baby Don't Scold Me"; matrix no. ends '1' stereo) | 70 |
| 67 | Atlantic 587 070 | BUFFALO SPRINGFIELD (LP, plum label, plays "For What It's Worth", mono) | 50 |
| 67 | Atlantic 588 070 | BUFFALO SPRINGFIELD (LP, plum label, plays "For What It's Worth", stereo) | 40 |
| 68 | Atlantic 587 091 | BUFFALO SPRINGFIELD AGAIN (LP, plum label, mono) | 70 |
| 68 | Atlantic 588 091 | BUFFALO SPRINGFIELD AGAIN (LP, plum label, stereo) | 50 |
| 69 | Atco 228 024 | LAST TIME AROUND (LP, plum label, gatefold sleeve) | 40 |
| 69 | Atco 228 012 | RETROSPECTIVE (LP, plum label) | 25 |
| 70 | Atlantic 2464 012 | EXPECTING TO FLY (LP, plum label) | 25 |
| 72 | Atlantic K 40014 | BUFFALO SPRINGFIELD AGAIN (LP, reissue, green & orange label) | 15 |
| 72 | Atlantic K 40077 | LAST TIME AROUND (LP, reissue, green & orange label, gatefold sleeve) | 15 |
| 73 | Atlantic K 30028 | BUFFALO SPRINGFIELD - ATLANTIC MASTERS: THE BEGINNNING (LP) | 15 |

*(see also Neil Young, Stephen Stills, Au-Go-Go Singers, Crosby Stills Nash & Young)*

## BUFFALO TOM
| 89 | Caff CAFF 6 | Enemy/Deep In The Ground (p/s) | 20 |
| 92 | Situation 2 SITU 36 | LET ME COME OVER (LP) | 15 |
| 93 | Beggars Banquet BBQLP 142 | BIG RED LETTER DAY (LP) | 15 |

## BUFF MEDWAYS
| 00 | Friends Of...FOBMFA 2 | Fire/Manic Depression (die-cut sleeve) | 8 |
| 01 | Vinyl Japan PAD 74 | Into Your Dreams/Highway Chile (p/s) | 8 |
| 01 | Hangman 10237 | Sally Sensation/Dawn Said What Have I Done | 8 |
| 02 | Transcopic TRAN 012 | A Strange Kind Of Happyness/BILLY CHILDISH: Hound Dog (p/s, 500 only) | 8 |
| 02 | Transcopic TRAN 015 | Troubled Mind/BILLY CHILDISH: Leave My Kitten Alone (p/s, 500 only) | 10 |
| 02 | Transcopic TRAN 017 | Strood Lights/You Make Me Die (p/s) | 10 |
| 03 | Transcopic TRAN 025 | Just 15/The Doo Rek (p/s) | 8 |
| 03 | Damaged Goods DAMGOOD 228 | Merry Christmas Fritz/Stille Nacht (p/s, swirly white vinyl, 1000 only) | 5 |
| 05 | Damaged Goods DAMGOOD 238 | (I'm A) Lie Detector/Dear Lorna (p/s) | 5 |
| 01 | Vinyl Japan ASKLP 132 | THIS IS THIS (LP) | 25 |
| 02 | Transcopic TRANLP 016 | STEADY THE BUFFS (LP) | 25 |
| 03 | Transcopic TRANLP 026 | 1914 (LP, as the Buffs) | 20 |

*(see also Billy Childish, Wild Billy Childish & Buff Medways, Nilkshakes, Thee Headcoats)*

## BUFFOONS
| 67 | Columbia DB 8317 | My World Fell Down/Tomorrow Is Another Day | 18 |

## BUG CENTRAL
| 99 | Dole Office/DHSS 1 | Gotta Get A Real Job/No Free Records (Unreleased, white label test pressings only) | 35 |
| 99 | Helen Of Oi HOO 48 | THE MEEK WILL INHERIT NOTHING (LP, with inserts) | 15 |

## JAKE BUGG
| 12 | Kitchenware JAKE 01 | Trouble Town/Someone Told Me (p/s) | 50 |
| 13 | EMI (No Cat/ No.) | What Doesn't Kill You (1-sided, die-cut sleeve) | 20 |
| 14 | Secret 7 S717 | Secret Creatures (1-sided, 100 only) | 40 |
| 12 | Mercury 3717304 | JAKE BUGG (LP) | 15 |

## THE BUGGER ALL STARS
| 81 | Bead Records BEAD 19 | THE BUGGER ALL STARS (LP) | 20 |
| 83 | Bead Records BEAD 21 | BONZO BITES BACK (LP) | 20 |

**BUGGY**
70   Parlophone R5832 — The Rolly Pole Coaster/Harry The Keeper ....................................................... 15

**BUKKSHEE**
86   Lyntone BUK 13 — In The Country/Sting In The Tail ................................................................ 10

**SANDY BULL**
69   Vanguard 19040 — E PLURIBUS UNUM (LP) ........................................................................ 25

**BULLAMAKANKA**
83   BBC REL 454 — Dr Who Is Gonna Fix It/Harlequin ............................................................ 10

**BULLDOG**
72   MCA MU1166 — No/Good Times Are Comin' ....................................................................... 5

**BULLDOG BREED**
69   Deram DM 270 — Portcullis Gate/Halo In My Hair ........................................................... 150
70   Deram Nova DN 5 — MADE IN ENGLAND (LP, mono) ........................................................... 350
70   Deram Nova SDN 5 — MADE IN ENGLAND (LP, stereo) ......................................................... 300
02   Acme ADLP 1036 — MADE IN ENGLAND (LP, reissue with free 7") ...................................... 15
(see also Flies)

**BULLDOGS**
64   Mercury MF 808 — John, Paul, George And Ringo/What Do I See ....................................... 20

**BULLET (1)**
71   Purple PUR 101 — Hobo/Sinister Minister ......................................................................... 20
75   Polydor 2058 548 — Hanged Man/The Contract Man .......................................................... 10
75   Contour 2870 437 — THE HANGED MAN (LP, TV soundtrack) ............................................... 40
(see also Hard Stuff, Quatermass, Atomic Rooster)

**BULLET (2)**
78   Pennine PSS 138 — Don't Go/Streetcrawler (500 only) ...................................................... 20

**BULLFROG**
74   Cube BUG 44 — Clancy/In The City ................................................................................... 8

**JOHN BULL BREED**
66   Polydor BM 56065 — Can't Chance A Breakup/I'm A Man ................................................. 375

**BULL MINSTRELS**
73   Boston Sound/Guildhall GHS HORNCASTLE FAYRE (LP) ..................................................... 20
     9

**BULLRING**
70   CBS 4881 — Birmingham Brass Band/Lady Of The Morning Sun ........................................ 15

**BULLSEYE**
80   Kennet K1 — No. 10,553/Why Don't You Let Me Know ....................................................... 8

**BULLY BOYS BAND**
70   Stateside SSL 5032 — MOVIE SCENE - HEAVY SOUNDS FROM TODAY'S FILMS (LP) ............ 20

**BULLY WEE (BAND)**
75   Folksound — BULLYWEE (LP) ......................................................................................... 20
76   Red Rag RRR 007 — THE ENCHANTED LADY (LP) ............................................................. 15
81   Jigsaw SAW 1 — THE MADMAN OF GOTHAM (LP) .............................................................. 20

**B. BUMBLE & STINGERS**
61   Top Rank JAR 561 — Bumble Boogie/School Day Blues ...................................................... 5
62   Top Rank JAR 611 — Nut Rocker/Nautilus .......................................................................... 5
62   Stateside SS 113 — Apple Knocker/The Moon And The Sea ............................................... 5
62   Stateside SS 131 — Dawn Cracker/Scales ......................................................................... 8
63   Stateside SS 192 — Baby Mash/Night Time Madness ......................................................... 8
67   Mercury MF 977 — Silent Movies/Twelfth Street Rag ......................................................... 8
(see also Kim Fowley)

**BUMBLE BEE SLIM**
60s  Fontana 688 138ZL — BEE'S BACK IN TOWN (LP) ........................................................... 25

**BUMBLEBEE UNLIMITED**
79   Sky SKY1004 — Love Bug/Disco Version ........................................................................... 15
14   Groove Line GLR12 0003 — Love Bug (Disco Mix)/Love Bug (Disco Remix) (12", reissue) ... 10

**BUMBLES**
72   Purple PUR 107 — Beep Beep/Buzz Off (promo only p/s) ................................................. 25
72   Purple PUR 107 — Beep Beep/Buzz Off ............................................................................. 8
(see laos Hard Stuff, Atomic Rooster, Curtis Muldoon)

**BUNCH**
67   CBS 202506 — We're Not What We Appear To Be/You Never Came Home ......................... 70
69   Beacon BEA 128 — Red Rover, Red Rover/Happy Like This .............................................. 10
72   Island WIP 6130 — When Will I Be Loved/Willie And The Hand Jive .................................. 10
67   CBS 2740 — Don't Come Back To Me/You Can't Do This .................................................... 25
67   CBS 3060 — Looking Glass Alice/Spare A Shilling ............................................................ 200
68   CBS 3692 — Birthday/Still ................................................................................................ 30
68   CBS 3709 — Birthday/Still (reissue) .................................................................................. 15
72   Island ILPS 9189 — ROCK ON (LP, with 1-sided flexi attached to die-cut sleeve: "Let There Be Drums" [WI 4002]) ........................................................................................................... 75
72   Island ILPS 9189 — ROCK ON (LP, without 1-sided flexi: "Let There Be Drums" [WI 4002]) ... 25
(see also Peter & The Wolves, Sounds Around, John Pantry)

**BUNCH OF FIVES**
66   Parlophone R 5494 — Go Home Baby/At The Station ......................................................... 120
(see also Viv Prince, Egg, Hullaballoos, Junior's Eyes, Outsiders [U.K.])

**BUNDLE**
70   Polydor 2058 029 — Dirty La Rue/Progressive Underground ............................................. 15

MINT VALUE £

### DAVE BUNDY
| | | | |
|---|---|---|---|
| 72 | UK UK 10 | Inside A Hole/Nicer Out | 5 |

### ROGER BUNN
| | | | |
|---|---|---|---|
| 70 | Major Minor SMLP 70 | PIECE OF MIND (LP, red/white/black label) | 200 |

*(see also Pete Browns Pitlokto, Roxy Music)*

### BUNNIES (OF LONDON)
| | | | |
|---|---|---|---|
| 68 | Decca LK4951 | CAUGHT LIVE AT THE PLAYBOY CLUB (LP) | 20 |
| 69 | Decca SKL5026 | THE BUNNIES AGAIN SINGIN' AND SWINGIN' AT THE LONDON PLAYBOY CLUB (LP) | 20 |

### BUNNY & RICKY
| | | | |
|---|---|---|---|
| 75 | Attack ATT 8107 | Too Bad Bull (as Bunnie And Rickey)/UPSETTERS: Bad Cow | 30 |
| 75 | Attack ATT 8109 | Bushwood Contrash/UPSETTERS: Callying Butt | 30 |

### BUNNY & RUDDY
| | | | |
|---|---|---|---|
| 68 | Nu Beat NB 007 | Rhythm & Soul/MONTY MORRIS: True Romance | 35 |
| 68 | Nu Beat NB 011 | On The Town/MONTY MORRIS: Simple Simon | 40 |

### BINGY BUNNY
| | | | |
|---|---|---|---|
| 82 | Cha Cha CHAD 46 | Keep It In The Family (with MORWELLS)/SCIENTIST : Extended Dub/Me & Jane (with MORWELLS)/SCIENTIST : Extended Dub (12") | 40 |
| 82 | Cha Cha CHAD 48 | Street Lover (with MORWELLS)/NICODEMUS : How You Look Girl 'Pon The Street (12") | 20 |
| 82 | Cha Cha CHALP 015 | ME & JANE (LP) | 40 |

### BINGY BUNNY & BONGO LES
| | | | |
|---|---|---|---|
| 73 | Ackee ACK 506 | International Scout/International Scout Version | 12 |

*(see also Bongo Les, Mediators)*

### BUNNY BROWN
| | | | |
|---|---|---|---|
| 72 | Songbird SB 1073 | Fat Boy/Fat Boy - Version | 20 |
| 78 | JCB JCB 002 | I Love The Way You Love/Version | 18 |

*(see also Noel Brown, Winston Scotland)*

### BUNNY LION
| | | | |
|---|---|---|---|
| 77 | M&M MM03 | Introducing Bunny Lion/REVOLUTIONARIES: Version (12", as Linval Thompson) | 20 |
| 79 | Starlight SLP 900 | RED (LP) | 25 |

### BUNNY MACK
| | | | |
|---|---|---|---|
| 80 | Rokel MACK 1 | Let Me Love You/Love You Forever (12") | 20 |

### BOB BUNTING
| | | | |
|---|---|---|---|
| 68 | Transatlantic TRA 166 | YOU'VE GOT TO GO DOWN THIS WAY (LP) | 40 |

### VASHTI BUNYAN
| | | | |
|---|---|---|---|
| 70 | Philips 6308 019 | JUST ANOTHER DIAMOND DAY (LP) | 1200 |
| 00 | Spinney SPINNEY 001 | JUST ANOTHER DIAMOND DAY (LP, reissue, gatefold) | 20 |
| 05 | Fat Cat FATLP 38 | LOOKAFTERING (LP) | 20 |

*(see also Vashti, Fairport Convention, Dave Swarbrick, Robin Williamson)*

### BUOYS
| | | | |
|---|---|---|---|
| 70 | Wand WN7 | Timothy/It Feels Good | 20 |
| 71 | Wand MSW 8296 | Give Up Your Guns/The Prince Of Thieves | 15 |

### DONI BURDICK
| | | | |
|---|---|---|---|
| 10 | Outta Sight/Ron's OSV006 | Candle (!n The Window)/Whatcha Gonna Do (reissue) | 10 |

### ERIC BURDON (BAND)
| | | | |
|---|---|---|---|
| 75 | Capitol E-ST 11426 | STOP (LP, as Eric Burdon Band) | 15 |
| 78 | Polydor 2302 078 | SURVIVOR (LP, with 5 inserts with lyrics and drawings) | 25 |

### ERIC BURDON & THE ANIMALS
| | | | |
|---|---|---|---|
| 66 | Decca F 12502 | Mama Told Me Not To Come/See See Rider (unreleased) | 0 |
| 66 | Decca F 12502 | Help Me Girl/See See Rider (amended issue with new A-side) | 8 |
| 67 | MGM MGM 1340 | When I Was Young/A Girl Named Sandoz | 8 |
| 67 | MGM MGM 1344 | Good Times/Ain't That So | 8 |
| 67 | MGM MGM 1359 | San Franciscan Nights/Gratefully Dead | 10 |
| 68 | MGM MGM 1373 | Sky Pilot (Parts 1 & 2) | 10 |
| 68 | MGM MGM 1412 | Monterey/Anything | 8 |
| 69 | MGM MGM 1461 | Ring Of Fire/I'm An Animal | 8 |
| 69 | MGM MGM 1481 | River Deep Mountain High/Help Me Girl | 8 |
| 67 | MGM C(S) 8052 | WINDS OF CHANGE (LP, yellow/black label with "sold in the U.K." label text) | 80 |
| 68 | MGM C(S) 8074 | THE TWAIN SHALL MEET (LP, yellow black labels with "sold in the U.K." text) | 80 |
| 68 | MGM C(S) 8105 | LOVE IS (LP, blue/gold labels with "sold in the U.K." text) | 100 |
| 71 | MGM 2619 002 | LOVE IS (2-LP; individual LP nos.: 2354 006/7) | 50 |

*(see also Animals, Stud, Zoot Money's Big Roll Band)*

### ERIC BURDON & WAR
| | | | |
|---|---|---|---|
| 70 | Polydor 2001 072 | Spill The Wine/Magic Mountain | 7 |
| 71 | Liberty LBF 15434 | They Can't Take Away Our Music/Home Cookin' | 5 |
| 71 | United Artists UP 35217 | Paint It Black/Spirit | 5 |
| 70 | Polydor 2310 041 | ERIC BURDON DECLARES WAR (LP) | 35 |
| 70 | Liberty LDS 8400 3/4 | BLACKMAN'S BURDON (2-LP, gatefold, with banned track "P.C. 3") | 45 |
| 70 | Liberty LDS 8400 | BLACKMAN'S BURDON (2-LP, gatefold, without banned track "P.C. 3") | 20 |

*(see also War)*

### ERIC BURDON & JIMMY WITHERSPOON
| | | | |
|---|---|---|---|
| 71 | United Artists UP 35287 | Soledad/Headin' For Home | 6 |
| 71 | United Artists UAG 29251 | GUILTY! (LP, gatefold sleeve) | 18 |

*(see also Jimmy Witherspoon)*

### DAVE BURGESS (TRIO)
| | | | |
|---|---|---|---|
| 55 | London HLB 8175 | I Love Paris/Five Foot Two, Eyes Of Blue (Has Anybody Seen My Girl) | 10 |
| 58 | Oriole CB 1413 | I'm Available/Who's Gonna Cry? | 20 |

### SONNY BURGESS
| 60 | London HLS 9064 | Sadie's Back In Town/A Kiss Goodnight | 200 |
|---|---|---|---|

### JIM BURGETT
| 61 | Philips PB 1133 | Let's Investigate/The Living Dead | 40 |
|---|---|---|---|

### BURGUNDY BLOOD
| 13 | Chopped Herring CHBURG 001 | THE CORDIAL STANCE EP (black vinyl) | 15 |
|---|---|---|---|
| 13 | Chopped Herring CHBURG 001 | THE CORDIAL STANCE EP (burgundy vinyl) | 20 |
| 13 | Chopped Herring CHBURG 001 | THE CORDIAL STANCE EP (white vinyl) | 20 |
| 14 | Chopped Herring FHBURGLP01 | SUEDE COMET (LP) | 18 |
| 14 | Chopped Herring FHBURGLP01 | SUEDE COMET (LP, burgundy vinyl) | 25 |
| 14 | Chopped Herring FHBURGLP01 | SUEDE COMET (LP, clear vinyl) | 30 |
| 14 | Chopped Herring FHBURGLP01 | SUEDE COMET (LP, Instrumental version) | 20 |

### ELPEDO BURKE
| 75 | Black Wax WAX 3 | Madgie/MIGHTY CLOUD: Madgie Dub | 15 |
|---|---|---|---|

### KEVIN BURKE
| 78 | Rockburgh ROC 105 | IF THE CAP FITS (LP) | 15 |
|---|---|---|---|

### SOLOMON BURKE
| 61 | London HLK 9454 | Just Out Of Reach/Be Bop Grandma | 40 |
|---|---|---|---|
| 62 | London HLK 9512 | Cry To Me/I Almost Lost My Mind | 50 |
| 62 | London HLK 9560 | Down In The Valley/I'm Hanging Up My Heart For You | 20 |
| 63 | London HLK 9715 | If You Need Me/You Can Make It If You Try | 20 |
| 63 | London HLK 9763 | Can't Nobody Love You/Stupidity | 40 |
| 64 | London HLK 9849 | He'll Have To Go/Rockin' Soul | 20 |
| 64 | London HLK 9887 | Goodbye Baby (Baby Goodbye)/Someone To Love Me | 20 |
| 64 | Atlantic AT 4004 | Everybody Needs Somebody To Love/Looking For My Baby | 30 |
| 64 | Atlantic AT 4014 | The Price/More Rockin' Soul | 15 |
| 65 | Atlantic AT 4022 | Got To Get You Off My Mind/Peepin' | 20 |
| 65 | Atlantic AT 4030 | Maggie's Farm/Tonight's The Night | 20 |
| 65 | Atlantic AT 4044 | Someone Is Watching/Dance, Dance, Dance | 18 |
| 65 | Atlantic AT 4061 | Only Love (Can Save Me Now)/Little Girl That Loves Me | 22 |
| 66 | Atlantic AT 4073 | Baby Come On Home/No, No, No, I Can't Stop Lovin' You Now | 18 |
| 66 | Atlantic 584 005 | I Feel A Sin Comin' On/Mountain Of Pride | 10 |
| 66 | Atlantic 584 026 | Keep Lookin'/Suddenly | 10 |
| 67 | Atlantic 584 100 | Keep A Light In The Window Till I Come Home/Time Is A Thief | 10 |
| 67 | Atlantic 584 122 | Take Me (Just As I Am)/I Stayed Away Too Long | 10 |
| 68 | Atlantic 584 191 | I Wish I Knew (How It Would Feel To Be Free)/It's Just A Matter Of Time | 10 |
| 68 | Atlantic 584 204 | Save It/Meet Me In Church | 10 |
| 68 | Bell BLL 1047 | Uptight Good Woman/I Can't Stop (No No No) | 10 |
| 69 | Bell BLL 1062 | Proud Mary/What Am I Living For | 10 |
| 74 | Anchor ABC 4002 | Midnight And You/I Have A Dream | 5 |
| 63 | London REK 1379 | TONIGHT MY HEART SHE IS CRYING (EP) | 70 |
| 65 | Atlantic AET 6008 | ROCK'N'SOUL (EP) | 60 |
| 63 | London HA-K 8018 | SOLOMON BURKE'S GREATEST (LP) | 70 |
| 64 | Atlantic ATL 5009 | ROCK'N'SOUL (LP) | 50 |
| 66 | Atlantic 587/588 016 | THE BEST OF SOLOMON BURKE (LP) | 30 |
| 68 | Atlantic 587 105 | KING SOLOMON (LP) | 35 |
| 68 | Atlantic 587/588 117 | I WISH I KNEW (LP) | 30 |
| 69 | Bell MBLL/SBLL 118 | PROUD MARY (LP) | 20 |
| 72 | MGM 2315 048 | THE ELECTRONIC MAGNETISM (LP) | 15 |

*(see also Soul Clan)*

### SONNY BURKE (U.K.)
| 62 | Island WI 155 | Let And Let Live/Our Love Is True | 25 |
|---|---|---|---|
| 64 | Black Swan WI 457 | I Love You Still/It's Always A Pleasure | 15 |
| 64 | Black Swan WI 458 | City In The Sky/Everyday I Love You More | 15 |
| 65 | Black Swan WI 469 | Glad/Jeanie | 15 |
| 65 | Black Swan WI 470 | Dance With Me/My Girl Can't Cook | 15 |
| 65 | Black Swan WI 471 | Wicked People/Good Heaven Knows | 15 |
| 66 | Blue Beat BB 363 | Blue Island/You Came And Left | 40 |
| 67 | Blue Beat BB 371 | Look In Her Eyes/LLOYD CLARKE: Love Is Strange | 40 |
| 67 | Ska Beat JB272 | Have Faith/Guinea Pig | 40 |
| 68 | Island ILP 972 | THE SOUNDS OF SONNY BURKE (LP, mono only) | 125 |

*(see also Bob Andy, Gaylads, Ken Parker, Eddie Thornton Outfit, Glen Adams, Stranger Cole, Gaylads, Sonny & Yvonne)*

### SONNY BURKE OUTFIT
| 68 | Instant IN 003 | Baby Be My Girl/All You | 120 |
|---|---|---|---|

*(see also Sonny Burke)*

### DAVE BURLAND
| 71 | Trailer LER 2029 | A DALESMAN'S LITANY (LP, red label) | 25 |
|---|---|---|---|
| 72 | Trailer LER 2082 | DAVE BURLAND (LP) | 20 |
| 75 | Rubber RUB 012 | SONGS AND BUTTERED HAYCOCKS (LP) | 18 |
| 79 | Rubber RUB 036 | YOU CAN'T FOOL THE FAT MAN (LP) | 15 |
| 80 | Rubber RUB 012/036 | DOUBLE TAKE (2-LP, reissue) | 18 |

### BURLITZ
| 84 | Spartan SP 13 | Sleep Softly Mary/In The Dead Of The Night (p/s) | 8 |
|---|---|---|---|

### PETER BURMAN
| | | | |
|---|---|---|---|
| 62 | Columbia 33SX 1452 | JAZZ TETE A TETE (LP) | 200 |

### BURMOE BROTHERS
| | | | |
|---|---|---|---|
| 85 | Wild Blue Yonder WBY 121 | Skin/Leber Oder Lippenstift/Under The Blanket Of Love (12", p/s) | 15 |

*(see also Marc Almond, Nick Cave)*

### BURN
| | | | |
|---|---|---|---|
| 00s | Virgin HUTCDP 146 | Facing The Music (1-sided, numbered gold-embossed p/s, 1000 only) | 20 |

### CHRIS BURN & JOHN BUTCHER
| | | | |
|---|---|---|---|
| 85 | Bead Records BEAD 24 | FONETIKS (LP) | 20 |

### JEAN-JACQUES BURNEL
| | | | |
|---|---|---|---|
| 79 | United Artists UP 36500 | Freddie Laker (Concorde And Eurobus)/Ozymandias (p/s) | 5 |
| 80 | United Artists BP 361 | Girl From The Snow Country/Ode To Joy (live)/Do The European (live) (p/s, unissued) | 350 |

### JEAN-JACQUES BURNEL & DAVE GREENFIELD
| | | | |
|---|---|---|---|
| 84 | Epic EPCA 4076 | Rain And Dole And Tea/Consequences (p/s) | 5 |

*(see also, Blue Maxi, Stranglers)*

### BURNER
| | | | |
|---|---|---|---|
| 84 | High Roller 7HRR0132007 | Hammer Of The Gods/Time Is On My Side/Old Enough To Know Better (EP, p/s) | 10 |

### JOHN BURNESS
| | | | |
|---|---|---|---|
| 69 | Columbia DB8536 | Theresa/I Don't Want You Anymore | 10 |

### CHARMAINE BURNETT
| | | | |
|---|---|---|---|
| 81 | Pro PROD 001 | (Am I The) Same Girl/Direct Response (12") | 25 |

### FRANCES BURNETT
| | | | |
|---|---|---|---|
| 59 | Coral Q 72374 | Please Remember Me/How I Miss You So (triangular centre) | 60 |
| 59 | Coral Q 72374 | Please Remember Me/How I Miss You So (round centre) | 30 |

### KING BURNETT
| | | | |
|---|---|---|---|
| 75 | Dip DL 5056 | I Man Free/UPSETTERS: Version | 20 |
| 75 | Dip DL 5073 | Key Card/UPSETTERS: Domino Game | 20 |

### WATTY BURNETT
| | | | |
|---|---|---|---|
| 82 | Dread At The Controls DATC 007 | Dancing Shoes/Congo Dubba (12") | 30 |

### DORSEY BURNETTE
| | | | |
|---|---|---|---|
| 60 | London HLN 9047 | Juarez Town/(There Was A) Tall Oak Tree | 5 |
| 60 | London HLN 9160 | Hey Little One/Big Rock Candy Mountain | 10 |
| 61 | London HLN 9365 | (It's No) Sin/Hard Rock Mine | 10 |
| 65 | Tamla Motown TMG 534 | Jimmy Brown/Everybody's Angel | 225 |
| 65 | Tamla Motown TMG 534 | Jimmy Brown/Everybody's Angel ( DJ copy) | 250 |
| 63 | London RE-D 1402 | DORSEY BURNETTE SINGS (EP) | 20 |
| 63 | London HA-D 8050 | DORSEY BURNETTE (LP) | 30 |

*(see also Johnny & Dorsey Burnette)*

## JOHNNY BURNETTE (TRIO)
### SINGLES
| | | | |
|---|---|---|---|
| 56 | Vogue Coral Q 72177 | Tear It Up/You're Undecided (as Johnny Burnette & Rock'N'Roll Trio) | 500 |
| 56 | Vogue Coral Q 72177 | Tear It Up/You're Undecided (as Johnny Burnette & Rock'N'Roll Trio) (78) | 60 |
| 57 | Vogue Coral Q 72227 | Honey Hush/Lonesome Train (as Johnny Burnette Trio) | 500 |
| 57 | Vogue Coral Q 72227 | Honey Hush/Lonesome Train (as Johnny Burnette Trio) (78) | 70 |
| 57 | Vogue Coral Q 72283 | Touch Me/Eager Beaver Baby (as Johnny Burnette Trio) | 200 |
| 57 | Vogue Coral Q 72283 | Touch Me/Eager Beaver Baby (as Johnny Burnette Trio) (78) | 60 |
| 60 | London HLG 9172 | Dreamin'/Cincinnati Fireball | 10 |
| 60 | London HLG 9172 | Dreamin'/Cincinnati Fireball (78) | 250 |
| 60 | London HLG 9254 | You're Sixteen/I Beg Your Pardon | 5 |
| 61 | London HLG 9315 | Little Boy Sad/Pledge Of Love | 5 |
| 61 | London HLG 9388 | Girls/I've Got A Lot Of Things To Do | 5 |
| 61 | London HLG 9453 | God Country And My Baby/Honestly I Do (withdrawn) | 50 |
| 61 | London HLG 9458 | Settin' The Woods On Fire/I'm Still Dreaming | 5 |
| 61 | London HLG 9473 | Big Big World/The Fool | 5 |
| 62 | Liberty LIB 55416 | Clown Shoes/The Way I Am | 5 |
| 62 | Liberty LIB 55489 | Damn The Defiant/Lonesome Waters | 5 |
| 66 | Liberty LIB 10235 | Dreamin'/Little Boy Sad | 5 |
| 62 | Pye International 7N 25158 | I Wanna Thank Your Folks/The Giant | 10 |
| 63 | Pye International 7N 25187 | Remember Me/Time Is Not Enough | 10 |
| 63 | Capitol CL 15322 | All Week Long/It Isn't There | 20 |
| 64 | Capitol CL 15347 | Sweet Suzie/Walking Talking Doll | 35 |

### EPs
| | | | |
|---|---|---|---|
| 60 | London RE-G 1263 | DREAMING | 15 |
| 61 | London RE-G 1291 | LITTLE BOY SAD | 15 |
| 61 | London RE-G 1309 | BIG BIG WORLD | 15 |
| 61 | London RE-G 1327 | GIRLS | 15 |
| 63 | Liberty LEP 2091 | HIT AFTER HIT | 15 |
| 64 | Capitol EAP 20645 | FOUR BY BURNETTE | 60 |

### ALBUMS
| | | | |
|---|---|---|---|
| 56 | Coral LVC 10041 | ROCK AND ROLL TRIO (10", as Johnny Burnette Trio) | 500 |
| 61 | London HA-G 2306 | DREAMIN' | 20 |
| 61 | London HA-G 2349 | YOU'RE SIXTEEN | 20 |
| 61 | London HA-G 2375 | JOHNNY BURNETTE SINGS (mono) | 20 |
| 61 | London SAH-G 6175 | JOHNNY BURNETTE SINGS (stereo) | 20 |
| 62 | Liberty LBY 1006 | BURNETTE'S HITS AND OTHER FAVOURITES | 20 |

| | | |
|---|---|---|
| 64 | Liberty LBY 1231 | THE JOHNNY BURNETTE STORY .................................................................. 20 |
| 66 | Ace Of Hearts AH 120 | ROCK AND ROLL TRIO (reissue, as Johnny Burnette Trio) ................................ 20 |
| 68 | Coral CP 10 | TEAR IT UP (as Johnny Burnette Trio)........................................................ 20 |

*(see also Johnny & Dorsey Burnette)*

## JOHNNY & DORSEY BURNETTE
| | | |
|---|---|---|
| 63 | Reprise R 20153 | Hey Sue/It Don't Matter Much ................................................................ 70 |

*(see also Johnny Burnette, Dorsey Burnette)*

## SMILEY BURNETTE
| | | |
|---|---|---|
| 54 | London HL 8071 | Lazy Locomotive/That Long White Line ...................................................... 25 |
| 54 | London HL 8085 | Chuggin' On Down "66"/Mucho Gusto ........................................................ 25 |

## ALAN BURNHAM
| | | |
|---|---|---|
| 80 | Cherry Red CHERRY 15 | Music To Save The World/Science Fiction (p/s)............................................. 12 |

## BURNIN' RED IVANHOE
| | | |
|---|---|---|
| 70 | Warner Bros WS 3013 | BURNIN' RED IVANHOE (LP, green label) ...................................................... 70 |
| 72 | Dandelion 2310 145 | W.W.W. (LP, gatefold sleeve) ................................................................ 70 |

## BURNING SAVIORS
| | | |
|---|---|---|
| 06 | Rise Above RISE 7/084 | The Giant/The Clown .......................................................................... 10 |

## BURNING SKIES OF ELYSIUM
| | | |
|---|---|---|
| 87 | Crisis EL 3 | THE LAST REVOLVING DOOR (LP)................................................................ 25 |

## BURNING SOUND
| | | |
|---|---|---|
| 82 | Right Track BURN 001 | Shining Through/Fit To Burn .................................................................. 6 |

## BURNING SPEAR
| | | |
|---|---|---|
| 70 | Bamboo 50 | SOUND DIMENTION : Soul Food/BURNING SPEAR : Door Peeper ...................... 60 |
| 75 | Fab FAB 240 | Foggy Road/Version ............................................................................ 20 |
| 76 | Island WIP 6346 | Lion/Door Peep ................................................................................ 10 |
| 78 | Island Pre IPR 2027 | Civilised Reggae/Social Living (12") .......................................................... 20 |
| 79 | Burning Spear BS 001 | Free The Whole Wide World/Jah Jah No Dead (12") ...................................... 30 |
| 79 | Tribesman TM 20 | Free The Whole Wide World/Jah Jah No Dead (12") ...................................... 30 |
| 82 | Radic 12RIC114 | Jah Is My Driver/Driver Dub/Distance/Forever .......................................... 15 |
| 75 | Island ILPS 9377 | MARCUS GARVEY (LP, 1st pressing has stickered sleeve)................................ 25 |
| 76 | Island ILPS 9377 | GARVEY'S GHOST (LP) .......................................................................... 35 |
| 76 | Island ILPS 9412 | MAN IN THE HILLS (LP, gatefold) ............................................................ 15 |
| 77 | Island MPLS 9431 | DRY AND HEAVY (LP) .......................................................................... 15 |
| 77 | Island ILPS 9513 | LIVE (LP)........................................................................................ 15 |
| 78 | 1 Stop STOP 1001 | SOCIAL LIVING (LP) ............................................................................ 15 |
| 79 | Island PRELP 3 | LIVING DUB VOL 1 (LP) ........................................................................ 25 |
| 80 | EMI RDC 2003 | HAIL H.I.M (LP) ................................................................................ 15 |
| 82 | Island SVLP 191 | MARCUS GARVEY/GARVEY'S GHOST (2-LP, reissue) ...................................... 20 |
| 04 | Soul Jazz SJRLP 101 | SOUNDS FROM BURNING SPEAR (2-LP) .................................................... 20 |

*(see also Irving Brown, King Cry Cry)*

## JAN BURNNETTE
| | | |
|---|---|---|
| 62 | Oriole CB 1716 | I Could Have Loved You So Well/The Miracle Of Life ...................................... 5 |

## EDDIE 'GUITAR' BURNS
| | | |
|---|---|---|
| 72 | Action ACMP 100 | BOTTLE UP AND GO (LP) ...................................................................... 30 |
| 75 | Big Bear BEAR 7 | DETROIT BLACKBOTTOM (LP) ................................................................ 20 |

## GILLIAN BURNS
| | | |
|---|---|---|
| 69 | Fontana TF 1044 | Hop Skip And Jump/Merry Go Round ........................................................ 10 |

## JACKIE BURNS & BELLES
| | | |
|---|---|---|
| 63 | MGM MGM 1226 | He's My Guy/I Do The Best I Can .............................................................. 100 |

## JIMMY BURNS
| | | |
|---|---|---|
| 79 | Grapevine GRP 118 | I Really Love You/I Love You Girl .............................................................. 25 |
| 79 | Grapevine GRP 118 | I Really Love You/I Love You Girl (DJ Copy) ................................................ 30 |

## LISA BURNS
| | | |
|---|---|---|
| 78 | MCA MCF 2849 | LISA BURNS (LP) ................................................................................ 15 |

## RANDY BURNS
| | | |
|---|---|---|
| 68 | Fontana STL 5520 | EVENING OF THE MAGICIAN (LP) ............................................................ 50 |

*(see also Blue Cheer)*

## RAY BURNS
| | | |
|---|---|---|
| 53 | Columbia SCM 5077 | Rags To Riches/Begorrah ...................................................................... 5 |
| 54 | Columbia SCM 5153 | I Can't Tell A Waltz From A Tango/Lonely Nightingale .................................. 5 |
| 56 | Columbia DB 3811 | Condemned For Life (With A Rock And Roll Wife)/The Mare Piccola.................. 35 |
| 57 | Columbia DB 3966 | Wonderful! Wonderful!/Bernadine .......................................................... 5 |
| 57 | Columbia DB 3998 | Dapper Dan/The Little Hut .................................................................... 5 |
| 58 | Columbia DB 4107 | Are You Sincere/The Best Dream Of All ..................................................... 5 |
| 55 | Columbia SEG 7594 | RAY BURNS (EP) ................................................................................ 20 |

*(see also Ruby Murray, Ronnie Harris, Diana Decker, Ray Martin)*

## HAROLD BURRAGE
| | | |
|---|---|---|
| 65 | Sue WI 353 | I'll Take One/A Long Ways Together .......................................................... 50 |
| 68 | President PT 130 | You Made Me So Happy/Take Me Now ...................................................... 10 |
| 81 | Flywright FLY 579 | SHE KNOCKS ME OUT - ORIGINAL COBRA BLUES (LP)................................... 15 |

## KENNY BURRELL
| | | |
|---|---|---|
| 61 | Esquire 32-140 | ALL NIGHT LONG (LP, as Kenny Burrell All Stars) ........................................ 40 |
| 64 | Verve VLP 9058 | BLUE BLASH (LP, with Jimmy Smith)........................................................ 25 |
| 65 | Verve VLP 9099 | GUITAR FORMS (LP) ............................................................................ 20 |
| 67 | Transatlantic PR 7315 | SOUL CALL (LP) ................................................................................ 15 |
| 66 | Stateside SL 10163 | CRASH! (LP, with Brother Jack McDuff) .................................................... 30 |
| 68 | Verve (S)VLP 9217 | BLUES, THE COMMON GROUND (LP) ...................................................... 20 |

MINT VALUE £

| | | | |
|---|---|---|---|
| 69 | Verve SVLP 9246 | NIGHT SONG (LP) | 15 |

*(see also Brother Jack McDuff, Jimmy Smith)*

## ROLAND BURRELL
| | | | |
|---|---|---|---|
| 84 | C&E CEDI 105 | Rip Off/Version (12") | 80 |

## WILLIAM S. BURROUGHS
| | | | |
|---|---|---|---|
| 80 | Industrial IR 0016 | NOTHING HERE NOW BUT THE RECORDINGS (LP) | 80 |

## TONY BURROWS
| | | | |
|---|---|---|---|
| 70 | Bell BLL 1103 | Melanie Makes Me Smile/I'll Get Along Somehow Girl | 5 |
| 70 | Bell BLL 1124 | Every Little Move She Makes/I've Still Got My Heart, Joe | 8 |

## CHINA BURTON
| | | | |
|---|---|---|---|
| 79 | Logo GO 354 | You Don't Care (About Our Love)/(Instrumental Version) | 30 |
| 79 | Logo GO 354 | You Don't Care (About Our Love)/(Instrumental Version) (DJ Copy) | 50 |
| 79 | Logo GO(T) 354 | You Don't Care (About Our Love) (Long Version)/(Short Version)/(Instrumental Version) (12") | 80 |

## GARY BURTON (QUARTET)
| | | | |
|---|---|---|---|
| 68 | RCA Victor SF 7923 | LOFTY FAKE ANAGRAM (LP) | 20 |
| 69 | RCA SF 7980 | IN CONCERT (LP) | 15 |
| 69 | RCA Victor SF 8015 | GENUINE TONGUE FUNERAL (LP) | 18 |
| 71 | Atlantic 2400 107 | GOOD VIBES (LP) | 18 |

*(see also Michael Gibbs)*

## HAL BURTON
| | | | |
|---|---|---|---|
| 58 | Embassy WB 308 | Move It/Susie Darling | 8 |

## JAMES BURTON
| | | | |
|---|---|---|---|
| 71 | A&M AMLS 64293 | THE GUITAR SOUNDS OF JAMES BURTON (LP) | 50 |

*(See also Jim & Joe, Shindogs)*

## JOHNNY BURTON
| | | | |
|---|---|---|---|
| 72 | Philips 60006 238 | Polevault Man/The Polythene Doll | 25 |

## TOMMY BURTON COMBO
| | | | |
|---|---|---|---|
| 64 | Blue Beat BB 237 | Lavender Blue/I'm Walking | 25 |

## TREVOR BURTON
| | | | |
|---|---|---|---|
| 71 | Wizard WIZ 103 | Fight For My Country/Janie Slow Down | 30 |

*(see also B,L&G; Uglys, Move, Balls, Denny Laine, Danny King's Mayfair Set, Magic Christians, Idle Race)*

## BURU
| | | | |
|---|---|---|---|
| 83 | CSA CSALP 04 | BURO (LP) | 30 |

## BURZUM
| | | | |
|---|---|---|---|
| 93 | Misanthropy Amazon 001 | HVIS LYSET TAR OSS (LP, marbled vinyl) | 200 |
| 94 | Misanthropy Amazon 002 | DET SOM ENGANG VAR (LP, with stickered sleeve, inner sleeve and poster) | 200 |
| 95 | Misanthropy Amazon 003 | BURZUM/ASKE (2-LP, gatefold sleeve) | 100 |
| 96 | Misanthropy Amazon 009 | FILOSOFEM (2-LP, 1 side etched, stickered gatefold sleeve) | 100 |
| 97 | Misanthropy Amazon 013 | DAUOI BALDRS (LP, with postcards and booklet, 1,000 only) | 25 |
| 99 | Misanthropy Amazon 021 | HILOSKJALF (LP, booket and insert, 1,000 only) | 50 |
| 08 | Back On Black BOBV 089LP | FILOSOFEM (LP, reissue, gatefold) | 18 |
| 10 | Back On Black BOBV 215LP | BELUS (LP, white vinyl) | 50 |
| 10 | Back On Black BOBV 215LP | BELUS (LP, black vinyl) | 20 |
| 11 | Back On Black BOBV 293LP | FALLEN (LP, clear vinyl) | 20 |

## LOU BUSCH & HIS ORCHESTRA
| | | | |
|---|---|---|---|
| 56 | Capitol CL 14504 | Zambesi/Rainbow's End | 5 |

*(see also Joe 'Fingers' Carr, Four Preps)*

## KATE BUSH
| | | | |
|---|---|---|---|
| 78 | EMI EMI 2719 | Wuthering Heights/Kite (p/s) | 30 |
| 78 | EMI EMI 2806 | The Man With The Child In His Eyes/Moving (p/s) | 15 |
| 79 | EMI PSR 442/3 | KATE BUSH ON STAGE (EP, double pack, gatefold sleeve, promo only) | 60 |
| 81 | EMI EMI 5201 | Sat In Your Lap/Lord Of The Reedy River (p/s) | 5 |
| 82 | EMI EMI 5350 | There Goes A Tenner/Ne T'Enfuis Pas (thick card, p/s) | 5 |
| 82 | EMI IEMI 9001 | Night Of The Swallow/Houdini (pressed in England for export to Ireland, p/s) | 100 |
| 84 | EMI KBS 1 | THE SINGLE FILE (13 x 7" box set with lyric booklet) | 70 |
| 85 | EMI KB 1 | Running Up That Hill/Under The Ivy (gatefold p/s) | 10 |
| 90 | EMI TRIB02 | Rocket Man/Candle In The Wind (poster p/s) | 8 |
| 93 | EMI EM 280 | Eat The Music/Big Stripey Lie (p/s, picture labels, release cancelled, 17 copies only) | 1600 |
| 93 | EMI 12EMPD 280 | Eat The Music/Eat The Music (Madagascan Remix)/Big Stripey Lie (12", picture disc, unissued) | 0 |
| 93 | EMI CDEM 280 | Eat The Music/(Madagascan Remix)/Big Stripey Lie (CD, unissued) | 0 |
| 93 | EMI MUSIC 1 | Eat The Music (CD, 1-track promo for unissued single, no inlay, withdrawn) | 150 |
| 94 | EMI EMPD 355 | And So Is Love/Rubberband Girl (USA Mix) (picture disc, PVC sleeve, with 60" x 40" poster, unnumbered or 5,000 numbered) | 10 |
| 78 | EMI EMA 787 | LIONHEART (LP, gatefold with gold embossed titles, inner) | 15 |
| 78 | EMI EMC 3223 | THE KICK INSIDE (LP, laminated sleeve) | 20 |
| 79 | EMI EM CP 3223 | THE KICK INSIDE (LP, picture disc, stickered sleeve) | 50 |
| 79 | EMI EM CP 3223 | THE KICK INSIDE (LP, picture disc, stickered sleeve, second pressing with "manufactured in the U.K. by EMI Records Ltd" wording) | 20 |
| 79 | EMI EM CP 3223 | THE KICK INSIDE (LP, picture disc, mispress with same picture both sides) | 150 |
| 80 | EMI EMA 794 | NEVER FOR EVER (LP, gatefold) | 15 |
| 82 | EMI EMC 3419 | THE DREAMING (LP, inner) | 15 |
| 85 | EMI KAB 1 | THE HOUNDS OF LOVE (LP, with inner and insert) | 20 |
| 86 | EMI KBTV1 | THE WHOLE STORY (LP, gatefold) | 15 |
| 89 | EMI EMD 1010 | THE SENSUAL WORLD (LP) | 15 |
| 90 | EMI KBBX 1 | THIS WOMAN'S WORK (9-LP, box set) | 120 |
| 90 | EMI CDKBBX 1 | THIS WOMAN'S WORK (CD, box set) | 80 |

| 93 | EMD 1047 | THE RED SHOES (LP, lyric inner) | 75 |
| 93 | EMI (No Cat. No) | THE RED SHOES (CD, video, slide transparency, fountain pen, parchment discography & red ribbon box set, promo) | 200 |
| 97 | EMI LPCENT5 | THE KICK INSIDE (LP, reissue, EMI Centenary, stickered sleeve) | 30 |
| 97 | EMI CENT 34 | THE HOUNDS OF LOVE (LP, reissue, EMI 100 Centenary, stickered sleeve) | 30 |
| 05 | EMI 343960-1 | AERIAL (2-LP, gatefold, booklet, stickered sleeve) | 125 |
| 11 | Fish People FPLP 001 | DIRECTOR'S CUT (2-LP, booklet) | 18 |
| 11 | Fish People FPLP 007 | 50 WORDS FOR SNOW (2-LP, booklet, CD) | 20 |

*(see also Peter Gabriel & Kate Bush, Lesley Duncan)*

## RAY BUSH & AVON CITIES' SKIFFLE

| 56 | Tempo A 146 | Hey Hey Daddy Blues/Green Corn | 25 |
| 56 | Tempo A 149 | Fisherman's Blues/This Little Light Of Mine | 25 |
| 57 | Tempo A 156 | How Long, How Long, Blues/Julian Johnson | 25 |
| 57 | Tempo A 157 | Lonesome Day Blues/I Don't Know | 25 |
| 57 | Tempo EXA 40 | RAY BUSH & AVON CITIES' SKIFFLE (EP) | 25 |
| 57 | Tempo EXA 50 | RAY BUSH & AVON CITIES' SKIFFLE NO. 2 (EP) | 25 |

*(see also Avon Cities Jazz Band)*

## BUSH CHEMISTS

| 98 | Conscious Sounds DNC 1203 | Collie Weed/Collie Dub/Earth Rocker/Rocker Dub (12") | 30 |
| 06 | Jah Tubbys JT10025 | Star Dub/Waters Edge (10") | 18 |

*(see also King General, King General & Bush Chemists)*

## BUSHKILLER

| 92 | Danger 001 | 92 Salute/Bushkiller Draw (12") | 12 |
| 94 | Danger 002 | TROUBLEMAKERS (EP) | 30 |

## BUSH TETRAS

| 81 | Fetish FET 007 | Things That Go Boom In The Night/Das Ah Riot (p/s) | 10 |
| 82 | Fetish FE 15 | Can't Be Funky (unissued, stamped white label only, custom plain sleeve) | 10 |
| 82 | Fetish FET 16EP | RITUALS (12" EP) | 15 |

## BUSINESS

| 81 | Secret SHH 123 | Harry May/National Insurance Blacklist (p/s) | 12 |
| 82 | Secret SHH 132 | SMASH THE DISCOS EP: Day-O (The Banana Boat Song)/Disco Girls/ Smash The Disco (p/s) | 10 |
| 83 | Secret SHH 150 | OUT OF BUSINESS (12" EP, unissued, white label promo, 10 copies only) | 100 |
| 85 | Wonderful World Of... 121 | Get Out Of My House/All Out Tonight/Foreign Girl/Outlaw (12", p/s) | 25 |
| 85 | Diamond DIA 001 | Drinking N Driving/H-Bomb (live) (p/s) | 15 |
| 85 | Diamond DIA 001T | Drinking N Driving/H-Bomb (live)/Hurry Up Harry/Drinking 'N' Driving (original version) (12", p/s) | 25 |
| 80s | Link LINK 1201 | DO A RUNNER (12" EP) | 12 |
| 83 | Secret SEC 11 | SUBURBAN REBELS (LP) | 15 |
| 83 | Syndicate SYNLP 2 | 1980-81 OFFICIAL BOOTLEGS (LP) | 15 |
| 84 | Syndicate SYNLP 6 | LOUD, PROUD 'N' PUNK, LIVE (LP) | 20 |
| 85 | Harry May SE 13 | SATURDAY HEROES (LP) | 15 |
| 86 | Dojo DOJO LP 35 | SINGALONGABUSINESS (LP) | 15 |
| 80s | Wonderful World WOWDLP 4 | OFFICIAL BUSINESS 1980-81 (LP) | 20 |
| 80s | Wonderful World WOWDLP 5 | SUBURBAN REBELS/SMASH THE DISCOS - BACK TO BACK VOL 2. (2xLP) | 25 |
| 90 | Link LRMO 1 | IN AND OUT OF BUSINESS (LP, mail-order, 550 only) | 20 |

## BUSKERS

| 70 | RCA 2023 | If I Rules The World/Joey Friendship | 5 |
| 73 | Rubber RUB 007 | LIFE OF A MAN (LP) | 18 |
| 75 | Hawk HALPX 142 | THE BUSKERS (LP) | 15 |

## GEORGE HENRY BUSSEY/JIM BUNKLEY

| 71 | Revival RVS 1003 | GEORGE HENRY BUSSEY/JIM BUNKLEY (LP) | 15 |

## BUSTER

| 71 | Parlophone R5881 | Pasadena/Priscilla | 8 |
| 73 | Bradleys BRAD 310 | Motor Machine/Ring Around | 25 |
| 74 | Bradleys BRAD 7401 | Superstar/Rainbows & Colours | 20 |

## BUSTERS

| 63 | Stateside SS 231 | Bust Out/Astronauts | 25 |

## BUSTER('S) ALLSTARS

| 64 | Blue Beat BB 244 | Prince Royal/COSMO: One God | 40 |
| 64 | Blue Beat BB 269 | The Tickler/COSMO: Rice And Badge | 40 |
| 65 | Blue Beat BB 294 | Eye For Eye/South Virginia | 35 |
| 65 | Blue Beat BB 322 | Happy Independence 65/STRANGER COLE: When The Party Is Over | 25 |
| 65 | Blue Beat BB 325 | Congo Revolution/Little Darlin' - No One | 150 |
| 65 | Blue Beat BB 333 | When The Party Is Over/Matilda (with Stranger Cole) | 30 |
| 66 | Blue Beat BB 342 | Cincinnatti Kid/Sammy Dead | 50 |
| 67 | Blue Beat BB 372 | Sounds And Pressure/My Darling (both actually by Hopeton Lewis) | 45 |
| 67 | Blue Beat BB 384 | Take It Easy/Why Must I Cry (both actually by Hopeton Lewis) | 25 |
| 69 | Fab FAB 101 | Pum Pum A Go Kill You/Oh Lady Oh | 15 |
| 70 | Fab FAB 124 | The Rebel/The Preacher | 15 |

*(see also Prince Buster, Teddy King, Little Darling, Khandars, Higgs & Wilson, Owen Gray, Charmers, Fitzroy D Long, Maytals, Derrick Morgan, Eric Morris, Personalities, Roy & Millie, Zoot Simms, Spanish Boys, Spanish Town Skabeats)*

## BUSTER'S GROUP

| 61 | Starlite ST45 052 | Buster's Shack/ERIC MORRIS: Search The World | 40 |
| 65 | Blue Beat BB 395 | This Gun For Hire/Yes Daddy | 60 |

*(see also Prince Buster, Rico, Owen Gray)*

## BUSTY & COOL
| | | | |
|---|---|---|---|
| 62 | Blue Beat BB 144 | Mr Policeman/What A World | 20 |

## TONY BUTALA
| | | | |
|---|---|---|---|
| 62 | Salvo SLO 1801 | Long Black Stockings/Rumors (99 copies only) | 40 |

## BUTCHER
| | | | |
|---|---|---|---|
| 82 | Inept INEPT 002 | On The Ground/Grow Up Don't Blow Up (p/s) | 5 |
| 83 | Inept INEPT 003 | Stand And Fight (p/s, red vinyl) | 5 |

*(see also Intestines)*

## STAN BUTCHER
| | | | |
|---|---|---|---|
| 67 | CBS 3007 | Fortuosity/Birds Meet Brass | 5 |
| 66 | CBS SS62838 | HIS BIRDS AND BRASS (LP) | 20 |
| 67 | CBS 63072 | SWING LIKE A BASTARD (LP) | 35 |

## SAM BUTERA (& WITNESSES)
| | | | |
|---|---|---|---|
| 58 | HMV POP 476 | Good Gracious Baby/It's Better Than Nothing At All | 70 |
| 58 | Capitol CL 14913 | Bim Bam/Twinkle In Your Eye (as Sam Butera & Witnesses) | 250 |
| 59 | Capitol CL 14988 | Handle With Care/French Poodle | 20 |
| 64 | Prima PR 1003 | Skinnie Minnie/Little Liza Jane | 18 |
| 81 | Capitol CL 16179 | Bim Bam/Twinkie In Your Eyes (reissue) | 10 |
| 56 | HMV 7EG 8087 | SAX SERENADE (EP) | 20 |
| 60 | London HA-D 2288 | THE RAT RACE (LP, as Sam Butera & Witnesses) | 20 |

*(see also Louis Prima)*

## BILLY BUTLER (& ENCHANTERS)
| | | | |
|---|---|---|---|
| 69 | Soul City SC 113 | The Right Track/Boston Monkey | 15 |
| 74 | Epic S EPC 2508 | The Right Track/Can't Live Without Her (Yellow label) | 10 |
| 78 | Epic S EPC 2508 | The Right Track/Can't Live Without Her (Orange label) | 8 |

## CHAMP BUTLER
| | | | |
|---|---|---|---|
| 56 | Vogue Coral Q 72163 | The Joshua Tree/Down In Mexico | 5 |

## HAROLD BUTLER
| | | | |
|---|---|---|---|
| 77 | Charmers 3 | GOLD CONNECTION (LP) | 50 |

## JERRY BUTLER
| | | | |
|---|---|---|---|
| 58 | London HL 8697 | For Your Precious Love/Sweet Was The Wine (as Jerry Butler & the Impressions) | 200 |
| 58 | London HL 8697 | For Your Precious Love/Sweet Was The Wine (as Jerry Butler & the Impressions) (78 rpm) | 100 |
| 60 | Top Rank JAR 389 | I Found A Love/A Lonely Soldier | 45 |
| 60 | Top Rank JAR 531 | He Will Break Your Heart/Thanks To You | 55 |
| 61 | Top Rank JAR 562 | Find Another Girl/When Trouble Calls | 40 |
| 61 | Columbia DB 4743 | Moon River/Aware Of Love | 25 |
| 62 | Stateside SS 121 | Make It Easy On Yourself/It's Too Late | 25 |
| 63 | Stateside SS 158 | You Can Run But You Can't Hide/I'm The One | 30 |
| 63 | Stateside SS 170 | You Go Right Through Me/The Wishing Star | 20 |
| 63 | Stateside SS 195 | Whatever You Want/You Won't Be Sorry | 20 |
| 64 | Stateside SS 252 | Need To Belong/Give Me Your Love | 25 |
| 64 | Stateside SS 300 | Giving Up On Love/I've Been Trying | 20 |
| 65 | Fontana TF 553 | Good Times/I've Grown Accustomed To Her Face | 20 |
| 65 | Fontana TF 588 | I Can't Stand To See You Cry/Nobody Needs Your Love | 15 |
| 65 | Mercury MF 932 | Love (Oh, How Sweet It Is)/Loneliness | 15 |
| 66 | Sue WI 4003 | I Stand Accused/I Don't Want To Hear Anymore | 50 |
| 66 | Sue WI 4009 | Just For You/Believe In Me | 50 |
| 67 | Mercury MF 964 | I Dig You Baby/Some Kinda Magic | 8 |
| 67 | Mercury MF 1005 | Mr. Dream Merchant/'Cause I Love You So | 8 |
| 68 | Mercury MF 1035 | Never Give You Up/Beside You | 10 |
| 68 | Mercury MF 1058 | Hey Mr Western Union Man (Send A Telegram)/Just Can't Forget About You | 10 |
| 69 | Mercury MF 1078 | Are You Happy/Strange I Still Love You | 8 |
| 69 | Mercury MF 1094 | Only The Strong Survive/Just Because I Really Love You | 10 |
| 69 | Mercury MF 1122 | Moody Woman/Go Away And Find Yourself | 20 |
| 69 | Mercury MF 1122 | Moody Woman/Go Away And Find Yourself (DJ copy) | 100 |
| 69 | Mercury MF 1132 | A Brand New Me/What's The Use Of Breaking Up | 10 |
| 70 | President PT 299 | Make It Easy On Yourself/Moon River | 8 |
| 72 | Mercury 6052 036 | One Night Affair/What's So Good About It (You're My Baby) | 8 |
| 72 | Mercury 6052 119 | Moody Woman/A Brand New Me | 15 |
| 72 | Mercury 6052 155 | I Only Have Eyes For You/Ain't Understanding Mellow | 5 |
| 72 | Mercury 6052 168 | One Night Affair/What's So Good About It (You're My Baby) (reissue) | 5 |
| 63 | Stateside SL 10032 | HE WILL BREAK YOUR HEART (LP) | 100 |
| 63 | Stateside SL 10050 | FOLK SONGS (LP) | 40 |
| 68 | Fontana (S)TL 5246 | LOVE ME (LP) | 45 |
| 68 | Mercury 20118 (S)MCL | MR. DREAM MERCHANT (LP) | 30 |
| 69 | Mercury 20144 (S)MCL | SOUL GOES ON (LP) | 35 |
| 69 | Mercury 20154 (S)MCL | THE ICE MAN COMETH (LP) | 35 |

*(see also Betty Everett & Jerry Butler, Impressions)*

## LESLIE BUTLER (& FUGITIVES)
| | | | |
|---|---|---|---|
| 67 | Island WI 3069 | Hornpipe Rock Steady/You Don't Have To Say You Love Me | 35 |
| 67 | Doctor Bird DB 1083 | Winchester Rocksteady (with Fugitives)/ASTON CAMPBELL & CONQUERORS : Ramona | 35 |
| 68 | High Note HS 008 | Top Cat/WEBBER SISTERS: Stars Above | 25 |
| 68 | High Note HS 009 | Revival/GAYLADS: Over The Rainbow's End | 12 |
| 75 | Trojan TRLS 112 | JA-GAN (LP) | 30 |

*(see also Ken Boothe, Fugitives, Gaylads)*

## BUTTERCUPS
| | | | |
|---|---|---|---|
| 68 | Pama PM 742 | If I Love You/Loving You | 15 |
| 69 | Pama PM 760 | Come Put My Life In Order/If I Love You | 15 |

## BILLY BUTTERFIELD & HIS ORCHESTRA
| | | | |
|---|---|---|---|
| 55 | London HLF 8181 | The Magnificent Matador/Sugar Blues Mambo | 35 |

## PAUL BUTTERFIELD BLUES BAND
| | | | |
|---|---|---|---|
| 66 | London HLZ 10100 | Come On In/I Got A Mind To Give Up Living | 35 |
| 67 | Elektra EKSN 45007 | All These Blues/Never Say No | 10 |
| 67 | Elektra EKSN 45020 | Run Out Of Time/One More Heartache | 20 |
| 68 | Elektra EKSN 45047 | Get Yourself Together/Mine To Love | 12 |
| 69 | Elektra EKSN 45069 | Where Did My Baby Go/In My Own Dream | 10 |
| 70 | Elektra 2101 012 | Love March/Love Disease | 6 |
| 65 | Elektra EKL/EKS 294 | PAUL BUTTERFIELD BLUES BAND (LP, with rare gold 'guitar player' label) | 200 |
| 65 | Elektra EKL/EKS 294 | PAUL BUTTERFIELD BLUES BAND (LP, orange label) | 50 |
| 66 | Elektra EKL/EKS 315 | EAST - WEST (LP, orange label) | 50 |
| 67 | Elek. EKL 4015/EKS 74015 | THE RESURRECTION OF PIGBOY CRABSHAW (LP, orange label) | 35 |
| 68 | Elektra EKL 4025 | IN MY OWN DREAM (LP, orange label, also stereo EKS 74025) | 40 |
| 69 | Elektra EKS 74053 | KEEP ON MOVIN' (LP) | 20 |
| 71 | Elektra EKD 2001 | LIVE (2-LP) | 20 |
| 72 | Elektra K 62011 | GOLDEN BUTTER (LP, gatefold sleeve) | 18 |

*(see also John Mayall's Bluesbreakers, Mike Bloomfield)*

## BUTTERFLIES
| | | | |
|---|---|---|---|
| 68 | President PT 192 | Love Me Forever/He's Got Everything | 15 |

## BUTTERFLYS
| | | | |
|---|---|---|---|
| 64 | Red Bird RB 10009 | Goodnight Baby/The Swim | 22 |

## BUTTERSCOTCH
| | | | |
|---|---|---|---|
| 70 | RCA 1937 | Don't You Know (She Said Hello)/The Closer To You | 7 |
| 70 | RCA 1983 | Surprise, Surprise/In This World Of Loving You | 6 |
| 72 | Jam 15 | Can't You Hear A Song/All I Ever Wanna Do | 7 |
| 70 | RCA LSA 5000 | BUTTERSCOTCH (LP, with insert and music book) | 20 |

## BUTTERSCOTCH CABOOSE
| | | | |
|---|---|---|---|
| 68 | Bell BLL 1023 | Melinda/Let A Little Sunshine In | 8 |

## BUTTHOLE SURFERS
| | | | |
|---|---|---|---|
| 85 | Fundamental SAVE 5 | PSYCHIC...POWERLESS...ANOTHER MAN'S SAC (LP) | 15 |
| 91 | Rough Trade R 2081 2601 | PIOUGHD (LP, with bonus 12") | 15 |
| 93 | Capitol 0777 7 98798 1 6 | INDEPENDENT WORM SALOON (LP) | 25 |

## BUTTONDOWN BRASS
| | | | |
|---|---|---|---|
| 68 | Fontana TF 950 | March Of The Little Brown Jugs/Frere Jacques | 7 |
| 67 | Fontana LPS 16255 | HA HA HA (HEE-HEE-HEE) (LP) | 15 |
| 76 | DJM DJS 22046 | FUNK IN HELL (LP) | 40 |
| 76 | DJM DJSLM2023 | FIREDOG (LP) | 15 |
| 77 | DJM DJS 22076 | COPS N'ROBBERS (LP) | 15 |

## BUTTS BAND
| | | | |
|---|---|---|---|
| 75 | ABC ABC4050 | Get Up, Stand Up/Mike's Blues | 12 |

## SHEILA BUXTON
| | | | |
|---|---|---|---|
| 55 | Columbia SCM 5193 | Thank You For The Waltz/Just Between Friends | 7 |
| 57 | Columbia DB 3887 | Perfect Love/I Love You Baby (My Baby Loves Me) | 7 |
| 57 | Columbia DB 4051 | The In-Between Age/Charm | 6 |
| 59 | Top Rank JAR 144 | The Valley Of Love/The Wonder Of You | 6 |
| 59 | Top Rank JAR 240 | All I Do Is Dream Of You/Shakedown | 5 |
| 60 | Top Rank JAR 356 | Sixteen Reasons/Goodnight, God I Love You | 10 |

*(see also Craig Douglas)*

## BUY OFF THE BAR
| | | | |
|---|---|---|---|
| 88 | Bi-Joopiter BIJOOP 023 | PARBOILED (LP, screen printed sleeve with insert) | 20 |

## BUZZ & BUCKY
| | | | |
|---|---|---|---|
| 65 | Stateside SS 428 | Tiger A Go Go/Bay City | 50 |

*(see also Ronny & The Daytonas)*

## BUZZ (1)
| | | | |
|---|---|---|---|
| 66 | Columbia DB 7887 | You're Holding Me Down/I've Gotta Buzz | 250 |
| 76 | Polydor2058 714 | Motorway Madness/Love Games | 10 |

*(see also Boston Dexters, Tam White)*

## BUZZ (2)
| | | | |
|---|---|---|---|
| 79 | Redball RR 06 | Insanity/Him Not Me/Sick At Heart (p/s) | 30 |

## BUZZARD
| | | | |
|---|---|---|---|
| 85 | PTO MSPT01 | Catch Me Alone/Raven Eyed Queen | 45 |

## BUZZCOCKS
| | | | |
|---|---|---|---|
| 77 | New Hormones ORG 1 | SPIRAL SCRATCH (EP, plastic labels, p/s doesn't credit Howard Devoto) | 60 |
| 77 | United Artists UP 36316 | Orgasm Addict/Whatever Happened To...? (p/s) | 10 |
| 77 | United Artists UP 36316B | Whatever Happened To? (1-sided test pressing) | 50 |
| 78 | United Artists UP36348 | What Do I Get/Oh Shit | 7 |
| 78 | United Artists UP36348 | What Do I Get?/Oh Shit (Mispress, plays Stranglers Peaches) | 75 |
| 78 | United Artists UP 36386 | I Don't Mind/Autonomy | 5 |
| 78 | United Artists UP 36433 | Love You More/Noise Annoys (p/s) | 6 |
| 78 | United Artists UP 36455 | Ever Fallen In Love (With Someone You Shouldn't've?)/Just Lust | 5 |
| 78 | United Artists UP 36455 | Ever Fallen In Love (With Someone You Shouldn't've?)/Just Lust (p/s mispressed with Gerry Rafferty track on B-side) | 20 |
| 78 | United Artists UP 36471 | Promises/Lipstick (p/s) | 7 |

| | | | MINT VALUE £ |
|---|---|---|---|

**BUZZIN CUZZINS**

| 78 | New Hormones ORG 1 | SPIRAL SCRATCH (EP, reissue, p/s credits Howard Devoto, paper label) | 10 |
| 78 | United Artists UALP 15 | Moving Away From The Pulsebeat (12", 1-sided, die-cut co. sl., promo only) | 20 |
| 79 | United Artists UP 36499 | Everybody's Happy Nowadays/Why Can't I Touch It? (p/s, available in 3 different colours) | 5 |
| 79 | United Artists UP 36541 | Harmony In My Head/Something's Gone Wrong Again (p/s) | 5 |
| 79 | United Artists BP 316 | You Say You Don't Love Me/Raison D'etre | 5 |
| 80 | United Artists BP 365 | Why She's A Girl From The Chainstore/Are Everything (p/s) | 6 |
| 80 | United Artists BP 365 DJ | Why She's A Girl From The Chainstore/Are Everything (DJ promo) | 5 |
| 80 | United Artists BP371 | Strange Thing/Airwaves Dream (p/s) | 5 |
| 87 | Strange Fruit SFPS044 | PEEL SESSION EP (12") | 10 |
| 89 | EMI EM104 | Ever Fallen In Love/Promises/Everybody's Happy Nowdays/Harmony in My Head (p/s) | 8 |
| 91 | New Hormones ORG 1 | SPIRAL SCRATCH (EP, 2nd reissue, promo only 7") | 10 |
| 91 | New Hormones DV1T | SPIRAL SCRATCH (12" EP, reissue, numbered) | 12 |
| 95 | One Stop Music ONE 7001 | Noise Annoys/Isolation (live) (p/s, 1,500 only) | 5 |
| 95 | United Artists ESP001 | What Do I Get?/Mad Mad Judy/Raison D'Etre (Demo) | 10 |
| 78 | United Artists UAG 30159 | ANOTHER MUSIC IN A DIFFERENT KITCHEN (LP, black inner sleeve, in printed carrier bag) | 30 |
| 78 | United Artists UAG 30159 | ANOTHER MUSIC IN A DIFFERENT KITCHEN (LP) | 15 |
| 78 | United Artists UAG 30159 | ANOTHER MUSIC IN A DIFFERENT KITCHEN (LP, mispressing without "I Need") | 20 |
| 78 | United Artists UAG 30197 | LOVE BITES (LP, with embossed sleeve with insert) | 20 |
| 79 | United Artists UAG 30260 | A DIFFERENT KIND OF TENSION (LP, with inner sleeve) | 20 |
| 89 | Strange Fruit SFRLP 104 | PEEL SESSIONS (LP) | 15 |
| 89 | EMI LP PRODT 1 | PRODUCT (5xLP boxed set with booklet) | 40 |
| 89 | Absolutely Free FREELP 02 | LIVE AT THE ROXY (LP) | 15 |
| 91 | Document DLP 2 | TIME'S UP (LP, mock bootleg, with bonus 33rpm interview single [FDLP 2]) | 20 |

*(see also Pete Shelley, Things, Stevie's Buzz)*

**BUZZIN CUZZINS**

| 94 | Azuli Records AZNY 024 | Let Me Show You Love (12") | 60 |

**JAKI BYARD**

| 67 | Transatlantic PR 7419 | LIVE! VOL 1 (LP, white purple label) | 20 |
| 68 | Transatlantic PR 7463 | FREEDOM TOGETHER! (LP) | 20 |
| 68 | Transatlantic PR 7550 | SUNSHINE OF MY SOUL (LP) | 20 |

**DON BYAS & HIS RHYTHM**

| 56 | Vogue V 2390 | On The Way To Your Heart/The Portuguese Washerwomen | 10 |
| 64 | Realm RM 230 | ON 52ND STREET (LP) | 15 |

**BYE LAWS**

| 68 | Pye 7N 17481 | Then You Can Tell Me Goodbye/Come On Over To My Place | 8 |
| 69 | Pye 7N 17701 | Run Baby Run/To Sir With Love | 20 |

**ANN BYERS**

| 75 | Power Exchange 108 | This Man Is X-Rated/Gotta Get You Back | 5 |

**TREVOR BYFIELD**

| 80 | Ethnic Fight EF 086 | Jah Guide/TREVOR & CLIVE: Sea Of Love (12") | 35 |

**ANTHONY BYGRAVES**

| 74 | Pye 7N 45429 | Painted Lady/Love Star Ship | 15 |

**JUNIOR BYLES**

| 71 | Bullet BU 499 | Beat Down Babylon/UPSETTERS: Version | 25 |
| 71 | Upsetter US 365 | Place Called Africa/UPSETTERS: Earthquake | 25 |
| 72 | Upsetter US 387 | Festival Da Da/UPSETTERS: Version | 25 |
| 72 | Pama PM 857 | Fever/GROOVERS: Soul Sister (B-side actually by Heptones) | 40 |
| 72 | Dynamic DYN 432 | Pharaoh Hiding/UPSETTERS: Hail To Power | 15 |
| 72 | Randy's RAN 523 | King Of Babylon/UPSETTERS: Nebuchadnezzer | 20 |
| 72 | Punch PH 109 | Pharaoh Hiding/UPSETTERS: Hail To Power | 20 |
| 73 | Pama PM 878 | Education Rock/KEN McKAY: Nobody Knows | 10 |
| 73 | Count Shelley CS 31 | Break Up To Make Up/YOUTH MAN (DILLINGER): Plat Skank | 15 |
| 74 | Magnet MAG 27 | Curly Locks/Now Generation | 8 |
| 74 | Dip DL 5035 | Curly Locks/Now Generation | 20 |
| 75 | Dip DL 5074 | Long Way/All The Way | 15 |
| 75 | Ethnic ETH 26 | Mumbling And Grumbling/King Size Mumble | 15 |
| 76 | Jessus JI 006 | Know Where You Are Going/JESSUS EXPERIENCE: Going To Zion | 12 |
| 76 | Ethnic Fight EF 042 | Bury O Boy/THE THING MUSIC CO: Version | 8 |
| 76 | Black Wax WAX 17 | Pitchy Patchy/THE JA-MAN ALL STARS: 129 Beat Street | 6 |
| 72 | Trojan TRL 52 | BEAT DOWN BABYLON (LP, beware of Canadian imports) | 50 |
| 87 | Trojan TRLS 253 | BEAT DOWN BABYLON: THE UPSETTER YEARS (LP) | 15 |
| 88 | Trojan TRLS 269 | WHEN WILL BETTER COME (LP) | 15 |

*(see also King Chubby, Lloyd Terrell, Dennis Alcapone, Upsetters, Bob Marley, Lee & Junior)*

**JUNIOR BYLES & RUPERT REID**

| 76 | Black Wax WAX 15 | Chant Down Babylon/THE JA-MAN ALL STARS: Version | 20 |

**JAMES BYNUM**

| 79 | Grapevine GRP 117 | Time Passes By/Love You | 10 |

**BOBBY BYRD**

| 71 | Mojo 2001 118 | I Need Help Parts 1 & 2 | 8 |
| 71 | Mojo 2027 003 | I Know You Got Soul/If You Don't Work You Can't Eat | 8 |
| 71 | Mojo 2093 004 | Hot Pants ... I'm Coming, I'm Coming, I'm Coming/Hang It Up | 10 |
| 72 | Mojo 2093 013 | Keep On Doin' What You're Doin'/Let Me Know | 8 |
| 72 | Mojo 2093 017 | If You Got A Love You'd Better Keep Hold Of It/ You've Got To Change Your Mind | 8 |
| 72 | Mojo 2093 020 | Never Get Enough/My Concerto | 8 |
| 73 | Warner Bros K 16291 | Try It Again/I'm On The Move | 6 |
| 73 | Mojo 2093 028 | Saying It And Doing It Are Two Different Things/VICKI ANDERSON: Don't Throw Your Love In Garbage/In The Land Of Milk & Honey | 10 |

| | | | |
|---|---|---|---|
| 87 | Urban URB 8 | I Know You Got Soul/Hot Pants ........................................................................ | 7 |
| 87 | Urban URBX 8 | I Know You Got Soul/Hot Pants ... I'm Coming, I'm Coming, I'm Coming/I Know You Got Soul (Version) (12", die-cut company sleeve) ................................................ | 10 |

*(see also JB's, James Brown, Anna King & Bobby Byrd, Vicki Anderson)*

### C. BYRD & SIR D.'S GROUP

| | | | |
|---|---|---|---|
| 60 | Blue Beat BB 49 | Baa Baa Black Sheep/LLOYD & CECIL: Come Over Here ............................ | 12 |

### CHARLIE BYRD

| | | | |
|---|---|---|---|
| 84 | Riverside RLP 9451 | THE GUITAR ARTISTRY OF CHARLIE BYRD (LP, Nimbus Supercut, mail oder only through Practical Hi Fi magazine) ..................................................................... | 40 |

### DONALD BYRD

| | | | |
|---|---|---|---|
| 65 | Verve VS 532 | Boom Boom/See See Rider ........................................................................... | 10 |
| 73 | Blue Note 35564 | Black Byrd/Slop Jar Blues ............................................................................ | 7 |
| 80 | United Artists UP 622 | Dominoes/Wind Parade ................................................................................ | 7 |
| 80 | Blue Note 12 UP 622 | Dominoes/Wind Parade (12") ....................................................................... | 30 |
| 55 | Esquire 32-013 | BYRD'S EYE VIEW (LP) .................................................................................. | 50 |
| 55 | Esquire 32-019 | BYRD JAZZ (THE MOTOR CITY SCENES) (LP, as Donald Byrd Sextet) ............ | 80 |
| 56 | Esquire 32-032 | JAZZ FOR THE CARRIAGE TRADE (LP) ............................................................. | 50 |
| 60s | Esquire 32-039 | INFORMAL JAZZ (LP) ..................................................................................... | 25 |
| 70s | Blue Note BI 7243187515 | KOFI (LP) ...................................................................................................... | 20 |
| 73 | Blue Note BN-LA047 | BLACKBYRD (LP) ........................................................................................... | 15 |
| 75 | Blue Note UAG 20001 | PLACES AND SPACES (LP) .............................................................................. | 25 |

*(see also Blackbyrds, Art Farmer)*

### RUSSELL BYRD

| | | | |
|---|---|---|---|
| 64 | Sue WI 305 | Hitch Hike Parts 1 & 2 .................................................................................. | 50 |

### ESTHER BYRDE

| | | | |
|---|---|---|---|
| 79 | Survival SUR 1 | Touch Me Take Me/Tracks Of Love ............................................................... | 50 |

### BYRDS

**SINGLES**

| | | | |
|---|---|---|---|
| 65 | CBS 201765 | Mr. Tambourine Man/I Knew I'd Want You ................................................... | 8 |
| 65 | CBS 201796 | All I Really Want To Do/Feel A Whole Lot Better .......................................... | 8 |
| 65 | CBS 202008 | Turn! Turn! Turn! (To Everything There Is A Season)/ She Don't Care About Time | 8 |
| 66 | CBS 202037 | Set You Free This Time/It Won't Be Wrong ................................................... | 12 |
| 66 | CBS 202067 | Eight Miles High/Why ................................................................................... | 15 |
| 66 | CBS 202259 | 5D (Fifth Dimension)/Captain Soul ............................................................... | 10 |
| 66 | CBS 202295 | Mr Spaceman/What's Happening?!?! ............................................................ | 20 |
| 67 | CBS 202559 | So You Want To Be A Rock'n'Roll Star/Everybody's Been Burned ................... | 12 |
| 67 | CBS 2648 | My Back Pages/Renaissance Fair .................................................................. | 12 |
| 67 | CBS 2924 | Lady Friend/Don't Make Waves..................................................................... | 20 |
| 67 | CBS 3093 | Goin' Back/Change Is Now ........................................................................... | 12 |
| 68 | CBS 3411 | You Ain't Goin' Nowhere/Artificial Energy ................................................... | 8 |
| 68 | CBS 3752 | I Am A Pilgrim/Pretty Boy Floyd .................................................................. | 8 |
| 69 | CBS 4055 | Bad Night At The Whiskey/Drug Store Truck Drivin' Man .............................. | 12 |
| 69 | CBS 4284 | Lay Lady Lay/Old Blue (p/s) ......................................................................... | 12 |
| 69 | CBS 4572 | Wasn't Born To Follow/Child Of The Universe ............................................. | 8 |
| 70 | CBS 4753 | Jesus Is Just Alright/It's All Over Now Baby Blue.......................................... | 8 |
| 71 | CBS 5322 | Chestnut Mare/Just A Season ....................................................................... | 7 |
| 71 | CBS 7253 | I Trust/This Is My Destiny ............................................................................. | 10 |
| 72 | CBS 7712 | America's Great National Pastime/Farther Along (unreleased) ...................... | 0 |
| 73 | Asylum AYM 516 | Things Will Be Better/For Free (promos in p/s) ............................................ | 12 |
| 73 | Asylum AYM 516 | Things Will Be Better/For Free (promos without p/s)..................................... | 6 |
| 73 | Asylum AYM 517 | Full Circle/Long Live The King ...................................................................... | 6 |

**EPs**

| | | | |
|---|---|---|---|
| 66 | CBS EP 6069 | THE TIMES THEY ARE A' CHANGIN' (EP) ......................................................... | 25 |
| 66 | CBS EP 6077 | EIGHT MILES HIGH (EP)................................................................................. | 30 |

**ALBUMS**

| | | | |
|---|---|---|---|
| 65 | CBS BPG 62571 | MR TAMBOURINE MAN (LP, mono) ............................................................... | 45 |
| 65 | CBS (S)BPG 62571 | MR TAMBOURINE MAN (LP, stereo) .............................................................. | 35 |
| 66 | CBS BPG 62652 | TURN! TURN! TURN! (LP, mono) .................................................................... | 45 |
| 66 | CBS (S)BPG 62652 | TURN! TURN! TURN! (LP, stereo) ................................................................... | 40 |
| 66 | CBS BPG 62783 | FIFTH DIMENSION (LP, mono) ...................................................................... | 40 |
| 66 | CBS (S)BPG 62783 | FIFTH DIMENSION (LP, stereo) ..................................................................... | 35 |
| 67 | CBS BPG 62988 | YOUNGER THAN YESTERDAY (LP, mono) ...................................................... | 40 |
| 67 | CBS (S)BPG 62988 | YOUNGER THAN YESTERDAY (LP, stereo)...................................................... | 35 |
| 68 | CBS BPG 63107 | THE BYRDS' GREATEST HITS (LP, mono) ....................................................... | 15 |
| 68 | CBS BPG 63169 | THE NOTORIOUS BYRD BROTHERS (LP, mono, Ernest J, Day on rear) ............ | 50 |
| 68 | CBS (S)BPG 63169 | THE NOTORIOUS BYRD BROTHERS (LP, stereo) ............................................ | 30 |
| 68 | CBS 63353 | SWEETHEART OF THE RODEO (LP, mono) ..................................................... | 40 |
| 68 | CBS 63353 | SWEETHEART OF THE RODEO (LP, stereo) .................................................... | 45 |
| 69 | CBS 63545 | DR BYRDS & MR HYDE (LP, mono) ............................................................... | 40 |

*(Original copies of the above LPs were issued with rough-textured, plain orange labels & laminated sleeves; later copies are worth two-thirds these values.)*

| | | | |
|---|---|---|---|
| 69 | CBS S 63545 | DR BYRDS & MR HYDE (LP, stereo) ............................................................... | 25 |
| 71 | Bumble GEXP 8001 | PRE-FLYTE (LP) ............................................................................................. | 25 |
| 73 | Asylum SYLA 8754 | THE BYRDS (LP, gatefold sleeve)................................................................... | 15 |
| 75 | CBS 63353 | SWEETHEARTS OF THE RODEO (LP, reissue) ................................................. | 15 |
| 99 | Sundazed 5059 | 5th DIMENSION (LP, reissue, gatefold) .......................................................... | 15 |
| 99 | Simply Vinyl 62571 | MR TAMBOURINE MAN (LP, reissue) ............................................................. | 15 |
| 99 | Simply Vinyl SVLP 007 | YOUNGER THAN YESTERDAY (LP, reissue) ..................................................... | 15 |

| | | | |
|---|---|---|---|
| 02 | Simply Vinyl SVLP 375 | THE VERY BEST OF (2-LP) | 15 |

*(see also Beefeaters, Roger McGuinn, David Crosby, Gene Clark, Gram Parsons, Gene Parsons, Skip Battin, Flying Burrito Brothers, Evergreen Blueshoes, Dillard & Clark, Kentucky Colonels)*

### JERRY BYRNE
| | | | |
|---|---|---|---|
| 76 | Specialty SON 5011 | Lights Out/Honey Baby | 5 |

### PACKIE BYRNE (& BONNIE SHALJEAN)
| | | | |
|---|---|---|---|
| 69 | EFDSS LP 1009 | PACKIE BYRNE (LP) | 20 |

### EDD/EDWARD BYRNES
| | | | |
|---|---|---|---|
| 60 | Warner Bros WB 5 | Kookie, Kookie (Lend Me Your Comb) (with Connie Stevens)/You're The Top | 5 |
| 60 | Warner Bros WB 27 | Lonely Christmas/Yulesville (as Edd Byrnes) | 5 |
| 60 | Warner Bros WEP 6010 | KOOKIE (EP, mono) | 10 |
| 60 | Warner Bros WSEP 2010 | KOOKIE (EP, stereo) | 10 |
| 63 | Warner Bros W(S)EP 6108 | KOOKIE VOLUME 2 (EP) | 10 |

*(see also Connie Stevens)*

### MARTIN BYRNES
| | | | |
|---|---|---|---|
| 70 | Leader LEA 2004 | BYRNES (LP) | 15 |

### DAVID BYRON
| | | | |
|---|---|---|---|
| 75 | Bronze ILPS 9342 | TAKE NO PRISONERS (LP, lyric inner sleeve) | 15 |
| 78 | Arista SPART 1077 | BABY FACED KILLER (LP) | 25 |
| 81 | Creole CRX 2 | ON THE ROCKS (LP, as BYRON BAND) | 20 |

*(see also Uriah Heep)*

### SOL BYRON & IMPACTS
| | | | |
|---|---|---|---|
| 60s | Flamingo PR 5027 | Pride And Joy/Thou Shall Not Steal | 15 |

### BYSTANDERS (1)
| | | | |
|---|---|---|---|
| 65 | Pylot WD 501 | That's The End/This Time | 150 |
| 66 | Piccadilly 7N 35330 | (You're Gonna) Hurt Yourself/Have I Offended The Girl | 25 |
| 66 | Piccadilly 7N 35351 | My Love - Come Home/If You Walk Away | 30 |
| 67 | Piccadilly 7N 35363 | 98.6/Stubborn Kind Of Fellow | 20 |
| 67 | Piccadilly 7N 35382 | Royal Blue Summer Sunshine Day/Make Up Your Mind | 30 |
| 67 | Piccadilly 7N 35399 | Pattern People/Green Grass | 15 |
| 68 | Pye 7N 17476 | When Jezamine Goes/Cave Of Clear Light | 50 |
| 68 | Pye 7N 17540 | This World Is My World/Painting The Time | 15 |

*(see also Man)*

### BYSTANDERS (2)
| | | | |
|---|---|---|---|
| 81 | Uncle Robert UR 001 | Nowhere To Hide/Sweet Fanny Adams/True Blue/I Wonder (EP) | 20 |

### BYZANTIUM
| | | | |
|---|---|---|---|
| 73 | A&M AMS 7064 | What A Coincidence/My Seasons Changing With The Sun | 7 |
| 72 | Private pressing | LIVE AND STUDIO ('BLACK AND WHITE') (LP, 100 only with insert) | 300 |
| 72 | A&M AMLH 68104 | BYZANTIUM (LP, with poster, brown label) | 100 |
| 72 | A&M AMLH 68104 | BYZANTIUM (LP, without poster) | 40 |
| 73 | A&M AMLH 68163 | SEASONS CHANGING (LP, poster sleeve, brown labels) | 100 |

*(see also Ora)*

### B.Z.N.
| | | | |
|---|---|---|---|
| 73 | Birth RAB 1003 | Rolling Round The Band/Superman | 12 |

## C

### ANDY C
| | | | |
|---|---|---|---|
| 92 | RAM RAMM 001 | SOUR MASH EP (12") | 40 |
| 93 | RAM RAMM 003 | BASS LOGIC EP (12") | 30 |
| 93 | RAM RAMM 006 | Slip 'N' Slide/Bass Constructor (Sonz Of A Loop Da Loop Era Remix) (12") | 25 |
| 95 | RAM RAMM 12 | Cool Down/Roll On (12") | 15 |

*(See also Randall and Andy C.)*

### ERROL C
| | | | |
|---|---|---|---|
| 76 | Concrete Jungle CJ 601 | Jah For I/4TH STREET ORCHESTRA: Version | 35 |

### FANTASTIC JOHNNY C
| | | | |
|---|---|---|---|
| 67 | London HL 10169 | Boogaloo Down Broadway/Look What Love Can Make You Do | 15 |
| 68 | London HL 10212 | Hitch It To The Horse/Cool Broadway | 15 |
| 69 | Action ACT 4543 | Is There Anything Better Than Making Love/New Love | 18 |
| 75 | Island USA 8 | Don't Depend On Me (Parts 1 & 2) | 8 |
| 69 | Action ACLP 6001 | BOOGALOO DOWN BROADWAY (LP) | 40 |

### ROY C
| | | | |
|---|---|---|---|
| 66 | Island WI 273 | Shotgun Wedding/I'm Going To Make It | 20 |
| 66 | Island WI 273 | Shotgun Wedding/High School Dropout (different B-side) | 12 |
| 67 | Ember EMB S 230 | Twistin' Pneumonia/Tear Avenue | 15 |
| 66 | Ember NR 5055 | THE SHOTGUN WEDDING MAN (LP) | 30 |
| 75 | Mercury 9100 017 | SEX AND SOUL (LP) | 15 |

### C. STAR
| | | | |
|---|---|---|---|
| 73 | Jam JAM 56 | Bad Boy/Alex | 10 |

### CABARET VOLTAIRE
| | | | |
|---|---|---|---|
| 78 | Rough Trade RT 003 | EXTENDED PLAY EP ( paper p/s) | 12 |
| 79 | Rough Trade RT 018 | Nag Nag Nag/Is That Me (p/s) | 8 |
| 79 | Rough Trade RT 035 | Silent Command/Chance Versus Causality (p/s) | 6 |

| 80 | Rough Trade RT 060 | Seconds Too Late/Control Addict (p/s) | 6 |
| 79 | Rough Trade ROUGH 4 | MIX UP (LP) | 15 |
| 80 | Rough Trade ROUGH 11 | VOICE OF AMERICA (LP) | 15 |
| 80 | Industrial IRC 35 | 1974-1976 (LP, cassette) | 30 |
| 92 | Plasticity EXL LP03 | PLASTICITY (2-LP) | 25 |

*(see also Richard H. Kirk, Hafler Trio,,, Wicky Wacky)*

### CABINET
| 82 | Sharp CAL 1 | Still Tears/Future In Your Hand (p/s) | 5 |
| 83 | Sharp CAL 2 | Language And Words/Language And Words (Extended) (p/s) | 6 |

### CABLES
| 68 | Coxsone CS 7072 | What Kind Of World?/My Broken Heart | 70 |
| 68 | Coxsone CS 7082 | Soul Power/HEPTONES: Love Me Alway | 125 |
| 68 | Studio One SO 2060 | Baby Why?/Be A Man | 50 |
| 68 | Studio One SO 2071 | Love Is A Pleasure/Cheer Up | 80 |
| 69 | Studio One SO 2085 | Got To Find Someone/ALEXANDER HENRY: Please Be True | 50 |
| 69 | Bamboo BAM 12 | So Long/PRESSURE BOYS: More Love | 40 |
| 70 | Bamboo BAM 19 | How Can I Trust You?/SOUND DIMENSIONS: How Can I Trust You? (Inst.) | 40 |
| 70 | Trojan TR 7792 | Salt Of The Earth/Ring A Bell | 10 |
| 70 | Harry J. HJ 6614 | Didn't I/JAY BOYS: Tilly | 20 |
| 70 | Harry J. HJ 6620 | Feel Alright/Equal Rights | 10 |
| 71 | Big Shot BI 598 | A Sometime Girl/IN CROWD BAND: A Sometime Girl Version | 10 |
| 71 | Duke DU 124 | Mixing/IN CROWD BAND: In Orbit | 8 |
| 72 | Jackpot JP 787 | Come On/Come On Version | 6 |
| 73 | Attack ATT 8053 | Give Me A Chance/JAH FISH: King Of Zion | 8 |
| 91 | Studio One PSOL 002 | WHAT KIND OF WORLD (LP, repressing by Peckings Shop, red and white labels) | 35 |

*(see also K. Drummond, Dingle Brothers, Alton Ellis)*

### CABOOSE
| 70 | Stax STAX 151 | Black Hands, White Cotton/In My Hour Of Need | 6 |

### CACHE
| 81 | Groove GP 111 | Where Is My Sunshine/Jazzin' And Crusin' | 6 |
| 81 | Groove GP 111 T | Where Is My Sunshine/Jazzin' And Crusin' (12") | 30 |

### CACTUS
| 70 | Atco 2400 020 | CACTUS (LP) | 50 |
| 71 | Atco 2400 114 | ONE WAY ... OR ANOTHER (LP, reissue of above LP) | 30 |
| 72 | Atlantic K 40307 | RESTRICTIONS (LP) | 20 |
| 72 | Atlantic K 50013 | 'OT AND SWEATY (LP) | 18 |

*(see also Vanilla Fudge, Leaf Hound, Beck Bogert Appice, Atomic Rooster)*

### BILL CADDICK
| 76 | Park SHP 102 | ROUGH MUSIC (LP) | 15 |
| 77 | Leader LER 2097 | SUNNY MEMORIES (LP) | 15 |
| 79 | Highway SHY 7006 | REASONS BRIEFLY SET DOWN (LP) | 15 |

### ALAN CADDY
| 64 | HMV POP 1286 | Tornado/Workout | 35 |

*(see also Tornados)*

### CADETS (U.K.)
| 63 | Decca F 11677 | Hello Trouble/Our First Quarrel | 5 |
| 64 | Pye 7N 15693 | Chapel Of Love/I Gave My Wedding Dress Away | 5 |
| 65 | Pye 7N 15769 | Are You Teasing Me?/My Heart Skips A Beat | 5 |
| 65 | Pye 7N 15852 | Jealous Heart/Right Or Wrong | 20 |
| 65 | Pye 7N 15947 | Baby Roo/Raining In My Heart | 10 |
| 66 | Pye 7N 17024 | If I Had My Life To Live Over/Best Of All | 5 |
| 66 | Pye 7N 17167 | At The Close Of A Long Long Day/True Love | 5 |
| 69 | Pye 7N 17762 | Dying Ranger/Storeen Bawn | 5 |

### CADETS (U.S.)
| 56 | London HLU 8313 | Stranded In The Jungle/I Want You (gold label lettering) | 500 |
| 56 | London HLU 8313 | Stranded In The Jungle/I Want You (silver label lettering) | 250 |
| 56 | London HLU 8313 | Stranded In The Jungle/I Want You (78) | 20 |

### CADILLAC
| 86 | CBS A 7180 | Valentino/Valentino (p/s) | 8 |

### CADILLACS (1)
| 59 | London HLJ 8786 | Peek-A-Boo/Oh, Oh, Lolita | 40 |

### CADILLACS (2)
| 80 | Red Eye | Billy/Who Dat Man (p/s) | 8 |

### BOBBY CADMAN
| 74 | Regal Zonophone RZ3008 | A Magic Spell/Own Up Time | 25 |

### CADO BELLE
| 76 | Anchor 1033 | Got To Love/Paper In The Rain | 15 |
| 76 | Anchor 1038 | Stone Throw From Nowhere/Airport Shutdown | 8 |

### SUSAN CADOGAN
| 70 | Magnet MAG 23 | Hurt So Good/Hurt So Good (Instrumental) | 10 |
| 74 | Dip DL 5030 | Hurt So Good/UPSETTERS: Loving Is Good | 15 |
| 75 | Lucky LY 5078 | Feeling Right/Congratulations | 7 |
| 75 | Black Wax WAX 2 | Love My Life/MR. VIBES: Love Vibes | 8 |
| 77 | Trojan TR9028 | Nice And Easy/You Need Me | 10 |
| 76 | Trojan TRLS 122 | SUSAN CADOGAN (LP) | 25 |

### CAEDMON
| 78 | Private pressing | CAEDMON (LP, with insert, with bonus 7": Beyond The Second Mile/Give Me Jesus) | 250 |

| | | |
|---|---|---:|
| 78 | Private pressing | CAEDMON (LP, with insert, without bonus 7": Beyond The Second Mile/Give Me Jesus) ........ 100 |
| 97 | Engliah Garden ENG 1014 | CAEDMON (LP, reissue) ........ 25 |

**CAESAR & CLEO**

| | | |
|---|---|---:|
| 65 | Reprise R 20419 | Love Is Strange/Let The Good Times Roll (in p/s) ........ 25 |
| 65 | Reprise R 30056 | CAESAR AND CLEO (EP, 2 tracks each by Caesar & Cleo and Sonny & Cher) ........ 20 |

*(see also Sonny & Cher)*

**CAESARS**

| | | |
|---|---|---:|
| 65 | Decca F 12251 | On The Outside Looking In/Can You Blame Me? ........ 15 |
| 66 | Decca F 12462 | Five In The Morning/It's Superman ........ 10 |

**CAFE SOCIETY**

| | | |
|---|---|---:|
| 75 | Konk KOS 5 | Whitby Two-Step/Maybe It's Me ........ 6 |
| 75 | Konk KONK 102 | CAFE SOCIETY (LP, with inner sleeve) ........ 20 |

*(see also Tom Robinson Band, Claire Hamill)*

**BUTCH CAGE/MABEL LEE WILLIAMS**

| | | |
|---|---|---:|
| 60s | Storyville SLP 129 | COUNTRY BLUES (LP) ........ 20 |

**CAGES PLAY**

| | | |
|---|---|---:|
| 81 | SSM 031 | Midnight In Katowice/Abstraction (p/s) ........ 10 |

**AUBREY CAGLE**

| | | |
|---|---|---:|
| 62 | Starlite ST45 082 | Come Along Little Girl/Blue Lonely World ........ 75 |

**CAGLIOSTRO**

| | | |
|---|---|---:|
| 86 | él GPO 22 | Libera Me/Madmen And Lovers (p/s) ........ 8 |

**JEREMY CAHILL**

| | | |
|---|---|---:|
| 70s | Solent | September Blues/Yesterday ........ 15 |

*(see also Shide & Acorn)*

**PATRICIA CAHILL**

| | | |
|---|---|---:|
| 70 | Deram Nova SDN 22 | SUMMER'S DAUGHTER (LP) ........ 30 |

**DAVID CAIN**

| | | |
|---|---|---:|
| 69 | BBC RESR7 | THE SEASONS (LP) ........ 50 |

**CAIN (1)**

| | | |
|---|---|---:|
| 68 | Page One POF 054 | Her Emotion/Take Me Back One Time ........ 35 |
| 78 | SHP 103 | VISITOR 2035 (2-LP, fold-out lyric sheet) ........ 20 |

**CAIN (2)**

| | | |
|---|---|---:|
| 80s | private pressing | CAIN (2-LP) ........ 30 |

**CHRISTOPHER CAINE**

| | | |
|---|---|---:|
| 67 | Decca F12586 | Saturday Night People/Turn The World Around The Other Way ........ 10 |

**TUBAL CAINE**

| | | |
|---|---|---:|
| 70 | Attack ATT 8023 | I'm A Drifter Part 1/CIMARONS: I'm A Drifter Part 2 ........ 30 |

**AL CAIOLA (ORCHESTRA)**

| | | |
|---|---|---:|
| 56 | London HLC 8285 | Flamenco Love/From The Heart ........ 15 |
| 61 | London HLT 9294 | The Magnificent Seven/The Lonely Rebel ........ 5 |
| 61 | London HLT 9325 | Bonanza/Bounty Hunter ........ 5 |
| 61 | HMV POP 884 | Bonanza/Bounty Hunter (as Al Caiola Orchestra, reissue) ........ 5 |
| 61 | HMV POP 889 | The Magnificent Seven/The Lonely Rebel (as Al Caiola Orchestra) ........ 5 |
| 62 | Oriole CB 1732 | Mambo Jambo/Twistin' At The Woodchoppers Mill ........ 5 |
| 62 | United Artists UP 1003 | Big Guitar/Guns Of Navarone ........ 5 |
| 66 | United Artists (S)ULP 1115 | SOUNDS FOR SPIES AND PRIVATE EYES (LP) ........ 20 |

*(see also Hugo Montenegro)*

**CAIRN**

| | | |
|---|---|---:|
| 70s | GES 1015 | A COLLECTION OF SCOTCH FOLK (LP) ........ 15 |

**JOHN CAIRNEY**

| | | |
|---|---|---:|
| 57 | HMV POP 424 | Two Strangers/A Certain Girl I Know (with Sammy San) ........ 5 |
| 68 | Waverley SLP 543 | Please/Deep Purple ........ 5 |

**CAIRO (1)**

| | | |
|---|---|---:|
| 80 | Absurd ASK 15 | Movie Stars/Cuthbert's Birthday Treat (p/s) ........ 5 |

**CAIRO (2)**

| | | |
|---|---|---:|
| 83 | Tunnel TUN 01 | Seconds & Hours/Green Light (p/s) ........ 6 |

**CAIROS**

| | | |
|---|---|---:|
| 03 | Shrine 101 | Stop Overlooking Me/Don't Fight It ........ 8 |
| 03 | Shrine L2AS | Stop Overlooking Me/CAUTIONS: Watch Your Step (reissue) ........ 7 |

**CAIR PARAVEL**

| | | |
|---|---|---:|
| 76 | Koala KOA PO 16 | SOME OTHER MORNING (LP, insert) ........ 600 |

**CAJUN MOON**

| | | |
|---|---|---:|
| 76 | Polydor 2058 801 | No Honey No Love/Version ........ 6 |

*(see Allan Taylor)*

**CAKE**

| | | |
|---|---|---:|
| 68 | MCA MUPS 303 | THE CAKE (LP) ........ 30 |
| 69 | MCA MUPS 390 | A SLICE OF CAKE (LP) ........ 30 |

**J.J. CALE**

| | | |
|---|---|---:|
| 66 | Liberty LIB 55881 | Outside Lookin' In/In Our Time ........ 18 |
| 79 | Shelter ISA 5018 | FIVE (LP, with bonus single "Katy Cool"/"Juan And Maria Juarez Blues" [JJ-1]) ........ 15 |
| 92 | Silvertone ORE 532 | NUMBER TEN (LP) ........ 20 |

*(see also Leathercoated Minds)*

**JOHN CALE**

| | | |
|---|---|---:|
| 74 | Island WIP 6202 | The Man Who Couldn't Afford To Orgy/Sylvia Said ........ 10 |
| 77 | Illegal IL 006 | Jack The Ripper In The Moulin Rouge/Memphis (unissued, test pressings only) ........ 25 |
| 81 | A&M AMS 8130 | Dead Or Alive/Honi Soit ........ 5 |

| | | | |
|---|---|---|---|
| 83 | Ze IS 113 | Close Watch/I Keep A Close Watch (p/s) | 5 |
| 84 | Ze IS 157 | Caribbean Sunset/(same) (unissued, promo only) | 8 |
| 84 | Ze IS 197 | Ooh La La/Magazines (p/s) | 5 |
| 77 | Illegal IL 003 | ANIMAL JUSTICE (12" EP) | 10 |
| 71 | CBS 64256 | VINTAGE VIOLENCE (LP, orange label) | 25 |
| 71 | CBS 64259 | CHURCH OF ANTHRAX (LP, with Terry Riley) | 20 |
| 72 | Reprise K 44212 | ACADEMY IN PERIL (LP) | 20 |
| 73 | Reprise K 44239 | PARIS 1919 (LP, with lyric insert) | 20 |
| 74 | Island ILPS 9301 | FEAR (LP, pink rim) | 18 |
| 75 | Island ILPS 9350 | HELEN OF TROY (LP) | 20 |
| 77 | Island ILPS 9459 | GUTS (LP) | 15 |
| 07 | EMI 37760 | CIRCUS (3-LP with free 7", sealed) | 20 |

(see also Velvet Underground, Nico, Terry Riley, Ayers Cale Nico & Eno, Judy Nylon)

**CALEB (QUAYE)**

| | | | |
|---|---|---|---|
| 67 | Philips BF 1588 | Baby Your Phrasing Is Bad/Woman Of Distinction (300-500 pressed) | 950 |
| 00s | Philips BF 1588 | Baby Your Phrasing Is Bad/Woman Of Distinction (limited edition reissue) | 7 |

(see also Mirage, Hookfoot, Bread & Beer Band, Elton John)

**CALEDONIANS**

| | | | |
|---|---|---|---|
| 69 | Fab FAB 103 | Funny Way Of Laughing/Don't Please | 40 |

(see also Clarendonians, Prince Buster)

**CALENDAR CROWD**

| | | | |
|---|---|---|---|
| 82 | Romantic RR002 | Perfect Hideaway/Perfect Hideaway Dub (p/s) | 20 |

**CALIFORNIA IN-CROWD**

| | | | |
|---|---|---|---|
| 66 | Fontana TF 779 | Questions And Answers/Happiness In My Heart | 70 |

**CALIFORNIA MUSIC**

| | | | |
|---|---|---|---|
| 74 | RCA RCA 2488 | Don't Worry Baby/Ten Years Harmony | 12 |
| 76 | RCA RCA 2661 | Jamaica Farewell/California Farewell | 12 |
| 78 | RSO 014 | I Can Hear Music/Love's Supposed To Be That Way (as California) | 10 |

(see also Bruce Johnston, Beach Boys)

**CALIFORNIA PINES**

| | | | |
|---|---|---|---|
| 67 | CBS 3074 | Two Weeks In September Part 1/Part 2 | 10 |

**CALIFORNIAN LICENSE**

| | | | |
|---|---|---|---|
| 70 | Philips 6006052 | The Cage/Easter Song | 12 |

**CALIFORNIANS**

| | | | |
|---|---|---|---|
| 67 | CBS 2263 | Golden Apples/Little Ship With A Red Sail | 75 |
| 67 | Decca F 12678 | Follow Me/What Love Can Do | 20 |
| 67 | Decca F 12712 | Sunday Will Never Be The Same/Can't Get You Out Of My Mind | 10 |
| 68 | Decca F 12758 | Congratulations/What Is Happy, Baby? | 10 |
| 68 | Decca F 12802 | Out In The Sun/The Sound | 20 |
| 69 | Fontana TF 991 | Mandy/The Cooks Of Cake And Kindness | 100 |
| 69 | Fontana TF 1052 | Sad Old Song/Weep No More | 15 |
| 69 | Chapter One CH 112 | You've Got Your Troubles/Early Morning Sun | 7 |

(see also Warren Zevon)

**CALLAN & JOHN**

| | | | |
|---|---|---|---|
| 69 | CBS 4447 | House Of Delight/Long Shadow Day | 40 |

**CALL GIRLS**

| | | | |
|---|---|---|---|
| 88 | 53rd & 3rd AGAR 001 | Primal World/VATICAN SHOTGUN SCARE: Thick Fat Heat Source (p/s) | 8 |

**CALLICOTT, (MISSISSIPPI) JOE**

| | | | |
|---|---|---|---|
| 68 | Blue Horizon 7-63227 | PRESENTING THE COUNTRY BLUES (LP) | 110 |
| 71 | Revival RVS 1002 | DEAL GONE DOWN (LP, as Joe Callicott) | 25 |

**CALLIES**

| | | | |
|---|---|---|---|
| 71 | Rubber RUB 002 | ON YOUR SIDE (LP, gatefold sleeve) | 15 |

**CALLINAN-FLYNN**

| | | | |
|---|---|---|---|
| 72 | Mushroom 50 MR 17 | We Are The People (The Road To Derry Town)/The Old Man And The Flower | 30 |
| 72 | Mushroom 150 MR 18 | FREEDOM'S LAMENT (LP) | 200 |

**CALLING HEARTS**

| | | | |
|---|---|---|---|
| 91 | Illuminated ILL 6 | Return To Base/In The Jungle (p/s) | 15 |

**CALLIOPE**

| | | | |
|---|---|---|---|
| 69 | Uni UN 514 | Clear Mud/Wiser | 15 |
| 68 | Buddah 203 016 | STEAMED (LP) | 25 |

**JO CALLIS**

| | | | |
|---|---|---|---|
| 81 | Pop: Aural POP 12 | Woah Yeah/Sinistrale/Dodo Boys (p/s) | 5 |

(see also Rezillos, Shake, Human League)

**CALOOGIE**

| | | | |
|---|---|---|---|
| 68 | CBS 1095 | Bleeker Street/Benedictus | 10 |

**GEORGE CALSTOCK**

| | | | |
|---|---|---|---|
| 78 | Hit Run DD2 | The Ungodly (Feat. U Black)/DOCTOR PABLO: Righteous Melody (12") | 35 |

**ROBERT CALVERT**

| | | | |
|---|---|---|---|
| 72 | United Artists UP 35543 | Ejection/Catch A Falling Starfighter (p/s) | 25 |
| 79 | Wake Up WUR 5 | Cricket Star (p/s, 33rpm flexidisc, as Robert Calvert & 1st XI) | 10 |
| 80 | Flicknife FLS 204 | Lord Of The Hornets/The Greenfly & The Rose (purple print p/s) | 10 |
| 81 | Flicknife FLS 204 | Lord Of The Hornets/The Greenfly & The Rose (reissue, black print p/s) | 5 |
| 74 | United Artists UAS 29507 | CAPTAIN LOCKHEED AND THE STARFIGHTERS (LP, embossed gatefold sleeve, with attached booklet and inner sleeve) | 40 |
| 75 | United Artists UAS 29852 | LUCKY LIEF AND THE LONGSHIPS (LP, gatefold sleeve) | 20 |
| 81 | A-Side IF 0311 | HYPE (SONGS OF TOM MAHLER) (LP) | 15 |
| 88 | Beat Goes On BGOLP 2 | LUCKY LIEF AND THE LONGSHIPS (LP, gatefold sleeve, reissue) | 20 |

MINT VALUE £

| 89 | Clear BLACK 1 | ROBERT CALVERT AT THE QUEEN ELIZABETH HALL (LP, mail order only, with badge, poster & T-shirt, gatefold sleeve) | 40 |

*(see also Hawkwind, Imperial Pompadours, Catapilla, Adrian Wagner, John Stevens Away)*

## TABBY CALVIN & ROUNDERS
| 56 | Capitol CL 14640 | False Alarm/I Came Back To Say I'm Sorry | 10 |

## CALYPSO JOE
| 69 | Escort ES 801 | Adults Only/Calalue | 30 |

## CAMALEONTI
| 68 | CBS 3968 | Applause/Applausi | 20 |

## CAMARQUE
| 83 | Clubland SJP 848 | Howl Of The Pack/Someone Just Like You (in p/s) | 75 |
| 83 | Clubland SJP 848 | Howl Of The Pack/Someone Just Like You | 30 |

## CAMBERWELL NOW
| 86 | Ink 19 | GHOST TRADE (LP) | 18 |

*(see also This Heat)*

## CAMBODIANS
| 70 | Duke DU 101 | Coolie Man/J.J. ALLSTARS: Coolie Version | 25 |

## CAMEL
| 73 | MCA MUPS 1177 | Never Let Go/Curiosity | 8 |
| 75 | Decca FR 13581 | Flight Of The Snow Goose/Rhayader | 5 |
| 75 | Decca FR 13606 | The Snow Goose/Freefall | 5 |
| 76 | Decca FR 13656 | Another Night/Lunar Sea (live) | 5 |
| 77 | Decca FR 13729 | Highways Of The Sun/Tell Me | 5 |
| 79 | Decca FR 13879 | Remote Romance/Rainbows End/Tell Me | 5 |
| 80 | Decca FR 13871 | Your Love Is Stranger Than Mine/Neon Magic (p/s) | 6 |
| 84 | Decca CAMEL 1 | Cloak And Dagger Man/Pressure Point (p/s) | 5 |
| 73 | MCA MUPS 473 | CAMEL (LP, black/blue hexagon label) | 175 |
| 74 | Deram SML 1107 | MIRAGE (LP, with insert, red/white label, small Deram logo) | 60 |
| 73 | MCA MUPS 473 | CAMEL (LP, later rainbow label) | 30 |
| 75 | Decca SKL-R 5207 | THE SNOW GOOSE (LP, laminated sleeve, insert) | 40 |
| 76 | Decca TXS-R 115 | MOON MADNESS (LP, 1st pressing with textured gatefold sleeve and P1 matrixes) | 20 |
| 77 | Decca TXS-R 124 | RAIN DANCES (LP, with inner) | 15 |
| 78 | Decca TXS R 132 | BREATHLESS (LP, insert) | 15 |
| 78 | Decca DBC-R 7/8 | A LIVE RECORD (2-LP, gatefold) | 15 |
| 79 | Decca TXS R 137 | I CAN SEE YOUR HOUSE FROM HERE (LP, insert) | 15 |

*(see also Pete Bardens, Gong/Camel, Caravan, Hatfield & The North)*

## CAMEL DRIVERS
| 68 | Pye International 7N 25471 | Sunday Morning 6 O'Clock/Give It A Try | 15 |

## CAMEOS (1)
| 63 | Columbia DB 7092 | Powercut/High Low And Lonesomely | 30 |
| 64 | Columbia DB 7201 | My Baby's Coming Home/Where E'er You Walk | 30 |

## CAMEOS (2)
| 67 | Toast TT 503 | A Pretty Shade Of Blue/You Didn't Have To Be So Nice | 8 |
| 68 | Toast TT 508 | On The Good Ship Lollipop/The Love Of A Boy | 8 |

## CAMERA OBSCURA (1)
| 80 | Small Wonder SMALL 28 | Destitution/Race In Athens (p/s) | 12 |

## CAMERA OBSCURA (2)
| 98 | Andmoresounds AND 0945 | Park And Ride/Swimming Pool | 25 |
| 98 | Andmoresounds AND 1145 | Your Sound/Autumn Tides/Annawaltzerpose | 25 |
| 01 | Andmoresounds AND 1645 | Eighties Fan/Shine Like A New Pin/Let's Go Bowling | 10 |
| 06 | Elefant ER-1123LP | LET'S GET OUT OF THIS COUNTRY (LP) | 18 |
| 01 | Andmoresounds AND 1733 | BIGGEST BLUEST HI-FI (LP) | 35 |

## CAMERAS IN CARS
| 80 | In Cinc CINC 1 | Time Room/Avoid A Void/Bright Boy/The Author (p/s) | 15 |

## DION CAMERON & THREE TOPS
| 66 | Rio R 111 | Lord Have Mercy/Get Ready | 25 |

*(see also Dion & Three Tops)*

## G.C. CAMERON
| 76 | Tamla Motown TMG 1033 | Me And My Life/Act Like A Shotgun | 10 |
| 80 | Flamingo FM-11 | Live For Love/If I Love You | 50 |
| 80 | Flamingo FM T-11 | Live For Love/If I Love You (12") | 60 |
| 89 | Ardent ADS 9002 | Wait Until Tomorrow/Shadows | 18 |

*(see also Detroit Spinners)*

## ISLA CAMERON
| 64 | Transatlantic TRAEP 109 | LOST LOVE (EP) | 12 |

*(see also Ewan MacColl)*

## JOHN CAMERON (QUARTET)
| 67 | Columbia DB 8120 | You Owe Me/Walk Small (solo) | 8 |
| 69 | Deram DM 256 | Troublemaker/Off Centre | 60 |
| 67 | Columbia SCX 6116 | COVER LOVER (LP) | 30 |
| 68 | Columbia Studio Two TWO 197 | WARM & GENTLE (LP) | 20 |
| 69 | Deram DML/SML 1044 | OFF CENTRE (LP) | 100 |
| 01 | Trunk KES 001 LP | KES (1-sided LP, 500 only) | 20 |
| 03 | Trunk JBH 002 | PSYCHOMANIA (LP, 1000 only, as John Cameron & Frog) | 60 |

*(see also Frog)*

## JOHNNY CAMERON
| 60 | Top Rank JAR 396 | I Double Dare You/Fantasy | 8 |

## KEN CAMERON
| | | | |
|---|---|---|---|
| 73 | DJM DJS 5281 | Land Of Love/Don't Bring Me Down | 10 |

## RAY CAMERON
| | | | |
|---|---|---|---|
| 67 | Island WIP 6003 | Doin' My Time/Getaway, Getaway Car | 12 |
| 75 | A&M AMS 7168 | Dynamite Party Part 1/Part 2 | 5 |

## AL CAMPBELL
| | | | |
|---|---|---|---|
| 78 | Chanan Jah TUFF 12 | Sister Soul/Footstool | 30 |
| 78 | Phil Pratt SS 1009 | Gee Baby/Where Were You (12") | 15 |
| 78 | Deb DEB 018 | Love The Way It Should Be/Version (12") | 20 |
| 79 | Saferno SOF 004 | Gone Down The Drain/One More Chance (12") | 25 |
| 79 | Nigara NADD 103 | La-La Means I Love You (12") | 40 |
| 70s | Ethnic ETH DD 2244 | Down In A Babylon/Babylon Dub (12") | 30 |
| 80 | Strong Like Sampson SLSD 14 | Jah Shine On Me/SUGAR MINOTT: Hall Of Love (12") | 35 |
| 80 | JB JBD 019 | You Jamming/You Jamming (Part 2) (12") | 30 |
| 81 | Greensleeves GRED 51 | Unfaithful Children/WAILING SOULS: Who No Waan Come (12") | 60 |
| 81 | JB JBD 029 | Feedback/Part 2 (12") | 25 |
| 82 | Greensleeves GRED 94 | Dance Hall Stylee/Fight I Down (12") | 20 |
| 82 | Silver Camel SC 014 | Lambs Bread/I Was Born A Loser (10") | 15 |
| 78 | Sunshot SS 1002 | GEE BABY (LP) | 50 |
| 78 | Terminal TMLP 1002 | NO MORE RUNNING (LP) | 100 |
| 78 | ITAL IT001 | LOVING MOODS OF (LP) | 40 |
| 78 | D.E.B. DBLP07 | SHOWCASE (LP) | 70 |
| 79 | Burning Sounds BS 1036 | DIAMONDS (LP) | 20 |
| 79 | Hawkeye HLD 03 | RAINY DAYS (LP) | 50 |
| 80 | Ethnic Fight ETH 2236 | MORE SHOWCASE (LP) | 40 |
| 80 | JB JBLP 002 | LATE NIGHT BLUES (LP) | 40 |
| 80 | JB JBLP 005 | WORKING MAN (LP) | 60 |

## AL CAMPBELL & TRINITY
| | | | |
|---|---|---|---|
| 78 | Deb DEB 013 | Reggae Dance/Dragon Dance/AL CAMPBELL: Roots Man Style (12") | 20 |

## ALEX CAMPBELL
| | | | |
|---|---|---|---|
| 65 | Transatlantic TRASP 4 | Been On The Road So Long/The Night Visiting Song (in p/s) | 10 |
| 65 | Transatlantic TRASP 4 | Been On The Road So Long/The Night Visiting Song | 5 |
| 68 | Saga OPP 2 | Victoria Dines Alone/Pack Up Your Sorrows | 30 |
| 64 | Xtra XTRA 1014 | ALEX CAMPBELL (LP, with Martin Carthy) | 25 |
| 65 | Polydor 623 035 | IN COPENHAGEN (LP) | 18 |
| 67 | Saga ERO 8021 | ALEX CAMPBELL AND HIS FRIENDS (LP, with Sandy Denny) | 15 |
| 71 | Ad-Rhythm/Tepee ARPS 1 | THIS IS ALEX CAMPBELL VOL. 1 (LP) | 15 |
| 71 | Ad-Rhythm/Tepee ARPS 2 | THIS IS ALEX CAMPBELL VOL. 2 (LP) | 15 |
| 87 | Sundown SDLP 2048 | WITH THE GREATEST RESPECT (2-LP, reissue of "This Is..." Vols. 1 & 2) | 18 |

*(see also Sandy Denny)*

## AMBROSE CAMPBELL
| | | | |
|---|---|---|---|
| 66 | Columbia SX 6081 | HIGH LIFE TODAY (LP) | 40 |

## BILL & PETE CAMPBELL
| | | | |
|---|---|---|---|
| 71 | Duke DU 123 | Come On Home Girl/You Are Mine | 7 |

## CAT CAMPBELL & NICKY THOMAS
| | | | |
|---|---|---|---|
| 72 | Pressure Beat PB 5511 | Hammering/PETER TOSH: Medicine Man | 20 |

## CHOKER CAMPBELL
| | | | |
|---|---|---|---|
| 65 | Tamla Motown TMG 517 | Mickey's Monkey/Pride And Joy (as Choker Campbell's Big Band) | 140 |
| 65 | Tamla Motown TMG 517 | Mickey's Monkey/Pride And Joy (as Choker Campbell's Big Band) (DJ copy) | 250 |
| 65 | Tamla Motown TML 11011 | HITS OF THE SIXTIES (LP, as Choker Campbell & His 16-Piece Band) | 125 |

## CORNELL CAMPBELL
| | | | |
|---|---|---|---|
| 63 | Island WI 039 | Rosabelle/Turndown Date (B-side actually "Under The Old Oak Tree") | 30 |
| 63 | Island WI 083 | Each Lonely Night/ROLAND ALPHONSO: Steamline | 20 |
| 64 | Port-O-Jam PJ 4008 | Jericho Road (with Dimple Hinds)/DON DRUMMOND & GROUP: Roll On Sweet Don | 80 |
| 64 | Rio R 38 | Gloria/I'll Be True | 25 |
| 72 | Dynamic DYN 446 | My Confession/AGGROVATORS: Version | 20 |
| 72 | Green Door GD 4042 | Dearest Darling/Star Dust | 20 |
| 72 | Jackpot JP 801 | Queen And The Minstrel/Put Yourself In My Place | 25 |
| 72 | Bullet BU 515 | For Once In My Life/Didn't I? | 25 |
| 73 | Jackpot JP 809 | Pity The Children/You're No Good | 20 |
| 73 | Jackpot JP 814 | Harry Hippy/Just One Kiss | 12 |
| 73 | Green Door GD 4057 | Give Me Love/Help Them O Lord | 20 |
| 73 | Duke DU 158 | Shotgun Wedding/Girl Of My Dreams | 15 |
| 73 | Duke DU 159 | The Very Best I Can/Heading For The Mountains | 15 |
| 73 | Ackee ACK 513 | Give Me A Love/SHORTY PERRY: Message Of Love | 10 |
| 73 | Gayfeet GS 209 | My Baby Just Care For Me/Jah Jah Me Horn Ya | 20 |
| 75 | Action ACT 102 | Natty In A Greenwich Farm/Natty Version | 12 |
| 75 | Angen ANG 101 | Talking Love/AGGROVATORS: Gorgon Dub | 12 |
| 75 | Angen ANG 105 | The Gorgon Speaks/AGGROVATORS: Version | 12 |
| 76 | Angen ANG 122 | A Tear Fell/My True Destination | 12 |
| 76 | Attack ATT 8125 | I Will Never Change/Version | 12 |
| 77 | Third World TW57 | The Investigator/Version | 12 |
| 70s | Rocket VR 001 | Many Rivers To Cross/Many Dub | 10 |
| 76 | Daddy Kool DK001 | I Heart Is Clean/KING TUBBY AND THE OBSERVERS : Zinc Fence | 10 |
| 77 | Nationwide 1018 | Let Me Go Girl/Version | 7 |
| 77 | Terminal TM 104 | I Am A King/Watch And Peep | 10 |
| 78 | Cactus CT 118 | My Country/ Part 2 | 20 |

| 78 | D-Roy 3 | Listen Dread/Version | 10 |
|----|---------|----------------------|-----|
| 78 | Third World 7529 | Blessed Are They/New York City (With I ROY) | 10 |
| 79 | Lord Koos EQ 1001 | Mash You Down/Sweet Talking (12") | 15 |
| 80 | Cha Cha CHAD25 | Rainbow/PETER BROGGS: Never Forget Jah (12") | 30 |
| 80s | Live & Love LLDIS0022 | Nothing Don't Come Easy/Version (12") | 20 |
| 70s | Wambesi TW 004 | I'm A Man/Jah Jah GIve Us Love (12") | 15 |
| 80 | Papa D PD0167 | Rasta Come From Jail (with SASSAFRASS)/100 Pounds of Collie (with PAPA TULLO) | 18 |
| 72 | Trojan TBL 199 | CORNELL CAMPBELL (LP) | 50 |
| 75 | Groundnation GROL 503 | DANCE IN A GREENWICH FARM (LP) | 45 |
| 76 | Angen ANGL 03 | GORGON (LP) | 45 |
| 76 | Third World TWS 301 | STALOWATT (LP) | 40 |
| 78 | Justice JUSLP 09 | ROPIN (LP) | 30 |
| 79 | Striker Lee TSL 104 | NATTY DREAD IN A GREENWICH FARM (LP) | 40 |
| 79 | Burning Sounds BS 1034 | SWEET BABY (LP) | 18 |
| 82 | Starlight SDLP 908 | BOXING (LP) | 25 |
| 83 | Vista Sounds VSLP 4020 | FIGHT AGAINST CORRUPTION (LP) | 15 |
| 00 | Simply Vinyl SVLP 391 | I SHALL NOT REMOVE (2-LP) | 20 |

*(see also Eternals, Don Cornel & Eternals, Clarendonians, Charmers, Stranger & Patsy, GG Allstars)*

## DAVID CAMPBELL

| 67 | Transatlantic TRA 153 | YOUNG BLOOD (LP) | 20 |
|----|-----------------------|------------------|-----|
| 67 | Transatlantic TRA 141 | DAVID CAMPBELL (LP) | 30 |
| 72 | Decca SKL 5139 | SUN WHEEL (LP) | 25 |

## ERROL CAMPBELL

| 77 | Tempus 103 | Jah Man/Jah | 20 |
|----|------------|-------------|-----|
| 76 | Shebazz SHE 001 | Wolves/Follow | 30 |

## ETHNA CAMPBELL

| 64 | Mercury MF 804 | What's Easy For Two Is Hard For One/Again | 20 |
|----|----------------|-------------------------------------------|-----|
| 64 | Mercury MF 816 | Girls Like Boys/Five Minutes More | 10 |
| 74 | Philips 6382138 | FOR THE GOOD TIMES (LP) | 15 |

## GLEN CAMPBELL

| 61 | Top Rank JAR 596 | Turn Around, Look At Me/Brenda | 7 |
|----|------------------|--------------------------------|-----|
| 69 | Ember EMB S 263 | Galveston/Everytime I Itch I Wind Up Scratching You (p/s) | 5 |

*(see also Sagittarius, Jimmy Slade)*

## IAN CAMPBELL (FOLK) GROUP

| 68 | Transatlantic TRA 163 | THE CIRCLE GAME (LP) | 15 |
|----|-----------------------|----------------------|-----|
| 71 | Acorn CF 233 | HOPE IS A STAR (LP) | 30 |
| 71 | Argo ZFB 13 | THE SUN IS BURNING (LP) | 15 |

*(see also Dave Swarbrick)*

## ISOBEL CAMPBELL

| 03 | Snowstorm STORM 024LP | AMORINO (LP, 1500 only) | 20 |
|----|-----------------------|-------------------------|-----|
| 06 | V2 VVR1043451 | MILKWHITE SHEETS (LP) | 15 |

*(see also Belle & Sebastian)*

## ISOBEL CAMPBELL & MARK LANEGAN

| 06 | V2 VVR5036037 | Ramblin Man/Further Into The Night | 8 |
|----|---------------|------------------------------------|-----|
| 08 | V2 VVR5050637 | Who Built The Road/Wild Is The Night | 8 |
| 06 | V2 VVR1635821 | BALLAD OF THE BROKEN SEAS (LP) | 50 |
| 08 | V2 VVR 1050621 | SUNDAY AT DEVIL DIRT (LP) | 30 |
| 10 | V2 VVR 745755 | HAWK (LP) | 20 |

*(see also Mark Lanegan, Solusavers, Belle & Sebastian)*

## JIMMY CAMPBELL

| 69 | Fontana TF 1009 | On A Monday/Dear Marge (in p/s) | 35 |
|----|-----------------|---------------------------------|-----|
| 69 | Fontana TF 1009 | On A Monday/Dear Marge | 25 |
| 70 | Fontana TF 1076 | Lyanna/Frankie Joe | 6 |
| 70 | Fontana 6007 025 | Don't Leave Me Now/So Lonely Without You | 6 |
| 69 | Fontana STL 5508 | SON OF ANASTASIA (LP, black/silver label) | 120 |
| 70 | Vertigo 6360 010 | HALF BAKED (LP, gatefold sleeve, large swirl label) | 150 |
| 72 | Philips 6308 100 | JIMMY CAMPBELL'S ALBUM (LP, black/silver label) | 150 |

*(see also Kirkbys, 23rd Turnoff, Rockin' Horse)*

## JO-ANN CAMPBELL

| 58 | London HLU 8536 | Wait A Minute/It's True | 50 |
|----|-----------------|-------------------------|-----|
| 60 | HMV POP 776 | Bobby, Bobby, Bobby/A Kookie Little Paradise | 25 |
| 61 | HMV POP 873 | Motorcycle Michael/Puka Puka Pants | 20 |
| 62 | HMV POP 1003 | You Made Me Love You/I Changed My Mind Jack | 20 |
| 62 | Columbia DB 4889 | I'm The Girl From Wolverton Mountain/Sloppy Joe | 10 |
| 62 | Cameo Parkway CP 237 | Mr Fix It Man/Let Me Do It My Way | 15 |
| 63 | Cameo Parkway CP 249 | Mother Please/Waiting For Love | 15 |

## JUNIOR CAMPBELL

| 73 | Deram 387 | Sweet Illusion/Ode To Karen | 6 |
|----|-----------|-----------------------------|-----|
| 74 | Deram SML 1106 | SECOND TIME AROUND (LP) | 18 |

*(see also Marmalade, Clan, Dean Ford & Gaylords)*

## LLOYD CAMPBELL

| 76 | Love LOV 2 | FIGHTING DUB (LP, artist commonly listed as Skin, Flesh & Bone) | 50 |
|----|------------|----------------------------------------------------------------|-----|

## MARTIN CAMPBELL

| 95 | Raghga Delic LIC 1 | Wicked Rule/Dub/Version/Drums (12") | 20 |
|----|--------------------|-------------------------------------|-----|
| 97 | Channel 1 (UK) NXTB 007 | Wicked Rule/Remix Next Vs/Wicked Dub/Everywhere/I Walk/Next Version/Dub (12") | 18 |
| 90 | Jah Works JW 002T | Who Can We Run To?/SISTER NETIFA: Woman Determined (12") | 20 |
| 91 | Jah Works JW015 | Got To Pray/Praying Dub (12") | 20 |

| 98 | Channel 1 TBX 010 | ROOTSMAN - THE REAL THING (LP) | 25 |
| 90 | Jah Works JW008P | THE DREAM IS OVER (LP) | 15 |
| 02 | Channel 1 LOGLP 015 | HISTORICAL TRACKS (1978-1981) THE FOUNDATION (LP) | 15 |

## ROY CAMPBELL (& JAZZBO JASPERS)
| 68 | Giant GN 41 | Another Saturday Night/Wonderful World (with Jazzbo Jaspers) | 12 |
| 68 | Jolly JY 003 | Suzette/Engine Engine Number Nine | 15 |

## PATRICK CAMPBELL-LYONS
| 73 | Sovereign SOV 115 | Everybody Should Fly A Kite/I Think I Want Him Too | 15 |
| 73 | Sovereign SOV 119 | Out On The Road/Me And My Friend | 15 |
| 77 | Electric WOT 12 | That's What My Guru Said Last Night/The Whistling Fiddler | 5 |
| 73 | Sovereign SVNA 7258 | ME AND MY FRIEND (LP, gatefold sleeve) | 250 |
| 81 | Public PUBL 1 | THE ELECTRIC PLOUGH (LP) | 20 |

*(see also Nirvana [U.K.], Pica, Hat & Tie, Aquila, Informants)*

## CAMPER VAN BEETHOVEN
| 86 | Rough Trade ROUGH 95 | TELEPHONE FREE LANDSLIDE VICTORY (LP, with insert) | 18 |
| 86 | Rough Trade RT 161 | TAKE THE SKINHEADS BOWLING (LP) | 15 |
| 87 | Rough Trade RT 109 | CAMPER VAN BEETHOVEN (LP) | 15 |

## RAY CAMPI
| 74 | Injun EP 200 | ROCK 'N' ROLL (EP) | 10 |

## CAN
| 73 | United Artists UP 35596 | Moonshake/Future Days (Edit) | 20 |
| 73 | United Artists UP 35506 | Spoon/I'm So Green | 20 |
| 74 | United Artists UP 35749 | Dizzy Dizzy (Edit)/Splash (Edit) | 10 |
| 76 | Virgin VS 153 | I Want More/... And More | 6 |
| 76 | Virgin VS 166 | Silent Night/Cascade Waltz | 5 |
| 77 | Virgin VS 172 | Don't Say No/Return | 5 |
| 78 | Lightning LIG 545 | Can-Can/Can Can Disco | 5 |
| 83 | Cherry Red CHERRY 57 | Moonshake/Turtles Have Short Legs/One More Night (12") | 20 |
| 69 | United Artists UAS 29094 | MONSTER MOVIE (LP, burgundy label) | 150 |
| 70 | United Artists UAS 29283 | SOUNDTRACKS (LP) | 40 |
| 71 | Utd. Artists UAD 60009/10 | TAGO MAGO (2-LP, flip-top sleeve) | 150 |
| 72 | United Artists UAS 29414 | EGE BAMYASI (LP, with inner sleeve) | 60 |
| 73 | United Artists UAS 29505 | FUTURE DAYS (LP) | 50 |
| 74 | United Artists UAG 29673 | SOON OVER BABALUMA (LP, original silver sleeve) | 50 |
| 74 | United Artists USP 103 | LIMITED EDITION (LP) | 50 |
| 75 | Virgin V 2041 | LANDED (LP) | 20 |
| 76 | Caroline CAD 3001 | UNLIMITED EDITION (2-LP, gatefold sleeve) | 40 |
| 76 | Sunset SLS 50400 | OPENER (LP) | 20 |
| 76 | Virgin V 2071 | FLOW MOTION (LP, some stickered stating "featuring the hit single I Want More") | 18 |
| 77 | Virgin V 2079 | SAW DELIGHT (LP, with insert) | 20 |
| 78 | Lightning LIP 4 | OUT OF REACH (LP) | 15 |
| 78 | United Artists UDM 105/6 | CANNABALISM (2-LP, gatefold sleeve) | 20 |
| 89 | Mercury 838883 | RITE TIME (LP) | 18 |
| 97 | Mute SPOON39/40 | SACRILEGE (3-LP, gatefold) | 20 |
| 07 | Mute SPOON 008 | EGE BAMYASI (LP, reissue) | 15 |
| 12 | Mute SPOON 55 | THE LOST TAPES (5-LP box set, booklet) | 50 |
| 12 | Spoon CDSPOON5 | THE LOST TAPES (3-CD boxed set, booklet) | 25 |

## CANAAN
| 73 | Dovetail DOVE 3 | CANAAN (LP) | 25 |
| 76 | Myrrh MYR 1042 | OUT OF THE WILDERNESS (LP, with inner sleeve) | 20 |

## LOS CANARIOS
| 67 | Major Minor MM 502 | Three Two One Ah/What Can I Do For You | 50 |
| 67 | Major Minor MM 532 | Get On Your Knees/Keep On The Right Side | 35 |

## CANCER
| 90 | Vinyl Solution SOL 22 | TO THE GORY END (LP) | 25 |
| 91 | Vinyl Solution SOL 28 | DEATH SHALL RISE (LP) | 20 |
| 93 | Vinyl Solution SOL 35 | THE SINS OF MANKIND (LP) | 25 |

## CANDIDO
| 79 | Salsoul Sa 8520 | DANCIN AND PRANCIN (LP) | 18 |

## CANDLE FACTORY
| 77 | CAVS | NIGHTSHIFT (LP, private pressing) | 80 |

## CANDLELIGHT
| 67 | CBS 2002507 | That's What I Want/The Happy Days Of Summer | 25 |

## CANDLEMASS
| 87 | Active ATV 3 | NIGHTFALL (LP) | 15 |
| 89 | Music For Nations MFN 95 | TALES OF CREATION (LP) | 15 |
| 88 | Active Records ACT LP7 | ANCIENT DREAMS (LP, insert) | 20 |
| 03 | Powerline PRLP 010 | DIAMONDS OF DOOM (2-LP, white vinyl, gatefold sleeve with iron-on transfer, 1000 only) | 20 |

## CANDY
| 69 | Emerald MD 1119 | Little Bit Of Soul/Signs Of Love | 20 |
| 69 | Grape GR 3017 | Ace Of Hearts/BILLY JACK: Bet Yer Life I Do | 20 |
| 70 | Big Shot BI 599 | Ace Of Hearts/BILLY JACK: Bet Your Life | 10 |

## ICHO CANDY
| 88 | Selah DEX 007 | Cool Down Sufferer/FISH CLARKE: Carry You Woman Go A Dance (12") | 20 |
| 93 | Jah Shaka SHAKA 948 | GLORY TO THE KING (LP) | 18 |

## CANDY CHOIR
| 66 | Parlophone R 5472 | Silence Is Golden/Shake Hands (And Come Out Crying) | 15 |

# CANDY DATES

| | | | |
|---|---|---|---|
| 67 | CBS 3061 | Children And Flowers/Marianne | 10 |
| 68 | CBS 3305 | Alexander's Ragtime Band/No Grey Skies | 10 |
| 70 | Polydor 56369 | Why Do You Cry My Love/Lucky Jim | 5 |

*(see also Summer Set, Barry Ryan)*

## CANDY DATES
| | | | |
|---|---|---|---|
| 65 | Pye 7N 15944 | A Day Just Like That/Well I Do | 12 |

## CANDY FLOSS
| | | | |
|---|---|---|---|
| 72 | Polydor 2041360 | Delta Queen/Looking Over My Shoulder | 8 |

## CANDY & KISSES
| | | | |
|---|---|---|---|
| 65 | Cameo Parkway C 336 | The 81/Two Happy People | 150 |
| 65 | Cameo Parkway C 336 | The 81/Two Happy People (DJ copy) | 200 |
| 85 | Kent TOWN 104 | Mr Creator/CHUCK JACKSON: Hand It Over (withdrawn) | 40 |

## CANDYLAND
| | | | |
|---|---|---|---|
| 91 | Yes 1 | Bitter Moon/I'm A Good Girl (p/s) | 6 |

## CANDYMEN
| | | | |
|---|---|---|---|
| 67 | HMV POP 1612 | Georgia Pines/Movies In My Mind | 10 |

## PENNY CANDY
| | | | |
|---|---|---|---|
| 60 | Top Rank JAR 328 | Come On Over/They Said | 7 |

## CANDY ROCK
| | | | |
|---|---|---|---|
| 75 | Philips 6006 442 | Captain Captain/Pocahontas (some with photo) | 12 |

## CANE
| | | | |
|---|---|---|---|
| 78 | Lightning GIL 31 | 3 BY 3 EP (p/s) | 25 |

## CANIS MAJOR
| | | | |
|---|---|---|---|
| 80 | Gem GEMLP 109 | BUTTERFLY QUEEN (LP) | 30 |

*(see also Girlschool)*

## JAMES CANN BAND
| | | | |
|---|---|---|---|
| 82 | LJS LJS 001 | Love Don't Know Your Name/Hush Hush We Can Boogie | 15 |

## CANNED HEAT
| | | | |
|---|---|---|---|
| 68 | Liberty | Rollin' And Tumblin'/Bullfrog Blues (unreleased) | 0 |
| 68 | Liberty LBF 15090 | On The Road Again/The World In A Jug | 8 |
| 69 | Liberty LBF 15169 | Going Up The Country/One Kind Favour | 6 |
| 69 | Liberty LBF 15200 | Time Was/Low Down | 8 |
| 69 | Liberty LBF 15255 | Poor Moon/Sic 'Em Pigs | 8 |
| 69 | Liberty LBF 15302 | Let's Work Together/I'm Her Man | 6 |
| 70 | Liberty LBF 15350 | Sugar Bee/Shake It And Break It | 8 |
| 70 | Pye International 7N 25513 | Spoonful/Big Road Blues | 12 |
| 70 | Liberty LBF 15395 | Future Blues/Skat | 8 |
| 70 | Liberty LBF 15429 | Christmas Blues/Do Not Enter | 6 |
| 71 | Liberty LBF 15439 | Wooly Bully/My Time Ain't Long | 6 |
| 72 | United Artists UP 35348 | Rockin' With The King (with Little Richard)/I Don't Care What You Tell Me | 6 |
| 73 | United Artists UP 35562 | Keep It Clean/You Can Run But You Sure Can't Hide | 6 |
| 67 | Liberty LBL/LBS 83059E | CANNED HEAT (LP) | 70 |
| 68 | Liberty LBL/LBS 83103 | BOOGIE WITH CANNED HEAT (LP) | 30 |
| 69 | Liberty LDS 84001E | LIVING THE BLUES (2-LP, gatefold sleeve) | 30 |
| 69 | Liberty LBS 83239 | HALLELUJAH (LP, gatefold sleeve) | 25 |
| 70 | Pye Intl. NSPL 28129 | VINTAGE HEAT (LP) | 30 |
| 70 | Liberty LBS 83303 | CANNED HEAT COOKBOOK (LP) | 15 |
| 70 | Liberty LBS 83364 | FUTURE BLUES (LP, gatefold sleeve) | 20 |
| 71 | Liberty LPS 103/4 | HOOKER'N'HEAT (2-LP, gatefold sleeve, with John Lee Hooker) | 35 |
| 72 | United Artists UAG 29304 | HISTORICAL FIGURES AND ANCIENT HEADS (LP, gatefold sleeve) | 15 |
| 73 | United Artists UAS 29455 | THE NEW AGE (LP) | 15 |
| 76 | United Artists REM 407 | CANNED HEAT (EP) | 10 |

*(see also Harvey Mandel, John Lee Hooker)*

## CANNIBAL & HEADHUNTERS
| | | | |
|---|---|---|---|
| 65 | Stateside SS 403 | Land Of A Thousand Dances/I'll Show You How To Love Me | 30 |
| 67 | CBS 62942 | LAND OF A 1000 DANCES (LP) | 40 |

## CANNIBAL CORPSE
| | | | |
|---|---|---|---|
| 93 | Metal Blade MZORRO 57 | HAMMER SMASHED FACE EP (12") | 10 |
| 90 | Metal Blade ZORRO 12 | EATEN BACK TO LIFE (LP, inner) | 15 |

## CANNIBALS
| | | | |
|---|---|---|---|
| 78 | Big Cock F-UK 1 | Good Guys/Nothing Takes The Place Of You (printed paper bag sleeve) | 5 |
| 85 | Hit Records REEBEE 2 | Christmas Rock 'n' Roll/New Year's Eve Song (doublepack in stocking) | 6 |

*(see also Count Bishops)*

## PHIL CANNING
| | | | |
|---|---|---|---|
| 79 | Woodbine St. WSR 002 | Sell Out/Underground (p/s) | 40 |

## FREDDY CANNON
| | | | |
|---|---|---|---|
| 59 | Top Rank JAR 135 | Tallahassee Lassie/You Know | 12 |
| 59 | Top Rank JAR 135 | Tallahassee Lassie/You Know (78) | 25 |
| 59 | Top Rank JAR 207 | Okefenokee/Kookie Hat | 7 |
| 59 | Top Rank JAR 247 | Way Down Yonder In New Orleans/Fractured | 5 |
| 60 | Top Rank JAR 309 | California, Here I Come/Indiana | 5 |
| 60 | Top Rank JAR 334 | Chattanooga Shoeshine Boy/Boston (My Home Town) | 5 |
| 60 | Top Rank JAR 369 | The Urge/Jump Over | 5 |
| 60 | Top Rank JAR 407 | Happy Shades Of Blue/Guernavaca Choo Choo | 5 |
| 60 | Top Rank JAR 518 | Humdinger/My Blue Heaven | 7 |
| 61 | Top Rank JAR 548 | Muskrat Rumble/Two Thousand 88 | 5 |
| 61 | Top Rank JAR 568 | Buzz Buzz A Diddle It/Opportunity | 20 |

| 61 | Top Rank JAR 579 | Transistor Sister/Walk To The Moon | 5 |
|----|------------------|-----------------------------------|---|
| 61 | Top Rank JAR 592 | For Me And My Gal/Blue Plate Special | 5 |
| 62 | Top Rank JAR 609 | Teen Queen Of The Week/Wild Guy | 5 |
| 62 | Stateside SS 101 | Palisades Park/June July And August | 5 |
| 62 | Stateside SS 118 | What's Gonna Happen When Summer's Done/Broadway | 10 |
| 62 | Stateside SS 134 | If You Were A Rock & Roll Record/The Truth Ruth | 10 |
| 63 | Stateside SS 155 | Come On And Love Me/Four Letter Man | 10 |
| 63 | Stateside SS 183 | The Ups And Downs Of Love/It's Been Nice | 10 |
| 63 | Stateside SS 201 | Patty Baby/Betty Jean | 20 |
| 63 | Stateside SS 220 | Everybody Monkey/Oh Gloria | 5 |
| 64 | Stateside SS 260 | That's The Way Girls Are/Do What The Hippies Do | 5 |
| 64 | Warner Bros WB 123 | Abigail Beecher/All American Girl | 5 |
| 64 | Stateside SS 298 | Sweet Georgia Brown/What A Party | 5 |
| 65 | Warner Bros WB 5645 | Action/Beechwood City | 10 |
| 66 | Warner Bros WB 5693 | The Dedication Song/Come On Come On | 6 |
| 69 | London HLK 10252 | Beautiful Downtown Burbank/If You Give Me A Title | 5 |
| 79 | Hot Rock 003 | Hey Punk Rocker/At The Disco Down | 5 |
| 60 | Top Rank JKP 2058 | THE EXPLOSIVE FREDDY (BOOM! BOOM!) CANNON (EP) | 15 |
| 60 | Top Rank JKP 2066 | FOUR DIRECT HITS (EP) | 15 |
| 61 | Top Rank JKP 3010 | ON TARGET (EP) | 15 |
| 62 | Stateside SE 1002 | BLAST OFF WITH FREDDY CANNON (EP) | 15 |
| 60 | Top Rank 25/018 | THE EXPLOSIVE FREDDY CANNON (LP) | 20 |
| 61 | Top Rank 35/106 | FREDDY CANNON SINGS HAPPY SHADES OF BLUE (LP) | 25 |
| 61 | Top Rank 35/113 | FREDDY CANNON FAVOURITES (LP) | 25 |
| 63 | Stateside SL 10013 | BANG ON (LP) | 25 |
| 64 | Stateside SL 10062 | STEPS OUT (LP) | 25 |
| 64 | Warner Bros WM/WS 8153 | FREDDY CANNON (LP) | 20 |

*(see also Danny & Juniors)*

## JUDY CANNON
| 65 | Pye 7N 15900 | The Very First Day I Met You/Hello Heartache | 50 |
|----|--------------|----------------------------------------------|----|

## SEAN CANNON
| 77 | Cottage COT 411 | ROVING JOURNEYMAN (LP) | 30 |
|----|-----------------|------------------------|----|

## CONROY CANNON
| 69 | Pama PM 769 | Oh Happy Day/Can't Get Along Without You | 8 |
|----|-------------|------------------------------------------|---|
| 69 | Atlantic 584 305 | My Bunny/Good Boy | 8 |

## CANNON BALL & JOHNNY MELODY
| 69 | Big Shot BI 518 | Parapinto/Cool Hand Luke | 100 |
|----|-----------------|--------------------------|-----|

*(see also Carl Bryan, King Cannon, Johnny Moore, Jackie Mittoo, Royals)*

## CANNONBALLS
| 61 | Coral Q 72428 | Cannonball Caboose/New Orleans Beat | 5 |
|----|---------------|-------------------------------------|---|
| 61 | Coral Q 72431 | Lullaby Of Birdland/Calliope Boogie | 5 |

## CANNON BROTHERS
| 65 | Brit WI 1003 | Turn Your Eyes To Me/Don't Stop Now | 18 |
|----|--------------|-------------------------------------|----|

## CANNONS
| 60 | Decca F 11269 | I Didn't Know The Gun Was Loaded/My Guy's Come Back | 5 |
|----|---------------|-----------------------------------------------------|---|
| 61 | Columbia DB 4724 | Bush Fire/Juicy | 10 |

## CANNY FETTLE
| 75 | Tradition TSR 023 | VARRY CANNY (LP) | 30 |
|----|-------------------|------------------|----|
| 77 | Tradition TSR 027 | TRIP TO HARROGATE (LP) | 18 |

## CAN'T STOP
| 80 | Can't Stop CAN 1 | IT'S GETTING DARK AGAIN EP | 10 |
|----|------------------|----------------------------|----|

## CANYON
| 75 | RCA RCA 2112 | Top Of The World/Boogie Down Broadway | 15 |
|----|--------------|---------------------------------------|----|

## CAPABILITY BROWN
| 72 | Charisma CB 193 | Wake Up Little Sister/Windfall | 6 |
|----|-----------------|--------------------------------|---|
| 73 | Charisma CB 207 | Midnight Cruiser/Silent Sounds | 6 |
| 72 | Charisma BCP 7 | Liar/SPREADEAGLE: Nightingale Lane (demo in p/s) | 10 |
| 73 | Charisma CB 217 | Liar/Keep Death Off The Road (Drive On The Pavement) | 6 |
| 70s | Charisma BCP 7 | War (p/s) | 6 |
| 72 | Charisma CAS 1056 | FROM SCRATCH (LP, lyric inner sleeve, pink 'scroll' label) | 50 |
| 73 | Charisma CAS 1068 | VOICE (LP, gatefold sleeve, large 'Mad Hatter' label) | 30 |
| 74 | Charisma Perspective CS 5 | LIAR (LP) | 15 |

*(see also Unit 4+2, Tony Rivers & Castaways, Fuzzy Duck)*

## JIM CAPALDI
| 74 | Island WIP 6198 | It's All Up To You/Whale Meat Again | 5 |
|----|-----------------|-------------------------------------|---|
| 72 | Island ILPS 9187 | OH HOW WE DANCED (LP, gatefold sleeve, pink rim label) | 15 |
| 74 | Island ILPS 9254 | WHALE MEAT AGAIN (LP, pink rim label) | 15 |
| 77 | Island ILPS 9497 | PLAY IT BY EAR (LP) | 15 |

*(see also Hellions, Traffic)*

## CAPE KENNEDY CONSTRUCTION CO.
| 69 | President PT 265 | The First Steps On The Moon/Armageddon | 70 |
|----|------------------|----------------------------------------|----|

## CAPES & MASKS
| 65 | Fontana TL 5339 | COMIC BOOK HEROES (LP) | 50 |
|----|-----------------|------------------------|----|
| 65 | Nevis NEV R005 | COMIC BOOK HEROES (LP) | 18 |

## CAPES OF GOOD HOPE
| 66 | Stateside SS 577 | Winter's Children/If My Monique Could Only Dance | 15 |
|----|------------------|--------------------------------------------------|----|

## CAPITAL LETTERS
| | | |
|---|---|---|
| 77 | Greensleeves GRED 2 | Smoking My Ganja/Natty Walk (12")..................................30 |
| 79 | Greensleeves GRED 16 | UK Skanking/Run Run Run (12")...................................30 |
| 79 | Greensleeves GREL 7 | HEADLINE NEWS (LP)..............................................28 |

## CAPITOL K
| | | |
|---|---|---|
| 99 | Planet Mu ZIQ 015 | Postcard/JEGA: Untitled (100 in numbered p/s, those un-numbered = £4)..........10 |

## CAPITOLS (U.K.)
| | | |
|---|---|---|
| 66 | Pye 7N 17025 | Honey And Wine/Boulavogue........................................15 |

## CAPITOLS (U.S.)
| | | |
|---|---|---|
| 66 | Atlantic 584 004 | Cool Jerk/Hello Stranger.........................................25 |
| 72 | Atlantic 10205 | Ain't That Terrible/Zig-Zagging....................................8 |
| 76 | Contempo Rarities 9030 | Cool Jerk/Ain't That Terrible (reissue)..............................5 |

*(see also Three Caps)*

## CAPLO BANAAL
| | | |
|---|---|---|
| 83 | Rambert RAM THREE | She Loves The Money/Is This Love (p/s)..............................45 |

## CAPOEIRA TWINS
| | | |
|---|---|---|
| 99 | Blowpop Records BLOWP 001 | 4 x 3 (12")..................................................15 |

## CAPONE
| | | |
|---|---|---|
| 98 | Hardleaders HL 028 | Friday/Alaska (12")............................................30 |

## ANDY CAPP
| | | |
|---|---|---|
| 69 | Treasure Isle TI 7052 | Pop-A-Top/RICO: The Lion Speaks..................................18 |
| 70 | Duke DU 69 | The Law Parts 1 & 2............................................25 |
| 70 | Duke DU 71 | Poppy Show/Pop-A-Top (Part 2)..................................12 |

## CAPPO
| | | |
|---|---|---|
| 99 | Son Records SON011 | CAP 3000 (EP)................................................10 |
| 00 | Son Records SON016 | CODEX (EP)..................................................10 |
| 00 | Blunted Astronaut BAR 12 TWE 0007 | THOUSAND WORD EXODUS (EP)...................................10 |
| 14 | Boot BEP 011 | THE BOOT (EP, 100 copies only)..................................30 |
| 10 | Son 047 | GENGHIS (LP, 200 only).........................................20 |

## CAPPO & STYLY CEE
| | | |
|---|---|---|
| 11 | SON 050 | FALL OUT (LP, 200 only hand-sprayed sleeve).........................25 |

## AL CAPPS
| | | |
|---|---|---|
| 73 | Stateside SS 2214 | Shangri-La/Magician..............................................7 |

## CAPREEZ
| | | |
|---|---|---|
| 79 | Grapevine 113 | How To Make A Sad Man Glad/It's Good To Be Home Again..................8 |

## DANNY CAPRI
| | | |
|---|---|---|
| 55 | Capitol CL 14265 | Desirable/I Do, I Do..............................................7 |
| 55 | Capitol CL 14302 | Don't Make A Liar Out Of Me/Angelica................................7 |

## CAPRICORN
| | | |
|---|---|---|
| 70 | MCA MK 5050 | Liverpool Hello/How Did You Find Me.................................6 |

*(see also Marty Wilde)*

## CAPRIS
| | | |
|---|---|---|
| 61 | Columbia DB 4605 | There's A Moon Out Tonight/Indian Girl..............................80 |

## CAPTAIN BEEFHEART & HIS MAGIC BAND
### SINGLES
| | | |
|---|---|---|
| 68 | Pye International 7N 25443 | Yellow Brick Road/Abba Zabba.....................................40 |
| 68 | A&M AMS 726 | Moonchild/Who Do You Think You're Fooling..........................30 |
| 73 | Reprise K 14233 | Too Much Time/My Head Is My Only House Unless It Rains.................12 |
| 74 | Virgin VS 110 | Upon The My-Oh-My/Magic Be.......................................5 |
| 78 | Buddah BDS 466 | Sure 'Nuff 'N Yes I Do/Electricity...................................7 |
| 78 | MCA MCA 366 | Hard Workin' Man (Jack Nitzsche featuring Captain Beefheart)/ JACK NITZSCHE: Coke Machine...................................................................6 |
| 82 | Virgin VS 534 | Ice Cream For Crow/Light Reflected Off The Oceans Of The Moon............7 |

### EPs
| | | |
|---|---|---|
| 71 | A&M AME 600 | DIDDY WAH DIDDY (promo only in p/s)..............................250 |
| 79 | Virgin SIXPACK 1 | SIX-PACK/SIX TRACK (picture disc, die-cut p/s with stand, 5,000 only)........15 |
| 82 | Virgin VS 534 12 | LIGHT REFLECTED OFF THE OCEANS OF THE MOON (12" EP, p/s)...........12 |
| 84 | A&M AMY 226 | THE LEGENDARY A&M SESSIONS (12" EP/mini-LP, Diddy Wah Diddy EP plus "Here I Am, I Always Am")...........................................................15 |
| 86 | Edsel BLIMP 902 | THE LEGENDARY A&M SESSIONS (12" EP, reissue).......................15 |

### ALBUMS
| | | |
|---|---|---|
| 68 | Pye Intl. NPL 28110 | SAFE AS MILK (mono, flipback sleeve)..............................150 |
| 68 | Liberty LBL 83172 | STRICTLY PERSONAL (gatefold sleeve, mono).........................120 |
| 68 | Liberty LBS 83172 | STRICTLY PERSONAL (gatefold sleeve, stereo)........................80 |
| 69 | Straight STS 1053 | TROUT MASK REPLICA (2-LP, gatefold sleeve)........................200 |
| 69 | Buddah 623171 | SAFE AS MILK (LP, reissue, stereo)................................40 |
| 69 | Pye/Marble Arch MAL 1117 | SAFE AS MILK (LP, reissue, mono, 10 tracks not 12)...................40 |
| 70 | Straight STS 1063 | LICK MY DECALS OFF, BABY.......................................100 |
| 70 | Buddah 2349 002 | DROPOUT BOOGIE (stereo reissue of "Safe As Milk")...................30 |
| 71 | Buddah 2365 002 | MIRROR MAN (gatefold die-cut sleeve)..............................50 |
| 72 | Reprise K 44162 | THE SPOTLIGHT KID (tan 'riverboat' label, with lyric card insert)...........35 |
| 72 | Reprise K 44162 | THE SPOTLIGHT KID (tan 'riverboat' label, without lyric card insert).........15 |
| 72 | Reprise K 54007 | CLEAR SPOT (PVC sleeve with card insert)...........................40 |
| 73 | Reprise K 44244 | LICK MY DECALS OFF, BABY (reissue)...............................18 |
| 74 | Virgin V 2015 | UNCONDITIONALLY GUARANTEED ('two virgins' label)..................20 |

| 74 | Buddah BDLP 4004 | MIRROR MAN | 20 |
|---|---|---|---|
| 74 | Virgin V 2023 | BLUEJEANS & MOONBEAMS ('two virgins' label) | 20 |
| 75 | Reprise K 64026 | TROUT MASK REPLICA (2-LP, gatefold sleeve, tan 'riverboat' label, matt sleeve, 'Captain Beefhart' on labels) | 50 |
| 76 | Reprise K 84006 | TWO ORIGINALS OF CAPTAIN BEEFHEART (2-LP, reissue of Lick My Decals Off, Baby & "The Spotlight Kid") | 20 |
| 77 | Pye FILD 008 | THE FILE SERIES (2-LP, reissue of "Safe As Milk" & "Mirror Man", die-cut sleeve with inners) | 25 |
| 79 | Virgin V 2149 | SHINY BEAST (BAT CHAIN PULLER) | 20 |
| 80 | Virgin V 2172 | DOC AT THE RADAR STATION | 25 |
| 81 | PRT NCP 1004 | SAFE AS MILK (LP, reissue, 10 track version omits 'I'm Glad' and 'Grown So Ugly') | 15 |
| 70s | Reprise K 64026 | TROUT MASK REPLICA (2-LP, gatefold sleeve, 2nd re-pressing, tan 'riverboat' label, soft laminated sleeve) | 25 |
| 82 | Virgin V 2237 | ICE CREAM FOR CROW (with inner sleeve) | 18 |
| 84 | PRT NCP 1004 | SAFE AS MILK (LP, reissue) | 20 |
| 99 | Buddah 91751 | SAFE AS MILK (2-LP reissue) | 20 |
| 08 | Oz It Morpheus OZITLP 8006 | DUST SUCKER (2-LP) | 20 |

*(see also Mu, Frank Zappa, Jack Nitzsche)*

## CAPTAIN BEYOND
| 72 | Capricorn K 47503 | CAPTAIN BEYOND (LP) | 30 |
|---|---|---|---|

*(see also Deep Purple, Iron Butterfly)*

## CAPTAIN JESUS AND THE SUNRAY TEAM
| 92 | Criminal Jesus 2 | ALL THANKS TO THE LORD JESUS CHRIST AMEN (LP) | 40 |
|---|---|---|---|
| 94 | Criminal (No Cat. No.) | THE DAY THAT NEBULON EXPLODED (LP) | 40 |

*(see also Hawkwind)*

## CAPTAIN LOCKHEED & THE STARFIGHTERS
| 73 | United Artists UP 35543 | Ejection/Catch A Falling Starfighter (p/s) | 25 |
|---|---|---|---|
| 73 | United Artists UP 35543 | Ejection/Catch A Falling Starfighter (different mix of A-side, no p/s) | 10 |

*(see also Robert Calvert)*

## CAPTAIN MARRYAT
| 74 | Thor THOR 1007 S | CAPTAIN MARRYAT (LP, 200 only) | 2000 |
|---|---|---|---|
| 10 | Shadoks S114 | CAPTAIN MARRYAT (LP, reissue) | 35 |

## CAPTAIN MOG & PRIVATE SIGH
| 80 | Governor GOV 1 | Island Sea/Captains Protest Dub (p/s) | 5 |
|---|---|---|---|

## CAPTAIN ROCK & SKYRIDERS
| 72 | Crystal CR 7028 | Luppy Lu/Together | 8 |
|---|---|---|---|

## CAPTAIN SINBAD
| 83 | Oak Sound OSLP 002 | AGAIN (LP) | 25 |
|---|---|---|---|
| 84 | Greensleeves GREL 34 | THE SEVEN VOYAGES OF SINBAD (LP) | 25 |

## CAPTAIN ZERO
| 75 | Gull GULS 23 | Space Walk/I'm Only An Elf | 6 |
|---|---|---|---|

## CAPTAIN ZORRO
| 79 | Gem GEM 12 11 | Phantasm/Sure Can Boogie (12", yellow vinyl) | 12 |
|---|---|---|---|

## C.A. QUINTET
| 83 | Psycho PSYCHO 12 | TRIP THROUGH HELL (LP, reissue of U.S. 60s LP) | 15 |
|---|---|---|---|

## CARAVAN
| 69 | Verve VS 1518 | A Place Of My Own/Ride | 60 |
|---|---|---|---|
| 70 | Decca F 13063 | If I Could Do It All Over Again, I'd Do It All Over You/Hello, Hello | 20 |
| 71 | Decca F 23125 | Love To Love You (And Tonight Pigs Will Fly)/Golf Girl | 20 |
| 75 | Decca FR 13599 | Stuck In A Hole/Lover | 5 |
| 76 | BTM SBT 104 | All The Way (With John Wayne's Single-Handed Liberation Of Paris)/ Chiefs And Indians (p/s) | 6 |
| 77 | Arista ARIST 110 | Better By Far/Silver Strings | 5 |
| 80 | Kingdom KV 8009 | Heartbreaker/It's Never Too Late (p/s) | 6 |
| 68 | Verve VLP 6011 | CARAVAN (LP, 'pillar' sleeve, mono, brown/white label, with "sold in the U.K." text) | 500 |
| 68 | Verve SVLP 6011 | CARAVAN (LP, 'pillar' sleeve, stereo) | 400 |
| 70 | Decca SKL 5052 | IF I COULD DO IT ALL OVER AGAIN, I'D DO IT ALL OVER YOU (LP, boxed logo) | 80 |
| 71 | Deram SDL-R 1 | IN THE LAND OF GREY AND PINK (LP, gatefold sleeve, 1st pressing with brown/white label) | 120 |
| 71 | Deram SDL-R 1 | IN THE LAND OF GREY AND PINK (LP, gatefold sleeve, later pressing with red/white label) | 40 |
| 72 | Deram SDL 8 | WATERLOO LILY (LP, gatefold sleeve, 1st pressing brown/white large Deram labels. SDL8 on sleeve and label) | 150 |
| 72 | Deram SDL 8 | WATERLOO LILY (LP, gatefold sleeve later pressing with red/white labels and SDL-R 8 on labels and sleeves) | 20 |
| 72 | MGM 2353 058 | CARAVAN (LP, reissue, blue/gold label) | 25 |
| 73 | Deram SDL-R 12 | FOR GIRLS WHO GROW PLUMP IN THE NIGHT (LP, gatefold sleeve, red/white label) | 30 |
| 74 | Decca SML-R 1110 | CARAVAN AND THE NEW SYMPHONIA (LIVE AT DRURY LANE) (LP, red/white label) | 20 |
| 75 | Decca SKL-R 5210 | CUNNING STUNTS (LP) | 20 |
| 76 | Decca DKL-R 8/1 & 8/2 | CANTERBURY TALES (2-LP) | 18 |
| 76 | BTM BTM 1007 | BLIND DOG AT ST. DUNSTAN'S (LP) | 15 |
| 80 | Kingdom KVL 9003 | THE ALBUM (LP, laminated sleeve) | 20 |
| 11 | Music On Vinyl MOVLP 385 | CARAVAN (LP, reissue) | 18 |
| 11 | Decca 375 069-3 | IF I COULD DO IT ALL OVER AGAIN, I'D DO IT ALL OVER YOU (LP, reissue) | 18 |
| 11 | Deram 533 420 | IN THE LAND OF GREY AND PINK (2-LP reissue, 'splatter pink' vinyl) | 20 |

*(see also Gringo, Matching Mole, Hatfield & The North, Spiro Gyra)*

## CARAVELLES
| 64 | Fontana TF 466 | You Are Here/How Can I Be Sure? | 5 |
|---|---|---|---|
| 64 | Fontana TF 509 | I Don't Care If The Sun Don't Shine/I Like A Man | 5 |
| 64 | Polydor NH 59034 | True Love Never Runs Smooth/Georgia Boy | 5 |

# CARAVELLI

| | | | |
|---|---|---|---|
| 66 | Polydor 56137 | Hey Mama You've Been On My Mind/New York | 5 |
| 67 | Polydor 56156 | I Want To Love You Again/I Had To Walk Home Myself | 5 |
| 68 | Pye 7N 17654 | The Other Side Of Love/I Hear A New Kind Of Music | 5 |
| 63 | Decca LK 4565 | THE CARAVELLES (LP) | 15 |

*(see also Lois Lane)*

## CARAVELLI
| | | | |
|---|---|---|---|
| 69 | CBS 4275 | Theme From The Film Z/Isadora | 8 |

## GUY CARAWAN
| | | | |
|---|---|---|---|
| 58 | Pye Nixa 7N 15132 | Old Man Atom (Talking Atomic Blues)/Michael Row The Boat Ashore | 5 |
| 60 | Collector JEA 4 | SONGS FROM THE SOUTH (EP) | 12 |
| 58 | Topic 10T 24 | MOUNTAIN SONGS AND BANJO TUNES (10" LP) | 30 |
| 57 | 77 Records LP8 | GUY CARAWAN, HIS BANJO AND GUITAR (10" LP) | 50 |
| 67 | Columbia SX 6065 | A GUY CALLED CARAWAN (LP) | 30 |

*(see also Peggy Seeger & Guy Carawan)*

## CARBARETTA
| | | | |
|---|---|---|---|
| 78 | Ignition IR 1 | You Must Be Kidding Me/Scat (die-cut sleeve) | 20 |

## CARBON COPIES
| | | | |
|---|---|---|---|
| 02 | Grapevine 125 | Just Don't Love You/Baby I'm Coming Home | 8 |

## CARCASS
| | | | |
|---|---|---|---|
| 89 | Strange Fruit SFPS073 | PEEL SESSION (12") | 20 |
| 94 | Earache MOSH 108T | THE HEARTWORK EP (12") | 15 |
| 88 | Earache MOSH 06 | REEK OF PUTREFACTION (LP) | 30 |
| 89 | Earache MOSH 18 | SYMPHONIES OF SICKNESS (LP, picture disc) | 30 |
| 91 | Earache MOSH 42 | NECROTICISM - DESCANTING THE INSALUBRIOUS (LP) | 30 |

## CARDBOARD ORCHESTRA
| | | | |
|---|---|---|---|
| 69 | CBS 4176 | Zebady Zak/Mary Tell Me Why | 8 |
| 69 | CBS 4633 | Nothing But A Sad Sad Show/Yes I Heard A Little Bird | 8 |

*(see also Zior, Monument)*

## CARDIAC ARREST
| | | | |
|---|---|---|---|
| 79 | Another Record AN 1 | Running In The Street/T.V. Friends (p/s, 500 only) | 40 |
| 79 | Tortch TOR 002 | A BUS FOR A BUS ON A BUS (EP) | 20 |

## CARDIACS
| | | | |
|---|---|---|---|
| 86 | Alphabet ALPH 002 | SEASIDE TREATS (12" EP, with poster & lyric insert) | 25 |
| 87 | Alphabet ALPH 006 | THERE'S TOO MANY IRONS IN THE FIRE (12" EP, with poster) | 10 |
| 88 | Alphabet ALPH 008 | Is This The Life/I'm Eating In Bed (p/s) | 7 |
| 88 | Alphabet ALPHT 008 | Is This The Life/Loosefish Goosegash/I'm Eating In Bed (12", p/s) | 12 |
| 88 | Alphabet ALPH 009 | Susannah's Still Alive/Blind In Safety And Leafy In Love (p/s) | 6 |
| 91 | Alphabet ALPH 015 | DAY IS GONE (12" EP, with lyric sheet) | 12 |
| 87 | Alphabet ALPH 004 | BIG SHIP (mini LP, with lyric insert) | 18 |
| 87 | Alphabet ALPH 005 | RUDE BOOTLEG - LIVE AT READING '86 (LP, stamped sleeve with insert) | 18 |
| 88 | Alphabet ALPH 009T | Susannah's Still Alive/Blind In Safety And Leafy In Love/All His Geese Are Swans (12", p/s) | 10 |
| 89 | Alphabet ALPH 011 | Baby Heart Dirt/I Hold My Love In My Arms (p/s) | 7 |
| 88 | Night Tracks SFNT 013 | RADIO ONE EVENING SESSION: R.E.S./ Buds And Spawn/In A City Lining/ Is This The Life/Cameras (12" EP) | 18 |
| 88 | Alphabet ALPHLP 010 | CARDIACS LIVE (LP) | 18 |
| 88 | Alphabet ALPH 012 | ON LAND AND IN THE SEA (LP) | 18 |
| 91 | Alphabet ALPHLP 014 | SONGS FOR SHIPS AND IRONS (LP) | 15 |
| 92 | Alphabet ALPHLP 017 | HEAVEN BORN AND EVER BRIGHT (LP) | 15 |

*(see also Cardiac Arrest)*

## CARDIGAN BROTHERS
| | | | |
|---|---|---|---|
| 63 | London HLU 9740 | I Know Know Know/Let's Go To The Movies | 5 |

## CARDIGANS
| | | | |
|---|---|---|---|
| 95 | Trampoliene 523 556-1 | LIFE (LP) | 25 |
| 96 | Stockholm 533117-1 | FIRST BAND ON THE MOON (LP) | 40 |
| 03 | Stockholm 067 101-1 | LONG GONE BEFORE DAYLIGHT (LP) | 80 |
| 00 | Stockholm/Simply Vinyl SVLP 175 | GRAN TURISMO (LP, with inner sleeve) | 80 |

## CARDINAL
| | | | |
|---|---|---|---|
| 94 | Dedicated DEDLP 018 | CARDINAL (LP) | 25 |

## CARDINALS
| | | | |
|---|---|---|---|
| 71 | Nelmwood Audio NWA 1 | SWEET & REFRESHING (LP) | 30 |
| 72 | Nelmwood Audio | ON TOP OF THE WORLD (LP) | 22 |

## JACK CARDWELL
| | | | |
|---|---|---|---|
| 54 | Parlophone CMSP 24 | Whiskey, Women And Loaded Dice/Slap-Ka-Dab (export issue) | 20 |
| 54 | Parlophone CMSP 27 | Blue Love/Diddle Diddle Dumpling (export issue) | 20 |

## CARE
| | | | |
|---|---|---|---|
| 83 | Arista KBIRD 122 | Flaming Sword/Misericorde (12" p/s) | 10 |

*(see also Wild Swans, Lotus Eaters, Lightning Seeds)*

## CAREFREES
| | | | |
|---|---|---|---|
| 63 | Oriole CB 1916 | We Love You Beatles/Hot Blooded Lover | 25 |
| 64 | Oriole CB 1931 | Aren't You Glad You're You/Paddy Wack | 15 |

## CARELESS HANDS
| | | | |
|---|---|---|---|
| 81 | Flying Kite FKR 001 | Looking For A Secret/New Lamps For Old (p/s) | 6 |
| 81 | Flying Kite FKR 002 | Lawrence/Other (p/s) | 8 |

## THE CARETAKER
| | | | |
|---|---|---|---|
| 01 | V/VM Test Record OFFAL 07 | A STAIRWAY TO THE STARS (2-LP, blue vinyl) | 50 |

| 11 | History Always Favors The Winners HAFTW008-LP | AN EMPTY BLISS BEYOND THIS WORLD (LP, blue vinyl) | 45 |
| 11 | History Always Favors The Winners HAFTW008-LP | AN EMPTY BLISS BEYOND THIS WORLD (LP, repressing, clear vinyl) | 35 |

**CARETAKER/ELLIS BAND**

| 80s | Stonehouse 2 | Majority Rules/Two Steps Forward | 8 |

*(see also Alton Ellis)*

**DAVE CAREY (JAZZ BAND)**

| 53 | Columbia SCM 5030 | Broken Wings/Oh, Happy Day (as David Carey) | 5 |
| 56 | Tempo A 122 | Kater Street Rag/Kansas City Kitty | 7 |
| 56 | Tempo A 133 | I've Found A New Baby/Brown Skin Mama | 7 |
| 56 | Tempo A 138 | Sunset Cafe Stomp/Sweet Georgia Brown | 7 |
| 56 | Tempo A 150 | Ida, Sweet As Apple Cider/Button Up Your Overcoat | 5 |
| 56 | Tempo EXA 51 | DAVE CAREY JAZZ BAND (EP) | 10 |

**CAREY & LLOYD**

| 72 | Attack ATT 8032 | Do It Again (as Carey/Lloyd)/GARY RANGLIN: Watch It | 15 |
| 72 | Grape GR 3025 | Come Down Part 1/DYNAMITES: Come Down Part 2 | 15 |

*(see also Carey Johnson, Lloyd Young, Lloyd & Carey)*

**MARIAH CAREY**

| 92 | Columbia 657 941-7 | Make It Happen(radio edit)/Emotions (Special Motion Edit) (p/s) | 5 |
| 94 | Columbia 661070 7 | All I Want For Christmas Is You/Miss You Most (At Christmas Time) (jukebox issue) | 40 |
| 98 | Columbia MARIAH 1 | 12s (10x12" in box) | 50 |
| 97 | Columbia COL 488537-1 | BUTTERFLY (LP) | 40 |
| 98 | Columbia 4926041 | #1's (2-LP) | 30 |
| 99 | Columbia 495065-1 | RAINBOW (2-LP) | 30 |
| 01 | Virgin VUSLP 201 | GLITTER (2-LP) | 30 |

**TONY CAREY**

| 84 | MCA MCA 873 | Fine Fine Day/Say It's Over (p/s) | 6 |

*(see also Rainbow)*

**HENSON CARGILL**

| 68 | Monument MON 1015 | Skip A Rope/Very Well-Travelled Man | 6 |

**CARGO (1)**

| 70 | No Label, LS 1674 | Killing Time/Love Will Turn You Round (Unissued, white labels only) | 300 |

**CARGO (2)**

| 82 | Cargo Z38 | Holding On/It's Your Love | 6 |

**CARIBBEANS**

| 69 | Doctor Bird DB 1181 | Let Me Walk By/AMBLINGS: Tell Me Why | 50 |
| 69 | Crab CR 14 | Please Please/MATADORS: The Destroyer | 35 |

**CARIBBEATS**

| 66 | Ska Beat JB 246 | The Bells Of St. Mary's/WINSTON RICHARDS: Loki | 20 |
| 67 | Double D DD 101 | Highway 300/I Think Of You (actually by Merlene McKenzie) | 75 |
| 67 | Double D DD 103 | I'll Try/If I Did Look | 60 |
| 68 | Double D DD 111 | One Step/HAZEL WRIGHT: Please Help Me | 60 |

*(see also Bobby Aitken, Itals)*

**CARIBBENN (THE)**

| 65 | Pye 7N 15961 | Inside Out/Up My Street | 8 |

**CARIBOES**

| 71 | Bullet BU 479 | Let It Be Me/All I Have To Do Is Dream | 15 |

**CARIBOU**

| 05 | Leaf BAY 42V | THE MILK OF HUMAN KINDNESS (LP) | 20 |
| 14 | City Slang SLANG 500070LP | OUR LOVE (LP, CD) | 20 |

*(see also Manitoba)*

**CARIBS**

| 60 | Starlite ST45 012 | Taboo/Mathilda Cha Cha Cha! | 12 |

**CARIFTA ALLSTARS**

| 72 | Green Door GD 4040 | The Harder They Come (actually by Charlie Ace)/Time Is Still Here | 8 |

**CARL & COMMANDERS**

| 61 | Columbia DB 4719 | Farmer John/Cleanin' Up | 20 |

**DONOVAN CARLESS**

| 71 | Tropical ALO31 | How Can I Tell Her About It/Be Thankful For What You Got | 15 |

**CARLEW CHOIR**

| 69 | Spark SRL 1028 | Huma-Lama/Give A Hand To This Clown | 7 |

**TOM CARLILE**

| 67 | CBS 3249 | I Saw The Light/Nightingale | 7 |

**BILL CARLISLE & CARLISLES**

| 59 | Mercury AMT 1063 | Down Boy/Union Suit | 40 |
| 64 | Hickory 45-1254 | Shanghai Rooster/Big John Henry's Girl | 5 |

**JIM CARLISLE**

| 78 | Billy Goat 001 | Don't Start Crying Now/She Knows How To Rock Me | 15 |
| 79 | Billy Goat 003 | Train Whistle Boogie/Hillbilly Boogie | 15 |

**CARLISLE BROTHERS**

| 59 | Parlophone GEP 8799 | FRESH FROM THE COUNTRY (EP) | 20 |

**DON CARLOS ORCHESTRA**

| 54 | HMV 7 MC 4 | Delicado/Anything Can Happen (export issue) | 5 |
| 56 | HMV 7 MC 48 | The Bandit/Mexicana (export issue) | 5 |
| 60 | Top Rank JAR 376 | Mustapha/Josita | 5 |
| 58 | Pye Nixa NPT 19028 | CHA CHA CHA CARLOS (10" LP) | 12 |

## DON CARLOS

| | | | |
|---|---|---|---|
| 78 | Dove 511 | Plantation/Version ................................................................................ | 20 |
| 80 | Pirate PIR 001 | Nice Time/Get Up (12") .......................................................................... | 20 |
| 80 | Negus Roots NERT003 | I Love Jah/I Don't Care (12", as Don McCarlos) .......................................... | 40 |
| 80 | Ethnic ETH 2236 | Grief My Heart/Spread Out (12") ............................................................ | 15 |
| 81 | Negus Roots NERT 004 | Gimme Gimme Your Love/PAPA TULLO: Gimme More Love (12") ................ | 30 |
| 82 | Negus Roots NERT 015 | Magic Man/Magic Dub (12") ................................................................... | 15 |
| 82 | Cha Cha CHAD 52 | Can't Waste Time/PAPA BRUCE : No Time To Waste (10") ........................ | 20 |
| 83 | Shuttle SH 008 | Money & Women (with John Wayne)/CORNELL CAMPBELL/PURPLEMAN: Keep On Working (12") ................................................................................. | 20 |
| 83 | Blacker Dread SCOM 003 | From Creation/Versions (12") ................................................................. | 30 |
| 83 | Youth In Progress YP001 | Jordan River/LITTLE JOHN: Reasons/LADY ANNE AND SANTANA; Love Life (12") ........... | 20 |
| 85 | Blacker Dread SCOM 020 | Strictly Culture (Love We Culture Version)/MIKEY DREAD: Dubuling Mix (12") ............. | 30 |
| 80s | Rusty International RI 001 | Isabel/BILLY BOYO: One Morning/CAPTAIN SINBAD & ROOTS RADICALS: Radication Dehbout (12") ........................................................................................ | 20 |
| 81 | Blue Moon BM 001 | PROPHET (LP) ....................................................................................... | 40 |
| 82 | Negus Roots NERLP 001 | SUFFERING (LP) ..................................................................................... | 40 |
| 82 | Negus Roots NERLP 005 | HARVEST TIME (LP) ............................................................................... | 60 |
| 83 | Burning Sounds BRD 1053 | SPREAD OUT INA DANCEHALL STYLE (LP) ............................................... | 20 |
| 84 | Real Authentic Sound RAS 3008 | JUST A PASSING GLANCE (LP) ................................................................ | 15 |
| 84 | Saxon International 5550 | SAMMY DREAD MEETS DON CARLOS (LP, not released in sleeve) .............. | 25 |

*(see also Black Uhuru)*

## DAVE CARLSEN
| | | | |
|---|---|---|---|
| 73 | Spark SRLP 110 | A PALE HORSE (LP, yellow/blue label) ................................................... | 40 |

## RAY CARLSON
| | | | |
|---|---|---|---|
| 67 | MGM MGM 1362 | Speak No Sorrow/It's Getting Me Down Girl .......................................... | 6 |

## CARL CARLTON (LITTLE)
| | | | |
|---|---|---|---|
| 68 | Action ACT 4501 | Competition Ain't Nothin'/Three Way Love ........................................... | 50 |
| 68 | Action ACT 4514 | 46 Drums 1 Guitar/Why Don't They Leave Us Alone ............................... | 15 |
| 69 | Action ACT 4537 | Look At Mary Wonder/Bad For Each Other (as Carl Carlton) .................... | 20 |
| 75 | ABC ABC 4040 | Smokin' Room/Signed, Sealed, Delivered, I'm Yours (as Carl Carlton) ...... | 6 |
| 90s | Kent TOWN 105 | Competition Ain't Nothin'/HESITATIONS: I'm Not Built That Way ........... | 12 |

## EDDIE CARLTON
| | | | |
|---|---|---|---|
| 76 | Cream CRM 5001 | It Will Be Done (Parts 1 & 2) ............................................................... | 10 |

## CARLTON & HIS SHOES
| | | | |
|---|---|---|---|
| 68 | Coxsone CS 7065 | Love Me Forever/Happy Land ............................................................... | 175 |
| 68 | Studio One SO 2062 | This Feeling/You And Me (Love Is A Treasure) ....................................... | 100 |
| 80s | Live & Love LLDIS 116 | What A Day/Version (12") ..................................................................... | 40 |
| 79 | Studio One PSOL 003 | LOVE ME FOREVER (LP, laminated sleeve, 1st UK press through Peckings) .... | 80 |
| 85 | Studio One PSOL 002 | LOVE ME FOREVER (LP, reissue, Peckings) ............................................. | 20 |

*(see also Lee 'Scratch' Perry, Roy & Enid)*

## PAUL CARMAN
| | | | |
|---|---|---|---|
| 74 | DJM DJS 317 | In My World/School Love ...................................................................... | 6 |

## CARMEN
| | | | |
|---|---|---|---|
| 74 | Regal Zonophone RZ 3086 | Flamenco Fever/Lonely House .............................................................. | 10 |
| 74 | Regal Zonophone RZ 3090 | Bulerias/Stepping Stone ....................................................................... | 6 |
| 73 | R. Zonophone SRZA 8518 | FANDANGOS IN SPACE (LP, gatefold sleeve, red/silver label) ................. | 35 |
| 75 | R. Zonophone SLRZ 1040 | DANCING ON A COLD WIND (LP, with inner sleeve, red/silver label) ....... | 45 |

*(see also Jethro Tull)*

## ROGER CARMEN, ROCK KEELING, MO THOMAS & ANN & STEVE MITCHELL
| | | | |
|---|---|---|---|
| 71 | Mosart Music MM 1 | FROST LAND (LP) ................................................................................. | 25 |

## JEAN CARN
| | | | |
|---|---|---|---|
| 79 | Philadelphia Int. S PIR 13 8840 | Was That All It Was/Whats On Your Mind (12") ..................................... | 10 |

## CARNABY
| | | | |
|---|---|---|---|
| 65 | Piccadilly 7N 35272 | Jump And Dance/My Love Will Stay ...................................................... | 120 |

## CARNABY STREET POP ORCHESTRA & CHOIR
| | | | |
|---|---|---|---|
| 69 | Carnaby CNLS 6003 | THE LONDON THEME (LP) ..................................................................... | 40 |

## CARNAGE
| | | | |
|---|---|---|---|
| 84 | Creative Reality REAL 07 | FACE THE FACTS (LP) ............................................................................ | 20 |

## CARNATIONS
| | | | |
|---|---|---|---|
| 65 | Blue Beat BB 285 | Mighty Man/What Are You Selling ........................................................ | 22 |

## JUDY CARNE
| | | | |
|---|---|---|---|
| 61 | Decca F 11347 | Late Last Evening (with David Kernan)/A Plea For The Throne (with Betty Marsden & Pip Hinton) ('On The Brighter Side' cast) ........................................... | 5 |
| 69 | Reprise RS 20680 | Right, Said Fred/Sock It To Me ............................................................. | 8 |

## CARNEGY HALL
| | | | |
|---|---|---|---|
| 68 | Polydor 56224 | The Bells Of San Francisco/Slightly Cracked ......................................... | 6 |

## CARNIVAL
| | | | |
|---|---|---|---|
| 67 | Columbia DB 8255 | The Big Bright Green Pleasure Machine/Silver Dreams And Scarlet Memories............. | 10 |
| 70 | Liberty LBF 15252 | Son Of A Preacher Man/Walk On By ...................................................... | 6 |
| 70 | Liberty LBS 83305 | THE CARNIVAL (LP) .............................................................................. | 20 |

## SASHA CARO
| | | | |
|---|---|---|---|
| 67 | Decca F 12687 | Grade 3 Section 2/Little Maid Song ...................................................... | 12 |
| 68 | Decca F12744 | Molotov Molotov/Never Play A B Side .................................................. | 15 |

## BOBBI CAROL
| | | | |
|---|---|---|---|
| 63 | Fontana 267 260TF | Will You Love Me Tomorrow/It Doesn't Matter ...................................... | 5 |

**CAROL & MEMORIES**
66   CBS 202086                    Tears On My Pillow/Crying My Eyes Out................................................22

**CAROLE & SHERRY**
62   Fontana 270 107 TF            I Ain't Ready Yet/Like I Gotta Get Away.............................................5

**CAROLINA SLIM**
72   Flyright LP 4702              CAROLINA BLUES AND BOOGIE (LP)..............................................20

**CAROLINES**
65   Polydor BM 56027             Love Made A Fool Of Me/Believe In Me..........................................20

**CAROLLS**
65   Polydor BM 56046             Give Me Time/Darling I Want You So Much....................................20
*(see also Carrols)*

**CAROLS**
70   Revolution REV 013           Everyday I Have To Cry Some/FIRE SESSION: Sleeping Reggae...........10
*(see also Carolls)*

**CAROUSELS**
67   Pye 7N 17353                 Holiday Romance/The Run Run.......................................................15

**BOB CARPENTER**
76   Celtic Music CM 027          SILENT PASSAGE (LP)...................................................................20

**CARPENTER JOE**
87   Solo SOLO 2                  MAVERICK GENIUS (EP).................................................................20
*(See also Doubt)*

**THELMA CARPENTER**
61   Coral Q 72422                Yes, I'm Lonesome Tonight/Gimme A Little Kiss Will Ya, Huh?............10
61   Coral Q 72442                Back Street/I Ought To Know........................................................10

**CARPENTER'S APPRENTICE**
72   SRS 12107                    CHANGES (LP, with insert)..........................................................100

**CARPET BAGGERS**
67   Spin SP 2006                 Flea Teacher/On Sunday................................................................30

**CARPETTES**
77   Small Wonder SMALL 3         THE CARPETTES (EP)....................................................................15
78   Small Wonder SMALL 9         Small Wonder?/2 Ne 1 (p/s, 2,000 only)........................................35
79   Beggars Banquet BEG 27       I Don't Mean It/Easy Way Out (p/s)..............................................10
80   Beggars Banquet BEG 32       Johnny Won't Hurt You/Frustration Paradise//Keys To Your Heart/Total Insecurity
                                  (double pack).............................................................................10
80   Beggars Banquet BEG 47       Nothing Ever Changes/You Never Realise/Frustration Paradise (live) (p/s)........10
80   Beggars Banquet BEG 49       The Last Lone Ranger/Love So Strong/Fan Club (p/s)........................12
79   Beggars Banquet BEGA 14      FRUSTRATION PARADISE (LP)......................................................18
80   Beggars Banquet BEGA 21      FIGHT AMONGST YOURSELVES (LP)..............................................20

**CATHY CARR**
56   London HLH 8274              Ivory Tower/Please, Please Believe Me............................................15
56   Vogue Coral Q 72175          Heartbroken/I'll Cry At Your Wedding..............................................6
63   Stateside SS 147             Sailor Boy/The Next Time The Band Plays A Waltz............................12

**JAMES CARR**
66   Stateside SS 507             You've Got My Mind Messed Up/That's What I Want To Know..............80
66   Stateside SS 507             You've Got My Mind Messed Up/That's What I Want To Know (DJ Copy).....150
66   Stateside SS 535             Love Attack/Coming Back To Me Baby..............................................40
66   Stateside SS 535             Love Attack/Coming Back To Me Baby (DJ copy)................................70
66   Stateside SS 545             You're Pouring Water On A Drowning Man/Forgetting You....................20
67   Stateside SS 2001            The Dark End Of the Street/Loveable Girl........................................30
67   Stateside SS 2038            Let It Happen/A Losing Game........................................................15
67   Stateside SS 2052            I'm A Fool For You/Gonna Send You Back To Georgia..........................25
68   Bell BLL 1004                A Man Needs A Woman/Stronger Than Love......................................20
69   B&C CB 101                   Freedom Train/That's The Way Love Turned Out For Me......................12
69   B&C CB 101                   Freedom Train/That's The Way Love Turned Out For Me (DJ Copy).......50
72   Mojo 2092 053                Freedom Train/That's What I Want To Know........................................8
11   Goldwax ITDEP 012            IN MUSCLE SHOALS EP (p/s)........................................................10
67   Stateside SL 10205           YOU GOT MY MIND MESSED UP (LP)............................................100
69   Bell MBLL/SBLL 113           A MAN NEEDS A WOMAN (LP)......................................................20

**JOE 'FINGERS' CARR**
55   Capitol CL 14372             Give Me A Band And My Baby/Zig-A-Zig (with Joy-Riders)....................6
*(see also Lou Busch, Vicki Young)*

**JOHNNY CARR (& CADILLACS)**
64   Decca F 11854                Remember That Night/Respectable..................................................20
65   Fontana TF 600               Do You Love That Girl?/Give Him A Little Time...................................15
66   Fontana TF 681               Then So Do I/I'm Just A Little Bit Shy (solo)....................................10
67   Fontana TF 823               Things Get Better/You Got Me Baby (solo)......................................35

**LEROY CARR**
63   CBS BPG 62206                BLUES BEFORE SUNRISE (LP).....................................................50

**LINDA CARR**
67   Stateside SS 2058            Everytime/Trying To Be Good For You.............................................40

**LODY CARR**
60   Top Rank 35-111              LADYBIRD (LP)............................................................................15

**MIKE CARR**
62   Decca F11448                 That Certain Something/The Girl In The Mountains............................10
68   Columbia SCX 6248            UNDER PRESSURE (LP).................................................................20
73   Ad-Rhythm ARPS 1020          MIKE CARR (LP)...........................................................................18

MINT VALUE £

**PETER CARR**
69   DJM DJS213   Angel And The Woman/Imagine Yourself ........................ 20

**ROMEY CARR**
70   Columbia DB 8710   These Things Will Keep Me Loving You/Stand Up And Fight ........ 30
70   Columbia DB 8710   These Things Will Keep Me Loving You/Stand Up And Fight (DJ Copy) ... 50

**VALERIE CARR**
58   Columbia DB 4083   You're The Greatest/Over The Rainbow ........................ 5
58   Columbia DB 4131   When The Boys Talk About The Girls/Padre .................... 5
58   Columbia DB 4225   Bad Girl/Look Forward ...................................... 5
59   Columbia DB 4365   The Way To My Heart/I'm Only Asking ......................... 5
61   Columbia 33SCX 3307   EV'RY HOUR, EV'RY DAY OF MY LIFE (LP, stereo) ............. 15

**VIKKI CARR**
68   CBS 5161   Ain't No Mountain High Enough/Call My Heart Your Home ...... 10
64   Liberty LBY 1208   DISCOVERY (LP) ....................................... 15

**WYNONA CARR**
61   Reprise R 20033   I Gotta Stand Tall/My Faith ............................. 15

**CARRAIG AONAIR**
77   Gwerin   CARRAIG AONAIR (LP, insert) ................................. 25

**CARRIAGE COMPANY**
70   CBS 5209   In Your Room/Feel Right ................................ 30
71   CBS 7059   Paint The City Red/Jubilee ............................. 12

**CARRICK FOLK FOUR**
65   Thistle TM 90   Radio Scotland/Blue Nose ........................... 5

**ANDREA CARROLL**
63   London HLX 9772   It Hurts To Be Sixteen/Why Am I So Shy (some copies have Why Am I So Sorry as the B-side) ........ 25

**BARBARA CARROLL**
59   London HLR 8981   North By Northwest/Far Away ........................ 8

**BERNADETTE CARROLL**
64   Stateside SS 311   Party Girl/I Don't Wanna Know ..................... 20

**BOB CARROLL**
55   MGM SP 1132   I Love You So Much It Hurts/My Dearest, My Darling, My Love ... 10
56   London HLU 8299   Red Confetti, Pink Balloons And Tambourines/Handwriting On The Wall ... 25
58   London HLT 8724   Hi Yo Silver/Tonto The Brave ....................... 15
59   London HLT 8888   I Can't Get You Out Of My Heart/Since I'm Out Of Your Arms ... 10

**CATHY CARROLL**
62   Warner Bros WB 72   Poor Little Puppet/Love And Learn .............. 10

**DON CARROLL**
57   Capitol CL 14812   At Your Front Door/The Gods Were Angry With Me ... 10
58   Capitol CL 14823   In My Arms/The Things I Might Have Been ....... 5

**GINA CARROLL**
65   Decca F 12297   Bye Bye Big Boy/Down The Street ............... 20

**JOHNNY CARROLL & HOT ROCKS**
56   Brunswick 05580   Corrine Corrina/Wild Wild Women ................. 800
56   Brunswick 05580   Corrine Corrina/Wild Wild Women (78) ........... 50
56   Brunswick 05603   Crazy, Crazy Lovin'/Hot Rock .................. 800
56   Brunswick 05603   Crazy, Crazy Lovin'/Hot Rock (78) ............ 50
74   UK USA 1   Black Leather Rebel/Be-Bop-A-Lula (as Johnny Carroll & Blue Caps) ... 10

**LISA CARROLL**
69   CBS 4428   You Made Me What I Am/Don't Count The Days ...... 6

**PAT CARROLL**
72   Pye International 7N 25592   To The Sun/Out Of My Mind ........... 5

**TONI CARROLL**
58   MGM MGM 987   Dreamsville/I've Never Felt This Way Before ..... 10
58   MGM EP 689   THIS ONE IS TONI (EP) ....................... 15

**VIVIAN CARROLL**
12   Goldmine Soul Supply GS 051   Oh Yeah Yeah Yeah/Instrumental Version ... 6

**CARROLLS**
66   Polydor BM 56081   Surrender Your Love/The Folk I Love ........... 25
66   Polydor BM 56081   Surrender Your Love/The Folk I Love (DJ Copy) ... 50
68   CBS 3710   Ever Since/Come On .............................. 5
68   CBS 3875   A Lemon Balloon And A Blue Sky/Make Me Belong To You ... 20
69   CBS 4401   We're In This Thing Together/We Know Better ... 15
67   CBS 3414   So Gently Falls The Rain/Nice To See You Darling ... 15
67   CBS 3414   So Gently Falls The Rain/Nice To See You Darling (DJ Copy) ... 25
*(see also Carols, Carolls, Faith Brown, Brotherly Love)*

**BEN CARRUTHERS & DEEP**
65   Parlophone R 5295   Jack O' Diamonds/Right Behind You ......... 50

**CHAD CARSON**
63   HMV POP 1156   They Were Wrong/Stop Picking On Me ......... 50

**DEL CARSON**
59   Decca F 11135   Jean/I Told Myself A Lie ..................... 5

**JOE CARSON**
63   Liberty LIB 55578   I Gotta Get Drunk (And I Shore Do Dread It)/Who Will Buy My Memories ... 25

**KEN CARSON**
55   London HLF 8213   Hawkeye/I've Been Working On The Railroad ...... 70

| | | |
|---|---|---|
| 56 | London HLF 8237 | Let Her Go, Let Her Go/The Song Of Daniel Boone (The Daddy Of Them All) ................ 60 |

**KIT CARSON**

| 56 | Capitol CL 14524 | Band Of Gold/Cast Your Bread Upon The Waters ................................................. 10 |

**MINDY CARSON & GUY MITCHELL**

| 53 | Columbia SCM 5022 | That's A Why/Train Of Love ....................................................................... 15 |

(see also Guy Mitchell)

**VINCE CARSON**

| 55 | HMV 7M 313 | Sweetie, Sweet, Sweet Sue/My Possession ...................................................... 5 |

**CARSTAIRS**

| 79 | Inferno Heat 7 | It Really Hurts Me Girl (re-mix 1)/It Really Hurts Me Girl (re-mix 2) (reissue) ............ 8 |
| 12 | Inferno 1001 | It Really Hurts Me Girl (Unreleased Mix)/Original Mix (reissue) ............................ 8 |

**CARTE BLANCHE**

| 79 | Pye 7NL46193 | Get Up On Your Feet/Do It Like You Like It (p/s) ............................................. 15 |

**ANITA CARTER**

| 58 | London HLA 8693 | Blue Doll/Go Away Johnnie ........................................................................ 10 |
| 60 | London HLW 9102 | Moon Girl/Mama Don't Cry At My Wedding ..................................................... 10 |

**BENNY CARTER**

| 54 | HMV 7M 189 | Blue Mountain/Sunday Afternoon ............................................................... 5 |
| 62 | HMV CLP 1624/CSD1480 | FURTHER DEFINITIONS (LP, mono/stereo) ....................................................... 20 |
| 66 | HMV CLP/CSD 3576 | FURTHER DEFINITIONS (LP, mono/stereo) ....................................................... 20 |

(see also Helen Humes)

**BETTY CARTER**

| 63 | London HLK 9748 | The Good Life/Nothing More To Look Forward To ............................................... 7 |

(see also Ray Charles)

**CAROLINE CARTER**

| 65 | Decca F 12239 | The Ballad Of The Possibilities/We Want Love ................................................. 20 |

**CAROLYN CARTER**

| 65 | London HL 9959 | It Hurts/I'm Thru ................................................................................... 40 |

**CLARENCE CARTER**

| 68 | Atlantic 584 154 | Thread The Needle/Don't Make My Baby Cry ................................................... 18 |
| 68 | Atlantic 584 176 | Looking For A Fox/I Can't See Myself (Crying About You) ................................... 20 |
| 68 | Atlantic 584 187 | Funky Fever/Slip Away .............................................................................. 15 |
| 68 | Atlantic 584 223 | Too Weak To Fight/Let Me Comfort You ......................................................... 15 |
| 69 | Atlantic 584 248 | Snatchin' It Back/Making Love (At The Dark End Of The Street) ............................. 15 |
| 69 | Atlantic 584 272 | The Feeling Is Right/You Can't Miss When You Can't Measure ................................ 10 |
| 70 | Atlantic 584 309 | Take It Off Him And Put It On Me/The Few Troubles I've Had ................................ 10 |
| 70 | Atlantic 2091 030 | Patches/I Can't Leave Your Love Alone .......................................................... 10 |
| 71 | Atlantic 2091 045 | It's All In Your Mind/Willie And Laura Mae Jones .............................................. 10 |
| 71 | Atlantic 2091 093 | The Court Room/Getting The Bills (But No Merchandise) ..................................... 10 |
| 71 | Atlantic 2091 139 | Slipped, Tripped And Fell In Love/I Hate To Love And Run ................................... 10 |
| 74 | ABC 4037 | Warning/On Your Way Down ..................................................................... 8 |
| 83 | Certain ACENT 1 | Messin' With My Mind/Messin' (Instrumental Version) ....................................... 15 |
| 68 | Atlantic 588 152 | THIS IS CLARENCE CARTER (LP) ................................................................ 20 |
| 69 | Atlantic 588 172 | THE DYNAMIC CLARENCE CARTER (LP) ........................................................ 20 |
| 69 | Atlantic 588 191 | TESTIFYIN' (LP) ................................................................................... 20 |
| 70 | Atlantic 2400 027 | PATCHES (LP) ...................................................................................... 15 |

**HAL CARTER FIVE**

| 62 | Oriole CB 1709 | Come On And Twist Me/Twistin' Time Is Here .................................................. 10 |

**HERBIE CARTER**

| 68 | Duke DU 4 | Happy Time (actually by Keble Drummond)/BOYS: Smashville .............................. 50 |

**JACK CARTER**

| 70 | Penny Farthing PEN 739 | Morning/Fanny ..................................................................................... 8 |

**JEAN CARTER & CENTREPIECES**

| 68 | Stateside SS 2114 | No Good Jim/And None ........................................................................... 15 |
| 68 | Stateside SS 2114 | No Good Jim/And None (DJ Copy) ............................................................... 30 |

**JOHN CARTER & RUSS ALQUIST**

| 68 | Spark SRL 1017 | The Laughing Man/Midsummer Dreaming ..................................................... 30 |

(see also Carter-Lewis & Southerners, Ivy League, Flowerpot Men)

**JOHN CARTER**

| 72 | Spark SRL 1069 | One More Mile To Freedom/The Saddest Word I Know ....................................... 6 |

**LYNDA CARTER**

| 73 | EMI 2005 | It Might As Well Stay Monday/I Believe In Music .............................................. 6 |
| 80 | Motown TMG 1207 | The Last Song/What's A Little Love Between Friends (p/s) ................................... 7 |
| 78 | CBS EPC 83052 | LYNDA CARTER (LP, as aka WONDER WOMAN) ............................................... 18 |

**MARTIN CARTER**

| 71 | Tradition TSR 008 | SOMEONE NEW (LP) ............................................................................. 30 |
| 72 | Tradition TSR 012 | UPS & DOWNS (LP) ............................................................................... 25 |

**MEL CARTER**

| 63 | Pye International 7N 25212 | When A Boy Falls In Love/So Wonderful .............................................. 50 |
| 66 | Liberty LIB 66113 | Hold Me, Thrill Me, Kiss Me/Sweet Little Girl ................................................. 20 |
| 65 | Liberty LIB 66138 | (All Of A Sudden) My Heart Sings/When I Hold The Hand Of The One I Love ............ 10 |
| 66 | Liberty LIB 66148 | Love Is All We Need/I Wish I Didn't Love You So .............................................. 10 |
| 66 | Liberty LIB 66165 | Band Of Gold/Detour ............................................................................. 10 |
| 66 | Liberty LIB 66183 | You You You/If You Lose Her ..................................................................... 10 |

**MIKE CARTER (& DRAGONFLY)**

| 84 | Button BTN 117 | My True Love/Talk To Me ......................................................................... 6 |

See also Dragonfly

## NELL CARTER
| 74 | RCA 2503 | Dreams/Send Him Back To Me | 15 |
| 74 | RCA 2503 | Dreams/Send Him Back To Me (DJ Copy) | 25 |

## NICK CARTER
| 79 | NC 001 | ABSTRACTS & EXTRACTS (LP) | 100 |

## SHEILA CARTER & EPISODE SIX
| 66 | Pye 7N 17194 | I Will Warm Your Heart/Incense | 30 |

*(see also Episode, Episode Six)*

## SONNY CARTER WITH EARL BOSTIC & HIS ORCHESTRA
| 55 | Parlophone MSP 6167 | There Is No Greater Love/Oh Baby | 20 |

*(see also Earl Bostic)*

## CARTER STEPHENS CHORALE
| 68 | Fontana TF 936 | Peace! (Dream Of The Common Man)/The Promised Land | 15 |

## ERROL CARTER
| 73 | Cactus CT 71 | Hold Up Your Head/SUCCESS ALL STARS: Tank Skank | 30 |
| 76 | Cactus CT 96 | Ram Goat Malish Water/Ranking Dub | 60 |

## CARTER-LEWIS & SOUTHERNERS
| 61 | Piccadilly 7N 35004 | So Much In Love/Back On The Scene | 30 |
| 61 | Ember EMB S 145 | Two Timing Baby/Will It Happen To Me? | 50 |
| 62 | Piccadilly 7N 35085 | Here's Hopin'/Poor Joe | 30 |
| 62 | Ember EMB S 165 | Tell Me/My Broken Heart | 50 |
| 63 | Oriole CB 1835 | Sweet And Tender Romance/Who Told You? | 20 |
| 63 | Oriole CB 1868 | Your Momma's Out Of Town/Somebody Told My Girl | 20 |
| 64 | Oriole CB 1919 | Skinny Minnie/Easy To Cry | 40 |

*(see also Ivy League, Flowerpot Men, White Plains, John Carter & Russ Alquist, Jimmy Page, Dawn Chorus)*

## MARTIN CARTHY
| 65 | Fontana (S)TL 5269 | MARTIN CARTHY (LP, black/silver label) | 30 |
| 71 | Philips 6308 049 | LANDFALL (LP, black/silver label) | 30 |
| 72 | Peg PEG 12 | SHEARWATER (LP, with insert, purple label) | 25 |
| 74 | Deram SML 1111 | SWEET WIVELSFIELD (LP, red/white label) | 15 |

## MARTIN CARTHY & DAVE SWARBRICK
| 67 | Fontana TE 17490 | NO SONGS (EP) | 30 |
| 66 | Fontana STL 5362 | SECOND ALBUM (LP, black/silver label) | 30 |
| 67 | Fontana STL 5434 | BYKER HILL (LP) | 30 |
| 68 | Fontana STL 5477 | BUT TWO CAME BY (LP) | 30 |
| 70 | Fontana STL 5529 | PRINCE HEATHEN (LP, black/silver label) | 35 |
| 71 | Pegasus PEG 6 | SELECTIONS (LP, gatefold sleeve) | 30 |

*(see also Dave Swarbrick, Three City Four, Steeleye Span, Leon Rosselson, Alex Campbell, Nigel Denver)*

## CARTOONE
| 69 | Atlantic 584 240 | Knick Knack Man/A Penny For The Sun | 12 |
| 69 | Atlantic 588 174 | CARTOONE (LP) | 25 |

*(see also Jimmy Page)*

## CARTOONS (1)
| 80 | Hot HOT 001 | Lunchtime Love Affair/Dark Alleys (p/s) | 15 |
| 81 | Hot HOT 002 | Beep Beep Love/Thomas Cadillac (p/s) | 10 |

## CARTOONS (2)
| 84 | Cage CAGE 2 | Once The Victor/Instrumental Version (p/s) | 10 |

## CARTOONS (3)
| 83 | Stiletto SO 1 | Gee George/Love Is The Drug (p/s) | 7 |

## DAVE CARTWRIGHT
| 73 | DJM DJS 10750 | Band Of Hope/Queen Of The May (promo) | 10 |
| 70 | Harmony DB 0001 | MIDDLE OF THE ROAD (LP, private pressing, 99 only, with insert) | 200 |
| 72 | Transatlantic TRA 255 | A LITTLE BIT OF GLORY (LP, with inner sleeve) | 20 |
| 73 | Transatlantic TRA 267 | BACK TO THE GARDEN (LP, with lyric inner sleeve) | 20 |
| 74 | Transatlantic TRA 284 | DON'T LET YOUR FAMILY DOWN (LP, with lyric insert) | 20 |

*(see also Bev Pegg, Away From The Sand)*

## DICK CARUSO
| 60 | MGM MGM 1077 | Two Long Years/Yes Sir, That's My Baby | 5 |
| 60 | MGM MGM 1099 | Pretty Little Dancin' Doll/We've Never Met | 5 |

## ALAN CARVELL
| 76 | United Artists UP 36124 | Georgia On My Mind/Never Give Your Love (To A New York Woman) | 5 |

*(see also Carvells, Five Sapphires, Telegrams)*

## CARVELLS
| 78 | Rocket ROKN 540 | Skateboard Queen/Skateboard Surfing | 5 |
| 78 | Rocket ROKN 544 | Skateboard Riders/Skateboard King | 5 |

*(see also Alan Carvell, Five Sapphires,Telegrams)*

## MIKE CARVER
| 79 | Venom SRTS/79/CUS 396 | THE MURDER OF BLAIR PEACH | 8 |
| 81 | SRTS/CUS1139 | Ordinary People/Brixton (p/s) | 7 |

## TRISTRAM CARY
| 70 | Galliard GAL 4006 | 3 4 5 (LP, with booklet) | 100 |
| 70 | Galliard GAL 4007 | NARCISSIS (LP, gatefold, with insert) | 100 |
| 71 | EMS (No Cat No) | TRIOS (2-LP, with booklet/instructions, most warped and they are worth half this price) | 400 |
| 10 | Trunk JBH 035 LP | IT'S TIME FOR TRISTRAM CARY (LP, 500 only, black vinyl) | 18 |
| 10 | Trunk JBH 035 LP | IT'S TIME FOR TRISTRAM CARY (LP, reissue, 300 only, clear vinyl) | 20 |

## CASABLANCA
| | | | |
|---|---|---|---|
| 74 | Rocket PIGL 7 | CASABLANCA (LP, die-cut sleeve with inner lyric sleeve) | 20 |

*(see also Trees, Ginger Bakers Airforce)*

## JULIAN CASABLANCAS
| | | | |
|---|---|---|---|
| 09 | Rough Trade RTRADS 563 | I Wish It Was Christmas Today/Old Hollywood (p/s, 500 only) | 8 |

*(see also Strokes)*

## CASANOVAS
| | | | |
|---|---|---|---|
| 00s | Singles Society 7STAS 3320 | Nasty/Too Cool (numbered die-cut p/s, 500 only) | 10 |

## CASCADES
| | | | |
|---|---|---|---|
| 63 | Warner Bros WB 88 | Rhythm Of The Rain/Let Me Be | 5 |
| 63 | Warner Bros WB 98 | Shy Girl/The Last Leaf | 5 |
| 63 | Warner Bros WB 103 | I Wanna Be Your Lover/My First Day Alone | 5 |
| 63 | RCA Victor RCA 1358 | Cinderella/A Little Like Loving | 5 |
| 64 | RCA Victor RCA 1378 | Jeannie/For Your Sweet Love | 5 |
| 65 | Liberty LIB 55822 | I Bet You Won't Stay/She'll Love Again | 5 |
| 66 | Stateside SS 515 | Cheryl's Goin' Home/Truly Julie's Blues | 10 |
| 69 | Uni UN 508 | Maybe The Rain Will Fall/Naggin' Cries | 5 |
| 63 | Warner Bros WEP 6106 | RHYTHM OF THE RAIN (EP, mono) | 20 |
| 63 | Warner Bros WSE 6106 | RHYTHM OF THE RAIN (EP, stereo) | 20 |
| 63 | Warner Bros WM 8127 | RHYTHM OF THE RAIN (LP, mono) | 30 |
| 63 | Warner Bros WM 8127 | RHYTHM OF THE RAIN (LP, stereo) | 30 |

## AL CASEY & K.C. ETTES
| | | | |
|---|---|---|---|
| 63 | Pye International 7N 25215 | Surfin' Hootenanny/Easy Picking | 12 |

*(see also Sanford Clark, Duane Eddy)*

## HOWIE CASEY & SENIORS
| | | | |
|---|---|---|---|
| 62 | Fontana H 364 | Double Twist/True Fine Mama | 25 |
| 62 | Fontana H 381 | I Ain't Mad At You/Twist At The Top | 20 |
| 63 | Fontana TF 403 | The Boll Weevil Song/Bony Moronie | 20 |
| 62 | Fontana TFL 5180 | TWIST AT THE TOP (LP, mono) | 80 |
| 62 | Fontana STFL 592 | TWIST AT THE TOP (LP, stereo) | 100 |

*(see also Freddie Starr)*

## ALVIN CASH (& REGISTERS)
| | | | |
|---|---|---|---|
| 65 | Stateside SS 386 | Twine Time/The Bump (as Alvin Cash & Crawlers) | 30 |
| 65 | Stateside SS 386 | Twine Time/The Bump (as Alvin Cash & Crawlers) (DJ Copy) | 60 |
| 66 | Stateside SS 543 | Philly Freeze/No Deposits, No Returns (as Alvin Cash & Registers) | 25 |
| 66 | Stateside SS 543 | Philly Freeze/No Deposits, No Returns (as Alvin Cash & Registers) (DJ Copy) | 50 |
| 68 | President PT 115 | Philly Freeze/No Deposits, No Returns (as Alvin Cash & Registers) (reissue) | 5 |
| 68 | President PT 119 | Alvin's Boo-Ga-Loo/Let's Do Some Good Timing (as Alvin Cash & Registers) | 10 |
| 68 | President PT 129 | Doin' The Ali Shuffle/Feel So Good | 10 |
| 68 | President PT 147 | Charge/Diff'rent Strokes For Diff'rent Folks | 10 |
| 71 | President PT 351 | Twine Time/Twine Awhile | 8 |
| 72 | President PT 383 | Barracuda/Do It One More Time (as Alvin Cash & Crawlers) | 8 |
| 67 | President PTL 1000 | THE PHILLY FREEZE (LP) | 35 |

## JOHNNY CASH (SOLO & WITH TENNESSEE TWO)
### 78s
| | | | |
|---|---|---|---|
| 57 | London HL 8358 | I Walk The Line/Get Rhythm | 20 |
| 57 | London HLS 8427 | Train Of Love/There You Go | 20 |
| 57 | London HLS 8461 | Next In Line/Don't Make Me Go | 20 |
| 57 | London HLS 8514 | Home Of The Blues/Give My Love To Rose | 20 |
| 58 | London HLS 8586 | Ballad Of A Teenage Queen/Big River (with Tennessee Two) | 20 |
| 58 | London HLS 8656 | Guess Things Happen That Way/Come In, Stranger | 20 |
| 59 | Philips PB 874 | All Over Again/What Do I Care | 20 |
| 59 | Philips PB 897 | Don't Take Your Guns To Town/I Still Miss Someone | 20 |
| 59 | London HLS 8789 | It's Just About Time/I Just Thought You'd Like To Know | 20 |
| 59 | London HLS 8847 | Luther Played The Boogie/Thanks A Lot | 40 |
| 59 | Philips PB 928 | Frankie's Man, Johnny/You Dreamer You | 20 |
| 59 | London HLS 8928 | Katy Too/I Forgot To Remember To Forget | 40 |
| 59 | Philips PB 953 | I Got Stripes/Five Feet High And Rising | 40 |
| 59 | London HLS 8979 | You Tell Me/Goodbye, Little Darlin', Goodbye | 40 |
| 59 | Philips PB 979 | The Little Drummer Boy/I'll Remember You | 40 |

### SINGLES
| | | | |
|---|---|---|---|
| 57 | London HL 8358 | I Walk The Line/Get Rhythm (gold label lettering) | 80 |
| 57 | London HL 8358 | I Walk The Line/Get Rhythm (silver label lettering) | 20 |
| 57 | London HLS 8427 | Train Of Love/There You Go | 30 |
| 57 | London HLS 8461 | Next In Line/Don't Make Me Go | 50 |
| 57 | London HLS 8514 | Home Of The Blues/Give My Love To Rose | 40 |
| 58 | London HLS 8586 | Ballad Of A Teenage Queen/Big River (with Tennessee Two) | 20 |
| 58 | London HLS 8656 | Guess Things Happen That Way/Come In, Stranger (with Tennessee Two) | 20 |
| 58 | London HLS 8709 | The Ways Of A Woman In Love/You're The Nearest Thing To Heaven (with Tennessee Two) | 15 |
| 59 | Philips PB 874 | All Over Again/What Do I Care | 10 |
| 59 | Philips PB 897 | Don't Take Your Guns To Town/I Still Miss Someone | 10 |
| 59 | London HLS 8789 | It's Just About Time/I Just Thought You'd Like To Know (with Tennessee Two) | 20 |
| 59 | London HLS 8847 | Luther Played The Boogie/Thanks A Lot | 20 |
| 59 | Philips PB 928 | Frankie's Man, Johnny/You Dreamer You | 10 |
| 59 | London HLS 8928 | Katy Too/I Forgot To Remember To Forget | 20 |
| 59 | Philips PB 953 | I Got Stripes/Five Feet High And Rising | 5 |
| 59 | London HLS 8979 | You Tell Me/Goodbye, Little Darlin', Goodbye | 5 |

MINT VALUE £

| | | | |
|---|---|---|---|
| 59 | Philips PB 979 | The Little Drummer Boy/I'll Remember You | 6 |
| 60 | London HLS 9070 | Straight A's In Love/I Love You Because | 10 |
| 60 | Philips PB 1017 | Seasons Of My Heart/Smiling Bill McCall | 5 |
| 60 | London HLS 9182 | Down The Street To 301/Story Of A Broken Heart | 15 |
| 60 | Philips PB 1075 | Going To Memphis/Loading Coal | 15 |
| 61 | London HLS 9314 | Oh Lonesome Me/Life Goes On | 10 |
| 61 | Philips PB 1148 | Forty Shades Of Green/he Rebel - Johnny Yuma | 5 |
| 61 | Philips PB 1200 | Tennessee Flat-Top Box/Tall Man | 5 |
| 63 | CBS AAG 159 | Ring Of Fire/I'd Still Be There | 5 |
| 63 | CBS AAG 173 | The Matador/Still In Town | 5 |
| 63 | CBS AAG 200 | Understand Your Man/Dark As A Dungeon | 5 |
| 65 | CBS 201741 | Orange Blossom Special/All God's Children Ain't Free | 5 |
| 65 | CBS 201760 | It Ain't Me Babe/Time And Time Again | 5 |
| 68 | CBS 3549 | Folsom Prison Blues (live)/The Folk Singer | 5 |

## EXPORT SINGLES

| | | | |
|---|---|---|---|
| 57 | London HL 7020 | Next In Line/Don't Make Me Go | 30 |
| 57 | London HL 7023 | Home Of The Blues/Give My Love To Rose | 30 |
| 58 | London HL 7032 | Ballad Of A Teenage Queen/Big River | 25 |
| 58 | London HL 7053 | The Ways Of A Woman In Love/You're The Nearest Thing To Heaven | 20 |
| 57 | London HL 7131 | Folsom Prison Blues/I Walk The Line | 40 |

## EPs

| | | | |
|---|---|---|---|
| 58 | London RES 1120 | JOHNNY CASH (triangular centre) | 25 |
| 58 | London RES 1120 | JOHNNY CASH (round centre) | 15 |
| 59 | London RES 1193 | JOHNNY CASH SINGS HANK WILLIAMS (triangular centre) | 25 |
| 59 | London RES 1193 | JOHNNY CASH SINGS HANK WILLIAMS (round centre) | 15 |
| 59 | London RES 1212 | COUNTRY BOY (triangular centre) | 25 |
| 59 | London RES 1212 | COUNTRY BOY (round centre) | 15 |
| 59 | London RES 1230 | JOHNNY CASH NO. 2 (triangular centre) | 25 |
| 59 | London RES 1230 | JOHNNY CASH NO. 2 (round centre) | 15 |
| 60 | Philips BBE 12377 | THE TROUBADOR | 20 |
| 60 | Philips BBE 12318 | GRANDFATHER'S CLOCK | 15 |
| 60 | Philips BBE 12395 | SONGS OF OUR SOIL | 15 |
| 61 | Philips BBE 12494 | STRICTLY CASH | 15 |
| 69 | CBS EP 6601 | FOLSOM PRISON BLUES | 10 |

## ALBUMS

| | | | |
|---|---|---|---|
| 59 | London HA-S 2157 | SINGS THE SONGS THAT MADE HIM FAMOUS | 40 |
| 59 | London HA-S 2179 | WITH HIS HOT AND BLUE GUITAR | 40 |
| 59 | Philips BBL 7298 | THE FABULOUS JOHNNY CASH (mono) | 20 |
| 59 | Philips SBBL 554 | THE FABULOUS JOHNNY CASH (stereo) | 20 |
| 59 | Philips BBL 7353 | SONGS OF OUR SOIL | 15 |
| 60 | Philips BBL 7358 | NOW THERE WAS A SONG! (mono) | 15 |
| 60 | Philips SBBL 580 | NOW THERE WAS A SONG! (stereo) | 15 |
| 60 | Philips BBL 7417 | RIDE THIS TRAIN | 15 |
| 61 | CBS (S)BPG 62042 | THE FABULOUS JOHNNY CASH (mono/stereo) | 15 |
| 62 | CBS (S)BPG 62073 | THE SOUND OF JOHNNY CASH (mono/stereo) | 15 |
| 63 | CBS BPG 62119 | BLOOD SWEAT AND TEARS | 15 |
| 63 | CBS (S)BPG 62171 | RING OF FIRE (mono/stereo) | 15 |
| 69 | CBS LP 63629 | LIVE AT SAN QUENTIN (LP) | 15 |
| 84 | Charly SUN BOX-105 | THE SUN YEARS (5-LP box set) | 25 |
| 94 | American 0731458679028 | AMERICAN RECORDINGS (LP, inner) | 30 |
| 96 | American 51011 2793-1 | UNCHAINED (LP, inner) | 30 |
| 00 | American 51011 279-14 | AMERICAN III: SOLITARY MAN (LP) | 25 |
| 06 | American 0602517005099 | AMERICAN V: A HUNDRED HIGHWAYS (LP) | 25 |

## CASHMAN, PISTILLI & WEST
| | | | |
|---|---|---|---|
| 70 | Capitol CL 15633 | Goodbye Jo/She Never Looked Better | 6 |

## CASHMERES
| | | | |
|---|---|---|---|
| 90s | Soul City 133 | Showstopper/Let The Door Hit Your Back (reissue) | 8 |

## CASH PUSSIES
| | | | |
|---|---|---|---|
| 79 | The Label TLR 010 | 99% Is Shit/Cash Flow (p/s) | 6 |

*(see also Sex Pistols)*

## CASINO
| | | | |
|---|---|---|---|
| 81 | Ellie Jay EJSP 9609 | More Than Ever/Tonight (p/s) | 10 |

## CASINO ROYALE
| | | | |
|---|---|---|---|
| 72 | Nest NRS 125 | Come On Down To The Beach/Jig-A-Jag | 10 |

## CASINO ROYALES
| | | | |
|---|---|---|---|
| 67 | London HLU 10122 | When I Tell You That I Love You/Love In The Open Air | 6 |

## CASINOS
| | | | |
|---|---|---|---|
| 67 | Ember EMB S 241 | That's The Way/Too Good To Be True | 30 |
| 67 | President PT 123 | Then You Can Tell Me Goodbye/I Still Love You | 10 |
| 68 | President PT 140 | To Be Loved/Tailor Made | 10 |
| 68 | President PT 156 | When I Stop Dreaming/Please Love Me | 10 |
| 68 | President PTL 1007 | THEN YOU CAN TELL ME GOODBYE (LP) | 18 |

## TONY CASO
| | | | |
|---|---|---|---|
| 68 | London HL 10178 | Shadow On The Ground/I Don't Care Who Knows It | 5 |

## CASPAR
| | | | |
|---|---|---|---|
| 79 | Rock Steady MICK 007 | Messin' Around/Make You Feel Like You're Mine (p/s) | 20 |

*(see also 10cc)*

**PAUL CASS**
| | | | |
|---|---|---|---|
| 75 | Rainbow Records RBW 2000 | Mini Marianne/Riverboat Rock | 30 |

**CASSANDRA**
| | | | |
|---|---|---|---|
| 76 | Lucky LY 6034 | Love Me Sweeter Tonight/Albatross | 15 |
| 79 | D Roy DRDD 19 | Sitting In The Park/D ROY BAND: Hyde Park Dub | 30 |
| 80 | D Roy DRDD 29 | My Angel Baby/Thank You For The Many Things You've Done (12") | 30 |
| 80 | D Roy DRDD 31 | I Must Be Dreaming/Trading Dub (12") | 30 |

**TOMMY CASSELL**
| | | | |
|---|---|---|---|
| 70 | Injun 114 | Rockin' Rock A Rollin' Stone/Go Ahead On | 10 |

**CASSETTE**
| | | | |
|---|---|---|---|
| 79 | 1 track CAS 001 | THE FAST FORWARD EP: What's The Point/Product/All The Rage | 35 |

**CASSETTES (1)**
| | | | |
|---|---|---|---|
| 81 | Zip ZIP 101 | Reverberate/Don't Label Me (die-cut sleeve) | 50 |

**CASSETTES (2)**
| | | | |
|---|---|---|---|
| 82 | X-Ray X 001 | Call On Me/Fast Forward | 20 |

**CASSIBER**
| | | | |
|---|---|---|---|
| 84 | Recommended RE 0110 | BEAUTY AND THE BEAST (LP) | 15 |

**DITCH CASSIDY**
| | | | |
|---|---|---|---|
| 71 | Decca F13240 | Pisces Apple Lady/Hamburger Midnight | 20 |

**STEVE CASSIDY**
| | | | |
|---|---|---|---|
| 63 | Ember EMB S 177 | Ecstasy/I'm A Worrying | 5 |

**TED CASSIDY**
| | | | |
|---|---|---|---|
| 65 | Capitol CL 15423 | The Lurch/Wesley | 30 |
| 65 | Capitol CL 15423 | The Lurch/Wesley (DJ Copy) | 40 |

**CAST**
| | | | |
|---|---|---|---|
| 95 | Polydor INV137 LP COL | ALL CHANGE (2-LP) | 20 |
| 99 | Polydor 547 176-1 | MAGIC HOUR (2-LP) | 18 |

*(see also La's)*

**CASTANARC**
| | | | |
|---|---|---|---|
| 74 | Peninsula PENCIL 10 | JOURNEY TO THE EAST (LP, private pressing) | 18 |

**CASTAWAYS**
| | | | |
|---|---|---|---|
| 65 | London HL 10003 | Liar Liar/Sam | 50 |
| 65 | London HL 10003 | Liar Liar/Sam (DJ Copy) | 80 |

**CASTE**
| | | | |
|---|---|---|---|
| 68 | President PT 211 | Don't Cast Aside/One Step Closer | 6 |

**JOEY CASTELL**
| | | | |
|---|---|---|---|
| 57 | Decca F 10966 | I'm Left, You're Right, She's Gone/Tryin' To Get To You | 250 |
| 57 | Decca F 10966 | I'm Left, You're Right, She's Gone/Tryin' To Get To You (78) | 25 |

**LACKSLEY CASTELL**
| | | | |
|---|---|---|---|
| 79 | Sufferers Heights SUFF 01 | What A Great Day/PRINCE JAMMY: Slaughter House 5 (12") | 50 |
| 79 | Sound Off SOFD 003 | My Collie Tree/RISING SUN: Stop Cheating (12") | 50 |
| 80 | Negus Roots NERT 001 | African Queen/Queen In Dub (12") | 25 |
| 80 | Negus Roots NERT 003 | I Love Jah/Version | 40 |
| 81 | Negus Roots NERT 005 | Jah Is Watching You/PAPA TULLO: Sweet Reggae Music (12") | 25 |
| 80 | Black Joy DH 805 | Jah Love Is Sweeter/ROCKERS BAND: Sweeter Rockers (12") | 50 |
| 81 | Negus Roots NERT 008 | Government Man/P. TULLO: Straight To The Government (12" blue/black vinyl) | 40 |
| 82 | Negus Roots NERT 013 | Speak Softly/Money A The Remedy (with PAPA TULLO/Take This Message To My Woman (12") | 30 |
| 83 | Negus Roots NERT 019 | Johnny Brown/Mrs Brown (12") | 20 |
| 83 | Csa SPCSA 12006 | Tug A War Game/EARL SIXTEEN: Rise In The Morning (12") | 50 |
| 82 | Negus Roots NERT LP 002 | MORNING GLORY (LP) | 60 |
| 83 | Negus Roots NERT LP 008 | AFRICAN LADY (LP) | 50 |

**CASTELLS**
| | | | |
|---|---|---|---|
| 61 | London HLN 9392 | Sacred/I Get Dreamy | 20 |
| 62 | London HLN 9551 | So This Is Love/On The Street Of Tears | 25 |
| 67 | Masquerade MA 500 | Two Lovers/Jerusalem | 8 |

**BEBETO CASTILHO**
| | | | |
|---|---|---|---|
| 02 | Whatmusic.com WMLP 0016 | BEBETO (LP) | 15 |

**LEE CASTLE & BARONS**
| | | | |
|---|---|---|---|
| 64 | Parlophone R 5151 | A Love She Can Count On/Foolin' | 10 |

**ROY CASTLE**
| | | | |
|---|---|---|---|
| 60 | Philips PB 1087 | Little White Berry/Crazy Little Thorn | 5 |
| 65 | CBS 201736 | Doctor Terror's House Of Horrors/Voodoo Girl (with Tubby Hayes) | 50 |
| 68 | Olga OLE 12 | Wonderful World/For All The World | 5 |

**CASTLE SISTERS (JAMAICA)**
| | | | |
|---|---|---|---|
| 66 | Ska Beat JB 257 | Stop Your Lying/Don't Be A Fool | 30 |

**CASTLE SISTERS (USA)**
| | | | |
|---|---|---|---|
| 59 | Columbia DB 4335 | Drifting And Dreaming/Lucky Girl | 5 |

**CASTLE FARM**
| | | | |
|---|---|---|---|
| 72 | Farm FARM 1 | Hot Rod Queen/Mascot | 60 |

**CAST OF THOUSANDS**
| | | | |
|---|---|---|---|
| 66 | Stateside SS 546 | My Jenny Wears A Mini/Girl Do What You Gonna Do | 40 |

**CASTON & MAJORS**
| | | | |
|---|---|---|---|
| 75 | Tamla Motown TMG 938 | Child Of Love/No One Will Know | 15 |

*(see also Radiants)*

MINT VALUE £

## JIMMY CASTOR (BUNCH)
| | | | |
|---|---|---|---|
| 66 | Philips BF 1543 | Hey Leroy, Your Mama's Callin'/Ham Rock's Espanol | 20 |
| 67 | Philips BF 1590 | Magic Saxophone/Just You Girl | 25 |
| 71 | Mercury 6052 110 | Hey Leroy, Your Mama's Callin'/Ham Rock's Espanol (reissue) | 5 |
| 73 | RCA Victor APD1 0103 | DIMENSION III (LP, quadrophonic) | 20 |

## MARIO CASTRO NEVES & HIS ORCHESTRA
| | | | |
|---|---|---|---|
| 73 | Decca PFS 4294 | BRAZILIAN MOOD (LP) | 15 |

## CASUAL FOUR
| | | | |
|---|---|---|---|
| 70s | Specially Made For Us 102 | I Can Tell/Love Potion No. 9 | 20 |

## CASUALEERS
| | | | |
|---|---|---|---|
| 74 | Pye Disco Demand DDS 103 | Dance Dance Dance/Something About This Girl | 6 |

## CASUALS
| | | | |
|---|---|---|---|
| 65 | Fontana TF 635 | If You Walk Out/Please Don't Hide | 5 |
| 68 | Decca F 12737 | Adios Amor (Goodbye My Love)/Don't Dream Of Yesterday | 5 |
| 68 | Decca F 22784 | Jesamine/I've Got Something Too | 5 |
| 68 | Decca F 22852 | Toy/Touched (p/s) | 10 |
| 68 | Decca F 22852 | Toy/Touched | 5 |
| 69 | Decca F 22900 | Fools Paradise/7 X 7 | 5 |
| 69 | Decca F 22943 | Sunflower Eyes/Never My Love | 5 |
| 69 | Decca F 22969 | Caroline/Naughty Boy | 5 |
| 70 | Decca F 23027 | My Name Is Love/I Can't Say | 5 |
| 71 | Decca F 23112 | Someday Rock 'n' Roll Lady/A Letter Every Day | 5 |
| 72 | Parlophone R 5959 | Tara Tiger Girl/Nature's Girl | 10 |
| 74 | Dawn DNS 1069 | Witch/Good Times | 20 |
| 69 | Decca LK-R/SKL-R 5001 | HOUR WORLD (LP, large unboxed logo on label) | 50 |

*(see also American Jam, Kansas Hook)*

## JOHNNY CASWELL
| | | | |
|---|---|---|---|
| 85 | Kent TOWN 106 | You Don't Love Me No More/STEINWAYS: You've Been Leading Me On | 20 |

## CATAPILLA
| | | | |
|---|---|---|---|
| 71 | Vertigo 6360 029 | CATAPILLA (LP, gatefold sleeve, small swirl label) | 600 |
| 72 | Vertigo 6360 074L | CHANGES (LP, die-cut gatefold sleeve, small swirl label) | 1500 |

*(see also Jon Stevens, Liar)*

## CATAPULT
| | | | |
|---|---|---|---|
| 75 | Box BOX 7 | Put On The Lights/Linda | 15 |

## CATATONIA
| | | | |
|---|---|---|---|
| 98 | Blanco Y Negro 20834-1 | INTERNATIONAL VELVET (LP, 1,000 only, with free 12") | 18 |

## CATCH
| | | | |
|---|---|---|---|
| 77 | Logo GO 103 | Borderline/Black Blood (company sleeve) | 40 |

*(see also Tourists, Eurythmics)*

## CATE BROTHERS
| | | | |
|---|---|---|---|
| 76 | Asylum 13062 | Where Can We Go/Instrumental | 15 |

## CATFISH
| | | | |
|---|---|---|---|
| 70 | CBS 64006 | GET DOWN (LP, orange label) | 15 |
| 71 | Epic 64408 | LIVE CATFISH (LP) | 15 |

## CATHEDRAL
| | | | |
|---|---|---|---|
| 92 | Earache MOSH 40T | Soul Sacrifice/Autumn Twilight/Frozen Rapture/Golden Blood (Flooding) | 12 |
| 94 | Earache MOSH 106T | STATIK MAJIK EP (12", p/s) | 10 |
| 95 | Earache MOSH 152 | HOPKINS (THE WITCHFINDER GENERAL) EP (12", p/s) | 12 |
| 11 | Rise Above ROSE 12 141 | A NEW ICE AGE EP: Open Mind Surgery/Sabbadaius Sabbatum (12", poster 100 clear/100 white or 100 transluscent blue vinyl, sold at farewell gig) | 60 |
| 91 | Earache MOSH 43 | FOREST OF EQUILIBRIUM (LP, gatefold) | 30 |
| 93 | Earache MOSH 77C | THE ETHEREAL MIRROR (LP, blue vinyl, 1000 copies) | 80 |
| 94 | Rise Above RISE 8 | IN MEMORIAM (LP, purple vinyl) | 25 |
| 95 | Earache MOSH 130 | THE CARNIVAL BIZARRE (2 x 10" LP, gatefold sleeve) | 20 |
| 96 | Earache MOSH 156 | SUPERNATURAL BIRTH MACHINE (2 x 10" test pressings, 10 copies only, release cancelled) | 350 |

## CATHERINE WHEEL
| | | | |
|---|---|---|---|
| 92 | Fontana 510 903-1 | FERMENT (LP, initially with free 12") | 35 |
| 92 | Fontana 510903-1 | FERMENT (LP, without free 12") | 20 |
| 93 | Fontana 518 039-1 | CHROME (LP with inner sleeve) | 60 |
| 97 | Chrysalis 7243 4 93099 1 3 | ADAM & EVE (2-LP) | 40 |
| 00 | Chrysalis 7243526776 1 0 | WISHVILLE (LP) | 15 |

## RAY CATHODE (BBC RADIOPHONICS)
| | | | |
|---|---|---|---|
| 62 | Parlophone R 4901 | Time Beat/Waltz In Orbit | 10 |

*(see also BBC Radiophonic Workshop, George Martin)*

## CATHY LA CREME
| | | | |
|---|---|---|---|
| 80 | Ovation OVS 12 | I Married A Cult Figure From Salford/CROTONES: Tea Machine Dub | 6 |

## CAT IRON
| | | | |
|---|---|---|---|
| 69 | Xtra XTRA 1087 | CAT IRON (LP) | 25 |

## CAT MOTHER & ALL NIGHT NEWSBOYS
| | | | |
|---|---|---|---|
| 69 | Polydor 56543 | Good Old Rock'N'Roll/Bad News | 8 |
| 70 | Polydor 2066 026 | I Must Be Dreaming/Last Go Round | 6 |
| 69 | Polydor 184 300 | THE STREET GIVETH AND THE STREET TAKETH AWAY (LP) | 30 |
| 70 | Polydor 2425 021 | ALBION DOO-WAH (LP, gatefold sleeve) | 15 |
| 72 | United Artists UAG 29313 | CAT MOTHER & ALL NIGHT NEWS BOYS (LP, gatefold sleeve) | 20 |
| 73 | United Artists UAG 29381 | LAST CHANCE DANCE (LP) | 15 |

*(see also Jimi Hendrix)*

## CATS 'N' JAMMER KIDS
| | | | |
|---|---|---|---|
| 77 | Ebony EYE 3 | Disco Drum/Disco Drum (Part 5) | 6 |
| 77 | Ebony EYEC 3 | Disco Drum/Disco Drum (Part 5) (12") | 30 |

## CATS EYES
| | | | |
|---|---|---|---|
| 68 | Deram DM 190 | Smile Girl For Me/In A Fantasy World | 10 |
| 68 | Deram DM 209 | I Thank You Marianne/Turn Around | 10 |
| 69 | Deram DM 251 | Where Is She Now?/Tom Drum | 25 |
| 70 | MCA MK 5028 | The Loser/Circus | 12 |
| 70 | MCA MK 5043 | Circus/Come Away Melinda | 5 |
| 70 | MCA MK 5056 | The Wizard/Hey (Open Your Eyes) | 20 |

## CATS EYES (2)
| | | | |
|---|---|---|---|
| 11 | Polydor 2763913 | BROKEN GLASS EP (2 x 7") | 20 |
| 11 | Polydor 2766263 | CAT'S EYES (LP) | 20 |

*(see also Horrors)*

## CAT'S PYJAMAS
| | | | |
|---|---|---|---|
| 68 | Direction 58-3235 | Virginia Water/Baby I Love You | 40 |
| 68 | Direction 58-3482 | Camera Man/House For Sale | 40 |

*(see also Kenny Bernard)*

## CATS (1)
| | | | |
|---|---|---|---|
| 67 | Parlophone R 5558 | What A Crazy Life/Hopeless Try | 7 |
| 68 | Parlophone R 5663 | What Is The World Coming To/How Could I Be So Blind? | 10 |
| 69 | Columbia DB 8524 | I Gotta Know What's Going On/Lea | 10 |
| 69 | Columbia DB 8571 | Why/Mandy, My Dear | 5 |
| 70 | Columbia DB 8655 | Marian/Somewhere Up There | 5 |
| 71 | Columbia DB 8748 | I Love You, I Do/Where Have I Been Wrong | 5 |
| 71 | Columbia DB 8816 | One Way Mind/Country Woman | 5 |
| 72 | Columbia DB 8850 | Dance, Dance, Dance/My Friend Joe | 5 |
| 72 | Columbia DB 8909 | Let's Dance/I've Been In Love Before | 5 |

## CATS (2)
| | | | |
|---|---|---|---|
| 69 | Baf BAF 1 | Swan Lake/Swing Low | 10 |
| 69 | Baf BAF 2 | My Girl/The Hog | 10 |
| 69 | Baf BAF 3 | The Hig/Blues For Justice | 10 |
| 69 | Baf BAF 4 | William Tell/Love Walk Right In | 10 |
| 70 | Crystal CR 7009 | Sherman/What Can I Do | 40 |

## CLEM CATTINI ORK
| | | | |
|---|---|---|---|
| 65 | Decca F 12135 | No Time To Think/Impact | 50 |

*(see also Tornados, Aquarian Age, Rumplestiltskin, Spaghetti Head, Sounds Nice)*

## NADIA CATTOUSE
| | | | |
|---|---|---|---|
| 60s | Church Miss. Soc. LIV/SP/81 | The Larder/PAULINE FILBY: I'm Hungry | 5 |
| 66 | Reality RY 1001 | NADIA CATTOUSE (LP) | 40 |
| 70 | RCA Victor SF 8070 | EARTH MOTHER (LP, orange/white label) | 30 |

## CATWAX AXE CO
| | | | |
|---|---|---|---|
| 81 | Waxwalk CAT 001 | Waxwalk/Jumbo Jet (Hey! I Wany Your Crazy Wild) | 10 |
| 81 | Waxwalk CAT 001 | Waxwalk/Jumbo Jet (Hey! I Wany Your Crazy Wild) (reissue) | 6 |

## THE CAUSE
| | | | |
|---|---|---|---|
| 82 | Rising Sun RS 001 | METRO POLICE EP (original copies with insert sleeve) | 30 |
| 82 | Rising Sun RS 001 | METRO POLICE EP (without insert sleeve) | 15 |

## CAUSE N EFFECT
| | | | |
|---|---|---|---|
| 90 | Foxadelic JTF1 | Hype/That's What It Is | 25 |
| 91 | Foxadelic JTF2 | Some Bite The Bullet (EP) | 30 |

## CAUSTIC WINDOW
| | | | |
|---|---|---|---|
| 92 | Rephlex CAT 004 | JOYREX J4 EP (12", 6-track) | 40 |
| 92 | Rephlex CAT 005 | JOYREX J5 EP (12, 4-track, black vinyl) | 40 |
| 92 | Rephlex CAT 005 | JOYREX J5 EP (12, 4-track, white vinyl) | 30 |
| 93 | Rephlex CAT 009 i | JOYREX J9 EP (10", picture disc, with bonus track "HMNA", 300 only) | 100 |
| 93 | Rephlex CAT 009 ii | JOYREX J9 EP (12" 4-track, initial 100 in card mailer with bag of "space dust") | 70 |
| 93 | Rephlex CAT 009 ii | JOYREX J9 EP (12" 4-track) | 50 |
| 94 | Rephlex CAT 023 | CAUSTIC WINDOW (2-LP, test pressing only, 5 known copies) | 2500 |

*(see also Aphex Twin)*

## CAVALIERS
| | | | |
|---|---|---|---|
| 86 | él GPO 11 | It's A Beautiful Game/The I.T. Man (p/s) | 10 |
| 86 | él ACME 4 | A PERFECT ACTION (LP) | 18 |

## EDDIE CAVE & FYX
| | | | |
|---|---|---|---|
| 66 | Pye 7N 17161 | Fresh Out Of Tears/It's Almost Good | 35 |

## NICK CAVE (& BAD SEEDS)
| | | | |
|---|---|---|---|
| 84 | Mute 7 MUTE 32 | In The Ghetto/The Moon Is In The Gutter (p/s) | 8 |
| 85 | Mute 7 MUTE 38 | Tupelo/The Six Strings That Drew Blood (p/s) | 8 |
| 86 | Mute MUTE 47 | The Singer/Running Scared/Black Betty | 6 |
| 86 | Lyntone LYN 18038 | Scum (green vinyl flexidisc, with poster, concert freebie) | 18 |
| 86 | Lyntone LYN 18038 | Scum (green vinyl flexidisc, without poster, concert freebie) | 12 |
| 88 | Mute MUTE 52 | The Mercy Seat/New Day | 10 |
| 88 | Muite 12MUTE 52 | The Mercy Seat (Full Length Version)/New Day/The Mercy Seat (Video Mix) (12", p/s) | 12 |
| 88 | Mute MUTE 86 | Oh Deanna/The Girl At The Bottom Of My Glass (no p/s, DJ-only) | 12 |
| 88 | Mute 12MUTE86 | Deanna/The Girl At The Bottom Of My Glass (12". with poster and postcard) | 10 |
| 90 | Mute MUTE 118 | The Weeping Song/Cocks 'n' Asses | 8 |
| 92 | Mute LMUTE 140 | Straight To You/Jack The Ripper (Acoustic Version) (limited issue, p/s) | 8 |
| 92 | Mute MUTE 148 | I Had A Dream, Joe/The Good Son (live) (numbered p/s, 7,000 only) | 8 |

MINT VALUE £

| 94 | Mute PMUTE 172 | Red Right Hand (1-sided promo, with postcard and press release) | 20 |
|---|---|---|---|
| 94 | Mute MUTE 160 | Do You Love Me? (Single Version)/Cassiel's Song/Sail Away (silver vinyl, p/s, 1,000 copies) | 10 |
| 94 | Mute MUTE 169 | Loverman (Single Version)/(I'll Love You) Till The End Of The World (picture disc, 2,000 only) | 10 |
| 94 | Mute MUTE 172 | Red Right Hand/That's What Jazz Is To Me (red vinyl, p/s, with 2 different stickers & labels, 2,000 only) | 15 |
| 97 | Mute MUTE 192 | Into My Arms/Little Empty Boat | 10 |
| 04 | Mute MUTE 329 | Breathless (alternative mix)/These She Goes, My Beautiful World (edit)/She's Leaving You | 6 |
| 08 | Mute MUTE 403 | Midnight Man/Hey Little Firing Squad | 10 |
| 08 | Mute MUTE 377 | Dig Lazarus Dig!!!/Accidents Will Happen | 5 |
| 08 | Mute MUTE 390 | More News From Nowhere/Fleeting Love | 5 |
| 84 | Mute STUMM 17 | FROM HER TO ETERNITY (LP, with inner sleeve) | 30 |
| 85 | Mute STUMM 21 | THE FIRSTBORN IS DEAD (LP, with inner sleeve) | 30 |
| 86 | Mute STUMM 28 | KICKING AGAINST THE PRICKS (LP) | 25 |
| 86 | Mute STUMM 34 | YOUR FUNERAL...MY TRIAL (2-LP, gatefold sleeve, with inner sleeves) | 25 |
| 88 | Mute LSTUMM 52 | TENDER PREY (LP, with bonus spoken word 12" And The Ass Saw The Angel [P STUMM 52]: "Autumn"/"Animal Static/Mah Sanctum/Lamentation, 5,000 only) | 40 |
| 88 | Muite STUMM 52 | TENDER PREY (LP, without bonus spoken word 12") | 25 |
| 90 | Mute LSTUMM 76 | THE GOOD SON (LP, with bonus 7" "Acoustic Versions From Tender Prey" [P STUMM 76]: "The Mercy Seat"/"City Of Refuge"/"Deanna") | 35 |
| 90 | Mute STUMM 76 | THE GOOD SON (LP, inner sleeve, without free 7") | 18 |
| 92 | Mute STUMM 92 | HENRY'S DREAM (LP, with inner sleeve and art print) | 25 |
| 94 | Mute LSTUMM 123 | LET LOVE IN (LP, with set of postcards or poster) | 35 |
| 96 | Mute STUMM 138 | MURDER BALLADS (LP, with insert) | 40 |
| 97 | Mute STUMM 142 | THE BOATMANS CALL (LP) | 50 |
| 98 | Mute MUTEL4 | THE BEST OF NICK CAVE AND THE BAD SEEDS (2-LP, inners) | 50 |
| 01 | Mute STUMM 164 | NO MORE SHALL WE PART (2-LP, with inner sleeves) | 50 |
| 03 | Mute STUMM 207 | NOCTURAMA (2-LP, inners) | 20 |
| 04 | Mute STUMM 233 | ABBATOIR BLUES/THE LYRE OF ORPHEUS (2-LP, inner sleeves and insert) | 80 |
| 08 | Mute STUMM 277 | DIG LAZARUS DIG (LP, inners, booklet, and free 7") | 25 |
| 13 | Bad Seed Ltd. BS001 DLX | PUSH THE SKY AWAY (2-LP, 2x7", DVD, book numbered and signed box set) | 100 |
| 13 | Bad Seed Ltd. BS001 DLX | PUSH THE SKY AWAY (2-LP, 2x7", DVD, book numbered and unsigned box set) | 70 |

*(see also Birthday Party, Annie Hogan, Burmoe Brothers)*

## STUART & SANDY CAVE
| 77 | Profile GMOR 143 | DAWN ON SUNDAY (LP) | 60 |
|---|---|---|---|

## ANDY CAVELL
| 62 | HMV POP 1024 | Hey There Cruel Heart/Lonely Soldier Boy | 40 |
|---|---|---|---|
| 62 | HMV POP 1080 | Always On Saturday/Hey There, Senorita | 40 |
| 63 | Pye 7N 15539 | Andy/There Was A Boy | 30 |
| 64 | Pye 7N 15610 | Shut Up/Tell The Truth | 30 |

## JIMMY CAVELLO & HIS HOUSE ROCKERS
| 57 | Vogue Coral Q 72226 | Rock, Rock, Rock/The Big Beat | 250 |
|---|---|---|---|
| 57 | Vogue Coral Q 72240 | Foot Stompin'/Ooh-Wee | 250 |

*(see also Alan Freed)*

## CAVE OF THE LIVING STREAMS
| 74 | Indigo Sound Studios UHC 1 | SIXTEEN SONGS (LP, private pressing with booklet) | 40 |
|---|---|---|---|

## MONTE CAZAZZA
| 79 | Industrial IR 0005 | To Mom On Mother's Day/Candy Man (p/s, with outer polystyrene sleeve & insert, 2,500 only) | 20 |
|---|---|---|---|
| 80 | Industrial IR 0010 | SOMETHING FOR NOBODY (EP) | 20 |

*(see also Psychic TV)*

## C.C.S. (COLLECTIVE CONSCIOUSNESS SOCIETY)
| 71 | Rak 109 | Walking/Salome | 5 |
|---|---|---|---|
| 71 | Rak 119 | Tap Turns On The Water/Save The World | 6 |
| 72 | Rak 126 | Brother/Mister What You Can't Have I Can Get | 5 |
| 73 | Rak RAK 154 | The Band Played The Boogie/Hang It On Me | 5 |
| 70 | Rak SRAK 6751 | C.C.S. (LP, gatefold sleeve) | 25 |
| 72 | Rak SRAK 503 | C.C.S. (LP) | 25 |
| 73 | Rak SRAK 504 | THE BEST BAND IN THE LAND (LP) | 15 |

*(see also Alexis Korner)*

## CEDARS
| 68 | Decca F 22720 | For Your Information/Hide If You Want To Hide | 50 |
|---|---|---|---|
| 68 | Decca F 22772 | I Like The Way/I Don't Know Why | 50 |

*(see also Seaders)*

## TONY CEE
| 81 | Cheeseman CT 1 | Holiday/One Way Street | 50 |
|---|---|---|---|

## CELEBRATION FEATURING MIKE LOVE
| 73 | MCA 365 | Almost Summer/Lookin' Good | 8 |
|---|---|---|---|

*(see also Beach Boys)*

## ADRIANO CELENTANO
| 72 | Epic EPC 1886 | Prisencohnensinaincusol/Disc Jockey | 6 |
|---|---|---|---|

## CELIA & THE MUTATIONS
| 77 | United Artists UP 36262 | Mony Mony/Mean To Me (p/s) | 6 |
|---|---|---|---|
| 77 | United Artists UP 36318 | You Better Believe Me/Round And Around (p/s) | 10 |

*(see also Stranglers, Tonight)*

## CELIBATES
| 81 | ALPLP 1001 | A SHAMELESS FASHION (LP) | 40 |
|---|---|---|---|

## CELTIC F.C.
| 67 | Thistle | Celtic Celtic (p/s) ................................................................ | 12 |
| 73 | Polydor 2058332 | Celtic Your Favourites In Green/Saturday ........................................ | 5 |

## CELTIC FROST
| 84 | Noise N 0017 | MORBID TALES (mini LP, with poster) ............................................ | 40 |
| 84 | Noise N 0017 | MORBID TALES (mini LP, without poster) ......................................... | 25 |
| 86 | Combat MX 8091 | TO MEGA THERION (LP, gatefold, with inner sleeve) .............................. | 25 |
| 87 | NOISE NOISE 065 | INTO THE PANDEMONIUM (LP, gatefold sleeve, with insert) ........................ | 25 |
| 06 | Century Media 9979951 | MONOTHEIST (2-LP, gatefold, brown marbled vinyl, 100 only) ..................... | 50 |

## CENOTAPH CORNER
| 76 | Cottage COT 501 | UPS AND DOWNS (LP) ............................................................. | 20 |
| 79 | Cottage COT 031 | EVERY DAY BUT WEDNESDAY (LP) ................................................... | 25 |

## CENTIPEDE
| 71 | RCA Neon NE 9 | SEPTOBER ENERGY (2-LP, gatefold sleeve, black inner sleeve) .................... | 80 |
| 74 | RCA DPS 2054 | SEPTOBER ENERGY (2-LP, reissue, different cover) .............................. | 20 |

*(see also Mark Charig, Elton Dean, Zoot Money, Alan Skidmore, Keith Tippett, Julie Tippetts, Mike Patto, Robert Wyatt)*

## CENTRY
| 80s | Conscious Sounds DPS 001 | Stepping Time/Stepping Dub (12") ............................................. | 10 |
| 93 | Conscious Sounds DNC 002 | THUNDER MOUNTAIN : CENTRY IN DUB (LP) ........................................ | 25 |
| 95 | Conscious Sounds DNC 005 | RELEASE THE CHAINS (LP) ...................................................... | 15 |

## CENTURION
| 82 | Centurion 0001 | Two Wheels/Bitch (private pressing) ........................................... | 50 |
| 82 | Centurion 0001 | Two Wheels/Bitch (private pressing, mislabelled 'Nikki') ...................... | 30 |

## CENTURY 21 (GERRY ANDERSON TV SPIN-OFFS)
| 65 | Century 21 MA 100 | JOURNEY TO THE MOON (EP) ...................................................... | 15 |
| 65 | Century 21 MA 101 | INTO ACTION WITH TROY TEMPEST (EP) ........................................... | 12 |
| 65 | Century 21 MA 102 | A TRIP TO MARINEVILLE (EP) .................................................... | 15 |
| 65 | Century 21 MA 103 | INTRODUCING THUNDERBIRDS (EP) ................................................. | 15 |
| 65 | Century 21 MA 104 | MARINA SPEAKS (EP) ............................................................ | 15 |
| 65 | Century 21 MA 105 | TV CENTURY 21 THEMES (EP) ..................................................... | 15 |
| 66 | Century 21 MA 106 | THE DALEKS (EP) ............................................................... | 50 |
| 66 | Century 21 MA 107 | F.A.B. (EP) ................................................................... | 18 |
| 66 | Century 21 MA 108 | THUNDERBIRD 1 (EP) ............................................................ | 18 |
| 66 | Century 21 MA 109 | THUNDERBIRD 2 (EP) ............................................................ | 18 |
| 66 | Century 21 MA 110 | THE STATELY HOME ROBBERIES (EP) ............................................... | 25 |
| 66 | Century 21 MA 111 | LADY PENELOPE & OTHER TV THEMES (EP) .......................................... | 25 |
| 66 | Century 21 MA 112 | THUNDERBIRD 3 (EP) ............................................................ | 25 |
| 66 | Century 21 MA 113 | THUNDERBIRD 4 (EP) ............................................................ | 25 |
| 66 | Century 21 MA 114 | THE PERILS OF PENELOPE (EP) ................................................... | 30 |
| 66 | Century 21 MA 115 | TOPO GIGIO IN LONDON (EP) ..................................................... | 45 |
| 67 | Century 21 MA 116 | GREAT THEMES FROM GERRY ANDERSON'S THUNDERBIRDS (EP) .......................... | 30 |
| 67 | Century 21 MA 117 | SPACE AGE NURSERY RHYMES (EP) ................................................. | 35 |
| 67 | Century 21 MA 118 | LADY PENELOPE AND PARKER (EP) ................................................. | 35 |
| 67 | Century 21 MA 119 | BRAINS AND TIN TIN (EP) ....................................................... | 35 |
| 67 | Century 21 MA 120 | INTERNATIONAL RESCUE (EP) ..................................................... | 35 |
| 67 | Century 21 MA 121 | THUNDERBIRDS (EP) ............................................................. | 35 |
| 67 | Century 21 MA 122 | LADY PENELOPE (EP) ............................................................ | 35 |
| 67 | Century 21 MA 123 | BRAINS (EP) ................................................................... | 35 |
| 67 | Century 21 MA 124 | BRINK OF DISASTER (EP) ........................................................ | 35 |
| 67 | Century 21 MA 125 | ATLANTIC INFERNO (EP) ......................................................... | 35 |
| 67 | Century 21 MA 126 | RICOCHET (EP) ................................................................. | 35 |
| 67 | Century 21 MA 127 | TINGHA & TUCKER & THE WOMBAVILLE BAND (EP) .................................... | 35 |
| 67 | Century 21 MA 128 | ONE MOVE & YOU'RE DEAD (EP) ................................................... | 35 |
| 67 | Century 21 MA 129 | 30 MINUTES AFTER NOON (EP) .................................................... | 35 |
| 67 | Century 21 MA 130 | TINGHA & TUCKER IN NURSERY RHYME TIME (EP) .................................... | 35 |
| 67 | Century 21 MA 131 | INTRODUCING CAPTAIN SCARLET (EP) .............................................. | 30 |
| 67 | Century 21 MA 132 | CAPTAIN SCARLET AND THE MYSTERONS (EP) ........................................ | 30 |
| 67 | Century 21 MA 133 | CAPTAIN SCARLET IS INDESTRUCTIBLE (EP) ........................................ | 25 |
| 67 | Century 21 MA 134 | CAPTAIN SCARLET OF SPECTRUM (EP) .............................................. | 20 |
| 67 | Century 21 MA 135 | CAPTAIN SCARLET VS. CAPTAIN BLACK (EP) ........................................ | 25 |
| 67 | Century 21 MA 136 | THEMES FROM GERRY ANDERSON'S CAPTAIN SCARLET (EP) ............................. | 25 |
| 65 | Century 21 LA 100 | JOURNEY TO THE MOON (LP) ...................................................... | 70 |
| 66 | Century 21 LA 1 | THE WORLD OF TOMORROW (LP) .................................................... | 50 |
| 66 | Century 21 LA 2 | LADY PENELOPE PRESENTS (LP) ................................................... | 50 |
| 66 | Century 21 LA 3 | JEFF TRACY INTRODUCES INTERNATIONAL RESCUE (LP) ............................... | 50 |
| 66 | Century 21 LA 4 | LADY PENELOPE INVESTIGATES (LP) ............................................... | 50 |
| 66 | Century 21 LA 5 | THE TINGHA & TUCKER CLUB SONG BOOK (LP) ....................................... | 50 |
| 67 | Century 21 LA 6 | FAVOURITE TELEVISION THEMES (LP) .............................................. | 50 |
| 68 | Marble Arch MAL 770 | TV FAVOURITES VOL. 1 (LP) ..................................................... | 20 |
| 68 | Marble Arch MAL 771 | TV FAVOURITES VOL. 2 (LP) ..................................................... | 20 |

*(see also Barry Gray, Dr. Who)*

## CEOLBEG
| 90 | Ceolbeg Music CB 001 | NOT THE BUNNY HOP (LP) ........................................................ | 20 |

## CERTAIN LIONS & TIGERS
| 70 | Polydor 2344 002 | SOUL CONDOR (LP) .............................................................. | 40 |

## CEYLEIB PEOPLE
| 68 | Vocalion SAVL 8072 | TANYET (LP) ................................................................... | 200 |

## ERNIE CHAFFIN

| | | | |
|---|---|---|---|
| 57 | London HLS 8409 | Feelin' Low/Lonesome For My Baby | 150 |
| 57 | London HLS 8409 | Feelin' Low/Lonesome For My Baby (78) | 30 |

## CHAIN REACTION

| | | | |
|---|---|---|---|
| 77 | Gull GULS 43 | This Eternal Flame/Never Lose, Never Win | 15 |
| 77 | Gull GULS 53 | Why Can't We Be Lovers/Hogtied | 15 |
| 77 | Gull GULS 77 | Never Lose Never Win/Chase A Miracle | 15 |

## CHAIN OF STRENGTH

| | | | |
|---|---|---|---|
| 91 | First Strike FS010 | WHAT HOLDS US APART (EP, blue vinyl) | 30 |
| 91 | First Strike FS010 | WHAT HOLDS US APART (EP, white vinyl) | 40 |

## CHAINSAW

| | | | |
|---|---|---|---|
| 80 | Square SQSP 2 | Police And Politicians/Hole In The Road (p/s) | 45 |
| 80 | Pot Belly EJSP 9462 | Lonely Without You/On The Highway | 35 |
| 84 | GMC CS 001 | Long Legged Woman/Midnight Blue | 30 |

## CHAIRMAN YOUTH

| | | | |
|---|---|---|---|
| 81 | Last Ditch TRENCH 1 | Uncertainty/Business Partners (p/s) | 6 |

## CHAIRMEN OF THE BOARD

| | | | |
|---|---|---|---|
| 70 | Invictus INV 501 | Give Me Just A Little More Time/Since The Days Of Pigtails | 8 |
| 70 | Invictus INV 501 | Give Me Just A Little More Time/Since The Days Of Pigtails (DJ Copy) | 20 |
| 70 | Invictus INV 504 | You've Got Me Dangling On A String/Patches | 6 |
| 70 | Invictus INV 504 | You've Got Me Dangling On A String/Patches (DJ Copy) | 20 |
| 71 | Invictus INV 507 | Everything's Tuesday/Bless You | 6 |
| 71 | Invictus INV 507 | Everything's Tuesday/Bless You (DJ Copy) | 15 |
| 71 | Invictus INV 511 | Pay To The Piper/When Will She Tell Me She Needs Me? | 5 |
| 71 | Invictus INV 511 | Pay To The Piper/When Will She Tell Me She Needs Me? (DJ Copy) | 15 |
| 71 | Invictus INV 516 | Chairman Of The Board/Hanging On To A Memory | 5 |
| 71 | Invictus INV 516 | Chairman Of The Board/When Will She Tell Me She Needs Me? (different B-side) | 5 |
| 72 | Invictus INV 519 | Working On A Building Of Love/Try On My Love For Size | 5 |
| 72 | Invictus INV 524 | Elmo James/Bittersweet | 5 |
| 72 | Invictus INV 527 | I'm On My Way To A Better Place/So Glad You're Mine | 5 |
| 73 | Invictus INV 530 | Finders Keepers/Finders Keepers (Instrumental) | 5 |
| 70 | Invictus SVT 1002 | CHAIRMEN OF THE BOARD (LP) | 20 |
| 71 | Invictus SVT 1003 | IN SESSION (LP) | 20 |
| 72 | Invictus SVT 1006 | BITTERSWEET (LP) | 15 |
| 74 | Invictus SVT 65868 | SKIN I'M IN (LP) | 15 |

*(see also Showmen, General Johnson, Norman Johnson)*

## CHAKA KHAN

| | | | |
|---|---|---|---|
| 80 | Warner Bros. 17617T | Clouds/What You Did (12") | 10 |
| 81 | Warner Bros. LV 48 | Wha'cha Gonna Do For Me/We Got The Love/I'm Every Woman (12", p/s) | 12 |

*(see also Rufus, Rufus & Chaka Khan)*

## CHAKACHAS

| | | | |
|---|---|---|---|
| 61 | RCA RCA 1264 | Twist Twist/Baila La Bamba | 5 |
| 72 | Polydor 2121 064 | Jungle Fever/Chaka Cha | 10 |
| 72 | Polydor 2489 050 | JUNGLE FEVER (LP) | 20 |
| 73 | Young Blood SYB 3003 | CHAKACHAS (LP) | 20 |

## GEORGE CHAKIRIS

| | | | |
|---|---|---|---|
| 60 | Triumph RGM 1010 | Heart Of A Teenage Girl/I'm Always Chasing Rainbows | 20 |

## CHALAWA

| | | | |
|---|---|---|---|
| 78 | Skynote SKYLP 14 | EXODUS DUB (LP) | 40 |

## CHALICE

| | | | |
|---|---|---|---|
| 80 | Galactic GALD 002 | I'm Gonna Get You/Oi Nayga (12") | 12 |

## CHALK GIANTS

| | | | |
|---|---|---|---|
| 91 | SRT 91 LS 2856 | THROW IT ALL AWAY EP (12", p/s) | 10 |

## BRYAN CHALKER('S NEW FRONTIER)

| | | | |
|---|---|---|---|
| 70 | Amity OTS 502 | Ned Kelly/Four Girls From The Town Of Boston | 6 |
| 72 | Columbia DB 8883 | Daddy Sang Bass/Lot 69 | 6 |
| 72 | Chapter One SCH 179 | Help Me Make It Through The Night/Eskimo Song | 6 |
| 73 | Chapter One SCH 185 | Daisy A Day/Life Gets Tee-jus, Don't It | 6 |
| 71 | Avenue AVE 071 | THE HANGING OF SAMUEL HALL (LP, textured sleeve, as Bryan Chalker's New Frontier) | 15 |

## CHALLENGER

| | | | |
|---|---|---|---|
| 81 | CMC CM 0001 | So Sure Of Yourself/Out To Kill | 40 |

## CHALLENGERS (U.K.)

| | | | |
|---|---|---|---|
| 61 | Parlophone R 4773 | Cry Of The Wild Goose/Deadline | 10 |

## CHALLENGERS (U.S.)

| | | | |
|---|---|---|---|
| 63 | Stateside SS 177 | Torquay/Bulldog | 10 |
| 65 | Vocalion V 9253 | The Man From U.N.C.L.E./The Streets Of London | 20 |
| 66 | Vocalion V 9270 | Walk With Me/How Could I | 10 |
| 63 | Stateside SL 10030 | SURFBEAT (LP) | 50 |
| 67 | Vocalion VA-N 8069 | WIPE OUT (LP, mono) | 50 |
| 67 | Vocalion SAV-N 8069 | WIPE OUT (LP, stereo) | 55 |

## CHAMBER POP ENSEMBLE

| | | | |
|---|---|---|---|
| 68 | Decca F 12789 | Walk Away Renee/59th Street Bridge Song (Feeling Groovy) | 5 |

## CHAMBERPOT

| | | | |
|---|---|---|---|
| 76 | Bead Records BEAD 2 | CHAMBERPOT (LP) | 50 |

## JAMES CHAMBERS

| | | | |
|---|---|---|---|
| 71 | Summit SUM 8523 | Bongo Man/KEN BOOTHE: Now I Know | 10 |

*(see also Jimmy Cliff)*

## CHAMBERS BROTHERS

| | | | |
|---|---|---|---|
| 66 | Vocalion VL 9267 | Love Me Like The Rain/Pretty Girls Everywhere | 20 |
| 66 | Vocalion VL 9276 | Call Me/Seventeen | 20 |
| 67 | CBS 202565 | All Strung Out Over You/Falling In Love | 10 |
| 68 | Direction 58-3215 | Up Town/Love Me Like The Rain | 7 |
| 68 | Direction 58-3671 | Time Has Come Today/Dinah | 12 |
| 68 | Direction 58-3760 | Time Has Come Today/Dinah (reissue) | 8 |
| 68 | Direction 58-3865 | I Can't Turn You Loose/Do Your Thing | 8 |
| 69 | Direction 58-4098 | Are You Ready/You Got The Power To Turn Me On | 6 |
| 69 | Direction 58-4318 | People Get Ready/No, No, No, Don't Say Goodbye | 6 |
| 69 | Direction 58-4367 | Wake Up/Everybody Needs Someone | 10 |
| 70 | Direction 58-4846 | Love Peace And Happiness/If You Want Me To | 7 |
| 70 | Direction 58-5033 | Let's Do It/To Love Somebody | 7 |
| 71 | CBS 5389 | Funky/Love, Peace And Happiness | 15 |
| 71 | CBS 7689 | By The Hair On My Chinny Chin Chin/Heaven | 6 |
| 66 | Vocalion VA-L/SAV-L 8058 | PEOPLE GET READY (LP) | 60 |
| 68 | Liberty LBS 83272 | SHOUT! (LP, blue label) | 30 |
| 68 | Direction 8-63407 | THE TIME HAS COME (LP) | 30 |
| 69 | Direction 8-63451 | A NEW TIME - A NEW DAY (LP) | 30 |
| 70 | Direction 8-66228 | LOVE PEACE AND HAPPINESS (Live At Bill Graham's Fillmore West) (2-LP) | 30 |
| 70 | Liberty LBS 83276 | FEELIN' THE BLUES (LP) | 15 |
| 71 | CBS 64156 | A NEW GENERATION (LP) | 15 |

## CHAMELEON

| | | | |
|---|---|---|---|
| 71 | CBS 5428 | Who Am I/Coogans Keep | 20 |

## CHAMELEONS

| | | | |
|---|---|---|---|
| 82 | Epic EPCA 2210 | In Shreds/Less Than Human (p/s) | 15 |
| 83 | Statik STAT 30 | As High As You Can Go/Pleasure And Pain (p/s) | 6 |
| 83 | Statik STAT 3012 | As High As You Can Go/Pleasure And Pain/Paper Tigers (12", p/s) | 10 |
| 83 | Statik TAK 6 | A Person Isn't Safe Anywhere These Days/Thursday's Child (p/s) | 7 |
| 85 | Statik TAK 29 | In Shreds/Nostalgia (p/s) | 6 |
| 85 | Statik TAK 29/12 | In Shreds/Less Than Human/Nostalgia (12", p/s) | 10 |
| 86 | Geffen GEF 4F/SAM 287 | Tears/Paradiso//Swamp Thing/Inside Out (double pack, gatefold p/s) | 7 |
| 86 | Geffen GEF 10 | Swamp Thing/John, I'm Only Dancing | 6 |
| 90 | Glass Pyramid EMC 1 | TONY FLETCHER WALKED ON WATER (12" EP) | 25 |
| 90 | Strange Fruit SFRLP 114 | PEEL SESSIONS (LP) | 15 |
| 83 | Statik STATLP 17 | SCRIPT OF THE BRIDGE (LP, 1st pressing, textured sleeve, insert) | 15 |
| 85 | Statik STATLP 17 | SCRIPT OF THE BRIDGE (LP, picture disc) | 20 |
| 86 | Geffen 924119 | STRANGE TIMES (LP, pink or blue sleeves) | 15 |
| 90 | Glass Pyramid EMC 2 | TRIPPING DOGS (LP) | 20 |
| 93 | Imaginary ILLUSION 042 | AUFFUHRUNG IN BERLIN (LP) | 20 |

*(see also Sun & Moon, Reegs)*

## TEDDY CHAMES

| | | | |
|---|---|---|---|
| 68 | Blue Cat BS 141 | I Want It Girl/She Is Gone (actually by Teddy Charmes) | 100 |

## DES CHAMP ORCHESTRA

| | | | |
|---|---|---|---|
| 70 | Page One POF 172 | It Takes A Thief/My Own Thing | 10 |

## CHAMPIONS OF NATURE

| | | | |
|---|---|---|---|
| 00 | White FOFF 1 | The Fuck Off Song/An Undercurrent/360/Carpe Diem (EP) | 30 |
| 00 | White FOFF 2 | Finalisation/Cold Dessert/Breakfast Of Champions (EP) | 30 |
| 01 | White SALSA001 | Salsa Smurph/Jazzy Styles (12") | 12 |

## CHAMPS (JAMAICA)

| | | | |
|---|---|---|---|
| 64 | Blue Beat BB 267 | Walk Between Your Enemies/Do What I Say | 20 |

## CHAMPS (U.S.)

| | | | |
|---|---|---|---|
| 58 | London HLU 8580 | Tequila/Train To Nowhere | 10 |
| 58 | London HL 8655 | Midnighter/El Rancho Rock | 10 |
| 58 | London HL 8715 | Chariot Rock/Subway | 10 |
| 59 | London HLH 8811 | Beatnik/Gone Train | 10 |
| 59 | London HLH 8864 | Caramba/Moonlight Bay | 10 |
| 60 | London HLH 9052 | Too Much Tequila/Twenty Thousand Leagues | 8 |
| 61 | London HLH 9430 | Cantina/Panic Button | 8 |
| 62 | London HLH 9506 | Tequila Twist/Limbo Rock | 8 |
| 62 | London HLH 9539 | Experiment In Terror/La Cucaracha | 8 |
| 62 | London HLH 9604 | Limbo Dance/Latin Limbo | 8 |
| 59 | London RE 1176 | FOUR BY THE CHAMPS (EP) | 25 |
| 59 | London RE-H 1209 | ANOTHER FOUR BY THE CHAMPS (EP) | 25 |
| 59 | London RE-H 1223 | STILL MORE BY THE CHAMPS (EP) | 25 |
| 61 | London RE-H 1250 | KNOCKOUTS! (EP) | 25 |
| 58 | London HA-H 2152 | GO CHAMPS GO! (LP) | 50 |
| 59 | London HA-H 2184 | EVERYBODY'S ROCKIN' WITH THE CHAMPS (LP) | 50 |
| 62 | London HA-H 2451 | GREAT DANCE HITS (LP, early issue with flipback cover) | 30 |

## ROB CHANCE & CHANCES-R

| | | | |
|---|---|---|---|
| 67 | CBS 3130 | At The End Of The Day/I've Got The Power | 15 |

*(see also Chances-R)*

## CHANCES ARE

| | | | |
|---|---|---|---|
| 67 | Columbia DB 8144 | Fragile Child/What Went Wrong | 40 |

## CHANCES-R

| | | | |
|---|---|---|---|
| 67 | CBS 202614 | Talking Out The Back Of My Head/I Aimed Too High | 20 |
| 67 | CBS 2940 | Do It Yourself/Turn A New Leaf Over | 12 |

*(see also Rob Chance & Chances-R)*

## CHANCIS
| | | | |
|---|---|---|---|
| 64 | Decca F 11860 | Everybody's Laughing/Tell Me | 15 |

## CHANDELIERS
| | | | |
|---|---|---|---|
| 73 | Penny Farthing PEN 809 | Can't You Hear My Heartbreak/One Way Street | 6 |

## TIM CHANDELL
| | | | |
|---|---|---|---|
| 78 | Orbitone 05 | Keep Me/Let's Make Love | 20 |

## DANY CHANDELLE
| | | | |
|---|---|---|---|
| 65 | Columbia DB 7540 | Lying Awake/I Love You | 30 |

## BARBARA CHANDLER
| | | | |
|---|---|---|---|
| 63 | London HLR 9823 | Do You Really Love Me Too?/I Live To Love You | 30 |
| 64 | London HLR 9861 | I'm Going Out With The Girls/Lonely New Year | 30 |

## GENE CHANDLER
| | | | |
|---|---|---|---|
| 62 | Columbia DB 4793 | Duke Of Earl/Kissing In The Kitchen | 20 |
| 63 | Stateside SS 185 | Rainbow/You Threw A Lucky Punch | 40 |
| 64 | Stateside SS 331 | Just Be True/A Song Called Soul | 25 |
| 64 | Stateside SS 364 | Bless Our Love/London Town | 25 |
| 65 | Stateside SS 388 | What Now/If You Can't Be True (Find A Part Time Love) | 35 |
| 65 | Stateside SS 401 | You Can't Hurt Me No More/Everybody Let's Dance | 25 |
| 65 | Stateside SS 425 | Nothing Can Stop Me/The Big Lie | 60 |
| 65 | Stateside SS 425 | Nothing Can Stop Me/The Big Lie (DJ copy) | 150 |
| 65 | Stateside SS 458 | Good Times/No One Can Love You (Like I Do) | 35 |
| 66 | Stateside SS 500 | (I'm Just A) Fool For You/Buddy Ain't It A Shame | 35 |
| 66 | Chess CRS 8047 | I Fooled You This Time/Such A Pretty Thing | 40 |
| 66 | Chess CRS 8047 | I Fooled You This Time/Such A Pretty Thing (DJ copy) | 100 |
| 67 | Coral Q 72490 | The Girl Don't Care/My Love | 20 |
| 68 | Soul City SC 102 | Nothing Can Stop Me/The Big Lie (reissue) | 15 |
| 69 | Action ACT 4551 | I Can't Save It/I Can Take Care Of Myself | 60 |
| 69 | President PT 234 | Duke Of Earl/Stand By Me | 8 |
| 70 | Mercury 6052 033 | Groovy Situation/Not The Marrying Kind | 6 |
| 71 | Mercury 6052 098 | You're A Lady/Stone Cold Feeling | 15 |
| 76 | Brunswick BR 39 | There Was A Time/ARTISTICS: I'm Gonna Miss You | 15 |
| 65 | Fontana TL 5247 | DUKE OF EARL (LP) | 80 |
| 67 | Coral LVA 9236 | THE GIRL DON'T CARE (LP) | 60 |
| 69 | MCA MUPS 367 | THERE WAS A TIME (LP) | 30 |
| 69 | Action ACLP 6010 | LIVE ON STAGE (LP) | 50 |
| 71 | Mercury 6338 037 | SITUATION (LP) | 20 |
| 74 | Joy JOYS 136 | A GENE CHANDLER ALBUM (LP) | 15 |
| 86 | Kent 049 | 60s SOUL BROTHER (LP) | 15 |

## GENE CHANDLER & BARBARA ACKLIN
| | | | |
|---|---|---|---|
| 74 | Brunswick BR 30 | From The Teacher To The Preacher/Little Green Apples | 8 |

*(see also Barbara Acklin)*

## GEORGE CHANDLER
| | | | |
|---|---|---|---|
| 82 | Polydor 436 | This Could Be The Night/Can't Go Back No More | 15 |

## JEFF CHANDLER
| | | | |
|---|---|---|---|
| 54 | Brunswick 05264 | I Should Care/More Than Anyone | 7 |
| 58 | London HA-U 2100 | JEFF CHANDLER SINGS TO YOU (LP) | 20 |

## KAREN CHANDLER
| | | | |
|---|---|---|---|
| 55 | Vogue Coral Q 72091 | The Price You Pay For Love/The Man In The Raincoat | 6 |
| 56 | Brunswick 05570 | Love Is The $64,000 Question/(I'm Just A) Beginner | 10 |
| 56 | Brunswick 05596 | Tonight You Belong To Me/Crazy Arms (with Jimmy Wakely) | 10 |
| 57 | Brunswick 05662 | Your Wild Heart/It's An International Language | 6 |
| 62 | Salvo SLO 1803 | My Own True Love/You Made Me Love You (99 copies only) | 10 |

*(see also Jimmy Wakely)*

## KENNY CHANDLER
| | | | |
|---|---|---|---|
| 63 | Stateside SS 166 | Heart/Wait For Me | 15 |
| 68 | Stateside SS 2110 | Beyond Love/Charity | 40 |
| 68 | Stateside SS 2110 | Beyond Love/Charity (DJ Copy) | 60 |

## LEN CHANDLER
| | | | |
|---|---|---|---|
| 67 | CBS 62931 | TO BE A MAN (LP) | 20 |

## LORRAINE CHANDLER
| | | | |
|---|---|---|---|
| 75 | Black Magic BM 105 | Love You Baby/What Can I Do | 8 |
| 97 | Kent 6T 13 | You Only Live Twice/METROS: My Imagination | 30 |
| 11 | Outta Sight OSV 032 | I Can't Change/You Only Live Twice | 6 |

## CHANDONS
| | | | |
|---|---|---|---|
| 68 | RCA RCA 1704 | Timber/Never Been Loved Before | 6 |

## ALLEN CHANEY
| | | | |
|---|---|---|---|
| 82 | Albion ION 1027 | The Sound Of Musak/It Is Nowhere (p/s) | 12 |

## CHANG AND VOYLE
| | | | |
|---|---|---|---|
| 86 | Cottage Industry CIR 001 | Chinese Eyes/If You Were Here | 8 |

## CHANGE
| | | | |
|---|---|---|---|
| 73 | Orange OAS 221 | Lazy London Lady/Arkmaker | 40 |
| 73 | Orange OAS 222 | Sunshine/Get Your Gun | 25 |
| 73 | Orange OAS 210 | Yaketty Yak, Smacketty Smack/When The Morning Comes | 8 |
| 74 | EMI EMI 2354 | Wildcat/Hold On | 10 |

## CHANGIN' TIMES
| | | | |
|---|---|---|---|
| 65 | Phillips BF 1442 | Pied Piper/Thank You Babe | 25 |

| 68 | Bell BLL 1009 | When The Good Sun Shines/Show Me The Way To Go Home ........................ 6 |

## BRUCE CHANNEL
| 62 | Mercury AMT 1171 | Hey! Baby/Dream Girl ........................................................ 8 |
| 62 | Mercury AMT 1177 | Number One Man/If Only I Had Known ........................................ 10 |
| 62 | Pye International 7N 25137 | Run Romance Run/Don't Leave Me ...................................... 15 |
| 63 | London HLU 9776 | I Don't Wanna/Blue And Lonesome .......................................... 15 |
| 64 | London HLU 9841 | Going Back To Louisiana/Forget Me Not .................................... 10 |
| 67 | Stateside SS 2066 | Mr. Bus Driver/It's Me .................................................. 10 |
| 68 | Bell BLL 1010 | Keep On/Barbara Allen ...................................................... 5 |
| 68 | Bell BLL 1030 | Try Me/Water The Family Tree ............................................... 5 |
| 68 | Bell BLL 1038 | Mr. Bus Driver/Trouble With Sam ............................................ 6 |
| 72 | UK USA 3 | Kiss And Run/Don't Let Go ..................................................... 5 |
| 62 | Mercury MMC 14104 | HEY! BABY! (LP) ....................................................... 25 |
| 68 | Bell MBLL/SBLL 110 | KEEP ON (LP) ........................................................ 20 |

## CHANNEL 4
| 79 | Ripping RIP 1 | Vampire/Channel 4 (numbered p/s with insert) ............................... 6 |

## CHANNEL 3
| 82 | No Future OI 11 | I've Got A Gun/Manzanar/Mannequin (p/s) ................................... 10 |
| 82 | No Future PUNK 2 | I'VE GOT A GUN (LP) ................................................... 18 |

## CHANTAYS
| 63 | London HLD 9696 | Pipeline/Move It ........................................................... 6 |
| 64 | King KG 1018 | Beyond/I'll Be Back Someday ............................................... 15 |
| 63 | London RED 1397 | PIPELINE (EP) ........................................................ 35 |
| 63 | London HA-D 8087 | PIPELINE (LP, mono) .................................................. 25 |
| 63 | London SH-D 8087 | PIPELINE (LP, stereo) ................................................. 25 |

## CHANTELLES
| 65 | Parlophone R 5271 | I Want That Boy/London My Home Town ..................................... 25 |
| 65 | Parlophone R 5303 | The Secret Of My Success/Sticks And Stones ............................... 15 |
| 65 | Parlophone R 5350 | Gonna Get Burned/Gonna Give Him Some Love ............................. 15 |
| 66 | Parlophone R 5431 | I Think Of You/Please Don't Kiss Me ...................................... 15 |
| 66 | Polydor 56119 | There's Something About You/Just Another Fool ............................ 20 |
| 67 | CBS 2777 | Blue Mood/The Man I Love .................................................. 25 |
*(see also Lana Sisters)*

## CHANTELS
| 58 | London HLU 8561 | Maybe/Come My Little Baby .............................................. 250 |
| 58 | London HLU 8561 | Maybe/Come My Little Baby (78) ......................................... 35 |
| 62 | London HLL 9428 | Look In My Eyes/Glad To Be Back .......................................... 60 |
| 62 | London HLL 9480 | Well I Told You/Still ................................................... 60 |
| 62 | London HLL 9532 | Here It Comes Again/Summertime .......................................... 40 |
| 63 | Capitol CL 15297 | Swamp Water/Eternally .................................................. 40 |
| 70 | Roulette RO 514 | Maybe/He's Gone .......................................................... 5 |
*(see also Richard Barrett)*

## CHANTERS (1)
| 66 | CBS 202454 | Every Night (I Sit And Cry)/Where ........................................ 30 |
| 67 | CBS 202616 | You Can't Fool Me/All Day Long ........................................... 20 |
| 68 | CBS 3400 | What's Wrong With You/Right By Your Side .................................. 6 |
| 68 | CBS 3668 | My Love Is For You/Mississippi Paddleboat ................................. 8 |
*(see also Birds Of A Feather)*

## CHANTERS (2)
| 79 | Burning Rockers BRD 011 | Mash Down Babylon/I Told You So (12") .............................. 25 |

## CHANTS (U.K.)
| 63 | Pye 7N 15557 | I Don't Care/Come Go With Me ............................................. 15 |
| 64 | Pye 7N 15591 | I Could Write A Book/A Thousand Stars .................................... 15 |
| 64 | Pye 7N 15643 | She's Mine/Then I'll Be Home ............................................. 15 |
| 64 | Pye 7N 15691 | Sweet Was The Wine/One Star ............................................. 15 |
| 66 | Fontana TF 716 | Come Back And Get This Loving Baby/Love Light ........................... 20 |
| 67 | Decca F 12650 | A Lover's Story/Wearing A Smile .......................................... 20 |
| 67 | Page One POF 016 | Ain't Nobody Home/For You ............................................. 15 |
| 68 | RCA Victor RCA 1754 | A Man Without A Face/Baby I Don't Need Your Love ................... 100 |
| 68 | RCA Victor RCA 1754 | A Man Without A Face/Baby I Don't Need Your Love (DJ Copy) ......... 130 |
| 69 | RCA Victor RCA 1823 | I Get The Sweetest Feeling/Candy .................................... 25 |
| 76 | Chipping Norton CHIP 2 | I've Been Trying/Lucky Old Me ...................................... 30 |
*(see also Real Thing)*

## CHANTS (U.S.)
| 58 | Capitol CL 14876 | Close Friends/Lost And Found ........................................... 25 |

## CHAOS & JULIA SET
| 93 | Recoil RCL 001 | VOL. 1 ATMOSPHERE EP (12", plain sleeve) ................................. 10 |
| 93 | Recoil RCL 002 | VOL. 2 - FEAR OF THE FUTURE (12", plain sleeve) .......................... 12 |
*(see also Global Communications)*

## CHAOS U.K.
| 79 | Chaotic Records VD 1 | Summer Of Hate/I Wanna To Be Left Alone (p/s, 500 only) ............. 200 |

## CHAOS U.K. (BRISTOL)
| 82 | Riot City RIOT 6 | BURNING BRITAIN (EP) ................................................. 10 |
| 82 | Riot City RIOT 12 | LOUD, POLITICAL AND UNCOMPROMISING (EP) ............................. 10 |
| 85 | C.O.R. GURT 1 | SHORT SHARP SHOCK (LP) ................................................. 20 |
| 86 | Manic Ears ACHE 1 | RADIOACTIVE (LP, with inner, split with EXTREME NOISE TERROR) ......... 20 |

## CHAOTIC DISCHORD
| 81 | Riot City 12 ROT 30 | Don't Throw It Away (12") ............................................ 15 |

MINT VALUE £

| | | | |
|---|---|---|---|
| 83 | Riot City RIOT RIOT 22 | Never Trust A Friend/Are Students Safe? (p/s) | 12 |
| 82 | Riot City RIOT 10 | FUCK THE WORLD (EP) | 10 |
| 83 | Riot City CITY 004 | FUCK RELIGION, FUCK POLITICS, AND FUCK THE LOT OF YOU (LP) | 15 |
| 84 | Syndicate SYNLP 12 | FUCK OFF YOU CUNT WHAT A LOAD OF BOLLOCKS (LP) | 15 |

## CHAOTIC YOUTH
| | | | |
|---|---|---|---|
| 83 | Beat The System YOUTH 1 | SAD SOCIETY (EP) | 50 |

## HARRY CHAPIN
| | | | |
|---|---|---|---|
| 73 | Elektra 7E 1012 | VERITIES & BALDERDASH (LP) | 15 |
| 74 | Elektra K 42155 | SHORT STORIES (LP, gatefold sleeve) | 15 |
| 78 | Elektra K 52089 | LIVING ROOM SUITE (LP) | 15 |
| 79 | Elektra K 62026 | LEGENDS OF THE LOST & FOUND (LP) | 18 |
| 79 | Elektra ELK 62017 | HARRY CHAPIN GREATEST STORIES LIVE (2xLP) | 18 |
| 70s | Elektra FW 36872 | IN SEQUEL (LP) | 15 |
| 70s | Elektra K 42107 | HEADS & TALES (LP) | 15 |
| 70s | Elektra E1082 | ON THE ROAD TO KINGDOM COME (LP) | 15 |
| 70s | Elektra K 62021 | DANCE BAND ON THE TITANIC (2xLP, gatefold sleeve) | 20 |
| 70s | Ekektra 7E 1041 | PORTRAIT GALLERY (LP, gatefold sleeve) | 15 |

## PAUL CHAPLAIN & HIS EMERALDS
| | | | |
|---|---|---|---|
| 60 | London HLU 9205 | Shortnin' Bread/Nicotine | 10 |

## CHARLIE CHAPLIN
| | | | |
|---|---|---|---|
| 84 | Vista VSLP 4063 | ROOTS & CULTURE (LP) | 20 |

## CHAPMAN AND WHITNEY
| | | | |
|---|---|---|---|
| 74 | Reprise K54017 | STREETWALKERS (LP, with inner) | 20 |

*(see also Streetwalkers)*

## COLIN CHAPMAN
| | | | |
|---|---|---|---|
| 60s | CCLP 1001 | FOLK SONGS VOL 1 (LP) | 15 |

## GENE CHAPMAN
| | | | |
|---|---|---|---|
| 63 | Starlite ST45 102 | Oklahoma Blues/Don't Come Crying | 25 |

## GRADY CHAPMAN
| | | | |
|---|---|---|---|
| 60 | Mercury AMT 1107 | Sweet Thing/I Know What I Want | 30 |

## MICHAEL CHAPMAN
| | | | |
|---|---|---|---|
| 74 | Deram DM 407 | The Bento Song/Dumplings | 7 |
| 69 | Harvest HAR 5002 | It Didn't Work Out/Mozart Lives Upstairs | 18 |
| 69 | Harvest SHVL 755 | RAINMAKER (LP, gatefold sleeve, with "Sold in U.K..." label text on 4 lines, No EMI on label) | 100 |
| 69 | Harvest SHVL 755 | RAINMAKER (LP, gatefold sleeve, later pressing with EMI on label) | 40 |
| 69 | Standard ESL 146 | SOLO GUITAR (LP, library issue) | 60 |
| 70 | Harvest SHVL 764 | FULLY QUALIFIED SURVIVOR (LP, gatefold sleeve, 1st pressing with no EMI on label) | 90 |
| 70 | Harvest SHVL 764 | FULLY QUALIFIED SURVIVOR (LP, gatefold sleeve, later pressing with EMI on label) | 30 |
| 70 | Harvest SHVL 786 | WINDOW (LP, gatefold sleeve, with no EMI on label) | 80 |
| 70 | Harvest SHVL 786 | WINDOW (LP, gatefold sleeve, with EMI on label) | 25 |
| 71 | Harvest SHVL 798 | WRECKED AGAIN (LP, gatefold sleeve, EMI on label) | 60 |
| 73 | Deram SML 1105 | MILLSTONE GRIT (LP, red/white label) | 20 |
| 74 | Deram SML 1114 | DEAL GONE DOWN (LP) | 20 |
| 76 | Decca SKL-R 5242 | SAVAGE AMUSEMENT (LP, with lyric sheet, blue/silver label) | 20 |
| 77 | Decca SKL-R 5290 | THE MAN WHO HATED MORNINGS (LP) | 15 |
| 78 | Criminal STEAL 2 | PLAYING GUITAR THE EASY WAY (LP) | 15 |
| 79 | Criminal TAKE 3 | FULLY QUALIFIED SURVIVOR (LP, reissue) | 15 |

## CHAPS
| | | | |
|---|---|---|---|
| 62 | Parlophone R 4979 | Poppin' Medley (Parts 1 & 2) | 10 |

*(see also Outlaws)*

## CHAPTER FIVE
| | | | |
|---|---|---|---|
| 66 | CBS 202395 | Anything You Do Is Alright/You Can't Mean It | 750 |
| 67 | CBS 2696 | One In A Million/Hey Hey (unissued, demos only) | 250 |
| 00s | Goldmine Soul Supply GS 009 | You Can't Mean It/One In A Million (reissue) | 15 |

## CHAPTER FOUR (U.K.)
| | | | |
|---|---|---|---|
| 60s | GSP 11009/10 | CHAPTER FOUR (EP, no p/s) | 90 |

## CHAPTER FOUR (U.K.)
| | | | |
|---|---|---|---|
| 80 | Bridge BR 001 | HANGING AROUND STERLING (LP) | 35 |

## CHAPTER FOUR (U.S.)
| | | | |
|---|---|---|---|
| 66 | United Artists UP 1143 | In My Life/In Each Other's Arms | 250 |

*(see also Jay & Americans)*

## CHAPTER ONE
| | | | |
|---|---|---|---|
| 84 | Wag 4 | I Know That She Knows/Take My Advice | 6 |
| 86 | Wag 5 | When The Summer Comes/Stephanie Powers/Girl On The Phone | 6 |

## CHAPTER THREE (U.K.)
| | | | |
|---|---|---|---|
| 67 | CBS 2971 | Cold And Lonely Hours/Wrecking Crew | 7 |
| 67 | CBS BPG 63007 | RAMBLE AWAY (LP) | 25 |

## CHAPTERHOUSE
| | | | |
|---|---|---|---|
| 91 | Chapterhouse HOUSE 002 | Losing Touch With My Mind/It won't Be Wrong (flexi) | 12 |
| 91 | Dedicated DEDLP 001 | WHIRLPOOL (LP with bonus 12") | 30 |
| 91 | Dedicated DEDLP 001 | WHIRLPOOL (LP, without free 12") | 20 |
| 93 | Dedicated DEDLP 011D | BLOOD MUSIC (2-LP) | 35 |

*(see also Slowdive)*

## CHAPTERS
| | | | |
|---|---|---|---|
| 65 | Pye 7N 15815 | Can't Stop Thinking About Her/Dance Little Lady | 60 |

## CHARACTERS
| | | | |
|---|---|---|---|
| 86 | BEM BEM 101 | Love Talk/Where Has All The Love Gone (500 only) | 30 |

## ERIC CHARDON
| | | | |
|---|---|---|---|
| 69 | Major Minor MM596 | One Love One Life/Sorrow Is My Name | 8 |

## CHARGE (1)
| | | | |
|---|---|---|---|
| 73 | SRT private pressing | CHARGE (LP, 1 known copy) | 750 |
| 92 | Kissing Spell KSLP 9205 | CHARGE (LP, reissue, revised sleeve, 500 only) | 20 |

## CHARGE (2)
| | | | |
|---|---|---|---|
| 70 | private pressing | Zeugma/Boring Song (art sleeve) | 20 |

## CHARGE (3)
| | | | |
|---|---|---|---|
| 80 | YCAFO Records | You Get What You Deserve/Rather B Crazy/Angel Deceast (foldout p/s) | 65 |
| 81 | Test Pressing | You Deserve More Than A Maybe (p/s, 500 only, existence unconfirmed) | 30 |
| 82 | Test Pressing TP 3 | Kings Cross/Brave New World (p/s) | 12 |

## CHARGERS
| | | | |
|---|---|---|---|
| 84 | Charge BCSK 01 | Desperaroes/Are You Out There (p/s) | 60 |

## MARK CHARIG
| | | | |
|---|---|---|---|
| 77 | Ogun OG 710 | PIPEDREAM (LP) | 15 |

*(see also Bluesology, B.B. Blunder, Reg King, Centipede, Keith Tippett, Julie Tippett, Brotherhood Of Breath, Elton Dean, Ninesense)*

## CHARIOT
| | | | |
|---|---|---|---|
| 84 | Shades SHADE 2 | ALL ALONE AGAIN (EP) | 12 |
| 84 | Shades SHADE 1 | THE WARRIOR (LP) | 15 |
| 86 | Shades SHADE 4 | BURNING AMBITION (LP) | 15 |

## CHARIOTS
| | | | |
|---|---|---|---|
| 62 | Piccadilly 7N 35061 | Problem Girl/Song Of A Broken Heart | 10 |

## CHARLATANS (U.K.)
| | | | |
|---|---|---|---|
| 91 | Beggars Banquet CHAR 2 | Happen To Die (7" 1-sided promo) | 5 |
| 90 | Situation Two SITU 30L | SOME FRIENDLY (LP, 'some friendly edition' in white PVC sleeve with inner) | 15 |
| 92 | Situation Two SITU 37 | BETWEEN 10TH AND 11TH (LP) | 15 |
| 91 | Live Live Good CB 2 | ISOLATION 21.2.91 (LP, official live bootleg, sold via fan club, 1,000 only) | 20 |
| 94 | Beggars Banquet BBQLP 147 | UP TO OUR HIPS (LP, textured sleeve) | 25 |
| 95 | Beggars Banquet BBQLP 174 | THE CHARLATANS (2-LP) | 25 |
| 97 | Beggars Banquet BBQLP 190 | TELLIN' STORIES (LP) | 25 |
| 98 | Beggars Banquet BBQLP 198 | MELTING POT (2-LP) | 35 |
| 01 | Universal 014911-1 | WONDERLAND (2-LP) | 25 |
| 99 | Universal 1538650-1 | US & US ONLY (LP) | 30 |

*(see also Electric Crayons, Makin' Time)*

## CHARLATANS (U.S.)
| | | | |
|---|---|---|---|
| 69 | Philips SBL 7903 | THE CHARLATANS (LP) | 90 |

*(see also Mike Wilhelm, Tongue & Groove, Dan Hicks & His Hot Licks)*

## BOBBY CHARLES
| | | | |
|---|---|---|---|
| 56 | London HLU 8247 | See You Later, Alligator/On Bended Knee | 1500 |
| 56 | London HLU 8247 | See You Later, Alligator/On Bended Knee (78) | 250 |

## BOBBY CHARLES
| | | | |
|---|---|---|---|
| 78 | Bearsville J 15508 | Small Town Talk/Grow Too Old | 10 |
| 72 | Bearsville K 45516 | BOBBY CHARLES (LP) | 15 |

## DON CHARLES
| | | | |
|---|---|---|---|
| 62 | Decca F 11424 | Walk With Me My Angel/Crazy Man, Crazy | 8 |
| 62 | Decca F 11464 | The Hermit Of Misty Mountain/Moonlight Rendezvous | 8 |
| 62 | Decca F 11528 | It's My Way Of Loving You/Guess That's The Way It Goes | 5 |
| 63 | Decca F 11602 | Angel Of Love/Lucky Star | 5 |
| 63 | Decca F 11645 | Heart's Ice Cold/Daybreak | 5 |
| 64 | HMV POP 1307 | If You Don't Know I Ain't Gonna Tell Ya/Voice On The Phone | 5 |
| 63 | HMV POP 1271 | Tower Tall/Look Before You Love | 5 |
| 64 | HMV POP 1332 | Big Talk From A Little Man/She's Mine | 10 |
| 68 | Parlophone R 5688 | The Drifter/Great To Be Livin' | 60 |
| 68 | Parlophone R 5688 | The Drifter/Great To Be Livin' (DJ Copy) | 100 |
| 68 | Parlophone R 5712 | Your Name Is On My Heart/How Can I | 15 |
| 63 | Decca DFE 8530 | DON CHARLES (EP) | 50 |
| 67 | Parlophone PMC/PCS 7021 | HAVE I TOLD YOU LATELY (LP, mono/stereo) | 25 |

## GARY CHARLES
| | | | |
|---|---|---|---|
| 71 | B & C CB 159 | You've Been Away Too Long/Lovely Linda | 6 |

## JIMMY CHARLES
| | | | |
|---|---|---|---|
| 60 | London HLU 9206 | A Million To One/Hop Scotch Hop | 25 |
| 63 | Windsor WPS 120 | Pitter Pitter Patter/How You Gonna Treat Me Now | 10 |

## JOHN CHARLES
| | | | |
|---|---|---|---|
| 60 | Cetra SP 785 | Sixteen Tons/Love In Portofino | 5 |
| 60 | Cetra SP 786 | La Fine (The End)/Non Dimenticar | 5 |

## RAY CHARLES
### 78s
| | | | |
|---|---|---|---|
| 58 | London HLE 8768 | Rockhouse (Parts 1 & 2) | 25 |
| 59 | London HLE 8917 | What'd I Say (Parts 1 & 2) | 30 |
| 59 | London HLE 9009 | I'm Movin' On/I Believe To My Soul | 40 |
| 60 | HMV POP 792 | Georgia On My Mind/Carry Me Back To Old Virginny | 50 |

### SINGLES
| | | | |
|---|---|---|---|
| 58 | London HLE 8768 | Rockhouse (Parts 1 & 2) | 30 |
| 59 | London HLE 8917 | What'd I Say (Parts 1 & 2) | 25 |

# Ray CHARLES

| 59 | London HLE 9009 | I'm Movin' On/I Believe To My Soul | 20 |
|---|---|---|---|
| 60 | London HLE 9058 | Let The Good Times Roll/Don't Let The Sun Catch You Cryin' | 20 |
| 60 | HMV POP 774 | Sticks And Stones/Worried Life Blues | 15 |
| 60 | London HLK 9181 | Tell The Truth/You Be My Baby | 15 |
| 60 | HMV POP 792 | Georgia On My Mind/Carry Me Back To Old Virginny | 5 |
| 60 | London HLK 9251 | Come Rain Or Come Shine/Tell Me You'll Wait For Me | 5 |
| 61 | HMV POP 825 | Ruby/Hard Hearted Hannah | 5 |
| 61 | HMV POP 838 | Them That Got/I Wonder | 25 |
| 61 | London HLK 9364 | Early In The Mornin'/A Bit Of Soul | 15 |
| 61 | HMV POP 862 | One Mint Julep/Let's Go | 15 |
| 61 | HMV POP 935 | Hit The Road Jack/The Danger Zone | 10 |
| 61 | London HLK 9435 | I Wonder Who/Hard Times | 10 |
| 62 | HMV POP 969 | Unchain My Heart/But On The Other Hand Baby | 7 |
| 62 | HMV POP 1017 | Hide Nor Hair/At The Club | 10 |
| 63 | HMV POP 1133 | Don't Set Me Free/The Brightest Smile In Town | 5 |
| 63 | HMV POP 1161 | Take These Chains From My Heart/No Letter Today | 5 |
| 63 | HMV POP 1202 | No One/Without Love (There Is Nothing) | 5 |
| 63 | HMV POP 1221 | Busted/Making Believe | 7 |
| 64 | HMV POP 1251 | That Lucky Old Sun/Mississippi Mud | 5 |
| 64 | HMV POP 1272 | Baby Don't You Cry/My Heart Cries For You | 5 |
| 64 | HMV POP 1315 | My Baby Don't Dig Me/Something's Wrong | 10 |
| 64 | HMV POP 1333 | No One To Cry To/A Tear Fell | 5 |
| 64 | HMV POP 1350 | Smack Dab In The Middle/I Wake Up Crying | 5 |
| 65 | HMV POP 1383 | Makin' Whoopee/Move It On Over | 5 |
| 65 | HMV POP 1392 | Cry/Teardrops From My Eye | 5 |
| 65 | HMV POP 1414 | Light Out Of Darkness/Please Forgive And Forget | 5 |
| 65 | HMV POP 1437 | I Gotta Woman/Without A Song | 5 |
| 65 | HMV POP 1457 | Love's Gonna Live Here/I'm A Fool To Care | 5 |
| 65 | HMV POP 1484 | The Cincinnati Kid/That's All I Am To You | 5 |
| 66 | HMV POP 1502 | Crying Time/When My Dreamboat Comes Home | 6 |
| 66 | HMV POP 1519 | Together Again/You're Just About To Lose Your Clown | 20 |
| 66 | HMV POP 1537 | Let's Go Get Stoned/The Train | 20 |
| 66 | HMV POP 1551 | I Chose To Sing The Blues/Hopelessly | 25 |
| 66 | HMV POP 1566 | Please Say You're Fooling/I Don't Need No Doctor | 50 |
| 66 | HMV POP 1566 | Please Say You're Fooling/I Don't Need No Doctor (DJ Copy) | 80 |
| 67 | Atlantic 584 093 | What'd I Say/I Got A Woman | 5 |
| 67 | HMV POP 1589 | You Win Again/Bye Bye Love | 5 |
| 67 | HMV POP 1595 | Somebody Oughta Write A Book About It/Here We Go Again | 5 |
| 67 | HMV POP 1607 | In The Heat Of The Night/Something's Got To Change | 6 |
| 67 | Stateside SS 2071 | Yesterday/Never Had Enough Of Nothing Yet | 5 |
| 68 | Stateside SS 2120 | Eleanor Rigby/Understanding | 5 |
| 71 | Tangerine 6121 001 | Booty Butt/Zig Zag | 5 |

## EPs

| 59 | London Jazz EZK 19043 | THE GREAT RAY CHARLES | 15 |
|---|---|---|---|
| 59 | London Jazz EZK 19048 | SOUL BROTHERS (with Milt Jackson) | 15 |
| 61 | London REK 1306 | WHAT'D I SAY | 20 |
| 61 | London REK 1317 | RAY CHARLES AT NEWPORT | 15 |
| 62 | HMV 7EG 8729 | HIT THE ROAD JACK | 15 |
| 62 | HMV 7EG 8781 | I CAN'T STOP LOVING YOU | 15 |
| 63 | HMV 7EG 8783 | THE BALLAD STYLE OF RAY CHARLES | 10 |
| 63 | HMV 7EG 8801 | THE SWINGING STYLE OF RAY CHARLES | 10 |
| 63 | HMV 7EG 8807 | BABY IT'S COLD OUTSIDE (with Betty Carter) | 10 |
| 63 | HMV 7EG 8812 | TAKE THESE CHAINS FROM MY HEART | 10 |
| 63 | London REB 1407 | THE ORIGINAL RAY CHARLES VOLUME ONE | 10 |
| 63 | London REB 1408 | THE ORIGINAL RAY CHARLES VOLUME TWO | 10 |
| 63 | London REB 1409 | THE ORIGINAL RAY CHARLES VOLUME THREE | 10 |
| 64 | HMV 7EG 8841 | BUSTED | 10 |
| 64 | HMV 7EG 8861 | RAY CHARLES SINGS | 10 |
| 64 | Realm REP 4001 | THE YOUNG RAY CHARLES | 10 |
| 66 | HMV 7EG 8932 | RAY CHARLES LIVE IN CONCERT | 10 |
| 66 | HMV 7EG 8951 | RAY CHARLES SINGS SONGS OF BUCK OWENS | 10 |

## ALBUMS

| 58 | London Jazz LTZ-K 15134 | THE GREAT RAY CHARLES | 50 |
|---|---|---|---|
| 59 | London Jazz LTZ-K 15146 | SOUL BROTHERS (with Milt Jackson, mono) | 25 |
| 59 | London Jazz SAH-K 6030 | SOUL BROTHERS (with Milt Jackson, stereo) | 25 |
| 59 | London Jazz LTZ-K 15149 | RAY CHARLES AT NEWPORT (mono) | 25 |
| 59 | London Jazz SAH-K 6008 | RAY CHARLES AT NEWPORT (stereo) | 25 |
| 59 | London HA-E 2168 | YES INDEED | 50 |
| 59 | London HA-E 2226 | WHAT'D I SAY | 40 |
| 60 | London Jazz LTZ-K 15190 | THE GENIUS OF RAY CHARLES | 40 |
| 60 | HMV CLP 1387/CSD 1320 | THE GENIUS HITS THE ROAD (mono) | 15 |
| 60 | HMV CLP 1387/CSD 1320 | THE GENIUS HITS THE ROAD (stereo) | 18 |
| 60 | London HA-K 2284 | RAY CHARLES IN PERSON | 30 |
| 61 | HMV CLP 1449/CSD 1362 | DEDICATED TO YOU (mono) | 15 |
| 61 | HMV CLP 1449/CSD 1362 | DEDICATED TO YOU (stereo) | 20 |
| 61 | HMV CLP 1475/CSD 1384 | GENIUS + SOUL = JAZZ (mono) | 15 |
| 61 | HMV CLP 1475/CSD 1384 | GENIUS + SOUL = JAZZ (stereo) | 20 |
| 62 | HMV CLP 1520/CSD 1414 | RAY CHARLES AND BETTY CARTER (mono) | 15 |
| 62 | HMV CLP 1520/CSD 1414 | RAY CHARLES AND BETTY CARTER (stereo) | 18 |

| 62 | London Jazz LJZ-K 15238 | THE GENIUS SINGS THE BLUES | 25 |
| 62 | HMV CLP 1580/CSD 1451 | MODERN SOUNDS IN COUNTRY & WESTERN (mono) | 15 |
| 62 | HMV CLP 1580/CSD 1451 | MODERN SOUNDS IN COUNTRY & WESTERN (stereo) | 18 |
| 63 | HMV CLP 1613/CSD 1477 | MODERN SOUNDS IN COUNTRY & WESTERN VOL. TWO (mono) | 15 |
| 63 | HMV CLP 1613/CSD 1477 | MODERN SOUNDS IN COUNTRY & WESTERN VOL. TWO (stereo) | 15 |
| 63 | London HA-K 8022 | THE ORIGINAL RAY CHARLES | 15 |
| 63 | London HA-K 8035 | THE GENIUS AFTER HOURS | 15 |
| 63 | London HA-K/SH-K 8045 | SOUL MEETING (with Milt Jackson) | 15 |
| 63 | HMV CLP 1678 | INGREDIENTS IN A RECIPE FOR SOUL | 20 |

*(see also Raelets, Milt Jackson)*

## ROGER CHARLES
| 73 | Dawn DNS 1038 | Understand Each Other/Can't Forget | 6 |

## SONNY CHARLES (& CHECKMATES LTD)
| 67 | Ember EMB S 240 | Mastered The Art Of Love/Please Don't Take My World Away | 40 |
| 69 | A&M AMS 752 | Black Pearl/Lazy Susan | 10 |
| 70 | A&M AMS 787 | It Takes A Little Longer/Welfare Man | 6 |

*(see also Checkmates Ltd)*

## TINA CHARLES
| 69 | CBS 4015 | Nothing In The World/Millions Of Hearts | 15 |
| 69 | CBS 4307 | In The Middle Of The Day/Rich Girl | 40 |
| 69 | CBS 4658 | Good To Be Alive/Same Old Story | 50 |

## CHILI CHARLES
| 75 | Virgin V 2028 | QUICKSTEP (LP) | 15 |

## CHARLES, PAULETTE & GEE
| 71 | G.G. GG 4515 | Shock And Shake (Version 3)/WINSTON WRIGHT: Roll On (Version 2) (as Charlie, Paulette & Gee) | 10 |
| 71 | G.G. GG 4517 | Rock And Shake (Version 3) (actually "Lover's Affair" by Charlie Ace & Maytones)/Roll On (Version 2) (actually "My Love And I" by Winston Wright) | 10 |

*(see also Charlie Ace)*

## CHARLIE
| 72 | Bumble GE 111 | Dream Hero/Lament | 15 |
| 73 | Decca F 13451 | I Need Your Love/I'm So Happy | 20 |

## CHARLIE BOY
| 71 | Trojan TR 7823 | Funky Strip/UPSETTERS: Mellow Mood | 25 |

*(see also Lee Perry/Upsetters)*

## CHARLIE & FAY
| 72 | Pama 853 | Big Seven (Punnany)/YOUTH PROFESSIONAL BAND : Version | 12 |

## CHARLIE PARKAS
| 80 | Paranoid Plastics PPS 1 | The Ballad Of Robin Hood/Space Invaders (mock 2-Tone die cut p/s) | 10 |

*(see also Alberto Y Lost Trios Paranoias)*

## CHARLIES BROTHER
| 84 | Lost Moment LMO 100 | Wishing Tree/Further Adventures Of | 25 |

## CHARLY & THE BOURBON FAMILY
| 71 | Decca F 23164 | Acapulco Gold/Boogachi | 15 |

## CHARMAINES
| 98 | Kent 6T 18 | I Idolize You/M&M & THE PEANUTS: Can't Say No | 25 |

## CHARMERS (JAMAICA)
| 61 | Blue Beat BB 42 | Lonely Boy/I Am Going Back Home | 20 |
| 62 | Blue Beat BB 114 | Crying Over You/Now You Want To Cry | 20 |
| 63 | Blue Beat BB 157 | Time After Time/Done Me Wrong (with Prince Buster's Band) | 15 |
| 60s | Blue Beat | How Could I Forget/Why Won't You Come Home? (with Prince Buster's Band) (white label only) | 75 |
| 63 | R&B JB 118 | Angel Love/My Heart | 20 |
| 63 | R&B JB 121 | Oh Why Baby/ROLAND ALPHONSO: Perhaps | 30 |
| 64 | R&B JB 151 | What's The Use/I Am Through | 20 |
| 64 | R&B JB 156 | In My Soul/Beware | 20 |
| 64 | Blue Beat BB 204 | I'm Back/It's A Dream | 20 |
| 64 | Blue Beat BB 238 | Waiting For You/You Are My Sunshine | 20 |
| 64 | Blue Beat BB 251 | Dig Then Prince (actually Dip Them Prince)/Girl Of My Dreams (as The Charmer) | 25 |
| 65 | Blue Beat BB 279 | Nobody Takes My Baby Away From Me/ BUSTER ALLSTARS: Mules Mules Mules | 75 |
| 66 | Blue Beat BB 345 | Oh My Baby/STRANGER COLE: When The Party Is Over | 20 |
| 66 | Ska Beat JB 237 | Best Friend/MAYTALS: My Darling | 25 |
| 66 | Rio R 78 | You Don't Know/CORNELL CAMPBELL & ROY PANTON: Sweetest Girl | 20 |
| 68 | Coxsone CS 7043 | Things Going Wrong/KEN BOOTHE: You Keep Me Hanging On | 300 |
| 68 | Treasure Isle TI 7036 | Keep On Going (actually by Lloyd Charmers)/SILVERTONES: Don't Say No | 20 |
| 70 | Duke DU 87 | Colour Him Father/Version | 30 |
| 70 | Trojan TR 7773 | Sweeter She Is (actually by Lloyd Charmers, Dave Barker & Slim Smith)/ Fire Fire (actually by Lloyd Charmers) | 12 |
| 70 | Explosion EX 2026 | Can I Get Next To You?/Big Five | 10 |
| 70 | Explosion EX 2035 | Sweet Back/Music Talk (actually by Lloyd Charmers) | 12 |
| 71 | Bullet BU 473 | Reggae In Wonderland/Wonder (Version) | 10 |
| 71 | Explosion EX 2045 | Skinhead Train/TONY & CHARMERS: Everstrong (B-side with Tony Binns) | 125 |
| 71 | Explosion EX 2055 | Reggae In Wonderland/Wonder - Version (both actually by Byron Lee & Dragonaires) | 7 |
| 71 | Supreme SUP 220 | Just My Imagination/Gotta Get A Message To You (actually by Dave Barker) | 25 |
| 71 | Green Door GD 4000 | Rasta Never Fails (actually by Lloyd Charmers & Ken Boothe)/CHARMERS ALL STARS: Rasta Version | 7 |
| 71 | Green Door GD 4001 | One Big Unhappy Family/CONSCIOUS MINDS: Africa Is Paradise | 12 |
| 71 | Pama Supreme PS 340 | Red Head Duck/Jingle Jangle | 6 |

*(see also Spanishtown Skabeats, Lloyd & Ken, Lloydie & Lowbites, Lloyd Terrell)*

## LLOYD CHARMERS

| | | | |
|---|---|---|---|
| 67 | Coxsone CS 7023 | Time Is Getting Hard/TONY GREGORY: I Sit By The Shore | 100 |
| 69 | Duke DU 15 | Cooyah/UNIQUES: Forever | 30 |
| 69 | Duke DU 16 | Follow This Sound/Why Pretend | 30 |
| 69 | Duke DU 25 | 5 To 5/SOUL STIRRERS: Come See About Me | 35 |
| 69 | Duke DU 36 | Safari (The Far East)/Last Laugh | 30 |
| 69 | Songbird SB 1001 | Ling Ting Tong/LLOYD ROBINSON: Sweet Sweet | 20 |
| 69 | Songbird SB 1007 | Duckey Luckey/In The Spirit | 50 |
| 69 | Camel CA 30 | Confidential/TOMMY COWAN: House In Session | 35 |
| 69 | Explosion EX 2001 | Death A Come/Zylon | 40 |
| 70 | Explosion EX 2032 | Vengeance/Look A-Py-Py | 40 |
| 70 | Explosion EX 2034 | Ready Talk/There Is Something About You | 18 |
| 70 | Trojan TR 7788 | Oh Me Oh My/I Did It | 20 |
| 70 | Bullet BU 435 | Dollars And Bonds/Sounds Familiar | 50 |
| 70 | Bullet BU 442 | Reggae A Bye Bye/DAVE BARKER:Doctor Jekyll | 40 |
| 70 | Escort ES 820 | Soul Of England/Shang I | 30 |
| 70 | Escort ES 836 | Hi Shan/Soul At Large | 30 |
| 70 | Smash SMA 2302 | Big Red Bum Ball/BUNNIE LEE ALLSTARS: Big Bum Ball Version | 7 |
| 71 | Black Swan BW 1405 | Love You The Most/LOW BITES:Version | 15 |
| 73 | Green Door GD 4064 | Save The People (as L. Charmers)/SCOTTY: Salvation Train | 10 |
| 74 | Harry J. HJ 6662 | I'm Gonna Love You Just A Little Bit More/Have I Sinned | 6 |
| 71 | Pama Supreme PS 339 | Shaft/Harry's Mood | 10 |
| 71 | Pama Supreme PS 346 | Show Business/DEBBY & LLOYD: Gloria | 8 |
| 72 | Pama Supreme PS 355 | Desiderata/Desiderata Music | 10 |
| 11 | Explosion THB 7009 | The Premises/JOKERS: Brixton | 50 |
| 70 | Trojan TTL 25 | REGGAE IS TIGHT (LP, orange/white label) | 40 |
| 70 | Trojan TTL 30 | REGGAE CHARM (LP) | 30 |
| 70 | Pama SECO 25 | HOUSE IN SESSION (LP, with Hippy Boys) | 175 |
| 72 | Trojan TRLS 86 | BEST OF (LP) | 20 |
| 73 | Trojan TBL 201 | IN SESSION (LP) | 20 |

*(see also Charmers, Lloyd Tyrell/Terrell, Ken Boothe, Hippy Boys, Wayne Howard, Martia Riley, Eric Donaldson)*

## CHARMERS (U.S.)

| | | | |
|---|---|---|---|
| 58 | Vogue V 9095 | He's Gone/Oh! Yes | 300 |
| 58 | Vogue V 9095 | He's Gone/Oh! Yes (78) | 20 |

## CHARMETTES

| | | | |
|---|---|---|---|
| 63 | London HLR 9820 | Please Don't Kiss Me Again/What Is A Tear | 40 |

## CHARMS (JAMAICA)

| | | | |
|---|---|---|---|
| 64 | Island WI 154 | Carry, Go, Bring Home (actually by Justin Hinds & Dominoes)/Hill And Gully (actually by L. Reid's Group) | 20 |
| 66 | Rio R 98 | Everybody Say Yeah/This World Is Yours | 20 |

## CHARMS (U.S.)

| | | | |
|---|---|---|---|
| 55 | Parlophone MSP 6155 | Hearts Of Stone/Ko Ko Mo (I Love You So) | 250 |
| 55 | Parlophone R3988 | Hearts Of Stone/Ko Ko Mo (I Love You So) (78) | 20 |
| 55 | Parlophone DP 412 | Hearts Of Stone/Bazoom, I Need Your Lovin' (78) (export issue) | 20 |
| 55 | Parlophone DP 423 | Two Hearts/The First Time We Met (78) (export issue) | 20 |

*(see also Otis Williams & Charms, Harmonizing Four)*

## CHARTBUSTERS

| | | | |
|---|---|---|---|
| 64 | London HLU 9906 | She's The One/Slippin' Thru Your Fingers | 15 |
| 64 | London HLU 9934 | Why/Stop The Music | 5 |

## CHARTERED HURRICANE

| | | | |
|---|---|---|---|
| 83 | SRTS 83 CUS 1695 | Cathy Come Home/All Smashed Up (stamped plain white sleeve) | 25 |

## CHASE

| | | | |
|---|---|---|---|
| 71 | Epic EPC 7301 | Get It On In The Morning/River | 6 |
| 71 | Epic EPCS 7506 | Handbags And Gladrags/Open Up Wide | 10 |

## LINCOLN CHASE

| | | | |
|---|---|---|---|
| 57 | London HLU 8495 | Johnny Klingeringding/You're Driving Me Crazy (What Did I Do) | 20 |
| 61 | Philips PB 1103 | Miss Orangutang/Walking Slowly | 20 |

## CHASERS

| | | | |
|---|---|---|---|
| 65 | Decca F 12302 | Hey Little Girl/That's What They Call Love | 50 |
| 66 | Parlophone R 5451 | Inspiration/She's Gone Away | 150 |
| 67 | Philips BF 1546 | The Ways Of A Man/Summer Girl | 15 |

## CHASERS

| | | | |
|---|---|---|---|
| 84 | SRT SRT4KS 304 | Raiders/Final Stand (300 only) | 60 |

## CHATEAUX

| | | | |
|---|---|---|---|
| 82 | Ebony EBON 9 | Young Blood/Fight To The Last | 20 |
| 83 | Ebony EBON 13 | CHAINED AND DESPERATE (LP) | 20 |
| 84 | Ebony EBON 18 | FIRE POWER (LP) | 15 |
| 85 | Ebony EBON 31 | HIGHLY STRUNG (LP) | 15 |

## CHEAP BOOTS

| | | | |
|---|---|---|---|
| 70 | Fontana 6001 020 | Baby I Do Need You/Come And Stay With Me | 6 |

## CHEAP TRICK

| | | | |
|---|---|---|---|
| 78 | Epic S EPC 6199 | So Good To See You/You're All Talk (withdrawn) | 20 |
| 79 | Epic S EPC 7144 | Voices/Surrender (withdrawn) | 5 |
| 79 | Epic S EPC 7258 | I Want You To Want Me (live)/I Want You To Want Me (studio) (DJ only) | 6 |
| 79 | Epic CT-1 | Dream Police/Voice/I'll Be With You Tonight (sampler, promo only) | 10 |

## CHEATERS

| | | | |
|---|---|---|---|
| 80 | Parlophone R6041 | Nuthin' Ever Happens On Saturday/Hard Work/Stop Pushing (p/s) | 5 |

| 80 | Pre Fab Z 01 | I Wanna Be A Policeman/Baby What Do You Want Me To Do/From The Hip (foldout p/s) ............ 8 |

## CHEATIN' HEARTS
| 66 | Columbia DB 8048 | Zip-Tease/The Bad Kind ............ 10 |

## CHUBBY CHECKER
| 59 | Top Rank JAR 154 | The Class/Schooldays, Oh, Schooldays ............ 30 |
| 60 | Columbia DB 4503 | The Twist/Toot ............ 8 |
| 60 | Columbia DB 4541 | The Hucklebuck/Whole Lotta Shakin' Goin' On ............ 15 |
| 61 | Columbia DB 4591 | Pony Time/Oh Susanna ............ 8 |
| 61 | Columbia DB 4652 | Good Good Loving/Mess Around ............ 15 |
| 61 | Columbia DB 4691 | Let's Twist Again/Everything's Gonna Be All Right ............ 5 |
| 61 | Columbia DB 4728 | The Fly/That's The Way It Goes ............ 10 |
| 62 | Columbia DB 4808 | Slow Twistin'/The Lose Your Inhibitions Twist ............ 5 |
| 62 | Columbia DB 4876 | Dancin' Party/Gotta Get Myself Together ............ 5 |
| 62 | Pye International 7N 25160 | Dancin' Party/Gotta Get Myself Together (reissue) ............ 5 |
| 62 | Cameo Parkway P 806 | What Do You Say/Something To Shout About ............ 5 |
| 62 | Cameo Parkway P 849 | Limbo Rock/Hitch Hiker ............ 5 |
| 63 | Cameo Parkway P 862 | Let's Limbo Some More/Twenty Miles ............ 5 |
| 63 | Cameo Parkway P 873 | Black Cloud/Birdland ............ 5 |
| 63 | Cameo Parkway P 879 | Twist It Up/Surf Party ............ 5 |
| 63 | Cameo Parkway P 890 | Loddy Lo/Hooka Tooka ............ 8 |
| 64 | Cameo Parkway P 907 | Hey Bobba Needle/Spread Joy ............ 10 |
| 64 | Cameo Parkway P 920 | Lazy Elsie Molly/Rosie ............ 5 |
| 64 | Cameo Parkway P 922 | She Wants T'Swim/You Better Believe It Baby ............ 15 |
| 65 | Cameo Parkway P 936 | Lovely, Lovely/The Weekend's Here ............ 20 |
| 65 | Cameo Parkway P 949 | (At The) Discotheque/Do The Freddie (DJ copy) ............ 150 |
| 65 | Cameo Parkway P 949 | (At The) Discotheque/Do The Freddie ............ 50 |
| 65 | Cameo Parkway P 959 | Everything's Wrong/Cu Ma La Be Stay (DJ copy) ............ 120 |
| 65 | Cameo Parkway P 959 | Everything's Wrong/Cu Ma La Be Stay ............ 50 |
| 65 | Cameo Parkway P 965 | Two Hearts Make One Love/You Just Don't Know (What You Do To Me) (DJ Copy) ..... 300 |
| 65 | Cameo Parkway P 965 | Two Hearts Make One Love/You Just Don't Know (What You Do To Me) ............ 200 |
| 65 | Cameo Parkway P 989 | Hey You Little Boogaloo/Pussy Cat ............ 30 |
| 65 | Cameo Parkway P 989 | Hey You Little Boogaloo/Pussy Cat (DJ Copy) ............ 60 |
| 73 | Pye Int 25620 | Reggae My Way/Gypsy ............ 25 |
| 76 | London HLU 10515 | (At The) Discotheque/Slow Twistin'. ............ 5 |
| 78 | London HLU 10557 | You Just Don't Know (What You Do To Me)/ Two Hearts Make One Love (reissue) (DJ Copy) ............ 30 |
| 78 | London HLU 10557 | You Just Don't Know (What You Do To Me)/ Two Hearts Make One Love (reissue) ............ 15 |
| 93 | Kent 6T 9 | You Can't Lose Something You've Never Had/TEARDROPS: Here Comes The Lonliness . 10 |
| 71 | London SHZ 8419 | CHEQUERED (LP) ............ 20 |

## CHUBBY CHECKER & DEE DEE SHARP
| 62 | Cameo Parkway C 1029 | DOWN TO EARTH (LP) ............ 20 |

*(see also Dream Lovers, Bobby Rydell, Dee Dee Sharp)*

## CHECKMATES
| 61 | Piccadilly 7N 35010 | Rockin' Minstrel/Pompeii ............ 5 |
| 63 | Decca F 11603 | You've Gotta Have A Gimmick Today/Westpoint ............ 10 |
| 64 | Decca F 11844 | Sticks And Stones/Please Listen To Me ............ 15 |
| 65 | Decca F 12114 | Around/I've Got To Know Now ............ 10 |
| 65 | Parlophone R 5337 | Stop That Music/I've Been In Love Before ............ 10 |
| 66 | Parlophone R 5402 | (You Got) The Gamma Goochie/It Ain't Right ............ 10 |
| 66 | Parlophone R 5495 | Every Day Is Just The Same/I'll Be Keeping The Score ............ 15 |
| 61 | Pye NPL 18061 | THE CHECKMATES (LP) ............ 25 |

*(see also Original Checkmates, Emile Ford)*

## CHECKMATES LTD
| 67 | Ember EMB S 235 | Do The Walk (The Temptation Walk)/Glad For You ............ 5 |

*(see also Sonny Charles & Checkmates Ltd)*

## CHEE CHEE AND PEPPY
| 71 | Buddah 2011 083 | I Know I'm In Love/My Love Will Never Fade Away ............ 5 |

## CHEEKY
| 80 | Woodbine St. WSR 005 | Don't Mess Around/Get Outa My 'Ouse (no p/s) ............ 40 |

## CHEERS
| 54 | Capitol CL 14189 | Bazoom (I Need Your Lovin')/Arrivederci ............ 15 |
| 55 | Capitol CL 14248 | Bernie's Tune/Whadaya Want? ............ 10 |
| 55 | Capitol CL 14280 | Blueberries/Can't We Be More Than Friends ............ 10 |
| 55 | Capitol CL 14337 | I Must Be Dreaming/Fancy Meeting You Here ............ 10 |
| 55 | Capitol CL 14377 | Black Denim Trousers And Motorcycle Boots/Some Night In Alaska ............ 30 |
| 55 | Capitol CL 14377 | Black Denim Trousers And Motorcycle Boots/Some Night In Alaska (78) ............ 8 |
| 56 | Capitol CL 14561 | Chicken/Don't Do Anything ............ 20 |
| 56 | Capitol CL 14601 | Que Pasa Muchacha/BERT CONVY: Heaven On Earth ............ 5 |
| 56 | Capitol EAP1 584 | THE CHEERS (EP) ............ 15 |

*(see also Bert Convy [& Thunderbirds])*

## CHEETAHS
| 64 | Philips BF 1362 | Mecca/Goodnight Kiss ............ 20 |
| 65 | Philips BF 1383 | Soldier Boy/Johnny ............ 20 |
| 65 | Philips BF 1412 | Goodbye Baby (Baby Goodbye)/That's How It Goes ............ 15 |
| 65 | Philips BF 1453 | Whole Lotta Love/The Party ............ 15 |
| 66 | Philips BF 1499 | The Russian Boat Song/Gamble ............ 15 |

*(see also Carl Wayne & Cheetahs)*

MINT VALUE £

## CHEFS
| | | | |
|---|---|---|---|
| 80 | Attatrix RB 10 | SWEETIE EP | 15 |
| 81 | Graduate GRAD 11 | 24 Hours/Thrush | 15 |

## CHELMSFORD COUNTY HIGH SCHOOL FOLK GROUP
| | | | |
|---|---|---|---|
| 70 | Private Pressing | CHELMSFORD COUNTY HIGH SCHOOL FOLK GROUP (LP) | 20 |

## CHELSEA
| | | | |
|---|---|---|---|
| 77 | Step Forward SF 2 | Right To Work/The Loner (p/s, original pressing in card p/s) | 15 |
| 77 | Step Forward SF 2 | Right To Work/The Loner (p/s) | 8 |
| 77 | Step Forward SF 5 | High Rise Living/No Admission (p/s) | 10 |
| 78 | Step Forward SF 8 | Urban Kids/No Flowers (p/s) | 8 |
| 80 | Step Forward SF 14 | No One's Coming Outside/What Would You Do (p/s) | 6 |
| 80 | Step Forward SF 15 | Look At the Outside/Don't Get Me Wrong (p/s) | 6 |
| 80 | Step Forward SF 16 | No Escape/Decide (p/s) | 6 |
| 82 | Step Forward SF 22 | Stand Out/Last Drink (p/s) | 5 |
| 84 | Chelsea CH 001 | Give Me More/Sympathy For The Devil (p/s) | 5 |
| 79 | Step Forward SFLP 2 | CHELSEA (LP, with inner sleeve) | 30 |
| 81 | Step Forward SFLP 5 | ALTERNATIVE HITS (LP) | 20 |
| 82 | Step Forward SFLP 7 | EVACUATE (LP) | 15 |

## CHEMICAL ALICE
| | | | |
|---|---|---|---|
| 81 | Acidic GNOME 1 | The Judge/Goodnight Vienna/Lands Of Home/Henry The King (12", p/s) | 40 |

*(see also Marillion)*

## CHEMICAL BROTHERS
| | | | |
|---|---|---|---|
| 91 | Eastern Bloc | Sea Of Beats/Sea Of Beats (Justin Robertson Mix) (12", p/s, as Ariel) | 80 |
| 91 | Deconstruction PT 44888 | Rollercoaster/Mustn't Grumble/Mustn't Grumble (God's Grumble Mix) (12", as Ariel) | 30 |
| 93 | Dust Brothers DB's 333 | Song To The Siren (12", as Dust Brothers, no p/s, 500 only) | 60 |
| 93 | Junior Boys Own JBO 10 | Song To The Siren/Song To The Siren (Sabres Of Paradise Mixes) (12", p/s) | 30 |
| 94 | Boys Own COLLECT 004 | 14TH CENTURY SKY EP (12", no p/s, as Dust Brothers) | 20 |
| 94 | Junior Boys Own JBO 20 | MY MERCURY MOUTH EP (12", JBO sleeve, as Dust Brothers) | 30 |
| 95 | Junior Boys Own CHEMS TI | Leave Home/Leave Home (Sabres Of Paradise)/Let Me In Mate (12", p/s) | 15 |
| 95 | Junior Boys Own | Leave Home (Underworld Mix One)/Leave Home (Underworld Mix Two) (12", p/s) | 15 |
| 95 | Junior Boys Own XDUSTLP1 | EXIT PLANET DUST (2-LP, inners) | 25 |
| 97 | Freestyle Dust XDUSTLP2 | DIG YOUR OWN HOLE (2-LP) | 25 |
| 99 | Freestyle Dust XDUST LP4 | SURRENDER (2-LP, gatefold) | 20 |
| 02 | Virgin XDUST LP5 | COME WITH US (2-LP) | 20 |
| 03 | Freestyle Dust XDUSTLP 6 | SINGLES 93-03 (4-LP box set) | 40 |
| 04 | Virgin XDUST LP7 | PUSH THE BUTTON (2-LP) | 20 |

## CHEMICAL (1)
| | | | |
|---|---|---|---|
| 92 | Head Press SRT 92LS 3170 | Distrurbance/Paranoia (12") | 10 |
| 92 | Head Press HP 002 | THE VIRUS EP (12") | 12 |
| 92 | Basement BRSS 017 | Hex/Sub Sector (12") | 10 |

*(see also Two Dark Troopers, DJ Chemistry Meets Jack Smooth)*

## CHEMICAL (2)
| | | | |
|---|---|---|---|
| 96 | Acme AC 8014LP | CHEMICAL (LP, 500 only) | 15 |

## CHEMISTRY SET
| | | | |
|---|---|---|---|
| 11 | Fruits De Mer Winkle1 | Impossible Love/We Luv You (folded p/s, inserts) | 15 |
| 12 | Regal Crambone Winkle 8 | Time To Breathe/Come Kiss Me Vibrate And Smile/Hallucinations (p/s, blue vinyl) | 7 |

## CLIFTON CHENIER
| | | | |
|---|---|---|---|
| 69 | Action ACT 4550 | Black Gal/Frogs Legs | 15 |
| 70 | Specialty SNTF 5012 | BAYOU BLUES (LP) | 20 |
| 70 | Harvest MHSP 4002 | CLIFTON CHENIER'S VERY BEST (LP) | 50 |
| 79 | Flyright FLY 539 | ZYDECO BLUES (LP, with other artists) | 20 |

## CHEQUERED PAST
| | | | |
|---|---|---|---|
| 85 | Heavy Metal America | CHEQUERED PAST (LP, picture disc, 1,000 only) | 30 |

*(see also Steve Jones)*

## CHEQUERS (1)
| | | | |
|---|---|---|---|
| 76 | Creole CRLP 504 | CHECK US OUT (LP) | 40 |

## CHEQUERS (2)
| | | | |
|---|---|---|---|
| 80 | Matthias MT 101 | Midnight Hour/Move Up | 15 |
| 83 | Matthias MT 102 | Hard Times/If You Want My Love (no p/s) | 200 |

## CHER
| | | | |
|---|---|---|---|
| 69 | Atlantic 584 278 | Walk On Gilded Splinters/Tonight I'll Be Staying Here With You | 15 |
| 66 | Liberty LBY 3081 | CHER (LP, mono) | 15 |
| 66 | Liberty (S)LBY 3081 | CHER (LP, stereo) | 15 |

*(see also Sonny & Cher, Caesar & Cleo, Nilsson)*

## VIVIENNE CHERING
| | | | |
|---|---|---|---|
| 66 | Decca F 12360 | I'll Do My Crying Tomorrow/Make My Dreams Come True | 10 |

*(see also Flip & Dateliners)*

## CHEROKEE
| | | | |
|---|---|---|---|
| 71 | Probe PRO 550 | Girl, I've Got News For You/Write To You | 10 |

## CHEROKEES (U.K.)
| | | | |
|---|---|---|---|
| 64 | Decca F 11915 | You've Done It Again Little Girl/Girl Girl Girl | 7 |
| 64 | Columbia DB 7341 | Seven Daffodils/Are You Back In My World Now | 8 |
| 65 | Columbia DB 7473 | Wondrous Place/Send Me All Your Love | 10 |
| 65 | Columbia DB 7704 | I Will Never Turn My Back On You/Dig A Little Deeper | 10 |
| 66 | Columbia DB 7822 | Land Of A 1000 Dances/Everybody's Needs | 20 |

*(see also Lee Diamond)*

## CHEROKEES (U.S.)
61   Pye International 7N 25066   Cherokee/Harlem Nocturne ........................................................................ 15

## CHERRY
80s   Crashed Records CAR 91   He's A Bum/He Rides With Me ...................................................................... 10

## CHERRY BOYS
81   Open Eye OE5   Man To Man/So Much Confusion (p/s) ................................................................ 6

## DON CHERRY (1)
56   Brunswick 05538   Wanted Someone To Love/The Thrill Is Gone .......................................................... 6
57   Philips JK 1013   The Last Dance/Don't You Worry (jukebox edition) ..................................................... 7

## DON CHERRY (2)
73   JCOA/Virgin J2001   RELATIVITY SUITE (LP) ........................................................................... 25
74   Sonet SNTF 653   ETERNAL NOW (LP) ............................................................................... 25
78   Sonet SNFF 669   LIVE IN ANKARA (LP) ............................................................................ 25

## CHERRY ORCHARD
88   Red Honey (No Cat. No)   So Blind (p/s, 1-sided flexi) ....................................................................... 15
89   Red Honey ORCHARD 1   SING SISTER GLORY (12" EP) ....................................................................... 18
90   Red Honey ORCHARD 3   For What It's Worth/For What It's Worth (Version) (12", no p/s, promo only) ............. 18
90   Red Honey ORCHARD 2   HEALING FAITH LIKE FIRE (LP) ................................................................. 15

## CHERRY PEOPLE
68   MGM MGM 1438   And Suddenly/Imagination ......................................................................... 40
68   MGM MGM 1438   And Suddenly/Imagination (DJ copy) .............................................................. 60
69   MGM MGM 1472   Gotta Get Back/I'm The One Who Loves You ..................................................... 15
69   MGM MGM 1489   Light Of Love/On To Something New ................................................................ 8
69   MGM MGM 1489   Light Of Love/I'm The One Who Loves You .......................................................... 8
75   Black Magic BM 112   And Suddenly/Imagination (reissue) ................................................................. 8

## CHERRY PIES
64   Black Swan WI 448   Do You Keep Dreaming/Sweeter Than Cherry Pie .......................................... 25

## CHERRY POPPERS
80   Hiroshima HRH 1   Money In My Pocket/Hiroshima ................................................................... 20

## CHERRY SMASH
67   Track 604 017   Sing Songs Of Love/Movie Star ..................................................................... 20
68   Decca F 12838   Goodtime Sunshine/Little Old Country Home Town ........................................ 25
69   Decca F 12884   Fade Away Maureen/Green Plant ................................................................. 60

## JIMMY CHERRY
76   Gull GULS 36   Capella/Slow Burning ............................................................................... 8

## FRANKIE CHERVAL
62   MGM MGM 1183   How Come/Tag Along ................................................................................ 5

## VIC CHESNUTT
96   PLR 005-1   ABOUT TO CHOKE (LP) ............................................................................ 15

## PETE CHESTER
60   Pye 7N 15305   Ten Swinging Bottles/Whole Lotta Shakin' On The Range (with Consulates) ........... 15
61   Pye International 7N 25074   Three Old Maids/Forest Fire (as Pete Chester & Group) ........................... 15
(see also Five Chesternuts)

## VIC CHESTER
57   Decca F 10882   Rock-A-Billy/First Date, First Kiss, First Love ....................................................... 12

## CHESTERFIELDS (1)
86   Subway Org. SUBWAY 7   Completely & Utterly/Girl On A Boat (foldover p/s with insert in poly bag) ............ 5

## CHESTERFIELDS (2)
03   Grapevine 45-134   Think It Over/Why Did You Leave Me Baby? (reissue) .......................................... 15

## MORRIS CHESTNUT
79   Grapevine GRP 128   Too Darn Soulful/You Don't Love Me Anymore ............................................. 20
79   Grapevine GRP 128   Too Darn Soulful/You Don't Love Me Anymore (DJ Copy) ................................. 35

## CHEVLONS
66   Pye 7N 17145   Too Long Alone/It's My Problem ..................................................................... 5

## CHEVRONS (1)
60   Top Rank JAR 308   Lullaby/Day After Forever .......................................................................... 5

## CHEVRONS (2)
79   Shy Talk   Sindy's Got An Action Man/No More Tears (p/s) ..................................................... 25

## CHEVY
80   Avatar AAA 104   Too Much Loving/See The Light (company sleeve) ........................................... 15
80   Avatar AAA 107   The Taker/Life On The Run (p/s) .................................................................. 15
81   Avatar AAA 114   Just Another Day/Rock On ......................................................................... 12
80   Avatar AALP 5001   THE TAKER (LP, with inner sleeve) ................................................................ 18

## CHEYNES (1)
63   Columbia DB 7153   Respectable/It's Gonna Happen To You ..................................................... 120
64   Columbia DB 7368   Going To The River/Cheyne-Re-La ............................................................ 120
65   Columbia DB 7464   Down And Out/Stop Running Around ........................................................ 120
(see also Peter Bardens, Peter B's, Fleetwood Mac, Mark Leeman Five, Bo Street Runners)

## CHEYNES (2)
71   Bell BLL 1144   April Fool/Gotta Get Back ............................................................................. 6

## CHIC
78   Atlantic K 11209   Le Freak/Savoir Faire (12") ......................................................................... 10
79   Atlantic K11385T   My Forbidden Lover/What About Me? (12") ...................................................... 10
78   Atlantic K50565   C'EST CHIC (LP, inner) ............................................................................. 15

## CHICAGO
69   CBS 4381   Questions 67 And 68/Listen ........................................................................... 6

| | | | |
|---|---|---|---|
| 69 | CBS 4503 | I'm A Man (Parts 1 & 2) (withdrawn) | 20 |
| 69 | CBS 4715 | I'm A Man/Does Anyone Really Know What Time It Is? (promo p/s) | 20 |
| 69 | CBS 66221 | CHICAGO TRANSIT AUTHORITY (2-LP, orange label) | 18 |
| 71 | CBS 66405 | IV (AT CARNEGIE HALL) (4-LP, orange label) | 20 |

## CHICAGO LINE
| | | | |
|---|---|---|---|
| 66 | Philips BF 1488 | Shimmy Shimmy Ko Ko Bop/Jump Back | 200 |

*(see also Mike Patto, Bo Street Runners, Viv Prince)*

## CHICAGO LOOP
| | | | |
|---|---|---|---|
| 66 | Stateside SS 564 | (When She Needs Good Lovin') She Comes To Me/This Must Be The Place (DJ Copy) | 40 |
| 66 | Stateside SS 564 | (When She Needs Good Lovin') She Comes To Me/This Must Be The Place | 15 |

## CHICANES
| | | | |
|---|---|---|---|
| 81 | Dinosaur Discs DD 003 | Cry A Little/Further Thoughts (p/s) | 20 |
| 88 | Bam Caruso NRIC 039 | Cry A Little/Further Thoughts (p/s) | 20 |

## CHICK WITH TED CAMERON & D.J.'S
| | | | |
|---|---|---|---|
| 60 | Pye 7N 15292 | Early In The Morning/Cool Water | 40 |

## CHICKEN SHACK
| | | | |
|---|---|---|---|
| 67 | Blue Horizon 57-3135 | It's OK With Me Baby/When My Left Eye Jumps | 20 |
| 68 | Blue Horizon 57-3143 | Worried About My Woman/Six Nights In Seven | 20 |
| 68 | Blue Horizon 57-3146 | When The Train Comes Back/Hey Baby | 15 |
| 69 | Blue Horizon 57-3153 | I'd Rather Go Blind/Night Life | 8 |
| 69 | Blue Horizon 57-3160 | Tears In The Wind/The Things You Put Me Through | 10 |
| 70 | Blue Horizon 57-3168 | Maudie/Andalucian Blues | 10 |
| 70 | Blue Horizon 57-3176 | Sad Clown/Tired Eyes | 15 |
| 73 | Deram DM 381 | Time Goes Passing By/Poor Boy | 10 |
| 73 | Deram DM 396 | You Know You Could Be Right/The Loser | 10 |
| 74 | CBS 1832 | I'd Rather Go Blind/Sad Clown | 5 |
| 68 | Blue Horizon 7-63203 | FORTY BLUE FINGERS FRESHLY PACKED AND READY TO SERVE (LP, 1st pressing with 'stereo' sticker on sleeve) | 100 |
| 68 | Blue Horizon 7-63203 | FORTY BLUE FINGERS FRESHLY PACKED AND READY TO SERVE (LP, 1st pressing, mono) | 40 |
| 69 | Blue Horizon 7-63209 | O.K. KEN? (LP, gatefold sleeve, 1st pressing with 'stereo' sticker on sleeve) | 100 |
| 69 | Blue Horizon 7-63209 | O.K. KEN? (LP, gatefold sleeve, 1st pressing, mono) | 60 |
| 69 | Blue Horizon 7-63218 | 100 TON CHICKEN (LP, gatefold, 1st pressing with 'stereo' sticker on sleeve) | 100 |
| 70 | Blue Horizon 7-63861 | ACCEPT CHICKEN SHACK (LP, gatefold sleeve) | 75 |
| 71 | Deram SDL 5 | IMAGINATION LADY (LP, gatefold sleeve, brown/white label with large Deram label) | 75 |
| 72 | Deram SDL 5 | IMAGINATION LADY (LP, gatefold sleeve, later pressing with red/white label) | 30 |
| 73 | Deram SML 1100 | UNLUCKY BOY (LP) | 40 |

*(see also Errol Dixon, Fleetwood Mac, Christine Perfect, Carmen Macrae, Broken Glass)*

## CHICKEN SHED
| | | | |
|---|---|---|---|
| 77 | Colby AJ 370 | ALICE (LP, hand-made sleeves) | 120 |

## CHICKS
| | | | |
|---|---|---|---|
| 63 | Oriole CB 1828 | What Are Boys Made Of?/Over The Mountain | 20 |

## CHICORY TIP
| | | | |
|---|---|---|---|
| 71 | CBS 7118 | My Girl Sunday/Doctor Man | 15 |
| 71 | CBS 7595 | I Love Onions/Don't Hang Jack | 12 |

## CHIEF
| | | | |
|---|---|---|---|
| 81 | Swamp WAM 114 | Don't Touch The Receiver/Icebreaker (not released in p/s) | 25 |

## CHIEF CHECKER
| | | | |
|---|---|---|---|
| 79 | Original WBA 102 | Impossibilities/Possibility (dub) (12", die cut sleeve) | 40 |
| 79 | Original WBL 101 | THE SOUND OF CHIEF CHECKER (LP) | 100 |

## CHIEFS
| | | | |
|---|---|---|---|
| 58 | London HLU 8624 | Apache/Dee's Dream | 20 |
| 58 | London HLU 8720 | Enchiladas!/Moments To Remember | 20 |

## CHIFFONS
| | | | |
|---|---|---|---|
| 63 | Stateside SS 172 | He's So Fine/Oh! My Lover | 10 |
| 63 | Stateside SS 202 | One Fine Day/Why Am I So Shy | 10 |
| 63 | Stateside SS 230 | A Love So Fine/Only My Friend | 15 |
| 64 | Stateside SS 254 | I Have A Boyfriend/I'm Gonna Dry Your Eyes | 15 |
| 64 | Stateside SS 332 | Sailor Boy/When Summer's Through | 20 |
| 65 | Statside SS 437 | Nobody Knows What's Going On (In My Mind But Me)/The Real Thing (DJ copy) | 60 |
| 65 | Stateside SS 437 | Nobody Knows What's Going On (In My Mind But Me)/The Real Thing | 40 |
| 66 | Stateside SS 512 | Sweet Talkin' Guy/Did You Ever Go Steady | 10 |
| 66 | Stateside SS 533 | Out Of This World/Just A Boy | 15 |
| 66 | Stateside SS 559 | Stop, Look And Listen/March | 25 |
| 67 | Stateside SS 578 | My Boyfriend's Back/I Got Plenty Of Nuttin' | 22 |
| 64 | Stateside SE 1012 | THEY'RE SO FINE (EP) | 60 |
| 63 | Stateside SL 10040 | THE CHIFFONS - HE'S SO FINE (LP) | 80 |
| 66 | Stateside S(S)L 10190 | SWEET TALKIN' GUY (LP) | 80 |
| 85 | Impact ACT 007 | FLIPS FLOPS & RARITIES (LP) | 15 |

*(see also Four Pennies)*

## ANTHONY CHILD/ANDREW READ
| | | | |
|---|---|---|---|
| 99 | Fat Cat 12FAT 031 | Speedranch/Jansky Noise (12" EP, 'bullet hole' sleeve) | 12 |

## LORRAINE CHILD
| | | | |
|---|---|---|---|
| 64 | Decca F 11969 | You/Not This Time | 5 |

## ALAN CHILDE
| | | | |
|---|---|---|---|
| 76 | Epic SEPC 4183 | Rainmaker/Mind Blowing Love | 6 |

## SONNY CHILDE (& T.N.T.)
| | | | |
|---|---|---|---|
| 65 | Decca F 12218 | Giving Up On Love/Mighty Nice (Of You To Call) | 150 |
| 65 | Decca F12218 | Giving Up On Love/Mighty Nice (Of You To Call) (DJ Copy) | 300 |

| | | | |
|---|---|---|---|
| 66 | Polydor 56108 | Two Lovers/Ain't That Good News | 15 |
| 66 | Polydor 56141 | Heartbreak/I Still Love You (as Sonny Childe & T.N.T.) | 30 |
| 66 | Polydor 582 003 | TO BE CONTINUED (LP) | 40 |

**CHILD HAROLDS**

| | | | |
|---|---|---|---|
| 68 | Trident TRA 201 | Diary Of My Mind/Loophole | 30 |

**WILD BILLY CHILDISH**

| | | | |
|---|---|---|---|
| 87 | Hangman HANG 13 UP | I REMEMBER (LP) | 20 |
| 87 | Hangman HANG 2 UP | I'VE GOT EVERYTHING INDEED (LP) | 35 |

**BILLY CHILDISH**

| | | | |
|---|---|---|---|
| 93 | Damaged Books DAMBOOK 1 | TREMBLING OF LIFE (3 x 7" box set with book & 2 postcards) | 20 |
| 87 | Hangman HANG 9-UP | THE 1982 CASSETTES (LP, blue & white sleeve, with poster) | 30 |
| 87 | Hangman HANG 9-UP | THE 1982 CASSETTES (LP, blue & white sleeve, without poster) | 30 |
| 88 | Hangman HANG 16-UP | POEMS OF LAUGHTER & VIOLENCE (LP) | 30 |
| 91 | Hangman HANG 37 UP | 50 ALBUMS GREAT (LP) | 30 |
| 08 | Aquarium AQU 000l-13 | LIVE AT THE AQUARIUM (2-LP, 150 only, numbered and signed) | 100 |

**WILD BILLY CHILDISH & HIS FAMOUS HEADCOATS**

| | | | |
|---|---|---|---|
| 00 | Buff Medway COCK 1-UP | I AM THE OBJECT OF YOUR DESIRE (LP) | 15 |

**BILLY CHILDISH & THE BLACKHANDS**

| | | | |
|---|---|---|---|
| 93 | Hangman 53 UP | LIVE IN THE NETHERLANDS (LP) | 20 |

**BILLY CHILDISH & THE NATURAL BORN LOVERS**

| | | | |
|---|---|---|---|
| 89 | Hangman 30 UP | LONG LEGGED BABY (LP) | 20 |

**BILLY CHILDISH & SEXTON MING**

| | | | |
|---|---|---|---|
| 87 | Hangman HANG 05 UP | WHICH DEAD DONKEY DADDY (LP, poster) | 15 |
| 87 | Hangman HANG 10 UP | PLUMP PRIZES & LITTLE GEMS (LP) | 15 |
| 87 | Hangman HANG 12 UP | YPRES 1917 OVERTURE(LP) | 20 |
| 98 | Damaged Goods DAMGOOD 159LP | THE CHEEKY CHEESE (LP) | 15 |

**BILLY CHILDISH & THE SINGING LOINS**

| | | | |
|---|---|---|---|
| 93 | Hangmans Daughter SCRAG 1 | AT THE BRIDGE (LP) | 20 |

**WILD BILLY CHILDISH & THE BLACKHANDS**

| | | | |
|---|---|---|---|
| 88 | Hangman HANG-21 UP | PLAY CAPT'N CALYPSO'S HOODOO PARTY | 20 |

*(see also Milkshakes, Thee Mighty Caesars and Billy Childish & entries)*

**WILD BILLY CHILDISH & BIG RUSS WILKINS**

| | | | |
|---|---|---|---|
| 87 | Empire CPO 195 | LAUGHING GRAVY (10" LP) | 20 |

**WILD BILLY CHILDISH & BUFF MEDWAYS**

| | | | |
|---|---|---|---|
| 03 | Aquarium (No Cat. No) | You Are All Phonys (p/s, 1-sided, white label other side etched, 100 numbered and signed by Childish) | 50 |
| 03 | Aquarium (No Cat. No) | You Are All Phonys (p/s, 1-sided, white label other side etched, 400 unsigned) | 20 |
| 04 | Aquarium (No Cat. No) | (I'm Not Going To Your Boring) Private View (p/s, 1-sided other side etched, 100 numbered and signed by Childish) | 50 |
| 04 | Aquarium (No Cat. No) | (I'm Not Going To Your Boring) Private View (p/s, 1-sided other side etched, 400 unsigned) | 20 |
| 05 | Damaged Goods DAMGOOD 239LP | MEDWAY WHEELERS (LP, 50 copies with numbered 'The Poundlands Poets' booklet | 30 |
| 05 | Damaged Goods DAMGOOD 239LP | MEDWAY WHEELERS (LP, without booklet) | 15 |

*(see also Buff Medways)*

**CHILDREN**

| | | | |
|---|---|---|---|
| 82 | C391/1 | Demon Blues/Nightland (promo version - different catalogue number) | 15 |
| 82 | INT 002 | Nightland/Demon Blues | 10 |

**CHI-LITES**

| | | | |
|---|---|---|---|
| 69 | Beacon BEA 119 | Pretty Girl/Love Bandit | 70 |
| 71 | MCA 1143DJ | What Do I Wish For (1-sided DJ copy) | 15 |
| 72 | Brunswick 55489 | We Need Order/Living In The Footsteps Of Another Man | 6 |

*(see also Jackie Wilson)*

**CHILLIWACK**

| | | | |
|---|---|---|---|
| 71 | London HLU 10327 | Everyday/Sundown | 5 |
| 71 | London SHU 8418 | CHILLIWACK (LP, U.K. issue of US 1970 issue) | 25 |
| 71 | A&M AMLH 63509 | CHILLIWACK (LP) | 15 |

*(see also Collectors, Electric Prunes)*

**CHILLI WILLI & RED HOT PEPPERS**

| | | | |
|---|---|---|---|
| 75 | Mooncrest MOON 40 | Breathe A Little/Friday Song | 6 |
| 72 | Revelation REV 002 | KINGS OF THE ROBOT RHYTHM (LP, with lyric insert, inner sleeve and sticker) | 60 |
| 72 | Revelation REV 002 | KINGS OF THE ROBOT RHYTHM (LP, with lyric insert, but without inner sleeve and sticker) | 30 |
| 74 | Mooncrest CREST 21 | BONGOS OVER BALHAM (LP, with inner sleeve) | 25 |

*(see also Brinsley Schwarz, Jo-Ann Kelly, Mighty Baby, Hapshash And The Coloured Coat, Attractions, Action)*

**CHILLS**

| | | | |
|---|---|---|---|
| 85 | Normal 43 | LOST EP (12") | 15 |
| 84 | Flying Nun Europe FNE 13 | KALEIDOSCOPE WORLD (LP, with free 7") | 30 |
| 84 | Flying Nun Europe FNE 13 | KALEIDOSCOPE WORLD (LP, without free 7") | 20 |
| 90 | Slash 828191 | SUBMARINE BELLS (LP, with inner sleeve) | 15 |

**CHILLUM**

| | | | |
|---|---|---|---|
| 71 | Mushroom 100 MR 11 | CHILLUM (LP, with photo insert) | 150 |

*(see also Secondhand)*

**ALEX CHILTON**

| | | | |
|---|---|---|---|
| 80 | Aura AUS 117 | Hey! Little Child/No More The Moon Shines Lorena (p/s) | 8 |

*(see also Box Tops, Big Star)*

MINT VALUE £

## CHIMES FEATURING DENISE (U.K.)
| | | | |
|---|---|---|---|
| 63 | Decca F 11783 | Say It Again/Can This Be Love? | 5 |
| 64 | Decca F 11885 | I'll Be Waiting, I'll Be Here/Hello Heartache | 5 |

*(see also Little Frankie)*

## CHIMES (U.S.)
| | | | |
|---|---|---|---|
| 61 | London HLU 9283 | Once In A While/Summer Night | 25 |

## CHIMNEYS
| | | | |
|---|---|---|---|
| 80 | Tagmemics 45-003 | Do The Big Baby/Take Your Brain Out For A Walk (p/s, 500 only) | 15 |

## CHINA DOLL
| | | | |
|---|---|---|---|
| 80 | Wessex WEX 273 | Oysters And Wine/Past Tense (p/s) | 150 |

## CHINA DOLLS
| | | | |
|---|---|---|---|
| 82 | Speed FIRED 1 | One Hit Wonder/Ain't Love Ain't Bad (p/s) | 35 |

*(see also Slade, Dummies)*

## CHINA DRUM
| | | | |
|---|---|---|---|
| 93 | No label or Cat. No. | Simple/On My Way/Meaning (Acoustic) (p/s, 550 only gig freebie) | 12 |
| 96 | Mantra MNTLP1002 | GOOSE FAIR (LP) | 15 |
| 97 | Mantra MNTLP1009 | SELF MADE MANIAC (LP) | 15 |

## CHINA SOUL
| | | | |
|---|---|---|---|
| 09 | Foofar FF 001 | Cold/Be My Husband (signed sleeve) | 15 |
| 09 | Foofar FF 001 | Cold/Be My Husband (unsigned sleeve) | 10 |

## CHINA STREET
| | | | |
|---|---|---|---|
| 78 | Criminal CRM 1 | You're A Ruin/(I Wanna Be) Your M.P. (foldout lyric p/s in poly bag & badge) | 10 |

## CHINATOWN
| | | | |
|---|---|---|---|
| 81 | Airship AP 138 | Short And Sweet/How Many Times (p/s) | 60 |
| 81 | Airship AP 343 | PLAY IT TO DEATH (LP) | 85 |

## CHINAWITE
| | | | |
|---|---|---|---|
| 83 | Future Earth FER 014 | Blood On The Streets/Ready To Satisfy (p/s) | 30 |

## KES CHINS
| | | | |
|---|---|---|---|
| 62 | Starlite ST45 089 | Annie/Moody | 8 |

## CHIPS
| | | | |
|---|---|---|---|
| 75 | Decca FR 13574 | Love Matters/Gentle Teacher | 5 |
| 75 | Decca FR 13604 | Twice A Week/Reelin In The Years | 8 |

## CHISEL
| | | | |
|---|---|---|---|
| 70 | Ariel AR 003 | Turn To The Sun/Nightingale | 35 |

## GEORGE CHISHOLM & BLUENOTES
| | | | |
|---|---|---|---|
| 56 | Beltona BL 2671 | Honky Tonk/D.R. Rock (with Bert Weedon) | 10 |

*(see also Bert Weedon)*

## CHITINIOUS ENSEMBLE
| | | | |
|---|---|---|---|
| 71 | Deram SML 1093 | CHITINOUS ENSEMBLE (LP) | 300 |

## CHOC
| | | | |
|---|---|---|---|
| 70 | Decca F23106 | Way Of Life/I Want You To Be My Girl | 30 |

## CHOC ICE
| | | | |
|---|---|---|---|
| 71 | Polydor 2056189 | Groovy Situation/Look At It My Way | 20 |

## CHOCOLATE BOYS
| | | | |
|---|---|---|---|
| 74 | Decca F 13556 | El Bimbo/Voltaire Pier | 25 |
| 74 | Decca F 13556 | El Bimbo/Voltaire Pier (DJ Copy) | 35 |

## CHOCOLATE FROG
| | | | |
|---|---|---|---|
| 68 | Atlantic 584 207 | Butchers And Bakers/I Forgive You | 45 |

*(see also Fleur De Lys)*

## CHOCOLATE MILK
| | | | |
|---|---|---|---|
| 75 | RCA RCA 2592 | Action Speaks Louder Than Words/Ain't Nothing But A Thing | 10 |
| 79 | RCA RCAT 2592 | I'm Your Radio/Actions Speak Louder Than Words (12") | 15 |
| 77 | RCA PL 11830 | COMIN' (LP) | 15 |

## CHOCOLATE WATCH BAND
| | | | |
|---|---|---|---|
| 67 | Decca F 12649 | The Sound Of The Summer/The Only One In Sight | 50 |
| 67 | Decca F 12704 | Requiem/What's It To You | 40 |
| 84 | Big Beat WIK 25 | 44 (LP) | 15 |

## CHOCOLATS
| | | | |
|---|---|---|---|
| 76 | Aquarius AQ 1 | Voltaire Pier/Brasilia Carnival | 40 |

*(see also chocolate Boys)*

## CHOICE FOUR
| | | | |
|---|---|---|---|
| 74 | RCA APBO 0311 | The Finger Pointers Part 1/The Finger Pointers Part 2 | 5 |

## CHOICE OF COLOUR
| | | | |
|---|---|---|---|
| 00 | Goldmine G2K 45 102 | Your Love/Love Is Gone (with Ron Henderson) (no p/s) | 8 |

## CHOIR
| | | | |
|---|---|---|---|
| 68 | Major Minor MM 537 | It's Cold Outside/I'm Going Home | 40 |
| 68 | Major Minor MM 557 | When You Were With Me/Changin' My Mind | 30 |

## CHOPPER
| | | | |
|---|---|---|---|
| 71 | Decca F 13161 | Singer Wihout A Song/Think I'm A Man | 50 |

## CHOPYN
| | | | |
|---|---|---|---|
| 75 | Jet LPO 8 | GRAND SLAM (LP) | 20 |

*(see also Ann Odell, Ray Russell, Simon Phillips, C.M.U.)*

## CHORALE
| | | | |
|---|---|---|---|
| 85 | Towerbell TVP 4 | Mountain Men/Mountain Men (Remix) (p/s) | 5 |

## CHORALERNA
| | | | |
|---|---|---|---|
| 70s | Key KL 018 | POWER (LP) | 20 |

| | | | |
|---|---|---|---|
| 70s | Myrrh MYRRH 1047 | LET THERE BE LIGHT (LP) | 25 |

## CHORDETTES
| | | | |
|---|---|---|---|
| 54 | Columbia SCM 5158 | Mr. Sandman/I Don't Wanna See You Cryin' | 70 |
| 55 | London HLA 8169 | Humming Bird/Lonely Lips | 15 |
| 56 | London HLA 8217 | Dudelsack Polka/I Told A Lie | 25 |
| 56 | London HLA 8264 | Eddie My Love/Our Melody (triangular centre) | 25 |
| 56 | London HLA 8264 | Eddie My Love/Our Melody (round centre) | 10 |
| 56 | London HLA 8302 | Born To Be With You/Love Never Changes | 10 |
| 56 | London HA 7011 | Born To Be With You/Love Never Changes (export issue) | 10 |
| 56 | London HLA 8323 | Lay Down Your Arms/Teenage Goodnight | 10 |
| 57 | London HLA 8473 | Echo Of Love/Just Between You And Me | 10 |
| 57 | London HLA 8497 | Like A Baby/Soft Sands | 10 |
| 58 | London HLA 8566 | Baby Of Mine/Photographs | 10 |
| 58 | London HLD 8584 | Lollipop/Baby, Come-A-Back-A | 10 |
| 58 | London HLA 8654 | Love Is A Two-Way Street/I Don't Know, I Don't Care | 7 |
| 59 | London HLA 8809 | We Should Be Together/No Other Arms, No Other Lips | 7 |
| 59 | London HLA 8926 | A Girl's Work Is Never Done/No Wheels (B-side with Jeff Crom & Jackie Ertel) | 10 |
| 61 | London HLA 9400 | Never On Sunday/Faraway Star | 6 |
| 62 | London HLA 9519 | The White Rose Of Athens/Adios (Goodbye My Love) | 6 |
| 60 | London RE-A 1228 | THE CHORDETTES (EP) | 30 |
| 58 | London HA-A 2088 | THE CHORDETTES (LP) | 60 |
| 62 | London HA-A 2441 | THE CHORDETTES SING (LP) | 25 |

## CHORDS (U.K.)
| | | | |
|---|---|---|---|
| 79 | Polydor 2059 141 | Now It's Gone/Don't Go Back (p/s) | 5 |
| 80 | Polydor POSP 101 | Maybe Tomorrow/I Don't Wanna Know/Hey Girl (p/s) | 6 |
| 80 | Polydor POSP 146 | Something's Missing/This Is What They Want (p/s) | 5 |
| 80 | Polydor 2059 258 | The British Way Of Life/The Way It's Got To Be (p/s) | 6 |
| 80 | Polydor POSP 185 | In My Street/I'll Keep On Holding On (p/s) | 6 |
| 81 | Polydor POSP 270 | One More Minute/Who's Killing Who (p/s) | 6 |
| 81 | Polydor POSP 288 | Turn Away Again/Turn Away Again (Again) (p/s) | 8 |
| 80 | Polydor Super POLS 1019 | SO FAR AWAY (LP, with stickered sleeve & 7" Now It's Gone/Things We Said [KRODS 1]) | 20 |

*(see also Rage)*

## CHORDS (U.S.)
| | | | |
|---|---|---|---|
| 54 | Columbia SCM 5133 | Sh-Boom (Life Could Be A Dream)/Little Maiden | 2000 |
| 54 | Columbia DB 3512 | Sh-Boom (Life Could Be A Dream)/Little Maiden (78) | 100 |

## CHORDS FIVE
| | | | |
|---|---|---|---|
| 67 | Island WI 3044 | I'm Only Dreaming/Universal Vagrant | 100 |
| 68 | Polydor 56261 | Same Old Fat Man/Hold On To Everythin' You've Got | 40 |
| 69 | Jay Boy BOY 6 | Some People/Battersea Fair | 80 |

*(see also Smoke)*

## CHOSEN FEW (JAMAICA)
| | | | |
|---|---|---|---|
| 70 | Songbird SB 1031 | Time Is Hard/CRYSTALITES: Time Is Hard Part Two | 15 |
| 70 | Songbird SB 1032 | Going Back Home/CRYSTALITES: Going Back Home Part Two | 10 |
| 70 | Songbird SB 1046 | Why Can't I Touch You/INNER CIRCLE BAND: Touch You Version | 15 |
| 71 | Songbird SB 1061 | Shaft/Shaft (Version) | 15 |
| 71 | Songbird SB 1067 | Everybody Just A Stall/Everybody (Version) | 10 |
| 72 | Songbird SB 1070 | Do Your Thing/Your Thing (Version) | 20 |
| 72 | Trojan TR 7864 | Ebony Eyes/Ebony Eyes (Version) | 10 |
| 72 | Trojan TR 7882 | Everybody Plays The Fool/You're A Big Girl Now | 12 |
| 72 | Grape | You're A Big Girl Now/Version | 12 |
| 73 | Trojan TR 7894 | Am I Black Enough For You/Message From A Blackman | 12 |
| 73 | Duke DU 162 | Children Of The Night/LLOYD CHARMERS: For The Good Times | 20 |
| 73 | Duke DU 163 | Stoned In Love/MIKE CHUNG & NOW GENERATION: Stoned In Love (Version) | 12 |
| 73 | Duke DU 164 | It's Too Late/MIKE CHUNG & NOW GENERATION: It's Too Late (Version) | 12 |
| 73 | Trojan TRLS 56 | HIT AFTER HIT (LP) | 40 |
| 75 | Trojan TRLS 106 | EVERYBODY PLAYS THE FOOL (LP) | 50 |

## CHOSEN FEW (U.K.) (1)
| | | | |
|---|---|---|---|
| 65 | Pye 7N 15905 | It Won't Be Around You Anymore/Big City | 20 |
| 65 | Pye 7N 15942 | So Much To Look Forward To/Today, Tonight & Tomorrow | 20 |

*(see also Alan Hull, Lindisfarne, Skip Bifferty)*

## CHOSEN FEW (U.K.) (2)
| | | | |
|---|---|---|---|
| 74 | Action ACT 4623 | Funky Butter/Wondering | 70 |
| 76 | Polydor 2058 721 | I Can Make Your Dreams Come True/Pretty Face | 20 |
| 76 | Miami MIA401 | Night And Day/Funky Buttercup | 60 |
| 78 | Polydor 2058 975 | You Mean Everything To Me/It Won't Be Long | 30 |
| 77 | Polydor 2058 752 | Miracle Worker/Young And Foolish | 25 |

## CHOSEN PEOPLE
| | | | |
|---|---|---|---|
| 69 | Royalty RT 01 | When A Dream Ends/Firefly | 35 |

## CHOU PAHROT
| | | | |
|---|---|---|---|
| 79 | Klub KEP 101 | Buzgo Tram Chorus/Gwizgweela Gwamhnoo/Lemons (p/s) | 10 |

## CHRIS AND MAXINE
| | | | |
|---|---|---|---|
| 67 | Philips BF 1587 | Only A Thousand Times A Day/I've Made You My Mind | 15 |

## CHRIS & COSEY/CREATIVE TECHNOLOGY INSTITUTE
| | | | |
|---|---|---|---|
| 81 | Rough Trade RT 078 | October (Love Song)/Little Houses (p/s) | 5 |
| 84 | Intl. One CTI 002 | Conspiracy International/The Gift Of Tongues/The Need (p/s) | 6 |
| 91 | World Serpent WS7 004 | Passion (p/s, 1-sided, other side etched) | 5 |
| 81 | Rough Trade ROUGH 34 | HEARTBEAT (LP, with insert) | 20 |

MINT VALUE £

| 82 | Rough Trade ROUGH 44 | TRANCE (LP) | 20 |
| 84 | Rough Trade ROUGH 64 | SONGS OF LOVE AND LUST (LP) | 15 |
| 10 | Conspiracy International CTILP016 | EXOTICA (LP, reissue) | 15 |

*(see also Throbbing Gristle, Eurythmics, Cosey Fanni Tutti)*

## PETER CHRIS & OUTCASTS
| 66 | Columbia DB 7923 | Over The Hill/The Right Girl For Me | 40 |

## CHRIST CHILD
| 78 | Barak BAR 5 | Let Them Eat Rock/Five Finger Exercise | 8 |

## CHRISTEL & THE GOLDMASTER
| 98 | Goldmaster GM 002 | Government Man/Version | 25 |

## CHRISTIAN
| 71 | Decca F 23137 | Other Side Of Life/She | 15 |

## CHARLIE CHRISTIAN
| 57 | Philips BBL 7172 | CHARLIE CHRISTIAN (LP) | 20 |

## FUD CHRISTIAN ALL STARS
| 71 | Big Shot BI 571 | Never Fall In Love (actually by Winston Heywood)/Never Fall In Love Version | 15 |

## HANS CHRISTIAN
| 68 | Parlophone R 5676 | All Of The Time/Never My Love | 80 |
| 68 | Parlophone R 5698 | (The Autobiography Of) Mississippi Hobo/Sonata Of Love | 100 |

*(see also Jon Anderson, Yes)*

## JOHN CHRISTIAN DEE
| 68 | Pye 7N 17566 | Take Me Along/The World Can Pack Its Bags And Go Away | 15 |
| 70 | London HLH 10317 | Come Forward The Man/Mr. & Mrs. Jones | 5 |
| 69 | Decca F12901 | The World Can Pick Up Its Bags And Go Away/Stick To Your Guns | 15 |

## LIZ CHRISTIAN
| 67 | CBS 202520 | Suddenly You Find Love/Make It Work Out | 90 |
| 67 | CBS 202520 | Suddenly You Find Love/Make It Work Out (DJ copy) | 120 |
| 69 | Spark SRL 1004 | Call My Name/Think Of You Baby | 8 |

*(see also James Royal)*

## MARIA CHRISTIAN
| 85 | MCA MCA 974 | Wait Until The Weekend Comes/(Instrumental) (p/s) | 15 |

## NEIL CHRISTIAN (& CRUSADERS)
| 61 | Private Pressing | Restless/Red Sails In The Sunset/Your Cheating Heart/Danny (1-sided 4 track 12" demo acetate, 6 made, Jimmy Page's first studio recording) | 3000 |
| 62 | Columbia DB 4938 | The Road To Love/The Big Beat Drum | 40 |
| 63 | Columbia DB 7075 | A Little Bit Of Someone Else/Get A Load Of This (with Crusaders) | 20 |
| 66 | Strike JH 301 | That's Nice/She's Got The Action | 15 |
| 66 | Strike JH 313 | Oops/She Said Yeah | 10 |
| 66 | Strike JH 319 | Two At A Time/Wanna Lover | 10 |
| 67 | Pye 7N 17372 | You're All Things Bright And Beautiful/I'm Gonna Love You Baby | 15 |
| 73 | Youngblood YB 1044 | That's Nice/She's Got The Action | 6 |
| 76 | Satril SAT 106 | She's Got The Power/Someone Following Me Around | 20 |
| 66 | Columbia SEG 8492 | A LITTLE BIT OF SOMETHING ELSE (EP) | 80 |

*(see also Christian's Crusaders, Guy Hamilton, Jimmy Page, Nicky Hopkins, Miki Dallon, Screaming Lord Sutch)*

## CHRISTIAN DEATH
| 83 | Future FL 2 | ONLY THEATRE OF PAIN (LP, with insert) | 25 |

## CHRISTIAN'S CRUSADERS
| 64 | Columbia DB 7289 | Honey Hush/One For The Money | 60 |

*(see also Neil Christian & Crusaders)*

## CHRISTIE
| 71 | CBS 9130 | Everything's Gonna Be Alright/Freewheelin' Man/Magic Highway (p/s) | 6 |
| 72 | CBS S 8403 | Fools Gold/Born To Lose | 10 |
| 70 | CBS 64108 | CHRISTIE (LP) | 15 |
| 71 | CBS 64397 | FOR ALL MANKIND (LP, gatefold sleeve, orange label) | 20 |

*(see also Acid Gallery, Epics)*

## DAVE CHRISTIE
| 68 | Mercury MF1028 | Love And The Brass Band/Penelope Breedlove | 15 |

## JOHN CHRISTIE
| 74 | Polydor 2058 441 | Everybody But Me/Childhood | 7 |
| 74 | Polydor 2058 496 | 4th Of July (written by Paul McCartney)/Old Enough To Know Better (in p/s) | 30 |
| 74 | Polydor 2058 496 | 4th Of July (written by Paul McCartney)/Old Enough To Know Better | 15 |
| 74 | Polydor 2058 528 | Everybody Knows/How Does It Feel (p/s) | 6 |

## KEITH CHRISTIE
| 54 | Esquire 20-047 | HOMAGE TO THE DUKE (LP) | 20 |

## LOU CHRISTIE
| 63 | Columbia DB 4983 | The Gypsy Cried/Red Sails In The Sunset | 10 |
| 63 | Columbia DB 7031 | Two Faces Have I/All That Glitters Isn't Gold | 10 |
| 63 | Columbia DB 7096 | How Many Teardrops/You And I (Have A Right To Cry) | 10 |
| 66 | MGM MGM 1297 | Lightnin' Strikes/Cryin' In The Streets | 20 |
| 66 | MGM MGM 1297 | Lightnin' Strikes/Cryin' In The Streets (DJ Copy) | 50 |
| 66 | MGM MGM 1308 | Rhapsody In The Rain/Trapeze | 5 |
| 66 | MGM MGM 1317 | Painter/Du Ronda | 6 |
| 66 | MGM MGM 1325 | If My Car Could Only Talk/Song Of Lita | 20 |
| 66 | Colpix PX 735 | Merry Go Round/Guitars And Bongos | 10 |
| 67 | King KG 1036 | Outside The Gates Of Heaven/All That Glitters Isn't Gold | 8 |
| 67 | CBS 2718 | Shake Hands And Walk Away Cryin'/Escape | 15 |
| 67 | CBS 2922 | Gina/Back To The Days Of The Romans | 10 |

| | | | |
|---|---|---|---|
| 66 | MGM MGM-C(S) 8008 | LIGHTNIN' STRIKES (LP) | 25 |
| 66 | Colpix PXL 551 | STRIKES AGAIN (LP) | 25 |

**SUSAN CHRISTIE**
| 66 | CBS 202261 | I Love Onions/Take Me As You Find Me | 15 |

**TONY CHRISTIE (& TRACKERS)**
| 66 | CBS 202097 | Life's Too Good To Waste/Just The Two Of Us | 8 |
| 67 | MGM MGM 1365 | Turn Around/When Will I Ever Love Again? | 8 |
| 68 | MGM MGM 1386 | I Don't Want To Hurt You Anymore/Say No More | 8 |
| 68 | MGM MGM 1440 | My Prayer/I Need You | 8 |

**CHRISTIEN BROTHERS**
| 69 | Major Minor MM 628 | I Reached For You/Answer Me | 7 |

**DEREK CHRISTIEN**
| 70 | Major Minor MM 676 | When A Woman Has A Baby/Please Don't Go Away | 30 |
| 70 | Major Minor MM 713 | Suddenly There's A Valley/I'll Be Coming Home | 100 |

*(see also Christien Brothers)*

**CHRISTINES'S CAT**
| 89 | Sarah SARAH 13 | Your Love Is.... (5" flexi with two fanzines 'Lemonade: A Fanzine' and 'Cold: A Lie') | 50 |

**KEITH CHRISTMAS**
| 69 | RCA Victor SF 8059 | STIMULUS (LP, with Mighty Baby, orange/white label) | 200 |
| 70 | B&C CAS 1015 | FABLE OF THE WINGS (LP) | 80 |
| 71 | B&C CAS 1041 | PIGMY (LP, gatefold sleeve) | 70 |
| 74 | Manticore K 53503 | BRIGHTER DAY (LP. with inner sleeve) | 20 |
| 76 | Manticore K 53509 | STORIES FROM THE HUMAN ZOO (LP, with insert) | 20 |

*(see also Mighty Baby, Magic Muscle)*

**CHRISTOPHER**
| 70 | Chapter One CH121 | Sharkey/The Race | 20 |

**JORDAN CHRISTOPHER**
| 66 | United Artists UP 1140 | Hello Lover/What That I Was | 20 |

**CHARA CHRISTOU**
| 71 | Somerville SVL 1 | CELEBRATE HIS LOVE (LP) | 25 |

**JUNE CHRISTY**
| 55 | Capitol CL 14355 | Pete Kelly's Blues/Kicks | 6 |

*(see also Stan Kenton)*

**CHROME**
| 80 | Red RS 12007 | READ ONLY MEMORY (12" EP, with poster) | 20 |
| 80 | Red RS 12007 | READ ONLY MEMORY (12" EP, without poster) | 12 |
| 80 | Beggars Banquet BEG 36 | New Age/Information (p/s) | 12 |
| 81 | D. F. O. T. Mountain Y3 | INWORLDS (12") | 15 |
| 82 | D. F. O. T. Mountain Z17 | Firebomb/Shadows Of A Thousand Years (p/s) | 12 |
| 80 | Beggars Banquet BEGA 15 | RED EXPOSURE (LP, with inner sleeve) | 25 |
| 80 | Beggars Banquet BEGA 18 | HALF MACHINE LIP MOVES (LP, with poster insert) | 25 |
| 80 | Beggars Banquet BEGA 18 | HALF MACHINE LIP MOVES (LP, without poster insert) | 15 |
| 81 | D. F. O. T. Mountain X6 | BLOOD ON THE MOON (LP, with inner sleeve) | 18 |
| 82 | D. F. O. T. Mountain X18 | 3RD FROM THE SUN (LP, with insert) | 15 |

**CHEETAH CHROME**
| 85 | Children Of The Revolution GURT 3 | I REFUSE IT! (Split LP with MOTHERFUCKERS) | 35 |

**CHROMING ROSE**
| 90 | EMI 5667 93774 | LOUIS XIV (LP, some as picture disc) | 12 |

**CHRON GEN**
| 81 | Gargoyle GRGL 780 | PUPPETS OF WAR (EP, with sticker) | 15 |
| 81 | Step Forward SF 19 | Reality/Subway Sadist (p/s) | 5 |
| 82 | Secret SHH 129 | Jet Boy Jet Girl/Abortions/Subway Sadist (p/s) | 5 |
| 82 | Secret SHH 139 | Outlaw/Behind Closed Doors/Disco (p/s) | 6 |
| 83 | Secret SEC 3 | CHRONIC GENERATION (LP, with free 7") | 15 |

**CHRYSTAL BELLE SCRODD**
| 86 | United Dairies | BELLE DE JOUR (LP with insert) | 25 |

*(see also Nurse With Wound)*

**CHUBBY & HONEYSUCKERS**
| 65 | Venus VE 3 | Come On Home/What Shall I Do? | 12 |
| 66 | Rio R 75 | Emergency Ward/LEN & HONEYSUCKERS: One More River | 12 |

**CHUCK & BETTY**
| 59 | Brunswick 05815 | Sissy Britches/Come Back Little Girl | 20 |

**CHUCK (JOSEPHS) & DOBBY (DOBSON)**
| 60 | Blue Beat BB 19 | Til The End Of Time (as Chuck & Darby)/DUKE REID & HIS GROUP: What Makes Honey | 20 |
| 60 | Blue Beat BB 23 | Cool School/DUKE REID & HIS GROUP: Joker | 20 |
| 61 | Starlite ST45 043 | Sad Over You/Sweeter Than Honey | 20 |
| 61 | Starlite ST45 044 | Lovey Dovey/Sitting Square | 20 |
| 61 | Blue Beat BB 39 | Du Du Wap/I Love My Teacher (with Aubrey Adams & Du Droppers) | 18 |
| 61 | Blue Beat BB 59 | Oh Fanny/Running Around | 18 |
| 64 | Blue Beat BB 246 | Tell Me/I'm Going Home | 15 |

**CHUCK & GARY**
| 58 | HMV POP 466 | Teenie Weenie Jeanie/Can't Make Up My Mind | 30 |

**CHUCK & GIDEON**
| 63 | Parlophone R 5011 | Cherry Berry Lips/The Tender Touch | 5 |

MINT VALUE £

## CHUCKA
| | | |
|---|---|---|
| 74 | Lemmy LMY2 | Switch On The Heat/My Oh My ........................................................................ 30 |

## CHUCKLES (1)
| | | |
|---|---|---|
| 69 | Bullet BU 416 | Run Nigel Run/Come On Home ........................................................................ 30 |

## CHUCKLES (2)
| | | |
|---|---|---|
| 72 | Duke DU 144 | Reggae Limbo/ZAP POW: Broken Contract ...................................................... 30 |

## CHUMBAWAMBA
| | | |
|---|---|---|
| 88 | Agit Prop AGIT 3 | Smash Clause 28/Fight The Alton Bill (with booklet)......................................... 6 |
| 86 | Agit Prop PROP 1 | PICTURES OF STARVING CHILDREN SELL RECORDS (LP, with inner) ............... 20 |
| 87 | Agit Prop PROP 2 | NEVER MIND THE BALLOTS... (LP, gatefold) ..................................................... 15 |
| 88 | Agit Prop PROP 3 | ENGLISH REBEL SONGS 1381-1914 (10" LP, with die-cut sleeve) ................... 15 |
| 95 | One Little Indian TPLP056 | SHOWBUSINESS (LP) .................................................................................... 15 |

## MIKIE CHUNG & NOW GENERATION
| | | |
|---|---|---|
| 72 | Green Door GD 4032 | Breezing/NOW GENERATION: Breezing - Version ............................................... 5 |
| 73 | Duke DU 163 | Stoned In Love/CHOSEN FEW: Stoned In Love ................................................... 7 |
| 73 | Duke DU 164 | It's Too Late/CHOSEN FEW: It's Too Late .......................................................... 7 |

## CHUNKY
| | | |
|---|---|---|
| 73 | Orange OAS 214 | Albatross Baby/Road Runner Girl ................................................................... 30 |

## CHURCH
| | | |
|---|---|---|
| 82 | Carrere CAR 212 | Unguarded Moment/Busdriver (p/s) ................................................................. 5 |
| 82 | Carrere CAR 247 | Almost With You/Life Speeds Up (p/s) ............................................................... 5 |
| 82 | Carrere CAR EP 257 | Unguarded Moment/Interlude/Golden Dawn/Sisters (10", p/s) ...................... 8 |
| 83 | Carrere CHURCH R5A | Different Man/I Am A Rock (no p/s) ................................................................... 7 |
| 83 | Carrere CHURCH 5 | SING SONGS (12" EP) .................................................................................... 10 |
| 88 | Arista 208895 | STARFISH (LP, with bonus 5-track numbered 12") .......................................... 15 |

## EUGENE CHURCH
| | | |
|---|---|---|
| 59 | London HL 8940 | Miami/I Ain't Goin' For That (round centre) ..................................................... 50 |

## CHICK CHURCHILL
| | | |
|---|---|---|
| 73 | Chrysalis CHR 1051 | YOU AND ME (LP) ......................................................................................... 15 |

*(see also Ten Years After, Cozy Powell, Jethro Tull)*

## SAVANNAH CHURCHILL
| | | |
|---|---|---|
| 60 | London HLW 9273 | I Want To Be/Time Out For Tears ...................................................................... 5 |

## CHVRCHES
| | | |
|---|---|---|
| 12 | National Anthem ANTHEM 003 | The Mother We Share/(AJD Optimo Remix)/(Miaoux Miaoux Remix) (10" 500 only).... 60 |
| 13 | Goodbye GR001V | Recover/ZVVL/Recover (Cim Rim Remix)/Recover Curxes 1996 Remix) (12" orange vinyl) .......................................................................................................... 20 |
| 13 | Virgin V3116 | THE BONES OF WHAT YOU BELIEVE (LP) ......................................................... 15 |

## CIGARETTES
| | | |
|---|---|---|
| 78 | Dead Good KEVIN 1 | THE CIGARETTES (EP, unreleased) ..................................................................... 0 |
| 79 | Company CIGCO 008 | They're Back Again, Here They Come/I've Forgot My Number/All We Want Is Your Money (gatefold p/s, initial pressing with red labels) ...................................... 100 |
| 79 | Company CIGCO 008 | They're Back Again, Here They Come/I've Forgot My Number/All We Want Is Your Money (gatefold p/s, later pressing with black labels) ...................................... 60 |
| 80 | Dead Good DEAD 10 | Can't Sleep At Night/It's The Only Way To Live (Die) (p/s) ............................... 40 |
| 02 | Detour DRLP 029 | WILL DAMAGE YOUR HEALTH (2-LP) ............................................................... 30 |

## CIM(M)AR(R)ONS
| | | |
|---|---|---|
| 70 | Hot Rod HR 105 | Grandfather Clock/Kick Me Or I Kick You (as Cimarrons) ............................... 100 |
| 70 | Reggae REG 3003 | Bad Day At Black Rock (with Cimmaron Kid)/Fragile ........................................ 70 |
| 71 | Big Shot BI 562 | Funky Fight/You Turned Me Down ................................................................... 30 |
| 71 | Spinning Wheel SW 107 | Soul For Sale/Bogus-ism ................................................................................ 30 |
| 71 | Downtown DT 486 | Oh Mammy Blue/Oh Mammy Blue - Version ................................................... 15 |
| 71 | Downtown DT 487 | Holy Christmas/Silent Night/White Christmas ................................................ 12 |
| 71 | Bullet BU 457 | Call Me/Call Me (Part 2) ................................................................................... 8 |
| 71 | Bullet BU 458 | Leave Me A Little Love/My Baby ....................................................................... 8 |
| 74 | Trojan TR7919 | Over The Rainbow/We Are Not The Same ........................................................ 15 |
| 75 | Vulcan VUL 1005 | Tradition/Wicky Wacky ................................................................................... 15 |
| 78 | Cimarak CR002 | Paul Bogle/Greedy Man (12") .......................................................................... 20 |
| 82 | IMP IMPS 50 | With A Little Luck/Peggy Sue ............................................................................ 5 |
| 82 | Safari/MPL SAFE 49 | Big Girls Don't Cry/How Can I Prove Myself To You? .......................................... 5 |
| 83 | MPL/Cimarons CIM 001 | Love And Affection ........................................................................................ 12 |
| 83 | MPL/Cimarons 12CIM 001 | Love And Affection (12", less than 1000 pressed) ........................................... 30 |
| 74 | Trojan TRLS 77 | IN TIME (LP) .................................................................................................. 20 |
| 78 | Polydor 2383512 | MAKA (LP, green vinyl) .................................................................................. 15 |

*(see also Reaction, Winston Groovy)*

## CINCH
| | | |
|---|---|---|
| 80 | SRTS/80/CUS 622 | SELL OUT EP ................................................................................................ 20 |

## CINDERELLAS (1)
| | | |
|---|---|---|
| 59 | Brunswick 05794 | Mister Dee-Jay/Yum Yum Yum ........................................................................ 10 |
| 60 | Philips PB 1012 | The Trouble With Boys/Puppy Dog ................................................................... 25 |

## CINDERELLAS (2)
| | | |
|---|---|---|
| 64 | Colpix PX 11026 | Baby, Baby (I Still Love You)/Please Don't Wake Me .......................................... 60 |
| 64 | Colpix PX 11026 | Baby, Baby (I Still Love You)/Please Don't Wake Me (DJ Copy) ........................ 100 |

*(see also Cookies)*

## CINDERS
| | | |
|---|---|---|
| 63 | Warner Bros WB 86 | The Cinnamon Cinder/C'mon Wobble ............................................................. 10 |

*(see also Darlene Love)*

## CINDI AND THE BARBI DOLLS
| 79 | A Not Major Production NOTEM 1 | ISN'T SHOWBIZ WONDERFUL EP (hand-made p/s) | 15 |

## CINEMA
| 82 | Floppy FLOPPY 1 | Donor Donor/Cinema Star (p/s) | 8 |

## CINEMATIC ORCHESTRA
| 99 | Ninja Tune ZEN12 084 | Channel 1 Suite/Ode To The Big Sea (12") | 15 |
| 99 | Ninja Tune ZEN 45 | MOTION (2xLP) | 30 |
| 00 | Ninja Tune ZEN 50 | REMIXES 98 - 2000 (2xLP) | 20 |
| 02 | Ninja Tune ZEN 59 | EVERY DAY (2xLP) | 35 |
| 03 | Ninja Tune ZEN 78 | MAN WITH A MOVIE CAMERA (2xLP) | 40 |
| 07 | Ninja Tune ZEN 122 | MA FLEUR (2xLP) | 25 |

## CINEMATICS
| 82 | Pulsebeat CINE 001 | FAREWELL TO THE PLAYGROUND (EP, foldover p/s) | 30 |

*(see also Razorcuts)*

## CINNAMON
| 69 | Beacon BEA 111 | You Won't See Me Leaving/Leaves Of Love | 6 |
| 69 | President PT 258 | So Long Sam/Broken Hearted Me, Evil Hearted You | 6 |

## CINNAMON QUILL
| 69 | Morgan MRS 17 | Girl On A Swing/Take It Or Leave It | 20 |
| 69 | Morgan MRS 21 | Candy/Hello, It's Me | 50 |

## CIRCLE (1)
| 60s | Circle GR 1 | IN AID OF THE MILLFIELD BUILDING FUND (EP, private pressing) | 150 |

## CIRCLE (2)
| 02 | Static Caravan/Resonance Staticresonance 6 | PROSPEKT (2-LP, gatefold sleeve, black vinyl and green vinyl, 1000 only) | 30 |

## CIRCLES (1)
| 66 | Island WI 279 | Take Your Time/Don't You Love Me No More | 100 |

*(see also Plastic Penny, Savages, Tony Dangerfield & Thrills, Screaming Lord Sutch)*

## CIRCLES (2)
| 72 | Sioux SIOUX 017 | Mammy Blue/POOCH JACKSON & HARRY J. ALLSTARS: King Of The Road | 12 |

*(see also Bob Andy)*

## CIRCLES (3)
| 79 | Graduate GRAD 4 | Opening Up/Billy (p/s) | 20 |
| 80 | Vertigo ANGRY 1 | Angry Voices/Summer Nights (p/s) | 20 |
| 80 | Chrysalis CHS 2418 | Opening Up/Billy (p/s, reissue) | 8 |
| 85 | Graduate GRAD 17 | Circles/Summer Nights (p/s) | 40 |

## CIRCUIT 7
| 84 | Micro Rapp MIC 1 RAPP 023459 | Video Boys/The Force (p/s red vinyl) | 40 |
| 84 | Rapp 023462 | Modern Story/Eastern Dream (p/s, blue vinyl) | 25 |

## CIRCULUS
| 05 | Rise Above RISE 7/064 | Mirl It Is (Moog Up Mix)/WITCHCRAFT: Chylde Of Fire | 18 |
| 05 | Rise Above RISE 7/065 | Swallow/My Body Is Made Of Sunlight | 5 |
| 06 | Rise Above RISE 7/094 | Song Of Our Despair/Honeycomb (clear or purple vinyl) | 6 |
| 05 | Rise Above RISELP 63 | THE LICK ON THE TIP OF MY ENVELOPE YET TO BE SENT (LP, clear vinyl gatefold sleeve, poster, 100 only) | 30 |
| 06 | Rise Above RISELP 093 | CLOCKS ARE LIKE PEOPLE (LP, white vinyl, free 1-sided 7", "Tapestry", 500 only) | 25 |
| 06 | Rise Above RISELP 093 | CLOCKS ARE LIKE PEOPLE (LP, 700 on blue vinyl, 500 on black vinyl) | 18 |

## CIRCUS
| 67 | Parlophone R 5633 | Gone Are The Songs Of Yesterday/Sink Or Swim | 25 |
| 68 | Parlophone R 5672 | Do You Dream/House Of Wood | 45 |
| 69 | Transatlantic TRA 207 | CIRCUS (LP, gatefold sleeve, white/lilac label with 'T' logo) | 120 |

*(see also Philip Goodhand-Tait, King Crimson)*

## CIRCUS MAXIMUS
| 67 | Vanguard VSD 79260 | CIRCUS MAXIMUS (LP) | 20 |
| 68 | Vanguard VSD 79274 | NEVERLAND REVISITED (LP) | 20 |

## CIRKUS
| 80 | Guardian GRCA 4 | Melissa/Amsterdam/Pick Up A Phone (EP) | 20 |
| 73 | RCB 1 | CIRKUS ONE (LP, private pressing with gatefold sleeve, black/white label) | 250 |
| 77 | Shock SHOCK 1 | FUTURE SHOCK (LP) | 90 |

## CITATIONS
| 63 | Columbia DB 7068 | Moon Race/Slippin' And Slidin' | 30 |

## CITIZEN FISH
| 90 | Bluurg FISH 24 | FREE SOULS IN A TRAPPED ENVIRONMENT (LP, with cartoon insert) | 15 |
| 91 | Bluurg FISH 26 | WIDER THAN A POSTCARD (LP) | 15 |

## CITIZENS
| 80 | Cavalcade CAV 1 | Satisfy The Citizens/TV Woman (p/s) | 6 |

## CITIZENS OF ROME
| 82 | Someone Elses Music SOM 1 | Someone Elses World/St Malo (p/s) | 15 |

## CITY GENTS
| 73 | Triumph TR02 | Shake/Turn It Down | 15 |

## CITY GIANTS
| 87 | Give It A Blast BLA 001 | Little Next To Nothing/Where Love's Concerned/Have You Got Any Idea? (p/s) | 15 |

## CITY LIMITS
| 79 | Luggage RRP 1003 | Morse Code Signals/If I Had Time/I Just Can't Say (EP) | 125 |

## CITY RAMBLERS SKIFFLE GROUP

| | | | |
|---|---|---|---|
| 57 | Tempo A 158 | Ella Speed/2.19 Blues | 15 |
| 57 | Tempo A 161 | Mama Don't Allow/Tom Dooley | 15 |
| 57 | Tempo A 165 | Delia's Gone/Boodle-Am Shake | 15 |
| 57 | Storyville SEP 327 | I WANT A GIRL (EP) | 25 |
| 57 | Storyville SEP 345 | I SHALL NOT BE MOVED (EP) | 25 |
| 57 | Tempo EXA 59 | I WANT A GIRL (EP) | 25 |
| 57 | Tempo EXA 71 | GOOD MORNING BLUES (EP) | 25 |
| 57 | Tempo EXA 77 | DELIA'S GONE (EP) | 25 |

*(see also Henrik Johansen)*

## CITY SMOKE
| 66 | Mercury MF 971 | Sunday Morning/A Little Bit Of Love | 7 |
|---|---|---|---|

## CITY TALK
| 80 | PAD PAD 001 | Trick Of The Light/Nightmare | 12 |
|---|---|---|---|

## CITY WAITES
| | | | |
|---|---|---|---|
| 74 | EMI EMI 2149 | The Fox/One Of My Aunts | 5 |
| 74 | EMI EMC 3027 | A GORGEOUS GALLERY OF GALLANT INVENTIONS (LP) | 20 |
| 76 | Decca SKL 5264 | THE CITY WAITES (LP) | 20 |
| 81 | Hyperion A 66008 | HOW THE WORLD WAGS (LP, gatefold sleeve, some with Hyperion insert) | 40 |

## CIVILIANS
| 79 | Arista ARIST 318 | MADE FOR TELEVISION EP | 60 |
|---|---|---|---|

## CIVILISED SOCIETY?
| | | | |
|---|---|---|---|
| 86 | Manic Ears ACHE 2 | SCRAP METAL (LP, with inner) | 15 |
| 87 | Manic Ears ACHE 6 | VIOLENCE SUCKS (LP, with lyric inner) | 15 |

## C-JAM BLUES
| 66 | Columbia DB 8064 | Candy/Stay At Home Girl | 40 |
|---|---|---|---|

## CLAGGERS
| | | | |
|---|---|---|---|
| 71 | DJM DJS 235 | Train Song/Mr Sun | 6 |
| 71 | DJM DJS 242 | Ania/Primo | 6 |
| 71 | DJM DJS 260 | Some One/Umber Rag | 15 |
| 73 | Jam 57 | Primo/Ania (reissue) | 8 |

## CLAGUE
| | | | |
|---|---|---|---|
| 69 | Dandelion S 4493 | Mandy Lee/Bottle Up And Go (with Kevin Coyne) | 12 |
| 69 | Dandelion 4494 | The Stride/I Wonder Where | 12 |

*(see also Coyne-Clague, Kevin Coyne, Claque, Siren)*

## CLAIM
| | | | |
|---|---|---|---|
| 89 | Esurient Comms PACE 04 | Wait & See/Business Boy/God, Cliffe & Me | 12 |
| 90 | Esurient Comms PACE 07 | Losers Corner/Picking Up The Bitter Little Pieces | 12 |
| 90 | Caff CAFF 008 | Birth Of A Teenager/Mike The Bike | 20 |
| 91 | Esurient Comms PACE 10 | Sunday/Sporting Life | 12 |
| 92 | A Turntable Friend TURN 08 | Say So/Plastic Grip/Waiting For Jesus | 12 |
| 87 | Trick Bag CU 0388 | THIS PENCIL WAS OBVIOUSLY SHARPENED BY A LEFT-HANDED INDIAN KNIFE THROWER (EP) | 18 |
| 85 | Trick Bag TBR 001 | ARMSTRONG'S REVENGE AND ELEVEN OTHER SHORT STORIES (LP) | 30 |
| 88 | Esurient Comms PACE 003 | BOOMY TELLA (LP) | 30 |

## CLAIR OBSCUR
| | | | |
|---|---|---|---|
| 86 | Cathexi CRC 69 | SMURF IN THE GULAG (12" EP p/s) | 12 |
| 86 | All The Madmen MAD 10 | THE PILGRIM'S PROGRESS (LP) | 15 |

## CLAN (1)
| | | | |
|---|---|---|---|
| 70 | Bullet BU 419 | Copycats/BUNNY LEE ALLSTARS: Hot Lead | 40 |
| 70 | Bullet BU 430 | Na Na Hay Hay Goodbye/KING STITT: Musical Bop | 40 |

## CLAN (2)
| 72 | Deram DM 356 | Pretty Belinda/Ode To Karen | 7 |
|---|---|---|---|

*(see also Junior Campbell)*

## CLANCY'S ALLSTARS
| 68 | Pama PM 722 | C.N. Express Parts 1 & 2 (B-side actually "You Were Meant For Me" by Lee Perry) | 40 |
|---|---|---|---|

*(see also Owen Gray)*

## CLANDESTINE
| 86 | Market Trader PITCH 1 | I'm All Over You (Like Jam On A Scone)/The Valley Of The Larne | 6 |
|---|---|---|---|

## CLANNAD & BONO
| 89 | RCA PA42995A | In A Lifetime (7" picture disc) | 10 |
|---|---|---|---|

*(see also U2, Bono & Gavin Friday, The Passengers)*

## CLAN OF XYMOX
| | | | |
|---|---|---|---|
| 85 | 4AD BAD 504 | A Day/Stranger (12") | 10 |
| 85 | 4AD CAD 503 | CLAN OF XYMOX (LP) | 15 |

## JIMMY CLANTON
| | | | |
|---|---|---|---|
| 58 | London HLS 8699 | Just A Dream/You Aim To Please (as Jimmy Clanton & His Rockets) | 20 |
| 58 | London HL 7066 | A Letter To An Angel/A Part Of Me (as Jimmy Clanton & Aces) (export issue) | 20 |
| 59 | London HLS 8779 | A Letter To An Angel/A Part Of Me (as Jimmy Clanton & Aces) | 20 |
| 59 | Top Rank JAR 189 | My Own True Love/Little Boy In Love | 15 |
| 60 | Top Rank JAR 269 | Go, Jimmy, Go/I Trusted You | 15 |
| 60 | Top Rank JAR 382 | Another Sleepless Night/I'm Gonna Try | 10 |
| 60 | Top Rank JAR 509 | Come Back (To Me)/Wait | 10 |
| 61 | Top Rank JAR 544 | What Am I Gonna Do/If I | 10 |
| 62 | Stateside SS 120 | Venus In Blue Jeans/Highway Bound | 10 |
| 63 | Stateside SS 159 | Darkest Street In Town/Dreams Of A Fool | 5 |
| 65 | Stateside SS 410 | Hurting Each Other/Don't Keep Your Friends Away | 20 |

| | | | |
|---|---|---|---|
| 65 | Stateside SS 140 | Hurting Each Other/Don't Keep Your Friends Away (DJ Copy) | 40 |
| 69 | London HLP 10289 | Curly/I'll Never Forget Your Love | 5 |
| 59 | London RES 1224 | JUST A DREAM (EP) | 30 |

## CLAP
| | | | |
|---|---|---|---|
| 79 | SRTS SRTS/79/CUS | Hey Little Girl/20 Watts Of Power (p/s) | 20 |

## CLAPHAM SOUTH ESCALATORS
| | | | |
|---|---|---|---|
| 81 | Upright UP YOUR 1 | Get Me To The World On Time/Leave Me Alone/Cardboard Cut Outs (p/s) | 12 |

*(see also Meteors, Escalators, Tall Boys)*

## ERIC CLAPTON
| | | | |
|---|---|---|---|
| 66 | Purdah 45-3502 | Lonely Years/Bernard Jenkins (with John Mayall, 500 copies only) | 400 |
| 70 | Polydor 2001 096 | I Am Yours (unissued) | 0 |
| 70 | Polydor 2001 096 | After Midnight/Easy Now | 10 |
| 74 | RSO 2090 139 | Willie And The Hand Jive/I Can't Hold Out Much Longer (p/s) | 5 |
| 76 | RSO 2090 208 | Hello Old Friend/All Our Pastimes (p/s) | 8 |
| 80 | RSO JON 1 | Wonderful Tonight (live)/Further On Up The Road (live) (promo only) | 10 |
| 80 | RSO JONX 1 | Wonderful Tonight (live)/Further On Up The Road (live) (12", numbered p/s) | 10 |
| 81 | RSO RSO 75 | Another Ticket/Rita Mae (p/s) | 5 |
| 87 | Duck W 8461F | Behind The Mask/Grand Illusion//Crossroads (live)/White Room (live) (double pack, gatefold p/s) | 10 |
| 87 | Duck W 8397F | It's In The Way That You Use It/Bad Influence//Behind The Mask/ Grand Illusion (double pack, shrinkwrapped with sticker) | 8 |
| 89 | Duck W 2644B | Bad Love/I Shot The Sheriff (live) (box set with family tree & 2 colour prints) | 6 |
| 70 | Polydor 2383 021 | ERIC CLAPTON (LP, laminated sleeve, red label) | 25 |
| 73 | RSO 2479 702 | CLAPTON (LP, withdrawn) | 60 |
| 74 | RSO QD 4801 | 461 OCEAN BOULEVARD (LP, quadrophonic) | 20 |
| 82 | RSO RSDX 3 | TIME PIECES (2-LP, unissued) | 0 |
| 84 | Aston PD 20118 | TOO MUCH MONKEY BUSINESS (LP, picture disc, with Yardbirds) | 15 |

*(see also Yardbirds, John Mayall, Cream, Blind Faith, Delaney & Bonnie, Derek & The Dominos, Viv Stanshall, King Curtis, Randy Crawford)*

## ALAN CLARE GROUP
| | | | |
|---|---|---|---|
| 62 | Parlophone R 4938 | Screwball/Love For Sale | 5 |
| 65 | Pye 7N 15764 | Dog's Body/Mulligatawny | 5 |
| 56 | Decca DFE 6368 | THE IMPROVISATIONS OF... (EP) | 20 |
| 56 | Decca DFE 6391 | ALAN CLARE TRIO WITH BOB BURNS (EP) | 20 |
| 58 | Decca LK 4260 | JAZZ AROUND THE CLOCK (LP) | 20 |

## KENNY CLARE & RONNIE STEPHENSON
| | | | |
|---|---|---|---|
| 67 | Columbia SCX 6168 | DRUM SPECTACULAR (LP, with Tubby Hayes, stereo) | 40 |
| 67 | Columbia SX 6168 | DRUM SPECTACULAR (LP, with Tubby Hayes, mono) | 30 |
| 72 | Sounds Superb SPR90057 | DRUM SPECTACULAR (LP, reissue with Tubby Hayes and Stan Tracey) | 18 |

## CLARENDONIANS
| | | | |
|---|---|---|---|
| 65 | Ska Beat JB 219 | Muy Bien (My Friend)/You Are A Fool | 40 |
| 66 | Ska Beat JB 261 | Doing The Jerk/You Won't See Me | 40 |
| 66 | Island WI 284 | Try Me One More Time/Can't Keep A Good Man Down | 40 |
| 66 | Island WI 3005 | I'll Never Change/Rules Of Life | 40 |
| 67 | Island WI 3032 | Shoo-Be-Doo-Be (I Love You)/Sweet Heart Of Beauty | 40 |
| 67 | Island WI 3041 | You Can't Be Happy/Goodbye Forever | 40 |
| 67 | Studio One SO 2004 | The Table's Going To Turn/I Can't Go On | 40 |
| 67 | Studio One SO 2007 | He Who Laughs Last/GAYLADS: Just A Kiss From You | 50 |
| 67 | Studio One SO 2017 | Love Me With All Your Heart/Love Don't Mean Much To Me | 40 |
| 67 | Rio R 112 | Rudie Bam Bam/Be Bop Boy | 30 |
| 67 | Rio R 115 | Musical Train/Lowdown Girl | 30 |
| 68 | Caltone TONE 114 | Baby Baby/Bye Bye Bye | 80 |
| 69 | Duke DU 97 | Come Along/Try To Be Happy | 20 |
| 69 | Gas GAS 131 | When I Am Gone/She Brings Me Joy | 20 |
| 70 | Trojan TR 7714 | Lick It Back/BEVERLEY'S ALLSTARS: Busy Bee | 20 |
| 70 | Trojan TR 7719 | Baby Don't Do It/BEVERLEY'S ALLSTARS: Touch Down | 50 |
| 71 | Green Door GD 4009 | Seven In One (Medley) (both sides) | 12 |
| 72 | Attack ATT 8039 | Bound In Chains/STUD ALLSTARS: Version | 12 |
| 72 | Pama PM 847 | This Is My Story/VAL BENNETT: Caledonia | 25 |
| 73 | Pama PM 856 | Good Hearted Woman/CORNELL CAMPBELL: What Happens | 12 |
| 73 | Techniques TE 925 | Just One Look/Sinner Man | 12 |
| 73 | Dragon DRA 1006 | Walking Up A One Way Street/DYNAMITES: Instrumental | 30 |

*(see also Lee & Clarendonians, Desmond Baker & Clarendonians, Four Aces, Prince Buster, Dennis Walks)*

## ALICE CLARK
| | | | |
|---|---|---|---|
| 69 | Action ACT 4520 | You Got A Deal/Say You'll Never | 40 |
| 04 | Acid Jazz 01716 | Don't You Care/Never Did I Stop Loving You | 15 |

## CHRIS CLARK (1)
| | | | |
|---|---|---|---|
| 67 | Tamla Motown TMG 591 | Love's Gone Bad/Put Yourself In My Place | 150 |
| 67 | Tamla Motown TMG 591 | Love's Gone Bad/Put Yourself In My Place (DJ Copy) | 200 |
| 67 | Tamla Motown TMG 624 | From Head To Toe/The Beginning Of The End | 45 |
| 67 | Tamla Motown TMG 624 | From Head To Toe/The Beginning Of The End (DJ Copy) | 80 |
| 68 | Tamla Motown TMG 638 | I Want To Go Back There Again/I Love You | 30 |
| 68 | Tamla Motown TMG 638 | I Want To Go Back There Again/I Love You (DJ Copy) | 60 |
| 68 | T. Motown STML 11069 | SOUL SOUNDS (LP, stereo) | 90 |
| 68 | T. Motown TML 11069 | SOUL SOUNDS (LP, mono) | 100 |

## CHRIS CLARK (2)
| | | | |
|---|---|---|---|
| 01 | Warp WARPLP86 | CLARENCE PARK (LP) | 18 |
| 03 | Warp WARPLP107 | EMPTY THE BONES OF YOU (2-LP) | 20 |
| 06 | Warp WARLP149 | BODY RIDDLE (LP, 2 x 12") | 18 |
| 08 | Warp WARLP162 | TURNING DRAGON (2-LP) | 18 |

## CLAUDINE CLARK
| 62 | Pye International 7N 25157 | Party Lights/Disappointed | 20 |
|----|----|----|----|
| 63 | Pye International 7N 25186 | Walk Me Home From The Party/Who Will You Hurt? | 20 |
| 67 | Sue WI 4039 | The Strength To Be Strong/Moon Madness | 75 |

## DAVE CLARK FIVE
| 62 | Ember EMB S 156 | Chaquita/In Your Heart (grey/pink labels) | 40 |
|----|----|----|----|
| 62 | Ember EMB S 156 | Chaquita/In Your Heart (red/yellow labels) | 30 |
| 62 | Piccadilly 7N 35088 | First Love/I Walk The Line | 30 |
| 62 | Piccadilly 7N 35500 | That's What I Said/I Knew It All The Time | 30 |
| 63 | Columbia DB 7011 | The Mulberry Bush/Chaquita | 20 |
| 63 | Columbia DB 7112 | Do You Love Me/Doo-Dah | 10 |
| 64 | Columbia DB 7291 | Can't You See That She's Mine/Because | 5 |
| 64 | Columbia DB 7335 | Thinking Of You Baby/Whenever You're Around | 6 |
| 64 | Columbia DB 7377 | Any Way You Want It/Crying Over You | 7 |
| 65 | Columbia DB 7453 | Everybody Knows/Say You Want Me | 10 |
| 65 | Columbia DB 7503 | Reelin' And Rockin'/Little Bitty Pretty One | 6 |
| 65 | Columbia DB 7580 | Come Home/Mighty Good Loving (in p/s) | 18 |
| 65 | Columbia DB 7580 | Come Home/Mighty Good Loving | 6 |
| 65 | Columbia DB 7625 | Catch Us If You Can/Move On | 6 |
| 65 | Columbia DB 7744 | Over And Over/I'll Be Yours | 10 |
| 66 | Columbia DB 7863 | Try Too Hard/All Night Long | 6 |
| 66 | Columbia DB 7909 | Look Before You Leap/Please Tell Me Why | 6 |
| 66 | Columbia DB 8028 | Nineteen Days/I Need Love | 5 |
| 67 | Columbia DB 8152 | You Got What It Takes/Sitting Here Baby | 5 |
| 67 | Columbia DB 8194 | Tabatha Twitchit/Man In A Pin-Striped Suit (in export p/s) | 20 |
| 67 | Columbia DB 8194 | Tabatha Twitchit/Man In A Pin-Striped Suit | 6 |
| 67 | Columbia DB 8286 | Everybody Knows/Concentration Baby | 5 |
| 68 | Columbia DB 8342 | No One Can Break A Heart Like You/You Don't Want My Lovin' | 5 |
| 68 | Columbia DB 8465 | The Red Balloon/Maze Of Love | 6 |
| 69 | Columbia DB 8591 | Get It On Now/Maze Of Life (unreleased, acetates exist) | 0 |
| 70 | Columbia DB 8681 | Julia/Five By Five | 10 |
| 72 | Columbia DB 8963 | All Time Greats Medley (Glad All Over/Do You Love Me/Bits & Pieces/ Glad All Over)/ Wild Weekend (p/s) | 15 |
| 64 | Columbia SEG 8289 | THE DAVE CLARK FIVE (EP) | 10 |
| 65 | Columbia SEG 8381 | THE HITS OF THE DAVE CLARK FIVE (EP) | 10 |
| 65 | Columbia SEG 8447 | WILD WEEKEND (EP) | 10 |
| 64 | Columbia 33SX 1598 | SESSION WITH THE DAVE CLARK FIVE (LP, blue/black label, with "sold in the U.K..." label text) | 20 |
| 64 | Ember FA 2003 | DAVE CLARK FIVE AND THE WASHINGTON D.C.'s (LP) | 20 |
| 65 | EMI Regal REG 2017 | IN SESSION (LP, export issue) | 20 |
| 65 | Columbia SX 1756 | CATCH US IF YOU CAN (LP, soundtrack, blue/black label) | 20 |
| 67 | Columbia SX 6105 | THE DAVE CLARK FIVE'S GREATEST HITS (LP, blue/black label) | 20 |
| 68 | Columbia SX 6207 | EVERYBODY KNOWS (LP, blue/black label) | 20 |
| 69 | Columbia SX 6309 | 5 BY 5 1964-69: 14 TITLES BY THE DAVE CLARK FIVE (LP, blue/black label) | 30 |
| 70 | Columbia SCX 6437 | IF SOMEBODY LOVES YOU (LP) | 20 |
| 72 | Columbia SCX 6494 | DAVE CLARK AND FRIENDS (LP, boxed logo on label) | 25 |

*(see also Dave Clark & Friends, Smith D'Abo, Mike Smith, Washington D.C.s)*

## DEE CLARK
| 59 | London HL 8802 | Nobody But You/When I Call On You | 30 |
|----|----|----|----|
| 59 | London HL 8915 | Just Keep It Up (And See What Happens)/ Whispering Grass(Don't Tell The Trees) | 15 |
| 59 | Top Rank JAR 196 | Hey, Little Girl/If It Wasn't For Love | 15 |
| 60 | Top Rank JAR 284 | How About That/Blues Get Off My Shoulder | 10 |
| 60 | Top Rank JAR 373 | At My Front Door/Cling-A-Ling | 25 |
| 60 | Top Rank JAR 501 | Gloria/You're Looking Good | 10 |
| 61 | Top Rank JAR 551 | Your Friends/Because I Love You | 10 |
| 61 | Top Rank JAR 570 | Raindrops/I Want To Love You | 15 |
| 62 | Columbia DB 4768 | Don't Walk Away From Me/You're Telling Our Secrets | 40 |
| 63 | Stateside SS 180 | I'm A Soldier Boy/Shook Up Over You | 25 |
| 64 | Stateside SS 355 | Heartbreak/Warm Summer Breeze | 15 |
| 65 | Stateside SS 400 | T.C.B./It's Impossible | 20 |
| 70 | Liberty LBF 15334 | Where Did All The Good Times Go?/24 Hours Of Loneliness | 10 |
| 60 | Top Rank BUY 044 | HOW ABOUT THAT! (LP) | 30 |
| 70 | Joy JOYS 130 | YOU'RE LOOKING GOOD (LP) | 20 |

## DOTTY CLARK
| 61 | London HLX 9418 | It's Been A Long, Long Time/That's A Step In The Right Direction | 5 |
|----|----|----|----|

## DUANE CLARK
| 77 | Spark SRL 1152 | Stop Come Down Come Around/Gettin It | 15 |
|----|----|----|----|

## GENE CLARK
| 67 | CBS 202523 | Echoes/I Found You | 50 |
|----|----|----|----|
| 74 | Asylum AYM 536 | No Other/The True One | 6 |
| 74 | Asylum AYM 540 | Life's Greatest Fool/From A Silver Phial | 6 |
| 67 | CBS 62934 | GENE CLARK WITH THE GOSDIN BROTHERS (LP) | 60 |
| 72 | A&M AMLS 64297 | WHITE LIGHT (LP) | 25 |
| 74 | Asylum SYL 9020 | NO OTHER (LP) | 20 |

*(see also Byrds, Dillard & Clark)*

## GUY CLARK
| 75 | RCA Victor APL1-1303 | OLD NO. 1 (LP) | 15 |
|----|----|----|----|
| 76 | RCA Victor RS 1097 | TEXAS COOKIN' (LP) | 15 |

**J. CLARK**
80   Cha Cha CHAD 17                        Babylon/One Man Live (12") .......................................................................... 40

**JIMMY 'SOUL' CLARK**
76   Black Magic BM 115                      Sweet Darlin'/Sweet Darlin' (Instrumental) ................................................. 20

**LARENA CLARK**
66   Topic 12T 140                           A CANADIAN GARLAND (LP) ........................................................................ 15

**MICHAEL CLARK**
66   Liberty LIB 5893                        None Of These Girls/Work Out .................................................................. 15

**MICKY CLARK**
65   HMV POP 1400                            You Want My Love Again/Do You Ever Feel Lonely? ................................. 7

**NOBBY CLARK**
76   Epic S EPC 4381                         Steady Love/Give Me The Heart ............................................................... 10
78   Mercury 6007164                         Shake It Down/Lifes Long Highway ........................................................... 10

**PAUL CLARK & FRIENDS**
77   Myrrh MYR 1054                          GOOD TO BE HOME (LP, with inner sleeve) .............................................. 20
78   Myrrh MYR 1059                          HAND TO THE PLOUGH (LP) ...................................................................... 20

**PETULA CLARK**
**ALBUMS**
56   Pye Nixa NPT 19002                      PETULA CLARK SINGS (10") ....................................................................... 60
56   Pye Nixa NPT 19014                      A DATE WITH PET (10") ............................................................................ 60
57   Pye Nixa NPL 18007                      YOU ARE MY LUCKY STAR .......................................................................... 60
59   Pye Nixa NPL 18039                      PETULA CLARK IN HOLLYWOOD .................................................................. 50
62   Pye NPL 18070                           IN OTHER WORDS - PETULA CLARK .............................................................. 15
63   Pye NPL 18098                           PETULA ................................................................................................... 15
64   Pye-Vogue VRL 3001                      LES JAMES DEAN ...................................................................................... 25

**ROBIN CLARK**
61   Capitol CL 15230                        It's Love/The Butterfly Tree ..................................................................... 6

**ROY CLARK**
59   HMV POP 581                             Please Mr. Mayor/Puddin' ...................................................................... 100
63   Capitol CL 15288                        In The Mood/Texas Twist .......................................................................... 15
63   Capitol CL 15317                        Tips Of My Fingers/Spooky Movies ........................................................... 15
62   Capitol (S)T 1780                       THE LIGHTNING FINGERS OF ROY CLARK (LP) ............................................ 30

**SANFORD CLARK**
56   London HLD 8320                         The Fool/Lonesome For A Letter (with Al Casey) (gold label print) ......... 200
56   London HLD 8320                         The Fool/Lonesome For A Letter (with Al Casey) (later silver print label) ........ 50
56   London HL 7014                          The Fool/Lonesome For A Letter (with Al Casey) (export issue) ............... 20
59   London HLW 8959                         Run, Boy Run/New Kind Of Fool (triangular centre) ................................ 10
59   London HLW 8959                         Run, Boy Run/New Kind Of Fool (round centre) ....................................... 5
59   London HLW 8959                         Run, Boy Run/New Kind Of Fool (78) ....................................................... 20
60   London HLW 9026                         Son-Of-A-Gun/I Can't Help It (If I'm Still In Love With You) (tri centre) ...... 20
60   London HLW 9026                         Son-Of-A-Gun/I Can't Help It (If I'm Still In Love With You) (round centre) ...... 5
60   London HLW 9095                         Go On Home/Pledging My Love ............................................................... 20
68   Ember EMB S 250                         Shades/Once Upon A Time ....................................................................... 5
57   London RED 1105                         PRESENTING SANFORD CLARK (EP) ............................................................ 40
60   London REW 1256                         LOWDOWN BLUES (EP) .............................................................................. 40
*(see also Al Casey)*

**TERRY CLARK**
70   Myrrh MYR 1071                          WELCOME (LP) ......................................................................................... 15

**ALLAN CLARKE**
72   RCA RCA 2244                            You're Losing Me/A Coward By Name ....................................................... 10
75   EMI 2352                                Born To Run/Why Don't You Call .............................................................. 5
72   RCA SF 8283                             MY REAL NAME IS 'AROLD (LP, lyric insert, orange/white label) ............. 20
73   EMI EMA 752                             HEADROOM (LP, gatefold sleeve, lyric inner sleeve) ................................ 15
*(see also Hollies)*

**ANNETTE CLARKE**
73   Techniques TE 925                       Just One Look/Sinner Man ....................................................................... 18

**AUGUSTUS 'GUSSIE' CLARKE**
78   Hawkeye HALP 001                        DREAD AT THE CONTROLS DUB (LP) .......................................................... 25
*(see also Black Foundation)*

**BOB CLARKE**
70   CBS 7435                                Haunted/Run Colorado ............................................................................ 30
72   CBS 17741                               Sad/Some Ones Slipping Into My Mind .................................................... 10

**BRYAN CLARKE**
75   Safari SF 1107                          What Am I to Do/So Good To See You ...................................................... 12

**DAVE CLARKE**
94   Bush 1012                               Red 1 (of 3) (Protective Custody)/Zeno Xero (12", p/s, red vinyl) .......... 15
94   Bush 1015                               Red 2 (of 3) (Wisdom To The Wise)/Gonk (12", p/s, red vinyl) ............. 12

**ERIC CLARKE**
78   Baal BAL 89004                          LOVE THAT GROWS AND GROWS BAAL (LP) ............................................... 60

**FREDDIE CLARKE**
81   Main Line MLD6                          Home We Wanna Go/THE CIRCLE: Legend (12") ...................................... 50

**JAMES CLARK(E) + SOUNDS**
68   Fontana TF 918                          A Man Of Our Times T.V. Series Theme/Spring Bossa ............................... 8
68   Fontana SFJL 966                        A MAN OF OUR TIMES (LP) ....................................................................... 40

**JOHN COOPER CLARKE**
79   Epic S EPC 12 7009                      ¡Gimmix!/I Married A Monster From Outer Space (Third Version) (p/s, triangular disc, orange vinyl) ...... 6

## Johnny CLARKE

| 79 | Epic S EPC 7982 | Splat/Twat/Sleepwalk (double-grooved A-side, p/s, with Epic inner sleeve) .................. 5 |
| 78 | CBS 83132 | DISGUISE IN LOVE (LP) ........................... 20 |
| 80 | Epic EPC 84083 | SNAP, CRACKLE [&] BOP (LP, with 48-page book in sleeve pocket) .......... 20 |
| 81 | Epic EPC 84979 | ME AND MY BIG MOUTH (LP) ........................... 15 |

## JOHNNY CLARKE

| 74 | Explosion EX 2089 | None Shall Escape The Judgement/Every Rasta Is A Star ........................... 15 |
| 74 | Pyramid PYR 7013 | My Desire/Lemon Tree ........................... 15 |
| 74 | Lord Koos KOOS42 | Enter Into This Gate With Praise/KING TUBBY & THE AGGROVATORS : This Is The Hardest Version ........................... 15 |
| 74 | Atra ATRA019 | Everyday Wondering/Julie ........................... 10 |
| 74 | Cactus CTEP32 | Jump Back Baby ........................... 15 |
| 74 | Harry J HJ6706 | Move Out A Babylon/Move Out A Babylon (Instrumental) ........................... 10 |
| 75 | Horse HOSS86 | Move out Of Babylon/AGGROVATORS : Version ........................... 7 |
| 75 | Horse HOSS100 | Too Much War/AGGROVATORS : Version ........................... 8 |
| 75 | Vulcan VUL 1001 | I'm Gonna Put It On/KING TUBBY AND THE AGGROVATORS - Version ........................... 6 |
| 75 | Attack ATT 8100 | Rock With Me Baby/KING TUBBYS AND THE AGGROVATORS: A Crabit Version ........................... 6 |
| 75 | Attack ATT 8118 | Cold I Up/Cold I Up (Version) ........................... 15 |
| 76 | Virgin VS159 | Crazy Baldhead/Version ........................... 8 |
| 77 | Virgin VS173 | Roots, Natty Roots, Natty Congo/Version ........................... 8 |
| 77 | Third World TW 70 | Age is growing/Version ........................... 15 |
| 78 | Star PTP1009 | Every Knee Shall Bow/Version (With U Roy) (12") ........................... 25 |
| 78 | Justice JUDIS 109 | Pity Fool Fe Get Wise/Satisfaction (12") ........................... 40 |
| 78 | Third World TW 92 | Riding For A Fall/CLINT EASTWOOD AND THE AGROVATORS: Version ........................... 8 |
| 79 | Greensleeves GRED20 | Jah Love Is With I/Bad Days Are Going (12") ........................... 35 |
| 80 | Jah Shaka 842 | Got To Be Strong/Babylon (12") ........................... 20 |
| 80 | Cha Cha CHAD17 | Babylon/One Man Live (as J. Clark) (12") ........................... 40 |
| 81 | Chrysalis 122849 | Babylon/Than You For The Many Things You've Done - Cassandra (12") ........................... 20 |
| 81 | Art & Craft ACD 007 | Can't Get Enough/Version (12') ........................... 20 |
| 81 | Art & Craft ACD 014 | Guide Us Jah/Version (12") ........................... 40 |
| 81 | Art & Craft ACD 015 | Rude Boy/Version (12") ........................... 20 |
| 82 | Art & Craft ACD 018 | You Better Try/Version (12") ........................... 20 |
| 82 | Black Joy DH822 | Stop Them Jah/Too Much War ........................... 12 |
| 82 | Cha Cha CHAD 49 | Give Me Love/Version (10") ........................... 12 |
| 82 | Red Nail RN 039 | Guidance/DUB BAND: Protection (12") ........................... 30 |
| 83 | Top Notch TOP005 | Young Rebel/Version (10") ........................... 20 |
| 84 | Ariwa ARISL002 | Nuclear Weapon/Reggae Music (12") ........................... 20 |
| 89 | Jah Shaka SHAKA 876 | Rosie/Rosie Dub (12") ........................... 12 |
| 90 | Justice JS 008 | Give Up The Badness/Version ........................... 6 |
| 03 | Attack Gold ATT10 001 | Jah Love Is With I/KING TUBBY: Dub/LEROY SMART: I Don't Like It/DILLINGER: Jah Show Them The Way (10") ........................... 12 |
| 75 | Attack ATLP 1015 | ENTER INTO HIS GATES WITH PRAISE (LP) ........................... 50 |
| 75 | Vulcan VULP 001 | PUT IT ON (LP) ........................... 40 |
| 76 | Virgin V2076 | AUTHORISED VERSION (LP, mono) ........................... 20 |
| 76 | Virgin V2058 | ROCKERS TIME NOW (LP, mono credits on label) ........................... 30 |
| 77 | Justice JUSLP 001 | GIRL I LOVE YOU (LP) ........................... 40 |
| 77 | Paradise PDLP 001 | DON'T STAY OUT LATE (LP) ........................... 25 |
| 78 | Third World TWS 932 | KING IN A ARENA (LP, as Johnie Clark) ........................... 40 |
| 79 | Paradise PDLP 008 | SHOWCASE (LP) ........................... 35 |
| 79 | Third World TDWD 4 | SATISFACTION (LP) ........................... 20 |
| 82 | Art & Craft ACDLP001 | CAN'T GET ENOUGH (LP) ........................... 50 |
| 83 | Ariwa ARI 007 LP | YARD STYLE (LP) ........................... 30 |
| 83 | Vista VSLP 4016 | MEETS CORNEL CAMPBELL (LP) ........................... 30 |
| 85 | Ariwa ARI LP 022 | GIVE THANKS (LP) ........................... 15 |
| 89 | Attack ATLP 105 | ENTER INTO HIS GATES WITH PRAISE (LP, reissue) ........................... 15 |

## KENNY CLARKE

| 56 | London LTZC 15004 | KENNY CLARKE SEXTET (LP) ........................... 25 |
| 56 | London LTZC 15008 | KENNY CLARKE AND ERNIE WILKINS (LP) ........................... 20 |
| 57 | London LTZC 15038 | KENNY CLARKE (LP) ........................... 25 |
| 57 | London LTZC 15047 | KENNY CLARKE (LP) ........................... 20 |
| 57 | Vogue LAE 12029 | JAZZ INTERNATIONAL (LP) ........................... 25 |

## KENNY CLARKE (WITH FRANCY BOLAND BIG BAND)

| 56 | London LTZ C 15047 | BOHEMIA AFTER DARK (LP) ........................... 15 |
| 57 | Columbia SEG 7830 | KENNY CLARKE QT. (EP) ........................... 10 |
| 63 | London HA-K 8085 | JAZZ IS UNIVERSAL (LP, with Francy Boland Big Band) ........................... 15 |
| 66 | CBS SBPG 62567 | NOW HEAR OUR MEANIN' (LP) ........................... 18 |
| 68 | Polydor 583726 | LATIN KALEIDOSCOPE (LP) ........................... 20 |
| 69 | Polydor 583727 | ALL SMILES (LP) ........................... 20 |
| 69 | Polydor 583738 | FELLINI 712 (LP) ........................... 20 |
| 69 | Polydor 583054 | LIVE AT RONNIE SCOTT'S - THE FIRST SET (LP) ........................... 20 |
| 69 | Polydor 583055 | LIVE AT RONNIE SCOTT'S - THE SECOND SET (LP) ........................... 20 |
| 70 | Polydor 583739 | FACES (LP) ........................... 15 |
| 70 | Polydor 2310 147 | OFF LIMITS (LP, reflective sleeve) ........................... 30 |

*(see also Francey Boland, Kenny Clarke)*

## LINDA CLARKE

| 67 | Decca F 12709 | Your Hurtin' Kinda Love/Send Me The Pillow You Dream On ........................... 15 |
| 68 | Decca F 12787 | Society's Child/Rain In My Heart ........................... 20 |

## LLOYD CLARKE

| 62 | Blue Beat BB 99 | Good Morning/Now I Know A Reason (with Smithie's Sextet) ........................... 12 |
| 62 | Blue Beat BB 104 | Fool's Day/You're A Cheat (with Reco's All Stars) ........................... 15 |

| 62 | Island WI 007 | Love You The Most/LLOYD ROBINSON: You Said You Loved Me | 20 |
| 62 | Island WI 045 | Japanese Girl/He's Coming | 20 |
| 63 | Rio R 16 | Love Me/Half As Much | 20 |
| 64 | Rio R 23 | Stop Your Talking/A Penny | 20 |
| 64 | Rio R 24 | Fellow Jamaican/PATRICK & GEORGE: My Love | 20 |
| 68 | Island WI 3116 | Summertime/VAL BENNETT: Soul Survivor | 100 |
| 68 | Blue Cat BS 136 | Young Love/UNTOUCHABLES: Wall Flower | 50 |
| 70 | Escort ERT 849 | Chicken Thief/STRANGER COLE: Tomorrow | 15 |

*(see also Derrick & Lloyd, Theo Beckford, Soulettes, Delroy Wilson, Laurel Aitken, Sonny Burke, Uniques)*

## MICKEY CLARKE
| 66 | HMV 1483 | Help Me/For Me | 20 |

## PAULA CLARKE
| 83 | Oak Sound OSD 013 | University/Didn't I Blow Your Mind (12") | 40 |

## RONA CLARKE
| 67 | Westwood WRS 067 | UTOPIAN DREAM (LP) | 30 |

## TERRY CLARKE
| 72 | Polydor 2058191 | Lady/Army Captains Daughter | 10 |

## TONY CLARKE
| 64 | Pye International 7N 25251 | Ain't Love Good, Ain't Love Proud/Coming Back Strong | 22 |
| 65 | Chess CRS 8011 | The Entertainer/This Heart Of Mine | 30 |
| 65 | Chess CRS 8011 | The Entertainer/This Heart Of Mine (DJ Copy) | 50 |
| 69 | Chess CRS 8091 | The Entertainer/Ain't Love Good, Ain't Love Proud | 8 |
| 74 | Chess 6145 030 | Landslide/The Entertainer | 8 |

## FREDDY CLARKE
| 78 | Jungle Beat JBDC 805 | Troubles/I Man (12" with I ROY) | 80 |
| 81 | Jungle Beat JBDC801 | Fight I Down/VIN GORDON: Fire Horns (12", red vinyl) | 40 |

*(see also Freddie Clarke)*

## CLARK-HUTCHINSON
| 68 | Decca LK-R 5006 | CLARK-HUTCHINSON (LP, one known copy, red Decca labels, no sleeve Matrix: ARL-8968.P-1A/1B | 500 |
| 70 | Decca Nova DN-R 2 | A = MH2 (LP, mono) | 150 |
| 70 | Decca Nova DN-R 2 | A = MH2 (LP, stereo) | 100 |
| 70 | Deram SML 1076 | RETRIBUTION (LP) | 80 |
| 71 | Deram SML 1090 | GESTALT (LP) | 80 |

*(see also Vamp, Upp)*

## CLARO INTELECTO
| 02 | Ai Ai 003 | PEACE OF MIND (12", first pressings in blue p/s) | 15 |

## CLASH
### SINGLES
| 77 | CBS S CBS 5058 | White Riot/1977 (p/s, 'The Clash' or 'The CLASH' on label) | 20 |
| 77 | CBS CL 1 | CAPITAL RADIO (EP, NME freebie, p/s) | 50 |
| 77 | CBS S CBS 5293 | Remote Control/London's Burning (live) (p/s) | 10 |
| 77 | CBS S CBS 5664 | Complete Control/The City Of The Dead (p/s) | 10 |
| 78 | CBS CBS 5834 | Clash City Rockers/Jail Guitar Doors (p/s) | 5 |
| 78 | CBS S CBS 6383 | (White Man) In Hammersmith Palais/The Prisoner (initially green, then pink, blue or yellow die-cut sleeve) | 12 |
| 78 | CBS S CBS 6788 | Tommy Gun/1 - 2 Crush On You (p/s) | 8 |
| 78 | CBS CBS 7082 | English Civil War/Pressure Drop (p/s) | 8 |
| 79 | CBS S CBS 7324 | THE COST OF LIVING (EP, gatefold p/s & inner sleeve) | 12 |

*(All the early Clash singles were re-pressed in 1979 with picture sleeves.)*

| 79 | CBS S CBS 8087 | London Calling/Armagideon Time (p/s, green or red shaded sleeve, white or yellow/orange label) | 10 |
| 79 | CBS 12 8087 | London Calling/Armagidion Time/Armagidion Time (version) | 15 |
| 80 | CBS 8323 | Bankrobber/Rockers Galore (p/s) | 7 |
| 80 | CBS S CBS 9339 | The Call Up/Stop The World (p/s) | 5 |
| 81 | CBS A 1133 | The Magnificent Seven/The Magnificent Dance (die cut sleeve) | 5 |
| 81 | CBS A12 1133 | The Magnificent Seven/The Magnificent Dance (12", p/s) | 15 |
| 81 | CBS S CBS 9480 | Hitsville U.K./Radio One (die cut sleeve) | 5 |
| 81 | CBS A 1797 | This Is Radio Clash/Radio Clash (p/s) | 5 |
| 81 | CBS S 2309 | Know Your Rights/First Night Back In London (p/s, with free sticker) | 10 |
| 82 | CBS A 2479 | Rock The Casbah/Long Time Jerk (p/s, with free stickers) | 10 |
| 82 | CBS A 13 2479 | Rock The Casbah/Mustapha Dance | 18 |
| 82 | CBS A 2646 | Should I Stay Or Should I Go/Straight To Hell (p/s, with dragon sticker) | 10 |
| 82 | CBS A 12 2646 | Should I Stay Or Should I Go/Straight To Hell (12") | 12 |
| 88 | CBS CLASHB 2 | London Calling/Brand New Cadillac/Rudie Don't Fail (box set) | 12 |
| 06 | Sony 82876 876287 | THE SINGLES (Box set 19 x 7" singles) | 60 |
| 11 | Columbia 88697890297 | The Magnificent Seven/The Cool Out (red vinyl, numbered, die-cut sleeve) | 12 |
| 12 | Columbia 88691959247 | London Calling (2012 Mix)/London Calling (2012 Instrumental) (p/s) | 10 |

### ALBUMS
| 77 | CBS 82000 | THE CLASH (LP, 10,000 only with sticker on inner sleeve for free NME Capital Radio EP freebie) | 80 |
| 77 | CBS 82000 | THE CLASH (LP, 1st issue with orange/yellow labels) | 25 |
| 78 | CBS 82431 | GIVE 'EM ENOUGH ROPE (LP, promo-only package with poster in folder) | 500 |
| 78 | CBS 82431 | GIVE 'EM ENOUGH ROPE (LP) | 20 |
| 79 | CBS CLASH 3 | LONDON CALLING (2-LP, stickered, with inner sleeves, 1st issue with black & white labels) | 40 |
| 80 | CBS FSLN | SANDINISTA (3-LP, stickered sleeve with 'Armagideon Times' insert) | 35 |
| 82 | CBS 32232 | THE CLASH (LP, reissue) | 15 |
| 82 | CBS FMLN2 | COMBAT ROCK (LP, inner sleeve and poster) | 30 |

MINT VALUE £

| 85 | CBS 26601 | CUT THE CRAP (LP, with inner) | 15 |
|----|-----------|-------------------------------|-----|
| 88 | CBS 460244 1 | THE STORY OF THE CLASH (2-LP) | 20 |
| 92 | CBS 32787 | COMBAT ROCK (LP, reissue, has barcode on sleeve) | 15 |
| 99 | CBS 49 5344-1 | THE CLASH (LP, reissue) | 15 |
| 99 | Simply Vinyl SVLP 134 | GIVE 'EM ENOUGH ROPE (LP, reissue) | 15 |
| 99 | CBS 495347 - 1 | LONDON CALLING (2-LP, reissue) | 20 |
| 99 | CBS 495348-1 | SANDINISTA (3-LP, reissue) | 25 |
| 99 | CBS 495349-1 | COMBAT ROCK (LP, 2nd reissue) | 18 |
| 99 | Sony 496183-1 | FROM HERE TO ETERNITY (2-LP, gatefold with inners) | 60 |
| 13 | Columbia 88725460002 | SOUND SYSTEM (Box set, 11 x CD, DVD, book, 5 badges, 3 stickers, notebook, booklet & poster) | 100 |

### PROMOS

| 77 | CBS S CBS 5058 | White Riot/1977 (A label promo, The Clash on label, p/s) | 70 |
|----|----------------|----------------------------------------------------------|-----|
| 77 | CBS S CBS 5293 | Remote Control/London's Burning (Studio Version) ('A' Label Promo) | 50 |
| 77 | CBS S 5664 | Complete Control/The City Of The Dead (A label promo, p/s) | 50 |
| 78 | CBS S CBS 5834 | Clash City Rockers/Jail Guitar Doors (A label promo, p/s) | 50 |
| 78 | CBS S CBS 6383 | (White Man) In Hammersmith Palais/The Prisoner (A label demo - small black A - in die-cut sleeve) | 60 |
| 78 | CBS S CBS 6788 | Tommy Gun/1 - 2 Crush On You (A label promo, p/s) | 50 |
| 78 | CBS S CBS 7082 | English Civil War/Pressure Drop (A label promo, p/s) | 50 |
| 79 | CBS S CBS 7324 | I Fought The Law/Gates Of The West (2-track promo for COST OF LIVING EP) | 40 |
| 80 | CBS S CBS 9339 | The Call Up/Stop The World (A label promo, p/s) | 50 |
| 80 | CBS S CBS 9480 | Hitsville U.K./Radio One (A label promo, die cut sleeve) | 60 |
| 82 | CBS A2309 | Know Your Rights/First Night Back In London ("promo copy not for sale" , no A, p/s) | 30 |
| 82 | CBS A2479 | Rock The Casbah/Long Time Jerk (promo with small "A", p/s) | 30 |
| 82 | CBS A 2646 | Should I Stay Or Should I Go/Straight To Hell (edit) (A label promo, p/s) | 40 |

*(see also 101'ers, Janie Jones & Lash, Tymon Dogg, Ellen Foley, Futura 2000, Joe Strummer)*

### CLASS 50

| 77 | Electric WOT 13 | Freerider/Time Machine | 12 |
|----|-----------------|------------------------|-----|

### CLASSICS IV

| 66 | Capitol CL 15470 | Pollyanna/Cry Baby (issued as if by the "Classics" | 40 |
|----|------------------|---------------------------------------------------|-----|
| 68 | Liberty LBF 15051 | Spooky/Poor People | 8 |
| 69 | Liberty LBF 15177 | Stormy/Twenty Four Hours Of Loneliness | 15 |
| 69 | Liberty LBF 15196 | Traces/Mary, Mary Row Your Boat | 5 |
| 69 | Liberty LBF 15231 | Everyday With You Girl/Sentimental Lady | 5 |

*(see also Dennis Yost & Classics IV)*

### CLASSICS (JAMAICA)

| 69 | Doctor Bird DB 1190 | Worried Over Me/LAUREL AITKEN: Rice And Peas | 40 |
|----|---------------------|----------------------------------------------|-----|
| 70 | New Beat NB 061 | Same Old Feeling/So Much Love | 12 |
| 70 | New Beat NB 071 | History Of Africa/Honeybee | 12 |
| 70 | Pama PM 830 | Sex Education/POWER: Soul Flash | 12 |
| 71 | Punch PH 79 | Cheerio Baby/Civilization | 40 |
| 71 | Banana BA331 | Mr Fire Coal Man/SOUND DIMENSION: Version | 40 |

### CLASSICS (U.S.)

| 61 | Mercury AMT 1152 | Life Is But A Dream/That's The Way | 100 |
|----|------------------|------------------------------------|-----|
| 63 | Stateside SS 215 | Till Then/Enie Minie Mo | 40 |

### CLASSIC SULLIVANS

| 74 | Kwanza K19501 | Paint Yourself Into A Corner/I Don't Want To Loose You | 10 |
|----|---------------|--------------------------------------------------------|-----|

### CLASSIFIED INFO

| 84 | Dead Dog DOG 02 | Drug Called Love/Drug Called Love Dub (p/s) | 12 |
|----|-----------------|---------------------------------------------|-----|

### CLASSMATES

| 63 | Decca F 11736 | Let's Get Together Tonight/It's No Game | 5 |
|----|---------------|-----------------------------------------|-----|
| 63 | Decca F 11779 | Go Tell It On The Mountain/Give Me A Girl | 5 |
| 64 | Decca F 11806 | In Morocco/I Feel | 5 |
| 64 | Decca F 12047 | Go Away/Pay Day | 5 |

### CLAUDETTE (& CORPORATION)

| 69 | Jackpot JP 712 | Let's Fall In Love/PROPHETS: Purple Moon | 30 |
|----|----------------|------------------------------------------|-----|
| 70 | Grape GR 3020 | Skinheads A Bash Them (with Corporation)/ CORPORATION: Walkin' Thru Jerusalem | 200 |
| 12 | Grape THB 701 | Hot Bread And Butter/Ashes To Ashes | 25 |

*(see also Corporation)*

### CASSIUS CLAY

| 64 | CBS AAG 190 | Stand By Me/I Am The Greatest | 5 |
|----|-------------|-------------------------------|-----|
| 63 | CBS BPG 62274 | I AM THE GREATEST! (LP) | 15 |

### JUDY CLAY

| 67 | Stax 601 022 | You Can't Run Away From Your Heart/It Takes A Lotta Good Love | 10 |
|----|--------------|--------------------------------------------------------------|-----|

*(see also Billy Vera & Judy Clay, Booker T. & M.G.'s)*

### JUDY CLAY & WILLIAM BELL

| 68 | Stax STAX 101 | Private Number/Love-Eye-Tis | 5 |
|----|---------------|------------------------------|-----|
| 69 | Stax STAX 115 | My Baby Specialises/Left Over Love | 8 |

*(see also William Bell, Billy Vera & Judy Clay)*

### OTIS CLAY

| 67 | President PT 121 | It's Easier Said Than Done/Flame In Your Heart | 8 |
|----|------------------|------------------------------------------------|-----|
| 68 | President PT 132 | I'm Satisfied/I Testify | 8 |
| 68 | President PT 148 | That's How It Is/Show Place | 10 |
| 68 | President PT 176 | A Lasting Love/Got To Find A Way | 10 |
| 69 | Atlantic 584 282 | Baby Jane/You Hurt Me For The Last Time | 80 |
| 72 | London HLU 10397 | Trying To Live My Life Without You/Let Me Be The One | 12 |
| 74 | London HLU 10467 | You Did Something To Me/It Was Jealousy | 12 |

| 76 | President PT 456 | All I Need Is You/Special Kind Of Love .................................................................. | 12 |
| 73 | London SH-U 8446 | TRYING TO LIVE MY LIFE WITHOUT YOU (LP) ......................................................... | 30 |

**TOM CLAY**

| 72 | Tamla Motown TMG 801 | What The World Needs Now Is Love/The Victors........................................................ | 12 |

**CLAY FAV**

| 79 | Own label | CONSIGNMENT STOCK (EP, 1,000, 200 with stamped "consignment Stock' sleeve, no p/s) ...................................................................................................................... | 150 |
| 79 | Own label | CONSIGNMENT STOCK (EP, 1,000, 800 without stamped "consignment Stock' sleeve, no p/s) ...................................................................................................................... | 50 |

**ALASDAIR CLAYRE**

| 67 | Elektra EUK 255 | ALASDAIR CLAYRE (LP, some with mail order insert) ............................................. | 60 |
| 76 | Acorn CF 252 | ADAM AND THE BEASTS (LP) ............................................................................... | 25 |

**ADAM CLAYTON & LARRY MULLEN**

| 96 | Mother MUM 75 | Theme From Mission: Impossible/Theme From Mission: Impossible (Junior's Hard Mix Edit) (jukebox issue, no p/s, promo only) ......................................................... | 5 |

*(see also U2)*

**DOCTOR CLAYTON**

| 65 | RCA Victor RCX 7177 | RCA RACE SERIES VOLUME 6 (EP) ......................................................................... | 10 |
| 70 | RCA Intl. INTS 1176 | PEARL HARBOUR BLUES (LP) ............................................................................... | 15 |

**MERRY CLAYTON**

| 70 | A&M AMS 802 | Gimme Shelter/Good Girls ................................................................................... | 20 |
| 70 | A&M AMS 802 | Gimme Shelter/Good Girls (DJ Copy) ................................................................... | 30 |
| 73 | Ode ODS 66301 | Acid Queen/Underture (p/s) ................................................................................ | 10 |
| 75 | Ode 66110 | Keep Your Eye On The Sparrow/Love Creeps Up Slowly ........................................ | 6 |
| 70 | A&M AMLS 995 | GIMME SHELTER (LP) .......................................................................................... | 20 |
| 72 | A&M AMLS 67012 | MERRY CLAYTON (LP) ......................................................................................... | 20 |

*(see also Raelets)*

**PAUL CLAYTON**

| 61 | London HLU 9285 | Wings Of A Dove/So Long (It's Been Good To Know You) .................................... | 5 |
| 61 | London REU 1276 | PAUL CLAYTON (EP) ............................................................................................ | 30 |

**VIKKI CLAYTON**

| 88 | Dambuster DAM 021 | LOST LADY FOUND (LP).................................................................................... | 20 |

*(see also Fairport Convention)*

**CLAYTON SQUARES**

| 65 | Decca F 12250 | Come And Get It/And Tears Fell ........................................................................ | 40 |
| 66 | Decca F 12456 | There She Is/Imagination ................................................................................... | 175 |

*(see also Liverpool Scene, Andy Roberts, Mike Hart)*

**CLAYTOWN TROUPE**

| 92 | EMI 12 88007) | SKYBOUND (LP, withdrawn) ............................................................................... | 20 |

**CLEAN**

| 94 | Dark Beloved Cloud DBC 020 | Late Last Night/Psychedelic Clown (p/s) ................................................... | 8 |
| 86 | Flying Nun FNE 29 | COMPILATION (LP) .......................................................................................... | 25 |
| 89 | Flying Nun Europe FNE 29 | IN-A-LIVE (Mini-LP) .............................................................................. | 20 |
| 90 | Rough Trade ROUGH 143 | VEHICLE (LP)......................................................................................... | 25 |

**CLEANERS FROM VENUS**

| 87 | Ammunition JANGLE 1 | Illya Kurayakin Looked At Me/Black And White And Blue All Over (p/s) ............. | 25 |
| 87 | Ammunition JANGLE 1T | Illya Kurayakin Looked At Me/Albion's Daughter/Black And White And Blue All Over/Illya Kuryakin Looked At Me (Full Version) (12", p/s) .............................. | 15 |
| 87 | Ammunition JANGLE 2 | Living With Victoria Grey/Sunday Afternoon (p/s) ............................................. | 20 |
| 87 | Ammunition JANGLE 2T | Living With Victoria Grey/Sunday Afternoon/She's Checking You Out (12", p/s) ........... | 15 |
| 88 | Ammunition JANGLE 3 | Mercury Girl/Gamma Ray Blues .......................................................................... | 20 |
| 88 | Ammunition JANGLE 3T | Mercury Girl/Gamma Ray Blues/The Iceberg Unicorn (12", p/s) .......................... | 15 |
| 87 | Ammunition CLEAN LP 1 | GOING TO ENGLAND (LP) ............................................................................ | 30 |
| 88 | Ammunition CLEAN LP 2 | TOWN AND COUNTRY (LP) ........................................................................... | 30 |

*(see also Gypp, Martin Newall, Brotherhood of Lizards)*

**CLEAN LOOKING BOYS**

| 83 | DJW 001 | Sent To Coventry/I Like Your Feel (no p/s) ......................................................... | 12 |

**CLEAR BLUE SKY**

| 70 | Vertigo 6360 013 | CLEAR BLUE SKY (LP, gatefold sleeve, large swirl label) ..................................... | 500 |
| 90 | Saturn SRLP 101 | DESTINY (LP) ..................................................................................................... | 15 |

**CLEAR LIGHT**

| 67 | Elektra EKSN 45019 | Black Roses/She's Ready To Be Free ................................................................... | 10 |
| 68 | Elektra EKSN 45027 | Night Sounds Loud/How Many Days Have Passed ............................................ | 30 |
| 67 | Elektra EKL 4011 | CLEAR LIGHT (LP, orange label, also stereo EKS 74011) ..................................... | 140 |

**CLEARLIGHT**

| 75 | Virgin V 2029 | SYMPHONY (LP, stickered sleeve) ....................................................................... | 20 |
| 75 | Virgin V 2039 | FOREVER BLOWING BUBBLES (LP) ...................................................................... | 20 |

*(see also Gong, Steve Hillage)*

**CLEARWAYS**

| 64 | Columbia DB 7333 | I'll Be Here/I've Just Got A Letter ...................................................................... | 10 |

**CLEFS**

| 62 | Salvo SLO 1810 | Don't Cry/The Dream Train Special (99 copies only) ........................................... | 20 |

**CLEFS OF LAVENDER HILL**

| 66 | CBS 202230 | Stop, Get A Ticket/First Tell Me Why .................................................................. | 20 |

**CLEFTONES**

| 56 | Columbia SCM 3801 | You Baby, You/Little Girl Of Mine ....................................................................... | 250 |
| 61 | Columbia DB 4678 | Heart And Soul/How Do You Feel ....................................................................... | 100 |
| 61 | Columbia DB 4720 | (I Love You) For Sentimental Reasons/Deed I Do ................................................ | 100 |

MINT VALUE £

| 63 | Columbia DB 4988 | Lover Come Back To Me/There She Goes | 50 |

## PAT CLEMENCE
| 64 | HMV POP 1360 | While I Live/Since I Don't Have You | 5 |

## JACK CLEMENT
| 58 | London HLS 8691 | Ten Years/Your Lover Boy | 150 |
| 58 | London HLS 8691 | Ten Years/Your Lover Boy (78) | 40 |

## SOUL JOE CLEMENTS
| 69 | Plexium PXM 10 | Smoke And Ashes/Ever, Ever | 200 |

## CLEO
| 64 | Decca F 11817 | To Know Him Is To Love Him/ANDREW OLDHAM ORCHESTRA: There Are But Five Rolling Stones | 25 |

*(see also Andrew Oldham Orchestra, This 'N' That)*

## CLERKS
| 79 | Rok ROK VIII/VII | No Good For Me/HAZARD: Gotta Change My Life (company sleeve) | 15 |
| 84 | Puddisc SRT8 KS 1538 | Dancing With My Girl/On The Telephone/All I Want Is You (p/s) | 5 |

## CLEVELANDS
| 64 | Philips BF 1315 | Big Town/Lonely, Weary And Blue | 5 |

## CLICHE
| 80 | Carrere CAR 133 | I Know Your Name/Drawing The Line | 100 |

## CLIENTELE
| 98 | Pointy POINT 001 | What Goes Up/Five Day Morning (p/s) | 15 |
| 99 | Johnny Kane KANE 002 | Reflections After Jane/An Hour Before The Light (p/s) | 15 |
| 99 | Pointy POINT 002 | I Had To Say This/Monday's Rain (p/s) | 15 |
| 02 | Pointy POINT 008 | Haunted Melody/Fear Of Falling (p/s) | 5 |
| 00 | Pointy POINT 004LP | SUBURBAN LIGHT (LP) | 20 |
| 03 | Pointy POINT 011LP | THE VIOLET HOUR (LP) | 15 |

## CLIENTELLE
| 79 | Quest BRS 003 | Can't Forget/Skyline (p/s) | 125 |
| 81 | Banana BANANA 505 | DESTINATION UNKNOWN (LP, with insert) | 100 |

## JIMMY CLIFF
| 62 | Blue Beat BB 78 | I'm Sorry (with Cavaliers Combo)/BLUE BEATS: Roarin' (with Red Price) | 30 |
| 62 | Island WI 012 | Hurricane Hatty/Dearest Beverley | 18 |
| 62 | Island WI 016 | Miss Jamaica/Gold Digger | 25 |
| 62 | Island WI 025 | Since Lately/I'm Free | 25 |
| 63 | Island WI 062 | My Lucky Day/One-Eyed Jacks | 25 |
| 63 | Island WI 070 | King Of Kings/SIR PERCY: Oh Yeah | 30 |
| 63 | Island WI 112 | Miss Universe/The Prodigal | 18 |
| 63 | Black Swan WI 403 | The Man (vocal version)/You Are Never Too Old | 20 |
| 63 | Black Swan WI 403 | The Man (Instrumental version)/You Are Never Too Old | 20 |
| 64 | Stateside SS 342 | One Eyed Jacks/King Of Kings | 20 |
| 67 | Island WIP 6004 | Aim And Ambition/Give And Take | 15 |
| 66 | Fontana TF 641 | Call On Me/Pride And Passion | 15 |
| 67 | Island WIP 6011 | I Got A Feeling/Hard Road To Travel | 15 |
| 67 | Island WIP 6024 | That's The Way Life Goes/Thank You | 10 |
| 68 | Island WIP 6039 | Waterfall/Reward | 35 |
| 69 | Trojan TR 690 | Wonderful World, Beautiful People/Hard Road To Travel (in p/s) | 7 |
| 69 | Trojan TR 690 | Wonderful World, Beautiful People/Hard Road To Travel | 5 |
| 70 | Trojan TR 7722 | Vietnam/She Does It Right | 5 |
| 70 | Trojan TR 7745 | Suffering/Come Into My Life | 5 |
| 70 | Trojan TR 7745 | Those Good Good Old Days/Pack Up Hang Ups | 5 |
| 70 | Trojan TR 7767 | You Can Get It If You Really Want/Be Aware | 5 |
| 70 | Island WIP 6087 | Wild World/Be Aware | 5 |
| 70 | Island WIP 6097 | Synthetic World/I Go To Pieces | 5 |
| 71 | Island WIP 6103 | Goodbye Yesterday/Breakdown | 5 |
| 71 | Island WIP 6110 | Sitting In Limbo/The Bigger They Come | 5 |
| 72 | Island WIP 6132 | Trapped/Struggling Man | 5 |
| 68 | Island ILP 962 | HARD ROAD TO TRAVEL (LP) | 60 |
| 69 | Trojan TRLS 16 | JIMMY CLIFF (LP) | 20 |
| 71 | Island ILPS 9159 | ANOTHER CYCLE (LP) | 18 |
| 72 | Island ILPS 9202 | THE HARDER THEY COME (LP, pink rim palm tree label) | 18 |

*(see also Jackie Edwards & Jimmy Cliff, James Chambers)*

## CLIFF DWELLERS
| 66 | Polydor BM 56707 | Hang On Stupid/I'm A Superman For You | 15 |

## CLIFFORD
| 73 | Satril SAT 10 | Drink Wine Susan/Looking Upon The Day | 7 |

## BUZZ CLIFFORD
| 61 | Fontana H 297 | Baby Sittin' Boogie/Driftwood | 5 |
| 61 | Fontana H 312 | Three Little Fishes/Simply Because | 5 |
| 62 | Columbia DB 4903 | More Dead Than Alive/Nobody Loves Me Like You | 5 |

## JOHN & JULIA CLIFFORD
| 77 | Topic 12TS 311 | THE HUMOURS OF LISHEEN (LP) | 20 |

## LINDA CLIFFORD
| 74 | Paramount PARA 3051 | After Loving You/Check Out Your Heart | 30 |
| 78 | Curtom K17078 | From Now On/You Can Do It | 8 |
| 78 | Curtom K 17163T | If My Friends Could See Me Now/Runaway Love (12") | 12 |

## MIKE CLIFFORD
| 61 | Philips PB 1175 | Pretty Little Girl In The Yellow Dress/At Last | 5 |
| 62 | United Artists UP 1006 | Close To Cathy/She's Just Another Girl | 5 |

## CLIFFTERS
| | | |
|---|---|---|
| 62 | Philips PB 1242 | Django/Amapola (Pretty Little Poppy) ....................................................... 5 |

## BILL CLIFTON
| | | |
|---|---|---|
| 60 | Melodisc 1554 | You Don't Think About Me/Mail Carrier's Warning ................................. 5 |
| 63 | Decca F 11793 | Beatle Crazy/Little Girl Dressed In Blue ............................................. 5 |

## PAUL CLIFTON
| | | |
|---|---|---|
| 09 | Kent Select CITY 029 | She Wobbles When She Walks/BOYCE CUNNINGHAM: Too Young ........... 10 |

## CLIMAX (CHICAGO) BLUES BAND
| | | |
|---|---|---|
| 69 | Parlophone R 5809 | Like Uncle Charlie/Loving Machine ................................................... 30 |
| 70 | Harvest HAR 5029 | Reap What I've Sowed/Spoonful ..................................................... 12 |
| 71 | Harvest HAR 5041 | Towards The Sun/Everyday (as Climax Chicago) ................................ 10 |
| 72 | Harvest HAR 5065 | Mole On The Dole/Like Uncle Charlie ............................................... 12 |
| 69 | Parlophone PMC/PCS 7069 | CLIMAX CHICAGO BLUES BAND (LP, yellow/black label, with "sold in the UK.." text) .. 150 |
| 70 | Parlophone PCS 7084 | PLAYS ON (LP, yellow/black labels) .................................................. 250 |
| 70 | Parlophone PCS 7084 | PLAYS ON (LP, later issue with boxed Parlophone logo) ..................... 70 |
| 70 | Harvest SHSP 4009 | A LOT OF BOTTLE (LP, no EMI logo on label, fully laminated sleeve) .... 60 |
| 71 | Harvest SHSP 4015 | TIGHTLY KNIT (LP, with EMI logo on label, flipback sleeve)................. 40 |
| 72 | Harvest SHSP 4024 | RICH MAN (LP) ............................................................................ 18 |
| 74 | Polydor 2383259 | LIVE (LP) ..................................................................................... 15 |

*(see also Hipster Image)*

## CLIMAX INVASION
| | | |
|---|---|---|
| 77 | Top Secret TS1 | The Advertiser (one-sided) ............................................................. 30 |

## CLIMAX (1)
| | | |
|---|---|---|
| 71 | Voice VC1 | I'm A Man/I'm A Man Part 2............................................................. 45 |

## CLIMAX (2)
| | | |
|---|---|---|
| 72 | Bell 1219 | Precious And Few/Park Preserve ...................................................... 6 |

## CLIMB
| | | |
|---|---|---|
| 81 | Pinnacle PIN 510 | I Can't Forget/Only A Human (p/s) ..................................................... 8 |
| 81 | Pinnacle 12 PIN 510 | I Can't Forget (A Mother's Crime)/Your Hell (12", p/s) ...................... 15 |
| 82 | Pinnacle PIN 511 | Touch Me (Heaven)/A Lower Class Of Heaven (p/s) .............................. 7 |
| 84 | Second Vision SV 004 | Poacher Is (As Poacher Does)/The Woodcutter (p/s) ......................... 20 |

## PATSY CLINE
| | | |
|---|---|---|
| 57 | Brunswick 05660 | A Poor Man's Roses (Or A Rich Man's Gold)/Walkin' After Midnight........... 20 |
| 63 | Brunswick 05888 | Sweet Dreams/Back In My Baby's Arms ........................................... 10 |
| 63 | Decca 31262 | Blue Moon Of Kentucky/Faded Love (export) ................................... 20 |
| 62 | Brunswick OE 9490 | SWEET DREAMS (EP) ................................................................... 15 |
| 62 | Brunswick LAT 8394 | SHOWCASE (LP)........................................................................... 15 |

## CLINIC
| | | |
|---|---|---|
| 97 | Aladdin's Cave Of Golf GOLF001 | IPC Subeditors Dictate Our Youth/Porno/D.I.Y. (p/s, 500 copies only) ........... 12 |
| 98 | Aladdin's C.O.G. GOLF002 | Monkey On Your Back/D.T. (p/s, 500 copies only) ............................... 8 |
| 98 | Aladdin's C.O.G. GOLF003 | Cement Mixer/Kimberley (p/s, 1,000 copies only) ............................... 8 |
| 99 | Domino WIGLP 64 | CLINIC (LP) ................................................................................. 25 |
| 00 | Domino WIGLP 78 | INTERNATIONAL WRANGLER (LP) ................................................. 15 |
| 01 | Domino WIGLP 100 | WALKING WITH THEE (LP) ............................................................ 18 |
| 10 | Domino WIGLP 261X | BUBBLEGUM (2-LP, pink vinyl, transfer, sticker, poster & badge) ........... 20 |

## BUDDY CLINTON
| | | |
|---|---|---|
| 60 | Top Rank JAR 287 | Across The Street From Your House/How My Prayers Have Changed ........... 15 |

## DAVY CLINTON
| | | |
|---|---|---|
| 68 | NEMS 56-3855 | Can I Bring Back Yesterday/The Girl With The Sun In Her Hair ........... 35 |
| 68 | President PT 290 | House Of The Rising Sun/On A Rooftop In Memphis............................ 6 |

## GEORGE CLINTON
| | | |
|---|---|---|
| 79 | ABC ABC 4053 | Please Don't Run From Me/Life And Breath ...................................... 5 |
| 79 | ABC ABC 4053 | Please Don't Run From Me/Life And Breath (DJ Copy) ...................... 15 |

*(do not see also Parliament, Funkadelic)*

## LARRY CLINTON
| | | |
|---|---|---|
| 79 | Grapevine GRP 120 | She's Wanted In Three States/If I Knew ............................................ 25 |
| 79 | Grapevine GRP 120 | She's Wanted In Three States/If I Knew (DJ Copy) ............................ 45 |

## CLINTONES
| | | |
|---|---|---|
| 73 | Ackee ACK 515 | Equal Rights/Version ...................................................................... 6 |

## CLIQUE (U.K.) (1)
| | | |
|---|---|---|
| 65 | Pye 7N 15786 | She Ain't No Good/Time Time Time ................................................. 100 |
| 65 | Pye 7N 15853 | We Didn't Kiss, Didn't Love, But Now We Do/You've Been Unfair ........... 175 |
| 60s | private pressing | THE CLIQUE (EP, no p/s)................................................................ 550 |
| 95 | Dig The Fuzz DIG 003 | THE COMPLETE RECORDINGS 1964/1965 (LP) ................................ 20 |

*(see also Hammersmith Gorillas)*

## CLIQUE (U.K.) (2)
| | | |
|---|---|---|
| 91 | Guild GUIEP 001 | INTRODUCING...THE CLIQUE (EP) .................................................. 20 |
| 94 | Detour DR 014 | Reggie/She Doesn't Need You Anymore (p/s, red vinyl)...................... 10 |
| 94 | Detour DR 014 | Reggie/She Doesn't Need You Anymore (pic disc, 200 only) ............... 15 |
| 93 | Detour DR 006 | THE EARLY DAYS (EP) .................................................................. 15 |

## CLIQUE (U.S.)
| | | |
|---|---|---|
| 69 | London HLU 10286 | Sugar On Sunday/Superman ........................................................... 20 |

## JOHNNY CLIVE
| | | |
|---|---|---|
| 62 | Oriole CB 1793 | Lazy Boy/Swiss Twistin' Baby ........................................................... 5 |
| 63 | Oriole CB 1820 | China Girl/Sue............................................................................... 5 |

## CLIVE & DOREEN
| | | |
|---|---|---|
| 68 | Treasure Isle TI 7033 | What Can I Do/TOMMY MCCOOK: Black Power ........................................... 45 |

## CLIVE & GLORIA
| | | |
|---|---|---|
| 63 | R&B JB 113 | Change Of Plan/Little Gloria ............................................... 20 |
| 64 | R&B JB 173 | Money Money Money/Have I Told You Lately ................... 20 |
| 64 | King KG 1004 | Do The Ska/You Made Me Cry ......................................... 20 |

## CLIVE & NAOMI
| | | |
|---|---|---|
| 65 | Ska Beat JB 181 | You Are Mine/Open The Door ...................................... 20 |

*(see also Desmond Dekker)*

## CLOCK DVA
| | | |
|---|---|---|
| 81 | Fetish FET 008 | Four Hours (Re-mixed)/Sensorium (p/s) ...................... 6 |
| 81 | Industrial IRC 31 | WHITE SOULS IN BLACK SUITS (cassette, with booklet) ........ 20 |

## CLOCKHOUSE
| | | |
|---|---|---|
| 83 | Picturesque PIC 1 | Vanishing Point/Everyman (p/s) .................................. 7 |

## CLOCKWORK CRIMINALS
| | | |
|---|---|---|
| 82 | Ace ACE 38 | YOUNG AND BOLD (EP) ............................................. 150 |

## CLOCKWORK ORANGES
| | | |
|---|---|---|
| 66 | Ember EMB S 227 | Ready Steady/After Tonight ...................................... 40 |

## CLOCKWORK SOLDIERS
| | | |
|---|---|---|
| 84 | Rot ASS 5 | Wet Dreams/Suicide/In The Name Of Science (p/s) .......... 15 |

## CLONE 81
| | | |
|---|---|---|
| 81 | FMR 058 | Product Of Society/Into The Recess (hand-made p/s) ........ 25 |

## BETTY CLOONEY
| | | |
|---|---|---|
| 55 | HMV 7M 311 | I Love You A Mountain/Can't Do Without You .................. 5 |

*(see also Rosemary Clooney)*

## ROSEMARY CLOONEY
| | | |
|---|---|---|
| 53 | Columbia SCM 5019 | Half As Much/Botch-A-Me (Ba-Ba-Baciami Piccina) ........... 10 |
| 53 | Columbia SCM 5027 | If I Had A Penny/You're After My Own Heart ..................... 8 |
| 53 | Columbia SCM 5028 | On The First Warm Day/If Teardrops Were Pennies ............ 5 |
| 53 | Columbia SCM 5040 | (Remember Me) I'm The One Who Loves You/Lover's Gold ..... 5 |
| 53 | Columbia SCM 5049 | Blues In The Night/Who Kissed Me Last Night? ................. 5 |

*(see also Bing Crosby)*

## CLOSE LOBSTERS
| | | |
|---|---|---|
| 89 | Caff CAFF 4 | Just Too Bloody Stupid/All The Little Boys And Girls (fold-out, p/s, insert) ................... 20 |

## CLOSE SHAVE
| | | |
|---|---|---|
| 99 | Helen Of Oi! H 003 | Attack/We Hate You (p/s, first pressing, 200 numbered copies) ............ 8 |

## CLOSE RIVALS
| | | |
|---|---|---|
| 81 | Hyped BMRB 52 | Short Sharp Kick In The Teeth/You've Got To Make Mistakes ........ 6 |

## CLOUD
| | | |
|---|---|---|
| 75 | Kingsway DOVE 16 | FREE TO FLY (LP) ................................................... 20 |
| 77 | Kingsway DOVE 44 | WATERED GARDEN (LP, gatefold sleeve) ...................... 30 |
| 78 | Dove 62 | THE RESTING PLACE (LP) ........................................... 20 |
| 85 | Songs Of Fellow. SFR103 | THE PROMISE (LP) ............................................. 15 |

## CLAUDE CLOUD
| | | |
|---|---|---|
| 55 | MGM MGM 820 | Cloudburst/One Bone (78, as Claude Cloud & Thunderclaps) ........ 10 |
| 57 | MGM MGM 946 | The Beat/Around The Horn (as Claude Cloud & His Orchestra) ....... 15 |
| 55 | MGM MGM-EP 517 | LET'S GO CATSTATIC NO. 1 (EP, as Claude Cloud & Thunderclaps) .... 15 |
| 56 | MGM MGM-D 142 | ROCK 'N' ROLL (10" LP) ......................................... 150 |

*(see also Sonny Thompson, Sam 'The Man' Taylor)*

## CLOUD NINE
| | | |
|---|---|---|
| 90s | Acid Jazz JAZID 87P | I Feel It (12", p/s, promo-only, withdrawn) ................... 18 |
| 90s | Acid Jazz JAZID 78 | MILLENNIUM (LP, withdrawn) .................................. 30 |

## CLOUDS (1)
| | | |
|---|---|---|
| 69 | Island WIP 6055 | Heritage/Make No Bones About It ............................. 20 |
| 69 | Island WIP 6067 | Scrapbook/Carpenter .......................................... 20 |
| 69 | Island ILPS 9100 | THE CLOUDS SCRAPBOOK (LP, gatefold sleeve, first pressing with black/orange circle logo) ................... 250 |
| 69 | Island ILPS 9100 | THE CLOUDS SCRAPBOOK (LP, second pressing, circle logo) ......... 100 |
| 69 | Island ILPS 9100 | THE CLOUDS SCRAPBOOK (LP, later pressing 'pink rim palm tree') .... 25 |
| 71 | Chrysalis ILPS 9151 | WATERCOLOUR DAYS (LP, gatefold sleeve, green label with Island logo and Island address in white) ................... 50 |

## CLOUDS (2)
| | | |
|---|---|---|
| 88 | Subway Org. SUBWAY 12 | Tranquil/Get Out Of My Dream (p/s) ........................ 5 |

*(see also Boy Hairdressers, Teenage Fanclub)*

## CLOUT
| | | |
|---|---|---|
| 90 | Mooncrest JWL 1000 | We'll Bring The House Down/Jim Jam (p/s) ................... 7 |

*(see also Slade)*

## CLOVEN HOOF
| | | |
|---|---|---|
| 82 | Elemental EM 001 | OPENING RITUAL (12" EP) ........................................ 80 |
| 84 | Neat NEAT 1013 | CLOVEN HOOF (LP) ............................................... 20 |
| 86 | Trojan CH 002 | FIGHTING BACK (LP, with poster) .............................. 25 |
| 86 | Trojan CH 002 | FIGHTING BACK (LP, without poster) ........................... 20 |

## CLOVER
| | | |
|---|---|---|
| 70 | Liberty LBF 15341 | Wade In The Water/Stealin' .................................. 10 |
| 69 | Liberty LBS 83340 | CLOVER (LP) ................................................... 30 |
| 71 | Liberty LBS 83487 | FORTY-NINER (LP) ............................................. 30 |

*(see also Huey Lewis & News)*

## CLOVERLEAFS
| | | | |
|---|---|---|---|
| 56 | MGM MGM 933 | Step Right Up And Say Howdy/With Plenty Of Money And You (Gold Digger's Lullaby) | ..8 |

*(see also Art Mooney)*

## CLOVERS
| | | | |
|---|---|---|---|
| 56 | London HLE 8229 | Nip Sip/If I Could Be Loved By You (gold label lettering) | 500 |
| 56 | London HLE 8229 | Nip Sip/If I Could Be Loved By You (silver label lettering) | 200 |
| 56 | London HLE 8229 | Nip Sip/If I Could Be Loved By You (78) | 35 |
| 56 | London HLE 8314 | Love, Love, Love/Hey, Doll Baby | 300 |
| 56 | London HLE 8314 | Love, Love, Love/Hey, Doll Baby (78) | 35 |
| 56 | London HLE 8334 | From The Bottom Of My Heart/Your Tender Lips | 200 |
| 56 | London HLE 8334 | From The Bottom Of My Heart/Your Tender Lips | 20 |
| 58 | London HL 7048 | Wishing For Your Love/All About You (export issue) | 150 |
| 58 | HMV POP 542 | In The Good Old Summertime/Idaho | 30 |
| 59 | London HLT 8949 | Love Potion No. 9/Stay Awhile (triangular centre) | 50 |
| 59 | London HLT 8949 | Love Potion No. 9/Stay Awhile (round centre) | 35 |
| 60 | London HLT 9122 | Lovey/One Mint Julep | 30 |
| 60 | London HLT 9154 | Easy Lovin'/I'm Confessin' (That I Love You) | 40 |
| 61 | HMV POP 883 | Honey Dripper/Have Gun | 25 |
| 68 | Atlantic 584 160 | Your Cash Ain't Nothin' But Trash/I've Got My Eyes On You | 15 |
| 69 | Atlantic 587 162 | LOVE BUG (LP) | 50 |

## CLOWN
| | | | |
|---|---|---|---|
| 72 | CBS 7906 | Lord Of The Ringside/Rumania | 40 |

## CLOX ITALIA
| | | | |
|---|---|---|---|
| 82 | B Flat FLAT 2 | LookingThe Part/Leave It in (p/s, as Clox) | 15 |
| 84 | B Flat FLAT 3 | Ageing Agent/You Belong To Me | 8 |
| 84 | B Flat FLAT 4 | Follow Me Into The Water/This (p/s, as Clox) | 7 |

## CLUB TANGO
| | | | |
|---|---|---|---|
| 81 | Dining Out TUX 15 | FTN/Get The Picture (p/s) | 5 |
| 81 | Dining Out TUX 7 | Performance/Fun Specialists (p/s) | 5 |

## CLUES
| | | | |
|---|---|---|---|
| 81 | Clues CLU 001 | NO VACANCIES (EP) | 10 |

## CLUTCH
| | | | |
|---|---|---|---|
| 73 | EMI 2010 | Black Angel/The Frightners | 8 |

## CLUTHA (FOLK GROUP)
| | | | |
|---|---|---|---|
| 71 | Argo ZFB 18 | SCOTIA! (LP, as Clutha Folk Group) | 15 |

## CMETRIC
| | | | |
|---|---|---|---|
| 94 | B12 B1210 | Cmetric (12") | 30 |

## C.M.J.
| | | | |
|---|---|---|---|
| 68 | Impression IMP 102 | I Can't Do It All By Myself/Nothing At All | 45 |
| 71 | Mother MOT 3 | La La La/Step Around It | 50 |
| 65 | Impression EPIM 501 | THE C.M.J. TRIO (EP) | 50 |
| 69 | Impression IMPL 1001 | C.M.J. LIVE AT THE BANKHOUSE (LP, private pressing) | 80 |

## C.M.U. (CONTEMPORARY MUSIC UNIT)
| | | | |
|---|---|---|---|
| 72 | Transatlantic BIG 508 | Heart Of The Sun/Doctor Am I Normal? | 15 |
| 71 | Transatlantic TRA 237 | OPEN SPACES (LP, gatefold sleeve, clear plastic with foam inner, this price for mint record that has not reacted and been marked by plastic/foam inner) | 150 |
| 71 | Transatlantic TRA 237 | OPEN SPACES (LP, gatefold sleeve, clear plastic with foam inner, this price for mint sleeve with record that has been marked by chemical reaction to the plastic/foam inner) | 30 |
| 72 | Transatlantic TRA 259 | SPACE CABARET (LP, with lyric insert) | 100 |

*(see also Chopyn)*

## COACHMEN
| | | | |
|---|---|---|---|
| 59 | Vogue V 9154 | Those Brown Eyes/Bald Mountain | 5 |

## COACHMEN
| | | | |
|---|---|---|---|
| 66 | Columbia DB 8057 | Gabrielle/Seasons In The Sun | 8 |

## COACHOUSE RHYTHM SECTION
| | | | |
|---|---|---|---|
| 77 | Ice ICE 3 12 | Nobody Got Time/Time Warp (12") | 25 |

*(see also Eddy Grant)*

## COALESCE
| | | | |
|---|---|---|---|
| 95 | Earache MOSH 140 | 002: 73-C/Grain Of Salt (p/s) | 5 |

## COASTERS
| | | | |
|---|---|---|---|
| 57 | London HLE 8450 | Searchin'/Young Blood | 75 |
| 57 | London HL 7021 | Searchin'/Young Blood (export issue) | 30 |
| 58 | London HLE 8665 | Yakety Yak/Zing! Went The Strings Of My Heart | 15 |
| 58 | London HLE 8729 | The Shadow Knows/Sorry But I'm Gonna Have To Pass | 50 |
| 59 | London HLE 8819 | Charlie Brown/Three Cool Cats | 10 |
| 59 | London HL 7073 | Charlie Brown/Three Cool Cats (export issue) | 10 |
| 59 | London HLE 8882 | Along Came Jones/That Is Rock And Roll (silver top label) | 15 |
| 59 | London HLE 8938 | Poison Ivy/I'm A Hog For You | 15 |

*(The above 45s were originally issued with triangular centres, later round centre copies are worth half to two-thirds these values.)*

| | | | |
|---|---|---|---|
| 60 | London HLE 9020 | What About Us/Run Red Run | 20 |
| 60 | London HLK 9111 | Besame Mucho (Parts 1 & 2) | 50 |
| 60 | London HLK 9111 | Besame Mucho (Parts 1 & 2) (78) | 50 |
| 60 | London HLK 9151 | Wake Me, Shake Me/Stewball | 20 |
| 60 | London HLK 9208 | Shoppin' For Clothes/The Snake And The Bookworm | 25 |
| 61 | London HLK 9293 | Wait A Minute/Thumbin' A Ride | 15 |
| 61 | London HLK 9349 | Little Egypt/Keep On Rolling | 15 |
| 61 | London HLK 9413 | Girls! Girls! Girls! (Parts 1 & 2) | 15 |

# COASTERS (Jamaica)

| | | | |
|---|---|---|---|
| 62 | London HLK 9493 | (Ain't That) Just Like Me/Bad Blood | 15 |
| 64 | London HLK 9863 | T'Ain't Nothin' To Me/Speedo's Back In Town | 15 |
| 66 | Atlantic 584 033 | She's A Yum Yum/Saturday Night Fish Fry | 12 |
| 67 | Atlantic 584 087 | Searchin'/Yakety Yak | 10 |
| 67 | CBS 2749 | Soul Pad/Down Home Girl | 15 |
| 68 | Direction 58-3701 | She Can/Everybody's Woman | 10 |
| 71 | Parlophone R 5931 | Love Potion No. 9/D.W. Washburn | 5 |
| 72 | Stateside SS 2201 | Cool Jerk/Talkin' 'Bout A Woman | 30 |
| 72 | London HLZ 10437 | Love Potion No. 9/D. W. Washburn | 5 |
| 59 | London REE 1203 | THE COASTERS (EP) | 25 |
| 60 | London HA-E 2237 | GREATEST HITS (LP) | 50 |
| 63 | London HA-K 8033 | COAST ALONG WITH THE COASTERS (LP) | 50 |
| 66 | Atlantic 588 134 | COAST ALONG WITH THE COASTERS (LP, reissue) | 15 |
| 67 | Atlantic 590 015 | ALL TIME GREATEST HITS (LP) | 15 |
| 71 | Joy JOYS 189 | HUNGRY (LP) | 15 |

## COASTERS (JAMAICA)

| | | | |
|---|---|---|---|
| 69 | Doctor Bird DB 1182 | Stoney Hill/RICK RODRIGUES & JOHNNY MOORE : Continental Shuffle | 100 |

## COAST ROAD DRIVE

| | | | |
|---|---|---|---|
| 74 | Deram SML 1113 | DELICIOUS AND REFRESHING (LP) | 60 |

## COAST TO COAST

| | | | |
|---|---|---|---|
| 79 | Yorkie JB 102 | The Hucklebuck/Telephone Baby (special die-cut sleeve) | 10 |
| 82 | Polydor POSP 451 | The Bell/How Can I Be Sure | 8 |

*(see also Status Quo)*

## C.O.B. (CLIVE'S ORIGINAL BAND)

| | | | |
|---|---|---|---|
| 72 | Polydor 2058 260 | Blue Morning/Bones | 15 |
| 71 | CBS 69010 | SPIRIT OF LOVE (LP, gatefold sleeve, orange label) | 200 |
| 72 | Polydor Folk Mill 2383 161 | MOYSHE McSTIFF & THE TARTAN LANCERS OF THE SACRED HEART (LP, gatefold sleeve, red label) | 400 |

*(see also Famous Jug Band, Incredible String Band)*

## JIMMY COBB

| | | | |
|---|---|---|---|
| 00 | Expansion EXP 76 | So Nobody Else Can Hear/Pistachio | 10 |

## COBBLERS

| | | | |
|---|---|---|---|
| 70 | Emblem JDR 314 | WARM ARE THE SOUNDS (LP) | 30 |

## COBBLERS LAST

| | | | |
|---|---|---|---|
| 79 | Banshee BAN 1012 | BOOT IN THE DOOR (LP, with insert) | 80 |

## COBBS

| | | | |
|---|---|---|---|
| 69 | Amalgamated AMG 845 | Hot Buttered Corn/COUNT MACHUKI: It Is I | 20 |
| 69 | Amalgamated AMG 849 | Space Doctor/LLOYD & DEVON: Baby Reggae | 100 |

## BILLY COBHAM

| | | | |
|---|---|---|---|
| 73 | Atlantic K40506 | SPECTRUM (LP, gatefold) | 20 |

## COBRA (1)

| | | | |
|---|---|---|---|
| 78 | Rip Off RIP 3 | Graveyard Boogie/Looking For A Lady (p/s) | 35 |

*(see also Speed)*

## COBRA (2)

| | | | |
|---|---|---|---|
| 85 | Criminal Response COBRA 2 | WARRIORS OF THE DEAD (LP) | 18 |
| 87 | Ebony EBON 39 | BACK FROM THE DEAD (LP) | 18 |

## COBWEB

| | | | |
|---|---|---|---|
| 71 | Private Pressing SJP 762 | You'll Go far/Broken Web | 10 |

## COCHISE

| | | | |
|---|---|---|---|
| 70 | United Artists UP 35134 | Watch This Space/59th St. Bridge Song | 6 |
| 70 | Liberty LBS 15425 | Love's Made A Fool Of You/Words Of A Dying Man | 6 |
| 71 | Liberty LBF 15460 | Why I Sing The Blues/Jed Colider | 6 |
| 70 | United Artists UAS 29117 | COCHISE (LP, gatefold sleeve, orange/pink label) | 30 |
| 70 | Liberty LBS 83428 | SWALLOW TALES (LP, black label) | 20 |
| 72 | United Artists UAS 29286 | SO FAR (LP) | 25 |

*(see also B.J. Cole, Mick Grabham)*

## DIB COCHRAN & EARWIGS

| | | | |
|---|---|---|---|
| 70 | Bell BLL 1121 | Oh Baby/Universal Love | 500 |

*(see also Marc Bolan, Tyrannosaurus Rex, Tony Visconti, Rick Wakeman)*

## EDDIE COCHRAN

### 78s

| | | | |
|---|---|---|---|
| 57 | London HLU 8386 | 20 Flight Rock/Dark Lonely Street | 50 |
| 57 | London HLU 8433 | Sittin' In The Balcony/Completely Sweet | 60 |
| 58 | London HLU 8702 | Summertime Blues/Love Again | 70 |
| 59 | London HLU 8792 | C'mon Everybody/Don't Ever Let Me Go | 90 |
| 59 | London HLU 8880 | Teenage Heaven/I Remember | 100 |
| 59 | London HLU 8944 | Somethin' Else/Boll Weevil Song | 100 |
| 60 | London HLW 9022 | Hallelujah, I Love Her So/Little Angel | 200 |
| 60 | London HLG 9115 | Three Steps To Heaven/Cut Across Shorty | 400 |
| 95 | Cruisin' The 50s CASS 001 | Three Steps To Heaven/Cut Across Shorty (reissue, 300 only) | 30 |
| 96 | Cruisin' The 50s CASB 004 | Week-End/Cherished Memories (reissue, 400 only) | 30 |

### SINGLES

| | | | |
|---|---|---|---|
| 57 | London HLU 8386 | 20 Flight Rock/Dark Lonely Street (triangular centre) | 100 |
| 57 | London HLU 8386 | 20 Flight Rock/Dark Lonely Street (silver-top label with triangular centre) | 125 |
| 57 | London HLU 8386 | 20 Flight Rock/Dark Lonely Street (round centre) | 50 |
| 57 | London HLU 8433 | Sittin' In The Balcony/Completely Sweet | 350 |
| 58 | London HLU 8702 | Summertime Blues/Love Again | 25 |

| 59 | London HLU 8792 | C'mon Everybody/Don't Ever Let Me Go | 25 |
| 59 | London HLU 8880 | Teenage Heaven/I Remember | 20 |
| 59 | London HL 7082 | Teenage Heaven/Boll Weevil Song (export issue) | 20 |
| 59 | London HLU 8944 | Somethin' Else/Boll Weevil Song | 20 |
| 60 | London HLW 9022 | Hallelujah, I Love Her So/Little Angel (triangular centre) | 25 |

*(The above 45s were originally issued with triangular centres, later round centre copies are worth half these values unless otherwise stated.)*

| 60 | London HLW 9022 | Hallelujah, I Love Her So/Little Angel (round centre) | 15 |
| 60 | London HLG 9115 | Three Steps To Heaven/Cut Across Shorty | 10 |
| 60 | London HLG 9196 | Sweetie Pie/Lonely | 40 |
| 61 | London HLG 9362 | Weekend/Cherished Memories | 20 |
| 61 | London HLG 9460 | Jeannie, Jeannie, Jeannie/Pocketful Of Hearts | 20 |
| 61 | London HLG 9464 | Pretty Girl/Teresa | 35 |
| 61 | London HLG 9467 | Undying Love/Stockin's 'n' Shoes | 50 |
| 62 | Liberty LIB 10049 | Never/Think Of Me | 20 |
| 63 | Liberty LIB 10088 | My Way/Rock And Roll Blues | 15 |
| 63 | Liberty LIB 10108 | Drive-In Show/I Almost Lost My Mind | 15 |
| 64 | Liberty LIB 10151 | Skinny Jim/Nervous Breakdown (black label) | 60 |
| 66 | Liberty LIB 10233 | C'mon Everybody/Summertime Blues | 10 |
| 66 | Liberty LIB 10249 | Three Stars/Somethin' Else | 20 |
| 67 | Liberty LIB 10276 | Three Steps To Heaven/Eddie's Blues | 20 |
| 68 | Liberty LBF 15071 | Summertime Blues/Let's Get Together | 10 |
| 68 | Liberty LBF 15109 | Somethin' Else/Milk Cow Blues | 10 |
| 70 | Liberty LBF 15366 | C'mon Everybody/Mean When I'm Mad | 10 |

## EPs

| 59 | London REU 1214 | C'MON EVERYBODY (orange sleeve, triangular centre) | 30 |
| 59 | London REU 1214 | C'MON EVERYBODY (orange sleeve, round centre) | 20 |
| 59 | London REU 1214 | C'MON EVERYBODY (yellow sleeve, silver-top label) | 30 |
| 59 | London REU 1214 | C'MON EVERYBODY (yellow sleeve, round centre) | 20 |
| 60 | London REU 1239 | SOMETHIN' ELSE (triangular centre) | 30 |
| 60 | London REU 1239 | SOMETHIN' ELSE (round centre) | 20 |
| 60 | London REG 1262 | EDDIE'S HITS | 30 |
| 61 | London REG 1301 | CHERISHED MEMORIES OF EDDIE COCHRAN | 30 |
| 62 | Liberty LEP 2052 | NEVER TO BE FORGOTTEN | 30 |
| 63 | Liberty LEP 2090 | CHERISHED MEMORIES (VOL.1) | 20 |
| 63 | Liberty LEP 2111 | C'MON EVERYBODY (reissue) | 15 |
| 63 | Liberty LEP 2122 | SOMETHIN' ELSE (reissue) | 15 |
| 63 | Liberty LEP 2123 | CHERISHED MEMORIES OF EDDIE COCHRAN (reissue) | 15 |
| 63 | Liberty LEP 2124 | EDDIE'S HITS (reissue) | 15 |
| 64 | Liberty LEP 2165 | C'MON AGAIN | 20 |
| 64 | Liberty LEP 2180 | STOCKIN'S 'N' SHOES | 25 |

## ALBUMS

| 58 | London HA-U 2093 | SINGIN' TO MY BABY (initial pressing with laminated rear sleeve) | 250 |
| 58 | London HA-U 2093 | SINGIN' TO MY BABY (without laminated rear sleeve) | 100 |
| 60 | London HA-G 2267 | THE EDDIE COCHRAN MEMORIAL ALBUM | 80 |
| 62 | Liberty LBY 1109 | CHERISHED MEMORIES | 50 |
| 63 | Liberty LBY 1127 | THE EDDIE COCHRAN MEMORIAL ALBUM (reissue) | 15 |
| 63 | Liberty LBY 1158 | SINGIN' TO MY BABY (reissue) | 20 |
| 64 | Liberty LBY 1205 | MY WAY | 40 |
| 88 | Liberty ECB 1 | THE EDDIE COCHRAN BOX SET (6-LP box set with booklet) | 40 |

## HANK COCHRAN

| 68 | Monument LMO 5020 | HEART OF HANK (LP) | 15 |

## JACKIE LEE COCHRAN

| 57 | Brunswick 05669 | Ruby Pearl (with Jimmy Pruett)/Mama Don't You Think I Know | 2500 |
| 57 | Brunswick 05669 | Ruby Pearl (with Jimmy Pruett)/Mama Don't You Think I Know (78) | 250 |

## COCK & WOODPECKERS

| 71 | Newbeat 93 | Every Day And Every Night/I Fall In Love Everyday | 15 |

## BRUCE COCKBURN

| 71 | True North WTN 003 | HIGH WINDS WHITE SKY (LP) | 15 |
| 71 | True North TNX 7 | SUNWHEEL DANCE (LP) | 15 |

## JARVIS COCKER

| 06 | Rough Trade RTRADLP 340 | THE JARVIS COCKER RECORD (LP, with bonus one-sided 7") | 35 |

*(see also Pulp)*

## JOE COCKER

| 64 | Decca F 11974 | I'll Cry Instead/Precious Words | 100 |
| 68 | Regal Zonophone RZ 3006 | Marjorine/New Age Of The Lily | 8 |
| 68 | Regal Zonophone RZ 3013 | With A Little Help From My Friends/Something's Coming On | 6 |
| 69 | Regal Zonophone RZ 3024 | Delta Lady/She's So Good To Me | 6 |
| 70 | Regal Zonophone RZ 3027 | The Letter/Space Captain | 6 |
| 70 | Fly BUG 3 | Cry Me A River/Give Peace A Chance (p/s) | 5 |
| 71 | Fly BUG 9 | High Time We Went/Black-Eyed Blues | 5 |
| 72 | Magni Fly ECHO 103 | With A Little Help From My Friends/Delta Lady/The Letter (p/s) | 5 |
| 72 | Cube BUG 25 | Woman To Woman/Midnight Rider (with Chris Stanton Band) | 5 |
| 83 | Island WIP 6818 | Ruby Lee/Talking Back To The Night (export issue) | 7 |
| 60s | Oak | JOE COCKER (EP, existence unconfirmed) | 500 |
| 67 | Action ACT 002 EP | RAG GOES MAD AT THE MOJO (33rpm EP, 2 tracks by Joe Cocker's Blues Band, in conjunction with Sheffield University rag magazine Twikker) | 50 |
| 69 | Regal Zono. LRZ 1006 | WITH A LITTLE HELP FROM MY FRIENDS (LP, mono, red/silver label with "sold in the U.K..." text) | 120 |

| | | | |
|---|---|---|---|
| 69 | Regal Zono. SLRZ 1006 | WITH A LITTLE HELP FROM MY FRIENDS (LP, stereo, red/silver label with "sold in the U.K..." text) | 70 |
| 69 | Regal Zono. SLRZ 1011 | JOE COCKER! (LP, red/silver label) | 30 |
| 70 | A&M AMLS 6002 | MAD DOGS & ENGLISHMEN (2-LP, multifold gatefold sleeve, brown label) | 20 |
| 71 | Fly HIFLY 3 | COCKER HAPPY (LP, gatefold sleeve) | 20 |

*(see also Grease Band, Made In Sheffield)*

## COCKERSDALE
| | | | |
|---|---|---|---|
| 85 | EFDSS ESLP 001 | PROSPECT PROVIDENCE (LP) | 20 |

## COCKNEY REJECTS
| | | | |
|---|---|---|---|
| 79 | Small Wonder SW 19 | Flares'N'Slippers/Police Star/I Wanna Be A Star (p/s) | 15 |
| 79 | EMI EMI 5008 | I'm Not A Fool/East End (p/s) | 6 |
| 80 | EMI EMI 5035 | Bad Man!/The New Song (p/s) | 6 |
| 80 | Zonophone Z 2 | The Greatest Cockney Rip-Off/Hate Of The City (p/s, yellow vinyl) | 7 |
| 80 | Zonophone Z 4 | I'm Forever Blowing Bubbles/West Side Boys (p/s) | 8 |
| 80 | Zonophone Z 6 | We Can Do Anything/15 Nights (p/s) | 6 |
| 80 | Zonophone Z 10 | We Are The Firm/War On The Terraces (p/s) | 8 |
| 81 | Zonophone Z 20 | Easy Life/Motorhead/Hang 'Em High (p/s) | 6 |
| 80 | Zonophone ZONO 101 | GREATEST HITS VOLUME 1 (LP) | 20 |
| 80 | Zonophone ZONO 102 | GREATEST HITS VOLUME 2 (LP, with inner sleeve & poster) | 15 |
| 81 | Zonophone ZEM 101 | GREATEST HITS VOLUME 3 (LIVE AND LOUD) (LP, gatefold) | 15 |
| 85 | Wonderful World WOW LP 2 | UNHEARD REJECTS (LP) | 15 |

## COCKNEYS
| | | | |
|---|---|---|---|
| 64 | Philips BF 1303 | After Tomorrow/I'll Cry Each Night | 10 |
| 64 | Philips BF 1338 | After Tomorrow/I'll Cry Each Night (reissue) | 5 |
| 64 | Philips BF 1360 | I Know You're Gonna Be Mine/Oh No You Won't | 10 |

## COCK SPARRER
| | | | |
|---|---|---|---|
| 77 | Decca FR 13710 | Runnin' Riot/Sister Suzie (demos in p/s) | 200 |
| 77 | Decca FR 13710 | Runnin' Riot/Sister Suzie (no p/s) | 40 |
| 77 | Decca FR 13732 | We Love You/Chip On My Shoulder (no p/s) | 20 |
| 77 | Decca LFR 13732 | We Love You/Chip On My Shoulder (12" p/s, with photo insert, 7,500 only) | 25 |
| 82 | Carrere CAR 255 | England Belongs To Me/Argy Bargy (p/s, beware of bootlegs With "fuzzy" looking label logo on sleeve) | 40 |
| 83 | Razor RAZ 9 | SHOCK TROOPS (LP) | 30 |
| 84 | Syndicate SYNLP 7 | RUNNIN' RIOT IN 84 | 35 |
| 86 | Razor RAZ 26 | TRUE GRIT (LP) | 25 |
| 87 | Link LP 005 | LIVE AND LOUD (LP) | 15 |

*(see also Little Roosters, Guttersnipes)*

## COCKTAIL CABINET
| | | | |
|---|---|---|---|
| 67 | Page One POF 046 | Puppet On A String/Breathalyser | 15 |

## COCOA TEA
| | | | |
|---|---|---|---|
| 88 | Live And Love LLD 87 | Lonesome Side/ADMIRAL TIBET: Reality Time (12") | 30 |

## COCONUT DOGS
| | | | |
|---|---|---|---|
| 80 | Mongrel Music MM 001 | Lipstick On The Glass/The Neighbours/Mannequin (no p/s, 1000 only) | 50 |
| 81 | Rialto TREB 136 | Officers Mess/Germinate (p/s) | 7 |

## COCTEAU TWINS
| | | | |
|---|---|---|---|
| 83 | 4AD AD 303 | Peppermint Pig/Laugh Lines (p/s) | 10 |
| 82 | 4AD CAD 411 | GARLANDS (LP) | 20 |
| 83 | 4AD CAD 313 | HEAD OVER HEELS (LP) | 15 |
| 84 | 4AD CAD 412 | TREASURE (LP, inner) | 20 |
| 86 | 4AD CAD 602 | VICTORIALAND (LP) | 20 |
| 88 | 4AD CAD 807 | BLUE BELL KNOLL (LP, tri-foldout sleeve) | 20 |
| 90 | 4AD CAD 0012 | HEAVEN OR LAS VEGAS (LP, with inner) | 20 |
| 91 | 4AD CT BOX 1 | SINGLE COLLECTION (10-CD box set) | 50 |
| 93 | Fontana 518259-1 | FOUR CALENDAR CAFE (LP) | 60 |
| 96 | Fontana 514-501-1 | MILK AND KISSES (LP) | 60 |
| 05 | 4AD CTBOX 2 | LULLABIES TO VIOLAINE (4-CD box set, tactile cover) | 40 |
| 10 | Vinyl 180 VIN180LP024 | BOX SET ONE (5-LP, 1 x 12", box set) | 80 |

*(see also This Mortal Coil, Felt, Massive Attack, Harold Budd, Lonely Is An Eyesore, The Future Sound Of London, Elizabeth Fraser)*

## BILL CODAY
| | | | |
|---|---|---|---|
| 01 | Grapevine G2K 45 117 | A Man Can't Be A Man (Without A Woman)/SANDRA WRIGHT: A Man Can't Be A Man (Without A Woman) | 10 |

## CODE 071
| | | | |
|---|---|---|---|
| 92 | Reinforced RIVET 1213 | A London Sumtin' (12") | 20 |

## CODEK
| | | | |
|---|---|---|---|
| 80 | MCA MCA 550 | Me Me Me/Demo (p/s) | 6 |
| 80 | MCA MCAT 550 | Me Me Me (Full Length Version)/Demo (12", p/s) | 25 |
| 82 | Island 12WIP 6764 | Tim Toum/Closer (12", p/s) | 25 |

## CODENAME JOHN
| | | | |
|---|---|---|---|
| 94 | Prototype PRO 001 | Deep Inside Of Me/(Inta) The Anthem (12") | 12 |
| 94 | Prototype PRO 002 | Kindred/Dreams Of Heaven (Shorty/s Mix) (12", as John) | 10 |

## CODE OF PRACTICE
| | | | |
|---|---|---|---|
| 95 | Certificate 18 CERT 1813 | Can We Change The Future/Remix (12") | 10 |

## C.O.D.S
| | | | |
|---|---|---|---|
| 66 | Stateside SS 489 | Michael (The Lover)/Cry No More | 25 |
| 66 | Stateside SS 489 | Michael (The Lover)/Cry No More (DJ copy) | 60 |

## CODY
| | | | |
|---|---|---|---|
| 71 | Polydor 2058-100 | I Belong With You/Wanna Make You Happy | 6 |

## TONY CODY
| | | | |
|---|---|---|---|
| 72 | Pye 7N 45153 | Walk On By/(Ain't It) Funny How Time Slips By | 30 |
| 72 | Pye 7N 45153 | Walk On By/(Ain't It) Funny How Time Slips By (DJ Copy) | 50 |

## JAMIE COE
| | | | |
|---|---|---|---|
| 59 | Parlophone R 4600 | Summertime Symphony/There's Gonna Be A Day | 150 |
| 60 | Parlophone R 4621 | School Day Blues/I'll Go On Loving You | 100 |
| 61 | HMV POP 991 | How Low Is Low/Little Dear Little Darling | 20 |
| 63 | London HLX 9713 | The Fool/I've Got That Feeling Again | 20 |

## PETER & CHRIS COE
| | | | |
|---|---|---|---|
| 72 | Trailer LER 2077 | OPEN THE DOOR AND LET US IN (LP) | 25 |
| 76 | Trailer LER 2098 | OUT OF SEASON, OUT OF RHYME (LP, yellow label) | 20 |
| 79 | Highway SHY 7007 | GAME OF ALL FOURS (LP) | 15 |

*(see also Bandoggs)*

## TONY COE (QUINTET)
| | | | |
|---|---|---|---|
| 61 | Philips B 10784L | SWINGIN' TILL THE GIRLS COME HOME (LP) | 50 |
| 67 | Columbia SCX 6170 | TONY'S BASEMENT (LP) | 100 |
| 78 | Lee Lambert LAM100 | COE-EXISTENCE (LP) | 20 |

## TONY COE & BRIAN LEMON TRIO
| | | | |
|---|---|---|---|
| 68 | '77' SEU 12/41 | TONY COE AND BRIAN LEMON TRIO (LP) | 30 |

*(see also Robert Farnon & Tony Coe)*

## JACK & CHARLIE COEN
| | | | |
|---|---|---|---|
| 77 | Topic 12TS 337 | THE BRANCH LINE (LP) | 22 |

## CARLTON COFFE
| | | | |
|---|---|---|---|
| 78 | Justice JUS 110 | Chant Away/Version (12") | 35 |

## COFFEE BAR SKIFFLERS
| | | | |
|---|---|---|---|
| 58 | Embassy WEP 1008 | SKIFFLE SESSION (EP) | 10 |

*(see also Chas McDevitt Skiffle Group)*

## CARLTON COFFEE
| | | | |
|---|---|---|---|
| 78 | Shebazz FME 003 | Music Revoluion/Music Revolution Part 2 | 15 |

## COFFEE SET
| | | | |
|---|---|---|---|
| 69 | Mercury MF 1113 | Happy Birthday/Our Anniversary | 6 |
| 69 | Fontana LPS 16503 | SAY IT WITH MUSIC (LP) | 15 |

## DENNIS COFFEY
| | | | |
|---|---|---|---|
| 72 | A&M AMS 7010 | Getting It On/Ride Sally Ride | 8 |
| 71 | A&M AMS 875 | Scorpio/Sad Song (with Detroit Guitar Band) | 20 |
| 70 | A&M AMLS 68035 | EVOLUTION (LP) | 15 |
| 71 | A&M AMLS 68072 | GOIN' FOR MYSELF (LP) | 15 |
| 74 | Sussex LPSX 9 | INSTANT COFFEY (LP) | 15 |

## ALMA COGAN
| | | | |
|---|---|---|---|
| 53 | HMV 7M 166 | Over And Over Again/Isn't Life Wonderful (with Les Howerd) | 15 |
| 53 | HMV 7M 106 | I Went To Your Wedding/You Belong To Me | 15 |
| 53 | HMV 7M 107 | To Be Loved By You/The Homing Waltz (B-side with Larry Day) | 15 |
| 54 | HMV 7M 173 | Ricochet (Rick-O-Shay)/The Moon Is Blue | 15 |
| 54 | HMV 7M 188 | Bell Bottom Blues/Love Me Again | 20 |
| 54 | HMV 7M 196 | Make Love To Me/Said The Little Moment | 15 |
| 54 | HMV 7M 219 | The Little Shoemaker/Chiqui-Chaqui (Chick-ee Chock-ee) | 15 |
| 54 | HMV 7M 228 | Little Things Mean A Lot/Canoodlin' Rag | 15 |
| 54 | HMV 7M 239 | Skinnie Minnie (Fishtail)/What Am I Going To Do, Ma (The Doo-Ma Song) | 20 |
| 54 | HMV 7M 269 | This Ole House/Skokiaan | 15 |
| 54 | HMV 7M 271 | I Can't Tell A Waltz From A Tango/Christmas Cards | 15 |
| 55 | HMV 7M 286 | Paper Kisses/Softly, Softly | 10 |
| 55 | HMV 7M 293 | Chee-Chee-Oo-Chee (Sang The Little Bird)/Tika Tika Tok | 10 |
| 55 | HMV 7M 301 | Tweedlee-Dee/More Than Ever Now | 15 |
| 55 | HMV 7M 316 | Got'n Idea/Give A Fool A Chance | 15 |
| 55 | HMV 7M 337 | Never Do A Tango With An Eskimo/Twenty Tiny Fingers | 15 |
| 56 | HMV 7M 367 | Love And Marriage/Sycamore Tree | 15 |
| 56 | HMV 7M 415 | Why Do Fools Fall In Love?/ (The Same Thing Happen With) The Birds And The Bees? | 20 |
| 56 | HMV POP 239 | Mama Teach Me To Dance/I'm In Love Again | 20 |
| 56 | HMV POP 261 | In The Middle Of The House/Two Innocent Hearts | 20 |
| 57 | HMV POP 284 | You, Me And Us/Three Brothers | 15 |
| 57 | HMV POP 317 | Whatever Lola Wants (Lola Gets)/Lucky Lips | 30 |
| 57 | HMV POP 336 | Chantez, Chantez/Funny, Funny, Funny | 10 |
| 57 | HMV POP 367 | Fabulous/Summer Love | 20 |
| 57 | HMV POP 392 | That's Happiness/What You've Done To Me | 10 |
| 57 | HMV POP 415 | Party Time/Please Mister Brown (Mister Jones, Mister Smith) | 20 |
| 58 | HMV POP 433 | The Story Of My Life/Love Is | 10 |
| 58 | HMV POP 450 | Sugartime/Gettin' Ready For Freddy | 15 |
| 58 | HMV POP 482 | Stairway Of Love/Comes Love | 15 |
| 58 | HMV POP 500 | Sorry, Sorry, Sorry/Fly Away Lovers | 10 |
| 58 | HMV POP 531 | There's Never Been A Night/If This Isn't Love | 10 |
| 59 | HMV POP 573 | Last Night On The Back Porch/Mama Says | 10 |
| 59 | HMV POP 608 | Pink Shoelaces/The Universe | 10 |
| 59 | HMV POP 670 | We Got Love/I Don't Mind Being All Alone | 8 |
| 60 | HMV POP 728 | O Dio Mio/Dream Talk | 10 |
| 60 | HMV POP 760 | The Train Of Love/The 'I Love You' Bit | 10 |
| 60 | HMV POP 815 | Must Be Santa/Just Couldn't Resist Her With Her Pocket Transistor | 5 |
| 61 | Columbia DB 4607 | Cowboy Jimmy Joe/Don't Read This Letter | 6 |
| 65 | Columbia DB 7652 | Snakes And Snails (And Puppy Dog Tails)/How Many Days, How Many Nights | 20 |

MINT VALUE £

| 65 | Columbia DB 7786 | Eight Days A Week/Help! | 10 |
|----|------------------|------------------------|----|
| 66 | Columbia DB 8088 | Now That I've Found You/More | 10 |
| 55 | HMV 7EG 8122 | THE GIRL WITH A LAUGH IN HER VOICE (EP, no picture sleeve) | 20 |
| 55 | HMV 7EG 8151 | THE GIRL WITH A LAUGH IN HER VOICE NO. 2 (EP) | 20 |
| 56 | HMV 7EG 8169 | THE GIRL WITH A LAUGH IN HER VOICE NO. 3 (EP) | 20 |
| 57 | HMV 7EG 8437 | SHE LOVES TO SING (EP) | 20 |
| 58 | HMV CLP 1152 | I LOVE TO SING (LP) | 30 |
| 61 | Columbia 33SX 1345 | ALMA SINGS WITH YOU IN MIND (LP, mono) | 20 |
| 62 | Columbia 33SX 1469 | HOW ABOUT LOVE! (LP, mono) | 20 |
| 61 | Columbia SCX 3391 | ALMA SINGS WITH YOU IN MIND (LP) | 20 |
| 62 | Columbia SCX 3459 | HOW ABOUT LOVE! (LP, stereo) | 20 |

*(see also Ronnie Hilton, Angela & Fans)*

### ALMA COGAN & FRANKIE VAUGHAN
| 54 | HMV 7M 226 | Do, Do, Do, Do, Do, Do, Do It Again/Jilted | 5 |
|----|-----------|-------------------------------------------|---|

*(see also Frankie Vaughan)*

### DON COGAN
| 58 | MGM MGM 984 | The Fountain Of Love/I'm Takin' Over | 25 |
|----|-------------|-------------------------------------|----|

### SHAYE COGAN
| 58 | Columbia DB 4055 | Billy Be Sure/Doodle Doodle Doo | 10 |
|----|------------------|--------------------------------|----|
| 60 | MGM MGM 1063 | Mean To Me/They Said It Couldn't Be Done | 25 |

*(see also Buddy Morrow)*

### ALAN COHEN BAND
| 72 | Argo ZDA 159 | BLACK, BROWN AND BEIGE (LP) | 80 |
|----|--------------|----------------------------|----|

### LEONARD COHEN
| 68 | CBS 3337 | Suzanne/So Long, Marianne | 7 |
|----|----------|--------------------------|---|
| 69 | CBS 4245 | Bird On The Wire/Seems So Long Ago, Nancy | 7 |
| 71 | CBS 7292 | Joan Of Arc/Diamonds In The Mine | 7 |
| 74 | CBS 2494 | Bird On The Wire (live)/Tonight Will Be Fine (live) | 7 |
| 74 | CBS 2699 | Lover Lover Lover/Who By Fire | 6 |
| 76 | CBS 4306 | Suzanne/Take This Longing | 6 |
| 77 | CBS 5882 | Memories/Don't Go Home With Your Hard-On | 6 |
| 78 | CBS 6095 | True Love Leaves No Traces/I Left A Woman Waiting | 6 |
| 68 | CBS BPG 63241 | SONGS OF LEONARD COHEN (LP, orange label, with stickered sleeve; mono) | 30 |
| 68 | CBS (S)BPG 63241 | SONGS OF LEONARD COHEN (LP, orange label, with stickered sleeve; stereo) | 20 |
| 68 | CBS 63241 | SONGS OF LEONARD COHEN (LP, orange label, re-pressing w/out prefix) | 15 |
| 69 | CBS M 63587 | SONGS FROM A ROOM (LP, mono) | 25 |
| 69 | CBS 63587 | SONGS FROM A ROOM (LP, stereo) | 20 |
| 71 | CBS S 69004 | SONGS OF LOVE & HATE (LP, orange label, with booklet) | 20 |
| 73 | CBS 65224 | LIVE SONGS (LP) | 15 |
| 77 | CBS 86042 | DEATH OF A LADIES MAN (LP, gatefold) | 20 |
| 84 | CBS 465569 | VARIOUS POSITIONS (LP) | 20 |
| 88 | CBS 460642 | I'M YOUR MAN (LP) | 15 |
| 92 | CBS 472498 | FUTURE (LP) | 25 |
| 97 | Simply Vinyl SVLP 008 | SONGS FROM A ROOM (LP, reissue, 180gm vinyl) | 20 |

### COIL (1)
| 79 | North'ton Wood H. HAV 1 | Motor Industry/Alcoholic Stork (p/s) | 25 |
|----|-------------------------|-------------------------------------|----|

### COIL (2)
| 85 | F & F/K.422 FFK 512 | Panic/Tainted Love/Aqua Regis (12", red vinyl, 'hair'-textured p/s) | 25 |
|----|--------------------|--------------------------------------------------------------------|----|
| 85 | F & F/K.422 FFK 512 | Panic/Tainted Love/Aqua Regis (12", black vinyl, 'hair'-textured p/s) | 15 |
| 86 | Force & Form/K.422 | The Anal Staircase/Blood From The Air/Ravenous (12", p/s, on clear vinyl) | 25 |
| 86 | Force & Form/K.422 ROTA 121 | The Anal Staircase/Blood From The Air/Ravenous (12", p/s) | 15 |
| 87 | Solar Lodge 001 | HELLRAISER (10" EP, coloured vinyl [clear or pink, 500 each]) | 25 |
| 90 | Shock SX 002 | Wrong Eye/Scope (pink p/s, signed & lettered A-Z, 26 only) | 45 |
| 90 | Shock SX 002 | Wrong Eye/Scope (974 with numbered white p/s) | 15 |
| 90 | Shock SX 002 | Wrong Eye/Scope (1,000 with un-numbered yellow p/s) | 10 |
| 90 | Shock SX 002 | Wrong Eye/Scope (green p/s, 300 only, some with gold/black sticker) | 25 |
| 92 | Clawfist 22 | Airborne Bells/Is Suicide A Solution (p/s, 1,250 only) | 25 |
| 94 | Loci S1 | Themes From Blue (p/s, 23 on yellow vinyl) | 60 |
| 94 | Loci S1 | Themes From Blue (p/s, 1,000 on blue vinyl) | 20 |
| 94 | Eskaton 001 | Nasa Arab/First Dark Ride (12", stickered plain black sleeve, 2,500 only) | 15 |
| 95 | Eskaton 003 | PHILM (10" EP, with poster, 50 on clear vinyl in handmade p/s) | 60 |
| 95 | Eskaton 003 | PHILM (10" EP, with poster, 2,000 only) | 12 |
| 86 | Threshold ROTA 1 | HORSE ROTORVATOR (LP, with A5 card insert & stickers) | 20 |
| 87 | Threshold House LOCI 1 | GOLD IS THE METAL (LP, red vinyl; with bonus 7": "The Wheel"/The Wheal, unfinished proof sleeve without writing, 25 only) | 200 |
| 87 | Threshold House LOCI 1 | GOLD IS THE METAL (LP, box set with 7", "The Wheel"/"The Wheal", poster & booklet in black linen folder, embossed sleeve, autographed, 55 only) | 300 |
| 87 | Threshold House LOCI 1 | GOLD IS THE METAL (LP, red vinyl [150 only] with inner sleeve; with bonus 7": "The Wheel"/"The Wheal") | 70 |
| 87 | Threshold House LOCI 1 | GOLD IS THE METAL (LP, clear vinyl [500 only], with inner sleeve; with bonus 7": "The Wheel"/"The Wheal") | 50 |
| 90 | Normal NORMAL 77 | GOLD IS THE METAL (LP, black vinyl re-pressing with 7": The Wheel/"Keel Hauler") | 18 |
| 95 | Eskaton 007 | WORSHIP THE GLITCH (2 x 10" LP, as Coil Vs. Elph, with insert, 50 with white optical plastic cover) | 55 |
| 95 | Eskaton 007 | WORSHIP THE GLITCH (2 x 10" LP, as Coil Vs. Elph, with insert, 2,000 only) | 25 |
| 99 | Acme/Prescription DRUG8 | ASTRAL DISASTER (LP, 99 copies signed and numbered by Balance And Christopherson, with insert, artwork in plastic bag) | 100 |
| 99 | Chalice GRAAL LP002 | MUSICK TO PLAY IN THE DARK VOL 1 (LP, 500 only, white vinyl) | 50 |
| 00 | Threshold House LOC114 | ASTRAL DISASTER (LP re-issue, 100 copies, grey vinyl signed lyric sheet and art | 60 |

| | | | |
|---|---|---|---|
| 00 | Chalice GRAAL LP004 | MUSICK TO PLAY IN THE DARK VOL 2 (2 x LP, white vinyl, one side etched) | 50 |
| 00 | Chalice GRAAL LP004 | MUSICK TO PLAY IN THE DARK VOL 2 (2 x LP, 100 copies with blue/green vinyl) | 50 |
| 00 | Chalice GRAAL LP004 | MUSICK TO PLAY IN THE DARK VOL 2 (2 x LP, translucent purple, 4th side etched with picture of moon and has 'gold leaf' attached, art print on cover, 2 part print inserts – signed – 60 copies only) | 300 |
| 00 | Chalice GRAAL LP004 | MUSICK VOL 2 (26 copy "trauma edition" lettered A-Z white sleeves smeared with Balance's blood.) | 70 |
| 02 | Eskaton 28 | TIME MACHINES (Coil as Time Machines) (2 x LP, 1,000 55 clear, signed) | 50 |
| 02 | Eskaton 28 | TIME MACHINES (Coil as Time Machines) (2 x LP, 1,000 only) | 40 |

*(see also Psychic TV, Throbbing Gristle, Current 93, Thighpaulsandra)*

## COINS
| | | | |
|---|---|---|---|
| 69 | Toast TT 513 | Love Power/You Can't Get Away From It | 8 |
| 69 | Toast TT 515 | Don't You Know It's Just A Game, Love? (actually by Miss White & Mr. Green)/Crying Over You | 6 |

## JAMES COIT
| | | | |
|---|---|---|---|
| 79 | Destiny DS 1004 | Black Power/Philadrine (p/s) | 5 |

## ALVADEAN COKER
| | | | |
|---|---|---|---|
| 55 | London HLU 8191 | Do Dee Oodle De Do I'm In Love/We're Gonna Bop | 750 |
| 55 | London HLU 8191 | Do Dee Oodle De Do I'm In Love/We're Gonna Bop (78) | 60 |

## SANDY COKER & HIS BAND
| | | | |
|---|---|---|---|
| 54 | London HL 8109 | Meadowlark Melody/Toss Over | 40 |

## COKI
| | | | |
|---|---|---|---|
| 05 | DMZ DMZ 004 | Officer/Mood Dub (12") | 20 |
| 07 | Big Apple BAM 009 | Red Eye/Beep/The Sign/Hidden Treasure (12") | 18 |
| 07 | SMZ DMZ 013 | Spongebob/The End (12") | 20 |

## RIC COLBECK QUARTET
| | | | |
|---|---|---|---|
| 70 | Fontana 6383 001 | THE SUN IS COMING UP (LP) | 75 |

## COLD BLOOD
| | | | |
|---|---|---|---|
| 70 | Atlantic 584 319 | You Got Me Hummin'/If You Will | 10 |
| 70 | Atlantic 588 218 | COLD BLOOD (LP, plum/red label) | 50 |
| 71 | Atlantic 2400 102 | SISYPHUS (LP, gatefold sleeve, plum/red label) | 18 |
| 74 | Warner Bros K 56047 | LYDIA (LP) | 15 |

## COLDCUT
| | | | |
|---|---|---|---|
| 91 | Ninja Tune ZEN12 004 | Jade (12") | 15 |
| 94 | Ninja Tune ZEN 12 | PHILOSOPHY (2xLP, promo, different mixes to commercial release) | 20 |

## COLD FISH
| | | | |
|---|---|---|---|
| 82 | CBS A2779 | Love Me Today/Strange Boy (p/s) | 6 |

## COLD FLY
| | | | |
|---|---|---|---|
| 73 | Bus Stop BUS 1007 | Caterpillar/Yesterday Started For Judy | 15 |

## COLD HAND BAND
| | | | |
|---|---|---|---|
| 82 | BK BK 12 | Tropicana/Instrumental | 12 |

## COLDPLAY
### SINGLES
| | | | |
|---|---|---|---|
| 98 | private pressing HGCD 633 | SAFETY EP: Bigger, Stronger/No More Keeping My Feet On The Ground/Such A Rush (CD, 500 only) | 400 |
| 99 | Fierce Panda NING 68 | Brothers And Sisters/Easy To Please (wraparound p/s, 1000 only) | 30 |
| 99 | Fierce Panda NING 68CD | Brothers And Sisters/Easy To Please/Only Superstition | 8 |
| 99 | EMI EMI CDR 6528 | THE BLUE ROOM EP (Bigger, Stronger/Don't Panic/See You Soon/High Speed/Such A Rush) (CD, digipak) | 30 |
| 99 | EMI EMI 12R 6528 | THE BLUE ROOM EP (Bigger, Stronger/Don't Panic/See You Soon/High Speed/Such A Rush) (12", numbered sleeve) | 30 |
| 00 | Parlophone R 6536 | Shiver/For You/Careful Where You Stand (p/s) | 8 |
| 00 | Parlophone R 6538 | Yellow/Help Is Around The Corner (7" ltd edn. Numbered single p/s) | 12 |
| 00 | Parlophone R 6549 | Trouble/Brothers And Sisters (p/s, numbered, stickered poly outer) | 10 |
| 01 | COLDXMAS01 | Mince Spies/Have Yourself A Merry Little Christmas/Yellow (Alpha Mix) (CD EP, 1000 only, given away with Coldplayground fanzine) | 120 |
| 01 | Parlophone 07243 879080-6-2 | Don't Panic/You Only Live Twice (live)/Bigger Stronger (live) (12" p/s, withdrawn) | 60 |
| 02 | Parlophone R 6588 | The Scientist/1:36/I Ran Away (p/s) | 7 |
| 03 | Parlophone R 6594 | Clocks/Crest Of Waves (p/s) | 7 |
| 03 | Parlophone 12 R 6594 | Clocks (Royksopp Trembling Heart Mix)/Royksopp Trembling Heart Instrumental Mix/God Put A Smile Upon Your Face (Def Inc. Remix feat. Mr. Thing) (12", die-cut sleeve, 1000 only) | 10 |
| 05 | Parlophone R6664 | Speed Of Sound/Things I Don't Understand/Proof (10", clear vinyl) | 5 |
| 07 | Parlophone 3883247 | THE SINGLES 1999 - 2006 (15 x 7" box set) | 50 |
| 09 | Parlophone R 676 | Life In Technicolour II/The Goldrush | 10 |
| 12 | Parlophone R6851 | Up With The Birds/UFO (die-cut sleeve) | 8 |
| 13 | Parlophone R6901 | Hurts Like Heaven/Up Against The World (live) (picture disc with comic) | 8 |

### ALBUMS
| | | | |
|---|---|---|---|
| 00 | Parlophone 5277831 | PARACHUTES (LP) | 15 |
| 02 | Parlophone 540 5041 | A RUSH OF BLOOD TO THE HEAD (LP, gatefold sleeve, with inner) | 18 |
| 05 | Parlophone 474 7861 | X&Y (LP, gatefold sleeve with slip case and poster) | 18 |
| 11 | Parlophone P 729 7262 | MYLO XYLOTO (LP in pop up sleeve with 12" picture disc and stencil) | 25 |
| 11 | EMI 087 5531 | MYLO XYLOTO (LP with poster) | 18 |

### PROMOS
| | | | |
|---|---|---|---|
| 98 | None | Ode To Deodorant/Brothers And Sisters (2-track cassette sent to concert promoters and radio DJ's. White label, attributed to The Coldplay with "contact Phil" and 0777 mobile no.) | 400 |
| 99 | Parlophone CDRDJ 6528 | THE BLUE ROOM EP (Bigger, Stronger/Don't Panic/See You Soon/High Speed/ Such A Rush) (CD digipak) | 40 |

MINT VALUE £

| 99 | Parlophone 12RDJ 6528 | THE BLUE ROOM EP (Bigger, Stronger/Don't Panic/See You Soon/High Speed/ Such A Rush) (12", blue vinyl) | 50 |
| 00 | Parlophone 12RDJ 6538 | Yellow/Help Is Round The Corner/No More Keeping My Feet On The Ground (12") | 15 |
| 06 | Parlophone (No cat no) | Talk (FK Dub Mix) 12" one-sided acetate 10 only DJ copies) | 40 |
| 05 | Parlophone COLDINT2 | X&Y (CD interview disc) | 25 |
| 06 | Parlophone (No cat. no) | Clocks (Royksopp remixes) (12" promo. die-cut sleeve) | 10 |
| 08 | Parlophone VIVA 001 | VIVA LA VIDA (OR DEATH AND ALL HIS FRIENDS) (LP, promo, 300 only) | 80 |
| 10 | Parlophone (No Cat No.) | Christmas Lights (CD-R, promo only) | 50 |

### COLD TURKEY
| 72 | Pye 7N 45142 | Nobody's Fool/Sesame Street | 15 |

### COLD WAR
| 83 | Namedrop NR 4 | The Machinist/Illusion (p/s) | 15 |

### ANN COLE
| 84 | Krazy Kat KK 782 | GOT MY MOJO WORKING (LP) | 15 |

### BILLY COLE
| 75 | Power Exchange 104 | Extra Careful/Bump All Night | 20 |

### B.J. COLE
| 73 | United Artists UAS 29418 | NEW HOVERING DOG (LP, laminated front sleeve) | 30 |
(see also Cochise)

### CINDY COLE
| 65 | Columbia DB 7519 | A Love Like Yours/He's Sure The Boy I Love | 25 |
| 66 | Columbia DB 7973 | Just Being Your Baby (Turns Me On)/Lonely City Blue Boy | 30 |
(see also Jeannie & Big Guys)

### CLAY COLE
| 62 | London HLP 9499 | Twist Around The Clock/Don't Twist (With Anyone Else But Me) | 10 |

### COZY COLE
| 58 | London HL 8750 | Topsy (Parts 1 & 2) | 10 |
| 58 | London HL 7065 | Topsy (Parts 1 & 2) (export issue) | 10 |
| 59 | Mercury AMT 1015 | St. Louis Blues/Father Co-operates | 5 |
| 59 | London HL 8843 | Turvy (Parts 1 & 2) | 10 |
| 62 | Coral Q 72457 | Big Noise From Winnetka (Parts 1 & 2) | 5 |

### DON COLE & ALLEYNE
| 65 | Fontana TF 522 | Gotta Find My Baby/Something's Gotta Hold Of Me | 5 |

### JERRY COLE
| 65 | Capitol CL 15397 | Every Window In The City/Come On Over To My Place | 5 |

### KEITH COLE
| 71 | Big BG 315 | Musical Attack/RUPIE EDWARDS ALLSTARS: Shack Attack | 8 |
| 71 | Big BG 316 | Music Alone Version 3/RUPIE EDWARDS ALLSTARS: Behold Another Version | 8 |

### LLOYD COLE & COMMOTIONS
| 84 | Welcome To L. Vegas LC 1 | Are You Ready To Be Heartbroken?/Down At The Mission (p/s, withdrawn) | 30 |
| 85 | Polydor COLET 5 | Lost Weekend (extended)/Big World/Lost Weekend - (7" version) (10" p/s) | 8 |
| 93 | Phonogram 518318-1 | BAD VIBES (LP, as Lloyd Cole) | 20 |

### NAT COLE
| 70 | Jackpot JP 717 | Pack Of Cards/RITA & NAT COLE: Spread Joy | 10 |
| 70 | Jackpot JP 718 | Love Making/SONNY BINNS & RITA: My Love | 20 |
| 70 | Jackpot JP 722 | Sugar Sugar/SONNY BINNS & RITA: Sign Off | 10 |
| 70 | Explosion EX 2022 | In The Summertime/Apollo Moon Walk | 12 |
| 70 | Creole CR 1002 | Me And My Life/Instrumental | 10 |
(see also Rita Alston)

### NIKKI COLE
| 70s | Dance Centre 023 | ELEMENTARY MODERN DANCE (LP) | 40 |
| 70s | Dance Centre DC020 | CONTEMPORARY DANCE - BEGINNERS VOL 1. (LP) | 40 |

### PATSY COLE
| 66 | Island WI 271 | Disappointed Bride/EARL BOSTIC: Honeymoon Night | 45 |

### ROCKY COLE
| 61 | Oriole CB 1635 | Heaven And Earth/Huey's Song | 5 |

### STRANGER COLE
| 63 | R&B JB 133 | Out Of Many/Nothing Tried | 25 |
| 63 | Island WI 110 | Stranger At The Door/Conqueror | 25 |
| 63 | Island WI 114 | Last Love/STRANGER & KEN: Hush Baby | 25 |
| 63 | Island WI 126 | We Are Rolling/Millie Maw | 25 |
| 64 | Island WI 137 | Goodbye Peggy (actually plays "Goodbye Peggy Darling" by Roy Panton)/ BABA BROOKS: Portrait Of My Love | 25 |
| 64 | R&B JB 129 | Morning Star/Beat Up Your Gum | 18 |
| 64 | Island WI 133 | Til My Dying Days/STRANGER & PATSY: I Need You | 20 |
| 64 | Black Swan WI 413 | Uno Dos Tres (act. with Ken Boothe)/Look (B-side actually by unknown artist) | 20 |
| 64 | Black Swan WI 415 | Summer Day/Loving You Always (both actually by Dottie & Bonnie) | 20 |
| 64 | Black Swan WI 435 | Little Boy Blue/ERIC MORRIS: Words Of Wisdom | 20 |
| 65 | Ska Beat JB 192 | Pussy Cat/MAYTALS: Sweet Sweet Jenny | 20 |
| 65 | Island WI 169 | Koo Koo Doo (with Owen & Leon)/GLORIA & DREAMLETTS: Stay Where You Are | 30 |
| 65 | Island WI 177 | Run Joe (with Baba Brooks)/Make Believe | 40 |
| 65 | Blue Beat BB 322 | When The Party Is Over/BUSTER'S ALLSTARS: Happy Independence '65 | 30 |
| 65 | Blue Beat BB 333 | Matilda (actually with Prince Buster)/BUSTER'S ALL STARS: When The Party Is Over | 35 |
| 66 | Doctor Bird DB 1025 | We Shall Overcome/Do You Really Love Me (as Stranger Cole & Seraphines) | 40 |
| 66 | Doctor Bird DB 1040 | Drop The Ratchet/Oh Yee Mahee (as Stranger Cole & Conquerors) | 25 |
| 67 | Doctor Bird DB 1066 | You Took My Love (actually by Patsy Todd)/FUGITIVES: Living Soul | 175 |
| 68 | Island WI 3154 | Jeboza Macoo/Now I Know (B-side actually with Gladdy Anderson) | 45 |
| 68 | Amalgamated AMG 801 | Just Like A River (as Stranger Cole & Gladdy)/LEADERS: Hope Someday | 30 |

| 69 | Amalgamated AMG 838 | What Mama Na Want She Get/We Two | 30 |
|----|---------------------|----------------------------------|----|
| 69 | Duke DU 27 | Glad You're Living/Help Wanted | 30 |
| 69 | Unity UN 501 | Last Flight To Reggae City (w/ Tommy McCook)/JUNIOR SMITH: Watch Dem Go | 30 |
| 69 | Unity UN 514 | When I Get My Freedom/Life Can Be Beautiful | 40 |
| 69 | Escort ES 810 | Pretty Cottage/To Me | 40 |
| 69 | Escort ES 811 | Why Did You/Do You Remember | 25 |
| 69 | Escort ES 819 | Leana Leana/Na Na Na | 25 |
| 69 | Escort ES 826 | Loneliness/Remember | 25 |
| 70 | Escort ES 830 | Little Things/Till The Well Runs Dry | 10 |
| 70 | Escort ES 831 | Everything With You/Picture On The Wall | 10 |
| 70 | Escort ES 832 | Pussy/Let Me In | 10 |
| 70 | Camel CA 54 | Everyday Tomorrow/Let Your Head Up High | 40 |
| 70 | Pama PM 790 | Come Dance With Me/Dance With Me | 10 |
| 71 | Bullet BU 488 | Soul Sop/Stranger Cole Medley | 15 |
| 71 | Camel CA 72 | Crying Every Night/DENNIS ALCAPONE & DELROY WILSON: It Must Come | 10 |
| 71 | Escort ERT 849 | Tomorrow/SONNY BURKE: Chicken Thief | 7 |
| 72 | Tropical AL 0011 | Mail Man (with Charlie Ace)/Mail Man (Version) | 7 |
| 72 | Jackpot JP 791 | My Confession/LASCELS & HORTENSE: The Might Organ | 6 |
| 72 | Pama PM 848 | The House Where Bombo Lives/Our High School Dance | 5 |

*(see also Stranger, Stranger & Gladys, Stranger & Patsy, Stranger & Ken, Rob Walker, Charmers, Lloyd Clarke, Don Drummond, Tommy McCook, Ernest Wilson, Delroy Wilson, Lester Sterling, Baba Brooks, Roland Alphonso)*

## TONY COLE
| 69 | Columbia DB 8604 | If I Were A Cat/Magdalena | 10 |
|----|------------------|---------------------------|----|

## BOBBY COLEMAN
| 66 | Pye International 7N 25365 | (Baby) You Don't Have To Tell Me/Pleasure Girl | 70 |
|----|---------------------------|-----------------------------------------------|----|
| 66 | Pye International 7N 25365 | (Baby) You Don't Have To Tell Me/Pleasure Girl (DJ Copy) | 100 |

## FITZROY COLEMAN
| 61 | Starlite ST45 064 | Lucilla/Caribbean Sunset | 6 |
|----|-------------------|--------------------------|---|

## LONNIE COLEMAN & JESSE ROBERTSON
| 56 | London HLU 8335 | Dolores Diane/Oh Honey, Why Don'tcha | 40 |
|----|-----------------|--------------------------------------|----|

## ORNETTE COLEMAN
| 60 | Contemporary LAC 12228 | TOMORROW IS THE QUESTION (LP) | 30 |
|----|------------------------|-------------------------------|----|
| 61 | London Jazz LTZ-K 15199 | CHANGE OF THE CENTURY (LP, mono) | 30 |
| 61 | London Jazz SAH-K 5099 | CHANGE OF THE CENTURY (LP, stereo) | 30 |
| 61 | London Jazz LTZ-K 15228 | THIS IS OUR MUSIC (LP, mono) | 30 |
| 62 | London Jazz LTZ-K 15241 | THE ORNETTE COLEMAN QUARTET (LP, mono) | 25 |
| 62 | London Jazz SAH-K 6235 | THE ORNETTE COLEMAN QUARTET (LP, stereo) | 35 |
| 62 | Atlantic 588121 | ORNETTE ON TENOR (LP) | 20 |
| 65 | Fontana SFJ 923 | TOWN HALL DECEMBER 1962 (LP) | 20 |
| 66 | Atlantic 588022 | THE SHAPE OF JAZZ TO COME (LP, mono/stereo) | 25 |
| 67 | CBS 66023 | CHAPPAQUA SUITE (2-LP) | 25 |
| 68 | Polydor 623 246/7 | AN EVENING WITH ORNETTE COLEMAN (2-LP) | 30 |
| 69 | Impulse SIPL 518 | ORNETTE AT 12 (LP) | 25 |
| 71 | Atlantic 2400 109 | THE AT OF THE IMPROVISERS (LP) | 20 |
| 72 | Atlantic K 40278 | TWINS (LP) | 25 |
| 77 | Blue Note BNS 40021 | AT THE GOLDEN CIRCLE STOCKHOLM (LP, reissue) | 20 |

## ROGER COLEMAN
| 60 | Top Rank JAR 311 | Nobody's Fool/Endlessly | 5 |
|----|------------------|-------------------------|---|

## COLETTE & BANDITS
| 65 | Stateside SS 416 | A Ladies Man/Lost Love | 20 |
|----|------------------|------------------------|----|

## COLEY
| 70s | Coley (Private Pressing) | GOODBYE BRAIN (LP) | 35 |
|-----|--------------------------|--------------------|----|

## COLLAGE
| 73 | Studio Two TWO 410 | MISTY (LP) | 30 |
|----|--------------------|------------|----|

*(see also Brian Bennett)*

## COLLECTIVE HORIZONTAL
| 79 | Dolmen DO 1 | COLLECTIVE HORIZONTAL EP (gatefold p/s, stickered white labels) | 20 |
|----|-------------|----------------------------------------------------------------|----|

## COLLECTORS (CANADA)
| 70 | London HLU 10304 | I Must Have Been Blind/The Beginning | 6 |
|----|------------------|--------------------------------------|---|
| 69 | Warner Bros WS 1774 | GRASS AND WILD STRAWBERRIES (LP) | 22 |

*(see also Chilliwack, Electric Prunes)*

## COLLECTORS (U.K.)
| 80 | Central Collection COL 1 | Different World/Talking Hands (p/s) | 15 |
|----|--------------------------|-------------------------------------|----|

## COLLEGE BOYS (JAMAICA)
| 64 | Blue Beat BB 202 | Love Is A Treasure/Someone Will Be There | 25 |
|----|------------------|------------------------------------------|----|

## COLLEGE BOYS (U.K.)
| 64 | Columbia DB 7306 | I Just Don't Understand/I'm Gonna Cry | 20 |
|----|------------------|---------------------------------------|----|
| 67 | Pye 7N 17294 | Good Times/San Antonio Rose | 10 |

## KEITH COLLEY
| 63 | Stateside SS 234 | Enamorado/No Joke | 8 |
|----|------------------|-------------------|---|

## GRAHAM COLLIER SEXTET/SEPTET
| 67 | Deram DML/SML 1005 | DEEP DARK BLUE CENTRE (LP) | 100 |
|----|--------------------|----------------------------|-----|
| 69 | Fontana SFJL 922 | DOWN ANOTHER ROAD (LP) | 90 |
| 70 | Fontana 6309 006 | SONGS FOR MY FATHER (LP, as Graham Collier Music featuring Harry Beckett) | 70 |
| 71 | Philips 6308 051 | MOSAICS (LP, live, as Graham Collier Music featuring Harry Beckett) | 45 |
| 72 | Saydisc SDL 244 | PORTRAITS (LP) | 25 |
| 75 | Mosaic GCM 751 | MIDNIGHT BLUE (LP) | 20 |

MINT VALUE £

75   Cambridge Univ 521205638   JAZZ LECTURE CONCERT (LP) ..................................................................... 40

*(see also Harry Beckett)*

## MITTY COLLIER
| | | | |
|---|---|---|---|
| 64 | Pye International 7N 25275 | I Had A Talk With My Man/Free Girl ............................................. | 20 |
| 64 | Pye International 7N 25275 | I Had A Talk With My Man/Free Girl (DJ Copy) ............................... | 40 |
| 69 | Peachtree P122 | I'd like To Change Places/Share What You Got ............................... | 20 |
| 15 | Outta Sight RSV 059 | Don't Let Her Take My Baby/BABY JEAN: If You Wanna ................... | 6 |

## ALBERT COLLINS
| | | | |
|---|---|---|---|
| 69 | Liberty LBS 585275 | TRASH TALKIN (LP) ......................................................................... | 30 |
| 69 | Liberty LBS 83238 | LOVE CAN BE FOUND ANYWHERE (LP) .............................................. | 40 |
| 73 | Tumbleweed TW 3501 | THERE'S GOTTA BE A CHANGE (LP) ................................................... | 30 |

## ANSEL(L) COLLINS
| | | | |
|---|---|---|---|
| 69 | Trojan TR 699 | Night Of Love/DERRICK MORGAN: Copy Cat .................................. | 15 |
| 69 | Trojan TR 7712 | Cotton Dandy/CARL DAWKINS: Don't Get Weary ........................... | 20 |
| 70 | Trojan TR 7729 | Moon Dust/Fat Cat ......................................................................... | 30 |
| 70 | Trojan TR 7730 | Monkey (Version I)/(Version II) (plays "High Voltage"/"High Voltage Version"; B-side actually by Beverley All Stars) ......................................................................... | 15 |
| 70 | J-Dan JDN 4401 | Cock Robin/KING DENNIS: Seven Zero .......................................... | 12 |
| 70 | Techniques TE 907 | Top Secret/Crazy Rhythm (both actually by Winston Wright) ......... | 15 |
| 71 | Techniques TE 913 | Nuclear Weapon/TECHNIQUES ALL STARS: La, La, La .................... | 15 |
| 11 | Techniques THB 7011 | Double Or Nothing/DANDY: Double Barrel Man ............................ | 18 |

*(see also Conquerors, Lloyd Young, Prince Buster, Les Foster, Ethiopians, Eternals, Pam Brooks, Dennis Alcapone, Rad Bryan, Immortals)*

## CLANCY COLLINS ALL STARS (ACTUALLY, LLOYD CHALMERS)
| | | | |
|---|---|---|---|
| 71 | Smash SMA 2321 | Sir Collins Special/Conqueror (Actually, LENNOX BROWN : Heart of Knights) ............... | 40 |

## DAVE & ANSELL COLLINS
| | | | |
|---|---|---|---|
| 72 | Techniques TE 915 | Karate/Doing Your Own Thing .......................................................... | 20 |
| 73 | Rhino RNO 111 | Hot Line/Sunshine Rock (label credits 'Dave Collins') ..................... | 15 |
| 71 | Trojan TBL 162 | DOUBLE BARREL (LP) ....................................................................... | 25 |
| 75 | Trojan TRLS12 | IN THE GHETTO (LP) ........................................................................ | 18 |

## DONIE COLLINS SHOWBAND
| | | | |
|---|---|---|---|
| 68 | Pye 7N 17682 | Get Down With It/I Can't Help Myself (Sugar Pie Honey Bunch) ...... | 10 |

## DOROTHY COLLINS
| | | | |
|---|---|---|---|
| 55 | Vogue Coral Q 72111 | My Boy - Flat Top/In Love .............................................................. | 30 |
| 56 | Vogue Coral Q 72116 | Moments To Remember/Love And Marriage ..................................... | 5 |
| 56 | Vogue Coral Q 72137 | Seven Days/Manuello ...................................................................... | 10 |
| 56 | Vogue Coral Q 72173 | Treasure Of Love/He's Got Me, Hook, Line And Sinker ..................... | 10 |
| 56 | Vogue Coral Q 72193 | Love Me As Though There Were No Tomorrow/Rock And Roll Train | 30 |
| 56 | Vogue Coral Q 72198 | The Italian Theme/Cool It, Baby ...................................................... | 30 |
| 56 | Vogue Coral Q 72208 | The Twelve Gifts Of Christmas/Mr. Santa ....................................... | 5 |
| 57 | Vogue Coral Q 72232 | Baby Can Rock/Would You Ever ...................................................... | 30 |
| 57 | Vogue Coral Q 72252 | Mr. Wonderful/I Miss You Already .................................................. | 5 |
| 57 | Vogue Coral Q 72262 | Four Walls/Big Dreams .................................................................... | 5 |
| 57 | Vogue Coral Q 72287 | Soft Sands/Sing It, Children, Sing It ................................................ | 5 |
| 59 | Top Rank JAR 259 | Baciare, Baciare/Everything I Have Is Yours ................................... | 5 |
| 60 | Top Rank JAR 401 | Banjo Boy/Tintarella Di Luna .......................................................... | 5 |
| 60 | Top Rank JAR 523 | Unlock Those Chains/I'll Be Yours, You'll be Mine ......................... | 5 |
| 55 | London REP 1025 | DOROTHY COLLINS SINGS (EP) ...................................................... | 30 |
| 57 | Coral LVA 9058 | AT HOME WITH DOROTHY AND RAYMOND (LP) ............................. | 20 |

## EDWYN COLLINS
| | | | |
|---|---|---|---|
| 87 | Creation CRE 047T | Don't Shilly Shally/If Ever You're Ready (7" white label test pressing only) ................... | 40 |
| 87 | Creation CRE 047T | Don't Shilly Shally/If Ever You're Ready (12", white label test pressing only) .............. | 35 |
| 87 | Elevation ACIDB 6 | My Beloved Girl/50 Shades Of Blue (Acoustic Version)/Clouds (Fogging Up My Mind)/What's The Big Idea? (box set with 3 postcards) ................ | 6 |
| 08 | Heavenly HVN 180 | Home Again/Searching For The Truth (7", 1500 copies in sealed brown envelope in PVC sleeve) ................ | 8 |
| 08 | Heavenly HVN 180 | Home Again/Searching For The Truth (7" one of 25 copies with hand decorated insert by 25 different people including John Squire, Nicky Wire, Billy Childish and Jarvis Cocker) ................ | 50 |
| 94 | Setanta SETLP14 | GORGEOUS GEORGE (LP, inner) .................................................... | 25 |
| 97 | Setanta SETLP039 | I'M NOT FOLLOWING YOU (LP, inner) .......................................... | 15 |

*(see also Orange Juice, Paul Quinn & Edwyn Collins)*

## GLENDA COLLINS
| | | | |
|---|---|---|---|
| 60 | Decca F 11280 | Take A Chance/Crazy Guy ............................................................... | 15 |
| 61 | Decca F 11321 | Oh How I Miss You Tonight/Age For Love ...................................... | 15 |
| 61 | Decca F 11417 | Head Over Heels In Love/Find Another Fool .................................. | 15 |
| 63 | HMV POP 1163 | I Lost My Heart In The Fairground/I Feel So Good .......................... | 60 |
| 63 | HMV POP 1233 | If You Gotta Pick A Baby/In The First Place ................................... | 80 |
| 64 | HMV POP 1283 | Baby It Hurts/Nice Wasn't It ........................................................... | 65 |
| 64 | HMV POP 1323 | Lollipop/Everybody's Got To Fall In Love ....................................... | 50 |
| 65 | HMV POP 1439 | Johnny Loves Me/Paradise for Two ................................................ | 50 |
| 65 | HMV POP 1475 | Thou Shall Not Steal/Been Invited To A Party ............................... | 50 |
| 66 | Pye 7N 17044 | Something I've Got To Tell You/My Heart Didn't Lie ...................... | 75 |
| 66 | Pye 7N 17150 | It's Hard To Believe It/Don't Let It Rain On Sunday ...................... | 75 |
| 90 | Document CSAP LP 108 | BEEN INVITED TO A PARTY (LP) ..................................................... | 20 |

## JOHNNY COLLINS
| | | | |
|---|---|---|---|
| 75 | Tradition TSR 020 | JOHNNY'S PRIVATE ARMY (LP) ..................................................... | 18 |

## JOHNNY COLLINS & FRIENDS
| | | | |
|---|---|---|---|
| 73 | Tradition TSR 014 | THE TRAVELLER'S REST (LP, dark blue label, laminated sleeve) ...... | 18 |

## JUDY COLLINS
| | | | |
|---|---|---|---|
| 66 | London HLZ 10029 | I'll Keep It With Mine/Thirsty Boots | 12 |
| 69 | Elektra EKSN 45077 | Turn, Turn, Turn/Mr. Tambourine Man | 5 |
| 65 | Elektra EKL 209 | MAID OF CONSTANT SORROW (LP) | 15 |

## KEANYA COLLINS
| | | | |
|---|---|---|---|
| 77 | Grapevine 105 | Barnabus Collins - Love Bandit/I Call You Daddy (reissue) | 8 |

## LYN COLLINS
| | | | |
|---|---|---|---|
| 64 | Sabre SA 0002 | What Am I Gonna Do Without You?/When A Girl Meets A Bad, Bad Boy | 20 |
| 74 | Polydor 2066 490 | Rock Me Again And Again And Again And Again And Again And Again/Wide Awake In A Dream | 15 |
| 74 | Mojo 2093 029 | Think (About It)/Me And My Baby Got Our Own Thing Going | 10 |
| 72 | Polydor 2918 006 | THINK (ABOUT IT) (LP) | 40 |

*(see also James Brown)*

## PETER COLLINS
| | | | |
|---|---|---|---|
| 70 | Decca F 13048 | Get In A Boat/Girl By The Sea | 6 |
| 70 | Decca Nova SDN 21 | PETER COLLINS (LP, blue/silver label) | 20 |

## RODGER COLLINS
| | | | |
|---|---|---|---|
| 67 | Vocalion VF 9285 | She's Looking Good/I'm Serving Time | 40 |
| 67 | Vocalion VF 9285 | She's Looking Good/I'm Serving Time (DJ copy) | 70 |
| 76 | Fantasy FTC 134 | She's Looking Good/I'm Serving Time (reissue) | 5 |

## SHIRLEY COLLINS
| | | | |
|---|---|---|---|
| 60 | Collector JEI 1508 | SINGS IRISH (EP) | 70 |
| 60 | Collector JEB 3 | THE FOGGY DEW (EP) | 70 |
| 60 | Collector JEB 5 | ENGLISH SONGS (EP) | 70 |
| 64 | Collector JEB 9 | ENGLISH SONGS VOL. 2 (EP, with Robin Hall) | 70 |
| 63 | Topic TOP 95 | HEROES IN LOVE (EP) | 70 |
| 59 | Folkways FG 3564 | FALSE TRUE LOVERS (LP) | 200 |
| 60 | Argo RG 150 | SWEET ENGLAND (LP, blue/silver label) | 300 |
| 64 | Decca LK 4652 | FOLK ROOTS, NEW ROUTES (LP, insert, with Davy Graham) | 320 |
| 67 | Topic 12T 170 | THE SWEET PRIMROSES (LP, original pressing with blue label) | 50 |
| 67 | Topic 12T 170 | THE SWEET PRIMROSES (LP) | 25 |
| 68 | Polydor 583 025 | THE POWER OF THE TRUE LOVE KNOT (LP, with Incredible String Band) | 250 |
| 71 | Pegasus PEG 7 | NO ROSES (LP, gatefold sleeve, with Albion Country Band) | 55 |
| 74 | Topic 12T 238 | ADIEU TO OLD ENGLAND (LP, original pressing with blue label) | 40 |
| 74 | Topic 12T 238 | ADIEU TO OLD ENGLAND (LP) | 25 |
| 75 | Deram SML 1117 | A FAVOURITE GARLAND (LP) | 50 |
| 76 | Harvest SHSM 2008 | AMARANTH (LP, textured sleeve) | 35 |
| 76 | Mooncrest CREST 011 | NO ROSES (LP, reissue, gatefold sleeve) | 25 |
| 78 | Topic 12T 380 | FOR AS MANY AS WILL (LP) | 20 |
| 81 | Righteous GDC 001 | FOLK ROOTS, NEW ROUTES (LP, reissue, with Davy Graham) | 20 |
| 83 | Hannibal HNBL 1327 | THE POWER OF THE TRUE LOVE KNOT (LP, reissue) | 20 |
| 91 | Mooncrest CREST 011 | NO ROSES (LP, reissue) | 15 |
| 05 | Boweavil WEAVIL 05 | FALSE TRUE LOVERS (LP, reissue) | 20 |
| 05 | Boweavil WEAVIL 06 | THE POWER OF THE TRUE LOVE KNOT (LP, reissue) | 20 |

## SHIRLEY & DOLLY COLLINS
| | | | |
|---|---|---|---|
| 69 | Harvest SHVL 754 | ANTHEMS IN EDEN (LP, gatefold sleeve, with "Sold in U.K..." text on 4 lines) | 175 |
| 69 | Harvest SHVL 754 | ANTHEMS IN EDEN (LP, gatefold sleeve, later issue with EMI logo on label) | 100 |
| 70 | Harvest SHVL 771 | LOVE, DEATH AND THE LADY (LP, gatefold sleeve, no EMI logo on label) | 140 |
| 87 | See for Miles SEE57 | ANTHEMS IN EDEN (LP, reissue) | 20 |
| 87 | Beat Goes On BGOLP1 | LOVE, DEATH AND THE LADY (LP, reissue, gatefold) | 25 |

*(see also Davy Graham, Albion Country Band, Conundrum)*

## STEVE COLLINS
| | | | |
|---|---|---|---|
| 73 | Big Shot BI 620 | Ding A Ling Ting A Ling/Run Rhythm Run | 15 |

## TERRY COLLINS
| | | | |
|---|---|---|---|
| 74 | Warner Bros. K16426 | I L.O.V.E. You/Action Speaks Louder | 7 |

## COLLINS BAND & BOB STACKIE
| | | | |
|---|---|---|---|
| 68 | Collins Downbeat | Bob Stackie In Soho/LORD CHARLES & HIS BAND: Jamaican Bits And Pieces | 45 |

## JOE COLMAN
| | | | |
|---|---|---|---|
| 90 | Blast First FU10 | INFERNAL MACHINE (LP, picture disc, 1,000 only) | 18 |

## COLONEL (1)
| | | | |
|---|---|---|---|
| 75 | Ring O' 2017 104 | Cokey Cokey/Away In A Manger (company sleeve) | 10 |

## COLONEL (2)
| | | | |
|---|---|---|---|
| 80 | Virgin VS 380 | Too Many Cooks (In The Kitchen)/I Need Protection (p/s) | 6 |

*(see also XTC)*

## COLONEL BAGSHOT
| | | | |
|---|---|---|---|
| 71 | Parlophone R 5893 | Georgia Fireball/Look In Her Eyes | 15 |

## COLORADOS
| | | | |
|---|---|---|---|
| 64 | Oriole CB 1972 | Lips Are Redder Than You/Who You Gonna Hurt? | 30 |

## COLOR TAPES
| | | | |
|---|---|---|---|
| 79 | Wavelength HURT 4 | Cold Anger/Leaves Of China (p/s) | 6 |

## COLOSSEUM
| | | | |
|---|---|---|---|
| 69 | Fontana TF 1029 | Walking In The Park/Those About To Die | 15 |
| 69 | Fontana STL 5510 | THOSE WHO ARE ABOUT TO DIE SALUTE YOU (LP, gatefold sleeve, black/silver labels) | 150 |
| 69 | Vertigo VO 1 | VALENTYNE SUITE (LP, gatefold sleeve, large swirl label with Philips credit & inner bag) | 150 |
| 70 | Vertigo 6360 017 | DAUGHTER OF TIME (LP, gatefold sleeve, with large swirl label & bag) | 200 |
| 70 | Vertigo 6360 017 | DAUGHTER OF TIME (LP, gatefold sleeve, small swirl label) | 30 |

MINT VALUE £

| 71 | Bronze ICD 1 | COLOSSEUM LIVE (2-LP, gatefold, plastic inner) | 40 |
| 72 | Bronze HELP 4 | VALENTYNE SUITE (LP, reissue with rarer HELP 4 cat no) | 20 |
| 72 | Bronze BRNA 214 | VALENTYNE SUITE (LP, reissue) | 15 |

*(see also Bakerloo, Dick Heckstall-Smith, Chris Farlowe, Greenslade, Humble Pie, John Mayall, Howard Riley Trio, Tempest, Mogul Thrash)*

## COLOSSEUM II
| 77 | Mercury MCF 2800 | ELECTRIC SAVAGE (LP) | 15 |

## COLOURBOX
| 82 | 4AD AD 215 | Breakdown/Tarantula (p/s) | 6 |
| 83 | 4AD AD 304 | Breakdown (Second Version)/Tarantula (Second Version) (different p/s) | 5 |
| 86 | 4AD 605 | The Official Colourbox World Cup Theme/Philip Glass (p/s) | 5 |
| 85 | 4AD CAD 508 | COLOURBOX (LP, stickered sleeve, 10,000 only, with bonus LP MAD 509) | 18 |

## COLOURED RAISINS
| 70 | Trojan TR 7700 | One Way Love/No More Heartaches | 7 |

*(see also Raisins)*

## COLOURFIELD
| 84 | Chrysalis COLF D2 | Thinking Of You/Wild Flames//Little Things/Thinking Of You (double pack) | 5 |
| 85 | Chrysalis COLF D4 | Castles In The Air/Your Love Was Smashing//I Can't Get Enough Of You Baby/Castles In The Air (Instrumental Mix) (double pack, gatefold p/s) | 5 |

*(see also Specials)*

## COLOURFUL SEASONS
| 68 | MGM MGM 1433 | Out Of The Blue/It's Gonna Break My Heart | 6 |

## COLO(U)RS OF LOVE
| 68 | Page One POF 060 | I'm A Train/Up On A Cotton Cloud | 8 |
| 68 | Page One POF 086 | Just Another Fly/Twenty Ten | 8 |
| 69 | Page One POF 124 | Mother Of Convention/Music Mother Made | 8 |
| 75 | DJM DJS 625 | I Can Dream Can't I?/I'll Be Seeing You | 6 |

## COLOURS (1)
| 68 | Dot 113 | Bad Day At Black Rock, Baby/Love Heals | 6 |

## COLOURS (2)
| 80 | See Saw Sounds SAW 1 | Dierdre Is An Artist/Over My Head/Facts Of Live (p/s) | 12 |

## COLOURS OUT OF TIME
| 81 | Minsters In Orbit TVEYE 1 | Dancing With Joy/Rock Section/Mambo Girls Mambo (hand-made pasted sleeve) | 10 |
| 82 | TVEYE 007 | She Spins/The Ocean Monsters In Orbit | 10 |

## CHRISTOPHER COLT
| 68 | Decca F 12726 | Virgin Sunrise/Girl In The Mirror | 40 |

## TONY COLTON('S BIG BOSS BAND)
| 64 | Decca F 11879 | Lose My Mind/So Used To Loving You (solo) | 30 |
| 65 | Pye 7N 15886 | I Stand Accused/Further On Down The Track (with Big Boss Band) | 200 |
| 66 | Pye 7N 17046 | You're Wrong There Baby/Have You Lost Your Mind | 40 |
| 66 | Pye 7N 17117 | I've Laid Some Down In My Time/Run Pony Rider | 50 |
| 68 | Columbia DB 8385 | In The World Of Marnie Dreaming/Who Is She? (solo) | 25 |

*(see also Poet & One Man Band, Head Hands & Feet, Real McCoy, Peter B's)*

## ALICE COLTRANE
| 76 | Impulse! AS 9156 | A MONASTIC TRIO (LP, reissue) | 20 |

## JOHN COLTRANE
| 58 | Esquire 32-079 | THE FIRST TRANE (LP) | 60 |
| 58 | Esquire 32-089 | SOUL TRANE (LP) | 100 |
| 59 | Esquire 32-091 | TRANEING IN (LP) | 40 |
| 60 | Esquire 32-101 | CATTIN' (LP) | 40 |
| 60 | London Jazz LTZ-K 15197 | GIANT STEPS (LP) | 150 |
| 61 | Esquire 32-129 | LUSH LIFE (LP) | 35 |
| 61 | London Jazz LTZ-K 15219 | COLTRANE JAZZ (LP, also stereo SAH-K 6162) | 25 |
| 62 | London Jazz LTZ-K 15232 | BAGS AND TRANE (LP, also stereo SAH-K 6192) | 25 |
| 62 | Columbia 33SX 1399 | THE BIRDLAND STORY VOL. 1: ECHOES OF AN ERA (LP) | 20 |
| 62 | London Jazz LTZ-K 15239 | OLE COLTRANE (LP, mono) | 20 |
| 62 | London Jazz SAH-K 6223 | OLE COLTRANE (LP, stereo) | 25 |
| 62 | HMV CLP 1548 | AFRICA/BRASS (LP, mono) | 30 |
| 62 | HMV SCD 1431 | AFRICA/BRASS (LP, stereo) | 45 |
| 62 | HMV CLP 1590 | LIVE AT THE VILLAGE VANGUARD (LP, mono) | 25 |
| 62 | HMV CSD 1456 | LIVE AT THE VILLAGE VANGUARD (LP, stereo) | 30 |
| 63 | United Artists (S)ULP 1018 | COLTRANE TIME (LP) | 26 |
| 63 | London HA-K/SH-K 8017 | COLTRANE PLAYS THE BLUES (LP, as John Coltrane Group) | 30 |
| 63 | Esquire 32-179 | STANDARD COLTRANE (LP) | 35 |
| 63 | HMV CLP 1629 | COLTRANE (LP, also stereo CSD 1483) | 30 |
| 63 | HMV CLP 1647 | BALLADS (LP, also stereo CSD 1496) | 25 |
| 63 | HMV CLP 1657 | DUKE ELLINGTON & JOHN COLTRANE (LP, mono) | 25 |
| 63 | HMV CSD 1502 | DUKE ELLINGTON & JOHN COLTRANE (LP, stereo) | 30 |
| 64 | HMV CLP 1695 | IMPRESSIONS (LP, mono) | 30 |
| 64 | HMV CSD 1509 | IMPRRESSIONS (LP, stereo) | 35 |
| 64 | HMV CLP 1700 | JOHN COLTRANE WITH JOHNNY HARTMAN (LP) | 30 |
| 64 | Realm RM 157 | ON WEST 42ND STREET (LP) | 25 |
| 64 | Realm RM 181 | TRANE RIDE (LP) | 25 |
| 64 | HMV CLP 1741 | LIVE AT BIRDLAND (LP, also stereo CSD 1544) | 30 |
| 65 | HMV CLP 1799 | CRESCENT (LP, mono) | 30 |
| 65 | HMV SCD 1567 | CRESCENT (LP, stereo) | 35 |
| 65 | Stateside SL 10124 | BLACK PEARLS (LP) | 30 |
| 65 | HMV CLP 1869 | A LOVE SUPREME (LP, mono) | 40 |
| 65 | HMV CSD 1605 | A LOVE SUPREME (LP, stereo) | 60 |

| 65 | Atlantic ATL/SAL 5022 | MY FAVOURITE THINGS (LP) | 25 |
|---|---|---|---|
| 65 | Realm RM 52226 | TANGANYIKA STRUT (LP) | 25 |
| 65 | HMV CLP 1897 | COLTRANE PLAYS (LP, also stereo CSD 1619) | 30 |
| 66 | Stateside SL 10162 | BAHIA (LP) | 30 |
| 66 | HMV CLP/CSD 3543 | ASCENSION (LP, as John Coltrane Orchestra) | 45 |
| 66 | HMV CLP/CSD 3551 | NEW THING AT NEWPORT (LP, with Archie Shepp) | 40 |
| 66 | Atlantic 587/588 004 | THE AVANT-GARDE (LP, with Don Cherry) | 40 |
| 66 | HMV CLP 3575 | MEDITATIONS (LP, mono) | 30 |
| 66 | HMV CSD 3575 | MEDITATIONS (LP, flipback sleeve stereo) | 35 |
| 67 | Atlantic 587/588 039 | COLTRANE'S SOUND (LP) | 30 |
| 67 | HMV CLP/CSD 3599 | COLTRANE LIVE AT THE VILLAGE VANGUARD AGAIN! (LP) | 30 |
| 67 | HMV CLP/CSD 3617 | OM (LP, withdrawn) | 50 |
| 67 | HMV CLP/CSD 3617 | KULU SE MAMA (LP) | 25 |
| 68 | Transatlantic PR 7280 | DAKAR (LP) | 30 |
| 68 | Transatlantic PR 7378 | LAST TRANE (LP) | 30 |
| 68 | Impulse MIPL 502 | EXPRESSION (LP, mono) | 30 |
| 68 | Impulse SIPL 502 | EXPRESSION (LP, stereo) | 20 |
| 69 | Atlantic 588 139 | THREE LITTLE WORDS (LP) | 25 |
| 69 | Impulse MIPL/SIPL 515 | COSMIC MUSIC (LP, by Alice & John Coltrane) | 35 |
| 70 | Impulse SIPL 522 | SELFLESSNESS (LP) | 25 |
| 71 | Probe SPB 1025 | AFRO BLUE (LP) | 25 |
| 72 | Prestige PR 24003 | JOHN COLTRANE (2-LP) | 25 |
| 74 | CBS PR 24037 | BLACK PEARLS (2-LP) | 25 |

*(see also Miles Davis, Thelonious Monk, Cannonball Adderley, Archie Shepp)*

## COLUMBIA BOYS
| 68 | Pye 7N 17513 | Baby Come Back/Born To Lose | 8 |
|---|---|---|---|
| 69 | Pye 7N 17763 | That's My Pa/She Thinks I Still Care | 7 |

## COLUMBUS
| 70 | Deram DM 294 | Ev'rybody Loves The U.S. Marshall/So Tired | 10 |
|---|---|---|---|

## RAY COLUMBUS INVADERS
| 60s | Zodiac AZ/1009 | She's A Mod/INVADERS : Cruel Sea | 20 |
|---|---|---|---|

## STEVE COLYER
| 75 | Polydor 2058 647 | Hey Mary/I Found My Sunshine | 6 |
|---|---|---|---|

## KEN COLYER'S SKIFFLE GROUP
| 55 | Decca F 10631 | Down By The Riverside/Take This Hammer | 20 |
|---|---|---|---|
| 56 | Decca FJ 10711 | Streamline Train/Go Down Old Hannah | 20 |
| 56 | Decca FJ 10751 | Down Bound Train/Mule Skinner | 20 |
| 56 | Decca FJ 10772 | Old Riley/Stack O'Lee Blues | 10 |
| 57 | Decca FJ 10889 | The Grey Goose/I Can't Sleep | 10 |
| 57 | Decca FJ 10926 | Sporting Life/House Rent Stomp | 10 |
| 57 | Decca FJ 10972 | Ella Speed/Go Down Sunshine | 10 |
| 55 | Decca DFE 6286 | KEN COLYER'S SKIFFLE GROUP (EP, various coloured sleeves) | 20 |
| 58 | Decca DFE 6444 | KEN COLYER'S SKIFFLE GROUP NO. 2 (EP) | 15 |
| 60 | Decca DFE 6563 | KEN COLYER'S SKIFFLE GROUP IN HAMBURG (EP) | 10 |

*(see also Crane Skiffle Group)*

## VEE COMA
| 62 | Pun PUN 001 | Piccadilly/Independence Day | 15 |
|---|---|---|---|

## COMBAT 84
| 82 | Victory VIC 1 | ORDERS OF THE DAY (EP, wraparound p/s) | 20 |
|---|---|---|---|
| 83 | Victory VIC 2 | Rapist/The Right To Choose/Barry Prudom (p/s) | 20 |

## PETER COMBE
| 78 | Voyage VOY 001 | Music Of The Day (Sing Birds Sing)/You Baby On My Mind | 6 |
|---|---|---|---|

## COMBINATIONS
| 72 | Punch PH 99 | 1 2 3 A B C/Zee | 15 |
|---|---|---|---|

## COMBO A
| 80 | Broderick BROD 1 | Smalltown/Lead By The Neck | 8 |
|---|---|---|---|

## COME
| 81 | Come Org. WDC 883012 | Come Sunday (cassette) | 60 |
|---|---|---|---|
| 79 | Come Org. WDC 88001 | Come Sunday/Shaved Slits (p/s) | 40 |
| 79 | Come Org. WDC 883001 | COME PRESENT RAMPTON (cassette) | 60 |
| 79 | Come Org. WDC 88203 | PRESENT RAMPTON (LP) | 100 |
| 81 | Come Org. WDC 881012 | I'M JACK (LP, orange vinyl with insert) | 80 |

*(see also Whitehouse, New Order)*

## COME ON
| 80 | Aura AUS 120 | Housewives Play Tennis/Howard After 6 (p/s) | 10 |
|---|---|---|---|

## COMET GAIN
| 94 | Soul Static SOUL 5 | HOLLOWAY SWEETHEARTS EP | 10 |
|---|---|---|---|
| 96 | Wiiija WIJ 50V | SAY YES TO INTERNATIONAL SOCIALISM EP | 10 |
| 97 | Wiiija WIJ 66 | Strength/A Film By Kenneth Anger/Letting Go (p/s) | 8 |
| 98 | Mei Mei MEI 001 | Jack Nance Hair/We Are All Rotten/Record Prayer (p/s) | 8 |
| 01 | Fortuna Pop! FPOP 26 | You Can't Hide Your Love Forever/Beatnik (p/s) | 10 |
| 95 | Wiiija WIJ 042V | CASINO CLASSICS (LP) | 25 |
| 02 | Milou Studios 2MILLP | REALISTES (LP) | 20 |

## COMETS SHOWGROUP
| 70 | LRC SCG 1 | COMETS ON LOCATION (LP, private pressing, handmade sleeve) | 50 |
|---|---|---|---|

## COMMANCHES
| 64 | Pye 7N 15609 | Tomorrow/Missed Your Loving | 10 |
|---|---|---|---|

MINT VALUE £

*(see also Bobby Allen)*

## COMMANDERS
| | | | |
|---|---|---|---|
| 55 | Brunswick 05366 | The Elephants' Tango/Commanders Overture | 5 |
| 55 | Brunswick 05433 | The Cat From Coos Bay/Camptown Boogie | 5 |
| 55 | Brunswick 05467 | The Monster/Cornball No. 1 | 5 |

## COMMENDABLES
| | | | |
|---|---|---|---|
| 80s | Lip CC 1 | London E1/Decaying House | 10 |

## COMMERCIAL ACROBATS
| | | | |
|---|---|---|---|
| 81 | Teesbeat TB1 | LITTLE MIXED UP (EP, front and back insert p/s with photo inside) | 10 |

## COMMERCIALS
| | | | |
|---|---|---|---|
| 81 | Fast Product COM 1 | Sixteen Again And Again/The Heroine Dies/Simon (p/s) | 8 |

## COMMITTED
| | | | |
|---|---|---|---|
| 79 | Ace ACE 006 | Crash Victim/British Crimes/Fast Lane/Advertising (500 only) | 100 |

## COMMITTEE (1)
| | | | |
|---|---|---|---|
| 68 | Liberty LBF 15154 | Hard Way/Hey You | 15 |

## COMMITTEE (2)
| | | | |
|---|---|---|---|
| 69 | Pye 7N 17826 | Sleep Tight Honey/Memories Of Melinda | 6 |

## COMMODORES (1)
| | | | |
|---|---|---|---|
| 55 | London HLD 8209 | Riding On A Train/Uranium | 200 |
| 56 | London HLD 8251 | Speedo/Whole Lotta Shakin' Goin' On | 200 |

## COMMODORES (2)
| | | | |
|---|---|---|---|
| 69 | Atlantic 584 273 | Keep On Dancing/Rise Up | 30 |

## COMMOTION UPSTAIRS
| | | | |
|---|---|---|---|
| 89 | Saucy SAUCY TT 17 | Lift Me Up/Not Like That/Too Bad/Fake (p/s) | 100 |

## COMMUTERS
| | | | |
|---|---|---|---|
| 79 | Long Corporation LONE 001 | Small Talk/Let's Talk About Girls/Angeline (p/s) | 5 |

## PERRY COMO
| | | | |
|---|---|---|---|
| 53 | HMV 7M 102 | The Ruby And The Pearl/My Love And Devotion | 8 |
| 53 | HMV 7M 110 | Some Enchanted Evening/Bali Ha'i | 8 |
| 53 | HMV 7M 118 | Don't Let The Stars Get In Your Eyes/To Know You (Is To Love You) (B-side with Fontane Sisters) | 12 |
| 53 | HMV 7M 124 | Wild Horses/Please Believe Me | 5 |
| 53 | HMV 7M 138 | My Lady Loves To Dance/A Bushel And A Peck (B-side with Betty Hutton) | 5 |
| 53 | HMV 7M 149 | My One And Only Heart/Say You're Mine Again | 5 |
| 53 | HMV 7M 155 | Hello, Young Lovers/We Kiss In A Shadow | 5 |
| 53 | HMV 7M 163 | Pa-Paya Mama/Why Did You Leave Me? | 5 |
| 54 | HMV 7M 175 | You Alone/Surprising | 5 |
| 54 | HMV 7M 200 | Idle Gossip/Look Out The Window | 5 |
| 54 | HMV 7M 215 | Wanted/Give Me Your Hand | 5 |
| 54 | HMV 7M 241 | Hit And Run Affair/If You Were Only Mine | 5 |
| 54 | HMV 7M 263 | There Never Was A Night So Beautiful/Papa Loves Mambo | 20 |
| 54 | HMV 7M 278 | Frosty The Snowman/The Twelve Days Of Christmas | 15 |
| 55 | HMV 7M 296 | Ko Ko Mo (I Love You So)/You'll Always Be My Lifetime Love | 15 |
| 55 | HMV 7M 305 | Door Of Dreams/Nobody | 5 |
| 55 | HMV 7M 326 | There's No Place Like Home For The Holidays/Tina Marie | 5 |
| 56 | HMV 7M 366 | Fooled/The Rose Tattoo | 5 |
| 56 | HMV 7M 404 | Hot Diggity (Dog Ziggity Boom)/My Funny Valentine | 15 |
| 56 | HMV 7MC 39 | Hot Diggity (Dog Ziggity Boom)/Juke Box Baby (export issue) | 10 |

*(see also Fontane Sisters, Betty Hutton)*

## COMPANY OF COWARDS
| | | | |
|---|---|---|---|
| 87 | Company Of Cowards COC 1 | 18 AGAIN EP (12") | 70 |

## COMPANY (1)
| | | | |
|---|---|---|---|
| 79 | United Artists BP 326 | We Wish You Well/Right Time For Love | 30 |

*(see also Whitesnake)*

## COMPANY (2)
| | | | |
|---|---|---|---|
| 80 | Incus INCUS 36 | FABLES (LP) | 50 |
| 80 | Incus INCUS 38 | FICTIONS (LP) | 50 |
| 82 | Incus INCUS 46 | EPIPHANY (LP) | 50 |
| 82 | Incus INCUS 47 | EPIPHANIES (LP) | 50 |
| 83 | Incus INCUS 51 | TRIOS (LP) | 50 |

## COMPASS
| | | | |
|---|---|---|---|
| 74 | MAM 115 | No More Whiskey/Maybe She Will | 7 |

## COMPLETE CYCLE
| | | | |
|---|---|---|---|
| 70 | Jay Boy BOY 23 | I'm On The Road Again/Back On The Road Again | 6 |

## COMPLETE CONTROL
| | | | |
|---|---|---|---|
| 85 | Oi! OIR 1 | BRICKS BLOOD N GUTS (mini-LP) | 20 |

## COMPLEX
| | | | |
|---|---|---|---|
| 70 | CLPM 001 | COMPLEX (LP, private pressing, 99 copies only) | 4000 |
| 71 | Deroy | THE WAY WE FEEL (LP, private pressing, 99 copies only) | 1000 |
| 98 | Tenth Planet TP 038 | COMPLEX (LP, reissue, 1000, no'd) | 30 |

*(see also Monsoon, Misfits)*

## COMPLEXXION
| | | | |
|---|---|---|---|
| 79 | UK Records INT 584 | So Much In Love/Weekend (in p/s with bonus floppy gold disc) | 8 |
| 79 | UK Records INT 584 | So Much In Love/Weekend | 5 |

## COMPROMISE
| | | | |
|---|---|---|---|
| 66 | CBS 202050 | You Will Think Of Me/Love Minus Zero | 7 |

## COMSAT ANGELS
| | | | |
|---|---|---|---|
| 79 | Junta JUNTA 1 | Red Planet/I Get Excited/Specimen No. 2 (1st pressing, black vinyl, 2000 copies p/s) | 6 |
| 79 | Junta JUNTA 1 | Red Planet/I Get Excited/Specimen No. 2 (p/s, later reissue on red vinyl) | 8 |

## BOBBY COMSTOCK (& COUNTS)
| | | | |
|---|---|---|---|
| 59 | Top Rank JAR 223 | The Tennessee Waltz/Sweet Talk (with Counts) | 10 |
| 60 | London HLE 9080 | Jambalaya/Let's Talk It Over (as Bobby Comstock & Counts) | 10 |
| 63 | Stateside SS 163 | Let's Stomp/I Want To Do It | 15 |
| 63 | Stateside SS 221 | Susie Baby/Take A Walk | 15 |
| 65 | United Artists UP 1086 | I'm A Man/I'll Make You Glad | 10 |

## COMUS
| | | | |
|---|---|---|---|
| 71 | Dawn DNX 2506 | Diana/In The Lost Queen's Eyes/Winter Is A Coloured Bird (p/s) | 100 |
| 71 | Dawn DNLS 3019 | FIRST UTTERANCE (LP, gatefold sleeve with lyric sheet, orange label) | 1000 |
| 74 | Virgin V 2018 | TO KEEP FROM CRYING (LP, twin Virgin label) | 60 |
| 10 | Rise Above Relics RARLP 006 | FIRST UTTERANCE (LP, reissue, limited edition with 10" and A2 poster, 300 only, black vinyl) | 50 |

*(see also Gong, Henry Cow, Esperanto Rock Orchestra)*

## CON-CHORDS
| | | | |
|---|---|---|---|
| 65 | Polydor BM 56059 | You Can't Take It Away/Let Me Walk With You | 25 |

## CONCORDE
| | | | |
|---|---|---|---|
| 70 | Attack ATT 8020 | Let Me Out/I Belong To You | 12 |

## CONCORDS (1)
| | | | |
|---|---|---|---|
| 66 | Emblem JDR 303 | SOUL PURPOSE (LP) | 30 |

## CONCORDS (2)
| | | | |
|---|---|---|---|
| 69 | Blue Cat BS 170 | Buttoo/I Need Your Loving | 40 |

## CONCRETE
| | | | |
|---|---|---|---|
| 81 | Concrete CON 001 | GHOULISH PRACTICES EP | 15 |

## CONCRETE GOD
| | | | |
|---|---|---|---|
| 87 | Phlox CGOD1 | FLOOR EP (12" p/s) | 15 |
| 87 | Phlox CGOD2 | TOYTOWN EP (12" p/s) | 25 |

## CONCRETE SOX
| | | | |
|---|---|---|---|
| 89 | Big Kiss KISS 1 | SEWERSIDE (LP, with inner) | 15 |
| 87 | Manic Ears ACHE 11 | WHOOPS, SORRY VICAR! (LP) | 15 |
| 88 | C.O.R GURT 10 | YOUR TURN NEXT (LP, with insert) | 15 |

## CONCRETES
| | | | |
|---|---|---|---|
| 04 | EMI LFLP 012 | CONCRETES (LP, stickered sleeve) | 20 |

## CONDEMNED
| | | | |
|---|---|---|---|
| 79 | Rock Against Racism TRAR 1 | Soldier Boys/Endless Revolution/PROLES: Stereo Love/Thought Crime(p/s) | 45 |

## CONDEMNED 84
| | | | |
|---|---|---|---|
| 86 | RFB SIN 2 | Oi Ain't Dead!/Under Her Thumb/Follow The Leader/The Nutter (12", p/s, blue vinyl) | 25 |
| 86 | RFB SIN 2 | Oi Ain't Dead!/Under Her Thumb/Follow The Leader/The Nutter (7", p/s, blue vinyl) | 20 |
| 87 | RFB SIN 3 | IN SEARCH OF THE NEW BREED (12" EP) | 30 |
| 88 | Oi! OIR 003 | BATTLE SCARRED (LP) | 22 |
| 88 | Grade 1 | FACE THE AGGRESSION (LP) | 22 |

## JEFF CONDON
| | | | |
|---|---|---|---|
| 63 | MGM MGM 1221 | (Walkin' In) Freddy's Footsteps/Never You Mind | 5 |

## HOWIE G. CONDOR
| | | | |
|---|---|---|---|
| 65 | Fontana TF 613 | Big Noise From Winnetka/The Fix | 5 |

## CONEY ISLAND KIDS
| | | | |
|---|---|---|---|
| 55 | London HLJ 8207 | Baby, Baby You/Moonlight Beach | 30 |

## CONFESSOR
| | | | |
|---|---|---|---|
| 91 | Earache MOSH 44 | CONDEMNED (LP) | 40 |

## CONFLICT
| | | | |
|---|---|---|---|
| 82 | Crass 221984/1 | THE HOUSE THAT MAN BUILT (EP, foldout poster p/s) | 10 |
| 83 | Corp. Christi CHRIST IT'S 4 | A Nation Of Animal Lovers/Liberate (fold-out poster p/s) | 8 |
| 83 | Mortarhate MORT 1 | The Serenade Is Dead EP ('Pay no mpre than 99p' on cover, with insert) | 8 |
| 83 | Mortarhate MORT EX001 | The Serenade Is Dead (12" with insert) | 15 |
| 85 | Mortarhate MORT 15 | The Battle Continues (both sides) (p/s, black or white sleeve, with lyric sheet) | 8 |
| 85 | Mortarhate MORT 20 | Custom Rock/Statement (Ungovernable Force Promo, white label) | 30 |
| 83 | Corpus Christi CHRIST'S 3 | IT'S TIME TO SEE WHO'S WHO (LP) | 15 |

## CONGO ASHANTI ROY
| | | | |
|---|---|---|---|
| 82 | On-U Sound DP 08 | Hands & Feet/African Blood (10") | 15 |
| 80 | Pre PREX 8 | SIGN OF THE STAR (LP) | 25 |

## CONGOS
| | | | |
|---|---|---|---|
| 77 | Black Swan BS 1 | Congo Man/Congo Man Chant (12") | 40 |
| 78 | Go-Feet FEET 5 | Fisherman/Can't Come In | 15 |
| 81 | Go-Feet BEAT 2 | HEART OF THE CONGOS (LP) | 40 |
| 96 | Blood & Fire BAFLP 009 | HEART OF THE CONGOS (2-LP, reissue) | 30 |

## CONGREGATION
| | | | |
|---|---|---|---|
| 73 | Columbia DB 9006 | Jubilation/Love Is The Sweetest Thing I know | 12 |

## ARTHUR CONLEY
| | | | |
|---|---|---|---|
| 67 | Atlantic 584 083 | Sweet Soul Music/Let's Go Steady | 10 |
| 67 | Atlantic 584 121 | Shake, Rattle And Roll/You Don't Have To See Me | 5 |
| 67 | Atlantic 584 143 | Whole Lotta Woman/Love Comes And Goes | 10 |
| 68 | Atlantic 584 175 | Funky Street/Put Our Love Together | 10 |
| 68 | Atlantic 584 197 | People Sure Act Funny/Burning Fire | 10 |
| 68 | Atlantic 584 224 | Aunt Dora's Love Soul Shack/Is That You Love | 10 |
| 69 | Atco 226 004 | Star Revue/Love Sure Is A Powerful Thing | 7 |

MINT VALUE £

| Year | Label & Number | Title | Value |
|---|---|---|---|
| 70 | Atco 226 011 | They Call The Wind Maria/Hurt | 5 |
| 70 | Atlantic 2091 025 | All Day Singing/God Bless | 5 |
| 71 | Atlantic 2091 106 | Sweet Soul Music/Shake, Rattle And Roll | 8 |
| 71 | Atlantic 2091 120 | I'm Living Good/I'm So Glad You're Here | 5 |
| 72 | Capricorn K 17506 | Rita/More Sweet Soul Music | 5 |
| 67 | Atlantic 587 069 | SWEET SOUL MUSIC (LP) | 35 |
| 68 | Atlantic 587 084 | SHAKE, RATTLE AND ROLL (LP) | 20 |
| 68 | Atlantic 587/588 128 | SOUL DIRECTION (LP) | 20 |
| 69 | Atco 228 019 | MORE SWEET SOUL (LP) | 15 |

*(see also Soul Clan)*

## CONNARD
| 68 | Spot JW 11 | Amadhan/Desdemona | 70 |

## CONNECTION
| 92 | Spare Beat SBRR 006 | THE CONNECTION EP (12") | 30 |
| 93 | Spare Beat SBRR 008 | THE CONNECTION EP VOL II (12") | 30 |

## BRIAN CONNELL & ROUND SOUND
| 66 | Mercury MF 956 | Just My Kind Of Loving/Something You've Got | 10 |
| 66 | Mercury MF 991 | The Same Thing's Happened To Me/Mister Porter | 10 |
| 68 | Philips BF 1661 | What Good Am I/Just Another Wedding Day | 10 |
| 68 | Philips BF 1718 | I Know/Mister Travel Company | 45 |

## RAY CONNIFF & ROCKIN' RHYTHM BOYS
| 55 | Vogue Coral QW 5001 | Piggy Bank Boogie/Short Stuff | 6 |

## TERRY CONNOLLY & THE TRIXONS
| 67 | Kinh KG 1069 | You're Gonna Wonder About Me/Mama, I'm Not The Boy I Used To Be | 20 |

## BRIAN CONNOLLY
| 82 | Carrere CAR 231 | Hypnotised/Fade Away (p/s) | 18 |

*(see also Sweet)*

## CHRIS CONNOR
| 60 | London LZ-N 14036 | THIS IS CHRIS (10" LP) | 10 |

## PAUL CONNOR
| 71 | Polydor 2121045 | Little Sparrow/I Don't Love You Any More | 35 |
| 71 | Polydor 2480072 | EASY TO REMEMBER (LP) | 40 |

## TIM CONNOR
| 60 | Decca F 11239 | Rosemary/Love What Took So Long | 5 |
| 62 | HMV POP 1007 | Lost Love/Down | 5 |
| 62 | HMV POP 1056 | Without A Shoulder To Cry On/I've Fallen In Love | 5 |
| 62 | HMV POP 1096 | Take This Message/Maybe | 5 |

## CAROL CONNORS
| 62 | London HLN 9619 | Big Big Love/Two Rivers | 20 |

*(see also Teddy Bears)*

## NORMAN CONNORS
| 74 | Buddah BDS 5611 | SLEWFOOT (LP) | 20 |
| 77 | Buddah BDLP 4043 | AQUARIAN DREAM (LP) | 40 |
| 77 | Buddah BDLP 4043 | YOU ARE MY STARSHIP (LP) | 20 |

## CONNY
| 61 | HMV POP 867 | Midi Midinette/CONNY & REX GILDO: Yes My Darling | 5 |
| 61 | Columbia DB 4714 | No One Can Tell Me I'm Too Young/Lovable | 6 |
| 62 | Columbia DB 4845 | Gino/Midi-Midinette | 6 |

## CONQUERORS
| 67 | Doctor Bird DB 1119 | Won't You Come Home Now?/Oh That Day | 50 |
| 67 | Treasure Isle TI 7035 | Lonely Street/I Fell In Love | 40 |
| 69 | Amalgamated AMG 832 | Secret Weapon (actually by Ansell Collins)/Jumpy Jumpy Girl | 40 |
| 69 | High Note HS 016 | If You Can't Beat Them/Anywhere You Want To Go | 50 |
| 69 | High Note HS 025 | National Dish/Mr D.J. | 50 |
| 72 | Fab FAB 22 | You Hold The Handles/SOUL REBELS : Bongo Skank | 150 |

*(see also Stranger Cole & Conquerors, Baba Brooks)*

## BOB CONRAD
| 61 | Warner Bros WB 54 | Bye Bye Baby/Love You | 5 |

## JESS CONRAD
| 62 | Decca DFE 6702 | TWIST MY WRIST (EP) | 10 |

*(see also Guvners)*

## TONI CONRAD & FAUST
| 73 | Caroline C 1501 | OUTSIDE THE DREAM SYNDICATE (LP, as Tony Conrad) | 45 |

*(see also Faust)*

## CONSCIOUS MINDS
| 71 | Big BG 318 | Jamaican Boy/Brainwash | 20 |
| 71 | Ackee ACK 141 | Paul, Marcus And Norman/Version | 15 |
| 71 | Punch PH 97 | Paul, Marcus And Norman/Version (reissue) | 6 |
| 71 | Escort ERT 857 | Peace Treaty/Brainwash | 15 |

*(see also Ken Boothe, Jamaicans, B.B.Seaton, Charmers)*

## CONSOLERS
| 67 | President PT165 | Someone Must Answer/Lord Bring Me Down | 8 |

## CONSORTIUM
| 68 | Pye 7N 17635 | All The Love In The World/Spending My Life Saying Goodbye | 10 |
| 69 | Pye 7N 17725 | When The Day Breaks/Day The Train Never Came | 30 |
| 69 | Pye 7N 17797 | Beggar Man/Cynthia Serenity | 20 |
| 69 | Pye 7N 17841 | I Don't Want Her Anymore/The House Upon The Hill | 7 |

| | | | |
|---|---|---|---|
| 70 | Trend TNT 52 | Melanie Cries Alone/Copper Coloured Years | 7 |

### CONSTRUCTION
| | | | |
|---|---|---|---|
| 90 | White SDT17 | Sudden Impact - In A State Of Experimentation | 60 |
| 90 | White SDT30 | Transmission/Revenge Of The Dragon (12") | 120 |
| 91 | White SDT37 | Change Your Attitude/Time To Get Raw (12") | 25 |

### CONSUMATES
| | | | |
|---|---|---|---|
| 68 | Coxsone CS 7054 | What Is It/SOUL VENDORS: Musical Happiness | 70 |

### CONTACT
| | | | |
|---|---|---|---|
| 79 | Object OM 11 | FUTURE/PAST EP | 18 |

### CONTACTS
| | | | |
|---|---|---|---|
| 81 | Small Operations S0001 | Young Girls/Boyfriends (p/s) | 12 |

### JOHN CONTEH
| | | | |
|---|---|---|---|
| 75 | Boxa KO 1 | The Boxer/Dance The Boxer (p/s) | 5 |

### CONTINENTALS (1)
| | | | |
|---|---|---|---|
| 62 | Oriole 1569 | Bye Bye Blackbird/Everybody Loves My Baby | 15 |
| 62 | Island WI 010 | Going Crazy/Give Me All Your Love | 25 |

### CONTINENTALS (2)
| | | | |
|---|---|---|---|
| 79 | CBS S 7476 | Fizz Pop (Modern Rock)/(I Lost My Love On A) 747 | 5 |

### CONTINENTAL UPTIGHT BAND
| | | | |
|---|---|---|---|
| 71 | Columbia SCX 6454 | BEAUTIFUL FRIENDSHIP (LP, black/silver/white boxed Columbia label) | 30 |

### CONTINUUM
| | | | |
|---|---|---|---|
| 70 | RCA Victor SF 8157 | CONTINUUM (LP, gatefold, orange labels) | 20 |
| 71 | RCA Victor SF 8196 | AUTUMN GRASS (LP, gatefold sleeve, orange label) | 40 |

### CONTOURS
| | | | |
|---|---|---|---|
| 62 | Oriole CB 1763 | Do You Love Me/Move Mister Man (DJ Copy) | 100 |
| 62 | Oriole CB 1763 | Do You Love Me/Move Mister Man | 40 |
| 63 | Oriole CB 1799 | Shake Sherry/You Better Get In Line | 60 |
| 63 | Oriole CB 1831 | Don't Let Him Be Your Baby/It Must Be Love | 75 |
| 64 | Stateside SS 299 | Can You Do It/I'll Stand By You | 60 |
| 64 | Stateside SS 299 | Can You Do It/I'll Stand By You (DJ Copy) | 100 |
| 65 | Stateside SS 381 | Can You Jerk Like Me/That Day She Needed Me | 60 |
| 65 | Stateside SS 381 | Can You Jerk Like Me/That Day She Needed Me (DJ Copy) | 100 |
| 65 | Tamla Motown TMG 531 | First I Look At The Purse/Searching For A Girl | 60 |
| 65 | Tamla Motown TMG 531 | First I Look At The Purse/Searching For A Girl (DJ Copy) | 120 |
| 66 | Tamla Motown TMG 564 | Determination/Just A Little Misunderstanding | 60 |
| 66 | Tamla Motown TMG 564 | Determination/Just A Little Misunderstanding (DJ Copy) | 150 |
| 67 | Tamla Motown TMG 605 | It's So Hard Being A Loser/Your Love Grows More Precious Every Day | 35 |
| 67 | Tamla Motown TMG 605 | It's So Hard Being A Loser/Your Love Grows More Precious Every Day (DJ Copy) | 70 |
| 70 | Tamla Motown TMG 723 | Just A Little Misunderstanding/First I Look At The Purse | 10 |
| 70 | Tamla Motown TMG 723 | Just A Little Misunderstanding/First I Look At The Purse (DJ Copy) | 40 |
| 65 | Tamla Motown TME 2002 | THE CONTOURS (EP) | 120 |
| 63 | Oriole PS 40043 | DO YOU LOVE ME (LP) | 250 |

### CONTRABAND
| | | | |
|---|---|---|---|
| 74 | Transatlantic BIG 518 | Lady For Today/On The Road | 6 |
| 74 | Transatlantic TRA 278 | CONTRABAND (LP, with lyric insert) | 20 |

### CONTRAST
| | | | |
|---|---|---|---|
| 69 | Orange OAS 202 | Hey That's No Way To Say Goodbye/We Can Make It If We Try | 10 |

### CONTRASTS FEATURING BOB MORRISON
| | | | |
|---|---|---|---|
| 68 | Monument MON 1018 | What A Day/Lonely Child | 6 |

*(see also Bill Forbes)*

### CONTROLLED BLEEDING
| | | | |
|---|---|---|---|
| 86 | Sterile SR 11 | HEADCRACK (LP) | 20 |

### CONTROLLERS
| | | | |
|---|---|---|---|
| 75 | President PT 448 | Is That Long Enough For You/Pictures And Memories | 6 |
| 86 | MCA 1052 | Stay/Undercover Lover (p/s) | 6 |

### CONUNDRUM & RICHARD HARVEY
| | | | |
|---|---|---|---|
| 78 | Streetsong No. 1 | Black Birds Of Brittany/SHIRLEY COLLINS & ANNIE POWER: The Mariners Farewell (poster p/s) | 18 |

*(see also Bert Jansch, Shirley Collins)*

### CONVAIRS
| | | | |
|---|---|---|---|
| 66 | HMV POP 1549 | Tomorrow Is A Long Time/Midnight Mary | 5 |

### BERT CONVY & THUNDERBIRDS
| | | | |
|---|---|---|---|
| 55 | London HLB 8190 | C'mon Back/Hoo Bop De Bow | 50 |
| 56 | Capitol CL 14601 | Heaven On Earth/CHEERS: Que Pasa Muchacha | 5 |

*(see also Cheers,Thunderbirds)*

### MIKE CONWAY
| | | | |
|---|---|---|---|
| 66 | Plexium PXM 1 | I'm Gonna Get Me A Woman/Reign Of King Sadness | 15 |

### PAUL CONWAY
| | | | |
|---|---|---|---|
| 64 | Piccadilly 7N 35215 | Come A Little Bit Closer/Be Lonely Little Girl | 7 |

### JIMMY CONWELL
| | | | |
|---|---|---|---|
| 72 | Jay Boy BOY 64 | Cigarette Ashes/Second Hand Happiness | 10 |
| 72 | Jay Boy BOY 64 | Cigarette Ashes/Second Hand Happiness (DJ Copy) | 30 |

### COO-COO RACHAS
| | | | |
|---|---|---|---|
| 59 | Capitol CL 15024 | Chili Beans/Track Down | 5 |

### RY COODER
| | | | |
|---|---|---|---|
| 71 | Reprise RS 23497 | How Can A Poor Man Stand Such Times And Live/Goin' To Brownsville | 7 |
| 71 | Reprise RSLP 6402 | RY COODER (LP) | 15 |

*(see also Captain Beefheart, Don Everly)*

**ENGLAND COOK**
| | | | |
|---|---|---|---|
| 72 | Explosion EX 2063 | Samba Girl/NOW GENERATION: Samba (Version) | 5 |

**LITTLE JOE COOK (U.K.)**
| | | | |
|---|---|---|---|
| 65 | Sue WI 385 | Stormy Monday Blues (Parts 1 & 2) | 50 |

*(see also Chris Farlowe, Beazers)*

**LITTLE JOE COOK (U.S.)**
| | | | |
|---|---|---|---|
| 68 | Sonet SON 2002 | Don't You Have Feelings?/Hold On To Your Money | 20 |
| 74 | Sonet SON 2041 | Hold On To Your Money/Don't You Have Feelings? (reissue, sides reversed) | 10 |
| 04 | Soul City SC 148 | I'm Falling In Love WIth You Baby/SHERRY'S: Put Your Arms Around Me | 5 |

**PETER COOK (1)**
| | | | |
|---|---|---|---|
| 65 | Pye 7N 15847 | Georgia/There And Bach Again | 20 |

*(see also Peter London)*

**PETER COOK (2)**
| | | | |
|---|---|---|---|
| 66 | Lyntone LYN 776 | Watney's Pale Ale (Flexi, p/s) | 10 |

**PETER COOK & DUDLEY MOORE**
| | | | |
|---|---|---|---|
| 62 | Parlophone R 4969 | Excerpts From "Beyond The Fringe": Sitting On The Bench/The End Of The World (with Alan Bennett & Jonathan Miller) | 5 |
| 65 | Decca F 12158 | Goodbyeee (& Dudley Moore Trio)/DUDLEY MOORE TRIO: Not Only But Also | 5 |
| 66 | Decca F 12380 | Isn't She A Sweetie/Bo Duddley | 5 |
| 67 | Decca F 12551 | The L.S. Bumble Bee/The Bee Side | 5 |
| 67 | Decca F 12710 | Bedazzled/Love Me | 70 |
| 68 | Decca SKL 4923 | BEDAZZLED (LP, stereo, soundtrack) | 90 |

*(see also Dudley Moore Trio)*

**ROGER NOEL COOK**
| | | | |
|---|---|---|---|
| 73 | Dart ART 2039 | Slick Go Getter/I Mean It You Know It | 8 |

**COOK COUNTY**
| | | | |
|---|---|---|---|
| 77 | Barak BAR 5 | Space Dancin'/Star Wars | 15 |

**PAUL COOKE**
| | | | |
|---|---|---|---|
| 71 | Ackee ACK 129 | That Girl Was Mine/No Harm | 12 |

**ROGER (JAMES) COOKE**
| | | | |
|---|---|---|---|
| 68 | Columbia DB 8458 | Skyline Pigeon/I'm Burning | 7 |
| 69 | Columbia DB 8510 | Not That It Matters Anymore/Paper Chase | 6 |
| 69 | Columbia DB 8556 | Stop/Someday | 6 |
| 69 | Columbia DB 8596 | Smiling Through My Tears/Ain't That A Wonderful Thing (with Eve Graham) | 8 |
| 70 | Columbia DB 8729 | Jubilation/Anticipation Grows | 6 |
| 71 | Columbia DB 8761 | If You Would Stay/Mama Packed A Picnic Tea | 6 |
| 71 | Columbia DB 8806 | People I Gotta Dream/Today I Killed A Man I Didn't Know | 6 |
| 70 | Regal Zonophone RZ 3005 | We Will Get By/My Home City (as Roger Cook) | 6 |
| 73 | Regal Zonophone RZ 3074 | She/Stay With Me (as Roger Cook) | 6 |
| 76 | Polto DR 2058 857 | Please Get My Name Right/Alright | 6 |
| 70 | Columbia SCX 6388 | STUDY (LP, boxed logo on label) | 25 |
| 72 | Regal Zono. SRZA 8508 | MEANWHILE ... BACK AT THE WORLD (As Roger Cook, LP, gatefold sleeve, red/silver label) | 30 |
| 73 | Regal Zono. SLRZ 1035 | MINSTREL IN FLIGHT (LP) | 20 |

*(see also David & Jonathan)*

**SAM COOKE**
| | | | |
|---|---|---|---|
| 57 | London HLU 8506 | You Send Me/Summertime | 40 |
| 57 | London HLU 8506 | You Send Me/Summertime (78) | 20 |
| 58 | London HLU 8615 | That's All I Need To Know/I Don't Want To Cry | 40 |
| 58 | London HLU 8615 | That's All I Need To Know/I Don't Want To Cry (78) | 20 |
| 58 | HMV POP 568 | Love You Most Of All/Win Your Love For Me | 40 |
| 58 | HMV POP 568 | Love You Most Of All/Win Your Love For Me (78) | 20 |
| 59 | HMV POP 610 | Everybody Likes To Cha Cha Cha/The Little Things You Do | 40 |
| 59 | HMV POP 610 | Everybody Likes To Cha Cha Cha/The Little Things You Do (78) | 25 |
| 59 | HMV POP 642 | Only Sixteen/Let's Go Steady Again | 10 |
| 59 | HMV POP 642 | Only Sixteen/Let's Go Steady Again (78) | 30 |
| 59 | HMV POP 675 | There, I've Said It Again/One Hour Ahead Of The Posse | 30 |
| 60 | London HLU 9046 | Happy In Love/I Need You Now | 25 |
| 60 | RCA RCA 1184 | Teenage Sonata/If You Were The Only Girl | 20 |
| 60 | HMV POP 754 | Wonderful World/Along The Navajo Trail | 10 |
| 60 | RCA RCA 1202 | Chain Gang/I Fall In Love Everyday | 10 |
| 61 | RCA RCA 1221 | Sad Mood/Love Me | 10 |
| 61 | RCA RCA 1230 | That's It, I Quit, I'm Movin' On/What Do You Say | 15 |
| 61 | RCA RCA 1242 | Cupid/Farewell, My Darling | 10 |
| 61 | RCA RCA 1260 | Feel It/It's Alright | 10 |
| 62 | RCA RCA 1277 | Twisting The Night Away/One More Time | 5 |
| 62 | RCA RCA 1296 | Bring It On Home To Me/Having A Party | 8 |
| 62 | RCA RCA 1310 | Nothing Can Change This Love/Somebody Have Mercy | 8 |
| 63 | RCA RCA 1327 | Send Me Some Loving/Baby Baby Baby | 20 |
| 63 | RCA RCA 1341 | Another Saturday Night/Love Will Find A Way | 5 |
| 63 | RCA RCA 1361 | Frankie And Johnny/Cool Train | 10 |
| 63 | RCA RCA 1367 | Little Red Rooster/Shake Rattle And Roll | 10 |
| 64 | RCA RCA 1386 | Good News/Basin Street Blues | 6 |
| 64 | RCA RCA 1405 | Good Times/Tennessee Waltz | 6 |
| 64 | RCA RCA 1420 | Cousin Of Mine/That's Where It's At | 10 |
| 65 | RCA RCA 1436 | Shake/A Change Is Gonna Come | 30 |
| 65 | RCA RCA 1452 | It's Got The Whole World Shakin'/Ease My Troublin' Mind | 20 |
| 65 | RCA RCA 1476 | Sugar Dumpling/Bridge Of Tears | 40 |

| 65 | RCA RCA 1476 | Sugar Dumpling/Bridge Of Tears (DJ Copy) | 70 |
| 68 | RCA RCA 1701 | Another Saturday Night/DUANE EDDY: Dance With The Guitar Man (w/drawn) | 10 |
| 63 | RCA RCX 7117 | HEART AND SOUL (EP) | 20 |
| 64 | RCA RCX 7128 | SWING SWEETLY (EP) | 25 |
| 58 | HMV CLP 1261 | SAM COOKE (LP, with Bumps Blackwell Orchestra) | 100 |
| 59 | HMV CLP 1273 | ENCORE (LP) | 70 |
| 61 | RCA RD 27190 | COOKE'S TOUR (LP, mono) | 35 |
| 61 | RCA SF 5076 | COOKE'S TOUR (LP, stereo) | 45 |
| 61 | RCA RD 27215 | HITS OF THE FIFTIES (LP, mono) | 25 |
| 61 | RCA RD SF 5098 | HITS OF THE FIFTIES (LP, stereo) | 40 |
| 61 | RCA RD 27222 | SWING LOW (LP) | 35 |
| 62 | RCA RD 27245 | MY KIND OF BLUES (LP, mono) | 30 |
| 62 | RCA SF 5120 | MY KIND OF BLUES (LP, stereo) | 30 |
| 62 | RCA RD 27263 | TWISTIN' THE NIGHT AWAY (LP, mono) | 30 |
| 62 | RCA RD SF 5133 | TWISTIN' THE NIGHT AWAY (LP, stereo) | 40 |
| 63 | RCA RDF 7539 | MR. SOUL (LP, mono) | 40 |
| 63 | RCA SF 7539 | MR. SOUL (LP, stereo) | 45 |
| 63 | RCA RD/SF 7583 | NIGHT BEAT (LP) | 40 |
| 63 | RCA RD/SF 7583 | NIGHT BEAT (LP) | 45 |
| 64 | RCA RD 7635 | AIN'T THAT GOOD NEWS (LP, mono) | 25 |
| 64 | RCA SF 7635 | AIN'T THAT GOOD NEWS (LP, stereo) | 30 |
| 65 | RCA RD 7674 | AT THE COPA (LP, mono) | 25 |
| 65 | RCA SF 7674 | AT THE COPA (LP, stereo) | 30 |
| 65 | RCA RD 7730 | SHAKE (LP, mono) | 40 |
| 65 | RCA SF 7730 | SHAKE (LP, stereo) | 55 |
| 65 | London HA-U 8232 | THE SOUL STIRRERS FEATURING SAM COOKE (LP) | 70 |
| 66 | RCA RD/SF 7764 | TRY A LITTLE LOVE (LP) | 30 |
| 66 | Immediate IMLP 002 | THE WONDERFUL WORLD OF SAM COOKE (LP) | 80 |
| 74 | BBC | SAM COOKE AND OTHERS (LP, for radio use) | 70 |

## COOKIES
| 62 | London HLU 9634 | Chains/Stranger In My Arms | 25 |
| 63 | London HLU 9704 | Don't Say Nothin' Bad About My Baby/Softly In The Night | 25 |
| 63 | Colpix PX 11012 | Will Power/I Want A Boy For My Birthday | 30 |
| 64 | Colpix PX 11020 | Girls Grow Up Faster Than Boys/Only To Other People | 30 |

*(see also Earl-Jean, Cinderellas, Dorothy Jones)*

## COOL
| 69 | DeWolfe DW/LP 3136 | POP SOUNDS (LP, music library only) | 40 |

*(see also Elastic Band)*

## COOL BREEZE
| 71 | Patheway PAT 103 | People Ask What Love Is/There'll Be No More Sad Tomorrows | 20 |
| 72 | Decca F 13324 | Summertime Sunshine/Sing Out Your Love | 6 |
| 75 | Bus Stop BUS 1023 | Do It Some More/Citizen Jones | 6 |
| 75 | Bus Stop BUS 1027 | You Gotta Love Me More/Turn On The Sun | 6 |

## COOL CATS
| 68 | Jolly JY 007 | What Kind Of Man/HEMSLEY MORRIS: Little Things | 125 |
| 69 | Jolly JY 009 | Hold Your Love/ALVA LEWIS: Hang My Head And Cry | 100 |

## COOLERS
| 73 | Bread BR 1112 | The Youth Of Today/TYRONE TAYLOR: Close Observation | 6 |

## EDDIE COOLEY & DIMPLES
| 57 | Columbia DB 3873 | Priscilla/Got A Little Woman | 150 |
| 57 | Columbia DB 3873 | Priscilla/Got A Little Woman (78) | 30 |

## COOL HAND FLEX
| 92 | De Underground UG 08 | Your Risk/Untitled/Untitled (12", white label) | 12 |
| 92 | Ruff Groove HN 05 | Lock Me Up/I Don't Want No (12", stamped white label) | 10 |
| 92 | Ruff Groove UG 10 | Welcome/Way Back Then/Woman (12") | 10 |
| 92 | In Touch INT 001 | On The Strength/Your Risk/Go Insane (12") | 25 |

## RITA COOLIDGE
| 83 | Scanlite BOND 1 | All Time High/All Time High (Extended Instrumental) (p/s) | 5 |

## COOLIES
| 77 | Electric WOT 14 | Geisha Girl/Calling Out Your Name | 25 |

## JOE COOL & KILLERS
| 77 | Ariola ARO 165 | I Just Don't Care/My Way | 6 |

*(see also Killers)*

## COOL MEN
| 58 | Parlophone GEP 8739 | COOL FOR CATS NO. 1 (EP) | 25 |
| 58 | Parlophone GEP 8752 | COOL FOR CATS NO. 2 (EP) | 25 |

## COOL NOTES
| 80 | Jama JADC 0008 | Billy The Kid/Kidnap My Baby (12") | 12 |
| 80 | Jama JADC 0024 | My Tune (Re-Mix)/Version (12") | 30 |
| 84 | Sour Grapes SG 116 | I Wanna Dance/Blowin It | 25 |
| 84 | Sour Grapes SGR 116 | I Wanna Dance (Extended)/Blowin It (12") | 80 |
| 84 | Mass Media | Forgot How To Love/Why Can't We Be Friends (12") | 30 |
| 85 | Abstract Dance 12AD 001 | You're Never Too Young/Sound Of Summer (12") | 15 |
| 84 | Mass Media MMLP 2 | DOWN TO EARTH (LP) | 60 |

## COOL RUNNERS
| 82 | MCA MCAT 760 | Play The Game (So You Think It Funny)/Hawaiian Dream (12", p/s) | 20 |
| 82 | MCA MCAT 893 | Checking Out/High On A Feeling (12", p/s) | 40 |
| 84 | Tai Wan TWD 1949 | Checking Out/High On A Feeling (12", p/s, reissue as Nat King Cool & Cool Runners) | 25 |

MINT VALUE £

## COOL SPOON (JEFF DIXON & ALTON ELLIS)
| | | | |
|---|---|---|---|
| 67 | Coxsone CS 7031 | Yakety Yak/SOUL VENDORS: Drum Song | 40 |

## COOL STICKY
| | | | |
|---|---|---|---|
| 68 | Amalgamated AMG 825 | Train To Soulsville/ERIC MONTY MORRIS: Cinderella (actually by Errol Dunkley) | 50 |

## CHRIS COOMBES
| | | | |
|---|---|---|---|
| 65 | Holyground HG 110 | WHERE IT'S AT (EP, 99 only) | 35 |

## NIGEL COOMBES & STEVE BERESFORD
| | | | |
|---|---|---|---|
| 80 | Bead Records BEAD 16 | IMPROVISED VIOLIN AND PIANO DUETS (LP) | 25 |

## ALICE COOPER
| | | | |
|---|---|---|---|
| 71 | Straight W 7209 | Eighteen/Body | 100 |
| 71 | Warner Bros K 16127 | Under My Wheels/Desperado | 6 |
| 72 | Warner Bros K 16188 | School's Out/Gutter Cat (p/s) | 7 |
| 72 | Warner Bros K 16214 | Elected/Luney Tune (p/s) | 8 |
| 73 | Warner Bros/Lyntone LYN 2585/6 | Slick Black Limousine/Extracts From: Unfinished Sweet/Elected/No More Mr Nice Guy/Billion Dollar Babies/I Love The Dead (33rpm flexi free with NME magazine) | 5 |
| 73 | Warner Brothers K16262 | No More Mr. Nice Guy/Raped And Freezin' (possibly export only) | 20 |
| 74 | Warner Bros K 16409 | School's Out/No More Mr. Nice Guy/Elected/Billion Dollar Babies (maxi-45) | 5 |
| 74 | Chrysalis CHS 2069 | I'm Flash/ELKIE BROOKS: Sacrifice (p/s, promo only) | 35 |
| 75 | Anchor ANC 1012 | Department Of Youth/Cold Ethyl (p/s) | 6 |
| 75 | Anchor ANE 12001 | Welcome To My Nightmare/Department Of Youth/Black Widow/ Only Women Bleed (12" EP, p/s) | 10 |
| 76 | Warner Bros K 16792 | I Never Cry/Got To Hell (p/s) | 5 |
| 77 | Warner Bros K 16935 | (No More) Love At Your Convenience/It's Hot Tonight (p/s, gothic type on label) | 5 |
| 80 | Warner Bros K 17598 | Clones (We're All)/Model Citizen (p/s) | 8 |
| 86 | MCA MCA 1090 | He's Back (The Man Behind The Mask)/Billion Dollar Babies (poster p/s) | 10 |
| 89 | Epic ALICE 3 | Bed Of Nails/I'm Your Gun (p/s, with poster) | 8 |
| 69 | Straight STS 1051 | PRETTIES FOR YOU (LP, purple label, gatefold sleeve) | 100 |
| 69 | Straight STS 1061 | EASY ACTION (LP, purple label, gatefold sleeve) | 100 |
| 71 | Straight STS 1065 | LOVE IT TO DEATH (LP, purple label, gatefold sleeve) | 80 |
| 71 | Warner Bros K 56005 | KILLER (LP, olive green label, A1/B1 Matrix numbers, gatefold sleeve with perforated foldout calendar that must have '1972' in bottom left hand corner. Any with '1973' are repressings) | 70 |
| 72 | Warner Bros K 56007 | SCHOOL'S OUT (LP, green label, 'desktop' gatefold sleeve, with 'paper panties' inner) | 60 |
| 73 | Warner Bros K 56013 | BILLION DOLLAR BABIES (LP, 1st pressing, A1/B1 matrixes, 'Pil' etched into dead wax side 2, olive green label, gatefold embossed sleeve with round corners and K56013 in top right corner, 'WEA records printed in England' in bottom right on rear, attached perforated cards, with $ billion note & inner sleeve with large thumb notch) | 40 |
| 73 | Warner Bros K 46177 | LOVE IT TO DEATH (LP, reissue, green label, gatefold sleeve) | 15 |
| 73 | Warner Bros K 66021 | SCHOOL DAYS (2-LP, gatefold sleeve, reissue of STS 1051 & 1061) | 18 |
| 74 | Warner Bros K 56018 | MUSCLE OF LOVE (LP, 'cardboard box' sleeve, with insert & inner sleeve) | 15 |

## BO COOPER
| | | | |
|---|---|---|---|
| 74 | Bell 1373 | Don't Call It Love/Christian | 15 |
| 74 | Bell 1373 | Don't Call It Love/Christian (DJ Copy) | 30 |

## GARNELL COOPER & KINFOLKS
| | | | |
|---|---|---|---|
| 63 | London HL 9757 | Green Monkey/Long Distance | 20 |

## HENRY COOPER
| | | | |
|---|---|---|---|
| 76 | DJM DJS 10734 | Knock Me Down With A Feather/Knocked Out For Your Love (p/s) | 6 |

## LES COOPER & SOUL ROCKERS
| | | | |
|---|---|---|---|
| 62 | Stateside SS 142 | Wiggle Wobble/Dig Yourself | 20 |

## MARTY COOPER CLAN
| | | | |
|---|---|---|---|
| 63 | RCA Victor RD 7596 | NEW SOUNDS - OLD GOODIES (LP) | 15 |

## MIKE COOPER
| | | | |
|---|---|---|---|
| 70 | Dawn DNX 2501 | Your Lovely Ways (Parts 1 & 2)/Watching You Fall (Parts 1 & 2) (p/s) | 7 |
| 71 | Dawn DNX 2511 | Too Late Now/The Ballad Of Fulton Allen/Good Times (p/s) | 7 |
| 72 | Dawn DNS 1022 | Time In Hand/Schwabisch Hall | 6 |
| 60s | Saydisc SD 137 | UP THE COUNTRY BLUES (EP) | 80 |
| 68 | Matchbox SDM 159 | THE INVERTED WORLD (LP, with Ian A. Anderson) | 70 |
| 69 | Pye NSPL 18281 | OH REALLY!? (LP, blue/black label with logo banner on top) | 40 |
| 70 | Dawn DNLS 3005 | DO I KNOW YOU? (LP, gatefold sleeve, orange label) | 30 |
| 70 | Dawn DNLS 3011 | TROUT STEEL (LP, with poster insert, gatefold sleeve, orange label) | 50 |
| 71 | Dawn DNLS 3026 | PLACES I KNOW (LP, with insert, lilac label) | 40 |
| 72 | Dawn DNLS 3031 | THE MACHINE GUN COMPANY (LP, lilac label) | 25 |
| 74 | Fresh Air 6370 500 | LIFE AND DEATH IN PARADISE (LP) | 20 |

*(see also Ian A. Anderson, Heron)*

## COOPERETTES
| | | | |
|---|---|---|---|
| 75 | Brunswick BR22 | Shing A Ling/Don't Trust Him (DJ Copy) | 20 |
| 75 | Brunswick BR22 | Shing A Ling/Don't Trust Him | 10 |

## COOPER TEMPLE CLAUSE
| | | | |
|---|---|---|---|
| 00s | private pressing | The Crayon Demos/Who Needs Enemies?/Let's Kill Music/Devil Walks In The Sand Demos (CD-R, in hand-crayoned sleeve, 120 only) | 40 |
| 01 | Morning MORNING 2 | THE HARDWARE EP (Way Out West/Sister Soul/The Devil Walks In The Sand/Solitude) (2 x 7", 1 black and 1 white vinyl, poly sleeves in box, 500 only) | 10 |
| 02 | Morning MORNING 20 | SEE THIS THROUGH AND LEAVE (6 x 7", limited, numbered box set) | 12 |

## JULIAN COPE
| | | | |
|---|---|---|---|
| 87 | Antar 4503 | Interview/Christmas Mourning/Transmitting (fan club box set, with card, biography, membership card, letter, photos & stickers) | 30 |
| 91 | Island JC 1 | Safesurfer/If You Love Me At All (33rpm, sold at gigs, stickered white sleeve) | 6 |
| 94 | K.A.K. (no cat. no.) | Paranormal In The West Country (Original Version)/(String Quartet Version)/(Acoustic Version)/(Krankenhausmusik Version)/(Acoustic Version)/(Krankenhausmusik Version) (Mail-order only via offer with "Queen Elizabeth" LP) | 10 |
| 84 | Mercury MERL 48 | FRIED (LP, with poster & promo 12" [MADOX 5]) | 18 |

| | | | |
|---|---|---|---|
| 87 | Island ILPS 9861 | SAINT JULIAN (LP, with free 12" interview LP [JCCLP 1]) | 15 |
| 89 | CopeCo JULP 89 | SKELLINGTON (LP, mail order only) | 25 |
| 90 | Mofoco MOFOCO 90 | DROOLIAN (LP, mail order only) | 20 |
| 91 | Island ILPSD 9977 | PEGGY SUICIDE (2-LP) | 20 |
| 92 | Island ILPSD 9997 | JEHOVAHKILL (2-LP, 4th side etched) | 25 |
| 93 | Ma-Gog MA-GOG 2 | THE SKELLINGTON CHRONICLES (LP, mail order only) | 18 |
| 94 | Echo ECHLP 1 | AUTOGEDDON (LP, gatefold sleeve) | 15 |
| 95 | Echo ECHLP 5 | 20 MOTHERS (2-LP, black or purple vinyl) | 25 |
| 96 | Echo ECHLP 12 | INTERPRETER (LP, with poster) | 18 |
| 01 | Head Heritage HH12 | DISCOVER ODIN (CD, mail order only, 10" x 5" package with booklet, signed & numbered, 1000 only) | 40 |

*(see also Teardrop Explodes, Brain Donor, Elizabeth, L.A.M.F, Universal Panzies)*

**SUZY COPE**

| | | | |
|---|---|---|---|
| 61 | HMV POP 941 | Teenage Fool/Juvenile Delinquent | 25 |
| 62 | HMV POP 1047 | Not Never Not Now/Kisses And Tears | 25 |
| 63 | HMV POP 1167 | Biggity Big/Doing What You Know Is Wrong | 25 |
| 65 | CBS 201792 | You Can't Say I Never Told You/And Now I Don't Want You | 25 |

**AL(L)AN COPELAND**

| | | | |
|---|---|---|---|
| 57 | Vogue Coral Q 72237 | Feeling Happy/You Don't Know | 10 |
| 57 | Vogue Coral Q 72277 | How Will I Know?/Will You Still Be Mine | 7 |
| 59 | Pye International 7N 25007 | Flip Flop/Lots More Love (as Allan Copeland) | 25 |

**JOHNNY COPELAND**

| | | | |
|---|---|---|---|
| 69 | Atlantic 10242 | Sufferin' City/It's My Own Tears That's Being Wasted | 12 |

**KEN COPELAND**

| | | | |
|---|---|---|---|
| 57 | London HLP 8423 | Pledge Of Love/MINTS: Night Air | 40 |

**BOB & RON COPPER**

| | | | |
|---|---|---|---|
| 63 | EFDSS 1002 | BOB & RON COPPER (LP) | 35 |

**COPPER FAMILY**

| | | | |
|---|---|---|---|
| 71 | Leader LED 2067 | A SONG FOR EVERY SEASON (LP, sampler, tracks from 4-LP set) | 40 |
| 71 | Leader LEAB 404 | A SONG FOR ALL SEASONS (4xLP) | 70 |

**COPPERFIELD**

| | | | |
|---|---|---|---|
| 69 | Instant IN 004 | Any Old Time/I'm No Good For Her | 15 |
| 69 | Parlophone R 5818 | I'll Hold Out My Hand/Far Away Love | 10 |

*(see also Quartz)*

**JOHNNY COPPIN**

| | | | |
|---|---|---|---|
| 87 | Rola RO 15 | FOREST & VALE (LP) | 20 |

**COPS 'N ROBBERS**

| | | | |
|---|---|---|---|
| 64 | Decca F 12019 | St. James Infirmary/There's Gotta Be A Reason | 50 |
| 65 | Pye 7N 15870 | I Could Have Danced All Night/Just Keep Right On | 25 |
| 65 | Pye 7N 15928 | It's All Over Now Baby Blue/I've Found Out | 25 |

*(see also Fairies)*

**COPY CATS**

| | | | |
|---|---|---|---|
| 69 | Bullet BU 419 | Copy Cat (with Derrick Morgan)/BUNNY LEE ALL STARRS: Hot Lead | 20 |

**CORAL**

| | | | |
|---|---|---|---|
| 02 | Deltasonic DLTLP006 | THE CORAL (LP) | 30 |
| 02 | Deltasonic DLTLP036 | THE INVISIBLE INVASION (2-LP, gatefold) | 20 |
| 04 | Deltasonic DLTLP014 | MAGIC AND MEDICINE (2-LP, orange vinyl) | 20 |
| 07 | Deltasonic DLTLP 069 | ROOTS & ECHOES (2-LP) | 20 |
| 08 | Deltasonic DLTLP 083 | SINGLES COLLECTION (3-LP) | 25 |
| 10 | Deltasonic DLTBX 08 | BUTTERFLY HOUSE (LP, 2-CD, DVD, box set) | 25 |
| 14 | Skeleton SKL 006 | THE CURSE OF LOVE (LP, CD) | 25 |

**CORBAN**

| | | | |
|---|---|---|---|
| 78 | Acorn AC 002 | A BREAK IN THE CLOUDS (LP, with insert) | 18 |

**HARRY H. CORBETT**

| | | | |
|---|---|---|---|
| 67 | Decca F 12714 | Flower Power Fred/(I'm) Saving All My Love (with Unidentified Flower Objects) | 15 |

*(see also & Harry H. Corbett, Faraway Folk)*

**MIKE CORBETT & JAY HIRSH**

| | | | |
|---|---|---|---|
| 71 | Atlantic 2091-126 | Gypsey Child/Butterfly Day | 6 |
| 71 | Atlantic 2400 141 | MIKE CORBETT & JAY HIRSH (LP, gatefold sleeve) | 20 |

*(see also Mr. Flood's Party)*

**JERRY CORBITT**

| | | | |
|---|---|---|---|
| 69 | Polydor 583 576 | CORBITT (LP) | 15 |

**CORBY & CHAMPAGNE**

| | | | |
|---|---|---|---|
| 66 | Pye 7N 17203 | Time Marches On/I'll Be Back | 5 |

**JASON CORD**

| | | | |
|---|---|---|---|
| 69 | Chapter One CH 102 | I've Got My Eyes On You/I Can't Take No More Of Your Lies | 6 |
| 69 | Chapter One CH 110 | Why Shouldn't I/Spring Never Came Twice | 6 |

**FRANK CORDELL & HIS ORCHESTRA**

| | | | |
|---|---|---|---|
| 68 | National (No cat. no.) | Theme One/Theme Two (with John Meyer Group) | 8 |

**PHIL CORDELL**

| | | | |
|---|---|---|---|
| 69 | Warner Bros WB 8001 | Pumping The Water/Red Lady | 35 |

*(see also Thursday's Children)*

**CORDES**

| | | | |
|---|---|---|---|
| 65 | Cavern Sound IMSTL 1 | Give Her Time/She's Leaving | 70 |

**LOUISE CORDET**

| | | | |
|---|---|---|---|
| 62 | Decca F 11476 | I'm Just A Baby/In A Matter Of Moments | 5 |
| 62 | Decca F 11476 | I'm Just A Baby/In A Matter Of Moments (export copy in p/s) | 15 |

## CORDUROYS

| | | | |
|---|---|---|---|
| 62 | Decca F 11524 | Sweet Enough/Someone Else's Fool | 5 |
| 62 | Decca F 11524 | Sweet Enough/Someone Else's Fool (export copy in p/s) | 15 |
| 63 | Decca F 11673 | Around And Around/Which Way The Wind Blows | 15 |
| 64 | Decca F 11824 | Don't Let The Sun Catch You Crying/Loving Baby | 15 |
| 64 | Decca F 11875 | Don't Make Me Over/Two Lovers | 20 |
| 62 | Decca DFE 8515 | THE SWEET BEAT OF LOUISE CORDET (EP) | 70 |

## CORDUROYS
| | | | |
|---|---|---|---|
| 66 | Planet PLF 122 | Tick Tock/Too Much Of A Woman | 50 |

## CHICK COREA (& RETURN TO FOREVER)
| | | | |
|---|---|---|---|
| 74 | People PLEO 9 | SUNDANCE (LP) | 15 |

## PADDY COREA
| | | | |
|---|---|---|---|
| 72 | Explosion EX 2066 | Soul And Inspiration/STAGS: You Must Be Trying My Faith | 6 |

## CORKSCREW
| | | | |
|---|---|---|---|
| 79 | Highway SHY 7005 | FOR OPENERS (LP) | 25 |

## CORNBREAD & JERRY
| | | | |
|---|---|---|---|
| 61 | London HLG 9352 | L'il Ole Me/Loco Moto | 10 |

## DON CORNEL & ETERNALS
| | | | |
|---|---|---|---|
| 70 | Moodisc MU 3506 | Christmas Joy/WINSTON & RUPERT: Musically Beat | 7 |

## CORNELIUS
| | | | |
|---|---|---|---|
| 98 | Matador OLE 3000 | FANTASMA (LP) | 20 |
| 02 | Matador OLE 332-1 | POINT (LP) | 20 |

## EDDIE CORNELIUS
| | | | |
|---|---|---|---|
| 80 | GB Records GB 001 | That's Love Making In Your Eyes/Hurry Up | 15 |

## DON CORNELL
| | | | |
|---|---|---|---|
| 54 | Vogue Coral Q 2013 | Hold My Hand/I'm Blessed | 15 |
| 54 | Vogue Coral Q 2037 | S'Posin'/I Was Lucky | 10 |
| 55 | Vogue Coral Q 72058 | No Man Is An Island/All At Once | 8 |
| 55 | Vogue Coral Q 72070 | Give Me Your Love/When You Are In Love | 8 |
| 55 | Vogue Coral Q 72071 | Athena/Size 12 | 8 |
| 55 | Vogue Coral Q 72073 | Stranger In Paradise/The Devil's In Your Eyes | 8 |
| 55 | Vogue Coral Q 72080 | Unchained Melody/Most Of All | 8 |
| 55 | Vogue Coral Q 72104 | Love Is A Many Splendored Thing/The Bible Tells Me So | 6 |
| 56 | Vogue Coral Q 72132 | There Once Was A Beautiful/Make A Wish | 6 |
| 56 | Vogue Coral Q 72144 | Teenage Meeting (Gonna Rock It Right)/I Still Have A Prayer | 30 |
| 57 | Vogue Coral Q 72234 | Let's Be Friends/Afternoon In Madrid | 6 |

## JERRY CORNELL
| | | | |
|---|---|---|---|
| 55 | London HL 8157 | Please Don't Talk About Me When I'm Gone/St. Louis Blues | 25 |

## LYN CORNELL
| | | | |
|---|---|---|---|
| 60 | Decca F 11227 | Like Love/Demon Lover | 20 |
| 60 | Decca F 11260 | Teaser/What A Feeling | 5 |
| 62 | Decca F 11430 | African Waltz/Moanin' | 5 |
| 62 | Decca F 11469 | I Sold My Heart To The Junkman/Step Up And Rescue Me | 15 |
| 63 | Decca F 11750 | Sally Go Round The Roses/You Can Kiss Me If You Like | 10 |

## CORNFLAKES
| | | | |
|---|---|---|---|
| 62 | Fontana 267 227TF | Oh, Listen To The Band/Moonstruck | 10 |

## BARRY CORNISH
| | | | |
|---|---|---|---|
| 73 | Jam 60 | Questions/Stones From The Wishing Well | 8 |

## ARNOLD CORNS
| | | | |
|---|---|---|---|
| 71 | B&C CB 149 | Moonage Daydream/Hang Onto Yourself (Demo copy as 'The Arnold Corns') | 75 |
| 71 | B&C CB 149 | Moonage Daydream/Hang Onto Yourself (as 'The Arnold Corns') | 60 |
| 72 | B&C CB 189 | Hang Onto Yourself/Man In The Middle (Demo copy) | 50 |
| 72 | B&C CB 189 | Hang Onto Yourself/Man In The Middle (reissue) | 40 |
| 74 | Mooncrest MOON 25 | Hang Onto Yourself/Man In The Middle (Demo copy) | 25 |
| 74 | Mooncrest MOON 25 | Hang Onto Yourself/Man In The Middle (reissue) | 20 |

*(see also David Bowie)*

## CORONADOS
| | | | |
|---|---|---|---|
| 64 | London HL 9895 | Love Me With All Your Heart/Querida | 10 |
| 67 | Stateside SS 2043 | Johnny B. Goode/Shook Me Down | 10 |

## CORONETS (1)
| | | | |
|---|---|---|---|
| 54 | Columbia SCM 5117 | Do, Do, Do, Do, Do, Do, Do It Again/I Ain't Gonna Do It No More | 15 |

*(see also Chris Sandford & Coronets, Tony Brent, Ronnie Harris, Eric Jupp, Lee Lawrence)*

## CORONETS (2)
| | | | |
|---|---|---|---|
| 68 | Stresa BEV SP 1104/1105 | I Wonder Why/You're Leaving Tomorrow | 45 |

## CORPORATION (JAMAICA)
| | | | |
|---|---|---|---|
| 70 | Grape GR 3022 | Sweet Musille/Walking Thru' Jerusalem | 22 |

*(see also Claudette & Corporation, Billy Jack)*

## CORPORATION (U.S.)
| | | | |
|---|---|---|---|
| 69 | Capitol E-T/E-ST 175 | THE CORPORATION (LP) | 25 |

## CORRIDOR ONE
| | | | |
|---|---|---|---|
| 81 | Hip HIP 1 | Working On The Papers/Corridor One (p/s) | 5 |

## CORRIE FOLK TRIO/CORRIES
| | | | |
|---|---|---|---|
| 63 | Waverley SLP 530 | Love Is Teasing/O, Waly Waly (p/s) | 8 |

## JAY C CORRY
| | | | |
|---|---|---|---|
| 76 | Decca FR 13680 | Love Me Or Leave Me/House Of Truth | 12 |

## CORSAIRS (JAMAICA)
| | | | |
|---|---|---|---|
| 70 | Unity UN 558 | Goodnight My Love/Lover Girl | 8 |

### CORSAIRS (U.K.)
| | | | |
|---|---|---|---|
| 67 | CBS 202624 | Pay You Back With Interest/I'm Going To Shut You Down | 20 |

### CORSAIRS (U.S.)
| | | | |
|---|---|---|---|
| 62 | Pye International 7N 25142 | I'll Take You Home/Sitting On Your Doorstep (with Jay 'Bird' Uzzel) | 15 |

### BOB CORT (SKIFFLE GROUP)
| | | | |
|---|---|---|---|
| 57 | Decca FJ 10831 | It Takes A Worried Man To Sing A Worried Blues/ Don't You Rock Me Daddy-O | 10 |
| 57 | Decca F 10892 | Six-Five Special/Roll Jen Jenkins | 10 |
| 57 | Decca F 10899 | Maggie May/Jessamine (with Liz Winters) | 10 |
| 57 | Decca F 10951 | 'Bob Cort Skiffle Party' Medley (Parts 1 & 2) | 5 |
| 57 | Decca F 10905 | Schoolday (Ring! Ring! Goes The Bell)/Ain't It A Shame (To Sing Skiffle On Sunday) | 12 |
| 60 | Decca F 11256 | Mule Skinner Blues/The Ballad Of Walter Williams (solo) | 10 |

(see also Liz Winters & Bob Cort)

### DAVE 'BABY' CORTEZ
| | | | |
|---|---|---|---|
| 60 | London HLU 9126 | Deep In The Heart Of Texas/You're Just Right | 15 |
| 62 | Pye International 7N 25159 | Rinky Dink/Getting Right | 15 |
| 66 | Roulette RK 7001 | Countdown/Summertime (Cha Cha Cha) | 5 |
| 60 | London RE-U 1233 | DAVE 'BABY' CORTEZ (EP) | 20 |
| 64 | London HA-U 8142 | THE GOLDEN HITS OF DAVE 'BABY' CORTEZ (LP) | 30 |

### CORTINAS (1)
| | | | |
|---|---|---|---|
| 68 | Polydor 56255 | Phoebe's Flower Shop/Too Much In Love | 15 |

### CORTINAS (2)
| | | | |
|---|---|---|---|
| 77 | Step Forward SF 1 | Fascist Dictator/Television Families (p/s, first 1,000 in card sleeve) | 20 |
| 77 | Step Forward SF 1 | Fascist Dictator/Television Families (p/s) | 15 |
| 78 | Step Forward SF 6 | Defiant Pose/Independence (p/s) | 12 |
| 78 | Step Forward SF 6 | Defiant Pose/Independence (12", pink die-cut sleeve) | 12 |
| 78 | CBS CBS 6759 | Heartache/Ask Mr. Waverley (p/s) | 8 |
| 78 | CBS CBS 82831 | TRUE ROMANCES (LP, with photo insert) | 20 |

### LEE CORVETTE
| | | | |
|---|---|---|---|
| 62 | Decca F11481 | The Heart You Break (May Be Your Own)/Tender Love | 10 |

### CORVETTES
| | | | |
|---|---|---|---|
| 82 | Bitchin BIT 100 | Surf, Don't Walk/She'll Be Blonde (p/s) | 15 |
| 84 | Bitchin BIT 101 | Girls Cars Girls Sun Girls Surf Girls Fun Girls/The Beach Is Not Enough (p/s) | 18 |

### LARRY CORYELL
| | | | |
|---|---|---|---|
| 70 | Vanguard 6359 005 | SPACES (LP) | 25 |
| 85 | Nimbus/Novus AN 3024 | STANDING OVATION (LP, NImbus Supercut, mail order only sold via Practical Hi Fi magazine) | 40 |

(see also Jazz Composers Orchestra)

### BILL COSBY
| | | | |
|---|---|---|---|
| 67 | Warner Bros WB 7072 | Little Ole Man (Uptight! Everything's Alright)/Don'cha Know (in p/s) | 10 |

### COSMETICS
| | | | |
|---|---|---|---|
| 81 | Panic SEC 31 | Closures/The Chain (p/s) | 8 |

### COSMIC BABY/VANGELIS
| | | | |
|---|---|---|---|
| 94 | East West SAM 1484 | A TRIBUTE TO BLADERUNNER (12", double pack, promo only) | 20 |

(see also Vangelis)

### COSMIC EYE
| | | | |
|---|---|---|---|
| 72 | Regal Zono. SLRZ 1030 | DREAM SEQUENCE (LP) | 220 |

### COSMIC PSYCHOS
| | | | |
|---|---|---|---|
| 88 | What Goes On GOES ON 23 | COSMIC PSYCHOS (LP) | 15 |

### COSMIC INTRUSION
| | | | |
|---|---|---|---|
| 78 | Seajay CW 01 | Celestine/Carol | 5 |

### COSMO
| | | | |
|---|---|---|---|
| 63 | Blue Beat BB 175 | Gypsy Woman/Do Unto Others | 10 |
| 64 | Blue Beat BB 244 | One God/BUSTER'S ALL STARS: Prince Royal (actually "Reincarnation") | 50 |
| 64 | Blue Beat BB 269 | Rice And Badgee/BUSTER'S ALL STARS: The Tickler | 50 |

(see also Cosmo & Dennis, Denzil Dennis)

### COSMO & DENNIS (ALIAS DENZIL)
| | | | |
|---|---|---|---|
| 62 | Blue Beat BB 145 | Bed Of Roses/Tonight And Evermore (as Cosmo & Denzil) | 10 |
| 65 | Blue Beat BB 296 | Sweet Rosemarie/Lollipop I'm In Love | 12 |
| 65 | Blue Beat BB 312 | Come On Come On/I Don't Want You (As COSMO & DENZIL) | 12 |

(see also Cosmo)

### FRANK COSMO
| | | | |
|---|---|---|---|
| 63 | Island WI 058 | Revenge/Laughin' At You (B-side actually with Bobby Aitken) | 15 |
| 63 | Island WI 073 | Dear Dreams/Go Go Go | 15 |
| 63 | Island WI 100 | Merry Christmas/Greetings From Beverley's | 20 |
| 63 | R&B JB 119 | I Love You/DON DRUMMOND: Close Of Play | 22 |
| 64 | Island WI 135 | Better Get Right/Ameletia | 20 |
| 64 | Black Swan WI 446 | Alone/Beautiful Book | 20 |

(see also Two Kings)

### COSMOTHEKA
| | | | |
|---|---|---|---|
| 70s | Shy SHY 7001 | WINES & SPIRITS (LP) | 35 |
| 85 | Dambuster DAM 1 | COSMOTHEKA (LP) | 18 |

### DON COSTA, HIS ORCHESTRA & CHORUS
| | | | |
|---|---|---|---|
| 55 | London HLF 8186 | Love Is A Many Splendoured Thing/Safe In The Harbour | 10 |

### JACK COSTANZO & TUBBY HAYES
| | | | |
|---|---|---|---|
| 62 | Fontana TFL 5190 | COSTANZO PLUS TUBBS - EQUATION IN RHYTHM (LP, mono) | 50 |
| 62 | Fontana STFL 598 | COSTANZO PLUS TUBBS - EQUATION IN RHYTHM (LP, stereo) | 40 |

(see also Tubby Hayes)

## CELIA COSTELLO
| | | | |
|---|---|---|---|
| 75 | Leader LEE 4054 | CELIA COSTELLO (LP, with insert) | 20 |

## DANNY COSTELLO
| | | | |
|---|---|---|---|
| 57 | Oriole CB 1393 | Like A Brook Gets Lost In A River/That's Where I Shine | 5 |

## DAY COSTELLO
| | | | |
|---|---|---|---|
| 71 | Spark SRL 1042 | The Long And Winding Road/Free (Unlimited Horizons) | 10 |

*(see also Ross McManus)*

## ELVIS COSTELLO (& ATTRACTIONS)
| | | | |
|---|---|---|---|
| 77 | Stiff BUY 11 | Less Than Zero/Radio Sweetheart (p/s) | 10 |
| 77 | Stiff Buy 14 | Alison/Welcome To The Working Week (p/s) | 10 |
| 77 | Stiff BUY 14 | Alison/Welcome To The Working Week (p/s, A-side mispress on white vinyl) | 300 |
| 77 | Stiff BUY 15 | (The Angels Wanna Wear My) Red Shoes/Mystery Dance (push-out centre) | 6 |
| 77 | Stiff BUY 15 | Red Shoes/Mystery Dance (p/s, mispress, plays "Dream Tobacco" by Max Wall) | 8 |
| 77 | Stiff BUY 20 DJ | Watching The Detectives (short version) /Blame It On Cain (live)/Mystery Dance (live) (promo copy) | 40 |
| 77 | Stiff BUY 20 | Watching The Detectives/Blame It On Cain (live)/Mystery Dance (live) (phone book p/s) | 8 |
| 78 | Radar ADA 24 | Radio Radio/Tiny Steps (12", promo-only, 500 pressed) | 15 |
| 78 | Radar RG 1 | Talking In The Dark/Wednesday Week (p/s, gig freebie) | 8 |
| 80 | 2-Tone CHS TT 7 | I Can't Stand Up For Falling Down/Girls Talk (unreleased, later a gig freebie, more common issue (see other price) has XX1 in run-off groove, 13,000 pressed) | 50 |
| 80 | 2-Tone CHS TT 7 | I Can't Stand Up For Falling Down/Girls Talk (unreleased, gig freebie, more common issue with XX1 in run-off groove, 13,000 pressed) | 20 |
| 80 | Stiff GRAB 3 | STIFF SINGLES FOUR PACK (BUY 11, 14, 15 & 20 in clear plastic wallet) | 20 |
| 81 | F-Beat XX 17 | A Good Year For The Roses/Your Angel Steps Out Of Heaven (withdrawn p/s) | 10 |
| 77 | Stiff Seez 3 | MY AIM IS TRUE (LP, 1st pressing with 'Help us hype Elvis' promo insert) | 150 |
| 77 | Stiff Seez 3 | MY AIM IS TRUE (LP) | 30 |
| 78 | Radar RAD 3 | THIS YEAR'S MODEL (LP, with free 7" "Stranger In The House"/"Neat Neat Neat" (live) [die-cut company sleeve, SAM 83], 50,000 pressed; 1st 5,000 shrinkwrapped and stickered) | 25 |
| 79 | Radar RAD 15 | ARMED FORCES (LP, foldout stickered sleeve with free EP Live At Hollywood High [p/s, SAM 90] & postcards) | 20 |
| 79 | Radar RAD 15 | ARMED FORCES (LP, mispress, plays "[What's So Funny 'Bout] Peace, Love & Understanding" instead of "Two Little Hitlers"; sticker on insert) | 25 |
| 82 | F-Beat EC CHAT 2 | A CONVERSATION WITH ELVIS COSTELLO (2-LP) | 20 |

*(see also Nick Lowe, George Jones, Coward Brothers)*

## COTERIE
| | | | |
|---|---|---|---|
| 69 | Emerald GEM 1026 | A SWING TO FOLK (LP) | 40 |

## JAMES COTTON (BLUES BAND)
| | | | |
|---|---|---|---|
| 78 | Buddah BDS 471 | Rock'n'Roll Music/Help Me | 5 |
| 68 | Vanguard SVRL 19035 | CUT YOU LOOSE! (LP, as James Cotton Blues Band) | 25 |

## JIMMY COTTON
| | | | |
|---|---|---|---|
| 62 | Columbia SEG 8141 | CHRIS BARBER PRESENTS JIMMY COTTON (EP) | 20 |
| 62 | Columbia SEG 8189 | CHRIS BARBER PRESENTS JIMMY COTTON NO. 2 (EP) | 20 |

*(see also James Cotton Blues Band, Alexis Korner)*

## JOSEPH COTTON
| | | | |
|---|---|---|---|
| 77 | Observer OB 001 | Fit And Ready/OBSERVER: Iron Fist (12") | 40 |

## MIKE COTTON JAZZMEN
| | | | |
|---|---|---|---|
| 61 | Columbia DB 4697 | Senorita/The Colonel's Tune | 5 |
| 62 | Columbia DB 4821 | The Cobbler's Song/African Twist | 5 |

## MIKE COTTON (SOUND)
| | | | |
|---|---|---|---|
| 62 | Columbia DB 4910 | The Tinker/Zulu Warrior (as the Mike Cotton Jazz Men) | 10 |
| 63 | Columbia DB 7029 | Swing That Hammer/Heartaches (as Mike Cotton Jazzmen) | 8 |
| 63 | Columbia DB 7134 | Midnite Flyer/One Mint Julep (as Mike Cotton Band) | 10 |
| 64 | Columbia DB 7267 | I Don't Wanna Know/This Little Pig | 60 |
| 64 | Columbia DB 7382 | Round And Round/Beau Dudley | 50 |
| 65 | Columbia DB 7623 | Make Up Your Mind/I've Got My Eye On You | 50 |
| 66 | Polydor BM 56096 | Harlem Shuffle/Like That | 40 |
| 62 | Columbia SEG 8144 | COTTON PICKING (EP) | 40 |
| 63 | Columbia SEG 8190 | THE WILD AND THE WILLING (EP) | 40 |
| 64 | Columbia 33SX 1647 | MIKE COTTON SOUND (LP) | 500 |

*(see also Lucas & Mike Cotton Sound, Satisfaction)*

## COTTON CASINO
| | | | |
|---|---|---|---|
| 03 | Riot Season REPOSE 701 | Fly High/Open The Shine (white vinyl, p/s) | 8 |

*(See also Acid Mothers Temple and the Melting Paraiso UFO)*

## COUGARS
| | | | |
|---|---|---|---|
| 63 | Parlophone R 4989 | Saturday Night At The Duckpond/See You In Dreamland | 10 |
| 63 | Parlophone R 5038 | Red Square/Fly-By-Nite | 10 |
| 64 | Parlophone R 5115 | Caviare And Chips/While The City Sleeps | 5 |
| 63 | Parlophone GEP 8886 | SATURDAY NIGHT WITH THE COUGARS (EP) | 20 |

## ROGER COULAM QUARTET
| | | | |
|---|---|---|---|
| 67 | CBS 52399 | ORGAN IN ORBIT (LP) | 20 |
| 70 | Fontana 16009 | BLOW HOT, BLOW COLD (LP) | 20 |

## DENIS COULDRY (& SMILE)
| | | | |
|---|---|---|---|
| 68 | Decca F 12734 | James In The Basement (solo)/DENIS COULDRY & NEXT COLLECTION: I Am Nearly There | 40 |
| 68 | Decca F 12786 | Penny For The Wind/Tea And Toast, Mr. Watson? (as Denis Couldry & Smile) | 20 |

*(see also Felius Andromeda)*

## COULSON, DEAN, MCGUINNESS, FLINT
| | | | |
|---|---|---|---|
| 72 | DJM DJS 267 | Lay Down Your Weary Tune/Tiny Montgomery/I Wanna Be Your lover | 6 |

| | | |
|---|---|---|
| 72 | DJM DJLPS 424 | LO AND BEHOLD (LP, gatefold sleeve) ........................................................................ 18 |

*(see also Manfred Mann, McGuinness Flint, Dennis Coulson, Lyle McGuinness Band)*

## DENNIS COULSON
| | | |
|---|---|---|
| 73 | Elektra K 42148 | DENNIS COULSON (LP, gatefold sleeve) ....................................................................... 15 |

## PHIL COULTER ORCHESTRA
| | | |
|---|---|---|
| 68 | Pye 7N 17511 | Congratulations/Gold Rush ........................................................................................ 20 |

## COUNT BISHOPS
| | | |
|---|---|---|
| 74 | Purple PUR 122 | Gazaroody/The So, So Song.......................................................................................... 10 |
| 77 | Chiswick S12 | Baby You're Wrong/Stay Free (p/s) ............................................................................. 8 |
| 78 | Chiswick NS 35 | Mr Jones/Human Bean/Route 66/Too Much Too Soon (unissued, test pressings only, as Bishops)................................................................................................................... 18 |
| 77 | Chiswick WIK 1 | THE COUNT BISHOPS (LP) ........................................................................................... 18 |

*(see also Cannibals)*

## COUNT BUSTY & RUDIES
| | | |
|---|---|---|
| 68 | Melody MRC 003 | You Like It/The Reggay ............................................................................................. 200 |

## COUNT DOWNE & ZEROS
| | | |
|---|---|---|
| 64 | Ember EMB S 189 | Hello My Angel/Don't Shed A Tear ............................................................................. 40 |

*(see also Peter & Headlines)*

## COUNT FIVE
| | | |
|---|---|---|
| 66 | Pye International 7N 25393 | Psychotic Reaction/They're Gonna Get You ............................................................... 75 |
| 87 | Edsel ED 225 | PSYCHOTIC REACTION (LP) ......................................................................................... 20 |

## COUNT HALA
| | | |
|---|---|---|
| 69 | Rude Boy RBH 005 | Cut Price Pussy/THE ATTACKERS : Police In Z Cars Blues........................................... 50 |
| 70 | Rude Boy RBH 006 | Gems Of Christies/Cut Price Meow ........................................................................... 25 |

## COUNT HOUSE FOLK MUSIC CLUB
| | | |
|---|---|---|
| 65 | Own label MSCH 2 | MORE SINGING AT THE COUNT HOUSE (LP, private pressing)................................... 250 |

## COUNT LASHER
| | | |
|---|---|---|
| 59 | Caribou 106 | Caribou Calabash/Dalvey Girl .................................................................................... 20 |

## COUNT MACHUKI
| | | |
|---|---|---|
| 10 | Randys THB 7002 | Pepper Pot/WINSTON SAMUELS: Lick It Back .......................................................... 18 |

## COUNT OSSIE & HIS MYSTIC REVELATION
| | | |
|---|---|---|
| 71 | Ashanti ASH 404 | Rasta Reggae/Samia.................................................................................................. 15 |
| 71 | Moodisc MU 3515 | Whispering Drums/SLIM SMITH & UNIQUES: Give Me Some More Loving................ 15 |
| 71 | Moodisc HM 105 | Whispering Drums/SLIM SMITH & UNIQUES: Give Me Some More Loving................ 15 |
| 74 | Ashanti NTI 1301 | GROUNATION (3-LP, with Mystic Revelation Of Rastafari)........................................ 50 |
| 76 | Dynamic DVLS 1001 | TALES OF MOZAMBIQUIE (LP)..................................................................................... 30 |

*(see also Jackie Estick, Gaylads, Soul Defenders)*

## COUNT OSSIE & THE REVOLUTIONARIES
| | | |
|---|---|---|
| 78 | Charmers CH 0012 | Hog Head/TRINITY: Dog Meat (12")........................................................................... 40 |

## COUNT STICKY
| | | |
|---|---|---|
| 68 | Amalgamated AMG 825 | Train To Soulsville/ERIC MORRIS : Cinderella ........................................................... 40 |

## COUNT SUCKLE
| | | |
|---|---|---|
| 70 | Q 2200 | Lavender Blues/Humpty Dumpty ............................................................................... 15 |
| 70 | Q 2201 | Please Don't Go/FREDDIE & THE NOTES: Bread On The Table .................................. 15 |

## COUNT VICTORS
| | | |
|---|---|---|
| 62 | Coral Q 72456 | Peepin' 'N' Hidin'/Don't Laugh At Me ('Cos I'm A Fool) ............................................... 8 |
| 63 | Coral Q 72462 | Road Runner/Lorie ...................................................................................................... 8 |

## COUNTDOWNS
| | | |
|---|---|---|
| 63 | United Artists UP 1024 | Mouse On The Moon/The Big Safari ........................................................................... 10 |

*(see also John Barry)*

## COUNTING CROWS
| | | |
|---|---|---|
| 94 | Geffen GFS 69 | Mr Jones/Raining In Baltimore/Mr Jones (live) (p/s) ................................................. 10 |
| 93 | Geffen GEF 24528 | AUGUST AND EVERYTHING AFTER (LP) ....................................................................... 70 |

## COUNTRY BOY
| | | |
|---|---|---|
| 64 | Blue Beat BB 236 | I'm A Lonely Boy (actually by Shenley Duffas)/EDWARD'S ALL STARS: He's Gone Ska .... 35 |

## COUNTRY EXPRESS
| | | |
|---|---|---|
| 70 | Lucky LU 104 | Watching Trains Go By/Blue Against Grey..................................................................... 8 |

## COUNTRY FEVER
| | | |
|---|---|---|
| 69 | Bell BLL 1052 | Too Much Of nothingTears Of Rage ............................................................................. 8 |
| 71 | Lucky LU 106 | Mental Revenge/My World Has Ended ....................................................................... 10 |

## COUNTRY FOLK
| | | |
|---|---|---|
| 70s | Thule SLP 101 | THE COUNTRY FOLK (LP, private pressing)................................................................ 180 |

## COUNTRY FUNK
| | | |
|---|---|---|
| 70 | Polydor 248 2018 | COUNTRY FUNK (LP)..................................................................................................... 18 |

## COUNTRY GAZETTE
| | | |
|---|---|---|
| 72 | United Artists UAG 29404 | TRAITOR IN OUR MIDST (LP) ....................................................................................... 15 |

*(see also Flying Burrito Brothers)*

## COUNTRY HAMS
| | | |
|---|---|---|
| 74 | EMI EMI 2220 | Walking In The Park With Eloise/Bridge On The River Suite (p/s, red & brown label) .... 50 |
| 82 | EMI EMI 2220 | Walking In The Park With Eloise/Bridge On The River Suite (p/s, reissue, beige label) .. 15 |

*(see also Paul McCartney/Wings, Chet Atkins, Floyd Cramer)*

## COUNTRY JOE & THE FISH
| | | |
|---|---|---|
| 67 | Fontana TF 882 | Not So Sweet Martha Lorraine/Love ........................................................................... 15 |
| 69 | Vanguard VA 3 | Here I Go Again/It's So Nice To Have Love .................................................................... 7 |
| 70 | Vanguard 6076 250 | I-Feel-Like-I'm-Fixin'-To-Die Rag/Maria...................................................................... 10 |
| 67 | Fontana TFL 6081 | ELECTRIC MUSIC FOR THE MIND AND BODY (LP, flipback sleeve, also Stereo STFL 6087) .......................................................................................................................... 40 |

MINT VALUE £

| 68 | Fontana TFL 6086 | I-FEEL-LIKE-I'M-FIXIN'-TO-DIE (LP, flipback sleeve) | 40 |
| 68 | Vanguard SVRL 19006 | TOGETHER (LP) | 20 |
| 69 | Vanguard SVRL 19026 | ELECTRIC MUSIC FOR THE MIND AND BODY (LP, reissue) | 30 |
| 69 | Vanguard SVRL 19029 | I-FEEL-LIKE-I'M-FIXIN'-TO-DIE (LP, reissue) | 15 |
| 69 | Vanguard SVRL 19048 | HERE WE ARE AGAIN (LP) | 20 |
| 70 | Vanguard 6359 002 | C.J. FISH (LP) | 20 |
| 72 | Vanguard VSD 79244 | ELECTRIC MUSIC FOR THE MIND AND BODY (LP, reissue, 'West Brothers' printing credit) | 18 |
| 73 | Vanguard VSD 27/28 | THE LIFE AND TIMES OF (2-LP, gatefold sleeve, quadrophonic) | 20 |
| 75 | Vanguard VSD 79244 | ELECTRIC MUSIC FOR THE MIND AND BODY (LP, reissue) | 15 |
| 80 | Piccadilly PIC 3009 | THE EARLY YEARS (LP, private pressing, withdrawn) | 40 |

(see also Country Joe McDonald)

## COUNTRY JUG
| 72 | Decca F 13270 | I'm Sorry/Do You Wanna?/Flying | 8 |

(see also Ray Dorset)

## COUNTRYMEN
| 69 | Jayboy BOY 3 | After All/White Rose Of Athens | 5 |

## WAYNE/JAYNE COUNTY (& ELECTRIC CHAIRS)
| 77 | Illegal IL 002 | Stuck On You/Paranoia Paradise/The Last Time (p/s) | 10 |
| 77 | Sweet F.A. WC 1 | Fuck Off/On The Crest (p/s) | 12 |
| 78 | Safari SAFE 1 | Eddie And Sheena/Rock And Roll Cleopatra (p/s, with cartoon insert) | 15 |
| 78 | Safari SAFE 1 | Eddie And Sheena/Rock And Roll Cleopatra (p/s, without cartoon insert) | 10 |
| 78 | Safari SAFE 6 | I Had Too Much To Dream Last Night/Fuck Off (unissued) | 0 |
| 78 | Safari WC 2 | BLATANTLY OFFENZIVE (EP, gold vinyl) | 10 |
| 78 | Safari SAFE 9 | Trying To Get On The Radio/Evil Minded Momma (p/s) | 5 |
| 79 | Illegal IL 005 | Thunder When She Walks/What You Got (p/s) | 6 |
| 79 | Safari SAFE 19 | So Many Ways/J'Attends Les Marines (p/s, as Electric Chairs) | 8 |
| 78 | Safari LONG 1 | ELECTRIC CHAIRS (LP) | 20 |
| 78 | Safari GOOD 1 | STORM THE GATES OF HEAVEN (LP, multicoloured or grey marbled vinyl) | 20 |
| 79 | Safari GOOD 2 | THINGS YOUR MOTHER NEVER TOLD YOU (LP) | 18 |

(see also Mystere Five's)

## DIANA COUPLAND
| 60 | HMV POP 690 | Love Him/I Am Loved | 5 |

## COURIERS
| 66 | Ember EMB S 218 | Take Away/Done Me Wrong (with p/s) | 80 |
| 66 | Ember EMB S 218 | Take Away/Done Me Wrong | 25 |

(see also William E. Kimber)

## COURIERS
| 69 | Ash ALP 201 | PACK UP YOUR SORROWS (LP) | 30 |

## COURTEENERS
| 07 | Loog LOOG 022 | Cavorting/No You Didn't, No You Don't (p/s, 750 only) | 20 |
| 10 | Polydor 2758403 | ELECTRIC LICK (EP, 10", numbered) | 10 |
| 13 | V2 VVR726589 | Lose Control/Chipping Away | 6 |
| 08 | Polydor 1767024 | ST. JUDE (LP) | 40 |
| 10 | Polydor 2729354 | FALCON (LP) | 40 |

## COURTIERS OF FASHION
| 83 | Sonar SON 1 | Courtiers Of Fashion/The Discussion (p/s) | 6 |

## COURT MARTIAL
| 82 | Riot City RIOT 11 | NO SOLUTION (EP) | 15 |

## DEAN COURTNEY
| 96 | Kent 6T 12 | Today Is My Day/SHARON SCOTT: (Putting My Heart) Under Lock And Key | 35 |

## COURTSHIPS
| 72 | UK USA 6 | Oops It Just Slipped Out/Love Ain't Love (Until You Give It To Somebody) | 10 |

## COURTYARD MUSIC GROUP
| 74 | Deroy | JUST OUR WAY OF SAYING HELLO (LP, private pressing) | 1500 |
| 15 | No Label or Cat no | JUST OUR WAY OF SAYING GOODBYE (LP, reissue, with 48 page booklet, 300 only) | 70 |

## COUSINS (BELGIUM)
| 61 | Palette PG 9011 | Kili Watch/Feugo | 10 |
| 61 | Palette PG 9017 | Bouddha/Kana Kapila | 10 |
| 62 | Palette PG 9035 | Anda/Danseuse | 10 |

## DAVE COUSINS
| 72 | A&M AMS 7032 | Going Home/Ways And Means | 6 |
| 72 | A&M AMLS 68118 | TWO WEEKS LAST SUMMER (LP, brown label) | 35 |
| 79 | Old School SLURP 1 | OLD SCHOOL SONGS (LP, private pressing with Brian Willoughby) | 35 |

(see also The Strawbs)

## COUSTEAU
| 00 | Palm PALMLP-58-1 | COUSTEAU (LP, numbered) | 18 |

## DON COVAY (& GOODTIMERS)
| 61 | Pye International 7N 25075 | Pony Time/Love Boat | 30 |
| 61 | Philips PB 1140 | Shake Wid The Shake/Every Which Way | 30 |
| 62 | Cameo Parkway C 239 | The Popeye Waddle/One Little Boy Had Money | 30 |
| 64 | Atlantic AT 4006 | Mercy, Mercy/Can't Stay Away | 20 |
| 65 | Atlantic AT 4016 | Take This Hurt Off Me/Please Don't Let Me Know | 20 |
| 65 | Atlantic AT 4056 | See Saw/I Never Get Enough Of Your Love | 20 |
| 66 | Atlantic AT 4078 | Sookie Sookie/Watching The Late Late Show | 15 |
| 66 | Atlantic 584 025 | You Put Something In Me/Iron Out The Rough Spots | 15 |
| 66 | Atlantic 584 059 | See Saw/Somebody's Got To Love You | 15 |
| 67 | Atlantic 584 082 | Shingaling '67/I Was There | 10 |

| | | | |
|---|---|---|---|
| 67 | Atlantic 584 094 | Sookie Sookie/Mercy Mercy | 10 |
| 67 | Atlantic 584 114 | 40 Days - 40 Nights/The Usual Place | 10 |
| 70 | Atlantic 2091 018 | Everything I Do Goin' Be Funky/Key To The Highway | 5 |
| 65 | Atlantic ATL 5025 | MERCY! (LP, plum label) | 80 |
| 67 | Atlantic 587 062 | SEE-SAW (LP) | 30 |
| 69 | Atlantic K 50225 | HOUSE OF BLUE LIGHT (LP) | 25 |

*(see also Soul Clan)*

## DAVID COVERDALE

| | | | |
|---|---|---|---|
| 77 | Purple PUR 133 | Hole In The Sky/Blindman | 5 |
| 78 | Purple PUR 136 | Breakdown/Only My Soul | 5 |
| 90 | Epic 656 292 7 | Last Note Of Freedom/HANS ZIMMER: Car Building (poster p/s) | 8 |
| 77 | Purple TPS 3509 | DAVID COVERDALE'S WHITESNAKE (LP, with inner) | 25 |
| 77 | Purple TPS 3509TC | DAVID COVERDALE'S WHITESNAKE (LP, white label promo, plain sleeve, with insert) | 40 |
| 78 | Purple TPS 3513 | NORTHWINDS (LP, with inner sleeve) | 20 |

*(see also Whitesnake, Deep Purple, Wizard's Convention, Roger Glover, Jimmy Page)*

## COVERDALE PAGE

| | | | |
|---|---|---|---|
| 93 | EMI EMD 1041 | COVERDALE PAGE (LP) | 40 |

*(see also David Coverdale, Jimmy Page, Led Zeppelin, Deep Purple, Whitesnake)*

## COVERS

| | | | |
|---|---|---|---|
| 80 | Small Operations SO 001 | Young Girls/Boyfriend (p/s) | 20 |
| 79 | Decca FR 13880 | Modern Girls/Head Out On The Road | 30 |
| 81 | Polydor POSP 233 | Too Hot To Handle/Tinted Windows (p/s) | 6 |
| 81 | Polydor POSP 320 | Lonely Diamond/Shoot Shoot | 6 |

## JULIEN COVEY & MACHINE

| | | | |
|---|---|---|---|
| 67 | Island WIP 6009 | A Little Bit Hurt/Sweet Bacon | 50 |
| 78 | Island WIP 6442 | A Little Bit Hurt/Sweet Bacon (reissue) | 15 |
| 87 | Sunset | A Little Bit Hurt/Sweet Bacon (reissue) | 12 |

## JULIE COVINGTON

| | | | |
|---|---|---|---|
| 70 | Columbia DB 8649 | The Magic Wasn't There/The Way Things Ought To Be | 15 |
| 70 | Columbia DB 8705 | Tonight Your Love Is Over/If I Had My Time Again | 15 |
| 72 | RCA RCA 2181 | Day By Day/With Me It Goes Deeper | 6 |
| 71 | Columbia SCX 6466 | THE BEAUTIFUL CHANGES (LP) | 150 |

*(see also Rock Follies)*

## COWBOY

| | | | |
|---|---|---|---|
| 71 | Atlantic 2466 022 | REACH FOR THE SKY (LP) | 15 |
| 72 | Atlantic K 40312 | 5'LL GETCHA TEN (LP, with insert) | 20 |

## COWBOY COPAS

| | | | |
|---|---|---|---|
| 54 | Parlophone CMSP 10 | I Can't Go On/A Wreath On The Door Of My Heart (export issue) | 10 |
| 54 | Parlophone MSP 6079 | Tennessee Senorita/If You Will Let Me Be Your Love | 10 |
| 55 | Parlophone MSP 6164 | I'll Waltz With You In My Dreams/Return To Sender | 10 |
| 60 | Melodisc M 1566 | Alabam/I Can | 6 |

*(see also Johnny Bond)*

## COWBOY JUNKIES

| | | | |
|---|---|---|---|
| 88 | Cooking Vinyl COOK 011 | THE TRINITY SESSIONS (LP) | 15 |

## COWBOYS INTERNATIONAL

| | | | |
|---|---|---|---|
| 79 | Virgin VS 253 | Aftermath/Pt. 2 (orange vinyl, p/s) | 10 |
| 79 | Virgin V2136 | THE ORIGINAL SIN (LP, stickered PVC outer sleeve) | 15 |

*(see also Public Image Ltd.)*

## STANLEY COWELL

| | | | |
|---|---|---|---|
| 72 | Freedom FLP40104 | BRILLIANT CIRCLES (LP) | 25 |

## COWSILLS

| | | | |
|---|---|---|---|
| 67 | MGM MGM 1353 | The Rain, The Park And Other Things/River Blue | 30 |
| 68 | MGM MGM 1383 | We Can Fly/A Time For Remembrance | 15 |
| 68 | MGM MGM 1400 | In Need Of A Friend/Mr. Flynn | 6 |
| 68 | MGM MGM 1424 | Indian Lake/Newspaper Blanket | 6 |
| 68 | MGM MGM 1441 | Poor Baby/Meet Me At The Wishing Well | 5 |
| 69 | MGM MGM 1469 | Hair/What Is Happy | 5 |
| 69 | MGM MGM 1484 | The Prophecy Of Daniel And John The Divine/Gotta Get Away From It All | 5 |
| 69 | MGM MGM 1490 | Love American Style/Silver Threads And Golden Needles | 5 |
| 71 | London HLU 10329 | On My Side/There Is A Child | 5 |
| 67 | MGM C/CS 8059 | THE COWSILLS (LP) | 25 |
| 68 | MGM CS 8077 | WE CAN FLY (LP) | 20 |
| 68 | MGM CS 8095 | CAPTAIN SAD AND HIS SHIP OF FOOLS (LP) | 15 |

## BILLY COX

| | | | |
|---|---|---|---|
| 71 | Pye Intl. NSPL 25158 | NITRO FUNCTION (LP, blue/black label with logo-banner on left) | 100 |

*(see also Jimi Hendrix)*

## HARRY COX

| | | | |
|---|---|---|---|
| 65 | EFDSS LP 1004 | ENGLISH FOLK SINGER (LP) | 25 |
| 65 | DTS Records LFX 4 | ENGLISH FOLK SINGER (LP) | 15 |

## IDA COX

| | | | |
|---|---|---|---|
| 54 | London AL 3517 | SINGS THE BLUES (10" LP) | 40 |
| 75 | Gannet GEN 5371-5376 | PARAMOUNT RECORDINGS (6-LP box set) | 20 |

*(see also Ma Rainey)*

## IDA COX/ETHEL WATERS

| | | | |
|---|---|---|---|
| 50s | Poydras 104 | IDA COX AND ETHEL WATERS (EP) | 25 |

## MICHAEL COX

| | | | |
|---|---|---|---|
| 59 | Decca F 11166 | Boy Meets Girl/Teenage Love | 20 |

MINT VALUE £

| | | | |
|---|---|---|---|
| 59 | Decca F 11182 | Too Hot To Handle/Serious | 20 |
| 60 | Triumph RGM 1011 | Angela Jones/Don't Want To Know | 8 |
| 60 | Ember EMB S 103 | Angela Jones/Don't Want To Know (export issue) | 20 |
| 60 | HMV POP 789 | Along Came Caroline/Lonely Road | 10 |
| 61 | HMV POP 830 | Teenage Love/Linda | 10 |
| 61 | HMV POP 905 | Sweet Little Sixteen/Cover Girl | 25 |
| 62 | HMV POP 972 | Young Only Once/Honey Cause I Love You | 8 |
| 62 | HMV POP 1065 | Stand Up/In April | 5 |
| 63 | HMV POP 1137 | Don't You Break My Heart/Hark Is That A Cannon I Hear | 5 |
| 63 | HMV POP 1220 | Gee What A Party/See That Again | 10 |
| 64 | HMV POP 1293 | Rave On/Just Say Hello | 15 |
| 65 | HMV POP 1417 | Gypsy/It Ain't Right | 10 |
| 66 | Parlophone R 5436 | I Hate Getting Up In The Morning/Love 'Em And Leave 'Em | 5 |
| 67 | Parlophone R 5580 | I'll Always Love You/You Never Can Tell (Till You Try) | 5 |

**SONNY COX**

| | | | |
|---|---|---|---|
| 70 | Pama PM 815 | Choking Kind/Chocolate Candy | 12 |

**WALLY COX**

| | | | |
|---|---|---|---|
| 61 | Vogue V 9175 | I Can't Help It/The Heebie Jeebees | 15 |
| 74 | Pye Disco Demand DDS 105 | This Man/I've Had Enough | 8 |
| 74 | Pye Disco Demand DDS 105 | This Man/I've Had Enough (DJ Copy) | 15 |
| 89 | Kent 6T 5 | This Man Wants You/SIX TEASERS: Doing The Hundred | 15 |

**LOL COXHILL**

| | | | |
|---|---|---|---|
| 78 | Chiltern Sound CS 100 | MURDER IN THE AIR (12" EP) | 35 |
| 71 | Dandelion DSD 8008 | EAR OF THE BEHOLDER (2-LP, gatefold sleeve) | 90 |
| 71 | Dandelion DSD 69001 | EAR OF THE BEHOLDER (2-LP, gatefold sleeve) | 50 |
| 72 | Mushroom 150 MR 23 | TOVERBAL SWEET (LP) | 80 |
| 73 | Caroline C 1503 | COXHILL MILLER (LP, with Stephen Miller) | 20 |
| 74 | Caroline C 1507 | THE STORY SO FAR ... OH REALLY? (LP, with Stephen Miller) | 25 |
| 75 | Caroline C 1514 | LOL COXHILL & WELFARE STATE (LP) | 18 |
| 75 | Caroline C 1515 | FLEAS IN THE CUSTARD (LP) | 18 |
| 76 | Ogun OG 510 | DIVERSE (LP) | 15 |
| 78 | Ogun OG 525 | THE JOY OF PARANOIA (LP) | 15 |
| 78 | Ictus 0008 | MOOT (LP) | 25 |
| 80 | Pipe PIPE 1 | SLOW MUSIC (LP) | 30 |

*(see also Stephen Miller & Lol Coxhill, Kevin Ayers, Steve York's Camelo Pardalis)*

**COXHILL BEDFORD DUO**

| | | | |
|---|---|---|---|
| 71 | Polydor 2001 253 | Pretty Little Girl (Parts 1 & 2) | 25 |
| 72 | Dandelion 2058 214 | Mood/WILL DANDY & DANDYLETTES: Sonny Boy/Oh Mein Papa | 20 |

*(see also David Bedford, Lol Coxhill)*

**GRAHAM COXON**

| | | | |
|---|---|---|---|
| 00 | Transcopic 10 RDJ 6541 | Oochy Woochy/That's When I Reach For My Revolver (10" promo p/s) | 6 |
| 06 | Parlophone R 6721 | What Ya Gonna Do Now?/Bloody Annoying | 6 |
| 04 | EMI R 6632 | Freakin' Out/Feel Right (numbered p/s) | 5 |
| 07 | Regal SCO16 | This Old Town (with Paul Weller)/Each New Morning/Black River (7" die-cut sleeve) | 5 |
| 98 | Transcopic TRANLP 005 | THE SKY IS TOO HIGH (LP, inner sleeve, 4 postcards) | 20 |
| 01 | Transcopic TRANLP 010 | CROW SIT ON BLOOD TREE (2-LP, with inners & print, signed, 1,000 only) | 30 |
| 01 | Transcopic TRANLP 010 | CROW SIT ON BLOOD TREE (2-LP, with inners & print, 1,000 only) | 20 |
| 02 | Transcopic TRANLP 018 | THE KISS OF MORNING (2-LP, 10" x 10" picture book) | 20 |
| 04 | EMI 5775191 | HAPPINESS IN MAGAZINES (LP) | 25 |
| 06 | Parlophone 350 5191 | LOVE TRAVELS AT ILLEGAL SPEEDS (2-LP) | 20 |

*(see also Blur)*

**KEVIN COYNE**

| | | | |
|---|---|---|---|
| 72 | Dandelion 2001 357 | Cheat Me/Flowering Cherry | 7 |
| 72 | Dandelion 2310 228 | CASE HISTORY (LP) | 150 |
| 73 | Virgin VD 251/2 | MARJORY RAZORBLADE (2-LP, gatefold sleeve with "130 Notting Hill Gate" credit, black/white label) | 25 |
| 73 | Virgin VD 2501 | MARJORY RAZORBLADE (2-LP, gatefold sleeve, later pressing without "130 Notting Hill Gate" credit) | 15 |
| 74 | Virgin V 2012 | BLAME IT ON THE NIGHT (LP, lyric insert, coloured 'twin Virgin' label) | 15 |
| 75 | Virgin V 2033 | MATCHING HEAD AND FEET (LP, laminated sleeve, lyric poster, coloured "twin-Virgin" label) | 15 |
| 80 | Dandelion BUTBOX 1 | DANDELION YEARS (3-LP, re-issue of Siren LP's Siren, Strange Locomotion and Coynes Case History) | 25 |

*(see also Clague, Coyne-Clague, Siren, Gordon Smith)*

**COYNE-CLAGUE**

| | | | |
|---|---|---|---|
| 69 | Dandelion S 4494 | The Stride/I Wonder Where | 8 |

**CRABBY APPLETON**

| | | | |
|---|---|---|---|
| 70 | Elektra 2101 006 | Go Back/Try | 12 |
| 71 | Elektra EK 45716 | Grab On/Can't Live My Life | 8 |
| 70 | Elektra EKS 74067 | CRABBY APPLETON (LP) | 20 |
| 71 | Elektra EKS 74106 | ROTTEN TO THE CORE (LP) | 20 |

**CRACK (1)**

| | | | |
|---|---|---|---|
| 80 | JSO EAT 4 | Making The Effort/Easy Street | 8 |

**CRACK (2)**

| | | | |
|---|---|---|---|
| 82 | RCA RCA 214 | Don't You Ever Let Me Down/I Can't Take It (die-cut 'Battle of the Bands' sleeve) | 25 |
| 82 | RCA RCA 255 | Going Out/The Troops Have Landed (p/s) | 15 |
| 83 | RCA CRACK 1 | All Or Nothing/I Caught You Out (p/s) | 30 |
| 83 | Link LP073 | IN SEARCH OF THE CRACK (LP) | 20 |

### CRACKED MIRROR
| | | | |
|---|---|---|---|
| 83 | CMLP 001 | CRACKED MIRROR (LP, private pressing, 200 only) | 80 |

### CRACKERS
| | | | |
|---|---|---|---|
| 69 | Fontana TF 995 | Honey Do/It Happens All The Time | 15 |

*(see also Merseys)*

### CRACKLES
| | | | |
|---|---|---|---|
| 74 | Filo FL2 | Keep Shaking/Hey Hey Little Girl | 20 |

### SARAH CRACKNELL
| | | | |
|---|---|---|---|
| 87 | 3 Bears TED 001 | Love Is All You Need/Coastal Town (p/s) | 100 |

*(see also St. Etienne, 50 Year Void, Lovecut D.B.)*

### CRACK THE SKY
| | | | |
|---|---|---|---|
| 76 | Lifesong ELS 45016 | We Want Mine/Invaders From Mars | 8 |
| 76 | Lifesong LSLP 6005 | ANIMAL NOTES (LP, with inner sleeve) | 15 |

### (BILLY) 'CRASH' CRADDOCK
| | | | |
|---|---|---|---|
| 59 | Philips PB 966 | Boom Boom Baby/Don't Destroy Me (as 'Crash' Craddock) | 30 |
| 60 | Philips PB 1006 | Since She Turned Seventeen/I Want That (as 'Crash' Craddock) | 30 |
| 60 | Philips PB 1092 | Good Time Billy (Is A Happiness Fool)/Heavenly Love | 15 |
| 61 | Mercury AMT 1146 | How Lonely He Must Be/Truly True | 8 |

### CRADLE OF FILTH
| | | | |
|---|---|---|---|
| 96 | Cacophonous NIHIL 6LP | VEMPIRE (mini-LP) | 30 |
| 94 | Cacophonous NIHIL1 | THE PRINCIPLE OF EVIL MADE FLESH (LP) | 25 |
| 96 | Music For Nations MFN 108 | DUSK AND HER EMBRACE (LP, with poster) | 30 |
| 98 | Music For Nations MFN 242 | CRUELTY AND THE BEAST (LP, stickered sleeve) | 25 |
| 00 | Music For Nations MFN 666 | MIDIAN (2-LP) | 20 |
| 01 | AbraCadaver COF 001LP | BITTER SUITES TO SUCCUBI (LP) | 15 |

### CARL CRAIG
| | | | |
|---|---|---|---|
| 94 | Open OPENT-001 | Throw/Remake Uno (as CARL CRAIG PRESENTS PAPERCLIP PEOPLE) (12") | 15 |
| 94 | Open OPENT-004 | Throw (The Remixes) (as CARL CRAIG PRESENTS PAPERCLIP PEOPLE (12") | 12 |
| 04 | Carl Craig (White) CCR002 | Volume Two (2x12") | 25 |
| 95 | Blanco Y Negro 509-99865-1 | LANDCRUISING (2xLP) | 20 |
| 01 | Obsessive EVSLP20 | ABSTRACT FUNK THEORY (as CARL CRAIG PRESENTS...) (2xLP) | 20 |

### DESMOND CRAIG
| | | | |
|---|---|---|---|
| 78 | Jah Lion HLDC 602 | African Children/Coming From Jamaica/Jack The Ripper (12") | 12 |

### PAUL CRAIG
| | | | |
|---|---|---|---|
| 66 | CBS 202406 | Midnight Girl/Autumn | 10 |

### CRAIG (1)
| | | | |
|---|---|---|---|
| 65 | King KG 1022 | Ain't That A Shame/International Blues | 18 |
| 66 | Fontana TF 715 | I Must Be Mad/Suspense | 250 |

### CRAIG (2)
| | | | |
|---|---|---|---|
| 66 | Fontana TF 665 | A Little Bit Of Soap/Ready Steady Let's Go | 80 |

*(see also Galliard)*

### DON CRAINE'S NEW DOWNLINERS SECT
| | | | |
|---|---|---|---|
| 67 | Pye 7N 17261 | I Can't Get Away From You/Roses | 250 |

*(see also Downliners Sect)*

### FLOYD CRAMER
| | | | |
|---|---|---|---|
| 54 | London HL 8012 | Fancy Pants/Five Foot Two Eyes Of Blue | 20 |
| 54 | London HL 8062 | Jolly Cholly/Oh! Suzanna | 20 |
| 55 | London HLU 8195 | Rag-A-Tag/Aunt Dinah's Quiltin' Party | 30 |
| 58 | RCA RCA 1050 | Flip Flop And Bop/Sophisticated Swing | 40 |
| 55 | London REP 1023 | PIANO HAYRIDE (EP, with Louisiana Hayride Band) | 30 |

*(see also Country Hams)*

### CRAMP
| | | | |
|---|---|---|---|
| 78 | Rip Off RIP 7 | She Doesn't Love Me/Suzy Lie Down (p/s) | 10 |

### CRAMPS
| | | | |
|---|---|---|---|
| 79 | Illegal ILS 12013 | GRAVEST HITS (12" EP, blue vinyl) | 30 |
| 79 | Illegal ILS 12013 | GRAVEST HITS (12" EP, black vinyl) | 15 |
| 80 | Illegal ILS 0017 | Fever/Garbage Man (withdrawn 1st 'full band' p/s) | 20 |
| 80 | Illegal ILS 0017 | Fever/Garbage Man (p/s; re-pressing in different p/s with 4 separate shots) | 15 |
| 80 | Illegal ILS 0017 | Garbage Man/Mystery Plane (Unreleased test pressing) | 150 |
| 80 | Illegal ILS 021 | Drug Train/Love Me/I Can't Hardly Stand It (p/s) | 15 |
| 81 | IRS PFS 1003 | Goo Goo Muck/She Said (p/s, yellow vinyl) | 15 |
| 81 | IRS PFSX 1008 | The Crusher/Save It/New Kind Of Kick (12", p/s) | 15 |
| 85 | Big Beat NS 110 | Can Your Pussy Do The Dog?/Blue Moon Baby (p/s, orange see-through vinyl) | 8 |
| 86 | Big Beat NS 115 | What's Inside A Girl/Give Me A Woman (p/s, purple vinyl) | 10 |
| 86 | Big Beat NS 115 | What's Inside A Girl/Get Off The Road/Give Me A Woman (12", p/s, white vinyl) | 12 |
| 90 | Enigma 12ENV22 | Creature From The Black Leather Lagoon/Jailhouse Rock/Beat Out My Love (12") | 15 |
| | | *(shrinkwrapped inner with sticker)* | |
| 80 | Illegal ILP 005 | SONGS THE LORD TAUGHT US (LP, white label with "Drug Train" in place of "T.V. Set") | 175 |
| 80 | Illegal ILP 005 | SONGS THE LORD TAUGHT US (LP, with "T.V. Set") | 30 |
| 81 | IRS SP 70016 | PSYCHEDELIC JUNGLE (LP) | 25 |
| 83 | Illegal ILP 012 | OFF THE BONE (LP, white label, with different mix of "Drug Train", around 50 copies pressed, unreleased) | 100 |
| 83 | Illegal ILP 012 | OFF THE BONE (LP, with 3-D sleeve & glasses) | 35 |
| 83 | Illegal ILP 012 | OFF THE BONE (LP, picture disc with extra track) | 15 |
| 84 | Big Beat NED 6 | SMELL OF FEMALE (LP, red see-through vinyl) | 20 |
| 84 | Big Beat BEDP 6 | SMELL OF FEMALE (LP, picture disc) | 20 |
| 84 | Big Beat NED 6 | SMELL OF FEMALE (LP, 2nd issue, black vinyl) | 15 |

MINT VALUE £

| 86 | Big Beat WIKA 46 | A DATE WITH ELVIS (LP, with poster) | 15 |
| 86 | Big Beat WIKA 46 | A DATE WITH ELVIS (LP, blue vinyl) | 25 |
| 90 | Enigma ENVLP 1001 | STAY SICK (LP, inner) | 15 |
| 91 | Big Beat WIKDP 101 | LOOK MOM NO HEAD (LP) | 15 |
| 91 | Big Beat WIKPD 101 | LOOK MOM NO HEAD (LP, picture disc) | 15 |
| 90 | Illigal ILP 5 | SONGS THE LORD TAUGHT US (LP, reissue) | 15 |
| 91 | Windsong WINDSONG 4 | LUX (3 x 12" box set, with poster, T-shirt & book, numbered, withdrawn) | 50 |

*(see also Beast)*

## CRANBERRIES

| 91 | Xeric XER 014 | Uncertain/Nothing Left At All (p/s) | 15 |
| 91 | Xeric XER 014T | Uncertain/Nothing Left At All/Pathetic Senses/Them (12", p/s) | 20 |
| 91 | Xeric XER 014CD | Uncertain/Nothing Left At All/Pathetic Senses/Them (CD) | 40 |
| 94 | Island IS 559 | Linger/Pretty (p/s, 2nd issue with b/w picture) | 6 |
| 92 | Island ILPS 8003 | EVERYBODY ELSE IS DOING IT... (LP) | 35 |
| 94 | Island ILPS 8029 | NO NEED TO ARGUE (LP) | 50 |
| 96 | Island ILPS 8048 | TO THE FAITHFUL DEPARTED (LP, yellow vinyl, poster) | 40 |
| 99 | Mercury/Island 524 644 1 | BURY THE HATCHET (2-LP) | 80 |

## CRANE/FARLOWE

| 73 | Dawn DNS 1034 | Can't Find A Reason/Moods | 7 |

*(see also Atomic Rooster, Crazy World Of Arthur Brown, Chris Farlowe)*

## LES CRANE

| 71 | Warner Bros K16119 | Desiderata/A Different Drummer | 7 |

## TONY CRANE

| 65 | Polydor BM 56008 | Ideal Love/Little You | 15 |
| 66 | CBS 202022 | Even The Bravest/I Still Remember | 20 |
| 67 | Pye 7N 17337 | Anonymous Mr Brown/In This World | 15 |
| 68 | Pye 7N 17517 | Scratchin' Ma Head/Patterns In The Sky | 20 |

*(see also Bob Miller, Merseys/Merseybeats)*

## CRANES

| 89 | Bite Back! BB! 017 | SELF NON SELF (LP) | 15 |
| 91 | Dedicated DEDLP 003S | WINGS OF JOY (LP with free 12") | 15 |
| 93 | Dedicated DEDLP 009S | FOREVER (LP, with free 12") | 15 |
| 94 | Dedicated DEDLP 016 | LOVED (LP) | 20 |

## CRANIUM PIE

| 09 | Fruits De Mer crustacean 08 | Baby You're A Rich Man/Madman Running Through The Fields (poster p/s, 300 only | 60 |
| 11 | Regal Crabmophone WINKLE 002 | MECHANISMS (PART 1) LP, red vinyl card inserts) | 30 |
| 11 | Regal Crabmophone WINKLE 002 | MECHANISMS (PART 1) (LP, black vinyl, 100 only) | 80 |
| 12 | Lunartica LUNAR LP 001 | THE GEOMETRY OF THISTLES (LP, 'down under' edition, 25 copies, hand-numbered, hand-painted/decorated insert and slightly different cover to standard issue) | 60 |
| 12 | Lunartica LUNAR LP 001 | THE GEOMETRY OF THISTLES (LP) | 30 |

## CRANNOG

| 76 | Crannog CR 1 | CRANNOG (LP) | 25 |

## CRASH

| 82 | Crash EJSP 9819 | FIGHT FOR YOUR LIFE (EP, no p/s) | 30 |

## CRASH COURSE IN SCIENCE

| 79 | Go Go ROO1 | Kitchen Motors/Mechanical Breakdown/Cakes In The Home (p/s) | 15 |

## CRASHERS

| 69 | Amalgamated AMG 834 | Hurry Come Up/Off Track | 100 |

## CRASS

| 78 | Small Wonder WEENY 2 | THE FEEDING OF THE 5000 (12" EP, with 4-page insert with 621984 on front & poster) | 50 |
| 78 | Small Wonder WEENY 2 | THE FEEDING OF THE 5000 (12" EP, reissue, please note that booklet has 521984 on front with the 6 crossed out) | 20 |
| 79 | Crass 521984/1 | Reality Asylum/Shaved Women (brown cardboard gatefold p/s) | 20 |
| 79 | Crass 521984/1 | Reality Asylum/Shaved Women (later pressing in white newspaper foldout sleeve) | 10 |
| 80 | Crass/Xntrix 421984/1 | Bloody Revolutions/POISON GIRLS: Persons Unknown (foldout p/s) | 10 |
| 80 | Crass 421984/5 | Nagasaki Nightmare/Big A Little A (foldout p/s, with patch) | 20 |
| 80 | Crass 421984/5 | Nagasaki Nightmare/Big A Little A (foldout p/s, without patch) | 10 |
| 81 | Crass 421984/6 | Rival Tribal Rebel Revel/Bully Boys Out Fighting (flexidisc with Toxic Graffiti fanzine) | 20 |
| 81 | Crass 421984/6 | Rival Tribal Rebel Revel/Bully Boys Out Fighting (flexidisc without Toxic Graffiti fanzine) | 10 |
| 81 | Crass 421984/6 | Rival Tribal Rebel Revel/Bully Boys Out Fighting (hard vinyl promo, p/s) | 60 |
| 81 | Crass COLD TURKEY 1 | Merry Crassmass/Merry Crassmass - Have Fun (p/s) | 10 |
| 81 | Crass 321984/IF flexi | Our Wedding (free flexi sent to readers of Loving -'for the price of a Stamp'. By Creative Recording And Sound Services – CRASS' with mailer envelope) | 300 |
| 82 | Crass 221984/6 | How Does It Feel (To Be The Mother Of 1000 Dead?)/The ImmortalDeath/Don't Tell Me You Care (foldout p/s) | 10 |
| 83 | Crass 121984/3 | Sheep Farming In The Falklands/Gotcha! (p/s with lyric insert) | 6 |
| 83 | (no label) | Gotcha! (clear flexidisc) | 10 |
| 83 | Crass 121984/4 | Who Dunnit? (Parts 1 & 2) (p/s, brown vinyl) | 6 |
| 84 | Crass 1984 | YOU'RE ALREADY DEAD EP | 7 |
| 79 | Crass 521984 | STATIONS OF THE CRASS (2-LP, fold-out sleeve, black and white inners, original issue with "Pay no more than £3.00" on sleeve) | 25 |
| 81 | Crass 321984 | PENIS ENVY (LP, original issue with "pay no more than £2.25 on sleeve) | 25 |
| 82 | Crass BOLLOX 2U2 | CHRIST THE ALBUM (2-LP, box set with booklet) | 25 |
| 83 | Crass 121984 | YES SIR, I WILL (LP, fold-out sleeve, original issue with "Pay no more than £2.75" on sleeve) | 15 |
| 84 | Crass CAT 5 | BEST BEFORE 1984 (2-LP, gatefold, 2 inners) | 20 |

*(see also Anne Anxiety, Joy De Vivre, Eve Libertine, Poison Girls)*

## CRATOR
79   Recordiau Lloer SEL 0001   Blas Da/Fy Mreuddwyd I/Gelyn Yr Awyr (EP, 1000 only, no p/s) ................................ 20

## CRAVATS
78   The Cravats CH 004   Gordon/Situations (p/s) .................................................................................. 25
79   Small Wonder SMALL 15   The End/Burning Bridges/I Hate The Universe (p/s) ........................ 10
80   Small Wonder SMALL 25   You're Driving Me Mad/I Am The Dregs (p/s) .................................. 10
81   Small Wonder SMALL 26   Off The Beach/And The Sun Shone On (p/s) ...................................... 8
82   Crass 221984/2   RUB ME OUT (EP, 21" x 14" poster p/s)............................................... 12
85   Reflex 12 RE 10   THE LAND OF THE GIANTS (12" EP) ..................................................... 12
80   Small Wonder CRAVAT 1   THE CRAVATS IN TOYTOWN (LP, with inner sleeve) ...................... 25
*(see also Very Things)*

## CAROLYN CRAWFORD
65   Stateside SS 384   When Someone's Good To You/My Heart ............................................. 175
65   Stateside SS 384   When Someone's Good To You/My Heart (DJ copy) ............................ 250

## JAMES 'SUGARBOY' CRAWFORD
73   Chess 6145 024   BOBBY CHARLES: See You Later, Alligator/Jock-o-mo (Iko Iko)................. 6

## JIMMY CRAWFORD
60   Columbia DB 4525   Long Stringy Baby/Unkind ......................................................... 50

## JOHNNY CRAWFORD
62   Pye International 7N 25145   Cindy's Birthday/Patti Ann ....................................................... 10
62   London RE 1343   JOHNNY CRAWFORD (EP) ................................................................ 20
64   London RE 1416   WHEN I FALL IN LOVE (EP) ............................................................ 20
63   London HA 8060   RUMORS (LP) .............................................................................. 20
64   London HA 8197   JOHNNY CRAWFORD - HIS GREATEST HITS (LP) ................................ 15

## CRAWFORD BROTHERS
57   Vogue V 9077   Midnight Mover Groover/Midnight Happenings ...................................... 250
57   Vogue V 9077   Midnight Mover Groover/Midnight Happenings (78) ............................... 50
59   Vogue V 9140   It Feels Good/I Ain't Guilty (triangular or round centre) ........................ 250
59   Vogue V 9140   It Feels Good/I Ain't Guilty (triangular or round centre) (78) ................. 50

## CRAWLING CHAOS
80   Factory FAC 17   Sex Machine/Berlin (p/s) ............................................................. 20

## PEE WEE CRAYTON
71   Vanguard VSD 6566   THINGS I USED TO DO (LP) ......................................................... 15

## CRAZE
79   Cobra COB 3   Motions/Spartans (p/s) ................................................................... 6
80   Harvest HAR 5200   Motions/Spartans (reissue in different p/s) ..................................... 5
80   Harvest HAR 5205   Lucy/Stop Living In The Past (p/s) .............................................. 6
80   Harvest SHSP 4114   SPARTANS (LP, unissued, test pressings only) ................................ 50
*(see also Skunks, Hard Corps, Beasts In Cages)*

## CRAZY CAVAN AND THE RHYTHM ROCKERS
73   Crazy Rhythm CR 01   Teddy Boy Boogie/Bop Little Baby ................................................. 8
74   Crazy Rhythm CR 02   Teddy Boy Rock'N'Roll/Rockabilly Star/Wildest Cat In Town/Little Teddy Girl ............. 10

## CRAZY ELEPHANT
69   Major Minor MM 609   Gimme Gimme Good Lovin'/Dark Part Of My Mind ................................ 6
69   Major Minor MM 623   Sunshine Red Wine/Pam ............................................................... 5
70   Major Minor MM 672   There's A Better Day Coming/Space Buggy ....................................... 5
69   Major Minor SMLP 62   CRAZY ELEPHANT (LP, red/white/black label) ................................ 60

## CRAZY FEELINGS
67   Polydor NH 56723   Please Lie/Time Is Running Out ..................................................... 6

## CRAZY HORSE
72   Reprise RSLP 6438   CRAZY HORSE (LP) ..................................................................... 25
72   Reprise K 44171   LOOSE (LP, gatefold sleeve) .......................................................... 15
*(see also Neil Young, Jack Nitzsche)*

## CRAZY HOUSE
82   TW 105   The First Time/A Memorial For Love (hand-made p/s)............................... 5
82   T.W. PROP 2   THEY DANCE LIKE THIS FROM AS FAR OFF AS THE CRAZY HOUSE (LP, insert) ............. 15

## CRAZY PAVING
70   MCA KM55057   Anytime Sunshine/Sweet Brandy ..................................................... 12

## CRAZY ROCKERS
64   King KG 1001   Third Man Theme/Mama Papa ......................................................... 5

## CRAZY ENGLISH
82   Crazy English CH 001   Crazy English/Lose Or Win ......................................................... 40

## CREAM
66   Reaction 591 007   Wrapping Paper/Cat's Squirrel ..................................................... 20
66   Reaction 591 011   I Feel Free/N.S.U. ....................................................................... 12
67   Reaction 591 015   Strange Brew/Tales Of Brave Ulysses ........................................... 15
68   Polydor 56258   Anyone For Tennis (The Savage Seven Theme)/Pressed Rat And Warthog ........... 10
68   Polydor 56286   Sunshine Of Your Love/SWLABR ................................................... 10
68   Polydor 56300   White Room/Those Were The Days ................................................. 8
69   Polydor 56315   Strange Brew/Wrapping Paper (unissued) ....................................... 0
69   Polydor 56315   Badge/What A Bringdown ............................................................. 7
71   Polydor 2058 120   I Feel Free/Wrapping Paper .......................................................... 6
72   Polydor 2058 285   Badge/What A Bringdown (reissue) ................................................ 6
66   Reaction 593 001   FRESH CREAM (LP, mono) ........................................................... 150
66   Reaction 594 001   FRESH CREAM (LP, stereo) .......................................................... 100

MINT VALUE £

| 67 | Reaction 593 003 | DISRAELI GEARS (LP, 1st pressing, with label miscredits to 'Windfall Music' and 'Apple Publishing' , '1967' on side 2 label, A1/B1 matrix, sleeve laminated on front & back, mono) | 250 |
|---|---|---|---|
| 67 | Reaction 593 003 | DISRAELI GEARS (LP, 2nd pressing, with label credits of 'Immediate Music' and 'Copyright Control' , sleeve laminated on front & back, mono) | 100 |
| 67 | Reaction 594 003 | DISRAELI GEARS (LP, sleeve laminated on front & back, stereo) | 90 |
| 68 | Reaction 593 003 | DISRAELI GEARS (LP, sleeve laminated on front only, mono) | 40 |
| 68 | Reaction 594 003 | DISRAELI GEARS (LP, sleeve laminated on front only, stereo) | 30 |
| 68 | Polydor 582 031/2 | WHEELS OF FIRE (2-LP, gatefold sleeve, mono; set no. 2612 001) | 70 |
| 68 | Polydor 583 031/2 | WHEELS OF FIRE (2-LP, gatefold sleeve, stereo; set no. 2612 001) | 50 |
| 68 | Polydor 582/583 033 | WHEELS OF FIRE - IN THE STUDIO (LP, mono) | 40 |
| 68 | Polydor 583 033 | WHEELS OF FIRE - IN THE STUDIO (LP, stereo) | 30 |
| 68 | Polydor 582/583 040 | WHEELS OF FIRE - LIVE AT THE FILLMORE (LP, mono) | 40 |
| 68 | Polydor 582/583 040 | WHEELS OF FIRE - LIVE AT THE FILLMORE (LP, stereo) | 30 |
| 69 | Polydor 583 053 | GOODBYE (LP, gatefold sleeve) | 18 |
| 70 | Polydor 2383 016 | LIVE CREAM (LP) | 15 |
| 71 | Polydor 2855 002 | CREAM ON TOP (LP, mail-order compilation) | 35 |
| 80 | RSO 2658 142 | CREAM (7-LP set including "Fresh Cream", "Disraeli Gears", "Wheels Of Fire", Goodbye, "Live Cream" & "Live Cream Vol. 2") | 40 |
| 97 | Simply Vinyl SVLP 202 | WHEELS OF FIRE (2-LP, reissue) | 20 |
| 14 | Polydor/Back To Black 0600753548417 | CREAM 1966 - 1972 (7-LP box set) | 100 |

(see also Eric Clapton, Jack Bruce, Ginger Baker, Blind Faith)

## CREAMERS
| 89 | Fierce FRIGHT 045 | Sunday Head/Think I'm Gonna Be Sick (p/s) | 10 |
|---|---|---|---|

## JOAN CREARY
| 71 | Fab FAB 181 | Your Best Friend/Version | 7 |
|---|---|---|---|

## CREATION (U.K.)
| 66 | Planet PLF 116 | Making Time/Try And Stop Me (with Planet sleeve) | 50 |
|---|---|---|---|
| 66 | Planet PLF 116 | Making Time/Try And Stop Me (without Planet sleeve) | 35 |
| 66 | Planet PLF 119 | Painter Man/Biff Bang Pow (with Planet sleeve) | 45 |
| 66 | Planet PLF 119 | Painter Man/Biff Bang Pow (without Planet sleeve) | 35 |
| 67 | Polydor 56177 | If I Stay Too Long/Nightmares | 50 |
| 67 | Polydor 56207 | Life Is Just Beginning/Through My Eyes | 100 |
| 68 | Polydor 56230 | How Does It Feel To Feel/Tom Tom | 75 |
| 68 | Polydor 56246 | Midway Down/The Girls Are Naked | 50 |
| 73 | Charisma CB 213 | Making Time/Painter Man | 8 |
| 77 | Raw RAW 4 | Making Time/Painter Man (reissue, p/s) | 10 |
| 84 | Edsel E 5006 | Making Time/Uncle Bert (p/s) | 10 |
| 73 | Charisma Perspective CS 8 | THE CREATION '66-67 (LP) | 50 |
| 82 | Edsel ED 106 | HOW DOES IT FEEL TO FEEL (LP, with foldout insert) | 15 |

(see also Mark Four, Birds, Ashton Gardner & Dyke, Kennedy Express, Eddy Phillips, Smiley, Spectrum)

## CREATION (U.S.)
| 72 | Stateside SS 2205 | I Got The Fever/Soul Control | 12 |
|---|---|---|---|

(see also Prophets)

## CREATION REBEL
| 79 | Hit Run HIT DD8 | Beware/Natty Conscience Free (12") | 50 |
|---|---|---|---|
| 81 | On-U Sound DP3 | Independent Man Dub/CREATION REBEL : Dub (10") | 30 |
| 78 | Hit Run APLP 9001 | DUB FROM CREATION (LP) | 70 |
| 79 | Hit Run APLP 9004 | REBEL VIBRATIONS (LP) | 70 |
| 78 | Hit Run APLP 9008 | CLOSE ENCOUNTERS OF THE THIRD WORLD (LP) | 45 |
| 81 | 4D Rhythms 4DLP1 | STARSHIP AFRICA (LP) | 40 |
| 81 | Static STATLP 04 | PSYCHOTIC JONKANOO (LP) | 30 |
| 82 | On-U Sound ON-U LP08 | STARSHIP AFRICA (LP) | 30 |
| 82 | Cherry Red BRED 21 | THREAT TO CREATION (LP, With the New Age Steppers) | 15 |
| 82 | Cherry Red/On-U BRED 33 | LOWS & HIGHS (LP) | 15 |

## CREATIONS
| 67 | Rio R 133 | Meet Me At Eight/Searching | 35 |
|---|---|---|---|
| 68 | Amalgamated AMG 818 | Holding Out/Get On Up | 50 |
| 69 | Punch PH 2 | Mix Up Girl/Qua Kue Shut | 200 |

(see also Little Roys)

## CREATION STEPPER
| 79 | Tribesman TM 22 | What You Are Not Supposed To Do/Children Obey Your Parents (12") | 18 |
|---|---|---|---|
| 79 | Tribesman TM 006 | Stormy Night (with Ranking Jahman)/Stepper Now (12", p/s as Creation Stoppers) | 70 |
| 80 | Nationwide NWD 015 | Homeward Bound/Version (12") | 80 |
| 81 | Moa Anbassa MA005 | Treat Me Unkind/Unkind Dub (12") | 15 |
| 04 | Jah Tubbys JT 10019 | King Nebuchadnezzar (with the Disciples Riddim Section)/The Nebuchadnezzar Skarock (with the Dread-UK Crew) (12") | 30 |

(see also Fred Locks)

## CREATIVE SOURCE
| 75 | Polydor 2066680 | Don't Be Afraid (Take My Love)/Pass The Feelin' On | 12 |
|---|---|---|---|
| 73 | Sussex LPSX6 | CREATIVE SOURCE (LP, gatefold) | 20 |

## CREATOR
| 80 | Seven Leaves SLPP 001 | Such Is Life/PRODIGAL CREATOR: Such Is Life (12") | 40 |
|---|---|---|---|

## CREATOR & NORMA
| 63 | Island WI 105 | We Will Be Lovers/Come On Pretty Baby | 15 |
|---|---|---|---|

## CREATORS
| 96 | Blind Side BS002 | HAVE A MASTER PLAN (EP) | 12 |
|---|---|---|---|

## CREATURES
| | | | |
|---|---|---|---|
| 66 | CBS 202048 | Turn Out The Light/It Must Be Love | 12 |
| 66 | CBS 202350 | String Along/Night Is Warm | 12 |
| 67 | CBS 2666 | Looking At Tomorrow/Someone Needs You | 12 |

## CREEDENCE CLEARWATER REVIVAL
| | | | |
|---|---|---|---|
| 69 | Liberty LBF 15223 | Proud Mary/I Put A Spell On You (withdrawn) | 20 |
| 69 | Liberty LBF 15223 | Proud Mary/Born On The Bayou | 6 |
| 69 | Liberty LBF 15230 | Bad Moon Rising/Lodi | 7 |
| 69 | Liberty LBF 15250 | Green River/Commotion | 6 |
| 70 | Liberty LBF 15283 | Down On The Corner/Fortunate Son | 7 |
| 70 | Liberty LBF 15310 | Travellin' Band/Who'll Stop The Rain | 8 |
| 70 | Liberty LBF 15354 | Up Around The Bend/Run Through The Jungle (in p/s) | 10 |
| 70 | Liberty LBF 15354 | Up Around The Bend/Run Through The Jungle | 6 |
| 70 | Liberty LBF 15384 | Long As I Can See The Light/Lookin' Out My Back Door (in p/s) | 10 |
| 69 | Liberty LBS 83259 | CREEDENCE CLEARWATER REVIVAL (LP, blue label) | 80 |
| 69 | Liberty LBS 83261 | BAYOU COUNTRY (LP, blue label) | 40 |
| 69 | Liberty LBS 83273 | GREEN RIVER (LP, blue label) | 40 |
| 70 | Liberty LBS 83338 | WILLY AND THE POORBOYS (LP, blue label) | 40 |
| 70 | Liberty LBS 83388 | COSMO'S FACTORY (LP) | 30 |
| 71 | Liberty LBG 83400 | PENDULUM (LP, gatefold sleeve) | 20 |
| 73 | Fantasy FT 506 | CREEDENCE CLEARWATER REVIVAL (LP, reissue) | 15 |
| 73 | Fantasy FT 507 | BAYOU COUNTRY (LP, reissue) | 15 |
| 73 | Fantasy FT 503 | WILLY AND THE POORBOYS (LP, reissue) | 15 |

*(see also Golliwogs, John Fogerty, Tom Fogerty, Blue Ridge Rangers)*

## CREEPERS
| | | | |
|---|---|---|---|
| 66 | Blue Beat BB 366 | Beat Of My Soul/LLOYD ADAMS: I Wish Your Picture Was You | 40 |

## CREEPIES
| | | | |
|---|---|---|---|
| 75 | Penny Farthing PEN 875 | Teach Me How To Rock N Roll/Legend Of The Creepies | 12 |

## CREERY SISTERS
| | | | |
|---|---|---|---|
| 70 | High Note BSLP 5004 | OH WHAT A GLORY (LP) | 20 |

## CREME CARAMEL
| | | | |
|---|---|---|---|
| 69 | Pye International 7N 25495 | My Idea/Excursion | 6 |
| 70 | Pye Int. 7N 25521 | Crying Eyes/It's A Life I Give To You | 5 |

## CRESCENDOS
| | | | |
|---|---|---|---|
| 58 | London HLU 8563 | Oh Julie/My Little Girl | 60 |

## CRESCENTS (1)
| | | | |
|---|---|---|---|
| 58 | Columbia DB 4093 | Wrong/Baby, Baby, Baby | 100 |

## CRESCENTS (2)
| | | | |
|---|---|---|---|
| 64 | London HLN 9851 | Pink Dominos/Breakout | 15 |

## CRESSIDA
| | | | |
|---|---|---|---|
| 70 | Vertigo VO 7 | CRESSIDA (LP, gatefold sleeve, large swirl label) | 750 |
| 71 | Vertigo 6360 025 | ASYLUM (LP, gatefold sleeve, large swirl label) | 900 |
| 11 | Record Collector RCLP 002 | TRAPPED IN TIME - THE LOST TAPES (LP) | 40 |

*(see also Uriah Heep, Black Widow)*

## CRESTAS
| | | | |
|---|---|---|---|
| 65 | Fontana TF 551 | To Be Loved/When I Fall In Love | 25 |

## CRESTERS
| | | | |
|---|---|---|---|
| 64 | HMV POP 1249 | I Just Don't Understand/I Want You | 10 |
| 64 | HMV POP 1296 | Put Your Arms Around Me/Do It With Me | 5 |

*(see also Mike Sagar & Cresters, Richard Harding)*

## CRESTS
| | | | |
|---|---|---|---|
| 59 | London HL 8794 | Sixteen Candles/Beside You | 30 |
| 59 | Top Rank JAR 150 | Flower Of Love/Molly Mae | 20 |
| 59 | Top Rank JAR 168 | Six Nights A Week/I Do | 25 |
| 59 | London HL 8954 | The Angels Listened In/I Thank The Moon | 40 |
| 60 | Top Rank JAR 302 | A Year Ago Tonight/Paper Crown | 25 |
| 60 | Top Rank JAR 372 | Step By Step/Gee (But I'd Give The World) | 25 |
| 60 | HMV POP 768 | Always You/Trouble In Paradise | 25 |
| 60 | HMV POP 808 | Isn't It Amazing/Molly Mae | 25 |
| 61 | HMV POP 848 | Model Love/We've Got To Tell Them | 20 |
| 62 | HMV POP 976 | Little Miracles/Baby I Gotta Know | 25 |
| 63 | London HLU 9671 | Guilty/Number One With Me | 25 |

*(see also Johnny Maestro)*

## CREW
| | | | |
|---|---|---|---|
| 69 | Plexium PXM 12 | Marty/Danger Signs | 10 |
| 70 | Decca F 13000 | Cecilia/1970 | 7 |

## CREW-CUTS
| | | | |
|---|---|---|---|
| 56 | Mercury 7MT 2 | Angels In The Sky/Seven Days (export issue) | 10 |
| 58 | RCA RCA 1075 | Hey, Stella!/Forever, My Darling | 10 |
| 56 | Mercury MEP 9002 | PRESENTING THE CREW-CUTS (EP) | 40 |
| 56 | Mercury MPT 7501 | THE CREW-CUTS ON PARADE (10" LP) | 20 |

## BOB CREWE (GENERATION)
| | | | |
|---|---|---|---|
| 60 | London HLI 9077 | Water Boy/Voglio Cantare (solo) | 5 |
| 64 | Stateside SS 356 | Maggie Maggie May/We Almost Made It | 6 |
| 67 | Stateside SS 582 | Music To Watch Girls By/Girls On The Rocks | 8 |
| 67 | Stateside SS 2032 | You Only Live Twice/A Lover's Concerto | 10 |
| 67 | Philips BL 7788 | PLAY THE FOUR SEASONS HITS (LP, as Bob Crewe Generation) | 25 |

MINT VALUE £

| | | | |
|---|---|---|---|
| 67 | Stateside SL 10210 | MUSIC TO WATCH GIRLS BY (LP) | 35 |
| 68 | Stateside S(S)L 10260 | BARBARELLA (LP, soundtrack) | 75 |

## CREWSKY FIXERS
| | | | |
|---|---|---|---|
| 80 | Big Mix ACE 22 | CREWSKY FIXERS EP (hand-made p/s, stamped white labels) | 12 |

## BERNARD CRIBBINS
| | | | |
|---|---|---|---|
| 67 | Parlophone R 5603 | When I'm Sixty-Four/Oh My Word | 20 |

## THE CRIBS
| | | | |
|---|---|---|---|
| 03 | Squirrel No 5 | Baby Don't Sweat/You and I (other 2 tracks by JEN SCHANDE) | 80 |
| 03 | Wichita WEBB 051S | Baby Don't Sweat/Another Number (p/s, yellow vinyl) | 6 |
| 04 | Wichita WEBB 059S | You Were Always The One/Song From Practice 1 (p/s) | 20 |
| 04 | B-Unique KAISER | Plays Kaiser Chiefs (gig only 7" given away free, stickered sleeve) | 15 |
| 04 | Wichita WEBB 061S | What About Me/Feelin' It (yellow vinyl, p/s) | 12 |
| 05 | Wichita WEBB 074 s | Hey Scenesters!/North Of England (p/s, clear vinyl) | 7 |
| 05 | Wichita WEBB 074 SX | Hey Scenesters!/You're Gonna Loose Us (p/s, clear vinyl) | 7 |
| 05 | Wichita WEBB 097S | COLLECTORS BOX SET (8 x 7" box set, coloured vinyl) | 45 |
| 10 | Wichita WEBB 271S | Housewife (1-sided) | 8 |
| 12 | Wichita WEBB 337S | Come On Be A No One/Don't Believe In Me (red vinyl) | 8 |
| 13 | Roots ROOTS 3 | Jaded Youth (Live)/THE BLACK BELLES: Leave You With A Letter (Live) (10" only sold in Jumbo Records, Leeds) | 15 |
| 12 | Wichita WEBB 338S | Glitters Like Gold/On A Hotel Wall (clear vinyl) | 15 |
| 06 | Wichita WEBB 082LP | THE NEW FELLAS (LP) | 30 |
| 07 | Wichita WEBB 126LP | MEN'S NEEDS, WOMAN'S NEEDS, WHATEVER (LP) | 20 |
| 09 | Wichita WEBB 220LP | IGNORE THE IGNORANT (LP) | 15 |
| 10 | Wichita WEBB 058 LPTEN | THE CRIBS (LP, reissue with CD) | 25 |
| 12 | Wichita WEBB 335LP | IN THE BELLY OF THE BRAZEN BULL (2-LP, one side etched with free 7") | 18 |

*(see also The Smiths)*

## CRICKETS FEATURING BUDDY HOLLY
### SINGLES
| | | | |
|---|---|---|---|
| 57 | Vogue Coral Q 72279 | That'll Be The Day/I'm Lookin' For Someone To Love | 25 |
| 57 | Coral Q 72298 | Oh Boy!/Not Fade Away | 20 |
| 58 | Coral Q 72279 | That'll Be The Day/I'm Lookin' For Someone To Love (2nd issue) | 5 |
| 58 | Coral Q 72307 | Maybe Baby/Tell Me How | 20 |
| 58 | Coral Q 72329 | Think It Over/Fool's Paradise | 20 |
| 58 | Coral Q 72343 | It's So Easy/Lonesome Tears | 20 |

*(Originally issued with triangular centres; later round centre copies are worth around half these values.)*

| | | | |
|---|---|---|---|
| 68 | Decca AD 1012 | Oh, Boy/That'll Be The Day (export issue) | 75 |

### EPs
| | | | |
|---|---|---|---|
| 58 | Coral FEP 2003 | THE SOUND OF THE CRICKETS (triangular or round centre) | 30 |
| 59 | Coral FEP 2014 | IT'S SO EASY (triangular or round centre) | 30 |
| 60 | Coral FEP 2060 | FOUR MORE BY THE CRICKETS | 30 |
| 60 | Coral FEP 2062 | THAT'LL BE THE DAY | 30 |

### ALBUMS
| | | | |
|---|---|---|---|
| 58 | Vogue Coral LVA 9081 | THE CHIRPING CRICKETS (Vogue-Coral labels & Coral sleeve) | 150 |
| 58 | Coral LVA 9081 | THE CHIRPING CRICKETS (re-pressing with Coral labels & sleeve) | 100 |

*(see also Buddy Holly)*

## CRICKETS
### SINGLES
| | | | |
|---|---|---|---|
| 59 | Coral Q 72365 | Love's Made A Fool Of You/Someone, Someone | 15 |
| 59 | Coral Q 72382 | When You Ask About Love/Deborah | 15 |
| 60 | Coral Q 72395 | More Than I Can Say/Baby My Heart | 15 |
| 61 | Coral Q 72417 | Peggy Sue Got Married/Don'tcha Know | 15 |
| 61 | Coral Q 72440 | I Fought The Law/A Sweet Love | 15 |
| 61 | London HLG 9486 | He's Old Enough To Know Better/I'm Feeling Better | 15 |

### EPs
| | | | |
|---|---|---|---|
| 60 | Coral FEP 2053 | THE CRICKETS (initial trangular centre) | 40 |
| 61 | Coral FEP 2064 | THE CRICKETS DON'T EVER CHANGE | 15 |
| 63 | Liberty (S)LEP 2094 | STRAIGHT NO STRINGS (mono/stereo) | 15 |
| 64 | Liberty LEP 2173 | COME ON | 15 |

### ALBUMS
| | | | |
|---|---|---|---|
| 61 | Coral LVA 9142 | IN STYLE WITH THE CRICKETS | 15 |
| 62 | Liberty LBY 1120 | SOMETHING OLD, SOMETHING NEW, SOMETHING BLUE, SOMETHING ELSE! (mono) | 15 |
| 62 | Liberty (S)LBY 1120 | SOMETHING OLD, SOMETHING NEW, SOMETHING BLUE, SOMETHING ELSE! (stereo) | 15 |

*(see also Buddy Holly, Jerry Allison & Crickets, Ivan, Sonny Curtis, Earl Sinks, Sinx Mitchell, David Box)*

## JIMMY CRIKIT
| | | | |
|---|---|---|---|
| 70 | MCA MK 5047 | Isabella/Love Is A See Saw | 8 |

## CRIME
| | | | |
|---|---|---|---|
| 80 | Punk Products PP 1 | Johnny Come Home/Generation Gap (p/s, beware of bootlegs) | 100 |

## CRIME (U.S.)
| | | | |
|---|---|---|---|
| 90 | Solar Lodge DOOMED 2 | SAN FRANCISCO'S DOOMED (LP) | 15 |

## THE CRIMEWATCH PROJECT
| | | | |
|---|---|---|---|
| 92 | Strategic Dance Initiative SDI 004 | Boomzabang/Kis My Neck/Friday Night Style (white label 12", stickered paper sleeve) | 80 |

## CRIMINAL CLASS
| | | | |
|---|---|---|---|
| 82 | Inferno HELL 7 | Fighting The System/Soldier (p/s) | 15 |

## CRIMINAL JUSTICE
| | | | |
|---|---|---|---|
| 85 | Endangered Music EDR 2 | HIERARCHY OF HELL (EP) | 12 |

## THE CRIMINAL MINDS
| | | | |
|---|---|---|---|
| 90 | TCM SRT90L2748 | GUILTY AS CHARGED (EP) | 150 |
| 91 | TCM EP002 | TALES FROM THE WASTELAND (EP) | 120 |
| 03 | Vinylstore Records VSR001 | BREAK SHIT UP (EP) | 25 |
| 01 | UK Rap Records UKR001 | WIDOWMAKER (LP) | 18 |

## CRIMINALS
| 81 | Crush CR 1 | No Pleasure/The Criminals Of This World | 100 |
|---|---|---|---|

## CRIMINAL SEX
| 85 | Flexi Tits | CRIMINAL SEX EP (whitle label inside p/s) | 20 |
|---|---|---|---|

## CRIMSON BRIDGE
| 72 | Myrrh Ms 6224 | FILL YOUR HEAD WITH (LP) | 25 |
|---|---|---|---|

## CRINKS
| 67 | Softspot SPO 1 | Pure And Simple/You Can't Cheat | 35 |
|---|---|---|---|

## CRISIS (1)
| | | | |
|---|---|---|---|
| 79 | Peckham Action NOTH 1 | No Town Hall (Southwark)/Holocaust/P.C. One Nine Eight Four (p/s) | 20 |
| 79 | Ardkor CRI 002 | UK '79/White Youth (p/s) | 20 |
| 80 | Ardkor CRI 003 | HYMNS OF FAITH (12" EP) | 20 |
| 81 | Ardkor CRI 004 | Alienation/Brückwood/Hospital (p/s, with insert) | 20 |
| 82 | Crisis NOTH 1/CRI 002 | HOLOCAUST UK (12" EP) | 15 |

(see also Death In June, Current 93, Theatre Of Hate)

## CRISIS (2)
| 70s | private pressing | ANOTHER FINE MESS (LP) | 35 |
|---|---|---|---|

## MARILYN CRISPELL
| 83 | Leo LR 118 | RHYTHMS HUNG IN UNDRAWN SKY (LP) | 15 |
|---|---|---|---|
| 85 | Leo LR 126 | AND YOUR IVORY VOICE SINGS (LP) | 15 |

## CRISPY AMBULANCE
| | | | |
|---|---|---|---|
| 79 | Aural Assault AAR 001 | From The Cradle To The Grave/4 Minutes From The Frontline (glossy p/s) | 15 |
| 79 | Aural Assault AAR 001 | From The Cradle To The Grave/4 Minutes From The Frontline (matt p/s) | 8 |
| 81 | Factory FAC 32 | Unsightly And Serene: Not What I Expected/Deaf (10", p/s) | 12 |

## GARY CRISS
| | | | |
|---|---|---|---|
| 62 | Stateside SS 104 | Our Favourite Melodies/Welcome Home To My Heart | 12 |
| 62 | Stateside SS 123 | My Little Heavenly Angel/The Girl That I Told You About | 8 |
| 63 | Stateside SS 164 | Long Lonely Nights/I Still Miss You So | 8 |
| 63 | Stateside SS 265 | Sweet, Warm And Soft/Little Joe | 8 |
| 65 | Stateside SS 427 | Hands Off Buddy/If This Is Goodbye | 5 |

## PETER CRISS
| 79 | Casablanca CAN 139 | You Matter To Me/Hooked On Rock And Roll (p/s, green vinyl with mask) | 20 |
|---|---|---|---|
| 79 | Casablanca CAN 139 | You Matter To Me/Hooked On Rock And Roll (p/s, black vinyl) | 8 |

(see also Kiss)

## LINDA CRISTAL
| 59 | Coral Q 72350 | Strictly For Pleasure (A Perfect Romance)/It's Better In Spanish | 5 |
|---|---|---|---|

## CRISTINA
| | | | |
|---|---|---|---|
| 80 | Ze 12WIP 6560 | Is That All There Is/Jungle Love | 15 |
| 80 | Island/Ze 12WIP 6560 | Is That All There Is?/Jungle Love (12", p/s) | 15 |
| 80 | Ze ILPS 7004 | CRISTINA (LP) | 15 |

## BOBBY CRISTO & REBELS
| 64 | Decca F 11913 | The Other Side Of The Track/I've Got You Out Of My Mind | 45 |
|---|---|---|---|

## MARY CRISTY
| 76 | Polydor 2056 513 | Thank You For Rushing Into My Life/We Can't Hide This Time | 10 |
|---|---|---|---|

## CRITICS
| 81 | Moody Music 80C1 | Town Girl/Without You/Plastic Valentine (foldout p/s) | 35 |
|---|---|---|---|

## CRITICS & NYAH SHUFFLE
| 70 | Joe JRS 1 | Behold/SEXY FRANKIE: Tea, Patty, Sex And Ganja | 25 |
|---|---|---|---|

## CRITICS GROUP
| | | | |
|---|---|---|---|
| 66 | Argo ZDA 46 | A MERRY PROGRESS TO LONDON (LP, with insert) | 25 |
| 68 | Argo ZDA 82 | THE FEMALE FROLIC (LP, with insert) | 20 |
| 68 | Argo DA 86 | WATERLOO PETERLOO (LP, yellow label with insert) | 20 |
| 71 | Argo ZDA 138 | YE MARINERS ALL (LP) | 15 |

## CRITTERS
| | | | |
|---|---|---|---|
| 66 | London HLR 10047 | Younger Girl/Gone For Awhile | 15 |
| 66 | London HLR 10071 | Mr. Dieingly Sad/It Just Won't Be That Way | 15 |
| 66 | London HLR 10101 | Bad Misunderstanding/Forever Or No More | 25 |
| 67 | London HLR 10119 | Marryin' Kind Of Love/New York Bound | 25 |
| 67 | London HLR 10149 | Don't Let The Rain Fall Down On Me/Walk Like A Man Again | 15 |
| 67 | London HA-R 8302 | THE CRITTERS (LP) | 40 |

## JIM CROCE
| | | | |
|---|---|---|---|
| 72 | Vertigo 6073 251 | Operator/Rapid Roy | 6 |
| 72 | Vertigo 6360 700 | YOU DON'T MESS AROUND WITH JIM (LP, gatefold sleeve, swirl label) | 40 |
| 73 | Vertigo 6360 701 | LIFE & TIMES (LP, with spiral label) | 200 |
| 70s | Life Song 135004 | LIFE & TIMES (LP) | 15 |
| 70s | Life Song 135004 | GREATEST CHARATOR (LP) | 15 |

## CROCHETED DOUGHNUT RING
| | | | |
|---|---|---|---|
| 67 | Polydor 56204 | Two Little Ladies (Azalea And Rhododendron)/Nice | 40 |
| 67 | Deram DM 169 | Havana Anna/Happy Castle | 40 |
| 68 | Deram DM 180 | Maxine's Parlour/Get Out Your Rock And Roll Shoes | 25 |

(see also Force Five, Doughnut Ring, Daddy Lindberg)

## TONY CROCKET
82  Alternative ALT 010    Queen Of Hearts/Plane Jane (12", p/s).................................................................50

## CROCODILE RIDE
88  CROC 1    Kiss And Tell/Ride ..............................................................................................8

## CROCODILES
81  Aura AUS 126    New Wave Goodbye/Ribbons Of Steel ...............................................................10

## CROFT
71  Maple MP 1    The Dream/Henry And His Friends ...................................................................200

## CROFTERS
69  Say Disc SD 113    PILL FERRY (EP)................................................................................................10
69  Beltona SBE 103    CROFTERS (LP).................................................................................................15

## NICOLE CROISILLE
68  Polydor 56746    We Got A Thing/It's All Over ..............................................................................6
77  Decca F13708    The Loving Song/Tell Me What I Want To Hear/Telephone Moi ...........................6

## TONY CROMBIE
54  Decca F 10424    Stop It All/All Of Me (& His Orchestra) ...............................................................5
55  Decca F 10454    Perdido/Love You Madly (& His Orchestra)........................................................5
55  Decca F 10547    Early One Morning/Flying Home (& His Orchestra)..............................................5
55  Decca F 10592    Flying Hickory/String Of Pearls (& His Orchestra)...............................................5
55  Decca F 10637    I Want You To Be My Baby (with Annie Ross)/Three Little Words..........................5
56  Columbia DB 3822    Teach You To Rock/Short'nin' Bread Rock (as Tony Crombie & Rockets) ............50
56  Columbia DB 3859    Sham Rock/Let's You And I Rock (as Tony Crombie & Rockets) ..........................40
57  Columbia DB 3881    Lonesome Train (On A Lonesome Track)/We're Gonna Rock Tonight (78, as Tony Crombie & Rockets)..............................................................................................20
57  Columbia DB 3921    London Rock/Brighton Rock (as Tony Crombie & Rockets) ................................30
57  Columbia DB 4000    Sweet Beat/Sweet Georgia Brown (as Tony Crombie & His Sweet Beat)............10
58  Columbia DB 4076    Dumplin's/Tw'on Special ..................................................................................10
58  Columbia DB 4145    Unguaua/Piakukaungchung (as Tony Crombie Men)...........................................5
58  Columbia DB 4189    Rock-Cha-Cha/The Gigglin' Gurgleburp (as Tony Crombie Men) .........................5
59  Columbia DB 4253    Champagne Cha Cha/Shepherd's Cha Cha (as Tony Crombie Men).......................5
59  Top Rank JAR 182    Man From Interpol Theme/Interpol Cha Cha & Chase (as Tony Crombie Orchestra) .5
62  Ember JBS 706    Gutbucket/Just Like Old Times .........................................................................5
57  Columbia SEG 7676    ROCK ROCK ROCK (EP).....................................................................................60
57  Columbia SEG 7686    LET'S YOU AND I ROCK (EP) ..............................................................................60
61  Decca DFE 6670    FOUR FAVOURITE FILM THEMES (EP)..................................................................10
59  Columbia SEG 7882    SWINGIN' DANCE BEAT NO. 1 (EP).....................................................................10
59  Columbia SEG 7896    SWINGIN' DANCE BEAT NO. 2 (EP).....................................................................10
59  Columbia SEG 7918    ATMOSPHERE (EP, as Tony Crombie & His Men) ................................................10
56  Columbia 33S 1117    TONY CROMBIE & HIS SWEETBEAT (10" LP) ......................................................40
57  Columbia 33S 1108    ROCKIN' WITH TONY CROMBIE & ROCKETS (10" LP) .......................................150
58  Columbia SCX 3262    ATMOSPHERE (LP) ...........................................................................................30
59  Top Rank 35/043    MAN FROM INTERPOL (LP, TV series music, by Tony Crombie & Band)...............20
61  Tempo TAP 30    JAZZ INC. (LP) ................................................................................................175
60  Top Rank BUY 027    DRUMS! DRUMS! DRUMS! (LP, as Tony Crombie & His Band) ............................30
61  Decca SKL 4114    SWEET WIDE AND BLUE (LP).............................................................................30
61  Decca LK 4385    TWELVE FAVOURITE FILM THEMES (LP, also stereo SKL 4127).............................15
61  Ember EMB 3336    WHOLE LOTTA TONY (LP)..................................................................................40
*(see also Annie Ross, Ray Ellington, London Jazz Quartet)*

## CROMWELL
75  Cromwell WELL 006    First Day............................................................................................................20
75  Cromwell WELL 005    AT THE GALLOP (LP, private pressing)..............................................................120
*(see also Establishment)*

## LINK CROMWELL (LENNY KAYE)
66  London HLB 10040    Crazy Like A Fox/Shock Me ..............................................................................25
*(see also Patti Smith Group)*

## ANDREW CRONSHAW
74  Xtra XTRA 1139    A IS FOR ANDREW, Z IS FOR ZITHER (LP) ..........................................................15
77  Trailer LREP 1    CLOUD VALLEY (EP)..........................................................................................10
77  Trailer LER 2104    EARTHED IN CLOUD VALLEY (LP) ......................................................................15

## CROOKED OAK
76  Folkland FL 0102    FROM LITTLE ACORNS GROW (LP, 500 only) ...................................................200
79  Eron ERON 019    THE FOOT O'WOR STAIRS (LP).........................................................................25

## CROOKS
79  Blue Print BLU 2002    Modern Boys/The Beat Goes On (die-cut p/s) .....................................................6
80  Blue Print BLU 2006    All The Time In The World/Bangin' My Head (p/s) ..............................................10

## DAVID CROOKS
70  Jackpot JP 759    I Won't Hold It Against You (actually by Dave Barker)/ BOBBY JAMES: King Of Hearts...20
*(see also Dave Barker)*

## STEVE CROPPER
70  Stax STAX 147    Funky Broadway/Crop Dustin' ..........................................................................10
69  Stax SXATS 1008    WITH A LITTLE HELP FROM MY FRIENDS (LP) ....................................................30

## STEVE CROPPER & ALBERT KING
69  Stax SXATS 1020    JAMMED TOGETHER (LP, with Pops Staples) .....................................................20
*(see also Booker T. & M.G.'s, Albert King)*

## BING CROSBY
54  Brunswick 03384    White Christmas/Let's Start The New Year Right .................................................5
54  Brunswick 05224    What A Little Moonlight Can Do/Down By The Riverside (with Gary Crosby) .........5
67  Reprise RS 20645    What Do We Do With The World/Step To The Rear ...........................................15

*(see also Gary Crosby, Bob Hope, Peggy Lee)*

## BOB CROSBY & HIS BOBCATS
59  London HLD 8828    Petite Fleur/Such A Long Night ............................................................. 5

*(see also Modernaires)*

## DAVID CROSBY
71  Atlantic 2401 005    IF I COULD ONLY REMEMBER MY NAME (LP, gatefold sleeve, red/plum label) ............. 40

*(see also Byrds, Crosby [Stills] Nash [& Young])*

## GARY CROSBY
58  HMV POP 550    Judy, Judy/Cheatin' On Me ................................................................. 60
59  HMV POP 648    The Happy Bachelor/This Little Girl Of Mine ............................................. 5
57  Vogue VA 160118    GARY CROSBY (LP) ......................................................................... 15

*(see also Bing Crosby)*

## CROSBY & NASH
72  Atlantic K 10192    Southbound Train/Whole Cloth ............................................................. 7
72  Atlantic K 50011    GRAHAM NASH & DAVID CROSBY (LP, foldout sleeve) ....................................... 20

## CROSBY, STILLS & NASH
69  Atlantic 584 283    Marrakesh Express/Helplessly Hoping ...................................................... 10
69  Atlantic 584 304    Suite: Judy Blue Eyes/Long Time Gone ..................................................... 10
69  Atlantic 588 189    CROSBY, STILLS & NASH (LP, gatefold sleeve, with lyric sheet, plum/orange labels) ....... 25
72  Atlantic K40033    CROSBY, STILLS & NASH (LP, reissue, green/orange labels) ................................ 15

## CROSBY, STILLS, NASH & YOUNG
70  Atlantic 2091 002    Teach Your Children/Country Girl .......................................................... 7
70  Atlantic 2091 010    Woodstock/Helpless ........................................................................ 8
70  Atlantic 2091 023    Ohio/Find The Cost Of Freedom ............................................................. 7
70  Atlantic 2091 039    Our House/Deja Vu ......................................................................... 10
70  Atlantic 2401 001    DÉJA VU (LP, 1st pressing, 'copyright control/Warner Bros.' publishing credits, gatefold sleeve, pasted-on photo on front, plum/red label) ....................... 60
70  Atlantic 2401001    DÉJA VU (LP, 2nd pressing 'Goldhill/Giving Room/Guerilla/Kinney & Flamingo' publishing credits, gatefold sleeve, pasted-on photo on front, plum/red label) ........... 30
71  Atlantic 2657 004    FOUR WAY STREET (2-LP, gatefold sleeve with lyric sheet) ................................ 25
72  Atlantic K50001    DÉJA VU (LP, reissue, green/orange labels) .............................................. 15

*(see also David Crosby, Stephen Stills [Manassas], Graham Nash, Neil Young)*

## CROSS
90  Parlophone PCS 7342    MAD, BAD AND DANGEROUS TO KNOW (LP) ...................................................... 15

*(see also Roger Taylor, Queen)*

## JIMMIE CROSS
66  Red Bird RB 10042    Super Duper Man/Hey Little Girl .......................................................... 30
71  Decca F 13224    Can You Believe It?/Blind Willie Johnson ................................................. 7
72  Decca F 13316    Peace In The End/Prophets Guiders ........................................................ 7

*(see also T2)*

## SANDRA CROSS
11  Trunk JBH 040 LP    THE MMS BAR RECORDINGS (LP, 300 only) ..................................................... 30

## CROSS SECTION
74  Private Pressing AAMA/B    Loving Song/Rock N Roll Queen ......................................................... 50

## CROSS & ROSS
72  Decca EPS 1    CROSS & ROSS (EP) ......................................................................... 75
72  Decca SKL 5129    BORED CIVILIANS (LP, blue/silver labels) ................................................ 300

## CROSS COUNTRY
72  Atlantic K 10353    In The Midnight Hour/A Smile Song ........................................................ 6

*(see also Tokens)*

## CROSS TOWN TRAFFIC
83  Cross Town Traffic CTT 001    No For An Answer/Hanging On To You ................................................... 50

## ANDRAE CROUCH (& DISCIPLES)
70s  Light LS 7014    JUST ANDRAE (LP) .......................................................................... 25
70s  Light LS 7018    DISCIPLES LIVE AT CARNEGIE HALL (LP) ..................................................... 25
70s  Light LS 7019    KEEP ON SINGING (LP) ...................................................................... 25
70s  Light LS 7025    TAKE ME BACK (LP) ......................................................................... 25
70s  Myrrh MYR 1188    NO TIME TO LOSE (LP) ...................................................................... 25
78  Light LSD 7048    LIVE IN LONDON (LP) ....................................................................... 15
70s  Light LSD 7034    BEST OF (2xLP) ............................................................................ 30
70s  Light LS 7052    I'LL BE THINKING OF YOU (LP) ............................................................. 20

## CROW (1)
70  Stateside SS 2159    Evil Woman, Don't Play Your Games With Me/Gonna Leave A Mark ............................ 6
70  Stateside SS 2171    Slow Down/Cottage Cheese ................................................................. 10
70  Stateside SS 2180    Don't Try To Lay No Boogie Woogie On The King Of Rock And Roll/Satisfied ................ 6
70  Stateside SSL 10301    CROW MUSIC (LP) ........................................................................ 25
70  Stateside SSL 10310    CROW BY CROW (LP) ...................................................................... 20

## CROW (2)
78  Inferno HEAT 14    Uncle Funk/Your Autumn Of Tomorrow ....................................................... 20

## CROWBAR
84  Skinhead SKIN 1    Hippie Punks/White Riot (p/s) ............................................................ 45

## CROWD (1)
76  Tropical TST 108    Mango Walk/Beefy Dub ...................................................................... 15

## CROWD (2)
79  SRT SRTS/79/CUS 377    Ronnie (Is A Headbanger)/A Little Of What I Fancy/Let's Fly Together (p/s) ............. 6

## CROWDED HOUSE
91  Capitol 064-793559-1    WOODFACE (LP) .......................................................................... 20
93  Capitol SVLP 282    TOGETHER ALONE (LP) ...................................................................... 35

| 96 | Capitol EST 2283 | RECURRING DREAM - THE VERY BEST OF CROWDED HOUSE (2-LP) | 40 |
| 97 | EMI LPCENT 6 | WOODFACE (LP, reissue EMI 100 Centenary, stickered sleeve) | 25 |

*(see also Split Enz, Tim Finn, Liam Finn)*

## CROWFOOT
| 70 | Paramount PARA 3008 | California Rock 'N' Roll/Maybe I Can Learn To Live | 5 |

## DON CROWN & HIS BUSKING BUDGIES
| 70 | Orange OA 5507 | Budgerigar Man/Piper Call A Tune | 15 |
| 71 | President PT 340 | Mrs Wilson's Budgie/Flying Machines | 10 |

## JUDITH CROWNE
| 73 | Dart ART 2034 | Steamhammer/I Will Need Your Love | 10 |

## CROWNS
| 68 | Pama PM 725 | I Know, It's Alright/I Surrender | 25 |
| 68 | Pama PM 736 | Jerking The Dog/Keep Me Going | 35 |
| 68 | Pama PM 745 | She Ain't Gonna Do Right/I Need Your Loving | 25 |
| 68 | Pama PM 759 | Since You Been Gone/Call Me | 25 |
| 68 | Pama PMLP 6 | MADE OF GOLD (LP) | 45 |

## CROWS
| 54 | Columbia SCM 5119 | Gee/I Love You So | 1500 |
| 54 | Columbia DB 3478) | Gee/I Love You So (78) | 150 |

## STEVE CROWTHER BAND
| 82 | SMK Records SRTS 82 CUS 1584 | Red Herring/My Machine | 100 |

## TREVOR CROZIER'S BROKEN CONSORT
| 72 | Argo AFB 60 | PARCEL OF OLD CRAMS (LP) | 35 |

## CRUCIAL BUNNY
| 82 | Hawkeye HLP 008 | DUB DUAL (LP, as Crucial Bunny Vs Scientist) | 25 |

## CRUCIFIX
| 83 | Corpus Christi CHRIST ITS 11 | DEHUMANISATION (LP, poster sleeve) | 25 |

## CRUCIFIXION
| 80 | Miramar MIR 4 | The Fox/Death Sentence (no p/s) | 80 |
| 82 | Neat NEAT 19 | Take It Or Leave It/On The Run (p/s) | 10 |
| 84 | Neat NEAT 37 | Green Eyes/Moon Rising/Jailbait (p/s) | 10 |
| 84 | Neat NEAT 3712 | Green Eyes/Jailbait/Moon Rising (12", p/s, purple or green vinyl) | 20 |

## ARTHUR 'BIG BOY' CRUDUP
| 64 | RCA RCA 1401 | My Baby Left Me/I Don't Know It | 40 |
| 64 | RCA RCX 7161 | RHYTHM AND BLUES VOL. 4 (EP) | 15 |
| 69 | Blue Horizon 7-63855 | MEAN OLE FRISCO (LP) | 100 |
| 70 | Delmark DS 614 | LOOK ON YONDERS WALL (LP) | 25 |
| 71 | Delmark DS 621 | CRUDUP'S MOOD (LP) | 25 |
| 72 | RCA RD 8224 | THE FATHER OF ROCK 'N' ROLL (LP) | 30 |
| 74 | United Artists UAS 29092 | ROEBUCK MAN (LP) | 35 |

## CRUELLA DE VILLE
| 83 | EMI 5412 | Gypsy Girl/Blue Blue Blues (p/s) | 5 |
| 83 | EMI 12 EMI 5412 | Gypsy Girl/Blue Blue Blues/Gyspy Girl (Edit) (12") | 10 |
| 84 | EMI CDLP 1984 | I'll Do The Talking/Hollywood Hong Kong Swing/Oceans (p/s) | 5 |

## CRUISERS (1)
| 65 | Decca F 12098 | It Ain't Me Babe/Baby What You Want Me To Do | 30 |

*(see also Dave Berry, Godley & Creme)*

## CRUISERS (2)
| 73 | EMI 2202 | Schoolgirls/College Collage | 6 |

## CRUIZE
| 83 | Wait WAIT 1 | Strange Little Girl/Standing In The Rain | 35 |

## SIMON CRUM
| 58 | Capitol CL 14965 | Stand Up, Sit Down, Shut Your Mouth/Country Music Is Here To Stay | 8 |

*(see also Ferlin Husky)*

## RAY CRUMLEY
| 77 | Magnet MAG 103 | It's Uncanny/All The Way In Love With You | 10 |

## CRUNCH
| 72 | Youngblood YB 1064 | Let's Do It Again/Not Tonight Josephine | 7 |

## CRUSADERS
| 71 | Rare Earth SRE 3001 | OLD SOCKS NEW SHOES (LP) | 15 |

*(see also Jazz Crusaders)*

## CRUSH
| 80 | Carrere CAR 150 | JFC 105/He's A Rebel | 12 |

## CRUSHED BUTLER
| 69 | EMIDISC | Love Is All Around Me/Factory Grime (acetate) | 150 |

## BETTYE CRUTCHER
| 75 | Stax STXS 2031 | Sugar Daddy/As Long As You Love Me | 6 |
| 74 | Stax STX 1035 | LONG AS YOU LOVE ME (LP) | 18 |

## CRUX/CRASH
| 82 | No Future OI 18 | KEEP ON RUNNING (12" EP) | 16 |

## CRY SHARK
| 81 | Radical Wallpaper RD 002 | Protect And Survive/One Phone Call (p/s) | 15 |

## CRY (1)
| 80 | Sayonara S-3221083 | Looking To The Future/Alone (p/s) | 35 |

## CRY (2)
81   DATO DAT 1A           Love Is Necessary/Ends Are Split (no p/s) .......................................................... 80

## CRY (3)
87   Crazy Flowerpot CFP 001   Party After Dark (with p/s) ................................................................ 80
87   Crazy Flowerpot CFP 001   Party After Dark ................................................................................ 15
87   Crazy Flowerpot CFP 002   Give Her An Ice Cream (no p/s) .......................................................... 20

## CRYER
80   Happy Face MM 124       The Single/Hesitate (p/s, with 2 inserts) ............................................ 65

## BARRY CRYER
58   Fontana H 139            The Purple People Eater/Hey! Eula ...................................................... 5
58   Fontana H 151            Nothin' Shakin'/Seven Daughters ........................................................ 5
59   Fontana H 177            Angelina/Kissin' ................................................................................... 5

## CRYIN' SHAMES
66   Decca F 12340            Please Stay/What's News Pussycat ...................................................... 20
66   Decca F 12425            Nobody Waved Goodbye/You .............................................................. 30
*(see also Paul & Ritchie & Cryin' Shames, Gary Walker & Rain)*

## CRYING SHAMES
80   Logo GO 385              That's Rock'n'Roll/Too Late (p/s) ........................................................ 12

## CRY OF THE INNOCENT
82   Pagan CUS 1436          The Haunting/Still Forever (p/s) .......................................................... 25

## CRYPTIC SLAUGHTER
90   Metal Blade ZORRO 6      SPEAK YOUR PEACE (LP, inner)............................................................ 15

## CRYSBAS
79   Sain 66S                 Draenog Marw/Y Nhw (p/s) ................................................................ 25
79   Sain 72E                 Mae'di Bwrw/Blws Ty Golchi//Mor Gryg wr Morgrug/Amser (p/s) .............. 25

## CRYSTAL CASTLES
07   Merok ME 002            Alice Practice/Air War/Love And Caring (p/s) ...................................... 60
07   Trouble TROUBLE 1        XxzxcuZx Me/HEALTH: Crimewave (200 only, green vinyl white label promo) ............. 10
07   Trouble TROUBLE 1        XxzxcuZx Me/HEALTH: Crimewave (500 only, gig freebie, die-cut stamped sleeve) ....... 12
07   Trouble TROUBLE 001      XxzxcuZx Me/HEALTH: Crimewave (1000 only, p/s)................................... 8
07   Trouble DUDE 003         Air War/Air War (David Wolf Remix) (7" p/s) ...................................... 10
07   Rough Trade              Pre Untrust/S&MSMS (demo)/Fuck Nicole/And Prolapse (7" given away as 'ticket' to Rough Trade In-Store appearance, 500 only) .................................... 25
08   Play It Again Sam PIAS 451 1092 140 DIFB 1092   Courtship Dating/Trash Hologram (Demo) (p/s) ............................ 7
10   Polydor/Fiction LC06444/ 2735606   Doe Deer/Mother Knows Best/Insectica/Seed (12" EP, 500 only, p/s)........ 25
08   Different DIFB 1200PLP     CRYSTAL CASTLES (2-LP) ...................................................................... 18

## CRYSTAL CLEAR
75   Crystal Clear CC 1        Buena Sera/I Want To Make Clear To You .......................................... 15

## CRYSTAL JOY
70   Wren 0346               Little Dreamer/Bite Hard ...................................................................... 30

## CRYSTAL MANSION
70   Polydor 2058-070         Carolina in My Mind/If I Live ................................................................ 6

## CRYSTAL SET
81   Heart & Soul HSCS 001     Know How/Critical Town ...................................................................... 15
*(see also Al Foulcer)*

## CRYSTALITES
69   Big Shot BI 510           Biafra/Drop Pan ................................................................................... 40
69   Nu Beat NB 036           Splash Down/Finders Keepers ............................................................ 100
69   Songbird SB 1015         Musical Madness Parts 1 & 2................................................................ 20
69   Songbird SB 1016         The Bad Parts 1 & 2............................................................................. 20
69   Explosion EX 2002        Doctor Who (Parts 1 & 2) .................................................................... 30
69   Explosion EX 2003        Barefoot Brigade/Slippery ................................................................... 30
69   Explosion EX 2005        Bombshell/Bag-A-Wire (B-side actually by Bobby Ellis & Crystalites) ........ 50
69   Explosion EX 2006        A Fistful Of Dollars/The Emperor (B-side actually by Bobby Ellis & Crystalites) ............ 50
70   Explosion EX 2010        The Bad/The Bad Version ..................................................................... 20
70   Bullet BU 424             A Fistful Of Dollars/BOBBY ELLIS: Crystal ............................................ 15
70   Songbird SB 1017         The Undertaker/Stop That Man (B-side actually "Easy Ride" by Ike Bennett & Crystalites)................................................................................ 30
70   Songbird SB 1020         Lady Madonna/Ghost Rider ................................................................. 35
70   Songbird SB 1024         Isies/Isies (Version 2) ........................................................................... 20
70   Songbird SB 1025         Stranger In Town/Stranger In Town (Version 2)................................... 20
70   Songbird SB 1030         Sic Him Rover/Drop Pon ..................................................................... 25
70   Songbird SB 1034         Overtaker (Version I)/Overtaker (Version II) ........................................ 15
70   Songbird SB 1035         Undertaker's Burial/Ghost Rider .......................................................... 20
70   Songbird SB 1036         Short Story/No Baptism (Version 2)..................................................... 45
71   Songbird SB 1057         Earthly Sounds/Version ........................................................................ 12
73   Grape GR 3050            Blacula/Version ................................................................................... 25
*(see also Chosen Few, Ramon & Crystalites, Kingstonians, Bongo Herman, Denzil Laing, Derrick Harriot, Ethiopians, Dennis Brown, Glen Brown, Big Youth)*

## CRYSTALS
62   Parlophone R 4867       There's No Other Like My Baby/Oh Yeah Maybe Baby ...................... 150
62   London HLU 9611         He's A Rebel/I Love You Eddie ............................................................ 10
63   London HLU 9661         He's Sure The Boy I Love/Walking Along (La-La-La) ............................ 15
63   London HLU 9732         Da Doo Ron Ron/Git It.......................................................................... 10
63   London HLU 9773         Then He Kissed Me/Brother Julius ...................................................... 10
64   London HLU 9837         Little Boy/Uptown (withdrawn)........................................................... 150

MINT VALUE £

| 64 | London HLU 9852 | I Wonder/Little Boy | 50 |
| 64 | London HLU 9909 | All Grown Up/PHIL SPECTOR GROUP: Irving (Jaggered Sixteenths) | 15 |
| 65 | United Artists UP 1110 | My Place/You Can't Tie A Girl Down | 50 |
| 69 | London HLU 10239 | Da Doo Ron Ron/He's A Rebel | 5 |
| 74 | Warners/Spector K 19010 | Da Doo Ron Ron/Then Kissed Me (blue vinyl) | 5 |
| 76 | Phil Spector Intl. 2010 020 | All Grown Up/The Twist | 5 |
| 63 | London RE-U 1381 | DA DOO RON RON (EP) | 50 |
| 63 | London HA-U 8120 | HE'S A REBEL (LP) | 70 |

(see also Darlene Love, Bob B. Soxx & Blue Jeans, Phil Spector)

## CRYTUFF & THE ORIGINALS
| 79 | Hit Run APLP 9006 | DUB TO AFRICA (LP) (Pre-release) | 45 |

## CSA
| 78 | Goat GOAT 001 | STOCKADE (LP) | 40 |

## C.S.A.
| 96 | Squariel Records SQ003 | Don't/'Till I Waltz Again With You (p/s) | 6 |

## C-SAIM
| 83 | Summit SUM 3 T | Night Air/Give And Take (p/s) | 15 |

## C.U.B.
| 73 | Dart ART 2033 | I'm Going Home/You Have Come My way | 8 |

## JOE CUBA SEXTET
| 66 | Pye International 7N 25401 | Bang! Bang!/Push, Push, Push | 20 |

## CUBAN HEELS
| 78 | Housewives' Choice JY 1/2 | Downtown/Do The Smoke Walk (p/s) | 30 |

## CUBY & BLIZZARDS
| 68 | Philips BF 1638 | Distant Smile/Don't Know Which Way To Go | 15 |
| 68 | Philips BF 1719 | Windows Of My Eyes/Checkin' Up On My Baby | 10 |
| 69 | Philips BF 1827 | Apple Knocker's Flophouse/Go Down Sunshine | 25 |
| 69 | Philips (S)BL 7874 | DESOLATION (LP, black/silver labels) | 80 |
| 69 | Philips SBL 7918 | APPLE KNOCKERS FLOPHOUSE (LP) | 45 |

## 'CUDDLY' DUDLEY (HESLOP)
| 59 | HMV POP 586 | Lots More Love/Later | 20 |
| 60 | HMV POP 725 | Too Pooped To Pop/Miss In-Between | 25 |
| 61 | Ember EMB S 136 | Sitting On A Train/One Thing I Like | 10 |
| 62 | Piccadilly 7N 35090 | Monkey Party/The Ferryboat Ride (as Cudley Dudley) | 5 |
| 64 | Oriole International ICB 9 | Blarney Blues/Peace On Earth | 5 |
| 64 | Oriole International ICB 10 | Way Of Life/When Will You Say You'll Be Mine | 15 |

## CUDDLY TOYS
| 80 | Fresh FRESH 010 | Madman/Join The Girls (p/s) | 12 |
| 81 | Parole PURLE 9 | Astral Joe/Slowdown (p/s) | 12 |
| 81 | Fresh FRESH 10 | Mothman/Jo In The Girls (p/s, with 5 stickers) | 12 |
| 81 | Fresh FRESH 20 | Astral Joe/Slowdown (p/s, reissue) | 12 |
| 81 | Fresh FRESH 25 | Someone's Crying/Bring On The Ravers (p/s) | 8 |
| 82 | Fresh LP 6 | TRIALS AND CROSSES (LP) | 15 |

(see also Raped)

## CUES
| 56 | Capitol CL 14501 | Burn That Candle/O My Darlin' | 250 |
| 56 | Capitol CL 14651 | Crackerjack/The Girl I Love (featuring Jimmy Breedlove) | 200 |
| 57 | Capitol CL 14682 | Prince Or Pauper/Why | 150 |

(see also Jimmy Breedlove)

## CUFF-LINKS
| 69 | MCA MU 1101 | Tracy/Where Do You Go? | 5 |
| 70 | MCA MU 1112 | When Julie Comes Around/Sally Ann (You're Such A Pretty Girl) | 6 |
| 70 | MCA MU 1128 | Robin's World/Lay A Little Love On Me | 6 |
| 75 | Pye Int. 7N 25687 | Some Girls Do (Some Girls Don't)/Poppa's Theme | 5 |
| 70 | MCA MUP(S) 398 | TRACY (LP) | 5 |

## XAVIER CUGAT
| 63 | Mercury AMT 1202 | Watermelon Man/Swinging Shepherd Blues | 10 |

## CLIVE CULBERTSON
| 79 | Rip Off RIP 9 | Time To Kill/Busy Signal (initially came in brown paper bag sleeve) | 75 |
| 79 | Logo GO 364 | Time To Kill/Busy Signals (reissue) | 25 |
| 82 | Mint CHEW 66 | Kill Me/The Night's No Friend Of Mine | 30 |
| 84 | Mint CHEW 89 | Just A Little Bit/The Last Laugh | 30 |
| 85 | Mint CHEW 101 | I Can't Fight It/You Don't Have A Dream | 20 |

(see also No Sweat (1))

## ELI CULBERTSON
| 74 | EMI 2207 | I Need Your Love Tonight/Boogie Queen | 25 |

## CHRIS CULLEN
| 82 | Zim Zam Z1 | Coincidence/I'll See You Later (p/s) | 15 |

## CULPEPPER'S ORCHARD
| 72 | Polydor 2480 123 | SECOND SIGHT (LP) | 175 |

## CULT FIGURES
| 79 | Rather GEAR 4/RT 020 | Zip Nolan (Highway Patrolman)/P.W.T. (Playing With Toys)/ Zip Dub (gatefold p/s) | 8 |
| 80 | Rather GEAR 8 | In Love/Laura Kate/Almost A Love Song (p/s) | 8 |

(see also Swell Maps)

## CULT HERO
| 79 | Fiction FICS 006 | I'm A Cult Hero/I Dig You (p/s, 2,000 only) | 60 |

(see also Cure)

## CULT MANIAX
| | | | |
|---|---|---|---|
| 82 | Elephant Rock ROCK 001 | Blitz/Lucy Looe (p/s, with A3 lyric poster) | 30 |
| 82 | Elephant Rock ROCK 002 | American Dream/Elephant Rock | 15 |
| 82 | Next Wave NXT 2/BAK 1 | Frenzie/The Russians Are Coming/Black Horse/Death March (p/s, withdrawn most have band-inflicted scratch through Black Horse) | 60 |
| 84 | Xcentric SIXTH 1 | FULL OF SPUNK! (EP, fold-over p/s in polythene bag) | 6 |
| 84 | Xcentrix EIGTH 1 | THE AMAZING ADVENTURES OF JOHNNY THE DUCK AND THE BATH TIME BLUES (EP) | 6 |

## CULT (1)
| | | | |
|---|---|---|---|
| 80 | Anti-Hype DL 001 | It'll Take Time/Frontier/I Always Lose My Temper (p/s) | 100 |

## CULT (2)
| | | | |
|---|---|---|---|
| 80s | Beggars Banquet 235H | Sun King/Edie (Ciao Baby)/She Sells Sanctuary (12", holographic plastic sleeve.) | 12 |
| 84 | B. Banquet BEGA 57P | DREAMTIME (LP, picture disc) | 12 |
| 84 | B. Banquet BEGA 57 | DREAMTIME (white label test pressing, with unique version of "Go West") | 30 |
| 80s | Beggars Banquet | ELECTRIC (LP, gatefold sleeve gold vinyl, 5,000 only) | 25 |
| 91 | Beggars Banquet CBOX 1 | SINGLES COLLECTION (10-CD box set, picture discs with booklet) | 30 |
| 93 | Beggars Banquet BEGA 1230B | PURE CULT (4-LP box set) | 35 |
| 94 | Beggars Banquet BBQLP 164 | THE CULT (2-LP) | 40 |

*(see also Death Cult, Southern Death Cult, Lonesome No More, Theatre Of Hate, Studio Sweethearts)*

## CULTURAL ROOTS
| | | | |
|---|---|---|---|
| 82 | Reggae REG 01 | Ghetto Running/Version (12") | 25 |
| 80s | Up Front EX 718 | Mr Liar Man/People Com A Dance (12", with HUGH CHRIS) | 20 |
| 82 | Germain GLP 002 | DRIFT AWAY FROM EVIL (LP) | 30 |
| 84 | Greensleeves GREL 62 | HELL A GO POP (LP) | 15 |

## CULTURE
| | | | |
|---|---|---|---|
| 77 | Sky Note DD 003 | The Cultures Trod On/THE REVOLUTIONARIES, CULTURE AND RANKING TREVOR: Trod On In Dub (A-side as "The Cultures") (12" white pasted sleeve) | 25 |
| 78 | Lightning LIG 1978 | Two Sevens Clash/I'm Not Ashamed | 10 |
| 78 | Lightning LIG 515 | Jah Pretty Face/Natty Dread Taking Over | 5 |
| 87 | Strange Fruit SFPS 042 | PEEL SESSIONS (12") | 10 |
| 78 | Sky Note SKY LP 016 | IN DUB (LP) | 45 |
| 78 | Lightning LIP 1 | TWO SEVENS CLASH (LP) | 25 |
| 78 | Virgin FL 1016 | HARDER THAN THE REST (LP) | 18 |
| 79 | Virgin Frontline FL1047 | INTERNATIONAL HERB (LP) | 15 |
| 81 | Virgin VX1001 | VITAL SELECTION (LP) | 15 |
| 83 | Blue Moon BMLP 004 | TWO SEVENS CLASH (LP, reissue) | 15 |

## BOBBY CULTURE
| | | | |
|---|---|---|---|
| 82 | Leggo LG 003 | Health And Strength/Buenos Dias (12") | 40 |

## CULTURE CLUB
| | | | |
|---|---|---|---|
| 84 | Virgin VSY 694 | The War Song/La Cancion De Guerra (picture disc, withdrawn) | 30 |
| 82 | Virgin VP 2232 | KISSING TO BE CLEVER (LP, picture disc, with insert) | 12 |
| 83 | Virgin VP 2285 | COLOUR BY NUMBERS (LP, picture disc) | 12 |
| 84 | Virgin VP 2330 | WAKING UP WITH THE HOUSE ON FIRE (LP, picture disc, with insert) | 12 |

*(see also The Edge)*

## CULTURE PAUL
| | | | |
|---|---|---|---|
| 80s | Music House MH 2 | Mini Van Man (12") | 40 |

## PETER CULTURE
| | | | |
|---|---|---|---|
| 84 | Ariwa ARI 38 | The Counsel Of The Father/BLACK STEEL: Grooving In Love (12") | 20 |
| 84 | Ariwa ARILP 018 | FACING THE FIGHT (LP) | 15 |

## CULTURE SHOCK
| | | | |
|---|---|---|---|
| 82 | Bluurg FISH 20 | ONWARDS & UPWARDS (LP) | 15 |
| 87 | Bluurg FISH 19 | GO WILD (LP) | 15 |

## CULVER STREET PLAYGROUND
| | | | |
|---|---|---|---|
| 68 | President PT 145 | Alley Pond Park/A Decent Sort Of Guy | 12 |

## ANDREW CULVERWELL
| | | | |
|---|---|---|---|
| 71 | Polydor 2343 035 | WHERE IS THE LOVE? (LP) | 15 |

## DAVID CUMMING
| | | | |
|---|---|---|---|
| 67 | Philips BF 1545 | Rubber Rabbit/The Parrots Of Simple Street | 6 |

## BARBARA CUMMINGS
| | | | |
|---|---|---|---|
| 67 | London HLU 10110 | She's The Woman/There's Something Funny Going On | 7 |

## JON CUNDO
| | | | |
|---|---|---|---|
| 72 | Bamboo BAM 69 | Love Is Strange/When We Were Children | 10 |

*(see also Joncuno)*

## DAVID CUNNINGHAM
| | | | |
|---|---|---|---|
| 80 | Piano PIANO 001 | GREY SCALE (LP) | 40 |

## EARL CUNNINGHAM
| | | | |
|---|---|---|---|
| 70s | One Top OSM 002 | Got To Know That Place/Gates Are Wide Open (12") | 100 |
| 79 | Freedom Sounds FSD 016 | Vanity Woman/Best Things (12") | 15 |
| 80 | Freedom Sounds FSD 017 | Never Give Up/Follow Fashion (12") | 25 |
| 81 | Rusty International RI 012 | Cool Profile/School Girl (12") | 25 |
| 79 | Vista Sounds VSLP 4021 | EARL CUNNINGHAM (LP) | 25 |
| 84 | Time TRLP 002 | JOHN TOM (LP, insert) | 25 |

## H. CUNNINGHAM
| | | | |
|---|---|---|---|
| 71 | Tropical AL 004 | Ethiopian Son/TROPICAL ALLSTARS: Version 2 | 5 |

## CUPIDS
| | | | |
|---|---|---|---|
| 58 | Vogue V 9102 | Now You Tell Me/Lillie Mae | 900 |
| 58 | Vogue V 9102 | Now You Tell Me/Lillie Mae (78) | 100 |

## CUPID'S INSPIRATION

| | | | |
|---|---|---|---|
| 68 | NEMS 56-3500 | Yesterday Has Gone/Dream | 15 |
| 68 | NEMS 56-3702 | My World/Everything Is Meant To Be | 7 |
| 69 | Bell BLL 1069 | The Sad Thing/Look At Me | 7 |
| 69 | CBS 4509 | Boat Trip/Time Only Knows | 20 |
| 70 | CBS 4722 | Without Your Love/Different Guy | 8 |
| 70 | CBS 4994 | Are You Growing Tired Of My Love/Sunshine | 8 |
| 74 | DJM DJS 300 | Yesterday Has Gone/My World | 6 |
| 69 | NEMS 6-63553 | YESTERDAY HAS GONE (LP, gatefold, as Cupid's Inspiration Featuring T. Rice-Milton) | 20 |

*(see also Gordon Haskell, Paper Blitz Tissue)*

## CUPOL

| | | | |
|---|---|---|---|
| 80 | 4AD BAD 9 | Like This For Ages/Kluba Cupol (12", p/s, 45/33rpm) | 12 |

*(see also Wire)*

## CUPPA T

| | | | |
|---|---|---|---|
| 67 | Deram DM 144 | Miss Pinkerton/Brand New World | 25 |
| 68 | Deram DM 185 | Streatham Hippodrome/One Man Band | 20 |

*(see also Overlanders)*

## CUPS

| | | | |
|---|---|---|---|
| 68 | Polydor 56777 | Good As Gold/Life And Times | 40 |

*(see also Gallagher & Lyle)*

## CURE

### SINGLES

| | | | |
|---|---|---|---|
| 78 | Small Wonder SMALL 11 | Killing An Arab/10.15 Saturday Night (p/s, 15,000 only, beware of counterfeits) | 60 |
| 79 | Fiction FICS 001 | Killing An Arab/10.15 Saturday Night (p/s, reissue) | 20 |
| 79 | Fiction FICS 002 | Boys Don't Cry/Plastic Passion ('soldier' p/s, typed matrix, 'but Bill does' on A side runout and 'land of 1000 motorhomes' on B) | 20 |
| 79 | Fiction FICS 005 | Jumping Someone Else's Train/I'm Cold (p/s, typed matrix) | 25 |
| 80 | Fiction FICS 010 | A Forest/Another Journey By Train (p/s) | 15 |
| 80 | Fiction FICS 10 | A Forest/Another Journey By Train (2nd pressing, "radiophonic" sleeve) | 8 |
| 80 | Fiction FICS 010 | A Forest/Another Journey By Train ('radiophonic' die-cut sleeve) | 10 |
| 80 | Fiction FICSX 010 | A Forest (Extended Version)/Another Journey By Train (12", p/s) | 30 |
| 81 | Fiction FICS 012 | Primary/Descent (p/s) | 15 |
| 81 | Fiction FICSX 012 | Primary (Extended)/Descent (12", p/s) | 25 |
| 81 | Fiction FICS 014 | Charlotte Sometimes/Splintered In Her Head (p/s) | 15 |
| 81 | Fiction FICSX 014 | Charlotte Sometimes/Splintered In Her Head/Faith (live) (12", p/s) | 18 |
| 82 | Fiction FICS 015 | The Hanging Garden/Killing An Arab (live) (p/s) | 10 |
| 82 | Fiction FICG 015 | The Hanging Garden/100 Years//A Forest/Killing An Arab (double pack, gatefold p/s, 5,000 only) | 15 |
| 82 | Lyntone LYN 12011 | Lament (1-sided flexidisc, red vinyl) | 40 |
| 82 | Lyntone LYN 12011 | Lament (1-sided flexidisc, green vinyl) | 15 |
| 82 | Lyntone LYN 12011 | Lament (1-sided flexidisc, red vinyl with Flexipop issue 22) | 50 |
| 82 | Lyntone LYN 12011 | Lament (1-sided flexidisc, green vinyl, with Flexipop issue 22) | 18 |
| 82 | Fiction FICS 17 | Let's Go To Bed/Just One Kiss (p/s) | 8 |
| 82 | Fiction FICSX 017 | Let's Go To Bed (Extended)/Just One Kiss (Extended) (12", p/s) | 12 |
| 83 | Fiction FICS 018 | The Walk/The Dream (paper labels, poster p/s) | 20 |
| 83 | Fiction FICSP 018 | The Walk/The Dream (picture disc) | 35 |
| 83 | Fiction FICSX 018 | Upstairs Room/The Dream/The Walk/Lament//Let's Go To Bed (Extended)/ Just One Kiss (Extended) (12" double pack, shrinkwrapped with sticker) | 30 |
| 83 | Fiction FICS 19 | Lovecats/Speak My Language (p/s) | 5 |
| 83 | Fiction FICSP 019 | The Lovecats/Speak My Language (picture disc, PVC sleeve) | 35 |
| 84 | Fiction FIXSP 020 | The Caterpillar/Happy The Man (picture disc, printed PVC sleeve) | 30 |
| 85 | Fiction 080182-2 | In Between Days/The Exploding Boy/A Few Hours After This/ Six Different Ways (live)/Push (live) (CD Video) | 40 |
| 85 | Fiction FICSG 23 | Close To Me (Remix)/A Man Inside My Mouth (poster p/s; some copies with blue & white 'Head On The Door' sticker) | 15 |
| 85 | Fiction FICST 23 | HALF AN OCTOPUS: Close To Me (Remix)/A Man Inside My Mouth/New Day/ Stop Dead (10" EP, p/s) | 18 |
| 85 | Fiction 080180-2 | Close To Me (12" Remix)/A Man Inside My Mouth/Stop Dead/ New Day (CD Video) | 45 |
| 87 | Fiction FICSG 25 | Why Can't I Be You?/A Japanese Dream//Six Different Ways (live)/ Push (live) (numbered double pack, gatefold p/s) | 12 |
| 87 | Fiction FICS 26 | Catch/Breathe (p/s, in carrier bag) | 8 |
| 87 | Fiction FICSP 26 | Catch/Breathe (clear vinyl, printed PVC sleeve) | 18 |
| 87 | Fiction 080186-2 | Catch/Breathe/A Chain Of Flowers/Icing Sugar (Remix) (CD Video) | 45 |
| 87 | Fiction FICS 27 | Just Like Heaven/Snow In Summer (p/s, numbered, white vinyl) | 8 |
| 87 | Fiction FICS 27 | Just Like Heaven/Snow In Summer (p/s, mispress, A-side plays both sides) | 20 |
| 87 | Fiction FICSP 27 | Just Like Heaven/Snow In Summer (picture disc in custom PVC sleeve) | 20 |
| 87 | Fiction FIXCD 27 | Just Like Heaven (Remix)/Snow In Summer/Sugar Girl (CD, card sleeve) | 25 |
| 88 | Strange Fruit SFPS 050 | PEEL SESSIONS EP (12") | 12 |
| 89 | Fiction FICSG 29 | Lullaby (Remix)/Babble (gatefold p/s, numbered with sticker) | 8 |
| 89 | Fiction FICSP 29 | Lullaby (Remix)/Babble (clear vinyl, numbered printed 'spider web' PVC sleeve) | 18 |
| 89 | Fiction FICVX 29 | Lullaby (Remix)/Babble/Out Of Mind (12", pink vinyl, numbered with stickers) | 18 |
| 89 | Fiction FICSG 30 | Lovesong/2 Late ('The Love Box' set with linen print) | 12 |
| 90 | Fiction FICPA 34 | Pictures Of You (Remix)/Last Dance (live) (p/s, green vinyl, no'd sticker) | 6 |
| 90 | Fiction FICPA 34 | Pictures Of You (Remix)/Last Dance (live) (p/s, green vinyl, mispress, plays "Last Dance" both sides) | 30 |
| 90 | Fiction FICPB 34 | Pictures Of You (Remix)/Prayers For Rain (p/s, purple vinyl, numbered sticker) | 10 |
| 90 | Fiction FICXA 34 | Pictures Of You (Extended Remix)/Last Dance (Live)/Fascination Street (Live) (12") | 18 |
| 90 | Fiction 080184-2 | Why Can't I Be You? (12" Remix)/A Japanese Dream (5.40 Remix)/Hey You!!! (CD Video) | 45 |
| 92 | Fiction FICS 42 | Friday I'm In Love/Halo (p/s) | 5 |

| 92 | Fiction FICCD 42 | Friday I'm In Love/Halo/Scared Of You/Friday I'm In Love (Strangelove Mix) (12", p/s, different coloured or marbled vinyl) .................... 25 |
|----|----|----|
| 92 | Fiction FICS 46 | A Letter To Elise/The Big Hand (p/s) ............................................. 5 |
| 12 | Secret 7 S74 | Friday I'm In Love (1-sided RSD 7" in unique individual art sleeve, 100 only) .............. 80 |

## ALBUMS

| 79 | Fiction FIX 1 | THREE IMAGINARY BOYS (with inner sleeve, postcard & badge) .................. 50 |
|----|----|----|
| 79 | Fiction FIX 1 | THREE IMAGINARY BOYS (LP, with inner sleeve and "Limited edition special price" stamped in gold on cover) ........................ 20 |
| 80 | Fiction FIXD 004 | SEVENTEEN SECONDS (LP, textured sleeve, 1st pressing has FIX 004 on rear of sleeve)) 25 |
| 80 | Fiction FIX 4 | SEVENTEEN SECONDS (LP, reissue) ............................................ 18 |
| 81 | Fiction FIX 6 | FAITH (LP, inner) ..................................................... 20 |
| 82 | Fiction FIX D7 | PORNOGRAPHY (LP, with inner sleeve) ................................... 20 |
| 84 | Fiction FIXS 9 | THE TOP (with badge & poster, green inner sleeve) ................... 20 |
| 84 | Fiction FIXS 9 | THE TOP (with promo plastic snake & top) ................................ 35 |
| 85 | Fiction FIXH 11 | HEAD ON THE DOOR (LP, inner) ............................................ 20 |
| 86 | Fiction 815 011-2 | BOYS DON'T CRY (CD, original non-picture disc, with "Object" & "World War" & without "So What") ........................ 30 |
| 86 | Fiction FIXH 12 | STANDING ON A BEACH - THE SINGLES (LP, gatefold with inner sleeve) ............ 20 |
| 87 | Fiction FIXH 13/FIXHA 13 | KISS ME, KISS ME, KISS ME (with bonus orange vinyl 6-track 12" [FIXHA 13], in custom PVC sleeve) ........................ 50 |
| 89 | Fiction FIXH 14 | DISINTEGRATION (LP, with inner sleeve) ................................ 20 |
| 89 | Fiction FIXHP 14 | DISINTEGRATION (picture disc, printed PVC sleeve) ................... 30 |
| 90 | Fiction FIXLP 18 | MIXED UP (2-LP, inners) .............................................. 20 |
| 90 | Fiction FIXCD 17 | ENTREAT (CD, exclusive to HMV, card p/s, yellow photo) ............ 25 |
| 92 | Fiction FIXH 20 | WISH (2-LP) .......................................................... 25 |
| 92 | Fiction 513 600-0 | LIMITED EDITION CD BOX (15 x CD hinged box set, 2,500 only) ............ 200 |
| 96 | Fiction FIXLP 28 | WILD MOOD SWINGS (2-LP) ................................................ 60 |
| 97 | Fiction FIXLP 30 | GALORE (2-LP, inners) ................................................. 30 |
| 00 | Fiction FIX 31 | BLOODFLOWERS (2-LP) .................................................... 40 |
| 04 | Fiction 981463 | JOIN THE DOTS: B-SIDES AND RARITIES 1978-2001 (4-CD box set) ............ 20 |

## PROMOS

| 79 | Fiction | Boys Don't Cry ............................................................ 45 |
|----|----|----|
| 79 | Fiction CUR 1 | Grinding Halt/Meat Hook (12", stickered sleeve) ..................... 150 |
| 81 | Fiction FICS 12 | Primary (1-sided, no p/s) .................................................. 25 |
| 82 | Fiction CURE 1 | One Hundred Years/The Hanging Garden (12", p/s, promo/gig freebie) .......... 70 |
| 82 | Lyntone LYN 12011 | Lament (hard vinyl test pressing, no p/s) ............................ 400 |
| 84 | Fiction KAREN 1 | THE TOP (12", 1-sided, 3-track sampler) ............................. 55 |
| 88 | Fiction FICSDJ 28 | Hot Hot Hot!!! (Remix)/Hey You!!! (Remix) (die-cut title p/s) ......... 15 |
| 89 | Fiction CIFCD 3 | STRANGER THAN FICTION (CD, 6-track sampler, 1000 only) ............... 100 |
| 90 | Fiction CUREPROCD 3 | THE CURE - AN INTERVIEW (CD) ....................................... 25 |
| 80s | Fiction FICS DJ 42 | Friday I'm In Love (Promo in die-cut Fiction sleeve) ............... 20 |
| 92 | Fiction CURE 1 | CLASSIC CURE: Love Cats/Close To Me (Closer Mix)/Lovesong/ Charlotte Sometimes/Lullaby/Why Can't I Be You/A Forest (CD, sampler, inlay) ............ 25 |
| 96 | Fiction FIXCD 20 | Wish (CD promo, digipak) ............................................. 25 |
| 96 | Fiction FICSTX 53 | Gone! (Ultraliving Mix) (12", same track both sides, with 'DJ' insert) ......... 12 |
| 97 | Fiction FICSX 54 | Wrong Number (Single Mix)/(ISDN Mix)/(Digital Exchange Mix)/(Dub Analogue Exchange Mix)/(Crossed Line Mix)/(Engaged Mix)/(P2P Mix) (12", double pack, p/s promo only) ............ 25 |
| 97 | Fixtion FIXCD.COM 1 | FIVE SWING LIVE (CD, 5-track sampler, available via the internet, 5,000 only) .............. 30 |

*(see also Cult Hero, Siouxsie & Banshees, Glove, Fools Dance, Tim Pope, Lockjaw, Obtainers)*

## MARTIN CURE & PEEPS

| 67 | Philips BF 1605 | It's All Over Now/I Can Make The Rain Fall Up .......................... 40 |
|----|----|----|

*(see also Peeps, Rainbows)*

## CURFEW

| 70 | Brent BN 001 | Visions/Look Behind You .................................................. 200 |
|----|----|----|

## CURIOSITY SHOPPE

| 68 | Deram DM 220 | Baby I Need You/So Sad ..................................................... 100 |
|----|----|----|

## JOHNNY CURIOUS & STRANGERS

| 78 | Illegal IL 009 | In Tune/Road To Cheltenham/Pissheadsville/Jennifer (p/s) ............ 20 |
|----|----|----|
| 79 | Bugle BLAST 2 | Someone Else's Home/Backwards In The Night (p/s) .................... 12 |

## CURLY

| 75 | EPIC EPC 3145 | High Flying Bird/Breakout ................................................. 6 |
|----|----|----|
| 71 | Pye 25570 | Funky Yeah/Shelly's Rubber Band .......................................... 12 |

## TERRY CURRAN

| 80 | Norwood NR 2004 | Singing The Blues/Wednesday Chant ....................................... 6 |
|----|----|----|

## CURRANT KRAZE

| 70 | Deram DM 292 | Lady Pearl/Breaking The Heart Of A Good Man .......................... 6 |
|----|----|----|

## CURRENT 93

| 98 | Durtro DURTRO 042 | SOFT BLACK STARS (LP, clear vinyl with free 12" and insert, 2000 only) ........ 25 |
|----|----|----|
| 83 | L.A.Y.L.A.H. L.A.Y. 1 | Lashtal/Salt/Caresse (12", white p/s) ................................ 22 |
| 83 | L.A.Y.L.A.H. L.A.Y. 1 | Lashtal/Salt/Caresse (12", white p/s [reissue from in 1988 with dark p/s and "1988" on label]) ........................ 18 |
| 85 | L.A.Y.L.A.H. L.A.Y. 14 | NIGHTMARE CULTURE (12" EP, with Sickness Of Snakes [i.e. Coil feat. Boyd Rice]; matt black & red sleeve) ........................ 22 |
| 87 | L.A.Y.L.A.H. L.A.Y. 18 | HAPPY BIRTHDAY PIGFACE CHRISTUS (12" EP) ............................. 22 |
| 87 | Maldoror MAL 108 | Crowleymass/Christmassacre/Crowleymass (Mix Mix Mix) (12", p/s) ......... 28 |
| 88 | Yangki 002 | FAITH'S FAVOURITES EP (Ballad Of The Pale Girl/NURSE WITH WOUND: Swamp Rat) (12", laminated p/s) ........................ 28 |
| 88 | Maldoror MAL 088 | The Red Face Of God/The Breath And The Pain Of God (12", p/s, with insert, 666 only) ........................ 40 |
| 89 | Yangki 003 | DEATH OF THE CORN (12" EP, with Sol Invictus; 'art' sleeve) ............ 18 |

| 90 | Harbinger 001 | No Hiding From The Blackbird/NURSE WITH WOUND: Burial Of The Stoned Sardine (p/s, remixed reissue of giveaway 7") .................................................................................. 12 |
|---|---|---|
| 90 | Shock SX 003 | She Is Dead And All Fall Down/God Has Three Faces And Wood Has No Name (folded sleeve in bag, 1,000 only, this price for 26 copies that were signed/lettered) ....................... 45 |
| 90 | Shock SX 003 | She Is Dead And All Fall Down/God Has Three Faces And Wood Has No Name (folded sleeve in bag, 1,000 only) ................................................................................................. 22 |
| 90 | Cerne 004 | This Ain't The Summer Of Love (live) (with Sol Invictus, gig freebie, printed labels, this price for 93 copies with ticket) ................................................................................... 30 |
| 90 | Cerne 004 | This Ain't The Summer Of Love (live) (with Sol Invictus, gig freebie, printed labels) ....... 20 |
| 92 | Durtro DURTRO 004 | LOONEY RUNES (12", live EP, 2,000 only, with poster) ................................................. 20 |
| 94 | Ptolemaic Terrascope POT6 | Broken Birds Fly/RANDY CALIFORNIA: The American Society/The Whale Song (free with Ptolemaic Terrascope mag) ...................................................................................... 10 |
| 94 | Ptolemaic Terrascope POT6 | Broken Birds Fly/RANDY CALIFORNIA: The American Society/The Whale Song (without Ptolemaic Terrascope mag) ...................................................................................... 8 |
| 94 | Durtro DURTRO 022 | THE FIRE OF THE MIND (CD EP, free with book 'Simply Being') ..................................... 55 |
| 95 | Durtro DURTRO 025 | Tamlin/How The Great Satanic Glory Faded (12", numbered with insert, 2,000 only) ... 28 |
| 95 | Durtro DURTRO 028 | Where The Long Shadows Fall (12", 1-sided clear vinyl with insert, 2,000 only) ........... 18 |
| 84 | L.A.Y.L.A.H. LAY 008 | DOGS BLOOD RISING (LP) ................................................................................................ 25 |
| 86 | Maldoror UDO 22M | IN MENSTRUAL NIGHT (LP, 25 with handmade inserts & cover) ................................... 100 |
| 86 | Maldoror UDO 22M | IN MENSTRUAL NIGHT (LP) .............................................................................................. 20 |
| 86 | United Dairies UD 022 | IN MENSTRUAL NIGHT (LP, picture disc) ......................................................................... 20 |
| 87 | L.A.Y.L.A.H. LAY 20 | SWASTIKAS FOR NODDY (LP, with insert) ........................................................................ 25 |
| 88 | Maldoror MAL 666 | CHRIST AND THE PALE QUEENS MIGHTY IN SORROW (3-sided LP, with inserts, 93 copies only) ....................................................................................................................... 100 |
| 88 | Maldoror MAL 777 | IMPERIUM (LP, black label, with insert) .......................................................................... 28 |
| 88 | Maldoror MAL 777 | IMPERIUM (LP, later pressing with white label) .............................................................. 18 |
| 89 | Maldoror MAL 093 | DAWN (LP) ....................................................................................................................... 60 |
| 89 | Durtro DURTRO 001 | LIVE AT BAR MALDOROR (LP, white label, 1,000 only) ................................................... 55 |
| 80s | Maldoror MAL 123 | NATURE UNVEILED (LP, with insert & free 7": "No Hiding From The Blackbird/NURSE WITH WOUND: Burial Of The Sardine") ............................................................................ 30 |
| 80s | Maldoror MAL 123 | NATURE UNVEILED (LP, with insert) ................................................................................ 20 |
| 88 | United Dairies UD 029 | EARTH COVERS EARTH (mini-LP) ..................................................................................... 35 |
| 90 | Dutro 048 | I HAVE A SPECIAL PLAN FOR THIS WORLD (LP, limited edition on red vinyl) ................. 50 |
| 90 | Dutro 048 | I HAVE A SPECIAL PLAN FOR THIS WORLD (LP, limited edition on clear vinyl) .............. 30 |
| 90 | Cerne 00123 | THE CERNE BOX SET (3-LP set, includes "Horse"; other LPs by Sol Invictus & Nurse With Wound, 2,000 only) ................................................................................................. 70 |
| 90 | NER BADVC 693 | 1888 (LP, split with Death In June, 500 each on clear & red vinyl) ................................ 35 |
| 90 | NER BADVC 693 | 1888 (LP, split with Death In June, black vinyl) .............................................................. 25 |
| 92 | Durtro DURTRO 006 | ISLAND (LP, with insert, 2,000 only) ............................................................................... 20 |
| 92 | Durtro DURTRO 011 | THUNDER PERFECT MIND (2-LP, with insert) .................................................................. 20 |
| 94 | Durtro DURTRO 018 | OF RUINE, OR SOME BLAZING STARRE (LP, blue vinyl w/insert, 2,000 only) ................. 20 |
| 94 | Durtrohoho 019 | LUCIFER OVER LONDON (LP, red vinyl with insert, 2,000 only) ....................................... 20 |
| 96 | Durtro DURTRO 026 | ALL THE PRETTY LITTLE HORSES (LP, clear vinyl with insert, 2,000 only) ...................... 20 |

*(see also Nurse With Wound, 23 Skidoo, Psychic TV, Crisis, Death In June, Sol Invictus, Steven Stapleton & David Tibet, Tibet & Stapleton)*

## DAVID CURRIE
| 71 | Philips 6006165 | I Don't Want To Talk About It/The Question ................................................................... 10 |
|---|---|---|

## CLIFFORD CURRY
| 69 | Action ACT 4549 | She Shot A Hole In My Soul/We're Gonna Hate Ourselves In The Morning ...................... 10 |
|---|---|---|
| 69 | Pama PM 793 | You Turn Out The Light/Good Humour Man ................................................................... 10 |
| 69 | Pama PM 797 | I Can't Get A Hold Of Myself/Ain't No Danger ............................................................... 50 |

## TIM CURRY
| 74 | Ode ODE 66103 | Sweet Transvestite/Time Warp (in p/s) ............................................................................ 8 |
|---|---|---|
| 74 | Ode ODE 66103 | Sweet Transvestite/Time Warp ........................................................................................ 5 |

## TED CURSON QUARTET
| 64 | Fontana 688310 ZL | TEARS FOR DOLPHY (LP) .................................................................................................. 35 |
|---|---|---|

## CURTAINS
| 95 | Detour DR 025 | In My Street/Family Affair (p/s, blue vinyl, 100 only) ...................................................... 7 |
|---|---|---|

## DAN CURTIN
| 94 | Peacefrog PF 018X | PARALLEL EP (12", sampler, plain sleeve) ....................................................................... 10 |
|---|---|---|
| 95 | Peacefrog PF 023 | PURVEYORS OF FINE FUNK - HEIGHTS TRAX VOL 1 EP (12", plain sleeve) ...................... 15 |
| 95 | Peacefrog PF 024 | DREAMS NOT OF TODAY EP (12", plain sleeve) .............................................................. 10 |
| 95 | Peacefrog PF 032 | PURVEYORS OF FINE FUNK - HEIGHTS TRAX VOL 2 EP (12", plain sleeve) ...................... 10 |
| 96 | Peacefrog PF 058 | PURVEYORS OF FINE FUNK VOL 3 EP (12", plain sleeve) ................................................. 10 |
| 94 | Peacefrog PF 018 | THE SILICON DAWN (2-LP) ............................................................................................... 18 |
| 95 | Peacefrog PF 038 | WEB OF LIFE (2-LP) ......................................................................................................... 18 |

## ALLEN CURTIS
| 64 | Hickory 45-1226 | Fireball Mail/The Hole He Said He'd Dig For Me .............................................................. 5 |
|---|---|---|

## CHRIS CURTIS
| 66 | Pye 7N 17132 | Aggravation/Have I Done Something Wrong .................................................................... 35 |
|---|---|---|

*(see also Searchers)*

## CLEM CURTIS & FOUNDATIONS
| 72 | Pye 7N 45150 | I've Never Found A Girl (To Love Me Like You)/Point Of No Return .................................. 20 |
|---|---|---|
| 75 | Riverdale RS 105 | Sweet Happiness/Lady Luck ............................................................................................ 20 |

*(See also the Foundations)*

## DENNY CURTIS
| 68 | Plexium PXM 2 | Crying Over You/You Don't Love Me No More .................................................................. 6 |
|---|---|---|
| 69 | Plexium PXM 6 | Message/You Gotta Be Mine ............................................................................................ 6 |

## EDDIE CURTIS
| 63 | Oriole CB 1852 | Leavin Town/Faithful Kind (with Hellions) ...................................................................... 10 |
|---|---|---|

## JOE CURTIS
72  Spiral DIT 4      Black Is Beautiful/This Is Love ............................................................... 8

## JOHNNY CURTIS
66  Parlophone R 5529      Our Love's Disintegrating/(I'd Be) A Legend In My Time ....................... 70
67  Parlophone R 5582      Jack And The Beanstalk/Go On Back ...................................................... 30
68  Major Minor MM 564      Pickin' Up Pebbles/Gentle On My Mind ................................................. 7

## LEE CURTIS (& ALL STARS)
63  Decca F 11622      Little Girl/Just One More Dance (solo) ................................................... 10
63  Decca F 11690      Let's Stomp/Poor Unlucky Me ................................................................ 15
64  Decca F 11830      What About Me/I've Got My Eyes On You ............................................. 15
64  Philips BF 1385      Ecstasy/A Shot Of Rhythm And Blues .................................................... 15
*(see also Pete Best Four)*

## LYNNE CURTIS
64  Decca F11869      House For Sale/My Little Boy ................................................................... 8

## MAC CURTIS
57  Parlophone R 4279      The Low Road/You Ain't Treatin' Me Right ....................................... 2000
57  Parlophone R 4279      The Low Road/You Ain't Treatin' Me Right (78) ................................. 275
74  Polydor 2310 293      ROCKABILLY KINGS (LP, with Charlie Feathers) .................................... 30

## SONNY CURTIS
60  Coral Q 72400      The Red Headed Stranger/Talk About My Baby ................................... 40
64  Colpix PX 11024      A Beatle I Want To Be/So Used To Loving You ...................................... 12
64  Liberty LIB 55710      I Pledged My Love To You/Bo Diddley Bach ......................................... 15
*(see also Crickets)*

## T.C. CURTIS
82  Romantic RR 0001      Party Down/Party Down (Instrumental) ................................................. 6
82  Romantic RR 0001/12      Party Down/Party Down (Instrumental) (12") ...................................... 10

## WINSTON CURTIS
77  Empire EMP 901      WINSTON'S GREATS (LP) ......................................................................... 40
77  Diamond DMLP 401      INSTRUMENTAL EXPLOSION (LP) ........................................................... 80
81  Empire EMP 906      PORTRAIT (LP) ........................................................................................ 80

## DAVE CURTISS & TREMORS
63  Philips BF 1257      You Don't Love Me Any More/Sweet Girl Of Mine ............................. 10
63  Philips BF 1285      What Kind Of Girl Are You?/Dreamer's Funfair ................................... 10
64  Philips BF 1330      Summertime Blues/I'm A Hog For You Baby ....................................... 10

## CURTISS MALDOON
71  Regal Zonophone 3038      You Make Me Happy (And You Make Me Sad)/Amber Man ................... 5
72  Purple PUR 106      One Way Ticket/Next Time ..................................................................... 7
71  Purple TPS 3501      CURTISS MALDOON (LP) .......................................................................... 30
73  Purple TPS 3502      MALDOON (LP) ....................................................................................... 15

## ROCKY CURTISS & HARMONY FLAMES
59  Fontana TFE 17172      U.S.A. HIT PARADE (EP) .......................................................................... 40

## BOBBY CURTOLA (& MARTELLS)
61  Columbia DB 4672      Don't You Sweetheart Me/My Heart's Tongue-Tied (solo) .................. 15
62  London HL 9577      Fortune Teller/Johnny Take Your Time (solo) ...................................... 15
62  London HL 9639      Aladdin/I Don't Want To Go On Without You (solo) ............................ 15
63  Decca F 11670      Gypsy Heart/I'm Sorry ........................................................................... 15
63  Decca F 11725      Three Rows Over/Indian Giver .............................................................. 15

## CURVE
93  Anxious      FALLING FREE - APHEX TWIN REMIX (12", 1-sided promo only, 500 only) ..................... 15
92  Anxious ANXLP 77      DOPPELGANGER (LP) .............................................................................. 15
93  Anxious ANXLP 81      CUCKOO (LP) .......................................................................................... 20

## CURVED AIR
71  Warner Bros WB 8023      It Happened Today/What Happens When You Blow Yourself Up/Vivaldi ............... 7
72  Warner Bros K 16164      Sarah's Concern/Phantasmagoria .......................................................... 6
71  Warner Brothers K 16092      Backstreet Luv/Everdance ...................................................................... 5
84  Pearl Key PK 07350      Renegade/We're Only Human (p/s) ...................................................... 15
70  Warner Bros K 56004      AIR CONDITIONING (LP, picture disc, with booklet, 10,000 only) ....... 70
70  Warner Bros K 56004      AIR CONDITIONING (LP, picture disc) .................................................... 30
70  Warner Bros WSX 3012      AIR CONDITIONING (LP, green label, laminated sleeve) ...................... 40
71  Warner Bros K 46092      SECOND ALBUM (LP, die-cut 'leaves' fold-out sleeve, green label) ..... 40
72  Warner Bros K 46158      PHANTASMAGORIA (LP, green label, with inner lyric card) .................. 20
73  Warner Bros K 46224      AIR CUT (LP, green label, gatefold sleeve) ........................................... 25
75  Deram SML 1119      LIVE (LP, red/white label) ...................................................................... 20
*(see also Kirby, Sonja Kristina, [Darryl Way's] Wolf, Trace, Legs, Stretch, Police)*

## PETER CUSACK
77  Bead Records BEAD 5      AFTER BEING IN HOLLAND FOR TWO YEARS (LP) .................................. 40
84  Bead Records BEAD 22      BIRD JUMPS INTO WOOD (LP, with Clive Bell) ...................................... 20

## SUE CUSS
79  Orchid OR 101      You Really Got Me/Physical Love (no p/s) ............................................. 10

## CUSTERS TRACK
70  Major Minor MM698      On The Run/Hello Heaven ..................................................................... 12

## IVOR CUTLER TRIO
67  Parlophone R 5624      I Had A Little Boat/A Great Grey Grasshopper .................................... 12
59  Fontana TFE 17144      OF Y'HUP (EP) ........................................................................................ 20
61  Decca DFE 6677      GET AWAY FROM THE WALL (EP) ........................................................... 20
89  Strange Fruit SFPS 068      PEE SESSIONS (12") ............................................................................... 15
61  Decca LK 4405      WHO TORE YOUR TROUSERS? (LP) ........................................................ 60

| 67 | Parlophone PCS 7040 | LUDO (LP) | 100 |
| 74 | Virgin V2021 | DANDRUFF (LP, as Ivor Cutler) | 30 |
| 75 | Virgin V2037 | VELVET DONKEY (LP) | 20 |
| 76 | Virgin V2056 | JAMMY SMEARS (LP) | 20 |
| 78 | Harvest SHSP4084 | LIFE IN A SCOTCH SITTING ROOM VOL 2 (LP) | 20 |
| 84 | Rough Trade ROUGH 59 | PRIVILEGE (LP with Linda Hirst) | 25 |
| 85 | Virgin OVED 12 | JAMMY SMEARS (LP, reissue) | 15 |
| 86 | Virgin OVED 34 | VELVET DONKEY (LP, reissue) | 15 |
| 86 | Rough Trade ROUGH 89 | PRINCE IVOR (2-LP) | 25 |
| 86 | Rough Trade ROUGH 98 | GRUTS (LP) | 20 |

## T. TOMMY CUTRER (& GINNY WRIGHT)
| 54 | London HL 8093 | Mexico Gal/Wonderful World (B-side with Ginny Wright) | 40 |

*(see also Ginny Wright)*

## CUTTERS
| 59 | Decca F 11110 | I've Had It/Rockaroo | 10 |

*(see also Neville Taylor & Cutters)*

## CYAN THREE
| 66 | Decca F 12371 | Since I Lost My Baby/Face Of A Loser | 20 |

## CYANIDE
| 78 | Pye 7N 46048 | I'm A Boy/Do It (p/s) | 25 |
| 78 | Pye 7N 46094 | Mac The Flash/Hate The State (demo copies in p/s) | 60 |
| 78 | Pye 7N 46094 | Mac The Flash/Hate The State (demo copies no p/s) | 15 |
| 79 | Pinnacle PIN 23 | Fireball/Your Old Man (p/s) | 40 |
| 78 | Pye NSPL 18554 | CYANIDE (LP) | 40 |

## CYBERMEN
| 78 | Rockaway AERE 101 | THE CYBERMEN (EP, available in 2 different sleeves with info sheet) | 100 |
| 78 | Rockaway AERE 101 | THE CYBERMEN (EP, available in 2 different sleeves without info sheet) | 40 |
| 79 | Rockaway LUV 002 | You're To Blame/It's You I Want (with inserts) | 45 |

## CYBERNETIC SERENDIPITY GROUP
| 68 | ICA ICA 1/2 | CYBERNETIC SERENDIPITY MUSIC (LP, private pressing) | 150 |

## CYBOTRON FEATURING DILLINJA
| 96 | Prototype PRO 004 | Threshold/Hot To (12") | 10 |
| 98 | Prototype PRO 010 | Light Years/Revelations (12") | 10 |
| 00 | Valve CYBX 001 | NASTY WAYZ (EP) | 15 |

*(see also Dillinja)*

## CYCLONE
| 79 | Magnet MAG 159 | Palisades Park/Crazy Haze (p/s) | 8 |

*(see also Matchbox)*

## CYCLONES (1)
| 64 | Oriole CB 1898 | Nobody/Little Egypt | 60 |

## CYCLONES (2)
| 71 | Banana BA 338 | My Sweet Lord/DENNIS BROWN: Silky (B-side actually by Monty Alexander & Cyclones) | 12 |

## CYCLOP'S EYE
| 72 | Phoenix PHO12 | Rolling Thunder/Kentucky Freeway | 12 |

## CYGNUS
| 78 | Greensleeves GRED 4 | Jah Man/Babylon (12") | 25 |

## CYLOB
| 95 | Rephlex CAT 015 | INDUSTRIAL FOLKSONGS (12", initially in polystyrene sleeve) | 12 |

## CYMANDE
| 73 | Alaska ALA 4 | The Message/Zion I | 10 |
| 73 | Alaska ALA 10 | Bra/Ras Tafarian Folk Song | 10 |
| 74 | Contempo CS 2019 | Brothers On The Slide/Pon De Dungle | 30 |
| 73 | Alaska ALKA 100 | CYMANDE (LP) | 30 |
| 74 | Contempo CLP 508 | PROMISED HEIGHT (LP) | 25 |
| 93 | Sequel NEXLP 202 | CYMANDE (LP, reissue) | 15 |
| 99 | Sequel NEMLP 428 | CYMANDE (LP, reissue) | 18 |
| 99 | Sequel NEMLP 429 | SECOND TIME AROUND (LP, reissue) | 20 |
| 99 | Sequel NEMLP 430 | PROMISE HEIGHTS (LP, reissue) | 20 |

## JOHNNY CYMBAL
| 60 | MGM MGM 1106 | It'll Be Me/Always, Always | 25 |
| 63 | London HLR 9682 | Mr Bass Man/Sacred Lovers Vow | 7 |
| 63 | London HLR 9731 | Teenage Heaven/Cinderella Baby | 20 |
| 63 | London HLR 9762 | Dum Dum Dee Dum/Surfing At Tijuana | 20 |
| 64 | London HLR 9911 | Mitsou/Robinson Crusoe On Mars | 10 |
| 65 | United Artists UP 1093 | Go V.W. Go/Sorrow And Pain | 10 |
| 63 | London RER 1375 | MISTER BASS MAN (EP) | 40 |
| 64 | London RER 1406 | CYMBAL SMASHES (EP) | 20 |

*(see also Derek)*

## CYMBALINE
| 65 | Pye 7N 15916 | Please Little Girl/Coming Home Baby | 35 |
| 65 | Mercury MF 918 | Top Girl/Can You Hear Me? | 25 |
| 66 | Mercury MF 961 | I Don't Want It/Where Did Love Go Wrong | 8 |
| 66 | Mercury MF 975 | Peanuts And Chewy Macs/Found My Girl | 10 |
| 67 | Philips BF 1624 | Matrimonial Fears/You Will Never Love Me | 70 |
| 68 | Philips BF 1681 | Down By The Seaside/Fire | 25 |
| 69 | Philips BF 1749 | Turn Around/Come Back Baby | 5 |

## CYMERONS
| | | | |
|---|---|---|---|
| 64 | Decca F 11976 | I'll Be There/Making Love To Another | 15 |
| 66 | Polydor 56098 | Everyday (Will Change)/I Can See You | 7 |

## CYNIC
| | | | |
|---|---|---|---|
| 83 | Cynic CYN 1 | Suicide/No Time At All (no p/s) | 75 |

## CYNICS
| | | | |
|---|---|---|---|
| 85 | Sounds Cynical CYNIC 1 | Don't Give In (Fight to Win)/Breaking Out/One Way Out (foldout p/s) | 8 |

## CYNTHIA & ARCHIE
| | | | |
|---|---|---|---|
| 64 | R&B JB 168 | Every Beat/DELROY WILSON: Sammy Dead | 25 |

## CYPRESS HILL
| | | | |
|---|---|---|---|
| 93 | Columbia 474075 | BLACK SUNDAY (2-LP, gatefold, inners) | 25 |
| 95 | Columbia 478127-1 | CYPRESS HILL III (TEMPLES OF BOOM) (2-LP, gatefold) | 25 |

## CYRKLE
| | | | |
|---|---|---|---|
| 66 | CBS 202064 | Red Rubber Ball/How Can I Leave Her | 8 |
| 66 | CBS 202246 | Turn Down Day/Big Little Woman | 8 |
| 67 | CBS 202516 | Bony Maronie/Please Don't Ever Leave Me | 8 |
| 67 | CBS 202577 | I Wish You Could Be There/The Visit (She Was Here) | 8 |
| 67 | CBS 2790 | We Had A Good Thing Goin'/Two Rooms | 8 |
| 67 | CBS 2917 | Penny Arcade/Words | 8 |
| 67 | CBS 62977 | NEON (LP) | 40 |

## CZAR
| | | | |
|---|---|---|---|
| 70 | Philips 6006 071 | Oh Lord I'm Getting Heavy/Why Don't We Be A Rock'n'Roll Band | 40 |
| 70 | Fontana 6309 009 | CZAR (LP, black/silver label, laminated sleeve) | 1200 |
| 11 | Sunbeam SBR2LP5040 | CZAR (2-LP, reissue) | 20 |

*(see also Hungry Wolf)*

## HOLGER CZUKAY
| | | | |
|---|---|---|---|
| 79 | EMI EMC 3319 | MOVIES (LP) | 15 |
| 81 | EMI EMC 3384 | ON THE WAY TO THE PEAK OF NORMAL (LP) | 15 |

*(see under Jah Wobble, Can)*

# D

## KIM D
| | | | |
|---|---|---|---|
| 65 | Pye 7N 15953 | The Real Thing/Come On Baby | 30 |

*(see also Kim Davis)*

## ROB D
| | | | |
|---|---|---|---|
| 95 | Mo' Wax MW 037 | Clubbed To Death/(Mixes) (12", p/s) | 25 |

## SCHOOLLY D
| | | | |
|---|---|---|---|
| 86 | Flame MELT LP 1 | SCHOOLLEY D (LP) | 15 |

## TONY D & SHAKEOUTS
| | | | |
|---|---|---|---|
| 64 | Piccadilly 7N 35168 | Is It True/Never Let Her Go | 25 |

## DA BAND
| | | | |
|---|---|---|---|
| 78 | Rip Off RIP 2 | I Like It/Pirate's Lullaby (p/s) | 20 |

## DA BIZ
| | | | |
|---|---|---|---|
| 80 | Small Operations SO 002 | On The Beach/This Is No Audition (p/s) | 10 |
| 80 | Sire SIR 4045 | On The Beach/This Is No Audition (p/s, reissue) | 6 |

## DAB HAND
| | | | |
|---|---|---|---|
| 85 | Celtic Music CM 025 | HIGH ROCK AND LOWATER (LP) | 18 |

## MIKE D'ABO
| | | | |
|---|---|---|---|
| 69 | Immediate IM 075 | See The Little People — Gulliver's Travels/Anthology Of Gulliver's Travels Part 2 (withdrawn) | 30 |
| 70 | Uni UNS 525 | Let It Roar/California Line | 7 |
| 70 | Bell BLL 1134 | Miss Me In The Morning/Arabella, Cinderella | 6 |
| 72 | A&M AMS 7016 | Belinda/Little Miss Understood | 6 |
| 74 | A&M AMS 7121 | Fuel To Burn/Hold On Darlin' | 6 |
| 70 | Uni UNLS 114 | D'ABO (LP, gatefold sleeve) | 40 |
| 72 | A&M AMLH 68097 | DOWN AT RACHEL'S PLACE (LP, with lyric insert) | 15 |
| 74 | A&M AMLH 63634 | BROKEN RAINBOWS (LP) | 15 |

*(see also Manfred Mann, Band Of Angels, Gulliver's Travels, Smith & D'Abo)*

## TERESA D'ABREAU BAND
| | | | |
|---|---|---|---|
| 80 | Miss Chief MC 1 | Sister Revoluton/Carry It Through | 7 |

## KAREN D'ACHE
| | | | |
|---|---|---|---|
| 89 | SRT KDA 2 | Spin And Cry/Divide And Rule | 6 |

## RITA DACOSTA
| | | | |
|---|---|---|---|
| 75 | Contempo CS 2060 | Don't Bring Me Down/No! No! No! | 10 |

## DADA
| | | | |
|---|---|---|---|
| 71 | Atco 2400 030 | DADA (LP, mustard/blue label) | 50 |

*(see also Elkie Brooks, Paul Korda, Vinegar Joe)*

## DADDY COLONEL
| | | | |
|---|---|---|---|
| 85 | Bubblers UKMC7 | Take A Tip From Me/Lyric Banton (12") | 20 |

## DADDY DEWDROP
| | | | |
|---|---|---|---|
| 71 | Stateside SS2192 | Foxhunting On The Weekend/March Of The White Corpuscles | 8 |

MINT VALUE £

**DADDY FREDDY**
| | | | |
|---|---|---|---|
| 89 | Fashion FAD 7707 | Yes We A Blood/Version | 25 |

**DADDY JUNGLE**
| | | | |
|---|---|---|---|
| 80s | Daddy Jungle DJ001 | Flash It Operator/Jungle Dub | 20 |

**DADDY LONGLEGS**
| | | | |
|---|---|---|---|
| 70 | Warner Bros WB 8012 | High Again/To The Rescue (Wet Putso) | 5 |
| 70 | Warner Bros WS 3004 | DADDY LONGLEGS (LP) | 30 |
| 71 | Vertigo 6360 038 | OAKDOWN FARM (LP, gatefold sleeve, swirl label) | 250 |
| 72 | Polydor 2371 261 | THREE MUSICIANS (LP) | 15 |
| 73 | Polydor 2371 323 | SHIFTING SANDS (LP) | 25 |

*(see also Daylight)*

**DADDY MAXFIELD**
| | | | |
|---|---|---|---|
| 73 | Pye 7N 45266 | Rave 'N' Rock/Smilin' Again | 50 |

**DADDY TAR**
| | | | |
|---|---|---|---|
| 90 | Umbra | Zigawya/Full Up The Style (12" with Aytonbridge) | 15 |

**DADDY'S ACT**
| | | | |
|---|---|---|---|
| 67 | Columbia DB 8242 | Eight Days A Week/Gonna Get You | 18 |

**DAD'S ARMY PLATOON**
| | | | |
|---|---|---|---|
| 71 | Columbia DB 8766 | Dad's Army March/What Did You Do In The War? | 6 |
| 72 | Columbia DB 8952 | We Stood Alone/Down Our Way (AS DAD'S ARMY CHOIR) | 6 |

**DAEMION**
| | | | |
|---|---|---|---|
| 82 | SiJenn MSP1001 | Dizzy/Human Arcade (p/s) | 50 |

**D.A.F. (DEUTSCHE AMERIKANISCHE FREUNDSCHAFT)**
| | | | |
|---|---|---|---|
| 81 | Mute MUTE005 | Kebabtraume/Gewalt (p/s) | 6 |
| 80 | Mute MUTE 011 | Der Rauber Und Der Prinz/Tanz Mit Mir (p/s) | 6 |
| 81 | Virgin VS 418 | Der Mussolini/Der Räuber Und Der Prinz (co. sleeve) | 8 |
| 81 | Virgin VS 418-12 | Der Mussolini/Der Räuber Und Der Prinz (12", p/s, original issue) | 10 |
| 80 | Mute STUMM 1 | DIE KLEINEN UND DIE BOSEN (LP) | 15 |

**CALVIN DAFOS**
| | | | |
|---|---|---|---|
| 66 | Blue Beat BB 347 | Brown Sugar/I'm Gone | 22 |
| 69 | Doctor Bird DB 1174 | Lash Them/CDs: Medicine Master | 35 |

**DAFT PUNK**
| | | | |
|---|---|---|---|
| 94 | Soma 014 | Alive/The New Wave (12" EP, company sleeve) | 12 |
| 95 | Soma 025 | Da Funk/Rollin' And Scratchin' (12" EP, company sleeve) | 10 |
| 96 | Virgin V 2821 | HOMEWORK (2-LP) | 30 |
| 01 | Virgin V 2940 | DISCOVERY (2-LP) | 30 |
| 01 | Virgin V 2952 | ALIVE 1997 (LP) | 30 |
| 05 | Virgin V 2996 | HUMAN AFTER ALL (2-LP, gatefold) | 20 |
| 10 | Warner Bros. 5099909792012 | TRON LEGACY (2-LP, soundtrack) | 45 |

**DAGABAND**
| | | | |
|---|---|---|---|
| 80 | Rutland RX 100 | Test Flight/Images (p/s) | 5 |
| 83 | MHM A-M 094 | Second Time Around/Reds Under The Beds/I Can See For Miles (p/s) | 25 |

**DAGGERMEN**
| | | | |
|---|---|---|---|
| 86 | Empire UPW 258J | INTRODUCING THE DAGGERMEN (EP, die-cut company sleeve) | 10 |
| 86 | Own Up DAG 001 | DAGGERS IN MY MIND (LP) | 15 |

*(see also James Taylor Quartet)*

**DAGGERS (1)**
| | | | |
|---|---|---|---|
| 74 | Scotty SC 003 | Live Your Life Alone/Circles Of Dust | 50 |

**DAGGERS (2)**
| | | | |
|---|---|---|---|
| 07 | Fandango/Galagos 18 | Money/Magazine (die cut sleeve) | 12 |

*(see also Hurts)*

**DAILY FLASH**
| | | | |
|---|---|---|---|
| 84 | Psycho PSYCHO 32 | I FLASH DAILY (LP) | 20 |

**DAISY CLAN**
| | | | |
|---|---|---|---|
| 70 | Pye Intl. 7N 25532 | Love Needs Love/Glory Be | 30 |
| 71 | Decca F23169 | San Francisco China Town/Ridin' A Rainbow | 30 |

**DAISY HILL**
| | | | |
|---|---|---|---|
| 88 | Lakeland LKND 006 | POPPY FARM EP | 10 |

**DAISY PLANET**
| | | | |
|---|---|---|---|
| 60s | Oak (no cat. no.) | DAISY PLANET (EP, no p/s) | 70 |

**DAKOTA JIM**
| | | | |
|---|---|---|---|
| 66 | Blue Beat BB 358 | Only Soul Can Tell (actually by Slim Smith)/DAKOTA'S ALLSTARS: Call Me Master (actually by Prince Buster All Stars) | 150 |

*(see also Slim Smith)*

**DAKOTAS**
| | | | |
|---|---|---|---|
| 63 | Parlophone R 5044 | The Cruel Sea/The Millionaire | 10 |
| 63 | Parlophone R 5064 | Magic Carpet/Humdinger | 12 |
| 64 | Parlophone R 5203 | Oyeh/Hello Josephine | 30 |
| 67 | Page One POF 018 | I'm 'N 'Ardworkin' Barrow Boy/Seven Pounds Of Potatoes | 35 |
| 68 | Philips BF 1645 | I Can't Break The News To Myself/The Spider And The Fly | 100 |
| 63 | Parlophone GEP 8888 | MEET THE DAKOTAS (EP) | 40 |

*(see also Billy J. Kramer & Dakotas)*

**ALAN DALE**
| | | | |
|---|---|---|---|
| 55 | Vogue Coral Q 72072 | Cherry Pink And Apple Blossom White/I'm Sincere | 6 |
| 55 | Vogue Coral Q 72089 | Sweet And Gentle/You Still Mean The Same To Me | 6 |
| 55 | Vogue Coral Q 72105 | Rockin' The Cha-Cha/Wham! (There I Go In Love Again) | 12 |

| 57 | Vogue Coral Q 72225 | Don't Knock The Rock/Your Love Is My Love | 30 |
| 57 | Vogue Coral Q 72231 | The Girl Can't Help It/Lonesome Road | 30 |

*(see also Johnny Desmond)*

## DICK DALE & HIS DELTONES
| 63 | Capitol CL 15296 | Peppermint Man/Surf Beat | 20 |
| 63 | Capitol CL 15320 | The Scavenger/Wild Ideas | 20 |
| 88 | Pulch Wave PSC 666 | Pick And Play/The Wedge (p/s) | 5 |
| 63 | Capitol T 1886 | SURFERS' CHOICE (LP) | 30 |
| 63 | Capitol T/ST 1930 | KING OF THE SURF GUITAR (LP, mono/stereo) | 30 |

## GLEN DALE
| 66 | Decca F 12475 | Good Day Sunshine/Make Me Belong To You | 8 |
| 68 | Page One POF 059 | I've Got You On My Mind/Now I See You | 10 |
| 68 | Page One POF 105 | I've Got Something Too/Something's Gotten Hold Of My Heart | 5 |

*(see also Fortunes)*

## DALE & GRACE
| 63 | London HL 9807 | I'm Leaving It Up To You/That's What I Like About You | 15 |
| 64 | London HL 9857 | Stop And Think It Over/Bad Luck | 15 |
| 69 | London HL 10249 | I'm Leaving It Up To You/Love Is Strange | 10 |
| 64 | London RE 1428 | DALE AND GRACE NO. 1 (EP) | 30 |
| 64 | London RE 1429 | DALE AND GRACE NO. 2 (EP) | 30 |
| 64 | London RE 1430 | DALE AND GRACE NO. 3 (EP) | 35 |

## JACKIE DALE
| 78 | Freedom Sounds FSD 020 | Stop And Think Me Over/Bucket Bottom (12", with Prince Allah) | 15 |

## JIM DALE
| 57 | Parlophone R 4329 | Piccadilly Line/I Didn't Mean It | 6 |
| 57 | Parlophone R 4343 | Be My Girl/You Shouldn't Do That | 7 |
| 57 | Parlophone R 4356 | All Shook Up/Wandering Eyes (with Vipers & King Brothers) | 10 |
| 57 | Parlophone R 4376 | Just Born (To Be Your Baby)/Crazy Dream | 5 |
| 57 | Parlophone GEP 8656 | JIM DALE (EP) | 20 |
| 58 | Parlophone PMD 1055 | JIM (10" LP) | 40 |

## PAUL DALE BAND
| 82 | KA KA 6/PAUL 1 | Alright On The Night/Hold On (p/s, clear vinyl) | 12 |
| 82 | KA KA 6/PAUL 1 | Alright On The Night/Hold On (p/s) | 6 |

## SYD DALE ORCHESTRA
| 65 | Decca F 22300 | C'mon In/Disc A Go Go | 10 |
| 01 | Trunk JBH 01 | Theme To Screen Test (Marching There & back) (1-sided 7", 500 only) | 30 |

## DALEK I LOVE YOU
| 79 | Vertigo DALEK 1 | Freedom Fighters/Two Chameleons (p/s, as Dalek I) | 6 |
| 83 | Korova KOW 31 | Horrorscope/These Walls We Build | 7 |

## DALEKS
| 80 | Exterminated Products EXPS 1 | Rejected/Man Of The World/This Life (fold-out, p/s) | 15 |

## DALES
| 75 | Deroy 953 | LUCKY THIRTEEN (LP) | 30 |

## DALE SISTERS
| 60 | HMV POP 781 | The Kiss/Billy Boy, Billy Boy | 5 |
| 61 | Ember EMB S 140 | My Sunday Baby/All My Life | 10 |
| 62 | Ember EMB S 151 | Secrets/Road To Love | 10 |

## DÄLEX
| 81 | Dodgy DODGY 1 | Juvenile/Action Man/Touched (p/s) | 30 |

## BASIL DALEY
| 68 | Studio One SO 2054 | Hold Me Baby/HEPTONES: I Got A Feeling | 60 |

## JIMMY DALEY & DING-A-LINGS
| 57 | Brunswick 05648 | Rock, Pretty Baby/Can I Steal A Little Love | 100 |

## GRAHAM DALLEY
| 66 | Hollick & Taylor HT/LP 1068 | GRAHAM DALLEY AT THE BARN (LP) | 15 |

## SALVADOR DALI
| 62 | Decca SET 230 | DALI IN VENICE (LP, gatefold sleeve with booklet. Dali does not sing or talk - he just did the cover) | 30 |

## DALIDA
| 60 | HMV POP 793 | Never On A Sunday/MILKO PAPAYAKI: Parle Doucement | 7 |
| 57 | Felsted ESD 3043 | DALIDA IS HER NAME (EP) | 20 |
| 59 | Felsted ESD 3077 | PARDON MY ENGLISH (EP) | 25 |
| 57 | Felsted SDL 86053 | THE GLAMOUROUS DALIDA (10" LP) | 50 |
| 66 | Fontana TL 5348 | DALIDA (LP) | 18 |

## DALLAS BOYS
| 67 | Major Minor MM 534 | He Won't Love You (Like I Do)/What Do You Know About Losin' | 5 |

*(see also Five Dallas Boys)*

## DALLIONS
| 62 | Oriole CB 1794 | Teardrops In The Rain/Loop De Loop | 6 |

## MIKI DALLON
| 65 | RCA RCA 1438 | Do You Call That Love?/Apple Pie | 20 |
| 65 | RCA RCA 1478 | I Care About You/I'll Give You Love | 40 |
| 66 | Strike JH 306 | Cheat And Lie/(I'm Gonna Find A) Cave | 40 |
| 66 | Strike JH 318 | What Will Your Mama Say Now?/Two At A Time | 8 |

*(see also Neil Christian & Crusaders)*

MINT VALUE £

## DAVID & MARIANNE DALMOUR
| | | | |
|---|---|---|---|
| 65 | Columbia 33SX 1715 | INTRODUCING (LP) | 20 |
| 66 | Columbia SCX 6005 | STRANGE ENCHANTMENT (LP) | 25 |

## KAREN DALTON
| | | | |
|---|---|---|---|
| 71 | Paramount SPFL 271 | IN MY OWN TIME (LP) | 60 |

## DALTONS
| | | | |
|---|---|---|---|
| 67 | Fab FAB 30 | Never Kiss You Again/RIGHTEOUS FLAMES: When A Girl Loves A Boy | 60 |

*(see also Prince Buster)*

## ROGER DALTREY
| | | | |
|---|---|---|---|
| 73 | Track 2094 014 | Thinking/There Is Love | 6 |
| 75 | A&M AMS 7206 | Orpheus Song/Love's Dream | 6 |
| 75 | Lyntone LYN 3176/7 | Wagner's Dream/Love's Theme/RICK WAKEMAN: Count Your Blessings (flexidisc with 19 magazine) | 10 |
| 77 | Polydor 2058 896 | One Of The Boys/You Better Put Something Inside Me (p/s) | 6 |
| 77 | Polydor 2058 948 | Say It Ain't So Joe/Satin And Lace (withdrawn, existence unconfirmed) | 20 |
| 77 | Polydor 2121 319 | Written On The Wind/Dear John | 8 |
| 78 | Polydor 2058 986 | Say It Ain't So Joe/The Prisoner | 8 |
| 73 | Track 2406 107 | DALTREY (LP, gatefold sleeve) | 15 |

*(see also Who, High Numbers, McEnroe & Cash)*

## TONI DALY
| | | | |
|---|---|---|---|
| 66 | Columbia DB 8043 | Like The Big Man Said/You Can't Get No Water | 7 |

*(see also Antoinette)*

## DALYS
| | | | |
|---|---|---|---|
| 65 | Fontana TF 546 | Me Japanese Boy/Never Kind Of Love | 5 |
| 65 | Fontana TF 637 | She's My Girl/When Love Has Gone | 5 |
| 66 | Strike JH 317 | Don't Go Breaking My Heart/Little Stranger | 6 |
| 67 | Fontana TF 809 | Sweet Maria/Leaving Time | 5 |
| 67 | Fontana TF 841 | A Fistful Of Dollars/Man With No Name | 6 |
| 68 | Fontana TF 907 | Let Me Go Lover/A Place In The Sun | 5 |
| 69 | Fontana TF 988 | Early Morning Rain/Chanson D'Amour | 5 |

## DAMARIS
| | | | |
|---|---|---|---|
| 83 | CBS 4172 | What About My Love/Hooray For Love | 12 |
| 83 | CBS 4172 | What About My Love/Hooray For Love (12") | 30 |

## DAMASCUS
| | | | |
|---|---|---|---|
| 80s | Private pressing | OPEN YOUR EYES (12" EP, with insert) | 100 |
| 80s | Private pressing | OPEN YOUR EYES (12" EP, later with different back sleeve, with insert) | 75 |

*(see also Thin End Of The Wedge)*

## DAMBALA
| | | | |
|---|---|---|---|
| 78 | Isis ISIS 001 | Rebel/MILITANT BARRY : Version | 20 |
| 78 | Music Hive MH001 | Zimbabwe/GUS ANYIA : Visions Of War | 40 |
| 79 | Radic RIC 107 | Babylon/No Go (As Dambala featuring Gus Anyia) | 40 |
| 81 | Blank IS 1002 | Rally Round/Version (12" p/s) | 40 |
| 83 | Dada Music DLP 1 | AZANIA (LP) | 40 |

## DAMITA JO
| | | | |
|---|---|---|---|
| 54 | HMV 7MC 2 | I'd Do It Again/Do I, Do I, Do I (B-side with Steve Gibson)(export issue) | 20 |
| 60 | Mercury AMT 1085 | Widow Walk/Dearest Darling | 5 |
| 60 | Mercury AMT 1116 | I'll Save The Last Dance For You/Forgive | 5 |
| 60 | Mercury AMT 1133 | Keep Your Hands Off Him/Hush, Somebody's Calling My Name | 5 |
| 61 | Mercury AMT 1141 | Do What You Want/Sweet Georgia Brown | 5 |
| 61 | Mercury AMT 1155 | I'll Be There/Love Laid Its Hands On Me | 5 |
| 61 | Mercury ZEP 10118 | I'LL SAVE THE LAST DANCE FOR YOU (EP) | 10 |

## DAMNED (1)
| | | | |
|---|---|---|---|
| 74 | Youngblood YB 1067 | Morning Bird/Theta | 40 |

*(see also Motordamn)*

## DAMNED (2)
### SINGLES
| | | | |
|---|---|---|---|
| 76 | Stiff BUY 6 | New Rose/Help! (first pressing with push-out centre, 'Street music co' credit on label, 'is this a record' & 'a bilbo boppa' on A side run out, 'Damned Beatles & 'Bilbo master room' on B. 'Delga' credit on p/s) | 30 |
| 76 | Stiff BUY 6 | New Rose/Help! (p/s, 2nd pressing, with Rock Music Co Ltd/Street Music Co credit on A side, push-out centre) | 12 |
| 76 | Stiff BUY 6 | New Rose/Help! (3rd pressing, solid centre) | 7 |
| 77 | Stiff BUY 10 | Neat Neat Neat/Stab Yor Back/Singalongascabies (glossy p/s, no 'Island' logo on sleeve, first pressing solid centre) | 25 |
| 77 | Stiff BUY 10 | Neat Neat Neat/Stab Yor Back/Singalongascabies (glossy p/s, no 'Island' logo on sleeve, second pressing push-out centre) | 25 |
| 77 | Stiff BUY 10 | Neat Neat Neat/Stab Yor Back/Singalongascabies (glossy p/s, 'Island' logo on rear, later pressing, push-out/solid centre) | 10 |
| 77 | Stiff DAMMED 1 | Stretcher Case Baby/Sick Of Being Sick (p/s, NME competition & gig freebie) | 125 |
| 77 | Stiff BUY 18 | Problem Child/You Take My Money (p/s, originally with press-out centre) | 10 |
| 77 | Stiff BUY 18 | Problem Child/You Take My Money (p/s) | 5 |
| 77 | Stiff BUY 24 | Don't Cry Wolf/One Way Love (promo grey label with small "A") | 30 |
| 77 | Stiff BUY 24 | Don't Cry Wolf/One Way Love (20,000 on pink vinyl, no p/s) | 12 |
| 77 | Stiff BUY 24 | Don't Cry Wolf/One Way Love (push-out centre, black vinyl) | 15 |
| 78 | Dodgy Demo Co. SGS 105 | Love Song/Burglar (mail order issue/gig freebie, plain sleeve, stickered labels) | 60 |
| 79 | Chiswick CHIS 112 | Love Song/Noise Noise Noise/Suicide (red vinyl, 4 different sleeves) | 8 |
| 79 | Chiswick CHIS 112 | Love Song/Noise Noise Noise/Suicide (4 different sleeves) | 5 |
| 79 | Chiswick CHIS 116 | Smash It Up/Burglar (p/s) | 5 |
| 79 | Chiswick CHIS 120 ADJ-1 | I Just Can't Be Happy Today/Ballroom Blitz ('A' Label DJ promo copy) | 200 |

| 79 | Chiswick CHIS 120 | I Just Can't Be Happy Today/Ballroom Blitz/The Turkey Song (p/s) | 5 |
|---|---|---|---|
| 80 | Chiswick CHIS 130 | White Rabbit/Rabid (Over You)/Seagulls (unissued in U.K., Europe-only, 2 x 1-sided white-label test pressings exist, hand-written labels) | 400 |
| 80 | Chiswick CHIS 135 | The History Of The World Part 1/I Believe The Impossible/Sugar And Spite (p/s) | 5 |
| 80 | Chiswick CHIS 139 DJ | There Ain't No Sanity Clause/Hit Or Miss (double A side demo) | 30 |
| 80 | Chiswick CHIS 139 | There Ain't No Sanity Clause/Hit Or Miss/Looking At You (live) (p/s) | 5 |
| 81 | Stiff GRAB 2 | Four Pack (4 x 7" [BUY 6, 10, 18 & 24], in a plastic wallet) | 50 |
| 82 | Big Beat NS 75 | Love Song/Noise Noise Noise/Suicide (3 different sleeves, blue vinyl) | 6 |
| 82 | Big Beat NS 76 | Smash It Up/Burglar (p/s, red vinyl) | 6 |
| 82 | Big Beat NS 77 | Wait For The Blackout/CAPTAIN SENSIBLE & SOFTIES: Jet Boy, Jet Girl (p/s, red/black 'Damned' labels) | 5 |
| 82 | Big Beat NS 80 | Lively Arts/Teenage Dream (p/s, green vinyl) | 10 |
| 82 | Bronze BRO 149 | Lovely Money/Lovely Money (Disco Mix)/I Think I'm Wonderful (p/s) | 6 |
| 82 | Bronze BRO 156 | Dozen Girls/Take That/Mine's A Large One, Landlord/Torture Me (p/s) | 5 |
| 82 | Bronze BRO 159 | Generals/Disguise/Citadel Zombies (p/s) | 8 |
| 83 | Big Beat NS 85 | White Rabbit/Rabid (Over You)/Seagulls (p/s) | 5 |
| 84 | Plus One DAMNED 1 | Thanks For The Night/Nasty (p/s, 1,000 each on red, white & blue vinyl) | 10 |
| 84 | Plus One DAMNED 1T | Thanks For The Night/Nasty/Do The Blitz (12", no'd p/s, multicoloured vinyl) | 15 |
| 84 | Plus One DAMNED 1T | Thanks For The Night/Nasty ('woman'-shaped pic disc w/ plinth, 1,000 only) | 25 |
| 85 | MCA GRIM 1 | Grimly Fiendish/Edward The Bear (autographed gatefold p/s, 1,000 only) | 8 |
| 85 | MCA GRIMT 1 | Grimly Fiendish (Spic'n'Span Mix)/Edward The Bear (12", autographed p/s) | 10 |
| 85 | MCA GRIM 2/GRIMY 2 | Edition Premier: The Shadow Of Love/Nightshift/Let There Be Rats/ Wiped Out (double pack) | 5 |
| 85 | MCA GRIM 3 | Is It A Dream (Wild West End Mix)/Street Of Dreams (live) (p/s, with 5 badges) | 5 |
| 85 | Stiff BUY DJ 238 | New Rose/Help!/I'm So Bored (promo reissue) | 20 |
| 86 | Stiff BUY DJ 238 | New Rose/Neat Neat Neat (promo) | 12 |
| 86 | Stiff BUY 6/BUY DJ 6A | New Rose/Help!/I'm So Bored (1-sided) (double pack, stickered PVC sleeve with insert, 1st disc on white vinyl, 2nd disc actually plays "I Fall" (live)) | 20 |
| 86 | Stiff BUY 6 | New Rose/Help! (reissue, red vinyl, PVC sleeve, with card insert) | 8 |
| 86 | Strange Fruit SFPS002 | PEEL SESSIONS (12") | 10 |
| 87 | Strange Fruit SFPS 040 | PEEL SESSIONS 2 (12") | 10 |
| 90s | Sugar & Spite SS 01 | History Of The World Part 1 (Psychedelic Mix) (1-sided flexi credited to 'The Dimmed' wraparound p/s free with Sugar & Spite fanzine) | 12 |
| 02 | Stiff FBUPC 004 | New Rose/Help! (reissue with free CD single) | 15 |
| 05 | Lively Arts LADAM 1 | Little Miss Disaster/Anti-Pope (live) (p/s, red splatter vinyl) | 20 |

## ALBUMS

| 77 | Stiff SEEZ 1 | DAMNED DAMNED DAMNED (LP) | 75 |
|---|---|---|---|
| 77 | Stiff SEEZ 1 | DAMNED DAMNED DAMNED (LP, 2,000 with Eddie & Hot Rods photograph on rear sleeve; shrinkwrapped with title sticker) | 350 |
| 77 | Stiff SEEZ 1 | DAMNED DAMNED DAMNED (LP, 2,000 with Eddie & Hot Rods photograph on rear sleeve; not shrinkwrapped with title sticker) | 150 |
| 77 | Stiff SEEZ 2 | MUSIC FOR PLEASURE (LP) | 25 |
| 79 | Chiswick CWK 3011 | MACHINE GUN ETIQUETTE (LP, with inner sleeve) | 35 |
| 80 | Chiswick CWK 3015 | THE BLACK ALBUM (2-LP) | 20 |
| 81 | Ace DAM 1 | THE BEST OF THE DAMNED (LP, red or blue vinyl) | 15 |
| 82 | Bronze BRON 542 | STRAWBERRIES (LP, with scratch and sniff insert) | 15 |
| 82 | Ace DAM 3 | THE BLACK ALBUM (LP, single reissue, 12,000 with lyrics & poster) | 15 |
| 82 | Ace DAM 2 | MACHINE GUN ETIQUETTE (LP, reissue, blue or white/clear vinyl with inner) | 15 |
| 83 | Stiff MAIL 2 | DAMNED DAMNED DAMNED/MUSIC FOR PLEASURE (2-LP, reissue, gatefold sleeve, mail-order, 5000 only) | 25 |
| 83 | Damned DAMU 2 | LIVE IN NEWCASTLE (LP, 5,000 by mail-order only) | 15 |
| 83 | Damned PDAMU 2 | LIVE IN NEWCASTLE (LP, picture disc, 5,000 only) | 15 |
| 85 | MCA MCFW 3275 | PHANTASMAGORIA (LP, white vinyl, with inner) | 15 |
| 86 | Stiff MAIL 2 | DAMNED, DAMNED, DAMNED/MUSIC FOR PLEASURE (2-LP, reissue, yellow vinyl, 4000 by mail-order only) | 25 |
| 86 | Dojo DOJOPD 46 | STRAWBERRIES (LP, reissue picture disc) | 15 |
| 86 | Stiff GET 4 | THE CAPTAIN'S BIRTHDAY PARTY — LIVE AT THE ROUNDHOUSE (mini-LP, 45rpm, blue vinyl, stickered plain white sleeve) | 15 |
| 87 | Demon FIEND 91 | DAMNED DAMNED DAMNED (LP, reissue) | 15 |
| 87 | Demon PFIEND 91 | DAMNED DAMNED DAMNED (LP, reissue picture disc) | 15 |
| 87 | Demon FIEND 108 | MUSIC FOR PLEASURE (LP, reissue, orange vinyl) | 15 |
| 89 | Essential ESCLP 008 | FINAL DAMNATION (LP, green vinyl, with poster) | 15 |
| 92 | Reciever RRLP 159 | LIVE AT THE LYCEUM (LP, clear vinyl) | 15 |

*(see also Bartok, Captain Sensible, Rat Scabies, Rat & Whale, Edge, Magic Michael, Maxim's Thrash, Naz Nomad & Nightmares, Auntiepus, Phantom Chords, Tank, Eddie & Hot Rods, U.F.O., Tanz Der Youth)*

## KENNY DAMON

| 65 | Mercury MF 907 | While I Live/Fountain In Capri | 8 |
|---|---|---|---|
| 66 | Mercury MF 936 | World Of No Return/You Are Everything That's Beautiful | 5 |
| 67 | Mercury MF 959 | Only Your Love/Sold To The Man With The Broken Heart | 5 |
| 68 | Mercury MF 1014 | Turn Her Away/Till Then My Love | 5 |

*(see also Kenny Roberts)*

## RUSS DAMON

| 64 | Stateside SS 258 | Hip Huggers/Heaven Sent | 12 |
|---|---|---|---|

## STUART DAMON

| 70 | Reflection REF L7 | STUART 'CHAMPION' DAMON (LP) | 20 |
|---|---|---|---|

## DAMON & NAOMI

| 97 | Earworm WORM 3 | The Navigator/Awake In A Muddle (p/s) | 8 |
|---|---|---|---|

*(see also Galaxie 500)*

## VIC DAMONE

| 57 | Mercury MPT 7514 | ALL-TIME SONG HITS (10" LP) | 12 |
|---|---|---|---|

*(see also Easy Riders)*

## DAN
| | | | |
|---|---|---|---|
| 89 | Meantime COX 013c | KICKING ASS AT TJ'S (LP, with flexi) | 15 |

## RUPIE DAN
| | | | |
|---|---|---|---|
| 82 | Flag FLG 101 | My Black Race/Black Race Dub (12") | 40 |

## JONAH DAN
| | | | |
|---|---|---|---|
| 96 | Inner Sanctuary ACT10-004 | Meditation Rock/Dub 1/Dub 2 (10") | 20 |
| 89 | Conscious Sounds JKPD 001 | MEETS THE BUSH CHEMISTS AT CONSCIOUS SOUNDS (LP) | 25 |

## DANCE CHAPTER
| | | | |
|---|---|---|---|
| 80 | 4AD AD 18 | Anonymity/New Dance (p/s, with card insert) | 10 |
| 80 | 4AD AD 18 | Anonymity/New Dance (p/s) | 6 |
| 81 | 4AD BAD 115 | CHAPTER II (12" EP, most with mismatched A&B-side labels) | 10 |

## DANCE SQUAD
| | | | |
|---|---|---|---|
| 93 | Mendoza MEN 0026 | Everybody (Vocal Mix)/Everybody (Instrumental)/Bad Boy (Hard Mix) (12", as Dance Squad featuring Camilla) | 25 |
| 94 | Wicked Sounds WS 02 | Yu-a Raggamuffin/Ganjaman (12") | 25 |

## DANCELAND ROCK GROUP
| | | | |
|---|---|---|---|
| 62 | Danceland Y 2032 | Anytime/Because They're Young | 10 |
| 63 | Danceland Y 2043 | William Tell/Last Night Was Made For Love | 10 |

## DANCER
| | | | |
|---|---|---|---|
| 75 | Dawn DNS 1118 | Hate Generator/Love Seeds | 12 |

## DANCETTE
| | | | |
|---|---|---|---|
| 83 | Bel BEL 45 | Going Green/He's Clever | 30 |

## GRAHAM PHILIP D'ANCEY
| | | | |
|---|---|---|---|
| 81 | Blue September BSEP 005 | Sacred Heart/Lament Of The Winged Warrior (p/s) | 40 |
| 83 | Shibui SHS 001 | Freedom/False Prophet (p/s) | 30 |
| 83 | Shibui SHS 001 | ALLUMA (LP) | 30 |

## DANCING DID
| | | | |
|---|---|---|---|
| 79 | Fruit & Veg F&V 1 | Dancing Did/Lorry Pirates (p/s) | 18 |
| 80 | Fruit & Veg F&V 2 | The Haunted Tearooms/Squashed Things On The Road (p/s) | 10 |
| 82 | Stiff BUY 136 | The Lost Platoon/The Human Chicken (withdrawn 'cavalry' p/s) | 15 |
| 82 | Stiff BUY 136 | The Lost Platoon/The Human Chicken (sunset p/s) | 5 |
| 82 | Kamera Records KAM 009 | AND DID THOSE FEET (LP, with insert) | 25 |

## DANDO SHAFT
| | | | |
|---|---|---|---|
| 70 | Youngblood YB 1012 | Cold Wind/Cat Song | 15 |
| 72 | RCA RCA 2246 | Sun Clog Dance/This Gift | 10 |
| 70 | Youngblood SSYB 6 | AN EVENING WITH DANDO SHAFT (LP, white/red label) | 120 |
| 71 | RCA Neon NE 5 | DANDO SHAFT (LP, gatefold sleeve, black inner sleeve) | 175 |
| 72 | RCA Victor SF 8256 | LANTALOON (LP, with poster, orange label) | 175 |
| 72 | RCA Victor SF 8256 | LANTALOON (LP, without poster, orange label) | 80 |
| 77 | Rubber RUB 034 | KINGDOM (LP) | 60 |

*(see also Hedgehog Pie)*

## DANDY (& SUPERBOYS)
| | | | |
|---|---|---|---|
| 64 | Dice CC 21 | Rudie Don't Go/It's Just Got To Be | 15 |
| 65 | Dice CC 24 | You Got To Pray/I Got To Have You (as Dandy & Barbara) | 15 |
| 65 | Blue Beat BB 308 | To Love You/I'm Looking For Love | 15 |
| 65 | Blue Beat BB 319 | Hey Boy Hey Girl/So Long Baby (as Dandy & Del) | 15 |
| 65 | Blue Beat BB 327 | My Baby/I'm Gonna Stop Loving You | 15 |
| 65 | Blue Beat BB 336 | I Found Love/You've Got Something Nice | 15 |
| 66 | Dice CC 29 | The Operation/A Little More Ska | 15 |
| 66 | Ska Beat JB 247 | The Fight/Do You Know | 15 |
| 67 | Ska Beat JB 269 | One Scotch One Bourbon One Beer/Maximum Pressure | 20 |
| 67 | Ska Beat JB 273 | Rudie A Message To You/Til Death Do Us Part | 18 |
| 67 | Ska Beat JB 279 | You're No Hustler/No No | 15 |
| 67 | Giant GN 3 | My Time Now/East Of Suez (with Superboys) | 35 |
| 67 | Giant GN 5 | Puppet On A String/Have Your Fun (with Superboys) | 15 |
| 67 | Giant GN 7 | We Are Still Rude/Let's Do Rocksteady (with Superboys) | 15 |
| 67 | Giant GN 10 | Somewhere My Love/My Kind Of Love (with Superboys) | 15 |
| 67 | Giant GN 15 | There Is A Mountain/This Music Got Soul (with Superboys) | 15 |
| 68 | Giant GN 20 | Charlie Brown/Groovin' At The Cue | 15 |
| 68 | Giant GN 23 | Propagandist/Giant March | 20 |
| 68 | Giant GN 27 | Sweet Ride/Up The Hill (with Superboys) | 10 |
| 68 | Giant GN 30 | Tears On My Pillow/Mad Them (with Superboys) | 10 |
| 68 | Giant GN 36 | I'm Back With A Bang Bang/Jungle Walk (with Superboys) | 80 |
| 68 | Trojan TR 618 | The Toast/Kicks Out | 12 |
| 69 | Columbia Blue Beat DB 112 | Play It Cool/Rude With Me | 8 |
| 68 | Downtown DT 401 | Move Your Mule/Reggae Me This | 20 |
| 69 | Downtown DT 402 | Come Back Girl/Shake Me Wake Me | 20 |
| 69 | Downtown DT 404 | Tell Me Darling/Cool Hand Luke | 30 |
| 69 | Downtown DT 405 | Copy Your Rhythm/BROTHER DAN ALL STARS: Lovely Lady | 20 |
| 69 | Downtown DT 406 | Doctor Sure Shot/Put On Your Dancing Shoes | 20 |
| 69 | Downtown DT 410 | Reggae In Your Jeggae/DREAMERS: Reggae Shuffle | 20 |
| 69 | Downtown DT 411 | You Don't Care/Tryer (both sides with Audrey) | 20 |
| 69 | Downtown DT 415 | Rocksteady Gone/Walking Down | 20 |
| 69 | Downtown DT 416 | I'm Your Puppet/Water Boy | 25 |
| 69 | Downtown DT 421 | Games People Play/AUDREY: One Fine Day | 7 |
| 69 | Downtown DT 429 | People Get Ready/RUDIES: Near East | 50 |
| 69 | Downtown DT 434 | Be Natural, Be Proud/Who Do You Want To Run To | 15 |
| 69 | Downtown DT 437 | Come On Home/Love Is All You Need | 20 |

| | | | |
|---|---|---|---|
| 69 | Downtown DT 442 | Everybody Loves A Winner/Try Me One More Time | 20 |
| 69 | Downtown DT 445 | Let's Come Together (with Israelites)/JAKE WADE: Music Fever | 20 |
| 69 | Downtown DT 453 | Won't You Come Home/Baby Make It Soon | 20 |
| 70 | Downtown DT 456 | Raining In My Heart/First Note | 15 |
| 70 | Downtown DT 458 | Build Your Love (On Solid Foundation)/Let's Talk It Over (p/s) | 15 |
| 70 | Downtown DT 458 | Build Your Love (On Solid Foundation)/Let's Talk It Over | 8 |
| 70 | Downtown DT 462 | Morning Side Of The Mountain (as Dandy & Audrey)/AUDREY: Show Me Baby | 15 |
| 70 | Downtown DT 468 | How Glad I Am/I'm So Glad (as Dandy & Audrey) | 12 |
| 70 | Trojan TR 7800 | Take A Letter Maria/You're Coming Back | 6 |
| 71 | Downtown DT 483 | Could It Be True/Your Eyes Are Dreaming (as Dandy & Jackie) | 15 |
| 71 | Downtown DT 484 | Daddy's Home/Everyman | 10 |
| 71 | Trojan TR 7816 | Same Old Fashioned Way/Out Of Many, One People | 6 |
| 72 | Trojan TR 7857 | What Do You Want To Make Those Eyes At Me For/Talking About Sally | 6 |
| 67 | Giant GNL 1000 | ROCKSTEADY WITH DANDY (LP) | 100 |
| 68 | Trojan TRL 2 | DANDY RETURNS (LP) | 75 |
| 69 | Trojan TRL 17 | I NEED YOU (LP, with Audrey) | 40 |
| 70 | Trojan TTL 26 | YOUR MUSICAL DOCTOR (LP) | 40 |
| 70 | Trojan TBL 118 | MORNING SIDE OF THE MOUNTAIN (LP, with Audrey) | 40 |

*(see also Bobby Thompson, Sugar & Dandy, Rub A Dubs, Don Martin,, Little Sal with Dandy & Superboys)*

## DANDY & AUDREY
| | | | |
|---|---|---|---|
| 69 | Downtown DT 411 | You Don't Care/Tryer (both sides with Audrey) | 20 |
| 70 | Downtown DT 462 | Morning Side Of The Mountain (as Dandy & Audrey)/AUDREY: Show Me Baby | 15 |
| 69 | Downtown TRLS 17 | I NEED YOU (LP) | 40 |
| 70 | Downtown TBL 118 | MORNING SIDE OF THE MOUNTAIN (LP) | 40 |

## CHRIS DANE
| | | | |
|---|---|---|---|
| 55 | London HLA 8165 | Cynthia's In Love/My Ideal | 30 |

## JERRY DANE
| | | | |
|---|---|---|---|
| 60 | Decca F 11234 | You're My Only Girl/Nothing But The Truth | 5 |
| 60 | Decca F 11284 | Let's/Awhile In Love | 5 |
| 63 | Windsor WPS 127 | Everybody Go Wild/Watcha Want (p/s) | 10 |
| 63 | Windsor WPS 127 | Everybody Go Wild/Watcha Want | 5 |

## D'ANGELO
| | | | |
|---|---|---|---|
| 95 | Cooltempo CTLP46 | BROWN SUGAR (LP) | 30 |
| 00 | EMI 523373 1 | VOODOO (2-LP) | 30 |

## CAL DANGER
| | | | |
|---|---|---|---|
| 62 | Fontana 267 225 TF | Restless/Teenage Girlie Blues | 100 |

*(see also Tony Dangerfield)*

## DANGERDOOM
| | | | |
|---|---|---|---|
| 05 | Lez LEX 036LP | MOUSE AND THE MASK (2-LP, printed plastic sleeve, inner & insert) | 50 |

## A.P. DANGERFIELD
| | | | |
|---|---|---|---|
| 68 | Fontana TF 935 | Conversations (In A Station Light Refreshment Bar)/Further Conversations | 30 |

## KEITH DANGERFIELD
| | | | |
|---|---|---|---|
| 68 | Plexium P 1237 | No Life Child/She's A Witch | 200 |

## TONY DANGERFIELD & THRILLS
| | | | |
|---|---|---|---|
| 64 | Pye 7N 15695 | I've Seen Such Things/She's Too Way Out | 70 |

*(see also Savages, Circles, Cal Danger)*

## DANGEROUS BROTHERS
| | | | |
|---|---|---|---|
| 80 | Sheep Worrying TMS 002 | False Nose/County Councillor (p/s) | 15 |

## DANGEROUS GIRLS
| | | | |
|---|---|---|---|
| 78 | Happy Face MM 115 | Dangerous Girls/I Don't Want To Eat (With The Family) (p/s) | 10 |
| 80 | Human HUM 1 | Man In The Glass/MO75 (p/s) | 6 |
| 81 | Human HUM 6 | Step Out/Sidekick Phenomenon/Men In Suits (p/s) | 6 |

## PINO D'ANGIO
| | | | |
|---|---|---|---|
| 82 | System 12 STEM 2 | Ma Quale Idea/Lezione D'Amore (12") | 20 |

## DANI
| | | | |
|---|---|---|---|
| 74 | Pye International 7N 25667 | La Vie A 25 Ans/Pour Que Ça Dure (p/s) | 6 |
| 74 | Pye International 7N 25667 | That Old Familiar Feeling/Pour Que Ça Dure | 12 |

## ERROLL DANIEL
| | | | |
|---|---|---|---|
| 69 | Paradox PAR 45902 | No Excuses/Go Back | 20 |

## DANIEL IN THE LION'S DEN
| | | | |
|---|---|---|---|
| 70 | Trojan TR 7797 | Dancing In The Sun/LION'S DEN: Chick A Bow | 6 |

## DANIELLE
| | | | |
|---|---|---|---|
| 66 | Philips BF 1532 | I'm Gonna Marry The Boy/Magic Carpet Of Love | 8 |
| 67 | Philips BF 1574 | Oh Mama/Come A Little Closer | 7 |

## JULIUS DANIELS
| | | | |
|---|---|---|---|
| 65 | RCA RCX 7175 | R.C.A. VICTOR RACE SERIES VOL. 4 (EP) | 15 |

## MAXINE DANIELS
| | | | |
|---|---|---|---|
| 57 | Oriole CB 1366 | Coffee-Bar Calypso/Cha-Cha Calypso | 8 |
| 58 | Oriole CB 1402 | I Never Realised/Moonlight Serenade | 5 |
| 58 | Oriole CB 1440 | You Brought A New Kind Of Love To Me/Somebody Else Is Taking My Place | 5 |
| 58 | Oriole CB 1449 | When It's Springtime In The Rockies/My Summer Heart | 5 |
| 58 | Oriole CB 1462 | Passionate Summer/Lola's Heart | 5 |

## MIKE DANIELS & HIS BAND
| | | | |
|---|---|---|---|
| 57 | Parlophone R 4285 | Hiyawatha/Don't You Think I Love You | 8 |
| 57 | Columbia 33SX 1256 | MIKE ON MIKE (LP) | 40 |

## ROLY "YO YO" DANIELS
| | | | |
|---|---|---|---|
| 60s | Stardisc SD 101 | Yo Yo Boy/The Teacher (p/s, features Don Rendell) | 50 |

MINT VALUE £

| 61 | Parlophone R 4759 | Late Last Evening/Bella Bella Marie | 5 |
| 62 | Decca F 11501 | Yo Yo Boy/The Teacher (reissue) | 10 |

## SAM DANIELS
| 63 | Sway SW 003 | Tell Me Baby/ERNIE FAULKENER: Beautiful Girl (both with Planets) | 8 |

## JOHNNY DANKWORTH ORCHESTRA
| 53 | Parlophone MSP 6026 | Honeysuckle Rose (with Cleo Laine)/Swingin' | 10 |
| 53 | Parlophone MSP 6032 | Moon Flowers/Two Ticks | 10 |
| 53 | Parlophone MSP 6037 | I Get A Kick Out Of You (with Frank Holder)/Easy Living (with Cleo Laine) | 10 |
| 54 | Parlophone MSP 6067 | S' Wonderful/Younger Every Day | 10 |
| 54 | Parlophone MSP 6077 | The Slider/It's The Talk Of The Town | 10 |
| 54 | Parlophone MSP 6083 | The Jerky Thing/My Buddy | 10 |
| 54 | Parlophone MSP 6092 | Runnin' Wild/Oo-Be-Doop | 10 |
| 54 | Parlophone MSP 6113 | Perdido/Four Of A Kind | 10 |
| 54 | Parlophone MSP 6139 | Bugle Call Rag/You Go To My Head | 10 |
| 55 | Capitol CL 14285 | Singin' In The Rain/Non-Stop London | 10 |
| 56 | Parlophone MSP 6255 | Experiments With Mice/Applecake | 15 |
| 57 | Parlophone R 4274 | All Clare/Melbourne Marathon | 5 |
| 57 | Parlophone R 4294 | Duke's Joke/Coquette | 5 |
| 57 | Parlophone R 4321 | Big Jazz Story/Firth Of Fourths | 5 |
| 58 | Parlophone R 4456 | The Colonel's Tune/Jim And Andy's | 5 |
| 59 | Top Rank JAR 209 | We Are The Lambeth Boys/Duet For 16 | 5 |
| 61 | Columbia DB 4695 | The Avengers/Chano | 15 |
| 61 | Columbia DB 4751 | String Of Camels/Winter Wail | 5 |
| 62 | No label 19517 | Music For The New Prestige Film (1-sided white label) | 15 |
| 62 | Columbia DB 4852 | Cannonball/S.O. Blues | 5 |
| 62 | Fontana TF 396 | Hoe Down/Sing Sing Sing | 6 |
| 63 | Fontana TF 422 | The Avengers/Off The Cuff | 15 |
| 64 | Fontana TF 512 | Beefeaters/Down A Tone | 35 |
| 65 | Fontana TF 643 | Sands Of The Kalahari/Night Thoughts | 6 |
| 66 | Fontana TF 675 | Return From The Ashes/Piano Theme | 5 |
| 66 | Fontana TF 700 | Modesty Blaise Theme/The Frost Report | 10 |
| 67 | Fontana TF 805 | (Ain't That) Just Like A Woman/Accident | 10 |
| 73 | Philips 6006 337 | Tomorrows World/Bitter Lemons | 10 |
| 78 | BBC RESL 63 | Telford's Change/Serenade For Sylvia (p/s) | 8 |
| 61 | Columbia SEG 8137 | AFRICAN WALTZ (EP) | 12 |
| 58 | Parlophone GEP 8653 | DANKWORTH WORKSHOP NO. 1 (EP) | 20 |
| 58 | Parlophone GEP 8697 | DANKWORTH WORKSHOP NO. 2 — EXPERIMENTS WITH DANKWORTH (EP) | 15 |
| 60 | Columbia SEG 8037 | THE CRIMINALS (EP, soundtrack; also stereo ESG 7825) | 15 |
| 56 | Parlophone PMD 1042 | JOURNEY INTO JAZZ (10" LP) | 20 |
| 58 | Parlophone PMC 1076 | THE VINTAGE YEARS (LP) | 20 |
| 59 | Parlophone PMC 1043 | FIVE STEPS TO DANKWORTH (LP) | 20 |
| 60 | Top Rank 30/019 | LONDON TO NEWPORT (LP) | 40 |
| 62 | Columbia 33SX 1280 | JAZZ ROUTES (LP, also stereo SCX 3347) | 30 |
| 62 | Columbia | COLLABORATION! (LP, with London Philharmonic) | 15 |
| 63 | Columbia 33SX 1572 | CURTAIN UP (LP) | 15 |
| 64 | Fontana TL/STL 5203 | WHAT THE DICKENS! (LP) | 20 |
| 64 | Encore ENC 165 | FROM 7 ON (LP) | 20 |
| 65 | Fontana TL 5229 | THE ZODIAC VARIATIONS (LP, mono) | 25 |
| 65 | Fontana STL 5229 | THE ZODIAC VARIATIONS (LP, stereo) | 30 |
| 67 | Stateside S(S)L 10213 | FATHOM (LP, soundtrack) | 40 |
| 68 | Fontana TL 5445 | THE $1,000,000 COLLECTION (LP) | 20 |
| 69 | Fontana LPS 16261 | OFF DUTY (LP) | 18 |
| 72 | Philips 6308 122 | FULL CIRCLE (LP) | 15 |
| 73 | Philips 6308 169 | LIFELINE (LP) | 15 |

*(see also Cleo Laine, Philip Green, Tony Mansell, Kenny Wheeler & Johnny Dankworth)*

## DANLEERS
| 58 | Mercury AMT 1003 | One Summer Night/Wheelin' And A-Dealin' | 200 |
| 58 | Mercury AMT 1003 | One Summer Night/Wheelin' And A-Dealin' (78) | 40 |

## DANNY & NOGOODNIKS
| 82 | Chrysalis CHS 2667 | Bike/Spaghetti (p/s) | 10 |

*(see also Adam Ant, Adam & The Ants)*

## DANNY BOYS
| 89 | Ugly Man UG 1 | Days Of The Week (12" EP) | 15 |

## DANNY & THE JUNIORS
| 58 | HMV POP 436 | At The Hop/Sometimes (When I'm All Alone) | 15 |
| 58 | HMV POP 467 | Rock And Roll Is Here To Stay/School Boy Romance | 40 |
| 58 | HMV POP 504 | Dottie/In The Meantime | 30 |
| 60 | Top Rank JAR 510 | Twistin' U.S.A./Thousand Miles Away | 15 |
| 61 | Top Rank JAR 552 | Pony Express/Daydreamer | 15 |
| 61 | Top Rank JAR 587 | Back To The Hop/The Charleston Fish | 15 |
| 62 | Top Rank JAR 604 | Twistin' All Night Long/Twistin' England (with Freddy Cannon) | 15 |
| 63 | London HL 9666 | Oo-La-La-Limbo/Now And Then | 5 |
| 68 | Stateside SS 2117 | At The Hop/LLOYD PRICE: (You've Got) Personality | 5 |

## DANNY & JOE/TOMMY McCOOK'S BAND
| 12 | Jackpot THB 7018 | Please Be Mine/More Strings | 8 |

## C. DANOVAN (ACTUALLY DON CARLOS)
| 73 | Randy's RAN 529 | Sweet Caroline/IMPACT ALL STARS: Caroline (Version) | 5 |

## DANSE MACABRE
| | | | |
|---|---|---|---|
| 88 | Wild West/Alchemy 1 | THINK ABOUT DEATH EP | 20 |

## DANSE SOCIETY
| | | | |
|---|---|---|---|
| 81 | Society SOC 3-81 | The Clock/Continent (brown, black & white foldout p/s) | 15 |
| 81 | Society SOC 3-81 | The Clock/Continent (re-pressing, black & white foldout p/s) | 5 |
| 81 | Pax PAX 2 | There Is No Shame In Death/Dolphins/These Frayed Edges (12", p/s, blue vinyl) | 20 |
| 82 | Pax SOC 5 | Woman's Own/We're So Happy (p/s) | 8 |
| 82 | Pax SOC 5 | Woman's Own/Continent/We're So Happy/Belief (12", with spined p/s) | 10 |
| 84 | Society SOC V 127 | 2,000 Light Years From Home (12" blue vinyl, 50-150 pressed) | 60 |

## DANSETTE DAMAGE
| | | | |
|---|---|---|---|
| 78 | Shoestring LACE 001 | New Musical Express/The Only Sound (p/s, Robert Plant on backing vocals) | 150 |
| 79 | Pinnacle PIN 30 | 20013/4 Approximately/Must Be Love (p/s) | 8 |
| 94 | Shoestring BLOO 2LP | SOLD AS SEEN (LP, gatefold sleeve, 500 only) | 30 |

## DANTA
| | | | |
|---|---|---|---|
| 72 | Epic EPC 7776 | Freeway/Mau Mau | 15 |
| 73 | Epic SEPC 1466 | Crossfire/Daddy's Gone | 15 |

## DANTALIAN'S CHARIOT
| | | | |
|---|---|---|---|
| 67 | Columbia DB 8260 | The Madman Running Through The Fields/Sun Came Bursting Through My Cloud | 120 |
| 95 | Tenth Planet TP 015 | CHARIOT RISING (LP, numbered, 1,000 only) | 25 |

*(see also Zoot Money's Big Roll Band)*

## DANTE (1)
| | | | |
|---|---|---|---|
| 61 | Brunswick 05857 | Bye Bye Baby/That's Why | 12 |

## DANTE (2)
| | | | |
|---|---|---|---|
| 71 | CBS 7382 | Queen Of Sheba/Feelin' The Heat | 15 |

## RON DANTE
| | | | |
|---|---|---|---|
| 68 | MCA MK5003 | It's About Time/Behold | 8 |
| 70 | RCA 1992 | Let Me Bring You Up/How Do You Know | 8 |

## RONNIE DANTE
| | | | |
|---|---|---|---|
| 64 | Stateside SS 351 | Don't Stand Up In A Canoe/If You Love Me Laurie | 5 |

## TROY DANTE (& INFERNOS)
| | | | |
|---|---|---|---|
| 63 | Decca F 11639 | The Face/Give Me Some More | 5 |
| 63 | Decca F 11746 | It's Alright/Tell Me (as Troy Dante & Infernos) | 5 |
| 64 | Fontana TF 445 | Tell Me When/It Had To Be (as Troy Dante & Infernos) | 5 |
| 64 | Fontana TF 477 | This Little Girl/Loving Eyes (as Troy Dante & Infernos) | 5 |

## DANTE & EVERGREENS
| | | | |
|---|---|---|---|
| 60 | Top Rank JAR 402 | Alley-Oop/The Right Time | 12 |

## DANZIG
| | | | |
|---|---|---|---|
| 88 | Def American 838 487-1 | DANZIG (LP, gatefold sleeve) | 45 |
| 90 | Def American 846 374-1 | DANZIG II - LUCIFUGE (LP, with inner) | 30 |
| 92 | Def American 512 270-1 | DANZIG III - HOW THE GODS KILL (LP, gatefold, stickered sleeve) | 40 |

## DAPHINE
| | | | |
|---|---|---|---|
| 79 | My Records MY 12 | The World Is Moving On/Just Another Flirt (p/s) | 8 |

## STEVE DARBYSHIRE
| | | | |
|---|---|---|---|
| 65 | Decca F12261 | That's The Reason Why/She's Got Quality | 10 |
| 66 | Decca F 12512 | Trains Trains/Alma Jones (as Steve Darbishire) | 7 |
| 67 | Decca F 12553 | Just A Little Lovin' Changes Things/Holiday In Waikiki | 6 |

## JOE DARENSBOURG & HIS DIXIE FLYERS
| | | | |
|---|---|---|---|
| 58 | Vogue V 2409 | Yellow Dog Blues/Careless Love | 5 |

## DARIEN SPIRIT
| | | | |
|---|---|---|---|
| 73 | Charisma CAS 1065 | ELEGY TO MARILYN (LP, large "Mad Hatter" label, with lip intact!) | 30 |

## BOBBY DARIN
### 78s
| | | | |
|---|---|---|---|
| 56 | Brunswick 05561 | Rock Island Line/Timber (as Bobby Darin & Jaybirds) | 20 |
| 58 | London HLE 8737 | Queen Of The Hop/Lost Love | 25 |
| 59 | London HLE 8793 | Mighty Mighty Man/You're Mine (as Bobby Darin with Rinky Dinks) | 25 |
| 59 | London HLE 8815 | Plain Jane/While I'm Gone | 30 |
| 59 | London HLE 8867 | Dream Lover/Bullmoose | 20 |
| 59 | London HLK 8939 | Mack The Knife/Was There A Call For Me | 25 |
| 60 | London HLK 9034 | La Mer (Beyond The Sea)/That's The Way Love Is | 40 |
| 60 | London HLK 9086 | Clementine/Down With Love | 50 |
| 60 | London HLK 9142 | Bill Bailey Won't You Please Come Home/Tall Story | 60 |

### SINGLES
| | | | |
|---|---|---|---|
| 56 | Brunswick 05561 | Rock Island Line/Timber (as Bobby Darin & Jaybirds) | 30 |
| 58 | London HLE 8666 | Splish Splash/Judy Don't Be Moody | 25 |
| 58 | London HLE 8679 | Early In The Morning/Now We're One (as Rinky-Dinks featuring Bobby Darin) | 25 |
| 58 | London HLE 8737 | Queen Of The Hop/Lost Love | 30 |
| 58 | London HL 7060 | Queen Of The Hop/Lost Love (export issue) | 20 |
| 59 | London HLE 8793 | Mighty Mighty Man/You're Mine (as Bobby Darin with Rinky Dinks) | 25 |
| 59 | London HLE 8815 | Plain Jane/While I'm Gone | 30 |
| 59 | London HL 7078 | Plain Jane/Dream Lover (export issue) | 25 |
| 59 | London HLE 8867 | Dream Lover/Bullmoose | 5 |
| 58 | London HLK 8939 | Mack The Knife/Was There A Call For Me | 5 |
| 60 | London HLK 9034 | La Mer (Beyond The Sea)/That's The Way Love Is | 5 |

*(The above 45s were originally issued with triangular centres, later round centre pressings are worth around two thirds these values.)*

| | | | |
|---|---|---|---|
| 60 | London HLK 9086 | Clementine/Down With Love | 5 |
| 60 | London HLK 9142 | Bill Bailey Won't You Please Come Home/Tall Story | 5 |
| 60 | Brunswick 05831 | Hear Them Bells/The Greatest Builder | 5 |

MINT VALUE £

| | | | |
|---|---|---|---|
| 60 | London HLK 9197 | Beachcomber/Autumn Blues (credited to 'Bobby Darin At The Piano') | 5 |
| 60 | London HLK 9215 | Somebody To Love/I'll Be There | 5 |
| 61 | London HLK 9303 | Lazy River/Oo-Ee-Train | 5 |
| 61 | London HLK 9375 | Nature Boy/Look For My True Love | 5 |
| 61 | London HLK 9407 | Theme From "Come September"/Walk Bach To Me (with Orchestra) | 5 |
| 61 | London HLK 9429 | You Must Have Been A Beautiful Baby/Sorrow Tomorrow | 5 |
| 61 | London HLK 9474 | Multiplication (From "Come September")/Irresistible You | 5 |
| 62 | London HLK 9540 | What'd I Say/Ain't That Love | 5 |
| 62 | London HLK 9575 | Things/Jailer Bring Me Water | 5 |
| 62 | Atlantic HLK 9575 | Things/Jailer Bring Me Water | 20 |
| 62 | Capitol CL 15272 | If A Man Answers/A True, True Love | 5 |
| 62 | London HLK 9624 | Baby Face/You Know How | 5 |
| 63 | London HLK 9663 | I've Found A New Baby/Keep A-Walkin' | 5 |
| 63 | Capitol CL 15286 | You're The Reason I'm Living/Now You're Gone | 5 |
| 63 | Capitol CL 15306 | Eighteen Yellow Roses/Not For Me | 10 |
| 63 | Capitol CL 15328 | Be Mad Little Girl/Since You've Been Gone | 6 |
| 64 | Capitol CL 15338 | I Wonder Who's Kissing Her Now/As Long As I'm Singing | 5 |
| 64 | Atlantic AT 4002 | Milord/Golden Earrings | 6 |
| 64 | Capitol CL 15360 | The Things In This House/Wait By The Water | 5 |
| 65 | Capitol CL 15401 | When I Get Home/Lonely Road | 5 |
| 65 | Capitol CL 15414 | Gyp The Cat/That Funny Feeling | 5 |
| 65 | Atlantic AT 4046 | We Didn't Ask To Be Brought Here/Funny What Love Can Do | 10 |
| 66 | Atlantic 584 014 | Mame/Walking In The Shadow Of Love | 6 |
| 66 | Atlantic 584 051 | If I Were A Carpenter/Rainin' | 6 |
| 67 | Atlantic 584 063 | The Girl That Stood Beside Me/Reason To Believe | 6 |
| 67 | Atlantic 584 079 | Lovin' You/Amy | 6 |
| 67 | Atlantic 584 105 | The Lady Came From Baltimore/I Am | 6 |
| 67 | Atlantic 584 147 | At The Crossroads/She Knows | 5 |
| 68 | Bell BLL 1040 | Change/Long Line Rider | 5 |
| 69 | Bell BLL 1090 | Sugar-Man/Jive | 5 |
| 70 | Major Minor MM 697 | Maybe We Can Get It Together/RX-Pyro (Prescription: Fire) (as Bob Darin) | 5 |
| 74 | Mowest MW 3014 | Blue Monday/Moritat: Mack The Knife | 5 |

**EPs**

| | | | |
|---|---|---|---|
| 59 | London REE 1173 | BOBBY DARIN (tri centre) | 30 |
| 59 | London REE 1173 | BOBBY DARIN (round centre) | 10 |
| 59 | London REE 1225 | BOBBY DARIN NO. 2 (tri centre) | 30 |
| 59 | London REE 1225 | BOBBY DARIN NO. 2 (round centre) | 10 |
| 60 | London REK 1243 | THAT'S ALL | 10 |
| 61 | London REK 1286 | FOR TEENAGERS ONLY | 25 |
| 62 | London REK 1338 | TWIST WITH BOBBY DARIN | 10 |

**ALBUMS**

| | | | |
|---|---|---|---|
| 58 | London HA-E 2140 | BOBBY DARIN | 30 |
| 59 | London HA-E 2172 | THAT'S ALL | 15 |
| 59 | London HA-K 2235 | THIS IS DARIN (mono) | 15 |
| 59 | London SAH-K 6067 | THIS IS DARIN (stereo) | 18 |
| 60 | London HA-K 2311 | FOR TEENAGERS ONLY | 50 |
| 61 | London HA-K 2394 | LOVE SWINGS (mono) | 20 |
| 61 | London SAH-K 6194 | LOVE SWINGS (stereo) | 15 |
| 62 | London HA-K 2456 | DARIN SINGS RAY CHARLES (mono) | 15 |
| 62 | London SAH-K 6243 | DARIN SINGS RAY CHARLES (stereo) | 15 |
| 63 | London SH-K 8102 | IT'S YOU OR NO-ONE (stereo) | 15 |
| 63 | Capitol (S)T 1942 | EIGHTEEN YELLOW ROSES & 11 OTHER HITS (stereo) | 15 |
| 64 | Capitol (S)T 2007 | GOLDEN FOLK HITS (stereo) | 15 |
| 67 | Atlantic 587 073 | SOMETHING SPECIAL | 20 |

*(see also Rinky Dinks)*

**DARK (1)**

| | | | |
|---|---|---|---|
| 72 | SIS 0102 | DARK ROUND THE EDGES (LP, private pressing, 12 copies with colour gatefold sleeve & booklet) | 6000 |
| 72 | SIS 0102 | DARK ROUND THE EDGES (LP, private pressing, 8 copies with black & white gatefold sleeve) | 4000 |
| 72 | SIS 0102 | DARK ROUND THE EDGES (LP, private pressing, 40 copies with single black & white sleeve) | 3000 |
| 90 | Swank/Darkside 001 | DARK ROUND THE EDGES (LP, reissue, U.K. pressing marketed in U.S.) | 40 |
| 91 | Swank/Darkside 001 | DARK ROUND THE EDGES (LP, as above, with different insert, 225 only) | 30 |
| 95 | Acme AC 8009LP | ARTEFACTS FROM THE BLACK MUSEUM (LP, 500 only, with insert) | 20 |

**DARK (2)**

| | | | |
|---|---|---|---|
| 79 | Fresh FRESH 2 | My Friends/John Wayne (p/s) | 8 |
| 80 | Fresh FRESH 13 | Hawaii Five O/Don't Look Now (/s) | 20 |

**DARK ANGEL**

| | | | |
|---|---|---|---|
| 86 | Under One Flag FLAG 6 | DARKNESS DESCENDS (LP) | 15 |
| 91 | Under One Flag FLAG 54 DM | TIME DOES NOT HEAL (2-LP) | 20 |

**DARKER SHADE OF BLACK**

| | | | |
|---|---|---|---|
| 71 | Jackpot JP 758 | War/JEFF BARNES: People's Version | 8 |

**DARK & MOODY**

| | | | |
|---|---|---|---|
| 93 | Dark & Moody DARK T 001 | VOLUME 1 (12") | 12 |

**DARKNESS**

| | | | |
|---|---|---|---|
| 03 | Must Destroy DESTROYER 6 | Get Your Hands Off My Woman (Clean Version)/(Dirty Version)/Best Of Me (p/s, 2000 only) | 10 |
| 03 | Atlantic 745217 | PERMISSION TO LAND (LP, gatefold, poster) | 15 |

*(see also Hot Leg)*

## DARKSIDE
| | | | |
|---|---|---|---|
| 90 | Situation 2 SITU 29P | ALL THAT NOISE (LP, picture disc, die-cut sleeve) | 12 |

*(see also Spacemen 3)*

## DARK STAR
| | | | |
|---|---|---|---|
| 81 | Avatar AAA 105 | Lady Of Mars/Rock 'N' Romancin' (company sleeve) | 12 |
| 81 | Steel Strike no cat. no. | Lady Of Mars/Rock 'N' Romancin' (12", 250 pressed) | 90 |
| 81 | Avatar AALP 5003 | DARK STAR (LP, with patch) | 20 |
| 81 | Avatar AALP 5003 | DARK STAR (LP) | 15 |
| 87 | FM WKFMLP 97 | REAL TO REEL (LP) | 15 |

## DARKTHRONE
| | | | |
|---|---|---|---|
| 91 | Peaceville VILE 22 | SOULSIDE JOURNEY (LP, picture disc) | 50 |
| 92 | Peaceville VILE 28 | A BLAZE IN THE NORTHERN SKY (LP) | 50 |
| 93 | Peaceville VILE 35 | UNDER A FUNERAL MOON (LP) | 50 |
| 94 | Peaceville VILE 43 | TRANSILVANIAN HUNGER (LP) | 80 |

## DARLETTES
| | | | |
|---|---|---|---|
| 70 | President PT 317 | Lost/Sweet Kind Of Loneliness | 15 |

## DARLING BUDS
| | | | |
|---|---|---|---|
| 87 | Darling Buds DAR 1 | If I Said/Just To Be Seen (p/s, with insert, 2,000 only) | 12 |
| 87 | Darling Buds DAR 1 | If I Said/Just To Be Seen (p/s, without insert, 2,000 only) | 6 |
| 87 | Bonk On 001 | Spin/BUBBLEGUM SPLASH: If Only (flexidisc free with So Naive fanzine) | 10 |
| 90 | Native NTV 54 | Shame On You/Valentine//It's All Up To You/Spin/Think Of Me/That's The Reason (triple-pack in envelope sleeve) | 6 |

## DARLINGS
| | | | |
|---|---|---|---|
| 67 | CBS 2932 | Saturday Town/Wish You Were Here | 20 |

## BILL DARNEL
| | | | |
|---|---|---|---|
| 55 | London HLU 8204 | My Little Mother/Bring Me A Bluebird (with Frank Weir & His Orchestra) | 15 |
| 56 | London HLU 8234 | The Last Frontier/Rock-A-Boogie Baby | 25 |
| 56 | London HLU 8267 | Guilty Lips/Ain't Misbehavin' | 10 |
| 56 | London HLU 8292 | Tell Me More/Satin Doll | 10 |

*(see also Frank Weir & His Orchestra)*

## DARONDO
| | | | |
|---|---|---|---|
| 12 | Kent Select CITY 027 | Didn't I/Saving My Love (reissue) | 8 |

## GUY DARRELL (& MIDNIGHTERS)
| | | | |
|---|---|---|---|
| 63 | Oriole CB 1932 | Go Home Girl/You Won't Come Home (as Guy Darrell & Midnighters) | 15 |
| 64 | Oriole CB 1964 | Sorry/Sweet Dreams (as Guy Darrell & Midnighters) | 15 |
| 65 | CBS 201806 | Stupidity/One Of These Days | 10 |
| 66 | CBS 202033 | Somewhere They Can't Find Me/It Takes A Lot To Laugh | 10 |
| 66 | CBS 202082 | I've Been Hurt/Blessed | 25 |
| 66 | CBS 202082 | I've Been Hurt/Blessed (demo) | 40 |
| 66 | CBS 202296 | Big Louie/My Way Of Thinking | 5 |
| 67 | CBS 202510 | Hard Lovin'/I've Never Had A Love Like That | 10 |
| 67 | CBS 202642 | Crystal Ball/Didn't I | 5 |
| 67 | Piccadilly 7N 35406 | Evil Woman/What You Do About That | 20 |
| 67 | Pye 7N 17435 | Cupid/What's Happened To Our Love | 5 |
| 68 | Pye 7N 17586 | Skyline Pigeon/Everything | 5 |
| 69 | Page One POF 120 | Turn To Me/What's Her Name | 5 |
| 69 | Page One POF 141 | Birds Of A Feather/Keep The Rain From My Door | 5 |
| 69 | Page One POF 155 | How Are You/Turtle Turquoise And The Hare (as Guy Darrell Syndicate) | 5 |
| 72 | CBS 53364 | GUY DARRELL (LP) | 25 |
| 73 | Santa Ponsa PNL 502 | I'VE BEEN HURT (LP) | 15 |

## JAMES DARREN
| | | | |
|---|---|---|---|
| 59 | Pye International 7N 25019 | Gidget/There's No Such Thing (as Jimmy Darren) | 5 |
| 59 | Pye International 7N 25034 | Angel Face/I Don't Wanna Lose You (as Jimmy Darren) | 5 |
| 60 | Pye International 7N 25059 | Because They're Young/Let There Be Love | 5 |
| 61 | Pye International 7N 25116 | Goodbye Cruel World/Valerie | 5 |
| 62 | Pye International 7N 25125 | Her Royal Majesty/If I Could Only Tell You | 5 |
| 62 | Pye International 7N 25138 | Conscience/Dream Big | 5 |
| 62 | Pye International 7N 25155 | Mary's Little Lamb/The Life Of The Party | 5 |
| 62 | Pye International 7N 25168 | Hail To The Conquering Hero/Too Young To Go Steady | 5 |
| 63 | Pye International 7N 25170 | Pin A Medal On Joey/I'll Be Loving You | 5 |
| 63 | Colpix PX 708 | Backstage/Gegetta | 5 |
| 65 | Warner Bros WB 5648 | Because You're Mine/Millions Of Roses | 5 |
| 66 | Warner Bros WB 5689 | Tom Hawk/I Want To Be Lonely | 5 |
| 67 | Warner Bros WB 5874 | All/Misty Morning Eyes | 5 |
| 59 | Pye Intl. NEP 44004 | P.S. I LOVE YOU (EP) | 25 |
| 62 | Pye Intl. NEP 44008 | JAMES DARREN HIT PARADE (EP) | 12 |
| 63 | Pye Intl. NPL 28021 | LOVE AMONG THE YOUNG (LP) | 30 |

## JEANNIE DARREN & SECOND CITY SOUND
| | | | |
|---|---|---|---|
| 69 | Major Minor MM 611 | River Deep, Mountain High/Julie | 7 |

## MAXINE DARREN
| | | | |
|---|---|---|---|
| 65 | Pye 7N 15796 | How Can I Hide It From My Heart/Don't You Know | 10 |

## CHRIS DARROW
| | | | |
|---|---|---|---|
| 73 | United Artists UAG 29453 | CHRIS DARROW (LP, gatefold) | 20 |
| 74 | United Artists UAG 29634 | UNDER MY OWN DISGUISE (LP) | 20 |

*(see also Kaleidoscope, Nitty Gritty Dirt Band)*

## DARTELLS
| | | | |
|---|---|---|---|
| 63 | London HLD 9719 | Hot Pastrami/Dartell Stomp | 20 |

## BARRY DARVELL
60    London HL 9191       Geronimo Stomp/How Will It End? ..................................................... 50

## DARWIN'S THEORY
67    Major Minor MM 503       Daytime/Hosanna ..................................................... 50

## NITAE DASGUPTA
72    Mushroom 100 MR 22       SONGS OF INDIA (LP) ..................................................... 35

## DAS KABINETTE
83    Klosette PL0026       The Cabinet/Fudge It (p/s, 500 only) ..................................................... 100

## DAS SCHNITZ
79    Ellie Jay EJSP 9249       4 AM (EP, custom sleeve) ..................................................... 70

## DATE WITH SOUL
67    Stateside SS 2062       Yes Sir, That's My Baby/PRISCILLA: He Noticed Me ..................................................... 50
(see also Jack Nitzsche, Brian Wilson, Sonny & Cher, Darlene Love/Blossoms, Jackie De Shannon, the Paris Sisters)

## DAT POLITICS
04    Chicks On Speed COSR 15       GO PET GO (LP) ..................................................... 15

## DAUGHTERS OF ALBION
69    Fontana STL 5486       DAUGHTERS OF ALBION (LP) ..................................................... 30

## DAVANI & RYAN
72    Philips 6308 132       FUNKY COUNTRY (LP) ..................................................... 20

## DAVE DAVANI & D MEN
63    Columbia DB 7125       Don't Fool Around/She's The Best For Me ..................................................... 15
64    Decca F 11896       Midnight Special/Sho' Know A Lot About Love ..................................................... 20
(see also Davani & Ryan)

## DAVE DAVANI (FOUR)
65    Parlophone R 5329       Top Of The Pops/Workin' Out ..................................................... 40
66    Parlophone R 5490       Tossin' And Turnin'/Jupe ..................................................... 50
66    Parlophone R 5525       One Track Mind/On The Cooler Side ..................................................... 35
72    Philips 6006 195       King Kong Blues/Come Back Baby (solo) ..................................................... 12
65    Parlophone PMC 1258       FUSED (LP) ..................................................... 100
(see also Davani & Ryan)

## DAVE & DIAMONDS
65    Columbia DB 7692       I Walk The Lonely Night/You Do Love (p/s) ..................................................... 35
65    Columbia DB 7692       I Walk The Lonely Night/You Do Love ..................................................... 15
(see also Dave Russell)

## DAVE & DON
67    Polydor 56212       What A Feeling/That's My Way ..................................................... 6

## BOB DAVENPORT (& RAKES)
60    Collector JEB 4       GEORDIE SONGS (EP) ..................................................... 15
62    Topic TOP 83       WOR GEORDIE (EP, with Rakes) ..................................................... 15
66    Columbia SX 1786       BOB DAVENPORT AND THE RAKES (LP, with Rakes) ..................................................... 40
71    Trailer LER 3008       BOB DAVENPORT& THE MARSDEN RATTLERS (LP, red label) ..................................................... 22
73    Trailer LER 2088       PAL OF MY CRADLE DAYS (LP, red label) ..................................................... 18
77    Topic 12TS 318       POSTCARDS HOME (LP, with lyric sheet) ..................................................... 15

## D.A.V.E. THE DRUMMER
90s    Yolk YOLK 05       Steamliner/Jaws (12", with Jerome Hill) ..................................................... 40
00    Smitten SMT 46       DIG YOUR OWN GRAVE EP (2x12", p/s) ..................................................... 10
00    Smitten SMTLTD 02       Effective Therapy (1-sided 12", green vinyl) ..................................................... 15

## ALAN DAVEY
87    Hawkfan HWFB 3/4       THE ELF EP (double pack, 2 x 7" with insert in wraparound p/s in poly bag) ................. 20
(see also Hawkwind)

## (SHAUN) DAVEY & (JAMES) MORRIS
73    York FYK 417       DAVEY AND MORRIS (LP, with insert) ..................................................... 400
(see also Strawbs)

## DAVID
69    Philips BF 1776       Light Of Your Mind/Please Mister Policeman ..................................................... 200
69    President PT286       The Who The Why/President ..................................................... 6
70    Fontana TF 1081       I'm Going Back/Selppin ..................................................... 60

## ALAN DAVID
64    Decca F 11956       I Want So Much To Know You/I Can't Go Wrong ..................................................... 10
65    Decca F 12084       Hurt/I Found Out Too Late ..................................................... 50
65    Decca F 12130       Crazy 'Bout My Baby/A Thousand Tears Ago ..................................................... 10
67    Polydor BM 56201       Flower Power/Completely Free ..................................................... 30
69    Page One POF116       Oh What A Naughty Man/I've Got To Know ..................................................... 10
65    Decca LK 4674       ALAN DAVID (LP) ..................................................... 40

## DAVID & DAVID
70    Columbia DB8678       In The City/Good Morning Morning ..................................................... 10

## DAVID & EMBERS
63    Decca F 11717       What Is This/Teddy Bear Special ..................................................... 5
(see also Embers)

## DAVID & GIANTS
68    Capitol CL 15915       Ten Miles High/Super Love ..................................................... 10

## DAVID & GOLIATH
71    Concord CON 025       Why Do You Pretend/I Wonder Where ..................................................... 8

## DAVID & JONATHAN
66    Columbia DB 7950       Lovers Of The World Unite/Oh My World ..................................................... 5
67    Columbia DB 8208       She's Leaving Home/One Born Every Minute ..................................................... 5

| | | | |
|---|---|---|---|
| 67 | Columbia S(C)X 6031 | DAVID AND JONATHAN (LP) | 15 |

*(see also Roger Cook, Edison Lighthouse, White Plains)*

### DAVID & ROZAA
| | | | |
|---|---|---|---|
| 70 | Philips 6006 040 | Time Of Our Life/We Can Reach An Understanding | 20 |
| 71 | Philips 6006 094 | The Spark That Lights The Flame/Two Can Share | 20 |

*(see also David Essex, Rozaa & Wine)*

### DIANNE DAVIDSON
| | | | |
|---|---|---|---|
| 72 | Janus 6146 019 | Sympathy/All I Wanted | 8 |
| 72 | Janus 6146 021 | Ain't Gonna Be Treated This Way/All I Wanted (All The Time) | 5 |
| 72 | Janus 6310 209 | BACKWOODS WOMAN (LP) | 18 |

### TOMMY DAVIDSON
| | | | |
|---|---|---|---|
| 56 | London HLU 8219 | Half Past Kissing Time/I Don't Know Yet But I'm Learning | 20 |

### HUTCH DAVIE
| | | | |
|---|---|---|---|
| 58 | London HLE 8667 | At The Woodchopper's Ball/Honky Tonk Train Blues (& Honky Tonkers) | 7 |
| 60 | London HLE 9076 | Sweet Georgia Brown/Heartaches | 5 |
| 62 | Pye International 7N 25149 | But I Do/Time Was (& Orchestra) | 5 |

### ALUN DAVIES
| | | | |
|---|---|---|---|
| 65 | Parlophone R 5384 | Girls Were Made To Love And Kiss/Rose Marie | 6 |
| 68 | Mercury MF 1043 | One Day Soon/Pretend You Don't See Her | 6 |
| 72 | CBS 58302 | Waste Of Time/Portobello Road | 6 |
| 72 | CBS 65108 | DAYDO (LP, gatefold sleeve) | 30 |

*(see also Cat Stevens, Sweet Thursday)*

### BARRY DAVIES
| | | | |
|---|---|---|---|
| 70 | Beacon BEA 114 | I Wish It Would Rain/Strange Days | 30 |
| 71 | Beacon BEA 185 | Strange Days/My Song My Whisky and Me (A-side different version from previous release) | 40 |

### BAZ DAVIES
| | | | |
|---|---|---|---|
| 80 | BAT EJSP 9397 | Back In 1969/Easy On My Mind | 8 |

### BOB DAVIES
| | | | |
|---|---|---|---|
| 63 | London HLU 9767 | Rock'N'Roll Show/With You Tonight | 25 |

### CYRIL DAVIES (R&B ALLSTARS)
| | | | |
|---|---|---|---|
| 63 | Pye International 7N 25194 | Country Line Special/Chicago Calling | 25 |
| 63 | Pye International 7N 25221 | Preachin' The Blues/Sweet Mary | 40 |
| 69 | Pye 7N 17663 | Country Line Special/Sweet Mary | 15 |
| 64 | Pye Intl. NEP 44025 | THE SOUND OF CYRIL DAVIES (EP) | 75 |
| 57 | '77' LP 2 | THE LEGENDARY CYRIL DAVIES (10" LP, 99 only, with Alexis Korner) | 300 |
| 70 | Folklore F-LEAT 9 | THE LEGENDARY CYRIL DAVIES (LP, reissue) | 50 |

*(see also Alexis Korner, Beryl Bryden)*

### DAVE DAVIES
| | | | |
|---|---|---|---|
| 67 | Pye 7N 17356 | Death Of A Clown/Love Me Till The Sun Shines | 8 |
| 67 | Pye 7N 17429 | Susannah's Still Alive/Funny Face | 10 |
| 68 | Pye 7N 17514 | Lincoln County/There's No Life Without Love | 20 |
| 69 | Pye 7N 17678 | Hold My Hand/Creeping Jean | 25 |
| 68 | Pye NEP 24289 | DAVE DAVIES HITS (EP) | 300 |

*(see also Kinks)*

### GLYN DAVIES
| | | | |
|---|---|---|---|
| 89 | Eyewitness SRT 9KS 1968 | Everyone Will Benefit In The End/Building Bridges To Another World | 8 |

### MARION DAVIES
| | | | |
|---|---|---|---|
| 69 | Columbia DB 8589 | Walk Out Of My Mind/This Is My Lonely Life | 7 |

*(see also Ladybirds)*

### MIAR DAVIES
| | | | |
|---|---|---|---|
| 64 | Decca F 11805 | Ten Good Reasons/I Won't Remember You | 10 |
| 64 | Decca F 11894 | I Hear You Knocking/Navy Blue | 10 |

### NICOLA DAVIES
| | | | |
|---|---|---|---|
| 68 | SNB 55-3627 | Infatuation/My Boy | 10 |

### RAY DAVIES
| | | | |
|---|---|---|---|
| 86 | Virgin VS 865 | Quiet Life/Voices In The Dark (p/s) | 5 |

*(see also Kinks)*

### RON DAVIES
| | | | |
|---|---|---|---|
| 70 | A&M AMS 799 | It Ain't Easy/Silent Song Through The Land | 6 |
| 70 | A&M AMLS 993 | SILENT SONG THROUGH THE LAND (LP, green label) | 30 |

### TYRONE DAVIES
| | | | |
|---|---|---|---|
| 69 | Trojan TR 677 | If This World Were Mine/You Done Me Wrong (as Tyrone Davis) | 300 |
| 77 | D-Roy FORCE 2012 | Mind Blowing Decisions/Trenchtown Skank | 20 |

### BARRINGTON DAVIS
| | | | |
|---|---|---|---|
| 72 | Montague MONS 2 | TRACKS OF MIND (LP, with lyric inner sleeve) | 60 |

### BETTE DAVIS (& DEBBIE BURTON)
| | | | |
|---|---|---|---|
| 63 | London HLU 9711 | Whatever Happened To Baby Jane?/ DEBBIE BURTON:I've Written A Letter To Daddy | 8 |
| 76 | EMI EMA 778 | MISS BETTE DAVIS (LP) | 15 |

### BETTY DAVIS
| | | | |
|---|---|---|---|
| 75 | Island USA 2011 | Shut Off The Light/He Was A Big Freak | 6 |
| 75 | Island ILPS 9329 | NASTY GAL (LP) | 25 |

### BILLIE DAVIS
| | | | |
|---|---|---|---|
| 63 | Decca F 11572 | Tell Him/I'm Thankful | 10 |
| 63 | Decca F 11572 | Tell Him/I'm Thankful (export copies with p/s) | 20 |
| 63 | Decca F 11658 | He's The One/V.I.P. | 10 |
| 63 | Decca F 11658 | He's The One/V.I.P. (export copies with p/s) | 15 |

MINT VALUE £

| 63 | Columbia DB 7115 | Bedtime Stories/You And I | 15 |
|----|------------------|---------------------------|----|
| 64 | Columbia DB 7195 | That Boy John/Say Nothin' Don't Tell | 15 |
| 64 | Columbia DB 7246 | School Is Over/Give Me Love | 15 |
| 64 | Columbia DB 7346 | Whatcha Gonna Do/Everybody Knows (as Billie Davis & Le Roys) | 35 |
| 65 | Piccadilly 7N 35227 | Last One To Be Loved/You Don't Know | 10 |
| 65 | Piccadilly 7N 35266 | No Other Baby/Hands Off | 18 |
| 66 | Piccadilly 7N 35308 | Heart And Soul/Don't Take All Night | 10 |
| 66 | Piccadilly 7N 35350 | Just Walk In My Shoes/Ev'ry Day | 100 |
| 67 | Decca F 12620 | Wasn't It You?/Until It's Time For You To Go | 10 |
| 67 | Decca F 12696 | Angel Of The Morning/Darling Be Home Soon | 10 |
| 68 | Decca F 12823 | I Want You To Be My Baby/Suffer | 10 |
| 69 | Decca F 12870 | Make The Feeling Go Away/I'll Come Home | 10 |
| 69 | Decca F 12923 | I Can Remember/Nobody's Home To Go Home To | 20 |
| 69 | Decca F 12977 | Nights In White Satin/It's Over | 18 |
| 70 | Decca F 13049 | Venid Con Migo/Love (Spanish export issue) | 7 |
| 70 | Decca F 13085 | There Must Be A Reason/Love | 20 |
| 72 | Regal Zonophone RZ 3050 | I Tried/Touch My Love | 8 |
| 76 | United Artists UP 36117 | Any Way That You Want Me/Somewhere Along The Line | 5 |
| 76 | United Artists UP 46066 | I've Been Loving Someone Else/Beyond The Pale | 5 |
| 78 | Magnet MAG 124 | Run Joey Run/East Come Easy Go | 5 |
| 70 | Decca LK 5029 | BILLIE DAVIS (LP, mono) | 50 |
| 70 | Decca SKL 5029 | BILLIE DAVIS (LP, stereo) | 45 |

*(see also Le Roys, Mike Sarne)*

## BLIND GARY DAVIS/REVEREND GARY DAVIS

| 63 | '77' LA 12-14 | PURE RELIGION AND BAD COMPANY (LP) | 30 |
|----|---------------|-------------------------------------|----|
| 60s | Fontana 688 303 ZL | HARLEM STREET SINGER (LP) | 45 |
| 64 | Xtra XTRA 1009 | REV. GARY DAVIS/SHORT STUFF MACON (LP, 1 side each) | 22 |
| 66 | Xtra XTRA 5014 | SAY NO TO THE DEVIL (LP) | 25 |
| 67 | Xtra XTRA 5042 | A LITTLE MORE FAITH (LP) | 25 |
| 69 | Fontana SFJL 914 | BRING YOUR MONEY HONEY (LP) | 25 |
| 71 | Transatlantic TRA 244 | RAGTIME GUITAR (LP) | 15 |
| 71 | Transatlantic TRA 249 | CHILDREN OF ZION (LP) | 15 |
| 77 | Kicking Mule SNKF 103 | LET US GET TOGETHER (LP) | 18 |

## BOBBY DAVIS (JAMAICA)

| 71 | Banana BA 342 | Got To Get Away/We'll Cry Together (with BARBARA DUNKLEY) | 20 |
|----|---------------|-----------------------------------------------------------|----|
| 71 | Banana BA 344 | Return Your Love/RILEY'S ALLSTARS: Version | 20 |
| 71 | Beacon 114 | Strange Days/I Wish It would Rain | 12 |

*(see also Barbara Dunkley)*

## BOBBY DAVIS (U.S.)

| 61 | Starlite ST45 056 | I Was Wrong/Hype You Into Selling Your Head | 50 |
|----|-------------------|---------------------------------------------|----|

## BONNIE DAVIS

| 55 | Brunswick 05507 | Pepper-Hot Baby/For Always, Darling | 40 |
|----|-----------------|-------------------------------------|----|

## CLIFFORD DAVIS

| 69 | Reprise RS 27003 | Before The Beginning/Man Of The World | 20 |
|----|------------------|----------------------------------------|----|
| 70 | Reprise RS 27008 | Come On Down And Follow Me/Homework | 15 |
| 71 | Reprise K 14282 | Before The Beginning/Man Of The World (reissue) | 5 |

## DANNY DAVIS ORCHESTRA (U.S.)

| 65 | MGM MGM 1277 | Main Theme From "The Saint"/Little Bandits Of Juarez | 10 |
|----|--------------|-------------------------------------------------------|----|
| 64 | London HAR 8204 | THEY'RE PLAYING OUR SONG (LP, with Ruby & Romantics) | 20 |

*(see also Ruby & Romantics, Byron Lee)*

## DANNY DAVIS & BYRON LEE

| 64 | MGM 1256 | Night Train From Jamaica/Ska Dee Dah | 18 |
|----|----------|---------------------------------------|----|

## DANNY DAVIS (U.K.)

| 60 | Parlophone R 4657 | Love Me/You're My Only Girl | 20 |
|----|-------------------|------------------------------|----|
| 60 | Parlophone R 4796 | Talking In My Sleep/Lullaby Of Love | 15 |
| 61 | Pye 7N 15391 | Tell All The World/Rumours | 10 |
| 62 | Pye 7N 15427 | Rome Wasn't Built In A Day/Tell Me | 5 |
| 62 | Pye 7N 15470 | Patches/September In The Rain | 5 |

*(see also Marauders)*

## DEL DAVIS

| 71 | Bread BR-1105 | Baby Don't Wake Me/Wishing And Hoping | 150 |
|----|---------------|----------------------------------------|-----|
| 72 | Trojan 7870 | Baby Don't Wake Me/Sugarloaf Hill | 200 |
| 72 | Horse HOSS 13 | Love Sweet Love/Open The Door | 7 |
| 73 | Horse HOSS 26 | World Without Love/Bucket | 7 |

## EDDIE ('LOCKJAW') DAVIS

| 56 | Parlophone GEP 8587 | EDDIE 'LOCKJAW' DAVIS TRIO (EP) | 10 |
|----|---------------------|----------------------------------|----|
| 57 | Parlophone GEP 8678 | LOCKJAW (EP) | 10 |
| 58 | Parlophone GEP 8685 | EDDIE 'LOCKJAW' DAVIS TRIO (EP) | 10 |
| 59 | Esquire EP 217 | EDDIE 'LOCKJAW' DAVIS (EP) | 10 |
| 61 | Esquire EP 237 | EDDIE 'LOCKJAW' DAVIS QUARTET (EP) | 10 |
| 60 | Esquire 32-104 | THE EDDIE 'LOCKJAW' DAVIS COOK BOOK (LP) | 20 |
| 60 | Esquire 32-117 | VERY SAXY (LP, with Coleman Hawkins, Arnett Cobb & Bobby Tate) | 20 |
| 61 | Esquire 32-128 | JAWS IN ORBIT (LP) | 25 |
| 64 | Stateside SL 10102 | THE FIRST SET — LIVE AT MINTONS (LP, with Johnny Griffin) | 20 |

*(see also Coleman Hawkins, Johnny Griffin)*

## EDWARD H. DAVIS

| 74 | Sain SAIN 1016M | HEN FFORDD GYMREIG O FYW (LP) | 20 |
|----|-----------------|--------------------------------|----|
| 76 | Sain SAIN 1053M | SNEB YN BECSO DAM (LP, gatefold) | 15 |

## JACKIE DAVIS (& THE TROMBONES)
| | | | |
|---|---|---|---|
| 59 | Capitol CL 15005 | Frenesi/Gonna Get A Girl ............................................................ | 5 |

## JESSE DAVIS
| | | | |
|---|---|---|---|
| 71 | Atlantic 2400 106 | JESSE DAVIS (LP, features Gram Parsons and Eric Clapton) ........................ | 18 |

## JESSE (ED) DAVIS
| | | | |
|---|---|---|---|
| 71 | Atlantic 2091 076 | Every Night Is Saturday Night/Washita Love Child (as Jesse Davis)................ | 6 |
| 71 | Atco 2400 106 | JESSE 'ED' DAVIS (LP)............................................................. | 18 |
| 72 | Atlantic K 40329 | ULULU (LP)....................................................................... | 15 |

## JIMMY DAVIS
| | | | |
|---|---|---|---|
| 66 | Bounty BY 6009 | MAXWELL STREET (LP)............................................................. | 25 |

## KIM DAVIS
| | | | |
|---|---|---|---|
| 66 | Decca F 12387 | Don't Take Your Lovin' Away/Feelin' Blue ........................................ | 20 |
| 67 | CBS 202568 | Tell It Like It Is/Losing Kind ................................................. | 25 |
| 68 | CBS 3260 | Until It's Time For You To Go/I Hold No Grudge .................................. | 7 |
| 69 | CBS 4210 | Are You Ready For Love/Taste Of Excitement ..................................... | 7 |

*(see also Kim D, Kim & Kinetics)*

## LARRY DAVIS/FENTON ROBINSON
| | | | |
|---|---|---|---|
| 72 | Python PLP 24 | LARRY DAVIS AND FENTON ROBINSON (LP, 99 copies only) .......................... | 90 |

## MAXWELL DAVIS
| | | | |
|---|---|---|---|
| 66 | Ember FA 2040 | BATMAN THEME AND OTHER BAT SONGS (LP)........................................... | 30 |

## MELVIN DAVIS
| | | | |
|---|---|---|---|
| 69 | Action ACT 4531 | Save It/This Love Was Meant To Be .............................................. | 35 |

## MILES DAVIS
| | | | |
|---|---|---|---|
| 53 | Esquire 20-017 | MILES DAVIS PLAYS (10") ........................................................ | 50 |
| 53 | Esquire 20-021 | MILES DAVIS ALL STARS (10") .................................................... | 50 |
| 53 | Vogue LDE 028 | MILES DAVIS ALL STARS (10") .................................................... | 50 |
| 54 | Esquire 20-052 | MILES DAVIS ALL STARS (A HIFI MODERN JAZZ JAM SESSION) (10") ................... | 50 |
| 54 | Vogue LDE 064 | MILES DAVIS AND HIS ORCHESTRA (10") ............................................ | 50 |
| 54 | Esquire 20-056 | MILES DAVIS ALL STARS (A SECOND HIFI MODERN JAZZ JAM SESSION) (10")............. | 50 |
| 54 | Capitol LC 6683 | CLASSICS IN JAZZ (10") ......................................................... | 40 |
| 55 | Esquire 20-041 | MILES DAVIS QUINTET (10") ...................................................... | 50 |
| 55 | Esquire 20-062 | DIG (10") ...................................................................... | 50 |
| 55 | Esquire 20-072 | MILES DAVIS QUINTET (10") ...................................................... | 50 |
| 56 | Esquire 32-012 | THE MUSINGS OF MILES ........................................................... | 45 |
| 55 | Esquire 32-021 | HIS NEW QUINTET (10") .......................................................... | 80 |
| 56 | Philips BBL 7140 | 'ROUND ABOUT MIDNIGHT .......................................................... | 50 |
| 57 | Esquire 32-028 | CHANGES ........................................................................ | 30 |
| 57 | Esquire 32-030 | BIRTH OF THE COOL .............................................................. | 50 |
| 57 | Vogue LDE 191 | NATURE BOY ..................................................................... | 40 |
| 57 | Fontana TFL 5007 | MILES AHEAD .................................................................... | 50 |
| 58 | Fontana TFL 5035 | MILESTONES ..................................................................... | 50 |
| 58 | Esquire 32-048 | COOKIN' ........................................................................ | 60 |
| 58 | Esquire 32-068 | RELAXIN' WITH THE MILES DAVIS QUARTET........................................... | 60 |
| 59 | Esquire 32-090 | BAGS' GROOVE.................................................................... | 40 |
| 59 | Fontana TFL 5056 | PORGY AND BESS (mono) .......................................................... | 30 |
| 59 | Fontana STFL 507 | PORGY AND BESS (stereo) ........................................................ | 40 |
| 60 | Fontana TFL 5081 | JAZZ TRACK — "L'ANSCENSEUR POUR L'ECHAFAUD" .................................... | 20 |
| 60 | Fontana TFL 5089 | THE MOST OF MILES .............................................................. | 20 |
| 60 | Fontana TFL 5072 | KIND OF BLUE (mono) ............................................................ | 60 |
| 60 | Fontana STFL 513 | KIND OF BLUE (stereo) .......................................................... | 60 |
| 60 | CBS SBPG 62066 | KIND OF BLUE (stereo) .......................................................... | 60 |
| 60 | CBS BPG 62066 | KIND OF BLUE (mono) ............................................................ | 60 |
| 60 | Esquire 32-088 | BLUE HAZE ...................................................................... | 25 |
| 60 | Esquire 32-098 | WALKIN'......................................................................... | 40 |
| 60 | Esquire 32-100 | MILES DAVIS AND THE MODERN JAZZ GIANTS VOL. 2 .................................. | 40 |
| 60 | Esquire 32-108 | WORKIN' WITH THE MILES DAVIS QUINTET ........................................... | 40 |
| 61 | Font. TFL 5100/STFL 531 | SKETCHES OF SPAIN .............................................................. | 40 |
| 61 | Esquire 32-118 | EARLY MILES .................................................................... | 20 |
| 61 | Esquire 32-138 | STEAMIN' WITH THE MILES DAVIS QUINTET .......................................... | 50 |
| 61 | Fontana TFL 5163 | FRIDAY NIGHT AT THE BLACKHAWK, SAN FRANCISCO (VOL. 1) (with Cannonball Adderley & John Coltrane; also stereo STFL 580) ...................................... | 35 |
| 61 | Fontana TFL 5164 | SATURDAY NIGHT AT THE BLACKHAWK, SAN FRANCISCO (VOL. 2) (with Cannonball Adderley & John Coltrane; also stereo STFL 581) .................................... | 35 |
| 62 | Fontana TFL 5172 | SOMEDAY MY PRINCE WILL COME (also stereo STFL 587) ............................. | 40 |
| 62 | Transatlantic PR 7254 | THE ORIGINAL QUINTET ........................................................... | 20 |
| 63 | CBS CL 2106 | QUIET NIGHTS (LP) .............................................................. | 35 |
| 63 | CBS BPG 62389 | MILES AND MONK AT NEWPORT (with Thelonious Monk, also stereo SBPG 62389)....... | 30 |
| 64 | Vocalion LAEF 584 | BLUE MOODS ..................................................................... | 20 |
| 65 | Stateside SL 10111 | MILES DAVIS AND JOHN COLTRANE .................................................. | 35 |
| 66 | CBS 62577 | E.S.P........................................................................... | 40 |
| 66 | Stateside SL 10168 | MILES DAVIS PLAYS FOR LOVERS................................................... | 20 |
| 66 | Fontana FJL 135 | BACK TO BACK ................................................................... | 25 |
| 67 | CBS 62933 | MILES SMILES (LP, stereo/mono) ................................................. | 40 |
| 67 | CBS 963097 | SORCERER (LP) .................................................................. | 40 |
| 67 | CBS 63248 | NEFERTITI (LP) ................................................................. | 40 |
| 68 | CBS 63352 | MILES IN THE SKY (LP) .......................................................... | 45 |
| 69 | CBS 63551 | FILLES DE KILIMANJARO (stereo) ................................................. | 45 |
| 69 | CBS 63630 | IN A SILENT WAY ................................................................ | 50 |
| 70 | CBS 64010 | BITCHES BREW (2-LP) ............................................................ | 50 |

MINT VALUE £

| 70 | CBS 70089 | A TRIBUTE TO JACK JOHNSON | 40 |
|----|-----------|---------------------------|-----|
| 71 | CBS 66257 | MILES DAVIS AT FILLMORE (2-LP) | 40 |
| 72 | CBS 64575 | LIVE-EVIL (2-LP, gatefold) | 40 |
| 72 | CBS 65246 | ON THE CORNER | 40 |
| 72 | Prestige PR 24001 | MILES DAVIS (2-LP) | 20 |
| 72 | Prestige PR 24012 | TALLEST TREES (2-LP) | 35 |
| 73 | CBS CQ 30997/Q 66236 | BITCHES BREW (2-LP, quadrophonic) | 40 |
| 73 | CBS GQ 30954/Q 67219 | LIVE-EVIL (2-LP, quadrophonic) | 40 |
| 73 | CBS 68222 | IN CONCERT (2-LP) | 30 |
| 74 | Columbia 88024 | BIG FUN (LP, gatefold) | 40 |
| 74 | CBS S80476 | GET UP WITH IT (2-LP) | 35 |
| 85 | CBS 62066 | KIND OF BLUE (LP, Nimbus Supercut, mail order from Practical Hi Fi magazine) | 125 |
| 87 | CBS 4606031 | KIND OF BLUE (LP, remastered CBS Jazz masterpieces series) | 15 |
| 87 | CBS 450982-1 | IN A SILENT WAY (LP, reissue, CBS Jazz masterpieces series) | 15 |
| 89 | CBS 463351-1 | AURA (2-LP) | 15 |
| 97 | Columbia 069897-1 | PANTHALASSA: THE REMIXES (2-LP) | 25 |
| 98 | Sony C4K 65570 | COMPLETE BITCHES BREW SESSIONS (5-CD box set) | 40 |
| 07 | Legacy 88697062392 | COMPLETE ON THE CORNER SESSIONS (6-CD, Metal box sleeve) | 50 |

## MILES DAVIS/ART BLAKEY

| 66 | Fontana FJL 135 | L'ASCENSEUR POUR L'ECHAFAUD/LA FEMME DISPARAISSANTE (LP, soundtrack, 1 side each) | 30 |
|----|-----------------|---------|-----|

*(see also Art Blakey, Thelonius Monk, Dizzy Gillespie, Milt Jackson, Cannonball Adderley, Charlie Parker)*

## PAT DAVIS

| 75 | Black Wax WAX 8 | I'm Just A Girl/SKIN, FLESH & BONES: Girl Version | 10 |
|----|-----------------|---------|-----|

## RONNIE DAVIS

| 75 | Angen ANG 104 | The Good News/AGGROVATORS: Version | 8 |
|----|---------------|---------|-----|
| 75 | Angen ANG 110 | Maga Lion/AGGROVATORS: Version | 8 |
| 75 | Attack ATT 8088 | I Lost My Lover/MATADOR ALL STARS: Bula Dub | 8 |
| 75 | Attack ATT 8116 | Tradition/Tradition (Version) | 8 |
| 75 | Live & Love LAL 04 | Jah Jah Jehovah/Version | 15 |
| 77 | Third World TWDIS 005 | Anywhere Don't Watch Your Woman (with Dillinger)/BARRY BROWN : Mr Money Man (12") | 25 |
| 77 | Hawkeye HE 011 | Used To Be My Girl/HAWKEYE IN SESSION - My Dub | 10 |
| 76 | Dip DLP 5028 | BEAUTIFUL PEOPLE FROM JAMAICA (LP) | 70 |
| 77 | Third World TWS 917 | HARD TIMES (LP) | 20 |

## SAMMY DAVIS (JNR.)

| 63 | Reprise R 20227 | The Shelter Of Your Arms/Falling In Love With You | 15 |
|----|-----------------|---------|-----|
| 64 | Reprise R 20289 | Not For Me/Bang Bang | 10 |
| 69 | MCA MK 1072 | Rhythm Of Life/Pompeii Club/Rich Man's Frug | 30 |
| 76 | 20th Century BTC 2292 | Baretta's Theme/I Heard A Song | 10 |
| 70 | Tamla Motown STML 11160 | SOMETHING FOR EVERYONE (LP) | 30 |

*(see also Dean Martin)*

## SANDY DAVIS

| 75 | EMI EMC 3070 | BACK ON MY FEET AGAIN (LP) | 15 |
|----|--------------|---------|-----|

## SILKIE DAVIS

| 70 | Torpedo TOR 2 | Conversations/TWIZZLE & HOT ROD ALL-STARS: Peace & Tranquility | 20 |
|----|---------------|---------|-----|
| 70 | Torpedo TOR 12 | When I Was A Little Girl/I'm So Lonely | 5 |

## SKEETER DAVIS

| 65 | RCA Victor RCA 1474 | Sun Glasses/He Loved Me Too Little | 10 |
|----|---------------------|---------|-----|

## SKEETER DAVIS & BOBBY BARE

| 65 | RCA RD 7711 | TUNES FOR TWO (LP) | 20 |
|----|-------------|---------|-----|

## SMILEY DAVIS

| 53 | London L 1189 | Big Mamou/Play Girl (78, actually by Smiley Lewis) | 80 |
|----|---------------|---------|-----|

## SPENCER DAVIS (GROUP)

| 64 | Fontana TF 471 | Dimples/Sittin' And Thinkin' | 30 |
|----|----------------|---------|-----|
| 64 | Fontana TF 499 | I Can't Stand It/Midnight Train | 25 |
| 65 | Fontana TF 530 | Every Little Bit Hurts/It Hurts Me So | 15 |
| 65 | Fontana TF 571 | Strong Love/This Hammer | 20 |
| 65 | Fontana TF 632 | Keep On Running/High Time Baby | 7 |
| 66 | Fontana TF 679 | Somebody Help Me/Stevie's Blues | 7 |
| 66 | Fontana TF 739 | When I Come Home/Trampoline | 10 |
| 66 | Fontana TF 762 | Gimme Some Loving/Blues In F | 7 |
| 67 | Fontana TF 785 | I'm A Man/I Can't Get Enough Of It | 12 |
| 67 | Fontana TF 854 | Time Seller/Don't Want You No More | 15 |
| 67 | United Artists UP 1203 | Mr. Second Class/Sanity Inspector | 10 |
| 68 | United Artists UP 2213 | After Tea/Moonshine | 10 |
| 68 | United Artists UP 2226 | Short Change/Picture Of Heaven | 10 |
| 73 | Vertigo 6059 076 | Catch You On the Rebop/The Edge | 10 |
| 73 | Vertigo 6059 087 | Livin' In A Back Street/Sure Need A Helping Hand | 10 |
| 65 | Fontana TE 17444 | YOU PUT THE HURT ON ME (EP) | 25 |
| 65 | Fontana TE 17450 | EVERY LITTLE BIT HURTS (EP) | 25 |
| 66 | Fontana TE 17463 | SITTIN' AND THINKIN' (EP) | 40 |
| 65 | Fontana TL 5242 | THEIR FIRST LP (LP, laminated front, black/silver label) | 90 |
| 66 | Fontana TL 5295 | THE SECOND ALBUM (LP, laminated front cover, flipbacks, island) label on rear) | 80 |
| 66 | Fontana TL 5359 | AUTUMN '66 (LP, laminated front sleeve, flipbacks. black/silver label) | 60 |
| 67 | United Artists ULP 1186 | HERE WE GO ROUND THE MULBERRY BUSH (LP, soundtrack, with Traffic, mono) | 50 |
| 67 | United Artists (S)ULP 1186 | HERE WE GO ROUND THE MULBERRY BUSH (LP, soundtrack, with Traffic, stereo) | 40 |
| 68 | United Artists ULP 1192 | WITH THEIR NEW FACE ON (LP, mono, blue/silver label) | 60 |
| 68 | United Artists (S)ULP 1192 | WITH THEIR NEW FACE ON (LP, stereo) | 50 |

| | | | |
|---|---|---|---|
| 68 | Wing WL 1165 | EVERY LITTLE BIT HURTS (LP, reissue of "Their First LP") | 15 |
| 68 | Island ILP 970 9070 | THE BEST OF THE SPENCER DAVIS GROUP FEATURING STEVIE WINWOOD (LP, plain pink label, flipback sleeve; sleeve lists "Please Do Something" but plays "Together Till The End Of Time", mono) | 30 |
| 68 | Island ILPS 9070 | THE BEST OF THE SPENCER DAVIS GROUP FEATURING STEVIE WINWOOD (LP, plain pink label, flipback sleeve; sleeve lists "Please Do Something" but plays "Together Till The End Of Time", stereo) | 15 |
| 69 | CBS 63842 | LETTERS FROM EDITH (LP, unissued, 50 white label test pressings only) | 500 |
| 71 | United Artists UAS 29177 | IT'S BEEN SO LONG (LP, solo with Peter Jameson, 'envelope' cover) | 20 |
| 72 | United Artists UAS 29361 | MOUSETRAP (LP, solo) | 20 |
| 73 | Vertigo 6360 088 | GLUGGO (LP, die cut, gatefold sleeve, 'spaceship' label) | 30 |
| 74 | Vertigo 6360 105 | LIVIN' IN A BACK STREET (LP) | 15 |

*(see also Stevie Winwood, Traffic, Anglos, Blind Faith, Ray Fenwick, Pete York, Hardin & York, Murgatroyd Band, Mirage, Portobello Explosion, Shotgun Express)*

## STEVE DAVIS
| | | | |
|---|---|---|---|
| 68 | Fontana TF 922 | Take Time To Know Her/She Said Yeah | 75 |

## TYRONE DAVIS
| | | | |
|---|---|---|---|
| 68 | Stateside SS 2092 | What If A Man/Bet You Win | 45 |
| 69 | Atlantic 584 253 | Can I Change My Mind/A Woman Needs To Be Loved | 20 |
| 69 | Atlantic 584 265 | Is It Something You've Got?/Undying Love | 15 |
| 69 | Atlantic 584 288 | All The Waiting Is Not In Vain/Need Your Lovin' Everyday | 15 |
| 70 | Atlantic 2091 003 | Turn Back The Hands Of Time/I Keep Coming Back | 15 |
| 71 | Atlantic 2091 078 | Could I Forget You/Just My Way Of Loving You | 15 |
| 71 | Atlantic 2091 131 | One Way Ticket/We Got A Love | 12 |
| 72 | Atlantic K 10207 | Can I Change My Mind/Turn Back The Hands Of Time/One Way Ticket | 12 |
| 73 | Brunswick BR 4 | Without You In My Life/How Could I Forget You | 10 |
| 73 | Brunswick BR 6 | There It Is/You Wouldn't Believe | 10 |
| 74 | Brunswick BR 10 | I Wish It Was Me/You Don't Have To Beg To Stay | 10 |
| 76 | Brunswick BR 31 | Turning Point/Don't Let It Be Too Late | 10 |
| 77 | Brunswick BR 40 | Ever Lovin' Girl/Forever | 10 |
| 70 | Atlantic 588 209 | CAN I CHANGE MY MIND (LP) | 30 |
| 71 | Atlantic 2465 021 | TURN BACK THE HANDS OF TIME (LP) | 30 |
| 73 | Brunswick BRLS 3002 | I HAD IT ALL THE TIME (LP) | 35 |
| 73 | Brunswick BRLS 3005 | GREATEST HITS (LP) | 18 |

## WALTER DAVIS
| | | | |
|---|---|---|---|
| 64 | RCA RCX 7169 | R.C.A. VICTOR RACE SERIES VOL. 3 (EP) | 15 |
| 70 | RCA Intl. INTS 1085 | THINK YOU NEED A SHOT (LP) | 15 |

## WARREN DAVIS MONDAY BAND
| | | | |
|---|---|---|---|
| 60s | Island WI 353 | How Can You Forget/Best News (test pressings only) | 50 |
| 60s | Island WIP 354 | Strain On My Heart/Question (test pressings only) | 50 |
| 67 | Columbia DB 8190 | Wait For Me/I Don't Wanna Hurt You | 30 |
| 67 | Columbia DB 8270 | Love Is A Hurtin' Thing/Without Fear | 20 |

*(see also Boardwalkers)*

## BRIAN DAVISON
| | | | |
|---|---|---|---|
| 70 | Charisma CAS 1021 | BRIAN DAVISON'S EVERY WHICH WAY (LP, pink 'scroll' label) | 40 |

*(see also Habits, Nice, Every Which Way, Refuge)*

## DAVISON BROTHERS
| | | | |
|---|---|---|---|
| 60 | Philips PB 1053 | Journey Of Love/Seven Days A Week | 60 |

## WILD BILL DAVISON
| | | | |
|---|---|---|---|
| 55 | Melodisc MLP 501 | WILD BILL DAVISON (LP) | 15 |

## TIM DAWE
| | | | |
|---|---|---|---|
| 69 | Straight ST(S) 1058 | PENROD (LP) | 70 |

## CARL DAWKINS
| | | | |
|---|---|---|---|
| 67 | Rio R 136 | All Of A Sudden/Running Shoes | 20 |
| 67 | Rio R 137 | Baby I Love You/Hard Time | 20 |
| 68 | Blue Cat BS 114 | I Love The Way You Are/DERMOTT LYNCH: I Can't Stand It | 100 |
| 68 | Duke DU 3 | I'll Make It Up/J.J. ALL STARS: One Dollar Of Music | 30 |
| 69 | Nu Beat NB 030 | Rodney's History/DYNAMITES: Tribute To Drumbano | 45 |
| 70 | Duke DU 93 | Get Together/FAMILY MAN: Instalment Plan | 12 |
| 70 | Duke DU 95 | This Land/J.J. ALL STARS: Land Version | 12 |
| 70 | Trojan TR 7765 | Satisfaction/Things A Get Bad To Worse | 12 |
| 71 | Big Shot BI 570 | Perseverance/J.J. ALL STARS: Perseverance (Version) | 12 |
| 71 | Explosion EX 2051 | I Feel Good/J.J. ALL STARS: I Feel Good Version Two | 10 |
| 71 | Explosion EX 2059 | Make It Great/STONE: What A Day | 10 |
| 71 | New Beat NB 086 | Walk A Little Prouder/YOUTH PROFESSIONALS: Walk (Version) | 10 |
| 72 | Duke DU 133 | My Whole World/Men A Broken Heart | 10 |

*(see also Rass Dawkins, Untouchables, Winston Wright, Ansell Collins, Roland Alphonso, West Indians)*

## HORRELL DAWKINS
| | | | |
|---|---|---|---|
| 66 | Ska Beat JB 240 | Cling To Me/Butterfly | 25 |

## JIMMY DAWKINS
| | | | |
|---|---|---|---|
| 73 | Mojo 2027 011 | The Things I Used To Do/Put It On The Hawg | 8 |
| 71 | Delmark DS 623 | FAST FINGERS (LP) | 30 |
| 78 | Sonet SNTF 758 | TRANSATLANTIC 770 (LP) | 15 |
| 82 | JSP 1042 | PLAY MY BLUES (LP) | 18 |
| 86 | JSP 1102 | ALL BLUES (LP) | 15 |
| 88 | JSP 1085 | FEEL THE BLUES (LP) | 15 |

## RASS DAWKINS (& WAILERS)
| | | | |
|---|---|---|---|
| 71 | Upsetter US 368 | Picture On The Wall/UPSETTERS: Picture Version | 25 |

*(see also Bob Marley/Wailers, Carl Dawkins)*

## DAWN AND CHRISTINE
78    Burning Rockers BRD 002    We Love Collie Weed (with Clint Eastwood)/LAWES ROCKERS: Collie Weed Version (12") ........................................................................................ 30

## JULIE DAWN
53    Columbia SCM 5035    Wild Horses/A Whistling Kettle And A Dancing Cat ...................... 10
*(see also Tony Brent & Julie Dawn, Cyril Stapleton)*

## DAWN TRADER
80    AFE 1980    NO ONE GONNA BETTER ME (EP, private pressing) ......................... 40

## DAWNBREAKERS
65    Decca F 12110    Let's Live/Lovin' For You ........................................................ 15

## DAWN CHORUS (1)
69    MCA MK 5004    A Night To Be Remembered/Crying All Night ........................... 15
*(see also Carter-Lewis)*

## DAWN CHORUS (2)
85    Dawn DAWN 1    Teenage Kicks/Dream Lover (p/s) ........................................... 18

## DAWN & DEEJAYS
65    RCA RCA 1470    These Are The Things About You/I Will Think Of You ............... 18

## DAWNWATCHER
80    Dawnwatcher DWS 001    Spellbound/Hall Of Mirrors ................................................. 75
82    Dawnwatcher DWS 002    Salvadors Dream/Backlash ................................................. 20

## DAWNWIND
76    Amron ARN 5003    LOOKING BACK ON THE FUTURE (LP, private pressing) ........... 80

## DONNA DAWSON
73    Trojan TR 7892    You Can't Buy Me Love/First Cut Is The Deepest ..................... 10

## LESLEY DAWSON
66    Mercury MF 924    Pastel Shades Of Love/The Time Has Come .............................. 5
67    Mercury MF 946    Just Say Goodbye/Just A Passing Phase ................................... 8
67    Mercury MF 965    Run For Shelter/I'll Climb On A Rainbow ................................. 35

## DANIELLE DAX
83    Initial IRC 009    POP-EYES (LP, with 'Meat Harvest' cover & lyric sheet) ........... 40
*(see also Lemon Kittens)*

## DAY
94    Detour DR 019    Another Country/Gospel (p/s, 100 on green vinyl) ..................... 7

## BING DAY
59    Mercury AMT 1047    I Can't Help It/Mama's Place .............................................. 60

## BOBBY DAY (& SATELLITES)
57    HMV POP 425    Little Bitty Pretty One/When The Swallows Come Back To Capistrano (as Bobby Day & Satellites) ........................................................................ 150
57    HMV POP 425    Little Bitty Pretty One/When The Swallows Come Back To Capistrano (as Bobby Day & Satellites) (78) ................................................................. 25
58    London HL 8726    Rockin' Robin/Over And Over .............................................. 10
59    London HL 8800    The Bluebird, The Buzzard And The Oriole/Alone Too Long ...... 40
59    London HL 8964    Love Is A One Time Affair/Ain't Gonna Cry No More ............... 10
60    London HLY 9044    My Blue Heaven/I Don't Want To ....................................... 15
61    Top Rank JAR 538    Over And Over/Gee Whiz .................................................. 20
65    Sue WI 388    Rockin' Robin/Over And Over (reissue) .................................... 15

## DORIS DAY & JOHNNIE RAY
53    Columbia SCM 5033    Ma Says, Pa Says/A Full Time Job ..................................... 20
*(see also Johnnie Ray)*

## HELEN DAY
76    Philips 6006 503    You Can Do It Better Than Me/I Got The Catch (with Catch) ....... 7
76    Philips 6006 531    Butter Wouldn't Melt In Your Mouth/Posessed (p/s) ............... 7

## JACKIE DAY
67    Sue WI 4040    Before It's Too Late/Without A Love ...................................... 250
09    Kent 6T 25    Get To Steppin/LARRY BANKS: My Life Is No Better ................. 20

## JILL DAY
55    Parlophone MSP 6169    Sincerely/Chee-Chee-Oo Chee (Sang The Little Bird) ........... 8
55    Parlophone MSP 6177    Promises/Whistlin' Willie ................................................. 8
56    HMV 7M 362    I Hear You Knocking/Far Away From Everybody ..................... 8
56    HMV 7M 391    A Tear Fell/Holiday Affair ..................................................... 8

## JOHNNY DAY
69    Stax STAX 111    Stay Baby Stay/I Love Love (listed as Johnny Daye on demos) ..... 20

## KENNY DAY
60    Top Rank JAR 339    Teenage Sonata/My Love Doesn't Love Me At All (p/s) ............ 10
61    Top Rank JAR 400    Why Don't We Do This More Often/The Sheik Of Morocco (p/s) ... 10

## MURIEL DAY
66    Pye 7N 17197    A Petal From A Faded Rose/I Wear His Heart .......................... 10
69    CBS 4115    The Wages Of Love/Thinking Of You ........................................ 15
69    Page One POF 151    Optimistic Fool/Nine Times Out Of Ten .............................. 60
69    Page One POF 151    Optimistic Fool/Nine Times Out Of Ten (DJ copy) ............... 100

## SYLVIA DAY
68    SNB 55-3859    You Don't Understand/Show A Little Love ............................... 10

## TANYA DAY & NU-NOTES
64    Polydor NH 52331    His Lips Get In The Way/I Get So Lonely .............................. 8

## TERRY DAY
62    CBS AAG 104    That's All I Want/I Waited Too Long ........................................ 20
*(see also Rip-Chords, Rogues)*

**DAYBREAKERS**
| | | | |
|---|---|---|---|
| 67 | John Hassell 814/5 | DAYBREAKERS (LP) | 60 |
| 67 | John Hassell HAS LP 1126 | VOL 2 (LP) | 60 |

**DAY BROTHERS**
| | | | |
|---|---|---|---|
| 60 | Oriole CB 1575 | Angel/Just One More Kiss | 20 |

**JOEL DAYDE**
| | | | |
|---|---|---|---|
| 71 | Barclay BAR 7 | Mammy Blue/You've Got Freedom | 25 |

**JENNIFER DAYE**
| | | | |
|---|---|---|---|
| 80 | Arawak ARK DD 018 | Together/Version (12") | 10 |

**DAYLIGHT**
| | | | |
|---|---|---|---|
| 71 | RCA RCA 2106 | Lady Of St. Clare/Wednesday People | 10 |
| 71 | RCA SF 8194 | DAYLIGHT (LP, gatefold sleeve, orange label) | 80 |

*(see also Daddy Longlegs)*

**DAYLIGHTERS**
| | | | |
|---|---|---|---|
| 64 | Sue WI 343 | Oh Mom! (Teach Me How To Uncle Willie)/Hard-Headed Girl | 45 |

**DAY N NIGHT**
| | | | |
|---|---|---|---|
| 70 | DJM DJS 220 | I Just Need Somebody/Such A Lot To Talk About | 12 |

**DAY OF THE PHOENIX**
| | | | |
|---|---|---|---|
| 70 | Greenwich GSLP 1002 | WIDE OPEN N-WAY (LP) | 100 |
| 72 | Chapter One CHS-R 812 | THE NEIGHBOUR'S SON (LP, red/silver label) | 70 |

**DAYSHIFT**
| | | | |
|---|---|---|---|
| 80 | Wot WOT 1 | Living In The UK/Cedric Wazza Superstar/Yeah Eh Oh Yeah (p/s) | 20 |

**DAYS OF 29**
| | | | |
|---|---|---|---|
| 85 | Trigger Happy TH 271284AA | DESTINATION D-DAY EP (12", p/s) | 12 |

**DAYS OF GRACE**
| | | | |
|---|---|---|---|
| 82 | DJM DJS 10988 | My Life Is A Video/21st Century (p/s) | 6 |

**DAYTRIPPERS**
| | | | |
|---|---|---|---|
| 71 | Trojan TR 7839 | The Birds And The Bees/My Family | 5 |

**DAZE (1)**
| | | | |
|---|---|---|---|
| 79 | Motor City Rhythm MCR10S | I Wanna Be A Star/At The Seaside | 300 |

**DAZE (2)**
| | | | |
|---|---|---|---|
| 83 | Mynah SDM 001 | Deep South/Made In America | 20 |

**BOBBY DAZZLER**
| | | | |
|---|---|---|---|
| 76 | Bigbear BB1 | Dance Dance Dance/Easy Lovin' Lady | 8 |

**DAZZLERS**
| | | | |
|---|---|---|---|
| 78 | Charisma CB 325 | Phonies/Kick Out (5,000 copies in fold-out p/s with poly bag) | 8 |
| 79 | Charisma CB 330 | Lovely Crash/Feeling In Your Heart (p/s) | 7 |
| 79 | Charisma CB 338 | Feeling Free/No One Ever Knows (p/s) | 10 |

**DBX**
| | | | |
|---|---|---|---|
| 93 | Peacefrog PF 015 | Alien EP (12", plain sleeve) | 15 |
| 94 | Peacefrog PF 022 | Losing Control/Beat Phreak/Live Wire/Spock's Brain (12", plain sleeve) | 22 |
| 95 | Peacefrog PR 025 | Losing Control Remixes (12", plain sleeve) | 20 |

**D.C. 10'S**
| | | | |
|---|---|---|---|
| 80 | Certain Euphoria ACE 451 | Bermuda/I Can See Through Walls | 10 |

**DDR**
| | | | |
|---|---|---|---|
| 90s | Smitten SMTLTD 05 | The Gift (12", 1-sided yellow vinyl, 500 only) | 60 |

**BOBBY DEACON**
| | | | |
|---|---|---|---|
| 60 | Pye 7N 15270 | A Fool Was I/Where's My Love? | 6 |
| 60 | Pye 7N 15299 | I Love You So/Your Kisses Are Fine | 5 |

**GEORGE DEACON & MARION ROSS**
| | | | |
|---|---|---|---|
| 73 | Xtra XTRA 1130 | SWEET WILLIAM'S GHOST (LP, with lyric insert) | 60 |

**DEAD PARROTS SOCIETY**
| | | | |
|---|---|---|---|
| 92 | Private Press MDNLP 001 | MUSIC OF A BYGONE AGE (LP) | 20 |

**DEADBEATS**
| | | | |
|---|---|---|---|
| 80 | Red Rhino RED 3 | Choose You/Julie's New Boyfriend (p/s) | 10 |

**DEAD BOYS**
| | | | |
|---|---|---|---|
| 77 | Sire SRE 1004 | Sonic Reducer/Down In Flames (no p/s) | 25 |
| 77 | Sire 6078 609 | Sonic Reducer/Little Girl/Down In Flames (12", p/s) | 15 |
| 78 | Sire SRE 1029 | Tell Me/Not Anymore/Ain't Nothin' To Do (p/s) | 25 |
| 77 | Sire 9103 329 | YOUNG, LOUD & SNOTTY (LP) | 25 |
| 78 | Sire SRK 6054 | WE HAVE COME FOR YOUR CHILDREN (LP) | 25 |
| 87 | Line LILP 400200 | NIGHT OF THE LIVING DEAD BOYS (LP) | 15 |
| 99 | Rude LP00010 | 3RD GENERATION NATION (LP, clear vinyl, mail order only) | 15 |

*(see also Stiv Bators, Lords Of The New Church, Wanderers)*

**DEAD CAN DANCE**
| | | | |
|---|---|---|---|
| 96 | 4AD DCD 2 | Nierika/Dedicace Outo/The Snake And The Moon (12", promo red vinyl, PVC sleeve) | 12 |
| 84 | 4AD CAD 404 | DEAD CAN DANCE (LP) | 20 |
| 85 | 4AD CAD 512 | SPLEEN AND IDEAL (LP) | 20 |
| 87 | 4AD CAD 705 | WITHIN THE REALM OF A DYING SUN (LP) | 25 |
| 88 | 4AD CAD 808 | THE SERPENT'S EGG (LP) | 25 |
| 90 | 4AD CAD 0007 | AION (LP) | 25 |
| 93 | 4AD DAD 3013 | INTO THE LABYRINTH (2-LP) | 40 |
| 94 | 4AD DAD 4015 | TOWARDS THE WITHIN (2-LP) | 35 |
| 96 | 4AD DAD 608 | SPIRITCHASER (2-LP) | 45 |
| 05 | The Show (No Cat. No.) | CHICAGO: 12th OCTOBER 2005 (3-LP, 500 only, signed and numbered) | 80 |
| 08 | Vinyl 180 VIN180LP003 | DEAD CAN DANCE (LP, reissue on 180gm vinyl, with free 12" on black or clear vinyl) | 20 |

| 08 | Vinyl 180 VIN180LP007 | SPLEEN AND IDEAL (LP, reissue 180gm vinyl) | 20 |
| 09 | Vinyl 180 VIN180LP011 | WITHIN THE REALMS OF A DYING SUN (LP, reissue, 180gm vinyl) | 20 |
| 09 | Vinyl 180 VIN180LP016 | THE SERPENTS EGG (LP, reissue 180gm vinyl) | 30 |
| 11 | Vinyl 180 VIN180LP028 | AION (LP, reissue 180gm vinyl) | 20 |
| 12 | PIAS PIAS R3313LP | IN CONCERT (3-LP box set) | 40 |
| 12 | PIAS PIASR311DLP | ANASTASIS (2-LP) | 20 |

## DEAD FINGERS TALK
| 79 | Pye 46156 | This Crazy World/The Boyfriend (p/s) | 20 |

## DEAD FLOWERS
| 87 | Lout 001 | TV/Fallout | 10 |
| 91 | Mystic Stones RUNE 2 | SMELL THE FRAGRANCE, FREE YOUR MIND (LP) | 15 |
| 92 | Mystic Stones RUNE 12 | MOONTAN (LP) | 15 |
| 94 | Delerium DELEC LP 022 | ALTERED STATE CIRCUS (LP) | 15 |

## DEAD KENNEDYS
| 80 | Fast Products FAST 12 | California Uber Alles/Man With The Dogs (p/s, moulded or paper labels) | 6 |
| 81 | Statik STAT EP 2 | IN GOD WE TRUST (12" EP, with insert) | 10 |
| 81 | Cherry Red CHERRY 13 | Holiday In Cambodia/Police Truck ('digger' p/s) | 5 |
| 81 | Cherry Red CHERRY 13 | Holiday In Cambodia/Police Truck ('burning man' p/s, with lyric sheet) | 6 |
| 81 | Cherry Red CHERRY T13 | Holiday In Cambodia/Police Truck (12") | 10 |
| 81 | Cherry CHERRY 16 | Kill The Poor/In-Sight (p/s) | 8 |
| 81 | Cherry CHERRY 24 | Too Drunk To Fuck/The Prey (p/s, with lyric sheet) | 5 |
| 82 | Statik STAT 24 | Nazi Punks Fuck Off/Moral Majority (p/s) | 7 |
| 82 | Statik STAT 22 | Bleed for Me/Life Sentence (p/s) | 7 |
| 82 | Statik STAT 27 | Halloween/Saturday Night Holocaust (p/s) | 7 |
| 81 | Cherry Red B RED 10 | FRESH FRUIT FOR ROTTING VEGETABLES (LP, with insert & 'Heads' pic on rear) | 25 |
| 80 | Cherry Red B RED 10 | FRESH FRUIT FOR ROTTING VEGETABLES (LP, with insert & without 'Heads' pic on rear) | 20 |
| 85 | Statik/Alternative Tentacles VIRUS 45 | FRANKENCHRIST (LP, with poster) | 20 |
| 86 | Statik/Alternative Tentacles VIRUS 50 | BEDTIME FOR DEMOCRACY (LP) | 15 |
| 87 | Alternative Tent. VIRUS 57 | GIVE ME CONVENIENCE... (LP, with booklet and "Buzzbomb From Pasadena" flexidisc) | 15 |

*(see also East Bay Ray, Lard)*

## DEADLINE
| 60s | Hollick & Taylor HT 137 | Glass Man/I'm In My Element | 300 |

## DEADLY HEADLEY
| 82 | On U Sound ONULP 14 | 35 YEARS FROM ALPHA (LP) | 30 |

## DEADLY TOYS
| 79 | Bonhard/Hunt DT 1 | Nice Weather/Roll On Doomsday/I'm Logical/Deadly Mess Around (EP, in hand-made gatefold sleeve) | 100 |
| 79 | Bonhard/Hunt DT 1 | Nice Weather/Roll On Doomsday/I'm Logical/Deadly Mess Around (EP) | 30 |

## DEAD MANS SHADOW
| 81 | Pig Records HOG 1 | Neighbours/Morons With Power/Poxy Politics/War Ploys (p/s and sticker) | 20 |
| 81 | Subversive Anarcho 1 | HEATHROW TOUCHDOWN (Shared EP with ACTION PACT) | 20 |
| 82 | Rondelet ROUND 16 | Bomb Scare/Another Hiroshima/Fighting For Reality (p/s) | 10 |
| 83 | Expulsion OUT 4 | Toleration Street/In My Dream (p/s) | 5 |

## DEAD MEADOW
| 03 | Matador OLE 566-1 | SHIVERING KING AND OTHERS (2-LP) | 35 |

## DEAD OR ALIVE
| 80 | Inevitable INEV 005 | I'm Falling/Flowers (foldout p/s) | 12 |
| 81 | Inevitable INEV 008 | Number Eleven/Name Game (live) (p/s) | 8 |
| 82 | Black Eyes BE 1 | It's Been Hours Now/Whirlpool/Nowhere To Nowhere/ It's Been Hours Now (Alternative Mix) (12", p/s) | 20 |
| 82 | Black Eyes BE 2 | The Stranger/Some Of That (p/s) | 8 |
| 83 | Epic A 3399 | Misty Circles/Misty Circles (Instrumental) (p/s) | 8 |
| 83 | Epic TA 3399 | Misty Circles (Dance Mix)/Misty Circles (Dub Mix)/Selfish Side (12", p/s) | 10 |
| 83 | Epic A 3676 | What I Want/The Stranger (Remix) (white 'floppy hat' p/s, withdrawn) | 35 |
| 83 | Epic TA 3676 | What I Want (Dance Mix)/The Stranger (12", p/s, with poster) | 15 |
| 84 | Epic XPR 1257 | MIGHTY MIX: Wish You Were Here/What I Want/Do It/Misty Circles/ Absolutely Nothing/Sit On It/You Make Me Wanna/That's The Way (I Like It) (12", white label, promo only) | 15 |
| 85 | Epic A 6086 | Lover Come Back To Me/Far Too Hard (blue p/s, withdrawn) | 150 |
| 87 | Epic XPR 1328 | CLEAN AND DIRTY: Something In My House (Mortevicar Mix)/Something In My House (Naughty XXX Mix) (12", white label, plain white sleeve) | 40 |
| 88 | Epic BURNSQ 4 | Turn Around And Count 2 Ten (I Had A Disco Dream Mix)/Something In My House (Instru-Mental)/Then There Was You/Come Inside (12", p/s autographed) | 15 |

*(see also Nightmares In Wax, Sisters Of Mercy, Pauline Murray & Invisible Girls, International Chrysis, Mission)*

## DEAD PREZ
| 99 | Epic 668986 | Hip Hop (Real Version)/It's Bigger Than Hip Hop (Real Version)/Selling D.O.P.E. (12", p/s) | 12 |
| 00 | Epic 496864-1 | LET'S GET FREE (2-LP) | 35 |

## DEAD SEA FRUIT
| 67 | Camp 602 001 | Kensington High Street/Put Another Record On | 20 |
| 68 | Camp 602 004 | Love At The Hippiedrome/My Naughty Bluebell | 20 |
| 67 | Camp 603 001 | DEAD SEA FRUIT (LP) | 100 |

## DEAD WEATHER
| 09 | Third Man TMR 001 | Hang You From The Heavens/Are Friends Electric? (luminous vinyl, 'Halloween' cover, 100-only) | 100 |

*(see also The Kills/White Stripes/Raconteurs)*

## DEADWOOD
| | | | |
|---|---|---|---|
| 71 | Decca F13109 | The Turning Of Them All/They Don't Help Me None | 45 |
| 71 | Decca F13179 | Me And My Friends/Little Joe | 12 |

## DEAD WRETCHED
| | | | |
|---|---|---|---|
| 82 | Inferno HELL 5 | Convicted/Infiltrator (p/s) | 5 |
| 82 | Tempest HELL 2 | NO HOPE FOR ANYONE EP | 20 |

## DEAF AIDS
| | | | |
|---|---|---|---|
| 79 | Regana REG 1 | DO IT AGAIN EP (250 copies only) | 100 |
| 80 | Conspiracy CONS1 | Heroes/Bored Christine (p/s) | 15 |

## BILL DEAL & RHONDELLS
| | | | |
|---|---|---|---|
| 69 | MGM MGM 1466 | May I/Day By Day My Love Grows Stronger | 6 |
| 69 | MGM MGM 1479 | I've Been Hurt/I've Got My Needs | 15 |
| 69 | MGM MGM 1488 | What Kind Of Fool Do You Think I Am/Are You Ready For This | 10 |

## MICHAEL DE ALBUQUERQUE
| | | | |
|---|---|---|---|
| 74 | RCA SF 8383 | WE MAY BE CATTLE BUT WE ALL HAVE NAMES (LP, with lyric sheet) | 20 |

*(see also E.L.O., Michael Albuquerque)*

## DEALER
| | | | |
|---|---|---|---|
| 83 | Windrush WR 1030 | Better Things To Do/Suspected Foul Play (p/s) | 100 |

## DEALERS
| | | | |
|---|---|---|---|
| 76 | Private Stock PVT 73 | Midnight Dog/Higher Than God's Hat | 6 |

## ALAN DEAN
| | | | |
|---|---|---|---|
| 57 | Columbia DB 3932 | Rock 'n' Roll Tarantella/Life Is But A Dream | 10 |

## ALAN DEAN & HIS PROBLEMS
| | | | |
|---|---|---|---|
| 64 | Decca F 11947 | The Time It Takes/Dizzy Heights | 40 |
| 65 | Pye 7N 15749 | Thunder And Rain/As Time Goes By | 60 |

## LITTLE BILLY DEAN
| | | | |
|---|---|---|---|
| 67 | Strike JH 325 | That's Always Like You/Tic Toc | 20 |

## DEREK DEAN & FRESHMEN
| | | | |
|---|---|---|---|
| 66 | Pye 7N 17037 | So This Is Love/King Cole Yenka | 5 |

*(see also Derek & Freshmen)*

## ELTON DEAN
| | | | |
|---|---|---|---|
| 71 | CBS 64539 | ELTON DEAN (LP) | 60 |
| 77 | Ogun OG 610 | THE CHEQUE IS IN THE MAIL (LP, with Joe Gallivan & Kenny Wheeler) | 20 |
| 78 | Ogun OG 530 | THE BOLOGNA TAPE (LP) | 25 |

*(see also Bluesology, Soft Machine, Centipede, Ninesense, Julie Tippetts, Hugh Hopper, Mike Hugg, Reg King, Keith Tippett)*

## EMIL DEAN
| | | | |
|---|---|---|---|
| 67 | CBS 3106 | Ave Maria/Now You're Gone | 6 |
| 68 | Island WIP 6033 | This Is Our Anniversary/Lonely Boy | 12 |
| 69 | Mercury MF 1071 | It's Only Make Believe/One Broken Heart For Sale | 6 |

*(see also Nirvana [UK])*

## HAZELL DEAN
| | | | |
|---|---|---|---|
| 75 | Decca F 13613 | Our Day Will Come/Instrumental | 6 |
| 76 | Decca F 13668 | Got You Where I Want You/You Were There | 6 |
| 77 | Decca F 13683 | Look What I've Found At The End Of A Rainbow/Where Are We Going | 6 |
| 77 | Decca F 13736 | No One's Ever Gonna Love You (The Way That I Love You)/Just One More Time | 6 |
| 77 | Decca F 13751 | Who Was That Lady (I Saw You With)/One Bad Mistake | 6 |
| 81 | Carlin Music Corp. CMC 1004 | THE SOUND OF BACHARACH & DAVID (LP, promo only) | 25 |

## JIMMY DEAN
| | | | |
|---|---|---|---|
| 59 | Philips PB 940 | Weekend Blues/Sing Along | 5 |
| 60 | Philips PB 984 | There's Still Time, Brother/Thanks For The Dream | 5 |

## NORA DEAN
| | | | |
|---|---|---|---|
| 69 | Upsetter US 322 | The Same Thing You Gave To Daddy/UPSETTER PILGRIMS: A Testimony | 60 |
| 70 | Trojan TR 7735 | Barbwire/BRONS: Calypso Mama | 40 |
| 71 | Randy's RAN 508 | Want Man/RANDY'S ALL STARS: Man | 25 |
| 71 | High Note HS 050 | I Must Get A Man/The Valet | 20 |
| 71 | Bullet BU 472 | Peace Begins Within/SLICKERS: Go Back Home | 100 |
| 71 | Gas GAS 165 | Greedy Boy/KEITH: Please Stay (B-side actually by Slim Smith) | 20 |
| 72 | Big Shot BI 611 | Night Food Reggae/PROPHETS: Jaco | 20 |
| 73 | Bread BR 1117 | Mama/Man A Walk And Talk | 20 |
| 74 | Harry j HJ6668 | Eddie My Love/What Is Your Plan (with Jackie Brown) | 12 |
| 76 | Attack ATT 8126 | Scorpion/Version | 20 |
| 11 | Harry J THB 7013 | Mama/SOUL SYNDICATE: Natty In Hong Kong | 25 |
| 79 | Nationwide NWLP 007 | PLAY ME A LOVE SONG (LP) | 30 |

*(see also Hugh Roy)*

## PAUL DEAN (& SOUL SAVAGES)
| | | | |
|---|---|---|---|
| 65 | Decca F 12136 | You Don't Own Me/Hole In The Head (as Paul Dean & Thoughts) | 18 |
| 66 | Reaction 591 002 | She Can Build A Mountain/A Day Gone By (as Paul Dean & Soul Savages) | 15 |

*(see also Oscar, Thoughts)*

## PAULA DEAN & NYAH SHUFFLE
| | | | |
|---|---|---|---|
| 70 | Joe's JRS 2 | Since I Met You Baby/Jug Head | 20 |

## ROGER DEAN'S LYSIS
| | | | |
|---|---|---|---|
| 77 | Mosaic GCM 762 | LYSIS LIVE (LP) | 15 |
| 77 | Mosaic GCM 774 | CYCLE (LP) | 15 |

## TRACEY DEAN
| | | | |
|---|---|---|---|
| 74 | Decca FR 13497 | Moonshiner/Boy On The Ball | 10 |

## DEAN & JEAN
| | | | |
|---|---|---|---|
| 64 | Stateside SS 249 | Tra La La La Suzy/I Love The Summertime | 20 |

| | | | |
|---|---|---|---|
| 64 | Stateside SS 283 | Hey Jean Hey Dean/Please Don't Tell Me How | 20 |
| 64 | Stateside SS 313 | Thread Your Needle/I Wanna Be Loved | 20 |

*(see also Brenda Lee Jones)*

**DEAN & MARK**

| | | | |
|---|---|---|---|
| 64 | Hickory 45-1227 | With Tears In My Eyes/Kissin' Games | 10 |
| 64 | Hickory 45-1249 | When I Stop Dreaming/There Oughta Be A Law | 10 |
| 65 | Hickory 45-1294 | Just A Step Away/Fallen Star | 10 |

*(see also Newbeats, Larry Henley)*

**JASON DEANE**

| | | | |
|---|---|---|---|
| 66 | King KG 1049 | Make Believe/Don't Ever Want To See You No More | 30 |
| 67 | King KG 1060 | Down In The Street/Ain't Got No Love | 40 |

*(see also Jason Dene)*

**DEANO**

| | | | |
|---|---|---|---|
| 65 | Columbia DB 7728 | Just A Child In This World/Little Miss With-It | 10 |
| 66 | Columbia DB 7898 | Starlight, Starbright/I'm So Happy | 10 |
| 66 | Columbia DB 7965 | Please Don't Talk To The Lifeguard/When You Wish Upon A Star | 15 |
| 67 | Columbia DB 8233 | What's The Matter With The Matador?/Baby, Let Me Be Your Baby | 10 |
| 65 | Columbia SEG 8470 | DEANO (EP) | 40 |

**BLOSSOM DEARIE**

| | | | |
|---|---|---|---|
| 66 | Fontana TF 719 | I'm Hip/Wallflower Lonely, Cornflower Blue | 8 |
| 67 | Fontana TF 788 | Sweet Georgie Fame/One Note Samba | 8 |
| 67 | Fontana TF 886 | Once I Loved/Sunny | 8 |
| 67 | Fontana TF 934 | The Music Played/Discover Who I Am | 8 |
| 68 | Fontana TF 986 | Hey John/59th Street Bridge Song | 8 |
| 67 | Fontana TL 5399 | SWEET BLOSSOM DEARIE (LP) | 45 |
| 67 | Fontana TL 5352 | BLOSSOM TIME AT RONNIE'S (LP) | 55 |
| 67 | Fontana STL 5454 | SOON IT'S GONNA RAIN (LP) | 40 |
| 70 | Fontana 6309 015 | THAT'S THE WAY I WANT IT TO BE (LP) | 80 |

**DEAR MR. TIME**

| | | | |
|---|---|---|---|
| 70 | Square SQ 3 | Prayer For Her/Light Up A Light | 50 |
| 71 | Square SQA 101 | GRANDFATHER (LP, black/white label) | 200 |

**DEATH**

| | | | |
|---|---|---|---|
| 87 | Under One Flag FLAG 12 | SCREAM BLOODY GORE (LP, with inner sleeve) | 15 |
| 88 | Under One Flag FLAG 24 | LEPROSY (LP, inner) | 20 |
| 90 | Under One Flag FLAG 38 | SPIRITUAL HEALING (LP) | 20 |
| 90 | Under One Flag FLAG 38 | SPIRITUAL HEALING (LP, picture disc) | 25 |
| 92 | Under One Flag M FLAG 71 | FATE (LP) | 15 |
| 07 | Back On Black BOBV 055 | SCREAM BLOODY GORE (2-LP, reissue, orange vinyl, 500 only) | 20 |
| 07 | Back On Black BOBV 056 | LEPROSY (LP, reissue, red and white splatter vinyl, gatefold p/s) | 15 |
| 07 | Back On Black BOBV 058 | HUMAN (LP, reissue, red splatter vinyl) | 15 |
| 07 | Back On Black BOBV 059 | INDIVIDUAL THOUGHT PATTERNS (LP, reissue, red splatter vinyl) | 15 |
| 07 | Back On Black BOBV 059 | INDIVIDUAL THOUGHT PATTERNS (LP, reissue, clear vinyl) | 15 |
| 08 | Back On Black BOBV 071 | THE SOUND OF PERSEVERANCE (2-LP, reissue, red splatter vinyl, gatefold) | 18 |
| 09 | Black Sleeves BLACK 113 | LIVE IN L.A. (DEATH & RAW) (2-LP reissue) | 18 |

**DEATH ADDICT**

| | | | |
|---|---|---|---|
| 83 | Stench STN 1 | Killing Time/Dead And Buried (p/s) | 12 |

**DEATH ANGEL**

| | | | |
|---|---|---|---|
| 87 | Under One Flag FLAG 14 | THE ULTRA-VIOLENCE (LP) | 20 |

**DEATH CAB FOR CUTIE**

| | | | |
|---|---|---|---|
| 02 | Fierce Panda NING 116 | I Was A Kaleidoscope/405 (Acoustic) (p/s) | 6 |
| 02 | Fierce Panda NING 126 | We Laugh Indoors (New Mix)/Debate Exposed Doubt (Acoustic SBN Session Track) (p/s) | 8 |
| 03 | Fierce Panda NING 149 | The New Year/TV Trays (p/s) | 8 |
| 04 | Fierce Panda NING 158 | The Sound Of Settling/This Charming Man (p/s) | 10 |
| 06 | Atlantic AT 0246X | I Will Follow You Into The Dark/Brothers On A Hotel Bed (Rolling Stone Originals Session) (Orange vinyl, poster p/s) | 5 |
| 06 | Atlantic AT 0246 | I Will Follow You Into The Dark/Photobooth (Rolling Stone Originals Session) blue vinyl, poster p/s) | 5 |
| 11 | Atlantic 7567 88268-4 | In Living Stereo (1-sided, white die-cut sleeve, Record Store Day release, 300 only) | 5 |
| 98 | Sonic Boom SBR 002 | SOMETHING ABOUT AIRPLANES (LP) | 25 |
| 03 | Sonic Boom SBR 012 | TRANSATLANTICISM (2-LP) | 30 |

**DEATH CULT**

| | | | |
|---|---|---|---|
| 83 | Situation 2 SIT 29 | God's Zoo/God's Zoo (These Times) (p/s) | 5 |

*(see also Cult, Southern Death Cult)*

**DEATH IN JUNE**

| | | | |
|---|---|---|---|
| 84 | New European SA 29634 | Heaven Street/We Drive East/In The Night Time (12", 2,000 with brown/gold embossed/textured sleeve) | 60 |
| 84 | New European SA 29634 | Heaven Street/We Drive East/In The Night Time (12", later pressing of 2,000 with blue/white sleeve) | 50 |
| 84 | New European SA 30634 | State Laughter/Holy Water (p/s) | 40 |
| 84 | New European BADVC 6 | She Said Destroy/The Calling (p/s) | 25 |
| 84 | New European 12BADVC 6 | The Calling/She Said Destroy/Doubt To Nothing (12", p/s with insert) | 35 |
| 85 | New European BADVC 69 | Born Again/The Calling (Mk II)/Carousel (Bolt Mix) (12", p/s) | 25 |
| 85 | New European BADVC 73 | ...And Murder Love/A.M.L. (Instrumental) (p/s) | 25 |
| 85 | New European 12BADVC73 | Come Before Christ And Murder Love/Torture By Roses (12", p/s) | 25 |
| 87 | New European BADVC 10 | To Drown A Rose/Zimmerit/Europa/The Gates Of Heaven (10", p/s) | 20 |
| 88 | Cenaz CENAZ 09 | Born Again/The Calling (Mk II)/Carousel (Remix) (12" picture disc, 1st pressing with silver print & rim, 970 only) | 25 |
| 88 | Cenaz CENAZ 09 | Born Again/The Calling (Mk II)/Carousel (Remix) (12" picture disc, 2nd pressing bronze print & rim) | 20 |

MINT VALUE £

| 94 | Twilight Command NERO I | SUNDOGS (Rose Clouds Of Holocaust/13 Years Of Carrion) (p/s with sticker) | 7 |
| 92 | New European BADVC 8 | CATHEDRAL OF TEARS (12" EP, picture disc with sticker) | 25 |
| 93 | New European BADVC 63 | PARADISE RISING (12" EP) | 18 |
| 96 | Twilight. Command NERO XIII | Kapo!/Occidental Martyr (p/s) | 18 |
| 85 | New European BADVC 3 | THE GUILTY HAVE NO PRIDE (LP) | 40 |
| 92 | Leprosy UBADVC 4 | BURIAL (LP, standard sleeve, green vinyl) | 40 |
| 80s | Leprosy UBADVC 4 | BURIAL (LP, 'quilted' sleeve, brown, pink, white & other coloured vinyl) | 60 |
| 90s | Leprosy UBADVC 4 | BURIAL (LP, textured sleeve, various coloured vinyl) | 35 |
| 85 | New European BADVC 13 | NADA (LP, blue sleeve) | 40 |
| 85 | New European BADVC 13 | NADA (LP, brown sleeve) | 25 |
| 85 | New European BADVC 13 | NADA (LP, picture disc) | 15 |
| 86 | New European BADVC 726 | LESSON ONE: MISANTHROPY (LP, embossed sleeve with insert) | 25 |
| 87 | New European BADVC 11 | BROWN BOOK (LP, textured sleeve with inner & insert; export copies with extra inserts & postcards) | 35 |
| 87 | New European BADVC 11 | BROWN BOOK (LP, textured sleeve with inner & insert) | 25 |
| 88 | New European BADVC 9 | THE WORLD THAT SUMMER (2-LP, gatefold textured sleeve) | 30 |
| 88 | New European BADVC 88 | WALL OF SACRIFICE (LP, red sleeve) | 70 |
| 88 | New European BADVC 88 | WALL OF SACRIFICE (LP, green/yellow sleeve) | 40 |
| 89 | New European BADVC 93 | 93 DEAD SUN WHEELS (mini-LP, with Current 93) | 20 |
| 92 | Leprosy LEPER 2 | NIGHT AND FOG (LP, red vinyl, 1,000 only) | 30 |
| 93 | New European BADVC 36 | BUT WHAT ENDS WHEN THE SYMBOLS SHATTER (LP, with inner & insert, 500 on purple vinyl) | 40 |
| 93 | New European BADVC 36 | BUT WHAT ENDS WHEN THE SYMBOLS SHATTER (LP, with inner & insert, 3,000 on black vinyl) | 20 |
| 93 | New European BADVCCD 96 | SOMETHING IS COMING (2-CD, digipak, 5,000 only) | 25 |
| 95 | New European BADVC 39 | BLACK WHOLE OF LOVE (box set with 12", 10", 7" & CDs with inserts) | 30 |
| 99 | New European BAD VC44 | OPERATION HUMMINGBIRD (LP, with inner and postcards) | 25 |

*(see also Crisis, Current 93, Boyd Rice & Friends, Sol Invictus)*

## DEATH IN VEGAS
| 03 | Concrete HARD 550 | So You Say You've Lost Your Baby (7", pink vinyl, white labels featuring Paul Weller) | 25 |
| 97 | Concrete HARD 22 LP 12 | DEAD ELVIS (2-LP) | 20 |
| 99 | Concrete HARD 41 LP | CONTINO SESSIONS (2-LP) | 30 |
| 02 | Concrete HARD 5312 | SCORPIO RISING (2-LP, gatefold sleeve with inners) | 20 |
| 04 | Drone DRONELP ONE | SATAN'S CIRCUS (3-LP) | 25 |
| 11 | Portabello PORT 1 LP | TRANS-LOVE ENERGIES (2-LP) | 18 |

## DEATH SENTENCE
| 82 | Beat The System DEATH 1 | DEATH & PURE DESTRUCTION (EP) | 10 |

## DEATH FROM ABOVE
| 05 | 679 LO78X | Blood On Our Hands/Better Off Dead (p/s, red vinyl) | 5 |

## DEB MUSIC PLAYERS
| 78 | Deb DEB LP 003 | UMOJA - LOVE AND UNITY (LP) | 45 |

## DE BLANC
| 75 | Arista 35 | Oh No, Not My Baby/Guava Jelly | 6 |

## DEBONAIRES (U.K.)
| 66 | Pye 7N 17151 | A Love Of Our Own/The Night Meets The Dawn | 5 |
| 66 | Pye 7N 17204 | Crying Behind Your Smile/Forever More | 5 |

## DEBONAIRES (U.S.)
| 70 | Track 604 035 | I'm In Love Again/Headache In My Heart | 50 |

## DEBONAIRS
| 63 | Parlophone R 5054 | That's Right/When True Love Comes Your Way | 5 |

## DEBS
| 65 | Mercury MF 888 | Sloopy's Gonna Hang On/Under A Street Light | 10 |

## DEB-TONES
| 59 | RCA RCA 1137 | Knock, Knock — Who's There?/I'm In Love Again | 25 |

## DEBUTANTES
| 80 | Rok ROK XVII/XVIII | Man In The Street/INNOCENT BYSTANDERS: Where Is Johnny (company sleeve) | 6 |

## DECADES BY NIGHT
| 81 | Slip 001 | Life Spiral/SONS OF MONKEYS: Me And Mr. Suzuki | 50 |

## DECAMERON
| 73 | Vertigo 6360 097 | SAY HELLO TO THE BAND (LP) | 18 |
| 73 | Mooncrest CREST 19 | MAMMOTH SPECIAL (LP, lyric insert) | 30 |
| 75 | Transatlantic TRA 304 | THIRD LIGHT (LP) | 20 |
| 76 | Transatlantic TRA 325 | TOMORROW'S PANTOMIME (LP) | 25 |

## YVONNE DE CARLO
| 55 | Capitol CL 14380 | Take It Or Leave It/Three Little Stars | 8 |

## PAULO DE CARVALHO
| 74 | Pye International 7N 25647 | (And Then) After Love/E Depois Do Adeus (p/s) | 10 |

## DE CASTRO SISTERS
| 54 | London HL 8104 | Teach Me Tonight/It's Love | 20 |
| 55 | London HL 8137 | Boom Boom Boomerang/Let Your Love Walk In | 20 |
| 55 | London HL 8158 | I'm Bewildered/To Say You're Mine | 15 |
| 55 | London HLU 8189 | If I Ever Fall In Love/Cuckoo In The Clock | 20 |
| 55 | London HLU 8212 | Christmas Is A-Comin'/Snowbound For Christmas | 15 |
| 56 | London HLU 8228 | Give Me Time/Too Late Now | 15 |
| 56 | London HLU 8296 | No One To Blame But You/Cowboys Don't Cry | 15 |
| 58 | HMV POP 527 | Who Are They To Say?/When You Look At Me | 5 |
| 59 | HMV POP 583 | Teach Me Tonight Cha Cha/The Things I Tell My Pillow | 5 |

MINT VALUE £

## DECEMBER
| | | |
|---|---|---|
| 96 | Elfenblut SAG 44 | River Of Blood/Venus In Chains (red vinyl, p/s, 1000 only) ........................ 10 |

## DECISION
| | | |
|---|---|---|
| 68 | MCA MU 1027 | In The Shade Of Your Love/Constable Jones ........................ 7 |

## DECISIONS
| | | |
|---|---|---|
| 71 | A&M 844 | It's Love That Really Counts In The Long Run/I Can't Forget About You ........................ 18 |

## DIANA DECKER
| | | |
|---|---|---|
| 54 | Columbia SCM 5083 | Oh, My Papa/Crystal Ball ........................ 10 |
| 54 | Columbia SCM 5096 | The Happy Wanderer/Till We Two Are One ........................ 10 |
| 54 | Columbia SCM 5120 | Jilted/The Man With The Banjo ........................ 10 |
| 54 | Columbia SCM 5123 | Kitty In The Basket/Never Never Land ........................ 10 |
| 54 | Columbia SCM 5130 | Mama Mia/Percy The Penguin ........................ 10 |
| 54 | Columbia SCM 5145 | Sisters/Abracadabra ........................ 15 |
| 55 | Columbia SCM 5166 | Open The Window Of Your Heart/The Violin Song ........................ 6 |
| 55 | Columbia SCM 5173 | Apples, Peaches And Cherries/Paper Valentine ........................ 6 |
| 56 | Columbia SCM 5246 | Rock-A-Boogie Baby/Willie Can ........................ 30 |

*(see also Ray Burns, Ruby Murray)*

## DECLINO
| | | |
|---|---|---|
| 85 | Children Of the Revolution GURT 7 | MUCCHIO SELVAGGIO (split LP with NEGAZIONE) ........................ 75 |

## DECORATORS
| | | |
|---|---|---|
| 81 | New Hormones ORG 5 | Twilight View/Reflections (p/s) ........................ 5 |

## NINA DECOSTA
| | | |
|---|---|---|
| 80 | Rokel ROK 12 | Don't Want To Lose You/Instrumental Version (12") ........................ 40 |

## DECOYS
| | | |
|---|---|---|
| 64 | Studio 36 KEP 108 | DECOYS (EP, 500 only) ........................ 30 |

## DE DANAAN
| | | |
|---|---|---|
| 82 | Cara CARA 1 | Hey Jude/St. Jude's Hornpipe/Trip To Taum Reel/Teetoaller ........................ 5 |
| 75 | Polydor 2904 005 | DE DANAAN (LP) ........................ 15 |
| 77 | Decca SKL-R 5287 | DE DANAAN — SELECTED JIGS AND REELS (LP) ........................ 18 |

## DEDICATED MEN'S JUG BAND
| | | |
|---|---|---|
| 65 | Piccadilly 7N 35245 | Boodle-Am-Shake/Come On Boys ........................ 5 |
| 66 | Piccadilly 7N 35283 | Don't Come Knocking/One Time Blues ........................ 5 |

## DEDRINGER
| | | |
|---|---|---|
| 80 | DinDisc DIN 10 | Sunday Drivers/We Don't Mind (p/s) ........................ 5 |
| 80 | DinDisc DIN 11 | Innocent 'Till Proven Guilty/Maxine//Took A Long Time/We Don't Mind (double pack) . 8 |
| 81 | DinDisc DIN 12 | Direct Line/She's Not Ready (p/s) ........................ 5 |
| 82 | Neat NEAT 18 | Hot Lady/Hot Licks And Rock'N'Roll (p/s) ........................ 5 |

## DAVE DEE, DOZY, BEAKY, MICK & TICH
| | | |
|---|---|---|
| 65 | Fontana TF 531 | No Time/Is It Love ........................ 25 |
| 65 | Fontana TF 586 | All I Want/It Seems A Pity ........................ 25 |
| 65 | Fontana TF 630 | You Make It Move/I Can't Stop ........................ 10 |
| 66 | Fontana TL 5350 | DAVE DEE, DOZY, BEAKY, MICK & TICH (LP) ........................ 20 |
| 66 | Fontana TL 5388 | IF MUSIC BE THE FOOD OF LOVE PREPARE FOR INDIGESTION (LP, mono) ........................ 20 |
| 66 | Fontana STL 5388 | IF MUSIC BE THE FOOD OF LOVE PREPARE FOR INDIGESTION (LP, stereo) ........................ 25 |
| 67 | Fontana (S)TL 5441 | GOLDEN HITS OF DAVE DEE, DOZY, BEAKY, MICK & TICH (LP) ........................ 15 |
| 68 | Fontana (S)TL 5471 | IF NO-ONE SANG (LP) ........................ 15 |

*(see also Dozy Beaky Mick & Tich [D,B,M & T])*

## JAY DEE
| | | |
|---|---|---|
| 74 | Warner Bros. 7798 | Strange Games And Funky Things/Intrumental ........................ 7 |

## JEANNIE DEE
| | | |
|---|---|---|
| 69 | Beacon BEA 115 | Come Into My Arms/Sun Shine On Me ........................ 7 |
| 69 | Beacon BEA 142 | Don't Go Home My Little Darling/Come See About Me ........................ 15 |

## JOEY DEE & STARLI(GH)TERS
| | | |
|---|---|---|
| 61 | Columbia DB 4758 | Peppermint Twist (Parts 1 & 2) ........................ 5 |
| 62 | Columbia DB 4803 | Hey, Let's Twist/Roly Poly ........................ 5 |
| 62 | Columbia DB 4842 | Shout (Parts 1 & 2) ........................ 5 |
| 62 | Columbia DB 4862 | Ya Ya/Fanny Mae ........................ 5 |
| 62 | Columbia DB 4905 | What Kind Of Love Is This?/Wing Ding ........................ 5 |
| 63 | Columbia DB 4955 | I Lost My Baby/Keep Your Mind On What You're Doin' ........................ 5 |
| 63 | Columbia DB 7005 | Baby You're Driving Me Crazy/Help Me Pick Up The Pieces ........................ 5 |
| 63 | Columbia DB 7055 | Hot Pastrami With Mashed Potatoes (Parts 1 & 2) ........................ 5 |
| 63 | Columbia DB 7102 | Dance, Dance, Dance/Let's Have A Party (features Ronettes uncredited) ........................ 5 |
| 63 | Columbia DB 7277 | Down By The Riverside/Getting Nearer (features Ronettes uncredited) ........................ 5 |
| 61 | Columbia 33SX 1406 | DOIN' THE TWIST LIVE AT THE PEPPERMINT LOUNGE (LP) ........................ 15 |
| 62 | Columbia 33SX 1461 | BACK AT THE PEPPERMINT LOUNGE (LP) ........................ 15 |
| 62 | Columbia 33SX 1502 | ALL THE WORLD IS TWISTIN' (LP) ........................ 15 |
| 63 | Columbia 33SX 1532 | JOEY DEE (LP) ........................ 15 |
| 63 | Columbia 33SX 1607 | DANCE DANCE DANCE (LP, with Starlighters, also with Ronettes uncredited) ........................ 15 |

*(see also Young Rascals)*

## JOHNNIE DEE
| | | |
|---|---|---|
| 65 | Columbia DB 7612 | Frankie's Angel/Everything's Upside Down ........................ 7 |

## JOHNNY DEE
| | | |
|---|---|---|
| 57 | Oriole CB 1367 | Sittin' In The Balcony/A-Plus Love ........................ 150 |
| 57 | Oriole CB 1367 | Sittin' In The Balcony/A-Plus Love (78) ........................ 20 |

*(see also John D. Loudermilk)*

## KIKI DEE

| | | | |
|---|---|---|---|
| 63 | Fontana TF 394 | Early Night/Lucky High Heels | 25 |
| 63 | Fontana TF 414 | Don't Put Your Heart In His Hand/I Was Only Kidding | 12 |
| 64 | Fontana TF 443 | Miracles/That's Right, Walk On By | 18 |
| 64 | Fontana TF 490 | (You Don't Know) How Glad I Am/Baby I Don't Care | 15 |
| 65 | Fontana TF 596 | Runnin' Out Of Fools/There He Goes | 10 |
| 66 | Fontana TF 669 | Why Don't I Run Away From You?/Small Town | 30 |
| 67 | Fontana TF 792 | I'm Going Out (The Same Way I Came In)/We've Got Everything Going For Us | 20 |
| 67 | Fontana TF 833 | I/Stop And Think | 10 |
| 67 | Fontana TF 870 | Excuse Me/Patterns | 10 |
| 68 | Fontana TF 926 | Can't Take My Eyes Off You/Hungry Heart | 10 |
| 68 | Fontana TF 983 | Now The Flowers Cry/On A Magic Carpet Ride | 200 |
| 70 | Tamla Motown TMG 739 | The Day Will Come Between Sunday And Monday/My Whole World Ended (The Moment You Left Me) | 25 |
| 72 | Philips 6006 352 | Excuse Me/Patterns | 8 |
| 73 | Rocket PIG 2 | Lonnie And Josie/The Last Good Man In My Life | 7 |
| 65 | Fontana TE 17443 | KIKI DEE (EP) | 40 |
| 66 | Fontana TE 17470 | KIKI DEE IN CLOVER (EP) | 30 |
| 68 | Fontana (S)TL 5455 | I'M KIKI DEE (LP) | 45 |
| 70 | Tamla Motown STML 11158 | GREAT EXPECTATIONS (LP) | 45 |

*(see also Elton John)*

## LENNY DEE
| | | | |
|---|---|---|---|
| 55 | Brunswick 05440 | Plantation Boogie/Birth Of The Blues | 7 |

## RICKY DEE & EMBERS
| | | | |
|---|---|---|---|
| 62 | Stateside SS 136 | Workout/JOHN MOBLEY: Tunnel Of Love | 15 |

## SANDRA DEE
| | | | |
|---|---|---|---|
| 61 | Brunswick 05858 | Tammy Tell Me True/Let's Fall In Love | 10 |

## TAMMI DEE
| | | | |
|---|---|---|---|
| 71 | Downtown DT 479 | Val/MUSIC DOCTORS: Bank Raid | 12 |

## TOMMY DEE
| | | | |
|---|---|---|---|
| 59 | Melodisc 1516 | Three Stars/TEEN JONES (TONES): I'll Never Change (tri centre) | 20 |
| 59 | Melodisc 1516 | Three Stars/TEEN JONES (TONES): I'll Never Change (round centre) | 10 |

## DEE & DYNAMITES
| | | | |
|---|---|---|---|
| 60 | Philips PB 1081 | Blaze Away/South Bound Gasser | 5 |

## DEE AND THE QUOTIUM
| | | | |
|---|---|---|---|
| 69 | Jay Boy Boy 8 | Someday You'll Need Someone/Send Some Flowers To Jule | 45 |

## DEEE LITE
| | | | |
|---|---|---|---|
| 90 | Elektra EKR 114T | Groove Is In The Heart/(Peanut Butter Mix)/What Is Love? (Holographic Goatee Mix)/(Rainbow Beard Mix) (12" original pressing with "EW" in centre of label) | 10 |

## DEEJAY FRIENDLY
| | | | |
|---|---|---|---|
| 96 | Deejay Friendly PK 01 | Piano Me Softly (12" promo) | 8 |

## DEEJAYS
| | | | |
|---|---|---|---|
| 65 | Polydor BM 56034 | Dimples/Coming On Strong | 60 |
| 65 | Polydor BM 56501 | Blackeyed Woman/I Just Can't Go To Sleep | 110 |

## ANTHONY DEELEY
| | | | |
|---|---|---|---|
| 68 | Pama PM 728 | Anytime Man/Don't Change Your Mind About Me | 20 |

## ANGELA DEEN
| | | | |
|---|---|---|---|
| 64 | Fontana TF 491 | There's So Much About My Baby That I Love/Gotta Hand It To The Boy | 8 |

## CAROL DEENE
| | | | |
|---|---|---|---|
| 61 | HMV POP 922 | Sad Movies (Make Me Cry)/Don't Forget | 10 |
| 62 | HMV POP 973 | Norman/On The Outside Looking In | 5 |
| 62 | HMV POP 1027 | Johnny Get Angry/Somebody's Smiling (While I'm Crying) | 7 |
| 62 | HMV POP 1058 | Some People/Kissin' | 5 |
| 62 | HMV POP 1086 | James(Hold The Ladder Steady)/It Happened Last Night | 6 |
| 63 | HMV POP 1123 | Let Me Do It My Way/Growin' Up | 5 |
| 63 | HMV POP 1200 | Oh Oh Oh Willie/I Want To Stay Here | 5 |
| 64 | HMV POP 1275 | Who's Been Sleeping In My Bed?/Love Is Wonderful | 5 |
| 64 | HMV POP 1337 | Very First Kiss/Hard To Say Goodnight | 5 |
| 65 | HMV POP 1405 | Most People Do/I Can't Forget Someone Like You | 5 |
| 65 | Columbia DB 7743 | He Just Don't Know/Up In The Penthouse | 15 |
| 66 | Columbia DB 7890 | Dancing In Your Eyes/Please Don't Be Unfaithful Again | 8 |
| 67 | Columbia DB 8107 | Love Not Have I/Time | 8 |
| 68 | CBS 3206 | When He Wants A Woman/I'm Not Crying | 15 |
| 69 | Conquest CXT 102 | One More Chance/Invisible Tears | 5 |
| 79 | RIM 003 | Ready For The Times To Get Better/It's So Easy | 5 |

## DEEP END
| | | | |
|---|---|---|---|
| 78 | Private pressing | BEGGED AND BORROWED (LP, listed as CPLP 016) | 15 |

## DEEP FEELING
| | | | |
|---|---|---|---|
| 69 | Page One POF 160 | Oh Darlin'/Feelin' | 40 |
| 70 | DJM DJS 231 | Do You Wanna Dance/The Day My Lady Cried | 6 |
| 70 | Page One POF 165 | Do You Love Me/Move On | 6 |
| 70 | Page One POF 177 | Skyline Pigeon/We've Thrown It All Away | 6 |
| 71 | DJM DJS 237 | Sweet Dust And Red Wine/Turn Around | 6 |
| 74 | Santa Ponsa PN 512 | Lets Spend The Night Together/Avalon | 8 |
| 71 | DJM DJLPS 419 | DEEP FEELING (LP) | 200 |

*(see also Raw Material)*

## DEEP FREEZE
| | | | |
|---|---|---|---|
| 70s | Guardian GRL 43 | Keeping You In Furs/Don't Look Back | 5 |

## DEEP FREEZE MICE

| | | | |
|---|---|---|---|
| 86 | Cordelia ERICAT 002 | Zoology/These Floors Are Smooth (500 copies, no sleeve) | 15 |
| 86 | Cordelia ERICAT 016 | NEURON MUSIC (12" EP, also featuring Mr. Concept, Yung Analysts and Rimarimba) | 20 |
| 93 | Farce 042 | Slow Shiny Bricks/George Bailey Lassoes A Refrigerator (Remix) (300 numbered copies) | 10 |
| 79 | Mole Embalming MOLE 1 | MY GERANIUMS ARE BULLETPROOF (LP, 1st 250 copies with paste-on sleeve, 8-page booklet & various A4 inserts) | 120 |
| 79 | Mole Embalming MOLE 1 | MY GERANIUMS ARE BULLETPROOF (LP, printed sleeve, 1500 only) | 70 |
| 81 | Mole Embalming MOLE 2 | TEENAGE HEAD IN MY REFRIGERATOR (LP, 400 copies with red cover) | 45 |
| 81 | Mole Embalming MOLE 2 | TEENAGE HEAD IN MY REFRIGERATOR (LP, 800 printed) | 50 |
| 81 | Inedible MOLE 3 | GATES OF LUNCH (LP, 1,000 pressed, various inserts) | 40 |
| 82 | Mole Embalming MOLE C1 | TEENAGE HEAD IN MY REFRIGERATOR/LED ZEPPELIN 2 (cassette, around 30 copies) | 50 |
| 83 | Mole Embalming MOLE 4 | SAW A RANCH BURNING LAST NIGHT (LP, 120 in wraparound sleeve) | 40 |
| 83 | Mole Embalming MOLE 4 | SAW A RANCH BURNING LAST NIGHT (LP, 1000 copies) | 40 |
| 84 | Inedible MOLE 3 | GATES OF LUNCH (LP, 1,000 pressed, these 150 copies with wraparound poster sleeve with insert) | 55 |
| 84 | Cordelia ERICAT 001 | I LOVE YOU LITTLE BOBO WITH YOUR DELICATE GOLDEN LIONS (2 x LP) | 60 |
| 84 | Cordelia ERICAT 004 | HANG ON CONSTANCE, LET ME HEAR THE NEWS (LP, 120 wraparound poster sleeve with insert) | 20 |
| 84 | Cordelia ERICAT 004 | HANG ON CONSTANCE, LET ME HEAR THE NEWS (LP, 1000 copies) | 20 |
| 84 | Mole Embalming MOLE C2 | MY GERANIUMS ARE BULLETPROOF (cassette, 30 copies only) | 50 |
| 84 | Mole Embalming MOLE C3 | TEENAGE HEAD IN MY REFRIGERATOR (cassette, around 30 copies) | 50 |
| 86 | Cordelia/Unlikely CERICAT 001 | I LOVE YOU LITTLE BOBO WITH YOUR DELICATE GOLDEN LIONS (double cassette, around 25 copies) | 25 |
| 87 | Cordelia ERICAT 013 | RAIN IS WHEN THE EARTH IS TELEVISION (LP, 1000 copies only) | 20 |
| 87 | Cordelia ERICAT 024 | WAR, FAMINE, DEATH, PESTILENCE & MISS TIMBERLAKE (LP, 1000 copies) | 20 |
| 88 | Cordelia ERICAT 027 | THE TENDER YELLOW PONIES OF INSOMNIA (LP, 1000 copies) | 20 |
| 89 | Logical Fish 1 | I LIVE IN SWITZERLAND (LP, 500 copies) | 15 |

## DEEP POCKETS

| | | | |
|---|---|---|---|
| 74 | Stadium S77 | Loose Change/Run Back To Me | 30 |

## DEEP PURPLE

### SINGLES

| | | | |
|---|---|---|---|
| 68 | Parlophone R 5708 | Hush/One More Rainy Day (in promo-only p/s) | 350 |
| 68 | Parlophone R 5708 | Hush/One More Rainy Day | 40 |
| 68 | Parlophone R 5745 | Kentucky Woman/Wring That Neck (withdrawn) | 60 |
| 69 | Parlophone R 5763 | Emmaretta/Wring That Neck | 40 |
| 69 | Harvest HAR 5006 | Hallelujah (I Am The Preacher)/April Part 1 (in promo-only p/s) | 250 |
| 69 | Harvest HAR 5006 | Hallelujah (I Am The Preacher)/April Part 1 | 30 |
| 70 | Harvest PSR 325 | Concerto, 1st Movement (edit)/Concerto, 2nd Movement (edit) (promo, possibly some commercial) | 40 |
| 70 | Harvest HAR 5020 | Black Night/Speed King | 6 |
| 71 | Harvest HAR 5033 | Strange Kind Of Woman/I'm Alone | 6 |
| 71 | Harvest HAR 5045 | Fireball/Demon's Eye | 6 |
| 72 | Purple PUR 102 | Never Before/When A Blind Man Cries | 6 |
| 74 | Purple PUR 117 | Might Just Take Your Life/Coronarias Redig | 8 |
| 76 | Purple PUR 130 | You Keep On Moving/Love Child | 8 |
| 77 | Purple PUR 132 | Smoke On The Water/Woman From Tokyo/Child In Time (10,000 with p/s) | 7 |
| 85 | Polydor POSPP 719 | Perfect Strangers (edit)/Son Of Alerik (edit) (picture disc) | 10 |
| 87 | Polydor POSPP 843 | Call Of The Wild/Strange Ways (12", picture disc) | 12 |
| 88 | Polydor POC 4 | Hush ('88 Re-recording)/Dead Or Alive (Live) (black vinyl, p/s) | 7 |
| 88 | Polydor POC 4 | Hush ('88 Re-recording)/Dead Or Alive (Live) (blue vinyl, p/s) | 5 |
| 11 | EMI 266987 8 HAR 5304 | Hush (1969 BBC Session)/Speed King (1969 BBC Session) (p/s) | 20 |
| 12 | EMI PURRSD 138 | Smoke On The Water/Smoke On The Water (p/s, 1000 only) | 10 |

### EPs

| | | | |
|---|---|---|---|
| 77 | Purple PUR 135 | NEW LIVE AND RARE VOL. 1 (EP, 15,000 on purple vinyl) | 12 |
| 78 | Purple PUR 137 | NEW LIVE AND RARE VOL. 2 (EP) | 10 |
| 80 | Harvest SHEP 101 | NEW LIVE AND RARE VOL. 3 (EP) | 10 |

### ALBUMS : PARLOPHONE

| | | | |
|---|---|---|---|
| 68 | Parlophone PMC 7055 | SHADES OF DEEP PURPLE (LP, yellow/black label, mono, with "sold in U.K..." text) | 600 |
| 68 | Parlophone PCS 7055 | SHADES OF DEEP PURPLE (LP, yellow/black label, stereo, with "sold in U.K..." text) | 400 |
| 69 | Parlophone PCS 7055 | SHADES OF DEEP PURPLE (LP, stereo repressing, laminated sleeve, white/black label) | 35 |

### ALBUMS : HARVEST

| | | | |
|---|---|---|---|
| 69 | Harvest SHVL 751 | THE BOOK OF TALIESYN (LP, laminated gatefold sleeve, first pressing with "sold in U.K." text spread over 4 lines, no EMI on label) | 200 |
| 69 | Harvest SHVL 751 | THE BOOK OF TALIESYN (LP, laminated sleeve, second pressing with "sold in U.K." text spread over 5 lines) | 70 |
| 69 | Harvest SHVL 751 | THE BOOK OF TALIESYN (LP, laminated sleeve, third pressing without "sold in U.K." text) | 40 |
| 69 | Harvest SHVL 759 | DEEP PURPLE (LP, laminated gatefold sleeve, no EMI logo on label) | 150 |
| 69 | Harvest SHVL 759 | DEEP PURPLE (LP, laminated gatefold sleeve, later pressing with EMI logo on label) | 25 |
| 70 | Harvest SHVL 767 | CONCERTO FOR GROUP AND ORCHESTRA (LP, laminated gatefold sleeve, no EMI logo on label) | 40 |
| 70 | Harvest SHVL 767 | CONCERTO FOR GROUP AND ORCHESTRA (LP, laminated gatefold sleeve, later pressing with EMI logo on label) | 20 |
| 70 | Harvest SHVL 777 | IN ROCK (LP, laminated gatefold sleeve with "file under popular: pop groups", "Printed and Made by Garrod & Lofthouse Ltd." A2, B1 matrix, "The Gramophone Co" text around label rim not "EMI Records" no EMI logo on label, advertising inner sleeve with "Patent no's 1,125,555 & 1,072,844" at bottom) | 100 |
| 70 | Harvest SHVL 777 | IN ROCK (LP, laminated gatefold sleeve, later pressing with EMI logo on label) | 20 |
| 71 | Harvest SHVL 759 | DEEP PURPLE (LP, laminated gatefold sleeve, non EMI pressing with indented circular groove around spindle hole) | 20 |
| 71 | Harvest SHVL 793 | FIREBALL (LP, textured gatefold sleeve, with lyric insert) | 125 |

| 71 | Harvest SHVL 751 | THE BOOK OF TALIESYN (LP, laminated gatefold sleeve with 'Ernest J. Day' printing credit, fourth pressing with EMI logo on label) | 40 |
|---|---|---|---|
| 75 | Harvest SHVL 751 | THE BOOK OF TALIESYN (LP, laminated gatefold sleeve, fifth pressing with EMI logo) | 15 |
| 76 | Harvest SHVL 751 | THE BOOK OF TALIESYN (LP, laminated gatefold sleeve with 'Garrod & Lofthouse Ltd' printing credit, sixth pressing with EMI logo on slightly more yellow label) | 15 |
| 78 | Harvest SHSM 2026 | THE SINGLES A's AND B's (LP, purple vinyl) | 20 |
| 80 | Harvest SHSM 2016 | SHADES OF DEEP PURPLE (LP, 'dismembered doll-limb' sleeve, withdrawn) | 200 |
| 80 | Harvest SHDW 412 | IN CONCERT (2-LP) | 22 |
| 82 | Harvest SHSP 4124 | LIVE IN LONDON (LP) | 15 |
| 99 | Harvest 7243 4 99469 10 | BOOK OF TALIESYN (LP, 180gm vinyl, gatefold sleeve in stickered PVC outer) | 20 |

## ALBUMS : PURPLE

| 72 | Purple TPSP 3511/12 | MADE IN JAPAN 2-LP, First pressing, "Gramophone Co" on label rim, MATRIX TPS 3511 A-1U/TPS 3512 A-1U/B1-U, "Porky" (side 1), "Delta Pork" (side 2), "Pecko" (side 3), "Peckie" (Side 4) etched into dead wax, double gatefold sleeve, many originals with £3.25 price sticker) | 40 |
|---|---|---|---|
| 72 | Purple TSPS 3511/12 | MADE IN JAPAN 2-LP, Contract pressing, no mother or stamper details at 3 and 9 'o' clock, (just number "3" at 9 "o" clock. Ridge around inside of label half an inch from the rim, no "Made in Gt. Britain" at foot of label, no brackets on "Made In Japan" on labels,double gatefold sleeve) | 40 |
| 72 | Purple TPSA 7504 | MACHINE HEAD (LP, laminated gatefold sleeve, with fold-out lyric insert) | 30 |
| 73 | Purple TPSA 7508 | WHO DO WE THINK WE ARE (LP, 1st pressing with 'The Gramophone Co' on rim of label, -1U matrix numbers on both sides, laminated gatefold sleeve with 'File under popular: pop groups', with lyric insert) | 25 |
| 74 | Purple Q4TPS 7504 | MACHINE HEAD (LP, laminated gatefold sleeve, quadrophonic) | 60 |
| 74 | Purple TPS 3505 | BURN (LP, First Pressing: "The Gramophone Co" on rim, MATRIX TPS 3505 A-1U/B-1U, "Porky & Mel * Trish" etched into dead wax side 1/"Pecko" etched into dead wax on side 2. Spine wording on top edge as well as spine) | 30 |
| 74 | Purple TPS 3505 | BURN (LP, Second Pressing: "EMI Records" on rim, -1U Matrixes) | 15 |
| 74 | Purple TPS 3505 | BURN (LP, hybrid pressing with: "The Gramophone Co" on one label and "EMI Records" on the other) | 20 |
| 74 | Purple TPS 3508 | STORMBRINGER (LP, 1st pressing, matrixes TPS3508 A-1U/B-1U, 'Kendun' stamped in dead wax, "EMI Records Ltd" on label rim, spine wording on top edge and spine, "7411 Garrod & Lofthouse Ltd" on bottom right corner of sleeve) | 20 |
| 75 | Purple TPSA 7515 | COME TASTE THE BAND (LP, laminated gatefold sleeve with inner) | 15 |
| 79 | Purple TPS 3514 | THE MARK 2 PURPLE SINGLES (LP, purple vinyl) | 15 |
| 12 | EMI 50999 463275 1 2 | MACHINE HEAD (LP, gatefold sleeve, 180gram 40th anniversary edition with bonus 7") | 22 |

## ALBUMS : OTHER LPS

| 84 | Polydor POLHP 16 | PERFECT STRANGERS (LP, picture disc, with extra track & die-cut sleeve) | 15 |
|---|---|---|---|
| 84 | Polydor DEEP 1A | DEEP PURPLE INTERVIEW (LP, 1-sided, promo-only, stickered white sleeve) | 18 |
| 85 | EMI EJ 26 0343 0 | IN ROCK (LP, picture disc with poster) | 20 |
| 85 | EMI EJ 34 0344 0 | FIREBALL (LP, picture disc with poster) | 20 |
| 85 | EMI EG 26 0345 0 | MACHINE HEAD (LP, picture disc with poster) | 20 |
| 85 | EMI PUR 1/E 2606131 | DEEP PURPLE — ANTHOLOGY (2-LP, blue vinyl) | 25 |
| 86 | Polydor DEEP 2A | HOUSE OF BLUE LIGHT (interview LP, promo-only, plays same both sides, stickered black sleeve) | 15 |
| 88 | Connoisseur VSOP 125 | SCANDINAVIAN NIGHTS (2-LP, gatefold sleeve, with booklet) | 18 |
| 90 | RCA PL 90535 | SLAVES AND MASTERS (LP) | 15 |
| 91 | EMI 96129 | ANTHOLOGY (3-LP, gatefold sleeve) | 30 |
| 93 | BMG 74321 15420-1 | THE BATTLE RAGES ON (LP, with inner sleeve) | 20 |
| 95 | EMI 7243 8 34019 18 | DEEP PURPLE IN ROCK (2-LP, purple vinyl, gatefold sleeve with inners) | 35 |
| 97 | EMI DEEPP 3 | MACHINE HEAD (2-LP, 'EMI 100' remixed anniversary edition, purple vinyl, gatefold sleeve, with insert) | 40 |
| 97 | EMI LPCENT 25 | SHADES OF DEEP PURPLE (LP, 'EMI 100', 180gm vinyl edition, yellow/black label) | 30 |
| 97 | EMI DEEPP 2 | FIREBALL (2-LP, gatefold sleeve with inners & limited edition print) | 30 |
| 98 | EMI PP 074 | VERY BEST OF (2-LP, purple vinyl) | 30 |
| 98 | EMI 7243 8 57864 19 | MADE IN JAPAN (2-LP, numbered, purple vinyl, gatefold sleeve with inners) | 30 |
| 03 | EMI 7243 5 91048 12 | BANANAS (LP, gatefold sleeve) | 20 |

*(see also Rainbow, Gillan, [David Coverdale's] Whitesnake, Tommy Bolin, [Sheila Carter &] Episode Six, Jon Lord, Roger Glover, Green Bullfrog, Wizard's Convention, Elf, M.I. Five, Warhorse, Captain Beyond, John Lawton, Hell Preachers Inc., Glen Hughes, Trapeze, Leading Figures, Paice Ashton & Lord, Silverhead, Pete York Percussion Band)*

## DEEP RIVER BOYS

| 54 | HMV 7M 174 | Sweet Mama Tree Top Tall/A Kiss And Cuddle Polka | 10 |
|---|---|---|---|
| 54 | HMV 7M 280 | Shake, Rattle And Roll/St. Louis Blues | 40 |
| 56 | HMV 7M 361 | Rock-A-Beatin' Boogie/Just A Little Bit More! | 40 |
| 56 | HMV POP 263 | That's Right/Honey Honey | 20 |
| 57 | HMV POP 395 | Whole Lotta Shakin' Goin' On/There's A Goldmine In The Sky | 30 |
| 58 | HMV POP 449 | Not Too Old To Rock And Roll/Slow Train To Nowhere | 15 |
| 58 | HMV POP 537 | Itchy Twitchy Feeling/I Shall Not Be Moved | 10 |

*(see also Fats Waller, Harry Douglass & Deep River Boys)*

## DEEP SET

| 68 | Pye 7N 17594 | That's The Way Life Goes/Hello Amy | 60 |
|---|---|---|---|
| 69 | Major Minor MM 607 | I Started A Joke/Spicks And Specks | 8 |
| 70 | Target 7N 45018 | Cinnamon Girl/You'll Never Know | 100 |

## DEEP SIX

| 66 | Liberty LIB 55882 | Counting/When Morning Breaks | 8 |
|---|---|---|---|

## DEEP SWITCH

| 86 | SWITCH 1 | NINE INCHES OF GOD (LP, private pressing) | 40 |
|---|---|---|---|

## DEEP THROATS

| 78 | Limp LMP 1 | Rock N Roll Discharge/Miami Connection | 15 |
|---|---|---|---|

## DEEP TIMBRE

| 72 | Westwood WR 5006 | DEEP TIMBRE (LP) | 40 |
|---|---|---|---|

MINT VALUE £

## DEEP WATER
70    Pye 7N 17946                          Take A Look Around/Poor Little Me ...................................................................... 6

## DEERHUNTER
07    4AD CAD 2822                          MICROCASTLE/WEIRD ERA CONT. (LP, CD) ............................................... 25

## SAM DEES
69    Major Minor MM 655                    If It's All Wrong (It's All Right)/Don't Keep Me Hangin' On ............................ 50
75    Atlantic K 10676                      Fragile, Handle With Care/Save The Love At Any Cost.............................. 100
89    RCA PB 43129                          After All/Always Something (p/s) ....................................................... 10
80s   Soul City 137                         Lonely For You Baby/I Need You Girl (reissue) ....................................... 8
97    Soul Supply GS0002                    Lonely For You Baby/SAM FLETCHER: I'd Think It Over (promos [GS 0002X] £12) ... 8
10    Outta Sight OSV 008                   Lonely For You Baby (original version)/Lonely For You Baby (alternative version) (reissue) ....................................................................................... 6
75    Atlantic K 50142                      THE SHOW MUST GO ON (LP) ............................................................ 30

## SAM DEES & BETTYE SWANN
76    Atlantic K 10719                      Storybook Children/Just As Sure ..................................................... 15
*(see also Bettye Swann)*

## DEE SET
68    Blue Cat BS 146                       I Know A Place/ROY BENNETT: I Dangerous......................................... 50

## DEF J
92    Kold Sweat KS122                      Just Save It (12") ...................................................................... 15
*(see also Encona Coarse)*

## DEF LEPPARD
79    Bludgeon Riffola SRT/CUS/232          THE DEF LEPPARD EP: Ride Into The Sun/Getcha Rocks Off/The Overture (red label, p/s with lyric insert, 150 only) ................................................ 350
79    Bludgeon Riffola SRT/CUS/232          THE DEF LEPPARD EP: Ride Into The Sun/Getcha Rocks Off/The Overture (red label, with p/s, 850 only) ............................................................ 250
79    Bludgeon Riffola SRT/CUS/232          THE DEF LEPPARD EP: Ride Into The Sun/Getcha Rocks Off/The Overture (red label, /without p/s, 850 only) ..................................................... 60
79    Bludgeon Riffola MSB 001              Ride Into The Sun/Getcha Rocks Off/The Overture (reissue, yellow label, 15,000 pressed, no p/s) ...................................................................... 18
79    Phonogram 6059 240                    Getcha Rocks Off/Ride Into The Sun/The Overture (2nd reissue, no p/s) ......... 10
79    Phonogram 6059 240                    Getcha Rocks Off/Ride Into The Sun/The Overture (mispressing, both sides play "The Overture") ................................................................ 40
79    Phonogram 6059 247                    Wasted/Hello America (p/s)............................................................ 12
80    Phonogram LEPP 1                      Hello America/Good Morning Freedom (p/s)....................................... 12
81    Phonogram LEPP 2                      Let It Go/Switch 625 (p/s, 10,000 shrinkwrapped with patch)..................... 15
81    Phonogram LEPP 2                      Let It Go/Switch 625 (p/s) ............................................................. 12
82    Phonogram LEPP 3                      Bringin' On The Heartbreak/Me And My Wine (p/s).............................. 35
82    Phonogram LEPP 312                    Bringin' On The Heartbreak/Me And My Wine/You Got Me Runnin' (12", p/s) ... 18
83    Phonogram VER 5                       Photograph/Bringin' On The Heartbreak (p/s) ...................................... 10
83    Phonogram VERP 5                      Photograph/Bringin' On The Heartbreak (camera-shaped fold-out/pop-up sleeve, 500 only) .................................................................... 25
83    Phonogram VERX 5                      Photograph/Bringin' On The Heartbreak/Mirror, Mirror (12", p/s) ............... 20
83    Phonogram VER 6                       Rock Of Ages/Action! Not Words (p/s) ................................................ 7
83    Phonogram VERP 6                      Rock Of Ages/Action! Not Words (guitar-shaped picture disc) .................... 35
83    Phonogram VERQ 6                      Rock Of Ages/Action! Not Words (foldout 'rock box' cube sleeve, 500 only) ...... 40
83    Phonogram VERX 6                      Rock Of Ages/Action! Not Words (12", p/s) ........................................ 18
83    Phonogram VERDJ 8                     Too Late/Foolin' (p/s, DJ-only promo with rear band photo in football kit) ...... 150
83    Phonogram VER 8                       Too Late For Love/Foolin' (p/s) ...................................................... 12
83    Phonogram VERX 8                      Too Late For Love/Foolin'/High And Dry (12", p/s) ............................... 20
84    Phonogram VER 9                       Photograph/Bringin' On The Heartbreak (reissue, 'wallet' p/s).................. 10
84    Phonogram VERG 9                      Photograph/Bringin' On The Heartbreak (g/fold printed 'wallet' p/s, 500 only) ... 35
84    Phonogram VERX 9                      Photograph/Bringin' On The Heartbreak/Mirror, Mirror (12", p/s) ............... 15
87    Phonogram LEPC 1                      Animal/Animal (Extended Mix)/Tear It Down (12", p/s, red vinyl) ............... 15
87    Phonogram LEPS 2                      Pour Some Sugar On Me/I Wanna Be Your Hero (tri-shaped picture disc in silver 12" foldout p/s with tour dates) ........................................................... 10
87    Phonogram LEPPX 2                     Pour Some Sugar On Me (Extended Version)/Pour Some Sugar On Me (Extended)/I Wanna Be Your Hero (12", picture disc, unissued) ............................ 0
87    Phonogram LEPS 3                      Hysteria/Ride Into The Sun (1987 Version) (p/s, shrinkwrapped with patch) ...... 10
87    Phonogram LEPX 313                    Hysteria/Ride Into The Sun (1987 Version)/Love And Affection (live) (12", envelope box sleeve with poster & international discography, 5,000 only) ............... 15
88    Phonogram LEPP 4                      Armageddon It! (The Atomic Mix)/Ring Of Fire (poster p/s)........................ 7
88    Phonogram LEPXB 4                     Armageddon It!/Armageddon It! (The Atomic Mix)/Ring Of Fire (12", numbered box set with poster, enamel badge & 5 postcards, 5,000 only) ................... 18
88    Phonogram LEPG 5                      Love Bites/Billy's Got A Gun (live) (no'd gatefold p/s with 8-page lyric book)...... 8
88    Phonogram LEPXB 5                     Love Bites/Billy's Got A Gun (live)/Excitable (Orgasmic Mix) (12", box set with 4 cardboard inserts, 5,000 only) ......................................................... 15
89    Phonogram LEPC 6                      Rocket/Release Me (foldout 'Brit' pack, envelope sleeve with 3 inserts)........... 15
89    Phonogram LEPXP 6                     Rocket (The Lunar Mix)/(Radio Edit)/Release Me (12", picture disc, numbered) ... 15
89    Phonogram LEPXC 6                     Rocket (The Lunar Mix)/Release Me/Rock Of Ages (live) (12", calendar pack) ...... 10
92    Phonogram DEFXP 7                     Let's Get Rocked/Only After Dark/Too Late For Love (live) (12", picture disc, with insert) ............................................................................... 10
83    Vertigo VERS 2                        PYROMANIA (LP)....................................................................... 15
87    Phonogram HYSPD 1                     HYSTERIA (LP)......................................................................... 15
87    Phonogram HYSPD 1                     HYSTERIA (LP, picture disc)........................................................... 15
92    Phonogram 510 978-1                   ADRENALIZE (LP, picture disc, 5,000 only, numbered, die-cut sleeve)............. 15
94    Phonogram (no cat. no.)               ADRENALIZE — MAHOGANY BOX SET (CD, picture disc, with interview picture CD, 3 booklets, signed/no'd certificate, signed photo & plectrum, 1,000 only) ........ 200
95    Mercury 528 656-1                     VAULT 1980 - 1995 (2-LP, inners).................................................... 20
96    Mercury 532 486-1                     SLANG (LP, inner) .................................................................... 50

*(see also Lucy, Gogmagog, Johnny Kalendar Band)*

## DEF TEX

| | | | |
|---|---|---|---|
| 91 | Sound Clash SCR 003 | MASTER BLASTER (EP) | 70 |
| 92 | Sound Clash SCR 001 | TUTORIAL SESSIONS (EP) | 10 |
| 99 | Son SON008 | Poetic Speech Techniques (12") | 12 |
| 01 | Monkey Face MF01 | Sing Sad Songs (7") | 8 |
| 11 | Son 049 | Stop, Pause, Reflect/Get Respect (with Chrome, 10", 150 copies only) | 10 |
| 01 | Son SONCD018 | SERENE BUG (LP) | 15 |

## DEFECTS

| | | | |
|---|---|---|---|
| 81 | Casualty CR 001 | Dance 'Til You Drop/Guilty Conscience/Brutality (p/s) | 20 |
| 82 | WXYZ ABCD-3 | Survival/Brutality (p/s) | 5 |
| 85 | WXYZ LMNOP2 | DEFECTIVE BREAKDOWN (LP, with insert) | 15 |

## DEFENDANTS

| | | | |
|---|---|---|---|
| 80s | Edible EAT 001 | Headmaster/Such A Spiv (stickered insert cover & stickered labels) | 12 |

## DEFENDERS

| | | | |
|---|---|---|---|
| 68 | Doctor Bird DB 1104 | Set Them Free/Don't Blame The Children (actually by Lee Perry & Sensations) | 50 |

*(see also Lee Perry)*

## DEFIANT POSE

| | | | |
|---|---|---|---|
| 81 | Groucho Marxist WH 4 | Someone Else's War/After The Bang (p/s) | 15 |

## ZION DE GALLIER

| | | | |
|---|---|---|---|
| 68 | Parlophone R 5686 | Me/Winter Will Be Cold | 25 |
| 68 | Parlophone R 5710 | Dream Dream Dream/Geraldine | 20 |

*(see also Mark Wirtz)*

## GLORIA DE HAVEN

| | | | |
|---|---|---|---|
| 55 | Brunswick 05369 | So This Is Paris/The Two Of Us | 5 |
| 55 | Brunswick 05457 | Red Hot Pepper Pot/Won't You Save Me? | 10 |
| 59 | Oriole CB 1524 | Dearly Beloved/Life | 5 |

## DE-HEMS

| | | | |
|---|---|---|---|
| 72 | President PT 388 | Don't Cross That Line/Lover Let Me Go | 20 |

## DEIGHTON TASK FORCE

| | | | |
|---|---|---|---|
| 89 | White REACT1 | Neighbourhood (12") | 100 |

*(see also Unique 3)*

## JACK DE JOHNETTE

| | | | |
|---|---|---|---|
| 70 | CBS 64076 | COMPLEX (LP) | 20 |

## DE JOHN SISTERS

| | | | |
|---|---|---|---|
| 57 | Mercury MT 174 | What Am I/Where Would I Be | 5 |
| 60 | London HLT 9127 | Yes Indeed/Be Anything (But Be Mine) | 5 |

## DEK & JERRY

| | | | |
|---|---|---|---|
| 66 | Philips BF 1494 | What's The Matter With Me?/Don't Waste Your Time | 8 |

## DESMOND DEKKER (& ACES)

| | | | |
|---|---|---|---|
| 63 | Island WI 054 | Honour Your Mother And Father (as Desmond Decker & Beverley's Allstars)/ Madgie ('63) (with Beverley's Allstars) | 20 |
| 63 | Island WI 111 | Parents/Labour For Learning (solo) | 30 |
| 64 | Island WI 158 | Jeserine/King Of Ska (as Desmond Dekkar & His Cherry Pies) | 30 |
| 64 | Black Swan WI 455 | Dracula (as Desmond Dekkar)/DON DRUMMOND: Spitfire | 50 |
| 65 | Island WI 181 | Get Up Adine (as Desmond Dekkar, actually with Four Aces)/Be Mine Forever (as Patsy & Desmond; song is act. "Down Down Down" by Clive & Naomi) | 50 |
| 65 | Island WI 202 | This Woman (as Desmond Dekker & Four Aces)/LEE PERRY & UPSETTERS: Si Senora (B-side actually by Ossie & Upsetters) | 25 |
| 67 | Pyramid PYR 6003 | Wise Man/ROLAND ALPHONSO: Middle East | 30 |
| 67 | Pyramid PYR 6004 | 007 (Shanty Town)/ROLAND ALPHONSO: El Torro | 10 |
| 67 | Pyramid PYR 6006 | It's A Shame/ROLAND ALPHONSO: On The Move | 25 |
| 67 | Pyramid PYR 6008 | Rudy Got Soul/ROLAND ALPHONSO: The Cat | 30 |
| 67 | Pyramid PYR 6011 | Rude Boy Train/ROLAND ALPHONSO: Nothing For Nothing | 25 |
| 67 | Pyramid PYR 6012 | Mother's Young Girl/SOUL BROTHERS: Confucious | 35 |
| 67 | Pyramid PYR 6017 | Unity/Sweet Music | 20 |
| 67 | Pyramid PYR 6020 | Sabotage/Pretty Africa | 20 |
| 67 | Pyramid PYR 6020 | Sabotage/It Pays | 15 |
| 67 | Pyramid PYR 6026 | It Pays/Young Generation | 15 |
| 68 | Pyramid PYR 6031 | Beautiful And Dangerous/I've Got The Blues | 20 |
| 68 | Pyramid PYR 6035 | Bongo Gal/Shing A Ling | 15 |
| 68 | Pyramid PYR 6037 | To Sir, With Love/Fu Manchu | 175 |
| 68 | Pyramid PYR 6044 | Mother Pepper/Don't Blame Me | 18 |
| 68 | Pyramid PYR 6045 | Try Me/I'm Leaving | 15 |
| 68 | Pyramid PYR 6047 | Hey Grandma/Young Generation | 15 |
| 68 | Pyramid PYR 6051 | Music Like Dirt (Intensified)/Coconut Water | 15 |
| 68 | Pyramid PYR 6054 | it Mek/Writing On The Wall | 8 |
| 68 | Pyramid PYR 6058 | Israelites/BEVERLEY'S ALLSTARS: The Man | 7 |
| 68 | Pyramid PYR 6058 | Christmas Day/I've Got The Blues | 10 |
| 69 | Pyramid PYR 6068 | It Miek/Problems | 5 |
| 69 | J.J. PYR 6058 | Israelites/BEVERLEY'S ALLSTARS: The Man (reissue, mis-labelled copy) | 5 |
| 70 | Trojan TR 7777 | You Can Get It If You Really Want/Perseverance | 10 |
| 70 | Trojan TR 7802 | The Song We Used To Sing/Get Up Little Suzie | 5 |
| 71 | Trojan TR 7847 | Lightning Stick/Troubles And Miseries | 5 |
| 72 | Trojan TR 7876 | It Gotta Be So/The First Time For A Long Time | 5 |
| 73 | Rhino RNO 115 | Sing A Little Song/I'm A Busted Lad | 5 |
| 80 | Stiff BUY 70 | Israelite/Why Fight? | 6 |
| 10 | Trojan THB 7001 | Sugar & Spice/Sentimental Reasons | 15 |
| 10 | Trojan THB 7005 | Dancing Time/Beverley's Special (Nothing For Nothing) | 15 |

MINT VALUE £

| | | | |
|---|---|---|---|
| 13 | Island WI 3161 | 007/Wise Man | 10 |
| 67 | Doctor Bird DLM 5007 | 007 SHANTY TOWN (LP) | 150 |
| 69 | Doctor Bird DLM 5013 | THE ISRAELITES (LP, solo) | 150 |
| 69 | Trojan TTL 4 | THIS IS DESMOND DEKKAR (LP, label credits Dekker) | 30 |
| 70 | Trojan TBL 146 | YOU CAN GET IT IF YOU REALLY WANT (LP) | 30 |
| 80 | Stiff SEEZ 26 | BLACK AND DEKKER (LP) | 15 |
| 85 | Trojan TRLS 226 | ORIGINAL REGGAE HITSOUND (LP) | 15 |
| 91 | Trojan TRLS 292 | KING OF SKA (LP) | 18 |
| 93 | Trojan TRLS 324 | KING OF KINGS (LP, with the Specials) | 15 |

*(see also Al Barry, Skatalites, Maytals)*

## GEORGE DEKKER
| | | | |
|---|---|---|---|
| 71 | Trojan TR 7879 | Time Hard/SYDNEY, GEORGE & JACKIE: Fall In Love | 6 |

## HOWARD DEKKER
| | | | |
|---|---|---|---|
| 74 | A Rover AR 01 | Me Throw Me Corn/On The Fire | 12 |

## DEL
| | | | |
|---|---|---|---|
| 73 | Uk UK 40 | Motorbike Annie/Gypsy Girl (some in p/s) | 20 |

## DELACARDOS
| | | | |
|---|---|---|---|
| 61 | HMV POP 890 | Hold Back The Tears/Mister Dillon | 30 |

## SIMON DE LACY
| | | | |
|---|---|---|---|
| 68 | Spark 1001 | Baby Come Back To Me/Goodbye Love | 25 |

## JUNIOR DELAHAYE
| | | | |
|---|---|---|---|
| 80s | Solid Groove SG 015 | Love/I Love You (12") | 10 |

## DE LAINE SISTERS
| | | | |
|---|---|---|---|
| 62 | Piccadilly 7N 35070 | It Might As Well Rain Until September/Puppet On A String | 10 |

*(see also Ladybirds, Breakaways)*

## DEL AMITRI
| | | | |
|---|---|---|---|
| 83 | No Strings NOSP 1 | Sense Sickness/The Difference Is (p/s) | 30 |
| 89 | A&M AM 527 | Stone Cold Sober/The Return Of Maggie Brown/Talk It To Death (p/s) | 6 |
| 90 | A&M AMX 589 | Spit In The Rain/Scared To Love/The Return Of Maggie Brown/Talk It To Death (10", in box with lyric insert) | 8 |
| 95 | A&M 540 311-1 | TWISTED (LP, with poster) | 25 |
| 97 | A&M 540 705-1 | SOME OTHER SUCKER'S PARADISE (LP) | 25 |

## DELANEY & BONNIE (& FRIENDS)
| | | | |
|---|---|---|---|
| 69 | Elektra EKSN 45066 | Get Ourselves Together/Soldiers Of The Cross (withdrawn) | 20 |
| 69 | Atlantic 584 308 | Comin' Home/Groupie (Superstar) | 8 |
| 70 | Stax 139 | Just Plain Beautiful/Hard To Say Goodbye | 6 |
| 69 | Apple SAPCOR 7 | THE ORIGINAL DELANEY & BONNIE (LP, unreleased, no sleeve) | 1500 |
| 69 | Elektra EKS 74039 | THE ORIGINAL DELANEY & BONNIE — ACCEPT NO SUBSTITUTE (LP, commercial release of above LP) | 25 |
| 69 | Stax SXATS 1029 | HOME (LP) | 20 |
| 70 | Atlantic 2400 013 | ON TOUR WITH ERIC CLAPTON (LP) | 25 |
| 71 | Atco 2400 029 | TO BONNIE FROM DELANEY (LP) | 15 |

*(see also Eric Clapton, Delaney Bramlett, King Curtis with Delaney & Friends, Shindogs)*

## ERIC DELANEY BAND
| | | | |
|---|---|---|---|
| 60 | Parlophone R 4646 | Bass Drum Boogie/Let's Get Organised | 5 |
| 62 | Parlophone R 4925 | Manhattan Spiritual/Down Home | 5 |
| 57 | Pye Nixa NEP 24066 | AT THE BBC FESTIVAL (EP) | 10 |
| 56 | Pye NIAX NP 19018 | HI-FI DELANEY (10" LP) | 20 |

## SIMON DELANO
| | | | |
|---|---|---|---|
| 70 | Jay Boy JSX2001 | BANGARANG REGGAE (LP, with the Gassers) | 20 |

## DEL-BYZANTEENS
| | | | |
|---|---|---|---|
| 82 | Don't Fall Off The Mountain Z 16 | Draft Riot/Sally Go Round The Roses (p/s) | 6 |

## DEL-CAPRIS
| | | | |
|---|---|---|---|
| 79 | Grapevine GRP 112 | Hey Little Way Out Girl (actually by Construction)/EULA COOPER: Beggars Can't Be Choosey (p/s) | 10 |

## DELEGATION
| | | | |
|---|---|---|---|
| 77 | State 25 | The Promise Of Love/It Only Happens | 25 |

## DELFONICS
| | | | |
|---|---|---|---|
| 68 | Bell BLL 1005 | La La Means I Love You/Can't Get Over Losing You | 7 |
| 68 | Bell BLL 1016 | Together We Can Make Such Sweet Music/Bad Bad Weather | 5 |
| 68 | Bell 1028 | Break Your Promise/Alfie | 6 |
| 68 | Bell BLL 1042 | Ready Or Not Here I Come/Somebody Loves You | 8 |
| 69 | Bell BLL 1066 | You Can't Be Loving Him/Let It Be Me | 10 |
| 69 | Bell BLL 1073 | Funny Feeling/You Got Yours And I'll Get Mine | 6 |
| 70 | Bell BLL 1099 | Didn't I (Blow Your Mind This Time)/Down is Up, Up Is Down | 5 |
| 70 | Bell BLL 1467 | With These Hands/Let It Be Me | 20 |
| 68 | Bell SBLL 106 | LA-LA MEANS I LOVE YOU (LP) | 25 |
| 69 | Bell SBLL 121 | THE SOUND OF SEXY SOUL (LP) | 15 |
| 71 | Bell SBLL 137 | THE DELFONICS (LP) | 15 |
| 72 | Bell SBLL 217 | TELL ME THIS IS A DREAM | 20 |
| 74 | Bell BELLS 245 | ALIVE AND KICKING (LP) | 15 |

## TERESA DEL FUEGO
| | | | |
|---|---|---|---|
| 81 | Satril HH 155 | Don't Hang Up/Wonder Wonder (no p/s) | 8 |

## DELGADOS
| | | | |
|---|---|---|---|
| 96 | Boa HISS 4 | Liquidation Girl/VAN IMPE: Piranha (hand-painted brown paper bag p/s, 500 only) | 12 |
| 96 | Chemikal Underground CHEM 009 | DOMESTIQUES (LP, inner) | 20 |

| | | | |
|---|---|---|---|
| 98 | Chemikal Underground CHEM 024 | PELOTON (LP, inner) | 20 |
| 00 | Chemikal Underground CHEM 040 | THE GREAT EASTERN (LP) | 25 |

## DELICATES
| | | | |
|---|---|---|---|
| 59 | London HLT 8953 | Ronnie Is My Lover/Black And White Thunderbird | 50 |
| 60 | London HLT 9176 | Too Young To Date/The Kiss | 30 |

## DELICATESSAN
| | | | |
|---|---|---|---|
| 67 | Vocalion VN 9286 | The Red Baron's Revenge/The Dog Fight (Der Hundtkampf) | 10 |

## DE LITE
| | | | |
|---|---|---|---|
| 89 | Circa YRTPRX 35 | Wild Times (12") | 30 |

## DE-LITES
| | | | |
|---|---|---|---|
| 79 | Destiny 1022 | Lover/Do The Zombie | 20 |
| 80 | Grapevine GRP 127 | Lover/Tell Me Why | 20 |

## JOHNNY DE LITTLE
| | | | |
|---|---|---|---|
| 61 | Columbia DB 4578 | Not Guilty/They | 6 |
| 62 | Columbia DB 4907 | Lover/You Made Me Love You | 6 |
| 63 | Columbia DB 7023 | Days Of Wine And Roses/Ride On | 5 |
| 63 | Columbia DB 7044 | The Wind And The Rain/Unchained Melody | 5 |
| 65 | CBS 201790 | The Knack/What To Do With Laurie | 5 |

*(see also John Barry)*

## DELIVERANCE
| | | | |
|---|---|---|---|
| 92 | European Rhyme ERR001 | Serious Public Disorder/Do Not Disturb (12") | 20 |
| 94 | Nut Cracker NUT001 | Dead Funny/Up And Down The Country (12") | 35 |
| 95 | Nut Cracker NUT002 | INJECT INTELLECT (EP) | 10 |
| 96 | Nut Cracker NUT003 | Twisted Mystics/Sedating Your Aims (12") | 8 |
| 87 | Metalworks VOV 664 | DEVIL'S MEAT (LP) | 15 |
| 89 | Metalworks VOV 673 | EVIL FRIENDSHIP (LP, lyric inner) | 15 |
| 90 | Metalworks VOV 679 | THE BOOK OF LIES (LP) | 15 |

## DELKOM
| | | | |
|---|---|---|---|
| 91 | Wau! Mr Modo MWS 034R | Superjack — Orbital Infusion 2000/Neutron 9000 Mix (12", 500 only) | 12 |

## DENNIS D'ELL
| | | | |
|---|---|---|---|
| 67 | CBS 202605 | It Breaks My Heart In Two/Better Use Your Head (withdrawn) | 400 |
| 67 | CBS 202605 | It Breaks My Heart In Two/Better Use Your Head (withdrawn: DJ copy) | 300 |
| 67 | Decca F 12647 | A Woman Called Sorrow/The Night Has A Thousand Eyes (as Denny D'ell) | 15 |
| 76 | Polydor 2058 715 | Home Is Home/Morning Without You (as Denis D'ell) | 7 |

*(see also Honeycombs)*

## JIMMY DELL
| | | | |
|---|---|---|---|
| 58 | RCA RCA 1066 | Teeny Weeny/BARRY DE VORZON: Barbara Jean | 50 |
| 58 | RCA RCA 1066 | Teeny Weeny/BARRY DE VORZON: Barbara Jean (78) | 20 |

## DELL-VIKINGS
| | | | |
|---|---|---|---|
| 57 | London HLD 8405 | Come Go With Me/How Can I Find A True Love (gold label lettering) | 100 |
| 57 | London HLD 8405 | Come Go With Me/How Can I Find A True Love (silver label lettering) | 20 |
| 57 | London HLD 8464 | Whispering Bells/Little Billy Boy | 30 |
| 58 | Mercury 7MT 199 | The Voodoo Man/Can't Wait | 10 |
| 59 | Mercury AMT 1027 | Flat Tyre/How Could You | 40 |
| 62 | HMV POP 1072 | Kilimanjaro/Confession Of Love | 5 |
| 63 | HMV POP 1145 | An Angel Up In Heaven/The Fishing Chant | 5 |

*(see also Chuck Jackson)*

## DELLINGER
| | | | |
|---|---|---|---|
| 77 | Carib Gems GG 004 | Melting Pot/Version | 7 |

*(see also Dillinger)*

## PETE DELLO & FRIENDS
| | | | |
|---|---|---|---|
| 71 | Nepentha 6437 001 | INTO YOUR EARS (LP, gatefold sleeve) | 750 |
| 89 | See For Miles 257 | INTO YOUR EARS....PLUS (2-LP, reissue) | 40 |

*(see also Honeybus, Lace, Red Herring, Leah, John Killigrew, Magic Valley, Grant Tracy & Sunsets, Sunsets)*

## DELLS
| | | | |
|---|---|---|---|
| 63 | Pye International 7N 25178 | The (Bossa Nova) Bird/Eternally | 25 |
| 67 | Chess CRS 8066 | O-O I Love You/There Is | 15 |
| 68 | Chess CRS 8071 | Wear It On Our Face/Please Don't Change Me Now | 20 |
| 68 | Chess CRS 8079 | Stay In My Corner/Love Is So Simple | 8 |
| 68 | President PT 223 | It's Not Unusual/Stay In My Corner | 15 |
| 68 | Chess CRS 8084 | Always Together/I Want My Momma | 8 |
| 69 | Chess CRS 8099 | I Can Sing A Rainbow/Love Is Blue-Hallelujah Baby | 6 |
| 69 | Chess CRS 8102 | Oh What A Night/Believe Me | 7 |
| 69 | President PT 270 | Oh What A Night/Moving On | 7 |
| 69 | Chess CRS 8105 | On The Dock Of The Bay/When I'm In Your Arms | 7 |
| 71 | Chess 6145 001 | The Love We Had Stays On My Mind/Freedom Means | 7 |
| 72 | Chess 6145 008 | It's All Up To You/Oh, My Dear | 6 |
| 73 | Chess 6145 022 | Give Your Baby A Standing Ovation/Run For Cover | 20 |
| 74 | Philips 6145037 | Bring Back The Love Of Yesterday/Learning To Love You Was Easy | 10 |
| 80 | 20th Century TC 2403 | All That Paper/I Touched A Dream | 10 |
| 80 | 20th Century TC 2478 | Your Song/Look At Us Now | 40 |
| 68 | Chess CRLS 4554 | GREATEST HITS (LP) | 25 |
| 69 | Chess CRLS 4555 | LOVE IS BLUE/OH, WHAT A NIGHT (LP) | 30 |
| 71 | Joy JOYS 186 | OH WHAT A NIGHT (LP) | 15 |

## ELAINE DELMAR
| | | | |
|---|---|---|---|
| 59 | Fontana H 227 | I Loves You Porgy/Porgy | 5 |

MINT VALUE £

| | | | |
|---|---|---|---|
| 67 | CBS 3191 | What Love Can Do/Too Much Loneliness | 5 |
| 68 | CBS 63511 | Sneakin' Up On You | 40 |
| 68 | CBS 3876 | Shadow Of The Evening/When I Learn To Love Again | 5 |
| 69 | CBS 4408 | The World Is Ours/The Rhythm Of Life | 5 |
| 69 | CBS 4017 | Why Can't I Go To Him/Those Were The Days | 5 |
| 70 | CBS 5329 | Hurt So Bad/The Train | 5 |
| 60 | Columbia SEG 8060 | A SWINGING CHICK (EP) | 20 |
| 68 | EMI SX6222 | LA BELLE ELAINE (LP) | 20 |
| 68 | CBS 63511 | SNEAKIN' UP ON YOU (LP) | 35 |

## DEL MONAS

| | | | |
|---|---|---|---|
| 85 | Empire JLM 14 | Sally Sue Brown/Dangerous Charms (7" die cut sleeve) | 15 |
| 84 | Big Beat SW 101 | COMIN' HOME BABY - VOLUME ONE (7" EP) | 12 |
| 84 | Big Beat SW 102 | HELLOW WE LOVE YOU - VOLUME TWO (7" EP) | 12 |
| 85 | Big Beat WIK 35 | DANGEROUS CHARMS (LP) | 20 |
| 85 | Empire SYF 95 | 5 (LP) | 25 |
| 88 | Hangman HANG 20 UP | 5 (LP, reissue) | 15 |
| 89 | Hangman HANG 28 UP | DEL MONAS (LP) | 18 |
| 99 | Vinyl Japan ASKLP 107 | DANGEROUS CHARMS (LP, reissue) | 15 |

## DANNY DELMONTE

| | | | |
|---|---|---|---|
| 63 | Oriole CB 1894 | John Kennedy/Come Summer | 5 |
| 64 | Oriole CB 1958 | Worry/Till I'm Back With You Darlin' Again | 5 |

## DELMONTES

| | | | |
|---|---|---|---|
| 80s | Rational RATE 3 | Don't Cry Your Tears/So It's Not To Be (yellow or blue p/s) | 8 |

## DELMONTS

| | | | |
|---|---|---|---|
| 71 | Spiral DIT 1 | A Ra Chicera/Sorry For My Jealousy | 6 |
| 72 | Spiral DIT 2 | Gimmie Gimmie Your Loving/Now Is The Time For Love | 15 |

## AL DE LORY

| | | | |
|---|---|---|---|
| 65 | London HLU 9999 | Yesterday/Traffic Jam | 20 |
| 70 | Capitol CL 15644 | Song From MASH/Feeling Of Love | 5 |

## LANA DEL REY

| | | | |
|---|---|---|---|
| 11 | Stranger 2783433 | Video Games/Blue Jeans (picture disc, 100 copies signed) | 20 |
| 12 | Polydor 2793424 | BORN TO DIE (2-LP) | 18 |

## DELROY & SPORTY

| | | | |
|---|---|---|---|
| 71 | Banana BA 322 | Lovers Version/DUDLEY SIBLEY: Having A Party | 20 |

## DELROY & TENNORS

| | | | |
|---|---|---|---|
| 71 | Camel CA 62 | Donkey Shank/MURPHY'S ALL STARS: Donkey Track | 20 |

## DELTA 5

| | | | |
|---|---|---|---|
| 79 | Rough Trade RT 31 | Mind Your Own Business/Now That You've Gone (p/s) | 10 |
| 80 | Rough Trade RT 41 | Anticipation/You (p/s) | 7 |
| 81 | Rough Trade RT 61 | Try/Colour (p/s) | 7 |
| 81 | Pre PRE 16 | Shadow/Leaving (p/s) | 5 |
| 82 | Pre PRE 24 | Powerlines/The Heart Is A Lonely Hunter (p/s) | 6 |
| 81 | PRE PREX 6 | SEE THE WHIRL (LP) | 15 |

## DELTA CATS

| | | | |
|---|---|---|---|
| 69 | Bamboo BAM 3 | I Can't Re-Live (song actually "I Can't Believe")/I've Been Hurt | 75 |

*(see also Thrillers)*

## DELTA RHYTHM BOYS

| | | | |
|---|---|---|---|
| 54 | Brunswick 05353 | Mood Indigo/Have A Hope, Have A Wish, Have A Prayer | 10 |
| 52 | Esquire 15-001 | DELTA RHYTHM BOYS WITH THE METRONOME ALLSTARS (10" LP) | 15 |

## DELTAS

| | | | |
|---|---|---|---|
| 64 | Blue Beat BB 265 | Georgia/The Party | 20 |
| 65 | Blue Beat BB 275 | The Visitor/SKATALITES: Hanging The Beam | 40 |

## DELTA SKIFFLE GROUP

| | | | |
|---|---|---|---|
| 58 | Esquire EP 162 | DELTA SKIFFLE GROUP (EP) | 40 |

## DELTONES (JAMAICA)

| | | | |
|---|---|---|---|
| 71 | Green Door GD 4010 | Chopsticks/DES BRYAN: Belmont Street | 8 |
| 72 | Trojan TRM 9001 | Chopsticks/I Got It/Put It On | 6 |

## DELTONES (U.K.)

| | | | |
|---|---|---|---|
| 70 | Columbia DB 8719 | Gimme Some Lovin'/Have A Little Talk With Myself | 20 |

## DEL-TONES (U.S.)

| | | | |
|---|---|---|---|
| 59 | Top Rank JAR 171 | Moonlight Party/Rockin' Blues | 100 |
| 59 | Top Rank JAR 171 | Moonlight Party/Rockin' Blues (78) | 20 |

*(see also Beau-Marks)*

## MILTON DE LUGG ORCHESTRA

| | | | |
|---|---|---|---|
| 65 | Columbia DB 7474 | The Addams Family Theme/The Alfred Hitchcock Theme | 8 |
| 66 | Columbia DB 7762 | The Munsters Theme/The Addams Family Theme | 8 |

*(see also Beau-Marks)*

## DELUSION

| | | | |
|---|---|---|---|
| 79 | Wizzo WIZZO 2 | Pessimists Paradise/Desert Island (gatefold p/s) | 8 |

## DELUSIONS OF GRANDEUR

| | | | |
|---|---|---|---|
| 86 | Music Factory GRAND 1 | We Are The Humans/Colour Me/Destiny (12", p/s) | 10 |

## LEO DE LYON

| | | | |
|---|---|---|---|
| 54 | MGM SP 1087 | The Band Played On/Say It Isn't So | 7 |
| 60 | Oriole CB 1561 | Rich In Love/The Blue Train | 5 |

## ARIN DEMAIN

| | | | |
|---|---|---|---|
| 90s | Goldmine/Soul Supply GS 028 | Silent Treatment/PARIS: Sleepless Nights | 8 |

**RALPH DE MARCO**
| | | | |
|---|---|---|---|
| 59 | London HLL 9010 | Old Shep/More Than Riches | 7 |

**DEMENSIONS**
| | | | |
|---|---|---|---|
| 60 | Top Rank JAR 505 | Over The Rainbow/Nursery Rhyme Rock | 40 |
| 61 | Coral Q 72437 | Count Your Blessings Instead Of Sheep/Again | 10 |

*(see also Wheels, James Brothers, Fox)*

**DEMENTED ARE GO**
| | | | |
|---|---|---|---|
| 86 | ID NOSE 9 | IN SICKNESS AND IN HEALTH (LP) | 20 |
| 88 | ID NOSE 21 | KICKED OUT OF HELL (LP) | 20 |
| 89 | Link MLP 084 | THE DAY THE EARTH SPAT BLOOD (LP, as the Demon Teds) | 15 |
| 90 | Link LRM 05 | GO GO DEMENTED (LP, blue vinyl) | 15 |
| 91 | Fury F 3016 | ORGASMIC NIGHTMARE (LP, blue vinyl) | 15 |
| 93 | Fury DAGLP 1 | TANGENTAL MADNESS ON A PLEASANT SIDE OF HELL (LP, white vinyl) | 15 |

**(ROD) DEMICK & (HERBIE) ARMSTRONG**
| | | | |
|---|---|---|---|
| 70 | Decca F 13056 | We're On The Right Track/Dreaming (as Demick-Armstrong) | 6 |
| 71 | Mam MAM 10 | If I Ever Get To You/Girl | 5 |
| 71 | Mam MAM-AS 1001 | LITTLE WILLY RAMBLE (LP, black/silver labels) | 25 |
| 72 | A&M AMLH 68908 | LOOKIN' THROUGH (LP, inner sleeve, brown label) | 50 |

**DEMOB**
| | | | |
|---|---|---|---|
| 81 | Round Ear ROUND 1 | Anti Police/Teenage Adolescence (foldout p/s) | 15 |
| 81 | Round Ear ROUND 1 | Anti Police/Teenage Adolescence (later standard p/s) | 10 |
| 81 | Round Ear EAR 3 | No Room For You/Think Straight/New Breed (p/s) | 18 |

**DEMOLITION**
| | | | |
|---|---|---|---|
| 81 | Demolition Rock ZEL SPS 296 | Hooker Hater/Axeman (p/s) | 250 |

**DEMON**
| | | | |
|---|---|---|---|
| 81 | Clay CLAY 4 | Liar/Wild Woman (p/s, red vinyl) | 8 |
| 83 | Clay CLAY 25 | The Plague/The Only Sane Man (p/s) | 6 |
| 84 | Clay CLAY 41 | Wonderland/Blackheath (p/s) | 6 |
| 88 | Clay CLAY 48D | Tonight (The Hero Is Back)/Hurricane/Night Of The Demon/Don't Break The Circle (double pack) | 5 |
| 81 | Carrere CA 651 | NIGHT OF THE DEMON (LP, pressed in France) | 20 |
| 83 | Clay CLAYLP 6 | THE PLAGUE (LP, gatefold sleeve, with insert) | 15 |
| 83 | Clay CLAYLP 6P | THE PLAGUE (LP, picture disc) | 20 |
| 90 | Sonic SONICLP 1 | NIGHT OF THE DEMON (LP, reissue) | 15 |
| 90 | Flametrader LP 1 | ONE HELLUVA NIGHT (2-LP) | 18 |

**DEMON BOYZ**
| | | | |
|---|---|---|---|
| 88 | Music Of Life NOTE 013 | Northside/Rougher Than An Animal | 10 |
| 89 | Music Of Life NOTE 26 | Recognition/Lyrical Culture (12") | 5 |
| 92 | Tribal Bass Tribe4 | DETT (12") | 10 |
| 92 | Tribal Bass Tribe9 | Glimity Glamity/Junglist (12") | 12 |
| 89 | Music Of Life DEMON1 | RECOGNITION (LP) | 15 |
| 92 | Tribal Bass Tribe11 | ORIGINAL GUIDANCE – THE SECOND CHAPTER (LP) | 40 |

**DEMON D**
| | | | |
|---|---|---|---|
| 95 | Voyager VOD 94 | Let The Jazz Take You/Together (12") | 18 |

**DEMON FUZZ**
| | | | |
|---|---|---|---|
| 70 | Dawn DNX 2504 | I Put A Spell On You/Message To Mankind/Fuzz Oriental Blues (p/s) | 50 |
| 70 | Dawn DNX 2504 | I Put A Spell On You/Message To Mankind/Fuzz Oriental Blues | 10 |
| 70 | Dawn DNLS 3013 | AFREAKA! (LP, gatefold sleeve, orange label) | 200 |

**DEMON PACT**
| | | | |
|---|---|---|---|
| 81 | Slime PACT 1 | Eaten Alive/Raiders (p/s) | 50 |
| 81 | Slime PACT 2 | Escape/Demon Pact (unreleased, labels only) | 0 |

**DEMON PREACHER**
| | | | |
|---|---|---|---|
| 78 | Illegal SRTS/CUS/78110 | Royal Northern (N7)/Laughing At Me/Steal Your Love/Dead End Kidz (numbered p/s) | 125 |
| 78 | Small Wonder SMALL TEN | Little Miss Perfect/Perfect Dub (p/s) | 20 |

*(see also Demons, Alien Sex Fiend, Fenzyx)*

**DEMON ROCKA**
| | | | |
|---|---|---|---|
| 82 | Unity UN 001 | Iron Lady/Stick Together | 12 |

**DEMONS (JAMAICA)**
| | | | |
|---|---|---|---|
| 69 | Big Shot BI 523 | You Belong To My Heart/Bless You | 20 |

**DEMONS (U.K.)**
| | | | |
|---|---|---|---|
| 80 | Crypt Music DEM 1 | Action By Example/I Wish I Was A Dog (p/s) | 12 |

*(see also Alien Sex Fiend, Demon Preacher)*

**DEMONSTRATORS**
| | | | |
|---|---|---|---|
| 64 | Warner Bros WB 132 | Sweet Violets/Ultra Violet | 12 |

**JASON DENE**
| | | | |
|---|---|---|---|
| 66 | Parlophone R 5485 | Opportunity/It's Me | 8 |

*(see also Jason Deane)*

**TERRY DENE**
| | | | |
|---|---|---|---|
| 57 | Decca F 10895 | A White Sport Coat/The Man In The Phone Booth | 7 |
| 57 | Decca F 10914 | Start Movin'/Green Corn | 7 |
| 57 | Decca F 10938 | Come And Get It/Teenage Dream | 7 |
| 57 | Decca F 10964 | Lucky Lucky Bobby/Baby, She's Gone | 7 |
| 58 | Decca F 10977 | The Golden Age/C'Min And Be Loved | 7 |
| 58 | Decca F 11016 | Stairway Of Love/Lover, Lover! | 5 |
| 58 | Decca F 11037 | Seven Steps To Love/Can I Walk You Home | 7 |
| 58 | Decca F 11076 | Who Baby Who/Pretty Little Pearly | 5 |
| 59 | Decca F 11100 | I've Got A Good Thing Going/Bimbombey | 5 |

MINT VALUE £

| | | | |
|---|---|---|---|
| 59 | Decca F 11136 | There's No Fool Like A Young Fool/I've Come Of Age | 5 |
| 59 | Decca F 11154 | Thank You Pretty Baby/A Boy Without A Girl | 5 |
| 60 | Oriole CB 1562 | Geraldine/Love Me Or Leave Me | 10 |
| 61 | Oriole CB 1594 | Like A Baby/Next Stop Paradise | 15 |
| 63 | Aral PS 107 | The Feminine Look/Fever (all in p/s) | 15 |
| 57 | Decca DFE 6459 | THE GOLDEN DISCS (EP) | 10 |
| 57 | Decca DFE 6507 | TERRY DENE NO. 1 (EP) | 10 |
| 66 | Herald ELR 107 | TERRY DENE NOW (EP) | 10 |

## DENE BOYS
| | | | |
|---|---|---|---|
| 57 | HMV POP 374 | Bye Bye Love/Love Is The Thing | 20 |
| 58 | HMV POP 455 | Skylark/I Walk Down The Street | 8 |

## DENE FOUR
| | | | |
|---|---|---|---|
| 59 | HMV POP 666 | Hush-a-bye/Something New | 25 |

*(see also Dene Boys)*

## DENIGH
| | | | |
|---|---|---|---|
| 80 | Ace ACE 16 | No Way/Running (no p/s) | 50 |

## DENIM
| | | | |
|---|---|---|---|
| 92 | Boys Own BOI 12 | Middle Of The Road/Ape Hangers | 8 |
| 92 | Boys Own BOIX 12 | Middle Of The Road/Ape Hangers/Robin's Nest/The Great Grape Ape Hangers (12") | 10 |
| 97 | EMI RADIODJ 1 | Summer Smash (promo, withdrawn) | 20 |
| 92 | Boys Own 82849 | BACK IN DENIM (LP) | 40 |
| 96 | Echo ECH LP8 | DENIM ON ICE (LP) | 30 |
| 97 | EMI ADISC 001 | NOVELTY ROCK (LP) | 15 |

*(see also Felt, Go-Kart Mozarts)*

## DENIMS
| | | | |
|---|---|---|---|
| 65 | CBS 201807 | I'm Your Man/Ya Ya | 70 |

## ROGER DENISON
| | | | |
|---|---|---|---|
| 66 | Parlophone R 5545 | I'm On An Island/I'm Running Out Of Time | 12 |
| 67 | Parlophone R 5566 | It Just Doesn't Seem To Be My Day/She Wanders Through My Mind | 50 |

## DENIZENS
| | | | |
|---|---|---|---|
| 79 | Big SOLD 5 | People Of The Night/Ammonia Subway (p/s) | 10 |
| 80 | Citizen | IN THE CROWD EP (with 16-page booklet) | 12 |

## SUE DENNING
| | | | |
|---|---|---|---|
| 65 | Columbia DB 7486 | Kiss Me Once Again/Goodtime Johnny | 20 |

## WADE DENNING & PORT WASHINGTONS
| | | | |
|---|---|---|---|
| 67 | MGM MGM 1339 | Tarzan's March/Batman | 15 |

## D.D. (DENZIL) DENNIS
| | | | |
|---|---|---|---|
| 70 | Crab CRAB 53 | Rain Is Ginna Fall/This Game Ain't Free | 25 |
| 70 | Crab CRAB 60 | Having A Party/Man With Ambition | 25 |
| 70 | Pama Supreme PS 301 | My Way/Happy Days | 25 |
| 71 | Punch PH 93 | Christmas Message/Cool It Girl | 15 |
| 71 | Pama Supreme PS 330 | I'm A Believer/I'll Make The Way Easy | 15 |
| 74 | Pama Supreme PS 391 | Women And Money/UPSETTERS: Ten Cent Skank | 15 |

*(see also Denzil Dennis)*

## D D DENNIS - BROTHER LLOYD'S ALL STARS
| | | | |
|---|---|---|---|
| 68 | Mercury MF 1064 | Save The Last Dance For Me/Will You Still Love Me Tomorrow | 15 |

## DENZIL DENNIS
| | | | |
|---|---|---|---|
| 63 | Blue Beat BB 181 | Seven Nights In Rome/Love Is For Fools (as DENZIL) | 15 |
| 68 | Trojan TR 614 | Donkey Train/Down By The Riverside | 15 |
| 68 | Trojan TR 615 | Me Nah Worry/Hush Don't You Cry | 15 |
| 68 | Jolly JY 011 | Oh Carol/Where Has My Little Girl Gone | 15 |
| 70 | Mary Lyn ML 100 | I Guess I'd Better Start Believing/When Will You Ever Learn | 15 |
| 70 | Pama Supreme PS 304 | Painful Situation/Nothing Has Changed | 8 |
| 71 | Pama Supreme PS 350 | South Of The Border/GRAHAM: Long Island | 15 |
| 72 | Pama Supreme PS 375 | Mama We're All Crazy Now/ROY SHIRLEY: A Lady's A Man's Best Friend | 7 |
| 72 | Duke DU 142 | I Forgot To Be Your Lover/I've Got To Settle Down | 5 |
| 73 | Grape GR 3059 | People Got To Be Friends/Ups And Downs (actually by Pat Rhoden) | 5 |
| 74 | Arrow AR 003 | If/How Can I Touch You | 8 |

*(see also D.D. Dennis, Cosmo & Dennis, Denzil & Pat, Denzil & Jennifer, Les & Silkie)*

## JACKIE DENNIS
| | | | |
|---|---|---|---|
| 58 | Decca F 10992 | La Dee Dah/You're The Greatest | 5 |
| 58 | Decca F 11011 | Miss Valerie/My Dream | 5 |
| 58 | Decca F 11033 | The Purple People Eater/You-Oo | 10 |
| 58 | Decca F 11060 | More Than Ever (Come Prima)/Linton Addie | 5 |
| 58 | Decca F 11090 | Gingerbread/Lucky Ladybug | 5 |
| 59 | Top Rank JAR 129 | Summer Snow/Night Bird | 5 |
| 58 | Decca DFE 6513 | JACKIE DENNIS NO. 1 (EP) | 10 |

## DENNIS & LIZZY
| | | | |
|---|---|---|---|
| 70 | Camel CA 56 | Everybody Bawlin'/Mr Brown | 10 |
| 73 | Pyramid PYR 7002 | Ba-Ba-Ri-Ba-Shank/TOMMY McCOOK ALL STARS: Buck And The Preacher | 12 |

*(see also Dennis Alcapone, Lizzy & Dennis)*

## DENNISONS
| | | | |
|---|---|---|---|
| 63 | Decca F 11691 | (Come On) Be My Girl/Little Latin Lupe Lu | 10 |
| 64 | Decca F 11880 | Walkin' The Dog/You Don't Know What Love Is | 15 |
| 64 | Decca F 11990 | Nobody Like My Babe/Lucy (You Sure Did It This Time) | 20 |

## SANDY DENNY
| | | | |
|---|---|---|---|
| 72 | Island WIP 6141 | Here In Silence/Man Of Iron (theme from Pass Of Arms film, in p/s) | 50 |

| 72 | Island WIP 6141 | Here In Silence/Man Of Iron (theme from Pass Of Arms film) | 25 |
| 72 | Island WIP 6142 | Listen Listen/Tomorrow Is A Long Time | 8 |
| 73 | Island WIP 6176 | Whispering Grass/Friends (p/s) | 8 |
| 73 | Island WIP 6176 | Whispering Grass/Friends | 5 |
| 74 | Island WIP 6195 | Like An Old Fashioned Waltz (unissued) | 0 |
| 76 | Mooncrest MOON 54 | Make Me A Pallet On Your Floor/This Train | 6 |
| 77 | Island WIP 6391 | Candle In The Wind/Still Waters Run Deep (unissued, promo only) | 30 |
| 11 | Island 276-797-3 | I'm A Dreamer (Second Demo)/Who Knows Where The Time Goes? (First Demo) | 8 |
| 67 | Saga EROS 8041 | SANDY AND JOHNNY (LP, with Johnny Silvo, black/silver label) | 30 |
| 70 | Saga EROS 8153 | SANDY DENNY (LP) | 30 |
| 71 | Island ILPS 9165 | THE NORTH STAR GRASSMAN AND THE RAVENS (LP, gatefold sleeve, 'pink rim palm tree' label) | 60 |
| 72 | Island ILPS 9207 | SANDY (LP, gatefold sleeve, original pressing with 'pink rim palm tree' label) | 50 |
| 73 | Island ILPS 9258 | LIKE AN OLD FASHIONED WALTZ (LP, gatefold sleeve, 'pink rim palm tree' label) | 40 |
| 73 | Hallmark SHM 813 | ALL OUR OWN WORK (LP, with Strawbs) | 15 |
| 77 | Island ILPS 9433 | RENDEZVOUS (LP, with lyric inner sleeve) | 25 |
| 78 | Mooncrest CREST 28 | THE ORIGINAL SANDY DENNY (LP) | 25 |
| 97 | Strange Fruit SFRSCD 006 | THE BBC SESSIONS 1971-73 (CD, limited edition, withdrawn – beware of bootlegs) | 30 |
| 85 | Island SDSP 100 | WHO KNOWS WHERE THE TIME GOES (4-LP, box set with booklet) | 60 |

*(see also Fairport Convention, Strawbs, Fotheringay, Alex Campbell, Trevor Lucas, Richard Thompson)*

## SUSAN DENNY
| 65 | Melodisc MEL 1596 | Don't Touch Me/Johnny | 35 |

## DENNY & WILSON
| 72 | Hillcrest HCT 6 | Hey Hey Girl/CARLTON ALPHONSO: Girl I Love You | 6 |

## DENTISTS
| 85 | Spruck SP 003 | Strawberries Are Growing In My Garden (And It's Wintertime)/Burning The Thoughts From My Skin/Doreen (p/s) | 12 |
| 85 | Spruck SP 004 | YOU AND YOUR BLOODY ORANGES (12" EP, p/s) | 10 |
| 86 | Tambourine SP 006 | DOWN AND OUT IN PARIS AND CHATHAM (12" EP, brown/white or group p/s) | 10 |
| 87 | Tambourine URINE 3 | Writhing On The Shagpile/Just Like Oliver Reed/A Strange Way To Go About Things/Calm You Down/The Turquoise Castle (12", p/s) | 10 |
| 85 | Spruck SPR 001 | SOME PEOPLE ARE ON THE PITCH THEY THINK IT'S ALL OVER IT IS NOW (LP) | 15 |

## MICKEY DENTON
| 61 | London HLX 9398 | The Steady Kind/Now You Can't Give Them Away | 8 |

## NIGEL DENVER
| 64 | Decca DFE 8580 | FOLK SINGER (EP) | 15 |
| 66 | Decca LK 4728 | MOVIN' ON (LP, featuring Martin Carthy) | 40 |
| 67 | Decca LK 4844 | REBELLION (LP) | 20 |

## DENYM
| 82 | Occult S 82 CUS 1351 | Beauty/Selassie Hi | 30 |
| 83 | Real Wax RW003 | Why Boy/Why Dub (12") | 50 |

## DENZIL & JENNIFER
| 70 | Escort ES 824 | Young, Gifted And Black/OWEN GRAY: I Am Satisfied | 100 |

## DENZIL (DENNIS) & PAT (RHODEN)
| 69 | Downtown DT 403 | Dream/Sincerely | 15 |

## WILBUR DE PARIS' NEW ORLEANS BAND
| 59 | London HLE 8816 | Petite Fleur/Over And Over Again | 5 |

## DEPECHE MODE
### SINGLES
| 81 | Lyntone LYN 10209 | Sometimes I Wish I Was Dead/FAD GADGET: King Of The Flies (test pressing) | 150 |
| 81 | Lyntone LYN 10209 | Sometimes I Wish I Was Dead/FAD GADGET: King Of The Flies (red flexidisc free with Flexipop magazine, issue 11) | 25 |
| 81 | Lyntone LYN 10209 | Sometimes I Wish I Was Dead/FAD GADGET: I Wish I Was Dead (red vinyl flexidisc free without Flexipop magazine, issue 11) | 15 |
| 81 | Mute MUTE 013 | Dreaming Of Me/Ice Machine (p/s) | 5 |
| 84 | Mute L12BONG 6 | Master And Servant (On-U-Sound Science Fiction Dancehall Classic)/Are People People?/(Set Me Free) Remotivate Me (12", numbered p/s) | 25 |
| 87 | Mute CDBONG 14 | Never Let Me Down Again (Split Mix)/Pleasure Little Treasure (Join Mix)/ To Have And To Hold (Spanish Taster)/Never Let Me Down Again (Aggro Mix) (CD in pouch) | 8 |
| 87 | Mute P12 BONG 14 | Never Let Me Down Again (7" Mix)/Pleasure Little Treasure (7" Mix)/Never Let Me Down Again (12" Split Mix) (12") | 50 |
| 89 | Mute 10BONG 16 | Everything Counts (Absolute Mix)/(1983 12" Mix)/Nothing (US 7" Mix) (10", envelope p/s, with 2 postcards & window sticker) | 10 |
| 89 | Mute LCDBONG 16 | Everything Counts (Tim Simenon & M. Saunders Remix)/Nothing (Justin Strauss Remix)/Strangelove (Tim Simenon & M. Saunders Remix) (3" CD 'filofax' page- p/s) | 15 |
| 89 | Mute L12BONG 17 | Personal Jesus (Mixes)/Dangerous (Hazchemix) (12", p/s) | 15 |
| 00 | Mute 12 BONG 22 | Walking In My Shoes (Grungy Gonads Mix)/(Seven Inch Mix)/My Joy (Seven Inch Mix)/(Slow Slide Mix) (12", p/s, repressing with 'Olympus Studios' misprint)) | 20 |

### ALBUMS
| 82 | Mute STUMM 5 | SPEAK AND SPELL (LP) | 15 |
| 85 | Mute MUTEL1 | SINGLES 81-85 (LP, gatefold, inner) | 20 |
| 87 | Mute STUMM 47 | MUSIC FOR THE MASSES (LP, clear vinyl) | 50 |
| 87 | Mute STUMM 47 | MUSIC FOR THE MASSES (LP, with bonus 12" "Strangelove (Maximix)"/"Never Let Me Down Again (Split Mix)" [HMV1]) | 40 |
| 89 | Mute STUMM 101 | 101 (2-LP, stickered gatefold sleeve, inner sleeves and booklet) | 20 |
| 90 | Mute STUMM 64 | VIOLATOR (LP, inner) | 30 |
| 90 | Mute STUMM 47 | MUSIC FOR THE MASSES (LP, reissue, withdrawn, 'budget' sleeve) | 2000 |
| 93 | Mute STUMM 106 | SONGS OF FAITH AND DEVOTION (LP, inner) | 20 |
| 97 | Mute STUMM 148 | ULTRA (LP, inner sleeve with transfer) | 40 |
| 98 | Mute P12MUTEL5 | REMIXES 86-98 (3-LP) | 40 |
| 98 | Mute MUTEL 5 | THE SINGLES 86-98 (3 x LP, box set with booklet, numbered) | 40 |

# DEPECHE MODE

MINT VALUE £

| 01 | Mute STUMM 190 | EXCITER (2-LP) | 30 |
|----|----------------|----------------|----|
| 04 | Mute MUTEL 8 | MUTE REMIXES 81-04 (6 x LP box set, numbered) | 50 |
| 09 | Mute STUMM 300 | SOUNDS OF THE UNIVERSE (2-LP) | 20 |
| 09 | Mute BXSTUMM300 | SOUNDS OF THE UNIVERSE (4-CD/DVD set) | 40 |

## PROMOS

| 82 | Mute 12MUTE 018 | See You/This Is Fun (12", white label promo) | 40 |
|----|-----------------|-----------------------------------------------|----|
| 82 | Mute 12 BONG 1 | Leave In Silence (Stripped Mix)/Instrumental (12" white label promo) | 50 |
| 84 | Mute 12 BONG 8 | Blasphemous Rumours/Somebody (Live)/Two Minute Warning (Live)/Ice Machine (Live)/Everything Counts (Live) (12" white label promo) | 60 |
| 86 | Mute BONG 10 | Stripped/But Not Tonight (white label test pressing) | 250 |
| 86 | Mute RR BONG 10 | Breathing In Fumes/Stripped (Highland Mix) (12", white labels, some stamped) | 80 |
| 86 | Mute 7BONG 12 | A Question Of Time (Edited)/Black Celebration (Live) (white label) | 100 |
| 86 | Mute L12 BONG 12 | A Question Of Time (New Town Mix)/A Question Of Time (Live)/Black Celebration (Black Tulip Mix)/More Than A Party (Live) (12", printed labels with stamped number, plain black die-cut sleeve) | 30 |
| 87 | Mute BONG 14R | Never Let Me Down Again/Pleasure Little Treasure | 80 |
| 87 | Mute R BONG 13 | Strangelove (Radio Edit)/Strangelove (p/s) | 100 |
| 87 | Mute DANCE BONG 13 | Strangelove (Blind Mix)/(Fresh Ground Mix) (12", promo-only remix some on blue vinyl) | 80 |
| 87 | Mute CLUB BONG 13 | Strangelove (12 Inch Maxi Mix)/Strangelove (Pain Mix) (12", promo) | 80 |
| 87 | Mute 12BONG 14 | Never Let Me Down Again (Split Mix)/Pleasure Little Treasure (Glitter Mix)/ Never Let Me Down Again (Aggro Mix) (12") | 40 |
| 87 | Mute DJBONG 15 | Behind The Wheel (DJ Remix)/Behind The Wheel (LP Mix) | 300 |
| 87 | Mute D BONG 15 | Behind The Wheel (Shep Mix)/Behind The Wheel (LP Mix)/Route 66 (7" Mix) (12") | 30 |
| 87 | Mute (no cat. no.) | THE B-SIDES (4-LP test pressings in title box) | 800 |
| 87 | Mute (no cat. no.) | THE B-SIDES (4-cassette set) | 200 |
| 89 | Mute PP12BONG 16 | Strangelove (Hijack Mix)/Nothing (12") | 18 |
| 89 | Mute BONG 16R | Everything Counts (Live – Radio Edit)/Nothing (Live Mix) (stickered p/s) | 20 |
| 89 | Mute P12 BONG 16 | Everything Counts (Tim Simenon/Mark Saunders Remix)/(Alan Moulder Remix) (12", black die-cut sleeve) | 20 |
| 89 | Mute P12 BONG 17 | Personal Jesus (Pump Mix)/Dangerous (Hazchemix) (12", black die-cut sleeve) | 20 |
| 89 | Mute BONG 17 | Personal Jesus/Dangerous (censored black rear p/s) | 60 |
| 90 | Mute BONG 18 | Enjoy The Silence/Memphisto ('A' label) | 50 |
| 90 | Mute P12 BONG 18 | Enjoy The Silence (Bass Line)/(Ricki Tik Tik Mix)/(7" Mix) (12", die-cut Mute sleeve) | 20 |
| 90 | Mute R7 BONG 19 | Policy Of Truth (Radio Edit)/Kaleid (p/s) | 20 |
| 90 | Mute P12 BONG 19 | Policy Of Truth (Capitol Mix)/(Pavlov's Dub)/(Trancentral)/Kaleid (Remix) (12", die-cut Mute sleeve) | 15 |
| 90 | Mute 12BONG 20 | World In My Eyes (Oil Tank Mix)/Happiest Girl (Kiss-A-Mix)/Sea Of Sin (Sensoria) (12", white label, numbered, stickered sleeve) | 30 |
| 90 | Mute BONG 20R | World In My Eyes (7" Version)/Happiest Girl (Jack Mix)/Sea Of Sin (Tonal Mix) (p/s, 33rpm) | 20 |
| 90 | Mute PSTUMM 64 | VIOLATOR (12" EP, 4-track sampler) | 30 |
| 90 | Mute (no cat. no.) | VIOLATOR (LP, CD & cassette in 12" x 12" picture box with insert) | 400 |
| 90 | Mute P12 BONG 20 | World In My Eyes (Mayhem Mode Mix)/Happiest Girl (The Pulsating Orbital Mix) (12", die-cut Mute sleeve) | 20 |
| 93 | Mute P12 BONG 21 | I Feel You (Throb Mix)/(Seven Inch Mix)/(Babylon Mix)/One Caress (12", die-cut Mute sleeve) | 20 |
| 93 | Mute BONG 22 | Walking In My Shoes/My Joy (large centre hole) | 20 |
| 93 | Mute BONG 23 | Condemnation (Paris Mix)/Death's Door (Jazz Mix) (large centre hole) | 30 |
| 93 | Mute PL12BONG 23 | Rush (Spiritual Guidance Mix)/Rush (Amylnitrate Mix)/Rush (Wild Planet Vocal Mix) (12") | 40 |
| 93 | Mute P12 BONG 22 | Walking In My Shoes (Grungy Gonads Mix)/(Seven Inch Mix)/My Joy (Seven Inch Mix)/(Slow Slide Mix) (12", die-cut Mute sleeve) | 20 |
| 93 | Mute P 12 BONG 23 | Condemnation (Paris Mix)/Death's Door (Jazz Mix)/Rush (Spiritual Guidance Mix) (12". die-cut Mute sleeve) | 30 |
| 93 | Mute VERBONG 1 | SONGS OF FAITH & DEVOTION (interview CD) | 20 |
| 93 | Mute (no cat. no.) | SONGS OF FAITH & DEVOTION (4-CD box set) | 300 |
| 94 | Mute P12 BONG 24 | In Your Room (The Jeep Rock Mix)/Higher Love (Adrenaline Mix)/In Your Room (Extended Zephyr Mix) (12", die-cut Mute sleeve) | 25 |
| 94 | Mute DEPRO 1 | DEPRO 1 (13-track compilation CD) | 50 |
| 97 | Mute BONG 26 | It's No Good (Club 69 Future Mix)/It's No Good (Club 69 Future Dub)/It's No Good (Club 69 Funk Dub) (12") | 35 |
| 97 | Mute PL12BONG 26 | It's No Good (Club 69 mixes) (12") | 40 |
| 97 | Mute P12BONG26 | It's No Good (Hardfloor Mix)/(Speedy J Mix)/(Motor Bass Mix)/(Andrea Parker Mix)/ (Dom T Mix) (12") | 8 |
| 97 | Mute XLCDBONG 26 | It's No Good (Live) (CD) | 70 |
| 97 | Mute P12 BONG 27 | Home (Jedi Knights Remix [Drowning In Time])/(Air "Around The Golf" Remix)/ (Meant To Be)/(Grantby Mix) (12", 33rpm, die-cut p/s) | 12 |
| 97 | Mute P12BONG 28 | Useless (CJ Bolland Funky Sub Mix)/Useless (the Kruder & Dorfmeister Session™) (12", die-cut p/s) | 20 |
| 97 | Mute BXSTUMM 148 | ULTRA (box set, with CD, T-shirt, stickers & EPK video, soap box pack) | 80 |
| 98 | Mute (no cat. no.) | THE SINGLES 86>98 (15" x 6" box set, with 3 CDs, video tape & cards) | 120 |
| 01 | Mute PL12BONG 30 | Dream On (Octagon Man Mix)/(Octagon Man Dub)/(Dave Clarke Acoustic Mix)/(Kid 606 Mix) 12" p/s | 12 |
| 01 | Mute PL12BONG 32 | Freelove (Deep Dish Freedom Mix)/Freelove (Josh Wink Vocal Interpretation)/ Freelove (Deep Dish Freedom Dub)/Freelove (Power Productions Remix) (12", doublepack, p/s) | 15 |
| 01 | Mute PXL 12 BONG 31 | I Feel Loved (Umek Mix)/(Thomas Brinkman Remix)/(Chamber's Remix) (12", p/s) | 12 |
| 01 | Mute !PKSTUMM 190 | EXCITER (interview CD with bonus multimedia disc) | 30 |
| 01 | Mute BCDSTUMM 190 | EXCITER (interview CD with bonus multimedia disc, in long box) | 60 |
| 04 | Mute P12BONG 34 | REMIXES 81 – 04 SAMPLER : Enjoy The Silence (Richard X Extended Mix)/(Ewan Pearson Extended Instrumental)/Timo Maas Extended Remix)/Ewan Pearson Extended Remix) (2 x 12") | 20 |
| 04 | Mute ACD MUTEL8 | REMIXES 81 – 04 (3 x CD, insert & press release) | 30 |
| 06 | Mute PXL12 BONG 39 | Just Can't Get Enough – (Dirty South Mix)/Personal Jesus (Timo Maas Remix) | 5 |

| | | | |
|---|---|---|---|
| 06 | Mute DMINT06CD | THE BEST OF VOLUME 1 - Interview Disc CD (p/s) | 25 |

## DEPRESSIONS
| | | | |
|---|---|---|---|
| 77 | Barn 2014 112 | Living On Dreams/Family Planning (p/s) | 10 |
| 78 | Barn 2014 119 | Messing With Your Heart/Street Kid (p/s) | 10 |
| 78 | Barn 2014 122 | Get Out Of This Town/Basement Daze (p/s) | 10 |
| 78 | Barn 2314 105 | THE DEPRESSIONS (LP) | 30 |

## DEPUTIES
| | | | |
|---|---|---|---|
| 66 | Strike JH 305 | Given Half A Chance/Where Do People Go | 12 |

## DEPUTY DAWG
| | | | |
|---|---|---|---|
| 96 | Peacefrog P F053 | GUN SLINGER EP (12", plain sleeve) | 10 |

*(see also Luke Slater)*

## DEREK
| | | | |
|---|---|---|---|
| 68 | London HLZ 10230 | Cinnamon/This Is My Story | 12 |

*(see also Johnny Cymbal)*

## DEREK & THE DOMINOES
| | | | |
|---|---|---|---|
| 70 | Polydor 2058 057 | Tell The Truth/Roll It Over (withdrawn) | 80 |
| 70 | Polydor 2058 130 | Layla/Bell Bottom Blues (original, red paper label) | 6 |
| 74 | RSO 2090 104 | Why Does Love Got To Be Sad?/Presence Of The Lord | 5 |
| 82 | RSO RSO 87 | Layla/ERIC CLAPTON: Wonderful Tonight (p/s) | 5 |
| 71 | Polydor 2625 005 | LAYLA AND OTHER ASSORTED LOVE SONGS (2-LP, gatefold sleeve) | 30 |
| 11 | Universal 0600753314326 | LAYLA AND OTHER ASSORTED LOVE SONGS (box set, 4-CD, DVD, Book, art print and badge) | 45 |

*(see also Eric Clapton, Bobby Whitlock)*

## DEREK & FRESHMEN
| | | | |
|---|---|---|---|
| 65 | Oriole CB 305 | Gone Away/I Stand Alone | 15 |

*(see also Derek Dean & Freshmen)*

## FRANK DE ROSA & HIS ORCHESTRA
| | | | |
|---|---|---|---|
| 58 | London HLD 8576 | Big Guitar/Irish Rock | 10 |

## DERRICK (MORGAN) & JENNIFER
| | | | |
|---|---|---|---|
| 70 | Crab CRAB 47 | Need To Belong/Let's Have Some Fun | 20 |
| 70 | Crab CRAB 54 | Rocking Good Way/Wipe These Tears | 20 |

*(see also Derrick Morgan)*

## DERRICK (MORGAN) & LLOYDS (CLARKE)
| | | | |
|---|---|---|---|
| 62 | Blue Beat BB 135 | Love And Leave Me (actually by Lloyd Clarke)/Merry Twist (actually "Whistle Stop Tour" by Roy Richards) | 15 |

*(see also Derrick Morgan, Lloyd Clarke)*

## DERRICK (MORGAN) & NAOMI (CAMPBELL)
| | | | |
|---|---|---|---|
| 65 | Island WI 193 | Two Of A Kind/I Want A Lover (credited to Derrick Morgan) | 20 |
| 65 | Ska Beat JB 185 | Heart Of Stone/DERRICK MORGAN: Let Me Go | 18 |
| 65 | Ska Beat JB 188 | I Wish I Were An Apple/DERRICK MORGAN: Around The Corner | 18 |

*(see also Derrick Morgan, Naomi, Don Drummond)*

## DERRICK (MORGAN) & PATSY (TODD)
| | | | |
|---|---|---|---|
| 61 | Blue Beat BB 57 | Feel So Fine/ROLAND ALPHONSO & GROUP: Mean To Me | 18 |
| 61 | Blue Beat BB 65 | Baby Please Don't Leave Me/Let The Good Times Roll | 20 |
| 62 | Blue Beat BB 97 | Love Not To Brag/DRUMBAGO'S ALL STARS: Duck Soup | 20 |
| 62 | Blue Beat BB 100 | In My Heart (actually by Derrick Morgan)/BELL'S GROUP: Kingston 13 | 30 |
| 62 | Blue Beat BB 106 | Oh Shirley/BASIL GABIDON'S GROUP: Sam The Fisherman (B-side actually by Roland Alphonso) | 18 |
| 62 | Blue Beat BB 121 | Crying In The Chapel/Come Back My Love | 15 |
| 62 | Blue Beat BB 123 | Oh My Love/Let's Go To The Party | 15 |
| 62 | Island WI 018 | Housewife's Choice/Gypsy Woman | 18 |
| 63 | Blue Beat BB 152 | Little Brown Jug/Mow Sen Wa (with Lloyd Clarke) | 15 |
| 63 | Blue Beat BB 160 | Trying To Make You Mine (actually "Baby Please Don't Leave Me" by Derrick Morgan)/Hold Me | 15 |
| 63 | Island WI 055 | Sea Wave/Look Before You Leap | 20 |
| 64 | Blue Beat BB 207 | Lover Boy/The Moon | 15 |
| 64 | Blue Beat BB 224 | Steal Away/Money | 15 |
| 64 | Blue Beat BB 247CD | Troubles/Right (B-side actually "Baby Face") | 15 |
| 65 | Blue Beat BB 291 | You I Love/Let Me Hold Your hand (song actually "Steal Away") | 15 |
| 65 | Blue Beat BB 318 | Eternity/Want My Baby | 15 |
| 65 | Island WI 224 | The National Dance/DESMOND DEKKER & FOUR ACES: Mount Zion | 25 |
| 66 | Island WI 288 | I Found A Queen/It's True My Darling | 18 |
| 68 | Nu Beat NB 008 | Hey Boy, Hey Girl/Music Is The Food Of Life | 15 |

*(see also Derrick Morgan, Patsy Todd)*

## DERRICK (MORGAN) & PAULETT
| | | | |
|---|---|---|---|
| 69 | Nu Beat NB 027 | I'll Do It/Give You My Love | 20 |

*(see also Derrick Morgan, Paulette)*

## DERRICK (MORGAN) & PAULINE (MORGAN)
| | | | |
|---|---|---|---|
| 68 | Pyramid PYR 6027 | You Never Miss Your Water/DERRICK MORGAN: Got You On My Mind | 18 |
| 68 | Pyramid/J.J. PYR 6063 | Don't Say/DERRICK MORGAN: Johnny Pram Pram | 40 |

*(see also Derrick Morgan, Patsy Todd, Basil Gabbidon)*

## DERRICK & SOUNDS
| | | | |
|---|---|---|---|
| 68 | Pye 7N 17601 | Power Of Love/I'll Take You Home | 5 |
| 69 | Pye 7N 17709 | My Sly Sadie/I Can't Lose That Girl | 5 |
| 69 | Pye 7N 17801 | Morning Papers And Margarine/Winter Of Your Love | 12 |

## DERRINGERS
| | | | |
|---|---|---|---|
| 61 | Capitol CL 15189 | (If You Cry) True Love, True Love/Sheree | 10 |

## DES ALLSTARS
| | | | |
|---|---|---|---|
| 79 | Black Joy DH807 | Gone West/West Side (12", yellow/green vinyl) | 10 |

## DES (BRYAN) ALLSTARS
| | | | |
|---|---|---|---|
| 70 | Grape GR 3014 | Night Food Reggae/Walk With Des | 50 |
| 70 | Grape GR 3015 | If I Had A Hammer/Hammer Reggae | 20 |
| 70 | Grape GR 3016 | Henry The Great/Black Scorcher | 25 |

## HENRI DES
| | | | |
|---|---|---|---|
| 70 | United Artists UP 35109 | Return/Retour | 18 |

## SUGAR PIE DE SANTO
| | | | |
|---|---|---|---|
| 64 | Pye International 7N 25249 | Soulful Dress/Use What You Got | 25 |
| 64 | Pye International 7N 25267 | I Don't Wanna Fuss/I Love You So Much | 30 |
| 66 | Chess CRS 8034 | There's Gonna Be Trouble/In The Basement (B-side with Etta James) | 30 |
| 69 | Chess CRS 8093 | Soulful Dress/There's Gonna Be Trouble | 20 |

*(see also Etta James & Sugar Pie De Santo)*

## MICHAEL DES BARRES
| | | | |
|---|---|---|---|
| 74 | Purple PUR 123 | Leon/New Moon Tonight | 8 |

*(see also Silverhead)*

## DESCENDANTS
| | | | |
|---|---|---|---|
| 67 | CBS 202545 | Garden Of Eden/Lela | 50 |

## DESECTORS
| | | | |
|---|---|---|---|
| 70 | GAS GAS 137 | King Kong/Please Stay | 6 |

## DESERT SESSIONS (JOSH HOLME)
| | | | |
|---|---|---|---|
| 03 | Island IS 835 | Crawl Home/The Whores Hustle And The Hustlers Whore (p/s) | 20 |

*(see also P J Harvey)*

## DESERT WOLVES
| | | | |
|---|---|---|---|
| 87 | Ugly Man UGLY 6 | Love Scattered Lives/Stopped In My Tracks (p/s) | 20 |
| 87 | Ugly Man UGLY 6T | Love Shattered Lives/Stopped In My Tracks/Desolation/ Sunday Morning (12", p/s) | 25 |
| 88 | Ugly Man UGLY 9 | Speak To Me Rochelle/Besotted (p/s) | 15 |
| 88 | Ugly Man UGLY 9T | Speak To Me Rochelle/Mexico/Besotted/La Petite Rochelle (12", p/s) | 20 |

## JACKIE DE SHANNON
| | | | |
|---|---|---|---|
| 62 | Liberty LIB 55497 | You Won't Forget Me/I Don't Think So Much | 20 |
| 63 | Liberty LIB 55563 | Needles And Pins/Did He Call Today Mama? | 20 |
| 64 | Liberty LIB 55645 | When You Walk In The Room/Till You Say You'll Be Mine | 20 |
| 64 | Liberty LIB 10165 | Dancing Silhouettes/Hold Your Head High | 15 |
| 64 | Liberty LIB 10175 | Don't Turn Your Back On Me/Be Good Baby | 18 |
| 65 | Liberty LIB 10192 | She Don't Understand Him Like I Do/The Prince | 12 |
| 65 | Liberty LIB 10202 | What The World Needs Now Is Love/It's Love Baby | 7 |
| 65 | Liberty LIB 12019 | A Lifetime Of Loneliness/I Remember The Boy | 10 |
| 66 | Liberty LIB 66171 | Come And Get Me/Splendour In The Grass | 5 |
| 66 | Liberty LIB 66202 | I Can Make It With You/To Be Myself | 5 |
| 66 | Liberty LIB 66224 | Come On Down/Find Me Love | 20 |
| 68 | Liberty LBF 15133 | The Weight/Effervescent Blue | 6 |
| 69 | Liberty LBF 15238 | Put A Little Love In Your Heart/Always Together | 8 |
| 65 | Liberty LEP 2233 | JACKIE (EP) | 40 |
| 64 | Liberty LBY 1182 (S) | JACKIE DE SHANNON (LP) | 25 |
| 65 | Liberty LBY 1245 | DON'T TURN YOUR BACK ON ME (LP) | 25 |
| 65 | Liberty LBY 3063 | THIS IS JACKIE DE SHANNON (LP) | 20 |
| 66 | Liberty SLBY 3085 | ARE YOU READY FOR THIS? (LP) | 25 |
| 68 | Liberty LBS 83117E | GREAT PERFORMANCES (LP) | 20 |
| 69 | Liberty LBS 83148E | ME ABOUT YOU (LP) | 20 |
| 70 | Liberty LBS 83304 | PUT A LITTLE LOVE IN YOUR HEART (LP) | 20 |
| 72 | Atlantic K 40396 | JACKIE (LP) | 15 |

*(see also Date With Soul)*

## DESIGN FOR LIVING
| | | | |
|---|---|---|---|
| 84 | Anthem 3 | Hold Me Closer/The Girl Who Knew Too Much | 18 |

## DESIGN (1)
| | | | |
|---|---|---|---|
| 70 | CBS 5112 | Willow Stream/Coloured Mile | 7 |
| 71 | Epic EPC 7119 | Jet Song/Minstrel's Theme | 15 |
| 72 | Regal Zonophone RZ 3044 | Colour All The World/Lazy Song | 7 |
| 72 | Regal Zonophone RZ 3060 | Mayday/Yellow Bird (Have You No Home) | 6 |
| 73 | Regal Zonophone RZ 3082 | One Sunny Day/End Of The Party | 6 |
| 76 | EMI 2430 | Michaelangelo/Never Need Another Love | 6 |
| 71 | Epic EPC 64322 | DESIGN (LP) | 15 |
| 71 | Epic EPC64653 | TOMORROW IS SO FAR AWAY (LP, with lyric insert, stickered sleeve) | 20 |
| 73 | Regal Zono. SLRZ 1037 | DAY OF THE FOX (LP, textured sleeve, red/silver label) | 15 |

## DESIGN (2)
| | | | |
|---|---|---|---|
| 86 | Dental 12DENT001 | I Want You I Need You/Never Gonna Give You Up (12") | 40 |

## DESIRE
| | | | |
|---|---|---|---|
| 79 | Carrere CAR 124 | Boogie Airlines/Lifting Off | 7 |

## DESI ROOTS
| | | | |
|---|---|---|---|
| 79 | Hawkeye HD 018 | Hung-Up/Up-Town Rebel (12") | 20 |
| 80 | Hawkeye HD 025 | Weed Fields/Hawkeye All Stars – Burning (12") | 40 |
| 80 | Hawkeye HD 033 | Go Deh Right/Revolutionaries Go Right Deh (12") | 30 |
| 80 | Hawkeye HLP 007 | DO IT RIGHT (LP) | 40 |

## ANDY DESMOND
| | | | |
|---|---|---|---|
| 74 | Konk KOS2 | So It Goes/She Can Move Mountains | 5 |
| 75 | Konk KOS4 | Beware/Only Child | 5 |
| 75 | Konk KONK 103 | LIVING ON A SHOESTRING (LP) | 40 |

*(see also Gothic Horizon)*

## JOHNNY DESMOND
| 55 | Vogue Coral Q 72099 | Yellow Rose Of Texas/You're In Love With Someone | 7 |
|----|---------------------|--------------------------------------------------|---|
| 56 | Vogue Coral Q 72115 | Sixteen Tons/Ballo Italiano | 7 |
| 57 | Vogue Coral Q 72261 | A White Sports Coat (And A Pink Carnation)/Just Lookin' | 7 |
| 57 | Vogue Coral Q 72269 | Shenandoah Rose/Consideration | 5 |
| 58 | Philips PB 890 | Willingly/Apple (when Ya Gonna Fall From The Trees?) | 5 |
| 58 | MGM MGM 994 | Hot Cha Cha/I'll Close My Eyes | 5 |
| 60 | Coral Q 72398 | The Most Happy Fella/LANCERS: Joey, Joey, Joey | 5 |
| 60 | Philips PB 1044 | Hawk/Playing The Field | 25 |
| 62 | Top Rank JAR 612 | Twistin' Rose Of Texas/ Hello Honey | 6 |
| 66 | Polydor BM 56703 | My Melancholy Baby/The Common Touch | 5 |
| 67 | Stateside SS 373 | Rio Conchos/Fate In The Hunter | 7 |

## LORRAE DESMOND (& REBELS)
| 54 | Decca F 10375 | Hold My Hand/On The Waterfront | 10 |
|----|---------------|--------------------------------|----|
| 54 | Decca F 10398 | Far Away (My Love Is Far Away)/No One But You | 10 |
| 54 | Decca F 10404 | I Can't Tell A Waltz From A Tango/For Better, For Worse (with Johnston Brothers) | 10 |
| 55 | Decca F 10461 | A Boy On Saturday Night/Why — Oh Why? | 10 |
| 55 | Decca F 10510 | Don't/Where Will The Baby's Dimple Be? | 10 |
| 55 | Decca F 10533 | Stowaway/Heartbroken (B-side with Johnston Brothers) | 10 |
| 55 | Decca F 10612 | You Should Know/Wake The Town And Tell The People | 6 |
| 56 | Parlophone R 4239 | Written On The Wind/A House With Love In It | 6 |
| 57 | Parlophone R 4287 | You Won't Be Around/Play The Music (as Lorrae Desmond & Rebels) | 8 |
| 57 | Parlophone R 4320 | Kansas City Special/Preacher, Preacher (as Lorrae Desmond & Rebels) | 6 |
| 57 | Parlophone R 4361 | Ding-Dong Rock-a-billy Weddin'/Cabin Boy (as Lorrae Desmond & Rebels) | 10 |
| 58 | Parlophone R 4400 | Two Ships/Little David | 8 |
| 58 | Parlophone R 4430 | Down By The River/The Secret Of Happiness | 6 |
| 58 | Parlophone R 4463 | Soda Pop Hop/Blue, Blue Day | 20 |
| 59 | Parlophone R 4534 | Tall Paul/Wait For It | 10 |
| 60 | Parlophone R 4670 | Tell Me Again/Get Your Daddie's Car Tonight | 10 |

## MIKE DESMOND
| 57 | Columbia DB 3954 | Young And In Love/Two Loves (as Michael Desmond) | 6 |
|----|------------------|--------------------------------------------------|---|
| 57 | Columbia DB 4018 | Chances Are/If You're Not Completely Satisfied (as Michael Desmond) | 6 |

## DESOLATION ANGELS
| 84 | AM AM 266 | Valhalla/Boadicea (p/s) | 40 |
|----|-----------|-------------------------|----|
| 85 | Thameside TRR 111 | DESOLATION ANGELS (LP) | 50 |

## DESPERATE BICYCLES
| 77 | Refill RR 1 | Smokescreen/Handlebars (p/s, same tracks both sides) | 40 |
|----|-------------|------------------------------------------------------|----|
| 77 | Refill RR 2 | The Medium Was Tedium/Don't Back The Front (p/s, same tracks both sides) | 40 |
| 78 | Refill RR 3 | NEW CROSS NEW CROSS (EP) | 40 |
| 78 | Refill RR 4 | Occupied Territory/Skill (p/s) | 20 |
| 78 | Refill RR 7 | Grief Is Very Private/Obstructive/Conundrum | 20 |
| 80 | Refill RR 6 | REMORSE CODE (LP) | 50 |

## DESSIE & JOHN
| 69 | Downtown DT 440 | Boss Sound/Everything Is Alright | 30 |
|----|-----------------|----------------------------------|----|

## DESSUS
| 81 | Ellie Jay EJSP 9710 | Ghetto Children/Dessus Jammin' (with p/s) | 25 |
|----|---------------------|-------------------------------------------|----|
| 81 | Ellie Jay EJSP 9710 | Ghetto Children/Dessus Jammin' (without p/s) | 12 |

## DESTROY ALL MONSTERS
| 79 | Cherry Red CHERRY 3 | Bored/You're Gonna Die (p/s, red vinyl) | 5 |
|----|---------------------|-----------------------------------------|---|
| 79 | Cherry Red CHERRY 7 | Meet The Creeper/November 22nd 1963 (p/s) | 5 |
| 79 | Cherry Red CHERRY 9 | Nobody Knows/What Do I Get? (p/s) | 5 |

*(see also MC5)*

## DESTROYER (1)
| 81 | Clean Kill SJP 829 | Evil Place/Stand And Deliver (no p/s) | 50 |
|----|--------------------|---------------------------------------|----|

## DESTROYER (2)
| 13 | Dead Oceans DOC 088 | FIVE SPANISH SONGS EP (12") | 10 |
|----|---------------------|----------------------------|----|
| 14 | Dead Oceans DOC 046 | KAPUTT (2-LP, white vinyl reissue) | 20 |

## DESTROYERS
| 70 | Amalgamated AMG 856 | Niney Special/Danger Zone | 25 |
|----|---------------------|---------------------------|----|
| 70 | Pressure Beat PR 5505 | Pressure Tonic/Machuki's Cooking (B-side actually with Count Machuki) | 35 |

*(see also Soul Brothers, Nicky Thomas)*

## DESTRUCTORS
| 82 | KILL 3 | Electronic Church/Khymer Rouge Boogie (rubber-stamped white label, 500 only given away with copies of Trees And Flowers punkzine) | 50 |
|----|--------|-----------------------------------------------------------------------|----|
| 82 | Carnage BOOK 2 | Meaningless Names/AK 47/Police State/Dachau/Death Squad (p/s) | 5 |
| 82 | Carnage Benelux KILL 2 | Religion/Soldier Boy/Agent Orange/Corpse Gas (p/s) | 5 |
| 82 | Illuminated ILL 14 | Jailbait/Kalgsnocov/Sewage Worker/Image (p/s) | 10 |
| 82 | Carnage Records BOOK 2 | SENSELESS VIOLENCE (EP) | 10 |
| 82 | Death DEATH 1 | MERRY XMAS & FUCK OFF (LP) | 20 |
| 83 | Radical Change RCLP 2 | ARMAGEDDON IN ACTION (LP) | 20 |

*(see also Blanks)*

## DETAILS
| 80 | Energy NRG 2 | Keep On Running/Run'ins (p/s) | 5 |
|----|--------------|-------------------------------|---|

## FRANK DETAILS
| 80 | Buzz Bomb BB 1 | False Pretences/Stranger On A Train (p/s) | 10 |
|----|----------------|-------------------------------------------|----|

## DETENTE
| 82 | SRTS 82 CUS 1411 | Feel Like Crying/On My Own | 6 |
|----|------------------|----------------------------|---|

## DETERGENTS
| | | | |
|---|---|---|---|
| 65 | Columbia DB 7513 | Leader Of The Laundromat/Ulcers | 12 |
| 65 | Columbia DB 7591 | I Don't Know/The Blue Kangaroo | 6 |

## DETONATORS (1)
| | | | |
|---|---|---|---|
| 78 | Local LR 1 | Need Love Tonight/Great Big Ghetto/Shoob Shooby Do/Give Me A Helping Hand (p/s) | 6 |

## DETONATORS (2)
| | | | |
|---|---|---|---|
| 79 | Burning Rockers BR 1008 | GANGSTER (LP) | 20 |

## DETOURS (1)
| | | | |
|---|---|---|---|
| 68 | CBS 3213 | Run To Me Baby/Hangin' On | 50 |
| 68 | CBS 3401 | Whole Lotta Lovin'/Pieces Of You | 200 |

*(see also Gene Latter)*

## DETOURS (2)
| | | | |
|---|---|---|---|
| 76 | MCA 249 | Try To Hold On/Love To | 5 |

## DETRIUS
| | | | |
|---|---|---|---|
| 90 | Under One Flag FLAG 55 | PERPETUAL DEFIANCE (LP, with inner sleeve) | 15 |

## DETROIT WITH MITCH RYDER
| | | | |
|---|---|---|---|
| 72 | Paramount PARA 3022 | It Ain't Easy/Long Neck Goose | 5 |
| 72 | Paramount SPFL 277 | DETROIT (LP) | 20 |

*(see also Mitch Ryder)*

## DETROIT EMERALDS
| | | | |
|---|---|---|---|
| 71 | Pye International 7N 25544 | Do Me Right/Just Now And Then | 6 |
| 71 | Janus 6146 004 | Wear This Ring/I Bet You Get The One | 5 |
| 72 | Janus 6146 007 | You Want It, You Got It/Till You Decide To Come Home | 5 |
| 72 | Janus 6146 015 | Do Me Right/Baby Let Me Take You In My Arms | 5 |
| 72 | Janus 6146 020 | Feel The Need In Me/And I Love Her | 5 |
| 73 | Westbound 6146108 | You're Getting A Little Too Smart/Lee | 5 |

## DETROIT ESCALATOR CO.
| | | | |
|---|---|---|---|
| 96 | Ferox FERLP 2 | SOUNDTRACK (313) (LP) | 20 |

## DETROIT MAGNIFICENTS
| | | | |
|---|---|---|---|
| 06 | Grapevine GRP 161 | Is This A Woman's Way/Where Can I Find Love | 10 |

## DETROIT SPINNERS
| | | | |
|---|---|---|---|
| 65 | Tamla Motown TMG 514 | Sweet Thing/How Can I? (demo credited to 'Spinners') | 425 |
| 65 | Tamla Motown TMG 514 | Sweet Thing/How Can I? (demo credited to 'Detroit Spinners') | 250 |
| 65 | Tamla Motown TMG 514 | Sweet Thing/How Can I? (stock copies credited to 'Spinners') | 425 |
| 65 | Tamla Motown TMG 523 | I'll Always Love You/Tomorrow May Never Come (as 'Spinners') | 110 |
| 65 | Tamla Motown TMG 523 | I'll Always Love You/Tomorrow May Never Come (as 'Detroit Spinners') | 75 |
| 65 | Tamla Motown TMG 523 | I'll Always Love You/Tomorrow May Never Come (as 'Spinners' or 'Detroit Spinners' DJ Copy) | 250 |
| 67 | Tamla Motown TMG 627 | For All We Know/I'll Always Love You (1st pressing with tall, narrow print) | 25 |
| 67 | Tamla Motown TMG 627 | For All We Know/I'll Always Love You (2nd pressing) | 18 |
| 70 | Tamla Motown TMG 755 | It's A Shame/Together We Can Make Such Sweet Music (unissued) | 0 |
| 70 | Tamla Motown TMG 755 | It's A Shame/Sweet Thing (as Motown Spinners) | 7 |
| 71 | Tamla Motown TMG 766 | Together We Can Make Such Sweet Music/Truly Yours (as Motown Spinners) | 7 |
| 74 | Tamla Motown TMG 871 | Together We Can Make Such Sweet Music/Bad Bad Weather | 5 |
| 75 | Atlantic K10571 | Living A Little, Laughing A Lot/I've Got To Make It On My Own | 20 |
| 80 | Atlantic K 11558 | Split Decision/Now That You're Mine Again | 5 |
| 80 | Atlantic K 11558 | Split Decision/Now That You're Mine Again (12") | 12 |
| 82 | Atlantic 9891 | I'll Be Around/City Full Of Memories | 6 |
| 68 | T. Motown TML 11060 | THE DETROIT SPINNERS (LP, mono) | 50 |
| 68 | T. Motown STML 11060 | THE DETROIT SPINNERS (LP, stereo) | 60 |
| 71 | T. Motown STML 11182 | SECOND TIME AROUND (LP, as Motown Spinners) | 20 |

*(see also G.C. Cameron)*

## DEUCE
| | | | |
|---|---|---|---|
| 86 | 1986 Powermetal VB004 | Backs To The Ball/Queen Of The Night/Jealousy | 10 |

## DEUCE COUP
| | | | |
|---|---|---|---|
| 67 | Mercury MF 1013 | A Clown In One Town/Angela (in p/s) | 12 |
| 67 | Mercury MF 1013 | A Clown In One Town/Angela (no p/s) | 6 |

## DEUCE OF HEARTS
| | | | |
|---|---|---|---|
| 66 | CBS 202345 | Closer Together/The Times They Are A Changin' | 10 |

## JIMMY DEUCHAR
| | | | |
|---|---|---|---|
| 54 | Esquire EP 53 | JIMMY DEUCHAR (EP) | 50 |
| 55 | Tempo EXA 18 | JIMMY DEUCHAR ENSEMBLE (EP) | 50 |
| 56 | Esquire EP 93 | JIMMY DEUCHAR QUARTET (EP) | 50 |
| 56 | Esquire EP 103 | JIMMY DEUCHAR QUARTET (EP) | 50 |
| 58 | Tempo EXA 79 | OPUS DE FUNK (EP, as Jimmy Deuchar Sextet) | 50 |
| 58 | Tempo EXA 81 | SWINGIN' IN STUDIO TWO (EP) | 50 |
| 59 | Tempo EXA 88 | WAIL (EP, with Victor Feldman Quintet) | 50 |
| 54 | Esquire 20-059 | DIG DEUCHAR, DON'T DANCE (LP) | 125 |
| 55 | Tempo LAP 2 | JIMMY DEUCHAR ENSEMBLE (10" LP) | 275 |
| 56 | Tempo TAP 4 | TOP TRUMPETS (LP) | 250 |
| 56 | Vogue LDE | SHOWCASE (LP) | 80 |
| 58 | Tempo TAP 20 | PAL JIMMY (LP) | 750 |

*(see also Victor Feldman)*

## BIG PETE DEUCHAR/DUKER
| | | | |
|---|---|---|---|
| 63 | Fontana 267 278 TF | Google Eye/There's A Hand Leading Me (as Big Pete Deuchar) | 8 |
| 63 | Fontana TF 423 | It Comes And Goes/Married By The Bible | 8 |
| 65 | Columbia DB 7763 | Goin' In Training/I Saw Your Face In The Moon (as Big Pete Duker) | 8 |

## DEUS
| | | | |
|---|---|---|---|
| 94 | Island 155981854 018-7 | Suds & Soda/Secret Hell (limited edition, numbered) | 25 |
| 94 | Island 1215598854-019-1 | Suds And Soda (Extended Version)/Texan Coffee/Secret Hell/Furniture In The Far West (12") | 20 |
| 94 | Island 15599/854 150 7 | Via/Violins And Happy Endings | 12 |
| 95 | Island 15603/854 188-7 | Hotel Lounge (Be The Death Of Me)/Jigsaw You (Live) (limited edition, die-cut sleeve) | 8 |
| 96 | Island 630/854 682-7 | Theme From Turnpike/Overflow/My Little Contessa (7" picture disc) | 10 |
| 96 | Island 1015630/854 682-0 | Theme From Turnpike/Overflow/My Little Contessa (10", gatefold sleeve) | 10 |
| 96 | Island IS 663 | Little Arithmetics/Fell Off The Floor, Man (Dust Brothers Edit) (picture disc) | 10 |
| 99 | Island 15750/562-109-7 | Sister Dew (Album Version)/Thirteen (Live) (with poster) | 6 |
| 99 | Island IS 714 | Instant Street/Dream Sequence 1 (Demo) (p/s) | 6 |
| 94 | Island ILPS 8028/524-0451 | WORST CASE SCENARIO (LP, limited edition with postcard and CD booklet) | 70 |
| 96 | Island ILPS 8052/52429-1 | IN A BAR UNDER THE SEA (LP, with inner sleeve) | 40 |
| 99 | Island ILPS 8082/524 643-1 | THE IDEAL CRASH (LP) | 40 |
| 05 | V2 VVR 1034711 | POCKET REVOLUTION (2-LP) | 30 |

## DEUX FILLES
| | | | |
|---|---|---|---|
| 82 | Papier PULP 31 | DEUX FILLES (LP) | 25 |
| 83 | Papier PULP 32 | DOUBLE HAPPINESS (LP) | 25 |

## DEVASTATING AFFAIR
| | | | |
|---|---|---|---|
| 73 | Mowest 3010 | That's How It Was (Right From The Start)/It's So Sad | 10 |
| 73 | Mowest 3010 | That's How It Was (Right From The Start)/It's So Sad (DJ copy) | 20 |

## DEVASTATION
| | | | |
|---|---|---|---|
| 84 | Creative Reality REAL 8 | DRAG YOU DOWN EP | 20 |

## DEVIANTS
| | | | |
|---|---|---|---|
| 68 | Stable STA 5601 | You Got To Hold On/Let's Loot The Supermarket | 20 |
| 67 | Underground Imp. IMP 1 | PTOOFF! (LP, foldout sleeve, private pressing via IT magazine) | 400 |
| 68 | Stable SLP 007 | DISPOSABLE (LP, gatefold sleeve, red/black label) | 300 |
| 69 | Transatlantic TRA 204 | THE DEVIANTS (LP, with booklet, white/lilac label with 't' logo) | 300 |
| 69 | Transatlantic TRA 204 | THE DEVIANTS (LP, without booklet, white/lilac label with 't' logo) | 150 |
| 69 | Decca LK-R/SKL-R 4993 | PTOOFF! (LP, reissue, large unboxed logo on label) | 90 |
| 78 | Logo MOGO 4001 | THE DEVIANTS (LP, reissue) | 15 |
| 84 | Psycho PSYCHO 25 | HUMAN GARBAGE (LIVE AT DINGWALLS '84) (LP) | 15 |

*(see also Mick Farren, Pink Fairies, Larry Wallis)*

## DEVIATED INSTINCT
| | | | |
|---|---|---|---|
| 86 | Peaceville WARP 2 | WELCOME TO THE ORGY EP | 15 |
| 88 | Peaceville VILE 3 | ROCK 'N' ROLL CONFORMITY (LP, inner) | 25 |
| 90 | Prophecy PRO 004 | NAILED EP (12", p/s) | 20 |
| 90 | Peaceville VILE 16 | GUTTURAL BREATH (LP) | 20 |

## DEVIL'S HOLE GANG
| | | | |
|---|---|---|---|
| 70s | Slow Burning Fuse SSSS 1 | Free The People/Isn't It/Something To Look Forward To (p/s, with insert) | 12 |

## JOHNNY DEVLIN (& DETOURS)
| | | | |
|---|---|---|---|
| 64 | Pye 7N 15598 | Sometimes/If You Want Someone (as Johnny Devlin & Detours) | 6 |
| 66 | CBS 202085 | Hung On You/Prove It | 5 |
| 66 | CBS 202339 | My Strength; Heart Of Soul/I Can't Get You Off My Mind | 5 |
| 67 | CBS 202452 | Tender Lovin' Care/Five O'Clock World | 5 |
| 67 | CBS 2751 | Hurtin'/You Gotta Tell Me | 5 |

## DEVO
| | | | |
|---|---|---|---|
| 78 | Stiff DEV 1 | Jocko Homo/Mongoloid (foldout p/s) | 10 |
| 78 | Stiff DEV 2/BOY 1 | (I Can't Get No) Satisfaction/Sloppy (I Saw My Baby Getting) (p/s) | 5 |
| 78 | Stiff BOY 2 | Be Stiff/Social Fools (clear vinyl) | 5 |
| 79 | Elevator NICE 1 | Mechanical Man/Blockhead/Blackout/Auto-Modern (official bootleg, red/yellow stamped sleeves) | 8 |
| 85 | Warner Bros W9119 | Shout/C'mon (p/s) | 5 |
| 78 | Virgin V 2106 | Q: ARE WE NOT MEN? (LP, various coloured vinyl) | 20 |
| 78 | Virgin VP 2106 | Q: ARE WE NOT MEN? (LP, picture disc, with 'Flimsy Wrap' 33rpm 1-sided flexidisc [VDJ 27/Lyntone LYN 6260]) | 15 |
| 79 | Stiff ODD 1 | B-STIFF (Mini-LP, 6 tracks released as Stiff singles) | 15 |
| 79 | Virgin V2125 | DUTY NOW FOR THE FUTURE (LP, promo version with stock LP but different sleeve from official release) | 20 |
| 79 | Virgin V2125 | DUTY NOW FOR THE FUTURE (LP, with red or blue band on front sleeve) | 15 |
| 80 | Virgin V 2162 | FREEDOM OF CHOICE (LP, stickered sleeve with poster) | 15 |

## DEVON (RUSSELL) & SEDRIC (MYTON)
| | | | |
|---|---|---|---|
| 69 | Blue Cat BS 158 | What A Sin Thing/Short Up Dress | 60 |

## DEVON (RUSSELL) & TARTANS
| | | | |
|---|---|---|---|
| 68 | Nu Beat NB 021 | Let's Have Some Fun/Making Love | 25 |

*(see also Tartans)*

## DEVONNES
| | | | |
|---|---|---|---|
| 75 | UK USA 5 | I'm Gonna Pick Up My Toys/Limits | 5 |
| 06 | Kent 6T 21 | Doin The Gittin' Up/MAYBERRY MOVEMENT: I See Him Making Love To You | 20 |

## BARRY DE VORZON
| | | | |
|---|---|---|---|
| 58 | RCA RCA 1066 | Barbara Jean/JIMMY DELL: Teeny Weeny | 50 |
| 60 | Philips PB 993 | Betty Betty (Go Steady With Me)/Across The Street | 25 |

*(see also Barry & Tamerlanes, Jimmy Dell)*

## DEVOTED
| | | | |
|---|---|---|---|
| 68 | Page One POF 076 | I Love George Best/United (p/s) | 35 |
| 68 | Page One POF 076 | I Love George Best/United | 15 |

## DEVOTION
| | | | |
|---|---|---|---|
| 79 | Sapphire | Devotion/Acid/Energy For The Universe (no p/s) | 50 |

## DEVOTIONS
64  Columbia DB 7256     Rip Van Winkle/(I Love You) For Sentimental Reasons ........................................ 100

## DEWDROPS
67  Blue Beat BB 381     Somebody's Knocking/By And By ........................................ 25

## BRIAN DEWHURST
75  Folk Heritage FHR 075     THE HUNTER & THE HUNTED (LP, black label and laminated sleeve) .................... 20

## HARRY DE WIT
79  Bead Records BEAD 11     APRIL '79 (LP) ........................................ 25
79  Bead Records BEAD 12     FOR HARM (LP, with Philipp Wachsmann) ........................................ 25

## DANNY DEXTER
63  London HLU 9690     Sweet Mama/Go On ........................................ 8

## EDDIE DEXTER & HIS BAND
55  Capitol CL 14371     Moonlight/The Verse Of Stardust ........................................ 5

## LEVI DEXTER (AND THE RIPCHORDS)
80  Mistral BLOW 1     IN THE BEGINNING... (EP) ........................................ 10
81  Fresh 40     I Get So Excited/The Other Side Of Midnight ........................................ 5

## RAY DEXTER & LAYABOUTS
62  Decca F 11538     The Coalman's Lament/Lonely Weekend ........................................ 30

## TRACEY DEY
64  Stateside SS 287     Go Away/Gonna Get Along Without You Now ........................................ 18

## DEZIGN
84  EN AY DZ 256     Love Myth/Let's Go (no p/s) ........................................ 10

## DEZZI D
05  Vibes House VH008     Judas/Dub Version ........................................ 15

## BOBBY D'FANO
63  Palette PG 9038     Message Of Love/The Kiss That Broke My Heart ........................................ 10

## DHARMA BLUES BAND
69  Major Minor SMCP 5017     DHARMA BLUES (LP, yellow/white/black label) ........................................ 125
*(see also Hawkwind)*

## ALI BEN DHOWN
67  Piccadilly 7N 35395     Musapha/Turkish Delight ........................................ 30

## DIABOLIKS
00  Vinyl Japan ASKLP P116     THREE FUR BURGERS...AND A HOT CHILLI DOG TO GO! (LP) ........................................ 15

## DIAGONAL
10  Rise Above 127 FREE     Stop/ASTRA: Empty Spaces (300 only, gig freebie) ........................................ 12

## DIAGRAM BROTHERS
80  Construct CON 1     We Are All Animals/There Is No Shower/Would I Like To Live In Prison ........................................ 15
81  New Hormones ORG 9     Bricks/Postal Bargains (p/s) ........................................ 8
82  New Hormones ORG 21     DISCORDO EP ........................................ 10

## DIALS (JAMAICA)
69  Duke DU 48     Bye Bye Love/It's Love ........................................ 12
69  Duke DU 49     Love Is A Treasure/DIAMONDS: I Want To Be ........................................ 12

## DIALS (U.K.)
79  Wessex WEX 266     Maxine/Hey Denise (p/s) ........................................ 7
79  Scene ACT1     All I Hear/Running (p/s) ........................................ 10

## BRIAN DIAMOND & THE CUTTERS
63  Decca F 11724     Jealousy Will Get You Nowhere/Brady Brady ........................................ 15
64  Fontana TF 452     Shake, Shout And Go/Wotcha Gonna Do Now Pretty Baby ........................................ 150
65  Pye 7N 15779     Big Bad Wolf/See If I Care ........................................ 15
65  Pye 7N 15952     Bone Idol/Sands Of Time ........................................ 15

## GREGG DIAMOND'S BIONIC BOOGIE
79  Urban URBX 16     Hot Butterfly/Mess Up The Boogie/When The Shit Hits The Fan (12", p/s) ........................................ 10
79  Polydor PB 50     Chains/Hot Butterfly ........................................ 5
79  Polydor POSPX 50     Chains/Hot Butterfly (12") ........................................ 15

## JERRY DIAMOND
57  London HLE 8496     Sunburned Lips/Don't Trust Love ........................................ 20

## LEE DIAMOND (& CHEROKEES)
61  Fontana H 310     I'll Step Down/Josephine (as Lee Diamond & Cherokees) ........................................ 10
61  Fontana H 345     Stop Your Crying/You'll Want Me ........................................ 10
*(see also Cherokees)*

## NEIL DIAMOND
66  London HLZ 10049     Solitary Man/Do It ........................................ 10
66  London HLZ 10072     Cherry, Cherry/I'll Come Running ........................................ 10
67  London HLZ 10126     Girl, You'll Be A Woman Soon/You'll Forget ........................................ 5
66  London HA-Z 8307     THE FEEL OF NEIL DIAMOND (LP) ........................................ 20

## DIAMOND BOYS
62  Parlophone GIB 102     Fool In Love/New Orleans (export issue) ........................................ 25
63  RCA RCA 1351     Hey Little Girl/What'd I Say ........................................ 15
*(see also Albert Ammons)*

## DIAMOND HEAD
80  Happy Face MMDH 120     Shoot Out The Lights/Helpless (p/s) ........................................ 15
80  Media SCREEN 1     Sweet And Innocent/Streets Of Gold (p/s) ........................................ 15
81  DHM DHM 004     Waited Too Long/Play It Loud (p/s) ........................................ 7
81  DHM DHM 005     DIAMOND LIGHTS EP (Diamond Lights/ We Won't Be Back/I Don't Got/It's Electric) (12", p/s) ........................................ 20
82  MCA DHMT 101     FOUR CUTS (12" EP, with insert) ........................................ 12

| 83 | MCA DHM 103 | Makin' Music/(Andy Peebles Interview) (p/s).............................................................................8 |
| 83 | MCA DHMT 103 | Makin' Music/(Andy Peebles Interview) (12", p/s) ...............................................................15 |
| 83 | MCA DHM 104 | Out Of Phase/The Kingmaker (p/s)..........................................................................................5 |
| 83 | MCA DHMT 104 | Out Of Phase/The Kingmaker/Sucking My Love (live) (12", p/s) ....................................25 |
| 80 | DHM MMDHLP 105 | LIGHTNING TO THE NATIONS (LP, plain or printed white labels, plain white sleeve, sold at gigs, signed in blue ink & available via Sounds) ....................................................100 |
| 80 | DHM MMDHLP 105 | LIGHTNING TO THE NATIONS (LP, plain or printed white labels, plain white sleeve, sold at gigs) ..................................................................................................................................50 |
| 81 | MCA DH 1001 | LIVING ON BORROWED TIME (LP, gatefold sleeve with inner sleeve, with poster & fan club insert) ...............................................................................................................................25 |
| 81 | MCA DH 1001 | LIVING ON BORROWED TIME (LP, gatefold sleeve with inner sleeve) ..............................15 |
| 82 | MCA DH1001 | BORROWED TIME (LP, with poster)..........................................................................................20 |
| 83 | MCA DH 1002 | CANTERBURY (LP, with lyric and tour dates sheet, first pressing faulty and jumps) ....15 |
| 86 | Metal Masters METALP 110 | BEHOLD THE BEGINNING (LP, remixed reissue of 1st LP) ................................................20 |
| 87 | FM WKFMLP 92 | AM I EVIL (LP, with inner sleeve)..............................................................................................20 |

## DIAMONDS (JAMAICA)
| 72 | Songbird SB 1079 | Mash Up/DYNAMITES: Mash Up (Version) ..............................................................................10 |
| 75 | Attack ATT 8108 | Jah Jah Bless Your Dreadlocks/Version ..................................................................................15 |
| 75 | Attack ATT 8113 | Just Can't Figure Out/Just Can't Figure Out (Version) ......................................................12 |
| 75 | Black Wax WAX 5 | Country Living/A Living Version ..............................................................................................12 |
| 78 | Virgin V2102 | PLANET EARTH (LP) .....................................................................................................................20 |

*(see also Dymonds, Sir Collins Band)*

## DIAMONDS (U.K.)
| 63 | Philips BF 1264 | The Lost City/Chasey Chasey (John Peel) ..................................................................................6 |

## DIAMONDS (U.S.)
| 55 | Vogue Coral Q 72109 | Black Denim Trousers And Motorcycle Boots/Nip Sip ........................................................20 |
| 58 | Mercury 7MT 187 | Silhouettes/Honey Bird ...........................................................................................................20 |
| 58 | Mercury 7MT 195 | The Stroll/Land Of Beauty .......................................................................................................10 |
| 58 | Mercury 7MT 207 | Don't Let Me Down/High Sign .................................................................................................10 |
| 58 | Mercury 7MT 208 | Straight Skirts/Patsy .................................................................................................................50 |
| 58 | Mercury 7MT 233 | Where Mary Go?/Kathy-O..........................................................................................................5 |
| 58 | Mercury AMT 1004 | Eternal Lovers/Walking Along ..................................................................................................5 |
| 59 | Mercury AMT 1024 | She Say (Oom Dooby Doom)/From The Bottom Of My Heart............................................5 |
| 60 | Mercury AMT 1086 | Tell The Truth/Real True Love .................................................................................................30 |
| 61 | Mercury AMT 1156 | One Summer Night/It's A Doggone Shame ...........................................................................15 |
| 57 | Mercury MEP 9515 | PRESENTING THE DIAMONDS (EP) ........................................................................................20 |
| 57 | Mercury MEP 9523 | THE DIAMONDS VOL. 1 (EP) ...................................................................................................20 |
| 58 | Mercury MEP 9527 | THE DIAMONDS VOL. 2 (EP) ...................................................................................................20 |
| 58 | Mercury MEP 9530 | THE DIAMONDS VOL. 3 (EP) ...................................................................................................20 |
| 59 | Mercury ZEP 10003 | DIG THE DIAMONDS (EP).........................................................................................................20 |
| 59 | Mercury ZEP 10020 | THE DIAMONDS MEET PETE RUGOLO (EP) .........................................................................15 |
| 60 | Mercury ZEP 10053 | STAR STUDDED DIAMONDS (EP) ..........................................................................................15 |
| 59 | Mercury ZEP 10026 | DIAMONDS ARE TRUMPS (EP) ...............................................................................................15 |
| 61 | Mercury ZEP 10097 | PETE RUGOLO LEADS THE DIAMONDS (EP, mono) ...........................................................10 |
| 61 | Mercury SEZ 10912 | PETE RUGOLO LEADS THE DIAMONDS (EP, stereo) .........................................................10 |
| 57 | Mercury MPT 7526 | THE DIAMONDS (10" LP) ........................................................................................................40 |

*(see also Pete Rugolo)*

## DIAMOND TWINS
| 66 | HMV POP 1508 | Crying The Night Away/Start The World Spinning Again ...................................................6 |

*(see also Sonia Kent)*

## ALENA DIANE
| 06 | Names NAMES 25 | SONGS WHISTLED THROUGH WHITE TEETH (EP, 10", 500 only)......................................12 |

## DIANE & JAVELINS
| 66 | Columbia DB 7819 | Heart And Soul/Who's The Girl ...............................................................................................55 |

## (PAUL) DI'ANNO
| 84 | FM VHF 1 | Heart User/Road Rat (p/s).........................................................................................................8 |
| 84 | FM WKFM LP1 | DI'ANNO (LP, blue vinyl, stickered sleeve).............................................................................15 |
| 84 | FM WKFM PD1 | DI'ANNO (LP, picture disc) .......................................................................................................18 |

*(see also Gogmagog, Iron Maiden)*

## DIATONES
| 61 | Starlite ST45 057 | Ruby Has Gone/Oh Baby Come Dance With Me ...............................................................100 |

## DIATRIBE
| 84 | Criminal Damage CRI 12 123 | DIATRIBE EP ....................................................................15 |

## DANNY DIAZ & THE CHECKMATES
| 69 | Pye 7N 17690 | Solomon Grundy/Goodbye Baby ............................................................................................15 |

## MANU DIBANGO
| 73 | London HL 10423 | Soul Makossa/Lily .....................................................................................................................10 |
| 73 | London SH 8451 | O BOSO (LP) ...............................................................................................................................20 |
| 75 | Creole CRLP 503 | MAKOSSA MUSIC (LP) .............................................................................................................15 |
| 78 | Decca SKL-R 5296 | AFROVISION (LP) .....................................................................................................................15 |

## BILLY DICE & SHENLEY DUFFUS
| 73 | Pama 874 | Women Smarter/Standing On The Hill .....................................................................................8 |

## DICE THE BOSS
| 69 | Joe DU 50 | Brixton Cat Big And Fat/JOES ALL STARS : Solitude............................................................55 |
| 69 | Duke/Joe DU 51 | Gun The Man Down/JOE MANSANO: The Thief ..................................................................50 |
| 69 | Duke/Joe DU 52 | But Officer/JOE'S ALL STARS: Reggae On The Shore ........................................................50 |
| 70 | Duke/Joe DU 57 | Your Boss D.J./TITO SIMON: Read The News ......................................................................80 |
| 70 | Joe's JRS 17 | The Informer/Cool It .................................................................................................................40 |
| 70 | Explosion EX 2017 | Funky Monkey/JOE'S ALL STARS: Funky Monkey Version ..............................................15 |

# Lloyd DICE

| | | | |
|---|---|---|---|
| 70 | Explosion EX 2020 | Funky Duck/Dunkier Than Duck | 15 |

*(see also Joe The Boss, Ray Martel)*

## LLOYD DICE
| | | | |
|---|---|---|---|
| 70 | Joe JRS 5 | Trial Of Pama Dice/JOE: Jughead Returns | 25 |

*(see also Trevor Lloyd)*

## PAMA DICE
| | | | |
|---|---|---|---|
| 70 | Reggae 3002 | Brixton Pum Pum Wrecker/JOE ALLSTARS: Version (White label, possibly unreleased) | 100 |
| 69 | Jackpot JP 715 | Honky Tonk Popcorn/Bongo Man | 40 |
| 69 | Jackpot JP 715 | Bongo Man/Bear De Pussy | 30 |
| 69 | Jackpot JP 716 | Sin, Sun And Sex/Reggae Popcorn | 30 |
| 70 | Reggae REG 3001 | Brixton Fight/OPENING: Tea House | 150 |

*(see also Dice The Boss, Joe The Boss)*

## DICEMEN
| | | | |
|---|---|---|---|
| 83 | Random MCPS RR1 | Number 19/A Year Without You/Sunrise/Today | 15 |

## CHARLES DICKENS
| | | | |
|---|---|---|---|
| 65 | Pye 7N 15887 | That's The Way Love Goes/In The City | 25 |
| 65 | Pye 7N 15938 | I Stand Alone/Hey Little Girl | 10 |
| 66 | Immediate IM 025 | So Much In Love/Our Soul Brothers | 40 |

*(see also Habits)*

## DOLES DICKEN'S BAND
| | | | |
|---|---|---|---|
| 58 | London HLD 8639 | Piakukaungchung (Pie-ah-coo-ka-ung-chung)/Our Melody | 10 |

## LITTLE JIMMY DICKENS
| | | | |
|---|---|---|---|
| 54 | Columbia DC 670 | Then I Had To Turn Around/Hot Diggity Dog (78, export issue) | 8 |

## DICKIES
| | | | |
|---|---|---|---|
| 78 | A&M AMS 7351 | Give It Back/You Drive Me Ape (white vinyl, p/s) | 5 |
| 78 | A&M AMS 7368 | Paranoid/I'm OK, You're OK (p/s, milky vinyl) | 5 |
| 78 | A&M AMS 7403 | Silent Night/The Sounds Of Silence (p/s, white vinyl) | 6 |
| 79 | A&M AMS 7431 | Banana Splits/Hideous/Got It At The Store (yellow vinyl, p/s) | 5 |
| 79 | A&M AMS 7491 | Manny, Moe And Jack/She Loves Me Not (p/s, black vinyl only) | 8 |
| 80 | A&M AMS 7504 | Fan Mail/Tricia Toyota (I'm Stuck In A Pagoda) (opaque or translucent red vinyl, poster p/s) | 6 |
| 80 | A&M AMS 7544 | Gigantor/Bowling With Bedrock Barney (yellow vinyl, p/s with full colour or b&w reverse) | 8 |
| 90 | Overground OVER 12 | Just Say Yes/Ayatollah You So (p/s with lyric sheet, mauve, blue or white vinyl, 2,000 of each colour) | 7 |
| 95 | Plastic Head HOLE 008 | Make It So/Oh Baby (p/s, black vinyl, 1,000 only) | 5 |
| 79 | A&M AMLE 64742 | THE INCREDIBLE SHRINKING DICKIES (LP, black or yellow vinyl) | 20 |
| 79 | A&M AMLE 64742 | THE INCREDIBLE SHRINKING DICKIES (LP, blue vinyl, with black or red-and-black on sleeve) | 20 |
| 79 | A&M AMLE 64742 | THE INCREDIBLE SHRINKING DICKIES (LP, orange vinyl, with black or red-and-black on sleeve) | 20 |
| 79 | A&M AMLH 68510 | DAWN OF THE DICKIES (LP, blue vinyl) | 20 |
| 79 | A&M AMLH 68510 | DAWN OF THE DICKIES (LP, black vinyl) | 15 |

*(see also Chuck Wagon)*

## BRUCE DICKINSON
| | | | |
|---|---|---|---|
| 90 | EMI EM 138 | Tattooed Millionaire/Ballad Of Mutt (paper label, glossy p/s) | 5 |
| 90 | EMI EMPD 138 | Tattooed Millionaire/Ballad Of Mutt (shaped picture disc) | 10 |
| 90 | EMI EMPD 138 | Tattooed Millionaire/Ballad Of Mutt (uncut shaped picture disc) | 40 |
| 90 | EMI EMPD 142 | All The Young Dudes/Darkness Be My Friend (shaped picture disc with plinth) | 10 |
| 90 | EMI EMPD 142 | All The Young Dudes/Darkness Be My Friend (uncut shaped picture disc) | 25 |
| 90 | EMI EMPD 151 | Dive! Dive! Dive!/Riding With The Angels (live)/Sin City (live)/ Black Night (live) (12", picture disc) | 10 |
| 94 | EMI EM 341 | Shoot All The Clowns/Over And Out (p/s, clear vinyl with insert) | 5 |
| 94 | EMI EMD 1057 | BALLS TO PICASSO (LP, gatefold sleeve) | 15 |
| 95 | Raw DV 102 | ALIVE IN STUDIO (2-LP, gatefold with inners) | 20 |
| 96 | Raw Power RAWLP 106 | SKUNKWORKS (LP, gatefold, inner) | 15 |
| 97 | Raw Power RAWLP 124 | ACCIDENT OF BIRTH (LP) | 15 |

*(see also Iron Maiden, Samson, Xero, Speed)*

## BARBARA DICKSON
| | | | |
|---|---|---|---|
| 74 | RSO 2090 144 | Here Comes The Sun/The Long And Winding Road | 5 |
| 70 | Decca SKL 5041 | THRO' RECENT YEARS (LP, with Archie Fisher) | 40 |
| 71 | Decca SKL 5058 | DO RIGHT WOMAN (LP) | 40 |
| 72 | Decca SKL 5116 | FROM THE BEGGAR'S MANTLE FRINGED WITH GOLD (LP) | 35 |
| 74 | RSO 2394 141 | JOHN, PAUL, GEORGE, RINGO AND BERT (LP, with London cast) | 30 |

## DICK TURPIN
| | | | |
|---|---|---|---|
| 70 | Evolution E 2446 | If You've Got The Time/Madeline | 180 |

## DICTATORS WITH TONY & HOWARD
| | | | |
|---|---|---|---|
| 63 | Oriole CB 1934 | So Long Little Girl/Say Little Girl | 20 |

*(see also Tony & Howard)*

## DICTATORS
| | | | |
|---|---|---|---|
| 77 | Asylum K 13091 | Search And Destroy/Sleepin' With The TV On | 5 |
| 75 | Epic S EPC 80767 | GO GIRL CRAZY (LP) | 20 |
| 77 | Asylum K 53061 | MANIFEST DESTINY (LP, lyric inner) | 15 |
| 78 | Asylum K 53083 | BLOOD BROTHERS LP, inner) | 15 |

## BO DIDDLEY
| | | | |
|---|---|---|---|
| 59 | London HLM 8913 | The Great Grandfather/Crackin' Up | 50 |
| 59 | London HLM 8913 | The Great Grandfather/Crackin' Up (78) | 20 |
| 59 | London HLM 8975 | Say Man/The Clock Strikes Twelve | 70 |
| 59 | London HLM 8975 | Say Man/The Clock Strikes Twelve (78) | 20 |

| 60 | London HLM 9035 | Say Man, Back Again/She's Alright | 80 |
| 60 | London HLM 9112 | Road Runner/My Story | 50 |
| 62 | Pye Intl. 7N 25165 | You Can't Judge A Book By The Cover/I Can Tell | 20 |
| 63 | Pye Intl. 7N 25193 | Who Do You Love?/The Twister | 20 |
| 63 | Pye Intl. 7N 25210 | Bo Diddley/Detour | 20 |
| 63 | Pye Intl. 7N 25216 | You Can't Judge A Book By The Cover/I Can Tell (reissue) | 10 |
| 63 | Pye Intl. 7N 25217 | Pretty Thing/Road Runner | 10 |
| 63 | Pye Intl. 7N 25227 | Bo Diddley Is A Lover/Doin' The Jaguar | 10 |
| 64 | Pye Intl. 7N 25235 | Memphis/Monkey Diddle | 10 |
| 64 | Pye Intl. 7N 25243 | Mona/Gimme Gimme | 15 |
| 64 | Pye Intl. 7N 25258 | Mama Keep Your Big Mouth Shut/Jo-Ann | 10 |
| 65 | Chess CRS 8000 | Hey Good Lookin'/You Ain't Bad (As You Claim To Be) | 10 |
| 65 | Chess CRS 8014 | Somebody Beat Me/Mush Mouth Millie | 12 |
| 65 | Chess CRS 8021 | Let The Kids Dance/Let Me Pass | 10 |
| 66 | Chess CRS 8026 | 500% More Man/Stop My Monkey | 10 |
| 66 | Chess CRS 8036 | We're Gonna Get Married/Easy | 10 |
| 67 | Chess CRS 8053 | Ooh Baby/Back To School | 12 |
| 67 | Chess CRS 8057 | Wrecking My Love Life/Boo-Ga-Loo Before You Go | 20 |
| 68 | Chess CRS 8078 | Another Sugar Daddy/I'm High Again | 10 |
| 69 | Chess CRS 8088 | Bo Diddley 1969/Soul Train | 10 |
| 72 | Chess 6145 002 | I Said Shut Up Woman/I Love You More Than You'll Ever Know | 5 |
| 56 | London RE-U 1054 | RHYTHM AND BLUES WITH BO DIDDLEY (EP, gold label lettering) | 200 |
| 63 | Pye Intl. NEP 44014 | HEY! BO DIDDLEY (EP) | 20 |
| 64 | Pye Intl. NEP 44019 | THE STORY OF BO DIDDLEY (EP) | 20 |
| 64 | Pye Intl. NEP 44031 | BO DIDDLEY IS A LUMBERJACK (EP) | 20 |
| 64 | Pye Intl. NEP 44036 | DIDDLING (EP) | 20 |
| 65 | Chess CRE 6008 | I'M A MAN (EP) | 20 |
| 66 | Chess CRE 6023 | ROOSTER STEW (EP) | 20 |
| 59 | London HA-M 2230 | GO BO DIDDLEY (LP) | 350 |
| 62 | Pye Jazz NJL 33 | BO DIDDLEY IS A GUNSLINGER (LP) | 50 |
| 63 | Pye Intl. NPL 28025 | HEY! BO DIDDLEY (LP) | 25 |
| 63 | Pye Intl. NPL 28026 | BO DIDDLEY (LP) | 25 |
| 63 | Pye Intl. NPL 28029 | BO DIDDLEY RIDES AGAIN (LP) | 25 |
| 63 | Pye Intl. NPL 28032 | BO DIDDLEY'S BEACH PARTY (LP) | 25 |
| 64 | Pye Intl. NPL 28034 | BO DIDDLEY IN THE SPOTLIGHT (LP) | 25 |
| 64 | Pye Intl. NPL 28049 | 16 ALL-TIME HITS (LP) | 15 |
| 64 | Chess CRL 4002 | HEY GOOD LOOKIN' (LP) | 20 |
| 65 | Chess CRL 4507 | LET ME PASS (LP) | 25 |
| 67 | Chess CRL 4525 | THE ORIGINATOR (LP) | 25 |
| 68 | Chess CRL 4529 | SUPER BLUES (LP, with Muddy Waters & Little Walter) | 20 |
| 68 | Chess CRL 4537 | THE SUPER SUPER BLUES BAND (LP, with Muddy Waters & Howlin' Wolf) | 20 |
| 71 | Chess 6310107 | ANOTHER DIMENSION (LP) | 20 |

*(see also Chuck Berry & Bo Diddley)*

## DIDJITS
| 95 | Touch & Go RCRPA 11 | Pigs (1-sided white label) | 5 |

## DIDO
| 00 | Cheeky 74321 86823 1 | NO ANGEL (LP, gatefold) | 30 |

## DIE ELECTRIC EELS
| 78 | Rough Trade RT 008 | Agitated/Cyclotron (p/s) | 15 |

## DIE LAUGHING
| 80 | Ocean OC 003 | Hard Living Man/You Got The Power (p/s) | 50 |

## DIESEL M
| 94 | Choci's Chewns CCB 001 | M for Multiple (12", blue vinyl, 666 only) | 25 |
| 95 | Choci's Chewns DDL 001 | M For Mangoes (12", red vinyl, 666 only) | 25 |

## DIF JUZ
| 81 | 4AD BAD 109 | HU/RE/MI/CS (12" EP) | 10 |
| 81 | 4AD BAD 116 | VIBRATING AIR: Heset/Diselt/Gunet/Soarn (12" EP) | 15 |

## DIFFERENT EYES
| 79 | Tuzmadoner TUZMADONER 001 | Open The Box/Uncomfortable//ROYSTON: Snake's Song/Gerald's Eyes (stapled photocopied cover, rubber-stamped labels) | 100 |

## DIGA RHYTHM BAND
| 76 | United Artists UAG 29975 | DIGA RHYTHM BAND (LP) | 25 |

*(see also Grateful Dead, Mickey Hart, Jerry Garcia)*

## DIGABLE PLANETS
| 94 | Pendulum 7243 8 30654 1 7 | BLOWOUT COMB (2-LP) | 30 |

## DIG DIG DIG
| 81 | No Cure DIG 001/DIG 002 | Our Money/625 Lines/Four Five | 8 |

## STEVE DIGGLE
| 80 | Faulty Products FEP 7000 | Fifty Years Of Comparative Wealth/Shut Out The Light/ Here Comes The Fire Brigade (unreleased) | 0 |

*(see also Buzzcocks, Flag Of Convenience)*

## DIGITAL MYSTIKZ
| 04 | Big Apple BAM 004 | Pathways/Ugly/Mawo Dub/Da Wrath (12") | 20 |
| 05 | DMZ DMZ 005 | Neverland/Struck (12") | 25 |
| 06 | DMZ DMZ 005 | Haunted/Anti War Dub (12") | 60 |
| 06 | DMZ DMZ 008 | Ancient Memories/Ancient Memories (Skream Remix) (12") | 25 |
| 10 | DMZ DMZLP 001 | RETURN II SPACE (3-LP) | 18 |
| 10 | DMZ DMZLP 001 | RETURN II SPACE (3-LP, picture discs, 200 only but no indication on sleeve if you get picture discs or black vinyl!) | 40 |

## DIGITAL MYSTIKZ & LEOFAH
| 04 | DMZ DMZ 001 | Twisup/B/Chainba (with Leofah) (12" white labels) | 45 |
| 04 | DMZ DMZ 002 | Lost City/Jah Fire/Horror Show/Dread Commands (EP) | 25 |

## DILLARD & CLARK
| 69 | A&M AMS 764 | Radio Song/Why Not Your Baby | 40 |
| 69 | A&M AMLS 939 | THE FANTASTIC EXPEDITION OF DILLARD & CLARK (LP) | 18 |
| 69 | A&M AMLS 966 | THROUGH THE MORNING, THROUGHTHENIGHT (LP) | 18 |

*(see also Gene Clark, Byrds, Dillards)*

## MOSES & JOSHUA (DILLARD)
| 67 | Stateside SS 2059 | My Elusive Dreams/What's Better Than Love (as Moses & Joshua Dillard) | 25 |
| 67 | Stateside SS 2059 | My Elusive Dreams/What's Better Than Love (as Moses & Joshua Dillard) (DJ Copy) | 40 |
| 68 | Bell BELL 1018 | Get Out Of My Heart/They Don't Want Us Together (as Moses & Joshua) | 25 |
| 72 | Mojo 2092 054 | My Elusive Dreams/Get Out Of My Heart | 15 |

## DILLARDS
| 65 | Capitol CL 15420 | Nobody Knows/Ebo Walker | 8 |
| 69 | Elektra EKSN 45048 | Reason To Believe/Nobody Knows | 6 |
| 69 | Elektra EKSN 45062 | She Sang Hymns Out Of Tune/Single Saddle | 5 |
| 69 | Elektra EKSN 45081 | Rainmaker/West Montana Hanna | 5 |
| 66 | Bounty BY 6019 | BACK PORCH BLUEGRASS (LP) | 20 |
| 68 | Elektra EKS 7265 | LIVE!!! ALMOST!!! (LP) | 15 |
| 72 | United Artists UAG 29366 | ROOTS AND BRANCHES (LP, textured gatefold sleeve) | 15 |

*(see also Dillard & Clark)*

## DILLINGER
| 73 | Duke DU 149 | Headquarters (as Dellenger)/CHENLEY DUFFAS: Black Girl In My Bed | 10 |
| 73 | Downtown DT 512 | Tighten Up Skank/Middle East Rock | 20 |
| 76 | Black Swan WIP 6355 | Bionic Dread/Eastman Skank | 10 |
| 79 | Island ISL 976 | Cokane In My Brain/Power | 5 |
| 77 | Black Swan WIP 6380 | Natty BSc/Buckingham Palace | 10 |
| 77 | Black Swan WIP 6416 | Cocaine In My Brain/Buckingham Palace/Ragnampiza | 10 |
| 77 | Black Swan BS 7 | Cocaine In My Brain/Buckingham Palace/Ragnampiza (12") | 20 |
| 76 | Black Swan ILPS 9385 | CB200 (LP) | 20 |
| 76 | Black Swan ILPS 9455 | BIONIC DREAD (LP) | 25 |
| 76 | Island ILPS 9385 | CB200 (LP, reissue) | 15 |
| 77 | Magnum DEAD 1001 | TALKIN' BLUES (LP) | 30 |
| 77 | Magnum BB27 | TALKIN' BLUES (LP, reissue) | 20 |
| 77 | Third World TWS 919 | TOP RANKING (LP) | 30 |
| 78 | Third World TWS 928 | ANSWER ME QUESTION (LP) | 30 |

*(see also David Isaacs)*

## DILLINGER V TRINITY
| 78 | Burning Sounds BSLP 1003 | CLASH (LP) | 30 |

## DILLINJA
| 93 | Cybotron DILL 01 | Steal The Way/Forever Fierce (1-sided 12") | 20 |
| 93 | Cybotron DILL 03 | From Beyond/Ride It Hard (1-sided 12") | 20 |
| 93 | Cybotron DILL 04 | Sine/Dark Science (1-sided 12") | 30 |
| 93 | Tough Toonz TT 02 | DILLINJA EP (12", promo only, four untitled tracks) | 20 |
| 93 | Wave Form DIL 08 | TEST [2] EP (12", as Dillinger) | 15 |
| 94 | Deadly Vinyl D2 | Deadly Ceremonies/Sovergin Melody (12") | 30 |
| 94 | Deadly Vinyl D3 | Deadly Deep Subs/Calculus Beats (12") | 30 |
| 94 | Logic Productions DM 003 | You Don't Know (Remix)/Heavenly Bass (12") | 15 |
| 94 | Deadly Vinyl DIL 06 | MAJESTIC B-LINE EP (12") | 12 |
| 94 | IQ IQ 001 | 3.01 In The Morning/Catch The Vibe (12", as Dillinja And Mr E) | 10 |
| 94 | Logic Productions DM 001 | Moods/Deep Love (Remix) (12", as Dillinja And Mystery) | 12 |
| 94 | Logic Productions DM 002 | You Don't Know/Warrior (12") | 12 |
| 94 | Heavyweight HW 003 | VOL 3 (10", two untitled tracks, as Dillinja And Ruffkut) | 12 |
| 94 | JA 1 | South Side (Riffin Mix)/Stompers Delight (12") | 15 |
| 95 | Deadly Vinyl D4 | Deadly Deep Subs (Remix)/Perfect Match (12") | 12 |
| 95 | Philly Blunt PB 005 | Muthaf*cka/Sky (12") | 12 |
| 95 | Metalheadz MET 006 | The Angel Fell/Ja Know Ya Big/Brutal Bass (12") | 18 |

*(See also Cybotron featuring Dillinja)*

## LEONARD DILLON
| 66 | Island WI 285 | Beggars Have No Choice (by Leonard Dillon & Wailers)/ MARCIA GRIFFITHS: Funny | 100 |

## PHYLLIS DILLON
| 66 | Doctor Bird DB 1061 | Don't Stay Away (as Phillis Dillon)/TOMMY McCOOK & SUPERSONICS: What Now | 70 |
| 67 | Trojan TR 006 | This Is A Lovely Way/Thing Of The Past (as Phyllis Dellon) | 70 |
| 67 | Treasure Isle TI 7003 | This Is A Lovely Way/Thing Of The Past | 40 |
| 67 | Treasure Isle TI 7015 | Perfidia/It's Rocking Time | 40 |
| 68 | Treasure Isle TI 7041 | I Wear This Ring/Don't Touch Me Tomato | 15 |
| 69 | Trojan TR 651 | Love Is All I Had/Boys And Girls Reggae (as Phillis Dylon) | 50 |
| 69 | Trojan TR 671 | The Right Track/TOMMY McCOOK & SUPERSONICS: Moonshot | 15 |
| 69 | Trojan TR 686 | Lipstick On Your Collar (as Phillis Dillon)/TOMMY McCOOK & SUPERSONICS: Tribute To Rameses | 25 |
| 70 | Duke Reid DR 2508 | This Is Me/Skabuvie (act. "If Your Name Is Andy"/"Ska Vovi" by Dorothy Reid) | 12 |
| 70 | Duke DU 76 | Walk Through This World/The Rooster | 8 |
| 71 | Treasure Isle TI 7058 | One Life To Live, One Love To Give/TOMMY McCOOK: My Best Dress | 20 |
| 71 | Treasure Isle TI 7070 | Midnight Confession/TOMMY McCOOK & SOUL SYNDICATE: Version | 20 |
| 72 | Sioux SI 009 | In The Ghetto/NYAH EARTH: Knight Of The Long Knives | 20 |
| 72 | Trojan TRL 41 | ONE LIFE TO LIVE (LP) | 60 |

## DIMENSIONS
65   Parlophone R 5294          Tears On My Pillow/You Don't Have To Whisper.................................................25

## DIMPLES & EDDIE WITH RICO'S COMBO
62   Planetone RC 3             Fleet Street/Good Bye World.............................................................20

## DIMPLES (1)
66   Decca F 12537              The Love Of A Lifetime/My Heart Is Tied To You...........................................40
*(see also Gospel Garden, Amazing Blondel)*

## DIMPLES (2)
76   Hybrid HB09                Doctor Dark Eyes/Devil You..............................................................20

## DINGER
85   Face Value FVRA 221        Air Of Mystery/I Love To Love (no p/s)...................................................35
*(see also Erasure)*

## DINGLE BROTHERS
71   Dynamic DYN 418            You Don't Know/CABLES: Rich Man, Poor Man.................................................6

## MARK DINNING
60   MGM MGM 1053               Teen Angel/Bye Now Baby.................................................................8
60   MGM MGM 1069               You Win Again/A Star Is Born (A Love Is Dead)...........................................5
60   MGM MGM 1101               The Lovin' Touch/Come Back To Me (My Love).............................................5
61   MGM MGM 1125               Top Forty, News, Weather And Sport/Suddenly............................................15
62   MGM MGM 1148               In A Matter Of Moments/What Will My Mary Say...........................................5
62   MGM MGM 1155               All Of This For Sally/The Pickup.......................................................5
65   Hickory 45-1293            Dial Al 1-4883/I'm Glad We Fell In Love................................................5

## DINNING SISTERS
55   London HLF 8179            Drifting And Dreaming/Truly...........................................................20
56   London HLF 8218            Hold Me Tight/Uncle Joe...............................................................20
*(see also Tennessee Ernie Ford)*

## DINO
65   RCA 1494                   Now I Know/Loeeg Negli Occhi...........................................................6

## DINO, DESI & BILLY
65   Reprise R 20367            I'm A Fool/So Many Ways.................................................................8
66   Reprise R 23047            Not The Loving Kind/Chimes Of Freedom..................................................8

## KENNY DINO
61   HMV POP 960                Your Ma Said You Cried In Your Sleep Last Night/Dream A Girl..........................15

## DINOSAUR JR
88   Blast First BFFP 30        Freak Scene (censored)/Keep The Glove (plain white labels, no p/s, promo only)..........5
92   Warner Bros. NEG61TEP      START CHOPPIN' (10" EP numbered picture disc).........................................12
97   Trade 2 TRDSC 009          I'm Insane (2000 copies pressed).......................................................5
06   Blast First PIL 0713       Been There All The Time/Back To Your Heart.............................................6
89   Blast First BFFP 31        BUG (LP)..............................................................................18
91   Blanco Y Negro BYN 24      GREEN MIND (LP).......................................................................15
93   Blanco Y Negro BYN 28      WHERE YOU BEEN (LP)...................................................................15
94   Blanco Y Negro 4509        WITHOUT A SOUND (LP).................................................................15
     96933-1
12   PIAS PIASR575LP            I BET ON SKY (LP, purple vinyl).......................................................15

## DINOSAUR L
86   City Beat CBE 1205         Go Bang! 5/Clean On Your Bean 1 (12", p/s)............................................10
*(see also Arthur Russell)*

## DIO
75   Purple PUR 128             Sitting In A Dream (as Ronnie Dio featuring Roger Glover & Guests)/JOHN LAWTON:
                                Little Chalk Blue.....................................................................15
85   Vertigo DIOD 5             Rock'n'Roll Children/Sacred Heart (gatefold p/s)........................................5
85   Vertigo DIOFP 6            Hungry For Heaven/King Of Rock And Roll (p/s, with poster & sticker)....................5
93   Vertigo 518486-1           STRANGE HIGHWAYS (LP, on 'swirl' label, with inner sleeve)............................15
*(see also Elf, Rainbow, Roger Glover, Black Sabbath, John Lawton)*

## DION (& BELMONTS)
### 78s
58   London HL 8646             I Wonder Why/Teen Angel (as Dion & Belmonts).........................................20
58   London HL 8718             I Can't Go On (Rosalie)/No One Knows (as Dion & Belmonts)............................20
59   London HL 8799             Don't Pity Me/Just You (as Dion & Belmonts).........................................20
59   London HL 8874             A Teenager In Love/I've Cried Before (as Dion & Belmonts)............................20
59   Pye International 7N 25038  A Lover's Prayer/Every Little Thing I Do (as Dion & Belmonts)........................40
60   London HLU 9030            Where Or When/That's My Desire (as Dion & Belmonts).................................50

### SINGLES
58   London HL 8646             I Wonder Why/Teen Angel (as Dion & Belmonts).........................................40
58   London HL 8718             I Can't Go On (Rosalie)/No One Knows (as Dion & Belmonts)............................40
59   London HL 8799             Don't Pity Me/Just You (as Dion & Belmonts).........................................40
59   London HL 8874             A Teenager In Love/I've Cried Before (mispressing as Dion & Delmnts).................30
59   London HLU 8874            A Teenager In Love/I've Cried Before (as Dion & Belmonts)............................30
*(The above 45s were originally issued with triangular centres, round-centre re-pressings are worth half to two-thirds of these values.)*
59   Pye International 7N 25038  A Lover's Prayer/Every Little Thing I Do (as Dion & Belmonts)........................50
60   London HLU 9030            Where Or When/That's My Desire (as Dion & Belmonts).................................25
60   Top Rank JAR 368           When You Wish Upon A Star/My Private Joy (as Dion & Belmonts)........................20
60   Top Rank JAR 503           In The Still Of The Night/Swinging On A Star (as Dion & Belmonts)....................20
60   Top Rank JAR 521           Lonely Teenager/Little Miss Blue.....................................................20
61   Top Rank JAR 545           Havin' Fun/North-East End Of The Corner..............................................15
61   Top Rank JAR 586           Runaround Sue/Runaway Girl...........................................................10
62   HMV POP 971                The Wanderer/The Majestic............................................................10

## DION (Cameron) & THREE TOPS

| | | | |
|---|---|---|---|
| 62 | HMV POP 1020 | Lovers Who Wander/(I Was) Born To Cry | 10 |
| 62 | Stateside SS 115 | Little Diane/Lost For Sure | 10 |
| 62 | Stateside SS 139 | Love Came To Me/Little Girl | 10 |
| 63 | CBS AAG 133 | Ruby Baby/He'll Only Hurt You | 10 |
| 63 | Stateside SS 161 | Sandy/Faith | 20 |
| 63 | CBS AAG 145 | This Little Girl/The Loneliest Man In The World | 5 |
| 63 | Stateside SS 209 | Come Go With Me/King Without A Queen | 15 |
| 63 | CBS AAG 161 | Be Careful Of Stones That You Throw/I Can't Believe (That You Don't Love Me Anymore) | 5 |
| 63 | CBS AAG 169 | Donna, The Prima Donna/You're Mine (credited to Dion) | 5 |
| 63 | CBS AAG 177 | Drip Drop/No One's Waiting For Me | 5 |
| 64 | CBS AAG 188 | I'm Your Hoochie Coochie Man/The Road I'm On (Gloria) | 10 |
| 64 | CBS AAG 224 | Johnnie B. Goode/Chicago Blues | 10 |
| 65 | CBS 201728 | Sweet, Sweet Baby/Unloved, Unwanted Me (as Dion Di Mucci) | 10 |
| 65 | CBS 201780 | Spoonful/Kickin' Child | 10 |
| 66 | HMV POP 1565 | Berimbau (as Dion & Belmonts)/My Girl The Month Of May | 10 |
| 67 | HMV POP 1586 | Movin' Man/For Bobbie (as Dion & Belmonts) | 10 |

### EPs

| | | | |
|---|---|---|---|
| 62 | HMV 7EG 8745 | SWINGALONG WITH DION | 30 |
| 63 | Stateside SE 1006 | DION'S HITS | 15 |

### ALBUMS

| | | | |
|---|---|---|---|
| 59 | London HA-U 2194 | PRESENTING DION AND THE BELMONTS (as Dion & Belmonts) | 150 |
| 60 | Top Rank 25-027 | THE TOPPERMOST — VOL. 1 (as Dion & Belmonts, with others) | 40 |
| 61 | HMV CLP 1539 | RUNAROUND SUE | 50 |
| 63 | Stateside SL 10034 | LOVERS WHO WANDER | 40 |
| 63 | CBS (S) BPG 62137 | RUBY BABY (mono/stereo) | 25 |
| 64 | CBS (S) BPG 62203 | DONNA THE PRIMA DONNA (mono/stereo) | 25 |
| 67 | HMV CLP 3618 | TOGETHER AGAIN (as Dion & Belmonts, also stereo CSD 3618) | 20 |

*(see also Belmonts)*

## DION (CAMERON) & THREE TOPS

| | | | |
|---|---|---|---|
| 67 | Doctor Bird DB 1101 | Miserable Friday/This World Has A Feeling | 50 |
| 72 | Big BG 331 | Three Tops Time/UNDERGROUND PEOPLE: Tops (Version) | 10 |

*(see also Three Tops)*

## CELINE DION

| | | | |
|---|---|---|---|
| 93 | Columbia 474743 | COLOUR OF MY LOVE (LP) | 25 |

## DIOS MALOS

| | | | |
|---|---|---|---|
| 06 | Full Time Hobby FTH 012S | I Want It All/Asshole (p/s, 500 only) | 8 |

## DIPLOMATS (1)

| | | | |
|---|---|---|---|
| 67 | Caltone TONE 108 | Meet Me At The Corner/Do It To Me Baby (by Lloyd & Groovers) | 50 |
| 68 | Caltone TONE 109 | Going Alone/My Heart My Soul (by Lloyd & Groovers) | 60 |
| 68 | Caltone TONE 112 | Strong Man/Listen To The Music (by Lloyd & Groovers) | 60 |
| 68 | Direction 58-3899 | I Can Give You Love/I'm So Glad I Found You | 20 |

## DIPLOMATS (2)

| | | | |
|---|---|---|---|
| 82 | Exchange EX 1 | Memories Of You/I'll Keep Holding On (p/s) | 7 |

*(see also Scene)*

## DIPLOMATS (3)

| | | | |
|---|---|---|---|
| 98 | Kent 6T 19 | I Really Love You/DEBRA JOHNSON: To Get Love | 30 |

## DIRECT ACTION

| | | | |
|---|---|---|---|
| 85 | Second Coming SCP 78501 | THE ALBUM (LP, with booklet) | 18 |

## DIRECT CURRENT MCS

| | | | |
|---|---|---|---|
| 90 | Underground Recordz TUBE1 | Keep In Step/Gangland Rap (12") | 45 |

## DIRECT HITS

| | | | |
|---|---|---|---|
| 82 | Whaam! WHAAM 007 | Modesty Blaise/Sunny Honey Girl (p/s) | 60 |
| 85 | Direct POP 001 | Christopher Cooper/She Really Didn't Care (p/s) | 7 |
| 80 | Bootleg BOOT 004 | COLLISIONS AT TEEN JUNCTION (LP, white card sleeve with home made printed front and back, lyric insert) | 30 |
| 84 | Whaam! BIG 7 | BLOW UP (LP) | 30 |

*(see also Exits)*

## DIRECTION

| | | | |
|---|---|---|---|
| 93 | Detour DR 003 | Yesterday/The Kids Wanna New Direction (p/s, 1,000 only) | 6 |

## DIRECTIONS

| | | | |
|---|---|---|---|
| 79 | Tortch TOR 004 | Three Bands Tonite/On The Train (p/s, with badge) | 80 |
| 79 | Tortch TOR 004 | Three Bands Tonite/On The Train (p/s) | 75 |

*(see also Big Sound Authority)*

## DIRECTIONS IN JAZZ UNIT

| | | | |
|---|---|---|---|
| 64 | Philips BL 7625 | DIRECTIONS IN JAZZ (LP) | 50 |

## DIRE STRAITS

| | | | |
|---|---|---|---|
| 80 | Vertigo MOVIE 1 | Romeo And Juliet/Solid Rock | 5 |
| 85 | Vertigo DSPIC 10 | Money For Nothing/Love Over Gold (live) (shaped picture disc with plinth) | 12 |
| 85 | Vertigo DSPIC 11 | Brothers In Arms/Going Home — Theme From 'Local Hero' (Live Version) (oblong picture disc in stickered PVC sleeve) | 10 |
| 85 | Vertigo 884 285-2 | Brothers In Arms (short)/Going Home (live)/Brothers In Arms (long)/ Why Worry (CD, promo only) | 30 |
| 85 | Vertigo DSTRD 11 | Brothers In Arms/Going Home — Theme From 'Local Hero' with free copy of Sultans Of Swing/Earthbound Train (live) in stickered PVC pack) | 7 |
| 78 | Vertigo 9102 021 | DIRE STRAITS (LP) | 20 |
| 82 | Vertigo HS 6359 034 | MAKING MOVIES (LP, half-speed master recording) | 30 |
| 82 | Vertigo HS 9102 021 | DIRE STRAITS (LP, half-speed master recording) | 30 |

*(see also Mark Knopfler, Notting Hillbillies)*

## DIRK & STIG
| | | | |
|---|---|---|---|
| 78 | Ring O' 2017 109/DIB 1 | Ging Gang Goolie/Mr. Sheene (unissued) | 0 |
| 79 | EMI EMI 2852 | Ging Gang Goolie/Mr. Sheene (p/s, khaki vinyl) | 18 |
| 79 | EMI EMI 2852 | Ging Gang Goolie/Mr. Sheene (p/s, black vinyl) | 10 |

*(see also Rutles, Neil Innes)*

## DIRT
| | | | |
|---|---|---|---|
| 82 | Crass 221984/7 | NEVER MIND THE DIRT HERE'S THE BOLLOCKS (LP, inner) | 18 |
| 85 | Dirt DIRT 1 | JUST AN ERROR (LP) | 25 |
| 95 | Dirt DIRT 3 | DRUNKS IN RUSTY TRANSITS (LP) | 15 |

## DIRTY BLUES BAND
| | | | |
|---|---|---|---|
| 68 | Stateside S(S)L 10234 | DIRTY BLUES BAND (LP) | 50 |
| 69 | Stateside S(S)L 10268 | STONE DIRT (LP) | 45 |

*(see also Bacon Fat and Juicy Lucy)*

## DIRTY DOG
| | | | |
|---|---|---|---|
| 78 | Lightning GIL 511 | Let Go Of My Hand/Shouldn't Do It/Gonna Quit/Guitar In My Hand (p/s) | 25 |

## DIRTY HARRY
| | | | |
|---|---|---|---|
| 73 | Unity UN 573 | Big Haire/YOUNG DOUG: Skank In Skank | 12 |
| 76 | Treble C CCC 015 | Djamballa (with Bobby Ellis)/BIG JOE: Rock Up A Zion | 8 |

## DIRTY PRETTY THINGS
| | | | |
|---|---|---|---|
| 06 | Mercury 9856418 | WATERLOO TO ANYWHERE (LP, with free 7") | 25 |
| 08 | Vertigo 177 236-7 | ROMANCE AT SHORT NOTICE (LP) | 18 |

*(see also Libertines)*

## DIRTY STRANGERS
| | | | |
|---|---|---|---|
| 89 | Thrill TH 3 | Bathing Belles/Oh Yeah/Hands Up (p/s, featuring Keith Richards) | 8 |

*(see also Rolling Stones)*

## DIRTY TRICKS
| | | | |
|---|---|---|---|
| 75 | Polydor 2383351 | DIRTY TRICKS (LP, red label) | 30 |

## DIRTY BEACHES
| | | | |
|---|---|---|---|
| 10 | Italian Beach Babes IBB 006 | Golden Desert Sun/Night Drive (p/s, 300 only) | 20 |
| 10 | Italian Beach Babes IBB 010 | No Fun/No Where Fast (100 hand-numbered copies, risograph cover) | 20 |
| 10 | Italian Beach Babes IBB 010 | No Fun/No Where Fast (p/s, 500 only) | 10 |
| 11 | Zoo ZM 010 | BADLANDS (LP) | 20 |

## DIRTY PROJECTORS
| | | | |
|---|---|---|---|
| 11 | Domino RUG 418T | MOUNT WITTENBERG (LP, with Bjork, 3D sleeve, insert, first 500 hand-numbered with signed print) | 20 |

## DISASTER
| | | | |
|---|---|---|---|
| 91 | Tone Deaf TONE DEAF 1 | WAR CRY (LP) | 50 |

## DISCHARGE (1)
| | | | |
|---|---|---|---|
| 80 | Clay CLAY 1 | Realities Of War/They Declare It/But After The Gig/Society's Victim (p/s) | 12 |
| 80 | Clay CLAY 3 | Fight Back/War's No Fairy Tale/Always Restrictions/You Take Part In Creating This System/Religion Instigates (p/s) | 12 |
| 80 | Clay CLAY 5 | Decontrol/It's No TV Sketch/Tomorrow Belongs To Us (p/s) | 12 |
| 81 | Clay CLAY 6 | Never Again/Death Dealers/Two Monstrous Nuclear Stock-Piles (p/s) | 9 |
| 81 | Clay PLATE 2 | WHY (12" EP) | 15 |
| 82 | Clay CLAY 14 | State Violence, State Control/Doomsday (p/s) | 10 |
| 83 | Clay CLAY 29 | Price Of SIlence/Born To Die In The Gutter (p/s) | 7 |
| 84 | Caly CLAY 34 | The More I See/Protest And Survive (p/s) | 8 |
| 85 | Clay CLAY 45 | Ignorance/No Compromise (p/s) | 6 |
| 82 | Clay CLAYLP 3 | HEAR NOTHING, SEE NOTHING, SAY NOTHING (LP, original issue has "Pay no more than £3.99" on top right of sleeve) | 30 |
| 84 | Clay CLAYLP 12 | NEVER AGAIN (LP, red vinyl) | 20 |
| 86 | Clay CLAY LP 19 | GRAVE NEW WORLD (LP) | 15 |
| 89 | Clay CLAY LP 103 | LIVE AT THE CITY GARDEN NEW JERSEY (LP, red vinyl) | 15 |
| 91 | Clay CLAY LP 110 | MASSACRE DIVINE (LP) | 15 |
| 03 | Earmark 40024 | DISCHARGE (LP) | 15 |

*(see also Broken Bones)*

## DISCHARGE (2)
| | | | |
|---|---|---|---|
| 80 | Go Round ROUND 001 | DISCHARGE/THE FILTH (split 7, no p/s) | 75 |

*(not the Discharge that punks know and love!)*

## DISCIPLE (1)
| | | | |
|---|---|---|---|
| 69 | Parlophone R 5760 | Cherie Alamayonaika/Caucasoid Junkie | 45 |

## DISCIPLES
| | | | |
|---|---|---|---|
| 93 | Boom Shacka Lacka BSL 001 | Prowling Lion/Downbeat Rock (12") | 30 |
| 94 | Boom Shacka Lacka BSL 002 | Return To Addis Ababa/Africa Macka (12") | 30 |
| 94 | Boom Shacka Lacka BSL 003 | Dub Revolution/(Innovation Mix)/Chamber Of Echoes Mix (10") | 15 |
| 94 | Topatop TOP 001 | Prowling Lion (Original Cut)/Fourth Cut (Unreleased)Return To Addis Ababa (Original Cut)/Next Cut (Unreleased) (10") | 12 |
| 95 | Boom Shacka Lacka BSL 004 | Chant Of Freedom/Unshackled Version (10") | 20 |
| 95 | Boom Shacka Lacka BSL 005 | Sunrise/Message (12") | 45 |
| 02 | Boom Shacka Lacka BSL 006 | Ilodica Theme Pt.1/Ilodica Theme Pt.2/Fearless Dub Pt.1/Fearless Dub Pt.2 (12") | 15 |
| 04 | Boom Shacka Lacka BSL 009 | Almighty Dub/Zion Rock Dub (12") | 20 |
| 95 | Cloak & Dagger NLX5 004 | RESONATIONS (LP) | 20 |
| 96 | Boom Shacka Lacka BSL 101 | FOR THOSE WHO UNDERSTAND (LP) | 30 |

## DISCIPLES OF BELIAL
| | | | |
|---|---|---|---|
| 95 | Praxis PRAXIS 17 | GOAT OF MENDES EP (12") | 40 |
| 97 | Praxis PRAXIS 7 | Lucifer We Praise Thee/Sell Your Soul To The Devil/One God (p/s) | 50 |

## DISCIPLES RIDDIM SECTION
| | | | |
|---|---|---|---|
| 03 | Jah Tubbys JT 10018 | Roots Workout/Mission Of Dub (10") | 25 |

### DISCO DUB BAND
76   Movers MO 1     For the Love Of Money/For The Love Of Money Part 2 ................................................. 20

### DISCO 2000
87   KLF Comms. D 2000     I Gotta CD/I Love Disco 2000 (12", p/s)........................................................ 12

*(see also KLF, Timelords, Bill Drummond, Space)*

### DISCO DREAD
93   Dub Jockey DJ 023     Ancient Vibrations/Modern Dub ................................................................. 10

### DISCO DREAM AND ANDROIDS
79   Wake UP WUR 2     DISCO DREAM AND THE ANDROIDS (LP)........................................................ 25

### DISCO INFERNO
91   Che CHE 2     OPEN DOORS (LP) ................................................................................ 15
94   Rough Trade R 3071     D.I. GO POP (LP) ................................................................................ 35

### DISCORDS
91   Hangman 41 UP     SECOND TO NO-ONE (LP) ...................................................................... 15

### DISCO STUDENTS
79   Yeah Yeah Yeah UHHUH 1     South Africa House/Kafkaesque (no p/s) ................................................... 15
80   Yeah Yeah Yeah UHHUH 2     A Boy With A Penchant For Open-Necked Shirts/Pink Triangles/Credit (no p/s)........... 15

### DISCO VOLANTE
84   Catalyst Box CBR 001     No Motion/Click Punishment Tank Live! (p/s) .............................................. 40

### DISCO ZOMBIES
79   South Circular SGS 106     Drums Over London/Heartbeats Love (black, white & pink or black, white & green handmade wraparound p/s).......................................................................... 40
79   Uptown/Wizzo WIZZO 1     THE INVISIBLE (EP) ............................................................................ 25
81   Dining Out TUX 2     Here Come The Buts/Mary Millington (p/s) ............................................... 15

*(see also Fifty Fantastics)*

### DISCS
65   Columbia DB 7477     Not Meant To Be/Come Back To Me ........................................................ 10

### BABA DISE
69   Gas GAS 118     Wanted/SENSATIONS: I'll Always Love You ............................................... 30

### DISGUISE
78   Chiswick CHIS 107     Hey Baby/Juvenile Delinquent ............................................................... 30

### DISORDER (1)
80   Ace ACE 12     Air Raid/Law And Disorder (1st 100 in custom 'War Book' p/s) .................... 200
80   Ace ACE 12     Air Raid/Law And Disorder .................................................................... 70
80   Durham Book Centre BOOK 1     Reality Crisis/1984 (over sized p/s) ........................................................ 30

### DISORDER (2)
81   Disorder ORDER 1     Complete Disorder/Insane Youth/Today's World/Violent Crime (p/s)................... 8
81   Disorder ORDER 2     Distortion To Deafness/More Than Fights/Daily Life/You've Got To Be Someone (p/s).... 8
84   Disorder AARGH 1     UNDER THE SCALPEL BLADE (LP, with poster) ........................................... 15
84   Disorder 12 ORDER 5     THE SINGLES COLLECTION (12" EP) .......................................................... 10
85   Disorder AARGH 2     GI FAEN I NASJONALITENTEN DIN (LP) ..................................................... 15
86   Disorder AARGH 3     ONE DAY SON ALL THIS WILL BE YOURZ (split LP with KAFKA PROCESS)............... 15

### DISRUPTERS
81   Radical Change RC 1     Young Offender/U.K. Solider/No Place For You (p/s) .................................... 8
82   Radical Change RC 2     Shelters For The Rich/Animal Farm/Self Rule (p/s) .................................... 10
83   Radical Change RC 6     Bomb Heaven/Die With Mother (p/s) ...................................................... 8
85   Radical Change 12 RC 8     ALIVE IN THE ELECTRIC CHAIR (12" EP, with insert) ................................... 20
83   Radical Change RCLP1     UNREHEARSED WRONGS (LP)................................................................... 30
84   Radical Change RCLP3     PLAYING WITH FIRE (LP) ...................................................................... 20

### TOM DISSEVELT
62   Philips 430 736 PE     ELECTRONIC MOVEMENTS (EP) ............................................................... 20
65   Philips BL 7681     FANTASY IN ORBIT (LP) ........................................................................ 60

### DISTAINERS
79   Beck 885     Say Goodbye/Spies In Your Eyes (no p/s, 300 copies)................................. 60

### DISTANT COUSINS
66   CBS 202352     She Ain't Loving You/Here Today, Gone Tomorrow ..................................... 18
67   CBS 2800     Mister Sebastian/Empty House .............................................................. 10

### DISTANT DRUMS
82   Rhythmic RMNS 3     Perfect Eyes/Halloween (p/s) ............................................................... 25

### DISTANT MEMORIES
72   N&G 01     Someone Who Knows/Escape From Reality ............................................... 60

### DISTINCTIVE DRONE
79   No label, no cat no     DISTINCTIVE DRONE (cassette LP, 20 only) ............................................... 40

### DISTORHAUS
94   Mystic MRD 99401     PLASTIC ANGEL EP (12") ...................................................................... 20

### DISTORTED WAVES OF OHM
94   Eurk 12EK 001     ZYRCON (12" EP) ................................................................................ 50
95   Eurk 12EK 002     STRANGE ROTATION (12" EP) ................................................................ 30
95   Eurk 12EK 003     WITH INTENT TO DISTORT (12" EP) ........................................................ 20
96   Eurk 12EK 004     SURREAL SKETCH SHOW (12" EP) ........................................................... 10

### DISTRACTIONS
79   TJM TJM 2     YOU'RE NOT GOING OUT DRESSED LIKE THAT (12" EP) .................................. 12
79   Factory FAC 12     Time Goes By So Slow/Pillow Fight (p/s) .................................................. 18
80   Island WIP 6533     It Doesn't Bother Me/One Way Love ....................................................... 10
80   Island WIP 6568     Boys Cry (Where No One Can See Them)/Paracetamol Paralysis (p/s) ............... 6
80   Island ILPS 9604     NOBODY'S PERFECT (LP, sleeve designed by Peter Saville) ............................ 15

## DISTRAINERS
79   DJ Records BECK 885   Say Goodbye/Spies In Your Eyes (no p/s, 300 only) ...................................................... 125

## DISTRIBUTORS
80   Tap TAP 1   TV Me/Wireless (various foldover p/s) .............................................................. 8

## DISTURBED
79   Parole PURL: 3   I Don't Believe/Betrayed (p/s) .................................................................. 10

## DIVINE COMEDY
92   Setanta SET 011   Europop: New Wave/Intifada/Monitor/Timewatch/Jerusalem/ The Rise And Fall (12", p/s) ........................................ 15
93   Setanta CAO 008   Lucy/The Pop Singer's Fear Of The Pollen Count/I Was Born Yesterday (mail order, p/s) . 8
93   Setanta DC 001   Indulgence No. 1: Hate My Way/Untitled Melody/Europe By Train (picture disc) ......... 20
94   Setanta DC 002   Indulgence No. 2: A Drinking Song/When The Lights Go Out All Over Europe/Tonight We Fly (handfinished wraparound p/s, stamped labels) ....................................... 15
90   Setanta SETLPM 002   FANFARE FOR THE COMIC MUSE (LP, with inner sleeve) ......................................... 40
90   Setanta SETCD 002   FANFARE FOR THE COMIC MUSE (CD, beware of counterfeits) ................................. 30
93   Setanta SET LP 11   LIBERATION (LP) ................................................................................. 40
94   Setanta SETLP13   PROMENADE (LP) ................................................................................ 45
96   Setanta SETLP 25   CASSANOVA (LP) ................................................................................ 35
97   Setanta SETLP 036   A SHORT ALBUM ABOUT LOVE (LP) .......................................................... 30
98   Setanta SETLP 57   FIN DE SIECLE (LP) ............................................................................ 40
10   Divine Comedy DCRP 101LP   BANG GOES THE KNIGHTHOOD (LP) ..................................................... 30

## DIVISION
72   Wren WR1   Under Your Influence/Dark Dreams ............................................................. 35

## DIVORCE BROTHERS
87   Separation   To Understand/That First Kiss/Walk Out Of The Door/The Divorce/The Liquidator (12" p/s) .................................................. 20

## DIXIE BELLES
64   London REU 1434   THE DIXIE BELLES (EP) ......................................................................... 25
64   London HA-U/SH-U 8152   DOWN AT PAPA JOE'S (LP, with Cornbread & Jerry) ..................................... 30

## DIXIE CUPS
64   Pye International 7N 25245   Chapel Of Love/Ain't That Nice ....................................................... 15
64   Red Bird RB 10006   People Say/Girls Can Tell (some copies on Pye label) ................................... 10
64   Red Bird RB 10012   You Should Have Seen The Way He Looked At Me/No True Love ....................... 15
64   Red Bird RB 10017   Little Bell/Another Boy Like Mine ...................................................... 15
65   Red Bird RB 10024   Iko Iko/Gee Baby Gee ................................................................. 12
65   Red Bird RB 10032   Gee The Moon Is Shining Bright/I'm Gonna Get You Yet ............................. 20
65   HMV POP 1453   Two Way Poc A Way/That's Where It's At ............................................. 15
66   HMV POP 1524   What Kind Of Fool/Danny Boy .......................................................... 25
66   HMV POP 1557   Love Ain't So Bad (After All)/Daddy Said No .......................................... 25
71   Buddah 2011 079   Chapel Of Love/People Say ............................................................. 5
65   Red Bird RB 20100   CHAPEL OF LOVE (LP) ................................................................... 60
66   HMV CLP 1916   RIDING HIGH (LP) ........................................................................ 50
79   Charly CRM 2004   TEEN ANGUISH (LP) .................................................................... 15

## DIXIE DRIFTER
65   Columbia DB 7710   Soul Heaven/Three Chairs Theme ...................................................... 12

## DIXIE FOUR
60s   Rarities RA 3   THE DIXIE FOUR (EP) ................................................................... 25

## DIXIE HUMMINGBIRDS
64   Vogue V 2422   Have A Talk With Jesus/In The Morning ............................................... 10
64   Vogue LAE-P 588   PRAYER FOR PEACE (LP) ............................................................... 20

## DIXIELANDERS
63   Vocalion V 9209   Cyclone/Mardyke ..................................................................... 35

## DIXIELAND JUG BLOWERS
54   HMV 7M 223   Memphis Shake/Boodle-Am-Shake ..................................................... 10
54   HMV 7M 233   Hen Party Blues/Carpet Alley Breakdown .............................................. 10

## DIXIE PEACH
85   Jah Tubbys JT 005   Just Worries/Pure Worries (12") ...................................................... 60
85   Jah Tubbys JT 014   Spin Spin/Spin Style (12", with the Offbeat Posse) .................................. 40
86   Jah Tubbys JT 018   Slaughter/Slaughter Mix (12") ....................................................... 45
86   Y&D YDD 0102   Raggamuffin And Rambo/Raggamuffin Style (12") .................................... 40
87   Y&D YDD 0106   Get Up And Skank/LONG MAN AND THE OFFBEAT POSSE: Skank With Me/OFFBEAT POSSE: The Skank (12") .................................... 40
87   Y&D YDD 0112   Hold Onto Your Man/Tonight Is The Night (12") ...................................... 30
88   Y&D YDD 0119   Running Around/Run Come Follow Me Now (12") ...................................... 30
00   Jah Tubbys JT 7003   Every Step/DISCIPLES RIDDIM SECTION: Step Dub .................................. 20
01   Jah Tubbys JT 7008   I Heard Them Bawling/OFFBEAT POSSE: Bawling For Riddim .................... 18
03   Jah Tubbys JT 10013   Sufferers Time/What Am I to Do? (10", with the Offbeat Posse) ................. 30
03   Jah Tubbys JT 10017   Jah Jah Army/Who's Gonna Stop Us? (10", with the Offbeat Posse) ............. 30
06   Jah Tubbys JT 10027   Roots Vibration (with the Roots Squad)/Got To Be Humble (with WD Production) ....... 20

## THE DIXIES
64   Parlophone R 5223   Love Made A Fool/Valley Of Tears ..................................................... 10

## ERROL DIXON
60   Blue Beat BB 27   Midnight Track/Anytime Anywhere ..................................................... 15
61   Blue Beat BB 46   Mama Shut Your Door/Too Much Whisky ............................................. 15
62   Blue Beat BB 86   Bad Bad Woman/Early This Morning ................................................... 15
62   Island WI 017   Morning Train/Lonely Heart ........................................................... 20
63   Island WI 069   I Love You/Tell Me More ............................................................... 20
63   Carnival CV 7001   Oo Wee Baby/Twisting And Shaking .................................................. 10

| | | | |
|---|---|---|---|
| 63 | Carnival CV 7004 | Mean And Evil Woman/Tutti Frutti | 10 |
| 64 | Oriole CB 1945 | Rocks In My Pillow/Give Me More Time (as Errol Dixon & Bluebeaters) | 70 |
| 66 | Blue Beat BB 337 | Gloria/Heavy Shuffle | 15 |
| 66 | Blue Beat BB 344 | You're No Good/Midnight Bus | 20 |
| 66 | Rainbow RAI 104 | I Need Someone To Love/I Want (as Errol Dixon & Goodtime Band) | 30 |
| 66 | Fab EP 1 | I Need Someone To Love/I Want (reissue) | 20 |
| 67 | Ska Beat JB 271 | Midnight Party/It Makes No Difference | 18 |
| 67 | Direct DS 5002 | I Don't Want/The Hoop | 60 |
| 67 | Decca F 12613 | Six Questions/Not Again | 15 |
| 67 | Decca F 12717 | True Love Never Runs Smooth/What Ya Gonna Do (B-side with Judy Kay) | 8 |
| 68 | Decca F 12826 | Back To The Chicken Shack (as Big City Blues Of Errol Dixon)/ I Done Found Out | 20 |
| 69 | Doctor Bird DB 1197 | Why Hurt Yourself/She Started To Scream | 20 |
| 60s | Carnival CU 7002 | Crazy Baby/Our First Love (with Maynell Wilson) | 10 |
| 70 | Gas GAS 148 | Something On Your Mind/I Need Love | 8 |
| 72 | Transatlantic BIG 503 | Let The Love Shine into Your Heart/In A Moment Of Weakness | 10 |
| 65 | Decca DFE 8626 | SINGS FATS (EP, with Honeydrippers) | 60 |
| 68 | Decca LK/SKL 4962 | BLUES IN THE POT (LP, with Chicken Shack) | 100 |
| 70 | Transatlantic TRA 225 | THAT'S HOW YOU GOT KILLED BEFORE (LP) | 30 |

*(see also Chicken Shack)*

**JEFF DIXON**

| | | | |
|---|---|---|---|
| 67 | Coxsone CS 7015 | The Rock/HAMBOYS: Harder On The Rock | 40 |
| 68 | Studio One SO 2051 | Tickle Me/ENFORCERS: Forgive Me | 60 |

**WILLIE DIXON & ALLSTARS**

| | | | |
|---|---|---|---|
| 56 | London HLU 8297 | Walking The Blues/Crazy For My Baby | 1500 |
| 56 | London HLU 8297 | Walking The Blues/Crazy For My Baby (78) | 150 |
| 64 | Pye International 7N 25270 | Crazy For My Baby/Walkin' The Blues (reissue) | 25 |

**TEX DIXSON**

| | | | |
|---|---|---|---|
| 70 | Ackee ACK 111 | Funky Trombone/Crying Horn | 10 |
| 70 | Ackee ACK 112 | My Ring/Here I Am | 10 |

**DIXXY SISTERS**

| | | | |
|---|---|---|---|
| 54 | Columbia SCM 5105 | Spin The Bottle Polka/The Game Of Broken Hearts | 10 |

**DIZZY MANS BAND**

| | | | |
|---|---|---|---|
| 70 | Warner Bros WB 8015 | Tickatoo/My Love | 5 |

**DJ B AND EZM.**

| | | | |
|---|---|---|---|
| 92 | Industrial Noize DE 001 | Can't Beat Ruff Beats/Shockin' To The Break Of Dawn (12", stamped white label) | 35 |

**DJ CHEMISTRY MEETS JACK SMOOTH**

| | | | |
|---|---|---|---|
| 94 | Homegrown HG 015 | Alchemy/Freefall (12") | 12 |

*(see also Chemistry, Jack Smooth)*

**DJ CRYSTL**

| | | | |
|---|---|---|---|
| 92 | Lucky Spin LSR 001 | Suicidal/Drop XTC (12") | 20 |
| 93 | Dee Jay Recordings DJX 008 | Crystalize/Deep Space (12") | 15 |
| 93 | Dee Jay Recordings DJX 010 | Meditation/Warpdrive (12") | 20 |
| 93 | Force Ten FTR 001 | The Dark Cryst/Inna Year 3000 (12") | 15 |
| 94 | Dee Jay Recordings DJX 020 | Let It Roll/Paradise (12") | 12 |

**DJ CRYSTL & SLIPMASTER J**

| | | | |
|---|---|---|---|
| 92 | Lucky Spin LSR 004 | Frantic Situation/Drop XTC (12") | 25 |

**DJ CYCLONE**

| | | | |
|---|---|---|---|
| 96 | Acid Fever MDMA 9612 | 909 TRAX EP: Trak 101/Trak 3/4/Trak 303/Trak 23 (12") | 20 |
| 96 | Acid Fever MDMA 9613 | Innersense (Halfcore Remix)/Innersense (Original Hardcore Mix)/Mushroom Of Fire/Non-sense (12") | 20 |
| 96 | Acid Fever MDMA 9614 303 | Joy Ride/Cycloid Spiral Motion/Circular Motion/Cycloid Spiral Slow Motion (12") | 20 |
| 97 | Acid Fever MDMA 9703 | STATE OF THE PLANET EP (12" two tracks, other two tracks by OCTODRED) | 15 |

**DJ DADO**

| | | | |
|---|---|---|---|
| 96 | Steppin' Out IAN 045T | Face It (Club Mix)/(Radio Edit)/(Alternative Mix)/(Status Mix) (12") | 15 |

**DJ EXCEL**

| | | | |
|---|---|---|---|
| 91 | (No company) EDUC 2 | Just When You Thought It Was Safe/Breakbeat 1/Breakbeat 2/Breakbeat 3/Breakbeat 4 (12") | 30 |

**DJ FOOD**

| | | | |
|---|---|---|---|
| 00 | Ninja Tune ZEN12 015/021 | Classic House Tracks From The Vaults (12") | 10 |
| 90 | Ninja Tune ZEN 02 | JAZZ BRAKES VOL. 1 (LP) | 15 |
| 91 | Ninja Tune ZEN 03 | JAZZ BRAKES VOL. 2 (LP) | 20 |

**DJ FORCE & EVOLUTION**

| | | | |
|---|---|---|---|
| 93 | Knifeforce KF 003 | Fall Down On Me/The Force Will Be With You/Escape The Feeling/Mine All Mine (12") | 30 |
| 93 | Knifeforce KF 003 | Fall Down On Me/The Force Will Be With You/Escape The Feeling/Mine All Mine (12", red vinyl, 200 only) | 35 |
| 93 | Knifeforce KF 011 | Twelve Midnight/Lost It (12") | 20 |
| 93 | Knifeforce KF 16 | Poltergeist/Perfect Dreams (10", some on clear vinyl) | 20 |
| 93 | Knifeforce KF 019 | Perfect Dreams (Citadel Of Kaos Remix)/Perfect Dreams (Original Mix)/Fall Down On Me (Remix) (12") | 10 |

**DJ GOLLUM**

| | | | |
|---|---|---|---|
| 96 | UK44 UK44 07 | Pleasant Experience/Mystic Fusion (12") | 30 |
| 98 | UK44 UK44 15 | The Energy (Trance Mix)/The Energy (Rave Mix)/The Energy (Mix Mix) (12", p/s) | 10 |

*(see also Gollum & Gary D, M-Zone & DJ Gollum)*

**DJ GUNSHOT**

| | | | |
|---|---|---|---|
| 93 | GOD 1 | Untitled/Untitled (White label with Dread Or Dead stamp) (12") | 15 |
| 94 | No U Turn NUT 009 | Wheel N Deal/Marble Mix (10") | 15 |
| 95 | No U Turn NUT 010 | Soundboy/Soundtest (12") | 12 |
| 95 | DAT II DISC D2D 001 | Bad Boy/(Smooth Mix) (12") | 15 |

## DJ HARVEY
| | | | |
|---|---|---|---|
| 96 | Noid Recordings NOID 0066 | I Am A Man/MONSIEUR D: Hot Love (12") | 20 |
| 98 | Black Cock Records BK 016 | LOVE HOTEL EP (12") | 12 |
| 00 | Weekend Inc WKD 069 | Done Turn Me/Protect And Survive (Fuck Loop) (12") | 20 |

*(see also Ersatz)*

## DJ JINX
| | | | |
|---|---|---|---|
| 92 | Music Madness MM 003 | Devotion/Paradise Project/Paradise Project (Bounty Remix) (12") | 40 |

## DJ KRUSH
| | | | |
|---|---|---|---|
| 95 | Mo' Wax MWLP 039 | MEISO (2-LP, inner sleeves) | 18 |
| 98 | Mo' Wax MW 088 LP | HOLONIC (LP) | 15 |

*(see also DJ Shadow)*

## DJ LJT
| | | | |
|---|---|---|---|
| 93 | KIN 2 | Untitled/Untitled (stamped white labels "DJ LJT FEATURING KINETIC") (12") | 20 |

## DJ MAYHEM
| | | | |
|---|---|---|---|
| 92 | Basement BRSS 008 | Damage/Metrix: The Remix/Signal Generator (12") | 15 |
| 92 | Basement BRSS 016 | Storm Trooper/Cold Acid (12") | 15 |

*(see also Two Dark Troopers)*

## DJ MINK FEAT. 2WICE THE TROUBLE
| | | | |
|---|---|---|---|
| 89 | FON T18 | Hey Hey Can You Relate (4 mixes) (12") | 12 |

## DJ NUT NUT
| | | | |
|---|---|---|---|
| 93 | Virtual Motion VM 001 | Forbidden Planet/Set My Mind Free (12") | 12 |
| 94 | Production House PNT 058 R | The Rumble (Remixes) (12") | 25 |
| 94 | Babylon BR 001 | Press Up (VIP Mix)/Press Up (Dub Mix) (12", stamped white labels) | 15 |
| 94 | Hard Step HRD 001 | Special Dedication (Ladies Mix)/Bloodclart Hour (12") | 20 |
| 96 | London Some 'ting LS 006 | Special Dedication (DJ Ron Remix)/Special Dedication (The Dream Team Remix) (12") | 10 |

## DJ PESHAY
| | | | |
|---|---|---|---|
| 93 | Reinforced RIVET 1248 | PROTÉGÉ EP (12") | 20 |

## DJ RON
| | | | |
|---|---|---|---|
| 92 | Pure BR001 | Crackman (Mix 1)/Crackman (Mix 2)/Bad Boy/Untitled (12", stamped white label) | 15 |
| 93 | Rough Tone RT007 | Crackman The Return (Remix D.J. Ron)/Crackman The Return (Booyaka Mix) (E.Q.P. Mix) (12") | 35 |

## DJ SHADOW
| | | | |
|---|---|---|---|
| 93 | Mo' Wax MW 014 | In/ Flux/Hindsight (12", plain sleeve, with obi sticker, with the Groove Robbers) | 12 |
| 93 | Mo' Wax MW 014 | In/ Flux/Hindsight (12" picture disc, plastic sleeve, with the Groove Robbers) | 25 |
| 95 | Mo' Wax MW 027 P1/2/3 | What Does Your Soul Look Like Inside (3 x 10" forming DJ Shadow tag) | 70 |
| 94 | Mo' Wax MW 027 | What Does Your Soul Look Like (parts 1, 3 & 4) (12" p/s) | 10 |
| 97 | Mo' Wax MW 063s | High Noon/Organ Donor (Extended Overhaul) (stickered p/s) | 8 |
| 02 | none | Monosylabik/First Letter From Home (acetate, with letter, 10 copies only) | 100 |
| 06 | Gabacradabra CT 010 | Gabracadabra/Acappella Version (7", 500 only hand-stamped white label given away at door of London Indig02 gig 2007) | 70 |
| 10 | TNF-1 | Def Surrounds Us/I've Been Trying (100 only, hand-made cover) | 70 |
| 10 | New Futility TNF2 | Def Surrounds Us/Def Surrounds US (Neil Landstrumm Remix) (12" promo, 100 only electric blue sleeve, green vinyl) | 40 |
| 12 | A&M/Talenthouse S75 | Come On Riding (Through The Cosmos) (1-sided, 100 only) | 70 |
| 98 | Mo' Wax MW 059 | ENDTRODUCING (2-LP, gatefold, spine opening sleeve) | 20 |
| 96 | Mo' Wax MW059LP | ENDTRODUCING (2-LP, gatefold, centre opening sleeve) | 25 |
| 12 | Island 3708138 | RECONSTRUCTED (6-CD, DVD, 12" in perspex box with signed certificate, 500 only) | 80 |
| 02 | Island ILPSD8118586981-1 | THE PRIVATE PRESS (2-LP, gatefold) | 30 |
| 02 | none | PRESS CUTTINGS ('The Private Press' Compacted, 5 copies only) | 200 |
| 06 | Island 1704960 | THE OUTSIDER (2-LP) | 25 |

*(see also Q-Bert, U.N.K.L.E.)*

## DJ SIDE PHONE/DJ CYDER CLONE
| | | | |
|---|---|---|---|
| 97 | Acid Fever MDMA 9705 | ACID FLUFF EP (12", three tracks each) | 20 |

## DJ TOKEN PACE & TOXIC KEV
| | | | |
|---|---|---|---|
| 92 | Face The Bass FBR 001 | Losing You/Dreamers Revenge (12") | 40 |

## DJ TRACE
| | | | |
|---|---|---|---|
| 91 | Orbital 12 ORBIT 11 | Inception/Ain't Gonna Wait No More/Love Dove Sound (12") | 20 |
| 92 | (No company, no number) | Rudeboy Hardcore/Untitled/Untitled (white label 12" with 'DJ Trace' and phone number stamped on labels. A-side samples 'Orinoco flow') | 10 |
| 92 | Orbital 12OUT 997 | Teach Me To Fly/Inception (After Dark Remix) (12") | 18 |
| 93 | Lucky Spin LSR 003 | Lost Entity (London side)/Lost entity (New York side) (12") | 20 |

## DJ TRACE & ED RUSH
| | | | |
|---|---|---|---|
| 93 | Lucky Spin LSR 008 | Don Bad Man/Clean Gun (12") | 10 |

## DJ TREMA & THE AVENGER
| | | | |
|---|---|---|---|
| 93 | DBS 22 | Untitled/Untitled (12", white label, "DBS 22" etched in run-out groove) | 45 |

## DJ VADIM
| | | | |
|---|---|---|---|
| 98 | Ninja Tune ZEN 31/2 | U.S.S.R. RECONSTRUCTION (2 x 12") | 15 |

## DJAGO
| | | | |
|---|---|---|---|
| 72 | Duke DU 134 | Rebel Train/Babylon Version | 10 |

## DJANGO DJANGO
| | | | |
|---|---|---|---|
| 09 | Shadazz SHAD 09 | Storm/Love's Dart | 15 |
| 10 | Bonhour Branch BONBRA 002 | WOR/Skies Over Cairo | 10 |
| 13 | Because ILMVF004 | Love's Dart (Sal P Liquid Liquid Remix) (12" 1-sided, 50 copies only) | 25 |

## D'JURANN JURANN
| | | | |
|---|---|---|---|
| 74 | Dawn DNS 1068 | Streakin'/Oh! Janine | 10 |

*(see also Paul King, King Earl Boogie Band, Mungo Jerry)*

**D-LIVIN**
92   D-Livin DL01                          Why/Up Their Head/Make A Joyful Noize/Yard An Gorage (12") ..................... 25

**JED(RZEZ) DMOCHOWSKI**
83   Whaam! WHAAM 009             Sha-La-La-La (Dance With Me)/Ruined City (with 'Jed' on p/s) ..................... 8
83   Whaam! WHAAM 009             Sha-La-La-La (Dance With Me)/Ruined City (without 'Jed' on p/s) ............... 10
*(see also V.I.P.'s)*

**DMS**
91   Production House PNT 032     Exterminate (12") ............................................................................. 15
92   Production House PNT 039     Vengeance/Love Overdose (Remix) (12") .......................................... 15

**D.N.A.**
80   CPEP 002                              SHOCK ROCK EP ................................................................................. 30

**DNA (1)**
81   Rough Trade RTO 86             A TASTE OF DNA (12" EP, p/s) ........................................................... 15

**DNA (2)**
81   DNA 1                                  Do The Shopping/Zoo Tango (p/s) ...................................................... 6
82   DNA 2                                  Atlantic Flyer/What A Way To Go (p/s) ............................................... 6
81   DNA 3                                  The Road To Kong Kong/Praying Mantis (p/s) .................................. 6

**DNA (3)**
83   Confidential FILE 001            EXTENDED PLAY ................................................................................. 15

**DNV**
79   New Pleasures Z2                 Mafia/Death In Venice/Goodbye 70s (foldout p/s) ........................... 20
*(see also Another Pretty Face, Funhouse, TV21)*

**D.O.A.**
93   Alt. Tentacles VIRUS 120     It's Not Unusual/Dead Men Tell No Tales (yellow vinyl) .................... 5
83   Alt. Tentacles VIRUS 31       BLOODIED BUT UNBOWED — THE DAMAGE TO DATE 1978-84 (LP) ........ 15

**CARL DOBKINS JNR.**
59   Brunswick 05804                  My Heart Is An Open Book/My Pledge To You .................................. 6
60   Brunswick LAT 8329             CARL DOBKINS JNR. (LP) ................................................................... 20

**BOBBY DOBSON**
69   Punch PH 4                          Strange/Your New Love ..................................................................... 10
*(see also Dobby Dobson)*

**BONNIE DOBSON**
69   RCA RCA 1901                     I'm Your Woman/I Got Stung ............................................................. 8
70   RCA SF 8079                       BONNIE DOBSON (LP) ....................................................................... 35
72   Argo ZFB 79                       BONNIE DOBSON (LP) ....................................................................... 30
76   Polydor 2383 400                MORNING DEW (LP) ......................................................................... 15

**DOBBY DOBSON (& DELTAS)**
65   King KG 1008                      Cry A Little Cry/Diamonds And Pearls (as Dobby Dobson & Deltas) ...... 15
67   Trojan TR 011                     Loving Pauper/TOMMY McCOOK & SUPERSONICS: Sir Don .......... 35
68   Studio One SO 2068           Walking In The Footsteps/SOUL VENDORS: Studio Rock .............. 50
68   Coxsone CS 7058                Seems To Me I'm Losing You/GAYLADS: Red Rose ........................ 40
69   Blue Cat BS 171                  Strange/Your New Love ..................................................................... 25
69   Punch PH 12                       The Masquerade Is Over/Love For Ambition .................................. 10
70   Success RE 906                   Crazy/RUPIE EDWARDS ALL STARS: Your New Love ................... 6
70   Big BG 303                         That Wonderful Sound/I Wasn't Born Yesterday ........................... 6
70   Big BG 310                         Halfway To Paradise/Utopia .............................................................. 5
71   Dynamic DYN 426               Carry That Weight/More Weight ...................................................... 5
69   Pama SECO 33                    STRANGE (LP) .................................................................................... 70
70   Trojan TBL 145                   THAT WONDERFUL SOUND (LP) ....................................................... 50
*(see also Bobby Dobson, Chuck & Dobby, Bruce Bennett, Ernest Wilson & Freddy)*

**LYN DOBSON**
74   Fresh Air 6370 501             JAM SANDWICH (LP) .......................................................................... 40
*(see also Manfred Mann, Soft Machine, Miller Anderson)*

**DOC SCOTT**
91   Absolute 2 ABS 001DJR       Surgery (Remix) (12") ........................................................................ 8
92   Absolute 2 ABS 006DJ        The N.H.S. EP Vol 2 - The Second Chapter EP (12") ...................... 10
92   Absolute 2 ABS 006DJR      The N.H.S. EP Vol 2 - The Second Chapter (Remix) EP (12") ......... 60
94   Metalheadz MET 004           Far Away (Fourteen Flavors Of Funk)/It's Yours (12") .................. 20
95   Metalheadz METH 015         Drumz '95 (Nasty Habits Remix)/Blue Skies (12") ........................ 15
94   Reinforced RIVET 1256        Last Action Hero EP (12") ............................................................... 15
94   Metalheadz MH 001            Doc Scott/GOLDIE : Unreleased Metal (12") .................................. 20

**ROY DOCKER**
68   Domain D3                         Mellow Moonlight/MUSIC THROUGH SIX: Riff Raff ...................... 30
69   Pama PM 750                      When/Go ............................................................................................ 15
69   Pama PM 756                      Everyday Will Be Like A Holiday/I'm An Outcast ........................... 8

**DR. ATOMIC**
93   Guerilla GRRR42                  Schudelfloss (12") ............................................................................ 20

**DOCTOR BROWN**
95   Magic Gnome                     ANOTHER REALM (LP, 500 only) ...................................................... 15

**DOCTOR DARK**
76   Target TGT 102                   Red Hot Passion/Instrumental (no p/s) ............................................ 7
*(see also Snivelling Shits)*

**DOCTOR FATHER**
70   Pye 7N 17977                    Umbopo/Roll On ................................................................................ 10
*(see also 10cc, Godley & Creme, Hotlegs)*

**DR. FEELGOOD & THE INTERNS (U.S.)**
62   Columbia DB 4838              Dr. Feelgood/Mister Moonlight ........................................................ 25

| 64 | Columbia DB 7228 | Blang Dong/The Doctor's Doogie | 25 |
| 66 | CBS 202099 | Don't Tell Me No Dirty/Where Did You Go | 20 |
| 68 | Capitol CL 15569 | Sugar Bee/You're So Used To It | 20 |
| 64 | Columbia SEG 8310 | DR. FEELGOOD AND THE INTERNS (EP) | 70 |

*(see also Piano Red)*

## DR. FEELGOOD (U.K.)
| 74 | United Artists UP 35760 | Roxette/(Get Your Kicks On) Route 66 (no p/s) | 5 |
| 75 | United Artists UP 35815 | She Does It Right/I Don't Mind (no p/s) | 5 |
| 75 | United Artists UP 35857 | Back In The Night/I'm A Man | 5 |
| 77 | United Artists UP 36304 | She's A Windup/Hi-Rise (p/s) | 5 |
| 77 | United Artists UP 36332 | Baby Jane/Looking Back (p/s) | 6 |
| 79 | United Artists XUP 36506 | As Long As The Price Is Right/Down At The (Other) Doctors (p/s, either black, blue, brown or violet vinyl, 3 different p/s designs) | 5 |
| 86 | Stiff BUY 253 | Don't Wait Up/Something Good (shrink-wrapped with bonus 45: "Back In The Night"/"Milk And Alcohol" [FBUY 56]) (p/s) | 5 |
| 75 | United Artists UAS 29727 | DOWN BY THE JETTY (LP, mono only) | 20 |
| 75 | United Artists UAS 29880 | MALPRACTICE (LP) | 20 |
| 76 | United Artists UAS 29990 | STUPIDITY (LP, with stickered covers & bonus 7": "Riot In Cell Block No. 9"/"Johnny B. Goode" [FEEL 1]) | 20 |
| 79 | United Artists UAK 30239 | AS IT HAPPENS (LP, with inner sleeve & bonus 7": "Riot In Cell Block No. 9"/"The Blues Had A Baby And They Named It Rock'N'Roll"/"Lights Out"/"Great Balls Of Fire" [p/s, FEEL 2], with inner sleeve | 20 |

*(see also Wilko Johnson, Lew Lewis, Oil City Sheiks)*

## DR. HOOK
| 73 | CBS 1037 | The Cover Of "Radio Times" (1-sided, promo only, by Dr. Hook & Friends) | 10 |

## DR. JOHN (THE NIGHT TRIPPER)
| 70 | Atco 2091 019 | Wash Mama Wash/Mama Roux | 12 |
| 72 | Atlantic K 10158 | Iko Iko/Huey Smith Medley | 6 |
| 72 | Atlantic K 10214 | Wang Dang Doodle/Big Chief | 5 |
| 73 | Atlantic K 10291 | Right Place, Wrong Time/I Been Hoodooed | 10 |
| 73 | Atlantic K 10329 | Such A Night/Life | 6 |
| 68 | Atlantic 587/588 147 | GRIS GRIS (LP, plum label, mono/stereo) | 60 |
| 69 | Atco 228 018 | BABYLON (LP, plum label) | 25 |
| 70 | Atco 2400 015 | REMEDIES (LP, plum label) | 25 |
| 71 | Atlantic 2400 161 | THE SUN, MOON AND HERBS (LP, plum label, gatefold sleeve with insert) | 30 |
| 72 | Atlantic K 40384 | GUMBO (LP, green & orange label, gatefold sleeve) | 20 |
| 72 | Atlantic K 40168 | GRIS GRIS (LP, reissue, green & orange label) | 20 |
| 72 | Atlantic K 40250 | THE SUN, MOON AND HERBS (LP, reissue, green & orange label, gatefold sleeve with insert) | 20 |
| 73 | Atco K 50017 | IN THE RIGHT PLACE (LP, U.K. disc in U.S. stickered 3-way gatefold sleeve) | 25 |
| 73 | CBS 65659 | TRIUMVIRATE (LP, with John Hammond & Mike Bloomfield) | 18 |
| 74 | Atlantic K 50035 | DESITIVELY BONNAROO (LP) | 18 |
| 75 | DJM DJSLM 2019 | CUT ME WHILE I'M HOT (LP) | 22 |
| 75 | United Artists UAG 29902 | HOLLYWOOD BE THY NAME (LP, with inner sleeve) | 20 |

## DR. K'S BLUES BAND
| 68 | Spark SRLP 101 | DR. K'S BLUES BAND (LP, red/silver label) | 120 |

## DR. MARIGOLD'S PRESCRIPTION
| 68 | Pye 7N 17493 | My Old Man's A Groovy Old Man/People Get Ready | 6 |
| 69 | Pye 7N 17832 | You've Got To Build Your Love/My Picture Of Love | 6 |
| 70 | Bell BLL 1096 | Breaking The Heart Of A Good Man/Night Hurries On By | 6 |
| 70 | Bell BLL 1126 | Sing Along, Sing Along, Sing Along/Father Jim | 6 |
| 71 | Bell BLL 1149 | Muddy Water/Come With Me | 6 |

## DR. MIX & THE REMIX
| 79 | Rough Trade ROUGH 6 | Wall Of Noise (12") | 20 |

## DR. OCTAGON
| 96 | Mo' Wax MW 046LP | ECOLOGYST (3-LP) | 25 |
| 96 | Mo' Wax MWLP 046 | OCTAGONECOLOGYST (3-LP) | 25 |
| 96 | Mo' Wax MW064LP | INSTRUMENTALYST (OCTAGON BEATS) (LP) | 25 |

## DOCTOR PABLO
| 84 | On U Sound ON U 30 | NORTH OF THE RIVER THAMES (LP) | 25 |

## DOCTOR ROCKIT
| 96 | Clear CLR 416 | D For Doktor EP (12", p/s) | 12 |

## DR. STRANGELY STRANGE
| 69 | Island ILPS 9106 | KIP OF THE SERENES (LP, pink label, with black/orange circle logo) | 400 |
| 69 | Island ILPS 9106 | KIP OF THE SERENES (LP, later 'palm-tree' label with remix) | 100 |
| 70 | Vertigo 6360 009 | HEAVY PETTING (LP, gatefold sleeve, large swirl label; original pressing has machine etched matrix in the run out grooves, beware of counterfeits) | 600 |
| 86 | Timeless TIME 702 | KIP OF THE SERENES (LP, reissue) | 20 |

*(see also Sweeney's Men, Gary Moore)*

## DR. TECHNICAL & MACHINES
| 83 | Hawkfan HWFB 1 | Zones/Processed (1-sided with insert, mail-order issue, no p/s) | 25 |

*(see also Dave Brock, Hawkwind)*

## DR. WEST'S MEDICINE SHOW & JUNK BAND
| 67 | CBS 202492 | The Eggplant That Ate Chicago/You Can't Fight City Hall Blues | 10 |
| 67 | CBS 202658 | Gondoliers, Shakespeares, Overseers/Daddy I Know | 8 |
| 68 | Page One POF 061 | Bullets La Verne/Jigsaw | 50 |
| 70 | Page One POF 176 | Gondoliers, Shakespeares, Overseers/Daddy I Know (reissue) | 6 |
| 69 | Page One POLS 017 | THE EGGPLANT THAT ATE CHICAGO (LP) | 25 |

*(see also Norman Greenbaum)*

## DR. WHO

| | | | |
|---|---|---|---|
| 76 | Argo ZSW 564 | DR. WHO AND THE PESCATONS (LP, spoken word, read by Tom Baker & Elizabeth Sladen) | 18 |
| 79 | BBC REC 364 | GENESIS OF THE DALEKS (LP, spoken word) | 15 |
| 81 | RNIB | TALKING BOOK (reel-to-reel tape, read by Gabriel Wolf) | 20 |
| 82 | BBC 2LP-22001 | DOCTOR WHO COLLECTOR'S EDITION (2-LP, includes "Genesis Of The Daleks" [BBC 22364], "Sound Effects" [BBC 22316], & bonus 7" "Doctor Who"/"The Astronauts" [RESL 451], with poster) | 30 |

*(see also BBC Radiophonic Workshop, Century 21, Jon Pertwee)*

## DR. Z

| | | | |
|---|---|---|---|
| 70 | Fontana 6007 023 | Lady Ladybird/People In The Street | 100 |
| 71 | Vertigo 6360 048 | THREE PARTS TO MY SOUL (LP, gatefold sleeve, small swirl label) | 2000 |

*(see also Gorilla Grip)*

## DOCTOR BIRDS

| | | | |
|---|---|---|---|
| 77 | JS JSM 001 | Smoking (Smoking My Ganja)/Rock With Me (12") | 30 |

## DOCTORS OF MADNESS

| | | | |
|---|---|---|---|
| 77 | Polydor 2058 921 | Bulletin/Waiting (p/s) | 6 |

## CLEMENT 'COXSONE' DODD

| | | | |
|---|---|---|---|
| 89 | Trojan TRLD 408 | MUSICAL FEVER (2-LP, gatefold) | 20 |

## PAT DODD

| | | | |
|---|---|---|---|
| 59 | Pye International 7N 25030 | Stag Party/Odds'n'Dodds | 5 |

## DODD'S ALLSTARS

| | | | |
|---|---|---|---|
| 69 | Coxsone CS 7096 | Mother Aitken (actually by Lord Power)/What A Love (actually by Denzil Laing) | 70 |

## NELLA DODDS

| | | | |
|---|---|---|---|
| 65 | Pye 7N 25281 | Come See About Me/You Don't Love Me Anymore | 50 |
| 65 | Pye 7N 25281 | Come See About Me/You Don't Love Me Anymore (DJ Copy) | 75 |
| 65 | Pye 7N 25291 | Finders Keepers, Losers Weepers/A Girl's Life | 35 |
| 65 | Pye 7N 25291 | Finders Keepers, Losers Weepers/A Girl's Life (DJ Copy) | 60 |

## DODGEMS

| | | | |
|---|---|---|---|
| 80 | Criminal SWAG 12 | Lord Lucan Is Missing/Gotta GIve It Up | 8 |

## DODGERS (1)

| | | | |
|---|---|---|---|
| 60 | Downbeat CHA 2 | Let's Make A Whole Lot Of Love/You Make Me Happy | 25 |

## DODGERS (2)

| | | | |
|---|---|---|---|
| 70 | S & S SC 002 | True Love/TONY SEXTON: Baby I Will Be Yours | 12 |

## DODGERS (3)

| | | | |
|---|---|---|---|
| 76 | Island WIP 6342 | Just Wanna Love You/Don't Know What You're Doing | 8 |
| 78 | Polydor 2059028 | Love On The Rebound/Come Out Fighting | 8 |
| 78 | Polydor 2059046 | Don't Let Me Be Wrong/Come Out Fighting | 8 |

## DODO'S

| | | | |
|---|---|---|---|
| 67 | Polydor BM 56153 | I Made Up My Mind/Can't Make It Out | 30 |

## DOES IT OFFEND YOU, YEAH?

| | | | |
|---|---|---|---|
| 07 | Private Pressing | LIVE AT THE FEZ CLUB (12" white label) | 20 |

## DOGFEET

| | | | |
|---|---|---|---|
| 71 | Reflection HRS 7 | Sad Story/On The Road | 15 |
| 71 | Reflection HRS 12 | Since I Went Away/Evil Woman | 35 |
| 70 | Reflection REFL 8 | DOGFEET (LP, white/brown label) | 1000 |
| 94 | Kissing Spell CA 36001 | DOGFEET (LP, reissue) | 25 |

## TYMON DOGG

| | | | |
|---|---|---|---|
| 81 | Ghost Dance GHO 1 | Lose This Skin (featuring the Clash)/Indestructible (p/s) | 10 |

*(see also Timon, Clash)*

## DOGGEREL BANK

| | | | |
|---|---|---|---|
| 73 | Charisma CAS 1079 | SILVER FACES (LP, gatefold sleeve, large "Mad Hatter" label) | 25 |
| 75 | Charisma CAS 1102 | MISTER SKILLCORN DANCES (LP, small "Mad Hatter" label) | 30 |

## BILL DOGGETT

| | | | |
|---|---|---|---|
| 56 | Parlophone CMSP 39 | Honky Tonk (Parts 1 & 2) (gold label lettering, export issue) | 25 |
| 56 | Parlophone R 4231 | Honky Tonk (Parts 1 & 2) (gold label lettering, later silver) | 15 |
| 57 | Parlophone R 4265 | Slow Walk/Peacock Alley | 10 |
| 57 | Parlophone R 4306 | Ram-Bunk-Shush/Blue Largo | 10 |
| 57 | Parlophone R 4379 | Hot Ginger/Soft | 10 |
| 58 | Parlophone R 4413 | Leaps And Bounds (Parts 1 & 2) | 10 |
| 60 | Parlophone R 4629 | Smokie/Evening Dreams | 10 |
| 61 | Warner Bros WB 32 | The Hully Gully Twist/Jackrabbit | 10 |
| 61 | Warner Bros WB 46 | You Can't Sit Down (Parts 1 & 2) | 15 |
| 57 | Parlophone GEP 8644 | HONKY TONK (EP) | 20 |
| 57 | Parlophone GEP 8674 | PLAYS DUKE ELLINGTON (EP) | 10 |
| 58 | Parlophone GEP 8711 | BILL DOGGETT (EP) | 10 |
| 58 | Parlophone GEP 8727 | RAINBOW RIOT (EP) | 10 |
| 59 | Parlophone GEP 8771 | A JOLLY CHRISTMAS (EP) | 10 |
| 58 | Parlophone PMD 1067 | DAME DREAMING (10" LP) | 15 |
| 59 | Parlophone PMD 1073 | DANCE AWHILE WITH DOGGETT (10" LP) | 20 |
| 60 | Parlophone PMC 1118 | DOGGETT'S BIG CITY DANCE PARTY (LP) | 20 |
| 60 | Parlophone PMC 1124 | ON TOUR (LP) | 20 |

*(see also Ella Fitzgerald, Earl Bostic)*

## DOGGS

| | | | |
|---|---|---|---|
| 71 | Chapter 1 CH156 | Billy's Gotta Run/Why Do I Lie | 5 |

## DOGHEAD

| | | | |
|---|---|---|---|
| 73 | Sacred SC 01 | Come Out Shooting/Passing The Buck | 20 |

## DOGMATIC ELEMENT
| | | |
|---|---|---|
| 82 | Cattle Company CC001/ 562CUS 1412 | Strange Passion/Just Friends (p/s, 1000 only) .................... 15 |
| 84 | Cattle Company CC002/ SRT4KS128 | False Emotions/Not Now (p/s, 1000 only) .................... 10 |

## DOG ON A ROPE
| | | |
|---|---|---|
| 98 | Chase Out DAN 1 | SPIKE (LP) .................... 15 |

## DOGROSE
| | | |
|---|---|---|
| 72 | Satril SAT 2 | Paradise Row/Sunday Morning .................... 15 |
| 73 | Satril SAT 6 | All For The Love Of City Lights/All Of The Love Of Each Other .................... 20 |
| 72 | Satril SATL 4002 | ALL FOR THE LOVE OF DOGROSE (LP) .................... 30 |

## DOGS
| | | |
|---|---|---|
| 05 | Fallout IS874/986 | London Bridge/End Of An Era (Custom printed parcel tape label) .................... 5 |

## DOGS D'AMOUR
| | | |
|---|---|---|
| 88 | China WOL 7 | THE (UN)AUTHORISED BOOTLEG (LP) .................... 30 |

## DOG SOLDIER
| | | |
|---|---|---|
| 75 | United Artists UA 29769 | DOG SOLDIER (LP) .................... 20 |

*(see also Miller Anderson, Keef Hartley)*

## THE DOG THAT BIT PEOPLE
| | | |
|---|---|---|
| 71 | Parlophone R 5880 | Lovely Lady/Merry-Go-Round .................... 45 |
| 71 | Parlophone PCS 7125 | THE DOG THAT BIT PEOPLE (LP, black/silver label with boxed logo) .................... 800 |

*(see also Norman Haines, Locomotive)*

## DOGWATCH
| | | |
|---|---|---|
| 79 | Bridgehouse BHLP 002 | PENFRIEND (LP, with insert) .................... 20 |

## NED DOHENY
| | | |
|---|---|---|
| 81 | CBS 9481 | To Prove My Love/On The Swing Shift (p/s) .................... 8 |
| 81 | CBS 13-9481 | To Prove My Love/On The Swing Shift (12", p/s) .................... 10 |

## JIM DOHERTY TRIO
| | | |
|---|---|---|
| 65 | Decca LK 4684 | EXECUTIVE SUITE (LP) .................... 60 |

## DOKKEN
| | | |
|---|---|---|
| 82 | Carrere CAR 229 | We're Illegal/Paris Is Burning (p/s) .................... 5 |

## DAVE DOLBY
| | | |
|---|---|---|
| 73 | Bell 1418 | Shine A Light/Your Weight Is Your Mind .................... 6 |

## DOLE
| | | |
|---|---|---|
| 78 | Ultimate ULT 402 | New Wave Love/Hungry Men No Longer Steal Sheep But Are There Hanging Judges? (die-cut p/s) .................... 30 |

## MICKY DOLENZ
| | | |
|---|---|---|
| 67 | London HLH 10152 | Huff Puff/OBVIOUS: Fate .................... 8 |

*(see also Monkees)*

## DOLL
| | | |
|---|---|---|
| 78 | Beggars Banquet BEG 4 | Don't Tango On My Heart/Trash .................... 5 |

## ANDY DOLL
| | | |
|---|---|---|
| 62 | Starlite ST45 068 | Wild Desire/Wyat .................... 10 |
| 63 | Starlite STLP II | ON STAGE (LP, by Andy Doll Band & Guests) .................... 15 |

## LINDA DOLL & SUNDOWNERS
| | | |
|---|---|---|
| 64 | Piccadilly 7N 35166 | Bonie Maronie/He Don't Want Your Love Anymore .................... 15 |

## DOLLIES
| | | |
|---|---|---|
| 65 | CBS 201788 | You Touch Me Baby/I Can't Go On .................... 10 |

## DOLLY MIXTURE
| | | |
|---|---|---|
| 80 | Chrysalis CHS 2459 | Baby It's You/New Look Baby (p/s) .................... 30 |
| 81 | Respond RESP 1 | Been Teen/Honky Honda/Ernie Ball (p/s) .................... 25 |
| 82 | Respond RESP 4 | Everything And More/You And Me On The Sea Shore (p/s) .................... 15 |
| 83 | Dead Good Dolly Platters DMS 1 | Remember This/Listening Pleasure/Borinda's Lament (p/s) .................... 18 |
| 84 | Cordelia ERICAT 017 | FIRESIDE EP (12" p/s) .................... 30 |
| 84 | DM 1 | DEMONSTRATION TAPES (2-LP, rubber stamped, hand-numbered signed sleeves with insert) .................... 70 |
| 11 | For Us FU 043 | REMEMBER THIS: THE SINGLES 1980-1984 (LP, black or white vinyl) .................... 18 |

## DOLPHIN
| | | |
|---|---|---|
| 76 | Private Stock PVT 52 | Then I Kissed Her/The Glyderes .................... 6 |
| 76 | Private Stock PVT 67 | Goin' Back/Think Ahead .................... 10 |
| 77 | Private Stock PVT 91 | Only Seventeen/Take Care Of The Ocean .................... 5 |
| 77 | Private Stock PVT 122 | Imagination Dancing/The Actress .................... 6 |
| 78 | Private Stock PVT 154 | Carry Me Away/Linda Lovelace .................... 6 |
| 80 | Gale 5 | Hey Joe/Dubby Dubby .................... 5 |

## DOLPHINS
| | | |
|---|---|---|
| 65 | Stateside SS 375 | Hey Da Da Dow/I Don't Want To Go On Without You .................... 15 |

## ERIC DOLPHY
| | | |
|---|---|---|
| 60 | Esquire 21-123 | OUTWARD BOUND (LP) .................... 90 |
| 61 | Esquire 32-153 | OUT THERE (LP) .................... 65 |
| 61 | Esquire 32-173 | AT THE 5 SPOT VOL. 1.(LP) .................... 65 |
| 64 | Fontana TL5284 | LAST DATE (LP) .................... 60 |
| 65 | Fontana 688521XL | MEMORIAL ALBUM (LP) .................... 35 |
| 69 | Transatlantic PR 7311 | OUTWARD BOUND (LP) .................... 20 |
| 67 | Xtra 5039 | SCREAMING THE BLUES (LP, with Oliver Nelson Sextet) .................... 25 |

## ERIC DOLPHY & BOOKER LITTLE
| | | |
|---|---|---|
| 66 | Stateside SL 10160 | ERIC DOLPHY AND BOOKER LITTLE MEMORIAL ALBUM (LP) .................... 15 |

## BILLY DOLTON
| | | | |
|---|---|---|---|
| 61 | Parlophone R 4733 | Winkie Doll/Girls | 10 |

## DO MAKE SAY THINK
| | | | |
|---|---|---|---|
| 99 | Resonant RES 001 | BESIDES (12" EP) | 12 |

## DOME
| | | | |
|---|---|---|---|
| 80 | Dome DOME 1 | DOME (LP) | 20 |
| 80 | Dome DOME 2 | DOME 2 (LP) | 20 |
| 81 | Dome DOME 3 | DOME 3 (LP) | 20 |

*(see also Wire, Gilbert & Lewis)*

## DOMINANT FORCE
| | | | |
|---|---|---|---|
| 91 | Gangster GAGR001 | Criminals/Raptivity (12") | 20 |

## ANNA DOMINO
| | | | |
|---|---|---|---|
| 86 | Factory FAC 158 | Summer (p/s) | 12 |

## FATS DOMINO
### 78s
| | | | |
|---|---|---|---|
| 54 | London HL 8007 | Rose Mary/You Said You Love Me | 40 |
| 54 | London HL 8063 | Little School Girl/You Done Me Wrong | 40 |
| 54 | London HL 8096 | Don't Leave Me This Way/Something's Wrong | 30 |
| 55 | London HL 8124 | Love Me/Don't You Hear Me Calling You | 30 |
| 55 | London HL 8133 | Thinking Of You/I Know | 25 |
| 59 | London HLP 8822 | When The Saints Go Marching In/Telling Lies | 20 |
| 59 | London HLP 8865 | Margie/I'm Ready | 20 |
| 59 | London HLP 8942 | I Want To Walk You Home/I'm Gonna Be A Wheel Some Day | 20 |
| 59 | London HLP 9005 | Be My Guest/I've Been Around | 40 |
| 60 | London HLP 9073 | Country Boy/If You Need Me | 40 |
| 60 | London HLP 9163 | Walking To New Orleans/Don't Come Knockin' | 60 |

### SINGLES
| | | | |
|---|---|---|---|
| 55 | London HL 8124 | Love Me/Don't You Hear Me Calling You | 175 |
| 55 | London HL 8133 | Thinking Of You/I Know | 125 |
| 55 | London HLU 8173 | Ain't That A Shame/La La | 80 |
| 56 | London HLU 8256 | Bo Weevil/Don't Blame It On Me | 100 |
| 56 | London HLU 8280 | I'm In Love Again/My Blue Heaven | 100 |
| 56 | London HLU 8309 | When My Dream Boat Comes Home/So Long | 50 |
| 56 | London HLU 8330 | Blueberry Hill/I Can't Go On (Rosalie) | 50 |
| 57 | London HLU 8356 | Honey Chile/Don't You Know | 100 |
| 57 | London HL 8377 | Blue Monday/What's The Reason I'm Not Pleasing You | 50 |

*(Originally issued with triangular centres & gold lettering labels; later silver-label re-pressings are worth around half these values.)*

| | | | |
|---|---|---|---|
| 57 | London HLP 8407 | I'm Walkin'/I'm In The Mood For Love | 15 |
| 57 | London HLP 8449 | The Valley Of Tears/It's You I Love | 15 |
| 57 | London HLP 8471 | What Will I Tell My Heart/When I See You | 12 |
| 57 | London HLP 8519 | Wait And See/I Still Love You | 15 |
| 58 | London HLP 8575 | The Big Beat (From The Film)/I Want You To Know | 20 |
| 58 | London HLP 8628 | Sick And Tired/No, No | 20 |
| 58 | London HLP 8663 | Little Mary/The Prisoner's Song | 20 |
| 58 | London HLP 8727 | Young School Girl/It Must Be Love | 30 |
| 58 | London HLP 8759 | Whole Lotta Loving/Coquette | 20 |
| 59 | London HLP 8822 | When The Saints Go Marching In/Telling Lies | 10 |

*(HLP 8407 through to 8822 45s were issued with triangular centres & silver lettering on all-black labels; later copies are worth around half these values.)*

| | | | |
|---|---|---|---|
| 59 | London HLP 8865 | Margie/I'm Ready (triangular centre & silver-top) | 10 |
| 59 | London HLP 8865 | Margie/I'm Ready (later round centre) | 5 |
| 59 | London HLP 8942 | I Want To Walk You Home/I'm Gonna Be A Wheel Some Day (round) | 10 |
| 59 | London HLP 9005 | Be My Guest/I've Been Around (triangular centre) | 20 |
| 59 | London HLP 9005 | Be My Guest/I've Been Around (round centre) | 5 |

*(All subsequent London 45s for Fats Domino after London HLP 9005 were issued with round centres & silver-top labels.)*

| | | | |
|---|---|---|---|
| 60 | London HLP 9073 | Country Boy/If You Need Me | 10 |
| 60 | London HLP 9133 | Tell Me That You Love Me/Before I Grow Too Old | 10 |
| 60 | London HLP 9163 | Walking To New Orleans/Don't Come Knockin' | 10 |
| 60 | London HLP 9198 | Three Nights A Week/Put Your Arms Around Me, Honey | 10 |
| 60 | London HLP 9244 | My Girl Josephine/Natural Born Lover | 10 |
| 61 | London HLP 9301 | What A Price/Ain't That Just Like A Woman | 10 |
| 61 | London HLP 9327 | Fell In Love On Monday/Shu-Rah | 10 |
| 61 | London HLP 9374 | It Keeps Rainin'/I Just Cry | 20 |
| 61 | London HLP 9415 | Let The Four Winds Blow/Good Hearted Man | 10 |
| 61 | London HLP 9456 | What A Party/Rockin' Bicycle | 10 |
| 62 | London HLP 9520 | Jambalaya/You Win Again | 8 |
| 62 | London HLP 9557 | My Real Name/My Heart Is Bleeding | 10 |
| 62 | London HLP 9590 | Dance With Mr. Domino/Nothing New (Same Old Thing) | 10 |
| 62 | London HLP 9616 | Did You Ever See A Dream Walking/Stop The Clock | 10 |
| 63 | London HLP 9738 | You Always Hurt The One You Love/Trouble Blues | 10 |
| 63 | HMV POP 1164 | There Goes My Heart Again/Can't Go On Without You | 10 |
| 63 | HMV POP 1197 | When I'm Walkin'/I've Got A Right To Cry | 8 |
| 63 | HMV POP 1219 | Red Sails In The Sunset/Song For Rosemary | 8 |
| 63 | HMV POP 1265 | Just A Lonely Man/Who Cares | 8 |
| 64 | HMV POP 1281 | I Don't Want To Set The World On Fire/Lazy Lady | 7 |
| 64 | HMV POP 1303 | If You Don't Know What Love Is/Something You Got Baby | 40 |
| 64 | HMV POP 1324 | Mary Oh Mary/Packin' Up | 8 |
| 64 | HMV POP 1370 | Kansas City/Heartbreak Hill | 8 |

| 65 | Mercury MF 869 | (I Left My Heart) In San Francisco/I Done Got Over It | 5 |
| 65 | Mercury MF 873 | What's That You Got?/It's Never Too Late | 5 |
| 65 | HMV POP 1421 | Why Don't You Do Right?/Wigs | 5 |
| 67 | HMV POP 1582 | I'm Livin' Right/I Don't Want To Set The World On Fire | 5 |
| 67 | Liberty LBF 12055 | It Keeps Rainin'/Blue Monday | 15 |
| 67 | Liberty LBF 12055 | It Keeps Rainin'/Blue Monday (DJ Copy) | 30 |
| 68 | Reprise RS 20696 | Honest Mamas Love Their Papas Better/One For The Highway | 20 |
| 68 | Reprise RS 20763 | Lady Madonna/One For The Highway | 10 |

## EXPORT SINGLES

| 57 | London HL 7028 | Wait And See/I Still Love You | 30 |
| 58 | London HL 7040 | Sick And Tired/No, No | 30 |
| 58 | London HL 7054 | The Big Beat (From The Film)/Little Mary | 30 |

## EPs

| 55 | London RE-P 1022 | BLUES FOR LOVE (1st pressing with gold lettering label) | 30 |
| 55 | London RE-P 1022 | BLUES FOR LOVE (2nd pressing with silver lettering label) | 20 |
| 56 | London RE-U 1062 | BLUES FOR LOVE VOL. 2 (1st pressing with gold label) | 30 |
| 56 | London RE-U 1062 | BLUES FOR LOVE VOL. 2 (2nd pressing with silver label) | 20 |
| 57 | London RE-U 1073 | FATS (export issue, plain sleeve) | 40 |
| 57 | London RE-P 1079 | HERE COMES FATS VOL. 1 | 30 |
| 58 | London RE-P 1080 | HERE COMES FATS VOL. 2 | 30 |
| 58 | London RE-P 1115 | CARRY ON ROCKIN' PART 1 | 60 |
| 58 | London RE-P 1116 | CARRY ON ROCKIN' PART 2 | 60 |
| 58 | London RE-P 1117 | BLUES FOR LOVE VOL. 3 | 30 |
| 58 | London RE-P 1121 | BLUES FOR LOVE VOL. 4 | 30 |
| 58 | London RE-P 1138 | HERE COMES FATS VOL. 3 | 30 |
| 59 | London RE-P 1206 | THE ROCKIN' MR. D VOL. 1 | 30 |
| 59 | London RE-P 1207 | THE ROCKIN' MR. D VOL. 2 | 30 |

*(The above EPs were originally issued with triangular centres; round-centre re-pressings are worth two-thirds these values.)*

| 60 | London RE-P 1261 | BE MY GUEST | 30 |
| 60 | London RE-P 1265 | THE ROCKIN' MR. D VOL. 3 | 30 |
| 62 | London RE-P 1340 | WHAT A PARTY | 30 |
| 64 | HMV 7EG 8862 | RED SAILS IN THE SUNSET | 15 |
| 65 | Liberty LEP 4026 | MY BLUE HEAVEN | 20 |
| 66 | Liberty LEP 4045 | ROLLIN' | 20 |

## ALBUMS

| 56 | London HA-U 2028 | FATS' ROCK AND ROLLIN' | 90 |
| 56 | London HA-P 2041 | CARRY ON ROCKIN' | 100 |
| 57 | London HA-P 2052 | HERE STANDS FATS DOMINO | 90 |
| 56 | London HA-P 2073 | THIS IS FATS DOMINO | 60 |
| 58 | London HA-P 2087 | THIS IS FATS | 60 |
| 58 | London HA-P 2135 | THE FABULOUS "MR. D" | 50 |
| 59 | London HA-P 2223 | LET'S PLAY FATS DOMINO | 50 |
| 60 | London HA-P 2312 | A LOT OF DOMINOES! | 40 |
| 61 | London HA-P 2364 | I MISS YOU SO | 40 |
| 61 | London HA-P 2420 | LET THE FOUR WINDS BLOW | 40 |
| 61 | London HA-P 2426 | WHAT A PARTY | 40 |
| 62 | London HA-P 2447 | TWISTIN' THE STOMP | 40 |
| 63 | London HA-P 8039 | JUST DOMINO | 40 |
| 63 | London HA-P 8084 | WALKING TO NEW ORLEANS | 40 |
| 63 | HMV CLP 1690 | HERE COMES FATS DOMINO (also stereo CSD 1520) | 25 |
| 63 | HMV CLP 1740 | FATS ON FIRE (also stereo CSD 1543) | 25 |
| 65 | HMV CLP 1821 | GETAWAY WITH FATS DOMINO (also stereo CSD 1580) | 18 |
| 65 | Mercury (S)MCL 20070 | DOMINO '65 (mono/stereo) | 15 |
| 68 | Stateside (S)SL 10240 | FANTASTIC FATS | 15 |

## DOMINOES (JAMAICA)

| 68 | Melody MRC 001 | Tears In Your Eyes/Johnny Darling | 10 |
| 68 | Melody MRC 002 | A Tribute (actually by Ann Reid)/Hooray (actually by Uniques) | 10 |

## DOMINOES (U.K.)

| 60 | Reading Rag LYN 545 | Bye Bye Johnny/Yakety Yak | 15 |

## DOMINOES (U.S.)

| 51 | Vogue V 9012 | Sixty Minute Man/I Can't Escape From You (78) | 50 |
| 52 | Vogue V 2135 | Have Mercy, Baby/That's What You're Doing To Me (78) | 40 |
| 67 | Vogue V 212 | Sixty Minute Man/I Can't Escape From You | 30 |

*(see also Billy Ward & Dominoes, Clyde McPhatter, Jackie Wilson)*

## DON DAVID AND DEAN

| 64 | United Artists UP 1064) | No Need to Cry/Fairy Tales | 10 |

## DON, DICK & JIMMY

| 54 | Columbia SCM 5110 | Brand Me With Your Kisses/Angela Mia | 12 |
| 55 | London HL 8117 | You Can't Have Your Cake And Eat It Too/That's What I Like | 20 |
| 55 | London HL 8144 | Make Yourself Comfortable/(Whatever Happened To The) Piano Players (That Played Like This) | 10 |
| 56 | HMV POP 280 | That's The Way I Feel/Two Voices In The Night | 6 |
| 56 | London RE-U 1043 | DON, DICK AND JIMMY (EP) | 20 |

## SAM DONAHUE & HIS ORCHESTRA

| 55 | Capitol CL 14349 | Saxaboogie/September In The Rain | 10 |

## TROY DONAHUE

| 63 | Warner Bros WB 111 | Live Young/Somebody Loves Me | 5 |

## MIKE DONALD & BOB SIDDALL
| 74 | Tradition Century TSC 2 | A BUG'S EYE VIEW (LP, 100 copies only) | 30 |

*(see also Mike Donald)*

## MIKE DONALD
| 71 | Folk Heritage FHR 021 | YORKSHIRE SONGS OF THE BROAD ACRES (LP, first pressing, textured sleeve with black and white photo) | 25 |
| 71 | Folk Heritage FHR 021 | YORKSHIRE SONGS OF THE BROAD ACRES (LP, second pressing, laminated sleeve with colour photo) | 15 |
| 72 | Galliard GAL 4020 | NORTH BY NORTH EAST (LP) | 15 |

## ERIC DONALDSON
| 71 | Dynamic DYN 420 | Cherry Oh Baby/LLOYD CHARMERS: Sir Charmers Special | 6 |
| 71 | Dynamic DYN 423 | Love Of The Common People/DRAGONAIRES: The Dragon's Net | 10 |
| 71 | Dynamic DYN 425 | Just Can't (Happen This Way)/Just Can't (Happen This Way) Version | 7 |
| 72 | Dynamic DYN 431 | I'm Indebted/I'm Indebted (Version) | 7 |
| 72 | Dynamic DYN 439 | Miserable Woman/The Lion Sleeps | 7 |
| 72 | Dynamic DYN 445 | Blue Boot/Blue Boot (Version) | 7 |
| 72 | Dynamic DYN 452 | Little Did You Know/Little Did You Know (Version) | 7 |
| 73 | Dragon DRA 1017 | What A Festival/I ROY & ERIC: Festival Version | 7 |
| 73 | Dragon DRA 1018 | The Way You Do The Things You Do/Version | 7 |
| 73 | Dragon DRA 1020 | Watch What You're Doing To Me/You Must Believe Me | 7 |
| 73 | Dragon DRA 1027 | A Weh We A Go Go/SOUL DEFENDERS: Version | 7 |
| 70s | Serengeti SGTI 01 | Penny Farthing/Evil Eyes (12") | 60 |
| 72 | Trojan TRL 42 | ERIC DONALDSON (LP) | 20 |

*(see also Prunes, Satchmo)*

## DON & DENNY
| 60s | Loop LOO 504 | (Ain't That)Just Like Me/Feeling Groovy | 40 |

## DON & DEWEY
| 64 | London HL 9897 | Get Your Hat/Annie Lee | 20 |
| 66 | Cameo Parkway CP 750 | Soul Motion/Stretchin' Out | 50 |
| 67 | Sue WI 4032 | Soul Motion/Stretchin' Out (reissue) | 30 |
| 71 | Specialty SNTF 5006 | DON AND DEWEY (LP) | 15 |

*(see also Dewey Terry)*

## DON & GOODTIMES
| 67 | Columbia DB 8199 | I Could Be So Good To You/And It's So Good | 12 |
| 67 | Columbia DB 8266 | Happy And Me/If You Love Her, Cherish Her And Such | 8 |

## DON & JUAN
| 62 | London HLX 9529 | What's Your Name?/Chicken Necks | 15 |

## DON & PETE
| 66 | Columbia DB 7881 | And I'm Crying Again/Time Will Tell | 5 |

## DONAYS
| 62 | Oriole CBA 1770 | Devil In His Heart/Bad Boy | 150 |

## DON CABALLERO
| 93 | City Slang 04929-08 | FOR RESPECT (LP) | 15 |

## LONNIE DONEGAN
### SINGLES
| 55 | Decca F 10647 | Rock Island Line/John Henry (as Lonnie Donegan Skiffle Group) (tri-centre) | 15 |
| 56 | Decca FJ 10695 | Diggin' My Potatoes/Bury My Body (as Lonnie Donegan Skiffle Group) (tri-centre) | 15 |
| 56 | Columbia DB 3850 | On A Christmas Day/Take My Hand, Precious Lord (as Lonnie Donegan with Chris Barber's Jazz Band) | 20 |
| 57 | Pye Nixa 7N 15116 | Jack O' Diamonds/Ham 'N' Eggs | 8 |
| 58 | Pye Nixa 7N 15129 | The Grand Coolie Dam/Nobody Loves Like An Irishman | 5 |
| 58 | Pye Jazz 7NJ 2006 | Midnight Special/When The Sun Goes Down | 25 |
| 58 | Pye Nixa 7N 15148 | Sally, Don't You Grieve/Betty, Betty, Betty | 8 |
| 62 | Pye 7N 3109 | The Comancheros/Medley (export, p/s) | 10 |

### ALBUMS
| 57 | Pye Nixa NPTs19027 | LONNIE (10" LP, stereo) | 20 |
| 58 | Pye Nixa NPT 19027 | LONNIE (10" LP) | 12 |

*(see also Chris Barber)*

## DONKEYS
| 80 | Rhesus GO APE 102 | What I Want/Four Letters (yellow or orange label, p/s) | 12 |
| 80 | Rhesus GO APE 3 | No Way/You Jane (p/s) | 10 |
| 80 | Rhesus GO APE 105 | Don't Go/Living Legends (p/s) | 10 |
| 80 | Back Door DOOR 006 | No Way/You Jane (reissue, p/s) | 7 |
| 80 | Deram DM-R 431 | What I Want/Four Letters (reissue, p/s) | 5 |
| 81 | MCA MCA 721 | Let's Float/Watched By Everyone (p/s) | 10 |
| 81 | MCA MCA 737 | Listen To Your Radio/Watched By Everyone (as Donkees) (p/s) | 10 |

## JIMMY DONLEY
| 57 | Brunswick 05715 | South Of The Border/The Trail Of The Lonesome Pine | 20 |
| 59 | Brunswick 05807 | The Shape You Left Me In/What Must I Do | 100 |
| 59 | Brunswick 05807 | The Shape You Left Me In/What Must I Do (78) | 20 |

## DONNA & FREEDOM SINGERS
| 70 | Bamboo BAM 53 | Oh Me Oh My (actually by Jerry Jones)/JACKIE MITTOO: Gold Mine | 20 |

## PAUL DONNER
| 78 | Wildfire WRP 22 | Yesterday's Roses - No More Baby/Carolina Feel It Burning (p/s) | 6 |

## RAL DONNER
| 61 | Parlophone R 4820 | You Don't Know What You've Got/So Close To Heaven | 8 |
| 61 | Parlophone R 4859 | Please Don't Go/I Didn't Figure On Him (To Come Back) | 10 |
| 62 | Parlophone R 4889 | I Don't Need You/She's Everything (I Wanted You To Be) | 10 |

| 62 | Stateside SS 109 | Bells Of Love/Loveless Life | 10 |
| 63 | Reprise R 20141 | I Got Burned/A Tear In My Eye | 30 |

**DONNIE & DREAMERS**

| 61 | Top Rank JAR 571 | Count Every Star/Dorothy | 50 |

**DONOVAN**

| 65 | Pye 7N 15801 | Catch The Wind/Why Do You Treat Me Like You Do | 5 |
| 65 | Pye 7N 15866 | Colours/To Sing For You | 5 |
| 65 | Pye 7N 15984 | Turquoise/Hey Gyp (Dig The Slowness) | 8 |
| 66 | Pye 7N 17067 | Josie/Little Tin Soldier | 10 |
| 66 | Pye 7N 17088 | Remember The Alamo/The Ballad Of A Crystal Man | 15 |
| 66 | Pye 7N 17241 | Sunshine Superman/The Trip | 7 |
| 67 | Pye 7N 17267 | Mellow Yellow/Preachin' Love | 6 |
| 67 | Pye 7N 17403 | There Is A Mountain/Sand And Foam | 6 |
| 68 | Pye 7N 17457 | Jennifer Juniper/Poor Cow | 6 |
| 68 | Pye 7N 17537 | Hurdy Gurdy Man/Teen Angel | 10 |
| 68 | Pye 7N 17660 | To Susan On The West Coast Waiting/Atlantis (unreleased) | 0 |
| 68 | Pye 7N 17660 | Atlantis/I Love My Shirt | 6 |
| 69 | Pye 7N 17778 | Goo Goo Barabajagal (Love Is Hot)/Bed With Me (with Jeff Beck Group) | 12 |
| 69 | Pye 7N 17778 | Barabajagal/Trudi (shortened A-side title & retitled B-side) | 10 |
| 70 | Dawn DNS 1006 | Ricki Ticki Tavi/Roots Of Oak (as Donovan with Open Road) | 6 |
| 70 | Dawn DNS 1006 | Riki Tiki Tavi (shortened spelling of A-side)/Roots Of Oak (with Open Road) | 6 |
| 70 | Dawn DNS 1007 | Celia Of The Seals (with Danny Thompson)/Mr. Wind | 6 |
| 72 | private pressing | The Music Makers (one-sided, paper sleeve, 50 only) | 50 |
| 73 | Epic EPC 1471 | I Like You/Earth Sign Man | 5 |
| 73 | Epic EPC 1644 | Maria Magenta/Intergalactic Laxative (p/s) | 6 |
| 73 | Epic EPC 1960 | Sailing Homeward/Lazy Daze (p/s) | 6 |
| 74 | Epic EPC 1960 | Sailing Homeward/Yellow Star (p/s, reissue with different B-side; some copies list both Donovan & Andrew Oldham as producers) | 6 |
| 75 | Epic EPC 2661 | Rock'n'Roll With Me/Divine Daze Of Deathless Delight (in p/s) | 20 |
| 75 | Epic EPC 2661 | Rock'n'Roll With Me/Divine Daze Of Deathless Delight | 6 |
| 75 | Epic EPC 3037 | Rock And Roll Souijer/Love Of My Life | 5 |
| 77 | Rak RAK 265 | The Light/The International Man (p/s) | 8 |
| 77 | Rak RAK 265 | The Light/The International Man | 5 |
| 81 | Luggage LUG 03 | Lay Down Lassie/Love Is Only A Feeling (p/s) | 7 |
| 65 | Pye NEP 24229 | COLOURS (EP) | 15 |
| 66 | Pye NEP 24239 | DONOVAN VOL. 1 (EP) | 15 |
| 68 | Pye NEP 24287 | CATCH THE WIND (EP) | 15 |
| 68 | Pye NEP 24299 | HURDY GURDY DONOVAN (EP) | 20 |
| 65 | Pye NPL 18117 | WHAT'S BIN DID AND WHAT'S BIN HID (LP, some with misprinted Side 2 label) | 35 |
| 65 | Pye NPL 18128 | FAIRYTALE (LP, some copies with blank rear sleeve) | 50 |
| 66 | World Records ST 951 | DONOVAN (LP) | 18 |
| 67 | Pye NPL 18181 | SUNSHINE SUPERMAN (LP) | 50 |
| 68 | Pye NPL 20000 | A GIFT FROM A FLOWER TO A GARDEN (2-LP, black or navy blue box set, separate halves or with taped hinge; with 12 inserts in folder, mono) | 125 |
| 68 | Pye N(S)PL 20000 | A GIFT FROM A FLOWER TO A GARDEN (2-LP, black or navy blue box set, separate halves or with taped hinge; with 12 inserts in folder, stereo) | 100 |
| 68 | Pye NPL 18237 | DONOVAN IN CONCERT (LP, mono) | 20 |
| 68 | Pye N(S)PL 18237 | DONOVAN IN CONCERT (LP, stereo) | 18 |
| 70 | Dawn DNLS 3009 | OPEN ROAD (LP, gatefold sleeve) | 30 |
| 71 | Dawn DNLD 4001 | H.M.S. DONOVAN (2-LP, First pressing, orange label, MATRIX: DNLP 4001 A-1 *T/B-1 *T/C-1*T/D-1*T :gatefold sleeve, with foldout poster) | 150 |
| 72 | Dawn DNLD 4001 | H.M.S. DONOVAN (2-LP, Second pressing, lilac label, gatefold sleeve, with foldout poster) | 60 |
| 72 | Dawn DNLD 4001 | H.M.S. DONOVAN (2-LP, Second pressing, lilac label, gatefold sleeve, without foldout poster) | 20 |
| 73 | Dawn DNLD 4001 | H.M.S. DONOVAN (2-LP, Third pressing, white label with pink and blue sunrise, gatefold sleeve) | 40 |
| 71 | Dawn DNLD 4001 | H.M.S. DONOVAN (2-LP, gatefold sleeve, without foldout poster) | 25 |
| 73 | Pye 11PP 102 | FOUR SHADES ("H.M.S. Donovan"/"Greatest Hits"/"Open Road") (4-LP box set) | 50 |
| 73 | Epic EPC 69050 | ESSENCE TO ESSENCE (LP, gatefold sleeve, lyric insert, with sticker) | 15 |

*(see also Jeff Beck, Open Road)*

**DONTELLS**

| 65 | Fontana TF 566 | In Your Heart/Nothing But Nothing | 50 |
| 74 | President PT 373 | In Your Heart/Nothing But Nothing (reissue) | 10 |

**DICKY DOO & DON'TS**

| 58 | London HLU 8589 | Click Click/Did You Cry | 12 |
| 58 | London HLU 8754 | Leave Me Alone/Wild, Wild Party (with Orchestra) | 12 |
| 60 | Top Rank JAR 318 | Wabash Cannonball/WEST TEXAS MARCHING BAND: The Drums Of Richard A Doo | 5 |

**DOOF**

| 80 | Namedrop NR1 | EXIST (10" mini-LP, with booklet) | 15 |

*(see also Exhibit A)*

**DOOKIE SQUAD**

| 94 | Dookie DS 001 | 6FT Under/Mad Shit (12") | 15 |
| 13 | 1st Bass DS002 | Deep Rising (12" red vinyl) | 10 |

**DOOLEY SISTERS**

| 55 | London HL 8128 | Ko Ko Mo (I Love You So)/Heart Throb | 30 |

**DOOM**

| 89 | Discard DISC 001 | POLICE BASTARD EP | 15 |
| 89 | Strange Fruit SFPMA 203 | DOUBLE PEEL SESSIONS (LP, with insert) | 15 |
| 88 | Peaceville VILE 4 | WAR CRIMES INHUMAN BEINGS (LP, white vinyl) | 20 |

| | | | | MINT VALUE £ |
|---|---|---|---|---|

**DOOM/CRESS** *(continued)*

| 89 | Peaceville VILE 11 | BURY THE DEBT NOT THE DEAD (split LP with NO SECURITY) | 18 |
|---|---|---|---|

**DOOM/CRESS**
| 98 | Flat Earth FE 27 | SPLIT 10" LP (with insert) | 10 |
|---|---|---|---|

**JOHN DOONAN**
| 72 | Leader LEA 2043 | FLUTE FOR THE FEIS (LP) | 15 |
|---|---|---|---|

**DOONICANS**
| 87 | Probe Plus PP 23T | THE FISHERMAN'S WAY (12" EP) | 10 |
|---|---|---|---|

**DOOR & THE WINDOW**
| 79 | NR NR 1 | Subculture/Fashion Slaves/Nostradamus/Don't Kill Colin/Wurst Ban | 25 |
|---|---|---|---|
| 79 | NB Records NB 3 | He Feels Like A Doris/I Like Sound/Innocent/Dig/Production Line (white label with stickers & insert p/s in poly bag) | 5 |
| 80 | NB Records NB 5 | DETAILED TWANG (LP, blank labels) | 18 |
| 80 | NB Records NB 9 | MUSIC AND MOVEMENT (live cassette) | 15 |

*(see also Alternative TV)*

## DOORS

**SINGLES**

| 67 | Elektra EKSN 45009 | Break On Through (To The Other Side)/End Of The Night | 50 |
|---|---|---|---|
| 67 | Elektra EKSN 45012 | Alabama Song (Whisky Bar)/Take It As It Comes | 25 |
| 67 | Elektra EKSN 45014 | Light My Fire/The Crystal Ship | 20 |
| 67 | Elektra EKSN 45017 | People Are Strange/Unhappy Girl | 20 |
| 67 | Elektra EKSN 45022 | Love Me Two Times/Moonlight Drive | 15 |
| 68 | Elektra EKSN 45030 | We Could Be So Good Together/The Unknown Soldier | 15 |
| 68 | Elektra EKSN 45037 | Hello, I Love You, Won't You Tell Me Your Name/Love Street | 10 |
| 69 | Elektra EKSN 45050 | Touch Me/Wild Child | 10 |
| 69 | Elektra EKSN 45059 | Wishful Sinful/Who Scared You? | 10 |
| 69 | Elektra EKSN 45065 | Tell All The People/Easy Ride | 10 |
| 70 | Elektra 2101 004 | You Make Me Real/The Spy | 10 |
| 70 | Elektra 2101 008 | Roadhouse Blues/Blue Sunday | 10 |
| 71 | Elektra EK 45726 | Love Her Madly//(You Need Meat) Don't Go No Further | 6 |
| 71 | Elektra K 12021 | Riders On The Storm/The Changeling | 6 |
| 72 | Elektra K 12036 | Tightrope Ride/Variety Is The Spice Of Life | 8 |
| 72 | Elektra K 12048 | Ship W/Sails/In The Eye Of The Sun | 5 |
| 72 | Elektra K 12059 | Get Up And Dance/Tree Trunks | 5 |
| 79 | Elektra K 12215/SAM 94 | Love Me Two Times/Hello, I Love You// Ghost Song/Roadhouse Blues (double pack) | 10 |
| 83 | Elektra E 9974T | Gloria/Love Me Two Times (12", p/s with poster) | 10 |
| 92 | Final Vinyl FV 1/2 | INTERVIEW TAPES (2 x 7" box set, with 7 inserts, numbered, 500 only) | 10 |
| 79 | Elektra K 12400 | The End (Edit)/Carmen B Francis Coppola: The Delta | 5 |

**ALBUMS**

| 67 | Elektra EKL 4007 | THE DOORS (orange label, mono) | 200 |
|---|---|---|---|
| 67 | Elektra EKS 4007 | THE DOORS (orange label, stereo) | 120 |
| 68 | Elektra EKL 4014 | STRANGE DAYS (textured orange label, inner sleeve, mono) | 200 |
| 68 | Elektra EKS 4014 | STRANGE DAYS (textured orange label, inner sleeve, stereo) | 150 |
| 68 | Elektra EKL 4024 | WAITING FOR THE SUN (orange label, gatefold sleeve with insert, mono) | 200 |
| 68 | Elektra EKS 4024 | WAITING FOR THE SUN (orange label, gatefold sleeve with insert, stereo) | 120 |
| 69 | Elektra EKS 75005 | THE SOFT PARADE (orange label, gatefold sleeve, with lyric sheet) | 150 |
| 70 | Elektra EKS 75007 | MORRISON HOTEL (orange label, gatefold sleeve) | 100 |
| 70 | Elektra 2665 002 | ABSOLUTELY LIVE (2-LP, red label, gatefold sleeve) | 50 |
| 71 | Elektra EKS 74079 | 13 ('butterfly' label, compilation) | 15 |
| 71 | Elektra K 42090 | L.A. WOMAN ('butterfly' label, round-cornered, die-cut PVC 'window' sleeve & yellow inner sleeve) | 50 |
| 71 | Elektra K 42090 | L.A. WOMAN ('butterfly' label, round-cornered sleeve but no PVC window) | 20 |
| 71 | Elektra K 42104 | OTHER VOICES ('butterfly' label, gatefold sleeve) | 15 |
| 72 | Elektra K 62009 | WEIRD SCENES INSIDE THE GOLDMINE (2-LP, 'butterfly' label, gatefold sleeve) | 20 |
| 72 | Elektra K 62116 | FULL CIRCLE ('butterfly', gatefold sleeve) | 15 |
| 76 | Elektra K42012 | THE DOORS (LP, reissue, 'Butterfly' label) | 15 |
| 76 | Elektra K42016 | STRANGE DAYS (LP, reissue, 'butterfly' label) | 15 |
| 76 | Elektra K42080 | MORRISON HOTEL (LP, reissue 'butterfly' label) | 15 |
| 76 | Elektra K42079 | THE SOFT PARADE (LP, reissue, 'butterfly' label) | 15 |
| 76 | Elektra K42041 | WAITING FOR THE SUN (LP, reissue, 'butterfly' label) | 15 |
| 76 | Elektra K 42090 | L.A. WOMAN (LP, reissue, square cornered sleeve) | 15 |
| 78 | Elektra K52111 | AN AMERICAN PRAYER ('Butterfly' label, gatefold sleeve, with 8-page booklet) | 20 |
| 76 | Elektra K62005 | ABSOLUTELY LIVE (2-LP, reissue) | 18 |

*(see also Ray Manzarek)*

**DOORS OF PERCEPTION**
| 91 | Lizard Nation LN 001 | SO JOIN MR. DREAMS (LP, with inner sleeve and booklet) | 15 |
|---|---|---|---|

**D.O.P.E.**
| 92 | Spare Beat SBRR 002 | When I Was Young (Original Mix)/RIchard's First Trip (12") | 12 |
|---|---|---|---|
| 93 | Rugged Vinyl RUGGED 1 | THE DOPE ON PLASTIC EP (12") | 10 |

**DOPE ON PLASTIC**
| 94 | Wave DJC 001 | Wave Dub/Out Of Time/East A Bit/It's A Dream (12") | 70 |
|---|---|---|---|

**M.J. DORANE**
| 74 | Dip DL 5023 | Loving You/Medley | 10 |
|---|---|---|---|

**MIKE DORANE & CIMARONS**
| 71 | Ackee ACK 144 | Penguin Funk/Ad-Lib | 12 |
|---|---|---|---|

**DOREEN (CAMPBELL) & ALL STARS**
| 67 | Rainbow RAI 114 | Rude Girls/Please Stay | 15 |
|---|---|---|---|

**DOREEN (SHAFFER) & JACKIE (OPEL)**
| 65 | Ska Beat JB 208 | Welcome Home/You And I | 35 |
|---|---|---|---|

*(see also Jackie & Doreen)*

**DORIAN**
70   Ember EMB S 285          Psychedelic Lipstick/Help For My Waiting ................................................8

**DORIS**
81   ABCD ABCD 1               Sitting Here Waiting (no p/s) .................................................10
82   ABCD ABCD 3               GYPSY LADY (LP, actually credited to A Band Called Doris) .................250
98   EMI/Mr. Bongo MRBLP 010   DID YOU GIVE THE WORLD SOME LOVE TODAY, BABY? (LP, reissue of Swedish 60s LP) ..15

**HAROLD DORMAN**
60   Top Rank JAR 357          Mountain Of Love/To Be With You ...........................................10
61   London HLS 9386           There They Go/I'll Stick By You ...........................................15

**STACY DORNING**
74   Scratchy CHS 2051         Catch A Falling Star/Time Is On My Side ....................................5

**DOROTHY**
80   Industrial IR 0014        I Confess/Softness (p/s) ..................................................15

**RALPH DORPER**
83   Operation Twilight OPT 18 THE ERASERHEAD EP (12") ...................................................20

*(see also Propaganda)*

**CHRIS DORS**
61   Fontana H 329             That's When Your Heartaches Begin/They Called It Love .......................6

**DIANA DORS**
60   Pye 7N 15242              April Heart/Point Of No Return ............................................10
64   Fontana TF 506            So Little Time/It's Too Late ..............................................50
66   Polydor BM 56111          Security/Gary .............................................................10
77   EMI EMI 2705              Passing By/It's A Small World ..............................................5
82   Nomis NOM 1               Where Did They Go/It's You Again (with Gary Dors) ..........................5
60   Pye NPL 18044             SWINGIN' DORS (LP, foldout sleeve, red vinyl) ............................100

**RAY DORSET (WITH MUNGO JERRY)**
72   Dawn DNS 1018             Cold Blue Excursion/I Need It (solo) .......................................5
79   Satellite RAY 001         Forgotten Land/New Way Of Life (solo, unreleased; 100 promos only) .........6
72   Dawn DNLS 3033            COLD BLUE EXCURSION (LP, solo; gatefold sleeve with lyric inner, lilac label) ....50

*(see also Mungo Jerry, County Jug,, Insiders, Panache, Made In England)*

**DORSETS**
65   Sue WI 391                Pork Chops/Cool It ........................................................50

**GERRY DORSEY**
59   Decca F 11108             Mister Music Man/Crazy Bells ..............................................15
59   Parlophone R 4595         I'll Never Fall In Love Again/Every Day Is A Wonderful Day ..................7
61   Parlophone R 4739         Big Wheel/The Sentimental Joker ............................................7
64   Pye 7N 15622              Baby I Do/Take Your Time ...................................................7
65   Hickory 45-1337           Baby Turn Around/Things I Wanna Do ........................................35

**JACK DORSEY ORCHESTRA**
64   Pye 7N 15730              Ringo's Dog/March Of The Gonks (as BIG BAND) ..............................10
65   Polydor 56020             Dance Of The Daleks/Likely Lads ...........................................10
66   Polydor 56090             Alfie's Theme/Alfie's Theme Too ...........................................15
68   Pye 7N 17501              Soul Coaxing/Elizabeth's Waltz ............................................10

**LEE DORSEY**
62   Top Rank JAR 606          Do-Re-Mi/People Gonna Talk ................................................25
65   Sue WI 367                Do-Re-Mi/Ya Ya ............................................................40
65   Stateside SS 441          Ride Your Pony/The Kitty Cat Song .........................................12
65   Stateside SS 465          Work Work Work/Can You Hear Me ............................................12
66   Sue WI 399                Messed Around/When I Meet My Baby .........................................40
66   Stateside SS 485          Get Out Of My Life, Woman/So Long .........................................10
66   Stateside SS 506          Confusion/Neighbour's Daughter .............................................8
66   Stateside SS 528          Working In A Coalmine/Mexico ..............................................10
66   Stateside SS 528          Working In A Coalmine/Mexico (yellow vinyl) ...............................50
66   Stateside SS 552          Holy Cow/Operation Heartache ..............................................7
67   Stateside SS 593          Rain Rain Go Away/Gotta Find A Job .........................................5
67   Stateside SS 2017         My Old Car/Why Wait Until Tomorrow .........................................6
67   Stateside SS 2055         Go-Go Girl/I Can Hear You Callin' .........................................10
68   President PT 226          Ya Ya/Give Me You ..........................................................5
68   Bell BLL 1006             Can You Hear Me/Cynthia ....................................................5
69   Bell BLL 1051             I'm Gonna Sit Right Down And Write Myself A Letter/Little Baby ..............5
69   Bell BLL 1060             Ride Your Pony/Get Out Of My Life, Woman ...................................5
69   Bell BLL 1074             Everything I Do Gonna Be Funky/There Should Be A Book .....................15
71   Mojo 2066 063             Occapella/Yes We Can Part 1 ................................................5
72   Mojo 2093 009             Freedom For The Stallion/If She Won't (Find Someone Who Will) ..............5
66   Stateside SE 1038         RIDE YOUR PONY (EP) .......................................................30
66   Stateside SE 1043         YOU'RE BREAKING ME UP (EP) ................................................30
65   Sue ILP 924               THE BEST OF LEE DORSEY (LP) ...............................................60
66   Stateside S(S)L 10177     LEE DORSEY — RIDE YOUR PONY (LP) ..........................................30
66   Stateside S(S)L 10192     THE NEW LEE DORSEY (LP) ...................................................25
71   Polydor 2489 006          YES WE CAN (LP) ...........................................................25

**LEE DORSEY & BETTY HARRIS**
69   Buffalo BFS 1002          Love Lots Of Lovin'/Take Care Of Your Love ................................20

*(see also Betty Harris)*

**D.O.S.E.**
95   Colosseum TOGA 001TJX     Plug Myself In (with Mark E. Smith) (p/s, numbered, 1-sided, 500 only) ......10

*(see also Fall)*

## DOSSERS
| 83 | Secret SHH 168-12 | Red Night/Punk Rocker/Running Running/Armada (12" in Secret records house bag) ..25 |

## JOHNNY DOT & DASHERS
| 62 | Salvo SLO 1805 | I Love An Angel/Just For You (99 copies only) ......50 |

## DOTTY & BONNIE
| 64 | Rio R 43 | I'm So Glad/DOUGLAS BROTHERS: Got You On My Mind ......12 |
| 64 | Island WI 143 | Your Kisses/Why Worry ......18 |
| 64 | Island WI 148 | Dearest/Tears Are Falling ......15 |
| 65 | Ska Beat JB 183 | Foul Play/ROLAND ALPHONSO & GROUP: Yard Broom ......30 |
| 67 | Ska Beat JB 274 | I'll Know/Love Is Great ......15 |
| 70 | Ackee ACK 110 | I'm So Glad/Lonely Road ......20 |

*(see also Bonnie Frankson, Eric Morris, Don Drummond, Skatalites, Baba Brooks)*

## DOUBLE FEATURE
| 67 | Deram DM 115 | Baby Get Your Head Screwed On/Come On Baby ......70 |
| 67 | Deram DM 165 | Handbags And Gladrags/Just Another Lonely Night ......10 |

## DOUBLE VISION
| 97 | Big Drum BDRUM 01 | HOW SHOULD I START EP (12") ......25 |

## DOUBLES WITH GAY BLADES
| 59 | HMV POP 613 | Hey Girl!/Little Joe ......100 |

## DOUBT
| 80 | Solo SOLO 1 | Fringes/Lookaway/Contrast Disorder/Time Out (EP, with no p/s but insert) ......20 |

*(See also Carpenter Joe)*

## SUZANNE DOUCET
| 68 | Liberty LBF 15150 | Swan Song/Cry My Heart ......12 |

## DOUGHNUT RING
| 68 | Deram DM 215 | Dance Around Julie/The Bandit ......35 |

*(see also Crocheted Doughnut Ring)*

## JOHNNY DOUGHTY
| 77 | Topic 12TS 324 | ROUND RYE BAY FOR MORE (LP, with insert) ......15 |

## CARL DOUGLAS (& BIG STAMPEDE)
| 66 | Go AJ 11401 | Crazy Feeling/PETER PERRY SOUL BAND: Keep It To Myself ......35 |
| 67 | Go AJ 11408 | Let The Birds Sing/Something For Nothing ......50 |
| 67 | United Artists UP 1206 | Nobody Cries/Serving A Sentence Of Life ......200 |
| 67 | United Artists UP 1206 | Nobody Cries/Serving A Sentence Of Life (DJ Copy) ......250 |
| 68 | United Artists UP 2227 | Sell My Soul To The Devil/Good Hard Worker ......30 |
| 68 | Pye 7N 45551 | Witchfinder General/Crazy Feeling ......20 |
| 71 | CBS 7101 | Do You Need My Love (To Get Better)/Lean On Me ......70 |
| 72 | Blue Mountain BM 1007 | Somebody Stop This Madness/Ain't No Use (as Karl Douglas) ......10 |
| 79 | Pye 7N 46155 | Choose Between Two Lovers/Shame (red vinyl) ......6 |

## CHIC DOUGLAS
| 58 | Fontana H 121 | I'm Not Afraid Anymore/Jo-Ann ......6 |

## CRAIG DOUGLAS
| 58 | Decca F 11055 | Nothin' Shakin'/Sitting In A Tree House ......10 |
| 58 | Decca F 11075 | Go Chase A Moonbeam/Are You Really Mine ......8 |
| 59 | Top Rank TR 5004 | Battle Of New Orleans/Dream Lover/SHEILA BUXTON: Personality/ Where Were You On Our Wedding Day/BERT WEEDON: I Need Your Love Tonight ('King-Size' 7", special sleeve) ......5 |
| 61 | Top Rank JAR 555 | A Hundred Pounds Of Clay/Hello Spring ......5 |
| 61 | Top Rank JAR 556 | A Hundred Pounds Of Clay (censored version)/Hello Spring (p/s) ......10 |
| 62 | Top Rank JAR 603 | Another You/A Change Of Heart ......10 |
| 62 | Top Rank JAR 610 | When My Little Girl Is Smiling/Ring A Ding ......5 |
| 62 | Columbia DB 4854 | Our Favourite Melodies/Rainbows ......5 |
| 63 | Decca F 11575 | Town Crier/I'd Be Smiling Now ......5 |
| 63 | Decca F 11665 | Danke Shoen/Teenage Mona Lisa ......5 |
| 63 | Decca F 11722 | I'm So Glad I Found Her/Love Her While She's Young ......5 |
| 63 | Decca F 11763 | Counting Up The Kisses/From Russia With Love ......7 |
| 64 | Fontana TF 458 | Silly Boy/Love Leave Me Alone ......7 |
| 64 | Fontana TF 475 | Come Closer/She's Smiling At Me (as Craig Douglas & Tridents) ......8 |
| 65 | Fontana TF 525 | Across The Street/Party Girl ......7 |
| 65 | Fontana TF 580 | Around The Corner/Find The Girl ......5 |
| 69 | Pye 7N 17746 | How Do You Feel About That/Then ......12 |
| 60 | Decca DFE 6633 | CRAIG (EP) ......12 |
| 62 | Decca DFE 8509 | CUDDLE UP WITH CRAIG (EP) ......12 |
| 63 | Columbia SEG 8219 | CRAIG MOVIE SONGS (EP) ......12 |
| 62 | Columbia 33SX 1468 | OUR FAVOURITE MELODIES (LP) ......20 |

*(see also Bert Weedon)*

## DEV DOUGLAS
| 65 | Parlophone R 5237 | I Don't Know/How Does It Feel ......6 |
| 66 | Parlophone R5462 | What Am I Doing Here/I've Got Lovin' ......12 |

## DONNA DOUGLAS
| 58 | Fontana H 158 | The Shepherd/I'm Dancing With Tears In My Eyes ......5 |
| 59 | Fontana H 223 | Six Boys And Seven Girls/Into Each Life Some Rain Must Fall ......5 |
| 61 | Piccadilly 7N 35014 | Tammy Tell Me True/Memory Lane ......5 |
| 62 | Piccadilly 7N 35031 | The Message In A Bottle/If This Is Love ......7 |
| 62 | Piccadilly 7N 35042 | Matelot/All The Other Girls ......6 |
| 63 | Piccadilly 7N 35111 | It's A Pity To Say Goodnight/Do I Know ......5 |
| 63 | Piccadilly 7N 35135 | He's So Near/Turn Around ......5 |
| 64 | Pye 7N 15654 | Blue Star/Java Jones ......6 |

### JACK DOUGLAS
| | | | |
|---|---|---|---|
| 68 | Columbia DB 8393 | Swanee River/Call Alf (Why Does Love Pass Me By) | 8 |

### JAN DOUGLAS
| | | | |
|---|---|---|---|
| 64 | Vocalion V 9226 | More And More/Walkin' In The Rain | 10 |

### JOHNNY DOUGLAS (& HIS ORCHESTRA/COMBO)
| | | | |
|---|---|---|---|
| 54 | Decca F 10276 | Ballet Of The Bells/Solfeggio (as Johnny Douglas & His Orchestra) | 5 |
| 63 | Speyside SK 1501 | Ski Jump/Clementine (as Johnny Douglas Combo) | 5 |
| 65 | RCA 1444 | Crack In The World/Time | 10 |

### KEITH DOUGLAS
| | | | |
|---|---|---|---|
| 84 | Zip ZIP001 | Frontline/Dub Version (12") | 25 |

### KIRK DOUGLAS & MELLOMEN
| | | | |
|---|---|---|---|
| 55 | Brunswick 05408 | A Whale Of A Tale/And The Moon Grew Brighter And Brighter | 5 |

### LEW DOUGLAS & HIS ORCHESTRA
| | | | |
|---|---|---|---|
| 54 | MGM SP 1093 | Caesar's Boogie/Turn Around Boy | 10 |

### MARK DOUGLAS
| | | | |
|---|---|---|---|
| 62 | Ember EMB S 166 | It Matters Not/Upside Down | 75 |

### NORMA DOUGLAS
| | | | |
|---|---|---|---|
| 57 | London HLZ 8475 | Be It Resolved/Joe He Gone | 15 |

### DOUGLAS BROTHERS
| | | | |
|---|---|---|---|
| 66 | Rio R 57 | Valley Of Tears/CHARMERS: Where Do I Turn | 15 |
| 66 | Rio R 63 | Down And Out/RONALD WILSON: Lonely Man | 125 |

*(see also Dotty & Bonnie)*

### ROBB & DEAN DOUGLAS
| | | | |
|---|---|---|---|
| 67 | Deram DM 132 | I Can Make It With You/Phone Me | 50 |

### HARRY DOUGLASS & DEEP RIVER BOYS
| | | | |
|---|---|---|---|
| 60 | Top Rank JAR 352 | Dum Dum De Dum/Go Galloway, Go | 7 |

*(see also Deep River Boys)*

### RONNIE DOVE
| | | | |
|---|---|---|---|
| 64 | Stateside SS 314 | Sweeter Than Sugar/I Believed In You | 8 |
| 64 | Stateside SS 346 | Say You/Let Me Stay Today | 8 |
| 64 | Stateside SS 366 | Right Or Wrong/Baby, Put Your Arms Around Me | 6 |
| 65 | Stateside SS 392 | Hello Pretty Girl/Keep It A Secret | 6 |
| 65 | Stateside SS 412 | One Kiss For Old Times' Sake/Bluebird | 7 |
| 65 | Stateside SS 436 | A Little Bit Of Heaven/If I Live To Be A Hundred | 7 |
| 65 | Stateside SS 462 | I'll Make All Your Dreams Come True/I Had To Lose You To Find That I Need You | 6 |
| 65 | Stateside SS 480 | Kiss Away/Where In The World | 6 |
| 66 | Stateside SS 492 | When Liking Turns To Loving/I'm Learning How To Smile Again | 6 |
| 66 | Stateside SS 510 | Let's Start All Over Again/That Empty Feeling | 6 |
| 66 | Stateside SS 524 | Happy Summer Days/Long After | 6 |
| 66 | Stateside SS 542 | I Really Don't Want To Know/Years Of Tears | 6 |
| 66 | Stateside SS 571 | Cry/Autumn Rhapsody | 6 |
| 70 | Stateside SS 2003 | One More Mountain To Climb/All | 6 |
| 67 | Stateside SS 2018 | My Babe/Put My Mind At Ease | 6 |
| 68 | Stateside SS 2119 | Mountain Of Love/Never Gonna Cry (The Way I'll Cry Tonight) | 10 |
| 70 | Stateside SS 2047 | I Want To Love You For What You Are/I Thank You For Your Love | 6 |
| 70 | Stateside SS 2086 | Dancin' Out Of My Heart/Back From Baltimore | 6 |
| 65 | Stateside SL 10149 | RONNIE DOVE (LP) | 40 |

### DOVELLS
| | | | |
|---|---|---|---|
| 61 | Columbia DB 4718 | The Bristol Stomp/Out In The Cold Again | 20 |
| 62 | Columbia DB 4810 | Do The New Continental/Mopitty Mope Stomp | 20 |
| 62 | Columbia DB 4877 | Bristol Twistin' Annie/The Actor | 20 |
| 62 | Cameo Parkway P 845 | Hully Gully Baby/Your Last Chance | 10 |
| 63 | Cameo Parkway P 861 | You Can't Run Away From Yourself/Save Me Baby | 10 |
| 63 | Cameo Parkway P 867 | You Can't Sit Down/Stompin' Everywhere | 25 |
| 63 | Cameo Parkway P 882 | Betty In Bermudas/Dance The Froog | 10 |
| 63 | Cameo Parkway P 901 | Be My Girl/Dragster On The Prowl | 25 |
| 79 | London HAU 8515 | CAMEO PARKWAY SESSIONS (LP) | 15 |

*(see also Len Barry)*

### DOVES
| | | | |
|---|---|---|---|
| 98 | Manchester MANC 9 | Seven Day Smile (with Jane Weaver)/ANDY VOTEL & JANE WEAVER: Gutter Girl (p/s) | 6 |
| 99 | Casino CHIP 003 | Here It Comes/Meet Me At The Pier/(Acoustic Version) (10", p/s) | 10 |
| 98 | Casino CHIP 001 | CEDAR EP: Cedar Room/Rise/Zither (10", wraparound p/s) | 30 |
| 99 | Casino CHIP 002 | SEA EP (10", p/s) | 20 |
| 00 | Heavenly HVNLP 26 | LOST SOULS (2-LP) | 60 |
| 02 | Heavenly HVNLP 35 | THE LAST BROADCAST (2-LP) | 50 |
| 05 | Heavenly HVNLP 50 | SOME CITIES (2-LP) | 50 |

*(see also Badly Drawn Boy, Sub Sub, Jane Weaver v Doves)*

### NICK DOW
| | | | |
|---|---|---|---|
| 79 | Dingles DIN 306 | BURD MARGARET (LP) | 15 |

### BRENT DOWE
| | | | |
|---|---|---|---|
| 71 | Summit SUM 8521 | Knock Three Times/GAYLADS: This Time I Won't Hurt You | 6 |
| 71 | Summit SUM 8525 | Put Your Hand In The Hand/Miracle (B-side actually "It Took A Miracle Version" by Beverley's All Stars) | 6 |
| 71 | Summit SUM 8530 | Freedom Train/BEVERLEY'S ALL STARS: Freedom Train (Version) | 6 |
| 73 | Green Door GD 4061 | Reggae Makossa/No Nola (B-side actually by Melodians) | 12 |
| 76 | Student STU 1006 | It was Love/Version | 8 |
| 74 | Trojan TRLS 76 | BUILD ME UP (LP) | 15 |

*(see also Melodians)*

MINT VALUE £

### JOE DOWELL
| | | | |
|---|---|---|---|
| 61 | Mercury AMT 1161 | The Bridge Of Love/Just Love Me | 5 |
| 62 | Mercury AMT 1180 | Little Red Rented Rowboat/The One I Left For You | 5 |

### JOHN DOWIE
| | | | |
|---|---|---|---|
| 81 | Factory FAC 19 | It's Hard To Be An Egg/Mind Sketch (white vinyl, clear sleeve, with white feather) | 15 |

### DOWLANDS
| | | | |
|---|---|---|---|
| 62 | Oriole CB 1748 | Little Sue/Julie (as Dowlands & Soundtracks) | 50 |
| 62 | Oriole CB 1781 | Big Big Fella/Don't Ever Change | 100 |
| 63 | Oriole CB 1815 | Break Ups/A Love Like Ours | 50 |
| 63 | Oriole CB 1892 | Lonely Johnny (song actually titled "Lucky Johnny")/Do You Have To Have Me Blue? | 500 |
| 64 | Oriole CB 1897 | All My Loving/Hey Sally (as Dowlands & Soundtracks) | 15 |
| 64 | Oriole CB 1926 | I Walk The Line/Happy Endings | 40 |
| 64 | Oriole CB 1947 | Wishing And Hoping/You Will Regret It | 80 |
| 65 | Columbia DB 7547 | Don't Make Me Over/Someone Must Be Feeling Sad | 40 |

### DOWNBEATS
| | | | |
|---|---|---|---|
| 61 | Starlite ST45 051 | Thinkin' Of You/Midnight Love | 200 |

### BRUCE DOWNER
| | | | |
|---|---|---|---|
| 71 | Summit SUM 8524 | Free The People (actually by Bruce Ruffin)/BEVERLEY'S ALL STARS: Free The People (Version) | 6 |

### ROLAND DOWNER & COUNT OSSIE
| | | | |
|---|---|---|---|
| 68 | Doctor Bird DB 1130 | Ethiopian Kingdom/A Ju Ju Wah | 90 |

### BOB DOWNES
| | | | |
|---|---|---|---|
| 70 | Vertigo 6059 011 | No Time Like The Present/Keep Off The Grass | 35 |
| 70 | Philips SBL 7922 | BOB DOWNES' OPEN MUSIC (LP) | 200 |
| 70 | Vertigo 6360 005 | ELECTRIC CITY (LP, gatefold sleeve, large swirl label) | 300 |
| 70 | Music For Pleasure MFP 1412 | DEEP DOWN HEAVY (LP, red/silver label) | 25 |
| 73 | Ophenian BDOM 001 | DIVERSIONS (LP) | 25 |
| 74 | Ophenian BDOM 002 | EPISODES AT 4AM (LP, with insert) | 22 |
| 75 | Ophenian BDOM 003 | HELLS ANGELS (LP) | 30 |

*(see also Rock Workshop)*

### DEIRDRE DOWNES & BROADSIDERS
| | | | |
|---|---|---|---|
| 69 | Pye 7N 17781 | Lady Mary/Did He Mention My Name | 5 |

### DOWNHILL
| | | | |
|---|---|---|---|
| 79 | Bead Records BEAD 8 | DOWNHILL (LP) | 30 |

### BIG AL DOWNING
| | | | |
|---|---|---|---|
| 64 | Sue WI 341 | Yes I'm Loving You/Please Come Home | 45 |

### DOWNLINERS SECT
| | | | |
|---|---|---|---|
| 64 | Columbia DB 7300 | Baby What's Wrong/Be A Sect Maniac | 30 |
| 64 | Columbia DB 7347 | Little Egypt/Sect Appeal | 15 |
| 64 | Columbia DB 7415 | Find Out What's Happening/Insecticide | 35 |
| 65 | Columbia DB 7509 | Wreck Of The Old '97/Leader Of The Sect | 30 |
| 65 | Columbia DB 7597 | I Got Mine/Waiting In Heaven Somewhere | 35 |
| 65 | Columbia DB 7712 | Bad Storm Coming/Lonely And Blue | 35 |
| 66 | Columbia DB 7817 | All Night Worker/He Was A Square | 30 |
| 66 | Columbia DB 7939 | Glendora/I'll Find Out | 70 |
| 66 | Columbia DB 8008 | The Cost Of Living/Everything I've Got To Give | 25 |
| 64 | Contrast Sound RBCSP 1 | NITE IN GREAT NEWPORT STREET (EP) | 300 |
| 65 | Columbia SEG 8438 | THE SECT SING SICK SONGS (EP) | 100 |
| 64 | Columbia 33SX 1658 | THE SECT (LP) | 200 |
| 65 | Columbia 33SX 1745 | THE COUNTRY SECT (LP) | 150 |
| 66 | Columbia SX 6028 | THE ROCK SECT'S IN (LP, mono, black/blue label with "sold in the U.K..." text) | 200 |
| 66 | Columbia S(C)X 6028 | THE ROCK SECT'S IN (LP, stereo, blue/black label with "sold in the U.K..." text) | 250 |
| 93 | Hangman HANG 42 UP | BIRTH OF SUAVE (LP) | 15 |

*(see also Don Crane's Downliners Sect)*

### DOWN TO EARTH
| | | | |
|---|---|---|---|
| 71 | Downtown DT 485 | Under The Boardwalk/Under The Boardwalk (Version) (B-side actually "Double Barrel Version") | 10 |

### DOWNTOWN ALL STARS
| | | | |
|---|---|---|---|
| 69 | Downtown DT 426 | Everybody Feel Good/RUDIES: Downtown Jump | 50 |

### GENE DOZIER & UNITED FRONT
| | | | |
|---|---|---|---|
| 74 | Mercury 6167 007 | Give The Women What They Want/The Best Girl I Ever Had | 10 |

### LAMONT DOZIER
| | | | |
|---|---|---|---|
| 74 | Probe PRO 618 | Trying To Hold On To My Woman/We Don't Want Nobody To Come | 5 |
| 74 | Anchor ABC 4003 | Fish Ain't Bitin'/Breaking Out All Over | 5 |
| 75 | Anchor ABC 4056 | All Cried Out/Rose | 5 |
| 77 | Warner Bros K 16942 | Going Back To My Roots/Going Back To My Roots (Version) | 8 |
| 81 | CBS A 1235 | To Cool Me Out/Starting Over | 10 |
| 74 | ABC ABCL 5042 | OUT HERE ON MY OWN (LP) | 15 |

*(see also Holland & Dozier)*

### DOZY, BEAKY, MICK & TICH (D.B.M.&T.)
| | | | |
|---|---|---|---|
| 69 | Fontana TF 1061 | Tonight Today/Bad News | 5 |
| 70 | Fontana 6007 022 | Mr. President/Frisco Annie (as D.B.M.&T) | 6 |
| 70 | Fontana 6006 066 | Festival/Leader Of A Rock 'N' Roll Band | 6 |
| 70 | Philips 6308 029 | FRESH EAR (LP, gatefold sleeve, credited to D.B.M.&T) | 25 |

*(see also Dave Dee Dozy Beaky Mick & Tich)*

### DP'S
| | | | |
|---|---|---|---|
| 78 | Barn 2314107 | IF YOU KNOW WHAT I MEAN (LP) | 15 |

(see also The Depressions)

**DR. DOG**

| 05 | Rough Trade RTRADLP 258 | EASY BEAT (LP, textured sleeve, inner) | 15 |

**DRAGON**

| 76 | Acorn CF 268 | DRAGON (LP, gatefold sleeve) | 60 |

**DRAGONFLY**

| 74 | Retreat RTS 257 | Gondola/Almost Abandoned (demo) | 15 |
| 75 | Retreat RTS 261 | Driving Around The World/Since I Left My Home | 8 |
| 74 | Retreat RTL 6002 | ALMOST ABANDONED (LP) | 25 |
| 80s | Dragonfly DF 001 | SILENT NIGHTS EP (p/s, private pressing) | 150 |

**DRAGONS**

| 69 | Page One | Heart Transplantation/Hello I Love Maria | 40 |

**DRAGONSFIRE**

| 82 | Belltree BTR 001 | RISING PHOENIX (LP, with insert) | 20 |

(see also Spinning Wheel)

**DRAGONSLAYER**

| 83 | Cavalier CAV 017 | Broken Hearts/Satan Is Free/I Want Your Life (Early copies with band name as 'Slayer'. NO STICKER) | 120 |
| 83 | Cavalier CAV 017 | Broken Hearts/Satan Is Free/I Want Your Life (Early copies had band name as 'Slayer', these later copies have sticker with new name – Dragonslayer – covering it) | 80 |

**DRAG SET**

| 66 | Go AJ 11405 | Get Out Of My Way/Day And Night | 250 |

(see also Open Mind)

**DRAGSTER**

| 81 | Heavy Metal HEAVY 4 | Ambition/Won't Bring You Back (p/s) | 30 |

**CHARLES DRAIN**

| 75 | RCA 2750 | Is This Really Love/Only You | 15 |

**CHARLIE DRAKE**

| 59 | Parlophone R 4552 | Sea Cruise/Starkle, Starkle Little Twink | 8 |
| 64 | Parlophone R 5209 | Charles Drake 007/Bumpanology (Bump Head Blues) | 8 |
| 67 | Pye 7N 17269 | Who Is Sylvia/I Wanna Be In A Group | 6 |
| 73 | EMI 2079 | Someone Opened Watergate And They All Got Wet/'Ello Erf | 6 |
| 75 | Charisma CB 270 | You Never Know/I'm Big Enough For Me (produced by Peter Gabriel) | 10 |
| 76 | Sol Doon SDRO 24S | Super Punk/Someone | 8 |
| 58 | Parlophone GEP 8720 | HELLO MY DARLINGS (EP) | 10 |
| 60 | Parlophone GEP 8812 | NAUGHTY CHARLIE DRAKE (EP) | 12 |
| 64 | Parlophone GEP 8903 | HITS FROM THE MAN IN THE MOON (EP) | 10 |

**NICK DRAKE**

| 79 | Island RSS 7 | Introduction/Hazy Jane II/Time Has Told Me/Fruit Tree/Rider On The Wheel ("Fruit Tree" sampler, 1-sided promo only) | 200 |
| 04 | Island IS 854 | Magic/Northern Sky | 12 |
| 04 | Island IS 871 | River Man/River Man (1968 Recording) | 12 |
| 12 | Antar 11 | Plaisir D'Amour (1-sided, die cut sleeve) | 20 |
| 13 | Secret 7 S713 | Rider On The Wheel (1-sided, 100 only, each sleeve decorated by different artist) | 80 |
| 14 | Antar ANTARSP012 | Cello Song (Peel session version, 1-sided, p/s, booklet) | 25 |
| 69 | Island ILPS 9105 | FIVE LEAVES LEFT (LP, 1st pressing, pink label, black 'circle' logo, matrix numbers ILPS 9105 A//2/ILPS 9105 B//2, gatefold sleeve printed by Ernest J. Day, track order of Day Is Done and Way To Blue reversed) | 800 |
| 69 | Island ILPS 9105 | FIVE LEAVES LEFT (LP, gatefold sleeve, 2nd pressing, 'pink rim label', 'palm tree' logo) | 100 |
| 70 | Island ILPS 9134 | BRYTER LAYTER (LP, 1st pressing, 'pink rim label', 'palm tree' logo, 'stereo' on label and Joe Boyd credit on one line, Matrixes: ILPS 9134 A-1U/ILPS 9134 B-1U) | 400 |
| 71 | Longman (no cat. No.) | INTERPLAY ONE (2xLP, educational recording for schools, Drake plays guitar on three tracks, 2 booklets and 'teachers' notes) | 450 |
| 72 | Island ILPS 9134 | BRYTER LAYTER (LP, 2nd pressing 'pink rim label', 'palm tree' logo, no 'stereo' on right hand side of label and Joe Boyd credit on two lines) | 150 |
| 72 | Island ILPS 9184 | PINK MOON (LP, 'pink rim label', 'palm tree' logo, gatefold sleeve) | 400 |
| 76 | Island ILPS 9184 | PINK MOON (LP, reissue, blue rim, palm tree logo) | 50 |
| 76 | Island ILPS 9134 | BRYER LATER (LP, reissue, 3rd pressing, blue rim palm tree label, textured sleeve) | 50 |
| 78 | Island ILPS 9134 | BRYER LATER (LP, reissue, blue label) | 30 |
| 78 | Island ILPS 9184 | PINK MOON (LP, reissue) | 25 |
| 76 | Island ILPS 9105 | FIVE LEAVES LEFT (LP, reissue, 3rd pressing blue rim palm tree label) | 50 |
| 79 | Island NDSP 100 | FRUIT TREE (3-LP, box set with booklet) | 70 |
| 85 | Island ILPS 9826 | HEAVEN IN A WILD FLOWER (THE BEST OF NICK DRAKE) (LP) | 20 |
| 86 | Hannibal HNBX 5302 | FRUIT TREE (4-LP, expanded reissue with booklet) | 90 |
| 86 | Hannibal HNBL 1318 | TIME OF NO REPLY (LP) | 20 |
| 89 | Island ILPS 9105 | FIVE LEAVES LEFT (LP, reissue, 'blue with white palm tree' label) | 35 |
| 89 | Island ILPS 9134 | BRYTER LAYTER (LP, reissue, 'blue with white palm tree' label) | 35 |
| 89 | Island ILPS 9184 | PINK MOON (LP, reissue, 'blue with white palm tree' label) | 35 |
| 91 | Hannibal HNCD 5402 | FRUIT TREE (4-CD, with booklet in 12" x 12" box) | 70 |
| 99 | Simply Vinyl SVLP 094 | BRYTER LAYTER (LP, Simply vinyl 180gm repressing) | 25 |
| 00 | Simply Vinyl SVLP 172 | PINK MOON (LP, Simply Vinyl 180gm repressing) | 20 |
| 00 | Simply Vinyl SVLP 163 | FIVE LEAVES LEFT (LP, Simply Vinyl 180gm repressing) | 20 |
| 04 | Island ILPS 8141 | MADE TO LOVE MAGIC (LP, gatefold with inner sleeve) | 30 |
| 07 | Sunbeam SBR2LP 5041 | FAMILY TREE (2-LP) | 20 |

**PETE DRAKE**

| 63 | Philips BF 1332 | Forever/Sleep Walk | 8 |

**DRAMA**

| 82 | Orbit TRIP 1 | Been Too Long/Do You Love Me (no p/s) | 10 |

**DRAMATICS**

| 72 | Stax 2025 053 | Whatcha See Is Whatcha Get/Thankful For Your Love | 8 |

# Barry DRANSFIELD

| | | | |
|---|---|---|---|
| 72 | Stax 2025 101 | In The Rain/Get Up And Get Down | 6 |
| 73 | Stax 2025 117 | Toast To A Fool/Your Love Was Strange | 12 |
| 73 | Stax 2025 181 | Hey You, Get Off My Mountain/Devil Is Dope | 6 |
| 76 | ABC ABC 4101 | You're Fooling You/I'll Make It So Good | 6 |
| 72 | Stax 2362 025 | WHATCHA SEE IS WHATCHA GET (LP) | 15 |

## BARRY DRANSFIELD
| | | | |
|---|---|---|---|
| 72 | Polydor Folk Mill 2383 160 | BARRY DRANSFIELD (LP, red label) | 300 |
| 78 | Topic 12TS 386 | BOWIN' AND SCRAPIN' (LP) | 25 |
| 02 | Spinney SPINNEY 003 | BARRY DRANSFIELD (LP, reissue) | 20 |

(see also Robin & Barry Dransfield)

## ROBIN DRANSFIELD
| | | | |
|---|---|---|---|
| 80 | Topic 12TS 414 | TIDEWAVE (LP) | 15 |

(see also Robin & Barry Dransfield)

## ROBIN & BARRY DRANSFIELD
| | | | |
|---|---|---|---|
| 70 | Trailer LER 2011 | THE ROUT OF THE BLUES (LP, first pressing, white Trailer 'test' label) | 50 |
| 70 | Trailer LER 2011 | THE ROUT OF THE BLUES (LP, second pressing, dark red label/silver logo and text) | 40 |
| 71 | Trailer LER 2026 | LORD OF ALL I BEHOLD (LP) | 40 |
| 75 | Trailer LER 2011 | THE ROUT OF THE BLUES (LP, 70s repressing, red and black or yellow labels) | 30 |
| 82 | Highway | THE ROUT OF THE BLUES (LP, 80s repressing, black and white 'Highwayman' labels) | 15 |
| 82 | Highway/Trailer LER 2011 | THE ROUT OF THE BLUES (LP, Trailer labels and sleeves with 'Highway Records' stickers over 'Trailer' logo on sleeve) | 15 |

(see also Robin Dransfield, Barry Dransfield)

## RUSTY DRAPER
| | | | |
|---|---|---|---|
| 58 | Mercury 7MT 211 | Gamblin' Gal/That's My Doll | 10 |
| 58 | Mercury 7MT 229 | Chicken-Pickin' Hawk/June, July And August | 15 |
| 59 | Mercury AMT 1019 | Shoppin' Around/With This Ring | 30 |
| 59 | Mercury AMT 1034 | The Sun Will Always Shine/Hey Li Lee Li Lee Li | 5 |
| 60 | Mercury AMT 1101 | Mule Skinner Blues/Please Help Me, I'm Falling | 10 |
| 61 | Mercury AMT 1127 | Jealous Heart/Ten Thousand Years Ago | 7 |
| 63 | London HLU 9786 | Night Life/That's Why I Love You Like I Do | 5 |
| 65 | London HLU 9989 | Folsom Prison Blues/You Can't Be True, Dear | 5 |
| 56 | Mercury MEP 9506 | PRESENTING RUSTY DRAPER (EP) | 40 |
| 59 | Mercury ZEP 10016 | RUSTY DRAPER (EP) | 20 |
| 60 | Mercury ZEP 10059 | RUSTY IN GAMBLING MOOD (EP) | 20 |
| 60 | Mercury ZEP 10095 | MULE SKINNER BLUES (EP) | 25 |
| 64 | London RE-U 1431 | RUSTY DRAPER NO. 1 (EP) | 20 |
| 64 | London RE-U 1432 | RUSTY DRAPER NO. 2 (EP) | 20 |

## MIKEY DREAD (AKA MICKEY CAMPBELL )
| | | | |
|---|---|---|---|
| 79 | Do It DUNE 24 | Heavyweight Style/Rub A Dub (12") | 20 |
| 79 | Warrior WAR 125 | Barber Saloon/CARLTON PATTERSON: Wash Wash (12") | 20 |
| 80 | Dread At The Controls DREAD 1 | Break Down The Walls/Jumping Master (12") | 15 |
| 81 | Dread At The Controls DATC 003 | Warrior Stylee/Israel Stylee (12") | 25 |
| 82 | Dread At The Controls DATCD 008 | Roots & Culture/Jungle Dread (12") | 25 |
| 82 | Dread At The Controls DATCD10 | Warning/Death Squad/Manslaughter (12") | 10 |
| 77 | Hawkeye HALP 001 | DUB (LP) | 15 |
| 79 | Dread At The Controls DTCLP 002 | AFRICAN ANTHEM – THE MIKEY DREAD SHOW DUBWISE (LP) | 30 |
| 79 | Trojan TRLS178 | DREAD AT THE CONTROLS (LP) | 15 |
| 80 | Dread At The Controls DTCLP 006 | WORLD WAR III (LP) | 18 |
| 80 | Dread At The Controls DTLP 001 | MASTER SHOWCASE (LP) | 30 |
| 82 | Dread At The Controls DATCD 005 | DUB CATALOGUE VOLUME 1 (LP) | 20 |
| 82 | Dread At The Controls DATCLP 008 | JUNGLE SIGNAL (LP) | 30 |
| 82 | Dread At The Controls RIDE 19 | SWALK (LP) | 15 |
| 83 | Dread At The Controls DTLP 009 | DUB MERCHANT (LP) | 30 |

## DREAD & FRED
| | | | |
|---|---|---|---|
| 89 | Jah Shaka SHAKA 870 | Warriors Stance/Warriors Advance (12") | 12 |
| 89 | Jah Shaka SHAKA 875 | IRON WORKS (LP) | 20 |

## DREADZONE
| | | | |
|---|---|---|---|
| 93 | Creation CRELP 162 | 360 DEGREES (LP) | 20 |
| 94 | Totem TTPLP 002 | PERFORMANCE (LP) | 15 |
| 95 | Virgin V 2778 | SECOND LIGHT (2-LP) | 18 |

## DREAMBOYS
| | | | |
|---|---|---|---|
| 80 | St Vitus SV1 | Bela Lugosi's Birthday/Outer Limits/Shall We Dance | 25 |

## DREAM CYCLE 7
| | | | |
|---|---|---|---|
| 82 | SRT 82 CUS 1041 | I'll Please Myself/Who's To Blame | 10 |

## DREAMERS
| | | | |
|---|---|---|---|
| 68 | Columbia DB 8340 | The Maybe Song/The Long Road | 10 |
| 69 | Downtown DT 407 | Sweet Chariot/Let's Go Downtown | 20 |

(see also Freddie & Dreamers)

## DREAMERS
| | | | |
|---|---|---|---|
| 69 | Downtown DT 408 | I Second That Emotion/Dear Love | 10 |

**DREAMLETS**
| | | | |
|---|---|---|---|
| 65 | Ska Beat JB 182 | Really Now/SKATALITES: Street Corner | 50 |

**DREAMLOVERS**
| | | | |
|---|---|---|---|
| 61 | Columbia DB 4711 | When We Get Married/Just Because | 200 |

*(see also Chubby Checker)*

**DREAM MERCHANTS**
| | | | |
|---|---|---|---|
| 67 | Decca F 12617 | Rattler/I'll Be With You In Apple Blossom Time | 10 |

**DREAM POLICE**
| | | | |
|---|---|---|---|
| 70 | Decca F 12998 | I'll Be Home (In A Day Or So)/Living Is Easy | 10 |
| 70 | Decca F 13078 | Our Song/Much Too Much | 8 |
| 70 | Decca F 13105 | I've Got No Choice/What's The Cure For Happiness? | 8 |

*(see also Average White Band)*

**DREAMS**
| | | | |
|---|---|---|---|
| 68 | United Artists UP 2249 | I Will See You There/A Boy Needs A Girl | 35 |
| 69 | CBS 4247 | Baby I'm Your Man/Softly, Softly | 25 |
| 69 | Dolphin 4432 | Casatschok/Don't You Ask Me | 7 |
| 70 | CBS 64203 | DREAMS (LP) | 20 |
| 72 | CBS 64597 | IMAGINE MY SURPRISE (LP) | 20 |

**DREAM THEATER**
| | | | |
|---|---|---|---|
| 94 | East West A 5835 | Lie/Space-Dye Vest/To Live Forever/Another Day (live) (p/s) | 8 |
| 94 | East West A 5835 T | Lie/Take The Time (Demo)/Space-Dye Vest (12", p/s) | 10 |
| 92 | Atco 7567 92148 1 | IMAGES AND WORDS (LP) | 15 |

**DREAMTIMERS**
| | | | |
|---|---|---|---|
| 61 | London HLU 9368 | The Dancin' Lady/An Invitation | 20 |

**DREAM WEAVERS**
| | | | |
|---|---|---|---|
| 56 | Brunswick 05515 | It's Almost Tomorrow/You've Got Me Wondering (gold label lettering) | 30 |
| 56 | Brunswick 05515 | It's Almost Tomorrow/You've Got Me Wondering (silver label lettering) | 10 |
| 56 | Brunswick 05568 | A Little Love Can Go A Long, Long Way/Into The Night (featuring Wade Buff) | 12 |
| 56 | Brunswick 05607 | You're Mine/Is There Somebody Else? (featuring Wade Buff) | 8 |

**MIKE DRED**
| | | | |
|---|---|---|---|
| 90 | Machine Codes DH VOL 1 | THE MIGHTY DRED EP (12") | 12 |
| 93 | Machine Codes CODE A | FU-CHIN-RA EP (12") | 10 |

**DRED & FRED**
| | | | |
|---|---|---|---|
| 92 | Ironworks D&F 001 | Down Too Long/CREATIVE STEPPERS: Creative Version (12") | 30 |

**DREGS**
| | | | |
|---|---|---|---|
| 79 | Disturbing DRO 1 | THE DREGS EP (p/s, numbered, stamped sleeve, 500 only) | 50 |

**LEN DRESSLAR**
| | | | |
|---|---|---|---|
| 56 | Mercury 7MT 3 | Chain Gang/These Hands (export issue) | 10 |

**JOHN DREVAR('S EXPRESSION)**
| | | | |
|---|---|---|---|
| 67 | MGM MGM 1367 | The Closer She Gets/When I Come Home | 200 |
| 67 | MGM MGM 1367 | The Closer She Gets/When I Come Home (DJ Copy) | 300 |
| 68 | Polydor BM 56290 | What Greater Love/I've Decided (solo) | 10 |

**ALAN DREW**
| | | | |
|---|---|---|---|
| 63 | Columbia DB 7090 | Here Comes The Rain/Always The Lonely One | 5 |

**PATTI DREW**
| | | | |
|---|---|---|---|
| 68 | Capitol CL 15557 | Workin' On A Groovy Thing/Without A Doubt | 15 |
| 68 | Capitol CL 15575 | Hard To Handle/Just Can't Forget About You | 8 |

**DREXCIYA**
| | | | |
|---|---|---|---|
| 93 | Rephlex Cat 017 | 3 - MOLECULAR ENHANCEMENT EP (12", 4-track) | 25 |
| 95 | Warp WAP 57 | THE JOURNEY HOME EP (12", company sleeve) | 25 |

**DRIFTERS (U.K.)**
| | | | |
|---|---|---|---|
| 59 | Columbia DB 4263 | Feelin' Fine/Don't Be A Fool (With Love) | 50 |
| 59 | Columbia DB 4263 | Feelin' Fine/Don't Be A Fool (With Love) (78) | 50 |
| 59 | Columbia DB 4325 | Driftin'/Jet Black | 45 |

*(see also Shadows, Cliff Richard, Jet Harris, Tony Meehan)*

**DRIFTERS (U.S.)**

**78s**
| | | | |
|---|---|---|---|
| 56 | London HLE 8344 | Soldier Of Fortune/I Gotta Get Myself A Woman | 50 |
| 58 | London HLE 8686 | Moonlight Bay/Drip-Drop | 50 |
| 59 | London HLE 8892 | There Goes My Baby/Oh, My Love | 70 |
| 59 | London HLE 8988 | Dance With Me/True Love, True Love | 80 |
| 60 | London HLE 9081 | This Magic Moment/Baltimore | 100 |

**SINGLES**
| | | | |
|---|---|---|---|
| 56 | London HLE 8344 | Soldier Of Fortune/I Gotta Get Myself A Woman | 1000 |
| 58 | London HLE 8686 | Moonlight Bay/Drip-Drop | 150 |
| 59 | London HLE 8892 | There Goes My Baby/Oh, My Love | 30 |
| 59 | London HLE 8988 | Dance With Me/True Love, True Love | 15 |
| 60 | London HLE 9081 | This Magic Moment/Baltimore | 18 |
| 60 | London HLK 9145 | Lonely Winds/Hey Senorita | 18 |
| 60 | London HLK 9201 | Save The Last Dance For Me/Nobody But Me | 5 |
| 61 | London HLK 7114 | Save The Last Dance For Me/This Magic Moment (export issue) | 10 |
| 61 | London HLK 7115 | I Count The Tears/Dance With Me (export issue) | 20 |
| 61 | London HLK 9287 | I Count The Tears/Sadie My Lady | 25 |
| 61 | London HLK 9326 | Some Kind Of Wonderful/Honey Bee | 15 |
| 61 | London HLK 9382 | Please Stay/No Sweet Lovin' | 15 |
| 61 | London HLK 9427 | Sweets For My Sweet/Loneliness Or Happiness | 10 |

|  |  |  | MINT VALUE £ |
|---|---|---|---|
| 62 | London HLK 9500 | Room Full Of Tears/Somebody New Dancin' With You | 10 |
| 62 | London HLK 9522 | When My Little Girl Is Smiling/Mexican Divorce | 10 |
| 62 | London HLK 9554 | Stranger On The Shore/What To Do | 8 |
| 62 | London HLK 9626 | Up On The Roof/Another Night With The Boys | 10 |
| 63 | London HLK 9699 | On Broadway/Let The Music Play | 15 |
| 63 | London HLK 9750 | Rat Race/If You Don't Come Back | 15 |
| 63 | London HLK 9785 | I'll Take You Home/I Feel Good All Over | 8 |
| 64 | London HLK 9848 | Vaya Con Dios/In The Land Of Make Believe | 8 |
| 64 | London HLK 9886 | One Way Love/Didn't It | 10 |
| 64 | Atlantic AT 4001 | Under The Boardwalk/I Don't Want To Go On Without You | 12 |
| 64 | Atlantic AT 4008 | I've Got Sand In My Shoes/He's Just A Playboy | 12 |
| 64 | Atlantic AT 4012 | Saturday Night At The Movies/Spanish Lace | 15 |
| 65 | Atlantic AT 4019 | At The Club/Answer The Phone | 12 |
| 65 | Atlantic AT 4023 | Come On Over To My Place/Chains Of Love | 15 |
| 65 | Atlantic AT 4034 | Follow Me/The Outside World | 12 |
| 65 | Atlantic AT 4040 | I'll Take You Where The Music's Playing/Far From The Maddening Crowd | 15 |
| 66 | Atlantic AT 4062 | We Gotta Sing/Nylon Stockings | 12 |
| 66 | Atlantic AT 4084 | Memories Are Made Of This/My Island In The Sun | 15 |
| 66 | Atlantic 584 020 | Up In The Streets Of Harlem/You Can't Love 'Em All | 15 |
| 67 | Atlantic 584 065 | Baby What I Mean/Aretha | 15 |
| 68 | Atlantic 584 152 | I'll Take You Where The Music's Playing/On Broadway | 20 |
| 68 | Atlantic 584 195 | Still Burning In My Heart/I Need You Now | 12 |
| 69 | Atlantic 584 246 | Saturday Night At The Movies/Under The Boardwalk | 10 |
| 71 | Atlantic 2091 064 | A Rose By Any Other Name/Be My Lady | 6 |
| 75 | Atlantic K10700 | You Gotta Pay Your Dues/One Way Love | 7 |
| 77 | Arista 94 | I'll Know When True Love Really Passes By/A Good Song Never Dies | 10 |
| 78 | Arista 202 | Closely Guarded Secret/I Can't Believe It's Over | 18 |
| 79 | Epic EPC 7806 | Pour Your Little Heart Out Parts 1 & 2 | 10 |

**EPs**

| 61 | London RE-K 1282 | THE DRIFTERS' GREATEST HITS | 50 |
|---|---|---|---|
| 61 | London RE-K 1282 | THE DRIFTERS' GREATEST HITS | 20 |
| 63 | London RE-K 1355 | THE DRIFTERS | 20 |
| 63 | London RE-K 1385 | DRIFTIN' | 20 |
| 64 | Atlantic AET 6003 | DRIFTIN' VOL. 2 | 20 |
| 65 | Atlantic AET 6012 | TONIGHT | 20 |

## ALBUMS

| 60 | London HA-K 2318 | THE DRIFTERS' GREATEST HITS | 50 |
|---|---|---|---|
| 62 | London HA-K 2450 | SAVE THE LAST DANCE FOR ME | 30 |
| 65 | Atlantic ATL 5015 | OUR BIGGEST HITS | 20 |
| 65 | Atlantic ATL/STL 5023 | THE GOOD LIFE WITH THE DRIFTERS (mono/stereo) | 20 |
| 66 | Atlantic ATL/STL 5039 | I'LL TAKE YOU WHERE THE MUSIC'S PLAYING (mono/stereo) | 20 |
| 67 | Atlantic 587 038 | BIGGEST HITS | 15 |
| 67 | Atlantic 590 010 | SOUVENIRS | 18 |
| 68 | Atlantic 587 123 | ROCKIN' AND DRIFTIN' | 35 |
| 68 | Atlantic 587 144 | GOOD GRAVY (as Clyde McPhatter & Drifters) | 45 |
| 69 | Atlantic 587/588 160 | UP ON THE ROOF | 15 |

*(see also Clyde McPhatter, Ben E. King, Bobby Hendricks)*

## DRIFTING SLIM
| 66 | Blue Horizon 45-1005 | Good Morning Baby/My Sweet Woman (99 copies only) | 175 |
|---|---|---|---|

## DRIFTWOOD
| 70 | Decca F 13084 | Shylock Bay/The Wind Cries Above You | 6 |
|---|---|---|---|
| 71 | Decca F 13139 | Say The Right Things/Still I'll Stay With You | 6 |
| 70 | Decca SKL 5069 | DRIFTWOOD (LP, blue/silver label with boxed logo) | 100 |

*(see also Neil Harrison)*

## DRINKING ELECTRICITY
| 80 | Pop Aural POP 004 | Shaking All Over China (p/s) | 5 |
|---|---|---|---|
| 80 | Pop Aural POP 005 | Shake Some Action/Shake Some Action (Cheap Version) | 8 |
| 80 | Pop Aural POP 008 | Cruising Missiles/Shaking All Over (Dub) (p/s) | 8 |
| 81 | Survival SUR 001 | Subliminal/Random Particles | 8 |
| 82 | Survival SUR 122 | Subliminal/Breakout (12") | 10 |
| 82 | Survival SUR LP 001 | OVERLOAD (LP) | 20 |

## JULIE DRISCOLL
| 63 | Columbia DB 7118 | Take Me By The Hand/Stay Away From Me | 30 |
|---|---|---|---|
| 65 | Parlophone R 5296 | Don't Do It No More/I Know You | 30 |
| 66 | Parlophone R 5444 | I Didn't Want To Have To Do It/Don't Do It No More | 25 |
| 67 | Parlophone R 5588 | I Know You Love Me Not/If You Should Ever Leave Me | 20 |
| 67 | Marmalade 598 005 | Save Me Pts 1 & 2 | 30 |
| 71 | Polydor 2383077 | JULIE DRISCOLL — 1969 (LP) | 60 |

## JULIE DRISCOLL, BRIAN AUGER & TRINITY
| 68 | Marmalade 598 006 | This Wheel's On Fire/A Kind Of Love In (3-print push out or large centre, Marmalade sleeve) | 8 |
|---|---|---|---|
| 68 | Marmalade 598 011 | Road To Cairo/Shadows Of You | 8 |
| 69 | Marmalade 598 018 | Take Me To The Water/Indian Rope Man | 8 |
| 67 | Marmalade 607002 | OPEN (mono, first pressing, with 1-sided insert and non laminated cover produced by "Upton Printing") | 175 |
| 67 | Marmalade 607 002 | OPEN (LP, mono) | 125 |
| 67 | Marmalade 608 002 | OPEN (LP, stereo) | 100 |
| 68 | M. For Pleasure MFP 1265 | JOOLS/BRIAN (LP, tracks shared by Julie Driscoll & Brian Auger) | 20 |
| 69 | Marmalade 608 005/6 | STREET NOISE (2-LP, gatefold sleeve) | 300 |
| 69 | Marmalade 608 014 | STREET NOISE PART 1 (LP) | 35 |

| 69 | Marmalade 608 015 | STREET NOISE PART 2 (LP) | 35 |
| 70 | Polydor 2334004 | BEST OF (LP, 99p series) | 20 |

(see also Brian Auger & Trinity, Working Week, Julie Tippetts, B.B. Blunder)

## DRIVE
| 77 | NRG NE 467 | Jerkin'/Push'N'Shove (no p/s) | 50 |

## DRIVER
| 79 | Rods ROD 1 | Like A Mirror/Here I Am (p/s) | 20 |
| 79 | Rods ROD 2 | I'm Not Dreaming/So They Say | 15 |
| 80 | Rods HOT 1 | YOU BETTER TAKE IT (LP, 300 only) | 60 |

## DRIVERS
| 83 | Greyhound GRK 701 | Talk All Night/Sister (p/s) | 6 |
| 84 | Nouveau NMS 5 | Things/Stolen Treasure (p/s) | 6 |

(see also Nick Van Eede)

## DRIVESHAFT
| 80 | Undercover DC 02 | Cold As Ice/I Know What You Are After (features Noel Redding who also produced the single) | 50 |
| 82 | Undercover DC 03 | Heartbreaker/Now That It's Over (p/s) | 25 |

## DRIZABONE
| 91 | 4th & Broadway BRW 223 | Real Love/Real Love (Instrumental) | 5 |
| 94 | 4th & Broadway 12 BRW 264 | Pressure (Roger's Soul Sensation Mix)/Pressure (Album version)/Pressure (Bonus Beats Mix)/Pressure (Bone Idol Remix)/Pressure (Nu Solution Mix)/Pressure (Underground Network Mix) (12", p/s) | 30 |

## D-ROK
| 91 | Warhammer DROK 08722 | Get Out Of My Way (D-Mix)/Renegade/Get Out Of My Way (Airnix) (12", p/s) | 10 |

(see also Brian May)

## FRANK D'RONE
| 59 | Mercury ART 1040 | Fascinating Rhythm/Yesterdays | 5 |
| 60 | Mercury AMT 1123 | Strawberry Blonde (The Band Rocked On)/Time Hurries By | 6 |
| 59 | Mercury ZEP 10116 | THE BAND ROCKED ON (EP) | 10 |

## DRONES (1)
| 77 | Valer VRS 1 | Bone Idle/I Just Wanna Be Myself (gatefold p/s, made in France) | 12 |
| 77 | Valer VRS 1 | Bone Idle/I Just Wanna Be Myself (gatefold p/s, made in England) | 6 |
| 77 | Valer VRSP 1 | Be My Baby/Lift Off The Bans (12", white label, unreleased) | 50 |
| 77 | Valer | Be My Baby (Take Two)/The Clique (white label, unrel., many autographed) | 20 |
| 77 | Ohms GOOD MIX 1 | TEMPTATIONS OF A WHITE COLLAR WORKER (EP, different coloured sleeves, some with writing on inner sleeve) | 15 |
| 80 | Fabulous JC 4 | Can't See/Fooled Today (p/s) | 7 |
| 77 | Valer VRLP 1 | FURTHER TEMPTATIONS (LP) | 35 |

## DRONES (2)
| 06 | ATP ATPRLP 22 | GALA MILL (2-LP) | 30 |

## DRONGOS FOR EUROPE
| 81 | Kite DFE 001 | ADVERSE CHORUS EP | 40 |
| 82 | Inferno HELL 3 | DEATH'S A CAREER (EP, p/s with insert) | 10 |
| 82 | Inferno HELL 6 | ETERNITY EP (p/s) | 8 |

## DROP
| 81 | Dropped SRTS/81/CUS 929 | He Doesn't Know He's Trendy/Death In The Afternoon/I'm Wearing An Appliance | 20 |

## DROP NINETEENS
| 92 | Hut HUTLP 4 | DELAWARE (LP) | 25 |

## DROWNING CRAZE
| 81 | Situation 2 SIT 3 | Storage Case/Damp Bones (p/s) | 8 |
| 81 | Situation 2 SIT 13 | Trance/I Love The Fjords (p/s) | 8 |
| 82 | Situation 2 SIT 16 | Heat/Replays (p/s) | 8 |

## DRUDGE
| 90 | Deaf DEAF 01 | SUPPOSE IT WAS YOU (split LP with Agathocles) | 20 |

## DRUG ADDIX
| 78 | Chiswick SW 39 | MAKE A RECORD (EP) | 12 |

(see also Kirsty MacColl)

## DRUID
| 76 | EMI SPSR 395 | Barnaby- Kestrel/Nothing But Morning | 12 |
| 75 | EMI EMC 3081 | TOWARDS THE SUN (LP, textured, with inner sleeve) | 20 |
| 76 | EMI EMC 3128 | FLUID DRUID (LP, with inner sleeve) | 20 |

## DRUID CHASE
| 67 | CBS 3053 | Take Me In Your Garden/I Wanna Get My Hands On You | 30 |

## DRUIDS (1)
| 63 | Parlophone R 5097 | Long Tall Texan/Love So Blue | 20 |
| 64 | Parlophone R 5134 | It's Just A Little Bit Too Late/See What You've Done | 20 |

## DRUIDS (2)
| 71 | Argo ZFB 22 | BURNT OFFERING (LP) | 80 |
| 73 | Argo ZFB 39 | PASTIME WITH GOOD COMPANY (LP) | 60 |

(see also Giles Farnaby's Dream Band)

## DRUM CLUB
| 93 | Butterfly BFLT10A | Sound System Volume 1 (12") | 10 |
| 93 | Big Life DC PROMO 2 | Big Life (2 x 12" promo) | 15 |

## DRUMBAGO
| 63 | Island WI 085 | I Am Drunk (actually by Raymond Harper & Drumbago's Group)/Sea Breeze (actually by Sammy & Drumbago's Group) | 20 |
| 68 | Blue Cat BS 145 | Reggae Jeggae (with Blenders)/TYRONE TAYLOR: Delilah | 60 |
| 69 | Trojan TR 638 | Dulcemania (with Dynamites)/CLANCY ECCLES: China Man | 40 |

MINT VALUE £

*(see also Derrick Patsy, Dennis Walks)*

## BILL DRUMMOND
| | | | |
|---|---|---|---|
| 87 | Creation CRE 039T | King Of Joy/The Manager (12", p/s) | 25 |
| 86 | Creation CRELP 014 | THE MAN (LP) | 20 |

*(see also Big In Japan, Lori & Chameleons, KLF, Disco 2000, Timelords)*

## DON DRUMMOND
| | | | |
|---|---|---|---|
| 62 | Island WI 021 | Schooling The Duke/Bitter Rose (as Don Drummond Orchestra; B-side is actually by Shenley Duffus) | 30 |
| 63 | Black Swan WI 406 | Scrap Iron/DRAGONAIRE: Prevention | 25 |
| 63 | Blue Beat BB 179 | Reload/Far East | 30 |
| 63 | Island WI 094 | Scandal/My Ideal (B-side actually by W. Sparks) | 25 |
| 63 | R&B JB 103 | Royal Flush/MAYTALS: Matthew Mark | 25 |
| 63 | R&B JB 105 | The Shock/TONETTES: Tell Me You're Mine | 25 |
| 64 | Ska Beat JB 178 | Silver Dollar/TOMMY McCOOK: My Business | 30 |
| 64 | Island WI 149 | Eastern Standard Time/DOTTY & BONNIE: Sun Rises | 25 |
| 64 | Island WI 153 | Musical Storeroom/STRANGER COLE: He Who Feels | 25 |
| 64 | Island WI 162 | Garden Of Love/STRANGER COLE: Cherry May | 40 |
| 65 | Island WI 192 | Stampede (with Drumbago)/JUSTIN HINDS & DOMINOES: Come Bail Me | 25 |
| 65 | Island WI 204 | Coolie Baby/LORD ANTICS: You May Stray | 25 |
| 65 | Island WI 208 | Man In The Street/RITA & BENNY: You Are My Only Love | 40 |
| 65 | Island WI 242 | University Goes Ska/DERRICK & NAOMI: Pain In My Heart | 40 |
| 69 | Studio One SO 2078 | Heavenless/GLEN BROWN & DAVE BARKER: Lady Lovelight | 45 |
| 69 | Trojan TR 678 | Memory Of Don/JOHN HOLT: Darling I Love You | 15 |
| 69 | Coxsone CSL 8021 | IN MEMORY OF DON DRUMMOND (LP) | 150 |
| 69 | Studio One SO 9008 | THE BEST OF DON DRUMMOND (LP) | 200 |
| 69 | Trojan TTL 23 | MEMORIAL ALBUM (LP) | 40 |

*(see also Joe White, Rhythm Aces, Roy & Millie, Movers, Desmond Dekker, Shenley Duffas, Hi-Tones, Duke Reid, Soul Brothers, Baba Brooks, Bonnie & Skitto, Eric Morris, Pioneers, Stranger & Patsy, Techniques, Winston Wright)*

## DON DRUMMOND JUNIOR
| | | | |
|---|---|---|---|
| 67 | Caltone TONE 104 | Sir Pratt Special/HEMSLEY MORRIS: Love Is Strange | 90 |
| 68 | Caltone TONE 124 | Dirty Dozen/PHIL PRATT: Reach Out | 90 |
| 70 | Jackpot JP 710 | Memory Of Don Drummond/TOBIES: Resting | 20 |
| 82 | Rush NIBZ 001 | The Clash And The Specials Go To Jail/Jailbird Dub/Rudies Ska (12", p/s) | 25 |

*(see also Vincent Gordon)*

## JOHN DRUMMOND
| | | | |
|---|---|---|---|
| 68 | Page One POF 084 | Break My Mind/Molly Bye Bye | 7 |

## K. DRUMMOND
| | | | |
|---|---|---|---|
| 73 | Jackpot JP 810 | Your Pretty Face/Your Pretty Face (Version) | 5 |

*(see also Cables)*

## KEITH DRUMMOND
| | | | |
|---|---|---|---|
| 82 | Bengad | Love Grows/(Version) (12") | 20 |

## LEE DRUMMOND
| | | | |
|---|---|---|---|
| 66 | Fontana TF 728 | Messrs Lindsay, Parker & Flynn/Sitting And Drinking Alone | 8 |

## PETE DRUMMOND & THE VHF BAND
| | | | |
|---|---|---|---|
| 72 | Warner Bros K 16232 | Rocking At The BBC/Goodbye (vinyl 78) | 20 |

## DRUNKEN MASTER
| | | | |
|---|---|---|---|
| 93 | Kold Sweat KSEP209 | DEVIL IN DISGUISE (EP) | 12 |

*(see also SLR/Dashy D & Cue Tips)*

## REGINA DRUTTON
| | | | |
|---|---|---|---|
| 68 | CBS 5684 | A Hard Man Is Good To Hold Onto/Tell Me Lies Again | 5 |

## DRY FRUIT
| | | | |
|---|---|---|---|
| 70 | Staple ST 004 | Magic Thimble/The Die Is Cast | 40 |

## DRY ICE
| | | | |
|---|---|---|---|
| 69 | B&C CB 115 | Running To The Convent/Nowhere To Go | 25 |

*(see also Pluto)*

## DRY RIB
| | | | |
|---|---|---|---|
| 79 | Clockwork COR 001 | THE DRY SEASON (EP, 33rpm, photocopied foldover p/s, screen-printed labels) | 30 |

*(see also Television Personalities, Times, L'Orange Mechanik)*

## DRY WATERS
| | | | |
|---|---|---|---|
| 72 | Denby DEN 003 | Crystal Ball/The Magic Valley | 150 |

## AMANCIO D'SILVA
| | | | |
|---|---|---|---|
| 69 | Columbia S(C)X 6322 | INTEGRATION (LP) | 600 |
| 71 | Columbia SCX 6465 | REFLECTIONS (LP) | 30 |

*(see also Cosmic Eye, Joe Harriott)*

## D.S.K.F.
| | | | |
|---|---|---|---|
| 92 | WG 001 | NEW SCIENCE EP (12", stickered white label) | 70 |

## D.S.P.
| | | | |
|---|---|---|---|
| 92 | FX FXUKT 10 | Obsession/Revenge Attack/Intravenus/Kebab (12") | 20 |

## D TO THE K
| | | | |
|---|---|---|---|
| 88 | BPM BP12004 | Hard But Live/Ease Up Your Mind (12") | 25 |

## DTS
| | | | |
|---|---|---|---|
| 81 | Marvo MVO 002 | Bsa Rocket 111/Lonesome | 10 |
| 84 | Marvo AM 130 | Willy & The Hand Jive/Roadrunner | 10 |

## DUALS
| | | | |
|---|---|---|---|
| 61 | London HL 9450 | Stick Shift/Cruising | 25 |

## DUB JUDAH
| | | | |
|---|---|---|---|
| 90 | Dub Jockey DJ0012 | No Tresspassers/FOUNDATION PLAYERS: Version (12") | 15 |

| | | | |
|---|---|---|---|
| 92 | Dub Jockey DJ021 | Babylon Is A Trap/Version | 15 |
| 93 | Dub Jockey DJO24 | Fishers Of Men/Dub Fisher | 12 |
| 94 | Dub Jockey DJO30 | Revolution Revelation/Rev Dub | 12 |
| 95 | Dub Jockey DJO31 | Never Slumber/Ever Alert Dub | 10 |
| 92 | Dub Jockey DJLP 002 | BABYLON IS A TRAP (LP) | 30 |
| 93 | Dub Jockey DJLP 003 | DUBTECH DUB (LP) | 20 |
| 94 | Dub Jockey DJLP 004 | BETTER TO BE GOOD (LP) | 30 |

## DUB PLATE VIBE CREW
| | | | |
|---|---|---|---|
| 96 | Solar Dub SOLD 12003 | Respect Jah/Dub/Jah Putting On The Press (12") | 12 |

## DUBBING IN THE U.K.
| | | | |
|---|---|---|---|
| 81 | Star Light SDLP 902 | DUBBING IN THE U.K.(LP) | 30 |

## DUB FACTORY
| | | | |
|---|---|---|---|
| 95 | Dub Factory GEMCD 001 | VOYAGE INTO DUB - THE 1st JOURNEY (LP) | 18 |

## DUBKASM
| | | | |
|---|---|---|---|
| 04 | Sufferah's Choice DUBK02 | Displaced African/Higher Judgement (12") | 20 |
| 05 | Sufferah's Choice DUBK03 | Deh Inna De Lion's Den/Iration Steppas MIx (12" featuring Iration Steppas) | 20 |

## DUBS
| | | | |
|---|---|---|---|
| 57 | London HLU 8526 | Could This Be Magic/Such Lovin' | 250 |
| 57 | London HLU 8526 | Could This Be Magic/Such Lovin' (78) | 40 |
| 58 | London HL 8684 | Gonna Make A Change/Beside My Love | 200 |
| 58 | London HL 8684 | Gonna Make A Change/Beside My Love (78) | 30 |

## DUB SYNDICATE
| | | | |
|---|---|---|---|
| 84 | On-U Sound ON-U LP 18 | POUNDING SYSTEM (LP) | 15 |
| 86 | On-U Sound ON-U LP 38 | TUNES FROM THE MISSING CHANNEL (LP) | 20 |
| 89 | On-U Sound ON-U LP4 | STRIKE THE BALANCE (LP) | 15 |
| 91 | On-U Sound ON-U LP5 | STONED IMMACULATE (LP) | 15 |

## DIANE DUCANE
| | | | |
|---|---|---|---|
| 79 | Contact WN 2 | Better Late Than Never/One Day | 30 |

## JOHN DU CANN
| | | | |
|---|---|---|---|
| 77 | Arista ARIST 128 | Throw Him In Jail/Street Stutter | 5 |
| 77 | Arista ARIST 145 | Where's The Show/Hang Around | 5 |
| 79 | Vertigo 6059 241 | Don't Be A Dummy/If I'm Makin' (p/s) | 5 |

*(see also Attack, Andromeda, Five Day Week Straw People, Atomic Rooster, Hard Stuff, Status Quo)*

## DUCHESS OF BEDFORD
| | | | |
|---|---|---|---|
| 56 | HMV POP 361 | Luck's In Love With You/MRS GERALD LEGGE: I'm In Love | 8 |

## DUCKS DELUXE
| | | | |
|---|---|---|---|
| 73 | RCA RCA 2438 | Coast To Coast/Bring Back That Packard Car | 6 |
| 74 | RCA 2477 | Love's Melody/Two Times Twister | 6 |
| 75 | RCA RCA 2531 | I Fought The Law/Cherry Pie | 6 |
| 74 | RCA LPL1 5008 | DUCKS DELUXE (LP) | 15 |
| 74 | RCA SF 8402 | TAXI TO THE TERMINAL ZONE (LP) | 15 |

*(see also Tyla Gang, Brinsley Schwarz)*

## DUDLEY
| | | | |
|---|---|---|---|
| 60 | Vogue V 9171 | Lone Prairie Rock/El Pizza | 10 |

## DAVE DUDLEY
| | | | |
|---|---|---|---|
| 63 | United Artists UP 1029 | Six Days On The Road/I Feel A Cry Coming On | 10 |
| 67 | Mercury MF 1003 | Trucker's Prayer/Don't Come Cryin' To Me | 5 |
| 68 | Mercury MF 1037 | There Ain't No Easy Run/Why Can't I Be With You? (It's A Shame) | 5 |

## ROBERTA DUDLEY
| | | | |
|---|---|---|---|
| 51 | Poydras 3 | Krooked Blues/When You're Alone (shellac 45) | 8 |

*(see also Kid Ory)*

## DUET EMMO
| | | | |
|---|---|---|---|
| 81 | Mute MUTE 25 | OR SO IT SEEMS (12" EP) | 12 |

*(see also Dome, Wire)*

## DU-ETTES
| | | | |
|---|---|---|---|
| 72 | President PT 382 | Every Beat Of My Heart/Sugar Daddy | 8 |
| 72 | President PT 398 | Please Forgive Me/Lonely Days | 8 |

## D DUFFUS
| | | | |
|---|---|---|---|
| 79 | Jay Dee JD 009 | Is It Just A Dream/Cheaters (12") | 50 |

## SHENLEY DUFFAS
| | | | |
|---|---|---|---|
| 62 | Island WI 036 | Give To Get/What You Gonna Do (as S. Duffas; B-side actually with Millie Small) | 18 |
| 63 | Island WI 063 | Fret Man Fret/Doreen | 20 |
| 63 | Island WI 093 | What A Disaster/I Am Rich | 20 |
| 63 | Island WI 115 | Know The Lord/TOMMY McCOOK: Ska Ba | 45 |
| 63 | Island WI 125 | Easy Squeal/Things Ain't Going Right | 20 |
| 63 | R&B JB 134 | No More Wedding Bells/Let Them Fret | 15 |
| 64 | R&B JB 146 | Big Mouth/FRANKIE ANDERSON: Peanut Vendor | 25 |
| 64 | R&B JB 152 | Christopher Columbus/CARL BRYAN ORCHESTRA: Barber Chair | 18 |
| 64 | R&B JB 154 | Mother-In-Law/DON DRUMMOND & GROUP: Festival | 18 |
| 64 | Black Swan WI 440 | Digging A Ditch/He's Coming Down | 18 |
| 64 | Black Swan WI 443 | Gather Them In/Crucifixion | 20 |
| 64 | Rio R 41 | I Will Be Glad/Heariso (as Shandly Duffas) | 18 |
| 65 | Island WI 182 | La La La/UPCOMING WILLOWS: Jonestown Special | 40 |
| 65 | Island WI 184 | You Are Mine/UPCOMING WILLOWS: Red China | 30 |
| 65 | Island WI 186 | Rukumbine/One Morning | 35 |
| 72 | Upsetter US 380 | Bet You Don't Know/UPSETTERS: Ring Of Fire | 30 |
| 72 | Dynamic DYN 451 | Peace (with Soul Avengers)/UPSETTERS: Peace — Version | 7 |

# Chris DUFFIN

| | | | |
|---|---|---|---|
| 72 | Pama PM859 | At The End/Good Night My Love | 20 |
| 72 | Grape GR 3031 | Sincerely/Sincerely — Version (with Upsetters) | 8 |

*(see also Chenley Duffus, Billy Dyce)*

## CHRIS DUFFIN
| | | | |
|---|---|---|---|
| 76 | Deroy ADM LP 864 | HEY SANDY (LP) | 250 |

## DUFFO
| | | | |
|---|---|---|---|
| 79 | Beggars Banquet BEG 15 | Give Me Back My Brain/Duff Record | 5 |

## CHENLEY DUFFUS
| | | | |
|---|---|---|---|
| 72 | Upsetter US-386 | To Be A Lover/Baby Lose Burning | 10 |
| 72 | Pama PM 859 | At The End/Good Night My Love | 8 |

*(see also Shenley Duffas)*

## DUFFY (1)
| | | | |
|---|---|---|---|
| 73 | Chapter One SCHR 184 | The Joker/Running Away | 18 |
| 70 | Chapter One CHS-R 814 | SCRUFFY DUFFY (LP, red/silver label) | 300 |

## DUFFY (2)
| | | | |
|---|---|---|---|
| 04 | Awen REG150 CD | Dim Dealltwriaeth/Hedfan Angel/Cariad Dwi'n Unig (CD single as Aimee Duffy) | 25 |
| 07 | A&M 175 410-6 | Rockferry/Oh Boy (p/s, 1,500 only) | 10 |
| 08 | A&M Records 176 178-2 | Mercy/Save It For Your Prayers | 10 |

## CHRIS DUFFY
| | | | |
|---|---|---|---|
| 68 | SNB 55-3681 | Mr Jones Mr Brown Mr Smith And Not Forgetting Charlie Green/Something For Now | 10 |

## STEPHEN 'TIN TIN' DUFFY
| | | | |
|---|---|---|---|
| 85 | 10 | She Loves Me/She Loves It (p/s, withdrawn) | 40 |
| 85 | 10 | Baby Impossible (p/s, withdrawn) | 40 |

*(see also Hawks, Lilac Time)*

## DUFFY'S NUCLEUS
| | | | |
|---|---|---|---|
| 67 | Decca F 22547 | Hound Dog/Mary Open The Door | 50 |

*(see also Duffy Power, Pentangle, John McLaughlin)*

## DON DUGGAN
| | | | |
|---|---|---|---|
| 68 | Pye 7N 17633 | Let Her Dance/Westmeath Bachelor (with Savoys) | 6 |

## DUGZ
| | | | |
|---|---|---|---|
| 14 | Time and Matter T&M 015 | The Berlin Lights : Caught In A War/Hit The Floor | 20 |

## BILLY DUKE
| | | | |
|---|---|---|---|
| 62 | Ember EMB S 153 | Walking Cane/Amen | 5 |
| 62 | Ember EMB S 160 | Ain't She Pretty/Timbuctu | 5 |
| 64 | London HLU 9907 | While The Bloom Is On The Rose/I'm The Lonesomest Guy In Town | 5 |
| 65 | London HLU 9960 | Sugar'N'Spice/Prisoner Of Love | 5 |

## DENVER DUKE & JEFFREY NULL BLUEGRASS BOYS
| | | | |
|---|---|---|---|
| 63 | Starlite STEP 33 | DENVER DUKE & JEFFREY NULL BLUEGRASS BOYS (EP) | 15 |

## DORIS DUKE
| | | | |
|---|---|---|---|
| 71 | Mojo 2092 005 | To The Other Woman/I Don't Care Anymore | 8 |
| 71 | Mojo 2092 017 | If She's Your Wife Who Am I?/It Sure Was Fun | 15 |
| 73 | Mainstream MSS 302 | Business Deal/Nobody But You | 8 |
| 74 | Contempo CS2037 | Grasshopper/Please Come Back | 8 |
| 76 | Contempo CX15 | Woman Of The Ghetto/TAMIKO JONES: Let It Flow | 5 |
| 71 | Mojo 2916 001 | I'M A LOSER (LP) | 25 |
| 71 | Mojo 2916 006 | A LEGEND IN HER OWN TIME (LP) | 25 |
| 75 | Contempo CRM 111 | A LEGEND IN HER OWN TIME (LP, reissue) | 15 |
| 75 | Contempo CLP 519 | WOMAN (LP) | 20 |

## GEORGE DUKE
| | | | |
|---|---|---|---|
| 75 | MPS MC 25671 | I LOVE THE BLUES SHE HEARD ME CRY (LP) | 15 |

## PATTY DUKE
| | | | |
|---|---|---|---|
| 65 | United Artists UP 1103 | Don't Just Stand There/Everything But Love | 10 |
| 65 | United Artists UP 1116 | Say Something Funny/Funny Little Butterflies | 5 |
| 66 | United Artists UP 1131 | Whenever She Holds You/Nothing But You | 10 |
| 65 | United Artists (S)ULP 1123 | DON'T JUST STAND THERE (LP, mono/stereo) | 50 |

## DUKE SPIRIT
| | | | |
|---|---|---|---|
| 05 | Loog 987099 | CUTS ACROSS THE LAND (LP, textured gatefold sleeve) | 20 |
| 12 | Fiction 3700883 | DRESDEN LIVE (LP, 300 only) | 30 |

## JAMES DUKE
| | | | |
|---|---|---|---|
| 86 | Creole CRT 93 | Hold On/Zyzafon (12", p/s) | 250 |

## DUKE ALL STARS
| | | | |
|---|---|---|---|
| 68 | Blue Cat BS 111 | Letter To Mummy And Daddy (Parts 1 & 2) | 30 |

## DUKE & DUCHESS
| | | | |
|---|---|---|---|
| 55 | London HLU 8206 | Borrowed Sunshine/Get Ready For Love (with Sir Hubert Pimm) | 40 |

*(see also Sir Hubert Pimm)*

## DUKE OF BURLINGTON
| | | | |
|---|---|---|---|
| 71 | Decca F23120 | Flash/Slot Machine | 15 |

## AGGIE DUKES
| | | | |
|---|---|---|---|
| 57 | Vogue V 9090 | John John/Well Of Loneliness | 250 |
| 57 | Vogue V 9090 | John John/Well Of Loneliness (78) | 40 |

## DUKES NOBLEMEN
| | | | |
|---|---|---|---|
| 69 | Philips BF 1691 | City Of Windows/Thank You For Your Loving | 25 |

## DUKES OF ILLYRIA
| | | | |
|---|---|---|---|
| 70 | IAMBIG 0001 | Food Of Love/Come Away Death | 20 |

## DUKES OF STRATOSPHEAR
| | | | |
|---|---|---|---|
| 87 | Virgin VSY 982 | You're A Good Man Albert Brown/Vanishing Girl (p/s, 5,000 on multi-coloured vinyl) | 8 |

| | | |
|---|---|---|
| 85 | Virgin WOW 1 | 25 O'CLOCK (LP) ....................................................................................................... 20 |
| 87 | Virgin VP 2440 | PSONIC PSUNSPOT (LP, gatefold sleeve, 5,000 on multi-coloured vinyl) ...................... 30 |

*(see also XTC)*

## DULCIMER
| | | |
|---|---|---|
| 71 | Nepentha 6437 003 | AND I TURNED AS I HAD TURNED AS A BOY (LP, gatefold sleeve) ............................ 300 |
| 80 | Happy Face MMLP 1021 | A LAND FIT FOR HEROES (LP, private pressing)........................................................... 15 |

## LIZA DULITTLE
| | | |
|---|---|---|
| 68 | Pye 7N 17590 | I've Got To Get A Grip Of Myself/Did You Hear A Heart Break Last Night?..................... 8 |

*(see also Margo & Marvettes)*

## DUM
| | | |
|---|---|---|
| 74 | RAK RAK 179 | In The Mood/Watching The Clock .................................................................................. 5 |

*(see also Mud)*

## DUM DUM
| | | |
|---|---|---|
| 72 | Phillips 6414-318 | Peter Gunn/Cosa Nostra............................................................................................... 15 |

## JOHNNY DUMAR
| | | |
|---|---|---|
| 68 | CBS 3545 | Illusion/You Went Away ................................................................................................. 5 |

## DUMB ANGELS
| | | |
|---|---|---|
| 88 | Fierce FRIGHT 033 | Love And Mercy/Love And Mercy (p/s, numbered) ...................................................... 55 |

*(see also Pooh Sticks)*

## DUMBELLES
| | | |
|---|---|---|
| 80 | Polydor POSP 209/EGO 3 | Giddy Up/A Christmas Dream (no p/s) .......................................................................... 10 |

*(see also Roxy Music)*

## JOHN DUMMER (BLUES BAND)
| | | |
|---|---|---|
| 68 | Mercury MF 1040 | Travelling Man/40 Days (as John Dummer Blues Band) ................................................ 20 |
| 69 | Mercury MF 1119 | Try Me One More Time/Riding At Midnight (as John Dummer Blues Band) ................... 15 |
| 70 | Fontana 6007 027 | Happy/Nightingale (unissued in U.K.; France-only)........................................................ 0 |
| 70 | Philips 6006 111 | Nine By Nine/Going In The Out (credited to either Famous Music Band or John Dummer Band).......................................................................................................... 8 |
| 71 | Philips 6006 176 | Medicine Weasel/The Endgame (with Nick Pickett) ...................................................... 5 |
| 73 | Vertigo 6059 074 | Ooblee-Dooblee Jubilee/The Monkey Speaks His Mind (as John Dummer Oobleedooblee Band)................................................................................................. 5 |
| 69 | Mercury SMCL 20136 | CABAL (LP, black/silver label) ................................................................................... 200 |
| 69 | Mercury SMCL 20167 | JOHN DUMMER BAND (LP, black/silver label) ........................................................ 200 |
| 70 | Philips 6309 008 | FAMOUS MUSIC BAND (LP, gatefold sleeve, black/silver labels) ........................... 150 |
| 72 | Philips 6382 039 | THIS IS THE JOHN DUMMER BLUES BAND (LP) ...................................................... 20 |
| 73 | Philips 6382 040 | VOLUME II — TRY ME ONE MORE TIME (LP) .......................................................... 20 |
| 72 | Vertigo 6360 055 | BLUE (LP, gatefold sleeve, small swirl label) ........................................................... 500 |
| 73 | Vertigo 6360 083 | OOBLEEDOOBLEE JUBILEE (LP, as John Dummer Oobleedooblee Band, small swirl label)....................................................................................................................... 250 |

*(see also Nick Pickett, Dave Kelly, Famous Music Band, Tony McPhee)*

## DUMMIES
| | | |
|---|---|---|
| 79 | Cheapskate FWL 001 | When The Lights Are Out/She's The Only Woman (no p/s) ............................................ 8 |
| 80 | Pye 7P 163 | When The Lights Are Out/She's The Only Woman (no p/s, reissue) ............................... 5 |
| 80 | Cheapskate CHEAP 003 | Didn't You Used To Use To Be You?/Miles Out To Sea (p/s) ......................................... 8 |
| 81 | Cheapskate CHEAP 014 | Maybe Tonite/When I'm Dancin' I Ain't Fightin' (p/s) ................................................. 10 |

*(see also China Dolls, Slade)*

## DUNAMIS
| | | |
|---|---|---|
| 79 | Daybreak DB 2602 | I CAN FLY (LP, signed)................................................................................................. 60 |
| 79 | Daybreak DB 2602 | I CAN FLY (LP, un-signed) ........................................................................................... 15 |

## AYNSLEY DUNBAR (RETALIATION)
| | | |
|---|---|---|
| 67 | Blue Horizon 3109 | Warning/Cobwebs (in p/s) ........................................................................................... 60 |
| 67 | Blue Horizon 3109 | Warning/Cobwebs ....................................................................................................... 30 |
| 68 | Liberty LBF 15132 | Watch 'N' Chain/Roamin' And Ramblin'....................................................................... 15 |
| 68 | Liberty LBL/LBS 83154 | AYNSLEY DUNBAR RETALIATION (LP, mono/stereo) ............................................. 100 |
| 68 | Liberty LBL/LBS 83177 | DR. DUNBAR'S PRESCRIPTION (LP, mono/stereo) ................................................. 100 |
| 69 | Liberty LBS 83223 | TO MUM FROM AYNSLEY AND THE BOYS (LP)....................................................... 100 |
| 70 | Liberty LBS 83316 | REMAINS TO BE HEARD (LP) .................................................................................... 100 |
| 71 | Warner Bros WS 3010 | BLUE WHALE (LP, green label)..................................................................................... 70 |

*(see also John Mayall & Bluesbreakers, Heavy Jelly, Annette & Victor Brox, Excheckers)*

## SCOTT DUNBAR
| | | |
|---|---|---|
| 71 | Ahura Mazda AMS SDS 1 | FROM LAKE MARY (LP)................................................................................................ 30 |

## JOHNNY DUNCAN (& BLUE GRASS BOYS)
| | | |
|---|---|---|
| 57 | Columbia DB 3925 | Kaw-Liga/Ella Speed (gold label lettering)................................................................... 20 |
| 57 | Columbia DB 3925 | Kaw-Liga/Ella Speed (silver label lettering) .................................................................. 5 |
| 57 | Columbia DB 3959 | Last Train To San Fernando/Rock-A-Billy Baby (gold label lettering) ............................ 20 |
| 57 | Columbia DB 4029 | Footprints In The Snow/Get Along Home, Cindy............................................................ 6 |
| 57 | Columbia 33S 1122 | TENNESSEE SONG BAG (10" LP) ................................................................................ 30 |
| 58 | Columbia 33S 1129 | JOHNNY DUNCAN SALUTES HANK WILLIAMS (10" LP) ........................................... 30 |
| 61 | Columbia 33SX 1328 | BEYOND THE SUNSET (LP) ......................................................................................... 15 |

## LESLEY DUNCAN (& JOKERS)
| | | |
|---|---|---|
| 63 | Parlophone R 5034 | I Want A Steady Guy/Movin' Away (as Lesley Duncan & Jokers) .................................. 15 |
| 64 | Parlophone R 5106 | Tell Me/You Kissed Me Boy ......................................................................................... 15 |
| 64 | Mercury MF 830 | When My Baby Cries/Did It Hurt? ................................................................................ 10 |
| 65 | Mercury MF 847 | Just For The Boy/See That Guy ..................................................................................... 20 |
| 65 | Mercury MF 876 | Run To Love/Only The Lonely And Me ......................................................................... 20 |
| 65 | Mercury MF 939 | Hey Boy/I Go To Sleep.................................................................................................. 60 |
| 68 | RCA 1746 | Lullaby/I Love You, I Love You........................................................................................ 6 |
| 69 | CBS 4585 | Sing Children Sing/Exactly Who Are You ....................................................................... 7 |
| 79 | CBS 8061 | Sing Children Sing/Rainbow Games (p/s, with Kate Bush) ........................................... 10 |

## Tommy DUNCAN

| | | | |
|---|---|---|---|
| 71 | CBS 64202 | SING CHILDREN SING (LP, gatefold sleeve, orange labels) | 20 |
| 72 | CBS 64807 | EARTH MOTHER (LP, gatefold sleeve, orange labels) | 15 |
| 74 | GM GML 1007GM | EVERYTHING CHANGES (LP) | 15 |

*(see also Mitchell/Coe Mysteries, Pete Townshend, Phil Lynott, Madeline Bell, Joe Brown & Vicki Brown)*

## TOMMY DUNCAN
| | | | |
|---|---|---|---|
| 66 | Sue WI 4002 | Dance, Dance, Dance/Let's Try It Over Again | 40 |

## DIANE DUNCANE
| | | | |
|---|---|---|---|
| 79 | Contact 2 | Better Late Than Never/One Day (We're Gonna Do It Again) | 15 |

## DUNCANS
| | | | |
|---|---|---|---|
| 81 | Impact IMP 3 | Too Damn Hot/Communication (12") | 12 |

## DUNDEEVILLE PLAYERS
| | | | |
|---|---|---|---|
| 65 | Stateside SS451 | Wheels/Woodpecker | 7 |

## BARBARA DUNKLEY
| | | | |
|---|---|---|---|
| 71 | Banana BA 342 | We'll Cry Together/BOBBY DAVIS: Got To Get Away | 7 |

## DELROY DUNKLEY
| | | | |
|---|---|---|---|
| 70 | Hot Rod HR 109 | I Wish You Well/TONY & DELROY: Impossible Love | 20 |

## ERROL(L) DUNKLEY
| | | | |
|---|---|---|---|
| 67 | Rio R 109 | Love Me Forever/VIETNAM ALLSTARS: The Toughest | 100 |
| 67 | Rio R 131 | You're Gonna Need Me/Seek And You'll Find | 35 |
| 68 | Island WI 3150 | Once More/I'm Not Your Man | 35 |
| 68 | Amalgamated AMG 800 | Please Stop Your Lying/Feel So Fine (B-side actually by Tommy McCook & Band) | 35 |
| 68 | Amalgamated AMG 805 | I'm Going Home/I'm Not Your Man | 30 |
| 68 | Amalgamated AMG 807 | The Scorcher/Do It Right Tonight | 80 |
| 68 | Amalgamated AMG 820 | Love Brother/I Spy | 20 |
| 69 | Fab FAB 117 | I'll Take You In My Arms/KING CANNON: Daphney Reggae | 30 |
| 70 | Unity UN 554 | My Special Prayer/Never Hurt The One You Love | 7 |
| 70 | Banana BA 302 | Satisfaction/CECIL LOCKE: Sing Out Loud | 15 |
| 71 | Big BG 324 | Deep Meditation/RUPIE EDWARDS ALL STARS: Meditation Version | 20 |
| 71 | Big BG 327 | Three In One/RUPIE EDWARDS ALL STARS: One In Three | 8 |
| 71 | Nu Beat NB 091 | Three In One/RUPIE EDWARDS ALL STARS: One In Three | 10 |
| 71 | Explosion EX 2053 | O Lord/KEITH with IMPACT ALL STARS: Raindrops (B-side actually "My Baby" by Lloyd Charmers) | 8 |
| 72 | Camel CA 87 | Black Cinderella/PHIL PRATT ALLSTARS: Our Anniversary (B-side actually Tropic Shadows) | 12 |
| 73 | Grape GR 3039 | Why Did You Do It/One Love | 10 |
| 73 | Count Shelley CS 3039 | Girl You Cried/Where Must I Go | 10 |
| 73 | Ackee 507 | Keep The Pressure Down/Version | 10 |
| 75 | Kiss KISS 11 | Praise Jah All The Time/KISS ALLSTARS : Jah Rockers (12") | 45 |
| 76 | Daddy Kool DK 002 | Eunoch Power/INTIMIDATORS: Straight To Him Chest | 6 |
| 77 | Aries ARI 001 | Hard Luck Story/To Hell And Forward (p/s both with Jah Steach, actually Jah Stitch) | 100 |
| 78 | Arawak ARK DD 002 | Little Way Different/Differentiah (with Dreadful Julio) (12") | 25 |
| 79 | Success SRLD 004 | Down Below/The End/Untitled (12") | 15 |
| 79 | Burning Sounds BDS 022 | Holding On/Ranking Dub (12" with Ranking Dread) | 12 |
| 80 | Third World TW DIS 01 | Little Angel/GENE RONDO: Rebel Woman (12") | 10 |
| 81 | Natty Congo NCDM 005 | Happiness Forgets/Happy Dub (12", some on yellow vinyl) | 10 |
| 81 | Natty Congo NCDM007 | Jah Apple/Little Green Apple/Hell And Sorrow (12") | 10 |
| 82 | Success SRLD 014 | If You Say So/AFRICAN BROTHERS: Mystery Or Nature | 10 |
| 80s | PC Music PCDD 006 | You Have Been Bad/Militant Man (12") | 20 |
| 70s | Attack AT 1003 | YOU NEVER KNOW (LP) | 30 |
| 73 | Attack ATLP 1003 | DARLING OOH! (LP) | 40 |
| 79 | Black Joy DH 802 | DISCO SHOWCASE (LP) | 30 |
| 76 | Third World TWLP 101 | SIT AND CRY OVER YOU (LP) | 40 |
| 79 | Trojan TR 179 | DARLING OOH! (LP, reissue) | 20 |
| 91 | Attack ATLP 116 | DARLING OOH! (LP, reissue) | 15 |

*(see also Errol & His Group, Gaynor & Erroll], Mister Versatile, Don Lee, Ken Parker, Bongo Herman)*

## CLIVE DUNN
| | | | |
|---|---|---|---|
| 62 | Parlophone R 4873 | Too Old/Such A Beauty | 5 |

## GEORGE DUNN
| | | | |
|---|---|---|---|
| 73 | Leader LEE 4042 | GEORGE DUNN (LP, with insert) | 18 |

## TONY DUNNING (& TREMELOS)
| | | | |
|---|---|---|---|
| 60 | Palette PG 9006 | Seventeen Tomorrow/Be My Girl | 10 |
| 61 | Palette PG 9018 | Pretend/Don't Bother To Call | 12 |
| 61 | Palette PG 9027 | Under Moscow Skies/Sixteen Candles | 10 |

## DUNNO
| | | | |
|---|---|---|---|
| 71 | M&M FFMS 100013 | Sunday Girl/Magic Beat | 20 |

## BLIND WILLIE DUNN'S GIN BOTTLE FOUR WITH KING OLIVER
| | | | |
|---|---|---|---|
| 54 | Columbia SCM 5100 | Jet Black Blues/Blue Blood Blues | 25 |

*(see also Eddie Lang & Lonnie Johnson)*

## PETE DUNTON
| | | | |
|---|---|---|---|
| 73 | Rockfield ROC3 | Taking Time/Still Confused | 12 |

## DUPARS
| | | | |
|---|---|---|---|
| 76 | Contempo 2104 | Love Cookin'/Instrumental | 30 |

## DUPLICATES
| | | | |
|---|---|---|---|
| 79 | Stiff BUY 54 | I Want To Make You Very Happy/Call Of The Faithful (no p/s) | 5 |

## CHAMPION JACK DUPREE
| | | | |
|---|---|---|---|
| 51 | Jazz Parade B 16 | Fisherman's Blues/County Jail Special (78) | 30 |
| 62 | Storyville A 45051 | Whiskey Head Woman/Shirley May | 20 |
| 67 | Decca F 12611 | Barrelhouse Woman/Under Your Hood | 25 |

| | | | |
|---|---|---|---|
| 67 | Blue Horizon 45-1007 | Get Your Head Happy/Easy Is The Way (with T.S. McPhee) | 120 |
| 68 | Blue Horizon 57-3140 | I Haven't Done No-One No Harm/How Am I Doing It (with Stan Webb) | 20 |
| 69 | Blue Horizon 57-3152 | Ba'la Fouche/Kansas City | 30 |
| 69 | Blue Horizon 57-3158 | I Want To Be A Hippy/Goin' Back To Louisiana | 25 |
| 61 | Storyville SEP 381 | BLUES ANTHOLOGY VOL. 1 (EP) | 15 |
| 64 | RCA RCX 7137 | RHYTHM AND BLUES VOL. 1 (EP) | 15 |
| 64 | Decca DFE 8586 | LONDON SPECIAL (EP, with Keith Smith Climax Band) | 60 |
| 65 | Ember EMB 4564 | JACK DUPREE (EP) | 25 |
| 59 | London Jazz LTZ-K 15171 | BLUES FROM THE GUTTER (LP) | 50 |
| 61 | London Jazz LTZ-K 15217 | CHAMPION JACK'S NATURAL AND SOULFUL BLUES LP, mono) | 65 |
| 61 | London Jazz SAH-K 6150 | CHAMPION JACK'S NATURAL AND SOULFUL BLUES LP, stereo) | 75 |
| 65 | Storyville SLP 145 | TROUBLE TROUBLE (LP) | 25 |
| 65 | Xtra XTRA 1028 | CABBAGE GREENS (LP) | 25 |
| 65 | Storyville SLP 161 | PORTRAITS IN BLUES (LP) | 40 |
| 66 | Decca LK/SKL 4747 | FROM NEW ORLEANS TO CHICAGO (LP) | 100 |
| 67 | Storyville 670 194 | CHAMPION JACK DUPREE (LP) | 25 |
| 67 | Decca SKL 4871 | CHAMPION JACK DUPREE AND HIS BIG BLUES BAND (LP) | 125 |
| 68 | Blue Horizon 7-63206 | WHEN YOU FEEL THE FEELING YOU WAS FEELING (LP) | 90 |
| 69 | Blue Horizon 7-63214 | SCOOBYDOOBYDOO (LP) | 120 |

(see also T.S. McPhee)

## CHAMPION JACK DUPREE/JIMMY RUSHING
| | | | |
|---|---|---|---|
| 64 | Ember CJS 800 | TWO SHADES OF BLUE (LP) | 18 |

(see also Jimmy Rushing)

## SIMON DUPREE & BIG SOUND
| | | | |
|---|---|---|---|
| 66 | Parlophone R 5542 | I See The Light/It Is Finished | 10 |
| 67 | Parlophone R 5574 | Reservations/You Need A Man | 15 |
| 67 | Parlophone R 5594 | Day Time, Night Time/I've Seen It All Before | 10 |
| 67 | Parlophone R 5646 | Kites/Like The Sun Like The Fire (with Jacqui Chan) | 6 |
| 68 | Parlophone R 5670 | For Whom The Bell Tolls/Sleep | 10 |
| 68 | Parlophone R 5697 | Part Of My Past/This Story Never Ends | 10 |
| 68 | Parlophone R 5727 | Thinking About My Life/Velvet And Lace | 10 |
| 69 | Parlophone R 5757 | Broken Hearted Pirates/She Gave Me The Sun | 10 |
| 69 | Parlophone R 5816 | The Eagle Flies Tonight/Give It All Back | 10 |
| 67 | Parlophone PMC/PCS 7029 | WITHOUT RESERVATIONS (LP, yellow & black label, with "sold in the U.K..." text, laminated sleeve) | 125 |

(see also Moles, Gentle Giant, Shape Of The Rain)

## DUPREES
| | | | |
|---|---|---|---|
| 62 | HMV POP 1073 | You Belong To Me/Take Me As I Am | 25 |
| 62 | Stateside SS 143 | My Own True Love/Ginny | 15 |
| 63 | London HLU 9678 | I'd Rather Be Here In Your Arms/I Wish I Could Believe You | 15 |
| 63 | London HLU 9709 | Gone With The Wind/Let's Make Love Again | 15 |
| 63 | London HLU 9774 | Why Don't You Believe Me?/My Dearest One | 15 |
| 63 | London HLU 9813 | Have You Heard?/Love Eyes | 15 |
| 64 | London HLU 9843 | It's No Sin/The Sand And The Sea | 15 |
| 65 | CBS 201803 | Around The Corner/They Said It Couldn't Be Done | 15 |
| 66 | CBS 202028 | She Waits For Him/Norma Jean | 15 |
| 68 | MGM MGM 460 | My Special Angel/Ring Of Love | 10 |
| 70 | Polydor 2058 077 | Check Yourself/The Sky's The Limit | 35 |
| 75 | State 22 | Delicious/The Skys The Limit | 10 |

## DURAN DURAN
| | | | |
|---|---|---|---|
| 93 | Parlophone 7988761 | THE WEDDING ALBUM (LP, inner) | 50 |
| 95 | Parlophone 72438518981 | THANK YOU (LP, with poster) | 35 |

(see also Arcadia)

## JIMMY DURANTE
| | | | |
|---|---|---|---|
| 69 | Paramount PARA 3002 | Monte Carlo Or Bust/They're Playing Chester's Song | 5 |

(see also Ethel Merman, Groucho Marx)

## ALLISON DURBIN
| | | | |
|---|---|---|---|
| 69 | Decca LK-R/SKL-R 4996 | I HAVE LOVED ME A MAN (LP) | 40 |

## JUDITH DURHAM
| | | | |
|---|---|---|---|
| 67 | Columbia DB 8290 | Again And Again/Memories | 8 |
| 70 | A&M AMS 777 | The Light Is Dark Enough/Wander Love | 6 |
| 74 | Pye 7N 45312 | I Wanna Dance To Your Music/Mama's Got The Blues | 6 |
| 74 | Pye NSLP 18431 | THE HOTTEST BAND IN TOWN (LP) | 15 |

(see also Seekers, Keith Potger)

## TERRY DURHAM
| | | | |
|---|---|---|---|
| 69 | Deram DML/SML 1042 | CRYSTAL TELEPHONE (LP, with insert, red/white label with large logo) | 40 |

(see also Storyteller)

## LAWRENCE DURRELL
| | | | |
|---|---|---|---|
| 70 | Turret TRT 102 | ULYSSES COME BACK (LP) | 40 |

## DURUTTI COLUMN
| | | | |
|---|---|---|---|
| 82 | Factory FAC 64 | I Get Along Without You Very Well/Prayer (p/s) | 7 |
| 80 | Factory FACT 14 | THE RETURN OF THE DURUTTI COLUMN (LP, with sandpaper sleeve, with Martin Hannett's "Testcard" flexidisc [FACT 14C] | 250 |
| 80 | Factory FACT 14 | THE RETURN OF THE DURUTTI COLUMN (LP, with sandpaper sleeve, without Martin Hannett's "Testcard" flexidisc [FACT 14C] | 200 |
| 80 | Factory FACT 14 | THE RETURN OF THE DURUTTI COLUMN (reissue, different sleeve) | 20 |
| 82 | Factory FACT 44 | LC (LP, with inner) | 20 |
| 83 | Factory FACT 74 | ANOTHER SETTING (LP, with perfumed cut-out insert) | 20 |
| 83 | VU VINI 1 | LIVE AT THE VENUE LONDON (LP) | 25 |

# Ian DURY (& THE BLOCKHEADS)

| | | | |
|---|---|---|---:|
| 84 | Factory FACT 84 | WITHOUT MERCY (LP, pasted on picture) | 20 |
| 86 | Factory FACT 164c | VALUABLE PASSAGES (cassette in box with insert) | 35 |
| 86 | Factory FACT 14C | THE RETURN OF THE DURUTTI COLUMN (reissue, cassette in box with insert) | 35 |
| 86 | Factory FACT 44c | LC (reissue, cassette in box with insert) | 35 |
| 86 | Factory FACT 74c | ANOTHER SETTING (reissue, cassette in box with insert) | 35 |
| 86 | Factory FACT 84c | WITHOUT MERCY (reissue, cassette in box with insert) | 35 |
| 87 | Factory FACT 204 | THE GUITAR AND OTHER MACHINES (LP, inner) | 15 |
| 88 | Factory FACT 244 | VINI REILLY (LP, with free p/s 7" "I Know Very Well How I Got My Note Wrong" [FAC 244++] by Vincent Gerard & Steven Patrick) | 45 |
| 88 | Factory FACD 244 | VINI REILLY (CD, with 3" CD "I Know Very Well How I Got My Note Wrong" [FAC CD 244++] by Vincent Gerard & Steven Patrick) | 40 |
| 88 | Factory FACT 244 | VINI REILLY (LP, without 7") | 20 |
| 90 | Factory FACT 274 | OBEY THE TIME (LP) | 18 |

*(see also Nosebleeds, Morrissey)*

## IAN DURY (& THE BLOCKHEADS)

| | | | |
|---|---|---|---:|
| 77 | Stiff BUY 17 | Sex & Drugs & Rock & Roll/Razzle In My Pocket (p/s) | 5 |
| 77 | Stiff BUY 23 | Sweet Gene Vincent/You're More Than Fair (p/s) | 5 |
| 77 | Stiff BUY 23 | Sweet Gene Vincent/You're More Than Fair (promo pressing small "A" on label) | 10 |
| 78 | Stiff BUY 2712 | What A Waste/Wake Up (12", plain white sleeve, 100 only) | 100 |
| 78 | Stiff BUY 38 | Hit Me With Your Rhythm Stick/There Ain't Half Been Some Clever Bastards (red vinyl, p/s, one copy known) | 300 |
| 78 | Stiff FREEBIE 1 | Sex And Drugs And Rock And Roll/England's Glory/Two Steep Hills (p/s, free at NME party/competition, 1500 only) | 10 |
| 80 | Stiff BUY 90 | I Want To Be Straight/That's Not All (Band photo p/s) | 7 |
| 77 | Stiff SEEZ 4 | NEW BOOTS AND PANTIES!! (LP, with bonus track 'Sex And Drugs And Rock And Roll'). | 20 |
| 77 | Stiff SEEZ 4 | NEW BOOTS AND PANTIES!! (LP, limited edition gold vinyl) | 25 |

*(see also Kilburn & The High Roads, Greatest Show On Earth, Loving Awareness, Davey Payne)*

## ANDREW DURYER

| | | | |
|---|---|---|---:|
| 75 | Real RR 2003 | BALLADS OF A WANDERER (LP) | 25 |

## JEAN DUSHON

| | | | |
|---|---|---|---:|
| 65 | Chess CRL 4000 | MAKE WAY FOR JEAN DUSHON (LP) | 40 |

## DUSK

| | | | |
|---|---|---|---:|
| 71 | Bell BLL 1167 | I Hear Those Church Bells Ringing/I Cannot See To See You | 12 |

## PAT DUSKY AND MARINES

| | | | |
|---|---|---|---:|
| 67 | Stardust STP 1 | I Fall To Pieces/This Can Be The Night | 6 |

## LA DÜSSELDORF

| | | | |
|---|---|---|---:|
| 78 | Radar ADA 5 | La Düsseldorf/Silver Cloud (unissued, white label promo only) | 25 |
| 80 | Teldec | Dampfrieman/Individuellos (12", p/s) | 10 |
| 81 | Albion ION 1025 | Tintarella Di (some might have p/s) | 10 |
| 78 | Radar RAD 7 | DUSSELDORF (LP) | 20 |
| 78 | Radar RAD 10 | VIVA (LP, with lyric inner) | 15 |
| 80 | Albion ALB 107 | INDIVIDUELLOS (LP) | 20 |

*(see also Neu!)*

## DUST BROTHERS

| | | | |
|---|---|---|---:|
| 93 | Diamond DBS 333 | Song To The Siren (12" single sided) | 40 |
| 93 | Diamond DB's 333 | Song To The Siren (12", no p/s, 500 only) | 40 |
| 93 | Junior Boys Own JBO 10 | Song To The Siren/Song To The Siren (Sabres Of Paradise Mixes) (12", p/s) | 15 |
| 94 | Dust Up Beats NS 1 | Loops Of Fury (12") | 25 |
| 94 | Boys Own COLLECT 004 | 14TH CENTURY SKY EP (12", no p/s) | 15 |
| 94 | Junior Boys Own JBO 20 | MY MERCURY MOUTH EP (12", JBO sleeve) | 15 |

*(see also Chemical Brothers)*

## DUST (1)

| | | | |
|---|---|---|---:|
| 68 | Full Stop FS 039 | Before Time/There You Are | 45 |

## DUST (2)

| | | | |
|---|---|---|---:|
| 72 | Kama Sutra 2319 | DUST (LP) | 20 |
| 75 | 20th Century BTC 1009 | Rebound/Pieces | 7 |

## DUSTY LEDGE

| | | | |
|---|---|---|---:|
| 71 | Axes AX 114 | Sign Here/Look To The Sun | 50 |

## DUSTY SHELF

| | | | |
|---|---|---|---:|
| 74 | Sprint SP 2 | Jacobs Ladder/You Don't Realise | 25 |

## DUTCH

| | | | |
|---|---|---|---:|
| 68 | Phillips | What Is Soul/Down Here | 12 |

## DUTCH SWING COLLEGE BAND

| | | | |
|---|---|---|---:|
| 51 | Saturn EGX 106 | Alexander's Ragtime Band/Birthday Blues (78 picture disc, probably the first issued in the UK) | 15 |

## DUTCHESS

| | | | |
|---|---|---|---:|
| 81 | B'kreig Waxworks EJSP 9580 | Your Love/Dead And Gone | 150 |

## JACQUES DUTRONC

| | | | |
|---|---|---|---:|
| 66 | Vogue VRS 7015 | Et Moi, Et Moi, Et Moi/Mini-Mini-Mini | 15 |
| 66 | Vogue VRS 7021 | Les Cactus/L'Espace D'Une Fille | 12 |
| 66 | Vogue VRS 7024 | J'Aime Les Filles/L'Idole | 12 |
| 67 | Vogue VRS 7027 | Le Plus Difficile/Les Rois De La Reforme | 12 |
| 67 | Vogue VRL 3029 | JACQUES DUTRONC (LP) | 60 |

## JOSE DUVAL

| | | | |
|---|---|---|---:|
| 57 | London HLR 8458 | Message Of Love/That's What You Mean To Me | 25 |

## D&V

| | | | |
|---|---|---|---:|
| 83 | Crass 121984/1 | Jekyll And Hyde/Wake Up/High Above/Today's Conclusion/Step Inside/DignityS21RN (fold-out sleeve) | 15 |

| | | | |
|---|---|---|---|
| 85 | Crass CATNO 1 | INSPIRATION GAVE THEM THE MOTIVATION TO MOVE OUT OF THEIR ISOLATION (LP, inner) | 15 |

## DYAKS
| | | | |
|---|---|---|---|
| 78 | Bonaparte BONE 2 | Gutter Kids/It's A Game (p/s) | 7 |

## JUDY DYBLE
| | | | |
|---|---|---|---|
| 06 | Fungus 006 | SONGS FROM THE SPINDLE AND THE WHORL (LP, hand-made sleeves, 250 only, numbered) | 30 |

## BILLY DYCE
| | | | |
|---|---|---|---|
| 72 | G.G. GG 4532 | Be My Guest/HUGH ROY: Way Down South | 15 |
| 72 | G.G. GG 4534 | Take Warning/TYPHOON ALL STARS: Warning (Version) | 8 |
| 72 | G.G. GG 4537 | Time Is Still Here/G.G. ALL STARS: Time — Version | 7 |
| 72 | Pama PM 835 | Be My Guest/HUGH ROY: Way Down South | 15 |
| 73 | Pama PM 874 | Woman Smarter/SHENLEY DUFFAS: Standing On The Hill | 6 |
| 73 | Bread BR 1115 | You Need Love (with Millions)/G.G. ALL STARS: Love — Dub | 6 |

## DYKE & BLAZERS
| | | | |
|---|---|---|---|
| 67 | Pye International 7N 25413 | Funky Broadway (Parts 1 & 2) | 20 |

## MICHAEL DYKE
| | | | |
|---|---|---|---|
| 70s | Attack ATT 8112 | Saturday Night Special/CHINNA : Saturday Night Version | 20 |

## BOB DYLAN
### SINGLES
| | | | |
|---|---|---|---|
| 65 | CBS 201751 | The Times They Are A-Changin'/Honey, Just Allow Me One More Chance | 10 |
| 65 | CBS 201753 | Subterranean Homesick Blues/She Belongs To Me | 10 |
| 65 | CBS 201781 | Maggie's Farm/On The Road Again | 10 |
| 65 | CBS 201811 | Like A Rolling Stone/Gates Of Eden | 10 |
| 65 | CBS 201824 | Positively 4th Street/From A Buick 6 | 10 |
| 66 | CBS 201900 | Can You Please Crawl Out Your Window/Highway 61 Revisited | 15 |
| 66 | CBS 202053 | One Of Us Must Know (Sooner Or Later)/Queen Jane Approximately | 20 |
| 66 | CBS 202307 | Rainy Day Women Nos. 12 & 35/Pledging My Time | 10 |
| 66 | CBS 202258 | I Want You/Just Like Tom Thumb's Blues (live) | 15 |
| 66 | CBS 2700 | Leopard-Skin Pill-Box Hat/Most Likely You Go Your Way And I'll Go Mine (p/s) | 45 |
| 66 | CBS 2700 | Leopard-Skin Pill-Box Hat/Most Likely You Go Your Way And I'll Go Mine | 10 |
| 67 | CBS 2476 | Mixed Up Confusion/Corrine Corrina (unissued in U.K.) | 0 |
| 69 | CBS 4219 | I Threw It All Away/The Drifter's Escape | 6 |
| 70 | CBS 5122 | Wigwam/Copper Kettle (The Pale Moonlight) | 5 |
| 71 | CBS 7329 | Watching The River Flow/Spanish Is The Loving Tongue | 5 |
| 71 | CBS 7688 | George Jackson (Acoustic)/George Jackson (Big Band Version) | 8 |
| 73 | CBS 1158 | Just Like A Woman/I Want You (p/s, 'Hall Of Fame Hits' series) | 6 |
| 74 | CBS 2006 | A Fool Such As I/Lily Of The West | 6 |
| 74 | Island WIP 6188 | On A Night Like This/Forever Young | 5 |
| 75 | CBS 3160 | Tangled In Blue/If You See Her, Say Hello | 6 |
| 75 | CBS 3665 | Million Dollar Bash/Tears Of Rage | 6 |
| 76 | CBS SCBS 3878 | Hurricane (Part 1)/(Full Version) (some list 'Pt 1'/'Pt 2'; with p/s) | 8 |
| 76 | CBS SCBS 3878 | Hurricane (Part 1)/(Full Version) (some list 'Pt 1'/'Pt 2'; without p/s) | 5 |
| 76 | CBS 3945 | Lay Lady Lay/I Threw It All Away (p/s) | 5 |
| 76 | CBS 4859 | Stuck Inside Of Mobile With The Memphis Blues Again/Rita May (p/s; demos have "Rita May" as A-side) | 12 |
| 76 | CBS 4859 | Rita May/Stuck Inside Of Mobile With The Memphis Blues Again (demos with "Rita May" as A-side) | 8 |
| 78 | CBS 6935 | Changing Of The Guard/Sènor | 5 |
| 81 | CBS A 1406 | Heart Of Mine/Let It Be Me | 5 |
| 83 | CBS A 3916 | Union Sundown/Angels Flying Too Close To The Ground (p/s) | 5 |
| 84 | CBS A 4055 | Jokerman/Licence To Kill (p/s, embossed or standard label) | 5 |
| 84 | CBS A 4055 | Jokerman (Special Faded Radio Version)/Licence To Kill (p/s, promo only) | 15 |
| 85 | CBS GA 5020 | Highway 61 Revisited (live)/It Ain't Me Babe (live) (gatefold p/s) | 8 |
| 88 | CBS 6514066 | Silvio/When Did You Leave Heaven? (p/s) | 6 |
| 89 | CBS 6553588 | Everything Is Broken/Dead Man, Dead Man/I Want You (Live) (12" with limited edition album sleeve print) | 20 |
| 89 | CBS 6553587 | Everything Is Broken/Death Is Not The End (p/s) | 6 |
| 90 | CBS 6556436 | Political World/Ring Them Bells/Silvio/ All Along The Watchtower (Live) (12" p/s) | 6 |
| 90 | CBS 6563047 | Unbelievable/10,000 Men (p/s grey shaded not laminated/brown shaded laminated) | 6 |
| 00 | Columbia 6693797 | Things Have Changed/Blind Willy McTell (numbered p/s) | 6 |

### EPs
| | | | |
|---|---|---|---|
| 64 | CBS 6051 | DYLAN (Bob Dylan below song titles, solid/push-out centre, designer credits in bottom right corner, p/s) | 60 |
| 64 | CBS 6051 | DYLAN (Bob Dylan vertically on left: 'EXTENDED PLAY' on 1 line above 'EP 6051', push out centre – no designer credits, p/s) | 45 |
| 65 | CBS 6051 | DYLAN (Bob Dylan vertically on left: 'EXTENDED PLAY' on 2 lines above 'EP 6051', solid centre, no designer credits, p/s) | 45 |
| 66 | CBS 6070 | ONE TOO MANY MORNINGS (Only EP in Europe with five songs, p/s) | 50 |
| 66 | CBS 6070 | MR. TAMBOURINE MAN (length of EP on both sides: 27mm 'EXTENDED PLAY' on 1 line, 'Blossom Music LTD' on both sides. Solid/push-out centre, p/s) | 50 |
| 66 | CBS 6078 | MR. TAMBOURINE MAN (length of EP on side 1, 'EXTENDED PLAY' divided over 2 lines, 'Blossom Music' (side 1) 'Blossom Music Ltd' (side 2), | 50 |
| 65 | Fontana TFE 18009 | WITH GOD ON OUR SIDE (Joan Baez and Bob Dylan title track)/PETE SEEGER: The Bells of Rhymney/JOAN BAEZ: Waggoner's Lad, p/s) | 75 |
| 65 | Fontana TFE 18010 | BLOWIN' IN THE WIND (BOB DYLAN: Blowin' In The Wind/JOAN BAEZ: Oh Freedom/PETE SEEGER: Careless Love, p/s) | 75 |
| 65 | Fontana TFE 18011 | YE PLAYBOYS AND PLAYGIRLS (Bob Dylan and Pete Seeger title track/JOAN BAEZ: Te Ador, Te Manha/PETE SEEGER: This Land Is Mine, p/s) | 75 |

### ALBUMS
| | | | |
|---|---|---|---|
| 62 | CBS BPG 62022 | BOB DYLAN (mono) | 60 |

| | | | MINT VALUE £ |
|---|---|---|---|
| 62 | CBS SBPG 62022 | BOB DYLAN (stereo) | 60 |
| 63 | CBS BPG 62193 | THE FREEWHEELIN' BOB DYLAN (mono) | 60 |
| 63 | CBS SBPG 62193 | THE FREEWHEELIN' BOB DYLAN (stereo) | 50 |
| 63 | CBS BPG 62251 | THE TIMES THEY ARE A-CHANGIN' (mono) | 60 |
| 63 | CBS SBPG 62251 | THE TIMES THEY ARE A-CHANGIN' (stereo) | 50 |
| 64 | CBS BPG 62429 | ANOTHER SIDE OF BOB DYLAN (mono) | 60 |
| 64 | CBS SBPG 62429 | ANOTHER SIDE OF BOB DYLAN (stereo) | 50 |
| 65 | CBS BPG 62515 | BRINGING IT ALL BACK HOME (mono, flipback sleeve) | 50 |
| 65 | CBS SBPG 62515 | BRINGING IT ALL BACK HOME (stereo, flipback sleeve) | 60 |
| 65 | CBS BPG 62572 | HIGHWAY 61 REVISITED (mono) | 50 |
| 65 | CBS SBGP 62572 | HIGHWAY 61 REVISITED (stereo) | 60 |
| 66 | CBS BPG 66012 | BLONDE ON BLONDE (2-LP, 8 or 9 photos on inside gatefold sleeve, mono) | 50 |
| 66 | CBS (S)BPG 66012 | BLONDE ON BLONDE (2-LP, 8 or 9 photos on inside gatefold sleeve, stereo) | 100 |
| 67 | CBS BPG 62847 | BOB DYLAN'S GREATEST HITS (mono) | 65 |
| 68 | CBS BGP 63252 | JOHN WESLEY HARDING (mono) | 18 |
| | | | 40 |

*(The above LPs were originally issued with rough textured orange labels & flipback sleeves, without 'CBS Records' credit on rear sleeve & with inner sleeves advertising other CBS LPs. First pressings of Bob Dylan, The Freewheelin Bob Dylan, The Times They Are A-Changin', Another Side Of Bob Dylan, Bringing It All Back Home and Blond On Blond have '33' on the labels rather than 33 and a third which denote later 60s repressings. These copies are worth around half the value of the above LPs.)*

| 68 | CBS (S)BGP 63252 | JOHN WESLEY HARDING (stereo) | 20 |
| 69 | CBS (M) 63601 | NASHVILLE SKYLINE (mono) | 30 |
| 69 | CBS (S) 63601 | NASHVILLE SKYLINE (stereo) | 15 |
| 71 | CBS S 67239 | MORE BOB DYLAN GREATEST HITS | 15 |
| 73 | CBS S 69049 | DYLAN | 15 |
| 74 | Island ILPS 9261 | PLANET WAVES ('pink rim palm tree' label, with inner sleeve) | 15 |
| 74 | Island IDBD-1 | BEFORE THE FLOOD (2-LP, gatefold) | 15 |
| 75 | CBS 69097 | BLOOD ON THE TRACKS (orange label, red inner with painting on rear sleeve) | 20 |
| 75 | CBS 69097 | BLOOD ON THE TRACKS (orange label, red inner with liner notes on rear sleeve) | 25 |
| 75 | CBS S 88147 | THE BASEMENT TAPES | 20 |
| 76 | CBS S 86003 | DESIRE | 15 |
| 76 | CBS CBS 86016 | HARD RAIN (with inner) | 15 |
| 78 | CBS CBS 86067 | STREET LEGAL | 15 |
| 79 | CBS CBS 96004 | AT BUDOKAN (with poster and 16 page booklet) | 25 |
| 91 | Columbia 468086 | THE BOOTLEG SERIES VOLUMES 1-3 (5-LP box set, booklet) | 125 |
| 98 | CBS CK265759-1 | LIVE 1966 (2-LP) | 40 |
| 12 | Sony No Cat No | THE 50th ANNIVERSARY COLLECTION (4xCD-R, barcode 88765460722, 100 copies only, beware of bootlegs) | 600 |
| 13 | Sony 88883799701 | 50th ANNIVERSARY COLLECTION (6-LP box set) | 200 |

## ALBUMS : REISSUES

| 67 | CBS SBGP 62572 | HIGHWAY 61 REVISITED (LP, reissue, flipback sleeve, stereo with 33 and a third on the label) | 25 |
| 68 | CBS BPG 62193 | THE FREEWHEELIN' BOB DYLAN (LP, reissue, not flipback sleeve witth 33 and a third on the label) | 18 |
| 68 | CBS 62515 | BRINGING IT ALL BACK HOME (LP, reissue, non-flipback sleeve, orange label) | 18 |
| 70 | CBS SBPG 62251 | THE TIMES THEY ARE A-CHANGIN' (LP, reissue, orange/yellow labels) | 15 |
| 70 | CBS SBPG 62572 | HIGHWAY 61 REVISITED (LP, 2nd reissue, orange/yellow labels, stereo) | 18 |
| 98 | Simply Vinyl SVLP 063 | BLONDE ON BLOND (2-LP, reissue) | 20 |

*(see also Dick Farina, Band, George Harrison, Traveling Wilburys, Doug Sahm)*

## DYMONDS
| 71 | Big BG 326 | Girl You Are Too Young/RUPIE EDWARDS ALL STARS: Version | 6 |

## DYNAMIC CONCEPT
| 74 | Power Exchange PX 103 | California Part 1/California Part 2 | 5 |

## DYNAMIC CORVETTES
| 75 | Contempo CS 2059 | Funky Music Is The Thing (Parts 1 & 2) | 7 |

## DYNAMIC GANG (BOB ANDY & MARCIA GRIFFITHS)
| 71 | Moodisc MU 3511 | I'll Never Believe In You/LLOYD WILLIS: Black Attack | 12 |

## DYNAMIC MCS
| 87 | Tuff Groove TUFF002 | I Feel Dynamic (12") | 80 |

## DYNAMIC SUPERIORS
| 77 | Motown PSLP 233 | Nowhere To Run/MANDRE: Solar FLight (Opus 1) (12") | 80 |

## DYNAMICS (JAMAICA)
| 68 | Blue Cat BS 104 | My Friends/NEVILLE IRONS: Soul Glide | 45 |
| 69 | Punch PH 1 | The Burner/Juckie Juckie (B-side actually by Tommy McCook & Carl Bryan) | 25 |

## DYNAMICS (U.S.)
| 63 | London HLX 9809 | Misery/I'm The Man | 50 |
| 64 | King KG 1007 | So In Love With Me/Say You Will | 25 |
| 69 | Atlantic 584 270 | Ice Cream Song/The Love That I Need | 20 |

## DYNAMITES
| 69 | Duke DU 30 | John Public/CLANCY ECCLES: Fire Corner (B-side actually by King Stitt) | 20 |
| 69 | Duke DU 31 | I Don't Care (actually by Dingle Brothers)/CLANCY ECCLES: Shoo-Be-Do | 40 |
| 69 | Clandisc CLA 200 | Mr. Midnight (Skokiaan)/KING STITT: Who Yeah | 15 |
| 70 | Clandisc CLA 212 | Black Beret/BARRY & AFFECTIONS: Love Me Tender | 12 |
| 70 | Clandisc CLA 219 | Sha La La La/Pop It Up | 8 |
| 71 | Clandisc CLA 237 | Hello Mother/FABULOUS FLAMES: Hi-De-Ho | 5 |
| 72 | Duke DU 147 | Get In The Groove/Version | 6 |
| 69 | Trojan/Clandisc TTL 21 | FIRE CORNER (LP, with King Stitt) | 35 |

*(see also Clancy Eccles & Dynamites, Baba Brooks, Dennis Alcapone, Diamonds, Joe Higgs, Silvertones, Carl Dawkins, Chris Leon, Hopeton Lewis, Melodians, Cynthia Richards, Soul Twins, Stranger & Gladys, Carey & Lloyd)*

**DYNASTY**
| | | | |
|---|---|---|---|
| 72 | Top Nix 134 | Tutankhamen/Let's Boogie | 15 |

**DYNATONES**
| | | | |
|---|---|---|---|
| 59 | Top Rank JAR 149 | Steel Guitar Rag/The Girl I'm Searching For | 10 |
| 59 | Top Rank JAR 149 | Steel Guitar Rag/The Girl I'm Searching For (78) | 20 |
| 66 | Pye International 7N 25389 | The Fife Piper/And I Always Will | 50 |

**ALAN DYSON**
| | | | |
|---|---|---|---|
| 68 | Pye NPL 18218 | THE STILL SMALL VOICE OF...(LP) | 20 |

**RONNIE DYSON**
| | | | |
|---|---|---|---|
| 70 | CBS 5285 | She's Gone/I Don't Wanna Cry | 6 |
| 71 | CBS 7449 | When You Get Right Down To It/Sleeping Sun | 6 |
| 73 | CBS 1659 | Just Don't Want To Be Lonely/Point Of Mo Return | 7 |
| 74 | CBS 2430 | We Can Make It Last Forever/Just A Little Love From Me | 8 |
| 76 | CBS 4462 | The More You Do It/You And Me | 6 |

**E, THE**
| | | | |
|---|---|---|---|
| 88 | SUN 57 | Kites/Kites (Instrumental) p/s | 5 |

**VINCE EAGER (& THE VAGABONDS)**
| | | | |
|---|---|---|---|
| 58 | Decca F 11023 | Tread Softly Stranger & Yea Yea (as Vince Eager & The Vagabonds; unissued, 2 x 1-sided demos only) | 30 |
| 58 | Parlophone R 4482 | Five Days, Five Days/No More | 30 |
| 59 | Parlophone R 4531 | When's Your Birthday, Baby?/The Railroad Song | 10 |
| 59 | Parlophone R 4550 | This Should Go On Forever/No Other Arms, No Other Lips | 10 |
| 59 | Top Rank JAR 191 | Makin' Love/Primrose Lane | 5 |
| 60 | Top Rank JAR 275 | Why/El Paso | 5 |
| 60 | Top Rank JAR 307 | Lonely Blue Boy/No Love Have I | 5 |
| 61 | Top Rank JAR 539 | (I Wanna) Love My Life Away/I Know What I Want | 5 |
| 61 | Top Rank JAR 593 | The World's Loneliest Man/Created In A Dream | 5 |
| 63 | Piccadilly 7N 35110 | Any Time Is The Right Time/Heavenly | 5 |
| 63 | Piccadilly 7N 35157 | I Shall Not Be Moved/It's Only Make Believe | 5 |
| 11 | Stateside SS 2242 | MORRISSEY: Glamorous Glue (2011 remaster)/VINCE EAGER: The World's Loneliest Man (Retro A label 'Stateside' promo in die-cut 'Stateside' sleeve, 150 only) | 150 |
| 58 | Decca DFE 6504 | VINCE EAGER AND THE VAGABONDS NO. 1 (EP) | 100 |

**EAGLE**
| | | | |
|---|---|---|---|
| 70 | Pye International 7N 25530 | Kickin' It Back To You/Come In, It's All For Free | 15 |
| 69 | Pye Intl. NSPL 28138 | COME UNDER NANCY'S TENT (LP) | 40 |

**EAGLES (JAMAICA)**
| | | | |
|---|---|---|---|
| 69 | Songbird SB 1006 | Rudam Bam/Prodigal Boy (B-side actually "Any Little Bit" by Crystals) | 8 |
| 72 | Duke Reid DR 2522 | Your Enemies Can't Hurt You/Version | 7 |
| 73 | Techniques TE 927 | Rub It Down/TOMMY McCOOK ALL STARS: Rub It Down — Version | 6 |

*(see also Jamaican Eagles, Roy Richards)*

**EAGLES (U.K.)**
| | | | |
|---|---|---|---|
| 62 | Pye 7N 15451 | Bristol Express/Johnny's Tune | 5 |
| 62 | Pye 7N 15473 | Exodus: The Main Theme/March Of The Eagles | 5 |
| 62 | Pye 7N 15503 | The Desperados/Special Agent | 5 |
| 63 | Pye 7N 15550 | Come On Baby (To The Floral Dance)/Theme From Station Six Sahara | 5 |
| 63 | Pye 7N 15571 | Eagles Nest/Poinciana (unreleased) | 0 |
| 64 | Pye 7N 15613 | Andorra/Moonstruck | 5 |
| 64 | Pye 7N 15650 | Write Me A Letter/Wishin' And Hopin' | 5 |
| 62 | Pye NEP 24166 | NEW SOUND T.V. THEMES (EP) | 10 |
| 63 | Pye NPL 18084 | SMASH HITS (LP) | 30 |

*(see also Valerie Mountain)*

**EAGLES (U.S.)**
| | | | |
|---|---|---|---|
| 72 | Asylum AYM 505 | Take It Easy/Get You In The Mood (promo only p/s) | 8 |
| 75 | Asylum K 53003 | DESPERADO (LP, audiophile pressing, mail-order via Hi-Fi Today mag) | 100 |
| 98 | Simply Vinyl SVLP 050 | HELL FREEZES OVER (2-LP, reissue) | 100 |

**SNOOKS EAGLIN**
| | | | |
|---|---|---|---|
| 60s | Storyville A 45056 | Country Boy/Alberta (some with p/s) | 15 |
| 60s | Storyville SEP 386 | BLUES ANTHOLOGY VOL. 6 (EP) | 20 |
| 61 | Heritage HLP 1002 | SNOOKS EAGLIN (LP, 99 only) | 100 |
| 63 | Storyville SLP 119 | NEW ORLEANS STREET SINGER (LP) | 25 |
| 64 | Storyville SLP 140 | VOL. 2 — BLUES FROM NEW ORLEANS (LP) | 15 |
| 70s | Storyville 670 146 | PORTRAITS IN BLUES VOLUME 1 (LP) | 18 |

**JIM EANES**
| | | | |
|---|---|---|---|
| 59 | Melodisc 1530 | Christmas Doll/It Won't Seem Like Christmas | 10 |

**EARCANDY**
| | | | |
|---|---|---|---|
| 93 | Poor Person Prod. PPPR 1 | SPACE IS JUST A PLACE (LP, handmade sleeve, 500 only) | 20 |
| 94 | Poor Person Prod. PPPR 2 | TIME IS JUST A STATE OF MIND (LP, handmade sleeve) | 20 |
| 95 | Poor Person Prod. PPPR 5 | SOUND IS JUST THE WAY YOU EAR IT (LP, handmade sleeve with insert, numbered, 600 only) | 20 |
| 95 | Poor Person Prod. PPPR 8 | TASTING 1,2,3, TASTING (LP, handmade sleeve & insert, numbered, 500 only) | 20 |

MINT VALUE £

## EARGASM
| | | | |
|---|---|---|---|
| 81 | Venture EAR 26 | This Is Lovers Rock/Name That Tune (as Eargasm, P Pop & Beagle) | 20 |
| 80 | Venture CUT 007 | LOVERS DUB (LP) | 40 |

## CHARLES EARLAND
| | | | |
|---|---|---|---|
| 78 | Mercury 9199831 | Let The Music Play/Broken Heart (12") | 15 |

## EARL & DEAN
| | | | |
|---|---|---|---|
| 66 | Strike JH 323 | Slowly Goin' Out Of My Head/Little Buddy | 7 |

## KENNETH EARLE
| | | | |
|---|---|---|---|
| 60 | Decca F 11205 | The New Frankie And Johnny/40-30-40 | 10 |
| 60 | Decca F 11224 | Standing On The Corner/Put Your Arms Around Me, Honey | 5 |

## EARL-JEAN
| | | | |
|---|---|---|---|
| 64 | Colpix PX 729 | I'm Into Somethin' Good/We Love And Learn | 30 |
| 64 | Colpix PX 748 | Randy/They're Jealous Of Me | 30 |

(see also Cookies)

## JOSEPH EARLOCKS
| | | | |
|---|---|---|---|
| 80s | Freedom Sounds FSD014 | Free Up The Blackman/JAMAICANS & I DAUGHTER : Country Life (12") | 20 |

## EARLS
| | | | |
|---|---|---|---|
| 63 | Stateside SS 153 | Remember Then/Let's Waddle | 40 |
| 63 | London HL 9702 | Never/I Keep-A Tellin' You | 50 |
| 71 | Atlantic 2091 129 | Remember Then/I Believe | 10 |

## EARLY B
| | | | |
|---|---|---|---|
| 82 | Black Solidarity BSI 001 | Imitator/Mi Huh Know (with Papa San) | 40 |

## EARTH
| | | | |
|---|---|---|---|
| 69 | CBS 4671 | Resurrection City/Comical Man | 40 |
| 69 | Decca F 22908 | Everybody Sing The Song/Stranger Of Fortune | 15 |

## EARTH & FIRE
| | | | |
|---|---|---|---|
| 70 | Penny Farthing PEN 741 | Mechanical Lover/Ruby Is The One | 5 |
| 70 | Polydor 56790 | Seasons/Paradise | 15 |
| 71 | Nepentha 6129 001 | Invitation/Wild And Exciting | 15 |
| 72 | Polydor 2001 356 | Memories/From The End To The Beginning | 8 |
| 73 | Polydor 2001-435 | Maybe Tomorrow, Maybe Tonight/Theme From Atlantis | 8 |
| 71 | Nepentha 6437 004 | EARTH AND FIRE (LP, gatefold sleeve, artwork by Roger Dean) | 800 |
| 73 | Polydor 2310 262 | ATLANTIS (LP, laminated sleeve) | 30 |

## EARTH & STONE
| | | | |
|---|---|---|---|
| 78 | Different HAED 5 | Back To Africa/Still In Slavery (12") | 15 |
| 79 | Cha Cha CHAD 09 | Sweet Africa/Dance With Me (12") | 35 |
| 79 | Cha Cha CHAD 013 | False Ruler/Don't Let Them Fool You (12") | 50 |
| 79 | Cha Cha CHAD 015 | Slave Driver/Magic Woman (12") | 50 |
| 77 | Different DIFF 105 | BACK TO AFRICA (LP) | 30 |
| 79 | Cha Cha CHADLP 007 | KOOL ROOTS (LP, gatefold) | 80 |

## EARTHBOUND
| | | | |
|---|---|---|---|
| 78 | Archway S/79/CUS 308 | The Robot/Liberated Lady (7", different p/s) | 10 |
| 79 | Archway AR 17945 | The Robot/Liberated Lady/Song For South Kensington (12" p/s with inserts) | 25 |

## EARTH BOYS
| | | | |
|---|---|---|---|
| 59 | Capitol CL 14979 | Barbara Ann/Space Girl | 25 |

## EARTH LEAKAGE TRIP
| | | | |
|---|---|---|---|
| 91 | Moving Shadow SHADOW 1 | PSYCHOTRONIC EP (12", p/s) | 15 |

## EARTHLING SOCIETY
| | | | |
|---|---|---|---|
| 11 | Fruits De Mer Crustacean 19 | The Green Manalishi (With The Two-Prong Crown)/And I Heard The Fire Sing (orange vinyl, folded p/s, inserts) | 15 |

## EARTHLINGS
| | | | |
|---|---|---|---|
| 65 | Parlophone R 5242 | Landing Of The Daleks/March Of The Robots | 50 |

## EARTH MAN
| | | | |
|---|---|---|---|
| 80 | Feast | Life Is For Living/Love Is For Giving | 100 |

## EARTH OPERA
| | | | |
|---|---|---|---|
| 68 | Elektra EKSN 45035 | Close Your Eyes And Shut The Door/Dreamless | 8 |
| 69 | Elektra EKSN 45049 | American Eagle Tragedy/When You Were Full Of Wonder | 7 |
| 69 | Elektra EKSN 45061 | Alfie Finney/Home To You | 7 |
| 68 | Elektra EKS 74016 | EARTH OPERA (LP, gatefold sleeve) | 35 |
| 69 | Elektra EKS 74038 | GREAT AMERICAN EAGLE TRAGEDY (LP) | 30 |

(see also Rowan Brothers)

## EARTHQUAKE
| | | | |
|---|---|---|---|
| 74 | Cloud One HIT 4 | Friday On My Mind/Madness (p/s) | 10 |

## EARTHQUAKERS
| | | | |
|---|---|---|---|
| 67 | Stateside SS 2050 | Whistling In The Sunshine/Dreaming In The Moonlight | 10 |

## EARTHQUAKES
| | | | |
|---|---|---|---|
| 69 | Duke DU 54 | Pair Of Wings/I Can't Stop Loving You | 50 |
| 69 | Duke DU 56 | Earthquake/Simmering | 20 |

(see also Sir Collins & Earthquakes)

## EARWIG
| | | | |
|---|---|---|---|
| 74 | DJM DJS 310 | Sun Comes Up/Water It Down | 7 |

## TIM EASLEY
| | | | |
|---|---|---|---|
| 68 | Bell BLL 1036 | Susie Q (Parts 1 & 2) | 10 |

## EAST BAY RAY
| | | | |
|---|---|---|---|
| 84 | Alt. Tentacles VIRUS 34 | Trouble In Town/Poisonheart (p/s) | 5 |

(see also Dead Kennedys)

## EAST COAST ANGELS
| | | | |
|---|---|---|---|
| 77 | Ruby RUB 207 | Punk Rockin'/To Nite's The Nite (Irish pressing, no p/s) | 60 |

## EASTER AND THE TOTEM
| | | | |
|---|---|---|---|
| 88 | TOTEM III | Co-Conspirator/Chasing The Whale (p/s) | 10 |
| 88 | TOTEM IV | Act Of Faith/Tomb Of the Kings (p/s) | 10 |
| 82 | Ark Music (No Cat. No.) | HIP REPLACEMENT (LP) | 25 |
| 86 | Ideologically Sound ET 1 | THE SUM IS GREATER THAN ITS PARTS (LP) | 15 |

## EASTER MONDAY
| | | | |
|---|---|---|---|
| 89 | SRT TTWW001 | EASTER MONDAY EP (numbered foldover p/s, 500 only) | 15 |

## EAST MAIN ST. EXPLOSION
| | | | |
|---|---|---|---|
| 69 | Fontana TF 1039 | Hop, Skip And Jump/Little Jackie Horner | 6 |

## EAST OF EDEN
| | | | |
|---|---|---|---|
| 68 | Atlantic 584 198 | King Of Siam/Ballad Of Harvey Kaye | 100 |
| 69 | Deram DM 242 | Northern Hemisphere/Communion | 10 |
| 70 | Deram DM 297 | Jig-A-Jig/Marcus Junior | 8 |
| 71 | Deram DM 338 | Ramadhan/In The Snow For A Blow/Better Git It In Your Soul/ Have To Whack It Up A Bit | 10 |
| 72 | Harvest HAR 5055 | Boogie Woogie 'Flu/Last Dance Of The Clown (p/s) | 8 |
| 73 | United Artists UP 35567 | Sin City Girls/All Our Yesterdays | 5 |
| 69 | Deram DML 1038 | MERCATOR PROJECTED (LP, mono, red/white label with large logo) | 150 |
| 69 | Deram SML 1038 | MERCATOR PROJECTED (LP, stereo, red/white label with large logo) | 100 |
| 70 | Deram SML 1050 | SNAFU (LP, stereo, red/white label with small logo) | 80 |
| 70 | Deram SML 1050 | SNAFU (LP, mono, red/white label with small logo - existence unconfirmed) | 0 |
| 71 | Decca SPA 157 | WORLD OF EAST OF EDEN (LP, credited on sleeve and blue/silver label as a Deram release) | 15 |
| 71 | Harvest SHVL 792 | EAST OF EDEN (LP, gatefold sleeve, early copies with EMI box on side 1 label but no EMI box on side 2) | 80 |
| 71 | Harvest SHVL 792 | EAST OF EDEN (LP, gatefold sleeve) | 50 |
| 72 | Harvest SHVL 792 | EAST OF EDEN (LP, gatefold sleeve, non EMI 2nd pressing with indented centre perimeter) | 50 |
| 71 | Harvest SHVL 796 | NEW LEAF (LP, gatefold sleeve, with EMI on label) | 70 |

## EAST RIVER PIPE
| | | | |
|---|---|---|---|
| 93 | Sarah SARAH 75 | Helmet On/Happytown/Axl Or Iggy (foldover p/s, insert) | 12 |
| 93 | Sarah SARAH 78 | She's A Real Good Time/My Life Is Wrong/Times Square Go-Go Boy (foldover p/s in poly bag, insert) | 12 |
| 93 | Sarah SARAH 405 | GOODBYE CALIFORNIA (10" LP) | 20 |
| 94 | Sarah SARAH 621 | POOR FRICKY (LP) | 25 |
| 95 | Sarah SARAH 407 | EVEN THE SUN WAS AFRAID (10" LP) | 30 |

## EASTWOOD
| | | | |
|---|---|---|---|
| 70 | SRT SRTS7332 | Little Miss Lucy/Living To Learn | 200 |
| 71 | CBS 7076 | I Am Free/Gypsy | 45 |
| 72 | CBS 7325 | Orphan/Another Day In My Life | 25 |

## ALAN JAMES EASTWOOD
| | | | |
|---|---|---|---|
| 68 | President PT 209 | Blackbird Charlie/My Sun (as Bugsy Eastwood) | 6 |
| 71 | President PT 320 | Seeds/Boston | 6 |
| 72 | President PT 379 | Closer To The Truth/Strange News | 20 |
| 71 | President PTLS 1037 | SEEDS (LP) | 40 |

## CLINT EASTWOOD (1)
| | | | |
|---|---|---|---|
| 62 | Cameo Parkway C 240 | Rowdy/Cowboy Wedding Song (in p/s) | 10 |
| 62 | Cameo SC 1056 | COWBOY FAVOURITES... (LP) | 30 |

## CLINT EASTWOOD (2)
| | | | |
|---|---|---|---|
| 79 | Greensleeves GRED 25 | True True Love/Me Go Deh Already (12") | 15 |
| 77 | Jamaica Sounds JSLP 0010 | JAH LIGHTS SHINING (LP) | 15 |
| 78 | Live & Love LAP 011 | STEP IT IN A ZION! (LP) | 15 |
| 78 | Cha Cha CHALP003 | DEATH IN THE ARENA (LP) | 45 |
| 78 | Third World TWS933 | AFRICAN YOUTH (LP) | 35 |
| 79 | Burning Vibrations BV 1001 | LOVE AND HAPPINESS (LP) | 20 |

## EASTWOOD & POWELL
| | | | |
|---|---|---|---|
| 71 | President PT 352 | Beautiful/Opal Blue Sunday | 8 |

## ALAN EASTWOOD
| | | | |
|---|---|---|---|
| 73 | President PT 403 | Moonchild/Red Shoe Truckin' | 8 |

## EASYBEATS
| | | | |
|---|---|---|---|
| 66 | United Artists UP 1144 | Come And See Her/Make You Feel Alright (Women) | 20 |
| 66 | United Artists UP 1157 | Friday On My Mind/Made My Bed, Gonna Lie In It | 8 |
| 66 | United Artists UP 1175 | Who'll Be The One?/Saturday Night | 10 |
| 67 | United Artists UP 1183 | Heaven And Hell/Pretty Girl | 10 |
| 67 | United Artists UP 1201 | The Music Goes Round My Head/Come In, You'll Get Pneumonia | 12 |
| 68 | United Artists UP 2219 | The Land Of Make-Believe/We All Live Happily | 6 |
| 68 | United Artists UP 2209 | Hello, How Are You?/Falling Off The Edge Of The World | 6 |
| 68 | United Artists UP 2243 | Good Times/Lay Me Down And Die | 6 |
| 69 | Polydor 56335 | St. Louis/Can't Find Love | 6 |
| 70 | Polydor 2001 028 | (Who Are My) Friends?/Rock'n'Roll Boogie | 6 |
| 67 | United Artists (S)ULP 1167 | GOOD FRIDAY (LP) | 175 |
| 68 | United Artists (S)ULP 1193 | VIGIL (LP) | 100 |
| 70 | Polydor Special 2482 010 | FRIENDS (LP) | 80 |

*(see also Paintbox, Haffy's Whisky Sour, Harry Vanda, Grapefruit)*

## EASY RIDERS
| | | | |
|---|---|---|---|
| 58 | Philips PB 823 | Salute To Windjammer/Kari Waits For Me | 5 |
| 60 | London HLR 9204 | Young In Love/Saturday's Child | 5 |

*(see also Terry Gilkyson & Easy Riders, Vic Damone, Frankie Laine)*

## EASY STREET
| | | | |
|---|---|---|---|
| 76 | Polydor 2058807 | Feels Like Heaven/Shadows On The Wall (no p/s) | 10 |
| 70s | Muscle Music AP 591 | Person To Person/Easy Come Easy Go | 30 |
| 77 | Polydor 2058873 | Flying/Blame The Love | 12 |

## EATER
| | | | |
|---|---|---|---|
| 77 | The Label TLR 001 | Outside View/You (p/s) | 10 |
| 77 | The Label TLR 003 | Thinkin' Of The USA/Space Dreamin'/Michael's Monetary System (p/s) | 10 |
| 77 | The Label TLR 004 | Lock It Up/Jeepster (p/s) | 10 |
| 78 | The Label TLR 007 | GET YOUR YO-YO'S OUT (12" EP, white vinyl; (blue, green or red p/s) | 10 |
| 78 | The Label TLR 009 | What She Wants She Needs/Reaching For The Sky (p/s) | 6 |
| 78 | The Label TLRLP 001 | THE ALBUM (LP, with inner sleeve) | 30 |

*(see also Andy Blade)*

## EATHOPIANS
| | | | |
|---|---|---|---|
| 69 | Nu Beat NB 038 | Buss Your Mouth (actually "Contention" by Ethiopians)/REGGAE BOYS: Rough Way Ahead (B-side actually by Keith Blake & Hi-Tals) | 45 |
| 68 | Crab 4 | Reggie Hit The Town/Ding Dong Bell | 40 |

*(see also Ethiopians)*

## KOOKIE EATON
| | | | |
|---|---|---|---|
| 68 | Condor PS 1002 | Cream Machine/Joke B Side | 15 |

## EAZIE RYDER
| | | | |
|---|---|---|---|
| 78 | Graduate GRAD 1 | Motorbikin'/City Lights (p/s) | 15 |

## EAZYSTREET
| | | | |
|---|---|---|---|
| 84 | Private Pressing | Quest For Glory/Let 'Em Rock (no p/s) | 100 |

## EBONIES
| | | | |
|---|---|---|---|
| 68 | Philips BF 1648 | Never Gonna Break Your Heart Again/Shoeshine Boy | 10 |

## EBONY
| | | | |
|---|---|---|---|
| 84 | Touched TOUCH 1 | Dream Girl/We'll Fight Back (p/s) | 15 |

## EBONY DUBSTERS
| | | | |
|---|---|---|---|
| 03 | Ebony EBR 028 | EBONY DUBS VOL. 2 (12", p/s one side etched) | 20 |

## EBONY SISTERS
| | | | |
|---|---|---|---|
| 69 | Bullet BU 401 | Let Me Tell You Boy/RHYTHM RULERS: Mannix | 12 |
| 70 | Bullet BU 420 | Each Time/BUNNY LEE ALLSTARS: Boss Walk | 20 |

*(see also Sister)*

## EBONYS
| | | | |
|---|---|---|---|
| 71 | CBS 7384 | You're The Reason Why/Sexy Ways | 5 |

## KATJA EBSTEIN
| | | | |
|---|---|---|---|
| 70 | Liberty LBF 15317 | No More Love For Me/Without Love | 25 |

## ECCENTRICS
| | | | |
|---|---|---|---|
| 65 | Pye 7N 15850 | What You Got/Fe Fi Fo Fum | 45 |

## CLANCY ECCLES (& DYNAMITES)
| | | | |
|---|---|---|---|
| 61 | Blue Beat BB 34 | River Jordan/I Live And I Love (with Hersan & His City Slickers) | 15 |
| 61 | Blue Beat BB 67 | Freedom/More Proof | 25 |
| 63 | Island WI 044 | Judgement/Baby Please (B-side actually with Paulette) | 25 |
| 63 | Island WI 098 | Glory Hallelujah/Hot Rod (B-side actually by Roland Alphonso) | 25 |
| 65 | Ska Beat JB 194 | Sammy No Dead/Roam Jerusalem | 20 |
| 65 | Ska Beat JB 198 | Miss Ida/KING ROCKY: What Is Katty | 20 |
| 67 | Doctor Bird DB 1156 | Feel The Rhythm/Easy Snapping (B-side actually by Theo Beckford) | 30 |
| 67 | Pama PM 701 | What Will Your Mama Say/Darling Don't Do That | 25 |
| 67 | Pama PMB 703 | Western Organ/Mother's Advice (actually by The Clancy Set) | 20 |
| 68 | Pama PM 712 | The Fight/Great | 20 |
| 68 | Nu Beat NB 006 | Festival '68/I Really Love You | 25 |
| 69 | Trojan TR 639 | Sweet Africa/Let Us Be Lovers | 30 |
| 69 | Trojan TR 647 | Bangarang Crash/DYNAMITES: Rahthid | 100 |
| 69 | Trojan TR 648 | Constantinople/Deacon Sun | 40 |
| 69 | Trojan TR 649 | Demonstration/VAL BENNETT: My Girl | 30 |
| 69 | Trojan TR 658 | Fattie Fattie/SILVERSTARS: Last Call | 30 |
| 69 | Duke DU 9 | Auntie Lulu/SLICKERS: Bag A Boo | 100 |
| 69 | Duke DU 31 | Shoo-Be-Do/DYNAMITES: I Don't Care (B-side actually by Dingle Brothers) | 40 |
| 69 | Clandisc CLA 201 | The World Needs Loving/DYNAMITES: Dollar Train (B-side actually by Clancy Eccles) | 20 |
| 69 | Clandisc CLA 206 | Dance Beat/KING STITT: The Ugly One | 45 |
| 70 | Clandisc CLA 209 | Open Up/HIGGS & WILSON: Agane (B-side actually "Again") | 10 |
| 70 | Clandisc CLA 211 | Promises/Real Sweet (both sides with Dynamites) | 8 |
| 70 | Clandisc CLA 212 | Black Beret (with Dynamites)/BARRY & AFFECTIONS: Love Me Tender | 12 |
| 70 | Clandisc CLA 213 | Phantom/Skank Me (both sides with Dynamites) (B-side actually by Barry & Affections) | 12 |
| 70 | Clandisc CLA 214 | Africa/Africa Part Two (both sides with Dynamites) | 6 |
| 70 | Clandisc CLA 221 | Unite Tonight/Uncle Joe | 6 |
| 70 | Clandisc CLA 227 | Credit Squeeze/DYNAMITES: Credit Squeeze | 6 |
| 71 | Clandisc CLA 231 | Sweet Jamaica/DYNAMITES: Going Up West | 6 |
| 71 | Clandisc CLA 232 | Rod Of Correction/Rod Of Correction Version | 6 |
| 71 | Clandisc CLA 235 | John Crow Skank/KING STITT: Merry Rhythm | 15 |
| 71 | Clandisc CLA 236 | Power For The People/DYNAMITES: Power For The People — Version | 8 |
| 71 | Pama Supreme PS 332 | What Will Your Mama Say/TIGER: United We Stand | 10 |
| 72 | Clandisc CLA 239 | Hallelujah, Free At Last/DYNAMITES: Sha-La-La | 8 |
| 72 | Attack ATT 8037 | Ganja Free/DYNAMITES: Ganja (Version) | 12 |
| 69 | Clandisc TTL 22 | FREEDOM (LP) | 40 |
| 69 | Trojan TTL 22 | FREEDOM (LP) | 50 |

| | | | |
|---|---|---|---|
| 70 | Clandisc TBL 124 | HERBSMAN REGGAE (LP) | 60 |
| 73 | Big Shot BILP 101 | TOP OF THE LADDER (LP) | 30 |
| 88 | Trojan TRLS 262 | FATTY FATTY (LP) | 15 |

*(see also Dynamites, Drumbago, Marlene Webber, Westmorelites)*

## JIMMY ECHO
| | | | |
|---|---|---|---|
| 65 | Columbia DB 7629 | After Tonight/Practise What You Preach | 6 |

## ECHO & BUNNYMEN
| | | | |
|---|---|---|---|
| 79 | Zoo CAGE 004 | Pictures On My Wall/Read It In Books (p/s, 4000 only) | 8 |
| 85 | Korova KODE 13 | SONGS TO LEARN AND SING (LP, with lyric booklet & 7": "The Pictures On My Wall"/ "Read It In Books" [p/s, yellow/blue labels, CAGE 004], no "Voodoo Billy" run-off groove message; signed) | 30 |
| 01 | Cooking Vinyl COOK 208 | FLOWERS (LP) | 30 |
| 06 | Let Them Eat Vinyl LEN 007LP | SIBERIA (2-LP) | 30 |

*(see also Will Sergeant)*

## ECHO BASE
| | | | |
|---|---|---|---|
| 84 | DEP International DEP 14 | Out Of My Reach/Splash Down (p/s) | 12 |
| 85 | DEP International DEP 19 | Puppet At The Go Go/Genius + Soul = Jazz (p/s) | 12 |
| 85 | DEP International LPDEP 9 | BUY ME (LP) | 15 |

*(see also Ocean Colour Scene)*

## ECHOES (U.K.)
| | | | |
|---|---|---|---|
| 68 | Philips BF 1687 | Searchin' For You Baby/Listen To Me Baby | 10 |

## ECHOES (U.S.)
| | | | |
|---|---|---|---|
| 60 | Top Rank JAR 399 | Born To Be With You/My Guiding Light | 15 |
| 61 | Top Rank JAR 553 | Baby Blue/Boomerang | 15 |

## ECHOES & CELESTIALS (JAMAICA)
| | | | |
|---|---|---|---|
| 61 | Hornet H 1004 | Are You Mine/I'll Love You Forever | 18 |
| 62 | Blue Beat BB 89 | Are You Mine/I'll Love You Forever (reissue) | 10 |

## BILLY ECKSTINE
| | | | |
|---|---|---|---|
| 53 | MGM SP 1011 | Kiss Of Fire/I Apologise | 5 |
| 54 | MGM SP 1101 | No One But You/I Let A Song Go Out Of My Heart | 10 |
| 65 | Tamla Motown TMG 533 | Had You Been Around/Down To Earth | 100 |
| 65 | Tamla Motown TMG 533 | Had You Been Around/Down To Earth (DJ copy) | 150 |
| 57 | Parlophone GEP 8672 | A DATE WITH RHYTHM (EP, with His All Star Band) | 10 |
| 66 | T. Motown TML 11025 | THE PRIME OF MY LIFE (LP, mono) | 55 |
| 66 | T. Motown STML 11025 | THE PRIME OF MY LIFE (LP, stereo) | 65 |
| 67 | T. Motown TML 11046 | MY WAY (LP, mono) | 50 |
| 67 | T. Motown STML 11046 | MY WAY (LP, stereo) | 60 |
| 69 | T. Motown (S)TML 11101 | GENTLE ON MY MIND (LP, mono/stereo) | 45 |

## ECLECTION
| | | | |
|---|---|---|---|
| 68 | Elektra EKSN 45033 | Nevertheless/Mark Time | 12 |
| 68 | Elektra EKSN 45040 | Another Time, Another Place/Betty Brown | 12 |
| 68 | Elektra EKSN 45042 | Please/Saint George And The Dragon | 12 |
| 68 | Elektra EKSN 45046 | Please (Mark II)/In The Early Days | 10 |
| 76 | Elektra K 12196 | Nevertheless/Please | 5 |
| 68 | Elektra EKL 4023 | ECLECTION (LP, gatefold sleeve, also stereo EKS 74023) | 100 |

*(see also Fotheringay, Dorris Henderson, Trevor Lucas, Mogul Thrash)*

## ECLIPSE
| | | | |
|---|---|---|---|
| 78 | Baal BAL 89005 | ECLIPSED (LP) | 50 |

## ECOLOGY
| | | | |
|---|---|---|---|
| 92 | Vicious Pumpin' | THE COMMUNAL MIND EP (12", stamped white label) | 20 |
| 92 | Vicious Pumpin' OBS 004 | ECOLOGY EP (12", stamped white label) | 30 |
| 92 | Vicious Pumpin' VIC 002 | THE SMOKIN' JAM EP (12", stamped white label) | 20 |
| 93 | Vicious Pumpin' VIC 010 | Vicious House/Take Me Higher (12", stamped white label) | 15 |

## ECSTASY CLUB
| | | | |
|---|---|---|---|
| 88 | Swordfish DROP 1 | JESUS LOVES THE ACID (EP, 12") | 15 |
| 88 | Flim Flam FFR1207 | JESUS LOVES THE ACID (EP, 12") | 20 |
| 88 | Flim Flam FFR1207 | JESUS LOVES THE ACID (EP, 12" picture disc) | 20 |
| 89 | LD Records | JESUS LOVES THE ACID (EP, 12") | 20 |

## ECSTASY, PASSION & PAIN
| | | | |
|---|---|---|---|
| 74 | Pye International 7N 25641 | Don't Burn Your Bridges Behind You/I Wouldn't Give You Up | 5 |
| 74 | Pye International 7N 25660 | Good Things Don't Last Forever/Born To Lose You | 8 |
| 74 | Pye International 7N 25669 | Ask Me/I'll Take The Blame | 5 |

## ECTOMORPH
| | | | |
|---|---|---|---|
| 90s | Woronzow WOO 15 | THE FURIOUS SLEEPER (LP, with poster & inserts, 500 only) | 20 |

## EDDIE & THE CRAZY JETS
| | | | |
|---|---|---|---|
| 64 | King KG 1000 | Come On Let's Slop/Down By The Riverside | 6 |

## EDDIE & THE HOT RODS
| | | | |
|---|---|---|---|
| 76 | Island WIP 6270DJ | Writing On The Wall/Cruisin' (In The Lincoln) (promos in generic title p/s) | 25 |
| 76 | Island WIP 6270 | Writing On The Wall/Cruisin' (In The Lincoln) (in black & white p/s) | 15 |
| 76 | Island WIP 6270 | Writing On The Wall/Cruisin' (In The Lincoln) | 5 |
| 76 | Island WIP 6306 | Wooly Bully/Horseplay (Weary Of The Schmaltz) (p/s) | 8 |
| 76 | Island WIP 6333 | Get Out Of Denver/96 Tears (with 'Collectors item' and 'jukebox special' on label) | 80 |
| 76 | Island WIP 6354 | Teenage Depression/Shake (p/s) | 10 |
| 77 | Island WIP 6388 | I Might Be Lying/Ignore Them (p/s) | 10 |
| 77 | Island WIP 6411 | Quit This Town/Distortion May Be Expected (p/s) | 5 |
| 77 | Island 12WIP 6438 | Life On The Line/Do Anything You Wanna Do (live)/(I Don't Know) What's Really Going On (live)/Why Can't It Be (live) (12", p/s) | 10 |
| 76 | Island ILPS 9457 | TEENAGE DEPRESSION (LP, with poster) | 25 |

| | | | MINT VALUE £ |
|---|---|---|---|
| 76 | Island ILPS 9457 | TEENAGE DEPRESSION (LP, without poster) ..................................................... | 15 |

*(see also Engineers, Rob Tyner & Hot Rods, Lew Lewis)*

## JASON EDDIE & THE CENTREMEN
| | | | |
|---|---|---|---|
| 65 | Parlophone R 5388 | Whatcha Gonna Do Baby/Come On Baby (as Jason Eddie & the Centremen) ............. | 175 |
| 66 | Parlophone R 5473 | Singing The Blues/True To You (as Jason Eddy & the Centremen) ........................ | 175 |
| 69 | Tangerine DP 0010 | Heart And Soul/Playing The Clown (solo) .......................................................... | 50 |

## EDDIE & JERRY
| | | | |
|---|---|---|---|
| 72 | Hillcrest HCT 4 | Hail Rasta Man Hail/UPSETTERS: Scorcher ......................................................... | 8 |

## EDDIE'S CROWD
| | | | |
|---|---|---|---|
| 66 | CBS 202078 | Baby Don't Look Down/Take It Easy Baby ........................................................ | 90 |

## DUANE EDDY (& THE REBELS)
### 78s
| | | | |
|---|---|---|---|
| 59 | London HLW 8821 | The Lonely One/Detour ................................................................................ | 20 |
| 59 | London HLW 8879 | Peter Gunn/Yep! ......................................................................................... | 40 |
| 59 | London HLW 8929 | Forty Miles Of Bad Road/The Quiet Three ...................................................... | 30 |
| 59 | London HLW 9007 | Some Kind-A Earthquake/First Love, First Tears .............................................. | 30 |
| 60 | London HLW 9050 | Bonnie Came Back/Movin 'N' Groovin' ............................................................ | 40 |
| 60 | London HLW 9104 | Shazam!/The Secret Seven ........................................................................... | 60 |
| 60 | London HLW 9162 | Because They're Young/Rebel Walk ................................................................ | 80 |

### SINGLES
| | | | |
|---|---|---|---|
| 58 | London HL 8669 | Rebel-Rouser/Stalkin' (initially with triangular centre) ..................................... | 15 |
| 58 | London HL 8669 | Rebel-Rouser/Stalkin' (later round centre) ..................................................... | 5 |
| 58 | London HL 8723 | Ramrod/The Walker (as Duane Eddy & Rebels, actually by Al Casey tri-centre centre) | 10 |
| 58 | London HL 8723 | Ramrod/The Walker (as Duane Eddy & Rebels, actually by Al Casey round centre) ....... | 5 |
| 58 | London HL 8764 | Cannonball/Mason-Dixon Lion (as Duane Eddy & Rebels, tri centre) ...................... | 10 |
| 58 | London HL 8764 | Cannonball/Mason-Dixon Lion (as Duane Eddy & Rebels, round centre)................... | 5 |
| 59 | London HLW 8821 | The Lonely One/Detour (triangular centre) ...................................................... | 10 |
| 60 | London HLW 9050 | Bonnie Came Back/Movin 'N' Groovin' (tri centre) ............................................ | 15 |
| 59 | London HLW 8821 | The Lonely One/Detour (round centre) ........................................................... | 5 |
| 59 | London HLW 8879 | Peter Gunn/Yep! (triangular centre) ............................................................... | 8 |
| 59 | London HLW 8929 | Forty Miles Of Bad Road/The Quiet Three (triangular centre)............................. | 10 |
| 59 | London HLW 8929 | Forty Miles Of Bad Road/The Quiet Three (round centre).................................. | 5 |
| 59 | London HLW 9007 | Some Kind-A Earthquake/First Love, First Tears (tri centre) ............................... | 15 |
| 59 | London HLW 9007 | Some Kind-A Earthquake/First Love, First Tears (round centre) ........................... | 5 |
| 60 | London HLW 9050 | Bonnie Came Back/Movin 'N' Groovin'. ........................................................... | 5 |
| 60 | London HLW 9104 | Shazam!/The Secret Seven. .......................................................................... | 5 |
| 60 | London HLW 9162 | Because They're Young/Rebel Walk. ............................................................... | 5 |
| 60 | London HLW 9225 | Kommotion/Theme For Moon Children ........................................................... | 5 |
| 61 | London HLW 9257 | Pepe/Lost Friend ....................................................................................... | 5 |
| 61 | London HLW 9324 | Theme From Dixie/The Battle. ...................................................................... | 5 |
| 61 | London HLW 9370 | Ring Of Fire/Gidget Goes Hawaiian ............................................................... | 5 |
| 61 | London HLW 9406 | Drivin' Home/My Blue Heaven ...................................................................... | 5 |
| 61 | London HLW 9477 | The Avenger/Londonderry Air ...................................................................... | 6 |
| 61 | Parlophone R 4826 | Caravan (Parts 1 & 2) (actually by Al Casey) ................................................... | 10 |
| 62 | RCA RCA 1288 | Deep In The Heart Of Texas/Saints And Sinners .............................................. | 6 |
| 62 | RCA RCA 1300 | The Ballad Of Paladin/Wild Westerner ........................................................... | 5 |
| 63 | RCA RCA 1329 | Boss Guitar/Desert Rat (with Rebelettes) ....................................................... | 6 |
| 63 | RCA RCA 1344 | Lonely Boy, Lonely Guitar/Joshin'. ............................................................... | 6 |
| 63 | RCA RCA 1357 | You're Baby's Gone Surfin'/Shuckin'. ............................................................. | 10 |
| 63 | RCA RCA 1369 | My Baby Plays The Same Old Song On His Guitar All Night Long/ Guitar'd And Feather'd ..................................................................................................... | 8 |
| 64 | RCA RCA 1389 | The Son Of Rebel Rouser/The Story Of Three Loves .......................................... | 8 |
| 64 | RCA RCA 1425 | Guitar Star/The Iguana ................................................................................ | 15 |
| 65 | Colpix PX 779 | Trash/South Phoenix .................................................................................. | 15 |
| 65 | Colpix PX 788 | The House Of The Rising Sun/Don't Think Twice, It's All Right ............................ | 15 |
| 66 | Reprise RS 20504 | Daydream/This Guitar Was Made For Twangin'. ................................................ | 10 |
| 67 | Reprise RS 20557 | Monsoon/Roarin'. ...................................................................................... | 10 |
| 68 | Reprise RS 20690 | Niki Hoeky/Velvet Nights (Theme From "Elvira Madigan") ................................. | 10 |
| 68 | RCA RCA 1701 | Dance With The Guitar Man/SAM COOKE: Another Saturday Night (withdrawn)........ | 10 |
| 68 | London HLW 10191 | Peter Gunn/Rebel-Rouser ............................................................................ | 5 |
| 69 | CBS 3962 | Break My Mind/Loving Bird ......................................................................... | 10 |
| 75 | Target 101 | Love Confusion/Love Is A Warm Emotion ....................................................... | 5 |

### EXPORT SINGLES
| | | | |
|---|---|---|---|
| 58 | London HL 7057 | Ramrod/The Walker (as Duane Eddy & Rebels) ................................................ | 20 |
| 59 | London HL 7072 | The Lonely One/Detour. .............................................................................. | 20 |
| 59 | London HL 7076 | Yep!/Three-30-Blues .................................................................................. | 30 |
| 59 | London SLW 4001 | Peter Gunn/Yep! (stereo) ............................................................................ | 90 |
| 59 | London HL 7080 | Forty Miles Of Bad Road/The Quiet Three ...................................................... | 15 |
| 60 | London HL 7090 | Bonnie Come Back/Lost Island ..................................................................... | 15 |
| 60 | London HL 7096 | Because They're Young/Rebel Walk ............................................................... | 15 |

### EPs
| | | | |
|---|---|---|---|
| 58 | London RE 1175 | REBEL ROUSER (as Douane Eddy) ................................................................ | 20 |
| 59 | London RE-W 1216 | THE LONELY ONE ..................................................................................... | 20 |
| 59 | London RE-W 1217 | YEP! ........................................................................................................ | 15 |
| 60 | London RE-W 1252 | BECAUSE THEY'RE YOUNG ........................................................................ | 15 |
| 60 | London RE-W 1257 | TWANGY .................................................................................................. | 10 |
| 61 | London RE-W 1287 | PEPE........................................................................................................ | 15 |
| 61 | London RE-W 1303 | DUANE EDDY PLAYS MOVIE THEMES ............................................................ | 15 |

| 61 | London RE-W 1341 | TWANGY NO. 2 | 15 |
| 63 | RCA RCX 7115 | A COUNTRY TWANG | 15 |
| 63 | RCA RCX 7129 | MR. TWANG | 15 |
| 64 | RCA RCX 7146 | TWANGIN' UP A SMALL STORM | 15 |
| 65 | Colpix PXE 304 | COTTONMOUTH | 30 |

**ALBUMS**

| 58 | London HA-W 2160 | HAVE 'TWANGY' GUITAR, WILL TRAVEL | 40 |
| 59 | London HA-W 2191 | ESPECIALLY FOR YOU (mono) | 20 |
| 59 | London SAH-W 6045 | ESPECIALLY FOR YOU (stereo with different version of "Tuxedo Junction") | 25 |
| 60 | London HA-W 2236 | THE "TWANG'S" THE "THANG!" (mono) | 20 |
| 60 | London SAH-W 6068 | THE "TWANG'S" THE "THANG!" (stereo) | 30 |
| 60 | London HA-W 2285 | SONGS OF OUR HERITAGE (gatefold sleeve, mono) | 20 |
| 60 | London SAH-W 6119 | SONGS OF OUR HERITAGE (gatefold sleeve, stereo) | 20 |
| 61 | London HA-W 2325 | A MILLION DOLLARS' WORTH OF TWANG | 25 |
| 61 | London HA-W 2373 | GIRLS, GIRLS, GIRLS (mono) | 25 |
| 61 | London SAH-W 6173 | GIRLS, GIRLS, GIRLS (stereo) | 30 |
| 62 | London HA-W 2435 | A MILLION DOLLARS' WORTH OF TWANG VOL. 2 | 25 |
| 62 | RCA RD 27264/SF 5134 | TWISTIN' AND TWANGIN' (mono/stereo) | 25 |
| 62 | RCA RD/SF 7510 | TWANGY GUITAR — SILKY STRINGS (mono) | 15 |
| 62 | RCA SF 7510 | TWANGY GUITAR — SILKY STRINGS (stereo) | 20 |
| 63 | RCA RD/SF 7545 | DANCE WITH THE GUITAR MAN (mono) | 20 |
| 63 | RCA SF 7545 | DANCE WITH THE GUITAR MAN (stereo) | 25 |
| 63 | RCA RD/SF 7560 | TWANG A COUNTRY SONG (mono) | 20 |
| 63 | RCA SF 7560 | TWANG A COUNTRY SONG (stereo) | 25 |
| 63 | RCA RD/SF 7568 | TWANGIN' UP A STORM (mono) | 20 |
| 63 | RCA SF 7568 | TWANGIN' UP A STORM (stereo) | 25 |
| 64 | RCA RD/SF 7621 | LONELY GUITAR (mono) | 20 |
| 64 | RCA SF 7621 | LONELY GUITAR (stereo) | 20 |
| 64 | RCA RD/SF 7656 | WATER SKIING (mono) | 25 |
| 64 | RCA SF 7656 | WATER SKIING (stereo) | 30 |
| 65 | RCA RD/SF 7689 | TWANGIN' THE GOLDEN HITS (mono) | 15 |
| 65 | RCA SF 7689 | TWANGIN' THE GOLDEN HITS (stereo) | 15 |
| 65 | RCA RD/SF 7754 | TWANGSVILLE (mono) | 20 |
| 65 | RCA SF 7754 | TWANGSVILLE (stereo) | 20 |
| 65 | Colpix PXL 490 | DUANE A-GO-GO-GO | 20 |
| 66 | Colpix PXL 494 | DUANE EDDY DOES BOB DYLAN | 20 |
| 67 | Reprise R(S)LP 6218 | THE BIGGEST TWANG OF THEM ALL (mono) | 15 |
| 67 | Reprise R(S)LP 6218 | THE BIGGEST TWANG OF THEM ALL (stereo) | 18 |
| 67 | Reprise RLP 6240 | THE ROARIN' TWANGIES (mono only) | 25 |

*(see also Lee Hazlewood)*

**PEARL EDDY**

| 54 | HMV 7M 262 | Devil Lips/That's What A Heart Is For | 12 |

**EDDY & TEDDY**

| 61 | London HLU 9367 | Bye Bye Butterfly/Star Crossed Lovers | 15 |

**EDDYSONS**

| 68 | Olga OLE 010 | Ups And Downs/Sweet Memories | 7 |

**DAVID EDE BAND**

| 60 | Pye 7N 15280 | Easy Go/The Blue Bird (as David Ede & Rabin Rock) | 15 |
| 61 | Pye 7N 15329 | Obsession/Bootnik (& Go Man Go, Men) | 10 |
| 61 | Pye 7N 15370 | Last Night/Ding Dong John (as David Ede & Go Man Go Men) | 20 |
| 61 | Pye 7N 15394 | Twelfth Street Rag/No Hats On Ilkley | 5 |
| 62 | Pye 7N 15417 | Twistin' Those Meeces To Pieces/Twistin' The Trad (as David Ede & Rabin Band) | 15 |

*(see also Oscar Rabin)*

**EDEN**

| 87 | Den 3DEN | FORM FOLLOWS FUNCTION EP | 35 |

**EDEN STREET SKIFFLE GROUP**

| 57 | Headquarter & General Stores | SKIFFLE ALBUM NO. 1 (10 x 7" 78rpm clear flexidiscs in p/s) | 50 |

**TONI EDEN**

| 60 | Columbia DB 4409 | Teen Street/No One Understands (My Johnny) | 25 |
| 60 | Columbia DB 4458 | Grown Up Dreams/Whad'ya Gonna Do | 20 |
| 60 | Columbia DB 4527 | Will I Ever/The Waitin' Game | 10 |
| 61 | Decca F 11342 | Send Me/Interesting Facts | 10 |

**EDEN'S CHILDREN**

| 68 | Stateside (S)SL 10235 | EDEN'S CHILDREN (LP) | 80 |

**EDGE**

| 78 | Albion ION 4 | Macho Man/I'm Cold (p/s) | 8 |
| 79 | Hurricane FIRE 3 | Downhill/American Excess (p/s, white vinyl) | 8 |
| 79 | Hurricane FIRE 6 | Watching You/Overtaking (p/s) | 7 |
| 96 | Volume VOL 19 | Little Girl Blue/The Hopeless Dreams Of Neville Been (p/s) | 8 |
| 79 | Chiltern Sound CSLP | UNEASY PEACE (LP) | 15 |
| 80 | Hurricane FLAK 102 | SQUARE 1 (LP) | 15 |

*(see also Damned, Culture Club)*

**THE EDGE WITH SINÉAD O'CONNOR**

| 86 | Virgin VS 897 | Heroine (Theme From "Captive")/Heroine (Mix II) (p/s) | 5 |

*(see also U2, Jah Wobble)*

**EDISON LIGHTHOUSE**

| 71 | Bell BLL 1136 | It's Up To You Petula/Let's Make It Up | 5 |

MINT VALUE £

| 71 | Bell BLL 1153 | What's Happening/Take A Little Time | 6 |
|---|---|---|---|
| 72 | Bell BLL 1206 | Find Mr. Zebedee?/Reconsider, My Belinda | 6 |
| 81 | Greenstone GRS 3441 | Endearing Young Charms/Livin' On A Roller | 6 |

*(see also Flowerpot Men, White Plains, David & Jonathan, First Class)*

## EDITORS

| 04 | Kitchenware SKCD77 | Bullets/You Are Fading/Dust In The Sunlight (CD, 500 only) | 35 |
|---|---|---|---|
| 04 | Kitchenware SKX77 | You Are Fading/Dust In The Sunlight (500 only) | 35 |
| 05 | Kitchenware SKX78 | Munich/Disappear (Numbered, p/s) | 6 |
| 07 | Kitchenware SKX 973 | Escape The Nest (Demo)/When Anger Shows (Demo) (Fan club 7", 1,000 only) | 10 |
| 13 | Independent Label Market ILMVF008 | A Ton Of Love (Acoustic) (12" 1-sided, 50 only) | 60 |
| 05 | Kitchenware KWX 34 | THE BACK ROOM (LP, gatefold sleeve) | 20 |
| 07 | Kitchenware KWX 37 | AN END HAS A START (LP, CD) | 20 |
| 11 | PIAS PIASR 250 BOX | UNEDITED (7-LP, 7-CD, book, box set 200 with hand-written insert) | 150 |
| 11 | PIAS PIASR 250 BOX | UNEDITED (7-LP, 7-CD, book, box set without hand-written insert) | 90 |

## LADA EDMUND JR

| 75 | MCA MU 172 | The Larue/Soul Au Go-Go | 10 |
|---|---|---|---|
| 75 | MCA MU 172 | The Larue/Soul Au Go-Go (DJ Copy) | 20 |

## DAVE EDMUNDS (& ROCKPILE)

| 71 | Regal Zonophone RZ 3032 | I'm-A Comin' Home/Country Roll | 10 |
|---|---|---|---|
| 71 | Regal Zonophone RZ 3037 | Blue Monday/I'll Get Along | 10 |
| 72 | Regal Zonophone RZ 3059 | Down, Down, Down/It Ain't Easy | 10 |
| 77 | Swan Song SSK 19411 | I Knew The Bride/Back To Schooldays | 6 |
| 90 | Capitol 10CL 568 | King Of Love/Stay With Me Tonight (45rpm)/King Of Love (78 rpm) (10", p/s) | 30 |
| 90 | Capitol 12CL 568 | King Of Love/Stay With Me Tonight/Every Time I See Her (12", p/s) | 10 |
| 71 | Regal Zono. SRZA 8503 | ROCKPILE COLLECTION (LP, unreleased) | 0 |
| 72 | Regal Zono. SLRZ 1026 | ROCKPILE (LP) | 60 |
| 75 | Rockfield RRL 101 | SUBTLE AS A FLYING MALLET (LP) | 20 |
| 82 | Arista SPART 1184 | DE 7TH (LP, with bonus EP "Live At The Venue" [JUKE 1]) | 15 |

*(see also Image, Human Beans, Love Sculpture, Rockpile, Andy Fairweather-Low)*

## EDOUARD

| 66 | CBS 202200 | My Name Is Edouard/N'aie Pas Peur Antoinette (p/s) | 8 |
|---|---|---|---|

## EDSELS

| 61 | Pye International 7N 25086 | Rama Lama Ding Dong/Bells | 60 |
|---|---|---|---|

## EDWARD & HARDING

| 71 | Stateside SS 2196 | Mr. Sunlight/Blackbird | 10 |
|---|---|---|---|

## J VINCENT EDWARD

| 69 | CBS 4388 | Run To The Sun/I Never Thought I'd Fall In Love | 15 |
|---|---|---|---|

## ADINA EDWARDS

| 72 | Dynamic DYN 454 | Talk About Love/Don't Forget To Remember | 6 |
|---|---|---|---|
| 60s | Tabernacle TLP 1005 | JESUS IS MINE (LP) | 15 |

*(see also Coxsone Dodd)*

## BOBBY EDWARDS

| 61 | Top Rank JAR 584 | You're The Reason/I'm A Fool Loving You | 5 |
|---|---|---|---|

## BRENT EDWARDS

| 63 | Pye International 7N 25197 | Pride/Over The Weekend | 8 |
|---|---|---|---|

## C EDWARDS & SYMBOLIC

| 80 | Symbolic BS 02 | Loving Jah/Loving One & All (12") | 80 |
|---|---|---|---|

## CHUCK EDWARDS

| 68 | Soul City SC 104 | Downtown Soulville/I Need You | 30 |
|---|---|---|---|
| 68 | Soul City SC 104 | Downtown Soulville/I Need You (DJ Copy) | 100 |

## DEE EDWARDS

| 98 | Goldmine Soul Supply GS 208 | All The Way Home/DONI BURDICK: Bari Track (reissue) | 10 |
|---|---|---|---|

## DEVON EDWARDS

| 82 | CF 12 | Bad Boy Lay Down Flat/JAH RUBAL : Burst Shot | 35 |
|---|---|---|---|

## GARY EDWARDS (COMBO)

| 62 | Oriole CB 1700 | Twist Or Bust/The Franz Liszt Twist (as Gary Edwards Combo) | 10 |
|---|---|---|---|
| 62 | Oriole CB 1717 | The Method/Twistful Thinkin' | 12 |
| 62 | Oriole CB 1733 | Africa/One Fifteen A.M. | 10 |
| 62 | Oriole CB 1759 | Hopscotch/Theme For A Broken Dream | 10 |

## IDIATER EDWARDS

| 85 | Pressure HAVE 2 | Loving Sweet Devotion/Version | 70 |
|---|---|---|---|

## (WILFRED) JACKIE EDWARDS

| 60 | Starlite ST45 016 | We're Gonna Love/Your Eyes Are Dreaming (as Wilfred Edwards & Caribs) | 25 |
|---|---|---|---|
| 60 | Starlite ST45 026 | I Know/Tell Me Darling (as Wilfred Edwards) | 25 |
| 61 | Starlite ST45 046 | Whenever There's Moonlight/Heaven Just Knows (as Wilfred Edwards) | 25 |
| 61 | Starlite ST45 062 | More Than Words Can Say/I Love You No More (as Wilfred Edwards) | 25 |
| 62 | Starlite ST45 076 | Little Bitty Girl/Never Go Away (as Wilfred Edwards) | 25 |
| 62 | Island WI 008 | All My Days/Hear Me Cry (as Wilfred Jackie Edwards) | 18 |
| 62 | Island WI 019 | One More Week/Tears Like Rain (as Wilfred Edwards) | 18 |
| 62 | Decca F 11547 | Lonely Game/Suddenly | 15 |
| 63 | Black Swan WI 404 | Why Make Believe/Do You Want Me (as Wilfred Jackie Edwards & Velvetts) | 15 |
| 64 | Black Swan WI 416 | The Things You Do/Little Smile (as Wilfred Jackie Edwards) | 20 |
| 64 | Black Swan WI 426 | Why Make Believe/Do You Want Me Again | 22 |
| 64 | Fontana TF 465 | Sea Cruise/Little Princess | 15 |
| 64 | Sue WI 329 | Stagger Lee/Pretty Girl | 40 |
| 65 | Aladdin WI 601 | He'll Have To Go/Gotta Learn To Love Again | 25 |

| 65 | Aladdin WI 605 | Hush/I Am In Love With You No More (p/s) | 12 |
|----|----------------|------------------------------------------|-----|
| 65 | Aladdin WI 611 | The Same One/I Don't Know | 15 |
| 65 | Island WI 255 | White Christmas/My Love And I | 20 |
| 66 | Island WI 270 | Sometimes/Come On Home | 40 |
| 66 | Island WI 274 | L-O-V-E/What's Your Name | 40 |
| 66 | Island WI 287 | Think Twice/Oh Mary | 20 |
| 66 | Island WI 3006 | I Feel So Bad/I Don't Want To Be Made A Fool Of | 250 |
| 66 | Island WI 3018 | Royal Telephone/It's No Secret | 15 |
| 67 | Island WI 3030 | Only A Fool Breaks His Own Heart/The End | 15 |
| 67 | Island WIP 6008 | Come Back Girl/Tell Him You Lied | 25 |
| 68 | Island WIP 6026 | Julie On My Mind/If This Is Heaven | 15 |
| 68 | Island WI 3157 | You're My Girl/Heaven Only Knows | 15 |
| 69 | Direction 58-4096 | Why Must I Be Alone/I'm Gonna Make You Cry | 6 |
| 69 | Direction 58-4402 | Too Experienced/Someone To Love | 6 |
| 69 | Direction 58-4630 | Oh Manio/Here We Go Again | 6 |
| 70 | CBS 5147 | Tell Me Why Say Goodbye/Walter Walter | 6 |
| 71 | Horse HOSS 1 | I Must Go Back/Baby I Want To Be Near You (in p/s) | 20 |
| 71 | Horse HOSS 1 | I Must Go Back/Baby I Want To Be Near You | 15 |
| 71 | Bread BR 1107 | Johnny Gunman/JACKIE'S BOYS: Johnny Gunman Version | 15 |
| 72 | Bread BR 1108 | I Do Love You/Who Told You So? | 8 |
| 76 | Island WIP 6285 | I Feel So Bad/Come On Home (reissue) | 20 |
| 11 | Island 009 | I Feel So Bad/JULIAN COVEY: Little Bit Hurt | 6 |
| 66 | St. Mary's IEP 701 | SACRED HYMNS VOL. 1 (EP, in p/s) | 40 |
| 66 | St. Mary's IEP 701 | SACRED HYMNS VOL. 1 (EP) | 15 |
| 66 | St. Mary's IEP 702 | SACRED HYMNS VOL. 2 (EP, with St. Mary's label, in p/s) | 40 |
| 66 | St. Mary's IEP 702 | SACRED HYMNS VOL. 2 (EP, with St. Mary's label) | 15 |
| 66 | St. Mary's IEP 702 | SACRED HYMNS VOL. 2 (EP, with red-and-white Island label; in p/s) | 40 |
| 66 | St. Mary's IEP 702 | SACRED HYMNS VOL. 2 (EP, with red-and-white Island label) | 15 |
| 66 | Island IEP 708 | HUSH! (EP) | 45 |
| 64 | Island ILP 906 | THE MOST OF WILFRED JACKIE EDWARDS (LP) | 50 |
| 64 | Island ILP 912 | STAND UP FOR JESUS (LP) | 50 |
| 66 | Island ILP 931 | COME ON HOME (LP) | 50 |
| 66 | Island ILP 936 | THE BEST OF JACKIE EDWARDS (LP) | 50 |
| 66 | Island ILP 940 | BY DEMAND (LP) | 50 |
| 67 | Island ILP(S) 960 | PREMATURE GOLDEN SANDS (LP) | 40 |
| 69 | Island IWPS 4 | PUT YOUR TEARS AWAY (LP) | 40 |
| 69 | Direction 8-63977 | LET IT BE ME (LP) | 20 |
| 70 | Trojan TTL 40 | THE MOST OF WILFRED JACKIE EDWARDS (LP, as Wilfred Jackie Edwards) | 25 |
| 70 | Trojan TTL 45 | COME ON HOME (LP) | 25 |
| 70 | Trojan TTL 46 | BY DEMAND (LP) | 25 |
| 70 | Trojan TTL 57 | PREMATURE GOLDEN SANDS (LP, reissue) | 25 |
| 72 | Trojan TRLS 47 | I DO LOVE YOU (LP) | 30 |
| 78 | Trojan TRLS 47 | SINCERELY (LP) | 15 |
| 82 | Black Music BMLP 801 | KING OF THE GHETTO (LP) | 60 |

*(see also Wilfred & Millicent, Wilfred & Millie, Jackie & Millie, Jackie's Boys)*

## JACKIE EDWARDS & JIMMY CLIFF

| 68 | Island WIP 6036 | Set Me Free/Here I Come | 10 |
|----|-----------------|-------------------------|-----|
| 68 | Island WIP 6042 | You're My Girl/Heaven Only Knows | 10 |

*(see also Jackie & Millie, Millie, Jimmy Cliff, Wilfred & Millie, Jackie's Boys)*

## JIMMY EDWARDS (& PROFILE)

| 79 | Warner Bros K 17415 | Nora's Diary/Call Me A Fraud (features Sham 69) (p/s) | 20 |
|----|---------------------|------------------------------------------------------|-----|
| 79 | Warner Bros K 17464 | Twentieth Century Time/Seven Hail Marys (features Pretenders) (p/s) | 6 |
| 80 | Polydor 2059 240 | Toys/Hard Heart (p/s) | 5 |
| 80 | Polydor 2059 256 | Cabaret/Drag It Back (p/s, solo) | 5 |
| 81 | Polydor POSP 240 | In The City/Five Minute Girl (p/s, solo) | 5 |

*(see also Time U.K., Sham 69)*

## JIMMY EDWARDS (U.S.)

| 58 | Mercury 7MT 193 | Love Bug Crawl/Honey Lovin' (demo - hand-written label) | 700 |
|----|-----------------|--------------------------------------------------------|------|
| 58 | Mercury 7MT 193 | Love Bug Crawl/Honey Lovin' | 500 |
| 58 | Mercury MT 193 | Love Bug Crawl/Honey Lovin' (78) | 50 |

## MILL EDWARDS

| 73 | Action ACT 4617 | I Found Myself/Don't Forget About Me | 25 |
|----|-----------------|--------------------------------------|-----|

## NOKIE EDWARDS

| 77 | Cream CR 9006 | NOKIE (LP) | 15 |
|----|---------------|------------|-----|

*(see also Ventures)*

## O.G. EDWARDS

| 88 | Dance Yard YARDT 4 | Only You (Know What I Like)/Only You (Know What I Like) (Extended Version) (12") | 40 |
|----|--------------------|--------------------------------------------------------------------------------|-----|

## PAUL EDWARDS

| 76 | Cottage COT 301 | LONGSTONE FARM (LP) | 18 |
|----|-----------------|---------------------|-----|

## R. EDWARDS & SOCIAL EAGLES

| 73 | Dip DL 5014 | One Sunday Morning/Version Sunday Morning (with Allstars) | 6 |
|----|-------------|-----------------------------------------------------------|-----|
| 73 | Dip DL 5014 | One Sunday Morning/AFRICAN BROTHERS: Mysterious Nature (2nd issue, different B-side) | 10 |

## RUPIE EDWARDS (ALL STARS)

| 62 | Blue Beat BB 90 | Guilty Convict/Just Because (as Rupert Edwards & Smithie's Sextet) | 25 |
|----|-----------------|-------------------------------------------------------------------|-----|
| 68 | Doctor Bird DB 1163 | I Can't Forget/I'm Writing Again | 25 |
| 69 | Crab CRAB 35 | Long Lost Love/Uncertain Love | 25 |
| 70 | Crab CRAB 41 | Sharp Pan Ya Machete/Redemption | 12 |

MINT VALUE £

| 70 | Explosion EX 2030 | Full Moon/Baby | 20 |
| 70 | Explosion EX 2031 | Love At First Sight/I Need Your Care | 8 |
| 70 | Success RE 902 | Grandfather Clock/Promoter's Grouse | 25 |
| 70 | Success RE 905 | Handicap/If You Can't Beat Them | 15 |
| 70 | Success RE 909 | Pop Hi (as Rupie Edwards All Stars)/VAL BENNETT AND BUNNY LEE ALL STARS: High Tide | 15 |
| 71 | Bullet BU 494 | I'm Gonna Live Some Life/RUPIE EDWARDS ALLSTARS: Rock 'In' | 6 |
| 71 | Nu Beat NB 082 | Black Man/Tell The People | 10 |
| 71 | Nu Beat NB 091 | One In Three/ERROLL DUNKLEY: Three In One | 8 |
| 71 | Big BG 320 | Soulful Stew/Soulful Stew — Version Two (as Rupie Edwards Allstars) | 10 |
| 71 | Big BG 324 | Deep Meditation (version)/ERROLL DUNKLEY: Deep Meditation | 20 |
| 71 | Big BG 327 | One In Three/ERROLL DUNKLEY: Three In One | 6 |
| 71 | Bullet BU 462 | My Love (actually by Gaylads)/Stronger Love (both as Rupie Edwards All Stars) | 8 |
| 72 | Big BG 333 | Press Along/Press Along — Version (as Rupie Edwards Allstars) | 6 |
| 72 | Big BG 335 | Jimmy As Job Card (actually titled "Jimmy Has A Job Card")/ Riot (as Rupie Edwards Allstars) | 25 |
| 72 | Big BG 337 | Christmas Parade (actually by Rupie Edwards Allstars)/ UNDERGROUND PEOPLE: Santa | 5 |
| 78 | Success SLD 016 | Oh Black People/NOEL TEMPO : It's Time To Be Free (12") | 30 |
| 75 | Cactus CTLP 106 | IRE FEELING (LP) | 20 |
| 75 | Cactus CTLP 107 | DUB BASKET (LP) | 80 |
| 76 | Cactus CTLP 117 | DUB BASKET CHAPTER 2 (LP) | 40 |
| 76 | Cactus CTLP 120 | JAMAICA SERENADE (LP) | 30 |
| 77 | Success SUCLP | 101 DUB CLASSICS (LP) | 60 |

*(see also R. Edwards & Social Eagles, Gaylads, Heptones, Ethiopians, Dymonds, Dobby Dobson, Keith Cole, Country Boy, Keith Cole, Laurel Aitken, Dennis Alcapone, Gregory Isaacs, Itals, Hugh Roy, Kingstonians, Little George, Winston Blake, Mediators, Max Romeo, I Roy)*

## SAMUEL EDWARDS
| 69 | Blue Cat BS 159 | Want It Want It/SPARKERS: Israel | 35 |

## SIMON EDWARDS
| 70 | Jayboy JSX 2001 | NO RETURN (LP) | 30 |

## TOM EDWARDS
| 57 | Vogue Coral Q 72236 | What Is A Teen Age Girl?/What Is A Teen Age Boy? | 6 |

## TOMMY EDWARDS
| 53 | MGM SP 1030 | (Now And Then, There's) A Fool Such As I/Take These Chains From My Heart | 8 |
| 56 | MGM SP 1168 | Baby, Let Me Take You Dreaming/MARION SISTERS: Life Could Not Be Better | 8 |
| 58 | MGM 989 | It's All In The Game/Please Love Me Forever | 5 |

## VINCE EDWARDS (U.K.)
| 67 | United Artists UP 1179 | I Can't Turn Back Time/The Lively One | 20 |
| 68 | United Artists UP 2230 | County Durham Dream/It's The Same Old Song | 6 |
| 68 | United Artists UP 2236 | Aquarius/Hair | 5 |

## VINCE EDWARDS (U.S.)
| 58 | Capitol CL 14825 | Widget/Lollipop | 10 |
| 62 | Brunswick 05872 | Don't Worry About Me/And Now | 8 |
| 64 | Colpix PX 771 | No Not Much/See That Girl (p/s) | 10 |

## WEBLEY EDWARDS
| 60 | Capitol ST1033 | FIRE GODDESS (LP) | 20 |

## WINSTON EDWARDS
| 75 | Studio 16 WE 0010 | DUB CONFERENCE (with BLACKBEARD) | 50 |

## JOHN EDWARDS
| 95 | Kent 6T 11 | Ain't That Good Enough/LOLEATTA HOLLOWAY: This Man's Arms | 25 |
| 14 | Kent Select CITY 34 | Cold Hearted Woman/Ain't That Good Enough | 8 |

## EDWARDS HAND
| 71 | RCA SF 8154 | STRANDED (LP, orange label) | 20 |
| 73 | Regal Zono. SRZA 8513 | RAINSHINE (LP, unissued, demos only) | 150 |

*(see also Picadilly Line)*

## WINSTON EDWARS
| 75 | Fay FLP 2004 | NATTY LOCKS DUB (LP) | 200 |

## EDWICK RUMBOLD
| 66 | CBS 202393 | Specially When/Come Back | 120 |
| 67 | Parlophone R 5622 | Shades Of Grey/Boggle Woggle | 300 |

## EEK A MOUSE
| 80 | Greensleeves GRED 42 | Noah's Ark/FLICK WILSON: My Lady (12", green vinyl) | 20 |
| 81 | Love Linch LL019 | No Wicked/Trying To Be Free (12") | 50 |
| 81 | Greensleeves GRED 58 | Wa-Do-Dem/Wild Inna Eighty-One Style (12", with ERROL SHORTER) | 10 |
| 81 | Greensleeves GRED 74 | Christmas A Come/LEE VAN CLEEF: Water Gone (12") | 15 |
| 82 | Greensleeves GRED 88 | Do You Remember/TOYAN : Strictly The Dread (12") | 15 |
| 82 | Echo 12 008 | Georgie Porgie (with LUI LEPKI)/Version (12") | 15 |
| 83 | Greensleeves GRED 98 | Anarexol/Teacher (12") | 15 |
| 81 | Greensleeves GREL 31 | WA-DO-DEM (LP) | 15 |
| 82 | Greensleeves GREL 41 | SKIDIP! (LP) | 15 |
| 83 | Greensleeves GREL 86 | ASSASSINATOR (LP) | 15 |
| 84 | Greensleeves GRED 65 | MOUSEKETEER (LP) | 15 |

## EELS
| 96 | Dreamworks DRMS 22174 | Novocaine For The Soul/Fucker (p/s) | 20 |
| 97 | Dreamworks DRMS 22277 | Your Lucky Day In Hell/Altar Boy (p/s) | 5 |
| 97 | Dreamworks DRMS 22238 | Susan's House/Stepmother (p/s) | 8 |
| 98 | Dreamworks DRMS 22346 | Last Stop: This Town/Funeral Parlour (p/s) | 6 |
| 00 | Dreamworks 450945-7 | Flyswatter/Vice President Fruitley (Picture disc, stickered PVC sleeve) | 10 |

| | | | |
|---|---|---|---|
| 05 | Vagrant 988-188-0 | Hey Man (Now You're Really Living)/After The Operation (yellow vinyl, stickered p/s) ...5 | |
| 96 | Dreamworks DRLP 50001 | BEAUTIFUL FREAK (LP) | 100 |
| 01 | Dreamworks 450 335-1 | SOULJACKER (LP) | 40 |
| 10 | Eworks CSDLP 1145 | TOMORROW MORNING (LP and free 7") | 18 |

**E.F. BAND**

| | | | |
|---|---|---|---|
| 80 | Rok ROK XI/XII | Another Day Gone/SYNCHROMESH: October Friday (die-cut co. sleeve) | 40 |
| 80 | Aerco/EF Band EF 1 | Night Angel/Another Day Gone (p/s) | 30 |
| 80 | Aerco/EF Band EF 1 | Night Angel/Another Day Gone | 15 |
| 80 | Redball RR 026 | Self Made Suicide/Sister Syne (with wraparound p/s) | 30 |
| 80 | Redball RR 026 | Self Made Suicide/Sister Syne | 7 |
| 80 | Redball RR 036 | The Devil's Eye/Comprende (with wraparound p/s) | 25 |
| 80 | Redball RR 036 | The Devil's Eye/Comprende | 7 |
| 82 | Bullet CULP 2 | DEEP CUT (LP) | 15 |

**WILLIE EGANS**

| | | | |
|---|---|---|---|
| 70s | Flyright LP 6000 | ROCKS, BOOGIES AND ROLLS (LP) | 15 |

**JULIE EGE**

| | | | |
|---|---|---|---|
| 71 | CBS 5431 | Love/In One Of Your Weaker Moments | 6 |

**JOSEPH EGER**

| | | | |
|---|---|---|---|
| 70 | Charisma CAS 1008 | CLASSICAL HEADS (LP, gatefold sleeve, "pink scroll" label) | 25 |

**EGG**

| | | | |
|---|---|---|---|
| 69 | Deram DM 269 | Seven Is A Jolly Good Time/You Are All Princes | 40 |
| 70 | Deram Nova (S)DN 14 | EGG (LP, red/silver labels, with sticker on rear sleeve correcting credits) | 175 |
| 70 | Deram Nova (S)DN 14 | EGG (LP, 2nd pressing, orange label with black print) | 80 |
| 71 | Deram SML 1074 | THE POLITE FORCE (LP, red/white label with small logo) | 100 |
| 74 | Caroline C 1510 | THE CIVIL SURFACE (LP, red/white/red "twin" label) | 50 |
| 85 | See For Miles SEE 47 | SEVEN IS A JOLLY GOD TIME (LP) | 18 |

*(see also Hatfield & The North, Arzachel, Bunch Of Fives, Khan)*

**EGGY**

| | | | |
|---|---|---|---|
| 69 | Spark SRL 1024 | Hookey/You're Still Mine | 40 |

**EG OBLIQUE GRAPH**

| | | | |
|---|---|---|---|
| 82 | Recloose LOOSE 2 | TRIPTYCH EP | 30 |

*(see also Muslim Gauze)*

**EGYPT**

| | | | |
|---|---|---|---|
| 88 | HTD 7HTD 1 | Crazy Horses /Got No Fear (p/s) | 10 |
| 88 | HTD HTD LP 1 | EGYPT (LP, with inner) | 15 |

*(see also Paul Samson)*

**EGYPTIAN EMPIRE**

| | | | |
|---|---|---|---|
| 91 | Fokus FKFR 1 | The Horn Track (Original Mix)/The Horn Track (Mickey Finn Fog Horn Mix) (12") | 20 |
| 92 | FFRR TABX 115 | The Horn Track (Original Mix)/The Horn Track (Foghorn Mix)/The Horn Track (Toxic 2 Mix) (12") | 15 |

**8-EYED SPY**

| | | | |
|---|---|---|---|
| 82 | Fetish FE 19 | Diddy Wah Diddy/Dead You Me B Side (p/s) | 12 |
| 81 | Fetish FR 2003 | 8-EYED SPY (LP, with inner sleeve) | 20 |

*(see also Lydia Lunch)*

**808 STATE**

| | | | |
|---|---|---|---|
| 89 | ZTT ZANG 2CD | THE EXTENDED PLEASURES OF DANCE EP (CD, withdrawn) | 30 |

*(see also Hit Squad)*

**EIGHTH WONDER**

| | | | |
|---|---|---|---|
| 88 | CBS SCARE Y1 | I'm Not Scared/I'm Not Scared (Disco Mix)/J'ai Pas Peur (10", p/s, with Pet Shop Boys) | 15 |

*(see also Pet Shop Boys)*

**EIGHTIES LADIES**

| | | | |
|---|---|---|---|
| 86 | Music Of Life MOLIF 6 | Turned On To You/Sing Me/And I Knew That Love 12", p/s) | 20 |

*(see also Roy Ayers)*

**EINSTÜRZENDE NEUBAUTEN**

| | | | |
|---|---|---|---|
| 85 | Some Bizzare BART 12 | Yü-Gung/Seelebrennt/Sand (12", p/s) | 10 |
| 83 | Mute STUMM 14 | STRATEGIES AGAINST ARCHITECTURE (LP) | 15 |
| 87 | Some Bizarre BART 332 | FUENF AUF NACH OBEN OFFEN RICHTERSKALA (LP) | 15 |
| 89 | Some Bizarre BART 333 | HAUS DER LUEGE (LP) | 15 |
| 04 | Mute STUMM 221 | PERPETUUM MOBILE (2-LP) | 25 |

**EIRE APPARENT**

| | | | |
|---|---|---|---|
| 67 | Track 604 019 | Follow Me/Here I Go Again | 25 |
| 69 | Buddah 201 039 | Rock'N'Roll Band/Yes I Need Someone | 20 |
| 72 | Buddah 2011 117 | Rock'N'Roll Band/Yes I Need Someone (reissue) | 10 |
| 69 | Buddah 203 021 | SUN RISE (LP, featuring Jimi Hendrix, black/silver labels) | 200 |

*(see also Ernie Graham, Henry McCulloch)*

**EJECTED**

| | | | |
|---|---|---|---|
| 82 | Riot City RIOT 14 | HAVE YOU GOT 10p? (EP) | 10 |
| 82 | Riot City RIOT 19 | NOISE FOR THE BOYS (EP) | 10 |
| 82 | Riot City CITY 003 | A TOUCH OF CLASS (LP) | 20 |
| 83 | Riot City CITY 007 | THE SPIRIT OF REBELLION (LP) | 25 |

**EKSEN TRICK BRICK BAND**

| | | | |
|---|---|---|---|
| 78 | Aerco AERL 17 | SKY STORY (LP, with insert) | 30 |

**EKSEPTION**

| | | | |
|---|---|---|---|
| 70 | Philips 318 992 BF | Air/Dharma For One | 5 |
| 72 | Philips 6012 219 | Ava Maria/Dharma For One | 5 |
| 69 | Philips 6314 001 | BEGGAR JULIAN'S TIME TRIP (LP) | 15 |
| 70 | Philips 6314 005 | EKSEPTION (LP) | 18 |

MINT VALUE £

## EL PAS(S)O
| | | | |
|---|---|---|---|
| 71 | Philips 6423 005 | EKSEPTION III (LP, laminated sleeve) | 15 |
| 72 | Philips 6423 019 | 00.04 (LP) | 15 |
| 72 | Philips 6423 042 | V (LP, gatefold sleeve) | 15 |

## EL PAS(S)O
| | | | |
|---|---|---|---|
| 71 | Big Shot BI 572 | Out De Light, Baby/Mosquito I (both actually by Dennis Alcapone) | 15 |
| 71 | Punch PH 61 | Mosquito One/Out De Light (reissue) | 12 |

*(see also Dennis Alcapone)*

## MARGARET ELAINA
| | | | |
|---|---|---|---|
| 73 | Bullet BU 522 | Ben/RICHIE & NOW GENERATION: Laughing Stock Version | 5 |

## ELAINE
| | | | |
|---|---|---|---|
| 63 | Columbia DB 7091 | I Never Wonder Where My Baby Goes/Look But Don't Touch | 12 |

## ELANO B
| | | | |
|---|---|---|---|
| 81 | Ellie Jay EJSP 9639 | Diane/Too Late (p/s, insert) | 20 |

## ELASTICA
| | | | |
|---|---|---|---|
| 93 | Deceptive BLUFF 003 | Stutter/Pussycat (numbered die-cut sleeve, 1,500 only) | 12 |
| 93 | Deceptive BLUFF 003 | Stutter/Pussycat (White label test pressing) | 6 |
| 94 | Deceptive BLUFF 004 | Line Up/Vaseline (numbered die-cut sleeve, 1,500 only) | 8 |
| 95 | Deceptive BLUFF 014LP | ELASTICA (LP, with flexidisc & booklet, no'd & stickered sleeve, 5,000 only, mispressed labels) | 40 |
| 95 | Deceptive BLUFF 014LP | ELASTICA (LP) | 15 |
| 00 | Deceptive BLUFF 075LP | THE MENACE (LP, inner, poster, stickered sleeve) | 25 |

*(see also Suede)*

## ELASTIC BAND
| | | | |
|---|---|---|---|
| 68 | Decca F 12763 | Think Of You Baby/It's Been A Long Time Baby | 45 |
| 68 | Decca F 12815 | Do Unto Others (From "Mr. Rose" T.V. Series)/81/2 Hours Of Paradise | 60 |
| 69 | Decca Nova (S)DN 6 | EXPANSIONS ON LIFE (LP, mono) | 300 |
| 69 | Decca Nova (S)DN 6 | EXPANSIONS ON LIFE (LP, stereo) | 200 |

*(see also Mayfield's Mule, Sweet, Andy Scott, Love Affair, Northwind)*

## ELASTICK BAND
| | | | |
|---|---|---|---|
| 67 | Stateside SS 2056 | Spazz/Papier Mache (unissued, demos only) | 300 |

## DONNIE ELBERT
| | | | |
|---|---|---|---|
| 58 | Parlophone R 4403 | Let's Do The Stroll/Wild Child | 100 |
| 58 | Parlophone R 4403 | Let's Do The Stroll/Wild Child (78) | 40 |
| 65 | Sue WI 377 | A Little Piece Of Leather/Do Wat'cha Wanna | 35 |
| 65 | Sue WI 396 | You Can Push It (Or Pull It)/Lily Lou | 30 |
| 67 | CBS 2807 | Get Ready/Along Came Pride | 30 |
| 68 | Polydor BM 56234 | In Between The Heartaches/Too Far Gone | 20 |
| 68 | Polydor BM 56265 | This Old Heart Of Mine (Is Weak For You)/Run Little Girl | 10 |
| 68 | New Wave NW 001 | Baby Please Come Home/Without You | 8 |
| 69 | Deram DM 235 | Without You/Baby Please Come Home (reissue) | 45 |
| 69 | R&B UP 2000 | Without You/(different B-side) (white label test pressing only) | 8 |
| 72 | Epic EPC 7943 | Get Ready/Alone Came Pride | 5 |
| 72 | Mojo 2092 040 | This Old Heart Of Mine (Is Weak For You)/Good To Me | 5 |
| 72 | Jay Boy BOY 70 | Half As Old/Baby Let Me Love You Tonite | 5 |
| 72 | London HLU 10352 | Where Did Our Love Go/That's If You Love Me | 5 |
| 73 | London HLU 10370 | A Little Piece Of Leather/If I Can't Have You | 6 |
| 79 | Echo EC 7001 | Are You Ready (Willing And Able)/You Keep Me Crying (With Your Lying) | 8 |
| 97 | Joe Boy JBV 1 | So Soon/Can't Get Over Losing You (p/s with numbered certificate, 300 only) | 20 |
| 69 | Polydor 236 560 | TRIBUTE TO A KING (LP) | 50 |
| 73 | Ember EMB 3421 | THE ROOTS OF DONNIE ELBERT (LP) | 20 |

## ELBOW
| | | | |
|---|---|---|---|
| 98 | Soft Records Softrec001 | NOISEBOX EP: Powder Blue/Red/George Lassoes The Moon (Original version)/Theme From Munroe Kelly/Can't Stop (CD, 200 copies – 150 numbered) | 100 |
| 98 | Soft Records Softrec001 | NOISEBOX EP: Powder Blue/Red/George Lassoes The Moon (Original version)/Theme From Munroe Kelly/Can't Stop (CD, 200 copies – 50 un-numbered) | 50 |
| 05 | V2 VVR 5032547 | Forgot Myself/McGregor (mis-press A side plays Madness' 'Shame and Scandal') | 5 |
| 08 | Fiction 1767731 | One Day Like This/Every Bit The Little Girl | 15 |
| 08 | Fiction 1773700 | One Day Like This/L'il Pissed Charmin' Tune | 15 |
| 01 | V2 VVR 1015881 | ASLEEP IN THE BACK (2-LP) | 40 |
| 03 | V2 VVR 102181-1 | CAST OF THOUSANDS (LP) | 50 |
| 05 | V2 VVR 103255-1 | LEADERS OF THE FREE WORLD (LP) | 40 |
| 11 | Fiction 2763747 | BUILD A ROCKET BOYS! (2-LP, mispressing side B and D have same labels) | 20 |
| 11 | Fiction 2763747 | BUILD A ROCKET BOYS! (2-LP) | 18 |
| 12 | Fiction 3711518 | THE DEFINITIVE VINYL ALBUM BOX SET (7 x 2-LP, USB stick box set) | 200 |

## EL CHICANO
| | | | |
|---|---|---|---|
| 72 | MCA MUPS 445 | REVOLUCION (LP) | 15 |

## ELCORT
| | | | |
|---|---|---|---|
| 66 | Parlophone R 5447 | Tammy/Searchin' | 20 |

## ERIC ELDER
| | | | |
|---|---|---|---|
| 70 | Philips 6006 081 | San Tokay/Sunflower | 5 |

## ELDORADOS (JAMAICA)
| | | | |
|---|---|---|---|
| 70 | Bullet BU 428 | Savage Colt/The Clea Hog | 25 |

## ELDORADOS (RHODESIA)
| | | | |
|---|---|---|---|
| 63 | Decca DFE 8543 | THE ELDORADOS (EP) | 100 |

## ELDORADOS (U.S.)
| | | | |
|---|---|---|---|
| 72 | Mojo 2092 050 | Loose Booty (Parts 1 & 2) | 10 |

## ROY ELDRIDGE QUINTET
| | | | |
|---|---|---|---|
| 55 | Columbia/Clef 33C 9005 | ROY ELDRIDGE QUINTET (LP) | 15 |

## ROY ELDRIDGE & CLAUDE BOLLING
| | | | |
|---|---|---|---|
| 56 | Vogue V 2373 | Wild Man Blues/Fireworks | 10 |

## ELECAMPANE
| 75 | Dame Jane ODJ 1 | WHEN GOD'S ON THE WATER (LP, private pressing with insert) | 50 |
|---|---|---|---|
| 78 | Dame Jane ODJ 2 | FURTHER ADVENTURES OF MR PUNCH (LP, private pressing with booklet) | 20 |

## ELECKTROIDS
| 95 | Warp WARPLP 35 | ELEKTROWORLD (2-LP) | 100 |
|---|---|---|---|

## ELECTRIC EXPRESS
| 71 | Atlantic 2091 165 | It's The Real Thing Part 1/Part 2 | 12 |
|---|---|---|---|
| 00 | Grapevine 2000 G2K 45 | Hearsay (Vocal)/Hearsay (Instrumental) | 10 |

## ELECTRIC BANANA
| 67 | De Wolfe DW/LP 3040 | ELECTRIC BANANA (LP, 10", original issue, tricolour label) | 100 |
|---|---|---|---|
| 67 | De Wolfe DWLP 3040 | ELECTRIC BANANA (LP, second issue, with other artists) | 50 |
| 68 | De Wolfe DWLP 3069 | MORE ELECTRIC BANANA (LP) | 150 |
| 69 | De Wolfe DWLP 3123 | EVEN MORE ELECTRIC BANANA (LP) | 60 |
| 73 | De Wolfe DWLP 3284 | HOT LICKS (LP) | 60 |
| 76 | De Wolfe DWLP 3381 | THE RETURN OF THE ELECTRIC BANANA (LP) | 25 |
| 79 | Butt NOTT 001 | THE SEVENTIES (LP) | 20 |
| 80 | Butt NOTT 003 | THE SIXTIES (LP) | 20 |
| 97 | Tenth Planet TP 031 | THE ELECTRIC BANANA BLOWS YOUR MIND (LP, numbered, 1,000 only) | 35 |

*(see also Pretty Things, Zac Zolar & Electric Banana)*

## ELECTRIC CIRCUS
| 90 | White Label Only | Rhythm & Rhyme/Time | 10 |
|---|---|---|---|

## ELECTRIC CRAYONS
| 89 | Emergency MIV 3 | Hip Shake Junkie/Happy To Be Hated (p/s) | 20 |
|---|---|---|---|

*(see also Charlatans)*

## ELECTRIC DOLLS
| 73 | DJM 345 | Dr. Love/Love A Little Longer | 8 |
|---|---|---|---|
| 73 | Jam JAM 52 | Dr. Love/Love A Little Longer | 8 |

## ELECTRIC FLAG
| 68 | CBS 3584 | Groovin' Is Easy/Over-Lovin' You | 10 |
|---|---|---|---|
| 69 | CBS 4066 | Sunny/Soul Searchin' | 7 |
| 68 | CBS 62394 | A LONG TIME COMIN' (LP) | 20 |
| 69 | CBS 63462 | THE ELECTRIC FLAG — AN AMERICAN MUSIC BAND (LP) | 15 |

*(see also Mike Bloomfield, Buddy Miles, Barry Goldberg)*

## ELECTRICIANS
| 67 | Columbia DB 8228 | Champion House Theme/DON HARPER & ELECTRICIANS: Shin Bone | 7 |
|---|---|---|---|

*(see also Don Harper)*

## ELECTRIC INDIAN
| 69 | United Artists UP 35039 | Keem-O-Sabe/Broad Street | 5 |
|---|---|---|---|

*(see also Len Barry)*

## ELECTRIC JOHNNY
| 61 | London HLU 9384 | Black-Eyes Rock/Johnny On His Strings | 25 |
|---|---|---|---|

## ELECTRIC LIGHT ORCHESTRA (E.L.O.)
| 72 | Harvest HAR 5053 | 10538 Overture/1st Movement (Jumping Biz) | 6 |
|---|---|---|---|
| 72 | Harvest HAR 5063 | Roll Over Beethoven/Manhattan Rumble (49th Street Massacre) (with withdrawn B-side) | 10 |
| 72 | Harvest HAR 5063 | Roll Over Beethoven/Queen Of The Hours | 5 |
| 73 | Harvest HAR 5077 | Showdown/In Old England Town (Boogie 2) (Instrumental) | 8 |
| 81 | Jet ELO 2 | Mr Blue Sky/Across The Border/Telephone Line/Don't Bring Me Down (withdrawn, in p/s) | 8 |
| 81 | Jet ELO 2 | Mr Blue Sky/Across The Border/Telephone Line/Don't Bring Me Down (withdrawn) | 5 |
| 71 | Harvest SHVL 797 | ELECTRIC LIGHT ORCHESTRA (gatefold sleeve, with inner sleeve & lyric insert) | 90 |
| 72 | Harvest SHVL 806 | ELO 2 (LP, gatefold sleeve with EMI box on label) | 25 |
| 73 | Harvest Q4SHVL 797 | ELECTRIC LIGHT ORCHESTRA (quadrophonic, promo only) | 100 |
| 74 | Harvest SHSP 4037 | SHOWDOWN (LP) | 15 |
| 76 | Jet JETLP 19 | OLE ELO (withdrawn) | 15 |
| 77 | Jet UAG 30091 | ON THE THIRD DAY (new mix, new sleeve & inner sleeve) | 15 |
| 78 | Jet JETBX 1 | THREE LIGHT YEARS (3-LP, boxed set of "On The Third Day", "Eldorado" & "Face The Music", with booklet & inserts) | 18 |
| 78 | Jet JETLP 200 | A NEW WORLD RECORD (red vinyl, with inner sleeve) | 15 |
| 78 | Jet JETLP 201 | FACE THE MUSIC (green vinyl, with inner sleeve) | 15 |
| 78 | Jet JETLP 202 | ON THE THIRD DAY (clear vinyl, with inner sleeve) | 15 |
| 78 | Jet JETLP 203 | ELDORADO (yellow vinyl, with inner sleeve) | 15 |
| 78 | Jet JETDP 400 | OUT OF THE BLUE (2-LP, clear or dark blue vinyl, with inner sleeves, with cut-out spaceship, poster & insert) | 40 |

*(see also Idle Race, Move, Roy Wood, Michael D'Albuquerque, Wilson Gale & Co., Tandy-Morgan)*

## ELECTRIC PRUNES
| 66 | Reprise RS 20532 | I Had Too Much To Dream (Last Night)/Luvin' | 35 |
|---|---|---|---|
| 67 | Reprise RS 20564 | Get Me To The World On Time/Are You Lovin' Me More (But Enjoying It Less) | 30 |
| 67 | Reprise RS 20607 | The Great Banana Hoax/Wind-Up Toys | 20 |
| 67 | Reprise RS 23212 | A Long Day's Flight/The King Is In His Counting House | 18 |
| 68 | Reprise RS 20652 | Everybody Knows You're Not In Love/You Never Had It Better | 30 |
| 73 | Elektra K 12102 | I Had Too Much To Dream (Last Night)/KNICKERBOCKERS: Lies | 7 |
| 79 | Radar ADA 16 | I Had Too Much To Dream (Last Night)/Luvin' (p/s) | 8 |
| 67 | Reprise R(S)LP 6248 | THE ELECTRIC PRUNES (LP, mono/stereo) | 200 |
| 68 | Reprise R(S)LP 6275 | MASS IN F MINOR (LP, mono/stereo) | 120 |
| 68 | Reprise RSLP 6316 | RELEASE OF AN OATH (LP) | 120 |
| 86 | Edsel ED 179 | LONG DAY'S FLIGHT (LP) | 15 |

| 97 | Heartbeat HB 67 | STOCKHOLM '67 (LP, gatefold sleeve with booklet) | 20 |

## ELECTRIC TOILET
| 83 | Psycho PSYCHO 8 | IN THE HANDS OF KARMA (LP, reissue of U.S. LP) | 15 |

## ELECTRIC WIZARD
| 95 | Rise Above RISE 11 | Demon Lung/OUR HAUNTED KINGDOM: Aquatic Fanatic (blue vinyl, p/s) | 60 |
| 98 | Bad Acid TRIP 1 | Supercoven/Burnout (12", p/s) | 80 |
| 08 | Rise Above RISE 12/116 | The Processean (Procession) (1-sided 12", 500 only sold at Rise Above 20th Anniversary Gig, ULU London 13th December 2008) | 60 |
| 08 | Rise Above RISE 12/116 | The House On The Border/REVEREND BIZARRE: The Gates Of Nanna (12", 500 clear, 500 purple, 500 silver and 500 black vinyl, censored p/s) | 20 |
| 08 | Rise Above RISE 12/116 | The House On The Border/REVEREND BIZARRE: The Gates Of Nanna (12", 350 red vinyl, uncensored p/s, poster) | 50 |
| 95 | Rise Above RISE 009 | ELECTRIC WIZARD (LP, green vinyl) | 50 |
| 04 | Rise Above RISELP 48 | WE LIVE (2-LP, purple vinyl) | 70 |
| 04 | Rise Above RISELP 52 | DOPETHRONE (2-LP, white vinyl, reissue, first issued on CD in 2000) | 70 |
| 06 | Rise Above RISELP 48 | WE LIVE (2-LP, gatefold sleeve, reissue on green vinyl with 1-sided 7" "The Living Dead At Manchester Morgue") | 60 |
| 07 | Rise Above RISELP 74 | LET US PREY (2-LP, 100 clear vinyl, reissue first issued on CD in 2002) | 60 |
| 07 | Rise Above RISELP 74 | LET US PREY (2-LP, 500 dark red, 500 black vinyl, reissue first issued on CD in 2002) | 40 |
| 07 | Rise Above RISELP 100 | WITCHCULT TODAY (2-LP, 200 green vinyl, foil gatefold sleeve, poster, patch) | 50 |
| 07 | Rise Above RISELP 100 | WITCHCULT TODAY (2-LP, 500 silver vinyl, foil gatefold sleeve, poster, patch) | 40 |
| 10 | Rise Above RISELP 130 BOX | BLACK MASSES (2-LP, gatefold p/s, poster, comic, embroidered patch in box, clear vinyl, 100 only) | 350 |
| 10 | Rise Above RISELP 130 | BLACK MASSES (2-LP, gatefold p/s, poster, comic, embroidered patch in box, 400 only) | 120 |

## ELECTRIX
| 79 | ELX 001 | HOLLAND (EP) | 30 |

## ELECTRO HIPPIES
| 87 | Strange Fruit SFPS 042 | PEEL SESSIONS (12", metallic finish with insert) | 10 |
| 88 | Peaceville VILE 02 | THE ONLY GOOD PUNK... IS A DEAD ONE (LP) | 15 |
| 89 | Peaceville VILE 13 | LIVE (LP, clear vinyl) | 15 |
| 89 | Necrosis NECR 0001 | PLAY FAST OR DIE (LP) | 15 |

## ELECTRONIC
| 99 | Parlophone 12R651 | Late At Night/Make It Happen (Original Version)/Make It Happen (Darren Price Mix) (12" withdrawn) | 20 |
| 91 | Factory FACT 290 | ELECTRONIC (LP) | 20 |
| 06 | Parlophone PCS 7382 | RAISE THE PRESSURE (LP) | 25 |

*(see also New Order, Smiths, Pet Shop Boys, Joy Division)*

## ELECTRONIC CIRCUS
| 81 | Scratch SCR 002 | Direct Lines/Le Chorale (p/s) | 20 |

## ELECTRONIC EXPERIENCED
| 93 | Basement BRSS 025 | V-10 Overload/No. 303 (12") | 25 |
| 94 | Basement BRSS 032 | I.Q./I.Q. More (12") | 25 |

## ELECTROTUNES
| 80 | Cobra COS 5 | If This Ain't Love/Bodywork (p/s) | 5 |

## ELEGANTS
| 58 | HMV POP 520 | Little Star/Getting Dizzy | 15 |
| 58 | HMV POP 551 | Please Believe Me/Goodnight | 40 |

## ELEKTRAS
| 63 | United Artists UP 1027 | All I Want To Do Is Run/It Ain't Easy | 30 |

## ELEKTRIC MUSIC
| 93 | East West YZ 755 | TV/Television (p/s) | 8 |
| 93 | East West SAM 1252 | Lifestyle (Edit-Style Mix)/(Club-Style Mix)/(Phoneme-Style Mix) (10", promo) | 20 |

*(see also Kraftwerk)*

## ELEKTROIDS
| 95 | Warp WARPLP35 | ELEKTROWORLD (2-LP) | 40 |

## ELEMENTS
| 81 | Look LK/LP 6649 | ELEMENTARY (LP) | 30 |

## ELENA
| 65 | Columbia DB 7598 | Evening Time/Road Of Love | 20 |

## ELEPHANT BAND
| 72 | Mojo 2092 036 | Stone Penguin/Groovin' At The Apollo | 45 |

## ELEPHANT NOISE
| 91 | Own Label | This song Is Our Friend/Halloween Day/Remember The Big Time/Cactus Talk (12" EP) | 100 |

## ELEPHANT'S MEMORY
| 69 | Buddah 201055 | Crossroads Of The Stepping Stones/Yoghurt Song | 6 |
| 69 | Buddah 201067 | Old Man Willow/Jungle Gym At The Zoo | 25 |
| 70 | CBS 5207 | Mongoose/I Couldn't Dream | 25 |
| 72 | Apple APPLE 45 | Power Boogie/Liberation Special | 20 |
| 69 | Buddah 203 022 | ELEPHANT'S MEMORY (LP) | 30 |
| 72 | Apple SAPCOR 22 | ELEPHANT'S MEMORY (LP, gatefold sleeve with inner sleeve) | 40 |

*(see also John Lennon, Yoko Ono)*

## ELERI, JANET & DIANE
| 70s | Fanfare FR 2196 | THE ANSWER (LP) | 100 |

## ELEVATORS
| 80 | Koala KOA 401 | Your I's Are Too Close Together/That's My Baby | 60 |

## 11.59
| 74 | Dovetail DOVE 4 | THIS IS OUR SACRIFICE OF PRAISE (LP, with insert) | 40 |

## ELF
| | | | |
|---|---|---|---|
| 74 | Purple PUR 118 | L.A. 59/Ain't It All Amusing | 10 |
| 74 | Purple TPS 3506 | CAROLINA COUNTRY BALL (LP) | 30 |

*(see also Roger Glover, Dio, Rainbow, Deep Purple, Black Sabbath)*

## ELFLAND ENSEMBLE
| | | | |
|---|---|---|---|
| 77 | Chrysalis CHS 2151 | Too Much Magic (feat. Derek Brimstone)/Lizarel (featuring Mary Hopkin) (p/s) | 6 |
| 77 | Chrysalis CHS 2193 | Beyond The Fields We Know/Alveric's Journey | 6 |

*(see also Mary Hopkin)*

## STEVE ELGIN
| | | | |
|---|---|---|---|
| 74 | Dawn DNS 1093 | Don't Leave Your Lover Lying Around (Dear)/Seductress | 10 |

## ELGINS
| | | | |
|---|---|---|---|
| 66 | Tamla Motown TMG 551 | Put Yourself In My Place/Darling Baby | 130 |
| 66 | Tamla Motown TMG 551 | Put Yourself In My Place/Darling Baby (DJ Copy) | 150 |
| 66 | Tamla Motown TMG 583 | Heaven Must Have Sent You/Stay In My Lonely Arms | 80 |
| 66 | Tamla Motown TMG 583 | Heaven Must Have Sent You/Stay In My Lonely Arms (DJ Copy) | 120 |
| 67 | Tamla Motown TMG 615 | It's Been A Long Long Time/I Understand My Man | 35 |
| 67 | Tamla Motown TMG 615 | It's Been A Long Long Time/I Understand My Man (DJ Copy) | 50 |
| 68 | Tamla Motown TMG 642 | Put Yourself In My Place/Darling Baby (reissue) | 25 |
| 71 | Tamla Motown TMG 771 | Heaven Must Have Sent You/Stay In My Lonely Arms (reissue) | 7 |
| 71 | Tamla Motown TMG 787 | Put Yourself In My Place/It's Gonna Be Hard Times | 7 |
| 68 | T. Motown (S)TML 11081 | DARLING BABY (LP, mono/stereo) | 100 |

## ELIAS HULK
| | | | |
|---|---|---|---|
| 70 | Youngblood SSYB 8 | UNCHAINED (LP, laminated front cover, red/white label) | 1000 |

*(see also Babe Ruth)*

## ELIFFANT
| | | | |
|---|---|---|---|
| 79 | Macym MACYM 1 | Seren I Seren/Lisa Lan (no p/s) | 6 |
| 79 | Sain 1130M | M.O.M. (LP) | 20 |

## ELIGIBLES
| | | | |
|---|---|---|---|
| 59 | Capitol CL 15067 | Faker, Faker/24 Hours (Till My Date With You) | 10 |
| 59 | Capitol CL 15098 | The Little Engine/My First Christmas With You | 10 |
| 60 | Capitol CL 15203 | Young Is My Lover/East Of West Berlin | 5 |

## ELIJAH
| | | | |
|---|---|---|---|
| 71 | Ackee ACK 121 | Selassie High/Mount Zion | 20 |

## ELIMINATORS (1)
| | | | |
|---|---|---|---|
| 66 | Pye NPL 18160 | GUITARS AND PERCUSSION (LP, pink black label) | 25 |

## ELIMINATORS (2)
| | | | |
|---|---|---|---|
| 99 | Soul Brother SBC 54 | LOVING EXPLOSION (LP, reissue) | 20 |

## ELITE
| | | | |
|---|---|---|---|
| 79 | Aerco LAS 102 | Take Away/Part Of My Life (no p/s) | 8 |
| 79 | L&S | ANY PORT IN A STORM (LP, 500 only) | 20 |

## ELIXIR
| | | | |
|---|---|---|---|
| 85 | Elixir ELIXIR 1 | Treachery (Ride Like The Wind)/Winds Of Time (folded p/s with insert) | 80 |
| 86 | Elixir ELIXIR 2 | THE SON OF ODIN (LP, private pressing with insert) | 60 |
| 90 | Sonic SONICLP 9 | LETHAL POTION (LP, features Clive Burr) | 15 |

*(see also Iron Maiden)*

## ELIZABETH (1)
| | | | |
|---|---|---|---|
| 73 | Paramount PARA 3032 | Stop Killing Me With Kindness/Oh Bird | 6 |
| 68 | Vanguard SVRL 19010 | ELIZABETH (LP) | 150 |

## ELIZABETH (2)
| | | | |
|---|---|---|---|
| 77 | Creole CR 139 | God Save The Sex Pistols/Silver Story | 15 |

## ELIZABETH (3)
| | | | |
|---|---|---|---|
| 94 | Echo Special Prods ESPLP2 | QUEEN ELIZABETH (LP, mail order only, with inner sleeve) | 18 |
| 97 | Head Heritage HH2 | QUEEN ELIZABETH 2 - ELIZABETH VAGINA (2-CD mail order, 1000 only) | 30 |
| 02 | Head Heritage HH100 | QUEEN ELIZABETH 2 - ELIZABETH VAGINA (2-CD reissue, mail order, different artwork) | 25 |

*(see also Julian Cope)*

## ELKI & OWEN & RIM RAM BAND
| | | | |
|---|---|---|---|
| 69 | Revolution REV 004 | Groovie Kinda Love | 8 |

*(see also Elkie Brooks, Owen Gray)*

## JIMMY ELLEDGE
| | | | |
|---|---|---|---|
| 62 | RCA RCA 1274 | Swanee River Rocket/Funny How Time Slips Away | 15 |
| 65 | Hickory 45-1363 | Pink Dally Rue/(I'd Be) A Legend In My Time | 10 |
| 64 | RCA RCX 7132 | FUNNY HOW TIME SLIPS AWAY (EP) | 20 |

## ELLI
| | | | |
|---|---|---|---|
| 67 | Parlophone R 5575 | Never Mind/I'll Be Looking Out For You | 20 |
| 99 | Dig The Fuzz DIG 038 | ELLI (LP, 500 only) | 18 |

## ELLIE
| | | | |
|---|---|---|---|
| 74 | Fresh Air 6121111 | Tip Of My Tongue/Someones Stolen My Marbles | 8 |
| 74 | Fresh Air 6121123 | My Love Is Your Love/Let Me Shout It Out | 8 |

## YVONNE ELLIMAN
| | | | |
|---|---|---|---|
| 71 | MCA MK 5063 | I Don't Know How To Love Him/Jesus Christ Superstar Overture | 5 |
| 73 | Purple PUR 114 | I Can't Explain/Hawaii | 25 |
| 73 | Purple TPS 3504 | FOOD OF LOVE (LP) | 15 |

## DUKE ELLINGTON & HIS (FAMOUS) ORCHESTRA
| | | | |
|---|---|---|---|
| 60 | Philips SBBL 514 | ANATOMY OF A MURDER (soundtrack) | 25 |

## MARC ELLINGTON
| | | | |
|---|---|---|---|
| 68 | Philips BF 1665 | I Shall Be Released/Mrs. Whittle | 8 |

## Ray ELLINGTON QUARTET

| 69 | Philips BF 1742 | Did You Give The World Some Love Today Baby/Bless The Executioner | 8 |
| 69 | Philips BF 1779 | Four In The Morning/Peggy Day | 8 |
| 71 | Charisma CB 161 | Alligator Man/Song For A Friend | 8 |
| 69 | Philips (S)BL 7883 | MARC ELLINGTON (LP, black/silver labels) | 100 |
| 71 | B&C CAS 1033 | RAINS, REINS OF CHANGES (LP, envelope cover with lyric insert) | 100 |
| 72 | Philips 6308 120 | A QUESTION OF ROADS (LP, gatefold sleeve, black/silver label) | 100 |
| 72 | Xtra XTRA 1154 | MARC TIME (LP, with Fairport Convention) | 40 |
| 73 | Philips 6308 143 | RESTORATION (LP, blue/silver label) | 80 |

*(see also Fairport Convention, Matthews Southern Comfort)*

## RAY ELLINGTON QUARTET

| 53 | Columbia SCM 5050 | The Little Red Monkey/Kaw-Liga | 20 |
| 54 | Columbia SCM 5088 | All's Going Well (My Lady Montmorency) (with Marion Ryan)/Ol' Man River | 20 |
| 54 | Columbia SCM 5104 | Rub-A-Dub-Dub/The Owl Song | 15 |
| 54 | Columbia SCM 5147 | A.B.C. Boogie/Christmas Cards | 20 |
| 55 | Columbia SCM 5177 | Ko Ko Mo (I Love You So)/Woodpecker | 20 |
| 55 | Columbia SCM 5187 | Play It Boy, Play/The Irish Were Egyptians Long Ago | 20 |
| 55 | Columbia SCM 5199 | Cloudburst/Pet | 15 |
| 56 | Columbia SCM 5250 | Hold Him Tight/Who's Got The Money? | 10 |
| 56 | Columbia SCM 5274 | Keep The Coffee Hot/Lucky 13 | 10 |
| 56 | Columbia DB 3821 | Stranded In The Jungle/Left Hand Boogie | 20 |
| 56 | Columbia DB 3838 | Giddy-Up-A Ding Dong/The Green Door | 20 |
| 57 | Columbia DB 3905 | Marianne/That Rock 'N' Rollin' Man | 20 |
| 57 | Columbia DB 4013 | Don't Burn Me Up/Swaller-Tail Coat | 10 |
| 58 | Columbia DB 4057 | Living Doll/Long Black Nylons (solo) | 20 |
| 58 | Pye Nixa 7N 15159 | The Sultan Of Bezaaz/You Gotta Love Somebody | 5 |
| 59 | Pye Nixa 7N 15189 | Chip Off The Old Block/Charlie Brown | 10 |
| 59 | Oriole CB 1512 | Carina/I Was A Little Too Lonely | 5 |
| 60 | Ember EMB S 102 | The Madison/Jump Over (with Tony Crombie Orchestra) (p/s with insert) | 10 |
| 60 | Ember EMB S 114 | Très Jolie/Dracula's Three Daughters | 10 |
| 63 | Ember EMB S 172 | Too Old To Cut The Mustard/She Lied | 5 |
| 64 | Ember EMB S 188 | Rhythm Of The World/If You Can't Say Something Nice | 5 |
| 59 | Pye Nixa NPL 83011 | THAT'S NICE (LP, with Judd Proctor, mono) | 20 |
| 59 | Pye Nixa NPL 18032 | THAT'S NICE (LP, with Judd Proctor, stereo) | 20 |

*(see also Tony Crombie, Marion Ryan)*

## ELLINGTONS

| 79 | Grapevine GRP 114 | (I'm Not) Destined To Become A Loser/MILLIONAIRES: You've Got To Love Your Baby | 10 |
| 79 | Grapevine GRP 114 | (I'm Not) Destined To Become A Loser/MILLIONAIRES: You've Got To Love Your Baby (DJ Copy) | 20 |

## BILL ELLIOT & ELASTIC OZ BAND

| 71 | Apple APPLE 36 | God Save Us/Do The Oz (initially with p/s) | 60 |
| 71 | Apple APPLE 36 | God Save Us/Do The Oz | 20 |

*(see also Splinter, John Lennon/Yoko Ono)*

## DEREK & DOROTHY ELLIOT

| 72 | Trailer LER 2023 | DEREK & DOROTHY ELLIOT (LP) | 15 |
| 76 | Tradition TSR 025 | YORKSHIRE RELISH (LP) | 15 |

## MAMA CASS (ELLIOT)

| 68 | Stateside S(S)L 5004 | DREAM A LITTLE DREAM (LP) | 20 |
| 69 | Stateside S(S)L 5014 | BUBBLEGUM, LEMONADE AND SOMETHING FOR MAMA (LP) | 18 |
| 72 | RCA SF 8306 | THE ROAD IS NO PLACE FOR A LADY (LP) | 15 |

*(see also Mamas & Papas, Big Three, Dave Mason & Cass Elliot, Mugwumps)*

## ELLIOT MANSIONS

| 71 | President PT 323 | Float On Up/Shades And Shadows | 12 |
| 72 | President PT 361 | Don't Want To Live Inside Myself/Three Score And Ten | 6 |

## BERN ELLIOTT (& FENMEN)

| 63 | Decca F 11770 | Money/Nobody But Me | 10 |
| 64 | Decca F 11852 | New Orleans/Everybody Needs A Little Love | 10 |
| 64 | Decca F 11970 | Good Times/What Do You Want With My Baby (as Bern Elliott & Klan) | 10 |
| 65 | Decca F 12051 | Guess Who/Make It Easy On Yourself (solo) | 12 |
| 65 | Decca F 12171 | Lipstick Traces/Voodoo Woman (solo) | 20 |
| 64 | Decca DFE 8561 | BERN ELLIOTT AND THE FENMEN (EP) | 30 |

*(see also Fenmen)*

## DAVID ELLIOTT

| 72 | Atlantic K40374 | DAVID ELLIOTT (LP, with lyric insert) | 20 |

## JACK ELLIOTT

| 69 | Leader LEA 4001 | JACK ELLIOTT OF BIRTLEY (LP, with booklet) | 20 |

*(see also Elliotts Of Birtley)*

## (RAMBLIN') JACK ELLIOTT

| 56 | Topic TRC 98 | Talking Miner Blues/Pretty Boy Floyd (78) | 20 |
| 57 | Topic TRC 103 | Old Blue/Rambling Blues (78) | 20 |
| 57 | Topic TRC 104 | Streets Of Laredo/Boll Weevil (78) | 20 |
| 65 | Fontana TF 575 | More Pretty Girls/Roll On Buddy (as Jack Elliott) | 5 |
| 65 | Columbia DB 7593 | Rusty Jigs And Sandy Sam/Rocky Mountain Belle (as Ramblin' Jack Elliott) | 6 |
| 58 | 77 Records EP/1 | JACK ELLIOTT SINGS Vol 1. (EP) | 100 |
| 58 | 77 Records EP/2 | JACK ELLIOTT SINGS Vol. 2. (EP) | 100 |
| 60 | Columbia SEG 8046 | KID STUFF (EP) | 10 |
| 61 | Collector JEA 5 | RAMBLING JACK ELLIOTT (EP) | 20 |
| 64 | Collector JEA 6 | BLUES AND COUNTRY (EP) | 20 |
| 55 | Topic T 5 | WOODY GUTHRIE'S BLUES (8" mini-LP) | 40 |

| 57 | Topic 10T 15 | JACK TAKES THE FLOOR (10" LP) | 40 |
| 59 | Columbia 33SX 1166 | RAMBLIN' JACK ELLIOT IN LONDON (LP) | 20 |
| 62 | Encore ENC 194 | IN LONDON (LP, reissue of Columbia 33SX 1166) | 20 |
| 60 | Columbia 33SX 1291 | RAMBLIN' JACK ELLIOTT SINGS WOODY GUTHRIE & JIMMIE RODGERS (LP) | 40 |
| 61 | 77 LP 1 | JACK ELLIOT SINGS (10" LP, spelt 'Elliot' on sleeve) | 175 |
| 65 | Fontana TFL 6044 | JACK ELLIOTT (LP) | 20 |
| 65 | Stateside SL 10143 | JACK ELLIOTT COUNTRY STYLE (LP) | 20 |
| 66 | Stateside SL 10167 | SINGS THE SONGS OF WOODY GUTHRIE (LP) | 20 |
| 57 | Topic 10T 14 | THE RAMBLING BOYS (10" LP, stickered Topic sleeve, insert) | 60 |
| 63 | Topic 12T 105 | THE RAMBLING BOYS (LP, reissue of above with 2 extra tracks) | 50 |
| 64 | Topic 12T 106 | MULESKINNERS (LP) | 30 |
| 67 | Bounty BY 6036 | ROLL ON BUDDY - THE JACK ELLIOTT AND DERROLL ADAMS STORY VOL. 1 (LP) | 50 |

## KEN ELLIOTT
| 79 | RCA PL 26262 | BODY MUSIC (LP) | 25 |

## MARI ELLIOTT
| 76 | GTO GT 58 | Silly Billy/Half Past One | 15 |

*(see also Poly Styrene, X Ray Spex)*

## MIKE ELLIOTT
| 72 | Ackee ACK 151 | Milk And Honey/Burst A Shirt | 7 |

## PETER ELLIOTT
| 57 | Parlophone R 4355 | To The Aisle/All At Once (You Love Her) | 5 |
| 58 | Parlophone R 4457 | Devotion/No Fool Like An Old Fool | 5 |
| 59 | Parlophone R 4514 | Call Me/Flamingo | 5 |
| 59 | Parlophone R 4529 | The Young Have No Time/Over And Over | 5 |
| 61 | Top Rank JAR 390 | Waiting For Robert E. Lee/Toot Toot Tootsie | 5 |
| 61 | Fontana 325 | Three Little Peggies/The Devil's Workshop | 5 |
| 66 | Strike JH 311 | Thinking/Song Is Love | 5 |

## SHAWN ELLIOTT
| 62 | Stateside SS 124 | Goodbye My Lover/Ain't That A Shame | 5 |
| 63 | Stateside SS 174 | Sincerely And Tenderly/Why Don't You Love Me Anymore | 8 |
| 64 | Rio R 51 | Shame And Scandal In The Family/My Girl | 8 |
| 64 | Columbia DB 7418 | My Girl/Shame And Scandal In The Family (reissue) | 8 |
| 71 | London HLK 10347 | Child Is Father To The Man/Any Dream Will Do | 12 |

## SIDNEY ELLIOTT
| 69 | Spark SRL 1021 | Who Dat Girl In The Mini Skirt/Strawberry Blonde | 12 |
| 71 | CBS 7448 | Man And Woman/Stolen Fruit | 8 |
| 71 | CBS 7683 | Desperation/Came To See Me Yesterday | 12 |

## ELLIOTTS OF BIRTLEY
| 69 | Xtra XTRA 1091 | A MUSICAL PORTRAIT OF A DURHAM MINING FAMILY (LP) | 15 |

*(see also Jack Elliott)*

## ELLIOTT'S SUNSHINE
| 68 | Philips BF 1649 | Is It Too Late/'Cos I'm Lonely | 10 |

## ELLIS
| 72 | Epic S EPC 64878 | RIDING ON THE CREST OF A SLUMP (LP) | 20 |
| 72 | Epic SEPC 1052 | El Doomo/Your Game | 6 |
| 73 | Epic SEPC 1627 | Open Road/Leaving In The Morning | 6 |

*(see also Steve Ellis)*

## ALTON ELLIS (& FLAMES)
| 65 | Island WI 239 | Dance Crasher (with Flames)/BABA BROOKS: Vitamin A | 50 |
| 65 | Island WI 241 | You Are Not To Blame/BABA BROOKS: Teenage Ska | 70 |
| 66 | Doctor Bird DB 1044 | Blessings Of Love/Nothing Sweeter (as Alton & Flames) | 60 |
| 66 | Doctor Bird DB 1049 | The Preacher (as Alton & Flames)/LYNN TAITT & COMETS: Tender Loving Care | 40 |
| 66 | Doctor Bird DB 1055 | Shake It (with Flames)/SILVERTONES: Whoo Baby | 45 |
| 66 | Doctor Bird DB 1059 | Girl I've Got A Date (with Flames)/LYN TAITT & TOMMY McCOOK: The Yellow Basket | 40 |
| 67 | Island WI 3046 | Cry Tough (with Flames)/TOMMY McCOOK & SUPERSONICS: Mr Solo | 150 |
| 67 | Treasure Isle TI 7004 | Rocksteady (with Flames)/TOMMY McCOOK & SUPERSONICS: Wall Street Shuffle | 40 |
| 67 | Treasure Isle TI 7010 | Duke Of Earl/All My Tears (with Flames) | 35 |
| 67 | Treasure Isle TI 7016 | Ain't That Loving You/TOMMY McCOOK/SUPERSONICS: Tommy's Rocksteady | 35 |
| 67 | Treasure Isle TI 7030 | Oowee Baby/How Can I (with Flames) | 25 |
| 67 | Treasure Isle TI 7044 | Willow Tree/I Can't Stop Now | 25 |
| 67 | Trojan TR 004 | Ain't That Loving You (with Flames)/TOMMY McCOOK & SUPERSONICS: Comet Rocksteady | 30 |
| 67 | Trojan TR 009 | Wise Birds Follow Spring/TOMMY McCOOK & SUPERSONICS: Soul Rock | 25 |
| 67 | Studio One SO 2028 | I Am Just A Guy/SOUL VENDORS: Just A Little Bit Of Soul | 60 |
| 67 | Studio One SO 2033 | Only Sixteen/Baby (both actually by Heptones) | 20 |
| 68 | Studio One SO 2037 | Live And Learn/HEPTONES: Cry Baby Cry | 35 |
| 68 | Trojan TR 630 | I Can't Stand It/Trying To Reach My Goal | 25 |
| 68 | Trojan TR 642 | Breaking Up/Party Time | 18 |
| 68 | Nu Beat NB 010 | I Can't Stand It/Tonight | 45 |
| 68 | Nu Beat NB 013 | Bye Bye Love/MONTY MORRIS: My Lonely Days | 50 |
| 68 | Nu Beat NB 014 | La La Means I Love You/Give Me Your Love | 15 |
| 68 | Pama PM 707 | The Message/Some Talk | 18 |
| 68 | Pama PM 717 | My Time Is The Right Time/JOHNNY MOORE: Tribute To Sir Alex | 45 |
| 68 | Coxsone CS 7071 | A Fool/SOUL VENDORS: West Of The Sun | 80 |
| 69 | Studio One SO 2084 | Change Of Plans/CABLES: He'll Break Your Heart (B-side act. by Mad Lads) | 40 |
| 69 | Gas GAS 105 | Diana/English Talk | 60 |
| 69 | Bamboo BAM 2 | Better Example/DUKE MORGAN: Lick It Back | 70 |
| 69 | Duke DU 14 | Diana/Personality | 25 |

# Alton ELLIS & THE HEPTONES

| 70 | Duke DU 72 | Remember That Sunday/TOMMY McCOOK & SUPERSONICS: Last Lick .................... 40 |
|----|-----------|-----|
| 70 | Gas GAS 151 | Suzie/Life Is Down In Denver (some copies credit Alton Ellis & Flames) ............... 12 |
| 70 | Gas GAS 161 | Deliver Us/NEVILLE HINDS: Originator ................................................... 10 |
| 70 | Duke Reid DR 2501 | What Does It Take To Win Your Love/TOMMY McCOOK: Reggae Meringue ............... 12 |
| 70 | Duke Reid DR 2512 | You Made Me So Very Happy/TOMMY McCOOK & SUPERSONICS: Continental ............ 25 |
| 70 | Bamboo BAM 29 | Tumbling Tears/SOUND DIMENSION: Today Version ................................. 18 |
| 70 | Techniques TE 903 | It's Your Thing/TECHNIQUES ALL STARS: Get Left ................................. 15 |
| 70 | Techniques TE 905 | I'll Be Waiting/TECHNIQUES ALL STARS: I'll Be Waiting Version ..................... 15 |
| 71 | Banana BA 318 | Sunday Coming/CARL BRYAN: Sunday Version ................................... 20 |
| 71 | Banana BA 330 | Bam Bye/Keep On Yearning ................................................... 18 |
| 71 | Banana BA 347 | Hey World/Harder And Harder .................................................. 20 |
| 71 | Gas GAS 164 | Back To Africa/NEVILLE HINDS: Originator ........................................ 10 |
| 71 | Fab FAB 165 | Good Good Loving/Since I Fell For You ........................................... 40 |
| 71 | Bullet BU 466 | Black Man's Pride/LEROY PALMER: Groove With It ................................ 18 |
| 71 | Bullet BU 485 | Don't Care/True Born African ................................................. 18 |
| 71 | Smash SMA 2319 | A Little Loving/DELROY WILSON & ALTON ELLIS: Loving Version ........................ 7 |
| 71 | Smash SMA 2320 | I'll Be There/ITALS: Rude Boy Train ............................................... 7 |
| 72 | Big Shot BI 589 | Be True/Be True — Version ...................................................... 5 |
| 72 | Big Shot BI 602 | I'm Trying/Luna's Mood ....................................................... 15 |
| 72 | Count Shelly CS 004 | Follow My Heart/KOOS ALL STARS: Sincerely ...................................... 10 |
| 72 | Spur SP 3 | All That We Need Is Love/KEITH HUDSON: Better Love ............................... 30 |
| 72 | Grape GR 3029 | Big Bad Boy/HUDSON'S ALLSTARS: Big Bad Version .................................. 7 |
| 72 | Ackee ACK 145 | Oppression/Oppression Version (both with Zoot Simms) .......................... 45 |
| 72 | Ackee ACK 148 | Let's Stay Together/Version .................................................... 30 |
| 72 | Ackee ACK 502 | Too Late To Turn Back Now/IMPACT ALLSTARS: Version ............................ 15 |
| 72 | Jackpot JP 796 | Play It Cool/AGGROVATORS: King Of The Zozas ..................................... 10 |
| 72 | Camel CA 94 | Wonderful World/FAB DIMENSION: Wonderful Version ............................... 6 |
| 72 | Pama PM 840 | Girl I've Got A Date/Eat Bread ................................................... 5 |
| 72 | Pama Supreme PS 347 | Moon River/I Can't Find Out ..................................................... 7 |
| 72 | Pama Supreme PS 361 | Working On A Groovy Thing/HARLESDEN SKANKERS: Version ........................ 12 |
| 73 | Ackee ACK 511 | Alton's Official Daughter/Aquarius Dub (both with Herman) ....................... 15 |
| 73 | Harry J. HJ 6653 | Deliver Us To Africa/Nyah Medley .................................................. 5 |
| 73 | Pyramid PYR 7003 | Truly/LLOYD COXSONE SIX: Cruising ................................................ 25 |
| 73 | A&M AMS 7093 | Shoo BeDoo Be Doo/I Love You True .............................................. 25 |
| 75 | Bam Bam BAM 02 | I'm Still In Love With You/Version ................................................ 25 |
| 75 | Atra ATRA 26 | Rasta Spirit/WILD BUNCH: Jal Dub ................................................. 40 |
| 77 | Venture VEN7709 | Confusion/Version ............................................................ 10 |
| 77 | Grove GMDM 13 | It's Hard To Be A Lover/Love Like Mine (12") ..................................... 10 |
| 79 | Cha Cha | Children Are Crying/Mr. Ska Beana ............................................... 15 |
| 83 | Fashion FAD 013 | Too Late To Turn Back Now/Party Mix (12") ....................................... 12 |
| 12 | Doctor Bird THB 7022 | Honey I Love/Don't Trouble People .............................................. 10 |
| 67 | Coxsone CSL 8008 | SINGS ROCK AND SOUL (LP) ..................................................... 150 |
| 69 | Coxsone CSL 8019 | THE BEST OF ALTON ELLIS (LP) ................................................... 100 |
| 71 | Bamboo BDLPS 214 | SUNDAY COMING (LP) ........................................................... 80 |
| 80 | Cha Cha | MR. SKABEANA (LP) ............................................................. 20 |
| 77 | Trojan HRLP 708 | STILL IN LOVE (LP) .............................................................. 25 |
| 73 | Count Shelly SSLO 02 | ALTON ELLIS'S GREATEST HITS (LP) ................................................ 45 |

*(see also Alton & Eddy, Hortense Ellis, Hortense & Alton, Flames [Jamaica], Righteous Flames,Tony Gordon)*

## ALTON ELLIS & THE HEPTONES

| 80 | Cha Cha CHAD 21 | Mr. Ska Beana/ALTON ELLIS: Ain't No Music (12") ................................. 25 |
|----|-----------|-----|

## BOBBY ELLIS

| 68 | Island WI 3136 | Dollar A Head (with Crystalites)/RUDY MILLS: I'm Trapped ......................... 45 |
|----|-----------|-----|
| 74 | Dragon DRA 1033 | Up Park Camp/Verse 4 ........................................................... 6 |

*(see also Derrick Harriot, Rudy Mills, Crystalites, Keith & Tex, Eric Morris, Roy Richards, Soul Vendors)*

## DAVE ELLIS

| 72 | Sonet SNTF 646 | ALBUM (LP) ................................................................... 25 |
|----|-----------|-----|

## ELLIS DEE PROJECT

| 92 | Ellis Dee Project LSD 001 | Do You Want Me/Rock To The Max (12") ......................................... 20 |
|----|-----------|-----|
| 92 | Ellis Dee Project LSD 003 | Dance Factor (1-sided 12") ..................................................... 20 |
| 92 | Ellis Dee Project LSD 004 | Dance Factor (Rennie P Remix)/Don't Stop Rocking (12") ......................... 10 |
| 92 | Ellis Dee Project LSD 005 | Desire/Renegade (12") ......................................................... 10 |

## DON ELLIS (ORCHESTRA)

| 69 | CBS 4518 | Eli's Comin'/House In The Country .............................................. 5 |
|----|-----------|-----|
| 68 | Liberty LBL 83060E | LIVE IN THREE QUARTER TIME (LP) ................................................ 20 |
| 68 | CBS 63230 | ELECTRIC BATH (LP) ............................................................ 25 |
| 68 | CBS 63356 | SHOCK TREATMENT (LP) ........................................................ 15 |
| 69 | CBS 63680 | THE NEW DON ELLIS BAND GOES UNDERGROUND (LP) ............................. 15 |

## HERB ELLIS-JIMMY GIUFFRE ALL STARS

| 60 | HMV POP 721 | Goose Grease/My Old Flame ..................................................... 6 |
|----|-----------|-----|

## HORTENSE ELLIS

| 63 | R&B JB 101 | I'll Come Softly/I'm In Love (with Alton Ellis) .................................... 20 |
|----|-----------|-----|
| 65 | Blue Beat BB 295 | I've Been A Fool/Hold Me Tenderly .............................................. 25 |
| 67 | Fab FAB 20 | Somebody Help Me (with Buster's All Stars)/ PRINCE BUSTER & ALL STARS: Rock & Shake ........................................................................ 80 |
| 68 | Coxsone SC 7033 | A Man Of Chances(as Tree Tops)/HORTENSE ELLIS: A Groovy Kind Of Love ........ 300 |
| 70 | Bullet BU 427 | Last Date/PAT SATCHMO: Cherry Pink ............................................ 45 |
| 70 | Gas GAS 160 | To The Other Man/MUSIC BLENDERS: Raindrops ................................... 7 |
| 70 | Techniques TE 908 | To The Other Man/TECHNIQUES ALL STARS: To The Other Man Version ............. 7 |
| 71 | Gas 166 | I Shall Sing/Stand By Your Man ................................................. 15 |

| 72 | Green Door GD 4035 | Bringing In The Sheaves (with Stranger Cole)/Version ........................................... 6 |
|----|---|---|
| 73 | Tropical AL020 | Woman in The Ghetto/Instrumental Version ................................................ 20 |
| 77 | Hawkeye HE 02 | Superstar/Superstick ........................................................ 12 |
| 78 | Hawk Eye HE 007 | Unexpected Places/Lovers Places .............................................. 10 |
| 76 | Third World TWS 918 | JAMAICA'S FIRST LADY OF SONG (LP) ............................................ 20 |

(see also Hortense & Alton, Hortense & Delroy, Hortense & Jackie, Alton Ellis, Duke Reid, Three Tops, Jackie Opal)

## JOHN ELLIS
| 80 | Rat Race RAT 1 | Babies In Jars/Photostadt (p/s) ............................................................ 5 |
|----|---|---|

(see also Vibrators)

## JO-JO ELLIS
| 72 | Fury FY 302 | The Fly/Perdona Mia .................................................... 30 |
|----|---|---|

## LARRY ELLIS
| 58 | Felsted AF 110 | Buzz Goes The Bee/Nothing You Can Do ................................... 15 |
|----|---|---|

## MATTHEW ELLIS
| 71 | Regal Zonophone RZ 3033 | Avalon/You Are ................................................... 15 |
|----|---|---|
| 71 | Regal Zonophone RZ 3039 | Birthday Song/Salvation ........................................ 10 |
| 72 | Regal Zonophone RZ 3045 | Palace Of Plenty/Two By Two ................................... 12 |
| 71 | Regal Zono. SRZA 8501 | MATTHEW ELLIS (LP, gatefold sleeve, red/silver labels) ........... 40 |
| 72 | Regal Zono. SRZA 8505 | AM I...? (LP, gatefold sleeve, red/silver labels) .................... 50 |

(see also Procol Harum, Chris Spedding)

## SHIRLEY ELLIS
| 63 | London HLR 9824 | The Nitty Gritty/Give Me A List ................................... 10 |
|----|---|---|
| 65 | London HLR 9946 | The Name Game/Whisper To Me Wind ......................... 10 |
| 65 | London HLR 9961 | The Clapping Song/This Is Beautiful ............................ 10 |
| 65 | London HLR 9973 | The Puzzle Song/I See It, I Like It, I Want It .................... 8 |
| 66 | London HLR 10021 | Ever See A Diver Kiss His Wife While The Bubbles Bounce About Above The Water?/Stardust ........................................... 8 |
| 67 | CBS 202606 | Soul Time/Waitin' (DJ copy) ..................................... 75 |
| 67 | CBS 202606 | Soul Time/Waitin' ................................................ 40 |
| 67 | CBS 2817 | Sugar Let's Shing-A-Ling/How Lonely Is Lonely ............... 15 |
| 71 | CBS 7463 | Soul Time/Waitin' (reissue) ..................................... 20 |
| 77 | CBS 4901 | Soul Time/Waitin' (2nd reissue, blue coloured vinyl) ........ 10 |
| 67 | CBS (S)BPG 63044 | SOUL TIME WITH SHIRLEY ELLIS (LP) ........................... 70 |

(see also Love Affair, Widowmaker, Zoot Money, Peter Bardens)

## (STEVE) ELLIS
| 70 | CBS 4992 | Loot/More More More .............................................. 70 |
|----|---|---|
| 70 | CBS 5199 | Evie/Fat Crow ..................................................... 5 |
| 71 | CBS 7037 | Take Your Love/Jingle Jangle Jasmine .......................... 5 |
| 71 | CBS 7411 | Hold On/Goody Goody Dancing Shoes ......................... 5 |
| 72 | Ariola ARO 107 | Rag And Bone/Save All Your Encores ........................... 5 |
| 72 | Epic EPC 64878 | RIDING ON THE CREST OF A SLUMP (LP, as Ellis) ............. 20 |
| 73 | Epic EPC 65650 | WHY NOT? (LP, as Ellis) .......................................... 20 |

(see also Ellis)

## TONY ELLIS
| 79 | Sonet SON 2182 | Punky Reggae/Our Music (no p/s) ............................... 5 |
|----|---|---|

## ANDY ELLISON
| 68 | Track 604 018 | It's Been A Long Time/JOHN'S CHILDREN: Arthur Green ...... 70 |
|----|---|---|
| 68 | CBS 3357 | Fool From Upper Eden/Another Lucky Lie ...................... 45 |
| 68 | S.N.B. 55-3308 | You Can't Do That/Casbah ....................................... 75 |
| 68 | S.N.B. 55-3308 | You Can't Do That/Cornflake Zoo (second issue, different B-side) ..... 85 |

(see also John's Children, Jet, Radio Stars, Beau Brummel)

## LORRAINE ELLISON
| 66 | Warner Bros WB 5850 | Stay With Me/I Got My Baby Back ............................... 15 |
|----|---|---|
| 66 | Warner Bros WB 5850 | Stay With Me/I Got My Baby Back (1969 re-pressing) ......... 5 |
| 68 | Warner Bros WB 2094 | Try (Just A Little Bit Harder)/In My Tomorrow ................ 5 |
| 70 | Warner Bros WB 7394 | You've Really Got A Hold On Me/You Don't Know Anything About Love ..... 10 |
| 71 | Mercury 6052 073 | Call Me Anytime You Need Some Lovin'/Please Don't Teach Me To Love You ..... 30 |
| 70 | Warner Bros WS 1821 | STAY WITH ME (LP) ............................................... 30 |

## ELMER HOCKETT'S HURDY GURDY
| 68 | Parlophone R 5716 | Fantastic Fair/MOOD MOSAIC: The Yellow Spotted Capricorn ........ 15 |
|----|---|---|

(see also Mood Mosaic, Mark Wirtz)

## IAN ELMS
| 82 | Squid Marks SMT 013 | GOOD NIGHT (LP, with insert) ................................. 180 |
|----|---|---|

## ELOY
| 83 | Heavy Metal HMPD 1 | Fools/Heartbeat (clear vinyl) .................................... 6 |
|----|---|---|
| 82 | Heavy Metal HMILP 1 | PLANETS (LP, clear vinyl with inner sleeve) ................... 15 |
| 82 | Heavy Metal HMIPD 1 | PLANETS (LP, picture disc) ...................................... 18 |
| 82 | Heavy Metal HMIPD 3 | TIME TO TURN (LP, picture disc) ............................... 18 |
| 83 | Heavy Metal HMIPD 12 | PERFORMANCE (LP, picture disc) ............................... 15 |
| 84 | Heavy Metal HMIPD 21 | METROMANIA (LP, picture disc) ................................ 18 |
| 89 | FM Revolver REV PD120 | RA (LP, picture disc) ............................................. 15 |

## RAS ELROY
| 81 | Arawak DD 030 | Stepping/Walking On (12") ...................................... 30 |
|----|---|---|

(see also Elroy Baily)

## JEFF ELROY & BOYS BLUE
| 66 | Philips BF 1533 | Honey Machine/Three Woman .................................. 30 |
|----|---|---|

(see also Boys Blue)

## EL 7
80   Pop 000            MAGNIFICO EP ...................................................................................................... 7

## ELTI-FITS
80   Worthing Street WSEF 1     GOING STRAIGHT (EP, various foldover picture sleeves) ............................. 10

## ELVES
70   MCA MU 1114         Amber Velvet/West Virginia ....................................................................... 7

## CAROL ELVIN
63   Columbia DB 7095       'Cos I Know/C'mon Over ............................................................................ 10
65   Parlophone R 5228      Don't Leave Me/'Cos I Love You ................................................................ 10

## LEE & JAY ELVIN
59   Fontana H 191         So The Story Goes/When You See Her ...................................................... 20
*(see also Jerry Lordan)*

## ELVIS HITLER
90   GWR GWLP 37         DISGRACELAND (LP) ................................................................................... 20

## EMANON
77   Clubland SJP 777        Raging Pain/Rip A Bough (stamped sleeve) ............................................. 30

## ROBERT EMANUEL
80   Black Roots BRD 1      Illiteracy/RANKING SIMEON: Cultural Dread/Unknown Artist: Progress Road Dub/
                              Don't Get Weary/RANKING SIMEON: Don't Get Jumpy/Unknown Artist: Strictly Rub-
                              A-Dub (12") ........................................................................................ 20
81   Black Roots BR 25      Never Get Away/Jah Is My Light (12" as Robert Emanuel & Ranking Simeon) .............. 45
85   CF CMF 02           Fashion Dread/No Beggy Beggy (12") ...................................................... 50
84   Black Roots BR 181262   Leave Natty Business/BARRINGTON LEVY & DARBAZ: Jah Black (12") ......... 20

## EMBASSY
90   Impact SRT 90LS 2554   You Can't Poison Me/Take Me Back/How Loud Is Too Loud/She's Got The Mind (12") .. 10

## BOBBIE EMBER
65   Polydor BM 56062      Why Can't You Bring Me Home/When Love Isn't There ............................. 10

## EMBERS
63   Decca F 11625         Chelsea Boots/Samantha ......................................................................... 20
*(see also David & Embers, Three's A Crowd)*

## EMBRACE
96   Fierce Panda NING 29    All You Good Good People/My Weakness Is None Of Your Business (p/s, 1,300 only,
                              numbered) ......................................................................................... 10
96   Fierce Panda NING 29    All You Good Good People/My Weakness Is None Of Your Business (p/s, 1,300 only, not
                              numbered) ........................................................................................... 5
98   BBC BOX SET          EMBRACE EP'S (6 x 12"s in black box, numbered, 100 only) ..................... 60
98   Hut HUTLP 46         THE GOOD WILL OUT (2-LP) .................................................................... 30
99   Hut HUTDX 103/CD 109   ABBEY ROAD SESSIONS (2xCD gatefold, one CD mail-order from fanclub) ......... 25
00   Hut HUTLP 60         DRAWN FROM MEMORY (LP) .................................................................... 18
01   Hut HUTLP 68         IF YOU'VE NEVER BEEN (LP) .................................................................... 20

## EMBRYO
80   Rampant RAM 001      I'm Different/You Know He Did (p/s) ........................................................ 15
*(see also Jump Squad)*

## EMCEE 5
62   Columbia SEG 8153     LET'S TAKE FIVE (EP) ............................................................................... 175
62   Alpha International DB 92   VOLUME ONE (EP) .................................................................................. 150
*(see also Rendell-Carr, Ian Carr's Nucleus)*

## EMERALD
78   Look LK/SP 6365       The Tempter/Rolling Stone (no p/s) ......................................................... 20

## EMERALDS (U.K.)
65   Decca F 12096         Don't Listen To Your Friends/Say You're Mine ......................................... 7
65   Decca F 12304         King Lonely The Blue/Someone Else's Fool ............................................... 40

## EMERALDS (U.S.)
64   London HL 9839        Donkey Kick Back/Sittin' Bull .................................................................. 10

## KEITH EMERSON
76   Manticore K 13513     Honky Tonk Train Blues/Barrel House Shake Down (p/s) ......................... 6
80   Atlantic K 11612       Taxi Ride (Rome)/Mater Tenebrarum (p/s) ............................................. 6
81   MCA MCA 697         I'm A Man/Nighthawks Main Title Theme (p/s) ....................................... 7
*(see also Emerson Lake & Palmer, Nice, V.I.P.'s)*

## EMERSON, LAKE & PALMER
74   Manticore K 13503     Jerusalem/When The Apple Blossoms Bloom In The WIndmills Of Your Mind, I'll Be
                              Your Valentine (with p/s) ..................................................................... 10
77   Atlantic K 10946       Fanfare For The Common Man/Brain Salad Surgery (p/s) ......................... 5
77   Atlantic K 10946T      Fanfare For The Common Man (Album Version)/Brain Salad Surgery (12", p/s) ......... 12
70   Island ILPS 9132       EMERSON, LAKE AND PALMER (LP, pink label) ........................................ 125
70   Island ILPS 9123       EMERSON, LAKE AND PALMER (LP, later 'pink rim palm tree') .................... 40
71   Island ILPS 9155       TARKUS (LP, gatefold sleeve, 'pink rim palm tree' label) ......................... 50
71   Island HELP 1         PICTURES AT AN EXHIBITION (LP, gatefold sleeve, black label and pink "i") .......... 50
72   Island ILPS 9186       TRILOGY (LP, gatefold sleeve. pink label) ................................................ 50
73   Manticore K 53501     BRAIN SALAD SURGERY (LP, fold-out die cut sleeve with poster) ............. 40
73   Epic S EPC 65450      WELCOME BACK MY FRIENDS TO THE SHOW THAT NEVER ENDS (3-LP, trifold sleeve) ... 20
92   Victory 828 318-1      BLACK MOON (LP) .................................................................................. 15
*(see also Emerson Lake & Powell, Nice, Keith Emerson, Shame, Asia, King Crimson, Stray Dog, Atomic Rooster)*

## EMERSON, LAKE & POWELL
86   Polydor POSP 804      Touch And Go/Learning To Fly (p/s) ......................................................... 5
*(see also Emerson Lake & Palmer, Cozy Powell)*

**KATHLEEN EMERY**
| | | | |
|---|---|---|---|
| 97 | Jazzman JM001 | Sometimes I Feel Like A Motherless Child/Evil Ways (hand numbered sticker on paper sleeve, 500 only) | 20 |

**ÉMIGRÉ**
| | | | |
|---|---|---|---|
| 79 | Chrysalis CHS 2291 | Poison/Trouble Shooter | 6 |

**EMILY (1)**
| | | | |
|---|---|---|---|
| 74 | Emily (No cat no) | If All The World/Long Tall Glasses/Smoke On The Water (p/s) | 70 |

**EMJAYS**
| | | | |
|---|---|---|---|
| 59 | Top Rank JAR 145 | All My Love All My Life/Cross My Heart | 50 |

**ENDAF EMLYN**
| | | | |
|---|---|---|---|
| 71 | Wren WRL 537 | HIRAETH (LP) | 300 |
| 74 | Sain 1012M | SALEM (LP) | 50 |

**DAVID EMMANUEL**
| | | | |
|---|---|---|---|
| 83 | White Lodge WLT 1 | Giving It Up For Love/Stir It Around (p/s) | 10 |
| 83 | White Lodge WLT 1 | Giving It Up For Love/Stir It Around (12") | 50 |

**EMMET SPICELAND**
| | | | |
|---|---|---|---|
| 68 | Page One POF 089 | Lowlands Low/Bunclody | 7 |
| 69 | Page One POF 143 | So Long Marianne/In Search Of Franklin | 7 |
| 68 | Page One POLS 011 | THE FIRST (LP, with stickered sleeve, blue/silver labels) | 60 |
| 68 | Page ONe POLS 011 | THE FIRST (LP, without sticker on sleeve, blue/silver labels) | 50 |
| 77 | Hawk HALP 166 | THE EMMET SPICELAND ALBUM (LP, reissue of above LP) | 35 |

**FRED EMNEY**
| | | | |
|---|---|---|---|
| 58 | Decca TRI DFE 6554 | FRED EMNEY (EP) | 20 |

**E-MOTIONS**
| | | | |
|---|---|---|---|
| 90s | Slammin 1 | E-MOTIONS (EP) | 20 |

**EMOTIONS**
| | | | |
|---|---|---|---|
| 69 | Downtown DT 446 | Give Me Love/HORACE FAITH: Daddy's Home | 20 |

**EMOTIONS (JAMAICA)**
| | | | |
|---|---|---|---|
| 66 | Ska Beat JB 263 | Rude Boy Confession/Heartbreaking Gypsy | 35 |
| 67 | Caltone TONE 100 | A Rainbow/TONY & DOREEN: Just You And I | 40 |
| 68 | Caltone TONE 118 | Soulful Music/No Use To Cry | 30 |
| 68 | Caltone TONE 120 | Careless Hands/TOMMY McCOOK & SUPERSONICS: Caltone Special | 60 |
| 69 | High Note HS 018 | The Storm/Easy Squeeze | 15 |
| 69 | High Note HS 026 | Rum Bay/PATSY: Find Someone | 8 |
| 70 | Supreme SUP 209 | Halleluiah/MATADOR ALLSTARS: Boat Of Joy | 15 |
| 71 | Prince Buster PB 22 | Walking Along/Sometimes | 15 |
| 11 | Big Shot THB 7010 | You Are The One/PHIL PRATT ALL STARS: Girls Like Dirt Stars | 18 |

*(see also Romeo & Emotions, Horace Faith)*

**EMOTIONS (U.K.)**
| | | | |
|---|---|---|---|
| 62 | London HLR 9640 | Echo/Come Dance Baby | 40 |
| 63 | London HLR 9701 | L-O-V-E/A Million Reasons | 30 |
| 63 | Stateside SS 237 | A Story Untold/One Life One Love One You | 20 |
| 65 | Polydor BM 56025 | Lonely Man/Line Shooter | 5 |

**EMOTIONS (U.S.)**
| | | | |
|---|---|---|---|
| 69 | Stax STAX 123 | So I Can Love You/Got To Be The Man | 7 |
| 69 | Stax STAX 134 | I Like It/Best Part Of A Love Affair | 8 |
| 69 | Deep Soul DS 9104 | Somebody New/Brushfire | 30 |
| 75 | Stax STXS 2020 | Baby I'm Through/I Wanna Come Back | 6 |
| 70 | Stax SXATS 1030 | SO I CAN LOVE YOU (LP) | 20 |

**EMPEROR (NORWAY)**
| | | | |
|---|---|---|---|
| 93 | Candlelight 002 | EMPEROR (LP) | 20 |
| 95 | Candlelight 008 | IN THE NIGHTSIDE ECLIPSE (LP) | 20 |
| 98 | Candlelight 023 | ANTHEMS TO THE WELKIN AT DUSK (LP, gatefold sleeve) | 20 |
| 99 | Candlelight 035 | IX :EQUILIBRIUM (LP, gatefold sleeve) | 20 |
| 01 | Candlelight 052 | EMPERIAL VINYL PRESENTATION (Numbered box set with 5 picture disc LPs and booklet. 3000 only) | 60 |

**EMPERORS**
| | | | |
|---|---|---|---|
| 66 | Stateside SS 565 | Karate/I've Got To Have Her | 30 |
| 68 | Pama 786 | I've Got To Have Her/Karate | 25 |

**EMPIRE**
| | | | |
|---|---|---|---|
| 81 | Dinosaur DE 004 | Hot Seat/All These Things (p/s) | 10 |

*(see also Generation X)*

**EMPTY POCKETS**
| | | | |
|---|---|---|---|
| 83 | S 83 CUS 1990 | Caroline/You Made It Right/Oh Sussanah/Go With The Crowd | 8 |

**EMPTY VESSELS**
| | | | |
|---|---|---|---|
| 79 | Empty Vessel SRTS/79/CUS 361 | Too Much Trouble/Loony (p/s) | 8 |

**EMS STUDIOS**
| | | | |
|---|---|---|---|
| 72 | (No label or cat no) | SOUNDS FROM EMS (7" flexi in printed sleeve) | 120 |
| 72 | EMS | EMS SYNTHI AND THE COMPOSER (LP) | 500 |

**EN ROUTE**
| | | | |
|---|---|---|---|
| 79 | Barn BARN 006 | Break Down Your Defences/Rusty Capri | 30 |

**ENCHANTED FOREST**
| | | | |
|---|---|---|---|
| 68 | Stateside SS 2080 | You're Never Gonna Get My Lovin'/Suzanne | 15 |

**ENCHANTERS**
| | | | |
|---|---|---|---|
| 67 | Warner Bros WB 2054 | We Got Love/I've Lost All Communications | 25 |

MINT VALUE £

## ENCONA COURSE (FEATURING DEF J)
| | | | |
|---|---|---|---|
| 91 | Edutainment EDUT001 | Rhyme Grenade/Taste Of The Future/Hit Men (EP) | 40 |
| 92 | White (No Cat. No.) | VIA COARSEVILLE (EP) | 40 |

## END RESULT
| | | | |
|---|---|---|---|
| 73 | Priory PRY 1 | Towards The Sun/Please Go | 175 |

## THE END
| | | | |
|---|---|---|---|
| 65 | Philips BF 1444 | I Can't Get Any Joy/Hey Little Girl | 30 |
| 68 | Decca F 22750 | Shades Of Orange/Loving, Sacred Loving | 50 |
| 69 | Decca LK-R/SKL-R 5015 | INTROSPECTION (LP, large unboxed logo on label) | 600 |
| 96 | Tenth Planet TP 025 | IN THE BEGINNING ... THE END (LP, gatefold sleeve, numbered, 1,000 only) | 20 |
| 97 | Tenth Planet TP 033 | RETROSPECTION (LP, numbered, 1,000 only) | 15 |

*(see also Tucky Buzzard, Bill Wyman, Innocents, Bobby Angelo, Tuxedo)*

## ENDEAVOURS
| | | | |
|---|---|---|---|
| 75 | Bradleys BRAD 7510 | Baby's Comin' Home/First Price To The Winner | 12 |

## ENDEVERS
| | | | |
|---|---|---|---|
| 68 | Decca F 12817 | Remember When We Were Young/Taking Care Of Myself | 30 |
| 68 | Decca F 12859 | She's My Girl/She's That Kind Of Girl | 30 |
| 69 | Decca F 12939 | Sunny And Me/I Really Hope You Do | 10 |

## ENDGAMES
| | | | |
|---|---|---|---|
| 83 | Virgin VS 640 | Miracle In My Heart/Miracle In My Heart (Instrumental) | 6 |
| 83 | Virgin VS 640 | Miracle In My Heart/Ecstacy (Centurion MIx) (12") | 20 |

## END PHENOMENA
| | | | |
|---|---|---|---|
| 70 | Hollick And Taylor | END PHENOMENA (LP) | 50 |

## SERGIO ENDRIGO
| | | | |
|---|---|---|---|
| 68 | Pye International 7N 25502 | Marianne/Il Dolce Paese | 10 |

## MELVIN ENDSLEY
| | | | |
|---|---|---|---|
| 57 | RCA RCA 1004 | I Like Your Kind Of Love/Is It True? | 25 |
| 58 | RCA RCA 1051 | I Got A Feelin'/There's Bound To Be | 20 |

## ENEMY (1)
| | | | |
|---|---|---|---|
| 81 | Tin Tin NM 1 | 50,000 Dead/Society's Fool/Neutral Ground (p/s) | 8 |
| 82 | Fallout FALL 001 | Fallen Hero/Tomorrow's Warning/Prisoner Of War (p/s, with inner) | 7 |
| 82 | Fallout FALL 004 | Punks Alive/Piccadilly Sidetracks/Twist And Turn (p/s, orange vinyl) | 7 |
| 83 | Fallout FALL 014 | Last Rites/Why Not (p/s) | 5 |
| 84 | Rot ASS 9 | Last But Not Least/Images (live) (p/s) | 6 |
| 83 | Fallout FALL LP 015 | THE GATEWAY TO HELL (LP) | 20 |

## ENERGETIC KRUSHER
| | | | |
|---|---|---|---|
| 89 | Vinyl Solution SOL 17 | PATH TO OBLIVION (LP, with insert, features Danny McCormack) | 20 |

*(see also Wildhearts)*

## ENERGY
| | | | |
|---|---|---|---|
| 81 | GRN 1 | CONQUER THE WORLD: Conquer The World/Make It/Law Breaker (EP, no p/s) | 75 |
| 80 | BIPS BECK 927 | ENERGISED (EP) | 50 |
| 83 | Aros AROS 11233 | Nowhere To Hide/Fight For Your Freedom (no p/s) | 50 |

## SCOTT ENGEL
| | | | |
|---|---|---|---|
| 58 | Vogue V 9125 | Blue Bell/Paper Doll | 150 |
| 58 | Vogue V 9125 | Blue Bell/Paper Doll (78) | 80 |
| 59 | Vogue V 9145 | The Livin' End/Good For Nothin' (with Count Dracula & Boys) | 400 |
| 59 | Vogue V 9145 | The Livin' End/Good For Nothin' (with Count Dracula & Boys) (78) | 60 |
| 59 | Vogue V 9150 | Charlie Bop/All I Do Is Dream Of You | 200 |
| 59 | Vogue V 9150 | Charlie Bop/All I Do Is Dream Of You (78) | 40 |
| 66 | Liberty LEP 2261 | SCOTT ENGEL (EP) | 35 |

*(see also Scott Walker, Walker Brothers)*

## SCOTT ENGEL & JOHN STEWART
| | | | |
|---|---|---|---|
| 66 | Capitol CL 15440 | I Only Came To Dance With You/Greens | 40 |

*(see also Scott Walker, Walker Brothers)*

## ENGINE
| | | | |
|---|---|---|---|
| 87 | Beak BEAK 1 | Getting Away From It All (p/s) | 5 |

## ENGINEERS
| | | | |
|---|---|---|---|
| 78 | Beserkley BZZ 16 | You Baby/Easy Street (p/s) | 6 |

*(see also Eddie & Hot Rods)*

## ENGLAND (1)
| | | | |
|---|---|---|---|
| 76 | Deroy DER 1356 | ENGLAND (LP, private pressing) | 250 |

## ENGLAND (2)
| | | | |
|---|---|---|---|
| 77 | Arista ARIST 88 | Pariffinalea/Nanagram | 6 |
| 77 | Arista ARTY 153 | GARDEN SHED (LP, allegedly with booklet) | 60 |
| 77 | Arista ARTY 153 | GARDEN SHED (LP, without alleged booklet) | 40 |

## ENGLAND FOOTBALL SQUAD
| | | | |
|---|---|---|---|
| 70 | Pye 7N 17920 | Back Home/Cinnamon Stick (some with 'football centre) | 6 |
| 70 | Pye 7N 17920 | Back Home/Cinnamon Stick (with 'football centre and p/s) | 15 |
| 70 | Pye 7N 17920 | Back Home/Cinnamon Stick (in promo 'BOAC' sleeve) | 50 |

## ENGLAND'S GLORY
| | | | |
|---|---|---|---|
| 73 | Venus VEN 105 | ENGLAND'S GLORY (LP, private pressing, pink label, 25 copies only, Venus VEN 105 in run-out groove; beware of white label counterfeits) | 1000 |

*(see also Only Ones)*

## ENGLAND SISTERS
| | | | |
|---|---|---|---|
| 60 | HMV POP 710 | Heartbeat/Little Child | 30 |

## ENGLISH
| | | | |
|---|---|---|---|
| 81 | Albion ION 1008 | Hooray For The English/When You Fly (p/s) | 10 |

## ENGLISH COUNTRY BLUES BAND
| | | | |
|---|---|---|---|
| 83 | Rogue FMSL 2004 | HOME AND DERANGED (LP) | 15 |

## ENGLISH DOGS
| | | | |
|---|---|---|---|
| 83 | Clay PLATE 6 | MAD PUNX AND ENGLISH DOGS (12") | 20 |
| 84 | Ros ASS 17 | TO THE ENDS OF THE EARTH (12" EP, p/s) | 20 |
| 86 | Under One Flag 12 FLAG 101 | METALMORPHOSIS (12" EP, p/s) | 10 |
| 83 | Clay LP 10 | INVASION OF THE PORKY MEN (LP, inner) | 20 |
| 85 | Rot ASS 20 | FORWARD INTO BATTLE (LP) | 15 |
| 86 | Under One Flag FLAG 4 | WHERE LEGEND BEGAN (LP) | 15 |

## ERROL(L) ENGLISH
| | | | |
|---|---|---|---|
| 70 | Big Shot BI 547 | I Don't Want To Love You/Love Is Pure | 6 |
| 70 | Big Shot BI 548 | Once In My Life/Rabbit In A Cottage | 10 |
| 70 | Torpedo TOR 8 | Open The Door To Your Heart/That Will Do | 6 |
| 70 | Torpedo TOR 9 | Where You Lead Me/Hitchin' A Ride | 6 |
| 70 | Torpedo TOR 16 | Sad Girl/Welcome Me Back Home | 6 |
| 70 | Torpedo TOR 22 | Sha La La La Lee/BOVVER BOYS: A.G.G.R.O. | 50 |
| 71 | Duke DU 99 | Sometimes (with Champions)/Sugar Cane | 6 |

*(see also Junior English, Errol & Champions)*

## MR JOE ENGLISH
| | | | |
|---|---|---|---|
| 69 | Fontana TF 3034 | Lay Lady Lay/Two Minute Silence | 15 |

## JUNIOR ENGLISH
| | | | |
|---|---|---|---|
| 69 | Camel CA 35 | Nobody Knows (with Tony Sexton)/Somewhere | 25 |
| 71 | Pama PM 828 | Jesamine/SYDNEY ALL STARS: The Flash | 8 |
| 72 | Pama PM 841 | Miss Playgirl/Once In My Life | 8 |
| 72 | Pama PM 866 | I Don't Want To Die/Land Of Sea And Sand | 8 |
| 72 | Pama PM 869 | Daniel/Perfidia | 8 |
| 72 | Banana BA 368 | Anniversary/Girls Like You | 8 |
| 73 | Pama Supreme PS 381 | Garden Party/Version | 8 |
| 78 | Ethnic Fight ETH 1228 | Keep On Trying/HERB VENDOR: Horse Mouth Wallace (12") | 35 |
| 79 | Burning Rockers BRD 004 | Love And Key/Key Down (12", red vinyl) | 20 |
| 79 | Burning Rockers BRD 009 | Natural High/In Loving You (12") | 12 |
| 81 | Cha Cha CHAD 35 | We Can Work It Out/Love Me Tonight (12") | 12 |
| 74 | Cactus CTLP 102 | THE DYNAMIC (LP) | 25 |
| 75 | Horse HRLP 707 | THE GREAT (LP) | 15 |
| 80 | Burning Rockers BR 1010 | LOVERS KEY (LP) | 25 |

*(see also Errol English, Tony Sexton)*

## ENGLISH ROSE
| | | | |
|---|---|---|---|
| 70 | Polydor 2058 040 | Yesterday's Hero/To Jackie | 10 |

*(see also Neat Change, Love Affair)*

## ENGLISH SUBTITLES
| | | | |
|---|---|---|---|
| 79 | Small Wonder SMALL 22 | Time Tunnel/Sweat/Reconstruction (p/s) | 7 |
| 82 | Glass 007/10 SEC 21 | Tannoy/Cars On Fire (folded p/s in bag with insert) | 7 |

## ENGLISH MCCOY
| | | | |
|---|---|---|---|
| 88 | Nowyertalkin' 7TALK 2 | Give Me Something To Believe In/Breaking Down (p/s) | 100 |
| 88 | Nowyertalkin' 12TALK 2 | GIVE ME SOMETHING TO BELIEVE IN (12" EP) | 200 |

## ENID
| | | | |
|---|---|---|---|
| 76 | Buk BUK 3002 | The Lovers/In The Region Of The Summer Stars | 8 |
| 77 | EMI International INT 540 | Golden Earrings/Omega (p/s) | 6 |
| 79 | Pye 7P 106 | Dambusters March — Land Of Hope And Glory/The Skye Boat Song (p/s, blue vinyl) | 6 |
| 80 | Pye 7P 187 | Fool/Tito (p/s) | 6 |
| 80 | EMI EMI 5109 | Golden Earrings/665 The Great Bean (p/s) | 6 |
| 81 | Bronze BRO 127 | When You Wish Upon A Star/Jessica (p/s) | 6 |
| 81 | Bronze BRO 134 | Heigh Ho/Twinkle Twinkle Little Star (p/s) | 6 |
| 82 | Rak RAK 349 | And Then There Were None/Letter From America (p/s) | 5 |
| 76 | Buk BULP 2014 | IN THE REGION OF THE SUMMER STARS (LP, 1st issue, white label, with insert, without mention of "Enid" on front cover; distributed by Decca) | 20 |
| 77 | Buk BULP 2014 | IN THE REGION OF THE SUMMER STARS (2nd issue, black label, with "Enid" on front cover) | 15 |
| 84 | The Stand LE 1 | "THE LIVERPOOL ALBUM" (untitled mini-album, sold at gigs, 800 only) | 20 |
| 84 | The Stand THE STAND 1 | THE STAND (fan club issue, 5,000 only, autographed) | 25 |
| 84 | The Stand THE STAND 1 | THE STAND (fan club issue, 5,000 only, some autographed) | 15 |
| 85 | The Stand THE STAND 2 | THE STAND 1985-1986 (fan club issue, 2,000 only, autographed) | 15 |
| 85 | The Stand THE STAND 2 | THE STAND 1985-1986 (fan club issue, 2,000 only) | 15 |

*(see also Robert John Godfrey, Godfrey & Stewart, William Arkle, Glen Baker, Kim Wilde)*

## ETHEL ENNIS
| | | | |
|---|---|---|---|
| 64 | RCA SF 7654 | ONCE AGAIN (LP) | 15 |

## RAY ENNIS & BLUE JEANS
| | | | |
|---|---|---|---|
| 68 | Columbia DB 8431 | What Have They Done To Hazel?/Now That You've Got Me (You Don't Seem To Want Me) | 25 |

*(see also Swinging Blue Jeans, Blue Jeans)*

## BRIAN ENO
| | | | |
|---|---|---|---|
| 74 | Island WIP 6178 | Seven Deadly Finns/Later On | 10 |
| 75 | Island WIP 6233 | The Lion Sleeps Tonight (Wimoweh)/I'll Come Running | 6 |
| 78 | Polydor 2001 762 | The King's Lead Hat/R.A.F. (B-side with Snatch) | 6 |
| 83 | EG EGO 12 | Silver Morning/Deep Blue Day (with Daniel Lanois & Roger Eno, with wraparound promo p/s with Eno notes on back) | 8 |
| 73 | Island ILPS 9268 | HERE COME THE WARM JETS (LP, pink rim, palm tree label, MATRIX A-1E/B-1E) | 40 |
| 74 | Island ILPS 9309 | TAKING TIGER MOUNTAIN (BY STRATEGY) (LP, gatefold sleeve, pink rim, Island label) | 30 |
| 75 | Island ILPS 9351 | ANOTHER GREEN WORLD (LP, 1st pressing, blue rim, palm tree label) | 25 |

# Brian ENO & DAVID BYRNE

MINT VALUE £

| | | | |
|---|---|---|---|
| 75 | Island HELP 22 | EVENING STAR (LP, as Fripp & Eno) | 20 |
| 75 | Obscure OBS 3 | DISCREET MUSIC (LP) | 20 |
| 76 | Editions EG EGM 1 | MUSIC FOR FILMS (LP, private pressing) | 100 |
| 77 | Polydor 2302 071 | BEFORE AND AFTER SCIENCE (LP, with 4 Peter Schmidt prints) | 30 |
| 77 | Polydor 2683082 | HERE COME THE WARM JETS/BEFORE & AFTER SCIENCE (2-LP reissue) | 25 |
| 77 | Polydor 2302 668 | TAKING TIGER MOUNTAIN (BY STRATEGY) (LP, reissue, red label) | 15 |
| 77 | Polydor 2302 069 | ANOTHER GREEN WORLD (LP, reissue, red label) | 15 |
| 78 | Polydor 2310623 | MUSIC FOR FILMS (LP) | 25 |
| 78 | EG AMB 001 | AMBIENT 1 - MUSIC FOR AIRPORTS (LP, inner) | 15 |
| 82 | EG EGED 20 | AMBIENT 4 (LP) | 20 |
| 83 | EG EGLP 53 | APOLLO (LP) | 18 |
| 83 | EG EGBS 002 | WORKING BACKWARDS 1983-1973 (9-LP box set with "Music For Films, Vol. 2" LP & "Rarities" 12") | 150 |
| 89 | Standard Music Library ESL 168 | TEXTURES (LP) | 400 |
| 89 | Standard Music Library SML ESL 003CD | TEXTURES (CD) | 50 |
| 93 | Virgin ENOBOX1 | INSTRUMENTAL (box set 3-CD, booklet) | 35 |

*(see also Ayers Cale Nico & Eno, Roxy Music, Passengers, Robert Fripp, Lady June, David Toop, Gavin Bryars, Toto)*

## BRIAN ENO & DAVID BYRNE

| | | | |
|---|---|---|---|
| 81 | EG EGO 1 | The Jezebel Spirit/Regiment (p/s) | 10 |
| 81 | EG EGLP 48 | MY LIFE IN THE BUSH OF GHOSTS (LP, 1st pressing, later pressings have barcode on sleeve) | 20 |

*(see also David Byrne, Talking Heads)*

## ENOS & SHEILA

| | | | |
|---|---|---|---|
| 68 | Blue Cat BS 138 | Tonight You're Mine/UNTOUCHABLES: Your Love | 60 |

*(see also Enos McLeod)*

## ENOUGH'S ENOUGH

| | | | |
|---|---|---|---|
| 68 | Tattoo TT 101 | Please Remember/Look Around You Baby | 700 |

## ENSEMBLE

| | | | |
|---|---|---|---|
| 82 | Stiff WIN 1 | Viva Scotland, England, Ireland/Viva Scotland, England, Ireland ("A" label promo) | 15 |

## ENSLAVED

| | | | |
|---|---|---|---|
| 90s | Candlelight 001MLP | HORDANES LAND (EP) | 60 |

## ENTICERS

| | | | |
|---|---|---|---|
| 72 | Atlantic 2091 136 | Calling For Your Love/Storyteller | 40 |

## JIMI ENTLEY SOUND

| | | | |
|---|---|---|---|
| 02 | Espionage Disk ESP 001 | Apache/Charlie's Theme | 25 |

*(see also Portishead)*

## ENTOMBED

| | | | |
|---|---|---|---|
| 91 | Earache 7 MOSH 38 | Crawl/Forsaken (p/s) | 10 |
| 91 | Earache MOSH 38T | Crawl/Forsaken/Bitter Loss (12" p/s) | 12 |
| 92 | Earache MOSH 52 T | Stranger Eons/Dusk/Shreds Of Flesh (12", p/s) | 10 |
| 93 | Earache 7 MOSH 114 | Out Of Hand/God Of Thunder/Black Breath (p/s) | 12 |
| 93 | Earache MOSH 114 T | Out Of Hand/God Of Thunder/Black Breath (12", p/s) | 12 |
| 93 | Earache 7 MOSH 94 T | HOLLOWMAN EP (6 track 12", p/s) | 15 |
| 95 | Earache 7 MOSH 132 | Night Of The Vampire/NEW BOMB TURKS: I Hate People (p/s) | 8 |
| 89 | Earache MOSH 21P | LEFT HAND PATH (LP, picture disc) | 20 |
| 90 | Earache MOSH 21 | LEFT HAND PATH (LP, insert) | 25 |
| 91 | Earache MOSH 21 | LEFT HAND PATH (LP, white vinyl, stickered sleeve, 2000 only) | 30 |
| 91 | Earache MOSH 37 | CLANDESTINE LP, embossed sleeve, insert) | 20 |
| 93 | Earache MOSH 82 | WOLVERINE BLUES (LP, lyric insert) | 50 |
| 97 | Music For Nations MFN 216 | TO RIDE, SHOOT STRAIGHT AND SPEAK THE TRUTH (LP, with "Family Favourites" 12") | 50 |
| 98 | Music For Nations MFN 244 | SAME DIFFERENCE (LP) | 40 |
| 07 | Back On Black BOBV 067 LP | SERPENT SAINTS/THE TEN AMENDMENTS (LP, red vinyl) | 15 |

## JOHN ENTWISTLE('S OX)

| | | | |
|---|---|---|---|
| 71 | Track 2094 008 | I Believe In Everything/My Size | 10 |
| 75 | Decca FR 13567 | Mad Dog/Cell No.7 (as John Entwistle's Ox) | 8 |
| 81 | WEA K 79249P | Too Late The Hero/I'm Coming Back (picture disc, autographed) | 10 |
| 71 | Track 2406 005 | SMASH YOUR HEAD AGAINST THE WALL (LP, gatefold, black/silver label) | 30 |
| 72 | Track 2406 104 | WHISTLE RYMES (LP, gatefold sleeve, black/silver labels) | 25 |
| 73 | Track 2406106 | RIGOR MORTIS SETS IN (LP, gatefold, inner) | 15 |
| 75 | Decca TXS 114 | MAD DOG (LP, as John Entwistle's Ox, with poster, lyric insert) | 25 |
| 75 | Decca TXS 114 | MAD DOG (LP, as John Entwistle's Ox, without poster, lyric insert) | 15 |

*(see also Who, Rigor Mortis)*

## ENYA

| | | | |
|---|---|---|---|
| 87 | BBC RESL 201 | I Want Tomorrow/The Celts Theme (p/s) | 7 |
| 87 | BBC CDRSL 201 | I Want Tomorrow/The Celts Theme/To Go Beyond I/To Go Beyond II (3" CD) | 25 |
| 91 | WEA YZ 635 T | How Can I Keep From Singing/O'che Chi'n (Silent Night) (12", metallic p/s) | 10 |
| 87 | BBC REB 605 | ENYA (LP) | 15 |
| 87 | BBC BBCCD 605 | ENYA (CD) | 25 |

## EPICS (JAMAICA)

| | | | |
|---|---|---|---|
| 70 | Bamboo BAM 37 | Your Love/Driving Me Crazy | 30 |

## EPICS (U.K.)

| | | | |
|---|---|---|---|
| 65 | Pye 7N 15829 | There's Just No Pleasing You/My Little Girl | 10 |
| 66 | Pye 7N 17053 | Just How Wrong Can You Be/Blue Turns To Grey | 10 |
| 68 | CBS 3564 | Travelling Circus/Henry Long | 20 |

*(see also Acid Gallery, Christie)*

## EPIDEMIC

| | | | |
|---|---|---|---|
| 89 | Metalcore CORE 4 | THE TRUTH OF WHAT WILL BE (LP) | 20 |

## EPILEPTICS

| | | | |
|---|---|---|---|
| 80 | Stortbeat/Mirror BEAT 8 | 1970'S EP (black & white p/s, stencilled white labels) | 20 |
| 81 | Spiderleg SDL 1 | 1970'S EP (re-recorded, printed labels, folded different printed b&w p/s) | 15 |
| 81 | Spiderleg SDL 2 | LAST BUS TO DEBDEN (EP, hand-written labels & photocopied p/s) | 12 |
| 81 | Spiderleg SDL 2 | LAST BUS TO DEBDEN (EP, printed labels & different photocopied p/s) | 8 |

*(see also Licks, Flux Of Pink Indians)*

## EPISODE

| | | | |
|---|---|---|---|
| 68 | MGM MGM 1409 | Little One/Wide Smiles | 30 |

*(see also Episode Six)*

## EPISODE FOUR

| | | | |
|---|---|---|---|
| 86 | Lenin & McCarthy LENM 001T | STRIKE UP MATCHES EP (p/s with insert, 500 only, many destroyed) | 150 |

*(see also East Village)*

## EPISODE SIX

| | | | |
|---|---|---|---|
| 66 | Pye 7N 17018 | Put Yourself In My Place/That's All I Want | 25 |
| 66 | Pye 7N 17110 | I Hear Trumpets Blow/True Love Is Funny That Way | 20 |
| 66 | Pye 7N 17147 | Here, There And Everywhere/Mighty Morris Ten | 20 |
| 67 | Pye 7N 17244 | Love, Hate, Revenge/Baby Baby Baby | 40 |
| 67 | Pye 7N 17330 | Morning Dew/Sunshine Girl | 25 |
| 67 | Pye 7N 17376 | I Can See Through You/When I Fall In Love | 40 |
| 68 | Chapter One CH 103 | Lucky Sunday/Mr. Universe | 20 |
| 69 | Chapter One CH 104 | Mozart Versus The Rest/Jak D'Or | 20 |
| 87 | PRT PYL 6026 | PUT YOURSELF IN MY PLACE (LP) | 15 |
| 97 | RPM RPM 178 | THE RADIO ONE CLUB SESSIONS LIVE 1968/69 (CD) | 25 |

*(see also Episode, Sheila Carter & Episode Six, Neo Maya, Roger Glover, Jon Lord, Gillan, Deep Purple, Quatermass)*

## EPMD

| | | | |
|---|---|---|---|
| 88 | Sleeping Bag SBUK LP 1 | STRICTLY BUSINESS (LP) | 15 |
| 89 | Sleeping Bag SBUK LP 8 | UNFINISHED BUSINESS (LP) | 15 |

## MINNIE EPPERSON

| | | | |
|---|---|---|---|
| 68 | Action ACT 4503 | Grab Your Clothes (And Get On Out)/No Love At All | 75 |

## PRESTON EPPS

| | | | |
|---|---|---|---|
| 60 | Top Rank JKP 2060 | RUSHING FOR PERCUSSION (EP, with Sandy Nelson) | 10 |

*(see also Sandy Nelson)*

## EQUA

| | | | |
|---|---|---|---|
| 83 | Mr Fox FOX 1 | In The Red/City Dub | 20 |
| 83 | Mr Fox FOX 1 | In The Red/City Dub/City Lights (12") | 60 |

## EQUALS

| | | | |
|---|---|---|---|
| 67 | President PT 117 | I Won't Be There/Fire | 8 |
| 67 | President PT 135 | Baby, Come Back/Hold Me Closer | 6 |
| 67 | President ZAM 2 | I'm A Poor Man/Can't Find A Girl To Love Me (Export only) | 30 |
| 67 | President PT 158 | Give Love A Try/Another Sad And Lonely Night | 7 |
| 68 | President PT 180 | I Get So Excited/The Skies Above | 6 |
| 68 | President PT 200 | Laurel And Hardy/The Guy Who Made Her A Star | 6 |
| 68 | President PT 222 | Softly Softly/Lonely Rita | 6 |
| 69 | President PT 240 | Michael And The Slipper Tree/Honey Gum | 6 |
| 69 | President PT 260 | Viva Bobby Joe/I Can't Let You Go | 6 |
| 69 | President PT 275 | Rub A Dub Dub/After The Lights Go Down Low | 6 |
| 70 | President PT 288 | Soul Brother Clifford/Happy Birthday Girl | 6 |
| 70 | President PT 303 | I Can See But You Don't Know/Gigolo Sam | 40 |
| 70 | President PT 325 | Black Skin Blue Eyed Boys/Ain't Got Nothing To Give You | 5 |
| 70 | President PT 345 | Help Me Simone/Love Potion | 6 |
| 70 | Presiden ZAM 1 | Let's Go To The Moon/Watching The Girls (export) | 25 |
| 72 | CBS 7874 | Stand Up And Be Counted/What Would You Do To Survive | 6 |
| 73 | President PT 405 | Honey Bee/Put Some Rock & Roll In Your Soul | 6 |
| 73 | President PT 414 | Diversion/Here Today Gone Tomorrow | 15 |
| 74 | President PT 422 | Hang Up My Rock & Roll Shoes/She Lives For Today | 6 |
| 75 | President PT 436 | Georgetown Girl/We've Got It All Worked Out | 6 |
| 76 | Mercury 6007 104 | Kaiwana Sunshine Girl/Soul Mother | 6 |
| 76 | Mercury 6007 106 | Funky Like A Train/If You Didn't Miss Me | 15 |
| 76 | Mercury 6007 107 | Funky Like A Train/If You Didn't Miss Me (12") | 12 |
| 77 | Mercury 6007 139 | Irma La Douce/Ar'e Harry | 6 |
| 77 | President PT 464 | Beautiful Clown/Daily Love | 6 |
| 78 | Ice GUY 5 | Red Dog/Something Beautiful | 6 |
| 88 | Club JAB 58 | Funky Like A Train/Born Ya!/Funky Like A Train (extended) (reissue) | 7 |
| 88 | Club JABX 58 | Funky Like A Train/Born Ya!/Funky Like A Train (extended) (12", reissue) | 20 |
| 68 | President PTE 1 | BABY COME BACK (EP) | 20 |
| 68 | President PTE 2 | THE EQUALS (EP) | 25 |
| 67 | President PTL 1006 | UNEQUALLED EQUALS (LP) | 22 |
| 68 | President PTL 1015 | EQUALS EXPLOSION (LP) | 20 |
| 68 | President PTL(S) 1020 | SENSATIONAL EQUALS (LP) | 20 |
| 68 | President PTL(S) 1025 | SUPREME (LP) | 18 |
| 69 | President PTLS 1030 | THE EQUALS STRIKE AGAIN (LP) | 18 |
| 69 | President PTLS 1050 | BEST OF THE EQUALS (LP) | 18 |
| 70 | President PTLS 1038 | AT THE TOP (LP, gatefold, poster) | 18 |
| 76 | Mercury 9109 601 | BORN YA! (LP) | 25 |
| 78 | Ice ICEL 1002 | MYSTIC SISTER (LP) | 25 |

*(see also Little Grants & Eddie, Pyramids, Hickory, Little Brother Grant, Zappata Schmitt, Seven Letters/Syramip, Thirty-Second Turn-Off)*

MINT VALUE £

## EQUATION
80   Dash 850101            Arcacia Avenue/Down The Avenue ..................................................................... 10

## EQUATIONS
69   Fontana TF 1035        Waiting On The Shores Of Nowhere/You Stood Beside Me ............................... 10

## EQUATORS
76   Klik KL 620              Father Oh Father/Version .................................................................................. 25

## EQUINOX
73   Boulevard BLVD 4118    HARD ROCK (LP, black/silver labels) .............................................................. 25

## EQUIPE 84
67   Major Minor MM 517    Auschwitz/Twenty Ninth Of September ........................................................... 20

## ERASMUS CHORUM
72   Chapter 1 SCM 173     Oh Lord, The Holy House On Sunday/Mary Jane............................................. 20
73   Alaska 19                I Don't Want Our Loving To Die/That Is Why................................................... 10
73   Alaska ALA 13          Jungle/That Is Why ............................................................................................ 40

## ERASURE
### SINGLES
85   Mute L12MUTE 40      Who Needs Love (Like That) (Mexican Mix)/Push Me Shove Me (Tacos Mix) (12", p/s). 20
85   Mute L12MUTE 42      Heavenly Action (Yellow Brick Mix)/Don't Say No (Ruby Red Mix) (12", p/s, L12 cat. no. must be listed on sleeve & label) ........................................................... 40
85   Mute DMUTE 42        Heavenly Action/Don't Say No (Ruby Red Mix)//Who Needs Love (Like That) (Mexican Mix)/Push Me Shove Me (Tacos Mix) (12" shrinkwrapped double pack) ..................... 15
86   Mute 12MUTE 45       Oh L'Amour/March On Down The Line/Gimme! Gimme! Gimme! (12", 'Thomas The Tank Engine' p/s, withdrawn) ......................................................................... 12
94   Mute MUTE 166         I Love Saturday/Dodo/Because You're So Sweet (unreleased, p/s only) ...................... 30

### ALBUMS
94   Mute STUMM 115       I SAY I SAY I SAY (LP, with booklet) ............................................................... 30
95   Mute STUMM 145       ERASURE (2-LP, inners) ..................................................................................... 40
97   STUMM 155             COWBOY (LP) ..................................................................................................... 25

### PROMOS
86   Mute P12MUTE 45     Oh L'Amour/March On Down The Line/Gimme! Gimme! Gimme! (12", plain white sleeve, dark blue vinyl) ..................................................................................... 20
89   Mute (no cat. no.)        WILD (CD, promo-only box set, with LP, 12", stickers, postcard, photo & info sheet) ..... 80
90   Mute ERAS 1            Push Me Shove Me (Moonbeam Mix)/(Catatonic Mix)/Senseless (Avalon Mix) (12", p/s) ....................................................................................................... 20
90   Mute ERAS 3            Sometimes (Danny Rampling Mix) (12", die-cut title sleeve) ......................... 20
90s   Mute P12MUTE 195   Don't Say Your Love Is Killing Me (Tall Paul Mix)/(John Pleased Wimmin Flashback Vox) Oh L'Amour (Tin Tin Out Remix)/(Matt Darey Mix) (12", white label test pressing with press release & release sheet, 10 copies only) ....................... 70
91   Mute CDSTUMM 95    CHORUS (promo CD, with and booklet) .......................................................... 60
92   Mute (no cat. no.)        POP! THE FIRST 20 HITS (CD, promo-only box set, with T-shirt, info sheets, 2-LP, video tape, & CD) ....................................................................................................... 70
94   Mute PL12 MUTE 166   Ghost (12", 1-sided) ............................................................................................ 8

*(see also Depeche Mode, Dinger)*

## ERAZERHEAD
81   Test Pressing TP 4      Ape Man/Wipeout/Rock And Roll Zombie (p/s) .............................................. 5
82   Flicknife FLS 208       Shell Shock/She Can Dance (p/s) .................................................................... 5
82   Flicknife FLS 210       Teenager In Love/All For Me (p/s) .................................................................... 5

## EREHWON
81   Harvest HAR 5213      Tiny Goddess/The Hero (p/s) ........................................................................... 5

*(see also Patrick Campbell-Lyons)*

## ERIC HYSTERIC & ESOTERICS
80   Wasted Vinyl WASTE 1   Tropical Vision/Dance And Sing (p/s)............................................................... 5

## ERIC & THE VIKINGS
86   Kool Kat 5               Hurting/My Baby Ain't No Play Thing (red vinyl) ........................................... 25

## ROKY ERICKSON (& THE ALIENS)
77   Virgin VS 180          Bermuda/The Interpreter (p/s) ....................................................................... 10
80   CBS 8888               Creature With The Atom Brain/The Wind And More (with The Aliens) ........... 8
80   CBS 9055               Mine Mine Mind/Bloody Hammer (Acoustic Version) (p/s, with The Aliens) ... 8
80   CBS SCBS 84463       ROKY ERICKSON & THE ALIENS (LP) ............................................................... 20
86   Demon FIEND 66       GREMLINS HAVE PICTURES (LP) .................................................................... 15
87   5 Hours Back TOCK 007   CASTING THE RUNES (LP) .............................................................................. 15
87   5 Hours Back TOCK 7P    CASTING THE RUNES (LP, picture disc) ......................................................... 25
92   Swordfish SFMD LP 1    MAD DOG (LP) ................................................................................................. 25
92   Swordfish SFMD LP 2    LOVE TO SEE YOU BLEED (LP) ...................................................................... 25

*(see also 13th Floor Elevators)*

## ROLF ERICSON
59   Pye Nixa NJL 14        SESSION IN STOCKHOLM (LP, with Freddie Redd)......................................... 100

## ERIN PERYGLUS
87   OFN OFN 3              Bronson/Y Dyn Newydd (p/s).......................................................................... 30
88   OFN OFN 6              Dafydd Yn Gwneud Teisen/Merthyr (p/s) ....................................................... 20
89   OFN OFN 07B          Y LLOSG (12" picture disc) .............................................................................. 20

## ERNIE & ED
72   Jay Boy BOY 58         Beautiful World/Indication............................................................................... 50

## ERROL (ENGLISH) & CHAMPIONS
70   Jackpot JP 732          Lonely Boy/Da Boo ........................................................................................... 7
70   Jackpot JP 738          Lonely Boy/TONY & CHAMPIONS: All Of My Life ............................................ 8

*(see also Errol English)*

## ERROL (DUNKLEY) & HIS GROUP
| | | | |
|---|---|---|---|
| 65 | Blue Beat BB 284 | Gypsy/Miss May (actually by Errol Dunkley & Roy Shirley) | 25 |

*(see also Errol Dunkley)*

## ERROL (DUNKLEY) & U ROY
| | | | |
|---|---|---|---|
| 72 | Punch PH 105 | Darling Ooh Wee/GOD SONS: Merry Up Version | 12 |

## E.R. & THE ROUGH RIDERS
| | | | |
|---|---|---|---|
| 69 | Polydor 56361 | Heya/I'm Alive | 15 |

## ERSATZ
| | | | |
|---|---|---|---|
| 81 | Raw RAW 35 | Motorbody Love/One Good Reason/Gimme A Chance (poster p/s) | 35 |
| 81 | Leisure Sounds SRS 32 | Smile In Shadow/House Of Cards (p/s) | 6 |

*(see also DJ Harvey)*

## BOOKER ERVIN
| | | | |
|---|---|---|---|
| 61 | Parlophone PMC 1170 | THE BOOK (LP) | 40 |

## DEE ERVIN
| | | | |
|---|---|---|---|
| 72 | Signpost SG 4356 | DEE ERVIN SINGS (LP) | 20 |

## BLUEGRASS ERWIN
| | | | |
|---|---|---|---|
| 59 | Top Rank JAR 252 | I Won't Cry Alone/I Can't Love You | 5 |

## ESCALATORS
| | | | |
|---|---|---|---|
| 83 | Big Beat NS 86 | Something's Missing/The Edge (p/s) | 8 |
| 83 | Big Beat NS 87 | The Munsters Theme/Monday (p/s) | 8 |
| 83 | Big Beat WIKM15 | MOVING STAIRCASES (LP) | 25 |

*(see also Clapham South Escalators, The Meteors)*

## ESCORTS (JAMAICA)
| | | | |
|---|---|---|---|
| 70 | Big Shot BI 535 | I'm So Afraid/Mother Nature | 40 |
| 74 | Fab FAB 245 | Sixpense/Loving Feeling | 15 |

*(see also Sensations)*

## ESCORTS (U.K.)
| | | | |
|---|---|---|---|
| 64 | Fontana TF 453 | Dizzy Miss Lizzy/All I Want Is You | 25 |
| 64 | Fontana TF 474 | The One To Cry/Tell Me Baby | 25 |
| 64 | Fontana TF 516 | I Don't Want To Go On Without You/Don't Forget To Write | 25 |
| 65 | Fontana TF 570 | C'Mon Home Baby/You'll Get No Lovin' That Way | 25 |
| 66 | Fontana TF 651 | Let It Be Me/Mad Mad World | 25 |
| 66 | Columbia DB 8061 | From Head To Toe/Night Time | 45 |

*(see also Big Three, Paddy Klaus & Gibson, Swinging Blue Jeans)*

## ESCORTS (U.S.)
| | | | |
|---|---|---|---|
| 63 | Coral Q 72458 | Submarine Race Watching/Somewhere | 25 |

## ESCORTS & KAY JUSTICE
| | | | |
|---|---|---|---|
| 54 | Columbia SCM 5132 | If You Took Your Love From Me/Yes, Indeed | 15 |

## ESCOURTS
| | | | |
|---|---|---|---|
| 76 | Alaska ALA 1014 | Disrespect Can Wreck/Bam A Lam A Boogie | 8 |

## ESG
| | | | |
|---|---|---|---|
| 81 | Factory FAC 34 | You're No Good/UFO (p/s) | 25 |

## ESKIMOS & EGYPT
| | | | |
|---|---|---|---|
| 81 | Village VILS 102 | The Cold/A Year/Screams And Whispers (EP, p/s) | 60 |

## ESOTERIC/ESOTERIK
| | | | |
|---|---|---|---|
| 96 | Club Craft OR 100 | Dancing With The Devil/Esoteric Vs. Hybrid (12") | 50 |
| 96 | Club Craft OR 200 | Ultimate Straightness/Playing With Voices (12") | 40 |
| 96 | Club Craft OR 300 | Elegant Panning/3 After That One (12") | 30 |
| 96 | Club Craft OR 400 | Odd Sins/Odd Sins (12") | 80 |
| 96 | Crowd Control CROWD 005T | Desert Planet/Mayhem (12", as Esoterik) | 80 |
| 96 | Utmostfear UTMOST 1301 | Falling, Floating, Flying/Ultimate Straightness (12") | 40 |
| 96 | Utmostfear UTMOST 1302 | Curley And Ramon/Mad Strings (12") | 40 |
| 97 | Crowd Control CROWD 006 | Mayhem/Purdey's Effect/In The Hills (12", as Esoterik) | 80 |
| 98 | Utmostfear UTMOST 1303 | Untitled/Untitled (12", label bears legend "Curley Truly Unique 1973-1998") | 40 |

*(See also Spiral Tribe)*

## ESOTERIC (2)
| | | | |
|---|---|---|---|
| 11 | Aesthetic Death ADLP 003 | EPISTEMOLOGICAL DESPONDENCY (2-LP, reissue of 1994 CD release, numbered gatefold sleeve, insert, 350 only) | 25 |

## ESP
| | | | |
|---|---|---|---|
| 89 | Radical DJ INT 14 | It's You (12") | 80 |

## ESPERANTO ROCK ORCHESTRA
| | | | |
|---|---|---|---|
| 73 | A&M AMLH 68175 | ESPERANTO ROCK ORCHESTRA (LP, gatefold sleeve, brown label) | 20 |
| 74 | A&M AMLH 63624 | DANSE MACABRE (LP, as Esperanto, silver/gold labels) | 15 |
| 75 | A&M AMLS 68294 | LAST TANGO (LP, as Esperanto, silver/brown labels) | 20 |

*(see also Keith Christmas, Comus)*

## ESPERS
| | | | |
|---|---|---|---|
| 03 | Wichita WEBB084LP | ESPERS (LP) | 50 |

## ESPRIT DE CORPS (1)
| | | | |
|---|---|---|---|
| 73 | Jam JAM 24 | If (Would It Turn Out Wrong)/Picture On The Wall | 15 |
| 73 | Jam JAM 32 | Lonely/Do You Remember Me (Like I Remember You) | 10 |

*(see also David Ballantyne, Just Plain Smith, Just Plain Jones)*

## ESPRIT DE CORPS (2)
| | | | |
|---|---|---|---|
| 81 | Come COME 1 | Anxiety/The Tea Cup Song (hand-made silk-screened sleeve) | 30 |

## ESQUERITA
| | | | |
|---|---|---|---|
| 58 | Capitol CL 14938 | Rockin' The Joint/Esquerita And The Voola | 100 |
| 72 | Specialty SPE 6603 | WILDCAT SHAKEOUT (LP) | 30 |

## ESQUIRES
| | | | |
|---|---|---|---|
| 67 | Stateside SS 2048 | Get On Up/Listen To Me | 20 |
| 68 | Stateside SS 2077 | And Get Away/Everybody's Laughing | 20 |
| 73 | Action ACT 4618 | My Sweet Baby/Henry Ralph | 50 |
| 68 | London HA-Q/SH-Q 8356 | GET ON UP AND GET AWAY (LP) | 40 |

## ESQUIVEL
| | | | |
|---|---|---|---|
| 63 | Reprise R 6046 | MORE OF OTHER WORLDS, OTHER SOUNDS (LP) | 15 |

## ESSENTIAL LOGIC
| | | | |
|---|---|---|---|
| 78 | Cells SELL ONE | Aerosol Burns/World Friction (p/s) | 8 |
| 79 | Rough Trade RT29 | Popcorn Boy/Flora Force (p/s) | 12 |
| 80 | Rough Trade RT50 | Eugene/Tame The Neighbours (p/s) | 10 |
| 81 | Rough Trade RT74 | Fanfare In The Garden/The Captain (p/s) | 7 |
| 79 | Rough Trade ROUGH 5 | BEAT RHYTHM NEWS (LP) | 15 |

*(see also X-Ray Spex, Lora Logic)*

## ESSEX
| | | | |
|---|---|---|---|
| 63 | Columbia DB 7077 | Easier Said Than Done/Are You Going My Way | 15 |
| 63 | Columbia DB 7122 | A Walkin' Miracle/What I Don't Know Won't Hurt Me (with Anita Humes) | 20 |
| 63 | Columbia DB 7178 | She's Got Everything/Out Of Sight, Out Of Mind | 20 |
| 63 | Columbia 33SX 1593 | EASIER SAID THAN DONE (LP) | 50 |
| 64 | Columbia 33SX 1613 | A WALKIN' MIRACLE (LP) | 50 |

## DAVID ESSEX
| | | | |
|---|---|---|---|
| 65 | Fontana TF 559 | And The Tears Came Tumbling Down/You Can't Stop Me Loving You | 50 |
| 65 | Fontana TF 620 | Can't Nobody Love You/Baby I Don't Mind | 45 |
| 66 | Fontana TF 680 | This Little Girl Of Mine/Brokenhearted | 45 |
| 66 | Fontana TF 733 | Thigh High/De Boom Lay Boom | 40 |
| 68 | Uni UN 502 | Love Story/Higher Than High | 20 |
| 68 | Pye 7N 17621 | Just For Tonight/Goodbye | 20 |
| 69 | Decca F 12935 | That Takes Me Back/Lost Without Linda | 40 |
| 69 | Decca F 12967 | The Day The Earth Stood Still/Is It So Strange? | 30 |
| 79 | Vertigo 6059 233 | M.O.D./M.O.D. (2) (as M.O.D., songwriting credited to D. Cook, p/s, allegedly mispressed on 2-Tone label) | 75 |
| 79 | Vertigo 6059 233 | M.O.D./M.O.D. (2) (as M.O.D., songwriting credited to D. Cook, p/s) | 7 |

*(see also David & Rozaa, Us)*

## ESSJAY
| | | | |
|---|---|---|---|
| 71 | DJM DJS 254 | Twins Of Evil/Fastback | 35 |

## ASTON ESSON
| | | | |
|---|---|---|---|
| 80 | Studio 16 STD 01 | Woman Of My Dreams/Version (12") | 30 |

## NEVILLE ESSON
| | | | |
|---|---|---|---|
| 61 | Blue Beat BB 37 | Lover's Jive/Wicked And Dreadful (with Clue J. & His Blues Busters) | 18 |

## ESTABLISHMENT
| | | | |
|---|---|---|---|
| 81 | Foetain | BAD CATHOLICS (LP) | 30 |

*(see also Cromwell)*

## 'SLEEPY' JOHN ESTES
| | | | |
|---|---|---|---|
| 66 | Delmark DJB 3 | SLEEPY JOHN'S GOT THE BLUES (EP) | 40 |
| 63 | Esquire 32-195 | THE LEGEND OF SLEEPY JOHN ESTES (LP) | 60 |
| 63 | '77' LA 12-27 | TENNESSEE JUG BUSTERS — BROKE AND HUNGRY (LP) | 40 |
| 65 | Storyville SLP 172 | PORTRAITS IN BLUES VOLUME 10 (LP) | 22 |
| 72 | Delmark DS 619 | ELECTRIC SLEEP (LP) | 20 |
| 71 | Delmark DS 613 | BROWNSVILLE BLUES(LP) | 25 |

## JOHN ESTES/FURRY LEWIS/WILL SHADE
| | | | |
|---|---|---|---|
| 71 | Revival RVS 1008 | OLD ORIGINAL TENNESSEE BLUES (LP) | 20 |

## JACKIE ESTREK
| | | | |
|---|---|---|---|
| 61 | Blue Beat BB 64 | Boss Girl/COUNT OSSIE & GROUP: Cassavubu | 30 |
| 63 | Island WI 042 | Since You've Been Gone/Daisy I Love You | 15 |
| 66 | Ska Beat JB 256 | The Ska/Daisy I Love You | 18 |

## ETCETERAS
| | | | |
|---|---|---|---|
| 64 | Oriole CB 1950 | Where Is My Love/Bengawan Solo | 15 |
| 64 | Oriole CB 1973 | Little Lady/Now I Know | 20 |

## ETERNAL
| | | | |
|---|---|---|---|
| 90 | Sarah SARAH 031 | Sleep/Breathe/Take Me Down (p/s) | 15 |

## ETERNALS (JAMAICA)
| | | | |
|---|---|---|---|
| 69 | Coxsone CS 7091 | Queen Of The Minstrels/Stars | 40 |
| 70 | Moodisc MU 3506 | Christmas Joy/WINSTON & RUPERT: Musically Beat | 7 |
| 71 | Moodisc MU 3507 | Push Me In The Corner/MUDIE'S ALL STARS: Mudie's Madness (B-side actually by Ansell Collins) | 18 |
| 71 | Moodisc MU 3508 | Keep On Dancing/HAZEL WRIGHT: My Jealous Eyes | 10 |

*(see also Don Cornel & Eternals)*

## ETERNALS (U.S.)
| | | | |
|---|---|---|---|
| 59 | London HL 8995 | Rockin' In The Jungle/Rock 'N' Roll Cha-Cha (triangular centre) | 150 |
| 59 | London HL 8995 | Rockin' In The Jungle/Rock 'N' Roll Cha-Cha (round centre) | 50 |
| 59 | London HL 8995 | Rockin' In The Jungle/Rock 'N' Roll Cha-Cha (78) | 35 |

## ETERNAL SCREAM
| | | | |
|---|---|---|---|
| 81 | Eternal 01 | Hypocrite/Action In My Life (p/s) | 15 |
| 81 | Eternal 02 | How I Wish/Child (p/s) | 20 |

## ETERNAL TRIANGLE
| | | | |
|---|---|---|---|
| 69 | Decca F 12979 | I Guess The Lord Must Be In New York City/Perfumed Candle | 6 |
| 69 | Decca F 12954 | Turn To Me/Window | 7 |

## ETERNITY'S CHILDREN
| | | |
|---|---|---|
| 68 | Capitol CL 15558 | Mrs Bluebird/Little Boy ............................................................. 25 |

## ETHEL THE FROG
| | | |
|---|---|---|
| 80 | Best SRTSFMR 014 | Eleanor Rigby/Whatever Happened To Love................................. 60 |
| 80 | EMI EMI 5041 | Eleanor Rigby/Fight Back (reissue) ........................................... 10 |
| 80 | EMI EMC 3329 | ETHEL THE FROG (LP, with Terry Hopkinson & Doug Sheppard)......... 22 |

## ETHIOPIAN IRATION BLOOD RELATIVE & IDREN
| | | |
|---|---|---|
| 79 | Greensleeves GRED 21 | This Foundation/Elders and Deacons/How Can A Man/Jah Children Come (12").......... 40 |

## ETHIOPIANS
| | | |
|---|---|---|
| 66 | Ska Beat JB 260 | Live Good (credited to the Etheopians)/SOUL BROTHERS: Soho........... 50 |
| 66 | Island WI 3015 | I Am Free/SOUL BROTHERS: Shanty Town ................................. 70 |
| 67 | Rio R 110 | Owe Me No Pay Me/SHARKS: I Wouldn't Baby ............................ 25 |
| 67 | Rio R 114 | I'm Gonna Take Over Now/JACKIE MITTOO: Home Made ................ 70 |
| 67 | Rio R 123 | What To Do/JACKIE MITTOO: Got My Bugaloo .......................... 150 |
| 67 | Rio R 126 | Dun Dead A'Ready/BOB ANDY: Stay In My Lonely Arms ................ 50 |
| 67 | Rio R 130 | Train To Skaville/You Are The Girl (B-side actually by Gladiators)....... 30 |
| 67 | Doctor Bird DB 1092 | I Need You/Do It Sweet ........................................................ 35 |
| 67 | Doctor Bird DB 1096 | The Whip/Cool It, Amigo ..................................................... 25 |
| 67 | Doctor Bird DB 1103 | Stay Loose, Mama/The World Goes Ska .................................... 50 |
| 68 | Doctor Bird DB 1141 | Come On Now/Sh'Boom ...................................................... 45 |
| 68 | Doctor Bird DB 1147 | Engine 54/Give Me Your Love ............................................... 150 |
| 68 | Doctor Bird DB 1148 | Train To Glory/You Got The Dough ........................................ 60 |
| 68 | Doctor Bird DB 1169 | Everything Crash/I'm Not Losing You ...................................... 22 |
| 68 | Crab CRAB 2 | Fire A Muss Tail/Blacker Black (B-side actually by Count Ossie) ........ 40 |
| 68 | Crab CRAB 5 | Reggie Hit The Town/Ding Dong Bell ....................................... 40 |
| 69 | Crab CRAB 7 | I Am A King/What A Big Surprise ............................................ 30 |
| 69 | Doctor Bird DB 1172 | Not Me/Cut Down ............................................................. 40 |
| 69 | J J Records DB 1185 | Hong Kong Flu/Clap Your Hands ............................................ 18 |
| 69 | J J Records DB 1186 | What A Fire/You............................................................... 20 |
| 69 | Doctor Bird DB 1199 | Everyday Talking/Sharing You ............................................... 20 |
| 69 | Trojan TR 666 | Woman Capture Man/One ................................................... 20 |
| 69 | Trojan TR 697 | Well Red/J.J. ALLSTARS: R.F.K. ............................................. 12 |
| 69 | Nu Beat NB 031 | My Testimony/J.J. ALL STARS: One Dollar Of Soul ....................... 20 |
| 69 | Nu Beat NB 038 | Buss Your Mouth/GLEN ADAMS (Actually REGGAE BOYS) Rough Way Ahead ...... 45 |
| 69 | Duke DU 35 | My Girl/ANSELL COLLINS: Bigger Boss ..................................... 60 |
| 70 | Duke DU 61 | Mek You Go On So/WINSTON WRIGHT & J.J. ALL STARS: Neck Tie ...... 50 |
| 70 | Duke Reid DR 2507 | Mother's Tender Care/TOMMY McCOOK: Soldier Man ...................... 5 |
| 70 | Bamboo BAM 26 | Walkie Talkie/SOUND DIMENSION: Moan And Groan ..................... 20 |
| 70 | Bamboo BAM 38 | You'll Want To Come Back/JACKIE MITTOO: Baby Why (Instrumental) (B-side actually by Sound Dimension) ............................................... 40 |
| 70 | J.J. JJ 3302 | Wreck It Up/Don't Go ........................................................ 80 |
| 70 | J.J. JJ 3303 | Hong Kong Flu/Everything Crash ............................................ 20 |
| 70 | Gas GAS 142 | Satan Girl/MATADORS: The Pum .............................................. 6 |
| 70 | High Note HS 042 | Praise For I (actually "Praise Fari")/GAYTONES: Charrie Part II ......... 12 |
| 70 | Songbird SB 1040 | No Baptism/CRYSTALITES: No Baptism (Version Two) ................... 15 |
| 70 | Songbird SB 1047 | Good Ambition/CRYSTALITES: Ambition Version .......................... 10 |
| 71 | Randy's RAN 509 | Mi Want Girl/RANDY'S ALL STARS: Girl — Version ...................... 10 |
| 71 | Randy's RAN 510 | True Man, Free Man/RANDY'S ALL STARS: Truthful — Version .......... 10 |
| 71 | Randy's RAN 512 | Mr. Tom/Sad News ............................................................ 10 |
| 71 | Fab FAB 180 | Monkey Money/Version ....................................................... 10 |
| 71 | Treasure Isle TI 7067 | Pirate/TOMMY McCOOK & SOUL SYNDICATE: Depth Charge ........... 10 |
| 71 | Songbird SB 1059 | What A Pain/CRYSTALITES: Pain Version .................................. 12 |
| 71 | Songbird SB 1062 | Lot's Wife/DERRICK HARRIOTT: Slave ..................................... 12 |
| 71 | Songbird SB 1064 | Best Of Five (Parts 1 & 2) .................................................. 12 |
| 71 | Big Shot BI 569 | He's Not A Rebel/J.J. ALL STARS: He's Not A Rebel — Version .......... 15 |
| 71 | Big Shot BI 574 | The Selah/Don't Let Me Go .................................................. 10 |
| 71 | Duke DU 102 | Drop Him/J.J. ALL STARS: Drop Him Version .............................. 12 |
| 71 | Duke DU 108 | Rim Bim Bam/RANDY'S ALL STARS: Rim Bim Bam Version ............. 10 |
| 71 | Explosion EX 2050 | Starvation/TROJAN ALL STARS: Starvation Version ...................... 10 |
| 71 | G.G. GG 4519 | Love Bug/Sound Of Our Forefathers ....................................... 10 |
| 71 | Supreme SUP 221 | Love Bug/Sound Of Our Forefathers ....................................... 10 |
| 71 | Supreme SUP 226 | Starvation/MAXIE & GLEN: Jordan River ..................................... 8 |
| 71 | Big BG 330 | Solid As A Rock/RUPIE EDWARDS ALL STARS: Solid As A Rock Version ..... 6 |
| 71 | Punch PH 96 | Solid As A Rock/RUPIE EDWARDS ALL STARS: Solid As A Rock Version ..... 6 |
| 72 | G.G. GG 4533 | Israel Want To be Free/TYPHOON ALL STARS: Israel (Version)......... 12 |
| 72 | Prince Buster PB 38 | You Are For Me/Playboy ....................................................... 8 |
| 72 | Techniques TE 919 | Promises/TIVOLIS: Promises — Version ..................................... 6 |
| 73 | Harry J. HJ 6646 | The Word Is Love/The Word Is Love — Version ............................. 5 |
| 74 | Harry J. HJ 6663 | Buy You A Ring/Pray Muma .................................................... 5 |
| 74 | Cactus CT 37 | Better Man/Skanking Man ..................................................... 6 |
| 74 | Cactus CT 46 | Conquering Lion/Lion Head .................................................... 8 |
| 75 | Dragon DRA 1032 | Knowledge Is Power/Power Version .......................................... 5 |
| 75 | Tropical ALO54 | Another Moses/Moses ........................................................ 10 |
| 76 | Attack ATT 8131 | Another Moses/SYLFORD WALKER: I Can't Understand ................. 10 |
| 78 | Sensation SSD015 | Hail Rasta/Version (12") ..................................................... 15 |
| 78 | Treasure Isle TRE 010 | The Whip/Cool It, Omigo/BOBBY ELLIS: Shank I Sheck (12") .......... 15 |
| 86 | Trojan TROT 9085 | Pirate/Version (12") .......................................................... 10 |
| 11 | Smash THB 7012 | I'm Shocking/Sign The Cheque .............................................. 10 |

# ETHNIC FIGHT BAND

| | | | |
|---|---|---|---|
| 68 | Doctor Bird DLM 5011 | THE ETHIOPIANS GO ROCK STEADY/ENGINE 54 (LP, this is a UK pressing in a Jamaican sleeve) | 400 |
| 69 | Trojan TTL 10 | REGGAE POWER (LP) | 40 |
| 70 | Trojan TBL 112 | WOMAN CAPTURE MAN (LP) | 60 |
| 77 | Third World TWS 15 | SLAVE CALL (LP) | 30 |
| 86 | Trojan TRLS 228 | ORIGINAL REGGAE HITSOUND (LP) | 15 |

*(see Eathopians, Soul Brothers, Soul Vendors, Hamliins)*

## ETHNIC FIGHT BAND
| | | | |
|---|---|---|---|
| 75 | Ethnic Fight EF 4416 | OUT OF ONE MAN COMES MANY DUBS (LP) | 80 |
| 77 | Ethnic Fight EF 4444 | MUSIC EXPLOSION DUB (LP) | 100 |

## ETIVES
| | | | |
|---|---|---|---|
| 81 | Ayrespin AYRC 106 | A BREATH OF FRESH AIR (LP) | 20 |
| 84 | Ayrespin AYRC 015 | AN GAOL A THUG MI OG (MY LOVE OF EARLY DAYS) (LP) | 20 |

## ETTA (JAMES) & HARVEY (FUQUA)
| | | | |
|---|---|---|---|
| 60 | London HLM 9180 | If I Can't Have You/My Heart Cries | 50 |

*(see also Etta James, Moonglows, Harvey & Moonglows)*

## E-TYPES
| | | | |
|---|---|---|---|
| 83 | Banana 507 | Don't Wanna Do Those Things | 6 |

## JACK EUBANK'S ORCHESTRA
| | | | |
|---|---|---|---|
| 61 | London HLU 9312 | What'd I Say/Chiricahua | 10 |
| 62 | London HLU 9501 | Searchin'/Take A Message To Mary | 5 |

## EUGENE & BURST
| | | | |
|---|---|---|---|
| 71 | Supreme SUP 225 | Let It Fall/DENZIL & BURST: Can't Change | 6 |

## EUGENIUS
| | | | |
|---|---|---|---|
| 92 | Paperhouse PAPLP 011 | OOMALAMA (LP) | 15 |
| 94 | August Rust 008 | MARY QUEEN OF SCOTS (LP) | 15 |

*(see also Teenage Fanclub)*

## EUROPEANS
| | | | |
|---|---|---|---|
| 79 | Heartbeat PULSE 2 | Europeans/Voices (p/s) | 5 |

## EUROPEAN TOYS
| | | | |
|---|---|---|---|
| 83 | SUBVERSIVE SUB 008 | I Am The Creator/Keep It All/So Look At Me Now (p/s) | 10 |
| 84 | Backs 12NCH 009 | KOREA EP (12") | 15 |

## EURYTHMICS
| | | | |
|---|---|---|---|
| 81 | RCA RCA 68 | Never Gonna Cry Again/Le Sinistre (p/s) | 8 |
| 81 | RCA RCAT 68 | Never Gonna Cry Again (Extended)/Le Sinistre (Extended) (12", p/s) | 25 |
| 81 | RCA RCA 115 | Belinda/Heartbeat, Heartbeat (p/s) | 15 |
| 82 | RCA RCA 199 | This Is The House/Home Is Where The Heart Is (p/s) | 15 |
| 82 | RCA RCAT 199 | This Is The House/Your Time Will Come (live)/Never Gonna Cry Again/4/4 In Leather (live)/Take Me To Your Heart (live) (12", p/s) | 35 |
| 82 | RCA RCA 230 | The Walk/Step On The Beast/The Walk (Part 2) (p/s) | 12 |
| 82 | RCA RCAT 230 | The Walk/Invisible Hands/Dr Trash/The Walk (Part 2) (12", printed die-cut sleeve) | 35 |
| 83 | RCA DA 4/EUC 001 | Right By Your Side/Right By Your Side (Party Mix) (stickered p/s with free shrinkwrapped (RCA EUC 001) | 25 |
| 85 | RCA BYTI 100 | I Love You Like A Ball And Chain (mono)/I Love You Like A Ball And Chain (stereo) (promo only) | 8 |
| 83 | RCA RCALP 6063 | SWEET DREAMS (LP, picture disc) | 12 |
| 84 | RCA PLP 70109 | TOUCH (LP, picture disc) | 30 |

*(see also ACatch, Tourists, Chris & Cosey, Stewart & Harrison)*

## JOHN EVAN BAND
| | | | |
|---|---|---|---|
| 90 | A New Day NRS/CD 1 | THE JOHN EVAN BAND LIVE '66 (CD, 500 only) | 30 |

*(see also Jethro Tull)*

## BARBARA EVANS
| | | | |
|---|---|---|---|
| 59 | RCA RCA 1122 | Souvenirs/Pray For Me, Mother (triangular centre) | 25 |
| 61 | Mercury AMT 1151 | Charlie Wasn't There/Nothing You Can Do | 5 |

## BILL EVANS
| | | | |
|---|---|---|---|
| 59 | Fontana FJL 104 | DIG IT (LP) | 20 |
| 59 | Riverside 12-315 | PORTRAIT IN JAZZ (LP) | 100 |
| 63 | Verve VLP 9054 | CONVERSATIONS WITH MYSELF (LP) | 30 |
| 67 | Verve VLP 9161 | A SIMPLE MATTER OF CONVICTION (LP) | 30 |

## BRIAN EVANS
| | | | |
|---|---|---|---|
| 71 | CBS 5392 | We're Going Wrong/Paradise Lost | 50 |
| 71 | CBS 7293 | This Is My Woman/If You Still Want Me (as Bryan Evans) | 10 |

## BRYAN EVANS
| | | | |
|---|---|---|---|
| 72 | Columbia DB 8911 | Turnaround Sunday/Re-United | 8 |

## CHRISTINE EVANS
| | | | |
|---|---|---|---|
| 65 | Philips BF 1406 | Growing Pains/Someone In Love | 5 |
| 66 | Philips BF 1496 | Somewhere There's Love/Right Or Wrong | 6 |
| 67 | Melodisc MEL 1620 | I'm Gonna Tell Tony/Someone In Love | 10 |

## DAVE EVANS
| | | | |
|---|---|---|---|
| 71 | Village Thing VTS 6 | THE WORDS IN BETWEEN (LP) | 40 |
| 72 | Village Thing VTS 14 | ELEPHANTASIA (LP) | 45 |
| 74 | Kicking Mule SNKF 107 | SAD PIG DANCE (LP, with booklet) | 20 |
| 74 | Kicking Mule SNKF 122 | TAKE A BITE OUT OF LIFE (LP) | 18 |

## GIL EVANS ORCHESTRA
| | | | |
|---|---|---|---|
| 60 | Vogue LAE 12234 | GREAT JAZZ STANDARDS (LP) | 20 |
| 61 | HMV CLP 1456 | OUT OF THE COOL (LP) | 20 |

## JOHN EVANS
| | | | |
|---|---|---|---|
| 62 | Palette PG 9040 | Melodie Pour Madame/Cry Me A River | 10 |

## LARRY EVANS
| | | | |
|---|---|---|---:|
| 56 | London HLU 8269 | Crazy 'Bout My Baby/Henpecked | 750 |
| 56 | London HLU 8269 | Crazy 'Bout My Baby/Henpecked (78) | 75 |

## MAUREEN EVANS
| | | | |
|---|---|---|---:|
| 58 | Embassy WB 300 | Carolina Moon/Stupid Cupid | 10 |
| 58 | Embassy WB 303 | Fever/Born Too Late | 10 |
| 58 | Embassy WB 309 | The Hula Hoop Song/Hoopa Hoola | 6 |
| 58 | Embassy WB 313 | I'll Get By/Someday (You'll Want Me To Want You) | 6 |
| 58 | Embassy WB 316 | The Day The Rains Came/You Always Hurt The One You Love | 6 |
| 58 | Embassy WB 319 | To Know Him Is To Love Him/Kiss Me, Honey Honey, Kiss Me | 10 |
| 59 | Embassy WB 344 | Goodbye Jimmy, Goodbye/May You Always | 6 |
| 59 | Embassy WB 348 | Lipstick On Your Collar/What A Diff'rence A Day Made | 10 |
| 59 | Embassy WB 356 | Broken-Hearted Melody/Plenty Good Lovin' | 6 |
| 59 | Embassy WB 371 | Among My Souvenirs/Happy Anniversary | 10 |
| 59 | Oriole CB 1517 | Don't Want The Moonlight/The Years Between | 6 |
| 60 | Oriole CB 1533 | The Big Hurt/I Can't Begin To Tell You | 10 |
| 60 | Oriole CB 1540 | Love, Kisses And Heartaches/We Just Couldn't Say Goodbye | 10 |
| 60 | Oriole CB 1550 | Paper Roses/Please Understand | 10 |
| 61 | Oriole CB 1563 | Mama Wouldn't Like It/My Little Corner Of The World | 5 |
| 61 | Oriole CB 1578 | As Long As He Needs Me/Where Is Love? | 5 |
| 61 | Oriole CB 1581 | Till/Why Don't You Believe Me | 5 |
| 61 | Oriole CB 1613 | My Foolish Heart/Oh Gypsy Oh Gypsy | 5 |
| 62 | Oriole CB 1743 | Never In A Million Years/We Had Words | 5 |
| 62 | Oriole CB 1760 | Like I Do/Starlight Starbright | 5 |
| 63 | Oriole CB 1804 | Pick The Petals/Melancholy Me | 6 |
| 63 | Oriole CB 1806 | Tomorrow Is Another Day/Acapulco Mexico | 10 |
| 63 | Oriole CB 1851 | What A Difference A Day Made/Oh What A Guy | 5 |
| 63 | Oriole CB 1875 | Like You Used To Do/As You Love Her | 5 |
| 64 | Oriole CB 1906 | I Love How You Love Me/John John | 5 |
| 64 | Oriole CB 1939 | He Knows I Love Him Too Much/Don't Believe Him | 6 |
| 64 | Oriole CB 1969 | Get Away/I've Often Wondered | 10 |
| 65 | CBS 201733 | All The Angels Sing/Speak Sugar Speak | 8 |
| 65 | CBS 201752 | Never Let Him Go/Poco Sole | 12 |
| 67 | CBS 202621 | Somewhere There's Love/It Takes A Little Time | 8 |
| 68 | CBS 3222 | I Almost Called Your Name/Searching For Home | 8 |
| 63 | Oriole EP 7076 | MELANCHOLY ME (EP) | 30 |
| 63 | Oriole PS 40046 | LIKE I DO (LP) | 30 |

## MILL EVANS
| | | | |
|---|---|---|---:|
| 01 | Kent 6T 17 | Ain't You Glad/MILLIONAIRES: I'm The One Who Loves You | 20 |

## PAUL EVANS (& CURLS)
| | | | |
|---|---|---|---:|
| 59 | London HLL 8968 | Seven Little Girls Sitting In The Back Seat/Worshipping An Idol (with Curls) | 7 |
| 60 | London HLL 9045 | Midnite Special/Since I Met You, Baby | 30 |
| 60 | London HLL 9129 | Happy-Go-Lucky Me/Fish In The Ocean | 5 |
| 60 | London HLL 9183 | Brigade Of Broken Hearts/Twins | 5 |
| 60 | London HLL 9239 | Hushabye Little Guitar/Blind Boy | 20 |
| 62 | London HLR 9636 | The Bell That Couldn't Jingle/Gilding The Lily | 6 |
| 63 | London HLR 9770 | Even Tan/Ten Thousand Years | 6 |
| 63 | London RE-R 1349 | PAUL EVANS (EP) | 40 |
| 60 | London HA-L 2248 | PAUL EVANS SINGS THE FABULOUS TEENS (LP) | 100 |

## RICHARD EVANS
| | | | |
|---|---|---|---:|
| 78 | A&M AMSP 7438 | Burning Spear/Do Re Me For Soul | 10 |
| 78 | AMS 7438 | Burning Spear/Do Re Me For Soul (12") | 20 |

## ROGER EVANS & SWANSEA CITY FOOTBALL CLUB
| | | | |
|---|---|---|---:|
| 79 | Rotor Pro 001 | Swansea City/The Ballad Of Swansea Jack | 8 |

## RUSSELL EVANS & NITEHAWKS
| | | | |
|---|---|---|---:|
| 66 | Atlantic 584 010 | Send Me Some Cornbread/The Bold | 30 |

## TONY EVANS BAND
| | | | |
|---|---|---|---:|
| 71 | Polydor 2058 101 | Hot Pants/Beach Bird | 15 |

## EVEN AS WE SPEAK
| | | | |
|---|---|---|---:|
| 90 | Sarah SARAH 37 | Nothing Ever Happens/Blue Suburban Skies/Bizarre Love Triangle/ Goes So Slow/A Stranger Calls (p/s, insert) | 10 |
| 91 | Sarah SARAH 49 | One Step Forward/Must Be Something Else/Best Kept Secret (p/s, insert) | 10 |
| 91 | Sarah SARAH 59 | Beautiful Day/Nothing Much At All (p/s, insert) | 6 |
| 93 | Sarah SARAH 79 | (All You Find Is) Air/Getting Faster/Blue Eyes Deceiving Me (p/s, insert) | 6 |
| 93 | Sarah SARAH 614 | FERAL POP FRENZY (LP) | 25 |

## EVEN DOZEN JUG BAND
| | | | |
|---|---|---|---:|
| 66 | Bounty BY 6023 | THE EVEN DOZEN JUG BAND (LP) | 25 |

*(see also Lovin' Spoonful, John Sebastian)*

## EVENING OUTS
| | | | |
|---|---|---|---:|
| 80 | Refill RR5 | Channel/Stammer (no p/s, hand stamped labels) | 100 |

## EVENSONG
| | | | |
|---|---|---|---:|
| 73 | Philips 6006 276 | I Was Her Cowboy/Gypsy | 15 |

## EVER RED
| | | | |
|---|---|---|---:|
| 88 | Supertone STR 007 | Dem No Ruff Like We/Hot Number (12") | 40 |

## BETTY EVERETT
| | | | |
|---|---|---|---:|
| 64 | Stateside SS 259 | You're No Good/Chained To Your Love | 20 |
| 64 | Stateside SS 280 | It's In His Kiss (The Shoop Shoop Song)/Hands Off | 20 |
| 64 | Stateside SS 321 | I Can't Hear You/Can I Get To Know You | 25 |

## Betty EVERETT & JERRY BUTLER

| | | | |
|---|---|---|---|
| 64 | Fontana TF 520 | Getting Mighty Crowded/Chained To A Memory | 20 |
| 64 | King KG 1002 | Happy I Long To Be/Your Loving Arms | 20 |
| 65 | Sue WI 352 | I've Got A Claim On You/Your Love Is Important To Me | 60 |
| 68 | President PT 215 | It's In His Kiss (The Shoop Shoop Song)/Getting Mighty Crowded | 8 |
| 69 | President PT 251 | You're No Good/Hands Off | 8 |
| 69 | MCA Soul Bag BAG 3 | I Can't Say No To You/Better Tomorrow Than Today | 10 |
| 69 | MCA MU 1055 | There'll Come A Time/Take Me | 8 |
| 70 | Uni UN 517 | Sugar/Hold On | 8 |
| 71 | Liberty LBF 15428 | I Got To Tell Somebody/Why Are You Leaving Me | 15 |
| 72 | President PT 372 | Trouble Over The Weekend/The Shoe Doesn't Fit | 10 |
| 65 | Fontana TL 5236 | IT'S IN HIS KISS (LP) | 60 |
| 68 | Joy JOYS 106 | IT'S IN HIS KISS (LP, reissue) | 15 |
| 69 | Uni UNLS 109 | THERE'LL COME A TIME (LP) | 25 |

## BETTY EVERETT & JERRY BUTLER

| | | | |
|---|---|---|---|
| 64 | Stateside SS 339 | Let It Be Me/Ain't That Lovin' You Baby | 10 |
| 65 | Fontana TF 528 | Smile/Love Is Strange | 8 |
| 68 | President PT 214 | Let It Be Me/Smile | 8 |
| 69 | President PT 252 | Our Day Will Come/Just Be True | 6 |
| 65 | Fontana TL 5237 | DELICIOUS TOGETHER (LP) | 50 |

*(see also Jerry Butler)*

## KENNY EVERETT

| | | | |
|---|---|---|---|
| 68 | MGM 1421 | It's Been So Long/Without Her | 10 |
| 69 | Deram DM 245 | And Now For A Little Train Number/Nice Time | 8 |
| 77 | DJM DJS 10810 | Captain Kremmen (Retribution)/Retribution | 5 |

## ROY EVERETT

| | | | |
|---|---|---|---|
| 70 | Parlophone R 5857 | Turn On You Own Heat/Look At That Old Bird | 10 |

## VINCE EVERETT

| | | | |
|---|---|---|---|
| 65 | Fontana TF 606 | Bless You/'Til I Lost You | 10 |
| 67 | Fontana TF 818 | Endlessly/Who's That Girl? | 10 |
| 68 | Fontana TF 915 | Every Now And Then/Barbarella | 10 |

## EVERGREEN BLUES

| | | | |
|---|---|---|---|
| 67 | Mercury MF 1012 | Midnight Confessions/(Yes) That's My Baby | 10 |
| 68 | Mercury MF 1025 | Laura (Keep Hangin' On)/Yesterday's Coming | 6 |
| 68 | Mercury 20122 SMCL | 7 DO ELEVEN (LP) | 20 |

## EVERGREEN BLUESHOES

| | | | |
|---|---|---|---|
| 69 | London HA-U/SH-U 8399 | THE BALLAD OF THE EVERGREEN BLUESHOES (LP) | 20 |

*(see also Skip Battin, Byrds)*

## EVERLY BROTHERS

### 78s

| | | | |
|---|---|---|---|
| 59 | London HLA 8863 | Poor Jenny/Take A Message To Mary | 20 |
| 59 | London HLA 8934 | ('Til) I Kissed You/Oh, What A Feeling | 30 |
| 60 | London HLA 9039 | Let It Be Me/Since You Broke My Heart | 60 |
| 60 | Warner Bros WB 1 | Cathy's Clown/Always It's You | 100 |
| 60 | London HLA 9157 | When Will I Be Loved/Be-Bop-A-Lula | 60 |
| 60 | Warner Bros WB 19 | Lucille/So Sad (To Watch Good Love Go Bad) | 200 |

### SINGLES

| | | | |
|---|---|---|---|
| 57 | London HLA 8440 | Bye Bye, Love/I Wonder If I Care As Much (triangular centre) | 10 |
| 57 | London HLA 8440 | Bye Bye, Love/I Wonder If I Care As Much (round centre) | 5 |
| 57 | London HLA 8498 | Wake Up Little Susie/Maybe Tomorrow (triangular centre) | 10 |
| 57 | London HLA 8498 | Wake Up Little Susie/Maybe Tomorrow (round centre) | 5 |
| 58 | London HLA 8554 | Should We Tell Him/This Little Girl Of Mine (triangular centre) | 20 |
| 58 | London HLA 8554 | Should We Tell Him/This Little Girl Of Mine (round centre) | 5 |
| 58 | London HLA 8618 | All I Have To Do Is Dream/Claudette (triangular centre) | 5 |
| 58 | London HLA 8685 | Bird Dog/Devoted To You (triangular centre) | 5 |
| 58 | London HLA 8781 | Problems/Love Of My Life (triangular centre) | 5 |
| 59 | London HLA 8863 | Poor Jenny/Take A Message To Mary (triangular centre) | 5 |
| 59 | London HLA 8934 | ('Til) I Kissed You/Oh, What A Feeling (triangular centre) | 5 |
| 60 | London HLA 9039 | Let It Be Me/Since You Broke My Heart (triangular centre) | 10 |
| 60 | Warner Bros WB 1 | Cathy's Clown/Always It's You | 5 |
| 60 | London HLA 9157 | When Will I Be Loved/Be-Bop-A-Lula | 5 |
| 60 | Warner Bros WB 19 | Lucille/So Sad (To Watch Good Love Go Bad) | 5 |
| 60 | London HLA 9250 | Like Strangers/Leave My Woman Alone | 5 |
| 61 | Warner Bros WB 33 | Walk Right Back/Ebony Eyes | 5 |
| 61 | Warner Bros WB 42 | Temptation/Stick With Me Baby | 5 |
| 61 | Warner Bros WB 50 | Muskrat/Don't Blame Me | 5 |
| 62 | Warner Bros WB 56 | Crying In The Rain/I'm Not Angry | 5 |
| 62 | Warner Bros WB 67 | How Can I Meet Her?/That's Old Fashioned | 5 |
| 62 | Warner Bros WB 79 | No One Can Make My Sunshine Smile/Don't Ask Me To Be Friends | 5 |
| 63 | Warner Bros WB 94 | So It Will Always Be/Nancy's Minuet | 5 |
| 63 | Warner Bros WB 99 | It's Been Nice/I'm Afraid | 5 |
| 63 | Warner Bros WB 109 | The Girl Sang The Blues/Love Her | 6 |
| 64 | Warner Bros WB 129 | Ain't That Lovin' You Baby/Hello Amy | 6 |
| 64 | Warner Bros WB 135 | The Ferris Wheel/Don't Forget To Cry | 6 |
| 64 | Warner Bros WB 143 | You're The One I Love/Ring Around My Rosie (withdrawn) | 20 |
| 64 | Warner Bros WB 146 | Gone, Gone, Gone/Torture | 6 |
| 65 | Warner Bros WB 154 | You're My Girl/Don't Let The Whole World Know | 6 |
| 65 | Warner Bros WB 158 | That'll Be The Day/Give Me A Sweetheart | 6 |
| 65 | Warner Bros WB 161 | The Price Of Love/It Only Costs A Dime | 5 |

| | | | | |
|---|---|---|---|---|
| 65 | Warner Bros | WB 5628 | The Price Of Love/It Only Costs A Dime (reissue) | 5 |
| 65 | Warner Bros | WB 5639 | I'll Never Get Over You/Follow Me | 5 |
| 65 | Warner Bros | WB 5649 | Love Is Strange/Man With Money | 6 |
| 66 | Warner Bros | WB 5682 | It's All Over/I Used To Love You (unissued) | 0 |
| 66 | Warner Bros | WB 5743 | (You Got) The Power Of Love/Leave My Girl Alone | 10 |
| 66 | Warner Bros | WB 5754 | I've Been Wrong Before/Hard Hard Year | 10 |
| 67 | Warner Bros | WB 7520 | Bowling Green/I Don't Want To Love You | 10 |
| 67 | Warner Bros | WB 7062 | Mary Jane/Talking To The Flowers | 10 |
| 67 | Warner Bros | WB 7088 | Love Of The Common People/A Voice Within | 10 |
| 68 | Warner Bros | WB 7192 | It's My Time/Empty Boxes | 10 |
| 68 | Warner Bros | WB 7226 | Milk Train/Lord Of The Manor | 10 |
| 69 | Warner Bros | WB 6056 | Cathy's Clown/Walk Right Back | 5 |
| 70 | Warner Bros | WB 6074 | Good Golly, Miss Molly/Oh, Boy! | 8 |
| 70 | Warner Bros | WB 7425 | Yves/Human Race | 10 |
| 72 | RCA Victor | RCA 2232 | Ridin' High/Stories We Could Tell | 10 |
| 73 | RCA Victor | RCA 2286 | Not Fade Away/Lay It Down | 7 |
| 77 | Warner Bros | K 17004 | Silent Treatment/Dancing On My Feet | 5 |
| 80 | Old Gold | SET 1 | THE EVERLY BROTHERS SINGLES SET (15 x p/s 7", box set with book) | 15 |

**EPs**

| | | | | |
|---|---|---|---|---|
| 58 | London | RE-A 1113 | THE EVERLY BROTHERS | 15 |
| 58 | London | RE-A 1148 | THE EVERLY BROTHERS — NO. 2 | 15 |
| 58 | London | RE-A 1149 | THE EVERLY BROTHERS — NO. 3 | 15 |
| 59 | London | RE-A 1174 | THE EVERLY BROTHERS — NO. 4 | 15 |
| 59 | London | RE-A 1195 | SONGS OUR DADDY TAUGHT US PART 1 | 15 |
| 59 | London | RE-A 1196 | SONGS OUR DADDY TAUGHT US PART 2 | 15 |
| 59 | London | RE-A 1197 | SONGS OUR DADDY TAUGHT US PART 3 | 15 |
| 60 | London | RE-A 1229 | THE EVERLY BROTHERS — NO. 5 | 15 |

*(The above EPs were originally issued with triangular centres, later round-centre editions are worth half to two-thirds of these values.)*

| | | | | |
|---|---|---|---|---|
| 61 | Warners | WEP 6034 | ESPECIALLY FOR YOU | 20 |
| 61 | Warners | W(S)EP 6034 | ESPECIALLY FOR YOU (stereo) | 20 |
| 61 | London | RE-A 1311 | THE EVERLY BROTHERS — NO. 6 | 15 |
| 62 | Warners | WEP 6049 | FOREVERLY YOURS (mono) | 15 |
| 62 | Warners | W(S)EP 6049 | FOREVERLY YOURS (stereo) | 15 |
| 62 | Warners | WEP 6056 | IT'S EVERLY TIME (mono) | 15 |
| 62 | Warners | W(S)EP 6056 | IT'S EVERLY TIME (stereo) | 15 |
| 63 | Warners | WEP 6107 | A DATE WITH THE EVERLY BROTHERS VOL. 1 (mono) | 15 |
| 63 | Warners | W(S)EP 6107 | A DATE WITH THE EVERLY BROTHERS VOL. 1 (stereo) | 15 |
| 63 | Warners | WEP 6109 | A DATE WITH THE EVERLY BROTHERS VOL. 2 (mono) | 15 |
| 63 | Warners | W(S)EP 6109 | A DATE WITH THE EVERLY BROTHERS VOL. 2 (stereo) | 18 |
| 63 | Warners | WEP 6111 | INSTANT PARTY VOL. 1 (mono) | 15 |
| 63 | Warners | W(S)EP 6111 | INSTANT PARTY VOL. 1 (stereo) | 20 |
| 63 | Warners | WEP 6113 | INSTANT PARTY VOL. 2 (mono) | 15 |
| 63 | Warners | W(S)EP 6113 | INSTANT PARTY VOL. 2 (stereo) | 20 |
| 63 | Warners | WEP 6115 | BOTH SIDES OF AN EVENING — FOR DANCING VOL. 1 (mono) | 15 |
| 63 | Warners | W(S)EP 6115 | BOTH SIDES OF AN EVENING — FOR DANCING VOL. 1 (stereo) | 18 |
| 64 | Warners | WEP 6117 | BOTH SIDES OF AN EVENING — FOR DREAMING VOL. 2 (mono) | 15 |
| 64 | Warners | W(S)EP 6117 | BOTH SIDES OF AN EVENING — FOR DREAMING VOL. 2 (stereo) | 18 |
| 64 | Warners | WEP 6128 | THE EVERLY BROTHERS SING GREAT COUNTRY HITS VOL. 1 | 15 |
| 64 | Warners | WEP 6131 | THE EVERLY BROTHERS SING GREAT COUNTRY HITS VOL. 2 | 15 |
| 64 | Warners | WEP 6132 | THE EVERLY BROTHERS SING GREAT COUNTRY HITS VOL. 3 | 15 |
| 65 | Warner Bros | WEP 6138 | BOTH SIDES OF AN EVENING — FOR FUN VOL. 3 | 10 |
| 65 | Warner Bros | WEP 604 | THE PRICE OF LOVE | 10 |
| 65 | Warner Bros | WEP 608 | ROCK'N'SOUL VOL. 1 | 10 |
| 65 | Warner Bros | WEP 609 | ROCK'N'SOUL VOL. 2 | 10 |
| 66 | Warner Bros | WEP 610 | LOVE IS STRANGE | 10 |
| 66 | Warner Bros | WEP 612 | PEOPLE GET READY | 10 |
| 66 | Warner Bros | WEP 618 | WHAT AM I LIVING FOR? | 10 |
| 67 | Warner Bros | WEP 622 | LEAVE MY GIRL ALONE | 10 |
| 67 | Warner Bros | WEP 623 | SOMEBODY HELP ME | 10 |

**ALBUMS**

| | | | | |
|---|---|---|---|---|
| 58 | London | HA-A 2081 | THE EVERLY BROTHERS | 40 |
| 58 | London | HA-A 2150 | SONGS OUR DADDY TAUGHT US | 30 |
| 60 | Warner Bros | WM 4012 | IT'S EVERLY TIME (Mono) | 30 |
| 60 | Warner Bros | WS 8012 | IT'S EVERLY TIME (Stereo) | 30 |
| 60 | London | HA-A 2266 | THE FABULOUS STYLE OF THE EVERLY BROTHERS | 30 |
| 60 | Warner Bros | WM 4028 | A DATE WITH THE EVERLY BROTHERS (mono) | 30 |
| 60 | Warner Bros | WS 8028 | A DATE WITH THE EVERLY BROTHERS (stereo) | 35 |
| 61 | Warner Bros | WM 4052 | BOTH SIDES OF AN EVENING (Mono) | 20 |
| 61 | Warner Bros | WS 8052 | BOTH SIDES OF AN EVENING (stereo) | 25 |
| 62 | Warner Bros | WM 4061 | INSTANT PARTY (also stereo WS 8061) | 20 |
| 62 | Warner Bros | WM 4061 | INSTANT PARTY (also stereo WS 8061) | 25 |
| 62 | Warner Bros | WM 8116 | CHRISTMAS WITH THE EVERLY BROTHERS AND THE BOYS TOWN CHOIR (mono) | 20 |
| 62 | Warner Bros | WS 8116 | CHRISTMAS WITH THE EVERLY BROTHERS AND THE BOYS TOWN CHOIR (stereo) | 25 |
| 63 | Warner Bros | WM 8138 | SING GREAT COUNTRY HITS (mono) | 20 |
| 63 | Warner Bros | WS 8138 | SING GREAT COUNTRY HITS (stereo) | 25 |
| 65 | Warner Bros | WM 8169 | GONE GONE GONE (mono) | 20 |
| 65 | Warner Bros | WS 8169 | GONE GONE GONE (stereo) | 25 |
| 65 | Warner Bros | WM 8171 | ROCK 'N' SOUL (mono) | 20 |
| 65 | Warner Bros | WS 8171 | ROCK 'N' SOUL (stereo) | 25 |

MINT VALUE £

| | | | |
|---|---|---|---|
| 65 | Warner Bros W(S) 1605 | BEAT 'N' SOUL | 15 |
| 65 | Warner Bros W 1620 | IN OUR IMAGE (mono) | 15 |
| 65 | Warner Bros W(S) 1620 | IN OUR IMAGE (stereo) | 18 |

*(see also Don Everly, Phil Everly)*

## DON EVERLY
| | | | |
|---|---|---|---|
| 74 | Ode ODS 66046 | Warmin' Up The Band/Evelyn Swing | 5 |

## PHIL EVERLY
| | | | |
|---|---|---|---|
| 73 | RCA RCA 2409 | The Air That I Breathe/God Bless Older Ladies | 5 |
| 74 | Pye 7N 45398 | Invisible Man/It's True | 5 |
| 74 | Pye 7N 45415 | Sweet Music/Goodbye Line | 5 |

*(see also Cliff Richard)*

## EVERREADY'S
| | | | |
|---|---|---|---|
| 80 | Taaga TAG 3 | Don't Do It Again/Martian Girl (gatefold p/s) | 15 |

## LENNY EVERSONG
| | | | |
|---|---|---|---|
| 57 | Vogue Coral Q 72255 | Jezebel/Jealousy | 6 |

## EVERTON FOOTBALL CLUB
| | | | |
|---|---|---|---|
| 72 | Philips 6006 253 | Forever Everton/March Of The Gwladys Street Gladiators | 7 |

## EVERVESSENCE
| | | | |
|---|---|---|---|
| 69 | Priory 02 | Strange One/My Illusive Life | 50 |

## EVERYBODY
| | | | |
|---|---|---|---|
| 70 | Page One POF 163 | The Shape Of Things To Come/Do Like The Little Children Do | 15 |

## EVERYBODY'S CHILDREN
| | | | |
|---|---|---|---|
| 70 | Fontana TF 1070 | The Time Is Now/Abide With Me | 5 |

## EVERY MOTHER'S SON
| | | | |
|---|---|---|---|
| 67 | MGM MGM 1341 | Come And Take A Ride In My Boat/I Believe In You | 25 |
| 67 | MGM MGM 1350 | Put Your Mind At Ease/Proper Four Leaf Clover | 25 |
| 67 | MGM MGM 1372 | Pony With The Golden Mane/Dolls In The Clock | 10 |
| 67 | MGM C(S) 8044 | EVERY MOTHER'S SON (LP) | 40 |
| 68 | MGM C(S) 8061 | EVERY MOTHER'S SON'S BACK (LP) | 35 |

## EVERYONE
| | | | |
|---|---|---|---|
| 71 | Charisma CB 146 | Trouble At The Mill/Radio Lady | 5 |
| 71 | B&C CAS 1028 | EVERYONE (LP, gatefold sleeve, attached envelope with booklet) | 40 |

*(see also Andy Roberts)*

## EVERYONE ELSE
| | | | |
|---|---|---|---|
| 79 | Woodbine St WSR 001 | Schooldays/Brainwashed/Out Of My Mind/Don't Call Us (p/s) | 100 |

## EVERYONE INVOLVED
| | | | |
|---|---|---|---|
| 72 | Arcturus ARC 3 | The Circus Keeps On Turning/Motor Car Madness | 30 |
| 72 | Arcturus ARC 4 | EITHER OR (LP, private pressing, embossed plain white sleeve with inserts) | 200 |

## EVERYTHING BUT THE GIRL
| | | | |
|---|---|---|---|
| 82 | Cherry Red CHERRY 37 | Night And Day/Feeling Dizzy/On My Mind (yellow p/s) | 5 |

*(see also Ben Watt, Marine Girls, Tracey Thorn)*

## EVERYTHING IS EVERYTHING
| | | | |
|---|---|---|---|
| 69 | Vanguard VA 1 | Witchi Tai To/Oooh Baby | 15 |
| 68 | Vanguard SVRL 19036 | EVERYTHING IS EVERYTHING (LP) | 25 |

## EVERY WHICH WAY
| | | | |
|---|---|---|---|
| 70 | Charisma BD 1 | Go Placidly/The Light | 12 |

*(see also Brian Davison, Griffin, Heavy Jelly, Skip Bifferty, Graham Bell, Bell & Arc)*

## EVIL ED
| | | | |
|---|---|---|---|
| 01 | YNR YNR4 | THE TOURNAMENT ROUND 1 (12", EP stickered black die-cut sleeve) | 12 |
| 02 | Hidden Identity HID1 | THE TOURNAMENT ROUND 2 (12" EP) | 15 |

## EVOLUTION
| | | | |
|---|---|---|---|
| 90 | Positive Vinyl PV 001 | Came Outa Nowhere (12") | 20 |
| 91 | Positive Vinyl PV 002 | Metropolis (12") | 20 |

## EWAN (MCDERMOTT) & DENVER
| | | | |
|---|---|---|---|
| 67 | Giant GN 17 | I Want You So Bad/ERIC McDERMOTT: I'm Gonna Love You | 10 |

## EWAN (MCDERMOTT) & JERRY (MCCARTHY)
| | | | |
|---|---|---|---|
| 67 | Blue Beat BB 385 | Oh Babe/Dance With Me (with Carib Beats) | 18 |
| 67 | Giant GN 5 | The Right Track/We Got To Be One | 10 |
| 67 | Giant GN 10 | Rock Steady Train/My Baby Is Gone | 15 |
| 67 | Giant GN 14 | Tennessee Waltz/You've Got Something | 15 |

## EX
| | | | |
|---|---|---|---|
| 86 | Ron Johnson ZRON 11 | '1936' THE SPANISH REVOLUTION (double pack with book) | 20 |

## EX/ALERTA
| | | | |
|---|---|---|---|
| 84 | CNT CNT 017 | THE RED DANCE PACKAGE (12", split EP) | 15 |

## EXCALIBUR
| | | | |
|---|---|---|---|
| 88 | Clay PLATE 1 | HOT FOR LOVE (Hot For Love/Early In The Morning/Come On And Rock/ Death's Door (12" EP) | 15 |
| 85 | Conquest QUEST 5 | THE BITTER END (mini-LP) | 20 |

## EXCEL
| | | | |
|---|---|---|---|
| 79 | ARSS XL1 | If It Rains/Rolling Home/She's One Of The Boys/Rock Show (EP, p/s) | 100 |
| 80 | Polydor POSP 110 | What Went Wrong?/Junita (p/s) | 8 |

## EXCELS
| | | | |
|---|---|---|---|
| 67 | Atlantic 584 133 | California On My Mind/The Arrival Of Mary | 25 |

## EXCELSIOR SPRING
| | | | |
|---|---|---|---|
| 69 | Instant IN 002 | Happy Miranda/It | 35 |

## EXCEPTIONS
65   Decca F 12100     What More Do You Want?/Soldier Boy ................................................. 25

*(see also Orchids)*

## EXCEPTION(S)
67   CBS 202632     The Eagle Flies On Friday/Girl Trouble ........................................... 70
67   CBS 2830     Gaberdine Saturday Night Street Walker/Sunday Night At The Prince Rupert ............... 30
68   President PT 181     Rub It Down/It's Snowing In The Desert ........................................... 6
68   President PT 205     Helicopter/Back Room ........................................................... 6
68   President PT 218     Tailor Made Babe/Turn Over The Soil ............................................. 6
69   President PT 236     Jack Rabbit/Keep The Motor Running ............................................. 8
69   President PT 271     Pendulum/Don't Torture Your Mind ............................................. 12
69   President PTLS 1026     THE EXCEPTIONAL EXCEPTION (LP, yellow/black labels) ........................ 40

*(see also Fotheringay, Fairport Convention)*

## EXCHANGE AND MART
72   President PT 385     Yeah My Friend/I Know That I'm Dreaming ..................................... 15

## EXCHECKERS
64   Decca F 11871     All The World Is Mine/It's All Over .............................................. 25

*(see also Aynsley Dunbar Retaliation)*

## EXCITER
85   Music For Nations MFN 47     LONG LIVE THE LOUD (LP, inner) ................................................ 15
86   Music For Nations MFN 61     UNVEILING THE WICKED (LP, with inner) ....................................... 15

## EXCITERS
63   United Artists UP 1011     Tell Him/Hard Way To Go ....................................................... 15
63   United Artists UP 1017     He's Got The Power/Drama Of Love ............................................. 15
63   United Artists UP 1026     Get Him/It's So Exciting ........................................................ 20
64   United Artists UP 1041     Do-Wah-Diddy/If Love Came Your Way ........................................... 25
65   Columbia DB 7479     I Want You To Be My Boy/Tonight, Tonight ..................................... 25
65   Columbia DB 7544     Just Not Ready/Are You Satisfied ............................................... 20
65   Columbia DB 7606     Run Mascara/My Father ......................................................... 20
66   London HLZ 10018     A Little Bit Of Soap/I'm Gonna Get Him Someday ............................... 20
66   London HLZ 10038     You Better Come Home/Weddings Make Me Cry .................................. 40
69   United Artists UP 2274     Do Wah Diddy Diddy/Hard Way To Go ........................................... 10
71   Jay Boy BOY 38     Soul Motion/You Know It Ain't Right ............................................ 20
74   Contempo CS 2033     Blowing Up My Mind (Vocal)/Blowing UP My Mind (Instrumental) ............... 5
75   20th Century BTC 1005     Reaching For The Best/Keep On Reaching ....................................... 6
65   United Artists UEP 1005     DO WAH DIDDY DIDDY (EP) ....................................................... 60
64   United Artists ULP 1032     THE EXCITERS (LP) ............................................................. 100

*(see also Jerry Allen)*

## EXCURSION
68   Morgan MX 7001     NIGHT TRAIN (LP) ............................................................... 30
69   Gemini GMX 5029     NIGHT TRAIN (LP, reissue) ...................................................... 18

*(see also Jerry Allen)*

## EXECUTE/INFERNO
86   Pusmort 0012-06     SPLIT LP ....................................................................... 20

## EXECUTE(S) (1)
64   Columbia DB 7323     March Of The Mods/Why, Why, Why ............................................. 10
64   Columbia DB 7393     Strictly For The Beat/No Room For Squares ..................................... 10
65   Columbia DB 7573     It's Been So Long/You're For Me (as Executives) ............................... 10
65   Columbia DB 7770     Return Of The Mods/How Sad .................................................. 10
66   Columbia DB 7919     Lock Your Door/In My Arms (as Executives) ..................................... 8

## EXECUTIVE(S) (2)
67   CBS 202652     Smokey Atmosphere/Sensation ................................................. 30
67   CBS 3067     Ginza Strip/I'll Always Love You ............................................... 25
68   CBS 3431     Tracy Took A Trip/Gardena Dreamer (as Executive, with promo only p/s) ...... 40
68   CBS 3431     Tracy Took A Trip/Gardena Dreamer (as Executive) ............................. 30
69   CBS 4013     I Ain't Got Nobody/To Kingdom Come (as Executive) ........................... 30

## EXECUTIVES (3)
80   Attrix RB 05     Shy Little Girl/Never Go Home/JONNIE & LUBES: I Got Rabies/Terror In The Parking
Lot (p/s) ...................................................................... 15

## EXECUTIVE SUITE
74   Cloud One HIT 1     When The Fuel Runs Out/When The Fuel Runs Out ............................... 7
74   Polydor 2310400     EXECUTIVE SUITE 1 (LP) ....................................................... 30

## EXHIBIT A
80   Irrelevant Wombat DAMP 1     NO ELEPHANTS THIS SIDE OF THE WATFORD GAP (EP, with insert) ............... 25
80   Irrelevant Wombat DAMP 2     DISTANCE (EP) ................................................................ 15

*(see also Doof)*

## EXILE
77   Boring BO 1     DON'T TAX ME (EP, 1,000 only p/s) ............................................ 30
78   Charly CYS 1033     The Real People/Tomorrow Today/Disaster Movie (p/s) ....................... 15

## EXILES
66   Topic 12T 143     FREEDOM, COME ALL YE (LP) .................................................... 15
67   Topic 12T 164     THE HALE AND THE HANGED (LP) ................................................ 15

## EXIT 13
82   Artlos Music LOS 001     CELIA'S LAST WEDNESDAY (LP) ................................................... 25

## EXIT (1)
80   Kik KIK 010     Look Inside/Three In A Bed ..................................................... 20

## EXIT (2)
83 Red Beret REB 1     Planetoid Passion/Social Graces ............................................................ 50

## EXITS (1)
78 Way Out WOO 1     YODELLING (EP, numbered, gatefold p/s, hand-stamped labels) ................ 60

## EXITS (2)
78 Red Lightning GIL 519     The Fashion Plague/Cheam (p/s, labels on wrong sides) ..................... 100
*(see also Direct Hits)*

## EXIT STANCE (1)
84 Mortarhate MORT 11     WHILE BACKS ARE TURNED (LP, with insert) ................................. 20
84 Fight Back FIGHT 4     CRIME AGAINST HUMANITY (EP) ............................................... 15

## EXIT STANCE (2)
84 Exit Stance ES 002     Esthetics/Conspiracy Of Silence .................................................. 30

## EXOCET
86 Exocet EXO 1PS12     STALEMATE (EP) .......................................................................... 50

## EXODUS
85 Music For Nations MFN 44     BONDED BY BLOOD (LP) .................................................. 20

## EXODUS (JAMAICA)
71 Duke DU 103     Pharoah's Walk/Little Caesar ........................................................... 12
72 Sioux SI 001     Pharaoh's Walk No. 9/SAMMY JONES: Worried Over You ....................... 6
72 Sioux SI 010     Julia Sees Me/LLOYD THE MATADOR: The Train (Engine 54) ................. 50

## EXORDIUM
70s Face To Face FTF 1001     TROUBLE WITH ADAM (LP, private pressing) ......................... 20

## EXOTICS (1)
64 Decca F 11850     Cross My Heart/Ooh La La .............................................................. 10
68 Columbia DB 8418     Don't Lead Me On/You Can Try ................................................... 25

## EXOTICS (2)
70 Pye 7N 17925     I Don't Want Nobody (To Lead Me On)/Driftaway ............................ 6

## EXPELAIRES
79 Zoo CAGE 007     To See You/Frequency (p/s) ............................................................ 5
*(see also Mission)*

## EXPELLED
82 Riot City RIOT 8     Dreaming/No Life, No Future/What Justice (p/s) ............................... 6
82 Riot City RIOT 17     Government Policy/Make It Alone (p/s) ...................................... 6

## EXPERIMENTAL AUDIO RESEARCH
99 Ochre OCH 009LV     PESTREPELLER EP ................................................................ 10

## EXPERIMENTS WITH ICE
81 United Dairies EX 001     EXPERIMENTS WITH ICE (LP) ........................................... 25

## EX PISTOLS
84 Cherry Red/Virgina Pistol 76p     Land Of Hope And Glory/The Flowers of Romansk (Picture disc) ... 10

## EXPLICIT CORPSE
81 Corpse 1     That Day Before.../I Gotta Gistol (stickered white labels, plastic gatefold p/s) .......... 8

## EXPLOITED
81 Exploited EXP 001     Army Life/Fuck The Mods/Crashed Out (p/s) .................................. 8
81 Exploited EXP 002     Exploited Barmy Army/I Believe In Anarchy/What You Gonna Do? (p/s) ...... 8
81 Secret SHH 110     Dogs Of War/Blown To Bits (live) (p/s) ......................................... 5
81 Secret SHH 112     Army Life/Fuck The Mods/Crashed Out (p/s, reissue) ........................ 5
81 Secret SHH 120     Dead Cities/Hitler's In The Charts Again/Class War (p/s) ................. 5
83 Blurg/Pax PAX 15     Rival Leaders/Army Style/Singalongabushell (p/s) ......................... 6
81 Exploited EXP 1001     PUNK'S NOT DEAD (LP) ...................................................... 15
81 Exploited EXP 1002     ON STAGE (LP, some on yellow vinyl) .................................... 15
83 Pax PAX 18     LET'S START A WAR (LP) ..................................................................... 15
86 Dojo DOJOLP 37     HORROR EPICS (LP) ............................................................... 15
87 Rough Justice JUST 6     DEATH BEFORE DISHONOUR (LP, inner) ............................... 15
90 Rough Justice JUST 15     THE MASSACRE (LP) ........................................................ 15
96 Rough Justice JUS 22     BEAT THE BASTARDS (LP, inner) ...................................... 25

## EXPLORER
84 Rock Shop RSR 006     EXPLODING (LP) .................................................................. 50

## EXPLOSIVE
68 President PT 221     Crying All Night/I Close My Eyes ............................................... 6
69 President PT 244     Cities Make The Country Colder/Step Out Of Line ....................... 20
69 President PT 262     Who Planted Thorns In Miss Alice's Garden?/I Get My Kicks From Living ......... 15
70 President PT 286     I'm Gonna Use What I Got To Get What I Need/Am I A Fool? (with Del Taylor) ...... 6
70 President PT 302     This Ain't The Road To Freedom/Today Is Today ........................ 6
71 Plexium PXM 20     Hey Presto, Magic Man/Get It Together ....................................... 60
71 Plexium PXM 24     Love Doesn't Come Easy/See You In The Morning ........................ 6
*(see also Watson T. Browne & Explosive)*

## EXPORT
79 Atlantic K 11344     Julie Bitch/Nice To Know You ..................................................... 15
80 His Master's Vice VICE 2     You've Got To Rock/Wheeler Dealer (title sleeve) ................. 18
80 His Master's Vice VICE 1     EXPORT (LP) ............................................................... 18

## EXPOSE
79 A&M AMS 7473     Teenage Girls/If You See Kay (red vinyl, p/s) ................................. 6
79 A&M AMS 7490     Pretty Women Walk All Over Me/Isn't Life A Mystery (withdrawn, A label promos only) ........... 10

## EXPOSURE
80 Angular Music ACUTE 1     Style & Fashion/Video Eyes (p/s) ...................................... 10

## EXPOZER
80　Hit Hard HARD 1　Rock Japan/On My Knees (p/s) :................................................................ 12

## EXPRESSION
82　A&M AM 149　With Closed Eyes/Nothing Changes (p/s)................................................ 6

## EXTERNAL MENACE
82　Beat The System!! MENACE　YOUTH OF TODAY (EP)........................................................... 15
　　1
83　Beat The System!! MENACE　NO VIEWS (EP) ............................................................................. 15
　　2

## EXTREEM
66　Strike JH 326　On The Beach/Don't You Ignore Me ........................................... 20

## EXTREME NOISE TERROR
88　Strange Fruit SFPS 048　PEEL SESSION (12" EP p/s)............................................... 18
88　Head Eruption HURT 1　A HOLOCAUST IN YOUR HEAD (LP, with inner) ..................... 20
91　Vinyl Japan/Discipline　PHONOPHOBIA (LP, insert)............................................... 15
　　DISC1T

## EXTREME NOISE TERROR/CHAOS U.K.
86　Manic Ears ACHE 01　EAR SLAUGHTER — RADIOACTIVE (LP) ............................. 15

## EXTREMES
87　SRT 6KS 1082　Eat My Dust/Salome ............................................................ 10

## EXUMA
71　Mercury 6052 080　Damn Fool/You Don't Know What's Going On ......................... 6
72　Kama Sutra 2013 053　Monkberry Moon Delight/Obeah Man Come Back.................. 8

## EYE DO IT
84　No Rip Off YAW 2　I Lost My MInd/Hold Back (p/s)........................................ 10

## EYE FULL TOWER
67　Polydor BM 56734　How About Me?/Carol Cartoon ........................................... 7

## EYE WITNESS
81　Prp PRO 002　Tax Exile/Boys In Blue (p/s) ........................................... 8

## EYEHATEGOD
00　People Like You 772521　SOUTHERN DISCOMFORT (LP, white vinyl with inner)............. 20

## EYELESS IN GAZA
80　Ambivalent Scale ASR 2　Kodak Ghosts Run Amok/China Blue Vision/The Feeling's Mutual (wraparound p/s).... 20
81　Cherry Red CHERRY 20　Invisibility/Three Kittens/Plague Of Years (p/s, with insert)........ 5
81　Cherry Red CHERRY 31　Others/Jane Dancing/Ever Present/Avenue With Trees (p/s)........ 5
82　Cherry Red CHERRY 47　Veil Like Calm/Taking Steps (p/s)........................................ 8
81　Cherry Red BRED 18　CAUGHT IN THE FLUX (LP, with bonus 12" EP [12 BRED 18], with inner)......... 15
*(see also Martyn Bates)*

## EYES OF BLUE
66　Deram DM 106　Heart Trouble/Up And Down................................................ 60
67　Deram DM 114　Supermarket Full Of Cans/Don't Ask Me To Mend Your Broken Heart....... 70
68　Mercury MF 1049　Largo/Yesterday ...................................................... 15
69　Mercury SMCL 20134　THE CROSSROADS OF TIME (LP, black/silver labels with 'Mercury' logo) .......... 200
69　Mercury SMCL 20164　IN FIELDS OF ARDATH (LP, black/silver label with Mercury logo)................ 200
*(see also Ancient Grease, Big Sleep, Man, Ritchie Francis, Gary Pickford-Hopkins, Gentle Giant)*

## EYES (1)
65　Mercury MF 881　When The Night Falls/I'm Rowed Out........................................ 200
66　Mercury MF 897　The Immediate Pleasure/My Degeneration .............................. 150
66　Mercury MF 910　Man With Money/You're Too Much ...................................... 175
65　Mercury MF 934　Good Day Sunshine/Please Don't Cry .................................. 100
66　Mercury 10035 MCE　THE ARRIVAL OF THE EYES (EP) ........................................ 350
84　Bam Caruso KIRI 028　BLINK (LP, 2 different sleeves) ........................................ 18
87　Bam Caruso MARI 038　SCENE BUT NOT HEARD (mini-LP) ...................................... 15
*(see also Pupils)*

## EYES (2)
78　Raw RAW 16　I Like It/Once Ain't Enough (p/s) ........................................ 5
78　Raw RAW 29　Once In A Lifetime/Hello I Love You (1000 only in p/s)................ 8
*(see also Doug Kane)*

## EYNESBURY GIANT
78　Ultimate URL 602　FROM THE CASK (LP, with insert)........................................ 20

## EZY MEAT
84　Electric Storm ES 0001　NOT FOR WIMPS (LP, with insert, Irish only)......................... 50
86　Electric Storm ES 0002　ROCK YOUR BRAINS OUT (LP, with insert, Irish only) ................ 40

## EZY RIDER
82　English Steel　POWER (LP)..................................................................... 150

# F

## SHELLEY FABARES
62　Pye International 7N 25132　Johnny Angel/Where's It Gonna Get Me? (blue label, later yellow label)....................... 8
62　Pye International 7N 25133　She Can't Find Her Keys/Very Unlikely (with Paul Peterson) ...................... 8
62　Pye International 7N 25151　Johnny Loves Me/I'm Growing Up................................................. 8
62　Pye International 7N 25166　The Things We Did Last Summer/Breaking Up Is Hard To Do....................... 8

MINT VALUE £

| | | | |
|---|---|---|---|
| 63 | Pye International 7N 25184 | Telephone (Won't You Ring)/Big Star | 8 |
| 63 | Pye International 7N 25207 | Ronnie Call Me When You Get A Chance/I Left A Note To Say Goodbye | 8 |
| 65 | Fontana TF 592 | My Prayer/Pretty Please | 10 |

*(see also Paul Peterson & Shelley Fabares)*

## FAB FOOD
| | | | |
|---|---|---|---|
| 80 | Smile SR 021 | Never Alone/Holiday | 10 |

## FABIAN
| | | | |
|---|---|---|---|
| 59 | HMV POP 587 | I'm A Man/Hypnotized | 20 |
| 59 | HMV POP 587 | I'm A Man/Hypnotized (78) | 20 |
| 59 | HMV POP 612 | Turn Me Loose/Stop Thief! | 20 |
| 59 | HMV POP 643 | Tiger/Mighty Cold (To A Warm, Warm Heart) | 12 |
| 59 | HMV POP 659 | Got The Feeling/Come On And Get Me | 12 |
| 60 | HMV POP 695 | Hound Dog Man/This Friendly World | 12 |
| 60 | HMV POP 724 | String Along/About This Thing Called Love | 10 |
| 60 | HMV POP 778 | I'm Gonna Sit Right Down And Write Myself A Letter/Strollin' In The Springtime | 8 |
| 60 | HMV POP 800 | Tomorrow/King Of Love | 10 |
| 60 | HMV POP 810 | Kissin' And Twistin'/Long Before | 10 |
| 61 | HMV POP 829 | You Know You Belong To Somebody Else/Hold On | 10 |
| 61 | HMV POP 869 | Grapevine/David And Goliath | 12 |
| 61 | HMV POP 934 | You're Only Young Once/The Love That I'm Giving To You | 10 |
| 82 | Revival 6017 | Tiger/Turn Me Loose | 5 |
| 59 | HMV CLP 1301 | HOLD THAT TIGER (LP) | 40 |
| 60 | HMV CLP 1345 | THE FABULOUS FABIAN (LP) | 40 |
| 61 | HMV CLP 1433 | YOUNG AND WONDERFUL (LP, mono) | 30 |
| 61 | HMV CSD 1352 | YOUNG AND WONDERFUL (LP, stereo) | 30 |

## FABIAN (JAMAICA)
| | | | |
|---|---|---|---|
| 77 | Tribesman TM 004 | Prophecy/Prophecy Dub | 30 |
| 78 | Tribesman TM 08 | Prophecy/JIMMY LINDSAY : Easy (12") | 40 |
| 78 | Island 12 WIP 6431 | Prophecy/JIMMY LINDSAY : Easy (12") | 25 |

## FABIONS
| | | | |
|---|---|---|---|
| 69 | Bullet BU 410 | V. Rocket/Smile (B-side actually "My Baby" by Tennors) | 180 |

## FABLE
| | | | |
|---|---|---|---|
| 70 | Penny Farthing PEN 725 | Minstrel Song/She Said Yes | 5 |
| 71 | Penny Farthing PEN 751 | With A Boy Like You/She Said Yes | 5 |
| 73 | Magnet MAG 5002 | FABLE (LP, gatefold sleeve, white/red labels) | 15 |

*(see also Trapeze, Uriah Heep)*

## FABRIC
| | | | |
|---|---|---|---|
| 94 | Whole Car WCAR 004 | BODY OF WATER (LP) | 15 |

## GREGORY FABULOUS
| | | | |
|---|---|---|---|
| 03 | Jah Tubbys JT 10015 | Get Up/Moving To Zion (10", with the Offbeat Posse) | 20 |
| 04 | Jah Tubbys JT 10022 | Love Jah/Tra-La-La (10", with Prof. Natty) | 20 |

## FABULOUS COUNTS
| | | | |
|---|---|---|---|
| 71 | Mojo 2092 021 | Get Down People/Lunar Funk | 8 |

## FABULOUS DIALS
| | | | |
|---|---|---|---|
| 63 | Pye International 7N 25200 | Bossa Nova Stomp/Forget Me Not | 25 |

## FABULOUS ECHOES
| | | | |
|---|---|---|---|
| 73 | Contempo CON 002 | Don't You Know I Love You/If You Move It You Lose It | 8 |

## FABULOUS FIVE INC.
| | | | |
|---|---|---|---|
| 73 | Ahanti SHAN 104 | FABULOUS FIVE INC. (LP) | 25 |

## FABULOUS FLAMES
| | | | |
|---|---|---|---|
| 70 | Clandisc CLA 224 | Holly Holy/LORD CREATOR: Kingston Town | 12 |
| 71 | Trojan TR 7822 | Growing Up/Lovitis | 6 |

*(see also Dynamites)*

## FABULOUS IMPACT
| | | | |
|---|---|---|---|
| 90 | Kent 6T 6 | Baby Baby, I Want You/HAMPTONS: No No No No No No No Not My Girl (100 Club 6T's All-nighter anniversary disc) | 30 |

## FABULOUS JADES
| | | | |
|---|---|---|---|
| 80s | Soul City 140 | Come On And Live/Planning The Moment | 8 |

## FABULOUS SHADES
| | | | |
|---|---|---|---|
| 71 | Tropical AL 005 | Lonely Man/Version 2 | 8 |

## FABULOUS SWINGTONES
| | | | |
|---|---|---|---|
| 58 | HMV POP 471 | Geraldine/You Know Baby | 250 |
| 58 | HMV POP 471 | Geraldine/You Know Baby (78) | 50 |

## FABULOUS TALBOT BROTHERS
| | | | |
|---|---|---|---|
| 50s | Melodisc M 1507 | Bloodshot Eyes/She's Got Freckles | 20 |

## FACES
| | | | |
|---|---|---|---|
| 70 | Warner Bros WB 8005 | Flying/Three-Button Hand-Me-Down | 10 |
| 70 | Warner Bros WB 8014 | Wicked Messenger/Nobody Knows (unissued) | 0 |
| 70 | Warner Bros WB 8018 | Had Me A Real Good Time/Rear Wheel Skid | 8 |
| 73 | Warner Bros K 16247 | Cindy Incidentally/Skewiff (Mend The Fuse) (with lyric insert, no p/s) | 8 |
| 73 | Warner Bros K 16281 | Borstal Boys (withdrawn, any pressed?) | 0 |
| 73 | NME SF1 139 | Dishevelment Blues/Ooh La La Preview (flexidisc free with NME) | 10 |
| 74 | Warner Bros K 16494 | You Can Make Me Dance, Sing Or Anything/As Long As You Tell Him (credited to Rod Stewart and the Faces, p/s) | 8 |
| 70 | Warner Bros WS 3000 | FIRST STEP (LP, orange label, gatefold sleeve) | 100 |
| 71 | Warner Bros WS 3011 | LONG PLAYER (LP, blue & silver label, stitched die-cut '78rpm' style sleeve) | 50 |
| 71 | Warner Bros K 46053 | FIRST STEP (LP, reissue, green label, gatefold sleeve) | 20 |
| 71 | Warner Bros K 56006 | A NOD IS AS GOOD AS A WINK ... TO A BLIND HORSE (LP, green label, with poster) | 40 |

| | | | |
|---|---|---|---|
| 72 | Warner Bros K 46064 | LONG PLAYER (LP, reissue, blue & silver label, stitched die-cut '78rpm'-style sleeve) | 20 |
| 73 | Warner Bros K 56011 | OOH-LA-LA (LP, green label, 'Faces' sleeve with lyric poster) | 25 |
| 74 | Warner Bros K 56011 | OOH-LA-LA (LP, 'Burbank' label, 'Faces' sleeve, with lyric poster) | 20 |
| 74 | Warner Bros K 56006 | A NOD IS AS GOOD AS A WINK ... TO A BLIND HORSE (LP, reissue, 'Burbank' label) | 15 |
| 75 | Warner Bros K 66027 | TWO ORIGINALS OF . . . (2-LP, reissue of "First Steps" & "Long Player", gatefold sleeve) | 20 |

*(see also Small Faces, Rod Stewart, Ronnie Lane & Slim Chance, Ron Wood, Jeff Beck Group, Kenney Jones)*

## FACE TO FACE
| 72 | Face To Face FTF 002 | FACE TO FACE (LP) | 50 |

## FACTION
| 81 | Inevitable INEV 007 | Faction/Wrong Again | 7 |
| 83 | Bluurg FISH 7 | YOU'VE GOT THE FIRE EP (fold-out p/s) | 5 |

## FACTOR FICTION
| 81 | TKS 001 | FACTOR FICTION EP (Pressed in Ireland but imported into U.K) | 15 |

## FACTORY FLOOR
| 08 | Outside OUT 0015 | Bipolar/You Were Always Wrong (p/s, orange vinyl, 500 only) | 25 |
| 08 | One Of One ON 01 | PLANNING APPLICATION EP (12" p/s, 500 only) | 25 |
| 10 | Blast First Petite PTYT 035 V | Lying/16-16-9-2--1-14-9-7/A Wooden Box/Solid Sound (10" clear vinyl with DVD, 2000 only) | 10 |
| 10 | Blast First Petite PTVT 048 | Lying (Stephen Morris Mix)/Lying (Original)/Lying (Chris Carter Mix)/A Wooden Box (Original) (2x12" in plastic sleeve, 200 only) | 15 |
| 14 | Vinyl Factory VF 079 | o/o/o/o//o/o/o/o/ (NVC Remix) (12" signed, numbered, 100 only) | 20 |
| 13 | DFA DFA 2392 | FACTORY FLOOR (2-LP, yellow vinyl, with CD and CD-R, 300 only) | 30 |
| 13 | DFA DFA 2392 | FACTORY FLOOR (2-LP, white vinyl, with CD and CD-R) | 25 |

## FACTORY (1)
| 68 | MGM MGM 1444 | Path Through The Forest/Gone | 1000 |
| 69 | CBS 4540 | Try A Little Sunshine/Red Chalk Hill | 1400 |

*(see also Peter & Wolves, Norman Conquest, John Pantry, Velvet Hush)*

## FACTORY (2)
| 70 | OAK RGJ718 | Time Machine/Castle On The Hill (99 copies only) | 450 |

## FACTORY (3)
| 82 | Future Earth FER 011 | You Are The Music/History Of The World (silver die-cut sleeve) | 20 |

## FACTORY (4)
| 86 | Strike Back SBR10 | Hold Out/Burn Me Up (p/s) | 20 |
| 86 | Strike Back SBR 10T | Hold Out (Extended)/Burn Me Up/Outcast (12", p/s) | 25 |

## FACTOTUMS
| 65 | Immediate IM 009 | In My Lonely Room/Run In The Green And Tangerine Flaked Forest | 40 |
| 65 | Immediate IM 022 | You're So Good To Me/Can't Go Home Anymore My Love | 30 |
| 66 | Piccadilly 7N 35333 | Here Today/In My Room | 22 |
| 66 | Piccadilly 7N 35355 | I Can't Give You Anything But Love/Absolutely Sweet Marie | 20 |
| 67 | Pye 7N 17402 | Cloudy/Easy Said, Easy Done | 15 |
| 69 | CBS 4140 | Mr And Mrs Regards/Driftwood | 20 |

## FADELA
| 88 | Factory FAC 197 | N'sel Fik/Ateni Bniti (12") | 10 |

## FADERS
| 79 | Rip Off RIP 8 | Cheatin'/Library Book (in bag p/s) | 60 |

## FAD GADGET
| 79 | Mute 002 | Back To Nature/The Box (p/s) | 5 |
| 81 | Lyntone LYN 10209 | King Of The Flies/DEPECHE MODE: Sometimes I Wish I Was Dead (red vinyl flexidisc free with Flexipop magazine, issue 11) | 25 |
| 81 | Lyntone LYN 10209 | King Of The Flies/DEPECHE MODE: Sometimes I Wish I Was Dead (red vinyl flexidisc free without Flexipop magazine, issue 11) | 15 |
| 80 | Mute STUMM 3 | FIRESIDE FAVOURITES (LP) | 20 |

## FADING COLOURS
| 66 | Ember EMB S 229 | (Just Like) Romeo And Juliet/Billy Christian | 20 |
| 67 | Ember EMB S 237 | Be With Me/You're No Use | 10 |

*(see also Orange Seaweed)*

## FAERIE SYMPHONY
| 77 | Decca F13735 | Dance Of The Enashee (Da Oine Sidhe)/The Unseelie Court | 8 |

## BRIAN FAHEY (& HIS ORCHESTRA)
| 59 | Parlophone R 4655 | Street Of A Thousand Bongos/Waltz For Beatniks | 8 |
| 60 | Parlophone R 4686 | At The Sign Of The Swingin' Cymbal/The Clanger | 20 |
| 62 | Parlophone R 4909 | At The Sign Of The Swingin' Cymbal/The Clanger (reissue, as Brian Faye & His Orchestra) | 10 |
| 65 | Parlophone R 5262 | Gidian's Way/Love Theme From "In Harm's Way" | 8 |
| 65 | United Artists UP 1115 | Twang/You Can't Catch Me | 8 |
| 67 | Parlophone R 5615 | The Plank/Stay On the Island | 8 |
| 67 | Parlophone R 5639 | With A Song In My Heart/Swinging Choice | 6 |
| 68 | Columbia DB 8447 | Late Night Extra/Oh The Pity Of It All | 8 |
| 69 | Major Minor MM 656 | Open House/Countdown | 25 |

## JOHN FAHEY
| 67 | Transatlantic TRA 173 | THE TRANSFIGURATION OF BLIND JOE DEATH (LP, with booklet) | 40 |
| 67 | Transatlantic TRA 173 | THE TRANSFIGURATION OF BLIND JOE DEATH (LP, without booklet) | 20 |
| 68 | Vanguard SVRL 19033 | YELLOW PRINCESS (LP) | 25 |
| 68 | Vanguard SVRL 19055 | REQUIA (LP) | 30 |
| 69 | Takoma SNTF 607 | BLIND JOE DEATH (LP) | 20 |
| 69 | Takoma SNTF 608 | DEATH CHANTS, WALTZES & MILITARY BREAKDOWNS) (LP) | 20 |
| 72 | Sonet SNTF 628 | AMERICA (LP) | 25 |
| 72 | Reprise K 44213 | OF RIVERS AND RELIGION (LP) | 20 |

# Jad FAIR

| | | | |
|---|---|---|---|
| 73 | Reprise K 44246 | AFTER THE BALL (LP) | 20 |
| 74 | Takoma SNTF 675 | JOHN FAHEY, PETER LANG AND LEO KOTTKE (LP) | 15 |
| 74 | Sonet SNTF 656 | FARE FORWARD VOYAGERS (LP) | 20 |
| 76 | Sonet SNTF 702 | THE NEW POSSIBILITY (LP) | 20 |
| 77 | Transatlantic TRA 173 | THE TRANSFIGURATION OF BLIND JOE DEATH (LP, reissue, picture label) | 25 |

## JAD FAIR
| | | | |
|---|---|---|---|
| 80 | Armageddon AEP 003 | THE ZOMBIES OF MORA-TAU (EP, die-cut p/s with insert) | 12 |

*(see also Half Japanese)*

## JAD FAIR & PASTELS
| | | | |
|---|---|---|---|
| 91 | Paperhouse PAPER 013T | THIS COULD BE THE NIGHT EP (12", p/s) | 15 |

*(see also Pastels)*

## YVONNE FAIR
| | | | |
|---|---|---|---|
| 74 | Tamla Motown TMG 913 | Funky Music Sho Nuff Turns Me On/Let Your Hair Down | 7 |
| 75 | Tamla Motown TMG 1025 | It's Bad For Me To See You/Walk Out The Door If You Wanna | 7 |
| 75 | Tamla Motown STML 12008 | THE BITCH IS BLACK (LP) | 15 |

## WERLY FAIRBURN & DELTA BOYS
| | | | |
|---|---|---|---|
| 56 | London HLC 8349 | I'm A Fool About Your Love/All The Time | 1000 |
| 56 | London HLC 8349 | I'm A Fool About Your Love/All The Time (78) | 150 |

## JOHNNY FAIRE
| | | | |
|---|---|---|---|
| 58 | London HLU 8569 | Bertha Lou/Till The Law Says Stop | 500 |
| 58 | London HLU 8569 | Bertha Lou/Till The Law Says Stop (78) | 150 |

## FAIRFIELD PARLOUR
| | | | |
|---|---|---|---|
| 70 | Vertigo 6059 003 | Bordeaux Rosé/Chalk On The Wall | 20 |
| 70 | Vertigo 6059 008 | Just Another Day/Caraminda/I Am All The Animals/Song For You | 40 |
| 76 | Prism PRI 1 | Bordeaux Rosé/Baby Stay For Tonight (as Fairfield Parlor) | 10 |
| 70 | Vertigo 6360 001 | FROM HOME TO HOME (LP, gatefold sleeve, large swirl label) | 400 |
| 91 | UFO BFTP 003 | FROM HOME TO HOME (LP, reissue) | 30 |
| 03 | Circle CPWL 104 | PLEASE LISTEN TO THE PICTURES (2-LP, BBC sessions, split release with Kaleidoscope) | 20 |

*(see also Kaleidoscope [U.K.], I Luv Wight)*

## FAIRIES
| | | | |
|---|---|---|---|
| 64 | Decca F 11943 | Don't Think Twice, It's Alright/Anytime At All | 125 |
| 65 | HMV POP 1404 | Get Yourself Home/I'll Dance | 200 |
| 65 | HMV POP 1445 | Don't Mind/Baby Don't | 175 |

*(see also Twink, Cops 'N Robbers)*

## FAIRPORT CONVENTION
### SINGLES
| | | | |
|---|---|---|---|
| 67 | Track 604 020 | If I Had A Ribbon Bow/If (Stomp) | 75 |
| 68 | Island WIP 6047 | Meet On The Ledge/Throwaway Street Puzzle (pink label) | 20 |
| 69 | Island WIP 6064 | Si Tu Dois Partir/Genesis Hall | 8 |
| 70 | Island WIP 6089 | Now Be Thankful/Sir B. McKenzie's Daughter's Lament | 10 |
| 70 | Polydor 2058 014 | If (Stomp)/Chelsea Morning | 12 |
| 71 | Island WIP 6128 | John Lee/The Time Is Near (in p/s) | 12 |
| 71 | Island WIP 6128 | John Lee/The Time Is Near | 6 |
| 73 | Island WIP 6155 | Rosie/Knights Of The Road | 6 |
| 75 | Island WIP 6241 | White Dress/Tears (in p/s) | 12 |
| 75 | Island WIP 6241 | White Dress/Tears | 6 |
| 78 | Hawk HASP 423 | Jam's O'Donnell's Jig/The Last Waltz (Irish-only) | 15 |
| 79 | Simons PMW 1 | Rubber Band/The Bonny Black Hare | 12 |
| 86 | Sunrise Bong 1 | Quazi B Goode/MIKE SILVER: Where Would You Rather Be Tonight | 10 |
| 87 | Island 12IF 324 | Meet On The Ledge (Re-recorded)/John Barleycorn (live)/ Sigh Bheg Sigh Mhor (live) (12", p/s, with poster) | 10 |

### ALBUMS : POLYDOR ALBUMS
| | | | |
|---|---|---|---|
| 68 | Polydor 582 035 | FAIRPORT CONVENTION (mono, laminated sleeve) | 300 |
| 68 | Polydor 582/583 035 | FAIRPORT CONVENTION (stereo, laminated sleeve) | 250 |
| 76 | Polydor Special 2384 047 | FAIRPORT CONVENTION (LP, reissue) | 15 |

### ALBUMS : ISLAND ALBUMS
| | | | |
|---|---|---|---|
| 69 | Island ILPS 9092 | WHAT WE DID ON OUR HOLIDAYS (1st pressing, laminated front cover, pink label with orange/black 'circle' ) | 250 |
| 69 | Island ILPS 9092 | WHAT WE DID ON OUR HOLIDAYS (2nd pressing, pink label with black 'block' logo) | 100 |
| 69 | Island ILPS 9092 | WHAT WE DID ON OUR HOLIDAYS (3rd pressing, pink label with 'i' logo) | 60 |
| 70 | Island ILPS 9092 | WHAT WE DID ON OUR HOLIDAYS (4th pressing, pink rim label with 'palm tree' logo) | 20 |
| 69 | Island ILPS 9102 | UNHALFBRICKING (1st pressing, pink label with black 'block' logo) | 250 |
| 69 | Island ILPS 9102 | UNHALFBRICKING (2nd pressing, pink label with 'i' logo) | 100 |
| 70 | Island ILPS 9102 | UNHALFBRICKING (3rd pressing, pink rim label with 'palm tree' logo) | 40 |
| 69 | Island ILPS 9115 | LIEGE AND LIEF (gatefold sleeve, 1st pressing, pink label with 'i' logo) | 150 |
| 70 | Island ILPS 9115 | LIEGE AND LIEF (gatefold sleeve, 2nd pressing, pink rim label with 'palm tree' logo) | 20 |
| 70 | Island ILPS 9130 | FULL HOUSE (white label test pressing, with "Poor Will & The Jolly Hangman") | 300 |
| 70 | Island ILPS 9130 | FULL HOUSE (1st pressing, pink 'i' label, gatefold sleeve lists "Poor Will & The Jolly Hangman") | 60 |
| 70 | Island ILPS 9130 | FULL HOUSE (2nd pressing, with pink 'i' label, gatefold sleeve without reference to "Poor Will & The Jolly Hangman") | 30 |
| 70 | Island ILPS 9130 | FULL HOUSE (gatefold sleeve, 3rd pressing, pink rim label with 'palm tree' logo) | 15 |
| 71 | Island ILPS 9162 | ANGEL DELIGHT (gatefold sleeve with 'stuck-on' photos, pink rim label) | 20 |
| 71 | Island ILPS 9176 | BABBACOMBE LEE (gatefold sleeve, with innersleeve and booklet, with sticker, pink rim label) | 35 |
| 71 | Island ILPS 9176 | BABBACOMBE LEE (gatefold sleeve, with innersleeve and booklet, without sticker) | 20 |
| 72 | Island ICD 4 | THE HISTORY OF FAIRPORT CONVENTION (2-LP, with 12-page booklet & blue ribbons) | 20 |
| 72 | Island ICD 4 | THE HISTORY OF FAIRPORT CONVENTION (2-LP, later pressing with book & green, red or light blue ribbons) | 18 |

| 73 | Island ILPS 9208 | ROSIE | 15 |
|----|------------------|-------|----|
| 73 | Island ILPS 9246 | FAIRPORT NINE (gatefold sleeve) | 18 |
| 74 | Island ILPS 9285 | LIVE CONVENTION (with insert) | 15 |
| 75 | Island ILPS 9313 | RISING FOR THE MOON (with insert, 'palm tree' label) | 15 |
| 75 | Island ISS 2 | FAIRPORT TOUR SAMPLER (free in NME competition, 500 only) | 150 |
| 76 | Island HELP 28 | LIVE AT THE L.A. TROUBADOR 1974 | 30 |

## ALBUMS : OTHER ALBUMS

| 77 | Vertigo 9102 015 | BONNY BUNCH OF ROSES (gatefold sleeve) | 18 |
|----|------------------|-------|----|
| 78 | Vertigo 9102 022 | TIPPLER'S TALES (with lyric insert) | 15 |
| 79 | Woodworm BEAR 22 | FAREWELL FAREWELL (gatefold sleeve) | 20 |
| 79 | Simons GAMA 1 | FAREWELL FAREWELL (reissue, gatefold sleeve) | 18 |
| 83 | Woodworm WRC 1 | AT 2 (AIRING CUPBOARD TAPES 2) () | 15 |
| 84 | Woodworm (no cat. no.) | THE BOOT (2- cassette in video box, 1,000 only) | 20 |
| 87 | Woodworm (no cat. no.) | THE OTHER BOOT (2-cassette in video box, 1,000 only) | 20 |
| 88 | Woodworm (no cat. no.) | THE THIRD LEG (2-cassette in video box, 1,000 only) | 20 |

*(see also Richard Thompson, Ian Matthews, Dave Swarbrick, Sandy Denny, Ashley Hutchings, Trevor Lucas, Albion Band. Bunch, Fotheringay. Vashti Bunyan, Trader Horne, Thieves, Allan Taylor, Krysia, Marc Ellington, Brian Maxine, Steeleye Span, Vikki clayton)*

## FAIRUZ

| 57 | Parlophone LPVD 1 | FAIRUZ SINGS (10" LP, Export) | 50 |
|----|-------------------|-------|----|
| 58 | Parlophone LPVD 4 | FAIRUZ SINGS AGAIN (10" LP, Export) | 60 |
| 66 | Parlophone LPVDX 106 | DAMASCUS FESTIVAL (LP) | 30 |

## FAIR WARNING

| 87 | Areba ERA 2 | Rocking At The Speed Of Light EP (12", p/s) | 30 |
|----|-------------|-------|----|

## FAIRWAYS (FEATURING GARY STREET)

| 69 | Mercury MF 1116 | Yoko Ono/I Don't Care | 8 |
|----|-----------------|-------|----|

## FAIR WEATHER

| 70 | RCA RCA 1977 | Natural Sinner/Haven't I Tried (To Be A Good Man) | 6 |
|----|--------------|-------|----|
| 70 | RCA RCA 2040 | Road To Freedom/Tutti Frutti | 8 |
| 71 | RCA Neon NE 1000 | Lay It On Me/Looking For The Red Label Pt 2 | 15 |
| 70 | RCA Victor SF 8155 | BEGINNING FROM AN END (LP, withdrawn, different cover and one less track than Neon issue) | 125 |
| 71 | RCA Neon NE 1 | BEGINNING FROM AN END (LP, gatefold sleeve, black inner sleeve) | 100 |

*(see also Andy Fairweather-Low, Amen Corner, Wynder K. Frog)*

## ANDY FAIRWEATHER-LOW

| 86 | Stiff BUY 252 | Bossa Nova/House Of Blue Light (p/s) | 5 |
|----|---------------|-------|----|

*(see also Amen Corner, Fair Weather, Gary Pickford-Hopkins & Friends, Dave Edmunds & Rockpile)*

## FAIRY'S MOKE

| 75 | Deroy 1175 | FAIRY'S MOKE (LP, private pressing, actually various artists LP) | 80 |
|----|------------|-------|----|

*(see also Baby Sunshine)*

## FAIRYTALE

| 67 | Decca F 12644 | Guess I Was Dreaming/Run And Hide | 125 |
|----|---------------|-------|----|
| 67 | Decca F 12665 | Lovely People/Listen To Mary Cry | 70 |

## ADAM FAITH (& ROULETTES)

### SINGLES

| 58 | HMV POP 438 | (Got A) Heartsick Feeling/Brother Heartache And Sister Tears | 80 |
|----|-------------|-------|----|
| 58 | HMV POP 438 | (Got A) Heartsick Feeling/Brother Heartache And Sister Tears (78) | 30 |
| 58 | HMV POP 557 | High School Confidential/Country Music Holiday | 80 |
| 58 | HMV POP 557 | High School Confidential/Country Music Holiday (78) | 30 |
| 59 | Top Rank JAR 126 | Ah, Poor Little Baby!/Runk Bunk (blue label) | 25 |
| 59 | Top Rank JAR 126 | Ah, Poor Little Baby!/Runk Bunk (blue label) (78) | 40 |
| 59 | Parlophone R 4591 | What Do You Want?/From Now Until Forever | 5 |
| 59 | Parlophone R 4591 | What Do You Want?/From Now Until Forever (78) | 30 |
| 60 | Parlophone R 4623 | Poor Me/The Reason (78) | 30 |
| 60 | Parlophone R 4665 | Made You/When Johnny Comes Marching Home | 5 |
| 60 | Parlophone R 4665 | Made You/When Johnny Comes Marching Home (78, existence unconfirmed) | 0 |
| 65 | Parlophone R 5289 | Someone's Taken Maria Away/I Can't Think Of Anyone Else (with Roulettes) | 5 |

### EPs

| 62 | Columbia SEG 8138 | BEAT GIRL (2 Faith tracks, with John Barry Orchestra) | 20 |
|----|-------------------|-------|----|
| 64 | Parlophone GEP 8893 | TOP OF THE POPS (with Roulettes) | 12 |

### ALBUMS

| 60 | Parlophone PMC 1128 | ADAM (mono) | 15 |
|----|---------------------|-------|----|
| 60 | Columbia 33SX 1225 | BEAT GIRL (soundtrack, with John Barry Orchestra) | 40 |
| 64 | Parlophone PMC 1228 | ON THE MOVE (with Roulettes) | 30 |
| 65 | Parlophone PMC 1249 | FAITH ALIVE! (with Roulettes) | 30 |

*(see also Roulettes, John Barry)*

## AUSTIN FAITH

| 71 | Dynamic DYN 407 | 634 5789/DYNAMIC BOYS: Warm And Tender Love | 7 |
|----|-----------------|-------|----|

*(see also Austin Faithful)*

## FAITH BROTHERS

| 67 | Tabernacle TS 1002 | I Am Saved Now/Too Near My Heavenly Home | 20 |
|----|--------------------|-------|----|

## GENE FAITH

| 75 | Power Station PW 109 | Call The FBI/Love Of A Woman Soul Of A Man | 5 |
|----|----------------------|-------|----|

## GEORGE FAITH

| 77 | Island IPR 2034 | Diana/To Be A Lover (12") | 15 |
|----|-----------------|-------|----|
| 77 | Black Swan BS 2 | To Be A Lover/UPSETTERS: Rastaman Shuffle (12") | 20 |
| 77 | Black Swan BS 3 | I've Got The Groove/Diana (12") | 20 |
| 77 | Black Swan BS 4 | Midnight Hour/Turn Back The Hands Of Time (12") | 20 |

MINT VALUE £

| | | | |
|---|---|---|---|
| 77 | Black Swan BS 5 | All The Love I've Got/So Fine (12") | 20 |
| 79 | Warrior WAR 134 | Don't Be Afraid/BUNNY SCOTT : What's The Use/Never Had It So Good (act. Jimmy Riley) (12") | 15 |
| 77 | Black Swan ILPS 9504 | TO BE A LOVER (LP) | 30 |

## HORACE FAITH
| | | | |
|---|---|---|---|
| 69 | B&C CB 104 | Spinning Wheel/Like I Used To Do | 10 |
| 69 | Downtown DT 446 | Daddy's Home/EMOTIONS: Give Me A Love | 10 |
| 70 | Trojan TR 7790 | Black Pearl/Help Me Help Myself | 7 |
| 70 | A&M AMS 817 | Shame And Scandal In The Family/REGGAE STRINGS: Reggae Strings | 6 |
| 76 | DJM DJS 10687 | I Can't Understand It/Gimme Good Lovin' | 30 |

## PALOMA FAITH
| | | | |
|---|---|---|---|
| 12 | RCA 88725412231 | FALL TO GRACE (2-LP) | 40 |
| 14 | RCA 88843043981 | A PERFECT CONTRADICTION (2-LP) | 40 |

## AUSTIN FAITHFUL
| | | | |
|---|---|---|---|
| 68 | Blue Cat BS 140 | Uncle Joe/Can't Understand | 250 |
| 68 | Pyramid PYR 6016 | I'm In A Rocking Mood/ROLAND ALPHONSO: Stream Of Life | 80 |
| 69 | Pyramid PYR 6028 | Eternal Love/ROLAND ALPHONSO: Goodnight My Love | 80 |
| 69 | Pyramid PYR 6042 | Ain't That Peculiar?/Miss Anti-Social | 40 |

*(see also Austin Faith)*

## FAITHFUL DAWN
| | | | |
|---|---|---|---|
| 94 | Dawn 001 | The Sequel (Original mix)/Dark Beat Mix (12", white label – 300 only | 20 |

## MARIANNE FAITHFULL
| | | | |
|---|---|---|---|
| 64 | Decca F 11923 | As Tears Go By/Greensleeves | 7 |
| 64 | Decca F 12007 | Blowin' In The Wind/The House Of The Rising Sun | 8 |
| 65 | Decca F 12075 | Come And Stay With Me/What Have I Done Wrong? | 8 |
| 65 | Decca F 12162 | This Little Bird/Morning Sun | 6 |
| 65 | Decca F 12193 | Summer Nights/The Sha La La Song | 7 |
| 65 | Decca F 12268 | Yesterday/Oh Look Around You | 7 |
| 66 | Decca F 12408 | Tomorrow's Calling/That's Right Baby | 10 |
| 66 | Decca F 12443 | Counting/I'd Like To Dial Your Number | 20 |
| 66 | Decca F 22524 | Is This What I Get For Loving You?/Tomorrow's Calling | 12 |
| 69 | Decca F 12889 | Something Better/Sister Morphine (withdrawn) | 50 |
| 75 | NEMS NES 004 | Dreamin' My Dreams/Lady Madalaine | 10 |
| 76 | NEMS NES 013 | All I Wanna Do In Life/Wrong Road Again | 10 |
| 77 | NEMS NES 014 | Wrong Road Again/The Way You Want Me To Be | 10 |
| 78 | NEMS NES 117 | The Way You Want Me To Be/That Was The Day (Nashville) | 10 |
| 79 | Island WIP 6491 | The Ballad Of Lucy Jordan/Brain Drain (p/s) | 7 |
| 80 | Island 12WIP 6542 | Broken English/Why D'Ya Do It? (12", p/s) | 10 |
| 80 | Decca F 13890 | As Tears Go By/Come And Stay With Me/This Little Bird/Summer Nights (p/s) | 6 |
| 65 | Decca DFE 8624 | GO AWAY FROM MY WORLD (EP) | 35 |
| 65 | Decca LK 4688 | COME MY WAY (LP) | 60 |
| 65 | Decca LK 4689 | MARIANNE FAITHFULL (LP) | 80 |
| 66 | Decca LK 4778 | NORTH COUNTRY MAID (LP) | 75 |
| 67 | Decca LK/SKL 4854 | LOVEINAMIST (LP) | 120 |
| 69 | Decca PA 17 | THE WORLD OF MARIANNE FAITHFULL (LP, mono) | 15 |
| 76 | NEMS NEL 6007 | DREAMIN' MY DREAMS (LP) | 15 |

## FAITH NO MORE
| | | | |
|---|---|---|---|
| 88 | Slash LASH 17 | We Care A Lot/Spirit (p/s) | 10 |
| 88 | Slash LASH 18 | Annie's Song (Remix)/Greed (p/s) | 10 |
| 88 | Slash LASHP 18 | Annie's Song (Remix)/Greed (picture disc) | 10 |
| 88 | Slash LASHX 18 | Anne's Song (Remix)/Greed (12", p/s) | 10 |
| 90 | Slash LASPD 21 | Epic/War Pigs (live) (shaped picture disc) | 10 |
| 92 | London LASH 44 | I'm Easy/Be Aggressive (red vinyl, p/s) | 8 |
| 90 | London/Slash 850 228 | KING FOR A DAY, FOOL FOR A LIFETIME (7 x 7" box set) | 40 |
| 89 | Slash 828 217-1 | THE REAL THING (LP, picture disc) | 25 |
| 92 | Slash LASHP18 | ANGEL DUST (LP, insert with free 12") | 20 |
| 95 | Slash 828 560-1 | KING FOR A DAY FOOL FOR A LIFETIME (2-LP, red vinyl) | 50 |
| 97 | Slash 828 901 | ALBUM OF THE YEAR (LP) | 40 |

## FAKES
| | | | |
|---|---|---|---|
| 79 | Deep Cuts DEEP TWO | Production/Look-Out/Tony Blackburn/Sylvia Clark (p/s) | 15 |

## FALCON
| | | | |
|---|---|---|---|
| 80 | Ellie Jay EJSP 9344 | FALCON EP (12", p/s, 500 only) | 10 |

## EDDIE FALCON
| | | | |
|---|---|---|---|
| 60 | Columbia DB 4420 | The Young Have No Time To Lose/My Thanks To You | 6 |
| 61 | Columbia DB 4646 | Linda Rose/If Ever I Should Fall In Love | 6 |

## FALCONS (U.K.)
| | | | |
|---|---|---|---|
| 64 | Philips BF 1297 | Stampede/Kazutzka | 20 |

## FALCONS (U.S.)
| | | | |
|---|---|---|---|
| 59 | London HLT 8876 | You're So Fine/Goddess Of Angels | 100 |
| 59 | London HLT 8876 | You're So Fine/Goddess Of Angels (78) | 70 |
| 62 | London HLK 9565 | I Found A Love/Swim (some labels credit B-side as "Swin") | 50 |

*(see also Wilson Pickett, Eddie Floyd)*

## FALL OUT BOY
| | | | |
|---|---|---|---|
| 04 | Sorepoint SORE 010S | Dead On Arrival/Dead On Arrival (acoustic) (blue vinyl, die-cut sleeve) | 10 |
| 05 | Sorepoint SORE 038S | Grand Theft Autumn/Where Is Your Boy/MY AWESOME COMPILATION: As Always (yellow vinyl, die-cut sleeve) | 8 |

## THE FALL

### SINGLES

| | | | |
|---|---|---|---|
| 78 | Step Forward SF 7 | Bingo-Masters' Breakout! (EP) | 20 |
| 78 | Step Forward SF 9 | It's The New Thing/Various Times (p/s) | 15 |
| 79 | Step Forward SF 11 | Rowche Rumble/In My Area (p/s) | 15 |
| 80 | Step Forward SF 13 | Fiery Jack/Second Dark Age/Psykick Dancehall 2 (black-and-white p/s) | 18 |
| 80 | Step Forward SF 13 | Fiery Jack/Second Dark Age/Psykick Dancehall 2 (yellow p/s) | 12 |
| 80 | Rough Trade RT 048 | How I Wrote Elastic Man/City Hobgoblins (p/s) | 10 |
| 80 | Rough Trade RT 056 | Totally Wired/Putta Block (p/s) | 10 |
| 81 | Rough Trade RT 071 | SLATES (10" EP, 33rpm) | 25 |
| 81 | Kamera ERA 001 | Lie Dream Of A Casino Soul/Fantastic Life (p/s) | 10 |
| 82 | Kamera ERA 004 | Look, Know/I'm Into C.B. (p/s) | 8 |
| 82 | Rough Trade RT 133 | The Man Whose Head Expanded/Ludd Gang (p/s) | 8 |
| 82 | Kamera ERA 014 | Marquis Cha Cha/Papal Visit (p/s, B-side plays "Room To Live", withdrawn) | 80 |
| 83 | Rough Trade RT 143 | Kicker Conspiracy/Wings//Container Drivers/New Puritan (g/fold double pack) | 12 |
| 84 | Beggars Banquet BEG 116 | C.R.E.E.P./Pat-Trip Dispenser (p/s) | 6 |
| 85 | Beggars Banquet BEG 150 | Cruiser's Creek (p/s) | 6 |
| 87 | Beggars Banquet BEG 187H | There's A Ghost In My House/Haf Found Bormann (hologram p/s) | 5 |
| 87 | Beggars Banquet BEG 206B | Victoria/Tuff Life Boogie (box set with inserts & badge) | 8 |
| 89 | Beggars Banquet BEG 226 | Cab It Up/Dead Beat Descendant (p/s) | 6 |
| 90 | Cog Sinister SINR 5 | Popcorn Double Feature/Zandra (p/s) | 6 |
| 91 | Cog Sinister FALL ! | So What About It/Edinburgh Man (promo only) | 20 |
| 92 | Cog Sinister SINS 8 | Free Range/Everything Hurtz (p/s) | 6 |
| 94 | Permanent 10SPERM 14 | 15 Ways (10", p/s) | 10 |
| 96 | Jet JET 500 | The Chiselers/Chilinist (p/s) | 8 |
| 01 | Flitwick MK45 1FG | I Wake Up In The City/Rude (All The Time) (500 only) | 50 |

### ALBUMS

| | | | |
|---|---|---|---|
| 79 | Step Forward SFLP 1 | LIVE AT THE WITCH TRIALS (LP) | 20 |
| 79 | Step Forward SFLP 4 | DRAGNET (LP, with insert) | 20 |
| 80 | Rough Trade ROUGH 10 | TOTALE'S TURNS (IT'S NOW OR NEVER) (LP) | 20 |
| 80 | Rough Trade ROUGH 18 | GROTESQUE (AFTER THE GRAMME) (LP) | 20 |
| 81 | Step Forward SFLP 6 | THE EARLY YEARS 1977-79 (LP) | 20 |
| 82 | Kamera KAM 005 | HEX EDUCATION HOUR (LP) | 40 |
| 83 | Rough Trade 062 | PERVERTED BY LANGUAGE (LP) | 25 |
| 84 | Beggars Banquet BEGA 58 | WONDERFUL AND FRIGHTENING WORLD OF (LP) | 15 |
| 85 | Beggars Banquet BEGA 67 | THIS NATIONS SAVING GRACE (LP, gatefold with inner sleeve) | 18 |
| 85 | Situation 2 SITU 13 | HIP PRIEST AND KAMERADAS (LP) | 15 |
| 86 | Beggars Banquet BEGA 75 | BEND SINISTER (LP) | 15 |
| 88 | Beggars Banquet BEGA 96 | I AM A KURIOUS ORANJE (LP, gatefold) | 18 |
| 90 | Cog Sinister 842204 | EXTRICATE (LP) | 15 |
| 91 | Cog Sinister COG 1 | PALACE OF SWORDS REVERSED - COMPILATION 1980-83 (LP) | 15 |
| 91 | Cog Sinister 848594 | SHIFT-WORK (LP) | 15 |
| 93 | Permanent PERMLP 12 | THE INFOTAINMENT SCAM (LP) | 15 |
| 95 | Cog Sinister PERMLP 36 | TWENTY SEVEN POINTS (2-LP, gatefold) | 25 |
| 97 | Artful ARTFUL LP 9 | LEVITATE (LP) | 70 |
| 99 | Artful ARTFULP 17 | THE MARSHALL SUITE (2-LP) | 80 |
| 02 | Cog Sinister COGVP 131 | ARE YOU ARE MISSING WINNER (LP, picture disc) | 40 |
| 05 | BBC CMXBX982 | COMPLETE PEEL SESSIONS (6-CD box set) | 30 |
| 08 | Sanctuary 1766796 | IMPERIAL WAX SOLVENT (LP) | 80 |

*(see also D.O.S.E., Fates)*

### FALLEN ANGELS (U.S.)

| | | | |
|---|---|---|---|
| 67 | London HL 10166 | I Don't Want To Fall/Most Children Do | 10 |
| 68 | London HA-Z/SH-Z 8359 | THE FALLEN ANGELS (LP) | 50 |

### JOHNNY FALLIN

| | | | |
|---|---|---|---|
| 59 | Capitol CL 15043 | Party Kiss/The Creation Of Love | 60 |
| 59 | Capitol CL 15091 | Wild Streak/If I Could Write A Love Song | 60 |

### FALLING LEAVES (1)

| | | | |
|---|---|---|---|
| 65 | Parlophone R 5233 | She Loves To Be Loved/Not Guilty | 75 |

### FALLING LEAVES (2)

| | | | |
|---|---|---|---|
| 66 | Decca F 12420 | Beggar's Parade/Tomorrow Night | 50 |

### FALLOUT (1)

| | | | |
|---|---|---|---|
| 81 | No label or Cat. No.) | Conscription/Democracy?/Nuclear Power/Them & Us/Laughable Attack/Sign Away (fold-out sleeve) | 15 |
| 83 | Mouth Too Small To F. F2 | SALAMI TACTICS (EP) | 12 |
| 83 | Own Label F3 LP 1 | HOME COOKED MEAT (LP, with 2 inserts) | 15 |

### FALLOUT (2)

| | | | |
|---|---|---|---|
| 90 | Azuli AZ001 | The Morning After (12") | 20 |

### FALLOUT CLUB

| | | | |
|---|---|---|---|
| 80 | Secret SHH104 | The Falling Years/The Beat Boys (p/s) | 15 |
| 81 | Happy Birthday UR 7 | Wanderlust/Desert Song (p/s) | 10 |
| 81 | Happy Birthday UR 3 | Dream Soldiers/Pedestrian Walk Way (p/s) | 15 |

### FALSE IDOLS (1)

| | | | |
|---|---|---|---|
| 78 | Old Knew Wave BOG 005 | Broken Judy/Marbled Hands/H-Brain (tri-fold p/s) | 12 |
| 78 | Old Knew Wave BOG 007 | Ego Wino/Good Night (p/s, pink vinyl) | 7 |

### FALSE IDOLS (2)

| | | | |
|---|---|---|---|
| 81 | Caveman CM 02 | Ten Seconds To Midnight/American Nightmare | 12 |

### AGNETHA FALTSKOG

| | | | |
|---|---|---|---|
| 82 | Epic EPC A 2824 | Never Again/Just For The Fun (p/s, with Tomas Ledin) | 12 |

# Georgie FAME (& THE BLUE FLAMES)

| | | | |
|---|---|---|---|
| 83 | Epic EPC A 3436 | The Heat Is On/Man (p/s) | 6 |
| 83 | Epic EPC WA 3436 | The Heat Is On/Man (picture disc) | 30 |
| 83 | Epic EPC A 3622 | Wrap Your Arms Around Me/Take Good Care Of The Children (p/s) | 6 |
| 83 | Epic EPC TA 3622 | Wrap Your Arms Around Me/The Heat Is On/ Take Good Care Of The Children (Extended) (12", p/s) | 12 |
| 83 | Epic EPC A 3812 | Can't Shake Loose/To Love (p/s) | 6 |
| 83 | Epic EPC A 3812 | Can't Shake Loose/To Love (poster p/s) | 15 |
| 83 | Epic EPC WA 3812 | Can't Shake Loose/To Love (picture disc) | 25 |
| 85 | Epic EPC A 6133 | I Won't Let You Go/You're There (p/s) | 6 |
| 85 | Epic EPC TA 6133 | I Won't Let You Go (Extended)/You're There (12", p/s) | 12 |
| 86 | Sonet SON 2317 | The Way You Are/Fly Like The Eagle (p/s, with Ola Hanansson) | 10 |
| 88 | WEA YZ 170 | The Last Time/Are You Gonna Throw It All Away (p/s) | 6 |
| 88 | WEA YZ 170T | The Last Time (Extended Remix)/The Last Time/ Are You Gonna Throw It All Away (12", p/s) | 12 |
| 88 | WEA YZ 177 | I Wasn't The One (Who Said Goodbye)/If You Need Somebody Tonight (p/s, with Peter Cetera) | 6 |
| 88 | WEA YZ 177T | I Wasn't The One (Who Said Goodbye) (Extended Version)/(Yo No Fui [Quien Dijo Adios])/If You Need Somebody Tonight (12", p/s, with Peter Cetera) | 12 |
| 88 | WEA YZ 300 | Let It Shine/Maybe It Was Magic (p/s) | 8 |
| 88 | WEA YZ 300T | Let It Shine (Extended)/('Bright' Mix)/Maybe It Was Magic (12", p/s) | 12 |
| 98 | Polydor POLPROCD 2 | The Queen Of Hearts (Nar Du Tar Mej I Din Fam) (CD, promo only) | 30 |
| 74 | Embassy EMB 31094 | AGNETHA (LP) | 40 |

*(see also Abba)*

## GEORGIE FAME (& THE BLUE FLAMES)
### SINGLES

| | | | |
|---|---|---|---|
| 64 | Columbia DB 7193 | Do The Dog/Shop Around | 25 |
| 64 | Columbia DB 7255 | Green Onions/Do-Re-Mi | 18 |
| 64 | Columbia DB 7328 | Bend A Little/I'm In Love With You (solo) | 20 |
| 64 | Columbia DB 7428 | Yeh Yeh/Preach And Teach (some copies list "Yeah, Yeah" on label) | 5 |
| 64 | Columbia DB 7428 | Yeh Yeh/Preach And Teach (99 promo copies only with p/s) | 75 |
| 65 | Columbia DB 7494 | In The Meantime/Telegram | 10 |
| 65 | Columbia DB 7633 | Like We Used To Be/It Ain't Right | 8 |
| 65 | Columbia DB 7727 | Something/Outrage | 8 |
| 66 | Columbia DB 7946 | Getaway/El Bandido | 8 |

*(The above 45s were credited to Georgie Fame & Blue Flames)*

| | | | |
|---|---|---|---|
| 66 | Columbia DB 8015 | Sunny/Don't Make Promises | 7 |
| 66 | Columbia DB 8096 | Sitting In The Park/Many Happy Returns | 8 |
| 67 | CBS 202587 | Because I Love You/Bidin' My Time (p/s) | 5 |
| 67 | CBS 2945 | Try My World/No Thanks (p/s) | 5 |
| 67 | CBS 3124 | The Ballad Of Bonnie And Clyde/Beware Of The Dog (p/s) | 5 |
| 68 | CBS 3526 | By The Time I Get To Phoenix/For Your Pleasure | 5 |
| 69 | CBS 4295 | Peaceful/Hideaway (with John Barry) | 5 |
| 69 | CBS 4659 | Seventh Son/Fully Booked | 5 |
| 70 | CBS 5035 | Entertaining Mr. Sloane/Somebody Stole My Thunder (DJ Copy) | 175 |
| 70 | CBS 5035 | Entertaining Mr. Sloane/Somebody Stole My Thunder | 150 |
| 70 | CBS 5131 | Fire And Rain/Someday Man | 5 |
| 77 | Island WIP 6384 | Daylight/Three Legged Mule | 40 |
| 77 | Island WIP 6384 | Daylight/Three Legged Mule (12") | 30 |

### EPs

| | | | |
|---|---|---|---|
| 64 | Columbia SEG 8334 | RHYTHM AND BLUEBEAT | 60 |
| 64 | Columbia SEG 8382 | RHYTHM AND BLUES AT THE FLAMINGO | 50 |
| 64 | Columbia SEG 8393 | FAME AT LAST | 25 |
| 65 | Columbia SEG 8406 | FATS FOR FAME | 25 |
| 65 | Columbia SEG 8454 | MOVE IT ON OVER | 25 |
| 66 | Columbia SEG 8518 | GETAWAY | 25 |
| 67 | CBS EP 6363 | KNOCK ON WOOD | 25 |
| 80 | RSO 2252 136 | BLUE BEAT | 10 |

### ALBUMS

| | | | |
|---|---|---|---|
| 64 | Columbia 33SX 1599 | RHYTHM AND BLUES AT THE FLAMINGO | 90 |
| 64 | Columbia 33SX 1638 | FAME AT LAST | 30 |
| 66 | Columbia SX 6043 | SWEET THINGS | 40 |
| 66 | Columbia SX 6076 | SOUND VENTURE | 40 |
| 67 | Columbia SX 6120 | HALL OF FAME | 20 |
| 67 | CBS (S)BPG 63018 | TWO FACES OF FAME | 20 |
| 68 | CBS (S) 63293 | THE THIRD FACE OF FAME (mono/stereo) | 15 |
| 69 | CBS S 63786 | SEVENTH SON | 15 |
| 69 | Regal Starline SRS5002 | GEORGIE FAME AND THE BLUE FLAMES | 15 |
| 71 | CBS S 64350 | GOING HOME | 15 |
| 72 | Reprise K 44183 | ALL ME OWN WORK (LP, gatefold sleeve) | 20 |
| 74 | Island ILPS 9293 | GEORGIE FAME | 20 |

*(see also Blue Flames, Jimmy Nicol, Perry Ford & Sapphires, Annie Ross)*

## GEORGIE FAME & ANNIE ROSS

| | | | |
|---|---|---|---|
| 81 | Bald Eagle | Drip Drop/One Morning In May (12" p/s 50 copies only) | 40 |

## FAMILY

| | | | |
|---|---|---|---|
| 88 | Strange Fruit SFPS 061 | PEEL SESSIONS (12") | 10 |
| 67 | Liberty LBF 15031 | Scene Through The Eye Of A Lens/Gypsy Woman (mispress, B-side plays "Let Me Be Good To You" by Otis Redding) | 150 |
| 67 | Liberty LBF 15031 | Scene Through The Eye Of A Lens/Gypsy Woman | 200 |
| 68 | Reprise RS 23270 | Me My Friend/Hey Mr. Policeman | 20 |

| 68 | Reprise RS 23315 | Second Generation Woman/Home Town............................................................15 |
| 69 | Reprise RS 27001 | No Mule's Fool/Good Friend Of Mine (p/s) ..................................................15 |
| 69 | Reprise RS 27001 | No Mule's Fool/Good Friend Of Mine...............................................................5 |
| 70 | Reprise RS 27005 | Today/Song For Lots (p/s) ...................................................................................15 |
| 70 | Reprise RS 27005 | Today/Song For Lots.............................................................................................5 |
| 70 | Reprise RS 27009 | The Weaver's Answer/Strange Band/Hung Up Down (first pressing with 'cream' label in p/s) .................................................................................................................8 |
| 70 | Reprise RS 27009 | The Weaver's Answer/Strange Band/Hung Up Down (later 'Steamboat' label in p/s) .....5 |
| 71 | Reprise K 14090 | In My Own Time/Seasons (in p/s) ........................................................................5 |
| 71 | Reprise SAM 1 | Larf And Sing/Children (promo only) ................................................................15 |
| 73 | Raft RA 18501 | Boom Bang/Stop This Car...................................................................................7 |
| 73 | Raft RA 18503 | Sweet Desiree/Drink To You ...............................................................................7 |
| 68 | Reprise RLP 6312 | MUSIC IN A DOLL'S HOUSE (LP, 1st pressing with 'Steamboat' label, insert, mono) .....250 |
| 68 | Reprise R(S)LP 6312 | MUSIC IN A DOLL'S HOUSE (LP, 1st pressing, with 'Steamboat' label, insert, stereo) ... 150 |
| 69 | Reprise RLP 6340 | FAMILY ENTERTAINMENT (LP, 1st pressing, with 'Steamboat' label mono, with poster)..........................................................................................................150 |
| 69 | Reprise RSLP 6340 | FAMILY ENTERTAINMENT (LP, 1st pressing with 'Steamboat' label, stereo, with poster) .................................................................................................................90 |
| 70 | Reprise RSLP 9001 | A SONG FOR ME (LP, 1st pressing with 'Steamboat' label, with lyric sheet)...........90 |
| 70 | Reprise RSX 9005 | ANYWAY (LP, custom polythene sleeve)...........................................................35 |
| 71 | Reprise RMP 9007 | OLD SONGS NEW SONGS (LP) ...........................................................................30 |
| 71 | Reprise K 54003 | FEARLESS (LP, multi gatefold sleeve, lyric insert)..........................................50 |
| 72 | Reprise K 54006 | BANDSTAND (LP, 'window' die-cut sleeve, lyric inner).....................................30 |
| 73 | Raft RA58501 | IT'S ONLY A MOVIE (LP, lyric inner and 'banger' insert) ..................................40 |
| 73 | Raft RA 58501 | IT'S ONLY A MOVIE (LP, lyric inner and no 'banger' insert) ............................15 |

*(see also Farinas, Stud, Mogul Thrash, Hellions, Ashton Gardner & Dyke, Revolution, Streetwalkers)*

## FAMILY AFFAIR
| 68 | Saga STFID 2124 | THE FAMILY AFFAIR (LP)......................................................................................15 |

## FAMILY CHOICE
| 78 | Union UN 005 | Used To Be My Girl/Long Time .........................................................................10 |

## FAMILY CIRCLE
| 69 | Attack AT 8001 | Phoenix Reggae/BIG L: Music Box .....................................................................20 |
| 69 | Attack AT 8002 | Reggae Krishna/Official ......................................................................................40 |
| 69 | JJ DB 1300 | Give Peace A Chance/GEORGE LEE: Reggae Groove ......................................15 |

## FAMILY DOGG
| 67 | MGM MGM 1360 | The Storm/Family Dogg......................................................................................20 |
| 68 | Fontana TF 921 | I Wear A Silly Grin/Couldn't Help It ................................................................15 |
| 68 | Fontana TF 968 | Brown-Eyed Girl/Let It Rain ................................................................................7 |
| 69 | Bell BLL 1055 | A Way Of Life/Throw It Away .............................................................................7 |
| 69 | Bell BLL 1077 | Arizona/The House In The Heather...................................................................6 |
| 72 | Buddah 2011-143 | Sweet America/Rikers Island ...........................................................................10 |
| 70 | Bell BLL 1100 | When Tomorrow Comes Tomorrow/This Unhappy Heart Of Mine .................6 |
| 69 | Bell SBLL 122 | A WAY OF LIFE (LP, with members of Led Zeppelin, gatefold) .......................30 |
| 72 | Buddah 2318 061 | THE VIEW FROM ROWLAND'S HEAD (LP, gatefold, lyric insert)......................20 |

*(see also Steve Rowland, Christine Holmes)*

## FAMILY FODDER
| 80 | Fresh FRESH 15 | Debbie Harry/Version (p/s) .................................................................................7 |
| 80 | Fresh FRESH 22 | Savoir Faire/Carnal Knowledge (p/s) .................................................................6 |
| 79 | Parole/Fresh PURL 4 | Playing Golf/My Baby Takes Valium (p/s) .........................................................5 |
| 79 | Fresh Records FRESH 9 | SUNDAY GIRLS (12")...........................................................................................15 |
| 82 | Fresh 42 | The Big Dig/Plant Life (p/s) ..............................................................................10 |

## FAMILY MAN (ASTON BARRETT)
| 70 | Escort ERT 834 | Midnight Sunshine/GREGORY & STICKY: You Are My Sunshine ......................8 |
| 72 | Downtown DT 491 | Herb Tree/STUDIO SOUND: Holy Poly (reissue) ............................................12 |

*(see also Hippy Boys, Upsetters, Bob Marley & Wailers, Carl Dawkins)*

## FAMILY ON HOLIDAY
| 81 | Fabidoo S81CUS 1140 | Who's A Pretty Boy Then/You're As Cute As A Dead Gerbil (p/s).................15 |

## FAMILY QUEST
| 84 | Jungle Rhythm SWE-T2 | Outerspace 84 Rap ............................................................................................15 |

## FAMOUS ECCLES & MISS FREDA THING
| 56 | Parlophone R 4251 | My September Love/COUNT JIM MORIARTY & GRAVELEY STEPHENS: You Gotta Go Oww! (with The Alberts) ...................................................................................10 |

*(see also Spike Milligan)*

## FAMOUS IMPOSTORS
| 85 | COR COR 7 | WOULD ANYTHING CHANGE (12" EP p/s) ........................................................10 |

## FAMOUS JUG BAND
| 69 | Liberty LBF 15224 | The Only Friend I Own/A Leaf Must Fall.........................................................10 |
| 69 | Liberty LBS 83263 | SUNSHINE POSSIBILITIES (LP, blue labels) .....................................................90 |
| 70 | Liberty LBS 83355 | CHAMELEON (LP, textured sleeve, blue labels) ...........................................100 |

*(see also Incredible String Band, C.O.B.)*

## FAMOUS MUSIC BAND
| 69 | Philips 6006 111 | Nine By Nine/Going In The Out (with John Dummer) .......................................8 |

*(see also John Dummer)*

## FAMOUS PLAYERS
| 80 | Page 45 AH 1001 | Who's Kissing You (p/s) ......................................................................................70 |

## FANATICS
| 89 | Chapter 22 12 CHAP 38 | SUBURBAN LOVE SONGS (12" EP)......................................................................18 |

*(see also Ocean Colour Scene)*

## FAN-CLUB
78  **M&S SJP 791B**    Avenue/Night Caller (p/s, photocopied insert) .................................................. 15

## FANCY
73  **Sticky STY 3**    Starlord/Brother John ....................................................................................... 30
74  **Antic K11514**    Touch Me/I Don't Need Your Love ....................................................................... 8
75  **Arista ARISTA 3**    She's Riding The Rock Machine Part 1/Part 2......................................................... 8
76  **Arista ARIST 32**    Music Maker/Bluebird ........................................................................................ 8
*(see also Ray Fenwick, Judas Priest)*

## FANDANGO
73  **York SYK 562**    High Class Girl/Sha La La ................................................................................... 12
*(see Nic Simper's Fandango, under 'S')*

## COSEY FANNI TUTTI
83  **Flowmotion**    TIME TO TELL (cassette with booklet) ................................................................. 50
*(see also Throbbing Gristle, Chris & Cosey)*

## FANS
79  **Fried Egg EGG 3**    Giving Me That Look in Your Eyes/Stay The Night/He'll Have To Go (p/s) .............. 50
79  **Albion ION 0004**    True (dayglo inner, inc bonus 7" & lyric sheet) ................................................... 20
80  **Albion FAN 01**    Cars And Explosions/Dangerous Goodbyes (p/s) .................................................. 20
81  **Fried Egg EGG 10**    You Don't Live Here Anymore/Following You (p/s) ............................................... 60

## FANTASIA (1)
67  **Stateside SS 2031**    Gotta Get Away/She Needs My Love .................................................................... 15

## FANTASIA (2)
89  **Greenwood SRT9KL2225**    PICTURES IN MY MIND (LP) ........................................................................... 100

## FANTASTIC BAGGYS
76  **United Artists UP 36142**    Summer Means Fun/JAN & DEAN: Surf City/Sidewalk Surfin' ............................ 10
*(see also Jan & Dean, Bruce Johnston)*

## FANTASTIC FOUR
68  **Tamla Motown TMG 678**    I Love You Madly/I Love You Madly (Instrumental) ....................................... 22
68  **T. Motown TML 11105**    THE FANTASTIC FOUR (LP, mono) ................................................................. 60
69  **T. Motown STML 11105**    THE FANTASTIC FOUR (LP, stereo) ............................................................... 50

## FANTASTIC PUZZLES
76  **Right On 106**    Come Back/Come Back Part 2 ............................................................................ 20

## FANTASTIC SOMETHING
84  **Cherry Red CHERRY 61**    If She Doesn't Smile (It'll Rain)/The Thousand Guitars Of St. Dominiques (p/s)...... 12

## FANTASTICS
68  **MGM MGM 1434**    Baby Make Your Own Sweet Music/Who Could Be Lovin' You ............................ 20
68  **MGM MGM 1434DJ**    Baby Make Your Own Sweet Music/ Who Could Be Lovin' You (DJ promo) ......... 30
69  **Deram DM 264**    Face To Face With Heartache/This Must Be My Rainy Day ................................... 6
70  **Deram DM 283**    Waiting Round For Heartaches/Ask The Lonely ................................................... 20
71  **Deram DM 334**    For Old Times Sake/Exodus Main Theme ............................................................ 6
71  **Mojo 2027 004**    Baby Make Your Own Sweet Music/Who Could Be Lovin' You? (reissue) ............. 5
*(see also Velours)*

## FANTASY
73  **Polydor 2058 405**    Politely Insane/I Was Once Aware...................................................................... 40
73  **Polydor 2383 246**    PAINT A PICTURE (LP, gatefold sleeve, red label)........................................... 800

## FANTOMS
83  **Ear To Ear GRIN 1**    Hearts Of Stone (Break Hearts OF Glass)/Really Mystified (p/s)............................ 10

## BARRY FANTONI
66  **Fontana TF 707**    Little Man In A Little Box/Fat Man ...................................................................... 35
67  **Columbia DB 8238**    Nothing Today/The Spanish Lady Tango ............................................................... 8

## FAPARDOKLY
83  **Psycho PSYCHO 5**    FAPARDOKLY (LP, 300 only) ........................................................................... 20
*(see also Mu)*

## FARAWAY FOLK
70s  **Tabitha TAB 3**    Shadow Of A Pie/Folsom Prison Blues/Rent A Man/Soulful Shade Of Blue.............. 12
70s  **RA EP 7001**    INTRODUCING THE FARAWAY FOLK (EP) ..................................................... 25
70s  **RA LP 6006ST**    LIVE AT THE BOLTON (LP) ............................................................................ 30
72  **RA LP 6012ST**    TIME AND TIDE (LP) ...................................................................................... 30
73  **RA LP 6019**    ON THE RADIO (LP) ....................................................................................... 30
74  **RA LP 6022**    ONLY AUTHORISED EMPLOYEES TO BREAK BOTTLES (LP, with Harry H. Corbett)............ 22
75  **RA LP 6029**    SEASONAL MAN (LP, gatefold sleeve with insert)......................................... 60
80s  **RA**    BATTLE OF THE DRAGONS (LP)..................................................................... 15
*(see also Harry H. Corbett)*

## FAR CRY
69  **Vanguard SVRL 19041**    THE FAR CRY (LP) ....................................................................................... 30

## DON FARDON
67  **Pye International 7N 25437**    (The Lament Of The Cherokee) Indian Reservation/Dreamin' Room ............. 10
69  **Pye International 7N 25483**    We Can Make It Together/Coming On Strong ................................................ 25
69  **Pye International 7N 25486**    Good Lovin'/Ruby's Pictures On My Wall....................................................... 8
69  **Youngblood YB 1003**    I'm Alive/Keep On Loving Me ...................................................................... 40
69  **Young Blood YB 1007**    It's Been Nice Loving You/Let The Love Live ................................................ 25
70  **Young Blood YB 1010**    Belfast Boy/Echoes Of The Cheers ............................................................. 20
70  **Young Blood YB 1013**    Delta Queen/Hometown Baby ...................................................................... 5
70  **Young Blood YB 1015**    Indian Reservation/Hudson Bay ................................................................. 10
71  **Young Blood YB 1021**    Girl/Sandiago.............................................................................................. 5
71  **Young Blood YB 1027**    Follow Your Drum/Get Away John ............................................................... 5
70  **Young Blood SSYB 4**    I'VE PAID MY DUES! (LP) ......................................................................... 20

| | | | |
|---|---|---|---|
| 70 | Young Blood SSYB 13 | RELEASED (LP) | 15 |

*(see also Sorrows)*

## FAR EAST FAMILY BAND
| | | | |
|---|---|---|---|
| 75 | Vertigo 6370 850 | NIPPONJIN (LP) | 40 |

## DICK FARINA & ERIC VON SCHMIDT
| | | | |
|---|---|---|---|
| 63 | Folklore F-LEUT/7 | DICK FARINA & ERIC VON SCHMIDT (LP, featuring 'Blind Boy Grunt') | 100 |

*(see also Bob Dylan, Richard & Mimi Farina, Four For Fun)*

## RICHARD & MIMI FARINA
| | | | |
|---|---|---|---|
| 65 | Fontana STFL 6060 | CELEBRATIONS FOR A GREY DAY (LP) | 30 |
| 65 | Fontana STFL 6075 | REFLECTIONS IN A CRYSTAL WIND (LP) | 30 |

*(see also Dick Farina & Eric Von Schmidt)*

## FARINAS
| | | | |
|---|---|---|---|
| 64 | Victor Buckland Sound Studio | Bye Bye Johnny/All You Gotta Do/Twist And Shout (as James King & Farinas) | 500 |
| 64 | Fontana TF 493 | You'd Better Stop/I Like It Like That | 80 |

## TAL FARLOW
| | | | |
|---|---|---|---|
| 57 | Columbia 33CX 10029 | THE INTERPRETATIONS OF (LP) | 15 |

## CHRIS FARLOWE (& THUNDERBIRDS)
| | | | |
|---|---|---|---|
| 62 | Decca F 11536 | Air Travel/Why Did You Break My Heart? | 60 |
| 63 | Columbia DB 7120 | I Remember/Push Push (as Chris Farlowe & Thunderbirds) | 40 |
| 64 | Columbia DB 7237 | Girl Trouble/Itty Bitty Pieces (as Chris Farlowe & Thunderbirds) | 40 |
| 64 | Columbia DB 7311 | Just A Dream/What You Gonna Do? (as Chris Farlow & Thunderbirds) | 40 |
| 64 | Columbia DB 7379 | Hey, Hey, Hey, Hey/Hound Dog (as Chris Farlow & Thunderbirds) | 30 |
| 65 | Columbia DB 7614 | Buzz With The Fuzz/You're The One (withdrawn, as Chris Farlow & Thunderbirds, demos more common £100) | 200 |
| 65 | Immediate IM 016 | The Fool/Treat Her Good | 15 |
| 66 | Immediate IM 023 | Think/Don't Just Look At Me | 20 |
| 66 | Immediate IM 035 | Out Of Time/Baby Make It Soon (3.13 version, CBS pressing, matrix 1F//1) | 7 |
| 66 | Immediate IM 035 | Out Of Time/Baby Make It Soon (3.28 version, Philips pressing, matrix 1F V2) | 7 |
| 66 | Columbia DB 7983 | Just A Dream/Hey, Hey, Hey, Hey | 15 |
| 66 | Immediate IM 038 | Ride On Baby/Headlines | 12 |
| 67 | Immediate IM 041 | My Way Of Giving/You're So Good To Me | 15 |
| 67 | Immediate IM 049 | Yesterday's Papers/Life Is But Nothing | 8 |
| 67 | Immediate IM 056 | Moanin'/What Have I Been Doin'? | 8 |
| 67 | Immediate IM 065 | Handbags And Gladrags/Everyone Makes A Mistake | 10 |
| 68 | Immediate IM 066 | The Last Goodbye/Paperman Fly In The Sky (B-side with Thunderbirds) | 15 |
| 68 | Immediate IM 071 | Paint It Black/I Just Need Your Loving | 10 |
| 69 | Immediate IM 074 | Dawn/April Was The Month | 15 |
| 70 | Polydor 2066 017 | Black Sheep Of The Family/Fifty Years (as Chris Farlowe with The Hill) | 6 |
| 70 | Polydor 2066 046 | Put Out The Light/Questions (as Chris Farlowe & Hill) | 10 |
| 75 | Polydor 2066 650 | We Can Work It Out/Only Women Bleed | 5 |
| 78 | Beeb BEEB 022 | Gangsters (as Chris Farlowe & Dave Greenslade)/DAVE GREENSLADE'S GANGSTERS: Sarah Gant Theme | 6 |
| 65 | Decca DFE 8665 | CHRIS FARLOWE (EP) | 100 |
| 65 | Immediate IMEP 001 | FARLOWE IN THE MIDNIGHT HOUR (EP) | 50 |
| 66 | Immediate IMEP 004 | CHRIS FARLOWE HITS (EP) | 40 |
| 66 | Island IEP 709 | STORMY MONDAY (EP) | 120 |
| 66 | Columbia SX 6034 | CHRIS FARLOWE AND THE THUNDERBIRDS (LP, black/blue labels with "sold in the U.K..." text) | 150 |
| 66 | Music For Pleasure MFP 1186 | STORMY MONDAY (LP, reissue of Chris Farlowe & Thunderbirds LP) | 20 |
| 66 | Immediate IMLP 005 | 14 THINGS TO THINK ABOUT (LP, lilac label) | 75 |
| 66 | Immediate IMLP 006 | THE ART OF CHRIS FARLOWE (LP, mono, lilac label) | 70 |
| 66 | Immediate IMSP 006 | THE ART OF CHRIS FARLOWE (LP, stereo, lilac label) | 100 |
| 67 | EMI Regal REG 2025 | CHRIS FARLOWE (LP, export issue) | 40 |
| 68 | Immediate IMCP 010 | THE BEST OF CHRIS FARLOWE VOLUME ONE (LP, lilac label) | 30 |
| 69 | Immediate IMLP 021 | THE LAST GOODBYE (LP, pink label with "sold in U.K..." text) | 100 |
| 70 | Polydor 2425 029 | FROM HERE TO MAMA ROSA (LP, as Chris Farlowe & Hill, gatefold sleeve, insert) | 60 |

*(see also Thunderbirds, Beazers, Little Joe Cook, Crane/Farlowe, Atomic Rooster, Colosseum, Dave Greenslade, Spectrum)*

## FARM
| | | | |
|---|---|---|---|
| 74 | Spark SRL1105 | Fat Judy/Gysy Mountain Woman | 30 |

## ART FARMER
| | | | |
|---|---|---|---|
| 54 | Esquire 20-033 | ART FARMER SEXTET — WORK OF ART (10" LP) | 40 |
| 55 | Esquire 32-037 | MUSIC FOR THAT WILD PARTY (LP) | 40 |
| 56 | Esquire 32-072 | TWO TRUMPETS (LP, with Donald Byrd) | 40 |
| 56 | Esquire 32-137 | FARMERS MARKET (LP) | 30 |
| 57 | Esquire 32-037 | WILD PARTY LP with Gigi Gryce | 40 |
| 59 | London SAH-T 6028 | MODERN ART (LP) | 25 |
| 60 | London Jazz LTZ-T 15184 | BRASS SHOUT (LP) | 20 |
| 60 | London Jazz LTZ-T 15198 | THE AZTEC SUITE (LP) | 20 |
| 60 | Pye Jazz NJL 45 | MEET THE JAZZTET (with Benny Golson) | 30 |
| 61 | Esquire 32-120 | EARTHY (LP) | 30 |
| 64 | London HA-K/SH-K 8135 | INTERACTION (LP, as Art Farmer Quartet featuring Jim Hall) | 25 |

*(see also Clifford Brown, Benny Golson, Donald Byrd)*

## JULES FARMER
| | | | |
|---|---|---|---|
| 59 | London HLP 8967 | Love Me Now/Part Of Me (Is Still With You) | 10 |

## MYLENE FARMER
| | | | |
|---|---|---|---|
| 89 | Polydor 080 360-2 | Ainsi Soit Je. . . (Maxi Remix)/Ainsi Soit Je. . . (Lamentations)/ Ainsi Soit Je. . . (Classic Bonus Beats) (CD Video, export only) | 45 |
| 91 | Polydor 873 738 7 | Desenchantee (Edited Version)/Desenchantee (Chaos Mix) (Promo only) | 20 |

447

MINT VALUE £

## FARMLIFE
| | | | |
|---|---|---|---|
| 82 | Dining Out TUX 19 | Susie's Party/Simple Men | 6 |
| 83 | Whaam! WHAAM 13 | Big Country 1 & 2 (unreleased; Echantillan test pressings only) | 40 |

## GILES FARNABY'S DREAM BAND
| | | | |
|---|---|---|---|
| 73 | Argo AFW 112 | Newcastle Brown/29th Of May | 12 |
| 73 | Argo ZDA 158 | GILES FARNABY'S DREAM BAND (LP) | 60 |

*(see also Druids)*

## FARNBOROUGH FIREWORK FACTORY
| | | | |
|---|---|---|---|
| 72 | Decca F13290 | Too Many People/She's Against The Law | 8 |

## ROBERT FARNON ORCHESTRA
| | | | |
|---|---|---|---|
| 56 | Decca F 10818 | Westminister Waltz/Poodle Parade | 6 |
| 63 | Philips BF 1299 | Charade/Gina Gina Don't You Cry | 6 |
| 72 | MCA MCA 117 | Colditz March/That Italian Summer | 5 |
| 55 | Decca LK 4119 | CANADIAN IMPRESSIONS (LP) | 20 |
| 56 | Vogue Coral LVA 9003 | GENTLEMEN MARRY BRUNETTES (LP, soundtrack) | 30 |
| 60 | Delyse ECB 3157/DS 6057 | CAPTAIN HORATIO HORNBLOWER (LP, soundtrack, mono) | 30 |
| 60 | Delyse DS 6057 | CAPTAIN HORATIO HORNBLOWER (LP, soundtrack, stereo) | 30 |
| 68 | Philips SBL 7867 | SHALAKO (LP, soundtrack) | 15 |

*(see also Jack Saunders)*

## ROBERT FARNON & TONY COE
| | | | |
|---|---|---|---|
| 70 | Chapter One CHS 804 | POP MAKES PROGRESS (LP) | 30 |

*(see also Tony Coe)*

## FARON'S FLAMINGOS
| | | | |
|---|---|---|---|
| 63 | Oriole CB 1834 | Do You Love Me?/See If She Cares | 25 |
| 63 | Oriole CB 1867 | Shake Sherry/Give Me Time | 30 |
| 79 | Raw RAW 28 | Bring It On Home/C'mon Everybody | 10 |

*(see also Big Three, Mojos)*

## WAYNE FARO'S SCHMALTZ BAND
| | | | |
|---|---|---|---|
| 69 | Deram DM 222 | There's Still Time/Give It Time | 40 |

## FARQUAHAR
| | | | |
|---|---|---|---|
| 71 | Elektra EK45713 | Hanging On By A Thread/Start Living | 6 |

## GARY FARR (& THE T-BONES)
| | | | |
|---|---|---|---|
| 65 | Columbia DB 7608 | Give All She's Got/Don't Stop And Stare (as Gary Farr & T-Bones) (demo in p/s) | 100 |
| 65 | Columbia DB 7608 | Give All She's Got/Don't Stop And Stare (as Gary Farr & T-Bones) | 50 |
| 68 | Marmalade 598 007 | Everyday/Green (with Kevin Westlake) | 25 |
| 69 | Marmalade 598 017 | Hey Daddy/The Vicar And The Pope | 25 |
| 71 | CBS 5430 | Revolution Of The Seasons/Old Man Boulder | 12 |
| 65 | Columbia SEG 8414 | DEM BONES, DEM BONES, DEM T-BONES (EP) | 120 |
| 69 | Marmalade 608 013 | TAKE SOMETHING WITH YOU (LP) | 300 |
| 71 | CBS 64138 | STRANGE FRUIT (LP, with Richard Thompson & Mighty Baby) | 150 |

*(see also T-Bones, Richard Thompson, Mighty Baby, Meic Stevens, Kevin Westlake & Gary Farr)*

## MARY ANN FARRAR & SATIN SOUL
| | | | |
|---|---|---|---|
| 76 | Brunswick BR 38 | Stoned Out Of My Mind/Living In The Footsteps Of Another Girl (DJ Copy) | 30 |
| 76 | Brunswick BR 38 | Stoned Out Of My Mind/Living In The Footsteps Of Another Girl | 20 |

## BILLY FARRELL
| | | | |
|---|---|---|---|
| 58 | Philips PB 828 | Yeah Yeah/Someday (You'll Want Me To Want You) | 22 |

## DO & DENA FARRELL
| | | | |
|---|---|---|---|
| 57 | HMV POP 427 | Young Magic/New Love Tonight | 15 |

## MICK FARREN
| | | | |
|---|---|---|---|
| 78 | Logo GO 321 | Half Price Drinks/I Don't Want To Go This Way (thick card p/s, black and yellow on front) | 6 |
| 70 | Transatlantic TRA 212 | MONA (THE CARNIVOROUS CIRCUS) (LP, lilac label with "t" logo) | 125 |
| 78 | Logo LOGO 2010 | VAMPIRES STOLE MY LUNCH MONEY (LP, with lyric insert) | 25 |
| 84 | Psycho PSYCHO 20 | MONA (THE CARNIVOROUS CIRCUS) (LP, reissue) | 20 |

*(see also Deviants, Twink)*

## FARRIERS
| | | | |
|---|---|---|---|
| 69 | Broadside BRO 112 | FARRIERS (LP) | 20 |
| 76 | Broadside BRO 119 | KEMPION BRUMMAGEM BALLADS (LP, featuring Dick Brice) | 50 |

## FARTZ
| | | | |
|---|---|---|---|
| 82 | Alternative Tentacles VIRUS 21 | BECAUSE THIS FUCKIN' WORLD STINKS (EP) | 10 |
| 82 | Alt. Tentacles VIRUS 17 | WORLD FULL OF HATE (12" EP with poster) | 25 |

## FASCINATIONS
| | | | |
|---|---|---|---|
| 67 | Stateside SS 594 | Girls Are Out To Get You/You'll Be Sorry | 75 |
| 67 | Stateside SS 594 | Girls Are Out To Get You/You'll Be Sorry (DJ copy) | 150 |
| 68 | Sue WI 4049 | Girls Are Out To Get You/You'll Be Sorry (reissue) | 40 |
| 71 | Mojo 2092 004 | Girls Are Out To Get You/You'll Be Sorry (2nd reissue) | 10 |
| 71 | Mojo 2092 018 | I'm So Lucky He Loves Me/Say It Isn't So | 8 |

## FASCINATORS (1)
| | | | |
|---|---|---|---|
| 58 | Capitol CL 14942 | Chapel Bells/I Wonder Who | 300 |
| 59 | Capitol CL 15062 | Oh, Rose Marie/Fried Chicken And Macaroni | 150 |

## FASCINATORS (2)
| | | | |
|---|---|---|---|
| 81 | Penthouse PENT 9 | Blue Movies/Monochrome Moon (p/s) | 70 |

## FASHION
| | | | |
|---|---|---|---|
| 79 | Fashion FM 001 | Steady Eddie Steady/Killing Time (p/s) | 5 |
| 79 | Fashion FM 002 | Citinite/Wastelife (p/s) | 5 |
| 80 | Fashion FM 003 | Silver Blades/Silver Blades (A Deeper Cut) (p/s) | 5 |
| 81 | Arista 12440 | Move On/Mutant Dance Move (p/s) | 10 |

| | | |
|---|---|---|
| 79 | Fashion FML001 | PRODUCT PERFECT (LP) ....................................................................................... 15 |

**FASHIONS**

| | | |
|---|---|---|
| 68 | Stateside SS 2115 | I.O.U. (A Lifetime Of Love)/When Love Slips Away............................................... 10 |
| 69 | Evolution E 2444 | I.O.U. (A Lifetime Of Love)/He Gives Me Love (La La La)........................................ 8 |

**FAST**

| | | |
|---|---|---|
| 76 | CBS SCBS 6236 | Boys Will Be Boys/Wow Pow Bash Crash ............................................................ 6 |

**FAST ACTION**

| | | |
|---|---|---|
| 80 | Instant M1 | United/Dining Out With Clients (1000 only, poster sleeve) ................................ 5 |

**FAST BREEDERS**

| | | |
|---|---|---|
| 82 | Breeder BMS 82001 S82 CUS 1570 | How Could You/Strange Party ............................................................................. 20 |

**FAST BREEDERS & RADIO ACTORS**

| | | |
|---|---|---|
| 78 | Nuke NUKE 235 | Nuclear Waste/Digital Love (in p/s, with insert) ................................................ 18 |
| 78 | Nuke NUKE 235 | Nuclear Waste/Digital Love ................................................................................. 10 |

*(see also Radio Actors)*

**FAST CARS**

| | | |
|---|---|---|
| 79 | Streets Ahead SA 3 | The Kids Just Wanna Dance/You're So Funny (1,000 only, p/s)......................... 250 |

**FAST EDDIE (1)**

| | | |
|---|---|---|
| 82 | Well Suspect BLAM 001 | My Babe/Help Me/Sweet Sensations (p/s)............................................................. 8 |

**FAST EDDIE (2)**

| | | |
|---|---|---|
| 88 | Westside DJINT 04 | Acid Thunder (12") ............................................................................................... 25 |
| 88 | Westside PROMO 18 | My Melody/Halloween House (12") (with Slick Master Rick) ............................... 20 |

**FAST LINE**

| | | |
|---|---|---|
| 70 | Highwire HW 001 | Look Into My Mind/A Nice Time To Die (p/s) ....................................................... 40 |

**FAST SET**

| | | |
|---|---|---|
| 80 | Axis AXIS 1 | Junction One/Children Of The Revolution (p/s) ................................................... 20 |

**FASTBACKS**

| | | |
|---|---|---|
| 89 | Subway SUBWAY 26 | Wrong Wrong Wrong/In America (p/s) .................................................................. 6 |

**FAT**

| | | |
|---|---|---|
| 71 | RCA LSA 3009 | FAT (LP) ................................................................................................................. 50 |

**FATAL CHARM**

| | | |
|---|---|---|
| 79 | Company CR 005 | Paris/Glitterbit/Out Of My Head ........................................................................... 8 |
| 87 | Native 7N TV 20 | Lucille/To Master A Plan (p/s) ............................................................................... 6 |
| 89 | Fatal 1 | THIS STRANGE ATTRACTION (LP) .......................................................................... 25 |

**FATAL MICROBES**

| | | |
|---|---|---|
| 79 | Small Wonder SMALL 20 | Violence Grows/Beautiful Pictures/Cry Baby (p/s) .............................................. 10 |

*(see also Pete Fender)*

**FATES**

| | | |
|---|---|---|
| 85 | Taboo HAG 1 | FURIA (LP) ............................................................................................................. 25 |

**FATHEAD**

| | | |
|---|---|---|
| 83 | Greensleeves GRED 118 | Champion/Stop All The Fight (12") ....................................................................... 20 |

**FATHER THOMAS**

| | | |
|---|---|---|
| 70 | Candidate 1 | Look For The Sun/There's A Dream ....................................................................... 70 |

**FATHER JOHN MISTY**

| | | |
|---|---|---|
| 15 | Bella union BELLA487V | I Loved You Honeybee/I've Never Been A Woman (heart-shaped red vinyl)................ 40 |
| 15 | Bella Union BELLA 476VX | I LOVE YOU HONEYBEAR (2-LP, CD coloured vinyl and musical pop up sleeve) ............ 50 |
| 15 | Bella Union BELLA 527V | LIVE AT ROUGH TRADE (LP) ................................................................................... 18 |

*(see also Fleet Foxes)*

**FATHER'S ANGELS**

| | | |
|---|---|---|
| 68 | MGM MGM 1459 | Don't Knock It/Bok To Bach ............................................................................... 250 |
| 68 | MGM MGM 1459 | Don't Knock It/Bok To Bach (DJ Copy)................................................................ 300 |
| 75 | Black Magic BM 103 | Back To Bach/Disco Trucking ................................................................................. 6 |

**FATHER'S BROWN**

| | | |
|---|---|---|
| 70 | Decca F23059 | Maybe/The Yellow Moon Is High........................................................................... 20 |

**FATMAN VERSUS JAH SHAKA**

| | | |
|---|---|---|
| 80 | Live & Love LAP12 | DUB CONFRONTATION (LP)..................................................................................... 15 |

**FAT MATTRESS**

| | | |
|---|---|---|
| 69 | Polydor 56352 | Naturally/Iridescent Butterfly .............................................................................. 10 |
| 69 | Polydor 56367 | Magic Forest/Bright New Way ............................................................................... 15 |
| 70 | Polydor 2058 053 | Highway/Black Sheep Of The Family ..................................................................... 15 |
| 69 | Polydor 582/583 056 | FAT MATTRESS (LP, open-out sleeve, red label) ................................................... 50 |
| 70 | Polydor 2383 025 | FAT MATTRESS II (LP, red label) ............................................................................ 50 |

*(see also Jimi Hendrix Experience, Flowerpot Men, Juicy Lucy)*

**FATS & CHESSMEN**

| | | |
|---|---|---|
| 62 | Pye International 7N 25122 | Big Ben Twist/Old Macdonald Had A Twist.............................................................. 6 |

**ERIC FATTER**

| | | |
|---|---|---|
| 69 | Camel CA 20 | Since You've Been Gone (actually Eric Fratter)/WINSTON HINES: Cool Down (B-side actually by Winston Hinds)................................................................................ 20 |

*(see also Eric Fratter, Afrotones)*

**FAT TULIPS**

| | | |
|---|---|---|
| 90 | Heaven HV 01 | Where's Clare Grogan Now?/To Put It Bluntly (p/s) ............................................... 6 |
| 90 | Heaven HV 02 | FOUR SONGS FOR SIMON EP .................................................................................. 6 |
| 90 | Heaven HV 04 | FERENSWAY EP (hand-painted sleeve) ................................................................... 6 |
| 91 | Marineville MARINE 1 | Passionate Friend/Treason/Reward (p/s, 'The Tulip Explodes' artwork).................... 6 |
| 88 | Sweet William BILLY 001 | You Opened My Eyes/ROSEHIPS: Ask Johnny Dee (33rpm flexi, p/s w/insert)............ 15 |

**ERNIE FAULKNER**

| | | |
|---|---|---|
| 63 | Sway SW 003 | Beautiful Girl/SAM DANIELS: Tell Me Baby (both with The Planets)..................... 8 |

## FAUST

| | | | |
|---|---|---|---|
| 72 | Faust/Polydor 2001-299 | It's A Bit Of A Pain/So Far | 25 |
| 79 | Recommended RR 2.5 | It's A Bit Of A Pain/So Far (p/s, reissue) | 8 |
| 96 | Die Stadt 011 | Right Between Yr Eyes (p/s, Uberschall Festival single,with Stereolab and Foetus) | 20 |
| 90 | Chemical Imbalance CI 08 | Live In Hamburg (issued free with Chemical Imbalance magazine) | 25 |
| 79 | Recommended RR 1.5 | EXTRACTS FROM FAUST PARTY 3: Extract 1/Extract 4 (EP) | 12 |
| 80 | Recommended RR 6.5 | EXTRACTS FROM FAUST PARTY 3: Extract 2/Extract 6 (EP) | 12 |
| 71 | Polydor 2310 142 | FAUST (LP, initial pressing on clear vinyl, with clear sleeve & clear insert) | 150 |
| 71 | Polydor 2310 142 | FAUST (LP, insert) | 70 |
| 72 | Polydor 2310 196 | SO FAR (LP, with 9 prints in wallet) | 130 |
| 73 | Virgin VC 501 | THE FAUST TAPES (LP) | 25 |
| 73 | Virgin V 2004 | FAUST IV (LP) | 30 |
| 79 | Recommended R.R. 2 | SO FAR (LP, reissue, with 10 insert prints, numbered, 600 only) | 50 |
| 80 | Recommended RR 6 | THE FAUST TAPES (LP, plastic bag cover) | 20 |
| 86 | Recommended RR 125 | MUNICH AND ELSEWHERE (LP) | 18 |
| 88 | ReR Megacorp Rer 36 | THE LAST LP (LP, numbered) | 20 |

*(see also Toni Conrad & Faust)*

## FAVOURITES

| | | | |
|---|---|---|---|
| 80 | 4 Play FOUR 002 | S.O.S./Favourite Shoes (p/s) | 25 |
| 80 | 4 Play FOUR 003 | Angelica/Cold (p/s) | 20 |

## FAVOURITE SONS

| | | | |
|---|---|---|---|
| 65 | Mercury MF 911 | That Driving Beat/Walkin' Walkin' Walkin' | 175 |

## WALLY FAWKES (& HIS TROGLODYTES)

| | | | |
|---|---|---|---|
| 57 | Decca FJ 10855 | Petite Fleur/Baby Brown (with Sandy Brown Quintet) | 5 |
| 57 | Decca FJ 10936 | Sent For You Yesterday And Here You Came Today/Why Can't You Behave | 5 |
| 58 | Decca F 11002 | The Pilot Fish And The Whale/Pale Blues | 10 |
| 57 | Decca DEF 6407 | AND HIS TROGLODYTES (EP) | 10 |
| 60 | Decca DFE 6600 | FLOOK DIGS JAZZ (EP) | 10 |
| 61 | Decca STO 136 | A NIGHT AT THE SIX BELLS (EP) | 10 |
| 58 | Decca LF 312 | FAWKES ON HOLIDAY (LP) | 15 |

*(see also Sandy Brown)*

## CHARLIE FAWN

| | | | |
|---|---|---|---|
| 79 | WEA K 17835 | Blue Skies/Dream World | 7 |
| 79 | WEA/Hansa K17430 | Hothead Handshake Tremble/Playthings | 7 |
| 80 | Warner Bros K 17566 | Always Something There To Remind Me/Poet For A Generation | 8 |

## BILL FAY

| | | | |
|---|---|---|---|
| 67 | Deram DM 143 | Some Good Advice/Screams In The Ears | 60 |
| 70 | Deram Nova SDN 12 | BILL FAY (LP, stereo) | 400 |
| 70 | Deram Nova DN 12 | BILL FAY (LP, mono) | 500 |
| 71 | Deram SML 1079 | TIME OF THE LAST PERSECUTION (LP, red/white label) | 1000 |

## FAY & BITTER SWEET

| | | | |
|---|---|---|---|
| 74 | A Rover AR 02 | You're A Pirate Lover/Message To You | 6 |

## ALMA FAYE

| | | | |
|---|---|---|---|
| 78 | Flamingo FM 5 | I Believed/Don't Fall In Love | 30 |

## FRANCIS FAYE

| | | | |
|---|---|---|---|
| 61 | Vogue V 9186 | I Wish I Could Shimmy Like My Sister Kate/Night And Day | 10 |
| 65 | Stateside SL 10129 | YOU GOTTA GO! GO! GO! (LP) | 20 |

## FAZED IDJUTS

| | | | |
|---|---|---|---|
| 00 | U Star USR 002 | Dust Of Life (12") | 20 |

## F.B.I. (FOLK BLUES INC.)

| | | | |
|---|---|---|---|
| 66 | Eyemark EMS 1006 | Don't Hide/When The Ship Comes In | 25 |
| 73 | A&M AMS 7050 | I Wonder What She's Doing Tonight/Boogaloo Boo-Boo | 10 |
| 76 | Good Earth GD 6 | F.B.I./The Time Is Right To Leave The City | 25 |
| 77 | Good Earth GDS 802 | F.B.I. (LP) | 50 |

## FEAR OF FLYING (1)

| | | | |
|---|---|---|---|
| 81 | Fear Of Flying 001 | Tired/This Thing | 8 |

## FEAR OF FLYING (2)

| | | | |
|---|---|---|---|
| 06 | Young And Lost YALC 0011 | Three's A Crowd/Forget-Me-Nots (p/s) | 7 |

## FEARN'S BRASS FOUNDRY

| | | | |
|---|---|---|---|
| 68 | Decca F 12721 | Don't Change It/John White | 50 |
| 68 | Decca F 12835 | Now I Taste The Tears/Love, Sink And Drown | 25 |

## FEAR OF FALLING

| | | | |
|---|---|---|---|
| 83 | Excellent XL 7 | Like A Lion/You My Prodigal Son (p/s) | 20 |

## CHARLIE FEATHERS

| | | | |
|---|---|---|---|
| 76 | Red Neck R 100 | Tongue Tied Jill/Gone Gone Gone | 10 |

## CHARLIE FEATHERS/MAC CURTIS

| | | | |
|---|---|---|---|
| 74 | Polydor 2310 293 | ROCKABILLY KINGS (LP) | 20 |

*(see also Mac Curtis)*

## FEATURES (1)

| | | | |
|---|---|---|---|
| 77 | Progress PR 01 | Drab City/Job Satisfaction | 50 |

## FEATURES (2)

| | | | |
|---|---|---|---|
| 80 | Double D DDEE 3 | Go Now/Make Me Wanna | 10 |
| 80 | ASM HIT 06 | She Makes Me Blue/Don't Let Them Know | 20 |
| 81 | AFM PET 01 | Monday-Friday/Cue The Next Army | 20 |

## FEDERALMEN

| | | | |
|---|---|---|---|
| 70 | London HLU 10303 | Soul Serenade/Scorcher | 8 |

## FEDERALS (JAMAICA)

| | | | |
|---|---|---|---|
| 67 | Island WI 3126 | Penny For Your Song/I've Passed This Way Before | 30 |
| 68 | Island WI 3152 | Shocking Love/By The River | 25 |
| 69 | High Note HS 024 | Wailing Festival/Me And My Baby (B-side actually "By The River") | 15 |
| 70 | Camel CA 40 | In This World/You Better Call On Me (B-side actually "Shocking Love") | 70 |

## FEDERALS (U.K.)

| | | | |
|---|---|---|---|
| 63 | Parlophone R 4988 | Brazil/In A Persian Market | 15 |
| 63 | Parlophone R 5013 | Boot Hill/Keep On Dancing With Me | 15 |
| 64 | Parlophone R 5100 | The Climb/Dance With A Dolly | 15 |
| 64 | Parlophone R 5139 | Marlena/Please Believe Me | 15 |
| 64 | Parlophone R 5193 | Twilight Time/Lost And Alone | 15 |
| 65 | Parlophone R 5320 | Bucket Full Of Love/Leah | 25 |

*(see also Winston's Fumbs, Yes)*

## FEDS

| | | | |
|---|---|---|---|
| 85 | FED rated NSFRED 1 | Don't Take My Love Away/Louise | 8 |

## FEEDER

| | | | |
|---|---|---|---|
| 96 | Echo ECS 13 | TWO COLOURS: Pictures Of Rain/Chicken On A Bone (p/s, clear vinyl) | 40 |
| 96 | Echo ECSCD 13 | TWO COLOURS: Pictures Of Rain/Chicken On A Bone (CD, 1,000 only) | 40 |
| 96 | Echo ECS 27 | Stereo World/My Perfect Day (p/s) | 10 |
| 97 | Echo ECS 32 | Tangerine/Rhubarb (die-cut p/s) | 10 |
| 97 | Echo ECS 42 | Crash/Here In The Bubble (clear vinyl, numbered p/s) | 5 |
| 01 | Echo ECS 121 | Just A Day/Early (orange vinyl, p/s) | 5 |
| 01 | Echo | Turn/Bad Hair Day (6-12 white label promo competition prizes. 7" die-cut sleeve) | 10 |
| 04 | Echo ECS157A/B -1 | Tumble and Fall/Victoria (12" white label promos auctioned for Warchild charity) | 15 |
| 96 | Echo ECHLP 9 | SWIM (LP, inner) | 30 |
| 97 | Echo ECHLP15 | POLYPHENE (LP, vinyl re-issue of original CD album, with free High 7") | 30 |
| 99 | Echo ECHLP 28 | YESTERDAY WENT TOO SOON (LP, top opening sleeve, inner) | 30 |
| 01 | Echo ECHLP 34 | ECHO PARK (LP, gatefold, inner) | 30 |
| 02 | Echo ECHLP 43 | COMFORT IN SOUND (LP) | 25 |
| 04 | Echo ECHLP52 | PICTURE OF PERFECT YOUTH (3xLP) | 40 |
| 05 | Echo ECHLP 60 | PUSHING THE SENSES (LP) | 20 |
| 08 | Echo ECHLP 79 | SILENT CRY (LP) | 25 |

## FEELIES

| | | | |
|---|---|---|---|
| 79 | Stiff (no cat. no.) | Fa Ce La/The Boy With Perpetual Nervousness/ Everybody's Got Something To Hide (Except Me And My Monkey) (flexidisc, promo only, free with Be Stiff fanzine issue 6, 5,000 only) | 6 |
| 79 | Rough Trade RT 24 | Fa Ce La/Raised Eyebrows (p/s) | 10 |
| 80 | Stiff BUY 65 | Everybody's Got Something To Hide/Original Love (p/s) | 7 |
| 80 | Stiff SEEZ 20 | CRAZY RHYTHMS (LP) | 25 |
| 86 | Rough Trade ROUGH 104 | THE GOOD EARTH (LP) | 18 |

## FEIST

| | | | |
|---|---|---|---|
| 12 | Roadrunner 5439 19780 0 | Black Tongue/MASTODON: A Commotion | 8 |

## FELDER'S ORIOLES

| | | | |
|---|---|---|---|
| 65 | Piccadilly 7N 35247 | Down Home Girl/Misty | 40 |
| 65 | Piccadilly 7N 35269 | Sweet Tasting Wine/Turn On Your Lovelight | 20 |
| 66 | Piccadilly 7N 35311 | I Know You Don't Love Me No More/Only Three Can Play | 20 |
| 66 | Piccadilly 7N 35332 | Back Street/Something You Got | 25 |

*(see also V.I.P.s, Mike Patto)*

## VICTOR FELDMAN BIG BAND/QUARTET

| | | | |
|---|---|---|---|
| 56 | Tempo A 142 | Big Top/Cabaletto | 15 |
| 57 | Tempo A 154 | Jackpot/You Are My Heart's Desire | 15 |
| 62 | Fontana 267233 | A Taste Of Honey/Valerie | 10 |
| 55 | Tempo EXA 29 | BIG BAND (EP) | 50 |
| 57 | Tempo EXA 57 | VICTOR FELDMAN IN LONDON -- THE QUARTET VOLUME 1 (EP) | 60 |
| 57 | Tempo EXA 67 | VICTOR FELDMAN IN LONDON VOLUME 2 (EP) | 60 |
| 58 | Tempo EXA 85 | MUTUAL ADMIRATION (EP, with Dizzy Reece) | 75 |
| 53 | Esquire EP 43 | MODERN JAZZ QUARTET (EP) | 40 |
| 53 | Esquire EP 54 | MODERN JAZZ QUARTET (EP) | 20 |
| 53 | Esquire EP 64 | MODERN JAZZ QUINTET/SEXTET (EP) | 25 |
| 53 | Esquire EP 84 | MODERN JAZZ QUARTET/SEXTET (EP) | 20 |
| 54 | Esquire EP 104 | MODERN JAZZ QUARTET (EP) | 40 |
| 54 | Esquire EP 114 | VIC FELDMAN ENCORE (EP) | 20 |
| 54 | Esquire 20 - 046 | MULTIPLE TALENTS (LP) | 60 |
| 55 | Esquire 20 - 064 | EXPERIMENT IN TIME (LP) | 60 |
| 55 | Tempo LAP 5 | VICTOR FELDMAN'S SEXTET (10" LP) | 300 |
| 56 | Tempo LAP 6 | VICTOR FELDMAN MODERN JAZZ QUARTET (10" LP) | 200 |
| 57 | Tempo TAP 8 | VICTOR FELDMAN IN LONDON VOL. 1 (LP) | 150 |
| 57 | Tempo TAP 12 | VICTOR FELDMAN IN LONDON VOL. 2 (LP) | 140 |
| 58 | Tempo TAP 19 | TRANSATLANTIC ALLIANCE (LP) | 350 |
| 59 | Contemporary LAC 12172 | THE ARRIVAL OF VICTOR FELDMAN (LP) | 20 |

*(see also Dizzy Reece, Tubby Hayes)*

## VICTOR FELDMAN, TERRY GIBBS & LARRY BUNKER

| | | | |
|---|---|---|---|
| 60 | Top Rank 30/007 | VIBES TO THE POWER OF THREE (LP) | 20 |

## JOSE FELICIANO

| | | | |
|---|---|---|---|
| 74 | RCA RCA PB10094 | Golden Lady/Virgo | 10 |

## FELIUS ANDROMEDA

| | | | |
|---|---|---|---|
| 72 | Cactus CT 2 | After The Storm/Rainbow Chasing (as Andromeda) | 15 |
| 67 | Decca F 12694 | Meditations/Cheadle Heath Delusions | 50 |

# Lennie FELIX, BRIAN LEMON, KEITH INGHAM, RALPH SUTTON

*(see also Denis Couldry)*

## LENNIE FELIX, BRIAN LEMON, KEITH INGHAM, RALPH SUTTON
| | | | |
|---|---|---|---|
| 75 | 77 77S 58 | PIANO SUMMIT (LP) | 20 |

## JULIE FELIX
| | | | |
|---|---|---|---|
| 65 | Decca F 12246 | Someday Soon/I've Got Nothing But Time | 5 |
| 66 | Fontana TF 734 | I Can't Touch The Sun/Rainy Day | 5 |
| 67 | Fontana TF 875 | The Magic Of The Playground/Somewhere There's Gotta Be Me | 5 |
| 68 | Fontana TF 969 | That's No Way To Say Goodbye/The World Goes Round And Round | 5 |
| 70 | RAK 101 | (Pasa El Condor) If I Could/Alone | 5 |
| 71 | RAK 108 | Snakeskin/Watching Waiting | 40 |
| 72 | RAK 14 | Clothos Web/Windy Morning | 25 |
| 65 | Decca DFE 8613 | SINGS BOB DYLAN & WOODY GUTHRIE (EP) | 10 |
| 66 | Fontana TE 17474 | SONGS FROM THE FROST REPORT (EP) | 10 |
| 64 | Decca LK 4626 | JULIE FELIX (LP) | 20 |
| 65 | Decca LK 4683 | SINGS DYLAN AND GUTHRIE (LP) | 20 |

## MIKE FELIX
| | | | |
|---|---|---|---|
| 66 | Pye 7N 17058 | You Belong To Me/Booga Dee | 25 |
| 67 | Decca F 12701 | Blueberry Hill/I Don't Think You Want Me Anymore | 8 |

*(see also Migel 5)*

## RORY FELLOWES
| | | | |
|---|---|---|---|
| 68 | S n B 55-3877 | Nina/Endlessly Friendlessly Blue | 20 |

## GRAHAM FELLOWS
| | | | |
|---|---|---|---|
| 79 | EMI INT 598 | Men Of Oats And Creosote/Rebecca (promo, in envelope p/s) | 40 |
| 83 | Toadstool AM 219 | Through The Line/Sleeping Beauty (p/s) | 6 |
| 85 | Wicked Frog FROG 01 | LOVE AT THE HACIENDA (LP) | 40 |

*(see also Jilted John)*

## FELT
| | | | |
|---|---|---|---|
| 79 | Shanghai S79/CUS 321 | Index/Break It (p/s, early copies have poem on rear sleeve, yellow labels) | 200 |
| 79 | Shanghai S79/CUS 321 | Index/Break It (p/s, no notes on rear sleeve) | 60 |
| 81 | Cherry Red CHERRY 26 | Something Sends Me To Sleep/Red Indians/Something Sends Me To Sleep (Version)/Red Indians (p/s) | 40 |
| 82 | Cherry Red CHERRY 45 | My Face Is On Fire/Trails Of Colour Dissolve (p/s) | 20 |
| 83 | Cherry Red CHERRY 59 | Penelope Tree/A Preacher In New England (p/s) | 12 |
| 83 | Cherry Red 12CHERRY 59 | Penelope Tree/A Preacher In New England/ Now Summer's Spread Its Wings Again (12", p/s) | 15 |
| 84 | Cherry Red CHERRY 78 | Mexican Bandits/The World Is As Soft As Lace (p/s) | 12 |
| 84 | Cherry Red CHERRY 81 | Sunlight Bathed The Golden Glow/Fortune (p/s) | 18 |
| 84 | Cherry Red 12CHERRY 81 | Sunlight Bathed The Golden Glow/Fortune/Sunlight Strings (12", p/s) | 12 |
| 85 | Cherry Red 12CHERRY 89 | Primitive Painters/Cathedral (12", p/s, with Liz Frazer) | 10 |
| 86 | Creation CRE 027 | Ballad Of The Band/I Didn't Mean To Hurt You (p/s) | 12 |
| 86 | Creation CRE 027T | Ballad Of The Band/I Didn't Mean To Hurt You/Candles In A Church/Ferdinand (12", p/s) | 15 |
| 86 | Creation CRE 032 | Rain Of Crystal Spires/I Will Die With My Head In Flames (p/s) | 12 |
| 86 | Creation CRE 032T | Rain Of Crystal Spires/Gather Up Your Wings And Fly/I Will Die With My Head In Flames/Sandman's On The Rise Again (12", p/s) | 12 |
| 87 | Creation CRE 048T | The Final Resting Of The Ark/Autumn/Fore Circle/There's No Such Thing As Victory/Buried Wild Blind (12", p/s) | 12 |
| 88 | Creation CRE 060 | Space Blues/Tuesday's Secret (ltd. ed. die-cut company sleeve) | 12 |
| 88 | Creation CRE 060T | Space Blues/Be Still/Female Star/Tuesday's Secret (12") | 25 |
| 89 | el GPO F44 | Get Out Of My Mirror (1-side flexi, in-store freebie) | 12 |
| 82 | Cherry Red MRED 25 | CRUMBLING THE ANTISEPTIC BEAUTY (LP) | 25 |
| 84 | Cherry Red MRED 57 | THE SPLENDOUR OF FEAR (LP) | 25 |
| 84 | Cherry Red BRED 63 | STRANGE IDOLS PATTERN (LP) | 20 |
| 85 | Cherry Red B-RED 65 | IGNITE THE SEVEN CANNONS AND SET SAIL FOR THE SUN (LP, textured sleeve with lyric insert) | 18 |
| 86 | Creation CRELP 009 | LET THE SNAKES CRINKLE THEIR HEADS TO DEATH (LP) | 20 |
| 86 | Creation CRELP 011 | FOREVER BREATHES THE LONELY WORD (LP, with inner sleeve) | 40 |
| 87 | Creation CRELP 017 | POEM OF THE RIVER (LP) | 25 |
| 87 | Cherry Red BRED 79 | GOLD MINE TRASH (LP, with inner) | 15 |
| 88 | Creation CRELP 030 | PICTORIAL JACKSON REVIEW (LP) | 20 |
| 88 | Creation CRELP 033 | TRAIN ABOVE THE CITY (LP) | 20 |
| 89 | el ACME 24 | ME AND A MONKEY ON THE MOON (LP) | 20 |
| 90 | Creation CRELP 069 | BUBBLEGUM PERFUME (LP) | 25 |

*(see also Denim, Versatile Newts, Cocteau Twins, Go-Kart Mozart)*

## NARVEL FELTS
| | | | |
|---|---|---|---|
| 75 | ABC 4062 | Reconsider Me/Foggy Mountain Morning | 6 |

## FEMININE TOUCH FEATURING DUKE DURRELL
| | | | |
|---|---|---|---|
| 76 | Paladin PAL 11 | You Make Me Come Alive/You Make Me Come Alive (Instrumental) | 5 |

## FENCE
| | | | |
|---|---|---|---|
| 80 | BFD BFD 2 | Thinking That I Shouldn't/Thru With You/Hey Girl (p/s) | 15 |

## JAYMES FENDA & VULCANS
| | | | |
|---|---|---|---|
| 64 | Parlophone R 5210 | Mistletoe Love/The Only Girl | 8 |

## JAN FENDER
| | | | |
|---|---|---|---|
| 71 | Prince Buster PB 5 | Sea Of Love/PRINCE BUSTER: Heaven Help Us All | 15 |
| 71 | Fab FAB 164 | Sweet P/CLIFF & ORGANIZERS: Mr Brown | 25 |
| 71 | Fab FAB 166 | Holly Holy Version/Old Kentrone Version (as Jal Fender) | 12 |

## PETE FENDER
| | | | |
|---|---|---|---|
| 81 | Xntrix 2002 | FOUR FORMULAS (EP, in 8" silk-screened book p/s) | 30 |

*(see also Fatal Microbes, Omega Tribe)*

## FENDER BENDERS
| | | | |
|---|---|---|---|
| 79 | Sticky SL 001 | Big Green Thing/Hillman Hunter Paranoia (textured p/s, various colours) | 6 |

## FENDERMEN
| | | | |
|---|---|---|---|
| 60 | Top Rank JAR 395 | Mule Skinner Blues/Torture | 8 |
| 60 | Top Rank JAR 513 | Don't You Just Know It/Beach Party | 10 |

## FENMEN
| | | | |
|---|---|---|---|
| 64 | Decca F 11955 | Rag Doll/Be My Girl | 20 |
| 65 | Decca F 12269 | I've Got Everthing You Need Babe/Every Little Day Now | 15 |
| 66 | CBS 202075 | California Dreamin'/Is This Your Way? | 12 |
| 66 | CBS 202236 | Rejected/Girl Don't Bring Me Down | 25 |

*(see also Bern Elliott & Fenmen, Pretty Things, Zac Zolar & Electric Banana)*

## DAVID FENTON
| | | | |
|---|---|---|---|
| 83 | Razor RZS 106 | Fresh Air/Buried In The Snow (p/s) | 20 |

## PETER FENTON
| | | | |
|---|---|---|---|
| 66 | Fontana TF 748 | Marble Breaks, Iron Bends/Small Town | 15 |
| 67 | Fontana TF 789 | I Was Lord Kitcheners Valet/Walking In Circles | 15 |

## SHANE FENTON (& FENTONES)
| | | | |
|---|---|---|---|
| 61 | Parlophone R 4827 | I'm A Moody Guy/Five Foot Two, Eyes Of Blue | 8 |
| 62 | Parlophone R 4866 | Walk Away/Fallen Leaves On The Ground | 8 |
| 62 | Parlophone R 4883 | It's All Over Now/Why Little Girl | 8 |
| 62 | Parlophone R 4921 | Cindy's Birthday/It's Gonna Take Magic | 8 |
| 62 | Parlophone R 4951 | Too Young For Sad Memories/You're Telling Me | 8 |
| 63 | Parlophone R 4982 | I Ain't Got Nobody/Hey Miss Ruby | 8 |
| 63 | Parlophone R 5020 | A Fool's Paradise/You Need Love (solo) | 8 |
| 63 | Parlophone R 5047 | Don't Do That/I'll Know (solo) | 8 |
| 64 | Parlophone R 5131 | Hey, Lulu/I Do, Do You? | 8 |
| 72 | Fury FY 305 | Eastern Seaboard/Blind Fool | 8 |
| 77 | EMI NUT 2696 | SHANE FENTON & THE FENTONES (EP) | 10 |
| 74 | Contour 2870 409 | GOOD ROCKIN' TONIGHT (LP) | 15 |

*(see also Fentones)*

## FENTONES
| | | | |
|---|---|---|---|
| 62 | Parlophone R 4899 | The Mexican/Lover's Guitar | 5 |
| 62 | Parlophone R 4937 | The Breeze And I/Just For Jerry | 10 |

*(see also Shane Fenton)*

## FENWAYS
| | | | |
|---|---|---|---|
| 65 | Liberty LIB 66082 | Walk/Whip And Jerk | 25 |

## RAY FENWICK
| | | | |
|---|---|---|---|
| 78 | Mercury 6007 176 | Queen Of The Night/I Wanna Boogie | 6 |
| 71 | Decca SKL 5090 | KEEP AMERICA BEAUTIFUL, GET A HAIRCUT (LP, blue/silver label with small logo) | 60 |

*(see also Spencer Davis Group, After Tea, Fancy, Ian Gillan Band, Wizard's Convention, Murgatroyd Band, Marlon, Forcefield, Syndicats, South Coast Ska Kings, Rupert's People)*

## FENWYCK
| | | | |
|---|---|---|---|
| 68 | ERA ERA 100 | State Of Mind/Away | 80 |

## FENZYX
| | | | |
|---|---|---|---|
| 81 | Ellie Jay EJSP 9655 | Soldiers/Angels Of Mercy (p/s) | 25 |

## FERDIA
| | | | |
|---|---|---|---|
| 78 | Polydor 2904 012 | A SIGH FOR OLD TIMES (LP) | 15 |

## FERDINAND & DILL
| | | | |
|---|---|---|---|
| 70 | Pama PM 805 | Take Back Your Nicklet/Blueberry Hill | 8 |

## WINSTON FERGUS
| | | | |
|---|---|---|---|
| 78 | Arawak ARK DD 001 | Fly Natty Dread/Loving Pauper (12") | 40 |
| 79 | Burning Rockers BRD 016 | Corner Girl/Corner Dub (12") | 20 |
| 82 | Burning Rockers BRD 037 | Pay To Live/Earth In Dub (12") | 40 |
| 82 | Fergie Music FM 002 | In Ting Sound/My Own Way Heart (12") | 150 |
| 85 | John Dread JPD 002 | I WILL SING (LP) | 15 |

## HELENA FERGUSON
| | | | |
|---|---|---|---|
| 67 | London HLZ 10164 | Where Is The Party?/My Terms | 50 |

## JESSIE LEE FERGUSON & OUTER LIMITS
| | | | |
|---|---|---|---|
| 69 | Pye International 7N 25492 | New Shoes/Puttin' It On, Puttin' It Off | 12 |

## JOHNNY FERGUSON
| | | | |
|---|---|---|---|
| 60 | MGM MGM 1059 | Angela Jones/Blue Serge And White Lace | 10 |
| 61 | MGM MGM 1119 | No One Can Love You/The Valley Of Love | 7 |

## MAYNARD FERGUSON ORCHESTRA
| | | | |
|---|---|---|---|
| 58 | Emarcy EJL 1270 | JAM SESSION (LP) | 15 |
| 58 | Emarcy EJL 1275 | AROUND THE HORN (LP) | 20 |
| 58 | Emarcy EJL 1287 | DIMENSIONS (LP) | 20 |
| 59 | Columbia 33SX 1146 | MESSAGE FROM NEWPORT (LP) | 20 |
| 60 | Mercury MMC 14050 | THE BOY WITH LOTS OF BRASS (LP, also stereo CMS 18034) | 20 |
| 60 | Columbia 33SX 1210 | MESSAGE FROM BIRDLAND (LP, also stereo SCX 3245) | 15 |
| 60 | Columbia 33SX 1270 | JAZZ FOR DANCING (LP, also stereo SCX 3338) | 20 |
| 61 | Columbia 33SX 1301 | NEWPORT SUITE (LP, also stereo SCX 3368) | 20 |
| 62 | Columbia 33SX 1439 | MAYNARD 62 (LP) | 20 |
| 66 | Fontana TL 5274 | BLUES ROAR (LP) | 20 |
| 66 | Fontana TL 5293 | COLOR HIM WILD (LP) | 20 |
| 67 | Fontana TL 5310 | SEXTET (LP) | 20 |
| 68 | Atlantic 2464008 | FREAKY (LP) | 20 |
| 69 | CBS 63514 | BALLAD STLYE OF MAYNARD FERGUSON (LP) | 40 |

MINT VALUE £

| | | | |
|---|---|---|---|
| 71 | CBS 64432 | ALIVE AND WELL IN LONDON (LP) | 20 |
| 72 | CBS 65027 | M.F. HORN 2 (LP, gatefold) | 15 |
| 73 | CBS 65589 | M.F. HORN 3 (LP) | 20 |
| 73 | CBS 65952 | M.F. HORN 4 (LIVE AT JIMMYS) (LP) | 20 |

## ALEX FERGUSSON
| | | | |
|---|---|---|---|
| 92 | Private Pressing AF 001 | ALEX FERGUSSON (LP, white label, 500 copies, no sleeve) | 25 |

*(see also Alternative TV, Psychic TV)*

## FERKO STRING BAND
| | | | |
|---|---|---|---|
| 55 | London HL 8140 | Alabama Jubilee/Sing A Little Melody | 25 |
| 55 | London HLF 8183 | Ma (She's Making Eyes At Me)/You Are My Sunshine | 25 |
| 55 | London HLF 8215 | Happy Days Are Here Again/Deep In The Heart Of Texas | 25 |
| 58 | London HL 7052 | Happy Days Are Here Again/Alabama Jubilee (export issue) | 18 |
| 56 | London RE-F 1041 | PHILADELPHIA MUMMERS PARADE VOL. 1 (EP) | 10 |
| 56 | London RE-F 1052 | PHILADELPHIA MUMMERS PARADE VOL. 2 (EP) | 10 |
| 57 | London HB-C 1064 | THE FERKO STRING BAND VOL. 1 (10" LP) | 15 |

## FERMENA
| | | | |
|---|---|---|---|
| 71 | Pama PM 839 | Come What May/Version (B-side with Ranny) | 8 |
| 73 | Pama PM 879 | Wonderful Dreams/Version | 8 |

## PHIL FERNANDO
| | | | |
|---|---|---|---|
| 58 | Pye Nixa 7N 15142 | Blonde Bombshell/Make Ready for Love | 10 |
| 62 | Palette PG 9029 | (Come On And) Do The High Life/High Life Girl | 10 |

## ANDY FERNBACH
| | | | |
|---|---|---|---|
| 69 | Liberty LBL/LBS 83233 | IF YOU MISS YOUR CONNEXION (LP, blue label) | 200 |

*(see also Groundhogs)*

## MAJA FERNICK
| | | | |
|---|---|---|---|
| 72 | Philips 6006 196 | Give Me Your Love Again/Flowers In The City | 20 |

## PIERRE FEROLDI
| | | | |
|---|---|---|---|
| 94 | Disco Magic DISK 001 | Moving Now (Extended)/Moving Now (Italian version) (12" featuring Linda Ray) | 20 |

## CHRISTIAN FERRAS
| | | | |
|---|---|---|---|
| 61 | HMV ASD 427 | MOZART VIOLIN CONCERTOS NO 4 & 6 (LP, stereo) | 400 |
| 63 | HMV ASD 531 | FERRAS & BARBIZET : ENESCO & DEBUSSY SONATAS ETC (LP, Stereo with Pierre Barbizel) | 800 |
| 64 | HMV ASD 572 | BERG: CONCERTO FOR VIOLIN AND ORCHESTRA (LP, stereo) | 150 |

## DIANE FERRAZ & NICKY SCOTT
| | | | |
|---|---|---|---|
| 66 | Columbia DB 7824 | Me And You/Don't Pretend | 8 |
| 66 | Columbia DB 7897 | You've Got To Learn/Like You As You Are | 5 |
| 66 | Columbia DB 7963 | Sh-Boom, Sh-Boom/Allah Mobish | 5 |

*(see also Nicky Scott, Ferris Wheel)*

## JOE FERRER & HIS DEVILS BOYS
| | | | |
|---|---|---|---|
| 61 | Oriole CB 1629 | Rockin' Crickets/Blue Guitar | 20 |

## FERRET
| | | | |
|---|---|---|---|
| 74 | Deram DM 412 | Hudson Bay/Henry's Song | 7 |

## EUGENE FERRIS
| | | | |
|---|---|---|---|
| 66 | Planet PLF 112 | There Was A Smile In Your Eyes/Soft Moonlight (without p/s) | 15 |
| 66 | Planet PLF 112 | There Was A Smile In Your Eyes/Soft Moonlight (with p/s) | 30 |

## GEORGE FERRIS
| | | | |
|---|---|---|---|
| 71 | Ackee ACK 117 | With Every Dream/Diana | 6 |

## FERRIS WHEEL
| | | | |
|---|---|---|---|
| 67 | Pye 7N 17387 | I Can't Break The Habit/Number One Guy | 25 |
| 68 | Pye 7N 17538 | Let It Be Me/You Look At Me | 8 |
| 68 | Pye 7N 17631 | The Na Na Song/Three Cool Cats | 8 |
| 69 | Polydor 56366 | Can't Stop Now/I Know You Well | 6 |
| 67 | Pye NPL 18203 | CAN'T BREAK THE HABIT (LP) | 60 |
| 70 | Polydor 583 066 | FERRIS WHEEL (LP, lyric insert, red label) | 40 |

*(see also Linda Lewis, West Five)*

## BRYAN FERRY
| | | | |
|---|---|---|---|
| 73 | Island IDJ 1 | These Foolish Things/Sympathy For The Devil/Baby I Don't Care/ Loving You Is Sweeter Than Ever (promo) | 30 |
| 74 | Island WIP 6196 | The 'In' Crowd/Chance Meeting (in p/s) | 8 |
| 75 | Island WIP 6234 | You Go To My Head/Re-Make, Re-Model (DJ copies in generic promo p/s) | 20 |
| 78 | Polydor PPSP 10 | Hold On I'm Coming/Take Me To The River (12", unissued, promo only, numbered stamped p/s) | 20 |
| 73 | Island ILPS 9239 | THESE FOOLISH THINGS (LP, unissued gatefold sleeve) | 400 |
| 76 | Island ILPS 9367 | LET'S STICK TOGETHER (LP, original issue) | 15 |
| 78 | Polydor POLD 5003 | THE BRIDE STRIPPED BARE (LP, original with A//3 P matrix, includes 'Broken Wings', white label test pressings only) | 200 |
| 94 | Virgin V2751 | MAMOUNA (LP) | 50 |
| 07 | Virgin V3026 | DYLANESQUE (LP, inner) | 30 |

*(see also Roxy Music)*

## CATHERINE FERRY
| | | | |
|---|---|---|---|
| 76 | Barclay BAR 42 | One, Two, Three/1, 2, 3 | 8 |

## MANFREDO FEST
| | | | |
|---|---|---|---|
| 79 | Bluebird BRT 1 | Jungle Kitten (5.30)/Jungle Kitten (3.36)/Send In The Clowns (12") | 10 |

## FESTIVAL
| | | | |
|---|---|---|---|
| 78 | Nevis NEV 107 | Something In Your Smile/Let's Make Love | 60 |

## FEVER
| | | | |
|---|---|---|---|
| 71 | Decca F23156 | The Moth And The Flame/It's So Peaceful | 10 |

## FEVER TREE
| | | | |
|---|---|---|---|
| 68 | MCA MU 1043 | San Francisco Girls/Come With Me | 10 |
| 68 | Uni UNLS 102 | FEVER TREE (LP) | 100 |
| 68 | MCA MUPS 347 | ANOTHER TIME, ANOTHER PLACE (LP) | 70 |

## FFWD
| | | | |
|---|---|---|---|
| 94 | Inter Modo INTA001 | FFWD (2-LP, inners) | 18 |

*(see also King Crimson, Orb)*

## FIAT LUX
| | | | |
|---|---|---|---|
| 83 | Polydor FIAT 1 | Photography/Aqua Vitae (p/s) | 5 |

## FICKLE FINGER
| | | | |
|---|---|---|---|
| 69 | Page One POF 150 | Fickle Lizzie-Anne/Cellophane Mary Jane | 10 |

*(see also Matchmakers, Mark Wirtz)*

## FICKLE PICKLE
| | | | |
|---|---|---|---|
| 70 | Fontana TF 1069 | Millionaire/Sam And Sadie | 15 |
| 70 | Philips 6006 038 | Maybe I'm Amazed/Sitting On A Goldmine | 10 |
| 72 | B & C CB 178 | California Calling/Doctor Octopus | 12 |

## EDDIE FICTION
| | | | |
|---|---|---|---|
| 79 | Absurd A2 | U.F.O. Part 1/U.F.O. Part 2 | 8 |

## FIDD
| | | | |
|---|---|---|---|
| 69 | Polydor 56320 | Guai Guai (From the film 'Baby Love')/Happy Walk | 25 |

## FI-DELS
| | | | |
|---|---|---|---|
| 72 | Jay Boy BOY 69 | Try A Little Harder/You Never Do Right ( | 15 |
| 72 | Jay Boy BOY 69 | Try A Little Harder/You Never Do Right (DJ Copy) | 30 |
| 70s | DJM DJS 689 | Try A Little Harder/KEYMAN STRINGS: Instrumental Version (DJ copy p/s £20) | 10 |

## KEITH FIELD
| | | | |
|---|---|---|---|
| 68 | Polydor 56278 | The Day That War Broke Out/Stop Thief | 30 |

## ALAN FIELDING
| | | | |
|---|---|---|---|
| 61 | Decca F 11404 | Scatter Brain/I've Got To Learn To Forget | 6 |
| 62 | Decca F11518 | Too Late To Worry, Too Blue To Cry/You Reap Just What You Sow | 5 |

## FENELLA FIELDING
| | | | |
|---|---|---|---|
| 66 | Columbia DB 8086 | Big Bad Mouse/Later | 7 |

## JERRY FIELDING & HIS ORCHESTRA
| | | | |
|---|---|---|---|
| 54 | London HL 8017 | When I Grow Too Old To Dream/Button Up Your Overcoat | 30 |
| 55 | London HL 7001 | Faintly Reminiscent/Blues Serenade (export issue) | 12 |
| 55 | London HL 7002 | Pea-nut Vendor/Can't Help Lovin' Dat Man (export issue) | 12 |
| 55 | London HL 7003 | Tea For Two/Here In My Arms (export issue) | 15 |
| 55 | London HL 7004 | I'm In Love/Blue Prelude (export issue) | 15 |
| 55 | Brunswick 05399 | The Gypsy In My Soul/The Glory Of Love | 10 |
| 54 | London H-APB 1022 | FAINTLY REMINISCENT (10" LP) | 12 |

## FIELD MICE
| | | | |
|---|---|---|---|
| 88 | Sarah SARAH 012 | Emma's House/When You Sleep/Fabulous Friend/The Last Letter (p/s) | 25 |
| 88 | Sarah SARAH 18 | Sensitive/When Morning Comes To Town/Penguins (foldout p/s, with poster) | 20 |
| 89 | Caff CAFF 2 | I Can See Myself Alone Forever/Everything About You (foldaround p/s in poly bag with insert) | 30 |
| 90 | Sarah SARAH 024 | Autumn Store Pt. 1/If You Need Someone/World In Me (p/s) | 15 |
| 90 | Sarah SARAH 025 | Autumn Store Pt. 2/Anyone Else Isn't You/Bleak (p/s) | 12 |
| 91 | Sarah SARAH 44 | September's Not So Far Away/Hello And Goodbye (p/s, with insert) | 20 |
| 91 | Sarah SARAH 57 | Missing The Moon/A Wrong Turn And Raindrops/An Earlier Autumn (12", p/s) | 10 |
| 90 | Sarah SARAH 38 | SO SAID KAY EP 10", p/s) | 18 |
| 90 | Sarah SARAH 402 | SNOWBALL (10" LP) | 20 |
| 90 | Sarah SARAH 601 | SKYWRITING (LP) | 20 |
| 90 | Sarah SARAH 606 | COASTAL (LP) | 45 |
| 91 | Sarah SR607 | FOR KEEPS (LP) | 30 |

## FIELD MUSIC
| | | | |
|---|---|---|---|
| 12 | Memphis Industries | Heart/Rent (white vinyl) | 8 |
| 05 | Memphis Industries NI 043LP | FIELD MUSIC (LP) | 18 |
| 07 | Memphis industries NI 074LP | TONES OF MUSIC (LP) | 25 |

## BILLY FIELDS
| | | | |
|---|---|---|---|
| 55 | MGM SP 1126 | Sincerely/Thrilled | 5 |
| 59 | Mercury AMT 1067 | The Greatest Love In The World/No Other Love | 7 |

## ERNIE FIELDS & HIS ORCHESTRA
| | | | |
|---|---|---|---|
| 59 | London HL 8985 | In The Mood/Christopher Columbus (with tri-centre) | 5 |
| 60 | London HL 9100 | Chattanooga Choo Choo/Workin' Out | 6 |
| 60 | London HL 9227 | Raunchy/My Prayer | 6 |
| 60 | London RE 1260 | SAXY (EP) | 30 |
| 60 | London HA 2263 | IN THE MOOD (LP) | 30 |

## FIELDS OF THE NEPHILIM
| | | | |
|---|---|---|---|
| 84 | Tower N1 | BURNING THE FIELDS (12" EP, red/black p/s) | 30 |
| 86 | Situation 2 SIT 42 | Power/Secrets (7", white label promos only, stickered plain sleeve) | 15 |
| 87 | Situation 2 SIT 46 | Preacher Man/Laura II (p/s, swith Beggars Banquet sticker) | 35 |
| 87 | Situation 2 SIT 46 | Preacher Man/Laura II (p/s) | 25 |
| 87 | Situation 2 SIT 48T | Blue Water (1 track 12" promo) | 20 |
| 87 | Situation 2 SIT 48 | Blue Water/In Every Dream Home A Heartache (p/s) | 10 |
| 87 | Situation 2 SIT 48T | Blue Water (Electrostatic)/In Every Dream Home A Heartache (live)/Blue Water (Hot Wire) (12", p/s, with poster) | 15 |
| 89 | Situation 2 SIT 57 | Psychonaut/Celebrate (Second Seal) (blue/green p/s) | 6 |

| | | | |
|---|---|---|---|
| 90 | Beggars Banquet BEG 250 | Sumerland/Phobia (live) (no p/s) ....................................................................................... | 5 |
| 88 | Situation 2 SITU 22L | THE NEPHILIM (LP, 2 x 45rpm 12", gatefold sleeve, numbered) ........................................ | 20 |

## FIELDS (1)
| | | | |
|---|---|---|---|
| 69 | Uni UNLS 104 | FIELDS (LP) .................................................................................................................... | 80 |

## FIELDS (2)
| | | | |
|---|---|---|---|
| 71 | CBS 7555 | A Friends Of Mine/Three Minstrels ............................................................................. | 15 |
| 71 | CBS 69009 | FIELDS (LP, with poster) ............................................................................................. | 125 |
| 71 | CBS 69009 | FIELDS (LP, without poster) ........................................................................................ | 50 |

(see also Rare Bird, Greenslade)

## FIEND
| | | | |
|---|---|---|---|
| 84 | Endangered EDR 1 | STAND ALONE EP ........................................................................................................ | 18 |

## FIESTAS
| | | | |
|---|---|---|---|
| 59 | London HL 8870 | So Fine/Last Night I Dreamed ..................................................................................... | 40 |
| 59 | London HL 8870 | So Fine/Last Night I Dreamed (78) .............................................................................. | 20 |
| 71 | Atlantic 2091 121 | So Fine/Broken Heart .................................................................................................. | 8 |

## FIFE REIVERS
| | | | |
|---|---|---|---|
| 69 | Columbia SCX 6371 | FIFE REIVERS (LP) ........................................................................................................ | 15 |

## 15 16 17
| | | | |
|---|---|---|---|
| 77 | Morpheus DEB 06 | Black Skin Boy/Version ................................................................................................ | 15 |
| 78 | DEB DEB 003 | Emotion/Castro Black (with Dennis Bovell) ................................................................. | 12 |
| 78 | DEB DEB 012 | Good Times/Black Skin Boys (12") ............................................................................... | 15 |
| 79 | DEB DBR 101 | Someone Special/Suddenly Happiness ........................................................................ | 8 |
| 06 | DEB DEB LP 101 | MAGIC TOUCH (LP, reissue) ........................................................................................ | 15 |

## FIFTH AVENUE
| | | | |
|---|---|---|---|
| 65 | Immediate IM 002 | The Bells Of Rhymney/Just Like Anyone Would Do (in blue/white Immediate sleeve) .. | 40 |
| 65 | Immediate IM 002 | The Bells Of Rhymney/Just Like Anyone Would Do (in black/white Immediate sleeve) . | 30 |

(see also Denny Gerrard, Warm Sounds)

## FIFTH AVENUE BAND
| | | | |
|---|---|---|---|
| 69 | Reprise RSPL 6369 | FIFTH AVENUE BAND (LP) ............................................................................................ | 35 |

## FIFTH COLUMN
| | | | |
|---|---|---|---|
| 66 | Columbia DB 8068 | Benjamin Day/There's Nobody Here ............................................................................ | 50 |

## 5TH DIMENSION
| | | | |
|---|---|---|---|
| 67 | Liberty LIB 12051 | Go Where You Wanna Go/Too Poor To Die .................................................................. | 35 |
| 67 | Liberty LIB 12051 | Go Where You Wanna Go/Too Poor To Die (DJ Copy) ................................................. | 45 |
| 67 | Liberty LIB 15037 | Paper Cup/Poor Side Of Town ..................................................................................... | 20 |
| 67 | Liberty LBF 15014 | Up Up And Away/Pattern People ................................................................................ | 6 |
| 67 | Liberty LIB 12056 | Another Day, Another Heartache/Rosecrans Blvd ....................................................... | 8 |
| 68 | Liberty LBF 15052 | Carpet Man/Magic Garden .......................................................................................... | 15 |
| 68 | Liberty LBF 15072 | Stoned Soul Picnic/Sailboat Song ............................................................................... | 10 |
| 68 | Liberty LBF 15081 | Ticket To Ride/Orange Air ........................................................................................... | 6 |
| 68 | Liberty LBF 15130 | California Soul/It'll Never Be The Same ....................................................................... | 12 |
| 68 | Liberty LBF 15143 | Sweet Blindness/Good News ....................................................................................... | 5 |
| 69 | Liberty LBF 15180 | California Soul/I'll Never Be The Same Again .............................................................. | 5 |
| 69 | Liberty LBF 15193 | Aquarius — Let The Sun Shine In/Don'tcha Hear Me Callin' To Ya .............................. | 5 |
| 69 | Liberty LBF 15288 | Wedding Bell Blues/Let It Be Me ................................................................................. | 5 |
| 69 | Liberty LBF 15243 | Sunshine Of Your Love/Working On A Groovy Thing .................................................. | 6 |
| 69 | Liberty LBF 15308 | Blowing Away/Skinny Man ........................................................................................... | 6 |
| 70 | Liberty LBF 15356 | I'll Be Lovin' You Forever/Train Keep On Movin' ........................................................ | 25 |
| 68 | Liberty LBL/LBS 83098E | MAGIC GARDEN (LP) .................................................................................................... | 15 |
| 67 | Liberty LBL/LBS 83038 | UP UP AND AWAY (LP) .................................................................................................. | 15 |
| 68 | Liberty LBL/LBS 83155E | STONED SOUL PICNIC (LP) ........................................................................................... | 15 |

## FIFTH ESTATE
| | | | |
|---|---|---|---|
| 67 | Stateside SS 2034 | Ding Dong The Witch Is Dead/Rub A Dub ................................................................... | 10 |
| 67 | Stateside SS 2068 | Heigh Ho/It's Waiting There For You ........................................................................... | 10 |
| 68 | Stateside SS 2105 | Do Drop In/That's Love ............................................................................................... | 7 |
| 69 | Stateside SS 2125 | Coney Island Sally/Tomorrow Is My Turn .................................................................... | 10 |

## FIFTY FANTASTICS
| | | | |
|---|---|---|---|
| 79 | South Circular SGS 108 | God's Got Religion/STEPPES: The Beat Drill (white label) ........................................... | 10 |
| 80 | Dining Out TUX 5 | God's Got Religion/The Beat Drill (reissue, foldout p/s, hand made labels) ............... | 10 |

(see also Disco Zombies)

## FIFTY FIVE DEGREES
| | | | |
|---|---|---|---|
| 79 | No label or cat number | There's Gonna Be A Showdown/There's Gonna Be A Showdown (p/s) ......................... | 20 |

## FIFTY FOOT HOSE
| | | | |
|---|---|---|---|
| 69 | Mercury SLML 4030 | CAULDRON (LP) ............................................................................................................ | 200 |

## 53 BUS
| | | | |
|---|---|---|---|
| 83 | Custom Cars 100MPH | Horizontal Dancing/Horizontal D.I.Y. .......................................................................... | 50 |

## 50 YEAR VOID
| | | | |
|---|---|---|---|
| 92 | BLADE 1 | Blade's Love Machine (1-sided 12", white label promo, 100 only) ............................... | 30 |

(see also St. Etienne, Sarah Cracknell)

## 57TH PARALLEL
| | | | |
|---|---|---|---|
| 81 | Rising sun RS 005 | In This Light/Psalm Fifty Seven ................................................................................... | 20 |

## FIGGY DUFF
| | | | |
|---|---|---|---|
| 80 | Dingles DIN 326 | FIGGY DUFF (LP) .......................................................................................................... | 25 |
| 85 | Celtic CM 023 | AFTER THE TEMPEST (LP, with insert) ......................................................................... | 30 |

## NESTOR FIGUERAS, DAVID TOOP & PAUL BURWELL
| | | | |
|---|---|---|---|
| 77 | Bead Records BEAD 6 | NESTOR FIGUERAS, DAVID TOOP & PAUL BURWELL (LP) ............................................... | 40 |

**PAULINE FILBY**
| | | | |
|---|---|---|---|
| 60s | Church Miss. Soc. LIV/SP/81 | I'm Hungry/NADIA CATTOUSE: The Larder | 8 |
| 68 | Herald ELR 1081 | MY WORLD BY PAULINE FILBY (EP) | 20 |
| 69 | Herald LLR 567 | SHOW ME A RAINBOW (LP) | 120 |

*(see also Narnia, Accolade, Gordon Giltrap)*

**PHILIP JOHN FILBY**
| | | | |
|---|---|---|---|
| 71 | Dart ART2007 | David McKenzie/Close My Eyes And Stick With Me | 20 |

**FILE UNDER POP**
| | | | |
|---|---|---|---|
| 79 | Rough Trade RT 011 | Heathrow/Corrugate/Heathrow SLB (p/s) | 6 |

*(see also AK Process)*

**FILM CAST**
| | | | |
|---|---|---|---|
| 79 | True Friends TF 001 | Life In A Film Cast/Stations And Answers | 8 |
| 80 | True Friends TF 002 | Admission (Yours)/Colour - Colour (as FILMCAST) | 8 |
| 84 | True Friends TF 004 | The Distant Heart/World Of Light | 25 |

**FILTHY RICH**
| | | | |
|---|---|---|---|
| 87 | JM TR 102 | She's 17/Love Ain't A Fool (p/s) | 20 |

*(see also Trident)*

**FINAL ACADEMY**
| | | | |
|---|---|---|---|
| 83 | Spectrum SPEC 005 | Night Cafe/The Collector | 40 |

**FINAL CONFLICT**
| | | | |
|---|---|---|---|
| 86 | Futuresound FS 001 | EP (EP) | 10 |
| 86 | Futuresound FS 002 | THE TIME HAS ARRIVED (EP, with 22-page booklet) | 10 |
| 89 | Futuresound VFS 001 | My England/Across The Room (stickered white sleeve) | 20 |

**FINAL PROGRAM**
| | | | |
|---|---|---|---|
| 81 | Program FINAL 001 | PROTECT AND SURVIVE (EP) | 15 |

**FINAL TOUCH**
| | | | |
|---|---|---|---|
| 70s | Myrrh MYR 1188 | LOVE SONG (LP) | 25 |

**FINCH**
| | | | |
|---|---|---|---|
| 78 | Rockburgh ROC 103 | GALLEONS OF PASSION (LP) | 18 |

**FINDERS KEEPERS (U.K.)**
| | | | |
|---|---|---|---|
| 66 | CBS 202249 | Light/Power Of Love (withdrawn, promos may exist) | 65 |
| 66 | CBS 202249 | Light/Come On Now | 20 |
| 67 | Fontana TF 892 | Friday Kind Of Monday/On The Beach | 40 |
| 68 | Fontana TF 938 | Sadie (The Cleaning Lady)/Without Her | 20 |

*(see also Trapeze, Glenn Hughes, News)*

**FINDERS KEEPERS (U.S.)**
| | | | |
|---|---|---|---|
| 67 | London HLH 10117 | Lavender Blue/MICKEY DOLENZ: Don't Do It | 12 |

**JEM FINER**
| | | | |
|---|---|---|---|
| 00s | no cat. no. | LONGPLAYER (LP, with book) | 15 |

**FINGERS (1)**
| | | | |
|---|---|---|---|
| 66 | Polydor | I Go To Sleep/Oh! | 10 |
| 66 | Columbia DB 8026 | I'll Take You Where The Music's Playing/My Way Of Thinking | 20 |
| 67 | Columbia DB 8112 | All Kinds Of People/Circus With A Female Clown | 45 |

*(see also Crocheted Doughnut Ring, Legend)*

**FINGERS (2)**
| | | | |
|---|---|---|---|
| 79 | Ratched RAT 101 | Marching Band/The Bandleader (Baz's Tune) (no p/s) | 40 |
| 79 | Ratchet RAT 102 | Saints Alive/We're Alright | 40 |

**FINGERS INC.**
| | | | |
|---|---|---|---|
| 87 | Jack Trax 12 J TRAX 8 | Distant Planet Club Mix/Distant Planet Dub MIx (12", stickered die-cut company sleeve) | 45 |
| 88 | Desire WANTX 6 | Can You Feel It/My House (Acapella) (12", die-cut p/s) | 30 |
| 88 | Jack Trax JTX 8 | Distant Planet (Remix, 4 Mixes) (12") | 60 |
| 88 | Jack Trax JTX 20 | Can You Feel It (4 Mixes) (12", p/s) | 25 |
| 89 | Jack Trax JTX 2 | Never No More Lonely/Music Takes Me Up/Distant Planet (Club MIx) (12") | 30 |
| 88 | Jack Trax FING 1 | ANOTHER SIDE (2-LP, gatefold sleeve) | 30 |

**FINI TRIBE (101)**
| | | | |
|---|---|---|---|
| 84 | Finiflex LT 1001 | CURLING & STRETCHING EP (12", p/s, original issue) | 10 |
| 88 | Finiflex FT 002 | DESTIMONY EP (12", p/s) | 10 |
| 91 | Finiflex/One Little Indian | 101: Sonic Shuffle (Edit)/101: 303 (3D Bass Edit) (promo only, plain stickered sleeve) | 5 |

**FINK BROTHERS**
| | | | |
|---|---|---|---|
| 85 | Zarjazz JAZZ S2 | Mutants In Mega-City One/Mutant Blues (shaped picture disc) | 10 |
| 85 | Zarjazz JAZZ2-12 | Mutants In Mega-City One/Mutant Blues (12", p/s with poster) | 12 |

*(see also Madness)*

**LEE FINN & RHYTHM MEN**
| | | | |
|---|---|---|---|
| 63 | Starlite ST45 103 | High Class Feelin'/Pour Me A Glass Of Wine | 50 |

**LIAM FINN**
| | | | |
|---|---|---|---|
| 08 | Transgressive TRANS 079 | Second Chance/I'm Liam And This Is Eliza-Jane | 8 |

**FINN MACCUILL**
| | | | |
|---|---|---|---|
| 77 | private pressing | SINK YE SWIM YE (LP) | 80 |

**SIMON FINN**
| | | | |
|---|---|---|---|
| 70 | Mushroom 100 MR 2 | PASS THE DISTANCE (LP, with lyric insert, white/brown labels) | 500 |

**TIM FINN**
| | | | |
|---|---|---|---|
| 83 | Epic A 3932 | Fraction Too Much Friction/Below The Belt (p/s) | 5 |

*(see also Split Enz, Crowded House)*

**LARRY FINNEGAN**
| | | | |
|---|---|---|---|
| 62 | HMV POP 1022 | Dear One/Candy Lips | 10 |
| 62 | London HLU 9613 | Pretty Suzy Sunshine/It's Walkin' Talkin' Time | 20 |

MINT VALUE £

| 65 | Ember EMB S 207 | The Other Ringo (A Tribute To Ringo Starr)/When My Love Passes By (p/s) | 20 |
| 65 | Ember EMB S 207 | The Other Ringo (A Tribute To Ringo Starr)/When My Love Passes By | 10 |

## ALBERT FINNEY
| 77 | Tamla Motown TMG 1084 | Those Other Men/What Have They Done (To My Home Town) | 7 |

## MIKE FINNIGAN
| 78 | CBS 6656 | Just One Minute More/Blood Is Thicker Than Water | 10 |

## FINS
| 81 | SRTS 81 CUS 1075 | Voice Of America/Omega Man | 25 |

## FIRE
| 68 | Decca F 12753 | Father's Name Is Dad/Treacle Toffee World | 500 |
| 68 | Decca F 12856 | Round The Gum Tree/Toothie Ruthie | 70 |
| 70 | Pye NSPL 18343 | THE MAGIC SHOEMAKER (LP, blue/black labels with logo banner at top) | 600 |
| 97 | Tenth Planet TP 029 | UNDERGROUND AND OVERHEAD: THE ALTERNATE FIRE (LP, gatefold sleeve, numbered, 1,000 only) | 18 |

*(see also Strawbs, Paul Brett's Sage)*

## LUTAN FIRE AND BUSH CHEMIST
| 03 | Conscious Sounds CD 1003 | 16 Years/King David's House (10") | 10 |

## FIREBALL
| 73 | Spark SRL 1093 | Bachonola/I Dunno | 10 |

## FIREBALLS
| 59 | Top Rank JAR 218 | Torquay/Cry Baby | 15 |
| 60 | Top Rank JAR 276 | Bulldog/Nearly Sunrise | 5 |
| 60 | Top Rank JAR 354 | Foot-Patter/Kissin' | 5 |
| 60 | Top Rank JAR 507 | Vaquero (Cowboy)/Chief Whoopin'-Koff | 5 |
| 61 | Pye International 7N 25092 | Quite A Party/Gunshot | 5 |
| 62 | Stateside SS 106 | Rik-A-Tik/Yacky Doo | 5 |
| 63 | Stateside SS 151 | Carioca/Find Me A Golden Street | 5 |
| 65 | Stateside SS 417 | Baby What's Wrong/Yummie Yama Papa | 5 |
| 67 | Stateside SS 2095 | Bottle Of Wine/Ain't That Rain | 5 |
| 68 | Stateside SS 2106 | Goin' Away/Groovy Motions | 15 |
| 69 | Stateside SS 2134 | Come On, React!/Woman Help Me | 5 |
| 69 | London HLZ 10260 | Long Green/Light In The Window | 5 |
| 61 | Top Rank 35/105 | VAQUERO (LP) | 25 |

*(see also Jimmy Gilmer, Buddy Holly)*

## FIREBIRD (1)
| 74 | Bell Bell 1370 | Two Wheels/Side Tracking | 5 |

## FIREBIRD (2)
| 79 | Rat SRTS79/CUS576 | Change/Nightride (in p/s) | 150 |
| 79 | Rat SRTS79/CUS576 | Change/Nightride | 40 |

## FIREBRAND
| 85 | What WR 71 | Never Felt This Way Before/I'm Leaving (p/s) | 50 |

## FIRECLOWN
| 83 | Fireclown FC 1001 | INVASION EP (Magic/Poor Man/Invasion) (10", no p/s) | 12 |

## FIRE ENGINES
| 80 | Codex Comms. CDX 01 | Get Up And Use Me/Everything's Roses (p/s) | 15 |
| 81 | Pop:Aural POP 010 | Candy Skin/Meat Whiplash (foldout p/s in poly bag) | 10 |
| 81 | Pop:Aural POP 013 | Big Gold Dream/Sympathetic Anaesthetic (p/s) | 6 |
| 81 | Pop:Aural POP 01312 | Big Gold Dream/Sympathetic Anaesthetic/New Thing In Cartons (12", non-gatefold p/s; gatefold p/s £5) | 10 |
| 81 | Accessory ACC 001 | LUBRICATE YOUR LIVING ROOM (LP, in plastic bag) | 20 |

## FIRE EXIT
| 79 | Time Bomb Explosion 1 | Timewall/Talkin' About Myself (p/s, stamped labels) | 40 |

## FIREFLIES
| 59 | Top Rank JAR 198 | You Were Mine/Stella Got A Fella | 20 |
| 59 | Top Rank JAR 198 | You Were Mine/Stella Got A Fella (78) | 20 |
| 60 | London HLU 9057 | I Can't Say Goodbye/What Did I Do Wrong | 35 |

## FIREFLY
| 71 | Decca F131192 | My Friend/Younger Days | 8 |

## FIRE HYDRANT MEN
| 85 | MCHMLP 3 | BACKS (LP) | 20 |

## FIRE KINGS
| 77 | Terminal TM 107 | Poor Man Cry/Version | 8 |

## FIREMAN
| 98 | Hydra HYPRO 12 007 | Rushes: Bison/Fluid/Appletree Cinnabar Amber (12" with massive fold-out poster) | 100 |
| 98 | Hydra HYPRO 12 007 | Rushes: Bison/Fluid/Appletree Cinnabar Amber (12" without massive fold-out poster) | 20 |
| 99 | Hydra HYPRO 12 008 | Fluid (12", p/s, promo only) | 35 |
| 93 | Parlophone FIRE 1 | STRAWBERRIES OCEANS SHIPS FOREST (2-LP, clear vinyl, numbered white sleeve, with inners, promo only) | 100 |
| 93 | Parlophone PCSD 145 | STRAWBERRIES OCEANS SHIPS FOREST (2-LP, clear vinyl, red sleeve, with inners) | 100 |
| 98 | Hydra 4970551 | RUSHES (2-LP, inners) | 100 |

*(see also Paul McCartney, Youth)*

## FIRE SESSION
| 70 | Revolution REV 10 | Souvenir/Bad Girl | 10 |
| 70 | Revolution REV 13 | Sleeping Reggae/CAROLS: Everyday I Have To Cry Some | 10 |
| 70 | Revolution REV 14 | Death Of The Ugly One/Big Feet | 20 |

## FIRESIGN THEATRE
| 72 | CBS CQ 30737 | FIRESIGN THEATRE (LP, quadrophonic) | 15 |

**FIRESTONE**
71   Flash FL002                              Turning Away From Me/Empty Pages ...................................................... 12

**FIRESTONES**
62   Decca F 11436                            Party Twist (Medley) (Parts 1 & 2) ..................................................... 6

**FIRING SQUAD (1)**
64   Parlophone R 5152                        A Little Bit More/Bull Moose .......................................................... 50

**FIRING SQUAD (2)**
80   Shattered SHAT 5                         Big Red Car/Night Manoeuvres (p/s) .................................................... 8

**FIRKIN THE FOX**
84   Woodworm WR 005                          BEHIND BARS (LP) ...................................................................... 25

**FIRM (1)**
80   SRTS 80 CUS 806                          Angry Young Man/Not Gonna Turn Back Anymore/Mainstream (stamped paper
                                              sleeve) ............................................................................... 20

**FIRST AID**
77   Decca TXS 117                            NOSTRADAMUS (LP) ...................................................................... 40

**FIRST AID KIT**
08   Wichita WEBB201LP                        DRUNKEN TREES EP (12" and CD, white vinyl) ............................................ 10
09   Wichita WEBB206S                         You're Not Coming Home Tonight/Tangerine ............................................. 12
09   Wichita WEBB234S                         Hard Believer/Waltz For Richard ...................................................... 10
11   Wichita WEBB319S                         The Lion's Road/Marianne's Son ........................................................ 8
14   Columbia 88843066611                     STAY GOLD (LP, CD gold vinyl) ........................................................ 20

**FIRST CHOICE**
73   Pye International 7N 25613               This Is The House Where Love Died/One Step Away (unissued, demos may exist, this
                                              price for acetate) .................................................................. 400
73   Bell 1297                                Armed And Extremely Dangerous/Gonna Keep On Lovin Him ................................. 5
74   Bell BLL 1376                            The Player (Parts 1 & 2) .............................................................. 8
73   Bell BELLS 229                           ARMED AND EXTREMELY DANGEROUS (LP) .................................................... 18

**FIRST CLASS**
74   Sunny EON 102                            Beach Baby/Surfer Queen ............................................................... 6
74   UK UKAL 1008                             THE FIRST CLASS (LP) ................................................................. 18
76   UK UKAL 1022                             S.S.T. (LP) ......................................................................... 18
*(see also White Plains, Edison Lighthouse, Brotherhood Of Man, Carter-Lewis & Southerners, Ivy League)*

**FIRST DOWN**
90   Cobden Capers FD1                        Jaw Warfare/From Now On/Dedication ................................................... 70
93   Ill Gotten Gains FD002                   LET THE BATTLE BEGIN (EP) ............................................................ 40
94   Blitz Vinyl EFA61008                     MAD DOGS AND ENGLISHMAN (EP) ......................................................... 12
94   Blitz Vinyl EFA61009                     WORLD SERVICE (LP) ................................................................... 18

**FIRST EDITION**
68   Reprise RS 20655                         Just Dropped In (To See What Condition My Condition Was In)/Shadow In The Corner
                                              Of Your Mind ......................................................................... 40
68   Reprise RS 20693                         Charlie The Fer'de Lance/Look Around I'll Be There .................................... 8
69   Reprise RS 20799                         But You Know I Love You/Homemade Lies ................................................. 5
68   Reprise RSLP 6276                        THE FIRST EDITION (LP) ............................................................... 15
*(see also Kenny Rogers)*

**FIRST GEAR**
64   Pye 7N 15703                             A Certain Girl/Leave My Kitten Alone ................................................ 200
65   Pye 7N 15763                             The 'In' Crowd/Gotta Make Their Future Bright ........................................ 70

**FIRST IMPRESSION/GOOD EARTH**
68   Saga FID 2117                            SWINGING LONDON (LP) ................................................................. 25
*(see also Mungo Jerry)*

**FIRST IMPRESSIONS**
65   Pye 7N 15797                             I'm Coming Home/Looking For Her ...................................................... 25
*(see also Legends)*

**FIRST LIGHT**
82   Oval FLIGHT 22/12                        Don't Be Mistaken/Horse With No Name (12" p/s) ....................................... 8

**FIRST NATIONAL NOTHING (FEATURING J MARKS)**
70   CBS 5120                                 Purple Song/I Got The Answer (purple vinyl) .......................................... 8

**FIRST OFFENCE**
88   Metal Other OTH 11                       FIRST OFFENCE (LP, with insert) ...................................................... 30
88   Metal Other OTH 11                       FIRST OFFENCE (LP, without insert) ................................................... 25

**1ST OFFENCE**
82   Chaos                                    NIGHT THE PUNKS TURNED UGLY EP (fold out sleeve) ..................................... 15

**FIRST STEPS**
80   English Rose ER I                        The Beat Is Back/She Ain't In Love/Let's Go Cuboids (p/s, with insert) ............... 30
81   English Rose ER III                      Anywhere Else But Here/Airplay/I Got The News (p/s) .................................. 20

**FIRST REFUSAL**
78   Rainbow RSL 015                          FIRST REFUSAL EP (500 only) .......................................................... 40

**CLARE FISCHER**
62   Fontana 688124 ZL                        FIRST TIME OUT (LP) .................................................................. 15

**WILD MAN FISCHER**
69   Reprise RSLP 6332                        AN EVENING WITH WILD MAN FISCHER (LP, gatefold sleeve) ............................... 60
*(see also Frank Zappa)*

**FISCHERMAN'S FRIEND**
91   EG OP 51                                 Money (12", with "Orb Clubmix", 500 only) ............................................ 12

**F F & Z (FISHBAUGH FISHBAUGH & ZORN)**
72   CBS 8163                                 Everybody Got Out Of Bed/Spaced On Happy ............................................. 20

MINT VALUE £

## ARCHIE FISHER
| 68 | Xtra XTRA 1070 | ARCHIE FISHER (LP) | 25 |
| 70 | Decca SKL 5057 | ORFEO (LP) | 50 |
| 76 | Topic 12TS 277 | WILL YE GANG LOVE (LP) | 20 |
| 82 | Celtic Music CM 007 | ARCHIE FISHER (LP, reissue) | 20 |

*(see also Barbara Dickson)*

## ARCHIE FISHER, BARBARA DICKSON & JOHN MACKINNON
| 69 | Trailer LER 3002 | THE FATE O' CHARLIE: SONGS OF THE JACOBITE REBELLIONS (LP, first pressing, white label) | 60 |
| 69 | Trailer LER 3002 | THE FATE O' CHARLIE: SONGS OF THE JACOBITE REBELLIONS (LP, second pressing, red label) | 30 |

## CHIP FISHER
| 59 | Parlophone R 4604 | Poor Me/No One | 15 |
| 59 | RCA RCX 143 | AT THE SUGAR BOWL (EP) | 80 |

## CILLA FISHER & ARTIE TREZISE
| 76 | Trailer LER 2100 | BALCANQUHAL (LP, yellow label) | 15 |
| 79 | Kettle KAC 1 | FOR FOUL DAY AND FAIR (LP) | 15 |

## EDDIE FISHER
| 53 | HMV 7M 101 | I'm Yours/That's The Chance You Take | 15 |
| 53 | HMV 7M 115 | Everything I Have Is Yours/You'll Never Know | 10 |
| 53 | HMV 7M 116 | Trust In Me/Forgive Me | 10 |
| 53 | HMV 7M 117 | Outside Of Heaven/Lady Of Spain | 15 |
| 53 | HMV 7M 125 | Even Now/If It Were Up To Me | 10 |
| 53 | HMV 7M 126 | Downhearted/Am I Wasting My Time On You | 10 |
| 53 | HMV 7M 133 | I'm Walking Behind You (with Sally Sweetland)/Hold Me | 12 |
| 53 | HMV 7M 146 | Just Another Polka/When I Was Young (Yes, Very Young) | 8 |
| 53 | HMV 7M 159 | Wish You Were Here/A Fool Was I | 10 |
| 53 | HMV 7M 168 | Many Times/With These Hands | 10 |
| 54 | HMV 7M 172 | Oh My Papa/(I Never Missed You) Until You Said "Goodbye" | 10 |

## FAYE FISHER
| 65 | Columbia DB 7575 | Our Love/I Just Don't Know What To Say | 7 |
| 65 | Columbia DB 7732 | Oh Heartache You're Bothering Me/It's You | 7 |

## MATTHEW FISHER
| 73 | RCA SF8380 | JOURNEY'S END (LP) | 18 |
| 74 | RCA APL 1 | I'LL BE THERE (LP) | 15 |

*(see also Procol Harum, Green Bullfrog)*

## RAY FISHER
| 72 | Trailer LER 2038 | THE BONNY BIRD (LP, red label) | 25 |

## TONI FISHER
| 60 | Top Rank JAR 261 | The Big Hurt/Memphis Belle | 6 |
| 60 | Top Rank JAR 341 | How Deep Is The Ocean/Blue, Blue, Blue (as Miss Toni Fisher) | 7 |
| 62 | London HLX 9564 | West Of The Wall/What Did I Do | 5 |

## WILLIE FISHER
| 77 | Jama JA 35 | Put Your Lovin' On Me/Take Time To Know Her | 30 |

## FISHER BROTHERS
| 64 | London HLN 9928 | Big Round Wheel/By The Time You Read This Letter | 10 |

## FISH TURNED HUMAN
| 79 | Sequel PART 1 | TURKEYS IN CHINA (EP) | 15 |

## FIST
| 80 | Neat NEAT 04 | Name Rank And Serial Number/You'll Never Get Me In One Of Those (p/s, with poster insert) | 10 |
| 80 | Neat NEAT 04 | Name Rank And Serial Number/You'll Never Get Me In One Of Those (p/s) | 8 |
| 80 | MCA MCA 615 | Name Rank And Serial Number/You'll Never Get Me (In One Of Those) (p/s, reissue, with poster insert) | 30 |
| 80 | MCA MCA 615 | Name Rank And Serial Number/You'll Never Get Me (In One Of Those) (p/s, reissue, without poster insert) | 20 |
| 80 | MCA MCA 640 | Forever Amber/Brain Damage (p/s) | 12 |
| 81 | MCA MCA 663 | Collision Course/Law Of The Jungle (p/s) | 100 |
| 81 | MCA MCA 663 | Collision Course/Law Of The Jungle | 30 |
| 82 | Neat NEAT 021 | The Wanderer/Too Hot (p/s) | 10 |
| 80 | MCA MCF 3082 | TURN THE HELL ON (LP) | 15 |
| 85 | Neat NEAT 1003 | BACK WITH A VENGEANCE (LP, yellow vinyl) | 30 |
| 85 | Neat NEAT 1003 | BACK WITH A VENGEANCE (LP) | 15 |

## JOHN FITCH & ASSOCIATES
| 71 | Beacon BEA 117 | Romantic Altitude/Stoned Out Of It | 90 |

## FITS
| 82 | Rondelet ROUND 13 | Think For Yourself: Burial/Straps (p/s) | 5 |
| 83 | Corpus Christi ITS 9 | Tears Of A Nation/Bravado/Breaking Point (p/s) | 6 |
| 84 | Trapper FIT 1 | Action/Achilles Heel (p/s) | 7 |
| 85 | Trapper FIT 2 | Fact Or Fiction/Give Away (p/s) | 5 |
| 81 | Beat The System FIT 1 | YOU SAID WE'D NEVER MAKE IT (EP, wraparound p/s) | 10 |
| 82 | Rondelet ABOUT 6 | YOU'RE NOTHING, YOU'RE NOWHERE (LP) | 15 |

## FITZ & COOLERS
| 68 | Nu Beat NB 003 | Cover Me/Darling | 12 |

## ELLA FITZGERALD
### SINGLES
| 66 | Stateside SS 569 | These Boots Were Made For Walkin'/Stardust (DJ Copy) | 50 |
| 66 | Stateside SS 569 | These Boots Were Made for Walkin'/Stardust | 8 |

| | | | |
|---|---|---|---|
| 69 | Reprise RS 20850 | Get Ready/Open Your Window | 30 |
| 69 | Polydor 56767 | Hey Jude/Sunshine Of Your Love | 10 |
| 71 | Reprise RS 23507 | I Heard It Through The Grapevine/Days Of Wine & Roses | 8 |

**ALBUMS**

| | | | |
|---|---|---|---|
| 68 | Polydor 583737 | SUNSHINE OF YOUR LOVE (LP) | 20 |

*(see also Count Basie)*

## ELLA FITZGERALD & LOUIS ARMSTRONG
| | | | |
|---|---|---|---|
| 56 | HMV CLP 1098 | ELLA AND LOUIS (LP) | 20 |

## ELLA FITZGERALD/BILLIE HOLIDAY
| | | | |
|---|---|---|---|
| 58 | Columbia Clef 33CX 10100 | AT NEWPORT (LP) | 15 |

## G.F. FITZGERALD
| | | | |
|---|---|---|---|
| 70 | Uni UNLS 115 | MOUSEPROOF (LP, gatefold sleeve, with insert, yellow swirl label) | 200 |

## PATRIK FITZGERALD
| | | | |
|---|---|---|---|
| 77 | Small Wonder SMALL 4 | SAFETY PIN STUCK IN MY HEART (EP, with lyrics) | 10 |
| 78 | Small Wonder SMALL 6 | Buy Me, Sell Me/The Little Dippers/Trendy/The Backstreet Boys (p/s) | 8 |
| 79 | Polydor 2059 091 | All Sewn Up/Hammersmith Odeons (p/s) | 8 |
| 79 | Polydor 2059 135 | Improve Myself/The Bingo Crowd/My New Family (p/s, as Patrik Fitzgerald) | 8 |
| 78 | Small Wonder WEENY ONE | THE PARANOID WARD/THE BEDROOM TAPES (12" EP) | 10 |
| 81 | Ellie Jay AHPF 001 | Without Sex/Pop Star, Pop Star | 5 |
| 82 | Red Flame RF 708 | Personal Loss/Straight Boy | 5 |
| 79 | Polydor 2383 533 | GRUBBY STORIES (LP) | 15 |

## MAGGIE FITZGIBBON
| | | | |
|---|---|---|---|
| 59 | Pye Int. 7N 25047 | Kooka Burra/The Right Kind Of Man | 7 |
| 68 | Page One PDF 057 | I'll Walk Alone/Girls Are Made Loving (p/s) | 8 |

## FITZROY (STERLING) & HARRY
| | | | |
|---|---|---|---|
| 70 | Bullet BU 439 | Reggae Sounds Are Boss/Goodbye My Love | 30 |
| 70 | Escort ERT 827 | Pop A Top Train/Doing The Moonwalk | 15 |

## FIVE AMERICANS
| | | | |
|---|---|---|---|
| 66 | Pye International 7N 25354 | I See The Light/The Outcasts | 25 |
| 66 | Pye International 7N 25373 | Evol — Not Love/Don't Blame Me | 20 |
| 67 | Stateside SS 2012 | Western Union/Now That It's All Over | 10 |
| 68 | Stateside SS 2036 | Sound Of Love/Sympathy | 7 |

## 5 A.M. EVENT
| | | | |
|---|---|---|---|
| 66 | Pye 7N 17154 | Hungry/I Wash My Hands (In Muddy Water) | 325 |

## FIVE & A PENNY
| | | | |
|---|---|---|---|
| 68 | Polydor 56282 | You Don't Know Where Your Interest Lies/Mary Go Round | 40 |
| 68 | Polydor 56282 | You Don't Know Where Your Interest Lies/Mary Go Round (2nd pressing injection moulded) | 5 |

## FIVE BLIND BOYS
| | | | |
|---|---|---|---|
| 64 | Vocalion EPVP 1276 | NEGRO SPIRITUALS (EP, 2 tracks by Spirits Of Memphis) | 20 |
| 64 | Vocalion EPVP 1282 | FIVE BLIND BOYS (EP) | 10 |

## FIVE BLOBS
| | | | |
|---|---|---|---|
| 58 | Philips PB 881 | The Blob/Saturday Night In Tijuana | 20 |

## FIVE BY FIVE
| | | | |
|---|---|---|---|
| 68 | Pye International 7N 25477 | Fire/Hang Up | 70 |

## FIVE CARD STUD
| | | | |
|---|---|---|---|
| 67 | Philips BF 1567 | Beg Me/Once | 15 |

## FIVE CHESTERNUTS
| | | | |
|---|---|---|---|
| 58 | Columbia DB 4165 | Jean Dorothy/Teenage Love | 200 |
| 58 | Columbia DB 4165 | Jean Dorothy/Teenage Love (78) | 100 |

*(see also Shadows, Pete Chester)*

## FIVE COUNTS
| | | | |
|---|---|---|---|
| 62 | Oriole CBA 1769 | Watermelon Walk/Spanish Nights | 30 |

## FIVE CRESTAS
| | | | |
|---|---|---|---|
| 66 | Excel ES SP 288/289 | How Sweet It Is (To Be Loved By You)/You Used To Love Me (private pressing) | 100 |

## FIVE DALLAS BOYS
| | | | |
|---|---|---|---|
| 60 | Columbia SEG 8035 | THE FIVE DALLAS BOYS (EP) | 12 |

*(see also Dallas Boys)*

## FIVE DAY RAIN
| | | | |
|---|---|---|---|
| 70 | Private pressing | FIVE DAY RAIN (LP, no sleeve, 20-30 copies only) | 800 |
| 93 | Private pressing | FIVE DAY RAIN (LP, re-pressing in signed, numbered sleeve, signed note in run-out groove & letter of authenticity, 25 only) | 80 |

*(see also Scots Of St. James, Hopscotch, One Way Ticket, Glencoe)*

## FIVE DAY WEEK STRAW PEOPLE
| | | | |
|---|---|---|---|
| 68 | Saga FID 2123 | FIVE DAY WEEK STRAW PEOPLE (LP, black/silver labels) | 150 |

*(see also Attack, Andromeda, John Du Cann)*

## FIVE DE MARCO SISTERS
| | | | |
|---|---|---|---|
| 53 | MGM SP 1043 | Bouillabasse/I'm Never Satisfied | 5 |
| 54 | Brunswick 05349 | Love Me/Just A Girl That Men Forget | 5 |
| 55 | Brunswick 05425 | Dreamboat/Two Hearts, Two Kisses (Make One Love) | 6 |
| 55 | Brunswick 05474 | The Hot Barcarolle/Sailor Boys Have Talk To Me In English | 5 |
| 56 | Brunswick 05526 | Romance Me/This Love Of Mine | 5 |

## FIVE DU-TONES
| | | | |
|---|---|---|---|
| 63 | Stateside SS 206 | Shake A Tail Feather/Divorce Court | 20 |
| 68 | President PT 134 | Shake A Tail Feather/Divorce Court (reissue) | 5 |

## FIVE EMPREES
| | | | |
|---|---|---|---|
| 65 | Stateside SS 470 | Little Miss Sad/Hey Lover | 20 |

## FIVE FINGER DEATH PUNCH

MINT VALUE £

| | | | |
|---|---|---|---|
| 09 | Park/Spinefarm SPI360LP.272045 | WAR IS THE ANSWER (2-LP, red vinyl) | 20 |

### FIVE FLEETS
| | | | |
|---|---|---|---|
| 58 | Felsted AF 103 | Oh What A Feeling/I Been Cryin' | 150 |
| 58 | Felsted AF 103 | Oh What A Feeling/I Been Cryin' (78) | 40 |

### FIVE FLIGHTS UP
| | | | |
|---|---|---|---|
| 70 | Bell BLL 1123 | Do What You Wanna Do/Black Cat | 6 |

### FIVE GO DOWN TO THE SEA
| | | | |
|---|---|---|---|
| 83 | Kabuki KAFIVE 5 | KNOT A FISH (EP) | 15 |

### FIVE KEYS
| | | | |
|---|---|---|---|
| 54 | Capitol CL 14184 | Ling, Ting, Tong/I'm Alone | 300 |
| 54 | Capitol CL 14184 | Ling, Ting, Tong/I'm Alone (78) | 50 |
| 55 | Capitol CL 14313 | The Verdict/Make Me Um Pow Pow (triangular centre) | 300 |
| 55 | Capitol CL 14313 | The Verdict/Make Me Um Pow Pow (78) | 50 |
| 55 | Capitol CL 14325 | (Close Your Eyes) Take A Deep Breath/Doggone It, You Did It(tri centre) | 300 |
| 55 | Capitol CL 14325 | (Close Your Eyes) Take A Deep Breath/Doggone It, You Did It (78) | 40 |
| 56 | Capitol CL 14545 | Gee Whittakers!/'Cause You're My Lover | 300 |
| 56 | Capitol CL 14545 | Gee Whittakers!/'Cause You're My Lover (78) | 300 |
| 56 | Capitol CL 14582 | She's The Most/I Dreamt I Dwelt In Heaven | 25 |
| 56 | Capitol CL 14582 | She's The Most/I Dreamt I Dwelt In Heaven (78) | 250 |
| 56 | Capitol CL 14639 | That's Right/Out Of Sight, Out Of Mind | 25 |
| 56 | Capitol CL 14639 | That's Right/Out Of Sight, Out Of Mind (78) | 150 |
| 57 | Capitol CL 14686 | The Wisdom Of A Fool/Now Don't That Prove I Love You? | 20 |
| 57 | Capitol CL 14686 | The Wisdom Of A Fool/Now Don't That Prove I Love You? (78) | 150 |
| 57 | Capitol CL 14736 | Four Walls/Let There Be You | 25 |
| 57 | Capitol CL 14736 | Four Walls/Let There Be You (78) | 100 |
| 57 | Capitol CL 14756 | The Blues Don't Care/This I Promise You | 30 |
| 57 | Capitol CL 14756 | The Blues Don't Care/This I Promise You (78) | 150 |
| 58 | Capitol CL 14829 | From Me To You/Whippety Whirl | 40 |
| 58 | Capitol CL 14829 | From Me To You/Whippety Whirl (78) | 150 |
| 58 | Capitol CL 14967 | One Great Love/Really-O Truly-O | 45 |
| 57 | Capitol T 828 | THE FIVE KEYS ON STAGE! (LP) | 150 |
| | | | 200 |

### FIVE MILES OUT
| | | | |
|---|---|---|---|
| 73 | Action ACT 4614 | Super Sweet Girl Of Mine/Set Your Mind Free | 25 |

### FIVE NITES
| | | | |
|---|---|---|---|
| 64 | Decca F 11963 | With A Loving Kiss/Let's Try Again | 15 |

### FIVE OF DIAMONDS
| | | | |
|---|---|---|---|
| 65 | Oak RGJ 150 FD | FIVE OF DIAMONDS (EP) | 400 |

### FIVE OR SIX
| | | | |
|---|---|---|---|
| 81 | Cherry Red CHERRY 19 | Another Reason/The Trial (p/s) | 5 |

### FIVE ROYALES
| | | | |
|---|---|---|---|
| 60 | Ember EMB S 124 | Dedicated To The One I Love/Miracle Of Love | 150 |

### FIVE SAPPHIRES
| | | | |
|---|---|---|---|
| 78 | Rocket ROKN 539 | Love Music/Where Did All The Good Times Go | 7 |
| 79 | Warner Bros K 17307 | Duke of Earl/Oh My Darlin' | 5 |
| 79 | Warner Bros K 17360 | Once In A While/Falling in Love | 5 |

*(see also Alan Carvell, Carvells, Telegrams)*

### FIVE SATINS
| | | | |
|---|---|---|---|
| 57 | London HL 8501 | To The Aisle/Wish I Had My Baby | 450 |
| 57 | London HL 8501 | To The Aisle/Wish I Had My Baby (78) | 40 |
| 59 | Top Rank JAR 199 | Wonderful Girl/Weeping Willow | 30 |
| 59 | Top Rank JAR 239 | Shadows/Toni My Love | 50 |
| 60 | MGM MGM 1087 | Your Memory/I Didn't Know | 60 |

### FIVE SMITH BROTHERS
| | | | |
|---|---|---|---|
| 54 | Decca F 10403 | A.B.C. Boogie/Veni-Vidi-Vici (with Dennis Wilson Quartet) | 20 |
| 55 | Decca F 10507 | Paper Valentine/You're As Sweet Today (As Yesterday) | 7 |
| 55 | Decca F 10527 | Don't Worry/I'm In Favour Of Friendship | 7 |
| 56 | Decca F 10698 | You Took My Heart (My Only Heart)/The Grass Is Green | 5 |
| 55 | Parlophone GEP 8667 | UP NORTH WITH THE FIVE SMITH BROTHERS (EP) | 10 |

### FIVE STAIRSTEPS (& CUBIE)
| | | | |
|---|---|---|---|
| 68 | Pye International 7N 25448 | A Million To One/Something's Missing (with Cubie) | 12 |
| 69 | Buddah 201 026 | Stay Close To Me/I Made A Mistake (with Cubie) | 12 |
| 69 | Buddah 201 070 | We Must Be In Love/Little Young Lovers (with Cubie) | 12 |
| 70 | Buddah 201 083 | Dear Prudence/O-o-h Child | 15 |
| 70 | Buddah 2011 036 | O-o-h Child/Who Do You Belong To? | 8 |

*(see also Stairsteps)*

### FIVE STEPS BEYOND
| | | | |
|---|---|---|---|
| 67 | CBS 202490 | Not So Young Today/Meanwhile Back In My Heart | 25 |
| 95 | Tenth Planet TP 019 | FAINT HEARTS AND FAIR MAIDS (LP, 600 only) | 15 |
| 96 | Tenth Planet TP 021 | SMILE (LP, with A4 booklet, 600 only) | 15 |

### FIVE THIRTY/5.30
| | | | |
|---|---|---|---|
| 87 | Other 12 OTH 2 | THE CATCHER IN THE RYE EP (12", p/s) | 20 |

### FIVE TOWNS
| | | | |
|---|---|---|---|
| 67 | Direction 58-3115 | It Isn't What You've Got/Advice | 10 |

### FIVE YEAR PLAN
| | | | |
|---|---|---|---|
| 87 | Breaking Down Break 3 | Hit The Bottle/Swallow Your Pride | 20 |

## FIVEPENNY PIECE
74   EMI 2187                    Butterflies And Songbirds/Save Your Last Kiss For Me ..................................................... 6

## FIVER
76   EMI 2401                    When Love Walks Out The Door/I Don't Wanna Be Alone Tonight ......................... 6

## FIVE'S COMPANY
66   Pye 7N 17118                Sunday For Seven Days/The Big Kill .............................................................................. 12
66   Pye 7N 17162                Some Girls/Big Deal ...................................................................................................... 6
66   Pye 7N 17199                Session Man/Dejection ................................................................................................ 18
69   Saga FID 2151               THE BALLAD OF FRED THE PIXIE (LP) ........................................................................... 18
*(see also Brunning Hall Sunflower Blues Band)*

## FIVE STAR GAS
79   Warp Records SRTS/79/CUS    Smokey Bubble Shoo Fly Pie/Sledge Hammer (500 only, no p/s) ................................. 20
  - 540WARP 001

## FIXED PENALTY
92   FPT 001                     Man Of Action/All Of Us (12") ...................................................................................... 18
92   FPT 002                     To You/Bubble Up (12") ................................................................................................ 20
92   FPT 004                     Party Rocker (12" ......................................................................................................... 10

## FIXER
78   Rainbow RSL 116             Bright And Rosy (no p/s) .............................................................................................. 40

## FIXIT
79   Ellie Jay SJSP9246          Eighteen Plus/April Fool ............................................................................................... 50

## FIZZBOMBS
87   Narodnik NRK 003            Sign On The Line/The Lines That (p/s) ........................................................................ 10

## FIZZLER
79   Aerco AERS 105              Brill Plus (You Know Us)/Margy's Song (no p/s, 500 only) ......................................... 10

## FK9
81   ABS 001                     Our Condition/These Children/All That Fall (p/s) ....................................................... 10
81   ABS SBS 2                   Stranger At The Heart/Complete Surveillance (p/s) ................................................... 10

## ROBERTA FLACK
69   Atlantic 584 294            Compared To What/Hey, That's No Way To Say Goodbye .......................................... 6
79   Atlantic 11481              Only Heaven Can Wait/Back Together Again (featuring Donny Hathaway) ............... 5
*(see also Donny Hathaway)*

## FLACK OFF
80   Sofa                        FLACK OFF EP: COCKTAILS AT SIX ............................................................................... 20

## FLAG OF CONVENIENCE
82   Sire SIR 4057               Life On The Telephone/The Other Man's Sin (no p/s) .................................................. 6
*(see also Steve Diggle, Buzzcocks)*

## FLAIRS
57   Oriole CB 1392              Swing Pretty Mama/I'd Climb The Hills And Mountains .......................................... 500
57   Oriole CB 1392              Swing Pretty Mama/I'd Climb The Hills And Mountains (78) ................................... 100

## LES FLAMBEAUX
71   Mushroom 100 MR 13          LES FLAMBEAUX (LP, 2 different sleeve designs) ...................................................... 30

## FLAME
70   Stateside SS 2183           See The Light/Get Your Mind Made Up ...................................................................... 18
71   Stateside SSL 10312         THE FLAME (LP) .............................................................................................................. 40
*(see also Flames [South Africa], Beach Boys)*

## GEORGE FLAME
76   Seville 1014                You're Gone/Where Did Your Love Come From ............................................................ 8

## FLAME 'N' KING & BOLD ONES
79   Grapevine GRP 123           Ho Happy Day/Ain't Nobody Jivin' ............................................................................. 20

## FLAMES (SOUTH AFRICA)
68   Flame FAN 101/1             Streamliner/Follow The Sun (p/s) ............................................................................... 20
68   Page One FOR(S) 009         BURNING SOUL (LP) ...................................................................................................... 50
*(see also Beach Boys)*

## FLAMES (1)
64   Island WI 130               He's The Greatest/Someone Going To Bawl (both actually by the Maytals) ................ 60
64   Island WI 136               Little Flea/Good Idea (both actually by the Maytals) ................................................ 40
64   Island WI 138               When I Get Home/Neither Silver Nor Gold (both actually by the Maytals) ............... 40
64   Island WI 139               Broadway Jungle/Beat Lied (both actually by the Maytals) ...................................... 70
64   Blue Beat BB 205            Helena Darling/My Darling (both actually by Plamers) ............................................. 20
*(see also Maytals, Vikings)*

## FLAMES (2)
68   Nu Beat NB 020              Mini Really Fit Dem/Soul Train (both actually by Alton Ellis & Flames) .................. 30
69   Nu Beat NB 028              You've Lost Your Date/Little Girl ................................................................................. 20
73   Ackee ACK 528               Feeling Good/Zig Zag ..................................................................................................... 6
*(see also Alton Ellis & Flames, Righteous Flames, Larry Marshall)*

## FLAMING GNOMES
09   Fruits De Mer Crustacean 05   Care Of Cell 44/Love Song With Flute (300 only, purple vinyl) .............................. 30

## FLAMING STARS
95   Vinyl Japan PAD 23          HOSPITAL, HEAVEN OR HELL (EP) ............................................................................... 10
95   Vinyl Japan PAD 28          The Face On The Bar Room Floor/Get Carter (p/s) ....................................................... 5
95   Vinyl Japan PAD 30          MONEY TO BURN (EP) .................................................................................................... 10
96   Vinyl Japan PAD 31          DOWNHILL WITHOUT BRAKES (EP) ............................................................................. 10
96   Vinyl Japan PAD 34          Ten Feet Tall/Spaghetti Junction (p/s) ......................................................................... 5
97   Vinyl Japan PAD 35          Bury My Heart At Pier 13/Down To You (Live In London) (p/s) .................................. 5
97   Vinyl Japan PAD 37          New Hope For The Dead/Are You Being Served (p/s) .................................................... 5
98   Vinyl Japan PAD 59          Sweet Smell Of Success/The Day The Earth Caught Fire (p/s, numbered, 2000 only) ....... 6

# FLAMING LIPS

| | | | |
|---|---|---|---|
| 00 | Vinyl Japan PAD 71 | You Don't Always Want What You Get/Saturday Night Special (p/s) | 6 |
| 01 | Vinyl Japan PAD 73 | Some Things You Don't Forget/Only Tonight (p/s) | 6 |
| 02 | Vinyl Japan PAD 79 | A Little Bit Like you/The Man Who Would Be King (p/s) | 6 |
| 04 | Vinyl Japan PAD 84 | Spilled Your Pint/Sixty Nine (p/s) | 5 |
| 05 | Vinyl Japan PAD 85 | Stranger On The Fifth Floor/New Hope For The Dead (Live In Germany) (p/s) | 5 |
| 96 | Vinyl Japan ASKLP 62 | SONGS FROM THE BAR ROOM FLOOR (LP) | 25 |
| 99 | Vinyl Japan ASKLP 83 | PATHWAY (LP) | 20 |
| 00 | Vinyl Japan ASKLP 121 | A WALK ON THE WIRED SIDE (LP) | 20 |
| 02 | Vinyl Japan ASKLP 139 | SUNSET & VOID (LP) | 20 |
| 04 | Vinyl Japan ASKLP 146 | NAMED AND SHAMED (LP) | 20 |

## FLAMING LIPS

| | | | |
|---|---|---|---|
| 89 | Glitterhouse EFA 40153 | Drug Machine In Heaven/Strychnine/What's So Funny (About Peace, Love And Understanding) (p/s) | 20 |
| 91 | City Slang 04063-05 | Unconsciously Screamin'/Ma, I Didn't Notice/Let Me Be It/Lucifer Rising (clear vinyl, hologram sleeve) | 8 |
| 92 | Warners PRO S 5452 | Ballrooms Of Mars/MR BUNGLE: Sudden Death (promo, grey vinyl, no p/s) | 15 |
| 94 | Warners SAM 1431 | She Don't Use Jelly/Translucent Egg/Turn It On (Bluegrass Version)/The Process (12" promo) | 15 |
| 86 | Enigma 2173-1 | HEAR IT IS (LP with poster) | 15 |
| 89 | Enigma ENVLP523 | TELEPATHIC SURGERY (LP) | 20 |
| 90 | City Slang SLANG 005 | IN A PRIEST DRIVEN AMBULANCE (2-LP) | 18 |
| 03 | Warner Brothers 9362481411 | YOSHIMI BATTLES THE PINK ROBOTS (LP, inner sleeve, pink vinyl) | 30 |
| 06 | Warner Bros. WEA 9362 49966-1 | AT WAR WITH THE MYSTICS (2-LP, one orange & one turquoise LP) | 25 |
| 10 | Warner Bros. 520857-1 | EMBRYONIC (2-LP, blue/yellow vinyl) | 20 |
| 10 | Warner Bros. 523541-1 | DOING THE DARK SIDE OF THE MOON (LP, green vinyl, CD, insert, 500 only) | 20 |

## JOHNNY FLAMINGO

| | | | |
|---|---|---|---|
| 57 | Vogue V 9089 | My Teen-Age Girl/When I Lost You | 100 |
| 57 | Vogue V 9089 | My Teen-Age Girl/When I Lost You (78) | 30 |
| 58 | Vogue V 9100 | So Long/Make Me A Present Of You | 75 |
| 58 | Vogue V 9100 | So Long/Make Me A Present Of You (78) | 40 |

## FLAMINGOS

| | | | |
|---|---|---|---|
| 57 | London HLN 8373 | Would I Be Crying?/Just For A Kick | 600 |
| 57 | London HLN 8373 | Would I Be Crying?/Just For A Kick (78) | 100 |
| 57 | Brunswick 05696 | The Ladder Of Love/Let's Make Up | 500 |
| 57 | Brunswick 05696 | The Ladder Of Love/Let's Make Up (78) | 80 |
| 59 | Top Rank JAR 213 | Love Walked In/Yours | 50 |
| 60 | Top Rank JAR 263 | I Only Have Eyes For You/I Was Such A Fool | 60 |
| 60 | Top Rank JAR 367 | Nobody Loves Me Like You/You, Me And The Sea | 40 |
| 60 | Top Rank JAR 519 | Mio Amore/At Night | 35 |
| 66 | Philips BF 1483 | Boogaloo Party/Nearness Of You | 25 |
| 69 | Philips BF 1786 | Boogaloo Party/Nearness Of You (reissue, in p/s) | 10 |
| 69 | Philips BF 1786 | Boogaloo Party/Nearness Of You (reissue) | 8 |
| 70 | Polydor 2066-007 | Buffalo Soldier/Fontaineau Combustion | 10 |
| 69 | Philips SBL 7906 | HITS NOW AND THEN (LP) | 30 |

## FLAMIN' GROOVIES

| | | | |
|---|---|---|---|
| 71 | Kama Sutra 2013 031 | Teenage Head/Evil-Hearted Ada | 12 |
| 72 | Kama Sutra 2013 042 | Gonna Rock Tonite/Keep A-Knockin'/SHA NA NA: Rock'n'Roll Is Here To Stay/At The Hop/Duke Of Earl | 8 |
| 72 | United Artists UP 35392 | Slow Death/Talahassie Lassie (in promo only p/s) | 40 |
| 72 | United Artists UP 35392 | Slow Death/Talahassie Lassie | 7 |
| 72 | United Artists UP 35464 | Married Woman/Get A Shot Of Rhythm And Blues | 10 |
| 76 | Sire 6198 086 | Don't You Lie To Me/She Said Yeah/Shake Some Action (p/s) | 7 |
| 76 | Sire 6078 602 | Shake Some Action/Teenage Confidential (p/s, 2 different versions of A-side) | 6 |
| 76 | Kama Sutra KSS 707 | Teenage Head/Headin' For The Texas Border | 5 |
| 78 | Sire 6078 619 | Feel A Whole Lot Better/Paint It Black/Shake Some Action (p/s) | 5 |
| 76 | United Artists REM 406 | SLOW DEATH (EP) | 10 |
| 71 | Kama Sutra 2683 003 | FLAMIN' GROOVIES (2-LP) | 20 |
| 76 | Sire 9103 251 | SHAKE SOME ACTION (LP) | 30 |
| 78 | Sire 9103 333 | THE FLAMIN' GROOVIES NOW! (LP) | 15 |

*(see also Mike Wilhelm)*

## FLAMING YOUTH

| | | | |
|---|---|---|---|
| 69 | Fontana TF 1057 | Guide Me Orion/From Now On (Immortal Invisible) | 20 |
| 70 | Fontana 6001 002 | Every Man, Woman And Child/Drifting | 18 |
| 70 | Fontana 6001 003 | From Now On/Space Child | 18 |
| 69 | Fontana STL 5533 | ARK II (LP, with laminated multifold plastic window sleeve) | 150 |
| 69 | Fontana STL 5533 | ARK II (LP, later sleeve pressing with unlaminated multifold plastic window sleeve) | 60 |
| 69 | Fontana STL 5533 | ARK II (LP, gatefold sleeve, white front, black/silver labels) | 50 |

*(see also Genesis, Jackson Heights)*

## FLAMMA-SHERMAN

| | | | |
|---|---|---|---|
| 68 | SNB 55-3488 | No Need To Explain/Bassa Love | 20 |
| 68 | SNB 55-3769 | Love Is In The Air/Super Day | 18 |
| 69 | SNB 55-4142 | Move Me/Where Is He | 18 |
| 69 | SNB 55-4142 | Move Me/Where Is He (DJ copy) | 50 |

## TOMMY FLANAGAN

| | | | |
|---|---|---|---|
| 59 | Esquire 32-156 | THE CATS (LP) | 50 |

## FLANAGAN BROTHERS

| | | | |
|---|---|---|---|
| 58 | Vogue Coral Q 72342 | Salton City/Early One Evening | 20 |

## TOMMY FLANDERS
| | | |
|---|---|---|
| 69 | Verve SVLP 6020 | MOONSTONE (LP) ........25 |

*(see also Blues Project)*

## FLARES
| | | |
|---|---|---|
| 61 | London HLU 9441 | Foot Stompin'/Hotcha Cha-Cha Brown ........25 |
| 63 | London HA-U 8034 | FOOT STOMPIN' HITS (LP) ........75 |

## FLASH
| | | |
|---|---|---|
| 72 | Sovereign SOV 105 | Small Beginnings/Morning Haze ........7 |
| 73 | Sovereign SOV 116 | Watch Your Step/Lifetime ........7 |
| 72 | Sovereign SVNA 7251 | FLASH (LP, laminated outer gatefold sleeve) ........35 |
| 72 | Sovereign SVNA 7255 | FLASH IN THE CAN (LP, in unissued 'band in studio' proof sleeve) ........25 |
| 72 | Sovereign SVNA 7255 | FLASH IN THE CAN (LP, gatefold sleeve) ........20 |
| 73 | Sovereign SVNA 7260 | OUT OF OUR HANDS (LP, gatefold sleeve) ........30 |

*(see also Peter Banks, Yes)*

## FLASH & BOARD OF DIRECTORS
| | | |
|---|---|---|
| 68 | Bell BLL 1007 | Busy Signal/Love Ain't Easy ........10 |

## FLASH CADILLAC & THE CONTINENTAL KIDS
| | | |
|---|---|---|
| 75 | Private Stock PVT 29 | Hot Summer Girls/Time Will Tell ........6 |
| 77 | Private Stock PVT 92 | See My Baby Jive/Brown Water (Apocalypse Blues) ........6 |
| 75 | Private Stock PVLP 1002 | SONS OF THE BEACHES (LP) ........15 |

## FLASH CATS
| | | |
|---|---|---|
| 82 | Lark LS 1 | Tonight/I Want You/Gene Vincent Can't Be Dead (p/s) ........7 |

## FLASHPOINT
| | | |
|---|---|---|
| 87 | Private pressing FP 01 | NO POINT OF REFERENCE (LP) ........40 |

## FLAT EARTH SOCIETY
| | | |
|---|---|---|
| 83 | Psycho PSYCHO 17 | WALEECO (LP) ........20 |

## FLATMATES
| | | |
|---|---|---|
| 86 | Subway Organisation SUBWAY 6 | I Could Be In Heaven/Tell Me Why/So In Love With You (foldaround p/s with insert in poly bag) ........6 |

## LINDA FLAVELL
| | | |
|---|---|---|
| 66 | Decca F 12312 | And The Trouble With Me Is You/Over And Over ........12 |

## FLAVOR
| | | |
|---|---|---|
| 68 | Direction 58-3597 | Sally Had A Party/Shop Around ........15 |

## FLAVOUR
| | | |
|---|---|---|
| 76 | Tamla Motown TMG 1079 | Don't Freeze Up/Instrumental Version ........6 |

## LOS FLECHAZOS
| | | |
|---|---|---|
| 94 | Detour Records DRO 13 | Try It/You Drove Me Crazy (p/s, 100 red vinyl) ........7 |

## FLEE REKEERS
| | | |
|---|---|---|
| 60 | Triumph RGM 1008 | Green Jeans/You Are My Sunshine (as Fabulous Flee-Rakkers) ........20 |
| 60 | Top Rank JAR 431 | Green Jeans/You Are My Sunshine (reissue, as Fabulous Flea-Rakkers) ........30 |
| 60 | Pye 7N 15288 | Sunday Date/Shiftless Sam ........20 |
| 60 | Pye 7N 15326 | Blue Tango/Bitter Rice ........10 |
| 61 | Piccadilly 7N 35006 | Lone Rider/Miller Like Wow ........10 |
| 62 | Piccadilly 7N 35048 | Stage To Cimarron/Twistin' The Chestnuts ........10 |
| 62 | Piccadilly 7N 35081 | Sunburst/Black Buffalo ........10 |
| 63 | Piccadilly 7N 35109 | Fireball/Fandango ........10 |
| 61 | Pye NEP 24141 | THE FABULOUS FLEE-REKKERS (EP) ........40 |
| 91 | C5 C5 564 | JOE MEEK'S FABULOUS FLEE REKKERS (LP) ........15 |

## FLEETWOOD MAC
### SINGLES
| | | |
|---|---|---|
| 67 | Blue Horizon 57-3051 | I Believe My Time Ain't Long/Rambling Pony (as Peter Green's Fleetwood Mac, with p/s) ........100 |
| 67 | Blue Horizon 57-3051 | I Believe My Time Ain't Long/Rambling Pony (as Peter Green's Fleetwood Mac) ........20 |
| 68 | Blue Horizon 57-3138 | Black Magic Woman/The Sun Is Shining ........10 |
| 68 | Blue Horizon 57-3139 | Need Your Love So Bad/Stop Messin' Around ........10 |
| 68 | Blue Horizon 57-3145 | Albatross/Jigsaw Puzzle Blues ........6 |
| 69 | Immediate IM 080 | Man Of The World/EARL VINCE & VALIANTS: Somebody's Gonna Get Their Head Kicked In Tonight ........10 |
| 69 | Blue Horizon 57-3157 | Need Your Love So Bad/Black Magic Woman (unissued) ........0 |
| 69 | Blue Horizon 57-3157 | Black Magic Woman/No Place To Go (unissued) ........0 |
| 69 | Blue Horizon 57-3157 | Need Your Love So Bad/No Place To Go ........6 |
| 69 | CBS 3051 | I Believe My Time Ain't Long/Rambling Pony (reissue) ........6 |
| 69 | Reprise RS 27000 | Oh Well (Parts 1 & 2) ........6 |
| 70 | Reprise RS 27007 | The Green Manalishi (With The Two-Prong Crown)/ World In Harmony (initially with p/s) ........30 |
| 70 | Reprise RS 27007 | The Green Manalishi (With The Two-Prong Crown)/ World In Harmony ........8 |
| 71 | Reprise RS 27010 | Dragonfly/The Purple Dancer ........5 |
| 71 | CBS/Blue Horizon 3145 | Albatross/Jigsaw Puzzle Blues (reissue) ........5 |
| 72 | Reprise K 14194 | Spare Me A Little Of Your Love/Sunny Side Of Heaven ........5 |
| 73 | Reprise K 14280 | Did You Ever Love Me?/The Derelict ........5 |
| 73 | CBS 1722 | Black Magic Woman/Stop Messin' Around ........5 |
| 73 | CBS 8306 | Albatross/Need Your Love So Bad (p/s, 'Hall Of Fame Hits' reissue) ........5 |
| 74 | Reprise K 14315 | For Your Love/Hypnotised ........5 |
| 75 | Reprise K 14388 | Heroes Are Hard To Find/Born Enchanter ........5 |
| 75 | DJM DJS 10620 | Man Of The World/DANNY KIRWAN: Second Chapter ........5 |
| 75 | Reprise K 14403 | Warm Ways/Blue Letter (with p/s) ........5 |
| 76 | Reprise K 14413 | Over My Head (Edit)/I'm So Afraid ........5 |
| 76 | Reprise K 14430 | Rhiannon/Sugar Daddy (with p/s) ........6 |

## ALBUMS

| | | | |
|---|---|---|---|
| 68 | Blue Horizon 7-63200 | PETER GREEN'S FLEETWOOD MAC (mono, laminated front cover) | 90 |
| 68 | Blue Horizon 7-63200 | PETER GREEN'S FLEETWOOD MAC (stereo, with stereo sticker, laminated front) | 80 |
| 68 | Blue Horizon 7-63205 | MR. WONDERFUL (LP, mono, gatefold sleeve) | 80 |
| 68 | (S)7-63205 | MR. WONDERFUL (LP, stereo, gatefold sleeve) | 50 |
| 69 | Blue Horizon S 7-63215 | THE PIOUS BIRD OF GOOD OMEN | 40 |
| 69 | Reprise RSLP 9000 | THEN PLAY ON (gatefold sleeve, 'steamboat' label) | 80 |
| 70 | Reprise RSLP 9004 | KILN HOUSE (gatefold sleeve, with insert) | 35 |
| 70 | Reprise RSLP 9004 | KILN HOUSE (gatefold sleeve, without insert) | 20 |
| 71 | CBS Blue Horizon 63875 | THE ORIGINAL FLEETWOOD MAC | 30 |
| 72 | Reprise K 44181 | BARE TREES | 20 |
| 77 | Reprise K 54043 | FLEETWOOD MAC (white vinyl with lyric sheet) | 18 |
| 77 | Warner Bros. K56344 | RUMOURS (LP, with gatefold lyric insert) | 35 |
| 77 | Warner Bros K 56344 | RUMOURS (white vinyl with lyric sheet) | 18 |
| 79 | Warner Bros. K66088 | TUSK (2-LP, embossed sleeve, 4 inners) | 18 |

(see also Peter Green, Buckingham-Nicks, Jeremy Spencer, Christine Perfect, Danny Kirwan, John Mayall, Otis Spann, Eddie Boyd, Duster Bennett, Chicken Shack, Shotgun Express, Bo Street Runners, Cheynes, Tramp, Brunning Hall Sunflower Blues Band)

## FLEETWOODS

| | | | |
|---|---|---|---|
| 59 | London HLU 8841 | Come Softly To Me/I Care So Much | 8 |
| 59 | London HLU 4003 | Come Softly To Me/I Care So Much (stereo export issue) | 15 |
| 59 | London HLU 8895 | Graduation's Here/Oh Lord Let It Be Me | 10 |
| 59 | Top Rank JAR 202 | Mr. Blue/You Mean Everything To Me | 10 |
| 60 | Top Rank JAR 294 | Outside My Window/Magic Star (in p/s) | 20 |
| 60 | Top Rank JAR 294 | Outside My Window/Magic Star | 10 |
| 60 | Top Rank JAR 383 | Runaround/Truly Do | 10 |
| 61 | London HLG 9341 | Tragedy/Little Miss Sad One | 10 |
| 61 | London HLG 9426 | He's The Great Imposter/Poor Little Girl | 10 |
| 62 | Liberty LIB 62 | They Tell Me It's Summer/Lovers By Night Strangers By Day | 10 |
| 63 | Liberty LIB 75 | Goodnight My Love Pleasant Dreams/Jimmy Beware | 10 |
| 64 | Liberty LIB 93 | Ruby Red Baby Blue/Lonesome Town | 10 |
| 65 | Liberty LIB 10191 | Almost There/Before And After (Losing You) | 10 |
| 60 | Top Rank BUY 028 | MR BLUE (LP, with 3 tracks by Little Bill & Bluenotes, Frantics and Bonnie Guitar) | 20 |
| 61 | London HA-G 2388 | SOFTLY (LP, mono) | 20 |
| 61 | London SAH-G 6188 | SOFTLY (LP, stereo) | 20 |
| 61 | London HA-G 2419 | DEEP IN A DREAM (LP) | 20 |

## DEBBIE FLEMING

| | | | |
|---|---|---|---|
| 75 | Bradleys BRAD 7519 | Long Gone/All About You | 6 |

## HELEN FLEMING

| | | | |
|---|---|---|---|
| 66 | Blue Beat BB 341 | Eve's Ten Commandments/Don't Take Your Love Away | 15 |

## JOY FLEMING

| | | | |
|---|---|---|---|
| 75 | Antic K 11518 | A Bridge Of Love/Divorcee | 10 |
| 76 | Private Stock PVT 54 | Are You Ready For Love/Alabama Standby | 10 |

## RAY FLEMING

| | | | |
|---|---|---|---|
| 63 | MGM MGM 1196 | I'm Glad I Have You/Humpty Dumpty | 10 |

## WADE FLEMONS

| | | | |
|---|---|---|---|
| 59 | Top Rank JAR 206 | Slow Motion/Walking By The River | 12 |
| 60 | Top Rank JAR 327 | What's Happening?/Goodnight, It's Time To Go | 12 |
| 60 | Top Rank JAR 371 | Easy Lovin'/Woops Now | 12 |

## FLESH

| | | | |
|---|---|---|---|
| 79 | Dancing Industries DI 001 | My Boy Lollipop/Flesh | 7 |

## FLESHEATERS

| | | | |
|---|---|---|---|
| 81 | Initial IRC 007 | A MINUTE TO PRAY, A SECOND TO DIE (LP) | 18 |

## FLESH VOLCANO

| | | | |
|---|---|---|---|
| 87 | Some Bizzare SLUT 1 | Slut/The Universal Cesspool/Bruisin' Chain (12", p/s) | 10 |

(see also Marc Almond, Foetus)

## AMELIA FLETCHER

| | | | |
|---|---|---|---|
| 91 | Fierce FRIGHT 052 | Can You Keep A Secret/Wrap My Arms Around Him (p/s) | 8 |

## DARROW FLETCHER

| | | | |
|---|---|---|---|
| 66 | London HLU 10024 | The Pain Gets A Little Deeper/My Judgement Day | 75 |
| 66 | London HLU 10024 | The Pain Gets A Little Deeper/My Judgement Day (DJ copy) | 150 |

## DON FLETCHER

| | | | |
|---|---|---|---|
| 66 | Vocalion VP 9271 | Two Wrongs Don't Make A Right/I'm So Glad | 25 |

## GUY FLETCHER

| | | | |
|---|---|---|---|
| 68 | Pye 7N 17523 | Keep On Loving Me/Loving Bird | 10 |
| 69 | Pye 7N 17765 | Magic Woman/All Fall Down | 6 |
| 71 | Philips 6303013 | GUY FLETCHER (LP, gatefold sleeve, black/silver lables) | 20 |

## LINDA FLETCHER

| | | | |
|---|---|---|---|
| 78 | Ariola AHA 532 | Hush/Fadin Away | 6 |

## FLEUR-DE-LYS

| | | | |
|---|---|---|---|
| 65 | Immediate IM 020 | Moondreams/Wait For Me | 300 |
| 66 | Immediate IM 032 | Circles/So Come On | 800 |
| 66 | Polydor 56124 | Mud In Your Eye/I've Been Trying | 800 |
| 67 | Polydor 56200 | I Can See A Light/Prodigal Son | 100 |
| 68 | Polydor 56251 | The Gong With The Luminous Nose/Hammer Head | 300 |
| 68 | Atlantic 584 193 | Stop Crossing The Bridge/Brick By Brick (Stone By Stone) | 65 |
| 69 | Atlantic 584 243 | Liar/One Girl City | 200 |

(see also John Bromley, Terry Durham, Tony & Tandy, Sharon Tandy, Rupert's People, Shyster, Quotations, Chocolate Frog, Gordon Haskell, Waygood Ellis)

## FLEURITY
| | | | |
|---|---|---|---|
| 94 | Aesthetic Death ADEP 001 | A DARKER SHADE OF EVIL EP (p/s) | 20 |
| 08 | Aesthetic Death ADLP 001 | MIN TID SKAL KOMME (2-LP, numbered sleeve, insert, 600 only) | 18 |

## VIC FLICK SOUND
| | | | |
|---|---|---|---|
| 70 | Chapter One CH 136 | Hang On/Wonderful World | 15 |
| 71 | Chapter One CH 155 | Quest For Love/Clarice | 6 |

## FLIES
| | | | |
|---|---|---|---|
| 66 | Decca F 12533 | I'm Not Your Stepping Stone/Talk To Me | 175 |
| 67 | Decca F 12594 | House Of Love/It Had To Be You | 80 |
| 68 | RCA RCA 1757 | The Magic Train/Gently As You Feel | 70 |

## FLIGHT 77
| | | | |
|---|---|---|---|
| 82 | Flight 77 | Looking For The Aliens/Stranger (p/s) | 25 |

## MICK FLINN BAND
| | | | |
|---|---|---|---|
| 78 | EMI EMI 2805 | Doin' It Right/Do What You Wanna Do | 20 |

(see also Mixtures)

## FLINT
| | | | |
|---|---|---|---|
| 03 | Cool Kills 989009-3 | ASTEROIDS (1-track 10", neon pink vinyl with inner sleeve) | 10 |

## SHELBY FLINT
| | | | |
|---|---|---|---|
| 61 | Warner Bros WB 30 | Angel On My Shoulder/Somebody | 12 |
| 66 | London HLT 10068 | Cast Your Fate To The Wind/The Lilly | 20 |

## FLINTSTONES
| | | | |
|---|---|---|---|
| 64 | HMV POP 1266 | Safari/Work Out | 20 |

## BUNNY FLIP
| | | | |
|---|---|---|---|
| 72 | Pressure Beat PB 5510 | Shanky Dog (actually "Skanky Dog" by Winston Scotland)/JOE GIBBS & NOW GENERATION: Boney Dog | 10 |

(see also Winston Scotland)

## FLIP & DATELINERS
| | | | |
|---|---|---|---|
| 64 | HMV POP 1359 | My Johnny Doesn't Come Around Anymore/Please Listen To Me | 60 |

(see also Vivienne Chering)

## FLIPPER
| | | | |
|---|---|---|---|
| 81 | Alt. Tentacles VIRUS 8 | Ha Ha Ha/Love Canal (p/s, with insert) | 15 |
| 82 | Subterranean SUB UK1 | ALBUM GENERIC FLIPPER (LP) | 25 |

## FLIPS
| | | | |
|---|---|---|---|
| 62 | London HLU 9490 | Rockin' Twist/Oh, You Beautiful Doll — Twist | 5 |

## FLIRTATIONS
| | | | |
|---|---|---|---|
| 68 | Deram DM 195 | Someone Out There/How Can You Tell Me? | 10 |
| 68 | Deram DM 216 | Nothing But A Heartache/Christmas Time Is Here Again | 25 |
| 69 | Deram DM 252 | What's Good About Goodbye My Love?/Once I Had A Love | 8 |
| 70 | Deram DM 281 | Keep On Searchin'/Moma I'm Coming Home | 8 |
| 70 | Deram DM 295 | Can't Stop Loving You/Everybody Needs Somebody | 8 |
| 71 | Deram DM 329 | Give Me Love/This Must Be The End Of The Line | 8 |
| 72 | Deram DM 351 | Need Your Lovin'/I Wanna Be There | 8 |
| 71 | Polydor 2058 167 | Little Darlin'/Take Me In Your Arms And Love Me | 20 |
| 73 | Mojo 2092 058 | Why Didn't I Think Of That?/Oh Mia Bamba | 6 |
| 72 | Polydor 2058 249 | Love A Little Longer/Hold On To Me Babe | 8 |
| 74 | Polydor 2058 295 | Dirty Work/No Such Thing As A Miracle | 6 |
| 75 | RCA 2554 | Mr. Universe/Somebody Cares For Me | 7 |
| 98 | London Traffic TRAF 1 | Nothing But A Heartache (1-sided, reissue promo, 500 only) | 40 |
| 69 | Deram DML/SML 1046 | SOUNDS LIKE THE FLIRTATIONS (LP) | 40 |
| 75 | RCA SF8448 | LOVE MAKES THE WORLD GO ROUND (LP) | 15 |

(see also Gypsies)

## FLO & EDDIE
| | | | |
|---|---|---|---|
| 73 | Reprise K 14261 | Afterglow/Carlos And De Bull | 5 |
| 72 | Reprise K 44201 | THE PHLORESCENT LEECH AND EDDIE (LP) | 15 |
| 73 | Reprise K 44234 | FLO AND EDDIE (LP) | 15 |

(see also Turtles, Frank Zappa/Mothers Of Invention)

## FLOATING BRIDGE
| | | | |
|---|---|---|---|
| 69 | Liberty LBS 83271 | FLOATING BRIDGE (LP) | 100 |

## FLOATING OPERA
| | | | |
|---|---|---|---|
| 74 | DJM DJS 321 | Keep On Streaking/Home Run | 20 |

## FLOCK
| | | | |
|---|---|---|---|
| 70 | CBS 4932 | Tired Of Waiting For You/Store Bought — Store Thought | 15 |
| 69 | CBS 63733 | THE FLOCK (LP, orange label) | 15 |
| 70 | CBS 64055 | DINOSAUR SWAMPS (LP, orange label, gatefold sleeve) | 20 |

(see also Mahavishnu Orchestra)

## THE FLOOD
| | | | |
|---|---|---|---|
| 84 | Midnight Music DING 7 | Cold Cold World/2 Shots Of Jealousy | 10 |

## FLORENCE AND THE MACHINE
| | | | |
|---|---|---|---|
| 08 | Moshi Moshi MOMO15 | Kiss With A Fist/Hospital Beds (p/s) | 15 |
| 09 | Moshi Moshi 2710003 | Rabbit Heart (Raise It Up)/Are You Hurting The One You Love? (p/s) | 10 |
| 08 | Moshi Moshi 171 | Dog Days Are Over/You've Got The Love (p/s) | 15 |
| 09 | Moshi Moshi 2718895 | Drumming Song (Acoustic)/My Boy Builds A Coffin (Acoustic) | 10 |
| 09 | Moshi Moshi 2726062 | You've Got The Love/You'Ve Got The Love (Jamie XX Re-Write) (p/s) | 10 |
| 10 | Moshi Moshi 2736273 | Dog Days Are Over/Dog Days Are Over (Optimo Mix) | 15 |

MINT VALUE £

| | | | |
|---|---|---|---|
| 10 | Moshi Moshi 2744152 | Cosmic Love/Cosmic Love (Isa Machine Mix) | 15 |
| 11 | Vinyl Factory VF 035 | Shake It Out/Shake It Out (Weekend Remix) (12" white vinyl, hand numbered, 500 copies) | 60 |
| 11 | Vinyl Factory VF-04X | Never Let Me Go/Never Let Me Go (Clams Casino Mix) (12" white vinyl, hand numbered, 500 only) | 60 |
| 11 | Vinyl Factory VF-04Y | Spectrum/Spectrum (Calvin Harris Mix)/Spectrum (Aluna George Mix)/Spectrum (Mary Jane Coles Mix) (12" white vinyl hand numbered, 500 only) | 70 |
| 12 | Universal/Talenthouse S76 | Only If For A Night (1-sided, 100 only) | 60 |
| 12 | Vinyl Factory VF 038 | No Light, No Light/No Light, No Light (DAS Mix) (12" white vinyl, hand numbered, 500 only) | 70 |

### FLORIBUNDA ROSE
| | | | |
|---|---|---|---|
| 67 | Piccadilly 7N 35408 | One Way Street/Linda Loves Linda | 60 |

*(see also Scrugg, John T. Kongos)*

### FLOWCHART
| | | | |
|---|---|---|---|
| 90s | Enraptured RAPT 4527 | NO. 7 IN THE STRESS FREE SERIES: Gip Part One/Gip Part 2 (in box) | 6 |

### FLOWERPOT MEN
| | | | |
|---|---|---|---|
| 67 | Deram DM 142 | Let's Go To San Francisco (Parts 1 & 2) | 5 |
| 67 | Deram DM 160 | A Walk In The Sky/Am I Losing You? | 8 |
| 68 | Deram DM 183 | A Man Without A Woman/You Can Never Be Wrong | 8 |
| 68 | Page One POF 065 | Mighty Quinn/Voices From The Sky | 10 |
| 69 | Deram DM 248 | In A Moment Of Madness/Young Birds Fly | 10 |

*(see also Ivy League, Friends, Carter-Lewis & Southerners, Edison Lighthouse, Fat Mattress, Gordon Haskell, Kestrels, One & One)*

### FLOWERS
| | | | |
|---|---|---|---|
| 79 | Pop Aural POP 1 | Confessions/(Life) After Dark | 5 |

### FLOWERS FOR AGATHA
| | | | |
|---|---|---|---|
| 85 | Leeds Independent 12 LIL 3 | THE FREEDOM CURSE EP (12" p/s) | 12 |
| 85 | Off Beat OB 10 | Presentation/The Thickest Head (p/s) | 20 |
| 86 | Leeds Independent 12 LIL 8 | YOUNG FOOLISH OLD AND STUPID EP (12" p/s) | 15 |

### FLOWERS & FROLICS
| | | | |
|---|---|---|---|
| 77 | Free Reed FRR 016 | BEES ON HORSEBACK (LP, featuring June Tabor & Bob Davenport) | 35 |

### FLOWERS IN THE DUSTBIN
| | | | |
|---|---|---|---|
| 84 | All The Madmen MAD 7 | FREAKS RUN WILD IN THE DISCO (12" EP) | 15 |
| 85 | Mortarhate MORT 16 | Nails Of The Heart/All Fools Day/The Reason Why | 12 |
| 86 | Cold Harbour COLD 1002 | Lick My Crazy Colours!/The Continuing Tragedy Of Mr. Smith/Stranger In A Strange Land | 12 |

### LLOYD FLOWERS & RECO'S RHYTHM GROUP
| | | | |
|---|---|---|---|
| 62 | Blue Beat BB 88 | I'm Going Home/Lover's Town | 15 |

### (LLOYD) FLOWERS & ALVIN (RANGLIN)
| | | | |
|---|---|---|---|
| 72 | Explosion EX 2067 | Howdy And Tenky/SHORTY PERRY: Sprinkle Some Water | 7 |
| 72 | Grape GR 3028 | In De Pum Pum/MAYTONES: If Loving You Was Wrong | 10 |
| 72 | Bullet BU 512 | Howdy And Tenky/SHORTY PERRY: Sprinkle Some Water | 7 |
| 73 | Duke DU 150 | Rastaman Going Back Home/LITTLE YOUTH: Barble Dove Skank | 6 |

### FLOWERS OF EVIL
| | | | |
|---|---|---|---|
| 82 | Marching Men MAME 001 | First Blood/Joy (p/s) | 20 |

### PHIL FLOWER(S)
| | | | |
|---|---|---|---|
| 69 | A&M AMS 766 | Like A Rolling Stone/Keep On Sockin' It Children | 20 |

### FLOWER SERMON
| | | | |
|---|---|---|---|
| 92 | Rough Trade 45REV 13 | Sugar Lullaby (p/s with insert) | 8 |

### FLOWER SHOPPE
| | | | |
|---|---|---|---|
| 72 | Polydor 2066 096 | You've Come A Long Way/Kill The Monster | 10 |

### FLOWER TRAVELLING BAND
| | | | |
|---|---|---|---|
| 71 | Atlantic 2091 128 | Satori (Enlightment) (Parts 1 & 2) | 20 |

### BOBBY FLOYD
| | | | |
|---|---|---|---|
| 72 | Pama PM 860 | Sound Doctor/YOUNG DILLINGER: Doctor Skank | 20 |

### EDDIE FLOYD
| | | | |
|---|---|---|---|
| 66 | Atlantic 584 041 | Knock On Wood/Got To Make A Comeback | 10 |
| 67 | Stax 601 001 | Raise Your Hand/I've Just Been Feeling Bad (dark blue label) | 10 |
| 67 | Stax 601 001 | Raise Your Hand/I've Just Been Feeling Bad (light blue label) | 8 |
| 67 | London HL 10129 | Set My Soul On Fire/Will I Be The One? | 8 |
| 67 | Speciality SPE 1001 | Never Get Enough Of Your Love/Bye Bye Baby | 8 |
| 67 | Stax 601 016 | Things Get Better/Good Love, Bad Love | 12 |
| 67 | Stax 601 024 | On A Saturday Night/Under My Nose | 12 |
| 68 | Stax 601 035 | Big Bird/Holding On With Both Hands | 12 |
| 68 | Stax STAX 104 | I've Never Found A Girl (To Love Me Like You Do)/I'm Just The Kind Of Fool | 12 |
| 69 | Stax STAX 108 | Bring It On Home To Me/Sweet Things You Do | 7 |
| 69 | Stax STAX 116 | I've Got To Have Your Love/Girl I Love You | 5 |
| 69 | Stax STAX 125 | Don't Tell Your Mama/Consider Me | 5 |
| 70 | Stax STAX 153 | My Girl/Laurie | 5 |
| 72 | Polydor 2025 098 | Yum Yum Yum/I Want Some/Tears Of Joy | 5 |
| 74 | Stax STXS 2005 | Soul Street/The Highway Man | 5 |
| 81 | I-Spy SEE 9 | The Beat Song/London ('I-Spy' sleeve) | 5 |
| 67 | Stax 589 006 | KNOCK ON WOOD (LP) | 35 |
| 68 | Stax (S)XATS 1003 | I'VE NEVER FOUND A GIRL (LP) | 25 |
| 69 | Stax SXATS 1023 | YOU'VE GOT TO HAVE EDDIE (LP) | 20 |
| 70 | Stax SXATS 1036 | CALIFORNIA GIRL (LP) | 20 |

*(see also Falcons, Primettes/Eddie Floyd)*

### FLUDD
| | | | |
|---|---|---|---|
| 75 | Private Stock PVT 30 | What An Animal/Boarding School | 6 |

**FLUFF**
70 DJM DJS 215      Make Believe/Love Machine ...................................................... 12

**FLUTTERS**
70s STEW 101      Haunted Staircase/Something For The Children (p/s) ..................... 10

**FLUX OF PINK INDIANS**
81 Crass 321984/2      NEU SMELL (EP, foldout poster sleeve) ......................................... 12
83 Spiderleg SDL 8      STRIVE TO SURVIVE CAUSING THE LEAST SUFFERING POSSIBLE (LP, with booklet) ........ 20
84 Spiderleg SDL 13      THE FUCKING CUNTS TREAT US LIKE PRICKS (2-LP)................................ 20
*(see also Epileptics, Licks)*

**FLY ON THE WALL**
79 Next Wave NEXT 1      DEVON DUMB (EP, numbered, 1000 only) ...................................... 30

**FLYING BRIX**
80 Modello MHMS 194      BLACK COLOURS EP (p/s, with booket, 500 only) ............................. 20

**FLYING BURRITO BROTHERS**
69 A&M AMS 756      The Train Song/Hot Burrito No. 1 ............................................... 6
70 A&M AMS 794      Older Guys/Down In The Churchyard ........................................... 5
70 A&M AMS 816      Tried So Hard/Lazy Days ........................................................... 5
72 A&M AMS 871      White Line Fever/Colorado ......................................................... 5
69 A&M AML(S) 931      THE GILDED PALACE OF SIN (LP) ................................................. 30
70 A&M AMLS 983      BURRITO DELUXE (LP)................................................................ 18
71 A&M AMLS 64295      THE FLYING BURRITO BROTHERS (LP)............................................ 15
*(see also Byrds, Gram Parsons, Gene Parsons, Stephen Stills & Manassas, Country Gazette, Skip Battin)*

**FLYING CIRCUS**
71 Harvest SHSP 4010      PREPARED IN PEACE (LP, no EMI box on label) .............................. 75

**FLYING COLOURS**
81 No Records NO 1      Abstract Art/Ape Notes (p/s) ...................................................... 25

**FLYING IS EASY**
70 High Key HK1      Stone Cross/Magic Pastures ....................................................... 50

**FLYING LIZARDS**
80 Virgin V2150      FLYING LIZARDS (LP) ................................................................. 20
81 Virgin V2190      FOURTH WALL (LP) ................................................................... 18

**FLYING LOTUS**
07 Warp WAP 228      Reset (12") ............................................................................. 15
10 Warp WAP 195      COSMOGRAMMA (2-LP, plastic sleeves and grease proof sleeve, MP3 download) ....... 18

**FLYING MACHINE**
69 Pye 7N 17722      Smile A Little Smile For Me/Maybe We've Been Loving Too Long........... 7
69 Pye 7N 17722      Baby Make It Soon/Smile A Little Smile For Me ............................... 6
69 Pye 7N 17811      Send My Baby Home Again/Look At Me, Look At Me ....................... 7
70 Pye 7N 17914      Hanging On The Edge Of Sadness/Flying Machine ........................... 7
70 Pye 7N 45001      The Devil Has Possession Of Your Mind/Hey Little Girl.................... 30
70 Pye 7N 45093      Yes I Understand/Pages Of Your Life ........................................... 6
70 Pye NSPL 18328      DOWN TO EARTH WITH THE FLYING MACHINE (LP, blue/black label with logo-banner on top)........ 40
*(see also Pinkertons, Pinkerton's Assorted Colours, Tony Newman)*

**FLYING SAUCER ATTACK**
92 Heartbeat FSA 6      Soaring High/Standing Stone (p/s, 500 only, 1st few with autographed postcards) ....... 25
92 Heartbeat FSA 6      Soaring High/Standing Stone (p/s, 500 only, with various different designs)................. 20
93 Heartbeat FSA 61      Wish/Oceans (p/s, 700 only)....................................................... 20
94 Domino RUG 23      Land Beyond The Sun/Everywhere Was Everything (p/s, hand-painted rear sleeve, 500 only) ..... 6
95 Domino RUG 41      Outdoor Miner/Psychic Driving (p/s)............................................ 5
95 Planet PUNK 008      Beach Red Lullaby/Second Hour (p/s, 1,300 only) .......................... 6
96 Enraptured RAPT 4505      At Night/JESSAMINE: From Hereto And Now Otherwise (500 on clear vinyl) ....... 12
96 Enraptured RAPT 4505      At Night/JESSAMINE: From Hereto And Now Otherwise (2500 on black vinyl) ....... 8
98 Earworm WORMSC 1      Land Beyond The Sun (2-Track Version)/Instrumental For Silence (green vinyl, 500 only) ....... 6
93 Heartbeat FSA 62      FLYING SAUCER ATTACK (LP, 1st pressing, 1,000 only, black and white sleeve, hand numbered, booklet insert) ........ 40
93 FSA FAS 62      FLYING SAUCER ATTACK (LP, 2nd pressing, 923 copies, coloured sleeve, insert)............. 25
93 FSA FAS 62      FLYING SAUCER ATTACK (LP, 3rd pressing, 1,000 only, blue vinyl, stamped white sleeve, photocopied insert) ........ 25
94 Domino WIGLP 12      DISTANCE (LP) ........................................................................ 15
94 Domino WIGLP 20      FURTHER (LP, gatefold sleeve, insert)........................................... 20
95 Domino WIGLP 22      CHORUS (LP, inert) .................................................................. 15
97 Domino WIGLP 38      NEW LANDS (LP) ..................................................................... 20

**FLYING SAUCERS**
75 Harbour HRB 12      Beer, Bourbon and Wine/Teenage Boogie ..................................... 5
76 Alaska ALA 2001      Fabulous/Fish On The Line ......................................................... 6
76 Alaska ALA 2003      Keep On Comming/Shadow Walk................................................. 6
76 Alaska ALA 2009      Oh Carol/I Need Your Love ........................................................ 8
76 Alaska ALA 2014      Texas Calls You Home/Pretty Baby (p/s) ...................................... 6
78 Alaska ALA 2014      Texas Calls You Home/Pretty Baby............................................... 6
91 Rawking Music      THE ROCKING SANDY FORD (LP) ............................................... 25

**FLYING SQUAD**
78 Epic S EPC 6375      Drive On/Baltimore Baby ........................................................... 5
78 Epic S EPC 6542      Backroom Boys (Night After Night)/Tell Me What To Do ................... 5
*(see also Status Quo)*

**STEVE FLYNN**
67 Parlophone R 5625      Mr Rainbow/Let's Live For Tomorrow........................................... 45

| | | | |
|---|---|---|---|
| 68 | Parlophone R 5689 | Your Life And My Life/Come Tomorrow | 10 |

*(see also Mark Wirtz)*

## FLYS

| | | | |
|---|---|---|---|
| 78 | EMI EMI 2747 | Love And A Molotov Cocktail/Can I Crash Here?/Civilisation (p/s) | 12 |
| 78 | EMI EMI 2795 | Fun City/E.C. 4 (p/s) | 10 |
| 78 | EMI EMIY 2867 | Waikiki Beach Refugees/We Don't Mind The Rave (p/s, yellow vinyl) | 10 |
| 79 | EMI EMI 2907 | Beverley/Don't Moonlight On Me (p/s) | 6 |
| 79 | EMI EMI 2936 | Name Dropping/Fly V Fly (p/s, some on green vinyl) | 15 |
| 79 | EMI EMI 2979 | We Are The Lucky Ones/Living In The Sticks (p/s) | 8 |
| 79 | Parlophone R 6030 | 16 Down/Night Creatures/Lois Lane/Today Belongs To Me (p/s) | 5 |
| 77 | Zama ZA 10 EP | BUNCH OF FIVE (33rpm EP, die-cut p/s) | 50 |
| 80 | Parlophone R 6063 | FOUR FROM THE SQUARE (demo copies) | 20 |
| 78 | EMI EMC 3249 | WAIKIKI BEACH REFUGEES (LP) | 15 |

## FLYTE REACTION

| | | | |
|---|---|---|---|
| 91 | Woronzow W0014 | SONGS IN A CIRCLE (LP) | 20 |

## FOALS

| | | | |
|---|---|---|---|
| 06 | Try Harder | Try This On Your Piano/Look At My Furrows Of Worry (700 only, hand-numbered) | 25 |
| 07 | Transgressive TRANS 049 | FOALS LIVE (12" promo, 1000 only p/s) | 25 |
| 07 | Transgressive TRANS 050 | Hummer/Astronauts And All (p/s, 1000 only) | 20 |
| 07 | Transgressive TRANS 053 | Mathletics/Big Big Love (1,500 only) | 20 |
| 08 | Transgressive TRANS 069 | Cassius/The Chronic (p/s) | 5 |
| 08 | Transgressive TRANS 069X | Cassius/A Song For You (p/s) | 5 |
| 08 | Transgressive TRANS 089.5 | Super Inuit/HOLY FUCK: Balloons (die cut sleeve decorated by band, 250 only) | 12 |
| 08 | Transgressive TRANS 071LP | ANTIDOTES (LP, insert, poster, stickered sleeve) | 20 |
| 13 | Warner Bros. 825646521388 | HOLY FIRE (Box set, marbled vinyl LP, CD, DVD, 7", numbered) | 60 |

## GREG FOAT GROUP

| | | | |
|---|---|---|---|
| 11 | Jazzman JMANLP 041 | DARK IS THE SUN (LP) | 40 |

## FOCAL POINT

| | | | |
|---|---|---|---|
| 68 | Deram DM 186 | Love You Forever/Sycamore Sid | 60 |

## FO'C'SLE

| | | | |
|---|---|---|---|
| 72 | Tradition TSC 1 | FROM THE FOREST (LP, 100 copies only) | 25 |

## FOCUS

| | | | |
|---|---|---|---|
| 71 | Polydor 2001 134 | House Of The King/Black Beauty | 5 |
| 71 | Blue Horizon 2094 006 | Hocus Pocus/Janis | 15 |
| 72 | Blue Horizon 2096 008 | Tommy/Focus II | 15 |
| 71 | Polydor 2344 003 | IN AND OUT OF FOCUS (LP, gatefold sleeve) | 15 |
| 71 | Blue Horizon 2096 2931 | MOVING WAVES (LP, 1st pressing, white/blue labels, Matrixes: Side 1, 2931002 A etched (with 2431011 crossed out) A//1 V 420 1 1 2, Side 2 2931002 B etched (243101 stamped not crossed out) B//1 V 420 11 4, Blue Horizon logo on rear of E.J. Group sleeve) | 25 |
| 76 | Harvest SHSP 4068 | SHIP OF MEMORIES (LP) | 15 |
| 73 | Polydor 2442 118 | AT THE RAINBOW (multifold sleeve) | 15 |

*(see also Jan Akkerman, Brainbox, Robin Lent)*

## FOCUS THREE

| | | | |
|---|---|---|---|
| 67 | Columbia DB 8279 | 10,000 Years Behind My Mind/The Sunkeeper | 80 |

## FOETUS UNDER GLASS

| | | | |
|---|---|---|---|
| 85 | Self Immolation. WOMB S201 | Spite Your Face/OKFM (p/s) | 15 |

*(see also You've Got Foetus On Your Breath, Philip & His Foetus Vibrations, Scraping Foetus Off The Wheel,*

## FOGCUTTERS

| | | | |
|---|---|---|---|
| 64 | Liberty LIB 55793 | Cry Cry Cry/You Say | 15 |

## JOHN FOGERTY

| | | | |
|---|---|---|---|
| 74 | Fantasy FTC 111 | Comin' Down The Road/Ricochet | 5 |
| 75 | Fantasy FTC 119 | Rockin' All Over The World/The Wall | 5 |
| 75 | Fantasy FTC 120 | Almost Saturday Night/Sea Cruise | 5 |
| 76 | Fantasy FTC 133 | You Got The Magic/Evil Thing | 5 |

*(see also Creedence Clearwater Revival, Blue Ridge Rangers)*

## TOM FOGERTY

| | | | |
|---|---|---|---|
| 71 | United Artists UP 35264 | Goodbye Media Man (Parts 1 & 2) | 5 |
| 72 | Fantasy F 680 | Cast The First Stone/Lady Of Fatima | 5 |
| 73 | Fantasy FTC 109 | Joyful Resurrection/Heartbeat | 5 |

*(see also Creedence Clearwater Revival, Ruby)*

## FOGG

| | | | |
|---|---|---|---|
| 74 | EMI EMI 2182 | Water In My Wine/Just Like Me | 8 |
| 75 | Warner Bros. K16622 | Rock N Roll Star/You Got Something | 6 |

## FOGGY

| | | | |
|---|---|---|---|
| 72 | York SYK 534 | How Come The Sun/Take Your Time | 10 |
| 73 | York SYK 542 | Kitty Starr/She's Far Away (p/s) | 15 |
| 73 | York SYK 542 | Kitty Star/She's far Away (no p/s) | 10 |
| 72 | York FYK 411 | SIMPLE GIFTS (LP, with insert, featuring Strawbs) | 30 |
| 75 | Canon CNN 5759 | PATCHWORK (LP) | 20 |

*(see also Strawbs, Foggy Dew-O)*

## FOGGY DEW-O

| | | | |
|---|---|---|---|
| 68 | Decca F 12776 | Reflections/Grandfather's Clock | 8 |
| 71 | York SYK 503 | Me And Bobby McGee/Feelin' Groovy | 6 |
| 68 | Decca LK/SKL 4940 | THE FOGGY DEW-O (LP, blue/silver labels with large unboxed logo) | 25 |
| 70 | Decca LK/SKL 5035 | BORN TO TAKE THE HIGHWAY (LP, blue/silver label with small boxed logo) | 15 |

*(see also Strawbs, Foggy)*

## FOGHAT
| | | | |
|---|---|---|---|
| 72 | Bearsville K15501 | What A Shame / Hole To Hide In | 6 |
| 74 | Bearsville K15511 | Long Way To Go / Ride Ride Ride | 6 |
| 74 | Bearsville K15517 | Step Outside (edit) /Mabellene | 5 |
| 76 | Bearsville K15522 | Slow Ride (edit) / Save Your Loving | 5 |
| 77 | Bearsville K15537 | I Just Want To Make Love To You (live edit) / Fool For The City (live edit) | 5 |
| 79 | Bearsville WIP6582 | Third Time Lucky / Somebody's Been Sleeping In My Bed | 5 |
| 72 | Bearsville K45503 | FOGHAT (LP) | 20 |

*(see also Black Cat Bones, Warren Philips & The Rockets)*

## ELLEN FOLEY (& CLASH)
| | | | |
|---|---|---|---|
| 81 | Epic EPC A 9522 | The Shuttered Palace/Beautiful Waste Of Time (p/s) | 6 |
| 81 | Epic EPC A 1160 | Torchlight/Game Of A Man (p/s) | 6 |
| 81 | Epic SEPC 84809 | SPIRIT OF ST. LOUIS (LP, with inner sleeve) | 15 |

*(see also Clash)*

## RED FOLEY
| | | | |
|---|---|---|---|
| 54 | Brunswick 05321 | Skinnie Minnie (Fishtail)/Thank You For Calling | 8 |
| 55 | Brunswick 05508 | Croce Di Oro (Cross Of Gold) (with Betty Foley)/The Night Watch | 8 |
| 55 | Brunswick 05363 | Hearts Of Stone/RED FOLEY & BETTY FOLEY: Never | 18 |

*(see also Roberta Lee)*

## RED FOLEY & ERNEST TUBB
| | | | |
|---|---|---|---|
| 55 | Brunswick OE 9148 | COUNTRY DOUBLE DATE (EP, with Minnie Pearl) | 15 |

*(see also Ernest Tubb)*

## SIMON FOLEY
| | | | |
|---|---|---|---|
| 77 | Look LKLP 6324 | TO STRIVE WITH PRINCES (LP, with booklet) | 20 |

## FOLKAL POINT
| | | | |
|---|---|---|---|
| 72 | Midas MR 003 | FOLKAL POINT (LP) | 1500 |

## FOLK DEVILS
| | | | |
|---|---|---|---|
| 84 | Ganges RAY 1 | Hank Turns Blue/Chewin' The Fat (with p/s) | 15 |
| 84 | Ganges RAY 1 | Hank Turns Blue/Chewin' The Fat | 8 |

## CALVIN FOLKES
| | | | |
|---|---|---|---|
| 63 | Rio R 5 | Someone/Kentucky Home | 10 |
| 63 | Rio R 8 | You'll Never Know/Is It Time? | 10 |
| 64 | Port-O-Jam PJ 4117 | My Bonnie/What A Day | 12 |
| 64 | Port-O-Jam PJ 4118 | Hello Everybody/IRVING SIX: King's Boogie | 15 |

## FOLKLANDERS
| | | | |
|---|---|---|---|
| 60s | Urban PB 001 | TWO LITTLE FISHES (EP) | 10 |

## FOLKLORE
| | | | |
|---|---|---|---|
| 77 | Tank BSS 210 | ROOM FOR COMPANY (LP) | 20 |

## FOLK(S) BROTHERS
| | | | |
|---|---|---|---|
| 61 | Blue Beat BB 30 | Carolina/I Met A Man (original, blue label, as Folks Brothers) | 18 |
| 60s | Fab BB 30 | Carolina (as Folks Brothers)/ERIC 'HUMPTY DUMPTY' MORRIS: Humpty Dumpty | 7 |
| 70s | Blue Beat BB 30 | Carolina/I Met A Man (reissue, white label, as Folk Brothers) | 6 |

## FOLK SONG CLUB
| | | | |
|---|---|---|---|
| 65 | white label (no cat. no.) | IMPERIAL COLLEGE (LP, private pressing) | 100 |

## EDDIE FONTAINE
| | | | |
|---|---|---|---|
| 55 | HMV 7M 304 | Rock Love/All My Love Belongs To You (with Neal Hefti & Excels) | 150 |
| 55 | HMV B 10852 | Rock Love/All My Love Belongs To You (with Neal Hefti & Excels) (78) | 20 |
| 56 | Brunswick 05624 | Cool It, Baby/Into Each Life Some Rain Must Fall | 100 |
| 56 | Brunswick 05624 | Cool It, Baby/Into Each Life Some Rain Must Fall (78) | 20 |
| 58 | London HLM 8711 | Nothin' Shakin' (But The Leaves On The Trees)/Don't Ya Know | 50 |

## FONTAINES
| | | | |
|---|---|---|---|
| 87 | 51st Parallel FONT 1 | I Want Everything/Bernadette (p/s) | 30 |

## ARLENE FONTANA
| | | | |
|---|---|---|---|
| 59 | Pye International 7N 25010 | I'm In Love/Easy | 7 |

## WAYNE FONTANA & THE MINDBENDERS
| | | | |
|---|---|---|---|
| 63 | Fontana TF 404 | Hello! Josephine/Road Runner | 25 |
| 63 | Fontana TF 418 | For You, For You/Love Potion No.9 | 15 |
| 64 | Fontana TF 436 | Little Darlin'/Come Dance With Me | 20 |
| 64 | Fontana TF 451 | Stop Look And Listen/Duke Of Earl | 10 |
| 64 | Fontana TF 497 | Um, Um, Um, Um, Um, Um/First Taste Of Love | 5 |
| 65 | Fontana TF 535 | The Game Of Love/Since You've Been Gone | 6 |
| 65 | Fontana TF 579 | It's Just A Little Bit Too Late/Long Time Comin' | 10 |
| 65 | Fontana TF 611 | She Needs Love/Like I Did | 8 |
| 69 | Fontana H 1022 | Um, Um, Um, Um, Um, Um/The Game Of Love (p/s) | 8 |
| 64 | Fontana TE 17421 | ROAD RUNNER (EP) | 50 |
| 64 | Fontana TE 17435 | UM, UM, UM, UM, UM, UM (EP) | 20 |
| 65 | Fontana TE 17449 | THE GAME OF LOVE (EP) | 15 |
| 65 | Fontana TE 17453 | WALKING ON AIR (EP) | 40 |
| 64 | Fontana TL 5230 | WAYNE FONTANA AND THE MINDBENDERS (LP) | 60 |
| 65 | Fontana TL 5257 | ERIC, RICK, WAYNE, BOB — IT'S WAYNE FONTANA AND THE MINDBENDERS (LP) | 65 |
| 67 | Wing WL 1166 | WAYNE FONTANA AND THE MINDBENDERS (LP, reissue) | 15 |

*(see also Wayne Fontana, Mindbenders)*

## WAYNE FONTANA
| | | | |
|---|---|---|---|
| 65 | Fontana TF 642 | It Was Easier To Hurt Her/You Made Me What I Am Today | 10 |
| 66 | Fontana TF 684 | Come On Home/My Eyes Break Out In Tears | 5 |
| 66 | Fontana TF 737 | Goodbye Bluebird/The Sun's So Hot Today | 6 |
| 66 | Fontana TF 770 | Pamela Pamela/Something Keeps Calling Me Back | 6 |

Rare Record Price Guide 2018

# FONTANE SISTERS

| | | | |
|---|---|---|---|
| 67 | Fontana TF 827 | 24 Sycamore/From A Boy To A Man | 6 |
| 67 | Fontana TF 866 | The Impossible Years/In My World | 12 |
| 67 | Fontana TF 889 | Gina/We All Love The Human Race | 6 |
| 68 | Fontana TF 911 | Storybook Children/I Need To Love You | 6 |
| 68 | Fontana TF 933 | The Words Of Bartholomew/Mind Excursion | 6 |
| 68 | Fontana TF 976 | Never An Everyday Thing/Waiting For A Break In The Clouds | 40 |
| 69 | Fontana TF 1008 | Dayton Ohio 1903/Say Goodbye To Yesterday | 7 |
| 69 | Fontana TF 1054 | Charlie Cass/Linda (withdrawn issue) | 25 |
| 69 | Fontana TF 1054 | We're Building A Love/Charlie Cass | 10 |
| 69 | Fontana TF 1027 | Come On Home/Pamela Pamela (p/s) | 10 |
| 70 | Philips 6006 035 | Give Me Just A Little More Time/I'm In Love | 10 |
| 70 | Philips 6006 035 | Give Me Just A Little More Time/I'm In Love (withdrawn) | 150 |
| 73 | Warner Bros K 16269 | Together/One Man Woman (withdrawn) (DJ Copy) | 100 |
| 66 | Fontana (S)TL 5351 | WAYNE ONE (LP, black/silver labels) | 6 |
| | | | 25 |

(see also Mindbenders)

## FONTANE SISTERS

| | | | |
|---|---|---|---|
| 54 | London HL 8099 | Happy Days And Lonely Nights/If I Didn't Have You | 30 |
| 55 | London HL 8113 | Hearts Of Stone/Bless Your Heart | 30 |
| 55 | London HL 8126 | Rock Love/You're Mine | 30 |
| 55 | London HLD 8177 | Seventeen/If I Could Be With You | 35 |
| 55 | London HLD 8211 | Rolling Stone/Daddy-O | 30 |
| 56 | London HLD 8225 | Adorable/Playmates | 20 |
| 56 | London HLD 8265 | Eddie My Love/Yum Yum | 20 |
| 56 | London HL 7009 | Eddie My Love/Yum Yum (export issue) | 20 |
| 56 | London HLD 8289 | I'm In Love Again/You Always Hurt The One You Love (gold lettering label) | 25 |
| 56 | London HLD 8289 | I'm In Love Again/You Always Hurt The One You Love (later silver lettering label) | 10 |
| 56 | London HLD 8318 | Voices (with narration by Pat Boone)/Willow Weep For Me (gold lettering label) | 20 |
| 56 | London HLD 8318 | Voices (with narration by Pat Boone)/Willow Weep For Me (later silver lettering label) | 10 |
| 56 | London HLD 8343 | Silver Bells/Nuttin' For Christmas | 10 |
| 57 | London HLD 8378 | The Banana Boat Song/Lonesome Lover Blues (gold lettering) | 10 |
| 57 | London HLD 8378 | The Banana Boat Song/Lonesome Lover Blues (silver lettering) | 5 |
| 57 | London HLD 8415 | Please Don't Leave Me/Still | 5 |
| 57 | London HLD 8488 | Fool Around/Which Way To Your Heart? | 5 |
| 58 | London HLD 8621 | Chanson D'Amour (Song Of Love)/Cocoanut Grove | 5 |
| 59 | London HLD 8861 | Billy Boy/Chanson D'Amour | 10 |
| 55 | London RE-D 1029 | FONTANE SISTERS NO. 1 (EP) | 15 |
| 55 | London RE-D 1037 | FONTANE SISTERS NO. 2 (EP) | 15 |
| 57 | London HA-D 2053 | THE FONTANES SING (LP) | 30 |

(see also Pat Boone, Perry Como)

## SAM FONTEYN

| | | | |
|---|---|---|---|
| 66 | Parlophone R 5519 | Lost In Space/BERNARD SHARPE: Jorrocks | 10 |

## BILLY FONTEYNE

| | | | |
|---|---|---|---|
| 63 | Oriole CB 1917 | Little Child/Look Before You Leap | 15 |

## FOO FIGHTERS

| | | | |
|---|---|---|---|
| 95 | Roswell CL 753 | This Is A Call/Winnebago (p/s) | 6 |
| 95 | Roswell 12CL 753 | This Is A Call/Winnebago/Podunk (12", luminous vinyl) | 20 |
| 95 | Roswell CL 757 | I'll Stick Around/How I Miss You (red vinyl, p/s) | 8 |
| 95 | Roswell 12CL 757 | I'll Stick Around/How I Miss You (12" p/s) | 15 |
| 95 | Roswell CL 762 | For All The Cows/Watershed (blue vinyl, p/s) | 8 |
| 95 | Roswell CL 768 | Big Me/Floaty/Gas Chamber (white vinyl, p/s) | 12 |
| 97 | Roswell CL 788 | Monkey Wrench/Up In Arms (red vinyl, p/s) | 12 |
| 97 | Roswell CL 792 | Everlong/Drive Me Wild (blue vinyl, p/s) | 25 |
| 97 | Roswell CL 796 | My Hero/Dear Lover (red vinyl, stickered poly sleeve, with insert) | 10 |
| 00 | RCA 74321 79012-7 | Breakout/Stacked Actors (live) (p/s) | 5 |
| 00 | RCA 74321 80926-7 | Next Year/Big Me (live) (p/s) | 6 |
| 02 | RCA 74321 97315-7 | All My Life/Sister Europe (numbered p/s) | 6 |
| 03 | RCA 74321 98955-7 | Times Like These/Lack Of Illision (numbered p/s) | 6 |
| 03 | RCA 82876 56370-7 | Have It All/Darling Nikki (p/s) | 5 |
| 03 | BMG 82876-52250-7 | Low/Never Talking To You Again (Live Version) (numbered p/s, 3,000 only) | 10 |
| 05 | RCA 82876 72279-7 | D.O.A./Razor (Acoustic) (p/s, yellow vinyl) | 6 |
| 05 | RCA 82876 74965-7 | Resolve/World (Demo) (p/s) | 5 |
| 05 | RCA 82876 70121-7 | Best Of You/Spill (p/s) | 5 |
| 07 | RCA 88697 13999-7 | The Pretender/Bangin' (clear vinyl, p/s) | 5 |
| 07 | RCA 88697 19036-7 | Long Road To Ruin/Holiday In Cambodia (p/s) | 5 |
| 95 | Roswell EST 2266 | FOO FIGHTERS (LP) | 40 |
| 97 | Roswell EST 2295 | THE COLOUR AND THE SHAPE (LP) | 60 |
| 99 | RCA 07863678921 | THERE IS NOTHING LEFT TO LOSE (LP, stickered gatefold sleeve, with tattoo transfer) | 40 |
| 02 | RCA 74321973481 | ONE BY ONE (LP, gatefold sleeve with inner) | 40 |
| 05 | BMG 82876680381 | IN YOUR HONOUR (4-LP) | 40 |
| 11 | Roswell 88697983211RE1 | FOO FIGHTERS (LP, reissue, download card) | 15 |

## FOOL

| | | | |
|---|---|---|---|
| 69 | Mercury MF 1111 | We Are One/Shining Light | 10 |
| 69 | Mercury SMCL 20138 | THE FOOL (LP, gatefold sleeve. black/silver labels) | 100 |

## FOOLS DANCE

| | | | |
|---|---|---|---|
| 87 | L. T. T. Slaughter LTS 22 | They'll Never Know/Empty Hours (p/s) | 10 |
| 87 | L. T. T. Slaughter LTS 22T | They'll Never Know/The Collector/Empty Hours/The Ring (12", p/s) | 15 |
| 85 | Top Hole Turn TURN 19 | FOOLS DANCE (mini-LP) | 20 |

(see also Cure, Stranglers)

## FOOT IN COLD WATER
| 73 | Island WIP 6162 | (Isn't Love Unkind) In My Life/Deep Freeze | 7 |
| 74 | Elektra K12164 | I Know What You Need/Para – Dice | 8 |
| 74 | Elektra K 52011 | OR ALL AROUND US (LP) | 20 |

## FOOT SOLDIER
| 93 | Blipton Factor Wreckords BLIP 002 | SO WHAT HAPPENS NOW EP (stamped white labels) | 18 |
| 93 | Blipton Factor Wreckords BLIP 004 | WE HAVE SUCH SIGHTS TO SHOW YOU EP (12" stamped white labels) | 35 |

## CHUCK FOOTE
| 62 | London HLU 9495 | You're Running Out Of Kisses/Come On Back | 10 |

## FOR CARNATION
| 00 | Domino WIGLP 77 | FOR CARNATION (LP, stickered sleeve) | 15 |

## FORBES
| 77 | Power Exchange PX 253 | The Beatles/Sweet Kiss Of Fire | 7 |

## BILL FORBES
| 58 | Columbia DB 4232 | My Cherie/God's Little Acre | 6 |
| 59 | Columbia DB 4269 | Once More/Believe In Me | 8 |
| 59 | Columbia DB 4386 | Too Young/It's Not The End Of The World | 5 |
| 61 | Columbia DB 4566 | You're Sixteen, You're Beautiful/Backward Child | 5 |
| 61 | Columbia DB 4619 | That's It, I Quit, I'm Moving On/Big City Boy | 5 |
| 61 | Columbia DB 4747 | Goodbye Cruel World/Next Time | 5 |
| 62 | Columbia DB 4855 | Laughter Or Tears/Like A Good Girl Should | 5 |
| 62 | Columbia DB 4945 | Poker Face/Marianne | 5 |

*(see also Contrasts)*

## SMOKY FORBES
| 71 | Beacon BEA 176 | My Kind Of Music/Loves Goes | 6 |

## FORBIDDEN
| 88 | Under One Flag FLAG 27 | FORBIDDEN EVIL (LP) | 15 |

## FORCE/CASH CREW
| 88 | Vinyl Lab VL04T | Mission Impossible/Microphone Maniac (12") | 15 |

## FORCEFIELD
| 87 | President PT 551 | Smoke On The Water/Shine It On Me (p/s) | 5 |
| 88 | President PT 578 | Heartache/I Lose Again (Instrumental Version) (p/s) | 5 |

*(see also Cozy Powell, Graham Bonnet, Ray Fenwick, Whitesnake)*

## FORCE FIVE
| 64 | United Artists UP 1051 | Don't Make My Baby Blue/Shaking Postman | 30 |
| 65 | United Artists UP 1089 | Yeah, I'm Waiting/I Don't Want To See You Again | 35 |
| 65 | United Artists UP 1102 | Baby Don't Care/Come Down To Earth | 35 |
| 65 | United Artists UP 1118 | I Want You Babe/Gee Too Tiger | 50 |
| 66 | United Artists UP 1141 | Don't Know Which Way To Turn/Baby Let Your Hair Down | 45 |

*(see also Crocheted Doughnut Ring)*

## FORCE MAJOR
| 82 | Harbour City 14 | Put It In Your Pipe/Say What You Feel | 15 |

## FORCE OF MUSIC
| 78 | Ballistic UAS 530190 | FREEDOM FIGHTERS DUB (LP) | 20 |

## FORCE WEST
| 65 | Decca F 12223 | I Can't Give What I Haven't Got/Why Won't She Stay | 12 |
| 66 | Columbia DB 7908 | Gotta Find Another Baby/Talkin' About Our Love | 15 |
| 66 | Columbia DB 7963 | When The Sun Comes Out (Weatherman)/Gotta Tell Somebody | 12 |
| 67 | Columbia DB 8174 | All The Children Sleep/Desolation | 15 |
| 68 | CBS 3632 | I'll Walk In The Rain/What's It To Be? | 8 |
| 68 | CBS 3798 | I'll Be Moving On/Like The Tide, Like The Ocean | 8 |
| 69 | CBS 4385 | Sherry/Mister Blue | 8 |

## FORD & THE COALITION
| 94 | Shot In The Dark COAL 2616 | The Coalition (12") | 10 |

## DEAN FORD (& GAYLORDS)
| 64 | Columbia DB 7264 | Twenty Miles/What's The Matter With Me? | 25 |
| 64 | Columbia DB 7402 | Mr Heartbreak's Here Instead/I Won't | 25 |
| 65 | Columbia DB 7610 | The Name Game/That Lonely Feeling | 25 |
| 76 | EMI 2717 | The Fever/You Are The One | 6 |
| 75 | EMI EMC 3079 | DEAN FORD (LP) | 15 |

*(see also Gaylords, Marmalade, Junior Campbell)*

## DEE DEE FORD
| 60 | London HLU 9245 | Good-Morning Blues/I Just Can't Believe | 40 |

*(see also Don Gardner & Dee Dee Ford)*

## DONETTE FORD
| 91 | Jah Works JW 007 | Rhythm Of Resistance/Dub Wilderness (10") | 15 |

## EDDIE/EDDY FORD
| 72 | Pressure Beat PB 5512 | You Wrong Fe Trouble Joshua/KENNETH POWER: Joshua Row Us Home | 7 |
| 73 | Duke Reid DR 2523 | Guess I This Riddle/Riddle Version (as Eddie Ford) | 5 |

## 'TENNESSEE' ERNIE FORD
| 54 | Capitol CL 14005 | Give Me Your Word/River Of No Return | 10 |
| 54 | Capitol CL 14006 | Catfish Boogie/Kiss Me Big | 25 |
| 55 | Capitol CL 14261 | His Hands/I Am A Pilgrim | 6 |
| 55 | Capitol CL 14273 | Losing You/There Is Beauty In Everything | 6 |
| 56 | Capitol CL 14500 | Sixteen Tons/You Don't Have To Be A Baby To Cry | 15 |

MINT VALUE £

| | | | |
|---|---|---|---|
| 56 | Capitol CL 14506 | The Ballad Of Davy Crockett/Farewell | 10 |
| 56 | Capitol CL 14557 | That's All/Bright Lights And Blonde-Haired Women | 6 |
| 61 | Capitol CL 15210 | Little Red Rockin' Hood/I Gotta Have My Baby Back | 20 |
| 52 | Capitol LC 6573 | CAPITOL PRESENTS (10" LP) | 20 |
| 58 | Capitol T 888 | OL' ROCKIN' ERN (LP) | 20 |

*(see also Dinning Sisters)*

## 'TENNESSEE' ERNIE FORD & BETTY HUTTON
| | | | |
|---|---|---|---|
| 54 | Capitol CL 14133 | This Must Be The Place/The Honeymoon's Over (green label) | 18 |

## FRANKIE FORD
| | | | |
|---|---|---|---|
| 59 | London HL 8850 | Sea Cruise/Roberta (with Huey 'Piano' Smith & Clowns) (black triangular centre) | 60 |
| 59 | London HL 8850 | Sea Cruise/Roberta (with Huey 'Piano' Smith & Clowns) (later silver-top triangular centre) | 30 |
| 59 | Top Rank JAR 186 | Alimony/Can't Tell My Heart (What To Do) (with Huey 'Piano' Smith & Clowns) | 12 |
| 60 | Top Rank JAR 282 | Cheatin' Woman/HUEY 'PIANO' SMITH & CLOWNS: Don't You Just Know Kokomo | 20 |
| 60 | Top Rank JAR 299 | Time After Time/I Want To Be Your Man | 10 |
| 60 | London HLP 9222 | You Talk Too Much/If You've Got Troubles | 20 |
| 65 | Sue WI 366 | Sea Cruise/Roberta (with Huey 'Piano' Smith & Clowns) (reissue) | 25 |
| 65 | Sue WI 369 | What's Going On?/Watchdog | 40 |

*(see also Huey Piano Smith)*

## JASON FORD & THE BULLDOGS
| | | | |
|---|---|---|---|
| 62 | Piccadilly 7N 35193 | Nobody Knows/Am I The One | 10 |

## JOHN FORD
| | | | |
|---|---|---|---|
| 73 | UK UKR31 | It's Alright Bill/Captain Of Your Ship | 8 |

## JON FORD
| | | | |
|---|---|---|---|
| 68 | Philips BF 1690 | Two's Company, Three's A Crowd/Place In Your Heart | 7 |
| 69 | Philips BF 1791 | I Know It's Love/Look Before You Leap | 6 |
| 69 | Philips BF 1817 | Ice Cream Man/This Was The Time | 6 |
| 70 | Philips BF 1833 | Yesterday When I Was Young/Running Around | 6 |
| 70 | Philips 6006 030 | You've Got Me Where You Want Me/You're All Alone Tonight | 100 |
| 70 | Philips 6006 030 | You've Got Me Where You Want Me/You're All Alone Tonight (DJ Copy) | 150 |

## MIKE FORD & THE CONSULS
| | | | |
|---|---|---|---|
| 63 | Piccadilly 7N 35127 | Jumping Jeremiah/The Greenman | 20 |

## PERRY FORD (& SAPPHIRES)
| | | | |
|---|---|---|---|
| 59 | Parlophone R 4573 | Bye, Bye Baby, Goodbye/She Came As A Stranger | 15 |
| 60 | Parlophone R 4633 | Crazy Over You/Garden Of Happiness | 15 |
| 60 | Parlophone R 4683 | Don't Weep (Little Lady)/Little Grown-Up | 15 |
| 62 | Decca F 11497 | Baby, Baby (Don't You Worry)/Prince Of Fools (with Sapphires & Blue Flames) | 15 |

*(see also Ivy League, Georgie Fame)*

## RICKY FORD (& TENNESSEANS)
| | | | |
|---|---|---|---|
| 63 | Parlophone R 5018 | Sweet And Tender Romance/Cheat Cheat | 10 |
| 64 | Parlophone R 5230 | You Are My Love/Long Way From Home (with Tennesseans) | 7 |

## SIR TED FORD
| | | | |
|---|---|---|---|
| 77 | Barak BAR 3 | I Wanna Be Near You/Ridin' Too High | 10 |
| 79 | Ardent ADS 9001 | Disco Music/I've Got A Goal | 65 |

## JOHN FORDE
| | | | |
|---|---|---|---|
| 77 | EMI EMI 2656 | Stardance/Flight Of The Jumping Bean (12", p/s, some on blue vinyl) | 25 |
| 77 | Sidewalk 12 YSID 107 | Woman/Stardance/Don't You Know Who Did It (12", p/s) | 25 |

## FORD WORKERS ON STRIKE
| | | | |
|---|---|---|---|
| 78 | WG 0001/S/78/CUS-182 | FORD WORKERS ON STRIKE EP (with insert) | 6 |

## EDDIE 'BUSTER' FOREHAND
| | | | |
|---|---|---|---|
| 69 | Action ACT 4519 | Young Boy Blues/You Were Meant For Me | 35 |

## FOREHEADS IN A FISHTANK
| | | | |
|---|---|---|---|
| 80 | Stuff Records FAB 4 | She Loves You, Yeah/Baby Love (p/s) | 8 |

## FOREIGN LEGION
| | | | |
|---|---|---|---|
| 86 | Rent-A-Racket RRR0001 | TRENCHLINE (EP) | 12 |
| 89 | Schlawiner SO5 | SURF CITY (EP, 350 copies only, black/green vinyl) | 10 |
| 90 | Venture VR/FL 100 | WELCOME TO FORT ZINDERNEUF (LP) | 15 |

## FOREIGN PRESS
| | | | |
|---|---|---|---|
| 80 | Streets Ahead SA 1 | Downpour/Crossfire/Behind The Glass (1st pressing, gatefold sleeve) | 15 |
| 80 | Streets Ahead SA1 | Downpour/Crossfire/Behind The Glass (2nd pressing, non-gatefold black and white or blue and white sleeve) | 6 |

## FOREIGN BODIES
| | | | |
|---|---|---|---|
| 84 | Alien 1 | Take A Look/Love By Love (p/s) | 25 |

## FORELAND
| | | | |
|---|---|---|---|
| 77 | Flams | FORELAND (LP) | 35 |

## JOHN FOREMAN
| | | | |
|---|---|---|---|
| 66 | Reality RY 1004 | THE 'OUSES IN BETWEEN (LP) | 15 |

## FORERUNNERS
| | | | |
|---|---|---|---|
| 64 | Solar SRP 100 | Bony Maronie/Pride | 60 |

## FORERUNNERS
| | | | |
|---|---|---|---|
| 60s | Key KL 008 | THE FORERUNNERS (LP) | 18 |
| 60s | Key KL 004 | RUNNING BACK (LP) | 18 |

## FOREST SWORDS
| | | | |
|---|---|---|---|
| 10 | No Pain In Pop NPIP 013 | Rattling Cage/Hjurt (p/s) | 10 |

## FOREST (1)
| | | | |
|---|---|---|---|
| 69 | Harvest HAR 5007 | Searching For Shadows/Mirror Of Life | 20 |
| 69 | Harvest SHVL 760 | FOREST (LP, gatefold sleeve, no EMI logo on label) | 400 |

| | | | |
|---|---|---|---|
| 70 | Harvest SHVL 784 | FULL CIRCLE (LP, gatefold sleeve, no EMI logo on label) | 700 |
| 88 | Zap! ZAP 3 | FULL CIRCLE (LP, reissue) | 25 |

### FOREST (2)
| | | | |
|---|---|---|---|
| 76 | Midland International MID 1 Do Ya (Do Ya Want My Love)/I'll Stay With You | | 8 |

### SHARON FORESTER
| | | | |
|---|---|---|---|
| 73 | Ashanti ASH 403 | Silly Wasn't I?/NOW-GEN: Silly Wasn't I? — Version | 6 |
| 74 | Ashanti SHAN 105 | SHARON (LP) | 20 |

### FOREVER AMBER
| | | | |
|---|---|---|---|
| 69 | Advance (no cat. no.) | THE LOVE CYCLE (LP, private pressing, 99 copies only) | 2500 |
| 07 | 10th Planet TP060 | THE LOVE CYCLE (LP, reissue) | 20 |

### FOREVER MORE
| | | | |
|---|---|---|---|
| 70 | RCA RCA 2024 | Put Your Money On A Pony/Yours | 6 |
| 70 | RCA SF 8016 | YOURS FOREVER MORE (LP, gatefold sleeve, orange label) | 50 |
| 71 | RCA LSA 3015 | WORDS ON BLACK PLASTIC (LP, laminated front sleeve) | 40 |

*(see also Scots Of St. James, Hopscotch)*

### FOREVER PEOPLE
| | | | |
|---|---|---|---|
| 92 | Sarah SARAH 54 | Invisible/Sometimes (p/s, insert) | 12 |

### FORK IN THE ROAD
| | | | |
|---|---|---|---|
| 70 | Ember EMB 311 | I Can't Turn Around/Skeleton In My Closet (test pressing) | 150 |
| 70 | Ember EMB S 311 | I Can't Turn Around/Skeleton In My Closet | 100 |

### FORMAT
| | | | |
|---|---|---|---|
| 69 | CBS 4600 | Maxwell's Silver Hammer/Music Man | 10 |

*(see also Fourmost)*

### FORMATIONS
| | | | |
|---|---|---|---|
| 68 | MGM MGM 1399 | At The Top Of The Stairs/Magic Melody | 120 |
| 68 | MGM MGM 1399 | At The Top Of The Stairs/Magic Melody (DJ Copy) | 220 |
| 71 | Mojo 2027 001 | At The Top Of The Stairs/Magic Melody (reissue) | 5 |

### FORMERLY FAT HARRY
| | | | |
|---|---|---|---|
| 71 | Harvest SHSP 4016 | FORMERLY FAT HARRY (LP, with EMI logo on label) | 100 |

*(see also Country Joe and the Fish)*

### FORMINX
| | | | |
|---|---|---|---|
| 65 | Vocalion V 9235 | Jenka Beat/Geronimo Jenka | 30 |

*(see also Aphrodite's Child, Vangelis)*

### FORMIX
| | | | |
|---|---|---|---|
| 72 | Tulip TP 001 | What Would You Want Of Me/Shake | 40 |

### FORMULA
| | | | |
|---|---|---|---|
| 65 | HMV POP 1438 | Close To Me/If Ever | 10 |

### FORMULA 1
| | | | |
|---|---|---|---|
| 65 | Warner Bros WB 155 | I Just Can't Go To Sleep/Sure Know A Lot About Love | 30 |

### FORMULA TWO
| | | | |
|---|---|---|---|
| 72 | CBS SCBS 8285 | Easy Times/Girl Who Lives Next Door | 6 |

### ANDY FORRAY
| | | | |
|---|---|---|---|
| 68 | Parlophone R 5715 | Sarah Jane/Don't Care Anymore | 10 |
| 68 | Parlophone R 5729 | The Proud One/Messin' Round With Me | 15 |
| 68 | Decca F 12733 | Epitaph To You/Dream With Me | 80 |
| 69 | Fontana TF 999 | Let The Sunshine In/Baby Is Coming | 10 |

### HELEN FORREST
| | | | |
|---|---|---|---|
| 56 | Capitol CL 14594 | Taking A Chance On Love/I Love You Much Too Much | 10 |
| 56 | Capitol LC 6834 | VOICE OF THE NAME BANDS (10" LP) | 15 |

### JANE FORREST
| | | | |
|---|---|---|---|
| 56 | Columbia SCM 5213 | Sincerely Yours/A Girl Can't Say | 10 |

### FOR(R)ESTERS
| | | | |
|---|---|---|---|
| 65 | Polydor 56038 | Broken Hearted Clown/Lonely Boy | 10 |
| 65 | Polydor 56057 | How Can I Tell Her/So Shy | 10 |
| 66 | Polydor 56104 | Early Morning Hours/World Is Mine | 8 |
| 66 | Columbia DB 8040 | Sometimes When You're Lonely/Today Or Tomorrow (as Forresters) | 7 |
| 66 | Columbia DB 8086 | Mr. Smith/Ship On The Sea (as Forresters) | 10 |
| 67 | Columbia DB 8176 | Comin' Home In The Evening/Sunshine's On Its Way (as Forresters) | 6 |

### THOMAS FORSTNER
| | | | |
|---|---|---|---|
| 89 | Ariola 112 298 | Song Of Love/Nur Ein Lied (p/s, withdrawn) | 5 |

### FORTES MENTUM
| | | | |
|---|---|---|---|
| 68 | Parlophone R 5684 | Saga Of A Wrinkled Man/Mr. Partridge Passed Away Today | 50 |
| 68 | Parlophone R 5726 | I Can't Go On Loving You/Humdiggle We Love You | 15 |
| 69 | Parlophone R 5768 | Gotta Go/Marrakesh | 15 |

*(see also Angel Pavement, Pussy)*

### FORTUNATE PEOPLE
| | | | |
|---|---|---|---|
| 69 | Dukesbury DB 002 | Simple Skies/Stop | 90 |

### JOHNNY FORTUNE
| | | | |
|---|---|---|---|
| 60s | Sonet SON 2139 | Soul Surfer/Dragster | 15 |

### LANCE FORTUNE
| | | | |
|---|---|---|---|
| 61 | Pye 7N 15347 | Who's Gonna Tell Me?/Love Is The Sweetest Thing | 15 |

### FORTUNES
| | | | |
|---|---|---|---|
| 63 | Decca F 11718 | Summertime Summertime/I Love Her Still (as Fortunes & Cliftones) (in p/s) | 30 |
| 63 | Decca F 11718 | Summertime Summertime/I Love Her Still (as Fortunes & Cliftones) | 15 |
| 64 | Decca F 11809 | Caroline/If You Don't Want Me Now | 30 |
| 64 | Decca F 11809 | Caroline/If You Don't Want Me Now (later repressing with boxed Decca logo) | 10 |

| | | | |
|---|---|---|---|
| 64 | Decca F 11912 | Come On Girl/I Like The Look Of You (curved logo) | 15 |
| 64 | Decca F 11985 | Look Homeward Angel/I'll Have My Tears To Remind Me | 15 |
| 66 | Decca F 12321 | This Golden Ring/Someone To Care | 6 |
| 66 | Decca F 12429 | You Gave Me Somebody To Love/Silent Street | 6 |
| 66 | Decca F 12485 | Is It Really Worth Your While?/Am I Losing My Touch | 6 |
| 67 | Decca F 12612 | Our Love Has Gone/Truly Yours | 6 |
| 67 | United Artists UP 1188 | The Idol/His Smile Was A Lie | 10 |
| 68 | United Artists UP 2218 | Loving Cup/Hour At The Movies | 6 |
| 68 | United Artists UP 2239 | Seasons In The Sun/Louise | 6 |
| 69 | United Artists UP 35027 | Ballad Of The Alamo/Save A Little Dream | 6 |
| 69 | United Artists UP 35054 | Lifetime Of Love/Sad Sad Sad (withdrawn, existence unconfirmed) | 0 |
| 69 | United Artists UP 35054 | Books And Films/Sad Sad Sad | 7 |
| 71 | Capitol CL 15671 | Here Comes That Rainy Day Feeling Again/Bad Side Of Town | 5 |
| 71 | Capitol CL 15693 | Freedom Come Freedom Go/There's A Man | 5 |
| 72 | Capitol CL 15707 | Storm In A Teacup/I'm Not Following You | 5 |
| 72 | Capitol CL 15719 | Baby By The Way/Long Way Home | 6 |
| 72 | Capitol CL 15732 | Everything Is Out Of Season/Don't Sing To Me | 6 |
| 72 | Capitol CL 15739 | Secret Love/I Can't Remember When The Sun Went In | 6 |
| 65 | Decca LK 4736 | THE FORTUNES (LP, mono) | 35 |
| 65 | Decca SKL 4736 | THE FORTUNES (LP, stereo) | 60 |
| 72 | Capitol ST 21891 | THE FORTUNES (LP) | 15 |

*(see also Glen Dale)*

## 48 CHAIRS
| | | | |
|---|---|---|---|
| 79 | Absurd Absurd 3 | Snap It Around/Psycle Sluts (p/s) | 5 |

## 45'S
| | | | |
|---|---|---|---|
| 79 | Chopper CHEAP 5 | Couldn't Believe A Word/Lonesome Lane (no p/s) | 7 |
| 79 | Stiff BUY 52 | Couldn't Believe A Word/Lonesome Lane (no p/s, reissue) | 5 |
| 81 | 45's Records ONE 45 | Secrets And Whispers/Driving/Little Honda (p/s) | 8 |

## 49 AMERICANS
| | | | |
|---|---|---|---|
| 80 | Choo Choo Train CHUG 2 | TOO YOUNG TO BE IDEAL (12" EP) | 10 |

## FORUM
| | | | |
|---|---|---|---|
| 67 | London HLM 10120 | The River Is Wide/I Fall In Love (All Over Again) | 15 |
| 70 | B&C CB 119 | The River Is Wide/I Fall In Love (All Over Again) (reissue) | 5 |

## FORWARD INTENSE
| | | | |
|---|---|---|---|
| 92 | Harm HARM1 | Stated/Imply The Calm (12") | 50 |

## SHIRLEY FORWOOD
| | | | |
|---|---|---|---|
| 57 | London HLD 8402 | Two Hearts (With An Arrow Between)/Juke Box Lovers | 20 |

## FOSSIL
| | | | |
|---|---|---|---|
| 74 | Pennine PSS14 | Black Night/For Your Love/Smile On Me/Wishing Well | 75 |

## BOBBY FOSTER
| | | | |
|---|---|---|---|
| 70 | Bread BR 1101 | Tell Me Why You Say Goodbye/YOUTH: I'll Make Him Believe In You | 6 |

## FRANK FOSTER
| | | | |
|---|---|---|---|
| 60s | Esquire 32 033 | WAIL FRANK WAIL (LP) | 18 |

## JACKIE FOSTER
| | | | |
|---|---|---|---|
| 63 | Sway SWAY 001 | Dry Up Your Tears/Try To Understand | 20 |
| 63 | Planetone RC 13 | Oh Leona/I Fell In Love | 15 |

## JOHN FOSTER
| | | | |
|---|---|---|---|
| 66 | Island ILP 939 | JOHN FOSTER SINGS (LP) | 40 |

## LARRY FOSTER & SOUL EXPLOSION
| | | | |
|---|---|---|---|
| 70 | Fab FAB 130 | Boom Biddy Boom/Next To Me (actually by Sugar Simone) | 10 |

*(see also Sugar Simone)*

## LES FOSTER
| | | | |
|---|---|---|---|
| 69 | Wolf WM 02 | You And Your Love/Turning Point (actually by D Dennis) | 12 |
| 70 | Torpedo TOR 7 | Run Like A Thief/Nobody's Fool | 12 |

## LES FOSTER & ANSELL COLLINS
| | | | |
|---|---|---|---|
| 73 | Camel CA 102 | The Man In Your Life/Version | 5 |

*(see also Sugar Simone, Lance Hannibal)*

## LESLIE FOSTER
| | | | |
|---|---|---|---|
| 69 | Jolly JY 022 | Muriel/Nowhere To Hide | 7 |

## VINCENT FOSTER
| | | | |
|---|---|---|---|
| 69 | Escort ES 803 | Shine Eye Gal/Who Nest (B-side actually "Who Next" by Carl Bryan) | 12 |

## FOTHERINGAY
| | | | |
|---|---|---|---|
| 70 | Island WIP 6085 | Peace In The End/Winter Winds | 15 |
| 70 | Island ILPS 9125 | FOTHERINGAY (LP, pink label/'i' logo, gatefold sleeve) | 150 |
| 70 | Island ILPS 9125 | FOTHERINGAY (LP, later issue, pink rim label/'palm tree' logo, gatefold sleeve) | 30 |
| 86 | Hannibal HNBL 4426 | FOTHERINGAY (LP, reissue) | 18 |

*(see also Sandy Denny, Trevor Lucas, Eclection, Exception[s], Fairport Convention, Mick Greenwood)*

## FOTOSTAT
| | | | |
|---|---|---|---|
| 79 | Sour Grape SG 112 | Fotostat/Fotostat II (p/s) | 20 |

## FOUL PLAY
| | | | |
|---|---|---|---|
| 92 | Oblivion OR 001 | VOLUME 1 EP: The Alchemist/Ragatere/Ricochet/Feel The Vibe (12") | 25 |
| 92 | Oblivion OR 002 | VOLUME 2 EP: Survival/Dubbing You/Ricochet (No Stopping The Remix)/Feel The Vibe (Again) (12") | 25 |
| 93 | Section 5 SECTION 04 | Finest Illusion/Screwface (12" white label) | 60 |
| 93 | Section 5 SECTION 4 | Finest Illusion/Screwface (12" printed labels) | 50 |
| 93 | Section 5 SECTION 4 | Finest Illusion/Screwface (12", 2nd pressing, black labels, actually no labels at all!) | 50 |
| 93 | Moving Shadow SHAD 29R2 | VOLUME III REMIXES PART 2: Open Your Mind (Nookie Remix)/Finest Illusion (Legal Mix)(10", p/s) | 10 |

## AL FOULCER
81  Heart & Soul FOU A1 — Video Man/Song For John .................................................................. 8

*(see also Crystal Set)*

## FOUNDATIONS
| 67 | Pye 7N 17366 | Baby, Now That I've Found You/Come On Back To Me .................................................. 5 |
| 68 | Pye 7N 17417 | Back On My Feet Again/I Can Take Or Leave Your Loving ............................................ 5 |
| 68 | Pye 7N 17503 | Any Old Time (You're Lonely And Sad)/We Are Happy People ...................................... 5 |
| 68 | Pye 7N 17636 | Build Me Up Buttercup/New Direction ...................................................................... 5 |
| 69 | Pye 7N 17702 | In The Bad Bad Old Days/Give Me Love ...................................................................... 5 |
| 69 | Pye 7N 17809 | Born To Live, Born To Die/Why Did You Cry .............................................................. 10 |
| 69 | Pye 7N 1784 | Baby I Couldn'tSee/Penny Sir ................................................................................. 10 |
| 70 | Pye 7N 17904 | Take A Girl Like You/I'm Gonna Be A Rich Man .......................................................... 10 |
| 70 | Pye 7N 17956 | I'm Gonna Be A Rich Man/Who Am I .......................................................................... 10 |
| 71 | MCA MCA 5075 | Stoney Ground/I'll Give You Love .............................................................................. 20 |
| 77 | Summit SU 100 | Where Were You When I Needed Your Love/Love Me Nice 'n Easy ............................... 6 |
| 78 | Psycho P 2603 | Closer To Loving You/Change My Life ...................................................................... 250 |
| 68 | Pye NEP 24297 | IT'S ALL RIGHT (EP) .............................................................................................. 25 |
| 67 | Pye NPL 18206 | FROM THE FOUNDATIONS (LP) ............................................................................... 20 |
| 68 | Pye NPL 18227 | ROCKING THE FOUNDATIONS (LP, mono) ................................................................ 20 |
| 68 | Pye NSPL 18227 | ROCKING THE FOUNDATIONS (LP, stereo) .............................................................. 25 |
| 69 | Pye N(S)PL 18290 | DIGGING THE FOUNDATIONS (LP, gatefold sleeve) ................................................ 20 |

*(see also Pluto)*

## FOUNDED
82  Heroes ER 02 — Looking For Love/Run To Hell ...................................................................... 60

## JAMES FOUNTAIN
76  Cream CRM 5002 — Seven Day Lover/Malnutrition ............................................................. 5

## THE 4
64  Decca F 11999 — It's Alright/There's Nothing Like It .............................................................. 20

## 4 BY FOUR
60s  Victor Buckland — Roll Over Beethoven/Till There Was You/You Better Move On/Chains ......... 75

## FOUR DYNAMICS
02  Grapevine 2002 122 — Things That A Lady Ain't Supposed To Do/That's What Girls Are Made For ...... 8

## FOUR GUNS
85  Gun 001 — Sign Of The Crimes/Spirit Of The Thing (no'd p/s, 500 only) .................................... 20

## FOUR IDLE HANDS
90  Good Vibrations GOT 21 — 99 Streets/Friday Man .................................................................. 12

## FOUR PLUGS
80  Disposable THROWAY ONE — Wrong Treatment/Biking Girl (p/s) ............................................ 20

## FOUR ACES (JAMAICA)
| 65 | Island WI 178 | Hoochy-Koochy-Kai-Po/River Bank Coberly Again .................................................. 25 |
| 65 | Island WI 178 | Hoochy-Koochy-Kai-Po/SKATALITES: Sucu Sucu (different B-side) ............................ 25 |
| 65 | Island WI 179 | Sweet Chariot/Peace And Love ............................................................................... 15 |
| 65 | Island WI 180 | Little Girl/CLARENDONIANS: Day Will Come .......................................................... 20 |

*(see also Desmond Dekker)*

## FOUR ACES (U.K.)
60s  Anton/E.R.S. EAG 178/179 — Why Do You/Fortune Teller (private pressing) ............................ 250

## FOUR ACES (U.S.)
| 54 | Brunswick 05256 | The Gang That Sang "Heart Of My Heart"/Heaven Can Wait ................................... 8 |
| 54 | Brunswick 05308 | Three Coins In The Fountain/Wedding Bells (Are Breaking Up This Gang Of Mine) ... 15 |
| 54 | Brunswick 05322 | It Shall Come To Pass/Dream ................................................................................ 8 |
| 54 | Brunswick 05355 | Mister Sandman/(I'll Be With You) In Apple Blossom Time ................................... 15 |
| 53 | Brunswick LA 8614 | JUST SQUEEZE ME (10" LP) .............................................................................. 12 |

## FOURBEATS (1)
63  Oxford University UTF 164 — Do You Love Me/Mr Postman/Baby Its Me/They Say (p/s) ............ 30

## FOURBEATS (2)
82  SRTS 82 CUS 1460 — Back Door/If Pigs Could Fly .................................................................. 20

## 4 DEGREES
65  Oak RGJ 187 — 4 DEGREES (LP, 1-sided, no sleeve) ............................................................ 425

## FOUR DOLLS
| 57 | Capitol CL 14778 | Three On A Date/Proud Of You ............................................................................. 10 |
| 58 | Capitol CL 14845 | Whoop-A-Lala/I'm Following You ......................................................................... 10 |

## FOUR ESCORTS
54  HMV 7M 277 — Loop De Loop Mambo/Love Me ................................................................... 10

## FOUR ESQUIRES
| 55 | London HL 8152 | The Sphinx Won't Tell/Three Things (A Man Must Do) ........................................... 20 |
| 56 | London HLA 8224 | Adorable/Thunderbolt ....................................................................................... 10 |
| 57 | London HL 8376 | Look Homeward Angel/Santo Domingo (78) (unreleased on both 78 and 45) ............ 0 |

## FOUR EVERS
66  CBS 202549 — A Lovely Way To Say Goodnight/The Girl I Wanna Bring Home ......................... 45

## FOUR FOR FUN
63  Waverley ELP 113 — FOUR FOR FUN (EP) ....................................................................... 60

*(see also Dick Farina, Carolyn Hester)*

## FOUR FULLER BROTHERS
69  MCA MU 1068 — Groupie/Bitter Honey ............................................................................... 10

## FOUR GEES
67  President PT 160 — Ethiopia/Rough Rider ......................................................................... 7

MINT VALUE £

## FOUR GIBSON GIRLS
| 58 | Oriole CB 1447 | No School Tomorrow/June, July And August | 20 |
| 58 | Oriole CB 1453 | Safety Sue/VARIOUS ARTISTS: Safety Sue | 15 |

## FOUR GUYS
| 55 | Vogue Coral Q 72054 | Half Hearted Kisses/Mine | 10 |

*(see also Modernaires)*

## 4 HERO
| 98 | Reinforced/Talking Loud | TWO PAGES (4x12") | 25 |
| 95 | Reinforced LP 004 | PARALLEL UNIVERSE (2-LP) | 40 |

## FOUR INSTANTS
| 66 | Society | DISCOTHEQUE (LP) | 40 |

## FOUR JACKS
| 58 | Decca F 10984 | Hey! Baby/The Prayer Of Love | 15 |
| 58 | Decca DFE 6460 | HEY! BABY (EP) | 50 |

## FOUR JACKS & A JILL
| 68 | RCA Victor RCA 1669 | Master Jack/I Looked Back | 7 |

## FOUR JONES BOYS
| 56 | Decca F 10717 | Tutti Frutti/Are You Satisfied? | 15 |

*(see also Jones Boys, Annette Klooger)*

## FOUR JUST MEN
| 64 | Parlophone R 5186 | That's My Baby/Things Will Never Be The Same | 80 |

*(see also Just Four Men, Wimple Winch)*

## FOUR KENTS
| 68 | RCA RCA 1705 | The Moving Finger Writes/Searchin' | 20 |

## FOUR KESTRELS
| 61 | Decca F 11333 | Sound Off (Duckworth's Chant)/Can't Say That I Do | 6 |

## FOUR KINSMEN
| 67 | Decca F 22671 | It Looks Like The Daybreak/Forget About Him | 15 |

*(see also Kinsmen)*

## FOUR KNIGHTS
| 54 | Capitol CL 14076 | I Get So Lonely/Till Then | 20 |
| 54 | Capitol CL 14154 | Easy Street/In The Chapel In The Moonlight | 15 |
| 54 | Capitol CL 14204 | I Don't Wanna See You Cryin'/Saw Your Eyes | 15 |
| 55 | Capitol CL 14244 | Honey Bunch/Write Me, Baby | 15 |
| 55 | Capitol CL 14290 | Inside Out/Foolishly Yours | 15 |
| 56 | Capitol CL 14516 | Guilty/You | 15 |
| 59 | Coral Q 72355 | Foolish Tears/O' Falling Star | 15 |
| 55 | Capitol EAP1 506 | THE FOUR KNIGHTS (EP) | 15 |
| 53 | Capitol LC 6604 | SPOTLIGHT SONGS (10" LP) | 20 |

## FOUR LEAVED CLOVER
| 65 | Oak RGJ 207 | Alright Girl/Why | 500 |

## FOUR MACS
| 64 | Parlophone R 5204 | Come Back Silly Girl/Darlin' | 8 |

*(see also Sands Of Time)*

## FOUR MATADORS
| 66 | Columbia DB 7806 | A Man's Gotta Stand Tall/Fast Cars And Money | 70 |

## FOURMOST
| 63 | Parlophone R 5056 | Hello Little Girl/Just In Case | 6 |
| 63 | Parlophone R 5078 | I'm In Love/Respectable | 6 |
| 64 | Parlophone R 5128 | A Little Loving/Waiting For You | 6 |
| 64 | Parlophone R 5157 | How Can I Tell Her/You Got That Way | 5 |
| 64 | Parlophone R 5194 | Baby I Need Your Loving/That's Only What They Say | 6 |
| 65 | Parlophone R 5304 | Everything In The Garden/He Could Never | 7 |
| 65 | Parlophone R 5379 | Girls Girls Girls/Why Do Fools Fall In Love? | 6 |
| 66 | Parlophone R 5491 | Here, There And Everywhere/You've Changed | 10 |
| 66 | Parlophone R 5528 | Auntie Maggie's Remedy/Turn The Lights Down | 10 |
| 68 | CBS 3814 | Apples, Peaches, Pumpkin Pie/He Could Never | 15 |
| 69 | CBS 4041 | Rosetta/Just Like Before | 40 |
| 69 | CBS 4461 | Easy Squeezy/Do I Love You? | 20 |
| 72 | Phoenix SNIX 126 | Goodnight Sweet Dreams/Memphis | 8 |
| 64 | Parlophone GEP 8917 | THE FOURMOST (EP) | 35 |
| 64 | Parlophone GEP 8892 | THE SOUND OF THE FOURMOST (EP) | 35 |
| 65 | Parlophone PMC 1259 | FIRST AND FOURMOST (LP) | 100 |
| 75 | Fourmost SOF 001 | THE FOURMOST (LP) | 15 |

*(see also Format)*

## FOURMYULA
| 69 | Columbia DB 8549 | Honey Chile/Come With Me | 20 |

## FOUR PALMS
| 58 | Vogue V 9116 | Jeanie, Joanie, Shirley, Toni/Consideration | 600 |
| 58 | Vogue V 9116 | Jeanie, Joanie, Shirley, Toni/Consideration (78) | 150 |

## FOUR PENNIES (U.K.)
| 63 | Philips BF 1296 | Do You Want Me To/Miss Bad Daddy | 6 |
| 64 | Philips BF 1322 | Tell Me Girl/Juliet | 5 |
| 64 | Philips BF 1322 | Juliet/Tell Me Girl (A- & B-sides supposedly flipped after original release) | 5 |
| 64 | Philips BF 1349 | I Found Out The Hard Way/Don't Tell Me You Love Me | 5 |
| 64 | Philips BF 1366 | Black Girl/You Went Away | 5 |
| 65 | Philips BF 1398 | The Way Of Love/A Place Where No-One Goes | 5 |

| 65 | Philips BF 1435 | Until It's Time For You To Go/Till Another Day | 5 |
|----|-----------------|-----------------------------------------------|---|
| 66 | Philips BF 1469 | Trouble Is My Middle Name/Way Out Love | 5 |
| 66 | Philips BF 1491 | Keep The Freeway Open/Square Peg | 5 |
| 66 | Philips BF 1519 | No Sad Songs For Me/Cats | 10 |
| 66 | Philips BL 7734 | MIXED BAG (LP) | 60 |

*(see also Lionel Morton, Fritz Mike & Mo)*

## FOUR PENNIES (U.S.)

| 63 | Stateside SS 198 | My Block/Dry Your Eyes | 40 |
|----|------------------|------------------------|-----|
| 63 | Stateside SS 244 | When The Boy's Happy (The Girl's Happy Too)/Hockaday Part 1 | 30 |
| 79 | Ensign ENY 23 | When The Boy's Happy/CARLO: Little Orphan Girl | 5 |

*(see also Chiffons)*

## FOUR + ONE

| 65 | Parlophone R 5221 | Time Is On My Side/Don't Lie To Me | 120 |
|----|-------------------|------------------------------------|-----|

*(see also In Crowd, Tomorrow, Keith West)*

## FOUR PREPS

| 57 | Capitol CL 14727 | Falling Star/Where Wuz You | 5 |
|----|------------------|----------------------------|---|
| 57 | Capitol CL 14747 | I Cried A Million Tears/Moonstruck In Madrid | 5 |
| 57 | Capitol CL 14768 | Again 'n' Again 'n' Again/Promise Me Baby | 5 |
| 57 | Capitol CL 14783 | Band Of Angels/How About That? | 5 |
| 58 | Capitol CL 14815 | 26 Miles (Santa Catalina)/Fools Will Be Fools | 5 |
| 58 | Capitol CL 14873 | Big Man/Stop, Baby | 5 |
| 60 | Capitol CL 15128 | Got A Girl/(Wait Till You) Hear It From Me | 5 |
| 61 | Capitol CL 15217 | More Money For You And Me (Medley)/Swing Down Chariot | 5 |

## 4 SAXOPHONES IN 12 TONES

| 56 | Vogue V 2355 | Fantastic/Frankly Speaking | 7 |
|----|--------------|----------------------------|---|

## FOUR SEASONS

### SINGLES

| 62 | Stateside SS 122 | Sherry/I've Cried Before | 6 |
|----|------------------|--------------------------|---|
| 63 | Stateside SS 145 | Big Girls Don't Cry/Connie-O | 6 |
| 63 | Stateside SS 169 | Walk Like A Man/Lucky Ladybug | 6 |
| 63 | Stateside SS 194 | Ain't That A Shame/Soon (I'll Be Home Again) | 8 |
| 63 | Stateside SS 216 | Candy Girl/Marlena | 10 |
| 63 | Stateside SS 241 | Santa Claus Is Coming To Town/Christmas Tears | 15 |
| 64 | Stateside SS 262 | Peanuts/Silhouettes | 15 |
| 64 | Philips BF 1317 | Dawn (Go Away)/No Surfin' Today | 7 |
| 64 | Philips BF 1334 | Ronnie/Born To Wander | 8 |
| 64 | Stateside SS 315 | Alone/Long Lonely Nights | 10 |
| 64 | Philips BF 1347 | Rag Doll/Silence Is Golden | 6 |
| 64 | Stateside SS 343 | Since I Don't Have You/Sincerely | 15 |
| 65 | Philips BF 1364 | Save It For Me/Funny Face | 8 |
| 65 | Philips BF 1372 | Big Man In Town/Little Angel | 7 |
| 65 | Philips BF 1395 | Bye Bye Baby (Baby Goodbye)/Searching Wind | 7 |
| 65 | Philips BF 1411 | Toy Soldier/Betrayed | 8 |
| 65 | Philips BF 1420 | Girl Come Running/Cry Myself To Sleep | 10 |
| 65 | Philips BF 1439 | Let's Hang On!/On Broadway Tonight | 6 |
| 66 | Philips BF 1474 | Working My Way Back To You/Too Many Memories | 5 |
| 66 | Philips BF 1493 | Opus 17 (Don't Worry 'Bout Me)/Beggar's Parade | 10 |
| 66 | Philips BF 1511 | I've Got You Under My Skin/Huggin' My Pillow | 8 |
| 67 | Philips BF 1538 | Tell It To The Rain/Show Girl | 10 |
| 67 | Philips BF 1556 | Beggin'/Dody (as the 4 Seasons) | 15 |
| 67 | Philips BF 1584 | C'mon Marianne/Let's Ride Again | 7 |
| 67 | Philips BF 1600 | Around And Around/WONDER WHO: Lonesome Road | 10 |
| 67 | Philips BF 1621 | Watch The Flowers Grow/Raven | 10 |
| 68 | Philips BF 1651 | Will You Love Me Tomorrow?/Silhouettes | 10 |
| 68 | Philips BF 1685 | Saturday's Father/Goodbye Girl | 10 |
| 69 | Philips BF 1743 | Electric Stories/Pity | 10 |
| 69 | Philips BF 1763 | Rag Doll/Working My Way Back To You (p/s) | 7 |
| 71 | Philips 6051 018 | Rag Doll/Let's Hang On/I've Got You Under My Skin (maxi-single) | 5 |
| 71 | Warner Bros K 16107 | Whatever You Say/Sleeping Man (withdrawn, 300 only) As Frankie Valli and the...) | 45 |
| 64 | Stateside SE 1011 | THE FOUR SEASONS SING (EP) | 40 |

### ALBUMS

| 63 | Stateside SL 10033 | SHERRY AND 11 OTHERS | 30 |
|----|--------------------|----------------------|-----|
| 63 | Stateside SL 10042 | AIN'T THAT A SHAME | 40 |
| 63 | Stateside SL 10051 | THE FOUR SEASONS' GREETINGS | 25 |
| 64 | Philips BL 7611 | BORN TO WANDER | 20 |
| 64 | Philips BL 7621 | DAWN (GO AWAY) AND 11 OTHER GREAT SONGS | 20 |
| 64 | Philips BL 7643 | RAG DOLL | 18 |
| 65 | Philips BL 7663 | ENTERTAIN YOU | 20 |
| 65 | Philips (S)BL 7687 | SING BIG HITS BY BURT BACHARACH ... HAL DAVID ... BOB DYLAN | 18 |
| 65 | Philips (S)BL 7699 | WORKING MY WAY BACK TO YOU | 18 |
| 67 | Philips (S)BL 7753 | CHRISTMAS ALBUM | 25 |
| 69 | Philips (S)BL 7880 | THE GENUINE IMITATION LIFE GAZETTE | 25 |

*(see also Beverly Hills Blues Band, Frankie Valli, Wonder Who)*

## FOUR SIGHTS

| 64 | Columbia DB 7227 | But I Can Tell/And I Cry | 15 |
|----|------------------|--------------------------|-----|

## 4-SKINS

| 81 | Clockwork Fun CF 101 | One Law For Them/Brave New World (p/s) | 15 |
|----|----------------------|----------------------------------------|-----|
| 81 | Secret SHH 125 | Yesterday's Heroes/Justice/Get Out Of My Life (p/s) | 10 |

# FOUR SPICES

| | | | |
|---|---|---|---|
| 82 | Secret SHH 141 | Lowlife/Bread Or Blood (p/s) | 10 |
| 82 | Secret SEC 4 | THE GOOD, THE BAD AND THE 4-SKINS (LP, with photo inner) | 18 |
| 83 | Syndicate SYN 1 | A FISTFUL OF ... 4-SKINS (LP) | 18 |
| 84 | Syndicate SYN LP 5 | FROM CHAOS TO 1984 (LP) | 20 |
| 01 | Captain Oi! AHOY PD3 | THE GOOD THE BAD AND THE 4-SKINS (LP, reissue, clear vinyl picture disc) | 15 |

*(see also Plastic Gangsters)*

## FOUR SPICES
| | | | |
|---|---|---|---|
| 57 | MGM MGM 944 | Armen's Theme (Yesterday And You)/Fire Engine Boogie | 100 |

## FOUR SQUARES
| | | | |
|---|---|---|---|
| 64 | Hollick & Taylor HT 1009 | FOUR SQUARES (EP) | 100 |

*(see also Pink People)*

## FOURTEEN (14)
| | | | |
|---|---|---|---|
| 68 | Olga OLE 002 | Through My Door/Meet Mr. Edgar | 20 |
| 68 | Olga OLE 006 | Umbrella/Drizzle (Rain) | 20 |
| 68 | Olga OLE 006 | Umbrella/Drizzle (Rain) (Demo) | 45 |
| 68 | Olga S 051 | Easy To Fool/Frosty Stars On A Window Pane | 15 |

## 14 ICED BEARS
| | | | |
|---|---|---|---|
| 86 | Frank COPPOLA 101 | Inside/Blue Suit/Cut (hand-printed paper bag sleeve) | 25 |
| 87 | Frank CAPRA 202 | Like A Dolphin/Balloon Song/Train Song/Lie To Choose (12", p/s) | 10 |
| 88 | Sarah SARAH 005 | Come Get Me/Unhappy Days/Sure To See (poster p/s) | 40 |
| 89 | Thunderball 7TBL 2 | Mother Sleep (7", unreleased, Mayking test pressings only) | 25 |
| 90s | Thunderball Surfacer 002 | Falling Backwards/World I Love/CROCODILE RIDE: Ex-Hipster/Satellite (Speed Mix) (numbered & stickered mailer, 1,000 only) | 8 |

## FOUR TET
| | | | |
|---|---|---|---|
| 98 | Output OPR 14 | THIRTYSIXTWENTYFIVE EP (2 one-sided 12", p/s) | 15 |
| 02 | Domino RUG 139 | I'm On Fire (Part 1)/I'm On Fire (Part 2) (p/s) | 8 |
| 09 | Text TEXT 006 | Wolf Cub (12", black label, plain black sleeve) | 15 |
| 99 | Output OPR21 | DIALOGUE (LP) | 30 |
| 01 | Domino WIGLP94 | PAUSE (LP) | 15 |
| 02 | Domino WIGLP126 | ROUNDS (2-LP) | 20 |
| 05 | Domino WIGLP 154 | EVERYTHING ECSTATIC (2xLP, one sided etched, with bonus CD) | 20 |
| 10 | Domino WIGLP 254 | THERE IS LOVE IN YOU (2-LP) | 18 |

*(see also Fridge, Thom Yorke)*

## FOUR TONES
| | | | |
|---|---|---|---|
| 58 | Decca F 11074 | Voom Ba Voom/Rickshaw Boy | 15 |

## FOUR TOPHATTERS
| | | | |
|---|---|---|---|
| 55 | London HLA 8163 | Leave-a My Gal Alone/Go Baby Go | 200 |
| 55 | London HLA 8198 | Forty Five Men In A Telephone Booth/Wild Rosie | 200 |

## FOUR TOPS
### SINGLES
| | | | |
|---|---|---|---|
| 64 | Stateside SS 336 | Baby I Need Your Lovin'/Call On Me | 50 |
| 64 | Stateside SS 336 | Baby I Need Your Lovin'/Call On Me (DJ Copy) | 70 |
| 65 | Stateside SS 371 | Without The One You Love (Life's Not Worthwhile)/Love Has Gone | 60 |
| 65 | Stateside SS 371 | Without The One You Love (Life's Not Worthwhile)/Love Has Gone (DJ Copy) | 130 |
| 65 | Tamla Motown TMG 507 | Ask The Lonely/Where Did You Go? | 90 |
| 65 | Tamla Motown TMG 507 | Ask The Lonely/Where Did You Go? (DJ copy) | 150 |
| 65 | Tamla Motown TMG 515 | I Can't Help Myself/Sad Souvenirs | 150 |
| 65 | Tamla Motown TMG 515 | I Can't Help Myself/Sad Souvenirs (DJ copy) | 25 |
| 65 | Tamla Motown TMG 528 | It's The Same Old Song/Your Love Is Amazing | 150 |
| 65 | Tamla Motown TMG 528 | It's The Same Old Song/Your Love Is Amazing (DJ copy) | 25 |
| 65 | Tamla Motown TMG 542 | Something About You/Darling I Hum Our Song | 100 |
| 65 | Tamla Motown TMG 542 | Something About You/Darling I Hum Our Song (DJ copy) | 30 |
| 66 | Tamla Motown TMG 553 | Shake Me, Wake Me (When It's Over)/Just As Long As You Need Me ) | 100 |
| 66 | Tamla Motown TMG 553 | Shake Me, Wake Me (When It's Over)/Just As Long As You Need Me (DJ copy) | 35 |
| 66 | Tamla Motown TMG 568 | Loving You Is Sweeter Than Ever/I Like Everything About You | 100 |
| 66 | Tamla Motown TMG 568 | Loving You Is Sweeter Than Ever/I Like Everything About You (DJ copy £100) | 30 |
| 66 | Tamla Motown TMG 579 | Reach Out, I'll Be There/Until You Love Someone (small print, later large print = £15) | 100 |
| 66 | Tamla Motown TMG 579 | Reach Out, I'll Be There/Until You Love Someone (DJ copy) | 18 |
| 67 | Tamla Motown TMG 589 | Standing In The Shadows Of Love/Since You've Been Gone (small print) | 100 |
| 67 | Tamla Motown TMG 589 | Standing In The Shadows Of Love/Since You've Been Gone (later large print) | 15 |
| 67 | Tamla Motown TMG 589 | Standing In The Shadows Of Love/Since You've Been Gone (DJ copy) | 8 |
| 67 | Tamla Motown TMG 601 | Bernadette/I Got A Feeling | 100 |
| 67 | Tamla Motown TMG 601 | Bernadette/I Got A Feeling (DJ copy) | 15 |
| 67 | Tamla Motown TMG 612 | Seven Rooms Of Gloom/I'll Turn To Stone | 100 |
| 67 | Tamla Motown TMG 612 | Seven Rooms Of Gloom/I'll Turn To Stone (DJ copy) | 15 |
| 67 | Tamla Motown TMG 623 | You Keep Running Away/If You Don't Want My Love | 65 |
| 67 | Tamla Motown TMG 623 | You Keep Running Away/If You Don't Want My Love (DJ copy) | 12 |
| 67 | Tamla Motown TMG 634 | Walk Away Renee/Mame | 65 |
| 67 | Tamla Motown TMG 634 | Walk Away Renee/Mame (DJ copy) | 12 |
| 68 | Tamla Motown TMG 647 | If I Were A Carpenter/Your Love Is Wonderful | 60 |
| 68 | Tamla Motown TMG 647 | If I Were A Carpenter/Your Love Is Wonderful (DJ copy) | 12 |
| 68 | Tamla Motown TMG 665 | Yesterday's Dreams/For Once In My Life | 60 |
| 68 | Tamla Motown TMG 665 | Yesterday's Dreams/For Once In My Life (DJ copy) | 15 |
| 68 | Tamla Motown TMG 675 | I'm In A Different World/Remember When | 60 |
| 68 | Tamla Motown TMG 675 | I'm In A Different World/Remember When (DJ copy) | 15 |
| 69 | Tamla Motown TMG 698 | What Is A Man?/Don't Bring Back Memories | 60 |
| 69 | Tamla Motown TMG 698 | What Is A Man?/Don't Bring Back Memories (DJ copy) | 12 |
| 69 | Tamla Motown TMG 710 | Do What You Gotta Do/Can't Seem To Get You Out Of My Mind | 70 |
| | | | 18 |

| | | | |
|---|---|---|---|
| 69 | Tamla Motown TMG 710 | Do What You Gotta Do/Can't Seem To Get You Out Of My Mind (DJ copy) | 70 |
| 70 | Tamla Motown TMG 736 | It's All In The Game/Love (Is The Answer) | 7 |
| 70 | Tamla Motown TMG 736 | It's All In The Game/Love (Is The Answer) (DJ copy) | 40 |
| 70 | Tamla Motown TMG 965 | It's All In The Game/Bernadette | 5 |
| 70 | Tamla Motown TMG 752 | Still Water (Love)/Still Water (Peace) | 7 |
| 70 | Tamla Motown TMG 752 | Still Water (Love)/Still Water (Peace) (DJ copy) | 40 |
| 71 | Tamla Motown TMG 770 | Just Seven Numbers (Can Straighten Out My Life)/I Wish I Were Your Mirror | 7 |
| 71 | Tamla Motown TMG 770 | Just Seven Numbers (Can Straighten Out My Life)/I Wish I Were Your Mirror (DJ copy) | 30 |
| 71 | Tamla Motown TMG 785 | Simple Game/You Stole My Love | 7 |
| 71 | Tamla Motown TMG 785 | Simple Game/You Stole My Love (DJ copy) | 30 |
| 72 | Tamla Motown TMG 803 | Bernadette/I Got A Feeling/It's The Same Old Song | 5 |
| 72 | Tamla Motown TMG 803 | Bernadette/I Got A Feeling/It's The Same Old Song (DJ copy) | 30 |
| 72 | Tamla Motown TMG 829 | I'll Turn To Stone/Love Feels Like Fire | 10 |
| 72 | Tamla Motown TMG 829 | I'll Turn To Stone/Love Feels Like Fire (DJ copy) | 30 |
| 72 | Probe PRO 575 | Keeper Of The Castle/Jubilee With Soul | 5 |
| 73 | Probe PRO 596 | Are You Man Enough/Peace Of Mind | 5 |
| 74 | Probe PRO 612 | I Just Can't Get You Out Of My Mind/Am I My Brother's Keeper | 15 |
| 75 | ABC ABC 4057 | Seven Lonely Nights/I Can't Hold On Much Longer | 5 |
| 75 | Tamla Motown TMG 1011 | Walk Away Renee/You Keep Running Away (reissue) | 6 |
| 83 | Tamla Motown TMG 1320 | Medley/TEMPTATIONS: Papa Was A Rolling Stone | 35 |
| 84 | Calibre 124 | Your Song/I'm Here Again (p/s, withdrawn) | 70 |
| 84 | Calibre 124 | Your Song/I'm Here Again (withdrawn) | 25 |

## EPs

| | | | |
|---|---|---|---|
| 66 | Tamla Motown TME 2012 | THE FOUR TOPS (EP, flipback sleeve) | 30 |
| 67 | Tamla Motown TME 2018 | FOUR TOP HITS | 35 |

## ALBUMS

| | | | |
|---|---|---|---|
| 65 | Tamla Motown TML 11010 | THE FOUR TOPS | 80 |
| 66 | Tamla Motown TML 11021 | SECOND ALBUM (mono) | 40 |
| 66 | Tamla Motown STML 11021 | SECOND ALBUM (stereo) | 50 |
| 66 | Tamla Motown TML 11037 | FOUR TOPS ON TOP (mono) | 35 |
| 66 | Tamla Motown STML 11037 | FOUR TOPS ON TOP (stereo) | 45 |
| 67 | Tamla Motown TML 11041 | FOUR TOPS LIVE! (mono) | 25 |
| 67 | Tamla Motown (S)TML 11041 | FOUR TOPS LIVE! (stereo) | 30 |
| 67 | Tamla Motown TML 11056 | REACH OUT (mono) | 25 |
| 67 | Tamla Motown STML 11056 | REACH OUT (stereo) | 30 |
| 68 | Tamla Motown STML 11061 | FOUR TOPS GREATEST HITS (stereo) | 25 |
| 68 | Tamla Motown TML 11061 | FOUR TOPS GREATEST HITS (mono) | 20 |
| 69 | Tamla Motown (S)TML 11087 | YESTERDAY'S DREAMS (mono/stereo) | 25 |
| 69 | Tamla Motown TML 11113 | FOUR TOPS NOW (mono) | 25 |
| 69 | Tamla Motown STML 11113 | FOUR TOPS NOW (stereo) | 20 |
| 70 | Tamla Motown TML 11138 | SOUL SPIN (mono) | 25 |
| 70 | Tamla Motown STML 11138 | SOUL SPIN (stereo) | 20 |
| 70 | Tamla Motown STML 11149 | STILL WATERS RUN DEEP | 20 |
| 71 | Tamla Motown STML 11173 | CHANGING TIMES | 20 |
| 73 | Probe SPB 1064 | KEEPER OF THE CASTLE | 15 |
| 73 | Probe SPB 1077 | SHAFT IN AFRICA (soundtrack, with Johnny Pate) | 40 |
| 74 | Probe SPBA 6283 | MEETING OF THE MINDS | 15 |
| 74 | ABC ABCL 5035 | SHAFT IN AFRICA (soundtrack, reissue) | 15 |

*(see also Supremes & Four Tops)*

## FOUR TUNES

| | | | |
|---|---|---|---|
| 55 | London HL 8151 | I Sold My Heart To A Junkman/The Greatest Feeling In The World | 100 |
| 55 | London HL 8151 | I Sold My Heart To A Junkman/The Greatest Feeling In The World (78) | 20 |
| 55 | London HLJ 8164 | Tired Of Waitin'/L'Amour, Toujours L'Amour (Love Everlasting) | 50 |
| 55 | London HLJ 8164 | Tired Of Waitin'/L'Amour, Toujours L'Amour (Love Everlasting) (78) | 20 |

## FOURUM

| | | | |
|---|---|---|---|
| 78 | Sirius SP 519 | FOURUM (LP) | 20 |
| 81 | Guardian GRC 95 | SINGING THE DALES (LP) | 20 |

## FOUR VOICES

| | | | |
|---|---|---|---|
| 58 | Philips PB 864 | Tell Me You're Mine/Tight Spot | 5 |

## FOUR WINDS

| | | | |
|---|---|---|---|
| 58 | London HLU 8556 | Short Shorts/Five Minutes More | 25 |

## HARRY FOWLER

| | | | |
|---|---|---|---|
| 61 | HMV POP 891 | Buddies (with Mario Fabrizl)/Flower Flogger | 8 |

## KIM FOWLEY

| | | | |
|---|---|---|---|
| 66 | Parlophone R 5521 | Lights/Something New And Different | 30 |
| 66 | CBS 202243 | They're Coming To Take Me Away Ha-Haaa!!/You Get More For Your Money On The Flip Side Of This Record Talking Blues | 15 |
| 66 | CBS 202338 | Lights (The Blind Can See)/Something New And Different (reissue) | 15 |
| 66 | Island WI 278 | The Trip/Beautiful People | 20 |
| 72 | Action ACT 4606 | Born To Make You Cry/Thunder Road | 7 |
| 73 | Capitol CL 15743 | International Heroes/E.S.P. Reader | 5 |
| 77 | Island WIP 278 | The Trip/Beautiful People (p/s, reissue) | 15 |
| 78 | Mercury 6005 009 | Control/Rubber Rainbow | 5 |
| 79 | Illegal ILS 012 | Rubber Rainbow/In My Garage (p/s) | 5 |
| 80 | Island WIP 6555 | 1989: Waiting For The Next Ten Years/1987: Lost Like A Lizard In Snow | 5 |
| 73 | Capitol E-ST 11159 | INTERNATIONAL HEROES (LP) | 25 |

*(see also Freaks Of Nature, Hollywood Argyles, Napoleon XIV, B. Bumble & Stingers)*

MINT VALUE £

**(THE) FOX**
68   CBS 3381                              Mister Carpenter/Seek And You Find................................................................. 300

**FOX (1)**
70   Fontana 6007 016                      Second Hand Love/Butterfly.......................................................................... 25
70   Fontana 6309 007                      FOR FOX SAKE (LP, laminated sleeve, black/silver labels) ........................... 300
03   RPM RPM 254LP                         FOR FOX SAKE (LP, gatefold, reissue) ........................................................... 15

**BOB FOX & STU LUCKLEY**
78   Rubber RUB 028                        NOWT SO GOOD'LL PASS (LP) ......................................................................... 15

**DON FOX**
60   Triumph RGM 1022                      T'ain't What You Do/Out There ...................................................................... 40

**PAUL FOX**
90   Sound Business SB 1                   Writing On The Wall/Version/LIBERATION TRIBE: African Mask (12") ......... 40
*(see also Tafari & Paul Fox)*

**UFFA FOX**
60   Parlophone PMC 1112                   UFFA SINGS (LP) ............................................................................................. 15

**FOX IN SOCKS**
81   Jest 001                              Sound Patterns/Lonely House (p/s) ............................................................... 25

**FOXTROT**
74   RCA APBO 0169                         Cave Man Billy/These Passing Days ................................................................. 5

**FOXX**
71   MCA MUPS 419                          REVOLT OF EMILY YOUNG (LP) ....................................................................... 15

**INEZ FOXX**
63   Sue WI 301                            Mockingbird/He's The One You Love (actually by Inez & Charlie Foxx)........... 25
64   Sue WI 304                            Jaybirds/Broken-Hearted Fool (actually by Inez & Charlie Foxx)..................... 25
64   Sue WI 314                            Ask Me/Hi Diddle Diddle (actually by Inez & Charlie Foxx)............................. 25
64   Sue WI 323                            Hurt By Love/Confusion (actually by Inez & Charlie Foxx)............................. 25
71   Pye International 7N 25546            You Shouldn't Have Set My Soul On Fire/Live For Today ............................... 10
73   Stax 2025 151                         You Hurt Me For The Last Time/Watch The Dog (That Brings The Bone) ......... 8

**INEZ & CHARLIE FOXX**
64   Sue WI 307                            Competition/Here We Go Round The Mulberry Bush (as Charlie & Inez Foxx) ............ 30
64   Sue WI 356                            La De Da I Love You/Yankee Doodle Dandy.................................................... 30
65   London HLC 9971                       My Momma Told Me/I Feel Alright.................................................................. 10
65   London HLC 10009                      Hummingbird/If I Need Anyone (Let It Be You) ............................................. 10
66   Stateside SS 556                      Come By Here/No Stranger To Love ............................................................... 30
67   Stateside SS 586                      Tightrope/My Special Prayer ......................................................................... 30
67   Stateside SS 586                      Tightrope/My Special Prayer (DJ copy) ......................................................... 75
67   Direction 58-2712                     I Ain't Goin' For That/Undecided ................................................................... 10
67   Direction 58-3192                     (1, 2, 3, 4, 5, 6, 7) Count The Days/A Stranger I Don't Know ......................... 12
68   Direction 58-3816                     Come On In/Baby Drop Your Dime ................................................................. 12
69   Direction 58-4042                     Baby Give It To Me/You Fixed My Heartache ................................................. 40
69   London HLC 10250                      Mockingbird/Hummingbird (unissued)............................................................ 0
69   United Artists UP 2269                Mockingbird/Hurt By Love .............................................................................. 8
69   United Artists UP 35013               La De Da I Love You/Don't Do It No More ...................................................... 10
71   Pye International 7N 25561            Tightrope/Baby Take It All ............................................................................. 10
83   Sue ENS 2                             Mockingbird (EP) ........................................................................................... 15
64   Sue ILP 911                           MOCKINGBIRD (LP) ....................................................................................... 100
65   London HA-C 8241                      INEZ AND CHARLIE FOXX (LP, plum label)....................................................... 70
65   London HA-C 8241                      INEZ AND CHARLIE FOXX (LP, later black label) ............................................ 40
68   Direction 8-63085                     COME BY HERE (LP) ....................................................................................... 30
68   Direction 8-63281                     GREATEST HITS (LP) ...................................................................................... 20
69   United Artists UA(S) 29025           MOCKINGBIRD (LP) ....................................................................................... 15

**JOHN FOXX**
80   Virgin VS 338                         No-One Driving (2.53 DJ Version)/Glimmer//This City/Mr. No (double pack, stickered gatefold p/s, matrix no. VS 338 A5DJ)................................................................ 15
82   Virgin VS 543                         Endlessly/Ghosts On Water//Dance With Me/A Kind Of Wave (double pack)................ 5
84   Virgin VS 615                         Your Dress/Woman On A Stairway//Lifting Sky/Annexe (double pack) .......................... 5
85   Virgin VS 771                         The Stars On Fire/What Kind Of Girl (p/s, with bonus single)........................... 5
80   Virgin V 2146                         METAMATIC (LP) ........................................................................................... 15
*(see also Ultravox)*

**FRABJOY & RUNCIBLE SPOON**
69   Marmalade 598 019                     I'm Beside Myself/Animal Song....................................................................... 30
*(see also Godley & Creme, Doctor Father, Hotlegs, Mockingbirds, 10cc)*

**FRAGILE FRIENDS**
83   KC KCT1                               NOVELTY WEARS OFF (12" EP) ....................................................................... 25
84   KC KC 001                             Paper Doll/What I Call Beautiful ..................................................................... 35

**FRAGMENTS**
79   Shattered SHAT 1                      Nutbush City Limits/Fragments ....................................................................... 5
80   Shattered SHAT 2                      Some Other Guy/Intro Mental (p/s) ............................................................... 10

**FRAME**
66   RCA RCA 1556                          My Feet Don't Fit In His Shoes/She................................................................. 18
67   RCA RCA 1571                          Doctor Doctor/I Can't Go On .......................................................................... 65
70   Pye 7N 45213                          Rockin' Machine/One More Time..................................................................... 10
74   Seven Sun SSUN 12                     Billy The Dreamer/Rocking Machine .............................................................. 20

**FRAMED**
82   Thunderbay TBR 021                    Into My Life/Wonderland ................................................................................ 20
*(see also Girlschool)*

## FRAMES
| | | | |
|---|---|---|---|
| 79 | Brain Booster BBC 2 | False Accusations/69 (no p/s) | 6 |

## FRAN & ALAN
| | | | |
|---|---|---|---|
| 66 | Mercury MF 95 | Seein' The Right Love Go Wrong/There's A place | 5 |
| 68 | MGM MGM 1428 | Such A Pity/Mrs Robinson | 8 |

## PETER FRANC
| | | | |
|---|---|---|---|
| 73 | Dawn DNS 1033 | I'll Move Along/Song For Every Season | 5 |
| 73 | Dawn DNS 1039 | Ballad Of the Superstar/Strange Kind Of Woman | 5 |
| 74 | Dawn DNS 1088 | Flag Of Convenience/At Home With You | 5 |

## FRANCIS
| | | | |
|---|---|---|---|
| 67 | Blue Beat BB 379 | Warn The People (actually by Willie Francis)/SWINGERS: Simpleton (actually by Peter Tosh & Crackers) | 40 |
| 72 | Fab FAB 182 | Rocking Machine/SOUL CLANS: Flying Rhythm | 20 |
| 73 | Fab FAB 251 | Locks/Version | 12 |

## B. FRANCIS
| | | | |
|---|---|---|---|
| 65 | Ska Beat JB 193 | Judy Crowned/Who Crunch | 15 |

## BOBBY FRANCIS
| | | | |
|---|---|---|---|
| 67 | JJ DB 1153 | Chain Gang/Venus | 175 |

*(see also Winston Francis)*

## CLAIRE FRANCIS
| | | | |
|---|---|---|---|
| 66 | Polydor 56079 | I've Got My Own Thing Going/Here I Go Again | 7 |
| 67 | Polydor 56142 | But I Don't Care/If You Don't Know | 7 |

## CONNIE FRANCIS
### SINGLES
| | | | |
|---|---|---|---|
| 56 | MGM SP 1169 | My First Real Love (with Jaybirds)/Believe In Me (Crede Mi) | 200 |
| 56 | MGM SP 1169 | My First Real Love (with Jaybirds)/Believe In Me (Crede Mi) (78) | 20 |
| 56 | MGM MGM 932 | My Sailor Boy/Everyone Needs Someone | 60 |
| 57 | MGM MGM 945 | Little Blue Wren/I Never Had A Sweetheart | 50 |
| 57 | MGM MGM 962 | Eighteen/Faded Orchid | 50 |
| 58 | MGM MGM 975 | Who's Sorry Now?/You Were Only Fooling (While I Was Falling In Love) | 5 |
| 58 | MGM MGM 982 | I'm Sorry I Made You Cry/Lock Up Your Heart | 5 |
| 58 | MGM MGM 993 | I'll Get By/Fallin' | 10 |
| 59 | MGM MGM 1012 | If I Didn't Care/Toward The End Of The Day | 5 |
| 59 | MGM MGM 1036 | Plenty Good Lovin'/You're Gonna Miss Me | 8 |
| 60 | MGM MGM 1070 | Mama/Teddy (withdrawn; demos more common) | 40 |
| 60 | MGM MGM 1070 | Mama/Teddy (withdrawn; demo copy) | 30 |
| 62 | MGM MGM 1165 | Vacation/It's Gonna Take Me Some Time | 6 |
| 65 | MGM MGM 1271 | My Child/No One Ever Sends Me Roses | 6 |
| 69 | MGM MGM 1471 | The Wedding Cake/Overhill Underground | 5 |
| 69 | MGM MGM 1493 | Mr. Love/Zingara | 7 |

### EPs
| | | | |
|---|---|---|---|
| 56 | MGM MGM-EP 658 | A GIRL IN LOVE | 15 |
| 58 | MGM MGM-EP 677 | HEARTACHES | 15 |
| 58 | MGM MGM-EP 686 | CONNIE FRANCIS | 15 |
| 59 | MGM MGM-EP 697 | IF I DIDN'T CARE | 15 |
| 60 | MGM MGM-EP 711 | YOU'RE MY EVERYTHING | 15 |
| 60 | MGM MGM-EP 717 | ROCK AND ROLL MILLION SELLERS NO. 1 | 15 |
| 60 | MGM MGM-EP 720 | ROCK AND ROLL MILLION SELLERS NO. 2 | 15 |
| 60 | MGM MGM-EP 731 | ROCK AND ROLL MILLION SELLERS NO. 3 | 15 |
| 60 | MGM MGM-EP 742 | FIRST LADY OF RECORD (laminated or matt rear sleeve) | 15 |
| 61 | MGM MGM-EP 756 | WHERE THE BOYS ARE | 15 |
| 61 | MGM MGM-EP 759 | CONNIE FRANCIS FAVOURITES | 15 |
| 61 | MGM MGM-EP 760 | SINGS ITALIAN FAVOURITES | 15 |
| 63 | MGM MGM-EP 769 | CONNIE'S AMERICAN HITS | 15 |
| 63 | MGM MGM-EP 773 | HEY RING-A-DING | 40 |
| 63 | MGM MGM-EP 775 | WHAT KIND OF FOOL AM I? | 20 |
| 63 | MGM MGM-EP 780 | MALA FEMMENA | 10 |
| 63 | MGM MGM-EP 783 | FROM ITALY ... WITH LOVE | 10 |

### ALBUMS
| | | | |
|---|---|---|---|
| 58 | MGM MGM-D 153 | WHO'S SORRY NOW? (10") | 30 |
| 59 | MGM MGM-C 782 | MY THANKS TO YOU | 15 |
| 59 | MGM MGM-C 786 | THE EXCITING CONNIE FRANCIS | 15 |
| 59 | MGM MGM-C 797 | CHRISTMAS WITH CONNIE | 15 |
| 60 | MGM MGM-C 804 | ROCK AND ROLL MILLION SELLERS NO. 1 | 40 |
| 60 | MGM MGM-C 812 | COUNTRY AND WESTERN GOLDEN HITS | 15 |
| 60 | MGM MGM-C 819 | FUN SONGS FOR CHILDREN | 15 |
| 61 | MGM MGM-C 879 | DO THE TWIST | 40 |
| 78 | United Artists ULP 30182 | WHO'S HAPPY NOW? (withdrawn sleeve with different lettering) | 40 |

## CONNIE FRANCIS & MARVIN RAINWATER
| | | | |
|---|---|---|---|
| 58 | MGM MGM 969 | The Majesty Of Love/You My Darling You | 35 |

*(see also Marvin Rainwater)*

## (KING) JOE FRANCIS
| | | | |
|---|---|---|---|
| 65 | Blue Beat BB 323 | Wicked Woman/King Joe's Ska (as King Joe Francis) | 15 |
| 65 | Ska Beat JB 184 | Waggling Tails/I Don't Want You No More | 20 |
| 66 | Ska Beat JB 262 | Scarborough Ska/I Got A Scar (as Joe Francis & Ricky Logan & Snowballs) | 20 |
| 66 | Rio R 90 | Have My Body (song actually "Have Mercy Baby")/Everybody's Got To Know (as King Joe Francis & Hijackers) | 15 |
| 66 | Rio R 94 | Days Are Lonely/My Baby | 25 |

MINT VALUE £

| | | | |
|---|---|---|---|
| 67 | Rainbow RAI 114 | My Granny/Pull It Out (as J. Francis & Rico's Boys) | 15 |

## JOHNNIE FRANCIS
| | | | |
|---|---|---|---|
| 55 | Decca F 10440 | Funny Thing/Give Me The Right | 5 |

## LEE FRANCIS (1)
| | | | |
|---|---|---|---|
| 65 | Decca F 12148 | Ciao/If He Wants Me | 5 |

*(see also Vernons Girls)*

## LEE FRANCIS (2)
| | | | |
|---|---|---|---|
| 79 | Lee & Roy L 2 | A Lonely I & I/Paradise (12") | 15 |
| 79 | Lee & Roy L 3 | Shadows Of My Youth/Deception Of Consciousness (12") | 15 |

## NAT FRANCIS
| | | | |
|---|---|---|---|
| 66 | Blue Beat BB 346 | Mama Kiss Him Goodnight/Tra La La (with Prince Buster Junior & Sunsets) | 20 |
| 66 | Blue Beat BB 361 | Just To Keep You (credited to B. Junior)/You Only Want My Money | 18 |
| 67 | Blue Beat BB 376 | Seven Nights Of Love/Feeling Blue | 20 |

## PAT FRANCIS
| | | | |
|---|---|---|---|
| 77 | Western Kingston WK 506 | Rasta Protest/Part 2 | 8 |

## RITCHIE FRANCIS
| | | | |
|---|---|---|---|
| 72 | Pegasus PEG 11 | SONGBIRD (LP, gatefold textured sleeve) | 25 |

*(see also Eyes Of Blue, Big Sleep)*

## STEVE FRANCIS
| | | | |
|---|---|---|---|
| 64 | King KG 1012 | Watch Your Step/Lovey Dovey | 8 |

## WILBERT FRANCIS & VIBRATORS
| | | | |
|---|---|---|---|
| 66 | Ska Beat JB 267 | Memories Of You/CHUCK JACQUES: Now That You're Gone | 25 |

*(see also Little Willie, Vibrators [Jamaica])*

## WILLIE FRANCIS
| | | | |
|---|---|---|---|
| 69 | Bullet BU 415 | Motherless Children/I Am Not Afraid | 90 |
| 71 | Escort ERT 848 | Burn Them/Poor Boy | 10 |
| 71 | Bullet BU 489 | Willie's Rouster/Rouster Version | 15 |
| 71 | Pama PM 829 | Oh What A Mini/Version | 10 |
| 74 | Magnet MA 38 | Quick March/Africa Melody (actually by Charlie Organaire) | 10 |

*(see also Martin Riley)*

## WINSTON FRANCIS
| | | | |
|---|---|---|---|
| 69 | Coxsone CS 7089 | Reggae And Cry/FREEDOM SINGERS: Easy Come Easy Go (B-side actually by Righteous Flames) | 150 |
| 69 | Studio One SO 2086 | The Games People Play/ALBERT GRIFFITHS: The Kicks | 125 |
| 69 | Punch PH 5 | Too Experienced/JACKIE MINTO: Mule Jerk (B-side actually by Jackie Mittoo) | 15 |
| 69 | Bamboo BAM 10 | The Same Old Song/SOUND DIMENSION: Rattle On | 45 |
| 70 | Bamboo BAM 46 | Turn Back The Hands Of Time/Soul Bowl | 25 |
| 70 | Bamboo BAM 48 | California Dreaming/JACKIE MITTOO & SOUND DIMENSION: Soul Stew | 30 |
| 72 | Camel CA 99 | Ten Times Sweeter Than You/Fat Boy | 20 |
| 72 | Rhino RNO 102 | A Little Today A Little Tomorrow/Love Thy Neighbour | 7 |
| 73 | Fab FAB 271 | Mr Fix It/Version | 8 |
| 74 | Ashanti ASH 415 | California Dreaming/SOUND DIMENSION: Soul Food (reissue) | 8 |
| 70 | Bamboo BDLP 207 | MR FIX IT (LP) | 60 |
| 71 | Bamboo BDLPS 216 | CALIFORNIA DREAMING (LP) | 80 |

*(see also Bobby Francis, Jerry & Freedom Singers, Zimm & Dee Dee)*

## CLAUDE FRANCOIS
| | | | |
|---|---|---|---|
| 66 | Fontana TF 725 | In My Memory/Gone From My Mind | 30 |
| 67 | Fontana TF 799 | Bench Number 3 Waterloo Station/Run To Daddy | 80 |
| 78 | EMI 2773 | Bordeaux Rose/Magnolias (demo in p/s) | 20 |
| 77 | EMI EMC 3189 | HIS HITS IN ENGLISH (LP) | 30 |

## JACKSON C. FRANK
| | | | |
|---|---|---|---|
| 78 | B&C BCS 0012 | Blues Run The Game/Milk & Honey | 20 |
| 65 | Columbia DB 7795 | Blues Run The Game/Can't Get Away From My Love | 100 |
| 65 | Columbia 33SX 1788 | JACKSON C. FRANK (LP) | 300 |
| 78 | B&C BCLP 4 | AGAIN (LP, reissue of above LP) | 40 |

## FRANK & BARBARIANS
| | | | |
|---|---|---|---|
| 62 | Oriole CB 1758 | The Bouncer/Concerto In The Stars | 15 |

## FRANKIE & CLASSICALS
| | | | |
|---|---|---|---|
| 67 | Philips BF 1586 | I Only Have Eyes For You/What Shall I Do? | 200 |
| 74 | Pye Intl. DDS 101 | What Shall I Do?/Goodbye Love, Hello Sadness | 5 |

## FRANKIE GOES TO HOLLYWOOD
### SINGLES
| | | | |
|---|---|---|---|
| 83 | ZTT 12 ZTAS 1 | Relax (Original Mix)/Ferry Across The Mersey/Relax Bonus (Again) (12", ZTT sleeve or standard p/s, some copies play at 33rpm but list 45rpm) | 10 |
| 83 | ZTT 12 ZTAS 1 (matrix no.: 1A 2U) | Relax (Sex Mix [alias 8.20 "New York Mix"])/Ferry Across The Mersey Relax Bonus (Again) (12", p/s, 45rpm) | 12 |
| 84 | ZTT CTIS 105 | The Power Of Love (Extended Version)/Trapped And Scrapped/Holier Than Thou (, picture 'envelope' box) | 8 |
| 86 | ZTT ZTD 22 | Rage Hard/(Don't Lose What's Left) Of Your Little Mind ('pop-up fists' p/s) | 5 |
| 83 | ZTT ZTAS 1DJ | Relax " The Last Seven Inches/One September Monday (white label, stamped label, no p/s) | 5 |
| 84 | ZTT XZTAS 3DJ | Two Tribes (Carnage)/Relax (U.S. Mix) (12", ZTT sleeve) | 10 |
| 84 | ZTT XZIP 1 | Two Tribes (Hibakusha)/War (Hide Yourself)/Two Tribes/ One February Friday (12", ZTT sleeve) | 15 |
| 84 | ZTT ZTAS 5 DJ-A | The Power Of Love (5.28)/The World Is My Oyster (12") | 10 |
| 86 | ZTT 12 ZTAK 25 | Warriors (The Attack Mix) (12", white label, featuring Gary Moore) | 10 |

*(see also Spitfire Boys)*

## FRANKIE & JOHNNY
| | | | |
|---|---|---|---|
| 66 | Decca F 22376 | Never Gonna Leave You/I'll Hold You | 250 |

| 66 | Decca F 22376 | Never Gonna Leave You/I'll Hold You (DJ Copy) | 250 |
| 66 | Parlophone R 5518 | Climb Ev'ry Mountain/I Wanna Make You Understand | 25 |
| 78 | Inferno HEAT 8 | I'll Hold You/Never Gonna Leave You (reissue) | 10 |

*(see also Maggie Bell)*

## FRANKIE & LARRY
| 60 | Capitol CL 15153 | Not Yet/A Fool For You | 12 |

## FRANKIE & THE PHANTOMS
| 74 | RCA LPBO 5013 | Rock 'N' Roll Band/Jamburger | 6 |

## FRANKIE & TIMEBREAKERS
| 68 | Philips BF 1696 | I'll Be Home/Is There Anybody | 7 |

## ARETHA FRANKLIN
### SINGLES
| 61 | Fontana H 271 | Love Is The Only Thing/Today I Sing The Blues (with Ray Bryant Combo) | 15 |
| 61 | Fontana H 343 | Rock-A-Bye Your Baby With A Dixie Melody/Operation Heartbreak | 10 |
| 65 | CBS 201732 | Can't You Just See Me/You Little Miss Raggedy Anne | 20 |
| 67 | CBS 202468 | Cry Like A Baby/Swanee | 6 |
| 67 | CBS 3059 | Take A Look/Lee Cross | 6 |
| 67 | Atlantic 584 084 | I Never Loved A Man (The Way I Love You)/Do Right Woman – Do Right Man | 8 |
| 67 | Atlantic 584 115 | Respect/Save Me | 10 |
| 67 | Atlantic 584 127 | Baby I Love You/Going Down Slow | 10 |
| 67 | Atlantic 584 141 | (You Make Me Feel Like A) Natural Woman/Never Let Me Go | 8 |
| 67 | Atlantic 584 157 | (I Can't Get No) Satisfaction/Night Life (withdrawn B-side) | 12 |
| 67 | Atlantic 584 157 | (I Can't Get No) Satisfaction/Chain Of Fools | 8 |
| 67 | Atlantic 584 157 | Chain Of Fools/(I Can't Get No) Satisfaction | 10 |
| 68 | Atlantic 584 172 | Since You've Been Gone/Ain't No Way | 10 |
| 68 | Atlantic 584 186 | Think/You Send Me | 8 |
| 68 | Atlantic 584 206 | I Say A Little Prayer/See-Saw | 10 |
| 69 | Atlantic 584 239 | Don't Let Me Lose This Dream/The House That Jack Built | 25 |
| 69 | Atlantic 584 252 | The Weight/The Tracks Of My Tears | 8 |
| 69 | Atlantic 584 285 | Share Your Love With Me/Pledging My Love/The Clock | 8 |
| 69 | Atlantic 584 306 | Eleanor Rigby/It Ain't Fair | 8 |
| 70 | Atlantic 584 322 | Call Me/Son Of A Preacher Man | 8 |
| 70 | Atlantic 2091 027 | Don't Play That Song/The Thrill Is Gone | 5 |
| 70 | Atlantic 2091 042 | Border Song (Holy Moses)/You And Me (unissued) | 0 |
| 70 | Atlantic 2091 044 | Oh No, Not My Baby/You And Me | 6 |
| 71 | Atlantic 2091 063 | You're All I Need To Get By/The Border Song | 6 |
| 71 | Atlantic 2091 111 | I Say A Little Prayer/(I Can't Get No) Satisfaction | 6 |
| 71 | Atlantic 2091 127 | A Brand New Me/Spirit In The Dark | 10 |
| 71 | Atlantic 2091 168 | Rock Steady/Oh Me, Oh My | 10 |
| 72 | Atlantic K 10154 | Daydreaming / I've Been Loving You Too Long | 8 |
| 72 | Atlantic K 10224 | Rock Steady/All The King's Horses | 8 |

### EPs
| 62 | Fontana TE 467217 | TODAY I SING THE BLUES | 50 |

### ALBUMS
| 61 | Fontana TFL 5173 | ARETHA | 70 |
| 65 | CBS (S)BPG 62566 | YEAH!!! — IN PERSON | 40 |
| 67 | CBS (S)BPG 62744 | SOUL SISTER | 40 |
| 67 | Atlantic 587/588 066 | I NEVER LOVED A MAN | 15 |
| 67 | CBS (S)BPG 62969 | TAKE IT LIKE YOU GIVE IT | 20 |
| 67 | CBS 63160 | LEE CROSS | 15 |
| 68 | CBS 63269 | TAKE A LOOK AT ARETHA FRANKLIN | 15 |
| 68 | Atlantic 587/588 149 | ARETHA IN PARIS — LIVE AT THE OLYMPIA | 15 |

## CAROLYN FRANKLIN
| 69 | RCA Victor RCA 1851 | Boxer/I Don't Want To Lose You | 8 |
| 70 | RCA Victor RCA 2009 | All I Want To Be Is Your Woman/You Really Didn't Mean It | 6 |
| 69 | RCA RD/SF 8035 | BABY DYNAMITE! (LP) | 30 |

## ERMA FRANKLIN
| 67 | London HLZ 10170 | Piece Of My Heart/Big Boss Man | 15 |
| 68 | London HLZ 10201 | Open Up Your Soul/I Just Ain't Ready For Love | 10 |
| 68 | London HLZ 10220 | The Right To Cry/Don't Catch The Dog's Bone | 10 |
| 69 | Soul City SC 118 | Don't Wait Too Long/Time After Time | 25 |
| 69 | MCA MU 1073 | Gotta Find Me A Lover (24 Hours A Day)/Change My Thoughts From You | 15 |
| 71 | Jay Boy BOY 36 | I Just Ain't Ready For Love/The Right To Cry | 10 |
| 71 | Jay Boy BOY 41 | Piece Of My Heart/Big Boss Man (reissue) | 10 |
| 70 | MCA MUP MUPS 394 | SOUL SISTER (LP) | 25 |

## MARIE FRANKLIN
| 68 | MGM MGM 1455 | You Ain't Changed/Don'tcha Bet No Money | 10 |

## JOHNNY FRANKS
| 55 | Melodisc P 230 | Tweedle Dee/Shake, Rattle And Roll (78) | 25 |
| 58 | Melodisc 1459 | Good Old Country Music/Cheatin' On Me | 7 |
| 58 | Melodisc 1459 | Good Old Country Music/Cheatin' On Me (78) | 20 |

## BONNIE (BLUE) FRANKSON
| 68 | Jolly JY 014 | Loving You/Shoo Be Do (both with Joe Nolan Band) | 12 |
| 69 | Jolly JY 021 | London City/Dearest (both with Joe Nolan & Dynamic Heatwave) | 12 |
| 69 | Columbia Blue Beat DB 114 | Dearest/London City | 15 |
| 70 | Ackee ACK 110 | I'm So Glad/Lonely Road (both with Dotty) | 8 |
| 73 | Ackee ACK 512 | Getting Things Together/Version | 6 |

# FRANK XEROX AND THE COPYCATS

*(see also Dotty & Bonnie)*

**FRANK XEROX AND THE COPYCATS**
78   Arista ARIST 160          Judy In Disguise/Rock Show ................................................................ 10

**FRANTIC ELEVATORS**
79   TJM TJM 5                 Voice In The Dark/Passion/Every Day I Die (p/s) .................................... 40
80   TJM TJM 6                 Hunchback Of Notre Dame/See Nothing And Everything/Don't Judge Me
                              (unreleased; demos only) ...................................................................... 150
80   Eric's ERIC'S 6           You Know What You Told Me/Production Prevention (p/s) ........................ 50
81   Crackin' Up CRAK 1        Searching For The Only One/Hunchback Of Notre Dame (p/s) ................. 20
82   No Waiting WAIT 1         Holding Back The Years/Pistols In My Brain (p/s) ................................. 20
87   TJM TJM 101               THE EARLY YEARS (mini-LP) .................................................................. 20
88   Receiver KNOB 2           THE EARLY YEARS (mini-LP, reissue with new sleeve & interview disc, as Mick Hucknall
                              & Frantic Elevators) ............................................................................ 15

**FRANZ FERDINAND**
03   Domino RUG164T            Darts Of Pleasure/Van Tango/Shopping For Blood (12", p/s 500 only) ...... 10
04   Domino RUG172             Take Me Out/Truck Stop (3,000 only, p/s) ............................................. 5
04   Domino PRINCIPP01         Take Me Out (Naum Gabo Remix) (7" white label promo) ....................... 5
06   Domino 001                Swallow Smile/Take Me Out (Acoustic) (fan club release) ...................... 20
03   Chateau CHAT001           LIVE 2003 (LP, 10-track official bootleg/promo 500 copies) ................... 15
09   Domino WIG 205X           TONIGHT: FRANZ FERDINAND (6 x 7", 2 x CD & DVD box set) ................ 20
*(see also The Ampheta Meanies)*

**ANDY FRASER BAND**
75   CBS 80731                 THE ANDY FRASER BAND (LP) .............................................................. 20
*(see also Free, Sharks)*

**ELIZABETH FRASER**
00   Blancy Y Negro SAM 00346  Underwater (Charlie May Mix)/Underwater (Charlie May Instrumental) (12", stamped
                              white label, 200 only) .......................................................................... 40
*(see also Cocteau Twins)*

**JOHN FRASER**
58   Pye 7N 15118              Trolley Stop/Don't Take Your Love From Me ........................................ 5
59   Pye 7N 15212              Bye Bye, Baby, Goodbye/Golden Cage ................................................. 7
58   Pye NEP 24068             PRESENTING JOHN FRASER (EP) ......................................................... 10

**PHILLIP FRASER**
78   White Rum/Red Stripe 102  Need To Be Loved/Loving Version ...................................................... 6

**TERRY FRASER**
69   Rude Boy RBH 001          Beng Beng Chitty/Soul Food ............................................................. 25

**FRATELLIS**
06   Island IS 924             THE FRATELLIS EP: Creeping Up The Backstairs/Stacie Anne/The Gutterati? (pink
                              vinyl) ................................................................................................. 12
06   No Label                  Cigarillo/Got Ma Nuts From A Hippy (Demo) (gig freebie, 500 only) ....... 15

**FRATERNITY BROTHERS**
59   HMV POP 582               Passion Flower/A Nobody Like Me (B-side with Gil Fields) .................... 6

**FRATERNITY OF MAN**
70   Stateside SS 2166         Don't Bogart Me/Wispy Paisley Skies ................................................. 12

**ERIC FRATTER**
69   Trojan TR 655             Since You've Been Gone/AFROTONES: Things I Love ............................ 8
*(see also Eric Fatter)*

**FRAYS**
65   Decca F 12153             Keep Me Covered/Walk On ............................................................... 150
65   Decca F 12229             My Girl Sloopy/For Your Precious Love ............................................... 50
*(see also Mike Patto)*

**DEAN FRAZER**
79   Cha Cha CHALP 006         PURE HORN (LP) ............................................................................... 40

**NORMA FRAZER**
65   Ska Beat JB 223           Heartaches/Everybody Loves A Lover ................................................. 120
67   Coxsone CS 7017           The First Cut Is The Deepest/BUMPS OAKLEY: Rag Doll ...................... 30
67   Studio One SO 2024        Come By Here/WAILERS: I Stand Predominate ................................... 250
68   Coxsone CS 7060           Respect/Time .................................................................................. 250
*(see also Sound Dimension, Righteous Homes, Viceroys, Tommy McCook)*

**PHILIP FRAZER**
76   Student STU 1003          Blue Bird/Dub .................................................................................. 8

**CALVIN FRAZIER AND SAMSON PITTMAN**
80   Flyright FLY LP 542       I'M IN THE HIGHWAY MAN (LP) ........................................................... 40

**DALLAS FRAZIER**
66   Capitol CL 15445          Elvira/That Ain't No Stuff .................................................................. 6
66   Capitol CL 15457          Just A Little Bit Of You/Walkin' Wonder ............................................. 5
59   Capitol EAP 1035          DALLAS FRAZIER (EP) ........................................................................ 10

**FREAKS OF NATURE**
66   Island WI 3017            People! Let's Freak Out/The Shadow Chasers ..................................... 90
*(see also Kim Fowley, Belfast Gypsies, Jackie McAuley)*

**STAN FREBERG**
54   Capitol CL 14187          Sh-Boom (Life Could Be A Dream) (with The Toads)/C'est Ci Bon ......... 8
55   Capitol CL 14316          The Lone Psychiatrist/The Honey-Earthers (with Daws Butler) ............. 8
56   Capitol CL 14509          The Yellow Rose Of Texas/Rock Around Stephen Foster ...................... 8
56   Capitol CL 14571          The Great Pretender/The Quest For Bridey Hammerschlaugen (B-side with June Foray).8
56   Capitol CL 14608          Heartbreak Hotel/Rock Island Line ..................................................... 8
57   Capitol CL 14712          Banana Boat (Day-O)/Tele-vee-shun .................................................. 8

| | | | |
|---|---|---|---|
| 58 | Capitol CL 14966 | Green Chri$tma$ (with Daws Butler)/The Meaning Of Christmas (with Jud Conlon Chorale) | 5 |
| 60 | Capitol CL 15122 | The Old Payola Roll Blues (with Jesse White)/ Sh-Boom (Life Could Be A Dream) | 10 |

## FRED BANANA COMBO

| | | | |
|---|---|---|---|
| 78 | Warm AWMR 2004 | No Destination Blues/Jerk Off All Nite Long (p/s) | 7 |

## FRED BLOGGS BAND

| | | | |
|---|---|---|---|
| 76 | Firebrand DMO 12 | Mr Sun/Seaside/Moonrock/The Tribe | 8 |

## JOHN FRED & HIS PLAYBOY BAND

| | | | |
|---|---|---|---|
| 67 | Pye International 7N 25442 | Judy In Disguise (With Glasses)/When The Lights Go Out | 6 |
| 68 | Pye International 7N 25453 | Hey Hey Bunny/No Letter Today | 20 |
| 68 | Pye International 7N 25462 | We Played Games/Lonely Are The Lonely | 7 |
| 68 | Pye International 7N 25470 | Little Dum Dum/Tissue Paper | 7 |
| 68 | CBS 3475 | Shirley/High Heel Sneakers | 10 |
| 69 | MCA MU 1088 | Silly Sarah Carter/Back In The USSR | 6 |
| 67 | Pye Intl. NPL 28111 | AGNES ENGLISH (LP) | 20 |

## FRED LOCKS

| | | | |
|---|---|---|---|
| 78 | Tribesman TM 20 | Love & Only Love/Stricker Ishion | 15 |
| 78 | Revelations FRW 375 | Love & Harmony/Joy & Harmony (featuring Brigadier Jerry) (p/s) | 25 |
| 78 | Lloyd Coxsone LC 001 | Voice Of The Poor/LEVI ROOTS: Poor Man's Story | 25 |
| 78 | Form FORM 1091 | LOVE & HARMONY (LP) | 30 |
| 80 | Rev 001 LP | NEBUCHADNEZZER KING OF BABYLON (FRED LOCKS MEETS CREATORS) (LP) | 60 |
| 82 | Regal RLP 002 | LOVE AND ONLY LOVE (LP, with CREATION STEPPERS) | 45 |
| 83 | Vulcan VULA 502 | BLACK STAR LINER (LP, with poster) | 20 |

## FREDDIE & THE DREAMERS

| | | | |
|---|---|---|---|
| 63 | Columbia DB 7032 | If You Gotta Make A Fool Of Somebody/Feel So Blue | 5 |
| 64 | Columbia DB 7322 | Just For You/Don't Do That To Me | 5 |
| 65 | Columbia DB 7526 | A Little You/Things I'd Like To Say | 5 |
| 65 | Columbia DC 763 | A Windmill In Old Amsterdam/A Love Like You (export issue) | 8 |
| 66 | Columbia DB 7857 | If You've Gotta Minute Baby/When I'm Home With You | 5 |
| 66 | Columbia DB 7929 | Playboy/Some Day | 10 |
| 66 | Columbia DB 8033 | Turn Around/Funny Over You | 5 |
| 67 | Columbia DB 8137 | Hello, Hello/All I Ever Want Is You | 5 |
| 67 | Columbia DB 8200 | Brown And Porter's (Meat Exporters) Lorry/Little Brown Eyes | 5 |
| 68 | Columbia DB 8496 | Little Big Time/FREDDIE GARRITY: You Belong To Me | 5 |
| 68 | Columbia DB 8517 | It's Great/Gaberdine Mac | 5 |
| 69 | Columbia DB 8606 | Get Around Downtown Girl/What To Do | 5 |
| 71 | Philips 6006 098 | Susan's Tuba/You Hurt Me Girl | 5 |
| 67 | EMI Regal | SEE YOU LATER ALLIGATOR (Export issue) | 20 |
| 63 | Columbia 33SX 1577 | FREDDIE AND THE DREAMERS (LP) | 15 |

*(see also Freddie Garrity, Dreamers)*

## FREDDIE & THE DREAMERS/PETER & GORDON

| | | | |
|---|---|---|---|
| 64 | Columbia SEG 8337 | JUST FOR YOU (EP, 2 tracks each) | 15 |

*(see also Peter & Gordon)*

## FREDDIE & FITZY

| | | | |
|---|---|---|---|
| 60s | Dr Bird 1033 | Do Good/SOUL BROTHERS: On The Town | 30 |

## DOTTY FREDERICK

| | | | |
|---|---|---|---|
| 59 | Top Rank JAR 106 | Ricky/Just Wait | 40 |

## TOMMY FREDERICK & HI-NOTES

| | | | |
|---|---|---|---|
| 58 | London HLU 8555 | Prince Of Players/I'm Not Pretending | 50 |
| 58 | London HLU 8555 | Prince Of Players/I'm Not Pretending (78) | 20 |

## BILL FREDERICKS

| | | | |
|---|---|---|---|
| 76 | Polydor 2058 946 | Lose Someone Like You/Love With You | 15 |
| 77 | Polydor 2058 895 | Lovers/It's Just A Matter Of Time | 30 |
| 78 | Polydor 2059 035 | Almost/Wind Of Change | 75 |

## DOLORES FREDERICKS

| | | | |
|---|---|---|---|
| 56 | Brunswick 05540 | Cha Cha Joe/Whole Lotta Shakin' Goin' On | 30 |

## MARC FREDERICKS

| | | | |
|---|---|---|---|
| 56 | London HLD 8281 | Mystic Midnight/Symphony To Anne | 20 |

## FREE (HOLLAND)

| | | | |
|---|---|---|---|
| 69 | Philips BF 1738 | Soul Party/Down To The Bone | 15 |
| 69 | Philips BF 1754 | Keep In Touch/Taking It Away | 40 |

## FREE (U.K.)

| | | | |
|---|---|---|---|
| 69 | Island WIP 6054 | Broad Daylight/The Worm | 60 |
| 69 | Island WIP 6062 | I'll Be Creepin'/Sugar For Mr Morrison | 60 |
| 70 | Island WIP 6082 | All Right Now/Mouthful Of Grass (pink label) | 8 |
| 70 | Island WIP 6093 | The Stealer/Lying In The Sunshine | 5 |
| 71 | Island WIP 6100 | My Brother Jake/Only My Soul | 5 |
| 72 | Island WIP 6129 | Little Bit Of Love/Sail On | 5 |
| 72 | Island WIP 6146 | Wishing Well/Let Me Show You | 5 |
| 73 | Island WIP 6082 | All Right Now/Mouthful Of Grass (reissue pink rim, palm tree label) | 8 |
| 73 | Island WIP 6160 | Travellin' In Style/Easy On My Soul | 5 |
| 76 | Island WIP 6082 | All Right Now/Mouthful Of Grass (reissue, orange palm tree label) | 10 |
| 76 | Island WIP 6351 | The Hunter/Worry | 5 |
| 78 | Island IEPJB 6 | All Right Now/Wishing Well (jukebox copy, short version) | 25 |
| 82 | Island PIEP 6 | THE FREE EP (12", picture disc) | 10 |
| 69 | Island ILPS 9089 | TONS OF SOBS (LP, gatefold sleeve, 1st pressing, pink label & black & orange 'circle' logo) | 300 |
| 69 | Island ILPS 9089 | TONS OF SOBS (LP, gatefold sleeve, 2nd pressing, pink label/black 'block' logo) | 90 |

MINT VALUE £

| | | | |
|---|---|---|---|
| 70 | Island ILPS 9089 | TONS OF SOBS (LP, gatefold sleeve, 3rd pressing, pink label/'i' logo) | 35 |
| 71 | Island ILPS 9089 | TONS OF SOBS (LP, gatefold sleeve, 4th pressing, pink rim label/ 'palm tree' logo) | 15 |
| 69 | Island ILPS 9104 | FREE (LP, gatefold sleeve, 1st pressing, pink label/'i' logo) | 200 |
| 70 | Island ILPS 9104 | FREE (LP, gatefold sleeve, 2nd pressing, pink rim label/'palm tree' logo) | 15 |
| 70 | Island ILPS 9120 | FIRE AND WATER (LP, 1st pressing, pink label/'i' logo) | 120 |
| 70 | Island ILPS 9120 | FIRE AND WATER (LP, 2nd pressing, pink rim label/'palm tree' logo) | 15 |
| 70 | Island ILPS 9138 | HIGHWAY (LP, pink rim, palm tree label) | 20 |
| 71 | Island ILPS 9160 | LIVE (LP, in envelope sleeve with inner, pink rim, palm tree label) | 40 |
| 72 | Island ILPS 9192 | FREE AT LAST (LP) | 25 |
| 72 | Island ILPS 9217 | HEARTBREAKER (LP, lyric inner sleeve, pink rim, palm tree label) | 20 |
| 74 | Island ISLD 4 | THE FREE STORY (2-LP, gatefold, with 4-page booklet, numbered) | 25 |
| 09 | Island 0600753181850 | FIRE AND WATER (LP, 180 gram reissue with Island pink 'i' logo on label) | 15 |
| 11 | Music On Vinyl MOVLP 415 | FREE (LP, reissue, single sleeve) | 15 |

*(see also Paul Kossoff, Rabbit, Kossoff Kirke Tetsu & Rabbit, Sharks, Andy Fraser Band, Black Cat Bones)*

**FREE WINDS**
| | | | |
|---|---|---|---|
| 66 | MJB REV LP 397 | FROM A NEW DIRECTION (LP) | 20 |

**FREE AGENTS**
| | | | |
|---|---|---|---|
| 80 | Groovy STP 1 | FREE AGENTS (LP, 1000 only, hand-made sleeve) | 20 |

*(see also Pete Shelley)*

**ALAN FREED & HIS ROCK'N'ROLL BAND**
| | | | |
|---|---|---|---|
| 57 | Vogue Coral Q 72219 | Teen Rock/Right Now, Right Now (with Alan Freed's Rock'n'Rollers) | 100 |
| 57 | Vogue Coral Q 72230 | Rock'n'Roll Boogie/Teener's Canteen (with Alan Freed's Rock'n'Rollers) | 100 |
| 56 | Vogue Coral LVA 9033 | ROCK'N'ROLL DANCE PARTY VOL. 1 (LP, featuring Modernaires) | 60 |
| 57 | Vogue Coral LVA 9066 | ROCK'N'ROLL DANCE PARTY VOL. 2 (LP, with Jimmy Cavello) | 60 |

*(see also Jimmy Cavello)*

**FREE DESIGN**
| | | | |
|---|---|---|---|
| 69 | Project 3 | HEAVEN/EARTH (LP) | 30 |

**BOB FREEDMAN ORCHESTRA**
| | | | |
|---|---|---|---|
| 63 | Island ILP 101 | MUSIC TO STRIP BY (LP, with free G string) | 40 |

**J.A. FREEDMAN**
| | | | |
|---|---|---|---|
| 69 | Decca F12963 | When You Walked Out Of My Life/Love's Got A Minf Of It's Own | 25 |
| 69 | Decca LK 5021 | MY NAME IS J.A. FREEDMAN, I ALSO SING (LP) | 40 |

**FREEDOM**
| | | | |
|---|---|---|---|
| 68 | Mercury MF 1033 | Where Will You Be Tonight/Trying To Get A Glimpse Of You (in p/s) | 45 |
| 68 | Mercury MF 1033 | Where Will You Be Tonight/Trying To Get A Glimpse Of You | 30 |
| 69 | Plexium PXM 3 | Escape While You Can/Kandy Kay | 10 |
| 70 | Probe PRO 504 | Frustrated Woman/Man Made Laws | 20 |
| 71 | Vertigo 6059 051 | Thanks/Miss Little Louise | 30 |
| 70 | Probe SPBA 6252 | FREEDOM (LP, gatefold sleeve, pink label) | 125 |
| 71 | Vertigo 6360 049 | THROUGH THE YEARS (LP, gatefold sleeve, small swirl label) | 300 |
| 72 | Vertigo 6360 072 | FREEDOM IS MORE THAN A WORD (LP, die cut gatefold sleeve, small swirl label) | 400 |

*(see also Mick Abrahams, Procol Harum, Snafu)*

**FREEDOM GROUP**
| | | | |
|---|---|---|---|
| 72 | Randy's RAN 525 | Sing A Song Of Freedom (actually by Max Romeo)/IMPACT ALLSTARS: Song Of Freedom (Version) | 7 |

**FREEDOM OF CHOICE**
| | | | |
|---|---|---|---|
| 70 | Wand | Doctor Tom/Rat Man | 10 |

**FREEDOM SINGERS (JAMAICA)**
| | | | |
|---|---|---|---|
| 67 | Studio One SO 2010 | Have Faith/Work Crazy | 40 |
| 70 | Bamboo BAM 21 | Give Peace A Chance/SOUND DIMENSION: In Cold Blood | 35 |

*(see also Winston Francis)*

**FREEDOM SINGERS (U.K.)**
| | | | |
|---|---|---|---|
| 70 | New Beat NB 059 | Election (with Live Stocks)/FLECE & LIVE SHOCKS: Tomorrow's World | 10 |
| 71 | New Beat NB 074 | Your Testimony/Train Coming | 8 |

**FREED UNIT**
| | | | |
|---|---|---|---|
| 99 | Out-There OTT 06 | MASONIC YOUTH (9" EP, triangular clear vinyl, 100 only) | 50 |
| 01 | Out-There OTT 09 | SIX SIDED (9" EP, clear vinyl, 100 only) | 25 |
| 98 | Out-There OTTLP 04 | FIELD REPORTS FROM OUT-THERE (LP, clear vinyl) | 18 |
| 98 | Enraptured RAPTLP 19 | THINGS ARE LOOKING UP... (LP, orange vinyl) | 15 |

**FREE FERRY**
| | | | |
|---|---|---|---|
| 69 | CBS 4456 | Mary, What Have You Become?/Friend | 8 |
| 70 | CBS 4647 | Haverjack Drive/Flying | 20 |

**FREEFORM**
| | | | |
|---|---|---|---|
| 95 | Skam SKA 3 | Fane/Recut/Rail/Siamese Telebox/The Brink/Many/Freeform Dub (12") | 25 |
| 95 | Skam SKA 4 | FREE EP (12") | 25 |

**FREELANCE**
| | | | |
|---|---|---|---|
| 83 | Chav KMG S 83 CUS 1765 | Writing On The Wall/Elinor/One More Time (die-cut cover) | 40 |

**ALAN FREEMAN AND THE TALMY STONE BAND**
| | | | |
|---|---|---|---|
| 62 | Decca F 11543 | Madison Time/Madison Time | 10 |

**ART FREEMAN**
| | | | |
|---|---|---|---|
| 66 | Atlantic 584 053 | Slippin' Around/Can't Get You Out Of My Mind | 200 |

**BOBBY FREEMAN**
| | | | |
|---|---|---|---|
| 58 | London HLJ 8644 | Do You Want To Dance?/Big Fat Woman | 30 |
| 58 | London HLJ 8721 | Betty Lou Got A New Pair Of Shoes/Starlight | 40 |
| 59 | London HLJ 8782 | Shame On You Miss Johnson/Need Your Love | 50 |
| 59 | London HLJ 8898 | Mary Ann Thomas/Love Me | 40 |
| 60 | London HLJ 9031 | Sinbad/Ebb Tide (The Sea) | 15 |

| | | | |
|---|---|---|---|
| 60 | Parlophone R 4684 | (I Do The) Shimmy Shimmy/You Don't Understand Me | 20 |
| 64 | Pye International 7N 25260 | C'mon And Swim (Parts 1 & 2) | 20 |
| 64 | Pye International 7N 25280 | S-W-I-M/That Little Old Heartbreaker Me | 25 |
| 66 | Pye International 7N 25347 | The Duck/Cross My Heart | 30 |
| 66 | Pye International 7N 25347 | The Duck/The Devil (2nd issue with different B-side) | 10 |

## BUD FREEMAN
| | | | |
|---|---|---|---|
| 66 | Fontana TL 5370 | BUD FREEMAN ESQ. (LP) | 20 |
| 68 | Fontana TL 5414 | FREEMAN & CO (LP) | 20 |

## CAROL FREEMAN
| | | | |
|---|---|---|---|
| 67 | CBS 202579 | The Rolling Sea/Leaving You Now | 15 |

## ERNIE FREEMAN
| | | | |
|---|---|---|---|
| 57 | London HLP 8523 | Raunchy/Puddin' | 20 |
| 57 | London HL 7029 | Dumplin's/Beautiful Weekend (export issue) | 15 |
| 58 | London HLP 8558 | Dumplin's/Beautiful Weekend | 15 |
| 58 | London HLP 8660 | Indian Love Call/Summer Serenade | 10 |
| 60 | London HLP 9041 | Big River/Night Sounds | 7 |
| 65 | London HLP 9944 | Raunchy '65/Jivin' Around | 10 |
| 56 | London RE-U 1059 | ERNIE FREEMAN AND HIS RHYTHM GUITAR (EP) | 30 |
| 59 | London RE-P 1210 | ERNIE FREEMAN VOL. 2 (EP) | 30 |

## EVELYN FREEMAN EXCITING VOICES
| | | | |
|---|---|---|---|
| 69 | London HLU 10287 | I Heard The Voice/I Dreamed Last Night | 5 |

## GEORGE FREEMAN
| | | | |
|---|---|---|---|
| 71 | Jay Boy BOY 54 | I'm Like A Fish/Why Are You Doing This To Me | 15 |

## LOUISE FREEMAN
| | | | |
|---|---|---|---|
| 74 | London HLM 10490 | I Can Do It (If I Can See It)/How Could You Run Away | 10 |

## MARGARET FREEMAN
| | | | |
|---|---|---|---|
| 61 | Starlite ST45 040 | Forbidden Fruit/Mister Ting A Ling | 15 |

## PAUL FREEMAN
| | | | |
|---|---|---|---|
| 71 | Punch PH 82 | Don't Give Up/UPSETTERS: Give Up (Version) | 15 |

## RUSS FREEMAN & CHET BAKER QUARTET
| | | | |
|---|---|---|---|
| 60 | Vogue EPV 1255 | RUSS FREEMAN & CHET BAKER QUARTET (EP) | 12 |

*(see also Chet Baker)*

## ELAINE FREEME
| | | | |
|---|---|---|---|
| 79 | Terrific TRIF 001 | Mister Its Your Lucky Day/THe Interview | 5 |

## FREE MOVEMENT
| | | | |
|---|---|---|---|
| 72 | CBS 7768 | The Harder I Try/Comin' Home | 30 |

## FREE 'N EASY (1)
| | | | |
|---|---|---|---|
| 68 | Oak RGJ 628 | FREE 'N EASY (LP, private pressing [Warren Coley W.C.P. 001]) | 100 |

## FREE 'N' EASY (2)
| | | | |
|---|---|---|---|
| 81 | SRT/Clovis S81 CUS 1222 | FOUR EASY MOVES EP | 30 |
| | BMC 003 | | |

## FREE SAMPLE
| | | | |
|---|---|---|---|
| 79 | Oblivion S/79/CUS 339 | Hello My Friend/Something In Her Eyes | 10 |

## FREE SOULS
| | | | |
|---|---|---|---|
| 64 | Blue Beat BB 264 | I Want To Be Free/Angel | 20 |

## FREE SPIRIT
| | | | |
|---|---|---|---|
| 74 | Chess 6145035 | Love You As Long As I Can/As Long As I Can | 10 |

## FREESTYLE ORCHESTRA
| | | | |
|---|---|---|---|
| 89 | SBK 12SBKDJ 7011 | Keep On Pumping It Up (12", promo only) | 15 |

## FREEWAY
| | | | |
|---|---|---|---|
| 79 | Decca F 13824 | I Love The Music/Sarah Girl (p/s) | 8 |
| 79 | Decca F 13843 | That Was The Greatest Song/Lost In A Dream (p/s) | 8 |
| 79 | Decca TXS 131 | FREEWAY (LP) | 18 |

*(see also Terry Melcher)*

## FREEWHEELERS
| | | | |
|---|---|---|---|
| 65 | HMV POP 1406 | Why Do You Treat Me Like A Fool?/Ad Lib Blues | 8 |

## FREEZE
| | | | |
|---|---|---|---|
| 79 | A1.A.1.1.A.1 | IN COLOUR (EP, p/s) | 15 |
| 80 | A1 A.1.1.S.1 | Celebration/Cross-Over | 8 |

## ACE FREHLEY
| | | | |
|---|---|---|---|
| 78 | Casablanca CAN 135 | New York Groove/Snow Blind (p/s, blue vinyl with mask) | 30 |
| 78 | Casablanca CAN 135 | New York Groove/Snow Blind (no p/s, black vinyl) | 5 |

*(see also Kiss)*

## DON FRENCH
| | | | |
|---|---|---|---|
| 59 | London HLW 8884 | Lonely Saturday Night/Goldilocks | 40 |
| 59 | London HLW 8989 | Little Blonde Girl/I Look Into My Heart | 100 |
| 59 | London HLW 8989 | Little Blonde Girl/I Look Into My Heart (78) | 20 |

## FRENCH REVOLUTION
| | | | |
|---|---|---|---|
| 69 | Decca F 22898 | Nine Till Five/Why? | 70 |

## ROBERT FRENCH
| | | | |
|---|---|---|---|
| 85 | Uptemp UTO 10 | Something On My Mind/Help Yourself (12") | 40 |

## FRENCH IMPRESSIONISTS
| | | | |
|---|---|---|---|
| 82 | Operation Twilight OPT 020 | Santa Baby/THICK PIGEON: Jingle Bell Rock/MONKS IN THE SNOW: A Theme For This Special Evening (P/s, last track uncredited) | 20 |
| 82 | Operation Twilight 12OPT 20 | Santa Baby/Jingle Bell Rock (12", p/s) | 10 |

*(see also Aztec Camera)*

## FRENZ
| | | | |
|---|---|---|---|
| 70 | Sugar SU 101 | Mee Lei Moi/I Hear Music | 12 |
| 71 | Sugar ESS 103 | It's A Secret/Dusty Shoes | 10 |

## FRENZY (1)
| | | | |
|---|---|---|---|
| 76 | DJM DJS 633 | Poser/Things You Do (To Me) | 15 |

## FRENZY (2)
| | | | |
|---|---|---|---|
| 81 | Frenzy FRENZY 1 | This Is The Last Time/Gypsy Dancer (no p/s) | 50 |
| 81 | Frenzy FRENZY 2 | Blackburn Rovers/Up The Rovers | 35 |
| 81 | Frenzy FRENZY 3 | Without You/Thanks For Nothing (no p/s) | 50 |
| 84 | Nervous NEP 002 | Robot Riot/All Alone (p/s) | 6 |
| 84 | Nervous 12 NEP 002 | Robot Riot/All Alone/Cry Or Die/Torment (12", p/s, 1st 500 on blue vinyl) | 10 |
| 86 | ABC EYE T7 | I See Red/Whose Life (p/s) | 10 |
| 86 | I.D. NOSE 8 | CLOCKWORK TOY (LP) | 15 |
| 87 | I.D. NOSE 19 | SALLY'S PINK BEDROOM (LP) | 15 |

## FRESH
| | | | |
|---|---|---|---|
| 70 | RCA RCA 2003 | Stoned In Saigon/Just A Note | 7 |
| 70 | RCA SF 8122 | FRESH OUT OF BORSTAL (LP) | 20 |
| 71 | RCA LSA 3027 | FRESH TODAY (LP) | 18 |

*(see also Paul Korda, Brother Bung, Fruit Machine)*

## FRESH AIR
| | | | |
|---|---|---|---|
| 69 | Pye 7N 17736 | Running Wild/Stop, Look, Listen | 200 |
| 71 | Philips 6006 163 | In The Sun/Too Many Reasons | 7 |
| 72 | Philips 6006 187 | It Takes Too Long/Here Comes Summer | 6 |
| 72 | Columbia DB 8872 | Bye Bye Jane/It's All Over | 6 |

## FRESH FLAVOUR
| | | | |
|---|---|---|---|
| 75 | Buddah BDS 427 | Without You Baby, I'm A Loser/Treat Here Like A Lady | 7 |
| 75 | Buddah BDS 427 | Without You Baby, I'm A Loser/Treat Here Like A Lady (DJ Copy) | 12 |

## FRESH GROUND
| | | | |
|---|---|---|---|
| 70 | Dortell DT1 | Inside Out/Ways Of Man | 80 |

## FRESH MAGGOTS
| | | | |
|---|---|---|---|
| 71 | RCA RCA 2150 | Car Song/What Would You Do | 40 |
| 71 | RCA SF 8205 | FRESH MAGGOTS (LP, orange label) | 750 |
| 07 | Sunbeam SBR2LP5002 | FRESH MAGGOTS - HATCHED (2-LP, reissue) | 18 |

## FRESH MEAT
| | | | |
|---|---|---|---|
| 73 | Deram DMR 384 | Never Mind The Money/Candy Eyes | 7 |
| 73 | Raft RA 18504 | Hobo/If You Can't Live (You're Dead) | 12 |

## FRESH SKI & MO ROCK
| | | | |
|---|---|---|---|
| 88 | Tuff GrooveTUFF003 | Talking Pays/Pick Up On This (12") | 100 |
| 91 | Conscious CON003 | THE LONG AWAITED PAROXYSM (EP) | 20 |
| 11 | Diggers With Gratitude DWG 010 | THE COARSE SELECTORS (EP) | 15 |

## FRESH WINDOWS
| | | | |
|---|---|---|---|
| 67 | Fontana TF 839 | Fashion Conscious/Summer Sun Shines | 200 |

## FRESHIES
| | | | |
|---|---|---|---|
| 78 | Razz RAZZXEP 1 | BAISER (EP, with Chris Sievey solo tracks, 33rpm, no'd, handwritten labels) | 40 |
| 79 | Razz RAZZXEP 2 | STRAIGHT IN AT NO. 2 (EP, handwritten labels with inserts, 1,000 only, numbered, green or orange p/s) | 30 |
| 79 | Razz RAZZ 3 | THE MEN FROM BANANA ISLAND WHOSE STUPID IDEAS NEVER CAUGHT ON IN THE WESTERN WORLD AS WE KNOW IT (EP, black & white photocopied p/s or numbered blue p/s) | 15 |
| 79 | Razz RAZZ 5 | We're Like You/CHRIS SIEVEY: Hey (p/s) | 15 |
| 80 | Absurd A9 | Octopus/Sheet Music | 10 |
| 80 | Razz RAZZ 6 | Yellow Spot/If It's News (p/s) | 10 |
| 80 | Razz RAZZ 7 | No Money/Oh Girl (p/s) | 10 |
| 80 | Razz RAZZ 8 | RED INDIAN MUSIC (EP, with Chris Sievey) | 18 |
| 80 | Razz RAZZ 11 | I'm In Love With The Girl On The Virgin Manchester Megastore Checkout Desk/Singalong Version (p/s, with free lyric book) | 15 |
| 80 | Razz RAZZ 12 | I'm In Love With The Girl On The Manchester Checkout Desk (Radio Version)/Singalong Version ('bleeped') (white label radio issue, 200 only) | 15 |
| 80 | Razz RAZZ 13 | One To One/House Beautiful (unreleased) | 0 |
| 81 | MCA MCA 693 | Wrap Up The Rockets And It's Gonna Get Better/Tell Her I'm Ill | 10 |
| 81 | CV CVS 1 | If You Really Love ... Buy Me A Shirt/I Am A Walrus (p/s) | 10 |
| 84 | HANNA 1 | Virgin Megastore/Wrap Up The Rockets/Buy Me A Shirt/Tell Her I'm Ill/ Frank Talks To Chris (Conversation) (12", white label, stickered sleeve) | 30 |
| 81 | Razz CS-5 | LONDON PLAYS (cassette, live & radio sessions, 1,000 only) | 12 |
| 85 | ETS 1 | JOHNNY RADAR STORY (20-track, with bonus Frank Sidebottom 8-track: "Firm Favourites") | 20 |

*(see also Chris Sievey, Going Red?)*

## FRESHMEN
| | | | |
|---|---|---|---|
| 67 | Pye 7N 17432 | Papa Oom Mow Mow/Let's Dance | 10 |
| 68 | Pye 7N 17592 | Go Granny Go (The Little Old Lady From Pasadena)/Look At The Sunshine | 10 |
| 69 | Pye 7N 17689 | Just To See You Smile/Indian Lake | 8 |
| 69 | Pye 7N 17757 | She Sang Hymns Out Of Tune/Mr. Beverly's Heavy Days | 6 |
| 70 | CBS 4842 | Halfway To Where/Time Hasn't Changed Her | 6 |
| 70 | CBS 5168 | Banquet For The World/Time Hasn't Changed Her | 6 |
| 71 | CBS 7241 | One Bad Thing/Everywhere There Is Love | 6 |
| 72 | CBS 7694 | Swanee River/Take The Time It Takes | 8 |
| 68 | Pye N(S)PL 18263 | MOVIN' ON (LP) | 100 |
| 70 | CBS 64099 | PEACE ON EARTH (LP) | 40 |

## STEPHEN FRETWELL
03  Tape Recordings TAPE 001   Something's Got To Give/Whenforever/Honey ........................................ 20

## FRIDA
82  Epic EPC A 2603   I Know There's Something Going On/Threnody (p/s) ................................. 10
82  Epic EPC A 2863   To Turn To Stone/I Got Something (p/s) ................................................. 10
82  Epic EPC A 2863   To Turn To Stone/I Got Something (p/s, clear vinyl) .............................. 10
83  Epic EPC A 3435   Here We'll Stay/Strangers (p/s) ............................................................ 10
83  Epic EPC A 3983   Time/I Am A Seeker (p/s, with B.A. Robertson) .................................... 8
84  Epic EPC A 4717   Shine/That's Tough (p/s) ..................................................................... 8
84  Epic EPC TA 4717   Shine (6.27 Version)/That's Tough (12", p/s) ...................................... 12
84  Epic EPC A 4886   Heart Of The Country/Slowly (p/s) ...................................................... 15
84  Epic EPC TA 4886   Heart Of The Country/Slowly/I Know There's Something Going On (Extended) (12", p/s) ............................................................................ 20

*(see also Abba)*

## CAROL FRIDAY
65  Parlophone R 5297   Gone Tomorrow/Show Me The Way ..................................................... 10
65  Parlophone R 5369   Everybody I Know/Wasted Days .......................................................... 30
67  Parlophone R 5567   Big Sister/I Look Around Me ............................................................... 10

## FRIDAY CLUB
85  2 Tone CHSTT28   Window Shopping/Window Shopping (instrumental) (p/s) ................... 40
85  2 Tone CHSTT1228   Window Shopping (extended version)/Window Shopping (instrumental) 12" (p/s) ...... 45

## FRIDAY KNIGHTS
60  Oriole CB 1579   Poor Man's Roses/Don't Open That Door ........................................... 10

## FRIDGE
97  Output OPR 06   CEEFAX (LP) ........................................................................................ 15
98  Output OPR 12   SEMAPHORE (2-LP) ............................................................................ 20
00  Text TEXT002LP   HAPPINESS (2-LP) ............................................................................. 18

*(see also Four Tet)*

## FRIDGES
80  Ink-Ink II 01   Lynn Freeze/Shower Of B's/That's Why I Took Up The Harmonica/ No Room! (p/s, with insert) .................................................................................................. 5

## BRIAN JOSEPH FRIEL
74  Dawn DNLS 3054   BRIAN JOSEPH FRIEL (LP, gatefold sleeve with insert, pink 'sun' label) ............. 20

## FRIEND & LOVER
68  Verve VS 1515   Reach Out Of The Darkness/Time Is On Your Side ............................. 15

## TERRY FRIEND & FRIENDS
77  Tramp (no cat. no.)   COME THE DAY (LP, private pressing, 100 only) ............................... 40

*(see also Stonefield Tramp)*

## FRIENDLY FIRES
07  Moshi Moshi MOMO 11   Paris/Ex-Lover ................................................................................... 10
08  XL XLS 387   Jump In The Pool (one-sided hand-numbered and stencilled sleeve, white labels, 250 only) ...... 8
08  XL XLT 395   Paris (Aeroplane Remix)/Paris (Justus Kohncke Remix) (12", p/s) ............... 15
10  XL XLT 486   Hold On (Instrumental)/HOLY GHOST: On Board/On Board (Instrumental) (12") ............ 8

## FRIENDS (1)
68  Deram DM 198   Piccolo Man/Mythological Sunday ...................................................... 30

*(see also Flowerpot Men, Ivy League)*

## FRIENDS (2)
70  United Artists UP 35146   Futz/Costa Del Sol ............................................................................... 7

## FRIENDS (3)
74  Merlin HF 4   FRIENDS (LP, white label test pressing, 1 copy only!) ................... 2000

*(see also Ithaca, Alice Through The Looking Glass, Agincourt, Tomorrow Come Someday, BBC Radiophonic Workshop)*

## FRIENDS (4)
75  Caroline C1511   FRIENDS (LP, stickered with £1.49 price tag and quote from Jazz Forum) ............. 20

## FRIENDS (5)
83  Rock Shop RSR 002   Night Walker/Wasted Time (no p/s) ................................................... 25

## FRIENDS AGAIN
83  Moonboot MOON 1   Honey At The Core/Lucky Star (p/s) .................................................... 6

## FRIENDS O' MINE
72  Westwood WRS 021   FRIENDS O' MINE (LP, 250 copies only) .......................................... 100

*(see also Mark Kjeldsen)*

## FRIENDS OF DISTINCTION
69  RCA 1838   Grazing In The Grass/I Really Hope You Do ....................................... 12
69  RCA SF 8032   GRAZIN' (LP) ....................................................................................... 20

## FRIENDS OF ST. FRANCIS
74  Charisma CB 229   The Man Who Turned On The World/How Is The World Today .............. 6

## FRIENDSHIP
70  B&C CB 133   The World Is Going To Be A Better Place/Million Hearts ..................... 5

## FRIENDSHIP LEAGUE
75  Luggage (no cat no)   FRIENDSHIP LEAGUE 5 TRACKS (plays at 33rpm) ........................... 35

## FRIGHTY
01  Jah Tubbys JT 7009   Call On Jah Name/OFFBEAT POSSE: Call On Dub ............................. 15
03  Jah Tubbys JT 10012   Jah Jah Is Coming/Fright Jah Jah Is Coming Version/Dub Is Coming (10", with the Offbeat Posse) ...... 20

## FRIJID PINK
70  Deram DM-R 288   The House Of The Rising Sun/Drivin' Blues ......................................... 6
70  Deram DM 309   Sing A Song Of Freedom/End Of The Line ........................................... 6
70  Deram DM 321   Heartbreak Hotel/Bye Bye Blues ........................................................ 6

# (robert) FRIPP & (Brian) ENO

| | | | |
|---|---|---|---|
| | | | |
| 71 | Deram DM 332 | Music For The People/Sloony | 6 |
| 71 | Deram DM 336 | We're Gonna Be There (When Johnny Comes Marching Home)/Shortly Kline | 7 |
| 71 | Deram DM 347 | Lost Son/I Love Her | 7 |
| 70 | Deram SML 1062 | FRIJID PINK (LP) | 100 |
| 70 | Deram SML 1077 | DEFROSTED (LP) | 100 |

## (ROBERT) FRIPP & (BRIAN) ENO
| | | | |
|---|---|---|---|
| 73 | Island HELP 16 | NO PUSSYFOOTING (LP, gatefold sleeve, black label with pink 'i' logo) | 25 |
| 75 | Island HELP 22 | EVENING STAR (LP, black label with pink 'i' logo) | 20 |

*(see also Giles Giles & Fripp, King Crimson, Brian Eno, Roxy Music)*

## JACKIE FRISCO
| | | | |
|---|---|---|---|
| 63 | Decca F 11566 | You Can't Catch Me/Sugar Baby | 15 |
| 63 | Decca F 11692 | When You Ask About Love/He's So Near | 10 |

## VONNIE FRITCHIE
| | | | |
|---|---|---|---|
| 55 | London HLU 8178 | Sugar Booger Avenue/There I Stood (To Throw Old Shoes And Rice) | 40 |

## FRED FRITH
| | | | |
|---|---|---|---|
| 74 | Caroline C 1508 | GUITAR SOLOS (LP) | 20 |
| 76 | Caroline C 1518 | GUITAR SOLOS 2 (LP) | 25 |

*(see also Henry Cow)*

## FRITZ, MIKE & MO
| | | | |
|---|---|---|---|
| 65 | Philips BF 1427 | Somebody Stole The Sun/Let Me Hear Your Voice | 10 |
| 65 | Philips BF 1441 | What Colour Is A Man?/So Now You're Gone | 8 |

*(see also Four Pennies)*

## FROCK
| | | | |
|---|---|---|---|
| 78 | Frock Music FM 7848 | SILKIE (LP, 250 only) | 40 |

## EDGAR FROESE
| | | | |
|---|---|---|---|
| 74 | Virgin V 2016 | AQUA (LP, gatefold) | 15 |
| 75 | Virgin V 2040 | EPSILON IN MALAYSIAN PALE (LP beige "mirror" girl label) | 15 |

*(see also Tangerine Dream)*

## FROG
| | | | |
|---|---|---|---|
| 73 | Jam JAM 39 | Witch Hunt (Theme From Psychomania)/Living Dead (die-cut company sleeve) | 150 |

*(see also John Cameron)*

## FROG ISLAND SKIFFLE GROUP
| | | | |
|---|---|---|---|
| 57 | 77 Records EP 4 | FROG ISLAND SKIFFLE GROUP (EP) | 200 |

## FROGMEN
| | | | |
|---|---|---|---|
| 61 | Oriole CB 1617 | Underwater/Mad Rush (withdrawn) | 100 |

## FROGMORTON
| | | | |
|---|---|---|---|
| 76 | Philips 6308 261 | AT LAST (LP, blue/silver labels) | 20 |

## JANE FROMAN
| | | | |
|---|---|---|---|
| 55 | Capitol CL 14208 | The Song From "Desiree" (We Meet Again)/Mine | 5 |
| 55 | Capitol CL 14209 | The Finger Of Suspicion Points At You/My Shining Hour | 5 |
| 55 | Capitol CL 14254 | I Wonder/I'll Never Be The Same | 5 |
| 56 | Capitol CL 14658 | You'll Never Walk Alone/One Little Candle | 5 |

## FROM WEST TO EAST
| | | | |
|---|---|---|---|
| 72 | Zella JHPS 128 | FROM WEST TO EAST (LP) | 20 |

## FRONT
| | | | |
|---|---|---|---|
| 77 | The Label TLR 005 | System/Queen's Mafia (p/s) | 8 |

## DOM FRONTIERE & HIS ORCHESTRA
| | | | |
|---|---|---|---|
| 57 | London HLU 8385 | Jet Rink Ballad/Uno Mas | 15 |

## FRONT LINE
| | | | |
|---|---|---|---|
| 65 | Atlantic AT 4057 | I Don't Care/Got Love | 40 |

## FRONTLINE ORCHESTRA
| | | | |
|---|---|---|---|
| 81 | Ice ICET 50 | Don't Turn You Back On Me/No Entry (12") | 40 |

## FROST
| | | | |
|---|---|---|---|
| 69 | Vanguard SVRL 19056 | ROCK AND ROLL MUSIC (LP) | 18 |
| 69 | Vanguard SVRL 19052 | FROST MUSIC (LP) | 18 |

*(see also Alice Cooper)*

## BERNIE FROST
| | | | |
|---|---|---|---|
| 74 | Vertigo 6059 108 | The House/What Do You Want To Hear Today | 50 |

*(see also Status Quo, Rossi & Frost, Boz Frost)*

## BOZ FROST
| | | | |
|---|---|---|---|
| 73 | Vertigo 6059 089 | Foreign Lady/Big White Seagull | 25 |

*(see also Status Quo, Rossi & Frost, Bernie Frost)*

## FROST LANE
| | | | |
|---|---|---|---|
| 71 | Cutty Wren MM 1 | FROST LANE (LP, actually various artists LP) | 45 |

## MAX FROST & TROOPERS
| | | | |
|---|---|---|---|
| 68 | Capitol CL 15565 | Shape Of Things To Come/Free Lovin' | 30 |

*(see also Millicent Martin)*

## FROZEN TEAR
| | | | |
|---|---|---|---|
| 69 | Ra RA 5001 | The Hunter/You Know What Has To Be (99 copies only) | 450 |

## FRUGAL SOUND
| | | | |
|---|---|---|---|
| 66 | Pye 7N 17062 | Norwegian Wood/Cruel To Be Kind | 15 |
| 66 | Pye 7N 17129 | Just Outside The Door/I'm On Your Side | 6 |
| 67 | RCA Victor RCA 1556 | Backstreet Girl/Reason To Believe | 6 |
| 67 | RCA Victor RCA 1595 | Abilene/Love Is A New Face | 5 |
| 68 | RCA Victor RCA 1659 | All Strung Out/Miss Mary | 5 |

## FRUIT EATING BEARS
| | | | |
|---|---|---|---|
| 78 | DJM DJS 857 | Door In My Face/Going Through The Motions (company sleeve) | 45 |
| 78 | Raw RAW 9 | Chevy Heavy (p/s) | 25 |
| 78 | Lightning G!L 509 | Chevy Heavy/Fifties Cowboy (p/s) | 40 |

## FRUIT GUMS
| | | | |
|---|---|---|---|
| 70 | Fab FAB 138 | Sweet Pork/Crying All Night | 6 |

## FRUIT MACHINE
| | | | |
|---|---|---|---|
| 69 | Spark SRL 1003 | Follow Me/Cuddly Toy | 80 |
| 69 | Spark SRL 1027 | I'm Alone Today/Sunshine Of Your Love (in title p/s) | 200 |
| 69 | Spark SRL 1027 | I'm Alone Today/Sunshine Of Your Love | 80 |

*(see also Rare Bird)*

## FRUMPY
| | | | |
|---|---|---|---|
| 71 | Philips 6003 133 | Life Without Pain/Morning | 20 |
| 71 | Philips 6305 067 | ALL WILL BE CHANGED (LP, black/silver labels) | 120 |
| 72 | Philips 6305 098 | FRUMP 2 (LP, black & blue vinyl) | 100 |

*(see also Atlantis)*

## FRUUPP
| | | | |
|---|---|---|---|
| 74 | Dawn DNS 1087 | Prince Of Heaven/Jaunting Car | 10 |
| 73 | Dawn DNLS 3053 | FUTURE LEGENDS (LP, gatefold sleeve) | 100 |
| 74 | Dawn DNLS 3058 | SEVEN SECRETS (LP, with lyric insert) | 80 |
| 74 | Dawn DNLH 2 | THE PRINCE OF HEAVEN'S EYES (LP, gatefold sleeve, with book) | 80 |
| 74 | Dawn DNLH 2 | THE PRINCE OF HEAVEN'S EYES (LP, gatefold sleeve, without book) | 30 |
| 75 | Dawn DNLS 3070 | MODERN MASQUERADES (LP, gatefold sleeve, with lyric insert) | 30 |

## MARK FRY
| | | | |
|---|---|---|---|
| 06 | Sunbeam SBRLPS 028 | DREAMING WITH ALICE (LP, 180 gram vinyl reissue of original 1972 Italian pressing) | 20 |

## FUCHSIA
| | | | |
|---|---|---|---|
| 71 | Pegasus PEG 8 | FUCHSIA (LP) | 400 |

## FUCKED UP
| | | | |
|---|---|---|---|
| 11 | Fucked Up FU 010 | The Other Shoe/The Truest Road (p/s, lyric sheet, original U.K. tour 7") | 20 |

## FUD (CHRISTIAN) & DEL
| | | | |
|---|---|---|---|
| 73 | Duke DU 165 | Beef Sticker/PRINCE HERON: Ten Commandments | 6 |
| 73 | Songbird SB 1086 | Dr. Fud/FUD CHRISTIAN ALLSTARS: La-Fud-Del Skank | 6 |

## FUD CHRISTIAN ALLSTARS
| | | | |
|---|---|---|---|
| 71 | Big Shot BI 571 | Never Fall In Love (actually by Winston Heywood)/Never Fall In Love Version | 8 |

*(see also Linkers, Ansel Linkers)*

## FUDGE TUNNEL
| | | | |
|---|---|---|---|
| 91 | Earach MOSH 36 | HATE SONGS IN E MINOR (LP, with free 7") | 15 |
| 94 | Earache MOSH 119LP | THE COMPLICATED FUTILITY OF IGNORANCE (LP) | 18 |

## FUGAZI
| | | | |
|---|---|---|---|
| 89 | Dischord DIS 44 | REPEATER (LP) | 15 |
| 91 | Dischord DIS 60V | STEADY DIET OF NOTHING (LP, inner) | 15 |
| 93 | Dischord DIS 60V | IN ON THE KILL TAKER (LP) | 15 |
| 95 | Dischord DIS 90V | RED MEDICINE (LP) | 15 |
| 98 | Dischord DIS 110V | END HITS (LP, gatefold) | 20 |

## FUGEES
| | | | |
|---|---|---|---|
| 96 | Columbia 483549-1 | THE SCORE (2-LP) | 40 |

## FUGI
| | | | |
|---|---|---|---|
| 71 | Blue Horizon 2096 005 | Red Moon (Parts 1 & 2) | 30 |

## FUGITIVE
| | | | |
|---|---|---|---|
| 81 | Private pressing FMR 050 | Need My Freedom | 20 |

## FUGITIVES (JAMAICA)
| | | | |
|---|---|---|---|
| 67 | Doctor Bird DB 1082 | Musical Pressure/LESLIE BUTLER & FUGITIVES: Winchester Rocksteady | 30 |
| 67 | Doctor Bird 1097 | Lecture/Canteloupe Rock | 40 |

*(see also Jo Jo Bennett & Fugitives, Two Kings, Jo Jo Bennett, Stranger Cole)*

## FUGITIVES (U.S.)
| | | | |
|---|---|---|---|
| 61 | Vogue V 9176 | Freeway/Fugitive | 30 |

## FUGS
| | | | |
|---|---|---|---|
| 68 | Big T BIG 115 | Crystal Liaison/When The Mode Of The Music Changes | 15 |
| 68 | Transatlantic TRA 180 | TENDERNESS JUNCTION (LP, with poster) | 55 |
| 68 | Transatlantic TRA 180 | TENDERNESS JUNCTION (LP, without poster) | 25 |
| 68 | Transatlantic TRA 181 | IT CRAWLED INTO MY HAND, HONEST (LP) | 40 |
| 69 | Fontana (S)TL 5501 | VIRGIN FUGS (LP) | 30 |
| 69 | Fontana (S)TL 5513 | THE FUGS ... FIRST ALBUM (LP) | 40 |
| 69 | Fontana (S)TL 5524 | FUGS II (LP) | 35 |
| 69 | Reprise RSLP 6359 | THE BELLE OF AVENUE A (LP) | 35 |
| 70 | Reprise 6396 | GOLDEN FILTH - LIVE AT THE FILLMORE EAST (LP) | 35 |

## FULHAM FURIES
| | | | |
|---|---|---|---|
| 78 | GM GMS 9050 | These Boots Are Made For Walking/Under Pressure (no p/s) | 35 |

*(see also Lurkers)*

## BLIND BOY FULLER
| | | | |
|---|---|---|---|
| 57 | Philips BBL 7512 | BLIND BOY FULLER 1935-40 (LP) | 25 |
| 68 | Matchbox SDR 143 | BLIND BOY FULLER ON DOWN VOLUME 1 (LP) | 15 |
| 69 | Matchbox SDR 168 | BLIND BOY FULLER ON DOWN VOLUME 2 (LP) | 15 |
| 60s | Flyright LP 105 | CAROLINA BLUES (LP) | 15 |

## BOBBY FULLER FOUR
| | | | |
|---|---|---|---|
| 66 | London HLU 10030 | I Fought The Law/Little Annie Lou | 30 |
| 66 | London HLU 10041 | Love's Made A Fool Of You/Don't You Ever Let Me Know | 15 |

## Curtis FULLER/TOMMY FLANAGAN

MINT VALUE £

| | | | |
|---|---|---|---|
| 73 | President PT 394 | Another Sad And Lonely Night/Only When I Dream | 10 |
| 67 | President PTL 1003 | MEMORIAL ALBUM (LP) | 40 |

*(see also Randy Fuller)*

## CURTIS FULLER/TOMMY FLANAGAN
| | | | |
|---|---|---|---|
| 58 | Pye NPL28009 | IT'S MAGIC (LP) | 30 |

## JERRY FULLER
| | | | |
|---|---|---|---|
| 59 | London HLH 8982 | The Tennessee Waltz/Charlene | 5 |
| 61 | London HLN 9439 | Guilty Of Loving You/First Love Never Dies | 5 |
| 62 | Salvo SLO 1802 | Lipstick And Rouge/Mother Goose At The Bandstand (99 copies only) | 150 |

## JESSE FULLER
| | | | |
|---|---|---|---|
| 65 | Good Time Jazz GV 2426 | San Francisco Bay Blues/New Midnight Special | 10 |
| 67 | Good Time Jazz GV 2427 | Runnin' Wild/The Monkey And The Engineer | 10 |
| 67 | Fontana TF 821 | Going Back To My Old Used To Be/Bye And Bye | 10 |
| 58 | Good Time Jazz LAG 12159 | JESSE FULLER (LP) | 25 |
| 60 | Good Time Jazz LAG 12279 | LONE CAT (LP) | 25 |
| 60 | Topic 10T 59 | WORKING ON THE RAILROAD (10" LP) | 35 |
| 63 | Good Time Jazz LAG 574 | SAN FRANCISCO BAY BLUES (LP) | 25 |
| 65 | Stateside SL 10154 | JESSE FULLER'S FAVOURITES (LP) | 20 |
| 66 | Fontana TL 5313 | SESSION WITH JESSE FULLER (LP) | 25 |
| 66 | Topic 12T 134 | MOVE ON DOWN THE LINE (LP) | 35 |
| 60s | Vocalion VRLP 574 | SAN FRANCISCO BAY BLUES (LP) | 20 |
| 60s | Evolution Z 1004 | LIVE IN LONDON (LP) | 20 |

## RANDY FULLER
| | | | |
|---|---|---|---|
| 67 | President PT 111 | It's Love, Come What May/The Things You Do | 10 |

*(see also Bobby Fuller Four)*

## FULL EXPERIENCE
| | | | |
|---|---|---|---|
| 12 | Attack THB 7016 | Young Gifted And Broke/Can't See You | 8 |

## FULL MOON (1)
| | | | |
|---|---|---|---|
| 79 | SRTS/79/CUS 279 | Stand Up/Fly Away (p/s) | 35 |

## FULL MOON (2)
| | | | |
|---|---|---|---|
| 87 | Luna SRT 7K51283 | The Eternal Now/Nemesis | 25 |
| 89 | Voices Of Wonder VOW11 | FULL MOON (LP, insert) | 25 |
| 92 | Demi Monde DMLP 1031 | EUPHORIA (LP) | 20 |

## LOWELL FULSON/FULSOM
| | | | |
|---|---|---|---|
| 65 | Sue WI 375 | Too Many Drivers/Key To Your Heart | 40 |
| 66 | Sue WI 4023 | Talking Woman/Blues Around Midnight | 40 |
| 66 | Outasite 45-502 | Stop And Think/Baby (with Leon Blue) | 70 |
| 66 | Polydor 56515 | Black Nights/Little Angel | 20 |
| 67 | Fontana TF 795 | Tramp/Pico | 20 |
| 76 | Jet JET 770 | Do You Love Me?/Monday Morning | 5 |
| 69 | Fontana SFJL 920 | SAN FRANCISCO BLUES (LP) | 30 |
| 69 | Polydor 2384 038 | IN A HEAVY BAG (LP, as Lowell Fulsom) | 20 |

## FUMBLE (1)
| | | | |
|---|---|---|---|
| 72 | Sovereign SOV 110 | Hullo Mary Lou/Hanging On | 5 |
| 73 | Sovereign SOV 118 | Million Seller/Get Up | 5 |
| 73 | Sovereign SOV 121 | Alexandra Park (Palisades Park)/Mama I Can't Tell You | 6 |

## FUMBLE (2)
| | | | |
|---|---|---|---|
| 74 | RCA 2479 | Not Fade Away/After The Dance | 6 |
| 76 | Decca F 13671 | Rock N Roll School/On The Raod To Fame | 6 |
| 77 | Decca F 13702 | Carol Please Come Home/Giving The Best Years Away | 6 |

## FUMME
| | | | |
|---|---|---|---|
| 83 | Sanity 12STY 008 | Only You (Make It Right)/Only You (Make It Right - Instrumental)/Only You (Make It Right - Instrumental) (12") | 30 |
| 83 | Sanity STY 008 | Only You (Make It Right)/(Only You (Makie It Right) Instrumental | 10 |

## FUN AND GAMES
| | | | |
|---|---|---|---|
| 69 | MCA MU 1083 | We/Got To Say Goodbye | 8 |

## FUNBOY FIVE
| | | | |
|---|---|---|---|
| 80 | Cool Cat Daddy-O PHUN 1 | Life After Death/Compulsive Eater (foldover green, yellow, pink, blue and white p/s) | 70 |

## FUNERAL FOR A FRIEND
| | | | |
|---|---|---|---|
| 02 | Mighty Atom MTY 338 | Between Order And Model/Juno/Red Is The New Black (CD) | 25 |
| 03 | Infectious EW 269 | Juneau/Getaway Plan (white vinyl, p/s) | 15 |
| 03 | Warner EW 274 | She Drove Me To Daytime TV/Bullet Theory (blue vinyl, p/s) | 15 |
| 03 | Infectious INFEC 126S | Four Ways — This Year's Most Open Heartbreak/She Drove Me To Daytime Television//Kiss And Make Up (All Bets Are Off)/Escape Artists Never Die (2 x 7" red vinyl, gatefold p/s) | 20 |

## FUN FOUR
| | | | |
|---|---|---|---|
| 80 | NMC NMC 010 | Singing In The Showers/By Products/Elevator Crush (p/s) | 25 |

*(see also Orange Juice)*

## FUN 4
| | | | |
|---|---|---|---|
| 80 | NMC 1 | Singing In the Shower/Elevator Crash | 40 |

## FUNGUS
| | | | |
|---|---|---|---|
| 73 | Fungus FUN 1 | Premonitions Parts 1 & 2 (LP, private pressing) | 100 |

*(see also Secondhand)*

## FUNHOUSE
| | | | |
|---|---|---|---|
| 82 | Ensign ENY 222 | Out Of Control/This Could Be Hell (p/s) | 6 |
| 82 | Ensign ENYT 222 | Out Of Control (Full Version)/This Could Be Hell (12", p/s) | 10 |

*(see also Another Pretty Face, DNV)*

## FUNKADELIC
| 70 | Pye International 7N 25519 | I Got A Thing, You Got A Thing, Everybody's Got A Thing/Fish, Chips & Sweat | 10 |
|----|---------------------------|------------------------------------------------------------------------------|-----|
| 71 | Pye International 7N 25548 | You & Your Folks, Me & Mine/Funky Dollar Bill | 10 |
| 71 | Janus 6146 001 | Can You Get To That/Back In Our Minds | 10 |
| 70 | Pye Intl. NSPL 28137 | FUNKADELIC (LP) | 100 |
| 71 | Pye Intl. NSPL 28144 | FREE YOUR MIND AND YOUR ASS WILL FOLLOW (LP) | 80 |
| 71 | Janus 6310 201 | MAGGOT BRAIN (LP) | 50 |
| 75 | 20th Century W 215 | LET'S TAKE IT TO THE STAGE (LP) | 20 |
| 78 | Warner Bros K 56299 | HARDCORE JOLLIES (LP) | 20 |
| 78 | Warner Bros K 56539 | ONE NATION UNDER A GROOVE (LP, with free 12" "One Nation Under A Groove") | 30 |

*(see also Parliament, Parlet, Bootsy's Rubber Band, Dolby's Cube, P-Funk Allstars)*

## FUNKALOO
| 79 | Rouge RMS 122 | ROBOT DANCER (LP) | 40 |
|----|---------------|--------------------|-----|

## FUNK BAND INC.
| 76 | Beeb 12 | Get It Off/Part 2 | 10 |
|----|---------|--------------------|-----|

## FUNKGUS
| 76 | Baal BDN 38032 | Get It Together/Spill The Wine | 8 |
|----|----------------|--------------------------------|----|
| 76 | Baal BAL 89002 | II (LP) | 25 |

## FUNKMASTERS
| 84 | Master Funk MF4 | It's Over/(Versions) (12") | 10 |
|----|-----------------|-----------------------------|-----|

## FUNKY BOTTOM CONGREGATION
| 69 | Beacon BEA 122 | Hare-Krishna/Things About Yourself | 20 |
|----|----------------|-------------------------------------|-----|

## FUNKY BROWN & INNER CIRCLE
| 74 | Rhino 128 | I See You/Song Of The Swallow | 10 |
|----|-----------|-------------------------------|-----|

## FINBAR & EDDIE FUREY
| 68 | Transatlantic TRA 168 | FINBAR AND EDDIE FUREY (LP, laminated front sleeve, white/lilac labels) | 15 |
|----|-----------------------|--------------------------------------------------------------------------|-----|
| 72 | Dawn DNLS 3037 | THE DAWNING OF THE DAY (LP, with lyric insert, lilac label) | 20 |

## FUR FUR
| 80s | Daark Inc. D.I. 7 | FUR FUR EP | 12 |
|-----|-------------------|------------|-----|

*(see also Karl Blake, Danielle Dax, Lemon Kittens, Gland Shrouds)*

## FURNITURE
| 80 | Para 1 | Shaking Story/Take A Walk Down Town (p/s) | 30 |
|----|--------|--------------------------------------------|-----|
| 80 | Survival SUR 023 | Dancing The Hard Bargain/Robert Nightmans Story | 7 |
| 86 | Stiff BUY 251 | Brilliant Mind/To Gus | 6 |
| 86 | Stiff BUY 254 | Love Your Shoes/Turnupspeed | 7 |
| 90 | Arista 12844 | One Step Behind You/It Continues (P/S) | 6 |
| 91 | Survival SURT 53 | Brilliant Mind (Extended)/Brilliant Mind (7" Version)/On A Bus With Peter Nero/Brilliant Strings (12", p/s) | 12 |
| 83 | Premonition PREM 4CA | WHEN THE BOOM WAS ON (Mini-LP) | 20 |
| 86 | Premonition PREM 6 | THE LOVEMONGERS (LP) | 20 |

## FURRY DICE
| 80 | White Line WHLS 001 | Rudi Don't Take Your Love To Town/K.G.B. (p/s) | 6 |
|----|---------------------|-------------------------------------------------|----|

## FURRY PHREAKS (FEATURING TERRA DEVA)
| 98 | FSUK FSUKT3P | SOOTHE (2 x 12" promo) | 10 |
|----|--------------|-------------------------|-----|

## TOMMY FURTADO
| 57 | London HLA 8418 | Sun Tan Sam/Isabella | 40 |
|----|-----------------|----------------------|-----|

## FURY
| 77 | Arista 150 | Miss Demeanor/Stay On Your feet | 6 |
|----|------------|----------------------------------|----|

## BILLY FURY
### 78s
| 59 | Decca F 11102 | Maybe Tomorrow/Gonna Type A Letter | 100 |
|----|---------------|------------------------------------|------|
| 59 | Decca F 11128 | Margo/Don't Knock Upon My Door | 150 |
| 59 | Decca F 11158 | Angel Face/Time Has Come | 200 |
| 59 | Decca F 11189 | My Christmas Prayer/Last Kiss | 250 |

### SINGLES
| 59 | Decca F 11102 | Maybe Tomorrow/Gonna Type A Letter (triangular centre) | 25 |
|----|---------------|---------------------------------------------------------|-----|
| 59 | Decca F 11102 | Maybe Tomorrow/Gonna Type A Letter (later pressing with round centre) | 15 |
| 59 | Decca F 11128 | Margo/Don't Knock Upon My Door (triangular centre) | 30 |
| 59 | Decca F 11128 | Margo/Don't Knock Upon My Door (later pressing with round centre) | 20 |
| 59 | Decca F 11158 | Angel Face/Time Has Come (triangular centre) | 30 |
| 59 | Decca F 11158 | Angel Face/Time Has Come (later pressing with round centre) | 20 |
| 59 | Decca F 11189 | My Christmas Prayer/Last Kiss (triangular centre) | 50 |
| 59 | Decca F 11189 | My Christmas Prayer/Last Kiss (later pressing with round centre) | 25 |
| 60 | Decca F 11200 | Colette/Baby How I Cried (triangular centre) | 40 |
| 60 | Decca F 11200 | Colette/Baby How I Cried (later pressing with round centre) | 15 |
| 60 | Decca F 11237 | That's Love/You Don't Know (as Billy Fury & Four Jays) | 20 |
| 60 | Decca F 11267 | Wondrous Place/Alright, Goodbye | 20 |
| 60 | Decca F 11311 | A Thousand Stars/Push Push | 12 |
| 61 | Decca F 11334 | Don't Worry/Talkin' In My Sleep (with Four Kestrels) | 15 |
| 61 | Decca F 11349 | Halfway To Paradise/Cross My Heart | 5 |
| 61 | Decca F 11384 | Jealousy/Open Your Arms | 6 |
| 61 | Decca F 11409 | I'd Never Find Another You/Sleepless Nights | 5 |
| 62 | Decca F 11437 | Letter Full Of Tears/Magic Eyes | 15 |
| 62 | Decca F 11458 | Last Night Was Made For Love/King For Tonight | 6 |
| 62 | Decca F 11485 | Once Upon A Dream/If I Lose You | 6 |
| 62 | Decca F 11508 | Because Of Love/Running Around | 6 |
| 63 | Decca F 11582 | Like I've Never Been Gone/What Do You Think You're Doing Of? | 6 |

| | | | MINT VALUE £ |
|---|---|---|---|
| 63 | Decca F 11655 | When Will You Say I Love You?/All I Wanna Do Is Cry | 5 |
| 63 | Decca F 11701 | In Summer/I'll Never Fall In Love Again | 5 |
| 63 | Decca F 11744 | Somebody Else's Girl/Go Ahead And Ask Her | 7 |
| 63 | Decca F 11792 | Do You Really Love Me Too?/What Am I Gonna Do? | 7 |
| 64 | Decca F 11888 | I Will/Nothin' Shakin' (But The Leaves On The Trees) (some B-sides list "Nothin' Shakin' ") | 15 |
| 64 | Decca F 11939 | It's Only Make Believe/Baby What Do You Want Me To Do? | 10 |
| 64 | Decca F 40719 | Hippy Hippy Shake/Glad All Over (export-only, with p/s) | 80 |
| 64 | Decca F 40719 | Hippy Hippy Shake/Glad All Over (export-only) | 50 |
| 65 | Decca F 12048 | I'm Lost Without You/You Better Believe It, Baby | 10 |
| 65 | Decca F 12178 | In Thoughts Of You/Away From You | 10 |
| 65 | Decca F 12230 | Run To My Lovin' Arms/Where Do You Run? | 8 |
| 66 | Decca F 12325 | I'll Never Quite Get Over You/I Belong To The Wind | 10 |
| 66 | Decca F 12409 | Don't Let A Little Pride Stand In Your Way/Didn't See The Real Thing Come Along | 10 |
| 66 | Decca F 12459 | Give Me Your Word/She's So Far Out She's In | 15 |
| 67 | Parlophone R 5560 | Hurtin' Is Loving/Things Are Changing | 30 |
| 67 | Parlophone R 5605 | Loving You/I'll Go Along With It Now | 20 |
| 67 | Parlophone R 5634 | Suzanne In The Mirror/It Just Don't Matter Now | 40 |
| 67 | Parlophone R 5658 | Beyond The Shadow Of A Doubt/Baby Do You Love Me? | 40 |
| 68 | Parlophone R 5681 | Silly Boy Blue/One Minute Woman | 40 |
| 68 | Parlophone R 5723 | Phone Box/Any Morning Now | 40 |
| 68 | Parlophone R 5747 | Lady/Certain Things | 40 |
| 69 | Parlophone R 5788 | I Call For My Rose/Bye Bye | 50 |
| 69 | Parlophone R 5819 | All The Way To The U.S.A./Do My Best For You | 50 |
| 70 | Parlophone R 5845 | Why Are You Leaving?/Old Sweet Roll (Hi-De-Ho) | 50 |
| 70 | Parlophone R 5874 | Paradise Alley/Well ... All Right | 50 |
| 72 | Fury FY 301 | Will The Real Man Please Stand Up/At This Stage | 40 |
| 74 | Warner Bros WB 16402 | I'll Be Your Sweetheart/Fascinating Candle Flame | 30 |
| 76 | NEMS NES 018 | Halfway To Paradise/Turn My Back On You | 10 |
| 81 | Polydor POSP 355 | Be Mine Tonight/No Trespassers (p/s) | 5 |
| 82 | Polydor POSP 488 | Love Or Money/Love Sweet Love (p/s) | 5 |
| 82 | Polydor POSP 528 | Devil Or Angel/Don't Tell Me Lies ('guitar' p/s) | 5 |
| 82 | Polydor POSP 528 | Devil Or Angel/Don't Tell Me Lies ('microphone' p/s) | 6 |
| 83 | Polydor POSP 558 | Forget Him/Your Words (p/s) | 5 |
| 83 | Polydor POSP 558 | Let Me Go Lover/Your Words (same p/s as above but diff. A-side, 500 only) | 20 |
| 83 | Lyntone LYN 13078/BF 1 | Devil Or Angel/Lost Without You (flexi free within memorial concert booklet) | 20 |
| 83 | Private pressing | BILLY FURY IN INTERVIEW WITH STUART COLEMAN (10", 500 white label copies only, 1st 200 numbered) | 30 |
| 83 | Private pressing | BILLY FURY IN INTERVIEW WITH STUART COLEMAN (10", 500 white label copies only, un-numbered) | 20 |

**EPs**

| | | | |
|---|---|---|---|
| 59 | Decca DFE 6597 | MAYBE TOMORROW (triangular centre, orange/red p/s) | 80 |
| 59 | Decca DFE 6597 | MAYBE TOMORROW (round centre, orange/red p/s) | 60 |
| 59 | Decca DFE 6597 | MAYBE TOMORROW (round centre, yellow p/s) | 100 |
| 61 | Decca DFE 6694 | BILLY FURY | 45 |
| 62 | Decca DFE 6699 | BILLY FURY NO. 2 | 45 |
| 62 | Decca DFE 6708 | PLAY IT COOL | 25 |
| 62 | Decca DFE 6708 | PLAY IT COOL (export issue, blue/green 'crouching' cover) | 70 |
| 62 | Decca DFE 8505 | BILLY FURY HITS | 20 |
| 63 | Decca DFE 8525 | BILLY FURY AND THE TORNADOS | 30 |
| 63 | Decca DFE 8558 | AM I BLUE | 50 |
| 65 | Decca DFE 8641 | BILLY FURY AND THE GAMBLERS | 100 |

**ALBUMS**

| | | | |
|---|---|---|---|
| 60 | Decca LF 1329 | THE SOUND OF FURY (10") | 200 |
| 60 | Ace Of Clubs ACL 1047 | BILLY FURY | 30 |
| 61 | Ace Of Clubs ACL 1083 | HALFWAY TO PARADISE | 30 |
| 63 | Decca LK 4533 | BILLY | 40 |
| 63 | Decca LK 4548 | WE WANT BILLY! (with Tornados, mono) | 40 |
| 63 | Decca SKL 4548 | WE WANT BILLY! (with Tornados, stereo) | 45 |
| 65 | Decca LK 4677 | I'VE GOTTA HORSE (soundtrack) | 40 |

*(see also Tornados, Gamblers)*

**FURYS**

| | | | |
|---|---|---|---|
| 63 | Stateside SS 182 | Never More/Zing! Went The Strings Of My Heart | 12 |
| 72 | Jay Boy BOY 61 | What Is Soul?/I Lost My Baby | 8 |
| 72 | Jay Boy BOY 68 | I'm Satisfied With You/Just A Little Mixed Up | 15 |
| 72 | Jay Boy BOY 68 | I'm Satisfied With You/Just A Little Mixed Up (DJ Copy) | 30 |

**FURY'S TORNADOES**

| | | | |
|---|---|---|---|
| 74 | Warner Bros K 16442 | Telstar '74/I Would Give You Anything | 8 |

*(see also Billy Fury)*

**F.U.S.E.**

| | | | |
|---|---|---|---|
| 93 | Warp WAP38 | Train Tracs (12", some white vinyl, p/s) | 10 |

**FUSION ORCHESTRA**

| | | | |
|---|---|---|---|
| 73 | EMI EMI 2056 | When My Mama's Not At Home/Nuthouse Rock | 8 |
| 73 | EMI EMA 758 | A SKELETON IN ARMOUR (LP, gatefold sleeve) | 100 |

**FUSION (1)**

| | | | |
|---|---|---|---|
| 80 | Telephone TEL 101 | TILL I HEAR FROM YOU (LP, blue vinyl) | 20 |

**FUSION (2)**

| | | | |
|---|---|---|---|
| 96 | Ferox FER 021 | GALAXY OF FUTURE VISIONS (12" EP) | 10 |

## FUT
70    Beacon BEA 160      Have You Heard The Word/Futting Around .................................................. 30
*(see also Graham Bonnet, Bee Gees, Marbles, Maurice Gibb, Steve & Stevie; this record has NO Beatles involvement)*

## FUTURE BEAT ALLIANCE
99    Ferox FER 035      ABACO (12" EP) ........................................................................................ 10

## FUTURE BODIES
80    SGS 111      Terrorist/Science Of Romance (p/s, lyric insert, rubber stamped labels) ...................... 45

## FUTURE DAZE
82    Polydor POSP 455      House On The Hill/Silent Room (p/s) ............................................................. 8

## FUTURE OF THE LEFT
06    Too Pure PURE 206LP      CURSES! (LP) ........................................................................................ 15
09    4AD CAD2913      TRAVELS WITH MYSELF AND ANOTHER (LP) ...................................................... 15
12    Xtra Mile Recordings –      THE PLOT AGAINST COMMON SENSE (LP) ......................................................... 15
     XMR058LP

## FUTURE PAST
91    B12 03      Our Paths Meet/Harmony Park/Your Hand In My Mind/Dance Intellect/ TV People
     (12", black vinyl) ................................................................................... 50

## FUTURE SOUND OF LONDON
91    Jumpin' & Pumpin' TOT 17      Papua New Guinea/Papua New Guinea (Andrew Weatherall Mix) (p/s) ...................... 6
91    Jumpin' & Pumpin' 12TOT 16   PULSE 3: Tingler/Owl/Bite The Bullet/Calcium ................................................ 12
91    Jumpin' & Pumpin' 12TOT 17   Papua New Guinea (Dali Mix)/(Dumb Child Of Q Mix)/ (Qube Mix) (p/s).................... 12
94    Virgin promo 500      Slider/Snake Hips/You're Creeping Me Out/Herd Killing/Live In New York (2 x 12" p/s,
     promo only, 500 copies, FSOL under different names) ........................................ 15
94    Virgin VST 1540P      Far Out Son Of Lung And The Ramblings Of A Madman/ Snake Hips/Smokin' Japanese
     Babe/Amoeba (white vinyl, promo only)...................................................... 20
95    Virgin SEMTEX DJ 1      Semtex (Part 1)/Semtex (Part 2)/We Have Explosive/Semtex (stamped sleeve, promo
     only, 500 copies) ................................................................................... 15
92    Jumpin'/Pumpin' LPTOT 2      ACCELERATOR (2-LP) ............................................................................... 20
94    Virgin V 2722      LIFEFORMS (2-LP, stickered gatefold sleeve with inner sleeves) .............................. 40
94    Virgin V 2755      ISDN (LP, embossed, fold-out black sleeve with insert) ...................................... 30
96    Virgin V 2814      DEAD CITIES (2-LP, gatefold sleeve with inners) .............................................. 30
*(see also Amorphous Androgynous, Art Science Technology, Humanoid,*

## FUTUREHEADS
02    Project C'naut PCOS 001      Nul Book Standard — Park Inn/Robot/My Rules/Stupid And Shallow (p/s) .............. 10
03    Private Pressing      Hounds Of Love (1-track white label: gig/fanclub 7").......................................... 8
04    Private Pressing      Meantime/Decent Days & Nights Remixes (1000, white label gig/fanclub 7") .............. 6

## FUTURES
74    Buddah BDS 477      You Better Be Certain/No One Could Compare (DJ Copy) ................................... 12
75    Buddah BDS 430      You Better Be Certain/No One Could Compare ............................................... 8

## FUZZ FACE
68    Page One POF 065      Mighty Quinn/Voices From The Sky.............................................................. 5

## FUZZ (1)
71    Mojo 2916 010      FUZZ (LP)............................................................................................. 20

## FUZZ (2)
74    Pye 104      I'm So Glad/All About Love ....................................................................... 5

## FUZZBIRD
95    Fuzzbird FR3      Can't Believe A Word/A Man Named Fly (p/s) ................................................. 8

## FUZZTONES
85    ABC S 006      She's Wicked/Epitaph For A Head (p/s) ......................................................... 6

## FUZZY DUCK
71    MAM MAM 37      Double Time Woman/Just Look Around You.................................................... 15
71    MAM MAM 51      Big Brass Band/One More Hour.................................................................. 15
90    Reflection MM50      Double Time Woman/One More Hour ........................................................... 8
71    MAM AS 1005      FUZZY DUCK (LP, laminated front sleeve, black/silver labels) .............................. 700
90    Reflection MM 05      FUZZY DUCK (LP, reissue with booklet & single "Double Time Woman"/ "One More
     Hour" [MMS 01]) ................................................................................... 25
*(see also Andromeda, Greatest Show On Earth, Alvin Lee, Capability Brown, Cockney Rebel))*

## FX
79    Southern Rock SR 4501      THE SOUTH'S GONNA RISE AGAIN (EP, oversized folding p/s) ........................... 100

## FYNN MCCOOL
70    RCA RCA 1956      U.S. Thumbstyle/Diamond Lil .................................................................... 8
70    RCA SF 8112      FYNN McCOOL (LP, gatefold sleeve) ........................................................... 200
*(see also Shakespears, Grapefruit, Sleepy)*

## G

## TOMMY G & CHARMS
67    London HLB 10107      I Know What I Want/I Want You So Bad .......................................................... 40

## WINSTON G (& WICKED)
65    Parlophone R 5266      Please Don't Say/Like A Baby ..................................................................... 35
66    Parlophone R 5330      Until You Were Gone/That Way Too (as Winston G. & Wicked)................................ 18
66    Decca F 12444      Cloud Nine/I'll Make You Cry Tomorrow ........................................................ 18
67    Decca F 12559      Mother Ferguson's Love Dust/Judge And Jury .................................................. 75
67    Decca F 12623      Riding With The Milkman/Bye Bye Baby ......................................................... 20

MINT VALUE £

## B(ASIL) GABBIDON

| | | | |
|---|---|---|---|
| 61 | Blue Beat BB 069-A | Warpaint Baby (miscredited to B. Cabbidon & Buster's Group)/ I Was Wrong (miscredited to Chuck & Dobbie with Buster's Group) | 20 |
| 62 | Blue Beat BB 111-A | Ivoree/Lover Man | 20 |
| 62 | Blue Beat BB 124 | Independence Blues/For My Love (as B. Gabbidon) | 20 |
| 62 | Blue Beat BB 129-A | Our Melody/Going Back To Ja (with Randy's All Stars) | 20 |
| 62 | Island WI 033 | I Found My Baby (actually by Roy Braham)/No Fault Of Mine | 30 |
| 63 | Island WI 076 | I Bet You Don't Know/3 x 7 | 30 |
| 63 | Island WI 089 | St. Louis Woman/Get On The Ball | 40 |
| 63 | Blue Beat BB 155-A | Eana Mena/Since You Are Gone (with Prince Buster All Stars) | 20 |
| 63 | Blue Beat BB 161 | I'll Find Love (with Prince Buster All Stars)/ MELLOW LARKS: What You Gonna Do? | 20 |
| 65 | Blue Beat BB 288 | Tick Tock (actually by Theo Beckford)/The Streets Of Glory (actually by Theo Beckford & Yvonne Harrison) | 20 |

*(see also Derrick Patsy & Basil, Mellow Larks, Derrick Morgan)*

## PETER GABRIEL

| | | | |
|---|---|---|---|
| 77 | Charisma CB 301 | Solsbury Hill/Moribund The Burgermeister (p/s) | 6 |
| 77 | Charisma CB 302 | Modern Love/Slowburn (no p/s, 'nude' picture label, withdrawn) | 30 |
| 78 | Charisma CB 311 | D.I.Y./Perspective (p/s, purple label, Irish-only sleeve) | 8 |
| 78 | Charisma CB 311 | D.I.Y./Perspective (p/s, silver label, possibly Irish-only sleeve) | 8 |
| 78 | Charisma CB 319 | D.I.Y. (Remix)/Mother Of Violence/Teddy Bear (no p/s, withdrawn) | 20 |
| 80 | Reformation RSR 113 | CHROMEDOME (LP) | 20 |
| 92 | Virgin PG 7 | US (2-LP, inners) | 18 |

*(see also Genesis, Youssou 'Ndour & Peter Gabriel, Colin Scot, Charlie Drake)*

## PETER GABRIEL & KATE BUSH

| | | | |
|---|---|---|---|
| 86 | Charisma/Virgin PGSP 2 | Don't Give Up/In Your Eyes (Special Mix) (poster p/s in stickered PVC sleeve) | 6 |

*(see also Kate Bush)*

## RUSS GABRIEL

| | | | |
|---|---|---|---|
| 93 | Ferox FER 002 | PEACE EP (12", plain sleeve) | 18 |
| 95 | Input Neuron INMD(X)1 | FUTURE FUNK VOL. 1 (12", double pack, p/s) | 10 |

*(see also Fusion, Too Funk)*

## RUSS GABRIEL & AFFIE YUSUF

| | | | |
|---|---|---|---|
| 94 | Ferox FER 005 | Sian's Tune/Deep Space (12") | 18 |

## GABRIEL & ANGELS

| | | | |
|---|---|---|---|
| 63 | Stateside SS 150 | That's Life (That's Tough)/Don't Wanna Twist No More | 20 |

## GABRIELLI BRASS

| | | | |
|---|---|---|---|
| 65 | Polydor 56031 | Angel Cake/Cat Walk | 10 |
| 65 | Polydor 56047 | Ride Your Pony/Anyone Who Had A Heart | 10 |
| 68 | Polydor 56252 | 'Canterbury Tales' Theme/Working My Way Back To You | 15 |

## GABY & CABLES

| | | | |
|---|---|---|---|
| 72 | Duke DU 129 | Only Love Can Make You Smile/Only Love Version | 15 |

*(see also Gaby & Wilton)*

## GABY & WILTON

| | | | |
|---|---|---|---|
| 72 | Camel CA 92 | Only Love/CHARLEY ACE: The Ten Commandments Of Joshua | 10 |

*(see also Gaby & Cables)*

## PABLO GAD

| | | | |
|---|---|---|---|
| 77 | Caribbean CBN 318 | International Dread/International Dub | 10 |
| 77 | Caribbean CBM 320 | Kunte Kinte/Jah Jah Say (with The Equators) | 10 |
| 78 | Burning Sounds BDS 009 | Bloodsuckers/Jail House Pressure (12", red vinyl) | 20 |
| 79 | Burning Rockers BRD 007 | Visions Of Pablo/Tru I De A Jail (12") | 20 |
| 79 | Burning Rockers BRD 008 | Natty Loving/Trodding On Home (12") | 20 |
| 79 | Burning Rockers BRD 020 | Riddle I Dis/Iration (12") | 20 |
| 79 | Burning Sounds BS 042 | Blood Suckers/Blood Suckers Dub | 6 |
| 79 | Burning Sounds BSD 015 | Throw Your Dreams/What Makes A Natty Dread Cry (12", red vinyl) | 20 |
| 79 | Burning Rockers BRD 014 | Trafalgar Square/Chereene (12", red vinyl) | 20 |
| 80 | Burning Rockers BRD 043 | Hard Time/Lighter Shade Of Black (12") | 20 |
| 80 | His Majesty HMD 010 | Crisis Time/Saddest Mistake (12") | 25 |
| 80 | Burning Rockers BRD 044 | Black Before Creation/Reggae Music (12") | 15 |
| 80 | Greensleeves GRED 33 | Fly Away Home/Well Insane (12") | 20 |
| 80 | His Majesty HMD 012 | Oh Jah/Little Young Girl (12") | 35 |
| 80 | FORM D001 | Gun Fever/Fever Dub (12", red vinyl) | 20 |
| 80 | FORM D003 | Nursery Rhyme/Bubbling Angelo (12", purple vinyl) | 10 |
| 81 | FORM D005 | P.G. In Love/RANKING SIMEON: Ranking Love (12") | 20 |
| 81 | FORM D017 | Beggarman's Child/Poor Man Versus Rich Man Dub (12") | 10 |
| 86 | Jah Shaka SHAKA 853 | King Of Kings/Lord Of Lords (12") | 15 |
| 96 | Reggae On Top ROT 013 | Sha Sha Mane/Dub (12") | 10 |
| 80 | Burning Sounds BS 1038 | TRAFALGAR SQUARE (LP) | 25 |
| 80 | Federation Of Reggae FORM LP 1099 | HARD TIMES (LP, red vinyl) | 30 |

## GADGETS

| | | | |
|---|---|---|---|
| 79 | Final Solution FSLP 001 | GADGETREE (LP, with insert, blue or beige picture on sleeve) | 20 |
| 80 | Final Solution FSLP 002 | LOVE, CURIOSITY, FRECKLES & DOUBT (LP) | 25 |
| 83 | Glass GLALP 006 | THE BLUE ALBUM (LP, with inner sleeve) | 15 |

*(see also The The, Matt Johnson, Colin Lloyd Tucker)*

## MEL GADSON

| | | | |
|---|---|---|---|
| 60 | London HLX 9105 | Comin' Down With Love/I'm Gettin' Sentimental Over You | 20 |

## GAFFA

| | | | |
|---|---|---|---|
| 77 | Cleverly Bros CBM 002 | NORMAL SERVICE WILL NEVER BE RESUMED EP (various hand-made p/s) | 20 |
| 79 | Gaffa ZZZZ S001 | Hearts Of Stone/You Know I Love You (But I Don't Know How I Know) (various p/s) | 15 |

| | | | |
|---|---|---|---|
| 79 | Gaffa ZZZZ S002 | ATTITUDE DANCING (LAND OF 1000 DUNCES)/LONG WEEKEND (four different p/s of 250 copies to go with pressing of 1000 records) | 15 |
| 80 | Gaffa ZZZZ 5003 | Man With A Motive/Your Side/My Side | 20 |
| 78 | ZZZZ 001 | NEITHER USE NOR ORNAMENT (LP) | 15 |

## GAGALACTYCA
| | | | |
|---|---|---|---|
| 90 | Holyground HG 1135/ Magic Mixture MM 3 | GAGALACTYCA (LP, with booklet, actually by Lightyears Away & Thundermother, 425 only) | 40 |

*(see also David John & Mood)*

## MAJOR YURI GAGARIN
| | | | |
|---|---|---|---|
| 61 | Britone MK 100 | CONQUEST OF SPACE (EP) | 20 |

## GAGS
| | | | |
|---|---|---|---|
| 79 | Look LKLP 6312 | DEATH IN BUZZARD'S GULCH (LP) | 30 |

## LITTLE SAMMY GAHA
| | | | |
|---|---|---|---|
| 73 | Decca FR 13436 | Rock 'N' Roll Is Back Again/Come 'N' On Strong | 10 |

## DAVID GAHAN
| | | | |
|---|---|---|---|
| 08 | Mute LSTUMM 288 | HOURGLASS REMIXES (2-LP & CD of remixes) | 18 |

*(see also Depeche Mode)*

## GAH-GA
| | | | |
|---|---|---|---|
| 85 | Everbimes EVB 003 | Give Your Love To Me/Transition (p/s) | 40 |

## BASIL GAIL
| | | | |
|---|---|---|---|
| 70 | Bullet BU 454 | I Wish/Black Is Black | 8 |

## SLIM GAILLARD (QUARTET/TRIO)
| | | | |
|---|---|---|---|
| 56 | Parlophone GEP 8595 | SLIM GAILLARD NO. 1 (EP) | 15 |
| 56 | Columbia Clef SEB 10046 | MUSICAL AGGREGATIONS (EP) | 15 |
| 60 | London RED 1251 | SLIM GAILLARD RIDES AGAIN (EP) | 25 |

*(see also Meade 'Lux' Lewis & Slim Gaillard)*

## DONNA GAINES
| | | | |
|---|---|---|---|
| 71 | MCA MK 5060 | Sally Go Round The Roses/So Said The Man | 50 |

*(see also Donna Summer)*

## PEGGY GAINES
| | | | |
|---|---|---|---|
| 98 | Kent 6T 14 | When The Boy That You Love/SAN FRANCISCO TKOS: Make Up Your Mind | 25 |

## GAINORS
| | | | |
|---|---|---|---|
| 58 | London HLU 8734 | The Secret/Gonna Rock Tonite | 100 |
| 58 | London HLU 8734 | The Secret/Gonna Rock Tonite (78) | 25 |

## SERGE GAINSBOURG
| | | | |
|---|---|---|---|
| 79 | Island ILPS 9581 | AUX ARMES ET CAETERA (LP) | 20 |

*(see also Jane Birkin and Serge Gainsbourg)*

## GAK
| | | | |
|---|---|---|---|
| 94 | Warp WAP 48 | GAK EP (12") | 40 |
| 94 | Warp WAP 48CD | GAK (CD) | 40 |

*(see also Aphex Twin)*

## GALACTIC FEDERATION
| | | | |
|---|---|---|---|
| 66 | Polydor BM 56093 | The March Of The Sky People/Moon Shot | 25 |

## GALACTIC SYMPOSIUM
| | | | |
|---|---|---|---|
| 80 | Vague VOG 2 | Money/In The Navy (gatefold p/s) | 15 |

## GALAHAD (1)
| | | | |
|---|---|---|---|
| 73 | Bell BLL 1273 | Rocket Summer/Elephant Stomp | 30 |
| 72 | Polydor 2058 215 | Let's Dance/Jellyroll | 10 |

## GALAHAD (2)
| | | | |
|---|---|---|---|
| 87 | Private pressing G 1001 | Dreaming From The Inside/The Opiate (p/s, 500 only) | 12 |

## DIAMANDA GALAS
| | | | |
|---|---|---|---|
| 82 | Y Y 18 | LITANIES DU SATAN (LP) | 30 |
| 92 | Mute STUMM 103 | SINGER (LP) | 18 |

## GALAXIE 500
| | | | |
|---|---|---|---|
| 90 | Rough Trade RTD 199.006.7 | Blue Thunder/Untitled (1-sided) | 6 |
| 90 | Caff CAFF 9 | Rain/Don't Let Your Youth Go To Waste (p/s, with insert in bag) | 40 |
| 89 | Shimmy Disc Europe SDE 8908 LP | TODAY (LP) | 25 |
| 89 | Rough Trade ROUGH 146 | ON FIRE (LP) | 30 |
| 90 | Rough Trade ROUGH 156 | THIS IS OUR MUSIC (LP, with sticker and 3 postcards) | 25 |
| 91 | Rough Trade ROUGH 146L | ON FIRE (LP, reissue with shrinkwrapped CD single) | 20 |
| 10 | Domino REWIGLP69 | TODAY (LP, reissue) | 15 |

*(see also Damon & Naomi, Luna)*

## GALAXIES
| | | | |
|---|---|---|---|
| 60 | Capitol CL 15158 | The Big Triangle/Until The Next Time | 15 |

## EDDIE GALE
| | | | |
|---|---|---|---|
| 69 | Blue Note BST 84294 | GHETTO MUSIC (LP) | 15 |

## ERICA GALE
| | | | |
|---|---|---|---|
| 83 | Cassia CAS 001 | Ain't Gonna Loose My Head/Instrumental Version (12") | 12 |

## SANDRA GALE
| | | | |
|---|---|---|---|
| 63 | Ember EMB S 162 | Hello Heartbreak/If She's Right For You | 7 |

## SUNNY GALE
| | | | |
|---|---|---|---|
| 53 | HMV 7M 147 | Teardrops On My Pillow/Send My Baby Back To Me | 8 |
| 54 | HMV 7M 243 | Goodnight, Well It's Time To Go/Close To Me | 8 |
| 55 | HMV 7M 344 | C'est La Vie/Looking Glass | 8 |
| 57 | Brunswick 05659 | Two Hearts (With An Arrow Between)/Maybe You'll Be There | 8 |
| 57 | Brunswick 05661 | Come Go With Me/Please Go | 8 |

| 58 | Brunswick 05753 | A Certain Smile/Just Friends | 8 |
| 61 | London HLU 9322 | Please Love Me Forever/Sunny | 8 |

## GALE BROTHERS
| 66 | Parlophone R 5535 | Every Day Of My Life/All Strung Out | 6 |

## GALENS
| 63 | London HLH 9804 | Baby I Do Love You/Love Bells | 30 |

## NOEL GALLAGHER'S HIGH FLYING BIRDS
| 12 | Sour Mash JDNC 11 | Dream On/Shoot A Hole Into The Sun (12" p/s, numbered) | 20 |
| 12 | Sour Mash JDNC 14T | SONGS FROM THE GREAT WHITE NORTH EP (12", p/s numbered) | 15 |

*(see also Oasis)*

## RORY GALLAGHER
| 71 | Polydor 2814 004 | It's You/Just The Smile | 20 |
| 71 | Polydor 2383 044 | RORY GALLAGHER (LP) | 35 |
| 71 | Polydor 2383 076 | DEUCE (LP) | 30 |
| 72 | Polydor 2383 112 | LIVE! IN EUROPE (LP, gatefold sleeve) | 20 |
| 73 | Polydor 2383 189 | BLUEPRINT (LP) | 18 |
| 73 | Polydor 2383 230 | TATTOO (LP) | 20 |

*(see also Taste, Killing Floor, Joe O'Donnell)*

## GALLAGHER-LYLE
| 67 | Polydor BM 56170 | Trees/In The Crowd | 18 |
| 72 | Capitol ST 21906 | GALLAGHER AND LYLE (LP) | 20 |
| 73 | A&M AMLH 68148 | WILLIE AND THE LAPDOG (LP, with booklet) | 18 |

*(see also James Galt, McGuinness Flint, Cups)*

## GALLAHADS
| 55 | Capitol CL 14282 | Ooh-Ah/Careless | 15 |

## RONNIE GALLANT
| 62 | Warner Bros WB 61 | In The Night/The Hole In The Wall | 20 |

## GALLANTS
| 64 | Capitol CL 15366 | Happy Beat/Rhino | 10 |
| 65 | Capitol CL 15408 | Man From U.N.C.L.E. Theme/Vagabond | 15 |

## GALLERY (1)
| 72 | Midas | THE WIND THAT SHAKES THE BARLEY (LP) | 800 |
| 78 | Look LK LP 6029 | EACH DAY THROUGH (LP) | 100 |

## GALLERY (2)
| 82 | Cobweb AP163/CWB814 | EGYPTIAN THEORY (LP, with insert) | 40 |

## GALLIARD
| 70 | Deram DM 306 | I Wrapped Her In Ribbons/The Hermit And The Knight | 10 |
| 70 | Deram Nova (S)DN 4 | STRANGE PLEASURE (LP, red/silver labels) | 300 |
| 70 | Deram SML 1075 | NEW DAWN (LP, white/red labels with small logo) | 450 |

*(see also Craig)*

## GALLIARDS
| 60 | Topic STOP 101 | Black And White/Bahnuah | 7 |

## BOB GALLION
| 59 | MGM MGM 1028 | Out Of A Honky Tonk/You Take The Table And I'll Take The Chairs | 7 |
| 60 | MGM MGM 1057 | Froggy Went A Courtin'/Hey! Joe | 7 |
| 65 | Hickory 45-1300 | I Don't Have The Right (To Disagree)/Thank The Devil For Hideaways | 5 |

## VINCENT GALLO
| 01 | Warp 7201 WAP01-7 | Honey Bunny (stereo)/Honey Bunny (Mono) | 8 |
| 01 | Warp WAPLP 87 | WHEN (LP, 'book' cover) | 70 |
| 02 | Warp WAPLP 99 | RECORDINGS OF MUSIC FOR FILMS (2-LP) | 25 |

## GALLON DRUNK
| 93 | Clawfist XPIG 21 | Known, Not Wanted/TINDERSTICKS: We Have All The Time In The World ('singles club' release, p/s, 1,400 only) | 15 |
| 91 | Clawfist HUNKA LP2 | TONITE...THE SINGLES BAR (LP) | 15 |
| 96 | City Slang EFA04982-1 | IN THE LONG STILL NIGHT (LP) | 15 |
| 02 | Sweet Nothing SNLP 012 | FIRE MUSIC (2-LP) | 18 |

## GALLOWS
| 07 | Holy Roar HRR 006V | DEMO 2005 (white vinyl, 500 only) | 40 |
| 07 | Holy Roar HRR 006V | Just Because You Sleep Next To Me Doesn't Mean You're Safe/Abandon Ship/Will Someone Shoot That Fucking Snake/Swarm Over Death (white vinyl, 500 only) | 12 |
| 07 | Warner Bros. WEA425X | In The Belly Of A Shark/Sick Of Feeling Sick (live) (p/s, blue vinyl) | 10 |
| 07 | Thirty Days Of Night TDON 015 | Sick Of Feeling Sick/If Credits What Matters I'll Take Credit/NOVEMBER COMING FIRE: Return Of The Black Dog/Bear Away (split 7", p/s, various coloured vinyl) | 15 |
| 10 | Thirty Days Of Night TDON015 | Sick Of Feeling Sick/If Credits What Matters I'll Take Credit/NOVEMBER COMING FIRE: Return Of The Black Dog/Bear Away (brown vinyl, repressing, 500 only) | 10 |
| 10 | Thirty Days Of Night TDON015 | Sick Of Feeling Sick/If Credits What Matters I'll Take Credit/NOVEMBER COMING FIRE: Return Of The Black Dog/Bear Away (repressing, white/blue vinyl, 20 only) | 15 |
| 07 | Warner Bros. 25646 9846 3 | ORCHESTRA OF WOLVES (LP & CD, green vinyl) | 30 |
| 09 | Reprise 519232-1 | GREY BRITAIN (LP, red/grey vinyl) | 35 |

## JAMES GALT
| 65 | Pye 7N 15936 | Comes The Dawn/My Own Way | 12 |
| 65 | Pye 7N 17021 | With My Baby/A Most Unusual Feeling | 75 |
| 65 | Pye 7N 17021 | With My Baby/A Most Unusual Feeling (DJ Copy) | 100 |

*(see also Gallagher-Lyle)*

## GAMBIT OF SHAME
| 82 | Dead Hedgehog DHE 7009 | No Bounds/18 Out Of 20 (p/s) | 15 |

## GAMBLERS
| 63 | Decca F 11780 | You've Really Got A Hold On Me/Can I See You Tonight? | 15 |

| | | | |
|---|---|---|---|
| 64 | Decca F 11872 | Nobody But Me (Kissin' Time)/It's So Nice | 15 |
| 65 | Decca F 12060 | Now I'm All Alone/Find Out What's Happening | 30 |
| 66 | Decca F 12399 | Doctor Goldfoot (And His Bikini Machine)/It Seems So Long | 20 |
| 67 | Parlophone R 5557 | Cry Me A River/Who Will Buy | 30 |

*(see also Billy Fury)*

**GAME**

| | | | |
|---|---|---|---|
| 65 | Pye 7N 15889 | But I Do/Gotta Keep On Moving Baby | 80 |
| 66 | Decca F 12469 | Gonna Get Me Someone/Gotta Wait | 200 |
| 67 | Parlophone R 5553 | The Addicted Man/Help Me Mummy's Gone (withdrawn) | 1000 |
| 67 | Parlophone R 5553 | The Addicted Man/Help Me Mummy's Gone (withdrawn) (demo copy) | 700 |
| 67 | Parlophone R 5569 | It's Shocking What They Call Me/Help Me Mummy's Gone | 500 |
| 97 | Dig The Fuzz DIG 026 | IT'S SHOCKING WHAT THEY CALL US (LP, gatefold, poster and free 7") | 20 |

**GAMES**

| | | | |
|---|---|---|---|
| 80 | Games 001 | Childsplay/First Law Of Games (p/s) | 80 |
| 82 | Open Eye OE 7 | Dance This Way/Love Canal (p/s) | 40 |

**GAMMA**

| | | | |
|---|---|---|---|
| 80 | Elektra K12480 | Something In The Air/Mayday | 10 |

**GAMMER**

| | | | |
|---|---|---|---|
| 77 | Pennine (EP) PSS 147 | Market Place - Your Alone/San Diego (no p/s) | 12 |

**GAMMITT**

| | | | |
|---|---|---|---|
| 73 | Solar SL1 | Queen Of Rock/We Dance | 15 |

**GANDALF THE GREY**

| | | | |
|---|---|---|---|
| 80s | Heyoka | THE GREY WIZARD AM I (LP, reissue of U.S. LP) | 25 |

**RON GANDERTON**

| | | | |
|---|---|---|---|
| 82 | Centridge CENT 2 | Giggle Amongst The Tears/Smothered In Love (p/s) | 8 |

**LITTLE JIMMY GANDY**

| | | | |
|---|---|---|---|
| 69 | Roulette RO 510 | Cool Thirteen/I'm Not Like The Others (Existence unconfirmed) | 20 |

**GANELIN TRIO**

| | | | |
|---|---|---|---|
| 80 | Leo LR 102 | CATALOGUE, LIVE IN EAST GERMANY (LP) | 15 |
| 83 | Leo LR 112 | NEW WINE...(LP) | 30 |

**GANG STARR**

| | | | |
|---|---|---|---|
| 90 | CBS 656377-7 | Jazz Thing (Video Mix)/Jazz Thing (Movie MIx) (p/s) | 10 |

**GANGBUSTERS**

| | | | |
|---|---|---|---|
| 63 | Fontana TF 419 | The Memory Of Your Face/When We Met | 5 |

**GANG OF FOUR**

| | | | |
|---|---|---|---|
| 80 | Fast Product FAST 5 | DAMAGED GOODS (EP, original with b&w labels, with sticker) | 20 |
| 80 | Fast Product FAST 5 | DAMAGED GOODS (EP, original with b&w labels, without sticker) | 12 |
| 79 | EMI 2956 | At Home He's A Tourist/It's Her Factory (p/s) | 6 |
| 86 | Strange Fruit SFPS 008 | PEEL SESSIONS (12") | 12 |
| 79 | EMI EMC 3313 | ENTERTAINMENT! (LP, with inner sleeve) | 20 |
| 81 | EMI EMC 3364 | SOLID GOLD (LP, with insert) | 15 |

**GANGSTERS (1)**

| | | | |
|---|---|---|---|
| 79 | Stortbeat A45/B45 | Harlow Town/Record Company | 20 |
| 79 | Stortbeat BEAT 3 | Best Friend/Best Friend Dub (p/s) | 10 |
| 79 | Stortbeat BEAT 2 | GANGSTERS (LP) | 20 |

**GANGSTERS (2)**

| | | | |
|---|---|---|---|
| 80 | Big Bear BB 25 | Rudi The Red Nose Reindeer/White Christmas | 5 |
| 80 | Big Bear BB 28 | Wooly Bully/We Are The Gangsters | 5 |

**GANIM'S ASIA MINORS**

| | | | |
|---|---|---|---|
| 58 | London HLE 8637 | Daddy Lolo/Halvah | 12 |

**ALAN GANLEY QUARTET**

| | | | |
|---|---|---|---|
| 58 | Pye Nixa NJE 1046 | GONE GANLEY (EP) | 100 |

**CLENTT GANT**

| | | | |
|---|---|---|---|
| 60 | Starlite ST45 023 | I'm Just A Lucky So-And-So/I Need You So | 5 |

**DON GANT**

| | | | |
|---|---|---|---|
| 65 | Hickory 45-1297 | Early In The Morning/Don't Ya Even Cry | 5 |

**ELMER GANTRY'S VELVET OPERA**

| | | | |
|---|---|---|---|
| 67 | Direction 58-3083 | Flames/Salisbury Plain | 20 |
| 68 | Direction 58-3481 | Mary Jane/Dreamy | 20 |
| 69 | Direction 58-3924 | Volcano/A Quick 'B' | 20 |
| 68 | Direction 8-63300 | ELMER GANTRY'S VELVET OPERA (LP, laminated front sleeve, yellow/black labels) | 175 |

*(see also Velvet Opera, Stretch, Strawbs, Hudson-Ford, Paul Brett's Sage)*

**GANTS**

| | | | |
|---|---|---|---|
| 65 | Liberty LIB 55829 | Road Runner/My Baby Don't Care | 35 |
| 67 | Liberty LIB 55940 | I Wonder/Greener Days | 15 |

**GARBAGE**

| | | | |
|---|---|---|---|
| 95 | Discordant CORD 001 | Vow/Torn Apart (embossed metal 'G' logo sleeve, with insert, 3,000 pressed [934 issued], stickered, sealed) | 20 |
| 95 | Discordant CORD 001 | Vow/Torn Apart (embossed metal 'G' logo sleeve, with insert, 3,000 pressed [934 issued], stickered, unsealed) | 20 |
| 95 | Discordant CORD 001 | Vow/Torn Apart (plain black embossed 'G' logo sleeve, with insert in poly bag, 500 only, sealed) | 12 |
| 95 | Discordant CORD 001 | Vow/Torn Apart (plain black embossed 'G' logo sleeve, with insert in poly bag, 500 only, unsealed) | 12 |
| 95 | Mushroom SX 1138 | Subhuman/1 Crush (embossed rubber 'G' logo sleeve, with SX 1138 insert, some in white 'G' logo carrier bag, 3,000 only; with incorrect insert [S1138]) | 15 |
| 95 | Mushroom S 1138 | Subhuman/1 Crush (embossed card 'G' logo sleeve, with insert, 2,000 pressed [1,000 issued]) | 10 |

MINT VALUE £

| 95 | Mushroom SX 1199 | Only Happy When It Rains/Girl Can't Come/Sleep (double-grooved B-side, stickered 'hologram prismaboard' 'G' logo sleeve, with inner sleeve & insert; some in blue 'G' logo carrier bag, 5000 only) | 5 |
|----|------------------|------|---|
| 95 | Mushroom L 31450 | GARBAGE (LP) (as 2 x 45rpm 12", with inner sleeves) | 20 |
| 95 | Mushroom LX 31450 | GARBAGE (LP) (as 6 x 7" singles in box set with 3 inserts [now import only], sealed) | 20 |
| 95 | Mushroom LX 31450 | GARBAGE (LP) (as 6 x 7" singles in box set with 3 inserts [now import only], unsealed) | 15 |
| 98 | Mushroom MUSH29LP | VERSION 2.0 (LP) | 40 |
| 99 | Simply Vinyl SVLP 140 | VERSION 2.0 (LP, 180 gram reissue) | 40 |
| 01 | Mushroom MUSH95LP | BEAUTIFUL GARBAGE (2-LP) | 40 |

*(see also Goodbye Mr. MacKenzie)*

## GARBO
| 82 | Rarn RARN 201 | Dancing Strange/Why Don't You Call Me?/Everyday Hallucinations (with p/s) | 200 |
|----|---------------|------|-----|
| 82 | Rarn RARN 201 | Dancing Strange/Why Don't You Call Me?/Everyday Hallucinations (without p/s) | 50 |

## GARBO'S CELLULOID HEROES
| 78 | Big Bear BB 13 | Only Death Is Fatal/Won't You Come to my Funeral (p/s) | 10 |
|----|----------------|------|----|

## JERRY GARCIA
| 71 | Douglas DGL 69013 | HOOTEROLL? (LP, with Howard Wales) | 20 |
|----|-------------------|------|----|
| 72 | Warner Bros K 46139 | GARCIA (LP) | 15 |

*(see also Grateful Dead, Diga Rhythm Band, Old & In The Way)*

## RUSS GARCIA ORCHESTRA
| 58 | London HAU 2141 | FANTASTICA! (LP) | 15 |
|----|-----------------|------|----|

## GARDEN ODYSSEY (ENTERPRISE)
| 69 | Deram DM 267 | Sad And Lonely/Sky Pilot (8/M/1) (as Garden Odyssey Enterprise) | 80 |
|----|--------------|------|----|
| 72 | RCA RCA 2159 | Joker/Have You Ever Been To Georgia (as Garden Odyssey) | 70 |

*(see also Graham Gouldman)*

## GARDEZ DARKX
| 78 | New Bristol NBR 02 | Freeze/Heartbeat (p/s) | 6 |
|----|--------------------|------|---|
| 79 | Big Dwarf HURT 2 | Bliss/Winter Scene | 6 |

## BORIS GARD(I)NER (& LOVE PEOPLE)
| 69 | High Note HS 010 | Lucky Is The Boy/Bobby Sox To Stockings | 100 |
|----|------------------|------|-----|
| 69 | Doctor Bird DB 1205 | Elizabethan Reggae/Hooked On A Feeling | 25 |
| 69 | Duke DU 21 | Never My Love/The Bold One | 35 |
| 69 | Duke 39 | Elizabethan Reggae/BYRON LEE : Soul Serenade | 15 |
| 70 | Treasure Isle TI 7056 | Hooked On A Feeling/MESSAGE: Turn Around Twice | 12 |
| 70 | Big Shot BI 537 | Sweet Soul Special/Memories Of Love (with Love People) | 30 |
| 70 | Big Shot BI 538 | Darkness/Watch This Music (B-side actually "Keep Out") (with Love People) | 30 |
| 70 | Big Shot BI 539 | Hot Shot/Watch This Music (with Love People) | 40 |
| 70 | Dynamic DYN 404 | Commanding Wife/Band Of Gold (as Boris Gardner & Happening) | 20 |
| 70 | Trojan TR 7753 | Dynamic Pressure/Reggae Me Dis, Reggae Me Dat | 7 |
| 70 | Trojan TBL 121 | REGGAE HAPPENING (LP) | 20 |

## PAUL GARDINER
| 81 | Beggars Banquet BEG 61 | Stormtrooper In Drag/Night Talk (p/s) | 5 |
|----|------------------------|------|---|
| 81 | Beggars Banquet BEG 61T | Stormtrooper In Drag/Night Talk (12", unreleased, white label promos only) | 700 |
| 84 | Numa NU 1 | Venus In Furs/No Sense (p/s) | 5 |
| 84 | Numa NUM 1 | Venus In Furs (Extended Mix)/No Sense/Venus In Furs (7" Mix) (12", p/s) | 10 |

*(see also Tubeway Army, Gary Numan)*

## REGINALD GARDINER
| 71 | Decca F 5278 | Trains/Trains (Continued) | 6 |
|----|--------------|------|---|

## AVA GARDNER
| 53 | MGM SP 1005 | Can't Help Lovin' Dat Man/Bill | 10 |
|----|-------------|------|----|

## DAVE GARDNER
| 58 | Brunswick 05740 | Hop Along Rock/All By Myself (B-side with Anita Kerr Singers) | 30 |
|----|-----------------|------|----|

## DON GARDNER & DEE DEE FORD
| 62 | Stateside SS 114 | I Need Your Loving/Tell Me | 20 |
|----|------------------|------|----|
| 62 | Stateside SS 130 | Don't You Worry/I'm Coming Home To Stay | 20 |
| 68 | Soul City SC 101 | Don't You Worry/I'm Coming Home To Stay (reissue) | 10 |

*(see also Baby Washington & Don Gardner, Dee Dee Ford)*

## JOHNNY GARFIELD
| 65 | Pye 7N 15758 | Stranger In Paradise/Anyone Can Lose A Heart | 45 |
|----|--------------|------|----|

*(see also Simon & Garfunkel, Tom & Jerry)*

## ART GARFUNKEL
| 74 | CBS CQ 31474/Q 69021 | ANGEL CLARE (LP, quadrophonic) | 20 |
|----|----------------------|------|----|

## FRANK GARI
| 60 | London HLU 9277 | I Ain't Got A Girl/Utopia | 10 |
|----|-----------------|------|----|
| 61 | London HL 9371 | Lullaby Of Love/Tonight Is Our Last Night | 7 |

## JUDY GARLAND
| 53 | MGM SP 1001 | A Couple Of Swells/Medley: I Love A Piano/Snooky Ookums/When The Midnight Choo Choo Leaves (with Fred Astaire) | 10 |
|----|-------------|------|----|
| 56 | MGM SP 1157 | Look For The Silver Lining/Who? | 6 |
| 57 | Capitol F17691 | It's Lovely To Be Back In London (1-sided 7" given to audience at Gala Premiere of extended engagement at Dominion Theatre (p/s with insert) | 10 |
| 63 | Capitol CL 15291 | I Could Go On Singing/Hello Bluebird | 6 |
| 59 | Capitol (S)T 1188 | THE LETTER (LP, with paste-on letter intact) | 25 |

## RED GARLAND
| 60 | Esquire 32-096 | MANTECA (LP) | 20 |
|----|----------------|------|----|
| 60 | Esquire 32-099 | ALL MORNING LONG (LP) | 75 |
| 61 | Esquire 32-116 | RED IN BLUES VILLE (LP) | 30 |
| 61 | Esquire 32-126 | AT THE PRELUDE (LP) | 20 |

MINT VALUE £

| | | | |
|---|---|---|---|
| 61 | Esquire 32-136 | SOUL JUNCTION (LP) | 35 |
| 62 | Esquire 32-146 | ROJO (LP) | 30 |
| 62 | Esquire 32-166 | HIGH PRESSURE (LP) | 30 |

## BILLY GARNER
| | | | |
|---|---|---|---|
| 00 | BGPS 006 | Brand New Girl/JACQUELINE JONES : Can't Stop The Show | 15 |

## KAY GARNER
| | | | |
|---|---|---|---|
| 64 | Oriole CB 1951 | I Still Get Jealous/Squeeze Me | 10 |

## REGGIE GARNER
| | | | |
|---|---|---|---|
| 76 | Capitol CL 15874 | Hot Line/Blessed Be The Name Of My Baby | 10 |
| 76 | Capitol CL 15874 | Hot Line/Blessed Be The Name Of My Baby (DJ Copy) | 15 |

## COL GARNET
| | | | |
|---|---|---|---|
| 66 | Page One POF 002 | With A Girl Like You/Monday Monday | 12 |

## GALE GARNETT
| | | | |
|---|---|---|---|
| 64 | RCA RCA 1418 | We'll Sing In The Sunshine/Prism Song | 10 |
| 65 | RCA RCA 1451 | I'll Cry Alone/Where Do You Go To Go Away? | 60 |
| 65 | RCA RCA 1451 | I'll Cry Alone/Where Do You Go To Go Away? (DJ Copy) | 100 |
| 65 | RCA RD 7726 | MY KIND OF FOLK SONGS (LP) | 30 |
| 66 | RCA RD 7750 | LOVIN' PLACE (LP) | 20 |

## RACHELLE GARNIEZ
| | | | |
|---|---|---|---|
| 09 | Third Man TMR 004 | My House Of Peace (1-sided, 100 only, luminous vinyl) | 40 |

## VERNON GARRETT
| | | | |
|---|---|---|---|
| 67 | Stateside SS 2006 | If I Could Turn Back The Hands Of Time/You And Me Together | 40 |
| 67 | Stateside SS 2006 | If I Could Turn Back The Hands Of Time/You And Me Together (DJ copy) | 80 |
| 67 | Stateside SS 2026 | Shine It On/Things Are Lookin' Better | 50 |
| 67 | Stateside SS 2026 | Shine It On/Things Are Lookin' Better (DJ copy) | 75 |
| 68 | Action ACT 4508 | Shine It On/Things Are Lookin' Better (reissue) | 30 |

## DAVID GARRICK
| | | | |
|---|---|---|---|
| 67 | Piccadilly NEP 34056 | DAVID (EP) | 30 |
| 66 | Piccadilly NPL 38024 | A BOY CALLED DAVID (LP, mono) | 20 |
| 66 | Piccadilly N(S)PL 38024 | A BOY CALLED DAVID (LP, stereo) | 25 |
| 67 | Piccadilly N(S)PL 38035 | DON'T GO OUT INTO THE RAIN, SUGAR (LP) | 25 |
| 68 | Pye NSPL 18223 | LIVE! (LP, blue/black label) | 30 |

## MICHAEL GARRICK
| | | | |
|---|---|---|---|
| 65 | Argo EAF/ZFA 92 | ANTHEM - MICHAEL GARRICK QUINTET (EP, mono/stereo with Shake Keane) | 75 |
| 66 | Argo EAF 115 | BEFORE NIGHT/DAY (EP) | 75 |
| 63 | Airborne | CASE OF JAZZ (EP, with Shake Keane) | 350 |
| 64 | Airborne | MOONSCAPE (LP) | 2000 |
| 64 | Argo ZDA 26/27 | POETRY AND JAZZ IN CONCERT (2-LP, with Norma Winstone) | 60 |
| 65 | Argo (Z)DA 33 | OCTOBER WOMAN (LP, as Michael Garrick Quintet, with Joe Harriott) | 150 |
| 65 | Argo (Z)DA 36 | PROMISES (LP, as Michael Garrick Sextet, with Ian Carr) | 150 |
| 68 | Argo (Z)DA 88 | BLACK MARIGOLDS (LP, as Michael Garrick Septet) | 150 |
| 68 | Airborne NBP 0021 | JAZZ PRAISES AT ST. PAULS (LP) | 50 |
| 69 | Argo ZPR 264/5 | POETRY AND JAZZ IN CONCERT 250 (2-LP, as Michael Garrick Quintet) | 80 |
| 69 | Erase EO 2545 | JAZZ CANTATA (LP, 'Farnham Festival' release) | 150 |
| 70 | Argo ZDA 135 | HEART IS A LOTUS (LP, as Michael Garrick Sextet with Norma Winstone) | 150 |
| 72 | Argo ZDA 153 | COLD MOUNTAIN (LP, as Michael Garrick Trio) | 250 |
| 72 | Argo ZDA 154 | HOME STRETCH BLUES (LP, as Michael Garrick Band with Norma Winstone) | 200 |
| 73 | Impulse AS 49 | ILLUMINATION (LP, as Michael Garrick Sextet) | 50 |
| 74 | Argo ZDA 163 | TROPPO (LP) | 100 |
| 81 | Hep Records HEP2011 | YOU'VE CHANGED (LP) | 20 |
| 07 | Trunk JBH 022 LP | MOONSCAPE (LP, reissue 500 only) | 30 |
| 11 | Trunk JBH 041 LP | RISING STARS (LP, with Shake Keane, 750 only) | 20 |

*(see also Norma Winstone, Joe Harriott, Garrick's Fairground, Shake Keane)*

## GARRICK'S FAIRGROUND
| | | | |
|---|---|---|---|
| 71 | Argo AFW 105 | Epiphany/Blessed Are The Peacemakers | 20 |
| 72 | Argo ZAGF 1 | MR. SMITH'S APOCALYPSE (LP) | 70 |

*(see also Michael Garrick)*

## FREDDIE GARRITY
| | | | |
|---|---|---|---|
| 68 | Columbia DB 8348 | Little Red Donkey/So Many Different Ways | 5 |
| 73 | UK 55 | I Know You Know We Know/I Understand (Just How You Feel) | 5 |
| 74 | Bus Stop BUS 1017 | Hello Kids/It's Good For You | 5 |
| 74 | Bus Stop BUS 1022 | The Chicken Song/Pooh Pooh Pooh | 5 |

*(see also Freddie & Dreamers)*

## ROBIN GARSIDE & PAUL GOUGH
| | | | |
|---|---|---|---|
| 77 | Northern Sound NSR 01 | SEA SONGS (LP) | 15 |

## MORT GARSON
| | | | |
|---|---|---|---|
| 69 | A & M AMLS 960 | ELECTRIC HAIRPIECES (LP) | 20 |

## ROBIN GARTON & HIS BAND
| | | | |
|---|---|---|---|
| 58 | Martello MC 100 | Topsy/Jump For Me | 5 |

## GARUDA
| | | | |
|---|---|---|---|
| 77 | EMI EMC 3174 | GARUDA (LP) | 40 |

## GUY GARVEY
| | | | |
|---|---|---|---|
| 15 | Fiction 4758702 | COURTING THE SQUALL (LP, lenticular sleeve) | 25 |
| 15 | Fiction 4758702 | COURTING THE SQUALL (LP, signed) | 30 |

## REX GARVIN & MIGHTY CRAVERS
| | | | |
|---|---|---|---|
| 66 | Atlantic 584 028 | Sock It To 'Em J.B. (Parts 1 & 2) | 25 |
| 67 | Atlantic 584 097 | I Gotta Go Now (Up On The Floor)/Believe It Or Not | 25 |

MINT VALUE £

### JOHN GARY
| | | | |
|---|---|---|---|
| 59 | Top Rank JAR 177 | Let Them Talk/Tell My Love | 5 |
| 60 | Top Rank JAR 392 | Little Things Mean A Lot/Ever Since I Met Lucy | 5 |

### SAM GARY
| | | | |
|---|---|---|---|
| 56 | Esquire 32 017 | SAM GARY SINGS (LP) | 20 |

### GARY & ARIELS
| | | | |
|---|---|---|---|
| 64 | Fontana TF 476 | Say You Love Me/Town Girl | 15 |

*(see also Garry Mills)*

### GARY & STU
| | | | |
|---|---|---|---|
| 72 | Carnaby 6151 003 | Sweet White Dove/Good Lady Fair | 8 |
| 72 | Carnaby 6302 012 | HARLAN FARE (LP, white label with 'crab' logo) | 100 |

*(see also Koobas, March Hare)*

### GAS
| | | | |
|---|---|---|---|
| 80 | Polydor POSP 192 | It Shows In Your Face/Tomorrow (p/s) | 15 |
| 81 | Polydor POSP 264 | Ignore Me/Do It, Don't Tell Me (p/s) | 15 |
| 81 | Polydor POSP 296 | Treatment/That's It (p/s) | 10 |
| 81 | Polydor POSP 344 | The Finger/Knock It Down (p/s) | 18 |
| 82 | Polydor POSP 411 | Breathless/Heartache/Hostage (p/s) | 7 |
| 81 | Polydor POLE 1052 | EMOTIONAL WARFARE (LP) | 15 |
| 83 | Good Vibrations GAS LP 1 | FROM THE CRADLE TO THE GRAVE (LP) | 15 |

### GASKIN
| | | | |
|---|---|---|---|
| 81 | Rondelet ROUND 7 | I'm No Fool/Sweet Dream Maker (p/s) | 25 |
| 82 | Rondelet ROUND 21 | Mony Mony/Queen Of Hams (p/s) | 18 |
| 81 | Rondelet ABOUT 4 | END OF THE WORLD (LP, gatefold sleeve) | 25 |
| 82 | Rondelet ABOUT 8 | NO WAY OUT (LP, with inner) | 20 |

### GASLIGHT
| | | | |
|---|---|---|---|
| 69 | Jay Boy BOY 17 | Move/And So To Sleep | 18 |
| 70 | SDE 32732 | GASLIGHT (2-LP, private pressing, gatefold sleeve with inserts, 2nd disc by Gaslight Choir) | 40 |

### GASLIGHT ANTHEM
| | | | |
|---|---|---|---|
| 09 | Side One Dummy SD 13827 | Great Expectations/Miles Davis & The Cool (Acoustic) (p/s) | 8 |
| 12 | Mercury B0016941-01 | HANDWRITTEN (LP, blue vinyl and free blue vinyl 7") | 20 |

### GASOLIN
| | | | |
|---|---|---|---|
| 71 | CBS 64685 | GASOLIN (LP, gatefold sleeve, orange/black label) | 50 |
| 72 | CBS 65229 | 2 (LP, gatefold sleeve, orange/black label) | 40 |
| 73 | CBS 65798 | 3 (LP, orange label) | 30 |
| 75 | Epic SEPC 81436 | WHAT A LEMON (LP, yellow/black label) | 40 |

### GASOLINE BAND
| | | | |
|---|---|---|---|
| 72 | Cube HIFLY 9 | GASOLINE BAND (LP, cube label) | 200 |

### GASP
| | | | |
|---|---|---|---|
| 79 | Storm SR 028 | Gaz's Boots/Jimmy The Fish (no p/s) | 20 |

### GASPAR NETSCHER ENSEMBLE
| | | | |
|---|---|---|---|
| 68 | Pye 7N 17556 | Get Out Of My Bed Darling/Until You're Here Beside Me | 8 |

### GASS
| | | | |
|---|---|---|---|
| 65 | Parlophone R 5344 | One Of These Days/I Don't Know Why | 30 |
| 66 | Parlophone R 5456 | The New Breed/In The City | 60 |
| 67 | CBS 202647 | Dream Baby (How Long Must I Dream?)/Jitterbug Sid | 30 |
| 71 | Polydor 2058 147 | Something's Got To Change Your Ways/Mr Banana | 10 |
| 70 | Polydor 2383 022 | JUJU (LP, featuring Peter Green) | 150 |
| 70 | Polydor 2383 022 | JUJU (LP, featuring Peter Green, alternative sleeve, black/gold with Gass logo on front and drawing on rear, record has same matrix as other issue and red Polydor labels) | 250 |
| 71 | Polydor 2383 035 | CATCH MY SOUL - THE ROCK-OTHELLO (LP, cast recording featuring Gass) | 30 |

*(see also Hummingbird, Humble Pie, Streetwalkers, Peter Green)*

### GASS COMPANY
| | | | |
|---|---|---|---|
| 68 | President PT 170 | Everybody Needs Love/Nightmare | 60 |

*(see also Wake)*

### GAS WORKS
| | | | |
|---|---|---|---|
| 73 | Regal Zonophone RZ 3075 | Standing Stiff/Keep On Rolling | 6 |
| 73 | Regal Zonophone RZ 3080 | God's Great Spaceship/Cider With Rosie | 6 |
| 73 | Regal Zono. SRLZ 1036 | GAS WORKS (LP) | 25 |

### DAVID GATES
| | | | |
|---|---|---|---|
| 60 | Top Rank JAR 504 | The Happiest Man Alive/The Road That Leads To Love | 30 |

*(see also Bread)*

### PEARLY GATES
| | | | |
|---|---|---|---|
| 70 | MCA MU 1109 | Free/Carole's Epic Song | 12 |
| 74 | Polydor 2058 443 | Johnny And The Juke-Box/They Were Good Times | 5 |
| 75 | RCA PD 2605 | Make It My Business/You're The One For Me | 10 |

*(see also Flirtations, Gypsies)*

### RAY GATES
| | | | |
|---|---|---|---|
| 66 | Decca F 12502 | It's Such A Shame/Have You Ever Had The Blues | 40 |

### GATES OF EDEN
| | | | |
|---|---|---|---|
| 66 | Pye 7N 17195 | Too Much On My Mind/I'm Warning You | 25 |
| 67 | Pye 7N 17252 | In Your Love/Snoopy Versus The Red Baron | 12 |
| 67 | Pye 7N 17278 | 1 To 7/Hey Now | 30 |

### GATHERERS
| | | | |
|---|---|---|---|
| 73 | Duke DU 153 | Words Of My Mouth/UPSETTERS: Version | 90 |

## GATOR CREEK
| | | | |
|---|---|---|---|
| 71 | Mercury 6052 058 | Danny's Song/Take A Look | 15 |
| 71 | Mercury 6338 035 | GATOR CREEK (LP) | 15 |

## DICK GAUGHAN
| | | | |
|---|---|---|---|
| 72 | Trailer LER 2072 | NO MORE FOREVER (LP, red label) | 25 |
| 76 | Rubber RUB 019 | FIVE HAND REEL (LP) | 20 |
| 78 | Topic 12TS384 | GAUGHAN (LP, tan label) | 15 |
| 81 | Topic 12TS419 | HANDFUL OF EARTH (LP) | 15 |

## GEORGES GAVARENTZ
| | | | |
|---|---|---|---|
| 69 | Philips SBL 7898 | THEY CAME TO ROB LAS VEGAS (LP, soundtrack) | 40 |

## JIMMY GAVIN
| | | | |
|---|---|---|---|
| 57 | London HLU 8478 | I Sit In My Window/Lonely Chair | 80 |

## JOHNNY GAVOTTE
| | | | |
|---|---|---|---|
| 60 | Parlophone R 4631 | It's Not Too Late/Can't Forget | 10 |

## ELAINE GAY
| | | | |
|---|---|---|---|
| 54 | Parlophone MSP 6140 | Love/Instantly | 12 |

## MAC GAYDEN
| | | | |
|---|---|---|---|
| 73 | EMI EMA 760 | McGAVOCK GAYDEN (LP) | 50 |

*(see also Area Code 615)*

## MARVIN GAYE
| | | | |
|---|---|---|---|
| 63 | Oriole CBA 1803 | Stubborn Kind Of Fellow/It Hurt Me Too | 100 |
| 63 | Oriole CBA 1803 | Stubborn Kind Of Fellow/It Hurt Me Too (DJ Copy) | 200 |
| 63 | Oriole CBA 1846 | Pride And Joy/One Of These Days | 100 |
| 63 | Oriole CBA 1846 | Pride And Joy/One Of These Days (DJ Copy) | 200 |
| 63 | Stateside SS 243 | Can I Get A Witness?/I'm Crazy 'Bout My Baby | 90 |
| 63 | Stateside SS 243 | Can I Get A Witness?/I'm Crazy 'Bout My Baby (DJ Copy) | 100 |
| 64 | Stateside SS 284 | You're A Wonderful One/When I'm Alone I Cry | 50 |
| 64 | Stateside SS 284 | You're A Wonderful One/When I'm Alone I Cry (DJ Copy) | 100 |
| 64 | Stateside SS 326 | Try It Baby/If My Heart Could Sing | 40 |
| 64 | Stateside SS 326 | Try It Baby/If My Heart Could Sing (DJ Copy) | 70 |
| 64 | Stateside SS 360 | How Sweet It Is (To Be Loved By You)/Forever | 30 |
| 64 | Stateside SS 360 | How Sweet It Is (To Be Loved By You)/Forever (DJ Copy) | 90 |
| 65 | Tamla Motown TMG 510 | I'll Be Doggone/You've Been A Long Time Coming | 40 |
| 65 | Tamla Motown TMG 510 | I'll Be Doggone/You've Been A Long Time Coming (DJ Copy) | 120 |
| 65 | Tamla Motown TMG 524 | Pretty Little Baby/Now That You've Won Me | 40 |
| 65 | Tamla Motown TMG 524 | Pretty Little Baby/Now That You've Won Me (DJ Copy) | 90 |
| 65 | Tamla Motown TMG 539 | Ain't That Peculiar?/She's Got To Be Real | 30 |
| 65 | Tamla Motown TMG 539 | Ain't That Peculiar?/She's Got To Be Real (DJ Copy) | 90 |
| 66 | Tamla Motown TMG 552 | One More Heartache/When I Had Your Love | 30 |
| 66 | Tamla Motown TMG 552 | One More Heartache/When I Had Your Love (DJ Copy) | 80 |
| 66 | Tamla Motown TMG 563 | Take This Heart Of Mine/Need Your Lovin' (Want You Back) | 35 |
| 66 | Tamla Motown TMG 563 | Take This Heart Of Mine/Need Your Lovin' (Want You Back) (DJ Copy) | 80 |
| 66 | Tamla Motown TMG 574 | Little Darling (I Need You)/Hey Diddle Diddle | 35 |
| 66 | Tamla Motown TMG 574 | Little Darlin' (I Need You)/Hey Diddle Diddle (DJ Copy) | 120 |
| 67 | Tamla Motown TMG 618 | Your Unchanging Love/I'll Take Care Of You | 20 |
| 67 | Tamla Motown TMG 618 | Your Unchanging Love/I'll Take Care Of You (DJ Copy) | 50 |
| 68 | Tamla Motown TMG 640 | You/Change What You Can | 20 |
| 68 | Tamla Motown TMG 640 | You/Change What You Can (DJ Copy) | 40 |
| 68 | Tamla Motown TMG 676 | Chained/At Last (I Found A Love) | 18 |
| 69 | Tamla Motown TMG 686 | I Heard It Through The Grapevine/Need Somebody | 7 |
| 69 | Tamla Motown TMG 686 | I Heard It Through The Grapevine/Need Somebody (DJ Copy) | 30 |
| 69 | Tamla Motown TMG 705 | Too Busy Thinking 'Bout My Baby/Wherever I Lay My Hat | 7 |
| 69 | Tamla Motown TMG 718 | That's The Way Love Is/Gonna Keep On Tryin' Till I Win Your Love | 8 |
| 70 | Tamla Motown TMG 734 | Abraham, Martin And John/How Can I Forget? | 7 |
| 70 | Tamla Motown TMG 734 | Abraham, Martin And John/How Can I Forget? (DJ Copy) | 30 |
| 71 | Tamla Motown TMG 775 | What's Going On?/God Is Love | 8 |
| 71 | Tamla Motown TMG 775 | What's Going On/God Is Love (DJ Copy) | 40 |
| 71 | Tamla Motown TMG 796 | Save The Children/Little Darling (I Need You) | 8 |
| 72 | Tamla Motown TMG 802 | Mercy Mercy Me (The Ecology)/Sad Tomorrows | 6 |
| 72 | Tamla Motown TMG 817 | Inner City Blues/Wholly Holy | 10 |
| 73 | Tamla Motown TMG 846 | Trouble Man/Don't Mess With Mister 'T' | 12 |
| 73 | Tamla Motown TMG 868 | Let's Get It On/I Wish It Would Rain (DJ Copy) | 10 |
| 74 | Tamla Motown TMG 882 | Come Get To This/Distant Lover | 15 |
| 78 | Tamla Motown 12TMG 1138 | A Funky Space Reincarnation/Got To Give It Up (12", p/s) | 10 |
| 86 | Tamla Motown ZB 40757 | Lonely Lover/The World Is Rated X (p/s) | 25 |
| 96 | Chriskings 81156 DJ | This Love Starved Heart Of Mine/This Love Starved Heart Of Mine (promo, 500 only) | 20 |
| 66 | Tamla Motown TME 2016 | MARVIN GAYE (EP) | 60 |
| 67 | Tamla Motown TME 2019 | ORIGINALS FROM MARVIN GAYE (EP) | 50 |
| 64 | Stateside SL 10100 | MARVIN GAYE (LP) | 200 |
| 65 | Tamla Motown TML 11004 | HOW SWEET IT IS TO BE LOVED BY YOU (LP) | 60 |
| 65 | Tamla Motown TML 11015 | HELLO BROADWAY (LP) | 80 |
| 66 | T. Motown TML 11022 | A TRIBUTE TO THE GREAT NAT KING COLE (LP, mono) | 65 |
| 66 | T. Motown STML 11022 | A TRIBUTE TO THE GREAT NAT KING COLE (LP, stereo) | 80 |
| 66 | T. Motown TML 11033 | MOODS OF MARVIN GAYE (LP, mono) | 50 |
| 66 | T. Motown STML 11033 | MOODS OF MARVIN GAYE (LP, stereo) | 60 |
| 68 | T. Motown TML 11065 | MARVIN GAYE'S GREATEST HITS (LP, mono) | 20 |
| 68 | T. Motown STML 11065 | MARVIN GAYE'S GREATEST HITS (LP, stereo) | 20 |
| 69 | T. Motown (S)TML 11091 | IN THE GROOVE (LP, mono/stereo) | 30 |

## Marvin GAYE & TAMMI TERRELL

| | | | |
|---|---|---|---:|
| 69 | T. Motown (S)TML 11119 | M.P.G. (LP, mono/stereo) | 25 |
| 69 | T. Motown TML 11123 | MARVIN GAYE AND HIS GIRLS (LP, mono, with T. Terrell, M. Wells & K. Weston) | 25 |
| 70 | T. Motown STML 11123 | MARVIN GAYE AND HIS GIRLS (LP, stereo, with T. Terrell, M. Wells & K. Weston) | 22 |
| 70 | T. Motown TML 11136 | THAT'S THE WAY LOVE IS (LP, mono) | 30 |
| 70 | T. Motown STML 11136 | THAT'S THE WAY LOVE IS (LP, stereo) | 20 |
| 71 | Tamla Motown STML 11190 | WHAT'S GOING ON? (LP, textured sleeve A1/B1 matrixes, with lyric sheet) | 25 |
| 73 | Tamla Motown STMA 8013 | LET'S GET IT ON (LP, gatefold) | 18 |
| 73 | Tamla Motown STML 11225 | TROUBLE MAN (LP, soundtrack) | 20 |
| 76 | Tamla Motown STML 12025 | I WANT YOU (LP) | 15 |
| 78 | Tamla Motown TMSP 6008 | HERE, MY DEAR (2-LP) | 25 |

## MARVIN GAYE & TAMMI TERRELL

| | | | |
|---|---|---|---:|
| 67 | Tamla Motown TMG 611 | Ain't No Mountain High Enough/Give A Little Love | 30 |
| 67 | Tamla Motown TMG 611 | Ain't No Mountain High Enough/Give A Little Love (DJ Copy) | 80 |
| 67 | Tamla Motown TMG 625 | Your Precious Love/Hold Me Oh My Darling | 25 |
| 67 | Tamla Motown TMG 625 | Your Precious Love/Hold Me Oh My Darling (DJ Copy) | 50 |
| 67 | Tamla Motown TMG 635 | If I Could Build My Whole World Around You/If This World Were Mine | 15 |
| 67 | Tamla Motown TMG 635 | If I Could Build My Whole World Around You/If This World Were Mine (DJ Copy) | 30 |
| 68 | Tamla Motown TMG 655 | Ain't Nothin' Like The Real Thing/Little Ole Boy, Little Ole Girl | 12 |
| 68 | Tamla Motown TMG 655 | Ain't Nothin' Like The Real Thing/Little Ole Boy, Little Ole Girl (DJ Copy) | 30 |
| 68 | Tamla Motown TMG 668 | You're All I Need To Get By/Two Can Have A Party | 8 |
| 69 | Tamla Motown TMG 681 | You Ain't Livin' Till You're Lovin'/Oh How I'd Miss You | 12 |
| 69 | Tamla Motown TMG 697 | Good Lovin' Ain't Easy To Come By/Satisfied Feelin' | 8 |
| 69 | Tamla Motown TMG 715 | The Onion Song/I Can't Believe You Love Me | 6 |
| 69 | Tamla Motown TMG 715 | The Onion Song/I Can't Believe You Love Me (demo in p/s) | 50 |
| 68 | T. Motown TML 11062 | UNITED (LP, mono) | 40 |
| 68 | T. Motown STML 11062 | UNITED (LP, stereo) | 40 |
| 68 | T. Motown (S)TML 11084 | YOU'RE ALL I NEED (LP, mono/stereo) | 40 |
| 70 | T. Motown TML 11132 | EASY (LP, mono) | 20 |
| 70 | T. Motown STML 11132 | EASY (LP, stereo) | 18 |
| 70 | T. Motown (S)TML 11153 | GREATEST HITS (LP) | 15 |

## MARVIN GAYE & MARY WELLS

| | | | |
|---|---|---|---:|
| 64 | Stateside SS 316 | Once Upon A Time/What's The Matter With You, Baby? | 35 |
| 64 | Stateside SS 316 | Once Upon A Time/What's The Matter With You, Baby? (DJ Copy) | 80 |
| 64 | Stateside SL 10097 | TOGETHER (LP) | 75 |

## MARVIN GAYE & KIM WESTON

| | | | |
|---|---|---|---:|
| 64 | Stateside SS 363 | What Good Am I Without You?/I Want You Around | 40 |
| 64 | Stateside SS 363 | What Good Am I Without You?/I Want You Around (DJ Copy) | 80 |
| 67 | Tamla Motown TMG 590 | It Takes Two/It's Got To Be A Miracle (This Thing Called Love) | 12 |
| 67 | Tamla Motown TMG 590 | It Takes Two/It's Got To Be A Miracle (This Thing Called Love) (DJ Copy) | 70 |
| 67 | T. Motown TML 11049 | TAKE TWO (LP, mono) | 40 |
| 67 | T. Motown STML 11049 | TAKE TWO (LP, stereo) | 45 |

*(see also Diana Ross, Tammi Terrell, Mary Wells, Kim Weston)*

## GAYLADS

| | | | |
|---|---|---|---:|
| 64 | R&B JB 159 | There'll Come A Day/BILLY COOKE: Iron Bar | 50 |
| 64 | R&B JB 165 | What Is Wrong With Me?/Whap Whap | 60 |
| 66 | Island WI 281 | Goodbye Daddy/Your Eyes | 30 |
| 66 | Island WI 291 | You Never Leave Him/Message To My Girl | 30 |
| 66 | Island WI 3002 | Stop Making Love/They Call Her Dawn | 40 |
| 66 | Doctor Bird DB 1014 | Lady With The Red Dress/Dinner For Two | 15 |
| 66 | Doctor Bird DB 1031 | You Should Never Do That/WINSTON STEWART: I Don't Know Why I Love You | 25 |
| 66 | Rymska RA 104 | You Should Never Do That/TECHNIQUES: So Many Times | 35 |
| 67 | Island WI 3022 | Don't Say No/SONNY BURKE: You Rule My Heart | 40 |
| 67 | Island WI 3025 | You No Good Girl/Yes Girl | 30 |
| 67 | Studio One SO 2002 | Tears From My Eyes/Never Let Your Country Down | 125 |
| 67 | Studio One SO 2009 | Won't You Come Home/PETER & HORTENSE : I've Been Lonely | 50 |
| 67 | Studio One SO 2013 | I Am Going To Cool It (actually by Little Roy)/ MELODIANS: Let's Join Together | 60 |
| 67 | Studio One SO 2017 | Love Me With All Your Heart/I Don't Care | 40 |
| 67 | Studio One SO 2021 | IF You Knew/Festival Day | 80 |
| 67 | Rio R 125 | Put On Your Style/SOUL BROTHERS: Soul Serenade | 50 |
| 68 | Blue Cat BS 110 | Go Away/SOUL VENDORS: Julie On My Mind | 40 |
| 68 | Doctor Bird DB 1124 | It's Hard To Confess/I Need Your Loving | 40 |
| 68 | Doctor Bird DB 1145 | She Want It/Joy In The Morning | 40 |
| 68 | Fab FAB 62 | Looking For A Girl/Aren't You The Guy | 100 |
| 68 | Hi Note HS 001 | A B C Rocksteady/LESLIE BUTLER & COUNT OSSIE: Soul Drums | 35 |
| 69 | Trojan TR 688 | You Had Your Chance/Wha' She Do Now | 12 |
| 69 | Upsetter US 323 | The Same Things/I Wear My Slanders | 20 |
| 70 | Trojan TR 7703 | There's A Fire/Last Time | 8 |
| 70 | Trojan TR 7738 | That's What Love Will Do/This Time I Won't Hurt You | 10 |
| 70 | Trojan TR 7743 | Young, Gifted And Black/BEVERLEY'S ALLSTARS: Moon Glow | 10 |
| 70 | Trojan TR 7763 | Tell The Children The Truth/Something Is Wrong Somewhere | 8 |
| 70 | Trojan TR 7771 | Soul Sister/BEVERLEY'S ALLSTARS: Soul Version | 15 |
| 70 | Trojan TR 7782 | It's All In The Game/BEVERLEY'S ALLSTARS: Version II | 8 |
| 70 | Trojan TR 7799 | Fire And Rain/Cold And Lonely Night | 8 |
| 71 | Ackee AC 141 | Accept My Apologies (actually by B.B. Seaton & Ken Boothe)/ My Version (actually by Conscious Minds) | 6 |
| 71 | Big BG 319 | Can't Hide The Feeling/RUPIE EDWARDS ALLSTARS: Version | 7 |
| 71 | Camel CA 79 | Seven In One Medley (Parts 1 & 2) | 6 |
| 71 | Summit SUM 8514 | My Jamaican Girl/BEVERLEY'S ALLSTARS: Version | 6 |
| 71 | Bullet BU 462 | My Love/Stranger Love | 7 |

| | | | |
|---|---|---|---|
| 74 | Dip DL 5009 | You Made A Mistake/Shower Of Blessings | 6 |
| 13 | Summit THB 7024 | Baby I'll Be Yours/Tribute To Prince Ruff | 8 |
| 67 | Coxsone CSL 8005 | ROCKSTEADY (LP) | 200 |
| 67 | Coxsone CSL 8006 | SUNSHINE IS GOLDEN (LP) | 100 |
| 79 | Ballistic UAG 30236 | UNDERSTANDING (LP) | 15 |

(see also Gaylords, Rockstones, Delano Stewart, Ken Boothe, B.B. Seaton, Brent Dowe, Dobby Dobson, Jackie Mittoo, Heptones, Clarendonians, Soul Vendors)

### VINLEY GAYLE
| 64 | Black Swan WI 453 | Go-Go/BABA BROOKS: Take Five | 30 |
|---|---|---|---|

### GAYLET(T)S
| 68 | Island WI 3129 | Silent River Runs Deep/You're Kind Of Man | 40 |
|---|---|---|---|
| 68 | Island WI 3141 | I Like Your World/Lonely Feeling | 25 |
| 68 | Big Shot BI 502 | If You Can't Be Good/Something About My Man | 12 |
| 69 | Big Shot BI 516 | Son-Of-A-Preacher-Man/That's How Strong My Love Is | 12 |
| 70 | London HLJ 10302 | Son-Of-A-Preacher-Man/I Like Your World | 7 |

(see also Bob Andy)

### GAYLORDS (JAMAICA)
| 66 | Island WI 269 | Chipmunk Ska/What Is Wrong? (both actually by Gaylads) | 25 |
|---|---|---|---|

(see also Gaylads)

### GAYLORDS (U.K.)
| 66 | Columbia DB 7805 | He's A Good Face But He's Down And Out/You Know It Too | 15 |
|---|---|---|---|

(see also Dean Ford & Gaylords, Marmalade)

### WILTON 'BOGEY' GAYNAIR QUARTET
| 61 | Tempo EXA 103 | BLUE BOGEY VOLUME ONE (EP) | 60 |
|---|---|---|---|
| 59 | Tempo TAP 25 | BLUE BOGEY (LP) | 500 |

### GAYNOR (JUNIOR ENGLISH) & ERROL (DUNKLEY)
| 65 | Blue Beat BB 286 | My Queen/ROLAND ALPHONSO: Roland Plays Prince (B-side actually "Hanging The Beam" by Skatalites) | 60 |
|---|---|---|---|

(see also Errol Dunkley)

### MEL GAYNOR
| 55 | Decca F 10497 | Just A Man/How Important Can It Be? | 5 |
|---|---|---|---|
| 55 | Decca F 10542 | With You Beside Me/Oh, My Love | 5 |
| 55 | Decca F 10618 | Bella Notte/Sweet Kentucky Rose | 5 |

(see also Oscar Rabin)

### ROSEMARY GAYNOR
| 55 | Columbia SCM 5196 | Ain't That A Shame/A Happy Song | 15 |
|---|---|---|---|

### PAUL GAYTEN
| 57 | London HL 8503 | Yo, Yo, Walk/TUNE WEAVERS: Happy Happy Birthday Baby | 80 |
|---|---|---|---|
| 59 | London HLM 8998 | The Hunch/Hot Cross Buns | 50 |

### GAYTONES (JAMAICA)
| 70 | High Note HS 037 | Target (actually "Musical Fight" by Crashers)/PATSY: Find Someone (song actually "True Love") | 30 |
|---|---|---|---|
| 70 | High Note HS 048 | Ten To One/Another Version | 12 |
| 71 | High Note HS 055 | Heart Of The Knights/One Toke Over The Line (B-side actually by Stranger & Gladdy) | 15 |
| 71 | Green Door GD 4016 | Jamaican Hilite (Parts 1 & 2) | 8 |
| 73 | Smash SMA 2330 | Blackman Kingdom Come/Swing And Dine (B-side actually by Melodians) | 10 |
| 73 | Action ACT 4610 | Soul Makossa/Soul Makossa Part 2 | 8 |

(see also Righteous Flames, Max Romeo, Ethiopians, Jackie Brown, Jean & Gaytones, Huxbrown & Scotty, Charlie Ace, Delano Stewart, Teddy & Conquerors)

### GAYTONES (U.S.)
| 73 | Action ACT 4610 | Soul Makossa/Soul Makossa (Version) | 15 |
|---|---|---|---|

### G BAND
| 76 | Bell 1481 | Tuna Biscuit/Don't Make Promises You Can't Keep | 10 |
|---|---|---|---|

### GBH
| 82 | Clay CLAY 8 | No Survivors/Self Destruct/Big Women (p/s) | 8 |
|---|---|---|---|
| 82 | Clay CLAY 11 | Sick Boy/Slit Your Own Throat/Am I Dead Yet? (p/s) | 8 |
| 82 | Clay CLAY 16 | Give Me Fire/Mantrap (p/s) | 8 |
| 83 | Clay CLAY 22 | Catch 23/Hellhole (p/s) | 8 |
| 84 | Clay CLAY 36 | Do What You Do/Four Men (p/s) | 8 |
| 81 | Clay PLATE 3 | LEATHER, BRISTLES, STUDS AND ACNE (LP) | 15 |
| 82 | Clay CLAYLP 4 | CITY BABY ATTACKED BY RATS (LP) | 20 |

### G-CLEFS
| 56 | Columbia DB 3851 | Ka-Ding Dong/Darla, My Darlin' | 750 |
|---|---|---|---|
| 56 | Columbia DB 3851 | Ka-Ding Dong/Darla, My Darlin' (78 rpm) | 35 |
| 62 | London HLU 9530 | A Girl Has To Know/(There Never Was A Dog Like) Dad | 10 |
| 62 | London HLU 9563 | Make Up Your Mind/Call Me Away | 15 |

### GEDDES AXE
| 80 | ACS ACS 1 | Return Of The Gods/Wildfire/Aftermath (p/s, with insert) | 20 |
|---|---|---|---|
| 81 | Steel City AXE 1 | Sharpen Your Wits/Rock 'N' Roll (p/s) | 50 |

### MICKEY GEE
| 77 | Sonet SON 2124 | Dr Livingstone/Jodi | 6 |
|---|---|---|---|

### RON GEESIN
| 65 | RRG 319/320 | RON GEESIN (EP, handmade p/s, 100 only) | 100 |
|---|---|---|---|
| 67 | Transatlantic (S)TRA 161 | A RAISE OF EYEBROWS (LP) | 50 |
| 72 | KPM KPM 1102 | ELECTROSOUND (LP, library issue, 1,000 only) | 60 |
| 73 | Ron Geesin RON 28 | AS HE STANDS (LP) | 30 |
| 75 | KPM KPM 1154 | ELECTROSOUND VOL. 2 (LP, library issue, 1,000 only) | 50 |
| 75 | Ron Geesin RON 31 | PATRUNS (LP) | 15 |

# Ron GEESIN & ROGER WATERS

| 77 | Ron Geesin RON 323 | RIGHT THROUGH (LP) | 18 |
| 77 | KPM KPM 1201 | ATMOSPHERES (LP, library issue, 1,000 only) | 30 |
| 08 | Glo Spot 1102 | ELECTROSOUND (LP, reissue, different sleeve art, blue vinyl) | 20 |

*(see also Bridget St. John, Pink Floyd, Original Downtown Syncopators, Amory Kane)*

## RON GEESIN & ROGER WATERS
| 70 | Harvest SHSP 4008 | MUSIC FROM THE BODY (LP, soundtrack; green labels with Waters/Geesin photos) | 50 |

*(see also Roger Waters, Pink Floyd)*

## HERB GELLER QUARTET
| 56 | London RE-U 1067 | SENSATIONAL SAX OF HERB GELLER (EP) | 15 |

## HERB GELLER
| 75 | Atlantic SD 1681 | RHYME & REASON (LP) | 25 |

## GEM
| 81 | SRTS 81 CUS 1147 | Toast Of The Town/Change In The Air (p/s) | 8 |

## GEMAGE
| 80 | Private pressing BGA 1 | Story So Far/Bring Me Death (no p/s) | 50 |

## GEMINI (PORTUGAL)
| 78 | Philips 6031 070 | Dal-Li-Dou (Falling In Love)/Dal-Li-Dou | 12 |

## GEMINI (U.K.) (1)
| 65 | Columbia DB 7638 | Space Walk/Goodbye Joe (demos may credit the 'Original Tornados') | 50 |

*(see also Tornados)*

## GEMINI (U.K.) (2)
| 69 | President PT 257 | Never Say Die/Something Special | 6 |

## GEMINI (U.K.) (3)
| 81 | Airship AP 345 | COUNTER BALANCE (LP) | 60 |

## GENE
| 94 | Costermonger COST 1 | For The Dead/Child's Body (p/s, 1,994 numbered copies only) | 8 |
| 96 | Costermonger GENE 1LP | OLYMPIAN (LP) | 15 |
| 96 | Polydor GENE 2LP | TO SEE THE LIGHTS (2-LP) | 20 |
| 97 | Polydor GENELP 3 | DRAWN TO THE DEEP END (2-LP) | 20 |
| 99 | Polydor GENELP 4 | REVELATIONS (LP, with booklet) | 20 |

## GENE & GARY
| 09 | Kent 6T 26 | Baby Without You/PARAMOUNT FOUR: Sorry Ain't The Word | 20 |

## GENE & DEBBE
| 67 | London HLE 10165 | Go With Me/Torch I Carry | 6 |
| 68 | London HLE 10179 | Playboy/I'll Come Running | 10 |
| 68 | London HLE 10203 | Lovin' Season/Love Will Give Us Wings | 6 |

## GENE & EUNICE
| 56 | Vogue V 9062 | I Gotta Go Home/Have You Changed Your Mind? | 200 |
| 56 | Vogue V 9062 | I Gotta Go Home/Have You Changed Your Mind? (78) | 40 |
| 57 | Vogue V 9066 | Move It Over, Baby/This Is My Story | 150 |
| 57 | Vogue V 9066 | Move It Over, Baby/This Is My Story (78) | 40 |
| 57 | Vogue V 9071 | Let's Get Together/I'm So In Love With You | 150 |
| 57 | Vogue V 9071 | Let's Get Together/I'm So In Love With You (78) | 30 |
| 57 | Vogue V 9083 | Doodle Doodle Doo/Don't Treat Me This Way | 150 |
| 57 | Vogue V 9083 | Doodle Doodle Doo/Don't Treat Me This Way (78) | 30 |
| 58 | Vogue V 9106 | I Mean Love/The Angels Gave You To Me | 150 |
| 58 | Vogue V 9106 | I Mean Love/The Angels Gave You To Me (78) | 30 |
| 58 | Vogue V 9126 | Strange World/The Vow | 50 |

*(The above 45s were originally issued with triangular centres; later issues with round centres are worth about half the values listed.)*

| 58 | Vogue V 9126 | Strange World/The Vow (78) | 30 |
| 59 | Vogue V 9136 | Bom Bom Lulu/Hi Diddle Diddle | 100 |
| 59 | Vogue V 9136 | Bom Bom Lulu/Hi Diddle Diddle (78) | 40 |
| 59 | London HL 8956 | Poco-Loco/Go-On Kokomo | 50 |
| 59 | London HL 8956 | Poco-Loco/Go-On Kokomo (78) | 40 |

## GENE & GENTS
| 68 | Pye 7N 17532 | C'mon Everybody/Hound Dog | 10 |

## GENE LOVES JEZEBEL
| 82 | Situation 2 SIT 20 | Screaming (For Emaline)/So Young (Heave Hard, Heave Ho) (p/s) | 8 |

## GENERAL DOGGIE & TENOR SAW
| 88 | Night Life Posse NP 001 | Chill Out Chill Out/Cool Out Dub/To Love Somebody/To Love Ya This Dub (12") | 10 |

*(see also Tenor Saw)*

## GENERAL HAVOC
| 91 | Chapati Heat BIRD 1 | Moonshine/Vacuum Cleaner/Another Cup Of Tea Arch Deacon? | 40 |

## GENERAL JOHNSON
| 73 | Invictus INV 531 | Only Time Will Tell/Only Time Will Tell (Instrumental Version) | 10 |
| 76 | Arista 45 | All In The Family/Ready Willing And Able | 7 |

## GENERAL LEVY
| 90 | Musik Street MS 005 | You Can't Hurry Love (with Junior Dunn)/JAZWAD: You Can't Hurry Dub (12", red or blue labels) | 70 |
| 93 | Ffrr/Fashion F214 | Monkey Man (Fashion Radio Edit)/Mad Them (p/s) | 20 |
| 93 | Ffrr/Fashion FX 214 | WICKEDER GENERAL EP (12", p/s) | 25 |
| 92 | Fashion FADLP 024 | THE WICKEDER GENERAL (LP) | 40 |

## MIKEY GENERAL
| 85 | Fashion FAD 043 | Sound Doctor/Jump And Shout (12") | 10 |

## GENERAL STRIKE
| 79 | Canal CANAL 01 | Part 1: My Body/Part 2: (Parts Of) My Body (p/s) | 5 |

## GENERAL T
| 88 | Realistic RR09 | Nah Tek De Coke/Version (12") | 30 |

## GENERATION GAP
| 69 | Pye 7N 17845 | She's Coming Home/Reach The Top | 8 |
| 70 | Pye 7N 17979 | Any Old Time You're Lonely And Sad/Rainbows 'N' Sorrows | 8 |

## GENERATION X
| 77 | Generation X GX 101 | Your Generation/Listen! (white label test pressing, official bootleg sold at gigs, no p/s) | 100 |
| 77 | Chrysalis CHS 2165 | Your Generation/Day By Day (p/s, original copies with 'A' on label with band credits on front) | 6 |
| 77 | Chrysalis CHS 2165 | Your Generation/Day By Day (p/s) | 5 |
| 77 | Chrysalis CHS 2165 | Your Generation/Day By Day (sleeve only, unissued, featuring 'pre-peroxide' Billy Idol; 1 copy known to exist) | 500 |
| 77 | Chrysalis CHS 2189 | Wild Youth/Wild Dub (Version) (p/s) | 5 |
| 77 | Chrysalis CHS 2189 | Wild Youth/Wild Dub (Version) (p/s, mispressing, plays "No No No", B-side matrix: CHS 2189 B/1) | 40 |
| 78 | Chrysalis CHS 2207 | Ready Steady Go/No No No (p/s) | 5 |
| 79 | Chrysalis CHS(A) 2261 | King Rocker/Gimme Some Truth (pink vinyl, Tony James p/s) | 5 |
| 79 | Chrysalis CHS(B) 2261 | King Rocker/Gimme Some Truth (red vinyl, Billy Idol p/s) | 5 |
| 79 | Chrysalis CHS(C) 2261 | King Rocker/Gimme Some Truth (yellow vinyl, Mark Laff p/s) | 7 |
| 79 | Chrysalis CHS(D) 2261 | King Rocker/Gimme Some Truth (orange vinyl, Bob Andrews p/s) | 6 |
| 79 | Chrysalis CHS 2261 | King Rocker/Gimme Some Truth (black vinyl, Bob Andrews p/s) | 5 |
| 79 | Chrysalis CHS 2310 | Valley Of The Dolls/Shakin' All Over (p/s) | 6 |
| 79 | Chrysalis CHS 2310 | Valley Of The Dolls/Shakin' All Over (multi-coloured vinyl, p/s) | 50 |
| 79 | Chrysalis CHS 2330 | Friday's Angels/Trying For Kicks/This Heat (p/s, black vinyl) | 15 |
| 81 | Chrysalis CHS 2488 | Dancing With Myself/Untouchables/King Rocker/Rock On (as Gen X, p/s, on clear vinyl) | 8 |
| 78 | Chrysalis CHR 1169 | GENERATION X (LP, with rare obi at bottom of sleeve) | 40 |
| 78 | Chrysalis CHR 1169 | GENERATION X (LP) | 20 |
| 79 | Chrysalis CHR 1193 | VALLEY OF THE DOLLS (LP, inner) | 15 |

*(see also Billy Idol, Empire, Westworld)*

## GENESIS (1)
### SINGLES
| 68 | Decca F 12735 | The Silent Sun/That's Me | 450 |
| 68 | Decca F 12735 | The Silent Sun/That's Me (promo copy) | 325 |
| 68 | Decca F 12775 | A Winter's Tale/One Eyed Hound | 400 |
| 68 | Decca F 12775 | A Winter's Tale/One Eyed Hound (promo copy) | 350 |
| 68 | London F12775 | A Winter's Tale/One Eyed Hound (export promo single) | 500 |
| 69 | Decca F 12949 | Where The Sour Turns To Sweet/In Hiding | 400 |
| 69 | Decca F 12949 | Where The Sour Turns To Sweet/In Hiding (promo copy) | 375 |
| 70 | Charisma GS 1/2 | Looking For Someone/Visions Of Angels (promo only) | 600 |
| 71 | Charisma CB 152 | The Knife (Parts 1 & 2) (in p/s) | 500 |
| 71 | Charisma CB 152 | The Knife (Parts 1 & 2) | 100 |
| 72 | Charisma CB 181 | Happy The Man/Seven Stones (some belated copies in p/s; beware counterfeits) | 450 |
| 72 | Charisma CB 181 | Happy The Man/Seven Stones | 100 |
| 72 | Charisma CB 181 | Happy The Man/Seven Stones (promo copy) | 150 |
| 73 | Charisma (no cat. no.) | Twilight Alehouse (1-sided flexidisc free with Zig Zag) | 35 |
| 73 | Charisma (no cat. no.) | Twilight Alehouse (1-sided flexidisc free with Zig Zag & later via fan club, without magazine) | 20 |
| 73 | Charisma (no cat. no.) | Twilight Alehouse (black vinyl, white label test pressings) | 70 |
| 73 | Charisma (no cat. no.) | Twilight Alehouse (1-sided flexidisc free via fan club, with letter, sticker, poster and Genesis "revolver") | 80 |
| 74 | Charisma CB 224 | I Know What I Like (In Your Wardrobe)/Twilight Alehouse | 8 |
| 74 | Charisma CB 224 | I Know What I Like (In Your Wardrobe)/Twilight Alehouse (promos with press release) | 100 |
| 74 | Charisma CB 238 | Counting Out Time/Riding The Scree | 12 |
| 74 | Charisma CB 238 | Counting Out Time/Counting Out Time (promo) | 60 |
| 75 | Charisma CB 251 | The Carpet Crawlers/The Waiting Room (Evil Jam) | 25 |
| 75 | Charisma CB 251 | The Carpet Crawlers/The Waiting Room (Evil Jam) (promos copies) | 65 |
| 76 | Charisma CB 277 | A Trick Of The Tail/Ripples (purple label) | 8 |
| 77 | Charisma CB 300 | Your Own Special Way/It's Yourself | 5 |
| 78 | Charisma CB 309 | Follow You, Follow Me/Ballad Of Big (p/s) | 6 |
| 78 | Charisma CB 315 | Many Too Many/The Day The Light Went Out/Vancouver (p/s) | 6 |
| 80 | Charisma CB 369 | Misunderstanding/Evidence Of Autumn (p/s) | 5 |
| 81 | Charisma CB 391 | Keep It Dark/Naminanu (p/s) | 5 |
| 82 | Charisma CB 393 | Man On The Corner/Submarine (rare blue label, with p/s) | 90 |
| 82 | Charisma CB 393 | Man On The Corner/Submarine (blue label, without p/s) | 5 |
| 82 | Lyntone LYN 11806 | The Lady Lies (live) (green flexidisc free with Flexipop mag, issue 21) | 10 |
| 83 | Lyntone LYN 13143 | Firth Of Fifth (live edit) (flexidisc, with numbered gatefold p/s) | 15 |
| 83 | Charisma/Virgin TATA Y-1 | That's All/Taking It All Too Hard (shaped picture disc) | 12 |
| 84 | Charisma/Virgin ALS 1 | Illegal Alien/Turn It On Again (live) (shaped picture disc) | 12 |
| 84 | Charisma/Virgin CB 300 | Your Own Special Way/It's Yourself (blue label reissue, no p/s) | 6 |
| 84 | Charisma/Virgin CB 356 | Turn It On Again/Behind The Lines Part 2 (blue label reissue, no p/s) | 6 |
| 84 | Charisma/Virgin CB 369 | Misunderstanding/Evidence Of Autumn (blue label reissue, no p/s) | 6 |
| 87 | Virgin CDEP 1 | Tonight, Tonight, Tonight (Edit)/In The Glow Of The Night/ Invisible Touch (12" Remix)/Tonight, Tonight, Tonight (CD, gatefold p/s) | 40 |
| 92 | Virgin GENS 10 | Invisible Touch (live)/Abacab (live) (no'd gatefold p/s) | 8 |
| 98 | Virgin SOLO2 | Live Rehearsal: Mama (live)/Calling All Stations (live)/Invisible Touch (live)/ Follow You, Follow Me (live)/Turn It On Again (live) (CD 5-track promo) | 40 |

MINT VALUE £

## ALBUMS

| 69 | Decca LK 4990 | FROM GENESIS TO REVELATION (mono, with 'mono' peephole, with red/pink lyric sheet, red/silver unboxed logo) | 1500 |
|---|---|---|---|
| 69 | Decca SKL 4990 | FROM GENESIS TO REVELATION (stereo, with stereo 'peephole', with lyric sheet, unboxed logo) | 500 |
| 70 | Decca SKL 4990 | FROM GENESIS TO REVELATION (stereo, with lyric sheet, blue/silver boxed logo) | 100 |
| 70 | Decca KSKC 4990 | FROM GENESIS TO REVELATION ( tape, boxed logo) | 35 |
| 70 | Charisma CAS 1020 | TRESPASS (original pink scroll label & gatefold sleeve with lyric sheet) | 150 |
| 71 | Charisma CAS 1052 | NURSERY CRYME (LP, textured sleeve, original pink scroll label, gatefold sleeve) | 150 |
| 72 | Charisma CAS 1058 | FOXTROT (LP, gatefold sleeve, large 'Mad Hatter' logo and B&C credit on label) | 30 |
| 73 | Charisma CAS 1074 | SELLING ENGLAND BY THE POUND (LP, insert, large 'Mad Hatter' logo) | 25 |
| 73 | Charisma CLASS 1 | LIVE (LP, non laminated sleeve, large 'Mad Hatter' logo, with 'Charisma Live Giants - £1.99' sticker on front cover) | 30 |
| 73 | Charisma CLASS 1 | LIVE (LP, non laminated sleeve, large 'Mad Hatter' logo) | 25 |
| 74 | Charisma CGS 101 | THE LAMB LIES DOWN ON BROADWAY (2-LP, small 'Mad Hatter; label, original pressing with "Marketed by B&C..." label text on both LPs and "Printed and Made by Bruin B.V. Zaandam/Holland" credit on sleeve, some with Gold Chase contest insert) | 100 |
| 74 | Decca SKL 4990 | IN THE BEGINNING (reissue of 1st LP, 'snake' sleeve with lyric insert) | 20 |
| 75 | Charisma CGS 102 | GENESIS COLLECTION VOLUME ONE (2-LP, boxed set of Trespass & "Nursery Cryme" in original sleeves, with poster) | 95 |
| 75 | Charisma CGS 103 | GENESIS COLLECTION VOLUME TWO (2-LP, boxed set of Foxtrot & "Selling England By The Pound", with poster) | 95 |
| 91 | Virgin Edits 1 | WE CAN'T DANCE (CD, 6 track promo - tour edition marketed by Volkswagon) | 50 |
| 91 | Virgin GEN CD | WE CAN'T DANCE (CD & tape, housed in custom promo box With three hand numbered watercolours) | 90 |
| 93 | Virgin GENBOX1 | LIVE: THE WAY WE WALK (2xCD in wooden box with certificate & badge (1000 only) | 120 |
| 97 | Virgin GENLP6 | CALLING ALL STATIONS (2xLP fourth sided etched with band picture) | 70 |
| 98 | Virgin CDBOX6 | GENESIS ARCHIVE 1967 – 1975 (4 CD Box Set) | 30 |
| 98 | Virgin CDBOX98 | GENESIS ARCHIVE 1967 - 1975 (CD 12-track promo digipack) | 30 |
| 97 | EMI LPCENT 17 | SELLING ENGLAND BY THE POUND (LP, reissue, EMI Centenary pressing, stickered sleeve) | 20 |
| 98 | Virgin VCDJBOX98 | GENESIS ARCHIVE 1967 - 1975 The Interviews (2xCD promo, p/s) | 65 |
| 99 | Virgin VGP 000270 | TURN IT ON AGAIN - THE HITS (CD, in store promo p/s - each song played for 1 min) | 50 |
| 00 | Virgin CDBOX7 | GENESIS ARCHIVE 2: 1976 - 1992 (3xCD Box Set) | 25 |
| 07 | EMI CDBOX12 | GENESIS 1976 - 1882 (2007 UK 12 disc set comprising of 6 Hybrid SA CD's) | 70 |
| 07 | EMI CDBOX13 | GENESIS 1983 - 1998 (2007 UK 10 disc set comprising of 5 Hybrid SA CD's) | 60 |
| 08 | Virgin LPBOX 14 | 1970 - 1975 (6-LP box set, inners & inserts) | 80 |
| 15 | Not Bad BADBOX001 | FROM GENESIS TO REVELATION (3-LP, 3 x 7" box set) | 60 |

*(see also Flaming Youth,, Peter Gabriel, Steve Hackett, Anthony Phillips, Quiet World)*

## GENEVA
| 80 | Valiant ROUND1 | 2.30/Geneva Street (p/s) | 10 |
|---|---|---|---|

## GENEVEVE
| 66 | CBS 202061 | Once/Just A Whisper (in p/s) | 25 |
|---|---|---|---|
| 66 | CBS 202061 | Once/Just A Whisper | 15 |
| 66 | CBS 202096 | Nothing In The World/Summer Days | 10 |
| 67 | CBS 202524 | That Can't Be Bad/I Love Him, I Need Him | 10 |

## GENGHIS KHAN (U.K.)
| 83 | Genghis Khan GK 1 | DOUBLE DEALIN' (If Heaven Is Hell/Highway Passion//Midnight Rendezvous Mean Streak) (EP, double pack) | 80 |
|---|---|---|---|
| 83 | Wabbit WAB 61/63 | Love You/Lady Lady/Mongol Nation/Gone For A Drive (double pack) | 40 |

## GENOCIDE
| 79 | Safari SAP 2 | IMAGES OF DELUSION (EP) | 10 |
|---|---|---|---|

## GENOCIDE EXIT
| 80 | Slam SEM 016 | FUTURE VIBES (EP) | 10 |
|---|---|---|---|

## GENOCIDES
| 82 | Action TAKE 1 | IS THAT ALRIGHT? - tracks are Come Again (You Make Me Wanna)/Born To Lose (p/s) | 5 |
|---|---|---|---|

## GENTILES (JAMAICA)
| 70 | High Note HS 046 | Your Destiny/Lock Love Away (actually by Melodians) | 10 |
|---|---|---|---|

*(see also Melodians)*

## GENTILES (U.K.)
| 68 | Pye 7N 17530 | Goodbye Baby/Marlena | 8 |
|---|---|---|---|

## GENTLE DESPITE
| 90 | Sarah SARAH 26 | THE DARKEST BLUE EP (p/s, insert) | 10 |
|---|---|---|---|
| 91 | Sarah SARAH 45 | Torment To Me/Bittersweet Kiss/Shadow Of A Girl (p/s, insert) | 10 |

## JOHNNY GENTLE
| 59 | Philips BBE 12345 | THE GENTLE TOUCH (EP) | 15 |
|---|---|---|---|

*(see also Darren Young)*

## TIM GENTLE & HIS GENTLEMEN
| 65 | Oriole CB 1988 | Without You/Someone's In The Kitchen With Dinah | 8 |
|---|---|---|---|

## GENTLE GIANT
| 73 | WWA WWP 1001 | In A Glass House/An Inmate's Lullaby | 12 |
|---|---|---|---|
| 74 | WWA WWS 017 | The Power And The Glory/Playing The Game | 12 |
| 77 | Chrysalis CHS 2160 | I'm Turning Around/Just The Same (live) | 6 |
| 70 | Vertigo 6360 020 | GENTLE GIANT (LP, 1st pressing, gatefold sleeve, large swirl label) | 400 |
| 71 | Vertigo 6360 020 | GENTLE GIANT (LP, 2nd pressing, gatefold sleeve, small swirl label) | 70 |
| 71 | Vertigo 6360 041 | ACQUIRING THE TASTE (LP, gatefold sleeve, small swirl label) | 300 |
| 72 | Vertigo 6360 070 | THREE FRIENDS (LP, 1st pressing, no "made in England" under 1972 on top right hand side of label, gatefold sleeve, small swirl label) | 200 |
| 72 | Vertigo 6360 070 | THREE FRIENDS (LP, 2nd pressing, "made in England" under 1972 on top right hand side of label, gatefold sleeve, small swirl label) | 50 |

| | | | |
|---|---|---|---|
| 72 | Vertigo 6360 080 | OCTOPUS (LP, gatefold sleeve, small swirl label) | 200 |
| 73 | WWA WWA 002 | IN A GLASS HOUSE (LP, silk-screen cover, with photo insert & lyric inner) | 50 |
| 74 | WWA WWA 010 | THE POWER AND THE GLORY (LP, with insert, sleeve has 2 rounded corners) | 40 |
| 75 | Vertigo 6360 020 | GENTLE GIANT (LP, reissue, gatefold sleeve, spaceship label) | 30 |
| 75 | Vertigo 6360080 | OCTOPUS (LP, reissue, 'spaceship' label) | 30 |
| 75 | Vertigo 6641 334 | GIANT STEPS - (THE FIRST FIVE YEARS) 1970-1975 (2-LP, gatefold sleeve, spaceship label) | 25 |
| 75 | Chrysalis CHR 1093 | FREE HAND (LP, lyric insert, green label) | 15 |
| 77 | Chrysalis CTY 1133 | LIVE (PLAYING THE FOOL) (2-LP, with 12-page booklet) | 20 |
| 77 | Chrysalis CHR 1152 | THE MISSING PIECE (LP, with inner sleeve) | 15 |
| 78 | Chrysalis CHR 1186 | GIANT FOR A DAY (LP, with mask insert & lyric inner sleeve) | 15 |
| 80 | Chrysalis CHR 1285 | CIVILIAN (LP, with lyric inner sleeve) | 15 |

*(see also Simon Dupree & Big Sound, Moles)*

**GENTLE INFLUENCE**

| | | | |
|---|---|---|---|
| 69 | Pye 7N 17666 | Never Trust In Tomorrow/Easy To Love | 15 |
| 69 | Pye 7N 17743 | Always Be A Part Of My Living/Captain Reale | 22 |

**GENTLE PEOPLE (1)**

| | | | |
|---|---|---|---|
| 67 | Columbia DB 8276 | It's Too Late/Sea Of Heartbreak | 12 |

**GENTLE POWER OF SONG**

| | | | |
|---|---|---|---|
| 67 | Polydor 56211 | Constant Penelope/A Court Garden Party, Circa 1580 | 8 |
| 67 | Polydor 2310 285 | CIRCUS | 25 |

**GENTLE RAIN**

| | | | |
|---|---|---|---|
| 73 | Polydor 2310 285 | MOODY (LP) | 200 |

**GENTLE RESPITE**

| | | | |
|---|---|---|---|
| 90 | Sarah SARAH 026 | DARKEST BLUE EP: Summer In Me/Darkest Blue/If I Touch (wraparound p/s, with insert) | 15 |

**BILL GENTLES**

| | | | |
|---|---|---|---|
| 69 | Gas GAS 104 | Long Life/SCHOOLBOYS: O Tell Me | 18 |
| 70 | Pama PM 801 | What A Woman/Sleepy Cat | 8 |
| 70 | Punch PH 54 | Fight The Good Fight/Fight Beat | 8 |
| 71 | Escort ERT 853 | Bachelor Boy/SCORPIONS: Colour Rites | 8 |
| 72 | Bullet BU 506 | Pure In Heart/Clean Hands | 6 |

*(see also Bill Jentles, Bill Jenties)*

**ERROL GENTLES**

| | | | |
|---|---|---|---|
| 79 | Attack TACK 11 | Tell Me Why/Far Far Away (12") | 20 |

**GENTLE TOUCH**

| | | | |
|---|---|---|---|
| 65 | London HLR 10175 | Among The First To Know/Merry Go Round | 7 |
| 83 | Tristar TRI3 | Dreams Of You/Dreams Of You (Instrumental) | 6 |

**GENTRY**

| | | | |
|---|---|---|---|
| 70 | Dolphin DO571 | Long Road/Sing Me A Sad Song/Attempt Contact (EP, Irish pressing) | 250 |
| 70 | Dolphin DOS 35 | Sing Me A Sad Song/Attempted Contact | 150 |

**ART GENTRY**

| | | | |
|---|---|---|---|
| 72 | Mojo 2092 048 | Breakthrough/Wonderful Dream | 15 |

**BO GENTRY & RITCHIE CORDELL**

| | | | |
|---|---|---|---|
| 69 | CBS 4299 | Stone Go-Getter/Hung Up | 5 |

**BOBBIE GENTRY**

| | | | |
|---|---|---|---|
| 67 | Capitol CL 15511 | Ode To Billie Joe/Mississippi Delta | 5 |
| 67 | Capitol (S)T 2830 | ODE TO BILLIE JOE (LP) | 15 |
| 68 | Capitol ST2964 | LOCAL GENTRY (LP) | 15 |
| 68 | Capitol (S)T 2842 | THE DELTA SWEETE (LP) | 15 |

**GENTRY ICE**

| | | | |
|---|---|---|---|
| 88 | Jack Trax JTX 15 | Do You Wanna Jack/Lost In The Sound (with Adonis) (12") | 20 |

**GENTRYS**

| | | | |
|---|---|---|---|
| 65 | MGM MGM 1284 | Keep On Dancing/Make Up Your Mind | 20 |
| 66 | MGM MGM 1296 | Brown Paper Sack/Spread It On Thick | 25 |
| 66 | MGM MGM 1312 | Everyday I Have To Cry/Don't Let It Be | 15 |
| 68 | Bell BLL 1012 | I Can't Go Back To Denver/You Better Come Home | 8 |

**GENTS**

| | | | |
|---|---|---|---|
| 81 | Posh POSH 001 | The Faker/The Pink Panther | 20 |
| 82 | Kosmic KOS 6886 | Schooldays/True Stories (p/s) | 8 |
| 83 | Posh POSH 007 | Revenge/Girl (p/s) | 5 |
| 85 | Posh no cat. no. | Lambs To The Slaughter/Friday On My Mind | 5 |
| 85 | Lambs To The Slaughter GN7 | Shout/The Faker (p/s) | 5 |
| 80s | Posh MEGA 1 | Revenge/Over Me/The Gent (p/s) | 5 |

**GEOFFREY**

| | | | |
|---|---|---|---|
| 78 | Music Bank BECK 694 | ABH (Who Wants To Listen To Punk Rock?)/Colt 45 Rock (p/s) | 15 |

**GEORDIE**

| | | | |
|---|---|---|---|
| 72 | Regal Zonophone RZ 3067 | Don't Do That/Francis Was A Rocker | 8 |
| 72 | EMI EMI 2031 | Can You Do It/Red Eyed Lady | 8 |
| 73 | EMI EMC 3001 | HOPE YOU LIKE IT (LP) | 30 |
| 74 | EMI EMA 764 | DON'T BE FOOLED BY THE NAME (LP) | 80 |
| 76 | EMI EMC 3134 | SAVE THE WORLD (LP) | 25 |
| 83 | Neat NEAT 1008 | NO SWEAT (LP) | 25 |

*(see also Influence, AC/DC)*

**BARBARA GEORGE**

| | | | |
|---|---|---|---|
| 62 | London HL 9513 | I Know (You Don't Love Me No More)/Love (Is Just A Chance You Take) | 25 |
| 64 | Sue WI 316 | Send For Me/Bless You | 50 |

MINT VALUE £

**EARL GEORGE**
| | | | |
|---|---|---|---|
| 73 | Count Shelly CS 025 | Gonna Give Her All The Love/PRINCE JAZZBO: Wise Shepherd | 6 |
| 76 | Terminal TM 103 | Love Depression/Love Is Something | 8 |
| 76 | Terminal TM 106 | So Many Ways/Part 2 | 8 |
| 78 | Burning Sounds BS 1015 | ONE AND ONLY (LP) | 20 |

**GEORGE GOLDEN**
| | | | |
|---|---|---|---|
| 64 | R&B JB145 | Fire In My Feet/ One More Chance | 15 |
| 64 | R&B JB157 | Don't You Know/ Nancy Tell Me | 15 |

**LLOYD GEORGE**
| | | | |
|---|---|---|---|
| 62 | London HLP 9562 | Lucy Lee/Sing Real Loud | 60 |

**GEORGETTES**
| | | | |
|---|---|---|---|
| 58 | London HL 8548 | Love Like A Fool/Oh Tonight | 50 |
| 58 | London HL 8548 | Love Like A Fool/Oh Tonight (78) | 30 |
| 60 | Pye International 7N 25058 | Down By The River/A Pair Of Eyes | 10 |

**GEORGIA SLIM/WALTER ROLAND**
| | | | |
|---|---|---|---|
| 59 | Jazz Collector JEL 2 | THE MALE BLUES VOL. 1 (EP) | 10 |

**GEORGIA TOM**
| | | | |
|---|---|---|---|
| 60s | Riverside RLP 8803 | GEORGIA TOM AND FRIENDS (LP) | 20 |

*(see also Paramount Allstars)*

**GEORGIE'S VARSITY 5**
| | | | |
|---|---|---|---|
| 61 | Vogue Pop V 9189 | When My Sugar Walks Down The Street/Five Foot Two, Eyes Of Blue | 10 |

**GERALDINE**
| | | | |
|---|---|---|---|
| 71 | Beltona Sword SBE 128 | GERALDINE (LP) | 150 |

**GERALDO 1969**
| | | | |
|---|---|---|---|
| 69 | Morgan MRS 22 | QE2/Hello Again | 8 |

**WESLEY GERMS**
| | | | |
|---|---|---|---|
| 72 | Upsetter US 390 | Whiplash/UPSETTERS: Whiplash Version | 15 |

**GERONIMO BLACK**
| | | | |
|---|---|---|---|
| 72 | Uni UNLS 126 | GERONIMO BLACK (LP) | 75 |

*(see also Frank Zappa/Mothers Of Invention)*

**DANIEL GERRARD**
| | | | |
|---|---|---|---|
| 72 | CBS 58064 | From Japan To America/Rain | 12 |

**DENNY GERRARD**
| | | | |
|---|---|---|---|
| 70 | Deram Nova DN 10 | SINISTER MORNING (LP, mono, with High Tide, Deram Nova on top right hand corner of sleeve with either Deram Nova or Decca Nova on label) | 300 |
| 70 | Deram Nova SDN 10 | SINISTER MORNING (LP, stereo, with High Tide, Deram Nova on top right hand corner of sleeve with either Deram Nova or Decca Nova on label) | 150 |

*(see also Warm Sounds, High Tide, Open Road, Fifth Avenue)*

**GERRY & THE HOLOGRAMS**
| | | | |
|---|---|---|---|
| 79 | Absurd ABSURD 4 | Gerry And The Holograms/Increased Resistance (p/s) | 15 |
| 79 | Absurd ABSURD 5 | The Emperor's New Music (unplayable record, glued into p/s) | 8 |

**GERRY & THE PACEMAKERS**
| | | | |
|---|---|---|---|
| 63 | Columbia DB 4987 | How Do You Do It?/Away From You | 5 |
| 63 | Columbia DB 7041 | I Like It/It's Happened To Me | 5 |
| 63 | Columbia DB 7126 | You'll Never Walk Alone/It's All Right | 5 |
| 64 | Columbia DB 7189 | I'm The One/You've Got What I Like | 5 |
| 64 | Columbia DB 7268 | Don't Let The Sun Catch You Crying/Show Me That You Care | 6 |
| 64 | Columbia DB 7353 | It's Gonna Be Alright/It's Just Because | 7 |
| 64 | Columbia DB 7437 | Ferry Cross The Mersey/You You You | 5 |
| 65 | Columbia DB 7504 | I'll Be There/Baby, You're So Good To Me | 6 |
| 65 | Columbia DB 7738 | Walk Hand In Hand/Dreams | 6 |
| 66 | Columbia DB 7835 | La La La/Without You | 8 |
| 66 | Columbia DB 8044 | Girl On A Swing/A Fool To Myself | 8 |
| 74 | DJM DJS 298 | Remember (The Days Of Rock And Roll)/There's Still Time | 10 |
| 63 | Columbia SEG 8257 | HOW DO YOU DO IT? (EP) | 12 |
| 64 | Columbia SEG 8295 | YOU'LL NEVER WALK ALONE (EP, in misprinted sleeve listing "It's All Right" instead of "Jambalaya" on front) | 25 |
| 64 | Columbia SEG 8295 | YOU'LL NEVER WALK ALONE (EP) | 15 |
| 64 | Columbia SEG 8311 | I'M THE ONE (EP) | 15 |
| 64 | Columbia SEG 8346 | DON'T LET THE SUN CATCH YOU CRYING (EP) | 15 |
| 64 | Columbia SEG 8367 | IT'S GONNA BE ALRIGHT (EP) | 20 |
| 65 | Columbia SEG 8388 | GERRY IN CALIFORNIA (EP) | 30 |
| 65 | Columbia SEG 8397 | HITS FROM 'FERRY CROSS THE MERSEY' (EP) | 30 |
| 65 | Columbia SEG 8426 | RIP IT UP (EP) | 35 |
| 63 | Columbia 33SX 1546 | HOW DO YOU LIKE IT? (LP, mono) | 20 |
| 63 | Columbia 33SCX 1546 | HOW DO YOU LIKE IT? (LP, stereo) | 30 |
| 65 | Columbia 33SX 1693 | FERRY CROSS THE MERSEY (LP, soundtrack, with Cilla Black & Fourmost, mono) | 25 |
| 65 | Columbia 33SCX 1693 | FERRY CROSS THE MERSEY (LP, soundtrack, with Cilla Black & Fourmost, stereo) | 35 |
| 65 | EMI Regal REG 2018 | YOU'LL NEVER WALK ALONE (LP, export issue) | 25 |

*(see also Gerry Marsden)*

**GERVASE**
| | | | |
|---|---|---|---|
| 68 | Decca F12822 | Pepper Grinder/Visions | 20 |

**GESCOM**
| | | | |
|---|---|---|---|
| 94 | Skam SKA 2 | Dan One/Five/Cicada/Sciew Spo (12", card folder p/s) | 35 |
| 95 | Skam SKA 3 | Snackwitch/Mag (12", bubblewrap sleeve with insert) | 40 |
| 95 | Skam SKA 3 | Snackwitch/Mag (12", second issue, black sleeve) | 20 |
| 95 | Clear CLR 408 | THE SOUNDS OF MACHINES OUR PARENTS USED (12", p/s) | 35 |
| 96 | Skam SKA 7 | KEY NELL 1/2/3/4 (12", bubblewrap sleeve) | 15 |

| | | | |
|---|---|---|---|
| 98 | Skam SKA010 THAT | THAT (EP) (12", p/s 2 inserts) | 15 |
| 98 | Skam SKA010 THIS | THIS (EP) (12", p/s) | 15 |
| 96 | Warp WAP 88 | Keynell/Keynell (12", p/s, remixes by Autechre) | 10 |

*(see also Autechre, Ad Vance Vs Gescom)*

## GESTURES
| | | | |
|---|---|---|---|
| 65 | Stateside SS 379 | Run Run Run/It Seems To Me | 25 |

## STAN GETZ (QUARTET/QUINTET)
| | | | |
|---|---|---|---|
| 53 | Esquire 20-007 | STAN GETZ PLAYS (LP, 10") | 25 |
| 54 | Vogue LDE 089 | AT STORYVILLE (LP, 10") | 25 |
| 55 | Vogue LDE 147 | STAN GETZ QUARTET (LP, 10") | 25 |
| 55 | Columbia Clef 33CX 10000 | AT THE SHRINE NO. 1 (LP, as Stan Getz Quintet) | 20 |
| 55 | Columbia Clef 33CX 10001 | AT THE SHRINE NO. 2 (LP, as Stan Getz Quintet) | 20 |
| 58 | HMV CLP 1292 | STAN GETZ/CHET BAKER (LP) | 20 |
| 62 | HMV CLP 1577 | FOCUS (LP, also stereo CSD 1448) | 15 |
| 63 | Verve (S)VLP 9013 | JAZZ SAMBA (LP, with Charlie Byrd, stereo) | 15 |
| 63 | Verve (S)VLP 9038 | JAZZ SAMBA ENCORE! (LP, with Luiz Bonfa, stereo) | 15 |
| 65 | MGM MGM-C 8001 | MICKEY ONE (LP, soundtrack, mono, with booklet) | 20 |
| 65 | MGM MGM-C(S) 8001 | MICKEY ONE (LP, soundtrack, stereo, with booklet) | 25 |

*(see also Dizzy Gillespie, Astrud Gilberto, Joao Gilberto, Johnny Smith)*

## GEZLIM
| | | | |
|---|---|---|---|
| 72 | Helm 001 | Dark Side Of Your Face (1-sided) | 200 |

## G-FORCE
| | | | |
|---|---|---|---|
| 80 | Jet JET 183 | Hot Gossip/Because Of Your Love (p/s) | 20 |
| 80 | Jet JET 194 | You/Trust Your Lovin' (no p/s) | 12 |
| 80 | Jet JET 7005 | White Knuckles/Rockin' And Rollin'/I Look At You (p/s) | 15 |
| 80 | Jet JETLP 229 | G-FORCE (LP, with inner sleeve and patch) | 20 |
| 80 | Jet JETPD 229 | G-FORCE (LP, picture disc) | 18 |

*(see also Gary Moore)*

## G.G. ALLSTARS
| | | | |
|---|---|---|---|
| 70 | Explosion EX 2014 | Barabus/This Kind Of Life | 10 |
| 70 | Explosion EX 2012 | Champion/MAYTONES: Funny Man | 25 |
| 70 | Explosion EX 2023 | Man From Carolina/Gold On Your Dress (B-side actually by Slickers) | 10 |
| 70 | Explosion EX 2024 | African Melody/Serious Love (B-side actually by Maytones) | 8 |
| 70 | Explosion EX 2025 | Ganja Plane/Deep River | 10 |
| 70 | Gas GAS 153 | So Alive/Mercy Mr D.J. | 8 |
| 70 | Escort ERT 835 | African Melody/Man From Carolina | 7 |
| 70 | G.G. GG 4505 | I Don't Like To Interfere/Version II | 20 |
| 70 | G.G. GG 4501 | Music Keep On Playing (actually by Cornell Campbell)/ Music Keep On Playing Version | 10 |
| 71 | G.G. GG 4508 | Cleanliness Version 2/MAYTONES: Cleanliness | 7 |
| 71 | G.G. GG 4510 | Rocking On The G.G. Beat (actually by Maytones)/WINSTON WRIGHT: Rocking On The G.G. Beat Version II | 15 |
| 71 | G.G. GG 4511 | Lonely Nights (actually by Eric Donaldson & West Indians)/MAYTONES: Let The Version Play | 10 |
| 71 | G.G. GG 4513 | All One Nation (actually by Maytones)/VAL BENNETT: Judgement Warrant | 8 |
| 71 | G.G. GG 4526 | Rod Of Righteousness (actually "Stretch Forth His Hand" by Jah Huntly)/ DENNIS ALCAPONE: King Of Kings (B-side actually "King Of Glory") | 20 |
| 72 | G.G. GG 4530 | Donkey Face Version/MAYTONES: Donkey Face | 8 |
| 72 | Pama PM 846 | I'm Feeling Lonely Version/MAYTONES: I'm Feeling Lonely | 6 |
| 73 | Bullet BU 528 | People Get Funny Version/MAYTONES: People Get Funny | 6 |
| 70 | Trojan TBL 129 | MAN FROM CAROLINA (LP) | 30 |

*(see also Paulette & Gee, Billy Dyce, Maytones, Charlie Ace, Monty Morris, Starlights, Lloyd & Carey, Gladdy & Stranger, Heptones, Shorty Perry, Barbara Jones)*

## G.G.F.H.
| | | | |
|---|---|---|---|
| 94 | Peaceville CC8 | Welcome To The Process/Too Much Punch/Dread (green vinyl, p/s) | 15 |

## G.G. RHYTHM SECTION
| | | | |
|---|---|---|---|
| 69 | Blue Cat BS 165 | T.N.T./MAYTONES: Botheration | 35 |

## AMOS GHERKIN QUARTET
| | | | |
|---|---|---|---|
| 70 | Parlophone R 5872 | Blakey And Me/Theme From An Unmade Silent Movie | 8 |

## GHETTO CHILDREN
| | | | |
|---|---|---|---|
| 73 | CBS 1450 | I Just Gotta Find Somebody To Love Me/Rat-A-Tat-Tat | 10 |

## GHETTO PRIEST
| | | | |
|---|---|---|---|
| 03 | On U Sound ON-ULP 1003 | VULTURE CULTURE (LP) | 15 |

## GHETTO TEARS
| | | | |
|---|---|---|---|
| 84 | Ghetto Tears GT 001 | Ghetto Children/Ghetto Prayers (12" p/s) | 80 |

## WESS & DORI GHEZZI
| | | | |
|---|---|---|---|
| 74 | Bradleys BRAD 7404 | Let It Be Free/Turn Around | 7 |
| 75 | Bradleys BRAD 7515 | Fallin'/Era | 8 |

## GHOST DANCE
| | | | |
|---|---|---|---|
| 86 | Karbon KAR 604 | The Grip Of Love/Where Spirits Fly (p/s) | 8 |
| 88 | Karbon KAR XL 303 | GATHERING DUST (LP) | 15 |

*(see also Skeletal Family, All About Eve, Sisters Of Mercy)*

## GHOST (1)
| | | | |
|---|---|---|---|
| 69 | Gemini GMS 007 | When You're Dead/Indian Maid | 40 |
| 70 | Gemini GMS 014 | I've Got To Get To Know You/For One Second | 30 |
| 70 | Gemini GME 1004 | WHEN YOU'RE DEAD - ONE SECOND (LP, laminated front cover, with extra track, "I've Got To Know Her") | 750 |
| 70 | Gemini GME 1004 | WHEN YOU'RE DEAD - ONE SECOND (LP, laminated front cover, without extra track, "I've Got To Get To Know Her") | 500 |

|  |  |  | MINT VALUE £ |
|---|---|---|---|
| 87 | Bam Caruso KIRI 077 | FOR ONE SECOND (LP, reissue of "When You're Dead" with extra track) | 20 |

*(see also Velvett Fogg, Shirley Kent, Virginia Tree, Wizzard)*

## GHOST (2)
| 10 | Rise Above RISELP 124 | OPVS EPONYMOVS (LP, 'Die Hard Edition', 300 only) | 200 |
|---|---|---|---|

## GHOSTS
| 80 | Arista ARIST 347 | My Town/I'm Your Man (no p/s) | 8 |
|---|---|---|---|

## GHOSTS OF DANCE
| 82 | Plastic Canvas PC001 | Ghosts Of Dance/Walking Through Gardens (p/s) | 20 |
|---|---|---|---|

## BILL GIANT
| 61 | MGM MGM 1135 | Better Let Her Go/When I Grow Too Old To Dream | 12 |
|---|---|---|---|

## BILLY GIANT
| 65 | Pye 25337 | Leave My Girl Alone/Nice Girls | 20 |
|---|---|---|---|

## GIANT CRAB
| 68 | Uni UN 509 | Hot Line Conversation/E.S.P. | 35 |
|---|---|---|---|

## GIANT HAYSTACKS
| 83 | BSB BSB 01 | Baby I Need You/Baby I Need You (Instrumental) (p/s) | 7 |
|---|---|---|---|

## GIANTS
| 60s | Polydor LPHM 46426 | IN GERMANY (LP, mono) | 25 |
|---|---|---|---|
| 60s | Polydor SLPHM 237626 | IN GERMANY (LP, stereo) | 30 |

## GIANT SIZE C
| 91 | Afrocentric AFRO 1 | Perspective (12") | 40 |
|---|---|---|---|
| 93 | Afrocentric AFRO 3 | Hate (12") | 12 |

## GIANT SUNFLOWER
| 67 | CBS 2805 | February Sunshine/Big Apple | 20 |
|---|---|---|---|
| 67 | CBS 3033 | Mark Twain/What's So Good About Goodbye? | 10 |

## BARRY GIBB
| 70 | Lyntone LYN 2375 | King Cathy/Summer Ends/I Can Bring Love | 100 |
|---|---|---|---|
| 70 | Polydor 2058 030 | I'll Kiss Your Memory/This Time | 8 |

*(see also Bee Gees)*

## MAURICE GIBB
| 70 | Polydor 2058 013 | Railroad/I've Come Back | 8 |
|---|---|---|---|
| 84 | Audiotrax ATX 05 | Hold Her In Your Hand/Instrumental (gatefold sleeve) | 15 |

*(see also Bee Gees, Fut)*

## ROBIN GIBB
| 69 | Polydor 56337 | Saved By The Bell/Mother And Jack | 6 |
|---|---|---|---|
| 69 | Polydor 56337 | Saved By The Bell/Alexandria Good Time (withdrawn) | 20 |
| 69 | Polydor 56368 | One Million Years/Weekend | 8 |
| 70 | Polydor 56371 | August October/Give Me A Smile | 7 |
| 84 | Polydor POSP 686 | Boys Do Fall In Love/Diamonds (p/s) | 5 |
| 69 | Polydor 583 085 | ROBIN'S REIGN (LP) | 25 |

*(see also Bee Gees)*

## DOUG GIBBONS
| 65 | Decca F 12122 | I Got My Tears To Remind Me/I Found Out | 6 |
|---|---|---|---|

## STEVE GIBBONS (BAND)
| 71 | Wizard WIZ 102 | Alright Now/Lay Some Lovin' Down | 10 |
|---|---|---|---|
| 76 | Polydor 2058 745 | Johnny Cool/Speed Kills | 10 |
| 77 | Polydor 2058 889 | Tulane/Now You Know Me | 7 |
| 71 | Wizard SWZA 5501 | SHORT STORIES (LP, gatefold sleeve, lyric insert, yellow vinyl) | 100 |
| 71 | Wizard SWZA 5501 | SHORT STORIES (LP, gatefold sleeve, lyric insert, black vinyl) | 30 |

*(see also Uglys, Magic Christians, B,L&G)*

## CALY GIBBS
| 71 | Amalgamated AMG 870 | Seeing Is Believing/JOE GIBBS ALLSTARS: Ghost Capturer | 30 |
|---|---|---|---|

*(see also Carlton Gibbs)*

## CARLTON GIBBS
| 70 | Amalgamated AMG 872 | Ghost Walk/Joy Stick | 30 |
|---|---|---|---|

## GEORGIA GIBBS
| 55 | Vogue Coral Q 72088 | Ballin' The Jack/I Still Feel The Same About You | 10 |
|---|---|---|---|
| 56 | Vogue Coral Q 72182 | If I Were A Bell/I'll Know | 10 |
| 57 | RCA RCA 1011 | Sugar Candy/I'm Walking The Floor Over You | 10 |
| 58 | RCA RCA 1029 | Great Balls Of Fire/I Miss You | 45 |
| 58 | Mercury 7MT 210 | Arriverderci Roma/24 Hours A Day | 10 |
| 58 | Columbia DB 4201 | The Hula Hoop Song/Keep In Touch | 8 |
| 59 | Columbia DB 4259 | The Hucklebuck/Better Loved You'll Never Be | 5 |
| 60 | London HLP 9098 | The Stroll That Stole My Heart/Seven Lonely Days | 7 |
| 65 | Stateside SS 423 | Let Me Cry On Your Shoulder/Venice Blues | 7 |
| 56 | Mercury MPT 7500 | SINGS THE OLDIES (10" LP) | 15 |
| 57 | Mercury MPT 7511 | HER NIBS MISS GIBBS (10" LP) | 15 |
| 57 | Mercury MPL 6508 | SWINGING WITH HER NIBS (LP) | 15 |

## JOE GIBBS (& DESTROYERS)
| 68 | Amslgamated AMG 822 | People Grudgeful (as Sir Joe)/Pan-Ya Machete (actually the Pioneers) | 50 |
|---|---|---|---|
| 70 | Amalgamated AMG 855 | Nevada Joe (act. by Johnny Lover)/Straight To The Head (act. by Destroyers) | 50 |
| 70 | Amalgamated AMG 858 | Franco Nero (actually by Count Machuki & Destroyers)/ Version Two (actually by Destroyers) | 25 |
| 70 | Amalgamated AMG 859 | Rock The Clock/Version Two | 50 |
| 70 | Amalgamated AMG 860 | Let It Be/Turn Back The Hands Of Time (both actually by Nicky Thomas) | 18 |
| 70 | Amalgamated AMG 861 | La La/Reggae Fever (as Joe Gibbs All Stars) | 40 |
| 70 | Amalgamated AMG 865 | Hijacked/Life Is Down In Denver | 50 |

| | | | |
|---|---|---|---|
| 70 | Amalgamated AMG 867 | Movements/Caesar | 40 |
| 70 | Amalgamated AMG 869 | Perfect Born Yah/Red Red Wine (as Jo Gibs All Stars) | 20 |
| 70 | Amalgamated AMG 868 | Gift Of God (actually by Lizzy)/The Rapper | 15 |
| 70 | Pressure Beat PR 5504 | News Flash/Version Two | 15 |
| 72 | Pressure Beat DB5513 | Money In My Pocket/Money Love | 25 |
| 73 | Jackpot JP 811 | Ration/Version (as Joe Gibbs All Stars) | 8 |
| 78 | Lightning LIP 10 | AFRICAN DUB ALMIGHTY (LP, with The Professionals) | 20 |
| 78 | Lightning LIP 11 | AFRICAN DUB ALMIGHTY - CHAPTER TWO (LP) | 15 |
| 78 | Lightning LIP 12 | AFRICAN DUB ALMIGHTY - CHAPTER THREE (LP) | 15 |
| 88 | Trojan TRLS 261 | REGGAE TRAIN 1968 - 71 (LP) | 15 |

*(see also Lizzy, Reggae Boys, Bunny Flip, Destroyers, Dennis Brown, Caly Gibbs, Nicky Thomas)*

## MICHAEL GIBBS
| | | | |
|---|---|---|---|
| 70 | Deram DML/SML 1063 | MICHAEL GIBBS (LP) | 50 |
| 71 | Deram SML 1087 | TANGLEWOOD '63 (LP) | 50 |
| 72 | Polydor 2683 011 | JUST AHEAD (2-LP) | 35 |
| 74 | Polydor 2383 252 | IN THE PUBLIC INTEREST (LP, with Gary Burton) | 35 |
| 70s | Bronze ILPS 9353 | ONLY CHROME ... WATERFALL (LP) | 15 |

*(see also Neil Ardley, Gary Burton)*

## TERRY GIBBS SEXTET
| | | | |
|---|---|---|---|
| 56 | Vogue Coral LVA 9013 | TERRY (LP) | 20 |
| 56 | Vogue Coral LVA 9009 | JAZZTIME USA (LP, as Terry Gibbs Quartet & Sextet) | 20 |

*(see also Terry Gibbs Big Band)*

## TERRY GIBBS BIG BAND
| | | | |
|---|---|---|---|
| 59 | Mercury CMS 18016 | LAUNCHING A NEW BAND (LP) | 15 |

## NICK GIBLER
| | | | |
|---|---|---|---|
| 76 | Chrysalis CHS 2104 | Roxy Roller/Prophet's Tale | 6 |

## DON GIBSON
| | | | |
|---|---|---|---|
| 56 | MGM SP 1177 | Sweet Dreams/The Road Of Life Alone | 125 |
| 58 | RCA RCA 1056 | Oh Lonesome Me/I Can't Stop Lovin' You | 15 |
| 58 | RCA RCA 1073 | Blue Blue Day/Too Soon | 12 |
| 58 | RCA RCA 1098 | Give Myself A Party/Look Who's Blue | 20 |
| 59 | RCA RCA 1110 | A Stranger To Me/Who Cares? | 10 |
| 59 | RCA RCA 1150 | Don't Tell Me Your Troubles/Heartbreak Avenue | 18 |
| 59 | RCA RCA 1158 | Big Hearted Me/I'm Movin' On | 15 |

*(Originally issued with triangular centres; later round-centre copies are worth half these values.)*

| | | | |
|---|---|---|---|
| 60 | RCA RCA 1183 | Just One Time/I May Never Get To Heaven | 8 |
| 60 | RCA RCA 1200 | Far Far Away/A Legend In My Time | 8 |
| 60 | RCA RCA 1217 | Sweet Dreams/The Same Street | 8 |
| 61 | RCA RCA 1243 | Sea Of Heartbreak/I Think It's Best (To Forget Me) | 8 |
| 62 | RCA RCA 1272 | Lonesome Number One/The Same Old Trouble | 10 |
| 60 | RCA RCX 1050 | BLUE AND LONESOME (EP) | 12 |
| 62 | RCA RCX 213 | LOOK WHO'S BLUE (EP) | 12 |
| 62 | RCA RCX 214 | THAT GIBSON BOY (EP) | 12 |
| 63 | RCA RCX 7122 | MAY YOU NEVER BE ALONE (EP) | 10 |
| 60 | RCA RD 27158 | THE GIBSON BOY (LP) | 70 |

## GINNY GIBSON
| | | | |
|---|---|---|---|
| 55 | MGM SP 1121 | Like Ma-a-d/Once There Was A Little Girl | 15 |
| 58 | MGM MGM 953 | Whatever Lola Wants (Lola Gets)/If Anything Should Happen | 15 |

## JODY GIBSON & MULESKINNERS
| | | | |
|---|---|---|---|
| 59 | Parlophone R 4579 | Kissin' Time/Man On My Trail | 15 |
| 60 | Parlophone R 4645 | If You Don't Know/So You Think You've Got Troubles | 15 |

## LORNE GIBSON TRIO
| | | | |
|---|---|---|---|
| 62 | Decca F 11519 | Little Black Book/What Kind Of Love Is This? | 5 |
| 63 | Decca F 11684 | Some Do, Some Don't (Some Will, Some Won't)/Heaven's Above | 5 |
| 64 | Decca F 11814 | Hang Up The Phone/I Think It's Best To Forget Me | 5 |
| 64 | Decca F 12005 | The Girl I Loved/Don't Go Near The Indians | 5 |
| 65 | Decca F 12102 | Red Roses For A Blue Lady/Talking To Your Picture | 5 |
| 66 | Decca F 12357 | A Little Lovin Light/When Baby Says Goodbye | 5 |
| 66 | Decca F12450 | Roses From A Stranger/Jingle Jangle | 20 |
| 69 | RCA 1917 | Eva Magdalena/A Thing Called Love | 7 |

## STEVE GIBSON & RED CAPS
| | | | |
|---|---|---|---|
| 57 | HMV POP 417 | Silhouettes/Flamingo | 150 |
| 57 | HMV POP 417 | Silhouettes/Flamingo (78) | 30 |

## WAYNE GIBSON (& DYNAMIC SOUNDS)
| | | | |
|---|---|---|---|
| 63 | Decca F 11713 | Linda Lu/Beachcomber | 20 |
| 64 | Decca F 11800 | Come On Let's Go/DYNAMIC SOUNDS : Pop The Whip | 20 |
| 64 | Pye 7N 15680 | Kelly/See You Later Alligator | 20 |
| 65 | Pye 7N 15798 | Portland Town/Please Baby Please | 10 |
| 65 | Parlophone R 5357 | Ding Dong The Witch Is Dead/In The Night | 8 |
| 65 | Columbia DB 7683 | One Little Smile/Baby, Baby, Baby Pity Me | 30 |
| 66 | Columbia DB 7911 | Under My Thumb/It Always Happens (Icey) (solo) | 60 |
| 66 | Columbia DB 7911 | Under My Thumb/It Always Happens (Icey) (solo) (DJ copy) | 120 |
| 66 | Columbia DB 7998 | For No One/He's Got The Whole World In his Hands (solo) | 10 |
| 72 | Kingdom KV 8002 | For No One/Come Around | 10 |
| 74 | Pye DDS 2001 | Under My Thumb/The Game | 10 |

## GIBSONS
| | | | |
|---|---|---|---|
| 65 | CBS 202015 | Any Time That You're Lonely/Born To Be Free | 7 |
| 66 | CBS 202063 | Come Summertime/Summer Affair | 7 |

MINT VALUE £

## GIDEANS LEAGUE *(continued)*
| | | | |
|---|---|---|---|
| 66 | Deram DM 103 | Two Kinds Of Lovers/Hey Girl | 8 |
| 67 | Deram DM 119 | The Magic Book/You Know I Need Your Lovin' | 12 |
| 67 | Major Minor MM 524 | Night And Day/City Life | 25 |
| 67 | Major Minor MM 538 | Lazy Summer Day/She's Not Like Any Girl | 25 |
| 67 | Major Minor MM 547 | Only When You're Lonely/Ode To A Dolls House | 7 |

## GIDEANS LEAGUE
| | | | |
|---|---|---|---|
| 72 | Parlophone R 5933 | Hey! Did You Know You've Got Your Face On Upside Down/You've Got A Mind Of Your Own | 6 |

## GIDIAN (& UNIVERSALS)
| | | | |
|---|---|---|---|
| 66 | Columbia DB 7826 | Try Me Out/There Isn't Anything | 20 |
| 66 | Columbia DB 7916 | Fight For Your Love/See If She Cares | 8 |
| 66 | Columbia DB 8041 | Feeling/Don't Be Sentimental (as Gidian & Universals) | 10 |
| 70 | UPC UPC 107 | That's Love/We Are The Happiest | 6 |

*(see also Universals, Chris Lamb & Universals)*

## COLIN GIFFIN
| | | | |
|---|---|---|---|
| 69 | CBS 4030 | Changes In Our Time/When I Was So Young | 40 |

## GIFT BOX
| | | | |
|---|---|---|---|
| 85 | Steed Steed 01 | Steiner's Lament/Worm Purple | 5 |

## GIFT (1)
| | | | |
|---|---|---|---|
| 81 | Venus ORBIT 1 | Crashing Down/It'll End In Tears (p/s) | 20 |

## GIFT (2)
| | | | |
|---|---|---|---|
| 88 | Red Communications RED 001 | You Don't Feel For Me/Torn Apart (p/s) | 20 |

## GIFTED CHILDREN
| | | | |
|---|---|---|---|
| 81 | Whaam! WHAAM 001 | Painting By Numbers/Lichtenstein Girl (p/s) | 60 |

*(see also Television Personalities)*

## GIGGETTY
| | | | |
|---|---|---|---|
| 78 | Pye 7N 46136 | Black Country Christmas/Motorway Mess | 6 |
| 75 | GE 100 | DAWN TO DUSK IN THE BLACK COUNTRY (LP, with insert, credited to Giggetty and Jim Wm. Jones) | 40 |
| 77 | Bridge GE 101 | TAMBOURINE (LP) | 30 |
| 80 | Bridge GE 103 | BLACK COUNTRY TIME (LP, also listed as Revolver REV LP1) | 30 |

## GIGGLES
| | | | |
|---|---|---|---|
| 74 | EMI 2212 | Maria (The Enchildas Song)/Your Mother Wouldn't Like It | 6 |
| 74 | EMI 2246 | Giggle Wiggle/For Just One Day | 100 |
| 75 | EMI EMI 2288 | Glad To Be Alive/High School Girls | 6 |
| 76 | EMI EMI 2512 | Just Another Saturday Night In The City/Bazooka (p/s) | 6 |
| 77 | EMI EMI 2640 | Reaching Out/Street Dancer | 6 |

## GILBERTO GIL
| | | | |
|---|---|---|---|
| 71 | Famous SFM 1001 | GILBERTO GIL (LP) | 40 |

## GILBERT
| | | | |
|---|---|---|---|
| 67 | CBS 3089 | Disappear/You | 15 |
| 68 | CBS 3399 | What Can I Do?/You | 15 |
| 69 | Major Minor MM 613 | Mister Moody's Garden/I Wish I Could Cry | 15 |

*(see also Gilbert O'Sullivan)*

## GEORGE GILBERT
| | | | |
|---|---|---|---|
| 74 | Mime LPMS 7041 | MEDWAY FLOWS SOFTLY (LP, with insert) | 15 |

## GILBERT & LEWIS
| | | | |
|---|---|---|---|
| 81 | 4AD AD 106 | Ends With The Sea/Hung Up To Dry Whilst Building An Arch (p/s) | 6 |

*(see also Wire, Dome, Cupol)*

## ASTRUD GILBERTO
| | | | |
|---|---|---|---|
| 65 | Verve VLP 9107 | THE SHADOW OF YOUR SMILE (LP) | 15 |
| 66 | Verve (S)VLP 9163 | A CERTAIN SMILE AND A CERTAIN SADNESS (LP) | 15 |
| 67 | Verve SVLP 9137 | BEACH SAMBA (LP) | 20 |
| 68 | Verve 2317 021 | WINDY (LP) | 15 |
| 69 | Verve (S)VLP 9242 | I HAVEN'T GOT ANYTHING BETTER TO DO (LP) | 15 |
| 72 | C.T.I. CTL 1 | GILBERTO WITH TURRENTINE (LP, with Stanley Turrentine) | 15 |

*(see also Stan Getz)*

## JOAO GILBERTO
| | | | |
|---|---|---|---|
| 61 | Parlophone PMC 1248 | BOSSA-FINADO (LP) | 15 |

*(see also Stan Getz)*

## GILCHRIST
| | | | |
|---|---|---|---|
| 75 | Route RT 03 | Guardian In The Sky/Heading For The Grave | 7 |

## GILDED CAGE
| | | | |
|---|---|---|---|
| 69 | Tepee TPR 1003 | Long Long Road (For The Broken Heart)/Baby Grumpling | 40 |

*(see also She Trinity)*

## COSMO GILE
| | | | |
|---|---|---|---|
| 60 | Top Rank JAR 410 | Bambina D'Amsterdam/Tintarella Di Luna | 6 |

## GILES, GILES & FRIPP
| | | | |
|---|---|---|---|
| 68 | Deram DM 188 | One In A Million/Newly-Weds | 100 |
| 68 | Deram DM 210 | Thursday Morning/Elephant Song | 80 |
| 68 | Deram DML 1022 | THE CHEERFUL INSANITY OF GILES, GILES AND FRIPP (LP, mono) | 150 |
| 68 | Deram SML 1022 | THE CHEERFUL INSANITY OF GILES, GILES AND FRIPP (LP, stereo) | 150 |
| 70 | Deram SPA 423 | THE CHEERFUL INSANITY OF GILES, GILES AND FRIPP (LP, stereo reissue) | 40 |

*(see also Brain, Trendsetters Ltd, League Of Gentlemen, King Crimson, Fripp & Eno, McDonald & Giles)*

## GILGAMESH
| | | | |
|---|---|---|---|
| 75 | Caroline CA 2007 | GILGAMESH (LP) | 30 |

*(see also Hugh Hopper, Colosseum, Whitesnake)*

## TERRY GILKYSON & EASY RIDERS

| | | | |
|---|---|---|---|
| 58 | Philips JK 1007 | Marianne/Goodbye Chaquita (jukebox issue) | 18 |
| 60 | Fontana TFE 17326 | STROLLING BLUES (EP) | 12 |
| 60 | Fontana TFE 17327 | LONESOME RIDER (EP) | 10 |
| 61 | London RER 1333 | ROLLIN' (EP) | 12 |
| 53 | Brunswick LA 8618 | GOLDEN MINUTES OF FOLK MUSIC (10" LP) | 25 |
| 61 | London HA-R 2301 | ROLLIN' (LP, also stereo SAH-R 6111) | 15 |
| 61 | London HA-R 2323 | REMEMBER THE ALAMO (LP, as Easyriders Including Terry Gilkyson) | 15 |

(see also Easy Riders)

## JONATHAN GILL

| | | | |
|---|---|---|---|
| 73 | Pye 7N 45206 | I've Got To Please You/Isandulu Road | 15 |

## (IAN) GILLAN (BAND)

| | | | |
|---|---|---|---|
| 78 | Island R 553-B | Twin Exhausted (live)/Smoke On The Water (live)/ILLUSION: Madonna Blue/ Revolutionary (12", promo only, as Ian Gillan Band) | 20 |
| 78 | Island WIP 6423 | Mad Elaine/Mercury High (as Ian Gillan Band, company sleeve) | 8 |
| 79 | Acrobat BAT 1212 | She Tears Me Down/Puget Sound/Vengeance/Mr. Universe (12", stickered card sleeve, promo only) | 20 |
| 79 | Acrobat BAT 12 | Vengeance/Smoke On The Water (p/s) | 5 |
| 80 | Virgin VS 377 | Trouble/Your Sister's On My List//Mr. Universe (live)/Vengeance (live)/Smoke On The Water (live) (7" double pack, gatefold) | 5 |
| 81 | Lyntone LYN 10599 | Higher And Higher/Spanish Guitar (same tracks both sides, hard vinyl test pressing, handwritten white labels) | 35 |
| 76 | Polydor/Oyster 2490 136 | CHILD IN TIME (LP, gatefold sleeve, as Ian Gillan Band) | 15 |
| 77 | Island ILPS 9511DJ | IAN GILLAN BAND SAMPLER (LP, 1-sided promo for "Scarabus", company sleeve) | 20 |
| 77 | Island ILPS 59511 | SCARABUS (LP, as Ian Gillan Band) | 15 |
| 78 | Island ILPS 9545 | LIVE AT THE BUDO-KAN (LP, unissued) | 0 |
| 79 | Acrobat ACRO 3 | MR UNIVERSE (LP, inner) | 15 |
| 80 | Virgin V 2171 | GLORY ROAD (LP, with bonus LP "For Gillan Fans Only" [VDJ 32], stickered, embossed sleeve & inner sleeves) | 15 |
| 82 | Virgin VP 2236 | MAGIC (LP, picture disc) | 15 |
| 81 | Virgin V2196 | FUTURE SHOCK (LP, gatefold sleeve, booklet) | 15 |
| 12 | Virgin VIN 180 LP P048 | FUTURE SHOCK (2-LP, reissue, hardback book edition) | 18 |
| 12 | Virgin VIN 180 LP P 055 | DOUBLE TROUBLE (2-LP, reissue, hardback book edition) | 18 |

(see also Episode Six, Deep Purple, Ray Fenwick, Split Knee Loons, John McCoy, Johnny Gustafson, Bernie Tormé, Thunderstick, Jerusalem, Quatermass, Colin Towns, White Spirit, Zzebra)

## DANA GILLESPIE

| | | | |
|---|---|---|---|
| 65 | Pye 7N 15872 | Donna Donna/It's No Use Saying If | 15 |
| 65 | Pye 7N 15962 | Thank You Boy/You're A Heartbreak Man | 15 |
| 67 | Pye 7N 17280 | Pay You Back With Interest/Adam Can You Beat That | 8 |
| 68 | Decca F 12847 | You Just Gotta Know My Mind/He Loves Me, He Loves Me Not | 60 |
| 74 | RCA RCA 0211 | Weren't Born A Man/All Gone | 5 |
| 74 | RCA RCA 2466 | Andy Warhol/Dizzy Heights | 8 |
| 75 | RCA RCA 2489 | Really Love That Man/Hold Me Gently | 5 |
| 69 | Decca LK 5012 | BOX OF SURPRISES (LP, mono) | 100 |
| 69 | Decca SLK 5012 | BOX OF SURPRISES (LP, stereo) | 150 |
| 73 | RCA APL1 0354 | WEREN'T BORN A MAN (LP) | 20 |
| 74 | RCA APL1 0682 | AIN'T GONNA PLAY NO SECOND FIDDLE (LP, gatefold sleeve) | 15 |

(see also David Bowie)

## DIZZY GILLESPIE & CHARLIE PARKER

| | | | |
|---|---|---|---|
| 61 | Vogue LAE 12252 | DIZ 'N BIRD IN CONCERT (LP) | 15 |

(see also Charlie Parker)

## DOBIE GILLIS

| | | | |
|---|---|---|---|
| 68 | United Artists UP 2212 | How Peculiar/I Wish I Was Harry | 8 |

## JIMMY GILMER & FIREBALLS

| | | | |
|---|---|---|---|
| 62 | London HLD 9632 | I'm Gonna Go Walkin'/Born To Be With You (as Chimmy Gilmer) | 15 |
| 64 | London HA-D/SH-D 8150 | SUGAR SHACK (LP) | 20 |
| 65 | Dot DLP 3577 | BUDDY'S BUDDY - BUDDY HOLLY SONGS BY JIMMY GILMER (LP) | 20 |

(see also Fireballs, Jim & Monica)

## DAVID GILMOUR

| | | | |
|---|---|---|---|
| 78 | Harvest HAR 5167 | There's No Way Out Of Here/Deafinitely (no p/s) | 7 |
| 84 | Harvest 12HAR 5226 | Blue Light (LP Version)/Cruise (12", p/s) | 10 |
| 84 | Harvest HAR 5229 | Love On The Air/Let's Get Metaphysical (p/s) | 5 |
| 84 | Harvest HARP 5229 | Love On The Air/Let's Get Metaphysical (shaped picture disc) | 12 |
| 06 | EMI 696 | Smile/Island Jam (clear vinyl) | 5 |
| 06 | EMI EMIDJ 733 | Take a Breath (1-sided clear vinyl promo) | 100 |
| 06 | EMI EM 717. 0946 384878 7 6 | Arnold Layne (vocal by David Bowie)/Arnold Layne (vocal by Richard Wright)//Dark Globe (p/s) | 10 |
| 78 | Harvest SHVL 817 | DAVID GILMOUR (LP, gatefold) | 15 |
| 06 | EMI 094635569513 | ON AN ISLAND (LP, gatefold sleeve) | 80 |

(see also Pink Floyd, Joker's Wild, Unicorn)

## BILL GILONIS & TIM HODGKINSON

| | | | |
|---|---|---|---|
| 79 | Woof WOOF 001 | I DO I DO I DON'T I DON'T (EP, silkscreened sleeve) | 12 |

## JAMES GILREATH

| | | | |
|---|---|---|---|
| 63 | Pye International 7N 25190 | Little Band Of Gold/I'll Walk With You | 10 |
| 63 | Pye International 7N 25213 | Lollipops, Lace And Lipstick/Mean Ole River | 12 |

## GORDON GILTRAP (BAND)

| | | | |
|---|---|---|---|
| 77 | Electric WOT 11 | Lucifer's Cage/The Echoing Green (demos only) | 10 |
| 78 | Electric WOT 19 | Heartsong/The Deserter (demos only) | 10 |
| 78 | Electric WOT 29 | Fear Of The Dark/Catwalks Blues/Inner Dream (12" picture disc) | 8 |
| 95 | Munchkin MRC 1 | THE BROTHERHOOD SUITE (cassette, 300 only) | 30 |

# GIMMICKS

| 73 | Philips 6006 344 | No Way Of Knowing/I See A Road | 15 |
| 68 | Transatlantic TRA 175 | GORDON GILTRAP (LP, lilac label with 't' logo) | 50 |
| 69 | Transatlantic TRA 202 | PORTRAIT (LP) | 45 |
| 71 | MCA MKPS 2020 | A TESTAMENT OF TIME (LP, red/pink 'dogbone' label) | 40 |
| 73 | Philips 6308 175 | GILTRAP (LP, with lyric insert, blue/silver label) | 20 |

(see also Accolade, Pauline Filby, Catherine Andrews)

## GIMMICKS
| 70 | Decca Eclipse ECS-R 2054 | BRAZILIAN SAMBA (LP) | 30 |

## W. GIMMICS
| 65 | Polydor EPH 27 125 | HOT RODS (EP, manufactured in Europe) | 60 |

## GIMMIX
| 79 | Elektra K 12377 | Too Much/Testing Testing 1 2 3 | 15 |

## GINGER JUG BAND
| 70s | GJB 001 | GINGER JUG BAND (LP, private pressing) | 25 |

## GINGER ALE
| 70 | Famous FAM 102 | In The Sand/Get Off My Life Woman | 8 |

## GINGERBREAD (1)
| 69 | B&C CB 113 | How Are You/Easy Girl | 6 |

## GINGERBREAD (2)
| 71 | Pye 7N 45054 | Pollution/Moody Trudy | 8 |

## GINGER SNAPS
| 65 | RCA RCA 1483 | The Sh Down Down Song/I've Got Faith In Him | 20 |

## GINGRINI
| 73 | Harry J. HJ 6647 | Zion 'Iah/Zion 'Iah (Version) | 6 |

## GINHOUSE
| 71 | Charisma CAS 1031 | GINHOUSE (LP, gatefold sleeve) | 200 |

(see also Kestrel. Mouse, Sammy)

## GINNUNGAGAP
| 06 | Aurora Borealis ABX 007 | REMEINDRE (LP, clear folder cover, white vinyl) | 15 |

## GINO & GINA
| 58 | Mercury 7MT 230 | Pretty Baby/Love's A Carousel | 20 |

## ALLEN GINSBERG
| 60s | Cape Goliard | Wales: A Visitation (single issued with book of same title) | 15 |
| 65 | Better Books (no cat. no.) | ALLEN GINSBERG READING AT BETTER BOOKS (LP) | 20 |
| 65 | Love Books Ltd. LB 0001 | ALLEN GINSBERG, LAURENCE FERLINGHETTI, GREGORY CORSO & ANDREI VOZNESENSKY READING AT THE ARCHITECTURAL ASSOCIATION (LP) | 20 |
| 68 | Transatlantic TRA 192 | GINSBERG'S THING (LP) | 15 |

(see also Ginsbergs)

## GINSBERGS
| 67 | Saga Psyche PSY 3002 | THE GINSBERGS AT THE ICA (LP) | 15 |

(see also Allen Ginsberg)

## GINSENG SPARTA
| 83 | Guardian GRC 210 | Forbidden Fruit/Lazy Hazy Day | 25 |

## GINTY
| 80 | Wild Dog DOG 25 | I Am The Walrus/A Little Understanding/Say You Don't Mind | 10 |

## MARCELLO GIOMBINI
| 70 | United Artists UP 35110 | Sabata - Main Title/Banjo Arrives | 10 |

## GIORGIO
| 66 | Page One POF 003 | Full Stop/Believe Me | 6 |
| 67 | Page One POF 028 | How Much Longer Must I Wait/Bla Bla Diddly | 12 |
| 69 | MCA MCA 1094 | Happy Birthday/Looky Looky | 5 |
| 69 | MCA 5025 | Moody Trudy/Stop | 20 |
| 71 | Parlophone R 5935 | Son Of My Father/I'm Free Now | 10 |
| 71 | A&M AMS 822 | Underdog/Watch Yourself | 6 |

(see also Giorgio Moroder, Giorgio & Marco's Men)

## GIORGIO & MARCO'S MEN
| 66 | Polydor 56101 | Run Run/Girl Without A Heart | 7 |
| 68 | Electratone EP 1003 | Baby I Need You/Maureen | 70 |

## GIPSY LOVE
| 72 | BASF BAP 5026 | GIPSY LOVE (LP) | 20 |

## CHUCK GIRARD
| 75 | Myrrh MYR 1025 | CHUCK GIRARD (LP) | 15 |
| 70s | Myrrh MYR 1065 | WRITTEN ON THE WIND (LP) | 15 |
| 70s | myrrh MYR 1089 | THE STAND (LP) | 15 |

## GIRL TALK (U.S.)
| 04 | Apostles 12AP03 | STOP CLEVELAND HATE EP (12") | 12 |

## GIRL
| 79 | Jet JET 159 | My Number/My Number (Version) (clear vinyl, PVC sleeve, with 2 stickers) | 5 |
| 80 | Jet 176 | Hollywood Tease/My Number | 8 |

(see also Def Leppard, Bernie Torme)

## GIRL GUIDED MISSILES
| 79 | Seandee CND 01 | Desperate Men/Fully Qualified Robot (p/s, 1000 only) | 80 |

## GIRL OF MY BEST FRIEND
| 89 | Ambition AMB 003 | Warm Around You/Seasons (p/s) | 8 |

## GIRL BAND
| 15 | Rough Trade RTRADS 763 | Pears For Lunch (7", 1-side etched, numbered) | 10 |

Rare Record Price Guide 2018        518

| | | | |
|---|---|---|---|
| 15 | Rough Trade RTRADST 736 | THE EARLY YEARS (12", 500 only) | 18 |
| 15 | Rough Trade RTRADLP770 | HOLDING HANDS WITH JAMIE (LP, yellow vinyl with booklet, signed) | 30 |
| 15 | Rough Trade RTRADLP770 | HOLDING HANDS WITH JAMIE (LP, yellow vinyl with booklet, unsigned) | 30 |

**GIRLFRIENDS**

| | | | |
|---|---|---|---|
| 63 | Colpix PX 712 | Jimmy Boy/For My Sake (DJ Copy) | 125 |
| 63 | Colpix PX 712 | Jimmy Boy/For My Sake | 60 |

**GIRLIE**

| | | | |
|---|---|---|---|
| 69 | Treasure Isle TI 7053 | Boss Cocky/LOVE SHOCKS: Musical True | 100 |
| 69 | Bullet BU 400 | Madame Straggae/LAUREL AITKEN: Stupid Married Man | 20 |
| 69 | Duke DU 42 | African Meeting (as Girlie & Junior)/JOSH: Higher And Higher | 15 |
| 70 | Joe JRS 7 | Small Change/Mind Your Business (as Girlie & Joe [Mansano]) | 15 |
| 70 | Ackee ACK 124 | Decimilization/Decimilization Version (as Girlie & Paul) | 15 |

*(see also Laurel Aitken & Girlie, Madame Dracula)*

**GIRLS**

| | | | |
|---|---|---|---|
| 09 | Fantasy Trashcan FANTASY 001 | Laura/Oh Boy (p/s, 500 only) | 5 |
| 09 | Fantasy Trashcan FANTASY 002 | Lust For Life/Life In San Francisco (p/s, 500 only) | 7 |
| 09 | Fantasy Trashcan FANTASY 004 | Hellhole Ratrace/Solitude (10" p/s) | 10 |

**GIRLS ALOUD**

| | | | |
|---|---|---|---|
| 03 | Polydor JUMP 2 | Jump (Almighty Vocal Mix)/Jump/Girls Allowed (Almighty Vocal Mix)/Jump (Almighty Dub Mix) (12" pink glitter promo) | 20 |
| 03 | Polydor NGA 2 | No Good Advice - Doublefunk Vocal Mix/Doublefunk Dub Mix/Dreadzone Vocal/Clean Version (12" promo, p/s) | 12 |
| 05 | Polydor 9874045 | Long Hot Summer/Long Hot Summer - Tony Lamezma Rides Again/Jump - Almighty Vocal Mix) (12", p/s) | 15 |
| 08 | Fascination/Polydor 1788935 | The Promise/Girl Overboard (7" picture disc, numbered) | 10 |
| 04 | Polydor WHATGA 3 | WHAT WILL THE NEIGHBOURS SAY? (LP, promo, pink vinyl) | 20 |

**GIRLS AT OUR BEST**

| | | | |
|---|---|---|---|
| 80 | Record Records RR 001 | Getting Nowhere Fast/Warm Girls (p/s) | 10 |
| 81 | Record Records RR 002 | Politics/It's Fashion (p/s) | 8 |
| 81 | Happy Birthday UR 4 | Go For Gold/I'm Beautiful Now (p/s) | 8 |
| 81 | Happy Birthday UR 6 | Fast Boyfriends/This Train (p/s) | 8 |
| 81 | Happy Birthday RULP 1 | PLEASURE (LP, with lyric insert, 1st 10,000 with free 'pleasure bag' with 2 postcards, sticker & stencil) | 20 |

**GIRLSCHOOL**

| | | | |
|---|---|---|---|
| 79 | City NIK 6 | Take It All Away/It Could Be Better (p/s, red vinyl, pink p/s, b&w front photo) | 7 |
| 79 | City NIK 6 | Take It All Away/It Could Be Better (p/s, black vinyl, orange p/s) | 5 |
| 79 | Mulligan LUNS 723 | Take It All Away/It Could Be Better (Irish version, no p/s, red vinyl) | 8 |
| 88 | GWR GWR14 | Head Over Heals/Action (unissued) | 10 |
| 82 | Bronze BRO 144 | WILDLIFE (EP, p/s. red vinyl) | 8 |
| 81 | Bronze BRON 534 | HIT AND RUN (LP, red vinyl) | 20 |

*(see also Motorhead, Killjoys, Framed)*

**GIRL SKWADD**

| | | | |
|---|---|---|---|
| 79 | Ariola Hansa AHA | Sweet Talk/Love Condition (p/s) | 5 |

**GIRL TALK (U.K.)**

| | | | |
|---|---|---|---|
| 84 | Innervision IVST 4 | Can The Rhythm (mixes) (12", p/s) | 12 |

**GIST**

| | | | |
|---|---|---|---|
| 81 | Rough Trade RT 58 | This Is Love/Yanks (p/s) | 8 |
| 81 | Rough Trade RT 85 | Love At First Sight/Light Aircraft (p/s) | 7 |
| 83 | Rough Trade RT 125 | Fool For A Valentine/Fool For A Version (p/s) | 7 |
| 83 | Rough Trade ROUGH 25 | EMBRACE THE HERD (LP) | 15 |

**GITS**

| | | | |
|---|---|---|---|
| 89 | Stig STIG 0019 | Too Many People/Happy Song (p/s) | 40 |

**GITTE**

| | | | |
|---|---|---|---|
| 64 | Columbia DB 7440 | The Heart That You Break (May Be Your Own)/Seems Just Like Old Times | 10 |

**JIMMY GIUFFRE**

| | | | |
|---|---|---|---|
| 55 | Capitol LC 6699 | JIMMY GIUFFRE (10" LP) | 20 |
| 57 | London Jazz LTZK 15059 | THE JIMMY GIUFFRE CLARINET (LP) | 15 |
| 58 | London Jazz LTZK 15130 | JIMMY GIUFFRE (LP) | 20 |
| 58 | London Jazz LTZK 15137 | TRAV'LIN' LIGHT (LP) | 20 |
| 58 | London LTZ-K 15130 | JIMMY GIUFFRE 3 (LP) | 25 |

*(see also Shelly Manne)*

**GIZMO**

| | | | |
|---|---|---|---|
| 75 | President PT 443 | Just Like Velvet/Jesus Help Me Sleep | 8 |

**GLADDY (ANDERSON) & FOLLOWERS**

| | | | |
|---|---|---|---|
| 69 | Blue Cat BS 172 | Judas/The World Come To An End | 40 |

*(see also Stranger & Glady)*

**GLADDY (ANDERSON) & STRANGER (COLE)**

| | | | |
|---|---|---|---|
| 73 | Pama PM 872 | Dedicated To Illiteracy/G.G. ALLSTARS: Dub | 8 |

*(see also Gladstone Anderson, Stranger Cole, Stranger & Glady)*

**GLADE**

| | | | |
|---|---|---|---|
| 72 | Glade 1 | Touching The Sky/Evil | 80 |

**GLADIATORS (1)**

| | | | |
|---|---|---|---|
| 63 | HMV POP 1134 | Bleak House/Tovaritch | 25 |

*(see also Nero & Gladiators)*

## GLADIATORS (2)

MINT VALUE £

| | | | |
|---|---|---|---|
| 68 | Direction 58-3854 | Girl Don't Make Me Wait/Can't Get Away From Heartbreak | 18 |
| 69 | Direction 58-4308 | Waiting On The Shores Of Nowhere/I'll Always Love You | 18 |
| 69 | Direction 58-4507 | As Long As I Live/Everything | 10 |
| 69 | Direction 58-4660 | Twelfth Of Never/Lovin' My Baby Back Home | 8 |

## GLADIATORS (JAMAICA)

| | | | |
|---|---|---|---|
| 69 | Studio One SO 2072 | Hello Carol/RICHARD ACE: More Reggae | 50 |
| 69 | Studio One SO 2086 | Kicks/Games People Play | 45 |
| 69 | Doctor Bird DB 1114 | The Train Is Coming/Feeling So Fine | 30 |
| 69 | Bamboo BAM 7 | Anywhere/SOUND DIMENSION: Baby Face | 30 |
| 70 | Rock Steady Rev. REVR 12 | Unusual Reggae/Andue | 20 |
| 70 | Duke DU 58 | My Girl (actually by Glen Adams)/You Were To Be | 20 |
| 72 | Ackee ACK 149 | Sonia/SOUND DIMENSION: Solas | 20 |
| 77 | Virgin VS 19312 | Pocket Money/Money Version Disco Mix/Evil Doers/Disco Mix (12") | 20 |
| 76 | Virgin V2062 | TRENCHTOWN MIX UP (LP) | 20 |
| 78 | Virgin Frontline FL 1002 | PROVERBIAL REGGAE (LP) | 20 |
| 78 | Virgin Frontline FL 1035 | NATURALITY (LP) | 25 |
| 79 | Virgin Frontline FL 1048 | SWEET SO TILL (LP) | 18 |
| 81 | Virgin VX 1003 | VITAL SELECTION (LP) | 18 |
| 82 | Nighthawk NIGHTHAWK | SYMBOL OF REALITY (LP) | 15 |

## GLADIOLAS

| | | | |
|---|---|---|---|
| 57 | London HLO 8435 | Little Darlin'/Sweetheart, Please Don't Go | 20 |
| 57 | London HLO 8435 | Little Darlin'/Sweetheart, Please Don't Go (78 rpm) | 100 |

*(see also Maurice Williams & Zodiacs)* .................. 25

## GLASGOW

| | | | |
|---|---|---|---|
| 84 | Neat NEAT 40 | Stranded/Heat Of The Night (p/s) | 15 |
| 84 | Clydebank CLY 001 | GLASGOW'S MILES BETTER (12" EP) | 12 |

## LUD GLASKIN

| | | | |
|---|---|---|---|
| 62 | UPC 3428 | To My Good Friend Jack Cotton, the 'Allo Twist (1-sided private pressing) | 25 |

## GLASS

| | | | |
|---|---|---|---|
| 82 | Glass GLASS1 | New Colours/Sweet Entropy (p/s) | 22 |

## GLASS MUSEUM

| | | | |
|---|---|---|---|
| 80 | Fflang NAFF 1 | Free Kings/Alternative Take | 8 |
| 82 | RGM RGM 001 | Going Towards Pleasure/You're Changing | 5 |

## PHILIP GLASS

| | | | |
|---|---|---|---|
| 70s | Chatham Square LP 1001/2 | MUSIC WITH CHANGING PARTS (2-LP) | 25 |
| 70s | Chatham Square LP 1003 | MUSIC IN FIFTHS/MUSIC IN A SIMILAR MOTION (LP) | 20 |
| 70s | Folkways FTS 33902 | TWO PAGES (LP) | 20 |
| 76 | Caroline CA 2010 | MUSIC IN 12 (PARTS 1 & 2) (LP, 1st pressing in matt textured sleeve) | 25 |
| 78 | Shandar SHAN 83515 | SOLO MUSIC (LP) | 15 |
| 79 | CBS M4 38875 | EINSTEIN ON THE BEACH (4-LP box set) | 25 |
| 82 | CBS 73640 | GLASSWORKS (LP) | 15 |
| 83 | Island ISTA 4 | KOYAANISQATSI (LP, soundtrack) | 20 |
| 85 | CBS 13M39672 | SATYAGRAHA (3-LP box set, booklet) | 20 |
| 86 | CBS M342457 | AKHNATEN (3-LP box set, booklet) | 20 |

*(see also Ray Manzarek)*

## GLASS HARP

| | | | |
|---|---|---|---|
| 72 | MCA MUPS 431 | GLASS HARP (LP) | 25 |
| 72 | MCA MUPS 449 | SYNERGY (LP) | 22 |

## GLASS HOUSE

| | | | |
|---|---|---|---|
| 70 | Invictus INV 506 | Stealing Moments From Another Woman's Life/If It Ain't Love, It Don't Matter | 8 |
| 71 | Invictus INV 510 | I Can't Be You/He's In My Life | 8 |

## GLASS MENAGERIE

| | | | |
|---|---|---|---|
| 68 | Pye 7N 17518 | She's A Rainbow/But That's When I Start To Love Her | 12 |
| 68 | Pye 7N 17568 | You Didn't Have To Be So Nice/Let's All Run To The Sun | 10 |
| 68 | Pye 7N 17615 | Frederick Jordan/I Said Goodbye To Me | 240 |
| 69 | Polydor 56318 | Have You Forgotten Who You Are/Do You Ever Think? | 10 |
| 69 | Polydor 56341 | Do My Thing Myself/Watching The World Pass By | 25 |

*(see also Paladin, Toe-Fat)*

## GLASS OPENING

| | | | |
|---|---|---|---|
| 68 | Plexium P 1236 | Silver Bells And Cockle Shells/Does It Really Matter | 250 |

## GLASS TORPEDOES

| | | | |
|---|---|---|---|
| 79 | Teen Beat TBR 1 | SOMEONE DIFFERENT EP | 6 |

## GLASVEGAS

| | | | |
|---|---|---|---|
| 04 | Rebelstance J 21091979 | I'm Gonna Get Stabbed/Ina Lvs Rab (CD-R, self release with lyric inner) | 80 |
| 06 | Waks WAKS 0035 | Go Square Go/Legs 'N' Show (400 only, with lyric insert) | 50 |
| 07 | Sane Man SAN 001 | Daddy's Gone/Flowers And Football Tops (p/s, 1,000 only, numbered) | 20 |
| 08 | Sane Man SAN 002 | It's My Own Cheating Heart That Makes Me Cry/Be My Baby (2,000 only) | 6 |
| 11 | Columbia GOWOW23 | Euphoria, Take My Hand/Georgia, Walk With Me | 8 |
| 08 | Columbia GOWOW012 | GLASVEGAS (LP) | 20 |

## GLAXO BABIES

| | | | |
|---|---|---|---|
| 79 | Heartbeat PULSE 5 | Christine Keeler/Nova Bossanova (p/s) | 10 |
| 79 | Heartbeat PULSE 3 | THIS IS YOUR LIFE (12" EP) | 15 |
| 80 | Cherry Red PULSE 8 | Shake (The Foundations)/She Went To Pieces (Live 28-03-79) | 7 |
| 80 | Rough Trade Y6 | LIMITED ENTERTAINMENT EP | 6 |
| 80 | Heartbeat HBM 3 | PUT ME ON THE GUEST LIST (LP) | 25 |
| 80 | Heartbeat HB 2 | NINE MONTHS TO THE DISCO (LP) | 20 |

**GLEN (BROWN) & LLOYD (ROBINSON)**
| | | | |
|---|---|---|---|
| 66 | Ska Beat JB 250 | Live And Let Others Live/Too Late | 45 |
| 67 | Doctor Bird DB 1099 | Feel Good Now/What You've Got (credited as Lloyd Glen) | 45 |

**GLENCOE**
| | | | |
|---|---|---|---|
| 72 | Epic EPC 8383 | Look Me In The Eye/Telephonia | 6 |
| 72 | Epic EPC 65207 | GLENCOE (LP) | 25 |
| 73 | Epic EPC 65717 | SPIRIT OF GLENCOE (LP) | 15 |

(see also Hopscotch, Five Day Rain, Greatest Show On Earth, Loving Awareness)

**GLENDALES**
| | | | |
|---|---|---|---|
| 79 | Pennine PS 143 | Morgan/Too Late To Change Your Mind/Toymaker (500 only, no p/s) | 6 |

**DARRELL GLENN**
| | | | |
|---|---|---|---|
| 54 | HMV 7MC 23 | In The Chapel In The Moonlight/Once And Only Once (export issue) | 8 |

**GLIDE**
| | | | |
|---|---|---|---|
| 95 | Ochre OCH 003 | EXCERPTS FROM A SPACE AGE FREAK OUT (Part 1) (orange vinyl, p/s) | 5 |
| 97 | Enraptured RAPT 4512 | Glide (Yosum Remix)/Grind Theme 3 (wraparound p/s) | 5 |

(see also Echo & Bunnymen)

**GLITTERHOUSE**
| | | | |
|---|---|---|---|
| 68 | Stateside SS 2129 | Barbarella/BOB CREWE: An Angel Is Love | 20 |
| 68 | Stateside SS 2129 | Barbarella/Love Drags Me Down (different B-side) | 18 |

**GLITTERS**
| | | | |
|---|---|---|---|
| 56 | Gala GSP 810 | Red River Rock/PROMINEERS: Poison Ivy | 8 |

**GLOBAL COMMUNICATIONS**
| | | | |
|---|---|---|---|
| 93 | Evolution EVO 04 | KEONGAKU EP (12", 4-track, plain sleeve) | 25 |
| 94 | Dedicated DEDLP 014L | 76: 14 (2-LP, gatefold sleeve with bonus 12" [DEDLP 0145]) | 30 |
| 94 | Dedicated DEDLP 014 | 76: 14 (2-LP, gatefold sleeve) | 25 |
| 96 | Dedicated DED 21LP | REMOTION - THE GLOBAL COMMUNICATIONS REMIX ALBUM (2-LP) | 20 |

(see also Mystic Institue, Link, Reload, Reload & E621, Chaos & Julia Set, Jedi Knights)

**GLOBAL METHOD**
| | | | |
|---|---|---|---|
| 92 | Not On Label GM1 | VIBE TRIBE (EP) | 110 |

**GLOBAL VILLAGE TRUCKING COMPANY**
| | | | |
|---|---|---|---|
| 76 | Caroline C 1516 | GLOBAL VILLAGE TRUCKING COMPANY (LP, with lyric insert, b/s & red label, twins logo) | 20 |

(see also Byzantium, Man)

**GLOBE SHOW**
| | | | |
|---|---|---|---|
| 69 | Page One POF 128 | Yes Or No/Gettin' On Back | 30 |

(see also Chris Shakespeare Globe Show)

**GLOBE TROTTERS**
| | | | |
|---|---|---|---|
| 54 | Parlophone CMSP 18 | At Sundown/My Gal Sal (export issue) | 10 |
| 54 | Parlophone GEP 8528 | SATURDAY NIGHT HOP (EP) | 15 |

**GLOBETROTTERS**
| | | | |
|---|---|---|---|
| 70 | RCA RCA 2017 | Gravy/Cheer Me Up | 10 |
| 71 | RCA SF 8158 | THE GLOBETROTTERS (LP) | 15 |

**GLOOMYS**
| | | | |
|---|---|---|---|
| 68 | Columbia DB 8391 | Daybreak/Queen And King | 15 |
| 71 | DJM DJS 240 | I'm A Bum/Let Me Dream | 10 |

**GLORIA**
| | | | |
|---|---|---|---|
| 69 | Columbia DB 8568 | The Last Seven Days/Merry Dance | 15 |

**GLORIA MUNDI**
| | | | |
|---|---|---|---|
| 78 | RCA PB 5068 | Fight Back/Do It (p/s) | 5 |
| 78 | RCA PB 5118 | Glory To The World/Nothing To Say (p/s) | 8 |
| 79 | RCA PB 5169 | YY?/Do You Believe (no p/s) | 7 |
| 79 | RCA PB 5193 | Dangerous To Dream/Temporary Hell Part 2 (no p/s) | 7 |
| 78 | RCA PL2 5157 | I INDIVIDUAL (LP, with inner sleeve) | 15 |
| 79 | RCA PL2 5244 | THE WORD IS OUT (LP, with lyric inner) | 15 |

**GLORIAS ALLSTARS**
| | | | |
|---|---|---|---|
| 70 | Camel CA 48 | Jumping Dick/News Room | 20 |

**GLORIES**
| | | | |
|---|---|---|---|
| 67 | CBS 2786 | I Stand Accused (Of Loving You)/Wish They Could Write A Song | 15 |
| 67 | CBS 2786 | I Stand Accused (Of Loving You)/Wish They Could Write A Song (DJ Copy) | 20 |
| 67 | Direction 58-3084 | (I Love You Babe But) Give Me My Freedom/Security | 20 |
| 68 | Direction 58-3300 | Sing Me A Love Song/Oh Baby That's Love | 15 |
| 68 | Direction 58-3646 | My Sweet Sweet Baby/Stand By (I'm Comin' Home) | 10 |

**GLORY HUNTER**
| | | | |
|---|---|---|---|
| 79 | Rock Hard CPS 027 | Thoughts Of Destiny/At The Crossroads (no p/s) | 800 |

**GLORY LANDERS**
| | | | |
|---|---|---|---|
| 69 | IBA SECC 1203 | VOLUME 1 (LP) | 15 |

**GLOVE**
| | | | |
|---|---|---|---|
| 83 | Wonderland SHE 3 | Like An Animal/Mouth To Mouth (p/s, some sleeves with centre holes) | 5 |
| 83 | Wonderland SHE 5 | Punish Me With Kisses/The Tightrope (p/s) | 8 |
| 83 | Wonderland SHELP 2 | BLUE SUNSHINE (LP, mispressing with double-printed sleeve) | 20 |

(see also Cure, Siouxsie & Banshees)

**ROGER GLOVER (& GUESTS)**
| | | | |
|---|---|---|---|
| 74 | Purple PUR 125 | Love Is All/Old Blind Mole/Magician Moth | 10 |
| 84 | Safari SAF EP 1 | Love Is All/Sitting In A dream/Little Chalk Blue/Homeward | 5 |
| 84 | Polydor POSP 678 | The Mask/So Remote (p/s, solo) | 8 |
| 74 | Purple TPSA 7514 | THE BUTTERFLY BALL (AND THE GRASSHOPPER'S FEAST) (LP, g/fold sleeve) | 15 |
| 84 | Polydor POLD 5139 | THE MASK (LP, solo, with insert) | 15 |

# Jeremy GLUCK

MINT VALUE £

(see also [Sheila Carter &] Episode [Six], Deep Purple, Elf, Eddie Hardin, Whitesnake, Rainbow, Glenn Hughes, John Lawton, Wizard's Convention, Marlon, Green Bullfrog, David Coverdale, Dio)

## JEREMY GLUCK
| | | | |
|---|---|---|---|
| 86 | Flicknife SHARP 037 | I KNEW BUFFALO BILL (LP) | 15 |

(see also Barracudas)

## G MEN
| | | | |
|---|---|---|---|
| 82 | Cro Magnon | G-MEN (EP, 1000 only) | 20 |

(see also Blue Cats, Beltane fire)

## GMT
| | | | |
|---|---|---|---|
| 91 | Mausoleum BONE 12-83102 | One By One (12", p/s) | 10 |

## GNAC
| | | | |
|---|---|---|---|
| 98 | Earworm WORM 29 | The Moustache/Armchair Thriller (p/s, black vinyl) | 6 |

## GNANK
| | | | |
|---|---|---|---|
| 99 | Gnank GNANK 01 | Gnank Gnank/Oi, Gnank (p/s) | 8 |

## GNASHER
| | | | |
|---|---|---|---|
| 74 | Purple PUR 119 | Medina Road/Easy Meat | 10 |

## GNIDROLOG
| | | | |
|---|---|---|---|
| 72 | RCA SF 8261 | IN SPITE OF HARRY'S TOE-NAIL (LP, gatefold sleeve, orange label) | 200 |
| 72 | RCA SF 8322 | LADY LAKE (LP, with lyric insert) | 350 |
| 72 | RCA SF 8322 | LADY LAKE (LP, without lyric insert) | 250 |

(see also Pork Dukes, Steeleye Span)

## GNOMES OF ZURICH
| | | | |
|---|---|---|---|
| 66 | Planet PLF 121 | Please Mr Sun/I'm Coming Down With The Blues (with custom 'Planet' sleeve) | 60 |
| 66 | Planet PLF 121 | Please Mr Sun/I'm Coming Down With The Blues (without custom 'Planet' sleeve) | 30 |
| 67 | CBS 202556 | Hang On Baby/Blues For My Baby | 30 |
| 67 | CBS 2694 | High Hopes/Pretender | 30 |
| 67 | RCA Victor RCA 1606 | Second Fiddle/Publicity Girl | 60 |

## G-NOTES
| | | | |
|---|---|---|---|
| 58 | Oriole CB 1456 | Ronnie (How I Wish He'd Notice Me)/I Would | 20 |

## GOBBLEDEGOOKS
| | | | |
|---|---|---|---|
| 64 | Decca F 12023 | Now And Again/Where Have You Been | 15 |

## GOBBLINZ
| | | | |
|---|---|---|---|
| 79 | Pinnacle P 8454 | London/Women In Love (p/s) | 80 |
| 79 | Bacon SLICE 01 | Love Me Too/All Of This And More (p/s) | 80 |

## GO-BETWEENS
| | | | |
|---|---|---|---|
| 80 | Postcard 80-4 | I Need Two Heads/Stop Before You Say It (brown label & brown co. sleeve) | 25 |
| 80 | Postcard 80-4 | I Need Two Heads/Stop Before You Say It (yellow label & cream co. sleeve) | 18 |
| 80 | Postcard 81-9 | Your Turn My Turn/World Weary (company sleeve) | 12 |
| 82 | Rough Trade RT 108 | Hammer The Hammer/By Chance (p/s) | 10 |
| 83 | Rough Trade RT 114 | Man O'Sand To Girl O'See/This Girl Black Girl (p/s) | 6 |
| 83 | Rough Trade RT 124 | Cattle And Cane/Heaven Says (p/s) | 15 |
| 86 | Beggars Banquet BEG 155 | Spring Rain/The Life At Hand/Little Joe (p/s) | 5 |
| 87 | Beggars Banquet BEG 183D | Right Here/When People Are Dead/A Little Romance//Don't Call Me Gone/ A Little Romance (live) (double pack) | 6 |
| 88 | Beggars Banquet BEG 218B | Streets Of Your Town/Wait Until June (box set) | 8 |
| 81 | Rough Trade ROUGH 45 | SEND ME A LULLABY (LP) | 15 |
| 82 | Rough Trade ROUGH 54 | BEFORE HOLLYWOOD (LP) | 15 |

## GOBLIN
| | | | |
|---|---|---|---|
| 79 | EMI EMC 3222 | SUSPIRIA (LP, soundtrack) | 35 |

## VIC GODARD (& SUBWAY SECT)
| | | | |
|---|---|---|---|
| 80 | Oddball/MCA 585 | Split Up The Money/Out Of Touch (p/s, with Subway Sect) | 5 |
| 81 | Rough Trade RT 068 | Stop That Girl/Instrumentally Scared/Vertical Integration (p/s, w/Subway Sect) | 5 |
| 81 | Club Left CLUB 1 | Stamp Of A Vamp/Hey Now (I'm In Love) (p/s, with Subway Sect) | 5 |
| 85 | El Benelux EL 4 | Holiday Hymn/Nice On The Ice (p/s) | 5 |
| 85 | El Benelux EL 4T | Holiday Hymn/Nice On The Ice/Stop That Girl/Ice On The Volcano/ T.R.O.U.B.L.E. (12", p/s) | 10 |
| 93 | Postcard DUBH 937 | Won't Turn Back/Won't Turn Back (Version) (p/s, 1,000 only) | 5 |
| 80 | Oddball/MCA MCF 3070 | WHAT'S THE MATTER BOY? (LP, with Subway Sect) | 20 |
| 82 | London SH 8549 | SONGS FOR SALE (LP, with Subway Sect) | 18 |
| 85 | Rough Trade ROUGH 56 | A RETROSPECTIVE (LP, inner sleeve, with Subway Sect) | 20 |
| 85 | MCA/EI 01 | HOLIDAY HYMN (LP, 10 test pressings only; abandoned issue of "T.R.O.U.B.L.E.") | 30 |

(see also Subway Sect, Spirit Of The Sect)

## KEITH & DONNA GODCHAUX
| | | | |
|---|---|---|---|
| 75 | Round RX 104 | KEITH & DONNA GODCHAUX (LP) | 18 |

(see also Grateful Dead)

## GEOFF GODDARD
| | | | |
|---|---|---|---|
| 61 | HMV POP 938 | Girl Bride/For Eternity | 50 |
| 62 | HMV POP 1068 | My Little Girl's Come Home/Try Once More | 50 |
| 63 | HMV POP 1160 | Saturday Dance/Come Back To Me | 40 |
| 63 | HMV POP 1213 | Sky Men/Walk With Me My Angel | 80 |

## GODFATHER DON
| | | | |
|---|---|---|---|
| 07 | Diggers With Gratitude DWG 002 | SLAVE OF NEW YORK (EP, 150 only) | 150 |
| 09 | Diggers With Gratitude DWG 005 | BILLY BATHGATE (12", 20 only, green vinyl) | 200 |
| 09 | Diggers With Gratitude DWG 005 | BILLY BATHGATE (12", 280 only, black vinyl) | 30 |

## GODFLESH
| | | | |
|---|---|---|---|
| 91 | Earache MOSH 30 T | SLAVESTATE (12", p/s) | 12 |

| | | | |
|---|---|---|---|
| 91 | Earache MOSH 47 | Slateman/Wound'91 (p/s) | 6 |
| 91 | Earache MOSH 56T | Cold World/Nihil/Nihil (Total Belief Mix)/Nihil (No Belief Mix) (12", p/s) | 15 |
| 94 | Earache MOSH 116 | Merciless/Blind/Unworthy/Flowers (2 x 7", white vinyl, gatefold p/s) | 15 |
| 88 | Swordfish FLESH LP 1 | GODFLESH (LP, textured sleeve, inner) | 15 |
| 89 | Earache MOSH 15 | STREETCLEANER (LP) | 15 |
| 92 | Earache MOSH 32 | PURE (LP, poster, insert) | 20 |
| 94 | Earache MOSH 85 | SELFLESS (LP, insert) | 20 |

### HUGH GODFREY
| | | | |
|---|---|---|---|
| 67 | Coxsone CS 7001 | A Dey Pon Dem/SOUL BROTHERS: Take Ten | 100 |
| 67 | Studio One SO 2008 | My Time/MARCIA GRIFFITHS: Hound Dog | 80 |
| 67 | Studio One SO 2015 | Go Tell Him/MARCIA GRIFFITHS: After Laughter | 80 |

*(see also Soul Brothers)*

### RAY GODFREY
| | | | |
|---|---|---|---|
| 78 | Grapevine GRP 111 | Come And Get These Memories/I'm The Other Half Of You | 5 |

### ROBERT JOHN GODFREY
| | | | |
|---|---|---|---|
| 74 | Charisma CAS 1084 | FALL OF HYPERION (LP) | 40 |

*(see also Enid, Godfrey & Stewart, Don Bradshaw)*

### GODFREY & STEWART
| | | | |
|---|---|---|---|
| 88 | The Enid ENID 11 | THE SEED AND THE SOWER (LP) | 15 |
| 80s | The Stand HEARTLP | JOINED BY THE HEART (LP, fan club issue, 2,000 only) | 20 |
| 80s | The Stand HEARTC | JOINED BY THE HEART (LP, fan club issue) | 12 |

*(see also Robert John Godfrey, Enid)*

### GODIEGO
| | | | |
|---|---|---|---|
| 79 | BBC RESL 66 | Gandhara/The Birth Of The Odyssey/Monkey Magic | 7 |

### GODLEY & CREME
| | | | |
|---|---|---|---|
| 68 | Blinkers 1215 | Goodnight Blinkers/Hello Blinkers (die-cut sleeve) | 250 |
| 79 | Mercury SAMP 017 | 5 O'Clock/The Flood//Lost Weekend/Honolulu (double pack sampler, promo) | 10 |

*(see also Mockingbirds, Hotlegs, 10cc, Dave Berry, Frabjoy & Runcible Spoon, Cruisers, Whirlwinds, Doctor Father)*

### GOD MACHINE
| | | | |
|---|---|---|---|
| 92 | Fiction FICSX 44 | Desert Song/Prostitute/Commitment/Pictures Of A Bleeding Boy (12", p/s) | 20 |
| 93 | Fiction FICSX 47 | Home/All My Colours/Train/Fever (12", p/s) | 20 |
| 93 | Fiction FIXH 23 | SCENES FROM THE SECOND STOREY (2-LP) | 40 |
| 94 | Fiction FIXH 27 | ONE LAST LAUGH IN A PLACE OF DYING (LP) | 80 |

### GODS
| | | | |
|---|---|---|---|
| 67 | Polydor 56168 | Come On Down To My Boat Baby/Garage Man | 180 |
| 68 | Columbia DB 8486 | Baby's Rich/Somewhere In The Street | 60 |
| 69 | Columbia DB 8544 | Hey! Bulldog/Real Love Guaranteed | 40 |
| 69 | Columbia DB 8572 | Maria/Long Time, Sad Time, Bad Time | 40 |
| 68 | Columbia SX 6286 | GENESIS (LP, mono, blue/black label with "sold in U.K..." text) | 600 |
| 70 | SCX 6286 | GENESIS (LP, stereo, silver/black label) | 350 |
| 70 | Columbia SCX 6372 | TO SAMUEL A SON (LP, black/silver labels with boxed logo) | 500 |
| 76 | Harvest SHSM 2011 | GODS (LP) | 30 |

*(see also Uriah Heep, Shame, Toe-Fat, Birds Birds, Carmen, Jethro Tull)*

### GODS GIFT
| | | | |
|---|---|---|---|
| 79 | Newmarket NEW 101 | THESE DAYS EP | 15 |

### GOD SONS
| | | | |
|---|---|---|---|
| 72 | Green Door GD 4024 | Merry Up/Merry Up - Version | 10 |

*(see also Errol & U Roy, Carl Masters, Glen Brown)*

### GODSONS
| | | | |
|---|---|---|---|
| 71 | Philips 6006155 | All Dressed In White/We've Not Made It | 15 |

*(see also Orange Bicycle)*

### GODZ
| | | | |
|---|---|---|---|
| 67 | Fontana STL 5500 | CONTACT WITH THE GODZ (LP) | 40 |
| 69 | Fontana STL 5512 | GODZ II (LP) | 40 |

### GOGMAGOG
| | | | |
|---|---|---|---|
| 85 | F. For Thought YUMT 109 | I Will Be There/Living In A Timewarp/It's Illegal, It's Immoral, It's Unhealthy But It's Fun (12", p/s & insert) | 35 |

*(see also Iron Maiden, Di'Anno, Def Leppard, Whitesnake, Gillan, White Spirit)*

### GO GO THUNDER
| | | | |
|---|---|---|---|
| 75 | RCA RCA 2494 | The Race/Mrs. Mann | 20 |

### GO-GO'S (U.K.)
| | | | |
|---|---|---|---|
| 64 | Oriole CB 1982 | I'm Gonna Spend My Christmas With A Dalek/Big Boss Man (in p/s) | 60 |
| 64 | Oriole CB 1982 | I'm Gonna Spend My Christmas With A Dalek/Big Boss Man | 40 |

### GO-GO'S (U.S.)
| | | | |
|---|---|---|---|
| 80 | Stiff BUY 78 | We Got The Beat/How Much More (p/s) | 10 |
| 81 | I.R.S. PFP 1007 | Our Lips Are Sealed/Surfing And Spying (p/s, pink vinyl) | 6 |

*(see also Jane Wiedlin)*

### GOING RED?
| | | | |
|---|---|---|---|
| 81 | Razz CLEAN 1 | Some Boys/Tune Kevin's Strings (p/s) | 12 |
| 81 | MCA MCA 673 | Some Boys/Tune Kevin's Strings (reissue, p/s) | 7 |

*(see also Freshies, Chris Sievey, Jilted John)*

### HERBIE GOINS & NIGHT-TIMERS
| | | | |
|---|---|---|---|
| 66 | Parlophone R 5478 | No. 1 In Your Heart/Cruisin' | 150 |
| 66 | Parlophone R 5478 | No. 1 In Your Heart/Cruisin' (DJ Copy) | 200 |
| 66 | Parlophone R 5533 | The Incredible Miss Brown/Comin' Home To You | 120 |
| 67 | Parlophone PMC 7026 | NUMBER ONE IN YOUR HEART (LP) | 200 |

*(see also Night-Timers, Alexis Korner's Blues Incorporated)*

# GO-KART MOZART

MINT VALUE £

### GO-KART MOZART
| 12 | West Midlands GLUM 2 | New World In The Morning/Gizmos Gadgets Unrock Electric Guitar Clock Tick Tock (100 only) | 6 |
| 99 | West Midlands Records BRUM 1 | INSTANT WIGWAM AND IGLOO MIXTURE (LP, 1,000 only, with poster and small sealing sticker over opening) | 25 |
| 04 | West Midlands BRUM 4 | ON THE HOT DOG STREETS (2-LP) | 18 |

*(see also Felt)*

### GOLANT PISTONS
| 78 | Sawmills/Sonet SON 2165 | I Can See Where I'm Going/Katy May (p/s) | 6 |
| 79 | Sawmills/Sonet SON 2184 | Friday On My Mind/Break The Spell | 7 |

### DAVID GOLD
| 97 | Fat Cat 10FAT 001 | Respect City Police (10") | 40 |

### GOLD MACHINE
| 80 | Auberge MH 29444 | Suspect/Twilight | 10 |

### BARRY GOLDBERG (REUNION)
| 68 | Pye International 7N 25465 | Another Day/Capricorn Blues (as Barry Goldberg Reunion) | 7 |
| 68 | Pye Intl. NSPL 28116 | BARRY GOLDBERG REUNION (LP) | 20 |
| 69 | Buddah 203 020 | TWO JEWS BLUES (LP, with Mike Bloomfield) | 15 |

*(see also Electric Flag, Mike Bloomfield)*

### GOLDEBRIARS
| 64 | Columbia DB 7384 | Sea Of Tears/I've Got To Love Somebody | 10 |

### GOLDEN APPLES OF THE SUN
| 65 | Decca F 12194 | Monkey Time/Chocolate Rolls, Tea And Monopoly (unissued, test pressings only) | 100 |
| 65 | Immediate IM 010 | Monkey Time/Chocolate Rolls, Tea And Monopoly | 70 |

### GOLDEN CRUSADERS
| 64 | Columbia DB 7232 | I'm In Love With You/Always On My Mind | 10 |
| 64 | Columbia DB 7357 | Hey Good Lookin'/Come On, Come On | 10 |
| 65 | Columbia DB 7485 | I Don't Care/That Broken Heart Is Mine | 10 |

### GOLDEN DAWN
| 88 | Sarah SARAH 009 | My Secret World/Spring-Heeled Jack/The Railway Track (p/s, with poster) | 35 |
| 89 | Sarah SARAH 017 | George Hamilton's Dead/The Sweetest Touch/Let's Build A Dyonsphere (p/s, with poster) | 15 |

### GOLDEN EARRING(S)
| 68 | Capitol CL 15552 | I've Just Lost Somebody/The Truth About Arthur (as Golden Earrings) | 25 |
| 68 | Capitol CL 15567 | Dong Dong Di Ki Di Gi Dong/Wake Up - Breakfast (as Golden Earrings) | 20 |
| 69 | Major Minor MM 601 | Just A Little Peace In My Heart/Remember My Friend (as Golden Earrings) | 20 |
| 69 | Major Minor MM 633 | It's Alright But It Could Be Better/Where Will I Be (as Golden Earrings) | 12 |
| 70 | Major Minor MM 679 | Another Forty-Five Miles/I Can't Get Hold Of Her | 25 |
| 70 | Polydor BM 56514 | That Day/Words I Need | 20 |
| 70 | Polydor 2001 073 | Back Home/This Is The Time Of Year | 8 |
| 72 | Polydor 2001 346 | Buddy Joe/Avalanche | 5 |
| 73 | Track 2094 116 | Radar Love/Just Like Vince Taylor | 6 |
| 74 | Track 2094 121 | Instant Poetry/From Heaven, From Hell | 5 |
| 74 | Track 2094 126 | Candy's Going Bad/She Flies On Strange Wings | 5 |
| 75 | Track 2094 130 | Ce Soir/Lucky Number | 5 |
| 69 | Major Minor SMLP 65 | EIGHT MILES HIGH (LP) | 150 |
| 70 | Polydor 2310049 | GOLDEN EARRING (LP, gatefold sleeve) | 70 |
| 71 | Polydor 2310 135 | SEVEN TEARS (LP) | 30 |
| 72 | Polydor 2310 210 | TOGETHER (LP) | 18 |
| 73 | Track 2406 109 | HEARING EARRING (LP, braille sleeve) | 18 |
| 73 | Track 2406 112 | MOONTAN (LP, gatefold sleeve with insert) | 18 |

### GOLDEN FLEECE
| 67 | Decca F 12669 | Athens 6 a.m./Girl From Syracuse | 6 |

### GOLDEN GATE STRINGS
| 65 | Columbia DB 7634 | Mr. Tambourine Man/With God On Our Side | 30 |

### GOLDEN HORDE
| 80s | Hot Wire HWS 855 | Young And Happy/Little UFO/Fiona (p/s) | 5 |

### GOLDFRAPP
| 00 | Mute P STUMM 188 | FELT MOUNTAIN ALBUM SAMPLER (12" promo, p/s) | 10 |
| 00 | Mute STUMM 188 | FELT MOUNTAIN (LP, with inner) | 60 |
| 03 | Mute STUMM 196 | BLACK CHERRY (LP) | 40 |
| 05 | Mute STUMM 250 | SUPERNATURE (LP) | 40 |
| 08 | Mute STUMM 280 | SEVENTH TREE (LP, with poster) | 40 |
| 10 | Mute STUMM 320 | HEAD FIRST (LP, with CD insert) | 20 |

### GOLDIE
| 95 | FFRR 828 614-1 | TIMELESS (2-LP, gatefold) | 18 |

### GOLDIE (& GINGERBREADS)
| 65 | Decca F 12070 | Can't You Hear My Heartbeat/Little Boy | 15 |
| 65 | Decca F 12126 | That's Why I Love You/The Skip | 15 |
| 65 | Decca F 12199 | Sailor Boy/Please Please | 15 |
| 66 | Immediate IM 026 | Goin' Back/Headlines (solo) | 30 |
| 66 | Fontana TF 693 | I Do/Think About The Good Times (solo) | 25 |
| 69 | Decca F 12931 | Can't You Hear My Heartbeat/That's Why I Love You | 5 |

*(see also Ten Wheel Drive)*

### JOHN GOLDING
| 74 | Cottage 101S | DISCARDED VERSE (LP, 2,000 only) | 20 |

### GOLD LEAF
| 73 | Pembrook PEM 1 | After The Rain/The Sun (p/s) | 200 |

| 73 | Pembrook PEM 1 | After The Rain/The Sun (no p/s) | 50 |

## VIVIEN GOLDMAN
| 81 | Window WIN 1 | Launderette/Private Armies (gatefold p/s, with PiL) | 20 |
| 81 | Window 12WIN 1 | Launderette/Private Armies (12", different p/s, with PiL) | 30 |

*(see also Public Image Ltd)*

## ANNA GOLDRICK
| 70s | Polydor 2384030 | IT'S HERSELF (LP) | 30 |

## GOLDRUSH
| 73 | Decca F13380 | For A Few Dollars More/No More - No Less | 6 |

## BOBBY GOLDSBORO
| 63 | Stateside SS 193 | The Runaround/The Letter | 20 |
| 63 | United Artists UP 1046 | See The Funny Little Clown/Hello Loser | 8 |
| 64 | United Artists UP 1054 | Whenever He Holds You/If She Was Mine | 10 |
| 65 | United Artists UP 1079 | Little Things/I Just Can't Go On Pretending | 15 |
| 65 | United Artists UP 1091 | Voodoo Woman/It Breaks My Heart | 12 |
| 65 | United Artists UP 1104 | If You Wait For Love/If You've Got A Heart | 10 |
| 66 | United Artists UP 1120 | Broomstick Cowboy/Ain't Got Time For Happy | 10 |
| 66 | United Artists UP 1128 | It's Too Late/I'm Goin' Home | 15 |
| 66 | United Artists UP 1128 | It's Too Late/I'm Goin' Home (DJ copy) | 30 |
| 66 | United Artists UP 1135 | I Know You Better Than That/When Your Love Has Gone | 7 |
| 66 | United Artists UP 1146 | Take Your Love/Longer Than Forever | 25 |
| 67 | United Artists UP 1156 | It Hurts Me/Pity The Fool | 10 |
| 67 | United Artists UP 1166 | No Fun At The Fair/Hold On | 35 |
| 67 | United Artists UP 1177 | Too Many People/Goodbye To All You Women | 50 |
| 67 | United Artists UP 1177 | Too Many People/Goodbye To All You Women (DJ copy) | 85 |
| 68 | United Artists UP 2223 | Autumn Of My Life/She Chased Me | 10 |
| 69 | United Artists UP 2264 | Love Arrester/Dissatisfied Man | 15 |
| 69 | United Artists UP 35034 | Muddy Mississippi Line/Richer Man Than I | 8 |
| 69 | United Artists UP 35053 | Letter To Emily/Tomorrow Is Forgotten | 5 |
| 73 | United Artists UP 35558 | Summer (The First Time)/Childhood - 1949 | 5 |
| 74 | United Artists UP 35705 | Hello Summertime/And Then There Was Gina | 5 |
| 65 | United Artists UEP 1006 | LITTLE THINGS (EP) | 45 |
| 66 | United Artists UEP 1016 | THE TALENTED BOBBY GOLDSBORO (EP) | 45 |
| 65 | United Artists ULP 1118 | I CAN'T STOP LOVING YOU (LP) | 35 |
| 66 | United Artists (S)ULP 1135 | IT'S TOO LATE (LP) | 35 |
| 67 | United Artists (S)ULP 1163 | SOLID GOLDSBORO - GREATEST HITS (LP) | 22 |
| 68 | United Artists (S)ULP 1195 | HONEY (LP, black label) | 15 |
| 68 | United Artists (S)ULP 1206 | WORD PICTURES (LP) | 20 |
| 69 | United Artists UAS 29008 | TODAY (LP) | 18 |

## GOLDSMITH
| 83 | Bedlam BLM 001 | Life Is Killing Me/Music Man (p/s) | 50 |

## GOL GAPPAS
| 86 | él GPO 21 | West 14/Roman (p/s) | 12 |

## GOLGOTHA
| 84 | Golgotha GOTH 002 | DANGEROUS GAMES (Dangerous Games/Old England's Green/Air/The Great Divide (EP, no p/s) | 90 |
| 90 | Communique CMGLP 003 | UNMAKER OF WORLDS (EP, p/s) | 15 |

## GOLIARD
| 76 | Broadside BRO 127 | FORTUNE MY FOE (LP, with booklet) | 18 |

## GOLIATH
| 70 | CBS 5312 | Port And Lemon Lady/I Heard About A Friend | 10 |
| 70 | CBS 64229 | GOLIATH (LP) | 200 |

## GOLINSKI BROTHERS
| 80 | Badge BAD 6 | Bloody/Toy | 20 |

## GOLLIWOGS
| 66 | Vocalion VF 9266 | Brown-Eyed Girl/You Better Be Careful | 50 |
| 67 | Vocalion VF 9283 | Fragile Child/Fight Fire | 50 |
| 72 | Fantasy FAN 5996 | GOLLIWOGS (LP, pressed in U.S. for U.K. distribution) | 15 |

*(see also Creedence Clearwater Revival)*

## GOLLUM & GARY D
| 97 | UK 44 RMX 3 | Black Arrows (Lord Of The Rings Mix)/Black Arrows (Poisoned Tip Mix)/Black Arrows (Original E.D.M. Mix) (12", p/s) | 10 |

*(see also DJ Gollum)*

## BENNY GOLSON
| 59 | Esquire 32-125 | GONE WITH GOLSON (LP) | 35 |
| 60 | Esquire 32-105 | GROOVIN' WITH GOLSON (LP) | 35 |

## GOMEZ
| 98 | Hut HUTDLP 49 | BRING IT ON (2-LP) | 40 |
| 99 | Hut HUTDLP 54 | LIQUID SKIN (2-LP, gatefold, inner) | 40 |
| 02 | Hut HUTDLP 72 | IN OUR GUN (2-LP, gatefold) | 20 |
| 04 | Hut HUTDLP 84 | SPLIT THE DIFFERENCE (LP) | 18 |

## GONDOLIERS
| 58 | Starlite ST45 001 | Fly, Seagull, Fly/God's Green Acres | 6 |

## GONG
| 71 | Philips 6332 033 | CONTINENTAL CIRCUS (LP, soundtrack) | 20 |
| 71 | Caroline C1520 | CAMEMBERT ELECTRIQUE (LP, 'twin' label) | 15 |
| 73 | Virgin V 2002 | RADIO GNOME INVISIBLE PART 1 - THE FLYING TEAPOT (LP, gatefold sleeve, 1st pressing original with black & white label design) | 50 |

MINT VALUE £

| 73 | Virgin V 2002 | RADIO GNOME INVISIBLE PART 1 - THE FLYING TEAPOT (LP, gatefold sleeve, 2nd pressing with colour girl and dragon label design) | 15 |
| 73 | Virgin V 2007 | RADIO GNOME INVISIBLE PART 2 - ANGEL'S EGG (LP, 1st pressing, stickered gatefold sleeve, initially with b&w label; with booklet) | 50 |
| 73 | Virgin V 2007 | RADIO GNOME INVISIBLE PART 2 - ANGEL'S EGG (LP, 1st pressing, gatefold sleeve, initially with b&w label; without booklet) | 30 |
| 74 | Virgin V 2007 | RADIO GNOME INVISIBLE PART 2 - ANGEL'S EGG (LP, 2nd pressing, coloured "girl/dragon label") | 15 |
| 74 | Caroline C 1505 | CAMEMBERT ELECTRIQUE (LP, unissued, released as Virgin VC 502 with 1505 matrix struck through and 502 added as well as a V in front of the C) | 0 |
| 74 | Virgin V 2019 | YOU (LP, 1st pressing, with lyric insert, coloured 'twin' label) | 15 |
| 75 | Virgin V 2046 | SHAMAL (LP, gatefold) | 15 |

(see also Gilli Smyth & , Daevid Allen, Steve Hillage, Clearlight, Radio Actors, Sphynx, Tim Blake, Comus)

## GONG/CAMEL/HENRY COW/GLOBAL TRUCKING COMPANY
| 73 | Greasy Truckers GT 4997 | GREASY TRUCKERS (2-LP, 1 side each; with insert) | 18 |

(see also Camel, Henry Cow, Global Trucking Company)

## GONJASUFI
| 10 | Warp WARPLP172 | A SUFI AND A KILLER (2-LP) | 25 |

## GONKS
| 64 | Decca F 11984 | The Gonk Song/That's All Right, Mamma | 30 |

(see also Twinkle)

## PAUL GONSALVES
| 64 | Vocalion LAE 587 | BOOM JACKIE BOOM CHICK (LP) | 1000 |
| 70 | Deram SML 1064 | HUMMINGBIRD (LP) | 100 |

(see also Tubby Hayes & Paul Gonsalves)

## GONZALEZ
| 74 | RAK 204 | Hole In My Soul/Re-Souled | 10 |
| 74 | EMI EMC 3046 | GONZALEZ (LP) | 40 |
| 75 | EMI EMC 3100 | OUR ONLY WEAPON IS OUR MUSIC (LP) | 18 |

## BELLE GONZALEZ
| 72 | Columbia DB 8852 | Bottles/I Hate Sunday | 10 |
| 65 | Jupiter JEPOC 37 | POETS SET IN JAZZ (EP, as Belle Gonzalez & Sextet) | 18 |
| 66 | Jupiter JEPOC 39 | CONTEMPORARY POETS SET IN JAZZ (EP) | 18 |
| 72 | Columbia SCX 6484 | BELLE (LP) | 100 |

(see also Mark Wirtz)

## DOUGLAS GOOD & GINNY PLENTY
| 68 | Stateside SS 2104 | Sunny And Me/Living In A World Of Make Believe | 5 |

## JACK GOOD'S FAT NOISE
| 60 | Decca F 11233 | The Fat Washerwoman/The Fat Noise | 10 |

## ELMER GOODBODY
| 76 | Charisma CB 279 | Do Ya/Mad About You | 8 |

## GOODBYE MR. MACKENZIE
| 84 | Scruples YTS 1 | Death Of A Salesman/LINDY BERGMAN: Locked Inside Your Prison (no p/s, 500 only) | 15 |
| 90 | Parlophone PCS 7345 | HAMMER AND TONGS (LP, unreleased, white label test pressings only) | 30 |

(see also Garbage)o

## GOOD GUYS
| 70 | Duke DU 82 | Death Rides/Destruction | 20 |
| 70 | Duke DU 83 | Wreck It Up/Dynamic Groove | 20 |
| 70 | Duke DU 84 | Happiness/Latissimo | 20 |

(see also Byron Lee & Dragonaires)

## PHILIP GOODHAND-TAIT (& STORMSVILLE SHAKERS)
| 66 | Parlophone R 5448 | I'm Gonna Put Some Hurt On You/It's A Lie (with Stormsville Shakers) | 20 |
| 66 | Parlophone R 5498 | No Problem/What More Do You Want (with Stormsville Shakers) | 25 |
| 66 | Parlophone R 5547 | You Can't Take Love/J.C. Greaseburger (solo) | 20 |
| 70 | DJM DJLPS 411 | REHEARSAL (LP) | 15 |
| 71 | DJM DJLPS 416 | I THINK I'LL WRITE A SONG (LP, gatefold) | 15 |
| 72 | DJM DJLPS 425 | SONGFALL (LP, gatefold) | 20 |

(see also Circus, Larry Williams, Love Affair)

## JOHNNY GOODISON
| 70 | Deram DM 319 | A Little Understanding/One Mistake | 20 |

(see also Quotations, Johnny B. Great)

## LEMME B GOOD
| 65 | Mercury MF 874 | I Can't Stop Myself/Mother May I | 8 |

## GOODLETTSVILLE FIVE
| 64 | London HLW 9854 | Eef/Bailey's Gone Eefing | 12 |

## JOHN GOODLUCK
| 74 | Tradition TSR 015 | SUFFOLK MIRACLE (LP, with insert) | 20 |
| 75 | Sweet Folk & Country SFA 047 | SPEED THE PLOUGH: TRADITIONAL SONGS OF SUFFOLK (LP) | 20 |

## DAVE GOODMAN & FRIENDS
| 78 | The Label TLR 008 | Justifiable Homicide/Take Down Your Fences (p/s, 1st 15,000 on red vinyl) | 8 |

## GOOD MISSIONARIES
| 80 | Unormality NORM 002 | DERANGED IN HASTINGS: Keep Going Backwards/Attitudes (hand made p/s) | 15 |
| 80 | Kif KIF'S 1 | Good Missionary (Parts 1 & 2) (p/s) | 5 |
| 80 | Unnormality NORM 001 | VIBING UP THE SENILE WORLD (The Good Missionary Part 1 [live]/The Good Missionary Part/Kif Kif's Free Freak Out [live]) (EP, 1,000 only) | 15 |
| 79 | Deptford Fun City DLP 04 | FIRE FROM HEAVEN (LP) | 15 |

(see also Mark Perry, Alternative TV)

## GOOD RATS
| | | | |
|---|---|---|---|
| 69 | London HLR 10237 | The Hobo/The Truth Is Gone | 15 |

## GOOD SHIP LOLLIPOP
| | | | |
|---|---|---|---|
| 69 | Ember EMB S 276 | Maxwell's Silver Hammer/How Does It Feel (in p/s) | 12 |
| 69 | Ember EMB S 276 | Maxwell's Silver Hammer/How Does It Feel | 6 |

## GOOD TIME LOSERS
| | | | |
|---|---|---|---|
| 67 | Fontana TF 791 | Trafalgar Square/Where Did My Heart Go | 6 |

## GOODTIMERS
| | | | |
|---|---|---|---|
| 62 | Fontana H 360 | It's Twistin' Time/Twisting Train | 10 |

## GOOD VIBRATIONS
| | | | |
|---|---|---|---|
| 70 | Ember EMB S 270 | Call Me Lightning/Nantucket Ferry | 6 |

## ROD GOODWAY
| | | | |
|---|---|---|---|
| 90 | Woronzow WOO 12 | ETHEREAL COUNTERBALANCE (LP) | 18 |

## RON GOODWIN CONCERT ORCHESTRA
| | | | |
|---|---|---|---|
| 53 | Parlophone MSP 6035 | Limelight/The Song From Moulin Rouge | 18 |
| 53 | Parlophone MSP 6044 | The Melba Waltz (Dreamtime)/Shane | 10 |
| 53 | Parlophone MSP 6055 | Tropical Mirage/The Man Between | 12 |
| 54 | Parlophone MSP 6064 | Grand Waltz Of The Flowers And Dragonflies/The Lobster Quadrille | 10 |
| 54 | Parlophone MSP 6103 | The Sons Of The High Seas/Guadalcanal March | 12 |
| 54 | Parlophone MSP 6115 | Cara Mia/Three Coins In The Fountain | 12 |
| 54 | Parlophone MSP 6136 | Midnight Blue/On The Waterfront | 12 |
| 55 | Parlophone MSP 6159 | Under The Linded Tree/Last Love | 10 |
| 56 | Parlophone MSP 6221 | Concetta/Handyman | 10 |
| 56 | Parlophone 45 R-4235 | War And Peace/The Christmas Tree | 10 |
| 57 | Parlophone R 4297 | Skiffling Strings (Swinging Sweetheart)/I'll Find You | 8 |
| 57 | Parlophone R 4349 | Swedish Polka/Lingering Lovers | 8 |
| 58 | Parlophone R 4391 | Colonel Bogey And The River Kwai March/Laughing Sailor | 8 |
| 58 | Parlophone R 4508 | Latin Lovers/Blue Grotto | 8 |
| 58 | Parlophone R 4608 | Lolita/All Strung Up | 8 |
| 59 | Parlophone R 4537 | The Whirlpool Theme/Herman's Theme From Whirlpool | 8 |
| 60 | Parlophone R 4632 | Tracey's Theme/My Girl | 7 |
| 60 | Parlophone R 4663 | Love Theme From Ben Hur/Theme From The Unforgiven | 7 |
| 60 | Parlophone R 4687 | Walkin' Down To Washington/Sunshine Cruise | 7 |
| 61 | Parlophone R 4821 | Murder She Says/Double Scotch | 25 |
| 63 | Parlophone R 5053 | Moonstrike/Midsummer Madness | 12 |
| 64 | Parlophone R 5146 | 633 Squadron/Love Them From 633 Squadron | 8 |
| 65 | Parlophone R 5239 | The Fat Man/Colonel Schmendrick | 8 |
| 65 | Parlophone R 5394 | Theme From The Early Birds/Theme From The Alphabet Murders | 8 |
| 69 | United Artists UP 35040 | Battle Of Britain Theme/Luftwaffe March | 8 |
| 54 | Parlophone PMD 1014 | FILM FAVOURITES (10" LP) | 15 |
| 56 | Parlophone PMD 1038 | MUSIC TO SET YOU DREAMING (10" LP) | 15 |
| 58 | Parlophone PCS 3002 | MUSIC FOR AN ARABIAN NIGHT (LP) | 15 |
| 58 | Parlophone PCS 3006 | OUT OF THIS WORLD! (LP) | 20 |
| 64 | United Artists ULP 1071 | 633 SQUADRON (LP, soundtrack) | 20 |
| 65 | Stateside SL 10136 | THOSE MAGNIFICENT MEN IN THEIR FLYING MACHINES (LP, soundtrack) | 20 |
| 66 | Polydor 582 004 | THE TRAP (LP, soundtrack) | 40 |
| 68 | Stateside (S)SL 10259 | DECLINE AND FALL ... OF A BIRDWATCHER (LP, soundtrack) | 100 |
| 69 | Paramount SPFL 255 | MONTE CARLO OR BUST! (LP, soundtrack) | 25 |

*(see also 20th Century Fox Orchestra, Parlophone Pops Orchestra)*

## PETER GOODWRIGHT
| | | | |
|---|---|---|---|
| 75 | MWS 002 | When Christmas Comes To The Zoo (Part 1)/Part 2 | 6 |

## GOOFERS
| | | | |
|---|---|---|---|
| 55 | Vogue Coral Q 72051 | Hearts Of Stone/You're The One | 50 |
| 55 | Vogue Coral Q 72074 | Flip, Flop And Fly/My Babe | 50 |
| 55 | Vogue Coral Q 72094 | Goofy Drybones/Nare | 30 |
| 56 | Vogue Coral Q 72124 | Sick! Sick! Sick!/Twenty One | 15 |
| 56 | Vogue Coral Q 72171 | Tear Drop Motel/Tennessee Rock And Roll | 25 |
| 57 | Vogue Coral Q 72267 | Wow!/Push, Push, Push Cart | 15 |
| 57 | Vogue Coral Q 72289 | The Dipsy Doodle/Take This Heart | 15 |

## GOOM
| | | | |
|---|---|---|---|
| 72 | Pye 7N 25587 | Massai Part 1/Massai Part 2 | 15 |

## DEREK GOOM
| | | | |
|---|---|---|---|
| 80 | BBC RESL 84 | Juliet Bravo/Madelena (p/s) | 6 |

## GOO.Q
| | | | |
|---|---|---|---|
| 80 | Rising Star PCD 1 | I'm A Computer/Love Outa Hate (paper p/s) | 5 |

## SAM GOPAL
| | | | |
|---|---|---|---|
| 69 | Stable STA 5602 | Horse/Back Door Man (unissued, existence unconfirmed) | 0 |
| 69 | Stable SLE 8001 | Escalator/Angry Faces/Cold Embrace/The Sky is Burning (LP sampler) | 70 |
| 69 | Stable SLE 8001 | ESCALATOR (LP, gatefold sleeve, black/silver label) | 400 |
| 68 | Stable SLE 8001 | ESCALATOR (LP, gatefold sleeve, label stating "DJ Copy not for resale") | 400 |

*(see also Hawkwind, Motorhead, Vamp, Isaac Guillory, Clark-Hutchinson, G. F. Fitzgerald)*

## PETE(R) GORDENO
| | | | |
|---|---|---|---|
| 61 | Fontana H 319 | Be My Girl/Haven't Got Time (as Pete Gordeno) | 8 |
| 62 | Parlophone R 4862 | I Got Eyes/You're Following Me | 8 |
| 62 | Parlophone R 4914 | Uptown/The Making Of A Man | 8 |
| 62 | Parlophone R 4931 | Down By The Riverside/The Boys Kept Hanging Around | 7 |
| 65 | Decca F 12088 | Have You Looked Into Your Heart?/Don't Come To Me | 6 |

MINT VALUE £

## ANITA GORDON
| | | | |
|---|---|---|---|
| 55 | Brunswick 05456 | Lonesome Like Nobody Knows/His Hands | 10 |

## BARRY GORDON
| | | | |
|---|---|---|---|
| 56 | MGM MGM 928 | I Can't Whistle/The Milkman's Polka | 7 |
| 56 | MGM MGM 935 | Rock Around Mother Goose/Nuttin' For Christmas | 12 |

## CHANCE GORDON
| | | | |
|---|---|---|---|
| 63 | Pye 7N 15475 | Instant Love/You Don't Want My Love | 20 |

## CHRIS GORDON
| | | | |
|---|---|---|---|
| 68 | Derpy ADMLP 390 | IN THE EARLY MORNING RAIN (LP) | 200 |

## DEXTER GORDON
| | | | |
|---|---|---|---|
| 66 | Fontana Jazz FJL 907 | MASTER SWINGERS (LP, with Wardell Gray) | 20 |

*(see also Wardell Gray)*

## JOE GORDON (FOLK FOUR)
| | | | |
|---|---|---|---|
| 59 | HMV POP 634 | Dream Lover/Dance To Your Daddy | 6 |

## PETER GORDON
| | | | |
|---|---|---|---|
| 62 | Parlophone R 4931 | Down By The Riverside/The Boys Kept Hanging Around | 10 |
| 65 | Decca F 12088 | Have You Looked Into Your Heart?/Don't Come To Me | 8 |
| 68 | MCA MU 1009 | Born To Be Wanted/Shout It From The Hilltop | 5 |
| 68 | MCA MU 1058 | My Girl Maria/I Appreciate So Much | 5 |

## PHIL GORDON
| | | | |
|---|---|---|---|
| 55 | Brunswick 05481 | Get A Load Of That Crazy Walk/Strip Polka | 10 |
| 56 | Brunswick 05545 | Down The Road Apiece/I'm Gonna Move To The Outskirts Of Town | 50 |

## ROBERT GORDON WITH LINK WRAY
| | | | |
|---|---|---|---|
| 77 | Private Stock PVTS 127 | Endless Sleep & The Fool/The Fool (12", B-side plays at 78rpm) | 10 |
| 77 | Private Stock PVLP 1027 | ROBERT GORDON WITH LINK WRAY (LP) | 15 |

*(see also Link Wray)*

## RONNIE GORDON
| | | | |
|---|---|---|---|
| 63 | R&B JB 127 | Shake Some Time/Comin' Home | 50 |

## ROSCO(E) GORDON
| | | | |
|---|---|---|---|
| 60 | Top Rank JAR 332 | Just A Little Bit/Goin' Home (as Rosco Gordon) | 25 |
| 63 | Stateside SS 204 | Just A Little Bit/What I Wouldn't Do | 25 |
| 65 | Vocalion V-P 9245 | Keep On Doggin'/Bad Dream | 30 |
| 65 | Island WI 256 | Surely I Love You/What You Do To Me | 25 |
| 66 | Island WI 272 | No More Doggin'/Goin' Home | 30 |

## TONY GORDON
| | | | |
|---|---|---|---|
| 73 | Grape GR 3056 | Be True (actually by Alton Ellis)/Navajo Trail | 15 |

*(see also Alton Ellis)*

## VINCENT GORDON
| | | | |
|---|---|---|---|
| 69 | Coxsone CS 7085 | Soul Trombone/LARRY & ALVIN: Your Cheating Heart | 150 |
| 69 | Duke DU 37 | Everybody Bawlin'/SILVERTONES: Come Look Here | 35 |
| 69 | Crab CRAB 16 | Walking By/VICEROYS: Promises Promises | 35 |
| 74 | Big Shot BI 630 | Come Go With Me/SKIN, FLESH & BONES: Dub Ali Dub | 10 |
| 79 | Attack TACK 10 | Liquid Horns (as Vin Gordon & Corner Shots)/JUNIOR & CORNER SHOTS: Liquidator (12") | 18 |
| 79 | Third World TWDIS 17 | Grass In The Sun/Split Second (12") | 20 |
| 79 | Third World TWDIS 18 | Vin Cosmic/Enforcement (12") | 20 |
| 70s | Trojan TRO 9058 | Liquid Horns/JUNIOR: Liquidator | 10 |
| 75 | DIP DLP 5001 | MUSICAL BONES (LP, plain sleeve, white label) | 300 |

*(see also Don Drummond Junior)*

## TREV GORDON
| | | | |
|---|---|---|---|
| 66 | Pye 7N 17168 | Floating/Everyone Knows (possibly demo only) | 15 |

## CHARLIE GORE
| | | | |
|---|---|---|---|
| 54 | Parlophone CMSP 19 | I'll Find Somebody/Heaven Sent You To Me (export issue) | 25 |
| 54 | Parlophone CMSP 26 | Two Of A Kind/It's A Long Walk Back To Town (export issue) | 20 |
| 54 | Parlophone CMSP 30 | I Didn't Know/Oh! Mis'rable Love (export issue) | 20 |

*(see also Hawkshaw Hawkins, Ruby Wright)*

## LESLEY GORE
| | | | |
|---|---|---|---|
| 63 | Mercury AMT 1205 | It's My Party/Danny | 10 |
| 63 | Mercury AMT 1210 | Judy's Turn To Cry/Just Let Me Cry | 10 |
| 63 | Mercury AMT 1213 | She's A Fool/The Old Crowd | 10 |
| 64 | Mercury MF 803 | You Don't Own Me/Run Bobby Run | 12 |
| 64 | Mercury MF 810 | That's The Way Boys Are/That's The Way The Ball Bounces | 12 |
| 64 | Mercury MF 821 | I Don't Wanna Be A Loser/It's Gotta Be You | 10 |
| 64 | Mercury MF 829 | Maybe I Know/Wonder Boy | 10 |
| 64 | Mercury MF 837 | Hey Now/Sometimes I Wish I Were A Boy | 10 |
| 65 | Mercury MF 846 | The Look Of Love/Little Girl Go Home | 20 |
| 65 | Mercury MF 862 | Sunshine Lollipops And Rainbows/You've Come Back | 15 |
| 65 | Mercury MF 872 | My Town, My Guy And Me/Girl In Love | 15 |
| 65 | Mercury MF 889 | I Won't Love You Anymore (Sorry)/No Matter What You Do | 15 |
| 66 | Mercury MF 902 | Young Love/I Just Don't Know If I Can | 10 |
| 66 | Mercury MF 963 | California Nights/I'm Going Out (The Same Way I Came In) | 10 |
| 66 | Mercury MF 984 | I'm Fallin' Down/Summer And Sandy | 20 |
| 68 | Mercury MF 1017 | Magic Colours/It's A Happening World | 10 |
| 75 | A&M AMS 7184 | Immortality/Give It To Me, Sweet Thing | 5 |
| 64 | Mercury 10017 MCE | LESLEY GORE (EP) | 35 |
| 63 | Mercury MMC 14127 | I'LL CRY IF I WANT TO (LP) | 40 |
| 63 | Mercury 20001 MCL | SINGS OF MIXED-UP HEARTS (LP) | 30 |
| 64 | Mercury 20020 MCL | BOYS BOYS BOYS (LP) | 30 |

| | | | |
|---|---|---|---|
| 64 | Mercury 20033 MCL | GIRL TALK (LP) | 30 |
| 65 | Mercury 20071 MCL | MY TOWN, MY GUY & ME (LP) | 30 |
| 65 | Mercury 20076 MCL | ALL ABOUT LOVE (LP) | 30 |

## GORGONI, MARTIN & TAYLOR

| | | | |
|---|---|---|---|
| 71 | Buddah 2011 102 | Sweet Dream Woman/Got The Feeling Something Got Away | 6 |
| 72 | Buddah 2011-137 | Toly Toly Guyluesha/I Can Make You Cry | 7 |
| 72 | Buddah 2318 067 | GORGONI, MARTIN AND TAYLOR (LP) | 15 |

## GORILLA GRIP

| | | | |
|---|---|---|---|
| 78 | Birnback KOM 019 | King Of The Pipes/Birnback Island (500 only no p/s) | 20 |

*(see also DR Z)*

## GORILLAS

| | | | |
|---|---|---|---|
| 75 | Chiswick NS 4 | She's My Gal/Why Wait 'Til Tomorrow | 6 |
| 78 | Chiswick NS 8 | Gatecrasher/Gorilla Got Me | 15 |
| 78 | Raw RAW 14 | It's My Life/My Son's Alive | 6 |
| 81 | Chiswick CHIS 151 | Move It/A Song For Rita | 6 |
| 78 | Raw RWLP 103 | MESSAGE TO THE WORLD (LP, with insert) | 20 |

*(see also Hammersmith Gorillas, Jesse Hector)*

## GORILLAZ

| | | | |
|---|---|---|---|
| 01 | 7RDJ 6552 | Clint Eastwood/Dracula (33 rpm dinked 7" - cartoon die-cut stickered sleeve) | 8 |
| 01 | Parlophone (no Cat no) | Tomorrow Comes Today/Tomorrow Dub (7" white label, stamped promo) | 8 |
| 06 | Parlophone R 6685 | Kids With Guns/El Manana (p/s, red vinyl, poster) | 7 |
| 11 | Parlophone P7300787 | THE SINGLES COLLECTION 2001-2011 (8 x 7" box set) | 30 |
| 01 | Parlophone 724353113810 | GORILLAZ (2-LP) | 30 |
| 05 | Parlophone 07243 873838 1 4 | DEMON DAYS (2-LP) | 120 |
| 05 | Parlophone 07243 873838 | DEMON DAYS INSTRUMENTALS (2-LP, promo die-cut stickered sleeve) | 50 |
| 10 | Parlophone 5099962616614 | PLASTIC BEACH (2-LP) | 30 |
| 11 | Parlophone 5099909758810 | THE FALL (LP, numbered) | 30 |
| 11 | Parlophone P730 0781 | THE SINGLES COLLECTION 2001-2011 (2-LP) | 40 |

*(see also Blur, Damon Albarn)*

## GORKY'S ZYGOTIC MYNCI

| | | | |
|---|---|---|---|
| 93 | Ankst ANKST/GZM 040 | PATIO (10" EP) | 15 |
| 94 | Ankst ANKST 048 | Merched Yn Neud Gwallt Eu Gilydd/Bocs Angelica/ When You Laugh At Your Own Garden In A Blazer (p/s) | 10 |
| 94 | Ankst ANKST 053 | Game Of Eyes/Pentref Wrth Y Mor (p/s) | 10 |
| 95 | Ankst ANKST 053 | Pentref Wrth Y Môr/The Game Of Eyes (p/s) | 15 |
| 95 | Ankst ANKST 058 | Gewn Ni Gorffen/12 Impressionistic Soundscapes (clear vinyl, die-cut p/s, mail order only, 1,000 copies) | 10 |
| 98 | Mercury ANKST GZM 5 | Let's Get Together (In Our Minds)/Billy And The Sugarloaf Mountain/Hwiangerdd Mar (numbered p/s) | 8 |
| 95 | Ankst ANKST 059 | BWYD TIME (LP, gatefold sleeve) | 20 |
| 97 | Fontana 534 769 | BARAFUNDLE (LP) | 30 |
| 98 | Fontana 558 822-1 | GORKY 5 (LP) | 25 |
| 99 | Mantra MNTPL 1015 | SPANISH DANCE TROUPE (LP) | 30 |
| 00 | Mantra MNTLPM 1023 | THE BLUE TREES (LP) | 25 |
| 01 | Mantra MNTLP 1025 | HOW I LONG TO FEEL THAT SUMMER IN MY HEART (LP) | 30 |

## ROBERT GORL

| | | | |
|---|---|---|---|
| 83 | Mute 12 MUTE 027 | Mit Dir (Extended)/Beruhut Verfuhrt (Remixed) (12", p/s) | 10 |
| 83 | Mute 7 MUTE 027 | Mit Dir/Beruhut Verfuhrt (p/s) | 5 |

*(see also D.A.F.)*

## JOHN GORMAN

| | | | |
|---|---|---|---|
| 73 | Island WIP 6151 | WPC Hodges/I Remember | 5 |
| 77 | DJM DJF 20491 | GO MAN GORMAN (LP) | 15 |

*(see also Scaffold, Grimms)*

## EYDIE GORMÉ

| | | | |
|---|---|---|---|
| 54 | Vogue Coral Q 2014 | Frenesi/Climb Up The Wall | 10 |
| 54 | Vogue Coral Q 2027 | Tea For Two/Sure | 10 |
| 55 | Vogue Coral Q 72092 | Give A Fool A Chance/A Girl Can't Say | 10 |
| 55 | Vogue Coral Q 72103 | Soldier Boy/What Is The Secret Of Your Success? | 10 |
| 56 | London HL 8227 | Sincerely Yours/Come Home | 15 |
| 63 | CBS AAG 163 | I Want To Stay Here/Ain't Love (as STEVE & EYDIE) | 6 |

*(see also Steve Lawrence)*

## GORP

| | | | |
|---|---|---|---|
| 83 | Beet Bop 1 | THE WILD MEN OF GORP (LP) | 15 |

## FRANK GORSHIN

| | | | |
|---|---|---|---|
| 66 | Pye International 7N 25402 | The Riddler/Never Let Her Go (in p/s) | 50 |
| 66 | Pye International 7N 25402 | The Riddler/Never Let Her Go | 25 |

## PETER GOSLING

| | | | |
|---|---|---|---|
| 70 | Sonet SON 2010 | Values/Peace | 10 |

## GOSPEL CLASSICS

| | | | |
|---|---|---|---|
| 68 | Chess CRS 8080 | More Love, That's What We Need/You Need Faith | 100 |
| 68 | Chess CRS 8080 | More Love, That's What We Need/You Need Faith (DJ copy) | 150 |

## GOSPELFOLK

| | | | |
|---|---|---|---|
| 69 | Emblem 7DR 324 | PRODIGAL (LP) | 150 |

## GOSPEL GARDEN

| | | | |
|---|---|---|---|
| 68 | Camp 602 006 | Finders Keepers/Just A Tear | 40 |

*(see also Dimples, Amazing Blondel)*

## GOSPEL OAK

| | | | |
|---|---|---|---|
| 70 | Uni UNS 527 | Recollections Of Jessica/Brown Haired Girl | 6 |

MINT VALUE £

| | | | |
|---|---|---|---|
| 70 | Uni UNLS 113 | GOSPEL OAK (LP) | 100 |

**GOSPEL PEARLS**

| | | | |
|---|---|---|---|
| 63 | Liberty LBY 1191 | THE GOSPEL PEARLS (LP) | 25 |

**GOTAN PROJECT**

| | | | |
|---|---|---|---|
| 01 | XL XLLP 148 | LA REVANCHA DEL TANGO (2-LP) | 25 |

**GOTHAM CITY WRECKERS**

| | | | |
|---|---|---|---|
| 86 | SRT 6KS 816 | Counterfeit/Tube City | 10 |

**GOTHIC GIRLS**

| | | | |
|---|---|---|---|
| 83 | Backs NCH 007 | Outrage/Devil (p/s) | 10 |
| 84 | Backs 12NCH 011 | GLASS BABY EP (12", p/s) | 15 |
| 84 | Backs NCHM LP2 | LILAC DREAMS EP (12", p/s) | 10 |

**GOTHIC HORIZON**

| | | | |
|---|---|---|---|
| 70 | Argo AFW 102 | The Jason Lodge Poetry Book/Wilhelmina Before Sunrise | 12 |
| 71 | Argo AFW 104 | Marjorie/Song | 10 |
| 72 | Argo AFW 107 | If You Can Smile/Thoughts | 8 |
| 72 | Argo AFW 108 | Girl With Guitar/Can't Bear To Think About You | 8 |
| 71 | Argo ZFB 26 | THE JASON LODGE POETRY BOOK (LP) | 65 |
| 72 | Argo ZDA 150 | TOMORROW IS ANOTHER DAY (LP) | 60 |

**GOTH TRAD**

| | | | |
|---|---|---|---|
| 07 | Deep Medi Musik MEDI 05 | Cut End/Flags (12") | 20 |
| 07 | Skud SKUD 001 | Back To Chill/Swamp/The Gate (12") | 10 |
| 08 | Skud SKUD 002 | Far East Assassin/Far East Assassin (DJ Distance Remix) (12") | 10 |

**DALE GOULDER & LIZ DYER**

| | | | |
|---|---|---|---|
| 70 | Argo ZFB 10 | JANUARY MAN (LP) | 40 |
| 71 | Argo ZFB 30 | RAVEN & CROW (LP) | 40 |

**GRAHAM GOULDMAN**

| | | | |
|---|---|---|---|
| 66 | Decca F 12334 | Stop! Stop! Stop! (Or Honey I'll Be Gone...)/Better To Have Loved And Lost | 150 |
| 68 | RCA Victor RCA 1667 | Upstairs, Downstairs/Chestnut | 40 |
| 69 | Spark SRL 1026 | Windmills Of Your Mind/Harvey's Theme (as Graham Gouldman Orchestra) | 15 |
| 72 | CBS 7739 | Nowhere To Go/Growing Older | 7 |

*(see also 10cc, Whirlwinds, Mockingbirds, High Society, Frabjoy & Runcible Spoon, Manchester Mob, Garden Odyssey Enterprise, Friday Browne, Doctor Father)*

**GOVE**

| | | | |
|---|---|---|---|
| 69 | London HLE 10295 | Sunday Morning Early/Death Letter Blues | 12 |
| 72 | UNI UNs547 | Carry On (Till The Band Adjourns)/I've Been Thinking Of You Lately | 8 |

**JOHN GRAAS SEPTET**

| | | | |
|---|---|---|---|
| 54 | London RE-P 1003 | FRENCH HORN VOL. 1 (EP) | 10 |

**MICK GRABHAM**

| | | | |
|---|---|---|---|
| 72 | United Artists UP 35391 | On Fire For You Baby/Sweet Blossom Woman | 5 |
| 72 | United Artists UAS 29341 | MICK THE LAD (LP, laminated front cove sleeve) | 20 |

*(see also Plastic Penny, Cochise, Procol Harum)*

**GRACE**

| | | | |
|---|---|---|---|
| 77 | Zipp ZB 003 | Old Stories/Rule Britannia (in p/s) | 60 |
| 77 | Zipp ZB 003 | Old Stories/Rule Britannia (no p/s) | 20 |
| 80 | MCA MCA 628 | Fire Of London/Beatnik (p/s) | 5 |
| 81 | MCA MCA 667 | Billy Boy/Ad Mad (p/s) | 15 |

**GRAME GRACE**

| | | | |
|---|---|---|---|
| 76 | RCA RCA 2633 | Flambouyant Freak/Don't Hang Around Like That | 6 |
| 75 | RCA SF 8418 | HAIL ME (LP, with insert) | 15 |

**CHARLIE GRACIE**

| | | | |
|---|---|---|---|
| 57 | Parlophone R 4290 | Butterfly/Ninety-Nine Ways (initially gold lettering on label) | 40 |
| 57 | Parlophone R 4290 | Butterfly/Ninety-Nine Ways (later pressing with silver lettering on label) | 20 |
| 57 | Parlophone R 4313 | Fabulous/Just Lookin' (initially gold lettering on label) | 40 |
| 57 | Parlophone R 4313 | Fabulous/Just Lookin' (later pressing with silver lettering on label) | 15 |
| 57 | London HL 8467 | Wandering Eyes/I Love You So Much It Hurts (tri-centre) | 12 |
| 57 | London HLU 8521 | Cool Baby/You Got A Heart Like A Rock (tri-centre) | 20 |
| 58 | London HLU 8596 | Crazy Girl/Dressin' Up (tri-centre) | 30 |
| 59 | Coral Q 72362 | Doodlebug/Hurry Up, Buttercup (tri-centre) | 30 |
| 59 | Coral Q 72362 | Doodlebug/Hurry Up, Buttercup (78) | 30 |
| 59 | Coral Q 72373 | Angel Of Love/I'm A Fool, That's Why (tri-centre) | 15 |
| 59 | Coral Q 72373 | Angel Of Love/I'm A Fool, That's Why (later round centre) | 10 |
| 59 | Coral Q 72373 | Angel Of Love/I'm A Fool, That's Why (78) | 20 |
| 59 | Coral Q 72381 | Oh-Well-A/Because I Love You So | 15 |
| 59 | Coral Q 72381 | Oh-Well-A/Because I Love You So (78) | 25 |
| 60 | Columbia DB 4477 | The Race/I Looked For You | 10 |
| 62 | London HLU 9603 | Pretty Baby/Night And Day, U.S.A. | 20 |
| 65 | Stateside SS 402 | He'll Never Love You Like I Do/Keep My Love Next To Your Heart | 75 |
| 65 | Stateside SS 402 | He'll Never Love You Like I Do/Keep My Love Next To Your Heart (DJ copy) | 150 |
| 78 | London HLU 10563 | Fabulous/Makin' Whoopie/Wow...w (tri centre) | 10 |
| 57 | Parlophone GEP 8630 | THE FABULOUS CHARLIE GRACIE (EP) | 40 |
| 83 | Rollercoaster ROLL 2005 | LIVE AT THE STOCKHOLM GLOBE AUGUST 26 1957 (LP) | 15 |

**GRACIOUS!**

| | | | |
|---|---|---|---|
| 68 | Polydor 56333 | Beautiful/What A Lovely Rain | 35 |
| 70 | Vertigo 6059 009 | Once On A Windy Day/Fugue In D Minor | 30 |
| 70 | Vertigo 6360 002 | GRACIOUS! (LP, gatefold sleeve, large swirl label) | 500 |
| 72 | Philips Intl. 6382 004 | THIS IS ... GRACIOUS!! (LP, black/silver labels) | 350 |
| 88 | Beat Goes On BGO LP 34 | GRACIOUS! (LP, reissue) | 15 |

## GRADUATE

| | | | |
|---|---|---|---|
| 80 | Precision PAR 100 | Elvis Should Play Ska/Julie Julie (p/s) | 5 |
| 80 | Precision PAR 104 | Ever Met A Day/Shut Up (p/s, 1980 issue PAR 117 with no p/s = £3) | 6 |
| 80 | Precision PAR 111 | Ambition/Bad Dreams (p/s) | 5 |
| 81 | Precision PAR 117 | Shut Up/Ever Met A Day (reissue, no p/s) | 5 |
| 80s | Blue Hat 5 BHR | Mad One/Somebody Put Out The Fire | 10 |

*(see also Tears For Fears)*

## GRADUATES

| | | | |
|---|---|---|---|
| 79 | Graduate GRAD 1 | If You Want It/Hey Young Girl (p/s) | 6 |

## GRAFFIA

| | | | |
|---|---|---|---|
| 81 | Magic 102 | Stop It Stop/Cymer Di (die-cut company sleeve) | 10 |

## GRAFITTI

| | | | |
|---|---|---|---|
| 76 | Beeb 19 | Dear Prudence/Come Together | 20 |

## BILLY GRAHAM & ESCALATORS

| | | | |
|---|---|---|---|
| 67 | Atlantic 584 073 | Ooh Poo Pah Doo/East 24th Avenue | 15 |

## BOB GRAHAM EXPERIENCE

| | | | |
|---|---|---|---|
| 78 | Anchor ANC 1055 | Blast Off (Percussion In Space)/Malfunction | 6 |

## BOBBY/BOBBIE GRAHAM

| | | | |
|---|---|---|---|
| 65 | Fontana TF 521 | Skin Deep/Zoom Widge And Wag (as Bobbie Graham) | 25 |
| 66 | Fontana TF 667 | Teensville/Grotty Drums (as Bobby Graham) | 15 |

*(see also Outlaws, Jimmy Page)*

## CHICK GRAHAM & COASTERS

| | | | |
|---|---|---|---|
| 64 | Decca F 11859 | Education/I Know | 12 |
| 64 | Decca F 11932 | A Little You/Dance Baby Dance | 12 |

## DAV(E)Y GRAHAM

| | | | |
|---|---|---|---|
| 68 | Decca F 12841 | Both Sides Now/Tristano | 12 |
| 62 | Golden Guinea GGL 0224 | THE GUITAR PLAYER (LP) | 50 |
| 64 | Decca LK 4649 | FOLK, BLUES AND BEYOND (LP) | 175 |
| 66 | Decca LK 4780 | MIDNIGHT MAN (LP) | 100 |
| 68 | Decca LK/SKL 4969 | LARGE AS LIFE AND TWICE AS NATURAL (LP) | 120 |
| 69 | Decca LK/SKL 5011 | HAT (LP) | 100 |
| 70 | Decca SKL 5056 | HOLLY KALEIDOSCOPE (LP, as Davy Graham & Holly) | 120 |
| 70 | Decca LK 4649 | FOLK, BLUES AND BEYOND (LP, second issue with boxed Decca logo and laminated front cover) | 100 |
| 70 | President PTLS 1039 | GODINGTON BOUNDARY (LP, with Holly) | 150 |
| 76 | Eron ERON 007 | ALL THAT MOODY (LP, private pressing) | 200 |

*(see also Shirley Collins)*

## DAVY GRAHAM/THAMESIDERS

| | | | |
|---|---|---|---|
| 63 | Decca DFE 8538 | FROM A LONDON HOOTENANNY (EP, 2 tracks each) | 18 |

## DAVY GRAHAM & ALEXIS KORNER

| | | | |
|---|---|---|---|
| 62 | Topic TOP 70 | 3/4 A.D. (EP, first pressing in mauve sleeve with cream label) | 90 |
| 62 | Topic TOP 70 | 3/4 A.D. (EP, later pressings with lilac sleeve and blue label) | 60 |
| 62 | Topic TOP 70 | 3/4 A.D. (EP, later pressings with bronze sleeve and blue label) | 30 |

*(see also Alexis Korner)*

## ERNIE GRAHAM

| | | | |
|---|---|---|---|
| 78 | Stiff OFF 2 | Romeo And The Lonely Girl/Only Time Will Tell (p/s) | 7 |
| 71 | Liberty LBS 83485 | ERNIE GRAHAM (LP, textured sleeve, black label) | 250 |

*(see also Clancy, Eire Apparent, Brinsley Schwarz, Help Yourself, Nick Lowe)*

## KENNY GRAHAM'S AFRO-CUBISTS

| | | | |
|---|---|---|---|
| 60 | Starlite ST45 013 | Bongo Chant/Beguine | 10 |
| 57 | Pye Jazz NJE 1053 | PRESENTING KENNY GRAHAM PART 1 (EP) | 20 |
| 57 | Esquire EP 34 | CARIBBEAN SUITE (EP) | 20 |
| 57 | Esquire EP 68 | KENNY GRAHAM'S AFRO CUBISTS (EP) | 20 |
| 57 | Esquire EP 83 | KENNY GRAHAM'S AFRO CUBISTS (EP) | 25 |
| 56 | MGM MGM-C 764 | MOONDOG AND SUNCAT SUITES (LP, as Kenny Graham & His Satellites) | 140 |
| 57 | Nixa NJL 12 | PRESENTING KENNY GRAHAM (LP) | 120 |
| 57 | Esquire 20-012 | KENNY GRAHAM AFRO CUBISTS (LP) | 90 |
| 57 | Esquire 20-023 | CARIBBEAN SUITE (LP) | 120 |
| 10 | Trunk JBH 036 LP | MOONDOG AND SUNCAT SUITES (LP, 800 only, as Kenny Graham And His Satellites) | 20 |
| 10 | Trunk JBH 036 LP | MOONDOG AND SUNCAT SUITES (LP, reissue, 500 only yellow vinyl, as Kenny Graham And His Satellites) | 20 |

*(see also Yolanda)*

## LEO GRAHAM

| | | | |
|---|---|---|---|
| 73 | Upsetter US 399 | News Flash/UPSETTERS: Flashing Echo | 18 |
| 73 | Summit SUM 8539 | Three Blind Mice/UPSETTERS: Mice Skank | 15 |

## LOU GRAHAM

| | | | |
|---|---|---|---|
| 58 | Coral Q 72322 | Wee Willie Brown/You Were Mean Baby | 400 |
| 58 | Coral Q 72322 | Wee Willie Brown/You Were Mean Baby (78) | 50 |

## LYNDA GRAHAM

| | | | |
|---|---|---|---|
| 62 | Philips 326 552BF | As Long As The River Flows/When I'm Sixteen | 8 |
| 63 | Philips BF 1249 | Without Your Love/Wait And See | 8 |
| 64 | Philips BF 1308 | You'd Better Believe It/That's The Last Thing I'd Do | 10 |

## GRAHAM CENTRAL STATION

| | | | |
|---|---|---|---|
| 74 | Warner Bros K 46206 | GRAHAM CENTRAL STATION (LP) | 15 |

*(see also Sly & Family Stone)*

## RON GRAINER ORCHESTRA

| | | | |
|---|---|---|---|
| 64 | HMV POP 1366 | Not So Much A Programme, More A Way Of Life/Ascot Gavotte | 10 |
| 67 | Pye 7N 17383 | A Man In A Suitcase/Andorra (pink label, later blue) | 12 |

## Ross GRAINER (continued)

| 67 | RCA Victor RCA 1635 | The Prisoner/Happening Sunday | 75 |
| 69 | RCA Victor RCA 1898 | The Paul Temple Theme/The Jazz Age | 10 |
| 79 | RK 1018 | Tales Of The Unexpected/Paul Temple | 7 |
| 79 | RK 1021 | Tales Of The Unexpected/Malice Aforethought (p/s) | 7 |
| 79 | Six Of One 6 OF 1 | THE PRISONER ARRIVAL (EP, fan club issue) | 30 |
| 69 | RCA Intl. INTS 1020 | THEMES LIKE... (LP) | 15 |
| 78 | RK LB 003 | TALES OF THE UNEXPECTED (LP) | 15 |

## ROSS GRAINER
| 79 | Music Factory MF102 | Cardiff Roses/Wind And The Trees | 12 |

## COLIN GRAINGER & THE FRANK CORDELL ORCHESTRA
| 58 | HMV POP 484 | This I Know/Are You? | 7 |
| 59 | HMV POP 639 | Love Only Me/Plain And Simple Girl | 7 |

## GLENDA GRAINGER
| 60s | Audio Fidelity AFSP 007 | Mr. Kiss Kiss Bang Bang/Who | 12 |

## BILLY GRAMMER
| 58 | London HLU 8752 | Gotta Travel On/Chasing A Dream | 7 |
| 59 | Felsted AF 121 | Bonaparte's Retreat/The Kissing Tree | 5 |
| 59 | Felsted AF 128 | Willy, Quit Your Playing/It Takes You | 5 |
| 61 | Brunswick 05851 | Rainbow Round My Shoulder/Columbus Stockade Blues | 5 |
| 59 | Felsted GEP 1005 | BILLY GRAMMER HITS (EP) | 15 |

## GERRY GRANAHAN
| 58 | London HL 8668 | No Chemise, Please/Girl Of My Dreams | 20 |
| 60 | Top Rank JAR 262 | It Hurts/RICHIE ROBIN: Strange Dream | 15 |

## GRANDADDY
| 98 | Big Cat ABB5003507 | A.M. 180/Here (p/s, stickered) | 10 |
| 98 | Big Cat – ABB 157 S | Everything Beautiful Is Far Away/For The Dishwasher (p/s) | 7 |
| 98 | Big Cat – ABB 161 S | Laughing Stock/G.P.C./12-PAK-599 (p/s) | 6 |
| 98 | Big Cat – ABB 162 S | Summer Here Kids/Levitz (Birdless)/My Small Love (p/s) | 6 |
| 98 | Big Cat ABB 152 | UNDER THE WESTERN FREEWAY (LP, inner, stickered sleeve) | 30 |
| 00 | V2 VVR 1012231 | SOPHTWARE SLUMP (LP, inner) | 18 |
| 03 | V2 VVR 1012251 | SUMDAY (2-LP, with inner sleeves) | 20 |

## GRAND FUNK RAILROAD
| 70 | Capitol CL 15632 | Heartbreaker/Please Don't Worry | 8 |
| 70 | Capitol CL 15661 | Closer To Home/Aimless Lady | 5 |
| 71 | Capitol CL 15668 | Inside Looking Out/Paranoid (33rpm) | 10 |
| 71 | Capitol CL 15689 | I Can Feel Him In The Morning/Are You Ready/Mean Mistreater (33rpm maxi-single) | 12 |
| 71 | Capitol CL 15705 | People, Let's Stop The War/Save The Land | 5 |
| 72 | Capitol CL 15738 | Rock And Roll Soul/Flight Of Phoenix | 5 |
| 76 | EMI International INT 523 | Can You Do It/1976 | 8 |
| 69 | Capitol E-ST 307 | ON TIME (LP) | 50 |
| 70 | Capitol E-ST 406 | GRAND FUNK (LP) | 40 |
| 70 | Capitol E-ST 471 | CLOSER THAN HOME (LP) | 40 |
| 71 | Capitol E-SW 764 | SURVIVAL (LP) | 25 |
| 72 | Capitol E-AS 853 | E PLURIBUS FUNK (LP, circular 'silver coin' sleeve) | 50 |
| 73 | Capitol E-AST 11099 | PHOENIX (LP, gatefold sleeve) | 18 |

## GRANDISONS
| 63 | RCA RCA 1339 | All Right/True Romance | 12 |

## GRAND PRIX
| 80 | RCA RCA 7 | Thinking Of You/Feels Good (p/s) | 15 |
| 83 | Chrysalis PRIX 2 | Shout/Keep On Believing (p/s, with patch) | 8 |
| 83 | Chrysalis PRIXX 2 | Shout (12", p/s) | 12 |

*(see also McAuley Schenker Group, Praying Mantis, Stratus, Uriah Heep)*

## GRAND UNION
| 68 | CBS 3956 | Slowly But Surely/She Said | 40 |

*(see also Enough's Enough)*

## GERRI GRANGER
| 63 | London HLX 9759 | Just Tell Him Jane Said Hello/What's Wrong With Me | 15 |

## GRANNIE
| 71 | SRT 71138 | GRANNIE (LP, private pressing of 99 copies only, homemade sleeve) | 1500 |
| 12 | SRT 71138 | GRANNIE (LP, reissue, hand-made sleeve, 750 only, insert, and signed numbered certificate) | 30 |

## GRANNY
| 73 | DJM DJS. 291 | Lady/Weirdie Deirdre's Dilemma | 15 |

## GRANNY'S INTENTIONS
| 67 | Deram DM 158 | The Story Of David/Sandy's On The Phone Again | 25 |
| 68 | Deram DM 184 | Julie Don't Love Me Anymore/One Time Lovers | 18 |
| 68 | Deram DM 214 | Never An Everyday Thing/Hilda The Bilda | 25 |
| 70 | Deram DM 293 | Take Me Back/Maybe | 20 |
| 70 | Deram SML 1060 | HONEST INJUN (LP, white/red label with small logo) | 125 |

*(see also Gary Moore)*

## AMY GRANT
| 82 | Myrrh MYR 1124 | AGE TO AGE (LP, with lyric insert) | 15 |

## CLINTON GRANT
| 75 | Circle 5 | I've Been Trying/Second Attempt | 10 |

## CY GRANT
| 62 | Melodisc 45-1433 | Heavy Weather/Lucky Oyster (tri centre) | 10 |

## DOMINIC GRANT
| | | | |
|---|---|---|---|
| 68 | Mercury MF 1032 | I've Been There/Don't Stop Girl | 50 |

## EARL GRANT
| | | | |
|---|---|---|---|
| 58 | Brunswick 05762 | The End/Hunky Dunky Doo | 7 |
| 60 | Brunswick 05824 | House Of Bamboo/Two Loves Have I | 10 |
| 62 | Brunswick 05870 | Swingin' Gently/Evening Rain | 7 |

## EDDY GRANT
| | | | |
|---|---|---|---|
| 74 | Torpedo TOR 30 | My Queen Tonight/Hello Africa | 5 |
| 75 | Torpedo TOR 53 | Nobody's Got Time (Part 1)/Nobody's Got Time (Part 2) | 15 |

*(see also Equals, Coach House Rhythm Section)*

## ERKEY GRANT & EARWIGS
| | | | |
|---|---|---|---|
| 63 | Pye 7N 15521 | I'm A Hog For You/I Can't Get Enough Of You | 25 |

## GOGI GRANT
| | | | |
|---|---|---|---|
| 55 | London HLB 8192 | Suddenly There's A Valley/Love Is | 10 |
| 56 | London HLB 8257 | Who Are We/We Believe In Love | 10 |
| 56 | London HLB 8282 | Wayward Wind/No More Than Forever | 10 |
| 57 | London HLB 8364 | You're In Love/When The Tide Is High | 10 |
| 58 | London HLB 8550 | The Golden Ladder/All Of Me | 8 |

*(see also Tony Martin)*

## JANIE GRANT
| | | | |
|---|---|---|---|
| 61 | Pye International 7N 25093 | Triangle/She's Going Steady With You | 18 |
| 62 | Pye International 7N 25148 | That Greasy Kid Stuff/Trying To Forget You | 18 |

## JOHN GRANT
| | | | |
|---|---|---|---|
| 13 | Bella Union BELLAV 395 | STRONGROOM EP (12") | 20 |
| 13 | Bella Union BELLAV 433 | GETS SCHOOLED (12") | 20 |
| 15 | Bella Union BELLA 514V | JOHN GRANT WITH ROYAL NORTHERN SINFONIA (12") | 15 |
| 13 | Bella Union BELLAV 377 | PALE GREEN GHOSTS (2-LP, CD, green vinyl) | 20 |
| 15 | Bella Union BELLA 478V | WITH THE BBC PHILHARMONIC LIVE IN CONCERT (2-LP, silver vinyl) | 50 |
| 15 | Bella Union BELLA 505V | GREY TICKLES, BLACK PRESSURE (2-LP, lavender vinyl) | 20 |

*(see also Midlake)*

## JULIE GRANT
| | | | |
|---|---|---|---|
| 62 | Pye 7N 15430 | Somebody Tell Him/Ev'ry Letter You Write | 10 |
| 62 | Pye 7N 15447 | So Many Ways/Unimportant Things | 10 |
| 62 | Pye 7N 15461 | When You're Smiling/Lonely Sixteen | 10 |
| 62 | Pye 7N 15483 | Up On The Roof/When You Ask About Love | 5 |
| 63 | Pye 7N 15508 | Count On Me/Then, Only Then | 5 |
| 63 | Pye 7N 15526 | That's How Heartaches Are Made/Cruel World | 10 |
| 63 | Pye 7N 15545 | Don't Ever Let Me Down/Somebody Cares | 10 |
| 63 | Pye 7N 15590 | Hello Love/It's Alright | 12 |
| 64 | Pye 7N 15684 | Come To Me/Can't Get You Out Of My Mind | 8 |
| 64 | Pye 7N 15615 | Every Day I Have To Cry/Watch What You Do With My Baby | 8 |
| 64 | Pye 7N 15652 | You Are Nobody 'Til Somebody Loves You/I Only Care About You | 8 |
| 65 | Pye 7N 15756 | Baby Baby (I Still Love You)/My World Is Empty Without You | 8 |
| 65 | Pye 7N 15812 | Giving Up/Cause I Believe In You | 8 |
| 65 | Pye 7N 15884 | Lonely Without You/As Long As I Know He's Mine | 8 |
| 65 | Pye 7N 15937 | Stop/When The Lovin' Ends | 15 |
| 62 | Pye NEP 24171 | THIS IS JULIE GRANT (EP) | 20 |

## LEE GRANT (& CAPITOLS)
| | | | |
|---|---|---|---|
| 66 | Parlophone R 5531 | Breaking Point/Don't Cry Baby (with Capitols) | 20 |
| 70 | Decca F 13029 | A Little Love And Understanding/I Got To Get You Out Of My Mind (solo) | 7 |

## LITTLE BROTHER (GRANT)
| | | | |
|---|---|---|---|
| 70 | Torpedo TOR 27 | Baby Don't Let Me Down/Brother Strong Man (as Little Brother) | 15 |
| 70 | Torpedo TOR 28 | Let's Do It Together/Hey Man, Why (as Little Brother Grant & Zapatta Schmidt) | 15 |

*(see also Equals)*

## NEVILLE GRANT
| | | | |
|---|---|---|---|
| 73 | Attack ATT 8058 | Baby Don't Get Hooked On Me/Happy Hippie | 20 |
| 73 | Downtown DT 509 | Sick And Tired/PRINCE DJANGO: Hot Tip | 80 |

## NORMAN GRANT ORCHESTRA
| | | | |
|---|---|---|---|
| 61 | Starlite ST45 060 | Jive Medley/Speak Low | 7 |

## TOP GRANT
| | | | |
|---|---|---|---|
| 62 | Island WI 034 | Searching/David & Goliath | 15 |
| 62 | Island WI 052 | Suzie/Jenny | 15 |
| 63 | Island WI 072 | Riverbank Coberley (as Top-Grant)/Nancy | 15 |
| 63 | Island WI 074 | Money Money Money/Have Mercy On Me | 18 |
| 63 | Island WI 077 | War In Africa/The Birds | 15 |

*(see also Rhythm Aces)*

## GRAPE
| | | | |
|---|---|---|---|
| 92 | Pencil Toast PENT 001 | Baby In A Plastic Bag/Listen To Your Heart (p/s) | 25 |

## GRAPEFRUIT
| | | | |
|---|---|---|---|
| 68 | RCA Victor RCA 1656 | Dear Delilah/The Dead Boot | 8 |
| 68 | RCA Victor RCA 1677 | Elevator/Yes | 25 |
| 68 | RCA Victor RCA 1716 | C'mon Marianne/Ain't It Good | 6 |
| 68 | Stateside-Dunhill SS 8005 | Someday Soon/Theme For Twiggy | 7 |
| 69 | Stateside-Dunhill SS 8011 | Round Going Round/This Little Man | 7 |
| 69 | RCA Victor RCA 1855 | Deep Water/Come Down To The Station | 7 |
| 70 | RCA Victor RCA 1907 | Lady Godiva (Come Home)/Thunder And Lightning | 6 |
| 71 | Deram DM 343 | Universal Party/Sha Sha | 6 |
| 69 | Stateside-Dunhill S(S)L 5008 | AROUND GRAPEFRUIT (LP, black/white/red label with "sold in the U.K..." text) | 100 |

MINT VALUE £

| | | | |
|---|---|---|---|
| 69 | RCA Victor SF 8030 | DEEP WATER (LP) | 80 |

*(see also Tony Rivers & Castaways, Easybeats, Fynn McCool, Sleepy)*

## GRAPEVINE
| | | | |
|---|---|---|---|
| 68 | Liberty LBF 15063 | Things Ain't What They Used To Be Anymore/Ace In The Hole | 8 |

## GRAPHIC DESIGN
| | | | |
|---|---|---|---|
| 83 | SRTS/83/CUS/1952 | Lonely Life/Shock (p/s) | 100 |

## GRAPHITE
| | | | |
|---|---|---|---|
| 72 | Beacon BEA 109 | Gimme Your Number/Chestnut Loke (possibly promo only) | 40 |

## GRASS CUTTERS
| | | | |
|---|---|---|---|
| 72 | Malbury MB 1 | Inside A Dream/The Silence Is Over (p/s) | 25 |

## GRASSROOTS
| | | | |
|---|---|---|---|
| 66 | RCA Victor RCA 1532 | Where Were You When I Needed You/These Are Bad Times | 10 |
| 67 | Pye International 7N 25422 | Let's Live For Today/Depressed Feeling | 10 |
| 67 | Pye International 7N 25431 | Things I Should Have Said/Tip Of My Tongue | 6 |
| 68 | RCA Victor RCA 1682 | Melody For You/Hey Friend | 5 |
| 68 | RCA Victor RCA 1737 | Midnight Confessions/Who Will You Be Tomorrow | 15 |
| 69 | Stateside-Dunhill SS 8006 | Bella Linda/Hot Bright Lights | 5 |
| 69 | Stateside-Dunhill SS 8012 | All Good Things Come To An End/Melody For You | 5 |
| 69 | Stateside-Dunhill SS 8018 | The River Is Wide/(You Gotta) Live For Love | 5 |
| 69 | Stateside-Dunhill SS 8023 | Who Will You Be Tomorrow/Midnight Confessions | 8 |
| 69 | Stateside-Dunhill SS 8029 | I'd Wait A Million Years/Fly Me To Havana | 12 |
| 69 | Stateside-Dunhill SS 8033 | Heaven Knows/Don't Remind Me | 7 |
| 71 | Probe PRO 515 | Temptation Eyes/Keepin' Me Down | 10 |
| 69 | Stateside S(S)L 5005 | GOLDEN GRASS (LP) | 25 |
| 70 | Stateside SSL 5012 | LEAVING IT ALL BEHIND (LP) | 25 |

*(see also P.F. Sloan)*

## GRATEFUL DEAD
| | | | |
|---|---|---|---|
| 67 | Warner Bros WB 7186 | Born Cross-Eyed/Dark Star | 50 |
| 70 | Warner Bros WB 7410 | Uncle John's Band/New Speedway Boogie | 12 |
| 71 | Warner Bros. | Truckin'/Johnny B. Goode (unissued) | 0 |
| 72 | Warner Bros K 16167 | One More Saturday Night (as Grateful Dead with Bobby Ace)/Bertha | 7 |
| 73 | Atlantic K 19301 | Let Me Sing Your Blues Away/Here Comes Sunshine | 7 |
| 74 | United Artists UP 36030 | U.S. Blues/Loose Lucy | 6 |
| 77 | Warner Bros SAM 79 | Dark Star/Born Cross-Eyed (p/s, mail-order issue with Dark Star magazine) | 40 |
| 79 | Arista ARIST 236 | Good Lovin'/Stagger Lee | 6 |
| 87 | Arista RIS 35 | Touch Of Grey/My Brother Esau (grey vinyl, p/s) | 6 |
| 67 | Warner Bros W 1689 | THE GRATEFUL DEAD (LP, mono) | 100 |
| 67 | Warner Bros W(S) 1689 | THE GRATEFUL DEAD (LP, stereo) | 70 |
| 68 | Warner Bros W 1749 | ANTHEM OF THE SUN (LP, mono) | 80 |
| 68 | Warner Bros WS 1749 | ANTHEM OF THE SUN (LP, stereo) | 70 |
| 69 | Warner Bros WS 1790 | AOXOMOXOA (LP) | 60 |
| 70 | Warner Bros WS 1830 | LIVE/DEAD (2-LP) | 50 |
| 70 | Warner Bros WS 1869 | WORKINGMAN'S DEAD (LP, matt sleeve) | 40 |
| 71 | Warner Bros WS 1893 | AMERICAN BEAUTY (LP) | 30 |
| 71 | Warner Bros K 66009 | LIVE DEAD (SKULL AND ROSES) (2-LP) | 30 |
| 71 | Warner Bros. K66002 | LIVE DEAD (LP, reissue) | 20 |
| 72 | Polydor 2310 171 | HISTORIC DEAD (LP) | 25 |
| 72 | Polydor 2310 172 | VINTAGE DEAD (LP) | 25 |
| 72 | Warner Bros K 66019 | EUROPE '72 (3-LP, triple fold-out sleeve) | 25 |
| 73 | Warner Bros K 49301 | WAKE OF THE FLOOD (LP) | 15 |
| 74 | Warner Bros K 56024 | SKELETONS FROM THE CLOSET: THE BEST OF GRATEFUL DEAD (LP) | 15 |
| 74 | Warner Bros K 59302 | FROM THE MARS HOTEL (LP) | 15 |
| 75 | United Artists UA 29895 | BLUES FOR ALLAH (LP) | 15 |
| 76 | United Artists UAD 60131/2 | STEAL YOUR FACE (2-LP, gatefold sleeve, with sampler LP For Dead Heads Only [FREE 2] in inner sleeve) | 20 |
| 77 | Arista 1016 | TERRAPIN STATION (LP) | 18 |

*(see also Jerry Garcia, Mickey Hart, Kingfish, Robert Hunter, Bob Weir, Keith & Donna Godchaux, Silver [U.S.], Diga Rhythm Band)*

## GRATIS
| | | | |
|---|---|---|---|
| 79 | B.P.M. BPM 1 | Downtown/Please Call My Number (1000 only, p/s) | 30 |

## GRATTITUDE
| | | | |
|---|---|---|---|
| 70 | Moth NT 1 | Dark Approaches/Sit Still (p/s) | 100 |

## GRAVE
| | | | |
|---|---|---|---|
| 03 | Century Media | MORBID WAYS TO DIE (Numbered box set with 6 picture disc LPs and booklet, 2000 only) | 60 |

## GRAVEDIGGAZ
| | | | |
|---|---|---|---|
| 94 | Gee Street GEEA 14 | NIGGAMORTIS (LP, with inner sleeve) | 20 |

## NICK GRAVENITES
| | | | |
|---|---|---|---|
| 69 | CBS 63818 | MY LABORS (LP) | 22 |

*(see also Big Brother & Holding Company)*

## BILLY GRAVES
| | | | |
|---|---|---|---|
| 59 | Felsted AF 119 | The Shag (Is Totally Cool)/Uncertain (export issue) | 25 |

## CARL GRAVES
| | | | |
|---|---|---|---|
| 75 | A&M AM 7151 | Baby Hang Up The Phone/Walk Softly | 6 |
| 76 | A&M AMS 7235 | My Whole World Ended (The Moment You Left Me)/Baby Don't Knock | 6 |

## TERESA GRAVES
| | | | |
|---|---|---|---|
| 69 | RCA 1948 | We're On Our Way/I Spent My Last Dream On You | 10 |

## GRAVY TRAIN
| | | | |
|---|---|---|---|
| 71 | Vertigo 6059049 | Alone In Georgia/Can Anybody Hear Me | 30 |

| | | | |
|---|---|---|---|
| 73 | Dawn DNS 1036 | Strength Of A Dream/Tolpuddle Episode | 8 |
| 74 | Dawn DNS 1058 | Starbright Starlight/Good Time Thing | 8 |
| 75 | Dawn DNS 1115 | Climb Aboard The Gravy Train/Sanctuary | 8 |
| 70 | Vertigo 6360 023 | GRAVY TRAIN (LP, gatefold sleeve, large swirl label) | 400 |
| 71 | Vertigo 6360 051 | BALLAD OF A PEACEFUL MAN (LP, gatefold sleeve, small swirl label) | 900 |
| 73 | Dawn DNLS 3046 | SECOND BIRTH (LP) | 125 |
| 74 | Dawn DNLH 1 | STAIRCASE TO THE DAY (LP, gatefold sleeve, pink 'sun' label) | 125 |

*(see also Mandalaband)*

## BARRY GRAY (ORCHESTRA)

| | | | |
|---|---|---|---|
| 62 | Lyntone LYN 249/250 | Sabotage/Supercar Song/Supercar Twist (flexi, with p/s may exist) | 30 |
| 62 | Lyntone LYN 249/250 | Sabotage/Supercar Song/Supercar Twist (flexi) | 15 |
| 64 | Melodisc MEL 1591 | Fireball/Zero G (by Barry Gray & His Spacemakers; in p/s) | 55 |
| 64 | Melodisc MEL 1591 | Fireball/Zero G (by Barry Gray & His Spacemakers) | 20 |
| 65 | Pye 7N 17016 | Thunderbirds/Parker - Well Done (in p/s) | 35 |
| 65 | Pye 7N 17016 | Thunderbirds/Parker - Well Done | 15 |
| 67 | Pye 7N 17391 | Captain Scarlet/The Mysterons Theme (in p/s) | 35 |
| 67 | Pye 7N 17391 | Captain Scarlet/The Mysterons Theme | 15 |
| 68 | Pye 7N 17625 | Joe 90 - Title Theme/Joe 90 - Hijacked (in p/s) | 50 |
| 68 | Pye 7N 17625 | Joe 90 - Title Theme/Joe 90 – Hijacked | 25 |
| 62 | Golden Guinea GGL 0106 | SUPERCAR - FLIGHT OF FANCY (LP, with Edwin Astley) | 50 |
| 67 | United Artists ULP 1159 | THUNDERBIRDS ARE GO! (LP, soundtrack, mono) | 100 |
| 67 | United Artists (S)ULP 1159 | THUNDERBIRDS ARE GO! (LP, soundtrack, stereo) | 120 |
| 87 | Fanderson MAF 1 | MUSIC FROM THE 21st CENTURY (7" mail order only mini-album, 33prm) | 10 |
| 98 | Fanderson FANSP 7 | SPACE 1999: YEAR ONE (2-CD, mail order only) | 25 |
| 98 | Fanderson FANSF6 | SUPERCAR & FIREBALL XL5 (CD, mail order only) | 30 |

*(see also Century 21, Mary Jane with Barry Gray, Richard Harvey)*

## BARRY GRAY

| | | | |
|---|---|---|---|
| 04 | Trunk JBH 010 | UFO: THE ORIGINAL TELEVISION SERIES SOUNDTRACK (LP, 500 on clear vinyl) | 40 |
| 04 | Trunk JBH 010 | UFO: THE ORIGINAL TELEVISION SERIES SOUNDTRACK (LP, 500 on black vinyl) | 40 |

## DOBIE GRAY

| | | | |
|---|---|---|---|
| 65 | London HL 9953 | The "In" Crowd/Be A Man | 10 |
| 65 | London HL 9953 | The "In" Crowd/Be A Man (DJ Copy) | 40 |
| 65 | Pye International 7N 25307 | See You At The Go Go/Walk With Love | 25 |
| 65 | Pye International 7N 25307 | See You At The Go Go/Walk With Love (DJ Copy) | 50 |
| 69 | London HL 10268 | The "In" Crowd/Be A Man (reissue) | 5 |
| 73 | MCA MU 1184 | Drift Away/City Stars | 5 |
| 73 | MCA MU 1221 | Now That I'm Without You/Loving Arms | 6 |
| 75 | Black Magic BM 107 | Out On The Floor/Be A Man | 8 |
| 75 | Black Magic BM 107 | Out On The Floor/Be A Man (DJ Copy) | 12 |
| 74 | Sydna SYD 5028 | Good Old Days/Never Ending Love | 8 |

## DOLORES GRAY

| | | | |
|---|---|---|---|
| 55 | Brunswick 05382 | Heat Wave/After You Get What You Want, You Don't Want It | 15 |
| 55 | Brunswick 05407 | Rock Love/One | 30 |
| 57 | Capitol CL 14732 | There'll Be Some Changes Made/Fool's Errand | 7 |
| 57 | Capitol T 897 | WARM BRANDY (LP) | 15 |

## DORIAN GRAY

| | | | |
|---|---|---|---|
| 67 | Parlophone R 5612 | Behind The Tear/Walking Down A Back Street | 5 |
| 68 | Parlophone R 5667 | I've Got You On My Mind/Move On | 12 |
| 68 | Parlophone R 5705 | Love Is All That It Should Be/Let Me Go Home | 5 |
| 68 | Parlophone R 5732 | Jingle Down A Hill/Get Goin' Baby | 8 |

## HERBIE GRAY

| | | | |
|---|---|---|---|
| 68 | Giant GN 38 | We're Staying Here/Life Ska | 30 |

*(see also Gene Rondo, Owen & Dandy, Tony Tribe)*

## JIMMIE GRAY

| | | | |
|---|---|---|---|
| 82 | JKO 12JKO 100 | The Kool People (Vocal)/The Kool People (Instrumental) (12") | 40 |

## JOHNNIE 'THE GASH' GRAY

| | | | |
|---|---|---|---|
| 58 | Fontana H 123 | Big Guitar/Tequila | 10 |
| 58 | Fontana H 134 | Apache/Zach's Tune | 10 |

## LORRAINE GRAY

| | | | |
|---|---|---|---|
| 64 | Fontana TF 435 | Are You Getting Tired Of Your Little Toy?/ The Boy That I Want Doesn't Want Me | 10 |
| 64 | Fontana TF 484 | The Little Girl That Cries/Talk To Him | 6 |

## MAUREEN GRAY

| | | | |
|---|---|---|---|
| 61 | HMV POP 944 | I Don't Want To Cry/Come On And Dance | 10 |

## OWEN GRAY

| | | | |
|---|---|---|---|
| 60 | Starlite ST45 015 | Far Love/Please Let Me Go | 35 |
| 60 | Starlite ST45 019 | Jenny Lee/The Plea | 40 |
| 60 | Blue Beat BB 8 | Cutest Little Woman/Running Around (with Ken Richards Band) | 20 |
| 61 | Blue Beat BB 43 | Sinners Weep/Get Drunk (with Hersan & His City Slickers) | 20 |
| 61 | Starlite ST45 032 | Mash It (Parts 1 & 2) | 40 |
| 62 | Starlite ST45 078 | I Feel Good/Someone To Help Me | 40 |
| 62 | Starlite ST45 088 | Let Me Go Free/In My Dreams | 40 |
| 62 | Blue Beat BB 75 | Rockin' In My Feet/Nobody Else (with Jets) | 20 |
| 62 | Blue Beat BB 91 | Millie Girl (with Buster's Group)/DERRICK MORGAN: Headache | 25 |
| 62 | Blue Beat BB 103 | Lonely Days/No Good Woman (with Sonny Bradshaw Quartet) | 18 |
| 62 | Blue Beat BB 108 | Keep It In Mind/Do You Want To Jump (with Les Dawson Combo) | 18 |
| 62 | Blue Beat BB 113 | Best Twist/Grandma-Grandpa (B-side with Hersan & His City Slickers) | 18 |
| 62 | Blue Beat BB 127 | Pretty Girl/Twist So Fine | 18 |
| 62 | Blue Beat BB 136 | They Got To Move/I Love Her | 18 |

MINT VALUE £

| 62 | Blue Beat BB 139 | Tree In The Meadow/Lizebella (with Buster's Group) | 18 |
|---|---|---|---|
| 62 | Island WI 002 | Patricia/Twist Baby | 20 |
| 62 | Island WI 020 | Audrey/Dolly Baby (with Ernest Rauglin [sic] Orchestra) | 20 |
| 62 | Island WI 030 | Midnight Trail/Time Will Tell | 20 |
| 62 | Island WI 048 | I'm Still Waiting/Last Night | 10 |
| 62 | Chek TD 101 | Come On Baby/My One Desire | 15 |
| 62 | Dice CC 3 | On The Beach/Young Lover | 30 |
| 63 | Blue Beat BB 147 | Big Mabel/Don't Come Knocking (with Edwards' Groupe) | 15 |
| 63 | Blue Beat BB 188 | Call Me My Pet/Give Me Your Love | 15 |
| 63 | Blue Beat BB 201 | Snow Falling/Oowee Baby (as Owen Gray & His Big Brother) | 15 |
| 64 | Blue Beat BB 217 | Draw Me Nearer/Daddy's Girl | 15 |
| 65 | Blue Beat BB 290 | Daddy's Gone/BUSTER'S ALLSTARS: Johnny Dark | 30 |
| 65 | Aladdin WI 603 | Gonna Work Out Fine/Dolly Baby | 20 |
| 65 | Aladdin WI 607 | Can I Get A Witness/Linda Lu | 20 |
| 65 | Island WI 252 | Shook Shimmy And Shake/I'm Going Back | 20 |
| 65 | Island WI 258 | You Don't Know Like I Do/Take Me Serious (with Sound System) | 15 |
| 65 | Venus VE 2 | Too Many Heartaches/Baby It's True | 10 |
| 66 | Island WI 252 | Shook, Shimmy And Shake/Gonna Work Out Fine | 30 |
| 66 | Island WI 267 | Paradise/Bye Bye Love | 10 |
| 66 | Blue Beat BB 365 | I'm Gonna Say So Long/The Days I'm Living | 12 |
| 67 | Island WIP 6000 | Help Me/Incense | 25 |
| 67 | Collins Downbeat CR 003 | Collins Greetings/Rock It Down (with Sir Collins & Band) | 60 |
| 67 | Collins Downbeat CR 004 | I'm So Lonely (with Sir Collins & Band)/EL RECO, SIR COLLINS & J. SATCH: Shock Steady | 90 |
| 68 | Collins Downbeat CR 007 | Am Satisfy (with Sir Collins & Band)/BOB STACKIE & SIR COLLINS & BAND: Sweet Music | 150 |
| 68 | Collins Downbeat CR 009 | Grab It, Hold It, Feel It (with Bob Stackie)/DAN SIMMONS: Way Out Sound | 65 |
| 68 | Collins Downbeat CR 010 | I'm Gonna Take You Back (with Bob Stackie)/GLEN ADAMS: King Sized | 90 |
| 68 | Coxsone CS 7047 | Give Me A Little Sign/Ain't Nobody Home | 300 |
| 68 | Coxsone CS 7053 | Give It To Me/Isn't It So | 90 |
| 68 | Blue Cat BS 123 | These Foolish Things/This I Promise | 80 |
| 69 | Blue Cat BS 156 | I Can't Stop Loving You/Tell Me Darling | 30 |
| 68 | Trojan TR 632 | Lovey Dovey/Grooving | 20 |
| 68 | Revolution REV 001 | Sitting In The Park/You've Got It | 12 |
| 69 | Fab FAB 90 | Three Coins In The Fountain/Tennessee Waltz | 15 |
| 69 | Fab FAB 120 | Understand My Love/Apollo 12 | 30 |
| 69 | Fab FAB 96 | Ay Ay Ay/Let It Be Me (with Rudies) | 25 |
| 69 | Fab FAB 126 | Swing Low/Release Me | 20 |
| 69 | Trojan TR 650 | I Can't Stop Loving You/Tell Me Darling | 12 |
| 69 | Trojan TR 670 | Too Experienced/I Really Loved You Baby | 12 |
| 69 | Duke DU 12 | Reggae Dance/I Know | 10 |
| 69 | Duke DU 33 | Seven Lonely Days/He Don't Love You Like I Do | 8 |
| 69 | Downtown DT 423 | Groovin'/HERBIE GRAY & RUDIES: These Memories | 15 |
| 69 | Downtown DT 428 | Lovey Dovey (with Dandy)/HERBIE GRAY & RUDIES: Kitty Wait | 5 |
| 69 | Camel CA 25 | Girl What You Doing To Me/Woman A Grumble | 25 |
| 69 | Camel CA 34 | Don't Take Your Love Away/Two Lovers | 25 |
| 69 | Camel CA 37 | Every Beat Of My Heart/Don't Cry | 20 |
| 70 | Camel CA 50 | Don't Sign The Paper/Packing Up Loneliness | 20 |
| 70 | Camel CA 51 | Bring Back Your Love/Got To Come Back | 20 |
| 70 | Upfront UPF 3 | Dream Lover/Mudda-Granma-Reggae (with Maximum Breed) | 20 |
| 70 | Bamboo BAM 47 | I Can Feel It/I Don't Want (To Lose Your Love) | 12 |
| 70 | Crab CRAB 52 | Just A Little Loving/DERRICK MORGAN: Take A Letter Maria | 10 |
| 70 | Pama PM 810 | Sugar Dumpling/I Don't Know Why | 8 |
| 70 | Pama Supreme PS 299 | I Am In Love Again/RANDY WILLIAMS: Version | 6 |
| 70 | Pama Supreme PS 302 | Candida/When Will I Find My Way | 6 |
| 70 | Pama Supreme PS 310 | You Gonna Miss Me/I Hear You Knocking | 6 |
| 70 | Supreme SUP 206 | Surfin'/All The Love | 6 |
| 70 | Ackee ACK 102 | No More/Don't Leave Me (both as Owen Gray & Omen) | 15 |
| 71 | Ackee ACK 123 | Whispering Bells/CLANCY'S ALLSTARS: Whiplash (B-side actually "Jacket" by Dave Barker) | 10 |
| 71 | Camel CA 60 | Groove Me/No Other One | 20 |
| 71 | Camel CA 73 | Nothing Can Separate Us/Girl I Want You To Understand | 35 |
| 71 | Punch PH 87 | Sincerely/Hold On I'm Coming | 10 |
| 71 | Pama Supreme PS 325 | Summer Sand/Something To Remind Me | 10 |
| 71 | Pama Supreme PS 332 | Greatest Hits (Parts 1 & 2) | 10 |
| 72 | Pama Supreme PS 351 | Time/GRAHAM: Harlesden High Street | 10 |
| 72 | Pama Supreme PS 358 | Hail The Man/I'll Follow You | 6 |
| 72 | Pama Supreme PS 360 | Amazing Grace (with Graham Hawk)/SKETTO RICH: Don't Stay Out Late | 6 |
| 78 | Bushranger BAR 101 | The Greatest Love Of All (with RANKING JAH SON)/TONY SEXTON & SUPERSTAR: Segregation (12") | 25 |
| 70s | Rock Steady Rev. REV 004 | Groovy Kind Of Love (with Elki & Rim Ram Band)/RIM RAM BAND: The Whistler | 5 |
| 76 | Angen ANG 121 | Blazing Fire/Version | 6 |
| 76 | Conflict CFT 1 | Rizla/Rizla Version | 10 |
| 61 | Starlite STLP 5 | OWEN GRAY SINGS (LP) | 120 |
| 63 | Melodisc MLP 12-153 | CUPID (LP) | 45 |
| 69 | Trojan TTL 24 | REGGAE WITH SOUL (LP) | 30 |
| 77 | Trojan TRLS 139 | FIRE AND BULLETS (LP) | 20 |
| 78 | Trojan TRLS 150 | DREAMS OF OWEN GRAY (LP) | 15 |

(see also Laurel & Owen, Gray Brothers, Elki & Owen, Owen & Milie, Owen & Dandy, Dennis Lowe, Survivors, Denzil & Jennifer, Brother Dan, Glen Adam)

**SHANE GRAY**
68  Page One POF 102  Sing Out Loud/Come Back To My Heart Again ........................ 10

**VERA GRAY**
66  HMV CLP3531  LISTEN, MOVE & DANCE 4 (LP) ................................. 25

**WARDELL GRAY**
54  Brunswick LA 8646  THE CHASE (LP, with Dexter Gordon) ............................ 25

**LARRY GRAYSON**
72  York MYK 602  WHAT A GAY DAY (LP)........................................ 15

**MILTON GRAYSON**
60  London HLU 9068  Forget You/The Puppet ...................................... 8

**RUDY GRAYZELL**
54  London HL 8094  Looking At The Moon And Wishing On A Star/The Heart That Once Was Mine .......... 200
54  London HL 8094  Looking At The Moon And Wishing On A Star/The Heart That Once Was Mine (78) ...... 30

**GRAZINA**
62  HMV POP 1094  Lover Please Believe Me/So What ............................. 12
63  HMV POP 1149  Don't Be Shy/Another Like You............................... 12
63  HMV POP 1212  Be My Baby/I Ain't Gonna Knock On Your Door ................. 20
64  Giv-A-Disc LYN 568  Stay Awhile/Let Me Go Lover (with magazine) .................. 10
*(see also Lady Murray, Mr & Mrs Murray, Le Roys, Cliff Richard)*

**GREASE BAND**
72  Harvest HAR 5052  Laughed At The Judge/All I Want To Do/Jesse James ............ 6
75  Goodear EAR 602  New Morning/Pontardawe Hop ............................... 5
71  Harvest SHVL 790  THE GREASE BAND (LP, textured sleeve first pressing) .......... 60
72  Harvest SHVL 790  THE GREASE BAND (LP, second pressing with EMI boxed logo) .... 20
75  Goodear EAR 2902  AMAZING GREASE (LP) ...................................... 15
*(see also Joe Cocker, Wynder K. Frog, Made In Sheffield)*

**JOHNNY B. GREAT (& GOODMEN)**
63  Decca F 11740  School Is In/She's A Much Better Lover Than You (with Goodmen) ..... 10
*(see also Quotations, Johnny Goodison)*

**GREAT ACES**
72  Fab FAB 191  Gold And Silver/Liberty Rock................................ 12
72  Fab FAB 200  Liberty Rock/Rock My Soul .................................. 12
72  Fab FAB 201  I Didn't Mean It/Boots And Shoes ........................... 12
72  Fab FAB 202  Baby Girl/Version .......................................... 12
73  Fab FAB 203  Banana/My Sweet Lord....................................... 12

**GREAT AWAKENING**
69  London HLU 10284  Amazing Grace/Silver Waterfall............................... 6

**GREAT BRITISH HEROES (AKA GBH)**
78  Lightning Records GIL 534  Eric Miller/Don't Give A Damn (unreleased, 1 known only) ..... 1000

**GREATEST SHOW ON EARTH**
70  Harvest HAR 5012  Real Cool World/Again And Again ............................ 20
70  Harvest HAR 5026  Tell The Story/Mountain Song .............................. 6
77  Harvest HAR 5129  Magic Touch Woman/Again And Again ......................... 8
70  Harvest SHVL 769  HORIZONS (LP, gatefold sleeve, no EMI on label) ............. 150
70  Harvest SHVL 783  THE GOING'S EASY (LP, gatefold sleeve, no EMI logo on label) .. 150
75  Harvest SHSM 2004  THE GREATEST SHOW ON EARTH (LP) ........................... 15
*(see also Ian Dury & Blockheads, Fuzzy Duck, Glencoe, Naturals)*

**GREAT EXPECTATIONS**
72  Polydor 2058241  I'm So Glad I Gotcha/Time And Place ........................ 8
73  Polydor 2058348  Devils Gun/Bigger And Better............................... 8
81  Phillips (no cat no)  Midnight Man/Pt. 2 ........................................ 15

**GREAT METROPOLITAN STEAM BAND**
69  MCA MNP/S 403  THE GREAT METROPLITAN STEAM BAND (LP) ..................... 25

**GREAT SOCIETY**
68  CBS 63476  CONSPICUOUS ONLY IN ITS ABSENCE (LP)....................... 35
*(see also Jefferson Airplane)*

**GREAT UNCLE FRED**
67  Strike JH 324  I'm In Love With An Ex-Beauty Queen/Singalong Version ........ 20

**JOE GRECH**
71  Electro ES 152  Marija L-Maltija/In-Nassab (export issue) ................... 6

**BUDDY GRECO**
57  London HLR 8452  With All My Heart/Game Of Love (with B-G Skiffle Band)....... 10
*(see also Johnny Desmond)*

**JULIETTE GRECO**
58  Philips BBE 12219  TV SERIES (EP) ............................................ 10

**GREEDIES**
80  Vertigo GREED 1  A Merry Jingle/A Merry Jangle (p/s) ........................ 6
*(see also Professionals, Thin Lizzy, Sex Pistols)*

**AL GREEN(E)**
68  Stateside SS 2079  Back Up Train/Don't Leave Me (as Al Greene & Soul Mates)...... 25
68  Stateside SS 2079  Back Up Train/Don't Leave Me (as Al Greene & Soul Mates) (DJ copy) .... 40
69  Action ACT 4540  Don't Hurt Me No More/Get Yourself Together (by Al Greene) .... 20
70  London HLU 10300  You Say It/Gotta Find A New World .......................... 7
71  London HLU 10324  I Can't Get Next To You/Ride Sally Ride .................... 7
71  Bell BLL 1188  Back Up Train/Don't Leave Me (as Al Green & Soul Mates, reissue) .... 12
71  London HLU 10337  Tired Of Being Alone / Right Now, Right Now ................ 5
71  London HLU 10348  Let's Stay Together/Tomorrow's Dream....................... 5

MINT VALUE £

| 72 | London HLU 10369 | Look What You've Done For Me/I've Never Found A Girl | 5 |
|---|---|---|---|
| 72 | London HLU 10382 | I'm Still In Love With You/Old Time Relovin' | 5 |
| 72 | London HLU 10393 | You Ought To Be With Me/What Is This Feeling | 5 |
| 73 | London HLU 10406 | Call Me/What A Wonderful Thing Love Is | 5 |
| 73 | London HLU 10419 | Love And Happiness/So You're Leaving | 5 |
| 73 | London HLU 10426 | Here I Am/I'm Glad You're Mine | 5 |
| 74 | London HLU 10443 | Living For You/It Ain't No Fun To Me | 5 |
| 74 | London HLU 10452 | Let's Get Married/So Good To Be Here | 5 |
| 74 | London HLU 10470 | Sha La La (Make Me Happy)/School Days | 5 |
| 75 | London HLU 10482 | L.O.V.E./I Wish You Were Here With Me | 5 |
| 75 | London HLU 10493 | Oh Me Oh My/Strong As Death | 5 |
| 75 | London HLU 10511 | Full Of Fire/Could I Be The One | 5 |
| 76 | London HLU 10527 | Let It Shine/There's No Way | 5 |
| 76 | London HLU 10542 | Keep Me Crying/There Is Love | 5 |
| 77 | London STO U 8685 | I TRIED TO TELL MYSELF (EP) | 10 |
| 69 | Action ACLP 6008 | BACK UP TRAIN (LP) | 60 |
| 71 | London SHU 8424 | AL GREEN GETS NEXT TO YOU (LP) | 20 |
| 72 | London SHU 8430 | LET'S STAY TOGETHER (LP) | 20 |
| 72 | London SHU 8443 | I'M STILL IN LOVE WITH YOU (LP) | 15 |
| 73 | London SHU 8457 | CALL ME (LP) | 15 |
| 74 | London SHU 8464 | LIVIN' FOR YOU (LP) | 15 |
| 74 | London SHU 8479 | EXPLORES YOUR MIND (LP) | 15 |

**BRIAN GREEN**
| 68 | Fontana SFJL 912 | BRIAN GREEN DISPLAY (LP) | 40 |

**CARL GREEN AND THE SCENE**
| 79 | Sirius SP 516 | RECORD NOT FOUND EP | 20 |
| 80 | Benton Fun/Ginnis Bucka GRCGCS1 | All The Tea In China/Business Aquaintance/Fish In The Sea (p/s, double sided insert) | 100 |
| 81 | RCA PB5335 | Wam!/The Girl From The Barrengarth House | 5 |

**GREEN EYE**
| 73 | Whirl WH01 | Sinister Jack/Run Run Run | 25 |

**GARLAND GREEN**
| 69 | MCA Soul Bag BAG 9 | Jealous Kinda Fella/I Can't Believe You Quit Me | 10 |
| 98 | Kent 6T 16 | Come Through Me/JUNIOR MCCANTS: Try Me For Your New Love | 40 |

**GRANT GREEN**
| 65 | Verve VLP 9111 | HIS MAJESTY KING FUNK (LP) | 25 |
| 93 | Blue Note 89622 | STREET FUNK AND JAZZ GROOVES (2-LP) | 20 |

**IAN GREEN (REVELATION)**
| 67 | Polydor 56194 | Last Pink Rose/Green Blues (solo) | 30 |
| 69 | CBS 3997 | When You Love A Man/Santa Maria | 6 |
| 69 | CBS 4623 | Revelation/Groover's Grave | 6 |
| 70 | CBS 63840 | REVELATION (LP) | 30 |

*(see also Madeline Bell, Rosetta Hightower)*

**JIMMY GREEN**
| 73 | Duke DU 155 | Suspicion/LLOYD'S ALL STARS: Suspicion - Version | 10 |
| 73 | Green Door GD 4062 | I'll Be Standing By/LLOYD'S ALL STARS: I'll Be Standing By "Version" | 10 |

*(see also Jimmy London)*

**KATHE GREEN**
| 69 | Deram DM 279 | If I Thought You'd Ever Change Your Mind/Primrose Hill | 7 |
| 69 | Deram SML 1039 | RUN THE LENGTH OF YOUR WILDNESS (LP, white/red label) | 35 |

**KEITH GREEN**
| 60s | Bird 118 | NO COMPROMISE (LP) | 30 |

**LLOYD GREEN**
| 75 | Monument S MNT 81245 | STEEL RIDES (LP) | 20 |

**GREEN PAJAMAS**
| 89 | Ubik Records BAKTUN 1 | SUMMER OF LUST (LP, reissue) | 15 |
| 99 | Woronzow WOO 36 LP | SEVEN FATHOMS DOWN AND FALLING (LP) | 20 |

**PETER GREEN**
| 71 | Reprise RS 27012 | Heavy Heart/No Way Out | 25 |
| 72 | Reprise K 14141 | Beast Of Burden/Uganda Woman (with Nigel Watson) | 25 |
| 78 | PVK PV 16 | Apostle/Tribal Dance | 8 |
| 79 | PVK PV 24 | In The Skies/Proud Pinto (p/s) | 5 |
| 80 | PVK PV 36 | Walking In The Road/Woman Don't | 5 |
| 80 | PVK PV 41 | Loser Two Times/Momma Doncha Cry | 5 |
| 81 | PVK PV 103 | Give Me Back My Freedom/Lost My Love | 5 |
| 81 | PVK PV 112 | Promised Land/Bizzy Lizzy | 5 |
| 70 | Reprise RSLP 9006 | THE END OF THE GAME (LP, with Nigel Watson) | 60 |

*(see also Fleetwood Mac, Peter B's, Shotgun Express, John Mayall & Bluesbreakers, Gass, Peter Bardens, Gass)*

**PHILIP GREEN & PINEWOOD STUDIO ORCHESTRA**
| 60 | Top Rank JAR 355 | League Of Gentlemen March/"Golden Fleece" Theme | 10 |

**SALLY GREEN**
| 62 | Philips PB 1243 | It Hurts Too Much To Laugh/When's He Gonna Kiss Me | 15 |

**TEDDY GREEN**
| 63 | Piccadilly 7N 35131 | Can I Take You Out Tonight/Talk | 5 |
| 63 | Piccadilly 7N 35146 | Gee What A Party/Dream Chaser | 6 |

**TOM GREEN**
| 74 | Action ACT 4621 | Rock Springs Railroad Station/Endless Confusion | 100 |

## GREEN ANGELS
| | | | |
|---|---|---|---|
| 65 | Parlophone R 5390 | Rockin' Red Wing/Let It Happen | 15 |
| 66 | Parlophone R 5512 | An Exile's Dream/Hanningan's Hooley | 6 |

## NORMAN GREENBAUM
| | | | |
|---|---|---|---|
| 70 | Reprise RS 20885 | Spirit In The Sky/Milk Cow | 5 |
| 70 | Reprise RS 20846 | Jubilee/Skyline | 8 |
| 70 | Reprise RS 20919 | Canned Ham/Junior Cadillac | 8 |
| 71 | Reprise RS 21008 | California Earthquake/Rhode Island Red | 8 |
| 70 | Reprise RSLP 6365 | SPIRIT IN THE SKY (LP) | 20 |
| 70 | Page One POLS 017 | WITH DR. WEST'S MEDICINE SHOW & JUNK BAND (LP) | 22 |

*(see also Dr. West's Medicine Show & Junk Band)*

## GREEN BEAN
| | | | |
|---|---|---|---|
| 69 | Regal Zonophone RZ 3017 | The Garden's Lovely/Sittin' In The Sunshine | 7 |

## GREENBEATS
| | | | |
|---|---|---|---|
| 64 | Pye 7N 15718 | If This World Were Mine/You Must Be The One | 5 |
| 65 | Pye 7N 15843 | So Sad/I'm On Fire | 5 |
| 67 | Spin SP 2007 | Pretty Woman/Thing | 15 |

## GREEN BULLFROG
| | | | |
|---|---|---|---|
| 72 | MCA MKPS 2021 | GREEN BULLFROG (LP, black/blue 'hexagon' label) | 175 |

*(see also Deep Purple, Roger Glover, Matthew Fisher)*

## GREEN DAY
| | | | |
|---|---|---|---|
| 94 | Reprise W 0247 | Longview/On The Wagon (p/s) | 10 |
| 94 | Reprise W 0247 T | Longview/Going To Pasalacqua (Infatuation)/FOD (Live)/ Christy Road (Live) (10", green vinyl, stickered PVC sleeve) | 20 |
| 94 | Reprise W 0257 | Basket Case/Tired Of Waiting For You (Green vinyl, numbered p/s) | 15 |
| 94 | Reprise W 0269 T | Welcome To Paradise/Chump (Live)/Emenius Sleepus (green vinyl 12", stickered PVC sleeve) | 15 |
| 95 | Reprise W 0279 X | Basket Case/2,000 Light Years Away (Live) (numbered poster p/s, green vinyl) | 12 |
| 95 | Reprise W 0287X | Longview/Welcome To Paradise (live) (2nd issue with sticker sheet, p/s) | 8 |
| 95 | Reprise W 0327 | Stuck With Me/When I Come Around (Live) (p/s) | 10 |
| 98 | Reprise W 0438 | Redundant/The Grouch (live) (p/s) | 10 |
| 94 | Reprise 9362 45529 1 | DOOKIE (LP, with crowd photo on back cover, green vinyl, numbered sticker) | 30 |
| 95 | Reprise 9362 46046 1 | INSOMNIAC (LP, with inner) | 30 |
| 97 | Reprise 9362 46794 1 | NIMROD (LP, with inner) | 40 |
| 01 | Reprise 48145 | INTERNATIONAL SUPERHITS! (LP, insert, purple vinyl) | 30 |
| 04 | Reprise 9362-41777-1 | AMERICAN IDIOT (2-LP) | 20 |

## CLAUDE 'FATS' GREENE & ORCHESTRA
| | | | |
|---|---|---|---|
| 66 | Island WI 290 | Fats Shake 'Em Up Parts 1 & 2 (actually with Al Thomas) | 15 |

## JEANIE GREENE
| | | | |
|---|---|---|---|
| 69 | Atlantic 584 226 | Sure As Sin/I've Been A Long Time Loving You | 10 |

## KELLIE GREENE
| | | | |
|---|---|---|---|
| 64 | Stateside SS 303 | Madrigal/Foggy Day | 12 |

## LAURA GREENE
| | | | |
|---|---|---|---|
| 79 | Grapevine GRP 135 | Can't Help Loving Dat Man/It's A Good Day For A Parade | 5 |

*(see also Diane Renay)*

## GREENFIELD
| | | | |
|---|---|---|---|
| 71 | Philips 6113002 | Sweet America/Dorothys Daughter | 15 |

## GREENFIELD & COOK
| | | | |
|---|---|---|---|
| 72 | Polydor 2121-105 | Only Lies/You Return | 8 |

## GREENGAGE
| | | | |
|---|---|---|---|
| 74 | Philips 6006393 | Real Nice Time/SingSing a Song | 8 |
| 78 | RCA PB 5069 | Rosie/River | 8 |

## GREEN GINGER THREE
| | | | |
|---|---|---|---|
| 65 | Decca DFE 8623 | FROM THE LAND OF GREEN GINGER (EP) | 15 |

## GREEN JELLY
| | | | |
|---|---|---|---|
| 93 | Z 74321 15142-7 | Three Little Pigs/Joey The Cowboy (p/s) | 6 |

## LEE GREENLEE
| | | | |
|---|---|---|---|
| 59 | Top Rank JAR 226 | Cherry, I'm In Love With You/Starlight | 7 |

## GREEN LINES
| | | | |
|---|---|---|---|
| 80 | CMS MR 016X | A PIECE OF THE NIGHT (EP, folded p/s) | 15 |

## GREEN MAN
| | | | |
|---|---|---|---|
| 75 | Private pressing | WHAT AILS THEE? (LP) | 100 |

## GREEN RIVER
| | | | |
|---|---|---|---|
| 85 | Homestead HMS 031 | COME ON DOWN (EP, with insert) | 20 |

*(see also Mudhoney)*

## GREENSLADE
| | | | |
|---|---|---|---|
| 73 | Warner Bros K 16264 | Temple Song/An English Western | 5 |
| 73 | Warner Bros K 46207 | GREENSLADE (LP, gatefold sleeve, green label) | 25 |
| 73 | Warner Bros K 46259 | BEDSIDE MANNERS ARE EXTRA (LP, gatefold sleeve 'Burbank' label) | 20 |
| 74 | Warner Bros K 56055 | SPYGLASS GUEST (LP, gatefold sleeve) | 15 |
| 76 | Warner Bros K 56306 | CACTUS CHOIR (LP, lyric insert) | 15 |
| 80 | EMI EMSP 332 | THE PENTATEUCH OF THE COSMOGONY (2-LP, with 47-page book, as Dave Greenslade) | 40 |

*(see also Wes Minster Five, Alan Price Set, Geno Washington & Ram Jam Band, Chris Farlowe, Colosseum, Samurai, Web, King Crimson, Stackridge)*

## ARTHUR GREENSLADE (& GEE MEN)
| | | | |
|---|---|---|---|
| 61 | Decca F 11363 | Rockin' Susannah/Eclipse (with Gee Men) | 10 |
| 66 | Columbia DB 7865 | Watermelon Man/Serenade To A Broken Jaw | 10 |

MINT VALUE £

### GREEN TELESCOPE
| | | |
|---|---|---|
| 86 | Imaginary MIRAGE 001 | Two By Two/Make Me Stay/Thinkin' About Toady (p/s, various designs)......8 |
| 86 | Wump BIF 4811 | Face In The Crowd/Thoughts Of A Madman (p/s) ......5 |

### GREEN VELVET
| | | |
|---|---|---|
| 95 | Open OPENP 017 | Flash (The Relief Remixes) (12") ......15 |

### ELLIE GREENWICH
| | | |
|---|---|---|
| 67 | United Artists UP 1180 | I Want You To Be My Baby/Goodnight, Goodnight......25 |
| 68 | United Artists UP 2214 | Sunshine After The Rain/A Long Time Comin' ......12 |
| 70 | Bell BLL 1105 | I Don't Wanna Be Left Outside/Ain't That Peculiar ......12 |
| 73 | MGM 2006 306 | Maybe I Know/Goodnight Baby/Baby I Love You ......8 |
| 73 | MGM 2315 243 | LET IT BE WRITTEN, LET IT BE SUNG (LP) ......30 |

*(see also Popsicles, Raindrops [U.S.])*

### GREEN WILLOW
| | | |
|---|---|---|
| 80 | Cotswold Music SFA 115 | COTSWOLD MUSIC (LP) ......30 |

### GREEN WINDOWS
| | | |
|---|---|---|
| 73 | Decca F 13427 | Twenty Years/Story Of A Man ......8 |

### JONNY GREENWOOD
| | | |
|---|---|---|
| 03 | Parlophone 5951471 | BODYSONG (LP) ......25 |

*(see also Radiohead)*

### MICK GREENWOOD
| | | |
|---|---|---|
| 71 | MCA MDKS 8003 | THE LIVING GAME (LP, gatefold sleeve, pink/orange 'dogbone' label) ......30 |
| 72 | MCA MKPS 2026 | TO FRIENDS (LP, black/blue 'hexagon' label) ......20 |

*(see also Fotheringay)*

### NICHOLAS GREENWOOD
| | | |
|---|---|---|
| 72 | Kingdom KVLP 9002 | COLD CUTS (LP) ......1000 |

*(see also Crazy World Of Arthur Brown, Khan, Bryn Howarth)*

### STOCKER GREENWOOD & FRIENDS
| | | |
|---|---|---|
| 79 | Changes | BILLY + NINE (LP) ......20 |

### GINNY GREER
| | | |
|---|---|---|
| 57 | Brunswick 05673 | Five Oranges, Four Apples/Kiss Me Hello (But Never Goodbye) ......6 |

### GREGER
| | | |
|---|---|---|
| 66 | Polydor 249 1103 | IN THE NIGHT (LP) ......25 |

### BOBBY GREGG & FRIENDS
| | | |
|---|---|---|
| 62 | Columbia DB 4825 | The Jam (Parts 1 & 2) ......15 |

### JOEY GREGORASH
| | | |
|---|---|---|
| 71 | Polydor 2121 032 | Jodie/The Key ......7 |

### GREGORY
| | | |
|---|---|---|
| 66 | Pye 7N 17128 | Walk With Faith In Your Heart/More Than Yesterday......5 |

### BRIAN GREGORY
| | | |
|---|---|---|
| 65 | HMV POP 1412 | Give Me Your Word/The Ballad Of Dick Turpin ......5 |

### IA(I)N GREGORY
| | | |
|---|---|---|
| 60 | Pye 7N 15295 | Time Will Tell/The Night You Told A Lie (as Ian Gregory) ......30 |
| 61 | Pye 7N 15397 | Can't You Hear The Beat Of A Broken Heart/Because ......25 |
| 62 | Pye 7N 15435 | Mr. Lovebug/Pocketful Of Dreams ......35 |
| 63 | Columbia DB 7085 | Yellow Teddy Bear/How Many Times ......12 |

### JANE GREGORY
| | | |
|---|---|---|
| 84 | D Sharp DSS 1004 | Do Not Go/After A Dream (p/s) ......150 |

### JOHNNY GREGORY & HIS ORCHESTRA
| | | |
|---|---|---|
| 62 | Fontana TFE 17389 | THE T.V. THRILLERS (EP) ......10 |
| 74 | United Artists UAG 29546 | A MAN FOR ALL SEASONS (LP) ......25 |
| 74 | United Artists QUAG 29546 | A MAN FOR ALL SEASONS (LP, quadrophonic)......75 |

*(see also Chaquito)*

### TONY GREGORY
| | | |
|---|---|---|
| 66 | Doctor Bird DB 1007 | Baby Come On Home/Marie Elena ......30 |
| 66 | Doctor Bird DB 1016 | Give Me One More Chance/I've Lost My Love ......30 |
| 67 | Island WI 3029 | Get Out Of My Life/SOUL BROTHERS: Sugar Cane ......40 |
| 67 | Coxsone CS 7013 | Only A Fool (Breaks His Own Heart)/Pure Soul ......40 |
| 71 | Horse HOSS 3 | Bouncing All Over The World/Tell Me......10 |
| 67 | Coxsone CSL 8011 | TONY GREGORY SINGS (LP) ......60 |

*(see also Lloyd Charmers)*

### STAN GREIG'S JAZZ BAND
| | | |
|---|---|---|
| 59 | Tempo EXA 90 | STAN GREIG'S JAZZ BAND (EP) ......25 |
| 80s | Calligraph CLGLP 004 | BLUES EVERY TIME (LP) ......20 |

### GREMLINS
| | | |
|---|---|---|
| 66 | Mercury MF 981 | The Coming Generation/That's What I Want ......20 |
| 67 | Mercury MF 1004 | You Gotta Believe It/I Can't Say ......20 |

### JOEL GREY
| | | |
|---|---|---|
| 54 | MGM SPC 1 | Last Night In The Back Porch/Two-Faced (export issue) ......18 |
| 57 | Capitol CL 14779 | Everytime I Ask My Heart/Moonlight Swim......7 |
| 58 | Capitol CL 14832 | Be My Next/Shoppin' Around (demos is picture sleeves = £40) ......20 |
| 61 | London HLX 9442 | Brigitte Bardot/BURT AND THE BACKBEATS: Felicidade ......6 |

### MAL GREY AND FLIGHT 56
| | | |
|---|---|---|
| 75 | Arista 8 | Look Out For Love/Ballroom Queen ......10 |

### RONNIE GREY & JETS
| | | |
|---|---|---|
| 55 | Capitol CL 14329 | Run, Manny, Run/Sweet Baby ......20 |

## SARAH GREY & ELLIE ELLIS
86   Greenwich Village GVR 231   YOU GAVE ME A SONG (LP, with insert) ...................................... 15

## GREY BROTHERS
68   Blue Cat BS 124   Always/Big Man.............................................................................. 80

*(see also Owen Gray)*

## GREYHOUND
71   Trojan TR 7820   Black And White/Sand In Your Shoes........................................... 6
71   Trojan TR 7834   Follow The Leader/Funky Jamaica................................................ 6
71   Trojan TR 7848   Moon River/I've Been Trying/Pressure Is Coming On (solid or push-out centre) .......... 6
72   Trojan TRLS 27   BLACK AND WHITE (LP) .................................................................. 20

*(see also Tillermen)*

## GREY PARADE
85   Plan B GREY 1   THE REASON (LP)................................................................................ 25

## ANDREW GRIDLEY
83   ADG 001   Lost In Time/Reflections/Taking A Chance On Love/I'm A Fool In Love ............. 10

## GRIDS
80   Kings Head   NEW ANTHEMS (EP) ......................................................................... 20

## ROOSEVELT GRIER
68   Action ACT 4515   People Make The World/Hard To Forget...................................... 15
69   Pama PM 774   Who's Got The Ball............................................................................ 15
69   Pama PM 784   C'mon Cupid/High Society Woman................................................ 20

## GRANT GRIEVES
70   Injun 106   Four On The Floor/M1 Automatic..................................................... 10

## GRIFFIN
69   Bell BLL 1075   I Am The Noise In Your Head/Don't You Know ........................... 35
72   MGM 2006 088   What Happens In The Darkness/Calling You ............................... 10

*(see also Heavy Jelly, Skip Bifferty, Every Which Way, Bell & Arc, Happy Magazine, Ginger Baker's Airforce)*

## JOHNNY GRIFFIN
69   Polydor 583734   THE MAN I LOVE (LP) ...................................................................... 35
70   Youngblood SSYB 11   FOOT PATTING (LP)........................................................................ 40

## JOHNNY GRIFFIN BIG SOUL BAND
61   Riverside REP 3203   THE BIG SOUL BAND (EP, with Clark Terry & Bobby Timmons) ............. 10
61   Riverside RLP 12-3331   THE BIG SOUL BAND (LP, also stereo [RLP 9331] ........................ 20

*(see also Eddie 'Lockjaw' Davis)*

## MERV GRIFFIN
61   London HLL 9339   The Charanga/Along Came Joe ..................................................... 10

## SYLVIA GRIFFIN
88   Rocket BLAST 7   Love's A State Of Mind/Forgive The Girl (p/s, features George Harrison) ........... 8
88   Rocket BLAST 712   Love's A State Of Mind/Forgive The Girl/Lonely Heart (12", p/s, features George Harrison)........... 12

## ANDY GRIFFITH
55   Capitol CL 14263   Ko Ko Mo (I Love You So)/Make Yourself Comfortable ............. 10
56   Capitol CL 14619   No Time For Sergeants/Make Yourself Comfortable .................. 5
57   Capitol CL 14766   Mama Guitar/A Face In The Crowd................................................ 5
58   Capitol CL 14936   Midnight Special/She's Bad, Bad Business (with Dixie Seven)........... 8

## JOE GRIFFITHS
69   Philips SBL 7902   OUT OF THE HEAD OF...(LP, black/silver labels) ........................ 20

## MARCIA GRIFFITHS
66   Island WI 285   Funny/KING SPARROW: Beggars Have No Choice (B-side actually by Leonard Dillon & Wailers; some copies credit Marcia Griffiths on both sides) ........... 100
67   Studio One SO 2008   Hound Dog (actually by Norma Fraser)/HUGH GODFREY: My Time ........... 100
67   Studio One SO 2015   After Laughter/HUGH GODFREY: Go Tell Him .............................. 80
68   Coxsone CS 7035   Mojo Girl (actually Nora Dean)/HAMLINS: Tell Me That You Love Me ............ 200
68   Coxsone CS 7055   Feel Like Jumping/HORACE TAYLOR: Thundering Vibrations ........... 50
68   Coxsone CS 7062   Hold Me Tight/BASIES: Home Sweet Home (B-side actually by Basses)........... 400
68   Studio One SO 2047   Words (as Marcia Griffiths & Jeff Dixon)/SHARKS: How Could I Live ........... 40
68   Studio One SO 2059   Truly/SIMMS & ROBINSON: Drought ............................................ 50
69   Gas GAS 111   Tell Me Now/STAN HOPE: The Weight .......................................... 100
69   High Note HS 029   Talk (Parts 1 & 2) (correct title is actually "Toil") ......................... 15
69   Escort ES 808   Don't Let Me Down/REGGAEITES: Romper Room (B-side actually by Peter Tosh)........ 100
69   Trojan TR 693   Put A Little Love In Your Heart/J BOYS: Jay Fever ..................... 15
70   Harry J. HJ 6613   Put A Little Love In Your Heart/JAY BOYS: Bah Oop Ah ........... 15
70   Harry J. HJ 6623   Band Of Gold/JAY BOYS: Cowboy (Version II)............................. 15
70   Bamboo BAM 59   Shimmering Star/SOUND DIMENSION: Mun-Dun-Gu (B-side actually Im & David)...... 100
75   Torpedo TOR 47   Survival/Version................................................................................ 40
70   Trojan TRLS 94   SWEET BITTER LOVE (LP) ............................................................... 40
74   Trojan TRLS 94   SWEET BITTER LOVE (LP, orange/white label) ........................... 30
79   Sky Note SKYLP 09   NATURALLY (LP)................................................................................ 25

*(see also Bob & Marcia, Peter Touch/Tosh, Roy Richards, Soul Vendor, Bob Andy, Della Humphrey, Mr. Foundation, Bob Marley)*

## VICTOR GRIFFITHS
70   Punch PH 29   I Am Proud Of You/KING VICTOR ALL STARS: Version ............. 10

## JOHNNY GRIGGS
83   Hit HLS 3   When You Go Away/Eldorado Theme (p/s) .................................. 5

## FERRE GRIGNARD
68   Atlantic 584 158   Yellow You Yellow Me/La Si Do.................................................... 7

## CAROL GRIMES (& DELIVERY)
70   B&C CB 129   Harry Lucky/Homemade Ruin (with Delivery) ........................... 12

| | | | |
|---|---|---|---|
| 74 | Virgin VS 109 | You're The Only One/Southern Boogie | 7 |
| 76 | Decca FR 13674 | I Betcha Didn't Know/Dynamite | 6 |
| 70 | Charisma CAS 1023 | FOOLS MEETING (LP, with Delivery, gatefold sleeve) | 250 |
| 74 | Caroline CA 2001 | WARM BLOOD (LP, black/white/red 'twins' labels) | 25 |
| 75 | Decca SKL-R 5268 | CAROL GRIMES (LP, blue/silver labels) | 20 |

*(see also Uncle Dog, Babylon)*

## GRIMMS
| | | | |
|---|---|---|---|
| 73 | Island ILPS 9248 | ROCKIN' DUCK (LP, die cut 'duck' sleeve outside single sleeve, pink rim, palm tree logo) | 20 |
| 76 | DJM DJLPS 470 | SLEEPERS (LP) | 15 |

*(see also Neil Innes, Liverpool Scene, Scaffold, Mike McGear, McGough & McGear, John Gorman, Zoot Money, Patto, Viv Stanshall, Andy Roberts, Bashers)*

## GRIM REAPER
| | | | |
|---|---|---|---|
| 83 | Ebony EBON 16 | SEE YOU IN HELL (LP) | 20 |
| 85 | Ebony EBON 32 | FEAR NO EVIL (LP) | 20 |

## GRIN
| | | | |
|---|---|---|---|
| 71 | CBS 5239 | We All Sung Together/See What A Love Can Do | 5 |
| 71 | CBS 7405 | Everybody's Missin' The Sun/18 Faced Lover | 5 |
| 76 | CBS 4339 | Soft Fun/Slippery Fingers | 5 |

## GRINDERMAN
| | | | |
|---|---|---|---|
| 07 | Mute MUTE 370 | Get It On (1-sided 7" other side etched, p/s) | 15 |
| 07 | Mute MUTE 373 | No Pussy Blues (edit)/Chain Of Flowers (numbered, stickered p/s, poster) | 8 |
| 07 | Mute MUTE 381 | (I Don't Need You To) Set Me Free (embossed p/s, one-sided etched disc) | 8 |
| 07 | Mute 12 MUTE 449 | PALACES OF MONTEZUMA EP (12", splatter vinyl) | 10 |
| 10 | Mute 12 MUTE 441 | Heathen Child/Star Charmer/Super Heathen Child (12", red vinyl, poster, first pressing with black sticker) | 10 |
| 07 | Mute STUMM 272 | GRINDERMAN (LP) | 18 |
| 11 | Mute STUMM 299 | GRINDERMAN 2 (LP & CD with poster and print) | 15 |

*(see also Nick Cave)*

## GRINDERSWITCH
| | | | |
|---|---|---|---|
| 76 | Capricorn 2089 030 | Picking The Blues/The Best I Can | 7 |

## JANNY GRINE
| | | | |
|---|---|---|---|
| 70s | Sparrow BIRD 104 | FREE INDEED (LP) | 25 |

## GRINGO
| | | | |
|---|---|---|---|
| 71 | MCA MKS 5067 | I'm Another Man/Soft Mud | 6 |
| 71 | MCA MKPS 2107 | GRINGO (LP, red/pink 'dogbone' label) | 80 |

*(see also Caravan)*

## JOE GRINNE
| | | | |
|---|---|---|---|
| 69 | Coxsone CS 7098 | Mr Editor/How I Feel (both sides actually by Melodians) | 250 |

## GRIPPIN
| | | | |
|---|---|---|---|
| 72 | Priory PR1 | I See What You See/Times Over | 80 |

## GRISBY DYKE
| | | | |
|---|---|---|---|
| 69 | Deram DM 232 | The Adventures Of Miss Rosemary La Page/Mary Anne She | 30 |

## GRISSLE
| | | | |
|---|---|---|---|
| 74 | Roach RC 3 | Crazy Lady/She Goes | 40 |

## GRIZZARDS
| | | | |
|---|---|---|---|
| 98 | Baban GRIZ 5 | Grizzling/The Green Griz (p/s) | 8 |

## GROBBERT & DUFF
| | | | |
|---|---|---|---|
| 72 | Sunlamp GRA 101 | I Am I Think/The Man From Naz | 100 |

## DEWEY GROOM
| | | | |
|---|---|---|---|
| 62 | Starlite ST45 085 | Butane Blues/That's All I Want Out Of Life | 20 |
| 63 | Starlite ST45 095 | You're Tearing My Heart Out Of Me/Walking Papers | 10 |
| 63 | Starlite ST45 105 | Heartaches For Sale/Sometimes If I'm Lucky | 8 |

## GROOP (1)
| | | | |
|---|---|---|---|
| 68 | CBS 3204 | Woman You're Breaking Me/Mad Over You | 30 |
| 78 | CBS 3351 | Lovin' Tree/Night Life | 20 |

## GROOP (2)
| | | | |
|---|---|---|---|
| 69 | Bell BLL 1070 | A Famous Myth/Tears And Joys | 15 |
| 69 | Bell BLL 1080 | The Jet Song (When The Weekend's Over)/Nobody At All | 18 |

## GROOVE FARM
| | | | |
|---|---|---|---|
| 87 | Raving Pop Blast RPBGF 2 | ONLY THE MOST IGNORANT GUTLESS SHEEP-BRAINED POLTROON CAN DENY THEM NOW (EP) | 12 |
| 88 | Subway Organisation | Driving In Your New Car (Mini Mix)/Expanding Reindeer/I Can't Dance With You/ Epistle To Duppy (12", white label promos only, with press release) | 10 |

## GROOVE TUNNEL
| | | | |
|---|---|---|---|
| 95 | Detour DR 023 | Rainy Day/How Do You Feel (p/s, white vinyl) | 7 |

## GROOVE (1)
| | | | |
|---|---|---|---|
| 69 | Parlophone R 5783 | The Wind/Play The Song | 50 |

## GROOVE (2)
| | | | |
|---|---|---|---|
| 80 | Trendy WHIP 1 | Heart Complaint/I Wanna Be Your Pygmy | 15 |

## GROOVERS
| | | | |
|---|---|---|---|
| 71 | Camel CA 83 | Put Me Down Easy/I Want To Go Back Home | 15 |
| 71 | Escort ERT 863 | Bend Down Low/The Burning Feeling | 20 |

*(see also Lloyd & Groovers, Alva Lewis, Junior Byles, Dennis Walks)*

## WINSTON GROOV(E)Y
| | | | |
|---|---|---|---|
| 69 | Grape GR 3005 | Leaving Me Standing/Little Girl | 20 |
| 69 | Grape GR 3008 | Merry X-mas/I Am Lonely | 15 |
| 69 | Nu Beat NB 041 | Island In The Sun/Work It Up | 15 |

MINT VALUE £

| 69 | Nu Beat NB 042 | Josephine/Champagne And Wine | 12 |
|----|----------------|-------------------------------|----|
| 70 | New Beat NB 053 | Standing At The Corner/You Send Me | 12 |
| 70 | New Beat NB 055 | Yellow Bird/For Your Love | 12 |
| 70 | New Beat NB 058 | Here Is My Heart/Birds And Flowers | 12 |
| 70 | New Beat NB 066 | Groovin'/Sugar Mama | 12 |
| 70 | New Beat NB 073 | Tennessee Waltz/Old Man Trouble | 10 |
| 70 | Attack ATT 8018 | I Can't Go On/Only You | 10 |
| 70 | Attack ATT 8019 | You Can't Turn Your Back On Me/PAMA DICE: The Worm | 20 |
| 70 | Jackpot JP 708 | Funky Chicken/CIMARRONS: Part 2 (B-side actually unknown instrumental) | 20 |
| 70 | Jackpot JP 709 | Funny/CIMARRONS: Funny Version Two | 10 |
| 70 | Torpedo TOR 11 | Please Don't Make Me Cry/Motion On The Ocean | 12 |
| 70 | Crab CRAB 63 | I Like The Way/Tell Me Why | 10 |
| 71 | Crab CRAB 64 | I've Got The Find A Way To Win Mary Back/Wanna Be There | 10 |
| 71 | Bullet BU 471 | I Wanna Be Loved/Get Back Together | 10 |
| 71 | Pama PM 827 | Don't Break My Heart/How Long Will This Go On | 10 |
| 71 | Pama Supreme PS 323 | Free The People/Not Now | 8 |
| 72 | Pama Supreme PS 349 | What You Gonna Do/Why Did You Leave | 8 |
| 72 | Pama Supreme PS 364 | Sylvia's Mother/Here Is My Heart | 8 |
| 73 | Explosion EX 2086 | Nose For Trouble/RHYTHM RULERS: Version | 8 |
| 74 | Explosion EX 2088 | Please Don't Make Me Cry/So Easy | 8 |
| 69 | Pama PMP 2011 | FREE THE PEOPLE (LP) | 40 |
| 78 | Trojan TRLS 155 | THE GROOVEY COLLECTION (LP) | 15 |

*(see also King Horror, Upsetters)*

## PAUL GROOVY AND THE POP ART EXPERIENCE
| 87 | Bite Back! – BB!012 | Andy Watch Out!/Take Away The Pain (wrap-around p/s, sticker, lyric sheet) | 30 |

## GROSS CLUB
| 81 | Caveman CMR 01 | Second Chance/Look Away (sleeve is a paper insert glued on white inner sleeve) | 100 |

## WALTER GROSS
| 54 | MGM SP 1070 | Blue Moon/Tenderly | 5 |
| 54 | MGM SP 1071 | You Won't Forget Me (with India Adams)/Follow Me | 5 |

## G.G. GROSSETT
| 69 | Crab CRAB 10 | Run Girl Run/DENNIS WALKS: The Drifter | 100 |
| 69 | Crab CRAB 33 | Greater Sounds/Live The Life I Love | 40 |

## STEFAN GROSSMAN
| 70 | Big T BIG 133 | Pretty Little Tune/Little Sally Walker | 7 |
| 71 | Big T BIG 140 | 'Joe Hill' - Themes | 7 |
| 68 | Fontana (S)TL 5463 | AUNT MOLLY'S MURRAY FARM (LP) | 25 |
| 69 | Fontana STL 5485 | THE GRAMERCY PARK SHEIK (LP) | 20 |
| 70 | Transatlantic TRA 217 | YAZOO BASIN BOOGIE (LP) | 15 |
| 71 | Transatlantic TRA 246 | THOSE PLEASANT DAYS (LP, with lyric insert) | 15 |

*(see also John Renbourn)*

## LUTHER GROSVENOR
| 71 | Island WIP 6109 | Here Comes The Queen/Heavy Day | 6 |
| 72 | Island WIP 6124 | All The People/Waiting | 6 |
| 71 | Island ILPS 9168 | UNDER OPEN SKIES (LP, gatefold sleeve pink rim palm tree logo) | 50 |

*(see also Hellions, Revolution, Art, Spooky Tooth, Mott The Hoople, Widowmaker)*

## CARL GROSZMANN
| 70 | Decca F 13065 | Thunderbird/Missouri Woman | 6 |
| 75 | Ring O' 2017 103 | I've Had It/C'mon And Roll | 15 |
| 77 | Ring O' 2017 107 | Face Of A Permanent Stranger/Your Own Affair (promo p/s) | 15 |
| 77 | Ring O' 2017 107 | Face Of A Permanent Stranger/Your Own Affair (company sleeve) | 10 |
| 75 | Ring O' 2320 102 | CARL GROSZMANN (LP, unreleased) | 0 |

## GROUND ATTACK
| 81 | Ground Attack GAR 001 | THE RED LION EP (Red Lion/Every Mother's Son) (gatefold p/s) | 100 |
| 81 | Ground Attack GAR 001 | THE RED LION EP (Red Lion/Every Mother's Son) (later pressing with no p/s) | 20 |

## GROUNDHOGS
| 68 | Liberty LBF 15174 | You Don't Love Me/Still A Fool | 30 |
| 69 | Liberty LBF 15263 | B.D.D./TONY McPHEE: Gasoline | 35 |
| 70 | Liberty LBF 15346 | Eccentric Man/Status People | 20 |
| 73 | W. Wide Artists WWS 006 | Sad Go Round/Over Blue | 6 |
| 74 | W. Wide Artists WWS 012 | Plea Sing, Plea Sing/TONY McPHEE: Dog Me Bitch | 6 |
| 76 | United Artists UP 36095 | Live A Little Lady/Boogie Withus | 6 |
| 76 | United Artists UP 36177 | Pastoral Future/Live Right (as Tony McPhee & Groundhogs) | 6 |
| 68 | Liberty LBL 83199E | SCRATCHING THE SURFACE (LP, mono, blue label) | 125 |
| 68 | Liberty LBS 83199E | SCRATCHING THE SURFACE (LP, stereo, blue label) | 75 |
| 69 | Liberty LBS 83253 | BLUES OBITUARY (LP, blue label) | 80 |
| 70 | Liberty LBS 83295 | THANK CHRIST FOR THE BOMB (LP, gatefold sleeve, 1st pressing blue label) | 90 |
| 70 | Liberty LBS 83295 | THANK CHRIST FOR THE BOMB (LP, gatefold sleeve, 2nd pressing black label) | 30 |
| 71 | Liberty LBG 83401 | SPLIT (LP, gatefold sleeve, black label) | 30 |
| 72 | United Artists UAG 29347 | WHO WILL SAVE THE WORLD... (LP, gatefold sleeve) | 30 |
| 72 | United Artists UAG 29419 | HOGWASH (LP, tri-fold sleeve) | 25 |
| 74 | W. Wide Artists WWA 004 | SOLID (LP, with lyric insert) | 15 |
| 76 | United Artists UAS 29917 | CROSSCUT SAW (LP) | 15 |
| 84 | Psycho PSYCHO 24 | HOGGIN' THE STAGE (2-LP, with EP, stickered gatefold sleeve) | 18 |

*(see also Tony McPhee, Herbal Mixture, Home, Andy Fernbach, John Lee Hooker)*

## GROUP
| 72 | Charisma CB 197 | Bovver Boys/Piraeus Football Club/An Open Letter To George Best | 6 |

*(see also Neil Innes)*

## GROUP B
| | | |
|---|---|---|
| 67 | Vocalion VF 9284 | I Know Your Name Girl/I Never Really Knew ...................................................... 25 |

*(see also Blue Cheer)*

## GROUP 1850
| | | |
|---|---|---|
| 69 | Philips SBL 7884 | AGEMO'S TRIP TO MOTHER EARTH (LP, gatefold sleeve) .......................................... 600 |

## GROUP IMAGE
| | | |
|---|---|---|
| 69 | Stable SLE 8005 | A MOUTH IN THE CLOUDS (LP) ........................................................................ 90 |

## GROUP ONE
| | | |
|---|---|---|
| 58 | HMV POP 463 | She's Neat/Made For Each Other ..................................................................... 30 |
| 58 | HMV POP 492 | Chanson D'Amour/Londonderry Air .................................................................. 5 |

## GROUP SIX
| | | |
|---|---|---|
| 59 | Oriole CB 1488 | Rock-A-Boogie/Rockin' The Blues ................................................................... 20 |

## GROUP THERAPY
| | | |
|---|---|---|
| 69 | Philips BF 1744 | River Deep Mountain High/Remember What You Said .......................................... 6 |
| 69 | Philips BF 1792 | Can't Stop Lovin' You Baby/I Must Do ............................................................. 6 |
| 69 | Philips SBL 7888 | YOU'RE IN NEED OF GROUP THERAPY (LP) ....................................................... 20 |

## GROUP TWO
| | | |
|---|---|---|
| 68 | Columbia DB 8374 | It's Raining Outside/Western Man, Eastern Lady ................................................ 7 |

## GROUP X
| | | |
|---|---|---|
| 63 | Fontana 267 274 TF | There Are 8 Million Cossack Melodies - And This Is One Of Them/Teneriffe (in p/s) ...... 10 |
| 63 | Fontana 267 274 TF | There Are 8 Million Cossack Melodies - And This Is One Of Them/Teneriffe .................. 5 |
| 63 | Fontana TF 417 | Roti Calliope/Cross Beat .............................................................................. 10 |

## GROUT
| | | |
|---|---|---|
| 79 | Urinating Vicar | DO IT YOURSELF (EP) (100 only, sound quality very poor) ................................... 400 |

## GROW UP
| | | |
|---|---|---|
| 80 | Object Music OM12 | JOANNA EP ............................................................................................. 10 |
| 79 | Object OM 05 | GROW UP (EP) .......................................................................................... 12 |
| 79 | Object Music OBJ 5 | THE BEST THING (LP) ................................................................................ 20 |
| 81 | UP Records GROWL 1 | WITHOUT WINDS (LP) ................................................................................ 15 |

## GRUDGE
| | | |
|---|---|---|
| 73 | Black Label BL 002 | When Christine Comes Around/I'm Gonna Smash Your Face In .............................. 50 |

## GRUMBLEWEEDS
| | | |
|---|---|---|
| 71 | Phillips 78434 | Never Before/Fiona McLaughlin ..................................................................... 15 |
| 72 | Phillips 6006208 | String Of Beads (Good Old Leeds)/Simple Little Things ....................................... 12 |
| 73 | Decca F 13416 | Trees/I Am A Grumbleweed .......................................................................... 6 |
| 74 | Decca F13513 | (Hey Babe) Follow Me/Won't Say No Again ....................................................... 20 |

## GRUNT FUTTOCK
| | | |
|---|---|---|
| 72 | Regal Zonophone RZ 3042 | Rock 'N' Roll Christian/Free Sole .................................................................. 40 |

*(see also Move, Roy Wood)*

## DAVE GRUSIN
| | | |
|---|---|---|
| 85 | Arista GRP 5610 | MOUNTAIN DANCE (LP, Nimbus Supercut, mail order only through Practical Hi Fi magazine) ................................................................................................. 40 |

## GRUVY BEATS
| | | |
|---|---|---|
| 70 | Nu Beat NB 048 | Share Your Popcorn/LAUREL AITKEN: Mr. Popcorn ............................................ 15 |
| 70 | Nu Beat NB 049 | Blue Mink/LAUREL AITKEN: I've Got Your Love .................................................. 15 |

## GIGI GRYCE
| | | |
|---|---|---|
| 60 | Esquire 32-151 | SAYIN' SOMETHIN' (LP) .............................................................................. 20 |
| 60 | Esquire | RAT RACE BLUES (LP) ................................................................................. 30 |

## GRYPHON
| | | |
|---|---|---|
| 77 | Harvest HAR 5125 | Spring Song/Fall Of The Leaf ........................................................................ 6 |
| 73 | Transatlantic TRA 262 | GRYPHON (LP, gatefold sleeve) ..................................................................... 25 |
| 74 | Transatlantic TRA 282 | MIDNIGHT MUSHRUMPS (LP) ...................................................................... 15 |
| 74 | Transatlantic TRA 287 | RED QUEEN TO GRYPHON THREE (LP) ............................................................ 15 |
| 75 | Transatlantic TRA 302 | RAINDANCE (LP) ...................................................................................... 15 |
| 77 | Harvest SHSP 4063 | TREASON (LP, with lyric inner sleeve) ............................................................ 20 |

*(see also Richard Harvey, The Banned)*

## G.T.O.'S
| | | |
|---|---|---|
| 67 | Polydor 56721 | She Rides With Me/Rudy Vadoo .................................................................... 75 |

*(see also Joey & Continentals)*

## G.T.O.'S (GIRLS TOGETHER OUTRAGEOUSLY)
| | | |
|---|---|---|
| 70 | Straight STS 1059 | PERMANENT DAMAGE (LP) ......................................................................... 150 |

*(see also Jeff Beck, Frank Zappa)*

## G.T.R.
| | | |
|---|---|---|
| 86 | Arista GTR 1 | When The Heart Rules The Mind/Reach Out (poster sleeve) ................................. 6 |

*(see also Steve Hackett)*

## GT'S
| | | |
|---|---|---|
| 79 | Stiff BUY 60 | Boys Have Feelings Too/Be Careful (p/s) ......................................................... 5 |

## GUANA BATZ
| | | |
|---|---|---|
| 84 | Big Beat SW 89 | You're So Fine/Rockin' In My Coffin/Jungle Rumble/Guana Rock (p/s) ..................... 6 |
| 84 | Big Beat NS 96 | The Cave/Werewolf Blues (p/s) ..................................................................... 5 |

## GUARDIANS OF THE RAINBOW
| | | |
|---|---|---|
| 68 | President PT 186 | What Do You Do When You've Lost Your Love/Cry Alone ..................................... 6 |

## GUERNICA
| | | |
|---|---|---|
| 87 | Idol 12 ID 2 | ORANGE AND RED EP (12") ......................................................................... 30 |

## LENNIS GUESS
| | | |
|---|---|---|
| 75 | Route RT 11 | Just Ask Me/Workin' For My Baby .................................................................. 5 |

## GUESS WHO

| 65 | Pye International 7N 25305 | Shakin' All Over/Till We Kissed | 25 |
| 66 | King KG 1044 | His Girl/It's My Pride | 25 |
| 67 | Fontana TF 831 | This Time Long Ago/There's No Getting Away From You | 15 |
| 67 | Fontana TF 861 | Miss Felicity Grey/Flying On The Ground Is Wrong | 10 |
| 70 | RCA 1870 | Laughing/Undu | 5 |
| 70 | RCA 1943 | American Woman/No Sugar Tonight | 6 |
| 69 | RCA SF 8037 | WHEATFIELD SOUL (LP) | 15 |
| 70 | RCA SF 8107 | AMERICAN WOMAN (LP) | 15 |

## EARL GUEST

| 62 | Columbia DB 4707 | Honky Tonk Train Blues/Winkle Picker Stomp | 6 |
| 62 | Columbia DB 4926 | The Girl From The Fair Isle/Twistin' John | 5 |
| 64 | Columbia DB 7212 | Begin The Beguine/Foxy | 20 |

## GUEST & EDWARDS

| 72 | Phillips 6006231 | All Alone/Sing You A Picture | 20 |

## REG GUEST SYNDICATE

| 65 | Mercury MF 927 | Underworld/Guys, Guns, Dolls And Danger | 125 |
| 66 | Mercury 20089MCL | UNDERWORLD (LP) | 40 |

## GUGGENHEIM

| 72 | Indigo GOLP 7001 | GUGGENHEIM (LP, private pressing) | 75 |

## GUIDED BY VOICES

| 96 | Fear & Loathing RCRPA 17 | BRIGHTON ROCKS: Hot Freaks/Game Of Pricks (50 copies on blue vinyl with fanzine) | 50 |
| 96 | Fear & Loathing RCRPA 17 | BRIGHTON ROCKS: Hot Freaks/Game Of Pricks (450 copies on black vinyl with fanzine) | 20 |
| 99 | Creation CRE 325 | Teenage FBI/Flying Into Ashes/Tropical Robots (p/s) | 10 |

## GUILLEMOTS

| 05 | Fantastic Plastic FPS050 | I SAW SUCH THINGS IN MY SLEEP EP (10", 300 only p/s) | 15 |
| 05 | Fantastic Plastic FPTEN055 | Trains To Brazil/My Chosen One/Go Away (10", 1,000 only p/s) | 8 |
| 06 | Polydor IC00309 | THROUGH THE WINDOWPANE (2-LP, gatefold sleeve, inner sleeves & booklet) | 25 |

## ISAAC GUILLORY

| 74 | Atlantic K 40521 | ISAAC GUILLORY (LP) | 18 |

*(see also Shames)*

## GUILLOTEENS

| 65 | Pye International 7N 25324 | I Don't Believe/Hey You | 60 |

## GUILT EDGE

| 79 | Fragile FRAG 001 | Bye Bye/Wires (p/s) | 15 |

## BONNIE GUITAR

| 58 | London HLD 8591 | A Very Precious Love/Johnny Vagabond | 15 |
| 59 | Top Rank JAR 260 | Candy Apple Red/Come To Me, I Love You | 6 |
| 58 | London HA-D 2122 | MOONLIGHT AND SHADOWS (LP) | 15 |

## GUITAR CRUSHER WITH JIMMY SPURRILL

| 69 | Blue Horizon 57-3149 | Since My Baby Hit The Numbers/Hambone Blues | 45 |

*(see also Wild Jimmy Spurrill)*

## GUITAR RED

| 63 | Pye International 7N 25219 | Just You And I/Old Fashioned Love | 35 |

## GUITAR SHORTY

| 72 | Flyright LP 500 | CAROLINA SLIDE GUITAR (LP) | 15 |

## GUITAR GANGSTERS

| 89 | Link LP 105 | PROHIBITION (LP) | 20 |

## GULLIVER

| 70 | Elektra 2101 011 | Every Day's A Lovely Day/Angelina | 6 |
| 70 | Elektra 2101 017 | Angelina/Christine | 5 |
| 70 | Elektra 2410 006 | GULLIVER (LP) | 18 |

## GULLIVER'S PEOPLE

| 66 | Parlophone R 5435 | Splendor In The Grass/Took This Land | 20 |
| 66 | Parlophone R 5464 | Fi Fo Fum/Over The Hills | 10 |
| 68 | Parlophone R 5709 | On A Day Like This/My Life | 10 |
| 69 | Columbia DB 8588 | Somehow, Somewhere/I Found Love | 10 |

## GULLIVER'S TRAVELS

| 69 | Instant INLP 003 | GULLIVER'S TRAVELS (LP, withdrawn, front laminated sleeve, flipbacks) | 200 |

*(see also Mike D'Abo, Andrew Oldham)*

## GUMBAE CULTURE

| 85 | Leyson LR 0105 | Take It Easy/Ghetto Youth (12") | 15 |

## GUN

| 68 | CBS 3764 | Race With The Devil/Sunshine | 5 |
| 68 | CBS 3764 | Race With The Devil/3-4 In The Middle (different B-side) | 10 |
| 69 | CBS 4052 | Drives You Mad/Rupert's Travels | 7 |
| 69 | CBS 4443 | Hobo/Don't Look Back | 7 |
| 69 | CBS 4443 | Hobo/Long Hair Wild Man (different B-side) | 10 |
| 70 | CBS 4952 | Runnin' Wild/Drown Yourself In The River | 6 |
| 69 | CBS M63552 | GUN (LP, mono, laminated front sleeve, orange label) | 200 |
| 69 | CBS 63552 | GUN (LP, stereo, laminated front sleeve, orange label) | 100 |
| 69 | CBS 63683 | GUNSIGHT (LP) | 60 |

*(see also Baker-Gurvitz Army, Parrish & Gurvitz, Rupert's People, Three Man Army, Knack)o*

## GUN CLUB

| 82 | Animal/Chrysalis CHCAT 2635 | The Fire Of Love/Walking With The Beast (p/s) | 6 |

MINT VALUE £

| 82 | Beggars Banquet BEG 80 | Ghost On The Highway/Sex Beat (p/s) | 20 |
| 83 | Animal/Chrysalis GUN 1 | Death Party/House On Highland Avenue/The Lie (p/s) | 8 |
| 83 | Animal/Chrysalis GUN 12 | Death Party/House On Highland Avenue/The Lie/Light Of The World/ Come Back Jim (12", p/s) | 10 |
| 88 | Red Rhino RED 89 | The Breaking Hands/Crabdance (p/s) | 8 |
| 88 | Red Rhino RED 89 12 | The Breaking Hands/Crabdance/Nobody's City (12", p/s) | 10 |
| 90 | Fire BLAZE 47T | The Great Divide/Crabdance/St. John's Divine Part 2 (p/s) | 12 |
| 81 | Beggars Banquet BEGA 37 | THE FIRE OF LOVE (LP) | 25 |
| 82 | Animal CHR 1398 | MIAMI (LP) | 20 |
| 83 | ABC ABC LP 1 | THE BIRTH THE DEATH THE GHOST (LP) | 20 |
| 84 | Animal CHR 1398 | LAS VEGAS STORY (LP) | 15 |
| 87 | Red Rhino REDLP 84 | MOTHER JUNO (LP) | 20 |
| 85 | Castle DOJOLP 8 | TWO SIDES OF THE BEAST (LP) | 15 |
| 90 | Fire FIRELP 28 | PASTORAL HIDE AND SEEK (LP) | 15 |
| 08 | Retro Delux RDBX 004 | THE LIFE AND TIMES OF JEFFREY LEE PIERCE AND THE GUN CLUB (4-CD box set) | 30 |

*(see also Jeffrey Lee Pierce)*

## JON GUNN
| 67 | Deram DM 133 | I Just Made Up My Mind/Now It's My Turn | 10 |
| 67 | Deram DM 166 | If You Wish It/I Don't Want To Get Hung Up On You Babe | 10 |

## JIM GUNNER
| 60 | Decca F 11276 | Hoolee Jump/Footloose (as Jim Gunner & Echoes) | 15 |
| 61 | Fontana H 313 | Desperado/Baghdad (as Jim Gunner & His Sidekicks) | 20 |

## TONY GUNNER
| 62 | London HLU 9492 | Rough Road/You Gotta Get Home | 20 |

## SARAH OGAN GUNNING
| 67 | Topic 12T 171 | A GIRL OF CONSTANT SORROW (LP, mono, blue label) | 20 |

## GUNS FOR HIRE
| 80 | Korova KOW 6 | I'm Gonna Rough My Girlfriend's New Boyfriend Up/I'm Famous Now (p/s) | 10 |

*(see also Main T. Possee)*

## GUNSHOT
| 94 | Vinyl Solution STORM78L | Mind Of A Razor (10") | 12 |
| 94 | Vinyl Solution STEAM 92 | SINGLES CONNECTION (LP, red vinyl) | 15 |

## GUNSLINGER
| 84 | Clyde CLY 001 | Never A Dull Moment/Shake Some Action (no p/s) | 20 |

## GUNS N' ROSES
| 87 | Geffen GEF 22 | It's So Easy/Mr Brownstone (p/s) | 10 |
| 87 | Geffen GEF 22T | It's So Easy/Mr Brownstone/Shadow Of Your Love/Move To The City (12", p/s) | 12 |
| 87 | Geffen GEF 22TP | It's So Easy/Mr Brownstone/Shadow Of Your Love/ Move To The City (12", picture disc with stickered PVC sleeve) | 40 |
| 87 | Geffen GEF 30 | Welcome To The Jungle/Whole Lotta Rosie (live) (red p/s) | 8 |
| 87 | Geffen GEF 30T | Welcome To The Jungle/Whole Lotta Rosie (live)/It's So Easy (live)/Knockin' On Heaven's Door (live) (12", red p/s) | 20 |
| 87 | Geffen GEF 30TW | Welcome To The Jungle/Whole Lotta Rosie (live)/It's So Easy (live)/Knockin' On Heaven's Door (live) (12", poster p/s) | 10 |
| 87 | Geffen GEF 30P | Welcome To The Jungle/Whole Lotta Rosie (live)/It's So Easy (live)/Knockin' On Heaven's Door (live) (12", picture disc) | 40 |
| 88 | Geffen GEF 43 | Sweet Child O' Mine/Out Ta Get Me (p/s, with wraparound sticker) | 5 |
| 88 | Geffen GEF 43TE | Sweet Child O' Mine/Out Ta Get Me/Rocket Queen (10", revolving p/s) | 15 |
| 88 | Geffen GEF 43TV | Sweet Child O' Mine/Out Ta Get Me/Rocket Queen (12", metallic p/s) | 10 |
| 88 | Geffen GEF 47 | Welcome To The Jungle/Nightrain (p/s) | 5 |
| 88 | Geffen GEF 47TP | Welcome To The Jungle/Nightrain/You're Crazy (Acoustic Version) (12", picture disc) | 10 |
| 89 | Geffen GEF 50P | Paradise City/I Used To Love Her (gun-shaped clear picture disc) | 12 |
| 89 | Geffen GEF 50P | Paradise City/I Used To Love Her (gun-shaped white picture disc in 'holster' sleeve) | 15 |
| 89 | Geffen GEF 50X | Paradise City/I Used To Love Her (p/s, slotted in holster p/s) | 7 |
| 89 | Geffen GEF 55W | Sweet Child O' Mine (Remix)/Out Ta Get Me (with tattoo) | 10 |
| 89 | Geffen GEF 55 X | Sweet Child O' Mine/Out Ta Get Me (Limited edition sticker pack) | 10 |
| 89 | Geffen GEF 55P | Sweet Child O' Mine/Out Ta Get Me/Rocket Queen (shaped pic disc & sticker) | 12 |
| 89 | Geffen GEF 55P | Sweet Child O' Mine/Out Ta Get Me/Rocket Queen (12" uncut shaped pic disc) | 100 |
| 89 | Geffen GEF 55T | Sweet Child O' Mine (Remix)/Move To The City/Whole Lotta Rosie (live)/ It's So Easy (live) (12", p/s) | 10 |
| 89 | Geffen GEF 60X | Nightrain/Reckless Life (live) (p/s, with patch) | 7 |
| 89 | Geffen GEF 60P | Nightrain/Reckless Life (live) (case-shaped picture disc, stickered PVC sleeve) | 12 |
| 91 | Geffen GFS 18 | November Rain (LP version)/Sweet Child O' Mine (LP version) (p/s) | 5 |
| 93 | Geffen GFS 70 | Since I Don't Have You/You Can't Put Your Arms Around A Memory (p/s, orange vinyl) | 6 |
| 08 | Geffen 0602517906075 | Chinese Democracy/Shackler's Revenge (p/s, promo) | 10 |
| 87 | Geffen 9240 148 | APPETITE FOR DESTRUCTION (LP, withdrawn 'robot' sleeve, with stickers) | 30 |
| 91 | Geffen GEF 24415 | USE YOUR ILLUSION I (2 x LP) | 25 |
| 91 | Geffen GEF 24420 | USE YOUR ILLUSION II (2 x LP) | 25 |
| 93 | Geffen GEF24617 | THE SPAGHETTI INCIDENT? (LP) | 25 |

## ARTHUR GUNTER
| 72 | Blue Horizon 2431 012 | BLUES AFTER HOURS (LP) | 75 |
| 70s | Contempo COLP 119 | BLACK AND BLUES (LP) | 25 |

## HARDROCK GUNTER
| 55 | Brunswick OE 9167 | MOUNTAIN MUSIC (EP) | 25 |

*(see also Red Foley, Roberta Lee)*

## GURU GURU
| 73 | Atlantic K 50022 | DON'T CALL US WE'LL CALL YOU (LP) | 15 |
| 74 | Atlantic K 50044 | DANCE OF THE FLAMES (LP) | 18 |

## GURU GURU/ULI TREPTE
80s United Dairies UDT 07    LIVE 72 & 73 (LP, 1 side each) ........................................... 18

## GURU JOSH
90   Deconstruction PT 44140    Freaky Dreamer (12") ........................................... 15

## GURUS
66   United Artists UP 1160    Blue Snow Night/Come Girl ........................................... 30

## GUS GUS
97   4AD DAD 7005    POLYDISTORTION (2-LP, inners) ........................................... 20

## JOHNNY GUSTAFSON
65   Polydor 56022    Just To Be With You/Sweet Day ........................................... 20
65   Polydor 56043    Take Me For A Little While/Make Me Your Number One ........................................... 35
*(see also Big Three, Merseybeats, Quotations, Hard Stuff, Johnny & John, Ian Gillan Band, G-Force)*

## CARL GUSTAV & 84'S
81   Convulsive CN 001    I Want To Kill Russians/Through Birds, Through Fire, But Not Through Glass (p/s) ........ 10

## ARLO GUTHRIE
67   Reprise RS 20644    Motorcycle Song/Now And Then ........................................... 8
70   Reprise RS 20877    Alice's Rock'N'Roll Restaurant/Coming In To Los Angeles ........................................... 5
70   Reprise RS 20951    Valley To Pray/Gabriel's Mother's Hiway Ballad No. 16 Blues (demo-only) ........................................... 7
67   Reprise RSLP 6267    ALICE'S RESTAURANT (LP, mono) ........................................... 20
67   Reprise RLP 6267    ALICE'S RESTAURANT (LP, stereo) ........................................... 20
68   Reprise RSLP 6269    ARLO (LP) ........................................... 20
69   Reprise RSLP 6346    RUNNING DOWN THE ROAD (LP) ........................................... 15
70   Reprise RSLP 6411    WASHINGTON COUNTY (LP) ........................................... 15

## SHEILA GUTHRIE
63   Fontana TF 399    Mirror Mirror/It Doesn't Mean A Thing ........................................... 8

## WOODY GUTHRIE
55   Melodisc EPM7 84    HARD AIN'T IT HARD (EP) ........................................... 20
55   Melodisc EPM7 85    WORRIED MAN BLUES (EP) ........................................... 20
55   Melodisc EPM7 91    HEY LOLLY LOLLY (EP) ........................................... 20
55   Melodisc MLP 12-106    MORE SONGS BY GUTHRIE (LP) ........................................... 40
58   Topic 12T 31    BOUND FOR GLORY (LP) ........................................... 35
64   RCA RD 7642    DUST BOWL BALLADS (LP) ........................................... 25

## GUTTERSNIPES
88   Razor GUTT 1    Addicted To Love/Love's Young Dream (p/s) ........................................... 8
*(see also Cocksparrer)*

## GUTTERSNYPES
94   Liberty Grooves LIB004    The Trials Of Life (Green vinyl radio edit) (12") ........................................... 15
94   Liberty Grooves LIB005    The Trials Of Life (Blue, Red) (12") ........................................... 10
94   Liberty Grooves LIB005    The Trials Of Life (White vinyl, promo version, limited edition, personalised by band) (12") ........................................... 25
94   Liberty Grooves LIB006    The Trials Of Life (Clear vinyl, instrumentals) (12") ........................................... 15
94   Liberty Grooves LIB006    The Trails Of Life (Instrumentals) ........................................... 18

## GUV'NERS
63   Piccadilly 7N 35117    Let's Make A Habit Of This/The Kissing Had To Stop ........................................... 10
*(see also Jess Conrad, Dickie Pride, Nelson Keene)*

## GUV'NORS
75   Cambrian CSP 740    Fly To The Sun/I'm With You To The End ........................................... 10

## BARRY GUY
76   Incus INCUS 22    STATEMENTS V-XI FOR DOUBLE BASS AND VIOLONE (LP) ........................................... 50
*(see also Derek Bailey Barry Guy & Paul Rutherford)*

## BUDDY GUY
65   Chess CRS 8004    Let Me Love You Baby/Ten Years Ago ........................................... 20
68   Fontana TF 951    Mary Had A Little Lamb/Sweet Little Angel ........................................... 18
72   Atlantic K 10195    Honey Dripper/Man Of Many Words ........................................... 6
91   Silvertone ORE 30    Mustang Sally/Trouble Don't Last (with Jeff Beck, p/s) ........................................... 5
65   Chess CRE 6004    CRAZY MUSIC (EP) ........................................... 40
68   Vanguard SVRL 19001    COMING AT YOU (LP) ........................................... 30
68   Vanguard SVRL 19002    MAN AND HIS BLUES (LP) ........................................... 30
68   Vanguard SVRL 19004    BLUES TODAY (LP) ........................................... 30
69   Vanguard SVRL 19008    THIS IS BUDDY GUY! (LP) ........................................... 30
69   Vanguard SVRL 79290    HOT AND COOL (LP) ........................................... 30
69   Chess CRL(S) 4546    I LEFT MY BLUES IN SAN FRANCISCO (LP) ........................................... 30
69   Python KM 2    FIRST TIME I MET THE BLUES (LP) ........................................... 70
70   Harvest SHSP 4006    BUDDY AND THE JUNIORS (LP, with Junior Mance & Junior Wells) ........................................... 65
70   Red Lightnin' RL 001    IN THE BEGINNING (LP) ........................................... 15
72   Atlantic K 40240    PLAY THE BLUES (LP, with Junior Wells) ........................................... 20
73   Vanguard VSD 79323    HOLD THAT PLANE (LP) ........................................... 20
*(see also Junior Wells, Eddie Boyd/Buddy Guy)*

## GUYS
69   Tepee TPR SP 1001    You Go Your Way/Little Girl ........................................... 20
*(see also Beat Six)*

## GEORGE GUZMAN
68   London SH 8384    INTRODUCING GEORGE GUZMAN (LP) ........................................... 30

## GWENNO
14   Peski PESK1030    Y DYFF OLAF (LP) ........................................... 20
15   Heavenly HVNLP 118B    Y DYDD OLAF (LP, CD) ........................................... 18
*(see also Pipettes)*

**GYGAFO**

| | | | |
|---|---|---|---|
| 75 | Look LK SP 6061 | Broken Smiles/Wing | 40 |
| 89 | Holyground HG 1155 | LEGEND OF THE KINGFISHER (LP, 160 copies only, posthumously designed semi-gatefold sleeve with insert) | 60 |

**GYMSLIPS**

| | | | |
|---|---|---|---|
| 82 | Abstract ABS 011 48 | Crash/Miss Nunsweeta (p/s) | 5 |
| 83 | Abstract ABS 014 | Big Sister/Yo Yo/Pie And Mash (p/s) | 5 |
| 83 | Abstract ABS 016F | Robot Man/Multi-Coloured Sugar/Take Away (p/s) | 5 |
| 83 | Abstract ABT 006 | ROCKING WITH THE RENEES (LP, with insert) | 20 |

**GYNAECOLOGISTS**

| | | | |
|---|---|---|---|
| 81 | Teesbeat TB 2 | The Red Pullover/The Offence (hand made p/s, 500 only) | 12 |

(see also Basczax, Blitzkrieg Bop)

**GYPP**

| | | | |
|---|---|---|---|
| 79 | Shy Talk AC 1065 | YAAH EP: Marigoldz/Titania/Sister Darling (p/s) | 20 |

(see also Martin Newell, Cleaners From Venus, Brotherhood Of Lizards)

**GYPPO**

| | | | |
|---|---|---|---|
| 79 | United Artists | High Rise Love/Free Enterprise | 100 |

**GYPSIES**

| | | | |
|---|---|---|---|
| 67 | CBS 201785 | Jerk It/Diamonds, Rubies, Gold And Fame | 40 |

(see also Flirtations)

**GYPSY QUEEN**

| | | | |
|---|---|---|---|
| 72 | Cactus CT1 | Love Is In The Air/Everybody's Searching | 10 |

**GYPSY (1)**

| | | | |
|---|---|---|---|
| 71 | United Artists UP 35202 | What Makes A Man A Man/I Want To Be Beside You | 6 |
| 72 | United Artists UP 35272 | Changes Coming/Don't Cry On Me | 6 |
| 71 | United Artists UAG 29155 | GYPSY (LP) | 15 |
| 72 | United Artists UAS 29420 | BRENDA AND THE RATTLESNAKE (LP) | 15 |

(see also Legay)

**GYPSY (2)**

| | | | |
|---|---|---|---|
| 84 | Private Pressing | We Came To Be Free/Get It Right | 50 |

# H

**HABIBIYYA**

| | | | |
|---|---|---|---|
| 72 | Island HELP 7 | IF MAN BUT KNEW (LP, with inner sleeve, black/silver label, pink 'i' logo) | 25 |

(see also Mighty Baby)

**HABITS**

| | | | |
|---|---|---|---|
| 66 | Decca F 12348 | Elbow Baby/Need You | 40 |

(see also Charles Dickens, Nice, Brian Davison)

**HACKENSACK**

| | | | |
|---|---|---|---|
| 72 | Island WIP 6149 | Moving On/River Boat | 12 |
| 71 | Polydor 2383 263 | UP THE HARD WAY (LP, with inner sleeve) | 100 |
| 74 | Zel UZ 003 | HERE COMES THE JUDGE (LP, private pressing, as Hack & Sack) | 125 |

(see also Megaton, Tiger [U.K.], Nicky Moore Band, Samson)

**STEVE HACKETT**

| | | | |
|---|---|---|---|
| 78 | Charisma CB 312 | How Can I?/Kim (with Ritchie Havens) | 10 |
| 78 | Charisma CB 318 | Narnia (Remix)/Please Don't Touch | 7 |
| 79 | Charisma CB 334 | Every Day/Lost Time In Cordoba | 5 |
| 79 | Charisma CB 341 | Clocks - The Angel Of Mons/Acoustic Set | 5 |
| 80 | Charisma CB 357 | The Show/Hercules Unchained (p/s) | 5 |
| 80 | Charisma CB 368 | Sentimental Institution/The Toast (p/s) | 5 |
| 81 | Charisma CB 385 | Hope I Don't Wake/Talkes Of The Riverbank (p/s) | 5 |

(see also Peter Banks, Genesis, GTR, Quiet World)

**VERNON HADDOCK'S JUBILEE LOVELIES**

| | | | |
|---|---|---|---|
| 65 | Columbia SX 6011 | VERNON HADDOCK'S JUBILEE LOVELIES (LP) | 125 |

**IDA HAENDEL**

| | | | |
|---|---|---|---|
| 58 | HMV CLP 1021 | IDA HAENDEL WITH GERALD MOORE AT THE PIANO (LP) | 800 |
| 59 | HMV CLP 1032 | BRAHMS VIOLIN CONCERTO (LP) | 250 |
| 60 | HMV DLP 1190 | TCHAIKOVSKY VIOLIN CONCERTO (LP) | 450 |
| 77 | HMV ASD 3352 | A CLASSICAL RECITAL (LP) | 150 |
| 80 | EMI ASD 3785 | BRAVISSIMA! (LP) | 200 |

**HAFFY'S WHISKY SOUR**

| | | | |
|---|---|---|---|
| 71 | Deram DM 345 | Shot In The Head/Bye Bye Bluebird | 10 |

(see also Easybeats, Paintbox)

**HAFLER TRIO**

| | | | |
|---|---|---|---|
| 84 | Doublevision DVR 4 | BANG! - AN OPEN LETTER (LP, with insert) | 25 |
| 86 | Charrm 3 | THREE WAYS OF SAYING TWO - THE NETHERLANDS LECTURES (LP, stickered sleeve with booklet) | 25 |
| 86 | Touch T 05 | THE SEA ORG (10", 'audio/visual' package with booklet) | 20 |

(see also Cabaret Voltaire)

**HAGALAZ RUNEDANCE**

| | | | |
|---|---|---|---|
| 97 | Elfenblut SAG III | When The Trees Were Silenced/A Tale Of Fate (Folkswang Awaits) (p/s, insert) | 10 |

## HAGAR THE WOMB
| | | | |
|---|---|---|---|
| 84 | Abstract Sounds 12ABS 029 | FUNNERY IN THE NUNNERY (12" EP) ................................................ | 15 |
| 84 | Mortarhate MORT 2 | WORD OF THE WOMB (12" EP) ................................................ | 15 |

## EARLE HAGEN
| | | | |
|---|---|---|---|
| 64 | Colpix PX 740 | Nancy's Theme/New Interns Watusi ................................................ | 5 |

## HA HA HA
| | | | |
|---|---|---|---|
| 85 | Hobby Horse SRTSKS 387 | HA HA HA EP ................................................ | 10 |

## HA HA MONO
| | | | |
|---|---|---|---|
| 82 | SRTS 82 CUS 1481 | Run For Miles/Snakes (p/s) ................................................ | 60 |

## JOYCE HAHN
| | | | |
|---|---|---|---|
| 57 | London HLA 8453 | Gonna Find Me A Bluebird/I Saw You, I Saw You ................................................ | 10 |

## PAUL HAIG
| | | | |
|---|---|---|---|
| 82 | Operation Twilight OPT 03 | Running Away/Time (p/s) ................................................ | 5 |
| 89 | Circa YRT 25 | Something Good (Extended Version)/Over You/Free To Go (Technology)/Something Good (Radio Edit) (12") ................................................ | 10 |
| 98 | Syntactic NICE 49 | Listen To Me (Looking/Irresponsible) (handmade p/s, with Billy McKenzie) ................................................ | 20 |

*(see also Josef K, Rhythm Of Life, Juggernauts, Billy McKenzie)*

## ROBERT HAIGH
| | | | |
|---|---|---|---|
| 85 | Laylah LAY 09 | JULIET OF THE SPIRITS EP (12") ................................................ | 25 |
| 86 | Laylah LAY 21 | MUSIC FROM THE ANTE CHAMBER EP (12") ................................................ | 25 |
| 87 | United Dairies UDT 034 | THE BEST OF ROBERT HAIGH (cassette) ................................................ | 20 |
| 88 | United Dairies UD 026 | VALENTINE OUT OF SEASON (LP) ................................................ | 40 |
| 89 | Le Rey LR 103 | A WALTZ IN PLAIN C (CD) ................................................ | 50 |

*(see also SEMA)*

## NORMAN HAINES (BAND)
| | | | |
|---|---|---|---|
| 70 | Parlophone R 5871 | Daffodil/Autumn Mobile (as Norman Haynes Band) ................................................ | 25 |
| 71 | Parlophone SPSR 338 | Den Of Iniquity/Everything You See (Mr. Armageddon) (promo only) ................................................ | 60 |
| 72 | Parlophone R 5960 | Give It To You Girl/Elaine (as Norman Haines) ................................................ | 20 |
| 71 | Parlophone PCS 7130 | DEN OF INIQUITY (LP, black/silver label with boxed logo) ................................................ | 1250 |
| 94 | Shoestring BL001 | DEN OF INIQUITY (LP, reissue) ................................................ | 30 |

*(see also Avalanche, Brumbeats, The Dog That Bit People, Locomotive)*

## HAIR (1)
| | | | |
|---|---|---|---|
| 69 | Pye NSPL 18314 | RAVE UP (LIVE FROM THE SHAFTESBURY THEATRE) (LP) ................................................ | 70 |

*(see also Alex Harvey, Hairband)*

## HAIR (2)
| | | | |
|---|---|---|---|
| 70 | Columbia SCX 6452 | HAIRPIECE (LP, black/silver labels with boxed logo) ................................................ | 350 |

## HAIRBAND
| | | | |
|---|---|---|---|
| 69 | Bell BLL 1076 | Big Louis/Travelling Song ................................................ | 18 |
| 69 | Bell SBLL 69 | BAND ON THE WAGON (LP, blue/silver/black label with "sold in on the U.K..." text) ................................................ | 60 |

*(see also Alex Harvey, Hair)*

## HAIRPOWER
| | | | |
|---|---|---|---|
| 70 | CBS 4961 | Royal International Love-in/Be There, Be Hair ................................................ | 10 |

## HAIR & SKIN TRADING COMPANY
| | | | |
|---|---|---|---|
| 96 | Aquese AQR 711 | CROUCH END EP ................................................ | 6 |
| 94 | Beggars Banquet BBQLP 141 | OVER VALENCE (LP with free 12") ................................................ | 15 |

## HAL
| | | | |
|---|---|---|---|
| 05 | Heavenly HVN 147 | Keep Love As Your Golden Rule/THE MAGIC NUMBERS: Animla Sola (Double A side tour single - 500 only p/s) ................................................ | 10 |

## I. HALCIDEONS AND I. JARZIF
| | | | |
|---|---|---|---|
| 78 | Greensleeves GRED 7 | Rise Ethiopians/Signs Of The Messiah (12") ................................................ | 40 |

## DENNIS HALE
| | | | |
|---|---|---|---|
| 55 | Parlophone MSP 6153 | The Butterscotch Mop/S'posin' ................................................ | 10 |

*(see also Jack Parnell)*

## TERENCE HOLDERWAY HALE
| | | | |
|---|---|---|---|
| 60 | Fontana H 285 | Beauty And The Beast/My New Year's Eve ................................................ | 7 |

## TONY HALE AND ROGER PERKS
| | | | |
|---|---|---|---|
| 70 | TET 135 | A Lament For A Lost Soul/Plea For Public Support ................................................ | 8 |

## BILL HALEY (& HIS COMETS)
### 78s
| | | | |
|---|---|---|---|
| 53 | London L 1190 | Crazy Man, Crazy/Whatcha Gonna Do (as Bill Haley with Haley's Comets) (gold label lettering) ................................................ | 30 |
| 53 | London L 1216 | Pat-A-Cake/Fractured (as Bill Haley with Haley's Comets, gold label) ................................................ | 30 |
| 54 | London HL 1190 | Crazy Man, Crazy/Whatcha Gonna Do (as Bill Haley with Haley's Comets) (reissue, silver label lettering) ................................................ | 20 |
| 54 | London HL 1216 | Pat-A-Cake/Fractured (reissue, silver label lettering, as Bill Haley with Haley's Comets) ................................................ | 20 |
| 56 | Melodisc 1376 | I'm Gonna Dry Ev'ry Tear With A Kiss/Why Do I Cry Over You ................................................ | 40 |
| 59 | Brunswick 05788 | I Got A Woman/Charmaine ................................................ | 20 |
| 59 | Brunswick 05805 | Shaky/Caldonia ................................................ | 20 |
| 59 | Brunswick 05810 | Joey's Song/Ooh! Look-A There, Ain't She Pretty ................................................ | 20 |

### SINGLES
| | | | |
|---|---|---|---|
| 54 | Brunswick 05317 | (We're Gonna) Rock Around The Clock/Thirteen Women (gold lettering on label) ................................................ | 60 |
| 54 | Brunswick 05317 | (We're Gonna) Rock Around The Clock/Thirteen Women (silver lettering on label) ................................................ | 25 |
| 54 | Brunswick 05338 | Shake, Rattle And Roll/A.B.C. Boogie (gold lettering on label) ................................................ | 40 |
| 54 | Brunswick 05338 | Shake, Rattle And Roll/A.B.C. Boogie (silver lettering on label) ................................................ | 20 |
| 55 | Brunswick 05373 | Happy Baby/Dim, Dim The Lights (I Want Some Atmosphere) (gold lettering on label) | 40 |
| 55 | Brunswick 05373 | Happy Baby/Dim, Dim The Lights (I Want Some Atmosphere) (silver lettering on label) ................................................ | 20 |

# Bill HALEY (& HIS COMETS)

| | | | |
|---|---|---|---|
| 55 | Brunswick 05405 | Birth Of The Boogie/Mambo Rock (gold lettering on label) | 40 |
| 55 | Brunswick 05405 | Birth Of The Boogie/Mambo Rock (silver lettering on label) | 20 |
| 55 | London HL 8142 | Green Tree Boogie/Sundown Boogie (gold lettering on label) | 150 |
| 55 | London HL 8142 | Green Tree Boogie/Sundown Boogie (silver lettering on label) | 50 |
| 55 | Brunswick 05453 | Two Hound Dogs/Razzle Dazzle (gold lettering on label) | 40 |
| 55 | Brunswick 05453 | Two Hound Dogs/Razzle Dazzle (silver lettering on label) | 20 |
| 55 | London HLF 8161 | Farewell, So Long, Goodbye/I'll Be True (gold lettering on label) | 100 |
| 55 | London HLF 8161 | Farewell, So Long, Goodbye/I'll Be True (silver lettering on label) | 50 |
| 55 | London HLF 8194 | Ten Little Indians/Rocking Chair On The Moon (gold lettering on label) | 100 |
| 55 | London HLF 8194 | Ten Little Indians/Rocking Chair On The Moon (silver lettering on label) | 50 |
| 55 | Brunswick 05509 | Rock-A-Beatin' Boogie/Burn That Candle (gold lettering on label) | 40 |
| 55 | Brunswick 05509 | Rock-A-Beatin' Boogie/Burn That Candle (silver lettering on label) | 20 |
| 56 | Brunswick 05530 | See You Later, Alligator/The Paper Boy (On Main Street, USA) (gold lettering on label) | 40 |
| 56 | Brunswick 05530 | See You Later, Alligator/The Paper Boy (On Main Street, USA) (silver lettering on label) | 20 |
| 56 | Brunswick 05565 | The Saints Rock 'N' Roll/R-O-C-K | 15 |
| 56 | Brunswick 05582 | Rockin' Through The Rye/Hot Dog Buddy Buddy | 15 |
| 56 | Brunswick 05615 | Rip It Up/Teenager's Mother | 15 |
| 56 | Brunswick 05616 | Rudy's Rock/Blue Comet Blues | 15 |
| 57 | Brunswick 05640 | Don't Knock The Rock/Calling All Comets | 15 |
| 57 | Brunswick 05641 | Hook, Line And Sinker/Goofin' Around | 15 |
| 57 | London HLF 8371 | Rock The Joint/Yes Indeed! (gold label) | 150 |
| 57 | London HLF 8371 | Rock The Joint/Yes Indeed! (silver label) | 50 |
| 57 | Brunswick 05658 | Forty Cups Of Coffee/Choo Choo Ch'Boogie | 15 |
| 57 | Brunswick 05688 | (You Hit The Wrong Note) Billy Goat/Rockin' Rollin' Rover | 15 |
| 57 | Brunswick 05719 | Miss You/The Dipsy Doodle | 15 |
| 58 | Brunswick 05735 | Mary, Mary Lou/It's A Sin | 15 |
| 58 | Brunswick 05742 | Skinny Minnie/How Many | 20 |
| 58 | Brunswick 05752 | Lean Jean/Don't Nobody Move | 15 |
| 58 | Brunswick 05766 | Whoa Mabel!/Chiquita Linda | 15 |
| 59 | Brunswick 05788 | I Got A Woman/Charmaine | 15 |
| 59 | Brunswick 05805 | Shaky/Caldonia | 15 |
| 59 | Brunswick 05810 | Joey's Song/Ooh! Look-A There, Ain't She Pretty | 15 |

*(The above 45s were originally issued with triangular centres; later round centres are worth two-thirds of these values.)*

| | | | |
|---|---|---|---|
| 60 | Brunswick 05818 | Puerto Rican Peddler/Skokiaan | 10 |
| 60 | Warner Bros WB 6 | Candy Kisses/Tamiami | 10 |
| 61 | London HLU 9471 | Spanish Twist/My Kind Of Woman | 10 |
| 63 | Stateside SS 196 | Tenor Man/Up Goes My Love | 10 |
| 64 | Warner Bros WB 133 | Rock Around The Clock/Love Letters In The Sand | 10 |
| 64 | Brunswick 05910 | Happy Baby/Birth Of The Boogie | 15 |
| 64 | Brunswick 05917 | The Green Door/Yeah! She's Evil | 15 |
| 68 | Pye International 7N 25455 | Crazy Man, Crazy/Dance With A Dolly (With A Hole In Her Stocking) | 15 |

## EXPORT SINGLES

| | | | |
|---|---|---|---|
| 54 | Decca BM 05317 | (We're Gonna) Rock Around The Clock/Thirteen Women | 60 |
| 55 | Decca BM 05405 | Birth Of The Boogie/Mambo Rock | 40 |
| 55 | Decca BM 05509 | Rock-A-Beatin' Boogie/Burn That Candle | 40 |
| 56 | Decca BM 05530 | See You Later Alligator/The Paper Boy (On Main Street, USA) | 40 |
| 56 | Decca BM 31163 | The Saints Rock 'N' Roll/R-O-C-K | 30 |
| 56 | Decca BM 31164 | Rockin' Through The Rye/Hot Dog Buddy Buddy | 30 |
| 56 | Decca BM 31171 | Rip It Up/Teenager's Mother | 30 |
| 57 | Decca BM 31174 | Don't Knock The Rock/Choo Choo Ch'Boogie | 30 |
| 68 | Decca AD 1010 | (We're Gonna) Rock Around The Clock/Shake, Rattle And Roll | 20 |

## EPs

| | | | |
|---|---|---|---|
| 55 | Brunswick OE 9129 | DIM, DIM THE LIGHTS (gold lettering label, 'stage' p/s, various colours) | 40 |
| 55 | Brunswick OE 9129 | DIM, DIM THE LIGHTS (silver lettering label, 'stage' or 'cameo' p/s) | 25 |
| 55 | London REF 1031 | ROCK AND ROLL | 50 |
| 56 | London REF 1049 | LIVE IT UP PART 1 | 30 |
| 56 | London REF 1050 | LIVE IT UP PART 2 | 30 |
| 56 | Brunswick OE 9214 | ROCK AND ROLL WITH BILL HALEY | 25 |
| 56 | Brunswick OE 9250 | ROCK AROUND THE CLOCK | 20 |
| 56 | Brunswick OE 9250 | ROCK AROUND THE CLOCK (round centre, different sleeve, same design as "Bill Haley" [OE 9459]) | 35 |
| 56 | London REF 1058 | LIVE IT UP PART 3 | 35 |
| 56 | Brunswick OE 9278 | ROCK'N'ROLL STAGE SHOW PART 1 | 20 |
| 56 | Brunswick OE 9279 | ROCK'N'ROLL STAGE SHOW PART 2 | 20 |
| 56 | Brunswick OE 9280 | ROCK'N'ROLL STAGE SHOW PART 3 | 20 |
| 58 | Brunswick OE 9349 | ROCKIN' THE OLDIES PART 1 | 25 |
| 58 | Brunswick OE 9350 | ROCKIN' THE OLDIES PART 2 | 25 |
| 58 | Brunswick OE 9351 | ROCKIN' THE OLDIES PART 3 | 25 |

*(Originally issued with triangular centres, later round-centre copies are worth two-thirds this value.)*

| | | | |
|---|---|---|---|
| 59 | Brunswick OE 9446 | ROCKIN' AROUND THE WORLD | 60 |
| 59 | Brunswick OE 9459 | BILL HALEY | 50 |

*(The above EPs were originally issued with triangular centres, later round-centre copies are worth half to two-thirds these values.)*

| | | | |
|---|---|---|---|
| 60 | Warners WEP 6001 | BILL HALEY AND HIS COMETS | 20 |
| 61 | Warners WEP 6025 | BILL HALEY'S JUKE BOX (mono) | 20 |
| 61 | Warners WSEP 6025 | BILL HALEY'S JUKE BOX (stereo) | 30 |
| 64 | Warners WEP 6133 | BILL HALEY VOLUME 1 | 20 |
| 64 | Warners WEP 6136 | BILL HALEY VOLUME 2 | 20 |

## ALBUMS

| | | | |
|---|---|---|---|
| 55 | London H-APB 1042 | LIVE IT UP (10", gold lettering on label) | 80 |
| 55 | London H-APB 1042 | LIVE IT UP (10", silver lettering on label) | 25 |
| 56 | Brunswick LAT 8117 | ROCK AROUND THE CLOCK | 30 |
| 56 | Brunswick LAT 8139 | ROCK AND ROLL STAGE SHOW | 30 |
| 57 | London HA-F 2037 | ROCK THE JOINT | 80 |
| 57 | Brunswick LAT 8219 | ROCKIN' THE OLDIES | 60 |
| 57 | Brunswick LAT 8268 | ROCKIN' THE JOINT | 60 |
| 59 | Brunswick LAT 8295 | BILL HALEY'S CHICKS (mono) | 60 |
| 59 | Brunswick STA 3011 | BILL HALEY'S CHICKS (stereo) | 70 |
| 60 | Brunswick LAT 8326 | STRICTLY INSTRUMENTAL | 40 |
| 62 | Columbia 33SX 1460 | TWISTIN' KNIGHTS AT THE ROUNDTABLE (LIVE!) | 30 |
| 65 | Warner Bros W 1391 | BILL HALEY'S JUKE BOX | 20 |

*(see also Kingsmen, Jodimars, Nick Nantos & His Fireballs)*

## HALF JAPANESE

| | | | |
|---|---|---|---|
| 81 | Armageddon ABOX 1 | 1/2 GENTLEMEN NOT BEASTS (3-LP box set with poster, booklet & lyric insert) | 50 |
| 81 | Armageddon ARM 7 | LOUD (LP) | 15 |

*(see also Jad Fair)*

## HALFBREED

| | | | |
|---|---|---|---|
| 75 | United Artists UAG 29877 | HALFBREED (LP, fold out sleeve) | 20 |

## HALF PINT

| | | | |
|---|---|---|---|
| 85 | Greensleeves GRED 178 | Freedom Fighter/Hold On (12") | 25 |

## HAL HOPPERS

| | | | |
|---|---|---|---|
| 54 | London HL 8107 | More Love/Do Nothin' Blues | 40 |
| 55 | London HL 8129 | Mother Of Pearl/Baby I've Had It | 40 |

## ADELAIDE HALL

| | | | |
|---|---|---|---|
| 60 | Oriole CB 1556 | Common Sense/Blue Bird On My Shoulder | 10 |

## BARBARA HALL

| | | | |
|---|---|---|---|
| 75 | EMI INT 514 | You Brought It On Yourself/Drop My Heart Off At The Door | 10 |

## BOB HALL & ALEXIS KORNER

| | | | |
|---|---|---|---|
| 78 | Logo GO 331 | Pinetop's Boogie Woogie/All I Got Is You | 12 |

*(see also Brunning Hall Sunflower Blues Band, Alexis Korner)*

## CAROLINE HALL

| | | | |
|---|---|---|---|
| 70 | Major Minor MM 689 | Dream Boy/Julie | 5 |
| 71 | Decca F 13146 | Hold My Hand/Put A Light In The Window | 6 |

## DARYL HALL & SOUNDS OF BLACKNESS

| | | | |
|---|---|---|---|
| 94 | Mercury MERMC 404 | Gloryland/(mixes) (picture disc, in poster sleeve) | 10 |

## DEREK HALL & MIKE COOPER

| | | | |
|---|---|---|---|
| 60s | Kennet KRS 766 | OUT OF THE SHADES (EP) | 35 |

## DOLORES HALL

| | | | |
|---|---|---|---|
| 72 | Jay Boy BOY 77 | Good Lovin' Man/W-O-M-E-N | 8 |

*(see also Jackie Lee & Dolores Hall)*

## DORA HALL

| | | | |
|---|---|---|---|
| 64 | King KG 1003 | Hello Faithless/You've Got Me Cryin' Again | 5 |

## GERRI HALL

| | | | |
|---|---|---|---|
| 66 | Sue WI 4026 | Who Can I Run To/I Lost A Key (unissued) | 0 |
| 04 | Grapevine 2000 143 | Who Can I Run To/JADES: Lucky Fellow (reissue) | 18 |

## JIMMY GRAY HALL

| | | | |
|---|---|---|---|
| 74 | Epic EPC 2312 | Be That Way/Possessed By The Moon | 20 |

## JUANITA HALL

| | | | |
|---|---|---|---|
| 62 | Storyville SEP 382 | STORYVILLE BLUES ANTHOLOGY VOL. 2 (EP) | 10 |

## LANI HALL

| | | | |
|---|---|---|---|
| 83 | A&M AM 159 | Never Say Never Again/MICHAEL LEGRAND: Un Chanson D'Amour (p/s) | 8 |

## LARRY HALL

| | | | |
|---|---|---|---|
| 60 | Parlophone R 4625 | Sandy/Lovin' Tree | 15 |
| 62 | Salvo SLO 1811 | Ladder Of Love/The One You Left Behind (99 copies only) | 20 |

## RENE HALL'S ORCHESTRA

| | | | |
|---|---|---|---|
| 58 | London HLU 8581 | Twitchy/Flippin' | 30 |

## ROBIN HALL (& JIMMY MACGREGOR)

| | | | |
|---|---|---|---|
| 60 | Collector JDS 3 | Football Crazy/Rosin The Beau (with p/s) | 10 |
| 60 | Collector JDS 3 | Football Crazy/Rosin The Beau | 6 |
| 60 | Decca F 11266 | Football Crazy/Rosin The Beau (reissue, p/s) | 7 |

*(see also Galliards)*

## RONNIE HALL

| | | | |
|---|---|---|---|
| 61 | Piccadilly 7N 35001 | The Code Of Love/Who Cares | 5 |
| 61 | Piccadilly 7N 35015 | She's Mine/My Heart Is The Lover | 5 |
| 62 | Piccadilly 7N 35040 | My Very First Love/The Day After Forever | 5 |
| 65 | Fontana TF 569 | I'll Stand Aside/I'm Getting Nowhere | 5 |

## ROY HALL

| | | | |
|---|---|---|---|
| 56 | Brunswick 05531 | See You Later, Alligator/Don't Stop Now (gold label lettering) | 500 |
| 56 | Brunswick 05531 | See You Later, Alligator/Don't Stop Now (78) | 50 |
| 56 | Brunswick 05555 | Blue Suede Shoes/Luscious | 300 |
| 56 | Brunswick 05627 | Diggin' The Boogie/Three Alley Cats | 500 |
| 56 | Brunswick 05627 | Diggin' The Boogie/Three Alley Cats (78) | 50 |
| 70 | Injun 105 | One Monkey Don't Stop The Shop/Flood Of love | 10 |

MINT VALUE £

**TONY HALL**
77   Free Reed FRR 012                    FIELDVOLE MUSIC (LP, with insert) ................................................................. 20

**CHANCE HALLADAY**
62   Vogue V 9203                          John Henry/Thirteen Women ..................................................................... 25

**HALLELUJAH SKIFFLE GROUP**
58   Oriole CB 1429                        I Saw The Light/A Closer Walk With Thee (with Clinton Ford) ................. 20

**HALLIARD**
67   Saga SOC 1058                         IT'S THE IRISH IN ME (LP) ........................................................................ 30
68   Broadside BRO 106                     THE HALLIARD AND JON RAVEN (LP) ........................................................ 50
*(see also Jon Raven, Nic Jones)*

**DICK HALLMAN**
56   Brunswick 05608                       Two Different Worlds/Love Me As Though There Were No Tomorrow ......... 5
60   Vogue V 9162                          Born To Be Loved/Just Squeeze Me But Don't Teeze Me ......................... 6

**TERRY HALL AND MUSHTAQ**
03   Honest Jons HJRLP5                    THE HOUR OF TWO LIGHTS (2-LP, inners) ............................................... 18
*(see also Specials)*

**GERRY HALLOM**
84   Fellside FE 036                       A RUN A MINUTE (LP) ............................................................................... 15

**JOHNNY HALLYDAY**
62   Philips BF 1238                       Shake The Hand Of A Fool/Hold Back The Sun ...................................... 10
63   Philips 373 012BF                     Hey Little Girl/Caravan Of Lonely Men ................................................... 10
65   Philips BF 1449                       Pour Moi Tu Es La Seule/They Call Him A Man ...................................... 10
62   Philips 432 813BE                     ROCKING (EP) ........................................................................................ 100
66   Vogue VRE 5013                        JOHNNY HALLYDAY (EP) ........................................................................ 100
61   Philips BBL 7556                      SINGS AMERICA'S ROCKIN' HITS (LP) ...................................................... 100

**HALOS**
61   London HLU 9424                       Nag/Copycat ........................................................................................... 30

**STUART HAMBLEN**
54   HMV 7MC 20                            This Ole House/When My Lord Picks Up The 'Phone (export issue) ......... 25
55   HMV 7MC 30                            Go On By/Just A Man (export issue) ........................................................ 10
56   HMV 7M 394                            Hell Train/A Few Things To Remember ................................................... 15

**BILLY HAMBRIC**
79   Grapevine GRP 139                     She Said Goodbye/I Found True Love ..................................................... 12

**CLAIRE HAMILL**
72   Island WIP 6122                       When I Was A Child/Alice In The Streets Of Darlington .......................... 6
72   Island WIP 6133                       Baseball Blues/Smile Your Blues Away ................................................... 6
81   WEA K 18440                           First Night In New York/Ultraviolet Light (B-side with Gary Numan) (p/s) ... 7
72   Island ILPS 9182                      ONE HOUSE LEFT STANDING (LP, lyric inner sleeve) ............................... 40
73   Island ILPS 9225                      OCTOBER (LP, gatefold sleeve, pink rim palm tree label) ...................... 20
74   Konk KONK 101                         STAGE DOOR JOHNNIES (LP, gatefold sleeve, blue label) ..................... 15
75   Konk KONK 104                         ABRACADABRA (LP, featuring Cafe Society, with lyric insert, blue label) ... 15
*(see also Cafe Society, Gary Numan, Wishbone Ash)*

**HAMILTON**
79   Muscle SJP 806/MUS 001               Jet Set Girl/Methodone And Coconuts (500 only, no p/s) ................... 100

**BILLY HAMILTON & STRANDSMEN**
67   Philips BF 1622                       Try To Remember/Don't You Believe It .................................................... 7
*(see also Strandsmen)*

**CHICO HAMILTON QUINTET**
57   Decca DL 8614                         SWEET SMELL OF SUCCESS (LP) .............................................................. 15
58   Vogue LAE 12045                       CHICO HAMILTON QUINTET IN HIFI (LP) ................................................ 20
64   HMV CLP 1807                          MAN FROM TWO WORLDS (LP) .............................................................. 20

**DAVE HAMILTON**
12   Kent TOWN 144                         Pisces Pace/BARRINO BROTHERS: The Bad Things You Said To Me ......... 8

**ED HAMILTON**
70   Evolution E 3003                      Emily's Eyes/All I Needed Was The Rain .................................................. 8

**EDWARD HAMILTON & ARABIANS**
80   Grapevine GRP 134                     Baby Don't You Weep/I'm Gonna Love You ........................................... 20

**GARY HAMILTON**
67   Decca F 12697                         Let The Music Play/Don't Ask ................................................................. 12
69   CBS 4674                              Easy Rider/Hare Krishna ......................................................................... 6
*(see also Hamilton & [Hamilton] Movement)*

**GAVIN HAMILTON**
67   King KG 1067                          It Won't Be The Same/Turn The Key Softly ........................................... 150

**GEORGE HAMILTON IV**
57   London HL 8361                        A Rose And A Candy Bar/If You Don't Know (gold label print) ............ 125
57   London HL 8361                        A Rose And A Candy Bar/If You Don't Know (later silver label print) ..... 30
57   HMV POP 429                           Why Don't They Understand/Even Tho' ................................................... 5
72   Uni UNS 480                           Evel Knievel/Boy From The Country ........................................................ 5
59   HMV CLP 1263                          SING ME A SAD SONG - A TRIBUTE TO HANK WILLIAMS (LP) ................. 20

**GUY HAMILTON**
65   HMV POP 1418                          A Lifetime Of Loneliness/Give The Game Away ..................................... 15
*(see also Neil Christian)*

**(KINGSIZE) HAMILTON & PLATTERMEN**
66   Emerald MD 1048                       Shake/I Got To Know .............................................................................. 25

**LITTLE JOHNNY HAMILTON**
90   Horace's HRH 006                      Oh How I Love You/ENTERTAINERS IV: Gettin' Back Into Circulation ...... 10

| | | | |
|---|---|---|---|
| 99 | Jay Boy 10 | Keep On Moving/Oh How I Love You (DJ copy) | 12 |

**M. HAMILTON**
| | | | |
|---|---|---|---|
| 67 | Ska Beat JB 265 | Something Gotta Ring/DENNIS LYNWARD & HIS GROUP: Jazz Session | 20 |

**MILTON HAMILTON**
| | | | |
|---|---|---|---|
| 73 | Explosion EX 2069 | Long Long Road/Version | 8 |
| 77 | Wolf WM 005 | Children Are You Ready/Part 2 | 8 |

**ROY HAMILTON (1)**
| | | | |
|---|---|---|---|
| 58 | Fontana H 113 | Don't Let Go/The Right To Love | 25 |
| 58 | Fontana H 143 | Crazy Feelin'/In A Dream | 15 |
| 59 | Fontana H 180 | Pledging My Love/My One And Only Love | 15 |
| 59 | Fontana H 193 | I Need Your Loving/Somewhere Along The Way | 15 |
| 61 | Fontana H 298 | You Can Have Her/Abide With Me | 15 |
| 61 | Fontana H 320 | You're Gonna Need Magic/To The One I Love | 15 |
| 63 | MGM MGM 1210 | Theme From "The VIPs"/The Sinner | 15 |
| 64 | MGM MGM 1251 | There She Is/The Panic Is On | 175 |
| 64 | MGM MGM 1251 | There She Is/The Panic Is On (DJ copy) | 600 |
| 65 | MGM MGM 1268 | A Thousand Tears Ago/Sweet Violet | 15 |
| 66 | RCA RCA 1500 | And I Love Her/Tore Up Over You | 15 |
| 69 | Deep Soul DS 9106 | Dark End Of The Street/100 Years Ago | 40 |
| 59 | Fontana TFE 17160 | WHY FIGHT THE FEELING (EP) | 20 |
| 60 | Fontana TFE 17163 | THE MOOD MOVES (EP) | 20 |
| 61 | Fontana TFE 17170 | COME OUT SWINGING (EP) | 20 |
| 63 | Columbia 33SX 1473 | GREATEST HITS (LP) | 40 |
| 64 | MGM MGM-C 960 | WARM SOUL (LP) | 60 |

**ROY HAMILTON (2)**
| | | | |
|---|---|---|---|
| 83 | HBS K CAP 1 | Turn Up The Music/Instrumental Version (12", with Capiche) | 20 |

**RUSS HAMILTON**
| | | | |
|---|---|---|---|
| 58 | Oriole MG 20031 | WE WILL MAKE LOVE (LP) | 20 |

**SCOTT HAMILTON**
| | | | |
|---|---|---|---|
| 65 | Parlophone R5341 | When Things Go Wrong/I Wonder | 6 |
| 66 | Parlophone R 5492 | Good Day Sunshine/For No One | 10 |

**HAMILTON & MOVEMENT**
| | | | |
|---|---|---|---|
| 65 | Polydor BM 56026 | Really Saying Something/I Won't See You Tonight | 80 |
| 67 | CBS 202573 | I'm Not The Marrying Kind/My Love Belongs To You | 40 |

*(see also Gary Hamilton)*

**HAMLET**
| | | | |
|---|---|---|---|
| 67 | Decca F12571 | She Won't See The Light/Go Play In Your Own Yard | 20 |

**HAMLETT**
| | | | |
|---|---|---|---|
| 72 | Pye 7N45171 | Where'd The Day Go/Vampire Man | 20 |

**HAMLINS**
| | | | |
|---|---|---|---|
| 67 | Coxsone CS 7021 | Trying To Keep A Good Man Down/SUMMERTAIRS: Oh My Darling | 90 |
| 67 | Coxsone CS 7022 | Soul And Inspiration/ETHIOPIANS: Let's Get Together | 35 |
| 68 | Coxsone CS 7048 | Sentimental Reasons/SOUL VENDORS: Last Waltz | 200 |
| 68 | Blue Cat BS 115 | Sugar And Spice/SOUL VENDORS: Mercy Mercy Mercy | 200 |

*(see also Minstrels)*

**JACK HAMMER**
| | | | |
|---|---|---|---|
| 61 | Oriole CB 1634 | Young Only Once/Juliette | 15 |
| 62 | Oriole CB 1645 | Kissin' Twist/Melancholy Boy | 10 |
| 62 | Oriole CB 1728 | Crazy Twist/Twist Talk | 10 |
| 62 | Oriole CB 1753 | Don't Let Baby Know/Number 2539 | 15 |
| 66 | Polydor 56091 | Thanks/Love Ladder | 20 |
| 67 | Polydor 56158 | Joe Poor Loves Daphne Rich/Ode To A Discotheque | 50 |
| 69 | United Artists UP 35029 | What Greater Love/The Mason Dixon Line | 30 |
| 71 | Youngblood B 1023 | Swim/Colour Combination | 40 |
| 63 | Oriole PS 40020 | HAMMER + BEAT = TWIST (LP) | 80 |
| 66 | Polydor 582001 | BRAVE NEW WORLD (LP) | 120 |

**HAMMER (1)**
| | | | |
|---|---|---|---|
| 73 | Vertigo 6059084 | Rock Off/Rock And Roll Band | 5 |

**HAMMER (2)**
| | | | |
|---|---|---|---|
| 85 | Ebony EBON 29 | CONTRACT WITH HELL (LP) | 15 |

**HAMMERHEAD**
| | | | |
|---|---|---|---|
| 81 | Linden Sounds LS 009 | Time Will Tell/Lonely Man (p/s) | 60 |

**HAMMERS**
| | | | |
|---|---|---|---|
| 69 | President PT 247 | Baby And Me/Little Butterfly | 5 |
| 69 | President PT 276 | Sugar Baby/Power Of Love | 5 |

**HAMMERS (JAMAICA)**
| | | | |
|---|---|---|---|
| 70 | Gas GAS 162 | Hotter Than Scorcher/Someday Could See You | 30 |

*(see also Joan Ross)*

**HAMMERSMITH GORILLAS**
| | | | |
|---|---|---|---|
| 74 | Penny Farthing PEN 849 | You Really Got Me/Leavin' 'Ome (p/s) | 25 |
| 77 | Raw RAW 2 | You Really Got Me/Leavin' 'Ome (reissue, company sleeve) | 15 |

*(see also Gorillas, Helter Skelter, Jesse Hector)*

**PETER HAMMILL**
| | | | |
|---|---|---|---|
| 75 | Charisma CB 245 | Birthday Special/Shingle Song | 8 |
| 78 | Charisma CB 339 | The Polaroid (credited to Ricky Nadir)/The Old School Tie | 10 |
| 78 | Charisma PH 001 | Crying Wolf/This Side Of The Looking Glass (promo only) | 30 |
| 81 | Virgin VS 424 | My Experience/Glue (p/s) | 5 |

MINT VALUE £

| 82 | Naive NAV 3 | Paradox Drive/Now More Than Ever (p/s) | 6 |
| 83 | Naive NAV 8 | Film Noir/Seven Wonders | 6 |
| 84 | Charisma CB 414 | Just Good Friends/Just Good Friends (Instrumental) (p/s) | 5 |
| 86 | Foundry FOUND 3 | Painting By Numbers/You Hit Me Where I Live (p/s) | 5 |
| 71 | Charisma CAS 1037 | FOOL'S MATE (LP, gatefold sleeve, pink 'scroll' label) | 100 |
| 73 | Charisma CAS 1067 | CHAMELEON IN THE SHADOW OF THE NIGHT (LP, gatefold sleeve, large 'Mad Hatter' label) | 40 |
| 74 | Charisma CAS 1083 | THE SILENT CORNER AND THE EMPTY STAGE (LP, gatefold sleeve., with lyric inner, large 'Mad Hatter' label) | 20 |
| 74 | Charisma CAS 1089 | IN CAMERA (LP, with inner sleeve, small 'Mad Hatter' label) | 20 |
| 75 | Charisma CAS 1099 | NADIR'S BIG CHANCE (LP, laminated sleeve, with inner sleeve small 'Mad Hatter' label) | 15 |
| 77 | Charisma CAS 1125 | OVER (LP, with inner lyric sleeve, small 'Mad Hatter' label) | 15 |
| 78 | Charisma CAS 1137 | THE FUTURE NOW (LP, with insert) | 18 |
| 79 | Charisma CAS 1146 | PH7 (LP) | 15 |
| 84 | Foundry FOUND 1 | THE MARGIN LIVE (LP, as Peter Hammill & K Group) | 20 |

*(see also Van Der Graaf Generator, Rikki Nadir, Colin Scot)*

## HAMMOND BROS.
| 74 | London 10464 | The Garbage Man/Soul Over Easy (featuring Maggie) | 8 |

## CLAY HAMMOND
| 72 | Jay Boy BOY 78 | Dance Little Girl/Twin Brother | 6 |

## JOHN HAMMOND
| 65 | Fontana TF 560 | Baby Won't You Tell Me/I Love The Life I Live | 15 |
| 68 | Atlantic 584 190 | Brown Eyed Handsome Man/Crosscut Saw | 18 |
| 64 | Fontana TFL 6046 | BIG CITY BLUES (LP) | 60 |
| 65 | Fontana TFL 6059 | SO MANY ROADS (LP) | 50 |
| 71 | CBS 64365 | SOURCE POINT (LP) | 25 |
| 72 | CBS 65051 | I'M SATISFIED (LP) | 25 |
| 72 | Vanguard VSD 11/12 | THE BEST OF JOHN HAMMOND - SOUTHERN FRIED (2-LP) | 20 |

## CURLEY HAMNER & COOPER BROTHERS
| 59 | Felsted SD 80061 | Twistin' And Turnin'/King And Queen | 10 |

## BILLY HAMON
| 78 | Bronze BRO 58 | Butch Things/Amusement Arcade (p/s) | 20 |

## HEATH HAMPSTEAD
| 68 | Polydor 56289 | I Started A Joke/The Beginning Of The Ending | 6 |

## SLIDE HAMPTON & HIS BAND
| 62 | London HA-K/SH-K 8008 | JAZZ WITH A TWIST (LP) | 18 |
| 62 | London LZT-K 15225 | LONDON JAZZ (LP, as Slide Hampton Octet) | 18 |

## HERBIE HANCOCK
| 63 | Blue Note 45-1887 | Blind Man, Blind Man (Parts 1 & 2) | 10 |
| 70 | Warner Bros WB 7358 | Fat Mama/Wiggle-Waggle | 8 |
| 74 | CBS 2329 | Chameleon/Vein Melter | 6 |
| 75 | CBS 3059 | Palm Grease/Butterfly | 6 |
| 71 | Warner Bros WS 1834 | FAT ALBERT ROTUNDA (LP) | 20 |
| 71 | Warner Bros K 46077 | MWANDISHI (LP) | 20 |
| 72 | Warner Bros K 46164 | CROSSINGS (LP) | 15 |
| 74 | Warner Bros K 46039 | FAT ALBERT ROTUNDA (LP, reissue) | 15 |
| 74 | CBS 60193 | THRUST (LP) | 20 |
| 74 | CBS 80546 | DEATH WISH (LP, soundtrack) | 15 |
| 74 | CBS 65582 | SEXTANT (LP) | 20 |
| 74 | CBS 65928 | HEADHUNTERS (LP) | 20 |
| 75 | CBS 69185 | MAN CHILD (LP) | 16 |

*(see also Headhunters)*

## OWEN HAND
| 61 | Transatlantic TRA 127 | SOMETHING NEW (LP) | 100 |
| 66 | Transatlantic TRA | I LOVED A LASS (LP) | 80 |

## JOHNNY HANDLE
| 61 | Topic TOP 78 | STOTTIN' DOON THE WAAL (EP) | 10 |
| 75 | Topic 12TS 270 | THE COLLIER LAD (LP) | 15 |

*(see also Louise Killen & Johnny Handle, High Level Ranters)*

## HANDLEY FAMILY
| 73 | GL 100 | Wam Bam/Rum Dum And Baccy | 8 |

## HANDSLIPS
| 81 | Victoria Park VICKY 1 | Too Young To Date (But Not To Masturbate)/Art School Is For Wankers | 6 |

## HANDSOME BEASTS
| 81 | Heavy Metal HEAVY 1 | All Riot Now/Mark Of The Beast (p/s) | 25 |
| 81 | Heavy Metal HEAVY 2 | Breaker/One In A Crowd/Crazy (wraparound p/s) | 8 |
| 82 | Heavy Metal HEAVY 11 | Sweeties/You're One Your Own (p/s, with card sheet) | 8 |
| 82 | Heavy Metal HMRLP 2 | BEASTIALITY (LP) | 20 |

## WAYNE HANDY
| 58 | London HL 8547 | Say Yeah/Could It Be (B-side with King Sisters) | 200 |

## PAUL HANFORD
| 60 | Parlophone R 4680 | Itsy Bitsy Teenie Weenie Little Polka Dot Bikini/Why Have You Changed Your Mind | 10 |
| 60 | Parlophone R 4694 | If You Ain't Got Love/Ev'ry Little Girl | 10 |
| 61 | Parlophone R 4745 | Everything/Cigarettes And Coffee Blues | 10 |
| 61 | Parlophone R 4813 | Memphis Address/Flutter Flutter | 10 |
| 62 | Oriole CB 1779 | Don't Be/Habit Of Loving You | 10 |
| 63 | Oriole CB 1830 | Just When I Need You Most/Judy | 10 |

| | | | |
|---|---|---|---|
| 63 | Oriole CB 1866 | The Minute You're Gone/High School Dance | 10 |

**HANG DAVID**

| | | | |
|---|---|---|---|
| 90 | Vacant HANG 01 | HANG DAVID (12" EP, p/s) | 18 |

**HANGMAN'S BEAUTIFUL DAUGHTERS**

| | | | |
|---|---|---|---|
| 87 | Dreamworld DREAM 11 | Love Is Blue/Popular Trend (p/s) | 7 |

**BOBBY HANNA**

| | | | |
|---|---|---|---|
| 67 | Decca F 12604 | Thanks To You/Here I Stand | 5 |
| 67 | Decca F 12695 | Blame It On Me/Goin' Where The Lovin' Is | 7 |
| 68 | Decca F 12738 | Too Much Love/What Do I Want For Tomorrow | 5 |
| 68 | Decca F 12783 | Written On The Wind/Everybody Needs Love | 10 |
| 68 | Decca F 12833 | To Wait For Love (Is To Waste Your Life Away)/Is It Wrong | 6 |
| 69 | Decca F 22917 | Winter Love (E' L'Amore)/Time | 6 |
| 70 | Philips 6006 029 | Better Men Than I/Look Into My Life | 6 |

**JOSH HANNA**

| | | | |
|---|---|---|---|
| 65 | Parlophone R 5385 | When I Love You/Love Me, Love Me | 6 |
| 66 | Decca F 12532 | Shut Your Mouth/Sweet To My Soul | 20 |

**PAUL HANNAH**

| | | | |
|---|---|---|---|
| 94 | Ferox FER 007 | CONTROL EP (12", plain sleeve) | 12 |

**ROSS HANNAMAN**

| | | | |
|---|---|---|---|
| 67 | Columbia DB 8217 | Down Thru' Summer/I'll Give All My Love To Southend | 5 |
| 67 | Columbia DB 8288 | 1969/Probably On A Thursday (with p/s) | 50 |
| 67 | Columbia DB 8288 | 1969/Probably On A Thursday | 40 |
| 74 | Bellwood BW1 | A NIGHT AT FACTOTUM (LP, 100 only, as John and Rosalind) | 20 |

**MARTIN HANNETT**

| | | | |
|---|---|---|---|
| 80 | Factory FACT 14C | First Aspect Of The Same Thing/Second Aspect Of The Same Thing (flexi, most included first/second pressing of THE RETURN OF THE DURUTTI COLUMN LP) | 25 |

*(see also Durutti Column)*

**HANNIBAL**

| | | | |
|---|---|---|---|
| 74 | B&C HB 1 | Winds Of Change/Winter | 6 |
| 70 | B&C CAS 1022 | HANNIBAL (LP, gatefold sleeve) | 125 |

*(see also Wizzard)*

**LANCE HANNIBAL**

| | | | |
|---|---|---|---|
| 69 | Blue Cat BS 148 | Read The News/RECO & RHYTHM ACES: Return Of The Bullet | 40 |

*(see also Sugar Simone, Les Foster)*

**JERRY HANSEN & RAMBLERS DANCE BAND**

| | | | |
|---|---|---|---|
| 67 | Decca WAP 24 | DANCE WITH THE RAMBLERS (LP) | 25 |

**ANNETTE HANSHAW**

| | | | |
|---|---|---|---|
| 65 | VJM VEP 31 | THAT'S ALL (EP) | 10 |

**HANSIE**

| | | | |
|---|---|---|---|
| 79 | Sonet SON 2195 | Automobile/Tu Es Belle (p/s) | 6 |

**HANSON**

| | | | |
|---|---|---|---|
| 73 | Manticore K43507 | NOW HEAR THIS (LP, gatefold sleeve) | 20 |

**HANSON & KARLSSON**

| | | | |
|---|---|---|---|
| 67 | Polydor 184 196 | SWEDISH UNDERGROUND (LP) | 15 |
| 69 | Polydor 462 60 | MONUMENT (LP) | 60 |
| 69 | Polydor 583 564 | MAN AT THE MOON (LP) | 60 |

*(see also Bo Hansson)*

**BO HANSSON**

| | | | |
|---|---|---|---|
| 72 | Charisma CAS 1059 | LORD OF THE RINGS (LP, insert, large 'Mad Hatter' label) | 20 |
| 73 | Charisma CAS 1073 | MAGICIANS'S HAT (LP, large 'Mad Hatter' label) | 15 |
| 76 | Charisma CAS 1113 | ATTIC THOUGHTS (LP, gatefold. 'Mad Hatter' label) | 15 |

**HAPPENINGS**

| | | | |
|---|---|---|---|
| 66 | Fontana TF 735 | See You In September/He Thinks He's A Hero | 10 |
| 66 | Fontana TF 766 | Go Away Little Girl/Tea Time | 8 |
| 67 | Pye International 7N 25501 | My Mammy/I Believe In Nothing | 7 |
| 67 | Stateside SS 587 | Goodnight My Love/Lillies By Monet | 8 |
| 67 | Stateside SS 2013 | I Got Rhythm/You're In A Bad Way | 8 |
| 67 | BT Puppy BTS 45532 | Why Do Fools Fall In Love/When The Summer Is Through | 7 |
| 67 | BT Puppy BTS 45530 | My Mammy/I Believe In Nothing | 5 |
| 68 | BT Puppy BTS 45538 | Music Music Music/When I Lock My Door | 6 |
| 68 | BT Puppy BTS 45540 | Randy/Love Song Of Mummy And Dad | 8 |
| 68 | BT Puppy BTS 45543 | Breaking Up Is Hard To Do/Anyway | 6 |
| 68 | BT Puppy BTS 45545 | Crazy Rhythm/Love Song Of Mummy And Dad | 5 |
| 69 | BT Puppy BTS 45546 | Where Do I Go, Go-Be-In (Hare Krishna)/New Day Comin' | 5 |
| 67 | Fontana TL 5383 | BYE BYE, SO LONG, FAREWELL ... SEE YOU IN SEPTEMBER (LP) | 35 |
| 67 | BT Puppy BTLP 1003 | PSYCLE (LP) | 40 |
| 68 | BT Puppy BTLPS 1004 | GOLDEN HITS (LP) | 20 |

**HAPPY CATS**

| | | | |
|---|---|---|---|
| 78 | Grapevine 110 | These Boots Are Made For Walkin'/Destroy That Boy | 20 |

**HAPPY CONFUSION**

| | | | |
|---|---|---|---|
| 69 | Penny Farthing PEN 706 | Yes Sir/Hereditary Impediment | 15 |

**HAPPY FAMILY**

| | | | |
|---|---|---|---|
| 82 | 4AD AD 204 | Puritans/Innermost Thoughts/The Mistake (p/s) | 15 |

*(see also Josef K, Momus)*

**HAPPY MAGAZINE**

| | | | |
|---|---|---|---|
| 68 | Polydor 56233 | Satisfied Street/Do Right Woman Do Right Man | 20 |
| 69 | Polydor 56307 | Who Belongs To You (Ooby Dooby Doo)/Beautiful Land | 10 |

## HAPPY MONDAYS

*(see also Griffin)*

| | | | |
|---|---|---|---|
| 85 | Factory FAC 129 | FORTY FIVE EP : Delightful/This Feeling/Oasis (12" p/s) | 12 |
| 86 | Factory FAC 142 | Freaky Dancing (Live)/The Egg (p/s) | 8 |
| 87 | Factory FACT 170 | SQUIRREL & G-MAN TWENTY FOUR HOUR PARTY PEOPLE PLASTIC FACE CARNT SMILE (WHITE OUT) (LP, with "Desmond", 5,000 in plastic sleeve) | 30 |
| 87 | Factory FACT 170 | SQUIRREL & G-MAN TWENTY FOUR HOUR PARTY PEOPLE PLASTIC FACE CARNT SMILE (WHITE OUT) (LP, with "Desmond") | 20 |
| 87 | Factory FACT 170c | SQUIRREL & G-MAN TWENTY FOUR HOUR PARTY PEOPLE PLASTIC FACE CARNT SMILE (WHITE OUT) (cassette, in box with insert) | 20 |
| 90 | Factory FACT 320 | PILLS 'N' THRILLS & BELLYACHES (LP, withdrawn 'sweet wrapper' sleeve) | 20 |
| 07 | Sequel SEQLP 012 | UNCLE DYSFUNKTIONAL (LP) | 15 |

## HAPPY REFUGEES

| | | | |
|---|---|---|---|
| 82 | Gymnasium REF no 1 | Warehouse Sound/Enshrined In A Memory (p/s) | 8 |
| 84 | Gymnasium HREF 002 | LAST CHANGE SALOON (LP) | 15 |

## HAPSHASH & THE COLOURED COAT

| | | | |
|---|---|---|---|
| 69 | Liberty LBF 15188 | Colinda/The Wall | 25 |
| 67 | Minit MLS 40001E | FEATURING THE HUMAN HOST AND THE HEAVY METAL KIDS (LP, with Art, red vinyl (MLL 40001) with insert) | 200 |
| 67 | Minit MLS 40001E | FEATURING THE HUMAN HOST AND THE HEAVY METAL KIDS (LP, with Art, later pressing on black vinyl) | 60 |
| 69 | Liberty LBL/LBS 83212R | THE WESTERN FLYER (LP, with Mike Batt, blue label) | 100 |

*(see also Tony McPhee, Warm Sounds, Marc Bolan/T. Rex, Art, Mike Batt)*

## HARBOUR LITES

| | | | |
|---|---|---|---|
| 65 | HMV POP 1426 | Come Back Silly Girl/Revenge | 8 |
| 65 | HMV POP 1465 | I Would Give All/They Call The Wind Maria | 8 |
| 66 | Fontana TF 682 | Run For Your Life/Lonely Journey | 8 |

## HARDBACK

| | | | |
|---|---|---|---|
| 86 | Streetwave 7 BOSS 3 | The Champ/Bust The Champ | 6 |

## HARD CORPS

| | | | |
|---|---|---|---|
| 84 | Hard Corps HC 01 | Dirty/To Breathe (12", hand-written white labels, numbered) | 20 |
| 84 | Survival SUR 026 | Dirty/Respirer (To Breathe) (white or printed labels, stickered plain black sleeve) | 10 |
| 84 | Survival SUR 12 026 | Dirty/Respirer (To Breathe) (12", with sticker in plain black sleeve) | 12 |
| 85 | Immaculate 12 IMMAC 2 | Je Suis Passée (Extended French Version)/(Extended Club Dub Mix) (12", p/s) | 12 |
| 85 | Polydor HARDA 1 | Je Suis Passée (Hard Mix)/(French Mix)/(Dub Mix) (12", gatefold PVC sleeve, various colours, with poster) | 20 |
| 85 | Polydor HARD 2 | To Breathe/Metal And Flesh (unreleased) | 20 |
| 85 | Polydor HARDX 2 | To Breathe/Metal And Flesh/To Breathe (Instrumental) (12", unreleased) | 25 |
| 90 | Concrete P. CPPRODLP 011 | METAL AND FLESH (LP, clear vinyl) | 18 |

*(see also Craze, Skunks, T.U.F.F.)*

## HARDFLOOR

| | | | |
|---|---|---|---|
| 92 | Harthouse HARTUK 1 | HARDTRANCE ACPERIENCE EP (12", 4-track) | 10 |

## HARD HORSE

| | | | |
|---|---|---|---|
| 71 | Dart ART 2001 | Let It Ride/Hang Old Freddy | 20 |
| 72 | Dart ART 2012 | (Get It) Up Down/So Long I'm Moving On | 30 |

## (EDDIE) HARDIN & (PETE) YORK

| | | | |
|---|---|---|---|
| 69 | Bell BLL 1064 | Tomorrow Today/Candlelight (as Hardin-York) | 30 |
| 69 | Bell SBLL 125 | TOMORROW TODAY (LP, gatefold sleeve, blue/silver/black label, with "Sold in the U.K..." text) | 30 |
| 70 | Bell SBLL 136 | HARDIN & YORK (THE WORLD'S SMALLEST BIG BAND) (LP, gatefold) | 30 |
| 71 | Bell SBLL 141 | FOR THE WORLD (LP, existence unconfirmed) | 20 |
| 71 | Decca SKL 5095 | FOR THE WORLD (LP, reissue, blue/silver label with boxed logo) | 15 |

*(see also Eddie Hardin, Pete York, Spencer Davis Group)*

## EDDIE HARDIN

| | | | |
|---|---|---|---|
| 72 | Decca F 13307 | Why Does Everybody Put Me Down/Spend Your Money Honey | 5 |
| 72 | Decca TXS 106 | HOME IS WHERE YOU FIND IT (LP, gatefold sleeve, green/silver label) | 25 |

*(see also Hardin-York, Spencer Davis Group, Roger Glover, Wizards Convention)*

## RICHARD HARDIN

| | | | |
|---|---|---|---|
| 61 | HMV POP 887 | Jezebel/Temptation | 25 |

*(see also Cresters, Mike Sagar & Cresters)*

## TIM HARDIN

| | | | |
|---|---|---|---|
| 66 | Verve VS 1504 | Hang On To A Dream/Reason To Believe | 12 |
| 67 | Verve VS 1511 | Lady Came From Baltimore/Black Sheep Boy | 10 |
| 68 | Verve VS 1516 | Don't Make Promises/Smugglin' Man | 7 |
| 69 | CBS 4441 | Simple Song Of Freedom/Question Of Birth | 5 |
| 71 | Verve 2009 006 | If I Were A Carpenter/Hang On To A Dream | 8 |
| 66 | Verve (S)VLP 5018 | TIM HARDIN 1 (LP) | 40 |
| 67 | Verve (S)VLP 6002 | TIM HARDIN 2 (LP) | 35 |
| 67 | Atlantic 587/588 082 | THIS IS TIM HARDIN (LP, plum label) | 25 |
| 68 | Verve (S)VLP 6010 | LIVE IN CONCERT (LP) | 30 |
| 69 | Verve (S)VLP 6016 | TIM HARDIN 4 (LP) | 25 |
| 69 | Verve (S)VLP 6019 | THE BEST OF (LP) | 20 |
| 69 | CBS (S/M) 63571 | SUITE FOR SUSAN MOORE AND DAMIAN (LP, gatefold sleeve, mono/stereo) | 20 |
| 70 | CBS 64335 | BIRD ON A WIRE (LP) | 15 |
| 72 | CBS 65209 | PAINTED HEAD (LP) | 18 |
| 74 | Verve 2683 048 | TIM HARDIN 1/2 (2-LP, gatefold reissue) | 20 |

*(see also Eddie Hardin, Pete York, Spencer Davis Group)*

## MIKE HARDING

| | | | |
|---|---|---|---|
| 86 | Moonraker M 003 | BOMBERS MOON (LP) | 20 |

## ROSEMARY HARDMAN (& BOB AXFORD)

| | | | |
|---|---|---|---|
| 69 | Folk Heritage no cat. no. | QUEEN OF HEARTS (LP) | 125 |
| 71 | Trailer LER 2075 | FIREBIRD (LP) | 20 |
| 71 | Trailer LER 3018 | SECOND SEASON CAME (LP, by Rosemary Hardman & Bob Axford) | 20 |
| 75 | Alida Star Cottage | JERSEY BURGER (LP) | 120 |

## HARD MEAT

| | | | |
|---|---|---|---|
| 69 | Island WIP 6066 | Rain/Burning Up Years | 15 |
| 70 | Warner Bros WB 8010 | Ballad Of Marmalade Emma And Teddy Grimes/Yesterday, Today, Tomorrow | 6 |
| 70 | Warner Bros WS 1852 | HARD MEAT (LP, gatefold sleeve with photo insert) | 100 |
| 70 | Warner Bros WS 1879 | THROUGH A WINDOW (LP, green label) | 100 |

## HARDNOISE

| | | | |
|---|---|---|---|
| 89 | White HNX001 | Untitled (different recording to Music Of Life version - 300 pressed) (12") | 75 |
| 90 | Music Of Life NOTE40 | Untitled (12") | 15 |
| 91 | Music Of Life NOTE48 | Serve Tea, Then Murder/Mice In The Presence Of The Lion (12") | 15 |
| 12 | Gibo GIB 001 | Pure Destructive Power (12") | 20 |
| 13 | Gibo GIB 002 | Pure Destructive Power (12", green vinyl, 50 pressed) | 30 |

## HARD RAIN

| | | | |
|---|---|---|---|
| 88 | London LON 185 | Diamonds/Monkey House (p/s) | 12 |
| 88 | London LONX 185 | Diamonds/Monkey House/Diamonds (7" Version) (12", p/s) | 15 |

## HARD ROAD

| | | | |
|---|---|---|---|
| 79 | Goodstuff LP 1002 | NO PROBLEM (LP, private pressing) | 15 |

## HARDSHIP POST

| | | | |
|---|---|---|---|
| 95 | Sub Pop SP 295 | Watching You/Your Sunshine (red vinyl) | 5 |

## HARD SKIN

| | | | |
|---|---|---|---|
| 96 | Helen Of Oi H0031LP | HARD NUTS AND HARD CUNTS (LP, green vinyl) | 15 |
| 07 | No Future OI 28 | New Age/FUCKED UP: Toronto FC (250 copies with fold-out sleeve, 50 with hard cover) | 15 |

## HARD STUFF

| | | | |
|---|---|---|---|
| 72 | Purple PUR 103 | Jay Time/The Orchestrator | 30 |
| 73 | Purple PUR 116 | Inside Your Life/(It's) How Do You Do It! | 10 |
| 72 | Purple TPSA 7505 | BULLETPROOF (LP, gatefold sleeve) | 70 |
| 73 | Purple TPSA 7507 | BOLEX DEMENTIA (LP, textured gatefold sleeve) | 75 |

*(see also Andromeda, Atomic Rooster, John Du Cann, Five Day Week Straw People, Johnny Gustafson, Bullet, Quatermass)*

## HARD TRAVELLIN'

| | | | |
|---|---|---|---|
| 71 | Flams Ltd PR 1065 | HARD TRAVELLIN' (LP, private pressing) | 125 |

## HARDWARE

| | | | |
|---|---|---|---|
| 85 | Reset 7REST 7 | Dance/Hey (p/s) | 8 |
| 85 | Reset 12REST 7 | Dance/Hey (12", p/s) | 15 |

## HARDWARE

| | | | |
|---|---|---|---|
| 79 | Narc NARC 001 | Speed Unit/Wall To Wall/Walking/Fire (folded p/s) | 8 |
| 79 | Narc NARC 002 | Rubberface/Face The Flag/The Seven Minutes (p/s) | 5 |

## HARDY

| | | | |
|---|---|---|---|
| 71 | Ackee ACK 131 | Glorious Morning/Hearing's Not Seeing | 6 |

## FRANCOISE HARDY

| | | | |
|---|---|---|---|
| 64 | Pye 7N 15612 | Catch A Falling Star/Only Friends | 8 |
| 64 | Pye 7N 15653 | Tous Les Garcons Et Les Filles/L'Amour S'en Va | 6 |
| 64 | Pye 7N 15696 | Pourtant Tu M'Aimes/Jaloux | 8 |
| 64 | Pye 7N 15740 | Et Meme/Le Temps De L'Amour | 8 |
| 65 | Pye 7N 15802 | All Over The World/Another Place | 7 |
| 66 | Vogue VRS 7001 | Just Call And I'll Be There/You Just Have To Say The Word | 7 |
| 66 | Vogue VRS 7004 | So Many Friends/However Much | 10 |
| 66 | Vogue VRS 7010 | This Little Heart/The Rose | 7 |
| 66 | Vogue VRS 7011 | La Maison Ou J'ai Grandi/Je Ne Suis La Pour Personne | 7 |
| 66 | Vogue VRS 7014 | Autumn Rendezvous/It's My Heart | 7 |
| 66 | Vogue VRS 7020 | Si C'est Ca/Je Serai La Pour Toi | 7 |
| 66 | Vogue VRS 7025 | Voila/Qui Peut Dire | 8 |
| 67 | Vogue VRS 7026 | On Se Quitte Toujours/Les Petits Garcons | 10 |
| 68 | United Artists UP 1208 | Now You Want To Be Loved/Tell Him You're Mine | 10 |
| 68 | United Artists UP 2253 | Will You Love Me Tomorrow/Loving You | 10 |
| 69 | United Artists UP 35011 | Comment Te Dire Adieu/La Mer, Les Etoiles Et Le Vent | 10 |
| 70 | United Artists UP 35070 | All Because Of You/Time Passing By | 10 |
| 70 | United Artists UP 35105 | Soon Is Slipping Away/The Bells Of Avignon (mispelling on label) | 50 |
| 64 | Pye NEP 24188 | C'EST FAB (EP) | 10 |
| 64 | Pye NEP 24192 | FRANCOISE SINGS IN ENGLISH (EP) | 10 |
| 64 | Pye NEP 24193 | C'EST FRANCOISE (EP) | 10 |
| 65 | Vogue VRE 5000 | FRANCOISE (EP) | 10 |
| 65 | Vogue VRE 5001 | FRANCOISE HARDY (EP) | 10 |
| 65 | Vogue VRE 5003 | DIS LUI NON (EP) | 10 |
| 66 | Vogue VRE 5008 | LE TEMPS DES SOUVENIRS (EP) | 12 |
| 66 | Vogue VRE 5012 | CHANTE EN ALLEMAND (EP) | 12 |
| 66 | Vogue VRE 5015 | L'AMITIE (EP) | 12 |
| 66 | Vogue VRE 5017 | MON AMIE LA ROSE (EP) | 12 |
| 67 | Vogue VRE 5018 | AUTUMN RENDEZVOUS (EP) | 12 |
| 64 | Pye NPL 18094 | FRANCOISE HARDY (LP) | 25 |
| 64 | Pye NPL 18099 | IN VOGUE (LP) | 25 |
| 65 | Vogue VRL 3000 | FRANCOISE HARDY (LP) | 25 |
| 66 | Vogue VRL 3021 | FRANCOISE HARDY (LP) | 25 |
| 66 | Vogue VRL 3023 | LE MEILLEUR DE FRANCOISE HARDY (LP) | 20 |

MINT VALUE £

| | | | |
|---|---|---|---|
| 66 | Vogue VRL 3025 | SINGS IN ENGLISH (LP) | 20 |
| 67 | Vogue VRL 3028 | FRANCOISE (LP) | 20 |
| 67 | Vogue VRL 3031 | VOILA! FRANCOISE HARDY (LP) | 20 |
| 68 | United Artists SULP 1191 | IL N'Y A PAS D'AMOUR HEUREUX (LP) | 20 |
| 68 | United Artists ULP 1207 | EN ANGLAIS (LP) | 25 |
| 70 | United Artists UAS 29046 | ONE-NINE-SEVEN-ZERO (LP) | 40 |

**LAVELL HARDY**
68  Direction 58-3261  Don't Lose Your Groove/Women Of The World ... 20

**COLIN HARE**
70  Penny Farthing PEN 736  Grannie, Grannie/For Where Have You Been ... 12
71  Penny Farthing PEN 750  Underground Girl/Fighting For Peace ... 10
72  Warner Bros K 16203  Didn't I Tell You/Seek Not In The Wide World ... 10
71  Penny Farthing PELS 516  MARCH HARE (LP) ... 350
(see also Honeybus)

**WINSTON HAREWOOD**
71  Camel CA 64  I Will Never Fall In Love Again (actually by Winston Heywood)/LA-FUD-DIL ALL-STARS: La-Fud-Dil (actually "La-Fud-Del") ... 15
(see also Winston Heywood)

**RON HARGRAVE**
58  MGM MGM 956  Latch On/Only A Daydream ... 1000
58  MGM MGM 956  Latch On/Only A Daydream (78) ... 100

**HARLAN COUNTY**
70  Nashville 6076 002  Dr. Handy's Dandy Candy/Big Heat ... 8
70  Nashville 6336 002  HARLAN COUNTY (LP, red/black label) ... 25

**HARLEM**
77  DJM 10743  It Takes A Fool Like Me/There I Go ... 8

**HARLEM SPEAKEASY**
68  Polydor 56270  Aretha/Sight Of Pegasus ... 15

**HARLESDEN MONKS**
72  Pama Supreme PS 352  Time/Harlesden High Street ... 12
72  Pama Supreme PS 352  Rock Me Mister Ping Wing/Breakdown Rock ... 35

**STEVE HARLEY (& COCKNEY REBEL)**
73  EMI EMI 2051  Sebastian/Rock And Roll Parade ... 5
74  EMI EMI 2191  Psychomodo/Such A Dream (unreleased) ... 0
74  EMI EMI 2191  Mr Soft/Such A Dream (with 'Orchestrated by Alan Powell' credit) ... 5
74  EMI EMI 2233  Big Big Deal/Bed In The Corner ... 5
77  EMI EMI 2922  Someone's Coming/Riding The Waves (For Virginia Woolf) ... 5
(see also Anderson Harley & Batt)

**IAN G HARLING**
80  P.T.O. PT 209/EJSP 9410  Heavy Breathing/Black & White (no p/s) ... 15

**HARLOW**
79  Pepper UP 36452  Harry De Mazzio/Nothing To You ... 100

**LEE HARMER'S POPCORN**
68  Page One POF 053  Love Is Coming/Hello Sunshine ... 20

**HARMONIANS**
70  Junior JR 112  Music Street/Version ... 15
70  Ackee ACK 107  Music Street/Group Of Girls ... 150
(see also Tony & Hippy Boys, Winston Shan)

**HARMONICA FATS**
63  Stateside SS 184  Tore Up/I Get So Tired ... 50
68  Action ACT 4507  Tore Up/I Get So Tired (reissue) ... 25

**HARMONISERS**
69  Duke DU 32  Mother Hen/WINSTON SINCLAIR: Chastise Them ... 20

**HARMONIZING FOUR**
66  Rymska RA 102  Who Knows/Heart Of Stone (actually by Charms) ... 20
(see also Charms)

**HARMONY BEACH**
83  Surf King SK 1  HARMONY BEACH (EP, private pressing) ... 18

**HARMONY GRASS**
68  RCA RCA 1772  Move In A Little Bit Closer Baby/Happiness Is Toy Shaped ... 10
69  RCA RCA 1828  First Time Loving/What A Groovy Day ... 8
69  RCA RCA 1885  I Remember/Summer Dreaming ... 7
70  RCA RCA 1928  Mrs. Richie/Teach Me How (withdrawn) ... 10
70  RCA RCA 1932  Cecilia/Mrs. Richie ... 7
70  RCA RCA 2011  Stand On Your Own Two Feet/Sing In The Sunshine ... 7
70  RCA SF 8034  THIS IS US (LP) ... 35
(see also Capability Brown, Tony Rivers & Castaways)

**HARMONY ROCKETS**
95  Big Cat ABB90  PARALYZED MIND OF THE ARCHANGEL VOID (LP) ... 30
(see also Mercury Rev)

**JOE HARNELL**
62  London HLR 9637  Fly Me To The Moon - Bossa Nova/Harlem Nocturne ... 6
78  MCA MCA 397  The Incredible Hulk Theme/Love Theme ... 15

**BILLY HARNER**
71  Kama Sutra 2013 029  What About The Music/Please Spare Me This Time ... 20
71  Kama Sutra 2013 029  What About The Music(instrumental)/Please Spare Me This Time (withdrawn) ... 1250

## BENNY HARPER
| | | | |
|---|---|---|---|
| 06 | Grapevine 2000 G2K 158 | My Prayer/It's Love (reissue) | 10 |

## BUD HARPER
| | | | |
|---|---|---|---|
| 65 | Vocalion VP 9252 | Mr. Soul/Let Me Love You | 40 |
| 65 | Vocalion VP 9252 | Mr. Soul/Let Me Love You (DJ copy) | 80 |

## CHARLIE HARPER
| | | | |
|---|---|---|---|
| 80 | Gem GEMS 35 | Barmy London Army/Talk Is Cheap (p/s, green or yellow vinyl) | 5 |
| 81 | Ramkup CAC 005 | Freaked/Jo (p/s) | 5 |

*(see also U.K. Subs, Long Tall Shorty, Urban Dogs)*

## CHARLIE HARPER AND CAPTAIN SENSIBLE
| | | | |
|---|---|---|---|
| 13 | Time & Matter T&M 009 | TOO MUCH REALITY EP (cream and purple splatter vinyl) | 40 |

*(see also U.K. Subs, Damned)*

## DON HARPER ORCHESTRA
| | | | |
|---|---|---|---|
| 68 | Columbia DB 8519 | World Of Sport March/England 88 | 15 |
| 73 | Columbia DB 9023 | World Of Sport/"Dr. Who" Theme (as Don Harper's Homo Electronicus) | 25 |
| 74 | Columbia SCX 6559 | HOMO ELECTRONICUS (LP) | 40 |

*(see also Electricians)*

## JANICE HARPER
| | | | |
|---|---|---|---|
| 57 | HMV POP 376 | Bon Voyage/Tell Me That You Love Me Tonight | 7 |
| 58 | Capitol CL 14899 | Devotion/In Time | 10 |
| 59 | Capitol CL 14977 | I Was Hoping You'd Ask Me/I'm Making Love To You | 6 |
| 59 | Capitol CL 15026 | Let Me Call You Sweetheart/Just Whistle ( | 5 |
| 60 | Capitol CL 15159 | Only Once/Love Me Now, Love Me Never | 5 |
| 59 | Capitol T 1195 | WITH FEELING (LP) | 15 |

## JEANETTE HARPER
| | | | |
|---|---|---|---|
| 83 | Soul Stop 3004 | (Pick Me Up And)Put Me In Your Pocket/HORSLEY'S GIANT: Falling | 5 |

## JESSIE HARPER
| | | | |
|---|---|---|---|
| 92 | Kissing Spell KSLP 9203 | GUITAR ABSOLUTION IN THE SHADE OF A MIDNIGHT SUN (LP, reissue of acetate-only album) | 20 |

*(see also Human Instinct)*

## JOE 'HARMONICA' HARPER
| | | | |
|---|---|---|---|
| 58 | MGM MGM 983 | Lazy Train/Her Lips Were Like Velvet | 8 |

## MIKE HARPER
| | | | |
|---|---|---|---|
| 70 | Concord CON 026 | You've Got Too Much Going For You/This Time | 10 |
| 75 | Tetreat RTS 264 | I'm Crying /Goodbye | 7 |

## ROY HARPER
### SINGLES
| | | | |
|---|---|---|---|
| 66 | Strike JH 304 | Take Me Into Your Eyes/Pretty Baby (in wraparound p/s) | 100 |
| 66 | Strike JH 304 | Take Me Into Your Eyes/Pretty Baby | 35 |
| 67 | CBS 203001 | Midspring Dithering/Zengem | 20 |
| 68 | CBS 3371 | Life Goes By/Nobody's Got Any Money In The Summer | 25 |
| 72 | Harvest HAR 5059 | Bank Of The Dead (Valerie's Song)/Little Lady (in p/s) | 10 |
| 72 | Harvest HAR 5059 | Bank Of The Dead (Valerie's Song)/Little Lady | 6 |
| 74 | Harvest HAR 5080 | (Don't You Think We're) Forever/Male Chauvinist Pig Blues | 6 |
| 74 | Harvest HAR 5089 | Home (live)/Home (studio) | 6 |
| 75 | Harvest HAR 5096 | When An Old Cricketer Leaves The Crease/Hallucinating Light (Acoustic Version) (p/s) | 6 |
| 75 | Harvest HAR 5102 | Grown-Ups Are Just Silly Children/Referendum (Legend) | 5 |
| 75 | EMI PSR 407 | Referendum/Another Day (live)/Tom Tiddler's Ground (live) (promo only) | 8 |
| 77 | Harvest HAR 5120 | One Of Those Days In England/Watford Gap (p/s) | 5 |
| 77 | EMI PSR 408 | One Of Those Days In England/Watford Gap/Naked Flame/Extract From One Of Those Days In England | 5 |
| 77 | Harvest HAR 5140 | Sail Away/Cherishing The Lonesome (as Roy Harper's Black Sheep) | 7 |
| 78 | Harvest HAR 5160 | When An Old Cricketer Leaves The Crease/Home (studio) (p/s) | 5 |
| 80 | Harvest HAR 5203 | Playing Games/First Thing In The Morning (p/s) | 6 |
| 80 | Harvest HAR 5207 | Short And Sweet/Water Sports (live)/Unknown Soldier (live) (p/s) | 6 |
| 82 | Public PUBS 1001 | No One Gets Out Here Alive/Casualty (live) (p/s) | 5 |
| 83 | Public PUBS 1002 | I Still Care/Goodbye Ladybird (p/s) | 6 |
| 85 | B. Banquet BEG 131 | Elizabeth (Short Version)/Advertisement (Short Version) (p/s) | 5 |
| 88 | Regal Zonophone HR 1 | Laughing Inside/Laughing Inside (p/s, promo only; as Harry Rope) | 10 |
| 88 | EMI EM 46 | Laughing Inside/Laughing Inside (Acoustic Version) (p/s) | 5 |

### ALBUMS : ORIGINAL LPS
| | | | |
|---|---|---|---|
| 66 | Strike JHL 105 | SOPHISTICATED BEGGAR | 500 |
| 67 | CBS BPG 63184 | COME OUT FIGHTING GHENGIS SMITH (mono, orange label) | 100 |
| 67 | CBS SBPG 63184 | COME OUT FIGHTING GHENGIS SMITH (stereo, orange label) | 120 |
| 69 | Liberty LBL 83231 | FOLKJOKEOPUS (mono, blue label) | 120 |
| 69 | Liberty LBS 83231 | FOLKJOKEOPUS (stereo, blue label) | 100 |
| 69 | Harvest SHVL 766 | FLAT, BAROQUE AND BERSERK (gatefold sleeve; first pressing with "H. Ash" label credit) | 100 |
| 71 | Harvest SHVL 789 | STORMCOCK (gatefold sleeve with lyric insert, no EMI logo on label) | 50 |
| 73 | Harvest SHVL 808 | LIFEMASK (foldout 'door' sleeve, with insert) | 30 |
| 74 | Harvest SHSP 4027 | VALENTINE (1st pressing, with 'Made in GT. Britain' on bottom of label, initially with lyric booklet) | 40 |
| 74 | Harvest SHSP 4027 | VALENTINE (1st pressing with 'Made in GT. Britain' at bottom of label, without lyric booklet) | 15 |
| 74 | Harvest SHDW 405 | FLASHES FROM THE ARCHIVES OF OBLIVION (2-LP, gatefold sleeve) | 35 |
| 75 | Harvest SHSP 4046 | HQ (with lyric inner sleeve, EMI logo on label) | 20 |
| 77 | Harvest SHSP 4060 | BULLINAMINGVASE (with inner sleeve & "Watford Gap"; some with 7" single, Referendum/"Another Day" (live)/"Tom Tiddler's Ground" [PSR 407]) | 20 |
| 77 | Harvest SHSP 4060 | BULLINAMINGVASE (2nd pressing with "Breakfast With You") | 15 |

MINT VALUE £

| | | | |
|---|---|---|---|
| 77 | Harvest SHSP 4077 | COMMERCIAL BREAK (unreleased; test pressing with proof sleeve) | 300 |
| 78 | Harvest | HARPER 1970-1975 (6-LP box set) | 100 |
| 84 | Hard Up PUB 5002 | BORN IN CAPTIVITY (880 only) | 30 |
| 92 | Hard Up HU 2 | BORN IN CAPTIVITY II (LIVE) (cassette) | 15 |

**ALBUMS : REISSUE ALBUMS**

| | | | |
|---|---|---|---|
| 71 | Harvest SHVL 766 | FLAT, BAROQUE AND BERSERK (gatefold sleeve; second pressing with "H. Ash" label credit and boxed EMI logo) | 25 |
| 70 | Young Blood SSYB 7 | RETURN OF THE SOPHISTICATED BEGGAR (LP, with "Hup Hup Spiral" closed run-out groove, different sleeve) | 20 |
| 71 | Harvest SHVL 789 | STORMCOCK (gatefold sleeve with lyric inner, with EMI logo on label) | 20 |
| 73 | Birth RAB 3 | RETURN OF THE SOPHISTICATED BEGGAR (LP, 2nd reissue, with "Hup Hup Spiral" closed run-out groove, different sleeve) | 15 |
| 74 | Harvest SHSP 4027 | VALENTINE (2nd pressing without 'Made in GT. Britain' at bottom of label, without lyric booklet) | 15 |
| 75 | Sunset SLS 50373 | FOLKJOKEOPUS (LP) | 15 |
| 77 | Big Ben BBX 502 | THE SOPHISTICATED BEGGAR (LP, different rear sleeve) | 20 |
| 80 | CBS (S) BPG 63184 | COME OUT FIGHTING GHENGIS SMITH (LP, reissue) | 15 |
| 86 | Awareness AWL 1002 | WORK OF HEART (LP, different sleeve with inner; 1st 1,000 with 2 x 7" "No One Gets Out Of Here Alive"/"Casualty (live) [PUBS 1001]) & "Still Care"/"Goodbye Ladybird" [PUBS2]) | 15 |
| 86 | Awareness AWL 1002 | WORK OF HEART (LP, different sleeve, 250 only on 'real time' quality tape) | 15 |

*(see also Rory Phare, Per Yarroh, Pink Floyd)*

**TONI HARPER**

| | | | |
|---|---|---|---|
| 65 | Vocalion VF 9239 | Never Trust A Stranger/As Time Goes By | 10 |

**ROY HARPER & JIMMY PAGE**

| | | | |
|---|---|---|---|
| 85 | Beggars Banquet BEGA 60 | WHATEVER HAPPENED TO JUGULA? (LP) | 15 |

**HARPER'S BIZARRE**

| | | | |
|---|---|---|---|
| 67 | Warner Bros WB 5890 | 59th Street Bridge Song (Feelin' Groovy)/Lost My Love Today | 8 |
| 67 | Warner Bros WB 7528 | Come To The Sunshine/The Debutante's Ball | 5 |
| 67 | Warner Bros WB 7063 | Anything Goes/Malibu U. | 8 |
| 67 | Warner Bros WB 7090 | Chattanooga Choo Choo/Hey You In The Crowd | 7 |
| 68 | Warner Bros WB 7172 | Cotton Candy Sandman (Sandman's Coming)/Virginia City | 5 |
| 68 | Warner Bros WB 7223 | Battle Of New Orleans/Green Apple Tree | 5 |
| 69 | Warner Bros WB 7238 | I Love You, Alice B. Toklas!/Look To The Rainbow | 5 |
| 70 | Warner Bros WB 7388 | Anything Goes/Virginia City | 5 |
| 67 | Warner Bros W 1693 | FEELIN' GROOVY (LP) | 15 |
| 67 | Warner Bros W 1716 | ANYTHING GOES (LP) | 20 |
| 68 | Warner Bros W(S) 1739 | THE SECRET LIFE OF HARPER'S BIZARRE (LP) | 15 |

**HARPO**

| | | | |
|---|---|---|---|
| 74 | DJM DJS 400 | Movie Star/Teddy Love | 5 |

**SLIM HARPO**

| | | | |
|---|---|---|---|
| 61 | Pye International 7N 25098 | Rainin' In My Heart/Don't Start Cryin' Now | 25 |
| 63 | Pye International 7N 25220 | Don't Start Cryin' Now/Rainin' In My Heart | 25 |
| 66 | Stateside SS 491 | Baby Scratch My Back/I'm Gonna Miss You (Like The Devil) | 30 |
| 66 | Stateside SS 527 | Shake Your Hips/Midnight Blues | 40 |
| 66 | Stateside SS 557 | I'm A King Bee/I Got Love If You Want It | 50 |
| 67 | Stateside SS 581 | I'm Your Breadmaker Baby/Loving You (The Way I Do) | 30 |
| 67 | President PT 164 | I'm Gonna Keep What I've Got/I've Got To Be With You Tonight | 10 |
| 68 | Liberty LBF 15176 | Something Inside Me/PAPPA LIGHTFOOT: Wine Whisky And Women | 30 |
| 68 | President PT 187 | Tip On In (Parts 1 & 2) | 15 |
| 70 | Blue Horizon 57-3175 | Folsom Prison Blues/Mutual Friend | 30 |
| 65 | Stateside SL 10135 | A LONG DRINK OF THE BLUES (LP, with Lightnin' Slim) | 50 |
| 68 | President PTL 1017 | TIP ON IN (LP) | 50 |
| 70 | Blue Horizon 7-63854 | HE KNEW THE BLUES (LP) | 150 |
| 72 | Blue Horizon 2431 013 | TRIGGER FINGER (LP) | 150 |
| 76 | Flyright LP 520 | BLUES HANGOVER (LP) | 18 |
| 78 | Sonet SNTF 769 | HE KNEW THE BLUES (LP) | 20 |
| 80 | Flyright FLY 558 | GOT LOVE IF YOU WANT IT (LP) | 18 |

*(see also Lightnin' Slim)*

**GEORGE HARRASSMENT & HOMOSEXUALS**

| | | | |
|---|---|---|---|
| 80s | Black Noise 12 NO 6 | MASAI SLEEP WALKING (LP) | 12 |

*(see also Homosexuals)*

**ROCQ-E HARRELL**

| | | | |
|---|---|---|---|
| 89 | Nightmare MARES 113 | My Heart Keeps Beating Faster/Instrumental Version | 10 |

**HARRIER**

| | | | |
|---|---|---|---|
| 84 | Black Horse HARR 1T | OUT ON THE STREET EP (Out On The Street/Nickels And Dimes/Shine On) (12", p/s) | 15 |

**DERRICK HARRIOT(T) (& CRYSTALITES)**

| | | | |
|---|---|---|---|
| 62 | Blue Beat BB 131 | I Care/Have Faith In Me (as Derrick Harriott & Vagabonds) | 15 |
| 63 | Blue Beat BB 178 | Be True/I Won't Cry | 15 |
| 64 | Island WI 157 | What Can I Do (The Wedding)/Leona | 12 |
| 65 | Island WI 170 | I Am Only Human (as Derak Harriott)/OWEN AND LEON SILVERA: I Want My Cock (probably withdrawn) | 50 |
| 65 | Island WI 170 | I Am Only Human (as Derak Harriott)/ROY PANTON: Good Man | 30 |
| 65 | Island WI 237 | My Three Loves/The Jerk | 30 |
| 65 | Island WI 245 | Together/Mama Didn't Lie | 30 |
| 65 | Ska Beat JB 199 | Monkey Ska/Derrick! | 30 |
| 66 | Doctor Bird DB 1002 | Jon Tom/AUDREY WILLIAMS: Solas Market | 20 |
| 67 | Island WI 3063 | The Loser/Bless You | 80 |
| 67 | Island WI 3064 | Happy Times/You My Everything | 50 |
| 67 | Island WI 3077 | Walk The Streets/BOBBY ELLIS: Step Softly (B-side with Desmond Miles Seven) | 80 |

| 67 | Island WI 3089 | Solomon/BOBBY ELLIS: The Emperor (B-side with Desmond Miles Seven) .................. 45 |
|---|---|---|
| 68 | Island WI 3135 | Do I Worry?/BOBBY ELLIS & CRYSTALITES: Shuntin' ....................................................... 150 |
| 68 | Island WI 3147 | Born To Love You/IKE & CRYSTALITES: Alfred Hitchcock ................................................ 40 |
| 68 | Island WI 3153 | Tang Tang Festival Song/CRYSTALITES: James Ray ....................................................... 40 |
| 69 | Big Shot BI 505 | Standing In/Bumble Bee ........................................................................................... 50 |
| 69 | Big Shot BI 511 | Another Lonely Night/Been So Long ........................................................................... 25 |
| 70 | Songbird SB 1013 | Riding For A Fall/I'm Not Begging .............................................................................. 10 |
| 70 | Songbird SB 1014 | Sitting On Top/You Were Meant For Me ..................................................................... 10 |
| 70 | Songbird SB 1022 | Go Bye Bye/Laugh It Off ........................................................................................... 12 |
| 70 | Songbird SB 1028 | Message From A Black Man/(Version II) ...................................................................... 10 |
| 70 | Songbird SB 1029 | Psychedelic Train (w/ Chosen Few)/Psychedelic Train (Pt. 2) (with Crystalites) ............ 12 |
| 70 | Songbird SB 1033 | No Man Is An Island/No Man Is An Island Part 2 .......................................................... 10 |
| 70 | Songbird SB 1042 | Groovy Situation/CRYSTALITES: The Crystal Groove ..................................................... 10 |
| 70 | Songbird SB 1043 | Psychedelic Train Chapter Three/CRYSTALITES: Groovy Situation Version II .................. 10 |
| 71 | Songbird SB 1052 | Candy/CRYSTALITES: Candy Version .............................................................................. 7 |
| 71 | Songbird SB 1055 | Lollipop Girl/CRYSTALITES: Lollipop Version ................................................................ 15 |
| 71 | Songbird SB 1063 | Medley In 5 (Parts 1 & 2) ............................................................................................ 7 |
| 72 | Songbird SB 1065 | Have You Seen Her/CRYSTALITES: Have You Seen Her - Version ...................................... 7 |
| 72 | Songbird SB 1068 | Over The River/River (Version) ..................................................................................... 7 |
| 72 | Songbird SB 1071 | Since I Lost My Baby/Baby (Version) ............................................................................. 7 |
| 72 | Songbird SB 1078 | Being In Love/Love (Version) ........................................................................................ 6 |
| 72 | Songbird SB 1084 | Don't Rock The Boat/Rock (Version) .............................................................................. 7 |
| 73 | Attack ATT 8056 | Brown Baby/CRYSTALITES: Brown Baby Version ............................................................ 6 |
| 73 | Explosion EX 2071 | Let Me Down Easy/Let Me Down Easy - Version ............................................................ 7 |
| 74 | Harry J. HJ 6675 | Some Guys Have All The Luck/Some Guys Have All The Luck - Version ............................. 6 |
| 65 | Island ILP 928 | THE BEST OF DERRICK HARRIOTT (LP) ....................................................................... 125 |
| 67 | Island ILP 955 | DERRICK HARRIOTT'S ROCKSTEADY PARTY (LP, actually v/a LP) ................................. 300 |
| 68 | Island ILP 983 | THE BEST OF VOLUME TWO (LP, as Derrick Harriott & Crystalites) ............................. 150 |
| 69 | Pama SECO 13 | SINGS JAMAICA REGGAE (LP) ..................................................................................... 150 |
| 70 | Trojan TTL 43 | THE BEST OF DERRICK HARRIOTT (LP) ......................................................................... 50 |
| 70 | Trojan TTL 54 | ROCKSTEADY PARTY (LP) ............................................................................................ 60 |
| 70 | Trojan TBL 114 | THE UNDERTAKER (LP, as Derrick Harriott & Crystalites) ............................................. 30 |
| 70 | Trojan TBL 141 | PSYCHEDELIC TRAIN (LP, as Derrick Harriott & Crystalites) .......................................... 35 |

## JOE HARRIOTT

| 56 | Jazz Today JTE 106 | WITH STRINGS (EP) .................................................................................................... 40 |
|---|---|---|
| 56 | Pye Jazz NJE 1003 | NO STRINGS (EP) ....................................................................................................... 80 |
| 50s | Melodisc EPM7 117 | COOL JAZZ WITH JOE (EP) .......................................................................................... 75 |
| 57 | Columbia SEG 7665 | JOE HARRIOTT QUARTET (EP) .................................................................................... 100 |
| 59 | Columbia SEG 7939 | BLUE HARRIOTT (EP) .................................................................................................. 60 |
| 61 | Columbia SEG 8070 | A GUY CALLED JOE (EP) .............................................................................................. 45 |
| 60 | Jazzland JLP 49 | FREE FORM (LP) ....................................................................................................... 200 |
| 62 | Columbia 33SX 1477 | ABSTRACT (LP) ........................................................................................................ 300 |
| 63 | Columbia 33SX 1627 | MOVEMENT (LP) ...................................................................................................... 500 |
| 64 | Columbia 33SX 1692 | HIGH SPIRITS (LP) .................................................................................................... 500 |
| 66 | Columbia S(C)X 6025 | DOUBLE QUINTET (LP, with John Mayer) ..................................................................... 75 |
| 67 | Melodisc SLP 12150 | SWINGS HIGH (LP) ................................................................................................... 150 |
| 67 | Columbia S(C) 6122 | INDO-JAZZ FUSIONS (LP, with John Mayer) ................................................................. 40 |
| 68 | Columbia S(C)X 6215 | INDO-JAZZ FUSIONS II (LP, with John Mayer) .............................................................. 45 |
| 68 | Columbia S(C)X 6249 | PERSONAL PORTRAIT (LP) .......................................................................................... 75 |
| 69 | Columbia SCX 6354 | HUM-DONO (LP, with Amancio D'Silva) .................................................................... 1000 |
| 73 | One Up OU 2011 | MEMORIAL 1973 (LP) ................................................................................................ 30 |

*(see also Tony Kinsey Trio & Joe Harriott, John Mayer, Michael Garrick)*

## JOE HARRIOTT/DON RENDELL QUARTET

| 57 | MGM MGM-EP 615 | JAZZ BRITANNIA (EP, 2 tracks each) ............................................................................. 60 |
|---|---|---|

*(see also Don Rendell)*

## ANITA HARRIS

| 61 | Parlophone R 4830 | I Haven't Got You/Mr One And Only ............................................................................ 10 |
|---|---|---|
| 64 | Vocalion V 9223 | Lies/Don't Think About Love ........................................................................................ 6 |
| 65 | Decca F 12082 | Willingly/At Last Love ................................................................................................. 6 |
| 65 | Pye 7N 15868 | Trains And Boats And Planes/Upside Down .................................................................... 6 |
| 65 | Pye 7N 15894 | I Don't Know Anymore/When I Look At You ................................................................... 6 |
| 65 | Pye 7N 15971 | London Life/I Run To Hide ........................................................................................... 8 |
| 66 | Pye 7N 17069 | Something Must Be Done/Funny Kind Of Feeling ......................................................... 10 |
| 67 | CBS 2991 | The Playground/B.A.D. For Me .................................................................................... 10 |
| 66 | CBS BGP/SBPG 62894 | SOMEBODY'S IN MY ORCHARD (LP) ........................................................................... 15 |

*(see also Brello Cabal)*

## ARTIE HARRIS & HIS BOYS

| 63 | Oriole CB 1816 | Go Go Gaudeamus/Mexicana ....................................................................................... 8 |
|---|---|---|

## BETTY HARRIS

| 63 | London HL 9796 | Cry To Me/I'll Be A Liar ............................................................................................. 20 |
|---|---|---|
| 65 | Stateside SS 475 | What A Sad Feeling/I'm Evil Tonight ........................................................................... 30 |
| 67 | Stateside SS 2045 | Nearer To You/12 Red Roses ...................................................................................... 20 |
| 69 | Action ACT 4535 | Ride Your Pony/Trouble With My Lover ....................................................................... 60 |
| 80 | Charly CTD 102 | BETTY HARRIS EP ...................................................................................................... 10 |
| 69 | Action ACLP 6007 | SOUL PERFECTION (LP) .............................................................................................. 80 |

*(see also Betty Harris & Lee Dorsey)*

## BOBBY HARRIS

| 73 | London 10435 | Sticky Sticky/Mr. Success ............................................................................................. 7 |
|---|---|---|

MINT VALUE £

## BRENDA JO HARRIS
| | | | |
|---|---|---|---|
| 69 | Roulette RO 503 | I Can Remember/Play With Fire | 7 |

## EDDIE HARRIS
| | | | |
|---|---|---|---|
| 69 | Atlantic 584 218 | Listen Here/Theme - In Search Of A Movie | 10 |
| 69 | Atlantic 584 232 | It's Crazy/Live Right Now (unissued) | 0 |
| 74 | Atlantic K 10513 | Is It In?/Funkarama | 7 |
| 75 | Atlantic K 10561 | I Need Some Money/Don't Want Nobody | 7 |
| 76 | Atlantic K 10741 | Get On Up And Dance/Why Must We Part | 5 |

## EMMYLOU HARRIS
| | | | |
|---|---|---|---|
| 95 | Gravevine GRALP 102 | WRECKING BALL (LP) | 50 |

## HAL HARRIS
| | | | |
|---|---|---|---|
| 78 | Ace NS 47 | Jitterbop Baby/I Don't Know When | 5 |

## JET HARRIS
| | | | |
|---|---|---|---|
| 62 | Decca F 11466 | Besame Mucho/Chills And Fever | 6 |
| 62 | Decca F 11488 | Main Title Theme (from The Man With The Golden Arm)/Some People | 6 |
| 64 | Decca F 11841 | Big Bad Bass/Rifka | 8 |
| 67 | Fontana TF 849 | My Lady/You Don't Live Twice | 25 |
| 75 | SRT SRT 75355 | Theme For A Fallen Idol/This Sportin' Life (initial pressing) | 8 |
| 75 | SRT SRT 75355 | Theme/This Sportin' Life (later pressing with shortened A-side title) | 5 |
| 78 | SRT SRT 77389 | Guitar Man/Theme | 5 |
| 62 | Decca DFE 8502 | JET HARRIS (EP) | 25 |
| 78 | Ellie Jay EJSP 8622 | INSIDE JET HARRIS - THE LAST CONCERT (LP, 2,500 only) | 20 |
| 70s | Q LPMM 1038 | ANNIVERSARY ALBUM (LP) | 20 |

*(see also Shadows, Jet Harris & Tony Meehan, Keith Meehan, Peter Rawes)*

## JET HARRIS & TONY MEEHAN
| | | | |
|---|---|---|---|
| 63 | Decca F 11563 | Diamonds/Footstomp | 5 |
| 63 | Decca F 11644 | Scarlett O'Hara/(Doing The) Hully Gully | 5 |
| 63 | Decca F 11710 | Applejack/The Tall Texan | 6 |
| 80 | Decca F 13892 | Diamonds/Scarlett O'Hara/Applejack/Man With The Golden Arm (p/s) | 5 |
| 63 | Decca DFE 8528 | JET AND TONY (EP) | 12 |

*(see also Shadows, Jet Harris, Tony Meehan, Vipers Skiffle Group)*

## JOHNNY HARRIS
| | | | |
|---|---|---|---|
| 65 | Mercury MF 942 | Mynah Hop/Here Comes The Boot | 15 |
| 69 | Warner Bros WB 8000 | Footprints On The Moon/Lulu's Theme | 10 |
| 70 | Warner Bros WB 8016 | Fragment Of Fear/Stepping Stones | 25 |
| 70 | Warner Bros WS 3002 | MOVEMENTS (LP, 1st pressing with orange labels) | 50 |
| 72 | Warner Bros K 46054 | MOVEMENTS (LP, reissue) | 20 |
| 73 | Warner Bros K 46187 | ALL TO BRING YOU MORNING (LP) | 15 |

## JUNE HARRIS
| | | | |
|---|---|---|---|
| 65 | CBS 201774 | Over And Over Again/Stand Back | 12 |

## LENNY HARRIS
| | | | |
|---|---|---|---|
| 84 | Soul Stop 3008 | Long After Tonight Is All Over/Impressions | 10 |

## MAX HARRIS
| | | | |
|---|---|---|---|
| 60 | Fontana H 282 | Gurney Slade/Hat And Cane | 5 |
| 61 | Fontana H 296 | Wheels/Regency Ride | 5 |
| 69 | Pye 7N 17730 | Theme From The Film 'Baby Love'/Roberts Theme From 'Baby Love' | 6 |

## OSCAR HARRIS
| | | | |
|---|---|---|---|
| 70 | Upfront UPF 6 | T.O.P/I Don't Wanna Listen | 10 |

## PAT HARRIS & BLACKJACKS
| | | | |
|---|---|---|---|
| 63 | Pye 7N 15567 | The Hippy Hippy Shake/You Gotta See Your Mama Ev'ry Night | 25 |

*(see also Blackjacks)*

## PHIL HARRIS
| | | | |
|---|---|---|---|
| 54 | HMV 7M 199 | I Know An Old Lady/Take Your Girlie To The Movies | 8 |
| 54 | HMV 7M 231 | I Guess I'll Have To Change My Plan/The Persian Kitten | 8 |
| 55 | HMV 7M 289 | I Wouldn't Touch You With A Ten-Foot Pole/There's A Lot More | 8 |

## RONNIE HARRIS (& CORONETS)
| | | | |
|---|---|---|---|
| 56 | Columbia DB 3836 | That's Right/A House With Love In It | 10 |
| 57 | Columbia DB 3877 | Armen's Theme (Yesterday And You)/Dancing Chandelier | 5 |
| 57 | Columbia DB 3934 | Dear To Me/It's Not For Me To Say (B-side with Russ Conway) | 5 |

*(see also Coronets, Ruby Murray, Ray Burns)*

## ROY HARRIS
| | | | |
|---|---|---|---|
| 72 | Topic 12TS 217 | THE BITTER AND THE SWEET (LP, blue label) | 15 |

## SCOTT HARRIS
| | | | |
|---|---|---|---|
| 68 | Morgan MR7S | Barry Johnson's Sad Eyes Inn/Morning Sun | 30 |

## SHAKEY JAKE HARRIS
| | | | |
|---|---|---|---|
| 69 | Liberty LBS 83217 | FURTHER ON UP THE ROAD (LP) | 50 |
| 73 | Polydor 2391 015 | THE DEVIL'S HARMONICA (LP) | 20 |

## HARRIS SISTERS
| | | | |
|---|---|---|---|
| 55 | Capitol CL 14232 | Kissin' Bug/We've Been Walkin' All Night | 20 |

## SUZANNE HARRIS
| | | | |
|---|---|---|---|
| 69 | Polydor 56354 | Sure That's What God Said/It's A Long Way From The Movies/Go Out And Multiply/Are You | 15 |
| 70 | R.F.S. Records RFS 8270 | Here Come The Beautiful People/We're Using Up The World (p/s) | 20 |

## THURSTON HARRIS (& SHARPS)
| | | | |
|---|---|---|---|
| 57 | Vogue V 9092 | Little Bitty Pretty One/I Hope You Won't Hold It Against Me (with Sharps) | 200 |
| 58 | Vogue V 9098 | Do What You Did/I'm Asking Forgiveness (as Thurston Harris & Sharps) | 250 |
| 57 | Vogue V 9092 | Little Bitty Pretty One/I Hope You Won't Hold It Against Me (with Sharps) (78) | 30 |

| 58 | Vogue V 9098 | Do What You Did/I'm Asking Forgiveness (as Thurston Harris & Sharps) (78) | 20 |
| 58 | Vogue V 9108 | Be Baba Leba/I'm Out To Getcha | 250 |
| 58 | Vogue V 9108 | Be Baba Leba/I'm Out To Getcha (78) | 20 |
| 58 | Vogue V 9122 | Smokey Joe's/Only One Love Is Blessed | 150 |
| 58 | Vogue V 9122 | Smokey Joe's/Only One Love Is Blessed (78) | 20 |
| 58 | Vogue V 9127 | Tears From My Heart/Over Somebody Else's Shoulder | 100 |
| 58 | Vogue V 9127 | Tears From My Heart/Over Somebody Else's Shoulder (78) | 20 |
| 59 | Vogue V 9139 | Purple Stew (as Thurston Harris & Masters)/I Hear A Rhapsody | 150 |
| 59 | Vogue V 9139 | Purple Stew (as Thurston Harris & Masters)/I Hear A Rhapsody (78) | 20 |
| 59 | Vogue V 9144 | You Don't Know How Much I Love You/In The Bottom Of My Heart | 100 |
| 59 | Vogue V 9144 | You Don't Know How Much I Love You/In The Bottom Of My Heart (78) | 20 |
| 59 | Vogue V 9146 | Hey Little Girl/My Love Will Last | 150 |
| 59 | Vogue V 9146 | Hey Little Girl/My Love Will Last (78) | 30 |
| 59 | Vogue V 9149 | Runk Bunk/Bless Your Heart | 150 |
| 59 | Vogue V 9149 | Runk Bunk/Bless Your Heart (78) | 30 |
| 59 | Vogue V 9151 | Slip-Slop/Paradise Hill | 200 |
| 59 | Vogue V 9151 | Slip-Slop/Paradise Hill (78) | 40 |
| 66 | Sue WI 4016 | Little Bitty Pretty One/I Hope You Won't Hold It Against Me (reissue) | 50 |

*(see also Sharps)*

## WEE WILLIE HARRIS

| 57 | Decca F 10970 | Rockin' At The Two 'I's/Back To School Again | 40 |
| 58 | Decca F 10980 | Love Bug Crawl/Rosie Lee | 40 |
| 58 | Decca F 11044 | Got A Match/No Chemise, Please! | 20 |
| 60 | Decca F 11217 | Wild One/Little Bitty Girl | 20 |
| 63 | HMV POP 1198 | You Must Be Joking/Better To Have Loved | 10 |
| 66 | Parlophone R 5504 | Someone's In The Kitchen With Diana/Walk With Peter And Paul (some A-sides list 'Dina') | 10 |
| 66 | Polydor 56140 | Listen To The River Roll Along/Try Moving Baby (writing in black or white) | 30 |
| 74 | Decca F 13516 | Together/Rock'n'Roll Jamboree | 5 |
| 58 | Decca DFE 6465 | ROCKING WITH WEE WILLIE (EP) | 150 |

## WYNONIE 'MR BLUES' HARRIS

| 56 | Vogue V 2127 | Bloodshot Eyes/Lollipop Mama (triangular centre) | 100 |
| 56 | Vogue V 2127 | Bloodshot Eyes/Lollipop Mama (round centre) | 40 |
| 56 | Vogue EPV 1103 | WYNONIE 'MISTER BLUES' HARRIS (EP) | 60 |
| 61 | Blue Beat BBEP 301 | BATTLE OF THE BLUES (EP) | 80 |

## WYNONIE HARRIS/EDDIE 'CLEANHEAD' VINSON

| 72 | Polydor 2343 048 | JUMP BLUES (LP) | 15 |

*(see also Tiny Bradshaw/Wynonie Harris, Eddie 'Cleanhead' Vinson)*

## HARRISON

| 84 | Skipping Rope SKIP 1 | There Is No Refrain/Simply This (p/s) | 40 |

## DANNY HARRISON

| 62 | Starlite ST45 77 | No One To Love Me/All The World is Lonely | 6 |
| 62 | Starlite ST45 91 | Broken Love Affair/Have I Wasted My Life | 6 |
| 63 | Starlite ST45 108 | Have You Ever Been Lonely/Mary Ann I'm Lonesome | 6 |
| 65 | Coral Q 72479 | Speak Of The Devil/I'm A Rollin' Stone | 15 |
| 62 | Starlite STEP 23 | INTRODUCING DANNY HARRISON (EP) | 20 |

## EARL HARRISON

| 67 | London HL 10121 | Humphrey Stomp/Can You Forgive Me | 50 |
| 67 | London HL 10121 | Humphrey Stomp/Can You Forgive Me (DJ Copy) | 100 |

## GEORGE HARRISON
### SINGLES

| 71 | Apple R 5884 | My Sweet Lord/What Is Life (in colour 'head' p/s) | 12 |
| 71 | Apple R5912 | Bangla-Desh/Deep Blue (Demo copy) | 70 |
| 71 | Apple R 5912 | Bangla-Desh/Deep Blue (with rare p/s [beware of new-looking counterfeits!]) | 80 |
| 71 | Apple R 5912 | Bangla-Desh/Deep Blue | 5 |
| 73 | Apple R 5988 | Give Me Love (Give Me Peace On Earth)/Miss O'Dell (Demo copy) | 70 |
| 73 | Apple R 5988 | Give Me Love (Give Me Peace On Earth)/Miss O'Dell | 5 |
| 74 | Apple R 6001 | Dark Horse/I Don't Care Anymore (unissued) | 0 |
| 74 | Apple R 6002 | Ding Dong, Ding Dong/I Don't Care Anymore (no p/s) | 5 |
| 75 | Apple R 6001 | Dark Horse/Hari's On Tour (Express) (p/s) | 10 |
| 75 | Apple R 6007 | You/World Of Stone (p/s) | 8 |
| 76 | Apple R 6012 | This Guitar (Can't Keep From Crying)/Maya Love (no p/s) | 35 |
| 76 | Apple R 5884 | My Sweet Lord/What Is Life (reissue, black & white 'gnome' p/s) | 10 |
| 76 | Dark Horse K 16856 | This Song/Learning How To Love You (issued with U.S. p/s) | 10 |
| 77 | Dark Horse K 16896 | True Love/Pure Smokey (no p/s) | 6 |
| 77 | Dark Horse K 16967 | It's What You Value/Woman Don't You Cry For Me (no p/s) | 15 |
| 79 | Dark Horse K 17284 | Love Comes To Everyone/Soft Hearted Hana | 15 |
| 79 | Dark Horse K 17327 | Blow Away/Soft Touch (p/s) | 5 |
| 79 | Dark Horse K 17423 | Faster/Your Love Is Forever (with charity stickered plain white die-cut sleeve) | 15 |
| 79 | Dark Horse K 17423 | Faster/Your Love Is Forever (picture disc, stickered PVC sleeve with insert) | 30 |
| 81 | Dark Horse K 17807 | All Those Years Ago/Writing On The Wall (p/s) | 5 |
| 81 | Dark Horse K 17837DJ | Teardrops (Edited Version)/Save The World (DJ promo only, no p/s) | 25 |
| 81 | Dark Horse K 17837 | Teardrops/Save The World (p/s) | 10 |
| 82 | Dark Horse 929 864-7 | Wake Up My Love/Greece (p/s) | 8 |
| 86 | Ganga Publishing B.V. | Shanghai Surprise (with Vicki Brown) (unreleased, 1-sided promo only; no catalogue number, matrix: SHANGHAI 1) | 500 |
| 87 | Dark Horse W 8178 | Got My Mind Set On You/Lay His Head (p/s, green label) | 5 |
| 87 | Dark Horse W 8178B | Got My Mind Set On You/Lay His Head (box set with 2 postcards) | 20 |

| 87 | Dark Horse W 8178T | Got My Mind Set On You (Extended Version)/Got My Mind Set On You (Single Version)/Lay His Head (12", p/s with poster) | 15 |
| 87 | Dark Horse W 8178TP | Got My Mind Set On You (Extended Version)/Got My Mind Set On You (Single Version)/Lay His Head (12", picture disc) | 20 |
| 88 | Dark Horse W 8131B | When We Was Fab/Zig Zag (box set with fold-out poster & cut-out) | 10 |
| 88 | Dark Horse W 8131T | When We Was Fab (Unextended Version)/Zig Zag/That's The Way It Goes (Remix)/When We Was Fab (Reverse End) (12", p/s) | 10 |
| 88 | Dark Horse W 8131TP | When We Was Fab (Unextended Version)/Zig Zag/That's The Way It Goes (Remix)/When We Was Fab (Reverse End) (12", picture disc) | 20 |
| 88 | Dark Horse W 7913 | This Is Love/Breath Away From Heaven (p/s) | 8 |
| 88 | Dark Horse W 7913T | This Is Love/Breath Away From Heaven/All Those Years Ago (12", p/s) | 15 |
| 89 | Dark Horse W 2696 | Cheer Down/That's What It Takes (p/s) | 8 |
| 89 | Dark Horse W 2696T | Cheer Down/That's What It Takes/Crackerbox Palace (12", p/s) | 15 |
| 88 | Genesis SGH 777 | SONGS BY GEORGE HARRISON (Limited Edition) (EP, 33rpm, issued with limited edition book Songs By George Harrison) | 900 |
| 88 | Genesis SGHCD 777 | SONGS BY GEORGE HARRISON (CD EP, issued with limited edition book) | 800 |
| 92 | Genesis SGH 778 | SONGS BY GEORGE HARRISON VOL. 2 (EP, with limited edition book Songs By George Harrison Vol. 2) | 400 |
| 92 | Genesis SGHCD 778 | SONGS BY GEORGE HARRISON VOL. 2 (CD EP, with limited edition book) | 600 |
| 03 | Parlophone R 6601 | Any Road/Marwa Blues (p/s) | 7 |

## ALBUMS

| 68 | Apple APCOR 1 | WONDERWALL MUSIC (soundtrack; with insert, black inner sleeve, mono) | 250 |
| 68 | Apple SAPCOR 1 | WONDERWALL MUSIC (soundtrack; with insert, black inner sleeve, stereo) | 100 |
| 69 | Zapple ZAPPLE 02 | ELECTRONIC SOUND (with inner sleeve) | 200 |
| 71 | Apple STCH 639 | ALL THINGS MUST PASS (3-LP box set with poster & lyric inner sleeves; initial batch in U.K. Box) | 100 |
| 71 | Apple STCH 639 | ALL THINGS MUST PASS (3-LP box set with poster & lyric inner sleeves; later batch in U.S. box) | 50 |
| 72 | Apple STCX 3385 | THE CONCERT FOR BANGLA DESH (3-LP box set, orange inside with BMI/ASCAP label credits, with booklet, featuring Bob Dylan) | 75 |
| 73 | Apple PAS 10006 | LIVING IN THE MATERIAL WORLD (gatefold sleeve with inner) | 18 |
| 74 | Apple PAS 10008 | DARK HORSE (LP, gatefold sleeve, inner sleeve, lyric insert) | 30 |
| 75 | Apple PAS 10009 | EXTRA TEXTURE (LP with inner) | 30 |
| 76 | Dark Horse K56319 | THIRTY THREE AND A THIRD (LP, gatefold with inner) | 20 |
| 82 | Dark Horse 923734-1 | GONE TROPPO (LP with inner) | 20 |
| 87 | Dark Horse 925643-1 | CLOUD NINE (LP, with inner) | 20 |
| 91 | EPIC EPC 468835 1 | THE CONCERT FOR BANGLA DESH (3-LP set in single sleeve) | 25 |
| 92 | Dark Horse 759926964-1 | LIVE IN JAPAN (2xLP in single sleeve) | 40 |
| 92 | Apple SAPCOR 1 | WONDERWALL MUSIC (reissue, gatefold sleeve with inner sleeve) | 20 |
| 96 | Zapple ZAPPLE 02 | ELECTRONIC SOUND (reissue, with inner sleeve) | 35 |
| 01 | Parlophone 5304741 | ALL THINGS MUST PASS (3-LP, reissue) | 20 |
| 02 | Dark Horse 5419691 | BRAINWASHED (Gatefold LP with sticker on cover) | 35 |

## ALBUMS : CDS

| 87 | Dark Horse WX 123 | CLOUD NINE | 25 |
| 89 | Dark Horse K 9257262 | THE BEST OF DARK HORSE 1976-1989 | 40 |
| 02 | Dark Horse 580 3450 | BRAINWASHED (CD box set) | 25 |

*(see also Beatles, Traveling Wilburys, Billy Connolly & Chris Tummings, Sylvia Griffin)*

## JAYE HARRISON

| 77 | Ember EMBS 351 | Value For Money/Instrumental Version | 8 |

## MIKE HARRISON

| 75 | Good Ear 611 | We Can Work It Out/Maverick Woman Blues | 8 |
| 71 | Island ILPS 9170 | MIKE HARRISON (LP, gatefold sleeve, pink rim, palm tree label) | 40 |
| 72 | Island ILPS 9209 | SMOKESTACK LIGHTNING (LP, laminated sleeve, pink rim, palm tree label) | 30 |
| 75 | Good Ear EAR 7002 | RAINBOW RIDER (LP) | 20 |

*(see also Art, Spirit, Spooky Tooth)*

## NEIL HARRISON

| 74 | Decca F13520 | Sad Eyes/Bicycle Driver | 10 |

*(see also Driftwood)*

## NOEL HARRISON

| 65 | Decca F 12001 | Trees/To Ramona | 6 |
| 66 | Decca F 12314 | A Young Girl Of Sixteen/Tomorrow Is My Turn | 6 |
| 66 | Decca F 12345 | It's All Over Now Baby Blue/Much As I Love You | 6 |
| 67 | Reprise RS 20615 | Suzanne/Life Is A Dream | 6 |
| 68 | Reprise RS 20758 | Windmills Of Your Mind/Leitch On The Beach | 5 |
| 69 | Reprise RS23395 | Sparrow/California Weekend | 10 |
| 69 | Decca F12878 | Young Girl (Of Sixteen)/She's A Woman | 7 |
| 69 | Decca F 12918 | Love Minus Zero/No Limit/Just Can't Wait | 6 |
| 57 | HMV 7EG 8383 | NOEL HARRISON (EP) | 15 |
| 65 | Decca DFE 8616 | NOEL HARRISON (EP) | 10 |
| 65 | Decca DFE 8639 | TO RAMONA (EP) | 12 |
| 60 | Philips BBL 7399 | AT THE BLUE ANGEL (LP) | 20 |
| 69 | Reprise RSLP 6321 | THE GREAT ELECTRIC EXPERIMENT IS OVER (LP) | 15 |

## REGGIE HARRISON

| 63 | Cameo Parkway P 863 | A Lonely Piano/HIPPIES: Memory Lane | 20 |

## WILBERT HARRISON

| 59 | Top Rank JAR 132 | Kansas City/Listen My Darling | 20 |
| 59 | Top Rank JAR 132 | Kansas City/Listen My Darling (78) | 30 |
| 62 | Island WI 031 | I'm Broke/Off To School | 20 |
| 65 | Sue WI 363 | Let's Stick Together/Kansas City Twist | 20 |
| 70 | London HL 10307 | Let's Work Together/Stagger Lee | 15 |

| | | | |
|---|---|---|---|
| 73 | Action ACT 4613 | Get It While You Can/Amen | 8 |
| 70 | London HA/SH 8415 | LET'S WORK TOGETHER (LP) | 40 |
| 85 | Charly CRB 1102 | LOVIN...PERATOR (LP) | 15 |

**YVONNE HARRISON**

| | | | |
|---|---|---|---|
| 67 | Caltone TONE 102 | The Chase/Take My Hand | 100 |
| 75 | Camel CA 2003 | Knotty Screw Face/UNDERGROUND PEOPLE: Face Dub | 12 |

**DEBBIE/DEBORAH HARRY**

| | | | |
|---|---|---|---|
| 93 | Chrysalis TC-CHS 4900 | I Can See Clearly/Standing In My Way (B-side with Joey Ramone) | 7 |

*(see also Wind In The Willows, Blondie, New York Blondes)*

**HARRY J. ALL STARS**

| | | | |
|---|---|---|---|
| 69 | Harry J TR 694 | Spyrone/JOHN HOLT: Have Sympathy | 40 |
| 69 | Harry J. TR 675 | Liquidator/GLEN & DAVE: La La Always Stay (green label) | 8 |
| 69 | Harry J. TR 675 | Liquidator/GLEN & DAVE: La La Always Stay (white label) | 5 |
| 70 | Harry J. HJ 6601 | The Big Three/Lavender (B-side actually "Lavender Blue" by Lloyd Robinson) | 6 |
| 70 | Harry J. HJ 6608 | Reach For The Sky/Interrogator | 6 |
| 70 | Harry J. HJ 6621 | Return Of The Liquidator (actually "Tons Of Gold" by Val Bennett)/All Day | 12 |
| 72 | Harry J. HJ 6641 | Down Side Up/Down Side Up - Version | 8 |
| 73 | Explosion EX 2073 | Chirpy Chirpy Cheep Cheep/Chirpy Chirpy (Instrumental) | 5 |
| 73 | Blue Mountain BM 1028 | U.F.O./Reggae With The Birds | 5 |
| 70 | Trojan TBL 104 | THE LIQUIDATOR (LP) | 20 |

*(see also Jay Boys, Bob Andy, John Holt, Lizzy)*

**HARRY & RADCLIFFE**

| | | | |
|---|---|---|---|
| 69 | Camel CA 26 | History/Just Be Alone | 60 |
| 69 | Punch PH 8 | History/Just Be Alone | 8 |

**WARREN HARRY**

| | | | |
|---|---|---|---|
| 76 | Sonet SON-2088 | I don't Care/Backwards Forwards | 15 |
| 78 | HAH 1/EJSP-8632 | 1965/Radio Show (500 only, no p/s) | 30 |

**HARSH REALITY**

| | | | |
|---|---|---|---|
| 68 | Philips PB 1710 | Tobacco Ash Sunday/How Do You Feel | 18 |
| 69 | Philips PB 1769 | Heaven And Hell/Praying For Reprieve | 18 |
| 69 | Philips (S)BL 7891 | HEAVEN AND HELL (LP, gatefold sleeve, blue/silver labels) | 500 |

*(see also Matthews Southern Comfort)*

**CAJUN HART**

| | | | |
|---|---|---|---|
| 69 | Warner Bros WB 7258 | Got To Find A Way/Lover's Prayer | 200 |
| 69 | Warner Bros WB 7258 | Got To Find A Way/Lover's Prayer (DJ Copy) | 300 |
| 06 | Warner Bros WB 7258 | Got To Find A Way/LINDA JONES: A Last Minute Miracle (A-label reissue) | 20 |

**DERRY HART & HARTBEATS**

| | | | |
|---|---|---|---|
| 59 | Decca F 11138 | Come On Baby/Nowhere In This World | 20 |

**MICKEY HART**

| | | | |
|---|---|---|---|
| 73 | Warner Bros. K 46182 | ROLLING THUNDER (LP) | 15 |

*(see also Grateful Dead, Diga Rhythm Band)*

**MIKE HART**

| | | | |
|---|---|---|---|
| 70 | Dandelion S 4781 | Yawney Morning Song/Almost Liverpool 8 | 7 |
| 74 | Deram DM 409 | Son Son/Bad News Man | 6 |
| 70 | Dandelion 63756 | MIKE HART BLEEDS (LP, black/red/silver labels) | 50 |
| 72 | Dandelion 2310 211 | BASHER, CHALKY, PONGO AND ME (LP, as Mike Hart & Comrades) | 50 |

*(see also Clayton Squares, Liverpool Scene)*

**STEVE HART**

| | | | |
|---|---|---|---|
| 68 | CBS 3732 | The Master Of Man/Without You | 5 |

**TIM HART**

| | | | |
|---|---|---|---|
| 79 | Chrysalis CHR 2335 | Overseas/Hillman Avenger (p/s) | 7 |

*(see also Steeleye Span)*

**TIM HART & MADDY PRIOR**

| | | | |
|---|---|---|---|
| 68 | Tepee TPRM 104 | FOLK SONGS OF OLDE ENGLAND VOL. 1 (LP, gatefold sleeve) | 100 |
| 69 | Tepee TPRM 105 | FOLK SONGS OF OLDE ENGLAND VOL. 2 (LP, gatefold sleeve) | 100 |
| 69 | Ad-Rhythm ARPS 3 | FOLK SONGS OF OLDE ENGLAND VOL. 1 (LP, reissue) | 25 |
| 69 | Ad-Rhythm ARPS 4 | FOLK SONGS OF OLDE ENGLAND VOL. 2 (LP, reissue) | 25 |
| 71 | B&C CAS 1035 | SUMMER SOLSTICE (LP, gatefold sleeve) | 30 |

*(see also Steeleye Span, Maddy Prior)*

**CIARAN HARTE**

| | | | |
|---|---|---|---|
| 80 | Glass 003 | Love Is Strange/Shimahero (p/s) | 20 |

**HARTLEPOOL FC**

| | | | |
|---|---|---|---|
| 72 | United Artists UP 35358 | Who Put The Sugar In My Tea/Never Say Die | 10 |

**KEEF HARTLEY (BAND)**

| | | | |
|---|---|---|---|
| 69 | Deram DM 250 | Leave It 'Till The Morning/Just To Cry | 12 |
| 69 | Deram DM 273 | Waiting Around/Not Foolish, Not Wise | 12 |
| 70 | Deram DM 316 | Roundabout (Parts 1 & 2) | 12 |
| 73 | Deram DM 380 | Dance To The Music/You And Me | 8 |
| 69 | Deram DML 1037 | HALFBREED (LP, mono, gatefold sleeve, 1st pressing has 'mono/stereo' holes on rear sleeve, white/red label) | 85 |
| 69 | Deram SML 1037 | HALFBREED (LP, stereo, gatefold sleeve, 1st pressing has 'mono/stereo' holes on rear sleeve, white/red label) | 65 |
| 69 | Deram DML 1054 | THE BATTLE OF N.W.6 (LP, mono, gatefold sleeve, 1st pressing with 'mono/stereo' holes on rear sleeve, white/red labels) | 65 |
| 69 | Deram SML 1054 | THE BATTLE OF N.W.6 (LP, stereo, gatefold sleeve, 1st pressing with 'mono/stereo' holes on rear sleeve, white/red labels) | 50 |
| 70 | Deram SML 1071 | THE TIME IS NEAR (LP, with booklet, white/red labels with small logo) | 45 |
| 70 | Deram SML 1071 | THE TIME IS NEAR (LP, without booklet, white/red labels with small logo) | 25 |
| 71 | Deram SDL 2 | OVERDOG (LP, gatefold sleeve, white/brown labels with small logo) | 35 |

MINT VALUE £

| 71 | Deram SDL 4 | LITTLE BIG BAND (LP, white/brown label, gatefold sleeve) | 60 |
| 72 | Deram SDL 9 | SEVENTY SECOND BRAVE (LP, gatefold sleeve) | 40 |
| 73 | Deram SDL 13 | LANCASHIRE HUSTLER (LP, gatefold sleeve, as Keeg Hartley) | 25 |
| 74 | Deram DPA 3011/2 | THE BEST OF (2-LP, gatefold sleeve) | 20 |
| 70s | Deram SDN 30251/2 | THE BATTLE OF N.W.6/THE TIME IS NEAR (2-LP, gatefold sleeve) | 20 |

*(see also Rory Storm & Hurricanes, Artwoods, John Mayall's Bluesbreakers, Miller Anderson, Dog Soldier, Henry Lowther, Wynder K. Frog)*

## TREVOR HARTLEY
| 80 | Matumbi MA 006 | Skip Away/Selassi (12") | 25 |

## HARVEST
| 80 | Secular Records SEC 001 | Fashion Parade/Will You Be The One | 70 |

## HARVEST MINISTERS
| 92 | Sarah SARAH 64 | You Do My World The World Of Good/Petticoats (p/s, insert) | 12 |
| 92 | Sarah SARAH 68 | Six O'Clock Is Rosary/The First Star (p/s, insert) | 15 |
| 93 | Sarah SARAH 84 | If It Kills Me And It Will/Can Go It Alone (p/s, insert) | 12 |
| 93 | Sarah SARAH 616 | LITTLE DARK MANSIONS (LP) | 20 |

## HARVESTERS
| 72 | Westwood WRS 015 | THE HARVESTERS (LP) | 25 |

## ALEX HARVEY (1) AKA THE SENSATIONAL ALEX HARVEY BAND
| 64 | Polydor NH 52264 | I Just Wanna Make Love To You/Let The Good Times Roll | 60 |
| 64 | Polydor NH 52907 | Got My Mojo Working/I Ain't Worried Baby (as Alex Harvey & His Soul Band) | 60 |
| 65 | Polydor BM 56017 | Ain't That Just Too Bad/My Kind Of Love (as Alex Harvey & His Soul Band) | 60 |
| 65 | Fontana TF 610 | Agent 00 Soul/Go Away Baby | 40 |
| 66 | Fontana TF 764 | Work Song/I Can Do Without Your Love | 25 |
| 67 | Decca F 12640 | The Sunday Song/Horizon's | 50 |
| 67 | Decca F 12660 | Maybe Some Day/Curtains For My Baby | 60 |
| 69 | Fontana TF 1063 | Midnight Moses/Roman Wall Blues | 70 |
| 72 | Vertigo 6059 070 | There's No Lights On The Christmas Tree Mother, (They're Burning Big Louie Tonight)/Harp | 40 |
| 75 | Vertigo ALEX 001 | Delilah (live)/Soul In Chains (p/s) | 5 |
| 75 | Vertigo ALEX 002 | Gamblin' Bar Room Blues/Shake That Thing (p/s) | 5 |
| 76 | Mountain PSLP 183 | Amos Moses/$25 For A Massage (promo only 12") | 12 |
| 77 | Mountain TOP 32 | Mrs Blackhouse/Engine Room Boogie (p/s) | 6 |
| 64 | Polydor LPHM 46424 | ALEX HARVEY AND HIS SOUL BAND (LP) | 250 |
| 64 | Polydor LPHM 46441 | THE BLUES (LP) | 200 |
| 69 | Fontana (S)TL 5534 | ROMAN WALL BLUES (LP) | 400 |
| 73 | Vertigo 6360 081 | FRAMED (LP, as The Sensational Alex Harvey Band, gatefold sleeve, small swirl label) | 200 |
| 72 | Vertigo 6360 081 | FRAMED (LP, as The Sensational Alex Harvey Band, gatefold sleeve, later spaceship label) | 30 |
| 73 | Vertigo 6360 103 | NEXT (LP, as The Sensational Alex Harvey Band, spaceship label, 1st pressing, side 1 Matrix 1Y//1 1 6 3) | 20 |
| 74 | Vertigo 6360 112 | THE IMPOSSIBLE DREAM (LP, gatefold sleeve, spaceship label) | 15 |
| 75 | Vertigo 9102 003 | TOMORROW BELONGS TO ME (LP, gatefold sleeve, spaceship label) | 15 |
| 77 | K-Tel NE 984 | ALEX HARVEY PRESENTS THE LOCH NESS MONSTER (LP, withdrawn, gatefold stickered sleeve, with 16-page 'descriptive diary') | 50 |
| 78 | Mountain TOPS 114 | ROCK DRILL (with 'No Complaints Department'.) | 35 |
| 78 | Mountain TOPS 114 | ROCK DRILL (Later copies with revised Track listing stickered on sleeve) | 15 |
| 83 | Power Supply AMP 2 | THE SOLDIER ON THE WALL (LP, solo) | 20 |
| 84 | Samurai SAH 117PD | S.A.H.B. LIVE (LP, reissue, picture disc) | 12 |

*(see also Tear Gas, Hairband, Rock Workshop, Nazareth, Michael Schenker Group, Tandoori )*

## ALEX HARVEY (2)
| 71 | Capitol E-ST 789 | ALEX HARVEY (LP) | 15 |

## CARL HARVEY MEETS THE DUB MASTER
| 78 | Cancer CANLP 003 | ECSTACY OF MANKIND (LP) | 40 |

## JANCIS HARVEY
| 73 | Pilgrim King KLPS 47 | DISTANCE OF DOORS (LP) | 45 |
| 73 | Westwood WRS 029 | WORDS YOU LEFT BEHIND (LP) | 55 |
| 74 | Westwood WRS 038 | JANCIS HARVEY (LP) | 55 |
| 75 | Westwood WRS 054 | TIME WAS NOW (LP) | 55 |
| 76 | Westwood WRS 107 | A PORTRAIT OF JANCIS HARVEY (LP) | 45 |
| 79 | Westwood WRS 144 | FROM THE DARKNESS CAME LIGHT (LP) | 40 |

## JANE HARVEY
| 60 | Pye International 7N 25046 | I'm Gonna Go Fishin'/Hundred Dreams From Now | 6 |

## LANCE HARVEY & KINGPINS
| 64 | Pye 7N 15647 | He's Telling You Lies/How Do You Fix A Broken Heart | 10 |
| 64 | Lyntone LYN 509 | SINCE YOU WALKED OUT ON ME (Keele Rag flexidisc EP, with The Escorts) | 15 |

## MICK HARVEY
| 97 | Mute STUMM 157 | PINK ELEPHANTS (LP, inner) | 25 |

*(see also Nick Cave)*

## HARVEY (FUQUA) & MOONGLOWS
| 58 | London HLM 8730 | Ten Commandments Of Love/Mean Old Blues | 300 |
| 58 | London HLM 8730 | Ten Commandments Of Love/Mean Old Blues (78) | 50 |

*(see also Moonglows, Etta & Harvey)*

## PETER HARVEY
| 62 | Columbia DB 4873 | Rainin' In My Heart/Please Don't Tell Joe | 7 |
| 63 | Columbia DB 7030 | Wishing You The Best Of Luck My Friend/Lovin' Can Be Lonesome | 5 |
| 64 | Columbia DB 7192 | Heart Of Ice/Trace Of A Heartache | 5 |
| 64 | Columbia DB 7331 | Big Man In A Big House/Date With A Heartache | 5 |

## P.J. HARVEY

| | | |
|---|---|---|
| 90 | Private Pressing | P. J. Harvey (3-track demo , 'wooden' p/s includes pictures of P. J. and lyrics to Dress) . 70 |
| 91 | Too Pure PURE 5 | Dress/Water (demo)/Dry (demo) (12") .......... 20 |
| 92 | Too Pure PURES 8 | Sheela-Na-Gig/Joe (p/s, 400 only) .......... 45 |
| 92 | Too Pure PURE 8 | Sheela-Na-Gig/Hair (demo)/Joe (demo) (12", p/s) .......... 25 |
| 93 | Island 12IS 538 | 50 Ft Queenie/Mansize (demo)/Hook (demo)/Reeling (12", p/s) .......... 12 |
| 93 | Island 12IS 569 | Mansize/Wang Dang Doodle/Daddy (12", p/s) .......... 20 |
| 95 | Island IS 607 | Down By the Water/Lying In The Sun/Somebody's Down Somebody's Name (p/s) .......... 8 |
| 95 | Island 12IS 614 | C'Mon Billy/Darling Be There/Maniac (12", p/s) .......... 10 |
| 95 | Island IS 610 | Send His Love To Me/Long Time Coming (Evening Session) (7" picture disc in 12" poster p/s) .......... 12 |
| 95 | Island CIDD J610 | Send His Love To Me (Promo-only CD, exclusive 'rose dress' sleeve) .......... 30 |
| 99 | Island IS 730 | The Wind/Rebecca/Nina In Ecstacy 2 .......... 8 |
| 00 | Island IS 769 | Good Fortune/66 Promises .......... 12 |
| 01 | Island IS 771 | A Place Called Home/Kick It To The Ground (demo) (humbered) .......... 12 |
| 01 | Island IS 785 | This Is Love/Angline (live) (p/s) .......... 12 |
| 04 | Island IS 873 | Shame/Dance (p/s) .......... 8 |
| 04 | Island IS 861 | The Letter/Bows And Arrows (p/s) .......... 8 |
| 07 | Island 1747513 | When Under Ether/Wait (p/s) .......... 6 |
| 07 | Island 1753491 | The Piano/Heaven (p/s) .......... 10 |
| 11 | Island 2768296 | The Glorious Land/The Nightingale .......... 10 |
| 11 | Island 2762434 | The Words That Maketh Murder/The Guns Called Me Back Again .......... 12 |
| 92 | Too Pure PURE(D) 10 | DRY (LP, 1st 5,000 with bonus LP, "Demonstrations", inner sleeve and no'd sticker) .....80 |
| 92 | Too Pure PURE 10 | DRY (LP with inner but without "Demonstrations") .......... 30 |
| 93 | Island 5146961 | RID OF ME (LP) .......... 60 |
| 93 | Island ILPM 2079 | 4 TRACK DEMOS (LP, with inner) .......... 30 |
| 95 | Island CIDZ 8035 | TO BRING YOU MY LOVE & THE B-SIDES CD (2-CD) .......... 40 |
| 95 | Island ILPS 8035 | TO BRING YOU MY LOVE (LP, 1st pressing, with inner and large photo on rear) .......... 30 |
| 98 | Island ILPS 8076 | IS THIS DESIRE? (LP, with inner) .......... 70 |
| 00 | Island ILPS 8099 | STORIES FROM THE CITY, STORIES FROM THE SEA (LP, with inner) .......... 60 |
| 04 | Island ILPS 8143 | UH HUH HER (LP, with inner) .......... 50 |
| 07 | Island 1740335 | WHITE CHALK (LP, inner) .......... 20 |

(see also Automatic Dlamini, Grape, John Parish & Polly Jean Harvey)

## RICHARD HARVEY

| | | |
|---|---|---|
| 83 | Anderburr HX 1010 | Theme From Terrahawks (3.00)/Variations On The Theme (3.17) (p/.s) .......... 10 |
| 83 | Anderburr HX 21010 | Theme From Terrahawks (4.50)/Variations On The Theme (7.25) (12", p/s with poster) .......... 12 |
| 75 | Transatlantic TRA 292 | DIVISIONS ON A GROUND (LP) .......... 15 |

(see also Gryphon, Barry Gray, The Banned)

## TINA HARVEY

| | | |
|---|---|---|
| 72 | UK UK 2 | Working My Way Back To You/Tina's Song .......... 6 |
| 73 | UK UK 24 | Nowhere To Run/Tina's Second Song .......... 25 |
| 73 | UK UKAL 1002 | TINA HARVEY (LP, bule/silver labels) .......... 25 |

## HARVEY BOYS

| | | |
|---|---|---|
| 57 | London HLA 8397 | Nothing Is Too Good For You/Marina Girl .......... 30 |

## HARVEY'S PEOPLE

| | | |
|---|---|---|
| 69 | Galliard GAL 4001 | LOVING AND LIVING (LP) .......... 15 |

## CHRISTINE HARWOOD

| | | |
|---|---|---|
| 70 | Birth RAB 1 | NICE TO MEET MISS CHRISTINE (LP, white 'rabbit' child' label) .......... 200 |

## GORDON HASKELL

| | | |
|---|---|---|
| 69 | CBS 4509 | Boat Trip/Time Only Knows .......... 8 |
| 70 | CBS 4795 | Oo-La-Di-Doo-Da-Day/Born To Be Together .......... 8 |
| 90 | Wilderness WLD 700 | Hambledon Hill/Mystical Illusion (p/s) .......... 6 |
| 69 | CBS 63741 | SAILIN' MY BOAT (LP) .......... 125 |
| 72 | Atlantic K 40311 | IT IS AND IT ISN'T (LP, with lyric insert) .......... 40 |
| 73 | RCA | SERVE AT ROOM TEMPERATURE (LP, unissued) .......... 250 |

(see also Fleur-De-Lys, Cupid's Inspiration, Flowerpot Men, King Crimson)

## JACK HASKELL (& HONEY-DREAMERS)

| | | |
|---|---|---|
| 57 | London HL 8426 | Around The World/Away Out West .......... 15 |
| 58 | Oriole CB 1442 | The Night Of The Senior Prom/Hungry For Love (with Honey-Dreamers) .......... 5 |

## MICHAEL HASLAM

| | | |
|---|---|---|
| 65 | Parlophone R 5267 | There Goes (The Forgotten Man)/My Heart Won't Say Goodbye .......... 5 |

## JON HASSELL

| | | |
|---|---|---|
| 83 | Editons EG EGED 31 | AKA/DARBARI/JAVA- MAGIC REALISM (LP) .......... 20 |

## JON HASSELL & BRIAN ENO

| | | |
|---|---|---|
| 80 | EG EGED 7 | POSSIBLE MUSICS (LP) .......... 15 |

(see also Roxy Music, Brian Eno, Fripp & Eno)

## JOE HASSELVANDER

| | | |
|---|---|---|
| 85 | Pentagram DEVIL 3 | LADY KILLER (LP) .......... 15 |

## HASSLES

| | | |
|---|---|---|
| 67 | United Artists UP 1199 | You Got Me Hummin'/I'm Thinkin' .......... 20 |

(see also Billy Joel)

## HAT & TIE

| | | |
|---|---|---|
| 66 | President PT 105 | Chance For Romance/California Jazz Club U.S.A. .......... 15 |
| 67 | President PT 122 | Bread To Spend/Finding It Rough (demos credit A-side as "Bread") .......... 150 |

(see also Patrick Campbell-Lyons, Nirvana (U.K.))

## TONY HATCH ORCHESTRA

| | | |
|---|---|---|
| 59 | Top Rank JAR 107 | Chick/Side Saddle .......... 6 |

| 59 | Top Rank JAR 165 | Rhoom Ba-Cha/Stetson | 5 |
| 61 | Pye International 7N 25085 | Rocking Waltz/Devil's Herd | 6 |
| 61 | Pye International 7N 25068 | Tim Frazer's Theme/Girls Of Copenhagen | 5 |
| 61 | Pye International 7N 25109 | La Paloma/Theme From Rosemary | 5 |
| 61 | Pye 7N 15316 | Two-Some/Last Summer | 5 |
| 61 | Pye 7N 15408 | The Ghost Squad/What's All That About | 7 |
| 62 | Pye 7N 15434 | Ben Casey Theme/Perry Mason Theme | 7 |
| 62 | Pye 7N 15440 | Theme From 'The Naked City'/In Party Mood | 5 |
| 62 | Pye 7N 15460 | Out Of This World Theme/Cyril's Tune (in p/s) | 10 |
| 62 | Pye 7N 15460 | Out Of This World Theme/Cyril's Tune | 5 |
| 62 | Pye 7N 15494 | Theme From The Dick Powell Show/Sharon | 5 |
| 63 | Pye 7N 15537 | The Wonderful World Of The Brothers Grimm/Spanish Main Theme | 5 |
| 63 | Pye 7N 15583 | Mondo Cane Theme/Girls Of Copenhagen | 5 |
| 65 | Pye 7N 15754 | Crossroads Theme/The Marie Celeste (in p/s) | 8 |
| 65 | Pye 7N 15754 | Crossroads Theme/Round Every Corner | 5 |
| 65 | Pye 7N15972 | Man Alive/Crosstown Commuter | 8 |
| 65 | Pye 7N 15930 | Maori/Sugar And Spice | 6 |
| 66 | Pye 7N 17169 | Crossroads Theme/Round Every Corner (in p/s) | 10 |
| 66 | Pye 7N 17169 | Crossroads Theme/Round Every Corner | 5 |
| 67 | Pye 7N 17263 | Comedy Tonight/You're Lovely | 10 |
| 67 | Pye 7N 17298 | Beautiful In The Rain/While The City Sleeps | 6 |
| 67 | Pye 7N 17340 | Fiddler On The Roof/El Payaso/Spanish Clown | 5 |
| 69 | Pye 7N 17814 | Theme From Who-Dun-It/The Champions | 30 |
| 69 | Pye 7N 17864 | The Doctors - Theme/Love Song | 6 |
| 73 | Pye 7N 45210 | Memories Of Summer/Best In Football | 6 |
| 74 | Pye 7N 45326 | The World At War/Sportsnight | 5 |
| 78 | EMI EMI 2780 | Sweeney 2/Regan's Key | 12 |
| 83 | Tube TUBE 003 | Airline/The HI-FA | 6 |

*(see also Jackie Trent)*

## GEORGE HATCHER BAND
| 77 | United Artists UP 36233 | Black Moon Rising/Find A New Lover (p/s) | 7 |

*(see also Budgie)*

## ROGER HATCHER
| 76 | Mint CHEW 5 | We Gonna Make It/High Blood Pressure | 10 |

## HATE
| 70 | Famous SFMA 5752 | HATE KILLS (LP, gatefold sleeve, orange labels) | 125 |

## BOBBY HATFIELD
| 68 | Verve VS 570 | Hang-Ups/Soul Cafe | 10 |
| 68 | Verve VS 576 | Only You/The Wonder Of You | 10 |
| 72 | Warner Bros K 16163 | Oo-Wee-Baby, I Love You/Rock'n'Roll Woman | 12 |

*(see also Righteous Brothers, Ringo Starr)*

## HATFIELD & THE NORTH
| 74 | Virgin VS 116 | Let's Eat (Real Soon)/Fitter Stoke Has A Bath | 8 |
| 74 | Virgin V 2008 | HATFIELD AND THE NORTH (LP, gatefold sleeve, red 'twin' label) | 40 |
| 76 | Virgin V 2008 | HATFIELD AND THE NORTH (LP, gatefold sleeve, repressing on "red mirror girl" label) | 25 |
| 75 | Virgin V 2030 | THE ROTTER'S CLUB (LP, red Virgin inner, coloured 'twin' label) | 30 |
| 79 | Virgin VR 5 | AFTERS (LP, withdrawn) | 35 |

*(see also Matching Mole, Egg, Khan, Camel, National Health, Caravan)*

## DONNY HATHAWAY
| 70 | Atco 226 010 | The Ghetto (Parts 1 & 2) | 10 |
| 72 | Atlantic K 10193 | The Ghetto (Parts 1 & 2)/Little Ghetto Boy | 8 |
| 73 | Atlantic K 10354 | Love Love Love/Someday We'll Be Free | 10 |
| 71 | Atco 2465 019 | EVERYTHING IS EVERYTHING (LP) | 18 |

*(see also Roberta Flack)*

## HAUSFRAUEN EXPERIMENT
| 10 | Fruits De Mer Crustacean 12 | Oscillations/Spirit Of The Age//Baby's On Fire/Sebastian (2x7", yellow/blue vinyl, foldover p/s) | 30 |

## HAVANA LETS GO
| 81 | Polydor POSP 364 | Spanish Cabaret/Continental Shelf (in p/s) | 18 |
| 81 | Polydor POSP 364 | Spanish Cabaret/Continental Shelf (no p/s) | 8 |

## ALAN HAVEN
| 62 | Fontana 267253 | My Mothers's Eyes/Lean Baby | 10 |
| 63 | Fontana TF 395 | I Feel Pretty/Haven's Haunts | 8 |
| 64 | United Artists UP 1057 | Theme From "A Jolly Bad Fellow"/Jee B'ees (with John Barry) | 10 |
| 65 | Fontana TF 542 | Image/Romance On The North Sea | 8 |
| 65 | Fontana TF 590 | The Knack/Satin Doll (with John Barry) | 15 |
| 66 | Fontana TF 658 | Flamingo/Shangri-La | 6 |
| 66 | Fontana TF 754 | Summer Samba/The Dachsund | 6 |
| 67 | Fontana TF 835 | Image/Romance Of The North Sea (reissue) | 8 |

## JIM HAVEN
| 75 | Penny Farthing PEN 868 | Do It In Slow Motion/Do It In Slow Motion (Part 2) | 10 |

## RICHIE HAVENS
| 69 | Big T BIG 119 | Oxford Town/My Own Way | 5 |
| 69 | Verve VS 1512 | Three Day Eternity/No Opportunity Necessary No Experience Needed | 5 |
| 69 | Verve VS 1519 | Lady Madonna/Indian Rope Man | 15 |
| 72 | Polydor 2121098 | What About Me/Fire And Rain | 6 |
| 68 | Verve (S)VLP 6005 | SOMETHIN' ELSE AGAIN (LP) | 20 |
| 68 | Verve (S)VLP 6008 | MIXED BAG (LP) | 20 |

| | | |
|---|---|---|
| 69 | Verve (S)VLP 6014 | 1983 (LP) ........ 20 |
| 69 | Verve (S)VLP 6021 | STONEHENGE (LP) ........ 15 |
| 69 | Transatlantic TRA 187 | ELECTRIC HAVENS (LP) ........ 15 |
| 69 | Transatlantic TRA 199 | THE RICHIE HAVENS RECORD (LP) ........ 15 |

**HAVENSTREET**

| | | |
|---|---|---|
| 76 | Rissole (no cat. no.) | THE END OF THE LINE (LP, private pressing with booklet) ........ 50 |

**CYRIL HAVERMANS**

| | | |
|---|---|---|
| 73 | MGM 2315 261 | CYRIL (LP, gatefold sleeve, blue/gold 'lion' label) ........ 25 |
| 74 | MGM 2315 311 | MIND WAVE (LP, blue/gold 'lion' label) ........ 18 |

**NICK HAWARD**

| | | |
|---|---|---|
| 83 | Cradle Music CMINH1 | Grey Day/Watching Through My Window (p/s) ........ 30 |

**PAT HAWES WITH DAVE CAREY'S RHYTHM**

| | | |
|---|---|---|
| 56 | Tempo A 141 | Snowy Morning Blues/Sheik Of Araby ........ 5 |
| 56 | Tempo LAP 9 | PAT HAWES (10" LP) ........ 20 |

**GRAHAM HAWK & OWEN GRAY**

| | | |
|---|---|---|
| 72 | Pama Supreme PS 360 | Amazing Grace/SKETTO RICH: Don't Stay Out Late ........ 5 |

**JACKSON HAWKE**

| | | |
|---|---|---|
| 76 | CBS 5034 | Into The Mystic/Fortune ........ 6 |

**TOMMY HAWKE**

| | | |
|---|---|---|
| 60 | Top Rank JAR 348 | Good Gravy (I'm In Love Again)/Umpteen Years (And A Million Tears) ........ 10 |

**HAWKEYES**

| | | |
|---|---|---|
| 57 | Capitol CL 14764 | Someone Someday/Who Is He? ........ 20 |

**BUDDY BOY HAWKINS/WILLIAM MOORE**

| | | |
|---|---|---|
| 50s | Heritage RE 102 | BUDDY BOY HAWKINS/WILLIAM MOORE (EP) ........ 60 |

*(see also Blind Lemon Jefferson)*

**CAROL HAWKINS**

| | | |
|---|---|---|
| 73 | Polydor 2058 387 | Listen/All For One ........ 8 |

**COLEMAN HAWKINS**

| | | |
|---|---|---|
| 53 | Capitol LC 6580 | CLASSICS IN JAZZ (10" LP) ........ 20 |
| 53 | Capitol LC 6650 | CAPITOL PRESENTS COLEMAN HAWKINS AND SONNY GREER (10" LP) ........ 20 |
| 54 | HMV DLP 1055 | TEN COLEMAN HAWKINS' SPECIALS (10" LP) ........ 20 |
| 59 | HMC CLP 1293 | GENIUS OF COLEMAN HAWKINS (LP) ........ 20 |
| 59 | Felsted FJA 7005 | THE HIGH AND MIGHTY HAWK (LP, also stereo SJA 2005) ........ 20 |
| 61 | Esquire 32-095 | SOUL (LP) ........ 25 |
| 61 | Esquire 32-102 | HAWK EYES (LP) ........ 25 |
| 61 | Moodsville MV 7 | COLEMAN HAWKINS (LP) ........ 20 |
| 62 | Swingsville SVLP 2001 | COLEMAN HAWKINS WITH THE RED GARLAND TRIO (LP) ........ 20 |
| 62 | Swingsville SVLP 2005 | THE COLEMAN HAWKINS ALL STARS (LP) ........ 20 |
| 62 | Swingsville SVLP 2013 | STASCH (LP) ........ 20 |
| 63 | HMV CLP 1630 | DESAFINADO (LP, also stereo CSD 1484) ........ 20 |
| 64 | Verve VLP 9044 | ALIVE! AT THE VILLAGE GATE (LP) ........ 20 |
| 64 | HMV CLP 1689 | TODAY AND NOW (LP) ........ 20 |
| 64 | CBS BPG 62157 | BACK IN BEAN'S BAG (LP, with Clark Terry) ........ 15 |
| 64 | Fontana FJL 102 | SWING' (LP) ........ 15 |
| 65 | Fontana TL 5273 | MEDITATION (LP) ........ 15 |
| 66 | Fontana SJL 131 | CATTIN' (LP) ........ 15 |

*(see also Milt Jackson & Coleman Hawkins, Eddie 'Lockjaw' Davis, Sir Charles Thompson)*

**COLEMAN HAWKINS GROUP**

| | | |
|---|---|---|
| 58 | London LTZC 15048 | COLEMAN HAWKINS GROUP (LP) ........ 18 |

*(see also Coleman Hawkins)*

**COLEMAN HAWKINS & LESTER YOUNG**

| | | |
|---|---|---|
| 65 | Stateside SL 10117 | CLASSIC TENORS (LP) ........ 20 |

**DALE HAWKINS**

| | | |
|---|---|---|
| 57 | London HL 8482 | Susie-Q/Don't Treat Me That Way ........ 500 |
| 57 | London HL 8482 | Susie-Q/Don't Treat Me That Way (78) ........ 80 |
| 58 | London HLM 8728 | La-Do-Dada/Cross Ties ........ 40 |
| 59 | London HLM 8842 | Yea-Yea (Glass Cutter)/Lonely Nights ........ 40 |
| 59 | London HLM 9016 | Liza Jane/Back To School Blues ........ 40 |
| 60 | London HLM 9060 | Hot Dog/Our Turn ........ 40 |
| 69 | Bell SBLL 127 | L.A., MEMPHIS AND TYLER, TEXAS (LP) ........ 15 |
| 73 | Checker 6467 301 | OH! SUSIE Q (LP) ........ 15 |

**ERSKINE HAWKINS QUINTET**

| | | |
|---|---|---|
| 60 | Brunswick LAT 8374 | THE HAWK BLOWS AT MIDNIGHT (LP, also stereo STA 3042) ........ 15 |

**HAWKSHAW HAWKINS**

| | | |
|---|---|---|
| 54 | Parlophone CMSP 1 | Betty Lorraine/CHARLIE GORE & LOUIS INNIS: Mexican Joe (export issue) ........ 30 |
| 63 | London HL 9737 | Lonesome 7-7203/Everything Has Changed ........ 10 |
| 58 | Parlophone GEP 8742 | COUNTRY AND WESTERN (EP) ........ 30 |
| 58 | Vogue VE 170117 | HAWKSHAW HAWKINS - COUNTRY AND WESTERN (EP) ........ 30 |
| 64 | London HA 8181 | THE ALL NEW HAWKSHAW HAWKINS (LP) ........ 20 |

*(see also Charlie Gore, Louis Innis)*

**RONNIE HAWKINS (& HAWKS)**

| | | |
|---|---|---|
| 59 | Columbia DB 4319 | Forty Days (To Come Back Home)/One Of These Days ........ 50 |
| 59 | Columbia DB 4345 | Mary Lou/Need Your Lovin' (Oh So Bad) ........ 50 |
| 60 | Columbia DB 4412 | Southern Love (Whatcha-Gonna' Do)/Love Me Like You Can ........ 20 |
| 60 | Columbia DB 4442 | Clara/Lonely Hours ........ 30 |
| 63 | Columbia DB 7036 | Bo Diddley/Who Do You Love? ........ 30 |
| 70 | Roulette RO 512 | Who Do You Love?/Bo Diddley ........ 5 |

# Screamin' JAY HAWKINS

| | | | |
|---|---|---|---|
| 70 | Atlantic 584 320 | Down In The Alley/Matchbox | 7 |
| 70 | Atlantic 2091 007 | Bitter Green/Forty Days | 5 |
| 72 | Monument MNT 8292 | Cora Mae/Ain't That A Shame | 5 |
| 60 | Columbia SEG 7983 | ROCKIN' WITH RONNIE (EP, mono) | 50 |
| 60 | Columbia ESG 7792 | ROCKIN' WITH RONNIE (EP, stereo) | 90 |
| 60 | Columbia SEG 7988 | ROCKIN' WITH RONNIE (EP, mono) | 50 |
| 60 | Columbia ESG 7795 | ROCKIN' WITH RONNIE (EP, stereo) | 90 |
| 60 | Columbia 33SX 1238 | MR. DYNAMO (LP, mono) | 50 |
| 60 | Columbia SCX 3315 | MR. DYNAMO (LP, stereo) | 90 |
| 60 | Columbia 33SX 1295 | THE FOLK BALLADS OF RONNIE HAWKINS (LP, mono) | 40 |
| 60 | Columbia SCX 3358 | THE FOLK BALLADS OF RONNIE HAWKINS (LP, stereo) | 50 |
| 70 | Roulette RCP 1003 | ARKANSAS ROCK PILE (LP, with The Band) | 20 |

*(see also Band, Levon & Hawks)*

## SCREAMIN' JAY HAWKINS

| | | | |
|---|---|---|---|
| 58 | Fontana H 107 | I Put A Spell On You/Little Demon (78) | 60 |
| 65 | Columbia DB 7460 | The Whammy/Strange | 40 |
| 65 | Sue WI 379 | I Hear Voices/Just Don't Care | 40 |
| 66 | Sue WI 4008 | I Put A Spell On You/Little Demon (unissued) | 0 |
| 69 | Direction 58-4097 | I Put A Spell On You/Little Demon | 20 |
| 80 | Polydor POSP 183 | I Put A Spell On You/Armpit 6 (with Keith Richards) | 10 |
| 66 | Planet PLL 1001 | THE NIGHT AND DAY OF SCREAMIN' JAY HAWKINS (LP) | 125 |
| 69 | Direction (S) 8-63481 | I PUT A SPELL ON YOU (LP, mono or stereo) | 70 |
| 69 | Mercury SMCL 20178 | WHAT THAT IS (LP) | 50 |

*(see also Keith Richards)*

## HAWKLORDS

| | | | |
|---|---|---|---|
| 78 | Charisma HL 1 | PSI Power/Death Trap (no p/s, promo only) | 12 |
| 78 | Charisma CB 323 | PSI Power/Death Trap (no p/s) | 8 |
| 79 | Charisma CB 332 | 25 Years/(Only) The Dead Dreams Of A Cold War Kid (no p/s) | 6 |
| 79 | Charisma CB 332 12 | 25 Years/(Only) The Dead Dreams Of A Cold War Kid/PXR 5 (12", grey vinyl) | 10 |
| 79 | Charisma CB 332 12 | 25 Years/(Only) The Dead Dreams Of A Cold War Kid/PXR 5 (12", mispressed on black vinyl) | 12 |
| 82 | Flicknife FLS 209 | Who's Gonna Win The War?/Time Of (p/s) | 6 |
| 78 | Charisma CDS 4014 | 25 YEARS ON (LP, with inner sleeve, sold with separate tour book) | 20 |
| 78 | Charisma CDS 4014 | 25 YEARS ON (LP, with inner sleeve) | 15 |

*(see also Hawkwind)*

## HAWKS (1)

| | | | |
|---|---|---|---|
| 69 | Stateside SS 2147 | The Grissle/SHEEP: Hide And Seek | 12 |

## HAWKS (2)

| | | | |
|---|---|---|---|
| 81 | Five Believers FB 001 | Words Of Hope/Sense Of Ending (p/s) | 12 |

*(see also Lilac Time, Stephen 'Tin Tin' Duffy)*

## ALAN HAWKSHAW

| | | | |
|---|---|---|---|
| 70 | Tangerine DP 0005 | Puppet On A String/Everybody Knows | 5 |
| 79 | BBC RESL 64 | Grange Hill/Stoned (credited to Deluxe) | 20 |
| 72 | Studio Two TWO 391 | 27 TOP TV THEMES AND COMMERCIALS (LP) | 30 |
| 72 | KPM 1080 | FLUTE FOR MODERNS (with Alan Parker and Joe Hailer) (LP) | 35 |

*(see also Shadows, Bizarre)*

## JOHNNY HAWKSWORTH (ORCHESTRA)

| | | | |
|---|---|---|---|
| 65 | Pye 7N 15969 | Lunar Walk/It's Murder (as Johnny Hawksworth Orchestra) | 15 |
| 66 | Columbia DB 8059 | Goal/"Goal - World Cup 1966" Theme (as Sounds Of Johnny Hawksworth) | 6 |
| 67 | Columbia DB 8129 | Wack Wack/On The Tiles | 8 |
| 64 | Columbia 33SX 1654 | I'VE GROWN ACCUSTOMED TO MY BASS (LP) | 50 |

*(see also Johnny's Jazz)*

## HAWKSWORTH-VERRELL JAZZ GROUP

| | | | |
|---|---|---|---|
| 56 | Decca FJ 10726 | Ring Dem Bells/Always | 6 |

## HAWKWIND

### SINGLES

| | | | |
|---|---|---|---|
| 70 | Liberty LBF 15382 | Hurry On Sundown/Mirror Of Illusion | 300 |
| 72 | United Artists UP 35381 | Silver Machine/Seven By Seven ('machine' art p/s) | 15 |
| 73 | United Artists (WD 3637) | Sonic Attack (1-sided promo in cloth sleeve) | 250 |
| 73 | United Artists UP 35566 | Urban Guerilla/Brainbox Pollution | 15 |
| 73 | United Artists USEP 1 | HURRY ON HAWKWIND (EP) | 50 |
| 74 | United Artists UP 35715 | The Psychedelic Warlords (Disappear In Smoke)/It's So Easy | 10 |
| 75 | United Artists UP 35808 | Kings Of Speed/Motorhead (in p/s) | 40 |
| 75 | United Artists UP 35808 | Kings Of Speed/Motorhead | 10 |
| 76 | Charisma CB 289 | Kerb Crawler/Honky Dorky | 10 |
| 77 | Charisma CB 299 | Back On The Streets/The Dream Of Isis (p/s) | 8 |
| 77 | Charisma CB 305 | Quark, Strangeness & Charm/Forge Of Vulcan | 8 |
| 78 | United Artists UP 35381 | Silver Machine/Seven By Seven (reissue, black-on-white p/s) | 6 |
| 78 | United Artists 12UP 35381 | Silver Machine/Seven By Seven (12", silver p/s) | 10 |
| 80 | Bronze BRO 98 | Shot Down In The Night/Urban Guerilla (p/s) | 5 |
| 80 | Bronze BRO 98 | Shot Down In The Night/Urban Guerilla (1-sided gold vinyl flexidisc) | 30 |
| 80 | Bronze BRO 109 | Who's Gonna Win The War?/Nuclear Toy (p/s, cream labels) | 12 |
| 80 | Bronze BRO 109 | Who's Gonna Win The War?/Nuclear Toy (p/s, green labels) | 5 |
| 81 | RCA RCA 137 | Angels Of Death/Trans-Dimensional Man (p/s) | 5 |
| 82 | RCA Active RCA 267 | Silver Machine/Silver Machine (Full Version)/Psychedelic Warlords (p/s) | 5 |
| 82 | RCA Active RCAP 267 | Silver Machine/(Full Version)/Psychedelic Warlords (picture disc) | 10 |
| 82 | Flicknife FLS 005 | Motorhead/Valium Ten (p/s) | 5 |
| 83 | United Artists UP 35381 | Silver Machine/Seven By Seven (reissue, white-on-black p/s) | 5 |

| | | | |
|---|---|---|---|
| 83 | Liberty UPP 35381 | Silver Machine/Seven By Seven (picture disc) | 12 |
| 83 | Liberty UPP 35381 | Silver Machine/Seven By Seven (mispressed picture disc, plays Beatles' "Ask Me Why") | 15 |
| 83 | Flicknife FLS 025 | Motorway City/Master Of The Universe (p/s) | 5 |
| 83 | Flicknife FLS 214 | Hawkwind And Co: Your Last Chance (p/s, sampler with Robert Calvert & Michael Moorcock) | 6 |
| 85 | Flicknife FLS 032 | Needle Gun/Arioch (p/s) | 5 |
| 85 | Flicknife FLST 032 | Needle Gun (extended)/Arioch (p/s) | 8 |
| 86 | Flicknife FLS 033 | Zarozinia/Assault And Battery (live) (p/s) | 5 |
| 86 | Samurai HW 001 | Silver Machine/Magnu (motorcycle-shaped picture disc) | 15 |
| 86 | Flicknife FLS 034-A | Motorhead/Hurry On Sundown (p/s with insert) | 5 |
| 90 | Receiver REPLAY 3014 | THE EARLY YEARS LIVE (12", p/s, blue vinyl) | 15 |
| 93 | 4 Real 4R 1 | SPIRIT OF THE AGE (SOLSTICE REMIXES) (12" EP) | 12 |
| 93 | 4 Real 4R 2 | DECIDE YOUR FUTURE (12" EP) | 10 |
| 94 | Emerg. Broadcast EBS 110 | QUARK, STRANGENESS & CHARM (12" EP, clear vinyl, 200 only) | 15 |

**ALBUMS**

| | | | |
|---|---|---|---|
| 70 | Liberty LBS 83348 | HAWKWIND (LP, gatefold sleeve; blue label) | 350 |
| 70 | Liberty LBS 83348 | HAWKWIND (LP, gatefold sleeve; black label) | 50 |
| 71 | United Artists UAG 29202 | IN SEARCH OF SPACE (LP in foldout 'door' sleeve, with 'log book') | 80 |
| 71 | United Artists UAG 29202 | IN SEARCH OF SPACE (LP in foldout 'door' sleeve, without 'log book') | 50 |
| 72 | United Artists UAG 29364 | DOREMI-FASOL-LATIDO (LP, with inner sleeve, with poster) | 80 |
| 72 | United Artists UAG 29364 | DOREMI-FASOL-LATIDO (LP, with inner sleeve, without poster) | 40 |
| 73 | Utd. Artists UAD 60037/8 | SPACE RITUAL ALIVE (2-LP, foldout sleeve with inners) | 40 |
| 74 | United Artists UAG 29672 | HALL OF THE MOUNTAIN GRILL (LP, with inner sleeve) | 25 |
| 75 | United Artists UAG 29766 | WARRIOR ON THE EDGE OF TIME (LP, foldout pop-up sleeve with inner) | 70 |
| 76 | United Artists UAK 29919 | ROADHAWKS (LP, gatefold sleeve with poster & sticker) | 20 |
| 76 | Mushroom | THE XENON CODEX (LP, with inner, gatefold sleeve) | 15 |
| 77 | Charisma CDS 4008 | QUARK STRANGENESS AND CHARM (LP) | 20 |
| 79 | Charisma CDS 4016 | P.X.R.5 (LP, with family tree poster, with picture of incorrectly wired plug on rear) | 30 |
| 79 | United Artists UAG 29766 | WARRIOR ON THE EDGE OF TIME (LP, reissue) | 20 |
| 79 | Charisma CDS 4016 | P.X.R.5 (LP, without family tree poster, but with uncensored wired plug on rear) | 15 |
| 80 | Bronze BRON 530 | LEVITATION (LP, blue vinyl) | 20 |
| 82 | RCA Active RCALP 9004 | CHURCH OF HAWKWIND (LP, with lyric booklet) | 15 |
| 84 | Liberty SLP 1972921 | HAWKWIND (LP, reissue, picture disc, die-cut) | 15 |
| 84 | Flicknife PSHARP 014 | ZONES (LP, picture disc) | 12 |
| 84 | Flicknife SHARP 022 | STONHENGE: THIS IS HAWKWIND DO NOT PANIC (LP, with 12", gatefold sleeve or single sleeve with poster) | 15 |
| 86 | Hawkfan HWFB 2 | HAWKFAN 12 (LP, with poster, sticker insert & carrier bag, 600 only) | 70 |
| 86 | Samurai SMR 046 | APPROVED HISTORY OF HAWKWIND 1967-1982 (3-LP, pic discs & booklet) | 45 |
| 87 | Flicknife HWBOX 01 | OFFICIAL PICTURE LOG BOOK (4-LP box set, [3 picture discs & interview disc] with badge & insert) | 35 |
| 92 | Essential ESSLP 181 | ELECTRIC TEPEE (2-LP, 5,000 only, numbered) | 35 |
| 94 | Emerg. Broadcast EBS 111 | THE BUSINESS TRIP (2-LP, clear vinyl, 1,500 only) | 25 |
| 95 | Emergency Broadcast System EBSLP 118 | ALIEN 4 (2-LP, gatefold sleeve) | 18 |
| 96 | Emergency Broadcast System EBSLP 120 | LOVE IN SPACE (2-LP, gatefold) | 30 |

*(see also Hawklords, Robert Calvert, Michael Moorcock, Inner City Unit, Sphynx, Dave Brock, Tim Blake, Huw Lloyd Langton Group, Alan Davey, Motorhead, Dr. Technical & Machines, Magic Muscle, Opal Butterfly, Widowmaker, Adrian Shaw, Captain Jesus And The Sunray Team)*

**DEANE HAWLEY**

| | | | |
|---|---|---|---|
| 61 | Liberty LIB 55359 | Pocketful Of Rainbows/That Dream Could Never Be | 10 |

**RICHARD HAWLEY**

| | | | |
|---|---|---|---|
| 05 | Mute 347 | The Ocean/Kelham Island | 5 |
| 05 | Mute 352 | Coles Corner/A Bird Never Flew On One Wing (p/s) | 5 |
| 06 | Mute 362 | Born Under A Bad Sign/I'm Just Here To Get My Baby Out Of Jail (numbered p/s) | 7 |
| 07 | Mute 282 | Tonight The Streets Are Ours/Vickers Road | 5 |
| 12 | Parlophone RHSCBOX | THE SINGLE CLUB 1-IV (4 x 10" box set) | 50 |
| 03 | Setanta SETLP 110 | LOWLEDGES (LP) | 70 |
| 05 | Mute STUMM 251 | COLES CORNER (LP) | 80 |
| 09 | Mute STUMM 312 | TRUELOVE'S GUTTER (2-LP, CD & signed print, 100 only) | 70 |
| 14 | Setanta SETLP 088 | LATE NIGHT FINAL (LP, reissue) | 20 |
| 14 | Setanta SETLP 153 | RICHARD HAWLEY (LP, reissue) | 20 |

**GOLDIE HAWN**

| | | | |
|---|---|---|---|
| 72 | Reprise K 14211 | Carey/I'll Be Your Baby Tonight | 6 |

**HAYDEN WOOD**

| | | | |
|---|---|---|---|
| 69 | NEMS 56 4499 | House Beside The Mine/Lady Wants More | 25 |
| 70 | NEMS 4803 | Sixty Years On/The Last One To Know | 25 |
| 73 | Jam JAM 46 | I Don't Want To Lose You/Hand Me Down | 6 |

**HAYDOCK'S ROCKHOUSE**

| | | | |
|---|---|---|---|
| 66 | Columbia DB 8050 | Cupid/She Thinks | 70 |
| 67 | Columbia DB 8135 | Lovin' You/Mix A Fix | 60 |

*(see also Hollies)*

**BILL HAYES**

| | | | |
|---|---|---|---|
| 53 | MGM SP 1036 | The Donkey Song/My Ever-Lovin' | 15 |
| 55 | London HL 8149 | The Berry Tree/Blue Black Hair | 25 |
| 56 | London HLA 8220 | Ballad Of Davy Crockett/Farewell | 25 |
| 56 | London HLA 8239 | Kwela Kwela/The White Buffalo | 20 |
| 56 | London HLA 8300 | Das Ist Musik/I Know An Old Lady | 20 |
| 56 | London HLA 8325 | The Legend Of Wyatt Earp/That Do Make It Nice | 15 |
| 57 | London HL 8430 | Wringle Wrangle/Westward Ho The Wagons | 15 |

# Isaac HAYES

| 59 | London HLR 8833 | Wimoweh/Goin' Down The Road Feelin' Bad (with Buckle Busters) | 5 |
|---|---|---|---|
| 56 | London RE-A 1051 | GREAT PIONEERS OF THE WEST (EP) | 15 |

## ISAAC HAYES
| 69 | Stax STAX 133 | Walk On By/By The Time I Get To Phoenix | 5 |
|---|---|---|---|
| 70 | Stax STAX 154 | I Stand Accused/I Just Don't Know What To Do With Myself | 5 |
| 71 | Stax 2025 020 | You've Lost That Lovin' Feelin'/Our Day Will Come | 5 |
| 71 | Stax 2025 029 | Never Can Say Goodbye/I Can't Help It (If I'm Still In Love With You) | 5 |
| 72 | Stax 2025 069 | Theme From "Shaft"/Cafe Regio's | 5 |
| 72 | Stax 2025 089 | Let's Stay Together/Ain't That Loving You (For More Reasons Than One) (with David Porter) | 5 |
| 72 | Stax 2025 146 | Theme From The Men/Type Thang | 5 |
| 74 | Stax STXS 2004 | Title Theme/Hung Up On My Baby (Instrumental) | 8 |
| 69 | Stax SXATS 1028 | HOT BUTTERED SOUL (LP) | 20 |
| 70 | Stax SXATS 1032 | THE ISAAC HAYES MOVEMENT (LP) | 18 |
| 70 | Stax 2465 016 | BLUE HAYES (LP) | 18 |
| 71 | Stax 2325 026 | TO BE CONTINUED (LP) | 20 |
| 72 | MGM 2315 115 | SHAFT'S BIG SCORE! (LP, soundtrack) | 35 |
| 72 | Stax 2628 004 | BLACK MOSES (2-LP, cruciform sleeve) | 50 |
| 73 | Stax 2362 032 | LIVE AT THE SAHARA TAHOE (2-LP) | 20 |

## LINDA HAYES
| 55 | Parlophone MSP 6174 | Please Have Mercy (with Platters)/Oochi Pachi (with Tony Williams) | 300 |
|---|---|---|---|
| 55 | Parlophone R 4038 | Please Have Mercy (with Platters)/Oochi Pachi (with Tony Williams) (78) | 50 |

(see also Platters)

## PETER LIND HAYES
| 60 | Brunswick 05821 | Life Gets Tee-jus Don't It/Sing Me A Happy Song | 8 |
|---|---|---|---|

(see also Peter & Mary)

## TUBBY HAYES
| 56 | Tempo A 148 | Ode To Ernie/No, I Woodyn't | 10 |
|---|---|---|---|
| 62 | Fontana H 397 | Sally/I Believe In You (as Tubby Hayes Quintet) | 25 |
| 55 | Tempo EXA 14 | THE LITTLE GIANT (EP) | 75 |
| 55 | Tempo EXA 17 | TUBBY HAYES AND HIS ORCHESTRA (EP) | 30 |
| 55 | Tempo EXA 27 | THE SWINGING GIANT NO. 1 (EP, as Tubby Hayes Quartet) | 50 |
| 56 | Tempo EXA 28 | THE SWINGING GIANT NO. 2 (EP, as Tubby Hayes Quartet) | 50 |
| 56 | Tempo EXA 36 | MODERN JAZZ SCENE (EP, as Tubby Hayes & His Orchestra) | 60 |
| 57 | Tempo EXA 55 | AFTER LIGHTS OUT (EP, as Tubby Hayes Quintet) | 60 |
| 57 | Tempo EXA 75 | TUBBY HAYES AND THE JAZZ COURIERS (EP) | 60 |
| 58 | Tempo EXA 82 | THE EIGHTH WONDER (EP, solo) | 60 |
| 09 | Trunk TTT005 | VOODOO SESSION (EP, 1st pressing 666 copies only) | 30 |
| 10 | Trunk TTT 005 | VOODOO SESSION (EP, reissue, different label, no p/s) | 10 |
| 57 | Tempo TAP 6 | AFTER LIGHTS OUT (LP, as Tubby Hayes Quintet) | 400 |
| 57 | Tempo TAP 15 | JAZZ COURIERS (LP) | 300 |
| 60 | Tempo TAP 29 | TUBBY'S GROOVE (LP, as Tubby Hayes Quartet) | 400 |
| 61 | Fontana TFL 5142 | TUBBS (LP, also stereo STFL 562) | 150 |
| 61 | Ember EMB 3337 | AN EVENING WITH MR. PERCUSSION (LP, with Tony Kinsey) | 70 |
| 61 | Fontana TFL 5183 | TUBBS IN NEW YORK (LP, also stereo STFL 595) | 120 |
| 63 | Fontana 680 998 TL | DOWN IN THE VILLAGE (LP, mono) | 350 |
| 63 | Fontana 886 163TY | DOWN IN THE VILLAGE (LP, stereo) | 250 |
| 64 | Fontana (S)TL 5195 | RETURN VISIT! (LP) | 140 |
| 64 | Fontana TL 5200 | LATE SPOT AT SCOTT'S (LP) | 250 |
| 66 | Fontana (S)TL 5221 | TUBBS' TOURS (LP, with Orchestra) | 70 |
| 66 | Fontana (S)TL 5410 | 100% PROOF (LP) | 70 |
| 67 | Wing WL 1162 | TUBBS IN NEW YORK (LP, reissue) | 15 |
| 69 | Fontana SFJL 911 | MEXICAN GREEN (LP) | 100 |
| 71 | Fontana 6309 002 | THE TUBBY HAYES ORCHESTRA (LP) | 30 |
| 72 | Philips 6382 041 | THIS IS JAZZ - 100% PROOF (LP) | 15 |
| 81 | Mole MOLE 2 | MEXICAN GREEN (LP, reissue) | 20 |
| 81 | Mole MOLE 4 | TUBBS' TOURS (LP, reissue) | 20 |
| 82 | Jasmine JASM 2015 | AFTER LIGHTS OUT (LP, reissue) | 20 |
| 90 | CBS Masterpieces CBS 466363-1 | TUBBY HAYES WITH CLARK TERRY THE NEW YORK SESSIONS (LP, reissue) | 25 |
| 90 | MMO 79 | 67 LIVE - FOR MEMBERS ONLY (LP) | 20 |
| 09 | Gearbox GB 1502 | BBC JAZZ FOR MODERNS (LP) | 30 |

(see also Jack Constanzo & Tubby Hayes, Jazz Couriers, London Jazz Quartet, Dave Lee, Ronnie Scott, Roy Castle)

## TUBBY HAYES & CLEO LAINE
| 61 | Fontana TFL 5151 | PALLADIUM JAZZ DATE (LP, also stereo STFL 570) | 20 |
|---|---|---|---|

(see also Cleo Laine)

## TUBBY HAYES & PAUL GONSALVES ALLSTARS
| 67 | Columbia SX 6003 | JUST FRIENDS (LP) | 110 |
|---|---|---|---|
| 60s | World Record Club T 631 | CHANGE OF SETTING (LP) | 120 |

(see also Paul Gonsalves)

## LOU HAYLES
| 77 | Myrrh MYR 1055 | DON'T HIDE AWAY (LP) | 22 |
|---|---|---|---|

## ROY HAYNES QUARTET
| 62 | HMV CLP 1628 | OUT OF THE AFTERNOON (LP) | 30 |
|---|---|---|---|

## ROY HAYNES, PHINEAS NEWBORN, PAUL CHAMBERS TRIO
| 61 | Esquire 32-103 | WE THREE (LP) | 30 |
|---|---|---|---|

## STEVE HAYNES BAND
| 78 | Black Bear BLA 2005 | Back In My Arms Again/Walk On By (p/s) | 20 |
|---|---|---|---|
| 78 | Black Bear BLA 2008 | Save Me Save Me/Strong Good Lovin' (p/s) | 15 |

### HAYSTACK
| | | | |
|---|---|---|---|
| 69 | United Artists UP 35024 | Letter To Josephine/Love You're Making A Fool Of Me | 6 |
| 69 | United Artists UP 35035 | Tahiti Farewell/Pantomime People | 6 |

### HAYSTACKS BALBOA
| | | | |
|---|---|---|---|
| 70 | Polydor | Spoiler/Bruce's Twist | 25 |
| 70 | Polydor 2489 002 | HAYSTACKS BALBOA (LP) | 100 |

### JUSTIN HAYWARD
| | | | |
|---|---|---|---|
| 65 | Pye 7N 17041 | London Is Behind Me/Day Must Come | 150 |
| 66 | Parlophone R 5496 | I Can't Face The World Without You/I'll Be Here Tomorrow | 200 |
| 77 | Deram DM 428 | One Lonely Room/Songwriter (Part 2) | 7 |
| 80 | CBS 11-7731 | The Eve Of The War/Horsell (12" picture disc) | 15 |

*(see also Wilde Three)*

### RICK HAYWARD
| | | | |
|---|---|---|---|
| 71 | Blue Horizon 2431 006 | RICK HAYWARD (LP) | 200 |

*(see also Accent, Christine Perfect)*

### SUSAN HAYWARD
| | | | |
|---|---|---|---|
| 62 | Fontana 267224 | You Bet I Would/I Won't Give My Lips To Anyone | 6 |

### JOE HAYWOOD
| | | | |
|---|---|---|---|
| 65 | Island WI 218 | Warm And Tender Love/I Would If I Could | 25 |

### LEON HAYWOOD
| | | | |
|---|---|---|---|
| 66 | Vocalion VL 9280 | Ain't No Use/Hey, Hey, Hey | 30 |
| 66 | Vocalion VL 9280 | Ain't No Use/Hey, Hey, Hey (DJ copy) | 50 |
| 67 | Vocalion VL 9288 | Ever Since You Were Sweet Sixteen/Skate Awhile | 30 |
| 69 | MCA Soul Bag BAG 5 | Mellow Moonlight/Tennessee Waltz | 10 |
| 70 | Capitol CL 15634 | I Wanna Thank You/I Was Sent To Love You | 15 |
| 73 | Pye International 7N 25611 | La La Song/There Ain't Enough Hate Around To Make Me Turn Around | 5 |
| 75 | 20th Century BTC 2191 | Come On And Get Yourself Some/BMF (Beautiful) | 5 |
| 75 | 20th Century BTC 2228 | I Wanta Do Something Freaky To You/I Know What Love Is | 6 |
| 78 | Fantasy FTC 151 | Baby Reconsider/Would I | 20 |
| 67 | Vocalion VAL 8064 | SOUL CARGO (LP) | 75 |
| 69 | MCA MUPS 369 | IT'S GOT TO BE MELLOW (LP) | 20 |
| 73 | Pye Intl. NSPL 28177 | BACK TO STAY (LP) | 25 |
| 75 | 20th Century BT 476 | COME AND GET YOURSELF SOME (LP) | 15 |

### HAZARD
| | | | |
|---|---|---|---|
| 79 | Rok ROK VII/VIII | Gotta Change My Life/CLERKS: No Good For Me | 15 |

### HAZE (1)
| | | | |
|---|---|---|---|
| 74 | Haze HAZE 00174 | HAZE (LP, 100 only) | 100 |

### HAZE (2)
| | | | |
|---|---|---|---|
| 81 | Mushroom MUSH 1 | The Night/Dig Them Mushrooms | 20 |
| 84 | Gabadon GABL 001 | C'EST LA VIE (LP) | 25 |

### HAZEL
| | | | |
|---|---|---|---|
| 93 | Sub Pop SP74 241 | Jilted (blue vinyl) | 5 |

### HAZEL & JOLLY BOYS
| | | | |
|---|---|---|---|
| 67 | Doctor Bird DB 1063 | Stop Them/Deep Down | 20 |

### HAMMOND HAZLEWOOD
| | | | |
|---|---|---|---|
| 67 | Pye 7N 17273 | I Can Make The Rain Fall Up/The Hawkmoth And The Flame | 12 |
| 69 | Columbia DB 8579 | Hey Love, Let Me In/Let The Sunshine In | 10 |

### LEE HAZLEWOOD
| | | | |
|---|---|---|---|
| 60 | London HLW 9223 | Words Mean Nothing/The Girl On Death Row (with Duane Eddy) | 35 |
| 66 | MGM MGM 1310 | Sand/My Autumn's Done Come | 10 |
| 67 | MGM MGM 1348 | My Baby Cried All Night Long/These Boots Are Made For Walkin' | 12 |
| 67 | Reprise RS 20613 | Ode To Billie Joe/Charlie Bill Nelson | 10 |
| 68 | Reprise RS 20667 | Rainbow Woman/I Am, You Are | 10 |
| 72 | RCA RCA 2185 | Big Red Balloon/Down From Dover (with Nancy Sinatra) | 10 |
| 73 | Stateside SS 2225 | Poet/Come Spend The Morning | 10 |
| 66 | MGM MGM-CS 8014 | THE VERY SPECIAL WORLD OF LEE HAZLEWOOD (LP) | 30 |
| 68 | Reprise RSLP 6297 | LOVE AND OTHER CRIMES (LP) | 25 |
| 69 | London HA-N/SH-N 8398 | TROUBLE IS A LONESOME TOWN (LP) | 40 |
| 72 | Reprise K 44161 | REQUIEM FOR AN ALMOST LADY (LP) | 35 |
| 74 | Stateside SSL 10315 | POET, FOOL OR BUM (LP) | 30 |

*(see also Nancy Sinatra & Lee Hazlewood, Duane Eddy)*

### OSTERWALK HAZY
| | | | |
|---|---|---|---|
| 72 | Jam JAM 22 | Oumbalo Oumbalo/Tai Weh | 15 |

### HAZZARD
| | | | |
|---|---|---|---|
| 81 | Rammy EJSP9600 | Snake In The Grass/Kicked To The Ground (p/s) | 100 |

### TONY HAZZARD
| | | | |
|---|---|---|---|
| 66 | Columbia DB 7927 | You'll Never Put Shackles On Me/Calling You Home | 20 |
| 68 | CBS 3452 | Sound Of The Candyman's Trumpet/Everything's Gone Wrong | 5 |
| 69 | CBS 63608 | TONY HARRARD SINGS (LP, orange label) | 60 |
| 71 | Bronze ILPS 9174 | LOUDWATER HOUSE (LP, gatefold sleeve, lyric inner sleeve) | 20 |
| 73 | Bronze ILPS 9222 | WAS THAT ALRIGHT THEN? (LP, gatefold sleeve, lyric inner sleeve) | 20 |

### MICHAEL HEAD & STRANDS
| | | | |
|---|---|---|---|
| 95 | Megaphone Music MEGA 01 | THE MAGICAL WORLD OF THE STRANDS (LP, gatefold sleeve) | 60 |

*(see also Pale Saints, Shack)*

### ROY HEAD (& TRAITS)
| | | | |
|---|---|---|---|
| 65 | Pye International 7N 25340 | Just A Little Bit/Treat Me Right | 20 |
| 65 | Vocalion VP 9248 | Treat Her Right/So Long, My Love | 20 |

| 66 | Vocalion VP 9254 | Apple Of My Eye/I Pass The Day | 15 |
| 66 | Vocalion VP 9269 | My Babe/Pain | 20 |
| 66 | Vocalion VP 9274 | Wigglin' And Gigglin'/Driving Wheel | 20 |
| 66 | London HLZ 10097 | To Make A Big Man Cry/Don't Cry No More | 15 |
| 70 | Stateside SS 8050 | Mama Mama/I'm Not A Fool Anymore | 7 |
| 75 | London HLD 10487 | The Most Wanted Woman In Town/Gingers Breadman | 8 |
| 66 | Pye Intl. NEP 44053 | JUST A LITTLE BIT OF ROY HEAD (EP) | 50 |
| 70 | Stateside SSL 5033 | SAME PEOPLE (LP) | 25 |

*(see also Traits)*

## HEAD (1)
| 75 | Canon CNN 5970 | RED DWARF (LP) | 40 |

## HEAD (2)
| 77 | HEAD HSLP333333333C | BLACKPOOL COOL (LP) | 60 |

## HEAD (3)
| 79 | Ellie Jay MB1 | Nothing To Do In A Town Like Leatherhead/University '79 | 60 |
| 96 | Headhunter HH 7 01 | Gnu/Demonizer 48/48 (p/s, 1000 only) | 15 |

## HEADACHE
| 77 | Lout 001 | Can't Stand Still/No Reason For Your Call (p/s) | 20 |

## HEAD ARSE FUSION BAND
| 00 | U-Star US 009 | UNTITLED EP (12") | 40 |

## HEADBOYS
| 79 | RSO 40 | The Shape Of Things To Come/The Mood I'm In (p/s) | 6 |
| 79 | RSO 49 | Stepping Stones/Before Tonight | 5 |

## HEADCLEANERS
| 83 | Xcentric Noise THIRD 1 | THE INFECTION GROWS EP | 70 |

## HEADCOATEES (THEE)
| 91 | Damaged Goods DAMGOOD 12 | Santa Claus/Evil Things (picture disc) | 5 |

*(see also Milkshakes, Headcoatees)*

## HEADCOATS (THEE)
| 89 | Hangman HANG 29 UP | HEADCOATS DOWN (LP) | 18 |
| 90 | Hangman HANG 32 UP | THE KIDS ARE ALL SQUARE (LP) | 18 |
| 91 | Hangman HANG 40 UP | W.O.A.H. (LP) | 18 |
| 01 | Hangman HANG 54 UP | LIVE AT THE DIRTY WATER CLUB (LP) | 18 |

*(see also Milkshakes, Thee Headcoats)*

## HEADHUNTERS
| 76 | Arista ARTY 116 | SURVIVAL OF THE FITTEST (LP) | 25 |

*(see also Herbie Hancock)*

## HEADLESS CHICKENS
| 89 | Hometown Atrocities 1 | THE HOMETOWN ATROCITIES EP (wraparound p/s with 3 inserts, 'kylie') | 100 |
| 89 | Hometown Atrocities 1 | THE HOMETOWN ATROCITIES EP (wraparound p/s, 'glossy') | 40 |
| 89 | Maelstrom Storm 1 | THE HOMETOWN ATROCITIES EP (repress of above) | 15 |

*(see also Radiohead)*

## HEADLINERS (1)
| 59 | Parlophone R 4593 | The Bubble Car Song/Andy's Theme | 7 |

## HEADLINERS (2)
| 65 | Decca F 12209 | That's The Way I Must Go/Four Seasons | 8 |
| 65 | Decca F 12279 | What Became Of Love/Even Though | 7 |

## HEAD MACHINE
| 70 | Major Minor SMLP 79 | ORGASM (LP, laminated front sleeve, red/white/black labels) | 400 |

*(see also Uriah Heep)*

## MURRAY HEAD
| 65 | Columbia DB 7635 | Alberta/He Was A Friend Of Mine | 8 |
| 65 | Columbia DB 7771 | The Bells Of Rhymney/Don't Sing No Sad Songs For Me | 10 |
| 67 | Columbia DB 8102 | Someday Soon/You Bore Me | 8 |
| 67 | Immediate IM 053 | She Was Perfection/Secondhand Monday | 70 |
| 69 | MCA MK 5019 | Superstar/John 1941 (p/s, with Trinidad Singers) | 7 |
| 71 | MCA MKS 5019 | Superstar/John 1941 (p/s, reissue) | 6 |
| 73 | CBS 65503 | NIGEL LIVED (LP, gatefold sleeve and booklet) | 30 |

## HEAD OF DAVID
| 89 | Blast First WANT 001 | WHITE ELEPHANT (LP, mail-order only) | 15 |

## HEADS
| 94 | Rooster ROOSTER 1 | Quad/Woke Up/Looking At You (p/s, 500 only, with "Rizla" papers) | 45 |
| 94 | Rooster ROOSTER 1 | Quad/Woke Up/Looking At You (p/s, 500 only, without "Rizla" papers) | 30 |
| 95 | Headhunter HED 718 | Television/Steamroller '95/Jellystoned Park (8.47 Edit) (p/s) | 20 |
| 95 | Rooster ROOSTER 2 | Coogan's Bluff/J Walking/Theme (p/s 1000 only) | 20 |
| 97 | Butchers Hook HOOK 003 | Dirty Water/MAGIC DIRT: Goofy Dumb (p/s, 1000 only) | 10 |
| 98 | Rocket LAUNCH 1 | You Can Lean Back/LILLYDAMWHITE: Master F (p/s, 550 only, insert) | 10 |
| 00 | Rocket LAUNCH 008 | Spliff Riff (Conga'd Out)/75 (All Of It) (p/s, 4 inserts, First press 100 yellow vinyl) | 20 |
| 00 | Rocket LAUNCH 008 | Spliff Riff (Conga'd Out)/75 (All Of It) (p/s, 4 inserts, First press 400 black vinyl) | 15 |
| 00 | Rocket LAUNCH 008 | Spliff Riff (Conga'd Out)/75 (All Of It) (p/s, 4 inserts, Second press, 300 purple vinyl) | 10 |
| 95 | Headhunter HUK 001 | RELAXING WITH... (LP) | 40 |
| 00 | Sweet Nothing SNLP 007 | EVERYBODY KNOWS WE GOT NOWHERE (2-LP) | 35 |
| 02 | Rocket LAUNCH 015 | SESSIONS 02 (LP, limited edition of 100, blue vinyl with free 7", 10 inserts) | 100 |
| 02 | Rocket LAUNCH 015 | SESSIONS 02 (LP, 900 copies, black vinyl) | 35 |
| 02 | Sweet Nothing SNLP 011 | UNDER SIDED (2-LP) | 30 |
| 03 | Rocket LAUNCH 018 | AT LAST (LP) | 35 |
| 05 | Invada INV 015 | 33 (LP, blue or black vinyl) | 20 |

| | | | |
|---|---|---|---|
| 05 | Invada INV 017 | DEAD IN THE WATER (2-LP, pink marbled vinyl) | 30 |
| 06 | Rocket/Invada LAUNCH 26/ INVLP 24 | UNDER THE STRESS OF A HEADLONG DIVE (2-LP) | 20 |
| 09 | Rocket LAUNCH 033LP | COLLISIONS V.1 (LP, one side Heads one side WHITE HILLS, 150 orange vinyl with poster) | 30 |
| 09 | Rocket LAUNCH 033LP | COLLISIONS V.1 (LP, one side Heads one side WHITE HILLS, 150 orange vinyl without poster) | 20 |

**HEADS TOGETHER**
| | | | |
|---|---|---|---|
| 74 | SRT SRTM 73345 | FUNKY STUFF (LP) | 35 |

**HEADS, HANDS & FEET**
| | | | |
|---|---|---|---|
| 71 | Island WIP 6115 | Warming Up The Band/Silver Mine | 5 |
| 71 | Island ILPS 9149 | HEADS, HANDS AND FEET (LP, gatefold, pink rim palm tree label) | 25 |
| 72 | Island ILPS 9185 | TRACKS (LP, gatefold, pink rim palm tree label) | 22 |
| 73 | Atlantic K40465 | OLD SOLIDERS NEVER DIE (LP, gatefold sleeve, lyric insert) | 15 |

(see also Don Everly, Tony Colton, Poet & One Man Band)

**HEADSTONE**
| | | | |
|---|---|---|---|
| 74 | EMI EMA 766 | BAD HABITS (LP, gatefold sleeve) | 20 |
| 75 | EMI EMC 3673 | HEADSTONE (LP) | 20 |

**HEALEY SISTERS**
| | | | |
|---|---|---|---|
| 64 | HMV POP 1313 | Give Me Back My Heart/After The Party | 8 |

**HEART BEATS**
| | | | |
|---|---|---|---|
| 80 | Red Shadow REDS 2 | Talk To Me/Don't Want Romance (p/s) | 5 |
| 81 | Nothing Shaking SHAD 1 | Go/One Of The People (p/s, blue vinyl) | 15 |

**HEART BOUND**
| | | | |
|---|---|---|---|
| 74 | Decca F 13510 | Baby Ruth/Sailor Man | 8 |

**HEART (1)**
| | | | |
|---|---|---|---|
| 76 | Arista Arista 80 | Crazy On You/Soul Of The Sea | 6 |
| 77 | Arista ARISTA 140 | Heartless/Here Song (withdrawn) | 8 |
| 87 | Capitol CLP 457 | Who Will You Run To?/Nobody Home (picture disc) | 10 |
| 77 | Arista SPART 1024 | MAGAZINE (LP, withdrawn) | 15 |
| 77 | Arista SPART 1024 | MAGAZINE (LP, picture disc) | 15 |
| 90 | Capitol HGIFT 1 | HEART BOX SET (3-LP: "Heart", "Bad Animals" & "Brigade" + 24pp booklet) | 18 |

**HEART (2)**
| | | | |
|---|---|---|---|
| 78 | On U Sound LP 20 | NOAH HOUSE OF DREAD (LP) | 30 |

**HEARTBEAT**
| | | | |
|---|---|---|---|
| 79 | Chancery CH 42 | Operator/Bounce Right Back (no p/s) | 8 |

**HEARTBREAKERS**
| | | | |
|---|---|---|---|
| 77 | Track 2094 135 | Chinese Rocks/Born To Lose (p/s) | 10 |
| 77 | Track 2094 135T | Chinese Rocks/Born To Lose (12", p/s) | 15 |
| 77 | Track 2094 137 | One Track Mind/Can't Keep My Eyes On You (live)/Do You Love Me (p/s) | 10 |
| 77 | Track 2094 142 | It's Not Enough/Let Go (p/s, withdrawn) | 250 |
| 79 | Beggars Banquet BEG 21 | Get Off The Phone (live)/I Wanna Be Loved (live) (p/s) | 5 |
| 77 | Track 2409 218 | L.A.M.F. (LP) | 35 |
| 79 | Beggars Banquet BEGA 9 | LIVE AT MAX'S KANSAS CITY (LP, with inner bag) | 15 |
| 81 | Jungle FREUD 1 | D.T.K. - LIVE AT THE SPEAKEASY (LP, white or pink vinyl) | 18 |
| 84 | Jungle FREUD 4 | L.A.M.F. REVISITED (LP, picture disc) | 18 |
| 84 | Jungle FREUD 4 | L.A.M.F. REVISITED (white label with withdrawn test proof sleeve) | 150 |
| 88 | Jungle FREUDP 1 | D.T.K. - LIVE AT THE SPEAKEASY (LP, reissue, picture disc) | 18 |

(see also New York Dolls, Johnny Thunders)

**HEARTS (U.K.)**
| | | | |
|---|---|---|---|
| 64 | Parlophone R 5147 | Young Woman/Black Eyes | 20 |

**HEARTS (U.S.)**
| | | | |
|---|---|---|---|
| 64 | Stateside SS 268 | Dear Abby/Dear Abby (Instrumental) | 22 |

**HEARTS & FLOWERS**
| | | | |
|---|---|---|---|
| 67 | Capitol CL 15492 | Rock'N'Roll Gypsies/Road To Nowhere | 12 |
| 68 | Capitol CL 15549 | She Sang Hymns Out Of Tune/Tin Angel | 8 |

**HEARTS OF SOUL**
| | | | |
|---|---|---|---|
| 70 | Columbia DB 8670 | Waterman/Fat Jack | 20 |

**HEAT EXCHANGE**
| | | | |
|---|---|---|---|
| 79 | EMI EMI 2988 | Shake Down/You're Gonna Love This (p/s) | 5 |

(see also Brian Bennett)

**HEATERS**
| | | | |
|---|---|---|---|
| 70 | Upsetter US 329 | Melting Pot/UPSETTERS: Kinky Mood | 20 |

**JIMMY HEATH**
| | | | |
|---|---|---|---|
| 60 | Riverside RLP 333 | REALLY BIG (LP) | 20 |

**HEATHCLIFFE**
| | | | |
|---|---|---|---|
| 68 | Tangerine DP 0001 | Holly Bush And Mistletoe/My World | 8 |

**HEATHER**
| | | | |
|---|---|---|---|
| 65 | King KG 1027 | I'll Come Softly/No One In The Whole Wide World | 7 |

**HEATHMORE**
| | | | |
|---|---|---|---|
| 69 | Pye 7N 17734 | Home Isn't Home Anymore/Blackmore Prison | 6 |
| 73 | Philips 6006 299 | Reaching For The Moon/I Love You | 6 |

**HEATWAVE (1)**
| | | | |
|---|---|---|---|
| 70 | Penny Farthing PEN 738 | Sister Simon (Funny Man)/Rastus Ravel | 30 |

**HEATWAVE (2)**
| | | | |
|---|---|---|---|
| 75 | Harp HSP 1055 | One-Eyed Man/999 | 50 |

MINT VALUE £

## HEAVEN
| | | | |
|---|---|---|---|
| 72 | CBS 7782 | Hangin On/Funny Lines | 25 |
| 71 | CBS 66293 | BRASS ROCK 1 (2-LP, ornate fold-out sleeve) | 100 |

## HEAVEN & EARTH
| | | | |
|---|---|---|---|
| 73 | London SHO 8448 | REFUGE (LP) | 50 |

## HEAVENLY
| | | | |
|---|---|---|---|
| 89 | Sarah SARAH 30 | I Fell In Love Last Night/Over And Over (p/s) | 15 |
| 91 | Sarah SARAH 41 | Our Love Is Heavenly/Wrap My Arms Around Him (p/s, insert) | 10 |
| 91 | Sarah SARAH 51 | So Little Deserve/I'm Not Scared Of You (p/s, insert) | 10 |
| 93 | Sarah SARAH 81 | P.U.N.K. Girl/Hearts And Crosses (p/s, insert) | 10 |
| 93 | Sarah SARAH 82 | Atta Girl/Dig Your Own Grave/So? (p/s, insert) | 15 |
| 96 | Wiiija WIJ 58 | Space Manatee/You Tore Me Down/Art School (p/s) | 10 |
| 92 | Sarah SARAH 610 | LE JARDIN DE HEAVENLY (LP) | 25 |
| 94 | Sarah SARAH 623 | THE DECLINE AND FALL OF HEAVENLY (LP) | 20 |
| 96 | Wiiija WIJLP 1053 | OPERATION HEAVENLY (LP) | 15 |

## HEAVEN 17
| | | | |
|---|---|---|---|
| 82 | Virgin VS 483 | Height Of The Fighting (He-La-Hu)/Honeymoon In New York (unissued, no p/s) | 15 |

*(see also B.E.F., Human League, Glenn Gregory & Claudia Brucken)*

## HEAVY COCHRAN
| | | | |
|---|---|---|---|
| 78 | Psycho P 2611 | I've Got Big Balls/Well, Fairly Big | 5 |
| 79 | Psycho P 2619 | I've Got A Little Prick/It's 12 Inches Long, But I Don't Use It As A Rule | 6 |

*(see also Lieutenant Pigeon)*

## HEAVY FEATHER
| | | | |
|---|---|---|---|
| 71 | Penny Farthing | Beautiful And Black/Ceilings | 10 |

## HEAVY JEFF
| | | | |
|---|---|---|---|
| 74 | Harry J HJ 6689 | Black Pepper/Pepper Rock | 8 |

## HEAVY JELLY
| | | | |
|---|---|---|---|
| 69 | Head HDS 4001 | Time Out Chewn In/The Long Wait | 20 |
| 69 | Island WIP 6049 | I Keep Singing The Same Old Song/Blue | 30 |
| 70 | Island HELP | HEAVY JELLY (LP, promo only) | 250 |

*(see also Jackie Lomax, Aynsley Dunbar Retaliation, Skip Bifferty, Griffin, Graham Bell, Arc)*

## HEAVY METAL KIDS
| | | | |
|---|---|---|---|
| 74 | Atlantic K 50047 | HEAVY METAL KIDS (LP, with poster) | 15 |
| 77 | Rak SRAK 523 | KITSCH (LP) | 15 |

*(see also Kids)*

## HEAVY PETTIN'
| | | | |
|---|---|---|---|
| 82 | Neat NEAT 17 | Roll The Dice/Love Times Love (p/s) | 10 |

## HEAVY PUKE
| | | | |
|---|---|---|---|
| 80 | (No label or cat no) | Spunk Bunny/Ozymandias (p/s, handwritten white labels) | 30 |

## HEAVYWEIGHT
| | | | |
|---|---|---|---|
| 91 | One After D ODE3 | The Way Of The Future (12") | 45 |

## HEAVYWEIGHTS
| | | | |
|---|---|---|---|
| 69 | Spark SRL 1033 | Utterly Funky/Shambala | 30 |

## BOBBY HEBB
| | | | |
|---|---|---|---|
| 66 | Philips BF 1503 | Sunny/Bread | 5 |
| 66 | Philips BF 1522 | A Satisfied Mind/Love Love Love | 40 |
| 67 | Philips BF 1541 | Love Me/Baby I'm Crazy | 10 |
| 67 | Philips BF 1570 | I Love Everything About You/Some Kinda Magic | 10 |
| 67 | Philips BF 1610 | Everything Is Coming Up Roses/Bound By Love | 8 |
| 68 | Philips BF 1702 | You Want To Change Me/Dreamy | 50 |
| 72 | Philips 6051 023 | Love Love Love/Sunny | 10 |
| 72 | Philips 6051 025 | Some Kind Of Magic/Good Lovin' | 6 |
| 66 | Philips BL 7740 | SUNNY (LP) | 30 |

## HEBREW CHILDREN & INNER CIRCLE
| | | | |
|---|---|---|---|
| 73 | Ackee ACK 508 | Dog And Bone/Version | 6 |

## DICK HECKSTALL-SMITH (QUINTET)
| | | | |
|---|---|---|---|
| 57 | Pye Jazz NJE 1037 | VERY SPECIAL OLD JAZZ (EP, as Dick Heckstall-Smith Quintet) | 40 |
| 72 | Bronze ILPS 9196 | DUST IN THE AIR SUSPENDED MARKS THE PLACE ... WHERE A STORY ENDED (LP, gatefold sleeve with lyric inner sleeve) | 50 |

*(see also Graham Bond Organisation, John Mayall & Bluesbreakers, Alexis Korner, Colosseum, Rocket 88)*

## HECTOR
| | | | |
|---|---|---|---|
| 73 | DJM DJS 289 | Wired Up/Ain't Got Time | 30 |
| 74 | DJM DJS 303 | Bye Bye Bad Days/Lady | 30 |

## JESSE HECTOR
| | | | |
|---|---|---|---|
| 92 | Clawfist HUNKA 15 | Leavin Town/I Need Lovin (with the Sound) | 5 |
| 99 | No Hit NO HIT EP 1961 | Fast Train To Memphis/My Bucket's Got A Hole In It/All By Myself/ Nightmares (p/s) | 6 |
| 98 | Dig The Fuzz DIG 029 | CRUSHED BUTLER : UNCRUSHED (10" LP gatefold) | 20 |

*(see also Hammersmith Gorillas, Gorillas, Helter Skelter)*

## HEDGEHOG AFFAIR
| | | | |
|---|---|---|---|
| 92 | Purple Heart PH 002 | RUSH TILL DAWN PRESENTS THE HEDGEHOG AFFAIR EP (12") | 12 |
| 92 | Basement BRSS 005 | RUSH TILL DAWN PRESENTS THE HEDGEHOG AFFAIR PT. 2 EP (12") | 12 |
| 92 | Basement BRSS 010 | RUSH TILL DAWN PRESENTS THE HEDGEHOG AFFAIR PT. 3 EP (12") | 12 |
| 93 | Sound Entity SENT 1203 | RUSH TILL DAWN PRESENTS THE HEDGEHOG AFFAIR PT. 4 EP (12") | 12 |
| 94 | Sound Entity SENT 1206 | RUSH TILL DAWN PRESENTS THE HEDGEHOG AFFAIR PT. 5 EP (12") | 20 |

## HEDGEHOG PIE
| | | | |
|---|---|---|---|
| 76 | Rubber ADUB 8 | Well I Know/Go With The Flow | 6 |

| | | | |
|---|---|---|---|
| 71 | Rubber RUB 004 | HIS ROUND (LP, with Tony Capstick, first pressing with black label on side 1 and white label on side 2) | 20 |
| 75 | Rubber RUB 009 | HEDGEHOG PIE (LP) | 25 |
| 75 | Rubber RUB 014 | GREEN LADY (LP) | 50 |
| 78 | Rubber RUB 024 | JUST ACT NORMAL (LP, with lyric insert) | 20 |

*(see also Dando Shaft)*

## HEDGEHOPPERS ANONYMOUS

| | | | |
|---|---|---|---|
| 65 | Decca F12241 | It's Good News Week/Afraid Of Love | 5 |
| 65 | Decca F 12298 | Don't Push Me/Please Don't Hurt Your Heart For Me | 6 |
| 66 | Decca F 12400 | Baby (You're My Everything)/Remember | 10 |
| 66 | Decca F 12479 | Daytime/That's The Time | 10 |
| 66 | Decca F 12530 | Stop Press/Little Memories | 8 |

*(see also Alan Avon & Toy Shop, Mick Tinsley)*

## HEDONE

| | | | |
|---|---|---|---|
| 84 | Omgowa Power HEAD 001 | Sensible/Everything's Going To Be Nice (no p/s) | 50 |

## HEERA

| | | | |
|---|---|---|---|
| 86 | Arishma ARI 004 | DIAMONDS FROM HEERA (LP) | 20 |

## HEFNER

| | | | |
|---|---|---|---|
| 97 | Boogie Wonderland BWL 023 | Lee Remick/Schoolgirls Knees (p/s) | 15 |
| 98 | Sticky STICKY 23 | A Hymn For The Alcohol/My Art College Days Are Over (p/s, 500 only) | 15 |
| 99 | Too Pure PURE 93S | The Hymn For The Cigarettes/Grandmother Dies (7") | 5 |
| 99 | Too Pure PURE 98S | I Took Her Love For Granted/A Belly Full Of Babies (7") | 6 |
| 97 | Boogie Wonderland BWL020 | A BETTER FRIEND EP (7" p/s with two inserts) | 15 |
| 98 | Too Pure PURE 83LP | BREAKING GOD'S HEART (LP) | 20 |
| 99 | Too Pure PURE 92LP | THE FIDELITY WARS (LP) | 30 |
| 00 | Too Pure PURE 99LP | BOXING HEFNER (LP) | 18 |
| 00 | Too Pure PURE 106LP | WE LOVE THE CITY (LP) | 25 |
| 01 | Too Pure PURE 105LP | DEAD MEDIA (LP) | 15 |

## NEAL HEFTI & ORCHESTRA

| | | | |
|---|---|---|---|
| 66 | CBS 201795 | Girl Talk/Lonely Girl | 7 |
| 66 | RCA Victor RCA 1521 | The Batman Theme/Batman Chase | 30 |
| 54 | Vogue/Coral LVC 10005 | SWINGIN' ON A CORAL REEF (10" LP) | 15 |
| 65 | Warner Bros W 1599 | HARLOW (LP, soundtrack) | 15 |
| 65 | United Artists (S)ULP 1098 | HOW TO MURDER YOUR WIFE (LP, soundtrack) | 15 |
| 67 | London HA-D 8337 | BAREFOOT IN THE PARK (LP, soundtrack) | 15 |
| 68 | Dot (S)LPD 514 | THE ODD COUPLE (LP, soundtrack) | 15 |

## LUCILLE HEGAMIN

| | | | |
|---|---|---|---|
| 73 | VJM VLP 50 | BLUE FLAME (LP) | 15 |

## DONALD HEIGHT

| | | | |
|---|---|---|---|
| 66 | London HLZ 10062 | Talk Of The Grapevine/There'll Be No Tomorrow | 130 |
| 66 | London HLZ 10062 | Talk Of The Grapevine/There'll Be No Tomorrow (DJ copy) | 175 |
| 67 | London HLZ 10116 | Three Hundred & Sixty Five Days/I'm Willing To Wait | 100 |
| 67 | London HLZ 10116 | Three Hundred & Sixty Five Days/I'm Willing To Wait (DJ copy) | 140 |
| 71 | Avco Embassy 6105 005 | Dancin' To The Music Of Love/Rags To Riches To Rags | 75 |
| 71 | Jay Boy BOY 32 | Talk Of The Grapevine/There'll Be No Tomorrow (reissue) | 15 |
| 72 | Jay Boy BOY 51 | Three Hundred & Sixty Five Days/I'm Willing To Wait (reissue) | 10 |
| 72 | Jay Boy BOY 60 | We Gotta Make Up/I Can't Get Enough | 10 |

## RONNIE HEIGHT

| | | | |
|---|---|---|---|
| 60 | London HLN 9144 | The One Finger Symphony/Mem'ries & Habits | 5 |

## HEINZ (& WILD BOYS)

| | | | |
|---|---|---|---|
| 63 | Decca F 11652 | Dreams Do Come True/Been Invited To A Party | 20 |
| 63 | Decca F 11693 | Just Like Eddie/Don't You Knock At My Door | 5 |
| 63 | Decca F 11768 | Country Boy/Long Tall Jack | 5 |
| 64 | Decca F 11831 | You Were There/No Matter What They Say | 10 |
| 64 | Decca F 11920 | Please Little Girl/For Loving Me This Way | 20 |
| 64 | Columbia DB 7374 | Questions I Can't Answer/The Beating Of My Heart | 20 |
| 65 | Columbia DB 7482 | Diggin' My Potatoes/She Ain't Comin' Back (with Wild Boys) | 40 |
| 65 | Columbia DB 7559 | Don't Think Twice, It's All Right/Big Fat Spider | 30 |
| 65 | Columbia DB 7656 | End Of The World/You Make Me Feel So Good | 40 |
| 65 | Columbia DB 7779 | Heart Full Of Sorrow/Don't Worry Baby | 40 |
| 66 | Columbia DB 7942 | Movin' In/I'm Not A Bad Guy | 40 |
| 70s | Cargo CPS 010 | Country Boy/Just Like Eddie | 10 |
| 63 | Decca DFE 8545 | HEINZ (EP) | 40 |
| 63 | Decca DFE 8559 | LIVE IT UP (EP) | 30 |
| 64 | Decca LK 4599 | TRIBUTE TO EDDIE (LP) | 50 |

*(see also Tornados, Saints)*

## HEISENBERG

| | | | |
|---|---|---|---|
| 89 | Uncertain HEI 5001 | No More Dreams/Rain (p/s) | 20 |

## HELDEN

| | | | |
|---|---|---|---|
| 83 | Zica ZICA 01 | Holding On/Once Upon A Time In The ... (p/s) | 5 |
| 83 | Zica 12 ZICA 01 | Holding On/Once Upon A Time In The ... (12", p/s) | 15 |

*(see also Ultravox)*

## HELICOPTER

| | | | |
|---|---|---|---|
| 72 | Maple Annie MA 102 | I Belong To Yesterday/Lonely Tonight | 25 |

*(see also Galliard)*

## HELL

| | | | |
|---|---|---|---|
| 83 | Deadly Weapons DWS 666 | Save Us From Those Who Would Save Us/Death Squad | 75 |

MINT VALUE £

## RICHARD HELL (& VOIDOIDS)

| | | | |
|---|---|---|---|
| 76 | Stiff BUY 7 | (I Could Live With You In) Another World/(I Belong To The) Blank Generation/ You Gotta Lose (with p/s, numbered, 5,000 only with 4 point press-out centre) | 30 |
| 76 | Stiff BUY 7 | (I Could Live With You In) Another World/(I Belong To The) Blank Generation/ You Gotta Lose (repressing for THE STIFF BOX SET & numbered 001) | 8 |
| 77 | Sire 6078 608 | Blank Generation/Liar's Beware/Who Says? (no p/s) | 8 |
| 77 | Sire 6078 608 | Blank Generation/Liars Beware/Who Says? (12", p/s) | 10 |
| 79 | Radar ADA 30 | The Kid With The Replaceable Head/I'm Your Man (p/s) | 8 |
| 94 | Overground OVER 36 | Another World/Blank Generation/Love Comes In Spurts (p/s, reissue, 2,000 only) | 5 |
| 77 | Sire 9103 327 | BLANK GENERATION (LP, with inner sleeve) | 30 |
| 83 | I.D. NOSE 2 | DESTINY STREET (LP) | 15 |

*(see also Neon Boys)*

## HELLACOPTERS

| | | | |
|---|---|---|---|
| 99 | Butcher's Hook HOOK 004 | A House Is Not A Motel/POWDER MONKEYS: Destination X (p/s) | 5 |
| 01 | Sweet Nothing 12SN007 | HIGH ENERGY ROCK 'N' ROLL (mini-LP) | 20 |
| 04 | Sweet Nothing SNLP 040 | STRIKES LIKE LIGHTNING (3 x 7" box set, cards, badge & pendant) | 30 |

*(see also Super$hit666)*

## HELLANBACH

| | | | |
|---|---|---|---|
| 80 | Guardian GR/HC56 | Out To Get You/Light Of The World/Let's Get This Show On The Road/Nobody's Fool | 40 |
| 84 | Neat NEAT 1006 | NOW HEAR THIS (LP, with inner sleeve) | 15 |
| 84 | Neat NEAT 1019 | THE BIG ... H (LP, with insert) | 15 |

## HELLHAMMER

| | | | |
|---|---|---|---|
| 84 | Noise N 008 | APOCALYPTIC RAIDS (12" EP, 45/33rpm) | 50 |
| 08 | Century Media 9977392 | DEMON ENTRAILS (3-LP, 180gm vinyl with booklet and poster) | 80 |

## DAVE HELLING

| | | | |
|---|---|---|---|
| 65 | Stateside SS 409 | It Ain't Me Babe/If You're Gonna Leave Me | 10 |
| 66 | Planet PLF 101 | Christine/The Bells | 40 |

## HELLIONS

| | | | |
|---|---|---|---|
| 65 | Piccadilly 7N 35213 | Daydreaming Of You/Shades Of Blue | 25 |
| 65 | Piccadilly 7N 35232 | Tomorrow Never Comes/Dream Child | 25 |
| 65 | Piccadilly 7N 35265 | A Little Lovin'/Think It Over | 25 |

*(see also Revolution, Traffic, Roaring Sixties, Jim Capaldi, Dave Mason, Luther Grosvenor, Spooky Tooth)*

## HELLO

| | | | |
|---|---|---|---|
| 72 | Bell BELL 1238 | You Move Me/Ask Your Mama | 15 |
| 72 | Bell BELL 1265 | C'mon/Wench | 5 |
| 73 | Bell BELL 1333 | Another School Day/C'mon Get Together (p/s) | 6 |
| 76 | Bell BELL 1479 | Teenage Revolution/Keeps Us Off The Streets (demo copies only) | 100 |
| 76 | Bell BELLS 263 | KEEP US OFF THE STREETS (LP) | 15 |

## HELLO PEOPLE

| | | | |
|---|---|---|---|
| 74 | ABC 4034 | Future Shock/Destiny | 6 |

## HELL PREACHERS INC.

| | | | |
|---|---|---|---|
| 69 | Marble Arch MALS 1169 | SUPREME PSYCHEDELIC UNDERGROUND (LP) | 40 |

## HELMET

| | | | |
|---|---|---|---|
| 92 | Interscope 7567 92162-1 | MEANTIME (LP, inner) | 20 |

## BOBBY HELMS

| | | | |
|---|---|---|---|
| 57 | Brunswick 05711 | Fraulein/(Got A) Heartsick Feeling | 10 |
| 57 | Brunswick 05721 | My Special Angel/Standing At The End of My World | 10 |
| 58 | Brunswick 05730 | No Other Baby/The Magic Song | 15 |
| 58 | Brunswick 05741 | Love My Lady/Just A Little Lonesome | 10 |
| 58 | Brunswick 05748 | Jacqueline/Living In The Shadow Of The Past | 10 |
| 58 | Brunswick 05754 | Schoolboy Crush/Borrowed Dreams | 15 |
| 58 | Brunswick 05765 | Jingle Bell Rock/Captain Santa Claus | 10 |
| 59 | Brunswick 05786 | Miss Memory/New River Train | 6 |
| 59 | Brunswick 05801 | Soon It Can Be Told/I Guess I'll Miss The Prom | 6 |
| 59 | Brunswick 05813 | My Lucky Day/Hurry Baby | 6 |
| 59 | Brunswick 05813 | My Lucky Day/Hurry Baby (78) | 20 |
| 61 | Brunswick 05852 | Sad Eyed Baby/You're The One | 8 |
| 60 | Brunswick OE 9461 | BOBBY HELMS (EP) | 20 |
| 57 | Brunswick LAT 8250 | SINGS TO MY SPECIAL ANGEL (LP) | 50 |

## JIMMY HELMS

| | | | |
|---|---|---|---|
| 73 | Capitol CL 15762 | My Little Devil/Magnificent Sanctuary Band | 6 |
| 73 | Fly BUG 27 | Gonna Make You An Offer You Can't Refuse/Words And Music | 6 |
| 74 | Pye 7N 45440 | Ragtime Girl/Romeo & Juliet | 60 |

## HELP

| | | | |
|---|---|---|---|
| 71 | MCA MWPS 4039 | SECOND COMING (LP) | 80 |

## HELP YOURSELF

| | | | |
|---|---|---|---|
| 71 | Liberty LBF 15459 | Running Down Deep/Paper Leaves | 20 |
| 72 | United Artists UP 35355 | Heaven Row/Brown Lady | 15 |
| 72 | United Artists UP35466 | Mommy Won't Be Home For Christmas/Johnny B. Goode (demo in picture sleeve) | 60 |
| 72 | United Artists UP 35466 | Mommy Won't Be Home For Christmas/Johnny B. Goode | 40 |
| 71 | Liberty LBS 83484 | HELP YOURSELF (LP) | 100 |
| 72 | United Artists UAS 29287 | STRANGE AFFAIR (LP, with inner sleeve) | 100 |
| 72 | United Artists UAS 29413 | BEWARE OF THE SHADOW (LP) | 35 |
| 73 | United Artists UDG 4001 [UAS 29487/FREE 1] | THE RETURN OF KEN WHALEY/HAPPY DAYS (2-LP set in envelope sleeve with LPs in individual sleeves) | 50 |
| 73 | United Artists UAS 29487 | THE RETURN OF KEN WHALEY (LP) | 20 |

*(see also Man, Deke Leonard, Tyla Gang, Wreckless Eric)*

### HELPLESS HUW
| | | |
|---|---|---|
| 78 | US US 001 | Still Love You (In My Heart) .................................................................... 5 |
| 80 | US US 002 | Sid Vicious Was Innocent/Going Through The Motions/ Baby We're Not In Love/ When You're Weary (p/s in bag) ................................................................ 15 |

### HELTER SKELTER (1)
| | | |
|---|---|---|
| 69 | Peach PO1 | Between Dreams/Run ................................................................................ 100 |

### HELTER SKELTER (2)
| | | |
|---|---|---|
| 77 | Sticky STY 102 | I Need You/Goodbye Baby ........................................................................ 40 |

*(see also Gorillas, Hammersmith Gorillas, Jesse Hector)*

### HEMLOCK
| | | |
|---|---|---|
| 73 | Deram DM 379 | Mr Horizontal/Beggar Man ...................................................................... 12 |
| 73 | Deram SML 1102 | HEMLOCK (LP, white/red label with small logo) ...................................... 150 |

*(see also Miller Anderson, Keef Hartley Band, Dog Soldier)*

### BILL HENDERSON
| | | |
|---|---|---|
| 60 | Top Rank JAR 412 | Sweet Pumpkin/Joey, Joey, Joey ............................................................... 8 |

### DORRIS HENDERSON
| | | |
|---|---|---|
| 65 | Columbia DB 7567 | The Hangman/Leaves That Are Green ....................................................... 15 |
| 67 | Fontana TF 811 | Message To Pretty/Watch The Stars .......................................................... 10 |
| 65 | Columbia SX 6001 | THERE YOU GO (LP, with John Renbourn) ................................................. 140 |
| 67 | Fontana (S)TL 5385 | WATCH THE STARS (LP, with John Renbourn) .......................................... 175 |

*(see also Eclection, John Renbourn)*

### FINIS HENDERSON
| | | |
|---|---|---|
| 83 | Motown TMGT 1304 | Skip To My Lou/I'd Rather Be Gone/Vina Del Mar (12") ............................ 10 |

### JOE HENDERSON
| | | |
|---|---|---|
| 62 | London HLU 9553 | Snap Your Fingers/If You See Me Cry ......................................................... 12 |
| 63 | London REU 1376 | JOE HENDERSON (EP) ............................................................................... 30 |

### LORNA HENDERSON
| | | |
|---|---|---|
| 60 | Oriole CB 1549 | Lollipops To Lipstick/Steady Eddie ............................................................ 25 |
| 60 | Oriole CB 1590 | A Thousand Stars/Murray, What's Your Hurry? ........................................ 10 |

### MARIAN HENDERSON
| | | |
|---|---|---|
| 70 | MCA MK 5046 | Antique Annies Magic Lantern Show/Lady Of Carlisle ................................. 8 |

### BOBBY HENDRICKS
| | | |
|---|---|---|
| 58 | London HL 8714 | Itchy Twitchy Feeling/A Thousand Dreams ............................................... 60 |
| 58 | London HL 8714 | Itchy Twitchy Feeling/A Thousand Dreams (78) ........................................ 30 |
| 59 | Top Rank JAR 193 | Little John Green/Sincerely, Your Lover .................................................... 20 |
| 61 | Mercury AMT 1163 | I'm Coming Home/Every Other Night ....................................................... 10 |
| 64 | Sue WI 315 | Itchy Twitchy Feeling/Thousand Dreams (reissue, as Bobby Henricks) ...... 35 |

*(see also Drifters)*

### HUGH HENDRICKS & UPSETTERS
| | | |
|---|---|---|
| 70 | Spinning Wheel SW 103 | Land Of Kinks/O'NEIL HALL: This Man ..................................................... 15 |

### JON HENDRICKS
| | | |
|---|---|---|
| 56 | Brunswick 05521 | Four Brothers/Cloudburst (with Dave Lambert Singers) ............................. 8 |
| 68 | Verve VS 572 | No More/Rainbow's End ............................................................................ 5 |
| 71 | Philips 6006 088 | I Got Soul/Slow Train ................................................................................ 5 |

*(see also Dave Lambert)*

### JIMI HENDRIX (EXPERIENCE)
**SINGLES**
| | | |
|---|---|---|
| 66 | Polydor 56139 | Hey Joe/Stone Free ................................................................................... 15 |
| 67 | Track 604 001 | Purple Haze (1-sided promo, white label with black text) ........................ 250 |
| 67 | Track 604 001 | Purple Haze/51st Anniversary (white label) .............................................. 20 |
| 67 | Track 604 001 | Purple Haze/51st Anniversary (black label) .............................................. 15 |
| 67 | Track 604 001 | Purple Haze/51st Anniversary (black label, alternative mix, but no way of telling from either label or matrix number) ) ....................................... 25 |
| 67 | Track 604 004 | The Wind Cries Mary/Highway Chile ........................................................ 12 |
| 67 | Track 604 007 | The Burning Of The Midnight Lamp/The Stars That Play With Laughing Sam's Dice ...... 15 |
| 67 | Decca F 22652 | How Would You Feel/You Don't Want Me (with Curtis Knight, test pressing, unreleased) ........................................................................... 500 |
| 67 | Track 604 009 | How Would You Feel/You Don't Want Me (with Curtis Knight) ................. 12 |
| 67 | London HL 10160 | Hush Now/Flashing (with Curtis Knight; in export p/s) .............................. 30 |
| 67 | London HL 10160 | Hush Now/Flashing (with Curtis Knight) .................................................... 10 |
| 68 | Track 604 025 | All Along The Watchtower/Long Hot Summer Night ................................. 12 |
| 69 | Track 604 029 | Crosstown Traffic/Gypsy Eyes .................................................................. 12 |
| 69 | Track 604 033 | Let Me Light Your Fire/The Burning Of The Midnight Lamp ...................... 10 |
| 70 | London HLZ 10321 | Ballad Of Jimi/Gloomy Monday (with Curtis Knight) .................................. 8 |
| 70 | London HL 7126 | Ballad Of Jimi/Gloomy Monday (with Curtis Knight, export issue) ........... 30 |
| 70 | Track 2095 001 | Voodoo Chile/Hey Joe/All Along The Watchtower (p/s; later copies have white border on sleeve) .............................................................. 15 |
| 70 | Track 2095 001 | Voodoo Chile/Hey Joe/All Along The Watchtower (p/s; later copies with white border on sleeve) ..................................................................... 8 |
| 70 | Track 2095 001 | Voodoo Chile/Hey Joe/All Along The Watchtower ..................................... 6 |
| 71 | RCA RCA 2033 | No Such Animal (Parts 1 & 2) (initially in p/s, with Curtis Knight uncredited) ............... 25 |
| 71 | RCA RCA 2033 | No Such Animal (Parts 1 & 2) (with Curtis Knight uncredited) ................... 8 |
| 71 | Track 2094 007 | Angel/Night Bird Flying ............................................................................. 7 |
| 71 | Track 2094 010 | Gypsy Eyes/Remember/Purple Haze/Stone Free (in p/s) .......................... 25 |
| 71 | Track 2094 010 | Gypsy Eyes/Remember/Purple Haze/Stone Free ....................................... 8 |
| 72 | Polydor 2001 277 | Johnny B. Goode/Little Wing ..................................................................... 6 |
| 73 | Reprise K 14286 | Hear My Train A-Comin/Rock Me Baby ...................................................... 6 |
| 73 | Polydor/Sound For Industry SFI 1572 | Red House/Spanish Castle Magic (1-sided flexidisc with Rolling Stone) ...... 15 |

# Jimi HENDRIX (EXPERIENCE)

| | | | |
|---|---|---|---|
| 80 | Polydor 260 8001 | 6 SINGLES PACK (6 plain sleeve singles [2141 275-280], open-out card p/s) | 20 |
| 82 | CBS CBS A 2749 | Fire/Are You Experienced? (p/s) | 8 |
| 88 | Strange Fruit SFPS065 | PEEL SESSIONS (12", p/s) | 10 |
| 89 | Polydor PO 33 | Purple Haze/51st Anniversary (p/s, reissue) | 5 |
| 90 | Polydor PO 71 | Crosstown Traffic/Voodoo Chile (p/s) | 5 |
| 90 | Polydor PO 100 | All Along The Watchtower/Voodoo Chile/Hey Joe (p/s) | 5 |

## ALBUMS : TRACK LPS

| | | | |
|---|---|---|---|
| 67 | Track 612 001 | ARE YOU EXPERIENCED (mono, laminated (front and back) sleeve) | 700 |
| 67 | Track 612 001 | ARE YOU EXPERIENCED (mono, matt sleeve) | 350 |
| 67 | Track 612 003 | AXIS: BOLD AS LOVE (laminated gatefold sleeve, with gatefold insert mono) | 750 |
| 67 | Track 612 003 | AXIS: BOLD AS LOVE (laminated gatefold sleeve, without gatefold insert, mono) | 150 |
| 67 | Track 613 003 | AXIS: BOLD AS LOVE (laminated gatefold sleeve, with gatefold insert, stereo) | 300 |
| 67 | Track 613 003 | AXIS: BOLD AS LOVE (laminated gatefold sleeve, without gatefold insert, stereo) | 120 |
| 68 | Track 612 004 | SMASH HITS (mono) | 60 |
| 68 | Track 613 004 | SMASH HITS (stereo) | 30 |
| 68 | Track 612 008/009 | ELECTRIC LADYLAND (2-LP, plain white non-gatefold sleeve, labels marked "Test Pressing", mono) | 1500 |
| 68 | Track 613 008/009 | ELECTRIC LADYLAND (2-LP, laminated gatefold sleeve, stereo, blue text inside sleeve) | 700 |
| 68 | Track 613 008/009 | ELECTRIC LADYLAND (2-LP, laminated gatefold sleeve, stereo, white text inside sleeve) | 300 |
| 68 | Track 613 010 | ELECTRIC LADYLAND PART 1 (stereo only) | 35 |
| 68 | Track 613 017 | ELECTRIC LADYLAND PART 2 (stereo only) | 35 |
| 70 | Track Super 2406 002 | BAND OF GYPSYS (original 'puppet' sleeve, beware of 'fake' copies on eBay) | 200 |
| 70 | Track Super 2406 002 | BAND OF GYPSYS (repressing, gatefold 'Isle Of Wight' sleeve) | 50 |
| 70 | Track Super 2406 002 | BAND OF GYPSYS (2nd repressing, single sleeve) | 20 |
| 70 | Track 2407 010 | BACKTRACK 10: ARE YOU EXPERIENCED? (budget reissue, mono, some state mono but play stereo) | 20 |
| 70 | Track 2407 010 | BACKTRACK 10: ARE YOU EXPERIENCED? (budget reissue, stereo, but in Mono sleeve) | 50 |
| 70 | Track 2407 011 | BACKTRACK 11: AXIS: BOLD AS LOVE (budget reissue, stereo) | 20 |
| 71 | Track 2856 002 | ELECTRIC JIMI HENDRIX (mail-order only Record Club release) | 800 |
| 71 | Track 2408 101 | THE CRY OF LOVE (gatefold sleeve) | 30 |
| 71 | Track 2408 101 | THE CRY OF LOVE (red vinyl, factory custom pressing, 5 known copies. The LP was pressed to test dealer reaction to coloured vinyl with a view to marketing the Pink Fairies LP Never Never Land. Although the Cry Of Love is on both sides only side A has the correct (black) Track label with the other side having a red Polydor label stating 'The Very Best Of Bert Kaempfert'. It appears that initially these Hendrix LPs were sleeved in Never Never Land sleeves but over time they have been re-sleeved by owners in Hendrix Cry Of Love sleeves.) | 3000 |
| 74 | Track 603003 | ARE YOU EXPERIENCED (LP, stereo with POLYDOR INT. GmbH on label, this is NOT the 1967 Stereo issue of ARE YOU EXPERIENCED) | 40 |
| 88 | Track/HMV C 881-16 | ARE YOU EXPERIENCED (LP, box set, ltd. ed. of 2,500, no'd, with certificate) | 30 |

## ALBUMS : POLYDOR LPS

| | | | |
|---|---|---|---|
| 71 | Polydor 2302 016 | ISLE OF WIGHT | 15 |
| 71 | Polydor 2302 018 | HENDRIX IN THE WEST (gatefold sleeve) | 15 |
| 72 | Polydor 2302 020 | WAR HEROES | 15 |
| 73 | Polydor ACB 00219 Super | SMASH HITS (LP, Audio Club Of Great Britain issue) | 20 |
| 73 | Polydor 2657 012 | ELECTRIC LADYLAND (2-LP, laminated gatefold sleeve, reissue) | 60 |
| 73 | Polydor 2310 271 | ELECTRIC LADYLAND PART 1 (reissue) | 15 |
| 73 | Polydor 2310 272 | ELECTRIC LADYLAND PART 2 (reissue) | 15 |
| 74 | Polydor 2310 301 | LOOSE ENDS | 15 |
| 75 | Polydor 2310 398 | CRASH LANDING | 15 |
| 78 | Polydor 2612 034 | THE ESSENTIAL JIMI HENDRIX (2-LP, with bonus 1-sided 33rpm 7" Gloria [JIMI 1] in special bag) | 20 |
| 78 | St. Michael 2102/0102 | JIMI HENDRIX (cat. no. also listed as Polydor 2891 139) | 50 |
| 78 | St. Michael/Poly. 2891 139 | JIMI HENDRIX (cassette) | 20 |
| 80 | Polydor 2625 040 | JIMI HENDRIX (13-LP box set [11 x LP + 1 x 2-LP]) | 75 |
| 80 | Polydor POLS 1023 | NINE TO THE UNIVERSE | 15 |
| 84 | Polydor SPDLP 3 | ELECTRIC LADYLAND (2-LP, non-laminated gatefold sleeve, 2nd reissue) | 40 |
| 87 | Polydor 833 004-1 | LIVE AT WINTERLAND (2-LP, with poster) | 18 |
| 90 | Polydor 847 2311 | CORNERSTONES: JIMI HENDRIX 1967-1970 | 15 |
| 83 | Polydor PODV6 | SINGLES ALBUM (2-LP, gatefold) | 20 |
| 91 | Polydor 847 234 1 | ARE YOU EXPERENCED? (LP, reissue with barcode on rear) | 15 |
| 93 | Polydor 847243 | AXIS: BOLD AS LOVE (LP, reissue) | 25 |

## ALBUMS : OTHER LPS

| | | | |
|---|---|---|---|
| 68 | London HA 8349 | GET THAT FEELING (Mono, with Curtis Knight) | 50 |
| 68 | London SH 8369 | GET THAT FEELING (Stereo, with Curtis Knight) | 40 |
| 68 | London HA 8369 | STRANGE THINGS (Mono, with Curtis Knight) | 50 |
| 68 | London SH 8369 | STRANGE THINGS (Stereo, with Curtis Knight) | 40 |
| 71 | Reprise K 40430 | LIVE AT THE MONTEREY INTERNATIONAL POP FESTIVAL (shared with Otis Redding) | 35 |
| 71 | Reprise K 44159 | RAINBOW BRIDGE (matt gatefold sleeve, 'steamboat' label, soundtrack) | 20 |
| 73 | Reprise K 64017 | SOUNDTRACK RECORDINGS FROM THE FILM JIMI HENDRIX (2-LP) | 18 |
| 73 | Ember NR 5068 | IN THE BEGINNING (textured gatefold sleeve) | 15 |
| 74 | Ember EMB 3428 | LOOKING BACK WITH JIMI HENDRIX | 15 |
| 75 | DJM DJLMD 8011 | FOR REAL (2-LP, gatefold sleeve) | 18 |
| 89 | Castle Comms. HBLP 100 | LIVE AND UNRELEASED - THE RADIO SHOW (5-LP) | 30 |
| 89 | Castle CCSLP 212 | RADIO ONE (2-LP, gatefold) | 20 |

## ALBUMS : CDS

| | | | |
|---|---|---|---|
| 84 | Track 821 993 2 | BAND OF GYPSYS | 35 |
| 88 | Polydor/HMV C88 LP 1-11 | ARE YOU EXPERIENCED? (box set via HMV stores, 1,500 only) | 25 |
| 89 | Castle Comms. HBCD 100 | LIVE AND UNRELEASED - THE RADIO SHOW (3-CD, box set) | 30 |

*(see also Eire Apparent, Jayne Mansfield, McGough & McGear, Fat Mattress, Curtis Knight, Billy Cox, Buddy Miles, Riot Squad)*

**MARGIE HENDRIX**
| | | |
|---|---|---|
| 66 | Mercury MF 976 | I Call You Lover But You Ain't Nothin' But A Tramp/The Question ........................ 25 |
| 67 | Mercury MF 1001 | Restless/On The Right Track ........................ 20 |

**TONY HENDRIX**
| | | |
|---|---|---|
| 69 | Pye Int. 7n 25485 | The Grooviest Girl In The World/Majestic World ........................ 8 |

**LARRY HENLEY**
| | | |
|---|---|---|
| 64 | Hickory 45-1272 | My Reasons For Living/Stickin' Up For My Baby ........................ 12 |

*(see also Newbeats, Dean & Mark)*

**CHRISTIE HENNESSY**
| | | |
|---|---|---|
| 73 | Westwood | CHRISTIE HENNESSY (LP) ........................ 35 |

**HENNESSYS**
| | | |
|---|---|---|
| 69 | Cambrian CLP 593 | THE ROADS AND THE MILES (LP) ........................ 80 |
| 60s | Music Factory MF 106 | KARDIFF AFTER DARK (LP) ........................ 90 |

**ADRIAN HENRI**
| | | |
|---|---|---|
| 60s | Charivari | ADRIAN HENRI (LP) ........................ 45 |
| 60s | Argo PLP 1194 | ADRIAN HENRI AND HUGO WILLIAMS (LP) ........................ 40 |

*(see also Liverpool Scene, McGough & McGear)*

**ANN HENRY**
| | | |
|---|---|---|
| 60 | Top Rank JAR 292 | Like Young/Sugar Blues ........................ 5 |

**BOB HENRY**
| | | |
|---|---|---|
| 65 | Philips BF 1450 | I Need Me Someone/Built Like A Man ........................ 18 |

*(see also Robert Henry)*

**CLARENCE ('FROGMAN') HENRY**
| | | |
|---|---|---|
| 57 | London HLN 8389 | Ain't Got No Home/Troubles Troubles (as Clarence Henry) (gold lettering on label).... 150 |
| 57 | London HLN 8389 | Ain't Got No Home/Troubles Troubles (as Clarence Henry) (silver lettering on label) .. 100 |
| 57 | London HLN 8389 | Ain't Got No Home/Troubles Troubles (as Clarence Henry) (78) ........................ 40 |
| 61 | Pye International 7N 25078 | But I Do/Just My Baby And Me........................ 10 |
| 61 | Pye International 7N 25089 | You Always Hurt The One You Love/Little Suzy ........................ 8 |
| 61 | Pye International 7N 25108 | Lonely Street/Why Can't You........................ 8 |
| 61 | Pye International 7N 25115 | Standing In The Need Of Love/On Bended Knees ........................ 8 |
| 62 | Pye International 7N 25123 | A Little Too Much/I Wish I Could Say The Same ........................ 12 |
| 62 | Pye International 7N 25141 | Dream Myself A Sweetheart/Lost Without You ........................ 10 |
| 62 | Pye International 7N 25169 | The Jealous Kind/Come On And Dance ........................ 15 |
| 64 | London HLU 9936 | Little Green Frog/Have You Ever Been Lonely? ........................ 30 |
| 66 | London HLU 10025 | Ain't Got No Home/Baby, Ain't That Love? ........................ 30 |
| 61 | Pye Intl. NEP 44007 | CLARENCE 'FROGMAN' HENRY HIT PARADE (EP) ........................ 30 |
| 61 | Pye Intl. NPL 28017 | YOU ALWAYS HURT THE ONE YOU LOVE (LP) ........................ 40 |

**MILTON HENRY**
| | | |
|---|---|---|
| 76 | Cactus CT85 | Gypsy Woman/Dub ........................ 25 |

**PIERRE HENRY**
| | | |
|---|---|---|
| 66 | Philips 4FE 8000 | LE VOYAGE FROM THE TIBETAN BOOK OF THE DEAD (LP) ........................ 20 |
| 66 | Philips 4FE 8504 | VARIATIONS FOR A DOOR AND A SIGH (LP, UK record in French sleeve) ........................ 20 |
| 68 | Philips 4FE 8004 | MASS FOR THE PRESENT TIME (LP) ........................ 40 |

**RICHARD HENRY**
| | | |
|---|---|---|
| 68 | Regal Zonophone RZ 3014 | Oh Girl/Lay Your Head Upon My Shoulder........................ 6 |

**ROBERT HENRY**
| | | |
|---|---|---|
| 66 | Philips BF 1476 | Walk Away Like A Winner/That's All I Want ........................ 70 |

*(see also Bob Henry)*

**HENRY III**
| | | |
|---|---|---|
| 67 | Island WI 3078 | Thank You Girl/Take Me Back ........................ 40 |
| 67 | Island WI 3081 | I'll Reach The End/Won't Go Away (B-side actually Lee's Special by Don Tony Lee) ....... 60 |
| 67 | RCA RCA 1568 | So Much Love/Sitting In The Park ........................ 20 |
| 70 | Dynamic DYN 402 | Out Of Time/VICEROYS: Love For Everyone (both with Hubcap & Wheels) ........................ 8 |

*(see also Uniques)*

**DANNY HENRY**
| | | |
|---|---|---|
| 81 | Three Kings TK50 | Sharon My Love/Version/African Gold (12") ........................ 40 |

**HENRY & LIZA**
| | | |
|---|---|---|
| 73 | Dragon DRA 1004 | Hole Under Cratches/TIVOLIS: Hole Under Cratches (Instrumental) (actually "Hole Under Crutches") ........................ 6 |

*(see also Max Romeo)*

**HENRY & LOUIS**
| | | |
|---|---|---|
| 80s | 2 Kings 2K7001 | Jah Jah Never Fail/Dub Never Fail I ........................ 15 |

**HENRY COW**
| | | |
|---|---|---|
| 73 | Virgin V 2005 | THE LEGEND (LP) ........................ 50 |
| 74 | Virgin V 2011 | UNREST (LP, gatefold sleeve, black/white 'twin' label) ........................ 30 |
| 75 | Virgin V 2027 | IN PRAISE OF LEARNING (LP) ........................ 30 |
| 76 | Caroline CAD 3002 | CONCERTS (LP) ........................ 30 |
| 79 | Broadcast BC 1 | WESTERN CULTURE (LP) ........................ 15 |

*(see also Slapp Happy, Art Bears, Fred Frith, Gong/Henry Cow/Global Trucking Company)*

**HENRY ESSENCE**
| | | |
|---|---|---|
| 79 | Ellie Jay Records EJSP9392 | Margarita/14 Year Old Lover (500 only, p/s) ........................ 150 |

**JUDY HENSKE**
| | | |
|---|---|---|
| 66 | Reprise RS 20485 | Road To Nowhere/Sing A Rainbow ........................ 15 |
| 65 | Reprise RS 6203 | DEATH DEFYING (LP)........................ 30 |

**JUDY HENSKE & JERRY YESTER**
| | | |
|---|---|---|
| 69 | Straight STS 1052 | FAREWELL ALDEBARAN (LP) ........................ 50 |

MINT VALUE £

### KEN HENSLEY

| | | | |
|---|---|---|---|
| 73 | Bronze ILPS 9223 | PROUD WORDS ON A DUSTY SHELF (LP, gatefold sleeve, lyric inner, Island credit on label) | 60 |
| 75 | Bronze ILPS 9307 | EAGER TO PLEASE (LP, lyric inner, Island credit on label) | 50 |
| 81 | Bronze BRON 533 | FREE SPIRIT (LP) | 35 |

*(see also Uriah Heep. Wasp)*

### ROBERT HENRY HENSLEY

| 68 | Polydor 56295 | You're Gonna See Me Cry/Montage | 8 |
|---|---|---|---|

### NICKY HENSON

| 63 | Parlophone R 4976 | Till I See You Cry/What Does It Mean? | 20 |
|---|---|---|---|

### DAVID HENTSCHEL

| 75 | Ring O' 2017 101 | Oh My My/Devil Woman | 8 |
|---|---|---|---|

### NAT HEPBURN

| 60s | Jump Up JU 516 | River/Political Girl | 6 |
|---|---|---|---|

### HEPBURNS

| | | | |
|---|---|---|---|
| 87 | Cherry Red 12CHERRY 98 | GOALMOUTH INCIDENT (12" EP) | 10 |
| 89 | Let's Zine! (No Cat. No.) | Where You Belong/WALTONES: She Looks Right Through Me (Demo Version) (1-sided flexi, with Zine fanzine issue 10) | 15 |
| 90 | Magic MAGIC 01T | Electrified (From Countryside To City)/London Welshman/Dive (12", p/s) | 25 |
| 88 | Cherry Red BRED 83 | THE MAGIC OF THE HEPBURNS (LP) | 15 |

### HEP STARS

| | | | |
|---|---|---|---|
| 66 | Decca F 22446 | Sunny Girl/No Response | 45 |
| 67 | Olga OLE 001 | Wedding/Consolation | 25 |
| 68 | Olga OLE 013 | Let It Be Me/Groovy Summertime (withdrawn, supposedly reissued 1969) | 45 |
| 68 | Olga OLE 014 | Malaika/It's Nice To Be Back (in export p/s) | 55 |
| 68 | Olga OLE 014 | Malaika/It's Nice To Be Back | 25 |

*(see also Abba)*

### HEPTONES

| | | | |
|---|---|---|---|
| 66 | Rio R 104 | Gunmen Coming To Town/TOMMY McCOOK & SUPERSONICS: Riverton City | 100 |
| 67 | Ska Beat JB 266 | We've Got Love/I Am Lonely | 80 |
| 67 | Caltone TONE 105 | Schoolgirls/Ain't That Bad? | 80 |
| 67 | Studio One SO 2005 | A Change Is Gonna Come/Nobody Knows | 60 |
| 67 | Studio One SO 2014 | Fat Girl/DELROY WILSON: Mother Word | 80 |
| 67 | Studio One SO 2021 | If I Knew/Festival Day | 30 |
| 67 | Studio One SO 2026 | Why Did You Leave?/GAYLADS: Don't Try To Reach Me | 50 |
| 67 | Studio One SO 2027 | Why Must I?/SLIM SMITH: Try Again | 30 |
| 67 | Studio One SO 2031 | Take Me (actually by The Soul Vendors)/DELROY WILSON: I'm Not A King | 40 |
| 67 | Studio One SO 2033 | Only Sixteen/Baby | 50 |
| 68 | Studio One SO 2040 | Tripe Girl/DELROY WILSON: Mr. D.J. | 30 |
| 68 | Studio One SO 2049 | Cry, Baby, Cry/Mama | 40 |
| 68 | Studio One SO 2052 | Dock Of The Bay/KING ROCKY (ELLIS): The Ruler | 150 |
| 68 | Studio One SO 2055 | Party Time/Oil In Your Lamp | 40 |
| 68 | Coxsone CS 7052 | Love Won't Come Easy/Gee Wee | 100 |
| 68 | Coxsone CS 7068 | Equal Rights/Ting-A-Ling | 60 |
| 68 | Coxsone CS 7082 | Soul Power/Love Me Always | 125 |
| 69 | Coxsone CS 7092 | Sweet Talking/Ob-La-Di | 40 |
| 69 | Studio One SO 2083 | I Shall Be Released/Love Me Always | 40 |
| 69 | Bamboo BAM 11 | I Shall Be Released/Love Me Always (Power) (reissue) | 20 |
| 70 | Bamboo BAM 28 | Young, Gifted and Black/SOUND DIMENSION: Joyland | 20 |
| 70 | Bamboo BAM 39 | Young Generation/You Turned Away | 20 |
| 70 | Bamboo BAM 43 | Message From A Blackman/SOUND DIMENSION: Jamaica Underground | 25 |
| 70 | Upsetter US 339 | Hurry Up/Thanks We Get | 20 |
| 70 | Banana BA 311 | Be A Man/U ROY: Shock Attack | 15 |
| 71 | Banana BA 325 | Suspicious Minds/Haven't You Any Fight Left? | 10 |
| 71 | Banana BA 349 | Freedom Line/SOUND DIMENSION: Version | 15 |
| 72 | Green Door GD 4020 | Hypocrite/JOHNNY LOVER: Straight To The Head | 12 |
| 72 | Prince Buster PB 37 | Our Day Will Come/PRINCE BUSTER: Protection | 12 |
| 72 | Ashanti ASH 411 | I'm In The Mood For Love/TOMMY McCOOK & NOW GENERATION: Eight Years After | 8 |
| 72 | Duke DU 143 | Save The Last Dance For Me/Be The One | 8 |
| 72 | Pama PM 843 | You've Lost That Lovin' Feelin'/RUPIE EDWARDS ALLSTARS: Feeling Version | 8 |
| 72 | Pama Supreme PS 367 | Save The Last Dance For Me/Save The Last Dance Version | 7 |
| 72 | Ackee ACK 407 | I Miss You (Parts 1 & 2) | 8 |
| 73 | Ackee ACK 414 | Let Me Hold Your Hand/Version | 8 |
| 73 | Jaguar JAG 103 | Drifting Away/BONGO LES: Zion Drum | 10 |
| 73 | Grape GR 3053 | Old Time/G.G. ALLSTARS: Dub | 7 |
| 73 | Smash SMA 2328 | Soul Sister/IMPACT ALLSTARS: Soul Sister (Version) | 7 |
| 73 | Count Shelley CS 017 | Now I Know/AUGUSTUS PABLO: Version | 15 |
| 74 | Pama Supreme PS 390 | Thanks We Get/Oppression (both actually by Delroy Butler) | 10 |
| 75 | Faith FA 012 | Party Time/Version | 5 |
| 76 | Cancer CAN 003 | Cool Rasta/Rasta Dub | 12 |
| 76 | Trojan Horse HOSS 124 | Cool Rasta/Dreadlock | 12 |
| 70s | Third World TWDIS 13 | Losing You/Mount Zion (12") | 15 |
| 67 | Studio One SOL 9002 | THE HEPTONES (LP) | 200 |
| 68 | Studio One SOL 9010 | ON TOP (LP) | 300 |
| 72 | Trojan TBL 183 | THE HEPTONES AND THEIR FRIENDS MEET THE NOW GENERATION (LP) | 35 |
| 75 | Island ILPS 9297 | BOOK OF RULES (LP) | 20 |
| 76 | Island ILPS 9381 | NIGHT FOOD (LP) | 20 |
| 76 | Trojan TRLS 128 | COOL RASTA (LP) | 20 |
| 78 | Third World TDWD1 | BETTER DAYS (LP) | 15 |

*(see also Barry Llewellyn, Soul Vendors, Ronald & Lloyd, Ed Nangle, Love Generation, Alton Ellis, Basil Daley, Ken Boothe, Jackie Mittoo)*

## HERB & KAY
| | | | |
|---|---|---|---|
| 54 | Parlophone MSP 6127 | This Ole House/Angels In The Sky | 20 |
| 54 | Parlophone CMSP 23 | This Ole House/Angels In The Sky (export issue) | 20 |
| 55 | Parlophone CMSP 31 | Coffee Blues/Juke Box Jig (export issue) | 20 |

## HERBAL MIXTURE
| | | | |
|---|---|---|---|
| 66 | Columbia DB 8021 | A Love That's Died/Tailor Made | 175 |
| 66 | Columbia DB 8083 | Machines/Please Leave My Mind | 250 |

*(see also Tony McPhee, Groundhogs)*

## HERBALISER
| | | | |
|---|---|---|---|
| 97 | Ninja Tune ZEN 28 | BLOW YOUR HEADPHONES (LP) | 18 |

## HERBIE & ROYALISTS
| | | | |
|---|---|---|---|
| 68 | Saga FID 2121 | SOUL OF THE MATTER (LP) | 15 |

## HERBIE'S PEOPLE
| | | | |
|---|---|---|---|
| 65 | CBS 202005 | Sweet And Tender Romance/You Thrill Me To Pieces | 25 |
| 66 | CBS 202058 | One Little Smile/You Never Know | 20 |
| 67 | CBS 202584 | Residential Area/Humming Bird | 12 |

## HERD
| | | | |
|---|---|---|---|
| 65 | Parlophone R 5284 | Goodbye Baby, Goodbye/Here Comes The Fool | 50 |
| 65 | Parlophone R 5353 | She Was Really Saying Something/It's Been A Long Time Baby | 50 |
| 66 | Parlophone R 5413 | So Much In Love/This Boy's Always Been True | 60 |
| 67 | Fontana TF 819 | I Can Fly/Diary Of A Narcissist | 15 |
| 67 | Fontana TF 856 | From The Underworld/Sweet William | 7 |
| 67 | Fontana TF 887 | Paradise Lost/Come On - Believe Me (in p/s) | 20 |
| 67 | Fontana TF 887 | Paradise Lost/Come On - Believe Me | 7 |
| 68 | Fontana TF 925 | I Don't Want Our Loving To Die/Our Fairy Tale | 6 |
| 68 | Fontana TF 975 | Sunshine Cottage/Miss Jones | 8 |
| 69 | Fontana TF 1011 | The Game/Beauty Queen | 10 |
| 71 | B&C CB 154 | You've Got Me Hangin' From Your Lovin' Tree/I Don't Wanna Go To Sleep Again | 6 |
| 72 | Bumble GEX 1 | From The Underworld/Paradise Lost/On My Way Home (maxi-single) | 5 |
| 73 | Bumble GE 120 | I Don't Want Our Loving To Die/The Game | 5 |
| 68 | Fontana (S)TL 5458 | PARADISE LOST (LP, flipback sleeve, black/silver labels) | 70 |
| 72 | Bumble GEMP 5001 | NOSTALGIA (LP) | 25 |

*(see also Humble Pie, Judas Jump, Andy Bown, Preachers)*

## HERE & NOW
| | | | |
|---|---|---|---|
| 78 | Charly CYS 1055 | End Of The Beginning/Choke A Koala (p/s) | 5 |
| 79 | Charly CEP 122 | A Dog In Hell/Floating Anarchy Radio (p/s) | 5 |
| 80 | Charly NOW 1 | Give And Take | 5 |
| 83 | Chick CHRL 003 | FANTASY SHIFT (LP) | 20 |

*(see also Daevid Allen)*

## HERESY
| | | | |
|---|---|---|---|
| 85 | Earache EAR 01 | NEVER HEALED EP (Flexi) | 20 |
| 89 | In Your Face FACE 4 | WHOSE GENERATION? EP (gatefold p/s) | 10 |
| 88 | In Your Face FACE 01 | FACE UP TO IT! (LP) | 15 |
| 89 | In Your Face FACE 07 | 13 ROCKING ANTHEMS (LP) | 15 |

## HERESY/CONCRETE SOX
| | | | |
|---|---|---|---|
| 87 | Manic Ears MOSH 2 | HERESY/CONCRETE SOX (LP, inner, 1 side each) | 15 |

## HERETIC
| | | | |
|---|---|---|---|
| 84 | Thunderbolt THBE 1004 | BURNT AT THE STAKE EP (Water Of Vice/Keep On Telling Those Lies/Fever Of Love/Watch Me Grow (12", p/s) | 25 |

## HERITAGE
| | | | |
|---|---|---|---|
| 81 | Rondelet ROUND 8 | Strange Place To Be/Misunderstood (p/s) | 20 |
| 82 | Rondelet ABOUT 12 | REMORSE CODE (LP, with lyric insert) | 35 |
| 82 | Plant Life PLR 040 | LIVING BY THE AIR (LP) | 15 |

## HERMAN (CHIN-LOY)
| | | | |
|---|---|---|---|
| 71 | Big Shot BI 573 | El Fishy/HERMAN'S ALLSTARS: Nightmare (B-side actually "In The Spirit" by Lloyd Charmers) | 15 |
| 71 | Big Shot BI 577 | Tar Baby (actually "Crazy Baby" by U. Roy Jr.)/TOMMY McCOOK: Archie | 10 |
| 71 | Big Shot BI 578 | New Love/AUGUSTUS PABLO: The Mood | 25 |
| 71 | Big Shot BI 579 | East Of The River Nile Version/AUGUSTO PABLO: East Of The River Nile | 40 |
| 71 | Duke DU 107 | To The Fields/HERMAN'S VERSION MEN: Fields Version | 40 |
| 71 | Ackee ACK 133 | Dunce Cap/AQUARIANS: Version Cap | 10 |
| 71 | Ackee ACK 140 | Youth Man/AQUARIANS: Version | 10 |
| 71 | Explosion EX 2049 | Love Brother/Uganda | 6 |
| 71 | Escort ERT 854 | Love Brother/Love Brother Version (B-side actually by Tommy McCook) | 7 |
| 71 | Punch PH 55 | Hold The Ghost/AQUARIUS SOUL BAND: Duppy Dance | 15 |
| 71 | Punch PH 58 | Listen To The Beat/AQUARIANS: Sounds Only | 7 |

*(see also Jimbilin)*

## PRIEST HERMAN
| | | | |
|---|---|---|---|
| 64 | Blue Beat BB 266 | We Are Praying/BUSTER'S ALLSTARS: Dallas, Texas | 40 |

## WOODY HERMAN
| | | | |
|---|---|---|---|
| 54 | London HL 8013 | Wooftie/Moten Stomp (as Woody Herman & New Third Herd) | 20 |
| 54 | London HL 8031 | Fancy Woman/Eight Babies To Mind (as Woody Herman's Woodchoppers) | 20 |
| 54 | Capitol CL 14183 | Muskrat Ramble/Woodchopper's Mambo (Woody Herman & His Orchestra) | 12 |
| 55 | London HL 8122 | Sorry 'Bout The Whole Darned Thing/Love's A Dog (with New Third Herd) | 15 |
| 66 | CBS 202522 | Sidewinder/Greasy Sack Blues | 30 |
| 69 | Chess CRS 8095 | Hush/Light My Fire | 10 |

*(see also David Rose Orchestra)*

## HERMAN'S HERMITS

| 64 | Columbia DB 7338 | I'm Into Something Good/Your Hand In Mine | 5 |
|---|---|---|---|
| 64 | Columbia DB 7408 | Show Me Girl/I Know Why | 5 |
| 65 | Columbia DB 7475 | Silhouettes/Can't You Hear My Heartbeat? | 5 |
| 65 | Columbia DB 7546 | Wonderful World/Dream On | 5 |
| 65 | Columbia DB 7670 | Just A Little Bit Better/Take Love, Give Love | 5 |
| 65 | Columbia DB 7791 | A Must To Avoid/The Man With The Cigar | 5 |
| 66 | Columbia DB 7861 | You Won't Be Leaving/Listen People | 6 |
| 66 | Columbia DB 7947 | This Door Swings Both Ways/For Love | 6 |
| 66 | Columbia DB 8012 | No Milk Today/My Reservation's Been Confirmed | 7 |
| 66 | Columbia DB 8076 | East-West/What Is Wrong, What Is Right? | 8 |
| 67 | Columbia DB 8123 | There's A Kind Of Hush (All Over The World)/Gaslite Street | 5 |
| 67 | Columbia DB 8235 | Museum/Moonshine Man | 6 |
| 68 | Columbia DB 8327 | I Can Take Or Leave Your Loving/Marcel's | 5 |
| 68 | Columbia DB 8404 | Sleepy Joe/Just One Girl | 5 |
| 68 | Columbia DB 8446 | Sunshine Girl/Nobody Needs To Know | 5 |
| 68 | Columbia DB 8504 | Something's Happening/The Most Beautiful Thing In My Life | 5 |
| 69 | Columbia DB 8563 | My Sentimental Friend/My Lady | 5 |
| 68 | EMI SLES 15 | No Milk Today/There's A Kind Of Hush (promo only, white label) | 10 |
| 68 | EMI SLES 16 | London Look (promo only, white label) | 8 |
| 69 | Columbia DB 8626 | Here Comes The Star/It's Alright Now | 8 |
| 74 | Buddah BDS 700 | Train/Ride On The Water (withdrawn) | 30 |
| 65 | Columbia 33SX 1727 | HERMAN'S HERMITS (LP) | 20 |
| 66 | Columbia SX 6084 | BOTH SIDES OF HERMAN'S HERMITS (LP) | 15 |
| 67 | Columbia S(C)X 6174 | THERE'S A KIND OF HUSH ALL OVER THE WORLD (LP) | 15 |

*(see also Peter Noone)*

## HERMITS

| 71 | RCA 2135 | She's A Lady (Say What You Want To Say)/Gold Mandela | 15 |
|---|---|---|---|
| 72 | RCA 2265 | The Man/Effen Curly | 50 |
| 75 | Private Stock PVT 19 | Ginny Go Softly/Blond Haired Blue Eyed Boy | 5 |

## ZIGGY HEROE

| 79 | Crypticts CRYPT 1 | The Apart Man/Neon Lights (p/s, 500 only) | 5 |
|---|---|---|---|

## HEROES

| 75 | United Artists UP 36016 | Growing Up/Losing You | 8 |
|---|---|---|---|

## TED HEROLD

| 60 | Polydor NH 66817 | I Don't Know Why/Moonlight | 15 |
|---|---|---|---|

## HERON

| 70 | Dawn DNS 1015 | Take Me Back Home/Minstrel And A King | 15 |
|---|---|---|---|
| 71 | Dawn DNX 2509 | Bye And Bye/Through Time/Only A Hobo/I'm Ready To Leave (p/s) | 25 |
| 71 | Dawn DNLS 3010 | HERON (LP, with insert, some with "this album was recorded live in a field" sticker) | 250 |
| 72 | Dawn DNLS 3025 | TWICE AS NICE & HALF THE PRICE (2-LP, with postcard) | 300 |
| 72 | Dawn DNLS 3025 | TWICE AS NICE & HALF THE PRICE (2-LP, without postcard) | 100 |

*(see also Mike Cooper)*

## DIANA HERON

| 79 | Ethnic Fight DD4432 | Be Thankful/Dub (12") | 15 |
|---|---|---|---|
| 79 | Ethnic Fight EF 088 | Sweeter He Is/TIT COLLINS: Hey Boy | 10 |

## MIKE HERON('S REPUTATION)

| 71 | Island WIP 6101 | Call Me Diamond/Lady Wonder (p/s) | 5 |
|---|---|---|---|
| 75 | Neighbourhood NBH 3109 | Evie/Down On My Knees After Memphis (as Mike Heron's Reputation) | 5 |
| 78 | Zoom ZUM 5 | Sold On Your Love/Portland Rose (p/s) | 5 |
| 71 | Island ILPS 9146 | SMILING MEN WITH BAD REPUTATIONS (LP, gatefold sleeve, pink rim, palm tree label) | 40 |
| 75 | Neighborhood 80637 | MIKE HERON'S REPUTATION (LP) | 20 |

*(see also Incredible String Band)*

## BERNARD HERRMAN

| 69 | Phase 4 Stereo PFS 4173 | THE GREAT MOVIE THRILLERS (LP) | 18 |
|---|---|---|---|
| 75 | Phase 4 Stereo PFS 4309 | THE FANTASY FILM WORLD OF BERNARD HERRMANN (LP) | 18 |
| 76 | Phase 4 Stereo PFS 4337 | THE MYSTERIOUS FILM WORLD OF BERNARD HERRMANN (LP) | 18 |

## KRISTIN HERSH

| 94 | 4AD CAD 4002 | HIPS & MAKERS (LP) | 20 |
|---|---|---|---|

*(see also Throwing Muses)*

## EVERIT HERTER

| 60 | Capitol CL 15142 | Don't Get Serious/Boys Were Made For Girls | 10 |
|---|---|---|---|

## PAT HERVEY & TIARAS & ART SNIDER

| 63 | RCA 1332 | Tears Of Misery/Brother, Can You Spare A Dime (as Pat Hervey) | 7 |
|---|---|---|---|
| 67 | President PT 110 | Can't Get You Out Of My Mind/Givin' In | 10 |

## HERZFELD

| 93 | Duophonic DS45 07 | Two Mothers/Who The Scroungers Are (p/s, mail order only) | 6 |
|---|---|---|---|

## HESITATIONS

| 68 | London HLR 10198 | The Impossible Dream (The Quest)/Nobody Knows You When You're Down And Out | 8 |
|---|---|---|---|
| 69 | London HLR 10180 | Born Free/Push A Little Bit Harder | 20 |
| 68 | London HA-R/SH-R 8360 | THE NEW BORN FREE (LP) | 20 |

## CAROLYN HESTER

| 65 | Dot DS 16750 | Ain't That Rain?/Ten Thousand Candles | 5 |
|---|---|---|---|
| 65 | Dot DS 16751 | Playboys And Playgirls/High Flyin' Bird | 8 |
| 65 | Dot DS 26750 | Come On Back/Three Young Men | 5 |
| 65 | Dot DS 26751 | What Does It Get You?/Now He's Gone | 10 |
| 66 | CBS 202409 | A Reason To Believe/Early Morning Rain | 5 |

| 66 | CBS (S)BPG 62033 | CAROLYN HESTER (LP) | 30 |
| 69 | Pye Intl. NSPL 28121 | THE CAROLYN HESTER COALITION (LP) | 20 |

*(see also Four For Fun)*

## HETHERINGTON
| 73 | Mowest MW 3007 | (It's Just A) Teenage Love Song/That Girl's Alright | 6 |
| 73 | Mowest MW 3007 | (It's Just A) Teenage Love Song/That Girl's Alright (demo in p/s) | 12 |

## JOHN HETHERINGTON
| 70 | RCA 1965 | It's Only Me/Dreamboat Avenue | 8 |

## HEWETT SISTERS
| 59 | HMV POP 567 | Baby-O/Jerri-Lee (I Love Him So) | 25 |

## KEVIN HEWICK
| 82 | Factory FAC 48 | Ophelia's Drinking Song/Cathy Clown//He Holds You Tighter (p/s) | 15 |

## BEN HEWITT
| 59 | Mercury AMT 1041 | You Break Me Up/I Ain't Givin' Up Nothin' | 50 |
| 59 | Mercury AMT 1055 | For Quite A While/Patricia June | 35 |
| 59 | Mercury AMT 1084 | I Want A New Girl Now/My Search | 50 |
| 60 | Mercury ZEP 10035 | BREAK IT UP WITH BEN HEWITT (EP) | 200 |
| 84 | Bear Family BFX 15150 | THEY WOULD CALL ME ELVIS (LP, gatefold) | 15 |
| 85 | Bear Family BFX 15187 | GOOD TIMES AND SOME MIGHTY FINE ROCK 'N' ROLL (LP, gatefold) | 15 |

## GARTH HEWITT
| 70s | Myrrh MYR 1051 | LOVE SONGS FOR THE EARTH (LP) | 30 |
| 78 | Myrrh MYR 1078 | I'M GRATEFUL (LP, insert) | 30 |

## RICHARD HEWSON ORCHESTRA
| 76 | Splash CPLP 1002 | LOVE IS (LP) | 30 |

## PETER HEWSON
| 83 | Reset RES 2 | Take My Hand/Her (p/s) | 40 |
| 83 | Reset REST 2 | Take My Hand/Her (12", p/s) | 60 |

## HEX
| 93 | Ninja Tune ZEN 05 | SOUNDTRACK TO GLOBAL CHAOS (LP) | 20 |
| 93 | Ninja Tune ZEN 07 | DIGITAL LOVE (LP) | 20 |

## EDDIE HEYWOOD
| 58 | Mercury 7MT 131 | Heywood's Bounce/Soft Summer Breeze | 8 |
| 64 | Stateside SS 264 | Theme From The Film "The Prize"/Li'l Darlin' | 6 |

*(see also Hugo Winterhalter)*

## WINSTON HEYWOOD (& HOMBRES)
| 71 | Dynamic DYN 424 | Bam-Sa-Bo/Version | 8 |
| 72 | Dynamic DYN 441 | Stop The War/Version | 10 |
| 72 | Dynamic DYN 457 | Seek And You'll Find/Version | 8 |
| 73 | Attack ATT 8046 | Da Doo Ron Ron/Version | 8 |
| 76 | Mango MAN 1013 | Long Long Time/UPSETTERS: Long Time Dub | 10 |

*(see also Winston Harewood, Fud Christian All Stars)*

## HGB
| 81 | Backshop BS 001 | Chase The Night Away/Keep Off The Grass (p/s) | 7 |

## LENNIE HIBBERT & COUNT OSSIE BAND
| 69 | Doctor Bird DB 1113 | Pure Sole/PATSY: A Man Is Two Faced | 120 |

*(see also Sound Dimension)*

## AL HIBBLER
| 55 | Brunswick 05420 | Unchained Melody/Daybreak (gold label) | 15 |
| 55 | Brunswick 05420 | Unchained Melody/Daybreak (silver label) | 8 |
| 55 | Brunswick 05454 | They Say You're Laughing At Me/I Can't Put My Arms Around A Memory | 10 |
| 55 | London HL 8184 | Now I Lay Me Down To Dream/Danny Boy | 35 |

## EDDIE HICKEY
| 59 | Decca F 11153 | Lady May/Cap And Gown | 7 |
| 60 | Decca F 11204 | Who Could Be Bluer?/Plain Jane | 7 |
| 60 | Decca F 11241 | Another Sleepless Night/Barbara | 7 |

## ERSEL HICKEY
| 59 | Fontana H 198 | You Threw A Dart/Don't Be Afraid Of Love | 70 |
| 59 | Fontana H 198 | You Threw A Dart/Don't Be Afraid Of Love (78) | 20 |

## DWAYNE HICKMAN
| 60 | Capitol CL 15164 | I'm A Lover, Not A Fighter/I Pass Your House | 10 |

## HICKORY
| 68 | Lyntone 1928 | Scottish Magic (Promo flexi for Tartan Ale, p/s) | 20 |
| 69 | CBS 3963 | Green Light/Key | 30 |

*(see also Equals)*

## HICKORY SIX
| 64 | Oak RGJ 149 | Feelin Blue/Hello My Darling | 80 |

## COLIN HICKS (& CABIN BOYS)
| 57 | Pye 7N 15114 | Wild Eyes And Tender Lips/Empty Arms Blues (with Cabin Boys) | 15 |
| 57 | Pye 7N 15125 | La Dee Dah/Wasteland | 10 |
| 58 | Pye 7N 15163 | Little Boy Blue/Jambalaya | 10 |

## DAN HICKS & HIS HOT LICKS
| 72 | Blue Thumb ILPS 9204 | STRIKING IT RICH (LP) | 18 |

*(see also Charlatans (U.S.))*

## JIMMY HICKS
| 72 | London HLU 10396 | I'm Mr. Big Stuff/Tell Her That I Love You | 15 |

## MARVA HICKS
| 78 | Infinity 102 | Looking Over My Shoulder/Here I Go Again | 15 |

MINT VALUE £

## HIDDEN CAMERAS
03  Rough Trade RTRADLP 077 THE SMELL OF OUR OWN (LP, hand stencilled sleeve) .................................................. 30

## HIDDEN IDENTITY
94  Pure Rudeness HIDBBB1 BLUNTED BUMPKIN BUSTERS (EP) .................................................. 30
*(see also Evil Ed)*

## HIDEAWAYS
69  Action ACT 4544 Hide Out/Jolly Joe .................................................. 25
71  Jay Boy BOY 29 Hide Out/Jolly Joe (reissue) .................................................. 8

## HI-FI
84  Butt MGLS 003 Louie Louie/Summertime .................................................. 8
*(see also Ian Matthews)*

## HI-FI FOUR
56  Parlophone MSP 6210 Band Of Gold/Davy, You Upset My Life .................................................. 70

## HI FI'S
63  Piccadilly 7N 35130 Take Me Or Leave Me/I'm Struck .................................................. 8
64  Pye 7N 15635 Will Yer Won't Yer/She's The One .................................................. 10
64  Pye 7N 15710 I Keep Forgettin'/Why Can't I Stop Loving You? .................................................. 35
65  Pye 7N 15788 Baby's In Black/Kiss And Run .................................................. 15
66  Alp 595 010 It's Gonna Be Morning/I Wanna Hear You Say Yeah .................................................. 70

## JOE HIGGS
67  Coxsone CS 7004 Neighbour Neighbour/MELODIANS: I Should Have Made It Up .................................................. 200
67  Island WI 3026 I Am The Song/Worry No More .................................................. 60
68  Island WI 3131 You Hurt My Soul/LYNN TAITT: Why Am I Treated So Bad? .................................................. 100
70  Clandisc CLA 208 Mademoiselle/DYNAMITES: Lion .................................................. 30
71  Big BG 312 Burning Fire/RUPIE EDWARDS ALL STARS: Version .................................................. 12
71  New Beat NB 087 Mother Radio/DAWN SHARON: Little Deeds .................................................. 12
71  Supreme SUP 215 Burning Fire/RUPIE EDWARDS ALL STARS: Push And Pull .................................................. 12
72  Sioux SI 005 The World Is Spinning Around/THE REACTION: Hallelujah .................................................. 20
72  Sioux SI 014 The Wave Of War/JUMBO STERLING: Shaft .................................................. 20
72  Sioux SI 021 Lay A Foundation/JACKIE ROWLAND: Lay A Foundation (Version) .................................................. 15
75  Grounation GRO 2021 More Slavery/Version .................................................. 10
76  Ethnic Fight EF 038 Creation/AUGUSTUS PABLO & SUPER 8 CORPORATION: Creative Version .................................................. 15
75  Grounation GROL 508 LIFE OF CONTRADICTION (LP) .................................................. 50
78  1 STOP STOP 1002 UNITY IS POWER (LP) .................................................. 15
*(see also Higgs & Wilson, Bob Marley/Wailers, Soul Vendors)*

## (JOE) HIGGS & (ROY) WILSON
60  Blue Beat (B)B 3 Manny Oh/When You Tell Me Baby (yellow label/blue writing [B3] or blue label/silver writing [BB 3]) (with Ken Richards & His Comets) .................................................. 20
61  Starlite ST45 035 Pretty Baby/I Long For The Day .................................................. 20
61  Starlite ST45 036 Lover's Song/It Is A Day .................................................. 20
61  Starlite ST45 042 Come On Home/The Robe .................................................. 20
61  Starlite ST45 053 Sha Ba Ba/Change Of Mind .................................................. 20
62  Blue Beat BB 95 How Can I Be Sure/Mighty Man .................................................. 25
63  R&B JB 109 Let Me Know/Bye And Bye .................................................. 25
63  Blue Beat BB 190 If You Want Pardon/BABA BROOKS BAND: Musical Communion .................................................. 20
63  Island WI 081 Last Saturday Morning/Praise The Lord .................................................. 20
64  Rio R 29 Love Is Not For Me/Gone Is Yesterday .................................................. 15
65  Blue Beat BB 277 Pain In My Heart/BUSTER ALL STARS: Going West .................................................. 25
70  Clandisc CLA 218 Don't Mind Me/GLEN AND ROY: Angel .................................................. 8
*(see also Clancy Eccles)*

## HIGH
69  CBS 4164 Long Live The High/Beggar Man Dan .................................................. 30

## HIGH & MIGHTY
66  HMV POP 1548 Tryin' To Stop Cryin'/Escape From Cuba .................................................. 35

## HIGH AUTHORITY
91  Optimisim OPT 12005 I'm The Man (12") .................................................. 10

## HIGH BROOM
70  Island WI 6088 Dancing In The Moonlight/Percy's On The Run .................................................. 15
73  Columbia DB 8969 Dancing In The Moonlight/Percy's On The Run (reissue) .................................................. 7
*(see also Leviathan, Jason Crest, Holy Mackerel)*

## HIGHBURY MARCHERS
72  Columbia DB 8930 The Official Arsenal March/Arsenal Boogie .................................................. 8

## HIGHGATE CHILDREN
62  Piccadilly 7N 25065 The Battle Of Highgate Hill/Pity The Poor Pedestrian .................................................. 6

## HIGH KEYS
63  London HLK 9768 Que Sera Sera/Daddy, Ooh Long Legs .................................................. 30

## HIGH LEVEL RANTERS
68  Topic 12TS 186 NORTHUMBERLAND FOR EVER (LP, blue label, 2 different sleeves) .................................................. 15
69  Leader/Trailer LER 2007 THE LADS OF NORTHUMBERLAND (LP) .................................................. 18
75  Topic 2-12TS 271/2 THE BONNY PIT LADDIE (2-LP, blue label) .................................................. 18
77  Broadside BRO 128 ENGLISH SPORTING BALLADS (LP, 1-side Martin Wyndham-Read, 2,000 only) .................................................. 25

## HIGHLY LIKELY
74  BBC RESL 10 Whatever Happened To You? (Likely Lads Theme)/God Bless Everyone .................................................. 10
*(see also Mike Hugg, Rodney Bewes)*

## HIGH NUMBERS
64  Fontana TF 480 Zoot Suit/I'm The Face (textured labels with "Mono" on labels) .................................................. 1000
80  Back Door DOOR 4 I'm The Face/Zoot Suit (reissue, picture sleeve, silver plastic labels) .................................................. 20

| | | |
|---|---|---|
| 92 | Fontana TF 480 | I'm The Face/Zoot Suit (reissue, smooth labels with "stereo" on labels, die-cut sleeve from Fontana Box) ......... 20 |

*(see also Who)*

**HIGH SHELF**
| 70 | Sprint SP 2 | Suddenly You/Wendy ......... 40 |

**HIGH SOCIETY (1)**
| 66 | Fontana TF 771 | People Passing By/Star Of Eastern Street ......... 22 |

*(see also Friday Browne, Graham Gouldman, Manchester Mob)*

**HIGH SOCIETY (2)**
| 70 | CBS 4746 | Only You Only You/Tell Me Now ......... 15 |

**HIGH STREET EAST**
| 69 | Rubber RUBBER ONE | Newcastle Brown/Everybody Knows (p/s) ......... 70 |
| 69 | Rubber RUBBER ONE | Newcastle Brown/Everybody Knows (no p/s) ......... 45 |

**HIGH TIDE (1)**
| 69 | Liberty LBS 83264 | SEA SHANTIES (LP, gatefold sleeve, blue label) ......... 200 |
| 70 | Liberty LBS 83294 | HIGH TIDE (LP, blue label) ......... 150 |

*(see also Hawkwind, Misunderstood, Denny Gerrard, Magic Muscle, Third Ear Band)*

**HIGH TIDE (2)**
| 81 | Sunday Morning (No Cat. No.) | Baby Dancing/Letter From A Coward (mail-order only) ......... 8 |

**DEAN HIGHTOWER**
| 60 | HMV CLP 1360 | TWANGY - WITH A BEAT (LP) ......... 50 |

**DONNA HIGHTOWER**
| 60 | Capitol ST 1273 | GEE BABY (LP) ......... 15 |

**ROSETTA HIGHTOWER**
| 68 | Toast TT 506 | Pretty Red Balloons/How Can You Mistreat (The One You Love)? ......... 30 |
| 68 | Toast TT 509 | I Can't Give Back The Love I Feel For You/Big Bird ......... 80 |
| 69 | CBS 4584 | One Heart For Sale/What Do I Do? ......... 10 |
| 70 | CBS 4758 | April Fools/I'll Hold Out My Hand ......... 6 |
| 70 | CBS 4988 | Persuader/Come Together ......... 6 |
| 71 | CBS 7068 | Go Pray For Tomorrow/Give Me Just A Little More Line ......... 6 |
| 73 | Philips 6006 291 | The Walls Fell Down/Captain's Army ......... 40 |
| 71 | CBS 64201 | HIGHTOWER (LP) ......... 40 |
| 71 | Rediffusion ZS 88 | ROSETTA HIGHTOWER (LP) ......... 15 |

*(see also Orlons, Ian Green [Revelation])*

**HIGH TREASON**
| 80 | Burlington BURLS 001 | Saturday Night Special/Waste My Love (p/s) ......... 140 |
| 80 | Burlington BURLS 001 | Saturday Night Special/Waste My Love (no p/s) ......... 80 |

**HIGHWAY**
| 74 | EMI EMC 3019 | HIGHWAY (LP) ......... 20 |
| 75 | EMI EMA 770 | SMOKING AT THE EDGE (LP, gatefold sleeve) ......... 35 |

**HIGHWAYMEN**
| 62 | United Artists UP 1001 | Birdman (with narration from Burt Lancaster)/Cindy Oh Cindy ......... 5 |

**HIGH WINDOWS**
| 68 | CBS 3208 | Maybe Someday/Your Eyes ......... 10 |
| 68 | CBS 3437 | Anybody Need A Lover/El El Israel ......... 10 |

**HIGSONS**
| 82 | Two Tone CHSTT21 | Tear The Whole Thing Down/Ylang Ylang (p/s, paper labels) ......... 10 |
| 82 | Two Tone CHSTT121 | Tear The Whole Thing Down/Ylang Ylang (12", p/s) ......... 12 |
| 83 | Two Tone CHSTT24 | Run Me Down/Put The Punk Back Into Funk (p/s, paper labels) ......... 10 |
| 83 | Two Tone CHSTT 1224 | Run Me Down (extended)/Instrumental/Put The Punk Back Into Funk (1 & 2) (12", p/s) ......... 15 |
| 82 | Two Tone CHS TT 1 | Tear The Whole Thing Down/Ylang Ylang (12" promo shared with Apollinaires) ......... 35 |

*(see also New York New York, Serious Drinking)*

**HIJACK**
| 88 | Music Of Life NOTE016 | Style Wars (12") ......... 15 |
| 88 | Syndicate 655517 6 | The Badman is Robbin'/Hold No Hostage/Doomsday (12" EP) ......... 12 |
| 88 | Music Of Life NOTE021 | Hold No Hostage/Doomsday Of Rap (12") ......... 15 |
| 89 | Music Of Life NOTE016R | Style Wars Revenge (12") ......... 12 |
| 91 | Rhyme Syndicate 6555176 | HORNS OF JERICHO (LP) ......... 35 |
| 96 | Reservoir RES 18 | THE ORIGINAL HORNS OF JERICHO (LP) ......... 80 |

**HILARY HILARY**
| 80 | Modern STP 2 | How Come You're So Dumb/Rich Kid Blues (p/s) ......... 60 |

*(see also Roger Taylor, Queen)*

**RAY HILDEBRAND**
| 70s | Myrrh MST 6508 | SPECIAL KIND OF MAN (LP) ......... 20 |

**DIANE HILDEBRANDE**
| 69 | Elektra EKSN 45055 | Jan's Blues/Early Morning Blues And Greens ......... 10 |
| 69 | Elektra EKL 4031 | EARLY MORNING BLUES AND GREENS (LP) ......... 20 |

**HI-LITERS**
| 58 | Mercury AMT 1011 | Dance Me To Death/Cha Cha Rock ......... 150 |
| 58 | Mercury AMT 1011 | Dance Me To Death/Cha Cha Rock (78) ......... 35 |

**HI LITES**
| 65 | London HL 9967 | Hey Baby/Groovey ......... 20 |

**BUNKER HILL & RAYMEN**
| 62 | Stateside SS 135 | Hide & Go Seek Parts 1 & 2 ......... 25 |

## DAVID HILL
| 57 | Vogue V 9076 | All Shook Up/Melody For Lovers (with Ray Ellis Orchestra, probably unreleased)....... 200 |
| 57 | Vogue V 9076 | All Shook Up/Melody For Lovers (78, with Ray Ellis Orchestra) .............................. 35 |
| 58 | RCA RCA 1041 | That's Love/Keep Me In Mind (with Joe Relsman's Orchestra & Chorus).................... 100 |
| 58 | RCA RCA 1041 | That's Love/Keep Me In Mind (78, with Joe Relsman's Orchestra & Chorus) .............. 30 |

## JEFF HILL BAND
| 77 | Chiswick NS 16 | I Want You To Dance WIth Me/Feel Like Loving You (p/s) ...................................... 10 |
| 79 | Baloon BLOW 1/SRTS/79/CUS-557 | Something's Wrong With My Baby/Whatever She Wanted (p/s, 500 only) ........... 60 |

## JESSIE HILL
| 60 | London HLU 9117 | Ooh Poo Pah Doo Parts 1 & 2 ............................................................................. 25 |

## RONNI HILL
| 77 | Creole CR 138 | You Keep Me Hanging On/I Wouldn't Give You Up (as Roni Hill) ................................ 10 |

## VINCE HILL
| 62 | Pye 7N 17373 | Not Any More/Just As Long (As You Belong To Me) ............................................... 7 |
| 62 | Piccadilly 7N 35043 | The Rivers Run Dry/Not Any More .................................................................... 8 |
| 62 | Piccadilly 7N 35068 | There You Go/Just As Long As (You Belong To Me)............................................... 8 |
| 63 | Piccadilly 7N 35108 | A Day At The Seaside/Tricks Of The Trade ......................................................... 8 |
| 63 | Piccadilly 7N 35118 | As It Was Written/Is There Anyone At Home ...................................................... 5 |
| 63 | Piccadilly 7N 35148 | Blue Velvet/Like Anything ............................................................................... 5 |
| 64 | Piccadilly 7N 35161 | If You Knew/Fools & Lovers ............................................................................. 5 |
| 64 | Piccadilly 7N 35192 | It's Only Make Believe/Let The Wind Blow ......................................................... 5 |
| 65 | Columbia DB 7781 | Take Me To Your Heart Again/Push Push ........................................................... 6 |
| 66 | Columbia SEG 8509 | FOUR SIDES OF VINCE HILL (EP) ...................................................................... 10 |

*(see also [Jackie &] Raindrops, Elmer Bernstein)*

## Z.Z. HILL
| 65 | R&B MRB 5005 | Someone To Love Me/Have Mercy Someone......................................................... 30 |
| 69 | Action ACT 4532 | Make Me Yours/What Am I Living For?............................................................... 100 |
| 71 | Mojo 2092 019 | Faithful And True/I Think I'd Do It .................................................................... 8 |
| 75 | United Artists UP 35727 | I Keep On Loving You/Whoever's Thrilling You..................................................... 8 |
| 77 | CBS 5553 | Love Is So Good When You're Stealin' It/Need You By My Side ................................ 8 |
| 66 | Sue IEP 711 | GIMME GIMME (EP, 2 tracks each by Z.Z. Hill & Intentions; in p/s)........................ 300 |
| 66 | Sue IEP 711 | GIMME GIMME (EP, 2 tracks each by Z.Z. Hill & Intentions) ................................. 100 |
| 69 | Action ACLP 6004 | WHOLE LOT OF SOUL (LP).............................................................................. 60 |
| 72 | Mojo 2916 013 | THE BRAND NEW Z.Z. HILL (LP)....................................................................... 20 |
| 75 | Contempo CLP 515 | THE BRAND NEW Z.Z. HILL (LP, reissue)............................................................ 15 |
| 84 | Kent KENT 018 | DUES PAID IN FULL (LP, compilation) ............................................................... 20 |

*(see also Intentions)*

## STEVE HILLAGE
| 77 | Virgin VDJ 23 | Leylines To Glassdome/GLEN PHILLIPS: Lies (p/s, gig freebie) ................................ 6 |
| 75 | Virgin V 2031 | FISH RISING (LP, lyric insert, coloured 'twin' label)............................................. 20 |
| 77 | Virgin VGD 3501 | LIVE HERALD (2-LP, with limited edition mail order lyric sheet in English, French or German) ................................................................................................... 30 |
| 78 | Virgin V 2098 | GREEN (LP, green vinyl, with insert)................................................................. 15 |
| 79 | Virgin VR1 | RAINBOW DOME MUSIC (LP, clear vinyl, stickered sleeve) ................................... 15 |

*(see also Gong, Khan, Arzachel, Clearlight, Radio Actors, System 7)*

## HILLER BROTHERS
| 60s | Honey Hit TB 124 | Little Darlin'/Changin' My Mind (with p/s) ....................................................... 10 |
| 60s | Honey Hit TB 124 | Little Darlin'/Changin' My Mind ....................................................................... 6 |

## JANE HILLERY
| 66 | Columbia DB 7918 | You've Got That Hold On Me/Take Me Away ....................................................... 40 |

*(see also Magistrates)*

## MABLE HILLERY
| 69 | Xtra XTRA 1063 | IT'S SO HARD TO BE A NIGGER (LP)................................................................... 20 |

## CHRIS HILLS
| 72 | Atlantic 2400208 | EVERYTHING IS EVERYTHING (LP) ..................................................................... 25 |

## GILLIAN HILLS
| 65 | Vogue VRS 7005 | Tomorrow Is Another Day/Look At Them ........................................................... 10 |

## HILLTOPPERS
| 54 | London HL 8026 | From The Vine Came The Grape/Time Will Tell..................................................... 15 |
| 54 | London HL 8070 | Poor Butterfly/Wrapped Up In A Dream ............................................................ 20 |
| 54 | London HL 8081 | Will You Remember?/The Old Cabaret .............................................................. 20 |
| 54 | London HL 8092 | If I Didn't Care/Bettina ................................................................................. 20 |
| 55 | London HL 8116 | Time Waits For No One/You Try Somebody Else ................................................. 20 |
| 55 | London HLD 8168 | The Kentuckian Song/I Must Be Dreaming ......................................................... 20 |
| 55 | London HLD 8208 | Searching/All I Need Is You ............................................................................. 35 |
| 56 | London HLD 8221 | Only You (And You Alone)/(It Will Have To Do) Until The Real Thing Comes Along (gold label lettering) .............................................................................................. 30 |
| 56 | London HLD 8221 | Only You (And You Alone)/(It Will Have To Do) Until The Real Thing Comes Along (silver label lettering) ........................................................................................... 15 |
| 56 | London HLD 8255 | My Treasure/Last Word In Love........................................................................ 50 |
| 56 | London HLD 8278 | Do The Bop/When You're Alone ...................................................................... 100 |
| 56 | London HLD 8298 | Tryin'/D-A-R-L-I-N' ....................................................................................... 30 |
| 56 | London HLD 8333 | So Tired/Faded Rose ..................................................................................... 30 |
| 57 | London HLD 8381 | Marianne/You're Wasting Your Time ................................................................ 15 |
| 57 | London HLD 8441 | I'm Serious/I Love My Girl .............................................................................. 15 |
| 57 | London HLD 8455 | A Fallen Star/Footsteps ................................................................................. 15 |
| 57 | London HLD 8528 | The Joker/Chicken, Chicken ............................................................................ 40 |
| 58 | London HLD 8603 | You Sure Look Good To Me/Starry Eyes ............................................................ 20 |

| | | | |
|---|---|---|---|
| 60 | London HLD 9038 | Alone/The Prisoner's Song | 10 |
| 55 | London RE-P 1012 | PRESENTING THE HILLTOPPERS | 20 |
| 55 | London RE-D 1030 | THE HILLTOPPERS VOL. 2 | 20 |
| 57 | London RE-D 1099 | THE HILLTOPPERS VOL. 3 | 20 |
| 57 | London HA-D 2029 | THE TOWERING HILLTOPPERS | 20 |
| 57 | London HA-D 2071 | TOPS IN POPS | 20 |

*(see also Sacca, Billy Vaughn)*

## NICKY HILTON
| | | | |
|---|---|---|---|
| 65 | Decca F 12099 | Give Us Your Blessing/Always In My Heart | 6 |

## RONNIE HILTON
| | | | |
|---|---|---|---|
| 55 | HMV 7M 285 | Prize Of Gold/A Blossom Fell | 15 |
| 55 | HMV 7M 303 | Just Say You Love Her/My Loving Hands | 10 |
| 56 | HMV 7M 336 | Bella Notte/He | 10 |
| 56 | HMV 7M 358 | Young And Foolish/Moments To Remember | 7 |
| 56 | HMV 7M 382 | The Last Frontier/Here Comes My Love | 6 |
| 56 | HMV 7M 390 | No Other Love/It's All Been Done Before (B-side with Alma Cogan) | 10 |
| 67 | HMV POP 1600 | If I Were A Rich Man/Laughing Gnome (Bowie penned B-side) | 40 |
| 68 | Columbia DB 8506 | Glory Glory Leeds United/We Shall Not Be Moved (with Leeds United AFC) | 6 |

*(see also Alma Cogan)*

## HILTONAIRES
| | | | |
|---|---|---|---|
| 67 | Coxsone CSL 8004 | THE BEST OF THE HILTONAIRES (LP) | 80 |

## HIM & THE OTHERS
| | | | |
|---|---|---|---|
| 66 | Parlophone R 5510 | I Mean It/She's Got Eyes That Tell Lies | 850 |

## JUSTIN HINDS/HINES (& DOMINOES)
| | | | |
|---|---|---|---|
| 64 | Ska Beat JB 176 | King Samuel/River Jordan | 25 |
| 65 | Ska Beat JB 187 | Mother Banner/DON DRUMMOND & HIS GROUP: Apanga | 55 |
| 65 | Island WI 171 | Botheration/Satan (as Justin Hines & Dominoes) | 30 |
| 65 | Island WI 174 | Jump Out Of The Frying Pan/Holy Dove (as Justin Hines & Dominoes) | 30 |
| 65 | Island WI 194 | Rub Up, Push Up/The Ark | 25 |
| 65 | Island WI 232 | Turn Them Back/TOMMY McCOOK: Rocket Ship | 60 |
| 65 | Island WI 236 | Peace And Love/Skalarama (B-side actually by Lyn Taitt & Comets) | 40 |
| 66 | Doctor Bird DB 1048 | The Higher The Monkey Climbs/Fight For Your Right | 30 |
| 67 | Island WI 3048 | On A Saturday Night/Save A Bread | 22 |
| 67 | Treasure Isle TI 7002 | Here I Stand/No Good Rudie | 20 |
| 67 | Treasure Isle TI 7005 | Carry Go Bring Come/Fight Too Much | 40 |
| 67 | Treasure Isle TI 7014 | On A Saturday Night/Save A Bread | 20 |
| 67 | Treasure Isle TI 7017 | Once A Man/TOMMY McCOOK & SUPERSONICS: Persian Cat | 20 |
| 68 | Treasure Isle TI 7063 | Botheration/VINCENT HINDS: Mouth Trombone | 15 |
| 68 | Treasure Isle TI 7068 | Mighty Redeemer (Parts 1 & 2) | 15 |
| 69 | Trojan TR 652 | You Should've Known Better/TOMMY McCOOK & SUPERSONICS: Third Figure | 15 |
| 70 | Duke Reid DR 2511 | Say Me Say/I Want It | 15 |
| 70 | Duke DU 67 | Drink Milk/Everywhere I Go (as Justin Hines & Dominoes) | 15 |
| 72 | Treasure Isle TI 7068 | Mighty Redeemer/DUKE REID'S ALL STARS: Version | 12 |
| 75 | Pama PM 4001 | Sinners Where You Going To Hide?/If It's Love You Need | 8 |
| 12 | Duke THB 7023 | Sufferation 1969/Warm Up | 12 |
| 76 | Island ILPS 9416 | JEZEBEL (LP) | 30 |

*(see also Lyn Taitt, Skatalites, Don Drummond)*

## NEVILLE HINDS
| | | | |
|---|---|---|---|
| 70 | Duke Reid DR 2503 | Sunday Gravy (as Neville Hines)/JOHN HOLT: Write Her A Letter | 20 |
| 70 | Camel CA 44 | London Bridge/SCORCHERS: Things And Time (B-side act. by Wailing Souls) | 20 |
| 70 | Gas GAS 126 | I Who Have Nothing/You Send Me | 8 |
| 71 | Explosion EX 2043 | Delivered/Specially For You (B-side actually by Blake Boy) | 6 |
| 72 | Upsetter US 384 | Blackman's Time/UPSETTERS: Version | 10 |
| 73 | Harry J HJ 6657 | Musical Splendour/JOHN CROW GENERATION: Musical Drum & Bass | 6 |

*(see also Neville Irons & Byron Lee & The Dragonaires, Lloyd Robinson, Marvels, Alton Ellis)*

## RUPERT HINE
| | | | |
|---|---|---|---|
| 72 | Purple PUR 105 | Hamburgers/A Varlet Lad T'was Samuel Green (Historical Moments - Part 7) | 6 |
| 76 | Electric WOT 8 | Snakes Don't Dance Fast/Hopi Smile | 6 |
| 71 | Purple TPSA 7502 | PICK UP A BONE (LP, with David MacIver, textured gatefold sleeve) | 50 |
| 73 | Purple TPSA 7509 | UNFINISHED PICTURE (LP, gatefold sleeve) | 50 |

*(see also Jon Pertwee, Quantum Jump)*

## FRAZER HINES
| | | | |
|---|---|---|---|
| 68 | Major Minor MM 579 | Who's Dr. Who?/Punch And Judy Man | 70 |

## HINES, HINES & DAD
| | | | |
|---|---|---|---|
| 68 | CBS 3667 | Something Extra/Hambone | 5 |

## SONNY HINES
| | | | |
|---|---|---|---|
| 65 | King KG 1009 | Anytime, Any Day, Anywhere/Nothing Like Your Love | 25 |

## HINGE
| | | | |
|---|---|---|---|
| 68 | RCA RCA 1721 | The Village Postman/You'd Better Go Home | 10 |

## MICAH P HINSON
| | | | |
|---|---|---|---|
| 04 | Sketchbook SKETCH XX3 | The Day Texas Sank To The Bottom Of The Sea/Can't Change A Thing/It's Hard To Look At You And Breathe At The Same Time (10") | 10 |
| 04 | Sketchbook SKETCH XX4 | Beneath The Rose/The Dreams Didn't Work Out Right | 8 |
| 06 | Sketchbook SKETCH XX6 | Jackeyed/Don't Leave Me Now! (Reprise) | 8 |
| 06 | Sketch 013LP | MICAH P HINSON AND THE OPERA CIRCUIT (LP) | 40 |
| 06 | Full Time Hobby FTH 056LP | MICAH P HINSON AND RED EMPIRE ORCHESTRA (LP) | 35 |
| 10 | Full Time Hobby FTH 093LP | MICAH P HINSON AND THE PIONEER SABOTEURS (2-LP) | 25 |

MINT VALUE £

**JOE HINTON**

| | | | |
|---|---|---|---|
| 64 | Vocalion VP 9224 | Funny How Time Slips Away/You Gotta Have Love | 30 |
| 66 | Vocalion VP 9258 | Just A Kid Named Joe/Pledging My Love | 10 |
| 66 | Vocalion VA-P 8043 | FUNNY HOW TIME SLIPS AWAY (LP) | 120 |

**HI-NUMBERS**

| | | | |
|---|---|---|---|
| 65 | Decca F 12233 | Heart Of Stone/Dancing In The Street | 60 |

**HIPPIES**

| | | | |
|---|---|---|---|
| 63 | Cameo Parkway P 863 | Memory Lane/REGGIE HARRISON: A Lonely Piano | 20 |

**HIPPOLYTES**

| | | | |
|---|---|---|---|
| 77 | Top Deck TD 003 | Don;t Make The Promises/I Love Sue | 7 |

**HIPPY BOYS**

| | | | |
|---|---|---|---|
| 69 | Trojan TR 668 | Love/The Whole Family | 25 |
| 69 | Trojan TR 669 | Michael Row The Boat Ashore/Who Is Coming To Dinner | 40 |
| 69 | Bullet BU 412 | Hog In A Me Minte/Lorna Run | 50 |
| 69 | Bullet BU 413 | What's Your Excuse?/Tell Me Tell | 50 |
| 69 | Camel CA 29 | Cat Nip/Cooyah (both as Hippie Boys) | 30 |
| 69 | High Note HS 021 | Doctor No Go/Sailing (B-side actually "Faberge" by Baba Brooks & Band) | 30 |
| 69 | High Note HS 030 | Chicken Lickin'/BABA BROOKS: Old Man Flint | 25 |
| 69 | High Note HS 035 | Reggae Pressure/SOUL RHYTHMS: It Hurts (B-side actually Soul Rhythms) | 30 |
| 69 | Unity UN 528 | Dreams To Remember/Peace Maker | 70 |
| 70 | High Note HS 038 | Piccadilly Hop/Nigeria | 70 |
| 70 | Duke DU 92 | Cloud Burst/LLOYD CHARMERS: Message From A Black Man | 80 |
| 70 | Explosion EX 2032 | Vengeance/Look-Ea-Py-Py | 40 |
| 71 | Big Shot 580 | Voodoo/LITTLE ROY: Hard Fighter | 10 |
| 69 | Big Shot BSLP 5005 | REGGAE WITH THE HIPPY BOYS (LP, actually on High Note label) | 175 |
| 11 | Sunspot LP 003 | REGGAE WITH THE HIPPY BOYS, (LP reissue, 350 only, signed insert) | 30 |

*(see also Upsetters, Family Man, Danny Williams, Tony, Hippy Boys, Cynthia Richards, Pioneers)*

**HIPSTER IMAGE**

| | | | |
|---|---|---|---|
| 65 | Decca F 12137 | Can't Let Her Go/Make Her Mine | 500 |
| 65 | Lyntone LYN 951 | KEELE RAG RECORD (4 tracks but 2 by Hipster Image - All For You/A Little Piece Of Leather) | 30 |
| 11 | Decca F 12133 | Can't Let Her Go/Make Her Mine (reissue) | 10 |

*(see also Climax Chicago Blues Band)*

**HIRSCHE NICHT AUFS SOFA**

| | | | |
|---|---|---|---|
| 86 | United Dairies UD 018 | MELCHIOR (LP, with insert) | 30 |

**AL HIRT**

| | | | |
|---|---|---|---|
| 63 | RCA 1380 | Java/I Can't Get Started | 6 |
| 67 | RCA RCA 1590 | Theme From "The Monkees"/Tarzan March | 5 |

*(see also Ann-Margret)*

**HI-SPOTS**

| | | | |
|---|---|---|---|
| 58 | Melodisc 1457 | Lend Me Your Comb/I Don't Hurt Anymore | 22 |
| 58 | Melodisc 1473 | Secretly/I Got | 22 |

**HIS WORD**

| | | | |
|---|---|---|---|
| 87 | Lyn 14747 | Loving In Degrees/Life + 1 = 3 | 60 |

**ALFRED HITCHCOCK**

| | | | |
|---|---|---|---|
| 58 | London HA-P 2130 | MUSIC TO BE MURDERED BY (LP, music by Jeff Alexander Orchestra, mono) | 20 |
| 58 | London SH-P 6012 | MUSIC TO BE MURDERED BY (LP, music by Jeff Alexander Orchestra, stereo) | 20 |
| 60 | Wonderland LP 89 | ALFRED HITCHCOCK PRESENTS GHOST STORIES FOR YOUNG PEOPLE (LP, read by Peter Allen) | 30 |

*(see Jeff Alexander)*

**ROBYN HITCHCOCK (& THE EGYPTIANS)**

| | | | |
|---|---|---|---|
| 81 | Armageddon AS 008 | The Man Who Invented Himself/Dancing On God's Thumb (p/s, some with flexidisc "It's A Mystic Trip"/"Grooving On An Inner Plane" [4 SPURT 1]) | 8 |
| 81 | Armageddon AS 008 | The Man Who Invented Himself/Dancing On God's Thumb (p/s, some without flexidisc "It's A Mystic Trip"/"Grooving On An Inner Plane" [4 SPURT 1]) | 6 |
| 82 | Albion ION 103 | America/It Was The Night/How Do You Work This Thing? (p/s) | 8 |
| 82 | Midnight Music DING 2 | Eaten By Her Own Dinner/Listening To The Higsons/Dr. Sticky (p/s) | 7 |
| 82 | Midnight Music DONG 2 | Eaten By Her Own Dinner/Grooving On An Inner Plane/Messages Of The Dark The Abandoned Brain/Happy The Golden Prince (12", p/s) | 10 |
| 83 | Albion 12 ION 1036 | Nightride To Trinidad (Long Version)/Kingdom Of Love/Midnight Fish (12", p/s) | 10 |
| 86 | Glass Fish OOZE 1 | If You Were A Priest/The Crawling (p/s) | 5 |
| 84 | Bucketfull/Brains BOB 8 | Happy The Golden Prince (hard vinyl white label test pressing, 20 only) | 30 |
| 81 | Armageddon ARM 4 | BLACK SNAKE DIAMOND RôLE (LP) | 15 |

*(see also Soft Boys, Knox)*

**HI-TONES**

| | | | |
|---|---|---|---|
| 62 | Island WI 029 | Going Steady/Darlin' Elaine | 25 |
| 62 | Wasp W 004 | I'm In Love With You/Singing A Song | 30 |
| 63 | Island WI 086 | Ten Virgins (actually by Angelic Brothers)/Too Young To Love (actually by Larry Marshall) | 25 |
| 63 | R&B JB 123 | You Hold The Key/DON DRUMMOND: Rock Away | 50 |

**HIT PACK**

| | | | |
|---|---|---|---|
| 65 | Tamla Motown TMG 513 | Never Say No To Your Baby/Let's Dance | 150 |
| 65 | Tamla Motown TMG 513 | Never Say No To Your Baby/Let's Dance (DJ copy) | 200 |

**HIT PARADE (1)**

| | | | |
|---|---|---|---|
| 84 | JSH JSH 1 | Forever/Stop (die-cut p/s) | 10 |
| 84 | JSH JSH 2 | My Favourite Girl/It Rained On Monday Morning (die-cut p/s) | 10 |
| 85 | JSH JSH 3 | The Sun Shines In Gerrards Cross/You Hurt Me Too (die-cut p/s) | 10 |
| 85 | JSH JSH 4 | You Don't Love Me Then/Huevo's Mexicana (die-cut p/s with card) | 10 |
| 86 | JSH JSH 5 | See You In Havana/Wipe Away The Tears (die-cut p/s) | 10 |

| | | | |
|---|---|---|---|
| 87 | JSH JSH 6 | I Get So Sentimental/Sue (die-cut p/s) | 10 |
| 90 | Sarah SARAH 90 | Autobiography/The Dispossessed/Now The Holiday's Over (p/s, insert) | 20 |
| 91 | Sarah SARAH 58 | In Gunnersbury Park/Harvey (ps, insert) | 12 |
| 91 | Vinyl Japan ASKLP 5 | MORE POP SONGS (LP) | 18 |

**HIT PARADE (2)**

| | | | |
|---|---|---|---|
| 82 | Crass 221984/12 | BAD NEWS (EP) | 25 |
| 84 | Crass 1984/2 | PLASTIC CULTURE : Product of The Troubles/Media Son (12") | 18 |
| 86 | Crass No 9 | NICK NACK PADDY WHACK (LP, with lyric inner) | 25 |

**HERMAN HITSON**

| | | | |
|---|---|---|---|
| 90s | Special Agent 9003 | You Are Too Much For The Human Heart/I Got That Will (reissue) | 8 |
| 04 | Goldmine G2K 149 | You Can't Keep A Good Man Down/Ain't No Other Way (reissue) | 8 |

**HIT SQUAD**

| | | | |
|---|---|---|---|
| 88 | Eastern Bloc EASTERN 01 | Wax On The Melt/SPM MC Tunes/Shure.4 (12", white label promo only, plain stickered sleeve) | 30 |

*(see also 808 State)*

**HITTERS**

| | | | |
|---|---|---|---|
| 73 | United Artists UP 35530 | Hypocrite/The Version | 22 |

*(see also Brinsley Schwarz)*

**HIVES**

| | | | |
|---|---|---|---|
| 01 | Poptones MC5055LP | YOUR NEW FAVOURITE BAND (LP) | 15 |
| 04 | Polydor 9866988 | TYRANNOSAURUS HIVES (LP, inner with free 7") | 20 |

**HMC**

| | | | |
|---|---|---|---|
| 93 | New Electronica ELEC 03P | Science Funktion (12", promo) | 30 |

**HOAX**

| | | | |
|---|---|---|---|
| 80 | Hologram HOAX 1 | ONLY THE BLIND CAN SEE IN THE DARK (EP, 2000 only) | 30 |
| 81 | Hologram HOAX 3 | SO WHAT (12" EP, p/s, blue vinyl, 2000 only) | 15 |
| 81 | Hologram HOAX 6 | BLIND PANIC EP (p/s, 2000 only) | 15 |
| 82 | Hologram HOAX 4 | QUIET IN THE SIXPENNY'S (p/s, 2000 only) | 15 |

**HOBBIES OF TODAY**

| | | | |
|---|---|---|---|
| 79 | Waxworks H.O.T. WAX 01 | Metal Boys/Tightrope Walker (p/s) | 30 |
| 85 | Rune CAST 02/LYN 16721/2 | In My Minds Eye/You (Company sleeve) | 15 |

**HOBBIT**

| | | | |
|---|---|---|---|
| 72 | Satril SAT 7 | Only Friends/Everything's Turning Out Fine | 10 |
| 71 | Deroy | FIRST AND LAST (LP, private pressing) | 80 |

**HOBBITS**

| | | | |
|---|---|---|---|
| 68 | Decca AD 1004 | Daffodil Days (The Affection Song)/Sunny Day Girl (export issue) | 20 |
| 68 | MCA MU 1002 | Daffodil Days (The Affection Song)/Sunny Day Girl | 8 |
| 67 | MCA MUP 301 | DOWN TO MIDDLE EARTH (LP) | 35 |

**HOBBS**

| | | | |
|---|---|---|---|
| 78 | Big SOLD 4 | Bop Around The Shop/(You've Got Me In A) Whirl Girl (gatefold p/s & insert) | 6 |

**CHRISTOPHER HOBBS/JOHN ADAMS/GAVIN BRYERS**

| | | | |
|---|---|---|---|
| 75 | Obscure OBS 2 | ENSEMBLE PIECES (LP) | 30 |

**HOBBY HORSE**

| | | | |
|---|---|---|---|
| 72 | Bell BELL 1248 | Summertime, Summertime/Sweet And Low | 12 |

*(see also Mary Hopkin)*

**HOBBY SHOP**

| | | | |
|---|---|---|---|
| 68 | Columbia DB 8395 | Why Must It Be This Way?/Talk To Me | 10 |

*(see also Danny Storm)*

**LES HOBEAUX**

| | | | |
|---|---|---|---|
| 57 | HMV POP 377 | Oh, Mary Don't You Weep/Toll The Bell Easy | 8 |
| 57 | HMV POP 403 | Mama Don't Allow/Hey, Hey, Daddy Blues | 8 |
| 58 | HMV POP 444 | Dynamo/Two Ships | 15 |
| 57 | HMV 7EG 8297 | SOHO SKIFFLE (EP) | 35 |

**HOBNAIL**

| | | | |
|---|---|---|---|
| 72 | Bell Bell 1250 | She's Just A Friend Of Mine/Boy Scout Jambouree | 8 |

**HOBO**

| | | | |
|---|---|---|---|
| 76 | United Artists UAS 29809 | HOBO (LP) | 15 |

**HOBOKEN**

| | | | |
|---|---|---|---|
| 73 | Oak | HOBOKEN (LP, 6 copies only) | 450 |

**HOBOKIN**

| | | | |
|---|---|---|---|
| 72 | CBS 8002 | Put The Blame On Easy/But Never Wine | 7 |

**GEORGE HOBSON**

| | | | |
|---|---|---|---|
| 01 | Grapevine 2000 G2K 109 | Let It Be Real/A Place In Your Heart (reissue) | 8 |

**TREVOR HOCKEY**

| | | | |
|---|---|---|---|
| 70s | Beau Brummie TET 120ST | Happy 'Cos I'm Blue/BLUES PLAYERS: Keep Right On To The End Of The Road (p/s) | 40 |

**HOCUS**

| | | | |
|---|---|---|---|
| 72 | Epic EPCS 8361 | He/The Swan | 5 |

**ARCHIE HODGE**

| | | | |
|---|---|---|---|
| 01 | Goldmine 2000 G2K 115 | I Really Want To See You Girl/If I Really Didn't Need You Woman (reissue) | 10 |

**CHRIS HODGE**

| | | | |
|---|---|---|---|
| 72 | Apple APPLE 43 | We're On Our Way/Supersoul (in p/s) | 30 |
| 72 | Apple APPLE 43 | We're On Our Way/Supersoul | 20 |
| 74 | RCA LPBO 5007 | Beautiful Love/Sweet Lady From The Sky | 6 |
| 74 | DJM DJS 10337 | I Love You/Old James Dean | 5 |

**MARVA HODGE**

| | | | |
|---|---|---|---|
| 70 | Polydor 56792 | The Ghetto/Sometimes | 8 |

MINT VALUE £

**CHARLES HODGES**
69  Major Minor MM 654  Try A Little Love/Someone To Love ............................ 20
*(see also Outlaws, Cliff Bennett's Rebellion)*

**EDDIE HODGES**
61  London HLA 9369  I'm Gonna Knock On Your Door/Ain't Gonna Wash For A Week ......... 10
62  London HLA 9505  Bandit Of My Dreams/Mugmates ............................. 10
62  London HLA 9576  (Girls, Girls, Girls) Made To Love/I Make Believe It's You ......... 10
63  MGM MGM 1232  Just A Kid In Love/Avalanche ............................. 10
65  Stateside SS 442  New Orleans/Hard Times For Young Lovers ............. 10
65  Stateside SS 469  Love Minus Zero - No Limit/The Water Is Over My Head ......... 10
62  London REA 1353  EDDIE HODGES (EP) ................................. 30
*(see also Hayley Mills & Eddie Hodges)*

**JOHNNY HODGES & HIS ORCHESTRA**
52  Vogue LD 011  JOHNNY HODGES (10" LP) ............................. 15

**INGFRIED HOFFMAN**
67  Polydor 583 015  SOUL BOND (LP) ................................. 15

**HOFFNER BROTHERS**
72  Bullet BU 513  The King Man Is Back/SHALIMAR ALL STARS: Version ......... 5
72  Green Door GD 4039  The King Man Is Back/SHALIMAR ALL STARS: Version (reissue) ...... 5
73  Ackee ACK 521  Open Up The Gates/Version ............................. 5
73  Grape GR 3042  Let Me Dream (Parts 1 & 2) ............................. 5

**ANNIE HOGAN**
85  Doublevision DVR 9  PLAYS KICKABYE (12" EP) ............................. 15
*(see also Marc Almond, Nick Cave, Soft Cell)*

**CLAIRE HOGAN**
59  Top Rank JAR 161  Sing A Smiling Song/I Wonder ............................. 10
*(see also Teresa Brewer)*

**SILAS HOGAN**
71  Blue Horizon 2431 008  TROUBLE AT HOME (LP) ............................. 125
70s  Flyright FLY 595  I'M A FREE-HEARTED MAN (LP) ............................. 15

**HOGARTH**
68  Liberty LBF 15156  Suzie's Getting Married/I've Been Dreaming ............. 10

**JAMES HOGG**
72  Regal Zonophone RZ 3054  Lovely Lady Rock/Happy Sad ............................. 15
72  Regal Zonophone RZ 3068  California Blues/Everybody Smile ............................. 10
73  Regal Zonophone RZ 3078  Gotta Be A Winner/Everybody Smile ............................. 10

**SMOKEY HOGG**
64  Realm RM 197  I'M SO LONELY (LP) ............................. 25
72  Ember EMB 3405  SINGS THE BLUES (LP) ............................. 20
70s  Specialty SNTF 5018  U BETTER WATCH THAT JIVE (LP) ............................. 15
*(see also John Lee Hooker/Lightnin' Hopkins/Smokey Hogg)*

**HOGGS**
80  Now PRR 2001  See It Now/Time On The Line (p/s) ............................. 20

**HOGIA R DOCIA**
80  Recordia Sur SER 001  Annwyl Ser/Ser ............................. 10

**HOGS**
69  Jay Boy BOY 5  It's All Coming To Me Now/Motor Cycle Rider ............. 15

**SUZI JANE HOKUM**
66  MGM MGM 1323  Need All The Help I Can Get/Home ............................. 50

**HOKUS POKE**
72  Vertigo 6360 064  EARTH HARMONY (LP, die-cut gatefold sleeve, small swirl label) ....... 450

**RON HOLDEN**
60  London HLU 9116  My Babe/Love You So ............................. 60

**MARK HOLDER & THE POSITIVES**
73  Atlantic K10280  Whatever's Fair/Why Dear Lord ............................. 20

**RAM HOLDER BROTHERS**
66  Parlophone R 5471  Just Across The River/Ram Blues ............................. 30
*(see also Ram Jam Band, Ram John Holder)*

**RAM JOHN HOLDER**
67  Columbia DB 8157  I Need Somebody/She's Alright ............................. 12
67  Columbia DB 8262  My Friend Jones/It Won't Be Long Before I Love You ......... 25
68  Beacon BEA 108  I Just Came To Get My Baby/I Do ............................. 10
69  Upfront UPF 2  Goodwill To All Mankind/BLACK VELVET: Goodwill Sermon ...... 8
70  United Artists UP 35117  Where Do The Dreams Go?/Miracle Happens Every Day ........ 6
75  Fresh Air 6121 124  Battering Ram/London Ghetto ............................. 6
63  Melodisc MLP 12-133  RAM BLUES GOSPEL AND SOUL (LP) ............................. 60
69  Beacon BEAS 2  BLACK LONDON BLUES (LP, white/black label with "Sold in U.K..." text) ...... 70
70  Beacon BEAS 17  BOOTLEG BLUES (LP, gatefold sleeve with lyric poster, white/black labels) ...... 80
70  Beacon BEAS 17  BOOTLEG BLUES (LP, gatefold sleeve without lyric poster, white/black labels) ...... 30
*(see also Ram Jam Band, Ram Holder Brothers, Geno Washington)*

**HOLE**
91  City Slang EFA 04070-45  Teenage Whore/Drown Soda (p/s, lilac, clear or green vinyl, 500 of each) ...... 15
93  City Slang EFA 04916-45  Beautiful Son/Old Age/20 Years In The Dakota (purple vinyl) ...... 6
94  City Slang EFA 04936-7  Miss World/Rock Star (Alternate Mix) (pink vinyl) ............. 6
95  Geffen GFS P94  Violet/Old Age (purple vinyl)//Violet/He Hit Me (And It Felt Like A Kiss) 7" double pack) ............................. 8

| | | | |
|---|---|---|---|
| 96 | Mirromax 573 164-7 | Gold Dust Woman/N.Y. LOOSE: Spit (gatefold p/s, 2 x 1-sided 7"s, with etched B-sides, 5,000 numbered) | 6 |
| 91 | City Slang SLANG 012 | PRETTY ON THE INSIDE (LP, blue vinyl) | 35 |
| 94 | City Slang EFA 04935-1 | LIVE THROUGH THIS (LP, 3000 on white vinyl) | 80 |
| 94 | City Slang EFA 04935-1 | LIVE THROUGH THIS (LP, black vinyl) | 30 |
| 98 | Geffen GEF 25164 | CELEBRITY SKIN (LP) | 50 |

## BILLIE HOLIDAY
| | | | |
|---|---|---|---|
| 59 | MGM MGM 1033 | Don't Worry About Me/Just One More Chance | 6 |
| 54 | Columbia 33S 1034 | BILLIE HOLIDAY (10" LP) | 30 |
| 54 | Brunswick LA 8676 | LOVER MAN (10" LP) | 30 |
| 55 | Philips BBR 8032 | FAVOURITES (10" LP) | 35 |
| 56 | Columbia Clef 33C 9023 | AT JAZZ AT THE PHILHARMONIC (10" LP) | 20 |
| 56 | Columbia Clef 33CX 10019 | MUSIC FOR TORCHING (LP) | 25 |
| 57 | Columbia Clef 33CX 10064 | VELVET MOOD (LP) | 25 |
| 57 | Columbia Clef 33CX 10076 | SOLITUDE (LP) | 20 |
| 57 | Columbia Clef 33CX 10092 | LADY SINGS THE BLUES (LP) | 20 |
| 59 | Columbia Clef 33CX 10145 | SONGS FOR DISTINGUÉ LOVERS (LP) | 20 |
| 66 | Island ILP 929 | LAST LIVE RECORDING (LP) | 30 |

## CHICO HOLIDAY
| | | | |
|---|---|---|---|
| 59 | RCA RCA 1117 | Young Ideas/Cuckoo Girl | 30 |
| 61 | Coral Q 72443 | God, Country And My Baby/Fools (withdrawn) | 30 |
| 59 | RCA RCX 171 | CHICO HOLIDAY (EP) | 80 |

## JIMMY HOLIDAY
| | | | |
|---|---|---|---|
| 63 | Vocalion POP V 9206 | How Can I Forget/Janet | 30 |
| 64 | London HLY 9868 | I Lied/Alison | 20 |
| 66 | Liberty LIB 12040 | Baby I Love You/You Won't Get Away | 20 |
| 67 | Liberty LIB 12048 | Give Me Your Love/The Turning Point | 20 |
| 67 | Liberty LIB 12053 | Everybody Needs Help/I'm Gonna Move To The City | 20 |
| 68 | Minit MLF 11008 | Give Me Your Love/The Beauty Of A Girl In Love | 15 |
| 69 | Minit MLL/MLS 40010 | SPREAD YOUR LOVE (LP) | 60 |

## JIMMY HOLIDAY & CLYDIE KING
| | | | |
|---|---|---|---|
| 67 | Liberty LIB 12058 | Ready, Willing And Able/We Got A Good Thing Goin' | 30 |
| 67 | Liberty LIB 12058 | Ready, Willing And Able/We Got A Good Thing Goin' (DJ copy) | 50 |
| 72 | United Artists UP 35371 | Ready, Willing And Able/JIMMY HOLIDAY: Give Me Your Love | 8 |

*(see also Clydie King)*

## HOLIDAYMAKERS
| | | | |
|---|---|---|---|
| 89 | Woosh WOOSH 4 | Cincinnati/Seventh Valley Girl (p/s) | 10 |

## HOLIDAYS
| | | | |
|---|---|---|---|
| 66 | Polydor 56720 | I'll Love You Forever/Makin' Up Time | 100 |

*(see also Edwin Starr)*

## BRIAN HOLLAND
| | | | |
|---|---|---|---|
| 74 | Invictus INV 2553 | I'm So Glad/I'm So Glad (Version) | 10 |

## (BRIAN) HOLLAND & (LAMONT) DOZIER
| | | | |
|---|---|---|---|
| 72 | Invictus INV 525 | Why Can't We Be Lovers/Don't Leave Me | 5 |
| 73 | Invictus INV 528 | Don't Leave Me Starvin' For Your Love (Parts 1 & 2) | 5 |

*(see also Lamont Dozier, Brian Holland)*

## EDDIE HOLLAND
| | | | |
|---|---|---|---|
| 62 | Fontana H 387 | Jamie/Take A Chance On Me | 400 |
| 63 | Oriole CBA 1808 | If It's Love (It's All Right)/It's Not Too Late | 500 |

## LYNN HOLLAND
| | | | |
|---|---|---|---|
| 64 | Ember EMB S 198 | And The Angels Sing/I Can't Read Your Writing (For My Tears) (in p/s) | 12 |
| 64 | Ember EMB S 198 | And The Angels Sing/I Can't Read Your Writing (For My Tears) | 6 |
| 65 | Polydor BM 56035 | Oh Darling How I Miss You/Before | 5 |
| 67 | Polydor 56166 | One Man In My Life/Wand'rin Boy | 20 |
| 67 | Polydor 56187 | Come And Love/May God Help You And Protect You | 25 |
| 66 | Polydor 56129 | All The Love In The World/Loneliness | 6 |
| 71 | Pye 7N 45041 | The Last Time/In A Railway Carriage | 8 |
| 67 | Polydor 236217 | OH DARLING HOW I MISS YOU (LP) | 25 |

*(see also Holly)*

## MALCOLM HOLLAND
| | | | |
|---|---|---|---|
| 70 | Fontana TF 1075 | Dawning Of the Day/Wndy | 10 |

## TONY HOLLAND
| | | | |
|---|---|---|---|
| 63 | HMV POP 1135 | Sidewalk/Time Goes By | 40 |

## MICHAEL HOLLIDAY
| | | | |
|---|---|---|---|
| 56 | Columbia SCM 5221 | Sixteen Tons/The Rose Tattoo | 10 |
| 56 | Columbia SCM 5273 | Hot Diggity (Dog Ziggity)/The Gal With The Yaller Shoes | 10 |
| 56 | Columbia DB 3813 | The Runaway Train/Ten Thousand Miles | 10 |

*(see also Edna Savage)*

## SU(SAN) HOLLIDAY
| | | | |
|---|---|---|---|
| 64 | Columbia DB 7363 | Dark Despair/The Other Side (demos list A-side as "[Street Of] Dark Despair") | 15 |
| 64 | Columbia DB 7403 | Any Day Now/Don't Come Knocking At My Door | 15 |
| 65 | Columbia DB 7616 | Sometimes/Long Haired Boy | 8 |
| 65 | Columbia DB 7709 | Nevertheless (I'm In Love With You)/Moonglow | 8 |
| 66 | Columbia SX 6067 | I WANNA SAY HELLO (LP, as Su Holliday) | 40 |

*(see also Susan Singer)*

## TIM HOLLIER
| | | | |
|---|---|---|---|
| 70 | Fontana TF 1080 | In This Room/Love Song | 6 |
| 71 | Philips 6006 130 | Circle Is Small/In A Corner Of My Life/Time Stood Still | 6 |

| | | | |
|---|---|---|---|
| 68 | United Artists (S)ULP 1211 | MESSAGE TO A HARLEQUIN (LP, laminated front sleeve, blue/silver labels) | 70 |
| 70 | Fontana 6309 003 | TIM HOLLIER (LP, laminated sleve, black/silver labels) | 225 |
| 71 | Philips 6308 044 | SKY SAIL (LP, laminated sleeve, black/silver labels) | 45 |

*(see also Amory Kane)*

## HOLLIES
### SINGLES

| | | | |
|---|---|---|---|
| 63 | Parlophone R 5030 | (Ain't That) Just Like Me/Hey, What's Wrong With Me | 15 |
| 63 | Parlophone R 5052 | Searchin'/Whole World Over | 10 |
| 63 | Parlophone R 5077 | Stay/Now's The Time | 8 |
| 64 | Parlophone R 5104 | Just One Look/Keep Off That Friend Of Mine | 7 |
| 64 | Parlophone R 5137 | Here I Go Again/Baby That's All | 7 |
| 64 | Parlophone R 5178 | We're Through/Come On Back | 6 |
| 65 | Parlophone R 5232 | Yes I Will/Nobody | 6 |
| 65 | Parlophone R 5287 | I'm Alive/You Know He Did | 6 |
| 65 | Parlophone R 5322 | Look Through Any Window/So Lonely | 7 |
| 65 | Parlophone R 5392 | If I Needed Someone/I've Got A Way Of My Own | 10 |
| 66 | Parlophone R 5409 | I Can't Let Go/Running Through The Night | 6 |
| 66 | Parlophone R 5469 | Bus Stop/Don't Run And Hide | 7 |
| 66 | United Artists UP 1152 | After The Fox (with Peter Sellers)/BURT BACHARACH: The Fox-Trot | 35 |
| 66 | Parlophone R 5508 | Stop! Stop! Stop!/It's You | 8 |
| 67 | Parlophone R 5562 | On A Carousel/All The World Is Love | 6 |
| 67 | Parlophone R 5602 | Carrie Anne/Signs That Will Never Change | 6 |
| 67 | Parlophone R 5637 | King Midas In Reverse/Everything Is Sunshine | 10 |
| 68 | Parlophone R 5680 | Jennifer Eccles/Open Up Your Eyes | 6 |
| 68 | Parlophone R 5733 | Listen To Me/Do The Best You Can | 7 |
| 69 | Parlophone R 5765 | Sorry Suzanne/Not That Way At All | 7 |
| 69 | Parlophone R 5806 | He Ain't Heavy, He's My Brother/'Cos You Like To Love Me | 6 |
| 70 | Parlophone R 5837 | I Can't Tell The Bottom From The Top/Mad Professor Blyth | 5 |
| 70 | Parlophone R 5862 | Gasoline Alley Bred/Dandelion Wine | 5 |
| 71 | Parlophone R 5905 | Hey Willy/Row The Boat Together | 5 |
| 72 | Polydor 2058 199 | The Baby/Oh Granny | 5 |
| 72 | Parlophone R 5939 | Long Cool Woman (In A Black Dress)/Cable Car | 6 |
| 72 | Polydor 2058 289 | Magic Woman Touch/Indian Girl | 5 |

### EPs

| | | | |
|---|---|---|---|
| 64 | Parlophone GEP 8909 | THE HOLLIES | 40 |
| 64 | Parlophone GEP 8911 | JUST ONE LOOK | 35 |
| 64 | Parlophone GEP 8915 | HERE I GO AGAIN | 35 |
| 64 | Parlophone GEP 8927 | WE'RE THROUGH | 35 |
| 65 | Parlophone GEP 8934 | IN THE HOLLIES STYLE | 50 |
| 65 | Parlophone GEP 8942 | I'M ALIVE | 35 |
| 66 | Parlophone GEP 8951 | I CAN'T LET GO | 50 |

### ALBUMS

| | | | |
|---|---|---|---|
| 64 | Parlophone PMC 1220 | STAY WITH THE HOLLIES (mono) | 100 |
| 64 | Parlophone PCS 3054 | STAY WITH THE HOLLIES (stereo, large 'stereo' on sleeve) | 175 |
| 65 | Parlophone PMC 1235 | IN THE HOLLIES STYLE (mid-sized mono on front sleeve, "Sold in U.K..." text) | 125 |
| 65 | Parlophone PMC 1261 | THE HOLLIES (small mono on front sleeve, "Sold in U.K..." text) | 125 |
| 66 | Parlophone PMC 7008 | WOULD YOU BELIEVE? (mono, with "Sold in U.K..." text) | 80 |
| 66 | Parlophone PCS 7008 | WOULD YOU BELIEVE? (stereo, "Sold in U.K..." text) | 150 |
| 66 | Parlophone PMC 7011 | FOR CERTAIN BECAUSE (gatefold sleeve, mono, with "Sold in U.K..." text) | 50 |
| 66 | Parlophone PCS 7011 | FOR CERTAIN BECAUSE (gatefold sleeve, stereo, with "Sold in U.K..." text) | 80 |
| 67 | Parlophone PMC 7022 | EVOLUTION (mono, with "Sold in U.K..." text) | 50 |
| 67 | Parlophone PCS 7022 | EVOLUTION (stereo, with "Sold in U.K..." text) | 100 |
| 67 | Parlophone PMC 7039 | BUTTERFLY (mono, with "Sold in U.K..." text) | 50 |
| 67 | Parlophone PCS 7039 | BUTTERFLY (stereo, with "sold in U.K..." text) | 100 |
| 67 | EMI Regal SREG 2024 | THE HOLLIES (export compilation) | 25 |
| 67 | World Records ST 979 | THE VINTAGE HOLLIES (stereo reissue of "In The Hollies Style") | 35 |
| 68 | World Records ST 1035 | STAY WITH THE HOLLIES (record club reissue) | 30 |
| 68 | Parlophone PCS 7057 | THE HOLLIES' GREATEST (stereo, with outtake version of Yes I Will) | 15 |
| 69 | Parlophone PMC 7078 | THE HOLLIES SING DYLAN (mono, with "Sold in U.K..." text) | 35 |
| 69 | Parlophone PCS 7078 | THE HOLLIES SING DYLAN (stereo, with "Sold in U.K..." text) | 30 |
| 69 | Parlophone PCS 7092 | HOLLIES SING HOLLIES (gatefold sleeve) | 20 |

*(All Parlophone LPs listed above were originally issued with yellow/black labels; 1970s pressings with silver & black labels are worth £8)*

| | | | |
|---|---|---|---|
| 70 | Parlophone PCS 7116 | CONFESSIONS OF THE MIND (with colour insert) | 20 |
| 71 | Parlophone PAS 10005 | DISTANT LIGHT (gatefold sleeve) | 20 |
| 72 | Parlophone PCS 7148 | THE HOLLIES' GREATEST HITS VOL. 2 | 18 |
| 72 | Polydor 2383 144 | ROMANY (gatefold sleeve) | 15 |
| 74 | Polydor 2383 262 | HOLLIES (with lyric insert) | 15 |
| 75 | Polydor 2442 128 | ANOTHER NIGHT (gatefold sleeve) | 15 |
| 76 | Polydor 2442 141 | WRITE ON (with lyric inner) | 15 |
| 76 | Polydor 2383 421 | RUSSIAN ROULETTE (with lyric inner) | 15 |

*(see also Allan Clarke, Graham Nash, Terry Sylvester, Haydock's Rockhouse, Peter Sellers & Sophia Loren)o*

## HOLLINGWORTH

| | | | |
|---|---|---|---|
| 71 | Columbia DB 8808 | Jump On My Wagon/This Town | 18 |

## MARK HOLLIS

| | | | |
|---|---|---|---|
| 03 | Polydor 537 688-1 | MARK HOLLIS (LP, reissue of 1997 CD-only album, 180gm pressing with inner) | 70 |

*(see also Talk Talk)*

## BRENDA HOLLOWAY

| | | | |
|---|---|---|---|
| 64 | Stateside SS 307 | Every Little Bit Hurts/Land Of A Thousand Boys | 80 |

| 64 | Stateside SS 307 | Every Little Bit Hurts/Land Of A Thousand Boys (DJ Copy) | 150 |
|----|------------------|---------------------------------------------------------|-----|
| 65 | Tamla Motown TMG 508 | When I'm Gone/I've Been Good To You | 100 |
| 65 | Tamla Motown TMG 508 | When I'm Gone/I've Been Good To You (DJ copy) | 200 |
| 65 | Tamla Motown TMG 519 | Operator/I'll Be Available | 100 |
| 65 | Tamla Motown TMG 519 | Operator/I'll Be Available (DJ copy) | 200 |
| 66 | Tamla Motown TMG 556 | Together Till The End Of Time/Sad Song | 150 |
| 66 | Tamla Motown TMG 556 | Together Till The End Of Time/Sad Song (DJ copy) | 200 |
| 66 | Tamla Motown TMG 581 | Hurt A Little Everyday/Where Were You (demos credit Brenda Holiday) | 90 |
| 66 | Tamla Motown TMG 581 | Hurt A Little Everyday/Where Were You (demos credit Brenda Holiday) (DJ copy) | 100 |
| 67 | Tamla Motown TMG 608 | Just Look What You've Done/Starting The Hurt All Over Again | 60 |
| 67 | Tamla Motown TMG 608 | Just Look What You've Done/Starting The Hurt All Over Again (DJ copy) | 100 |
| 67 | Tamla Motown TMG 622 | You've Made Me So Very Happy/I've Got To Find It | 45 |
| 69 | Tamla Motown TMG 700 | Just Look What You've Done/You've Made Me So Very Happy | 18 |
| 68 | T. Motown (S)TML 11083 | THE ARTISTRY OF BRENDA HOLLOWAY (LP, mono/stereo) | 100 |

## LAURIE HOLLOWAY

| 68 | CBS 3332 | Windy/Roundabout | 5 |
|----|----------|------------------|---|

## LOLEATTA HOLLOWAY

| 71 | United Artists UP 35273 | Bring It On Up/Rainbow '71' | 8 |
|----|-------------------------|----------------------------|---|
| 76 | Salsoul SZ 2022 | Dreamin'/Is It Just A Man's Way | 8 |
| 96 | Kent 6T 11 | This Mans Arms/JOHN EDWARDS: Ain't That Good Enough | 25 |

## PATRICE HOLLOWAY

| 66 | Capitol CL 15484 | Love And Desire/Ecstasy | 150 |
|----|------------------|-------------------------|-----|
| 66 | Capitol CL 15484 | Love And Desire/Ecstasy (DJ Copy) | 250 |

## HOLLOW GROUND

| 80 | Guardian GR/HG C57 | FLYING HIGH EP (Flying High/Warlord/Rock On/Don't Chase The Dragon) (in p/s) | 150 |
|----|--------------------|------------------------------------------------------------------------------|-----|
| 80 | Guardian GR/HG C57 | FLYING HIGH EP (Flying High/Warlord/Rock On/Don't Chase The Dragon) | 45 |

## BUDDY HOLLY

### 78s

| 56 | Brunswick 05581 | Blue Days - Black Nights/Love Me | 300 |
|----|-----------------|----------------------------------|-----|
| 57 | Vogue Coral Q 72293 | Peggy Sue/Everyday | 150 |
| 58 | Coral Q 72288 | Listen To Me/I'm Gonna Love You Too | 25 |
| 58 | Coral Q 72325 | Rave On/Take Your Time | 30 |
| 58 | Coral Q 72333 | Early In The Morning/Now We're One | 35 |
| 58 | Coral Q 72346 | Heartbeat/Well ... All Right | 50 |
| 59 | Coral Q 72360 | It Doesn't Matter Anymore/Raining In My Heart | 30 |
| 59 | Brunswick 05800 | Rock Around With Ollie Vee/Midnight Shift | 200 |
| 59 | Coral Q 72376 | Peggy Sue Got Married/Crying, Waiting, Hoping | 200 |
| 60 | Coral Q 72392 | Heartbeat/Everyday | 350 |

### SINGLES

| 56 | Brunswick 05581 | Blue Days - Black Nights/Love Me | 800 |
|----|-----------------|----------------------------------|-----|
| 57 | Vogue Coral Q 72293 | Peggy Sue/Everyday | 50 |
| 58 | Coral Q 72293 | Peggy Sue/Everyday | 20 |
| 58 | Coral Q 72288 | Listen To Me/I'm Gonna Love You Too | 25 |
| 58 | Coral Q 72325 | Rave On/Take Your Time | 25 |
| 58 | Coral Q 72333 | Early In The Morning/Now We're One | 25 |
| 58 | Coral Q 72346 | Heartbeat/Well ... All Right | 25 |
| 58 | Coral Q 72360 | It Doesn't Matter Anymore/Raining In My Heart | 10 |
| 59 | Brunswick 05800 | Rock Around With Ollie Vee/Midnight Shift | 40 |
| 59 | Coral Q 72376 | Peggy Sue Got Married/Crying, Waiting, Hoping | 25 |

*(The above 45s were originally issued with triangular centres; reissues with round centres are worth two-thirds these values.)*

| 60 | Coral Q 72392 | Heartbeat/Everyday | 20 |
|----|---------------|--------------------|-----|
| 60 | Coral Q 72397 | True Love Ways/Moondreams | 10 |
| 60 | Coral Q 72411 | Learning The Game/That Makes It Tough | 10 |
| 61 | Coral Q 72419 | What To Do/That's What They Say | 10 |
| 61 | Coral Q 72432 | Baby I Don't Care/Valley Of Tears | 10 |
| 61 | Coral Q 72445 | Look At Me/Mailman, Bring Me No More Blues | 15 |
| 62 | Coral Q 72449 | Listen To Me/Words Of Love | 15 |
| 62 | Coral Q 72455 | Reminiscing/Wait Till The Sun Shines, Nellie | 10 |
| 63 | Coral Q 72459 | Brown-Eyed Handsome Man/Slippin' And Slidin' | 10 |
| 63 | Coral Q 72463 | Bo Diddley/It's Not My Fault | 10 |
| 63 | Coral Q 72466 | Wishing/Because I Love You | 10 |
| 63 | Coral Q 72469 | What To Do/Umm Oh Yeah | 12 |
| 64 | Coral Q 72472 | You've Got Love/An Empty Cup (as Buddy Holly & The Crickets) | 25 |
| 64 | Coral Q 72475 | Love's Made A Fool Of You/You're The One | 20 |
| 66 | Coral Q 72483 | Maybe Baby/That's My Desire | 40 |
| 68 | Decca AD 1009 | Rave On/Peggy Sue (p/s, export reissue) | 40 |
| 69 | MCA MU 1059 | Love Is Strange/You're The One | 10 |
| 84 | MCA BHB 1 | THAT'LL BE THE DAY (10 x 7" box set, comprising BH1-10 in p/s) | 40 |

### EPs

| 58 | Coral FEP 2002 | LISTEN TO ME (brown cover, sleeve shows Holly without glasses; disc credits title as "Buddy Holly") | 400 |
|----|----------------|------------------------------------------------------------------------------------------------------|-----|
| 58 | Coral FEP 2002 | LISTEN TO ME (re-pressing, various shades of green/brown p/s, shows Holly with glasses; disc credits title as "Buddy Holly") | 40 |
| 58 | Coral FEP 2005 | RAVE ON (various shades of green/brown p/s) | 40 |
| 59 | Coral FEP 2014 | IT'S SO EASY | 40 |
| 59 | Coral FEP 2015 | HEARTBEAT | 40 |
| 59 | Coral FEP 2032 | BUDDY HOLLY | 40 |
| 59 | Brunswick OE 9456 | BUDDY HOLLY NO. 1 | 60 |

## Stevie HOLLY

| | | | MINT VALUE £ |
|---|---|---|---|
| 59 | Brunswick OE 9457 | BUDDY HOLLY NO. 2 ........................................................ | 60 |

*(The above EPs were originally issued with triangular centres; later pressings with round-centres are worth between half and two thirds of these values.)*

| 60 | Coral FEP 2044 | THE LATE GREAT BUDDY HOLLY (tri centre) .......................... | 50 |
|---|---|---|---|
| 60 | Coral FEP 2044 | THE LATE GREAT BUDDY HOLLY (round centre) ...................... | 15 |
| 64 | Coral FEP 2065 | BUDDY - BY REQUEST ...................................................... | 40 |
| 64 | Coral FEP 2066 | THAT TEX-MEX SOUND ..................................................... | 40 |
| 64 | Coral FEP 2067 | WISHING ...................................................................... | 50 |
| 64 | Coral FEP 2068 | SHOWCASE VOLUME 1 ..................................................... | 50 |
| 64 | Coral FEP 2069 | SHOWCASE VOLUME 2 ..................................................... | 40 |
| 65 | Coral FEP 2070 | BUDDY HOLLY SINGS ....................................................... | 40 |

### ALBUMS

| 58 | Vogue Coral LVA 9085 | BUDDY HOLLY (Vogue-Coral labels & Coral sleeve) .................. | 100 |
|---|---|---|---|
| 58 | Coral LVA 9085 | BUDDY HOLLY ................................................................ | 45 |
| 59 | Coral LVA 9105 | THE BUDDY HOLLY STORY('High Fidelity Coral' logo on sleeve) ... | 25 |
| 60s | Coral LVA 9105 | THE BUDDY HOLLY STORY (reissue, different 'roll-neck sweater' sleeve with small 'Coral' logo) .................................................. | 40 |
| 60 | Coral LVA 9127 | THE BUDDY HOLLY STORY VOL. II ....................................... | 20 |
| 61 | Ace Of Hearts AH 3 | THAT'LL BE THE DAY ....................................................... | 25 |
| 63 | Coral LVA 9212 | REMINISCING ................................................................ | 25 |
| 64 | Coral LVA 9222 | SHOWCASE .................................................................... | 25 |
| 65 | Coral LVA 9227 | HOLLY IN THE HILLS (with Bob Montgomery, withdrawn mispressing, sleeve & label list "Wishing", plays "Reminiscing"; matrix no's end with 1B both sides) .................... | 40 |
| 65 | Coral LVA 9227 | HOLLY IN THE HILLS (corrected edition, with Bob Montgomery, plays "Wishing", matrix numbers end with 1B on one side & 2B on other) ...... | 60 |
| 68 | MCA MUP 320 | WISHING (mono only, reissue of "Holly In The Hills") .............. | 18 |
| 69 | MCA MUPS 371 | GIANT ......................................................................... | 18 |

*(Originally issued with yellow labels; later variations exist with various twin-toned designs.)*

| 75 | World Records SM 301/5 | THE BUDDY HOLLY STORY (5-LP box set) .............................. | 20 |
|---|---|---|---|
| 79 | MCA Coral CDMSP 807 | THE COMPLETE BUDDY HOLLY (6-LP box set with sepia-tinted book) ... | 30 |

*(see also Crickets, Fireballs)*

### STEVIE HOLLY
| 66 | Planet PLF 107 | A Strange World/Little Man .............................................. | 30 |
|---|---|---|---|

### HOLLY (1)
| 65 | Fontana TF 980 | On With The Game/Paradise Lost ....................................... | 8 |
|---|---|---|---|

*(see also Lynn Holland)*

### HOLLY (2)
| 79 | Eric's ERIC'S 003 | Yankee Rose/Treasure Island/Desperate Dan (p/s) ................. | 25 |
|---|---|---|---|
| 79 | Eric's ERIC'S 007 | Hobo Joe/Stars Of The Bars (p/s) ...................................... | 20 |

*(see also Frankie Goes To Hollywood, Big In Japan)*

### HOLLY & JOEY
| 82 | Virgin VS 478 | I Got You Babe/HOLLY & THE ITALIANS: One More Dance (p/s) ... | 12 |
|---|---|---|---|

*(see also Ramones, Deborah Harry)*

### HOLLY & THE ITALIANS
| 80 | Oval OVAL 1016 | Tell That Girl To Shut Up/Chapel Of Love (p/s) ..................... | 5 |
|---|---|---|---|
| 81 | Virgin VS 411 | I Wanna Go Home/Fanzine (p/s) ....................................... | 15 |
| 81 | Virgin VS 429 | Just For Tonight/Baby Gets It All (p/s) ................................. | 7 |
| 81 | Virgin V 2186 | THE RIGHT TO BE ITALIAN (LP, with lyric insert) ................... | 15 |

### HOLLYRIDGE STRINGS
| 61 | Capitol CL 15233 | The Guns Of Navarone/Moon River ................................... | 6 |
|---|---|---|---|
| 61 | Capitol CL 15237 | The Comancheros/A Thunder Of Drums .............................. | 6 |

### HOLLYWOOD ARGYLES
| 60 | London HLU 9146 | Alley Oop/Sho' Know A Lot About Love ............................... | 7 |
|---|---|---|---|
| 60 | Top Rank JAR 530 | Gun Totin' Critter Called Jack/GARY PAXTON: Bug-Eye ............ | 20 |

*(see also Kim Fowley, Skip & Flip, Gary Paxton)*

### HOLLYWOOD BRATS
| 79 | Cherry Red CHERRY 6 | Then He Kissed Me/Sick On You (p/s) .................................. | 8 |
|---|---|---|---|
| 80 | Cherry Red A RED 6 | HOLLYWOOD BRATS (LP) ................................................. | 25 |

### HOLLYWOOD FLAMES
| 57 | London HL 7030 | Buzz Buzz Buzz/Crazy (export issue) .................................. | 50 |
|---|---|---|---|
| 58 | London HL 8545 | Buzz Buzz Buzz/Crazy ..................................................... | 75 |
| 59 | London HLW 8955 | Much Too Much/In The Dark ............................................ | 75 |
| 59 | London HLW 8955 | Much Too Much/In The Dark (78) ...................................... | 25 |
| 60 | London HLE 9071 | If I Thought You Needed Me/Every Day Every Way ................. | 50 |

### HOLLYWOOD FREEWAY
| 72 | Deram DM 359 | I've Been Moved/Cool Calamares ...................................... | 6 |
|---|---|---|---|
| 73 | Pye 7N 45273 | You're The Song (That I Can't Stop Singing)/This Feeling Called Love ... | 8 |

*(see also Tony Rivers)*

### HOLLYWOOD HURRICANES
| 64 | Prima PR 1009 | Beavershot/Have Love Will Travel ...................................... | 6 |
|---|---|---|---|

### KENNY HOLLYWOOD
| 62 | Decca F 11546 | Magic Star/The Wonderful Story Of Love ............................ | 25 |
|---|---|---|---|

### HOLLYWOOD KILLERS
| 78 | Rollerball ROLL 2 | Goodbye Suicide/Tramp .................................................. | 50 |
|---|---|---|---|

*(see also Jim Penfold & The Hollywood Killers)*

### HOLLYWOOD STARS
| 77 | Arista ARIST103 | All The Kids On The Streets/All For Love (p/s) ....................... | 5 |
|---|---|---|---|

## HOLLYWOOD VINES
61   Capitol CL 15191           When Johnny Comes Slidin' Home/Cruisin' ............................................. 8

## MIKE HOLM
70   Major Minor MM 659         Mendocino/Cutey Girl ................................................................. 6

## PETER HOLM
67   Major Minor MM504          This Is Not The Way/You Will Be Mine.............................................. 15

## BILL HOLMAN OCTET
54   Capitol KC 65000           Cousin Jack/Plain Folks ............................................................ 8

## EDDIE HOLMAN
65   Cameo Parkway P 960        This Can't Be True/A Free Country ................................................ 50
69   Action ACT 4547            I Love You/I Surrender ............................................................ 125
70   Stateside SS 2160          (Hey There) Lonely Girl/It's All In The Game .................................... 10
70   Stateside SS 2170          Since I Don't Have You/Don't Stop Now ............................................ 8
77   Salsoul SZ 2026            This Will Be A Night To Remember/Time Will Tell .................................. 6
04   Grapevine 2000 G2K 150     She's Wanted (In Three States)/MRS BAND: Sunset On Ridge (reissue) ............... 10
04   Grapevine 2000 G2K 160     Sweet Memories Are Haunting Me/Groovin' The Go Go (reissue)...................... 10

## CHRISTINE HOLMES
64   Mercury MF 813             This Is My Prayer/My Dream ....................................................... 10
64   Mercury MF 819             Play Me A Sad Song (Mr DJ)/Doesn't He Know ...................................... 10
64   Mercury MF 831             Goodbye Boys Goodbye/Is It Love .................................................. 10
65   Mercury MF 851             Many Things From Your Window/You'd Better Believe It ............................. 7
65   Mercury MF 887             Goin' Where The Lovin' Is/Where There's Some Smoke There's Fire ................. 12
*(see also Family Dogg)*

## DAVID HOLMES
97   Go Beat GOB 6              Don't Die Just Yet (Mogwai Mix)/Holiday Girl (Arab Strap Mix) (p/s, 500 only) .... 6
02   13 Amp APM 001LP           COME GET IT I GOT IT (2xLP)....................................................... 20
*(see also Mogwai)*

## ELDRIDGE HOLMES
68   Pama PM 746                Beverley/Wait For Me Baby ........................................................ 18

## IVAN HOLMES
67   Columbia DB 8119           The Light, The Love And The Life/Cocaine.......................................... 7

## JAKE HOLMES
69   Polydor 56547              How Are You (Parts 1 & 2) ........................................................ 5
70   Ember EMB S 269            Saturday Night/Diner Song (p/s) .................................................. 20
70   Polydor 2066 040           So Close/Django And Friend ....................................................... 5
70   Polydor 583 579            JAKE HOLMES (LP) ................................................................. 30
70   Polydor 2425 036           SO CLOSE SO VERY FAR TO GO (LP) .................................................. 22
72   CBS 64905                  HOW MUCH TIME (LP) ............................................................... 20

## LEROY HOLMES & ORCHESTRA
59   MGM 1044                   Sweet Leicani/Alice Blue Gown .................................................... 6
59   MGM 1058                   Theme From A Summer Place/Indiscreet.............................................. 6
68   United Artists UP 2222     The Good, The Bad And The Ugly/Live For Life ..................................... 5

## RICHARD 'GROOVES' HOLMES
66   CBS 202240                 Misty/Groove's Groove ............................................................ 7
67   Transatlantic PR 7435      SOUL MESSAGE (LP) ................................................................ 25
68   Transatlantic PR 7493      RICHARD 'GROOVES' HOLMES (LP) .................................................... 20

## HOLOCAUST (1)
80   Phoenix PSP 1              Heavy Metal Mania/Only As Young As You Feel (p/s) ................................ 20
80   Phoenix 12 PSP 1           Heavy Metal Mania/Love's Power/Only As Young As You Feel (12", p/s) .............. 30
80   Phoenix 12 PSP 2           Smokin' Valves/Friend Or Foe (p/s) ............................................... 10
80   Phoenix 12 PSP 2           Smokin' Valves/Friend Or Foe/Out My Book (12", p/s) ............................. 30
81   Phoenix PSP 3P             HOLOCAUST LIVE (EP) .............................................................. 25
82   Phoenix 12 PSP 4           Comin' Through/Don't Wanna Be A Loser/Good Thing Going (12", p/s)................ 30
81   Phoenix PSLP 1             THE NIGHTCOMERS (LP) ............................................................. 40
83   Phoenix PSPLP 4            LIVE (HOT CURRY AND WINE) (LP) ................................................... 25
84   Phoenix PSPLP 5            NO MAN'S LAND (LP) ............................................................... 20

## HOLOCAUST (2)
79   Pile Driver HOL 201        Slay That Dragon/Take Me To Your Lawyer/So Called Civilised Way (12", no p/s) .... 1000

## ERROL HOLT
77   Lior ROAR 111              Come Rock Me/Congo Dread (12") ................................................... 40
78   Star Time EHLF 427         I Am Not A King (with PRINCE FAR I)/Version (12") ................................ 40
79   Hit Run HIT DD16           Yes Yes Yes/ROD TAYLOR: No One Can Tell I About Jah (12") ....................... 80
79   Hit Run HIT DD25           Sweet Reggae Music/PRINCE FAR I: Hairdressing Salon ............................. 90
70s  Dread DDLP 102             VISION OF AFRICA (LP) ........................................................... 30

## JOHN HOLT
63   Island WI 041              I Cried A Tear/I'll Stay .......................................................... 30
68   Trojan TR 643              Tonight/Oh How It Hurts (B-side actually by Paragons)............................. 25
69   Trojan TR 661              Ali Baba/I'm Your Man ............................................................ 75
69   Trojan TR 674              What You Gonna Do Now/Have You Ever Been To Heaven ............................... 12
69   Harry J TR 694             Have Sympathy/HARRY J ALLSTARS: Spyrone ......................................... 40
69   Trojan TR 7702             Wooden Heart/All My Life ......................................................... 10
70   Duke Reid DR 2506          Come Out Of My Bed/WINSTON WRIGHT: Hide And Seek ................................ 12
70   Duke DU 73                 Stealing, Stealing/WINSTON WRIGHT: Stealing, Stealing (Volume 2) ................ 20
70   Duke DU 77                 The Working Kind/Open Jaw ........................................................ 15
70   Jackpot JP 735             A Little Tear/JEFF BARNS: Get In The Groove ..................................... 15
70   Bamboo BAM 44              A Love I Can Feel/JOHNNY LAST: Long Liver Man (B-side act. by Hugh Black) ........ 15
70   Bamboo BAM 55              A Stranger In Love/WAILERS: Jailhouse (Good Rudy) ............................... 40

## Roosevelt HOLTS

| 70 | Bamboo BAM 62 | Holly Holy/Do You Love Me? | 12 |
|---|---|---|---|
| 70 | Banana BA 314 | Why Can't I Touch You/SOUND DIMENSION: Touching Version | 10 |
| 70 | Smash SMA 2303 | My Heart Is Gone/PHIL PRATT ALL STARS: Version | 6 |
| 70 | Smash SMA 2305 | I Had A Talk With My Woman/MAXINE: Life Is Not The Same Anymore | 6 |
| 70 | Supreme SUP 212 | Share My Rest/AL BROWN: Allways | 40 |
| 70 | Unity UN 548 | Sometimes/BUNNY LEE ALL STARS: Lash-La-Rue | 30 |
| 70 | Unity UN 549 | Sea Cruise/LEE'S ALL STARS: Niney's Hop | 8 |
| 70 | Unity UN 552 | Walking Along/LEE'S ALL STARS: Warefare | 45 |
| 70 | Unity UN 556 | Give Her All The Love/BUSTY BROWN: Nobody But You | 6 |
| 70 | Success RE 903 | Fat Girl, Sexy Girl/Man And Woman | 20 |
| 71 | Banana BA 340 | O.K. Fred/Fancy Make-Up | 15 |
| 71 | Banana BA 345 | Build Our Dreams/LEROY SIBBLES: Love In Our Nation | 25 |
| 71 | Treasure Isle TI 7061 | Let's Build Our Dreams/TOMMY McCOOK & SUPERSONICS: Testify Version | 20 |
| 71 | Treasure Isle TI 7065 | Sister Big Stuff/TOMMY McCOOK & SUPERSONICS: Black River | 20 |
| 71 | Treasure Isle TI 7066 | Paragons Medley/TOMMY McCOOK & SUPERSONICS: Medley Version | 18 |
| 71 | Ashanti ASH 401 | Again/MUDIES ALL STARS: Ten Steps To Soul Version | 10 |
| 71 | Camel CA 78 | Linger A While/Version | 7 |
| 71 | Escort ERT 847 | Knock On Your Door/URIEL ALDRIDGE: Set Me Free | 6 |
| 71 | Jackpot JP 772 | Stick By Me/It's A Pleasure | 6 |
| 71 | Jackpot JP 774 | It's A Jam In The Streets/A Man Needs A Woman | 6 |
| 71 | Jackpot JP 784 | Anymore/Lost Love | 6 |
| 71 | Moodisc MU 3513 | It May Sound Silly/MUDIE ALL STARS: Instrumental | 6 |
| 71 | Moodisc HM 105 | It May Sound Silly/MUDIE ALL STARS: Instrumental (reissue) | 10 |
| 71 | Punch PH 60 | Strange Things/WINSTON WRIGHT: Want Money (B-side act. G.G. All Stars) | 25 |
| 71 | Smash SMA 2324 | Mother And Father Love/AGGROVATORS: Mother Love Version | 6 |
| 71 | Prince Buster PB 26 | All I Want From You/Version | 12 |
| 72 | Blue Beat BB 424 | O.K. Fred/BIG YOUTH: Chi Chi Run | 20 |
| 72 | Prince Buster PB 40 | Close To Me/Version | 7 |
| 72 | Prince Buster PB 41 | Get Ready/Version | 7 |
| 72 | Prince Buster PB 42 | Rain From The Skies/Version | 7 |
| 72 | Prince Buster PB 43 | The First Time/Version | 7 |
| 72 | Prince Buster PB 49 | For Your Love/Version | 7 |
| 72 | G.G. GG 4529 | Keep It Up/A Love Like Yours | 6 |
| 72 | Fab FAB 188 | A Little Happiness/DELROY WILSON: Diamond Rings | 10 |
| 72 | Jackpot JP 790 | Don't You Know/Riding For A Fall | 6 |
| 72 | Jackpot JP 807 | Looking Back/I'll Be There | 6 |
| 72 | Pama PM 845 | I'll Always Love You/SLIM SMITH: 3 x 7 Rock And Roll | 10 |
| 72 | Pama PM 852 | Pledging My Love/I Will Know What To Do | 10 |
| 73 | Fab FAB 224 | Let's Go Dancing/Version | 10 |
| 73 | Fab FAB 244 | Let's Go Dancing/Version (reissue) | 10 |
| 73 | Attack ATT 8045 | Time And The River/Version | 5 |
| 73 | Smash SMA 2329 | Don't Break Your Promise/I've Been Admiring You | 12 |
| 73 | Ackee ACK 513 | Ecstacy/Version | 6 |
| 83 | Greensleeves GRED 120 | Police In Helicopter/Youth Pon The Corner (12") | 20 |
| 70 | Bamboo BDLP 210 | A LOVE I CAN FEEL (LP) | 60 |
| 72 | Melodisc MLP 12170 | GREATEST HITS (LP) | 40 |
| 70s | Melodisc MLP 12180 | OK FRED (LP) | 45 |
| 70s | Melodisc MLP 12191 | JOHN HOLT & FRIENDS (LP) | 45 |
| 71 | Trojan TRL(S) 37 | STILL IN CHAINS (LP) | 15 |
| 74 | Attack ATLP 1010 | A LOVE I CAN FEEL (LP) | 15 |
| 80 | Lord Koos KLP 4 | DON'T BREAK YOUR PROMISE (LP, colour or black and white cover) | 40 |
| 83 | Greensleeves GRED 120 | POLICE IN HELICOPTER (LP) | 25 |

(see also Jay & Joya, Little John, Neville Hinds, Jeff Barnes, Danny Simpson, Hugh Roy, U Roy Junior, Don Drummond, Interns)

## ROOSEVELT HOLTS
| 68 | Blue Horizon 7-63201 | PRESENTING THE COUNTRY BLUES (LP) | 85 |
|---|---|---|---|

## HOLY FUCK
| 10 | YTO48S | Red Lights/Dr Dr E | 10 |
|---|---|---|---|

## HOLY MACKEREL
| 72 | CBS 8447 | Rock-A-Bye/New Black Shoes | 6 |
|---|---|---|---|
| 72 | CBS 65297 | HOLY MACKEREL (LP) | 20 |
| 93 | Tenth Planet TP 005 | CLOSER TO HEAVEN (LP, numbered, 500 only) | 15 |

(see also Jason Crest, High Broom)

## HOLY MODAL ROUNDERS
| 68 | Elektra EKL 4026 | THE MORAY EELS EAT THE HOLY MODALS (LP, mono) | 40 |
|---|---|---|---|
| 68 | Elektra EKS 74026 | THE MORAY EELS EAT THE HOLY MODALS (LP, stereo) | 40 |
| 70 | Transatlantic TRA 7451 | HOLY MODAL ROUNDERS (LP) | 40 |
| 70 | Transatlantic TRA | HOLY MODAL ROUNDERS 2 (LP) | 35 |

## HOMBRES
| 67 | Verve VS 1510 | Let It Out (Let It All Hang Out)/Go Girl Go | 15 |
|---|---|---|---|

## HOME
| 72 | CBS 7809 | Fancy Lady, Hollywood Child/Shady Lady | 6 |
|---|---|---|---|
| 72 | (No Cat No) | You'll Get A Helping Hand At Barclays/Dreamer (p/s) | 15 |
| 71 | CBS 64356 | PAUSE FOR A HOARSE HORSE (LP, gatefold sleeve) | 40 |
| 72 | CBS 64752 | HOME (LP) | 25 |
| 73 | CBS 65550 | THE ALCHEMIST (LP) | 30 |

(see also Groundhogs, AC/DC, WIshbone Ash, Blue Rondos)

## HOME AND ABROAD
| 89 | SRT Z003/SRT9KS2194 | Alison Please Don't Fall/Feel The Floor (p/s) | 10 |
|---|---|---|---|

## HOMERS KNODS
69  Pye 7N 17731          All She Said Was Goodbye/Mr Rainbow ......................................................... 20

## HOME SERVICE
84  Coda NAT 001          THE MYSTERIES (LP) ......................................................................................... 15

## HOMESICK JAMES
64  Sue WI 319            Crossroads/My Baby's Sweet ......................................................................... 75
65  Sue WI 330            Set A Date/Can't Afford To Do It ................................................................ 50

## HOMESICK JAMES/SNOOKY PRYOR
74  Caroline C 1502       HOMESICK JAMES AND SNOOKY PRYOR (LP) ............................................ 20

## HOMESTEAD
68  Road R3946            She/Will You Leave ........................................................................................ 15

## HOMOSEXUALS
78  L'Orelei PF 151       Hearts In Exile/South South Africans (p/s, with insert) ........................... 15
79  Black Noise F12 No. 2 Divorce Proceedings/Mecho Madness (12", plain sleeve with sticker) ...... 10
81  Black Noise BN 1      BIGGER THAN THE NUMBER YET MISSING THE DOT (EP, clear vinyl, fold-around hand-painted sleeve) ............................................................................................. 20
82  Black Noise BLACKNOISE 2  THE HOMOSEXUALS EP (12") ................................................................... 30
84  Recommended RR 18     THE HOMOSEXUALS RECORD (LP, with inserts) ....................................... 20

*(see also George Harrassment & Homosexuals, Ice La Bas, Nancy Sesay & Melodaires, L-Voag, Sir Alick & Phraser)*

## MINAKO HONDA
87  Columbia DB 9153      Golden Days (English Version)/Crazy Nights (English Version) (p/s, features Brian May) ................................................................................................................ 35

## HONDELLS
64  Mercury MF 834        Little Honda/Hot Rod High ........................................................................... 20
65  Mercury MF 925        Younger Girl/All American Girl ................................................................... 20
66  Mercury MF 967        Cheryl's Goin' Home/Show Me Girl ............................................................ 20

## HONEST MEN
69  Tamla Motown TMG 706  Cherie/Baby ................................................................................................... 50
69  Tamla Motown TMG 706  Cherie/Baby (DJ Copy) ................................................................................. 60

## HONEYBOY
71  Trojan TR 7835        Jamaica/ITALS: Sea Wave ............................................................................... 7
72  Banana BA 375         Homeward Bound/Peace In The Land ..................................................... 100
73  Cactus CT 16          Sweet Cherrie/Impossible Love ..................................................................... 7
75  B & C BC 002          Darlin' Coming Home/SIR COLLINS: We A Come Dread .......................... 25
73  Count Shelly SSLP 101 THIS IS HONEY BOY (LP) ............................................................................ 40
74  Cactus CTLP 101       IMPOSSIBLE LOVE (LP) ................................................................................ 25

## HONEYBUS
67  Deram DM 131          Delighted To See You/The Breaking Up Scene ........................................ 12
67  Deram DM 152          Do I Figure In Your Life?/Throw My Love Away ....................................... 12
68  Deram DM 182          I Can't Let Maggie Go/Tender Are The Ashes ............................................. 5
68  Deram DM 207          Girl Of Independent Means/How Long ...................................................... 12
69  Deram DM 254          She Sold Blackpool Rock/Would You Believe ........................................... 25
70  Deram DM 289          Story/The Right To Choose ............................................................................ 7
72  Bell BLL 1205         She Is The Female To My Soul/For Where Have You Been .......................... 6
73  Warner Bros K 16250   For You/Little Lovely One ............................................................................. 8
76  Decca F 13631         I Can't Let Maggie Go/Julie In My Heart ..................................................... 5
70  Deram DML/SML 1056    STORY (LP) ................................................................................................. 120
73  Warner Bros K 46248   RECITAL (LP, withdrawn, test pressings only) ....................................... 300
79  See For Miles SEE 264 AT THEIR BEST (LP) ..................................................................................... 15

*(see also Pete Dello, Colin Hare, Lace, Magic Valley, Red Herring)*

## HONEYCOMBAK
69  Carousel CAR 1        Sex Change Sadie/It's My Life ..................................................................... 50

## HONEYCOMBS
64  Pye 7N 15664          Have I The Right/Please Don't Pretend Again .............................................. 5
64  Pye 7N 15705          Is It Because/I'll Cry Tomorrow ..................................................................... 8
64  Pye 7N 15736          Eyes/If You've Got To Pick A Baby ............................................................... 10
65  Pye 7N 15781          Don't Love You No More/I'll See You Tomorrow (withdrawn, promo only) ... 120
65  Pye 7N 15827          Something Better Beginning/I'll See You Tomorrow .................................. 10
65  Pye 7N 15890          That's The Way/Can't Get Through To You .................................................. 6
65  Pye 7N 15979          This Year, Next Year/Not Sleeping Too Well Lately ..................................... 10
66  Pye 7N 17089          Who Is Sylvia?/How Will I Know ................................................................. 15
66  Pye 7N 17138          It's So Hard/I Fell In Love ............................................................................. 15
66  Pye 7N 17173          That Loving Feeling/Should A Man Cry ...................................................... 18
69  Pye 7N 17741          Have I The Right/Please Don't Pretend Again (stereo reissue) .................. 6
65  Pye NEP 24230         THAT'S THE WAY (EP) ................................................................................. 35
64  Pye NPL 18097         THE HONEYCOMBS (LP) .............................................................................. 40
65  Pye NPL 18132         ALL SYSTEMS GO! (LP) ............................................................................... 70

*(see also Lemmings, Dennis D'Ell, Martin Murray)*

## HONEYCONE
70  Hot Wax HWX 103       While You're Out Looking For Sugar/The Feeling's Gone ............................. 8
71  Hot Wax HWX 105       Girls It Ain't Easy/Take Me With You ........................................................... 6
71  Hot Wax HWX 107       Want Ads/We Belong Together .................................................................... 10
72  Hot Wax HWX 111       One Monkey Don't Stop No Show/Stick Up ................................................. 6
72  Hot Wax HWX 112       The Day I Found Myself/When Will It End .................................................. 10
72  Hot Wax HWX 116       Sittin' On A Time Bomb/It's Better To Have Loved And Lost ...................... 20
71  Hot Wax SHW 5002      HONEYCONE (LP) ........................................................................................ 15
71  Hot Wax SHW 5004      SWEET REPLIES (LP) ................................................................................... 15
72  Hot Wax SHW 5005      SOULFUL TAPESTRY (LP) ............................................................................ 15

| | | | MINT VALUE £ |
|---|---|---|---|

**HONEYCRACK** (continued)

| 73 | Hot Wax SHW 5010 | LOVE, PEACE AND SOUL (LP) | 18 |

**HONEYCRACK**

| 95 | PPP1 | King Of Misery/5 Minutes (numbered p/s, 1500 only sold at gigs) | 5 |

*(see also Wildhearts)*

**HONEYDEW**

| 70 | Argo AFW 101 | Part Of This Game/To Make You Mine | 20 |
| 70 | Argo ZFB 15 | HONEYDEW (LP) | 150 |

**HONEYDRIPPERS**

| 84 | Es Paranza SAM 220 | Sea Of Love/Rockin' At Midnight (7" radio promo) | 10 |

*(see also Robert Plant)*

**HONEYEND**

| 72 | Spark SRL 1072 | Heartbreaker/Beautiful Downtown | 20 |

**HONEYS**

| 63 | Capitol CL 15299 | Surfin' Down The Swanee River/Shoot The Curl | 50 |

*(see also American Spring, Beach Boys)*

**HONEYTONES**

| 58 | London HLX 8671 | Don't Look Now, But.../I Know, I Know | 60 |
| 58 | London HLX 8671 | Don't Look Now, But.../I Know, I Know (78) | 35 |

**HONEYTREE**

| 70s | Myrrh MYR 1039 | EVERGREEN (LP) | 20 |

**HONG GANG**

| 72 | Sioux SI 004 | Reggae Mento/MONTEGO MELON: Swan Lake | 12 |
| 73 | Sioux SI 025 | Smoking Wild/ROOSEVELT SINGERS: Heavy Reggae | 12 |

*(see also Bob Andy)*

**HOOD**

| 92 | Fluff HONEY 4 | Sirens/Fault/Your Sixth Sense (p/s, 500 only) | 12 |
| 93 | Fluff HONEY 6 | I Didn't Think You Were Going To Hit Me In The Face/In The Trap Of Doing/Choosing A Grimace (wraparound p/s, 500 only) | 10 |
| 95 | Orgasm ORGASM 08 | A Harbour Of Thoughts/Disappointed/Uneven Conversation Should Point To Cause/Forced By The Reasoning Hand/John Clyde-Evans/Silo Crash (p/s) | 7 |
| 96 | Love Train PUBE 11 | I've Forgotten How To Live/The Weather Side Of The Stone Mill Tower/Dimensions TBA | 8 |
| 98 | Rocket Racer ROCKET 04 | The Year Of Occasional Lull/Fog Projections (1000 only, numbered, 20 with red artwork) | 10 |
| 98 | Rocket Racer ROCKET 04 | The Year Of Occasional Lull/Fog Projections (1000 only, numbered, 980 with black artwork) | 5 |
| 98 | Happy Go Lucky HGL 12 | Filmed Initiative/As Evening Changed The Day (different photo on each p/s) | 12 |
| 98 | 555 Recordings 555 13 | (The) Weight/Fallen Farmer/We Are Not Promote/Impossible Calm/Feel The Rush (Coming In From The Avant Garde)/I Know What To Squander/Mast-On-Hill/Collapsing Climate Soul (p/s) | 6 |
| 00 | Jonathan Whiskey 04 | I Can't Find My Brittle Youth/Song Of The Sea/STEWARD: Silver Soda Pop/I'm A Woman Not Just A Toy/Flatter Me With Concern For Prejudice (envelope sleeve, 250 only) | 20 |
| 94 | Fluff ARC 01 | CABLED LINEAR TRACTION (LP, 200 only) | 40 |
| 98 | Domino WIGLP 42 | RUSTIC HOUSES FORLORN VALLEYS (LP) | 30 |
| 99 | Domino WIGL 61 | THE CYCLE OF DAYS AND REASONS (LP) | 25 |
| 01 | Domino WIGLP 102 | COLD HOUSE (LP) | 20 |
| 05 | Domino WIGLP 148 | OUTSIDE CLOSER (LP) | 18 |
| 12 | Domino REWIGLP85 | COLD HOUSE (reissue, 2x12") | 20 |

**ROBBIN HOOD**

| 56 | MGM SP 1178 | The Rock-A-Bye Blues/Beautiful, Beautiful Love | 15 |

**HOODOO RHYTHM DEVILS**

| 78 | Fantasy FTC 147 | Gotta Lot Of Love In My Soul/MDR Of Love | 15 |

**HOOK**

| 68 | Uni UN 507 | In The Beginning/Show You The Way | 10 |

**MARCUS HOOK ROLL BAND**

| 72 | Regal Zonophone RZ 3061 | Natural Man/Boogalooing Is For Wooing | 30 |
| 73 | Regal zonophone RZ 3072 | Louisina Lady/Ghoochie Coochie Har Kau | 8 |
| 74 | EMI 2119 | Can't Stand The Heat/Moonshine Blues | 20 |

**EARL HOOKER**

| 69 | Blue Horizon 57-3166 | Boogie Don't Blot/Funky Blues | 30 |
| 70 | Blue Horizon 7-63850 | SWEET BLACK ANGEL (LP) | 120 |
| 70 | Stateside SSL 10298 | DON'T HAVE TO WORRY (LP) | 60 |

*(see also John Lee Hooker)*

**JOHN LEE HOOKER**

**78s**

| 52 | Vogue V 2102 | Hoogie Boogie/Whistlin' And Moanin' Blues | 40 |
| 54 | London HL 8037 | Need Somebody/Too Much Boogie | 40 |

**SINGLES**

| 63 | Stateside SS 203 | Boom Boom/Frisco Blues | 25 |
| 64 | Stateside SS 297 | Dimples/I'm Leaving | 20 |
| 64 | Stateside SS 341 | I Love You Honey/Send Me Your Pillow | 20 |
| 64 | Pye International 7N 25255 | High Priced Woman/Sugar Mama | 20 |
| 64 | Polydor NH 52930 | Shake It Baby/Let's Make It Baby | 20 |
| 65 | Sue WI 361 | I'm In The Mood/Boogie Chillun | 40 |
| 66 | Chess CRS 8039 | Let's Go Out Tonight/In The Mood | 20 |
| 66 | Planet PLF 114 | Mai Lee/Don't Be Messing With My Bread (with Groundhogs) | 50 |
| 70 | President PT 295 | Dimples/Boom Boom | 8 |

### EPs

| | | | |
|---|---|---|---|
| 60 | Riverside REP 3202 | WEDNESDAY EVENING | 30 |
| 60 | Riverside REP 3207 | DEMOCRAT MAN | 30 |
| 64 | Stateside SE 1019 | THE BLUES OF JOHN HOOKER | 30 |
| 64 | Stateside SE 1023 | I'M JOHN LEE HOOKER | 30 |
| 64 | Ember EP 4561 | THINKING BLUES | 40 |
| 65 | Pye Intl. NEP 44034 | LOVE BLUES | 35 |
| 65 | Chess CRE 6000 | DOWN AT THE LANDING | 35 |
| 65 | Atlantic AET 6010 | JOHN LEE HOOKER | 35 |
| 66 | Chess CRE 6007 | WALKING THE BOOGIE | 30 |
| 66 | Chess CRE 6014 | THE JOURNEY | 30 |
| 66 | Chess CRE 6021 | REAL FOLK BLUES VOL. 3 | 30 |
| 73 | Impulse 9103 | SERVES YOU RIGHT TO SUFFER | 15 |

### ALBUMS

| | | | |
|---|---|---|---|
| 60 | Advent LP 2801 | JOHN LEE HOOKER AND HIS GUITAR | 80 |
| 62 | Riverside RLP 12-838 | THE FOLK BLUES OF JOHN LEE HOOKER | 45 |
| 62 | Stateside SL 10014 | THE FOLK LORE OF JOHN LEE HOOKER | 70 |
| 63 | London HA-K 8097 | DON'T TURN ME FROM YOUR DOOR | 80 |
| 64 | Stateside SL 10053 | THE BIG SOUL OF JOHN LEE HOOKER | 80 |
| 64 | Stateside SL 10074 | I WANT TO SHOUT THE BLUES | 60 |
| 64 | Pye Intl. NPL 28042 | HOUSE OF THE BLUES | 60 |
| 64 | Fontana 688 700 ZL | THE FOLK-BLUES OF HOOKER | 45 |
| 65 | Fontana FJL 119 | BLUE! | 70 |
| 65 | Ember EMB 3356 | SINGS THE BLUES | 35 |
| 65 | Riverside RLP 008 | BURNING HELL | 35 |
| 65 | Chess CRL 4500 | JOHN LEE HOOKER PLAYS AND SINGS THE BLUES | 60 |
| 66 | HMV CLP 5032 | IT SERVES YOU RIGHT TO SUFFER (mono) | 45 |
| 66 | HMV CSD 3542 | IT SERVES YOU RIGHT TO SUFFER (stereo) | 60 |
| 66 | Ember (ST)EMB 3371 | DRIFTIN' THROUGH THE BLUES | 25 |
| 67 | Chess CRL 4527 | THE REAL FOLK BLUES | 40 |
| 67 | HMV CLP/CSD 3612 | LIVE AT THE CAFE A GO GO | 40 |
| 67 | Atlantic Special 590 003 | DRIFTIN' BLUES | 18 |
| 68 | Joy JOY(S) 101 | I'M JOHN LEE HOOKER | 15 |
| 68 | Joy JOY(S) 124 | BURNIN' | 15 |
| 68 | Stateside (S)SL 10246 | URBAN BLUES | 40 |
| 69 | Stateside (S)SL 10280 | SIMPLY THE TRUTH | 50 |
| 69 | Joy JOYS 133 | THE FOLKLORE OF JOHN LEE HOOKER | 15 |
| 69 | Joy JOYS 142 | CONCERT AT NEWPORT | 15 |
| 69 | Joy JOYS 147 | THE BIG SOUL OF JOHN LEE HOOKER | 15 |
| 69 | Storyville 673 005 | YOU'RE LEAVIN' ME BABY | 15 |
| 69 | Joy JOYS 152 | IN PERSON | 15 |
| 70 | Storyville 673 020 | TUPELO BLUES | 30 |
| 70 | Stax SXATS 1025 | THAT'S WHERE IT'S AT | 20 |
| 71 | Probe SPB 1016 | IF YOU MISS 'IM . . . I GOT 'IM (with Earl Hooker) | 30 |
| 71 | Probe SPB 1034 | ENDLESS BOOGIE | 15 |
| 71 | Stax 2362 017 | THAT'S WHERE IT'S AT! | 20 |
| 71 | Xtra XTRA 1114 | JOHN LEE HOOKER | 40 |
| 71 | United Artists UAS 29235 | COAST TO COAST BLUES BAND | 22 |
| 72 | Probe SPB 1057 | NEVER GET OUT OF THESE BLUES ALIVE | 18 |
| 73 | Green Bottle GN 4002 | JOHNNY LEE | 18 |
| 75 | ABC ABCL 5059 | FREE BEER AND CHICKEN | 20 |
| 91 | Silvertone ZL 75087 | MR. LUCKY (LP) | 18 |
| 95 | Virgin VPBLP 22 | CHILL OUT (LP) | 25 |

*(see also Canned Heat, Carlos Santana & Buddy Miles)*

### JOHN LEE HOOKER/LIGHTNIN' HOPKINS/SMOKEY HOGG

| | | | |
|---|---|---|---|
| 73 | Specialty SNTF 5013 | HOOKER HOPKINS HOGG (LP) | 20 |

*(see also Lightnin' Hopkins, Smokey Hogg)*

### STEVE HOOKER & HEAT

| | | | |
|---|---|---|---|
| 77 | Takeaway TAKE 1/ EJR 577 | If You Don't Do The Business/Rock & Roll Doctor/I'm Hooked/ Marionette (stamped white sleeve with insert) | 8 |

### HOOKFOOT

| | | | |
|---|---|---|---|
| 69 | Page One POF 144 | Way Of The Musician/Hookfoot | 12 |
| 72 | DJM DJS 272 | Heart To Heart Talking/Red Man | 8 |
| 72 | DJM DJS 265 | Sweet Sweet Funky Music/The Opener | 8 |
| 73 | DJM DJS 293 | So You Want To Be A Rock And Roll Star/Mr. Money | 8 |
| 71 | DJM DJLPS 413 | HOOKFOOT (LP, gatefold sleeve) | 30 |
| 72 | DJM DJLPS 422 | GOOD TIMES A' COMIN' (LP, gatefold sleeve) | 25 |
| 73 | DJM DJLPS 428 | COMMUNICATION (LP, gatefold sleeve) | 20 |
| 75 | DJM DJLMD 8013 | HEADLINES (2XLP) | 18 |

*(see also Elton John, Loot, Caleb, Soul Agents)*

### MARSHALL HOOKS & CO.

| | | | |
|---|---|---|---|
| 71 | Blue Horizon 2096 002 | I Want The Same Thing Tomorrow/Hookin' It | 20 |
| 71 | Blue Horizon 2431 003 | MARSHALL HOOKS & CO. (LP) | 100 |

### HOOKY

| | | | |
|---|---|---|---|
| 72 | RCA Victor SF 8247 | THE COLLECTED TALES OF HOOKY NO.1 (LP, gatefold sleeve) | 20 |

### HOOTEN(ANNY) SINGERS

| | | | |
|---|---|---|---|
| 64 | United Artists UP 1082 | Gabrielle/Darling (most copies list artist as Hooten Singers) | 35 |

*(see also Abba, Hep Stars, Northern Lights)*

## BOB HOPE

MINT VALUE £

| | | | |
|---|---|---|---|
| 58 | London HLU 8593 | Paris Holiday/Nothing In Common (with Bing Crosby) | 10 |

*(see also Bing Crosby, Rosemary Clooney)*

## LYN(N) HOPE

| | | | |
|---|---|---|---|
| 57 | Vogue V 9081 | Blue Moon/Blues For Anna Bacca | 20 |
| 57 | Vogue V 9082 | Eleven Till Two/Blues For Mary | 20 |
| 60 | Blue Beat BB 21 | Shockin'/Blue And Sentimental | 20 |
| 57 | Vogue VE 170103 | LYNN HOPE AND HIS TENOR SAX (EP) | 40 |
| 60 | Vogue VE 170146 | LYNN HOPE AND HIS TENOR SAX (EP) | 40 |

## HOPE STREET

| | | | |
|---|---|---|---|
| 71 | Parlophone R5982 | Wait Until Tomorrow/Ladies At The Bottom Of the Garden | 12 |

## HOPE & KEEN

| | | | |
|---|---|---|---|
| 71 | Excello XLO2 | Crazy House/You Can Go My Way | 12 |

## HOPETOWN (LEWIS) & GLENMORE (BROWN)

| | | | |
|---|---|---|---|
| 68 | Fab FAB 43 | Skinny Leg Girl/Live Like A King | 80 |

## MARY HOPKIN

| | | | |
|---|---|---|---|
| 68 | Apple APPLE 2 | Those Were The Days/Turn Turn Turn (First pressing) | 10 |
| 68 | Apple APPLE 2 | Those Were The Days/Turn Turn Turn (later pressing crediting Mary Hopkins) | 8 |
| 68 | Apple APPLE 2 | Those Were The Days/Turn Turn Turn (blank Apple label on A-side) | 12 |
| 69 | Apple APPLE 7 | Lontana Dagli Occhi/Game (Europe-only, unreleased in U.K.) | 0 |
| 69 | Apple APPLE 9 | Prince En Avignon/The Game (France-only, unreleased in U.K.) | 0 |
| 69 | Apple APPLE 10 | Goodbye/Sparrow | 6 |
| 69 | Apple APPLE 16 | Que Sera Sera/Fields Of St. Etienne (unreleased) | 0 |
| 69 | Cambrian CSP 703 | Aderyn Llwyd/Y Blodyn Gwyn (p/s) | 18 |
| 70 | Cambrian CSP 712 | Pleserau Serch/Tyrd Yn Ôl (p/s) | 18 |
| 70 | Apple APPLE 22 | Temma Harbour/Lontano Dagli Occhi (black or green lettering on p/s) | 6 |
| 70 | Apple APPLE 26 | Knock, Knock Who's There?/I'm Going To Fall In Love Again (p/s) | 6 |
| 70 | Apple APPLE 27 | Que Sera Sera/Fields Of St. Etienne (unreleased in U.K., acetates only) | 0 |
| 70 | Apple APPLE 30 | Think About Your Children/Heritage (p/s) | 6 |
| 71 | Apple APPLE 34 | Let My Name Be Sorrow/Kew Gardens (p/s) | 6 |
| 71 | Apple APPLE 39 | Water, Paper And Clay/Jefferson (p/s) | 15 |
| 72 | Regal Zonophone RZ 3070 | Mary Had A Baby/Cherry Tree Carol | 20 |
| 76 | Good Earth GD 2 | If You Love Me (I Won't Care): (some copies list "If You Love Me")/Tell Me Now | 6 |
| 77 | Good Earth GD 11 | Wrap Me In Your Arms/Just A Dreamer (p/s) | 6 |
| 68 | Cambrian CEP 414 | LLAIS SWYNOL MARY HOPKIN (EP) | 10 |
| 69 | Cambrian CEP 420 | MARY AC EDWARD (EP, with Edward Morris Jones) | 15 |
| 69 | Apple APCOR 5 | POST CARD (LP, laminated sleeve, with black or white inner sleeve, mono) | 15 |
| 69 | Apple SAPCOR 5 | POST CARD (LP, laminated sleeve, with black or white inner sleeve, stereo) | 25 |
| 71 | Apple SAPCOR 21 | EARTH SONG - OCEAN SONG (LP, gatefold sleeve, 'Apple' inner sleeve) | 20 |
| 72 | Apple SAPCOR 23 | THOSE WERE THE DAYS (LP, with 'Apple' inner sleeve) | 50 |
| 77 | Decca SPA 546 | THE WELSH WORLD OF MARY HOPKIN (LP) | 90 |
| 89 | Trax Modem 1045 | SPIRIT (LP) | 30 |
| 91 | Apple SAPCOR 5 | POST CARD (LP, reissue, gatefold sleeve with bonus 12" [SAPCOR 52]) | 20 |
| 92 | Apple SAPCOR 21 | EARTH SONG/OCEAN SONG (LP, reissue, gatefold sleeve with inner) | 30 |

*(see also Hobby Horse, Sundance, Oasis, Elfland Ensemble, Bob Johnson & Pete Knight, Roy Budd, Elmer Bernstein)*

## JOEL & LIGHTNIN' HOPKINS

| | | | |
|---|---|---|---|
| 60 | Heritage H 1000 | BLUES FROM EAST TEXAS (LP, 99 copies only) | 120 |

*(see also Lightnin' Hopkins)*

## LIGHTNIN' HOPKINS

| | | | |
|---|---|---|---|
| 61 | Bluesville BVLP 1019 | LIGHTNIN' HOPKINS (LP) | 80 |
| 62 | '77' LA 12/1 | SAM LIGHTNIN' HOPKINS - THE ROOSTER CROWED IN ENGLAND (LP 99 copies only) | 150 |
| 63 | Stateside SL 10031 | LIGHTNIN' STRIKES (LP) | 90 |
| 63 | Realm RM 128 | LIGHTNIN' HOPKINS SINGS THE BLUES (LP) | 35 |
| 63 | Realm RM 171 | DIRTY HOUSE BLUES (LP) | 30 |
| 64 | Stateside SL 10076 | BLUES HOOT (LP, some tracks by Sonny Terry & Brownie McGhee) | 60 |
| 65 | Stateside SL 10110 | HOOTIN' THE BLUES (LP) | 60 |
| 65 | Stateside SL 10155 | DOWN HOME BLUES (LP) | 60 |
| 65 | Fontana AH 183 | THE BLUES (LP) | 60 |
| 65 | Fontana 688 301 ZL | LAST NIGHT BLUES (LP) | 40 |
| 65 | Fontana 688 801 ZL | BURNIN' IN L.A. (LP) | 40 |
| 66 | Fontana 688 803 ZL | BLUE BIRD BLUES (LP) | 40 |
| 66 | Fontana 688 807 ZL | BLUES PARTY (LP) | 40 |
| 66 | Ember EMB 3389 | A TIME FOR BLUES (LP) | 25 |
| 66 | Ember EMB 3416 | LIVE AT THE BIRD LOUNGE (LP) | 25 |
| 67 | Ember EMB 3423 | I'VE BEEN BUKED AND SCORNED (LP) | 25 |
| 66 | Verve (S)VLP 5003 | ROOTS OF HOPKINS (LP) | 25 |
| 66 | Verve (S)VLP 5014 | LIGHTNIN' STRIKES (LP, reissue) | 25 |
| 66 | Saga ERO 8001 | LIGHTNIN' HOPKINS (LP) | 18 |
| 67 | Xtra XTRA 5036 | BLUES IN MY BOTTLE (LP) | 15 |
| 68 | Xtra XTRA 5044 | GOT TO MOVE YOUR BABY (LP, reissue of Fontana 688 301 ZL) | 18 |
| 68 | Minit MLL/MLS 40006 | EARTH BLUES (LP) | 20 |
| 68 | Liberty LBL 83254 | KING OF DOWLING STREET (LP) | 40 |
| 69 | Joy JOY(S) 115 | LIGHTNIN' STRIKES (LP, 2nd reissue) | 30 |
| 69 | Polydor 545 019 | THAT'S MY STORY (LP) | 15 |
| 70 | Ace Of Hearts AH 183 | THE BLUES (LP) | 25 |
| 70 | Poppy PYS 11000 | LIGHTNIN'! VOLUME 1 (LP) | 15 |
| 70 | Poppy PYS 11002 | LIGHTNIN'! VOLUME 2 (LP) | 20 |
| 71 | Liberty LBS 83293 | THE CALIFORNIA MUDSLIDE (AND EARTHQUAKE) (LP) | 30 |

| 71 | Mayfair AMLB 4000 1/2 | LIGHTNIN' STRIKES (2-LP) | 18 |
|---|---|---|---|
| 71 | Blue Horizon 2431 005 | LET'S WORK AWHILE (LP) | 120 |
| 71 | Xtra XTRA 1127 | THE ROOTS OF LIGHTNIN' HOPKINS (LP) | 18 |
| 72 | Carnival 2941 005 | LONESOME LIGHTNIN' (LP) | 18 |

(see also Sonny Terry & Brownie McGhee, Joel & Lightnin' Hopkins, Lightnin' Hopkins & John Lee Hooker, Big Joe Williams)

## LIGHTNIN' HOPKINS & JOHN LEE HOOKER
| 69 | Storyville 616 001 | THERE'S GOOD ROCKIN' TONIGHT! (LP) | 35 |
|---|---|---|---|
| 72 | Storyville SLP 174 | LIGHTNIN' HOPKINS AND JOHN LEE HOOKER (LP) | 35 |

(see also John Lee Hooker/Lightnin' Hopkins/Smokey Hogg)

## LINDA HOPKINS
| 61 | Coral Q 72423 | I Diddle Dum Dum/All In My Mind | 20 |
|---|---|---|---|
| 62 | Coral Q 72448 | Mama's Doin' The Twist/My Mother's Eyes | 20 |

## LINDA HOPKINS & JACKIE WILSON
| 63 | Coral Q 72464 | Shake A Hand/Say I Do | 15 |
|---|---|---|---|
| 65 | Coral Q 72480 | Yes Indeed/When The Saints Go Marching In | 15 |

(see also Jackie Wilson)

## NICKY HOPKINS
| 66 | CBS 202055 | Mr Big/Jenni | 18 |
|---|---|---|---|
| 67 | Polydor 56175 | Mister Pleasant/Nothing As Yet | 18 |
| 68 | MGM MGM 1419 | Top Pops No. 1 (Medley)/(Part 2) | 8 |
| 68 | Fontana TF 906 | High On A Hill/Trumpet Serenade (actually by Nigel Hopkins) | 6 |
| 73 | CBS CBS 1328 | Speed On/Sundown In Mexico | 5 |
| 66 | CBS (S)BPG 62679 | THE REVOLUTIONARY PIANO OF NICKY HOPKINS (LP) | 70 |
| 73 | CBS 65416 | THE TIN MAN WAS A DREAMER (LP, gatefold sleeve) | 30 |

(see also Aquarian Age, Neil Christian & Crusaders, Cyril Davies R&B All-Stars, Poet & One Man Band, Quicksilver Messenger Service, Sweet Thursday)

## WASH HOPKINS SINGERS
| 69 | Action ACT 4546 | He's Got Blessing/Rock In A Weary Land | 20 |
|---|---|---|---|

## HOPKIRK AND LEE
| 98 | Rough Trade/For Us 001 | Beneath The Apple Tree (7" 1,000 copies) | 15 |
|---|---|---|---|

## HUGH HOPPER
| 73 | CBS 65466 | 1984 (LP) | 30 |
|---|---|---|---|
| 76 | Compendium FIDARDO 4 | CRUEL BUT FAIR (LP) | 20 |
| 77 | Compendium FIDARDO 7 | HOPPERTUNITY BOX (LP) | 20 |
| 78 | Ogun OG 527 | ROGUE ELEMENT (LP, as Hopper, Dean, Gowen, Sheen - 'Soft Heap') | 20 |

(see also Caravan, Elton Dean, Gilgamesh, Isotope, Matching Mole, Ninesense, Soft Machine)

## HOPSCOTCH
| 69 | United Artists UP 2231 | Look At The Lights Go Up/Same Old Fat Man | 140 |
|---|---|---|---|
| 69 | United Artists UP 35022 | Long Black Veil/Easy To Find | 10 |

(see also Scots Of St. James, Five Day Rain, Forever More, Glencoe)o

## HORACE & IMPERIALS
| 68 | Nu Beat NB 012 | Young Love/Days Like These | 15 |
|---|---|---|---|

## EDDIE HORAN
| 78 | London HLU 10565 | When I Fly With You/Turn My World Back Around | 10 |
|---|---|---|---|

## HORATIO
| 70 | Penny Farthing PEN 729 | I've Gotta Have You/A Sad Song With A Happy Soul | 5 |
|---|---|---|---|

## HORDEN RAIKES
| 73 | Folk Heritage FHR 042 | KING COTTON (LP) | 15 |
|---|---|---|---|
| 72 | Folk Heritage FHR 026 | HORDEN RAIKES (LP) | 20 |

## HORIZON (1)
| 81 | SRT SRTS 81432 | Stage Struck/Remember The Bad Boys | 10 |
|---|---|---|---|

## HORIZON (2)
| 83 | Orbit TRIP 4 | Sunshine Reggae/Nightlife | 6 |
|---|---|---|---|

(see also Mungo Jerry)

## PAUL HORN
| 68 | Liberty LBL 83084E | COSMIC CONSCIOUSNESS (LP) | 30 |
|---|---|---|---|

## LENA HORNE
| 65 | United Artists UP 1101 | The Sand And The Sea/It Had Better Be Tonight | 25 |
|---|---|---|---|

## HANK HORNSBY
| 57 | MGM MGM 955 | Pots And Pans/Cotton | 6 |
|---|---|---|---|
| 58 | MGM MGM 972 | The Legend Of The Birds And Bees/Girls Girls Girls | 6 |

## HORNSEY AT WAR
| 79 | War WAR 001 | DEAD BEAT REVIVAL (EP, numbered p/s) | 40 |
|---|---|---|---|

## HORRORCOMIC
| 77 | Lightning/B&C BVZ 0007 | I'm All Hung Up On Pierrepoint/The Exorcist/Sex In The Afternoon (p/s) | 40 |
|---|---|---|---|
| 78 | Lightning GIL 512 | I Don't Mind/England 77 (p/s) | 90 |
| 79 | B&C BCS 18 | Jesus Crisis/Cut Your Throat (p/s) | 400 |

## HORRORS
| 06 | Loog LOOG 18-7X | Count In Fives/A Knife In Their Eye (p/s, inner p/s, stickered PVC sleeve) | 15 |
|---|---|---|---|
| 06 | Loog LOOG 18-7 | Count In Fives/Who Says (black sleeve, barcode sticker, with sticker inside) | 18 |
| 06 | Loog LOOG 015 | Sheena Is A Parasite/Jack The Ripper (p/s, insert, 500 only) | 40 |
| 06 | Loog LOOG 016 | Death At The Chapel/Crawdaddy Simone (p/s, 500 only with sticker) | 12 |
| 07 | Loog 1725544 | Gloves/Kicking Kay (p/s) | 10 |
| 07 | Loog 1725539 | Gloves/Death At The Chapel (p/s) | 6 |
| 07 | Loog 1735625 | She Is The New Thing/Draw Japan (Dandi Wind Remix) p/s) | 6 |
| 07 | Loog 1735628 | She Is The New Thing/Sister Leonella (p/s) | 6 |
| 09 | XL XLS 468 | Whole New Way/Primary Colours (p/s) | 8 |

MINT VALUE £

| | | | |
|---|---|---|---|
| 13 | XL XLBX 587 | HIGHER (4 x 12", 2-CD, DVD box set) | 25 |
| 07 | Polydor 172 417-9 | STRANGE HOUSE (LP, stickered gatefold sleeve, inner) | 80 |
| 09 | XL XLLP 418 | PRIMARY COLOURS (2-LP, poster) | 20 |

*(see also Spider & The Flies)*

**FRANK HORROX**
| | | | |
|---|---|---|---|
| 60 | Embassy WEP 1038 | JAZZ SESSION (EP, featuring Don Rendell) | 20 |

**HORSE**
| | | | |
|---|---|---|---|
| 70 | RCA Victor SF 8109 | HORSE (LP) | 400 |

*(see also Saturnalia, Atomic Rooster)*

**HORSEPOWER**
| | | | |
|---|---|---|---|
| 79 | Square SQS 2 | Outrageous/Highway Robbery | 10 |

**HORSLIPS**
| | | | |
|---|---|---|---|
| 73 | Oats OAT 1 | High Reel/Furniture | 5 |
| 73 | Oats OAT 2 | Dearg Doom/The Shamrock Shore | 5 |
| 76 | DJM DJS 10754 | Warm Sweet Breath Of Love/King Of Morning, Queen Of Day | 6 |
| 73 | Oats MOO 3 | HAPPY TO MEET ... SORRY TO PART (LP, booklet octagonal sleeve) | 45 |
| 73 | Oats MOO 5 | THE TAIN (LP, gatefold sleeve, lyric inner sleeve) | 20 |
| 75 | RCA Victor SF 8432 | THE UNFORTUNATE CUP OF TEA (LP, orange label) | 15 |

**HORTENSE (ELLIS) & ALTON (ELLIS)**
| | | | |
|---|---|---|---|
| 65 | Island WI 230 | Don't Gamble With Love/Something You Got (B-side actually by Alton Ellis & Flames) | 25 |

*(see also Hortense Ellis, Alton Ellis, Mr. Foundation)*

**HORTENSE (ELLIS) & DELROY (WILSON)**
| | | | |
|---|---|---|---|
| 66 | Rio R 119 | We're Gonna Make It/SOUL BROTHERS: Ska Shuffle | 25 |

*(see also Hortense Ellis, Delroy Wilson)*

**HORTENSE (ELLIS) & JACKIE (OPEL)**
| | | | |
|---|---|---|---|
| 64 | R&B JB 138 | Stand By Me/JACKIE OPEL: Solid Rock | 50 |

*(see also Hortense Ellis, Jackie Opel)*

**JOHNNY HORTON**
| | | | |
|---|---|---|---|
| 59 | Philips PB 932 | The Battle Of New Orleans/All For The Love Of A Girl | 5 |
| 59 | Philips PB 951 | Sal's Got A Sugar Lip/Johnny Reb | 8 |
| 59 | Philips PB 976 | Take Me Like I Am/I'm Ready If You're Willing | 5 |
| 60 | Philips PB 995 | Sink The Bismarck!/The Same Old Tale The Crow Told Me | 10 |
| 60 | Philips PB 1062 | North To Alaska/The Mansion You Stole | 5 |
| 61 | Philips PB 1130 | When It's Springtime In Alaska/Mr. Moonlight | 5 |
| 61 | Philips PB 1132 | Sleepy Eyed John/They'll Never Take Her Love From Me | 5 |
| 61 | Philips PB 1170 | Miss Marcy/Ole Slew Foot | 7 |
| 62 | Philips PB 1226 | Words/Honky Tonk Man | 10 |
| 63 | CBS AAG 132 | All Grown Up/I'm A One Woman Man | 8 |
| 60 | Mercury ZEP 10074 | THE FANTASTIC JOHNNY HORTON (EP) | 40 |
| 64 | Mercury 10008 MCE | COUNTRY AND WESTERN ACES (EP) | 40 |
| 60 | Philips BBL 7464 | THE SPECTACULAR JOHNNY HORTON (LP) | 20 |
| 61 | Philips BBL 7536 | HONKY TONK MAN (LP) | 40 |
| 63 | London HA-U 8096 | DONE ROVIN' (LP) | 25 |

**WALTER 'SHAKEY' HORTON**
| | | | |
|---|---|---|---|
| 70 | London HAK/SHK 8405 | SOUTHERN COMFORT (LP, as Shakey Horton) | 100 |
| 74 | Xtra XTRA 1135 | WALTER 'SHAKEY' HORTON WITH HOT COTTAGE (LP) | 30 |
| 74 | Sonet SNTF 677 | BIG WALTER HORTON (LP, with Carey Bell) | 25 |

**JOHN HOSIER**
| | | | |
|---|---|---|---|
| 70 | Universal Editions LYN 2177 | NEW SOUNDS IN CLASS (with St. Anne's Girls School) | 30 |

**LA/THE HOST**
| | | | |
|---|---|---|---|
| 85 | Quiet QU 1 | The Big Sleep/Just Breaking Away (p/s) | 8 |

**HOT CHIP**
| | | | |
|---|---|---|---|
| 04 | Moshi Moshi HOTCHIP7 | Hittin Skittles/Back To The Future (300 only, hand-made sleeve) | 10 |
| 07 | EMI CHIPS 01 | Rehab (AMY WINEHOUSE: Hot Chip Remix)/In The Morning (JUNIOR BOYS: Hot Chip Remix) (12") | 12 |
| 09 | Parlophone 50999 69399176 | Transmission/JOY DIVISION: Transmission (demo) | 12 |
| 12 | Domino DNO 337 | Look At Where We Are (Major Lazer Remix)/Look At Where We Are (Major Lazer v Junior Blender Remix) 7", large hole, die cut sleeve, 1000 only) | 6 |
| 04 | Moshi Moshi MOSHILP 06 | COMING ON STRONG (LP, 500 only) | 25 |
| 06 | EMI 094634741811 | THE WARNING (2-LP with free 7", Won't Wash/Bally) | 25 |
| 08 | EMI 5099952057717 | MADE IN THE DARK (LP) | 15 |
| 10 | Vinyl Factory VF 012 | ONE LIFE STAND (2-LP with free 7" Bubble/Do Not Wait, no'd gatefold sleeve, 1000 only) | 25 |
| 12 | Domino WIGLP 293X | IN OUR HEADS (2-LP with 7") | 18 |

**HOT CHOCOLATE (BAND)**
| | | | |
|---|---|---|---|
| 69 | Apple APPLE 18 | Give Peace A Chance/Living Without Tomorrow (as Hot Chocolate Band) | 60 |
| 70 | Rak RAK 103 | Love Is Life/Pretty Girls (with promo p/s) | 5 |
| 73 | Rak RAK 139 | You'll Always Be A friend/Go Go Girl | 15 |

*(see also Errol Brown & Chosen Few, Tony Wilson)*

**HOT CITY**
| | | | |
|---|---|---|---|
| 71 | London HLU 10344 | Leaving/I Believe In Life | 15 |

**HOT CLUB**
| | | | |
|---|---|---|---|
| 82 | RAK 346 | The Dirt That She Walks On Is Sacred Ground To Me/Heat (p/s) | 12 |
| 82 | RAK 346 | The Dirt That She Walks On Is Sacred Ground To Me/Heat (12", p/s) | 10 |
| 82 | RAK 361 | It Ain't Me Girl/It Ain't Me Girl (Night Version) (p/s) | 6 |

*(see also Rich Kids, Spectres)*

**HOTFOOT GALE**
| | | | |
|---|---|---|---|
| 78 | Charly SYS 1044 | Washin' Machine Boogie/Everybody's Feelin' Allright | 6 |

## HOT LEG
09  Barbeque Rock BRR0003V  RED LIGHT FEVER (LP, red) .................................................. 25

*(see also Darkness)*

## HOTLEGS
| | | | |
|---|---|---|---|
| 70 | Fontana 6007 019 | Neanderthal Man/You Didn't Like It Because You Didn't Think Of It ........ 5 |
| 71 | Philips 6006 140 | Lady Sadie/The Loser ........................................ 8 |
| 71 | Philips 6308 047 | THINKS: SCHOOL STINKS (LP, gatefold sleeve, black/silver label)........ 50 |
| 71 | Philips 6308 080 | SONG (LP, gatefold sleeve, black/silver label) ................... 60 |

*(see also 10cc, Mindbenders, Godley & Creme,Tristar Airbus, Ramases)*

## HOT POTATO
73  PMTB 1  HOT POTATO (LP, private pressing) ............................. 25

## HOT RAIN
90  Pine Tree TWIG 002  STAY TRUE (12", EP) ....................................... 25

## HOT RATS
09  No label or cat no  Damaged Goods/Fight For Your Right To Party (tour 7", 150-only, die-cut sleeve, signed) ................................................ 12

*(see also Supergrass)*

## HOT ROCKS
73  Bell Bell 1326  Chopper/Roly Poly ............................................ 6

## HOT ROCKS & JAH LOXLEY
80s  Gemini GSM 025  Jah Jah No Parcial/Badda Badda.................................. 20

## HOT ROD
69  Joe's DU 41  The Judge/RON: Soul Of Soul Of Joel............................... 20
73  President PT 397  I Want You (All Night Long)/Love Is All Right (Hey) .............. 10

## HOT ROD ALLSTARS
| | | | |
|---|---|---|---|
| 69 | Duke DU 59 | Lick A Pop/Treasure ........................................ 40 |
| 70 | Duke DU 65 | Paint Your Wagon/Organ Man (Setters as artist on label) ........ 140 |
| 70 | Duke DU 66 | Return Of The Bad Man/Caysoe Reggae ....................... 25 |
| 70 | Trojan TR 7732 | Strong Man/Sentimental ................................ 25 |
| 70 | Trojan TR 7733 | Virgin Soldier/Brixton Reggae Festival ....................... 50 |
| 70 | Torpedo TOR 1 | Pussy Got Nine Life/BOSS SOUNDS: Lick It Back ............... 60 |
| 70 | Torpedo TOR 5 | Skinheads Don't Fear/Ten Commandments From The Devil ...... 125 |
| 70 | Torpedo TOR 10 | Moonhop In London/Skinhead Moondust ..................... 150 |
| 70 | Torpedo TOR 14 | Control Your Doggy/Follow The Stars ....................... 30 |
| 70 | Hot Rod HR 104 | Skinhead Speaks His Mind/CARL LEVEY: Carnaby Street ......... 150 |
| 70 | Hot Rod HR 107 | Strictly Invitation/PATSY & PEGGY: Dog Your Woman .......... 100 |
| 70 | Hot Rod HR 108 | Beautiful World/Shocks Of A Drugs Man .................... 15 |

*(see also Setters, Betty Sinclair)*

## HOTRODS
65  Columbia DB 7693  I Don't Love You No More/Ain't Coming Back No More ............ 50

## HOT SPRINGS
66  Columbia DB 7821  It's All Right/All I Know About Love ........................ 20

## HOT THUMBS O'RILEY
73  Charisma CAS 1071  HOT THUMBS O'RILEY (LP, gatefold sleeve, large 'Mad Hatter' label) ........ 30

## HOT-TODDYS
59  Pye International 7N 25020  Rockin' Crickets/Shakin' And Stompin' ................. 30

*(see also Rockin' Rebels)*

## HOT TUNA
72  Grunt 65-0502  Keep On Truckin'/Water Song ................................ 5
76  Grunt RCG 1002  It's So Easy/I Can't Be Satisfied ............................. 5
70  RCA SF 8125  HOT TUNA (LP) ............................................ 20

*(see also Jefferson Airplane)*

## HOT VULTURES
77  Red Rag RRR 015  THE EAST STREET SHAKES (LP) ............................. 20
79  Plant Life PLR 018  UP THE LINE (LP) ...................................... 20

*(see also Ian (A) Anderson)*

## HOT WATER
78  Duff  Different Morning/Premium Bondage ............................... 8
79  Duff DWR 101  Get Lost!/Bird's Eye View (p/s) ............................... 7

## HOUNDHEAD HENRY/FRANKIE JAXON
60  Jazz Collector JEL 10  THE MALE BLUES VOLUME 6 (EP) ......................... 18

## HOUR GLASS
68  Liberty LBL83129/LBS 83129E  THE HOUR GLASS (LP) .............................. 40
74  United Artists USD 303/4  THE HOUR GLASS (2-LP) ........................... 25

*(see also Allman Brothers)*

## HOUSE
72  Parlophone R 5962  Captain America/I Like It .................................. 7

## HOUSE CREW
| | | | |
|---|---|---|---|
| 91 | Production House PNT 029 | Keep The Fire Burning/Get On Up (12").............. 12 |
| 91 | Production House PNT 029R | Keep The Fires Burning (Remixes) (12") ........... 20 |
| 92 | Production House PNT 035 | We Are Hardcore/Maniac (Hypermix) (12") ......... 15 |
| 92 | Production House PNT 035R | We Are Hardcore/Maniac (Remixes) (12") .......... 15 |
| 93 | Production House PNT 047 | The Theme/Euphoria (12")....................... 25 |
| 93 | Production House PNT 047R | The Theme/Euphoria (Remixes) (12")............. 15 |
| 94 | Production House PNT 060 | Superhero (My Knight) (12") .................... 15 |
| 94 | Production House PNT 060R | Superhero (Remixes) (12") ..................... 15 |

| | | | MINT VALUE £ |
|---|---|---|---|
| 94 | Production House PNT 060RX | Superhero (Remixes II) (12") | 15 |

**HOUSEHOLD**
| 67 | United Artists UP 1190 | I Guess I'll Learn How To Fly/Nothing You Can Do But Cry | 6 |
| 68 | United Artists UP 2210 | Twenty First Summer/Winter's Coming On | 6 |

**HOUSEHOLD NAMES**
| 81 | Blue Chip BC 104 | White Light/Much Too Young To Love | 7 |

**HOUSEMARTINS**
| 85 | Go! Discs GOD 7 | Flag Day/Stand At Ease (p/s) | 5 |
| 85 | Go! Discs GOD 7/GOD 9 | Flag Day/Stand At Ease//Sheep/Drop Down Dead (shrinkwrapped double pack) | 6 |
| 86 | Go! Discs GODB 16 | THE HOUSEMARTINS' CHRISTMAS BOX SET (4 singles in foldout sleeve, signed) | 25 |
| 07 | Mercury 175 252-3 | SOUP ('deluxe Fan Edition', in sealed/stickered tin: CD, DVD, T-shirt and mug) | 60 |

*(see also Beautiful South)*

**HOUSEMASTER BALDWIN**
| 88 | Koolkat KOOLT 21 | DELTA HOUSE (12", p/s) | 10 |
| 88 | Koolkat KOOLT 22 | DON'T LEAD ME (12", p/s) | 10 |

**HOUSE OF LORDS**
| 69 | B&C CB 112 | In The Land Of Dreams/Ain't Gonna Wait Forever | 25 |

**HOUSE OF LOVE**
| 87 | Creation CRE 043T | Shine On/Love/Flow (12", p/s, 4,000 only) | 20 |
| 87 | Creation CRE 044T | Real Animal/Plastic/Nothing To Me (12", p/s, 4,000 only) | 20 |
| 88 | Creation CRE 053 | Christine/Loneliness Is A Gun (die-cut '99p' sleeve) | 10 |
| 88 | Creation CRE 057 | Destroy The Heart/Blind | 5 |
| 88 | Creation CRE 057T | Destroy The Heart/Blind/Mr Jo (12", p/s) | 5 |
| 89 | Fontana HOLR212 | I Don't Know Why I Love You/Clothes/Secrets/The Spy (12") | 10 |
| 89 | Fontana HOLG4 | The Beatles & The Stones/Love IV (fold-out flower p/s, numbered & poster) | 5 |
| 92 | Love 1 | ROYAL ALBERT HALL EP (10" gig freebie, stickered) | 5 |
| 88 | Creation CRELP 034 | HOUSE OF LOVE (LP, with free 7", "Shine On/Christine", matt sleeve) | 20 |

**BOBBI HOUSTON**
| 74 | Action ACT 4622 | I Want To Make It With You (Parts 1 & 2) | 12 |

**CISCO HOUSTON**
| 60 | Top Rank 30/028 | THE CISCO SPECIAL (LP) | 50 |
| 62 | Fontana TFL 6007 | CISCO SPECIAL! (LP) | 25 |
| 62 | Fontana TFL 6014 | SINGS SONGS OF WOODY GUTHRIE (LP) | 20 |
| 68 | Fontana FJL 412 | I AIN'T GOT NO HOME (LP) | 15 |
| 69 | Ember CW 135 | CISCO HOUSTON AND WOODY GUTHRIE (LP) | 15 |

**CISSY HOUSTON**
| 70 | Major Minor MM 700 | He/I Believe/I'll Be There | 5 |
| 70 | Major Minor MM 716 | The Long And Winding Road/Be My Baby | 5 |
| 70 | Pye International 7N 25537 | I Just Don't Know What To Do With Myself/This Empty Place | 5 |
| 71 | Pye International 7N 25545 | The Long And Winding Road/Be My Baby (reissue) | 45 |
| 71 | Janus 6146 003 | Darling Take Me Back/Hang On To A Dream | 5 |
| 72 | Janus 6146 027 | Midnight Train To Georgia/I'm So Glad I Can Love Again | 5 |
| 70 | Major Minor SMLP 80 | PRESENTING CISSY HOUSTON (LP) | 30 |

*(see also Sweet Inspirations)*

**DAVID HOUSTON**
| 55 | London HL 8147 | Blue Prelude/I'm Sorry I Made You Cry | 30 |
| 63 | Columbia DB 7159 | Mountain Of Love/Poor Little Angeline | 7 |
| 66 | Columbia DB 7997 | Almost Persuaded/We Got Love | 7 |

**DAVID HOUSTON & TAMMY WYNETTE**
| 67 | Columbia DB 8246 | My Elusive Dreams/Marriage On The Rocks | 8 |

**SAM HOUSTON**
| 65 | Island WI 172 | My Mother's Eyes/Danny Boy | 12 |

**THELMA HOUSTON**
| 69 | Stateside SS 8026 | Jumpin' Jack Flash/Sunshower | 5 |
| 72 | Tamla Motown TMG 799 | I Want To Go Back There Again/Pick Of The Week | 12 |
| 72 | Mowest MW 3001 | No One's Gonna Be A Fool Forever/What If | 7 |
| 73 | Mowest MW 3004 | Black California/I'm Letting Go (withdrawn) | 60 |

**BRIAN HOWARD & SILHOUETTES**
| 62 | Columbia DB 4914 | Somebody Help Me/Young And Evil | 25 |
| 63 | Columbia DB 7067 | The Worryin' Kind/Come To Me | 25 |
| 64 | Fontana TF 464 | Back In The U.S.A./Hooked | 20 |

**JAN HOWARD**
| 60 | London HL 7088 | The One You Slip Around With/I Wish I Could Fall In Love Again (export issue) | 25 |

**JOHN HOWARD**
| 75 | CBS 80473 | KID IN A BIG WORLD (LP, with insert) | 25 |

**JOHNNY HOWARD BAND**
| 60 | Decca F 11298 | Up The Wall/Orbit | 5 |
| 62 | Decca F 11423 | Mind Reader/Spanish Gipsy Dance | 8 |
| 64 | Decca F 11925 | Rinky Dink/Java | 8 |
| 65 | Decca F 12065 | El Pussy Cat/A Tune Called Harry | 5 |
| 65 | Decca LK 4735 | THE EASY BEAT SOUND (LP) | 15 |
| 67 | Deram DML/SML 1001 | THE VELVET TOUCH OF JOHNNY HOWARD (LP) | 15 |

**KEITH HOWARD**
| 80 | Rods HOT 2 | LOOKING FOR YOU (LP, some sleeves contain Driver artwork on opposite sides of sleeve) | 35 |

*(see also Victory)*

## LES HOWARD
| 53 | HMV 7M 127 | Love Evermore/I Lived When I Met You | 10 |
| 53 | HMV 7M 171 | Rags To Riches/From Here To Eternity | 10 |

## NOAH HOWARD
| 69 | Polydor Super 2383093 | THE BLACK ARK (LP) | 40 |

## ROLAND S. HOWARD & LYDIA LUNCH
| 86 | 4AD BAD 210 | Some Velvet Morning/I Fell In Love With A Ghost (12", p/s, with postcard) | 12 |

*(see also Lydia Lunch, Birthday Party)*

## ROWLAND S. HOWARD & NIKKI SUDDEN
| 87 | Creation CRE 040T | Wedding Hotel/Hello Wolf/Girl Without A Name/Wedding Hotel (Original Mix) (12", p/s) | 10 |

*(see also Swell Maps, Last Bandits, Jeremy Gluck)*

## WAYNE HOWARD
| 70 | Explosion EX 2042 | All Kinds Of Everything/Cool And Easy (B-side actually by Lloyd Charmers) | 7 |

## HOWDY BOYS
| 80 | Spectacle SP 1 | Spectacle/Dancing In The Depression (p/s) | 15 |

## CATHERINE HOWE
| 71 | Reflection HRS 11 | Nothing More Than Strangers/It Comes With The Breezes | 20 |
| 71 | Reflection REFL 11 | WHAT A BEAUTIFUL PLACE (LP, laminated front sleeve 'correction' sticker on rear sleeve) | 1000 |
| 75 | RCA Victor SF 8407 | HARRY (LP) | 18 |

## STEVE HOWE
| 75 | Atlantic K50151 | BEGINNINGS (LP, gatefold sleeve) | 15 |

*(see also Yes)*

## EDDIE HOWELL
| 76 | Warner Bros K 16701 | Man From Manhattan/Waiting In The Wings (features members of Queen) | 6 |
| 77 | Warner Bros K 16866 | Sweet On You/Miss Amerika (features Gary Moore) | 6 |

*(see also Queen, Gary Moore, Brian May, Freddie Mercury)*

## EDDY HOWELL
| 69 | Parlophone R5756 | Easy Street/Judy's Good | 45 |

## FRANKIE HOWERD
| 54 | Decca F 10420 | (Don't Let The) Kiddy Geddin/Abracadabra | 10 |
| 58 | Columbia DB 4230 | It's All Right With Me/Song And Dance Man | 7 |
| 64 | Decca F 12028 | Last Word On The Election/Last Word On The Election (Part 2) | 5 |
| 70 | Pye 7N 45061 | Up Je T'Aime/All Through The Night | 5 |
| 71 | Columbia DB 8757 | Up Pompeii/Salute! | 5 |
| 63 | HMV CLP 1685 | A FUNNY THING HAPPENED ON THE WAY TO THE FORUM (LP) | 15 |

## CHRIS HOWLAND
| 58 | Columbia DB 4114 | Mama (Ma, He's Making Eyes At Me)/Fraulein | 7 |
| 59 | Columbia DB 4194 | Susie Darlin'/The Rain Falls On Ev'rybody | 10 |

## HOWLIN' WOLF
| 61 | Pye International 7N 25101 | Little Baby/Down In The Bottom | 25 |
| 63 | Pye International 7N 25192 | Just Like I Treat You/I Ain't Superstitious | 25 |
| 64 | Pye International 7N 25244 | Smokestack Lightnin'/Going Down Slow ('Slow' on B-side label) | 25 |
| 64 | Pye International 7N 25244 | Smokestack Lightnin'/Going Down Slow ("South' on B-side label) | 20 |
| 64 | Pye International 7N 25269 | Little Girl/Tail Dragger | 22 |
| 64 | Pye International 7N 25283 | Love Me Darling/My Country Sugar Mama | 22 |
| 65 | Chess CRS 8010 | Killing Floor/Louise | 15 |
| 65 | Chess CRS 8016 | Ooh Baby/Tell Me What I've Done | 15 |
| 69 | Chess CRS 8097 | Evil/Tail Dragger | 15 |
| 56 | London REU 1072 | RHYTHM AND BLUES WITH HOWLIN' WOLF (EP) | 200 |
| 63 | Pye Intl. NEP 44015 | SMOKESTACK LIGHTNIN' (EP) | 40 |
| 64 | Pye Intl. NEP 44032 | TELL ME (EP) | 30 |
| 66 | Chess CRE 6017 | REAL FOLK BLUES (EP) | 30 |
| 64 | Chess CRL 4006 | MOANIN' IN THE MOONLIGHT (LP) | 100 |
| 65 | Chess CRL 4508 | POOR BOY (LP) | 45 |
| 66 | Ember EMB 3370 | BIG CITY BLUES (LP) | 25 |
| 69 | Chess CRLS 4543 | THE HOWLIN' WOLF ALBUM (LP) | 25 |
| 71 | Syndicate Chapter SC 003 | GOING BACK HOME (LP) | 20 |
| 71 | Chess 6310 108 | MESSAGE TO THE YOUNG (LP) | 22 |
| 71 | Rolling Stones COC 49101 | THE LONDON SESSIONS (LP) | 20 |
| 71 | Python PLP 13 | HOWLIN' WOLF (LP) | 60 |

*(see also Hubert Sumlin)*

## HOWLIN' WOLF/JUNIOR PARKER/BOBBY BLAND
| 74 | Polydor 2383 257 | BLUES FOR MR. CRUMP (LP) | 30 |

## HOWLIN' WOLF, MUDDY WATERS & BO DIDDLEY
| 68 | Chess CRL 4537 | THE SUPER SUPER BLUES BAND (LP) | 45 |

*(see also Muddy Waters, Bo Diddley)*

## LINDA HOYLE
| 70 | Vertigo 6059 018 | Eli's Coming/United States Of Mind (as Linda Hoyle & Affinity) | 40 |
| 71 | Vertigo 6360 060 | PIECES OF ME (LP, gatefold sleeve, small swirl label) | 1000 |

*(see also Affinity, Nucleus)*

## H.P. LOVECRAFT
| 67 | Philips BF 1620 | Wayfarin' Stranger/The Time Machine | 7 |
| 68 | Philips BF 1639 | The White Ship (Parts 1 & 2) (unissued) | 0 |
| 68 | Philips BF 1639 | The White Ship/I've Been Wrong Before | 15 |
| 67 | Philips (S)BL 7830 | H.P. LOVECRAFT (LP) | 80 |
| 68 | Philips SBL 7872 | H.P. LOVECRAFT II (LP, without watermark at start of each side) | 50 |

MINT VALUE £

| Year | Label | Title | Value |
|---|---|---|---|
| 68 | Philips SBL 7872 | H.P. LOVECRAFT II (LP, with watermark at start of each side) | 20 |
| 72 | Philips 6336 210 | THIS IS H.P. LOVECRAFT (LP) | 40 |
| 72 | Philips 6336 213 | H.P. LOVECRAFT VOL. 2 (LP) | 25 |
| 88 | Edsel DED 256 | AT THE MOUNTAINS OF MADNESS (2-LP) | 20 |

**HQ SQUAD**
| 89 | Music Of Life NOTE33 | Burial Proceedings In The Course Of Three Knights/Onslaught (12") | 15 |

**HRATCH**
| 70 | Decca F13007 | Beautiful Bare Back Rider/Ain't It Tough | 10 |
| 74 | EMI 2170 | You/Just In Case | 6 |
| 77 | DJM DJS 10765 | Another Way Of Going Home/Life (promo only in p/s) | 8 |

**HT**
| 66 | Polydor 56127 | You & Me/Love Can Wait | 10 |

**H.T. SPLIFF**
| 79 | Septic SP 002 | OUT OF THE EARTH'S WOMB (LP) | 60 |

**H2O**
| 81 | Spock PARA 2 | Hollywood Dream/Children (with lyric insert) | 6 |
| 66 | Polydor 56127 | You & Me/Love Can Wait | 10 |

**FREDDIE HUBBARD**
| 70 | CTI 6001 | RED CLAY (LP) | 25 |
| 74 | MSP/BASF BAP 5036 | THE HUB OF HUBBARD (LP) | 20 |

**HUBCAP & WHEELS**
| 70 | Dynamic DYN 403 | One Pound Weight/VICEROYS: Come Dance | 20 |
*(see also Byron Lee & Dragonaires)*

**WENDY HUBER**
| 65 | Philips BF 1446 | Come Away Melinda/I Belong To The Wind | 10 |

**HUDDERSFIELD TRANSIT AUTHORITY**
| 72 | Polydor 2001284 | Runaway/Bayou Farm | 15 |
| 72 | Polydor 2001344 | A Different Drum/One Of The Old Time Greats | 6 |

**AL HUDSON**
| 78 | ABC 5251 | Spread Love (slow start 3.25 version)/Spread Love (2.38 version) | 30 |

**HUDSON BROTHERS**
| 75 | Rocket PIG 18 | Rendezvous/Medley: These Things We Do/Home And Four Others | 6 |

**JACK HUDSON**
| 72 | Folk Heritage FHR 041 | SUMMER DAYS AND YOU (LP) | 20 |

**JOHNNY HUDSON & TEENBEATS**
| 63 | Decca F 11679 | Charms/Makin' Up Is So Much Fun | 10 |

**KEITH HUDSON (& CHUCKLES)**
| 69 | Big Shot BI 528 | Tambourine Man/Old Fashioned Way (both actually by Ken Boothe) | 20 |
| 70 | Smash SMA 2311 | Don't Get Me Confused/D. SMITH: Ball of Confusion (B-side actually by Dennis Alcapone) | 20 |
| 71 | Smash SMA 2526 | Light Of Day/I Thought You Knew | 20 |
| 72 | Spur SP 1 | Darkest Night On A Wet Looking Road/Version | 50 |
| 72 | Duke DU 145 | Satan Side (with Chuckles)/DON T. JUNIOR: Evil Spirit | 35 |
| 72 | Downtown DT 492 | True True To My Heart/BIG YOUTH: Ace 90 Skank | 18 |
| 73 | Summit SUM 8541 | Melody Maker/Uncover Me | 25 |
| 75 | Atra AT28 | Lost All Sense Of Direction/Jah Jah | 8 |
| 75 | Mamba MAM 101 | Wild Fire/Version | 6 |
| 75 | Faith FA 025 | Blackbelt Jones/Version | 20 |
| 77 | Tunde TR 1000 | I Wanna Be Where You Are/Still Water (12") | 25 |
| 78 | Greensleeves GRED 8 | Bloody Eyes/Dub | 25 |
| 78 | Greensleeves GRED 8 | Bloody Eyes/Dub (12") | 25 |
| 79 | Greensleeves GRED 26 | Nuh Skin Up/Felt We Felt The Strain (12") | 25 |
| 75 | Magnet MGT 007 | ENTER THE DRAGON (LP) | 200 |
| 75 | Mamba KH1 | FLESH OF MY SKIN, BLOOD OF MY BLOOD (LP) | 150 |
| 75 | Mamba MAM 002 | TORCH OF FREEDOM (LP) | 40 |
| 75 | Atra LP1001 | TORCH OF FREEDOM (LP) | 50 |
| 75 | ATRA ATLP 1002 | PICK A DUB (LP) | 80 |
| 76 | Third World TWL 106 | REBEL DUB (LP, produced by Keith Hudson) | 70 |
| 76 | Virgin V2056 | TOO EXPENSIVE (LP) | 25 |
| 77 | BRD 001 | BRAND (LP) | 50 |
| 79 | Greensleeves GREL 5 | RASTA COMMUNICATION (LP) | 25 |
| 88 | Atra LP 1004 | FLESH OF MY SKIN BLOOD OF MY BLOOD (LP, reissue) | 25 |
| 94 | Blood & Fire LP 003 | PICK A DUB (LP, reissue) | 20 |
| 01 | Simply Vinyl SVLP 283 | PICK A DUB (LP, reissue) | 15 |
*(see also Big Youth, Alton Ellis, Hugh Roy, Delroy Wilson)*

**KEITH HUDSON & I ROY**
| 73 | Randy's RAN 534 | Silver Platter/Jean You Change Everything | 20 |
*(see also I Roy)*

**MIKE HUDSON**
| 65 | Columbia DB 7622 | One Sided Love/I'll Wait Until Tomorrow | 15 |

**HUDSON-FORD**
| 73 | A&M AMS 7116 | Floating In The Wind/Revelations | 8 |
| 73 | A&M AMS 7078 | Pick Up The Pieces/This Is Not The Way (To End A War Or Die) | 5 |
| 74 | A&M AMS 7096 | Burn Baby Burn/Angels (p/s) | 5 |
| 73 | A&M AMLH 68208 | NICKELODEON (LP, lyric insert, brown label) | 15 |
| 77 | Arnakata ARN 5001 | REPERTOIRE (LP, for publishers' use) | 20 |
*(see also Strawbs, Monks, Elmer Gantry's Velvet Opera)*

**HUDSON PEOPLE**
| | | | |
|---|---|---|---|
| 79 | Ensign ENY 27 | Trip To Your Mind/Part 2 | 25 |
| 78 | Hithouse HIT 1 | Trip To Your Mind/Power To The Hour (12") | 60 |
| 79 | Ensign ENY 2712 | Trip To Your Mind/Power To The Hour (12", different mix) | 40 |

**HUEYS**
| | | | |
|---|---|---|---|
| 69 | London HLU 10264 | Coo-Coo Over You/You Ain't No Hippie | 12 |

**HUG**
| | | | |
|---|---|---|---|
| 75 | Polydor 2058 553 | Keep Pushing On/City | 6 |
| 75 | Polydor 2383 330 | NEON DREAM (LP) | 20 |

*(see also Mike Hugg)*

**MIKE HUGG**
| | | | |
|---|---|---|---|
| 72 | Polydor 2058 265 | Blue Suede Shoes Again/Fool No More | 5 |
| 73 | Polydor 2058 359 | Stress And Strain/Tonight | 5 |
| 72 | Polydor 2383 140 | SOMEWHERE (LP, gatefold sleeve) | 30 |
| 73 | Polydor 2383 213 | STRESS AND STRAIN (LP) | 30 |

*(see also Manfred Mann, Hug, Highly Likely, Elton Dean)*

**BOBBY HUGHES EXPERIENCE**
| | | | |
|---|---|---|---|
| 99 | Ultimate Diler UDRLP 008 | FUSA RIOT (2xLP) | 20 |

**CAROL HUGHES**
| | | | |
|---|---|---|---|
| 58 | Columbia DB 4094 | Lend Me Your Comb/First Date | 15 |

**DANNY HUGHES**
| | | | |
|---|---|---|---|
| 69 | Pye 7N 17750 | Hi Ho Silver Lining/I Washed My Hands In Muddy Water | 15 |

*(see also Orange Machine)*

**FRED HUGHES**
| | | | |
|---|---|---|---|
| 65 | Fontana TF 583 | Oo Wee Baby I Love You/Love Me Baby | 25 |
| 76 | Brunswick BR 37 | Baby Boy/JOHNNY JONES & KING CASUALS: Purple Haze | 10 |
| 76 | DJM DJS 10717 | Oo Wee Baby I Love You/My Cries Oh | 6 |

**GLENN HUGHES**
| | | | |
|---|---|---|---|
| 79 | Safari SAFE 14 | I Found A Woman/L.A. Cut Off (p/s) | 5 |
| 77 | Safari LONG 2 | PLAY ME OUT (LP, with inner sleeve) | 15 |

*(see also Deep Purple, News, Finders Keepers, Trapeze, Roger Glover, Hughes-Thrall)*

**GUY HUGHES**
| | | | |
|---|---|---|---|
| 79 | Admiral AMC 01 | The Last Admiral/Just Call Me (no p/s) | 25 |

**JIMMY HUGHES**
| | | | |
|---|---|---|---|
| 63 | London HL 9680 | I'm Qualified/My Loving Time | 30 |
| 64 | Pye International 7N 25254 | Steal Away/Lollipops, Lace And Lipstick | 50 |
| 66 | Sue WI 4006 | Goodbye My Love/It Was Nice | 25 |
| 66 | Atlantic 584 017 | Neighbour, Neighbour/It's A Good Thing | 22 |
| 67 | Atlantic 584 135 | Hi-Heel Sneakers/Time Will Bring You Back | 15 |
| 69 | Stax STAX 117 | Sweet Things You Do/Let 'Em Down Baby | 8 |
| 69 | Stax STAX 126 | I'm Not Ashamed To Beg Or Plead/Chains Of Love | 12 |
| 80 | Charly CTD 103 | JIMMY HUGHES EP | 10 |
| 67 | Atlantic 587 068 | WHY NOT TONIGHT? (LP) | 75 |
| 69 | Stax SXATS 1010 | SOMETHING SPECIAL (LP) | 30 |

**NIA HUGHES**
| | | | |
|---|---|---|---|
| 70 | Penny Farthing PEN 724 | Turn On The Sun/The Wind | 8 |

**RHETTA HUGHES**
| | | | |
|---|---|---|---|
| 11 | Shotgun 107 | Cry Myself To Sleep/Giving Up My Heartaches | 10 |
| 70s | Polydor 184 223 | RELIGHT MY FIRE (LP) | 80 |

**HUGHES-THRALL**
| | | | |
|---|---|---|---|
| 82 | Epic EPC 25052 | HUGHES-THRALL (LP, with inner sleeve) | 15 |

*(see also Glenn Hughes)*

**HUGO & LUIGI**
| | | | |
|---|---|---|---|
| 57 | Columbia DB 3978 | Rockabilly Party/Shenandoah Rose | 15 |

**ALAN HULL**
| | | | |
|---|---|---|---|
| 70 | Big T BIG 129 | We Can Swing Together/Obadiah's Grave | 10 |
| 73 | Charisma CB 211 | Just Another Sad Song/Waiting | 6 |
| 75 | Warner Brothers K16599 | One More Bottle Of Wine/Squire | 6 |
| 73 | Charisma CAS 1069 | PIPEDREAM (LP, gatefold sleeve, booklet, large 'Mad Hatter' label) | 20 |
| 75 | Warner Bros K56121 | SQUIRE (LP, 'Burbank' label) | 15 |

*(see also Lindisfarne, Chosen Few)*

**HULLABALLOOS**
| | | | |
|---|---|---|---|
| 64 | Columbia DB 7392 | I'm Gonna Love You Too/Why Do Fools Fall In Love | 10 |
| 65 | Columbia DB 7558 | I'll Show You How To Love/Did You Ever | 10 |
| 65 | Columbia DB 7626 | Don't Stop/I Won't Turn Away Now | 10 |

*(see also Bunch Of Fives)*

**GEORGE HULTGREEN**
| | | | |
|---|---|---|---|
| 70 | Warner Bros WB 8017 | Say Hello/Before You Say Goodbye | 6 |

**HUMAN BEANS**
| | | | |
|---|---|---|---|
| 67 | Columbia DB 8230 | Morning Dew (Take Me For A Walk)/It's A Wonder | 50 |

*(see also Love Sculpture)*

**HUMAN BEAST**
| | | | |
|---|---|---|---|
| 70 | Decca LK/SKL 5053 | VOLUME ONE (LP) | 900 |
| 07 | Sunbeam SBRLP 5044 | VOLUME ONE (LP, reissue) | 20 |

*(see also Bread Love & Dreams)*

**HUMAN BEINGS**
| | | | |
|---|---|---|---|
| 80 | Airship AP 159 | Amnesia/New Song/Mrs Marshall (p/s and sticker) | 12 |

## HUMAN BEINZ
| | | | |
|---|---|---|---|
| 67 | Capitol CL 15529 | Nobody But Me/Sueno | 60 |
| 67 | Capitol CL 15529 | Nobody But Me/Sueno (DJ Copy) | 100 |
| 68 | Capitol CL 15542 | Turn On Your Lovelight/It's Fun To Be Clean | 25 |
| 77 | Capitol CL 15529 | Nobody But Me/Sueno (reissue) | 12 |
| 86 | Decal LIK 5 | EVOLUTIONS (LP, reissue) | 15 |

## HUMAN CONDITION
| | | | |
|---|---|---|---|
| 81 | THC 1 | THE HUMAN CONDITION (Live at Collegiate Theatre 13th September 1981) (cassette, black inlay, white writing) | 25 |
| 81 | THC 1 | THE HUMAN CONDITION (Live in Europe November 1981) (cassette, white inlay, black writing) | 25 |

*(see also Jah Wobble)*

## HUMAN INSTINCT
| | | | |
|---|---|---|---|
| 65 | Mercury MF 951 | Can't Stop Around/I Want To Be Loved By You My Friend | 50 |
| 66 | Mercury MF 972 | The Rich Man/Illusions | 50 |
| 67 | Mercury MF 990 | Go-Go/I Can't Live Without You | 70 |
| 68 | Deram DM 167 | A Day In My Mind's Mind/Death Of The Seaside | 50 |
| 68 | Deram DM 177 | Renaissance Fair/Pink Dawn | 140 |

*(see also Jessie Harper)*

## HUMAN LEAGUE
| | | | |
|---|---|---|---|
| 78 | Fast Product FAST 4 | Being Boiled/Circus Of Death (p/s, original issue with b&w picture labels) | 15 |
| 79 | Fast Product FAST 10 | THE DIGNITY OF LABOUR (12" EP, with spoken-word flexidisc [F10x/VF 1]) | 20 |
| 79 | Virgin VS 294 | Empire State Human/Introducing (p/s) | 5 |
| 80 | Virgin VS 351 | Empire State Human/Introducing//Only After Dark/Toyota City (Long Version) (double pack, p/s, shrinkwrapped) | 20 |
| 80 | Virgin VS 351 | Only After Dark/Toyota City (Long Version) (p/s) | 6 |
| 80 | Virgin VS 351 | Empire State Human/Introducing (p/s, reissue) | 5 |
| 81 | Virgin VS 395 | Boys And Girls/Tom Baker (gatefold or non-gatefold p/s) | 5 |
| 81 | Virgin SV 105-12 | HOLIDAY '80 (12", 5-track EP, withdrawn) | 20 |
| 79 | Virgin VS 2133 | REPRODUCTION (LP) | 20 |
| 80 | Virgin VS 2160 | TRAVELOGUE (LP) | 15 |
| 95 | East West 4509 98750 1 | OCTOPUS (LP) | 35 |

*(see also Heaven 17, Men, Respect, Jo Callis)*

## HUMAN CABBAGES
| | | | |
|---|---|---|---|
| 81 | Boys and Girls BAG TWO | The Witch/Air Raid Shelter/One More Fool (p/s) | 40 |

## HUMANOID
| | | | |
|---|---|---|---|
| 88 | Westside WSR 7 | Stakker Humanoid (Part 1)/Stakker Humanoid (Part 2) (p/s) | 8 |

*(see also Future Sound Of London, Art Science Technology)*

## HUMANTE & RABBIT IN THE MOON
| | | | |
|---|---|---|---|
| 95 | Rising High RSN 106 | East (The Remixes) (12") | 15 |

## HUMBLEBUMS
| | | | |
|---|---|---|---|
| 69 | Big T BIG 122 | Saturday Roundabout Sunday/Bed Of Mossy Green | 6 |
| 69 | Big T BIG 127 | Coconut Tree/Her Father Didn't Like Me Anyway | 6 |
| 70 | Big T BIG 130 | Shoeshine Boy/My Apartment | 6 |
| 69 | Transatlantic TRA 201 | THE NEW HUMBLEBUMS (LP, lilac/white label with 't' logo) | 20 |
| 70 | Transatlantic TRA 218 | OPEN UP THE DOOR (LP, laminated sleeve) | 15 |
| 74 | Transatlantic TRA 288 | THE COMPLETE HUMBLEBUMS (3-LP, box set of above albums) | 20 |

## HUMBLE PIE
| | | | |
|---|---|---|---|
| 69 | Immediate IM 082 | Natural Born Bugie/Wrist Job | 6 |
| 69 | Immediate IM 082 | Natural Born Bugie/Wrist Job (later pressing in p/s) | 10 |
| 70 | A&M AMS 807 | Big Black Dog/Strange Days | 7 |
| 71 | A&M AMS 862 | I Don't Need No Doctor/A Sonig For Jennie | 7 |
| 72 | A&M AMS 7003 | Hot'n'Nasty/You're So Good For Me | 7 |
| 73 | A&M AMS 7052 | Black Coffee/Say No More | 7 |
| 73 | A&M AMS 7070 | Get Down To It/Honky Tonk Woman | 7 |
| 73 | A&M AMS 7090 | Oh La De Da/Outcrowd | 7 |
| 75 | A&M AMS 7185 | Rock'n'Roll Music/Scored Out | 7 |
| 80 | Jet JET 180 | Fool For A Pretty Face/You Soppy Pratt (p/s) | 7 |
| 69 | Immediate IMSP 025 | AS SAFE AS YESTERDAY IS (LP, lyric inner sleeve, pink label) | 80 |
| 69 | Immediate IMSP 027 | TOWN AND COUNTRY (LP, lyric inner sleeve, pink label) | 75 |
| 70 | A&M AMLS 986 | HUMBLE PIE (LP, textured gatefold sleeve, brown label) | 75 |
| 71 | A&M AMLS 2013 | ROCK ON (LP) | 25 |
| 71 | A&M AMLH 63506 | PERFORMANCE - ROCKIN' THE FILLMORE (2-LP) | 25 |
| 72 | A&M AMLS 64342 | SMOKIN' (LP) | 25 |
| 73 | A&M AMLD 6004 | EAT IT (2-LP, gatefold sleeve, booklet, brown label) | 25 |
| 74 | A&M AMLH 63611 | THUNDERBOX (LP) | 15 |
| 75 | A&M AMLS 68282 | STREET RATS (LP) | 15 |
| 79 | Jet LP231 | ON TO VICTORY (LP) | 20 |
| 80 | Atco SD 38 131 | GO FOR THE THROAT (LP) | 20 |

*(see also Steve Marriott, Small Faces, Herd, Natural Gas)*

## HUMBUG
| | | | |
|---|---|---|---|
| 70 | CBS 4811 | Groovin' With Mr Bloe/Marianna | 20 |
| 70 | CBS 5208 | I Got A Feeling (Vocal)/I Got A Feeling (Instrumental) | 20 |

## HELEN HUMES
| | | | |
|---|---|---|---|
| 56 | Vogue V 2048 | Million Dollar Secret/If I Could Be With You One Hour Of The Day | 10 |
| 59 | Contemporary CV 2415 | When The Saints Come Marching In/Bill Bailey, Won't You Please Come Home (with Benny Carter's All-Stars) | 5 |
| 61 | Contemporary LAC 12245 | HELEN HUMES AND THE BENNY CARTER ALL STARS (LP) | 15 |

*(see also Benny Carter, Jimmy Witherspoon/Helen Humes)*

MINT VALUE £

## DELLA HUMPHREY
| | | |
|---|---|---|
| 69 | Action ACT 4525 | Don't Make The Good Girls Go Bad/Your Love Is All I Need ........................ 50 |
| 72 | Fab FAB 183 | Dreamland (actually by Marcia Griffiths)/Version .................................. 45 |

## LES HUMPHRIES SINGERS
| | | |
|---|---|---|
| 75 | Antic K11519 | She's Really Something Else/Mexico ....................................................... 8 |
| 76 | Atlantic K11527 | Indian War/Little Sparrow ................................................................... 8 |

## HUMPY BONG
| | | |
|---|---|---|
| 70 | Parlophone R 5859 | Don't You Be Too Long/We're Alright 'Till Then ................................... 15 |

*(see also Bee Gees, Jonathan Kelly, Morgan)*

## HUNGER
| | | |
|---|---|---|
| 84 | Psycho PSYCHO 14 | STRICTLY FROM HUNGER (LP, reissue of U.S. LP) ................................. 15 |

## HUNGRY TOUCH
| | | |
|---|---|---|
| 88 | Firehorse HT 188 | Shake The System/She's Got The Hungry Touch/Riding High (12" p/s) ......... 50 |

## HUNGRY WOLF
| | | |
|---|---|---|
| 70 | Philips 6308 009 | HUNGRY WOLF (LP, laminated sleeve, black/silver labels) ................... 250 |

*(see also Czar, Alan Parker, Ugly Custard)*

## GLORIA HUNNIFORD
| | | |
|---|---|---|
| 69 | Tangerine 0012 | Are You Ready For Love/The Sound Of Love ........................................... 6 |

## FRED HUNT TRIO
| | | |
|---|---|---|
| 68 | 77 88LEU12/27 | PEARLS ON VELVET (LP) ..................................................................... 35 |

## GERALDINE HUNT
| | | |
|---|---|---|
| 69 | Roulette RO 515 | Never Never Leave Me/Push Sweep ..................................................... 10 |
| 75 | EMI EMI 2275 | You/It's All For You ............................................................................ 6 |

## MARSHA HUNT
| | | |
|---|---|---|
| 69 | Track 604 030 | Walk On Gilded Splinters/Hot Rod Poppa ............................................ 15 |
| 69 | Track 604 034 | Desdemona/Hippy Gumbo .................................................................. 20 |
| 70 | Track 604 037 | Keep The Customer Satisfied/Lonesome Holy Roller ............................. 10 |
| 73 | Vertigo 6059 080 | Beast Day/Somebody To Love (as Marsha Hunt's 22) ........................... 20 |
| 73 | Vertigo 6059093 | Medusa/Bop City (as Marsha Hunt's 22) ............................................. 20 |
| 76 | Electric WATT 1 | C'est La Vie/Do You Really Believe In Voodoo ...................................... 10 |
| 71 | Track 2410 101 | WOMAN CHILD (LP) ........................................................................ 100 |

## TOMMY HUNT
| | | |
|---|---|---|
| 62 | Top Rank JAR 605 | The Door Is Open/I'm Wondering .......................................................... 20 |
| 68 | Direction 58-3216 | I Need A Woman Of My Own/Searchin' For My Baby Looking Everywhere ......... 30 |
| 72 | Polydor 2058 236 | Mind, Body & Soul/One More Mountain To Climb ................................... 5 |
| 74 | Pye 7N 45325 | Sleep Tight Honey/Time Alone Will Tell .................................................. 5 |
| 75 | Spark SRL 1132 | Crackin' Up/Get Out ............................................................................ 5 |
| 76 | Spark SRL 1146 | Loving On The Losing Side/Sunshine Girl ................................................ 5 |
| 76 | Spark SRL 1148 | One Fine Morning/Sign On The Dotted Line/Loving You Is ....................... 5 |
| 78 | RK RK 1012 | The Bus/Susanna Baby ......................................................................... 5 |
| 81 | SRTS 81 CUS 1009 | Crackin Up/Loving On The Losing Side/The Hungry Years/Sweetest Feelings (EP) ........ 12 |
| 85 | Kent TOWN 103 | The Work Song/IVORYS: Please Stay .................................................... 10 |

*(see also Ivorys)*

## WILLIE AMOS HUNT
| | | |
|---|---|---|
| 67 | Camp 602 003 | Would You Believe/My Baby Wants To Dance ........................................ 75 |

## HUNT & TURNER
| | | |
|---|---|---|
| 72 | Village Thing VTS 11 | MAGIC LANDSCAPE (LP) ..................................................................... 60 |

## CAROL HUNTER
| | | |
|---|---|---|
| 73 | Purple PUR 115 | Look Out Cleveland/5/4 March .............................................................. 7 |
| 73 | Purple TPS 3503 | THE NEXT VOICE YOU HEAR (LP) ........................................................ 15 |

## DANE HUNTER
| | | |
|---|---|---|
| 65 | Oriole CB 1985 | The Evergreen Tree/Too Late ............................................................... 20 |
| 65 | CBS 201777 | Silly Little Girl/Cryin Sobbin Wailin ...................................................... 15 |
| 65 | CBS 202004 | Because You're Mine/Look The Other Way ............................................ 15 |

## DANNY HUNTER (& GIANTS)
| | | |
|---|---|---|
| 60 | HMV POP 722 | Make It Up/Little Girl (as Danny Hunter & Giants) ................................. 20 |
| 60 | HMV POP 775 | Who's Gonna Walk Ya Home?/Lonely And Blue ..................................... 20 |
| 61 | Fontana H 300 | Lost Weekend/Age For Love ................................................................. 15 |

## DAVE HUNTER
| | | |
|---|---|---|
| 68 | RCA RCA 1766 | Love Me A Lifetime/She's A Heartbreaker .............................................. 35 |
| 69 | RCA RCA 1841 | Don't Throw Your Love To The Wind/Hitchcock Railway ......................... 12 |

## GREG HUNTER
| | | |
|---|---|---|
| 66 | Parlophone R 5483 | Five O'Clock World/Away From Happiness ............................................ 10 |

## IAN HUNTER
| | | |
|---|---|---|
| 75 | CBS 3486 | Who Do You Love/Boy ........................................................................... 5 |
| 76 | CBS 4268 | All American Alien Boy (Version)/Rape ................................................... 5 |
| 76 | CBS 4479 | You Nearly Did Me In/A Letter From Britannia To The Union Jack ........... 15 |
| 77 | CBS 5229 | Justice Of The Peace/The Ballad Of Little Star (as Ian Hunter's Overnight Angels) ........ 8 |
| 77 | CBS 5497 | England Rocks/Wild 'N' Free (as Ian Hunter's Overnight Angels) ............... 5 |
| 79 | Chrysalis CHS 2324 | When The Daylight Comes/Life After Death (p/s, white vinyl with mask) ...... 5 |
| 79 | Chrysalis CHS 2346 | Ships/Wild East (p/s) ............................................................................ 5 |
| 79 | Chrysalis CHS 2390 | Cleveland Rocks/Bastard (p/s) ............................................................... 5 |
| 80 | Chrysalis CHS 2434 | We Gotta Get Out/Medley: Once Bitten Twice Shy/Bastard/Cleveland Rocks/ Sons And Daughters/One Of The Boys (live double pack, stickered gatefold p/s) ............... 5 |
| 81 | Chrysalis CHS 2542 | Lisa Likes Rock 'n' Roll/Noises (p/s, clear vinyl) ...................................... 5 |
| 83 | CBS A 3541 | All Of The Good Ones Are Taken/Death 'N' Glory Boys (p/s) ................... 5 |
| 83 | CBS TA 3541 | All Of The Good Ones Are Taken/Death 'N' Glory Boys/Traitor (12", p/s) ......... 10 |

| | | | MINT VALUE £ |
|---|---|---|---|
| 83 | CBS A 3855 | Somethin's Goin' On/All Of The Good Ones Are Taken (Slow Version) (p/s) | 5 |
| 83 | CBS A 3855 | Somethin's Goin' On (Radio Edit)/All Of The Good Ones Are Taken (Slow Version) (promo only, no p/s) | 5 |

*(see also Mott The Hoople, At Last The 1958 Rock & Roll Show, Apex Rhythm & Blues All Stars, Mick Ronson, Roger Taylor)*

## IVORY JOE HUNTER

| | | | |
|---|---|---|---|
| 50 | MGM MGM 271 | I Almost Lost My Mind/S.P. Blues (78, with Orchestra) | 20 |
| 56 | London HLE 8261 | A Tear Fell/I Need You By My Side | 300 |
| 56 | London HLE 8261 | A Tear Fell/I Need You By My Side (78) | 20 |
| 57 | Columbia DB 3872 | Since I Met You, Baby/You Can't Stop This Rockin' And Rollin' | 250 |
| 57 | Columbia DB 3872 | Since I Met You, Baby/You Can't Stop This Rockin' And Rollin' (78) | 20 |
| 57 | London HLE 8486 | Love's A Hurting Game/Empty Arms | 150 |
| 57 | London HLE 8486 | Love's A Hurting Game/Empty Arms (78) | 20 |
| 61 | Capitol CL 15220 | I'm Hooked/Because I Love You | 30 |
| 61 | Capitol CL 15226 | You Better Believe It, Baby/May The Man Win | 30 |

## ROBERT HUNTER

| | | | |
|---|---|---|---|
| 74 | Round RX 101 | TALES OF THE GREAT RUM RUNNERS (LP) | 15 |
| 80 | Dark Star DSLP 8001 | JACK O'ROSES (LP) | 15 |

*(see also Grateful Dead)*

## SUSAN HUNTER

| | | | |
|---|---|---|---|
| 55 | Brunswick 05458 | Not Yet/Was That The Right Thing To Do? | 8 |

## TAB HUNTER

| | | | |
|---|---|---|---|
| 57 | London HLD 8380 | Young Love/Red Sails In The Sunset (gold label) | 15 |
| 57 | London HLD 8380 | Young Love/Red Sails In The Sunset (silver label) | 5 |
| 57 | London HLD 8410 | Ninety-Nine Ways/I Don't Get Around Much Anymore | 8 |
| 61 | Warner Bros WSEP 2023 | TAB HUNTER (EP, stereo) | 15 |
| 60 | Warner Bros WS 8008 | TAB HUNTER (LP, stereo) | 15 |
| 61 | London HA-D 2401 | YOUNG LOVE (LP, mono) | 15 |
| 61 | London SAH-G 6201 | YOUNG LOVE (LP, stereo) | 15 |

## HUNTER MUSKETT

| | | | |
|---|---|---|---|
| 73 | Bradleys BRAD 303 | John Blair/Silver Coin (p/s) | 6 |
| 70 | Decca Nova SDN 20 | EVERY TIME YOU MOVE (LP, blue/silver labels) | 300 |
| 73 | Bradleys BRADL 1003 | HUNTER MUSKETT (LP, lyric inner sleeve) | 35 |

## HUNTERS (HOLLAND)

| | | | |
|---|---|---|---|
| 66 | RCA RCA 1541 | Russian Spy And I/Spring | 20 |

*(see also Jan Akkerman, Brainbox)*

## HUNTERS (U.K.)

| | | | |
|---|---|---|---|
| 60 | Fontana H 276 | Teen Scene/Santa Monica Flyer | 15 |
| 61 | Fontana H 303 | Golden Ear-rings/Tally Ho | 15 |
| 61 | Fontana H 323 | The Storm/How's M'Chicks? | 20 |
| 64 | Fontana TF 514 | Teen Scene/Someone Else's Baby | 15 |
| 61 | Fontana TFL 5140 | TEEN SCENE: THE HUNTERS PLAY THE BIG HITS (LP, mono) | 30 |
| 61 | Fontana STFL 561 | TEEN SCENE: THE HUNTERS PLAY THE BIG HITS (LP, stereo) | 50 |
| 62 | Fontana TFL 5175 | HITS FROM THE HUNTERS (LP, mono) | 50 |
| 62 | Fontana STFL 572 | HITS FROM THE HUNTERS (LP, stereo) | 50 |

*(see also Dave Sampson & Hunters, Maisie McDaniel)*

## HUNTING LODGE

| | | | |
|---|---|---|---|
| 85 | Sterile SER 04 | NOMAD SOULS (LP) | 20 |

## HURDY GURDY

| | | | |
|---|---|---|---|
| 72 | CBS 64781 | HURDY GURDY (LP, gatefold sleeve) | 200 |

## ARTHUR HURLEY & GOTTLIEB

| | | | |
|---|---|---|---|
| 73 | CBS 1779 | Sunshine Ship/Bobbys Song | 6 |

## RED VINCENT HURLEY

| | | | |
|---|---|---|---|
| 76 | Pye 7N 45583 | When/Just A Little Love (p/s) | 7 |

## HURRICANE STRINGS

| | | | |
|---|---|---|---|
| 63 | Columbia DB 7027 | Venus/In The Carrick | 15 |

## HURRICANES

| | | | |
|---|---|---|---|
| 71 | Upsetter US 363 | Got To Be Mine/UPSETTERS: Version | 20 |

*(see also Dave Barker)*

## MIKE HURST (& METHOD)

| | | | |
|---|---|---|---|
| 64 | Philips BF 1353 | Half Heaven Half Heartache/Look In Your Eyes | 5 |
| 65 | Philips BF 1389 | The Last Time You'll Walk Out On Me/Something Told Me | 6 |
| 65 | Philips BF 1424 | Show Me Around/I'm Running Away | 7 |
| 71 | Capitol CL 15681 | Show Me The Way To Georgia/Over Again | 6 |

*(see also Springfields, Remo Four, Ashton Gardner & Dyke, Sundance)*

## MISSISSIPPI JOHN HURT

| | | | |
|---|---|---|---|
| 65 | Vanguard SVRL 19005 | THE IMMORTAL MISSISSIPPI JOHN HURT (LP) | 35 |
| 66 | Vanguard SVRL 19032 | MISSISSIPPI JOHN HURT (LP) | 35 |
| 67 | Fontana TFL 6079 | MISSISSIPPI JOHN HURT (LP) | 35 |
| 71 | Spokane SPL 1001 | THE ORIGINAL 1928 RECORDINGS (LP) | 50 |
| 71 | Vanguard VSD 19/20 | THE BEST OF MISSISSIPPI JOHN HURT (2-LP) | 18 |
| 73 | Vanguard VSD 79327 | LAST SESSIONS (LP) | 20 |
| 72 | Vanguard VSD 79220 | TODAY (LP) | 20 |

## HURTS

| | | | |
|---|---|---|---|
| 10 | Sony 88697741857 | Better Than Love/Mother Nature (white label, p/s, 500 only) | 12 |
| 10 | Major MAJRE 017 | Wonderful Life/(Mantronix Remix) (p/s, no'd) | 15 |
| 10 | Major MAJREC031 | HAPPINESS (LP & CD) | 40 |

*(see also Daggers (2))*

## HUSH
| | | | |
|---|---|---|---|
| 68 | Fontana TF 944 | Elephant Rider/Grey | 500 |

## HÜSKER DÜ
| | | | |
|---|---|---|---|
| 84 | SST SST 025 | Eight Miles High/Masochism World (live) (p/s) | 12 |
| 85 | SST 051 | Makes No Sense At All/Love Is All Around (p/s) | 5 |
| 86 | Warner Bros W 8612 | Sorry Somehow/All This I've Done For You (p/s) | 5 |
| 86 | Warner Bros W 8612 | Sorry Somehow/All This I've Done For You//Celebrated Summer (Acoustic)/ Flexible Flyer (double pack in single sleeve) | 8 |
| 86 | Warner Bros W 8746 | Don't Want To Know If You're Lonely/All Work And No Play (p/s) | 5 |
| 86 | Warner Bros W 8746T | Don't Want To Know If You're Lonely/All Work And No Play/ Helter Skelter (live) (12", p/s) | 10 |
| 87 | Warner Bros W 8456 | Could You Be The One/Everytime (p/s) | 10 |
| 87 | Warner Bros W 8456T | Could You Be The One/Everytime/Charity, Chastity, Prudence, Hope (12", p/s) | 10 |
| 87 | Warner Bros W 8276 | Ice Cold Ice/Gotta Lotta (p/s) | 5 |
| 87 | Warner Bros W 8276T | Ice Cold Ice/Gotta Lotta/Medley (12", p/s) | 12 |
| 81 | Alternative Tentacles VIRUS 25 | LAND SPEED RECORD (LP) | 18 |
| 82 | Bespoke BES 03 LP | EVERYTHING FALLS APART (LP) | 20 |
| 83 | SST SST 020 | METAL CIRCUS (LP) | 20 |
| 84 | SST SST 027 | ZEN ARCADE (2-LP) | 20 |
| 86 | Warner Bros WX40 | CANDY APPLE GREY (LP) | 15 |
| 87 | Warner Bros WB 925544 | WAREHOUSE SONGS & STORIES (2-LP) | 18 |

## HUSKY
| | | | |
|---|---|---|---|
| 75 | Anchor ANC 1026 | Give It Up/Silence Of Dreams | 6 |
| 76 | Anchor ANC 1030 | Pretty Little Linda/Make It Turn Out Right | 6 |

## FERLIN HUSKY (& HIS HUSH PUPPIES)
| | | | |
|---|---|---|---|
| 57 | Capitol CL 14753 | A Fallen Star/Prize Possession | 8 |
| 58 | Capitol CL 14824 | Wang Dang Doo/What'cha Doin' After School | 20 |
| 60 | Capitol EAP2 1280 | FERLIN'S FAVOURITES (EP) | 10 |
| 58 | Capitol T 880 | BOULEVARD OF BROKEN DREAMS (LP) | 15 |

*(see also Simon Crum)*

## JACQUES HUSTIN
| | | | |
|---|---|---|---|
| 74 | EMI EMI 2143 | Fleur De Liberté/Freedom For The Man | 15 |

## HUSTLER
| | | | |
|---|---|---|---|
| 74 | Firefly AMS501 | Get Outa My 'Ouse/Happy Days | 5 |

## HUSTLERS
| | | | |
|---|---|---|---|
| 63 | Philips BF 1275 | Gimme What I Want/Not Much | 7 |
| 64 | Mercury MF 807 | Be True To You/You Can't Sit Down | 7 |
| 64 | Mercury MF 817 | Sick Of Giving/Easy To Find | 20 |

## WILLIE HUTCH
| | | | |
|---|---|---|---|
| 73 | Tamla Motown TMG 862 | Brother's Gonna Work It Out/I Choose You | 15 |
| 78 | ABC 4206 | Love Runs Out/BOBBY HUTTON: Lend A Hand (DJ copy) | 15 |
| 73 | Tamla Motown STMA 8003 | THE MACK (LP, soundtrack) | 15 |
| 73 | Tamla Motown STML 11247 | FULLY EXPOSED (LP) | 15 |
| 74 | Tamla Motown STML 11269 | FOXY BROWN (LP, soundtrack) | 15 |
| 74 | Tamla Motown STML 11280 | THE MARK OF THE BEAST (LP) | 20 |
| 75 | Tamla Motown STML 12015 | ODE TO MY LADY (LP) | 20 |
| 76 | Tamla Motown STML 12023 | CONCERT IN BLUES (LP) | 15 |

## ASHLEY HUTCHINGS
| | | | |
|---|---|---|---|
| 72 | Island HELP 5 | MORRIS ON (LP, actually by various folk artists) | 20 |
| 76 | Island HELP 24 | RATTLEBONE AND ROUGHJACK (LP) | 25 |
| 76 | Harvest SHSM 2012 | SON OF MORRIS ON (LP, actually by various folk artists) | 18 |

*(see also Albion Band, Fairport Convention, Steeleye Span)*

## HUTCH HUTCHINGS
| | | | |
|---|---|---|---|
| 77 | Goodwood GM 12324 | FEELS LIKE RAIN (LP) | 35 |

## SAM HUTCHINS
| | | | |
|---|---|---|---|
| 69 | Bell BLL 1044 | Dang Me/I'm Tired Of Pretending | 12 |

## LEROY HUTSON
| | | | |
|---|---|---|---|
| 75 | Warner Bros. K16536 | All Because Of You/All Because Of You (Theme Instrumental) | 30 |
| 74 | Buddah BDLP 4013 | THE MAN (LP) | 20 |
| 75 | Warner Bros K 56139 | HUTSON (LP) | 50 |

## J.B. HUTTO & HIS HAWKS
| | | | |
|---|---|---|---|
| 73 | Delmark DS 617 | HAWK SQUAT (LP) | 30 |

## BETTY HUTTON
| | | | |
|---|---|---|---|
| 53 | HMV 7M 103 | Somebody Loves Me/Jealous (B-side with Pat Morgan) | 5 |
| 56 | Capitol CL 14568 | Sleepy Head/Hit The Road To Dreamland | 5 |

*(see also Hutton Sisters, Perry Como, 'Tennessee' Ernie Ford)*

## BOBBY HUTTON
| | | | |
|---|---|---|---|
| 78 | ABC 4206 | Lend A Hand/WILLIE HUTCH: Love Runs Out (DJ copy) | 15 |

## DANNY HUTTON
| | | | |
|---|---|---|---|
| 66 | MGM MGM 1314 | Funny How Love Can Be/Dreamin' Isn't Good For You | 15 |
| 65 | Pye International 7N 25325 | Roses And Rainbows/Monster Shindig | 5 |

*(see also Three Dog Night)*

## HUTTON SISTERS (BETTY & MARION)
| | | | |
|---|---|---|---|
| 55 | Capitol CL 14250 | Ko Ko Mo (I Love You So)/Heart Throb | 25 |

*(see also Betty Hutton)*

## HYACINTH GIRLS
| | | | |
|---|---|---|---|
| 88 | Red RED 002 | HAPPY NOW? | 40 |

MINT VALUE £

### CHARLIE HYATT
| | | | |
|---|---|---|---|
| 65 | Island IEP 707 | RASS! (EP, as Bam & Charlie Hyatt) | 30 |
| 66 | Island ILP 932 | KISS ME NECK (LP) | 35 |

### LEON HYATT
| | | | |
|---|---|---|---|
| 76 | Nationwide NW 1014 | 40 Days And Nights/Third World Affairs | 15 |

### HYBRID KIDS
| | | | |
|---|---|---|---|
| 80 | Cherry Red BRED 11 | CLAWS (LP) | 15 |

### TANYA HYDE
| | | | |
|---|---|---|---|
| 79 | Waldo's DS 008 | Herr Wunderbar/Auf Der Anderen Seite (p/s) | 15 |

### HYDRA
| | | | |
|---|---|---|---|
| 74 | Capricorn 2089 008 | Glitter Queen/It's So Hard | 5 |

### HYGRADES
| | | | |
|---|---|---|---|
| 65 | Columbia DB 7734 | She Cared/We're Through | 15 |

### BRIAN HYLAND
| | | | |
|---|---|---|---|
| 60 | London HLR 9161 | Itsy Bitsy Teeny Weeny Yellow Polka Dot Bikini/Don't Dilly Dally, Sally (78) | 100 |
| 60 | London HLR 9113 | Rosemary/Library Love Affair | 20 |
| 60 | London HLR 9161 | Itsy Bitsy Teeny Weeny Yellow Polka Dot Bikini/Don't Dilly Dally, Sally | 5 |
| 60 | London HLR 9203 | Four Little Heels/That's How Much | 5 |
| 61 | London HLR 9262 | Lop Sided, Over Loaded/I Gotta Go ('Cause I Love You) | 5 |
| 61 | HMV POP 915 | Let Me Belong To You/Let It Die | 5 |
| 61 | HMV POP 955 | The Night I Cried/I'll Never Stop Wanting You | 5 |
| 62 | HMV POP 1013 | Ginny Come Lately/I Should Be Gettin' Better | 5 |
| 62 | HMV POP 1051 | Sealed With A Kiss/Summer Job | 5 |
| 62 | HMV POP 1079 | Warmed Over Kisses/Walk A Lonely Mile | 5 |
| 63 | HMV POP 1113 | I May Not Live To See Tomorrow/It Ain't That Way At All | 5 |
| 63 | HMV POP 1143 | If Mary's There/Remember Me | 5 |
| 63 | HMV POP 1169 | Somewhere In The Night/I Wish Today Was Yesterday | 5 |
| 63 | HMV POP 1188 | I'm Afraid To Go Home/Save Your Heart For Me | 5 |
| 63 | HMV POP 1237 | Let Us Make Our Own Mistakes/Nothing Matters But You | 5 |
| 64 | Philips BF 1326 | Here's To Our Love/Two Kinds Of Girls | 5 |
| 65 | Philips BF 1429 | Stay Away From Her/I Can't Keep A Secret | 5 |
| 65 | Philips BF 1486 | 3,000 Miles/Sometimes They Do | 5 |
| 66 | Philips BF 1508 | The Joker Went Wild/I Can Hear The Rain | 20 |
| 66 | Philips BF 1528 | Run Run Look And See/Why Did You Do It | 7 |
| 66 | Philips BF 1555 | Hung Up In Your Eyes/Why Mine | 5 |
| 67 | Philips BF 1569 | Holiday For Clowns/Yesterday I Had A Girl | 6 |
| 69 | Dot 124 | A Million To One/It Could All Begin Again (in You) | 7 |
| 67 | Philips BF 1601 | Get The Message/Kinda Groovy | 5 |
| 70 | Uni UN 530 | Gypsy Woman/You And Me | 5 |
| 72 | Uni UN 540 | I Love Every Little Thing About You/With My Eyes Wide Open | 5 |
| 62 | HMV 7EG 8780 | SEALED WITH A KISS (EP) | 20 |
| 61 | London HA-R 2289 | THE BASHFUL BLONDE (LP) | 80 |
| 62 | HMV CLP 1553 | LET ME BELONG TO YOU (LP) | 30 |
| 63 | HMV CLP 1759 | COUNTRY MEETS FOLK (LP) | 20 |
| 66 | Philips BL 7762 | THE JOKER WENT WILD (LP) | 20 |
| 68 | Fontana SFL 13008 | HERE'S TO OUR LOVE (LP) | 20 |

### C. HYMAN
| | | | |
|---|---|---|---|
| 65 | Ska Beat JB 200 | The Ska Rhythm/The Ska Is Moving On | 40 |

### DICK HYMAN TRIO
| | | | |
|---|---|---|---|
| 56 | MGM SP 1164 | Theme From The Threepenny Opera/Baubles, Bangles And Beads | 6 |
| 67 | Command SCMD 105 | BRAZILIAN IMPRESSIONS (LP) | 15 |
| 69 | Command SCMD 508 | MOOG - THE ELECTRIC ECLECTICS OF DICK HYMAN (LP) | 20 |
| 70 | Command SCMD 946 | THE AGE OF ELECTRONICUS (LP) | 30 |

### PHYLLIS HYMAN
| | | | |
|---|---|---|---|
| 79 | Arista ARIST 323 | You Know How To Love Me/Give A Little More | 15 |
| 79 | Arista ARIST 323 | You Know How To Love Me/Give A Little More (12", p/s) | 10 |

### HYPA KONCEPT
| | | | |
|---|---|---|---|
| 91 | No Label L8 001 | Party People (Come Together) (3 Mixes) (12", hand written labels) | 20 |
| 92 | Club State CSR 12001 | Love Addict (4 Mixes) (12", stamped white label) | 40 |

### HYPER ON EXPERIENCE
| | | | |
|---|---|---|---|
| 93 | Moving Shadow SHADOW 30 | DEAF IN THE FAMILY EP (12", white label stamped with cat. no. only as Hyper On exp.) | 60 |
| 93 | Moving Shadow SHADOW 30 | DEAF IN THE FAMILY EP (12", p/s as Hyper-On Experience) | 40 |
| 93 | Moving Shadow SHADOW 40 | THE FAMILY WE NEVER HAD EP (12", p/s, as Hyper-On Experience) | 15 |
| 94 | Moving Shadow SHADOW 40 | THE FAMILY WE NEVER HAD (12" picture disc) | 50 |

### HYPER VYPER
| | | | |
|---|---|---|---|
| 88 | SRTS SRT/DIY/NWOBHM | EASY LIVIN EP | 15 |

### HYSTERIA
| | | | |
|---|---|---|---|
| 84 | Sculpture SCT4-1 | BEHIND THE VEIL (12" EP, p/s) | 20 |

## I AM KLOOT
| | | | |
|---|---|---|---|
| 99 | Ugly Man UGLY 16 | Titanic/To You (7", 1,000 only in brown paper sleeve) | 12 |
| 00 | Ugly Man UGLY 17 | Twist/ 86 TDs (red vinyl) | 8 |
| 01 | We Love You AMOUR 5 | NATURAL HISTORY (LP) | 30 |
| 03 | Echo ECHLP 46A | I AM KLOOT (LP, gatefold, black or white vinyl) | 25 |
| 05 | Echo ECHLP 62 | GODS AND MONSTERS (LP) | 25 |
| 08 | Pias 556 4763.010 | PLAY MOOLAH ROUGE (LP) | 20 |
| 10 | Pias 556 A003 012 | B (2-LP) | 20 |
| 10 | PIAS PIASR 210 LP | SKY AT NIGHT (LP) | 25 |

(see also Johnny Dangerously)

## JANIS IAN
| | | | |
|---|---|---|---|
| 67 | Verve Folkways VS 1503 | Society's Child (Baby I've Been Thinking)/Letter To Jon | 20 |
| 67 | Verve Folkways VS 1506 | Society's Child (Baby I've Been Thinking)/Letter To Jon (reissue) | 5 |
| 68 | Verve Folkways VS 1513 | Sunflakes Fall, Snowrays Call/Insanity Comes Quietly To The Structured Mind | 10 |
| 67 | Verve F'ways (S)VLP 6001 | JANIS IAN (LP) | 30 |
| 67 | Verve Forecast (S)VLP 6003 | FOR ALL THE SEASONS OF YOUR MIND (LP) | 30 |
| 68 | Verve Forecast (S)VLP 6009 | THE SECRET LIFE OF J. EDDY FINK (LP) | 20 |
| 70 | Verve Folkways SVLP 6023 | WHO REALLY CARES? (LP) | 25 |
| 71 | Capitol E-ST 683 | PRESENT COMPANY (LP) | 20 |
| 77 | CBS 31879 | MIRACLE ROW (LP, gatefold) | 15 |
| 85 | CBS 60636 | BETWEEN THE LINES (LP, Nimbus Supercut, mail order only through Practical Hi Fi magazine) | 40 |

## IAN (EDWARD) & ZODIACS
| | | | |
|---|---|---|---|
| 63 | Oriole CB 1849 | Beechwood 4-5789/You Can Think Again | 35 |
| 65 | Fontana TF 548 | Just The Little Things/This Won't Happen To Me (as Ian Edward with Zodiacs) | 30 |
| 66 | Fontana TF 708 | No Money, No Honey/Where Were You? | 50 |
| 66 | Fontana TF 753 | Wade In The Water/Come On Along, Girl | 60 |
| 65 | Wing WL 1074 | GEAR AGAIN - 12 HITS (LP) | 20 |

(see also Koppykats, Wellington Wade)

## IAN (MEESON) & BELINDA (GILLET)
| | | | |
|---|---|---|---|
| 89 | Odeon ODO 112 | Who Wants To Live Forever?/Who Wants To Live Forever? (Instrumental) (p/s, feat. Brian May, handful signed by Brian May for Blood Transfusion staff) | 40 |

(see also Brian May)

## IAN & SYLVIA
| | | | |
|---|---|---|---|
| 63 | Fontana TF 426 | Four Strong Winds/Long Lonesome Road | 7 |
| 65 | Fontana TFL 6053 | EARLY MORNING RAIN (LP) | 30 |

## IAN AND THE MUSCLETONES
| | | | |
|---|---|---|---|
| 81 | Muscletone MS 01 | I Like It/Vampire State (p/s) | 8 |

## I BENJAHMAN
| | | | |
|---|---|---|---|
| 82 | Lion Kingdom LK 002 | Give Love A Try/Mind Blowing Dub/Version (12") | 40 |
| 83 | Lion Kingdom LKLP 01 | INTRODUCING A FRACTION OF JAH ACTION (LP) | 35 |

## IBM 7090 COMPUTER & DIGITAL TO SOUND TRANSCUDER
| | | | |
|---|---|---|---|
| 62 | Brunswick STA 8523 | MUSIC FOR MATHEMATICS (LP) | 40 |

## RAS IBUNA
| | | | |
|---|---|---|---|
| 85 | Studio Now SNT 01 | Diverse Doctrine/Version/COOL BREEZE: Wi Nuh Want Nun A Dat (12") | 12 |

## ICARUS
| | | | |
|---|---|---|---|
| 69 | Spark SRL 1012 | The Devil Rides Out/You're In Life | 175 |
| 72 | Pye Int. NSPL 28161 | THE MARVEL WORLD OF ICARUS (LP, laminated sleeve, blue/black labels) | 175 |

(see also Soft Machine)

## ICE BABIES
| | | | |
|---|---|---|---|
| 81 | Groove Digger GOD 1 | Genius Of Lies/Reason Not Rhyme | 20 |

## ICE CREAM
| | | | |
|---|---|---|---|
| 74 | Fontana 6007 039 | Shout It Out/Hold Yourself Tight | 25 |

## ICE FACTORY
| | | | |
|---|---|---|---|
| 83 | No Label | JERUSALEM EP | 35 |

## ICE (1)
| | | | |
|---|---|---|---|
| 67 | Decca F 12680 | Anniversary (Of Love)/So Many Times | 80 |
| 68 | Decca F 12749 | Ice Man/Whisper Her Name (Maria Laine) | 120 |

(see also Affinity)

## ICE (2)
| | | | |
|---|---|---|---|
| 79 | Storm SR 3307 | SAGA OF THE ICE KING (LP, private pressing with booklet) | 80 |

## ICEBREAKERS
| | | | |
|---|---|---|---|
| 78 | Virgin Frontline FL1010 | PLANET MARS DUB (LP, as Icebreakers with the Diamonds) | 20 |

## ICED EARTH
| | | | |
|---|---|---|---|
| 02 | Century Media | DARK GENESIS (5-CD box set, initial issues with mispressed labels) | 25 |

## ICE NINE
| | | | |
|---|---|---|---|
| 83 | Clockwork TIK 1 | Another Love Affair/For Some Strange Reason (p/s) | 10 |

## ICEPICK
| | | | |
|---|---|---|---|
| 97 | Backbone BR971AA | Phenomenal Criminal/Brixtonites Pt 1(12") | 20 |
| 98 | Backbone ICEEP1 BB002 | ICEPICK (EP) | 18 |

MINT VALUE £

*(see also Bodysnatchers)*

## ICE THE FALLING RAIN
| | | | |
|---|---|---|---|
| 83 | Future FS 7 | Lifes Illusion/Illusions (p/s) | 20 |

## ICICLE WORKS
| | | | |
|---|---|---|---|
| 82 | Troll Kitchen WORKS 1 | Nirvana/Love Hunt/Scirocco (p/s) | 5 |

*(see also Ian McNabb, Melting Bear)*

## ICI LA BAS
| | | | |
|---|---|---|---|
| 79 | Black Noise NO 4 | ICI LA BAS (12" EP, with booklet) | 45 |

*(see also Homosexuals)*

## ICON AD
| | | | |
|---|---|---|---|
| 82 | Radical Change RC 3 | DON'T FEED US SHIT!! (Fight For Peace/Face The Facts/What's Your Name (fold out p/s) | 10 |
| 83 | Radical Change RC 4 | LET THE VUTURES FLY : Say No/Medals/For The Dead/Trident 1 And 2 | 10 |

## ICONS OF FILTH
| | | | |
|---|---|---|---|
| 83 | Corpus Christi CHRIST ITS 7 | USED, ABUSED, UNAMUSED EP (fold-out p/s) | 10 |
| 84 | Mortarhate MORT 10 | BRAIN DEATH EP (p/s with insert) | 10 |
| 85 | Mortarhate MORT 18 | THE FILTH AND THE FURY EP (Fold-out p/s) | 10 |
| 97 | BBP/Yellow Fever BBPV3/YF1 | SHOW US YOU CARE EP (12 test pressings with red fold-out p/s and inserts) | 25 |
| 97 | BBP/Yellow Fever BBPV3/YF1 | SHOW US YOU CARE EP (fold-out p/s, inserts) | 6 |
| 84 | Mortarhate MORT 5 | ONWARD CHRISTIAN SOLDIERS (LP) | 20 |

## IDEAL HUSBANDS
| | | | |
|---|---|---|---|
| 80 | Discovery DIK 001 | Town Planning/Out Of The Factory And Into The Wood (p/s) | 25 |

## IDEALS
| | | | |
|---|---|---|---|
| 61 | Pye International 7N 25103 | Knee Socks/Mary's Lamb | 40 |

## DAVID IDEMA
| | | | |
|---|---|---|---|
| 72 | Buddah 2011 130 | House On Holy Road/Dream Weaver | 6 |

## IDES OF MARCH (2)
| | | | |
|---|---|---|---|
| 86 | RS RSA 3 | In Winters Land/Civilian (p/s) | 8 |

## IDES OF MARCH (1)
| | | | |
|---|---|---|---|
| 66 | London HLU 10058 | You Wouldn't Listen/I'll Keep Searching (as I'des Of March) | 15 |
| 68 | London HLU 10183 | Hole In My Soul/Girls Don't Grow On Trees | 12 |
| 70 | Warner Bros WB 7378 | Vehicle/Lead Me Home, Gently | 6 |
| 70 | Warner Bros WB 7403 | Superman/Home | 6 |
| 70 | Warner Bros WS 1863 | VEHICLE (LP) | 25 |

*(see also Survivors)*

## IDIOT DANCERS
| | | | |
|---|---|---|---|
| 81 | Retrospect HP 1001 | Glances/Up And Down/Imagination (hand-stamped die cut sleeve) | 15 |

## IDIOTS
| | | | |
|---|---|---|---|
| 80s | Blue Angle BLI 2 | Operation Julie/(Why Does Politics Turn Men Into) Toads (p/s) | 5 |

*(see also Tone Deaf & Idiots)*

## IDJUT BOYS
| | | | |
|---|---|---|---|
| 94 | U Star US 001 | IDJUT BOY EP (12") | 50 |
| 94 | U Star US 003 | PHANTOM SLASHER EP (12") | 40 |
| 96 | Noid NOID ONE | Girth Soup/Crouton Bonus/DJ HARVEY: Keep On Trying/Drums in 6 Twelve (12") | 15 |
| 98 | Noid NOIDLP 001 | NOID LONG PLAYER (2xLP) | 50 |

## IDJUT BOYS & LAJ
| | | | |
|---|---|---|---|
| 95 | U Star US 004 | Not Reggae (12") | 40 |
| 95 | U Star US 006 | Foolin' (12") | 20 |
| 95 | U star US 007 | BEARD LAW (EP) | 15 |

## IDLE FLOWERS
| | | | |
|---|---|---|---|
| 84 | Miles Ahead AHEAD 1 | All I Want Is You/Fizz Music (p/s) | 10 |

## IDLE RACE
| | | | |
|---|---|---|---|
| 67 | Liberty LBF 15026 | The Imposters Of Life's Magazine/Sitting In My Tree | 80 |
| 68 | Liberty LBF 15054 | The Skeleton And The Roundabout/Knocking Nails Into My House | 30 |
| 68 | Liberty LBF 15101 | The End Of The Road/The Morning Sunshine | 20 |
| 68 | Liberty LBF 15129 | I Like My Toys/The Birthday (unissued) | 0 |
| 69 | Liberty LBF 15218 | Days Of Broken Arrows/Warm Red Carpet (B-side act. "Worn Red Carpet") | 20 |
| 69 | Liberty LBF 15242 | Come With Me/Reminds Me Of You | 25 |
| 71 | Regal Zonophone RZ 3036 | Dancing Flower/Bitter Green | 12 |
| 76 | United Artists UP 36060 | The Skeleton And The Roundabout/Morning Sunshine | 5 |
| 68 | Liberty LBL 83132 | THE BIRTHDAY PARTY (LP, mono) | 125 |
| 68 | Liberty LBS 83132 | THE BIRTHDAY PARTY (LP, stereo) | 100 |
| 69 | Liberty LBS 83221 | THE IDLE RACE (LP) | 100 |
| 71 | Regal Zono. SLRZ 1017 | TIME IS (LP) | 200 |
| 73 | Sunset SLS 50354 | ON WITH THE SHOW (LP) | 15 |
| 76 | Sunset SLS 50381 | THE BIRTHDAY PARTY (LP, reissue) | 15 |

*(see also Mike Sheridan &, Mike Sheridan's Lot, Lemon Tree, Move, E.L.O., Trevor Burton, Steve Gibbons Band, Wizzard)*

## IDLEWILD
| | | | |
|---|---|---|---|
| 97 | Human Condition HC 0017 | Queen Of The Troubled Teens/Faster/Self Healer (p/s, 1,000 only) | 30 |
| 97 | Fierce Panda NING 42 | Chandelier/I Want To Be A Writer (p/s) | 10 |
| 97 | Deceptive BLUFF 057 | Satan Polaroid/House Alone (die-cut p/s, numbered, 1,500 only) | 8 |
| 98 | Food FOODLP 28 | HOPE IS IMPORTANT (LP) | 25 |
| 00 | Food FOODLP 32 | 100 BROKEN WINDOWS (LP) | 25 |
| 02 | Parlophone 5402431 | THE REMOTE PART (LP, with inner sleeve) | 30 |
| 09 | Diverse DIV 020LP | POST ELECTRIC BLUES (LP) | 25 |

**BILLY IDOL**
93   Chrysalis CHR 6000          CYBERPUNK (LP, inner) ................................................................ 25
*(see also Generation X)*

**IDOL DEATH**
80   ID Records ID DISY 1234     Ignorance Is Bliss/Sticky Death ................................................ 30

**IDOL RICH**
84   Dork URIDOL 3               Blaze Of Love/Peso Trail ............................................................ 12

**IDOLS (1)**
65   Mercury MF 840              Don't Walk Away/You Don't Care .............................................. 20
*(see also Mike Sax & Idols)*

**IDOLS (2)**
79   Ork NYC 2                   You/Girl That I Love (p/s) ............................................................. 8
*(see also New York Dolls)*

**I. E. M. (INCREDIBLE EXPANDING MINDFUCK)**
96   Chromatic CHR 001           I.E.M. (LP) ................................................................................ 30
03   Gates Of Dawn GOD 007       HAVE COME FOR YOUR CHILDREN (LP, 2 x 12" no sleeve with 2 postcard inserts, 90
                                 only, includes track not on CD version) ..................................... 35
*(see also Porcupine Tree)*

**IF**
70   Island WIP 6083             Raise The Level Of Your Conscious Mind/I'm Reaching Out On All Sides ........ 10
71   United Artists UP 35263     Far Beyond/Forgotten Roads ...................................................... 6
72   United Artists UP 35356     You In Your Small Corner/Waterfall ............................................ 6
70   Island ILPS 9129            IF (LP, 1st pressing, pink label/'i' logo) .................................... 75
71   Island ILPS 9129            IF (LP, 2nd pressing, pink rim label/'palm tree' logo) ............... 40
71   Island ILPS 9137            IF 2 (LP, pink label, pink rim label/'palm tree' logo) ............... 40
71   United Artists UAG 29158    IF 3 (LP, gatefold sleeve) ......................................................... 40
72   United Artists UAG 29315    IF 4 (LP, gatefold sleeve with inner) ......................................... 40
75   Gull GULP 1007              TEA BREAK OVER - BACK ON YOUR 'EADS (LP) .......................... 15
74   Gull GULP 1004              NOT JUST ANOTHER BUNCH OF PRETTY FACES (LP, with inner sleeve) ........ 15
*(see also Ferris Wheel, Terry Smith)*

**TECWYN IFAN**
76   Sain Sain 1071              DREF WEN (LP, with insert) ....................................................... 80

**KRIS IFE**
67   MGM MGM 1369                Hush/The Spectator .................................................................. 50
68   MGM MGM 1390                This Woman's Love/I Gotta Feeling .......................................... 12
68   Music Factory CUB 3         Give And Take/Sands Of Time .................................................. 20
68   Parlophone R 5741           Imagination/I'm Coming 'Round .............................................. 20
69   Parlophone R 5770           Haven't We Had A Good Time?/Will I Ever Fall In Love Again? ........ 10
73   Bumlade GE122               Wherever You Are/The Sun, The Sea, The Sand And The Wine ........ 25
*(see also Quiet Five, Judd)*

**I GAD**
92   Nuff Tuff TUF 006           Brutality/ENHANCERS: Brutal Dub/Wicked Man/MANDINKA: Rootsman Corner/
                                 ENHANCERS: Wicked Dub (12") ................................................ 50

**IGANDA**
79   021 Records OTO1            Slow Down/Mark Of Slavery (p/s) ............................................ 50

**'IGGINBOTTOM**
69   Deram SML 1051              'IGGINBOTTOM'S WRENCH (LP, stereo) ................................. 200
69   Deram DML 1051              'IGGINBOTTOM'S WRENCH (LP, mono) .................................. 250
*(see also Soft Machine)*

**IGNERANTS**
79   Rundown ACE 008             Radio Interference/Wrong Place, Wrong Time (p/s) ................... 30

**IGUANA**
72   Polydor 2383 108            IGUANA (LP, gatefold sleeve) ................................................. 25

**IGUANAS**
65   RCA RCA 1484                This Is What I Was Made For/Don't Come Runnin' To Me ........... 40

**I HAICIDEONS & I JARZIF**
78   Greensleeves GRED 7         Rise Ethiopians/Signs Of The Messiah (12") ........................... 40

**I JAH MAN (LEVI)**
76   Lucky LY 6016               Jah Heavy Load/Heavy Dub ...................................................... 80
76   Concrete CJ 756             I Am Levi/Part 2 ..................................................................... 100
77   Ghetto Rocker PRE 1         Africa/Afrodub (handwritten labels) ....................................... 40
78   Island WIP 6458             Heavy Load/I'm A Levi ............................................................. 40
85   Jahmani JM1 501             Moulding/Jah Is Coming Again (12") ....................................... 40

**I-JOG & TRACKSUITS**
79   Tracksuit JOG 1             Jah Jah Jah/Tao Tao Tao (p/s, as the TRACKSUITS) ................... 6
80   Tyger TYG 1                 Red Box/Worrying Man (p/s) .................................................... 20

**IKE (B) & CRYSTALITES**
68   Island WI 3134              Illya Kuryakin/Anne Marie (B-side miscredited to Bobby Ellis & Crystalites) ........ 60
68   Island WI 3151              Try A Little Merriness/Patricia (as Ike B & Crystalites) ........... 20

**IKETTES**
62   London HLU 9508             I'm Blue/Find My Baby .............................................................. 25
65   Stateside SS 407            Peaches'N'Cream/The Biggest Players ...................................... 40
65   Stateside SS 434            (He's Gonna Be) Fine Fine Fine/How Come .............................. 30
65   Sue WI 389                  Prisoner In Love/Those Words.................................................. 40
66   Polydor 56506               I'm So Thankful/Don't Feel Sorry For Me .................................. 20
66   Polydor 56516               (Never More) Lonely For You/Sally Go Round The Roses ........... 20
66   London HLU 10081            What'cha Gonna Do?/Down, Down .......................................... 80

MINT VALUE £

| | | | |
|---|---|---|---|
| 67 | Polydor 56533 | I'm So Thankful/Don't Feel Sorry For Me (reissue) | 8 |
| 73 | Mojo 2092 063 | Peaches'N'Cream/Sally Go Round The Roses | 8 |
| 85 | Kent 6T1 | MARY LOVE: Hey Stoney Face/IKETTES: It's Been So Long/ETTA JAMES: Wallflower | 20 |
| 65 | Stateside SE 1033 | FINE FINE FINE (EP) | 175 |

*(see also Ike & Tina Turner, P.P. Arnold)*

## ILANIT
| | | | |
|---|---|---|---|
| 77 | Pye International 7N 25739 | I'm No One (If You Leave Me)/I Can't Say I Love You (p/s) | 10 |

## I LIFE
| | | | |
|---|---|---|---|
| 64 | R&B JB 140 | Kiss You Gave Me/No More | 18 |

## ILLUSION
| | | | |
|---|---|---|---|
| 69 | Dot DOT 122 | Did You See Her Eyes?/Falling In Love | 8 |
| 70 | Dot DOT 133 | Together/Don't Push It | 5 |
| 70 | Dot DOT 137 | Let's Make Each Other Happy/Beside You (unissued) | 0 |
| 70 | Paramount PARA 3007 | Let's Make Each Other Happy/Beside You | 5 |
| 69 | Dot (S)LPD 531 | ILLUSION (LP) | 25 |
| 70 | Dot SLPD 537 | TOGETHER (AS A WAY OF LIFE) (LP) | 22 |
| 70 | Paramount SPFL 264 | IF IT'S SO (LP, originally planned for Dot SLPD 539) | 15 |

## ILLUSIONS
| | | | |
|---|---|---|---|
| 83 | Zella ZEL LPS 405 | ILLUSIONS (LP, 100 only, with insert) | 50 |

## ILLUSIVE DREAM
| | | | |
|---|---|---|---|
| 69 | RCA Victor RCA 1791 | Electric Garden/Back Again | 30 |

*(see also Christine Perfect)*

## ILLUSTRATION
| | | | |
|---|---|---|---|
| 69 | Pye Int. NSPL 28140 | ILLUSTRATION (LP) | 25 |

## SOLOMON ILORY
| | | | |
|---|---|---|---|
| 63 | Blue Note 45-1899 | Yabe E (Farewell) (Parts 1 & 2) | 12 |

## ERIK ILOTT, SHANTYMAN
| | | | |
|---|---|---|---|
| 73 | Folk'sle Records FOR 7 | SHIPSHAPE & BRISTOL FASHION (LP, card foldout sleeve, pasted on photo & 25 page booklet) | 40 |

## I LUV WIGHT
| | | | |
|---|---|---|---|
| 70 | Philips 6006 043 | Let The World Wash In/Mediaeval Masquerade (in p/s) | 75 |
| 70 | Philips 6006 043 | Let The World Wash In/Mediaeval Masquerade | 35 |

*(see also Kaleidoscope, Fairfield Parlour)*

## IMAGE
| | | | |
|---|---|---|---|
| 65 | Parlophone R 5281 | Come To The Party/Never Let Me Go | 40 |
| 65 | Parlophone R 5352 | Home Is Anywhere/I Hear Your Voice Again | 40 |
| 66 | Parlophone R 5442 | I Can't Stop Myself/Let's Make The Scene | 40 |

## IMAGES
| | | | |
|---|---|---|---|
| 65 | Polydor 56011 | I Only Have Myself To Blame/Head Over Heels | 30 |

## IMAGINATION (1)
| | | | |
|---|---|---|---|
| 68 | Status ST 001 | Flying/The Magic Wand | 50 |

## IM & COUNT OSSIE
| | | | |
|---|---|---|---|
| 71 | Banana CA 357 | So Long Rastafari Calling/Give Me Back My Language & Culture | 50 |

## IM (CEDRIC BROOKS) & DAVID
| | | | |
|---|---|---|---|
| 70 | Bamboo BAM 57 | Candid Eye/SOUND DIMENSION: Federated Backdrop | 40 |

## IMITATIONS
| | | | |
|---|---|---|---|
| 71 | Crystal CR 7013 | Walking Up A One Way Street/One Way Street - Version | 6 |

## IMMEDIATE
| | | | |
|---|---|---|---|
| 05 | Fierce Panda NING161 | Never Seen/Say This (p/s) | 7 |

## IMMORTALS (1)
| | | | |
|---|---|---|---|
| 69 | Amalgamated AMG 851 | Bongo Jah/ANSELL COLLINS: My Last Waltz | 40 |

## IMMORTALS (2)
| | | | |
|---|---|---|---|
| 86 | MCA MCA 1057 | No Turning Back/No Turning Back (The Chocks-Away Mix) (p/s) | 25 |
| 86 | MCA MCAT 1057 | No Turning Back (Joy Stick Mix)/No Turning Back/No Turning Back (The Chocks-Away Mix) (12", p/s) | 30 |

*(see also Queen)*

## IMPAC
| | | | |
|---|---|---|---|
| 66 | CBS 202402 | Too Far Out/Rat Tat Ta Tat | 80 |

## IMPACT
| | | | |
|---|---|---|---|
| 83 | Cyanide | PUNK CHRISTMAS EP | 20 |

## IMPACT ALL STARS
| | | | |
|---|---|---|---|
| 71 | Bullet BU 483 | Dandy Shandy Version 4/Go Back Version 3 | 12 |
| 71 | Randy's RAN 519 | Go Back Version 4/Version 3 | 12 |
| 71 | Supreme SUP 223 | Go Back/Version | 12 |

*(see also Randy's All Stars, Alton Ellis, Gregory Issacs, Errol Dunkley, C. Danovan, Heptones, Dennis Brown, Horace Andy)*

## IMPALAS
| | | | |
|---|---|---|---|
| 59 | MGM MGM 1015 | Sorry (I Ran All The Way Home)/Fool, Fool, Fool | 15 |
| 59 | MGM MGM 1015 | Sorry (I Ran All The Way Home)/Fool, Fool, Fool (78) | 25 |
| 59 | MGM MGM 1031 | Oh, What A Fool/Sandy Went Away | 30 |
| 60 | MGM MGM 1068 | Peggy Darling/'Bye Everybody | 30 |
| 59 | MGM MGM-EP 696 | SORRY (I RAN ALL THE WAY HOME) (EP) | 400 |

## IMPALERS
| | | | |
|---|---|---|---|
| 79 | Decca F 13862 | Gimme Some Lovin'/Wild About It | 10 |

## IMPERIAL POMPADOURS
| | | | |
|---|---|---|---|
| 80 | Pompadour POMP 001 | ERSATZ (LP, actually Inner City Unit with Robert Calvert & Barney Bubbles) | 40 |

*(see also Inner City Unit, Robert Calvert)*

## IMPERIALS (JAMAICA)
69 Bullet BU 417     Black Is Soul/Always With You ........................................ 40

## IMPERIALS (1)
72 Key KL 012     TIME TO GET IT TOGETHER (LP) ................................. 18
74 Key KL 025     FOLLOW THE MAN WITH THE MUSIC (LP) ................. 15

## IMPERIALS (2)
68 Nu Beat NB 012     Young Love/Days Like These ........................................ 25

## IMPERSONATORS
69 Big Shot BI 524     Make It Easy On Yourself/I've Tried Before .................. 12

*(see also Moffat Allstars)*

## IMPOSSIBLE DREAMERS
80 Merciful Release MR 1     Books Books Books/Not A Love Song/Waiting For The Girl/ What Can You Do When You See Someone As Beautiful As You? ........................... 8

## IMPOSSIBLE YEARS
85 Dreamworld DREAM 1     SCENES WE'D LIKE TO SEE (12" EP) ......................... 12

## IMPOSTERS
69 Mercury MF 1080     Apache '69/Q Three ..................................................... 20

## IMPRESSIONS
| | | |
|---|---|---|
| 58 | London HL 8697 | For Your Precious Love/Sweet Was The Wine (as Jerry Butler & Impressions) ............... 220 |
| 58 | London HL 8697 | For Your Precious Love/Sweet Was The Wine (78, as Jerry Butler & Impressions) ......... 80 |
| 61 | HMV POP 961 | Gypsy Woman/As Long As You Love Me ............................ 40 |
| 63 | HMV POP 1129 | I'm The One Who Loves You/I Need Your Love ................. 40 |
| 63 | HMV POP 1226 | It's Alright/You'll Want Me Back .................................. 25 |
| 64 | HMV POP 1262 | Talkin' About My Baby/Never Too Much Love ................ 20 |
| 64 | HMV POP 1295 | I'm So Proud/I Made A Mistake ................................... 20 |
| 64 | HMV POP 1317 | Keep On Pushing/I Love You (Yeah) ............................. 20 |
| 64 | HMV POP 1343 | You Must Believe Me/See The Real Me .......................... 18 |
| 65 | HMV POP 1408 | People Get Ready/I've Been Trying ............................... 18 |
| 65 | HMV POP 1429 | Woman's Got Soul/Get Up And Move ............................ 18 |
| 65 | HMV POP 1446 | A Meeting Over Yonder/I Found That I've Lost ............... 20 |
| 65 | HMV POP 1472 | I Need You/Never Could You Be .................................... 12 |
| 65 | HMV POP 1492 | Amen/Long Long Winter ............................................. 30 |
| 66 | HMV POP 1498 | You've Been Cheatin'/Just One Kiss From You ............... 30 |
| 66 | HMV POP 1498 | You've Been Cheatin'/Just One Kiss From You (DJ Copy) .. 75 |
| 66 | HMV POP 1516 | Since I Lost The One I Love/Falling In Love With You ...... 15 |
| 66 | HMV POP 1526 | Too Slow/No One Else ................................................. 15 |
| 66 | HMV POP 1545 | Can't Satisfy/This Must End ........................................ 40 |
| 66 | HMV POP 1545 | Can't Satisfy/This Must End (DJ Copy) ......................... 75 |
| 67 | HMV POP 1581 | You Always Hurt Me/Little Girl ................................... 22 |
| 68 | Stateside SS 2083 | We're A Winner/You've Got Me Runnin' ....................... 18 |
| 68 | Buddah 201 021 | Fool For You/I'm Loving Nothing ................................. 10 |
| 69 | Stateside SS 2139 | Can't Satisfy/You've Been Cheatin' .............................. 20 |
| 69 | Buddah 201 062 | Choice Of Colors/Mighty Mighty Spade And Whitey ...... 15 |
| 70 | Buddah 2011 030 | Check Out Your Mind/Can't You See? ........................... 10 |
| 70 | Buddah 2011 045 | (Baby) Turn On To Me/Soulful Love .............................. 8 |
| 71 | Buddah 2011 068 | Ain't Got Time/I'm So Proud ....................................... 8 |
| 71 | Buddah 2011 087 | Love Me/Do You Want Me To Win ................................ 8 |
| 71 | Buddah 2011 099 | Inner City Blues/Amen/Keep On Pushin' ....................... 6 |
| 72 | Buddah 2011 124 | Our Love Goes On And On/This Love's For Real ............ 8 |
| 73 | Probe PRO 584 | People Get Ready/We're Rolling On ............................. 8 |
| 74 | Buddah BDS 403 | Finally Got Myself Together/I'll Always Be Here ............. 6 |
| 76 | ABC 4148 | You've Been Cheating/Amen ...................................... 100 |
| 65 | HMV 7EG 8896 | IT'S ALL RIGHT (EP) ................................................. 100 |
| 66 | HMV 7EG 8954 | SOULFULLY (EP) ........................................................ 80 |
| 64 | HMV CLP 1743 | THE NEVER ENDING IMPRESSIONS (LP) ........................ 40 |
| 65 | HMV CLP 1935 | BIG SIXTEEN (LP, mono) ............................................. 50 |
| 65 | HMV CSD 1642 | BIG SIXTEEN (LP, stereo) ............................................ 60 |
| 66 | HMV CLP/CSD 3548 | RIDIN' HIGH (LP) ....................................................... 60 |
| 67 | HMV CLP/CSD 3631 | THE FABULOUS IMPRESSIONS (LP) ............................... 35 |
| 68 | Stateside (S)SL 10239 | WE'RE A WINNER (LP) ................................................ 15 |
| 68 | Joy JOYS 104 | FOR YOUR PRECIOUS LOVE (LP, with Jerry Butler) ......... 20 |
| 69 | Buddah 203 012 | THIS IS MY COUNTRY (LP) .......................................... 20 |
| 69 | Stateside (S)SL 10279 | BIG SIXTEEN (VOL. 2) (LP) ......................................... 30 |
| 70 | Buddah 2359 003 | THE YOUNG MOD'S FORGOTTEN STORY (LP) ................. 18 |
| 70 | Buddah 2359 009 | AMEN (LP) ................................................................ 20 |
| 71 | Buddah 2318 017 | CHECK OUT YOUR MIND (LP) ...................................... 18 |
| 72 | Buddah 2318 059 | TIMES HAVE CHANGED (LP) ....................................... 18 |
| 75 | ABC ABCL 5104 | BIG SIXTEEN (LP, reissue) .......................................... 15 |

*(see also Curtis Mayfield, Jerry Butler)*

## IMPROVING SILENCE
77 Perky Pat CS LP 145/6     IMPROVING SILENCE EP (1,000, p/s with 8 page book insert) ................. 40

## IMPS
58 Parlophone R 4398     Dim Dumb Blonde/Let Me Lie ..................................... 20

## IN CROWD (JAMAICA)
| | | |
|---|---|---|
| 71 | Spinning Wheel SW 105 | Bush Jacket/Soul Face ................................................ 25 |
| 78 | Savannah SVN 12-1 | Riding High/Version (12") .......................................... 12 |
| 78 | Cactus CT 111 | Back A Yard/Yard (12") .............................................. 15 |
| 78 | Cactus CTLP 125 | HIS MAJESTY IS COMING (LP) ..................................... 25 |

## IN CROWD (U.K.)
| | | | |
|---|---|---|---|
| 65 | Parlophone R 5276 | That's How Strong My Love Is/Things She Says | 80 |
| 65 | Parlophone R 5328 | Stop! Wait A Minute/You're On Your Own | 70 |
| 65 | Parlophone R 5364 | Why Must They Criticize?/I Don't Mind | 60 |

*(see also Tomorrow, Keith West, Steve Howe, Four + One)*

## INCROWD (U.K.)
| | | | |
|---|---|---|---|
| 69 | Deram DM 272 | Where In The World/I Can Make Love To You | 15 |

## IN EMBRACE
| | | | |
|---|---|---|---|
| 82 | Glass GLASS 024 | Sun Brings Smiles/Play In Light (p/s) | 8 |

## IN FLAMES
| | | | |
|---|---|---|---|
| 72 | Pama PM 842 | Rocket Man/I'm All Broke Up | 30 |

## INADEQUATES
| | | | |
|---|---|---|---|
| 59 | Capitol CL 15051 | Pretty Face/Audie | 25 |

## INCANDESCENT LUMINAIRE
| | | | |
|---|---|---|---|
| 82 | Clock House CHR 0501 | Famous Names/The Warning | 18 |

## INCAS (1)
| | | | |
|---|---|---|---|
| 65 | Lyntone LYN 765/6 | KEELE RAG RECORD (EP, flexidisc, with 3 other bands) | 30 |
| 66 | Parlophone R 5551 | One Night Stand/I'll Keep Holding On | 60 |

## INCAS (2)
| | | | |
|---|---|---|---|
| 75 | Tank BSS 112 | X CERTIFICATE (LP, private pressing) | 50 |

## ERROL INCE
| | | | |
|---|---|---|---|
| 65 | Ember EMB 3360 | DANCE TRINIDAD (LP, as Errol Ince and his Music Makers) | 18 |

## INCEE WINCEE SPIDER
| | | | |
|---|---|---|---|
| 88 | Overspill SPILL1 | Don't Know Anythin'/See My Love Shine (p/s) | 30 |

## INCH BY INCH
| | | | |
|---|---|---|---|
| 81 | Blue Of London BOL 1 | If It's Magic (We Don't Want It)/War's Not Inevitable (12". p/s) | 15 |

## INCOGNITO
| | | | |
|---|---|---|---|
| 80 | Ensign ENY 4412 | Parisienne Girls/Summers Ended (12") | 12 |

## INCREDIBLE BONGO BAND
| | | | |
|---|---|---|---|
| 73 | MGM 2006 161 | Bongo Rock/Bongolia | 8 |
| 72 | MGM 2315 255 | BONGO ROCK (LP) | 25 |
| 76 | DJM DJS 20452 | BONGO ROCK (LP, reissue) | 15 |

## INCREDIBLE HOG
| | | | |
|---|---|---|---|
| 73 | Dart ART 2026 | Lame/Tadpole | 15 |
| 73 | Dart 65372 | VOLUME 1 (LP, laminated sleeve, pink/white/black label) | 200 |

## INCREDIBLE KIDDA BAND
| | | | |
|---|---|---|---|
| 78 | Psycho P 2608 | Everybody Knows/No Nerve (in p/s) | 100 |
| 78 | Psycho P 2608 | Everybody Knows/No Nerve (no p/s) | 30 |
| 79 | Carrere CAR 119 | Fighting My Way Back/Saturday Night Fever (as KIDDA BAND) | 130 |

## INCREDIBLES
| | | | |
|---|---|---|---|
| 67 | Stateside SS 2053 | There's Nothing Else To Say/Heart And Soul | 150 |
| 67 | Stateside SS 2053 | There's Nothing Else To Say/Heart And Soul (DJ copy) | 200 |
| 74 | Contempo CS 9008 | There's Nothing Else To Say/Another Dirty Deal | 12 |
| 74 | Contempo CLP 512 | HEART AND SOUL (LP) | 25 |

## INCREDIBLE STRING BAND
### SINGLES
| | | | |
|---|---|---|---|
| 67 | Elektra EKSN 45013 | Way Back In The 1960s/Chinese White (white-label promo) | 60 |
| 68 | Elektra EKSN 45028 | Painting Box/No Sleep Blues | 15 |
| 69 | Elektra EKSN 45074 | Big Ted/All Writ Down | 12 |
| 70 | Elektra 2101 003 | This Moment/Black Jack Davy | 6 |
| 72 | Island WIP 6145 | Black Jack David/Moon Hang Low | 5 |
| 73 | Island WIP 6158 | At The Lighthouse Dance/Jigs | 5 |

### ALBUMS : ORIGINAL ALBUMS
| | | | |
|---|---|---|---|
| 66 | Elektra EUK 254 | THE INCREDIBLE STRING BAND (1st pressing, white label, green logo, black lettering) | 225 |
| 67 | Elektra EUK 257 | THE 5000 SPIRITS OR THE LAYERS OF THE ONION (mono, orange label) | 130 |
| 67 | Elektra EUKS 7257 | THE 5000 SPIRITS OR THE LAYERS OF THE ONION (LP, stereo, orange label, laminated sleeve) | 80 |
| 68 | Elektra EUKS 258 | THE HANGMAN'S BEAUTIFUL DAUGHTER (mono, orange label, with lyric insert) | 70 |
| 68 | Elektra EUKS 7258 | THE HANGMAN'S BEAUTIFUL DAUGHTER (stereo, orange label, with lyric insert) | 60 |
| 68 | Elektra EKL 4036/7 | WEE TAM/THE BIG HUGE (2-LP, orange label, laminated gatefold sleeve, with insert; also stereo EKS 74036/7) | 45 |
| 69 | Elektra EKS 74057 | CHANGING HORSES (red/white label, gatefold sleeve) | 45 |
| 70 | Elektra 2469 002 | I LOOKED UP (red/white label) | 50 |
| 70 | Elektra 2665 001 | U (2-LP, red/white label, gatefold sleeve, with foldover lyric insert) | 35 |
| 70 | Elektra 2665 001 | U (2-LP, red label, gatefold sleeve, without foldover lyric insert) | 25 |
| 70 | Island ILPS 9140 | BE GLAD FOR THE SONG HAS NO ENDING (pink rim label/'palm tree' logo) | 18 |
| 71 | Island ILPS 9172 | LIQUID ACROBAT AS REGARDS THE AIR (gatefold sleeve, with inner, pink rim/'palm tree' logo) | 30 |
| 72 | Island ILPS 9211 | EARTHSPAN (with lyric inner sleeve, pink rim label/'palm tree' logo) | 18 |
| 73 | Island ILPS 9229 | NO RUINOUS FEUD (with inner sleeve, pink rim label/'palm tree' logo) | 15 |
| 74 | Island ILPS 9270 | HARD ROPE AND SILKEN TWINE (with inner sleeve, pink rim label/'palm tree' logo) | 15 |
| 76 | Island ISLD 9 | SEASONS THEY CHANGE (2-LP, gatefold sleeve) | 25 |

### ALBUMS : REISSUE ALBUMS
| | | | |
|---|---|---|---|
| 66 | Elektra EUK 254 | THE INCREDIBLE STRING BAND (2nd pressing, orange label) | 60 |
| 68 | Elektra EKL 254 | THE INCREDIBLE STRING BAND (3rd pressing, red label) | 20 |
| 68 | Elektra EKS 7257 | THE 5000 SPIRITS OR THE LAYERS OF THE ONION (LP, stereo, red label) | 80 |

*(All other 'butterfly' label re-issues £8-£10 each)*

| 68 | Elektra EUK 257 | THE 5000 SPIRITS OR THE LAYERS OF THE ONION (LP, mono, red label)...................... 25 |
| 68 | Elektra EKL 4036 | WEE TAM (red label, also stereo EKS 74036) ........................................................ 15 |

*(All other 'butterfly' label re-issues £8-£10 each)*

| 68 | Elektra EKL 4037 | THE BIG HUGE (red label, also stereo EKS 74037) ................................................ 15 |

*(see also Robin Williamson, Mike Heron, Famous Jug Band, C.O.B., Shirley Collins)*

## INCUBUS
| 84 | Guardian GRC 2165 | TO THE DEVIL A DAUGHTER (LP) ........................................................................ 18 |

## PETER IND
| 61 | Esquire 32 159 | LOOKING OUT (LP) ........................................................................................ 120 |
| 68 | Wave LP 3 | IMPROVISATION (LP) ........................................................................................ 30 |
| 69 | Wave LP 4 | TIME FOR IMPROVISATION (LP) ...................................................................... 30 |
| 69 | Wave LP 5 | JAZZ AT THE RICHMOND FESTIVAL (LP, with Charlie Burchell, Bernie Cash & Derek Phillips) ...................................................................................................... 30 |
| 70 | Wave LP 20 | COTRA-BACH (LP, with Bernard Cash) ............................................................ 30 |
| 74 | Wave LP 29 | NO KIDDING (LP, with Chas Burchell, Tox Drohar & Dave Cliff) ...................... 30 |

## INDECENT EXPOSURE
| 84 | Index IS A1 | Riots (Single Version)/A Matter Of Time (no p/s) ................................................ 7 |

## INDEX (1)
| 78 | Index INDY 001 | Jetlag/Total Bland (1st pressing, 500 only, push out centre, die cut stickered sleeve).... 30 |
| 78 | Index INDY 001 | Jetlag/Total Bland (2nd pressing, 500 only, solid centre, die cut sleeve)................ 15 |

## INDEX (2)
| 81 | Record Shack SHACK 8 | Starlight/Starbright Instrumental Mic ................................................................ 7 |

## INDIAN SUMMER
| 71 | RCA Neon NE 3 | INDIAN SUMMER (LP, gatefold sleeve)............................................................ 200 |

*(see also Badfinger)*

## INDIFFERENT DANCE CENTRE
| 81 | Recluse RECLUSE 1 | Flight & Pursuit/Release (p/s) ...................................................................... 25 |

## INDO-BRITISH ENSEMBLE
| 69 | MFP 1307 | CURRIED JAZZ (LP) ........................................................................................ 15 |

## INDO JAZZMEN
| 68 | Saga FID 2145 | RAGAS AND REFLECTIONS (LP) ...................................................................... 15 |

## INEPT
| 90 | Woodhouse | Experience/Roller Coaster (flexidisc) .............................................................. 10 |

## INERTIA (1)
| 80 | ERT 2 | DANCEBEAT ATTITUDE EP ............................................................................ 50 |

## INERTIA (2)
| 80s | Inertial ERT 1 | The Screen/4 Submarine (p/s) ........................................................................ 5 |

## INEVITABLES
| 82 | Honk 1 | The Fourth Contender/The Puppeteer/Neutral News (p/s) ................................ 25 |

## INFANTES JUBILATE
| 68 | Music Factory CUB 5 | Exploding Galaxy/Take It Now ...................................................................... 60 |

## INFA RIOT
| 81 | Secret SHH 117 | Kids Of The 80s/Still Out Of Order (p/s) ........................................................ 10 |
| 82 | Secret SHH 133 | The Winner/School's Out (p/s) ........................................................................ 6 |
| 82 | Secret SEC 7 | STILL OUT OF ORDER (LP) ............................................................................ 15 |
| 88 | Link LINKLP 052 | LIVE AND LOUD!! (LP) .................................................................................. 15 |

*(see also Infas)*

## INFAS
| 84 | Panache PAN 101 | Sound And Fury/Triffic Spiff Ya O.K. (p/s) ...................................................... 8 |
| 84 | Panache PANLP 501 | SOUND AND FURY (LP) ................................................................................ 15 |

*(see also Infa Riot)*

## INFERNAL BLUES MACHINE
| 76 | London SHU 8496 | ADIOS AMIGOS (LP) ...................................................................................... 15 |

## INFINITY PROJECT
| 89 | Fabulous FABU 004 | HYPERACTIVE (12" EP, sponged cover) ........................................................ 10 |
| 90 | Fabulous FABU 005 | UPHOLD THE LAW (12" EP) .......................................................................... 10 |

## INFLUENCE
| 69 | Orange OAS 201 | I Want To Live/Driving Me Wild .................................................................... 25 |

*(see also John Miles, Geordie, Smokestack Crumble)*

## INFORMANTS
| 79 | Criminal SWAG 5 | My Radio/Grandpa (company sleeve) .............................................................. 7 |

*(see also Nirvana (U.K.))*

## INFORMATION
| 69 | Beacon BEA 121 | Orphan/Oh Strange Man.............................................................................. 30 |
| 70 | Evolution E 2461S | Lovely To See You/Face To The Sun .............................................................. 20 |

## INFRA RED HELICOPTERS
| 79 | 1979 | BRACKNELL (EP) ............................................................................................ 25 |

## NICK INGHAM
| 75 | EMI EMI 2452 | American Pie/Brass Knuckles/Terminator ........................................................ 10 |
| 75 | Studio Two TWOX 1045 | TERMINATOR (LP)........................................................................................ 20 |

## RED INGLE
| 59 | Capitol EAP 20052 | CIGAREETS, WHUSKY AND WILD WILD WOMEN (EP) .................................... 12 |

## JORGEN INGMANN
| 61 | Fontana H 311 | Cherokee/Anna.............................................................................................. 5 |
| 61 | Fontana H 353 | Hear My Song - Violetta/Pinetop's Boogie Woogie .......................................... 5 |
| 62 | Fontana 267 237 TF | Africa/Johnny's Tune...................................................................................... 5 |

MINT VALUE £

| | | | |
|---|---|---|---|
| 63 | Columbia DB 7013 | I Loved You (Dansevise)/Little Boy (as Grethe & Jorgen Ingmann) | 5 |
| 59 | Pye Int. NPT 29000 | GUITAR IN HI-FI (10" LP) | 25 |

## INGRAM
| | | | |
|---|---|---|---|
| 83 | Streetwave WAVE 3 | DJ's Delight/Smoothin Groovin (12") | 12 |
| 83 | Streetwave WAVLP 001 | WOULD YOU LIKE TO FLY (LP, with bonus 12") | 30 |
| 83 | Streetwave WAVLP 001 | WOULD YOU LIKE TO FLY (LP, without bonus 12") | 20 |

## LUTHER INGRAM
| | | | |
|---|---|---|---|
| 70 | Stax STAX 142 | My Honey And Me/Puttin' Game Down | 8 |
| 70 | Stax STAX 148 | Home Don't Seem Like A Home/Ain't That Lovin' You? | 8 |
| 08 | Kent Select CITY 007 | Baby Don't You Weep/CHET POISON' IVY: Mata Hari | 20 |
| 72 | Koko KOS 2202 | IF LOVING YOU IS WRONG I DON'T WANT TO BE RIGHT (LP, photo insert) | 20 |

## I 'N' I ONENESS MEETS UK PLAYERS
| | | | |
|---|---|---|---|
| 97 | Jah Works JW 018S | Further/Further Into Dub (12") | 20 |

## INITIALS
| | | | |
|---|---|---|---|
| 64 | London HLR 9860 | School Day/Song Is Number One | 18 |

## AUTREY INMAN
| | | | |
|---|---|---|---|
| 63 | Decca DFE 8571 | AMERICAN COUNTRY JUBILEE NO. 1 (EP) | 15 |

## INMATES
| | | | |
|---|---|---|---|
| 79 | Soho SH 7 | Dirty Water/Danger Zone (gatefold p/s) | 8 |
| 79 | Radar ADA 47 | The Walk/Talkin' Woman (p/s) | 5 |
| 81 | Radar ADA 63 | (I Thought I Heard A) Heartbeat/Tallahassie Lassie (p/s) | 5 |
| 79 | Radar RAD 25 | FIRST OFFENCE (LP) | 15 |

## INNER CIRCLE
| | | | |
|---|---|---|---|
| 74 | Trojan TRO 9008 | Duppy Gunman/None Shall Escape The Judgement | 10 |
| 75 | Trojan TR 7948 | Road Block/Forward Jah Jah Children | 10 |

## INNER CIRCLE & FATMAN
| | | | |
|---|---|---|---|
| 00 | Blood & Fire SVLP 293 | HEAVY WEIGHT DUB KILLER DUB (2-LP) | 20 |

## INNER CITY BAND
| | | | |
|---|---|---|---|
| 78 | Key KS 101 | Happiness/Night At The Disco | 25 |

## INNER CITY EXPRESS
| | | | |
|---|---|---|---|
| 78 | Ebony EYE 5 | Fat On Funk/Sho' Dig Dancin' (12") | 20 |

## INNER CITY UNIT
| | | | |
|---|---|---|---|
| 79 | Riddle RID 001/ICU 45 | Solitary Ashtray/So Try As Id (Dub Version) (plain sleeve with colour insert) | 8 |
| 79 | Riddle RID 003 | Paradise Beach/Amyl Nitrate (company die-cut sleeve) | 8 |
| 81 | Avatar AAA 113 | Beer, Baccy, Bingo And Benidorm/In The Mood (Nude) (red vinyl, no p/s) | 6 |
| 82 | Avatar AAA 119 | Bones Of Elvis/Sid's Song (no p/s) | 5 |
| 79 | Riddle RID 002 | PASS OUT (THE 360° PSYCHO DELERIA SOUND) (LP) | 15 |

*(see also Hawkwind, Sphynx, Radio Actors, Imperial Pompadours, Catherine Andrews, Big Amongst Sheep)*

## INNER MIND
| | | | |
|---|---|---|---|
| 70 | New Beat NB 067 | Witchcraft Man/Night In Cairo | 10 |
| 70 | New Beat NB 069 | Pum Pum Girl/Freedom | 15 |
| 71 | Bullet BU 465 | Arawak Version/Cuffy Cuffy | 10 |
| 71 | Shades SHA 11 | Dreams Of Yesterday/Never Over The Land | 10 |
| 72 | Shades SHA 12 | Jesse James Hits Back/Let Me In | 15 |

## NEIL INNES
| | | | |
|---|---|---|---|
| 72 | United Artists UP 35358 | Slush/Rawlinson's End (this is a different version from that on the Vivian Stanshall LP) | 30 |
| 73 | United Artists UP 35495 | How Sweet To Be An Idiot/The Age Of Desperation | 10 |
| 73 | United Artists UP 35639 | Momma B/Imoortal Invisible | 7 |
| 74 | United Artists UP 35676 | Re-cycled Vinyl Blues/Fluff On The Needle | 7 |
| 74 | United Artists UP 35745 | Lie Down And Be Counted/Bandwagon | 7 |
| 75 | United Artists UP 35772 | What Noise Annoys An Oyster/Oo-Chuck-A-Mao-Mao | 7 |
| 77 | Arista ARISTA 106 | Lady Mine/Crystal Balls | 6 |
| 77 | Arista ARISTA 123 | Silver Jubilee (A Tribute)/Drama On A Saturday Night | 6 |
| 78 | Warner Bros K 17182 | Protest Song/The Hard-To-Get | 6 |
| 79 | Polydor 2059 247 | Kenny And Liza/Human Race | 6 |
| 82 | MMC MMC 100 | Them/Rock Of Ages | 6 |
| 82 | MMC MMC 103 | Mr. Eurovision/Ungawa | 6 |
| 73 | United Artists UAG 29492 | HOW SWEET TO BE AN IDIOT (LP) | 30 |
| 82 | MMC MMC 001 | OFF THE RECORD (2-LP) | 30 |

*(see also Grimms, Bonzo Dog [Doo Dah] Band, Rutles, World, Dirk & Stig, Group)*

## INN KEEPERS
| | | | |
|---|---|---|---|
| 71 | Banana BA 328 | Duppy Serenade/Sunshine Version (actually by Dennis Alcapone) | 20 |

*(see also Winston Matthews)*

## INNOCENCE
| | | | |
|---|---|---|---|
| 66 | Kama Sutra KAS 203 | There's Got To Be A Word!/I Don't Wanna Be Around You | 8 |
| 66 | Kama Sutra KAS 206 | Mairzy Doats And Dozy Doats/Lifetime Of Lovin' You | 8 |

## INNOCENCE IN AFRICA
| | | | |
|---|---|---|---|
| 81 | S/81/KUS 1205 | Larger Than Life/Strangers Now (p/s) | 25 |

## INNOCENT BYSTANDERS
| | | | |
|---|---|---|---|
| 80 | Rok ROK XVII/XVIII | Where Is Johnny?/DEBUTANTES: The Man In The Street (company sleeve) | 6 |

## INNOCENT VICARS
| | | | |
|---|---|---|---|
| 80 | No Brain INV 001 | She's Here/Antimatter (p/s, hand-stamped labels) | 60 |

## INNOCENTS (U.K.)
| | | | |
|---|---|---|---|
| 63 | Columbia DB 7098 | Stepping Stones/Grazina | 15 |
| 63 | Columbia DB 7173 | A Fine, Fine Bird/Spanish Holiday | 15 |
| 64 | Columbia DB 7314 | Stick With Me Baby/Not More Than Everything | 10 |

*(see also Mike Berry, Innocents & Leroys)*

## INNOCENTS (U.K.)
80   Kingdom KV 8010          One Way Love/Every Wednesday Night At Eight (p/s) ...................................... 10

*(see also Woodentops, Advertising, Secret Affair)*

## INNOCENTS (U.S.)
60   Top Rank JAR 508          Honest I Do/My Baby Hully Gullys................................................................ 30
61   Top Rank JAR 541          Gee Whiz/Please Mr Sun........................................................................... 40

*(see also Kathy Young)*

## INNOCENTS & LEROYS
64   Regal Zonophone RZ 502   HOT SIX: Don't Throw Your Love Away/My Girl Lollipop/I Love You Because/Not Fade Away/Tell Me When/I Believe (maxi-single, plain sleeve)................................ 10

*(see also Innocents [U.K.], Le-Roys)*

## INQUISITIVE PEOPLE
67   Decca F 12699             Big White Chief/Rhapsody Of Spring ............................................................ 10

## INSANE
82   Insane INSANE 1           Why Die?/War And Violence (p/s)................................................................ 15
82   Riot City RIOT 3          Politics/Dead And Gone/Last Day (p/s) ........................................................ 10
82   No Future OI 10           El Salvador/Nuclear War/Chinese Rock (p/s, with Rising Free Fanzine)................... 25

## INSANE CLOWN POSSE
98   Island ISP 705            Hokus Pokus/Prom Queen (picture disc) ...................................................... 15

## INSANE MACBETH
01   Insane 1203               True Heart (12")................................................................................... 10
00   Insane LP1                THE RETARDATION PROJECT (LP, 100 only)................................................. 60

*(see also Kinetic Effect)*

## INSECT TRUST
69   Capitol E-(S)T 109        THE INSECT TRUST (LP) .......................................................................... 80

## INSERTS
80   Supermusic SUP 26         N.M.E/The Plague/Teenage Girls (with p/s)................................................. 35
80   Supermusic SUP 26         N.M.E/The Plague/Teenage Girls (without p/s) ........................................... 25

## INSEX
79   Dining Out TUX 3          Inner Sanction/Fractured (p/s) ................................................................. 12

## INSIDE OV A COFFIN
98   Out-There OTT 1           Banking On Death (7", existence unconfirmed) ............................................... 0

*(see also Freed Unit)*

## INSIDERS
80   Satellite SATS 1002       Rollin' & Strollin'/She Had To Go (features Ray Dorset)................................... 10

*(see also Ray Dorset)*

## INSPIRAL CARPETS
80s  Own label                 SONGS OF SHALLOW INTENSITY (p/s, demo) ............................................... 20
80s  Own label                 WAITING FOR OURS (p/s, demo ) ............................................................ 20
80s  Own label                 COW (p/s, demo ) ............................................................................... 20
88   Playtime AMUSE 2          Keep The Circle Around/Theme From Cow (p/s) .............................................. 8
88   Playtime AMUSE 4          Butterfly/You Can't Take The Truth (unreleased, white label promos only) .......... 10
88   Playtime AMUSE 4T         TRAIN SURFING (12" EP, unreleased, white label test pressings only) ............... 10
88   Playtime AMUSE 2T         PLANE CRASH EP ................................................................................. 20
87   Debris DEB 6              Garage Full Of Flowers/METRO TRINITY (flexi, 4000 pressed, free with Debris magazine) ......................................................................................... 10
14   Cherry Red CRDUNG4        DUNG 4 (LP, 7", reissue) ....................................................................... 20

## INSPIRATION
73   Tavern STA 1004           Love Don't Grow On Trees/Dambusters March/Guitar Man/America ................... 15

## INSPIRATIONS (JAMAICA)
69   Camel CA 11               Down In The Park/Love Oh Love................................................................ 60
69   Camel CA 21               Wonder Of Love/Cinderella...................................................................... 60
70   Amalgamated AMG 857       Take Back Your Duck/Nothing For Nothing ................................................. 35
70   Amalgamated AMG 861       La La/Reggae Fever ............................................................................. 35
70   Amalgamated AMG 862       The Train Is Coming/Man Oh Man .............................................................. 50
71   Upsetter US 355           Confusion/THE UPSETTERS: Confusion version ............................................. 25
70   Trojan TTL 27             REGGAE FEVER (LP) .............................................................................. 50

*(see also Untouchables, Niney)*

## INSPIRATIONS (U.S.)
67   Polydor 56730             Touch Me, Kiss Me, Hold Me/What Am I Gonna Do With You? ....................... 200

## INSTANT AGONY
82   Half Man Half Biscuit DUNK 1   Think Of England/Working Class Victim/News At Ten ............................... 10
83   Flicknife FLS 022         No Sign Of Life/Taste Of Power (p/s).......................................................... 5
83   Flicknife FLS 028         Nicely Does It/We Don't Need You (p/s)..................................................... 5
83   Half Man Half Biscuit DUNK 2   Fashion Parade/Anti Police/Dead End Kids ........................................... 10

## INSTANT AUTOMATONS
80   Deleted DEP 001           PETER PAINTS HIS FENCE EP (2x7", numbered, fold-out sleeve with inserts and stickers) ........................................................................................ 25

## INSTANT FUNK
79   Salsoul 118               Crying/Dark Vader ................................................................................ 5
79   Salsoul SSLP 1511         I GOT MY MIND MADE UP (LP) ............................................................... 15

## INSTITUTION
79   Industrial Accident SGS 112   Jane and John/Stephanie (500 only, hand stamped labels) ...................... 30

*(see also Jazz Butcher)*

MINT VALUE £

## INSYNC VS MYSTERON
| | | | |
|---|---|---|---:|
| 95 | Peacefrog PF 033 | AUDIBLE ILLUSION EP (12", plain sleeve) | 10 |
| 97 | Fat Cat 12FAT 004 | TALES FROM THE CRYPT (12", custom sleeve) | 15 |

## INTELLIGENT COMMUNICATIONS
| | | | |
|---|---|---|---:|
| 91 | Jumpin' & Pumpin' 12TOT 15 | PRINCIPLES OF MOTION EP (12", p/s) | 10 |

*(see also Future Sound Of London)*

## INTENSE DEGREE
| | | | |
|---|---|---|---:|
| 88 | Strange Fruits SFPS 053 | THE PEEL SESSIONS EP (12", p/s) | 10 |
| 88 | Earache MOSH 9 | WAR IN MY HEAD (LP, with inner) | 15 |

## INTENSITY
| | | | |
|---|---|---|---:|
| 73 | Eden EDEN LP 68 | TURN ABOUT INSIDE OUT PLASTIC COATED HUMANS (LP) | 150 |

## INTENSIVE CARE
| | | | |
|---|---|---|---:|
| 87 | Back To Back BTB 001 | REBELS, ROCKETS AND RUBBERMEN (12", p/s) | 12 |

## INTENTIONS (U.K.)
| | | | |
|---|---|---|---:|
| 72 | Pye 7N 45123 | There's Nobody I'd Sooner Love/Hurry On Home | 5 |

## INTENTIONS (U.S.)/Z.Z. HILL
| | | | |
|---|---|---|---:|
| 66 | Sue IEP 711 | GIMME GIMME (EP, 2 tracks each by Intentions & Z.Z. Hill; 2 tracks mistakenly credited to Jackie Day on sleeve; in p/s) | 300 |
| 66 | Sue IEP 711 | GIMME GIMME (EP, 2 tracks each by Intentions & Z.Z. Hill; 2 tracks mistakenly credited to Jackie Day on sleeve; no p/s) | 100 |

## INTERFACE
| | | | |
|---|---|---|---:|
| 81 | Blue Beat HIT 2358 | Automaton/Electric Dreamland (p/s) | 40 |

## INTERGALACTIC TOURING BAND
| | | | |
|---|---|---|---:|
| 77 | Charisma CB 306 | Lone Station/Space Command | 6 |

## INTERNATIONAL CHRYSIS
| | | | |
|---|---|---|---:|
| 94 | PWL PWLT 303 | Rebel Rebel (The Hole Mix)/Rebel Rebel (Extended Mix) (12", promo only) | 15 |

*(see also Dead Or Alive)*

## INTERNATIONAL PENPALS
| | | | |
|---|---|---|---:|
| 03 | Radical Wallpaper RADWAL 001 | Day They Ate Ronald Reagan (p/s) | 12 |

## INTERNATIONAL SPARES
| | | | |
|---|---|---|---:|
| 81 | Spare KF 001 | No Time At All/The Windmill | 50 |

## INTERNS (JAMAICA)
| | | | |
|---|---|---|---:|
| 70 | Jackpot JP 729 | See You At Sunrise/LITTLE WONDER: Out Of Reach (B-side actually "Just Out Of Reach" by John Holt) | 12 |
| 75 | Attack ATT 8097 | Nothing Is Impossible/HARDY BOYS: Black Out | 20 |
| 79 | Burning Rockers BR 1003 | DETOUR (LP) | 30 |

*(see also Viceroys, Bob Marley & Wailers)*

## INTERNS (U.K.)
| | | | |
|---|---|---|---:|
| 64 | Philips BF 1320 | Don't You Dare/Here There Everywhere | 15 |
| 64 | Philips BF 1345 | Cry To Me/There's Love For You | 15 |
| 66 | Parlophone R 5479 | Is It Really What You Want?/Just Like Me | 50 |
| 67 | Parlophone R 5586 | Ray Of Sunshine/Please Say Something Nice | 10 |

*(see also Shadows)*

## INTERPOL
| | | | |
|---|---|---|---:|
| 00 | CHEM047CD | fukd i.d #3 PDA/Precipitate/Roland/5 (CD, stickered card sleeve, 1,000 only) | 80 |
| 02 | Matador OLE 546-7 | INTERPOL EP: PDA/Specialist (p/s) | 25 |
| 00s | Matador OLE 582-7 | Say Hello To The Angels/NYC (p/s) | 6 |
| 07 | Capitol/Parlophone CL 894 | The Heinrich Maneuver/Concert Introduction (p/s) | 6 |
| 07 | Capitol/Parlophone CLS 894 | The Heinrich Maneuver/Wrecking Ball (p/s) | 8 |
| 02 | Matador OLE 541 | TURN ON THE BRIGHT LIGHTS (LP) | 20 |
| 03 | Black Sessions 1803 | LIVE - BLACK SESSIONS (LP, red splatter vinyl) | 25 |
| 04 | Matador OLE 616-1 | ANTICS (LP) | 15 |
| 04 | Matador (no. Cat. No) | ANTICS (5 x 7" box set, only from Interpol Space Art Gallery, London) | 35 |
| 05 | Matador OLE 675 | ANTICS - REMIXES (LP) | 30 |
| 07 | Capitol/Parlophone 0946 3 96248 1 | OUR LOVE TO ADMIRE (2-LP) | 25 |

## INTERSTATE ROAD SHOW
| | | | |
|---|---|---|---:|
| 69 | President PT 249 | Grindy Grind/All I Want To Do Is To Love You | 8 |

## INTESTINES
| | | | |
|---|---|---|---:|
| 81 | Alternative Capitalists AC51 | Life In A Cardboard Box/New Recruit (p/s) | 25 |

## IN THE GYM
| | | | |
|---|---|---|---:|
| 81 | Taaga Records TAG 2 | Playing The Fool/Don't Go Slow (no sleeve) | 50 |

## IN THE NURSERY
| | | | |
|---|---|---|---:|
| 84 | Paragon VIRTUE 5 | Witness To A Scream/1984 (p/s) | 15 |
| 85 | New European BADVC 55 | Sonority - A Strength (12" EP) | 10 |
| 83 | Paragon VIRTUE 2 | WHEN CHERISHED DREAMS COME TRUE (mini-LP, silk-screened g/fold p/s) | 25 |

## IN THE WOODS...
| | | | |
|---|---|---|---:|
| 96 | Misanthropy OVL 69 | White Rabbit/Mourning The Death Of Aase (p/s) | 10 |
| 98 | Misanthropy OVL 68 | Let There Be More Light/Child Of Universal Tongue (p/s) | 10 |
| 95 | Misanthropy AMAZON 4 | HEART OF THE AGES (LP, with booklet) | 70 |
| 97 | Misanthropy AMAZON 11 | OMNIO (2-LP, gatefold sleeve, 1-sided etched disc) | 50 |

## INTIMATE OBSESSIONS
| | | | |
|---|---|---|---:|
| 85 | Third Mind TMLP 11 | EREBUS TO HADES (LP) | 15 |

## INTIMATE STRANGERS
| | | | |
|---|---|---|---:|
| 75 | Alaska ALA 1005 | Love Sounds/The Track | 50 |

## INTRA VEIN
| | | | |
|---|---|---|---:|
| 79 | Bum FP 001 | Speed Of The City/Sick (printed PVC sleeve) | 45 |

79   Bum FP 001                    Speed Of The City/Sick (stamped plain sleeve) ........................................ 35
*(see also Veins)*

## INTRIGUE
82   Pressure PRESS D 1003         I Like It (Vocal)/I Like It (Instrumental) (12") ................................. 60
84   Music Power MPR(T) 1          No Turning Back/Call Of The Heart (12") ....................................... 25
86   Intrigue INT 12-001           One Touch/Touch Down (12") ....................................................... 15

## INTRIGUES
69   London HL 10293               In A Moment/Scotchman Rock ..................................................... 10

## INTRO
83   MCA MCA 794                   Haunted Cocktails/Departure (p/s) ................................................. 8
83   MCA MCA 819                   Lost Without Your Love/Epic (p/s, with postcard) ........................... 5

## INTRODUCING DRAGONS
81   Zebra ZEBRA 3001              Via Media/Time Hangs (p/s) ....................................................... 20

## INTROZE
82   Monarch MON 037               Doin' The Lambeth Walk/Kids In Uniform .................................... 50

## INTRUDERS (1)
59   Top Rank JAR 158              Frankfurters And Sauerkraut/Creepin' ........................................ 10

## INTRUDERS (2)
66   London HL 10069              Up And Down The Ladder/United ................................................ 40
69   Action ACT 4523              Slow Drag/So Glad I'm Yours ..................................................... 15
69   Ember EMB S 254              Cowboys To Girls/Turn Back The Hands Of Time ........................ 15
72   Ember EMB S 325              Cowboys To Girls/GOOD VIBRATIONS: Shake A Hand ................... 7

## IN2XS
81   XS IVE S81 CUS 1099          Cyberman/Amount To Nothing/In Khaki/Too Many ...................... 10

## INVADERS (JAMAICA)
67   Columbia Bluebeat DB 105     Limbo Girl/Soul Of The Jungle .................................................. 10
68   Columbia Bluebeat DB 109     Stop Teasing/Invaders At The Carnival ...................................... 10
68   Studio One SO 2044           Soulful Music/SOUL VENDORS: Happy Organ ............................. 70
71   G.G. GG 4527                 Got To Go Home/PAULETTE & GEE: How Long Will You Stay? ........ 7

## INVADERS (U.K.)
70s  Jovian ZIT 2                 Launderama/Plastic Nose ............................................................ 5

## INVESTIGATORS
80   Inner City 104               Baby I'm Yours/I Want Your Love (12") ..................................... 10

## INVICTAS
64   United Artists UP 1013       Green Bow Tie/Touch Of Orchid ................................................. 7

## INVISIBLE MAN
92   Timeless DJ 005              On A Mission/Twisted/Intro (Think About It)/ The End (Drug Induced Psychosis Mix)/
                                  Bonus Turbo Cut (12") ............................................................. 30
93   Timeless DJ 006             The Beginning/The End (12") ..................................................... 20
93   Timeless DJ 007             Skyliner/Power (12") ................................................................ 20
93   Timeless DJ 008             Skyliner (Remix)/MYSTERON: U Don't Know (12") ..................... 20
95   Timeless DJ 010             Skyliner (Top Buzz's 95 VIP Mix)/The Beginning (Innerspace Remix) (12") ..... 10

## INVITATIONS (JAMAICA)
71   Crab CRAB 66                Birmingham Cat/Now You're On Your Own ................................. 20

## INVITATIONS (U.S.)
65   Stateside SS 453            Hallelujah/Written On The Wall ............................................... 50
65   Stateside SS 478            What's Wrong With My Baby?/Why Did My Baby Turn Bad? ........ 150
65   Stateside SS 478            What's Wrong With My Baby?/Why Did My Baby Turn Bad? (DJ copy) ... 300
70   Jay Boy BOY 24              How'd We Ever Get This Way?/Picking Up ................................. 35
72   Mojo 2092 055               What's Wrong With My Baby?/Why Did My Baby Turn Bad? (reissue) ..... 8
74   Polydor 2066 366            Let's Love (And Find Together)/Love Has To Grow ..................... 10

## INVOGUE
82   Street Life S 82 CUS 1474   EXPRESSIONS OF YOUTH EP ...................................................... 50

## IONA
78   Silver Scales               CUCKOO (LP) ............................................................................ 35
70s  Celtic Music CM 001         IONA (LP) ................................................................................. 35

## I.O.W. CHEROKEES
66   69 69EP 001                 I.O.W. CHEROKEES (EP, private pressing) ................................... 40

## I.P.O.H
73   Pye 7N 45215                Caveman Billy/Doggy ................................................................. 8
75   CBS 3408                    In Pursuit Of Happiness/Spearhead ............................................ 7

## IPSISSIMUS
69   Parlophone R 5774           Hold On/Lazy Woman ................................................................ 70

## IPSO FACTO
84   IF IF 7 84                  Noir Dior/Craving ..................................................................... 15
84   IF IF 8 84                  LIFE IS A CABARET - IS IT? (12" EP) ........................................... 10

## IQ
84   Jim White/IQ PROMO 101      Awake And Nervous/Through The Corridors (12", no p/s, 500 only) ......... 30
84   IQFREEB 1                   Hollow Afternoon (1-sided, Marquee gig freebie) ....................... 30
86   STAL Other Boxer 1          Nomzamo (Demo) (1-sided fan club single) ................................ 18
86   Sahara IQSD 1               It All Stops Here/Intelligence Quotient (shaped picture disc) .......... 18
87   RLOG Another Boxer 1        Fascination/The Bold Grenadier Pt. 1 (fan club single) ................. 18
88   RLOG One More Boxer 1       A Different Magic Roundabout (Honest!)/The Big Balls Of Bert Christ (fan club single) . 12
85   STAL BOXER 1                NINE IN A POND IS HERE (2-LP, 1,000 copies only) ...................... 20
*(see also Niadem's Ghost)*

## IQ PROCEDURE (ROOTS MANUVA)
94   Bluntly Speaking PHAT2      Run Tings/Can U Get With This/Big Up (12") ............................. 10

MINT VALUE £

## IQ ZERO
| | | | |
|---|---|---|---|
| 79 | Object Music OM 9 | (Everybody Kills) Insects/Electromotion/Quirky Pop Music (p/s) | 20 |
| 80 | Phony Gram SRTS/80/CUS 623 | She's So Rare/Crazy Dolls | 25 |
| 79 | Logo GO 374 | She's So Rare/Crazy Dolls (p/s) | 15 |

## IRATION STEPPAS
| | | | |
|---|---|---|---|
| 94 | Iration Steppa BS 159 | Scud Missile/High Rise Vibrations (12") | 35 |
| 03 | Tandori Space TS 012 | Too Much War/Stop The War Dub/What's Wrong/What's Wrong Dub (10") | 25 |

*(see also Dubkasm)*

## IRATION STEPPAS & TENA STELIN
| | | | |
|---|---|---|---|
| 01 | Tandori Space TSR 001 | War Inna Babylon/Dub Version | 20 |
| 01 | Tandori Space TSR 002 | Jungle Jungle/Dub Version | 20 |

*(see also Tena Stelin)*

## DAVID IRELAND
| | | | |
|---|---|---|---|
| 73 | Sovereign SOV 120 | Shoot The Family Man/Coming Up Strong | 15 |

## CLEMENT IRIE
| | | | |
|---|---|---|---|
| 88 | Blue Mountain BMD 039 | Follow Me/SENYA: Trying Woman (12") | 12 |

## IRONBELLY
| | | | |
|---|---|---|---|
| 70 | Parlophone R5864 | Woha! Buck/Wild About My Loving | 10 |

## IRON BUTTERFLY
| | | | |
|---|---|---|---|
| 68 | Atco 2091 024 | In-A-Gadda-Da-Vida/Termination (first pressing with Atco label and Polydor Records Limited type) | 20 |
| 68 | Atlantic 584 188 | Possession/Unconscious Power | 15 |
| 69 | Atlantic 584 254 | Soul Experience/In The Crowds | 12 |
| 70 | Atlantic 2091 024 | In-A-Gadda-Da-Vida/Termination | 12 |
| 68 | Atco 2465 015 | HEAVY (LP) | 25 |
| 68 | Atlantic 587/588 116 | IN-A-GADDA-DA-VIDA (LP) | 50 |
| 69 | Atco 228 011 | BALL (LP, gatefold sleeve) | 25 |
| 70 | Atlantic 2400 014 | LIVE (LP) | 18 |
| 71 | Atlantic 2401 003 | METAMORPHOSIS (LP) | 50 |

*(see also Ramatam, Captain Beyond)*

## IRON CROSS
| | | | |
|---|---|---|---|
| 72 | Spark 1079 | Little Bit Of Soul/Sunshine | 6 |
| 74 | Spark 1112 | Everybody Rock On/All The Time | 20 |

## IRON HORSE
| | | | |
|---|---|---|---|
| 71 | Bell BLL1148 | The Obeah Man/Magic Love | 20 |

## IRON MAIDEN (1)
| | | | |
|---|---|---|---|
| 70 | Gemini GMS 006 | Falling/Ned Kelly | 45 |

## IRON MAIDEN (2)
### SINGLES
| | | | |
|---|---|---|---|
| 80 | EMI EMI 5032 | Running Free/Burning Ambition (p/s) | 25 |
| 80 | EMI EMI 5065 | Sanctuary/Drifter (live)/I've Got The Fire (live) (uncensored p/s) | 45 |
| 80 | EMI EMI 5065 | Sanctuary/Drifter (live)/I've Got The Fire (live) (censored p/s) | 15 |
| 80 | EMI EMI 5105 | Women In Uniform/Invasion (p/s) | 18 |
| 80 | EMI 12EMI 5105 | Women In Uniform/Phantom Of The Opera (live)/Invasion (12", p/s) | 15 |
| 81 | EMI EMI 5145 | Twilight Zone/Wrathchild (p/s) | 15 |
| 81 | EMI EMI 5145 | Twilight Zone/Wrathchild (p/s, clear vinyl) | 25 |
| 81 | EMI EMI 5145 | Twilight Zone/Wrathchild (p/s, red vinyl) | 30 |
| 81 | EMI EMI 5145 | Twilight Zone/Wrathchild (p/s, brown vinyl mispressing) | 800 |
| 81 | EMI TCEMI 5145 | Twilight Zone/Wrathchild | 8 |
| 81 | EMI EMI 5184 | Purgatory/Genghis Khan (p/s) | 35 |
| 82 | EMI EMI 5263 | Run To The Hills/Total Eclipse (p/s) | 6 |
| 82 | EMI EMIP 5263 | Run To The Hills/Total Eclipse (picture disc, mispressed with b-side picture on both sides) | 30 |
| 82 | EMI EMIP 5263 | Run To The Hills/Total Eclipse (picture disc) | 20 |
| 82 | EMI EMI 5287 | The Number Of The Beast/Remember Tomorrow (live) (p/s) | 5 |
| 82 | EMI EMI 5287 | The Number Of The Beast/Remember Tomorrow (live) (p/s, red vinyl) | 12 |
| 83 | EMI EMI 5378 | Flight Of Icarus/I've Got The Fire (p/s) | 5 |
| 83 | EMI 12EMIP 5378 | Flight Of Icarus/I've Got The Fire (12", picture disc) | 20 |
| 83 | EMI EMI 5397 | The Trooper/Cross-Eyed Mary (p/s) | 5 |
| 83 | EMI EMIP 5397 | The Trooper/Cross-Eyed Mary (soldier-shaped picture disc) | 25 |
| 83 | EMI EMIP 5397 | The Trooper/Cross-Eyed Mary (uncut shaped picture disc) | 800 |
| 84 | EMI EMI 5489 | 2 Minutes To Midnight/Rainbow's Gold (p/s) | 5 |
| 84 | EMI 12EMI 5489 | 2 Minutes To Midnight/Rainbow's Gold/Mission From 'Arry (12", picture disc) | 15 |
| 84 | EMI EMI 5502 | Aces High/King Of Twilight (p/s) | 8 |
| 84 | EMI EMI 5502 | Aces High/King Of Twilight (mispress, A side label on both sides) | 10 |
| 84 | EMI 12EMIP 5502 | Aces High/King Of Twilight/The Number Of The Beast (live) (12", picture disc) | 20 |
| 85 | EMI EMI 5532 | Running Free (live)/Sanctuary (live) (poster p/s) | 7 |
| 85 | EMI 12EMIP 5532 | Running Free (live)/Sanctuary (live)/Murders In The Rue Morgue (live) (12", picture disc) | 20 |
| 85 | EMI EMI 5542 | Run To The Hills (live)/Phantom Of The Opera (live) (with Xmas card) | 8 |
| 85 | EMI 12EMIP 5542 | Run To The Hills (live)/Phantom Of The Opera (live)/ Losfer Words (The Big 'Orra) (live) (12", picture disc) | 20 |
| 86 | EMI EMIP 5583 | Wasted Years/Reach Out (computer-shaped picture disc) | 20 |
| 86 | EMI EMIP 5583 | Wasted Years/Reach Out (uncut computer-shaped picture disc) | 1000 |
| 86 | EMI EMI 5589 | Stranger In A Strange Land/That Girl (foldout poster p/s) | 6 |
| 86 | EMI 12EMIP 5589 | Stranger In A Strange Land/That Girl/Juanita (12", picture disc) | 18 |
| 88 | EMI EMS 49 | Can I Play With Madness/Black Bart Blues (p/s, with sticker & transfer) | 5 |
| 88 | EMI EMP 49 | Can I Play With Madness/Black Bart Blues (shaped picture disc) | 18 |

MINT VALUE £

| 88 | EMI EMP 49 | Can I Play With Madness/Black Bart Blues (uncut shaped picture disc) | 400 |
|---|---|---|---|
| 88 | EMI EMP 64 | The Evil That Men Do/Prowler '88 (gatefold p/s) | 5 |
| 88 | EMI EMP 64 | The Evil That Men Do/Prowler '88 (shaped picture disc) | 10 |
| 88 | EMI EMP 64 | The Evil That Men Do/Prowler '88 (uncut shaped picture disc) | 200 |
| 88 | EMI CDEM 64 | The Evil That Men Do/Prowler '88/Charlotte The Harlot '88 (CD, picture disc) | 10 |
| 88 | EMI EMS 79 | The Clairvoyant (live)/The Prisoner (live) (clear vinyl, poster p/s) | 6 |
| 88 | EMI EMP 79 | The Clairvoyant (live)/The Prisoner (live) (shaped picture disc) | 15 |
| 88 | EMI EMP 79 | The Clairvoyant (live)/The Prisoner (live) (uncut shaped picture disc) | 200 |
| 89 | EMI EM 117 | Infinite Dreams (live)/Killers (live) (with free patch) | 5 |
| 89 | EMI EMPD 117 | Infinite Dreams (live)/Killers (live) (uncut shaped picture disc) | 200 |
| 90 | EMI 12EMPD153 | Holy Smoke/All In Your Mind/Kill Me Ce Soir (12" picture disc with insert) | 12 |
| 90 | EMI EMS 171 | Bring Your Daughter ... To The Slaughter/I'm A Mover (1-sided etched, p/s) | 6 |
| 90 | EMI 12EMP 171 | Bring Your Daughter ... To The Slaughter/I'm A Mover (12", calendar pack) | 10 |
| 90 | EMI 12EMPD 171 | Bring Your Daughter ... To The Slaughter/I'm A Mover/ Communication Breakdown (12", picture disc, die-cut sleeve) | 12 |
| 90 | EMI CDEM 171 | Bring Your Daughter...To The Slaughter/I'm A Mover (UK pressed CD single) | 100 |
| 92 | EMI 12EMP 229 | Be Quick ...Or Be Dead/Nodding Donkey Blues/Space station No.5 (12" picture disc, with insert) | 10 |
| 92 | EMI EMPD 240 | From Here To Eternity/I Can't See My Feeling (shaped picture disc with insert) | 10 |
| 92 | EMI EMPD 240 | From Here To Eternity/I Can't See My Feeling (uncut shaped picture disc) | 150 |
| 92 | EMI EMPD 263 | Fear Of The Dark (live)/Hooks In You (live) (shaped picture disc, with insert) | 10 |
| 92 | EMI EMP 263 | Fear Of The Dark (live)/Tailgunner (live) (poster p/s) | 8 |
| 92 | EMI EMPD 263 | Fear Of The Dark (live)/Hooks In You (live) (uncut shaped picture disc) | 150 |
| 92 | EMI EMPD 263 | Fear Of The Dark (live)/Hooks In You (live) (shaped picture disc, with mispressed B-side "Tailgunner" [live]) | 18 |
| 95 | EMI CDEMS 398 | Man On The Edge/The Edge of Darkness/Judgement Day/Blaze Bailey interview (CD) | 25 |
| 95 | EMI 12EM 398 | Man On The Edge/I Live My Way (12", picture disc, with poster, die-cut sleeve) | 15 |
| 95 | EMI CDMAN 2 | Man On The Edge/The Edge Of Darkness/Sign Of The Cross (CD) | 50 |
| 98 | EMI EM 507 | The Angel And The Gambler/Blood On The World's Hands (Live) (picture disc) | 15 |
| 98 | EMI 8860690 | Futureal/ The Evil That Men Do(live)/ Man On The Edge(live)/ The Angel And The Gambler (video) (CD digi-pack Fan Club only issue with poster) | 50 |
| 00 | EMI EM 576 | Out Of The Silent Planet/Aces High (live) (red vinyl, p/s insert) | 6 |
| 02 | EMI EM 612 | Run To The Hills/Total Eclipse (live) (red vinyl, p/s) | 6 |
| 03 | EMI EM 627 | Wildest Dreams/Pass The Jam (green vinyl, stickered p/s) | 8 |
| 03 | EMI EM 633 | Rainmaker/Dance Of Death (Orchestral version) (blue vinyl, stickered p/s) | 6 |
| 05 | EMI EM 662 | The Trooper (live)/Another Life (p/s, poster, blue vinyl) | 7 |
| 05 | EMI 12EM 662 | The Trooper (live)/The Trooper/Murders In The Rue MOrgue (live) (12", picture disc) | 12 |
| 05 | EMI 666A | The Number Of The Beast/The Number Of The Beast (live at Brixton) (red vinyl, p/s, poster) | 7 |
| 06 | EMI EM 714 | Different World/Fear Of The Dark (Live 2006) (Picture disc, insert in stickered PVC sleeve) | 8 |

## SINGLES : PROMOS

| 80 | EMI EMI 5032 DJ | Running Free (One-sided 7" DJ copy) | 50 |
|---|---|---|---|
| 80 | EMI EMI 5065 | Sanctuary/Drifter (live)/I've Got The Fire (live) (DJ copy, censored p/s) | 50 |
| 90 | EMI EMDJ 153 | Holy Smoke (1-sided 7" DJ copy, radio edit, censored) | 50 |
| 90 | EMI 12EMP 153 | Holy Smoke/All In Your Mind/Kill Me Ce Soir (12", gold vinyl test pressing, promo only) | 150 |
| 90 | EMI EM 171 | Bring Your Daughter ... To The Slaughter/I'm A Mover (Clear or white vinyl Test pressing for 12" picture disc) | 100 |
| 90 | EMI (no cat. no.) | NO PRAYER FOR THE DYING (CD, with interview , photos & bio, promo only) | 100 |
| 92 | EMI (no cat. No.) | FEAR OF THE DARK (CD, interview , EPK video, colour booklet, A4 poster in luminous flip top box) | 150 |
| 95 | EMI CDMAN 1 | Man On The Edge (CD 1-track promo, slim jewel case) | 12 |
| 96 | EMI BEST 001 | BEST OF THE BEAST (CD, Steve Harris interview disc, commercial CD, video, in 40cm x 30cm, flip-up 3D presentation box with 60-page book, 2 photographs, biography, promo only) | 200 |
| 97 | EMI CDINPROF 001 | In Profile (CD, 31 track edit band history picture disc custom sleeve) | 35 |
| 98 | EMI CDONPROF 001 | IN PROFILE (CD) | 30 |
| 98 | EMI VIRTCDXI 003 | Futureal (CD, 1-track in custom card sleeve) | 25 |
| 98 | EMI HELLROM001 | Maiden Hell promotional CD-Rom in full colour custom card sleeve | 25 |
| 99 | EMI EDHUNTER 666 | ED HUNTER DEMO (CD-Rom, card p/s with booklet, press info and photo) | 40 |
| 00 | EMI CDEMDJ 568 | The Wicker Man (CD, 1-track promo in slim jewel case) | 10 |
| 00 | EMI no cat. no. | Tommy Vance Previews: The Wicker Man/Ghost Of The Navigator/ Brave New World/ Dream Of Mirrors/The Nomad (CD-R with Thomas The Vance intros) | 50 |
| 00 | EMI CDIN 130 | BRAVE NEW WORLD (promo interview CD) | 25 |
| 02 | EMI RIOINTCD 001 | ROCK IN RIO (Promo interview CD, with colour booklet) | 50 |
| 02 | EMI CDSP255 | EDDIE'S ARCHIVE (CD, 8 track sampler in card sleeve) | 50 |
| 03 | EMI CDEMDJ633 | Rainmaker (CD, 1-track promo in custom card sleeve) | 10 |
| 03 | EMI CDEMDJ627 | Wildest Dreams (CD, 1-track promo in custom card sleeve) | 10 |
| 04 | EMI CDEMDJ636 | No More Lies (CD, 1-track promo in custom card sleeve) | 15 |
| 04 | BMG PUB049 | Int Iron Maiden 10 track promo CD in custom sleeve | 50 |

## EPs

| 79 | EMI EMCP 3400 | THE SOUNDHOUSE TAPES (EP mispressing with labels on wrong sides, Matrix numbers ROK-1A SA LYN 7627-1T/ROK-1B EG SA LYN 7628-1T, p/s) | 600 |
|---|---|---|---|
| 79 | Rock Hard ROK 1 | THE SOUNDHOUSE TAPES (EP, p/s; Matrix ROK-1A EG SA LYN 7627-1T/ ROK-1B EG SA LYN 7628-1T. counterfeits have slightly glossier sleeves. Any with different p/s and coloured vinyl are also counterfeit) | 200 |
| 81 | EMI 12EMI 5219 | MAIDEN JAPAN EP (12" EP, p/s) | 15 |
| 93 | EMI 12EMP 288 | HALLOWED BE THY NAME EP (12", picture disc) | 12 |

## ALBUMS

| 80 | EMI EMC 3330 | IRON MAIDEN (LP, with poster) | 40 |
|---|---|---|---|
| 80 | EMI EMC 3330 | IRON MAIDEN (LP, without poster) | 15 |

MINT VALUE £

| | | | |
|---|---|---|---|
| 82 | EMI EMCP 3400 | THE NUMBER OF THE BEAST (LP, picture disc, with inner) | 40 |
| 84 | EMI POWERP 1 | POWERSLAVE (LP, picture disc) | 40 |
| 85 | EMI ES 24 0426 3 | LIVE AFTER DEATH (2-LP, gatefold, inners & booklet) | 20 |
| 88 | EMI EMDP 1006 | SEVENTH SON OF A SEVENTH SON (LP, picture disc, with banner) | 35 |
| 90 | EMI EMD 1017 | NO PRAYER FOR THE DYING (LP, inner) | 15 |
| 90 | EMI EMPD 1017 | NO PRAYER FOR THE DYING (LP, picture disc, die cut sleeve) | 25 |
| 90 | EMI (no cat. no.) | THE FIRST TEN YEARS - UP THE IRONS (10 x 12" double packs, box set available by mail order with tokens from records) | 175 |
| 90 | EMI (no cat. no.) | THE FIRST TEN YEARS - UP THE IRONS (10 x CD, box set available by mail order with tokens from CDs) | 100 |
| 92 | EMI EMD 1032 | FEAR OF THE DARK (2-LP with merchandising leaflet) | 60 |
| 93 | EMI DON 1 | LIVE AT DONINGTON (3-LP, numbered) | 70 |
| 93 | EMI EMD 1042 | A REAL LIVE ONE (LP, gatefold sleeve with inner sleeve) | 20 |
| 93 | EMI EMD 1048 | A REAL DEAD ONE (LP, gatefold sleeve and inner sleeve) | 20 |
| 95 | EMI 724383581917 | THE X FACTOR (2-LP, clear vinyl, gatefold with poster) | 60 |
| 96 | EMI (no cat. No.) | THE STORY SO FAR PART 1 (5xCD box set, 1000 copies only) | 300 |
| 96 | EMI (no cat. no.) | THE STORY SO FAR PART 2 (5xCD box set, 1000 copies only) | 300 |
| 96 | EMI EMDX 1097 | BEST OF THE BEAST (4-LP box set, with inners, book and bonus tracks) | 100 |
| 97 | EMI LPCENT 35 | IRON MAIDEN (LP, reissue, EMI centenary, stickered sleeve) | 30 |
| 97 | EMI LPCENT 7 | THE NUMBER OF THE BEAST (LP, reissue, 180gm vinyl) | 30 |
| 98 | EMI LPCENT 35 | IRON MAIDEN (LP, reissue, 180gm vinyl) | 30 |
| 98 | EMI 4979990 | EDDIE'S HEAD (13 CD boxset, plastic skull with flashing eyes) | 175 |
| 98 | EMI 4939151 | VIRTUAL XI (2-LP gatefold, with inner sleeves) | 60 |
| 00 | EMI 526 6051 | BRAVE NEW WORLD (2-LP gatefold, inner sleeves) | 35 |
| 02 | EMI 538 64316 | ROCK IN RIO (3-LP, picture discs, trifold sleeve) | 70 |
| 02 | EMI 544 2772 | EDDIE'S ARCHIVE (6-CD, tin box with insert, shot glass, pewter ring and Parchment. 1st issue blue lining) | 100 |
| 02 | EMI 544 2772 | EDDIE'S ARCHIVE (6-CD, tin box with insert, shot glass, pewter ring and Parchment. 2nd issue red lining) | 80 |
| 03 | EMI 592 3401 | DANCE OF DEATH (2-LP, picture disc, gatefold sleeve and inner sleeves) | 40 |
| 05 | EMI 336 4371 | DEATH ON THE ROAD (2-LP, picture disc gatefold) | 30 |
| 06 | EMI 372 3211 | A MATTER OF LIFE AND DEATH (2-LP, picture disc, gatefold, inner sleeves) | 30 |

*(see also Bruce Dickinson, Di'Anno, Gogmagog, Samson, Urchin, Xero, Lionheart, Pat Travers, Stratus, Nicko McBrain, Money, White Spirit, McEnroe & Cash, Speed)*

## IRON VIRGIN
| | | | |
|---|---|---|---|
| 74 | Deram DM 408 | Jet/Midnight Hitcher | 15 |
| 74 | Deram DM 416 | Rebels Rule/Ain't No Clown | 25 |

## NEVILLE IRONS
| | | | |
|---|---|---|---|
| 68 | Blue Cat BS 104 | Soul Glide/DYNAMICS: My Friends | 45 |

*(see also Neville Hinds)*

## IRRESTIBLE FORCE
| | | | |
|---|---|---|---|
| 92 | Rising High RSNLP 5 | FLYING HIGH (2-LP) | 25 |

## ANDY IRVINE
| | | | |
|---|---|---|---|
| 80 | Tara 3002 | RAINY SUNDAYS, WINDY DREAMS (LP, lyric insert) | 15 |

## ANDY IRVINE & PAUL BRADY
| | | | |
|---|---|---|---|
| 76 | Mulligan LUN 008 | ANDY IRVINE & PAUL BRADY (LP) | 30 |

*(see also Dr. Strangely Strange)*

## LONNIE IRVING
| | | | |
|---|---|---|---|
| 60 | Melodisc MEL 1546 | Pinball Machine/I Got Blues On My Mind | 40 |

## IRVING 6
| | | | |
|---|---|---|---|
| 70s | Port O Jam PJ4116 | Ossie's Special/Trouble | 20 |

## (BIG) DEE IRWIN
| | | | |
|---|---|---|---|
| 64 | Stateside SS 261 | Donkey Walk/Someday You'll Understand Why | 10 |
| 64 | Colpix PX 11040 | Heigh-ho/It's My Birthday | 8 |
| 64 | Colpix PX 11050 | Personality/It's Only A Paper Moon | 8 |
| 65 | Stateside SS 450 | You Satisfy My Needs/I Wanna Stay Right Here With You | 125 |
| 65 | Stateside SS 450 | You Satisfy My Needs/I Wanna Stay Right Here With You (DJ copy) | 200 |
| 68 | Minit MLF 11013 | I Can't Stand The Pain/My Hope To Die Girl (as Dee Irwin) | 15 |

## BIG DEE IRWIN & LITTLE EVA
| | | | |
|---|---|---|---|
| 63 | Colpix PX 11010 | Swinging On A Star/Another Night With The Boys (Little Eva uncredited) | 5 |
| 63 | Colpix PXE 301 | SWINGING ON A STAR (EP) | 20 |

*(see also Little Eva, Suzi & Big Dee Irwin)*

## DAVID ISAACS
| | | | |
|---|---|---|---|
| 66 | Island WI 261 | I'd Rather Be Lonely/See That Man | 80 |
| 68 | Trojan TR 616 | Place In The Sun/UPSETTER ALL STARS: Handy-Cap | 50 |
| 69 | Upsetter US 302 | Good Father/SLIM SMITH: What A Situation | 30 |
| 69 | Upsetter US 305 | I've Got Memories/I'm Leaving | 30 |
| 69 | Upsetter US 311 | He'll Have To Go/Since You're Gone | 30 |
| 69 | Upsetter US 319 | Who To Tell/BUSTY BROWN: I Can't See Myself Cry | 30 |
| 69 | Punch PH 6 | I Can't Take It Anymore/LLOYD DOUGLAS: Anyway | 10 |
| 71 | Punch PH 84 | You'll Be Sorry/Knock Three Times | 12 |
| 71 | Bullet BU 459 | Just Enough/ROY PATIN: Standing (B-side actually by Roy Panton) | 12 |
| 71 | Tropical AL 006 | Love Has Join Us/MAX ROMEO: Cross Over The Bridge (correct title for A-side is 'Love Has Joined Us') | 8 |
| 73 | Upsetter US 400 | Stranger On The Shore/DILLINGER: John Devour | 70 |
| 73 | Bread BR 1118 | Just Enough/We Are Neighbours | 5 |
| 79 | Attack TACK 13 | Just Like A Sea (with Jah Thomas)/WITTY'S ALL STARS: Just Like A Sea (Version) (12") | 18 |

*(see also Upsetters)*

## GREGORY ISAACS

| | | | |
|---|---|---|---|
| 70 | Escort ERT 833 | While There Is Life/HARRY YOUNG: Come On Over | 15 |
| 70 | Success RE 914 | Too Late/KINGSTONIANS: You Can't Wine | 25 |
| 70 | Bullet BU 448 | Set Back/SYDNEY'S ALLSTARS: Version II | 15 |
| 71 | Big Shot BI 584 | Lonely Man/RUPIE EDWARDS ALL STARS: Lonely Man Version | 12 |
| 73 | Ackee ACK 522 | I'm Coming Home/Version | 5 |
| 73 | Green Door GD 4054 | Lonely Soldier/IMPACT ALL STARS: Version | 12 |
| 74 | Pyramid PYR 7012 | Innocent People Cry/Version | 8 |
| 74 | Attack ATT 8066 | Love Is Overdue Part 1/Love Is Overdue Part 2 | 8 |
| 74 | Attack ATT 8081 | Don't Go/Dubwise | 8 |
| 74 | Stop Points DL 0022 | End Of The World/Gregory Shuffle | 10 |
| 75 | Black Wax WAX 9 | Sunshine For Me/Version | 8 |
| 75 | Attack ATT 8095 | Bad Da/Ad Dab | 8 |
| 75 | Attack ATT 8106 | Fly Little Silver Bird/Dub | 8 |
| 75 | Camel CA 2008 | Lonely Days/Version | 8 |
| 75 | Bullet BU 555 | Lonely Days/Version | 8 |
| 76 | Morpheus MOR 1018 | Extra Classic/Version | 12 |
| 76 | Third World TW 032 | Look Before You Leap/K. SMILEY: Sata | 15 |
| 76 | Morpheus MOR 1016 | Rasta Business/Version | 15 |
| 76 | Morpheus MOR 1017 | Black Kill A Black/Version | 25 |
| 77 | Golden Age GAM 05 | Mr. Cop/Mr. Cop Dub | 15 |
| 77 | Observer OBMM-1000 | Soul On Fire/CHRISTINE: Saturday Night/TYRONE TAYLOR: Sufferation/ In Style (12") | 40 |
| 77 | GGs GG 040 | The Border/Out Of Rome (12", with U BROWN) | 10 |
| 78 | Observer | Rock On/Murder Observer Style/DENNIS BROWN & DILLINGER: Jah Is Watching/ Hustling (12") | 50 |
| 78 | DEB DEB 004 | Mr Know It All/OSSIE HIBBERT & REVOLUTIONARIES: War Of The Stars (12") | 25 |
| 78 | Hawkeye HE 008 | John Public/LEGGO ALL STARS: Enemy No 1 | 8 |
| 78 | Star PTP 1002 | Lonely Days/U ROY: Nanny Skank (12") | 15 |
| 79 | Front Line FLS 12112 | Soon Forward/Uncle Joe/Come Off Mi Toe (Feat. Prince Far I) (12") | 15 |
| 79 | Niagra NIADD 104 | Going Down Town/Motherless Children (12") | 10 |
| 80 | Pre PRES 8 | Poor And Clean/Tribute To Wada | 10 |
| 80 | African Museum (no number) | If You See My Mary/Mary's Special (12", blue vinyl) | 20 |
| 84 | Fu Manchu PC 15484 | No One But Me/Version (12", p/s) | 15 |
| 85 | African Museum AF 0050 | G.P./Version (12") | 25 |
| 80 | Solomonic SM 002 | Sunday Morning/DENNIS BROWN: Running Around (12") | 25 |
| 88 | Greensleeves GRED 221 | Rumours/More Rumours (12") | 30 |
| 88 | Greensleeves GRED 225 | Rough Neck/Version (12" with the Mighty Diamonds) | 30 |
| 89 | Jah Shaka SHAKA 874 | Just Infatuation/Just Dub (12") | 15 |
| 89 | Greensleeves GRED 256 | Report To Me/Report To Me (continued) (12") | 30 |
| 75 | Trojan TRLS 102 | IN PERSON (LP) | 15 |
| 76 | Trojan TRLS 121 | ALL I HAVE IS LOVE (LP) | 20 |
| 78 | Conflict COLP 2002 | EXTRA CLASSIC (LP) | 20 |
| 80 | Shack BITE 200 | EXTRA CLASSIC (LP, reissue) | 20 |
| 78 | Burning Sounds BS1010 | SLUM – GREGORY ISAACS IN DUB (LP) | 30 |
| 78 | DEB DEB LP 04 | MR ISAACS (LP) | 30 |
| 78 | Virgin Front Line FL 1020 | COOL RULER (LP) | 18 |
| 79 | Virgin Front Line FL 1044 | SOON FORWARD (LP) | 30 |
| 82 | Island 9721 | NIGHT NURSE (LP, blue vinyl with poster) | 18 |
| 83 | Burning Sounds BS 1051 | SLUM DUB (LP) | 25 |
| 83 | Pre PREX1 | THE LONELY LOVER (LP) | 15 |

## IKE ISAACS

| | | | |
|---|---|---|---|
| 68 | Morgan MR 116P | I LIKE IKE (LP) | 15 |

## ISCA FAYRE

| | | | |
|---|---|---|---|
| 76 | Candle CAN 761 | THEN AROUND ME YOUNG AND OLD (LP) | 15 |

## ISH

| | | | |
|---|---|---|---|
| 79 | TKS TKR 7540 | Faster Than A Speeding Bullet/Don't Stop | 6 |

## JON ISHERWOOD

| | | | |
|---|---|---|---|
| 70 | Decca LK/SKL 5051 | A LAUGHING CRY (LP) | 15 |

## ISHMAEL UNITED

| | | | |
|---|---|---|---|
| 79 | Kingsway 5NIL | Song Of The Last Generation/Crowd Trouble | 20 |

## ISHMAEL & ANDY

| | | | |
|---|---|---|---|
| 73 | Myrrh MYR 1005 | READY SALTED (LP) | 20 |

## ISLANDERS (1)

| | | | |
|---|---|---|---|
| 59 | Top Rank JAR 215 | The Enchanted Sea/Pollyanna | 8 |
| 60 | Top Rank JAR 305 | Blue Train/Tornado | 6 |

## ISLANDERS (2)

| | | | |
|---|---|---|---|
| 65 | Fontana TF 577 | It Ain't Me Babe/Four Strong Winds | 10 |
| 65 | Fontana TF 605 | Walkin' Away/Roberta Let Your Hair Hang Down | 5 |

## JIMMY ISLE

| | | | |
|---|---|---|---|
| 59 | London HLS 8832 | Diamond Ring/I've Been Waiting | 70 |
| 59 | London HLS 8832 | Diamond Ring/I've Been Waiting | 20 |
| 60 | Top Rank JAR 274 | Billy Boy/Oh Judy | 15 |

## ISLEY BROTHERS

| | | | |
|---|---|---|---|
| 59 | RCA RCA 1149 | Shout (Parts 1 & 2) (tri centre) | 30 |
| 59 | RCA RCA 1149 | Shout (Parts 1 & 2) (round centre) | 25 |
| 59 | RCA RCA 1149 | Shout (Parts 1 & 2) (78) | 200 |
| 60 | RCA RCA 1172 | Respectable/I'm Gonna Knock On Your Door | 20 |

# ISOLATION

| | | | |
|---|---|---|---|
| 60 | RCA RCA 1190 | How Deep Is The Ocean/He's Got The Whole World In His Hands | 20 |
| 60 | RCA RCA 1213 | Tell Me Who/Say You Love Me Too | 20 |
| 62 | Stateside SS 112 | Twist And Shout/Spanish Twist | 15 |
| 62 | Stateside SS 132 | Twistin' With Linda/You Better Come Home | 15 |
| 63 | Stateside SS 218 | Nobody But Me/I'm Laughing To Keep From Crying | 20 |
| 63 | United Artists UP 1034 | Tango/She's Gone | 18 |
| 64 | United Artists UP 1050 | Shake It With Me Baby/Stagger Lee | 20 |
| 64 | Atlantic AT 4010 | The Last Girl/Looking For A Love | 45 |
| 66 | Tamla Motown TMG 555 | This Old Heart Of Mine (Is Weak For You)/There's No Love Left (1st press with narrow print on label) | 20 |
| 66 | Tamla Motown TMG 555 | This Old Heart Of Mine (Is Weak For You)/There's No Love Left (2nd re-press - 1968 - with wider print) | 10 |
| 66 | Tamla Motown TMG 566 | Take Some Time Out For Love/Who Could Ever Doubt My Love | 35 |
| 66 | Tamla Motown TMG 572 | I Guess I'll Always Love You/I Hear A Symphony (1st pressing with "sold subject to" on centre piece) | 25 |
| 67 | Tamla Motown TMG 606 | Got To Have You Back/Just Ain't Enough Love | 25 |
| 68 | Tamla Motown TMG 652 | Take Me In Your Arms (Rock Me A Little While)/Why When Love Is Gone | 30 |
| 69 | Tamla Motown TMG 683 | I Guess I'll Always Love You/It's Out Of The Question | 8 |
| 69 | Tamla Motown TMG 693 | Behind A Painted Smile/One Too Many Heartaches | 7 |
| 69 | Major Minor MM 621 | It's Your Thing/Don't Give It Away | 10 |
| 69 | Tamla Motown TMG 708 | Put Yourself In My Place/Little Miss Sweetness | 7 |
| 69 | Major Minor MM 631 | I Turned You On/I Know Who You Been Socking It To | 6 |
| 69 | Tamla Motown TMG 719 | Take Some Time Out For Love/Who Could Ever Doubt My Love (reissue) | 7 |
| 70 | Stateside SS 2162 | Was It Good To You?/I Got To Get Myself Together | 6 |
| 71 | Stateside SS 2188 | Warpath/I Got To Find Me One | 6 |
| 71 | Stateside SS 2193 | Love The One You're With/He's Got Your Love | 10 |
| 73 | Tamla Motown TMG 877 | Tell Me It's Just A Rumour, Baby/Save Me From This Misery | 8 |
| 73 | Epic EPC 1980 | The Highways Of My Life/Don't Let Me Be Lonely Tonight | 5 |
| 74 | Epic EPC 2803 | Need A Little Taste Of Love/If You Were There | 5 |
| 76 | DJM DJS 640 | Twist And Shout/Time After Time (reissue) | 5 |
| 79 | RCA PC 9411 | Shout/Respectable/Tell Me Who (12", p/s) | 10 |
| 64 | RCA RCX 7149 | THE ISLEY BROTHERS (EP) | 80 |
| 60 | RCA RD 27165 | SHOUT (LP, mono) | 60 |
| 60 | RCA SF 7055 | SHOUT (LP, stereo) | 100 |
| 64 | United Artists ULP 1064 | THE FAMOUS ISLEY BROTHERS - TWISTING AND SHOUTING (LP) | 80 |
| 66 | Tamla Motown TML 11034 | THIS OLD HEART OF MINE (IS WEAK FOR YOU) (LP, mono) | 30 |
| 66 | STML 11034 | THIS OLD HEART OF MINE (IS WEAK FOR YOU) (LP, stereo) | 35 |
| 68 | T. Motown TML 11066 | SOUL ON THE ROCKS (LP, mono) | 30 |
| 68 | T. Motown STML 11066 | SOUL ON THE ROCKS (LP, stereo) | 35 |
| 69 | Major Minor SMLP 59 | IT'S OUR THING (LP) | 25 |
| 69 | T. Motown TML 11112 | BEHIND A PAINTED SMILE (LP, mono) | 25 |
| 69 | T. Motown (S)TML 11112 | BEHIND A PAINTED SMILE (LP, stereo) | 22 |
| 70 | Stateside SSL 10300 | THE BROTHERS: ISLEY (LP) | 22 |

## ISOLATION
| | | | |
|---|---|---|---|
| 73 | Riverside HASLP 2083 | ISOLATION (LP, private pressing with insert) | 300 |

## ISOTOPE
| | | | |
|---|---|---|---|
| 74 | Gull GULP 1002 | ISOTOPE (LP) | 20 |
| 74 | Gull GULP 1006 | ILLUSION (LP) | 20 |
| 75 | Gull GULP 1017 | DEEP END (LP, 1976 on both labels) | 20 |

*(see also Brian Auger, Hugh Hopper)*

## ISRAELITES
| | | | |
|---|---|---|---|
| 69 | Downtown DT 413 | Moma Moma/Melody For Two | 25 |
| 69 | Downtown DT 421 | Games People Play/AUDREY: One Fine Day | 25 |
| 69 | Downtown DT 433 | Seven Books/Chucka Beat | 20 |
| 70 | J-Dan JDN 4410 | Can't Help From Crying/Can't Get Used To Losing You | 8 |

*(see also Music Doctors)*

## ISRAEL VIBRATION
| | | | |
|---|---|---|---|
| 78 | Harvest HAR 184 | The Same Song/Weep And Moan | 15 |
| 79 | Harvest 12 HAR 5189 | Crisis/Crisis Dub (12", feat. Augustus Pablo) | 30 |
| 79 | Harvest SHSP 4099 | THE SAME SONG (LP, black and red Harvest label) | 25 |
| 88 | RAS RAS 3037 | STRENGTH OF MY LIFE (LP) | 30 |
| 90 | RAS RAS 3054 | PRAISES (LP) | 30 |
| 90 | Greensleeves GREL 148 | UNCONQUERED PEOPLE (LP, reissue) | 15 |

## HUGHIE ISSACHAAR
| | | | |
|---|---|---|---|
| 82 | House Of Asher HA2 | Don't Pretent You Love/Dub (12") | 15 |

## HUGHY ISSACHAR
| | | | |
|---|---|---|---|
| 86 | Melody Muzik MM 001 | Mountain Rock/ORIGINAL ROCKERS: So Shall It Be (12") | 50 |

## ITALS (JAMAICA)
| | | | |
|---|---|---|---|
| 67 | Giant GN 8 | New Loving (with Soul Brothers)/I Told You Little Girl | 40 |
| 67 | Giant GN 12 | Don't Throw It Away/Make Up Your Mind (both with Carib-Beats) | 60 |
| 70 | Big Shot BI-561 | Put It On/Rasta Isies (as Hitals) | 25 |
| 70 | Big BG304 | Everytime/Version | 15 |
| 71 | Big BG 325 | Ba-Da-Doo-Ba-Dey/RUPIE EDWARDS ALL STARS: Version | 10 |

*(see also Alton Ellis, Honeyboy)*

## ITALS (U.K.)
| | | | |
|---|---|---|---|
| 71 | Black Swan BW 1404 | Dawn Patrol/Whiskey Bonga (DJ and Rhythm) | 12 |
| 71 | Black Swan BW 1407 | Judgement Rock (actually by Charlie Ace)/Night West | 12 |

## ITHACA
| | | | |
|---|---|---|---|
| 73 | Merlin HF 6 | A GAME FOR ALL WHO KNOW (LP, with insert) | 750 |

| | | | |
|---|---|---|---|
| 93 | Background | A GAME FOR ALL WHO KNOW (LP, reissue) .................................................. | 25 |

*(see also Friends, Alice Through The Looking Glass, Agincourt, Tomorrow Come Someday, BBC Radiophonic Workshop)*

## IT'S A BEAUTIFUL DAY

| | | | |
|---|---|---|---|
| 69 | CBS 4457 | White Bird/Wasted Union Blues ................................................................ | 8 |
| 70 | CBS 4933 | Soapstone Mountain/Do You Remember The Sun ................................. | 15 |
| 73 | CBS 1625 | Ain't That Lovin' You Baby/Time ............................................................. | 5 |
| 69 | CBS 63722 | IT'S A BEAUTIFUL DAY (LP, gatefold sleeve) ........................................ | 35 |
| 70 | CBS 64065 | MARRYING MAIDEN (LP) ......................................................................... | 30 |
| 72 | CBS 64314 | CHOICE QUALITY STUFF - ANYTIME (LP, insert) .................................... | 25 |

## IT'S IMMATERIAL

| | | | |
|---|---|---|---|
| 80 | Hit Machine HIT 001 | Young Man (Seeks Interesting Job)/Doosha (A Success Story) (p/s) ............ | 6 |
| 81 | Inevitable Hit Machine IHM 002 | Imitate The Worm/The Worm Turns (p/s) ........................................... | 10 |
| 86 | Siren SIREN 15 | Driving Away From Home/Trains, Boats, Planes (p/s) ........................ | 6 |
| 84 | Eternal JF 4 | A Gigantic Raft In The Philipines/The Mermaid (p/s) ........................ | 10 |

## IT'S A TIGHTROPE

| | | | |
|---|---|---|---|
| 82 | TR 00112 | Soho/Loves Like That ............................................................................. | 8 |

## IVAN

| | | | |
|---|---|---|---|
| 58 | Coral Q 72341 | Real Wild Child/Oh, You Beautiful Doll ............................................... | 200 |
| 58 | Coral Q 72341 | Real Wild Child/Oh, You Beautiful Doll (78) ...................................... | 50 |

*(see also Jerry Allison, Crickets)*

## IVAN D. JUNIORS

| | | | |
|---|---|---|---|
| 63 | Oriole CB 1874 | Catch You If I Can/On My Mind .............................................................. | 20 |

## IVANS MEADS

| | | | |
|---|---|---|---|
| 65 | Parlophone R 5342 | A Little Sympathy/The Sins Of A Family ............................................. | 50 |
| 66 | Parlophone R 5503 | We'll Talk About It Tomorrow/The Bottle .......................................... | 40 |

## IVEYS

| | | | |
|---|---|---|---|
| 68 | Apple APPLE 5 | Maybe Tomorrow/And Her Daddy's A Millionaire ............................. | 60 |
| 69 | Apple APPLE 14 | Dear Angie/No Escaping Your Love (unreleased; Europe & Japan only) .......... | 0 |
| 68 | Apple SAPCOR 8 | MAYBE TOMORROW (LP, unissued; Europe & Japan only) ................. | 0 |
| 92 | Apple SAPCOR 8 | MAYBE TOMORROW (LP, reissue, gatefold sleeve & bonus 12" [SAPCOR 82]) ............. | 25 |

*(see also Badfinger, Pleasure Garden)*

## IVOR & SHEILA

| | | | |
|---|---|---|---|
| 81 | Eron 027 | CHANGING TIMES (LP, with insert) ....................................................... | 30 |

## IVORIES

| | | | |
|---|---|---|---|
| 85 | Kent TOWN 103 | Please Stay/TOMMY HUNT: The Work Song .................................... | 10 |

*(see also Tommy Hunt)*

## JACKIE IVORY

| | | | |
|---|---|---|---|
| 66 | Atlantic AT 4075 | Hi-Heel Sneakers/Do It To Death ....................................................... | 20 |
| 65 | Atlantic ATL 5046 | SOUL DISCOVERY (LP) ......................................................................... | 60 |
| 65 | Atlantic ATL 5046 | SOUL DISCOVERY (LP, 1966 reissue) .................................................. | 25 |

## IVORY SUN

| | | | |
|---|---|---|---|
| 70 | Jupiter | Another Yesterday/ Rainy Tomorrow/Black Gold ............................. | 60 |

## IVY

| | | | |
|---|---|---|---|
| 94 | Sarah SARAH 91 | Wish You Would/Nowhere To Mourn (p/s) ....................................... | 15 |
| 94 | Sarah SARAH 92 | Avenge/Sound The Deep Waters ......................................................... | 15 |

## IVY LEAGUE

| | | | |
|---|---|---|---|
| 64 | Piccadilly 7N 35200 | What More Do You Want?/Wait A Minute .......................................... | 10 |
| 65 | Piccadilly 7N 35222 | Funny How Love Can Be/Lonely Room .............................................. | 5 |
| 65 | Piccadilly 7N 35228 | That's Why I'm Crying/A Girl Like You .............................................. | 5 |
| 65 | Piccadilly 7N 35251 | Tossing And Turning/Graduation Day ............................................... | 5 |
| 65 | Piccadilly 7N 35267 | Our Love Is Slipping Away/I Could Make You Fall In Love ................. | 5 |
| 66 | Piccadilly 7N 35294 | Running Round In Circles/Rain Rain Go Away ................................... | 5 |
| 66 | Piccadilly 7N 35326 | Willow Tree/One Day ......................................................................... | 5 |
| 66 | Piccadilly 7N 35348 | My World Fell Down/When You're Young ......................................... | 8 |
| 67 | Piccadilly 7N 35365 | Four And Twenty Hours/Arrivederci Baby ........................................ | 7 |
| 67 | Piccadilly 7N 35397 | Suddenly Things/Tomorrow Is Another Day ..................................... | 7 |
| 67 | Pye 7N 17386 | Thank You For Loving Me/In The Not Too Distant Future ................. | 10 |
| 65 | Piccadilly NEP 34038 | FUNNY HOW LOVE CAN BE (EP) ......................................................... | 15 |
| 65 | Piccadilly NEP 34042 | TOSSING AND TURNING (EP) .............................................................. | 15 |
| 66 | Piccadilly NEP 34048 | OUR LOVE IS SLIPPING AWAY (EP) ..................................................... | 20 |
| 65 | Piccadilly NEP 34046 | THE HOLLY AND THE IVY LEAGUE (EP) ............................................... | 10 |
| 65 | Piccadilly NPL 38015 | THIS IS THE IVY LEAGUE (LP) ............................................................. | 30 |

*(see also Carter-Lewis, White Plains, Edison Lighthouse, Flowerpot Men, Kestrels, One & One, Johnny Shadow, Perry Ford, First Class, Friends, Warm Sensations)*

## IVY THREE

| | | | |
|---|---|---|---|
| 60 | London HLW 9178 | Yogi/Was Judy There .......................................................................... | 15 |

## DAFYDD IWAN

| | | | |
|---|---|---|---|
| 69 | Welsh Teldisc WD 904 | Croeso/Chwedeg Nain (p/s) ............................................................... | 8 |

## IWASACUBSCOUT

| | | | |
|---|---|---|---|
| 06 | Fear And (No Cat. No.) | We Were Made To Love/That's Not A Crate, It's A Box Of Heaven Part Two (500 only, p/s) ............ | 6 |

## IZZY POUND

| | | | |
|---|---|---|---|
| 69 | Plexium PXM 9 | Pumpkin Miny/Na Na Na Na ............................................................... | 40 |

MINT VALUE £

## CLUE J. & HIS BLUES BLASTERS
60   Blue Beat BB 15      Easy Snappin'/Goin' Home (with vocal by Theophilus Beckford) ....................12
61   Blue Beat BB 37      Lovers' Jive/Wicked And Dreadful (actually with Neville Esson) ..................12
61   Blue Beat BB 60      Little Willie/Pine Juice ....................12

## DAVID J. (& J. WALKERS)
81   4AD AD 112           Nothing/Armour (as David Jay & René Halkett) (p/s, with lyric sheet) ............5
*(see also Bauhaus)*

## TONY J.
75   Stonehouse 001       Telephone Line/Telephone Version ....................5

## JABBERWOCK
77   MCA MCA 264          Sneakin' Snaky/Fortune Teller ....................15

## JAB JAB MUSIC
81   Shades SH3           Loneliness Is Not Happiness/Sweet Socca Music ....................10

## JABULA
75   Caroline CA 2004     JABULA (LP) ....................20
78   Jabula JBL 2003      AFRIKA AWAKE (LP) ....................18

## JOY JACINTH
83   Zebratone ZTD 93     Baby Boy/Red Lights (12") ....................15

## JACK (BERNARD) & BEANSTALKS
69   Supreme SUP 203      Work It Up/Chatty Chatty ....................12
*(see also Kingstonians)*

## BILLY JACK (& CIMARONS)
70   Grape GR 3018        Let's Work Together/CORPORATION: Jam Monkey ....................15
70   Big Shot BI 558      Once A Man/Soul Mood (as Billy Jack & Cimarons) ....................7
70   Big Shot BI 559      Bet Your Life I Do/CANDY & CIMARONS: Ace Of Hearts ....................7
*(see also Candy)*

## BOBBY JACK
59   Top Rank JAR 190     Tempting Me/Early Mornin' ....................8

## JACKAL (1)
74   BASF BA 1009         The Year Of The Tiger/Big Star ....................10

## JACKAL (2)
86   Crim. Damage CRI 12-134   Underneath The Arches/Thunder Machine (12", p/s) ....................15
*(see also Renegade Soundwave)*

## JACKIE
78   Fashion FAD 002      It's Too Late Baby/Fashion On Fine Style (12") ....................20

## JACKIE & BRIDIE
68   Major Minor MM 562   Come Me Little Son/We Only Needed Time ....................6
64   Fontana TL 5212      HOLD BACK THE DAWN (LP) ....................25
70   Concord CONS 1002    FOLK WORLD OF JACKIE AND BRIDIE (LP) ....................15
71   Galliard GAL 4009    THE PERFECT ROUND (LP) ....................15
*(see also Jacqueline & Bridie)*

## JACKIE & DOREEN
64   Ska Beat JB 168      Every Beat Of My Heart ....................20
65   Ska Beat JB 209      The New Vow/Adorable You ....................50
*(see also Doreen Shaffer, Jackie Opel)*

## JACKIE (EDWARDS) & MILLIE (SMALL)
65   Island WI 253        This Is My Story/SOUND SYSTEM: Never Again ....................45
66   Island WI 265        My Desire/MILLIE: That's How Strong My Love Is ....................15
67   Island WIP 6012      In A Dream/Ooh Ooh ....................20
67   Island ILP 941       PLEDGING MY LOVE (LP, as Jackie Edwards & Millie Small) ....................60
68   Island ILP 963       THE BEST OF JACKIE AND MILLIE VOLUME TWO (LP) ....................60
70   Trojan TTL 52        THE BEST OF JACKIE AND MILLIE VOLUME TWO (LP, reissue) ....................20
70   Trojan TBL 155       JACKIE & MILLIE (LP) ....................40
*(see also Wilfred & Millicent, Jackie Edwards, Millie)*

## JACKIE & RAINDROPS
63   Philips BF 1283      Down Our Street/My Heart Is Your Heart ....................8
64   Philips BF 1328      Come On Dream, Come On/Here I Go Again ....................8
*(see under Jackie Lee & Raindrops)*

## JACKIE & ROY
58   Vogue V 9101         You Smell So Good/Let's Take A Walk Around The Block ....................20
59   Vogue VE 1-70131     JACKIE AND ROY (EP) ....................30
58   Vogue VA 1-60111     JACKIE AND ROY (LP) ....................40

## JACKIE AND NICKY
74   Bradleys BRAD 313    Break Out In The Morning/Children Of Love ....................15
*(see also Jackie Lee (& Raindrops))*

## DAVID JACKMAN
96   Speed Pig SP 001     TEN CUT (10" clear vinyl, serrated edge, signed, no'd 80 only) ....................50

## JACKPOTS
69   Sonet SON 2006       Jack In The Box/Henbanes Sacrifice ....................25

## ALEXANDER JACKSON & TURNKEYS
| | | |
|---|---|---|
| 65 | Sue WI 386 | The Whip/Tell It Like It Is (actually "Flea Pot"/"Sweetie Lester" by Lala Wilson) .........100 |

## CHRIS JACKSON
| | | |
|---|---|---|
| 70 | 444 Label | Since There's No Doubt/We Will Be Together (unissued, acetate only - 2 known copies).....................800 |
| 70 | Soul City 120 | Since There's No Doubt/We Will Be Together (unissued)..............0 |
| 69 | Soul City SC 112 | I'll Never Forget You/Forever I'll Stay With You...............50 |

## CHUBBY JACKSON'S BIG BAND
| | | |
|---|---|---|
| 60 | Top Rank TR 5015 | A Ballad For Jai/Hail, Hail, The Herd's All Here.................5 |

## CHUCK JACKSON
| | | |
|---|---|---|
| 61 | Top Rank JAR 564 | I Don't Want To Cry/Just Once................40 |
| 62 | Top Rank JAR 607 | The Breaking Point/My Willow Tree................40 |
| 62 | Stateside SS 102 | Any Day Now/The Prophet................30 |
| 62 | Stateside SS 127 | I Keep Forgettin'/Who's Gonna Pick Up The Pieces................30 |
| 63 | Stateside SS 171 | Tell Him I'm Not Home/Getting Ready For The Heartbreak ................25 |
| 64 | Pye International 7N 25247 | Beg Me/For All Time ................25 |
| 64 | Pye International 7N 25276 | Any Day Now/The Prophet (reissue) ................20 |
| 65 | Pye International 7N 25287 | Since I Don't Have You/Hand It Over................75 |
| 65 | Pye International 7N 25287 | Since I Don't Have You/Hand It Over (DJ Copy) ................150 |
| 65 | Pye International 7N 25301 | I Need You/Chuck's Soul Brothers Twist................20 |
| 65 | Pye International 7N 25321 | If I Didn't Love You/Just A Little Bit Of Your Soul................25 |
| 66 | Pye International 7N 25384 | Chains Of Love/I Keep Forgettin'................100 |
| 66 | Pye International 7N 25384 | Chains Of Love/I Keep Forgettin' (DJ copy)................150 |
| 67 | Pye International 7N 25439 | Shame On Me/Candy ................25 |
| 68 | Tamla Motown TMG 651 | Girls, Girls, Girls/(You Can't Let The Boy Overpower) The Man In You................30 |
| 70 | Tamla Motown TMG 729 | Honey Come Back/What Am I Gonna Do Without You ................20 |
| 73 | Probe PRO 595 | I Only Get The Feeling/Slowly But Surely ................10 |
| 74 | Probe PRO 617 | I Can't Break Away/Just A Little Tear ................10 |
| 75 | All Platinum 6146 310 | I've Got The Need/Beautiful Woman ................10 |
| 75 | Disco Demand DDS 116 | These Chains Of Love/Any Day Now ................8 |
| 85 | Kent TOWN 104 | Hand It Over/CANDY & KISSES: Mr Creator (withdrawn) ................30 |
| 86 | Kent 6T2 | MELBA MOORE: Magic Touch/CHUCK JACKSON: Little By Little ................20 |
| 80s | Inferno SIN 1 | Chains Of Love/Good Things Come To Those Who Wait/Hand It Over/Any Day Now ....20 |
| 92 | Kent 8 | What's With This Loneliness/Surf And Soul ................20 |
| 66 | Pye Intl. NPL 28082 | TRIBUTE TO RHYTHM AND BLUES (LP) ................60 |
| 68 | T. Motown (S)TML 11071 | CHUCK JACKSON ARRIVES! (LP, mono/stereo) ................45 |
| 69 | T. Motown TML 11117 | GOIN' BACK TO CHUCK JACKSON (LP, mono) ................50 |
| 69 | T. Motown STML 11117 | GOIN' BACK TO CHUCK JACKSON (LP, stereo) ................50 |
| 72 | Probe SPB 1084 | THROUGH ALL TIMES (LP) ................25 |
| 84 | Kent 003 | MR. EMOTION (LP) ................15 |

*(see also Del[l]-Vikings)*

## CHUCK JACKSON & MAXINE BROWN
| | | |
|---|---|---|
| 65 | Pye International 7N 25308 | Something You Got/Baby Take Me ................20 |
| 65 | Pye Intl. NPL 28091 | SAYING SOMETHING (LP)................50 |

*(see also Maxine Brown, Tammi Terrell)*

## DAVID JACKSON
| | | |
|---|---|---|
| 82 | Butt NOTT 5 | THE LONG HELLO VOLUME 3 (LP)................20 |

*(see also Van Der Graaf Generator)*

## DEON JACKSON
| | | |
|---|---|---|
| 66 | Atlantic AT 4070 | Love Makes The World Go Round/You Said You Loved Me................45 |
| 66 | Atlantic 584 012 | Love Takes A Long Time Growing/Hush Little Baby................25 |
| 68 | Atlantic 584 159 | Ooh Baby/All On A Sunny Day................30 |
| 76 | Contempo CS 9031 | Love Makes The World Go Round/I Can't Go On................25 |

## EARL JACKSON
| | | |
|---|---|---|
| 76 | ABC 410 | Soul Self Satisfaction/Looking Thru' The Eyes Of Love (DJ Copy) ................30 |
| 76 | ABC ABC 4110 | Soul Self Satisfaction/Looking Thru' The Eyes Of Love ................20 |

## GEORGE JACKSON
| | | |
|---|---|---|
| 69 | Capitol CL 15605 | Find 'Em, Fool 'Em And Forget 'Em/My Desires Are Getting The Best Of Me ................25 |
| 72 | London HLU 10373 | Aretha, Sing One For Me/I'm Gonna Wait ................12 |
| 73 | London HLU 10413 | Let 'Em Know You Care/Patricia................12 |

## GORDON JACKSON
| | | |
|---|---|---|
| 69 | Marmalade 598 010 | Me And My Zoo/A Day At The Cottage ................20 |
| 69 | Marmalade 598 021 | Song For Freedom/Sing To Me Woman ................25 |
| 69 | Marmalade 608 012 | THINKING BACK (LP)................250 |

*(see also Hellions, Jane Relf, Traffic)*

## HAROLD JACKSON & TORNADOES
| | | |
|---|---|---|
| 58 | Vogue V 9105 | Move It On Down The Line Parts 1 & 2 ................100 |
| 58 | Vogue V 9105 | Move It On Down The Line Parts 1 & 2 (78) ................40 |

## JACKIE JACKSON
| | | |
|---|---|---|
| 74 | T. Motown STML 11249 | JACKIE JACKSON (LP) ................15 |

*(see also Jacksons, Jackson 5)*

## JERRY JACKSON
| | | |
|---|---|---|
| 63 | London HLR 9689 | Gypsy Eyes/Turn Back ................40 |
| 66 | Cameo Parkway P 100 | It's Rough Out There/I'm Gonna Paint A Picture ................175 |
| 66 | Cameo Parkway P 100 | It's Rough Out There/I'm Gonna Paint A Picture (DJ copy) ................300 |

## JIM JACKSON
| | | |
|---|---|---|
| 66 | RCA RCX 7182 | R.C.A. VICTOR RACE SERIES VOL. 7 (EP) ................10 |

# JIMMY JACKSON('S ROCK 'N' ROLL SKIFFLE)

## JIMMY JACKSON('S ROCK 'N' ROLL SKIFFLE)
| | | | |
|---|---|---|---|
| 57 | Columbia DB 3898 | California Zephyr/I Shall Not Be Moved | 20 |
| 57 | Columbia DB 3937 | Sittin' In The Balcony/Good Morning Blues | 25 |
| 57 | Columbia DB 3957 | River Line/Lonely Road | 15 |
| 57 | Columbia DB 3988 | White Silver Sands/Build Your Love (On A Strong Foundation) (solo) | 5 |
| 58 | Columbia DB 4085 | Love-A Love-A Love A/Photographs (solo) | 10 |
| 58 | Columbia DB 4153 | Swing Down, Sweet Chariot/This Little Light Of Mine (solo) | 5 |
| 58 | Columbia SEG 7750 | ROCK 'N' SKIFFLE (EP) | 60 |
| 58 | Columbia SEG 7768 | COUNTRY AND BLUES (EP) | 60 |

## J.J. JACKSON (& GREATEST LITTLE SOUL BAND IN THE LAND)
| | | | |
|---|---|---|---|
| 67 | Polydor 56718 | But It's Alright/Do The Boogaloo | 20 |
| 67 | Strike JH 329 | Come See Me/Try Me | 20 |
| 67 | Warner Bros WB 2082 | Sho Nuff (Got A Good Thing Going)/Here We Go Again | 15 |
| 68 | Warner Bros WB 2090 | Down, But Not Out/Why Does It Take So Long? | 15 |
| 68 | Warner Bros WB 6029 | Courage Ain't Strength/You Do It 'Cause You Wanna | 15 |
| 69 | Warner Bros WB 7276 | Ain't Too Proud To Beg/But It's Alright | 10 |
| 70 | RCA RCA 1924 | Bow Down To The Dollar/Indian Thing (as J.J's DILEMMA) | 20 |
| 71 | Mojo 2092 014 | But It's Alright/Do The Boogaloo | 10 |
| 67 | Strike JLH 104 | J.J. JACKSON WITH THE GREATEST LITTLE SOUL BAND (LP) | 40 |
| 69 | MCA SKA 100 | GREATEST LITTLE SOUL BAND (LP) | 25 |
| 70 | RCA Victor SF 8093 | J.J. JACKSON'S DILEMMA (LP) | 30 |

*(see also Greatest Little Soul Band)*

## LEVI JACKSON
| | | | |
|---|---|---|---|
| 71 | Columbia DB 8807 | This Beautiful Day/Don't You Be A Sinner | 100 |
| 71 | Columbia DB 8807 | This Beautiful Day/Don't You Be A Sinner (DJ copy) | 150 |

*(see also Solomon King)*

## LLOYD JACKSON
| | | | |
|---|---|---|---|
| 71 | Pama Supreme PS 308 | Cracklin' Rosie/Little Deeds Of Kindness (B-side with Scorpions) | 5 |

## MICHAEL JACKSON
### SINGLES
| | | | |
|---|---|---|---|
| 72 | Tamla Motown TMG 797 | Got To Be There/Maria (You Were The Only One) | 5 |
| 79 | Epic 12EPC 7135 | You Can't Win (Part 1)/You Can't Win (Part 2) (12") | 10 |
| 79 | Epic S EPC 7135 | You Can't Win (Part 1)/You Can't Win (Part 2) (picture disc) | 12 |
| 79 | Epic 12EPC 7763 | Don't Stop 'Til You Get Enough/I Can't Help It (12") | 15 |
| 81 | Motown TMG 977 | We're Almost There/We've Got A Good Thing Going (p/s) | 5 |
| 82 | Epic EPCA 11-2729 | The Girl Is Mine (with Paul McCartney)/Can't Get Outta The Rain (picture disc) | 30 |
| 83 | Epic EPC 2906 | GREATEST ORIGINAL HITS: Don't Stop 'Til You Get Enough/ She's Out Of My Life/Off The Wall/Rock With You (EP) | 15 |
| 83 | Motown TMG 986 | Happy (Love Theme From 'Lady Sings The Blues')/We're Almost There (poster p/s) | 8 |
| 83 | Motown EPCA 112729 | Happy (Love Theme From 'Lady Sings The Blues')/We're Almost There (picture disc) | 12 |
| 83 | Epic EPCA 3643 | Thriller/JACKSONS: Things I Do For You (live) (poster p/s) | 8 |
| 83 | Epic TA 3643 | Thriller (Album Version)/Thriller (Remix Short Version)/JACKSONS: Things I Do For You (live) (12", 'calendar' p/s) | 50 |
| 83 | Epic MJ 1 (1-9) | MICHAEL JACKSON'S 9 SINGLES PACK (9 x 7", p/s, each on red vinyl, in PVC foldout wallet) | 40 |
| 87 | Epic 650 202-0 | I Just Can't Stop Loving You (with Siedah Garratt)/Baby Be Mine (poster p/s) | 10 |
| 87 | Epic 650 202-6 | I Just Can't Stop Loving You (with Siedah Garratt)/Baby Be Mine (12", p/s with poster) | 15 |
| 87 | Epic 651 275-7 | The Way You Make Me Feel/The Way You Make Me Feel (Instrumental) (p/s, with competition leaflet, stickered sleeve) | 5 |
| 87 | Epic 651 275-3 | The Way You Make Me Feel (7" Mix)/(A Capella)/(Dance Radio Edit)/ (Dub)/(Get Into The Groove -Put Either Side On The Turntable, Lower The Arm And See Which Your Needle Pix) (12", p/s double-groove) | 12 |
| 88 | Epic 651 389-9 | Man In The Mirror (Single Mix)/Man In The Mirror (Instrumental) (Uncut 12", square-shaped picture disc) | 250 |
| 88 | Epic 651 388-9 | Man In The Mirror (Single Mix)/Man In The Mirror (Instrumental) (square-shaped picture disc) | 35 |
| 88 | Epic 651 546-7 | Dirty Diana/Dirty Diana (p/s, with 13" cardboard figure) | 20 |
| 88 | Epic 652 864-6 | Dirty Diana/Dirty Diana (Instrumental)/Bad (Extended Dance Mix With False Fade) (12", with tour poster p/s) | 15 |
| 88 | Epic MJ 5 | THE MICHAEL JACKSON BAD SOUVENIR SINGLES PACK (5 x 7" square picture discs in foldout PVC wallet, with lyric book) | 45 |
| 88 | Epic 652 844-9 | Another Part Of Me/(Instrumental) (p/s, with Bad tour backstage pass) | 25 |
| 88 | Epic 652 844-0 | Another Part Of Me/Another Part Of Me (Instrumental) (poster p/s) | 8 |
| 88 | Epic 653 026-0 | Smooth Criminal/Smooth Criminal (Instrumental) (pack with 4 postcards) | 20 |
| 88 | Epic 653 170-6 | Smooth Criminal (Extended Dance Mix)/Smooth Criminal Extended (Dance Mix Dub Mix)/Smooth Criminal (A Capella) (12" with "Moonwalker" advert calendar) | 20 |
| 89 | Epic 654 672-0 | Leave Me Alone/Human Nature (pop-up p/s) | 30 |
| 89 | Epic 654 947-9 | Liberian Girl (Edit)/Girlfriend (star mobile foldout card pack) | 20 |
| 91 | Epic 6584887 | Prelude/Heal The World/She Drives Me Wild (poster sleeve) | 5 |
| 92 | Epic 658 360-7 | Jam (7" Edit)/Beat It (Moby's Sub Mix) ('picture frame' pack with 2 prints) | 5 |
| 92 | Epic 658360-7 | Jam (7" Edit)/Beat It (Moby's Sub Mix) ('Frame' p/s with 2 photo inserts) | 5 |
| 92 | Epic EPC 658179-7 | Who Is It/Rock With You (Masters At Work Remix) (limited edition, with free standing Jackson figure inserr) | 12 |
| 92 | Epic MJ 4 (658 281-1/4) | TOUR SOUVENIR PACK (CD, 4-picture disc, box set with booklet) | 40 |
| 95 | Epic 662 127 | Scream (Def Radio Mix)/Scream (Single Edit) (limited edition poster sleeve) | 5 |
| 95 | Epic 662 022 | Scream (Single Edit)/Childhood (p/s, with 2 page lyric insert) | 5 |
| 97 | Epic 665 130 6 | Smile/It It Scary (Deep Dish Dark And Scary Remix)/Is It Scary (Eddie's Love Mix)/Off The Wall (Junior Vasquez Remix) (12" p/s withdrawn. Beware of counterfeits with poor print quality on label, sleeve and especially the barcode) | 200 |
| 03 | Epic 674480-8 | One More Chance (Album Version)/Billie Jean (album version) (12" picture disc, numbered) | 15 |

| 03 | Epic XPR 3744 | TWELVES (7 x 12" p/s in box with insert) .................................................................. 60 |

**ALBUMS**

| 79 | Epic EPC 83458/83468 | OFF THE WALL (LP, gatefold sleeve, with 7" picture disc "You Can't Win (Parts 1)/(Part 2)" [S EPC 7135], some with information sheet) ............................................. 25 |
| 82 | Epic EPC 11-85930 | THRILLER (LP, picture disc in PVC sleeve) ................................................................. 30 |
| 83 | MCA MCA 70000 | E.T. - THE EXTRA TERRESTRIAL (LP, box set with booklet & poster, narration & "Someone In The Dark", with music by John Williams) ............................................ 30 |
| 87 | Epic 450 290-8 | BAD GIFT PACK (pack, with note pad, highlighter pen & calendar) ....................... 15 |
| 87 | Epic 450 290-0 | BAD (LP, picture disc) ................................................................................................. 30 |
| 87 | Epic 450 290-9 | BAD (CD, picture disc, sealed in long PVC blister pack) ....................................... 45 |
| 87 | Epic 450 290-9 | BAD (CD, picture disc, unsealed in long PVC blister pack) ................................... 25 |
| 08 | Sony 88697233441 | THRILLER (2-LP 25th Anniversary special edition) ................................................ 20 |
| 09 | Sony 88697616541 | THIS IS IT (4-LP box set with 36 page book, numbered) ...................................... 45 |

**PROMOS**

| 92 | Epic XPR 1814 | Jam: (More Than Enuff Mix)/(Roger's Club Mix)/(E-Smoov Jazzy Jam)/ (Atlanta Techno Mix)/(Roger's Underground Mix)/(Silky 12")/(More Than Enuff Dub)/(Maurice's Jammin' Dub Mix)/(Roger's Club Dub)/(Atlanta Techno Dub)/(Roger's Slam Jam Mix)/ (Silky Dub)/(A Capella Mix) (12", double pack, black & orange stickered white sleeve). 15 |
| 92 | Epic XPR 1797 | Who Is It (Patience Mix)/(Patience Beats)/(Most Patient Mix)/(HIS Mix)/ (The P-Man Dub) (12", company sleeve) ........................................................................................ 10 |
| 95 | Epic XPR 2184 | Scream: (Classic Club Mix)/(DM R&B Extended Mix)/(Naughty Main Mix)/(Naughty Main Mix No Rap)/(Dave 'Jam' Hall's Extended Urban Remix)/ (Pressurised Dub Part 1)/(Pressurised Dub Part 2)/(Album Version)/(Single Edit No. 2)/(Naughty Pretty-Pella)/(Naughty A Capella) (12" double pack, red title sleeve) ........ 20 |
| 95 | Epic XPR 2266 | DMC Megamix (15.40)/(11.18) (12", custom sleeve) ............................................ 12 |
| 95 | Epic XPR 2265 | The Classic Remix Series: Wanna Be Startin' Something (Brothers In Rhythm Mix)/ (Tommy D's Main Mix) (12", plain sleeve, sealed with title sticker) ....................... 10 |
| 95 | Epic XPR 2229 | The Classic Remix Series: Rock With You (Frankie's Favorite Club Mix)/ (The Masters At Work Mix) (12", plain sleeve, sealed with title sticker) ................................... 12 |
| 96 | Epic XPR 2207 | Mj Club Megamix (MJ Mega Remix)/(MJ Urban Megamix) (12", blue & purple title sleeve) ........................................................................................................................ 15 |
| 96 | Epic XPR 3030 | They Don't Care About Us (The R&B Mixes): Track Masters Remix/ Dallas Austin Main Mix/Charles' Full Dirty Mix/LP Edit/Love To Infinity's Walk in The Park/Track Master's Instrumental (12" p/s) .......................................................................................... 10 |
| 97 | Epic XPR 3159 | HIStory (Tony Moran's HIStory Lesson)/(Tony Moran's HIStorical Dub) Is It Scary (Eddie's Love Mix)/(Eddie's Rub-A-Dub Mix)/(Eddie's Love Mix)/ (Radio Edit) (12", white embossed title p/s) ............................................................................... 20 |
| 97 | Epic XPR 3196 | Is It Scary (Deep Dish Dark & Scary Remix)/(Deep Dish Double-O-Jazz Dub)/ (Deep Dish Dark & Scary Remix)/(Radio Edit) (12", black embossed title p/s) ................ 35 |
| 04 | Epic YPR 3829 | Cheater (Demo)/One More Chance (R Kelly Remix) (12" p/s) .............................. 40 |

*(see also Jackson 5, Paul McCartney, Jacksons)*

**MILLIE JACKSON**

| 72 | Mojo 2093 011 | A Child Of God/You're The Joy Of My Life ............................................................... 10 |
| 72 | Mojo 2093 015 | Ask Me What You Want/I Just Can't Stand It .......................................................... 10 |
| 72 | Mojo 2093 022 | My Man, A Sweet Man/I Gotta Get Away (From My Own Self) (paper label) .......... 6 |
| 73 | Polydor 2066 317 | Breakaway/Strange Things ......................................................................................... 5 |
| 75 | Polydor 2066 536 | If Loving You Is Wrong/The Rap ................................................................................ 5 |
| 75 | Polydor 2006 612 | Loving Arms/Left Over .............................................................................................. 5 |
| 76 | Spring 2066 713 | A House For Sale/There You Are ............................................................................. 15 |
| 72 | Mojo 2918 005 | MILLIE JACKSON (LP) .............................................................................................. 15 |

*(see also Elton John)*

**MILT JACKSON**

| 53 | Vogue LDE 044 | MILT JACKSON AND HIS NEW GROUP (10" LP) ..................................................... 20 |
| 55 | Esquire 20-042 | MILT JACKSON QUINTET (10" LP) ........................................................................... 20 |
| 55 | London Jazz LZ-C 14006 | MILT JACKSON QUARTET (10" LP) .......................................................................... 20 |

*(see also Ray Charles, Modern Jazz Quartet, Miles Davis/Art Blakey, Coleman Hawkins)*

**PAPA CHARLIE JACKSON**

| 60 | Heritage R 100 | PAPA CHARLIE JACKSON (EP) 99 only ..................................................................... 80 |
| 60 | Heritage HLP 1011 | PAPA CHARLIE JACKSON (LP) 99 only .................................................................. 100 |

*(see also Paramount Allstars, Blind Blake)*

**POOCH JACKSON**

| 72 | Sioux SI 013 | You Just Gotta Get Ready/BROTHER DAN: Django's Valley ................................... 15 |
| 72 | Sioux SI 017 | King Of The Road/Circles/Mammy Blue ................................................................. 15 |
| 72 | Sioux SI 016 | Once Bitten (with Harry J. Allstars)/KING REGGAE: Slave Driver ......................... 15 |

*(see also Circles)*

**PYTHON LEE JACKSON**

| 70 | Young Blood YB 1002 | In A Broken Dream/Doing Fine (p/s) ......................................................................... 6 |
| 72 | Young Blood YB 3001 | IN A BROKEN DREAM (LP, featuring Rod Stewart who is not credited on front or rear sleeve) ..................................................................................................................... 20 |

*(see under 'P')*

**RALPH 'SOUL' JACKSON**

| 69 | Atlantic 584258 | 'Cause I Love You/Sunshine Of Your Love .............................................................. 30 |

**RAY JACKSON**

| 76 | EMI EMI 2514 | Take Some Time/Working On ..................................................................................... 5 |
| 80 | Mercury MER 3 | In The Night/Waiting For The Time (p/s) ................................................................... 5 |
| 80 | Mercury MER 8 | Little Town Flirt/Make It Last (p/s) ............................................................................. 5 |

*(see also Lindisfarne)*

**ROOT & JENNY JACKSON**

| 69 | Beacon BEA 110 | Lean On Me/Please Come Home ............................................................................. 10 |
| 69 | Beacon BEA 136 | Let's Go Somewhere/If I Didn't Love You ................................................................. 8 |

*(see also Roots and Jenny Jackson)*

**SHIRLEY JACKSON**

| 63 | Decca F 11612 | Don't Play Me A Love Song/You Gotta Love And Be Loved ...................................... 7 |

MINT VALUE £

| | | | |
|---|---|---|---|
| 63 | Decca F 11661 | The Boy Of The Year/I Miss You Most Of All | 10 |
| 63 | Decca F 11788 | Broken Home/No Greater Love Than Mine | 7 |

### SHOVELVILLE K. JACKSON
| | | | |
|---|---|---|---|
| 60s | Melodisc MEL 1683 | Be Careful Of Stones That You Throw/Kentucky Blues | 12 |

### SIMONE JACKSON
| | | | |
|---|---|---|---|
| 62 | Piccadilly 7N 35087 | Pop Pop Pop Pie/He Ain't Got No Time For Love | 12 |
| 63 | Piccadilly 7N 35124 | Ain't Gonna Kiss Ya/Slow Motion | 12 |
| 63 | Piccadilly 7N 35149 | Tell Me What To Do/Doing What You Know Is Wrong | 12 |

### JACKSON & SMITH
| | | | |
|---|---|---|---|
| 65 | Polydor 56051 | Ain't That Loving You Baby/Every Day I Have The Blues | 10 |
| 66 | Polydor 56086 | Party '66/And That's It | 10 |

### TONY JACKSON (& VIBRATIONS)
| | | | |
|---|---|---|---|
| 64 | Pye 7N 15685 | Bye Bye Baby/Watch Your Step | 25 |
| 64 | Pye 7N 15745 | This Little Girl Of Mine/You Beat Me To The Punch | 40 |
| 65 | Pye 7N 15766 | Love Potion No. 9/Fortune Teller | 50 |
| 65 | Pye 7N 15876 | Stage Door/That's What I Want (as Tony Jackson Group) | 40 |
| 66 | CBS 202039 | You're My Number One/Let Me Know (as Tony Jackson Group) | 40 |
| 66 | CBS 202069 | Never Leave Your Baby's Side/I'm The One She Really Thinks A Lot Of (solo) | 40 |
| 66 | CBS 202297 | Follow Me/Walk Walk Walk Walk (solo) | 60 |
| 66 | CBS 202408 | Anything Else You Want/Come On And Stop (solo) | 40 |
| 91 | Strange Things STZ 5005 | JUST LIKE ME (LP) | 15 |

*(see also Searchers)*

### VIVIAN JACKSON & THE PROPHETS
| | | | |
|---|---|---|---|
| 78 | Roots TS 100 | 72 Nation Bow/Ya Be Yoo | 40 |
| 78 | Nationwide PRO 001 | CHANT DOWN BABYLON KINGDOM (LP) | 120 |
| 78 | Grove Music GMLP 4 | BEWARE (LP) | 40 |

*(See also Yabby U.)*

### WALTER JACKSON
| | | | |
|---|---|---|---|
| 65 | Columbia DB 7620 | Welcome Home/Blowin' In The Wind | 40 |
| 66 | Columbia DB 7949 | Tear For Tear/It's An Uphill Climb To The Bottom | 75 |
| 66 | Columbia DB 7949 | Tear For Tear/It's An Uphill Climb To The Bottom (DJ copy) | 125 |
| 66 | Columbia DB 8054 | A Corner In The Sun/Not You | 30 |
| 67 | Columbia DB 8154 | Speak Her Name/They Don't Give Medals (To Yesterday's Heroes) | 30 |
| 70 | Atlantic 584 311 | Any Way That You Want Me/Life Has Its Ups And Downs | 10 |
| 73 | Brunswick BR 5 | Easy Evil/I Never Had It So Good | 8 |

### WANDA JACKSON
| | | | |
|---|---|---|---|
| 59 | Capitol CL 15033 | You're The One For Me/A Date With Jerry | 20 |
| 59 | Capitol CL 15090 | Reaching/I'd Rather Have You | 20 |
| 60 | Capitol CL 15147 | Let's Have A Party/Cool Love | 25 |
| 61 | Capitol CL 15176 | Mean Mean Man/Honey Bop | 30 |
| 61 | Capitol CL 15223 | Right Or Wrong/Funnel Of Love | 15 |
| 62 | Capitol CL 15234 | In The Middle Of A Heartache/I'd Be Ashamed | 10 |
| 62 | Capitol CL 15249 | If I Cried Every Time You Hurt Me/Let My Love Walk In | 10 |
| 58 | Capitol EAP1 1041 | WANDA JACKSON (EP) | 75 |
| 62 | Capitol EAP1 20353 | A LITTLE BITTY TEAR (EP) | 60 |
| 58 | Capitol T 1041 | WANDA JACKSON (LP) | 150 |
| 60 | Capitol T 1384 | ROCKIN' WITH WANDA (LP) | 120 |
| 61 | Capitol T 1511 | THERE'S A PARTY GOIN' ON (LP, mono) | 80 |
| 61 | Capitol (S)T 1511 | THERE'S A PARTY GOIN' ON (LP, stereo) | 100 |
| 61 | Capitol T 1596 | RIGHT OR WRONG (LP, mono) | 50 |
| 61 | Capitol (S)T 1596 | RIGHT OR WRONG (LP, stereo) | 60 |
| 62 | Capitol T 1776 | WONDERFUL WANDA (LP) | 30 |
| 64 | Capitol T 2030 | TWO SIDES OF WANDA (LP, mono) | 50 |
| 64 | Capitol (S)T 2030 | TWO SIDES OF WANDA (LP, stereo) | 55 |
| 64 | Capitol (S)T 2306 | BLUES IN MY HEART (LP) | 15 |
| 66 | Capitol (S)T 2438 | SINGS COUNTRY SONGS (LP, black label) | 15 |
| 67 | Capitol (S)T 2606 | SALUTES THE COUNTRY MUSIC HALL OF FAME (LP, black label) | 15 |
| 67 | Capitol (S)T 2812 | YOU'LL ALWAYS HAVE MY LOVE (LP) | 15 |
| 69 | Capitol (S)T 2976 | CREAM OF THE CROP (LP, with Party Timers) | 15 |

### JACKSON BROTHERS
| | | | |
|---|---|---|---|
| 59 | London HLX 8845 | Tell Him No/Love Me | 25 |

### JACKSON 5
**SINGLES**
| | | | |
|---|---|---|---|
| 70 | Tamla Motown TMG 724 | I Want You Back/Who's Loving You | 5 |
| 70 | Tamla Motown TMG 738 | ABC/The Young Folks (promo only p/s) | 60 |
| 70 | Tamla Motown TMG 738 | ABC/The Young Folks | 5 |
| 70 | Tamla Motown TMG 746 | The Love You Save/I Found That Girl | 5 |
| 70 | Tamla Motown TMG 758 | I'll Be There/One More Chance | 5 |
| 71 | Tamla Motown TMG 769 | Mama's Pearl/Darling Dear (promo only p/s) | 60 |
| 71 | Tamla Motown TMG 769 | Mama's Pearl/Darling Dear | 6 |
| 71 | Tamla Motown TMG 778 | Never Can Say Goodbye/She's Good | 5 |
| 72 | Tamla Motown TMG 809 | Sugar Daddy/I'm So Happy | 5 |
| 72 | Tamla Motown TMG 825 | Little Bitty Pretty One/Maybe Tomorrow | 5 |
| 72 | Tamla Motown TMG 833 | Lookin' Through The Windows/Love Song (promo only p/s) | 15 |
| 72 | Tamla Motown TMG 833 | Lookin' Through The Windows/Love Song | 5 |
| 72 | Tamla Motown TMG 837 | THE CHRISTMAS EP: Santa Claus Is Coming To Town/ Someday At Christmas/ Christmas Won't Be The Same This Year | 12 |
| 73 | Tamla Motown TMG 842 | Doctor My Eyes/My Little Baby | 5 |

| | | | |
|---|---|---|---|
| 73 | Tamla Motown TMG 856 | Hallelujah Day/To Know | 5 |
| 73 | Tamla Motown TMG 865 | Skywriter/Ain't Nothin' Like The Real Thing (promo only p/s) | 20 |
| 73 | Tamla Motown TMG 865 | Skywriter/Ain't Nothin' Like The Real Thing | 5 |
| 73 | Tamla Motown TMG 878 | Get It Together/Touch | 5 |
| 74 | Tamla Motown TMG 895 | The Boogie Man/Don't Let Your Baby Catch You | 5 |
| 74 | Tamla Motown TMG 904 | Dancing Machine/It's Too Late To Change The Time | 5 |
| 74 | Tamla Motown TMG 927 | The Life Of The Party/Whatever You Got I Want | 5 |
| 74 | Lyntone LYN 2639 | Talk And Sing Personally To Valentine Readers (33rpm flexidisc free with 'Valentine' magazine) | 15 |
| 75 | Rice Krispies (no cat. Nos.) | Sugar Daddy/Goin' Back To Indiana/Who's Loving You/Mama's Pearl/ ABC/The Love You Save (6 different Rice Krispies cut-out card discs, price is for each) | 30 |
| 75 | Tamla Motown TMG 942 | I Am Love (Part 1)/I Am Love (Part 2) | 5 |
| 75 | Tamla Motown TMG 1001 | Forever Came Today/I Can't Quit Your Love | 5 |
| 80 | Motown SPTMG 2 | THE MOTOWN 20TH ANNIVERSARY SINGLES BOX (15 x 7") | 30 |

**ALBUMS**

| | | | |
|---|---|---|---|
| 70 | Tamla Motown TML 11142 | DIANA ROSS PRESENTS THE JACKSON 5 (flipback sleeve, mono) | 30 |
| 70 | Tamla Motown (S)TML 11142 | DIANA ROSS PRESENTS THE JACKSON 5 (flipback sleeve, /stereo) | 20 |
| 70 | Tamla Motown TML 11156 | ABC (flipback sleeve, mono, existence unconfirmed) | 40 |
| 70 | Tamla Motown STML 11156 | ABC (flipback sleeve, stereo) | 15 |
| 70 | Tamla Motown STML 11168 | THE JACKSON 5 CHRISTMAS ALBUM (flipback sleeve) | 20 |
| 71 | Tamla Motown STML 11174 | THIRD ALBUM (original with flipback sleeve) | 20 |
| 71 | Tamla Motown STML 11188 | MAYBE TOMORROW | 20 |
| 72 | Tamla Motown STML 11214 | LOOKIN' THROUGH THE WINDOWS | 20 |
| 73 | Tamla Motown STML 11243 | GET IT TOGETHER (with photo insert) | 20 |
| 74 | Tamla Motown STML 11275 | DANCING MACHINE | 15 |
| 75 | Tamla Motown STML 11290 | MOVING VIOLATIONS | 15 |
| 77 | Motown STMX 6006 | MOTOWN SPECIAL - THE JACKSON 5 | 15 |
| 79 | MFP MFP 50418 | ZIP-A-DEE-DOO-DAH | 15 |
| 81 | Motown PR 84 | JACKSON 5: HISTORY OF MOTOWN (4-LP box set, with 1 Michael Jackson LP) | 30 |

*(see also Michael Jackson, Jacksons)*

**JACKSON HEIGHTS**

| | | | |
|---|---|---|---|
| 70 | Charisma JH 1 | Doubting Thomas/Insomnia | 6 |
| 72 | Vertigo 6059 068 | Maureen/Long Time Dying | 25 |
| 70 | Charisma CAS 1018 | KINGS PROGRESS (LP, pink 'scroll' label) | 70 |
| 72 | Vertigo 6360 067 | 5TH AVENUE BUS (LP, gatefold sleeve, swirl label) | 225 |
| 72 | Vertigo 6360 077 | RAGAMUFFIN'S FOOL (LP, swirl label, with poster) | 225 |
| 72 | Vertigo 6360 077 | RAGAMUFFIN'S FOOL (LP, swirl label, without poster) | 80 |
| 73 | Vertigo 6360 092 | BUMP AND GRIND (LP, 'spaceship label') | 40 |

*(see also Nice)*

**JACKSONS**

| | | | |
|---|---|---|---|
| 81 | Epic EPC A 1294 | Walk Right Now/Your Ways (picture disc) | 15 |
| 84 | Epic WA 4431 | State Of Shock/Your Ways (7" picture disc) | 15 |
| 79 | Epic S XPR 1207 | EPIC HITS FROM THE JACKSONS & MICHAEL JACKSON (LP, promo only) | 20 |
| 84 | Epic EPC 86303 | VICTORY (LP, picture disc) | 35 |
| 85 | Epic SAI 7561 | A TASTE OF VICTORY (LP, picture disc, promo only via Kelloggs offer) | 60 |

*(see also Jackson 5, Michael Jackson)*

**JACKSON SISTERS**

| | | | |
|---|---|---|---|
| 74 | Mums SMUM 2896 | Boy, You're Dynamite/Shake Her Loose | 8 |
| 73 | Mums SMUM 1591 | (Why Can't We Be) More than Just Friends/Rockin' On My Porch | 10 |
| 73 | Mums SMUM 1829 | I Believe In Miracles/Day In The Blue | 50 |
| 87 | Urban URB 4 | I Believe In Miracles/Boy You're Dynamite | 8 |
| 87 | Urban URBX 4 | I Believe In Miracles/Boy You're Dynamite (12", p/s) | 20 |
| 87 | Urban URBX 4 | I Believe in Miracles/MACEO & THE MACS: Across The tracks/URBAN ALL STARS: It All Began In Africa (12" promo) | 25 |

**JACKSON SISTERS**

| | | | |
|---|---|---|---|
| 00 | Fab FAB 004 | Rocksteady/STOVELLS: Hang On In There | 5 |

**JACK THE LAD**

| | | | |
|---|---|---|---|
| 73 | Charisma CB 206 | One More Dance/Draught Genius (Polka) (p/s) | 6 |
| 73 | Charisma CB 218 | Why Can't I Be Satisfied/Make Me Happy | 5 |
| 75 | Charisma CB 242 | Home Sweet Home/Big Ocean Liner | 5 |
| 75 | Charisma CB 253 | Gentleman Soldier/Oakey Strike Evictions | 5 |
| 75 | Charisma CB 264 | My Friend The Drink/Rocking Chair | 5 |
| 76 | United Artists UP 36162 | Eight Ton Crazy/Watery Drop | 5 |
| 74 | Charisma CAS 1085 | IT'S JACK THE LAD (LP, small 'Mad Hatter' label) | 15 |
| 74 | Charisma CAS 1094 | OLD STRAIGHT TRACK (LP, with lyric sheet, Charsima inner) | 15 |

*(see also Lindisfarne)*

**JACKY**

| | | | |
|---|---|---|---|
| 68 | Philips BF 1647 | White Horses/Too Many Chiefs (Not Enough Indians) | 10 |
| 68 | Philips BF 1689 | We're Off And Running/Well That's Loving You | 6 |
| 69 | Page One POF 122 | Love Is Now/Never Will I Be | 7 |
| 68 | Philips SBL 7851 | WHITE HORSES (LP) | 35 |

*(see also Jackie & Raindrops, Raindrops, Jackie Lee, Emma Rede, Vince Hill)*

**DICK JACOBS (& HIS ORCHESTRA)**

| | | | |
|---|---|---|---|
| 56 | Vogue Coral Q 72147 | Saxophone/Never Come Sunday | 5 |
| 56 | Vogue Coral Q 72154 | The Man With The Golden Arm Theme/Butternut | 5 |
| 56 | Vogue Coral Q 72204 | Petticoats Of Portugal/East Of Eden | 5 |
| 57 | Vogue Coral Q 72245 | The Big Beat/The Tower Trot | 15 |
| 57 | Vogue Coral Q 72260 | Rock-a-billy Gal/The Golden Strings | 15 |

# Hank JACOBS

| | | | |
|---|---|---|---|
| 57 | Vogue Coral LVA 9076 | THE SKIFFLE SOUND (LP, as Dick Jacobs & His Skiffle Group) | 30 |
| 59 | Coral LVA 9102 | THEMES FROM HORROR MOVIES (LP) | 25 |

## HANK JACOBS
| | | | |
|---|---|---|---|
| 64 | Sue WI 313 | So Far Away/Monkey, Hips And Rice | 40 |
| 83 | Sue ENS 5 | SO FAR AWAY EP: So Far Away/Out Of Sight/Hank's Groove/Summertime | 10 |

## JACQUELINE & BRIDIE
| | | | |
|---|---|---|---|
| 64 | Fontana TF 473 | Roses/Roving Jack | 6 |
| 64 | Fontana TL 5212 | HOLD BACK THE DAWN (LP) | 20 |

*(see also Jackie & Bridie)*

## CHUCK JACQUES & LYNN TAITT & COMETS
| | | | |
|---|---|---|---|
| 67 | Ska Beat JB 264 | Dial 609/VIBRATORS & TOMMY McCOOK & COMETS: Wait For Me | 20 |

*(see also Wilbert Francis & Vibrators)*

## JADE
| | | | |
|---|---|---|---|
| 70 | DJM DJS 227 | Alan's Song/Amongst Anemones | 15 |
| 70 | DJM DJLPS 407 | FLY ON STRANGE WINGS (LP, gatefold sleeve) | 200 |

## JADE WARRIOR
| | | | |
|---|---|---|---|
| 72 | Vertigo 6059 069 | The Demon Trucker/Snake | 15 |
| 78 | Island JAD 1 | Way Of The Sun/Sun Ra | 5 |
| 71 | Vertigo 6360 033 | JADE WARRIOR (LP, gatefold sleeve, swirl label) | 200 |
| 71 | Vertigo 6360 062 | RELEASED (LP, multi-poster sleeve, small swirl label) | 500 |
| 72 | Vertigo 6360 079 | LAST AUTUMN'S DREAM (LP, gatefold sleeve, swirl label) | 175 |
| 74 | Island ILPS 9290 | FLOATING WORLD (LP, textured sleeve, pink rim palm tree label) | 30 |
| 75 | Island ILPS 9318 | WAVES (LP, pink rim palm tree label) | 20 |
| 76 | Island ILPS 9393 | KITES (LP) | 18 |
| 79 | Butt BUTT 001 | REFLECTIONS (LP, lyric inner) | 18 |

*(see also July, Joe O'Donnell)*

## JADIS
| | | | |
|---|---|---|---|
| 84 | Private pressing | BABOON ENQUIRIES EP | 12 |
| 87 | Private pressing DEM 1 | G13/Out Of Reach | 8 |
| 88 | Private pressing DEM 2 | Don't Keep Me Waiting/In The Dark | 8 |
| 89 | Private pressing | Lost For Words/This Changing Face | 8 |
| 90 | Back Beat 004-12 | THE JADIS ALBUM (LP, numbered) | 15 |

## JAFFREY
| | | | |
|---|---|---|---|
| 76 | Tank | ALICE AT JAFFREY (LP) | 100 |

## CHRIS JAGGER
| | | | |
|---|---|---|---|
| 73 | GM GMS 3 | Something New/Joy Of The Ride | 6 |
| 73 | GM GML 1003 | CHRIS JAGGER (LP) | 15 |

## MICK JAGGER
| | | | |
|---|---|---|---|
| 70 | Decca F 13067 | Memo From Turner/Natural Magic (in export p/s) | 40 |
| 70 | Decca F 13067 | Memo From Turner/Natural Magic | 15 |
| 70 | United Artists UAS 29108 | NED KELLY (LP, soundtrack) | 35 |
| 70 | Warner Bros WS 2554 | PERFORMANCE (LP, first pressing, orange label, soundtrack) | 40 |
| 70 | Warner Bros WS 2554 | PERFORMANCE (LP, second pressing, green label, soundtrack) | 30 |

*(see also Rolling Stones)*

## JAGS (1)
| | | | |
|---|---|---|---|
| 61 | Decca F 11397 | The Hunch/Cry Wolf | 8 |

## JAGS (2)
| | | | |
|---|---|---|---|
| 79 | Island WIP 6501 | Back Of My Hand/Double Vision (p/s) | 6 |
| 80 | Island WIP 6531 | Woman's World/Dumb Blonde (p/s) | 8 |
| 80 | Island WIP 6587 | Party Games/She's So Considerate (p/s) | 10 |
| 80 | Island WIP 6666 | I Never Was A Beach Boy/Tune Into Heaven (p/s) | 18 |
| 80 | Island WIP 6683 | The Sound Of G-O-O-D-B-Y-E/The Hurt (no p/s) | 10 |

## JAGUAR
| | | | |
|---|---|---|---|
| 81 | Heavy Metal HEAVY 10 | Back Street Woman/Chasing The Dragon (p/s) | 40 |
| 82 | Neat NEAT 16 | Axe Crazy/War Machine (p/s) | 20 |
| 83 | Neat NEAT 1007 | POWER GAMES (LP, some on purple vinyl) | 30 |
| 83 | Neat NEAT 1007 | POWER GAMES (LP, black vinyl) | 18 |
| 84 | Roadrunner RR 9851 | THIS TIME (LP) | 15 |

## JAGUARS
| | | | |
|---|---|---|---|
| 63 | Impression IMP 101 | Opus To Spring/The Beat (1,000 only) | 35 |
| 65 | Contest RGJ 152 | We'll Live On Happily/Now You Wonder Why | 300 |

*(see also Dave Mason)*

## JAGWA MA
| | | | |
|---|---|---|---|
| 12 | Blue Rider BLUS001 | Come Save Me/What Love | 6 |

## JAH BUNNY
| | | | |
|---|---|---|---|
| 77 | Mainline ML2 | Six And Seven Books/Version (actually by Reggae Scientist) | 12 |
| 80 | White Label | DUBBS INTERNATIONAL (LP) | 40 |

## JAH DAVE
| | | | |
|---|---|---|---|
| 85 | Solid Groove SG 019 | Informer/RANKING REUBEN: Taken Away (12") | 40 |

## JAH ELEMENT
| | | | |
|---|---|---|---|
| 86 | Jah Element JE 001 | Jah Alone/Summertime (12") | 35 |

## JAH FATTA & THE BLACK BROTHERS
| | | | |
|---|---|---|---|
| 79 | Rite Sound RS DD 002 | Free Rasta Free/BLACK BROTHER ALL STARS: Free Dub (12") | 60 |

## JAH FISH
| | | | |
|---|---|---|---|
| 72 | Grape GR 3034 | Vampire Rock/MOD STARS: El-Sisco Rock | 15 |

## JAH FRANKIE JONES
| | | | |
|---|---|---|---|
| 77 | Third World TWS 916 | SATTA & PRAISE JAH (LP) | 45 |

## JAH FREE
| | | |
|---|---|---|
| 93 | Jah Free | Lightning Clap/Lightning Dub/Jubilation/Jubilation Dub (12") ........ 25 |

## JAH LION
| | | |
|---|---|---|
| 83 | Congo COS 2 | Melody For Negus/Negus Dub ........ 30 |
| 76 | Island ILPS 9386 | COLUMBIA COLLY (LP) ........ 30 |
| 83 | Kongo KLP 001 | PRAISE JAH (LP) ........ 100 |

*(see also Jah Lloyd)*

## JAH LLOYD
| | | |
|---|---|---|
| 73 | Jaguar JAG 102 | Channel One (with Douglas Boothe)/SOUL SYNDICATES:Channel Two ........ 6 |
| 73 | Jaguar JAG 104 | Psalm Two/SOUL SYNDICATES: Channel Two ........ 6 |
| 75 | Treble C CCC 02 | Once Bitten/CHARLEY ACE & INSWINGS: Real Red ........ 6 |
| 76 | Attack ATT 8121 | World Class/World Class (Version) ........ 6 |
| 74 | DIP PL DL 1001 | HERBS OF DUB...MORE HERBS (LP) ........ 80 |
| 78 | Virgin Frontline FL 1005 | THE HUMBLE ONE (LP) ........ 25 |
| 79 | Virgin Frontline FL 1031 | BLACK MOSES (LP) ........ 15 |
| 70s | His Majesty MH 1004 | REGGAE STICK (LP) ........ 20 |
| 70s | His Majesty MH 1003 | DREAD LION DUB (LP) ........ 40 |

*(see also Jah Lion)*

## JAH PALM
| | | |
|---|---|---|
| 79 | Soul And Fire SF 7 | Cumbaya/Version (12") ........ 30 |

## JAH RUBY
| | | |
|---|---|---|
| 77 | Dynamic DYLP 3011 | DREAD AFFAIR (LP) ........ 25 |

## JAH SCOUSE
| | | |
|---|---|---|
| 85 | Better Things BETS 1 | Merge/Vegan Mix (foldout p/s) ........ 5 |

## JAH SHAKA
| | | |
|---|---|---|
| 82 | Jah Shaka 821 | Revelation 18/Revelation Dub (12", red vinyl) ........ 20 |
| 82 | Jah Shaka 823 | Jah Children (with Sister Pat)/SHAKA RIDIM SECTION : Jah Works (12") ........ 35 |
| 82 | Jah Shaka 828 | Lion Youth/MAD PROFESSOR : Beyond The Realms (12") ........ 20 |
| 82 | Jah Shaka LP 824 | THE COMMANDMENTS OF DUB (LP) ........ 25 |
| 82 | Rough trade ROUGH 50 | COMMANDMENTS OF DUB (LP) ........ 15 |
| 83 | Jah Shaka 833 | REVELATION SONGS (LP) ........ 15 |
| 84 | Jah Shaka SHAKA 845 | KINGS MUSIC (VOCALS AND DUBS) (LP) ........ 18 |
| 84 | Jah Shaka 847 | COMMANDMENTS OF DUB PART 2 (LP) ........ 15 |
| 84 | Jah Shaka SHAKA 848 | MESSAGE FROM AFRICA (LP) ........ 15 |
| 84 | Ariwa SALP 84 | JAH SHAKA MEETS MAD PROFESSOR (LP) ........ 20 |
| 85 | Jah Shaka 849 | JAH SHAKA MEETS PEPPER IN ADDIS ABABA STUDIOS (LP) ........ 15 |
| 85 | Jah Shaka 850 | JAH SHAKA MEETS ASWAD (LP) ........ 15 |
| 85 | Jah Shaka 851 | DUB ALMIGHTY - COMMANDMENTS OF DUB VOLUME 4 (LP) ........ 15 |
| 85 | Jah Shaka SHAKA 856 | JAH DUB CREATOR (LP) ........ 15 |
| 87 | Jah Shaka 860 | DELIVERANCE - COMMANDMENTS OF DUB 6 (LP) ........ 15 |
| 86 | Jah Shaka 867 | WARRIOR - COMMANDMENTS OF DUB 7 (LP) ........ 15 |
| 89 | Jah Shaka SHAKA 87 | DISCIPLES (LP) ........ 20 |
| 89 | Mango MPLM 1001 | PRESENTS DUB MASTERS VOL. 1 (LP) ........ 15 |
| 90 | Jah Shaka SHAK 872 | CORONATION DUB (LP) ........ 20 |
| 92 | Jah Shaka SHAKA 924 | DISCIPLES PART 2 - ADDIS ABABA (LP) ........ 15 |

## JAH SHAKA VS FATMAN
| | | |
|---|---|---|
| 80 | Live & Love LP 10 | LIVE (LP) ........ 30 |

## JAH STITCH
| | | |
|---|---|---|
| 77 | Penguin PEN 16 | Militant Man/Sugar Dandy ........ 10 |
| 77 | Third World TW 73 | Black Harmony Killer/Natty on Top (12") ........ 12 |
| 78 | Aries PFUS 6000 | Combination Three/Combine Version ........ 8 |
| 75 | Third World TWS 401 | NO DREAD CAN'T DEAD (LP) ........ 30 |
| 78 | Cancer CANSLP 002 | MY PRECIOUS LOCKS (LP) ........ 25 |

## JAH THOMAS
| | | |
|---|---|---|
| 78 | Greensleeves GRE 12 | Stop Yu Loafin'/Bicycle Skank ........ 10 |
| 78 | Greensleeves GREL 3 | STOP YU LOAFIN' (LP) ........ 25 |
| 80 | Daddy Kool DKLP 16 | DANCE HALL STYLEE (LP) ........ 25 |
| 83 | Silver Camel SCLP 03 | DANCE HALL CONNECTION (LP) ........ 15 |

## JAH WALTON
| | | |
|---|---|---|
| 81 | Music Force MFLP 02 | TOUCH HERE WHERE SHE WANT IT MOST (LP) ........ 80 |

## JAH WARRIOR
| | | |
|---|---|---|
| 97 | Jah Warrior JW 703 | Hiding From Reality/Reality Dub ........ 8 |
| 96 | Jah Warrior JWLP 005 | AFRICAN TRIBES DUB (LP) ........ 15 |

## JAH WOBBLE
| | | |
|---|---|---|
| 79 | Virgin VS 275 | Dan Macarthur/Dan Macarthur (p/s) ........ 7 |
| 78 | Virgin VOLE 9 | Dreadlock Don't Deal In Wedlock/Pthilius Pubis (p/s) ........ 5 |
| 80 | Virgin VS 337 | Betrayal/MR. X: Battle Of Britain (p/s) ........ 5 |
| 82 | Jah Wobble JAH 1 | Fading/Nocturnal (p/s, as Jah Wobble With Animal) ........ 5 |
| 94 | Island ILSD 8044 | HEAVEN & EARTH (2-LP) ........ 30 |

*(see also Bartok)*

## JAH WOBBLE, THE EDGE & HOLGER CZUKAY
| | | |
|---|---|---|
| 83 | Island WOB 1 | Snake Charmer/Hold On To Your Dreams (p/s) ........ 5 |

*(see also Don Letts & Jah Wobble, Joolz, Public Image Ltd, The Edge, Orb, Can)*

## JAH WOOSH
| | | |
|---|---|---|
| 74 | Cactus CT 39 | Judy Drownded/Crooked Skank ........ 8 |
| 75 | Lucky DL 5096 | Don't Do That/That Dub ........ 8 |
| 75 | Lucky DL 5094 | Rocking Blues/Version ........ 7 |

| | | | MINT VALUE £ |
|---|---|---|---|
| 75 | Tropical AL 057 | Iffie This Life/Iffie Version.................... | 10 |
| 76 | Sunshot SS002 | Religious Dread/Religious Dub ................ | 10 |
| 76 | Sunshot SS005 | Ital Feast/Dub Feast ....................... | 10 |
| 76 | Angen ANG 116 | Set Up Yourself Dread/Version ................ | 10 |
| 76 | Attack ATT 8124 | I'm Alright/Version........................ | 12 |
| 76 | Attack ATT 8129 | Show I The Way/Show I The Way (Version) ......... | 12 |
| 77 | Sunshot SS009 | Whip Them Jah/Version ..................... | 10 |
| 78 | Grove Music GMDM 7 | Pay Them Dues/Diverse Doctrine (with Ras Ibuna) (12") ... | 15 |
| 78 | Freedom Sounds FSD 001 | Ales Skank/Different Style (12") .............. | 15 |
| 78 | Attack ATT 8137 | Marcus Say/Take Heed ..................... | 8 |
| 79 | Yard International YI 02 | Jah Is The Ruler/Ruling Power/Jammys At The Control (12") ... | 30 |
| 74 | Cactus CTLP 103 | JAH WOOSH (LP)......................... | 25 |
| 76 | Student STULP 1003 | CHALIS BLAZE (LP)........................ | 25 |
| 76 | Trojan TRLS 133 | DREADLOCKS AFFAIR (LP)................... | 15 |
| 76 | Black Wax WAX LP2 | PSALMS OF WISDOM (LP).................... | 100 |
| 76 | Cactus CTLP 116 | JAH JAH DEY DEY (LP)...................... | 25 |
| 77 | K&B KBLP 002 | LICK HIM WITH THE DUSTBIN (LP) ............. | 25 |
| 78 | Trojan TRLS 157 | RELIGIOUS DREAD (LP).................... | 30 |
| 79 | Creation Rebel CRBLP900 | MARIJUANA WORLD TOUR (LP)................. | 20 |
| 79 | Dread & Dread 002 | GATHERING ISRAEL (LP, multi-coloured vinyl) ....... | 35 |
| 90 | Reggae Collectors RCLP 338 | JAH WOOSH (LP, reissue) .................... | 15 |

## JAH YOUTH
| | | | |
|---|---|---|---|
| 76 | Caribbean CBN 307 | Little Natty Dread/Little Natty Dread Version ........ | 6 |

## JAHFA CULTURE & THE OFFBEAT POSSE
| | | | |
|---|---|---|---|
| 86 | Jah Tubbys JT 017 | Listen To We/Listen Mix (12")................ | 175 |

## JAILHOUSE
| | | | |
|---|---|---|---|
| 72 | Pye 7N 45172 | Ya Hoo Hoo/Bad End ....................... | 12 |
| | *(see also Hamlett)* | | |

## JAILHOUSE RECIPES
| | | | |
|---|---|---|---|
| 89 | First Strike FS 01 | ENERGY IN AN EMPTY TANK WORLD (LP) ......... | 15 |

## JAKE & FAMILY JEWELS
| | | | |
|---|---|---|---|
| 70 | Polydor 2425 027 | JAKE AND THE FAMILY JEWELS (LP)............. | 15 |

## JAKLIN
| | | | |
|---|---|---|---|
| 69 | Stable SLE 8003 | JAKLIN (LP, laminated sleeve, black/silver labels) ....... | 400 |

## JAKOB
| | | | |
|---|---|---|---|
| 78 | SRTS 78 CUS 152 | I Am A Child/Day By Day ..................... | 25 |

## JAKPAK
| | | | |
|---|---|---|---|
| 81 | Dart ART 2063 | Soul In A Box/Star Struck ................... | 5 |

## (THE) JAM
### SINGLES : ORIGINAL SINGLES
| | | | |
|---|---|---|---|
| 73 | Fanfare | Blueberry Rock/Taking My Love (From Me) (acetate) ..... | 2500 |
| 73 | Fanfare | Some Kinda Lovin'/Making My Way Back Home (acetate 6 copies only) ......... | 2500 |
| 75 | Fanfare | When I Needed You/Please Don't Treat Me Bad/Taking My Love/Again (acetate) .... | 2500 |
| 77 | Polydor 2058 866 | In The City/Takin' My Love (side opening p/s, plastic silver label) ...... | 5 |
| 77 | Polydor 2058 903 | All Around The World/Carnaby Street ......... | 5 |
| 77 | Polydor 2058 945 | The Modern World/Sweet Soul Music/Back In My Arms Again/ Bricks And Mortar (Part) (B-sides live at 100 Club 11.9.77) ..... | 5 |
| 78 | Polydor 2058 995 | News Of The World/Aunties And Uncles (Impulsive Youths)/Innocent Man ...... | 5 |

*(The above singles were reissued in 1980 in picture sleeves; early originals have curved edges on sleeve openings wheras reissues are straight. Lettering on the reissue labels tends to be fatter, reissues are worth £2-3).*

| | | | |
|---|---|---|---|
| 78 | Polydor 2059 054 | David Watts/"A" Bomb In Wardour Street (double-A-sided 7"; A-side songwriter miscredited as "Ray Davis" without an "e") .......... | 15 |
| 78 | Polydor 2059 054 | David Watts/"A" Bomb In Wardour Street (double-A-sided 7"; side opening p/s, plastic moulded label, those with white paper labels are worth £8)............ | 5 |
| 78 | Polydor POSP 8 (2059 068) | Down In The Tube Station At Midnight/So Sad About Us/The Night (7"; misprinted with erroneous B-side ref. to All Mod Cons) ........ | 15 |
| 78 | Polydor POSP 8 (2059 068) | Down In The Tube Station At Midnight/So Sad About Us/The Night) ...... | 5 |
| 79 | Polydor POSP 83 | The Eton Rifles/See Saw ..................... | 5 |
| 80 | Polydor POSPJ 113 2816 024 | Going Underground/The Dreams Of Children/Away From The Numbers/The Modern World/Down In The Tube Station At Midnight................ | 8 |

*Note: All 7" singles prior to 'Beat Surrender' were re-pressed on 14th January 1983 in their picture sleeves, the second reissue for singles prior to 'Going Underground'.*

| | | | |
|---|---|---|---|
| 80 | Polydor 2059 266 | Start/Liza Radley ........................ | 5 |

### SINGLES : REISSUES & RETROSPECTIVE SINGLES
| | | | |
|---|---|---|---|
| 83 | Polydor 2059 482/POSP 482 | That's Entertainment/Down In The Tube Station At Midnight (Live Version) (UK reissue of earlier import) ........ | 5 |
| 83 | Polydor POSP 483 | Just Who Is The 5 O'Clock Hero/The Great Depression (UK reissue of earlier import) ..... | 5 |
| 89 | Old Gold OG 9895 | Beat Surrender/The Bitterest Pill (I Ever Had To Swallow) (generic Old Gold sleeve) ...... | 5 |
| 89 | Old Gold OG 9896 | The Eton Rifles/Down In The Tube Station At Midnight (in p/s) ...... | 7 |
| 89 | Old Gold OG 9896 | The Eton Rifles/Down In The Tube Station At Midnight ......... | 5 |
| 89 | Old Gold OG 9897 | Going Underground/Start! (in p/s) .............. | 7 |
| 89 | Old Gold OG 9897 | Going Underground/Start! ................... | 5 |
| 89 | Old Gold OG 9894 | Town Called Malice/Absolute Beginners (in p/s)......... | 7 |
| 89 | Old Gold OG 9894 | Town Called Malice/Absolute Beginners.......... | 5 |
| 92 | Polydor PO 199 | The Dreams Of Children/Away From The Numbers (live) ...... | 6 |
| 92 | Polydor POCS 199 | The Dreams Of Children/Away From The Numbers (live) (withdrawn)......... | 6 |

### ALBUMS
| | | | |
|---|---|---|---|
| 77 | Polydor 2383 447 | IN THE CITY (LP)......................... | 18 |
| 77 | Polydor 2383 475 | THIS IS THE MODERN WORLD (LP)............... | 18 |

| | | | |
|---|---|---|---|
| 82 | Polydor POLD 5055 | THE GIFT (LP, 12/3/82, initially in pink/white striped paper bag) | 15 |
| 83 | Polydor SNAP 1/ SNAPL 45 | SNAP! (2-LP, gatefold sleeve, with bonus 7" EP: Live! Wembley Arena 2 & 3.12.82 [SNAPL 45]) | 18 |
| 91 | Receiver RRLP 141 | LIVE AT THE ROXY (LP, unreleased, white label test pressings exist with printed proof sleeve shelved before release as the recording was actually only half a show from the 100 club 11/9/77) | 150 |
| 92 | Polydor 513 177-1 | EXTRAS (2-LP, single sleeve with picture inners) | 25 |
| 93 | Polydor 519 667-1 | LIVE JAM (2-LP, single sleeve with picture inners) | 20 |
| 02 | Simply Vinyl SVLP 108 | ALL MOD CONS (LP, 180g vinyl, PVC sleeve, 2002) | 18 |
| 02 | Simply Vinyl SVLP 209 | SETTING SONS (LP, 180g vinyl, PVC sleeve, 2002) | 18 |

**PROMOS**

| | | | |
|---|---|---|---|
| 78 | Polydor 2059 054DJ | David Watts/'A' Bomb In Wardour Street | 25 |
| 82 | Polydor POSP 400 | Precious (1-sided 7", company sleeve) | 25 |
| 82 | Polydor DEN 1 | Town Called Malice (Live at Hammersmith Palais 14.12.81)/ Precious (Extended Version) (12", white label promo) | 30 |
| 82 | Polydor PODJ 540 | Beat Surrender (Censored)/Shopping (7", radio promo) | 15 |
| 82 | Polydor POSPX 540 | Beat Surrender/Shopping/Move On Up/Stoned Out Of My Mind/War (12", white label promo) | 15 |
| 83 | Polydor LEE 1 | Medley of Jam Songs to promote SNAP LP. 1-sided, plain white label) | 40 |
| 83 | Polydor SNAPL 45 | LIVE! WEMBLEY ARENA (bonus Snap! EP, white label promo) | 30 |
| 97 | Polydor 2058 266/ | In The City (1-sided 7", "20th anniversary party invite", co. sleeve; some copies with 'tax disc'-style card invite (ADMITS 1) | 25 |
| 97 | Polydor 2058 266/ ADMITS 1 | In The City (1-sided 7", "20th anniversary party invite", co. sleeve; some copies with 'tax disc'-style card invite (ADMITS 1) | 15 |
| 02 | Polydor JAMDVD 1 | THE COMPLETE JAM (2-DVD) | 25 |

**MISPRESSINGS**

| | | | |
|---|---|---|---|
| 78 | Polydor 2058 995 | News Of The World/Aunties And Uncles (Impulsive Youths)/ Innocent Man (plays B-side on both sides) | 40 |
| 78 | Polydor POSP 8 | Down In The Tube Station At Midnight/So Sad About Us/The Night (A-side plays John Travolta's "Sandy") | 30 |
| 78 | Polydor POSP 6 | Sandy/Can't Let You Go (by John Travolta, B-side mispressed with "So Sad About Us") | 30 |
| 79 | Polydor POSP 69 | When You're Young/Smithers-Jones (plays B-side both sides) | 40 |
| 80 | Polydor 2059 266 | Start!/Liza Radley (A-side plays Village People's "Can't Stop The Music") | 10 |
| 82 | Polydor POSP 400 | Town Called Malice/Precious (7", both sides play "Precious") | 30 |

**FLEXIDISCS**

| | | | |
|---|---|---|---|
| 80 | Lyntone (no cat. no.) | When You're Young (live) (1-sided fan club flexi) | 25 |
| 80 | Lyntone LYN 9048 | Boy About Town/Pop Art Poem (hard vinyl white label test pressing, same tracks both sides, without mailer, 1980) | 40 |
| 80 | Lyntone LYN 9048 | Boy About Town/Pop Art Poem (hard vinyl white label test pressing, same tracks both sides, with mailer, 1980) | 50 |
| 82 | Lyntone (no cat. no.) | Tales From The Riverbank (re-recorded) (1-sided fan club flexi) | 15 |

*(see also Style Council, Paul Weller, Time U.K., Sharp)*

**JAMAICA BAND**

| | | | |
|---|---|---|---|
| 73 | Action ACT 4611 | Sticky Fingers Part 1/Part 2 | 20 |

**JAMAICA FATS**

| | | | |
|---|---|---|---|
| 66 | Blue Beat BB 368 | Jacqueline/Please Come Home (actually by Al T. Joe & Celestials) | 22 |

*(see also Al T. Joe)*

**JAMAICA JUBILEE STOMPERS**

| | | | |
|---|---|---|---|
| 67 | Amusicon AMU 1002 | Give Your Love To Me/I Cry To My Heart | 15 |

**JAMAICAN ACTIONS**

| | | | |
|---|---|---|---|
| 68 | Coxsone CS 7070 | Catch The Quinella/JACKIE MITTOO: Songbird | 80 |

**JAMAICAN EAGLES**

| | | | |
|---|---|---|---|
| 73 | Harry J HJ 6661 | Country Living/Country Living (Version) | 5 |

*(see also Eagles)*

**JAMAICAN FOUNDATIONS**

| | | | |
|---|---|---|---|
| 68 | Coxsone CS 7036 | Take It Cool/VICEROYS: Try Hard To Leave | 200 |

**JAMAICANS**

| | | | |
|---|---|---|---|
| 66 | Doctor Bird DB 1109 | Cool Night/Ma And Pa | 75 |
| 67 | Trojan TR 007 | Dedicated To You/The Things I Said To You | 35 |
| 67 | Treasure Isle TI 7007 | Things You Say You Love/I've Got A Pain | 35 |
| 67 | Treasure Isle TI 7012 | Baba Boom (Festival Song 1967) (actually by Baba Boom)/ TOMMY McCOOK & SUPERSONICS: Real Cool | 25 |
| 67 | Treasure Isle TI 7037 | Peace And Love/Woman Gone Home | 35 |
| 69 | Escort ES 806 | Early In The Morning/Mr. Lonely | 15 |
| 70 | Harry J. HJ 6604 | Fire Parts 1 & 2 | 10 |
| 71 | Dynamc DYN 410 | Love Uprising/My Love For You | 7 |
| 71 | Dynamic DYN 417 | Mary/CONSCIOUS MINDS: Soldier Boy | 7 |
| 71 | New Beat NB 084 | Mary/CONSCIOUS MINDS: Soldier Boy | 7 |
| 72 | Dynamic DYN 430 | I Believe In Music/Music (Version) | 5 |
| 72 | Dynamic DYN 442 | Are You Sure/Are You Sure (Version) | 5 |
| 72 | Dynamic DYN 456 | Sunshine Love/Sunshine Version | 5 |
| 74 | Dragon DRA 1029 | My Heart Just Keeps On Breaking/My Heart Just Keeps On Breaking (Inst'l) | 5 |

*(see also Norris Weir & Jamaicans, Tommy Cowan)*

**JAMAICAN SHADOWS**

| | | | |
|---|---|---|---|
| 67 | Coxsone CS 7005 | HUGH GODFREY : Have Mercy/Blending Love | 40 |
| 69 | Upsetter US 320 | Dirty Dozen (actually by Upsetters)/Crying Too Long | 40 |

**JAMAICA'S OWN VAGABONDS**

| | | | |
|---|---|---|---|
| 64 | Decca DFE 8588 | BEHOLD (EP) | 30 |
| 64 | Decca LK 4617 | SKA TIME (LP) | 50 |
| 70 | Decca Eclipse ECM 7028 | SKA TIME (LP, reissue) | 20 |

*(see also Vagabonds, Jimmy James & Vagabonds)*

## JAMES

| | | | |
|---|---|---|---|
| 84 | Factory FAC 78 | JIMONE EP: What's The World/Fire So Close/Folklore (p/s) | 12 |
| 85 | Factory FAC 119 | Hymn From A Village/If Things Were Perfect (p/s) | 15 |
| 85 | Factory FAC 138 | VILLAGE FIRE: What's The World/Fire So Close/Folklore/Hymn From A Village/If Things Were Perfect (12" EP) | 12 |
| 86 | Sire JIM 3T | Chain Mail/Uprising/Hup Springs (12", p/s) | 15 |
| 86 | Sire JIM 3 | Chain Mail/Hup Springs (p/s) | 6 |
| 86 | Sire JIM 4 | So Many Ways/Withdrawn (p/s) | 25 |
| 86 | Sire JIM 4T | So Many Ways/Just Hipper/Withdrawn (12", p/s) | 15 |
| 88 | Blanco Y Negro NEG 26 | Yaho/Mosquito (p/s) | 8 |
| 88 | Blanco Y Negro NEG 26T | Yaho/Mosquito/Left Out Of Her Will/New Nature (12", p/s) | 12 |
| 88 | Blanco Y Negro NEG 31 | What For/Island Swing (p/s) | 6 |
| 88 | Blanco Y Negro NEG 31T | What For (Climax Mix)/Island Swing/Not There (12", p/s) | 10 |
| 88 | Blanco Y Negro NEG 31C | What For (Climax Mix)/Island Swing/Not There (7", in video-style box) | 8 |
| 89 | Rough Trade RT 225 | Sit Down/Sky Is Falling (p/s) | 6 |
| 89 | Rough Trade RTT 225 | Sit Down/Goin' Away/Sky Is Falling (12", p/s, 1st 500 with postcard) | 10 |
| 89 | Rough Trade RT 245 | Come Home/Promised Land (p/s) | 6 |
| 89 | Rough Trade RTT 245 | Come Home (Long Version)/Come Home (7" Version)/Promised Land/ Slow Right Down (Demo Version) (12", p/s) | 10 |
| 90 | Fontana JIMM 512 | How Was It For You?/How Was It For You? (Different Mix)/Lazy/ Undertaker (12", p/s, with stencil) | 10 |
| 91 | Fontana JIM 812 | SIT DOWN (12" EP, recorded live at G-Mex) | 10 |
| 93 | Fontana JIM 14 | Laid / Wah Wah Kits (p/s) | 5 |
| 90s | Lyntone | Weather Change (Demo Version) (flexidisc, with tour programme) | 10 |
| 89 | Rough Trade ONEMAN 1LP | ONE MAN CLAPPING (LP, with inner sleeve) | 15 |
| 93 | Fontana 5149431 | LAID (LP, with mailing card insert) | 35 |
| 93 | Fontana 5149431 | LAID (LP, without mailing card insert) | 25 |
| 94 | Fontana 5228271 | WAH WAH (2-LP) | 25 |
| 97 | Fontana 534 3541 | WHIPLASH (LP) | 40 |
| 03 | Simply Vinyl SVLP 158 | LAID (2-LP, reissue) | 25 |
| 12 | Universal 2753129 | THE GATHERING SOUND (12", 3-CD, DVD, memory stick, book, badges, stickers, signed art print, 500 only box set) | 70 |

## BARNABY JAMES

| | | | |
|---|---|---|---|
| 71 | Decca F 13198 | Feeling Alright/Gone Fishing | 6 |

## B.B. JAMES

| | | | |
|---|---|---|---|
| 70 | Upsetter US 328 | Consider Me/Consider Me Version | 15 |

## BOB JAMES

| | | | |
|---|---|---|---|
| 76 | CTI 6063 | THREE (LP, gatefold) | 20 |

## BOBBY JAMES & DAVE (BARKER)

| | | | |
|---|---|---|---|
| 71 | Smash SMA 2314 | You Said It/AGGRO BAND: Hot Sauce | 40 |

## BRIAN JAMES (1)

| | | | |
|---|---|---|---|
| 68 | Olga OLE 005 | Come Back Silly Girl/It Just Happened That Way | 8 |

## CALVIN JAMES

| | | | |
|---|---|---|---|
| 65 | Columbia DB 7516 | Some Things You Never Get Used To/Remember | 25 |

## DANNY JAMES

| | | | |
|---|---|---|---|
| 72 | Southern Sound BT 100 | Your Gravy Train/Devil Made Me Say That | 7 |

## DAVID JAMES

| | | | |
|---|---|---|---|
| 69 | Crystal CR 7008 | Nothing Left To Lose/Go With The Times | 25 |

## DICK JAMES

| | | | |
|---|---|---|---|
| 53 | Parlophone MSP 6039 | Mother Nature And Father Time/Don't You Care | 5 |
| 53 | Parlophone MSP 6047 | The Joker/Guessing | 5 |
| 55 | Parlophone MSP 6170 | Unchained Melody/Come Back (Come Back To Me) | 5 |
| 55 | Parlophone MSP 6190 | He/So Must I Love You | 5 |
| 56 | Parlophone MSP 6199 | Robin Hood/The Ballad Of Davy Crockett | 10 |
| 56 | Parlophone MSP 6230 | Summer Sing-Song Medley | 5 |
| 56 | Parlophone R 4220 | I Only Know I Love You/Mirabelle | 5 |
| 56 | Parlophone R 4241 | Sing Song Time (No. 3) Medley | 5 |
| 57 | Parlophone R 4255 | The Garden Of Eden/I Accuse | 5 |
| 57 | Parlophone R 4314 | Westward Ho The Wagons!/The Gay Cavalier | 5 |
| 57 | Parlophone R 4375 | Skiffling Sing Song Medley | 6 |
| 58 | Parlophone R 4498 | Daddy's Little Girl/When You're Young | 5 |
| 59 | Parlophone R 4606 | There But For Your Love Go I/Minus One Heart | 5 |
| 64 | Parlophone R 5212 | Sing A Song Of Beatles With Dick James Medley (Parts 1 & 2) | 12 |

## ELMORE JAMES

| | | | |
|---|---|---|---|
| 64 | Sue WI 335 | Dust My Blues/Happy Home (as Elmore James & Broom Dusters) | 50 |
| 65 | Sue WI 383 | It Hurts Me Too/Bleeding Heart | 40 |
| 65 | Sue WI 392 | Knocking At Your Door/Calling The Blues (B-side actually by Junior Wells & Earl Hooker) | 120 |
| 66 | Sue WI 4007 | I Need You/Mean Mistreating Mama | 40 |
| 65 | Sue ILP 918 | THE BEST OF ELMORE JAMES (LP) | 80 |
| 65 | Sue ILP 927 | THE ELMORE JAMES MEMORIAL ALBUM (LP) | 80 |
| 68 | Blue Horizon 7-63204 | TOUGH (LP, with 4 tracks by John Brim) | 70 |
| 68 | Bell MBLL/SBLL 104 | SOMETHING INSIDE OF ME (LP) | 45 |
| 68 | Ember EMB 3397 | THE LATE FANTASTICALLY GREAT ELMORE JAMES (LP) | 25 |
| 70 | United Artists UAS 29109 | THE LEGEND OF ELMORE JAMES (LP) | 50 |
| 70 | Blue Horizon 7-66230 | TO KNOW A MAN (2-LP) | 75 |
| 73 | Polydor 2383 200 | COTTON PATCH HOTFOOTS (LP, shared with Walter Horton) | 20 |
| 75 | DJM DJLMD 8008 | ALL THEM BLUES (2-LP) | 18 |

**ETTA JAMES**

| | | | |
|---|---|---|---|
| 60 | London HLM 9139 | All I Could Do Was Cry/Tough Mary | 50 |
| 60 | London HLM 9234 | My Dearest Darling/Girl Of My Dreams | 30 |
| 61 | Pye International 7N 25079 | At Last/I Just Want To Make Love To You | 50 |
| 61 | Pye International 7N 25080 | Trust In Me/Anything To Say You're Mine | 20 |
| 61 | Pye International 7N 25113 | Dream/Fool That I Am | 20 |
| 62 | Pye International 7N 25131 | Something's Got A Hold On Me/Waiting For Charlie To Come Home | 40 |
| 62 | Pye International 7N 25162 | Stop The Wedding/Street Of Tears | 20 |
| 63 | Pye International 7N 25205 | Pushover/I Can't Hold It In Any More | 25 |
| 65 | Sue WI 359 | Roll With Me Henry/Good Rockin' Daddy | 60 |
| 67 | Chess CRS 8052 | I Prefer You/I'm So Glad (I Found Love In You) | 20 |
| 67 | Chess CRS 8063 | Tell Mama/I'd Rather Go Blind | 25 |
| 67 | Chess CRS 8069 | Security/I'm Gonna Take What He's Got | 15 |
| 68 | Chess CRS 8076 | I Got You Babe/I Worship The Ground You Walk On | 15 |
| 68 | Chess CRS 8082 | You Got It/Fire | 15 |
| 72 | Chess 6145 016 | Tell Mama/I'd Rather Go Blind/I Found A Love | 10 |
| 74 | Chess 6145 033 | Out On The Streets Again/Come A Little Closer | 8 |
| 78 | Warner Brothers K 17173 | Piece Of My Heart/Lovesick Blues | 8 |
| 85 | Kent 6T1 | MARY LOVE: Hey Stoney Face/IKETTES: It's Been So Long/ETTA JAMES: Wallflower | 20 |
| 65 | Chess CRL 4502 | ETTA JAMES ROCKS THE HOUSE (LP) | 75 |
| 67 | Chess CRL 4524 | AT LAST (LP) | 70 |
| 68 | Ember EMB 3390 | THE SOUL OF ETTA JAMES (LP) | 50 |
| 68 | Chess CRL 4536 | TELL MAMA (LP) | 40 |
| 73 | Chess 6671 003 | PEACHES (2-LP) | 25 |

*(see also Etta & Harvey)*

**ETTA JAMES & SUGAR PIE DESANTO**

| | | | |
|---|---|---|---|
| 65 | Chess CRS 8025 | Do I Make Myself Clear/Somewhere Down The Line | 30 |

*(see also Sugar Pie DeSanto)*

**GARY JAMES**

| | | | |
|---|---|---|---|
| 68 | Polydor 56134 | Nicole/You're Gone | 20 |
| 67 | Polydor S6208 | Teddy Bear/In The Rain | 15 |

**GRAHAM JAMES**

| | | | |
|---|---|---|---|
| 63 | Columbia DB 7128 | You Could Have Fooled Me/Why Can't You See It My Way? | 8 |

**HARRY JAMES & HIS ORCHESTRA**

| | | | |
|---|---|---|---|
| 65 | Dot DS 16729 | Love Theme From In Harm's Way/Green Onions | 5 |

*(see also Rosemary Clooney)*

**JASON JAMES**

| | | | |
|---|---|---|---|
| 67 | CBS 2705 | Miss Pilkington's Maid/Count Me Out | 30 |

**JERRY JAMES & BANDITS**

| | | | |
|---|---|---|---|
| 64 | Solar SRP 101 | Sweet Little Sixteen/Three Steps To Heaven | 15 |

**JESSE JAMES**

| | | | |
|---|---|---|---|
| 54 | Vocalion V 1037 | Southern Casey Jones/Lonesome Day Blues (78) | 20 |
| 71 | Mojo 2092 016 | Don't Nobody Want To Get Married/(Pt. 2) | 7 |
| 00 | Soul City 131 | Love Is All Right (stereo mix)/Love Is All Right (mono mix) | 8 |

**JIMMY JAMES (& THE VAGABONDS)**

| | | | |
|---|---|---|---|
| 62 | Dice CC 4 | Bewildered And Blue/I Don't Want To Cry (solo) | 20 |
| 63 | R&B JB 112 | Jump Children/Tell Me (solo) | 25 |
| 64 | Black Swan WI 437 | Thinking Of You/Shirley (solo) | 30 |
| 65 | Columbia DB 7653 | Shoo Be Doo You're Mine/We'll Never Stop Loving You | 20 |
| 66 | Ska Beat JB 242 | Your Love/Someday (solo) | 18 |
| 66 | Piccadilly 7N 35298 | I Feel Alright/I Wanna Be Your Everything (p/s) | 75 |
| 66 | Piccadilly 7N 35298 | I Feel Alright/I Wanna Be Your Everything | 30 |
| 66 | Piccadilly 7N 35320 | Hi Diddley Dee Dum Dum (It's A Good Good Feelin')/Come To Me Softly | 20 |
| 66 | Piccadilly 7N 35331 | This Heart Of Mine/I Don't Wanna Cry (p/s) | 100 |
| 66 | Piccadilly 7N 35331 | This Heart Of Mine/I Don't Wanna Cry | 75 |
| 66 | Piccadilly 7N 35349 | Ain't Love Good, Ain't Love Proud/Don't Know What I'm Gonna Do | 20 |
| 67 | Piccadilly 7N 35360 | I Can't Get Back Home To My Baby/Hungry For Love (solo) | 12 |
| 67 | Piccadilly 7N 35374 | No Good To Cry/You Showed Me The Way | 12 |
| 68 | Pye 7N 17579 | Red Red Wine/Who Could Be Loving You | 10 |
| 69 | Pye 7N 17719 | Close The Door/Why (solo) | 5 |
| 71 | Trojan TR 7806 | Help Yourself/Why | 25 |
| 72 | Bamboo BAM 67 | Riverboat Jenny/If I Wasn't Black | 7 |
| 72 | Stateside SS 2209 | A Man Like Me/Survival | 15 |
| 72 | Stateside SS 2209 | A Man Like Me/Survival (DJ copy) | 35 |
| 75 | Pye 7N 45524 | Whatever Happened To The Love We Knew/Let's Have Fun | 5 |
| 75 | Pye 7N 45472 | Hey Girl/I Am Somebody | 50 |
| 66 | Piccadilly NEP 34053 | JIMMY JAMES AND THE VAGABONDS (EP) | 40 |
| 66 | Piccadilly NPL 38027 | THE NEW RELIGION (LP) | 40 |
| 68 | Pye N(S)PL 18231 | OPEN UP YOUR SOUL (LP) | 25 |

**JIMMY JAMES & THE VAGABONDS/ALAN BOWN SET**

| | | | |
|---|---|---|---|
| 67 | Pye N(S)PL 18156 | LONDON SWINGS - LIVE AT THE MARQUEE CLUB (LP, 1 side each) | 30 |

*(see also Vagabonds, Jamaica's Own Vagabonds, Alan Bown Set)*

**JOHN JAMES**

| | | | |
|---|---|---|---|
| 70 | Transatlantic TRA 219 | MORNING BRINGS THE LIGHT (LP) | 30 |
| 71 | Transatlantic TRA 242 | JOHN JAMES (LP) | 20 |
| 76 | Kicking Mule SNKF 128 | DESCRIPTIVE GUITAR INSTRUMENTALS (LP) | 15 |
| 78 | Kicking Mule SNKF 136 | LIVE IN CONCERT (LP) | 18 |
| 84 | Stoptime STOP 101 | ACOUSTICA ECLECTICA (LP, signed) | 35 |

# JONI JAMES

| | | | MINT VALUE £ |
|---|---|---|---|
| 84 | Stoptime STOP 101 | ACOUSTICA ECLECTICA (LP) | 20 |

**JONI JAMES**

| 53 | MGM SP 1013 | Why Don't You Believe Me?/Wishing Ring | 10 |
|---|---|---|---|
| 60 | MGM MGM-EP 728 | THE SONGS OF HANK WILLIAMS (EP, mono) | 10 |
| 60 | MGM MGM-ES 3501 | THE SONGS OF HANK WILLIAMS (EP, stereo) | 10 |
| 54 | MGM MGM-D 127 | LET THERE BE LOVE (10" LP) | 15 |

**JOSE JAMES**

| 08 | Brownsville BWOOD026LP | THE DREAMER (LP) | 35 |
|---|---|---|---|

**MARK JAMES**

| 67 | Liberty LIB 55953 | Bimbo Knows/I Can't Let You Go | 5 |
|---|---|---|---|

**NICKY JAMES (MOVEMENT)**

| 63 | Pye 7N 15560 | My Colour Is Blue/Take Me Back | 80 |
|---|---|---|---|
| 65 | Columbia DB 7747 | Stagger Lee/I'm Hurtin' Inside (as Nicky James Movement) | 30 |
| 67 | Philips BF 1566 | I Need To Be Needed/So Glad We Made It | 7 |
| 68 | Philips BF 1635 | Would You Believe/Silver Butterfly | 18 |
| 68 | Philips BF 1694 | Lookin' Through Windows/Nobody But Me | 7 |
| 69 | Philips BF 1755 | Time/Little Bit Of Paper | 8 |
| 69 | Philips BF 1804 | Reaching For The Sun/No Life At All | 7 |
| 72 | Threshold TH 12 | Why/Foreign Shore | 6 |
| 73 | Threshold TH 16 | Black Dream/She Came To Me | 6 |
| 73 | Threshold TH 17 | I Guess I've Always Loved You/My Style | 8 |
| 71 | Philips 6308 069 | NICKY JAMES (LP, black/silver labels) | 100 |
| 73 | Threshold THS 10 | EVERY HOME SHOULD HAVE ONE (LP, gatefold sleeve) | 30 |
| 76 | Threshold THS 19 | THUNDERTHROAT (LP) | 15 |

*(see also Move)*

**OSCAR JAMES**

| 64 | Carnival CV 7007 | Louisa/Go 'Way | 7 |
|---|---|---|---|

**PHILIP JAMES & BLUES BUSTERS**

| 65 | Island WI 219 | Wide Awake In A Dream/MAYTALS: Tell Me The Reason | 75 |
|---|---|---|---|

*(see also Blues Busters)*

**RICKY JAMES**

| 57 | HMV POP 306 | Knee Deep in The Blues/Bluer Than Blue | 20 |
|---|---|---|---|
| 57 | HMV POP 334 | Party Doll/Ninety-Nine Ways | 20 |

**ROGER JAMES FOUR**

| 65 | Columbia DB 7556 | Letter From Kathy/Leave Me Alone | 10 |
|---|---|---|---|
| 66 | Columbia DB 7813 | Better Than Here/You're Gonna Come Home Cryin' (withdrawn) | 70 |
| 66 | Columbia DB 7829 | Better Than Here/You're Gonna Come Home Cryin' | 100 |

*(see also Danny Storm)*

**ROGER JAMES**

| 71 | NEMS 563719 | If I Didn't Have You/I Know It's Love | 20 |
|---|---|---|---|
| 72 | Chapter 1 SCH 165 | Gold/Something Wonderful | 7 |
| 71 | Chapter One CHS 807 | RIDING FREE (LP, red/silver labels) | 25 |

*(see also Danny Storm, Prestons)*

**RUBY JAMES**

| 69 | Fontana TF 1051 | Gettin' Mighty Crowded/Don't Play That Song | 20 |
|---|---|---|---|

**SALLY JAMES**

| 74 | Philips 6006 418 | Isn't It Good/Wake Me When It's Over (p/s) | 7 |
|---|---|---|---|

**SKIP JAMES**

| 65 | Vanguard VSD 79219 | SKIP JAMES TODAY (LP) | 40 |
|---|---|---|---|
| 67 | Private PR3 | 1964-67 (LP, 99 copies only) | 100 |
| 67 | Vanguard SVRP 19001 | SKIP JAMES TODAY (LP, reissue) | 30 |
| 68 | Vanguard VSD 79273 | DEVIL GOT MY WOMAN (LP) | 45 |
| 70 | Spokane SPL 1003 | THE ORIGINAL 1930/31 RECORDINGS (LP) | 50 |
| 78 | Vanguard VDP 20001 | I'M SO GLAD (LP) | 20 |
| 69 | Storyville 670 185 | THE GREATEST OF THE DELTA BLUES SINGERS (LP) | 18 |

**SONNY JAMES**

| 56 | Capitol CL 14635 | The Cat Came Back/Hello Old Broken Heart | 20 |
|---|---|---|---|
| 56 | Capitol CL 14664 | Twenty Feet Of Muddy Water/For Rent (One Empty Heart) | 15 |
| 57 | Capitol CL 14683 | Young Love/You're The Reason I'm In Love | 12 |
| 57 | Capitol CL 14708 | First Date, First Kiss, First Love/Speak To Me | 12 |
| 57 | Capitol CL 14742 | Dear Love/Lovesick Blues | 10 |
| 57 | Capitol CL 14788 | Love Conquered (Love Came, Love Saw)/A Mighty Lovable Man | 10 |
| 57 | Capitol CL 14814 | Uh-Huh-Mm/Why Can't They Remember? | 30 |
| 58 | Capitol CL 14848 | Kathaleen/Walk To The Dance | 15 |
| 58 | Capitol CL 14879 | Are You Mine/Let's Play Love | 5 |
| 58 | Capitol CL 14915 | You Got That Touch/I Can See It In Your Eyes | 6 |
| 58 | Capitol CL 14952 | I Can't Stay Away From You/Let Me Be The One To Love You | 5 |
| 59 | Capitol CL 14991 | Yo-Yo/Dream Big | 10 |
| 59 | Capitol CL 15022 | Talk Of The School/The Table | 5 |
| 59 | Capitol CL 15046 | Pure Love/This Love Of Mine | 5 |
| 59 | Capitol CL 15079 | Red Mud/Who's Next In Line | 5 |
| 60 | London HL 9132 | Jenny Lou/Passin' Through | 10 |
| 65 | Capitol CL 15377 | You're The Only World I Know/Tying The Pieces Together | 5 |
| 57 | Capitol EAP1 827 | YOUNG LOVE (EP) | 20 |
| 64 | Capitol EAP1 20654 | YOU'RE THE ONLY WORLD I KNOW (EP) | 20 |
| 57 | Capitol T 779 | SOUTHERN GENTLEMAN (LP) | 10 |
| 57 | Capitol T 867 | SONNY (LP) | 20 |
| 63 | London HA-D 8049 | YOUNG LOVE (LP) | 20 |

## STU(ART) JAMES (& MOJOS)
| | | | |
|---|---|---|---|
| 65 | Decca F 12231 | Wait A Minute/Wonder If She Knows (as Stu James & Mojos) | 12 |
| 74 | Bradleys BRAD 7406 | I Only Wish I Had The Time/Back To Basingstoke (Part 1) | 5 |
| 76 | Bradleys BRAD 7614 | I'm In The Mood/Firefly (as Stuart James) | 8 |

*(see also Mojos)*

## SULLIVAN JAMES BAND
| | | | |
|---|---|---|---|
| 66 | Parlophone R 5465 | Goodbye Mr. Heartache/We're Gonna Make It | 10 |

## TOMMY JAMES & SHONDELLS
| | | | |
|---|---|---|---|
| 66 | Roulette RK 7000 | Hanky Panky/SHONDELLS: Thunderbolt | 15 |
| 66 | Pye International 7N 25398 | It's Only Love/Ya! Ya! | 10 |
| 67 | Major Minor MM 511 | I Think We're Alone Now/Gone Gone Gone | 12 |
| 67 | Major Minor MM 548 | Out Of The Blue/Love's Closing In On Me | 5 |
| 68 | Major Minor MM 558 | Wish It Were You/Get Out Now | 8 |
| 68 | Major Minor MM 567 | Mony Mony/One, Two, Three And I Fell | 7 |
| 68 | Roulette RO 500 | Do Something To Me/Somebody Cares | 8 |
| 69 | Roulette RO 502 | Crimson And Clover/Some Kind Of Love | 10 |
| 69 | Roulette RO 506 | Sweet Cherry Wine/Breakaway | 5 |
| 69 | Roulette RO 507 | Crystal Blue Persuasion/I'm Alive | 12 |
| 69 | Roulette RO 511 | Ball Of Fire/Makin' Good Time | 6 |
| 70 | Roulette RO 513 | She/Loved One | 5 |
| 70 | Roulette RO 516 | Come To Me/Talkin' And Signifyin' | 5 |
| 70 | Roulette RO 518 | Ball And Chain/Candy Makers (solo) | 5 |
| 68 | Major Minor MMLP/SMLP 27 | SOMETHING SPECIAL (LP) | 35 |
| 68 | Roulette RRLP/SRLP 1 | MONY MONY (LP) | 30 |
| 68 | Roulette RRLP/SRLP 2 | CRIMSON AND CLOVER (LP) | 40 |
| 69 | Roulette RRLP/SRLP 3 | CELLOPHANE SYMPHONY (LP) | 20 |
| 72 | Roulette 2432 002 | THE BEST OF TOMMY JAMES & THE SHONDELLS (LP) | 15 |

## TONY JAMES
| | | | |
|---|---|---|---|
| 68 | Jolly JY 002 | Treat Me Right/Me Donkey's Dead | 20 |

## WINSTON JAMES
| | | | |
|---|---|---|---|
| 70 | Hot Rod HR 106 | Prison Sentence/JANET FERRON: Darling I Need You | 45 |
| 70 | Torpedo TOR 6 | I May Never/Longest Day | 45 |
| 70 | Torpedo TOR 4 | Gal You Think You Nice/White Silver Sands | 100 |

## JAMES BOYS (1)
| | | | |
|---|---|---|---|
| 63 | Direction 58-3721 | The Mule (Instrumental)/The Horse (Vocal) | 15 |

## JAMES BOYS (2)
| | | | |
|---|---|---|---|
| 73 | Penny Farthing PEN 806 | Over And Over/Same Old Way | 5 |
| 74 | Penny Farthing PEN 846 | I Love You/Pick A Bale Of Cotton | 5 |
| 74 | Penny Farthing PEN 857 | Up Until Now/Pick A Bale Of Cotton | 5 |

## JAMES BROTHERS
| | | | |
|---|---|---|---|
| 68 | Page One POF 077 | I Forgot To Give You Love/The Truth About It | 8 |
| 68 | Page One POF 088 | Does It Have To Be Me/You Don't Really Love Me | 8 |
| 74 | Penny Farthing PEN 857 | Up Until Now/Pick A Bale Of Cotton | 6 |

*(see also Wheels)*

## JAMES GANG
| | | | |
|---|---|---|---|
| 70 | Stateside SS 2158 | Funk No. 48/Collage | 15 |
| 70 | Stateside SS 2173 | Stop/Take A Look Around (withdrawn) | 15 |
| 70 | Probe PRO 502 | Funk 49/Thanks | 8 |
| 71 | Probe PRO 533 | Walk Away/Yadig? | 8 |
| 70 | Stateside SSL 10295 | YER' ALBUM (LP) | 20 |
| 70 | Probe SPB 6253 | RIDES AGAIN (LP) | 18 |
| 71 | Probe SPB 1038 | THIRDS (LP) | 15 |
| 71 | Probe SPB 1045 | LIVE IN CONCERT (LP, textured sleeve, flipback sleeve) | 15 |
| 72 | Probe SPB 1056 | STRAIGHT SHOOTER (LP) | 15 |

*(see also Tommy Bolin)*

## BOBBY JAMESON
| | | | |
|---|---|---|---|
| 64 | Decca F 12032 | All I Want Is My Baby/Each And Every Day | 40 |
| 64 | London HL 9921 | I Wanna Love You/I'm So Lonely | 30 |
| 65 | Brit WI 1001 | Rum-Pum/Please Mr. Mailman | 20 |
| 69 | Joy JOYS 193 | TOO MANY MORNINGS (LP) | 100 |

## STEPHEN JAMESON
| | | | |
|---|---|---|---|
| 70 | Pye 7N 45189 | Margie Make It March/Happiness Road | 5 |
| 73 | Dawn DNS 1035 | Don't Say/Back Together Once Again | 5 |
| 73 | Dawn DNLS 3044 | STEPHEN JAMESON (LP) | 15 |

## JAMESON RAID
| | | | |
|---|---|---|---|
| 80 | Blackbird BRAID 001 | The Hypnotist/The Raid/Gettin' Hotter/Straight From The Butchers (p/s) | 40 |
| 81 | GBH GBH 1 | Seven Days Of Splendour/It's A Crime/Catcher In The Rye (p/s, with lyric sheet, white sleeve) | 50 |
| 81 | GBH GBH 1 | Seven Days Of Splendour/It's A Crime/Catcher In The Rye (p/s, with lyric sheet, later pressing with black sleeve) | 30 |

## JAMIE JON & JERRY
| | | | |
|---|---|---|---|
| 67 | Decca F12642 | You've Still Got A Place In My Heart/One Time Lover (All Time Fool) | 6 |

## JAMIES
| | | | |
|---|---|---|---|
| 58 | Fontana H 153 | Summertime Summertime/Searching For You | 40 |
| 62 | Columbia DB 4885 | Summertime Summertime/Searching For You (reissue) | 20 |

## JAMIROQUAI
| | | | |
|---|---|---|---|
| 93 | Acid Jazz JAZID 46 | When You Gonna Learn/Too Young To Die | 8 |

MINT VALUE £

| 93 | Acid Jazz JAZID 46T | When You Gonna Learn/Didgin' Out (12", p/s) | 10 |
| 94 | Sony 477813 - 1 | THE RETURN OF THE SPACE COWBOY (2-LP) | 20 |
| 96 | Sony 4839991 | TRAVELLING WITHOUT MOVING (2-LP with bonus track Do You Know Where You're Coming From) | 20 |
| 99 | Sony S2 494517 1 | SYNKRONIZED (2-LP) | 20 |
| 01 | Sony 504069 1 | A FUNK ODYSSEY (LP) | 25 |
| 05 | Epic BL 96532 | DYNAMITE (LP) | 20 |

## JAMME
| 70 | Stateside-Dunhill SSL 5024 | JAMME (LP) | 25 |

## JOE JAMMER
| 73 | Regal Zono. SRZA 8514 | BAD NEWS (LP, gatefold sleeve, red/silver labels) | 40 |

*(see also Mitchell/Coe Mysteries)*

## JAM TODAY
| 81 | Stroppy Cow SCJT 1 | Stereotyping/Song About Myself (p/s, with insert) | 50 |

## JAN & ARNIE
| 58 | London HL 8653 | Jennie Lee/Gotta Getta Date | 40 |
| 58 | London HL 8653 | Jennie Lee/Gotta Getta Date (78) | 35 |

*(see also Jan & Dean)*

## JAN & DEAN
| 59 | London HLN 8936 | Baby Talk/Jeanette, Get Your Hair Done | 20 |
| 59 | London HLN 8936 | Baby Talk/Jeanette, Get Your Hair Done (78) | 20 |
| 59 | London HLU 8990 | There's A Girl/My Heart Sings | 25 |
| 59 | London HLU 8990 | There's A Girl/My Heart Sings (78) | 40 |
| 60 | London HLU 9063 | Clementine/You're On My Mind | 20 |
| 61 | London HLH 9395 | Heart And Soul/Midsummer Night's Dream | 15 |
| 62 | Liberty LIB 55397 | A Sunday Kind Of Love/Poor Little Puppet | 20 |
| 63 | Liberty LIB 55531 | Linda/When I Learn How To Cry | 15 |
| 63 | Liberty LIB 55580 | Surf City/She's My Summer Girl | 10 |
| 63 | Liberty LIB 55613 | Honolulu Lulu/Someday You'll Go Walkin' By | 10 |
| 64 | Liberty LIB 55641 | Drag City/Schlock Rod Pt 1 | 15 |
| 64 | Liberty LIB 55672 | Dead Man's Curve/The New Girl In School | 10 |
| 64 | Liberty LIB 55704 | The Little Old Lady From Pasadena/My Mighty GTO | 10 |
| 64 | Liberty LIB 55724 | Ride The Wild Surf/The Anaheim, Azusa And Cucamonga Sewing Circle, Book Review And Timing Association | 10 |
| 65 | Liberty LIB 55727 | Sidewalk Surfin'/When It's Over | 10 |
| 65 | Liberty LIB 55766 | (Here They Come) From All Over The World/Freeway Flyer | 12 |
| 65 | Liberty LIB 55792 | You Really Know How To Hurt A Guy/It's As Easy As 1, 2, 3 | 12 |
| 65 | Liberty LIB 55833 | I Found A Girl/It's A Shame To Say Goodbye | 10 |
| 66 | Liberty LIB 10225 | Norwegian Wood/A Beginning From An End | 20 |
| 66 | Liberty LIB 55860 | Batman/Bucket 'T' | 25 |
| 66 | Liberty LIB 10244 | Popsicle/The Joker Is Wild | 25 |
| 66 | Liberty LIB 55923 | The New Girl In School/School Day (Ring Ring Goes The Bell) | 8 |
| 66 | Liberty LIB 10252 | Tennessee/Horace The Swinging School Bus Driver | 12 |
| 67 | CBS 202630 | Yellow Balloon/A Taste Of Rain | 25 |
| 65 | Liberty LEP 2213 | SURF 'N' DRAG HITS (EP) | 30 |
| 66 | Liberty LEP 2258 | THE TITANIC TWOSOME (EP) | 30 |
| 63 | Liberty LBY 1163 | SURF CITY AND OTHER SWINGING CITIES (LP) | 30 |
| 64 | Liberty LBY 1220 | DEAD MAN'S CURVE/NEW GIRL IN SCHOOL (LP) | 35 |
| 64 | Liberty LBY 1229 | RIDE THE WILD SURF (LP) | 30 |
| 65 | Liberty LBY 1279 | GOLDEN HITS (LP) | 20 |
| 65 | Liberty LBY 1304 | FOLK 'N' ROLL (LP) | 20 |
| 66 | Liberty LBY 1309 | JAN AND DEAN MEET BATMAN (LP) | 40 |
| 66 | Liberty LBY 1339 | FILET OF SOUL (A LIVE ONE) (LP) | 20 |

*(see also Legendary Masked Surfers, Fantastic Baggys, Jan & Arnie)*

## BRUCE JANAWAY
| 78 | Deep Range SRT/CUS/216 | PURITANICAL ODES (LP, with insert) | 35 |

## JAN DUKES DE GREY
| 70 | Decca Nova (S)DN 8 | SORCERERS (LP) | 350 |
| 71 | Transatlantic TRA 234 | MICE AND RATS IN THE LOFT (LP, gatefold sleeve, plastic inner/foam opening) | 350 |

*(see also Noy's Band)*

## MARY JANE WITH BARRY GRAY & SPACEMAKERS
| 63 | Philips 326 587 BF | Robot Man/Just The Same As I Do (in p/s) | 25 |
| 63 | Philips 326 587 BF | Robot Man/Just The Same As I Do (no p/s) | 15 |

*(see also Barry Gray)*

## SARAH JANE
| 66 | Pye 7N 17114 | Listen People/The World Is Round | 7 |

## PETER JANES
| 67 | CBS 203004 | Emperors And Armies/Go Home Ulla (in p/s) | 10 |
| 67 | CBS 203004 | Emperors And Armies/Go Home Ulla | 6 |
| 68 | CBS 3299 | Do You Believe/For The Sake Of Time | 20 |

## BUSTER JANGLES' FLYING MATTRESS
| 72 | RCA RCA 2112 | Love Has Taken Over My Brain/The Little World I Knew | 25 |

## JANGLETTIES
| 81 | Eskimo Vinyl | Happy All The Time/Backseat (p/s) | 30 |

## JANIE
| 61 | Capitol CL 15180 | You Better Not Do That/Only Girls Can Tell | 12 |
| 70 | President PT 309 | Back On My Feet Again/Psycho | 20 |

*(see also Jeanne Black)*

**JANINE**
| | | | |
|---|---|---|---|
| 81 | Stiletto JAN 001 | Crazy On You/Candy (p/s) | 170 |

**JOHNNY JANIS**
| | | | |
|---|---|---|---|
| 58 | London HLU 8650 | The Better To Love You/Can This Be Love | 6 |
| 60 | Philips PB 1090 | Gina/If The Good Lord's Willin' | 6 |
| 58 | HMV 7EG 8365 | JOHNNY JANIS (EP) | 30 |
| 66 | London HA-U 8270 | ONCE IN A BLUE MOON (LP) | 20 |

**BERT JANSCH**
| | | | |
|---|---|---|---|
| 67 | Big T BIG 102 | Life Depends On Love/A Little Sweet Sunshine | 12 |
| 73 | Reprise K 14234 | Oh My Father/The First Time Ever I Saw Your Face | 7 |
| 74 | Charisma CB 240 | In The Bleak Midwinter/One For Jo | 6 |
| 75 | Charisma CB 267 | Dance Lady Dance/Build Another Band | 5 |
| 79 | Kicking Mule SCK 44 | Time And Time/Una Linea Di Dolcezza (as Bert Jansch Conundrum) | 5 |
| 82 | Logo GO 409 | Heartbreak Hotel/Up To The Stars (p/s) | 5 |
| 66 | Transatlantic EP 145 | NEEDLE OF DEATH (EP) | 40 |
| 65 | Transatlantic TRA 125 | BERT JANSCH (LP) | 50 |
| 65 | Transatlantic TRA 132 | IT DON'T BOTHER ME (LP) | 45 |
| 66 | Transatlantic TRA 143 | JACK ORION (LP) | 50 |
| 67 | Transatlantic TRA 157 | NICOLA (LP) | 50 |
| 69 | Transatlantic TRA 179 | BIRTHDAY BLUES (LP) | 50 |
| 69 | Vanguard VSD 79292 | STEPPING STONES (LP) | 30 |
| 69 | Transatlantic TRASAM 10 | THE BERT JANSCH SAMPLER (LP) | 15 |
| 71 | Transatlantic TRA 235 | ROSEMARY LANE (LP) | 25 |
| 72 | Transatlantic TRASAM 27 | BOX OF LOVE - THE BERT JANSCH SAMPLER VOL. 2 (LP) | 20 |
| 73 | Reprise K 44225 | MOONSHINE (LP, with lyric insert) | 20 |
| 74 | Charisma CAS 1090 | L.A. TURNAROUND (LP, with lyric insert) | 35 |
| 75 | Charisma CAS 1107 | SANTA BARBARA HONEYMOON (LP) | 15 |
| 77 | Charisma CAS 1127 | A RARE CONUNDRUM (LP, lyric inner) | 15 |
| 80 | Kicking Mule SNKF 162 | THIRTEEN DOWN (LP, as Bert Jansch Conundrum) | 30 |
| 88 | Demon TRANDEM1 | BERT JANSCH (LP, reissue) | 15 |

**BERT JANSCH & JOHN RENBOURN**
| | | | |
|---|---|---|---|
| 66 | Transatlantic TRA 144 | BERT AND JOHN (LP) | 50 |

*(see also Conundrum, Pentangle, John Renbourn)*

**JANUARY**
| | | | |
|---|---|---|---|
| 69 | CBS 4465 | It Sings For Me/Julie | 10 |

**JAPAN**
| | | | |
|---|---|---|---|
| 78 | Ariola Hansa AHA 510 | Don't Rain On My Parade/Stateline (solid or press-out centre, no p/s) | 15 |
| 78 | Ariola Hansa AHA 525 | The Unconventional/Adolescent Sex (with p/s) | 20 |
| 78 | Ariola Hansa AHA 525 | The Unconventional/Adolescent Sex | 6 |
| 78 | Ariola Hansa AHA 529 | Sometimes I Feel So Low/Love Is Infectious (p/s, initial pressing on blue vinyl) | 10 |
| 78 | Ariola Hansa AHA 529 | Sometimes I Feel So Low/Love Is Infectious (p/s) | 8 |
| 79 | Ariola Hansa AHA 540 | Life In Tokyo (Short Version)/Life In Tokyo Pt 2 (p/s, red vinyl) | 8 |
| 79 | Ariola Hansa AHAD 540 | Life In Tokyo (Long Version)/(Short Version) (12", p/s, red vinyl) | 12 |
| 80 | Ariola Hansa AHA 559 | I Second That Emotion/Quiet Life (dull red vinyl, card p/s) | 10 |
| 80 | Ariola Hansa AHA 559 | I Second That Emotion/Quiet Life (dull red vinyl, paper p/s) | 6 |
| 80 | Virgin VS 379 | Gentlemen Take Polaroids/The Experience of Swimming (fully autographed by band, p/s) | 75 |
| 80 | Virgin VS 379 | Gentlemen Take Polaroids/The Experience of Swimming//The Width Of A Room/Burning Bridges (double pack, gatefold p/s) | 12 |

*(see also David Sylvian)*

**JAPANESE TOY**
| | | | |
|---|---|---|---|
| 79 | Coma CUT 6 | Confusion/New Men | 5 |

**JOHNNY JAPES & HIS JESTICLES**
| | | | |
|---|---|---|---|
| 87 | Viz VIZ 1 | Bags Of Fun With Buster/Scrotal Scratch Mix (p/s) | 5 |

*(see also XTC, John Otway)*

**JARMAZ**
| | | | |
|---|---|---|---|
| 84 | Rash ITCH 1 | Night City Life/Night City Life (Disco Remix) (p/s) | 80 |

**JARMELS**
| | | | |
|---|---|---|---|
| 61 | Top Rank JAR 560 | She Loves To Dance/Little Lonely One | 30 |
| 61 | Top Rank JAR 580 | A Little Bit Of Soap/The Way You Look Tonight | 30 |

**JEAN-MICHEL JARRE**
| | | | |
|---|---|---|---|
| 85 | Polydor POSPG 740 | Zoolookologie (Remix)/Ethnicolor 2//Oxygene 4/Oxygene 6 (double pack) | 8 |
| 88 | Polydor C88 1-3 | OXYGENE (LP, HMV-only box set with booklet, 3,300 only) | 15 |
| 97 | Epic EPC 486984 1 | OXYGENE 7-13 (LP) | 18 |

**MAURICE JARRE**
| | | | |
|---|---|---|---|
| 65 | Fontana (S)TL 5259 | THE COLLECTOR (LP, soundtrack) | 25 |
| 66 | CBS (S)BPG 62843 | IS PARIS BURNING? (LP, soundtrack) | 18 |
| 67 | RCA RD 7848 | NIGHT OF THE GENERALS (LP, soundtrack) | 30 |
| 67 | RCA Victor RD/SF 7876 | THE PROFESSIONALS (LP, soundtrack) | 50 |
| 68 | Dot (S)LPD 515 | VILLA RIDES (LP, soundtrack) | 15 |

**ECCLETON JARRETT**
| | | | |
|---|---|---|---|
| 86 | CF CFD 010 | Greedy Girl/Fling It Up (12") | 40 |

**KILLERMAN JARRETT**
| | | | |
|---|---|---|---|
| 86 | Trojan TROT 9086 | War Ina South Africa/Dub/Bub 2 (12") | 30 |

**WAYNE JARRETT**
| | | | |
|---|---|---|---|
| 80 | Greensleeves GRED 41 | Saturday Night Jamboree (12") | 20 |
| 81 | Greensleeves GRED 61 | Chip In/You Were On My Mind (12") | 12 |
| 82 | Echo ECHO 011 | Satta Dread/Sadat (12") | 35 |

## Winston JARRETT

| | | | |
|---|---|---|---|
| 97 | Jah Shaka SHAKA 9772 | Praises Unto HIM/JAH SHAKA: Dub Of Praise | 10 |
| 82 | Wackies W 191 | BUBBLE UP (LP, blue label) | 25 |
| 98 | Wackies WR 191 | BUBBLE UP (LP, reissue, black label) | 15 |

### WINSTON JARRETT
| | | | |
|---|---|---|---|
| 77 | Carib Gems CG 012 | Sleepers/Sleepers Version (with the Righteous Flames) | 20 |
| 78 | Write Sounds WTS 1002 | Spanish Town Road/Version | 8 |
| 78 | Ballistic UP 36416 | War/Version (12") | 15 |
| 80 | Warrior WAR 144 | Wise Man/I Shen Galore (12") | 20 |
| 80 | Kingley Sounds REX 3 | Youth Man/Melodica (12") | 18 |
| 80 | Wambesi TWLP 1001 | WISE MAN (LP) | 25 |
| 84 | VSLP 5008 | ROCKING VIBRATION (LP) | 15 |

### MARIAN JARVIS
| | | | |
|---|---|---|---|
| 75 | Chelsea 2005 038 | A Penny For Your Thoughts/A Good Man To Wake Up To | 30 |

### JASMIN T
| | | | |
|---|---|---|---|
| 69 | Tangerine DP 13 | Some Other Guy/Evening (with p/s) | 50 |
| 69 | Tangerine DP 13 | Some Other Guy/Evening | 20 |

### JASMINE MINKS
| | | | |
|---|---|---|---|
| 84 | Creation CRE 004 | Think/Work For Nothing (p/s) | 10 |
| 84 | Creation CRE 008 | Where Traffic Goes/Mr. Magic (foldout p/s) | 15 |
| 85 | Creation CRE 018 | What's Happening/Black & Blue (p/s) | 6 |

### JASON CREST
| | | | |
|---|---|---|---|
| 68 | Philips BF 1633 | Turquoise Tandem Cycle/Good Life (in export p/s) | 175 |
| 68 | Philips BF 1633 | Turquoise Tandem Cycle/Good Life | 60 |
| 68 | Philips BF 1650 | Juliano The Bull/Two By The Sea | 40 |
| 68 | Philips BF 1687 | (Here We Go Round) The Lemon Tree/Patricia's Dream | 60 |
| 69 | Philips BF 1752 | Waterloo Road/Education | 40 |
| 69 | Philips BF 1809 | A Place In The Sun/Black Mass | 200 |

*(see also Holy Mackerel, High Broom)*

### JASON'S GENERATIONS
| | | | |
|---|---|---|---|
| 66 | Polydor BM 56042 | It's Up To You/Insurance Co.'s Are Very Unfair | 80 |

### JASPER
| | | | |
|---|---|---|---|
| 69 | Spark SRLP 103 | LIBERATION (LP, laminated front sleeve, blue/silver labels) | 750 |

### JEROME JASPER
| | | | |
|---|---|---|---|
| 82 | NYC 1 | I'll Do Anything/I'll Do Anything (Instrumental) (12" promo white label) | 25 |
| 82 | Rak 12RAK 354 | I'll Do Anything For You/Treasure The Moment (12") | 15 |

### JAVAROO
| | | | |
|---|---|---|---|
| 80 | Capitol 12CL 16142 | Breakin' In/Change It Up/Bring Out The Woman (12") | 50 |
| 80 | Capitol CL 16142 | Breakin' In/Change It Up | 10 |

### JAVELLS
| | | | |
|---|---|---|---|
| 77 | Pye Disco Demand DDS 2003 | Goodbye Nothin' To Say/Nothin' To Say | 6 |

### JAWBONE
| | | | |
|---|---|---|---|
| 70 | Carnaby CNS 4007 | How's Ya Pa?/Mister Custer | 10 |
| 70 | Carnaby CNS 4020 | Way Down Down/Bulldog Goes West | 10 |
| 72 | B&C CB 190 | Gotta Go/Automobile Blues | 6 |
| 70 | Carnaby CNLS 6004 | JAWBONE (LP) | 200 |

*(see also Mirage, Portobello Explosion)*

### BOB JAXON (& HI-TONES)
| | | | |
|---|---|---|---|
| 55 | London HL 8156 | Ali Baba/Why Does A Woman Cry (as Bob Jaxon & Hi-Tones) | 40 |
| 57 | RCA RCA 1019 | Beach Party/(Gotta Have Something In The) Bank Frank | 80 |

### FRANKIE JAXON/HOUNDHEAD HENRY
| | | | |
|---|---|---|---|
| 60 | Jazz Collector JEL 10 | THE MALE BLUES VOLUME 6 (EP) | 10 |

### JAY (BLACK)
| | | | |
|---|---|---|---|
| 64 | Coral Q 72471 | I Rise, I Fall/How Sweet It Is | 35 |
| 67 | United Artists UP 1174 | What Will My Mary Say/Return To Me (as Jay Black) | 10 |

*(see also Jay & The Americans)*

### ABNER JAY
| | | | |
|---|---|---|---|
| 63 | London HLN 9791 | Cleo/Thresher | 40 |

### ERIC JAY
| | | | |
|---|---|---|---|
| 59 | London HL 9004 | The Little Drummer Boy/Blue Champagne Cha Cha | 6 |

### LAURIE JAY COMBO
| | | | |
|---|---|---|---|
| 62 | Ember JBS 710 | Shades Of Red/Nevada Sunsets | 6 |
| 63 | HMV POP 1234 | Teenage Idol/Think Of Me (Demo copy) | 60 |
| 63 | HMV POP 1234 | Teenage Idol/Think Of Me | 75 |
| 64 | HMV POP 1300 | Love In My Heart/'Til You're Mine | 6 |
| 64 | HMV POP 1335 | Maybe/Be Good To Me | 6 |
| 65 | Decca F 12083 | A Song Called Soul/Just A Little Bit | 25 |

*(see also Nero & Gladiators)*

### LONNIE JAY & JAYNES
| | | | |
|---|---|---|---|
| 63 | Stateside SS 197 | Around And Around We Go/Somewhere | 10 |

### PETER JAY (& BLUE MEN)
| | | | |
|---|---|---|---|
| 60 | Triumph RGM 1000 | Just Too Late/Friendship (as Peter Jay & Blue Men) | 40 |
| 60 | Pye 7N 15290 | Paradise Garden/Who's The Girl? | 45 |

*(see also Blue Men)*

### PETER JAY & JAYWALKERS
| | | | |
|---|---|---|---|
| 62 | Decca F 11531 | Can Can '62/Redskins | 6 |
| 63 | Decca F 11593 | Totem Pole/Jaywalker | 7 |
| 63 | Decca F 11659 | Poet And Peasant/Oo La La | 10 |

| 63 | Decca F 11757 | Kansas City/The Parade Of Tin Soldiers .................................. 10 |
|----|---------------|------|
| 64 | Decca F 11840 | You Girl/If You Love Me.................................................. 10 |
| 64 | Piccadilly 7N 35199 | Where Did Our Love Go/Caroline .......................................... 8 |
| 64 | Piccadilly 7N 35212 | Tonight You're Gonna Fall In Love/Red Cabbage ............................ 8 |
| 65 | Piccadilly 7N 35220 | Parchman Farm/What's Easy For Two Is So Hard For One .................... 20 |
| 65 | Piccadilly 7N 35259 | Before The Beginning/Solitaire........................................... 10 |

*(see also Terry Reid, Miller, Big Boy Pete)*

## JAY (JOHN HOLT) & JOYA (LANDIS)
| 68 | Trojan TR 633 | I'll Be Lonely/SUPERSONICS: Second Fiddle ............................... 20 |
|----|---------------|------|

*(see also John Holt, Joya Landis)*

## JAY & TECHNIQUES
| 67 | Philips PB 1597 | Apples, Peaches, Pumpkin Pie/Stronger Than Dirt......................... 25 |
|----|-----------------|------|
| 67 | Philips PB 1618 | Keep The Ball Rollin'/Here We Go Again ................................. 15 |
| 67 | Mercury 6052 302 | Apples, Peaches, Pumpkin Pie/Contact .................................... 7 |
| 68 | Philips PB 1644 | Strawberry Shortcake/Still (In Love With You) .......................... 12 |
| 68 | Mercury MF 1034 | Baby Make Your Own Sweet Music/Help Yourself To All My Lovin' .......... 12 |
| 75 | Polydor 2066 473 | I Feel Love Comin' On/This World Of Mine ............................... 10 |
| 71 | Mercury MCF 127360 | Baby Make Your Own Sweet Music/Help Yourself To All My Lovin' (reissue) . 6 |
| 67 | Philips (S)BL 7834 | APPLES, PEACHES, PUMPKIN PIE (LP)....................................... 30 |

## JAY & THE AMERICANS
| 62 | HMV POP 1009 | She Cried/Dawning ...................................................... 40 |
|----|--------------|------|
| 63 | United Artists UP 1002 | This Is It/It's My Turn To Cry .......................................... 6 |
| 63 | United Artists UP 1018 | What's The Use/Strangers Tomorrow ....................................... 6 |
| 64 | United Artists UP 1039 | Come Dance With Me/Look Into My Eyes Maria ............................. 18 |
| 64 | United Artists UP 1069 | Come A Little Bit Closer/Goodbye Boys Goodbye ........................... 8 |
| 65 | United Artists UP 1075 | Let's Lock The Door (And Throw Away The Key)/I'll Remember You ......... 10 |
| 65 | United Artists UP 1088 | Think Of The Good Times/If You Were Mine Girl ........................... 8 |
| 65 | United Artists UP 1094 | Cara Mia/When It's All Over ............................................ 10 |
| 65 | United Artists UP 1108 | Some Enchanted Evening/Girl ............................................. 8 |
| 66 | United Artists UP 1119 | Sunday And Me/Through This Doorway ..................................... 12 |
| 66 | United Artists UP 1129 | Why Can't You Bring Me Home/Baby Stop Your Crying ...................... 20 |
| 66 | United Artists UP 1132 | Crying/I Don't Need A Friend ............................................ 8 |
| 66 | United Artists UP 1142 | Livin' Above Your Head/She's The Girl (That's Messing Up My Mind) ...... 30 |
| 66 | United Artists UP 1162 | (He's) Raining In My Sunshine/Reason For Living ......................... 7 |
| 67 | United Artists UP 1178 | You Ain't As Hip As All That Baby/Nature Boy .......................... 10 |
| 67 | United Artists UP 1191 | (We'll Meet In The) Yellow Forest/Got Hung Up Along The Way ............ 60 |
| 68 | United Artists UP 2211 | French Provincial/Shanghai Noodle Factory ............................. 10 |
| 69 | United Artists UP 2268 | This Magic Moment/Since I Don't Have You .............................. 10 |
| 69 | United Artists UP 35008 | When You Dance/So Much In Love .......................................... 6 |
| 69 | United Artists UP 35026 | Hushabye/No I Don't Know Her .......................................... 10 |
| 70 | United Artists UP 35074 | Walkin' In The Rain/For The Love Of A Lady ............................ 40 |
| 65 | United Artists UEP 1003 | COME A LITTLE BIT CLOSER (EP)........................................... 40 |
| 66 | United Artists UEP 1017 | LIVING WITH JAY AND THE AMERICANS (EP) ................................ 40 |
| 66 | United Artists (S)ULP 1117 | JAY AND THE AMERICANS (LP)............................................. 50 |
| 66 | United Artists (S)ULP 1128 | SUNDAY AND ME (LP)..................................................... 30 |
| 67 | United Artists (S)ULP 1150 | LIVIN' ABOVE YOUR HEAD (LP) ........................................... 40 |
| 67 | United Artists (S)ULP 1164 | TRY SOME OF THIS (LP) ................................................. 30 |

*(see also Jay, Chapter Four)*

## JAYBIRDS
| 66 | Sue WI 4013 | Somebody Help Me/The Right Kind (without writer credits) .............. 125 |
|----|-------------|------|
| 66 | Sue WI 4013 | Somebody Help Me/The Right Kind (with writer credits).................. 150 |

## JAYBIRDS (U.K.)
| 64 | Embassy WB 624 | Tell Me When/You Can't Do That........................................... 5 |
|----|----------------|------|
| 64 | Embassy WB 625 | Can't Buy Me Love/DEL MARTIN: I Love You Because ........................ 5 |
| 64 | Embassy WB 626 | Good Golly Miss Molly/............................................. 5 |
| 64 | Embassy WB 628 | Mockin' Bird Hill/Hubble Bubble (Toil And Trouble)....................... 5 |
| 64 | Embassy WB 632 | Baby Let Me Take You Home/BUD ASHTON & HIS GROUP: Rise And Fall Of Fingel Blunt . 5 |
| 64 | Embassy WB 635 | Juliet/Here I Go Again .................................................. 5 |
| 64 | Embassy WB 651 | She's Not There/PAUL RICH: I Wouldn't Trade You For The World ........... 5 |
| 64 | Embassy WB 663 | All Day And All Of The Night/Google Eye ................................. 6 |
| 64 | Embassy WB 672 | What Have They Done To The Rain/BUD ASHTON & HIS GROUP: Genie With The Light Brown Lamp ................................................... 5 |
| 65 | Embassy WB 673 | Go Now/TERRY BRANDON: Ferry 'Cross The Mersey .......................... 5 |

*(see also Ray Pilgrim & Beatmen)*

## JAY BOYS
| 69 | Trojan TR 665 | Splendour Splash/TREVOR SHIELD: Please ................................. 40 |
|----|---------------|------|
| 70 | Harry J. HJ 6602 | The Dog (Parts 1 & 2) ................................................. 12 |
| 70 | Harry J. HJ 6607 | Jack The Ripper/Don't Let Me Down ..................................... 80 |
| 70 | Harry J. HJ 6609 | Jay Moon Walk/Elcong .................................................. 20 |
| 70 | Harry J. HJ 6610 | Je T'Aime/It Ain't Me Babe ............................................ 15 |
| 70 | Harry J. HJ 6617 | Del Gago/Killer Version ............................................... 50 |
| 70 | Harry J. HJ 6618 | Can't Get Next To You/(Part 2) (both actually by Charmers)............. 10 |
| 71 | Harry J. HJ 6628 | The Arcade Walk/The Arcade Walk Vers. II .............................. 12 |
| 72 | Harry J. HJ 6644 | African People/HARRY J. ALL STARS: African (Version) .................. 15 |
| 72 | Ashanti AHS 407 | Rough Road/TREVOR SHIELD: Rough Road .................................. 12 |

*(see also Roy Panton, Bob & Marcia, Cables)*

## JERRY JAYE
| 67 | London HLU 10128 | My Girl Josephine/Five Miles From Home ................................ 40 |
|----|------------------|------|

## JAYE SISTERS

MINT VALUE £

| | | | |
|---|---|---|---|
| 59 | London HLT 9011 | Sure Fire Love/G-3 | 60 |
| 59 | London HLT 9011 | Sure Fire Love/G-3 (78) | 30 |

### JAYHAWKS (1)
| | | | |
|---|---|---|---|
| 56 | Parlophone R 4228 | Stranded In The Jungle/My Only Darling | 800 |
| 56 | Parlophone R 4228 | Stranded In The Jungle/My Only Darling (78) | 100 |

### JAYHAWKS (2)
| | | | |
|---|---|---|---|
| 92 | Def American 512.986-1 | HOLLYWOOD TOWN HALL (LP, with inner) | 100 |
| 03 | American B00000801 | RAINY DAY MUSIC (2-LP) | 20 |

### JAYLADS
| | | | |
|---|---|---|---|
| 71 | Punch PH 95 | Royal Chord (actually by Melodians)/Version (actually "In The Spirit" by Lloyd Charmers) | 15 |

*(see also Melodians)*

### JAYNETTS
| | | | |
|---|---|---|---|
| 63 | Stateside SS 227 | Sally Go Round The Roses/Sally Go Round The Roses (Instrumental) | 15 |

### JAYS
| | | | |
|---|---|---|---|
| 63 | Fontana 7F 403 | Shock A Boom/Across The Sea | 10 |

### JAYWALKERS
| | | | |
|---|---|---|---|
| 76 | Cream CRM 5003 | Can't Live Without You/Heartbroken Memories | 10 |

### JAZZ BUTCHER
| | | | |
|---|---|---|---|
| 83 | Glass GLASS 027 | Southern Mark Smith/Jazz Butcher Meets Count Dracula (p/s) | 20 |
| 85 | Glass GLASS 12041 | Real Men/The Jazz Butcher V The Prime Minister/Southern Mark Smith (Original) (12", p/s) | 20 |
| 86 | Glass HMMM 001 | Christmas With The Pygmies (p/s, promo freebie, given away at gigs) | 10 |

*(see also Institution)*

## JAZZ COMPOSERS ORCHESTRA
| | | | |
|---|---|---|---|
| 74 | JCOA/Virgin JDA 3001 | JAZZ COMPOSERS ORCHESTRA (2-LP, gatefold sleeve) | 20 |

*(see also Carla Bley, Mike Mantler, Larry Coryell)*

### JAZZ COURIERS
| | | | |
|---|---|---|---|
| 50s | (no cat. no.) | Top Spot Blues/Monk Was Here/Last Minute Blues (square flexi) | 100 |
| 57 | Tempo EXA 75 | JAZZ COURIERS (EP) | 60 |
| 59 | Tempo EXA 87 | JAZZ COURIERS (EP) | 60 |
| 58 | Tempo TAP 22 | IN CONCERT (LP) | 400 |
| 59 | Tempo TAP 26 | THE LAST WORD (LP) | 350 |
| 60 | London Jazz LTZ-L 15188 | THE COURIERS OF JAZZ! (LP) | 200 |
| 67 | M. For Pleasure MFP 1072 | IN CONCERT (LP) | 15 |
| 80s | Jasmine JASM 2004 | THE JAZZ COURIERS (LP, reissue) | 20 |
| 80s | Jasmine JASM 2024 | THE LAST WORD (LP, reissue) | 15 |

*(see also Tubby Hayes, Ronnie Scott)*

### JAZZ CRUSADERS
| | | | |
|---|---|---|---|
| 66 | Fontana 688 149 ZL | THE THING (LP) | 20 |
| 66 | Fontana 688 117 ZL | LOOKIN' AHEAD (LP) | 18 |

*(see also Crusaders)*

### JAZZ DEFEKTORS
| | | | |
|---|---|---|---|
| 87 | Factory FACT 205 | THE JAZZ DEFEKTORS (LP) | 15 |

### JAZZ FIVE
| | | | |
|---|---|---|---|
| 61 | Tempo TAP 32 | THE FIVE OF US (LP) | 400 |

*(see also Vic Ash Quartet, Harry Klein Quartet)*

### JAZZ HIP TRIO
| | | | |
|---|---|---|---|
| 67 | Major Minor MMLP 8 | JAZZ IN RELIEF (LP) | 125 |

### JAZZ MAKERS
| | | | |
|---|---|---|---|
| 66 | Ember FA 2023 | SWINGIN' SOUNDS (LP) | 20 |

### JAZZ MODES
| | | | |
|---|---|---|---|
| 60 | London Jazz LTZ-K 15191 | THE MOST HAPPY FELLA (LP) | 20 |

### JAZZ ROCK EXPERIENCE
| | | | |
|---|---|---|---|
| 70 | Deram Nova SDN 19 | JAZZ ROCK EXPERIENCE (LP) | 100 |

### JAZZATEERS
| | | | |
|---|---|---|---|
| 83 | Rough Trade RT 138 | Sixteen Reasons/Show Me The Door (p/s) | 5 |

### J & B
| | | | |
|---|---|---|---|
| 66 | Polydor 56095 | Wow Wow Wow/There She Goes | 50 |

*(see also State Of Micky & Tommy)*

### J BLAST & 100% PROOF
| | | | |
|---|---|---|---|
| 92 | Geek Street GEEK666JC001/ DJ D Zire | 2 The Break Of Dawn (12") | 15 |

### J.B.'S
| | | | |
|---|---|---|---|
| 71 | Mojo 2001 155 | These Are The J.B.'s (Parts 1 & 2) | 6 |
| 71 | Mojo 2027 002 | The Grunt (Parts 1 & 2) | 6 |
| 72 | Mojo 2093 007 | Gimme Some More/The Rabbit Got The Gun | 6 |
| 72 | Mojo 2093 016 | Hot Pants Road/Pass The Peas | 6 |
| 72 | Mojo 2093 021 | Givin' Up Food For Funk (Parts 1 & 2) | 6 |
| 72 | Mojo 2918 004 | PASS THE PEAS (LP) | 20 |
| 72 | Polydor 2391 034 | FOOD FOR THOUGHT (LP) | 20 |
| 74 | Polydor 2391 087 | DOING IT TO DEATH (LP) | 20 |
| 75 | Polydor 2391 194 | HUSTLE WITH SPEED (LP) | 20 |
| 76 | Polydor 2391 204 | GIVIN' UP FOOD FOR FUNK - THE BEST OF THE JB's (LP) | 20 |

*(see also Fred Wesley & JB's, James Brown, Bobby Byrd)*

### J.B'S ALLSTARS
| | | | |
|---|---|---|---|
| 85 | 2 Tone CHSTT29 | The Alphabet Army/Al Arm (p/s) | 30 |

| | | |
|---|---|---|
| 85 | 2 Tone CHSTT1229 | The Alphabet Army (extended mix)/The Alphabet Army (string mix)/The Alphabet Army/Al Arm (12" p/s) .................................................................................35 |

**JCB**
| 80 | Red Rat RR 401 | Camera .................................................................................................6 |

**JC001/DJ D ZIRE**
| 88 | Furious Fish FFDJD 001 | No MC No Comment (12")..................................................................12 |
| 91 | White JCDZ001 | Favourite Breaks (12")........................................................................18 |

**J.D. (THE ROC)**
| 72 | Sioux SI 008 | Superbad/MONTEGO MELON: Lucky Dip............................................20 |

*(see also Jeff Dixon)*

**BOBBI JEAN**
| 65 | Mercury MF 921 | Dry Your Tears/Pity The Man ..............................................................10 |

**JEAN & GAYTONES**
| 71 | Trojan TR 7817 | I Shall Sing (actually by Judy Mowatt & Gaytones)/GAYTONES: Target ..........15 |

**LANA JEAN**
| 63 | Pye International 7N 25214 | It Hurts To Be Sixteen/Bad Boy .....................................................25 |

**CATHY JEAN & ROOMATES**
| 61 | Parlophone R 4764 | Please Love Me Forever/Canadian Sunset .........................................60 |

**JEAN & STATESIDES**
| 64 | Columbia DB 7287 | Putty In Your Hands/One Fine Day .................................................40 |
| 64 | Columbia DB 7439 | You Won't Forget Me/Cold, Cold Winter .........................................30 |
| 65 | Columbia DB 7651 | Mama Didn't Lie/Just Let Me Cry ...................................................30 |

**JEAN-ETTES**
| 59 | Pye 7N 15185 | May You Always/I Saw A Light.........................................................10 |

**JEANNIE (& BIG GUYS)**
| 63 | Piccadilly 7N 35147 | Don't Lie To Me/Boys (as Jeannie & Big Guys).................................15 |
| 64 | Piccadilly 7N 35164 | I Want You/Sticks And Stones (as Jeannie & Big Guys) .....................15 |
| 65 | Parlophone R 5343 | I Love Him/With Any Other Girl......................................................10 |

*(see also Cindy Cole)*

**JEANNIE & REDHEADS**
| 64 | Decca F 11829 | Animal Duds/ANDREW OLDHAM GROUP: Funky And Fleopatra .........30 |

*(see also Andrew Oldham Orchestra)*

**AUDREY JEANS**
| 56 | Decca F 10768 | Ticky Ticky Tick (I'm Gonna Tell On You)/Will You, Willyum ...............10 |
| 56 | Decca F 10788 | It's Better In The Dark/The Bus Stop Song (A Paper Of Pins) .............10 |
| 58 | Decca F 11035 | Send A Letter To Jeanette - Yet!/Bad Pianna Rag..............................7 |
| 61 | HMV POP 876 | How Lovely To Be A Woman/What Did I See In Him .........................5 |

**JEDDAH**
| 83 | Death RIP 2001 | Eleanor Rigby/Ghosts (Never Leave You Behind) (with poster, no p/s).........25 |

**JEDI KNIGHTS**
| 95 | Clear CLR 406 | MAY THE FUNK BE WITH YOU (12" EP, p/s) ..................................10 |
| 95 | Clear CLR 406X | MAY THE FUNK BE WITH YOU (12" EP, clear vinyl, embossed sleeve) .......15 |

*(see also Global Communications)*

**JEEP**
| 80 | Airport AIRP 001 | Wild Rover/Lark In The Dark (over sized p/s) ..................................8 |

**JEEPS**
| 66 | Strike JH 308 | He Saw Eesaw/The Music Goes Round .............................................15 |
| 66 | Strike JH 315 | Ain't It A Great Big Laugh/I Put On My Shoes ..................................15 |

**JEFFERSON**
| 68 | Pye 7N 17634 | Montage/Did You Hear A Heartbreak Last Night...............................15 |
| 69 | Pye 7N 17706 | The Colour Of My Love/Look No Further ..........................................8 |
| 69 | Pye 7N 17810 | Baby Take Me In Your Arms/I Fell Flat On My Face ..........................8 |
| 69 | Pye 7N 17855 | Love And The World Loves You/I've Got To Tell Her .........................30 |
| 71 | Pye 7N 45022 | Spider/Can't Get You Out Of My Mind .............................................10 |
| 75 | Alaska ALA 1016 | Workin' My Way Back To You/Baby You've Got Everything I Need ........15 |
| 69 | Pye NSPL 18316 | THE COLOUR OF MY LOVE (LP) ...................................................15 |
| 73 | Philips 6308 166 | I LOVE YOU THIS MUCH (LP, blue/silver labels) .............................20 |

*(see also Rockin' Berries, Sight & Sound)*

**JEFFERSON AIRPLANE**
| 67 | RCA Victor RCA 1594 | Somebody To Love/She Has Funny Cars.........................................15 |
| 67 | RCA Victor RCA 1631 | White Rabbit/Plastic Fantastic Lover ............................................15 |
| 67 | RCA Victor RCA 1647 | Ballad Of You And Me and Pooneil/Two Heads .............................10 |
| 68 | RCA Victor RCA 1711 | Greasy Heart/Share A Little Joke (With The World) .........................12 |
| 68 | RCA Victor RCA 1736 | If You Feel Like China Breaking/Triad ...........................................10 |
| 70 | RCA RCA 1933 | Volunteers/We Can Be Together....................................................6 |
| 70 | RCA RCA 1964 | Somebody To Love/White Rabbit ..................................................8 |
| 70 | RCA RCA 1989 | Mexico/Have You Seen The Saucers?.............................................8 |
| 72 | Grunt 65-0500 | Pretty As You Feel/Wild Turkey .....................................................7 |
| 72 | Grunt 65-0506 | Long John Silver/Milk Train ..........................................................5 |
| 67 | RCA Victor RD 7889 | SURREALISTIC PILLOW (LP, black label, mono) .............................80 |
| 67 | RCA Victor SF 7889 | SURREALISTIC PILLOW (LP, black label, stereo) ............................50 |
| 68 | RCA Victor RD 7926 | AFTER BATHING AT BAXTERS (LP, black label, mono) .....................70 |
| 68 | RCA Victor SF 7926 | AFTER BATHING AT BAXTERS (LP, black label, stereo).....................40 |
| 68 | RCA Victor RD 7976 | CROWN OF CREATION (LP, black label, mono) ...............................70 |
| 68 | RCA Victor SF 7976 | CROWN OF CREATION (LP, black label, stereo)...............................30 |
| 69 | RCA RD/SF 8019 | BLESS ITS POINTED LITTLE HEAD (LP) ........................................20 |
| 69 | RCA Victor SF 7889 | SURREALISTIC PILLOW (LP, repressing, orange label) .....................35 |

# Blind LEMON JEFFERSON

| | | | |
|---|---|---|---|
| 69 | RCA Victor SF 7926 | AFTER BATHING AT BAXTERS (LP, repressing, orange label) | 25 |
| 69 | RCA Victor SF 7976 | CROWN OF CREATION (LP, repressing, orange label, 'SR Ltd' printing credit on sleeve)) | 40 |
| 70 | RCA SF 8076 | VOLUNTEERS (LP, gatefold sleeve) | 20 |
| 71 | Grunt FTR 1001 | BARK (LP, bag cover with lyric sheet & brown inner sleeve) | 15 |
| 71 | RCA SF 8195 | JEFFERSON AIRPLANE TAKES OFF (LP) | 18 |
| 72 | Grunt FTR 1007 | LONG JOHN SILVER (LP, open-out box cover with inner lyric sleeve) | 15 |

(see also Great Society, Paul Kantner, Hot Tuna)

## BLIND LEMON JEFFERSON

| | | | |
|---|---|---|---|
| 50 | Tempo R 38 | Weary Dog Blues/Change My Luck Blues (78) | 25 |
| 50 | Tempo R 39 | Lock Step Blues/Hangman's Blues (78) | 25 |
| 51 | Tempo R 46 | Shuckin' Sugar Blues/Rabbit Foot Blues (78) | 25 |
| 52 | Tempo R 54 | Gone Dead On You Blues/One Dime Blues (78) | 25 |
| 53 | Jazz Collector L 91 | Shuckin' Sugar Blues/Rabbit Foot Blues (78) | 25 |
| 53 | Jazz Collector L 103 | Jack O'Diamonds Blues/Clock House Blues (78) | 20 |
| 54 | Jazz Collector L 126 | Gone Dead On You Blues/One Dime Blues (78) | 20 |
| 50s | Poydras 99 | BLIND LEMON JEFFERSON (10" LP) | 20 |
| 53 | London Jazz AL 3508 | FOLK BLUES OF BLIND LEMON JEFFERSON (10" LP) | 50 |
| 55 | London Jazz AL 3546 | PENITENTIARY BLUES (10" LP) | 50 |
| 57 | London Jazz AL 3564 | SINGS THE BLUES (10" LP) | 50 |
| 69 | CBS 63738 | THE IMMORTAL (LP) | 50 |
| 70s | Roots Matchbox RL 301 | BLIND LEMON JEFFERSON VOLUME 1 (LP) | 20 |
| 70s | Roots Matchbox RL 306 | BLIND LEMON JEFFERSON VOLUME 2 (LP) | 20 |
| 70s | Roots Matchbox RL 331 | BLIND LEMON JEFFERSON VOLUME 3 (LP) | 18 |

(see also Paramount Allstars)

## BLIND LEMON JEFFERSON/ED BELL

| | | | |
|---|---|---|---|
| 60 | Jazz Collector JEL 13 | THE MALE BLUES VOLUME 7 (EP) | 10 |

## BLIND LEMON JEFFERSON/BUDDY BOY HAWKINS

| | | | |
|---|---|---|---|
| 59 | Jazz Collector JEL 8 | THE MALE BLUES VOLUME 5 (EP) | 10 |

## BLIND LEMON JEFFERSON/LEADBELLY

| | | | |
|---|---|---|---|
| 61 | Jazz Collector JEL 24 | THE MALE BLUES VOLUME 8 (EP) | 10 |

## BLIND LEMON JEFFERSON & RAMBLING THOMAS

| | | | |
|---|---|---|---|
| 50s | Heritage HLP 1007 | BLIND LEMON JEFFERSON AND RAMBLING THOMAS (LP, 99 only) | 100 |

## EDDIE JEFFERSON

| | | | |
|---|---|---|---|
| 67 | Stateside SS 591 | Some Other Time/When You Look In The Mirror | 10 |

## GEORGE PAUL JEFFERSON

| | | | |
|---|---|---|---|
| 68 | Fontana TF 923 | Looking For My Mind/Out Of Place | 45 |

## MARSHALL JEFFERSON

| | | | |
|---|---|---|---|
| 88 | ffrr FFRX 18 | Open Your Eyes (Celestial Mix)/(Spiritual Mix)/ (Marshall's Elevated Dub) (12", p/s) | 15 |

## JE FRENCHIE

| | | | |
|---|---|---|---|
| 80 | Guardian GFR 18 | JE FRENCHIE EP | 15 |

## JEGA

| | | | |
|---|---|---|---|
| 96 | Skam SKA 6 | Phlax/Nortom Midgate/Bluette/Ionic/Evil Lee Kirtcele/ Steel Drum/In With The In (12", custom sleeve) | 45 |
| 97 | Skam SKA 9 | Card Hore/Oak Hanger/Nausicaa/Stainless Steel Drum/Star/Houdini (12", p/s) | 10 |
| 98 | Planet Mu ZIQ 001 | TYPE XERO EP (12") | 20 |
| 00 | Planet Mu ZIQ 012 | GEOMETRY (2-LP) | 20 |

## JEHST

| | | | |
|---|---|---|---|
| 99 | Y n R Productions YNR 001 | PREMONITIONS EP: (12", stickered (white die-cut sleeve, first pressing blue text on label) | 80 |
| 99 | Y n R YNR 1 | PREMONITIONS (EP, second pressing black text on label) | 15 |
| 01 | Lowlife LOW 12 | THE HIGH PLAINS DRIFTER (EP, p/s) | 40 |
| 01 | Lowlife LOW 12 PRO | The Trilogy Remix (1-sided 12", 2 mixes 500 pressed) | 50 |
| 02 | Y n R YNR008 | Alcoholic Author/Night Breed (12", p/s) | 25 |
| 02 | Lowlife LOW 18 | The Return Of The Drifter/People Under The Weather (12", p/s, 3 mixes each) | 12 |
| 13 | Y n R YNR 055 | Game Over (7") | 7 |
| 14 | Y n R YNR 062 | Dolph Lundgren/Instrumental (gig-only 7" with STRANGE U) | 50 |
| 14 | Y n R YNR 062RDS | Dolph Lundgren/Instrumental (picture disc) | 10 |
| 03 | Lowlife LOW30 | FALLING DOWN (LP) | 50 |
| 05 | High Plains REPHP 001 | NUKE PROOF SUIT (LP) | 30 |
| 11 | YNR YNR 047LP | THE DRAGON OF AN ORDINARY FAMILY (LP, red & blue vinyl) | 90 |
| 12 | YNR YNR 052 | THE DRAGON OF AN ORDINARY FAMILY (LP, remixes 300 only) | 15 |

## JELLIES

| | | | |
|---|---|---|---|
| 81 | Jelli 1 | Jive Baby On A Saturday Night/Conversation (die-cut sleeve) | 80 |
| 10 | Trunk TTT 006 | JIVE BABY ON A SATURDAY NIGHT (12" EP) | 15 |

## JELLY

| | | | |
|---|---|---|---|
| 72 | Mother MOT9 | I'll Meet You Half Way/Chicago Calling | 40 |

## JELLY BABIES

| | | | |
|---|---|---|---|
| 81 | De Nada | DE NADA EP (hand-made p/s, white labels) | 60 |

## JELLY BEANS

| | | | |
|---|---|---|---|
| 64 | Pye International 7N 25252 | I Wanna Love Him So Bad/So Long | 30 |
| 64 | Red Bird RB 10011 | The Kind Of Boy You Can't Forget/Baby Be Mine | 30 |
| 75 | Right On R 102 | You Don't Mean Me No Good/I'm Hip To You | 10 |

## JELLYBREAD

| | | | |
|---|---|---|---|
| 69 | Blue Horizon 57-3162 | Chairman Mao's Boogaloo/No One Else | 15 |
| 70 | Blue Horizon 57-3169 | Comment/Funky Wasp | 15 |
| 70 | Blue Horizon 57-3174 | Rockin' Pneumonia And The Boogie-Woogie Flu/Readin' The Meters | 15 |
| 70 | Blue Horizon 57-3180 | Old Man Hank/Faded Grace | 15 |
| 71 | Blue Horizon 2096 001 | Creepin' And Crawlin'/The Loser/The Clergyman's Daughter | 15 |

MINT VALUE £

| 72 | Blue Horizon 2096 006 | Down Along The Cove/Sister Lucy | 15 |
| 72 | Liphook 1 | JELLYBREAD (mini-LP) | 325 |
| 69 | Blue Horizon 7-63853 | FIRST SLICE (LP) | 100 |
| 71 | Blue Horizon 2431 002 | SIXTY-FIVE PARKWAY (LP, with lyric insert) | 110 |
| 71 | Blue Horizon 2431 002 | SIXTY-FIVE PARKWAY (LP, without lyric insert) | 70 |
| 72 | Blue Horizon 2931 004 | BACK TO THE BEGINNING AGAIN (LP, gatefold sleeve) | 160 |

### DIANNE JENKINS
| 76 | Crystal CR 7025 | Tow-A-Way-Zone/Anniversary (as Diane Jenkins) | 10 |

### JOHNNY JENKINS
| 69 | Atco 226 009 | The Voodoo In You/Backside Blues | 10 |
| 71 | Atco 2400 033 | TON-TON MACOUTE (LP) | 25 |

### LEROY JENKINS
| 76 | JCOA/Virgin J 2005 | FOR PLAYERS ONLY (LP) | 15 |

### BARBARA JENKYNS
| 67 | Newbreed NB1 | Shoult About It/Groovy Boy | 50 |

### JENNIFER (WARNES)
| 69 | London HLU 10278 | Let The Sun Shine In/Easy To Be Hard | 7 |
| 70 | London HLU 10312 | Cajun Train/Old Folks (Les Vieux) | 8 |

### JENNIFERS
| 92 | Nude NUD 2T | Just Got Back Today/Rocks And Boulders/Danny's Song/Tomorrow's Rain (12") | 20 |
| 92 | Nude NUD 2CD | Just Got Back Today/Rocks And Boulders/Danny's Song/Tomorrow's Rain (CD) | 30 |

*(see also Supergrass)*

### BILL JENNINGS
| 55 | Parlophone MSP 6146 | Stuffy/Solitude (as Bill Jennings-Leo Parker Quintet) | 6 |
| 55 | Parlophone MSP 6156 | Soft Winds/What's New? (as Bill Jennings Quartet) | 6 |

### JENNORS
| 67 | Coxsone CS 7024 | Pressure And Slide (actually by Tennors)/SOUL BROTHERS: One Stop | 40 |

*(see also Tennors)*

### KRIS JENSEN
| 62 | Fontana 267 241 TF | Torture/Let's Sit Down | 15 |
| 63 | Fontana 267 267 TF | Don't Take Her From Me/Claudette | 15 |
| 64 | Hickory 45-1224 | Donna Donna/Big As I Can Dream | 15 |

### PAUL JENSEN & CAR THIEVES
| 78 | Albatross TIT 3 | Holiday In Spain/Always Arrive On Time (p/s) | 6 |

### JENSENS
| 68 | Philips BF 1686 | Deep Thinking/Marguerite | 12 |

*(see also Tempus Fugit)*

### BILL JENTIES
| 70 | Smash SMA 2307 | Stop Them (actually by Bill Gentles)/MAXINE: I Don't Care | 6 |

*(see also Bill Gentles/Bill Jentles)*

### BILL JENTLES
| 70 | Pama PM 809 | True True Train/JEFF BARNES: Give And Take | 15 |
| 70 | Pama PM 801 | What A Woman/Sleepy Cat | 10 |

*(see also Bill Jenties)*

### JEREMIAHS
| 85 | No Label or catalogue number | Over The Stove/Wipe Away Your Tears/Never Come Back (printed insert and photo stuck on cover 25-50 copies only) | 150 |
| 87 | Abstract ABCT 112 | DRIVING INTO THE SUN (12" EP) | 45 |
| 87 | Abstract ABS 053 | DRIVING INTO THE SUN EP | 25 |

### JERICHO (JONES)
| 71 | A&M AMS 833 | Time Is Now/Freedom | 5 |
| 72 | A&M AMS 883 | Don't Let Me Down/Mona Mona | 7 |
| 72 | A&M AMS 7017 | Hey Man/Champs | 7 |
| 72 | A&M AMS 7037 | Mama's Gonna Take You Home/So Come On | 7 |
| 71 | A&M AMLH 68050 | JUNKIES, MONKEYS & DONKEYS (LP, as Jericho Jones, gatefold, brown label) | 200 |
| 72 | A&M AMLS 68079 | JERICHO (LP, beware of counterfeits with slightly thicker sleeves) | 200 |

### JERKS
| 78 | Underground URA 1 | Get Your Woofing Dog Off Me/Hold My Hand (p/s) | 35 |
| 78 | Lightning GIL 549 | Cool/Jerkin' (p/s) | 30 |
| 80 | Laser LAS 25 | Come Back Bogart (I Wish You Would)/Are You Strong Enough?/The Strangest Man Of All (p/s) | 15 |
| 97 | Overground OVER 65 | JERK OFF (LP, 600 only pressed in U.K. for export to Japan) | 20 |

### JERMZ
| 78 | One Way EFP 1 | Power Cut/Me And My Baby (with p/s) | 200 |
| 78 | One Way EFP 1 | Power Cut/Me And My Baby (without p/s) | 80 |

### JERRY JEROME
| 55 | MGM SP 1118 | Honey/In A Little Spanish Town | 5 |

### JERONIMO
| 70 | Major Minor MM695 | Hey Ya/Na Na Hey Hey Kiss Him Goodbye | 8 |

### JERRY THE FERRET
| 78 | Jerry The Ferret EGH 919 | One Step Forward/I Think You're Lyin' (1000 only, no p/s) | 50 |
| 80 | Dead Horse | THE MUSIC GOES ON AND ON (EP) | 20 |

### JERRY & THE BLUEBELLS
| 75 | Torpedo TOR 44 | Girls/Girls Version | 15 |

### JERRY & FREEDOM SINGERS
| 70 | Banana BA 308 | It's All In The Game (pseudonym for Winston Francis)/ IM: The Way To My Heart (pseudonym for Cedric Brooks) | 60 |

MINT VALUE £

(see also Winston Francis)

## JERRY O
| | | | |
|---|---|---|---|
| 67 | London HLZ 10162 | Karate Boo-ga-loo/The Pearl | 12 |
| 71 | Jay Boy BOY 53 | Funky Boogaloo/Push Push | 8 |
| 71 | Jay Boy BOY 33 | Karate Boo-ga-loo/The Pearl (reissue) | 8 |
| 72 | Jay Boy BOY 62 | Dance What 'Cha Wanna/Afro-Twist Time | 8 |

## JERUSALEM (2)
| | | | |
|---|---|---|---|
| 72 | Deram DM 358 | Kamakazi Moth/Frustration | 40 |
| 72 | Deram SDL 6 | JERUSALEM (LP, gatefold sleeve, white/brown label with large 'Deram' logo) | 350 |
| 72 | Deram SDL 6 | JERUSALEM (LP, gatefold sleeve, later red/white label) | 150 |

(see also Pussy, Ian Gillan)

## JESS & JAMES
| | | | |
|---|---|---|---|
| 68 | MGM MGM 1389 | Move/What Was I Born For | 25 |
| 68 | MGM MGM 1420 | Something For Nothing/I Let The Day Go By (with J.J. Band) | 20 |
| 68 | MGM MGM 1454 | Thank You Show Biz/Motherless Child | 10 |

## STEVE JESSE
| | | | |
|---|---|---|---|
| 76 | President PT 502 | Shifting Sands/Post Hall Life | 6 |

## JESSUP
| | | | |
|---|---|---|---|
| 72 | Beacon BEA 108 | Little Friend/On The Run | 15 |

## JESTERS
| | | | |
|---|---|---|---|
| 62 | R&L RL 15/16 | Little Girl/Casa Pedro (blue and white labels) | 30 |
| 73 | Jam JAM 35 | Fool For A Day/Can't Live Without You | 15 |

## JESUS & MARY CHAIN
| | | | |
|---|---|---|---|
| 84 | Creation CRE 012 | Upside Down/Vegetable Man (black & white wraparound p/s in poly bag with address on rear & name in red) | 20 |
| 84 | Creation CRE 012 | Upside Down/Vegetable Man (red & white wraparound p/s in poly bag with address on rear & name in black) | 20 |
| 84 | Creation CRE 012 | Upside Down/Vegetable Man (pink, blue or yellow wraparound p/s in poly bag; with small T-shirt offer insert) | 15 |
| 84 | Creation CRE 012 | Upside Down/Vegetable Man (pink, blue or yellow wraparound p/s in poly bag; without small T-shirt offer insert) | 8 |
| 85 | Fierce FRIGHT 004 | RIOT (EP, with 'LSD bar' & badge; 2 different sleeves) | 40 |
| 85 | Blanco Y Negro NEG 008 | Never Understand/Suck (p/s) | 6 |
| 85 | Blanco Y Negro NEG 17 | Just Like Honey/Head (p/s) | 6 |
| 85 | Blanco Y Negro NEG 17F | Just Like Honey/Head//Inside Me/Just Like Honey (Demo Oct 84) (double pack, gatefold p/s) | 8 |
| 86 | Creation CRE 012 | Upside Down/Vegetable Man (reissue, different printed p/s) | 5 |
| 86 | Creation CRE 012T | Upside Down/Vegetable Man/Upside Down (demo) (12" white label, no sleeve) | 60 |
| 86 | Blanco Y Negro NEG 19 | SOME CANDY TALKING EP: Some Candy Talking/Psychocandy/Cut Dead/Psychocandy (acoustic)/You Trip Me Up/Some Candy (acoustic) (2x7" double pack) | 6 |
| 87 | Blanco Y Negro NEGB 25 | Happy When It Rains/Everything Is Alright When You're Down (box set with postcards) | 5 |
| 89 | Blanco Y Negro NEG 42/XB/Y/Z | Head On/Terminal Beach//Head On/Deviant Slice//Head On/I'm Glad I Never/Head On/In The Black (4 x 7" box set; each single sold separately) | 12 |
| 91 | Strange Fruit SFPMA210 | PEEL SESSIONS (12") | 15 |
| 94 | Blanco Y Negro NEG 73 | Come On/I'm In With The Out Crowd (orange vinyl, numbered limited edition) | 6 |
| 85 | Creation CRE(T) 1 | LIVE (100 only, numbered, with press sheet) | 100 |
| 85 | Blanco Y Negro BYN 7 | PSYCHOCANDY (LP, with inner) | 25 |
| 87 | Blanco Y Negro BY 11 | DARKLANDS (LP, with inner) | 20 |
| 89 | Blanco Y Negro BYN 20W | AUTOMATIC (LP, gatefold sleeve, with insert) | 20 |
| 92 | Blanco Y Negro BYN 26 | HONEY'S DEAD (LP) | 15 |
| 94 | Warner Bros. 4509-96717-4 | STONED & DETHRONED (LP) | 30 |
| 98 | Creation CRELP 232 | MUNKI (2-LP) | 25 |
| 00 | Strange Fruit SFRSLP092 | THE COMPLETE PEEL SESSIONS (LP) | 18 |
| 13 | Demon CANDY 1 | PSYCHOCANDY (LP, reissue, red splatter vinyl, poster) | 25 |
| 13 | Demon JAMCLPBOX 01 | THE VINYL COLLECTION (11-LP box set) | 80 |

(see also Acid Angels, Primal Scream, Meat Whiplash)

## JESUS LIZARD
| | | | |
|---|---|---|---|
| 91 | Touch & Go T&GLP #43 | PURE (EP purple vinyl, numbered sticker on sleeve, 1500 only) | 18 |
| 92 | Own label | Gladiator (Marquee gig freebie) | 8 |
| 93 | Touch & Go TG 83 | Puss/NIRVANA: Oh, The Guilt (p/s, blue vinyl, with poster) | 25 |
| 93 | Touch & Go TG 83 | Puss/NIRVANA: Oh, The Guilt (p/s, blue vinyl, without poster) | 12 |
| 90 | Touch & Go T&GLP 54 | HEAD (LP, red & white vinyl, numbered sticker on sleeve, 1500 only) | 18 |
| 91 | Touch & Go T&GLP 68 | GOAT (LP, orange vinyl, numbered stickeer on sleeve, 1000 only) | 40 |
| 91 | Touch & Go TG68P | GOAT (LP, picture disc) | 18 |
| 92 | Tough & Go TG100 PD | LIAR (LP, picture disc in PVC sleeve) | 10 |

(see also Nirvana)

## JET
| | | | |
|---|---|---|---|
| 75 | CBS S CBS 3317 | Nothing To Do With Us/Brian Damage | 8 |
| 75 | CBS S CBS 3143 | My River/Quandary | 8 |
| 75 | CBS 80699 | JET (LP, with lyric insert) | 20 |

(see also Andy Ellison,John's Children, Nice, Radio Stars, Sparks)

## JETHRO TULL
### SINGLES
| | | | |
|---|---|---|---|
| 68 | MGM MGM 1384 | Sunshine Day/Aeroplane (miscredited to 'Jethro Toe'; counterfeits credit 'Jethro Tull') | 500 |
| 68 | Island WIP 6043 | A Song For Jeffrey/One For John Gee | 40 |
| 68 | Island WIP 6048 | Love Story/A Christmas Song (2 different pink label designs) | 10 |
| 68 | Island WIP 6048 | Love Story/A Christmas Song (mispressing, B-side or both sides credited to Ian Henderson) | 18 |
| 69 | Island WIP 6056 | Living In The Past/Driving Song (2 different pink labels) | 15 |

| | | | |
|---|---|---|---|
| 69 | Chrysalis WIP 6070 | Sweet Dream/17 (push-out or large centre hole) | 7 |
| 70 | Chrysalis WIP 6077 | The Witch's Promise/Teacher (in p/s) | 20 |
| 70 | Chrysalis WIP 6077 | The Witch's Promise/Teacher | 15 |
| 70 | Chrysalis WIP 6081 | Inside/Alive And Well And Living In | 10 |
| 71 | Chrysalis WIP 6098 | Lick Your Fingers Clean/Up To Me (unissued) | 0 |
| 74 | Chrysalis CHS 2054 | Bungle In The Jungle/Back Door Angels | 6 |
| 75 | Chrysalis CHS 2075 | Minstrel In The Gallery/Summerday Sands | 5 |
| 76 | Chrysalis CHS 2086 | Too Old To Rock'n'Roll: Too Young To Die/Rainbow Blues | 5 |
| 77 | Chrysalis CHS 2135 | The Whistler/Strip Cartoon (in p/s) | 25 |
| 77 | Chrysalis CHS 2135 | The Whistler/Strip Cartoon (no p/s) | 8 |
| 78 | Chrysalis CHS 2214 | Moths/Life Is A Long Song (p/s) | 10 |
| 78 | Chrysalis CHS 2260 | A Stitch In Time (3.30 Version)/Sweet Dream (p/s, white vinyl) | 12 |
| 78 | Chrysalis CHS 2260 | A Stitch In Time (3.30 Version)/Sweet Dream (p/s, black vinyl) | 8 |
| 78 | Chrysalis CHS 2260 | A Stitch In Time (4.20 Version)/Sweet Dream (p/s, white vinyl) | 12 |
| 78 | Chrysalis CHS 2260 | A Stitch In Time (4.20 Version)/Sweet Dream (p/s, black vinyl) | 8 |
| 79 | Chrysalis CHS 2378 | North Sea Oil/Elegy (p/s) | 10 |
| 79 | Chrysalis CHS 2394 | Home/King Henry's Madrigal (Theme From Mainstream)/Warm Sporran (p/s) | 12 |
| 79 | Chrysalis CHS 2468 | Working John, Working Joe/Flyingdale Flyer (p/s) | 8 |
| 80 | Chrysalis CHS 2619 | Broadsword/Fallen On Hard Times (p/s) | 6 |
| 80 | Chrysalis CHSP 2619 | Broadsword/Fallen On Hard Times (picture disc) | 12 |
| 84 | Chrysalis TULLD 1 | Lap Of Luxury/Astronomy//Automotive Engineering/Tundra (double pack, gatefold p/s) | 10 |
| 84 | Chrysalis TULL X 1 | Lap Of Luxury/Astronomy/Automotive Engineering/Tundra (12", p/s) | 10 |
| 86 | Chrysalis TULL 2 | Coronach (with David Palmer)/Jack Frost And The Hooded Crow (p/s) | 7 |
| 86 | Chrysalis TULLX 2 | Coronach (with David Palmer)/Jack Frost And The Hooded Crow/ Living In The Past/ Elegy (12", p/s) | 40 |
| 87 | Chrysalis TULLP 3 | Steel Monkey/Down At The End Of Your Road (die-cut picture disc) | 20 |
| 87 | Chrysalis ZTULL 3 | Steel Monkey/Down At The End Of Your Road/Too Many Too/I'm Your Gun (numbered edition of 3,000 with competition pack & badge) | 15 |
| 87 | Chrysalis TULLX 3 | Steel Monkey/Down At The End Of Your Road/Too Many Too/I'm Your Gun (12", p/s) | 10 |
| 88 | Chrysalis TULLX 4 | Said She Was A Dancer/Dogs In The Midwinter/The Waking Edge (p/s) | 8 |
| 88 | Chrysalis TULLP 4 | Said She Was A Dancer/Dogs In The Midwinter (shaped picture disc) | 10 |
| 88 | Chrysalis TULLCD 4 | Said She Was A Dancer/Dogs In The Midwinter/Down At The End Of The Road/Too Many Too (CD, picture disc, limited issue) | 25 |
| 89 | Chrysalis TULL 5 | Another Christmas Song (p/s) | 10 |
| 89 | Chrysalis TULLX5 | Another Christmas Song/Intro-A Christmas Song/Cheap Day Return-Mother Goose/ Outro-Locomotive Breath (12" p/s) | 20 |

## ALBUMS

| | | | |
|---|---|---|---|
| 68 | Island ILP 985 | THIS WAS (1st pressing, pink label/black & orange 'circle' logo, mono) | 350 |
| 68 | Island ILPS 9085 | THIS WAS (1st pressing, pink label/black & orange 'circle' logo, stereo, laminated gatefold flipback sleeve, some sleeves as mono issues with stereo stickers) | 150 |
| 69 | Island ILPS 9103 | STAND UP (1st pressing, gatefold sleeve pop-up inside, pink label/black & orange 'circle' logo) | 225 |
| 70 | Chrysalis ILPS 9123 | BENEFIT (green Chrysalis or Island pink rim label) | 100 |
| 70 | Chrysalis ILPS 9123 | BENEFIT ( Island pink rim label 'palm tree' logo) | 45 |
| 71 | Island ILPS 9145 | AQUALUNG (1st pressing, Matrixes ILPS 9145 A//1U and ILPS B//3U, Chrysalis labels with white 'i' at top of label, with textured E.J. Day Group gatefold sleeve with ILPS 9145 on top right hand corner, inner bag) | 100 |
| 71 | Island ILPS 9145 | AQUALUNG (pink rim palm tree label, gatefold sleeve) | 150 |
| 72 | Chrysalis CHR 1003 | THICK AS A BRICK (LP, 1st pressing with white 'i' at top of label, Matrixes: CHR1003 A-3U/CHR1003 B-2U, 'Porky' etched into dead wax side 1, 'Pecko' etched into dead wax side 2, textured sleeve with fold-out newspaper sleeve) | 80 |
| 72 | Chrysalis CJT 1 | LIVING IN THE PAST (2-LP, with hard sleeve & booklet) | 30 |
| 73 | Chrysalis CHR 1040 | A PASSION PLAY (gatefold sleeve with matt finish, with Linwell theatre booklet, Matrix CHR1040 A4U/B4, green label without small white "i", later presses have red wording on rim and A2U matrix) | 45 |
| 78 | Chrysalis CHR 1175 | HEAVY HORSES (LP, with insert) | 15 |
| 84 | Chrysalis CDLP 1461 | UNDER WRAPS (picture disc) | 15 |
| 88 | Chrysalis Tbox1 | 20 YEARS OF JETHRO TULL (5-LP box set with 24-page booklet) | 75 |
| 88 | Chrysalis Tbox CD1 | 20 YEARS OF JETHRO TULL (3-CD box set with 24-page booklet) | 50 |
| 89 | Chrysalis CHRP 1708 | ROCK ISLAND (Picture disc) | 18 |
| 91 | Chrysalis DCHR 1886 | CATFISH RISING (Ltd edn. With 3-track 12" and lyric sheet inner sleeve) | 20 |
| 93 | Chrysalis CDCHR 6004 | JETHRO TULL 25th ANNIVERSARY (4-CD cigar box set with 48-page booklet) | 55 |
| 95 | Chrysalis CHR 6109 | ROOTS TO BRANCHES (2-LP) | 80 |

## ALBUMS : LP REPRESSINGS

| | | | |
|---|---|---|---|
| 68 | Island ILP 985 | THIS WAS (pink label/'i' logo, mono) | 70 |
| 69 | Island ILPS 9085 | THIS WAS (pink label/black 'block' logo, 1st mix) | 40 |
| 70 | Island ILPS 9085 | THIS WAS (pink label/'i' logo) | 20 |
| 70 | Chrysalis ILPS 9103 | STAND UP (pop-up sleeve, pink label/black 'block' logo or pink label/'i' logo) | 18 |
| 96 | Chrysalis LP25AQUA1 | AQUALUNG (2-LP, 25th anniversary edition) | 50 |
| 97 | EMI LPCENT 8 | STAND UP (LP, reissue, EMI centenary, stickered sleeve) | 30 |
| 97 | EMI LPCENT 31 | AS THICK AS A BRICK (LP, reissue, EMI centenary, stickered sleeve) | 30 |

## PROMOS

| | | | |
|---|---|---|---|
| 76 | Chrysalis CHS 3 PDJ | Ring Out/Solstice Bells/March, The Mad Scientist/Christmas Song/ Pan Dance (12", p/s) | 25 |
| 79 | Chrysalis CHS018-PDJ | Dark Ages (Special edited version) 12" promo | 15 |
| 84 | Chrysalis AS 1967 | Under Wraps#1 (electric)/Under Wraps#2 (acoustic) (12" promo) | 12 |
| 87 | Chrysalis VAS 1039 | Budapest (Special Radio Edit) (12" promo with illustrated sticker) | 12 |
| 87 | Chrysalis VAS 2796 | Steel Monkey (12" promo) | 12 |
| 87 | Chrysalis VAS 2866 | Farm On The Freeway (Special Rock Radio Edit) (12" promo) | 15 |
| 88 | Chrysalis VAS 1170 | Part Of The Machine/Part Of The Machine (Edit) (12" promo with tour dates sticker) | 18 |

*(see also Mick Abrahams, Blodwyn Pig, Wild Turkey, The John Even Band)*

MINT VALUE £

### JETLINERS
| | | | |
|---|---|---|---|
| 66 | Blue Beat BB 367 | Meditation (actually by Sugar & Dandy)/GIRL SATCHMO: Nature Of Love (actually with Jetliners) | 35 |

### JETS (1)
| | | | |
|---|---|---|---|
| 73 | Cube BUG 35 | Yeah!/Rusty Corinthian Pillar | 15 |
| 78 | Soho SH 3 | Rockabilly Baby/James Dean | 7 |

### JETS (2)
| | | | |
|---|---|---|---|
| 79 | Decca FR 13867 | Tearaway/Impossible | 100 |

### JETS (3)
| | | | |
|---|---|---|---|
| 79 | Good Vibrations GV 1002 | Block 4/Iceburn (p/s) | 7 |

### JET SET
| | | | |
|---|---|---|---|
| 62 | Delta DW 5001 | VC 10/Cruising 600 (some in p/s) | 15 |
| 64 | Parlophone R 5199 | You Got Me Hooked/True To You | 25 |

### JETSET
| | | | |
|---|---|---|---|
| 84 | Dance Network NET 1 | BEST OF THE JETSET (EP) | 10 |
| 85 | Dance Network NET 3 | APRIL, MAY, JUNE AND THE JETSET (12" EP) | 12 |
| 85 | Dance Network WORK 1 | THERE GOES THE NEIGHBOURHOOD (LP, pink sleeve, poster) | 20 |
| 86 | Dance Network WORK 4 | 4 GO BANANAS (LP, with lyric insert) | 20 |

### JETSTREAMS
| | | | |
|---|---|---|---|
| 59 | Decca F 11149 | Bongo Rock/Tiger | 15 |

### JETZ
| | | | |
|---|---|---|---|
| 78 | Pollen PBM 019 | Down By The River/Brother John/You Ain't Seen Nothing Yet/Easy Feeling | 25 |

### JEVUTSHTA
| | | | |
|---|---|---|---|
| 78 | Zel-La JHSPS 226 | Fight Your Way Out/Stomp | 30 |

### LEN JEWELL
| | | | |
|---|---|---|---|
| 09 | Soul City 144 | Betting On Love/All My Good Lovin' (reissue) | 10 |

### JEWELLS (JAMAICA)
| | | | |
|---|---|---|---|
| 77 | Observer OB 005 | Black is The Highest Culture (Culture Version)/One Little Lick Version (12") | 25 |
| 77 | Observer OB 1101 | Jah I/LEROY SMART: Jah Is My Light/I-ROY: Wicked Eat Dirt (12") | 25 |

### JEWELS
| | | | |
|---|---|---|---|
| 64 | Colpix PX 11034 | Opportunity/Gotta Find A Way | 30 |
| 65 | Colpix PX 11048 | But I Do/Smokey Joe | 18 |

### JFK
| | | | |
|---|---|---|---|
| 92 | Fourth Dimension FDS24 | Sexodus/Temple Of Set (p/s, 500 only numbered) | 6 |

### JIGSAW
| | | | |
|---|---|---|---|
| 68 | Polydor 56241 | I Need Your Love/I've Gotta Get Me Some Money (as Jig-Saw Band) | 15 |
| 68 | Music Factory CUB 4 | Mister Job/Great Idea | 15 |
| 68 | Music Factory CUB 6 | Let Me Go Home/Tumblin' | 80 |
| 68 | MGM MGM 1410 | One Way Street/Then I Found You | 80 |
| 70 | Philips 6006 112 | One Way Street/Coffucius Confusion | 100 |
| 70 | Fontana 6007 017 | Lollipop And Goody Man/Seven Fishes | 70 |
| 71 | Philips 6006 131 | Jesu Joy Of Man's Desiring/No Questions Asked | 40 |
| 71 | Philips 6006 182 | Keeping My Head Above Water/It's Nice But It's Wrong | 10 |
| 74 | BASF BA 1002 | I've Seen The Film I've Read The Book/Mention My Name | 7 |
| 75 | BASF BA 1013 | Baby Don't Do It/Stand Next To Me | 7 |
| 75 | Spalsh CPI 1 | Sky High/Brand New Love Affair | 7 |
| 71 | Philips 6308 033 | LETHERSLADE FARM (LP) | 5 |
| 72 | Philips 6308 072 | AURORA BOREALIS (LP) | 80 |
| 73 | BASF 29106-5 | BROKEN HEARTED (LP, gatefold sleeve) | 50 |

### JIH
| | | | |
|---|---|---|---|
| 88 | Jungle JUNG 32T/BOV 3 | Take Me To The Girl/Come Summer Come Winter/Wake Up (12", unissued, Mayking test pressings only, white proof p/s) | 15 |
| 88 | Jungle JUNG 32T/BOV 3 | Take Me To The Girl/Come Summer Come Winter/Wake Up (12", 'small photos' p/s, later blue art p/s) | 20 |
| | | | 10 |

*(see also Associates)*

### JILL & BOULEVARDS
| | | | |
|---|---|---|---|
| 62 | Columbia DB 4823 | And Now I Cry/Eugene | 25 |

### JILL & Y'VERNS
| | | | |
|---|---|---|---|
| 60s | Oak RGJ 503 | My Soulful Dress/Anything He Wants Me To Do | 100 |

### JILTED JOHN
| | | | |
|---|---|---|---|
| 78 | Rabid TOSH 105 | Jilted John/Going Steady (p/s) | 15 |
| 78 | EMI International INT 567 | Jilted John/Going Steady (p/s, reissue) | 5 |
| 78 | EMI International INT 577 | True Love/I Was A Pre-Pubescent (p/s) | 5 |
| 78 | EMI International INT 587 | The Birthday Kiss/Baz's Party (p/s) | 5 |
| 78 | EMI Intl. INS 3024 | TRUE LOVE STORIES (LP, with board game insert) | 20 |

*(see also Going Red?)*

### JIM & JEAN
| | | | |
|---|---|---|---|
| 68 | Verve Folkways VLP 5017 | CHANGES (LP) | 40 |

### JIM & JOE
| | | | |
|---|---|---|---|
| 64 | London HL 9831 | Fireball Mail/Daisy Mae | 20 |

*(see also James Burton)*

### JIM & MONICA
| | | | |
|---|---|---|---|
| 64 | Stateside SS 266 | Slippin' And Slidin'/Sing Along Without Jim & Monica | 20 |

*(see also Jimmy Gilmer & Fireballs)*

### JIMBILIN
| | | | |
|---|---|---|---|
| 71 | Bamboo BAM 68 | Human Race/Let Love In (both actually by Herman Chin-Loy & Aquarians) | 15 |
| 75 | Ashanti ASH 421 | Balaclava/Tacku | 15 |

**JOSE JIMINEZ**
61   London HLR 9434   The Astronaut Part 1/Part 2 ...... 6

**JIMMIE & NIGHT HOPPERS**
59   London HLP 8830   Cruisin'/Night Hop ...... 30
59   London HLP 8830   Cruisin'/Night Hop (78) ...... 30

**JIMMY AND THE DIMENSIONS**
69   Youngblood YB 1008   Sugar Man/Slow Down ...... 12
*(see also Jimmy Powell & Red Alligator)*

**JIMMY J & CRU-L-T**
94   Kniveforce KF 027   Take Me Away (Slipmatt Remix)/FUTURE PRIMITIVE: Life Me Up (Slammin' Vinyl Remix) (12", p/s) ...... 15

**JIV-A-TONES**
58   Felsted AF 101   Flirty Gertie/Fire Engine Baby ...... 150
58   Felsted AF 101   Flirty Gertie/Fire Engine Baby (78) ...... 50

**JIVE FIVE**
61   Parlophone R 4822   My True Story/When I Was Single ...... 150
62   Stateside SS 133   What Time Is It?/Begging You Please ...... 90
65   United Artists UP 1106   I'm A Happy Man/Kiss Kiss Kiss ...... 45

**JIVERS (JAMAICA)**
68   Trojan TR 604   Wear My Crown/Down On The Beach ...... 15
*(see also Brother Dan Allstars)*

**JIVERS (U.S.)**
56   Vogue V 9060   Little Mama/Cherie ...... 650
56   Vogue V 9060   Little Mama/Cherie (78) ...... 150
57   Vogue V 9068   Ray Pearl/Dear Little One ...... 600
57   Vogue V 9068   Ray Pearl/Dear Little One (78) ...... 150

**JIVING JUNIORS**
60   Blue Beat BB 4   Lollipop Girl/Dearest Darling ...... 30
60   Blue Beat BB 5   My Heart's Desire/I Love You ...... 40
60   Starlite ST45 028   Lovers Line/Tu-Woo-Up-Tu-Woo ...... 40
61   Starlite ST45 049   Slop & Mash/My Sweet Angel ...... 40
61   Blue Beat BB 36   Over The River/Hip Rub (with Hersan & His City Slickers) ...... 30
62   Island WI 003   Sugar Dandy/Valerie ...... 25
62   Island WI 027   Andrea/Don't Leave Me ...... 25
63   Island WI 129   Sugar Dandy/Valerie (reissue) ...... 20
73   United Artists UP 35494   Stay/Call Me ...... 5
*(see also Duke Reid)*

**J.J. ALLSTARS**
68   Duke DU 3   One Dollar Of Music/CARL DAWKINS: I'll Make It Up ...... 30
69   Trojan TR 691   Memphis Underground (Parts 1 & 2) ...... 20
70   Duke DU 94   Collecting Coins/Cabbage Leaf ...... 15
70   Duke DU 95   This Land (actually by Carl Dawkins)/Land Version ...... 12
70   Escort ES 821   Mango Tree/The Removers (both actually by Winston Wright & J.J. All Stars) ...... 20
71   Big Shot BI 570   Perseverence Version/CARL DAWKINS: Perseverance ...... 12
71   Explosion EX 2051   I Feel Good (Version 2)/CARL DAWKINS: I Feel Good ...... 10
71   Duke DU 135   Soup/Soup (Version) ...... 10
*(see also Lloyd Young, Bleechers, Ethiopians)*

**J.J. BAND**
71   CBS S 64396   THE J.J. BAND (LP) ...... 25

**JJ72**
01   Lakota LAK 70019   Snow/Wounded (p/s) ...... 5
00   Lakota LAKLP 0017   JJ72 (LP) ...... 20

**JJ'S POWERHOUSE**
83   Sillysybin COX 1657   Running For The Line/Blackrods (no p/s) ...... 250

**MARCY JO & EDDIE RAMBEAU**
63   Stateside SS 235   Lover's Medley/When You Wore A Tulip ...... 10
*(see also Eddie Rambeau)*

**JOANIE, JOHNNY & HAL**
60   Capitol CL 15126   When You Lose The One You Love/Miracles Are Always Happening ...... 6

**JOBELL (& ORCHESTRA DE SALSA)**
77   Pye N25736   Never Gonna Let You Go/Disco Version ...... 8

**JOBRIATH**
73   Elektra K 12129   Take Me I'm Yours/Earthling ...... 5
74   Elektra K 12156   Ooh La La/Gone Tomorrow ...... 5
74   Elektra K 12156   Ooh La La/Gone Tomorrow (demo) ...... 20
73   Elektra EKS 75070   JOBRIATH (LP) ...... 15
74   Elektra K 42163   CREATURES OF THE STREET (LP) ...... 15

**JO'BURG HAWK**
72   Charisma CB 194   Orang Utang/Dark Side Of The Moon ...... 5
73   Charisma CAS 1064   JO'BURG HAWK (LP, gatefold sleeve, large 'Mad Hatter' label) ...... 20

**JOCELYNE JOCYA**
69   CBS 4177   I Have Loved Me A Man/Time ...... 60
69   CBS 4177   I Have Loved Me A Man/Time (DJ copy) ...... 150

**JODEY**
79   Elliejay EJSP 9242   The Rocker/Front Man ...... 150

**JODIMARS**
56   Capitol CL 14518   Well Now, Dig This/Let's All Rock Together ...... 75

# JODY GRIND

| | | | MINT VALUE £ |
|---|---|---|---|
| 56 | Capitol CL 14627 | Rattle My Bones/Lotsa Love | 75 |
| 56 | Capitol CL 14641 | Rattle Shakin' Daddy/Eat Your Heart Out Annie | 75 |
| 56 | Capitol CL 14642 | Dance The Bop/Boom, Boom My Bayou Baby | 75 |
| 56 | Capitol CL 14663 | Midnight/Clarabella | 75 |
| 57 | Capitol CL 14700 | Cloud 99/Later | 75 |
| 70s | Bulldog BD 16 | Well Now, Dig This/Dance The Bop | 70 |
| 72 | Specialty SPE 6608 | WELL NOW DIG THIS (LP) | 5 |
| | *(see also Bill Haley & Comets)* | | 20 |

## JODY GRIND
| | | | |
|---|---|---|---|
| 69 | Transatlantic TRA 210 | ONE STEP ON (LP, gatefold sleeve, lilac label with 't' logo) | 175 |
| 70 | Transatlantic TRA 221 | FAR CANAL (LP, white/lilac label with 't' logo) | 175 |

*(see also Vinegar Joe, Hummingbird, Heads, Hands & Feet)*

## JODY ST
| | | | |
|---|---|---|---|
| 81 | Lips LIPS1 | Fight Back/Granny Did It (private pressing) | 150 |
| 81 | Private Pressing | STREET (LP, private pressing) | 75 |

## AL T. JOE (& CELESTIALS)
| | | | |
|---|---|---|---|
| 62 | Dice CC 9 | Rise Jamaica/I'm On My Own | 15 |
| 62 | Blue Beat BB 126 | You Cheated On Me/This Heart Of Mine (as Al T. Joe & Celestials) | 12 |
| 63 | Blue Beat BB 166 | Goodbye Dreamboat/Please Forgive Me | 15 |
| 63 | Blue Beat BB 169 | Fatso/Slow Boat | 12 |
| 70 | Duke DU 70 | It's A Shame/Desertion | 8 |
| 72 | Duke DU 148 | Vision/Young And Unlearned | 15 |
| 72 | Dynamic DYN 429 | Oh What A Price/The Prisoners Song | 15 |

*(see also Jamaica Fats)*

## JOE & ANN
| | | | |
|---|---|---|---|
| 65 | Black Swan WI 468 | Gee Baby/Wherever You May Be | 20 |

## BILLY JOE & CHECKMATES
| | | | |
|---|---|---|---|
| 61 | London HLU 9502 | Percolator/Round & Round & Round & Round | 8 |

## JOE COOL (& THE KILLERS)
| | | | |
|---|---|---|---|
| 77 | Ariola ARO 105 | I Just Don't Care/My Way (p/s) | 25 |

## JOE CROW
| | | | |
|---|---|---|---|
| 82 | Cherry Red CHERRY 48 | Compulsion/Absent Friends | 12 |

## JOE & DELLA
| | | | |
|---|---|---|---|
| 65 | Doctor Bird DB 1043 | So Close/BABA BROOKS : Eight Games | 20 |

## JOE & EDDIE
| | | | |
|---|---|---|---|
| 59 | Capitol CL 15038 | Green Grass/And I Believed | 7 |
| 64 | Vocalion V 9215 | There's A Meetin' Here Tonight/Lonesome Traveller | 5 |
| 65 | Vocalion V 9238 | Gabrielle/He's Got The Whole World In His Hands | 5 |
| 65 | Vocalion V 9242 | Depend On Yourself/With You In Mind | 5 |
| 65 | Vocalion V-N 9246 | Farewell/Hey Nelly Nelly | 5 |
| 65 | Vocalion V-P 9250 | Walkin' Down The Line/It Ain't Me Babe | 10 |
| 65 | Vocalion VAN 8046 | WALKIN' DOWN THE LINE (LP) | 30 |

## JOE 9T & THUNDERBIRDS
| | | | |
|---|---|---|---|
| 79 | Gemme JOE 9T/LYN 6526 | Joe 9T Theme/THEY MUST BE RUSSIANS: Psycho Analysis (p/s, stamped white label) | 15 |

*(see also They Must Be Russians)*

## JOE 90
| | | | |
|---|---|---|---|
| 92 | Full Effect FERT 112 | Good Times/New Found Strength (12") | 20 |

## JOE PUBLIC (1)
| | | | |
|---|---|---|---|
| 79 | Wavelength HURT 3 | Herman's Back/Travelling With Raymond/Like It (p/s) | 8 |

## JOE PUBLIC (2)
| | | | |
|---|---|---|---|
| 85 | Capital Class | Anti CND/Champagne Charlie | 30 |

## JOE (MANSANO) THE BOSS
| | | | |
|---|---|---|---|
| 70 | Joe JRS 6 | Son Of Al Capone/All My Enemies | 25 |
| 70 | Joe JRS 10 | If Life Was A Thing/LLOYD KINGPIN: Daisy Bothering | 120 |

*(see also Joe's Allstars, Joe Mansano, Dice The Boss)*

## BILLY JOEL
| | | | |
|---|---|---|---|
| 72 | Philips 6078 001 | She's Got A Way/Everybody Loves You Now | 8 |
| 74 | Philips 6078 018 | The Ballad Of Billy The Kid/If I Only Had The Words (To Tell You) (in p/s) | 35 |
| 74 | Philips 6078 018 | The Ballad Of Billy The Kid/If I Only Had The Words (To Tell You) | 25 |
| 79 | CBS 7150 | Honesty/Root Beer Rag (withdrawn) | 20 |
| 72 | Philips 6369 150 | COLD SPRING HARBOR (LP) | 15 |
| 73 | Philips 6369 160 | PIANO MAN (LP, withdrawn) | 20 |
| 78 | CBS H 82311 | THE STRANGER (LP, half-speed master version) | 20 |

*(see also Hassles)*

## JOE'S ALLSTARS
| | | | |
|---|---|---|---|
| 69 | Joe/Duke DU 24 | Hey Jude/Musical Feet | 75 |
| 69 | Joe/Duke DU 28 | Battle Cry Of Biafra/Funky Reggae Part 1 | 25 |
| 69 | Joe/Duke DU 50 | Brixton Cat/Solitude | 50 |
| 70 | Joe JRS 9 | Tony B's Theme/JOE THE BOSS: Skinhead Revolt | 125 |
| 72 | Sioux SI 012 | Tony B's Theme/RAY MARTELL: She Caught The Train | 12 |
| 70 | Trojan TBL 106 | BRIXTON CAT (LP) | 50 |

*(see also Joe The Boss, Dice The Boss, King Horror, Pattie La Donne)*

## JOE SOAP
| | | | |
|---|---|---|---|
| 73 | Polydor 2383 233 | KEEP IT CLEAN (LP, laminated sleeve, correction sticker on rear) | 150 |

## JOE SOPE
| | | | |
|---|---|---|---|
| 79 | Redball RR 022 | Gotta Be Something Else/Don't Understand | 40 |

## JOEY & GROUP
| | | |
|---|---|---|
| 13 | Blue Cat THB 7028 | Soul Love/LORD COMIC: What A Situation ........................................ 8 |

## JOEY & CONTINENTALS
| | | |
|---|---|---|
| 70 | Polydor 56520 | She Rides With Me/Rudy Vadoo............................................................ 85 |

*(see also G.T.O.'s)*

## JOEY & GENTLEMEN
| | | |
|---|---|---|
| 64 | Fontana TF 444 | Like I Love You/I'll Never Let You Go ................................................ 10 |
| 64 | Fontana TF 485 | Dummy Dum Song/Goodbye Little Girl............................................... 6 |

## JOHANNE & JIMMY
| | | |
|---|---|---|
| 64 | Fontana TF 447 | Everybody Knows/I Still Love you ...................................................... 8 |

## JOHN
| | | |
|---|---|---|
| 71 | Capitol CL 15678 | The Ten Lost Tribes Of Israel/Good Morning Old Man Time .................. 10 |

## ANDREW JOHN
| | | |
|---|---|---|
| 71 | CBS 7017 | Streets Of London/Rick Rack ............................................................. 10 |
| 72 | CBS 64835 | THE MACHINE STOPS (LP)..................................................................... 20 |

## BASIL JOHN
| | | |
|---|---|---|
| 60s | Planetone RC 12 | Drink And Drive/MIKE ELLIOTT: J.K. Shuffle ...................................... 10 |

## CLIVE JOHN
| | | |
|---|---|---|
| 75 | United Artists UAS 29733 | YOU ALWAYS KNOW WHERE YOU STAND WITH A BUZZARD (LP)............... 25 |

*(see also Man)*

## DAVID JOHN & MOOD
| | | |
|---|---|---|
| 64 | Vocalion V 9220 | To Catch That Man/Pretty Thing ....................................................... 220 |
| 65 | Parlophone R 5255 | Bring It To Jerome/I Love To See You Strut ....................................... 275 |
| 65 | Parlophone R 5301 | Diggin' For Gold/She's Fine .............................................................. 275 |

*(see also Gagalactyca, Astral Navigations, Little Free Rock)*

## ELTON JOHN
### SINGLES
| | | |
|---|---|---|
| 68 | Philips BF 1643 | I've Been Loving You/Here's To The Next Time ............................... 250 |
| 69 | Philips BF 1739 | Lady Samantha/All Across The Havens .............................................. 70 |
| 69 | DJM DJS 205 | It's Me That You Need/Just Like Strange Rain (in p/s) ...................... 100 |
| 69 | DJM DJS 205 | It's Me That You Need/Just Like Strange Rain ................................... 50 |
| 70 | DJM DJS 217 | Border Song/Bad Side Of The Moon .................................................. 25 |
| 70 | DJM DJS 222 | Rock And Roll Madonna/Grey Seal .................................................... 30 |
| 71 | DJM DJS 233 | Your Song/Into The Old Man's Shoes ................................................. 5 |
| 71 | DJM DJS 244 | Friends/Honey Roll .......................................................................... 10 |
| 72 | DJM DJX 501 | Rocket Man/Holiday Inn/Goodbye (gatefold p/s) ............................... 10 |
| 72 | DJM DJX 501 | Rocket Man/Holiday Inn/Goodbye (plain p/s) ..................................... 5 |
| 72 | DJM DJS 269 | Honky Cat/Lady Samantha/It's Me That You Need ............................... 6 |
| 72 | DJM DJS 271 | Crocodile Rock/Elderberry Wine ........................................................ 5 |
| 73 | DJM DJS 275 | Daniel/Skyline Pigeon ....................................................................... 5 |
| 73 | DJM DJ X502 | Saturday Night's Alright For Fighting/Jack Rabbit/Whenever You're Ready (We'll Go Steady Again) (non-laminated p/s) ................................. 20 |
| 73 | DJM DJX 502 | Saturday Night's Alright For Fighting/Jack Rabbit/Whenever You're Ready (We'll Go Steady Again) (laminated p/s) ..................................... 8 |
| 73 | DJM DJS 290 | Step Into Christmas/Ho! Ho! Ho! (Who'd Be A Turkey At Christmas)..... 6 |
| 73 | DJM DJS 10705 | Benny And The Jets/Rock 'N' Roll Madonna ........................................ 5 |
| 74 | DJM DJS 297 | Candle In The Wind/Benny And The Jets ............................................. 5 |
| 74 | DJM DJS 302 | Don't Let The Sun Go Down On Me/Sick City ...................................... 5 |
| 74 | DJM DJS 322 | The Bitch Is Back/Cold Highway ......................................................... 5 |
| 74 | DJM DJS 340 | Lucy In The Sky With Diamonds (featuring Dr. Winston O'Boogie [John Lennon] & His Reggae Guitars)/One Day At A Time ............................... 5 |
| 75 | DJM DJS 354 | Philadelphia Freedom/I Saw Her Standing There (as Elton John Band; B-side featuring John Lennon with Muscle Shoals Horns) (p/s) ................ 6 |
| 75 | DJM DJS 610 | Island Girl/Sugar On The Floor (p/s) .................................................. 5 |
| 78 | DJM DJS 10902 | Your Song/Border Song (p/s).............................................................. 5 |
| 78 | DJM DJS 10903 | Honky Cat/Sixty Years On (p/s) .......................................................... 5 |
| 78 | DJM DJS 10904 | Country Comfort/Crocodile Rock (p/s) ................................................ 5 |
| 78 | DJM DJS 10905 | Rocket Man/Daniel (p/s) .................................................................... 5 |
| 78 | DJM DJS 10908 | Candle In The Wind/I Feel Like A Bullet (In The Gun Of Robert Ford) (p/s, limited edition) ..................................................................... 10 |
| 78 | DJM DJS 10910 | Island Girl/Saturday Night's Alright For Fighting (p/s, limited edition) ..... 5 |
| 78 | DJM DJS 10911 | Philadelphia Freedom/Lucy In The Sky With Diamonds (reissue) ........... 5 |
| 78 | DJM DJS 10912 | Pinball Wizard/Benny And The Jets (p/s) ............................................. 5 |
| 78 | DJM EJ 12 | THE ELTON JOHN SINGLES COLLECTION (12 x 7" box set [DJS 10901-12]) ..... 50 |
| 78 | DJM DJT 15000 | FUNERAL FOR A FRIEND (12" EP) ....................................................... 10 |
| 80 | DJM DJS 10961 | Harmony/Mona Lisas And Mad Hatters (glossy p/s) .............................. 8 |
| 77 | Rocket GOALD 1 | The Goaldigger Song/Jimmy, Brian, Elton, Eric (mail-order, signed, 500 only, solid centre copies are counterfeits) ...................................... 250 |
| 77 | Rocket GOALD 1 | The Goaldigger Song/Jimmy, Brian, Elton, Eric (mail-order, unsigned, 500 only, solid centre copies are counterfeits) .................................... 150 |
| 79 | Rocket XPRES 20 | Mama Can't Buy You Love/Strangers (p/s; withdrawn, misspelt "Mamma") ............... 350 |
| 79 | Rocket XPRES 21 | Victim Of Love/Strangers (p/s) ........................................................... 7 |
| 79 | Rocket XPRES 2412 | Johnny B. Goode/Thunder In The Night (12", p/s) ............................... 10 |
| 80 | Rocket XPRES 45 | Dear God/Tactics (company sleeve) ................................................... 40 |
| 80 | Rocket ELTON 1 | Dear God/Tactics//Steal Away Child/Love So Cold (double pack, p/s)....... 6 |
| 82 | Rocket XPRPO 88 | All Quiet On The Western Front/Where Have All The Good Times Gone (poster p/s).... 10 |
| 83 | Rocket XPRES 91 | That's Why They Call It The Blues/Lord Choc Ice Goes Mental ('raised musical note' sleeve with shorter A-side title) .............................. 15 |
| 83 | Rocket EJPIC 1 | I'm Still Standing/Earn While You Learn (piano-shaped picture disc) ..... 15 |
| 83 | Rocket EJS 2/FREEJ 2 | Kiss The Bride/Dreamboat//Ego/Song For Guy (double pack, p/s)............ 10 |

| 83 | Rocket EJS 3/2 | Cold As Christmas/Crystal//Don't Go Breaking My Heart/Snow Queen (double pack, gatefold p/s, 2nd 45 with Kiki Dee) | 12 |
| 85 | Rocket EJS 8 | Act Of War (Part 1)/(Part 2) (with Millie Jackson, 'concertina pack' of video stills) | 8 |
| 85 | Rocket EJS 10/EJS 9 | Wrap Her Up/Restless (live)//Nikita/The Man Who Never Died (double pack, stickered gatefold PVC wallet with 2 separate p/s's) | 10 |
| 85 | Rocket EJSP 10 | Wrap Her Up/Restless (live) (with George Michael, oblong-shaped picture disc, with pictures on wrong sides) | 25 |
| 85 | Rocket EJS 1012/ELTON 1 | Wrap Her Up (Extended Remix) (with George Michael)/Restless (live)/ Nikita/Cold As Christmas (12", double pack in stickered PVC sleeve) | 10 |
| 86 | Rocket EJSP 13 | Slow Rivers (with Cliff Richard)/Billy & The Kids (picture disc) | 30 |
| 86 | Rocket EJS 13-12 | Slow Rivers (with Cliff Richard)/Billy & The Kids/Lord Of The Flies (12", p/s) | 12 |
| 88 | Rocket EJS 1512 | Candle In The Wind (live)/Sorry Seems To Be The Hardest Word (live)/ Your Song (live)/Don't Let The Sun Go Down On Me (live) (12", p/s) | 12 |
| 88 | Rocket EJSIP 16 | I Don't Wanna Go On With You Like That/Rope Around A Fool/ (Radio 1 interview) (33rpm, poster sleeve) | 10 |
| 88 | Rocket EJS 1612 | I Don't Wanna Go On With You Like That (Remix)/(7" Version)/ Rope Around A Fool (12", blue vinyl factory custom pressing, no p/s) | 150 |
| 90 | Rocket EJS 21 | Club At The End Of The Street/Give Peace A Chance (p/s, withdrawn) | 200 |
| 90 | Rocket EJS 2112 | Club At The End Of The Street/Give Peace A Chance (12", p/s, withdrawn) | 500 |
| 97 | Rocket EJSCD 41 | Something About The Way You Look Tonight (Edited Version)/ I Know Why I'm In Love/No Valentines/Something About The Way You Look Tonight (Album Version) (CD, card sleeve, unreleased) | 40 |
| 97 | Rocket EJSCX 41 | Something About The Way You Look Tonight (Edited Version)/ I Know Why I'm In Love/You Can Make History (Young Again)/Something About The Way You Look Tonight (Album Version) (CD, digipak, unreleased) | 75 |

**ALBUMS**

| 69 | DJM DJLP 403 | EMPTY SKY (gatefold sleeve, mono) | 150 |
| 69 | DJM DJLPS 403 | EMPTY SKY (gatefold sleeve, stereo, with 'stereo' sticker on sleeve) | 25 |
| 70 | DJM DJLPS 406 | ELTON JOHN (textured gatefold sleeve) | 18 |
| 70 | DJM DJLPS 406 | ELTON JOHN (later smooth gatefold sleeve) | 15 |
| 76 | DJM DJE 29001 | GOODBYE YELLOW BRICK ROAD (2-LP, yellow vinyl, triplefold sleeve) | 45 |
| 78 | DJM DJV 2300 | CAPTAIN FANTASTIC AND THE BROWN DIRT COWBOY (picture disc) | 40 |
| 78 | DJM LSP 14512 | ELTON JOHN (5-LP, box set) | 40 |
| 70 | Warlock Music WMM 101/2 | WARLOCK MUSIC SAMPLER (untitled publishing sampler, 7 tracks by Elton, 4 by Linda Peters) | 1000 |
| 91 | Rocket 848 236-2 | TO BE CONTINUED ... THE VERY BEST OF ELTON JOHN (4-CD, 12" x 8" box set with large colour booklet) | 100 |
| 93 | Happenstance HAPP 001 | PLAYS THE SIRAN (private pressing, 50 only) | 1000 |
| 93 | Happenstance HAPP 002 | THE FISHING TRIP (4-CD set, private pressing, 100 only, existence unconfirmed) | 700 |
| 97 | Rocket ELTON 50 | CELEBRATING ELTON JOHN'S 50TH BIRTHDAY (promo only) | 50 |
| 99 | Mercury ADV 1999/1 | AIDA (with Sir Tim Rice) (box set with wallet, plinth stand, interview CD, booklet and calender cards, promo only) | 50 |
| 99 | Mercury ADV 1999/1 | AIDA PRESS KIT (card box set with wallet, plinth stand, interview CD, booklet, calender cards, scented candle and broadcast CD-R, promo only) | 50 |

*(see also [Stu Brown &] Bluesology, Bread & Beer Band, Neil Sedaka, Kiki Dee, Aretha Franklin, Dionne Warwick Radio Heart, Argosy)o*

## JOHN LEE'S GROUNDHOGS

| 66 | Planet PLF 104 | Over You Baby/I'll Never Fall In Love Again | 100 |

*(see also Groundhogs, Tony McPhee)*

## LITTLE WILLIE JOHN

| 56 | Parlophone R 4209 | Fever/Letter From My Darling | 150 |
| 56 | Parlophone R 4209 | Fever/Letter From My Darling (78) | 20 |
| 58 | Parlophone R 4396 | Uh, Uh, Baby/Dinner Date (With His Girl Friend) | 50 |
| 58 | Parlophone R 4432 | Talk To Me, Talk To Me/Spasms | 40 |
| 58 | Parlophone R 4472 | Let's Rock While The Rockin's Good/You're A Sweetheart | 60 |
| 59 | Parlophone R 4571 | Leave My Kitten Alone/Let Nobody Love You | 50 |
| 60 | Parlophone R 4674 | Heartbreak (It's Hurtin' Me)/Do You Love Me | 30 |
| 60 | Parlophone R 4699 | Sleep/There's A Difference | 30 |
| 61 | Parlophone R 4728 | Walk Slow/HANK BALLARD: The Hoochie Coochie Coo | 40 |
| 11 | Kent CITY 011 | Home At Last/(I Need) Someone | 8 |
| 59 | Parlophone PMC 1163 | SURE THINGS (LP) | 175 |
| 64 | London HA 8126 | COME ON AND JOIN LITTLE WILLIE JOHN (LP) | 70 |

## MABLE JOHN

| 66 | Atlantic 584 022 | It's Catching/Your Good Thing (Is About To End) | 15 |
| 67 | Stax 601 010 | Same Time Same Place/Bigger And Better (dark blue label) | 15 |
| 67 | Stax 601 010 | Same Time Same Place/Bigger And Better (light blue label) | 10 |
| 68 | Stax 601 034 | Able Mable/Don't Get Caught | 15 |

## MICHAEL JOHN

| 83 | Loose LSE 48 | Love Will Tear Us Apart/We're Together (p/s) | 6 |

## ROBERT JOHN (1)

| 68 | CBS 3436 | If You Don't Want My Love/Don't | 15 |
| 68 | CBS 3730 | Don't Leave Me/Children | 5 |
| 68 | A&M AMS 835 | Raindrops Love And Sunshine/When The Party Is Over (DJ Copy) | 100 |
| 68 | A&M AMS 835 | Raindrops Love And Sunshine/When The Party Is Over | 50 |

## ROBERT JOHN (2)

| 80 | John 1 | The Aliens Stalk The Wrecked Planet/The Aliens Stalk The Wrecked Planet (same track both sides, no p/s) | 25 |

## SAMMIE JOHN

| 67 | Stateside SS 585 | Little John/Boss Bag | 20 |

## JOHN & JOHNNY

| 63 | Decca F 11719 | I Want You To Be My Girl/It's You | 6 |

## JOHN & PAUL

| 65 | London HLU 9997 | People Say/I'm Walkin' | 15 |

## JOHNNIE & JOE
| | | | |
|---|---|---|---|
| 58 | London HLM 8682 | Over The Mountain, Across The Sea/My Baby's Gone, On, On | 150 |
| 58 | London HLM 8682 | Over The Mountain, Across The Sea/My Baby's Gone, On, On (78) | 20 |

## JOHNNY DANGEROUSLY
| | | | |
|---|---|---|---|
| 90 | Village (no cat no) | Introducing Jane/Tear It Down/Subway Life (12" p/s) | 20 |
| 89 | Village (no cat no) | YOU, ME AND THE ALARM CLOCK (mini LP p/s with photo insert, 1,000 only) | 35 |

*(see also I Am Kloot)*

## JOHNNY G
| | | | |
|---|---|---|---|
| 78 | Beggars Banquet BEG 3 | Call Me Bwana!/Suzy Was A Girl From Greenford (p/s) | 5 |
| 78 | Beggars Banquet BEG 7 | The Hippys Graveyard/Miles And Miles (p/s) | 6 |

## JOHNNY & JAILBIRDS
| | | | |
|---|---|---|---|
| 79 | Duke WIRP 001 | Shang A-Lang A-Ding Dong/Slick Chick | 8 |

## LITTLE JOHNNY JONES
| | | | |
|---|---|---|---|
| 73 | Pressure Beat PB 5515 | More Dub/More Dub - Chapter Two | 8 |

*(see also Johnny Lover)*

## JOHNNY & THE ROCCOS
| | | | |
|---|---|---|---|
| 78 | SRT SRTX/78/CUS 212 | JOHNNY & THE ROCCOS (LP) | 40 |

## JOHNNY RONDO TRIO
| | | | |
|---|---|---|---|
| 78 | Chiltern Sound RONDO 1 | Las Bicicletas/Frog Dance (p/s, trio of Lol Coxhill, Chris Wood and Dave Holland) | 10 |

*(see also Lol Coxhill)*

## JOHNNY (OSBORNE) & ATTRACTIONS
| | | | |
|---|---|---|---|
| 67 | Doctor Bird DB 1118 | Young Wings Can Fly/DUDLEY WILLIAMSON: I'm Moving On | 200 |
| 68 | Doctor Bird DB 1117 | Coming On The Scene/Anything You Want | 400 |

## JOHNNY (STEVENS) & THE BLUE BEATS
| | | | |
|---|---|---|---|
| 64 | Blue Beat BB 229 | Shame/Ball And Chain | 15 |

## JOHNNY & CHAZ & GUNNERS
| | | | |
|---|---|---|---|
| 61 | Decca F 11365 | Bobby/Out Of Luck | 22 |

## JOHNNY & THE COPYCATS
| | | | |
|---|---|---|---|
| 64 | Norco AB 102 | I'm A Hog For You Baby/I Can Never See You | 60 |

*(see also My Dear Watson)*

## JOHNNY & THE HURRICANES
| | | | |
|---|---|---|---|
| 59 | London HL 8899 | Crossfire/Lazy (triangular-centre) | 20 |
| 59 | London HL 8899 | Crossfire/Lazy (later round centre) | 10 |
| 59 | London HL 8948 | Red River Rock/Buckeye (triangular-centre) | 10 |
| 59 | London HL 8948 | Red River Rock/Buckeye (later round centre) | 5 |
| 59 | London HL 9017 | Reveille Rock/Time Bomb (triangular-centre) | 10 |
| 59 | London HL 9017 | Reveille Rock/Time Bomb (later round centre) | 5 |
| 59 | London HL 9017 | Reveille Rock/Time Bomb (78) | 20 |
| 60 | London HLI 9072 | Beatnick Fly/Sand Storm | 5 |
| 60 | London HLI 9072 | Beatnick Fly/Sand Storm (78) | 20 |
| 60 | London HLX 9134 | Down Yonder/Sheba | 5 |
| 60 | London HLX 9134 | Down Yonder/Sheba (78) | 30 |
| 60 | London HLX 9190 | Rocking Goose/Revival | 5 |
| 60 | London HLX 9190 | Rocking Goose/Revival (78) | 60 |
| 60 | London HL 7099 | The Hep Canary/Catnip (export issue) | 25 |
| 61 | London HLX 9289 | Ja-Da/Mr. Lonely | 5 |
| 61 | London HLX 9378 | High Voltage/Old Smokie | 5 |
| 62 | London HLX 9491 | Farewell, Farewell/Traffic Jam | 10 |
| 62 | London HLX 7116 | You Are My Sunshine/Farewell, Farewell (export issue) | 30 |
| 62 | London HLX 9536 | Salvation/Misirlou | 10 |
| 62 | London HLX 9617 | Minnesota Fats/Come On Train | 15 |
| 63 | London HLX 9660 | Whatever Happened To Baby Jane/Greens And Beans | 12 |
| 64 | Stateside SS 347 | Money Honey/That's All | 15 |
| 61 | London REX 1284 | ROCKING GOOSE (EP) | 20 |
| 62 | London REX 1347 | JOHNNY AND THE HURRICANES (EP) | 20 |
| 64 | London REX 1414 | JOHNNY AND THE HURRICANES VOL. 2 (EP) | 20 |
| 60 | London HA 2227 | RED RIVER ROCK (LP, plum label) | 25 |
| 60 | London HA-I 2269 | STORMSVILLE (LP) | 25 |
| 61 | London HA-X 2322 | THE BIG SOUND OF JOHNNY AND THE HURRICANES (LP) | 25 |
| 61 | London HA 2227 | RED RIVER ROCK (LP, reissue, black label) | 25 |

## JOHNNY & JACK
| | | | |
|---|---|---|---|
| 54 | HMV 7MC 21 | Honey, I Need You/Goodnight, Well It's Time To Go (export issue) | 20 |
| 59 | RCA RCA 1145 | Sailor Man/Wild And Wicked World | 5 |
| 59 | RCA RCX 176 | COUNTRY GUITAR VOL. 10 (EP) | 10 |

## JOHNNY & JAMMERS
| | | | |
|---|---|---|---|
| 79 | Big Beat NS 55 | School Day Blues/You Know I Love You (p/s) | 5 |

*(see also Johnny Winter)*

## JOHNNY & JOHN
| | | | |
|---|---|---|---|
| 66 | Polydor 56087 | Bumper To Bumper/Scrape My Boot | 25 |

*(see also Johnny Gustafson, Big Three)*

## JOHNNY & JUDY
| | | | |
|---|---|---|---|
| 59 | Vogue Pop V 9128 | Bother Me Baby/Who's To Say | 500 |
| 59 | Vogue Pop V 9128 | Bother Me Baby/Who's To Say (78) | 150 |

*(see also John Walker)*

## JOHNNY & THE SELF ABUSERS
| | | | |
|---|---|---|---|
| 77 | Chiswick NS 22 | Saints And Sinners/Dead Vandals (p/s) | 40 |

*(see also Simple Minds)*

MINT VALUE £

## JOHNNY & VIBRATONES
63   Warner Bros WB 107      Bird Stompin'/Movin' The Bird ........................................................................... 12

## JOHNNY F & KLM
92   Liberty Grooves LIB003   TAKIN' LIBERTIES VOL 1 (LP)............................................................................. 15

## JOHNNY MOPED
76   Chiswick PROMO 3     BASICALLY, THE ORIGINAL JOHNNY MOPED TAPE (33rpm, no p/s) ................... 20
77   Chiswick S 15         No-One/Incendiary Device (first pressing has laminate p/s) ........................... 15
78   Chiswick NS 27       Darling, Let's Have Another Baby/Something Else/It Really Digs (p/s) ............. 6
78   Chiswick NS 41       Little Queenie/Hard Lovin' Man (p/s) .............................................................. 8
78   Chiswick WIK 8       CYCLEDELIC (LP, with free single [PROMO 3]) ................................................ 30
90   Deltic DELTLP 6      THE SEARCH FOR XERXES (LP) ......................................................................... 20
*(see also Slime, Maxim's Trash)*

## JOHNNY'S JAZZ
56   Decca FJ 10663      R.J. Boogie/Get Happy (featuring Johnny Hawksworth)..................................... 6

## BARRY JOHNS
58   HMV POP 472        Locked In The Arms Of Love/Are You Sincere...................................................... 7

## JOHN'S CHILDREN
66   Columbia DB 8030     The Love I Thought I'd Found/Strange Affair (very few in p/s) ..................... 500
66   Columbia DB 8030     The Love I Thought I'd Found/Strange Affair.............................................. 300
67   Columbia DB 8124     Just What You Want - Just What You'll Get/But She's Mine ......................... 160
67   Track 604 003         Desdemona/Remember Thomas A'Beckett (in p/s) ..................................... 150
67   Track 604 003         Desdemona/Remember Thomas A'Beckett .................................................... 60
67   Track 604 005         Midsummer Night's Scene/Sara Crazy Child (withdrawn) ......................... 4000
67   Track 604 005         Come And Play With Me In The Garden/Sara Crazy Child (in p/s) ............... 200
67   Track 604 005         Come And Play With Me In The Garden/Sara Crazy Child .............................. 90
67   Track 604 010         Go Go Girl/Jagged Time Lapse ....................................................................... 80
82   Cherry Red BRED 31   ORGASM (LP, with inner) ................................................................................. 20
87   Bam Caruso KIRI 095  MIDSUMMER NIGHT'S SCENE (LP) ................................................................. 30
*(see also Marc Bolan, Andy Ellison, Radio Stars, Jook, Tyrannosaurus Rex)*

## GLYN JOHNS
62   Decca F 11478        January Blues/Sioux Indian ............................................................................... 5
63   Decca F 11753        Old Deceiver Time/Dancing With You................................................................ 5
65   Immediate IM 013     Mary Anne/Like Grains Of Yellow Sand .......................................................... 25
65   Pye 7N 15818         I'll Follow The Sun/I'll Take You Dancing ......................................................... 5
60s  Westcot LYN 827/828  Today You're Gone/Such Stuff Of Dreams (freebie with jeans offer) ............. 5

## LYNDON JOHNS (& ISRAELITES)
69   Downtown DT 444     Don't Gamble With Love/Song Bird ................................................................ 40
69   Downtown DT 451     Oh Mama Oh Papa/Bring Back The Night (with The Israelites)....................... 30

## JOHN'S RADIO
82   Epidemic EPC 001     Song In My Head/Strange.................................................................................. 20

## AL JOHNSON & JEAN CARN
80   CBS 8545            I'm Back For More/You Are My Personal Angel................................................. 10
*(see also Jean Carn)*

## ALEC JOHNSON
79   RFP RFP 001         Busman's Holiday (no p/s) ................................................................................ 12
*(see also Nightwing)*

## ANTHONY JOHNSON
82   Rusty R 005         Dread Locks Fight/ANTHONY JOHNSON & RANKING TOYAN: Babyloving (12" ............. 35
81   Greensleeves GRED 76  Let Go This One/BILLY BOYO: One Spliff A Day (12")...................................... 20
89   Unity UNI 7          Dance Hall Vibe/Version//TONTO IRIE: Wrap It UP MIx (12") ......................... 20
83   Rusty RILP 003       I'M READY (LP) ............................................................................................... 25
82   Midnight Rock MRLP 002  GUN SHOT (LP) ......................................................................................... 30

## BETTY JOHNSON
56   London HLU 8307     I'll Wait/Please Tell Me Why............................................................................. 40
56   London HLU 8326     Honky Tonk Rock/Say It Isn't So, Joe ............................................................ 100
56   London HLU 8326     Honky Tonk Rock/Say It Isn't So, Joe (78)....................................................... 30
57   London HLU 8365     I Dreamed/If It's Wrong To Love You.............................................................. 20
57   London HLU 8432     1492/Little White Lies ...................................................................................... 10
58   London HLE 8557     Little Blue Man/Song You Heard When You Fell In Love ................................. 10
58   London HLE 8678     Dream/How Much ............................................................................................ 15
58   London HLE 8701     There's Never Been A Night/Mr. Brown Is Out Of Town ................................. 25
58   London HLE 8725     Hoopa Hoola/One More Time .......................................................................... 20
59   London HLE 8839     Does Your Heart Beat For Me?/You And Only You .......................................... 20
59   London HLE 8839     Does Your Heart Beat For Me?/You And Only You (78) ................................... 20
59   London RE-E 1221     DREAM (EP) ..................................................................................................... 75
59   London HA-E 2163     THE SONG YOU HEARD WHEN YOU FELL IN LOVE (LP) ................................... 40

## BLIND WILLIE JOHNSON
58   Fontana TFE 17052    TREASURES OF NORTH AMERICAN NEGRO MUSIC NO. 2 (EP) ......................... 10
70   Xtra XTRA 1098       BLIND WILLIE JOHNSON (LP) ........................................................................... 20

## BOB JOHNSON & PETE KNIGHT
77   Chrysalis CHR 1137    THE KING OF ELFLAND'S DAUGHTER (LP, lyric insert, green label) ................. 15
*(see also Steeleye Span, Mary Hopkin)*

## BOBBY JOHNSON & ATOMS
67   Ember EMB S 245     Do It Again A Little Bit Slower/Tramp (in p/s) ................................................ 20
67   Ember EMB S 245     Do It Again A Little Bit Slower/Tramp .............................................................. 10

## BROWNIE JOHNSON
62   Longhorn BLH 0004    Best Dressed Beggar/Just Pretending (estimated that atound 1000 pressed) ............... 40

**BUBBER JOHNSON**
57  Parlophone R 4259 ......... Confidential/Have A Little Faith In Me ............................................................. 35

**BUDDY JOHNSON**
59  Mercury ZEP 10009 ......... BUDDY JOHNSON WAILS (EP, with Ella Johnson) ................................................ 50
57  Mercury MPT 7515 ......... ROCK AND ROLL (10" LP, with Ella Johnson) ..................................................... 150

**CAREY JOHNSON**
72  Banana BA 369 ......... Correction Train/SOUL DEFENDERS: Version ..................................................... 25

**DOMINO JOHNSON**
72  Green Door GD 4045 ......... Summertime/SWANS: Grazing ........................................................................ 20
73  Count Shelly ......... I've Seen The Light/BARRY CRUBER: This Yah Daughter ...................................... 40

**DOMINO JOHNSON & CHAMPIONS**
70  Duke DU 89 ......... You Broke My Heart/TONY & CHAMPIONS: Tell Me The Reason ........................... 12

**GENERAL JOHNSON**
76  Arista ARIST 45 ......... All In The Family/Ready, Willing And Able ........................................................... 6
73  Invictus SVT 1008 ......... GENERALLY SPEAKING (LP) ............................................................................. 20
*(see also Norman Johnson, Showmen, Chairmen Of The Board)*

**GINGER JOHNSON AND HIS AFRICAN MESSENGERS**
67  Masquerade SM 02001 ......... AFRICAN PARTY (LP) ................................................................................... 125

**HOWARD JOHNSON**
71  Jay Boy BOY 47 ......... The Slide/That Magic Touch Can Send You Flying ............................................... 15

**JIMMY JOHNSON**
65  Sue WI 387 ......... Don't Answer The Door Parts 1 & 2 ................................................................. 35

**J.J. JOHNSON**
55  Vogue LDE 124 ......... J.J. JOHNSON SEXTET (10" LP) ...................................................................... 15
55  Vogue LDE 162 ......... J.J. JOHNSON QUINTET (10" LP) ................................................................... 15
73  United Artists UAS 29451 ......... ACROSS 110TH STREET (LP, soundtrack, with Bobby Womack) ......................... 20
*(see also Sonny Stitt)*

**(JOHNNY JOHNSON &) THE BANDWAGON**
68  Direction 58-3520 ......... Baby Make Your Own Sweet Music/On The Day We Fall In Love (as Bandwagon) ........... 7
68  Direction 58-3670 ......... Breaking Down The Walls Of Heartache/Dancin' Master (as Bandwagon) ............... 7
69  Direction 58-3923 ......... You/You Blew Your Cool And Lost Your Fool ....................................................... 7
69  Direction 58-4180 ......... Let's Hang On/I Ain't Lying (withdrawn) ............................................................ 12
69  Direction 58-4180 ......... Let's Hang On/Don't Let It In ........................................................................... 6
70  Bell BLL 128 ......... (Blame It) On The Pony Express/Never Let Me Go .................................................. 6
70  Bell BLL 1111 ......... Sweet Inspiration/Pride Comes Before A Fall ....................................................... 5
72  Stateside SS 2207 ......... Honey Bee/I Don't Know Why .......................................................................... 20
74  EMI EMI 2114 ......... Strong Love, Proud Love/Fast Running Out Of World .......................................... 25
69  Direction 8-63500 ......... JOHNNY JOHNSON AND THE BANDWAGON (LP) ............................................... 30
70  Bell SBLL 138 ......... SOUL SURVIVOR (LP) ................................................................................... 25

**JUDI JOHNSON (& PERFECTIONS)**
64  HMV POP 1371 ......... My Baby's Face/Make The Most Of It (solo) ....................................................... 15
65  HMV POP 1399 ......... How Many Times/A Way Out (as Judi Johnson & Perfections) ............................. 20

**LARRY JOHNSON**
70  Blue Horizon 7-63851 ......... PRESENTING THE COUNTRY BLUES (LP) ....................................................... 150

**LAURIE JOHNSON ORCHESTRA**
56  HMV 7MC 47 ......... Buttercup/Lullaby Of The Leaves (export issue) ................................................ 10
57  HMV POP 404 ......... The Moonraker/Call Of The Casbah .................................................................. 7
60  Pye 7N 15251 ......... No Hiding Place/The Deputy ........................................................................... 6
64  Pye 7N 15599 ......... Dr Strangelove Theme/Nevada ........................................................................ 6
64  Pye 7N 15715 ......... Call Me Irresponsible/The Beauty Jungle ........................................................... 6
65  Pye 7N 15933 ......... Latin Quarter/M1 (in p/s) ............................................................................... 8
65  Pye 7N 15933 ......... Latin Quarter/M1 ......................................................................................... 6
65  Pye 7N 17015 ......... The Avengers/Minor Bossa Nova (in p/s) ......................................................... 50
65  Pye 7N 17015 ......... The Avengers/Minor Bossa Nova ..................................................................... 30
69  MGM MGM 1457 ......... There Is Another Song/Caesar Smith .............................................................. 25
71  Columbia DB 8826 ......... The Jason King Theme/There Comes A Time ...................................................... 50
76  EMI EMI 2562 ......... The New Avengers Theme/A Flavour Of The Avengers (in p/s) ............................. 10
76  EMI EMI 2562 ......... The New Avengers Theme/A Flavour Of The Avengers ......................................... 6
80  Unicorn Kachana MCPS 5 ......... The Professionals Main Title/On Target/The New Avengers Main Title (p/s, by Laurie
Johnson & London Studio Orchestra) ................................................................. 6
67  Marble Arch MAL 695 ......... THE AVENGERS AND OTHER FAVOURITES (LP) ............................................... 25
69  MGM C(S) 8104 ......... THEMES AND ... (LP) ................................................................................... 25
70  Columbia SCX 6412 ......... LAURIE JOHNSON/LONDON JAZZ ORCHESTRA - SYNTHESIS (LP, with Joe Harriott,
Tubby Hayes, Stan Tracey & Tony Coe) ............................................................. 60
80  Unicorn Kachana KPM 7009 ......... MUSIC FROM THE AVENGERS, THE NEW AVENGERS AND THE PROFESSIONALS (LP,
gatefold sleeve, with London Studio Orchestra) .................................................. 20

**LINTON KWESI JOHNSON**
78  Virgin VX 1002 ......... DREAD BEAT AN' BLOOD (LP, as Poet & The Roots) .......................................... 15
79  Island ILPS 9566 ......... FORCES OF VICTORY (LP, with inner sleeve) .................................................... 15
80  Island ILPS 9605 ......... BASS CULTURE (LP) ................................................................................... 15
80  Island ILPS 9650 ......... LKJ IN DUB (LP) ........................................................................................ 15

**LONNIE JOHNSON**
57  Parlophone GEP 8635 ......... LONESOME ROAD (EP) ................................................................................. 20
57  Parlophone GEP 8663 ......... LONNIE'S BLUES (EP) ................................................................................... 20
58  Parlophone GEP 8693 ......... LONNIE'S BLUES NO. 2 (EP) ........................................................................ 20
64  Storyville SLP 162 ......... PORTRAITS IN BLUES VOL. 6 (LP) ................................................................. 20
64  Storyville 616 010 ......... SEE SEE RIDER (LP, with Otis Spann) ............................................................. 40
60s Xtra XTRA 1037 ......... LONNIE JOHNSON (LP) ................................................................................ 25

# Lou JOHNSON

*(see also Eddie Lang & Lonnie Johnson)*

## LOU JOHNSON
| | | | |
|---|---|---|---|
| 63 | London HLX 9805 | Reach Out For Me/Magic Potion | 50 |
| 63 | London HLX 9805 | Reach Out For Me/Magic Potion (DJ copy) | 100 |
| 64 | London HLX 9917 | (There's) Always Something There To Remind Me/Wouldn't That Be Something | 25 |
| 64 | London HLX 9929 | A Message To Martha (Kentucky Bluebird)/The Last One To Be Loved | 15 |
| 65 | London HLX 9965 | Please Stop The Wedding/Park Avenue | 20 |
| 65 | London HLX 9994 | A Time To Love, A Time To Cry/Unsatisfied | 80 |
| 65 | London HLX 9994 | A Time To Love, A Time To Cry/Unsatisfied (DJ copy) | 150 |
| 69 | London HLX 10269 | (There's) Always Something There To Remind Me/Message To Martha | 10 |
| 12 | Kent Select CITY 028 | The Panic Is On/You Better Let Him Go | 8 |
| 64 | London REX 1438 | THE MAGIC POTION OF LOU JOHNSON (EP) | 150 |

## LUTHER 'GEORGIA BOY SNAKE' JOHNSON
| | | | |
|---|---|---|---|
| 69 | Transatlantic TRA 188 | THE MUDDY WATERS BLUES BAND (LP, credits Muddy Waters on label) | 30 |

## MARV JOHNSON
| | | | |
|---|---|---|---|
| 59 | London HLT 8856 | Come To Me/Whisper (tri-centre) | 100 |
| 59 | London HLT 8856 | Come To Me/Whisper | 30 |
| 59 | London HLT 9013 | You Got What It Takes/Don't Leave Me (tri centre) | 20 |
| 59 | London HLT 9013 | You Got What It Takes/Don't Leave Me | 10 |
| 59 | London HLT 9013 | You Got What It Takes/Don't Leave Me (78) | 20 |
| 60 | London HLT 9109 | I Love The Way You Love/Let Me Love You | 20 |
| 60 | London HL 7095 | I Love The Way You Love/Let Me Love You (export issue) | 20 |
| 60 | London HLT 9165 | Ain't Gonna Be That Way/All The Love I've Got | 20 |
| 60 | London HLT 9187 | (You've Got To) Move Two Mountains/I Need You | 20 |
| 61 | London HLT 9265 | Happy Days/Baby, Baby | 20 |
| 61 | London HLT 9311 | Merry-Go-Round/Tell Me That You Love Me | 30 |
| 65 | Tamla Motown TMG 525 | Why Do You Want To Let Me Go/I'm Not A Plaything | 100 |
| 69 | United Artists UP 35010 | I Love The Way You Love/You Got What It Takes | 6 |
| 68 | Tamla Motown TMG 680 | I'll Pick A Rose For My Rose/You Got The Love I Love | 6 |
| 69 | Tamla Motown TMG 713 | I Miss You Baby (How I Miss You)/Bad Girl | 10 |
| 70 | Tamla Motown TMG 737 | So Glad You Chose Me/I'm Not A Plaything | 10 |
| 60 | London HA-T 2271 | MARVELLOUS MARV JOHNSON (LP) | 150 |
| 69 | T. Motown TML 11111 | I'LL PICK A ROSE FOR MY ROSE (LP, mono) | 30 |
| 69 | T. Motown STML 11111 | I'LL PICK A ROSE FOR MY ROSE (LP, stereo) | 25 |

## MATT JOHNSON
| | | | |
|---|---|---|---|
| 81 | 4AD CAD 113 | BURNING BLUE SOUL (LP, original 'psychedelic eye' cover) | 18 |

*(see also Gadgets, The The)*

## MIRRIAM JOHNSON
| | | | |
|---|---|---|---|
| 61 | London HLW 9337 | Lonesome Road/Young And Innocent | 15 |

## NORMAN JOHNSON (& SHOWMEN)
| | | | |
|---|---|---|---|
| 69 | Action ACT 4529 | You're Everything/Our Love Will Grow | 100 |
| 69 | Action ACT 4545 | Take It Baby/In Paradise | 50 |
| 71 | Action ACT 4601 | You're Everything/Our Love Will Grow (reissue) | 40 |

*(see also General Johnson, Chairmen Of The Board, Showmen)*

## PETE JOHNSON
| | | | |
|---|---|---|---|
| 56 | Vogue V 2007 | J.J. Boogie/Yancey Special | 35 |
| 56 | Vogue V 2008 | Swanee River Boogie/St. Louis Boogie | 30 |
| 55 | Vogue EPV 1039 | PETE JOHNSON (EP) | 30 |
| 59 | Top Rank JKR 8009 | ROLL 'EM BOY (EP) | 25 |
| 55 | London AL 3549 | JUMPIN' WITH PETE JOHNSON (10" LP) | 50 |
| 55 | Vogue Coral LRA 10016 | BOOGIE WOOGIE MOOD (LP) | 30 |

*(see also Joe Turner & Pete Johnson, Albert Ammons & Meade Lux Lewis)*

## PHILIP JOHNSON
| | | | |
|---|---|---|---|
| 82 | Namedrop NR3 | YOUTH IN MOURNING (LP, with 4 double sided A4 sheets) | 20 |

## PLAS JOHNSON (ORCHESTRA)
| | | | |
|---|---|---|---|
| 57 | Capitol CL 14772 | The Big Twist/Come Rain Or Come Shine | 20 |
| 57 | Capitol CL 14816 | Swanee River Rock/You Send Me | 20 |
| 58 | Capitol CL 14836 | Popcorn/Hoppin' Mad | 20 |
| 58 | Capitol CL 14903 | Little Rockin' Deacon/Dinah | 20 |
| 59 | Capitol CL 14973 | Robbins Nest Cha Cha/Plaz Jazz | 10 |
| 57 | London HB-U 1078 | BOP ME DADDY (10" LP) | 60 |

## PROFESSOR JOHNSON & HIS GOSPEL SINGERS
| | | | |
|---|---|---|---|
| 51 | Vocalion V 1013 | Give Me That Old Time Religion/Where Shall I Be (78) | 20 |
| 58 | Brunswick OE 9352 | PROFESSOR JOHNSON AND HIS GOSPEL SINGERS (EP) | 20 |

## RAY JOHNSON
| | | | |
|---|---|---|---|
| 57 | Vogue V 9073 | If You Don't Want Me Baby/Calypso Joe | 40 |
| 58 | Vogue V 9093 | Calypso Blues/Are You There | 40 |

## ROBERT JOHNSON
| | | | |
|---|---|---|---|
| 62 | Philips BBL 7539 | ROBERT JOHNSON 1936-1937 (LP) | 100 |
| 65 | CBS BPG 62456 | KING OF THE DELTA BLUES SINGERS (LP) | 60 |
| 67 | Kokomo K 1000 | ROBERT JOHNSON (LP) | 50 |
| 60s | Smokestack SS/LP 1 | BLUES LEGEND 1936-1937 (LP) | 40 |
| 70 | CBS 64102 | KING OF THE DELTA BLUES SINGERS VOL. 2 (LP) | 30 |
| 85 | Blue Diamond/CBS 22190 | KING OF THE DELTA BLUES SINGERS VOLUMES 1 & 2 (2-LP) | 20 |

## ROY LEE JOHNSON
| | | | |
|---|---|---|---|
| 69 | Action ACT 4518 | So Anna Just Love Me/Boogaloo No. 3 (Red label) | 40 |
| 69 | Action ACT 4518 | So Anna Just Love Me/Boogaloo No. 3 (Yellow label) | 30 |

**RUBY JOHNSON**
| | | | |
|---|---|---|---|
| 67 | Stax 601 020 | If I Ever Needed Love (I Sure Do Need It Now)/Keep On Keeping On | 30 |

**SPIDER JOHNSON & POPEYE BAND**
| | | | |
|---|---|---|---|
| 63 | Riverside RIF 106904 | Doin' The Popeye/The Gospel Truth | 5 |

**T J JOHNSON**
| | | | |
|---|---|---|---|
| 83 | Switch DSW 003 | I Can Make It/Good For You (12") | 50 |

**THEO JOHNSON**
| | | | |
|---|---|---|---|
| 65 | Aladdin WI 604 | Masters Of War/The Water Is Wide | 15 |

**TOMMY JOHNSON**
| | | | |
|---|---|---|---|
| 60s | Saydisc SDM 224 | THE LEGACY OF TOMMY JOHNSON (LP) | 20 |

**DEBRA JOHNSON**
| | | | |
|---|---|---|---|
| 98 | Kent 6T 19 | To Get Love/DIPLOMATS: I Really Love You | 30 |

**DANIEL JOHNSON**
| | | | |
|---|---|---|---|
| 65 | Island WI 250 | Come On My People/Brother Nathan | 15 |

**WILCO JOHNSONS SOLID SENDERS**
| | | | |
|---|---|---|---|
| 78 | Virgin VS 214 | Walking On The Edge/Dr. Dupree | 6 |
| 81 | Fresh FRESH 31 | Casting My Spell On You/Looked Out Of My Window | 6 |
| 78 | Virgin V 2105 | SOLID SENDERS (LP, with free 'Live LP' stickered sleeve) | 15 |
| 80 | Fresh FRESH LP 4 | ICE ON THE MOTORWAY (LP, with free 7", as Wilco Johnson) | 15 |

*(see also Dr. Feelgood)*

**BRUCE JOHNSTON**
| | | | |
|---|---|---|---|
| 77 | CBS 5514 | Pipeline/Disney Girls | 5 |

*(see also Beach Boys)*

**BRUCE JOHNSTON COMBO**
| | | | |
|---|---|---|---|
| 63 | London HL 9780 | Original Surfer Stomp/Pajama Party | 60 |

*(see also Beach Boys, California Music, Fantastic Baggys, Sagittarius)*

**DANIEL JOHNSTON**
| | | | |
|---|---|---|---|
| 92 | Seminal Twang TWANG 13 | Laurie/The Monster Inside Of Me/Whiz Kid/The Lennon Song (p/s) | 10 |
| 93 | Ay Carramba! EL BARTO 001 | RESPECT (10" LP) | 15 |
| 99 | Pickled Egg EGG 6 | Dream Scream/Funeral Girl | 8 |
| 03 | For Us FU 020 | Mountain Top/Living It For The Moment | 12 |
| 03 | Sketchbook SKETCH XX2 | Fish/Living It For The Moment | 6 |
| 02 | Pickled Egg EGG 22 | REJECTED UNKNOWN (2-LP) | 20 |
| 06 | Coppertree CTR 007 | FEAR YOURSELF (LP, 1000 only) | 25 |

**JOHNSTON BROTHERS**
| | | | |
|---|---|---|---|
| 54 | Decca F 10234 | The Creep/Crystal Ball | 10 |
| 54 | Decca F 10286 | Oh Baby Mine I Get So Lonely/My Love, My Life, My Own | 10 |
| 54 | Decca F 10302 | The Bandit/KEYNOTES: A Dime And A Dollar | 10 |
| 54 | Decca F 10364 | Sh-Boom (Life Could Be A Dream)/Crazy 'Bout Ya Baby | 15 |
| 54 | Decca F 10401 | Mambo In The Moonlight/Papa Loves Mambo (with Ted Heath Music) | 5 |
| 54 | Decca F 10414 | Join In And Sing Medley (both sides) | 5 |
| 55 | Decca F 10451 | Majorca/Heartbroken | 5 |
| 55 | Decca F 10490 | The Right To Be Wrong/Hot Potato Mambo | 5 |
| 55 | Decca F 10513 | Chee Chee-Oo Chee (Sang The Little Bird)/Hubble Bubble | 5 |
| 55 | Decca F 10526 | Dreamboat/Jim, Johnny And Jonas | 5 |
| 55 | Decca F 10608 | Hernando's Hideaway/Hey There | 15 |
| 55 | Decca F 10636 | Join In And Sing Again Medley (both sides) | 10 |
| 56 | Decca F 10721 | No Other Love/Flowers Mean Forgiveness | 10 |
| 56 | Decca F 10747 | How Little We Know/The Street Musician | 6 |
| 56 | Decca F 10781 | In The Middle Of The House (with Keynotes)/Stranded In The Jungle | 10 |
| 56 | Decca F 10814 | Join In And Sing, No. 3 Medley (both sides) | 10 |
| 56 | Decca F 10828 | Give Her My Love (When You Meet Her)/A Rose And A Candy Bar | 10 |
| 57 | Decca F 10860 | Whatever Lola Wants (Lola Gets)/Heart | 10 |
| 57 | Decca F 10939 | I Like Music - You Like Music/Seven Bar Blues | 7 |
| 57 | Decca F 10962 | Join In And Sing, No. 4 Medley (both sides) | 5 |
| 56 | Decca DFE 6249 | JOIN THE JOHNSTON BROTHERS (EP) | 10 |

*(see also Dennis Lotis, Vera Lynn, Joan Regan, Lita Roza, Suzi Miller, Ted Heath, Keynotes)*

**JOHNSTONS**
| | | | |
|---|---|---|---|
| 68 | Transatlantic TRA 169 | THE JOHNSTONS (LP) | 22 |
| 68 | Transatlantic TRA 184 | GIVE A DAMN (LP) | 18 |
| 68 | Transatlantic TRA 185 | THE BARLEYCORN (LP) | 18 |
| 70 | Transatlantic TRA 211 | BITTER GREEN (LP) | 20 |
| 71 | Transatlantic TRA 231 | COLOURS OF THE DAWN (LP) | 15 |

*(see also Adrienne Johnston)*

**JOINER, ARKANSAS, JUNIOR HIGH SCHOOL BAND**
| | | | |
|---|---|---|---|
| 60 | London HLG 9147 | Big Ben/National City | 7 |

**JO JO GUNNE (U.K.)**
| | | | |
|---|---|---|---|
| 68 | Decca F 12807 | Every Story Has An End/Should Live Like That | 7 |
| 69 | Decca F 12906 | Beggin' You Baby/Bad Penny | 7 |

**JO JO GUNNE (U.S.)**
| | | | |
|---|---|---|---|
| 72 | Asylum AYM 501 | Run Run Run/Shake That Fat or Take It Easy as B-side (withdrawn) | 10 |
| 72 | Asylum AYM 507 | Shake That Fat/I Make Love | 5 |
| 73 | Asylum AYM 518 | Ready Freddy/Wait A Lifetime | 5 |
| 73 | Asylum AYM 521 | Rock Around The Symbol/Take Me Down Easy | 5 |
| 74 | Asylum AYM 528 | I Wanna Love You/Neon City | 5 |
| 74 | Asylum AYM 534 | Where Is The Show/Single Man | 5 |

*(see also Spirit)*

## JOKE SHOP

MINT VALUE £

**JOKE SHOP**
72  Access ACC 01                Lame Dog/Tell Her To Leave (p/s) ........................................................ 15

**JOKER (1)**
84  Lost Moment LM 018           Back On The Road/Pusher (p/s) ........................................................ 10

**JOKER (2)**
93  Skanna 06                    The Joker/Roots (12") ........................................................ 40
*(see also Skanna)*

**JOKERS**
62  Salvo SLO 1806               Blue Moonbeam/Dog Fight (99 only) ........................................................ 35

**JOKER'S WILD**
66  Regent Sound RSR 0031        Don't Ask Me/Why Do Fools Fall In Love (handwritten labels, 50 only) ............... 500
66  Regent Sound RSLP 007        JOKER'S WILD: Don't Ask Me/Why Do Fools Fall In Love/You Don't Know What I
                                 Know/That's How Strong My Love Is (12", 1-sided, 50 copies only) ................. 1000
*(see also Dave Gilmour, Pink Floyd)*

**JOHN JOLLIFFE**
79  Rocket XPRESS 9              Follow The Wind/Dream Love ........................................................ 6

**JOLLIVER ARKANSAS**
69  Bell SBLL 119                HOME (LP) ........................................................ 30
*(see also Leslie West, Mountain)*

**JOLLY BOYS**
70  Moodisc MU 3504              On The Water/MUDIES ALL STARS: Cash Register ........................................................ 15

**JOLLY BROTHERS**
81  Seven Leaves SL 008          Have A Litte Faith/Right Before My Eyes (12") ........................................................ 12
78  Ballistic FORCE 2002         Conscious Man/PRODIGAL CREATOR: Life (actually dub to Lee Perry's Ne Jah Go Run)
                                 (12") ........................................................ 15
93  Roots RRLP 001               LEE PERRY PRESENTS THE JOLLY BROTHERS (LP) ........................................................ 20

**JOLT**
77  Polydor 2058 936             You're Cold/All I Can Do (p/s) ........................................................ 15
78  Polydor 2059 008             What'cha Gonna Do About It/Again And Again (die-cut p/s) ........................................................ 12
78  Polydor 2059 039             I Can't Wait/Route 66 (p/s) ........................................................ 12
79  Polydor 2229 215             Maybe Tonight/I'm In Tears/See Saw/Stop Look (p/s) ........................................................ 12
79  Polydor 2229 215DJ           Maybe Tonight/See Saw (promo only, no p/s) ........................................................ 12
78  Polydor 2383 504             THE JOLT (LP, flip-back sleeve) ........................................................ 30

**JON**
67  Parlophone R 5604            So Much For Mary/Polly Sunday (in p/s) ........................................................ 50
67  Parlophone R 5604            So Much For Mary/Polly Sunday ........................................................ 25
67  Columbia DB 8249             Is It Love/Sing Out ........................................................ 150
*(see also Titus Groan, Still Life)*

**JON & ALUN**
63  Decca LK 4547                RELAX YOUR MIND (LP, mono) ........................................................ 22
63  Decca SKL 4547               RELAX YOUR MIND (LP, stereo) ........................................................ 30

**JON & DAVE**
97  Earworm SS 1                 Land Beyond The Sun/Instrumental For Silence (p/s, pale green vinyl, 500 copies only) . 8

**JON & JEANNIE**
68  Beacon 3-105                 Lover's Holiday/Something You Got ........................................................ 10
69  Beacon BEA 113               Don't Sign The Papers/We Got Lovin' ........................................................ 10

**JON & ROBIN & IN-CROWD**
67  Stateside SS 2027            Do It Again A Little Bit Slower/If I Need Someone It's You ........................................................ 15

**JONAH**
85  MW MW 7853                   Tough/This Is Love (no p/s) ........................................................ 280

**JONATHAN & CHARLES**
69  Herald LLR 566               ANOTHER WEEK TO GO (LP) ........................................................ 30

**JONCUNDO**
72  Banana BA 366                I'd Like To Teach The World To Sing/Rope Of Sand ........................................................ 10

**A JONES**
04  Jah Tubbys JT 10020          Jah Bless I/MA-KAYA CREW: Iron Dub ........................................................ 25

**AL JONES**
58  HMV POP 451                  Mad, Mad, World/Lonely Traveller ........................................................ 200
58  HMV POP 451                  Mad, Mad, World/Lonely Traveller(78) ........................................................ 20
69  Parlophone PMC/PCS 7081      ALUN ASHWORTH JONES (LP, black/yellow label with "Sold in U.K..." text) ............... 175
72  Village Thing VTS 19         JONESVILLE (LP) ........................................................ 175

**ALAN JONES**
82  Vada ABER 4134               MUSIC BY SECRETS EP ........................................................ 6

**BARBARA JONES**
72  Bullet BU 516                Sad Movies/SIR HARRY: Deejay Version ........................................................ 20
74  Count Shelley CS 045         Baby I'm Yours/Don't Turn Your Back On Me ........................................................ 8
74  Attack ATT 8077              Changing Partners/Part 2 ........................................................ 8
75  Dip DL 5085                  Where Do I Turn/G.G. ALL STARS: Version ........................................................ 8

**BEVERLEY JONES (& PRESTONS)**
63  HMV POP 1109                 The Boy I Saw With You/When It Comes To Love ........................................................ 10
63  HMV POP 1140                 Why Do Lovers Break Each Other's Heart/I'm Just An In-Between ........................................................ 20
63  HMV POP 1201                 Wait 'Til My Bobby Gets Home/A Boy Like You ........................................................ 15
64  Parlophone R 5189            Heatwave/Hear You Talking (with Prestons) ........................................................ 20
*(see also Roger James)*

**B-LOU JONES & HIS JUPITERS**
61  London HLU 9373              Anchors Aweigh (Parts 1 & 2) ........................................................ 10

**BRENDA LEE JONES**
75   UK USA 8            You're The Love Of My Life/Thread Your Needle (paper label) ............................... 8
*(see also Dean & Jean)*

**CAROL JONES**
60   Triumph RGM 1012    The Boy With The Eyes Of Blue/I Gave Him Back His Ring ............................... 125

**CASEY JONES & THE ENGINEERS**
63   Columbia DB 7083    One Way Ticket/I'm Gonna Love .................................................. 35

**CASEY JONES & THE GOVERNERS**
64   Golden 12LP 106     DON'T HA HA (LP) ........................................................... 60
*(see also Casey Jones & The Engineers)*

**CURTIS JONES**
66   RCA RCX 7184        R.C.A. VICTOR RACE SERIES VOL. 9 (EP) ...................................... 15
64   Decca LK 4587       CURTIS JONES IN LONDON (LP) ................................................ 125
68   Blue Horizon 7-63207   NOW RESIDENT IN EUROPE (LP, mono) ....................................... 80
68   Blue Horizon (S)-63207  NOW RESIDENT IN EUROPE (LP, stereo) ..................................... 50

**DATHAN JONES**
05   Hayley 008          Contract On Love/Mysterious Desire (reissue) ............................... 8

**DAVIE JONES & THE KING BEES**
64   Vocalion V 9221     Liza Jane/Louie, Louie Go Home (Demo copy) ................................ 2000
64   Vocalion Pop V 9221 Liza Jane/Louie, Louie Go Home (beware of counterfeits without centres) .......... 1250
78   Decca F 13807       Liza Jane/Louie, Louie Go Home (reissue) ................................... 25
*(see also David Bowie, Davy Jones, Manish Boys, Calvin James)*

**DAVY JONES**
65   Philips BF 1410     For Your Love/Love Bug ..................................................... 10

**DAVY JONES (U.K.) (1)**
65   Parlophone R 5250   You've Got A Habit Of Leaving/Baby Loves That Way (Demo) .................... 700
65   Parlophone R 5315   You've Got A Habit Of Leaving/Baby Loves That Way .......................... 900
*(see also David Bowie)*

**DAVY JONES (U.K.) (2)**
65   Colpix PX 784       What Are We Going To Do/This Bouquet ....................................... 10
67   Pye 7N 17302        It Ain't Me Babe/Baby It's Me (in p/s) ..................................... 12
67   Pye 7N 17302        It Ain't Me Babe/Baby It's Me .............................................. 5
67   Pye 7N 17380        Theme For A New Love/Dream Girl (in p/s) ................................... 10
67   Pye 7N 17380        Theme For A New Love/Dream Girl ............................................ 6
67   Pye International 7N 25432   Theme For A New Love/Dream Girl (reissue, withdrawn) ................. 20
71   Bell BLL 1163       Rainy Jane/Welcome To My Love .............................................. 5
77   MCA MCA 348         Life Line/It's A Jungle Out There/Gotta Get Up (from 'The Point') (p/s, last track with
                          Micky Dolenz) ............................................................. 5
78   Warner Bros K 17161 (Hey Ra Ra) Happy Birthday Mickey Mouse/You Don't Have To Be A Country Boy To
                          Sing A Country Song (p/s) ................................................. 5
83   J.J. 2001           I'll Love You Forever/When I Look Back On Christmas .......................... 12
67   Pye NPL 18178       DAVY JONES (LP) ............................................................ 20
*(see also Davy Jones & Micky Dolenz, Monkees)*

**DAVY JONES (U.K.) & MICKY DOLENZ**
71   Bell BLL 986        Do It In The Name Of Love/Lady Jane ........................................ 12
*(see also Monkees, Davey Jones)*

**DAVY JONES (U.K.) & THE LOWER THIRD/MANISH BOYS**
79   EMI 2925            You've Got A Habit Of Leaving/Baby Loves That Way/MANISH BOYS: I Pity The Fool/
                          Take My Tip (Demo copy, p/s) .............................................. 20
79   EMI EMI 2925        You've Got A Habit Of Leaving/Baby Loves That Way/MANISH BOYS: I Pity The Fool/
                          Take My Tip (p/s) ......................................................... 6
82   Charly CYM 1        You've Got A Habit Of Leaving/Baby Loves That Way/MANISH BOYS: I Pity The Fool/
                          Take My Tip (10", p/s) .................................................... 20
*(see also David Bowie, Davie Jones & King Bees, Manish Boys, Calvin James)*

**DAVY JONES (U.S.)**
60   Pye 7N 15254        Amapola/Mighty Man ......................................................... 10
61   Pye 7N 15318        Shenandoah/Scenery ......................................................... 10
61   Pye International 7N 25072   Model Girl/Scarlet Woman ........................................... 10
61   Pye International 7N 25095   Bonnie Banks/Baby Baby ............................................. 10
62   Piccadilly 7N 35038 Jezebel/Don't Come Crying To Me ............................................ 10
*(see also Thelonious Monk)*

**DILL JONES TRIO**
61   Columbia DB 4635    St. David/The Preacher ..................................................... 6
56   Jazz Today JTE 104  PIANO MOODS VOL. 2 (EP) .................................................... 25
56   Pye Jazz NJE 1024   PIANO MOODS VOL. 5 (EP) .................................................... 10
57   Columbia SEG 7764   TOP OF THE POLL (EP) ....................................................... 60
60   Columbia 33SX 1336  JONES THE JAZZ (LP) ........................................................ 20
78   77 77SEU 12/45      UP JUMPED YOU WITH LOVE (LP) ...............................................

**DORIS JONES**
76   Tomorrow LE 008     Stranded In The Wilderness/Stranded In The Wilderness (Instrumental) (promo only) . 10

**DOROTHY JONES**
61   Philips PB 1169     Takin' That Long Walk Home/It's Unbearable ................................. 30
*(see also Cookies)*

**GARY JONES**
62   Piccadilly 7N 35084 It's Over/Little Miss Nose In The Air ...................................... 8

**GEORGE JONES**
59   Mercury AMT 1036    White Lightning/Long Time To Forget ........................................ 25
59   Mercury AMT 1058    Who Shot Sam/Into My Arms Again ............................................ 15
59   Mercury AMT 1078    Big Harlan Taylor/Money To Burn ............................................ 10

| | | | MINT VALUE £ |
|---|---|---|---|
| 60 | Mercury AMT 1100 | Sparkling Brown Eyes/Accidentally On Purpose.................................................. | 10 |
| 61 | Mercury AMT 1124 | Candy Hearts/The Window Up Above ................................................................ | 10 |
| 62 | United Artists POP 1037 | She Thinks I Still Care/Geronimo ...................................................................... | 10 |
| 63 | United Artists UP 1015 | I Saw Me/Not What I Had In Mind (as George Jones with Jones Boys) ............ | 10 |
| 64 | United Artists UP 1044 | Your Heart Turned Left (And I Was On The Right)/My Tears Are Overdue ........ | 10 |
| 65 | United Artists UP 1080 | The Race Is On/She's So Lonesome Again ........................................................ | 10 |
| 59 | Mercury ZEP 10036 | GEORGE JONES (EP)........................................................................................ | 15 |
| 59 | Melodisc EPM7 109 | COUNTRY SONG HITS (EP) .............................................................................. | 80 |
| 64 | Mercury 10009 MCE | C & W ACES (EP)............................................................................................... | 40 |
| 64 | Ember EMB 4548 | THE BEST OF AMERICAN COUNTRY MUSIC VOL. 4 (EP) .............................. | 20 |
| 62 | United Artists ULP 1007 | THE NEW FAVOURITES OF GEORGE JONES (LP) .......................................... | 10 |
| 63 | United Artists ULP 1014 | MY FAVOURITES OF HANK WILLIAMS (LP) ...................................................... | 20 |
| 63 | Ember CW 101 | THE CROWN PRINCE OF COUNTRY MUSIC (LP, original pressings have grey & orange label)................................................................................................................. | 20 |

*(see also Gene Pitney, Elvis Costello)*

## GEORGE JONES/JIMMIE SKINNER
| | | | |
|---|---|---|---|
| 59 | Mercury ZEP 10012 | COUNTRY AND WESTERN (EP, 2 tracks each) ................................................ | 10 |

## JONES GIRLS
| | | | |
|---|---|---|---|
| 82 | Philadelphia Intl. PIR 2031 | Nights Over Egypt/Love Don't Ever Say Goodbye ............................................. | 5 |
| 82 | Phil. Intl. PIR 12-2031 | Nights Over Egypt/Love Don't Ever Say Goodbye (12") .................................... | 15 |

## GLORIA JONES
| | | | |
|---|---|---|---|
| 66 | Capitol CL 15429 | Heartbeat (Parts 1 & 2) ..................................................................................... | 50 |
| 66 | Stateside SS 555 | Finders Keepers/Run One Flight Of Stairs ....................................................... | 80 |
| 74 | Tamla Motown TMG 910 | Tin Can People/So Tired (Of The Way You're Treating Our Love Baby)............ | 10 |
| 76 | EMI EMI 2437 | Get It On/Get It On (Version) ............................................................................. | 6 |
| 76 | EMI EMI 2522 | I Ain't Going Nowhere/Simplicity Blues ............................................................. | 10 |
| 77 | EMI 2570 | Go Now (album version)/Drive Me Crazy (12" demos only) ............................... | 65 |
| 77 | EMI EMI 2570 | Go Now/Drive Me Crazy ..................................................................................... | 6 |
| 77 | EMI EMI 2720 | Bring On The Love (Why Can't We Be Friends Again)/Cry Baby ...................... | 6 |
| 74 | Tamla Motown STML 11254 | SHARE MY LOVE (LP) ....................................................................................... | 6 |
| 76 | EMI EMC 3159 | VIXEN (LP, produced by Marc Bolan)................................................................ | 25 |

*(see also Marc Bolan & Gloria Jones)*

## HEATHER JONES
| | | | |
|---|---|---|---|
| 74 | Sain SAIN 1008M | MAE'R OLYWVN YN TROI (LP) ......................................................................... | 50 |

## HUW JONES
| | | | |
|---|---|---|---|
| 69 | Welsh Teldisc WD 912 | Y ffoadur/Dewch I Ganu (La, La, La) (p/s) ........................................................ | 6 |
| 69 | Sain SAIN 1 | Dwr/Fy Ngwlad Fy Hun ...................................................................................... | 10 |
| 70 | Sain SAIN 3 | Paid Digalonni/Ffoi (p/s) ................................................................................... | 6 |

## INDIGO JONES
| | | | |
|---|---|---|---|
| 70 | Columbia DB 8744 | Noel Highway/Prodigal Son .............................................................................. | 12 |

## JACK JONES
| | | | |
|---|---|---|---|
| 58 | Capitol CL 14969 | Laffin' At Me/Deeply Devoted ............................................................................ | 10 |

## JAKE JONES
| | | | |
|---|---|---|---|
| 71 | MCA MVPS 432 | JAKE JONES (LP) .............................................................................................. | 25 |

## JANET JONES
| | | | |
|---|---|---|---|
| 74 | Midas MR 005 | SING TO ME LADY (LP) ..................................................................................... | 200 |
| 74 | Midas MFHR 059 | JANET JONES (LP, released on Folk Heritage label) ....................................... | 200 |

## JANIE JONES (& LASH)
| | | | |
|---|---|---|---|
| 65 | HMV POP 1495 | Witches Brew/Take-A My Tip ............................................................................. | 15 |
| 66 | HMV POP 1514 | Gunning For You/Go Go Away From Me ........................................................... | 15 |
| 67 | Columbia DB 8173 | Tickle Me Tootsie Wootsies/High And Dry ........................................................ | 12 |
| 68 | Pye 7N 17550 | Charlie Smith/Nobody's Perfect ........................................................................ | 10 |
| 68 | Major Minor MM 577 | The Girl's Song/I've Never Met A Boy Like You ................................................ | 10 |
| 70 | President PT 309 | Back On My Feet Again/Psycho ......................................................................... | 10 |
| 83 | Big Beat NS 91 | House Of The Ju-Ju Queen/Sex Machine (as Janie Jones & Lash, p/s) .......... | 10 |

*(see also The Clash)*

## JERRY JONES
| | | | |
|---|---|---|---|
| 70 | Banana BA 316 | Still Waters (Love)/SOUND DIMENSION: Wig Wam ........................................ | 30 |
| 71 | Bamboo BAM 65 | Still Waters (Love)/BRENTFORD ALLSTARS: Wig Wam (reissue).................. | 40 |
| 71 | Bamboo BALPS 213 | LIVE AT THE KINGSTON HOTEL, JAMAICA (LP) ........................................... | 50 |

## JIMMY JONES
| | | | |
|---|---|---|---|
| 60 | MGM MGM 1051 | Handy Man/The Search Is Over ......................................................................... | 7 |
| 60 | MGM MGM 1051 | Handy Man/The Search Is Over (78) ................................................................. | 40 |
| 60 | MGM MGM 1078 | Good Timin'/Too Long Will Be Too Late ............................................................ | 7 |
| 60 | MGM MGM 1078 | Good Timin'/Too Long Will Be Too Late (78) ..................................................... | 80 |
| 60 | MGM MGM 1091 | I Just Go For You/That's When I Cried .............................................................. | 12 |
| 60 | MGM MGM 1103 | Ready For Love/For You ..................................................................................... | 15 |
| 61 | MGM MGM 1123 | I Told You So/You Got It ..................................................................................... | 15 |
| 61 | MGM MGM 1133 | Dear One/I Say Love .......................................................................................... | 12 |
| 61 | MGM MGM 1146 | Mr Music Man/Holler Hey .................................................................................. | 15 |
| 62 | MGM MGM 1168 | You're Much Too Young/Nights Of Mexico ........................................................ | 12 |
| 65 | Columbia DB 7592 | Walkin'/Pardon Me ............................................................................................. | 30 |
| 65 | Cameo Parkway P 988 | Don't You Just Know It ....................................................................................... | 15 |
| 67 | Stateside SS 2041 | 39-21-46/Personal Property ............................................................................... | 18 |
| 60 | MGM MGM-EP 745 | JIMMY HANDYMAN JONES (EP) ...................................................................... | 25 |
| 61 | MGM MGM-EP 787 | ORIGINAL HITS (EP) ......................................................................................... | 20 |
| 60 | MGM MGM-C 832 | GOOD TIMIN' (LP) ............................................................................................. | 40 |

**JO JONES TRIO**
| | | | |
|---|---|---|---|
| 59 | Top Rank 25/039 | JO JONES (LP) | 18 |

**JOE JONES**
| | | | |
|---|---|---|---|
| 60 | Columbia DB 4533 | You Talk Too Much/I Love You Still | 15 |

**JOHN PAUL JONES**
| | | | |
|---|---|---|---|
| 64 | Pye 7N 15637 | Baja/A Foggy Day In Vietnam (B-side by Andrew Oldham Orchestra, white label promo) | 150 |
| 64 | Pye 7N 15637 | Baja/A Foggy Day In Vietnam (B-side actually by Andrew Oldham Orchestra) | 150 |

*(see also Led Zeppelin, Tony Meehan, Andrew Oldham Orchestra )*

**JOHNNY JONES & KING CASUALS**
| | | | |
|---|---|---|---|
| 68 | MCA MU 1031 | Soul Poppin'/Blues For The Brothers | 10 |
| 76 | Cream CRM 5004 | Purple Haze/Horsing Around | 10 |
| 76 | Brunswick BR 37 | Purple Haze/FRED HUGHES: Baby Boy | 8 |

**JONAH JONES (QUARTET)**
| | | | |
|---|---|---|---|
| 58 | Capitol CL 14939 | Night Train/Lots Of Luck Charley | 7 |
| 59 | Capitol 15085 | I Dig Chicks/Cherry | 5 |
| 62 | Ember JBS 704 | Down By The Riverside/Stars Fell On Alabama | 7 |

**JUSTIN JONES**
| | | | |
|---|---|---|---|
| 61 | London HLU 9463 | Dance By Yourself/Love | 150 |

**KEN JONES (& HIS ROCK'N'ROLLERS)**
| | | | |
|---|---|---|---|
| 60 | Parlophone R 4628 | Two Way Stretch/Paper Chase | 8 |
| 61 | Parlophone R 4763 | Bluesville/On The Rebound | 7 |
| 61 | Parlophone R 4788 | Joxville/Just Rollin' | 6 |
| 58 | Embassy WEP 1004 | ROCK'N'ROLL TIME (EP, as Ken Jones & His Rock'n'Rollers) | 12 |

**KENNEY JONES**
| | | | |
|---|---|---|---|
| 74 | GM GMS 027 | Ready Or Not/Woman Trouble | 8 |

*(see also Small Faces, Faces, Who)*

**LESLIE JONES**
| | | | |
|---|---|---|---|
| 59 | Pye NSEP 85004 | FOUR FARNON FAVOURITES (EP, stereo) | 10 |
| 59 | Pye NSPL 83008/9 | THE MUSIC OF ROBERT FARNON (2-LP) | 20 |

**LINDA JONES**
| | | | |
|---|---|---|---|
| 67 | Warner Bros WB 2070 | Hypnotised/I Can't Stop Lovin' My Baby | 60 |
| 72 | London HLU 10368 | For Your Precious Love/Don't Go | 15 |
| 75 | Warner Bros WB 16621 | I Just Can't Live My Life/My Heart Will Understand | 20 |
| 15 | Soul Brother SB 701 | I Just Can't Live My Life/My Heart Needs A Break | 15 |

**LLOYD JONES**
| | | | |
|---|---|---|---|
| 70 | Bullet BU 429 | Rome/RHYTHM RULERS: Version | 30 |

**LOUIS JONES ROCK & ROLL BAND**
| | | | |
|---|---|---|---|
| 50s | Vogue VE1 70111 | ROCK AND ROLL (EP) | 100 |

**MAE JONES ENSEMBLE**
| | | | |
|---|---|---|---|
| 54 | Decca 45-F 10486 | Tenderly He Watches/I Walked Into The Garden | 7 |

**MAGGIE JONES**
| | | | |
|---|---|---|---|
| 70 | VJM VLP 23 | COLUMBIA RECORDINGS IN CHRONOLOGICAL ORDER VOL. 1 (LP) | 15 |
| 70 | VJM VLP 25 | COLUMBIA RECORDINGS IN CHRONOLOGICAL ORDER VOL. 2 (LP) | 15 |

**NIC JONES**
| | | | |
|---|---|---|---|
| 70 | Trailer LER 2014 | BALLADS AND SONGS (LP, white label) | 50 |
| 70 | Trailer LER 2014 | BALLADS AND SONGS (LP, red label) | 40 |
| 70 | Trailer LER 2014 | BALLADS AND SONGS (LP, later pressing with 'highway' label) | 15 |
| 71 | Trailer LER 2027 | NIC JONES (LP, yellow label) | 50 |
| 71 | Trailer LER 2027 | NIC JONES (LP, red label) | 40 |
| 77 | Trailer LER 2091 | NOAH'S ARK TRAP (LP) | 15 |
| 77 | Trailer LER 2091 | NOAH'S ARK TRAP (LP, reissue with Highway label) | 35 |
| 78 | Transatlantic LTRA 507 | FROM THE DEVIL TO A STRANGER (LP) | 35 |
| 80 | Topic 12TS411 | PENGUIN EGGS (LP) | 35 |

*(see also Jon Raven, Halliard)*

**NIGEL MAZLYN JONES**
| | | | |
|---|---|---|---|
| 76 | Isle Of Light IOL 666/1 | SHIP TO SHORE (LP) | 50 |
| 78 | Avada AVA 105 | SENTINEL (LP, with inner sleeve, b/w picture label) | 20 |
| 82 | Isle Of Light IOL 0230 | BREAKING COVER (LP) | 20 |
| 91 | Isle Of Light 1OL 0232LP | MAZLYN JONES (LP) | 20 |

**PALMER JONES**
| | | | |
|---|---|---|---|
| 68 | Direction 58-3603 | The Great Magic Of Love/Dancing Master | 30 |

**PATSY JONES**
| | | | |
|---|---|---|---|
| 67 | RCA 1600 | Colours Of Love/There's A time And Place For Everything | 7 |

**PAUL JONES**
| | | | |
|---|---|---|---|
| 66 | HMV POP 1554 | High Time/I Can't Hold On Much Longer | 5 |
| 67 | HMV POP 1576 | I've Been A Bad Bad Boy/Sonny Boy Williamson | 5 |
| 67 | HMV POP 1602 | Thinkin' Ain't For Me/Softly (La Vita) | 20 |
| 67 | HMV PSR 5307 | Privilege (1-sided demo) | 8 |
| 67 | Columbia DB 8303 | Sons And Lovers/Three Sisters | 25 |
| 68 | Columbia DB 8379 | And The Sun Will Shine/The Dog Presides | 10 |
| 68 | Columbia DB 8417 | When I Was Six Years Old/You Have No Idea | 6 |
| 68 | Columbia DB 8514 | Aquarius/Pisces | 8 |
| 69 | Columbia DB 8567 | It's Getting Better/Not Before Time | 8 |
| 71 | Vertigo 6059 053 | Life After Death/The Mighty Ship | 6 |
| 73 | Philips 6006 282 | Perfect Roadie/Mouth Organ | 6 |
| 78 | RSO RSO 003 | Sheena Is A Punk Rocker/Pretty Vacant (p/s) | 6 |

| | | | MINT VALUE £ |
|---|---|---|---|
| 67 | HMV 7EG 8975 | PRIVILEGE (EP) | 20 |
| 66 | HMV CLP 3586 | MY WAY (LP, mono) | 20 |
| 66 | HMV CSD 3586 | MY WAY (LP, stereo) | 25 |
| 67 | HMV CLP 3602 | LOVE ME, LOVE MY FRIENDS (LP, mono) | 30 |
| 67 | HMV CSD 3602 | LOVE ME, LOVE MY FRIENDS (LP, stereo) | 35 |
| 67 | HMV CLP/CSD 3623 | PRIVILEGE (LP, soundtrack, with George Bean Group & Mike Leander) | 40 |
| 69 | Columbia SX/SCX 6347 | COME INTO MY MUSIC BOX (LP, mono/stereo) | 40 |
| 71 | Vertigo 6360 059 | CRUCIFIX IN A HORSESHOE (LP, gatefold sleeve, swirl label) | 20 |
| 70 | President PTLS 1068 | DRAKE'S DREAM (LP, soundtrack) | 150 |
| | | | 30 |

*(see also Manfred Mann, Blues Band)*

## POPPA JONES
| | | | |
|---|---|---|---|
| 66 | Parlophone R 5404 | Birthday Cake Walk/The Street Parade | 6 |

## QUINCY JONES
| | | | |
|---|---|---|---|
| 62 | Mercury AMT 1195 | Soul Bossa Nova/On The Street Where You Live | 10 |
| 65 | Mercury MF 844 | Seaweed/Golden Boy Theme | 5 |
| 69 | RCA RCA 1850 | MacKenna's Gold/Soul Full Of Gold | 5 |
| 70 | A&M AMS 781 | Killer Joe/Oh Happy Day | 5 |
| 72 | A&M AMS 888 | Ironside/Cast Your Fate To The Wind | 5 |
| 72 | Reprise K 14150 | Money Runned | 15 |
| 72 | Atlantic K 10172 | Listen To The Melody/Hot Rock Theme | 8 |
| 60 | Mercury MMC 14038 | THE BIRTH OF A BAND (LP, mono) | 5 |
| 60 | Mercury CMS 18026 | THE BIRTH OF A BAND (LP, stereo) | 20 |
| 65 | Mercury 20047 MCL | GOLDEN BOY (LP) | 25 |
| 65 | Mercury 20063 SMCL | THE PAWNBROKER (LP, soundtrack) | 15 |
| 66 | Mercury 20072 (S)MCL | MIRAGE (LP, soundtrack) | 30 |
| 66 | Mercury 20078 (S)MCL | QUINCY'S GOT A BRAND NEW BAG (LP) | 25 |
| 66 | Fontana FJL 127 | FAB! (LP) | 15 |
| 67 | Mercury SMWL 30003 | TRAVELLIN' ON THE QUINCY JONES BANDWAGON (LP) | 15 |
| 68 | RCA Victor RD/SF 7931 | IN COLD BLOOD (LP, soundtrack) | 20 |
| 68 | United Artists (S)ULP 1181 | IN THE HEAT OF THE NIGHT (LP, soundtrack, with Ray Charles) | 25 |
| 69 | Uni UNLS 103 | LOST MAN (LP, soundtrack) | 25 |
| 69 | Paramount SPFL 256 | THE ITALIAN JOB (LP, soundtrack, with Matt Monro) | 75 |
| 70 | United Artists UAS 29128 | THEY CALL ME MISTER TIBBS (LP, soundtrack) | 60 |
| 72 | WEA K 44168 | THE HEIST (LP, soundtrack, with Little Richard) | 15 |
| 72 | Atlantic K 40371 | HOW TO STEAL A DIAMOND IN FOUR UNEASY LESSONS (LP, soundtrack) | 15 |
| 85 | Nimbus/A&M AMLH 64485 | SOUNDS AND STUFF LIKE THAT (LP, Nimbus Supercut, mail order only from Practical Hi Fi magazine) | 40 |

*(see also Annie Ross, Eddie Barclay & Quincy Jones, Diana Ross & Quincy Jones, John & Joan Shakespeare)*

## RICK JONES
| | | | |
|---|---|---|---|
| 72 | Argo AFW106 | Theme From The Aeronauts/Lovebug | 10 |
| 73 | Argo ZDA 156 | HIYA MAYA (LP) | 15 |

## RICKIE LEE JONES
| | | | |
|---|---|---|---|
| 84 | Warner Bros. K56628 | RICKIE LEE JONES (LP, Nimbus Supercut, mail order only through Practical Hi-Fi magazine) | 90 |

## ROBIN JONES & HIS QUINTET
| | | | |
|---|---|---|---|
| 71 | Apollo Sound APPS 5012 | DENGA (LP) | 40 |
| 71 | Apollo Sound APP S 5016 | EL MAJA (LP, as Robin Jones Seven) | 50 |

## RONNIE JONES
| | | | |
|---|---|---|---|
| 64 | Decca F 12012 | Let's Pin A Rose On You/I Need Your Loving (B-side with Night Timers) | 20 |
| 65 | Decca F 12066 | My Love/It's All Over | 40 |
| 65 | Decca F 12146 | Anyone Who Knows What Love Is/Nobody But You | 20 |
| 65 | Parlophone R 5326 | You're Lookin' Good/I'm So Clean (with Blue Jays) | 40 |
| 67 | CBS 2699 | Little Bitty Pretty One/Put Your Tears Away | 18 |
| 67 | Polydor 56222 | In My Love Mind/Mama Come On Home | 15 |
| 68 | CBS 3304 | Without Love (There Is Nothing)/Little Bitty Pretty One | 12 |

*(see also Night-Timers)*

## SALENA JONES
| | | | |
|---|---|---|---|
| 66 | Columbia DB 7818 | A Walk In The Black Forest (Our Walk Of Love)/As Long As I Live | 7 |
| 66 | Columbia DB 7991 | I Am Yours/I Only Know I Love You | 7 |
| 67 | Columbia DB 8212 | When I Tell You (That I Love You)/Respect | 8 |
| 67 | Decca F 12708 | I've Got The Blues/The Glory Of Love | 25 |
| 70 | CBS 4767 | This Is Love/Everybodys Talkin' | 6 |
| 71 | CBS 7542 | Baby Don't Ya Get Crazy/Fire And Rain | 15 |
| 73 | Indigo GOPOP | Live And Let Die/Some Other World (in p/s) | 15 |
| 73 | Indigo GOPOP | Live And Let Die/Some Other World | 6 |
| 75 | DJM DJS 381 | In Love Like You And Me/Tell It Like It Is | 6 |
| 65 | CBS 63613 | THE MOMENT OF TRUTH (LP) | 35 |
| 70 | CBS 63901 | EVERYBODY'S TALKIN' ABOUT SALENA JONES (LP) | 30 |
| 71 | CBS 64435 | PLATINUM (LP) | 20 |
| 73 | RCA Victor SF 8335 | ALONE & TOGETHER (LP) | 20 |
| 74 | RCA LPL 1 5025 | THIS'N'THAT (LP) | 20 |

## SALINA JONES
| | | | |
|---|---|---|---|
| 65 | Polydor 56012 | Longing/Too Late | 7 |

## SAM JONES
| | | | |
|---|---|---|---|
| 60 | Riverside 12-324 | SOUL SOCIETY (LP) | 20 |

## SAMANTHA JONES
| | | | |
|---|---|---|---|
| 65 | United Artists UP 1072 | It's All Because Of You/I Woke Up Crying | 15 |
| 65 | United Artists UP 1087 | Don't Come Any Closer/Just Call And I'll Be There | 15 |
| 65 | United Artists UP 1105 | Chained To A Memory/Just For Him | 10 |

| 66 | United Artists UP 1139 | That Special Way/Somebody Else's Baby ................................................. 10 |
|---|---|---|
| 67 | United Artists UP 1185 | Surrounded By A Ray Of Sunshine/How Do You Say Goodbye ......................... 80 |
| 67 | United Artists UP 1185 | Surrounded By A Ray Of Sunshine/How Do You Say Goodbye (DJ Copy) ......... 150 |
| 67 | United Artists UP 1200 | Why Can't I Remember/Live For Life ......................................................... 8 |
| 68 | United Artists UP 2248 | Lonely Lonely Man/Doll On A Music Box ................................................. 10 |
| 68 | United Artists UP 2258 | And Suddenly/Go Ahead And Love Me ..................................................... 50 |
| 69 | Penny Farthing PEN 703 | Today (Without You)/The Feelin' That I Get .............................................. 10 |
| 69 | Penny Farthing PEN 708 | Do I Still Figure In Your Life?/I'm Sorry, But I Think I Love You ....................... 10 |
| 70 | Penny Farthing PEN 734 | My Way/Darling Be Home Soon ............................................................... 10 |
| 70 | Penny Farthing PEN 746 | Best Of Both Worlds/Guilty Of Loving You ................................................ 10 |
| 74 | Columbia DB 9031 | I Believed It All/This I Find Is Beautiful .................................................... 8 |
| 80 | Ford SLE 19 | Ford Leads The Way/Go Ahead And Love Me (p/s, Ford cars promo disc) ........ 15 |
| 68 | United Artists | CALL IT SAMANTHA (LP) ......................................................................... 25 |
| 72 | Contour 2870 303 | MY WAY (LP) ....................................................................................... 15 |

*(see also Vernons Girls, Krimson Kake)*

**SAMMY JONES**

| 70 | Gas GAS 123 | You're My Girl/HONEYBOY MARTIN: Unchained Melody ............................... 10 |
|---|---|---|
| 72 | Sioux SI 002 | Mendicino/RUM RUNNERS: Sugar Brown ................................................. 10 |
| 72 | Sioux SI 003 | Little Caesar/TWINKLE BROTHERS: Happy Song ........................................ 10 |
| 72 | Sioux SI 011 | You're My Girl/HONEYBOY MARTIN: Unchained Melody ............................... 8 |

**SANDIE JONES**

| 72 | Polydor 2058 223 | Music Of Love/Ceol An Ghra ................................................................... 12 |
|---|---|---|

**SOLOMON JONES**

| 70 | Bullet BU 452 | Be Strong/Version ................................................................................. 10 |
|---|---|---|
| 70 | Pama PM 812 | Here Comes The Night/RECO RODRIQUEZ: Jaded Ramble ........................... 18 |

**SPIKE JONES**

| 53 | HMV 7M 121 | Hot Lips/Hotter Than A Pistol (as Spike Jones & His Country Cousins) .............. 10 |
|---|---|---|
| 53 | HMV 7M 160 | I Saw Mommy Kissing Santa Claus/Winter (as Spike Jones & His City Slickers) ... 10 |
| 54 | HMV 7MC 3 | Deep Purple/Dragnet (as Spike Jones & His City Slickers, export issue) ............ 10 |
| 54 | HMV 7MC 17 | I Wanna Go Back To West Virginia/Little Bo-Beep Has Lost Her Sheep (as Spike Jones & His City Slickers, export issue) ...................................................... 10 |
| 55 | HMV 7M 324 | Secret Love/I'm In The Mood For Love (as Spike Jones & His City Slickers) ........ 10 |

**STAN JONES**

| 58 | Pye Disneyland DPL 39000 | CREAKIN' LEATHER (LP) ...................................................................... 15 |
|---|---|---|

**STEVE JONES (1)**

| 84 | P flight PFD 01 | I Need You (12") .................................................................................. 80 |
|---|---|---|

**TAMIKO JONES**

| 76 | Contempo CX 15 | Let It Flow/DORIS DUKE: Woman Of The Ghetto ....................................... 15 |
|---|---|---|

**THAD JONES**

| 57 | Esquire 32-065 | OLIO (LP) ........................................................................................... 40 |
|---|---|---|
| 58 | Esquire 32-080 | AFTER HOURS (LP) ............................................................................... 60 |
| 59 | Pye Nixa NJL 13 | MAD THAD (LP) ................................................................................... 70 |

**THELMA JONES**

| 68 | Sue WI 4047 | Stronger/Never Leave Me ...................................................................... 60 |
|---|---|---|
| 69 | Soul City SC 110 | The House That Jack Built/Give It To Me Straight ....................................... 40 |
| 76 | CBS 4711 | Salty Tears/You're The Song .................................................................. 15 |

**TOM JONES**

| 64 | Decca F 11966 | Chills And Fever/Breathless .................................................................... 60 |
|---|---|---|
| 65 | Columbia DB 7566 | Little Lonely One/That's What We'll All Do ................................................ 20 |
| 65 | Columbia DB 7733 | Lonely Joe/I Was A Fool ........................................................................ 20 |
| 65 | Decca F 12292 | Thunderball/Key To My Heart ................................................................. 8 |
| 66 | Decca F 12315 | To Make A Big Man Cry/I'll Never Let You Go (export issue) ......................... 10 |
| 66 | Decca F 12349 | Stop Breaking My Heart/Never Give Away Love ......................................... 10 |
| 66 | Decca F 12461 | This And That/City Girl .......................................................................... 15 |
| 71 | Decca FR 13237 | Till/One Day Soon (export issue) ............................................................. 10 |

**JONES TOWN MALE QUARTET/FRANKLIN LADIES TOWN TRIO**

| 62 | Son TD 104 | We'll Never Say Goodbye/Living For J (split 45 rpm single) ........................... 25 |
|---|---|---|

**U.K. JONES**

| 69 | Deram DM 231 | Let Me Tell Ya/And The Rains Came Down ............................................... 15 |
|---|---|---|
| 70 | Ember EMB S 298 | Take Me For What I Am/Love Is Here To Stay ............................................ 6 |

*(see also Mike Berry)*

**VIVIAN JONES**

| 79 | White Rum/Red Stripe 101 PROOF | Jah Music/Vibes (as V. Jones) ................................................................ 10 |
|---|---|---|
| 80s | Virgo Stomach VG 1003 | Who's Gonna Get Caught/Horn Fingers (12", blue vinyl) .............................. 15 |
| 81 | Cha Cha CHAD 37 | One Of These Days/Dub (12") ................................................................ 18 |
| 86 | Jah Shaka 859 | Red Eye/Got A Light (12") ..................................................................... 12 |
| 92 | Imperial House IH 006 | Ethiopian Eyes African Smile/African Love/African Dub (12") ....................... 15 |
| 87 | Jah Shaka SHAKA 861 | JAH WORKS (LP) ................................................................................. 15 |
| 89 | Ruff Cutt RCLP 001 | BANK ROBBER (LP) .............................................................................. 35 |

**WINSTON JONES**

| 73 | Gayfeet GS 208 | You Make Me Cry/Version ...................................................................... 6 |
|---|---|---|

**WIZZ JONES**

| 69 | United Artists (S)ULP 1209 | WIZZ JONES (LP) ................................................................................ 175 |
|---|---|---|
| 70 | Village Thing VTS 4 | LEGENDARY ME (LP) ........................................................................... 100 |
| 72 | CBS 64809 | RIGHT NOW (LP) ................................................................................ 100 |
| 74 | Village Thing VTS 24 | WHEN I LEAVE BERLIN (LP) .................................................................. 90 |
| 77 | Plant Life PLR 009 | MAGICAL FLIGHT (LP, with insert) .......................................................... 25 |

*(see also Pete Stanley & Wizz Jones, Accolade)*                                                                MINT VALUE £

## GRACE JONES
| 77 | RCA 2058856 | Sorry/That's The Trouble | 15 |

## JONES BOYS
| 57 | Columbia DB 4046 | Cool Baby/Rock-A-Hula Baby (Ukulele Lady) | 15 |
| 58 | Columbia DB 4170 | A Certain Smile/Kathy-O | 5 |
| 58 | Columbia DB 4217 | The Day The Rains Came/Hideaway | 7 |
| 59 | Columbia DB 4278 | Dream Girl/Straight As An Arrow | 6 |

*(see also Four Jones Boys)*

## JONES BROTHERS
| 69 | Pye Intl. 7N 25696 | Lucky Lady/Good Old Days | 75 |
| 02 | Grapevine 2000 G2K 123 | Good Old Days/Lucky Lady (reissue) | 10 |

## JONESY
| 73 | Dawn DNS 1030 | Ricochet/Every Day's The Same | 20 |
| 72 | Dawn DNLS 3042 | NO ALTERNATIVE (LP, gatefold sleeve) | 20 |
| 73 | Dawn DNLS 3048 | KEEPING UP (LP, with lyric insert, lilac label) | 80 |
| 73 | Dawn DNLS 3048 | KEEPING UP (LP, without lyric insert, lilac label) | 100 |
| 73 | Dawn DNLS 3055 | GROWING (LP, gatefold sleeve, with lyric insert, pink 'sun' label) | 60 |
| 73 | Dawn DNLS 3055 | GROWING (LP, gatefold sleeve, without lyric insert, pink 'sun' label) | 80 |
| | | | 50 |

*(see also Alan Bown, Ray Thomas)*

## JONIE D
| 89 | Positive Beat PBEP 001 | WHICH BASE (EP) | 15 |

## JONJO
| 72 | Bumble GE 119 | Nine Years Old/Flash In The Pan | 80 |

## JONNIE & THE LUBES
| 79 | Attrix RB 05 | I Got Rabies/Terror In T/EXECUTIVES: Shy Little Girl/Never Go Home | 15 |

## HARLEM JONNS RESHUFFLE
| 68 | Fontana TF 970 | You Are The One I Love/Good Lovin' | 30 |
| 69 | Fontana TF 1004 | Everything Under The Sun/Let Love Come Between Us | 20 |
| 69 | Fontana (S)TL 5509 | HARLEM JONNS RESHUFFLE (LP) | 40 |

## JONSTON MCPHILBRY
| 66 | Fontana TF 663 | She's Gone/Woke Up At Eight | 75 |

## JON THE POSTMAN
| 78 | Bent BIG BENT 2 | PUERILE (12" EP, stamped brown paper bag p/s, with inserts) | 20 |
| 78 | Bent BIG BENT 4 | PSYCHEDELIC ROCK'N'ROLL FIVE SKINNERS (12" EP, white label, foldover p/s in bag) | 20 |

## JOOK
| 72 | RCA RCA 2279 | Alright With Me/Do What You Can | 15 |
| 73 | RCA RCA 2344 | Shame/City And Suburban Blues | 20 |
| 73 | RCA RCA 2368 | Oo-Oo-Rudi/Jook's On You | 15 |
| 73 | RCA RCA 2431 | King Capp/Rumble | 12 |
| 74 | RCA RCA 5024 | Bish Bash Bosh/Crazy Kids | 18 |
| 78 | Chiswick SW 30 | Watch Your Step/La La Girl/Aggravation Place/Everything I Do (EP) | 10 |

*(see also John's Children, Sparks)*

## JANIS JOPLIN
| 69 | CBS 3683 | Turtle Blues/Piece Of My Heart (withdrawn) | 30 |
| 71 | CBS 7019 | Me And Bobby McGee/Half Moon | 6 |
| 71 | CBS 7217 | Cry Baby/Mercedes Benz | 7 |
| 71 | CBS 9136 | Move Over/Cry Baby/Try/Piece Of My Heart (maxi-single) | 8 |
| 72 | CBS 8241 | Down On Me/Bye Bye Baby | 6 |
| 76 | CBS 3960 | Piece Of My Heart/Kozmic Blues (p/s) | 7 |
| 69 | CBS 63546 | I GOT DEM OL' KOZMIC BLUES AGAIN, MAMA! (LP) | 30 |
| 74 | CBS CQ 30322/Q 64188 | PEARL (LP, quadrophonic) | 25 |

*(see also Big Brother & Holding Company)*

## JORDAN BROTHERS
| 59 | London HLW 8908 | Never, Never/Please Tell Me Now | 30 |
| 59 | London HLW 8908 | Never, Never/Please Tell Me Now (78) | 25 |
| 60 | London HLW 9235 | Things I Didn't Say/Polly Plays Her Kettle Drum | 10 |
| 61 | London HLW 9308 | No Wings On My Angel/Living For The Day | 10 |

## DANNY JORDAN
| 61 | Mercury AMT 1159 | Jeannie/Boom Ditty Boom | 6 |

## DICK JORDAN
| 60 | Oriole CB 1534 | Hallelujah, I Love Her So/Sandy | 15 |
| 60 | Oriole CB 1548 | Little Christine/I'll Love You Forever | 15 |
| 60 | Oriole CB 1566 | Garden Of Eden/Alive, Alive Oh! | 6 |
| 60 | Oriole CB 1591 | Angel On My Shoulder/The Next Train Home | 6 |
| 61 | Piccadilly 7N 35035 | Some Of These Days/I Want Her Back | 6 |
| 62 | Piccadilly 7N 35057 | Fortune Teller/My Angel | 75 |
| 63 | Columbia DB 7016 | Stop The Music/Dream Chaser | 6 |
| 66 | Parlophone R5475 | Progress/Something's Going On In There | 25 |

## EARL JORDAN
| 72 | Sovereign SVN 6501 | JORDAN (LP, textured sleeve with flipbacks) | 30 |

## JACK JORDAN - HIS MUSIC
| 60 | Parlophone R 4677 | Golden Girl/Beauty And The Beach | 7 |

## LOUIS JORDAN (& HIS TYMPANY FIVE)
| 56 | Melodisc 1349 | Messy Bessy/I Seen What'cha Done (78) | 20 |
| 60 | Downbeat CHA 3 | Ooo-Wee/I'll Die Happy | 20 |
| 50s | Melodisc EPM7 66 | LOUIS JORDAN (EP, as Louis Jordan Tympany Five, 3 different covers) | 90 |

| 57 | Mercury MPT 7521 | SOMEBODY UP THERE DIGS ME (10" LP, with Tympany Five) | 100 |
| 58 | Mercury MPL 6541 | MAN, WE'RE WAILIN' (LP, with Tympany Five) | 60 |
| 64 | HMV CLP 1809 | HALLELUJAH, LOUIS JORDAN IS BACK (LP) | 40 |

## LOUIS JORDAN & CHRIS BARBER'S BAND
| 63 | Melodisc 45-1616 | Is She Is Or Is She Ain't Your Baby/Fifty Cents | 18 |

*(see also Chris Barber)*

## JORDANAIRES
| 57 | Capitol CL 14687 | Sugaree/Baby, Won't You Please Come Home? | 40 |
| 57 | Capitol CL 14773 | Summer Vacation/Each Day | 20 |
| 58 | Capitol CL 14921 | Little Miss Ruby/All I Need Is You | 20 |
| 63 | Capitol CL 15281 | Don't Be Cruel/Don't Worry | 20 |
| 62 | Capitol T 1742 | SPOTLIGHT ON THE JORDANAIRES (LP) | 20 |

*(see also Elvis Presley, Patsy Cline, Don Gibson, Marty Robbins)*

## JORGE
| 69 | Aurora 7984 | Everybody Wants To Be Loved/Tic Tac Toe | 10 |

## JOSEF K
| 79 | Absolute ABS 1 | Chance Meeting/Romance (p/s, 1,000 only) | 45 |
| 80 | Postcard 80-3 | Radio Drill Time/Crazy To Exist (live) (hand-coloured foldaround p/s, blue labels) | 30 |
| 80 | Postcard 80-3 | Radio Drill Time/Crazy To Exist (live) (brown sleeve & labels) | 10 |
| 80 | Postcard 80-3 | Radio Drill Time/Crazy To Exist (live) (cream/yellow sleeve & labels) | 8 |
| 80 | Postcard 80-5 | It's Kinda Funny/Final Request (in poly bag, with picture insert) | 25 |
| 80 | Postcard 80-5 | It's Kinda Funny/Final Request (in poly bag, without picture insert) | 10 |
| 80 | Postcard 80-5 | It's Kinda Funny/Final Request (2nd issue, brown label and brown company sleeve)) | 5 |
| 81 | Postcard 81-5 | Chance Meeting/Pictures (die-cut sleeve, with postcard) | 30 |
| 81 | Postcard 81-5 | Chance Meeting/Pictures (die-cut sleeve, without postcard) | 8 |
| 81 | Postcard 81-4/TWI 023 | Sorry For Laughing/Revelation (p/s) | 15 |
| 81 | Postcard 81-1 | SORRY FOR LAUGHING (LP, unreleased, a few with proof sleeve) | 400 |
| 81 | Postcard 81-7 | THE ONLY FUN IN TOWN (LP, with inner sleeve) | 40 |
| 87 | Supreme Intl. Edit. 87-6 | YOUNG AND STUPID (LP) | 15 |

*(see also Orange Juice, Paul Haig, Happy Family, Rhythm Of Life)*

## IRVING JOSEPH
| 60 | London HLT 9027 | I Left My Love/Lorena | 8 |

## MARGIE JOSEPH (& BLUE MAGIC)
| 72 | Stax 2025 052 | Medicine Bend/Same Thing | 10 |
| 73 | Atlantic K10380 | Ridin High/Come Lay Some Lovin On Me | 6 |
| 74 | Atlantic K10460 | Sweet Surrender/My Love | 5 |
| 75 | Atlantic K10649 | What's Come Over Me/You And Me (as Margie Joseph & Blue Magic) | 5 |
| 75 | Atlantic K10646 | I Can't Move No Mountains/Just As Soon As The Feelings Over | 15 |
| 72 | Stax 2362 008 | MAKES A NEW IMPRESSION (LP) | 15 |
| 73 | Atlantic K 40462 | MARGIE JOSEPH (LP) | 15 |

## NERIOUS JOSEPH
| 85 | Fashion FAD 042 | You're My Special Lady/Danger Man (12") | 25 |

## JOSH
| 69 | Duke DU 41 | Judge/RON: Soul Of Joemel | 15 |
| 70 | Hot Rod HR 111 | Leaving Everything/HOT ROD ALL STARS : Psychedelic Bird | 45 |

*(see also Girlie)*

## JOSH & HERBIE
| 60s | Kalypso AB 107 | I'm Nobody's Child/How Can I Believe In You | 6 |

## JOSHUA
| 73 | Key KL 014 | JOSHUA (LP) | 100 |

## MARVA JOSIE
| 66 | Polydor 56711 | Crazy Stockings/I'll Get By | 15 |

## JOURNEY
| 92 | Columbia 4728102 | TIME3 (3-CD) | 25 |

## JOY & DAVID/DAVE
| 58 | Parlophone R 4477 | Whoopee!/My Oh My! (as Joy & David) | 20 |
| 59 | Decca F 11123 | Rocking Away The Blues/If You Pass Me By (as Joy & David) | 20 |
| 59 | Decca F 11123 | Rocking Away The Blues/If You Pass Me By (78, as Joy & David) | 10 |
| 60 | Triumph RGM 1002 | Let's Go See Gran'ma/Believe Me (as Joy & David) | 25 |
| 60 | Decca F 11291 | My Very Good Friend The Milkman/Doopey Darling (as Joy & Dave) | 15 |
| 61 | Parlophone R 4855 | Joe's Been A-Gittin' There/They Tell Us Not To Love (as Joy & Dave) | 20 |
| 61 | Parlophone R 4855 | Joe's Been A-Gittin' There/They Tell Us Not To Love (demo copies with alternate take of B-side) | 30 |

## MABEL JOY
| 75 | Real RR 2004 | MABEL JOY (LP) | 25 |

## JOY OF LIFE
| 85 | New European BAD VC 62 | ENJOY EP (12", p/s) | 18 |
| 88 | Cadre CR JOL67 | HEAR THE CHILDREN (LP) | 20 |

## RODDIE JOY
| 65 | Red Bird RB 10021 | Come Back Baby/Love Hit Me With A Wallop | 60 |

## JOHNNY JOYCE
| 76 | Freedom FLP 99003 | JOYCE'S CHOICE MIXTURE (LP) | 22 |

*(see also Velvet Opera, Levee Breakers)*

## JOYCE'S ANGELS
| 67 | Major Minor MM 526 | Flowers For My Friends/Rodney Reginald Smithfield Harvey Jones | 15 |

*(see also Chris White)*

MINT VALUE £

## JOY DE VIVRE
| 81 | Crass CR & SS ENVY 1 | Our Wedding (flexidisc, white vinyl, no p/s, with mailer) | 300 |
| 81 | Crass CR & SS ENVY 1 | Our Wedding (flexidisc, white vinyl, no p/s, without mailer) | 200 |

*(see also Crass)*

## JOY DIVISION
### SINGLES
| 78 | Enigma PSS 139 | AN IDEAL FOR LIVING (Warsaw/No Love Lost/Leaders Of Men/Failures) (EP, 1,000 only, foldout p/s; beware of counterfeits) | 1750 |
| 78 | Anonymous ANON 1 | AN IDEAL FOR LIVING (Warsaw/No Love Lost/Leaders Of Men/Failures) (12" EP reissue, 1,200 only) | 700 |
| 79 | Factory FAC 13 | Transmission/Novelty (p/s) | 10 |
| 80 | Factory FAC 23 | Love Will Tear Us Apart/These Days (p/s) | 10 |
| 80 | Factory FACUS T2 | She's Lost Control/Atmosphere | 15 |
| 80 | Factory FAC23.12 | Love Will Tear Us Apart/These Days (12", laminated sleeve) | 18 |
| 80 | Factory FACUS 2/UK | Atmosphere/She's Lost Control (UK variant, 12", black vinyl) | 20 |
| 80 | Factory FACUS 2/UK | Atmosphere/She's Lost Control (UK variant, 12", red vinyl) | 12 |
| 82 | Factory FAC 13 12 | Transmission/Novelty (12") | 12 |
| 88 | Factory FAC 213/7 | Atmosphere/The Only Mistake (p/s) | 5 |
| 88 | Factory FAC213 | Atmosphere/The Only Mistake/Sound Of Music (12", p/s) | 12 |
| 86 | Strange Fruit SFPS 013 | PEEL SESSIONS (12", p/s recorded 31/01/79) | 15 |
| 87 | Strange Fruit SFPS 033 | PEEL SESSIONS (12" EP) | |
| 95 | London YOJX 1 | Love Will Tear Us Apart (Original Version)/Love Will Tear Us Apart (Radio Version)/ Love Will Tear Us Apart (Arthur Baker Remix)/Atmosphere (12", stickered p/s) | 10 |
| 11 | Rhino FAC .33 | Ceremony (Original Version)/In A Lonely Place (12" Version)//Ceremony (Heart & Soul Rehearsal Version)/In A Lonely Place (Unreleased Rehearsal Version) (12", 800 only) | 25 |
| 10 | Rhino 5186595937 | SINGLES 1978-80 (10 x 7", art piece, 2 x CD-R, box set, 500 only) | 200 |
| 14 | Warner Bros. JDPM11 | AN IDEAL FOR LIVING EP (reissue) | 10 |

### ALBUMS
| 79 | Factory FACT 10 | UNKNOWN PLEASURES (LP with inner sleeve, textured sleeve, 1st press turns a deep translucent red when held over a light) | 80 |
| 79 | Factory FACT 10 | UNKNOWN PLEASURES (LP with inner sleeve, textured sleeve, 2nd non transluscent issue) | 50 |
| 80 | Factory FACT 25 | CLOSER (LP, hard textured sleeve & inner, some 1st press turns a deep translucent red when held over a light) | 50 |
| 80 | Factory FACT 25 | CLOSER (LP, hard textured sleeve & inner, 1st press, solid black vinyl) | 35 |
| 81 | Factory FACT 40 | STILL (2-LP, hessian sleeve, card inners & white/blue ribbon) | 90 |
| 81 | Factory FAC 40 | STILL (2-LP, gatefold) | 35 |
| 85 | Factory FACT 10c | UNKNOWN PLEASURES (reissue, cassette in box with insert) | 30 |
| 85 | Factory FACT 25c | CLOSER (reissue, cassette in box with insert) | 30 |
| 85 | Factory FACT 40c | STILL (reissue, cassette in box with insert) | 30 |
| 88 | Factory FACT 250 | SUBSTANCE (LP) | 35 |
| 90 | Strange Fruit SFRLP 111 | PEEL SESSIONS (LP, reissue of both EPs) | 20 |
| 95 | London 828624 1 | PERMANENT (2-LP, insert) | 50 |
| 01 | Strange Fruit SFRSLP 094 | THE COMPLETE BBC RECORDINGS (LP) | 30 |
| 07 | London 2564699291 | JOY DIVISION: IN MEMORY (4xLP boxed set, 3000 only) | 100 |
| 07 | London 25646 40151 | UNKNOWN PLEASURES (LP, remastered reissue on 180gram vinyl) | 20 |
| 07 | London 25645 4014 1 | CLOSER (LP, remastered reissue on 180gram vinyl) | 20 |
| 07 | Ozit Morpheus OZIT 8797 | MARTIN HANNETT'S PERSONAL MIXES (2-LP) | 20 |

*(see also New Order)*

## COL JOYE & JOYBOYS
| 59 | Brunswick 05806 | (Rockin' Rollin') Clementine/Bye Bye Baby Goodbye | 20 |
| 60 | Top Rank JAR 529 | Be My Girl/Yes Sir, That's My Baby | 10 |

## JOYFUL SOUND
| 73 | SRT SRT 73278 | IT WILL BE WORTH IT ALL (LP) | 300 |

## JOYRIDE
| 69 | RCA SF 8027 | FRIEND SOUND (LP) | 20 |

## JOY UNLIMITED
| 69 | Page One POF 147 | Daytime Night Time/Mister Pseudonym | 30 |
| 69 | Page One POF 160 | Oh Darlin'/Feelin' | 40 |
| 70 | Page One POLS 028 | TURBULENCE (LP) | 80 |

## J P SUNSHINE
| 95 | Uncle Glitch Records UG 1 | UNCLE GLITCH PRESENTS (LP, 500 only) | 30 |

## JR. WILSON
| 89 | Blue Trac BTRD 035 | Speak Softly (with T. Sparks and Mystic Man)/CONROY SMITH: Problems (12") | 40 |

## J.S.D. BAND
| 73 | Cube BUG 29 | Sarah Jane/Paddy Stacks (p/s) | 6 |
| 74 | Cube BUG 49 | Hayes And Harlington Blues/Cuckoo | 8 |
| 71 | Regal Zono. SRLZ 1018 | COUNTRY OF THE BLIND (LP, textured sleeve, first press with flipbacks) | 90 |
| 71 | Regal Zono. SRLZ 1018 | COUNTRY OF THE BLIND (LP, textured sleeve, later press without flipbacks) | 50 |
| 72 | Cube HIFLY 11 | J.S.D. BAND (LP) | 15 |
| 73 | Cube HIFLY 14 | TRAVELLING DAYS (LP, fully laminated sleeve) | 15 |

## JUAN & JUNIOR
| 67 | CBS 2949 | The Chase/Nothing | 6 |
| 68 | CBS 3223 | To Girls/Andurina | 15 |

## JUBILEE STOMPERS
| 70 | Trojan TR 7725 | Luciana/I Really Like It | 6 |

## JUDAS JUMP
| 70 | Parlophone R 5828 | Run For Your Life/Beer Drinking Woman | 15 |

| | | | |
|---|---|---|---|
| 70 | Parlophone R 5838 | This Feelin' We Feel/Hangman's Playing | 8 |
| 70 | Parlophone R 5873 | Beer Drinking Woman/I Have The Right | 6 |
| 70 | Parlophone PAS 10001 | SCORCH (LP, gatefold sleeve, black/silver label with boxed logo) | 50 |

*(see also Herd, Amen Corner, Andy Bown)*

## JUDAS PRIEST

| | | | |
|---|---|---|---|
| 74 | Gull GULS 6 | Rocka-Rolla/Never Satisfied | 25 |
| 76 | Gull GULS 31 | The Ripper/Island Of Domination | 25 |
| 77 | CBS S CBS 5222 | Diamonds And Rust/Dissident Aggressor | 7 |
| 78 | CBS S CBS 6077 | Better By You, Better Than Me/Invader | 5 |
| 78 | CBS S CBS 6794 | Before The Dawn/Rock Forever | 5 |
| 79 | CBS S CBS 7312 | Evening Star/Beyond The Realms Of Death | 5 |
| 79 | Gull GULS 71 | The Ripper/Victims Of Change | 8 |
| 79 | Gull GULS 7112 | The Ripper/Never Satisfied/Victim Of Changes (12", p/s) | 12 |
| 80 | CBS TA 4298 | United/Grinder (poster p/s) | 12 |
| 82 | CBS A 2822 | (Take These) Chains/Judas Priest Audio File (p/s) | 5 |
| 83 | Gull GULS 7612 | Tyrant/Rocka-Rolla/Genocide (12", p/s, white vinyl) | 15 |
| 86 | CBS QTA 7144 | Locked In (Extended)/Reckless/Desert Plains (live)/Freewheel Burning (live) (12", poster p/s) | 10 |
| 91 | Columbia 656589 0 | A Touch Of Evil/Between The Hammer And The Anvil (shaped disc) | 12 |
| 74 | Gull GULP 1005 | ROCKA ROLLA (LP, original issue, 'bottle top' sleeve) | 30 |
| 76 | Gull GULP 1015 | SAD WINGS OF DESTINY (LP) | 15 |
| 76 | Gull PGULP 1015 | SAD WINGS OF DESTINY (LP, picture disc) | 22 |
| 77 | CBS 82008 | SIN AFTER SIN (LP) | 15 |
| 78 | CBS 82430 | STAINED CLASS (LP) | 15 |
| 78 | Gull PGULP 1026 | THE BEST OF JUDAS PRIEST (LP, picture disc) | 12 |
| 78 | CBS 83135 | KILLING MACHINE (LP, red vinyl) | 15 |
| 79 | CBS 83852 | UNLEASHED IN THE EAST (LP, with free single "Rock Forever"/ Hell Bent For Leather/ "Beyond The Realms Of Death" [SJP 1], and tour advertising flyer) | 25 |
| 79 | CBS 66357 | BOX SET (3-LP, reissue of "Sin After Sin"/"Stained Class"/"Killing Machine") | 25 |
| 86 | Shanghai PGLP 1026 | JUDAS PRIEST (LP, picture disc) | 12 |
| 93 | CBS 473050 | METAL WORKS (2xLP, gatefold sleeve) | 18 |
| 98 | SPV 0891 8542 | 98 LIVE MELTDOWN (2xLP) | 18 |
| 04 | Sony 5128933 | METALOGY (4xCD, DVD, booklet, leather studded box set) | 45 |
| 08 | Sony 88697315572 | NOSTRADAMUS (3-LP, 2-CD boxed set) | 30 |
| 11 | Sony 88697967872 | COMPLETE ALBUMS COLLECTION (19 x CD box set. booklet) | 50 |

*(see also Trapeze, Fancy)*

## JUDD

| | | | |
|---|---|---|---|
| 70 | Penny Farthing PEN 709 | Snarlin' Mumma Lion/Stronger Than A Man | 6 |
| 70 | Penny Farthing PELS 504 | JUDD (LP, die-cut sleeve, insert, red/black/yellow labels) | 175 |

*(see also Kris Ife)*

## F.C. JUDD

| | | | |
|---|---|---|---|
| 60 | Castle EFX 1 | ELECTRONIC SOUNDS AND MUSIC (EP) | 50 |
| 60 | Castle EFX 2 | ELECTRONIC THEMES AND MUSIQUE CONCRETE (EP) | 50 |
| 60 | Castle EFX 3 | RHYTHMIC ELECTRONIC MUSIC (EP) | 50 |
| 60 | Castle HMX 1 | HAUNTED HOUSE, MYSTERY SOUNDS AND MUISIC (EP) | 25 |
| 67 | (No label or cat no) | ELECTRONIC SOUNDS AND EFFECTS (flexi, free with Practical Electronics) | 15 |

## JUDGE HAPPINESS

| | | | |
|---|---|---|---|
| 85 | Mynah SCS 8501 | Hey Judge/Pig In Pink (very few with p/s) | 25 |
| 85 | Mynah SCS 8501 | Hey Judge/Pig In Pink | 10 |

*(see also Mock Turtles)*

## TERRY JUDGE & THE BARRISTERS

| | | | |
|---|---|---|---|
| 63 | Oriole CB 1896 | Hey Look At Her/Kind Of Girl You Can't Forget | 10 |
| 64 | Oriole CB 1938 | I Don't Care/Try To Forget | 10 |
| 65 | Fontana TF 599 | Come With Me And Love Me/Waitin' For The Night To Come | 10 |

## JUG TRUST

| | | | |
|---|---|---|---|
| 70 | Parlophone R5825 | Goodbye Train/Cat And Mouse (demos are in p/s) | 10 |

## JUGGERNAUTS

| | | | |
|---|---|---|---|
| 84 | Supreme Int. Editions 84-2 | Come Throw Yourself/My First Million (p/s) | 10 |

*(see also Paul Haig)*

## JUICE CREW

| | | | |
|---|---|---|---|
| 08 | Diggers With Gratitude DWG 002 | THE JUICE CREW (EP, 125 only, black vinyl) | 60 |
| 08 | Diggers With Gratitude DWG 003 | THE JUICE CREW (EP, 75 only, white vinyl) | 80 |
| 08 | Diggers With Gratitude DWG 004 | THE JUICE CREW (EP, 75 only, blue vinyl) | 80 |
| 08 | Diggers With Gratitude DWG 004 | THE JUICE CREW (EP, 75 only, red vinyl) | 80 |

## JUICY LUCY

| | | | |
|---|---|---|---|
| 70 | Fontana TF 1068 | Who Do You Love/Walking Down The Highway (unissued) | 0 |
| 70 | Vertigo V1/6059 001 | Who Do You Love/Walking Down The Highway | 10 |
| 70 | Vertigo 6059 015 | Pretty Woman/I'm A Thief | 18 |
| 72 | Polydor 2001 279 | It Ain't Easy/Promised Land | 7 |
| 69 | Vertigo VO 2 | JUICY LUCY (LP, first press with 'Philips' credit on large swirl label, gatefold sleeve) | 200 |
| 69 | Vertigo VO 2 | JUICY LUCY (LP, later press without 'Philips' credit on large swirl label, gatefold sleeve) | 70 |
| 70 | Vertigo 6360 014 | LIE BACK AND ENJOY IT (LP, large swirl label, gatefold poster sleeve) | 200 |
| 71 | Bronze ILPS 9157 | GET A WHIFF OF THIS (LP, textured sleeve, Island credit on label) | 30 |
| 72 | Polydor 2310 160 | PIECES (LP) | 25 |

*(see also Misunderstood, Van Der Graaf Generator, Ray Owen, Paul Williams' Big Roll Band)*

MINT VALUE £

## JIMMY JUKEBOX
| | | | |
|---|---|---|---|
| 75 | Sonet SON 2057 | Motorboat/25 Hours A Day | 40 |
| 77 | Sonet SON 2057 | Motorboat/25 Hours A Day (1977 re-issue with new Savage Pencil p/s sleeve but original 1975 records inside) | 20 |

*(see also Kim Fowley)*

## JULIAN (SCOTT)
| | | | |
|---|---|---|---|
| 59 | Pye Nixa 7N 15236 | Sue Saturday/Can't Wait | 30 |
| 59 | Pye Nixa N 15236 | Sue Saturday/Can't Wait (78) | 20 |

*(see also Brian Bennett)*

## JULIAN (JUDY MOWATT) & CHOSEN FEW
| | | | |
|---|---|---|---|
| 71 | High Note HS 054 | Joy To The World/Joyful Version | 12 |

## JULIAN (JUDY MOWATT) & GAYTONES
| | | | |
|---|---|---|---|
| 72 | High Note HS 059 | She Kept On Talking/Version | 15 |

## JULIAN'S TREATMENT
| | | | |
|---|---|---|---|
| 70 | Young Blood YB 1009 | Phantom City/Alda, Dark Lady Of The Outer Worlds | 25 |
| 70 | Young Blood SYB 2/3 | A TIME BEFORE THIS (2-LP, laminated gatefold sleeve, white/red labels) | 400 |

*(see also Julian Jay Savarin)*

## JULY
| | | | |
|---|---|---|---|
| 68 | Major Minor MM 568 | My Clown/Dandelion Seeds | 200 |
| 68 | Major Minor MM 580 | Hello, Who's There?/The Way | 80 |
| 68 | Major Minor MMLP 29 | JULY (LP, laminated front sleeve, red/white/black labels) | 1000 |
| 87 | Bam Caruso KIRI 097 | DANDELION SEEDS (LP, reissue of above LP with extra tracks & different sleeve) | 25 |
| 95 | Essex 1011LP | JULY (LP, reissue with bonus 7": "Hello Who's There?"/"The Way" [p/s, 10117]) | 20 |

*(see also Jade Warrior, Tom Newman)*

## JUMBLE LANE
| | | | |
|---|---|---|---|
| 71 | Holyground HG 115 | JUMBLE LANE (LP, 99 copies only) | 600 |

## JUMBO
| | | | |
|---|---|---|---|
| 72 | CBS 7820 | She Said/Wasting My Time | 8 |
| 72 | CBS S 8082 | Promises/Sitting Thinking | 12 |
| 72 | Epic EPC S 8057 | Round And Round/Sewing Circle | 12 |

## JUMP
| | | | |
|---|---|---|---|
| 80 | Caveman CLUB 1 | Shake Up/All In Vain (p/s) | 25 |

## JUMPBACKS
| | | | |
|---|---|---|---|
| 73 | Maxi M3 | Shake/Hello Stranger | 30 |

## JUMPIN' JACKS
| | | | |
|---|---|---|---|
| 58 | HMV POP 440 | My Girl, My Girl/Tried And Tested | 25 |

## JUMPLEADS
| | | | |
|---|---|---|---|
| 82 | Ock OC 001 | THE STAG MUST DIE (LP, with insert) | 15 |

## JUMP SQUAD
| | | | |
|---|---|---|---|
| 81 | 101 UR 2 | Lord Of The Dance/Debt (p/s) | 20 |

*(see also Embryo)*

## JUNCO PARTNERS
| | | | |
|---|---|---|---|
| 65 | Columbia DB 7665 | As Long As I Have You/Take This Hammer | 70 |
| 79 | Rigid JUNK 1028 | Swinging Sixties Boys/Peepin' And Hidin' | 6 |
| 81 | Energy NRG 4 | Tall Windows/Noizez In My Head (p/s) | 5 |
| 81 | Energy NRGX 4 | Tall Windows (Extended)/Noizez In My Head (Extended) (12", stickered white label, plain sleeve, promo only) | 10 |
| 71 | Philips 6308 032 | JUNCO PARTNERS (LP, laminated sleeve, black/silver labels) | 150 |

## JUNCTION
| | | | |
|---|---|---|---|
| 87 | New Youth NYJ 175 | PANDORAS BOX EP | 20 |

## JUNCTION 32
| | | | |
|---|---|---|---|
| 75 | Holyground HGS 119 | JUNCTION 32 (LP, 100 copies only) | 550 |

## JUNCUNO
| | | | |
|---|---|---|---|
| 71 | Banana BA 361 | The End (as Joncuno)/HORACE ANDY: See A Man's Face | 30 |

*(see also Jon Cundo)*

## ROSANNE JUNE
| | | | |
|---|---|---|---|
| 56 | London HLU 8352 | The Charge Of The Light Brigade/Broken Windows | 20 |
| 58 | Oriole CB 1430 | When A Woman Cries/The Great Chicago Fire | 8 |

## ROSEMARY JUNE
| | | | |
|---|---|---|---|
| 58 | Fontana H 141 | I'll Always Be In Love With You/Person To Person | 5 |

## JUNE BRIDES
| | | | |
|---|---|---|---|
| 84 | Pink PINKY 1 | In The Rain/Sunday To Saturday (p/s) | 10 |
| 84 | Pink PINKY 2 | Every Conversation/Disneyland (die-cut sleeve, with insert) | 8 |
| 84 | Pink PINKY 2 | Every Conversation/Disneyland (die-cut sleeve) | 7 |
| 85 | Pikn PINKY 5 | THERE ARE EIGHT MILLION STORIES... (LP, insert) | 15 |

*(see also Phil Wilson)*

## JUNG COLLECTIVE
| | | | |
|---|---|---|---|
| 02 | Nanny Tango NT 1 | Injustice/Street Preacher (Plaid Mix) (clear vinyl, poly sleeve w/sticker insert) | 20 |

## CARL GUSTAV JUNG
| | | | |
|---|---|---|---|
| 63 | Piccadilly FTF 38505 | FACE TO FACE (LP) | 20 |

## JUNIOR (SIMPSON)
| | | | |
|---|---|---|---|
| 68 | Giant GN 18 | I'm Gonna Leave You Girl/I Love You I Love You | 20 |
| 68 | Giant GN 25 | Come Cure Me/I Want Your Loving | 25 |

## JUNIOR B
| | | | |
|---|---|---|---|
| 92 | Eastern Sher ES 001 | Meditation/Black And White (12") | 40 |

## JUNIOR BROWN
| | | | |
|---|---|---|---|
| 78 | Tempus TEMD 01 | Jah Find Babylon Guilty (feat. Ranking Ruben)/Dub (12") | 18 |

| | | | |
|---|---|---|---|
| 80 | Jah Shaka SHAKA 829 | Fly Me Away/Travelling Dub (12") | 30 |
| 82 | Jah Shaka SHAKA 822 | Warrior/Right Fight (12") | 15 |
| 92 | Jah Shaka SHAKA 822 | Warrior/Right Fight (12", reissue) | 10 |

## JUNIOR DELGADO

| | | | |
|---|---|---|---|
| 77 | Deb TIC 1001 | Tiction/Tiction Volume 2 | 15 |
| 78 | Deb DEB 001 | Tonight & Tune In/Armed Robbery (12") | 20 |
| 78 | Deb DEB 019 | Trickster/CARLTON & HIS SHOES: Better Days (12") | 20 |
| 79 | Greensleeves GRED 15 | Love Tickles Like Magic/PRINCE JAMMY & AGGROVATORS : Prince Jammy's Magic (12") | 20 |
| 79 | Burning Sounds BRD 005 | Raiders/Warrior (12") | 20 |
| 79 | DEB 026 | Warrior (with Ras Bug)/DEB PLAYERS: Version (12") | 30 |
| 80 | Greensleeves GRED 39 | Midnight Raver/365 days (12", blue vinyl) | 15 |
| 80 | Niagra NIADD 108 | Fort Augustus/Escape Prisioners (12") | 30 |
| 82 | Incredible Jux 04 | Trouble Part 1/Trouble Part 2 (12") | 20 |
| 86 | Incredible IM001 | Poverty/Version (12") | 30 |
| 87 | Fashion FAD 040 | Hot Stuff/It Takes Two To Tango (12") | 15 |
| 88 | Mango IS 368 | Hanging Tree/Hey Good Looking (12") | 20 |
| 89 | Fashion FAD 066 | Dub School/We A Blood (12") | 25 |
| 79 | Deb DEBLP 05 | TASTE OF THE YOUNG HEART (LP) | 35 |
| 79 | Deb DEBLP 010 | EFFORT (LP) | 40 |
| 82 | Incredible Jux HBLP 001 | BUSHMAN REVOLUTION (LP) | 40 |
| 86 | Fashion FADLP 003 | IT TAKES TWO TO TANGO (LP) | 18 |

## JUNIOR DISPROL

| | | | |
|---|---|---|---|
| 01 | SFDB AO27658 | Fight Club/Junq Waffle | 25 |

## JUNIOR ENGLISH

| | | | |
|---|---|---|---|
| 79 | Ethnic Fight ETH 1328 | Keep On Trying/HORSEMOUTH: Herb Vendor (12") | 20 |

## JUNIOR'S EYES

| | | | |
|---|---|---|---|
| 69 | Regal Zonophone RZ 3009 | Mr. Golden Trumpet Player/Black Snake | 30 |
| 69 | Regal Zonophone RZ 3018 | Woman Love/White Light Part 2 (withdrawn B-side) | 30 |
| 69 | Regal Zonophone RZ 3018 | Woman Love/Circus Days | 20 |
| 69 | Regal Zonophone RZ 3023 | Star Child/Sink Or Swim | 20 |
| 69 | Regal Zono. SLRZ 1008 | BATTERSEA POWER STATION (LP, laminated front, flipbacks, "Sold in U.K..." label text) | 150 |

*(see also David Bowie, Tickle, Bunch Of Fives, Outsiders)*

## JUNIOR GEE

| | | | |
|---|---|---|---|
| 86 | Scorcher 1032 | The Truth (12") | 50 |

## JUNIOR GEE & THE CAPITAL BOYS

| | | | |
|---|---|---|---|
| 84 | Tai Wan 1948 | Check Us Out/The Break (12") | 15 |

## HUGH ROY JUNIOR

| | | | |
|---|---|---|---|
| 71 | Big BG 329 | Papcito/RUPIE EDWARDS: I'm Gonna Live Some Life | 12 |
| 71 | Supreme SUP 211 | Double Attack/MURPHY'S ALL STARS: Puzzle | 15 |
| 72 | Ashanti ASH 405 | King Of The Road/ROOSEVELT ALL STARS: Version | 15 |
| 72 | Jackpot JP 806 | Two Ton Guletto/Version | 15 |

*(see also U Roy Junior)*

## JUNIOR KEITHING

| | | | |
|---|---|---|---|
| 80 | Grand Masters GM 001 | Jah Wrote Me A Letter/Letter Dub (12") | 20 |

## JUNIOR MCCANTS

| | | | |
|---|---|---|---|
| 98 | Kent 6T 16 | Try Me For Your New Love/GARLAND GREEN: Come Through Me | 40 |

## JUNIOR MURVIN

| | | | |
|---|---|---|---|
| 68 | Doctor Bird DB 1112 | Miss Cushie (as Junior Soul)/LYNN TAITT & JETS: Dr. Paul | 250 |
| 68 | Big Shot BI 503 | Chattie Chattie/The Magic Touch | 300 |
| 69 | Big Shot BI 527 | The Hustler/The Magic Touch | 200 |
| 70 | Gayfeet GS 205 | Jennifer/Slipping | 12 |
| 76 | Island 12WIP 6539 | Police & Thieves/JAH LION: Soldier & Police War/GLEN DACASTA: Magic Touch/THE UPSETTER: Grumblin' Dub (12", p/s) | 12 |
| 76 | Island WIP 6316 | Junior Murvin/Grumblin Dub | 8 |
| 77 | Island IPR 2001 | Tedious/Memories | 30 |
| 77 | Island 12WIP 2010 | Upsetter Revue Feat. Junior Murvin: Dread Locks In Moonlight/Closer Together (12") | 12 |
| 80 | Black Ark ARK 007 | Cross Over/I Am In Love (12") | 15 |
| 82 | Dread At The Controls DATCD 009 | Bad Man Posse/Riddim Request To All Posse Smoker Posse (12") | 18 |
| 86 | Greensleeves GRED 199 | Apartheid/Jack Slick (12") | 15 |
| 82 | Dread At The Controls | BADMAN POSSE (LP) | 30 |
| 84 | Greensleeves GREL 70 | MUGGERS IN THE STREET (LP) | 20 |

## JUNIOR REID

| | | | |
|---|---|---|---|
| 80 | Negus Roots NERT 02 | Sister Dawn/Dub Version (12") | 20 |
| 81 | Negus Roots NERT 09 | IF I/Versions (12") | 40 |
| 82 | King Imperial KG 008 | Jail House/We Got To Leave (12") | 50 |
| 84 | Greensleeves GRED 163 | Boom Shack A Lack/Old Time Something (12") | 15 |
| 85 | Greensleeves GREL 78 | BOOM SHACK A LACK (LP) | 15 |

## JUNIOR ROOTS

| | | | |
|---|---|---|---|
| 81 | Black Roots BR 24 | Natty Dread Time/BLACK TRAP: Into The Light (12") | 15 |

## JUNIOR ROSS AND THE SPEARS

| | | | |
|---|---|---|---|
| 76 | K&B KB 5529 | Judgement Time/Version | 25 |

## TREVOR JUNIOR

| | | | |
|---|---|---|---|
| 84 | Tonos TON 002 | Ghetto Living/Have Faith In Jah (12") | 50 |

## JUNIORS

| | | | |
|---|---|---|---|
| 64 | Columbia DB 7339 | There's A Pretty Girl/Pocket Size | 55 |

MINT VALUE £

## JUNIPER GREEN
71   Columbia DB 8809                Dreams In The Sky/Cascade Of Ice.................................................................. 20

## LENA JUNOFF
68   Olga OLE 8                      Yesterday Has Gone/Good Kind Of Hurt ....................................................... 40

## JUNO'S CLAW
79   MPA EMP 081                     Barbara/The Master/Big City (EP, no p/s) ................................................... 100

## JUPITER
72   Parlophone R 5967               The Meteor Song/Life Is Getting Better Every Day ..................................... 25

## ERIC JUPP & HIS ORCHESTRA
53   Columbia SCM 5070               Jog Trot/Doina Voda........................................................................................ 7
54   Columbia SCM 5081               Ooop De Ooh (Lazy Mambo)/Footsteps In The Fog................................... 7
54   Columbia SCM 5140               They Were Doin' The Mambo/Skokiian (with Coronets) ............................. 7
56   Columbia DB 3817                Theme From 'East Of Eden'/When The Lilac Blooms Again ......................... 7
57   Columbia DB 4030                Bleep! Bleep!/Three-Two-One-Zero! ............................................................ 7
55   Columbia SEG 7589               ERIC JUPP AND HIS ORCHESTRA (EP) ........................................................ 12
*(see also Coronets, Rockin' Strings)*                                                                               10

## MICKEY JUPP
78   Stiff UPP1                      My Typewriter/Nature's Radio (as Mickey Jupp with Legend, promo) .......... 8
78   Stiff BUY 36                    Old Rock N Roller/S.P.Y. (p/s) ...................................................................... 6
*(see also Rossi & Frost, Legend)*

## JUS BADD
87   Tuff GrooveTUFF001              Freestyle/Proud (12").................................................................................. 100

## JUST A HE HE
84   PRT JH 1                        Lucky Day/Take Time (p/s) .......................................................................... 8

## JUST MEASURES
83   It's War Boy £5                 FLAGELLATION (LP)......................................................................................... 20

## JUST THE JOB
80   KIK 2                           Fears Of The Years/Street Feelings/London Lights (with p/s) ..................... 50
80   KIK 2                           Fears Of The Years/Street Feelings/London Lights (without p/s) ............... 30

## JUST WATER
78   Stiff BUY 31                    Singin In The Rain/Witness To The Crime (p/s) ............................................ 7

## JUST BROTHERS
80s  Soul City SC 127               Carlena/IVORIES: Please Stay (die-cut company sleeve) ............................. 8
01   Hayley HR 003                   Honey/Carlena................................................................................................ 8

## SAMANTHA JUSTE
66   Go AJ 11402                     No One Needs My Love Today/If Trees Could Talk ..................................... 25

## JUST FOUR MEN
64   Parlophone R 5186               That's My Baby/Things Will Never Be The Same (withdrawn, as Four Just Men)........... 80
64   Parlophone R 5208               That's My Baby/Things Will Never Be The Same........................................... 60
65   Parlophone R 5241               There's Not One Thing/Don't Come Any Closer .......................................... 60
*(see also Wimple Winch, Four Just Men, Pacific Drift)*

## JUST FRANK
79   Rok ROK III/IV                  You/SPLIT SCREENS: Just Don't Try (die-cut company sleeve)................... 35

## JIMMY JUSTICE
60   Pye 7N 15301                    I Understand Just How You Feel/Bloodshot Eyes (as Jimmy Justice & Jury) ....... 10
61   Pye 7N 15351                    When Love Has Left You/The Teacher ........................................................ 10
61   Pye 7N 15376                    A Little Bit Of Soap/Little Lonely One ...................................................... 10
62   Pye 7N 15443                    Ain't That Funny/One (with p/s)................................................................ 5
62   Pye 7N 15443                    Ain't That Funny/One................................................................................. 5
62   Pye 7N 15457                    Spanish Harlem/Write Me A Letter............................................................. 5
62   Pye 7N 15469                    Parade Of Broken Hearts/Dawning ........................................................... 5
63   Pye 7N 15502                    The World Of Lonely People/I Wake Up Crying ........................................ 5
63   Pye 7N 15509                    Little Cracked Bell/Lighted Windows ........................................................ 5
63   Pye 7N 15528                    The Guitar Player/Don't Let The Stars Get In Your Eyes.......................... 5
63   Pye 7N 15558                    You're Gonna Need My Lovin'/Since You've Been Gone (with Exchequers) ....... 5
63   Pye 7N 15601                    Don't Say That Again/Green Leaves Of Summer ...................................... 5
69   Decca F 12899                   Running Out Of Time/There Goes My World ............................................. 5
65   Pye 7N 15963                    Only Heartbreak For Me/Everything In The Garden ................................. 5
68   RCA Victor RCA 1681             I'm Past Forgetting You/Walking Away With My Heart ........................... 25
63   Pye NEP 24159                   HIT PARADE (EP) ......................................................................................... 10
62   Pye NPL 18080                   TWO SIDES OF JIMMY JUSTICE (LP)........................................................... 20
62   Pye NPL 18085                   SMASH HITS (LP) ......................................................................................... 15

## JUSTIFIED ANCIENTS OF MU MU (J.A.M.S)
87   KLF Comm. JAMS 23              All You Need Is Love (Original) (12", white label, 1-sided, 500 only).............. 50
87   KLF Comm. JAMS 23(s)          All You Need Is Love (Me Ru Con Mix)/(Ibo Version) (1,000 only, plain sleeve)............. 10
87   KLF Comm. JAMS 23T            All You Need Is Love/Ivum Naya/Rap, Rhyme And Scratch Yourself (12", 'James
                                    Anderton' p/s, 5,000 only).......................................................................... 15
87   KLF Comm. JAMS 24T            Whitney Joins The JAMs (120 bpm) (12", 1-sided, 'Scottish' issue, 500 only).......15
87   KLF Comm. JAMS 25T            1987 - The 45 Edits (12", p/s).................................................................... 15
87   KLF Comm. JAMS 26T            BURN THE BEAT (12" EP, 5,000 for export only) .................................... 10
87   KLF Comm. JAMS 27             Down Town/118 BPM 27 (p/s) .................................................................... 8
87   KLF Comm. JAMS 27             Down Town (A-side Mix) (12", 1-sided, white label, 500 only) .................... 12
87   KLF Comm. JAMS 27             Down Town (B-side Mix) (12", 1-sided, white label, 500 only) .................... 12
87   KLF Comm. JAMS 27             Down Town (A-side Mix)/(B-side Mix) (12", white label) ........................... 12
87   KLF Comm. JAMS 27T            Down Town (118 bpm)/Down Town (12", JAMs label, generic sleeve) .......... 10
87   KLF Comm. JAMS 27T            Down Town (118 bpm)/Down Town (12",mispressed 'album' label, generic sleeve) ..... 15
88   KLF Comm. JAMS 28T            It's Grim Up North (Original Vocal Mix) (12", grey vinyl, 1-sided, 350 only)................ 100

| | | | |
|---|---|---|---|
| 87 | KLF Comm. JAMS DS 1 | Deep Shit (flexidisc, unreleased) | 150 |
| 91 | KLF Comm. JAMS 028R | It's Grim Up North (Original Vocal Mix) (12", black vinyl, 1-sided promo) | 8 |
| 88 | Fierce FRIGHT 34(T) | 20 GREATEST HITS (12" EP; not actually by J.A.M.s!) | 12 |
| 87 | KLF Comm. JAMS LP 1 | 1987 (WHAT THE FUCK IS GOING ON?) (LP, withdrawn) | 100 |
| 88 | KLF Comm. JAMS LP 2 | WHO KILLED THE JAMS? (LP, stickered sleeve with insert) | 20 |
| 89 | KLF Comm. JAMS DLP 3 | SHAG TIMES (2-LP) | 50 |
| 89 | KLF Comm. JAMS CD 3 | SHAG TIMES (CD) | 40 |

*(see also KLF, Timelords, Disco 2000, Space, Orb, Bill Drummond)*

## JUSTIN CASE
| | | | |
|---|---|---|---|
| 80 | Rok ROK XIX | TV/STRAIGHT UP: One Out All Out (die-cut company sleeve) | 40 |

## DAVE JUSTIN
| | | | |
|---|---|---|---|
| 67 | Polydor 56221 | Everybody's Gone Home/Lincoln Green | 12 |
| 68 | Polydor 56253 | You Outside/Thinking Twice | 12 |

## JAY JUSTIN
| | | | |
|---|---|---|---|
| 68 | Columbia DB 8439 | I Sell Summertime/Time (withdrawn) | 10 |

## JUSTIN & KARLSSON
| | | | |
|---|---|---|---|
| 66 | Piccadilly 7N 35295 | Somewhere They Can't Find Me/What More Do You Want | 40 |

## JUSTINE
| | | | |
|---|---|---|---|
| 69 | Dot DOT 121 | Leave Me Be/Clown | 10 |
| 69 | Buffalo BFS 1001 | Right Now/Place Where Sorrow Hides | 30 |
| 70 | Uni UNS 528 | She Brings Back The Morning With Her/Back To Boulder | 8 |
| 70 | Uni UNLS 111 | JUSTINE (LP) | 90 |

## JUSTINS
| | | | |
|---|---|---|---|
| 71 | Punch PH 65 | Cholera/LLOYD ALL STARS: Black Bird | 20 |

## BILL JUSTIS & HIS ORCHESTRA
| | | | |
|---|---|---|---|
| 57 | London HLS 8517 | Raunchy/The Midnight Man | 20 |
| 58 | London HLS 8614 | College Man/The Stranger (B-side with Spinners) | 25 |
| 63 | Mercury AMT 1201 | I'm Gonna Learn To Dance/Tamoure | 10 |
| 69 | Sun 6094 003 | Raunchy/Flip, Flop And Bop | 10 |

## JUST LIKE THAT
| | | | |
|---|---|---|---|
| 76 | Tank BS 122 | JUST LIKE THAT (LP) | 20 |

## JUST PLAIN JONES
| | | | |
|---|---|---|---|
| 71 | CBS CBS 7480 | Crazy, Crazy/Should Have Stayed With Mary | 20 |

*(see also Just Plain Smith, Dave Ballantyne, Esprit De Corps)*

## JUST PLAIN SMITH
| | | | |
|---|---|---|---|
| 69 | Sunshine SUN 7702 | February's Child/Don't Open Your Mind (with p/s) | 135 |
| 69 | Sunshine SUN 7702 | February's Child/Don't Open Your Mind | 60 |

*(see also Just Plain Jones, Esprit De Corps)*

## JUST US
| | | | |
|---|---|---|---|
| 66 | CBS 202068 | I Can't Grow Peaches On A Cherry Tree/I Can Save You | 7 |

## JUST WILLIAM
| | | | |
|---|---|---|---|
| 68 | Spark SRL 1018 | I Don't Care/Cherrywood Green | 30 |

## JUVENILES
| | | | |
|---|---|---|---|
| 66 | Pye International 7N 25349 | Bo Diddley/Yes I Believe | 100 |

## JYNX
| | | | |
|---|---|---|---|
| 64 | Columbia DB 7304 | How/Do What They Don't Say | 75 |

## K

## CAROLINE K
| | | | |
|---|---|---|---|
| 87 | Earthly Delights EARTH 1 | NOW WAIT FOR LAST YEAR (LP, 1,500 only) | 15 |

## JOHNNY K
| | | | |
|---|---|---|---|
| 63 | Fontana TF 408 | Lemonade/Come Closer Melinda | 12 |

## MOSES K & PROPHETS
| | | | |
|---|---|---|---|
| 65 | Decca F 12244 | I Went Out With My Baby Tonight/So Long | 25 |

*(see also Them)*

## SIMON K
| | | | |
|---|---|---|---|
| 69 | B&C CB 111 | You Know I Do/Bring Your Love Back | 40 |

## ERNIE K-DOE
| | | | |
|---|---|---|---|
| 68 | Action ACT 4502 | Dancing Man/Later For Tomorrow | 25 |

## KABBALA
| | | | |
|---|---|---|---|
| 82 | Red Flame RF 1211 | Ashewo Ara/Voltan Dance (12") | 25 |

## KABUKI
| | | | |
|---|---|---|---|
| 82 | Kabaret Noir KAB 1 | I Am A Horse/My Hair (p/s) | 30 |

## KADDO STRINGS
| | | | |
|---|---|---|---|
| 80 | Grapevine GRP 146 | Nothing But Love/Crying Over You | 15 |

*(see also Duke Browner, Tartans)*

## KADENZA
| | | | |
|---|---|---|---|
| 82 | PRT 12P 247 | Let's Stay Together (Night Club Mix)/Let's Stay Together (Vocal 2)/Instrumental Version (12") | 30 |

## KADETTES
| | | | |
|---|---|---|---|
| 82 | Blank GET 1 | Fireball XL5/Mission Impossible | 8 |

MINT VALUE £

## KAINE & ABEL
66 Philips BF 1472 — Then You Must Know My Love/Crying In The Rain .......... 8

## KAISER CHIEFS
04 B-Unique BUN088-7 — I Predict A Riot/Take My Temperature (150 signed 7" with p/s) ........ 15
05 KAISERCRIBS001 — KAISER CHIEFS: Another Number/THE CRIBS: Modern Way (Double 'A' Side sold at gigs during 2005 tour dates. 1000 copies) .......... 10
05 No Label — You Can Have It All (1-sided Xmas 2005 single sent out to first 2000 website subscribers. Christmas card fold-out sleeve. B side with 'I predict Some Quiet' label ...... 6
07 No Label — The Angry Mob/The Angry Mob (Paul Emmanuel Off The Streets Mix) (mail-order only, with poster, 1,000 only) .......... 8
07 B-Unique BUN119-7 — Ruby/Admire You (red vinyl, p/s) .......... 6
05 B-Unique BUN093LP — EMPLOYMENT (LP) .......... 20

## KAISERS
94 No Hit Records NO HIT 14 — IN STEP WITH THE KAISERS (LP) .......... 15
93 No Hit NO HIT 012 — SQUAREHEAD STOMP! (LP) .......... 18

## KAJANUS/PICKETT
72 Signport SGA 5001 — HI HO SILVER (LP, sleeve with cut flap) .......... 20

## KAKKO
90 CBS 656023 — What Kind Of Fool (mixes)/I Pledge You My Heart (12", p/s) .......... 12
90 CBS 655 710 6 — We Should Be Dancing (mixes) (12", p/s) .......... 12
90 CBS 655 710 8 — We Should Be Dancing (mixes) (12", p/s) .......... 18

## KALA
73 Bradleys BRAD 302 — Travelling Home/Still Got Time .......... 5
73 Bradleys BRADL 1002 — KALA (LP) .......... 15
(see also Quintessence)

## ALAN KALANI
59 Vogue V 9147 — A Touch Of Pink/SURFERS: Mambo Jambo .......... 20
59 Vogue V 9147 — A Touch Of Pink/SURFERS: Mambo Jambo (78) .......... 20

## KALASANDRO!
60 Warner Bros WB 13 — Chi Chi/Forbidden City .......... 12

## KALEIDOSCOPE (U.K.)
67 Fontana TF 863 — Flight From Ashiya/Holidaymaker (in p/s) .......... 100
67 Fontana TF 863 — Flight From Ashiya/Holidaymaker .......... 60
68 Fontana TF 895 — A Dream For Julie/Please Excuse My Face .......... 40
68 Fontana TF 964 — Jenny Artichoke/Just How Much Are You .......... 50
69 Fontana TF 1002 — Do It Again For Jeffrey/Poem .......... 50
69 Fontana TF 1048 — Balloon/If You So Wish .......... 110
69 Decca (No Cat. No.) — Black Fjord (1-sided) .......... 130
67 Fontana (S)TL 5448 — TANGERINE DREAM (LP, unlaminated sleeve, flipbacks, black/silver label) .......... 1000
69 Fontana STL 5491 — FAINTLY BLOWING (LP, laminated gatefold sleeve; without watermark on beginning of each side) .......... 1000
69 Fontana STL 5491 — FAINTLY BLOWING (LP, laminated gatefold sleeve; with watermark on beginning of each side) .......... 400
87 5 Hours Back TOCK 005 — TANGERINE DREAM (LP, stereo reissue) .......... 20
87 5 Hours Back TOCK 006 — FAINTLY BLOWING (LP, reissue, single sleeve) .......... 20
03 Circle CPWL 104 — PLEASE LISTEN TO THE PICTURES (2-LP, BBC sessions, split LP with Fairfield Parlour) .... 20
(see also Fairfield Parlour, I Luv Wight)

## KALEIDOSCOPE (U.S.)
70 CBS 64005 — BERNICE (LP, as American Kaleidoscope) .......... 30

## JOHNNY KALENDAR BAND
79 CJMO PX 109` — FOOLING YOURSELF EP (p/s) .......... 50
(see also Def Leppard)

## KITTY KALLEN
54 Brunswick 05261 — Are You Looking For A Sweetheart/In The Chapel In The Moonlight .......... 15
54 Brunswick 05287 — Little Things Mean A Lot/I Don't Think You Love Me Anymore .......... 15
54 Brunswick 05357 — Heartless Heart/The Spirit Of Christmas .......... 15
54 Brunswick 05359 — I Want You All To Myself/(Don't Let The) Kiddy Geddin' .......... 12

## DICK KALLMAN
56 Brunswick 05608 — Two Different Worlds/Love Me As Though There Were No Tomorrow .......... 6
60 Vogue V 9162 — Born To Be Loved/Just Squeeze Me But Don't Teeze Me .......... 10
63 HMV POP 1118 — Say It Isn't So/From This Day On (A-side with John Barry & His Orchestra) .......... 5
63 HMV CLP 1642 — SPEAK SOFTLY (LP) .......... 20

## BOBBY KALPHAT
68 Nu Beat NB 007 — Rhythm And Soul/BUNNY & RUDDY: True Romance .......... 20
73 Tropical AL 049 — Natty Rock/Natty Dub .......... 15
74 Faith FA 008 — Zion Hill/Dub Hill .......... 20

## BOBBY KALPHAT & PHIL PRATT
76 Terminal TERM 001 — ZION HILL DUB (LP) .......... 350
79 Phil Pratt SSLP 1007 — THE WAR IS ON DUB STYLE (LP) .......... 75

## CAROL KALPHAT
78 Hit Run HIT DD 1 — African Land (featuring Clint Eastwood)/ DOCTOR PABLO AND THE CRYTUFF ALLSTARS -African Melody (12", title sleeve) .......... 70

## KAMARAS
69 CBS 4199 — Let This Moment Pass Away/I Just Can't Break Away From This Lovin' .......... 25

## KAMIKAZE PILOTS
83 Lowther 002 — Dark Night Of The Soul/Red Indian Song .......... 10
85 Lowther HCW 003 — Sharon Signs To Cherry Red/It Goes Boing (p/s) .......... 8

## INI KAMOZE
84 Island IMA 7 — INI KAMOZE (LP) .......... 20

### KANDAHAR
| | | | |
|---|---|---|---|
| 74 | Sounds Superb 4M048-97401 | LONG LIVE THE SLICED HAM (LP) | 30 |

### AMORY KANE
| | | | |
|---|---|---|---|
| 68 | MCA MU 1036 | Reflections Of Your Face/Four Ravens | 15 |
| 70 | CBS 5111 | Him Or Me/Forever Waiting | 10 |
| 70 | UNI UNS 518 | You Were On My Mind/All The Best Songs And Marches | 6 |
| 68 | MCA MUP(S) 348 | MEMORIES OF TIME UNWOUND (LP, with insert) | 50 |
| 70 | CBS 63849 | JUST TO BE THERE (LP) | 40 |

*(see also Ron Geesin)*

### DOUG KANE
| | | | |
|---|---|---|---|
| 80 | Video VIDEO 2 | ONE BETWEEN THE EYES (LP) | 35 |

*(see also Eyes (2))*

### EDEN KANE
| | | | |
|---|---|---|---|
| 60 | Pye 7N 15284 | Hot Chocolate Crazy/You Make Love So Well | 35 |
| 61 | Decca F 11353 | Well I Ask You/Before I Lose My Mind | 5 |
| 61 | Decca F 11381 | Get Lost/I'm Telling You | 5 |
| 62 | Decca F 11418 | Forget Me Not/A New Kind Of Lovin' | 5 |
| 62 | Decca F 11460 | I Don't Know Why/Music For Strings | 5 |
| 62 | Decca F 11504 | House To Let/I Told You | 5 |
| 63 | Decca F 11568 | Sounds Funny To Me/Someone Wants To Know | 6 |
| 63 | Fontana TF 398 | Tomorrow Night/I Won't Believe You (some in p/s) | 6 |
| 63 | Fontana TF 413 | Like I Love You/Come Back (with Earl Preston's TTs) | 8 |
| 64 | Fontana TF 438 | Boys Cry/Don't Come Crying To Me | 5 |
| 64 | Fontana TF 462 | Rain Rain Go Away/Guess Who It Is | 6 |
| 64 | Fontana TF 508 | Hangin' Around/Gonna Do Something About You | 6 |
| 65 | Fontana TF 582 | If You Want This Love/Have I Done Something Wrong | 10 |
| 69 | Fontana TF 1023 | Boys Cry/Don't Come Cryin' To Me (p/s, reissue) | 5 |
| 62 | Decca DFE 6696 | WELL I ASK YOU! (EP) | 10 |
| 62 | Decca DFE 8503 | HITS (EP) | 10 |
| 64 | Decca DFE 8567 | SIX GREAT NEW SWINGERS (EP) | 10 |
| 64 | Fontana TFE 17424 | IT'S EDEN (EP) | 15 |
| 62 | Ace Of Clubs ACL 1133 | EDEN KANE (LP) | 20 |
| 64 | Fontana TL 5211 | IT'S EDEN (LP) | 20 |

*(see also Brothers Kane, Sarstedt Brothers)*

### HELEN KANE
| | | | |
|---|---|---|---|
| 55 | MGM EP 549 | THE BOOP BOOP A DOOP GIRL (EP) | 15 |

### JEFF KANE
| | | | |
|---|---|---|---|
| 69 | Tangerine DP 0006 | Pretty Young Lady/On My Darkest Day | 35 |

### JON KANE
| | | | |
|---|---|---|---|
| 69 | Warner Bros WB 8003 | Soulful Lady/In Ancient Times (Jerusalem) | 10 |

### LEE KANE
| | | | |
|---|---|---|---|
| 55 | Capitol CL 14297 | Ev'ry Day/How Would You Have Me? | 8 |
| 55 | Capitol CL 14328 | Around And Around/Merci Beaucoup | 8 |

### MARIA KANE
| | | | |
|---|---|---|---|
| 65 | Decca F 12184 | Love Is Slipping Away/Love Is Strange | 10 |

### MILES KANE
| | | | |
|---|---|---|---|
| 10 | Columbia 8869784487 | Inhaler/Rainbow Woman (p/s, numbered, with poster) | 12 |
| 11 | Columbia 8597940117 | Inhaler/Hey Bulldog (live) (p/s, blue vinyl, different cover) | 6 |
| 11 | Columbia 88697843567/ 88697843607 | Come Closer/Come Closer (Steve Mason Remix)//Come Closer/Before Midnight (live) (2 x 7", edition of 500 with signed lyric sheet) | 8 |
| 11 | Columbia 88697856677 | Rearrange/Morning Comes | 5 |
| 11 | Columbia 88697888187 | A Girl Like You/Our Man Flint (p/s, numbered) | 6 |
| 12 | Columbia 88691976881 | First Of My Kind/Night Runner/Looking Out Of My Window/Colour Of The Trap (10") | 12 |

*(see also Arctic Monkeys, Rascals (2))*

### STEPHANIE KANE
| | | | |
|---|---|---|---|
| 64 | Oriole CB1908 | It's Love/Think Of Me | 25 |

### KAN KAN
| | | | |
|---|---|---|---|
| 80 | Kabaret Music TRAIN 1 | Film Noir/The Watchmaker | 20 |

### KANSAS
| | | | |
|---|---|---|---|
| 76 | Epic SEPC 4932 | Carry On Wayward Son/Questions Of My Childhood | 6 |

### KANSAS HOOK
| | | | |
|---|---|---|---|
| 70 | UNI UNI 5515 | Echo Park/Manhattan Woman | 10 |
| 71 | Decca F13117 | Nervous Shaking/Mr. Universe | 40 |

### PAUL KANTNER
| | | | |
|---|---|---|---|
| 71 | RCA Victor SF 8163 | BLOWS AGAINST THE EMPIRE (LP, gatefold sleeve with booklet, as Paul Kantner & Jefferson Starship) | 20 |
| 71 | Grunt FTR 1002 | SUNFIGHTER (LP, gatefold sleeve with booklet & inner sleeve; as Paul Kantner, Grace Slick & Jefferson Starship) | 15 |

*(see also Jefferson Airplane/Starship)*

### KAPLAN
| | | | |
|---|---|---|---|
| 68 | Philips BF 1636 | Do You Believe In Magic/I Like | 18 |
| 68 | Philips BF 1699 | I Love It/Trousers Down | 20 |

### KAPT. KOPTER & FABULOUS TWIRLY BIRDS
| | | | |
|---|---|---|---|
| 73 | Epic EPC 65381 | KAPT. KOPTER & THE FABULOUS TWIRLY BIRDS (LP) | 15 |

*(see also Spirit)*

### KAREEM
| | | | |
|---|---|---|---|
| 97 | Exploding Plastic EXP8 | Never Give Up On Love/Restless Soul (Peaktime Radio Mix)/Hipster Mix | 30 |

MINT VALUE £

## KENNY KAREN
| 61 | Philips PB 1213 | Oh Susie Forgive Me/The Light In Your Window | 15 |

## KARIBS
| 70s | Karibs KA1 | Aching Heart/Sugar Lips | 8 |

## KARINA
| 71 | United Artists UP 35205 | Tomorrow I'm Coming Your Way/Something | 15 |

## BILLY KARLOFF (& EXTREMES)
| 78 | Wanted CULT-45-001 | Crazy Paving/Back Street Billy (p/s) | 10 |
| 81 | Warner Bros K 17753 | Headbangers/Don't Keep Me Down (p/s) | 5 |

*(see also Tom Robinson Band, Stiff Little Fingers)*

## BORIS KARLOFF
| 60 | Caedmon CAL 102/1 | HANS CHRISTIAN ANDERSEN (LP) | 15 |
| 67 | Brunswick LAT 8678 | AN EVENING WITH BORIS KARLOFF AND FRIENDS (LP) | 30 |

## KARMA SUTRA
| 87 | Paradoxical PARODY 1 | DAYDREAMS OF A PRODUCTION LINE WORKER (LP, with booklet) | 40 |

## STEVE KARMEN BIG BAND
| 75 | United Artists UP 35770 | Breakaway/Breakaway (Vocal Version) (featuring Jimmy Radcliffe) | 10 |

*(see also Jimmy Radcliffe)*

## KAROO
| 65 | Oak RGJ 193 | Mamma's Out Of Town/Lonely Weekend | 200 |

## KARPET KETCHUP
| 85 | Newspaper KK1 | Penny Drops/Deep Inside | 15 |

## KARRIER
| 84 | Unit TRANS 101 | I'm Back/Dreaming (no p/s) | 30 |
| 86 | Status JEMS 101 | Poor Little Rich Girl/Endless Shadow | 30 |
| 85 | Unit | WAY BEYOND THE NIGHT (LP) | 15 |

## KARYN KARSH
| 66 | RCA Victor RCA 1740 | I Wasn't Born To Follow/Musty Dusty | 5 |

## KASABIAN
| 03 | BMG Paradise 02 | Processed Beats (10" 45 rpm screen print sleeve with elastic bands) | 25 |
| 04 | BMG Paradise 04 | Reason Is Treason (10" p/s 1,000 only) | 18 |
| 04 | BMG Paradise 06 | Club Foot (Jagz Kooner mix) (12" with man-shaped hole sleeve) | 20 |
| 04 | BMG Paradise 09 | Club Foot/(Jagz Kooner Vocal Mix)/(Paradise Mix) (with poster p/s) | 8 |
| 04 | BMG Paradise 15 | L.S.F (Lost Souls Forever)/Club Foot (Live @ Cabinet War Rooms)/(Jagz Kooner Mix (Full Version) (10" poster p/s) | 12 |
| 07 | No label | Fast Fuse/Thick As Thieves (10" 200 only die-cut sleeve, stamped labels given away at Somerset House gig 2007) | 35 |
| 11 | Sony BMG 88697523092 | Days Are Forgotten/Pistols At Dawn (10") | 12 |
| 04 | BMG Paradise 18 | KASABIAN (LP, 2 x 10", embossed gatefold sleeve) | 35 |
| 06 | Paradise PARADISE 38 | EMPIRE (LP, 2x10") | 18 |
| 09 | Paradise PARADISE 59 | WEST RYDER PAUPER LUNATIC ASYLUM (LP, 2x10") | 25 |
| 11 | Paradise PARADISE 72 | VELOCIRAPTOR! (2-LP) | 25 |

## MURRAY KASH
| 68 | RCA 1767 | Sleeping Beauty/Everything's OK | 6 |

## AL KASHA
| 60 | Coral Q 72410 | Teardrops Are Falling/No Matter Where You Are | 5 |
| 60 | Coral Q72429 | Where Thete's A Will There's A Way/My Arms, My Lips, My Heart | 6 |

## KASHMERE
| 02 | Receptor RR 001 | RAW STYLES (EP) | 12 |
| 04 | Receptor RR 002 | RAW STYLES VOL 2 (EP) | 12 |
| 06 | Receptor RR 004 | Playing With Fire (12") | 10 |
| 04 | Low Life LOW 35 LP | BACKHAND SLAP TALK/TECHNICAL ILLNESS (LP, with VERB T) | 30 |
| 10 | Boot BLP 003 | GALAKTUS: POWER COSMIC (LP) | 15 |

## EDWARD KA-SPEL
| 84 | In Phaze HAZ 6 | DANCE CHINA DOLL (EP 12") | 20 |
| 84 | In Phaze PHA 6 | EYES CHINA DOLL (LP) | 25 |

## KASUALS
| 81 | KAS 101 | Mr. O/A Girl I Know | 8 |

## KATATONIA
| 96 | Misanthropy AMAZON 010 | Scarlet Heavens/PRIMORDIAL: To Enter Pagan MCMXCVI (10", p/s) | 20 |

## KATCH 22 (1)
| 84 | Mynah BBM 841 | Workshop Life/Visions Of Freedom | 12 |

## KATCH-22
| 66 | Fontana TF 768 | Major Catastrophe/Hold Me | 90 |
| 67 | Fontana TF 874 | Makin' Up My Mind/While We're Friends | 25 |
| 68 | Fontana TF 930 | The World's Gettin' Smaller/Don't Bother | 20 |
| 68 | Fontana TF 984 | Pumpkin Mini/100,000 Years | 25 |
| 69 | Fontana TF 1005 | Out Of My Life/Baby Love | 15 |
| 69 | CBS 4644 | It's The Sunshine/Mrs. Jones | 20 |
| 68 | Saga EROS 8047 | IT'S SOFT ROCK & ALLSORTS (LP, with insert, Saga inner sleeve) | 20 |

## KATCHIES
| 79 | Chart PSS 162 | Shambles/To Be A Musician | 20 |

## KATE
| 68 | CBS 3631 | Strange Girl/I Don't Make A Sound | 100 |
| 68 | CBS 3815 | Hold Me Now/Empty World | 20 |
| 69 | CBS 4123 | Shout It/Sweet Little Thing | 70 |

*(see also Viv Prince, Pretty Things)*

**KATHY**
69　Morgan MR 14　Bonjour Monsieur/Long Night................................................................5

**KATINA**
72　Cactus CT 4　Don't Stick Stickers On My Paper Knickers/Version................................6
72　Cactus CT 3　Don't Stroke My Pussy/Don't Stroke My Pussy (Version) ......................8

**KATZ (1)**
60s　Tetlow TET 118　LIVE AT THE RUM RUNNER (EP) ....................................................75

**KATZ (2)**
79　SRTS/79/CUS/533　Talkin' About You/I'm So Nasty (no p/s, 200 only) ......................250

**ARTHUR KAY'S ORIGINALS**
80　Red Admiral NYMPH 1　Ska-Wars/Warska (p/s)..........................................................8
80　Red Admiral NYMPH 2　Sooty Is A Rudie/Play My Record (p/s) ..................................10

**BARBARA KAY**
65　Columbia DB 8009　The Power And The Glory/I Wanna Walk In Your Sun ................5
65　Pye 7N 15774　That's What Angels Are For/What's The Good Of Loving ..............6
65　Pye 7N 15914　Yes I'm Ready/Someone Has To Cry ..............................................20
66　Pye 7N 15997　Chips With Everything/A Lot About Love......................................5

**JANET KAY**
77　Stonehouse SH 003　Loving You/Version ..................................................................8

**JANET K(AY)**
78　Bushays BFM 108　Silhouette (with Rico)/PRINCE JAZEBO & RICO: Silhouette Gone Clear (12") .............20

**JOHN KAY**
73　Probe PRO 601　Easy Evil/Dance To My Song ......................................................5
78　Mercury 6167 683　Give Me Some Good News I Can use/Business Is Business................5
72　Probe SPB 1054　FORGOTTEN SONGS AND UNSUNG HEROES (LP) ......................15

*(see also Steppenwolf)*

**SHIRLEY KAY**
68　Trojan TR 015　Make Me Yours/We Have Happiness ..........................................75

**KAYAK**
74　Harvest SHSP 4033　SEE SEE THE SUN (LP) ..............................................................20
74　Harvest SHSP 4036　KAYAK (LP) ..............................................................................20

**CAB KAYE**
61　Melodisc MEL 1584　Everything Is Go/Don't You Go Away ....................................5

**DAVE KAYE (& DYKONS)**
64　Decca F 11866　A Fool Such As I/It's Nice Isn't It (as Davy Kaye) ....................35
65　Decca F 12073　In My Way/All The Stars In Heaven (as Dave Kaye) ..............25
69　Major Minor MM 641　Yesterday When I Was Young/Say You Love Me (as Dave Kaye & Dykons) ..........12

**KATHIE KAY(E)**
55　HMV 7M 335　Suddenly There's A Valley/Teddy Bear................................8
56　HMV 7M 363　Jimmy Unknown/Dreams Can Tell A Lie......................10
56　HMV POP 265　A House With Love In It/To Be Sure..........................7
57　HMV POP 352　We Will Make Love/Wind In The Willow ..................8

**LINDA KAYE**
66　Columbia DB 7915　I Can't Stop Thinking About You/When We Meet Again ........25

**TONY KAYE & HEARTBEATS**
67　Pye International 7N 25412　Hey, Hey Little Orphan Annie/Dream World ................8

**KAYES**
67　Major Minor MM 515　It's No Secret/Remember Me ........................................8

*(see also Kaye Sisters)*

**KAYE SISTERS**
58　Philips PB 806　Are You Ready, Freddy?/The Pansy........................15
58　Philips PB 832　Stroll Me/Torero ........................................10
59　Philips PB 892　Jerri-Lee (I Love Him So)/Deeply Devoted................10
60　Philips PB 1024　Paper Roses/If Only You'd Be Mine (in p/s) ............5
60　Philips PB 1088　Come To Me/A Whole Lot Of Lovin' (in p/s) ............5

*(see also Three Kayes/Three Kaye Sisters, Kayes, Frankie Vaughan)*

**LAINIE KAZAN**
69　MGM MGM 1476　Window Of My Mind/It's You..........................30

**KCF & SKELLA TON**
91　Kold Sweat KS112　Taken To Heart/In Session (12").........................10

**ERNIE K-DOE**
61　London HLU 9330　Mother-In-Law/Wanted, $10,000.00 Reward ........15
61　London HLU 9390　Te-Ta-Te-Ta-Ta/Real Man ..........................20
65　Vocalion VP 9233　My Mother In Law (Is In My Hair Again)/Looking Into The Future ............20
68　Action ACT 4512　Gotta Pack My Bags/How Sweet You Are....................25

**KEANE**
00　Zoomorphic (No cat. no)　Call Me What You Like/Rubbernecking/Closer Now (CD, 500 only) ............80
01　Zoomorphic ZOO12101　Wolf At The Door/Call Me What You Like/She Has No Time (CD, 500 only p/s) ............80
04　Island IS 880　This Is The Last Time/She Opens Here Eyes ............5
04　Island CID849　Somewhere Only We Know/Snowed Under (numbered, p/s) ............5
04　Universal IS 870　Bedshaped/Something Inside Me Was Dying ..............5
05　Island KEANE2　The Sun Ain't Gonna Shine Anymore/Your Eyes Open (Fan club issue 1000 only p/s) .... 40
06　Island (no cat no)　Nothing In My Way (512MB memory stick, 1500 only, numbered in title sleeve) ..........20
06　Universal KEANEBX1　Is it Any Wonder? Fan club box set 2 x 7" with Is It Any Wonder/Let It Slide (IS 934)
　　with art print and 1-sided Atlantic (ATLANTIC001), 2,500 copies)............15
06　Universal IS 934　Is It Any Wonder?/Let It Slide (with art print) ............5
06　Island 1704804　Crtstal Ball/Maybe I Can Change (with art print) ..........5

MINT VALUE £

| | | | |
|---|---|---|---|
| 06 | Island 1723054 | A Bad Dream (512MN memory stick, numbered in title sleeve) | 20 |
| 06 | Island KEANEBX1 | Atlantic (single sided 7" in box) | 15 |
| 07 | Island 1723058 | A Bad Dream/She Sells Sanctuary (with fold-out sleeve, numbered) | 12 |
| 07 | Universal 1751091 | The Night Sky/Put It Behind You (Ffrisco Mix) (with art print) | 5 |
| 08 | Universal PSBOX1 | Spiralling (1-sided 7" in box, 2,000 only, numbered) | 20 |
| 04 | Island ILPS 8145 | HOPES AND FEARS (LP, 1000 only) | 120 |
| 04 | Island (no cat no) | HOPES AND FEARS (CD promo, 200 only) | 120 |
| 04 | Island (no cat no) | HOPES AND FEARS (DVD sampler, jewel case, promo) | 30 |
| 05 | Island | SINGLES BOX SET (1000 only, 5x7" from HOPES AND FEARS LP) | 120 |
| 06 | Island (no cat no) | THE VIDEOS (Fan club issue only) | 50 |
| 06 | Island ILPS 8167 | UNDER THE IRON SEA (2-LP) | 70 |
| 08 | Island 1785966 | PERFECT SYMMETRY (LP) | 30 |

### SHAKE KEANE

| | | | |
|---|---|---|---|
| 55 | HMV 7MC 38 | Akinla/Fire, Fire (export issue) | 15 |
| 62 | Columbia SEG 8140 | IN MY CONDITION (EP) | 40 |
| 64 | Airborne MBP 002 | A CASE OF JAZZ (EP, as Shake Keane and Michael Garrick Quartette, 99 copies only) | 150 |
| 65 | Decca SKL 4720 | SHAKE KEANE WITH THE KEATING SOUND (LP) | 20 |
| 66 | Ace Of Clubs ACL 1219 | THAT'S THE NOISE (LP) | 25 |
| 69 | Phase 4 Stereo PFS 4154 | DIG IT (LP, with Ivor Raymonde Orchestra) | 40 |
| 70 | Pama SECO 30 | RISING STARS AT EVENING TIME (LP with Gordon Langford and Hastings Girl Choir) | 30 |

*(see also Marie Bryant, Michael Garrick)*

### JOHNNY KEATING ORCHESTRA

| | | | |
|---|---|---|---|
| 62 | Piccadilly 7N 35033 | Theme From Z Cars/Lost Patrol | 5 |
| 63 | Picadilly 7N 35113 | The Preacher/Whoop Up (with the Z men) | 10 |
| 57 | Oriole MG 20011 | BRITISH JAZZ (LP) | 60 |
| 58 | London LTZ-15122 | SWINGIN' SCOTS (LP) | 25 |
| 64 | Ace Of Clubs ACL 1160 | SIXTEEN HITS FOR YOUR DANCE PARTY (LP) | 20 |
| 64 | Decca PFS 4038 | SWING REVISITED (LP) | 25 |
| 64 | Decca PFS 4078 | STRAIGHT AHEAD (LP) | 30 |
| 72 | Studio Two TWO 393 | SPACE EXPERIENCE (LP) | 15 |
| 72 | Studio Two Q4 TWO 393 | SPACE EXPERIENCE (LP, quadrophonic) | 25 |
| 75 | Studio Two TWOX 1044 | SPACE EXPERIENCE 2 (LP) | 15 |

### KEEFERS KIDS

| | | | |
|---|---|---|---|
| 67 | King KG 1068 | Millions Of Hearts/KEEFERS: Lonely Hill | 5 |

### YVONNE KEELEY

| | | | |
|---|---|---|---|
| 74 | EMI 2206 | Tumbling Down/Loretta's Theme | 7 |

### KEEN

| | | | |
|---|---|---|---|
| 90 | Scaredy Cat PUR 003 | FELINE GROOVY EP (12") | 30 |

### JEFF KEEN

| | | | |
|---|---|---|---|
| 12 | Trunk JBH 047 LP | NOISE ART (LP, 500 only silkscreened sleeves. 100 black sleeve/clear vinyl, 100 red sleeve/red and clear vinyl, 100 yellow sleeve/clear/red/yellow vinyl, 100 blue sleeve/clear/red/yellow and 100 blue vinyl and silver sleeve with clear/red/yellow/blue and silver vinyl) | 20 |

### JOHN KEEN

| | | | |
|---|---|---|---|
| 72 | Track 2094 103 | Old Fashioned Girl/That's The Way It Is | 8 |
| 73 | Track 2094 108 | Let Us In/Keep On The Grass | 8 |

*(see also Speedy Keen, Thunderclap Newman)*

### SPEEDY KEEN

| | | | |
|---|---|---|---|
| 71 | Track 2406 105 | PREVIOUS CONVICTIONS (LP) | 15 |

*(see also John Keen, Thunderclap Newman)*

### MARION KEENE

| | | | |
|---|---|---|---|
| 56 | HMV 7M 395 | Fortune Teller/A Dangerous Age | 7 |
| 57 | HMV POP 375 | In The Middle Of An Island/It's Not For Me To Say | 6 |

### NELSON KEENE

| | | | |
|---|---|---|---|
| 60 | HMV POP 771 | Image Of A Girl/Ocean Of Love | 15 |
| 60 | HMV POP 814 | Keep Loving Me/Teenage Troubles | 15 |
| 61 | HMV POP 916 | Miracles Are Happening To Me/Poor Little Rich Boy | 15 |

*(see also Guv'ners)*

### REX KEENE

| | | | |
|---|---|---|---|
| 56 | Columbia DB 3831 | Rebel In Town/Happy Texas Ranger | 10 |

### KEETH

| | | | |
|---|---|---|---|
| 77 | SMR 018 | SPEEDWAY EP | 10 |

### KEETY ROOTS

| | | | |
|---|---|---|---|
| 94 | Black Legacy BL 003 | African Blood/TENASTELIN: Spirit of | 80 |

### ACE KEFFORD STAND

| | | | |
|---|---|---|---|
| 69 | Atlantic 584 260 | For Your Love/Gravy Booby Jam (small centre hole) | 50 |
| 69 | Atlantic 584 260 | For Your Love/Gravy Booby Jam (large centre hole) | 40 |

*(see also Move, Cozy Powell, Young Blood, Big Bertha, Bedlam, Carl Wayne)*

### KEITH

| | | | |
|---|---|---|---|
| 66 | Mercury MF 940 | Ain't Gonna Lie/It Started All Over Again | 8 |
| 67 | Mercury MF 955 | 98.6/The Teeny Bopper Song | 10 |
| 67 | Mercury MF 968 | Tell Me To My Face/I Can't Go Wrong | 10 |
| 67 | Mercury MF 989 | Daylight Savin' Time/Happy Walking Around | 15 |
| 67 | Mercury MF 1002 | Sugar Man/Easy As Pie (in p/s) | 12 |
| 67 | Mercury MF 1002 | Sugar Man/Easy As Pie | 6 |
| 67 | Mercury MCL 20103 | 98.6/AIN'T GONNA LIE (LP) | 30 |

### BRIAN KEITH

| | | | |
|---|---|---|---|
| 68 | Page One POF 072 | The Shelter Of Your Arms/C'est La Vie | 5 |

| | | | |
|---|---|---|---|
| 68 | Page One POF 103 | When The First Tear Shows/When My Baby Smiles At Me | 5 |
| 69 | Page One POF 152 | Till We Meet Again/Lady Butterfly | 5 |

*(see also Plastic Penny)*

**BRYAN KEITH**
| 63 | London HLU 9707 | Sad Sad Song/Mean Woman | 20 |
|---|---|---|---|

**RON KEITH**
| 76 | A&M AMS 7217 | Party Music/Gotta Go By What You Tell Me | 90 |
|---|---|---|---|

**KEITH (STEWART) & ENID (CUMBERLAND)**
| 60 | Blue Beat BB 6 | Worried Over You/Everything Will Be Alright | 10 |
|---|---|---|---|
| 60 | Blue Beat BB 11 | Send Me/TRENTON SPENCE GROUP: People Will Say We're In Love | 10 |
| 61 | Starlite ST45 047 | Never Leave My Throne/Only A Pity (as Keith & Enid with Caribs) | 12 |
| 61 | Starlite ST45 067 | You're Gonna Break My Heart/What Have I Done | 12 |
| 62 | Blue Beat BB 125 | When It's Spring/True Love (with Sonny Bradshaw Orchestra) | 10 |
| 63 | Dice CC 14 | Sacred Vow/My Dreams | 8 |
| 63 | Dice CC 20 | Just A Closer Walk/Don't Yield To Temptation | 8 |
| 64 | Black Swan WI 429 | Lost My Love/I Cried | 10 |
| 63 | Island ILP 901 | KEITH & ENID SING (LP) | 50 |
| 70 | Trojan TTL 37 | KEITH & ENID SING (LP, reissue) | 20 |

**KEITH (POPPIN) & IMPACT ALL STARS**
| 71 | Randy's RAN 515 | Down By The Riverside/IMPACT ALL STARS: Version Two | 6 |
|---|---|---|---|

**KEITH (LYN) & KEN (LAZARUS)**
| 65 | London HA-R/SH-R 8229 | YOU'LL LOVE JAMAICA (LP) | 40 |
|---|---|---|---|

**KEITH (ROWE) & TEX (DIXON)**
| 67 | Island WI 3085 | Tonight/LYN TAIT & JETS: You Have Caught Me | 175 |
|---|---|---|---|
| 68 | Island WI 3091 | Stop That Train/BOBBY ELLIS: Feeling Peckish (with Desmond Miles Seven) | 175 |
| 68 | Island WI 3137 | Hypnotizing Eyes/Lonely Man | 150 |
| 70 | Explosion EX 2008 | Tighten Up Your Gird/Look To The Sky | 40 |

**KEITHY**
| 77 | Xamayca XAD 002 | Struggling In A Babylon (with Imperial Hudson)/XAMAYCA BAND: Togetherness | 25 |
|---|---|---|---|

**ROGER KELLAWAY**
| 67 | Liberty LBS 583061E | SPIRIT FEEL (LP) | 25 |
|---|---|---|---|

**JERRY KELLER**
| 59 | London HLR 8890 | Here Comes Summer/Time Has A Way (triangular centre) | 10 |
|---|---|---|---|
| 59 | London HLR 8890 | Here Comes Summer/Time Has A Way (round centre) | 5 |
| 59 | London HLR 8980 | If I Had A Girl/Lovable | 5 |
| 60 | London HLR 9106 | Now, Now, Now/Lonesome Lullaby | 7 |
| 60 | London HA-R 2261 | HERE COMES JERRY KELLER (LP, mono) | 35 |
| 60 | London SAH-R 6083 | HERE COMES JERRY KELLER (LP, stereo) | 40 |

**PAT KELL(E)Y**
| 68 | Giant GN 37 | Little Boy Blue/You Are Not Mine (as Pat Kelley & Uniques) | 80 |
|---|---|---|---|
| 68 | Island WI 3121 | Somebodies Baby (as Pat Kelly)/BEVERLY SIMMONS: Please Don't Leave Me | 45 |
| 69 | Gas GAS 110 | The Workman Song/Never Give Up (as Pat Kelly) | 10 |
| 69 | Gas GAS 115 | How Long/Try To Remember (as Pat Kelly) | 20 |
| 69 | Gas GAS 124 | Festival Time (Parts 1 & 2) (as Pat Kelly) | 20 |
| 69 | Gas GAS 125 | If It Don't Work Out/I Am Coming Home (as Pat Kelley) | 8 |
| 70 | Gas GAS 144 | Tammy/I Am Not Your Guy (as Pat Kelley) | 15 |
| 70 | Gas GAS 145 | Striving For The Right/When A Boy Fall In Love (as Pat Kelley) | 15 |
| 70 | Gas GAS 157 | I Just Don't Know What To Do With Myself/What's He Got That I Ain't Got (B-side actually titled 'Lorna') (as Pat Kelley) | 8 |
| 70 | Jackpot JP 734 | I Just Don't Know What To Do With Myself/Lorna (as Pat Kelley) | 8 |
| 71 | Camel CA 65 | Talk About Love (as Pat Kelley)/PHIL PRATT ALL STARS: Version | 15 |
| 71 | Gas GAS 171 | Love/With All Your Heart (as Pat Kelley) | 6 |
| 71 | Punch PH 88 | Soulful Love (as Pat Kelly)/HUGH ROY & PARAGONS: One For All | 10 |
| 72 | Pama Supreme PS 353 | I'm Gonna Give Her All The Love I've Got (as Pat Kelly)/ MAYTONES: As Long As You Love Me | 8 |
| 73 | Pama Supreme PS 379 | Twelfth Of Never (as Pat Kelley)/JERRY LEWIS: 5000 Watts | 6 |
| 73 | Pama Supreme PS 384 | I Wish It Could Rain (as Pat Kelly)/PAT KELLY SINGERS: Hallelujah | 6 |
| 75 | Black Wax WAX 1 | Sunshine/Sunshine Version | 8 |
| 77 | Rainbow Stepper RK 231 | Carefree Girl/Version | 60 |
| 69 | Pama PMLP 12 | PAT KELLEY SINGS (LP) | 60 |
| 71 | Pama PMP 2013 | COOL BREEZING (LP) | 25 |
| 77 | Burning Rockers BR 007LP | SO PROUD (LP) | 20 |
| 78 | Burning Sounds BS1001 | LONELY MAN (LP) | 25 |
| 78 | KG Imperial KGLP 001 | TALK ABOUT LOVE (LP) | 30 |

**PETER KELLEY**
| 69 | London HAK 8402 | PATH OF THE WAVE (LP) | 40 |
|---|---|---|---|
| 71 | Polydor 2310 119 | DEALIN' BLUES (LP) | 25 |

**MURRAY KELLUM**
| 64 | London HLU 9830 | Long Tall Texan/GLEN SUTTON: I Gotta Leave This Town | 15 |
|---|---|---|---|

**KELLY**
| 66 | RCA RCA 1507 | Be My Man/Here Comes My Baby | 6 |
|---|---|---|---|
| 69 | Deram DM 277 | Mary Mary/Reverend Richard Baily | 30 |

**CHARLIE KELLY**
| 68 | Island WI 3155 | So Nice Like Rice/STRANGER & GLADDY: Over Again | 25 |
|---|---|---|---|

**CHRIS KELLY**
| 71 | CBS 7331 | Red Bird/Sweet Albuquerque | 7 |
|---|---|---|---|

**DAVE KELLY**
| 69 | Mercury 20151 SMCL | KEEPS IT IN THE FAMILY (LP, laminated sleeve, black/silver labels) | 200 |
|---|---|---|---|

MINT VALUE £

| | | | |
|---|---|---|---|
| 71 | Mercury 6310 001 | DAVE KELLY (LP, with Jo-Ann Kelly & Brunning-Hall Sunflower Band) | 250 |

*(see also John Dummer Blues Band, Brunning-Hall Sunflower Blues Band)*

## DAVID WILLIAM KELLY
| | | | |
|---|---|---|---|
| 83 | Ethereal ETH 1 | Heart Of Hearts/Chemistry Of Mind (no p/s) | 50 |

## FRANK KELLY & HUNTERS
| | | | |
|---|---|---|---|
| 62 | Fontana 267 242 TF | Send Me The Pillow That You Dream On/'Cept Me | 7 |
| 63 | Fontana 267 261 TF | I Saw Linda Yesterday/Good And True | 10 |
| 63 | Fontana 267 277 TF | What Do You Wanna Do/She Loves Me So | 8 |
| 64 | Fontana TF 454 | Some Other Time/Why Baby Why | 8 |

## GENE KELLY
| | | | |
|---|---|---|---|
| 53 | MGM SP 1012 | Singin' In The Rain/All I Do Is Dream Of You | 8 |
| 53 | MGM SP 1015 | 'S Wonderful (with Georges Guetary)/I Got Rhythm (with Children's Choir) | 7 |

## JO-ANN KELLY
| | | | |
|---|---|---|---|
| 64 | GW EP 1 | BLUES AND GOSPEL (EP, live at the Bridge House Club) | 150 |
| 66 | Harlequin HAL 1/HW 349 | NEW SOUNDS IN FOLK (LP, with other artists) | 80 |
| 69 | CBS 63841 | JO-ANN KELLY (LP, laminated front sleeve) | 200 |
| 76 | Red Rag RRR 006 | DO IT (LP, with Peter Emery) | 35 |

*(see also Chilli Willi & Red Hot Peppers, Dave Kelly, Tramp)*

## JO-ANN KELLY & TONY MCPHEE
| | | | |
|---|---|---|---|
| 72 | Sunset SLS 50209 | THE SAME THING ON THEIR MINDS (LP) | 30 |

*(see also Tony McPhee, Dave Kelly)*

## JONATHAN KELLY
| | | | |
|---|---|---|---|
| 69 | Parlophone R 5805 | Denver/Son John | 6 |
| 70 | Parlophone R 5830 | Make A Stranger Your Friend/Daddy Don't Take Me Down Fishing No More | 8 |
| 70 | Parlophone R 5851 | Don't You Believe It?/Billy (Eric Clapton on guitar) | 40 |
| 70 | Parlophone PCS 7114 | JONATHAN KELLY (LP, black/silver labels with boxed logo) | 100 |
| 72 | RCA SF 8262 | TWICE AROUND THE HOUSES (LP, laminated cover) | 20 |
| 73 | RCA SF 8353 | WAIT TILL THEY CHANGE THE BACKDROP (LP, gatefold sleeve) | 20 |

*(see also John Ledingham, Humpty Bong, Boomerang)*

## KEITH KELLY
| | | | |
|---|---|---|---|
| 60 | Parlophone R 4640 | (Must You Always) Tease Me/Ooh-La-La | 25 |
| 60 | Parlophone R 4676 | Listen Little Girl/Uh-Huh | 30 |
| 60 | Parlophone R 4713 | With You/You'll Break My Heart | 20 |
| 61 | Parlophone R 4797 | Cold White And Beautiful/When You First Fall In Love | 20 |
| 65 | CBS 201794 | Laurie/Save Your Love For Me | 10 |

## PAUL KELLY
| | | | |
|---|---|---|---|
| 65 | Atlantic AT 4053 | Chills And Fever/Only Your Love | 45 |
| 67 | Philips BF 1591 | Sweet Sweet Lovin'/Cryin' For My Baby | 25 |
| 72 | Atlantic K 10272 | Chills And Fever/Only Your Love (reissue) | 10 |

## PETE KELLY'S SOULUTION
| | | | |
|---|---|---|---|
| 68 | Decca F 12755 | Midnight Confessions/If Your Love Don't Swing | 30 |
| 68 | Decca F 22829 | Midnight Confessions/BERNIE & BUZZ BAND: The House That Jack Built (export issue) | 20 |

*(see also Bernie & Buzz Band, Rhythm & Blues Inc.)*

## PETER D KELLY
| | | | |
|---|---|---|---|
| 74 | DJM DJS 333 | Rock To The Juke Box/Brotherhood Within (promo p/s) | 10 |
| 74 | DJM DJS 333 | Rock To The Juke Box/Brotherhood Within | 6 |

## SALLY KELLY
| | | | |
|---|---|---|---|
| 59 | Decca F 11175 | Little Cutie/Come Back To Me | 12 |
| 60 | Decca F 11238 | He'll Have To Stay/Honey That's Alright | 7 |

## SEYMOUR KELLY
| | | | |
|---|---|---|---|
| 68 | Columbia DB8445 | Indian Scene/Worlds Apart | 15 |

## TABBY CAT KELLY
| | | | |
|---|---|---|---|
| 78 | Arawak ARK DD005 | Don't Call Us Immigrants/Version | 20 |

## WYNTON KELLY TRIO
| | | | |
|---|---|---|---|
| 65 | Verve VLP 9103 | UNDILUTED (LP) | 15 |

## KELLY BROTHERS
| | | | |
|---|---|---|---|
| 67 | Sue WI 4034 | Falling In Love Again/Crying Days Are Over | 150 |
| 68 | President PT 143 | You Put Your Touch On Me/Hanging In There | 25 |
| 70 | Blue Horizon 57-3177 | That's What You Mean To Me/Comin' On In | 30 |
| 68 | President PTL 1019 | SWEET SOUL (LP) | 100 |

## KELV
| | | | |
|---|---|---|---|
| 81 | Axis Industries AXLP1 | ATTACKING VESSELS (LP, 250 only, insert) | 18 |

## WAYNE KEMP
| | | | |
|---|---|---|---|
| 66 | Atlantic 584 006 | Watch That First Step/Little Home Wrecker | 12 |

## KEMPION
| | | | |
|---|---|---|---|
| 77 | Broadside BRO 123 | KEMPION (LP) | 18 |
| 77 | Sweet Folk & C. SFA 044 | CAM YE O'ER FRAE FRANCE (LP) | 15 |

## BOB KEN
| | | | |
|---|---|---|---|
| 80 | Square S2SP | Keep Me Warm This Winter/More Than Life | 6 |

## KEN & NEW ESTABLISHMENT
| | | | |
|---|---|---|---|
| 73 | Fab FAB 264 | Soul Mood/Golden Locks | 10 |

## KEN & STEPPING TONY
| | | | |
|---|---|---|---|
| 78 | Rama RMD 005 | Sticks Man Affair/ROCKA & DAVE & GIRL WONDER: Skip-A Dip (12") | 30 |

## JOHNNY KENDALL & HERALDS
| | | | |
|---|---|---|---|
| 64 | RCA RCA 1416 | St. James Infirmary/Little Girl | 10 |

**KENDALL SISTERS**
| | | | |
|---|---|---|---|
| 58 | London HLM 8622 | Won't You Be My Baby/Yea, Yea | 30 |
| 58 | London HLM 8622 | Won't You Be My Baby/Yea, Yea (78) | 20 |

**LINDA KENDRICK**
| | | | |
|---|---|---|---|
| 66 | Polydor 56076 | It's The Little Things/When Your Love Is Warm | 30 |
| 66 | Polydor 56076 | It's The Little Things/When Your Love Is Warm (DJ copy) | 50 |
| 69 | Philips BF 1750 | I Will See You There/Inside My Heart | 8 |
| 69 | Philips BF 1816 | Hold On/Fa La La La La La Le | 8 |
| 71 | Philips 6006-078 | Generation (Light Up The Sky)/Come With The Beautiful People | 25 |
| 70 | Philips SBL 7921 | LINDA KENDRICK (LP) | 15 |

**NAT KENDRICK & SWANS**
| | | | |
|---|---|---|---|
| 60 | Top Rank JAR 351 | (Do The) Mashed Potatoes Parts 1 & 2 | 30 |
| 60 | Top Rank JAR 387 | Dish Rag Parts 1 & 2 | 20 |

*(see also James Brown)*

**LORETTA KENDRICK**
| | | | |
|---|---|---|---|
| 01 | Hayley HR004 | Neither One Of Us/My Feelings Keep Getting In The Way | 12 |

**EDDIE KENDRICKS**
| | | | |
|---|---|---|---|
| 73 | Tamla Motown TMG 916 | Girl You Need A Change Of Mind Part 1/Part 2 | 8 |

**KENICKIE**
| | | | |
|---|---|---|---|
| 95 | Slampt U.O. SLAMPT 1 | CATSUIT CITY (EP) | 12 |

**CALUM KENNEDY**
| | | | |
|---|---|---|---|
| 62 | Ember EMB 5167 | The Celtic Chorus/Danny Boy | 25 |

**CHERYL KENNEDY**
| | | | |
|---|---|---|---|
| 67 | Columbia DB 8271 | Thoroughly Modern Millie/Cradle Song | 5 |
| 68 | Columbia DB 8347 | Love Is Blue/I Could Be Happy With You | 6 |

**DOUG KENNEDY**
| | | | |
|---|---|---|---|
| 65 | Columbia DB 7707 | Julie/Jailbreak Man | 5 |

**GENE KENNEDY**
| | | | |
|---|---|---|---|
| 65 | Hickory 45-1314 | You Better Take Home/Stand In Line | 5 |

**JOHN F. KENNEDY**
| | | | |
|---|---|---|---|
| 64 | Stateside SL 10064 | THE PRESIDENTIAL YEARS 1960-1963 (LP) | 15 |

**LOU KENNEDY**
| | | | |
|---|---|---|---|
| 55 | Columbia SCM 5198 | Stars Shine In Your Eyes/The Kentuckian Song | 10 |
| 56 | Columbia SCM 5216 | Whisper/Sincerely Yours | 10 |

**MIKE KENNEDY**
| | | | |
|---|---|---|---|
| 69 | Major Minor MM 614 | I'll Never Forget/I'll Never Get You | 6 |
| 69 | Major Minor MM 629 | Johnny Rebel/Golden Memories | 6 |
| 72 | Youngblood YB 1035 | Louisiana/Look Up In The Sky | 20 |

**CHRIS KENNER**
| | | | |
|---|---|---|---|
| 61 | London HLU 9410 | I Like It Like That Parts 1 & 2 | 35 |
| 65 | Sue WI 351 | Land Of 1,000 Dances/That's My Girl | 35 |
| 66 | Atlantic 587 008 | LAND OF 1000 DANCES (LP) | 40 |

**TONY KENNY & SANDS SHOWBAND**
| | | | |
|---|---|---|---|
| 67 | Major Minor MM 555 | Help Me Rhonda/Some Enchanted Evening | 5 |
| 68 | Major Minor MM 573 | Yummy Yummy Yummy/Peanuts | 5 |
| 71 | Hit HIT 1 | Knock Three Times/See You In September | 5 |

*(see also Sands)*

**KENNY (EVERETT) & (DAVE) CASH**
| | | | |
|---|---|---|---|
| 65 | Decca F 12283 | Knees/The B Side | 6 |

**KENNY & DENY**
| | | | |
|---|---|---|---|
| 65 | Decca F 12138 | Try To Forget Me/Little Surfer Girl | 70 |

*(see also Jimmy Page, Tony Rivers & The Castaways, Harmony Grass, Capability Brown)*

**KENNY & WRANGLERS**
| | | | |
|---|---|---|---|
| 64 | Parlophone R 5224 | Somebody Help Me/Who Do You Think I Am? | 25 |
| 65 | Parlophone R 5275 | Doobie Doo/Moonshine | 25 |

*(see also Kenny Bernard & Wranglers)*

**JERRI BO KENO**
| | | | |
|---|---|---|---|
| 75 | Phil Spector Intl. 2010 001 | Here It Comes (And Here I Go)/I Don't Know Why | 20 |

**AL KENT**
| | | | |
|---|---|---|---|
| 67 | Track 604 016 | You Got To Pay The Price/Where Do I Go From Here | 50 |
| 71 | Mojo 2092 015 | You Got To Pay The Price/Where Do I Go From Here (unissued) | 0 |

**BILL KENT**
| | | | |
|---|---|---|---|
| 58 | Decca F 10975 | The Prettiest Girl In School/Hasty Words | 5 |
| 58 | Decca F 10997 | Oh-Oh, I'm Falling In Love/In Love | 5 |

**CINDY KENT**
| | | | |
|---|---|---|---|
| 73 | York FYK 418 | I AM YOUR SERVANT (LP) | 125 |

**DAVE KENT**
| | | | |
|---|---|---|---|
| 88 | SRT/RANA SRT 8KS 1795 RANA 001 | Out Of My Mind/I Will Be A Stranger | 10 |

**ENOCH KENT**
| | | | |
|---|---|---|---|
| 59 | Top Rank JAR 238 | The Ballad Of Johnny Ramensky/The Bonny Lass Of Fyvie | 5 |
| 60 | Top Rank JAR 386 | The Smashing Of The Van/Sean South Of Garryowen | 5 |
| 62 | Topic TOP 81 | SINGS THE BUTCHER BOY AND OTHER BALLADS (EP) | 10 |

**KLARK KENT**
| | | | |
|---|---|---|---|
| 78 | Kryptone KK 1 | Don't Care/Office Girls/Thrills (p/s, green vinyl) | 5 |
| 78 | Kryptone KK 1 | Don't Care/Office Girls/Thrills (p/s, black vinyl) | 8 |
| 78 | A&M AMS 7376 | Don't Care/Office Girls/Thrills (p/s or die-cut sleeve, black vinyl) | 20 |

MINT VALUE £

| | | |
|---|---|---|
| 78 | Kryptone KMS 7390 | Too Kool To Kalypso/Theme For Kinetic Ritual (p/s, green vinyl) ........... 5 |

*(see also Police)*

**MARY KENT**

| | | |
|---|---|---|
| 69 | CBS 4510 | Lost Generation/Gentle Moments .......... 10 |

**PAUL KENT**

| | | |
|---|---|---|
| 71 | B&C CB 165 | Do You/Helpless Harry .......... 6 |
| 70 | RCA SF 8083 | P.C. KENT (LP) .......... 60 |
| 71 | B&C CAS 1044 | PAUL KENT (LP) .......... 50 |

**RICHARD KENT STYLE**

| | | |
|---|---|---|
| 66 | Columbia DB 7964 | No Matter What You Do/Go, Go Children .......... 200 |
| 66 | Columbia DB 8051 | You Can't Put Me Down/All Good Things .......... 150 |
| 67 | Columbia DB 8182 | Marching Off To War/I'm Out .......... 120 |
| 68 | MCA MU 1032 | Love Will Shake The World Awake/Crocodile Tears .......... 40 |
| 69 | Mercury MF 1090 | A Little Bit O' Soul/Don't Tell Lies .......... 40 |

**SHIRLEY KENT**

| | | |
|---|---|---|
| 80 | Tadpole TAD 001 | My Dad/Marianne .......... 6 |
| 66 | Keele University 103 | THE MASTER SINGERS AND SHIRLEY KENT SING FOR CHAREC 67 (EP) .......... 35 |

*(see also Ghost, Virginia Tree)*

**SONIA KENT**

| | | |
|---|---|---|
| 66 | Parlophone R 5401 | This Is My Wonderful Day/Somebody Must Care .......... 7 |

*(see also Diamond Twins)*

**KENT (BROWN) & DIMPLE (HINDS)**

| | | |
|---|---|---|
| 63 | Island WI 046 | Day Is Done/Linger A While .......... 20 |

**KENT (BROWN) & JEANNIE WITH CITY SLICKERS**

| | | |
|---|---|---|
| 62 | Blue Beat BB 98 | Daddy/Hello Love .......... 20 |

*(see also Kent Brown & Rainbows)*

**RIK KENTON**

| | | |
|---|---|---|
| 74 | Island WIP 6214 | Bungalow Love/Lay It On You (no p/s) .......... 5 |
| 76 | EMI EMI 2443 | The Libertine/Messin' Round .......... 6 |

*(see also Woody Kern, Roxy Music)*

**KEN-TONES**

| | | |
|---|---|---|
| 56 | Parlophone MSP 6229 | Get With It/In Port Afrique .......... 12 |
| 57 | Parlophone R 4257 | I Saw Esau/Yaller, Yaller Gold .......... 8 |

*(see also Benny Lee)*

**KENTUCKY BOYS**

| | | |
|---|---|---|
| 55 | HMV 7M 312 | Don't Fetch It/A Little Fella Like Me .......... 12 |

**KENTUCKY COLONELS**

| | | |
|---|---|---|
| 74 | United Artists UAS 29514 | THE KENTUCKY COLONELS (LP) .......... 18 |

*(see also Byrds)*

**BILL KENWRIGHT (& RUNAWAYS)**

| | | |
|---|---|---|
| 67 | Columbia DB 8239 | I Want To Go Back There Again/Walk Through Dreams (with Runaways) .......... 10 |
| 68 | MGM MGM 1430 | Giving Up/Love's Black And White (solo) .......... 6 |
| 69 | MGM MGM 1463 | Tiggy/House That Fell On Its Face .......... 5 |
| 69 | MGM MGM 1478 | Baby I Could Be So Good At Loving You/A Boy And A Girl .......... 6 |
| 69 | Fontana TF 1065 | Sugar Man/Epitaph (When Times Were Good) .......... 6 |

**PATRICK KERR**

| | | |
|---|---|---|
| 65 | Decca F 12069 | Magic Potion/It's No Trouble To Love You .......... 30 |

**RICHARD KERR**

| | | |
|---|---|---|
| 66 | Decca F12478 | Concrete Jungle/You Got Nothing To Loose .......... 12 |
| 66 | Decca F12538 | Hard Lovin'/Auntie's Insurance Policy .......... 15 |
| 67 | Deram DM 138 | Happy Birthday Blues/Mother's Blue-Eyed Angel .......... 20 |
| 69 | RCA RCA 1785 | Colour My World/For The Rest Of My Life .......... 5 |
| 75 | Epic SEPC 3662 | Somewhere In The Night/In The End .......... 5 |
| 73 | Warner Bros K 46206 | FROM NOW UNTIL THEN (LP, laminated cover, foldout lyric insert) .......... 15 |

**JOHN KERRUISH**

| | | |
|---|---|---|
| 70 | A&M AMS 604 | Time To Wander/Today, Tonight And Tomorrow Morning .......... 70 |

**CHRIS KERRY**

| | | |
|---|---|---|
| 65 | Mercury MF 957 | Seven Deadly Sins/The Place .......... 15 |
| 66 | Mercury MF 985 | Watermelon Man/I've Got My Pride .......... 25 |

**DOUG KERSHAW**

| | | |
|---|---|---|
| 69 | Warner Bros WB 7304 | Feed It To The Fish/You Fight Your Fight (I'll Fight Mine) .......... 8 |
| 70 | Warner Bros WB 7413 | Orange Blossom Special/Swamp Rat .......... 6 |

*(see also Rusty & Doug)*

**KEN KESEY**

| | | |
|---|---|---|
| 83 | Psycho PSYCHO 4 | THE ACID TEST (LP, 300 only) .......... 30 |

**BARNEY KESSEL**

| | | |
|---|---|---|
| 69 | Polydor 56765 | Frank Mills/Quail Bait .......... 5 |
| 54 | Vogue LDE 085 | BARNEY KESSEL (10" LP) .......... 20 |
| 55 | Contemporary LDC 153 | BARNEY KESSEL VOLUME 2 (10" LP) .......... 20 |
| 77 | Phil Spector Intl. 2307 011 | SLOW BURN (LP) .......... 15 |

*(see also Rick Nelson)*

**LARRY KESSLER**

| | | |
|---|---|---|
| 96 | Lissey's LISS 5S | Radar Eyes/Godz Mix (p/s) .......... 10 |

**KESTREL**

| | | |
|---|---|---|
| 75 | Cube HIFLY 19 | KESTREL (LP) .......... 300 |

*(see also Spiders From Mars)*

## KESTRELS

| | | | |
|---|---|---|---|
| 59 | Pye 7N 15234 | There Comes A Time/In The Chapel In The Moonlight | 10 |
| 60 | Pye 7N 15248 | I Can't Say Goodbye/We Were Wrong | 8 |
| 61 | Decca F 11391 | All These Things/That's It | 8 |
| 62 | Piccadilly 7N 35056 | Wolverton Mountain/Little Sacka Sugar | 8 |
| 62 | Piccadilly 7N 35079 | Don't Want To Cry/Love Me With All Your Heart | 8 |
| 63 | Piccadilly 7N 35104 | Walk Right In/Moving Up The King's Highway | 8 |
| 63 | Piccadilly 7N 35126 | There's A Place/Little Star | 8 |
| 63 | Piccadilly 7N 35144 | Love Me With All Your Heart/Lazy River | 6 |
| 60s | Donegal MAU 500 | THE KESTRELS (EP) | 20 |
| 63 | Piccadilly NPL 38009 | SMASH HITS (LP) | 30 |

*(see also Ivy League, Flowerpot Men, White Plains)*

## JACK KETCH & CROWMEN
| | | | |
|---|---|---|---|
| 87 | Hangmen HANG 19 UP | BRIMFULL OF HATE (LP) | 35 |

## KEY CHAINS
| | | | |
|---|---|---|---|
| 66 | London HLU 10055 | Morgan's Song/Scruggs | 5 |

## KEYBOARD
| | | | |
|---|---|---|---|
| 75 | Eyelett EYE 4 | Will You Shut Up/Move On | 20 |

## EBONY KEYES
| | | | |
|---|---|---|---|
| 66 | Piccadilly 7N 35358 | Sitting In The Ring/If You Knew | 100 |
| 67 | Piccadilly 7N 35375 | Cupid's House/If Our Love Should End | 10 |
| 67 | Piccadilly 7N 35390 | Country Girl/How Many Times | 10 |
| 67 | Piccadilly 7N 35407 | Don't/Sweet Mary (Sweeter Than A Rose) | 12 |

## KAROL KEYES
| | | | |
|---|---|---|---|
| 64 | Fontana TF 517 | You Beat Me To The Punch/No-One Can Take Your Place (in p/s) | 30 |
| 64 | Fontana TF 517 | You Beat Me To The Punch/No-One Can Take Your Place | 20 |
| 66 | Columbia DB 7899 | A Fool In Love/The Good Love, The Bad Love | 20 |
| 66 | Columbia DB 8001 | One In A Million/Don't Jump | 75 |
| 67 | Fontana TF 846 | Can't You Hear The Music/The Sweetest Touch | 12 |

*(see also Volunteers)*

## TROY KEYES
| | | | |
|---|---|---|---|
| 68 | Stateside SS 2087 | Love Explosions/I'm Crying (Inside) | 22 |
| 69 | Stateside SS 2149 | Love Explosions/I'm Crying (Inside) (reissue) | 10 |

## KEY LARGO
| | | | |
|---|---|---|---|
| 71 | Blue Horizon 57-3178 | Voodoo Rhythm/As The Years Go Passing By | 20 |
| 70 | Blue Horizon 7-63859 | KEY LARGO (LP) | 60 |

## KEY MASSIVE
| | | | |
|---|---|---|---|
| 89 | Hat Music HT 001 | Oh Girl/Sweet Sensi (12") | 25 |
| 97 | Wild Bunch WBRTDJ8 | Risingson/Instrumental/Single Mix/Neanderthal Mix/Darren Emerson Mix/Underdog Mix/Underdog Instrumental (2 x 12², clear vinyl promo) | 18 |

## KEYMEN
| | | | |
|---|---|---|---|
| 59 | HMV POP 584 | Gazackstahagen/Miss You | 6 |
| 62 | Columbia DB 4902 | Five Weeks In A Balloon/Secretly | 8 |
| 57 | Vogue Coral LVA 9048 | THE VOCAL SOUNDS OF THE KEYMEN (LP) | 15 |

## KEYNOTES
| | | | |
|---|---|---|---|
| 54 | Decca F 10302 | A Dime And A Dollar/JOHNSTON BROTHERS: Bandit | 10 |
| 55 | Decca F 10643 | Relax-Ay-Voo/Steam Heat | 10 |
| 56 | Decca F 10745 | Let's Go Steady/Chincherinchee | 8 |

*(see also Bobbie Britton, Johnston Brothers, Dave King, Suzi Miller)*

## KEYNOTES
| | | | |
|---|---|---|---|
| 63 | Planetone 14 | I'm In Love/In The Valley | 15 |

## BOBBY KEYS
| | | | |
|---|---|---|---|
| 75 | Ring O' Records 2017 102 | Gimmie The Key/Honky Tonk | 7 |
| 72 | Warner Bros K 46141 | BOBBY KEYS (LP) | 25 |

## EBONY KEYS
| | | | |
|---|---|---|---|
| 71 | Parlophone R 5909 | Brother Joe/Under The Apple Tree | 8 |

## KEYS (1)
| | | | |
|---|---|---|---|
| 64 | Oriole CB 1968 | Sleep Sleep My Baby/Colour Slide | 20 |
| 65 | CBS 201804 | Go Get Her/My Everything | 10 |

## KEYS (2)
| | | | |
|---|---|---|---|
| 80 | A&M AMS 7511 | Just A Camera/It Ain't So (p/s) | 15 |
| 81 | A&M AMS 8121 | One Good Reason/Saturday To Sunday Morning (p/s) | 10 |
| 81 | A&M AMS 8142 | I Don't Wanna Cry/Listening In (p/s) | 15 |
| 81 | A&M AMS 8236 | Greasy Money/Run Run Run (p/s) | 6 |
| 81 | A & M | THE KEYS ALBUM (LP) | 15 |

## KEYTONES
| | | | |
|---|---|---|---|
| 85 | Keytone KEY 3 | Good To Be Alive/Now's The Time | 15 |

## KEYWI
| | | | |
|---|---|---|---|
| 83 | Virgin VS 623 | Lets Get It Right/Dub Version/Short Version (12") | 15 |

## KGB
| | | | |
|---|---|---|---|
| 81 | A Major KGB 001 | The KGB/See Me (stamped die cut p/s) | 8 |

## K GROOVE
| | | | |
|---|---|---|---|
| 91 | The White Label KG 1 | The Future/On FB/10 To 10/BYS (12") | 60 |

## KHAN
| | | | |
|---|---|---|---|
| 72 | Deram SDL-R 11 | SPACE SHANTY (LP, gatefold, white/red label, small logo) | 70 |
| 72 | Deram SDL 11 | SPACE SHANTY (LP, gatefold, white/red label, small logo, later stickered sleeve) | 35 |

*(see also Steve Hillage, Egg, Nick Greenwood, Arzachel, Hatfield & The North)*

MINT VALUE £

**ASHISH KHAN**
68  Liberty LBL 83083E          ASHISH KHAN (LP) ..................................................................................................... 15

**USTAD ALI AKBAR KHAN**
69  HMV ASD 2367               MUSIC FROM INDIA NO. 5 (LP) ................................................................... 15
69  Transatlantic TRA 183        DHUN PALAS KAFI (LP) ................................................................................ 20
71  Mushroom 100 MR 14          THE PEACEFUL MUSIC OF USTAD ALI AKBAR KHAN (LP) .............. 35
*(see also Ravi Shankar)*

**USTAD VILAYET KHAN**
70  Transatlantic TRA 239         RAGA TILAKKAMOD (LP) ............................................................................. 15

**STEVE KHAN**
85  Nimbus AN 3023             EVIDENCE (LP, Nimbus Supercut, mail order only from Practical Hi Fi Magazine)........... 25

**KHANDARS**
65  Blue Beat BB 332             Don't Dig A Hole For Me/BUSTER'S ALL STARS: Skara ............................. 60

**KHANS**
62  London HLU 9555             New Orleans, 2 AM/Blue Mist ................................................................... 18

**KHARTOMB**
83  Whaam! WHAAM 14           Swahili Lullaby/Teekon Warriors ............................................................... 6

**KICK (1)**
79  EMI 2962                    ROUGH N SMOOTH EP ................................................................................ 15

**KICK (2)**
84  Footwear FWR 01             Let's Get Back Together/A Shot In The Dark/Don't Ever Change (p/s) .......... 10
86  Countdown VAIN 03           I Can't Let Go/Armchair Politician (p/s) ...................................................... 8

**KICKER BOYS**
89  Link LINKLP 071             KICKER BOYS (LP) ...................................................................................... 25

**KICK PARTNERS**
83  RAW 1                       Just My Imagination/Crazy World ............................................................... 6

**KICKS**
80  Carrere CAR 138             Get Off The Telephone/Big Boys Don't Cry (p/s) ........................................ 30
81  Blue Chip BC 102             If Looks Could Kill/Don't She Look Fab ...................................................... 70

**JOHNNY KIDD (& PIRATES)**
59  HMV POP 615                Please Don't Touch/Growl ......................................................................... 30
59  HMV POP 674                Feelin'/If You Were The Only Girl In The World (solo) ............................... 25
60  HMV POP 698                You Got What It Takes/Longin' Lips ............................................................ 18
60  HMV POP 753                Shakin' All Over/Yes Sir, That's My Baby ................................................... 15
60  HMV POP 790                Restless/Magic Of Love ............................................................................. 18
61  HMV POP 853                Linda Lu/Let's Talk About Us .................................................................... 20
61  HMV POP 919                Please Don't Bring Me Down/So What ....................................................... 20
62  HMV POP 978                Hurry On Back To Love/I Want That (with The Mike Sammes Singers) ........ 25
62  HMV POP 1088               A Shot Of Rhythm And Blues/I Can Tell (blue or black label) ................... 15
63  HMV POP 1173               I'll Never Get Over You/Then I Got Everything ........................................... 6
63  HMV POP 1228               Hungry For Love/Ecstasy ........................................................................... 8
64  HMV POP 1269               Always And Ever/Dr. Feelgood.................................................................. 10
64  HMV POP 1309               Jealous Girl/Shop Around ......................................................................... 15
64  HMV POP 1353               Whole Lotta Woman/Your Cheatin' Heart ................................................ 20
65  HMV POP 1397               The Birds And The Bees/Don't Make The Same Mistake As I Did ............. 20
65  HMV POP 1424               Shakin' All Over '65/Gotta Travel On ........................................................ 40
65  HMV POP 1520               It's Got To Be You/I Hate To Get Up In The Morning (solo) ..................... 30
66  HMV POP 1559               Send For That Girl/The Fool .................................................................... 40
60s HMV JO 674                Feelin'/If You Were The Only Girl In The World (export issue, black label) ........ 30
97  Cruisin' 50 CASB 005         Shakin' All Over/Please Don't Touch (78rpm, 300 only) .......................... 30
60  HMV 7EG 8628               SHAKIN' ALL OVER (EP) .......................................................................... 30
64  HMV 7EG 8834               JOHNNY KIDD AND THE PIRATES (EP) ................................................. 30
*(see also Pirates)*

**KIDDA BAND**
79  Carrere CAR 119             Fighting My Way Back/Saturday Night Fever ...................................... 130

**KID DYNAMITE**
73  Pye 7N 45274                Call Me Sunshine Superman/Breaking The Ice ........................................ 15

**KID GUNGO**
69  Escort ES 801               Hold The Pussy/KING CANNON: Wha Pen (B-side actually by Carl Bryan) .......... 18

**KID 'N' PLAY**
88  Cooltempo COOLXR 175        2 Hype (12" promo) ................................................................................. 20

**KIDROCK**
73  Youngblood YB 1058          Ice Cream Man/Dream Dream .................................................................. 35

**KIDS**
75  Atlantic K 50143            ANVIL CHORUS (LP, with inner, stickered sleeve) ................................... 25
*(see also Heavy Metal Kids)*

**KIDS NEXT DOOR**
65  London HLR 9993             Inky Dinky Spider/Goodbye Don't Cry ....................................................... 7

**BRENDAN KIDULIS**
80  Grey GR 001                Rusty Love/One First Kiss ........................................................................... 6

**KIDZ NEXT DOOR**
79  Warner Bros K 17492         What's It All About?/The Kidz Next Door (p/s) ....................................... 50

**PETE KIELY**
79  Elephant TUN 1              Forgotten Song/Troubadour (gatefold p/s) ................................................ 8

**KILBURN & HIGH ROADS**
74  Dawn DNS 1090               Rough Kids/Billy Bentley .......................................................................... 10

| | | | |
|---|---|---|---|
| 75 | Dawn DNS 1102 | Crippled With Nerves/Huffety Puff | 12 |
| 78 | Warner Bros K 17225 | Billy Bentley/Pam's Moods | 8 |
| 75 | Dawn DNLS 3065 | HANDSOME (LP, pink 'sun' label) | 40 |
| 78 | Warner Bros. K56513 | WOTABUNCH (LP) | 15 |

*(see also Ian Dury & Blockheads, 999, Nine Days Wonder, Davey Payne)*

## ROY KILDARE
| | | | |
|---|---|---|---|
| 64 | Blue Beat BB 226 | I Won't Leave/What About It | 15 |

## JUDY KILEEN
| | | | |
|---|---|---|---|
| 56 | London HLU 8328 | Just Walking In The Rain/A Heart Without A Sweetheart | 35 |

## MERLE KILGORE
| | | | |
|---|---|---|---|
| 54 | London HL 8103 | Seeing Double, Feeling Single/It Can't Rain All The Time | 300 |
| 54 | London HL 8103 | Seeing Double, Feeling Single/It Can't Rain All The Time (78) | 20 |
| 57 | London HLP 8392 | Ernie/Trying To Find (Someone Like You) | 100 |
| 57 | London HLP 8392 | Ernie/Trying To Find (Someone Like You) (78) | 29 |
| 60 | Melodisc MEL 1545 | Dear Mama/Jimmie Bring Sunshine | 10 |
| 62 | Mercury AMT 1193 | 42 In Chicago/A Girl Named Liz | 15 |

## THEOLA KILGORE
| | | | |
|---|---|---|---|
| 67 | Sue WI 4035 | I'll Keep Trying/He's Coming Back To Me | 40 |

## KILLA INSTINCT
| | | | |
|---|---|---|---|
| 92 | Music Of Life NOTE061 | The Bambi Murders (12") | 15 |
| 92 | Music Of Life NOTE063 | Den Of Thieves/Ununited Kingdom (12") | 15 |
| 93 | European Rhyme ERR02 | WHISPERS OF HATRED (EP) | 18 |
| 96 | Move MOVE7017 5 | THE PENULTIMATE SACRIFICE (EP) | 10 |

*(see also Total Fiasco)*

## KILLER
| | | | |
|---|---|---|---|
| 77 | Ariola ARL 5003 | KILLER (LP) | 35 |

*(see also Joe Cool & The Killers)*

## KILLERHERTZ
| | | | |
|---|---|---|---|
| 91 | Evasion EVA 1 | The Enforcer/X.XS (12", p/s) | 12 |
| 92 | FX FXUKT 9 | Distant Dream (X-Static Mix)/Love Byte (Apocalypse Mix)/Love Byte (Stronthium Mix)/Distant Dream (Flying Fader Mix) (12") | 40 |

## KILLERMETERS
| | | | |
|---|---|---|---|
| 79 | Psycho P 2620 | Why Should It Happen To Me/Cardiac Arrest (in p/s) | 100 |
| 79 | Psycho P 2620 | Why Should It Happen To Me/Cardiac Arrest | 30 |
| 80 | Gem GEMS 22 | Twisted Wheel/SX 225 (p/s, demo copies £50) | 90 |
| 97 | Detour DRLP 013 | METRIC NOISE (2xLP, gatefold, 'sparkly' clear vinyl) | 20 |

## KILLERS (1)
| | | | |
|---|---|---|---|
| 78 | Satril SAT 129 | Killer (On The Dancefloor)/No Surrender (no p/s) | 5 |

## KILLERS (2)
| | | | |
|---|---|---|---|
| 03 | Lizard King LIZARD007X | Mr Brightside/Smile Like You Mean It (white vinyl, 500 only p/s) | 80 |
| 04 | Lizard King LIZARD009X | Somebody Told Me/The Ballad Of Michael Valentine (pink vinyl, 2,000 only, p/s and poster) | 20 |
| 04 | Lizard King LIZARD010X | Mr Brightside/Who Let You Go (red vinyl, p/s and poster) | 25 |
| 04 | Lizard King LIZARD012X | All These Things That I've Done/Andy, You're A Star (Radio 1 session) yellow vinyl, 2,000 only, with poster) | 10 |
| 04 | Lizard King IND1ERR | Glamorous Indie Rock & Roll (1-sided promo, 400 only) | 15 |
| 05 | Lizard King LIZARD014X | Somebody Told Me (Mylo Remix)/Somebody Told Me (Glimmers Mix) (12") | 12 |
| 05 | Lizard King LIZARD015X | Smile Like You Mean It/Ruby, Don't Take Your Love To Town (Radio 1 Session) (p/s, red vinyl) | 12 |
| 06 | Vertigo 170 672-1 | When You Were Young/Where The White Boys Dance (numbered p/s) | 6 |
| 07 | Vertigo 17245686 | Read My Mind/Steve Bays Remix (numbered p/s) | 8 |
| 04 | Lizard King LIZARD011X | HOT FUSS (LP, blue vinyl) | 125 |
| 08 | Island 602517902534 | DAY & AGE (LP) | 30 |
| 12 | Island 602537118762 | BATTLE BORN (2-LP, red and black vinyl, 200 only autographed for Wembley concert) | 40 |

## KILLER WATT
| | | | |
|---|---|---|---|
| 87 | Raglan RGS 312 | DEATH (EP) | 25 |

## JOHN KILLIGREW
| | | | |
|---|---|---|---|
| 71 | Penny Farthing PELS 513 | JOHN KILLIGREW (LP, with Pete Dello, red/black/yellow labels) | 175 |

*(see also Pete Dello)*

## KILLING FLOOR
| | | | |
|---|---|---|---|
| 70 | Penny Farthing PEN 745 | Call For The Politicians/Acid Bean | 20 |
| 69 | Spark (S)RLP 102 | KILLING FLOOR (LP, blue/silver labels) | 500 |
| 70 | Penny Farthing PELS 511 | OUT OF URANUS (LP, gatefold sleeve, red/black/yellow label) | 450 |
| 73 | Spark Replay SRLM 2004 | ORIGINAL KILLING FLOOR (LP, reissue) | 30 |

*(see also Rory Gallagher)*

## KILLING JOKE
| | | | |
|---|---|---|---|
| 79 | Malicious Damage MD 410 | Nervous System/Turn To Red/Are You Receiving (10" EP in bag, with picture & 4 cards) | 20 |
| 79 | Malicious Damage MD 410 | Nervous System/Turn To Red/Are You Receiving (10" EP in bag, without picture & 4 cards) | 10 |
| 80 | Island WIP 6550 | Turn To Red/Nervous System (p/s) | 5 |
| 80 | Island WIP 6550 | Turn To Red/Nervous System ('A' label) | 15 |
| 80 | Island 12 WIP 6550 | Almost Red/Nervous System/Are You Receiving/Turn To Red (12", p/s) | 10 |
| 80 | Malicious Damage MD 540 | Wardance/Psyche (p/s, with 'call up paper' insert) | 15 |
| 80 | Malicious Damage MD 540 | Wardance/Psyche (p/s, without 'call up paper' insert) | 5 |
| 80 | Malicious Damage MD 540 | Wardance/Psyche (Mispressed B-side plays 'unknown artist', p/s) | 25 |
| 80 | E.G. EGMD 1.00 | Requiem/Change (p/s) | 5 |
| 80 | E.G. EGMX 1.00 | Requiem/Change/Change/Requiem (12", stamped sleeve) | 10 |
| 83 | E.G. EGOD 14/KILL 1/2 | Me Or You/Wilful Days//Feast Of Blaze (double pack, gatefold p/s) | 5 |

| | | | |
|---|---|---|---|
| 83 | E.G. EGOXD 14 | Me Or You/Feast Of Blaze/Wilful Days//Let's All Go (To The Fire Dances)/The Fall Of Because (live)/Dominator (Version) (12", sealed double pack) | 15 |
| 84 | E.G. DJ17 | A New Day/Dance Day (DJ promo) | 12 |
| 85 | E.G. EGOY 20 | Love Like Blood (Gestalt Mix)/Love Like Blood/Blue Feather (12", p/s) | 10 |
| 85 | E.G. EGOY 21 | Kings And Queens (Knave Mix) (12", p/s) | 10 |
| 85 | E.G. EGOX 21 | Kings And Queens (The Right Royal Mix)/The Madding Crowd/Kings And Queens (12", different withdrawn p/s) | 10 |
| 86 | E.G. EGOD 27 | Adorations/Exile//Ecstasy/Adorations (Instrumental Mix) (double pack) | 5 |
| 90 | ODIC1 | Beautiful Dead (1-sided fan club flexi) | 10 |
| 80 | E.G. EGM5.45 | KILLING JOKE (LP, gatefold) | 20 |

*(see also Youth, Peyr)*

**KILLJOYS (1)**

| | | | |
|---|---|---|---|
| 77 | Raw RAW 3 | Johnny Won't Get To Heaven/Naive (p/s, 4 different label designs) | 35 |
| 91 | Dam. Goods FNARR LP10 | NAIVE (LP, green vinyl) | 20 |

*(see also Girlschool)*

**KILLJOYS (2)**

| | | | |
|---|---|---|---|
| 82 | Clay CLAY 18 | This Is Not Love/In Your Light (p/s) | 5 |

**KILLS**

| | | | |
|---|---|---|---|
| 02 | Domino RUG 144T | BLACK ROOSTER EP (10") | 12 |
| 08 | Domino RUG 282 | Cheap And Cheerful/Kiss The Wrong Side | 8 |
| 03 | Domino WIGLP 124 | KEEP ON YOUR MEAN SIDE (LP, with fold-out insert) | 25 |
| 05 | Domino WIGLP 140 | NO WOW (LP, with DVD) | 20 |
| 08 | Domino WIGLP 184 | MIDNIGHT BOOM (LP) | 15 |
| 11 | Domino WIGLP 249 | BLOOD PRESSURES (LP, gatefold, download card) | 15 |

*(see also Dead Weather)*

**KILOWATTS**

| | | | |
|---|---|---|---|
| 68 | JJ DB 1140 | Bring It On Home/What A Wonderful World (with Doctor Bird label cat no) | 30 |

*(see also West Indians)*

**PAT KILROY**

| | | | |
|---|---|---|---|
| 67 | Elektra EKL 311 | LIGHT OF DAY (LP) | 80 |

**KILTIES**

| | | | |
|---|---|---|---|
| 56 | Beltona BL 2666 | Teach You To Rock/Giddy-Up-A Ding Dong | 15 |

**ANDY KIM**

| | | | |
|---|---|---|---|
| 69 | Dot DOT 125 | Baby I Love You/Gee Girl | 12 |

**KIM & KINETICS**

| | | | |
|---|---|---|---|
| 60s | Mortonsound 3032/3033 | Without A Song/Stormy Monday | 60 |
| 60s | Mortonsound 3036/3033 | Wee Wee Hours/Stormy Monday | 60 |

*(see also Kim Davis)*

**WILLIAM E. KIMBER**

| | | | |
|---|---|---|---|
| 68 | Parlophone R 5690 | Shilo/Emptiness | 5 |
| 68 | Parlophone R 5735 | Kilburn Towers/Goodbye (withdrawn) | 8 |
| 69 | Parlophone R 5796 | Black Sheep Boy/And The Sun Began To Shine | 6 |

*(see also E William)*

**STEVIE KIMBLE**

| | | | |
|---|---|---|---|
| 66 | Decca F 12378 | Some Things Take A Little Time/All The Time In The World | 18 |

**KINCADE**

| | | | |
|---|---|---|---|
| 72 | Penny Farthing PEN 796 | Jenny Jenny Dreams Are Ten A Penny/Counting Trains | 5 |

**KINDNESS**

| | | | |
|---|---|---|---|
| 70 | RCA 1942 | Light Of Love/Lindy Lou | 7 |

**KINESPHERE**

| | | | |
|---|---|---|---|
| 76 | Kinesphere KIN 5001 | ALL AROUND YOU (LP) | 100 |

**KINETIC EFFECT**

| | | | |
|---|---|---|---|
| 93 | Insane 1201 | Borderin' Insanity/Beyond The Parameters (12" green vinyl, 500 pressed) | 30 |
| 93 | Insane 1201 | Borderin' Insanity/Beyond The Parameters (12") | 18 |
| 97 | Insane 1202 | Man Bites Dog/The Effect Of Fear (12") | 18 |
| 12 | Insane 1001 | A Physical Exorcise/The Catalyst (clear vinyl 10") | 15 |

*(see also 2 The Top and Insane Macbeth)*

**AL KING**

| | | | |
|---|---|---|---|
| 68 | Sue WI 4045 | Think Twice Before You Speak/The Winner | 40 |

**ALBERT KING**

| | | | |
|---|---|---|---|
| 67 | Atlantic 584 099 | Crosscut Saw/Down Don't Bother Me | 20 |
| 67 | Stax 601 015 | Born Under A Bad Sign/Personal Manager | 10 |
| 68 | Stax 601 029 | Cold Feet/You Sure Drive A Hard Bargain | 10 |
| 68 | Stax 601 042 | (I Love) Lucy/You're Gonna Need Me | 8 |
| 73 | Stax 2025 162 | Breaking Up Somebody's Home/Little Brother (Make A Way) | 5 |
| 67 | Polydor 2343 026 | TRAVELLIN' TO CALIFORNIA (LP) | 40 |
| 68 | Stax (S)XATS 1002 | LIVE WIRE - BLUES POWER (LP) | 40 |
| 69 | Atlantic 588 173 | KING OF THE BLUES GUITAR (LP) | 40 |
| 69 | Stax SXATS 1017 | KING DOES THE KING'S THINGS (LP) | 35 |
| 69 | Stax SXATS 1022 | YEARS GONE BY (LP) | 35 |
| 71 | Stax 2363 003 | LIVE WIRE - BLUES POWER (LP, reissue) | 15 |
| 71 | Stax 2325 042 | LOVEJOY (LP) | 35 |
| 73 | Stax 2325 089 | I'LL PLAY THE BLUES FOR YOU (LP) | 20 |
| 74 | Stax STX 1003 | I WANNA GET FUNKY (LP) | 20 |

*(see also Steve Cropper & Albert King)*

**ALLAN KING**

| | | | |
|---|---|---|---|
| 73 | Duke DU 151 | Africa Wants Us All/JOE GIBBS: Liberation (B-side actually by Joe Gibbs' All Stars) | 6 |

**ANNA KING**

| 65 | Philips BF 1402 | If Somebody Told You/Baby, Baby, Baby (as Anna King & Bobby Byrd).............15 |
| 65 | Philips BBE 12584 | BACK TO SOUL (EP)...............................................40 |
| 65 | Philips (S)BL 7655 | BACK TO SOUL (LP)................................................60 |

*(see also Bobby Byrd)*

**ANTHONY KING**

| 70s | Peer Intl. | ELECTRICAL BAZAAR - SYNTHESIZERS UNLIMITED (LP, library issue) ..........20 |

**B.B. KING**

| 62 | HMV POP 1101 | Tomorrow Night/Mother's Love ........................................25 |
| 64 | Ember EMB S 196 | Rock Me Baby/I Can't Lose ..........................................25 |
| 65 | Sue WI 358 | The Letter/You Never Know ..........................................30 |
| 66 | HMV POP 1568 | Don't Answer The Door Parts 1 & 2 ...................................20 |
| 67 | HMV POP 1580 | Night Life/Waitin' On You ...........................................15 |
| 67 | HMV POP 1594 | I Don't Want You Cuttin' Your Hair/Think It Over ......................15 |
| 67 | Polydor 56735 | Jungle/Long Gone Baby ..............................................10 |
| 68 | Stateside SS 2112 | Paying The Cost To Be The Boss/Having My Say .......................20 |
| 68 | Blue Horizon 57-3144 | The Woman I Love/Blues For Me .....................................20 |
| 69 | Stateside SS 2141 | Don't Waste My Time/Get Myself Somebody .............................6 |
| 69 | Blue Horizon 57-3161 | Everyday I Have The Blues/Five Long Years ..........................20 |
| 70 | Stateside SS 2161 | The Thrill Is Gone/You're Mean ......................................10 |
| 70 | Stateside SS 2169 | So Excited/Confessin' The Blues ......................................7 |
| 70 | Stateside SS 2176 | Hummingbird/Ask Me No Questions ....................................5 |
| 71 | Probe PRO 516 | Chains And Things/King's Special ......................................5 |
| 71 | Probe PRO 528 | Ask Me No Questions/Help The Poor/Humming Bird .......................5 |
| 71 | Probe PRO 546 | Ain't Nobody Home/Alexis' Boogie (with Alexis Korner) ...............10 |
| 72 | Probe PRO 573 | Summer In The City/Found What I Need .................................5 |
| 65 | HMV CLP 1870 | LIVE AT THE REGAL (LP) ............................................50 |
| 66 | HMV CLP 3514 | CONFESSIN' THE BLUES (LP) .........................................30 |
| 67 | HMV CLP 3608 | BLUES IS KING (LP) .................................................20 |
| 67 | Ember EMB 3379 | THE R&B AND SOUL OF B.B. KING (LP) .................................20 |
| 68 | Stateside (S)SL 10238 | BLUES ON TOP OF BLUES (LP) .......................................25 |
| 68 | Blue Horizon 7-63216 | THE B.B. KING STORY CHAPTER 1 (LP) .................................50 |
| 69 | Stateside (S)SL 10272 | LUCILLE (LP) .......................................................40 |
| 69 | Stateside SSL 10284 | HIS BEST - THE ELECTRIC B.B. KING (LP) .............................20 |
| 69 | Blue Horizon 7-63226 | THE B.B. KING STORY CHAPTER 2 - BEALE STREET BLUES (LP) ...........75 |
| 70 | Stateside SSL 10297 | LIVE AND WELL (LP) .................................................20 |
| 70 | Stateside SSL 10299 | COMPLETELY WELL (LP) ..............................................15 |
| 70 | Probe SPBA 6255 | INDIANOLA MISSISSIPPI SEEDS (LP) ..................................100 |
| 71 | Blue Horizon 2431 004 | TAKE A SWING WITH ME (LP, mono) ...................................20 |
| 71 | Probe SPB 1032 | LIVE IN COOK COUNTY JAIL (LP) ......................................20 |

*(see also U2)*

**B.B. KING & BOBBY BLAND**

| 74 | ABC ABCD 605 | TOGETHER FOR THE FIRST TIME (2-LP)...................................18 |

*(see also Bobby Bland)*

**BEN E. KING**

| 61 | London HLK 9258 | Spanish Harlem/First Taste Of Love ..................................10 |
| 61 | London HLK 9358 | Stand By Me/On The Horizon ........................................15 |
| 61 | London HLK 9416 | Amor, Amor/Souvenir Of Mexico ......................................10 |
| 61 | London HLK 9457 | Here Comes The Night/Young Boy Blues ..............................15 |
| 62 | London HLK 9517 | Ecstasy/Yes .......................................................10 |
| 62 | London HLK 9544 | Don't Play That Song (You Lied)/The Hermit Of Misty Mountain (later copies have Atlantic labels instead of London Atlantic, this price is for both pressings)....................10 |
| 62 | London HLK 9586 | Too Bad/My Heart Cries For You .....................................15 |
| 63 | London HLK 9631 | I'm Standing By/Walking In The Footsteps Of A Fool ..................15 |
| 63 | London HLK 9691 | How Can I Forget/Gloria, Gloria .....................................10 |
| 63 | London HLK 9778 | I (Who Have Nothing)/The Beginning Of Time .........................10 |
| 63 | London HLK 9819 | I Could Have Danced All Night/Gypsy ...............................20 |
| 64 | London HLK 9840 | Around The Corner/Groovin' ........................................22 |
| 64 | Atlantic AT 4007 | It's All Over/Let The Water Run Down ...............................22 |
| 65 | Atlantic AT 4018 | Seven Letters/River Of Tears ........................................20 |
| 65 | Atlantic AT 4025 | The Record (Baby I Love You)/The Way You Shake It ..................40 |
| 65 | Atlantic AT 4043 | Cry No More/(There's) No Place To Hide .............................12 |
| 66 | Atlantic AT 4065 | Goodnight My Love, Pleasant Dreams/Tell Daddy ......................12 |
| 66 | Atlantic AT 4065 | Goodnight My Love, Pleasant Dreams/I Can't Break The News To Myself (demos with blank label on different B-side).........................................400 |
| 66 | Atlantic 584 008 | So Much Love/Don't Drive Me Away ..................................15 |
| 66 | Atlantic 584 046 | I Swear By The Stars Above/Get In A Hurry .........................12 |
| 67 | Atlantic 584 069 | What Is Soul?/They Don't Give Medals To Yesterday's Heroes ..........12 |
| 67 | Atlantic 584 090 | Save The Last Dance For Me (as Ben E. King & Drifters)/Stand By Me ....8 |
| 67 | Atlantic 584 106 | Tears, Tears, Tears/A Man Without A Dream .........................15 |
| 68 | Atlantic 584 149 | Seven Letters/Goodnight My Love ....................................10 |
| 68 | Atlantic 584 184 | Don't Take Your Love From Me/Forgive This Fool .....................25 |
| 68 | Atlantic 584 205 | It's Amazing/Where's The Girl ......................................12 |
| 69 | Atlantic 584 238 | 'Till I Can't Take It Any More/It Ain't Fair ..........................12 |
| 70 | Crewe CRW 2 | Goodbye My Old Gal/I Can't Take It Like A Man .......................5 |
| 71 | Atlantic 2091 100 | It's Amazing/Tears, Tears, Tears ....................................10 |
| 71 | CBS 7397 | White Moon/All Of Your Sorrows .....................................6 |
| 72 | CBS 7785 | Take Me To The Pilot/I Guess It's Goodbye ..........................6 |
| 75 | Atlantic K 10565 | Supernatural Thing (Parts 1 & 2) ...................................10 |

# Bob KING & THE COUNTRY KINGS

| | | | |
|---|---|---|---|
| 75 | Atlantic K 10618 | Happiness Is Where You Find It/Drop My Heart Off | 15 |
| 03 | Atco 67855 | I Can't Break The News Myself/BOBBY SHEEN: Something New To Do | 15 |
| 63 | London REK 1361 | BEN E. KING (EP) | 15 |
| 63 | London REK 1386 | I'M STANDING BY (EP) | 40 |
| 64 | Atlantic AET 6004 | WHAT NOW MY LOVE (EP) | 40 |
| 61 | London HA-K 2395 | SPANISH HARLEM (LP, mono) | 40 |
| 61 | London SAH-K 6195 | SPANISH HARLEM (LP, stereo) | 50 |
| 62 | London HA-K 8012 | DON'T PLAY THAT SONG! (LP) | 70 |
| 63 | London HA-K 8026 | SONGS FOR SOULFUL LOVERS (LP, cover credits Sings For Soulful Lovers; mono) | 50 |
| 63 | London SH-K 8026 | SONGS FOR SOULFUL LOVERS (LP, cover credits Sings For Soulful Lovers; stereo) | 70 |
| 65 | Atlantic ATL 5016 | GREATEST HITS (LP, plum label) | 50 |
| 65 | Atlantic ATL 5024 | SEVEN LETTERS (LP) | 40 |
| 66 | Atlantic 587/588 055 | SONGS FOR SOULFUL LOVERS (LP, cover credits Sings For Soulful Lovers; reissue) | 50 |
| 67 | Atlantic 587 072 | WHAT IS SOUL? (LP) | 18 |
| 70 | Crewe CRWS 203 | ROUGH EDGES (LP) | 25 |
| | | | 15 |

*(see also Drifters, Soul Clan)*

## BOB KING & THE COUNTRY KINGS
| | | | |
|---|---|---|---|
| 59 | Oriole CB 1497 | My Petite Marie/Hey Honey | 80 |
| 59 | Oriole CB 1497 | My Petite Marie/Hey Honey (78) | 20 |

## BRENTON KING
| | | | |
|---|---|---|---|
| 73 | Downtown DT 505 | Why Do People Have To Cry/Version | 6 |

## BUZZY KING
| | | | |
|---|---|---|---|
| 60 | Top Rank JAR 278 | Schoolboy Blues/Your Picture | 20 |

## CANNON BALL KING
| | | | |
|---|---|---|---|
| 69 | Camel CA 14 | Danny Boy/Reggae Happiness | 40 |
| 69 | Gas GAS 133 | Stagger Back/The Creeper | 45 |
| 70s | Junior JR 103 | Reggay Got Soul/Land Of Love (actually by Soul Cats) | 15 |

*(see also Carl Bryan, King Cannon, Cannon Ball & Johnny Melody)*

## CARL KING
| | | | |
|---|---|---|---|
| 66 | CBS 202407 | Out Of My Depth/Keep It Coming | 25 |
| 67 | CBS 202553 | You And Me/Satin Doll | 8 |

## CAROLE KING
| | | | |
|---|---|---|---|
| 62 | London HLU 9591 | It Might As Well Rain Until September/Nobody's Perfect | 7 |
| 66 | London HLU 10036 | Road To Nowhere/Some Of Your Lovin' | 40 |

## CLAUDE KING
| | | | |
|---|---|---|---|
| 61 | Philips PB 1173 | Big River Big Man/Sweet Loving | 6 |
| 61 | Philips PB 1199 | The Comancheros/I Can't Get Over The Way You Got Over Me | 6 |
| 62 | CBS AAG 108 | Wolverton Mountain/Little Bitty Heart | 10 |
| 62 | CBS AAG 119 | Burning Of Atlanta/Don't That Moon Look Lonesome | 6 |
| 65 | CBS EP 6067 | TIGER WOMAN (EP) | 15 |
| 62 | CBS BPG 62114 | MEET CLAUDE KING (LP) | 20 |

## CLYDIE KING
| | | | |
|---|---|---|---|
| 69 | Minit MLF 11014 | One Part, Two Part/Love Now Pay Later | 5 |

*(see also Jimmy Holiday & Clydie King, Raelets)*

## DANNY KING('S MAYFAIR SET)
| | | | |
|---|---|---|---|
| 64 | Columbia DB 7276 | Tossin' And Turnin'/Young Blood | 35 |
| 65 | Columbia DB 7456 | Pretty Things/Outside Of My Room | 40 |
| 65 | Columbia DB 7792 | Amen (My Teenage Prayer)/It's Such A Shame (as Danny King's Mayfair Set) | 25 |

*(see also Trevor Burton, Lemon Tree, Roy Wood)*

## DAVE KING
| | | | |
|---|---|---|---|
| 56 | Decca F 10684 | Memories Are Made Of This (& Keynotes)/I've Changed My Mind A 1000 Times | 6 |
| 56 | Decca F 10720 | You Can't Be True To Two/A Little Bit Independent | 6 |
| 56 | Decca F 10741 | The Birds And The Bees/Hot Chocolatta (with Keynotes) | 6 |

## DAVE KING REGGAE BAND
| | | | |
|---|---|---|---|
| 70 | Attack ATT 8014 | Hey Little Girl/Why Don't You Try Me | 12 |

## DEE KING
| | | | |
|---|---|---|---|
| 66 | Piccadilly 7N 35316 | Sally Go Round The Roses/It's So Fine | 12 |

## DENNIS KING
| | | | |
|---|---|---|---|
| 74 | EMI 2247 | Galloping Home/Within These Walls/Screen Scene | 6 |
| 77 | EMI EMI 2578 | Regan's Theme From The Film 'Sweeney'/F.J.'s Tune | 20 |
| 79 | Columbia DB 9061 | Dick Turpin/Belinda (as Denis King Orchestra) | 6 |

*(see also King Brothers)*

## DR. MARTIN LUTHER KING
| | | | |
|---|---|---|---|
| 68 | Pama PM 732 | I Have A Dream/Top Of The Mountain | 5 |
| 68 | Tamla Motown TML 11076 | THE GREAT MARCH TO FREEDOM (LP) | 60 |

## EDDIE KING
| | | | |
|---|---|---|---|
| 65 | Columbia DB 7572 | Always At A Distance/If You Wish | 8 |
| 65 | Columbia DB 7654 | I Wanna Love Her So Bad/If All You Need | 10 |

## KING FLOYD
| | | | |
|---|---|---|---|
| 71 | Atlantic 2091-051 | Groove Me/What Our Love Needs | 6 |

## FREDDY/FREDDIE KING
| | | | |
|---|---|---|---|
| 61 | Parlophone R 4777 | Hideaway/I Love The Woman | 50 |
| 65 | Sue WI 349 | Driving Sideways/Hideaway | 40 |
| 69 | Atlantic 584 235 | Play It Cool/Funky | 15 |
| 73 | A&M AMS 7076 | Woman Across The River/Help Me Through The Day | 5 |
| 69 | Atlantic 588 186 | FREDDIE IS A BLUES MASTER (LP) | 45 |
| 69 | Polydor 2343 009 | KING OF R&B VOL. 2 (LP) | 15 |

| 69 | Python PLP-KM 5 | FREDDY KING VOLUME 1 (LP, 99 copies only) | 100 |
| 69 | Python PLP-KM 7 | FREDDY KING VOLUME 2 (LP, 99 copies only) | 100 |
| 69 | Python PLP-KM 11 | FREDDY KING VOLUME 3 (LP, 99 copies only) | 100 |

*(Pre-1970 releases are usually credited to Freddy King, post-1970 releases to Freddie King.)*

| 72 | A&M AMLS 68113 | TEXAS CANNONBALL (LP) | 15 |
| 72 | Black Bear 904 | LIVE PERFORMANCES VOLUME 1 (LP) | 15 |
| 72 | Black Bear 905 | LIVE PERFORMANCES VOLUME 2 (LP) | 15 |

*(see also Lula Reed & Freddy King)*

## HAMILTON KING
| 64 | HMV POP 1289 | Not Until/I Wanna Live | 6 |
| 64 | HMV POP 1356 | Ain't It Time/Money, Money | 12 |
| 65 | HMV POP 1425 | Bird Without Wings/Shoppin' | 12 |
| 69 | Toast TT 511 | This Love Of Mine/The Cup Is Fuller | 5 |

## HANK KING
| 63 | Starlite STEP 41 | COUNTRY AND WESTERN (EP) | 25 |
| 66 | Starlite GRK 510 | COUNTRY AND WESTERN (EP, reissue, around 999 pressed) | 10 |

## KING IWAH
| 72 | Upsetter US 382 | Give Me Power # 2/UPSETTERS: Public Enemy Number One | 20 |

## JAY W. KING
| 66 | Stateside SS 505 | I'm So Afraid/I Don't Have To Worry (Not Anymore) | 15 |

## MORGAN KING
| 93 | OM Records 12OM006 | I Am Free (12" promo) | 10 |
| 93 | OM Records 12OM006 | I Am Free (12") | 10 |
| 93 | OM Records 12OM0006 T | I Am Free (8 Mixes) (2 x12") | 40 |

## P. KING
| 83 | Red Bus RBUS 79 | Hey Rosalyn/Lyin' Again | 6 |

*(see also Paul King)*

## P. RUFUS KING
| 73 | Dawn DNS 1031 | Look At Me Now/Nobody Knows | 25 |

*(see also Paul King, Mungo Jerry)*

## PAUL KING
| 72 | Dawn DNS 1023 | Whoa Buck/Zoe | 7 |
| 72 | Dawn DNLS 3035 | BEEN IN THE PEN TOO LONG (LP, textured sleeve with lyric insert) | 40 |

*(see also Mungo Jerry, P. King, P. Rufus King, King Earl Boogie Band, D'Jurann Jurran, Jigilo Jug Band, Russian Roulette)*

## PEE WEE KING & HIS BAND
| 54 | HMV 7MC 14 | Bimbo/Changing Partners (export issue) | 7 |

*(see also Hank Snow)*

## PETE KING CHORALE & ORCHESTRA
| 61 | London HLR 9437 | Hey! Look Me Over/Tall Hope | 5 |

## PETER KING (1)
| 68 | Crab CRAB 3 | Reggae Limbo/DERRICK MORGAN: River To The Bank | 20 |

## PETER KING (2)
| 78 | Miles Music MM 076 | BROTHER BERNARD (LP, with Alan Skidmore) | 20 |

## PETER KING (3)
| 75 | Orbitone OTLP 007 | MILIKI SOUND (LP) | 75 |
| 76 | Orbitone OTLP 010 | OMU LEWA (LP) | 100 |
| 77 | Orbitone OTLP 012 | A SOULFUL PETER KING (LP) | 20 |

## PETER KING (4)
| 85 | Fashion FAD 029 | Step On The Gas/Ten Commandments Of An MC (12") | 30 |
| 85 | Fashion FAD 045 | Bad Memory/Rewind/Jack It Up (12") | 30 |

## RAMONA KING
| 64 | Warner Bros WB 125 | It's In His Kiss/It Couldn't Happen To A Nicer Guy | 25 |

## RAY KING SOUL BAND
| 67 | Piccadilly 7N 35394 | Behold/Soon You'll Be Gone | 20 |
| 68 | Direction 8-63394 | LIVE AT THE PLAYBOY CLUB (LP) | 20 |

## REG KING
| 71 | United Artists UP 35204 | Little Boy/10,000 Miles (as Reg King & B.B. Blunder) | 25 |
| 71 | United Artists UAG 29157 | REG KING (LP) | 120 |

*(see also Action, Andy Leigh, B.B. Blunder, Mark Charig, Elton Dean, Mighty Baby)*

## ROBERT KING
| 82 | Charisma PRE 23 | Paper Heart/Theme For Love | 10 |

*(see also Scars)*

## SAMMY KING (& VOLTAIRS)
| 64 | HMV POP 1285 | What's The Secret/Great Balls Of Fire (as Sammy King & Voltairs) | 10 |
| 64 | HMV POP 1330 | Rag Doll/We're Through | 8 |
| 65 | HMV POP 1384 | Only You (And You Alone)/A Kiss, A Promise | 10 |
| 66 | HMV POP 1540 | If You Can Find Someone To Love You/Past Caring (with Voltairs) | 8 |

## SID KING & FIVE STRINGS
| 56 | Philips PB 589 | Booger Red/Oobie-Doobie (78) | 50 |

## SOLOMON KING
| 67 | Columbia DB 8306 | She Wears My Ring/Try Try (withdrawn B-side) | 10 |
| 70 | Columbia DB 8676 | Say A Prayer/This Beautiful Day | 100 |
| 70 | Columbia DB 8676 | Say A Prayer/This Beautiful Day (demo copy) | 150 |
| 72 | Polydor 2058258 | When You Gotta Go/Life Child | 30 |

*(see also Levi Jackson)*

## KING SPORTY
| 70 | Banana BA 321 | Inspiration/Choice Of Music | 15 |

MINT VALUE £

| 70 | Banana BA 322 | Lover's Version (as Sporty & Wilson)/DUDLEY SIBLEY: Having A Party..................22 |
| 70 | Punch PH 44 | For Our Desire/WINSTON WRIGHT: Version.................................................15 |
| 71 | Banana BA 323 | D.J. Special/RICHARD & MAD: Creation Version ........................................20 |
| 73 | Green Door GD 4063 | Yearful Of Sundays/Version ..............................................................6 |
| 86 | Dancefloor DFLP 3002 | MEET ME AT THE DISCO (LP)............................................................15 |

## TEDDI KING
| 56 | Vogue Coral Q 72142 | My Funny Little Lover/I'll Never Be The Same..........................................5 |
| 57 | Vogue EPV 1204 | STORYVILLE PRESENTS MISS TEDDI KING (EP) ........................................12 |
*(see also George Shearing)*

## TEDDY KING & BUSTER'S ALLSTARS
| 67 | Fab FAB 27 | Mexican Divorce/SOUL TOPS: Baby I Got News ......................................35 |

## TOBY KING
| 75 | President PT 430 | First Man To Die From The Blues/Country Bump .....................................6 |

## TONY KING (& HIPPY BOYS)
| 69 | Trojan TR 667 | Proud Mary/My Devotion (as Tony King & Hippy Boys) ...........................20 |
| 70 | Gas GAS 156 | Daddy, Daddy Don't Cry/I Like It...........................................................12 |
*(see also Maytals)*

## TRACY KING
| 86 | DMD 002 | Don't Stop/Love Again (12")...................................................................20 |

## KINGBEES
| 66 | Tempo TPO 103 | I'm A Kingbee/My Little Red Book (Irish-only, in p/s)..............................350 |
| 66 | Tempo TPO 103 | I'm A Kingbee/My Little Red Book (Irish-only)......................................250 |

## KING BISCUIT BOY
| 70 | Paramount SPFL 270 | OFFICIAL MUSIC (LP) .....................................................................18 |
| 71 | Paramount SPFA 7001 | GOODUNS (LP) ............................................................................18 |
*(see also Bobby Bland)*

## KING BROTHERS
| 57 | Parlophone R 4288 | Marianne/Little By Little ...................................................................10 |
| 59 | Parlophone R 4554 | Hop, Skip And Jump/Civilization (Bongo, Bongo, Bongo) .........................10 |
| 61 | Parlophone R 4825 | The Next Train Out Of Town/Sabre Dance ............................................5 |
| 61 | Parlophone R 4861 | The Language Of Love/Got Tell Her For Me.............................................5 |
| 57 | Parlophone GEP 8638 | HARMONY KINGS (EP).....................................................................10 |
| 64 | Oriole CB 1978 | Real Live Girl/Every Time It Rains .......................................................8 |
*(see also Jim Dale, Dennis King)*

## KING CANNON
| 69 | Trojan TR 663 | Soul Scorcher/GLEN & DAVE: Lucky Boy ...............................................60 |
| 69 | Harry J TR 664 | Soul Special/TREVOR SHIELD: Moon Is Playing Tricks On Me ....................60 |
| 69 | Crab CRAB 6 | Mellow Trumpet/VAL BENNETT: Reggae City .........................................45 |
| 71 | Hillcrest HCT 2 | Reggay Got Soul/SOUL CATS: Land Of Love ............................................7 |
| 71 | Moodisc HME 109 | Raw Deal (as King Cannon Allout; actually by Carl Bryan)/ MUDIE'S ALL STARS: Shirley's Hide Out.............................................................................12 |
*(see also Cannon Ball & Johnny Melody, Carl Bryan, Max Romeo, Lester Sterling, Kid Gungo, Erroll Dunkley)*

## KING CANNON (BALL)
| 68 | Trojan TR 636 | Thunderstorm/BURT WALTERS: Honey Love ..........................................40 |

## KING CHUBBY
| 70 | Pama Supreme PS 297 | What's The World Coming To/Live As One..............................................15 |
| 70 | Supreme PS 297 | What's The World Coming To/Live As One (reissue)..................................10 |
*(see also Junior Byles)*

## KING CRIMSON
| 69 | Island WIP 6071 | The Court Of The Crimson King (Parts 1 & 2)..........................................40 |
| 70 | Island WIP 6080 | Cat Food/Groon (in p/s) ...................................................................40 |
| 70 | Island WIP 6080 | Cat Food/Groon ............................................................................10 |
| 74 | Island WIP 6189 | The Night Watch/The Great Deceiver ....................................................7 |
| 76 | Island WIP 6274 | 21st Century Schizoid Man/Epitaph (in p/s) ..........................................30 |
| 76 | Island WIP 6274 | 21st Century Schizoid Man/Epitaph.....................................................10 |
| 81 | EG EGO 2 | Matte Kudasai/Elephant Talk ..............................................................5 |
| 82 | EG EGO 6 | Heartbeat/(Except From Requiem) (p/s) ................................................5 |
| 84 | EG EGO 15 | Sleepless/Nuages (That Which Passes, Passes Like Clouds) (p/s)...................5 |
| 69 | Island ILPS 9111 | IN THE COURT OF THE CRIMSON KING (LP, 1st pressing, Matrixes ILPS 9111 A 2 1 2 4/ILPS 9111B//4 1 1 1or ILPS 9111 A//3 1 1 3/ILPS 9111 B//3 123 gatefold sleeve, 'Printed and made by E.J. Day, London.' sleeve credit , pink label/'i' logo) ...............600 |
| 70 | Island ILPS 9111 | IN THE COURT OF THE CRIMSON KING (LP, gatefold sleeve no printer credits, 2nd pressing, pink rim label/'palm tree' logo) ...............................................70 |
| 70 | Island ILPS 9127 | IN THE WAKE OF POSEIDON (LP, textured gatefold sleeve made by E.J. Day, 1st pressing, A1/B1 matrixes deep pink lightly textutured label with 'i' logo) ...........150 |
| 70 | Island ILPS 9127 | IN THE WAKE OF POSEIDON (LP, 2nd pressing, pink rim label/'palm tree' logo) ...........30 |
| 70 | Island ILPS 9141 | LIZARD (LP, 1st pressing with E.J. Day Co sleeves, Matrix ILPS9141 A-2U/B-2U, laminated gatefold sleeve, pink rim label/'palm tree' logo) ...........................100 |
| 70 | Island ILPS 9141 | LIZARD (LP, 2nd pressing with Robor sleeves, laminated gatefold sleeve, pink rim label/'palm tree' logo)...................................................................30 |
| 71 | Island ILPS 9175 | ISLANDS (LP, pink rim label/'palm tree' logo, with fold-out gatefold inner)..................60 |
| 71 | Island ILPS 9111 | IN THE COURT OF THE CRIMSON KING (LP, 3rd pressing, pink rim palm tree label with rough finish, no printers credits, Matrixes: ILPS+9111+A2/ILPS+9111+B2, Basing Street London W11 address) .........................................................40 |
| 72 | Island ILPS 9111 | IN THE COURT OF THE CRIMSON KING (LP, 4th pressing, smooth labels, PRINTED in ENGLAND by ROBOR LIMITED sleeve credit, Matrixes ILPS 9111 A-4U PD 2/ILPS 9111 B-4U HM 2) ................................................................................30 |
| 72 | Island HELP 6 | EARTHBOUND (LP, 1st pressing, black/pink label, Matrixes: HELP 6A - 2U GM 1/HELP 6 B - 1U PR 1) ................................................................................60 |
| 73 | Island ILPS 9230 | LARKS' TONGUES IN ASPIC (LP, pink rim label/'palm tree' logo, with inner) ...............60 |

| | | | |
|---|---|---|---|
| 74 | Island ILPS 9275 | STARLESS AND BIBLE BLACK (LP, textured gatefold sleeve printed by Robor, palm tree' logo, matrixes: A/3U, B/3U, 'Garc' etched into dead wax side A, 'Sean & Ray' etched into dead wax side B, with inner) | 60 |
| 74 | Island ILPS 9308 | RED (LP, pink rim label/'palm tree' logo, with inner sleeve) | 45 |
| 75 | Island ILPS 9316 | U.S.A. (LP, pink rim label/'palm tree' logo, with inner) | 35 |
| 76 | Island ISLP 7 | A YOUNG PERSON'S GUIDE (2-LP, gatefold sleeve, with booklet) | 30 |
| 77 | Polydor 2683-080 | IN THE COURT OF THE CRIMSON KING/LARKS TONGUES IN ASPIC (2-LP) | 20 |
| 77 | Polydor 2302 059 | LIZARD (LP, reissue, gatefold sleeve) | 15 |
| 77 | Polydor 2302060 | ISLANDS (LP, reissue) | 15 |
| 77 | Polydor 2343 092 | EARTHBOUND (LP, reissue) | 15 |
| 77 | Polydor 2302 061 | LARKS TONGUES IN ASPIC (LP, reissue) | 15 |
| 77 | Polydor 2302 065 | STARLESS AND BIBLE BLACK (LP, reissue) | 15 |
| 77 | Polydor 2302 066 | RED (LP, reissue) | 15 |
| 81 | EG EGLP 49 | DISCIPLINE (LP) | 25 |
| 82 | EG EGLP 51 | BEAT (LP) | 25 |
| 84 | EG EGLP 55 | THREE OF A PERFECT PAIR (LP) | 15 |
| 87 | EG EGLP 5 | ISLANDS (LP, reissue) | 15 |
| 87 | EG EGLP 15 | RED (LP, reissue) | 15 |
| 89 | EG EGLP 4 | LIZARD (LP, reissue, gatefold sleeve) | 15 |
| 91 | EG EGLP 7 | LARKS TONGUE IN ASPIC (LP, reissue) | 15 |
| 10 | KCCBXLP1 | IN THE COURT OF THE CRIMSON KING (3-LP box set) | 50 |

*(see also Giles Giles & Fripp, Fripp & Eno, Gordon Haskell, Shame, McDonald & Giles, Emerson Lake & Palmer, Uriah Heep, Boz, Trendsetters Ltd., Pete Sinfield, Adrian Belew)*

## KING CRY CRY (PRINCE FAR I)
| | | | |
|---|---|---|---|
| 71 | Banana BA 356 | I Had A Talk/BURNING SPEAR: Zion Higher | 25 |

## KING CURTIS
| | | | |
|---|---|---|---|
| 62 | London HLU 9547 | Soul Twist/Twistin' Time (as King Curtis & Noble Knights) | 20 |
| 64 | Capitol CL 15346 | Soul Serenade/More Soul | 20 |
| 67 | Atlantic 584 109 | Good To Me/Hold On I'm Comin' | 12 |
| 67 | Atlantic 584 134 | Memphis Soul Stew/Blue Nocturne | 15 |
| 68 | Speciality SPE 1000 | Wiggle Wobble/Night Train | 8 |
| 69 | Atlantic 584 287 | Little Green Apples/La Jeanne | 10 |
| 70 | Atco 2091 012 | Teasin'/Soulin' (as King Curtis & Delaney Bramlett, Eric Clapton & Friends) | 15 |
| 60 | London RE-K 1307 | HAVE TENOR SAX, WILL BLOW (EP) | 40 |
| 60 | London HA-K 2247 | HAVE TENOR SAX, WILL BLOW (LP) | 70 |
| 62 | RCA RD 27252 | ARTHUR MURRAY'S MUSIC FOR DANCING - THE TWIST (LP) | 30 |
| 62 | Esquire 32-161 | THE NEW SCENE OF KING CURTIS (LP) | 40 |
| 67 | Atlantic 587 067 | PLAYS THE GREAT MEMPHIS HITS (LP) | 20 |
| 68 | Ember SPE/LP 6600 | SOUL SERENADE (LP) | 18 |
| 68 | Atlantic 587 093 | KINGSIZE SOUL (LP, as King Curtis & Kingpins) | 18 |
| 68 | Atlantic 587/588 115 | SWEET SOUL (LP) | 18 |
| 69 | Atco 228 027 | INSTANT GROOVE (LP) | 15 |

*(see also Champion Jack Dupree, Eric Clapton)*

## KING CURTIS, OLIVER NELSON & JIMMY FORREST
| | | | |
|---|---|---|---|
| 63 | Esquire 32-189 | SOUL BATTLE (LP) | 30 |

## KING DIAMOND
| | | | |
|---|---|---|---|
| 89 | Roadrunner RR 9461-1 | CONSPIRACY (LP, inner) | 15 |
| 89 | Roadrunner RR 94616 | CONSPIRACY (LP, picture disc) | 20 |

## KINGDOM
| | | | |
|---|---|---|---|
| 70 | United Artists UP 35145 | All I Need/Nothing Could Be Better | 25 |

## BOBBY KINGDOM/BLUE BEATS
| | | | |
|---|---|---|---|
| 61 | Blue Beat BB 44 | Honey Please/BLUE BEATS: That's My Girl | 25 |
| 62 | Blue Beat 45/BB/77 | Spanish Town Twist/Brand New Automobile | 12 |

## KINGDOM COME (U.K.)
| | | | |
|---|---|---|---|
| 71 | Polydor 2001 234 | Eternal Messenger/I D Side To B Side The C Side | 10 |
| 72 | Polydor 2001 416 | Spirit Of Joy/Come Alive | 10 |
| 72 | Polydor 2310 130 | GALACTIC ZOO DOSSIER (LP, gatefold sleeve, with poster) | 100 |
| 72 | Polydor 2310 130 | GALACTIC ZOO DOSSIER (LP, gatefold sleeve, without poster) | 30 |
| 72 | Polydor 2310 178 | KINGDOM COME (LP) | 30 |
| 73 | Polydor 2310 254 | JOURNEY (LP) | 25 |

*(see also Arcadium. Arthur Brown, Kiki Dee, Spirit Of John Morgan, Arcadium)*

## KING-EARL BOOGIE BAND
| | | | |
|---|---|---|---|
| 72 | Dawn DNS 1024 | Plastic Jesus/If The Lord Don't Get You | 6 |
| 72 | Dawn DNS 1028 | Starlight/Goin' To Germany | 6 |
| 72 | Dawn DNLS 3040 | TROUBLE AT MILL (LP, with poster) | 30 |
| 72 | Dawn DNLS 3040 | TROUBLE AT MILL (LP, without poster) | 20 |

*(see also Mungo Jerry, Paul King)*

## KING EDWARDS ALL STARS
| | | | |
|---|---|---|---|
| 66 | Rio R 077 | North Coast/Kingston 11 | 150 |

## (KING) EDWARDS GROUP
| | | | |
|---|---|---|---|
| 63 | Island WI 040 | Dear Hearts/Oh Mary (B-side actually by Ransford Barnett) | 25 |
| 63 | Island WI 047 | Russian Roulette (actually by King Edwards All Stars)/You're Mine (actually by Douglas Brothers) | 30 |
| 63 | Island WI 082 | He Gave You To Me/Kings Priests And Prophets (both actually by The Schoolboys) | 20 |
| 63 | Island WI 087 | Hey Girl/Skies Are Grey (both actually by Ransford Barnett) | 18 |

## KING FIGHTER
| | | | |
|---|---|---|---|
| 60s | Jump Up JU 518 | People Will Talk/Same Thing | 8 |

## KINGFISH
| | | | |
|---|---|---|---|
| 76 | United Artists UAG 29922 | KINGFISH (LP) | 15 |

| | | | MINT VALUE £ |
|---|---|---|---|
| 77 | Jet UA 30080 | LIVE AND KICKIN' (LP, early copies with picture inner sleeve) | 15 |

*(see also Grateful Dead, Bob Weir)*

**KING GENERAL**

| 96 | Conscious Sounds DNC EP 01 | Gunman/Dub/Conscious Ites Cut 5/CULTURE FREEMAN: The Fittest/High Speed Dubbing/C23000Dubbing (12") | 30 |

**KING GENERAL & BUSH CHEMISTS**

| 96 | Conscious Sounds DNC 006 | MONEY RUN TINGS (LP, 1st pressing) | 35 |

**KING GEORGE**

| 67 | RCA RCA 1573 | Drive On James/I'm Gonna Be Somebody Someday | 30 |

**KING HARVEST**

| 73 | Pye Int. 7N 25605 | Dancing in The Moonlight/Marty And The Captain | 8 |
| 73 | Pye NSPL 28174 | DANCING IN THE MOONLIGHT (LP) | 15 |

**KING HORROR**

| 69 | Joe/Duke DU 34 | Dracula Prince Of Darkness/JOE'S ALL STARS: Honky | 50 |
| 69 | Grape GR 3003 | Cutting Blade/Vampire | 50 |
| 69 | Grape GR 3006 | The Hole/WINSTON GROOVY: Lover Come Back | 30 |
| 69 | Grape GR 3007 | Lochness Monster/VISIONS: Zion I | 50 |
| 69 | Jackpot JP 713 | Wood In The Fire/The Naked City | 25 |
| 69 | Jackpot JP 714 | Police/PAMA DICE: Honky Tonk Popcorn | 40 |
| 70 | Nu Beat NB 051 | Frankenstein/WINSTON GROOVY: I Can't Stand It | 60 |
| 70 | Reggae REG 3005 | Slave Driver | 20 |

*(see also Laurel Aitken)*

**KING KONG**

| 85 | Now Generation NG 013 | Predominant/Version (12") | 12 |
| 86 | Greensleeves GRED 206 | Paro Them Paro/BUBBLERS COMPUTER STARS : Paranoia (12") | 30 |
| 87 | Gigikal DIG 006 | Digital We Digital/FRANKIE PAUL: Rambo (12") | 20 |

**KING KOSS**

| 69 | Polydor 56329 | Spinning Wheel/Louisiana | 8 |

**KING KURT**

| 82 | Thin Sliced TSR 2 | Zulu Beat/Rockin' Kurt (first pressing, orange vinyl with hand-painted sleeves by band members) | 125 |
| 82 | Thin Sliced TSR 2 | Zulu Beat/Rockin' Kurt (second, green vinyl, 159 copies, with hand-painted sleeves by band members) | 100 |
| 82 | Thin Sliced TSR 2 | Zulu Beat/Rockin' Kurt (second pressing, green vinyl, 1529 copies, sleeves not hand painted by band members)) | 40 |
| 82 | Thin Sliced TSR 2 | Zulu Beat/Rockin' Kurt (later pressings, yellow/gold/purple vinyl, different sleeves) | 30 |
| 84 | Stiff P BUY 206 | Banana Banana/Bo Diddley Goes East (shaped picture disc) | 8 |
| 85 | Stiff P BUY 235 | Slammers/Ape Hour (shaped picture disc) | 6 |

**KINGLY BAND**

| 69 | Decca F 12926 | The Bitter And The Sweet/Standing At The Crossroads | 7 |
| 69 | Decca LK 5002 | ROCKSTEADY (LP) | 20 |

**KING MIGUEL**

| 73 | Bullet BU 524 | The Word Is Black/Town Talk | 10 |

**KING OF LUXEMBOURG**

| 86 | él GPO 14 | Valleri/Sketches Of Luxembourg (p/s) | 12 |

**KINGPINS (U.K.)**

| 65 | Oriole CB 1986 | Two Right Feet/That's The Way It Should Be | 35 |

**KINGPINS (U.S.)**

| 58 | London HLU 8658 | Ungaua Parts 1 & 2 | 15 |

**KING ROCK & WILLOWS**

| 67 | Caltone TONE 111 | You Are The One/ALVA LEWIS: Return Home | 100 |

**KING ROCKY**

| 68 | Studio One SO 2045 | The King Is Back/THREE TOPS: Vex Till Yuh Buss | 40 |

*(see also Leroy & Rocky, Clancy Eccles, Heptones)*

**KINGS IV**

| 59 | London HLT 8914 | Some Like It Hot/The World Goes On | 10 |

**KINGS COUNTY CARNIVAL**

| 69 | United Artists UP 2267 | Don't Vote For Luke McCabe/The Proof Of The Pudding | 18 |

**KING SCRATCH**

| 70s | Ethnic ETH 16 | Spiritual Whip/Version | 18 |
| 70s | Ethnic ETH 30 | Mash Finger/Version | 20 |

*(see also Lee Perry/Upsetters, Skatalites)*

**KINGSFOLK FOLK GROUP**

| 67 | Outlet OUT 008 | Black Velvet Band/Love Is Teasin | 10 |

**KING'S HENCHMEN**

| 59 | Coral FEP 2025 | ALAN FREED PRESENTS VOL. 1 (EP) | 150 |

**KINGSIGHTER**

| 78 | Trojan TRLS 166 | THE ONE EYED GIANT (LP) | 15 |

**KING SISTERS**

| 57 | Capitol CL 14711 | While The Lights Are Low/In Hamburg (When The Nights Are Long) | 10 |
| 57 | Capitol CL 14729 | Imagination/You're My Thrill | 5 |
| 57 | Capitol CL 14777 | Easy To Love/That Old Feeling | 5 |
| 58 | Capitol CL 14865 | Deep Purple/Unbelievable | 6 |
| 58 | Capitol CL 14893 | What's New?/The Thrill Was New | 5 |
| 58 | Capitol CL 14934 | Autumn In Pleasant Grove/The Guy In The Foreign Sports Car | 5 |
| 59 | Capitol CL 15012 | Keep Smiling (Keep Laughin', Be Happy)/The Maids Of Cadiz | 5 |
| 59 | Capitol CL 15069 | Lovin' Up A Storm/What Would I Do Without You | 5 |
| 59 | Capitol CL 15096 | Over The River (And Through The Woods)/Holiday Of Love (with Their Family) | 5 |

| | | | |
|---|---|---|---|
| 57 | Capitol T 808 | ALOHA (LP) | 15 |
| 60 | Capitol ST 1333 | BABY THEY'RE SINGING OUR SONG (LP) | 15 |

## PADDY KINGSLAND
| | | | |
|---|---|---|---|
| 74 | EMI 2110 | Spinball/Wobulator Rock | 6 |
| 74 | Studio 2 TWOX 1024 | SUPERCHARGED (LP) | 20 |

## CHARLES KINGSLEY CREATION
| | | | |
|---|---|---|---|
| 65 | Columbia DB 7758 | Summer Without Sun/Still In Love With You | 70 |

## EVELYN KINGSLEY & TOWERS
| | | | |
|---|---|---|---|
| 58 | Capitol CL 14944 | To Know Him Is To Love Him/FRANK PERRY & TOWERS: Let Me Be The One | 20 |

*(see also Towers)*

## KINGSMEN (1)
| | | | |
|---|---|---|---|
| 58 | London HLE 8735 | Better Believe It/Week-End | 30 |
| 59 | London HLE 8812 | Conga Rock/The Cat Walk | 30 |
| 59 | London REE 1211 | THE KINGSMEN (EP) | 100 |

*(see also Bill Haley & Comets)*

## KINGSMEN (2)
| | | | |
|---|---|---|---|
| 63 | Pye International 7N 25231 | Louie Louie/Haunted Castle | 30 |
| 64 | Pye International 7N 25262 | Little Latin Lupe Lu/David's Mood | 15 |
| 64 | Pye International 7N 25273 | Death Of An Angel/Searching For Love | 10 |
| 65 | Pye International 7N 25292 | The Jolly Green Giant/Long Green | 8 |
| 65 | Pye International 7N 25311 | The Climb/Waiting | 10 |
| 65 | Pye International 7N 25322 | Annie Fanny/Something's Got A Hold On Me | 10 |
| 66 | Pye International 7N 25366 | Little Latin Lupe Lu/Louie Louie | 15 |
| 66 | Pye International 7N 25370 | Killer Joe/Little Green Thing | 10 |
| 67 | Pye International 7N 25406 | Daytime Shadows/Trouble | 10 |
| 71 | Wand WN 14 | Louie Louie/If I Needed Someone | 8 |
| 64 | Pye Intl. NEP 44023 | THE KINGSMEN (EP) | 30 |
| 65 | Pye Intl. NEP 44040 | MOJO WORKOUT (EP) | 30 |
| 66 | Pye Intl. NEP 44063 | FEVER (EP) | 30 |
| 63 | Pye Intl. NPL 28050 | THE KINGSMEN IN PERSON (LP, live) | 25 |
| 64 | Pye Intl. NPL 28054 | THE KINGSMEN VOLUME II (LP) | 25 |
| 65 | Pye Intl. NPL 28068 | THE KINGSMEN ON CAMPUS (LP) | 25 |
| 66 | Pye Intl. NPL 28085 | 15 GREAT HITS (LP) | 25 |

*(see also Touch)*

## KINGS OF CONVENIENCE
| | | | |
|---|---|---|---|
| 01 | Source SOURV 025 | Toxic Girl (Album Version)/Once Around The Block (p/s) | 5 |
| 01 | Source SOURLP 019 | QUIET IS THE NEW LOUD (LP) | 40 |
| 01 | Source SOURLP 040 | VERSUS (LP, gatefold sleeve) | 30 |
| 04 | Source SOURLP 099 | RIOT ON AN EMPTY STREET (LP) | 50 |

## KINGS OF LEON
| | | | |
|---|---|---|---|
| 03 | Handmedown HMD 20 | HOLY ROLLER NOVOCAINE EP: Molly's Chambers/California Waiting/Holy Roller Novocaine (10", clear red vinyl, numbered p/s, 1000 only) | 10 |
| 03 | Handmedown HMD 24 | What I Saw/Red Morning Light/Introducing The Band (audio/visual DVD single) | 10 |
| 03 | Handmedown HMD 28 | Molly's Chambers/Holy Roller Novocaine (10", limited issue, numbered p/s) | 10 |
| 04 | Handmedown HMD 43 | The Bucket/Trani (Live) (numbered p/s) | 8 |
| 05 | Handmedown HMD 50 | King Of The Rodeo/Soft (Live) (numbered p/s) | 6 |
| 07 | Handmedown HMD 54 | Charmer/My Party (Chad Hugo/Kenna Remix) (p/s) | 5 |
| 08 | RCA 88697 36890 7 | Sex On Fire/Beneath The Surface (p/s) | 6 |
| 03 | Handmedown HMD 26 | YOUTH & YOUNG MANHOOD (LP, 2 x 10", p/s with picture inners) | 30 |
| 04 | Handmedown HMD 40 | AHA SHAKE HEARTBREAK (2-LP, 10" clear vinyl, gatefold sleeve) | 20 |
| 12 | Music On Vinyl MOVLP 473 | BECAUSE OF THE TIMES (2-LP) | 18 |

## KING SOUNDS
| | | | |
|---|---|---|---|
| 78 | Grove Music GMDM 5 | Spend One Night In Babylon (feat. Trinity)/Keep Us Down In Poverty (feat. Jah Woosh) (12") | 25 |
| 79 | Grove Music GMDM 11 | They That Hate Us (wrongfully)/Ungrateful Bretheren (12") | 15 |
| 79 | Grove Music GMDM 20 | Kill Them Dead/Look Into Youself (12") | 20 |
| 79 | Grove GMLP 22 | COME ZION SIDE HAPPINESS (LP) | 15 |

## KING SPARROW
| | | | |
|---|---|---|---|
| 58 | Melodisc MEL 1447 | Leading Calypsonians/BILLY MOORE: Love Is Everywhere | 10 |
| 58 | Melodisc MEL 1475 | Familysize Cokes/Clara Honey Bunch | 10 |
| 59 | Melodisc MEL 1491 | Goaty/I Confess | 10 |

*(see also Mighty)*

## KING STITT
| | | | |
|---|---|---|---|
| 69 | Clandisc CLA 200 | Who Yea/DYNAMITES: Mr Midnight | 20 |
| 69 | Clandisc CLA 202 | Vigerton Two/On The Street | 20 |
| 69 | Clandisc CLA 203 | On The Street/CYNTHIA RICHARDS: Foolish Fool | 25 |
| 69 | Clandisc CLA 206 | The Ugly One/CLANCY ECCLES: Dance Beat | 45 |
| 70 | Clandisc CLA 207 | Herbsman Shuffle (with Andy [Capp])/HIGGS & WILSON: Don't Mind Me | 20 |
| 70 | Clandisc CLA 223 | King Of Kings/DYNAMITES: Reggaedelic | 20 |
| 71 | Clandisc CLA 235 | Merry Rhythm/CLANCY ECCLES: John Crow Skank | 15 |
| 71 | Banana BA 332 | Back Out Version/VEGETABLES: Holly Rhythm | 20 |
| 71 | Banana BA 334 | Rhyming Time/Reality | 20 |

*(see also Kurass)*

## KINGSTON JOE
| | | | |
|---|---|---|---|
| 64 | Blue Beat BB 253 | Time Is On My Friend (actually by Lloyd Barnes)/Wear And Tear (B-side actually by Lascelles Perkins) | 30 |

## KINGSTON PETE & BUSTER'S ALL STARS
| | | | |
|---|---|---|---|
| 67 | Blue Beat BB 403 | Little Boy Blue/I'm A Lover Try Me (actually by Larry Marshall) | 200 |

*(see also Larry Marshall)*

## KINGSTON ALLSTARS
| | | | |
|---|---|---|---|
| 66 | Dice CC 25 | Happy Hunter/LITTLE NORMA: Ten Commandments Of Woman | 80 |

## KINGSTONIANS
| | | | |
|---|---|---|---|
| 67 | Rio R 140 | Winey Winey/I Don't Care | 30 |
| 68 | Coxsone CS 7066 | Mother Miserable/I Make A Woman | 300 |
| 68 | Doctor Bird DB 1120 | Put Down Your Fire/Girls Like Dirt | 150 |
| 68 | Doctor Bird DB 1123 | Mummy And Daddy/False Witness | 100 |
| 68 | Doctor Bird DB 1126 | Fun Galore/Crime Don't Pay | 100 |
| 68 | Trojan TR 627 | Mix It Up/I'll Be Around | 40 |
| 69 | Big Shot BI 508 | Sufferer/Kiss A Little Finger | 75 |
| 69 | Big Shot BI 526 | Nice Nice/I'll Be Around | 80 |
| 69 | Crab CRAB 19 | Hold Down/BARRY YORK: Who Will She Be | 150 |
| 69 | Bullet BU 409 | I Am Just A Minstrel/Yesterday | 25 |
| 69 | Songbird SB 1011 | The Clip/BRUCE ANTHONY: Little Miss Muffett | 20 |
| 70 | Songbird SB 1019 | Singer Man/CRYSTALITES: Version | 15 |
| 70 | Songbird SB 1041 | Rumble Rumble/CRYSTALITES: Version | 20 |
| 70 | Songbird SB 1045 | Out There/CRYSTALITES: Out There Version II | 35 |
| 70 | Trojan TR 7708 | I'll Need You Tomorrow/I'm Gonna Make It | 10 |
| 70 | Duke DU 88 | You Can't Wine/RUPIE EDWARDS ALLSTARS: Bee Sting | 20 |
| 72 | Duke DU 126 | Lion's Den/Version | 15 |
| 70 | Trojan TBL 113 | SUFFERER (LP) | 40 |

*(see also Jack (Bernard) & Beanstalks, Gregory Isaacs)*

## KING TRUMAN
| | | | |
|---|---|---|---|
| 89 | Acid Jazz JAZID 9T | Like A Gun (Safe Sax Mix)/(Dub Version)/(Radio Edit) (12", p/s) | 75 |

*(see also Style Council, Paul Weller)*

## KING TUBBY
| | | | |
|---|---|---|---|
| 75 | Grounation GROL 502 | THE ROOTS OF DUB (LP) | 25 |
| 94 | Blood & Fire BAFLP 002 | DUB GONE CRAZY (LP) | 20 |
| 99 | Blood & Fire SVLP 260 | DUB LIKE DIRT (2-LP) | 25 |

## KING TUBBY & THE AGGROVATORS
| | | | |
|---|---|---|---|
| 82 | Black Music BMLP 804 | DUBBING IN THE BACKYARD (LP) | 50 |

## KING TUBBY & LEE PERRY
| | | | |
|---|---|---|---|
| 75 | Live & Love LALP 02 | MEETS THE AGGROVATORS AT THE DUB STATION (LP) | 75 |
| 76 | Prophets (no. cat. no.) | PROPHECY OF DUB (LP, in plain sleeve) | 120 |
| 76 | Fay FMLP 307 | SURROUNDED BY DREAD AT THE NATIONAL ARENA (LP) | 60 |
| 76 | Klik KLIP 9002 | SHALOM DUB (LP) | 45 |
| 77 | Fay Music FMLP 304 | KING TUBBY MEETS THE UPSETTER AT THE GRASS ROOTS OF DUB (LP) | 60 |
| 78 | Studio 16 WE 100 | KING TUBBY MEETS THE UPSETTER AT THE GRASS ROOTS OF DUB (LP, reissue) | 30 |
| 78 | Studio 16 WE 102 | SURROUNDED BY DREAD AT THE NATIONAL ARENA (LP, re-issue) | 35 |
| 79 | Star PTLP 1029 | MAJESTIC DUB (LP) | 25 |
| 81 | Live & Love LAP 015 | UPSETS THE UPSETTER (LP) | 35 |

## KING TUBBY, PRINCE JAMMY & SCIENTIST
| | | | |
|---|---|---|---|
| 81 | K&G Imperial KGLP 002 | FIRST, SECOND AND THIRD GENERATION OF DUB (LP) | 35 |

## KING TUBBY MEETS ROOTS RADICS
| | | | |
|---|---|---|---|
| 81 | Copasetic COPLP 5002 | DANGEROUS DUB (LP) | 30 |

## KINKS
### SINGLES : PYE SINGLES
| | | | |
|---|---|---|---|
| 64 | Pye 7N 15611 | Long Tall Sally/I Took My Baby Home | 120 |
| 64 | Pye 7N 15611 | Long Tall Sally/I Took My Baby Home (Demo copy) | 150 |
| 64 | Pye 7N 15636 | You Still Want Me/You Do Something To Me | 200 |
| 64 | Pye 7N 15636 | You Still Want Me/You Do Something To Me (Demo copy) | 125 |
| 64 | Pye 7N 15673 | You Really Got Me/It's All Right | 10 |
| 64 | Pye 7N 15714 | All Day And All Of The Night/I Gotta Move | 10 |
| 65 | Pye 7N 15759 | Tired Of Waiting For You/Come On Now | 8 |
| 65 | Pye 7N 15813 | Everybody's Gonna Be Happy/Who'll Be The Next In Line | 10 |
| 65 | Pye 7N 15854 | Set Me Free/I Need You | 8 |
| 65 | Pye 7N 15919 | See My Friend/Never Met A Girl Like You Before | 8 |
| 65 | Pye 7N 15981 | Till The End Of The Day/Where Have All The Good Times Gone | 10 |
| 66 | Pye 7N 17064 | Dedicated Follower Of Fashion/Sittin' On My Sofa | 8 |
| 66 | Pye 7N 17125 | Sunny Afternoon/I'm Not Like Everybody Else | 8 |
| 66 | Pye 7N 17222 | Dead End Street/Big Black Smoke (some labels list "Deadend") | 8 |
| 67 | Pye 7N 17321 | Waterloo Sunset/Act Nice And Gentle | 10 |
| 67 | Pye 7N 17400 | Autumn Almanac/Mr. Pleasant | 10 |
| 68 | Pye 7N 17468 | Wonderboy/Polly | 15 |
| 68 | Pye 7N 17573 | Days/She's Got Everything | 15 |
| 69 | Pye 7N 17724 | Plastic Man/King Kong | 15 |
| 69 | Pye 7N 17776 | Drivin'/Mindless Child Of Motherhood | 35 |
| 69 | Pye 7N 17812 | Shangri-La/Last Of The Steam-Powered Trains (unissued, acetates only) | 0 |
| 69 | Pye 7N 17812 | Shangri-La/This Man He Weeps Tonight | 25 |
| 69 | Pye 7N 17865 | Victoria/Mr Churchill Says | 15 |
| 70 | Pye 7N 17961 | Lola/Berkeley Mews | 6 |
| 70 | Pye 7N 45016 | Apeman/Rats | 8 |
| 71 | Pye PMM 100 | You Really Got Me/Set Me Free/Wonder Boy/Long Tall Shorty (maxi-single, no p/s) | 10 |
| 71 | Pye 7NX 8001 | PERCY (33rpm 4-track maxi-single, p/s) | 20 |
| 74 | Pye 7N 45313 | Where Have All The Good Times Gone/Lola (p/s) | 20 |
| 83 | PRT KPD 1 | You Really Got Me/Misty Water (picture disc) | 10 |
| 84 | PRT KIS 003 | All Day And All Of The Night/I Gotta Move (picture disc) | 10 |

## SINGLES : EXPORT SINGLES

| | | | |
|---|---|---|---|
| 65 | Pye 7N 15981 | Till The End Of The Day/Where Have All The Good Times Gone (export p/s) | 150 |
| 66 | Pye 7N 17100 | Well Respected Man/Milk Cow Blues | 120 |
| 67 | Pye 7N 17314 | Mr. Pleasant/This Is Where I Belong | 100 |
| 67 | Pye 7N 17405 | Autumn Almanac/David Watts | 100 |
| 71 | Pye 7N 8001 | God's Children/Moments (in p/s) | 60 |
| 71 | Pye 7N 8001 | God's Children/Moments | 30 |

## SINGLES : RCA SINGLES

| | | | |
|---|---|---|---|
| 72 | RCA RCA 2211 | Supersonic Rocket Ship/You Don't Know My Name | 6 |
| 72 | RCA RCA 2299 | Celluloid Heroes/Hot Potatoes | 8 |
| 73 | RCA RCA 2387 | Sitting In The Midday Sun/One Of The Survivors | 8 |
| 73 | RCA RCA 2418 | Sweet Lady Genevieve/Sitting In My Hotel | 8 |
| 74 | RCA RCA 5015 | Mirror Of Love/Cricket | 12 |
| 74 | RCA RCA 5042 | Mirror Of Love/He's Evil | 12 |
| 74 | RCA RCA 2478 | Holiday Romance/Shepherds Of The Nation | 10 |
| 75 | RCA RCA 2546 | Ducks On The Wall/Rush Hour Blues | 10 |
| 75 | RCA RCA 2567 | You Can't Stop The Music/Have Another Drink | 10 |
| 76 | RCA RCM 1 | No More Looking Back/Jack The Idiot Dunce/The Hard Way (p/s) | 12 |

## SINGLES : ARISTA SINGLES

| | | | |
|---|---|---|---|
| 79 | Arista ARIS 12240 | I Wish I Could Fly Like Superman/Low Budget | 5 |
| 77 | Arista ARIST 153 | Father Christmas/Prince Of The Punks (p/s) | 10 |
| 78 | Arista ARIST 189 | A Rock'n'Roll Fantasy/Artificial Light | 8 |
| 78 | Arista ARIST 210 | Black Messiah/Misfits (p/s) | 8 |
| 79 | Arista ARIST 300 | Moving Pictures/In A Space (p/s) | 8 |
| 80 | Arista ARIST 404 | Lola (live)/Celluloid Heroes (live) (export only) | 12 |
| 81 | Arista ARIST 415 | Better Things/Massive Reductions | 10 |
| 81 | Arista ARIST 415/KINKS 1 | Better Things/Massive Reductions//Lola (live)/David Watts (live) (double pack, gatefold p/s) | 8 |
| 83 | Arista ARIST 524 | Don't Forget To Dance/Bernadette (p/s) | 7 |
| 83 | Arista ARIST 524 | Don't Forget To Dance/Bernadette//Predictable/Back To Front (shrinkwrapped with free picture disc) | 12 |

## SINGLES : OTHER SINGLES

| | | | |
|---|---|---|---|
| 84 | Music Week LONF119 | How Are You/The Video (freebie with Music Week magazine) | 7 |
| 86 | London LON 119 | How Are You/Killing Time (p/s) | 12 |
| 88 | London LON 165 | The Road (7" Edit)/Art Lover (p/s) | 8 |
| 89 | London LON 239 | Down All The Days (Til 1992)/You Really Got Me (live) (p/s) | 6 |
| 90 | London LON 250 | How Do I Get Close/War Is Over (p/s)) | 6 |

## EPs

| | | | |
|---|---|---|---|
| 64 | Pye NEP 24200 | KINKSIZE SESSION | 30 |
| 64 | Pye NEP 24203 | KINKSIZE HITS | 40 |
| 65 | Pye NEP 24221 | KWYET KINKS | 45 |
| 66 | Pye NEP 24258 | DEDICATED KINKS | 120 |
| 68 | Pye NEP 24296 | THE KINKS | 275 |
| 75 | Pye AMEP 1001 | THE KINKS ('Yesteryear' export issue, red or blue vinyl) | 22 |

## ALBUMS : PYE ALBUMS

| | | | |
|---|---|---|---|
| 64 | Pye NPL 18096 | THE KINKS (mono) | 175 |
| 64 | Pye NSPL 83021 | THE KINKS (stereo, export only) | 250 |
| 65 | Pye NSPL 18096 | THE KINKS (stereo, export only, reissue) | 275 |
| 65 | Pye NPL 18112 | KINDA KINKS | 150 |
| 65 | Pye NPL 18131 | THE KINK KONTROVERSY | 100 |
| 65 | Pye NSPL 18131 | THE KINK KONTROVERSY (reprocessed stereo with stickered catalogue number, export only) | 270 |
| 66 | Pye NPL 18149 | FACE TO FACE (mono) | 120 |
| 66 | Pye NPL 18149 | FACE TO FACE (stereo, stickered sleeve "export only") | 225 |
| 66 | Pye NSLP 18149 | FACE TO FACE (LP original issue) | 100 |
| 67 | Golden Guinea GGL 0357 | THE KINKS (reissue, mono) | 25 |
| 67 | Golden Guinea GGGL 10357 | THE KINKS (reissue, stereo) | 30 |
| 67 | Pye NPL 18191 | LIVE AT KELVIN HALL (mono) | 100 |
| 67 | Pye N(S)PL 18191 | LIVE AT KELVIN HALL (stereo) | 150 |

*(The Pye LPs listed above were originally issued with laminated flipback sleeves, pink labels & light blue labels.)*

| | | | |
|---|---|---|---|
| 67 | Pye NPL 18193 | SOMETHING ELSE BY THE KINKS (mono) | 200 |
| 67 | Pye N(S)PL 18193 | SOMETHING ELSE BY THE KINKS (stereo) | 150 |
| 68 | Pye N(S)PL 18233 | THE KINKS ARE THE VILLAGE GREEN PRESERVATION SOCIETY (unissued, 12-track version, 2 test pressings only) | 800 |
| 68 | Pye NPL 18233 | THE KINKS ARE THE VILLAGE GREEN PRESERVATION SOCIETY (15-track version, mono) | 250 |
| 68 | Pye N(S)PL 18233 | THE KINKS ARE THE VILLAGE GREEN PRESERVATION SOCIETY (15-track version, stereo) | 200 |
| 69 | Pye NPL 18317 | ARTHUR (mono, gatefold sleeve "Quiien Victoria" insert) | 150 |
| 69 | Pye N(S)PL 18317 | ARTHUR (stereo, gatefold sleeve "Quiien Victoria" insert) | 90 |
| 70 | Pye NPL 18326 | THE KINKS (2-LP, gatefold sleeve) | 20 |
| 70 | Pye NSPL 18359 | THE KINKS PT 1 - LOLA VS POWERMAN & THE MONEY-GO-ROUND (gatefold sleeve) | 60 |
| 71 | Pye NSPL 18365 | SOUNDTRACK FROM THE FILM 'PERCY' (soundtrack) | 40 |
| 73 | Pye 11PP 100 | ALL THE GOOD TIMES (4-LP, box set) | 50 |
| 83 | PRT KINK 1 | GREATEST HITS (with bonus 10" EP of unreleased material) | 40 |

## ALBUMS : OTHER ALBUMS

| | | | |
|---|---|---|---|
| 71 | RCA SF 8243 | MUSWELL HILLBILLIES (gatefold sleeve) | 50 |
| 72 | RCA DPS 2035 | EVERYBODY'S IN SHOWBIZ, EVERYBODY'S A STAR (2-LP, gatefold sleeve) | 25 |
| 73 | RCA SF 8392 | PRESERVATION ACT 1 | 20 |

# Tony KINSEY (QUARTET)

| | | | |
|---|---|---|---|
| 74 | RCA LPL2 5040 | PRESERVATION ACT 2 (2-LP, gatefold sleeve) | 25 |
| 75 | RCA SF 8411 | SOAP OPERA (gatefold sleeve) | 15 |
| 75 | RCA RS 1028 | SCHOOLBOYS IN DISGRACE | 15 |
| 76 | RCA RS 1059 | CELLULOID HEROES | 15 |
| 93 | Sony 472489-1 | PHOBIA (omits 2 tracks from CD) | 15 |
| 94 | Konk Grapevine KNK LP 1 | TO THE BONE | 35 |
| 97 | Castle ORLP 005 | THE KINKS ARE THE VILLAGE GREEN PRESERVATION SOCIETY (LP, reissue, free 7") | 15 |
| 98 | Earmark 42004 | FACE TO FACE (LP, reissue) | 20 |

*(see also Dave Davies, Ray Davies, Maple Oak, Leapy Lee)*

## TONY KINSEY (QUARTET)

| | | | |
|---|---|---|---|
| 55 | Decca F 10548 | She's Funny That Way/Fascinatin' Rhythm | 15 |
| 55 | Decca F 10606 | Close Your Eyes/Pierrot | 15 |
| 55 | Decca F 10648 | Hey! There/Ballet | 25 |
| 56 | Decca F 10708 | Stompin' At The Savoy/China Boy (with Dill Jones) | 6 |
| 56 | Decca F 10709 | Moonglow/One O'Clock Jump | 6 |
| 56 | Decca FJ 10725 | Starboard Bow/Body And Soul | 6 |
| 56 | Decca FJ 10760 | Lullaby Of The Leaves/Isolation | 6 |
| 56 | Decca FJ 10773 | In A Ditch/A Smooth One | 12 |
| 57 | Decca FJ 10851 | Mean To Me/Supper Party | 8 |
| 57 | Decca F 10952 | The Midgets/Blue Eyes | 12 |
| 62 | Ember JBS 707 | Girl In Blue/Weber The Great | 6 |
| 56 | Decca DFE 6282 | PRESENTING THE TONY KINSEY QUARTET NO. 1 (EP) | 20 |
| 56 | Decca DFE 6285 | PRESENTING THE TONY KINSEY QUARTET NO. 2 (EP) | 40 |
| 58 | Decca DFE 6461 | MY FAIR LADY (EP) | 40 |
| 59 | Parlophone SGE 2004 | RED BIRD - JAZZ AND POETRY (EP, mono [GEP 8765]/stereo, with Christopher Logue) | 15 |
| 59 | Parlophone SGE 2008 | FOURSOME (EP, stereo, also mono GEP 8895) | 15 |
| 57 | Decca LK 4186 | INTRODUCING THE QUINTET (LP) | 100 |
| 57 | Decca LK 4207 | JAZZ AT THE FLAMINGO (LP) | 100 |
| 58 | Decca LK 4274 | TIME GENTLEMEN PLEASE (LP) | 150 |
| 61 | Ember EMB 3337 | AN EVENING WITH ... (LP) | 100 |
| 63 | Decca LK 4534 | HOW TO SUCCEED IN BUSINESS WITHOUT REALLY TRYING (LP, with Gordon Beck) | 70 |

## TONY KINSEY TRIO & JOE HARRIOTT

| | | | |
|---|---|---|---|
| 54 | Esquire EP 36 | TONY KINSEY TRIO & JOE HARRIOTT (EP) | 50 |
| 54 | Esquire EP 52 | TONY KINSEY TRIO & JOE HARRIOTT (EP) | 50 |
| 54 | Esquire EP 82 | TONY KINSEY TRIO & JOE HARRIOTT (EP) | 50 |

*(see also Joe Harriott)*

## KINSMEN

| | | | |
|---|---|---|---|
| 68 | Decca F 22724 | Glasshouse Green, Splinter Red/It's Started To Rain Again | 45 |
| 68 | Decca F 22777 | It's Good To See You/Always The Loser | 10 |

*(see also Four Kinsmen)*

## KIPPINGTON LODGE

| | | | |
|---|---|---|---|
| 67 | Parlophone R 5645 | Shy Boy/Lady On A Bicycle | 40 |
| 68 | Parlophone R 5677 | Rumours/And She Cried | 40 |
| 68 | Parlophone R 5717 | Tell Me A Story/Understand A Woman | 40 |
| 68 | Parlophone R 5750 | Tomorrow Today/Turn Out The Light | 40 |
| 69 | Parlophone R 5776 | In My Life/I Can See Her Face | 90 |
| 78 | EMI NUT 2894 | KIPPINGTON LODGE (EP) | 12 |

*(see also Brinsley Schwarz, Nick Lowe)*

## KIRBY

| | | | |
|---|---|---|---|
| 76 | Anchor ANC 1031 | Love Letters/Flasher | 12 |
| 78 | Hot Wax WAX 1/ANCHO 1 | Bottom Line/That's Some Dream | 10 |
| 78 | Hot Wax HW 2 | COMPOSITION (LP) | 75 |
| 94 | Backtrack Archive HW 2 | COMPOSITION (LP, reissue) | 30 |

*(see also Curved Air, Stretch)*

## KATHY KIRBY

| | | | |
|---|---|---|---|
| 60 | Pye 7N 15313 | Love Can Be/Crush Me | 20 |
| 61 | Pye 7N 15342 | Danny/Now You're Crying | 20 |
| 62 | Decca F 11506 | Big Man/Slowly | 7 |
| 66 | Decca F 12432 | The Adam Adamant Theme/Will I Never Learn? | 25 |
| 71 | Columbia DB 8795 | So Here I Go/Yes - I've Got (A-side titled "Here I Go Again" on demos) | 5 |
| 71 | Decca F 13228 | Bill/Can't Help Lovin' Dat Man | 5 |
| 72 | Columbia DB 8910 | Do You Really Have A Heart/Dream On, Dreamer | 5 |
| 73 | Columbia DB 8965 | Little Song For You/Here, There And Everywhere | 5 |
| 73 | Orange OAS 216 | Singer With The Band/Hello Morning | 5 |
| 76 | President PT 455 | My Prayer/Nobody Loves Me Like You Do | 60 |
| 81 | President PT 491 | He/Nobody Loves Me Like You | 5 |
| 63 | Decca DFE 8547 | KATHY KIRBY (EP) | 10 |
| 65 | Decca DFE 8596 | KATHY KIRBY VOL. 2 (EP) | 10 |
| 65 | Decca DFE 8611 | A SONG FOR EUROPE (EP) | 10 |
| 67 | Decca LK 4746 | MAKE SOMEONE HAPPY (LP) | 25 |
| 68 | Columbia S(C)X 6259 | MY THANKS TO YOU (LP) | 40 |

## LARRY KIRBY & ENCORES

| | | | |
|---|---|---|---|
| 59 | Top Rank JAR 143 | My Baby Don't Love Me/My Rose Of Kentucky | 15 |

## PAT KIRBY

| | | | |
|---|---|---|---|
| 56 | Brunswick 05560 | Happiness Is A Thing Called Joe/Don't Tell Me Not To | 7 |
| 56 | Brunswick 05575 | What A Heavenly Night For Love/Greensleeves | 7 |
| 57 | Brunswick 05697 | Tammy/Don't Keep Silent | 7 |
| 58 | Brunswick 05731 | Sayonara/Please Be Gentle With Me | 7 |

## BASIL KIRCHIN (BAND)
| | | | |
|---|---|---|---|
| 57 | Parlophone R 4344 | White Silver Sands/Waiting For The Robert E. Lee | 5 |
| 58 | Parlophone R 4511 | Cha Cha Bells/Oh Dear What Can The Cha Cha Be (with Rock-A-Cha Cha Band) | 5 |
| 59 | Parlophone R 4527 | Rock-A-Conga/Skin Tight (as Basil Kirchin Band) | 6 |
| 71 | Columbia SCX 6463 | WORLD WITHIN WORLDS (LP) | 800 |
| 74 | Island HELP18 | WORLD WITHIN WORLDS (not a reissue but second LP) | 80 |
| 03 | Trunk JBH 003 LP | QUANTUM LP, hand numbered, 500 only) | 50 |
| 04 | Trunk JBH 005 LP | CHARCOAL SKETCHES/STATES OF MIND (LP, 500 only) | 40 |
| 05 | Trunk JBH 012 LP | ABSTRACTIONS OF THE INDUSTRIAL NORTH (LP) | 50 |
| 06 | Trunk JBH 021 LP | PARTICLES (LP) | 20 |

*(see also Basil Kirchin, London Studio Group)*

## (IVOR & BASIL) KIRCHIN BAND
| | | | |
|---|---|---|---|
| 54 | Parlophone MSP 6144 | Mambo Macoco/Tangerine (as Kirchin Band) | 10 |
| 55 | Decca F 10434 | Minor Mambo/Mother Goose Jumps (as Kirchin Band) | 15 |
| 56 | Parlophone R 4222 | The Roller/St. Louis Blues (as Ivor & Basil Kirchin) | 7 |
| 56 | Parlophone R 4237 | Rockin' & Rollin' Thru The Darktown Strutters' Ball/Ambush | 20 |
| 57 | Parlophone R 4266 | Rock Around The World Medley (with Shani Wallis) | 18 |
| 57 | Parlophone R 4284 | Calypso!!/Jungle Fire Dance (as Ivor & Basil Kirchin with Wendy Windows) | 5 |
| 57 | Parlophone R 4335 | Teenage World/So Rare (as Kirchin Band & Bandits) | 10 |
| 55 | Psrlophone GEP 8556 | THE BIGGEST LITTLE BAND IN THE WORLD (EP) | 15 |
| 55 | Decca DFE 6237 | MEET THE KIRCHINS (EP) | 15 |
| 55 | Parlophone GEP 8531 | KIRCHIN BANDBOX (EP) | 15 |
| 56 | Parlophone GEP 8569 | THE IVOR AND BASIL KIRCHIN BAND (EP) | 30 |

## DEE KIRK
| | | | |
|---|---|---|---|
| 62 | Salvo SLO 1809 | I'll Cry/My Used To Be (99 copies only) | 15 |

## KEVIN KIRK
| | | | |
|---|---|---|---|
| 62 | Columbia DB 4909 | Sweet/Don't Waste Your Tears On Him | 6 |
| 62 | Columbia DB 4863 | Teenage Heartache/Midnight | 7 |

## RICHARD H. KIRK
| | | | |
|---|---|---|---|
| 81 | Industrial IRC 34 | DISPOSABLE HALF TRUTHS (cassette) | 20 |

*(see also Cabaret Voltaire)*

## (RAHSAAN) ROLAND KIRK
| | | | |
|---|---|---|---|
| 64 | Mercury 10015 MCE | THE KIRK QUARTET MEETS THE BENNY GOLSON ORCHESTRA (EP) | 10 |
| 65 | Mercury 10016 MCE | ROLAND SPEAKS (EP, with Benny Golson Orchestra) | 10 |
| 62 | Esquire 32-164 | KIRK'S WORK (LP, with Jack McDuff) | 30 |
| 63 | Mercury MMC 14126 | WE FREE KINGS (LP) | 30 |
| 64 | Mercury MCL 20002 | THE KIRK QUARTET MEETS THE BENNY GOLSON ORCHESTRA (LP) | 30 |
| 64 | Mercury MCL 20021 | KIRK IN COPENHAGEN (LP) | 20 |
| 64 | Mercury SMWL 21020 | GIFTS & MESSAGES (LP) | 15 |
| 65 | Mercury MCL 20045 | DOMINO (LP) | 20 |
| 65 | Fontana FJL 114 | HIP! (LP) | 20 |
| 66 | Mercury (S)LML 4005 | I TALK WITH THE SPIRITS (LP) | 15 |
| 66 | Mercury (S)LML 4015 | RIP, RIG AND PANIC (LP) | 15 |
| 67 | Mercury (S)LML 4019 | SLIGHTLY LATIN (LP) | 20 |
| 67 | Verve 9193 | NOW PLEASE DON'T YOU CRY BEAUTIFUL EDITH (LP) | 18 |
| 68 | Atlantic 588112 | THE INFLATED TEAR (LP) | 20 |
| 69 | Atlantic 588 207 | VOLUNTEERED SLAVERY (LP) | 20 |
| 70 | Atlantic 588178 | LEFT & RIGHT (LP) | 25 |

## KIRKBYS
| | | | |
|---|---|---|---|
| 66 | RCA RCA 1542 | It's A Crime/I've Never Been So Much In Love | 150 |

*(see also 23rd Turnoff, Jimmy Campbell, Rockin' Horse, Merseybeats)*

## KEN KIRKHAM
| | | | |
|---|---|---|---|
| 56 | Columbia SCM 5244 | It's Almost Tomorrow/No Not Much | 10 |
| 58 | Columbia DB 4116 | Now And For Always/Cathy | 6 |
| 61 | Decca F 11336 | A Kiss In Time (Can Save A Broken Heart)/Never | 6 |

## JOHN KIRKPATRICK (& SUE HARRIS)
| | | | |
|---|---|---|---|
| 72 | Trailer LER 2033 | JUMP AT THE SUN (LP, with Sue Harris, first pressing with red/black label) | 25 |
| 75 | Trailer LER 2033 | JUMP AT THE SUN (LP, with Sue Harris, repressing with yellow label) | 15 |
| 76 | Topic 12TS 295 | AMONG THE MANY ATTRACTIONS AT THE SHOW WILL BE A REALLY HIGH-CLASS BAND (LP, with Sue Harris) | 20 |

*(see also Jon Raven)*

## JULIAN KIRSCH
| | | | |
|---|---|---|---|
| 69 | Columbia DB 8541 | Clever Little Man/The Adventures Of A Young Cuckoo | 40 |

## DANNY KIRWAN
| | | | |
|---|---|---|---|
| 75 | DJM DJS 10783 | Hot Summer's Day/Love Can Always Bring You Happiness (demo in p/s) | 8 |
| 75 | DJM DJS 10783 | Hot Summer's Day/Love Can Always Bring You Happiness | 6 |
| 75 | DJM DJLPS 454 | SECOND CHAPTER (LP, gatefold sleeve) | 15 |

*(see also Fleetwood Mac, Tramp)*

## KISS
### SINGLES
| | | | |
|---|---|---|---|
| 75 | Casablanca CBX 503 | Nothin' To Lose/Love Theme From Kiss | 25 |
| 75 | Casablanca CBX 510 | Rock And Roll All Nite/Anything For My Baby | 25 |
| 76 | Casablanca CBX 516 | Shout It Out Loud/Sweet Pain | 15 |
| 76 | Casablanca CBX 519 | Beth/God Of Thunder | 18 |
| 77 | Casablanca CAN 102 | Hard Luck Woman/Calling Dr Love/Beth (in p/s) | 35 |
| 77 | Casablanca CAN 102 | Hard Luck Woman/Calling Dr Love/Beth | 10 |
| 77 | Casablanca CAN 110 | Then She Kissed Me/Hooligan/Flaming Youth | 15 |
| 77 | Casablanca CANL 110 | Then She Kissed Me/Hooligan/Flaming Youth (12", company sleeve) | 10 |

# KATIE KISSOON

| 78 | Casablanca CAN 117 | Rocket Ride/Love Gun (live) | 8 |
| 78 | Casablanca CANL 117 | Rocket Ride/Detroit Rock City (live)/Love Gun (live) (12", company sleeve) | 12 |
| 78 | Casablanca CAN 126 | Rock And Roll All Nite/C'Mon And Love Me (in p/s) | 25 |
| 78 | Casablanca CAN 126 | Rock And Roll All Nite/C'Mon And Love Me | 8 |
| 79 | Casablanca CAN 152 | I Was Made For Lovin' You/Hard Times | 8 |
| 79 | Casablanca CANL 152 | I Was Made For Lovin' You (extended)/Charisma (12", p/s) | 18 |
| 79 | Casablanca CAN 163 | Sure Know Something/Dirty Livin' (no p/s) | 6 |
| 80 | Casablanca NB 1001 | 2000 Man/I Was Made For Lovin' You/Sure Know Something (p/s) | 15 |
| 80 | Casablanca NBL 1001 | 2000 Man/I Was Made For Lovin' You/Sure Know Something (12", co. sleeve) | 12 |
| 80 | Casablanca MER 19 | Talk To Me/She's So European (p/s) | 10 |
| 80 | Casablanca KISS 1 | What Makes The World Go 'Round/Naked City (p/s) | 10 |
| 81 | Casablanca KISS 2 | A World Without Heroes/Mr Blackwell (p/s) | 5 |
| 82 | Casablanca KISS 3 | Killer/I Love It Loud (pull-out tongue p/s) | 12 |
| 82 | Casablanca KISS 312 | Killer/I Love It Loud/I Was Made For Lovin' You (12", p/s) | 15 |
| 82 | Casablanca KISS 4 | Creatures Of The Night/Rock And Roll All Nite (live) (p/s, picture label) | 10 |
| 82 | Casablanca KISS 412 | Creatures Of The Night/Rock And Roll All Nite (live) (p/s, silver label) | 8 |
| 82 | Casablanca KISSD 4 | Creatures Of The Night/War Machine/Rock And Roll All Nite (live) (12", p/s) | 15 |
| | | Creatures Of The Night/Rock And Roll All Nite (live) (12", double groove, autographs engraved on 1 side) | 20 |
| 83 | Vertigo KISSP 5 | Lick It Up/Not For The Innocent (poster p/s) | 6 |
| 83 | Vertigo KPIC 5 | Lick It Up/Not For The Innocent (tank-shaped picture disc) | 20 |

## ALBUMS

| 75 | Casablanca CBC 4003 | KISS (blue 'Bogart' label) | 25 |
| 75 | Casablanca CBC 4004 | DRESSED TO KILL (blue 'Bogart' label, embossed sleeve) | 20 |
| 76 | Casablanca CBC 4008 | DESTROYER (blue 'Bogart' label with inner sleeve) | 20 |
| 76 | Casablanca CBC 4011/2 | ALIVE! (2-LP, blue 'Bogart' label, gatefold sleeve with insert, sleeve also lists CBSP 401) | 20 |
| 77 | Casablanca CALH 2001 | ROCK AND ROLL OVER ('lovegun' label, red vinyl) | 40 |
| 77 | Casablanca CAL 2006 | KISS (reissue, 'lovegun' label, red vinyl) | 40 |
| 77 | Casablanca CAL 2007 | HOTTER THAN HELL ('lovegun' label, red vinyl) | 40 |
| 77 | Casablanca CAL 2008 | DRESSED TO KILL (reissue, 'lovegun' label, red vinyl) | 40 |
| 77 | Casablanca CAL 2009 | DESTROYER (reissue, different sleeve, 'lovegun' label, red vinyl) | 40 |
| 77 | Casablanca CALD 5001 | ALIVE! (2-LP, reissue, 'lovegun' label, red vinyl) | 50 |
| 77 | Casablanca CALH 2017 | LOVE GUN ('lovegun' label, red vinyl with picture inner sleeve) | 40 |
| 77 | Casablanca CALD 5004 | KISS ALIVE II (2-LP, 'lovegun' label, with colour booklet & transfer sheet) | 25 |
| 77 | Casablanca CALD 5004 | KISS ALIVE II (2-LP, 'lovegun' label, red vinyl with colour booklet) | 50 |
| 78 | Casablanca CALD 5005 | DOUBLE PLATINUM (2-LP, 'lovegun' label, silver foil embossed sleeve & insert; sleeve & insert pressed in U.S. with U.K. cat. no. sticker) | 20 |
| 79 | Casablanca CALH 2051 | DYNASTY ('lovegun' label, black vinyl, colour inner sleeve & poster) | 15 |
| 80 | Mercury 6302 032 | UNMASKED (with poster) | 15 |
| 81 | Casablanca 6302 163 | (MUSIC FROM) THE ELDER (single sleeve or gatefold) | 15 |
| 87 | Vertigo 832 903-1 | CRAZY NIGHTS (picture disc in stickered PVC wallet) | 12 |
| 98 | Mercury PLP 31453 8137-2 | PSYCHO CIRCUS (LP, promo only picture disc) | 40 |

*(see also Gene Simmons, Ace Frehley, Peter Criss, Paul Stanley)*

## KATIE KISSOON
| 69 | Columbia DB 8525 | Don't Let It Rain/Will I Never See The Sun | 6 |
| 83 | Jive T37 | You're The One/You're The One (Instrumental) (12") | 10 |

*(see also Peanut, Marionettes, Rag Dolls [U.K.])*

## MAC KISSOON
| 60s | Boulevard (no cat. no.) | Wear It On Your Face/In A Dream | 10 |
| 69 | Youngblood YB 1005 | Wear It On Your Face/In A Dream (reissue) | 5 |

*(see also Marionettes, Rag Dolls [U.K.])*

## KISS THE BLADE
| 85 | Incision CUT 1-7 | The Party's Begun/The Night Comes Down (p/s) | 15 |
| 85 | Incision CUT 1 | The Party's Begun/The Night Comes Down/The Bridge (12", p/s) | 25 |
| 86 | Incision CUT 3 | Young Soldier/The Love I Give (12" p/s) | 40 |

## KIT KATS
| 66 | London HLW 10075 | Won't Find Better Than Me/That's The Way | 18 |

*(see also New Hope)*

## KITCHENS
| 79 | Red Square RS 001 | DEATH OF ROCK AND ROLL EP | 30 |

## EARTHA KITT
| 54 | HMV 7M 191 | Under The Bridges Of Paris/Lovin' Spree | 10 |
| 54 | HMV 7M 198 | Somebody Bad Stole De Wedding Bell/Sandy's Tune | 8 |
| 54 | HMV 7M 234 | Santa Baby/Let's Do It (Let's Fall In Love) | 6 |
| 54 | HMV 7M 246 | Easy Does It/Mink Shmink | 5 |
| 55 | HMV 7M 282 | Monotonous/African Lullaby | 5 |
| 55 | HMV 7M 288 | C'est Si Bon (with Henri René)/Senor | 5 |
| 56 | HMV 7M 422 | Honolulu Rock-A-Roll-A/Je Cherche Un Homme (I Want A Man) | 20 |
| 56 | MGM SP 1153 | Please Do It/Lady Loves | 5 |
| 56 | MGM SP 1178 | Diamonds Are A Girl's Best Friend/Good Little Girls | 5 |
| 57 | HMV POP 309 | Just An Old-Fashioned Girl/If I Can't Take It With Me When I Go (gold label) | 10 |
| 57 | HMV POP 346 | There Is No Cure For L'Amour/Hey Jacque | 10 |
| 70 | Spark SRL 1039 | Hurdy Gurdy Man/Catch The Wind | 20 |
| 71 | CBS 7626 | A Knight For My Nights/Summer Storm | 5 |

## KITTENS
| 64 | Decca F 12036 | Round About Way/Don't Stop Now | 15 |

## KIX
| 80 | Creole CR 205 | Fear Of Flying/Werewolf Walking (p/s) | 6 |

**MARK KJELDSEN**
80   Back Door DOOR 2 — Are You Ready/Somethings Happening ........................................ 10

**KLAN**
62   Palette PG 9052 — Fifi The Fly/Already Mine ............................................................ 10

**KLAXON 5**
86   él GPO 20 — Never Underestimate The Ignorance Of The Rich/Great Railway Journeys (p/s) ..... 8

**KLAXONS**
06   Angular ARC 012 — Gravity's Rainbow/The Bouncer (500, white label, numbered) ............ 12
07   RINSELP1T — MYTHS OF THE NEAR FUTURE (2-LP, 1 side etched) ........................... 25
10   RINSELP2T — SURFING THE VOID (2-LP, 500 only, white vinyl) .......................... 20

**SUSIE KLEE**
66   Polydor BM 56082 — Mr Zero/Punch And Judy Girl ......................................... 15

**KLEENEX**
79   Rough Trade/Sunrise RT 9 — Ain't You/Hedi's Head (poster p/s) ...................... 15
79   Rough Trade RT 014 — You/U (p/s) ........................................................ 10

*(see also Liliput)*

**ALAN KLEIN**
62   Oriole CB 1719 — Striped Purple Shirt/You Gave Me The Blues ........................ 15
62   Oriole CB 1737 — Three Coins In The Sewer/Danger Ahead ............................. 15
65   Parlophone R 5292 — It Ain't Worth The Lonely Road Back/I've Cried So Many Tears .... 6
65   Parlophone R 5370 — Age Of Corruption/I'm Counting On You .......................... 5
69   Page One POF 119 — Honey Pie/You Turned A Nightmare Into A Dream ................ 8
70   Decca F 13033 — Dinner's In The Ice Box/Here I Am, There You Are ................ 7
64   Decca LK 4621 — WELL, AT LEAST IT'S BRITISH (LP) ................................. 15

**HARRY KLEIN QUARTET**
56   Jazz Today JTE 105 — BRASH BARITONE (EP) ........................................ 30
56   Nixa NJE 1009 — NEW SOUND (EP) ................................................... 25
56   Nixa NJE 1022 — HARRY KLEIN QUARTET (EP) ....................................... 25
57   Columbia SEG 7647 — BARITONE SAX (EP) ........................................... 20

*(see also Jazz Five)*

**KLEPTOMANIA**
92   Hypno-Genesis HG 001 — Amadeus (Martini Mix)/Amadeus (Stringi Wingi Mix)/Morf (Plastascene Mix)/Morf (Scratchi Waxi Mix) (12") ........................................ 70

**DEAN KLEVATT**
74   Decca F 13495 — Don't Bury Molly/The Story Of His Life ............................. 10

**KLF**
89   KLF Comms 004M — What Time is Love (Monster Attack Mix) (1-sided 12", 3 only) ..... 300
89   KLF Comms. KLF 004T — What Time Is Love? (Trance Mix)/What Time Is Love? (Mix 2) (12", 'Pure Trance 1', original issue with black/green p/s) .................. 12
89   KLF Comms. KLF 004R — What Time Is Love? ('89 Primal Remix)/What Time Is Love? (Techno Slam)/ What Time Is Love? (Trance Mix 1) (12", stickered p/s) ........... 12
89   KLF Comms. KLF 010IR — Deep Shit Deep Shit Part 3 (the Illegal Remix)/Deep Shit Part 2/The Lovers' Side (unreleased 12", 6 copies only) ............................ 700
90   KLF Comms. KLF 004P — What Time Is Love? (Live At Trancentral)/Wandafull Mix (12", w/l, 1,500 only) .... 10
90   KLF Comms. KLF 004X — What Time Is Love? (Live At Trancentral)/Techno Gate Mix (12", p/s, mispressing, B-side actually plays "Wandafull Mix", matrix no.: KLF 004X-B) ........... 25
90   KLF Comms. KLF 005R — 3AM Eternal 'Single Edit'/Blue Danube Orbital Mix/Moody Boys Version/ 3PM Electro (12", original issue with stickered p/s) .......................... 10
91   KLF Comms. KLF 005S — 3AM Eternal (Live At The S.S.L.) (Radio Freedom Edit) (white label, 500 only) .... 12
92   KLF Comms. KLF 5 TOTP — 3AM Eternal (Xmas Top Of The Pops Version) (1-sided, w/Extreme Noise Terror, mail-order only, with insert & mailing envelope; beware of bootlegs!) ........... 30
92   KLF Comms. KLF 5 TOTP — 3AM Eternal (Xmas Top Of The Pops Version) (1-sided, w/Extreme Noise Terror, mail-order only, without insert & mailing envelope; beware of bootlegs!) ....... 8
89   KLF Comms. KLF 008R — Last Train To Trancentral (Remixes 1 & 2) (12", p/s, 'Pure Trance 5', 2,000 pressed, some warped, price is for unwarped copy) ............................ 40
89   KLF PROMO 2 — Kylie Said To Jason (Full Length)/Kylie Said Trance (12", promo & press sheet) .... 15
89   KLF Comms. KLF 010(S) — Kylie Said To Jason (Edit)/Kylie Said Trance (p/s) ...... 8
89   KLF Comms. KLF 010T — Kylie Said To Jason (Full Length)/Kylie Said Trance (12", stickered p/s & pstr) .... 15
89   KLF Comms. KLF 010R — Kylie Said To Jason (Trance Kylie Express)/Kylie In A Trance/ Kylie Said Harder (12" remix, p/s, export issue) ................................. 15
89   KLF Comms. KLF 010RR — Kylie In A Trance/Kylie Said Mu (12", p/s, export edition, 500 only, shrinkwrapped with KLF 010R) ................................... 70
89   KLF Comms. KLF 010RR — Kylie In A Trance/Kylie Said Mu (12", p/s, export edition, 500 only) .... 40
89   KLF Comms. KLF 010CD — Kylie Said To Jason (Full Length)/Madrugada Eterna/Kylie Said Trance (CD) .... 40
89   KLF Comms. KLF 006T — Love Trance/What Time Is Love (12", p/s, 3 copies known) .... 500
90   KLF Comms. KLF 011T — Madrugada Eterna (Club Mix)/Madrugada Eterna (Edit)/Madrugada Eterna (Ambient House Mix) (12", 20 only, beware of counterfeits!) ................... 150
90   KLF Comms. ETERNA 1 — Madrugada Eterna (Club Mix) (12", 1-sided, white label, 6 pressed, beware of counterfeits!) .................................................. 200
91   KLF Comms. CHOC ICE 2 — Justified And Ancient (Stand By The J.A.M.s)/Justified And Ancient (Let Them Eat Ice Cream) (12", white label promo) .......................... 12
91   KLF Comms. CHOC ICE 3 — Justified And Ancient (Anti-Acapella Version) (12", 1-sided, w/l, 200 only) .... 50
91   KLF Comms. LP PROMO 1 — Make It Rain/No More Tears (12", promo only, 1,729 pressed) .... 20
91   KLF Comms. 92PROMO 2 — America: What Time Is January? (12", 1-sided, white label promo, 50 - 250 only) .... 100
91   KLF Comms. 3AM 1 — 3AM Eternal (feat. Extreme Noise Terror) (p/s, mail order only) .... 20
92   KLF Comms. 92PROMO 3 — What Time Is Love (Acid Mix) (12", 1-sided, w/l promo, perhaps 20 only) .... 300
92   KLF Comms. USA 4X/ CHOC ICE 2 — Justified And Ancient/America: What Time Is Love? (12", 'longboat' picture disc, export edition, 4,000 only) .......................... 30
97   KLF Comms. — Fuck The Millennium (4-track CD, in white carrier bag Fuck The Millennium kit, with T-shirt, window sticker, certificate) ............................... 50
                — [Fuck The Millennium CD only entry] ...................................... 20
89   KLF Comms. JAMS LP 4 — THE WHAT TIME IS LOVE STORY (LP) ..................... 20
89   KLF Comms. JAMS CD 4 — THE WHAT TIME IS LOVE STORY (CD) .................... 30

| | | | MINT VALUE £ |
|---|---|---|---|
| 89 | KLF Comms. JAMS LP 5 | CHILL OUT (LP) | 30 |
| 89 | KLF Comms. JAMS LP 6 | (TUNES FROM) THE WHITE ROOM (LP, 9-track white label, unreleased, promo only, beware of counterfeits!) | 50 |
| 91 | KLF Comm. JAMS LP 006 | THE WHITE ROOM (LP) | 25 |

*(see also Timelords, Disco 2000, Bill Drummond, Space, Orb)*

## TONY KLINGER & MICHAEL LYONS
| | | | |
|---|---|---|---|
| 72 | Deram SML 1095 | EXTREMES (LP, soundtrack) | 100 |

## KLINGONS
| | | | |
|---|---|---|---|
| 80 | Kang KLING001 | Dr. Jekyl And Mr Hyde/The First Question (p/s) | 15 |

## PETER KLINT (QUINTET)
| | | | |
|---|---|---|---|
| 66 | Mercury MF 997 | Walkin' Proud/Shake | 20 |
| 68 | Atlantic 584 208 | Hey Diddle Diddle/Just Holding On (solo) | 18 |

## KLO
| | | | |
|---|---|---|---|
| 83 | International INTER 1 | Fun/Weirdo | 6 |

## KLONES
| | | | |
|---|---|---|---|
| 80 | Red Hot RED 001 | Metal Man/Neon Age (stamped die-cut sleeve) | 8 |

## ANNETTE KLOOGER
| | | | |
|---|---|---|---|
| 56 | Decca F 10701 | The Rock And Roll Waltz/Rock Around The Island (with Ted Heath Music) | 15 |
| 56 | Decca F 10733 | The Magic Touch/We'll Love Again (with Four Jones Boys) | 15 |
| 56 | Decca F 10738 | Why Do Fools Fall In Love?/Lovely One (with Four Jones Boys) | 15 |
| 56 | Decca F 10776 | Mama, Teach Me To Dance/Mama, I Long For A Sweetheart (with Edmundo Ros Orchestra) | 10 |
| 57 | Decca F 10844 | The Wisdom Of A Fool/Tra La La | 10 |

*(see also Four Jones Boys)*

## KLUBS
| | | | |
|---|---|---|---|
| 68 | Cam CAM 681 | I Found The Sun/Ever Needed Someone | 200 |

## EARL KLUGH
| | | | |
|---|---|---|---|
| 85 | Blue Note UAG 20009 | LIVING INSIDE YOUR LOVE (LP, Nimbus Supercut, mail order only with Hi Fi Today magazine) | 50 |

## KNACK (U.K.)
| | | | |
|---|---|---|---|
| 65 | Decca F 12234 | She Ain't No Good/Who'll Be The Next In Line | 60 |
| 65 | Decca F 12278 | It's Love Baby (24 Hours A Day)/Time Time Time | 50 |
| 66 | Piccadilly 7N 35315 | Did You Ever Have To Make Up Your Mind?/Red Hearts | 15 |
| 66 | Piccadilly 7N 35322 | Stop! (Before You Get Me Going)/Younger Girl | 15 |
| 66 | Piccadilly 7N 35347 | Save All My Love For Joey/Take Your Love | 15 |
| 67 | Piccadilly 7N 35367 | (Man From The) Marriage Guidance And Advice Bureau/ Dolly Catch Her Man | 15 |

*(see also Gun, Sky)*

## BERNIE KNEE QUARTETTE
| | | | |
|---|---|---|---|
| 55 | HMV 7M 306 | Chocolate Whiskey And Vanilla Gin/Scrape Off De Bark | 7 |

*(see also Bernie Nee)*

## KNEES
| | | | |
|---|---|---|---|
| 74 | United Artists UP 35773 | Day Tripper/Slow Down | 10 |

*(see also Brinsley Schwarz)*

## KNICKERBOCKERS
| | | | |
|---|---|---|---|
| 66 | London HLH 10013 | Lies/The Coming Generation | 20 |
| 66 | London HLH 10035 | One Track Mind/I Must Be Doing Something Right | 20 |
| 66 | London HLH 10061 | High On Love/Stick With Me | 30 |
| 66 | London HLH 10093 | Rumours, Gossip, Words Untrue/Love Is A Bird | 18 |
| 67 | London HLH 10102 | Can You Help Me/Please Don't Love Him | 18 |
| 73 | Elektra K 12102 | Lies/ELECTRIC PRUNES: I Had Too Much To Dream (Last Night) | 5 |
| 66 | London HA-H 8294 | THE FABULOUS KNICKERBOCKERS (LP) | 60 |

## KNIFE
| | | | |
|---|---|---|---|
| 04 | Rabid Records RABIDT 020 | HEARTBEATS EP (12", p/s) | 10 |
| 06 | Brille BRILLP 103 | SILENT SHOUT (2-LP) | 35 |
| 06 | Brille BRILLP 105 | DEEP CUTS (2-LP, inners) | 70 |
| 13 | Brille BRILLP 117 | SHAKING THE HABITUAL (3-LP, 2 booklets, 2 x CD) | 20 |

## KNIFE EDGE
| | | | |
|---|---|---|---|
| 80 | No Hessle F001 | Favourite Girl/Say You Will | 75 |

## BAKER KNIGHT
| | | | |
|---|---|---|---|
| 66 | Reprise RS 20465 | Would You Believe It/Tomorrow's Good Time Girl | 12 |

## CURTIS KNIGHT (& ZEUS)
| | | | |
|---|---|---|---|
| 69 | RCA RCA 1888 | Fancy Meeting You Here/Love In | 12 |
| 70 | RCA RCA 1950 | Down In The Village/No Point Of View | 15 |
| 74 | Dawn DNS 1049 | Devil Made Me Do It/Oh Rainbow | 7 |
| 74 | Dawn DNS 1065 | People Places And Things/Mysterious Lady | 7 |
| 74 | Dawn DNLS 3060 | THE SECOND COMING (LP, laminated sleeve, lyric insert, pink 'sun' label) | 100 |
| 74 | Dawn DNLS 3060 | THE SECOND COMING (LP, laminated sleeve, no lyric insert, pink 'sun' label) | 45 |

*(see also Jimi Hendrix, Blue Goose)*

## GLADYS KNIGHT (& PIPS)
### SINGLES
| | | | |
|---|---|---|---|
| 64 | Stateside SS 318 | Giving Up/Maybe Maybe Baby | 35 |
| 64 | Stateside SS 352 | Lovers Always Forgive/Another Love | 35 |
| 65 | Sue WI 394 | Letter Full Of Tears/You Broke Your Promise | 40 |
| 66 | Tamla Motown TMG 576 | Just Walk In My Shoes/Stepping Closer To Your Heart | 60 |
| 66 | Tamla Motown TMG 576 | Just Walk In My Shoes/Stepping Closer To Your Heart (DJ copy) | 150 |
| 67 | Tamla Motown TMG 604 | Take Me In Your Arms And Love Me/Do You Love Me Just A Little Honey | 15 |
| 67 | Tamla Motown TMG 619 | Everybody Needs Love/Stepping Closer To Your Heart (demo-only B-side) | 100 |
| 67 | Tamla Motown TMG 619 | Everybody Needs Love/Since I've Lost You | 20 |

| 67 | Tamla Motown TMG 629 | I Heard It Through The Grapevine/It's Time To Go Now | 25 |
|---|---|---|---|
| 68 | Tamla Motown TMG 645 | The End Of Our Road/Don't Let Her Take Your Love From Me | 20 |
| 68 | Tamla Motown TMG 660 | It Should Have Been Me/You Don't Love Me No More | 18 |
| 68 | Tamla Motown TMG 674 | I Wish It Would Rain/It's Summer | 18 |
| 69 | Tamla Motown TMG 714 | The Nitty Gritty/Got Myself A Good Man | 10 |
| 70 | Tamla Motown TMG 728 | Didn't You Know (You'd Have To Cry Sometime)/Keep An Eye | 12 |
| 70 | Tamla Motown TMG 756 | Friendship Train/You Need Love Like I Do (Don't You) | 10 |
| 71 | Tamla Motown TMG 765 | If I Were Your Woman/The Tracks Of My Tears | 8 |
| 72 | Tamla Motown TMG 805 | Make Me The Woman That You Go Home To/I Don't Want To Do Wrong | 15 |
| 72 | Tamla Motown TMG 813 | Just Walk In My Shoes/I'm Losing You | 10 |
| 73 | Ember EMB S 326 | Every Beat Of My Heart/Room In Your Heart | 6 |
| 73 | Tamla Motown TMG 844 | The Look Of Love/You're My Everything | 6 |
| 73 | Tamla Motown TMG 864 | Take Me In Your Arms And Love Me/No One Could Love You More | 60 |
| 74 | Contempo CS 2021 | Why Don't You Leave Me/Maybe Baby | 6 |
| 75 | Tamla Motown TMG 945 | You've Lost That Loving Feeling/This Child Needs A Father | 15 |
| 89 | MCA MCASP 1339 | Licence To Kill/MICHAEL KAMEN: Pain (p/s with postcards & lyric sheet) | 6 |

**ALBUMS**

| 67 | T. Motown TML 11058 | EVERYBODY NEEDS LOVE (mono) | 35 |
|---|---|---|---|
| 67 | T. Motown STML 11058 | EVERYBODY NEEDS LOVE (stereo) | 40 |
| 68 | Bell MBLL 103 | TASTIEST HITS | 30 |
| 68 | T. Motown TML 11080 | FEELIN' BLUESY (mono) | 35 |
| 68 | T. Motown STML 11080 | FEELIN' BLUESY (stereo) | 40 |
| 69 | T. Motown TML 11100 | SILK 'N' SOUL (mono) | 35 |
| 69 | T. Motown STML 11100 | SILK'N'SOUL (stereo) | 30 |
| 69 | T. Motown TML 11135 | THE NITTY GRITTY (mono) | 22 |
| 69 | T. Motown (S)TML 11135 | THE NITTY GRITTY (stereo) | 20 |
| 70 | T. Motown STML 11148 | GREATEST HITS (original with flipback sleeve) | 20 |
| 71 | T. Motown STML 11187 | IF I WERE YOUR WOMAN | 20 |

*(see also Pips, Dionne Warwick)*

**JASON KNIGHT**

| 67 | Pye 7N 17399 | Love Is Getting Stronger/Standing In My Shoes | 120 |
|---|---|---|---|
| 67 | Pye 7N 17399 | Love Is Getting Stronger/Standing In My Shoes (DJ copy) | 200 |
| 73 | Pye 7N 45287 | Love Is Getting Stronger/Standing In My Shoes (reissue) | 5 |

**JEAN KNIGHT**

| 71 | Stax 2025 049 | Mr Big Stuff/Why Do I Keep Living These Memories | 8 |
|---|---|---|---|
| 72 | Stax 2025 103 | Carry On/Do You Think You're Hot Stuff | 5 |
| 73 | Stax 2025 161 | Do Me/Save The Last Kiss For Me | 5 |
| 72 | Stax 2362 022 | MR. BIG STUFF (LP) | 20 |

**MARIE KNIGHT**

| 61 | Fontana H 354 | Nothing/Come Tomorrow | 20 |
|---|---|---|---|
| 65 | Stateside SS 419 | Cry Me A River/Comes The Knight | 20 |
| 85 | Kent TOWN 102 | That's No Way To Treat A Girl/JACK MONTGOMERY: Dearly Beloved | 15 |

**PETER KNIGHT & KNIGHT RIDERS**

| 61 | Pye 7N 15388 | Lucky Stars/Double Trouble | 7 |
|---|---|---|---|
| 62 | Pye 7N 15472 | Camel Train/Scarlett | 7 |
| 64 | Pye 7N 15687 | Wonderful Day Like Today/It Isn't Enough | 8 |

**PETER KNIGHT ORCHESTRA/SINGERS**

| 55 | Parlophone MSP 6183 | Twenty Minutes South (Medley) (both sides, as Peter Knight Singers) | 6 |
|---|---|---|---|
| 67 | Mercury SML 30023 | SGT. PEPPER'S LONELY HEARTS CLUB BAND (LP) | 15 |

**ROBERT KNIGHT**

| 62 | London HLD 9496 | Free Me/The Other Half Of Man | 30 |
|---|---|---|---|
| 68 | Monument MON 1008 | Everlasting Love/Somebody's Baby | 15 |
| 68 | Monument MON 1016 | Blessed Are The Lonely/It's Been Worth It All | 8 |
| 68 | Monument MON 1017 | The Power Of Love/Love On A Mountain Top | 35 |
| 68 | Bell BLL 1029 | Isn't It Lonely Together/We'd Better Stop | 8 |
| 73 | Monument 1875 | Love On A Mountain Top/Power Of Love (reissue, push-out centre) | 5 |

**SONNY KNIGHT**

| 57 | London HLD 8362 | Confidential/Jail Bird (gold label print) | 200 |
|---|---|---|---|
| 57 | London HLD 8362 | Confidential/Jail Bird (silver label print) | 60 |
| 57 | London HLD 8362 | Confidential/Jail Bird (78 rpm) | 20 |
| 57 | London HLD 8362 | Confidential/Jail Bird (export issue) | 60 |
| 57 | London HL 7016 | But Officer/Dear Wonderful God | 150 |
| 59 | Vogue Pop V 9134 | But Officer/Dear Wonderful God | 40 |
| 59 | Vogue Pop V 9134 | But Officer/Dear Wonderful God (78) | 40 |

**TERRY KNIGHT & PACK**

| 66 | Cameo Parkway C 102 | I (Who Have Nothing)/Numbers | 60 |
|---|---|---|---|

*(see also Grand Funk Railroad)*

**TONY KNIGHT**

| 64 | Decca F 11989 | Did You Ever Hear The Sound?/I Feel So Blue (as Tony Knight & Live Wires) | 40 |
|---|---|---|---|
| 65 | Decca F 12109 | How Sweet/Surfer Street (as Tony Knight's Chessmen) | 35 |

**KNIGHT BROTHERS**

| 65 | Chess CRS 8015 | Sinking Low/Temptation 'Bout To Get Me | 30 |
|---|---|---|---|
| 66 | Chess CRS 8046 | That'll Get It/She's A1 | 30 |

**KNIGHTRIDER**

| 87 | Omega KS 1299 | Shout Out Loud | 30 |
|---|---|---|---|

**KNIGHTS OF THE ROUND TABLE**

| 68 | Pama PM 734 | Lament To Bobby Kennedy/If You Were My Girl | 7 |
|---|---|---|---|

## KNIGHTSBRIDGE STRINGS

| | | | |
|---|---|---|---|
| 60 | Top Rank JAR 304 | Tracey's Theme/Misty | 7 |
| 61 | Top Rank JAR 532 | The Singer Not The Song/Anacleto's Theme | 12 |

## K9'S

| | | | |
|---|---|---|---|
| 79 | Dog Breath WOOF 1 | The K9 Hassle/Idi Amin/Sweeney Todd (1st issue in numbered blue p/s, with insert, 1000 only) | 45 |
| 79 | Dog Breath WOOF 1 | The K9 Hassle/Idi Amin/Sweeney Todd (reissue, 500 only in stamped die cut sleeve) | 15 |

## KNOCKER JUNGLE

| | | | |
|---|---|---|---|
| 70 | Ember EMB S 293 | I Don't Know Why/Reality (p/s) | 6 |
| 71 | Ember NR 5052 | KNOCKER JUNGLE (LP, gatefold sleeve) | 75 |

## KNOCKOUTS

| | | | |
|---|---|---|---|
| 60 | Top Rank JAR 279 | Riot In Room 3C/Darling Lorraine | 25 |

## KNOCK UP

| | | | |
|---|---|---|---|
| 82 | Movie Music MM 002 | Telling Lies/Need Your Love (no p/s) | 30 |

## MARK KNOPFLER

| | | | |
|---|---|---|---|
| 84 | Vertigo DSDJ 7 | Joy (from 'Comfort And Joy') (unissued, 1-sided promo only) | 12 |
| 84 | Vertigo DSTR 712 | Joy (from 'Comfort And Joy')/Fistful Of Ice Cream (12", p/s) | 12 |
| 84 | Vertigo MARK ONE | Comfort And Joy (12", 1-sided promo) | 25 |
| 02 | Mercury 063292-1 | THE RAGPICKERS DREAM (2-LP, numbered) | 80 |
| 04 | Mercury 9867262 | SHANGRI-LA (2-LP) | 45 |

*(see also Dire Straits, Randy Newman, Chet Atkins)*

## KNOPOV'S POLITICAL PACKAGE

| | | | |
|---|---|---|---|
| 80 | White label | Misadventure/You're In The Army Now | 6 |

*(see also Mission)*

## KENNY KNOTS

| | | | |
|---|---|---|---|
| 86 | Unity UNO 18 | Watch How The People Dancing/ERROL BELLUT: A Weh Do She (12") | 18 |
| 88 | Unity UNO 22 | Ring Up My Number/MIKEY MURKA: We Try (12") | 15 |
| 02 | Honest Jon's HJP1 | Watch How The People Dancing/Watch How The People Dancing (Version)/Watch How The People Dancing (Dubplate)/MIKEY MURKA: We Try/We Try (Version) (12" reissue) | 12 |
| 06 | Jah Tubby's JT 10023 | Babylon Fall Down/Gully Bank Rock (10" with Bush Chemists) | 25 |

## KNOTT SISTERS

| | | | |
|---|---|---|---|
| 58 | London HLX 8713 | Undivided Attention/SHADES with KNOTT SISTERS: Sun Glasses | 40 |

## KNOWLEDGE

| | | | |
|---|---|---|---|
| 78 | A&M AMLH 68500 | HAIL DREAD (LP) | 30 |

## SONNY KNOWLES

| | | | |
|---|---|---|---|
| 72 | Rex R11077 | Do I Love You/I'm Just A Country Boy | 7 |

## KNOX

| | | | |
|---|---|---|---|
| 81 | Armageddon AS 003 | Gigolo Aunt/Alligator Man (p/s) | 5 |

*(see also the Vibrators, Beau Brummel)*

## BOBBY KNOX

| | | | |
|---|---|---|---|
| 70 | Penny Farthing PEN 714 | Kissin Walkin/Down A Back Street | 12 |

## BUDDY KNOX

| | | | |
|---|---|---|---|
| 57 | Columbia DB 3914 | Party Doll/My Baby's Gone (gold label print) | 50 |
| 57 | Columbia DB 3952 | Rock Your Little Baby To Sleep/Don't Make Me Cry (as Lieutenant Buddy Knox, gold label print) | 50 |
| 57 | Columbia DB 4014 | Hula Love/Devil Woman | 25 |
| 58 | Columbia DB 4077 | Swingin' Daddy/Whenever I'm Lonely | 25 |
| 58 | Columbia DB 4180 | Somebody Touched Me/C'mon Baby | 20 |
| 59 | Columbia DB 4302 | To Be With You/I Think I'm Gonna Kill Myself | 15 |
| 61 | London HLG 9268 | Lovey Dovey/I Got You | 10 |
| 61 | London HLG 9331 | Ling Ting Tong/The Kisses (They're All Mine) | 10 |
| 61 | London HLG 9472 | Three-Eyed Man/All By Myself | 10 |
| 62 | Liberty LIB 55411 | Chi-Hua-Hua/Open Your Loving Arms | 10 |
| 62 | Liberty LIB 55473 | She's Gone/Now There's Only Me | 10 |
| 63 | Liberty LIB 55592 | Shadaroom/Tomorrow Is Coming | 20 |
| 64 | Liberty LIB 55694 | All Time Loser/Good Loving | 10 |
| 69 | United Artists UP 35019 | God Knows I Love You/Night Runners | 10 |
| 70 | United Artists UP 35100 | Party Doll/God Knows I Love You | 6 |
| 57 | Columbia SEG 7732 | ROCK-A-BUDDY KNOX (EP) | 30 |

## KNUCKLEHEAD

| | | | |
|---|---|---|---|
| 93 | Saucerman ART 01 | Red Eye, Dead Eye/Spirit Matter (p/s, hand-painted label, 150 copies only) | 15 |

## FRANKIE KNUCKLES

| | | | |
|---|---|---|---|
| 89 | FFRR FX 102 | Tears (Classic Vocal)/(Accapella)/(Classic Instrumental) (with Satoshi Tomiie, 12", die-cut p/s (12") | 10 |
| 89 | Radical Records TRAXT 3 | Your Love/Baby Wants To Ride (12", p/s) | 25 |

## KOBALT 60

| | | | |
|---|---|---|---|
| 91 | Music Of Life NOTE57 | Chaos From Order/Concrete Show (12") | 15 |

## KOCK

| | | | |
|---|---|---|---|
| 83 | Hard ON 11 | One-Eyed Giant/Hickory Dickory Kock (p/s) | 6 |

## KODIAKS

| | | | |
|---|---|---|---|
| 69 | Decca F 12942 | All Because You Wanna See Me Cry/Tell Me Rhonda | 20 |

## (SPIDER) JOHN KOERNER

| | | | |
|---|---|---|---|
| 63 | Palette PG 9035 | Cool Ghoul/Sapphire | 7 |
| 67 | Elektra EKSN 45005 | Won't You Give Me Some Love/Don't Stop | 25 |
| 69 | Elektra EKSN 45063 | Friends And Lovers/Magazine Lady (with Willie Murphy) | 10 |
| 66 | Elektra EKL 267 | (LOTS MORE) BLUES RAGS AND HOLLERS (LP, with Dave Ray and Tony Glover, US sleeve but UK pressed record with golden Elektra "guitar player" logo) | 45 |

| | | | |
|---|---|---|---|
| 65 | Elektra EKL 290 | SPIDER BLUES (LP) | 50 |
| 68 | Elek. EKL 4041/EKS 74041 | RUNNING JUMPING STANDING STILL (LP, with Willie Murphy) | 30 |

## KOFFIE AND JAMES
| | | | |
|---|---|---|---|
| 69 | Philips BF 1800 | You're My Everything/Different Shades | 10 |

## MOE KOFFMAN
| | | | |
|---|---|---|---|
| 58 | London HLT 8633 | Little Pixie/Koko Mamey | 8 |
| 58 | London HLT 8549 | Swingin' Shepherd Blues/Hambourg Sound | 6 |
| 63 | Palette PG 9035 | Cool Ghoul/Sapphire | 6 |

## LEONID KOGAN
| | | | |
|---|---|---|---|
| 58 | Columbia 33CX 1562 | PAGANINI VIOLIN CONCERTO NO. 1 IN D MAJOR (LP, mono) | 150 |
| 60 | Columbia SAX 2307 | BRAHMS VIOLIN CONCERTO (LP, stereo) | 1000 |
| 60 | Columbia SAX 2329 | LALO: SYMPHONIE ESPAGNOLE/TCHAIKOVSKY: SERENADE MELANCOLIQUE, LP, stereo, turquiose/silver label) | 1500 |
| 60 | Columbia SAX 2323 | TCHAIKOVSKY: VIOLIN CONCERTO OP 35 & MEDITATION D MINOR OP 42 with Paris Conservatoire Orchestra, turquiose/silver label) LP, stereo) | 1500 |
| 60 | Columbia 33CX 1711 | TCHAIKOVSKY: VIOLIN CONCERTO OP 35 & MEDITATION D MINOR OP 42 with Paris Conservatoire Orchestra, LP, blue label, mono) | 50 |
| 60 | Columbia SAX 2386 | BEETHOVEN VIOLIN CONCERTO (LP, stereo, turquiose/silver label) | 2000 |
| 64 | Columbia SAX 2531 | SONATAS FOR TWO VIOLINS (with ELISABTH GILELS) (LP, stereo, turquiose/silver label) | 1500 |
| 64 | Odeon SAX 2388 | SONATAS FOR TWO VIOLINS (with ELISABTH GILELS) (LP, stereo export edition, black label) | 500 |

## KOKANE GUNS
| | | | |
|---|---|---|---|
| 82 | SRTS 82 CUS 1644 | Delta Woman/Crying Shame | 12 |

## KOKOMO
| | | | |
|---|---|---|---|
| 60 | London HLU 9305 | Asia Minor/Roy's Tune | 7 |

## KO KO TAYLOR
| | | | |
|---|---|---|---|
| 66 | Chess CRS 8035 | Wang Dang Doodle/Blues Heaven | 35 |
| 66 | Chess CRS 8035 | Wang Dang Doodle/Blues Heaven (DJ copy) | 60 |
| 72 | Chess 6145 018 | Violent Love/The Egg Or The Hen/Wang Dang Doodle | 8 |

## KOLETTES
| | | | |
|---|---|---|---|
| 64 | Pye International 7N 25278 | Who's That Guy?/Just How Much | 50 |
| 73 | Chess 6145 021 | Who's That Guy?/Just How Much (reissue) | 10 |

## BONNIE KOLOC
| | | | |
|---|---|---|---|
| 72 | London HLO 10377 | Jazz Man/Got To Get What You Can | 6 |
| 72 | London HLO 10392 | Burgundy Wine/We Are Ships | 6 |
| 72 | London SHO 8432 | AFTER ALL THIS TIME (LP) | 25 |
| 72 | London SHO 8440 | HOLD ON TO ME (LP) | 20 |

## JIMMIE KOMACK
| | | | |
|---|---|---|---|
| 54 | Vogue Coral Q 2031 | Cold Summer Blues/The Nic-Name Song | 10 |
| 55 | Vogue Coral Q 72061 | Wabash 4-7473/An Old Beer Bottle | 10 |
| 55 | Vogue Coral Q 72087 | Rock-A-Bye Your Baby With A Dixie Melody/This Is The Place | 10 |

## CHRISTOPHER KOMEDA
| | | | |
|---|---|---|---|
| 66 | Polydor 580001 | CUL DE SAC (soundtrack EP) | 150 |
| 68 | Dot (S)LPD 519 | ROSEMARY'S BABY (LP, as Kryzstophe Komeda) | 50 |

## JOHN (T.) KONGOS
| | | | |
|---|---|---|---|
| 66 | Piccadilly 7N 35341 | I Love Mary/Goodtime Party Companion (as John T. Kongos) | 10 |
| 69 | Dawn DNS 1002 | Flim Flam Pharisee/Blood | 6 |
| 71 | Fly BUG 8DJ | He's Gonna Step On You Again/Sometimes It's Not Enough (DJ copy in p/s) | 10 |
| 71 | Fly BUG 8 | He's Gonna Step On You Again/Sometimes It's Not Enough | 5 |
| 69 | Dawn DNLS 3002 | CONFUSIONS ABOUT A GOLDFISH (LP, with sticker) | 40 |
| 69 | Dawn DNLS 3002 | CONFUSIONS ABOUT A GOLDFISH (LP, without sticker) | 30 |
| 71 | Fly HIFLY 7 | KONGOS (LP, gatefold sleeve, insert, Fly label) | 20 |

*(see also Scrugg, Floribunda Rose)*

## V. KONGS
| | | | |
|---|---|---|---|
| 63 | Halagala HG 18 | Tomorrow Will Soon Be Here/Pretty Little Girl | 20 |

## LEE KONITZ
| | | | |
|---|---|---|---|
| 56 | London LTZK 15025 | LEE KONITZ WITH WAYNE MARSH (LP) | 20 |

## KONRADS
| | | | |
|---|---|---|---|
| 65 | CBS 201812 | Baby It's Too Late Now/I'm Over You | 50 |

## KONSTRUKTIVITS
| | | | |
|---|---|---|---|
| 83 | Flowmotion FM 001 | VOLUME 1 (cassette) | 60 |
| 83 | Flowmotion FM 002 | A DISSEMBLY (LP) | 35 |
| 83 | Third Mind TMLP 02 | PSYKO GENETIKA (LP) | 35 |
| 84 | Third Mind TMLP 05 | BLACK DECEMBER (LP) | 30 |
| 85 | Sterile SR 10 | GLENNASCAUL (LP) | 15 |

*(see also Whitehouse)*

## KOOBAS
| | | | |
|---|---|---|---|
| 65 | Pye 7N 17012 | Take Me For A Little While/Somewhere In The Night | 50 |
| 66 | Pye 7N 17087 | You'd Better Make Up Your Mind/A Place I Know | 60 |
| 66 | Columbia DB 7988 | Sweet Music/Face | 60 |
| 67 | Columbia DB 8103 | Sally/Champagne And Caviar | 35 |
| 67 | Columbia DB 8187 | Gypsy Fred/City Girl | 30 |
| 68 | Columbia DB 8419 | The First Cut Is The Deepest/Walking Out | 55 |
| 69 | Columbia S(C)X 6271 | THE KOOBAS (LP, black/silver label, boxed logo, "Sold in U.K..." text) | 1500 |
| 88 | Bam Caruso KIRI 047 | BARRICADES (LP) | 18 |

*(see also Kubas, Van Der Graaf Generator, Gary & Stu, Juicy Lucy, March Hare)*

## KOOGA
| | | | |
|---|---|---|---|
| 88 | Kooga KO 001 | Don't Break My Heart/Lay Down Your Love (p/s, private pressing) | 8 |

*(see also Skin)*

## KOOKS

| | | | |
|---|---|---|---|
| 05 | Private Pressing | Slave To The Game (1-sided, stamped label, tour single, 500 only) | 8 |
| 06 | Virgin (no Cat no) | Naive (1-sided promo, hand-stamped label) | 6 |
| 06 | Virgin VS 1911 | Naive/Tea & Biscuits (clear vinyl) | 12 |
| 06 | Virgin VS 1913 | She Moves In Her Own Way/I Already Miss You | 6 |
| 07 | Virgin VSDJ1968 | Pull Me In (1-sided promo) | 8 |
| 09 | Virgin VSDJ1908 | Slave To The Game (1-sided, white label, gig-only single, 500 pressed) | 10 |
| 06 | Virgin VX 3016 | INSIDE IN/INSIDE OUT (LP, with 'bonus' live LP) | 30 |
| 08 | Virgin V3043 | KONK (LP) | 20 |

## KOOL

| | | | |
|---|---|---|---|
| 67 | CBS 203003 | Look At Me, Look At Me/Room At The Top | 20 |
| 69 | CBS 2865 | Step Out Of Your Mind/Funny (What A Fool A Man Can Be) | 20 |
| 69 | MCA MU 1085 | Lovin'/Baby's Out Of Reach | 80 |

## KOOL KEITH/PHAROE MONCH/AKINYELLE

| | | | |
|---|---|---|---|
| 95 | Liberty Grooves | Freestyle Frenzy/Gotta Go Down (7") | 45 |

## KOOL & THE GANG

| | | | |
|---|---|---|---|
| 70 | London HLZ 10308 | Kool And The Gang/Raw Hamburgers | 10 |

## AL KOOPER

| | | | |
|---|---|---|---|
| 65 | Mercury MF 885 | Parchman Farm/You're The Lovin' End (as Alan Kooper) | 20 |
| 69 | CBS 4011 | You Never Know Who Your Friends Are/Soft Landing On The Moon | 6 |
| 69 | CBS 4160 | Hey Western Union Man/I Stand Alone | 8 |
| 71 | CBS 5146 | Brand New Lady/The Landlord (Love Theme) | 5 |
| 71 | CBS 7376 | John The Baptist (Holy John)/Back On My Feet | 5 |
| 72 | CBS 8084 | Monkey Time/Bended Knees (Please Don't Let Me Down) | 10 |
| 69 | CBS 63538 | I STAND ALONE (LP, orange label) | 25 |
| 69 | CBS 63651 | YOU NEVER KNOW WHO YOUR FRIENDS ARE (LP, orange label) | 20 |
| 70 | CBS 63797 | KOOPER SESSION - WITH SHUGGIE OTIS (LP, orange label) | 20 |
| 70 | CBS 66252 | EASY DOES IT (2-LP, orange label) | 20 |
| 71 | United Artists UAS 29120 | THE LANDLORD (LP, soundtrack, with Staple Singers & Lorraine Ellison) | 20 |
| 71 | CBS 64340 | NEW YORK CITY (YOU'RE A WOMAN) (LP, gatefold sleeve, orange label) | 15 |
| 72 | CBS 64208 | A POSSIBLE PROJECTION OF THE FUTURE/CHILDHOOD'S END (LP, orange label) | 15 |
| 73 | CBS 65193 | NAKED SONGS (LP) | 15 |

*(see also Blues Project, Blood Sweat & Tears, Shuggie Otis)*

## AL KOOPER, MIKE BLOOMFIELD & STEPHEN STILLS

| | | | |
|---|---|---|---|
| 68 | CBS 3770 | Season Of The Witch/Albert's Shuffle | 12 |
| 68 | CBS 63396 | SUPER SESSION (LP) | 20 |
| 73 | CBS CQ 30991 | SUPER SESSION (LP, quadrophonic) | 25 |

*(see also Mike Bloomfield & Al Kooper, Stephen Stills)*

## KOPPYKATS

| | | | |
|---|---|---|---|
| 68 | Fontana SFT 13052/3 | BEATLES' BEST (2-LP) | 35 |

*(see also Ian [Edward] & Zodiacs)*

## TAMARA KORAN WITH PERCEPTION

| | | | |
|---|---|---|---|
| 68 | Doman D7 | Veils Of Mourning Lace/Don't Throw Our Love Away (DJ copy) | 400 |
| 68 | Domain D7 | Veils Of Mourning Lace/Don't Throw Our Love Away | 350 |

## TOMMY KÖRBERG

| | | | |
|---|---|---|---|
| 69 | Sonet SON 2005 | Dear Mrs. Jones/Bird You Must Fly | 8 |

## PAUL KORDA

| | | | |
|---|---|---|---|
| 66 | Columbia DB 7994 | Go On Home/Just Come Closer To Me | 30 |
| 69 | Parlophone R5778 | Seagull (West Coast Oil Tragedy Of '68)/Night Of The Next Day (with p/s) | 30 |
| 69 | Parlophone R 5778 | Seagull (West Coast Oil Tragedy Of '68)/Night Of The Next Day | 15 |
| 71 | MAM MAM 20 | Between The Road/English Country Garden | 5 |
| 71 | MAM AS 1003 | PASSING STRANGER (LP, gatefold sleeve) | 75 |

*(see also Tim Andrews & Paul Korda, Dada)*

## KORN

| | | | |
|---|---|---|---|
| 95 | Epic KORN 1 | Blind/Fake/Sean Olson (10", p/s numbered) | 18 |
| 96 | Epic 6638450 | No Place To Hide/Proud (white vinyl, 7,500 only) | 12 |

## ALEXIS KORNER (BLUES INCORPORATED)

| | | | |
|---|---|---|---|
| 58 | Tempo A 166 | I Ain't Gonna Worry No More/County Jail (as Alexis Korner Skiffle Group) | 100 |
| 58 | Tempo A 166 | I Ain't Gonna Worry No More/County Jail (78) | 50 |
| 63 | Lyntone LYN 299 | Blaydon Races/Up-Town (as Blues Incorporated With Alexis Korner, free with women's magazine Trio) | 100 |
| 63 | Parlophone R 5206 | I Need Your Loving/Please Please Please (as Alexis Korner's Blues Inc.) | 40 |
| 65 | Parlophone R 5247 | Little Baby/Roberta (as Alexis Korner's Blues Inc.) | 40 |
| 65 | King KG 1017 | See See Rider/Blues A La King(as Alexis Korner's All Stars) | 45 |
| 66 | Fontana TF 706 | River's Invitation/Everyday (I Have The Blues) | 25 |
| 67 | Fontana TF 817 | Rosie/Rock Me | 25 |
| 75 | CBS 3520 | Get Off My Cloud/Strange'n'Deranged | 10 |
| 76 | CBS 3877 | Ain't That Peculiar/Tree Top Fever | 8 |
| 58 | Tempo EXA 76 | BLUES FROM THE ROUNDHOUSE VOL. 1 (EP, as Alexis Korner Skiffle Group) | 175 |
| 59 | Tempo EXA 102 | BLUES FROM THE ROUNDHOUSE VOL. 2 (EP, as Alexis Korner's Blues Inc.) | 300 |
| 62 | Topic TOP 70 | 3/4 A.D. (EP, with Davy Graham, first pressing in mauve sleeve with cream label) | 90 |
| 62 | Topic TOP 70 | 3/4 A.D. (EP, with Davy Graham, later pressing with lilac sleeve and blue label) | 60 |
| 62 | Topic TOP 70 | 3/4 A.D. (EP, with Davy Graham, later pressings with bronze sleeve and blue label) | 30 |
| 57 | '77' LP/2 | BLUES FROM THE ROUNDHOUSE (10" LP, 99 only, as Alexis Korner Breakdown Group) | 1000 |
| 62 | Ace of Clubs ACL 1130 | R&B FROM THE MARQUEE (LP, claret labels, with Long John Baldry) | 120 |
| 64 | Transatlantic TRA 117 | RED HOT FROM ALEX (LP, with Herbie Goins) | 150 |

| | | | |
|---|---|---|---|
| 64 | Oriole PS 40058 | AT THE CAVERN (LP, live, with Herbie Goins, laminated sleeve with flipbacks) | 375 |
| 65 | Ace of Clubs ACL 1187 | ALEXIS KORNER'S BLUES INCORPORATED (LP) | 100 |
| 65 | Spot JW 551 | SKY HIGH (LP, featuring Duffy Power) | 400 |
| 67 | Fontana TL 5381 | I WONDER WHO (LP, mono) | 150 |
| 67 | Fontana (S)TL 5381 | I WONDER WHO (LP, stereo) | 200 |
| 67 | Polydor Special 236 206 | BLUES INCORPORATED (LP, 1st issue, listing 4 tracks on Side A on sleeve/label) | 80 |
| 67 | Polydor Special 236 206 | BLUES INCORPORATED (LP, 2nd issue, listing 5 tracks on Side A on sleeve/label) | 50 |
| 68 | Liberty LBL/LBS 83147 | A NEW GENERATION OF BLUES (LP) | 75 |
| 69 | Transatlantic TRASAM 7 | ALEXIS KORNER'S ALL STAR BLUES INCORPORATED (LP, reissue of "Red Hot From Alex", different cover) | 30 |
| 71 | Rak SRAK 501 | ALEXIS KORNER (LP, textured sleeve) | 45 |
| 72 | Rak SRAKSP 51 | BOOTLEG HIM! (2-LP, with booklet) | 55 |
| 73 | Transatlantic TRA 269 | ACCIDENTALLY BORN IN NEW ORLEANS (LP, as Snape) | 35 |
| 75 | CBS 69155 | GET OFF MY CLOUD (LP) | 25 |

*(see also Cyril Davies, C.C.S., Bob Hall & Alexis Korner, Herbie Goins, Duffy Power, Long John Baldry, Rocket 88, Davy Graham, Beryl Bryden, Jimmy Cotton, Ken Colyer, Jack Bruce, Snape & Little Brother Montgomery)*

## ARTIE KORNFELD'S TREE

| | | | |
|---|---|---|---|
| 72 | Neighbourhood NBH 3 | Island Song/Feel | 5 |
| 70 | Probe SPB 1022 | A TIME TO REMEMBER (LP) | 20 |

## KORPERAYSHUN

| | | | |
|---|---|---|---|
| 89 | BPM BP12007 | K Factor/Non Stop (12") | 30 |

## KOSMIK KOMMANDO

| | | | |
|---|---|---|---|
| 94 | Rephlex CAT 007EP | Cat 007 (I)/Cat 007 (II)/Cat 007 (III)/Cat 007 (IV) (12", clear vinyl) | 12 |
| 93 | Rephlex MX 202 | UNIVERSAL INDICATOR YELLOW EP (12") | 18 |
| 01 | Machine Codes CODE 1010 | ANALOGUE ANDROID (LP, 100 only, signed insert) | 50 |

*(see also Aphex Twin)*

## LEE KOSMIN

| | | | |
|---|---|---|---|
| 78 | Polydor 2059034 | Ain't No Way/How Fine I Feel | 20 |

## DAVID KOSSOFF

| | | | |
|---|---|---|---|
| 61 | Oriole CB 1626 | Don't Have Any More Mrs. Moore/The Golden Wedding | 5 |

## PAUL KOSSOFF

| | | | |
|---|---|---|---|
| 73 | Island ILPS 9264 | BACK STREET CRAWLER (LP, pink rim palm tree label) | 15 |
| 83 | St. Tunes SDLP 0012PD | MR. BIG/BLUE SOUL (LP, picture disc) | 12 |
| 77 | DJM DJE 29002 | KOSS (2-LP) | 15 |

*(see also Free, Kossoff Kirke Tetsu & Rabbit, Creepy John Thomas)*

## KOSSOFF, KIRKE, TETSU & RABBIT

| | | | |
|---|---|---|---|
| 71 | Island ILPS 9188 | KOSSOFF, KIRKE, TETSU AND RABBIT (LP, gatefold sleeve, pink rim palm tree label) | 50 |

*(see also Paul Kossoff, Rabbit, Free)*

## CHIM KOTHARI

| | | | |
|---|---|---|---|
| 66 | Deram DM 108 | Sitar'N'Spice/Indian Bat | 12 |
| 66 | Deram DML 1002 | SOUND OF THE SITAR (LP) | 40 |

## KOUMBA

| | | | |
|---|---|---|---|
| 82 | Greensleeves GRED 105 | We Are Leggo/Billy (12") | 10 |

## JENNIFER KRAAL

| | | | |
|---|---|---|---|
| 69 | NEMS 56-4200 | The Men In My Life/Sinful Davey | 8 |

## KRACKER

| | | | |
|---|---|---|---|
| 73 | Rolling Stones RS 19106 | A Song For Polly/Medicated Goo | 12 |
| 74 | Rolling Stones COC 49102 | KRACKER BRAND (LP, gatefold sleeve) | 20 |

## KRAFTWERK

**SINGLES**

| | | | |
|---|---|---|---|
| 74 | Vertigo 6147 012 | Autobahn/Kometenmelodie 1 | 12 |
| 75 | Vertigo 6147 015 | Comet Melody 2/Kristallo | 20 |
| 76 | Capitol CL 15853 | Radio Activity/Antenna (in p/s) | 15 |
| 76 | Capitol CL 15853 | Radio Activity/Antenna | 8 |
| 77 | Capitol CL 104 | Showroom Dummies/Europe Endless | 8 |
| 77 | Capitol CLX 104 | Showroom Dummies/Europe Endless (12", 'train station' p/s) | 18 |
| 77 | Capitol CL 15917 | Trans-Europe Express/Europe Endless | 10 |
| 78 | Capitol CL 15981 | The Robots (edited version)/Spacelab (demo copy, special die cut sleeve) | 35 |
| 78 | Capitol CL 15981 | The Robots/Spacelab (foldout p/s) | 15 |
| 78 | Capitol CL 15981 | The Robots (alternative mix)/Spacelab (foldout p/s) | 30 |
| 78 | Capitol CL 15998 | Neon Lights/Trans-Europe Express/The Model | 8 |
| 78 | Capitol 12CL 15998 | Neon Lights/Trans-Europe Express/The Model (12", luminous vinyl, dayglo sleeve) | 30 |
| 78 | Capitol 12CL 16098 | Showroom Dummies/Spacelab/Europe Endless (12", reissue, 'red shirts' p/s) | 15 |
| 81 | EMI EMI 5175 | Pocket Calculator/Dentaku (p/s) | 8 |
| 81 | EMI TCEMI 5175 | Pocket Calculator/Numbers/Dentaku (cassette in cigarette'-pack style box) | 35 |
| 81 | EMI 12EMI 5175 | Pocket Calculator/Numbers/Dentaku (12", p/s) | 12 |
| 81 | Vertigo VER 3 | Kometenmelodie 2/Vom Himmel Hoch (p/s) | 15 |
| 81 | EMI EMI 5207 | Computer Love/The Model (p/s, original issue) | 5 |
| 81 | EMI 12EMI 5207 | Computer Love/The Model (12", p/s, original issue) | 12 |
| 82 | EMI EMI 5272 | Showroom Dummies/Numbers (p/s, some with mispressed B-side "The Model") | 8 |
| 82 | EMI EMI 5272 | Showroom Dummies/Numbers (p/s) | 5 |
| 83 | EMI EMI 5413 | Tour De France/Tour De France (Instrumental) (p/s, red or yellow labels) | 8 |
| 83 | EMI TCEMI 5413 | Tour De France/Tour De France (Short Version)/ Tour De France (2" Etape) | 15 |
| 83 | EMI 12EMI 5413 | Tour De France (Long Version)/(7" Version)/(2" Etape) (12", p/s, red or yellow labels) | 18 |
| 84 | EMI EMI 5413 | Tour De France (Kevorkian Remix)/Tour De France (Original 7" Version) (reissue, 'Breakdance' p/s) | 7 |
| 84 | EMI 12EMI 5413 | Tour De France (Kevorkian Remix)/Tour De France (Different Extended Version)/Tour De France (Original 7" Version) (12", reissue, 'Breakdance' p/s) | 18 |

MINT VALUE £

| Year | Label/Cat No | Title | Value |
|---|---|---|---|
| 86 | EMI EMI 5588 | Musique Non-Stop/Musique Non-Stop (Different Version) (p/s) | 5 |
| 86 | EMI 12EMI 5588 | Musique Non-Stop (6.15)/Musique Non-Stop (7" Version) (12", p/s) | 15 |
| 87 | EMI EMI 5602 | The Telephone Call/Der Telefon Anruf (p/s) | 6 |
| 87 | EMI 12EMI 5602 | The Telephone Call (Remix)/House Phone/Der Telefon Anruf (12", p/s) | 20 |
| 91 | EMI EM 192 | The Robots (re-recorded version)/Robotronik (p/s, red/black or white/black song title box) | 5 |
| 91 | EMI EM 201 | Radioactivity (Francois Kevorkian Remix)/(William Orbit Mix) (p/s) | 6 |
| 91 | EMI CDEM 201 | Radioactivity (Francois Kevorkian 7" Remix)/(Francois Kevorkian 12" Remix)/(William Orbit 12" Remix) (CD) | 20 |
| 97 | EMI KLANG BOX 101 | KRAFTWERK (4 x 12" box set, including "Trans Europe Express", Numbers, "Musique Non-Stop" & "Homecomputer"; with separate white or black T-shirt, promo only) | 100 |
| 97 | EMI KLANG BOX 101 | KRAFTWERK (4 x 12" box set, including "Trans Europe Express", "Numbers", Musique Non Stop & "Homecomputer"; without T-shirt, promo only) | 60 |

**ALBUMS**

| Year | Label/Cat No | Title | Value |
|---|---|---|---|
| 72 | Vertigo 6641 077 | KRAFTWERK (2-LP, gatefold sleeve, small 'swirl') | 350 |
| 72 | Vertigo 6641 077 | KRAFTWERK (2-LP gatefold sleeve, 'spacecraft' labels) | 100 |
| 74 | Vertigo 6360 616 | RALF AND FLORIAN (gatefold sleeve, 'spacecraft' label) | 120 |
| 74 | Vertigo 6360 616 | RALF AND FLORIAN ('spacecraft' label, no gatefold sleeve) | 60 |
| 74 | Vertigo 6360 620 | AUTOBAHN (embossed blue sleeve) | 40 |
| 75 | Vertigo 6360 629 | EXCELLER 8 (some with stickered sleeve) | 35 |
| 76 | Capitol E-ST 11457 | RADIOACTIVITY (with insert) | 25 |
| 77 | Capitol E-ST 11603 | TRANS-EUROPE EXPRESS (LP, inner) | 30 |
| 78 | Capitol E-ST 11728 | MAN MACHINE (LP) | 20 |
| 81 | EMI EMC 3370 | COMPUTER WORLD (LP) | 20 |
| 81 | Vertigo 6449 066 | ELEKTROKINETIK (LP) | 25 |
| 83 | EMI EMC 3407 | TECHNOPOP (unissued, sleeves only) | 0 |
| 85 | Fame FA4131181 | THE MAN MACHINE (LP, reissue, 'Fame' series) | 15 |
| 86 | EMI EMD 100130 | ELECTRIC CAFE (LP, gatefold) | 25 |
| 91 | EMI EM 1408 | THE MIX (2-LP, with inner sleeves) | 20 |
| 03 | EMI EMI 591 708 1 | TOUR DE FRANCE SOUNDTRACKS (2-LP, single stickered sleeve with inners) | 20 |
| 04 | EMI KLANG BOX 001 | THE CATALOGUE (8-CD, in card box, 1,000 only) | 80 |
| 05 | EMI 560 6111 | MINIMUM - MAXIMUM (4-LP box set) | 60 |
| 05 | EMI 45855 | MINIMUM - MAXIMUM (2-CD, DVD box set) | 35 |

*(see also Organisation, Elektric Music)*

## KRAFTY KUTS
| 99 | Southern Fried ECB17 | Gimme The Funk (12") | 10 |
| 99 | Lacerba CERBAL 14 | SLAM THE BREAKS ON (3-LP) | 20 |

## KRAKEN
| 80 | Knave EJSP 9370 | FANTASY REALITY (EP, no p/s) | 50 |

## BILLY J. KRAMER
| 67 | Parlophone R 5552 | Sorry/Going Going Gone | 10 |
| 68 | CBS 56-3396 | 1941/His Love Is Just A Lie | 10 |
| 68 | NEMS 56-3635 | A World Without Love/Going Through It | 8 |
| 69 | MGM MGM 1474 | The Colour Of My Love/I'm Running Away | 10 |
| 73 | Decca F 13426 | A Fool Like You/I'll Keep You Satisfied | 7 |
| 73 | Decca F 13442 | Darlin' Come To Me/Walking | 7 |
| 74 | BASF BA 1006 | Stayin' Power/Blue Jean Queen | 7 |
| 77 | EMI EMI 2661 | San Diego/Warm Summer Rain | 6 |
| 78 | EMI EMI 2740 | Ships That Pass In The Night/Is There Anymore At Home Like You | 6 |
| 79 | Hobo HOS 010 | Blue Christmas/Little Love (p/s, blue vinyl) | 10 |
| 80 | JM JM 1005 | Silver Dream/Lonely Lady | 5 |
| 82 | Runaway BJK 1 | Rock It/Dum Dum | 6 |
| 83 | Rak RAK 359 | You Can't Live On Memories/Stood Up (p/s) | 5 |

## BILLY J. KRAMER & THE DAKOTAS
| 63 | Parlophone R 5023 | Do You Want To Know A Secret/I'll Be On My Way | 5 |
| 63 | Parlophone R 5049 | Bad To Me/I Call Your Name | 5 |
| 63 | Parlophone R 5073 | I'll Keep You Satisfied/I Know | 5 |
| 64 | Parlophone R 5156 | From A Window/Second To None | 5 |
| 65 | Parlophone R 5234 | It's Gotta Last Forever/Don't You Do It No More | 5 |
| 65 | Parlophone R 5285 | Trains And Boats And Planes/That's The Way I Feel | 5 |
| 65 | Parlophone R 5362 | Neon City/I'll Be Doggone | 8 |
| 66 | Parlophone R 5408 | We're Doing Fine/Forgive Me | 10 |
| 66 | Parlophone R 5482 | You Make Me Feel Like Someone/Take My Hand | 10 |
| 67 | Reaction 591 014 | Town Of Tuxley Toymakers/Chinese Girl | 10 |
| 63 | Parlophone GEP 8885 | THE BILLY J. KRAMER HITS (EP) | 50 |
| 63 | Parlophone GEP 8895 | I'LL KEEP YOU SATISFIED (EP) | 10 |
| 64 | Parlophone GEP 8907 | LITTLE CHILDREN (EP) | 10 |
| 64 | Parlophone GEP 8921 | FROM A WINDOW (EP) | 10 |
| 65 | Parlophone GEP 8928 | BILLY J. PLAYS THE STATES (EP) | 15 |
| 63 | Parlophone PMC 1209 | LISTEN (LP, mono) | 50 |
| 65 | Regal REG 1057 | BILLY J (LP, export only) | 30 |

*(see also Dakotas)*

## WAYNE KRAMER
| 78 | Stiffwick DEA/SUK 1 | Ramblin' Rose/Get Some (numbered p/s) | 8 |
| 79 | Radar ADA 41 | The Harder They Come/East Side Girl (p/s) | 6 |

*(see also MC5)*

## KRAVIN AS
| 91 | Hangman HANG 39 UP | KRAVE ON! (LP) | 15 |

## KRAY CHERUBS
| | | | |
|---|---|---|---|
| 88 | Fierce FRIGHT 014 | No (p/s, 1-sided) | 20 |
| 89 | Snakeskin SS 002 | Rot In Hell Mom/SAUCERMAN: Motor Drag (numbered black p/s, 300 only) | 12 |
| 89 | Snakeskin SS 002 | Rot In Hell Mom/SAUCERMAN: Motor Drag (later reissue in purple p/s) | 8 |
| 89 | Forced Exposure FE 18 | Teen Camel/I Hate My Job (p/s) | 15 |

*(see also Art Attacks, Savage Pencil)*

## BILL KRENZ & HIS RAGTIMERS
| | | | |
|---|---|---|---|
| 56 | London HLU 8258 | There'll Be No New Tunes On This Old Piano/Goofus | 35 |

## KREW KATS
| | | | |
|---|---|---|---|
| 61 | HMV POP 840 | Trambone/Peak Hour | 10 |
| 61 | HMV POP 894 | Samovar/Jack's Good | 20 |

*(see also Shadows, Brian Bennett)*

## KRIMSON KAKE
| | | | |
|---|---|---|---|
| 69 | Penny Farthing PEN 707 | Feelin' Better/Waiter | 30 |

*(see also Samantha Jones, Vernons Girls)*

## KRIS
| | | | |
|---|---|---|---|
| 79 | V-KRIS VKR 1 | Okay/Trouble With The Law | 30 |

## KRISSI K
| | | | |
|---|---|---|---|
| 74 | People PEO110 | Stick Up/Who Do You Think You Are? | 10 |

## SONJA KRISTINA
| | | | |
|---|---|---|---|
| 68 | Polydor 56299 | Let The Sunshine In/Frank Mills | 15 |
| 80 | Chopper CHOP 101 | St Tropez/Mr Skin (p/s) | 10 |
| 80 | Chopper CHOPE 5 | SONJA KRISTINA (LP) | 35 |

*(see also Curved Air)*

## LEE KRISTOFFERSON
| | | | |
|---|---|---|---|
| 77 | Thrust RUFF 1 | Night Of The Werewolf/Dinner With Drac | 7 |

## KROKODIL
| | | | |
|---|---|---|---|
| 69 | Liberty LBS 83306 | KROKODIL (LP) | 50 |
| 70 | Liberty LBS 83417 | SWAMP (LP) | 50 |

## KROME & TIME
| | | | |
|---|---|---|---|
| 92 | Suburban Base SUBBASE 011 | This Sound Is For The Underground/Manic Stampede (12", p/s) | 25 |
| 92 | Suburban Base SUBBASE 11R | This Sound Is For The Underground (E.5 Remix)/Manic Stampede (DJ Hype's Sandringham Road Mix) (12") | 20 |
| 93 | Suburban Base SUBBASE 26 | The Slammer/Into The Night (12", p/s as DJ Krome & Mr Time) | 20 |

## KRONSTADT UPRISING
| | | | |
|---|---|---|---|
| 85 | Dog Rock SD 108 | Part Of The Game/The Horsemen (fold out p/s) | 5 |
| 80s | Spider SDL 12 | The Unknown Revolution (p/s) | 10 |

## HARDY KRUGER
| | | | |
|---|---|---|---|
| 59 | Top Rank TR 5005 | Blind Date (I'm A Lonely Man)/PINEWOOD ORCHESTRA: Blind Date (p/s) | 8 |

## KRU POPS
| | | | |
|---|---|---|---|
| 82 | Electric Bubble Gum EB 101 | Yummy Yummy Yummy/Gimme One More Dance | 40 |

## KRUZA
| | | | |
|---|---|---|---|
| 79 | Black Hole Records BHE 101 | Movies in The Night/Sun In My Eyes/Someone's There/All Stood Up (p/s) | 20 |

## KRYPTON TUNES
| | | | |
|---|---|---|---|
| 78 | Black & Red FIRE 1 | Behind Your Smile/Coming To See You (p/s) | 12 |
| 78 | Lightning GIL 546 | Limited Vision/All In Jail | 12 |
| 79 | Secret SR 009 | EXTENDED PLAY EP | 8 |

## KRYSIA (KOCJAN)
| | | | |
|---|---|---|---|
| 74 | RCA LPL1 5052 | KRYSIA (LP) | 18 |

*(see also Natural Acoustic Band, Fairport Convention)*

## KRYSTAL GENERATION
| | | | |
|---|---|---|---|
| 72 | Mercury 6052 120 | Wanted Dead Or Alive/Every Man Seems To Be For Himself | 10 |

## BOB KUBAN & INMEN
| | | | |
|---|---|---|---|
| 66 | Stateside SS 488 | The Cheater/Try Me Baby | 60 |
| 66 | Stateside SS 488 | The Cheater/Try Me Baby (DJ copy) | 110 |
| 66 | Stateside SS 514 | The Teaser/All I Want | 20 |
| 68 | Bell BLL 1027 | The Cheater/Try Me Baby (reissue) | 10 |

## KUBAS
| | | | |
|---|---|---|---|
| 65 | Columbia DB 7451 | I Love Her/Magic Potion | 60 |

*(see also Koobas)*

## DAVE KUBINEC
| | | | |
|---|---|---|---|
| 69 | Parlophone R5762 | Schopi/The Lady Loves | 20 |

## KUF-LINX
| | | | |
|---|---|---|---|
| 58 | London HLU 8583 | So Tough/What'cha Gonna Do | 80 |
| 58 | London HLU 8583 | So Tough/What'cha Gonna Do (78) | 25 |

## LENNY KUHR
| | | | |
|---|---|---|---|
| 69 | Philips BF 1777 | The Troubadour/Oh No Monsieur | 10 |

## KUKL
| | | | |
|---|---|---|---|
| 84 | Crass 1984/1 | THE EYE (LP, foldout sleeve) | 20 |
| 85 | Crass No. 4 | HOLIDAYS IN EUROPE (LP, with inner sleeve) | 20 |

*(see also Sugarcubes)*

## KULA SHAKER
| | | | |
|---|---|---|---|
| 96 | Columbia SHAKER 1LP | K (LP, inner) | 18 |
| 99 | Columbia SHAKER 2LP | PEASANTS, PIGS & ASTRONAUTS (LP, gatefold) | 25 |
| 10 | Strangefolk SFKS003LP | PILGRIM'S PROGRESS (LP, 300 only with signed screenprinted cover) | 20 |

## KULT
| | | | |
|---|---|---|---|
| 69 | CBS 4276 | No Home Today/Mister Number One | 300 |

MINT VALUE £

## CHARLIE KUNZ
| 54 | Decca F 10419 | Charlie Kunz Piano Medley, No. 114 | 10 |

## KURASS
| 70 | Escort ES 825 | Stampede/KING STITT: You Were Meant For Me (B-side actually by Lee Perry) | 40 |

## KURSAAL FLYERS
| 77 | CBS 5705 | TV Dinners/Revolver (A label demo only) | 12 |
| 77 | CBS 5771 | Television Generation/Revolver (p/s as Kursaals) | 7 |

## KUSTOM
| 82 | Red Bus RBUS 71 | Let The Girl Dance/Arrested | 20 |

## KUT
| 81 | Half Kut HKR 001 | Can't Sleep at Night/Faithful (no p/s) | 35 |

## FELA RANSOME KUTI (& AFRICA '70)
| 72 | Regal Zonophone RZ 3052 | Chop And Quench/Egbe Mi O (with Africa '70 & Ginger Baker) | 10 |
| 72 | Regal Zono. SLRZ 1023 | FELI RANSOME-KUTI & THE AFRICA '70 WITH GINGER BAKER LIVE! (LP) | 50 |
| 73 | Regal Zono. SLR2 103Y | AFRODISIAC (LP, red/silver labels with EMI boxed logo) | 200 |
| 75 | Decca/Aphrodisia DWAPS 2005 | UPSIDE DOWN (LP) | 25 |
| 75 | Creole CRLP 501 | SHAKARA (LP, with Africa '70) | 40 |
| 77 | Creole CRLP 509 | EVERYTHING SCATTER (LP) | 30 |
| 77 | Creole CRLP 511 | ZOMBIE (LP, with Africa '70) | 40 |
| 78 | Phase 4 Stereo PFS 4412 | YELLOW FEVER (LP) | 20 |
| 79 | Creole CRLP 502 | GENTLEMEN (LP) | 20 |
| 81 | Arista SPART 1167 | BLACK PRESIDENT (LP) | 30 |
| 82 | Arista SPART 1177 | ORIGINAL SUFFERHEAD (LP) | 30 |
| 83 | EMI EDP 1547203 | FELA ANIKULAPO KUTI (2-LP) | 25 |
| 97 | Talkin Loud 547 035-1 | BOX SET 1 (Box set, 6-LP, booklet, postcards) | 80 |

(see also Ginger Baker)

## BEN KWELLER
| 02 | 679 777201 | SHA SHA (LP) | 25 |

## JIM KWESKIN JUG BAND
| 65 | Fontana TFL 6036 | JIM KWESKIN JUG BAND (LP) | 20 |
| 67 | Fontana (S)TFL 6080 | SEE REVERSE SIDE FOR TITLE (LP) | 18 |
| 68 | Vanguard SVRL 19046 | WHATEVER HAPPENED TO THOSE GOOD OLD DAYS AT CLUB 47 (LP) | 18 |

## KYDD
| 75 | Dart ASRT 2052 | Voodoo Magic/You Need Love Love Love | 8 |

## (THE) KYDDS
| 69 | NEMS 56-4095 | The Sun Is A Laughing Child/Touch Of The Sun | 15 |

## CHARLES KYNARD
| 73 | Mainstream MSL 1017 | YOUR MAMA DON'T DANCE (LP) | 25 |

## KYODS
| 70 | President PT 289 | Judas In Blue/Where Did I Go Wrong | 6 |

## KYTES
| 66 | Pye 7N 17136 | Blessed/Call Me Darling | 15 |
| 66 | Pye 7N 17179 | Frosted Panes/I'll Give You Better Love | 35 |
| 68 | Island WI 6027 | Running In The Water/The End Of The Day | 80 |

## KYTTOCK KYND
| 70 | Dorian 4782 | KYTTOCK KYND (LP) | 40 |

**L**

## PATTI LA BELLE (& BLUE BELLES)
| 64 | Sue WI 324 | Down The Aisle/C'est La Vie | 30 |
| 65 | Cameo Parkway P 935 | Danny Boy/I Believe | 20 |
| 65 | Atlantic AT 4055 | All Or Nothing/You Forgot How To Love (as Patty La Belle & Her Belles) | 30 |
| 66 | Atlantic AT 4064 | Over The Rainbow/Groovy Kind Of Love (as Patty La Belle & Her Belles) | 15 |
| 66 | Atlantic 584 007 | Patti's Prayer/Family Man (as Patti La Belle & Her Belles) | 12 |
| 67 | Atlantic 584 072 | Take Me For A Little While/I Don't Want To Go On Without You | 12 |
| 66 | Atlantic 587 001 | OVER THE RAINBOW (LP) | 40 |

(see also Blue-Belles)

## LABRADFORD
| 95 | Flying Nun FN 329 | A STABLE REFERENCE (LP, reissue, numbered sleeve) | 18 |
| 96 | Blast First BFFP 136 | LABRADFORD (LP, die-cut sleeve, 2 inserts) | 18 |
| 97 | Blast First BFFP 144 | MI MEDIA NARANJA (LP) | 15 |

## LACE
| 68 | Columbia DB 8499 | People People/The Nun | 25 |
| 69 | Page One POF 135 | I'm A Gambler/Go Away | 10 |

(see also Universals, Pete Dello, Honeybus, Red Herring, Gary Walker & Rain)

## DAVE LACEY & CORVETTES
| 65 | Philips BF 1419 | That's What They All Say/I've Had Enough | 10 |

## LACKEY & SWEENEY
| 73 | Village Thing VTS 23 | JUNK STORE SONGS FOR SALE (LP) | 50 |

## LACK OF KNOWLEDGE
| 81 | LOK LOK 1 | The Uninvited/Ritual (with A4 photocopied inserts) | 30 |

| | | | |
|---|---|---|---|
| 83 | Crass Records 121984/6 | GREY (EP) | 20 |
| 85 | Chainsaw TEXT 7 | SENTINEL (EP) | 10 |
| 84 | Corpus Christi CHRIST 15 | SIRENS ARE BACK (LP) | 20 |

**JUNIOR LACY**
| 77 | Aries ARI 003 | You Will See Jah Light/Jah Love Version (12") | 25 |
|---|---|---|---|

**STEVE LACY**
| 57 | Esquire 32 143 | SOPRANO TODAY (LP) | 50 |
|---|---|---|---|
| 72 | Emanem 301 | SOLO (LP) | 25 |
| 73 | Emanem 304 | THE CRUST (LP) | 35 |

**STEVE LACY & DEREK BAILEY**
| 76 | Incus 26 | COMPANY 4 (LP) | 25 |
|---|---|---|---|

*(see also Derek Bailey)*

**LADDERS**
| 83 | Statik TAK 2 | Gotta See Jane/Krugerrands (p/s) | 6 |
|---|---|---|---|
| 83 | Statik TAK 2-12 | Gotta See Jane/Krugerrands (12", p/s) | 10 |

**LADD'S BLACK ACES**
| 56 | London AL 3556 | LADD'S BLACK ACES (10" LP) | 15 |
|---|---|---|---|

**LA-DE-DA BAND**
| 69 | Parlophone R 5810 | Come Together/Here Is Love | 18 |
|---|---|---|---|

**LADIES**
| 80s | Music Of Life MOLIS 6 | Turned On To You/I Knew That Love (12") | 15 |
|---|---|---|---|

**TOMMY LADNIER**
| 54 | London AL 3524 | BLUES AND STOMPS VOLUME ONE - TOMMY LADNIER (10" LP) | 20 |
|---|---|---|---|
| 55 | London AL 3548 | PLAYS THE BLUES WITH MA RAINEY & EDMONIA HENDERSON (10" LP) | 20 |

*(see also Ma Rainey)*

**PATTIE LA DONNE**
| 69 | Joe/Duke DU 23 | Friends And Lovers/JOE'S ALLSTARS: Hot Line | 12 |
|---|---|---|---|

**LADY GAGA**
| 08 | Interscope LGDANCEUP1 | JUST DANCE - THE REMIXES (LP, promo, pink vinyl) | 45 |
|---|---|---|---|

**LADY JANE**
| 84 | Schizoid SCHIZ 01 | For You Tonight/Out For The Count/Whisky And Leather (private pressing) | 60 |
|---|---|---|---|

**LADY JANE & VERITY**
| 59 | Pye International 7N 25036 | The Slow Look/Cry Baby | 8 |
|---|---|---|---|

**LADY JUNE**
| 74 | Caroline C 1509 | LADY JUNE'S LINGUISTIC LEPROSY (LP, with perforated lyric sheet) | 35 |
|---|---|---|---|

*(see also Kevin Ayers, Eno)*

**LADY LEE**
| 64 | Decca F 11961 | I'm Into Something Good/When Love Comes Along | 12 |
|---|---|---|---|
| 65 | Decca F 12147 | 99 Times Out Of 100/I Can Feel It | 8 |
| 65 | Columbia DB 7121 | My Whole World (Seems To Be Tumbling Down)/Girl | 10 |

**LADY LUCK & LULLABIES**
| 62 | Philips PB 1245 | Young Stranger/Dance | 5 |
|---|---|---|---|

**LADYBIRDS**
| 64 | Columbia DB 7197 | Lady Bird/I Don't Care Any More | 10 |
|---|---|---|---|
| 64 | Columbia DB 7250 | The White Cliffs Of Dover/It's Not The Same Without A Boy | 10 |
| 64 | Columbia DB 7351 | Memories/Try A Little Love | 10 |
| 65 | Columbia DB 7523 | I Wanna Fly/O.K. Fred | 10 |
| 70 | Decca F13014 | Love As High As A Mountain/Stand Up And Be Counted | 12 |

*(see also Sharades, Russ Loader, Marion Davies, De Laine Sisters)*

**LADYHAWKE**
| 12 | Modular MODVL 151 | Black White And Blue/(Big Pink Remix) (250 only) | 6 |
|---|---|---|---|
| 08 | Modular MODVL 104 | LADYHAWKE (LP, gatefold) | 20 |

**LADYTRON**
| 01 | Invicta Hi Fi LIQ 014 | 604 (2-LP, white vinyl) | 25 |
|---|---|---|---|
| 02 | Telstar TELP 3296 | LIGHT & MAGIC (LP) | 18 |

**LAFAYETTES**
| 62 | RCA RCA 1299 | Life's Too Short/Nobody But You | 10 |
|---|---|---|---|
| 62 | RCA RCA 1308 | Caravan Of Lonely Men/I Still Do | 10 |

**JACK LE FORGE**
| 65 | Stateside SS 444 | Our Crazy Affair/Bossa Bossa Nova (withdrawn) | 25 |
|---|---|---|---|

**FRANCIS LAI**
| 67 | Brunswick LAT/STA 8689 | I'LL NEVER FORGET WHAT'S 'ISNAME (LP, soundtrack) | 50 |
|---|---|---|---|
| 69 | United Artists SULP 1231 | HANNIBAL BROOKS (LP) | 30 |
| 69 | Philips SBL 7876 | MAYERLING (LP) | 20 |
| 70 | United Artists UAS 29137 | RIDER IN THE RAIN (LP) | 25 |

**LAIBACH**
| 84 | L.A.Y.L.A.H. LAY 002 | Boji/Sila/Brat Moj (12", p/s) | 12 |
|---|---|---|---|
| 84 | East West 12 EWS 3 | Panarama/Decree (12", p/s) | 10 |
| 85 | Cherry Red 12CHERRY 91 | Die Liebe/Die Liebe Ist Grösste Kraft, Die Alles Schafft (12", p/s) | 10 |
| 87 | Mute MUTE 62 | Life Is Life/Germania (p/s) | 5 |
| 86 | Cherry Red BRED 67 | NOVA AKROPOLA (LP) | 15 |
| 88 | Mute PMUTE 80T | SYMPATHY FOR THE DEVIL (12" EP, picture disc) | 10 |
| 86 | Side Effects SER 08 | OCCUPIED EUROPE TOUR '85 (LP) | 15 |
| 96 | Mute STUMM 136 | JESUS CHRIST SUPERSTARS (LP) | 15 |
| 03 | Mute STUMM 223 | WAT (2-LP) | 20 |

**Rare Record Price Guide 2018**

## LAIKA
| | | | |
|---|---|---|---|
| 94 | Too Pure PURE 42 | SILVER APPLES ON THE MOON (LP) | 18 |
| 97 | Too Pure PURE 62 | SOUNDS OF THE SATELLITES (2-LP) | 18 |
| 00 | Too Pure PURE 89 | GOOD LOOKING BLUES (2-LP) | 20 |

## CLEO LAINE
| | | | |
|---|---|---|---|
| 54 | Parlophone MSP 6107 | I Got Rhythm/I Know You're Mine (with Johnny Dankworth Orchestra) | 10 |
| 55 | Parlophone MSP 6147 | Ain't Misbehavin'/I Got It Bad, And That Ain't Good (with Johnny Dankworth Orchestra) | 10 |
| 71 | Philips 6006 077 | Model City's Programme/Night Owl | 50 |
| 57 | Pye Nixa Jazz NJE 1026 | THE APRIL AGE (EP, as Cleo Laine & Dave Lee Quintet) | 20 |
| 57 | Esquire EP 102 | CLEO LAINE (EP, as Cleo Laine & Keith Christie Quintet) | 20 |
| 57 | Esquire EP 122 | CLEO LAINE (EP, as Cleo Laine & Keith Christie Quintet) | 20 |
| 55 | Esquire 15-007 | CLEO LAINE (10" LP) | 40 |
| 58 | Pye Nixa NPT 19024 | CLEO'S CHOICE (10" LP) | 40 |
| 58 | MGM MGM-C 765 | SHE'S THE TOPS (LP) | 25 |
| 62 | Fontana 680 992 TL | ALL ABOUT ME (LP, also stereo 886 159 TY) | 15 |
| 64 | Fontana (S)TL 5209 | SHAKESPEARE AND ALL THAT JAZZ (LP) | 15 |
| 66 | Fontana (S)TL 5316 | WOMAN TALK (LP) | 15 |
| 68 | Fontana STL 5483 | SOLILOQUY (LP) | 15 |

(see also Johnny Dankworth, Tubby Hayes & Cleo Laine, Dudley Moore)

## DENNY LAINE
| | | | |
|---|---|---|---|
| 67 | Deram DM 122 | Say You Don't Mind/Ask The People | 15 |
| 68 | Deram DM 171 | Too Much In Love/Catherine's Wheel | 30 |
| 69 | Deram DM 227 | Say You Don't Mind/Ask The People (reissue) | 10 |
| 73 | Wizard WIZ 104 | Find A Way Somehow/Move Me To Another Place | 15 |
| 77 | EMI 2588 | Moondreams/Heartbeat | 6 |
| 77 | Palladin PAL 5014 | Caroline/Blues | 6 |
| 86 | President PT 555 | Land Of Peace/If I Tried | 6 |
| 73 | Wizard SW2 2001 | AHH...LAINE (LP, yellow labels) | 20 |

(see also Paul McCartney/Wings, Balls, Trevor Burton, Magic Christians, Ginger Baker's Airforce, BL&G)

## FRANKIE LAINE
### SINGLES
| | | | |
|---|---|---|---|
| 53 | Columbia SCM 5016 | The Ruby And The Pearl/The Mermaid | 10 |
| 53 | Columbia SCM 5017 | Jealousy/The Gandy Dancers' Ball | 10 |
| 53 | Columbia SCM 5031 | I'm Just A Poor Bachelor/Tonight You Belong To Me | 7 |

### ALBUMS
| | | | |
|---|---|---|---|
| 52 | Oriole/Mercury MG 10002 | SONGS BY FRANKIE LAINE (10") | 12 |
| 54 | Mercury MG 25097 | MR. RHYTHM SINGS (10", reissue) | 12 |
| 54 | Columbia 33S 1047 | ONE FOR MY BABY (10") | 12 |
| 55 | Philips BBR 8068 | MR. RHYTHM (10") | 12 |
| 57 | Philips BBL 7155 | ROCKIN' | 15 |

(see also Jo Stafford & Frankie Laine,, Easy Riders)

## FRANKIE LAINE & JOHNNIE RAY
| | | | |
|---|---|---|---|
| 57 | Philips JK 1026 | Up Above My Head, I Hear Music In The Air/Good Evening Friends (jukebox issue) | 10 |
| 57 | Philips BBE 12153 | FRANKIE AND JOHNNIE (EP, 1 track each, 2 together) | 10 |

(see also Johnnie Ray)

## LINDA LAINE (& SINNERS)
| | | | |
|---|---|---|---|
| 64 | Columbia DB 7204 | Doncha Know, Doncha Know, Doncha Know/Ain't That Fun | 20 |
| 64 | Columbia DB 7370 | Low Grades And High Fever/After Today | 20 |
| 65 | Columbia DB 7549 | Don't Do It Baby/All I Want To Do Is Run | 20 |

(see also Sinners)

## SCOTT LAINE
| | | | |
|---|---|---|---|
| 63 | Windsor WB 114 | Tearaway Johnnie/John Silver | 40 |

## DENZIL LAING
| | | | |
|---|---|---|---|
| 71 | Songbird SB 1054 | Medicine Stick/CRYSTALITES: Short Cut | 15 |

(see also Soul Vendors, Dennis Alcapone)

## LAKE
| | | | |
|---|---|---|---|
| 76 | CBS 5015 | Do I Love You/Key To The Rhyme | 6 |

## ALAN LAKE
| | | | |
|---|---|---|---|
| 70 | Ember EMB S 278 | Good Times/Got To Have Tenderness (p/s) | 15 |

## BONNIE LAKE & HER BEAUX
| | | | |
|---|---|---|---|
| 56 | Brunswick 05622 | Thirteen Black Cats/The Miracle Of Love | 20 |

(see also Jack Pleis)

## LAKELANDERS
| | | | |
|---|---|---|---|
| | 60s | THE LAKELANDERS IN CONCERT (LP, hand-typed labels) | 80 |

## LEE LAMAR & HIS ORCHESTRA
| | | | |
|---|---|---|---|
| 57 | London HLB 8508 | Teenage Pedal Pushers/Sophia | 75 |

## GENE LAMARR
| | | | |
|---|---|---|---|
| 72 | Injun 112 | You Don't Love Me Anymore/Crazy Little House On The Hill | 15 |

## LAMB
| | | | |
|---|---|---|---|
| 96 | Fontana PY 281 | LAMB (2-LP, inner) | 30 |
| 99 | Mercury 558 821-1 | FEAR OF FOURS (2-LP) | 30 |
| 01 | Mercury 586 4351 | WHAT SOUND (2-LP) | 45 |
| 03 | Mercury 986 591-7 | BETWEEN DARKNESS AND WONDER (LP) | 25 |

## CHRIS LAMB & UNIVERSALS
| | | | |
|---|---|---|---|
| 65 | Decca F 12176 | Mysterious Land/If You Ask Me | 15 |

(see also Universals, Gidian)

**KEVIN LAMB**
| 70 | Concord CON 23 | Who Is The Hero?/The Road To Antibes | 6 |
| 73 | Birth RAB 1004 | Who Is The Hero?/Who Stole The Ice | 5 |
| 72 | Birth RAB 4 | WHO IS THE HERO? (LP, white label with 'rabbit' child logo) | 40 |

**LAMBCHOP**
| 96 | City Slang 04974-45 | The Man Who Loved Beer/Alumni Lawn/Burly & Johnson (p/s) | 5 |
| 10 | City Slang SLANG 0680056 | TOUR BOX (8-CD, 2-DVD in canvas box, 1000 only sold on 2010 tour) | 90 |

**JEANNIE LAMBE**
| 67 | CBS 202636 | Miss Disc/Montano Blues (with Gordon Beck Orchestra) | 25 |
| 67 | CBS 2731 | Day After Day After Day/City At Night | 20 |
| 67 | CBS 3000 | This Is My Love/Where Have All The Endings Gone (as Jeanne Lam) | 8 |

**DAVE LAMBERT, JON HENDRICKS & ANNIE ROSS**
| 60 | Philips BBL 7368 | DAVE LAMBERT, JON HENDRICKS & ANNIE ROSS (LP, stereo SBBL 562) | 15 |

*(see also Jon Hendricks, Annie Ross)*

**TREVOR LAMBERT**
| 72 | Duke DU 132 | Bald Head Teacher (act. by Max Romeo)/HEADMASTERS: Bald Head Version | 5 |

**LAMBRETTAS**
| 79 | Rocket XPRES 23 | Go Steady/Listen Listen/Cortinas (p/s) | 15 |
| 80 | Rocket XPRES 25 | Poison Ivy/Runaround (with '2-Stroke' die-cut sleeve & label) | 20 |
| 80 | Rocket XPRES 25 | Poison Ivy/Runaround (with ROCKET die-cut sleeve & label) | 12 |
| 80 | Rocket XPRES 36 | Page 3/Steppin' Out (Of Line) (withdrawn; one copy known to exist with p/s) | 500 |
| 80 | Rocket XPRES 36 | Another Day (Another Girl)/Steppin' Out (Of Line) ('emergency' p/s) | 5 |
| 81 | Rocket XPRES 48 | Good Times/Lamba Samba (p/s) | 5 |
| 81 | Rocket XPRES 52 | Anything You Want/Ambience (Rocket die-cut sleeve) | 6 |
| 81 | Rocket XPRES 62 | Decent Town/Da-a-a-ance (p/s) | 6 |
| 81 | Rocket XPRES 6212 | Decent Town/Da-a-a-ance/Total Strangers/Young Girls (12", p/s) | 12 |
| 82 | Rocket XPRES 74 | Somebody To Love/Nobody's Watching Me (p/s) | 8 |
| 82 | Rocket XPRES 74 | Somebody To Love/Nobody's Watching Me (p/s, mispressing, crediting Leap Before You Look on label & sleeve) | 8 |
| 80 | Rocket TRAIN 10 | BEAT BOYS IN THE JET AGE (LP, with inner) | 15 |

**LAME DUCK**
| 73 | Perth PR 001 | Sitting Still/Hold Out Your Hand | 25 |

**LAMELLA**
| 80 | Direct DO B1 | When Julie Dances/Wasting Your Time (no p/s, 500 only) | 50 |

**L.A.M.F.**
| 01 | Head Heritage HH11 | AMBIENT METAL (CD, mail order, 1000 only) | 30 |

**TONI LAMOND**
| 68 | Philips BF 1722 | Silent Voices/They Don't Give Medals (To Yesterday's Heroes) | 15 |

**DUNCAN LAMONT**
| 68 | Morgan MRSAM 2 | THIS GUY (LP) | 15 |

**LA MORTGAGE**
| 79 | Metro 0501/EJSP 9289 | Fallin/The Shady Lane (p/s) | 30 |

**LAMPLIGHTERS**
| 55 | Parlophone DP 416 | Salty Dog/Ride Jockey Ride (78, export issue) | 40 |

*(see also Thurston Harris)*

**LAMP SISTERS**
| 68 | Sue WI 4048 | A Woman With The Blues/I Thought It Was All Over | 40 |

**LANA SISTERS**
| 58 | Fontana H 148 | Ring-A My Phone/Chimes Of Arcady | 25 |
| 59 | Fontana H 176 | Buzzin'/Cry, Cry, Baby | 25 |
| 59 | Fontana H 190 | Mister Dee-Jay/Tell Him No | 25 |
| 59 | Fontana H 221 | (Seven Little Girls) Sitting In The Back Seat (with Al Saxon)/ Sitting On The Sidewalk | 20 |
| 60 | Fontana H 235 | My Mother's Eyes/You've Got What It Takes | 12 |
| 60 | Fontana H 252 | Someone Loves You, Joe/Tinatarella Di Luna | 10 |
| 60 | Fontana H 283 | Two-some/Down South | 10 |

*(see also Al Saxon, Dusty Springfield, Chantelles)*

**CYNTHIA LANAGAN**
| 54 | Columbia SCMC 8 | Body And Soul/I Can't Believe You're In Love With Me (export issue) | 10 |
| 57 | Parlophone R 4316 | Jamie Boy/Silent Lips (as Cynthia Lanigan) | 7 |
| 57 | Parlophone R 4383 | I'm Available/(Don't Stop, Don't Stop) Tell Me More | 7 |

**LANCASHIRE FAYRE**
| 80 | Folk Heritage FHR 113 | LANCASHIRE FAYRE (LP) | 20 |

**STEVE LANCASTER**
| 67 | Polydor 56215 | San Francisco Street/Miguel Fernando San Sebastian Brown | 15 |

**LANCASTRIANS**
| 64 | Pye 7N 15732 | We'll Sing In The Sunshine/Was She Tall | 20 |
| 65 | Pye 7N 15791 | Let's Lock The Door (And Throw Away The Key)/If You're Goin' To Leave Me | 7 |
| 65 | Pye 7N 15846 | There'll Be No More Goodbyes/Never Gonna Come On Home | 7 |
| 65 | Pye 7N 15927 | Lonely Man/I Can't Stand The Pain | 40 |
| 66 | Pye 7N 17043 | The World Keeps Going Round/Not The Same Anymore | 5 |
| 66 | Pye 7N 17072 | The Ballad Of The Green Berets/My Little Rose | |

**MAJOR LANCE**
| 63 | Columbia DB 7099 | The Monkey Time/Mama Didn't Know | 35 |
| 63 | Columbia DB 7099 | The Monkey Time/Mama Didn't Know (DJ copy) | 60 |
| 63 | Columbia DB 7168 | Hey Little Girl/Crying In The Rain | 25 |
| 64 | Columbia DB 7205 | Um, Um, Um, Um, Um, Um/Sweet Music | 20 |
| 64 | Columbia DB 7271 | The Matador/Gonna Get Married | 30 |

# Rick LANCELOT & SEVEN KNIGHTS

| | | | MINT VALUE £ |
|---|---|---|---|
| 64 | Columbia DB 7365 | Rhythm/Please Don't Say No More | 30 |
| 65 | Columbia DB 7463 | I'm So Lost/Sometimes I Wonder | 25 |
| 65 | Columbia DB 7527 | Come See/You Belong To Me, My Love | 30 |
| 65 | Columbia DB 7609 | Pride And Joy/I'm The One | 60 |
| 65 | Columbia DB 7688 | Too Hot To Hold/Dark And Lonely | 75 |
| 65 | Columbia DB 7787 | Everybody Loves A Good Time/I Just Can't Help It | 30 |
| 65 | Columbia DB 7787 | Everybody Loves A Good Time/I Just Can't Help It (DJ Copy) | 75 |
| 66 | Columbia DB 7967 | Investigate/Little Young Lover | 75 |
| 66 | Columbia DB 7967 | Investigate/Little Young Lover (DJ copy) | 75 |
| 67 | Columbia DB 8122 | Ain't No Soul (Left In These Ole Shoes)/You'll Want Me Back | 125 |
| 67 | Columbia DB 8122 | Ain't No Soul (Left In These Ole Shoes)/You'll Want Me Back (DJ copy) | 60 |
| 69 | Atlantic 584 277 | Follow The Leader/Since You've Been Gone | 100 |
| 69 | Atlantic 584 302 | Sweeter As The Days Go By/Shadows Of A Memory | 15 |
| 69 | Soul City SC 114 | The Beat/You'll Want Me Back | 20 |
| 70 | Buddah 2011 046 | Gypsy Woman/Stay Away From Me | 25 |
| 72 | Stax 2025 124 | I Wanna Make Up/That's The Story Of My Life | 15 |
| 72 | Epic EPC 8404 | Um, Um, Um, Um, Um, Um/Sweet Music (reissue) | 6 |
| 73 | Contempo C 1 | The Right Track/Um, Um, Um, Um, Um | 6 |
| 73 | Contempo C 9 | Ain't No Soul (Left In These Ole Shoes)/Investigate | 8 |
| 73 | Contempo C 26 | Dark And Lonely/My Girl | 15 |
| 73 | Warner Bros K 16334 | Sweeter/Wild & Free | 20 |
| 74 | Warner Bros K 16385 | Without A Doubt/Open The Door To Your Heart | 8 |
| 74 | Contempo CS 2017 | Gimme Little Sign/How Can You Say Goodbye | 15 |
| 74 | Contempo CS 9015 | The Right Track/Ain't No Soul (Left In These Ole Shoes) | 25 |
| 75 | Contempo CS 2045 | Don't You Know I Love You (Parts 1 & 2) | 6 |
| 75 | Pye 7N 45487 | You're Everything I Need (Parts 1 & 2) | 20 |
| 76 | Pye International 7N 25705 | Nothing Can Stop Me/Follow The Leader | 10 |
| 64 | Columbia SEG 8318 | UM UM UM UM UM UM (EP) | 10 |
| 65 | Columbia 33SX 1728 | THE RHYTHM OF MAJOR LANCE (LP) | 100 |
| 73 | Contempo COLP 1001 | GREATEST HITS LIVE AT THE TORCH (LP, sitting under a tree is first pressing) | 170/40 |

# RICK LANCELOT & SEVEN KNIGHTS

| | | | |
|---|---|---|---|
| 66 | RCA RCA 1502 | Say Girl/Live Like A Lion | 15 |

# LANCERS

| | | | |
|---|---|---|---|
| 54 | London HL 8027 | Stop Chasin' Me Baby/Peggy O'Neil | 15 |
| 54 | London HL 8079 | So High, So Low, So Wide/It's You, It's You I Love | 15 |
| 54 | Vogue Coral Q 2038 | Mister Sandman/The Little White Light | 15 |
| 55 | Vogue Coral Q 72062 | Timberjack/C-r-a-z-y Music | 20 |
| 55 | Vogue Coral Q 72081 | Get Out Of The Car (as Lancers & Georgie Auld)/Close Your Eyes | 20 |
| 55 | Vogue Coral Q 72100 | Jo-Ann/The Bonnie Banks Of Loch Lomon' | 10 |
| 56 | Vogue Coral Q 72128 | Alphabet Rock/Rock Around The Island | 40 |
| 56 | Vogue Coral Q 72157 | Little Fool/A Man Is As Good As His Word | 8 |
| 56 | Vogue Coral Q 72183 | The First Travelling Saleslady/Free | 5 |
| 57 | Vogue Coral Q 72220 | Never Leave Me/I Came Back To Say I'm Sorry | 5 |
| 57 | Vogue Coral Q 72254 | It Happened In Monterey/Ramona/Freckled-Face Sara Jane | 5 |
| 57 | Vogue Coral Q 72282 | Charm Bracelet/And It Don't Feel Bad | 6 |
| 58 | Coral Q 72300 | The Stroll/Don't Go Near The Water | 6 |
| 60 | Coral Q 72398 | Joey, Joey, Joey/JOHNNY DESMOND: The Most Happy Fella | 5 |
| 61 | Warner Bros WB 39 | Young In Love/Lonesome Town | 5 |
| 55 | London REP 1027 | PRESENTING THE LANCERS (EP) | 20 |
| 54 | London H-APB 1029 | OH SWEET MAMA (10" LP) | 25 |
| 61 | London HA-P 2307 | CONCERT IN CONTRASTS (LP) | 15 |

# BILLY LAND

| | | | |
|---|---|---|---|
| 62 | Oriole CB 1750 | I Go Walking/You're Too Much | 10 |

# HAROLD LAND

| | | | |
|---|---|---|---|
| 58 | Contemporary LAC 12178 | HAROLD IN THE LAND OF JAZZ (LP) | 15 |

# LAND OF BARBARA

| | | | |
|---|---|---|---|
| 93 | Loble L02 | Alcohol/Phosphorus For The Mutiny (p/s) | 8 |

# BOB LANDER & SPOTNICKS

| | | | |
|---|---|---|---|
| 62 | Oriole CB 1784 | Midnight Special/My Old Kentucky Home | 15 |

*(see also Spotnicks)*

# BILL & BRETT LANDIS

| | | | |
|---|---|---|---|
| 59 | Parlophone R 4516 | Since You've Gone/Bright Eyes | 15 |
| 59 | Parlophone R 4551 | By You, By You/Forgive Me | 10 |
| 59 | Parlophone R 4570 | Baby Talk/Love Me True | 15 |

# JERRY LANDIS

| | | | |
|---|---|---|---|
| 62 | Oriole CB 1930 | Carlos Dominquez/He Was My Brother | 40 |

*(see also Paul Simon)*

# JOYA LANDIS

| | | | |
|---|---|---|---|
| 68 | Trojan TR 620 | Kansas City/Out The Light | 20 |
| 68 | Trojan TR 622 | Angel Of The Morning/ALTON PHILLIPS: Love Letters | 40 |
| 69 | Trojan TR 641 | Moonlight Lover/I Love You True | 45 |

*(see also Jay & Joya, Hugh Roy)*

# LANDLORD

| | | | |
|---|---|---|---|
| 90 | Debut DEBTX 3084 | I Like It (12") | 10 |

# HOAGY LANDS

| | | | |
|---|---|---|---|
| 67 | Stateside SS 2030 | The Next In Line/Please Don't Talk About Me When I'm Gone | 250 |
| 67 | Stateside SS 2030 | The Next In Line/Please Don't Talk About Me When I'm Gone (DJ copy) | 400 |
| 68 | Stateside SS 2085 | I'm Yours/Only You | 20 |

Rare Record Price Guide 2018          718

| | | | |
|---|---|---|---|
| 72 | Action ACT 4605 | Why Didn't You Let Me Know/Do You Know What Life Is All About | 35 |
| 75 | UK USA 13 | Friends And Lovers Don't Go Together/True Love At Last | 30 |
| 75 | UK USA 14 | The Next In Line/I'm Yours | 10 |

## NEIL LANDSTRUMM
| | | | |
|---|---|---|---|
| 95 | Mosquito MSQ 02 | PASCAL EP (12", custom sleeve) | 20 |

*(see also Blue Arsed Fly)*

## DES(MOND) LANE
| | | | |
|---|---|---|---|
| 56 | Decca F 10821 | Penny-Whistle Rock/Penny-Whistle Polka | 8 |
| 57 | Decca F 10847 | Rock Mister Piper/Plymouth Rock | 10 |
| 59 | Top Rank JAR 203 | Moonbird/The Clanger March (as Des Lane Orchestra, with John Barry) | 6 |
| 68 | Pye 7N 17546 | Sadie/No More Wild Oats (as Des Lane) | 5 |

*(see also Cyril Stapleton, John Barry)*

## GARY LANE & GARRISONS
| | | | |
|---|---|---|---|
| 61 | Fontana H 338 | Start Walking Boy/How Wrong Can You Be | 10 |
| 62 | Fontana 267221 TF | I'm A Lucky Boy/A Love Like You | 10 |

## LOIS LANE
| | | | |
|---|---|---|---|
| 67 | RCA RCA 1570 | One Little Voice/Sing To Me | 6 |
| 68 | Mercury MF 1042 | Punky's Dilemma/Lazy Summer Day | 6 |
| 69 | Mercury MF 1115 | Lovin' Time/Winds Of Heaven | 6 |
| 70 | Philips BF 1829 | Putting My Baby To Sleep/Far From The Madding Crowd | 5 |
| 70 | DJM DJS 2280 | Day By Day/Cloud Of Blue | 5 |
| 68 | Mercury SMCL 20125 | LOIS LANE (LP) | 20 |

*(see also Caravelles)*

## MICKEY LEE LANE
| | | | |
|---|---|---|---|
| 64 | Stateside SS 354 | Shaggy Dog/Oo Oo | 20 |
| 65 | Stateside SS 456 | Hey Sah-Lo-Ney/Of Yesterday | 75 |
| 65 | Stateside SS 456 | Hey Sah-Lo-Ney/Of Yesterday (DJ copy) | 150 |

## PENNY LANE
| | | | |
|---|---|---|---|
| 68 | Columbia DB 8377 | Loving Or Losing You/Deep Down Inside | 10 |
| 68 | CBS 3718 | The Boy Who Never Grew Up/I'm Going Back | 8 |
| 70 | CBS 4749 | Bouzouki/Make Up Or Break Up | 10 |
| 72 | CBS 7916 | Legend In Your Own Time/Driving Me Out Of My Mind | 8 |
| 70 | CBS 4905 | Heartbreak House/He's Got A Hold Of My Heart | 6 |
| 70 | CBS 5311 | Rock Me In The Cradle (Of Your Loving Arms)/I'm Free | 10 |

## RONNIE LANE & SLIM CHANCE
| | | | |
|---|---|---|---|
| 73 | GM GMS 011 | How Come/Tell Everyone/Done This One Before (p/s) | 8 |
| 77 | Polydor 2058 944 | Street In The City/Annie (with Pete Townshend) | 6 |
| 79 | Gem GEMS 12 | Kuschty Rye/You're So Right (p/s) | 8 |
| 74 | GM GMS 024 | The Poacher/Bye & Bye (Gonna See The King) | 5 |
| 74 | GM GMS 033 | Roll on Babe/Anymore For Anymore | 5 |
| 74 | Island WIP 6216 | What Went Down (That Night With You)/Lovely | 7 |
| 75 | Island WIP 6229 | Brother Can You Spare A Dime/Ain't No Lady | 7 |
| 76 | Island WIP 6258 | Don't Try And Change My Mind/Well, well, Hello (The Party) | 7 |
| 80 | GEM GEMS 19 | One Step/Lad's Got Money | 5 |
| 74 | GML 1013 | ANYMORE FOR ANYMORE (LP) | 30 |
| 75 | Island ILPS 9321 | RONNIE LANE AND SLIM CHANCE (LP, gatefold) | 30 |
| 75 | Island ILPS 9366 | ONE FOR THE ROAD (LP) | 20 |
| 76 | Atlantic K 50308 | MAHONEY'S LAST STAND (LP, with Ron Wood, soundtrack) | 15 |
| 80 | Gem GEMLP 107 | SEE ME (LP, with insert) | 15 |
| 88 | Thunderbolt THBL 067P | MAHONEY'S LAST STAND (LP, reissue, picture disc) | 12 |

*(see also Small Faces, Faces, Pete Townshend & Ronnie Lane)*

## ROSEMARY LANE
| | | | |
|---|---|---|---|
| 60 | Philips PB 1041 | Down By The River/My First Love Letter | 8 |

## TONY LANE & DELTONES
| | | | |
|---|---|---|---|
| 64 | Sabre SA-45-5 | It's Great/Now She's Mine | 30 |

## PATTIE LANE
| | | | |
|---|---|---|---|
| 68 | Polydor 56260 | Paper Dreams/My Four Walls | 40 |

## LANE BROTHERS
| | | | |
|---|---|---|---|
| 60 | London HLR 9150 | Mimi/Two Dozen And A Half | 10 |

## MARK LANEGAN
| | | | |
|---|---|---|---|
| 99 | Beggars Banquet BBQLP215 | I'LL TAKE CARE OF YOU (LP) | 50 |

*(see also Screaming Trees, Soulsavers, Isobel Campbell & Mark Lanegan)*

## LANE SISTERS
| | | | |
|---|---|---|---|
| 61 | Columbia DB 4671 | Peek A Boo Moon/Birmingham Rag | 10 |

## DON LANG (& HIS "FRANTIC" FIVE)
| | | | |
|---|---|---|---|
| 56 | HMV 7M 354 | Four Brothers/I Want You To Be My Baby (solo) | 30 |
| 56 | HMV 7M 381 | Rock Around The Island/Jumpin' To Conclusions (solo) | 30 |
| 56 | HMV 7M 416 | Rock And Roll Blues/Stop The World I Wanna Get Off (solo) | 30 |
| 56 | HMV POP 260 | Sweet Sue - Just You/Lazy Latin (solo) | 20 |
| 57 | HMV POP 289 | Rock Around The Cookhouse/Rock Mister Piper | 30 |
| 57 | HMV POP 335 | Rock-A-Billy/Come Go With Me (B-side with Skifflers) | 30 |
| 57 | HMV POP 350 | School Day (Ring! Ring! Goes The Bell)/Six-Five Special | 30 |
| 57 | HMV POP 382 | White Silver Sands/Again 'N' Again 'N' Again | 15 |
| 57 | HMV POP 414 | Red Planet Rock/Texas Tambourine | 25 |
| 58 | HMV POP 434 | Ramshackle Daddy/6-5 Hand Jive | 25 |
| 58 | HMV POP 465 | Tequila/Junior Hand Jive | 10 |
| 58 | HMV POP 488 | Witch Doctor/Cool Baby Cool | 10 |
| 58 | HMV POP 510 | Hey Daddy!/The Bird On My Head | 10 |

# Eddie LANG & LONNIE JOHNSON

| | | | |
|---|---|---|---|
| 58 | HMV POP 547 | Queen Of The Hop/La-Do-Da-Da (solo) | 15 |
| 59 | HMV POP 585 | Wiggle Wiggle/(You Were Only) Teasin' (solo) | 15 |
| 59 | HMV POP 623 | Percy Green/Phineas McCoy (solo) | 15 |
| 59 | HMV POP 649 | A Hoot An' A Holler/See You Friday | 15 |
| 59 | HMV POP 682 | Reveille Rock/Frankie And Johnny | 8 |
| 60 | HMV POP 714 | Sink The Bismarck!/They Call Him Cliff (solo) | 15 |
| 60 | HMV POP 805 | Time Machine/Don't Open That Door | 30 |
| 62 | Decca F 11483 | Wicked Women/Play Money (as Don Lang & Boulder Rollers) | 15 |
| 57 | HMV 7EG 8208 | ROCK 'N' ROLL (EP) | 10 |
| 57 | HMV DLP 1151 | SKIFFLE SPECIAL (LP, 10", by Don Lang & His Skiffle Group) | 100 |
| 58 | HMV DLP 1179 | INTRODUCING THE HAND JIVE (LP, 10") | 120 |
| 62 | Ace Of Clubs ACL 1111 | TWENTY TOP-TWENTY TWISTS (LP) | 150 |

*(see also Gordon Langhorn)*

## EDDIE LANG & LONNIE JOHNSON

| | | | |
|---|---|---|---|
| 67 | Parlophone PMC 7019 | BLUE GUITARS (LP) | 20 |
| 70 | Parlophone PMC 7106 | BLUE GUITARS VOLUME 2 (LP) | 20 |

*(see also Blind Willie Dunn's Gin Bottle Four)*

## STEVIE LANGE

| | | | |
|---|---|---|---|
| 81 | RCA RCA 152 | Remember My Name/I Don't Want To Know (1st issue, p/s) | 8 |
| 81 | RCA LIM 1 | Remember My Name/I Don't Want To Know (2nd issue, p/s) | 6 |

## GORDON LANGHORN

| | | | |
|---|---|---|---|
| 55 | Decca F 10591 | Give A Fool A Chance/Don't Stay Away Too Long | 15 |

*(see also Don Lang, Cyril Stapleton)*

## MARY LANGLEY

| | | | |
|---|---|---|---|
| 67 | CBS 2862 | Stay In My World/Summer Love | 12 |
| 67 | CBS 3032 | It Always Rains On Sunday/All My Life Is You | 6 |

*(see also Perpetual Langley, Langleys)*

## PERPETUAL LANGLEY

| | | | |
|---|---|---|---|
| 66 | Planet PLF 110 | We Wanna Stay Home/So Sad | 40 |
| 66 | Planet PLF 115 | Surrender/Two By Two | 40 |

*(see also Mary Langley, Langleys)*

## LANGLEYS

| | | | |
|---|---|---|---|
| 65 | Fontana TF 544 | Green Island/You Know I Love You | 6 |

*(see also Hawkwind, Widowmaker)*

## (HUW) LLOYD LANGTON (GROUP)

| | | | |
|---|---|---|---|
| 83 | Flicknife FLS 021 | Wind Of Change/Outside The Law (as Lloyd Langton Group, p/s) | 5 |
| 83 | Flicknife SHARP 015 | OUTSIDE THE LAW (LP, 1,000 with bonus 7": "Working Time"/ I See You [FREE 001], as Huw Lloyd Langton) | 15 |

*(see also Hawkwind, Widowmaker)*

## PHIL LANGTON TRIO

| | | | |
|---|---|---|---|
| 60s | Holyground | PHIL LANGTON TRIO (LP) | 18 |

## LANGUAGE FROM MEMORY

| | | | |
|---|---|---|---|
| 81 | Squad SQA 001 | Fortune/The Coat (1st pressing, p/s) | 10 |
| 81 | Towerbell TOW 15 | Fortune/The Coat (p/s) | 6 |

## SNOOKY LANSON

| | | | |
|---|---|---|---|
| 56 | London HLD 8223 | It's Almost Tomorrow/Why Don't You Write | 100 |
| 56 | London HLD 8236 | Stop (Let Me Off The Bus)/Last Minute Love | 200 |
| 56 | London HLD 8249 | Seven Days/Tippity Top | 200 |
| 56 | London HL 7005 | Seven Days/Tippity Top (export issue) | 80 |

*(see also Teresa Brewer)*

## JENNIFER LARA

| | | | |
|---|---|---|---|
| 79 | Hitrun HIT DD 14 | Jah Will Lead Us Home/RANKING PURPLE: Ah Fi We Jah (12") | 60 |

## LARD

| | | | |
|---|---|---|---|
| 90 | Alternative Tentacles VIRUS 84 | LAST TEMPTATION OF REID (LP, with free 12") | 15 |

## TOBI LARK

| | | | |
|---|---|---|---|
| 06 | Kent Select CITY 001 | True True Love/LITTLE ANN: Sweep It Out In The Shed (reissue) | 10 |
| 08 | Kent TOWN 116 | Challnge My Love/O.C. TOLBERT: You Got Me Turned Around (reissue) | 10 |

## PHILIP LARKIN

| | | | |
|---|---|---|---|
| 58 | Mervell Press | LESS DECEIVED (LP, 100 only, numbered) | 125 |
| 68 | Listen | LESS DECEIVED (LP) | 40 |
| 75 | Argo PLP 1202 | HIGH WINDOWS (LP) | 25 |

## LARKS

| | | | |
|---|---|---|---|
| 86 | Exalation 12 LARX 2 | All Or Nothing Girl/Whatever You Say/Teachers: Parents/Heartless (12", p/s) | 12 |

## LARKS (1)

| | | | |
|---|---|---|---|
| 64 | Pye International 7N 25284 | The Jerk/Forget Me | 50 |
| 64 | Pye International 7N 25284 | The Jerk/Forget Me (DJ copy) | 80 |

## LARKS (2)

| | | | |
|---|---|---|---|
| 87 | Exaltation 12LARX 3 | PAIN IN THE NECK EP (12", p/s) | 20 |
| 87 | Exaltation LARX 3 | Pain In The Neck/I Am A Clean Boy | 20 |

## LARO

| | | | |
|---|---|---|---|
| 60 | Kalypso XX 21 | Jamaican Referendum Calypso/Wrong Impressions Of A Soldier | 8 |

## WINSTON LARO

| | | | |
|---|---|---|---|
| 70 | Downtown DT 461 | Goodnight My Love/BOYSIE: I Don't Want To Be Hurt | 12 |

## JULIUS LA ROSA

| | | | |
|---|---|---|---|
| 55 | London HL 8154 | Mobile/Pass It On | 15 |
| 55 | London HLA 8170 | Domani/Mama Rosa | 15 |
| 55 | London HLA 8193 | Suddenly There's A Valley/Everytime I Kiss Carrie | 15 |

| | | | |
|---|---|---|---|
| 56 | HMV 7M 384 | Lipstick And Candy And Rubber-Sole Shoe/Winter In New England ............ | 7 |
| 56 | London HLA 8272 | No Other Love/Rosanne ............ | 15 |
| 56 | London HLA 8353 | Jingle Bells (Campanelle)/Jingle Dingle ............ | 5 |
| 57 | London HA-A 2031 | JULIUS LA ROSA (LP) ............ | 20 |

### LARRY'S ALL STARS
| | | | |
|---|---|---|---|
| 71 | Ackee ACK 125 | In The Fields/Teardrops Got The Feeling ............ | 15 |
| 71 | Ackee ACK 130 | Pre-Fight/The Prayer ............ | 20 |

*(see also Larry Lawrence, Delroy Wilson, Hugh Roy, Sensations)*

### LARRY (MARSHALL) & ALVIN
| | | | |
|---|---|---|---|
| 68 | Studio One SO 2065 | Nanny Goat/Smell You Crep ............ | 30 |
| 68 | Studio One SO 2067 | Can't You Understand/Hush Up ............ | 50 |
| 69 | Studio One SO 2080 | Lonely Room (No One To Give Me Love)/You Mean To Me ............ | 40 |
| 69 | Coxsone CS 7081 | Love Got Me/BOB ANDY: Lady With The Bright Light (both sides actually by Glen [Brown] & Dave [Barker]) ............ | 150 |
| 70 | Bamboo BAM 22 | Girl Of My Dream/SOUND DIMENTION: Give It Away ............ | 60 |

*(see also Larry Marshall, Sound Dimension, Vincent Gordon)*

### LARRY & JOHNNY
| | | | |
|---|---|---|---|
| 65 | Outasite 45 501 | Beatle Time Parts 1 & 2 (99 copies only) ............ | 150 |

*(see also Larry Williams & Johnny 'Guitar' Watson)*

### LARRY & LINDA
| | | | |
|---|---|---|---|
| 70 | Beacon BEA 146 | Most Peculiar Girl/Magnificent Opupouring ............ | 10 |

### LARRY & TOMMY
| | | | |
|---|---|---|---|
| 68 | Polydor 56741 | You've Gotta Bend A Little/Yo-Yo (A side written and produced by John Cale) ............ | 35 |

### KIM LARSEN & JUNGLE DREAMS
| | | | |
|---|---|---|---|
| 82 | CBS A 2232 | Rock 'N' Roll City/Time Bomb ............ | 20 |

### JACK LARSON
| | | | |
|---|---|---|---|
| 61 | Top Rank JAR 573 | I Love The Way She Laughs/The Hammer Bell Song ............ | 8 |

### LA'S
| | | | |
|---|---|---|---|
| 87 | Go! Discs GOLAS 1 | Way Out/Endless (p/s) ............ | 5 |
| 87 | Go! Discs GOLAR 112 | Way Out/Knock Me Down/Endless/Liberty Ship (Demo)/Freedom Song (Demo) (12", blue & silver stickered p/s listing 5 tracks) ............ | 10 |
| 88 | Go! Discs LASEP 2 | There She Goes/Way Out/Who Knows/Come In Come Out (EP, blue p/s, 5,000 only) ... | 12 |
| 88 | Go! Discs GOLAS 2 | There She Goes/Come In Come Out (red p/s) ............ | 10 |
| 89 | Go! Discs GOLAS 3 | Timeless Melody/Clean Prophet (p/s, unissued; 10 test pressings only) ............ | 60 |
| 89 | Go! Discs LASEP 3 | Timeless Melody (10", unissued) ............ | 0 |
| 89 | Go! Discs LASDJ 312 | Timeless Melody/Clean Prophet/Knock Me Down/Over (12", promo, 500 only) ............ | 15 |
| 90 | Go! Discs GOLAB 5 | There She Goes/Freedom Song (numbered box set with badge & 3 stickers) ............ | 10 |
| 91 | Go! Discs GOLAS 6 | Feelin'/Doledrum (p/s) ............ | 6 |
| 91 | Go! Discs GOLAB 6 | Feelin'/IOU (Alternate Version)/Feelin' (Alternate Version)/Doledrum (numbered box set with badge & 3 stickers) ............ | 10 |
| 91 | Go! Discs 828 202-1 | THE LA'S (LP) ............ | 25 |
| 99 | Viper VLP 002 | LOST LA's 1984-1986 BREAKLOOSE (LP) ............ | 15 |
| 10 | Polydor 5326495 | CALLIN' ALL (4-CD 'book' box set) ............ | 20 |

*(see also Cast)*

### BONGO LES (CHEN) & BUNNY (HERMAN)
| | | | |
|---|---|---|---|
| 72 | Attack ATT 8041 | Feel Nice (Version)/WINSTON SCOTLAND: Quick And Slick ............ | 20 |

*(see also Bongo Herman)*

### DENISE LASALLE
| | | | |
|---|---|---|---|
| 71 | Janus 6310206 | TRAPPED BY A THING CALLED LOVE (LP) ............ | 15 |

### COUNT LASHER
| | | | |
|---|---|---|---|
| 60s | Kalypso 100 AB | Calypso Cha Cha Cha/Perseverance ............ | 5 |
| 60s | Kalypso 105 AB | Slide Mongoose/Miss Constance ............ | 5 |

### EMMANUEL LASKEY
| | | | |
|---|---|---|---|
| 07 | Hayley 013 | (Put Your Name) In The Hall Of Fame/A Different Kind Of Different ............ | 8 |

### LAST BANDITS
| | | | |
|---|---|---|---|
| 89 | Solid ROK 722 | The Angels Are Calling/The Dalkey Rake (p/s) ............ | 10 |

*(see also Swell Maps, Nikki Sudden)*

### LAST CHANT
| | | | |
|---|---|---|---|
| 81 | Chicken Jazz JAZZ 4 | Run Of The Dove/Strength Alone/Tradition (p/s) ............ | 8 |

### LAST EXIT
| | | | |
|---|---|---|---|
| 75 | Wudwink WUD 01 | Whispering Voices/Evensong (no p/s, push-out centre) ............ | 60 |
| 79 | Wudwink WUD 01 | Whispering Voices/Evensong (reissue, solid centre) ............ | 30 |
| 75 | Wudwink WUD.C.101 | FIRST FROM LAST EXIT (cassette only, pink card insert, sold at gigs, only 3 copies known to exist) ............ | 500 |

*(see also Newcastle Big Band, Police, Sting)*

### LAST FLIGHT
| | | | |
|---|---|---|---|
| 81 | Heavy Metal HEAVY 5 | Dance To The Music/I'm Ready (p/s) ............ | 8 |

### LAST MAN IN EUROPE
| | | | |
|---|---|---|---|
| 85 | Cocteau CO 22 | A Certain Bridge/TV Addict (p/s) ............ | 18 |

### LAST POETS
| | | | |
|---|---|---|---|
| 72 | Douglas DGL 69012 | THIS IS MADNESS (LP) ............ | 30 |

### LAST RESORT (1)
| | | | |
|---|---|---|---|
| 78 | Red Meat RMRS 01 | Having Fun?/F.U.2 (die-cut printed paper sleeve) ............ | 30 |

### LAST RESORT (2)
| | | | |
|---|---|---|---|
| 82 | Last Resort LR 1 | SKINHEAD ANTHEMS (LP, red vinyl) ............ | 30 |
| 82 | Last Resort LR 1 | SKINHEAD ANTHEMS (LP, white vinyl) ............ | 30 |
| 82 | Last Resort LR 1 | SKINHEAD ANTHEMS (LP, blue vinyl) ............ | 30 |
| 82 | Last Resort LR 1 | SKINHEAD ANTHEMS (LP, black vinyl) ............ | 40 |

## LAST RITES
| | | |
|---|---|---|
| 83 | Flicknife FLS 219 | We Don't Care/Step Down (p/s) .................................................. 20 |
| 84 | Essential 004 | FASCISM MEANS WAR (No Right To Take/Convicted Without Trial/Protest And Survive/The Dreams Of Many) (EP, gatefold p/s) ......................... 25 |
| 84 | Essential 001 | THIS IS THE REACTION (LP) ....................................................... 30 |

## LAST ROUGH CAUSE
| | | |
|---|---|---|
| 85 | LRC 001 | THE VIOLENT FEW (EP, with lyric sheet) ................................... 40 |

## LAST STAND
| | | |
|---|---|---|
| 81 | Silly Symbol SJP 825 | Just A Number/Caviare (p/s) ................................................... 40 |

## LAST STRAW
| | | |
|---|---|---|
| 78 | Solent SS 049 | Oh Lady/Fly By Night (p/s) ...................................................... 50 |

## LAST WORD
| | | |
|---|---|---|
| 74 | Polydor 2066 429 | Keep On Bumping Before You Run Out Of Gas/Funky And Some ......... 8 |

## LAST WORDS
| | | |
|---|---|---|
| 79 | Rough Trade RT 022 | Animal World/No Music In The World Today (p/s) ..................... 10 |
| 79 | Remand REMAND 2 | Todays Kidz/There's Something Wrong (p/s) ............................. 6 |
| 80 | Armageddon AS 02 | Top Secret/Walk Away (p/s) .................................................... 8 |
| 81 | Armageddon ARM 2 | THE LAST WORDS (LP) ............................................................ 15 |

## LAST LAUGH
| | | |
|---|---|---|
| 85 | Hmmm! HA 1 | GLEE SWITCH EP ................................................................... 25 |

## LAST SHADOW PUPPETS
| | | |
|---|---|---|
| 08 | Domino RUG 288 | The Age Of The Understatement/Two Hearts In Two Weeks ........... 5 |
| 08 | Domino RUG 301 | Standing Next To Me/Gas Dance ............................................... 5 |
| 08 | Domino RUG 309X | My Mistakes Were Made For You/Seperate And Ever Deadly (Live From New Theatre Oxford) ........................................................... 8 |
| 08 | Domino RUG 309 | My Mistakes Were Made For You/Paris Summer (Live) ................. 8 |

(see also Arctic Monkeys)

## LAST WITNESS
| | | |
|---|---|---|
| 10 | Holy Roar HRR 043V | GIVE UP EP (150 copies, clear vinyl) ......................................... 5 |
| 10 | Purgatory | GIVE UP EP (150 copies, clear/blue vinyl) .................................. 5 |
| 10 | Thirty Days Of Night | GIVE UP EP (150 copies, red vinyl) ........................................... 5 |

## BILL LASWELL
| | | |
|---|---|---|
| 84 | Rough Trade ROUGH 51 | BASELINES (LP) ................................................................... 15 |
| 88 | Venture VE12 | HEAR NO EVIL (LP) .............................................................. 25 |

## LATE ARRIVALS
| | | |
|---|---|---|
| 67 | Highlight HL1 | No One Cares/Voices Above ................................................... 25 |

## LATE OF THE PIER
| | | |
|---|---|---|
| 07 | Wow 02 | Space And The Woods/Heartbeat, Flicker, Line (7", 500 only) ..... 10 |

## LATE ROAD LUNATICS
| | | |
|---|---|---|
| 86 | Star Dust SD 001 | THE LATE ROAD LUNATICS EP .................................................. 10 |

## LATE SHOW
| | | |
|---|---|---|
| 78 | Decca F 13777 | Drop Dead/Ain't Gonna Stamp On His Face (p/s) ....................... 15 |
| 78 | Decca F13788 | I Like It/I Wrote A Book .......................................................... 6 |
| 79 | Decca F 13835 | Chains/Screws On You (p/s) ...................................................... 7 |

## YUSEF LATEEF
| | | |
|---|---|---|
| 58 | Esquire 32-069 | THE SOUNDS OF YUSEF (LP) .................................................... 40 |
| 58 | Columbia Clef 33CX 10124 | BEFORE DAWN (LP) ............................................................. 50 |
| 59 | Esquire 32-139 | CRY! TENDER (LP) ................................................................ 60 |
| 64 | Realm RM 228 | FABRIC OF JAZZ (LP) ............................................................ 25 |
| 64 | Transatlantic PR 7319 | EASTERN SOUNDS (LP) ......................................................... 30 |
| 72 | Atlantic K 40359 | GENTLE GIANT (LP) ............................................................. 15 |
| 73 | Prestige PR 24007 | YUSEF LATEEF (LP) .............................................................. 15 |
| 74 | Atlantic K 50041 | PART OF THE SEARCH (LP) ..................................................... 15 |
| 76 | Impulse IMPL 8013 | CLUB DATE (LP) .................................................................. 15 |

## LATIMORE
| | | |
|---|---|---|
| 73 | President PTLS 1058 | S.T. (LP) ............................................................................ 15 |
| 74 | President PTLS 1062 | MORE MORE MORE (LP) ....................................................... 15 |

## MARCEL LATOUR
| | | |
|---|---|---|
| 69 | United Artists UP 350058 | Women In Love/Kes ............................................................... 8 |

## GENE LATTER
| | | |
|---|---|---|
| 66 | Decca F 12364 | Just A Minute Or Two/Dream Lover ........................................ 30 |
| 66 | Decca F 12397 | Mother's Little Helper/Please Come Back To Me Again ............... 25 |
| 67 | CBS 202483 | Something Inside Me Died/Don't Go .......................................... 8 |
| 67 | CBS 202655 | Always/A Woman Called Sorrow .............................................. 8 |
| 67 | CBS 2843 | A Little Piece Of Leather/Funny Face Girl ................................. 40 |
| 67 | CBS 2843 | A Little Piece Of Leather/Funny Face Girl (DJ copy) ................... 60 |
| 67 | CBS 2986 | With A Child's Heart/Ways ..................................................... 10 |
| 68 | Direction 58-3245 | A Tribute To Otis/Bring Your Love Home ................................. 10 |
| 68 | Spark SRL 1015 | My Life Ain't Easy/Angie (as Gene Latter & Detours) ................. 6 |
| 69 | Spark SRL 1022 | Sign On The Dotted Line/I Love You ........................................ 10 |
| 69 | Spark SRL 1031 | The Old Iron Bell/Holding A Dream ....................................... 170 |
| 69 | Parlophone R 5800 | Help Me Judy, Help Me/On The Highway ................................... 7 |
| 69 | Parlophone R 5815 | Tiger Bay/We Can Make Out .................................................. 10 |
| 70 | Parlophone R 5853 | Someday You'll Need My Love/Come On Home ........................... 6 |
| 71 | Parlophone R 5896 | Catch My Soul/Happiness ...................................................... 10 |
| 71 | Parlophone R 5913 | Sing A Song Of Freedom/Too Busy Thinking About My Baby ....... 10 |

(see also Detours)

**STANLEY LAUDAN**
| | | | |
|---|---|---|---|
| 58 | Oriole CB 1434 | Two Guitars/Blue Shawl | 8 |
| 57 | Oriole CB 1397 | Marushka/Bucharest | 5 |

**THE LAUGHING APPLE**
| | | | |
|---|---|---|---|
| 81 | Autonomy AUT 001 | HA HA HEE HEE (EP) | 15 |
| 81 | Autonomy AUT 002 | Participate!/Wouldn't You? (foldover p/s) | 15 |
| 82 | Essential ESS 001 | Precious Feeling/Celebration (p/s) | 15 |

*(see also Biff Bang Pow!, Revolving Paint Dream)*

**LAUGHING GAS**
| | | | |
|---|---|---|---|
| 70 | RCA RCA 2006 | All Shapes And Sizes/Opus No. 1 | 6 |

**LAUGHING MOTHERS**
| | | | |
|---|---|---|---|
| 85 | Motherkare MUM 1 | Tunnel/Cats Cradle (p/s) | 20 |

**LAUREL (AITKEN) & OWEN (GRAY)**
| | | | |
|---|---|---|---|
| 62 | Blue Beat BB 149 | She's Going To Napoli/Have Mercy Mr Percy | 10 |

*(see also Laurel Aitken, Owen Gray)*

**LAURELS**
| | | | |
|---|---|---|---|
| 68 | RCA Victor RCA 1741 | Sunshine Thursday/Threepence A Tune | 15 |
| 69 | RCA Victor RCA 1836 | Making It Groovy/Rainmaker | 40 |
| 70 | Pye 7N 17980 | Shame Shame/Make Believe | 10 |
| 71 | Pye 45034 | The Devil's Well/Underground | 60 |

**ROD LAUREN**
| | | | |
|---|---|---|---|
| 59 | RCA RCA 1165 | If I Had A Girl/No Wonder | 10 |

**LAURENT**
| | | | |
|---|---|---|---|
| 71 | Pye 7N 25566 | Sing Sing Barbara/Le Temple Bleu | 8 |

**JOHN LAURENZ**
| | | | |
|---|---|---|---|
| 55 | London HL 8138 | Goodbye, Stranger, Goodbye/Red Roses | 20 |
| 65 | Decca F 12147 | 99 Times Out Of 100/I Can Feel It | 5 |

**LAURI**
| | | | |
|---|---|---|---|
| 78 | Thelopian THEO1 | If We Can't Have It Neither Can You/Reconciling Trades (p/s) | 6 |

**LAURIE**
| | | | |
|---|---|---|---|
| 66 | Decca F 12347 | He Understands Me/Fools Never Learn | 5 |

**LAURIE SISTERS**
| | | | |
|---|---|---|---|
| 60 | MGM MGM 1083 | Don't Forget (To Sign Your Name With A Kiss)/I Surrender Dear | 5 |
| 61 | MGM MGM 1128 | Live It Up/Lonesome And Sorry | 5 |

**MISS LAVELL**
| | | | |
|---|---|---|---|
| 65 | Vocalion VP 9236 | Everybody's Got Somebody/The Best Part Of Me | 25 |

**LAVENDER FACTION**
| | | | |
|---|---|---|---|
| 90 | Lust LUST 5 | In My Mind/Harbour Me/Something I See | 5 |

**JUNE LAVERICK**
| | | | |
|---|---|---|---|
| 60 | Oriole CB 1537 | Stop/JOHNNY WEBB: Concertino | 6 |

*(see also Johnny Webb)*

**ROGER LA VERN & MICRONS**
| | | | |
|---|---|---|---|
| 63 | Decca F 11791 | Christmas Stocking/Reindeer Ride | 25 |

*(see also Tornados)*

**BETTY LAVETTE**
| | | | |
|---|---|---|---|
| 67 | Stateside SS 2015 | I Feel Good All Over/Only Your Love Can Save Me | 60 |
| 67 | Stateside SS 2015 | I Feel Good All Over/Only Your Love Can Save Me (DJ copy) | 75 |
| 68 | Pama PM 748 | Only Your Love Can Save Me/I Feel Good All Over (reissue) | 40 |
| 70 | Polydor 56786 | He Made A Woman Out Of Me/Nearer To You | 10 |
| 72 | Mojo 2092 030 | Let Me Down Easy/I Feel Good All Over/What I Don't Know Won't Hurt Me | 10 |
| 73 | Atlantic K 10299 | Your Turn To Cry/Soul Tambourine | 10 |
| 78 | Atlantic K 11198 | Doin' The Best I Can Parts 1 & 2 | 6 |
| 82 | Tamla Motown TMG 1265 | I Can't Stop/Either Way We Lose | 8 |

**PETER LAW**
| | | | |
|---|---|---|---|
| 67 | Major Minor MM 522 | Lingering On/Memories Of You | 6 |

**LAW (THE)**
| | | | |
|---|---|---|---|
| 79 | Smile SR011 | Be My Girl/Dead City Kicks/I Just Want Your Body (500 pressed) | 50 |

**GASPAR LAWAL**
| | | | |
|---|---|---|---|
| 80 | Cap | AJOMASE (LP) | 20 |

**AZIE LAWRENCE**
| | | | |
|---|---|---|---|
| 59 | Mezzotone ME 7001/7002 | West Indians In England/Jump Up | 12 |
| 59 | Mezzotone ME 7004 | Love In Every Land/No Dice | 8 |
| 60 | Starlite ST45 022 | West Indians In England/Jump Up (with Carib Serenaders) | 15 |
| 61 | Starlite ST45 041 | No Dice/Love In Every Land | 10 |
| 61 | Melodisc M 1563 | Jamaica Blues/Come Rumble & Tumble With Me | 8 |
| 61 | Melodisc M 1572 | You Didn't Want To Know/I Want To Be In Love | 8 |
| 61 | Blue Beat BB 71 | So Far Apart/Palms Of Victory (with Melobeats) | 12 |
| 64 | Blue Beat BB 222 | Pempelem/Lovers Understand | 400 |

**DIANE LAWRENCE**
| | | | |
|---|---|---|---|
| 67 | Doctor Bird DB 1075 | I Won't Hang Around Like A Hound Dog/Read It Over | 35 |
| 68 | Jolly JY 005 | Treat Me Nice/I've Been Loving You | 12 |

**EDDIE LAWRENCE**
| | | | |
|---|---|---|---|
| 59 | Coral Q 72361 | The Salesman's Philosopher/Mother Philosopher | 5 |

**GENE LAWRENCE**
| | | | |
|---|---|---|---|
| 67 | Jump Up JU 505 | Longest Day Meringue/Bachelor Boy | 10 |
| 67 | Jump Up JU 510 | Meringue Triniana/Devil Woman | 10 |

## LARRY LAWRENCE (JAMAICA)
| | | | |
|---|---|---|---|
| 63 | Island WI 091 | Garden Of Eden/DERRICK MORGAN: Sendin' This Message | 15 |

*(see also Larry's Allstars, McBean Scott & Champions)*

## LARRY LAWRENCE (U.S.)
| | | | |
|---|---|---|---|
| 59 | Pye International 7N 25042 | Goofin' Off/Bongo Boogie (as Larry Lawrence & Band Of Gold) | 10 |
| 60 | Ember EMB S 106 | Squad Car Theme/Jug-A-Roo (with Beatniks, in art p/s) | 10 |
| 60 | Ember EMB S 106 | Squad Car Theme/Jug-A-Roo (with Beatniks) | 15 |

## LEE LAWRENCE (& CORONETS)
| | | | |
|---|---|---|---|
| 54 | Decca F 10285 | The Little Mustard Seed/My Love For You | 6 |
| 54 | Decca F 10367 | The Story Of Tina/For You My Love | 6 |
| 54 | Decca F 10408 | The Things I Didn't Do/You Still Mean The Same To Me | 5 |
| 55 | Decca F 10422 | My Own True Love (Tara's Theme)/Beware Now! | 5 |
| 55 | Decca F 10438 | Lights Of Paris/A Love Like Ours | 5 |
| 55 | Decca F 10485 | Wedding Bells And Silver Horse-Shoes/Will You Be Mine Alone? | 5 |
| 55 | Columbia SCM 5175 | Beyond The Stars/Give Me Your Word | 5 |
| 55 | Columbia SCM 5181 | My World Stood Still/Don't Worry | 5 |
| 55 | Columbia SCM 5190 | More Than A Millionaire/Overnight | 5 |
| 55 | Columbia SCM 5201 | Suddenly There's A Valley/Mi Muchacha (Little Girl) | 10 |
| 56 | Columbia SCM 5228 | Young And Foolish/Don't Tell Me Not To Love You | 5 |
| 56 | Columbia SCM 5254 | We Believe In Love/Welcome To My Heart | 5 |
| 56 | Columbia SCM 5283 | Come Back, My Love/Valley Valparaiso | 5 |
| 56 | Columbia DB 3830 | From The Candy Store On The Corner/High Upon A Mountain | 5 |
| 57 | Columbia DB 3855 | Rock 'n' Roll Opera/Don't Nobody Move | 10 |
| 57 | Columbia DB 3885 | Your Love Is My Love/By You, By You, By You | 6 |
| 53 | Decca LF 1132 | PRESENTING LEE LAWRENCE (10" LP) | 15 |

## STEVE LAWRENCE
| | | | |
|---|---|---|---|
| 53 | Parlophone MSP 6038 | Say It Isn't True/This Night (Madalena) (as Steve & Bernie Lawrence) | 10 |
| 54 | Parlophone MSP 6080 | Remember Me (You Taught Me To Love)/Too Little Time | 10 |
| 54 | Parlophone MSP 6106 | You Can't Hold A Memory In Your Arms/King For A Day | 10 |
| 55 | Vogue Coral Q 72114 | Open Up The Gates Of Mercy/My Impression Of Janie | 10 |
| 56 | Vogue Coral Q 72133 | Speedo/The Chicken And The Hawk | 25 |
| 57 | Vogue Coral Q 72228 | The Banana Boat Song/If You Would Say You're Mine | 10 |
| 57 | Vogue Coral Q 72243 | Party Doll/Pum-Pa-Lum (The Bad Donkey) | 20 |
| 57 | Vogue Coral Q 72264 | Fabulous/Can't Wait For The Summer (with Dick Jacobs Band) | 20 |
| 57 | Vogue Coral Q 72281 | Fraulein/Blue Rememberin' You | 8 |
| 57 | Vogue Coral Q 72286 | Never Mind/Long Before I Knew You | 10 |
| 58 | Coral Q 72304 | Geisha Girl/I Don't Know | 6 |
| 58 | Coral Q 72335 | Those Nights At The Round Table (with Guinevere)/Stranger In Mexico | 6 |
| 59 | Coral Q 72353 | These Things Are Free/I Only Have Eyes For You | 7 |
| 59 | HMV POP 604 | Only Love Me (Angelina)/Loving Is A Way Of Living | 6 |
| 60 | HMV POP 689 | Pretty Blue Eyes/You're Nearer | 6 |
| 60 | HMV POP 726 | Footsteps/You Don't Know | 8 |
| 60 | Top Rank JAR 416 | Say It Isn't True/My Shawl | 6 |
| 60 | HMV POP 763 | Why, Why, Why/You're Everything Wonderful | 5 |
| 60 | London HLT 9166 | Girls, Girls, Girls/Little Boy Blue | 10 |

## STEVE LAWRENCE & EYDIE GORMÉ
| | | | |
|---|---|---|---|
| 55 | Vogue Coral Q 72044 | Make Yourself Comfortable/EYDIE GORME: Chain Reaction | 8 |
| 55 | Vogue Coral Q 72085 | Besame Mucho/Take A Deep Breath | 8 |
| 61 | London HLT 9290 | The Facts Of Life/I'm A Girl, You're A Boy | 5 |
| 63 | CBS AAG 163 | I Want To Stay Here/Ain't Love (in p/s) | 5 |

*(see also Eydie Gorme)*

## TERRY LAWRENCE
| | | | |
|---|---|---|---|
| 71 | Pye Int. 7N 25558 | Medicine Man/Let Me Be Free | 7 |

## VALERIE ANN LAWRENCE
| | | | |
|---|---|---|---|
| 65 | Decca F 12273 | My Love Loves Me/12A Heartache Square | 7 |

## VICKI LAWRENCE
| | | | |
|---|---|---|---|
| 73 | Stateside SS 2210 | The Night The Lights Went Out In Georgia/Dime A Dance | 7 |

## ZACK LAWRENCE
| | | | |
|---|---|---|---|
| 73 | Pemini Organisation | ASSASSIN EP (with p/s) | 70 |
| 73 | Pemini Organisation | ASSASSIN EP (without p/s) | 30 |

## LAWRENCE AND COMFORTABLE SOCIETY
| | | | |
|---|---|---|---|
| 86 | LCA LCS 1 | Sleeper/Heartache (hand-made sleeve) | 150 |

## BILLY (M.) LAWRIE
| | | | |
|---|---|---|---|
| 69 | Polydor 56363 | Roll Over Beethoven/Come Back Joanna (as Billy M. Lawrie) | 25 |
| 73 | RCA RCA 2439 | Rock And Roller/Shalee Shala | 6 |
| 73 | RCA SF 8395 | SHIP IMAGINATION (LP, die-cut gatefold sleeve) | 25 |

## ELOISE LAWS
| | | | |
|---|---|---|---|
| 77 | Invictus 5247 | Love Goes Deeper Than That/Camouflage | 5 |
| 00s | Inferno HEAT 15 | Love Factory/JUST BROTHERS: Sliced Tomatoes (reissue) | 10 |
| 13 | Outta Sight OSV 104 | Love Factory/JUST BROTHERS: Sliced Tomatoes (reissue) | 8 |

## JOHN LAWSON
| | | | |
|---|---|---|---|
| 79 | SRTX 79 CUS 617 FMR 024 | 1 X 6 (LP) | 25 |

## JULIET LAWSON
| | | | |
|---|---|---|---|
| 72 | Sovereign SOV 111 | Only A Week Away/Weeds In The Yard | 7 |
| 72 | Sovereign SVNA 7257 | BOO (LP, textured gatefold sleeve) | 200 |

*(see also Trees)*

**SHIRLEY LAWSON**
68   Soul City SC 108              The Star/One More Chance ....................................................... 200

**LAWSON-HAGGART ROCKIN' BAND**
59   Brunswick OE 9451            BOPPING AT THE HOP (EP) .......................................................... 15
59   Brunswick STA 3010          BOPPING AT THE HOP (LP) .......................................................... 30

**LOU LAWTON**
67   Ember EMB S 232              Doin' The Philly Dog/I Am Searching ............................................. 30
68   Speciality SPE 1005         I'm Just A Fool/Wrapped In A Dream .............................................. 30

**LAXTON & OLIVER**
69   Blue Cat BS 168             Wickeder/Stay In My Arms ......................................................... 20

**GRAHAM LAYDEN**
72   Penny Farthing PEN 792      Tiny Lover/All You Lovers ........................................................ 10

**OSSIE LAYNE**
65   R&B MRB 5006                Come Back/Never Answer That 'Phone .............................................. 35

**EDDIE LAYTON**
58   Mercury 7MT 221             Over The Waves/Bright Lights Over Brussels ....................................... 5
59   Mercury AMT 1064            Duck Walk/Doodles ................................................................. 10

**PAUL LAYTON**
68   Paradox PAR 45901           Mister Mister/Sing Sadman Sing (p/s) ............................................ 25

**KEN LAZ(A)RUS (& CREW)**
65   Island WI 220               Funny (as Ken Lazrus & Byron Lee Orchestra)/ BYRON LEE ORCHESTRA: Walk Like A
                                 Dragon ........................................................................... 15
70   London HLJ 10301            Monkey Man/Bongo Nyah .............................................................. 5
71   Explosion EX 2056           Girl/TOMORROW'S CHILDREN: Sister Big Stuff ....................................... 8
72   Explosion EX 2064           Hail The Man/Where Do I Go ........................................................ 7
72   London HLH 10379            Hail The Man/Where I Go ........................................................... 6
70   London HA-J 8412            REGGAE SCORCHER (LP, unissued) .................................................... 0
70   London ZGJ 107              REGGAE - GREATEST HITS VOL. 1 (LP) ............................................... 20

**PETER LAZONBY**
96   Brainiak BRAINK 40R         Wavespeech (12") .................................................................. 30

**LAZY FOUR**
79   SGS SGS 110                 Callow Capital/I Won't Shed A Tear ............................................... 15

**LAZY LATINS**
67   Morgan MR 110 P             LAZY LATIN (LP) ................................................................... 15

**LAZY SMOKE**
80s  Heyoka                      CORRIDOR OF FACES (LP, reissue of U.S. LP) ....................................... 15

**LCD SOUNDSYSTEM**
07   EMI 0094639493470           All My Friends (John Cale Version)/All My Friends (Album Version) ................. 7
07   EMI 0094639645374           All My Friends (Franz Ferdinand Version)/All My Friends (Edit) .................... 5
07   EMI 0094638505877           North American Scum/Hippie Priest Burn-Out (with free poster) ..................... 5
05   DFA DFAEMI2138LP            LCD SOUNDSYSTEM (2xLP) ............................................................ 25
07   EMI 0946 3 85114 1 0        SOUND OF SILVER (2xLP) ............................................................ 20

**BARBARA LEA**
56   London HB-U 1058            A WOMAN IN LOVE (10" LP) .......................................................... 20
56   Esquire 32/043              NOBODY ELSE BUT ME (LP) ........................................................... 20
57   Esquire 32/063              IN LOVE (LP) ...................................................................... 20

**JIMMY LEA**
85   Trojan KANE 001             Citizen Kane/Poland (p/s) ......................................................... 15
*(see also Slade)*

**LEADBELLY (HUDDIE LEDBETTER)**
**EPs**
56   Melodisc EPM7 63            THE MUSIC OF HUDDIE LEDBETTER ..................................................... 10
58   Melodisc EPM7 77            LEADBELLY ......................................................................... 10
58   Melodisc EPM7 82            SEE SEE RIDER ..................................................................... 10
59   Melodisc EPM7 87            PARTY PLAYS AND SONGS ............................................................. 10
59   RCA RCX 146                 ROCK ISLAND LINE .................................................................. 10
61   Capitol EAP1 1821           HUDDIE LEDBETTER'S BEST NO. 1 ..................................................... 10
61   Capitol EAP4 1821           HUDDIE LEDBETTER'S BEST NO. 2 ..................................................... 10
61   Capitol EAP1 20111          LEADBELLY ......................................................................... 10
61   Storyville SEP 337          LEADBELLY ......................................................................... 10
62   Storyville SEP 387          STORYVILLE BLUES ANTHOLOGY VOL. 7 ................................................. 15

**ALBUMS**
53   Capitol LC 6597             LEADBELLY SINGS CLASSICS IN JAZZ (10") ............................................ 40
57   Melodisc MLP 511            LEADBELLY VOL. 1 (10", green & silver labels) .................................... 30
57   Melodisc MLP 512            LEADBELLY VOL. 2 (10", green & silver labels) .................................... 30
58   Melodisc MLP 515            LEADBELLY VOL. 3 (10", green & silver labels) .................................... 30
58   Melodisc MLP 517            PLAYS PARTY SONGS (10", green & silver labels) ................................... 30
58   Melodisc MLP 12-107         THE SAGA OF LEADBELLY (green & silver or blue & black labels) ..................... 20
59   Melodisc MLP 12-113         LEADBELLY'S LAST SESSIONS VOLUME 2 PART 1 ......................................... 20
59   Melodisc MLP 12-114         LEADBELLY'S LAST SESSIONS VOLUME 2 PART 2 ......................................... 20
62   Storyville SLP 124          A DEMON OF A MAN - BLUES ANTHOLOGY ................................................ 20
63   Storyville SLP 139          LEADBELLY 2 - T.B. BLUES .......................................................... 20
63   Capitol T 1821              HIS GUITAR, HIS VOICE, HIS PIANO: HUDDIE LEDBETTER'S BEST .......................... 15
63   RCA Victor RD 7567          GOOD MORNING BLUES ................................................................ 20
65   Verve (S)VLP 5002           TAKE THIS HAMMER .................................................................. 20
66   Elektra EKL 301/2           THE LIBRARY OF CONGRESS RECORDINGS (3-LP) ........................................ 30
67   Verve (S)VLP 5011           KEEP YOUR HANDS OFF HER ........................................................... 15

# LEADBELLY & BLIND LEMON JEFFERSON

| | | | MINT VALUE £ |
|---|---|---|---|
| 69 | Xtra XTRA 1046 | LEADBELLY SINGS FOLK SONGS | 18 |
| 69 | Xtra XTRA 1126 | SHOUT ON | 15 |

## LEADBELLY & BLIND LEMON JEFFERSON
| | | | |
|---|---|---|---|
| 61 | Jazz Collector JEL 124 | THE MALE BLUES VOLUME 8 (EP) | 10 |

*(see also Blind Lemon Jefferson)*

## HARRY LEADER BAND
| | | | |
|---|---|---|---|
| 65 | Parlophone R 5386 | Dragon Fly/Rush Hour | 5 |

## LEADERBEATS
| | | | |
|---|---|---|---|
| 60 | Top Rank JAR 405 | Dance, Dance, Dance/Washington Square | 12 |

## LEADERS (JAMAICA)
| | | | |
|---|---|---|---|
| 68 | Amalgamated AMG 804 | Tit For Tat (actually by Lynn Taitt & Jets)/MARVETTS: You Take Too Long | 25 |

*(see also Pioneers, Stranger Cole)*

## LEADERS (U.K.)
| | | | |
|---|---|---|---|
| 65 | Fontana TF 602 | Night People/Love Will Find A Way | 10 |

## LEADING FIGURES
| | | | |
|---|---|---|---|
| 67 | Deram DML/SML 1006 | OSCILLATION 67! (LP) | 65 |
| 67 | Ace Of Clubs ACL 1225/SCL 1225 | SOUND AND MOVEMENT (LP, mono/stereo) | 65 |

*(see also Jon Lord, Deep Purple)*

## LEAF HOUND
| | | | |
|---|---|---|---|
| 05 | Rise Above 7/68 | Freelance Fiend/Too Many Rock N Roll Times | 40 |
| 71 | Decca SKL-R 5094 | GROWERS OF MUSHROOM (LP) | 2500 |

*(see also Brunning Sunflower Blues Band, Black Cat Bones, Atomic Rooster, Cactus)*

## LEAGUE
| | | | |
|---|---|---|---|
| 67 | President PT 167 | Nothing On/Hey Conductor | 25 |

## LEAGUE OF GENTLEMEN (1)
| | | | |
|---|---|---|---|
| 65 | Columbia DB 7666 | Each Little Falling Tear/And I Do Now | 70 |
| 66 | Planet PLF 109 | How Can You Tell/How Do They Know (with Planet company sleeve) | 80 |

## LEAGUE OF GENTLEMEN (2)
| | | | |
|---|---|---|---|
| 80 | EG/Virgin EGEDS 1 | Heptaparaparshinokh/Marriagemuzic | 6 |

*(see also Giles Giles & Fripp, Brain)*

## LEAGUE OF NATIONS
| | | | |
|---|---|---|---|
| 84 | Glaze GZLP 102 | MUSIC FOR THE NEW DEPRESSION (LP) | 50 |

## LEAH
| | | | |
|---|---|---|---|
| 73 | GM GMS 10 | Arise Sir Henry/Uptight Basil | 7 |

*(see also Pete Dello, Red Herring)*

## JOE LEAHY (ORCHESTRA)
| | | | |
|---|---|---|---|
| 55 | Parlophone MSP 6149 | Desiree/Milano | 5 |
| 55 | Parlophone MSP 6168 | Green Fire/Secretly Mine | 5 |
| 57 | London HBZ 1072 | LOVELY LADY (10" LP) | 12 |

## JOE LEAHY
| | | | |
|---|---|---|---|
| 65 | Capitol CL 15417 | Life/Pink Powder Puff | 8 |

## BOB LEAPER
| | | | |
|---|---|---|---|
| 65 | Pye 7N 15700 | High Wire (Theme From 'Danger Man')/The Lost World | 40 |
| 64 | Decca LK 4639 | BIG BAND, BEATLE SONGS (LP) | 20 |

## LEAPERS CREEPERS SLEEPERS
| | | | |
|---|---|---|---|
| 66 | Island WI 275 | Precious Words/Ba Boo | 30 |

## KEVIN 'KING' LEAR
| | | | |
|---|---|---|---|
| 67 | Polydor 56203 | Count Me Out/Pretty Woman | 15 |
| 68 | Page One POF 087 | Power Of Love/Mr. Pearly | 20 |
| 68 | Page One POF 109 | Cry Me A River/Shoe Shine Sam | 20 |
| 69 | Page One POF 132 | The Snake/Man In The Funnies | 15 |

## LEARGO
| | | | |
|---|---|---|---|
| 79 | Motor City DNS 87903 | The Artist/Played Out Angel (p/s) | 40 |

## TIMOTHY LEARY MEETS THE GRID
| | | | |
|---|---|---|---|
| 90 | Evolution EVO 1 | Origins Of Dance (Electronic Future Mix)/(Hi-Tec Pagan Mix) (12") | 10 |

*(see also the Grid)*

## LEATHERCOATED MINDS
| | | | |
|---|---|---|---|
| 67 | Fontana (S)TL 5412 | A TRIP DOWN THE SUNSET STRIP (LP) | 80 |

*(see also J.J. Cale)*

## LEATHERFACE
| | | | |
|---|---|---|---|
| 90 | Roughneck HYPE 1 | Razor Blades And Asprin/Colorado Joe, Leningrad Vlad/Post War Product Of A Fat Man's Wallet | 15 |
| 91 | Roughneck HYPE 14 | I Want The Moon/You Are My Sunshine/Dreaming | 10 |
| 92 | Clawfist XPIG 15 | Hops And Barley/Discipline/A Public House/Not Superstitious/James Whale (split release with Wat Tyler 2 x 7") | 10 |
| 90 | Meantime COXEP 3 | BEERPIG (EP, with insert) | 10 |
| 90 | Roughneck HYPE 6T | SMOKEY JOE (12" EP) | 30 |
| 91 | Roughneck HYPE 9T | NOT SUPERSTITIOUS (12" EP) | 10 |
| 92 | Roughneck HYPE 17T | COMPACT AND BIJOU (10" EP) | 10 |
| 89 | Meantime COX 017 | CHERRY KNOWLE (LP) | 10 |
| 90 | Roughneck NECKLP 1 | FILL YOUR BOOTS (LP, with insert) | 20 |
| 91 | Roughneck NECKLP 5 | MUSH (LP, inner) | 25 |
| 93 | Roughneck NECKLP 11 | MINX (LP) | 50 |
| 93 | Roughneck NECK 11LPS | MINX (LP, with bonus 7" Can't Help Falling In Love/Dreaming (HYPE 24) | 30 |

*(see also Frankie Stubbs)*

## LEATHERHEAD
| | | | |
|---|---|---|---|
| 74 | Philips 6006 371 | Gimme Your Money Please/Epitaph (die-cut 'Leatherhead' sleeve) | 20 |

## LEATHER NUN

| | | | |
|---|---|---|---|
| 79 | Industrial IR 0006 | SLOW DEATH (EP) | 20 |
| 84 | Subterranean SUB 40 | Prime Mover/F.F.A. (p/s) | 5 |
| 84 | Criminal Damage CRI MLP 113 | SLOW DEATH (Reissue, mini LP) | 25 |

## LEA VALLEY SKIFFLE GROUP

| | | | |
|---|---|---|---|
| 58 | Esquire EP 163 | LEA VALLEY SKIFFLE GROUP (EP) | 40 |

## LEAVES

| | | | |
|---|---|---|---|
| 66 | Fontana TF 713 | Hey Joe/Funny Little World | 40 |

## OTIS LEAVILL(E)

| | | | |
|---|---|---|---|
| 70 | Atlantic 2091 015 | I Love You/I Need You | 5 |
| 70 | Atlantic 2091 035 | Love Uprising/Glad I Met You | 5 |
| 71 | Atlantic 2091 160 | There's Nothing Better/I'm So Jealous | 8 |

## LECUONDA CUBAN BOYS

| | | | |
|---|---|---|---|
| 55 | Columbia 33S 1075 | BENEATH THE CUBAN MOON (10" LP) | 15 |

## JOHN LEDINGHAM

| | | | |
|---|---|---|---|
| 68 | Pye 7N 17488 | Love Is A Toy/Thank You Mrs. Gilbert | 6 |

*(see also Jonathan Kelly)*

## LED ZEPPELIN

### SINGLES

| | | | |
|---|---|---|---|
| 69 | Atlantic 584 268 | Good Times, Bad Times (unissued, 1-sided EMIdisc and LDC acetates only) | 2000 |
| 69 | Atlantic 584 269 | Communication Breakdown/Good Times, Bad Times (unissued, promo only) | 700 |
| 69 | Atlantic/Emidisc | Whole Lotta Love (Edit)/Whole Lotta Love (Edit) (Acetate) | 2000 |
| 69 | Atlantic 584 309 | Whole Lotta Love (Edit)/Livin' Lovin' Maid (She's A Woman) (withdrawn, large centre hole, clean label or "5th Dec 1969" stamp on label) | 600 |
| 69 | Atlantic 584 309 | Whole Lotta Love (Edit)/Livin' Lovin' Maid (She's A Woman) (withdrawn, solid centre with small centre hole, 1 copy known) | 1500 |
| 69 | Atlantic 584 309 | Whole Lotta Love (Edit)/Living Loving Maid (She's A Woman) (withdrawn, large centre hole, mispressing with Living Loving Maid labels on both sides) | 600 |
| 70 | Emidisc | Immigrant Song (unissued one sided acetate, scheduled to be released as Atlantic 2091 043 on 27th November 1970) | 3000 |
| 73 | Trident | D'Yer Mak'er (Unissued one sided acetate) | 1200 |
| 73 | Atlantic K 10296 | D'Yer Mak'er/Over The Hills And Far Away (unreleased, promo only) | 350 |
| 75 | Swan Song DC 1 | Trampled Underfoot/Black Country Woman (white label test pressing) | 350 |
| 75 | Swan Song DC 1 | Trampled Underfoot/Black Country Woman (Red label test pressing) | 500 |
| 75 | Swan Song SSK 19403 | Trampled underfoot/Black Country Woman (withdrawn first pressing) | 150 |
| 75 | Swan Song DC 1 | Trampled Underfoot/Black Country Woman (Limited edition dealer incentive promo, die-cut title sleeve) | 25 |
| 75 | Swan Song SSK 19403 | Trampled Underfoot/Black Country Woman (push mispressed cat. no.) | 150 |
| 79 | Swan Song SSK 19421 | Wearing And Tearing/Darlene (cancelled Knebworth 45, existence unconfirmed) | 0 |
| 90 | Atlantic LZ 3 | Stairway To Heaven/Whole Lotta Love (white label test pressing) | 350 |
| 90 | Atlantic LZ 2 | Stairway To Heaven/Immigrant Song/Whole Lotta Love/Good Times Bad Times (10", p/s, promo only) | 40 |
| 90 | Atlantic LZ 2 | Stairway To Heaven/Immigrant Song/Whole Lotta Love/Good Times Bad Times (10", test pressing, white labels) | 350 |
| 90 | Atlantic CD LZ 1 | Stairway To Heaven/Immigrant Song/Whole Lotta Love/Good Times Bad Times (CD, promo only, in Zeppelin-design long box) | 30 |
| 90 | Atlantic LZ 3 | Stairway To Heaven/Whole Lotta Love (with East West Records internal memo, 150 copies only, promo) | 175 |
| 90 | Atlantic LZ 3 LC | Stairway To Heaven/Whole Lotta Love (jukebox single, push-out centre) | 30 |
| 97 | Atlantic AT 0031LC | Whole Lotta Love (Edit)/Whole Lotta Love (Edit) (jukebox issue, with pushout centre) | 15 |
| 03 | Warner Vision PR 03945 | What Is And What Should Never Be/In My Time Of Dying/Rock And Roll (DVD, promo sampler) | 25 |

### ALBUMS

| | | | |
|---|---|---|---|
| 69 | Atlantic 588 171 | LED ZEPPELIN (LP, 1st pressing, red/maroon label, turquoise sleeve lettering, "Superhype" publishing credit) | 1500 |
| 69 | Atlantic 588 171 | LED ZEPPELIN (LP, 2nd pressing, red/maroon label, orange sleeve lettering, "Warner Bros" publishing credit) | 200 |
| 69 | Atlantic 588 171 | LED ZEPPELIN (LP, 2nd pressing, red/maroon label, orange sleeve lettering, "Superhype" publishing credit) | 200 |
| 69 | Atlantic 588 198 | LED ZEPPELIN II (LP, 1st pressing, red/maroon label, with "Living Loving Wreck" miscredit, light brown gatefold sleeve with blue-green edge) | 450 |
| 69 | Atlantic 588 198 | LED ZEPPELIN II (LP, 1st pressing, red/maroon label, with "The Lemon Song" credit, light brown gatefold sleeve with blue-green edge) | 100 |
| 70 | Atlantic 588 198 | LED ZEPPELIN II (LP, light brown sleeve, 2nd pressing, credits "Killing Floor" instead of "The Lemon Song" on label) | 40 |
| 70 | Atlantic Deluxe 2401 002 | LED ZEPPELIN III (LP, first pressing, red/maroon label, gatefold rotating-wheel sleeve, 'Do What Thou Wilt' in run-off side 1, "Produced by Jimmy Page" and "Executive Producer Peter Grant" on top of label. Catalogue number "2401002" on label) | 200 |
| 70 | Atlantic Deluxe 2401 002 | LED ZEPPELIN III (LP, second pressing, red/maroon label, gatefold rotating-wheel sleeve, no Peter Grant Credit. Catalogue number 2401 002 on label) | 50 |
| 70 | Atlantic K5002 | LED ZEPPELIN III (LP, reissue, gatefold, green/orange labels) | 25 |
| 71 | Atlantic Deluxe 2401 012 | LED ZEPPELIN IV (FOUR SYMBOLS) (1st pressing, 1st labels, LP, gatefold sleeve, red/maroon label with 2 'stickers' covering Peter Grant credit and also revised publishing details to "Kinney Music Ltd/Superhype Music Inc.") | 200 |
| 71 | Atlantic Deluxe 2401 012 | LED ZEPPELIN IV (FOUR SYMBOLS) (1st pressing, 1st labels, LP, gatefold sleeve, red/maroon label with Peter Grant credit, 'Led Zeppelin' at bottom, "Pecko Duck" etched onto run out groove on side 1 and "Porky" on side 2. Matrix numbers A//3 and B//3) | 300 |
| 71 | Atlantic Deluxe 2401 012 | LED ZEPPELIN IV (FOUR SYMBOLS) (1st pressing, 2nd labels, LP, gatefold sleeve, red/maroon label without Peter Grant credit, 'Led Zeppelin' at top, 'Atlantic Recording' credit in central white band, full 'Kinney Music Ltd/Superhype Music Inc' credit. 'Misty Mountain Hop' spelt as 'Misty Mountain Top') | 100 |
| 71 | Atlantic Deluxe 2401 012 | LED ZEPPELIN IV (FOUR SYMBOLS) (1st pressing, 3rd labels, with 'Misty Mountain Top' corrected to 'Misty Mountain Hop') | 65 |

MINT VALUE £

| | | | |
|---|---|---|---|
| 71 | Atlantic Deluxe 2401 012 | LED ZEPPELIN IV (FOUR SYMBOLS) (1st pressing, 4th labels, stickered sleeve, some corrected pressings with a sticker on the sleeve that has the Atlantic logo, K50008, audio information and record label credits) | 75 |
| 72 | Atlantic K50008 | LED ZEPPELIN IV (FOUR SYMBOLS) (2nd pressing, first green/orange labels, no four symbols, 'Misty Mountain Top' spelling error, matrix 2401012/K 50008 in run-out grooves) | 75 |
| 72 | Atlantic K50008 | LED ZEPPELIN IV (FOUR SYMBOLS) (2nd pressing mispressing on 'Asylum' label) | 150 |
| 72 | Atlantic K40037 | LED ZEPPELIN II (LP, first reissue on green/orange label) | 25 |
| 72 | Atlantic K40031 | LED ZEPPELIN (LP, repressing) | 25 |
| 73 | Atlantic K 50014 | HOUSES OF THE HOLY (LP, original pressing, unlaminated sleeve with 'obi' around the sleeve, textured inner sleeve with thumb notch, matrix A2/B2) | 150 |
| 73 | Atlantic K50014 | HOUSES OF THE HOLY (LP, original pressing, unlaminated sleeve without 'Obi') | 40 |
| 75 | Swan Song SSK 89400 | PHYSICAL GRAFFITI (2-LP, First pressing MATRIXES: SSK89400 A1/B5/C1/D1 (There are some with A1/B4/C1/D1). (Sleeve must have "Swan Song/484 Kings Road, London SW10", inner wraparound on thick card with a matt finish and a spine at the bottom, inner sleeves on thick card, labels have "Made in UK" at 9 "o" clock and NO Warners logo at 3 "o" clock. die-cut sleeve, inner sleeve, folded insert) | 60 |
| 76 | Swan Song SSK 59402 | PRESENCE (LP, shrinkwrapped gatefold sleeve with 'Led Zeppelin Presence' sticker) | 50 |
| 76 | Swan Song SSK59402 | PRESENCE (LP, shrinkwrapped gatefold sleeve without 'Led Zeppelin Presence' sticker) | 30 |
| 76 | Swan Song SSK 89402 | THE SONG REMAINS THE SAME (2-LP, textured gatefold sleeve with booklet) | 35 |
| 78 | Atlantic K 50008 | LED ZEPPELIN IV (FOUR SYMBOLS) (LP, purple vinyl testpressing or mispressing of lilac vinyl reissue) | 250 |
| 78 | Atlantic K 50008 | LED ZEPPELIN IV (FOUR SYMBOLS) (LP, lilac vinyl reissue) | 50 |
| 79 | Swan Song SSK 59410 A-F | IN THROUGH THE OUT DOOR (LP, 6 different covers with inner sleeves; set labelled 'A' to 'F', each in individual paper outer; available separately with paper outer £25 each) | 350 |
| 82 | Swansong A0051 | CODA (LP, embossed gatefold sleeve) | 40 |
| 88 | Atlantic K 50008/C 88 1-4 | FOUR SYMBOLS (LP, HMV 'Classic Collection' box set, with booklet, numbered) | 25 |
| 88 | Atlantic 250008/C 88 1-4 | FOUR SYMBOLS (CD, HMV 'Classic Collection' box set, with booklet, numbered) | 30 |
| 90 | Atlantic ZEP 1 | REMASTERS (3-LP, triple gatefold sleeve) | 30 |
| 90 | Atlantic 7567 82144-1 | LED ZEPPELIN (5-LP, box set) | 60 |
| 97 | Atlantic 7567 83061-1 | BBC SESSIONS (4-LP, box set) | 80 |
| 99 | Atlantic 7567 83268-1 | EARLY DAYS - THE BEST OF LED ZEPPELIN VOLUME 1 (LP) | 35 |
| 00 | Atlantic 7567 83278-1 | LATTER DAYS - THE BEST OF LED ZEPPELIN VOLUME 2 (LP) | 35 |
| 08 | Rhino/Atlantic/Swan Song 8122799489 | SOUNDTRACK FROM 'THE SONG REMAINS THE SAME' (4-LP, 180gm expanded edition) | 50 |
| 08 | Rhino/Atlantic/Swan Song 8122799489 | SOUNDTRACK FROM 'THE SONG REMAINS THE SAME' (4-LP 180 gm expanded edition, white vinyl, 200 only) | 600 |
| 08 | Rhino/Atlantic/Swan Song 8122799513 | MOTHERSHIP (4-LP, 180gm vinyl) | 70 |

*(see also Jimmy Page, Robert Plant, John Paul Jones, Dansette Damage, Listen, Family Dogg, Ian Whitcomb, P.J. Proby, Lord Sutch,Yardbirds, Coverdale Page)*

## ALVIN LEE
| | | | |
|---|---|---|---|
| 74 | Chrysalis CHS 2020 | The World Is Changing/Riffin' (with Myron Le Fevre) | 6 |
| 73 | Chrysalis CHR 1054 | ON THE ROAD TO FREEDOM (LP, with Myron Le Fevre) | 20 |

*(see also Ten Years After)*

## LEE & CLARENDONIANS
| | | | |
|---|---|---|---|
| 72 | Green Door GD 4038 | Night Owl/Night Owl Version | 15 |

## LEE (PERRY) & JIMMY (RILEY)
| | | | |
|---|---|---|---|
| 75 | Dip DL 5075 | Rasta Train/Yagga Yagga | 25 |

## LEE (PERRY) & JUNIOR (BYLES)
| | | | |
|---|---|---|---|
| 75 | Dip DL 5060 | Dreader Locks/Militant Rock | 20 |

## LEE & PAUL
| | | | |
|---|---|---|---|
| 59 | Philips PB 912 | The Chick/Valentina, My Valentina | 7 |

## ARTHUR LEE
| | | | |
|---|---|---|---|
| 72 | A&M AMLS 64356 | VINDICATOR (LP) | 20 |

*(see also Love)*

## BENNY LEE (& KEN-TONES)
| | | | |
|---|---|---|---|
| 56 | Parlophone R 4245 | Rock 'N' Rollin' Santa Claus/Life Was Made For Livin' (with Ken-Tones) | 10 |

*(see also Ken-Tones)*

## BRENDA LEE
### 78s
| | | | |
|---|---|---|---|
| 56 | Brunswick 05628 | I'm Gonna Lasso Santa Claus/Christy Christmas (as Little Brenda Lee) | 20 |
| 57 | Brunswick 05685 | Dynamite/Love You Til I Die | 20 |
| 57 | Brunswick 05720 | Ain't That Love/One Teenager To Another | 20 |
| 58 | Brunswick 05755 | Ring-A-My-Phone/Little Jonah (Rock On Your Little Steel Guitar) | 30 |
| 59 | Brunswick 05780 | Bill Bailey, Won't You Please Come Home/Hummin' The Blues Over You | 20 |
| 60 | Brunswick 05819 | Sweet Nuthin's/Weep No More My Baby | 70 |

### SINGLES
| | | | |
|---|---|---|---|
| 56 | Brunswick 05628 | I'm Gonna Lasso Santa Claus/Christy Christmas (triangular centre) | 200 |
| 57 | Brunswick 05685 | Dynamite/Love You Til I Die (with Anita Kerr Singers, triangular centre) | 150 |
| 57 | Brunswick 05720 | Ain't That Love/One Teenager To Another (w/ Anita Kerr Singers, tri-centre) | 150 |
| 58 | Brunswick 05755 | Ring-A-My-Phone/Little Jonah (Rock On Your Little Steel Guitar) (tri-centre) | 150 |
| 58 | Decca BM 31186 | Fairyland/One Step At A Time (export issue, triangular centre) | 50 |
| 59 | Brunswick 05780 | Bill Bailey, Won't You Please Come Home/Hummin' The Blues Over You (triangular centre) | 20 |
| 59 | Brunswick 05780 | Bill Bailey, Won't You Please Come Home/Hummin' The Blues Over You (tround centre) | 10 |
| 60 | Brunswick 05819 | Sweet Nuthin's/Weep No More My Baby (round centre) | 10 |
| 60 | Brunswick 05823 | Let's Jump The Broomstick/Rock-A-Bye Baby Blues | 10 |
| 60 | Brunswick 05833 | I'm Sorry/That's All You Gotta Do | 5 |
| 60 | Brunswick 05839 | I Want To Be Wanted/Just A Little | 5 |

| | | | |
|---|---|---|---|
| 61 | Brunswick 05847 | Emotions/I'm Learning About Love | 5 |
| 61 | Brunswick 05854 | Dum Dum/Eventually | 6 |
| 62 | Brunswick 05864 | Break It To Me Gently/So Deep | 5 |
| 62 | Brunswick 05867 | Speak To Me Pretty/Lover, Come Back To Me | 5 |
| 62 | Brunswick 05871 | Here Comes That Feeling/Everybody Loves Me But You | 5 |
| 62 | Brunswick 05876 | It Started All Over Again/Heart In Hand | 5 |
| 62 | Brunswick 05880 | Rockin' Around The Christmas Tree/Papa Noel | 5 |
| 63 | Brunswick 05886 | Losing You/He's So Heavenly | 5 |
| 63 | Brunswick 05896 | Sweet Impossible You/The Grass Is Greener | 10 |
| 64 | Brunswick 05915 | Is It True/What'd I Say | 35 |
| 66 | Brunswick 05957 | Too Little Time/Time And Time Again | 15 |
| 66 | Brunswick 05963 | Ain't Gonna Cry No More/It Takes One To Know One | 15 |
| 66 | Brunswick 05967 | Coming On Strong/You Keep Coming Back To You | 5 |
| 67 | Brunswick 05970 | Ride, Ride, Ride/Lonely People Do Foolish Things | 20 |
| 67 | Brunswick 05976 | Where's The Melody?/Born To Be By Your Side | 5 |
| 68 | Decca AD 1003 | That's All Right/Baby, Won't You Please Come Home (export issue) | 5 |

**EPs**

| | | | |
|---|---|---|---|
| 59 | Brunswick OE 9462 | ROCK THE BOP (green p/s & tri-centre) | 100 |
| 59 | Brunswick OE 9462 | ROCK THE BOP (blue p/s & round centre) | 50 |
| 62 | Brunswick OE 9482 | PRETEND | 25 |
| 62 | Brunswick OE 9488 | SPEAK TO ME PRETTY | 25 |
| 63 | Brunswick OE 9492 | ALL ALONE AM I | 15 |
| 64 | Brunswick OE 9499 | BRENDA LEE'S TRIBUTE TO AL JOLSON | 10 |
| 65 | Brunswick OE 9510 | FOUR FROM '64 | 10 |

**ALBUMS**

| | | | |
|---|---|---|---|
| 59 | Brunswick LAT 8319 | GRANDMA WHAT GREAT SONGS YOU SANG | 30 |
| 60 | Brunswick LAT 8347 | MISS DYNAMITE | 35 |
| 61 | Brunswick LAT 8360 | THIS IS BRENDA | 25 |
| 62 | Brunswick LAT/STA 8516 | BRENDA, THAT'S ALL (mono/stereo) | 15 |

## BUNNY LEE ALLSTARS

| | | | |
|---|---|---|---|
| 69 | Unity UN 541 | Daydream/Joy Ride | 25 |
| 69 | Unity UN 543 | Ivan Itler The Conqueror/The Spice | 50 |
| 70 | Camel CA39 | Three Stooge/Isle Of Love | 25 |
| 70 | Pama PM 803 | Annie Pama/Mr Magoo | 25 |
| 71 | Smash SMA 2304 | Stanley (Parts 1 & 2) (as Bunnie Lee Allstars) | 15 |
| 78 | Jamaica Sound JS 013 | SUPER DUB DISCO STYLE (LP, with the Aggrovators) | 50 |

*(see also Lloyd Charmers, Sonny Binns & Rudies, Copy Cats, John Holt, Lloyd & Doreen, Delroy Wilson)*

## BYRON LEE & DRAGONAIR(E)S

| | | | |
|---|---|---|---|
| 60 | Blue Beat B 2 | Dumplin's/Kissin' Gal (vocal: Buddy Davidson) (white label, blue print) | 20 |
| 60 | Blue Beat BB 2 | Dumplin's/Kissin' Gal (vocal: Buddy Davidson) (2nd pressing, blue label, silver print) | 15 |
| 61 | Blue Beat BB 28 | Mash! Mr. Lee/Help Me Forget (vocal: Keith Lyn) | 20 |
| 61 | Starlite ST45 045 | Joy Ride/Over The Rainbow | 15 |
| 64 | Parlophone R 5124 | River Bank/Musical Communion | 20 |
| 64 | Parlophone R 5125 | Sour Apples/Hanging Up My Heart | 20 |
| 64 | Parlophone R 5140 | Sammy Dead/Say Bye Bye (both actually by Eric Morris with Byron Lee) | 20 |
| 64 | Parlophone R 5177 | Beautiful Garden/Too Late | 20 |
| 64 | Parlophone R 5182 | Come Back/Jamaica Ska | 20 |
| 64 | MGM MGM 1256 | Night Train From Jamaica/Ska Dee Wah (with Danny Davis) | 20 |
| 66 | Doctor Bird DB 1003 | Sloopy/Gold Finger | 10 |
| 67 | Pyramid PYR 6015 | Sloopy/Gold Finger (reissue) | 8 |
| 68 | Trojan TR 624 | Soul Limbo/The Whistling Song | 8 |
| 68 | Trojan TR 631 | Mr Walker/Sunset Jump Up | 5 |
| 69 | Major Minor MM 615 | Every Day Will Be Like A Holiday/Oh What A Feeling | 15 |
| 70 | Trojan TR 7731 | Squeeze Up (Parts 1 & 2) | 10 |
| 70 | Trojan TR 7736 | Birth Control/Love At First Sight | 10 |
| 70 | Trojan TR 7747 | Bond In Bliss/Musical Scorcher | 5 |
| 70 | Trojan TR 7761 | Julianne/We Five | 10 |
| 70 | Duke DU 39 | Elizabethan Reggae/Soul Serenade | 6 |
| 70 | Duke DU 91 | Cashbox/WINSTON WRIGHT: Strolling Thru' The Park | 8 |
| 71 | Dynamic DYN 405 | Hitching A Ride/Hitching A Ride Version | 12 |
| 71 | Duke DU 69 | The Law Part 1/The Law Part 2 | 10 |
| 71 | Duke DUN 110 | One Bad Apple/Poop-A-Poom | 7 |
| 71 | Dynamic DYN 409 | My Sweet Lord/Shock Attack | 7 |
| 71 | Dynamic DYN 414 | Way Back Home/Version | 15 |
| 72 | Dynamic DYN 435 | Make It Reggae/DENNIS ALCAPONE: Go Johnny Go | 7 |
| 73 | Dragon DRA 1008 | In The Mood/Black On | 35 |
| 65 | Atlantic AET 6014 | SKA TIME (EP, as Byron Lee Ska Kings) | 35 |
| 64 | Island ILP 905 | CARIBBEAN JOY RIDE (LP) | 35 |
| 66 | Atlantic 587018 | JUMP UP (LP) | 40 |
| 69 | Trojan TTL 5 | ROCKSTEADY EXPLOSION (LP) | 20 |
| 69 | Major Minor SMLP 53 | BYRON LEE & THE DRAGONAIRES (LP) | 20 |
| 70 | Trojan TRLS 18 | REGGAE WITH BYRON LEE (LP) | 20 |

*(see also Mighty Avengers, Ken Lazarus, Hopeton Lewis, Danny Davis Orchestra, Good Guys, Neville Hinds, Hubcaps & Wheels, Mighty Sparrow, Blues Busters)*

## LITTLE MR. LEE & CHEROKEES

| | | | |
|---|---|---|---|
| 66 | Vocalion VP 9268 | Young Lover/I Don't Want To Go | 40 |

## CHRISTOPHER LEE

| | | | |
|---|---|---|---|
| 74 | Studio Two TWOA Q4 5001 | HAMMER PRESENTS DRACULA (LP, gatefold sleeve, quadrophonic) | 15 |

MINT VALUE £

## CURTIS LEE
| | | | |
|---|---|---|---|
| 60 | Top Rank JAR 317 | With All My Heart (I Love You)/Pure Love | 60 |
| 61 | London HLX 9313 | Pledge Of Love/Then I'll Know | 25 |
| 61 | London HLX 9397 | Pretty Little Angel Eyes/Gee How I Wish You Were Here | 20 |
| 61 | London HLX 9445 | Under The Moon Of Love/Beverly Jean | 20 |
| 62 | London HLX 9533 | A Night At Daddy Gee's/Just Another Fool | 20 |
| 67 | CBS 2717 | Get My Bag/Everybody's Going Wild (as Curtis Lee & K.C.P.s) | 40 |
| 67 | CBS 2717 | Get My Bag/Everybody's Going Wild (as Curtis Lee & K.C.P.s) (DJ copy) | 80 |
| 72 | Stateside SS 2208 | Under The Moon Of Love/Beverly Jean (reissue) | 6 |

## DAVE LEE (& STAGGERLEES)
| | | | |
|---|---|---|---|
| 63 | Decca F 11600 | Take Four/Five To Four On | 10 |
| 63 | Oriole CB 1864 | Dance Dance Dance/Love Me (as Dave Lee & Staggerlees) | 10 |
| 63 | Oriole CB 1907 | Sweet & Lovely/Forever And Always (as Dave Lee & Staggerlees) | 10 |
| 66 | Fontana TF 723 | Adam Adamant/Georgie's Theme (as Dave Lee & His Orchestra) | 15 |

## DAVE LEE
| | | | |
|---|---|---|---|
| 66 | Colpix PXL 550 | OUR MAN CRICHTON (LP, with Tubby Hayes) | 80 |

*(see also Tubby Hayes)*

## DAVID H. LEE
| | | | |
|---|---|---|---|
| 65 | Pye 7N 15809 | Heaven With No Angel | 8 |
| 69 | Morgan MR 1 | Johnny's Eyes/You're The Only One | 7 |

## DEBBIE LEE
| | | | |
|---|---|---|---|
| 64 | Decca F 11931 | For Every Man There's A Woman/Can't You See | 8 |

## DEREK LEE
| | | | |
|---|---|---|---|
| 66 | Parlophone R 5468 | Girl/You've Done Something To My Heart | 10 |

## DICK LEE
| | | | |
|---|---|---|---|
| 53 | Columbia SCM 5066 | All I Want Is A Chance/The Show Is Ended | 10 |
| 53 | Columbia SCM 5078 | I Thought You Might Be Lonely/Happy Bells | 10 |
| 54 | Columbia SCM 5094 | The Book/(Stay In My Arms)Cinderella | 12 |

## DICKIE/DICKEY LEE
| | | | |
|---|---|---|---|
| 59 | MGM MGM 1013 | A Penny A Kiss - A Penny A Hug/Bermuda (as Dick Lee) | 5 |
| 62 | Mercury AMT 1190 | Patches/More Or Less | 10 |
| 62 | Mercury AMT 1196 | I Saw Linda Yesterday/The Girl I Can't Forget | 10 |
| 62 | Mercury AMT 1200 | Don't Wanna Think About Paula/Just A Friend | 10 |
| 65 | Stateside SS 433 | Laurie (Strange Things Happen)/Party Doll (as Dickey Lee) | 7 |
| 65 | Stateside SS 464 | The Girl From Peyton Place/A Girl I Used To Know (as Dickey Lee) | 7 |

## DINAH LEE
| | | | |
|---|---|---|---|
| 65 | Aladdin WI 606 | I'll Forgive You Then Forget You/Nitty Gritty | 35 |
| 65 | Brit 1005 | I Can't Believe What You Say/Pushin' A Good Thing Too Far (unissued) | 0 |
| 65 | Aladdin WI 608 | I Can't Believe What You Say/Pushin' A Good Thing Too Far | 40 |

## DON (TONY) LEE
| | | | |
|---|---|---|---|
| 68 | Big Shot BI 504 | It's Reggae Time (as Don Tony Lee)/ERROL DUNKLEY: The Clamp Is On | 35 |
| 68 | Doctor Bird DB 1106 | Lee's Special (as Don Tony Lee)/LLOYD & GROOVERS: My Heart And Soul | 40 |
| 68 | Island WI 3160 | It's Reggae Time (as D. Tony Lee)/ERROL DUNKLEY: The Clamp Is On | 45 |
| 69 | Unity UN 519 | Peyton Place/Red Gal In The Ring (as Don Tony Lee) | 20 |
| 70 | Gas 163 | Work Out/Too Long (as Donald Lee) | 35 |

## EDNA LEE
| | | | |
|---|---|---|---|
| 68 | President PT 175 | I Really Think I'm Crying 'Cause I Love You/Don't Let My Friends See What You Do | 5 |

## (FREDDIE) 'FINGERS' LEE (& UPPER HAND)
| | | | |
|---|---|---|---|
| 65 | Fontana TF 619 | The Friendly Undertaker/Little Bit More (as 'Fingers' Lee) | 25 |
| 66 | Fontana TF 655 | I'm Gonna Buy Me A Dog/I Can't Drive (as 'Fingers' Lee) | 40 |
| 66 | Columbia DB 8002 | Bossy Boss/Don't Run Away (as Fingers Lee & Upper Hand) | 40 |
| 77 | Beeb 020 | Down On the Farm/My Bucket's Got A Hole In It | 8 |

*(see also At Last The 1958 Rock & Roll Show)*

## GEORGE LEE (& MUSIC DOCTORS)
| | | | |
|---|---|---|---|
| 69 | Downtown DT 443 | Talking Boss/Jungle Fever (solo) | 45 |
| 70 | J-Dan JDN 4407 | Johnny Dollar/Tough Of Poison (with Music Doctors) | 25 |

*(see also Desmond Riley)*

## HUBERT LEE
| | | | |
|---|---|---|---|
| 73 | Ackee ACK 504 | I Love Verona/Version | 5 |
| 73 | Downtown DT 498 | Something On Your Mind/IMPACT ALL STARS: Mind Version | 8 |
| 73 | Green Door GD 4050 | High School Dance/PRINCE TONY'S ALL STARS: Version | 5 |
| 74 | Ackee ACK 524 | Tonight Will You Still Love Me/IMPACT ALL STARS: Version | 6 |

## JACKIE LEE (U.K.) (FEMALE)
| | | | |
|---|---|---|---|
| 55 | Decca F 10550 | I Was Wrong/For As Long As I Live | 12 |
| 65 | Decca F 12068 | I Cry Alone/Cause I Love Him | 12 |
| 65 | Columbia DB 7685 | Lonely Clown/Love Is Gone | 12 |
| 66 | Columbia DB 7860 | I Know, Know, Know I'll Never Love/So Love Me | 12 |
| 66 | Columbia DB 8052 | The Town I Live In/You Too | 10 |
| 67 | Decca F 12663 | Born To Lose/Saying Goodbye | 12 |
| 69 | Pye 7N 17829 | Love Is a Gamble/Something Borrowed, Something Blue | 10 |
| 70 | Pye 7N 45003 | Rupert/Going To The Circus | 6 |

*(see also Jacky, Jackie Lee & Raindrops, Emma Rede)*

## JACKIE LEE & RAINDROPS (U.K.) (FEMALE)
| | | | |
|---|---|---|---|
| 62 | Oriole CB 1702 | I Was The Last One To Know/There's No One In The Whole World | 10 |
| 62 | Oriole CB 1727 | There Goes The Lucky One/I Built My Whole World Around You | 10 |
| 62 | Oriole CB 1757 | Party Lights/Midnight | 15 |
| 63 | Oriole CB 1800 | The End Of The World/Goodbye Is Such A Lonely Word | 10 |

| | | | |
|---|---|---|---|
| 63 | Philips BF 1283 | Down Our Street/My Heart Is Your Heart (as Jackie & Raindrops) | 10 |
| 64 | Philips BF 1328 | Here I Go Again/Come On Dream Come On (as Jackie & Raindrops) | 10 |
| 72 | ICI Pharmacuticals Division ICI 1 | Space Age Lullaby/Sleep (p/s) | 15 |

(see also Jacky, Jackie Lee [U.K.], Raindrops [U.K], Emma Rede, Boeing Duveen and the Beautiful Soup)

## JACKIE LEE (U.S.) (MALE)
| | | | |
|---|---|---|---|
| 60 | Top Rank JAR 286 | Rancho/Like Sunset | 10 |
| 72 | Jay Boy BOY 76 | African Boo-Ga-Loo/Bring It Home | 8 |
| 85 | Kent TOWN 107 | Darkest Days/EDDIE BISHOP: Call Me | 25 |

## JACKIE LEE (U.S.) (MALE)
| | | | |
|---|---|---|---|
| 65 | Fontana TF 646 | The Duck/Let Your Conscience Be Your Guide | 40 |
| 66 | Jay Boy BOY 28 | Would You Believe/You're Everything | 10 |
| 68 | London HLM 10233 | The Duck/Dancing In The Street | 15 |
| 70 | Jay Boy BOY 26 | Do The Temptation Walk/The Shotgun And The Duck | 10 |
| 72 | Jay Boy BOY 66 | Oh! My Darlin'/Don't Be Ashamed | 15 |
| 72 | Jay Boy BOY 66 | Oh! My Darlin'/Don't Be Ashamed (DJ copy) | 30 |
| 73 | Contempo CR 5 | The Duck (Parts 1 & 2) | 5 |
| 67 | London HA-M 8336 | THE DUCK (LP) | 50 |

(see also Bob & Earl, Earl Nelson, Jackie Lee & Delores Hall)

## JACKIE LEE & DELORES HALL
| | | | |
|---|---|---|---|
| 69 | B&C CB 105 | Whether It's Right Or Wrong/Baby I'm Satisfied | 10 |
| 72 | Jay Boy BOY 52 | Whether It's Right Or Wrong/Baby I'm Satisfied (reissue) | 6 |

(see also Jackie Lee [U.S.], Delores Hall)

## JAMIE LEE & ATLANTICS
| | | | |
|---|---|---|---|
| 63 | Decca F 11571 | In The Night/Little Girl In Blue | 45 |

## JIMMY LEE
| | | | |
|---|---|---|---|
| 61 | Starlite ST45 059 | All My Life/Chicago Jump | 30 |

## JOHN LEE
| | | | |
|---|---|---|---|
| 72 | Explosion EX 2060 | Stagger Lee/Musical Version (both sides actually by John Holt) | 5 |

## JOHNNIE LEE
| | | | |
|---|---|---|---|
| 59 | Pye 7N 15201 | Echo/It's-A Me, It's-A Me, It's-A Me My Love | 8 |
| 59 | Pye 7N 15233 | I'm Finally Free/I Fell (with The King's Men) | 8 |
| 60 | Fontana H 257 | They're Wrong/Cindy Lou | 8 |
| 60 | Fontana H 280 | Poetry In Motion/Let It Come True | 10 |
| 61 | Fontana H 306 | Lonely Joe/Nobody | 8 |
| 67 | CBS 202591 | Kiss Tomorrow Goodbye/Love No Longer Sounds | 5 |
| 67 | CBS 2802 | I Forgot What It Was Like/Lonely Is The Willow | 5 |
| 67 | CBS 3112 | Because You're Mine/I'll Not Forget | 5 |

## JULIA LEE (& HER BOYFRIENDS)
| | | | |
|---|---|---|---|
| 51 | Capitol LC 6535 | PARTY TIME (10" LP, 2 different sleeves) | 50 |

## LAURA LEE (U.K.)
| | | | |
|---|---|---|---|
| 60 | Triumph RGM 1030 | Tell Tommy I Miss Him/I'm Sending Back Your Roses | 50 |
| 62 | Decca F 11513 | Too Young To Be In Love/Brand New Heartbeat | 15 |
| 68 | Columbia DB 8495 | Love In Every Room/Master Jack | 12 |
| 71 | Columbia DB 8770 | Someone To Love Me/Look Left-Look Right | 8 |

## LAURA LEE (U.S.)
| | | | |
|---|---|---|---|
| 67 | Chess CRS 8062 | Dirty Man/It's Mighty Hard | 7 |
| 68 | Chess CRS 8070 | As Long As I Got You/A Man With Some Backbone | 10 |
| 72 | Tamla Motown TMG 831 | To Win Your Heart/So Will I | 10 |
| 72 | Tamla Motown TMG 831 | To Win Your Heart/So Will I (DJ copy) | 40 |
| 72 | Hot Wax HWX 115 | Rip Off/Two Lovely Pillows | 6 |
| 73 | Hot Wax HWX 118 | Wedlock Is A Padlock/Since I Fell For You | 6 |
| 73 | Hot Wax HWX 119 | You've Got The Love To Save Me/Crumbs Off The Table | 12 |
| 74 | Invictus INV 2654 | I Need It Just As Bad As You/If I'm Good Enough To Love | 5 |
| 71 | Hot Wax SHW 5006 | WOMEN'S LOVE RIGHTS (LP) | 15 |
| 73 | Hot Wax SHW 5009 | TWO SIDES OF LAURA LEE (LP) | 15 |

## LEAPY LEE
| | | | |
|---|---|---|---|
| 65 | Pye 7N 17001 | It's All Happening/In The Meantime | 5 |
| 66 | Decca F 12369 | King Of The Whole Wide World/Shake Hands (featuring the Kinks) | 50 |
| 67 | CBS 202550 | The Man On The Flying Trapeze/My Mixed-Up Mind | 5 |
| 68 | Pye 7N 17619 | It's All Happening/It's Great | 5 |

## LOCKS LEE
| | | | |
|---|---|---|---|
| 75 | Atra ATRA 28 | What Can I Do/Dreader Version | 8 |

## MANDY LEE
| | | | |
|---|---|---|---|
| 69 | Dandelion S 4494 | Bottle Up And Go (Parts 1 & 2) | 6 |

## MICHELLE LEE
| | | | |
|---|---|---|---|
| 68 | CBS 3350 | L. David Sloan/Everybody Loves My Baby | 6 |

## MICKEY LEE
| | | | |
|---|---|---|---|
| 73 | Smash SMA 2332 | Hello My Little Queen/AUGUSTUS PABLO: African Queen | 10 |

## NICKIE LEE
| | | | |
|---|---|---|---|
| 69 | Deep Soul DS 9103 | And Black Is Beautiful/Faith Within | 25 |

## NORMA LEE
| | | | |
|---|---|---|---|
| 67 | CBM CBM 002 | Hurt/Rollin' On | 6 |

## PEGGY LEE
### SINGLES
| | | | |
|---|---|---|---|
| 54 | Brunswick 05286 | Johnny Guitar/I Didn't Know What Time It Was | 8 |
| 54 | Brunswick 05345 | Love, You Didn't Do Right By Me/Sisters | 8 |

MINT VALUE £

| 55 | Brunswick 05360 | Let Me Go, Lover/Bouquet Of Blues | 8 |
|----|-----------------|-----------------------------------|---|
| 55 | Brunswick 05368 | Straight Ahead/It Must Be So (with Mills Brothers) | 8 |
| 55 | Brunswick 05421 | Baubles, Bangles And Beads/Summer Vacation | 8 |
| 55 | Brunswick 05435 | I Belong To You/How Bitter, My Sweet | 8 |
| 55 | Brunswick 05461 | Ooh That Kiss/Oh! No! (Please Don't Go) | 8 |
| 55 | Brunswick 05471 | Sugar/What Can I Say After I Say I'm Sorry | 8 |
| 55 | Brunswick 05472 | He Needs Me/Sing A Rainbow | 8 |
| 55 | Brunswick 05482 | He's A Tramp (with Pound Hounds)/The Siamese Cat Song (with Oliver Wallace) | 8 |
| 55 | Brunswick 05483 | Bella Notte/La La Lu | 8 |

*(Originally issued with gold label lettering; silver reissues are worth two-thirds these values.)*

| 58 | Capitol CL 14902 | Fever/You Don't Know | 8 |
| 65 | Capitol CL 15394 | Bewitched/Sneakin' Up On You | 7 |

**ALBUMS**

| 53 | Capitol LC 6584 | CAPITOL PRESENTS PEGGY LEE (10") | 20 |
| 53 | Brunswick LA 8629 | BLACK COFFEE (10") | 20 |
| 55 | Brunswick LA 8717 | SONGS IN AN INTIMATE STYLE (10") | 20 |

*(see also Bing Crosby, George Shearing)*

## ROBERT LEE
| 87 | Josiah KJ 008 | Easy Norman/MICHAEL MARTIN ALLSTARS: Version (12") | 40 |

## ROBERTA LEE
| 52 | Brunswick 04876 | The Little White Cloud That Cried/Tell Me Why (78, with Grady Martin) | 8 |
| 54 | HMV 7M 261 | True Love And Tender Care/When The Organ Played At Twilight | 10 |
| 55 | Brunswick 05388 | Ridin' To Tennessee/I'll Be There If Ever You Want Me | 10 |

*(see also Red Foley, Hardrock Gunter)*

## ROBIN LEE
| 62 | Reprise R 20068 | Gambling Man/An Angel With A Broken Wing | 12 |

## ROY LEE
| 61 | Decca F 11406 | Two Initials/Honey Lies | 6 |

## RUDY LEE & STEPPER
| 89 | Wau! Mr. Modo MOWLP 003 | TEAM WORKS PRESENTS (LP) | 25 |

## DAVE LEE SOUND
| 74 | Sea Cruise SCDL 100 | DAVE LEE SOUND EP | 20 |
| 73 | Southern Sound 401 | PLAY ROCK N ROLL REQUESTS (LP, white labels) | 20 |
| 73 | Southern Sound SSLP 204 | LIVE AT THE STARDUST (LP) | 30 |
| 75 | Throstle Nest TN 001 | CARRY ON (LP) | 20 |

## VINNY LEE & RIDERS
| 61 | HMV POP 856 | Mule Train/Gambler's Guitar | 15 |

## WARREN LEE
| 69 | Pama PM 762 | Underdog Backstreet/Come Put My Life In Order | 20 |

## WILMA LEE & STONEY COOPER
| 64 | Hickory 45-1257 | Big John's Wife/Pirate King | 7 |

## BRAD LEEDS
| 60 | Pye International 7N 25050 | A Teenage Love Is Born/I'm Walking Behind You | 6 |

## PHIL LEEDS
| 66 | London HLR 10044 | Would You Believe It?/FRANK GALLOP: The Ballad Of Irving | 8 |

## MARK LEEMAN FIVE
| 65 | Columbia DB 7452 | Portland Town/Gotta Get Myself Together | 20 |
| 65 | Columbia DB 7648 | Blow My Blues Away/On The Horizon | 25 |
| 66 | Columbia DB 7812 | Forbidden Fruit/Goin' To Bluesville | 25 |
| 66 | Columbia DB 7955 | Follow Me/Gather Up The Pieces | 20 |

*(see also Cheynes)*

## THOMAS LEER
| 78 | Oblique ER 101 | Private Plane/International (folded photocopied p/s, hand-stamped labels) | 40 |
| 78 | Company/Oblique OBCO 1 | Private Plane/International (reissue, printed p/s) | 20 |
| 82 | Cherry Red CHERRY 52 | All About You/Saving Grace (p/s) | 5 |
| 79 | Industrial IR 0007 | THE BRIDGE (LP, with Robert Rental) | 40 |

*(see also Act, Robert Rental)*

## JOHN LEES
| 74 | Polydor 2058 513 | Best Of My Love/You Can't Get It | 15 |
| 77 | Harvest HAR 5132 | Child Of The Universe/Kes (A Major Fancy) | 5 |
| 73 | Harvest SHVL 811 | A MAJOR FANCY (LP, released as SHSM 2018) | 20 |

*(see also Barclay James Harvest)*

## RAYMOND LEFEVRE & HIS ORCHESTRA
| 68 | Major Minor MM 559 | Soul Coaxing (Ame Caline)/When A Man Loves A Woman | 8 |

## LEFT BANKE
| 66 | Philips BF 1517 | Walk Away Renee/I Haven't Got The Nerve | 8 |
| 67 | Philips BF 1540 | Pretty Ballerina/Lazy Day | 8 |
| 67 | Philips BF 1575 | Ivy Ivy/And Suddenly | 8 |
| 67 | Philips BF 1614 | Desiree/I've Got Something On My Mind | 8 |
| 87 | Bam Caruso OPRA 023 | Walk Away Renee/Ivy Ivy (DJ/jukebox issue) | 7 |
| 67 | Philips (S)BL 7773 | WALK AWAY RENEE/PRETTY BALLERINA (LP) | 50 |

## LEFTFIELD
| 90 | Outer Rhythm FOOT 3 | Not Forgotten (12") | 15 |
| 92 | Hard Hands HAND 002R | Song Of Life (Remixes)/Release The Horns (12") | 10 |
| 92 | Hard Hands HAND 002T | Song Of Life/Dub Of Life/Fanfare Of Life (12") | 10 |
| 95 | Hard Hands HANDLP 2 | LEFTISM (2-LP, gatefold sleeve) | 20 |
| 95 | Hard Hands HANDLP 2T | LEFTISM (3-LP, gatefold sleeve) | 25 |

| | | | |
|---|---|---|---|
| 99 | Hard Hands HANDLP 4 | RHYTHM AND STEALTH (2-LP) | 20 |
| 99 | Hard Hands HANDLP 4T | RHYTHM AND STEALTH (5 x 10" box set, limited edition) | 25 |

*(see also Curve)*

## LEFT HAND DRIVE
| | | | |
|---|---|---|---|
| 77 | Bankrupt Records BECK 611 | Jailbait/Motorway Crow (1,000 only, no p/s) | 50 |
| 79 | Bankrupt BAN 012 | Who Said Rock & Roll Is Dead/I Know Where I Am (p/s) | 10 |

## LEFT-HANDED MARRIAGE
| | | | |
|---|---|---|---|
| 67 | Private pressing | ON THE RIGHT SIDE OF THE LEFT-HANDED MARRIAGE (LP) | 500 |
| 96 | Tenth Planet TP 022 | ON THE RIGHT SIDE OF THE LEFT-HANDED MARRIAGE (LP, reissue, gatefold sleeve) | 25 |

*(see also Queen)*

## LEFT SIDE
| | | | |
|---|---|---|---|
| 69 | Columbia DB 8575 | Welcome To My House/This Little Village | 6 |

## LEGAL AID
| | | | |
|---|---|---|---|
| 81 | Earshot ERA 1 | That's Life/Limbo | 15 |

## LEGAY
| | | | |
|---|---|---|---|
| 69 | Fontana TF 904 | No-One/The Fantastic Story Of The Steam Driven Banana | 175 |

*(see also Gypsy)*

## LEGEND!
| | | | |
|---|---|---|---|
| 83 | Creation CRE 001/Lyntone LYN 12903 | '73 In '83/You (Chunka Chunka) Were Glamorous (foldaround p/s in poly bag, with 33rpm flexidisc "I Wonder Why! (live)" by The Pastels/"Wouldn't You? By Laughing Apple) | 15 |
| 84 | Creation CRE 010 | The Legend Destroys The Blues/Arrogant Bastards (foldaround p/s in poly bag) | 6 |

## TOBI LEGEND
| | | | |
|---|---|---|---|
| 78 | RK RK 1004 | Time Will Pass You By/DEAN PARRISH: I'm On My Way/JIMMY RADCLIFFE: Long After Tonight Is All Over (with p/s) | 10 |
| 78 | RK RK 1004 | Time Will Pass You By/DEAN PARRISH: I'm On My Way/JIMMY RADCLIFFE: Long After Tonight Is All Over | 6 |

## LEGEND (1)
| | | | |
|---|---|---|---|
| 69 | Bell BLL 1048 | National Gas/Wouldn't You | 20 |
| 69 | Bell BLL 1082 | Georgia George Part 1/July | 15 |
| 70 | Vertigo 6059 021 | Life/Late Last Night | 20 |
| 71 | Vertigo 6059 036 | Don't You Know/Someday | 15 |
| 69 | Bell MBLL/SBLL 115 | LEGEND (LP, blue/silver labels with "Sold in U.K..." text) | 175 |
| 71 | Vertigo 6360 019 | LEGEND ('RED BOOT') (LP, gatefold sleeve, large swirl label) | 300 |
| 72 | Vertigo 6360 063 | MOONSHINE (LP, gatefold sleeve, small swirl label) | 400 |

*(see also Procol Harum, Mickey Jupp)*

## LEGEND (2)
| | | | |
|---|---|---|---|
| 81 | Legend LEG 1 | Hideaway/Heaven Sent (p/s) | 70 |

## LEGEND (3)
| | | | |
|---|---|---|---|
| 82 | Workshop WR 3478 | FRONTLINE EP (Frontline/Sabre & Chatila/ Stormers Of Heaven/Open The Skies (12") | 25 |
| 81 | Workshop WR 2007 | LEGEND (LP) | 90 |
| 82 | Workshop WR 3477 | DEATH IN THE NURSERY (LP, with insert) | 20 |

## LEGENDARY FLOBS
| | | | |
|---|---|---|---|
| 79 | Flobs FLO 1 | Dead Popes/You're In Danger (p/s) | 25 |

## LEGENDARY HEARTS
| | | | |
|---|---|---|---|
| 88 | Surfin' Pict | IN A WORLD LIKE THIS (12" EP) | 30 |

## LEGENDARY LONNIE
| | | | |
|---|---|---|---|
| 81 | Nervous NER 002 | Constipation Shake/Devil's Guitar (p/s) | 6 |

## LEGENDARY MASKED SURFERS
| | | | |
|---|---|---|---|
| 73 | United Artists UP 35542 | Gonna Hustle You/Summertime, Summertime | 18 |

*(see also Beach Boys, Jan & Dean)*

## LEGENDARY PINK DOTS
| | | | |
|---|---|---|---|
| 81 | Mirrordot MD 01 | ONLY DREAMING (cassette, all different hand-made covers) | 100 |
| 81 | Mirrordot MD02/03 | CHEMICAL PLAYSCHOOL 1/2 (double cassette, 24 copies all different handmade covers) | 120 |
| 81 | Cassetteking CK04 | DOTS ON THE EYE (cassette) | 45 |
| 82 | Flowmotion FMC 09 | PREMONITION (cassette, around 60 copies) | 45 |
| 82 | Mirrordot MD/03/II | CHEMICAL PLAYSCHOOL 2 EDITION 2 (cassette, 9 copies, different handmade copies) | 120 |
| 82 | Mirrordot MD 02-03 | CHEMICAL PLAYSCHOOL 3/4 (double cassette, 120 copies, different covers) | 75 |
| 82 | Mirrordot MD 04 | KLEINE KRIEG (cassette, 120 copies, individual hand-made covers) | 80 |
| 82 | In Phaze 4 | BRIGHTER NOW (cassette, 300 copies, different mixes on some tracks) | 45 |
| 82 | In Phaze IPNER 1 | BRIGHTER NOW (LP) | 25 |
| 83 | Third Mind TMT 08 | BASILISK (cassette, 1000 copies) | 30 |
| 83 | In Phaze PHA 2 | CURSE (LP, 2500 copies) | 20 |
| 84 | In Phaze PHA | THE TOWER (LP, 2500 copies) | 20 |

## LEGENDS
| | | | |
|---|---|---|---|
| 65 | Pye 7N 15904 | I've Found Her/Something's Gonna Happen | 20 |
| 67 | Parlophone R 5581 | Tomorrow's Gonna Be Another Day/Nobody Laughs Anymore | 40 |
| 67 | Parlophone R 5613 | Under The Sky/Twenty-Four Hours A Day | 20 |

*(see also First Impressions)*

## B. LEGGS
| | | | |
|---|---|---|---|
| 71 | Green Door GD 4004 | Drums Of Passion/Love And Emotion (Version) | 6 |

*(see also Morgan's All Stars)*

## LEGION
| | | | |
|---|---|---|---|
| 84 | Off Beat S LEG 003 | Yesterday/Anticks (p/s) | 15 |

## LEGION OF PARASITES
| | | | |
|---|---|---|---|
| 84 | Fight Back FIGHT 2 | UNDESIRABLE GUESTS (12" EP) | 15 |
| 85 | Thrash THRASH 1 | THE PRISON OF LIFE! (LP) | 15 |

| | | | MINT VALUE £ |
|---|---|---|---|
| 87 | Stud STUDLP 3 | DAWN TO DUST (LP) | 15 |

**LEGO FEET**
| 91 | Skam SKAM 1 | Untitled1/Untitled 2 (12", black die cut sleeve) | 100 |

**MICHEL LEGRAND**
| 73 | Tamla Motown TMG 848 | Love Theme From "Lady Sings The Blues"/Any Happy Home (demo in p/s) | 10 |
| 64 | Mercury SML 30020 | VIOLENT VIOLINS (LP) | 18 |
| 66 | Philips (S)BL 7792 | THE YOUNG GIRLS OF ROCHEFORT (LP, soundtrack) | 25 |
| 68 | United Artists SULP 1218 | THE THOMAS CROWN AFFAIR (LP, soundtrack) | 25 |
| 70 | Sunset SLS 50519 | THE THOMAS CROWN AFFAIR (LP, reissue) | 35 |
| 70 | United Artists UAS 29084 | THE HAPPY ENDING (LP, soundtrack) | 20 |

**LE GRIFFE**
| 83 | Bullet BOL 1 | Fast Bikes/Where Are You? (p/s) | 8 |
| 83 | Bullet BOLT 1 | Fast Bikes/Where Are You?/The Actor (12", p/s) | 8 |
| 84 | Bullet BOL 7 | You're Killing Me (p/s) | 15 |
| 83 | Bullet BOLT 7 | You're Killing Me/E.T.A. (12", p/s) | 8 |
| 84 | Bullet BULP 2 | BREAKING STRAIN (mini-LP) | 15 |

**LEGS**
| 74 | Warner Bros K 16317 | So Many Faces/You Bet You Have | 20 |

*(see also Curved Air, Stretch)* | | | 15 |

**TOM LEHRER**
| 60 | Decca F 11243 | Poisoning Pigeons In The Park/The Masochism Tango (in p/s) | 5 |

**LEIBER-STOLLER ORCHESTRA**
| 62 | HMV 1050 | Cafe Expresso/Blue Baion | 25 |

**LEIBSTANDARTE SS MB**
| 81 | Come Organisation WDC 881015 | TRIUMPH OF THE WILL (LP, 500 only) | 100 |
| 81 | Come Organisation WDC 881018 | WELTANSCHAUUNG (LP) | 100 |
| 82 | Come Organisation WDC 883023 | MENSES (cassette) | 70 |

**ANDREW LEIGH**
| 70 | Polydor 2343 034 | MAGICIAN (LP) | 75 |

*(see also Reg King, Spooky Tooth)*

**ROBERTA LEIGH**
| 58 | HMV EH 8339 | THE ADVENTURES OF TWIZZLE (EP) | 15 |

**BERNIE LEIGHTON**
| 63 | Pye International 7N 25177 | Lawrence Of Arabia Theme/The Wonderful World We Live In (in p/s) | 8 |

**LEISURE ADDICTS**
| 80 | Addictive ADIC 1 | Subway Suicide/Prefab 13 (no p/s) | 20 |

**LEISURE RESEARCH**
| 84 | Innocent INNOC 1 | Discontent/Reasons (p/s) | 20 |

**LEITMOTIV**
| 83 | Paragon VIRTUE 3 | CARESS AND CURSE EP (12") | 15 |
| 84 | Pax PAX 17 | Silent Run/(Living In A) Tin | 10 |

**LELU/LU'S**
| 86 | Possum POST 001 | Africa/Fragile Thigs/Blipverts (12", p/s) | 15 |
| 86 | Possum POST 001 | Africa/Fragile Thigs/Blipverts (p/s) | 12 |

**LE MAT**
| 82 | Whaam 008 | Waltz For A Fool/Every Dream | 10 |

**GARY LEMEL**
| 67 | London HLM 7124 | Beautiful People/Take Me With You (export issue) | 20 |

**LEMMINGS**
| 65 | Pye 7N 15837 | Out Of My Mind/My Little Girl | 20 |
| 65 | Pye 7N 15899 | You Can't Blame Me For Trying/Bring Your Heart With You | 20 |

*(see also Honeycombs, Martin Murray)*

**LEMMY & UPSETTERS WITH MICK GREEN**
| 90 | Sunnyside STYLE 777 | Blue Suede Shoes/Paradise (p/s) | 7 |

*(see also Motorhead, Rockin' Vickers)*

**LEMON D**
| 92 | Planet Earth PEDJ 01 | DJ ON WAX (12" EP) | 25 |
| 93 | Planet Earth PDJ 02 | PURSUIT OF A VISION (12" EP) | 20 |
| 93 | Planet Earth PDJ 03 | TOXIC RHYTHMS (12" EP) | 10 |
| 93 | Planet Earth PDJ 05 | THE REMIXES? (12" EP) | 10 |
| 95 | Conqueror OC 7 | I Feel It/Don't Make Me Wait/Bad Man (12") | 10 |
| 95 | Conqueror OC 9 | VOL II (12" EP) | 15 |

**LEMON DIPS**
| 69 | De Wolfe DW/LP 3114 | WHO'S GONNA BUY? (10" LP, library issue) | 75 |

**LEMONHEADS**
| 90 | Atlantic 82137 | LOVEY (LP) | 15 |
| 93 | Atlantic 82537 | COME ON FEEL (LP) | 20 |

**LEMON INTERRUPT**
| 93 | Junior Boys Own JBO 12002 | Eclipse/Bigmouth (12") | 15 |
| 93 | Junior Boys Own JBO 712 | Dirty/Minneapolis/Minneapolis (Airwaves) (12") | 15 |

*(see also Underworld)*

**LEMON JELLY**
| 01 | Soft Rock SOFTROCK 001 | Soft/Rock (blue vinyl, denim sleeve with condom, 1000 only) | 40 |
| 02 | XL IFXLT 147P | Space Walk/Return To Patagonia (10", leather title sleeve, 3000 only) | 10 |

| 03 | Rolled Oats RO 01 | Rolled/Oats (gold vinyl, hessian sleeve, 1200 only)..................................... | 15 |
| 98 | Impotent Fury IF 001 | THE BATH EP: In The Bath/Nervous Tension/A Tune For Jack (10", 1000 only, stickered cardboard sleeve, 1st 250 hand-printed p/s)........................... | 80 |
| 98 | Impotent Fury IF 001 | THE BATH EP: In The Bath/Nervous Tension/A Tune For Jack (10", 1000 only, stickered).................................................... | 30 |
| 99 | Impotent Fury IF 002 | THE YELLOW EP: His Majesty King Raam/The Staunton Lick/Homage To Patagonia (10", 1000 only, stickered cardboard sleeve, 1st 240 in hand-printed p/s)........ | 70 |
| 99 | Impotent Fury IF 002 | THE YELLOW EP: His Majesty King Raam/The Staunton Lick/Homage To Patagonia (10", 1000 only, stickered cardboard sleeve).................................. | 20 |
| 00 | Impotent Fury IF 003 | THE MIDNIGHT EP: Kneel Before Your God/Page One/Come (10", 1000 only, stickered cardboard sleeve, 1st 350 in hand-printed p/s)..................... | 80 |
| 00 | Impotent Fury IF 003 | THE MIDNIGHT EP: Kneel Before Your God/Page One/Come (10", 1000 only, stickered cardboard sleeve).................................................. | 20 |
| 00 | XL IXXLLP 139 | KY (2-LP gatefold sleeve with insert).................................................. | 40 |

## LEMON KITTENS
| 79 | Step Forward SF 10 | SPOONFED AND WRITHING (EP)............................................ | 25 |
| 81 | United Dairies UD 07 | CAKE BEAST (12" EP, with inner sleeve & insert)....................... | 25 |
| 80 | United Dairies UD 02 | WE BUY A HAMMER FOR DADDY (LP, with inner sheet).................. | 35 |
| 83 | Illuminated JAMS 131 | THE BIG DENTIST (LP)....................................................... | 35 |

*(see also Danielle Dax, Shock Headed Peters, Gland Shrouds, Karl Blake, Fur Fur)*

## LEMON LINE
| 67 | Decca F 12688 | For Your Precious Love/You Made Me See The Light...................... | 15 |

## LEMON MEN
| 69 | Polydor 56365 | I've Seen You Cut Lemons/Lemon Strip/Lemon Walk.................... | 15 |

## LEMON PIPERS
| 68 | Pye International 7N 25444 | Green Tambourine/No Help From Me................................... | 7 |
| 68 | Pye International 7N 25454 | Rice Is Nice/Blueberry Blue.......................................... | 10 |
| 68 | Pye International 7N 25464 | Jelly Jungle (Of Orange Marmalade)/Shoeshine Boy................. | 6 |
| 68 | Pye Intl. NPL 28112 | GREEN TAMBOURINE (LP)............................................ | 30 |
| 68 | Pye Intl. NSPL 28118 | JUNGLE MARMALADE (LP)........................................... | 20 |

*(see also Ram Jam)*

## LEMON PIPERS/1910 FRUITGUM CO.
| 68 | Pye Intl. NEP 44091 | PRESENTING ... (EP, 1 side each)..................................... | 15 |

*(see also 1910 Fruitgum Co.)*

## LEMONS
| 81 | RCAE RB 004 | My Favourite Band/English Summer...................................... | 20 |

## LEMON TREE
| 68 | Parlophone R 5671 | I Can Touch A Rainbow/William Chalker's Time Machine............. | 50 |
| 68 | Parlophone R 5739 | It's So Nice To Come Home/Come On Girl............................ | 40 |

*(see also Idle Race, Uglys, Danny King's Mayfair Set, Balls)*

## LEN & HIS SEXTET
| 63 | Melotone ME 100 | Blowin' The Top/Don't Stop............................................... | 25 |

## LEN & HONEYSUCKERS
| 66 | Rio R 75 | One More River/Emergency Ward........................................ | 10 |

## FREDDIE LENNON
| 66 | Piccadilly 7N 35290 | That's My Life (My Love And My Home)/The Next Time You Feel Important............. | 40 |

*(see also Loving Kind)*

## JIMMY LENNON & ATLANTICS
| 64 | Decca F 11825 | Louisiana Mama/I Learned To Yodel..................................... | 35 |

## JOHN LENNON/PLASTIC ONO BAND
### SINGLES
| 69 | Apple APPLE 13 | Give Peace A Chance/Remember Love (p/s, as Plastic Ono Band; with Parlophone catalogue number, dark green label, only second pressings have R5795 added to catalogue number).......................................................... | 18 |
| 69 | Apple APPLE 13 | Give Peace A Chance/Remember Love (p/s, as Plastic Ono Band, first press with "sold in UK..." label text)......................................................... | 40 |
| 69 | Apple APPLES 1001 | Cold Turkey/Don't Worry Kyoko (Mummy's Only Looking For A Hand In The Snow) (p/s, as Plastic Ono Band) ........................................................... | 15 |
| 69 | Apple APPLES 1002 | You Know My Name (Look Up The Number)/What's The New Mary Jane? (as Plastic Ono Band, unreleased; vinyl test pressings only with typed Apple 'Custom Recording' labels & hand written catalogue number)..................... | 3000 |
| 70 | Apple APPLES 1003 | Instant Karma!/Who Has Seen The Wind? (p/s, as Lennon/Ono with Plastic Ono Band).............................................................................. | 12 |
| 71 | Apple R 5892 | Power To The People/YOKO ONO & PLASTIC ONO BAND: Open Your Box (p/s, full apple label both sides or full/half apple label)...................................... | 15 |
| 72 | Apple R 5970 | Happy Xmas (War Is Over) (as John & Yoko/Plastic Ono Band with Harlem Community Choir)/YOKO ONO & PLASTIC ONO BAND: Listen, The Snow Is Falling (p/s green vinyl). | 15 |
| 72 | Apple R 5953 | Woman Is The Nigger Of The World/Sisters O Sisters (unreleased, test pressings only) ............................................................................... | 2500 |
| 73 | Apple R 5994 | Mind Games/Meat City (demo copy) .................................... | 30 |
| 73 | Apple R 5994 | Mind Games/Meat City (p/s) ........................................... | 7 |
| 74 | EMI PSR 369 | Interview With John Lennon By Bob Mercer And Message To The Salesmen/ Whatever Gets You Thru' The Night (promo only)........................... | 900 |
| 74 | Apple R5998 | Whatever Gets You Thru The Night/Beef Jerky (demo copy)............ | 40 |
| 74 | Apple R5998 | Whatever Gets You Thru The Night/Beef Jerky............................ | 7 |
| 75 | Apple R 6005 | Stand By Me/Move Over Ms. L (demo copy) .......................... | 45 |
| 75 | Apple R 6005 | Stand By Me/Move Over Ms. L.......................................... | 5 |
| 75 | Apple R 6003 | 9 Dream (Edited Version)/What You Got (demo only).................. | 80 |
| 75 | Apple R 6009 | Imagine/Working Class Hero (demo copy)............................... | 30 |
| 75 | Apple R 6009 | Imagine/Working Class Hero (p/s)....................................... | 12 |
| 80 | WEA Geffen K 79186 | (Just Like) Starting Over/ YOKO ONO : Kiss Kiss Kiss (Green vinyl, promo)..... | 500 |
| 80 | WEA Gefen K 79186 | (Just Like) Starting Over/YOKO ONO: Kiss Kiss Kiss .................... | 5 |

## John LENNON & BLEECHERS (Jamaica)

| | | | |
|---|---|---|---|
| 81 | Geffen K 79195 | Woman/YOKO ONO: Beautiful Boys | 5 |
| 81 | WEA K 79207 | Watching The Wheels/YOKO ONO: I'm Your Angel (Pink vinyl "in house" promo) | 500 |
| 81 | WEA K 79207 | Watching The Wheels/YOKO ONO: I'm Your Angel | 5 |
| 82 | Parlophone R6059 | Love/Give Me Some Truth | 5 |
| 84 | Polydor PODJ 700 | Nobody Told Me (1-sided white label promo) | 5 |
| 84 | Polydor POSP 700 | Nobody Told Me/YOKO ONO: O Sanity | 60 |
| 84 | Polydor POSP 712 | Every Man Has A Woman Who Loves Him/SEAN ONO LENNON: It's Alright (p/s, with poster) | 5 |
| 84 | Polydor POSP 712 | Every Man Has A Woman Who Loves Him/SEAN ONO LENNON: It's Alright (p/s) | 10 |
| 84 | Polydor PODJ 701 | Borrowed Time (Edited Version)/YOKO ONO: Your Hands (promo only) | 5 |
| 88 | Parlophone RP 6199 | Imagine/Jealous Guy (picture disc) | 25 |
| 88 | Parlophone 12R 6199 | Imagine/Jealous Guy/Happy Xmas (War Is Over) (12" p/s) | 15 |

### ALBUMS

| | | | |
|---|---|---|---|
| 68 | Apple APCOR 2 | UNFINISHED MUSIC NO. 1: TWO VIRGINS (with Yoko Ono, mono; black inner, no track listing, with "Merrie In England..." blurb on front sleeve) | 3000 |
| 68 | Apple SAPCOR 2/Track 613 012 | UNFINISHED MUSIC NO. 1: TWO VIRGINS (with Yoko Ono, stereo; black inner, with track listing & "Merrie In England..." blurb on back sleeve & Track Records logo on label, dark green label, "Sold in U.K..." "Mfd in UK" label text) | 700 |
| 69 | Zapple ZAPPLE 01 | UNFINISHED MUSIC NO. 2: LIFE WITH THE LIONS (with Yoko Ono, with inner sleeve, dark green label, "Sold in U.K..." "Mfd in UK" label text) | 250 |
| 69 | Apple SAPCOR 11 | WEDDING ALBUM (with Yoko Ono; gatefold sleeve in box set, includes wedding certificate glued to inside box lid, press booklet, poster, white 'Bagism' bag, passport photographs, postcard & picture of wedding cake) | 600 |
| 69 | Apple CORE 2001 | LIVE PEACE IN TORONTO 1969 (as Plastic Ono Band, with stapled calendar, sealed, 1st pressing with rough surface label and Apple publishing credit on side 2, dark green label "Sold in U.K..." text) | 175 |
| 69 | Apple CORE 2001 | LIVE PEACE IN TORONTO 1969 (as Plastic Ono Band, with stapled calendar, unsealed) | 40 |
| 70 | Apple PCS 7124 | JOHN LENNON : PLASTIC ONO BAND (LP, with inner) | 60 |
| 72 | Apple PAS 10004 | IMAGINE (LP, with inner sleeve, poster & postcard, 1st pressing with laminated sleeve/'sniped' spine edges) | 50 |
| 72 | Apple PAS 10004 | IMAGINE (LP, with inner sleeve, without poster & postcard) | 30 |
| 72 | Apple Q4PAS 10004 | IMAGINE (LP, quadrophonic, with inner sleeve, poster & postcard) | 150 |
| 72 | Apple PCSP 716 | SOMETIME IN NEW YORK CITY (2-LP, gatefold, inner sleeve & postcard) | 45 |
| 72 | Apple PCSP 716 | SOMETIME IN NEW YORK CITY (2-LP, gatefold, inner sleeve & without postcard) | 20 |
| 73 | Apple PCS 7165 | MIND GAMES (LP, inner, 1U/1U matrix) | 20 |
| 75 | Apple PCS 7169 | ROCK 'N' ROLL (LP) | 20 |
| 74 | Apple PCTC 253 | WALLS AND BRIDGES (LP, gatefold, with booklet and inner sleeve) | 25 |
| 75 | Apple PCS 7173 | SHAVED FISH (LP, lyric inner) | 25 |
| 81 | Parlophone JLB 8 | THE JOHN LENNON BOX (9-LP set, with insert) | 100 |
| 84 | Polydor POLH P5 | MILK AND HONEY (picture disc, original pressing, thin vinyl, 2,000 only) | 100 |
| 84 | Polydor POLH P5 | MILK AND HONEY (picture disc, 2nd pressing, thicker vinyl, 1,000 only) | 40 |
| 86 | Parlophone PCS 7301 | LIVE IN NEW YORK CITY (LP, with inner) | 50 |
| 86 | Parlophone PCS 7308 | MENLOVE AVENUE (LP, with inner) | 15 |
| 88 | Parlophone PCSP 722 | IMAGINE : JOHN LENNON (2xLP with inner) | 20 |
| 90 | Parlophone CDS 79 5220 | LENNON (4 x CD set) | 20 |
| 97 | Parlophone 8 21954 2 | LENNON LEGEND (2-LP with inner) | 70 |
| 97 | EMI LPCENT 9 | ROCK 'N' ROLL (LP, reissue, EMI Centenary, stickered sleeve) | 50 |
| 97 | EMI LPCENT 27 | IMAGINE (LP, reissue, EMI centenary, stickered sleeve) | 30 |
| 98 | Parlophone 8306142 | ANTHOLOGY (4-CDR, jewel cases with Abbey Road studio inlays, incorrect track listing and missing "Grow Old With Me" from CD4, promo only) | 80 |
| 99 | Capitol 497 6391 | WONSAPONEATIME (2-LP with inner) | 50 |
| 99 | Apple PCTC 253 | WALLS AND BRIDGES (LP, reissue, inner & booklet) | 18 |

*(see also Beatles, Yoko Ono, Bill Elliott/Elastic Oz Band, Elephant's Memory, Musketeer Gripweed, Elton John)*

## JOHN LENNON & BLEECHERS (JAMAICA)

| | | | |
|---|---|---|---|
| 70 | Punch PH 23 | Ram You Hard/UPSETTERS: Soul Stew | 100 |

## LENNON SISTERS

| | | | |
|---|---|---|---|
| 56 | Vogue Coral Q 72176 | Graduation Day/Toy Tiger | 8 |
| 57 | Vogue Coral Q 72259 | Young And In Love/Teenage Waltz | 8 |
| 57 | Vogue Coral Q 72285 | Shake Me I Rattle/Pocohontas | 8 |
| 61 | London HLD 9417 | Sad Movies/I Don't Know Why | 15 |

## MIKE LENNOX

| | | | |
|---|---|---|---|
| 68 | Decca F 12736 | Images Of You/Words I Like | 7 |

## LENNY AND THE LAWBREAKERS

| | | | |
|---|---|---|---|
| 79 | Rip Pff RIP 11 | Me And Bobby McGee/Suzy D (die cut p/s) | 50 |

## J.B. LENOIR (& AFRICAN HUNCH RHYTHM)

| | | | |
|---|---|---|---|
| 65 | Sue WI 339 | I Sing Um The Way I Feel/I Feel So Good (with His African Hunch Rhythm) | 50 |
| 65 | Bootleg 503 | Man Watch Your Woman/Mama Talk To Your Daughter (99 copies only) | 60 |
| 66 | Blue Horizon 45-1004 | Mojo Boogie/I Don't Care What Nobody Say (99 copies only) | 150 |
| 68 | Python PLP 25 | J.B. LENOIR (LP, 99 copies only) | 75 |
| 70 | Polydor 2482 014 | CRUSADE (LP) | 40 |
| 75 | Rarity LP 2 | J.B. LENOIR (LP) | 25 |
| 70s | CBS 62593 | ALABAMA BLUES (LP) | 40 |

## ROBIN LENT

| | | | |
|---|---|---|---|
| 71 | Nepentha 6347 002 | SCARECROW'S JOURNEY (LP, gatefold sleeve, with Focus) | 175 |

*(see also Focus, Jan Akkerman)*

## VAN LENTON

| | | | |
|---|---|---|---|
| 65 | Immediate IM 008 | Gotta Get Away/You Don't Care | 80 |

## LEON (SILVERA) & OWEN (GRAY)

| | | | |
|---|---|---|---|
| 62 | Blue Beat BB 117 | Murder (with Drumbago All Stars)/ROY PANTON: Forty Four | 15 |

*(see also Owen & Leon, Owen & Millie)*

**CHRIS LEON**
72   Dynamic DYN 450                    (Last Night) I Didn't Get To Sleep At All/DYNAMITES: Instrumental Version ................... 8

**DEKE LEONARD**
73   United Artists UAG 29464          ICEBERG (LP, gatefold sleeve) .......................................................................... 15
74   United Artists UAG 29544          KAMIKAZE (LP, gatefold sleeve) ...................................................................... 15
*(see also Man, Marty Wilde, Help Yourself, Pete Brown's Piblokto, Gary Pickford-Hopkins & Friends)*

**LEONARD FAMILY**
72   Beacon BEA 186                     Once You Understand/It Won't Happen Again ..................................................... 6

**ANN LEONARDO**
57   Capitol CL 14723                   Straws In The Wind/Travelling Stranger ............................................................ 15
57   Capitol CL 14755                   Lottery/One And Only .................................................................................. 10
57   Capitol CL 14797                   Three Time Loser/I'll Wait Till Monday .............................................................. 5

**LEONIE & JOE NOLAN BAND**
68   Jolly JY 015                       Move And Groove/Don't Let Me Do It ................................................................ 8

**LE ORME**
73   Charisma CAS 1072                  FELONA AND SORONA (LP, gatefold sleeve, large 'Mad Hatter' label) .................... 60
*(see under 'O')*

**LEO'S SUNSHIPP**
79   Grapevine RED 3                    Give Me The Sunshine/I'm Back For More ......................................................... 10
79   Grapevine REDC 3                   Give Me The Sunshine/I'm Back For More (12") ................................................ 10

**LE RITZ**
77   Breaker BS 2001                    Punker/What A Sucker (p/s) ......................................................................... 15

**MIKE LEROY**
64   Columbia DB 7316                   Five Hundred Miles/The Big City ..................................................................... 6
70   CBS 4998                           With A Little Love (Just A Little Love)/All I Need Is You ..................................... 8

**LEROY & ROCKY (ELLIS)**
68   Studio One SO 2042                 Love Me Girl/WRIGGLERS: Reel Up................................................................ 60
*(see also King Rocky)*

**LE ROYS**
64   HMV POP 1274                       Gotta Lotta Love (Ciribiribin)/Don't Cry Baby .................................................. 10
64   HMV POP 1312                       Chills/Lost Out On Love .............................................................................. 15
64   HMV POP 1368                       I Come Smiling On Through/California GL 903 .................................................. 10
*(see also Mike Sarne, Simon Scott, John Leyton, Mike Berry, Grazina, Billie Davis, Billy Boyle, Don Spencer)*

**LES & MITCH**
63   Fontana 267265 TF                  Why Can't We Love/Don't Wake Me Up ............................................................ 5

**LES & SILKIE**
70   Torpedo TOR 13                     I Don't Want To Tell You/DENZIL DENNIS: Come On In .................................... 5

**LES KITTIES**
81   Camille CAM 1                      What's That?/Little Claw (500 only, no p/s) ................................................... 15

**BILL LE SAGE**
64   World Records T/ST 346             PRESENTING THE BILL LESAGE/RONNIE ROSS QUARTET (LP, stereo sticker on front) ..... 40
*(see also Ronnie Ross)*

**LES CHANSONETTES**
03   Shrine SRG 105                     Don't Let Him Hurt You/Deeper (reissue) ........................................................ 10

**LORNE LESLEY**
59   Parlophone R 4518                  Some Of These Days/When Love Has Let You Down .......................................... 5
59   Parlophone R 4567                  Warm/You Ought To Be Mine ......................................................................... 5
59   Parlophone R 4581                  So High, So Low/I Don't Know ....................................................................... 5
60   Polydor NH 66928                   Take All My Love/Ritroviamoci (Till We Meet Again) ........................................ 7
60   Polydor NH 66956                   Bloodshot Eyes/We're Gonna Dance ............................................................... 5
65   Philips BF 1403                    Someone Like You/Where My Heart Never Wandered ...................................... 5
65   Philips BF 1434                    Rainy Days Were Made For Lonely People/Fire Down Below ............................. 5
66   Philips BF 1487                    Somebody's Gonna Be Sorry/(I'm Afraid) The Masquerade Is Over ................... 5

**DESMOND LESLIE**
05   Trunk JBH 014 LP                   MUSIC OF THE FUTURE (LP) ......................................................................... 25

**JOHN & CHRIS LESLIE**
76   Cottage COT 901                    THE SHIP OF TIME (LP) ................................................................................ 15

**MICHAEL LESLIE**
65   Pye 7N 15835                       Momma Didn't Know/I Don't Wanna Know ...................................................... 6
65   Pye 7N 15908                       Penny Arcade/Bye Bye Baby ........................................................................ 12
65   Pye 7N 15959                       Make Up Or Break Up/She Can't See Me ........................................................ 25
66   Decca F 12531                      Right Or Wrong/Office Girl (credited to Michael Leslie) .................................... 5

**LES ROCKETS**
77   Decca FR 13752                     Space Rock/Let's Be Sad (Please note demos, state Let's Be Sade)..................... 40
77   Decca FR 13752                     Space Rock (extended)/Don't Be Sad (12") .................................................... 20

**LESTER & DENWOOD**
73   Atlantic K10381                    America (What Have You Done)/Song For Joanne ............................................ 10

**HEDDY LESTER**
77   Sonet SON 2013                     The World Keeps Turning/Never Saw Him Laughing (p/s) ................................. 6

**KETTY LESTER**
62   London HLN 9527                    Love Letters/I'm A Fool To Want You .............................................................. 6
62   London HLN 9574                    But Not For Me/Moscow Nights...................................................................... 6
62   London HLN 9608                    You Can't Lie To A Liar/River Of Salt .............................................................. 7
62   London HLN 9635                    This Land Is Your Land/Love Belongs To Everyone ........................................... 6
63   London HLN 9698                    A Warm Summer Day/I'll Never Stop Loving You ............................................. 7
64   RCA Victor RCA 1394                Some Things Are Better Left Unsaid/The House Is Haunted ............................. 60

# LAZY LESTER

| 64 | RCA Victor RCA 1394 | Some Things Are Better Left Unsaid/The House Is Haunted (DJ copy) | 100 |
|---|---|---|---|
| 64 | RCA Victor RCA 1403 | Roses Grow With Thorns/Please Don't Cry Anymore | 40 |
| 64 | RCA Victor RCA 1421 | I Trust You Baby/Theme From "The Luck Of Ginger Coffey" | 15 |
| 65 | RCA Victor RCA 1460 | Looking For A Better World/Pretty Eyes | 7 |
| 65 | Capitol CL 15427 | West Coast/I'll Be Looking Back | 7 |
| 66 | Capitol CL 15447 | When A Man Loves A Woman/We'll Be Together Again | 30 |
| 62 | London RE-N 1348 | KETTY LESTER (EP) | 8 |
| 63 | London HA-N 2455 | LOVE LETTERS (LP) | 40 |
| 64 | RCA Victor RD 7669 | THE SOUL OF ME (LP) | 60 |
| 65 | RCA Victor RD 7712 | WHERE IS LOVE (LP) | 40 |
| 67 | Stateside S(S)L 10196 | WHEN A MAN LOVES A WOMAN (LP) | 40 |

## LAZY LESTER
| 64 | Stateside SS 277 | I'm A Lover Not A Fighter/Sugar Coated Love | 40 |
|---|---|---|---|
| 71 | Blue Horizon 2431 007 | MADE UP MY MIND (LP) | 150 |
| 77 | Flyright FLYLP 526 | THEY CALL ME LAZY (LP) | 15 |
| 79 | Flyright FLYLP 544 | POOR BOY BLUES (LP) | 15 |

## ROBIE LESTER
| 62 | Polydor NH 66963 | Ballad Of Cheating John/Miracle Of Love | 5 |
|---|---|---|---|

## LESTER AND THE BREW
| 81 | PL EP 001 | A BAD DAY AT THE CITY (EP) | 25 |
|---|---|---|---|

## LES YPER SOUND
| 69 | Philips TFE 8004 | MASS FOR THE PRESENT TIME (LP) | 100 |
|---|---|---|---|

## LETHAL
| 94 | White BAD 1 | Portrait Of A Young Man As An Artist (12") | 20 |
|---|---|---|---|

## JOE LETHAL
| 78 | Lethal CI 200526 | Don't Come Back/You Ain't Free (no p/s) | 35 |
|---|---|---|---|

## LETIMOV
| 85 | Reconciliation RECONCILE 2 | To The Suffering/The Gift Of Life (p/s) | 15 |
|---|---|---|---|

## LETS GET DRESSED
| 83 | Prededent LGP 003 | Love Another Way/Before You Take Everything (p/s) | 7 |
|---|---|---|---|

## LETTERMEN (1)
| 61 | Capitol CL 15222 | The Way You Look Tonight/That's My Desire | 5 |
|---|---|---|---|
| 62 | Capitol CL 15248 | Come Back Silly Girl/Song For Young Love | 6 |

## LETTERMEN (2)
| 74 | Stag SG 10075 | FIRST CLASS (LP, private pressing) | 90 |
|---|---|---|---|

## LETTERS
| 79 | Heartbeat PULSE 9 | Nobody Loves Me/Don't Want You Back (p/s) | 90 |
|---|---|---|---|

## DON LETTS & JAH WOBBLE
| 79 | Virgin VS 239 | Steel Leg: Stratetime & The Wide Man/Electric Dread: Haile Unlikely (p/s) | 10 |
|---|---|---|---|
| 79 | Virgin VS 239-12 | Steel Leg: Stratetime & The Wide Man/Electric Dread: Haile Unlikely (12", p/s) | 12 |

*(see also Jah Wobble)*

## LEVEE BREAKERS
| 65 | Parlophone R 5291 | Babe I'm Leaving You/Wild About My Loving | 25 |
|---|---|---|---|

*(see also Beverley, Johnny Joyce)*

## LEVEE CAMP MOAN
| 69 | County | LEVEE CAMP MOAN (LP, private pressing) | 750 |
|---|---|---|---|
| 69 | County | PEACOCK FARM (LP, private pressing) | 750 |

## LEVEL 42
| 79 | Elite DAZZ 4 | Sandstorm/Journey To The Powerline (Remix) (12", white label test pressing, no p/s) | 75 |
|---|---|---|---|
| 80 | Elite DAZZ 5 | Love Meeting Love/Instrumental Love (7", unreleased) | 0 |
| 80 | Elite DAZZ 5 | Love Meeting Love/Instrumental Love (12", company die-cut stickered sleeve) | 25 |
| 91 | Polydor 511 635-2 | THE COMPLETE LEVEL 42 (9-CD box set) | 40 |

## LEVELLERS
| 91 | On The Fiddle OTF EP 1 | Police On My Back/Where The Hell Are We Going To Love?/Travelogue (4am Mix) (12", fan club issue, p/s) | 15 |
|---|---|---|---|
| 92 | On The Fiddle OTF LP 2 | LIVE 1992 (LP, fan club issue, 2,000 only) | 18 |

## GERRY LEVENE (& AVENGERS)
| 64 | Decca F 11815 | It's Driving Me Wild (solo)/Dr. Feelgood | 40 |
|---|---|---|---|

## ANNABEL LEVENTON
| 69 | Morgan MR 20 | Easy To Be Hard/My Dear Friend | 8 |
|---|---|---|---|

## LEVERS
| 79 | Bead Records BEAD 10 | LEVERS (LP) | 25 |
|---|---|---|---|

## CARL LEV(E)Y & CIMARRONS
| 70 | Hot Rod HR 100 | Walk The Hot Street/PEGGY & CIMARRONS: You Say You Don't Love Me | 35 |
|---|---|---|---|
| 70 | Hot Rod HR 101 | Remember Easter Monday/PEGGY & JIMMY: Pum Pum Lover | 20 |

*(see also Hot Rod Allstars, Rita Alston, Peggy)*

## IJAHMAN LEVI
| 76 | Concrete CJ 756 | I Am A Levi/Part 2 | 60 |
|---|---|---|---|
| 80 | Jahmani JMI 304 | Moulding (as Ijahman)/HIS MAJESTERIANS: Jah Is Coming Again (12") | 60 |
| 85 | Jahmani JMI 501 | Moulding/Africa (12") | 50 |
| 78 | Island ILPS 9521 | HAILE I HYMN (LP) | 18 |

## FRANKIE LEVI
| 86 | Firm (no cat no) | Steady Rock/KEVIN GAD: Bloodlines Connections (12") | 150 |
|---|---|---|---|

## LEVIATHAN
| 68 | Elektra EKSN 45052 | Remember The Times/Second Production | 45 |
|---|---|---|---|
| 69 | Elektra EKSN 45057 | The War Machine/Time | 30 |

| 69 | Elektra EKSN 45052/45057 | (WAY IN) THE FOUR FACES OF LEVIATHAN (Remember The Times/ Second Production/The War Machine/Time)(2 x 7" press pack, A4 folder sleeve, some overprinted with 'Harrods' logo, with bio & photo, promo, some commercial) | 250 |
| 69 | Elektra EKSN 45075 | | 30 |
| | | Flames/Just Forget Tomorrow | 25 |
| 90s | (no cat.no.) | ELEKTRA DAZE (CD EP, private pressing) | |
| 69 | Elektra EKS 74046 | LEVIATHAN (2-LP, unissued, acetates only, 1 copy known) | 2000 |

*(see also High Broom)*

## HANK LEVINE ORCHESTRA
| 61 | HMV POP 947 | Image (Parts 1 & 2) | 10 |

## LEVITTS
| 69 | ESP Disk/Fontana STL 5518 | WE ARE THE LEVITTS (LP) | 25 |

## LEVON & HAWKS
| 65 | Atlantic AT 4054 | The Stones I Throw/He Don't Love You | 70 |

*(see also Band)*

## BARRINGTON LEVY
| 79 | JB JBD 009 | Call You On The Phone/RANKING TOYAN: London Girl (12") | 10 |
| 79 | Bushays BFM 128 | Sister Debby/Blacksin Dub (12", with Jah Thomas) | 20 |
| 70s | Burning Vibrations BVD 003 | A Ya We Deh/Give Thanks And Praise (12", with Trinity) | 20 |
| 79 | Burning Rockers BRD 033 | Shine Eye Gal/Dub version (12". Jah Thomas toasts on A-side but is uncredited) | 12 |
| 79 | Burning Sounds BRD 029 | Hunting Man (feat. Jah Thomas)/Hunting Dub (12") | 25 |
| 79 | Greensleeves GRED 27 | Lose Respect (feat. Trinity)/ROMAN STEWART & TRINITY: Since You're Gone (12") | 15 |
| 80 | Greensleeves GRED 28 | Englishman/SCORCHER & ROOTS RADICS BAND: The Daughter Them Ire (12") | 15 |
| 80 | Greensleeves GRED 40 | Crucifixion/Eventide Fire A Disaster (red vinyl 12") | 18 |
| 80 | Cha Cha CHAD 22 | Warm and Sunny Day/GENERAL SAINT - DJ cut (12") | 50 |
| 80 | His Majesty HMD 004 | Shaolin Temple/Version (12") | 20 |
| 80 | Strong Like Sampson SLSD8 | Wicked Intention/ROD TAYLOR (12") | 40 |
| 80 | Greensleeves GRED 32 | Sister Carol/Put On My Clarkes (12") | 12 |
| 80 | Greensleeves GRED 35 | Mary Long Tongue/Look Youthman (12") | 20 |
| 80 | Lovelinch LL 03 | Skylarking/HORTENSE ELLIS - You Done Me Wrong (12") | 25 |
| 82 | Greensleeves GRED 80 | Tomorrow Is Another Day/PAPA TULLO: Delaware (12") | 20 |
| 80 | Strong Like Sampson SLSD 017 | She Rob And Gorn/PAPPA TULLO: Cat Called Francella (12") | 15 |
| | | | 20 |
| 82 | Oak Sounds OSD 008 | Open Book/Open version (12") | 12 |
| 84 | Greensleeves GRED 136 | Prison Oval Rock (master mix)/Prison Oval Rock (dub plate mix) (12") | 18 |
| 84 | Greensleeves GRED 145 | Pon Your Toe/Girl I Love You (12") | 10 |
| 85 | MGR MGR 4 | Get Up Stand Up/Do The Dance (12") | 20 |
| 87 | Live & Learn LLD014 | Juggling Soldier/Version (12") | 8 |
| 87 | Time I TR 026 | Living Dangerously/Version | 8 |
| 87 | Time I 7TR 0200 | Struggler/Version | 10 |
| 95 | Time TR009 | Here I Come/Trouble A Come/Run Come Dub/Rub A Dub (12") | 30 |
| 79 | Greensleeves GREL 9 | ENGLISHMAN (LP) | 30 |
| 79 | Burning Sounds BS 1039 | SHINE EYE GAL (LP) | 40 |
| 80 | JB JBLP 01 | DOH RAY ME (LP) | 40 |
| 80 | Jah Guidance JA CC 14 | ROBIN HOOD (LP) | 15 |
| 82 | Trojan TRLS 209 | POOR MAN STYLE (LP) | 40 |
| 83 | GG's GG 0032 | BARRINGTON LEVY'S LIFE STYLE (LP) | 20 |
| 83 | Burning Sounds BS 1050 | HUNTER MAN (LP) | 20 |
| 85 | Time Records TRLP 003 | HERE I COME (LP) | 20 |

## BEN LEVY
| 66 | Ska Beat JB 245 | Doreen/Never Knew Love | 20 |
| 66 | Ska Beat JB 255 | I'll Make You Glad/Keep Smiling | 20 |

## JONA LEWIE
| 74 | Sonet SON 2048 | Piggy Back Sue/Papa Don't Go | 6 |
| 75 | Sonet SON 2056 | The Swan/Custer's Last Stand | 5 |
| 76 | Sonet SON 2081 | Hallelujah Europe Parts 1 & 2 | 5 |
| 77 | Sonet SON 2117 | Rocking Yobs/After We Swum | 5 |
| 78 | Stiff BUY 30 | The Baby, She's On The Street/Denny Laine's Valet (p/s) | 50 |
| 78 | Stiff BUY 37 | Halleluja Europe/Police Trap (Unreleased, test pressings only) | 6 |
| 80 | Stiff BUY 85-5 | Big Shot - Momentarily/I'll Get By In Pittsburg (5" single) | 15 |
| 79 | Stiff SEEZ 8 | ON THE OTHER HAND THERE'S A FIST (LP, yellow vinyl) | 15 |
| 78 | Stiff SEEZ 8 | ON THE OTHER HAND THERE'S A FIST (LP, picture disc) | 15 |

*(see also Brett Marvin & Thunderbolts)*

## CARL LEWIN
| 71 | Bullet BU 456 | Knock Three Times/SIDNEY ALL STARS: The Whealing Mouse | 12 |
| 71 | Punch PH 98 | Nobody Told Me/WING: Don't Play That Song Again (version) | 12 |

## ALVA (REGGIE) LEWIS
| 67 | Caltone TONE 111 | Return Home/KING ROCK & WILLOWS: You Are The One | 100 |
| 67 | Island WI 3080 | I'm Indebted/GROOVERS: You've Got To Cry | 50 |
| 68 | Jolly HY 009 | Hang My Head And Cry/COOL CATS: Hold Your Love | 100 |
| 72 | Upsetter US 391 | Natty Natty (as Alva Reggie Lewis)/UPSETTERS: Version | 20 |

*(see also Reggae Boys, Webber Sisters, Lester Sterling, Cool Cats)*

## LEWIS & CLARKE EXPEDITION
| 67 | RCA 1633 | Blue Revelations/I Feel Good (I Feel Bad) | 20 |

## ANDY LEWIS & PAUL WELLER
| 97 | Acid Jazz AJX 193S | Are You Trying To Be Lonely?/Tell Me Once Again You Love Me (7", blue vinyl, numbered blue-ish p/s, 1,000 only) | 5 |
| 97 | Acid Jazz AJX 193P | Are You Trying To Be Lonely?/Tell Me Once Again You Love Me (7" promo, A-label in Acid Jazz sleeve, 50 copies only) | 40 |

*(see also Paul Weller)*

MINT VALUE £

## BARBARA LEWIS

| 63 | London HLK 9724 | Hello Stranger/Think A Little Sugar | 25 |
|----|----|----|----|
| 63 | London HLK 9724 | Hello Stranger/Think A Little Sugar (DJ Copy) | 60 |
| 63 | London HLK 9779 | Straighten Up Your Heart/If You Love Her | 25 |
| 64 | London HLK 9832 | Snap Your Fingers/Puppy Love | 25 |
| 64 | Atlantic AT 4013 | Pushin' A Good Thing Too Far/Come Home | 40 |
| 65 | Atlantic AT 4031 | Baby I'm Yours/Hello I Say Love | 20 |
| 65 | Atlantic AT 4041 | Make Me Your Baby/Love To Be Loved | 20 |
| 66 | Atlantic AT 4068 | Don't Forget About Me/It's Magic | 20 |
| 66 | Atlantic 584 037 | Make Me Belong To You/Girls Need Loving Care | 20 |
| 67 | Atlantic 584 061 | Baby What Do You Want Me To Do/I Remember The Feeling | 60 |
| 68 | Atlantic 584 153 | Hello Stranger/Baby I'm Yours (reissue) | 8 |
| 68 | Atlantic 584 174 | Sho Nuff (It's Got To Be Your Love)/Thankful For What I Got | 20 |
| 71 | Atlantic 2091 143 | Someday We're Gonna Love Again/Baby I'm Yours | 15 |
| 72 | Atlantic K 10128 | Someday We're Gonne Love Again/Baby I'm Yours (reissue) | 10 |
| 65 | Atlantic AET 6015 | SNAP YOUR FINGERS (EP) | 70 |
| 66 | Atlantic ATL 5042 | BABY I'M YOURS (LP) | 40 |
| 66 | Atlantic 587 002 | IT'S MAGIC (LP, mono) | 50 |
| 66 | Atlantic 588 002 | IT'S MAGIC (LP, stereo) | 60 |
| 70 | Stax SXATS 1035 | THE MANY GROOVES OF BARBARA LEWIS (LP) | 40 |

## BOBBY LEWIS

| 61 | Parlophone R 4794 | Tossin' And Turnin'/Oh Yes, I Love You | 20 |
|----|----|----|----|
| 61 | Parlophone R 4831 | One Track Mind/Are You Ready | 25 |
| 62 | Stateside SS 126 | I'm Tossin' And Turnin' Again/Nothin' But The Blues | 25 |

## CAPPY LEWIS

| 61 | Vogue V 9184 | Bullfight/OLYMPICS: Little Pedro | 20 |
|----|----|----|----|

*(see also Olympics)*

## DAVE LEWIS (1)

| 66 | Pye Intl. NEP 44057 | GIVIN' GAS (EP) | 40 |
|----|----|----|----|
| 64 | Pye Intl. NPL 28053 | LITTLE GREEN THING(LP) | 30 |

## DAVE LEWIS (2)

| 76 | Polydor 2383 420 | FROM TIME TO TIME (LP, with lyric sheet) | 18 |
|----|----|----|----|

## DAVID LEWIS

| 70 | AX 1 | SONGS OF DAVID LEWIS (LP, private pressing, paste-on sleeve) | 400 |
|----|----|----|----|

*(see also Andwella['s Dream], David Baxter)*

## FURRY LEWIS

| 69 | Blue Horizon 7-63228 | PRESENTING THE COUNTRY BLUES (LP) | 80 |
|----|----|----|----|
| 70 | Matchbox SDR 190 | IN MEMPHIS (LP) | 30 |
| 71 | Xtra XTRA 1116 | FURRY LEWIS (LP) | 20 |
| 71 | Spokane SPL 1004 | THE EARLY YEARS 1927-1929 (LP) | 30 |

*(see also John Estes)*

## GARY LEWIS & PLAYBOYS

| 65 | Liberty LIB 10187 | This Diamond Ring/Tijuana Wedding | 10 |
|----|----|----|----|
| 65 | Liberty LIB 55778 | Count Me In/Little Miss Go-Go | 10 |
| 65 | Liberty LIB 55809 | Save Your Heart For Me/Without A Word Of Warning | 10 |
| 65 | Liberty LIB 55818 | Everybody Loves A Clown/Time Stands Still | 7 |
| 66 | Liberty LIB 55846 | She's Just My Style/I Won't Make That Mistake Again | 20 |
| 66 | Liberty LIB 55865 | Sure Gonna Miss Her/I Don't Wanna Say Goodnight | 5 |
| 66 | Liberty LIB 55880 | Green Grass/I Can Read Between The Lines | 5 |
| 66 | Liberty LIB 55898 | My Heart's Symphony/Tina | 20 |
| 66 | Liberty LIB 55914 | (You Don't Have To) Paint Me A Picture/Looking For The Stars | 10 |
| 67 | Liberty LIB 55933 | Where Will The Words Come From/The Best Man | 7 |
| 67 | Liberty LIB 55949 | Loser (With A Broken Heart)/Ice Melts In The Sun | 7 |
| 67 | Liberty LIB 55971 | Girls In Love/Let's Be More Than Friends | 7 |
| 67 | Liberty LBF 15025 | Jill/Needles And Pins | 10 |
| 68 | Liberty LBF 15131 | Sealed With A Kiss/Pretty Thing | 5 |
| 70 | Liberty LBF 15335 | Orangutan/Something Is Wrong | 5 |
| 75 | United Artists UP 35780 | My Heart's Symphony/I Won't Make That Same Mistake Again (reissue) | 6 |
| 65 | Liberty LBY 1259 | THIS DIAMOND RING (LP) | 30 |
| 66 | Liberty LBY 1322 | JUST OUR STYLE (LP) | 25 |

## GEORGE LEWIS/FREDDIE KOHLMAN

| 53 | Brunswick LA 8627 | NEW ORLEANS JAZZ CONCERT (10" LP) | 15 |
|----|----|----|----|

## HOPETON LEWIS

| 67 | Island WI 3054 | Rock Steady/Cool Collie | 150 |
|----|----|----|----|
| 67 | Island WI 3055 | Finder's Keepers/ROLAND ALPHONSO: Shanty Town Curfew | 100 |
| 67 | Island WI 3056 | Let Me Come On Home/Hardships Of Life (with Merritone All Stars) | 75 |
| 67 | Island WI 3057 | Run Down/Pick Yourself Up | 150 |
| 67 | Island WI 3059 | Let The Little Girl Dance/This Music Got Soul | 125 |
| 67 | Island WI 3068 | Rock A Shacka/I Don't Want Trouble | 125 |
| 68 | Island WI 3076 | Everybody Rocking/Stars Shining So Bright | 125 |
| 68 | Fab FAB 43 | Skinny Leg Girl/Live Like A King (as Hopetown Lewis & Glenmore Brown) | 80 |
| 70 | Duke Reid DR 2505 | Boom Shaka Lacka/TOMMY McCOOK QUINTET: Dynamite | 15 |
| 70 | Duke Reid DR 2516 | Testify/TOMMY McCOOK: Super Soul | 25 |
| 71 | Duke DU 112 | Grooving Out Of Life (with Byron Lee & Dragonaires) (actually titled Grooving Out On Life)/BYRON LEE & DRAGONAIRES: Fire Fire | 15 |
| 71 | Treasure Isle TI 7060 | To The Other Man/TOMMY McCOOK: Stampede | 15 |
| 72 | Treasure Isle TI 7071 | Judgement Day (actually by Hopeton Lewis & Dennis Alcapone)/ EARL LINDO: Version Day | 15 |
| 72 | Attack ATT 8035 | Starting All Over Again/DYNAMITES: Instrumental Version | 10 |

| 72 | Dynamic DYN 436 | Come Together/Going Back To My Hometown | 10 |
| 72 | Dynamic DYN 447 | Good Together/Version | 10 |
| 73 | Dragon DRA 1001 | City Of New Orleans/The Wind Cries Mary | 10 |
| 73 | Dragon DRA 1011 | Groovin' Out On Life/God Bless Whoever Sent You | 10 |
| 12 | Duke Reid THB 7015 | Live It Up/JOHN HOLD WITH TOMMY MCCOOK AND THE SUPERSONICS: Ali Baba/Dub | 18 |
| 67 | Island ILP 957 | TAKE IT EASY: ROCKSTEADY WITH HOPETON LEWIS (LP) | 200 |
| 71 | Trojan TRL 36 | GROOVING OUT ON LIFE (LP) | 30 |

(see also Glenmore Brown & Hopeton Lewis)

## HUGH X. LEWIS
| 66 | London HLR 10032 | Looking In The Future/Too Late | 10 |

## JEFFREY LEWIS
| 01 | Rough Trade RTRADES 20 | The Chelsea Hotel Oral Sex Song (1-sided promo, stamped label, with comic) | 10 |
| 01 | Rough Trade RTRADES 20 | The Chelsea Hotel Oral Sex Song (1-sided promo, stamped label, without comic) | 5 |
| 02 | Rough Trade RTRADES 055 | Back When I was 4/3.4 Moon (p/s) | 5 |

## JENNIFER LEWIS & ANGELA STRANGE
| 65 | Columbia DB 7662 | Bring It To Me/You Know | 10 |
| 66 | Columbia DB 7814 | I've Heard It All Before/Bad Storm Coming | 12 |

## JERRY LEWIS (JAMAICA)
| 72 | Pama PM 862 | The Godfather/ALTON ELLIS: Some Day | 20 |
| 73 | Explosion EX 2077 | Rhythm Pleasure/AGGROVATORS: Doctor Seaton | 20 |

(see also I Roy)

## JERRY LEE LEWIS
### 78s
| 57 | London HLS 8529 | Great Balls Of Fire/Mean Woman Blues | 20 |
| 58 | London HLS 8559 | You Win Again/I'm Feelin' Sorry | 20 |
| 58 | London HLS 8592 | Breathless/Down The Line | 20 |
| 58 | London HLS 8700 | Break-Up/I'll Make It All Up To You | 35 |
| 59 | London HLS 8780 | High School Confidential/Fools Like Me | 50 |
| 59 | London HLS 8840 | Lovin' Up A Storm/Big Blon' Baby | 50 |
| 59 | London HLS 8941 | Let's Talk About Us/The Ballad Of Billy Joe | 60 |
| 59 | London HLS 8993 | Little Queenie/I Could Never Be Ashamed Of You | 100 |
| 96 | Cruisin' The 50s CASB 002 | Wild One/Old Black Joe (numbered, 300 only) | 35 |

### SINGLES
| 57 | London HLS 8457 | Whole Lotta Shakin' Goin' On/It'll Be Me | 30 |
| 57 | London HLS 8529 | Great Balls Of Fire/Mean Woman Blues | 20 |
| 58 | London HLS 8559 | You Win Again/I'm Feelin' Sorry | 25 |
| 58 | London HLS 8592 | Breathless/Down The Line | 20 |
| 58 | London HLS 8700 | Break-Up/I'll Make It All Up To You | 20 |
| 59 | London HLS 8780 | High School Confidential/Fools Like Me | 20 |
| 59 | London HLS 8840 | Lovin' Up A Storm/Big Blon' Baby | 20 |
| 59 | London HLS 8941 | Let's Talk About Us/The Ballad Of Billy Joe (no triangular centre) | 20 |
| 59 | London HLS 8993 | Little Queenie/I Could Never Be Ashamed Of You (no triangular centre) | 20 |

(Originally issued with triangular centres; round-centre pressings are worth two-thirds of these values.)

| 60 | London HLS 9083 | I'll Sail My Ship Alone/It Hurt Me So | 20 |
| 60 | London HLS 9131 | Baby, Baby, Bye Bye/Old Black Joe | 20 |
| 60 | London HLS 9202 | John Henry/Hang Up My Rock And Roll Shoes | 10 |
| 61 | London HLS 9335 | What'd I Say?/Livin' Lovin' Wreck | 10 |
| 61 | London HLS 9414 | It Won't Happen With Me/Cold Cold Heart | 10 |
| 61 | London HLS 9446 | As Long As I Live/When I Get Paid | 10 |
| 62 | London HLS 9526 | I've Been Twistin'/Ramblin' Rose | 10 |
| 62 | London HLS 9584 | Sweet Little Sixteen/How's My Ex Treating You | 10 |
| 63 | London HLS 9688 | Good Golly Miss Molly/I Can't Trust Me (In Your Arms Anymore) | 10 |
| 63 | London HLS 9722 | Teenage Letter/Seasons Of My Heart (B-side with Linda Gail Lewis) | 10 |
| 63 | Mercury AMT 1216 | Hit The Road Jack/Pen And Paper | 10 |
| 64 | Philips BF 1324 | I'm On Fire/Bread And Butter Man | 20 |
| 64 | London HLS 9867 | Lewis Boogie/Bonnie B | 10 |
| 65 | Philips BF 1371 | Hi-Heel Sneakers/You Went Back On Your Word | 7 |
| 65 | Philips BF 1407 | Baby Hold Me Close/I Believe In You | 8 |
| 65 | Philips BF 1425 | Rockin' Pneumonia And The Boogie Woogie Flu/This Must Be The Place | 10 |
| 65 | London HLS 9980 | Carry Me Back To Old Virginia/I Know What It Means | 8 |
| 66 | Philips BF 1521 | Memphis Beat/If I Had It All To Do Over | 10 |
| 67 | Philips BF 1594 | It's A Hang-Up Baby/Holdin' On | 8 |
| 67 | Philips BF 1615 | Turn On Your Love Light/Shotgun Man | 8 |
| 68 | Mercury MF 1020 | Another Place, Another Time/Walking The Floor Over You | 6 |
| 69 | Mercury MF 1088 | To Make Love Sweeter For You/Let's Talk About Us | 5 |
| 69 | Mercury MF 1105 | Long Tall Sally/Jenny, Jenny (some in p/s) | 10 |
| 69 | Mercury MF 1105 | Long Tall Sally/Jenny, Jenny (some in p/s) | 5 |
| 69 | Mercury MF 1110 | Great Balls Of Fire/Whole Lotta Shakin' Goin' On (in p/s) | 10 |
| 72 | Mercury 6052 14 1 | Chantilly Lace/Think About It Darlin' | 7 |
| 73 | Mercury 6052 260 | Drinking Wine Spo Dee O Dee/Rock And Roll Medley | 6 |
| 73 | Mercury 6052 378 | (Taking My) Music To The Man/Jack Daniels (Old No. 7) (in p/s) | 8 |
| 79 | Elektra K 12374 | Rocking My Life Away/Rita May (p/s) | 8 |
| 80 | Elektra K 12399 | Everyday I Have To Cry/Who Will The Next Fool Be | 5 |
| 80 | Elektra K 12432 | Rockin' Jerry Lee/Good Time Charles Got The Blues | 5 |

### SINGLES : EXPORT SINGLES
| 58 | London HL 7050 | High School Confidential/Fools Like Me | 20 |
| 62 | London HL 7117 | Save The Last Dance For Me/Hello Josephine | 30 |

MINT VALUE £

| | | | |
|---|---|---|---|
| 63 | London HL 7120 | Good Golly Miss Molly/I Can't Trust Me (In Your Arms Anymore) | 20 |
| 63 | London HL 7123 | In The Mood/I'm Feelin' Sorry | 40 |

**EPs**

| | | | |
|---|---|---|---|
| 58 | London RE-S 1140 | JERRY LEE LEWIS - NO. 1 (with triangular centre) | 40 |
| 58 | London RE-S 1140 | JERRY LEE LEWIS - NO. 1 | 20 |
| 59 | London RE-S 1186 | JERRY LEE LEWIS - NO. 2 (with triangular centre) | 40 |
| 59 | London RE-S 1186 | JERRY LEE LEWIS - NO. 2 | 25 |
| 59 | London RE-S 1187 | JERRY LEE LEWIS - NO. 3 (with triangular centre) | 40 |
| 59 | London RE-S 1187 | JERRY LEE LEWIS - NO. 3 | 25 |
| 61 | London RE-S 1296 | JERRY LEE LEWIS - NO. 4 | 30 |
| 62 | London RE-S 1336 | JERRY LEE LEWIS - NO. 5 | 30 |
| 63 | London RE-S 1351 | JERRY LEE LEWIS - NO. 6 | 30 |
| 63 | London RE-S 1378 | FOUR MORE FROM JERRY LEE LEWIS | 30 |
| 66 | Philips BE 12599 | COUNTRY STYLE | 30 |

**ALBUMS**

| | | | |
|---|---|---|---|
| 59 | London HA-S 2138 | JERRY LEE LEWIS | 100 |
| 62 | London HA-S 2440 | JERRY LEE'S GREATEST | 50 |
| 64 | Philips (S)BL 7622 | GOLDEN HITS | 20 |
| 65 | Philips (S)BL 7646 | LIVE AT THE STAR CLUB, HAMBURG (with Nashville Teens) | 25 |
| 65 | Philips BL 7650 | THE GREATEST LIVE SHOW ON EARTH | 15 |
| 65 | Philips BL 7668 | THE RETURN OF ROCK | 15 |
| 65 | London HA-S 8251 | WHOLE LOTTA SHAKIN' GOIN' ON | 50 |
| 66 | Philips BL 7688 | COUNTRY SONGS FOR CITY FOLKS | 15 |
| 66 | Philips (S)BL 7706 | MEMPHIS BEAT | 15 |
| 67 | London HA-S 8323 | BREATHLESS | 30 |

*(Originally issued with plum labels; later black label reissues are worth £15-£20.)*

| | | | |
|---|---|---|---|
| 84 | Sun SUN 102 | THE SUN YEARS (12-LP, box set with booklet) | 25 |

*(see also Nashville Teens)*

**JIMMY LEWIS**

| | | | |
|---|---|---|---|
| 68 | Minit MLF 11002 | The Girls From Texas/Let Me Know | 20 |

**JOHN LEWIS**

| | | | |
|---|---|---|---|
| 60 | London Jazz LTZ-K 15186 | IMPROVISED MEDITATIONS AND EXCURSIONS (LP) | 15 |
| 61 | London Jazz LTZ-K 15218 | THE GOLDEN STRIKER (LP, also stereo SAH-K 6152) | 15 |

*(see also Modern Jazz Quartet)*

**JOHN LEWIS AND SACHA DISTEL**

| | | | |
|---|---|---|---|
| 59 | UK Oriole MG20036 | AFTERNOON IN PARIS (LP) | 25 |

**LEW LEWIS (REFORMER)**

| | | | |
|---|---|---|---|
| 76 | Stiff BUY 5 | Caravan Man/Boogie On The Street (p/s, with Dr. Feelgood, 1st pressing with push-out centre) | 8 |
| 77 | United Artists UP 36217 | Out For A Lark/Watch Yourself (p/s) | 5 |
| 78 | Lew Lewis LEW 1 | Lucky Seven/Night Talk (500 only, plain white sleeve, handwritten-style white label) | 20 |
| 78 | Stiff LEW 1 | Lucky Seven/Night Talk (handwritten-style green label) | 10 |
| 78 | Stiff LEW 1 | Lucky Seven/Night Talk (yellow label, p/s) | 5 |
| 79 | Stiff BUY 48 | Win Or Lose/Photo Finish ("A" label promo. p/s) | 5 |

*(see also Oil City Sheiks, Dr. Feelgood, Eddie & the Hot Rods)*

**LINDA LEWIS**

| | | | |
|---|---|---|---|
| 67 | Polydor 56173 | You Turned My Bitter Into Sweet/Do You Believe In Love | 50 |
| 71 | Reprise K 14096 | We Can Win/Hampstead Way | 6 |
| 72 | Reprise K 14209 | Old Smokey/It's The Frame | 6 |
| 75 | Arista ARIST 17 | It's In His Kiss/Walk About (p/s) | 6 |
| 73 | Raft RA 18502 | Rock A Doodle Doo/Reach For The Truth | 6 |
| 71 | Reprise K 44130 | SAY NO MORE (LP) | 20 |
| 72 | Reprise K 44208 | LARK (LP, textured gatefold sleeve) | 15 |

*(see also Ferris Wheel)*

**LOUISE LEWIS**

| | | | |
|---|---|---|---|
| 79 | Inferno HEAT 120 | Wee Oo I'll Let It Be You Babe/Instrumental Version (unissued and unconfirmed, this price for test pressings may exist) | 100 |

**MARGARET LEWIS**

| | | | |
|---|---|---|---|
| 62 | Starlite ST45 081 | Sometin's Wrong Baby/John De Lee | 30 |

**MEADE 'LUX' LEWIS**

| | | | |
|---|---|---|---|
| 55 | Vogue EPV 1065 | MEADE 'LUX' LEWIS (EP) | 15 |
| 56 | Melodisc EPM7 107 | BOOGIE WOOGIE AND BLUES (EP) | 15 |

*(see also Albert Ammons, [Big] Joe Turner)*

**MEADE 'LUX' LEWIS & SLIM GAILLARD**

| | | | |
|---|---|---|---|
| 56 | Columbia Clef 33C 9021 | JAZZ AT THE PHILHARMONIC (10" LP) | 20 |

*(see also Slim Gaillard)*

**MIA LEWIS**

| | | | |
|---|---|---|---|
| 65 | Decca F 12117 | Wish I Didn't Love Him/This Is The End | 10 |
| 65 | Decca F 12240 | It's Goodbye Now/The Luckiest Girl | 8 |
| 66 | Parlophone R 5526 | Nothing Lasts Forever/(Baby) I'm Feeling Good | 12 |
| 67 | Parlophone R 5585 | No Time For Lovin'/Onion | 6 |
| 67 | Parlophone R 5617 | Woman's Love/You Won't Get Away | 6 |

**MICHAEL LEWIS**

| | | | |
|---|---|---|---|
| 73 | United Artists UP 35569 | Theatre Of Blood Theme/Edwina's Theme | 15 |

**MONICA LEWIS**

| | | | |
|---|---|---|---|
| 56 | Parlophone R 4224 | I Wish You Love/Stay After School | 5 |

**NIGEL LEWIS**

| | | | |
|---|---|---|---|
| 86 | Media Burn MB10 | WHAT I FEEL NOW (LP) | 25 |

## NORMA LEWIS
| | | | |
|---|---|---|---|
| 82 | Jive JIVE 11 | This Feelings Killing Me/T.B.C. Magic Bullet (features Atmosfear uncredited) | 8 |
| 82 | Jive JIVE T 11 | This Feelings Killing Me/THe Girl's A Fool/T.B.C. Magic Bullet (features Atmosfear uncredited) (12") | 12 |

*(see also Atmosfear)*

## PATTI LEWIS
| | | | |
|---|---|---|---|
| 56 | Columbia DB 3825 | Earthbound/Happiness Street (Corner Sunshine Square) | 10 |
| 57 | Columbia DB 3923 | Your Wild Heart/A Poor Man's Roses (Or A Rich Man's Gold) | 8 |
| 57 | Columbia DB 3967 | Pull Down De Shade/Speak For Yourself John | 8 |

## PHILLIPPA LEWIS
| | | | |
|---|---|---|---|
| 65 | Decca F 12152 | Just Like In The Movies/Get Along Without You | 10 |

## RAMSEY LEWIS (TRIO)
| | | | |
|---|---|---|---|
| 65 | Chess CRS 8020 | The 'In' Crowd/Since I Fell For You (as Ramsey Lewis Trio) | 15 |
| 65 | Chess CRS 8024 | Hang On Sloopy/Movin' Easy (as Ramsey Lewis Trio) | 8 |
| 66 | Chess CRS 8029 | A Hard Day's Night/'Tout A Doubt (as Ramsey Lewis Trio) | 8 |
| 66 | Chess CRS 8031 | Hi-Heel Sneakers (Parts 1 & 2) (as Ramsey Lewis Trio) | 10 |
| 66 | Chess CRS 8041 | Wade In The Water/Ain't That Peculiar (as Ramsey Lewis Trio) | 40 |
| 66 | Chess CRS 8041 | Wade In The Water/Ain't That Peculiar (as Ramsey Lewis Trio) (DJ copy) | 120 |
| 66 | Chess CRS 8044 | Uptight (Everything's Alright)/Money In The Pocket | 10 |
| 67 | Chess CRS 8051 | Day Tripper/Hurt So Bad | 20 |
| 67 | Chess CRS 8055 | 1-2-3/Down By The Riverside | 8 |
| 67 | Chess CRS 8058 | Function At The Junction/Hey Mrs. Jones | 10 |
| 67 | Chess CRS 8060 | Saturday Night After The Movies/China Gate | 8 |
| 67 | Chess CRS 8061 | Girl Talk/Dancing In The Street | 8 |
| 67 | Chess CRS 8064 | Soul Man/Struttin' Lightly | 10 |
| 69 | Chess CRS 8096 | Cry Baby Cry/Wade In The Water | 20 |
| 69 | Chess CRS 8096 | Cry Baby Cry/Wade In The Water (DJ copy) | 45 |
| 70 | Chess CRS 8104 | Julia/Do What You Wanna | 10 |
| 72 | Chess 6145 004 | Wade In The Water/Ain't That Peculiar (paper label) | 15 |
| 72 | Chess 6145 013 | The 'In' Crowd/Soul Man | 6 |
| 72 | CBS 8280 | Slipping Into Darkness/Collage | 8 |
| 66 | Chess CRE 6019 | A HARD DAY'S NIGHT (EP, as Ramsey Lewis Trio) | 30 |
| 65 | Pye Jazz NJL 55 | AT THE BOHEMIAN CAVERNS (LP) | 20 |
| 65 | Chess CRL 4511 | THE 'IN' CROWD (LP) | 25 |
| 65 | Chess CRL 4518 | CHOICE! THE BEST OF RAMSEY LEWIS (LP) | 25 |
| 66 | Chess CRL 4520 | HANG ON RAMSEY! (LP) | 20 |
| 66 | Chess CRL 4522 | WADE IN THE WATER (LP) | 40 |
| 67 | Chess CRL 4528 | GOIN' LATIN (LP) | 25 |
| 67 | Chess CRL 4531 | THE MOVIE ALBUM (LP) | 20 |
| 68 | Chess CRL(S) 4533 | DANCIN' IN THE STREET (LP) | 25 |
| 68 | Chess CRLS 4535 | UP POPS RAMSEY LEWIS (LP) | 25 |
| 68 | Chess CRLS 4539 | MAIDEN VOYAGE (LP) | 30 |
| 69 | Chess CRLS 4545 | MOTHER NATURE'S SON (LP) | 20 |
| 68 | Fontana SFJL 962 | DOWN TO EARTH (LP) | 15 |
| 72 | Chess 6310 106 | BACK TO THE ROOTS (LP) | 15 |
| 72 | Chess 6310 114 | THE BEST OF RAMSEY LEWIS (LP) | 15 |
| 72 | Chess 6310 124 | TOBACCO ROAD (LP) | 20 |
| 73 | CBS 65307 | FUNKY SERENITY (LP) | 15 |
| 73 | CBS CQ 31096 | UPENDO NI PAMOJA (LP, quadrophonic) | 15 |
| 74 | CBS S80677 | SUN GODDESS (LP) | 18 |

*(see also Young-Holt Unlimited)*

## RICHARD LEWIS & HIS BAND
| | | | |
|---|---|---|---|
| 60 | Downbeat CHA 1 | Hey, Little Girl/Hey, Little Boy | 40 |

## SHIRLEY LEWIS
| | | | |
|---|---|---|---|
| 83 | High Energy | Loves Warming Up/Dub Mix (12") | 15 |

## SMILEY LEWIS
| | | | |
|---|---|---|---|
| 53 | London L 1189 | Big Mamou/Play Girl (78, some copies miscredited to Smiley Davis) | 100 |
| 56 | London HLU 8312 | One Night/Ain't Gonna Do It | 800 |
| 56 | London HLU 8312 | One Night/Ain't Gonna Do It (78) | 100 |
| 56 | London HLU 8337 | Down Yonder We Go Ballin'/Don't Be That Way (Please Listen To Me) | 800 |
| 56 | London HLU 8337 | Down Yonder We Go Ballin'/Don't Be That Way (Please Listen To Me) (78) | 100 |
| 57 | London HLP 8367 | Shame, Shame, Shame/No, No (gold lettering) | 500 |
| 57 | London HLP 8367 | Shame, Shame, Shame/No, No (silver lettering) | 400 |
| 57 | London HLP 8367 | Shame, Shame, Shame/No, No (78) | 70 |
| 70 | Liberty LBF 15337 | I Hear You Knocking/Play Girl | 10 |
| 70 | Liberty LBS 83308 | SHAME, SHAME, SHAME (LP) | 25 |
| 78 | United Artists UAS 30167 | I HEAR YOU KNOCKING (LP) | 15 |

## STEVIE LEWIS
| | | | |
|---|---|---|---|
| 65 | Mercury MF 871 | Take Me For A Little While/My Whole World Seems To Be Tumbling Down | 22 |
| 65 | Mercury MF 919 | Sometimes When You're Lonely/Under The Smile Of Love | 5 |
| 65 | Polydor 56003 | Heard It All Before/Wild | 7 |
| 69 | RCA RCA 1840 | Take A Little Warning/I Can Try | 5 |

## TAMALA LEWIS
| | | | |
|---|---|---|---|
| 79 | Destiny DS 1010 | You Won't Say Nothing/If You Can Stand Me | 8 |
| 79 | Destiny DS 1010 | You Won't Say Nothing/If You Can Stand Me (DJ) | 15 |

## TINA LEWIS
| | | | |
|---|---|---|---|
| 83 | Inferno BURN 5 | Back Street/The Way You've Been Acting Lately | 12 |

MINT VALUE £

## TINY LEWIS
| | | | |
|---|---|---|---|
| 60 | Parlophone R 4617 | Too Much Rockin'/I Get Weak | 150 |

## VIC LEWIS
| | | | |
|---|---|---|---|
| 63 | HMV POP 1127 | Bossa Nova Scotia/Vic's Tune | 5 |
| 68 | NEMS 56-3893 | Goodnight/Julia (as Vic Lewis, his Orchestra and singers) | 10 |
| 69 | NEMS 56 3712 | Sunshine Superman/Mellow Yellow | 8 |
| 69 | NEMS 56-4057 | Blackbird/I Will | 20 |
| 55 | Decca LF 1216 | PROGRESSIVE JAZZ (10" LP) | 30 |
| 62 | HMV CLP 1641 | PLAY BOSSA NOVA HOME AND AWAY (LP, features Tubby Hayes) | 50 |
| 70 | Ember CJS 807 | AT THE BEAULIEU FESTIVAL (LP) | 25 |
| 60s | Ember SE 8018 | BIG BAND EXPLOSION (LP) | 30 |
| 70s | DJM SPECB 103 | MY LIFE MY WAY (LP) | 15 |

## LEWIS SISTERS
| | | | |
|---|---|---|---|
| 65 | Tamla Motown TMG 536 | You Need Me/Moonlight On The Beach | 120 |
| 65 | Tamla Motown TMG 536 | You Need Me/Moonlight On The Beach (DJ Copy) | 150 |

## DAVE LEWRY
| | | | |
|---|---|---|---|
| 72 | Westwood WRS 019 | ALL I WANT TO DO IS PLAY GUITAR (LP) | 35 |

## MONIQUE LEYRAC
| | | | |
|---|---|---|---|
| 68 | SNB 55-3309 | Time Time/Love Is Blue | 7 |

## LEYTON BUZZARDS
| | | | |
|---|---|---|---|
| 78 | Small Wonder SMALL 7 | 19 And Mad/Villain/Youthanasia (p/s) | 8 |
| 79 | Chrysalis CHS 2288 | Saturday Night Beneath The Plastic Palm Trees/Through With You (p/s) | 5 |
| 79 | Chrysalis CHS 2328 | I'm Hanging Around/I Don't Want To Go/No Dry Ice And Flying Pigs (p/s, green vinyl) | 5 |
| 79 | Chrysalis CHR 1213 | JELLIED EELS TO RECORD DEALS (LP, as Buzzards) | 15 |

## JOHN LEYTON
| | | | |
|---|---|---|---|
| 60 | Top Rank JAR 426 | Tell Laura I Love Her/Goodbye To Teenage Love | 20 |
| 60 | HMV POP 798 | The Girl On The Floor Above/Terry Brown's In Love With Mary Dee | 30 |
| 61 | Top Rank JAR 577 | Johnny Remember Me/There Must Be | 5 |
| 61 | Top Rank JAR 585 | Wild Wind/You Took My Love For Granted | 5 |
| 61 | HMV POP 956 | Son This Is She/Six White Horses | 5 |
| 62 | HMV POP 992 | Lone Rider/Heart Of Stone | 10 |
| 62 | HMV POP 1014 | Lonely City/It Would Be Easy | 10 |
| 62 | HMV POP 1054 | Down The River Nile/I Think I'm Falling In Love | 7 |
| 62 | HMV POP 1076 | Lonely Johnny/Keep On Loving You | 8 |
| 63 | HMV POP 1122 | Cupboard Love/Land Of Love | 5 |
| 63 | HMV POP 1175 | I'll Cut Your Tail Off/The Great Escape | 7 |
| 63 | HMV POP 1204 | On Lover's Hill/Lovers Lane | 5 |
| 63 | HMV POP 1230 | I Guess You Are Always On My Mind/Beautiful Dreamer | 5 |
| 64 | HMV POP 1264 | Make Love To Me/Missing You (as John Leyton & Le Roys) | 10 |
| 64 | HMV POP 1338 | Don't Let Her Go Away/I Want A Love I Can See | 10 |
| 64 | HMV POP 1374 | All I Want Is You/Every Day Is A Holiday (with Grazina Frame & Mike Sarne) | 10 |
| 73 | York SYK 551 | Dancing In The Graveyard/Riversong | 10 |
| 74 | York YR 210 | Rock 'N' Roll/Highway Song | 10 |
| 62 | Top Rank JKP 3016 | JOHN LEYTON (EP) | 10 |
| 62 | HMV 7EG 8747 | HIT PARADE (EP) | 20 |
| 64 | HMV 7EG 8843 | BEAUTIFUL DREAMER (EP) | 15 |
| 64 | HMV 7EG 8854 | TELL LAURA I LOVE HER (EP) | 15 |
| 61 | HMV CLP 1497 | THE TWO SIDES OF JOHN LEYTON (LP) | 20 |
| 62 | HMV CLP 1664 | ALWAYS YOURS (LP, with Charles Blackwell's Orchestra) | 30 |

*(see also Le Roys)*

## LFB
| | | | |
|---|---|---|---|
| 78 | Family FAM 1 | Certain Politicians/Dreamteller (p/s) | 7 |

## L.F.O.
| | | | |
|---|---|---|---|
| 90 | Warp/Outer WAP5R | LFO Remix/Mentok 1/Quijard (12") | 10 |
| 90 | Warp WAP 5 | L.F.O. (The Leeds Warehouse Mix)/L.F.O. (Track 4)/Probe (The Cuba Edit) (12", p/s) | 15 |
| 91 | Warp WAP 14 | We Are Back/Nurture (12") | 10 |
| 92 | Warp WAP 17 | What Is House (LFO Remix)/Push/Tan Ta Ra (Moby Remix) (12") | 10 |
| 91 | Warp WARPLP3 | FREQUENCIES (LP) | 25 |
| 96 | Warp WARPLP39 | ADVANCE (2-LP) | 20 |
| 03 | Warp WARPLP110 | SHEATH (LP) | 15 |

## LG & LOPEZ
| | | | |
|---|---|---|---|
| 01 | Sit Tight STR001 | Life Long/Tempered Waters/Storming (EP) | 10 |
| 02 | Sit Tight STR002 | Rocket Fuel/City Breaks (EP) | 10 |
| 06 | Sit Tight STRLP 03 | SMOKE RINGS (LP) | 15 |

## LIAISON
| | | | |
|---|---|---|---|
| 82 | Catweazle CR 001 | Play It With A Passion/Caught In A ... (grey p/s) | 35 |
| 82 | Catweazle CR 001 | Play It With A Passion/Caught In A ... (yellow p/s) | 10 |
| 84 | Liaison LSN 0020 | Only Heaven Knows/Ease The Pain Away (p/s) | 100 |

## LIAISONS DANGEREUSES
| | | | |
|---|---|---|---|
| 82 | Mute 023 | Los Ninos Del Parque/Mystere Dans Le Broulard (p/s) | 7 |

## LIAR
| | | | |
|---|---|---|---|
| 77 | Decca F13689 | Straight From The Hip, Kid/Roll Me Down | 5 |
| 79 | Bearsville K 55524 | SET THE WORLD ON FIRE (LP, picture disc) | 15 |

## LIARS
| | | | |
|---|---|---|---|
| 04 | Mute STUMM 225 | THEY WERE WRONG SO WE DROWNED (LP, gatefold, white vinyl, booklet) | 15 |
| 05 | Mute STUMM 246 | DRUM'S NOT DEAD (LP with DVD) | 15 |
| 07 | Mute STUMM 287 | LIARS (LP, white vinyl, inner) | 15 |

| | | | |
|---|---|---|---|
| 13 | Mute STUMM 343 | WIXIW (LP & CD, all dipped in wax, 355 copies) | 50 |

**SVEN LIBAEK**
| | | | |
|---|---|---|---|
| 06 | Trunk JBH 020 LP | INNER SPACE: THE LOST FILM MUSIC OF SVEN LIBAEK (LP, 500 only) | 30 |

**LIBERACE COUGHS UP BLOOD**
| | | | |
|---|---|---|---|
| 81 | Vital VTL 0002 | Messerschmidt/Too Many Places/NIK TOWNEND: Gunslinger (p/s) | 15 |

**LIBERATION SUITE**
| | | | |
|---|---|---|---|
| 75 | Myrrh MYR 1027 | LIBERATION SUITE (LP) | 20 |

**LIBERATORS**
| | | | |
|---|---|---|---|
| 65 | Stateside SS 424 | It Hurts So Much/You Look So Fine | 15 |

*(see also Pinkerton's Assorted Colours)*

**EVE LIBERTINE & CRASS**
| | | | |
|---|---|---|---|
| 84 | Crass 1984/4 | ACTS OF LOVE (LP, with book) | 15 |

*(see also Crass)*

**LIBERTINES**
| | | | |
|---|---|---|---|
| 02 | Rough Trade RTRADES 054 | What A Waster/I Get Along (p/s, 2000 only) | 25 |
| 02 | Rough Trade RTRADES 064 | Up The Bracket/Boys In The Band (p/s) | 10 |
| 03 | Rough Trade RTRADES 074 | Time For Heroes/The 7 Deadly Sins (demo version) (p/s) | 12 |
| 03 | Rough Trade RTRADS 119 | Don't Look Back Into The Sun/Death On The Stairs (blue vinyl, fold-out poster sleeve in PVC slipcase, 3000 only) | 20 |
| 04 | Rough Trade RTRADS 163 | Can't Stand Me Now/The Tide That Left Never Came Back/(I've Got) Sweets (p/s) | 8 |
| 04 | Rough Trade RTRADS 215 | What Became Of The Likely Lads?/(Reworked)/Boys In The Band (Live at Brixton Sat 6/3/04) (Free LP poster p/s) | 8 |
| 02 | Rough Trade RTRADELP 065 | UP THE BRACKET (LP) | 18 |
| 04 | Rough Trade RTRADELPX166 | THE LIBERTINES (LP, gatefold 3000 only) | 30 |
| 04 | Rough Trade RTRADELP166 | THE LIBERTINES (White label test pressing, 10 only) | 50 |
| 07 | Rough Trade RTRADLP 421 | TIME FOR HEROES - THE BEST OF THE LIBERTINES (LP, red vinyl) | 30 |

*(see also Babyshambles, Wolfman)*

**LIBERTY**
| | | | |
|---|---|---|---|
| 80s | Mortarhate MORT 19 | Our Voices Tomorrow's Hope | 12 |
| 80s | Mortarhate MORT 25 | THE PEOPLE WHO CARE ARE ANGRY (LP) | 25 |

**LIBERTY BELLES**
| | | | |
|---|---|---|---|
| 71 | Jay Boy BOY 40 | Shing-A-Ling Time/Just Try Me | 10 |

**LIBIDO 1**
| | | | |
|---|---|---|---|
| 73 | Mooncrest MOON 2 | Hold On To Your Fire/Weren't Born A Man | 20 |

**LICKS**
| | | | |
|---|---|---|---|
| 79 | Stortbeat BEAT 8 | 1970S EP | 15 |

*(see also Epileptics, Flux Of Pink Indians)*

**JAMIE LIDELL**
| | | | |
|---|---|---|---|
| 97 | Mosquito MSQ 08 | FREEKIN' THE FRAME (12" EP) | 10 |

**LIDJ INCORPORATED**
| | | | |
|---|---|---|---|
| 95 | Eastern Sher ES 001 | BLACK LIBERATION (LP) | 18 |

**BUNNY LIE LIE**
| | | | |
|---|---|---|---|
| 81 | Greensleeves GRED 52 | Babylonian/WAYNE WADE: Poor And Humble (12") | 20 |

**LIEUTENANT PIGEON**
| | | | |
|---|---|---|---|
| 73 | Decca SKL 5154 | MOULDY OLD MUSIC (LP) | 20 |
| 73 | Decca SKL 5174 | PIGEON PIE (LP) | 20 |
| 74 | Decca SKL 5196 | PIGEON PARTY (LP) | 25 |

*(see also Shel Naylor, Stavely Makepeace, Heavy Cochran)*

**LIFE**
| | | | |
|---|---|---|---|
| 69 | Polydor 56778 | Hands Of The Clock/Ain't I Told You Before | 22 |
| 72 | Phillips 6006247 | Hold On (I'll Find You)/Love Nest | 30 |
| 73 | Philips 6006 280 | Cats Eyes/Death In The Family (paper label) | 20 |
| 73 | Philips 6006 280 | Cats Eyes/Death In The Family (moulded label) | 10 |
| 74 | Polydor 2058 500 | Woman/Bless My Soul | 6 |
| 74 | Polydor 2383 295 | LIFE AFTER DEATH (LP) | 60 |

**LIFE AFTER LIFE**
| | | | |
|---|---|---|---|
| 85 | Timetrack SRTSKL 453 | LIFE AFTER LIFE (LP, private pressing) | 120 |

**LIFE 'N' SOUL**
| | | | |
|---|---|---|---|
| 67 | Decca F 12659 | Ode To Billy Joe/Peacefully Asleep | 25 |
| 68 | Decca F 12851 | Here Comes Yesterday Again/Dear Paul | 15 |

**LIFE STUDIES**
| | | | |
|---|---|---|---|
| 83 | Occasion OCC 001 | Girl On Fire/Inside Out/Citizen Of Love | 20 |

**LIFE SUPPORT**
| | | | |
|---|---|---|---|
| 79 | Slug SLUG 1 | Leader Deceiver/Confusion (p/s, white labels) | 25 |

**LIFE WITHOUT BUILDINGS**
| | | | |
|---|---|---|---|
| 00 | Tugboat TUGS 016 | The Leanover/New Town (p/s) | 10 |
| 00 | Tugboat TUGS 019 | Is Is & The IRS/Let's Get Out (p/s) | 8 |
| 01 | Tugboat TUGS 026 | Young Offenders/Daylighting (p/s) | 5 |
| 00 | Tugboat TUGLP 023 | ANY OTHER CITY (LP) | 30 |

**LIFE OF RILEY**
| | | | |
|---|---|---|---|
| 74 | Enisgn 11 | Turn The Pages Over/I Love My Life (p/s) | 10 |

**LIFETIME**
| | | | |
|---|---|---|---|
| 70 | Polydor 2066 050 | One Word/Two Worlds | 20 |

*(see also Tony Williams [Lifetime], Jack Bruce, John McLaughlin)*

**LIFETONES**
| | | | |
|---|---|---|---|
| 83 | Tone Of Life LTM 001 | FOR A REASON (LP) | 100 |

MINT VALUE £

**LIFT TO EXPERIENCE**
01  Bella Union BELLAV 23    THE TEXAS JERUSALEM CROSSROADS (2-LP) ..................... 50

**JOE LIGES**
63  Blue Beat BB 172    Spit In The Sky/Tell Me What (both actually by Delroy Wilson) .................. 25
*(see also Delroy Wilson)*

**JOE LIGGINS & HONEYDRIPPERS**
76  Specialty SDN 5006    Pink Champagne/Honey Dripper ............................................ 5

**(THE) LIGHT**
96  AAA Recordings TRIP 002    Dusk (12") ....................................................... 15

**LIGHT BEARER**
11  Eyes Of Sound EOSLP 035    LAPSUS (2-LP, 'wings' cover, inserts, 200 only) ...................... 30

**BEN LIGHT**
56  HMV 7M 350    Bring Me A Bluebird/You ..................................................... 10

**ENOCH LIGHT**
59  Top Rank JAR 134    With My Eyes Wide Open/I Cried For You (as Enoch Light & Light Brigade) .... 5
59  Top Rank JAR 234    Scarlet Ribbons/Greensleeves (as Enoch Light & His Vibrant Strings) ...... 5
65  Pye Command PCLS 873    DISCOTHEQUE (LP) .................................................. 20
69  Studio Two TWO 312    SPACED OUT (LP) ....................................................... 20
70  Project 3    PERMISSIVE POLYPHONICS (LP) ................................................ 20

**LIGHT FANTASTIC**
73  MAM R 105    Love Is Everywhere/Gone Are The Days .......................................... 10
73  MAM 112    Alley Oop/Peace And Love To The World .......................................... 8
73  RCA RCA 2331    Jeanie/You Don't Care ....................................................... 20
74  Blue Jean BJS 701    Take Me, Shake Me/Don't Let Go ......................................... 8
75  Blue Jean BJS 704    We Are The Song/Raining ................................................. 6

**J.J. LIGHT**
69  Liberty LBF 15228    Heya/On The Road Now ................................................... 10

**LIGHT OF THE WORLD**
82  EMI EMC 3410    CHECK US OUT (LP) ......................................................... 20

**LIGHT YEARS**
87  Amanda AM 7006    No Matter Where I Go/You Won't Break Me Down ......................... 8

**GORDON LIGHTFOOT**
62  Decca F 11527    (Remember Me) I'm The One/Daisy-Doo (as Gord Lightfoot) ............... 20
63  Fontana 267 275TF    Negotiations/It's Too Late, He Wins (as Gordie Lightfoot) ........... 10
63  Fontana TF 405    The Day Before Yesterday/Take Care Of Yourself (as Gordie Lightfoot) .... 6
65  United Artists UP 1109    Just Like Tom Thumb's Blues/Ribbon Of Darkness .................. 5
66  Warner Bros WB 5621    I'm Not Sayin'/For Lovin' Me ....................................... 5
68  President PT 138    Adios Adios/Is My Baby Blue Tonight (as Gordie Lightfoot) ............ 5
68  United Artists UP 2216    Black Day In July/Pussy Willow's Cat Tails ..................... 5
69  United Artists UP 2272    The Circle Is Small/Does Your Mother Know ..................... 5
69  United Artists UP 35020    Bitter Green/May I ........................................... 5
70  Reprise RS 20974    If You Could Read My Mind/Poor Little Alison ...................... 5

**PAPA (GEORGE) LIGHTFOOT**
69  Liberty LBF 15176    Wine Whiskey And Woman/SLIM HARPO: Something Inside Me ........... 25
60s  Jan & Dil JR 451    MORE DOWN HOME BLUES (EP) ....................................... 35
71  Liberty LBS 83353    NATCHEZ TRACE (LP, as Papa George Lightfoot) .................... 30

**LIGHTHOUSE**
69  RCA RCA 1884    Eight Miles High/If There Ever Was A Time ............................. 7
70  RCA RCA 1982    The Chant (Nam Myo-Ho Renge' Kyo)/Could You Be Concerned ........... 10
71  Vertigo 6073 150    Hats Off (To The Strangers)/Sing Sing Sing ...................... 12
72  Philips 6073 152    One Fine Morning/Little Kind Words ............................... 12
72  Philips 6073 153    Take It Slow/Sweet Lullaby ....................................... 20
70  RCA SF 8103    SUITE FEELING (LP) ...................................................... 15
71  Vertigo 6342 010    ONE FINE MORNING (LP, gatefold sleeve, swirl label) ............ 150
71  Vertigo 6342 011    THOUGHTS OF MOVIN' ON (LP, gatefold sleeve, swirl label) ....... 100

**LIGHTNIN' SLIM**
72  Blue Horizon 2096 013    Just A Little Bit/You're Old Enough To Understand/Mind Your Own Business .... 30
65  Stateside SL 10135    A LONG DRINK OF BLUES (LP, with Slim Harpo) ................... 80
69  Python PLP 8    THE DOWNHOME BLUES PART 1 (LP, 99 copies only) ...................... 60
70  Blue Horizon 7-63863    ROOSTER BLUES (LP) ........................................... 85
72  Blue Horizon 2931 005    LONDON GUMBO (LP) ......................................... 150
78  Flyright FLYLP 533    TRIP TO CHICAGO (LP) .......................................... 18
79  Flyright FLYLP 583    THE FEATURE SIDES 1954 (LP) ................................... 15
80  Flyright FLYLP 612    WE GOTTA ROCK TONIGHT (LP) .................................... 18
*(see also Slim Harpo)*

**LIGHTNING LEON**
60s  Jan & Dil JR 450    DOWN HOME BLUES - SIXTIES STYLE (EP) .......................... 35

**LIGHTNING RAIDERS**
80  Arista ARIST 341    Psychedelik Musik ('adult' version)/Views (p/s) ................... 18
80  Arista ARIST 341DJ    Psychedelik Musik ('censored' version)/Views (promo only, no p/s) .... 35
81  Revenge REVS 200    Criminal World/Citizens (p/s) .................................... 10
81  Revenge RSS 39    Sweet Revenge/Rowdies/Addiction/Soul Rescue (12", promo only) ....... 45
*(see also Pink Fairies, Professionals)*

**LIGOTAGE**
84  Picasso PIKM005    FORGIVE AND FORGET (LP, lyric insert) ............................ 15

**LIKE**
10  Geffen 2740655    He's Not A Boy/Why When Love Is Gone ............................. 15

**LIKE A SONG**
73 De Wolfe DW/LP 3273    LIKE A SONG (LP, library issue) ........... 18

**LIKE ICE LIKE FIRE**
86 Maiden Country LILF 01    Executioners Song/Dark Rosaline ........... 12

**LIL LOUIS**
89 Rough TOUGH 4    Frequency (Remix) (12", 3,000 copies) ........... 15

**LILAC TIME**
88 Swordfish LILAC 1    Return To Yesterday/Trumpets From Montparnasse (no p/s) ........... 8
88 Swordfish 12 LILAC 1    Return To Yesterday/Railway Bazaar/Trumpets From Montparnasse/Reunion Ball (12", p/s) ........... 12
88 Fontana LILAC 4    Black Velvet/Black Dawn (p/s in Xmas card folder) ........... 5
90 Caff CAFF 12    Madresfield/Bird On The Wire (p/s, with insert) ........... 25
88 Swordfish SWF LP 6    THE LILAC TIME (LP, original issue) ........... 15
*(see also Hawks, Stephen Duffy)*

**LILIPUT**
80 Rough Trade RT 047    Spilt/Die Matrosen (p/s) ........... 12
81 Rough Trade RT 062    Eisiger Wind/When The Cat's Away Then The Mice Will Play ........... 15
82 Rough Trade ROUGH 43    LILIPUT (LP) ........... 20
*(see also Kleenex)*

**LILYS**
96 Ché CHE 51    Returns Every Morning/Touch The Water (white vinyl, p/s, 500 only) ........... 6
96 Ché CHE 65    A Nanny In Manhattan/More Than Is Deserved (coffee-coloured vinyl, p/s, 500 only) .... 6

**LIMELIGHT (1)**
75 United Artists UP 35779    I Should Have Known Better/Tell Me Why ........... 12
*(see also Brinsley Schwarz)*

**LIMELIGHT (2)**
80 Future Earth FER 006    Metal Man/Hold Me Touch Me (p/s) ........... 12
82 Future Earth FER 010    Ashes To Ashes/Knife In Your Back (p/s, with insert) ........... 12
82 Future Earth FER 010    Ashes To Ashes/Knife In Your Back (p/s, some with insert) ........... 10
80 Future Earth FER 008    LIMELIGHT (LP) ........... 22
81 Avatar AALP 5005    LIMITED LIMELIGHT (LP, with bonus single) ........... 20
81 Avatar AALP 5005    LIMITED LIMELIGHT (LP) ........... 15

**LIMEYS**
65 Pye 7N 15820    I Can't Find My Way Through/Don't Cry (My Love) ........... 5
65 Pye 7N 15909    Some Tears Fall Dry/Half Glass Of Wine ........... 5
66 Decca F 12382    Cara-Lin/Feel So Blue ........... 30
66 Decca F 12466    The Mountain's High/Lovin' Yourself ........... 5

**LIMIT (2)**
81 Survival 002    Shockwaves/Ok Go (p/s) ........... 15
81 Survival SUR 004    Taki It/Do It (p/s) ........... 15

**LIMIT (1)**
78 Private Stock PVT 156    Please Please Me/My World At Night (company sleeve) ........... 45

**LIMMIE**
78 Psycho P 2604    Saturday Night's The Night/Party ........... 50

**LIMPS/NO SUPPORT**
79 Matchbox Classics MC 1    OPPOSITE SIDES EP (Split 7" with 2 tracks by Limps and 2 tracks by No Support, p/s) ... 20
79 Matchbox Classics MC 2    ANOTHER MATCHBOX CLASSIC? (Split EP, 2 tracks by Limps and 2 by No Support, with folded p/s) ........... 40
79 Matchbox Classics MC 2    ANOTHER MATCHBOX CLASSIC? (Split EP, 2 tracks by Limps and 2 by No Support, without folded p/s, just die-cut stamped sleeve) ........... 15

**PETER LINCOLN**
67 Major Minor MM 520    In The Day Of My Youth/My Monkey Is A Junkie ........... 30
*(see also Peter Sarstedt, Sarstedt Brothers, Brothers Kane)*

**PHILAMORE LINCOLN**
68 NEMS 56-3711    Running By The River/Rainy Day ........... 70
70 CBS 5007    The County Jail Band/You're The One ........... 40

**LINCOLN TURNPIKE**
71 Polydor 2058109    Green On The Other Side Of The Mountain/You Can Call Everybody Your Friend ........... 8

**LINCOLN X**
63 Oriole CB 1823    Heartaches And Happiness/Stand In For Her Past ........... 5

**LINCOLNS**
66 Parlophone R 5418    Mister Loneliness/Only Love Will Break Your Heart ........... 6

**LINDA AND THE DARK**
80 Crash Point    Horror Movies/I Don't Want To See You Out With Somebody Else (p/s) ........... 20

**DADDY LINDBERG**
67 Columbia DB 8138    Shirl/Wade In The Shade ........... 120
*(see also Crocheted Doughnut Ring)*

**ANITA LINDBLOM**
62 Fontana 267223 TF    Uptown/Mr Big Wheel ........... 10

**KATHY LINDEN**
58 Felsted AF 102    Billy/If I Could Hold You In My Arms ........... 5
58 Felsted AF 105    You'd Be Surprised/Why Oh Why ........... 5
58 Felsted AF 108    Oh! Johnny, Oh! Johnny Oh!/Georgie ........... 5
58 Felsted AF 111    Kissin' Conversation/Just A Sandy Haired Boy Called Sandy ........... 5
59 Felsted AF 122    Goodbye Jimmy, Goodbye/Heartaches At Sweet Sixteen ........... 5
59 Felsted AF 124    So Close To My Heart/You Don't Know Girls ........... 5
60 Felsted AF 130    Think Love/Mary Lou Wilson And Johnny Brown ........... 5

| | | | MINT VALUE £ |
|---|---|---|---|
| 59 | Felsted GEP 1001 | KATHY (EP) ................................................................ | 15 |
| 59 | Felsted GEP 1002 | KATHY'S IN LOVE VOLUME ONE (EP) ................................. | 15 |
| 59 | Felsted GEP 1004 | KATHY'S IN LOVE VOLUME TWO (EP) ................................. | 15 |

## LINDISFARNE
| | | | |
|---|---|---|---|
| 70 | Charisma CB 137 | Clear White Light Part II/Knackers Yard Blues ..................... | 15 |
| 71 | Charisma CB 153 | Lady Eleanor/Nothing But The Marvellous Is Beautiful (with p/s) .. | 6 |
| 70 | Charisma CAS 1025 | NICELY OUT OF TUNE (LP, pink 'scroll' label) ....................... | 35 |
| 71 | Charisma CAS 1050 | FOG ON THE TYNE (LP, gatefold sleeve, pink 'scroll' label) ...... | 25 |
| 72 | Charisma CAS 1057 | DINGLY DELL (LP, with inner sleeve & poster) ...................... | 15 |

*(see also Alan Hull, Jack The Lad, Chosen Few, Radiator, Ray Jackson)*

## WILLIE LINDO
| | | | |
|---|---|---|---|
| 76 | Klik KLP 9019 | FAR AND DISTANT (LP) ................................................ | 15 |
| 78 | Black Wax WAX 21 | Midnight/After Midnight .............................................. | 35 |

## JIMMY LINDSAY AND THE BEANS
| | | | |
|---|---|---|---|
| 70 | Q 2203 | Peace To You Brother/Tribute To Jimi Hendrix ..................... | 15 |

## JIMMY LINDSAY
| | | | |
|---|---|---|---|
| 77 | Black Swan BS 8 | Easy/FABIAN: Prophecy (12") ........................................ | 30 |
| 77 | Tribesman TM 008 | Easy/FABIAN: Prophecy (12") ........................................ | 30 |
| 78 | Music Hive MH002 | Ain't No Sunshine/EXODUS : Take Six/DIMBALA : And Ting (12") .. | 30 |
| 82 | Music Hive MH004 | Turn Out The Lights/Dole Queue (12") .............................. | 30 |
| 80 | Gem GEMLP 110 | CHILDREN OF RASTAFARI (LP) ....................................... | 15 |

## MARK LINDSAY
| | | | |
|---|---|---|---|
| 69 | CBS 4699 | Arizona/Man From Houston ........................................... | 10 |
| 70 | CBS 5055 | Silver Bird/So Hard To Leave You .................................... | 8 |
| 70 | CBS 5219 | And The Grass Won't Pay No Mind/Funny How Little Men Care .... | 8 |
| 71 | CBS 5408 | Problem Child/Bookends ............................................... | 8 |
| 71 | CBS 7330 | Been Too Long On The Road/All I Really See Is You ................ | 8 |
| 71 | CBS 7551 | Are You Old Enough/Don't You Know ................................ | 8 |
| 71 | CBS 7690 | Something Big/Pretty Pretty .......................................... | 8 |

*(see also Paul Revere & Raiders)*

## TERRY LINDSEY
| | | | |
|---|---|---|---|
| 69 | President PT 232 | It's Over/One Day Up, Next Day Down ............................... | 15 |

## BJORN J. SON LINDT
| | | | |
|---|---|---|---|
| 83 | Sonet SON 2254 | Cloud Pump/From Here To Eternity (p/s) ............................ | 12 |

## DAVID LINDUP ORCHESTRA
| | | | |
|---|---|---|---|
| 66 | Columbia DB 7979 | Informer Theme/Blue Mountain ...................................... | 10 |
| 66 | Polydor 56106 | Survival Theme/New Forest ........................................... | 20 |
| 70 | Aristocrat AR 1021 | WHEN THE SAINTS GO (LP) .......................................... | 20 |

## LINDYS
| | | | |
|---|---|---|---|
| 60 | Decca F 11253 | The Train Of Love/You Know How Things Get Around .............. | 15 |
| 60 | Decca F 11272 | Boy With The Eyes Of Blue/Someone Else's Roses ................. | 15 |

## LINES
| | | | |
|---|---|---|---|
| 78 | Linear SJP 782 | White Night/Barbican (p/s) ............................................ | 12 |
| 79 | Illegal ILS 0011 | White Night/Barbican (p/s, reissue) .................................. | 7 |
| 79 | Red RS 001 | On The Air/Not Through Windows/Dance For A Drop Of Blood ... | 8 |
| 80 | Red Linear RL 007 | Nerve Pylon/Over The Brow (screen-printed p/s) .................. | 8 |
| 80 | Red Linear RL12 005 | COOL SNAP EP (12") .................................................. | 12 |
| 81 | Red RS 010 | Transit/Part II (p/s) ................................................... | 7 |
| 83 | Red ROUGE 3 | ULTRAMARINE (LP) .................................................... | 15 |

## BUZZY LINHART
| | | | |
|---|---|---|---|
| 72 | Kama Sutra 2013049 | You Got What It Takes/Tell Me True ................................. | 5 |
| 69 | Philips SBL 7885 | BUZZY (LP, laminated gatefold sleeve, black/silver labels) ....... | 40 |
| 71 | Kama Sutra 2319011 | THE TIME TO LIVE IS NOW (LP, textured gatefold sleeve, yellow/red labels) .. | 25 |
| 71 | Buddah 2318028 | MUSIC (LP) .............................................................. | 15 |

## LINK
| | | | |
|---|---|---|---|
| 92 | Evolution EVO 05 | THE FIRST LINK EP (12", plain sleeve) ............................... | 30 |
| 95 | Warp WAP 59 | ANTACID EP (12", p/s) ................................................ | 15 |
| 95 | Warp WAP 59R | ANTACID REMIXES EP (12", p/s as Link & E621) .................. | 10 |

*(see also Reload, Global Communications, Mystic Institute)*

## LINKERS
| | | | |
|---|---|---|---|
| 71 | Big Shot BI 567 | Bongo Man/FUD CHRISTIAN ALLSTARS: Creation Version ......... | 20 |

*(see also Links)*

## ANSEL LINKERS & FUD CHRISTIAN ALL STARS
| | | | |
|---|---|---|---|
| 73 | Summit SUM 8540 | Memories By The Score/FUD CHRISTIAN ALL STARS: Scorer ...... | 7 |

*(see also Links)*

## LINKS
| | | | |
|---|---|---|---|
| 72 | Tropical AL 0010 | Sing A Song Of Freedom/TROPICAL ALL STARS: Love Rhythm (A-side actually by Linkers) .. | 6 |

## LINN COUNTY
| | | | |
|---|---|---|---|
| 68 | Mercury SMCL 20142 | PROUD FLESH SOOTHSEER (LP) ..................................... | 25 |
| 69 | Mercury SMCL 20165 | FEVER SHOT (LP) ...................................................... | 20 |
| 70 | Philips SBL 7923 | TILL THE BREAK OF DAWN (LP) ..................................... | 18 |

## ELMO LINN
| | | | |
|---|---|---|---|
| 63 | Starlite ST45 101 | Another Man's Arms/Sam Houston ................................... | 18 |

## JOE LINTHECOME
| | | | |
|---|---|---|---|
| 50s | Poydras 87 | Pretty Mama Blues/Hummingbird Blues .............................. | 15 |

## LIONHEART
| | | |
|---|---|---|
| 85 | Epic A 5001 | Die For Love/Dangerous Games (p/s) .............................................. 7 |
| 84 | Epic EPC26214 | HOT TONIGHT (LP) ................................................................ 15 |

*(see also Iron Maiden,Wildfire)*

## LIONROCK
| | | |
|---|---|---|
| 92 | M.E.R.C. 002 | Roots'n'Culture (Part One)/Lionrock (12", original issue) ...................... 10 |
| 92 | De Construction 74321123381 | Lionrock - The Remixes: (Most Excellent Mix)/(Roots 'n' Culture)/(A Trumpet Jamboree In Edinburgh)/(A Dubtastic Jamboree In Edinburgh) (12") ............ 10 |
| 93 | Distort & Cavort | Dub Plate No. 1 (12") ............................................................ 10 |
| 98 | Concrete HARD 3112 | Rude Boy Rock/Best Foot Forward/Push Button Cocktail (p/s) .................... 8 |

## LIONS
| | | |
|---|---|---|
| 69 | Polydor 56757 | Twisted Nerve/My Friend The Blackbird ......................................... 30 |

## LIONS (JAMAICA)
| | | |
|---|---|---|
| 77 | Truth & Right L 001 | Natty Congo 1/Version ........................................................... 15 |

## LIONS OF JUDAH
| | | |
|---|---|---|
| 69 | Fontana TF 1016 | Our Love's A Growin' Thing/Katja ............................................... 20 |

## LION TAMERS
| | | |
|---|---|---|
| 68 | Polydor 56283 | Speak Your Mind/Light .......................................................... 50 |

## LION YOUTH
| | | |
|---|---|---|
| 81 | Virgo Stomach VG104 | Rat Cut A Bottle/Rub A Dub (12") .............................................. 15 |
| 81 | Virgo Stomach VGLP 001 | LOVE COMES AND GOES (LP) ..................................................... 18 |

## LIP MOVES
| | | |
|---|---|---|
| 79 | Tichonderoga HP 1 | Guest/What Is (p/s with insert, stickered white labels, signed) ................ 40 |
| 79 | Tichonderoga HP 1 | Guest/What Is (p/s with insert, stickered white labels) ........................ 30 |

## JOE LIPMAN ORCHESTRA
| | | |
|---|---|---|
| 54 | MGM SP 1108 | Looking Back To See/Stop ......................................................... 5 |

## THE LIPS
| | | |
|---|---|---|
| 78 | GTO GT 219 | Say Hello To My Girl/Be Cool From School (no p/s) ............................. 8 |

## PEGGY LIPTON
| | | |
|---|---|---|
| 70 | CBS 4779 | Lu/Let Me Pass By ............................................................... 15 |

## LIQUID CRYSTAL
| | | |
|---|---|---|
| 91 | Bizarre BIZZ 2 | Inner Sense/Dischord (12") ...................................................... 25 |
| 92 | Bizarre BIZZ 3 | The Power Within/Let It Go/Inner Sense ('92 remix) (12") ..................... 25 |
| 92 | Bizarre BIZZ 3R T | The Power Within (Remix)/Radiate/Inner Sense (Original) (12", p/s) ........... 25 |
| 92 | Ruff On Wax ROWT 1 | CHROMATIC EP (12", stickered plain sleeve) ................................... 70 |
| 92 | Ruff On Wax ROWTR 1 | CHROMATIC 2 EP: (12", stickered plain sleeve) ................................ 60 |

## LIQUID LIQUID
| | | |
|---|---|---|
| 97 | Mo Wax MW 078LP | LIQUID LIQUID (2-LP) ............................................................ 20 |
| 08 | Domino REWIGLP 34 | SLIP IN AND OUT OF PHENOMENON (LP, 12", CD) ............................... 20 |

## LIQUID SMOKE
| | | |
|---|---|---|
| 75 | Pye Int. 7N 25677 | Dance Dance Dance/Where Is Our Love ........................................... 8 |
| 70 | Avco Embassy 646 6003 | LIQUID SMOKE (LP) .............................................................. 35 |

## LIQUID STONE
| | | |
|---|---|---|
| 81 | Liquid Stone LIQ 001 | Here Comes The Weekend/Because Of You (no p/s, hand stickered labels) .... 350 |

## LIQUORICE
| | | |
|---|---|---|
| 78 | Perno PER 1 | It's Gonna Turn You On/This Is The B-Side .................................... 10 |

## LISTEN
| | | |
|---|---|---|
| 65 | CBS 202456 | You'd Better Run/Everybody's Gonna Say ...................................... 300 |

*(see also Robert Plant, Led Zeppelin)*

## LITMUS
| | | |
|---|---|---|
| 09 | Rise Above RISELP 125 | AURORA (2-LP, 1 side etched) ................................................... 20 |

## LITTER
| | | |
|---|---|---|
| 69 | Probe CLPS 4504 | EMERGE (LP) .................................................................... 75 |

## 'BIG' TINY LITTLE
| | | |
|---|---|---|
| 57 | Vogue Coral Q 72263 | School Day/That's The Only Way To Live ....................................... 40 |
| 57 | Vogue Coral Q 72263 | School Day/That's The Only Way To Live (78) .................................. 20 |
| 60 | Coral FEP 2058 | HONKY TONK PIANO VOL. 1 (EP) ............................................... 10 |
| 60 | Coral FEP 2059 | HONKY TONK PIANO VOL. 2 (EP) ............................................... 10 |

## SHARON LITTLE
| | | |
|---|---|---|
| 78 | One Love (no number) | Don't Mash Up Creation/Version (12") ......................................... 90 |

## LITTLE ANGELS
| | | |
|---|---|---|
| 87 | Little Angels LAN 001 | LITTLE ANGELS '87 (12" EP) .................................................... 30 |
| 87 | Powerstation AMP 14 | TOO POSH TO MOSH (mini-LP) ................................................. 18 |

## LITTLE ANN
| | | |
|---|---|---|
| 98 | Kent TOWN 111 | What Should I Do/O.C. TALBOT: I'm Shooting High (I Reach For The Sky) ..... 15 |
| 99 | Kent TOWN 112 | Who Are You Trying To Fool/I Got To Have You ............................... 20 |
| 09 | Kent CITY 010 | Lean Lanky Daddy/DAVID HAMILTON ORCHESTRA: Who Are You Trying To Fool (reissue) ........................................................................ 10 |

## LITTLE ANTHONY & IMPERIALS
| | | |
|---|---|---|
| 58 | London HLH 8704 | Tears On My Pillow/Two People In The World ................................... 40 |
| 58 | London HLH 8704 | Tears On My Pillow/Two People In The World (78) .............................. 30 |
| 59 | London HL 8848 | So Much/Oh Yeah ............................................................... 50 |
| 59 | London HL 8848 | So Much/Oh Yeah (78) .......................................................... 40 |
| 59 | Top Rank JAR 256 | Shimmy, Shimmy, Ko-Ko Bop/I'm Still In Love With You ....................... 20 |
| 60 | Top Rank JAR 366 | My Empty Room/Bayou, Bayou, Baby ........................................... 15 |
| 64 | United Artists UP 1065 | I'm On The Outside Looking In/Please Go ....................................... 15 |
| 64 | United Artists UP 1073 | Goin' Out Of My Head/Make It Easy On Yourself ............................... 15 |

# LITTLE ARCHIE

| | | | |
|---|---|---|---|
| 65 | United Artists UP 1083 | Hurt So Bad/Reputation | 25 |
| 65 | United Artists UP 1098 | Take Me Back/Our Song | 20 |
| 65 | United Artists UP 1112 | I Miss You/Get Out Of My Life | 15 |
| 66 | United Artists UP 1126 | Hurt/Never Again | 40 |
| 66 | United Artists UP 1137 | Better Use Your Head/The Wonder Of It All | 80 |
| 66 | United Artists UP 1137 | Better Use Your Head/The Wonder Of It All (DJ copy) | 150 |
| 66 | United Artists UP 1151 | Gonna Fix You Good (Every Time You're Bad)/You Better Take It Easy Baby | 75 |
| 67 | United Artists UP 1189 | My Love Is A Rainbow/You Only Live Twice | 5 |
| 68 | United Artists UP 2260 | Let The Sunshine In/The Gentle Rain (as Anthony) | 10 |
| 69 | United Artists UP 35017 | Anthem/Goodbye Goodtimes (as Anthony & Imperials) | 7 |
| 72 | United Artists UP 35345 | Gonna Fix You Good (Every Time You're Bad)/You Better Take It Easy Baby (reissue) | 10 |
| 76 | United Artists UP 36118 | Better Use Your Head/Gonna Fix You Good (Every Time You're Bad) | 10 |
| 76 | United Artists REM 405 | Goin' Out Of My Head/I'm On The Outside Looking In/Hurt So Bad/ Gonna Fix You Good (Every Time You're Bad) | 10 |
| 65 | United Artists UEP 1004 | LITTLE ANTHONY AND THE IMPERIALS (EP) | 100 |
| 64 | United Artists ULP 1089 | I'M ON THE OUTSIDE LOOKING IN (LP) | 100 |
| 66 | United Artists ULP 1100 | GOIN' OUT OF MY HEAD (LP) | 60 |

## LITTLE ARCHIE
| | | | |
|---|---|---|---|
| 68 | Atlantic 584 209 | I Need You/I Am A Carpet | 40 |

## LITTLE AXE
| | | | |
|---|---|---|---|
| 96 | Wired WIRED 133 | SLOW FUSE (2-LP) | 20 |

## LITTLE BEAVER
| | | | |
|---|---|---|---|
| 72 | President PTLS 1060 | JOEY (LP) | 25 |

## LITTLE BEVERLEY
| | | | |
|---|---|---|---|
| 68 | Pama PM 731 | What A Guy/You're Mine | 8 |

*(see also Beverley Simmons)*

## LITTLE BIG HORN
| | | | |
|---|---|---|---|
| 70 | Polydor 2058042 | Another Man's Song/Just A Game | 40 |

## LITTLE BILL & BLUE NOTES
| | | | |
|---|---|---|---|
| 59 | Top Rank JAR 176 | I Love An Angel/Bye, Bye Baby | 25 |
| 59 | Top Rank JAR 176 | I Love An Angel/Bye, Bye Baby (78) | 25 |

*(see also Blue Notes)*

## LITTLE BIRD
| | | | |
|---|---|---|---|
| 84 | Magus MGB 1 | Zola/Reaching Out For Gold (p/s) | 5 |

## LITTLE BO BITCH
| | | | |
|---|---|---|---|
| 79 | Cobra COB 1 | It's Only Love/I'm Confused (p/s) | 5 |
| 80 | Cobra COB 4 | Take It Easy (Lights Out Over London)/Lorraine, Lorraine (p/s) | 5 |

## LITTLE BOOTS
| | | | |
|---|---|---|---|
| 08 | 50 Bones 4BONES | Meddle/Meddle (Toddla T & Ross Orton Mix) (green vinyl with tattoo set, 500 only) | 15 |

## LITTLE BOY BLUE
| | | | |
|---|---|---|---|
| 69 | Jackpot JP 701 | Dark End Of The Street/MR VERSATILE: Apple Blossoms | 25 |

## LITTLE CLARKIE & THE OFFBEAT POSSE
| | | | |
|---|---|---|---|
| 86 | Jah Tubbys JT 015 | Selector Him Good/COLONEL MITE: Bless The Selector/JAH TUBBY: Select The Rhythm (12") | 80 |
| 86 | Jah Tubbys JT 20 | Live Stock Party/Bounty Hunter (12") | 50 |
| 87 | Y&D YDD 0107 | Bubble-N-Rock/Cowboy Stylee (12") | 50 |
| 88 | Y&D YDD 0134 | Can't Come A Dance And Stand Up/Never Give You Up (12") | 30 |

## LITTLE DARLING
| | | | |
|---|---|---|---|
| 65 | Blue Beat BB 325 | No One/BUSTER'S ALL STARS: Congo Revolution | 150 |

## LITTLE DARLINGS
| | | | |
|---|---|---|---|
| 65 | Fontana TF 539 | Little Bit O' Soul/Easy To Cry | 100 |

## LITTLE DES
| | | | |
|---|---|---|---|
| 70 | J-Dan JDN 4400 | Somebody's Baby/Spy Man | 7 |

## LITTLE DIPPERS
| | | | |
|---|---|---|---|
| 60 | Pye International 7N 25051 | Forever/Two By Four | 10 |
| 61 | London HLG 9269 | Lonely/I Wonder, I Wonder, I Wonder | 15 |

## LITTLE EVA
| | | | |
|---|---|---|---|
| 62 | London HL 9581 | The Locomotion/He Is The Boy | 5 |
| 62 | London HLU 9633 | Keep Your Hands Off My Baby/Where Do I Go | 6 |
| 63 | London HLU 9687 | Let's Turkey Trot/Old Smokey Locomotion | 5 |
| 63 | Colpix PX 11013 | The Trouble With Boys/What I Gotta Do (To Make You Jealous) | 10 |
| 63 | Colpix PX 11019 | Please Hurt Me/Let's Start The Party Again | 10 |
| 64 | Colpix PX 11035 | Run To Her/Making With The Magilla | 15 |
| 65 | Stateside SS 477 | Stand By Me/That's My Man | 20 |
| 63 | London HA-U 8036 | L-L-L-LOCO-MOTION (LP, original with plum label & laminated sleeve) | 30 |

*(see also Big Dee Irwin & Little Eva)*

## LITTLE FEAT
| | | | |
|---|---|---|---|
| 86 | Nimbus 80027 | FEAT DON'T FAIL ME NOW (LP, Nimbus Supercut, mail order only through Practical Hi Fi magazine) | 70 |

## LITTLE FISH
| | | | |
|---|---|---|---|
| 72 | Plant Life PLR 011 | HERTFORDSHIRE FOLK SONGS (EP, with insert) | 50 |

## LITTLE FOLK
| | | | |
|---|---|---|---|
| 71 | Studio Republic CR 1001 | LEAVE THEM A FLOWER (LP) | 18 |

## LITTLE FRANKIE (& COUNTRY GENTLEMEN)
| | | | |
|---|---|---|---|
| 65 | Columbia DB 7490 | The Kind Of Boy You Can't Forget/I'm Not Gonna Do It | 20 |
| 65 | Columbia DB 7578 | Make-A-Love/Love Is Just A Game (with Country Gentlemen) | 20 |
| 65 | Columbia DB 7681 | It Doesn't Matter Anymore/Happy, That's Me | 20 |

*(see also Chimes featuring Denise)*

### LITTLE FREDDY (MCGREGOR)
70 Unity UN 551     Why Did My Little Girl Cry/PETER AUSTIN: Change Partners .................. 10
*(see also Freddie McGregor, Ernest Wilson)*

### LITTLE FREE ROCK
69 Transatlantic TRA 208     LITTLE FREE ROCK (LP, laminated sleeve, white/lilac labels, 't' logo) ................ 175
*(see also David John & Mood)*

### LITTLE GEORGE
64 Rio R 45     Mary Anne/EDWARDS ALLSTARS: Blue Night ................ 20

### LITTLE GRANT
70 Torpedo TOR 27     Baby Don't Let Me Down/Brother Strong Man ................ 20
*(see also Equals, Pyramids, Eddy Grant)*

### LITTLE GRANTS & EDDIE (GRANT)
67 President PT 159     Rudy's Dead/Everything's Alright ................ 10
67 President PT 172     Rock Steady '67/Bingo ................ 7
*(see also Equals, Pyramids, Eddy Grant)*

### LITTLE HANK
66 London HLU 10090     Mr. Bang Bang Man/Don't You Know (withdrawn) ................ 150
66 London HLU 10090     Mr. Bang Bang Man/Don't You Know (withdrawn) (DJ copy) ................ 150
70 Monument MON 1045     Mr. Bang Bang Man/Don't You Know (reissue) ................ 15
01 Grapevine 2000 108     Try To Understand/Mr Bang Bang Man (reissue) ................ 8

### LITTLE HOWIE
85 Look To Afrika LTAF 03     Original Love Me/EARL ANTHONY Sensi Man Rock (12") ................ 100

### LITTLE JOE BLUE
78 Flyright FLY LP 534     DON'T TAX ME IN (LP) ................ 20

### LITTLE JOE (JAMAICA)
70 Torpedo TOR 15     Bad Blood/Maxi-Mini War ................ 30
*(see also Sexy Girls)*

### LITTLE JOE (& THRILLERS)
60 Fontana H 281     Stay (as Little Joe & Thrillers)/Cherry ................ 25
63 Reprise R 20142     Peanuts/No No I Can't Stop ................ 20

### LITTLE JOEY & FLIPS
62 Pye International 7N 25152   Bongo Stomp/Lost Love ................ 12

### LITTLE JOHN
67 Pama PM 702     Let's Get Married/Around The World ................ 20
70 Unity UN 561     No Love/A Little Tear (both sides actually by John Holt) ................ 15
84 Greensleeves GRELD 139     Form A Line/YELLOWMAN: Rub & Go Down (12") ................ 15
84 Music Hawk MH15     Walk Away/Version (12") ................ 20
*(see also John Holt)*

### LITTLE JOHN
84 Vista VSLP 4061     UNITE (LP) ................ 20

### LITTLE JOHN ANTHONY
60 Ember EMB 3302     TEENAGE DANCE PARTY (LP) ................ 20

### ALAN LITTLEJOHN BAND
62 Oriole CB 1734     Out Of The Blue/There Ain't No Sweet Man Worth The Salt Of My Tears ................ 10

### LITTLE JOHN & BILLY BOYO
82 Greensleeves GRELD 86     Bushmaster Connection/BILY BOYO: Little Girl (12") ................ 18
82 Greensleeves GRED 92     Janet Sinclair/Agony Column Dub (12") ................ 25

### LITTLE JOHNNY & THREE TEENAGERS
58 Decca F 10990     Baby Lover/Rickety Rackety Rendezvous ................ 20

### KENNY LITTLE & LITTLE PEOPLE
65 United Artists UP 1074     A Shot In The Dark/Never On A Sunday ................ 5

### LITTLE KIRK
70s Ruddys RM 004     Ghetto People Broke/Version (12") ................ 40
70s Ruddys RM 001     Weed Them Out/Version (12") ................ 50

### LITTLE LULU
72 FAB FAB 21     Love & Obey/AL CAMPBELL & FREDDIE MCGREGOR: Free Man ................ 200

### LITTLE LUMAN
64 Rio R 44     Hurry Harry/R. ALPHONSE: Hucklebuck (B-side actually by Roland Alphonso) ................ 15

### LITTLE LUTHER
64 Pye International 7N 25266   Eenie Meenie Minie Moe/Twirl ................ 70

### LITTLE MACK & BOSS SOUNDS
66 Atlantic 584 031     In The Midnight Hour/You Can't Love Me (In The Midnight Hour) ................ 25

### MARIE LITTLE
71 Argo ZFB 19     FACTORY GIRL (LP) ................ 150
73 Trailer LER 2084     MARIE LITTLE (LP) ................ 50

### LITTLE MILTON
65 Pye International 7N 25289   Blind Man/Blues In The Night ................ 15
65 Chess CRS 8013     We're Gonna Make It/Can't Hold Back The Tears ................ 20
65 Chess CRS 8013     We're Gonna Make It/Can't Hold Back The Tears (demo copy) ................ 35
65 Chess CRS 8018     Who's Cheating Who?/Ain't No Big Deal On You ................ 20
66 Sue WI 4021     Early In The Morning/Bless Your Heart (actually by Roy Milton) ................ 40
69 Chess CRS 8087     Grits Ain't Groceries/I Can't Quit You Baby ................ 25
69 Chess CRS 8100     Let's Get Together/I'll Always Love You ................ 15
72 Stax 2025 095     That's What Love Will Make You Do/I'm Living Off The Love You Give ................ 8
74 Stax STXS 2003     Behind Closed Doors/Bet You I Win ................ 8
75 Stax STA 100     If That Ain't A Reason/Mr. Mailman ................ 6

# LITTLE NELL

| | | | |
|---|---|---|---|
| 69 | Chess CRLS 4552 | GRITS AIN'T GROCERIES (LP) | 80 |
| 72 | Chess 6310 120 | GOLDEN DECADE (LP) | 15 |
| 74 | Stax STX 1013 | BLUES 'N' SOUL (LP) | 25 |

## LITTLE NELL
| | | | |
|---|---|---|---|
| 75 | A&M AMS 7351 | Do The Swim/Stilettos And Lipstick/Tropical Isle (red vinyl, p/s) | 8 |

## LITTLE RICHARD
### 78s
| | | | |
|---|---|---|---|
| 57 | London HLO 8446 | Lucille/Send Me Some Lovin' (as Little Richard & His Band) | 20 |
| 57 | London HLO 8470 | Jenny, Jenny/Miss Ann (as Little Richard & His Band) | 20 |
| 58 | London HLO 8560 | Good Golly Miss Molly/Hey-Hey-Hey-Hey | 25 |
| 58 | London HLO 8647 | Ooh! My Soul/True, Fine Mama | 30 |
| 59 | London HLU 8831 | By The Light Of The Silvery Moon/Early One Morning | 30 |
| 59 | London HLU 8868 | Kansas City/She Knows How To Rock | 50 |
| 60 | London HLU 9065 | Baby/I Got It | 90 |

### SINGLES
| | | | |
|---|---|---|---|
| 56 | London HLO 8336 | Rip It Up/Ready Teddy (gold label print) | 150 |
| 56 | London HLO 8336 | Rip It Up/Ready Teddy (later pressing with silver label print) | 30 |
| 50s | London HLO 8336 | Rip It Up/Ready Teddy (repressing, silver-top label, round centre) | 25 |
| 57 | London HLO 8366 | Long Tall Sally/Tutti Frutti (gold label print) | 125 |
| 57 | London HLO 8366 | Long Tall Sally/Tutti Frutti (later silver label print) | 40 |
| 50s | London HLO 8366 | Long Tall Sally/Tutti Frutti (repressing, silver-top label, round centre) | 20 |
| 57 | London HLO 8382 | The Girl Can't Help It/She's Got It (gold label print) | 125 |
| 57 | London HLO 8382 | The Girl Can't Help It/She's Got It (later silver label print) | 30 |
| 50s | London HLO 8382 | The Girl Can't Help It/She's Got It (repressing, silver-top label, round centre) | 20 |
| 57 | London HLO 8446 | Lucille/Send Me Some Lovin' (as Little Richard & His Band) | 30 |
| 57 | London HLO 8470 | Jenny, Jenny/Miss Ann (as Little Richard & His Band) | 30 |
| 57 | London HLO 8509 | Keep A Knockin'/Can't Believe You Wanna Leave | 30 |
| 58 | London HLO 8560 | Good Golly Miss Molly/Hey-Hey-Hey-Hey | 30 |
| 58 | London HLO 8647 | Ooh! My Soul/True, Fine Mama | 15 |
| 58 | London HLU 8770 | Baby Face/I'll Never Let You Go | 8 |
| 59 | London HLU 8831 | By The Light Of The Silvery Moon/Early One Morning | 8 |
| 59 | London HLU 8868 | Kansas City/She Knows How To Rock | 10 |

*(The above 45s were originally issued with triangular centres; later round-centres are worth around half to two-thirds these values.)*

| | | | |
|---|---|---|---|
| 60 | London HLU 9065 | Baby/I Got It | 15 |
| 61 | Mercury AMT 1165 | Joy Joy Joy (Down In My Heart)/He's Not Just A Soldier | 8 |
| 62 | Mercury AMT 1189 | He Got What He Wanted (But He Lost What He Had)/ Why Don't You Change Your Ways? | 8 |
| 63 | London HLK 9708 | Crying In The Chapel/Hole In The Wall | 8 |
| 63 | London HLK 9756 | Travelin' Shoes/It Is No Secret | 8 |
| 64 | London HL 9896 | Bama Lama Bama Loo/Annie's Back | 10 |
| 64 | Fontana TF 519 | Blueberry Hill/Cherry Red | 10 |
| 64 | Stateside SS 340 | Whole Lotta Shakin' Goin' On/Goodnight Irene | 10 |
| 64 | Mercury MF 841 | Joy, Joy, Joy (Down In My Heart)/Peace In The Valley | 10 |
| 66 | Fontana TF 652 | I Don't Know What You've Got But It's Got Me (Parts 1 & 2) | 30 |
| 66 | Stateside SS 508 | Holy Mackerel/Baby, Don'tcha Want A Man Like Me? | 20 |
| 66 | Sue WI 4001 | Without Love/Dance What You Wanna | 40 |
| 66 | Sue WI 4015 | It Ain't Watcha Do (It's The Way How You Do It)/Crossover | 40 |
| 66 | Columbia DB 7974 | Poor Dog/Well | 25 |
| 66 | Columbia DB 8058 | I Need Love/The Commandments Of Love | 20 |
| 66 | Columbia DB 8116 | Get Down With It/Rose Mary | 25 |
| 67 | Columbia DB 8240 | A Little Bit Of Something/Money | 50 |
| 67 | Columbia DB 8240 | A Little Bit Of Something/Money (DJ copy) | 75 |
| 67 | Columbia DB 8263 | I Don't Want To Discuss It/Hurry Sundown | 50 |
| 67 | Columbia DB 8263 | I Don't Want To Discuss It/Hurry Sundown (DJ copy) | 85 |
| 68 | MCA MU 1006 | She's Together/Try Some Of Mine | 10 |
| 68 | London HLU 10194 | Good Golly Miss Molly/Lucille | 10 |
| 68 | President PT 201 | Whole Lotta Shakin' Goin' On/Lawdy Miss Clawdy | 10 |
| 69 | Action ACT 4528 | Baby What Do You Want Me To Do (Parts 1 & 2) | 10 |
| 70 | Reprise RS 20907 | Dew Drop In/Freedom Blues | 10 |
| 71 | President PT 329 | Without Love/Talkin' 'Bout Soul | 5 |
| 71 | Reprise K 14124 | Green Power/Dancing In The Street | 10 |
| 72 | Reprise K 14150 | Money Is/Money Runner | 5 |

### SINGLES : EXPORT SINGLES
| | | | |
|---|---|---|---|
| 57 | London HL 7022 | Jenny, Jenny/Miss Ann (as Little Richard & His Band) | 30 |
| 58 | London HL 7049 | Ooh! My Soul/True, Fine Mama | 15 |
| 58 | London HL 7056 | Baby Face/I'll Never Let You Go | 15 |
| 59 | London HL 7074 | She Knows How To Rock/Early One Morning | 20 |
| 59 | London HL 7079 | By The Light Of The Silvery Moon/Kansas City | 20 |
| 59 | London HL 7085 | Whole Lotta Shakin' Goin' On/All Around The World | 40 |
| 68 | Decca AD 1006 | She's Together/Try Some Of Mine | 25 |

### EPs
| | | | |
|---|---|---|---|
| 57 | London RE-O 1071 | LITTLE RICHARD AND HIS BAND VOL. 1 (gold tri-centre) | 40 |
| 57 | London RE-O 1071 | LITTLE RICHARD AND HIS BAND VOL. 1 (later silver label) | 30 |
| 57 | London RE-O 1074 | LITTLE RICHARD AND HIS BAND VOL. 2 (later silver label) | 40 |
| 57 | London RE-O 1074 | LITTLE RICHARD AND HIS BAND VOL. 2 (gold tri-centre, later silver) | 20 |
| 57 | London RE-O 1103 | LITTLE RICHARD AND HIS BAND VOL. 3 | 25 |
| 57 | London RE-O 1106 | LITTLE RICHARD AND HIS BAND VOL. 4 | 25 |
| 59 | London RE-U 1208 | LITTLE RICHARD AND HIS BAND VOL. 5 | 25 |

| 60 | London RE-U 1234 | LITTLE RICHARD AND HIS BAND VOL. 6 | 30 |
| 60 | London RE-U 1235 | LITTLE RICHARD AND HIS BAND VOL. 7 | 35 |

*(The above EPs were originally issued with triangular centres; later round-centre pressings are worth between half to two thirds of these listed values.)*

| 63 | London REK 1400 | HE'S BACK | 40 |
| 64 | Vocalion VEP 170155 | MEMPHIS SLIM AND LITTLE RICHARD | 80 |
| 66 | Stateside SE 1042 | DO YOU FEEL IT | 60 |

## ALBUMS

| 57 | London HA-O 2055 | HERE'S LITTLE RICHARD (flipback, rear sleeve in gloss red) | 100 |
| 57 | London HA-O 2055 | HERE'S LITTLE RICHARD (flipback) | 50 |
| 57 | London HA-O 2055 | HERE'S LITTLE RICHARD (small flipback sleeve) | 55 |
| 57 | London HA-O 2055 | HERE'S LITTLE RICHARD (non-flipback sleeve) | 35 |
| 58 | London HA-U 2126 | LITTLE RICHARD VOL. 2 (flipback sleeve) | 75 |
| 58 | London HA-U 2126 | LITTLE RICHARD VOL. 2 (non-flipback sleeve) | 40 |
| 59 | RCA Camden CDN 125 | LITTLE RICHARD (8 tracks only; others by Buck Ram Orchestra, picture of Richard in "frame" on sleeve, brown wooden effect is first pressing) | 25 |
| 59 | London HA-U 2193 | THE FABULOUS LITTLE RICHARD (flipback sleeve) | 75 |
| 59 | London HA-U 2193 | THE FABULOUS LITTLE RICHARD (non-flipback sleeve) | 40 |
| 60 | Top Rank 25/025 | PRAY ALONG WITH LITTLE RICHARD VOL. 1: A CLOSER WALK WITH THEE (plain white sleeve, mail-order only) | 40 |
| 60 | Top Rank 25/026 | PRAY ALONG WITH LITTLE RICHARD VOL. 2: I'M QUITTING SHOW BUSINESS (plain white sleeve, mail-order only) | 80 |
| 64 | Stateside SL 10054 | SINGS GOSPEL | 25 |
| 64 | Coral LVA 9220 | COMING HOME | 25 |
| 65 | Mercury MCL 20036 | IT'S REAL | 15 |
| 65 | Fontana TL 5235 | IS BACK! | 25 |
| 67 | Columbia SX/SCX 6136 | THE EXPLOSIVE LITTLE RICHARD | 40 |
| 68 | Fontana SFL 13010 | KING OF THE GOSPEL SINGERS | 15 |
| 70 | Reprise RSLP 6406 | THE RILL THING | 15 |

*(see also Canned Heat, Sister Rosetta Tharpe, Buck Ram's Ramrocks)*

## LITTLE ROOSTERS
| 79 | Pye 7P 152 | She Cat Sister Floozie/Roostering With Intent (p/s) | 6 |
| 80 | Ami AIS 101 | That's How Strong My Love Is/Suspicious (p/s) | 6 |
| 80 | Ami AIS 107 | I Need A Witness/The Age Of Reason (p/s) | 6 |

*(see also Cocksparrer, Alison Moyet)*

## LITTLE ROY
| 69 | Crab CRAB 39 | Without My Love (actually by Roy & Joy)/WINSTON SAMUELS: Here I Come Again | 35 |
| 70 | Bullet BU 445 | Keep Trying/Version (actually by the Matadors) | 20 |
| 70 | Bullet BU 445 | Keep Trying/THE MATADORS: Version II | 15 |
| 70 | Camel CA 43 | Scrooge/In The Days Of Old | 20 |
| 70 | Camel CA 52 | Fight Them/Dreadlock | 20 |
| 70 | Camel CA 46 | You Run Come/THE LITTLE ROYS: Skank King (actually "Skank Me" by Little Roy) | 20 |
| 71 | Escort ERT 850 | Yester-Me Yester-You Yesterday/MATADOR ALL-STARS: Yes Sir | 10 |
| 71 | Punch PH 75 | Hard Fighter/COUNT OSSIE: Back To Africa Version | 12 |
| 81 | Copasetic COP 5001 | COLUMBUS SHIP (LP) | 20 |

## LITTLE ROYS
| 69 | Camel CA 36 | Bongonyah/CREATIONS: Dad Name (B-side actually "Bad Name") | 25 |
| 70 | Camel CA 42 | Gold Digger (actually by Wailing Soul)/MATADORS: The Mine | 25 |
| 70 | Camel CA 57 | Selassie Want Us Back/ROY AND JOY: Make It With You | 25 |

*(see also Little Roy, Hippy Boys)*

## LITTLE SAL WITH DANDY & SUPERBOYS
| 68 | Giant GN 19 | I'm In The Mood/I'm A Lover | 30 |

*(see also Dandy & Superboys, Superboys)*

## LITTLE SISTER
| 71 | Atlantic 2091053 | Somebody's Watching You/Stanga | 6 |

## LITTLE SISTERS
| 63 | MGM MGM 1192 | Goin' To Boston/Where Does It Lead | 7 |

## LITTLE SONNY
| 71 | Stax 2363 005 | NEW KING OF THE BLUES HARMONICA (LP) | 20 |

## LITTLE SUZIE
| 61 | Warner Bros WB 35 | Young Love/The Boy I Left Behind | 12 |

## LITTLE TONY
| 75 | RCA 2638 | Shakin' All Over/Together | 6 |

## LITTLE TONY & HIS BROTHERS
| 59 | Durium DC 16639 | Who's That Knockin'/The Beat | 25 |
| 59 | Durium DC 16657 | Four An' Twenty Thousand Kisses/Bella Marie | 20 |
| 59 | Decca F 11164 | I Can't Help It/Arrivederci Baby | 10 |
| 59 | Decca F 11169 | The Hippy Hippy Shake/Hey Little Girl | 10 |
| 59 | Decca F 11190 | Too Good/Foxy Little Mama | 8 |
| 60 | Decca F 21218 | I Love You/The Magic Of Love | 8 |
| 60 | Decca F 21223 | Princess/I Love You | 8 |
| 61 | Durium DC 16657 | Bella Marie/Four An' Twenty Thousand Kisses | 8 |
| 60 | Decca F 21247 | Teddy Girl/Kiss Me, Kiss Me | 10 |
| 66 | Durium DRS 54008 | Let Her Go/What Did I Do | 5 |
| 67 | Durium DRS 54012 | Long Is The Lonely Night/People Talk To Me About You (as Little Tony) | 5 |
| 58 | Durium U 20058 | PRESENTING LITTLE TONY AND HIS BROTHERS (EP) | 20 |

## LITTLE WALTER
| 60 | London HLM 9175 | My Babe/Blue Midnight | 50 |
| 64 | Pye International 7N 25263 | My Babe/You Better Watch Yourself | 20 |

# LITTLE WILBUR (& PLEASERS)

| 56 | London RE-U 1061 | LITTLE WALTER AND HIS JUKES (EP) | 200 |
|----|------------------|----------------------------------|-----|
| 64 | Pye Intl. NPL 28043 | LITTLE WALTER (LP) | 70 |
| 67 | Chess CRL 4529 | SUPER BLUES (LP, with Bo Diddley & Muddy Waters) | 45 |
| 68 | Marble Arch MAL 815 | LITTLE WALTER (LP, reissue) | 15 |
| 69 | Python PLP-KM 20 | LITTLE WALTER AND HIS DUKES (LP, 99 copies only) | 55 |

## LITTLE WILBUR (& PLEASERS)

| 57 | Vogue V 9091 | Plaything/I Don't Care | 500 |
|----|--------------|------------------------|-----|
| 57 | Vogue V 9091 | Plaything/I Don't Care (78) | 100 |
| 58 | Vogue V 9097 | Heart To Heart/Alone In The Night (solo) | 600 |
| 58 | Vogue V 9097 | Heart To Heart/Alone In The Night (solo) (78) | 150 |

*(see also Wilbur Whitfield)*

## LITTLE WILLIE (FRANCIS)

| 63 | Blue Beat BB 151 | Settle Down/I'm Ashamed | 12 |
|----|------------------|-------------------------|-----|

*(see also Wilbert Francis & Vibrators)*

## LITTLE WINSTON

| 79 | Crazy Lane SP 001 | Time And Time Again/Come Back Baby (no p/s) | 20 |
|----|-------------------|---------------------------------------------|-----|

## LIVELY ONES

| 63 | London HA 8082 | SURF DRUMS (LP) | 70 |
|----|----------------|-----------------|-----|
| 63 | London HA 8107 | SURF RIDER (LP, mono) | 70 |
| 63 | London SH 8107 | SURF RIDER (LP, stereo) | 85 |

## LIVELY SET

| 65 | Pye 7N 15880 | Don't Call My Name/What Kind Of Love | 6 |
|----|--------------|--------------------------------------|-----|
| 66 | Capitol CL 15472 | Let The Trumpets Sound/The Green Years | 6 |

## LIVERPOOL ECHO

| 73 | Spark | LIVERPOOL ECHO (LP) | 20 |
|----|-------|---------------------|-----|

*(see also Mandrake Paddle Steamers)*

## LIVERPOOL EXPRESS

| 76 | Warner Brothers K 56281 | TRACKS (LP) | 15 |
|----|-------------------------|-------------|-----|

## LIVERPOOL F.C.

| 78 | Logo GO 339 | Hail To The Kop/We Are Liverpool (p/s) | 5 |
|----|-------------|----------------------------------------|-----|
| 83 | Mean MEAN 102 | Liverpool We're Never Gonna Stop/Liverpool Anthem (red vinyl) | 5 |
| 77 | State STAT 50 | LIVERPOOL FOOTBALL TEAM 76/77 (EP) | 10 |
| 65 | Seddon SED 100 | EE AYE ADDIO: SEVENTY YEARS WAITING (LP) | 50 |
| 84 | Extra-Terrestrial KOP 1 | CONQUERING LIONS OF ANFIELD (LP, picture disc, gatefold sleeve, with booklet, stickers & photographs) | 25 |

## LIVERPOOL F.C. & LIVERPOOL SUPPORTERS

| 72 | Penny Farthing PEN 794 | Sing A Song For Liverpool/Liverpool, Liverpool | 8 |
|----|------------------------|------------------------------------------------|-----|

## LIVERPOOL FISHERMEN

| 71 | Mushroom 150 MR 9 | SWALLOW THE ANCHOR (LP) | 50 |
|----|-------------------|-------------------------|-----|

## LIVERPOOL SCENE

| 68 | RCA RCA 1762 | Son Son/Baby | 6 |
|----|--------------|--------------|-----|
| 69 | RCA RCA 1816 | The Woo-Woo/Love Is | 6 |
| 67 | CBS BPG 63045 | THE INCREDIBLE NEW LIVERPOOL SCENE (LP) | 40 |
| 68 | RCA SF 7995 | THE AMAZING ADVENTURES OF THE LIVERPOOL SCENE (LP) | 18 |
| 68 | RCA SF 7995 | THE AMAZING ADVENTURES OF THE LIVERPOOL SCENE (LP, unlaminated cover) | 18 |
| 69 | RCA SF 8057 | BREAD ON THE NIGHT (LP) | 18 |
| 70 | RCA SF 8100 | ST. ADRIAN AND CO. BROADWAY & 3RD (LP) | 18 |
| 70 | RCA SF 8134 | HEIRLOON (LP) | 18 |

*(see also Clayton Squares, Adrian Henri, Brian Patten, Mike Hart, Andy Roberts, Grimms)*

## LIVERPOOL SPINNERS

| 61 | Topic TOP 69 | SONGS SPUN IN LIVERPOOL (EP) | 10 |
|----|--------------|------------------------------|-----|

*(see also Spinners [U.K.])*

## LIVES OF ANGELS

| 86 | Fire FIRE LP 2 | ELEVATOR TO EDEN (LP) | 45 |
|----|----------------|-----------------------|-----|

## RICKY LIVID & TONE DEAFS

| 64 | Parlophone R 5136 | Tomorrow/Nuts And Bolts | 8 |
|----|-------------------|-------------------------|-----|

*(see also Bill Oddie)*

## LIVING DAYLIGHTS

| 67 | Philips BF 1561 | Let's Live For Today/I'm Real (B-side actually titled "It's Real") | 30 |
|----|-----------------|-------------------------------------------------------------------|-----|
| 79 | E.S.R. S/79/CUS 523 | HEARTSTOP EP (Personality Changes/Outdoor Girl/Don't Fit/Let Me Know (33 rpm, die-cut p/s, also listed as ESR 3) | 45 |
| 67 | Philips BF 1613 | Always With Him/Baila Maria | 40 |

*(see also Greatest Show On Earth, Naturals)*

## LIVING FORCE

| 84 | Chapter 1 SCH 161 | Ride Ride Ride/Some People | 20 |
|----|-------------------|----------------------------|-----|

## LIVING INTENTS

| 81 | Powerful Pierre PPP 01 | (All The) Nice Boys/Genine/Said It's So (p/s) | 20 |
|----|------------------------|-----------------------------------------------|-----|

## CARLTON LIVINGSTONE

| 84 | Greensleeves GRED 144 | 100 Weights Of Collie Weed/Soundman Clash (12") | 12 |
|----|-----------------------|-------------------------------------------------|-----|

## DANDY LIVINGSTONE

| 72 | Horse HOSS 16 | Suzanne Beware Of The Devil/Right On Brother | 6 |
|----|---------------|----------------------------------------------|-----|
| 79 | More Cuts RIC 109 | Instant Music/Living In Sus | 8 |
| 70s | Night Owl NOR 5002 | Calling Africa/Yee Fre Afrikafo Nde | 25 |
| 80 | Mint Music MMD2 | Fever/Righteous Man (12") | 40 |
| 81 | Trojan TMX 4008 | RUDY, A MESSAGE TO YOU (EP, p/s) | 15 |

## J C LIVINGSTONE

| 73 | Penny Farthing Pen 808 | Let's Spend The Summer Together/Viva La Eva | 6 |
|----|------------------------|---------------------------------------------|-----|

| | | |
|---|---|---|
| 73 | Penny Farthing Pen 824 | Momma Was A Steamroller Lady/OO La La Me .................................................. 15 |

**R D LIVINGSTONE**
76　B&C CB 291　　Roots Man/Mo' Roots .................................................................................. 10

**LIVIN STONES**
65　Oak　　I Can't Hold Out/The Music Played On (acetate only) ................................. 50

**LIZA & JET SET**
65　Parlophone R 5248　　How Can I Know?/Dancing Yet ................................................................. 15
*(see also Liza Strike)*

**LIZZARD**
76　Attack ATT 8130　　Fight Down/Jah Jah Bless I .......................................................................... 10
76　Black Wax WAX 14　　Satta I/I And Eye (p/s as Lizard) ............................................................... 25
76　Trojan TRLS 138　　SATTA (LP) ..................................................................................................... 30

**LIZZIE & DELROY WILSON**
71　Jackpot JP 771　　Double Attack/AGGRAVATORS: The Sniper ............................................... 20

**LIZZY**
70　Harry J HJ 6625　　More Heartaches/HARRY J ALL STARS: Version .................................. 20
70　Pressure Beat PB 5508　　Ten Feet Tall (actually "Wear You From The Ball"/JOE GIBBS & DESTROYERS: Chapter (actually "Harmony Hall" by Mr Nigel) ........................................ 15
73　Duke DU 161　　Love Is A Treasure/FREDDIE McKAY: Love Is A Treasure ..................... 20

**LIZZY & DENNIS (ALCAPONE)**
70　Ackee ACK 114　　Happy Go Lucky Girl/BOBBY & DAVE: Sammy .................................... 20

**LIZZY & PARAGONS**
71　Ackee ACK 118　　On The Beach/DAVE BARKER: Maria ...................................................... 30

**LJ IV**
69　CBS 63512　　AN ELIZABETHAN SONGBOOK (LP) ....................................................... 125
*(see also London Jazz Four)*

**LLAN**
66　CBS 202405　　Realise/Anytime ...................................................................................... 40
*(see also Vogues)*

**BARRY LLEWELLYN**
73　Downtown DT 515　　Meaning Of Life/MORWELL ESQ: Version Of Life ............................ 25
*(see also Heptones, Sound Dimension)*

**A.L. LLOYD**
62　Topic TOP 71　　A.L. LLOYD EWAN MACCOLL (EP) .......................................................... 12
57　Topic T7　　A.L. LLOYD EWAN MACCOLL (10" LP with insert) ............................... 30
57　Topic T8　　THE BLACK BALL LINE (8" EP, insert, with Ewan MaCColl) ............. 25
60　Topic 12T 51　　OUTBACK BALLADS (LP, blue label) ...................................................... 40
64　Topic 12T 103　　ENGLISH AND SCOTTISH FOLK BALLADS (LP, with Ewan MacColl, with blue label & booklet) ................................................................. 30
64　Topic 12T 103　　ENGLISH AND SCOTTISH FOLK BALLADS (LP, with Ewan MacColl) ...... 20
65　Topic 12T 135　　BIRD IN THE BUSH (LP, with Anne Briggs & Frankie Armstrong, blue label) ..... 60
66　Topic 12T 118　　FIRST PERSON (LP, blue label) .............................................................. 30
67　Topic 12T 174　　LEVIATHAN! (LP, blue label with booklet) ........................................... 35
*(see also Frankie Armstrong, Anne Briggs)*

**A.L. LLOYD & MARTYN WYNDHAM-READ**
71　Topic 12TS 203　　THE GREAT AUSTRALIAN LEGEND (LP, blue label with booklet) ........... 65
*(see also Ewan MacColl, Peggy Seeger, Martin Wyndham-Read)*

**LLOYD ALEXANDER REAL ESTATE**
67　President PT 157　　Whatcha Gonna Do/Gonna Live Again .................................................. 100

**LLOYD & BARBARA**
73　Grape GR 3045　　Dear Lonely Hearts/LLOYD BANTAM: I Tried To Love You ................... 6

**LLOYD & CAREY WITH G.G. ALL STARS**
72　Attack ATT 8029　　Scorpion/MAYTONES: Hands And Feet ................................................. 10
*(see also Carey & Lloyd, Pat Satchmo)*

**LLOYD & CLAUDETTE**
70　Big Shot BI 546　　Queen Of The World/PROPHETS: Top Of The World ........................... 50

**LLOYD (ROBINSON) & DEVON (RUSSELL)**
69　Punch PH 14　　Love Is The Key/VIRTUES: High Tide .................................................... 30
69　Blue Cat BS 151　　Out Of The Fire/Can't Understand (B-side actually by Austin Faithful) ..... 100
*(see also Cobbs, Derrick Morgan)*

**LLOYD & DOREEN**
71　Jackpot JP 762　　Midnight/BUNNY LEE'S ALL STARS: Midnight - Version ...................... 7
*(see also Lloyd Clarke/Doreen Shaeffer)*

**LLOYD (ROBINSON) & GLEN (BROWN)**
67　Coxsone CS 7011　　That Girl/You Got Me Wrong ............................................................... 200
67　Doctor Bird DB 1058　　Jezebel/TOMMY McCOOK & SUPERSONICS: Jam Session .................. 45
67　Doctor Bird DB 1071　　Keep On Pushing/BOBBY AITKEN & CARIBBEATS: You Won't Regret (B-side actually by Lloyd & Glen) .......................................... 60
67　Doctor Bird DB 1099　　Feel Good Now/What You've Got .......................................................... 40
68　Doctor Bird DB 1105　　Successful Man/I'll Give You Love ........................................................ 60

**LLOYD (JACKSON) & GROOVERS**
67　Caltone TONE 108　　Do It To Me Baby/DIPLOMATS: Meet Me At The Corner ...................... 50
68　Caltone TONE 109　　My Heart My Soul/DIPLOMATS with TOMMY McCOOK & SUPERSONICS: Going Along . 60
68　Caltone TONE 112　　Listen To The Music/DIPLOMATS: Strong Man ................................... 60
*(see also Groovers, Don Lett)*

**LLOYD & JOHNNY**
68　Island WI 3158　　My Argument (actually by Lloyd Terrell)/JOHNNY MELODY: Foey Man (actually by George Dekker) ..................................................... 300

# LLOYD & KEN

MINT VALUE £

(see also Lloyd Terrell)

### LLOYD & KEN
72    Punch PH 110            Have I Sinned/Version ...................................................................................... 10

(see also Lloyd Charmers/Ken Boothe)

### LLOYD & LARRY
71    New Beat NB 080        Monkey Spanner/LLOYD & LARRY'S ALL STARS: Version ............................... 20

### LLOYD & THE PROPHETS
70    Big Shot BI 553        Bush Beat/PATRICK & PROPHETS: Please Come Come ............................... 20
70    Big Shot BI 556        Jaco/Soul Reggae ......................................................................................... 20

(see also Prophets [Jamaica], Patrick & Lloyd)

### CHARLES LLOYD (QUARTET)
67    Atlantic 584 125       Sombrero Sam (Parts 1 & 2) ............................................................................ 6
66    Atlantic 588025        DREAMWEAVER (LP) ..................................................................................... 20
67    Atlantic 587/588 077   LOVE-IN (LP) ................................................................................................ 20
68    Atlantic 587/588 101   JOURNEY WITHIN (LP) .................................................................................. 20
68    Atlantic 588 108       IN EUROPE (LP) ............................................................................................ 15
70    MCA MUPS 421          MOON MAN (LP) .......................................................................................... 15
71    Atlantic 2400 108      IN THE SOVIET UNION (LP) ........................................................................... 20

### LLOYD, DICE & THE BARRISTER
70    Joe JRS 14             Appeal Of Pama Dice/BOSS ALL STARS: Young And Strong Version 2 ............ 20

### LLOYD, DICE & HIS MUM
70    Joe JRS 5              Trial Of Pama Dice/NYAH SHUFFLE: Jughead Returns Version 1 .................... 25
72    Sioux SI 022           Trial Of Pama Dice/Lonely Man (reissue) ...................................................... 15

### FRED LLOYD
65    Polydor BM 56055       Girl From Chelsea/You Kissed Him ................................................................ 8

### IAN LLOYD
74    Kama Sutra KSS 702     Another Love/THE STORIES: Love Is In Motion ............................................. 6

### JIMMY LLOYD
58    Philips PB 795         The Prince Of Players/Ever Since I Met Lucy ............................................... 10
58    Philips PB 827         Witch Doctor/For Your Love .......................................................................... 8
58    Philips PB 871         The End/Street In The Rain ............................................................................ 6
59    Philips PB 909         I Kneel At Your Throne/Sapphire ................................................................. 10
59    Philips PB 978         That's Why I Dream/Take A Giant Step ......................................................... 10
60    Philips PB 1010        Teenage Sonata/Falling ............................................................................... 10
60    Philips PB 1055        I Double Dare You/Just For A Thrill ............................................................... 8
61    Philips PB 1120        Pony Time/Three Handed Woman ................................................................ 10
61    Philips PB 1201        I'm Coming Home/You Are My Sunshine ...................................................... 5
62    Philips 326 527 BF     True Love/Mother Nature And Father Time ................................................... 5
63    Philips 326 568 BF     Call On Me/Humma Humma Humma Humming Bird ..................................... 5
59    Philips BBE 12186      FOCUS ON JIMMY LLOYD (EP) ..................................................................... 12
62    Philips BBE 12509      YOU ARE MY SUNSHINE (EP) ...................................................................... 12

### LLOYD & JOY
71    Explosion EX 2047      Back To Africa (actually by Alton Ellis)/Born To Lose ................................. 15

### KATHY LLOYD
54    Decca F 10386          It Worries Me/Tomorrow Night ..................................................................... 5
54    Decca F 10418          Teach Me Tonight/It's A Woman's World ...................................................... 5
55    Decca F 10464          Our Future Has Only Begun/Unsuspecting Heart .......................................... 5
55    Decca F 10567          Experience Unnecessary/This Must Be Wrong (with Ted Heath Music) ........ 5

### LLOYD (CAMPBELL) THE MATADOR
72    Sioux SI 010           The Train/Julia Sees Me (Exodus) ................................................................ 50

### RUE LLOYD
72    Green Door GD 4033     Loving You/Version ........................................................................................ 8
72    Green Door GD 4036     Cheer Up/Version .......................................................................................... 8

(see also Joe White)

### TREVOR LLOYD
70    Explosion EX 2018      Chinee Brush/DICE & CUMMIE: Real Colley .............................................. 40
70    Explosion EX 2019      Give Me Back Your Love/Hold Me ............................................................... 20

### ANDY LLOYD
78    Ariola/Hansa AHA 519   Back To School/It's Up To You ..................................................................... 12

### LLOYDIE & LOWBITES
73    Harry J HJ 6660        Pussy Cat/Skanky Pussy ............................................................................... 10
71    Lowbite LOW 001        CENSORED! (LP, green/silver label) ............................................................. 40

(see also Lloyd Tyrell/Charmers)

### LLOYD'S ALLSTARS
69    Doctor Bird DB 1178    Love Kiss Blue/UNIQUES: Secretly ............................................................. 80

(see also Justins, U Roy Junior, Jimmy Green, Victors)

### ELERI LLWYD
72    Cambrian CSP 730       Mae Bywyd Yn Galed/Breuddwyn (p/s) ......................................................... 8
77    Sain 1073              AM HEDDIW MAE NGHAN (LP) ..................................................................... 25

### LLYGOD FFYRNIG
78    Pwdwr PWDWR 1          N.C.B./Sais/Cariad Y Bus Stop (p/s, white rubber stamped labels) ............ 100
78    Pwdwr PWDWR 1          N.C.B./Sais/Cariad Y Bus Stop (p/s, printed green labels) ......................... 150

### LOADED FORTY-FOURS
81    X-S TL 44/1            Thunderbirds (Are Go!)/T.V. Child (p/s) ........................................................ 5

### DICKIE LOADER
61    Palette PG 9015        Heatwave/Happiness .................................................................................... 20

## RUSS LOADER
| | | | |
|---|---|---|---|
| 65 | Columbia DB 7522 | When Your Heart Is Broken/That Girl Of Mine (with Breakaways Orchestra) | 10 |
| 65 | Columbia DB 7643 | Just Lies/Mona Lisa | 8 |
| 65 | Columbia DB 7696 | Count The Stars/Triyng Too Hard (with Ladybirds) | 10 |
| 66 | Columbia DB 7839 | Too Soon/Just A Little Step To Heaven | 10 |
| 69 | Conquest CXT 2 | Just Lies/Take Me Tonight | 5 |

*(see also Mark Wirtz)*

## LOBO
| | | | |
|---|---|---|---|
| 71 | Phillips 6073 802 | She Didn't Do Magic/I'm The Only One | 6 |

## EDU LOBO
| | | | |
|---|---|---|---|
| 71 | A&M AMLS63035 | SERGIO MENDES PRESENTS (LP) | 20 |

## LOCAL HEROES
| | | | |
|---|---|---|---|
| 80 | Junior Records | Blast The Pop!/Tomorrow (p/s) | 50 |

## LOCKETS
| | | | |
|---|---|---|---|
| 63 | Pye International 7N 25232 | Don't Cha Know/Little Boy | 40 |

## LOCKJAW
| | | | |
|---|---|---|---|
| 77 | Raw RAW 8 | Radio Call Sign/The Young Ones (p/s) | 20 |
| 78 | Raw RAW 19 | Journalist Jive/I'm A Virgin/A Doonga Doonga (p/s, beware of counterfeits) | 100 |

*(see also the Cure)*

## GERRY LOCKRAN
| | | | |
|---|---|---|---|
| 69 | Decca F 12873 | Hey Jude/This Train | 6 |
| 69 | Decca F 12919 | Standing On Your Own/You're Not There | 20 |
| 67 | Planet PLL 1002 | HOLD ON, I'M COMING (LP) | 150 |
| 68 | Waverley ZLP 2091 | BLUES VENDETTA (LP) | 60 |
| 69 | Spark SRLP 104 | THE ESSENTIAL GERRY LOCKRAN (LP) | 50 |
| 72 | Polydor 2383 122 | WUN (LP) | 60 |
| 76 | Decca SKL-R 5257 | RAGS TO GLADRAGS (LP) | 40 |
| 80 | BML 2536 | ACROSS THE TRACKS (LP) | 15 |

## ANNA LOCKWOOD
| | | | |
|---|---|---|---|
| 70 | Tangent TGS 104 | THE GLASS WORLD OF ANNA LOCKWOOD (LP) | 40 |

## MALCOLM LOCKYER ORCHESTRA
| | | | |
|---|---|---|---|
| 61 | HMV POP 929 | The Pursuers T.V. Theme/Stranger Than Fiction | 10 |
| 65 | Columbia DB 7552 | The Intelligence Men/Brighton Run | 20 |
| 65 | Columbia DB 7663 | The Eccentric Dr. Who/Daleks And Thals | 60 |

## LOCOMOTIVE
| | | | |
|---|---|---|---|
| 67 | Direction 58-3814 | Rudy A Message To You/Broken Heart | 25 |
| 68 | Parlophone R 5718 | Rudi's In Love/Never Set Me Free | 20 |
| 69 | Parlophone R 5758 | Mr. Armageddon/There's Got To Be A Way (in promos p/s) | 30 |
| 69 | Parlophone R 5758 | Mr. Armageddon/There's Got To Be A Way | 15 |
| 69 | Parlophone R 5801 | I'm Never Gonna Let You Go/You Must Be Joking | 20 |
| 70 | Parlophone R 5835 | Movin' Down The Line/Roll Over Mary | 10 |
| 71 | Parlophone R 5915 | Rudi's In Love/You Must Be Joking | 20 |
| 69 | Parlophone PCS 7093 | WE ARE EVERYTHING YOU SEE (LP, laminated front sleeve) | 1000 |
| 95 | Shoestring BL004 | WE ARE EVERYTHING YOU SEE (CD reissue) | 25 |

*(see also Norman Haines Band, Dog That Bit People, Steam-Shovel)*

## LOCOMOTIVE GT
| | | | |
|---|---|---|---|
| 74 | Epic EPC 80229 | LOCOMOTIVE GT (LP) | 15 |

## LOEFAH
| | | | |
|---|---|---|---|
| 04 | Big Apple BAM 006 | Jungle Infiltrator/Jazz Lick/Indian Dub/Life Dub (12") | 60 |
| 05 | DMZ DMZ 006 | Root/The Goat Stare (12") | 40 |
| 05 | Tectonic TEC 003 | 28g/Fearless (12") | 15 |
| 06 | DMZ DMZ 009 | Mud/Rufage (12") | 50 |
| 06 | Six Six Slx 001 | Voodoo/Voodoo (Omen Mix) | 25 |
| 06 | Tectonic TEC 008 | System/DIGITAL MYSTIKZ: Molten (10") | 30 |

## LOFT
| | | | |
|---|---|---|---|
| 84 | Creation CRE 009 | Why Does The Rain/Like (foldaround p/s in poly bag) | 15 |
| 85 | Creation CRE 015 | Up The Hill And Down The Slope/Lonely Street (foldaround p/s in poly bag) | 10 |
| 06 | Static Caravan VAN 116 | Model Village/Rickety Frame (p/s) | 6 |

*(see also Weather Prophets, Wishing Stones)*

## CRIPPLE CLARENCE LOFTON
| | | | |
|---|---|---|---|
| 59 | Vogue EPV 1209 | CRIPPLE CLARENCE LOFTON (EP) | 50 |
| 54 | London AL 3531 | A LOST RECORDING DATE (10" LP) | 50 |
| 55 | Vogue LDE 122 | JAZZ IMMORTALS NO. 1 (10" LP) | 50 |

## LOFTUS ROADRUNNERS
| | | | |
|---|---|---|---|
| 77 | QPR QPR 1 | Queens Park Rangers/Drive Me Down To QPR | 10 |

## LORA LOGIC
| | | | |
|---|---|---|---|
| 81 | Rough Trade RT 087 | Wonderful Offer/Stereo | 6 |

*(see also Essential Logic)*

## LOGIC
| | | | |
|---|---|---|---|
| 83 | Okey Doke LOGIC 03 | Pied Piper/Backstabber | 20 |
| 83 | Okey DokeLOGIG 01 OD 3 | Hi Ho Hi Ho/Never Break My Love | 40 |

## LOGIC CONTROL MCS
| | | | |
|---|---|---|---|
| 90 | Conscious CONN2 | High Pursuit/Gangster Trip (12") | 12 |

## LOG 10
| | | | |
|---|---|---|---|
| 83 | Sonic SR 77 | In The Dark/Dark Step Dub (p/s, with insert) | 25 |
| 84 | Sonic SR 78 | You're Not There/Freefall (die-cut sleeve) | 20 |

**L.O.K.**
| | | | |
|---|---|---|---|
| 79 | Fetish FET 001 | Fun House/Starlet Love/Tell Me (p/s) | 7 |

**LOLITA**
| | | | |
|---|---|---|---|
| 60 | Polydor NH 66818 | Sailor (Your Home Is The Sea)/La Luna (Quanda La Luna) | 10 |

**LOLLIPOP SHOP**
| | | | |
|---|---|---|---|
| 85 | Big Beat WIK36 | JUST COLOUR (LP) | 15 |

**LOLLIPOPS**
| | | | |
|---|---|---|---|
| 71 | Atlantic 2091 114 | Nothing's Gonna Stop Our Love/I Believe In Love | 10 |

**LAURIE LOMAN**
| | | | |
|---|---|---|---|
| 54 | London HL 8101 | Whither Thou Goest/I Was The Last One To Know (gold triangular centre) | 50 |

**ALAN LOMAX (& RAMBLERS)**
| | | | |
|---|---|---|---|
| 56 | Decca F 10787 | Dirty Old Town/Hard Case (as Alan Lomax & Ramblers) | 10 |
| 56 | Decca DFE 6367 | OH LULA (EP) | 10 |
| 58 | Pye Jazz NJE 1055 | SINGS (EP, with Dave Lee's Bandits) | 12 |
| 58 | Pye Jazz NJE 1062 | MURDERER'S HOME PT. 1 (EP) | 12 |
| 58 | Pye Jazz NJE 1063 | MURDERER'S HOME PT. 2 (EP) | 12 |
| 58 | Pye Jazz NJE 1064 | MURDERER'S HOME PT. 3 (EP) | 12 |
| 58 | Pye Jazz NJE 1065 | MURDERER'S HOME PT. 4 (EP) | 12 |
| 59 | Melodisc EPM7 88 | SONGS FROM TEXAS (EP) | 15 |
| 57 | Nixa Jazz NJL 8 | PRESENTS BLUES IN THE MISSISSIPPI NIGHT (LP, with others + insert) | 15 |
| 57 | Nixa Jazz NJL 11 | MURDERER'S HOME (LP) | 15 |
| 58 | HMV CLP 1192 | GREAT AMERICAN BALLADS (LP, with Alexis Korner & Guy Carawan) | 25 |

**LOMAX ALLIANCE**
| | | | |
|---|---|---|---|
| 67 | CBS 2729 | Try As You May/See The People | 50 |

*(see also Jackie Lomax)*

**JACKIE LOMAX**
| | | | |
|---|---|---|---|
| 68 | CBS 2554 | Genuine Imitation Life/One Minute Woman | 20 |
| 68 | Apple APPLE 3 | Sour Milk Sea/The Eagle Laughs At You | 35 |
| 69 | Apple APPLE 11 | New Day/I Fall Inside Your Eyes | 15 |
| 70 | Apple APPLE 23 | How The Web Was Woven/Thumbin' A Ride (in p/s) | 30 |
| 70 | Apple APPLE 23 | How The Web Was Woven/Thumbin' A Ride | 15 |
| 69 | Apple APCOR 6 | IS THIS WHAT YOU WANT (LP, with inner sleeve, mono) | 125 |
| 69 | Apple (S)APCOR 6 | IS THIS WHAT YOU WANT (LP, with inner sleeve, stereo) | 80 |
| 91 | Apple SAPCOR 6 | IS THIS WHAT YOU WANT (LP, reissue, gatefold sleeve with bonus 12" [SAPCOR 62]) | 25 |

*(see also Lomax Alliance, Undertakers, Takers, Heavy Jelly, Badger)*

**AL LOMBARDY & HIS ORCHESTRA**
| | | | |
|---|---|---|---|
| 54 | London HL 8076 | The Blues/The Boogie | 40 |
| 55 | London HL 8127 | In A Little Spanish Town/Flying Home | 20 |

**LONDON**
| | | | |
|---|---|---|---|
| 78 | MCA MCF 2823 | ANIMAL GAMES (LP) | 15 |

**EDDIE LONDON & CHIMES**
| | | | |
|---|---|---|---|
| 57 | Decca F 10859 | Song Of The Moonlight/I'll Thank You | 5 |

**JIMMY LONDON**
| | | | |
|---|---|---|---|
| 71 | Randy's RAN 514 | Shake A Hand/CARL MURPHY: Lick I Pipe | 6 |
| 71 | Randy's RAN 517 | Bridge Over Troubled Waters/RANDY'S ALLSTARS: War | 20 |
| 71 | Randy's RAN 518 | Hip Hip Hooray/IMPACT ALLSTARS: Version | 5 |
| 71 | Randy's RAN 520 | A Little Love/IMPACT ALLSTARS: Version | 8 |
| 72 | Randy's RAN 521 | It's Now Or Never/IMPACT ALLSTARS: Version | 5 |
| 72 | Randy's RAN 527 | Jamaica Festival '72 (with Rocking Horse)/IMPACT ALLSTARS: Version | 5 |
| 73 | Explosion EX 2080 | I'll Never Find Another You/IMPACT ALLSTARS: Version | 5 |
| 73 | Dragon DRA 1010 | Jennie/I Wonder If I Care As Much (as Jimmi London) | 5 |
| 74 | Dragon DRA 1019 | No Letter Today/The Road Is Rough | 5 |
| 74 | Ackee ACK 531 | Till I Kiss You/Version | 5 |
| 75 | Black Wax WAX 4 | Am I That Easy To Forget/100 Years Of Dub | 8 |
| 72 | Trojan TRL 39 | BRIDGE OVER TROUBLED WATERS (LP) | 30 |
| 78 | Burning Sounds BS 1016 | WELCOME TO MY WORLD (LP) | 18 |
| 79 | Jama JALP 003 | JIMMY IN LONDON (LP) | 35 |
| 80 | JB JBLP 03 | CHILDREN CRYING IN THE GHETTO (LP) | 15 |

*(see also Jimmy Green, The Inspirations)*

**JOE LONDON**
| | | | |
|---|---|---|---|
| 59 | London HLW 9008 | Lonesome Whistle/It Might Have Been | 15 |

**JULIE LONDON**

**SINGLES**
| | | | |
|---|---|---|---|
| 56 | London HLU 8240 | Cry Me A River/S'Wonderful (gold label print) | 80 |
| 56 | London HLU 8240 | Cry Me A River/S'Wonderful (later silver label print) | 20 |
| 56 | London HLU 8279 | Baby, Baby All The Time/Shadow Woman (gold label print) | 40 |
| 57 | London HLU 8394 | The Meaning Of The Blues/Now! Baby, Now! (gold label print) | 30 |
| 57 | London HLU 8394 | The Meaning Of The Blues/Now! Baby, Now! (later silver label print) | 15 |
| 57 | London HLU 8414 | The Boy On A Dolphin/Tall Boy | 10 |
| 58 | London HLU 8602 | Saddle The Wind/It Had To Be You | 10 |
| 58 | London HLU 8657 | My Strange Affair/It's Easy | 10 |

**EPs**
| | | | |
|---|---|---|---|
| 57 | London RE-U 1076 | JULIE SINGS FILM SONGS (gold label print) | 20 |
| 57 | London RE-N 1092 | LONDON'S GIRL FRIENDS VOL. 1 | 20 |
| 58 | London RE-U 1151 | MAKE LOVE TO ME - PART ONE | 10 |
| 58 | London RE-U 1152 | MAKE LOVE TO ME - PART TWO | 10 |
| 58 | London RE-U 1153 | MAKE LOVE TO ME - PART THREE | 10 |

| 59 | London RE-U 1180 | JULIE - PART ONE | 10 |
| 59 | London RE-U 1181 | JULIE - PART TWO | 10 |
| 59 | London RE-U 1182 | JULIE - PART THREE | 10 |
| 63 | Liberty LEP 2103 | DESAFINADO | 10 |
| 66 | Liberty LEP 2260 | ALL THROUGH THE NIGHT | 10 |

## ALBUMS

| 56 | London HA-U 2005 | JULIE IS HER NAME | 30 |
| 57 | London HA-U 2038 | CALENDAR GIRL | 30 |
| 58 | London HA-U 2083 | MAKE LOVE TO ME | 30 |
| 58 | London HA-U 2091 | ABOUT THE BLUES | 30 |
| 58 | London HA-U 2112 | JULIE | 30 |
| 59 | London HA-U 2171 | LONDON BY NIGHT | 25 |
| 59 | London HA-U 2186 | JULIE IS HER NAME VOL. 2 (also stereo SAH-U 6042) | 30 |
| 60 | London HA-W 2225 | SWING ME AN OLD SONG | 20 |
| 60 | London HA-W 2229 | YOUR NUMBER PLEASE | 25 |
| 60 | London HA-G 2280 | JULIE AT HOME (mono) | 18 |
| 60 | London SAH-G 6097 | JULIE AT HOME (stereo) | 20 |
| 61 | London HA-G 2299 | AROUND MIDNIGHT | 20 |
| 61 | London HA-G 2353 | SEND FOR ME (mono) | 18 |
| 61 | London SAH-G 6154 | SEND FOR ME (stereo) | 20 |
| 62 | London HA-G 2405 | WHATEVER JULIE WANTS (mono) | 18 |
| 62 | London SAH-G 6205) | WHATEVER JULIE WANTS (stereo) | 20 |
| 63 | Liberty (S)LBY 1113 | LOVE ON THE ROCKS | 15 |
| 63 | Liberty (S)LBY 1136 | SINGS LATIN IN A SATIN MOOD | 15 |
| 67 | Liberty (S)LBY 1364 | NICE GIRLS DON'T STAY FOR BREAKFAST | 15 |

## LAURIE LONDON

| 57 | Parlophone R 4359 | He's Got The Whole World In His Hands/The Cradle Rock | 8 |
| 57 | Parlophone R 4388 | Handed Down/She Sells Sea Shells | 5 |
| 58 | Parlophone R 4408 | The Gospel Train/Boomerang | 5 |
| 58 | Parlophone R 4426 | I Gotta Robe/Casey Jones | 5 |
| 58 | Parlophone R 4450 | Basin Street Blues/Joshua (Fit The Battle Of Jericho) | 5 |
| 58 | Parlophone R 4474 | My Mother/Darktown Strutters' Ball | 5 |
| 58 | Parlophone R 4499 | Up Above My Head/Three O'Clock | 7 |
| 59 | Parlophone R 4557 | Pretty-Eyed Baby (with Gitte)/Boom-Ladda-Boom-Boom | 8 |
| 59 | Parlophone R 4601 | Old Time Religion/God's Little Acre | 5 |
| 60 | Parlophone R 4662 | Banjo Boy/Hear Them Bells | 7 |
| 61 | Parlophone R 4747 | Todays Teardrops/Darling Sue | 8 |
| 57 | Parlophone GEP 8664 | LAURIE LONDON (EP) | 10 |
| 58 | Parlophone GEP 8689 | LITTLE LAURIE LONDON No. 2 (EP) | 20 |

## MARK LONDON

| 65 | Pye 7N 15825 | Stranger In The World/Moanin' | 15 |

## MICHAEL LONDON

| 62 | HMV POP 1026 | Miracles Sometimes Happen/Stranger On The Shore (with Acker Bilk) | 8 |
| 62 | HMV POP 1085 | Mutiny On The Bounty Love Song/For The Very Young | 5 |

## PETER LONDON

| 65 | Pye 7N 15957 | Bless You/Baby I Like The Look Of You | 50 |

*(see also Peter Cook)*

## LONDONAIRES

| 66 | Decca F12379 | Dearest Emma/Bugles A Go-Go | 15 |

## LONDON & BRIDGES

| 66 | CBS 202056 | It Just Ain't Right/Leave Her Alone | 40 |

## LONDON FUNK ALLSTARS

| 96 | Ninja Tune ZEN 24 | FLESH EATING DISCO ZOMBIES VERSUS THE BIONIC HOOKERS FROM MARS (3xLP) | 30 |

## LONDON HOSPITAL

| 60s | Private Pressing WAD 9-1 | LONDON HOSPITAL CHRISTMAS FACTOR (EP) | 60 |

## LONDON JAZZ CHAMBER GROUP

| 72 | Ember CJS 823 | ADAM'S RIB SUITE (LP) | 20 |

*(see also Ken Moule's London Jazz Chamber Group, Ken Moule Seven)*

## LONDON JAZZ COMPOSERS ORCHESTRA

| 70s | Incus 7 | ODE (LP, with insert) | 50 |

## LONDON JAZZ FOUR

| 66 | Polydor 56092 | Norwegian Wood/I Feel Fine | 25 |
| 67 | Polydor 56214 | It Strikes A Chord/Song For Hilary | 30 |
| 67 | Polydor 582 005 | TAKE A NEW LOOK AT THE BEATLES (LP) | 60 |

*(see also London Jazz Quartet, LJ IV)*

## LONDON JAZZ QUARTET

| 60 | Tempo TAP 28 | LONDON JAZZ QUARTET (LP, with Tubby Hayes & Tony Crombie) | 350 |
| 60s | Ember EMB 3306 | LONDON JAZZ QUARTET (LP) | 150 |

*(see also London Jazz Four, Tubby Hayes, Tony Crombie)*

## LONDON POPS ORCHESTRA

| 68 | Pye 7N 17630 | Eleanor Rigby/If I Only Had Time | 6 |

## LONDON POSSE

| 88 | Justice JT003 | Money Mad (12") | 25 |
| 87 | Big Life BLR2T | London Posse/My Beatbox Reggae Style (12") | 15 |
| 96 | Bullet BULT 5 | Style (12") | 10 |

*(see also Rodney P)*

## LONDON PX

MINT VALUE £

### LONDON PX
| 80 | New Puritan NP 1 | Orders/Eviction (p/s) | 25 |
| 82 | Terrapyn SYD 1 | Arnold Layne/Indian Summer (1-sided flexidisc) | 12 |

### LONDON STRING CHORALE
| 72 | Polydor 2058 280 | Galloping Home/Vicky | 6 |

### LONDON STUDIO GROUP
| 66 | De Wolfe DW/LP 2974 | THE WILD ONE (10" LP, tricolour label) | 60 |

*(see also Ivor & Basil Kirchen Band)*

### LONDON UNDERGROUND
| 81 | Situation Two SIT 9 | Train Of Though/All Too Many (p/s) | 6 |
| 83 | On-U Sound LP 22 | AT HOME WITH THE LONDON UNDERGROUND (LP) | 20 |

### LONDON WAITS
| 66 | Immediate IM 030 | Softly Softly/Serenadio | 30 |

### LONDON ZOO
| 80 | Gramaphone STB 80 | Who's Driving This Car?/You And Your Great Ideas (stamped white labels, no p/s) | 6 |
| 80 | Zoom ZUM 12 | Receiving End/London Zoo (p/s) | 5 |

### LONE ARCHER
| 74 | Strand ST11 | I'll Come To You/Glass Web | 15 |

### LONE PIGEON
| 01 | Sketchbook SKETCH 001 | CONCUBINE RICE (LP) | 25 |
| 10 | Domino REWIGCD77X | TIME CAPSULE (7-CD box set) | 35 |

*(see also Beta Band)*

### LONE RANGER
| 79 | Island WIPDJ 6517 | Barnabus Collins/Dub Part 2 | 8 |
| 82 | Greensleeves GRED 85 | Johnny Make You Bad So/TAXI GANG: Outside Right (12") | 12 |

### LONE WOLF (1)
| 80 | Wolf Music LW 001 | Cash For Candy/Pipedream Mary (p/s) | 150 |
| 82 | Guardian GRC 144 | Leave Me Behind/High Class Hooker | 20 |
| 84 | Neat NEAT 44-12 | Nobody's Move/Town To Town/Leave Me Behind (12") | 20 |

### LONE WOLF (2)
| 81 | Kai KR 02 | Fighting For Sommerlund/Vonotar The Traitor (p/s) | 15 |

### LONELADY
| 06 | Filthy Home FHV 0101 | Army/Intuition | 8 |
| 07 | Too Pure PURE 211 S | Early The Haste Comes/Joy | 8 |

### LONELY HEARTS
| 84 | Tenacity TROIA | FM Fantasy/Young Girl (p/s) | 10 |

### LONERS
| 67 | Stone ST 1 | Visions Of You/Falling | 100 |

### LONESOME DRIFTER
| 70 | Injun 104 | Eager Boy/Teardrop Valley | 10 |

### JOHNNY LONESOME
| 61 | HMV POP 837 | Marie Marie/Doctor Heartache | 20 |

### LONESOME PINE FIDDLERS
| 64 | London HA-B 8143 | MORE BLUEGRASS (LP) | 15 |

### LONESOME STONE
| 73 | Reflection RL 306 | LONESOME STONE (LP, stage production recording) | 18 |

*(see also Sheep)*

### LONESOME SUNDOWN
| 71 | Blue Horizon 7-63864 | LONESOME LONELY BLUES (LP) | 100 |
| 70s | Flyright LP 529 | BOUGHT ME A TICKET (LP) | 18 |
| 70s | Flyright LP 587 | LONESOME WHISTLER (LP) | 18 |

### LONESOME TONE
| 81 | Stiff BUY DJ 111 | Mum Dad Love Hate And Elvis/Ghost Town (promo only) | 20 |
| 81 | Silent SSH 5 | Mum Dad Love Hate And Elvis/Ghost Town (p/s) | 5 |

### LONESOME TRAVELLERS
| 70 | Tradition TSR 004 | THE LONESOME TRAVELLERS (LP) | 25 |
| 70s | Nebula NEB 100 | THE LOST CHILDREN (LP) | 15 |

### LONG & SHORT
| 64 | Decca F 11964 | The Letter/Love Is A Funny Thing | 35 |
| 64 | Decca F 12043 | Choc Ice/Here Comes The Fool | 40 |

### LONG BLONDES
| 04 | Thee Sheffield SPC 005 | New Idols/Long Blonde (p/s pink vinyl, playing card & newsletter insert) | 20 |
| 04 | Angular Recording ARC 007 | Giddy Stratospheres/Polly/Darts (p/s, 500 only, blue vinyl) | 15 |

### FITZROY D. LONG & BUSTER ALL STARS
| 68 | Fab FAB 32 | Get A New Girl/BUSTER'S ALL STARS: Come And Do It With Me | 20 |

*(see also Larry Marshall)*

### LONG HELLO
| 73 | Private pressing | THE LONG HELLO (LP, mail-order only, numbered white sleeve) | 20 |

*(see also Van Der Graaf Generator)*

### SHORTY LONG
| 65 | Tamla Motown TMG 512 | Out To Get You/It's A Crying Shame | 125 |
| 65 | Tamla Motown TMG 512 | Out To Get You/It's A Crying Shame (DJ copy) | 200 |
| 66 | Tamla Motown TMG 573 | Function At The Junction/Call On Me | 45 |
| 66 | Tamla Motown TMG 573 | Function At The Junction/Call On Me (DJ copy) | 60 |
| 67 | Tamla Motown TMG 600 | Chantilly Lace/Your Love Is Amazing | 20 |
| 68 | Tamla Motown TMG 644 | Night Fo' Last (Vocal)/Night Fo' Last (Instrumental) | 25 |

| | | | |
|---|---|---|---|
| 68 | Tamla Motown TMG 663 | Here Comes The Judge/Sing What You Wanna | 18 |
| 68 | T. Motown (S)TML 11086 | HERE COMES THE JUDGE (LP, mono/stereo) | 45 |
| 70 | T. Motown STML 11144 | THE PRIME OF SHORTY LONG (LP) | 35 |

*(see also Art Mooney)*

**LONG TALL SHORTY**

| | | | |
|---|---|---|---|
| 79 | Warner Bros K 17491 | By Your Love/1970's Boy (p/s, withdrawn) | 80 |
| 81 | Dr Creation LYN 9904 | If I Was You/That's What I Want (flexidisc) | 12 |
| 81 | Ramkup CAC 007 | Win Or Lose/Ain't Done Wrong (p/s) | 50 |
| 85 | Diamond DIA 002 | On The Streets Again/I Fought The Law/Promises (p/s, with poster) | 25 |
| 85 | Diamond DIA 002 | On The Streets Again/I Fought The Law/Promises (p/s, without poster) | 12 |
| 86 | Diamond DIA 005 | What's Going On/Steppin' Stone/Win Or Lose/England (p/s) | 15 |
| 88 | no label or cat. no. | ROCKIN' AT THE SAVOY (LP, official bootleg, with poster) | 18 |
| 88 | no label or cat. no. | ROCKIN' AT THE SAVOY (LP, official bootleg, without poster) | 15 |

*(see also Case, Rage, Charlie Harper)*

**LONGBOATMEN**

| | | | |
|---|---|---|---|
| 66 | Polydor 56115 | Take Her Any Time/Only In Her Home Town | 500 |

**LONGDANCER**

| | | | |
|---|---|---|---|
| 73 | Rocket PIG 1 | If It Was So Simple/Silent Emotions (p/s) | 15 |
| 74 | Rocket PIG 11 | Puppet Man/Cold Love | 15 |
| 77 | Rocket PIGL 6 | TRAILER FOR A GOOD LIFE (LP, die cut gatefold sleeve) | 15 |

**CLAUDINE LONGET**

| | | | |
|---|---|---|---|
| 67 | A&M AMS 708 | Good Day Sunshine/The Look Of Love | 8 |
| 67 | A&M AML 903 | CLAUDINE (LP) | 20 |

**LONGPIGS**

| | | | |
|---|---|---|---|
| 96 | Mother MUM 77 | She Said/Flare Is Meteor//Far (live)/On And On (live) (p/s, reissue, pink vinyl, no'd and stickered sleeve) | 5 |
| 96 | Mother MUM 9602 | THE SUN IS OFTEN OUT (LP) | 20 |

**LONGPORT BUZZ**

| | | | |
|---|---|---|---|
| 78 | Buzz 13 | CANTERBURY POP EP (White labels, most handwritten) | 30 |
| 80 | Criminal Records SWAG 14 | Fun/Who Is He (different sleeve to Canterbury Pop version, with sticker) | 25 |

**LOOKALIKES**

| | | | |
|---|---|---|---|
| 80 | Riva RIVA 22 | Can I Take You Home Tonight/Radio/Don't Cry For Me (Irish pressing, imported into U.K.) | 5 |

**LOOK BACK IN ANGER**

| | | | |
|---|---|---|---|
| 81 | L.B.A. LBA 1 | Caprice/Mannequin (oversized card sleeve) | 25 |
| 84 | Criminal Damage CRI MLP 118 | CAPRICE (mini-LP) | 15 |

**LOOKING GLASS**

| | | | |
|---|---|---|---|
| 72 | Philips BF 1837 | Can You Believe/Freedom In Our Time | 8 |
| 72 | Epic 65041 | LOOKING GLASS (LP) | 20 |

**LOOP**

| | | | |
|---|---|---|---|
| 86 | Head HEAD 5 | 16 Dreams/Head On/Burning World (12", p/s) | 18 |
| 87 | Head HEAD 7L | Spinning Parts 1 & 2 (large centre, plain black die-cut sleeve) | 15 |
| 87 | Head HEAD 7 | Spinning/Deep Hit/I'll Take You There (12", p/s) | 20 |
| 88 | Chapter 22 12 CHAP 27 | COLLISION EP (12") | 10 |
| 88 | Chapter 22 12 CHAP 32 | BLACK SUN EP (12") | 10 |
| 88 | Chapter 22 CAT 065 | Torched (flexidisc, with The Catalogue magazine no. 65) | 12 |
| 88 | CHEREE Cheree 1 | TELESCOPES: Forever Close Your Eyes/LOOP: Soundhead (33rpm flexi, p/s, 1,000 only) | 10 |
| 89 | Situation 2 SIT 64T | ARC LITE EP (12", p/s) | 10 |
| 87 | Head HEAD LP 1 | HEAVEN'S END (LP, with inner sleeve) | 25 |
| 87 | Head HEAD LP 2 | WORLD IN YOUR EYES (LP) | 20 |
| 88 | Chapter 22 CHAPLLP 34 | FADE OUT (LP, 2 x 45rpm 12", gold stickered gatefold sleeve, signed) | 35 |
| 88 | Chapter 22 CHAPLLP 34 | FADE OUT (LP, 2 x 45rpm 12", gold stickered gatefold sleeve) | 20 |
| 88 | Chapter 22 CHAPL 44 | ETERNAL - SINGLES (LP) | 15 |
| 90 | Situation 2 SITU 27 | A GILDED ETERNITY (2-LP with free 7") | 25 |
| 91 | Reactor REACTORLP 3 | WOLF FLOW - JOHN PEEL SESSIONS 1987-90 (2-LP) | 18 |
| 92 | Reactor LP 5 | DUAL (LP, blue vinyl) | 20 |

**LOOPFLESH**

| | | | |
|---|---|---|---|
| 91 | Clawfist XPIG 07 | Like Rats/FLESHLOOP: Straight To Your Heart (foldover p/s in poly bag, actually by Loop and Godflesh) | 10 |

**LOOSE ENDS (1)**

| | | | |
|---|---|---|---|
| 66 | Decca F 12437 | Send The People Away/I Ain't Gonna Eat My Heart Out Anymore | 40 |
| 66 | Decca F 12476 | Taxman/That's It | 100 |

**LOOSE FITTINGS**

| | | | |
|---|---|---|---|
| 69 | Amber AM 01 | Sightings Of Emily/It's Down To Us | 50 |

**LOOSE RAIL**

| | | | |
|---|---|---|---|
| 68 | Denby DB 002 | Leave Me/A Place To Die (p/s) | 100 |
| 72 | Homewatch HW 1 | Silence In The Sky/Magic Well (p/s) | 75 |

**LOOSE SHOES**

| | | | |
|---|---|---|---|
| 81 | Applause CLAP 2 | Put The Blame On Me/Nobody's Clown | 8 |

**LOOSE TALK**

| | | | |
|---|---|---|---|
| 82 | Jet JET 7025 | Dan Dare/Home Planet (p/s) | 8 |

**LOOSE TIE**

| | | | |
|---|---|---|---|
| 73 | M&M 331 | Tie The Knot/Look Here You | 12 |

**LOOT**

| | | | |
|---|---|---|---|
| 66 | Page One POF 013 | Baby Come Closer/Baby | 15 |
| 67 | Page One POF 026 | I've Just Gotta Love You/You Need Someone To Love | 20 |

## LINDA LOPEZ MAMBO ORCHESTRA

| | | | |
|---|---|---|---|
| 67 | CBS 2938 | Whenever You're Ready/I Got What You Want | 18 |
| 68 | Page One POF 095 | She's A Winner/Radio City (withdrawn B-side) | 30 |
| 68 | Page One POF 095 | She's A Winner/Save Me | 22 |
| 68 | CBS 3231 | Don't Turn Around/You Are My Sunshine Girl | 25 |
| 69 | Page One POF 115 | Try To Keep It A Secret/Radio City | 40 |

*(see also Soul Agents, Hookfoot)*

### LINDA LOPEZ MAMBO ORCHESTRA
| | | | |
|---|---|---|---|
| 55 | Parlophone MSP 6179 | Limehouse Blues Mambo/Nursery Mambo | 7 |

### TRINI LOPEZ
| | | | |
|---|---|---|---|
| 63 | London HL 9808 | Jeanie Marie/Love Me Tonight | 6 |
| 07 | Kent TOWN 142 | Sinner Not A Saint/JOHNNY COPELAND: No Puppy Love | 8 |
| 65 | Stateside SE 1013 | SINNER NOT A SAINT (EP) | 30 |

### DENISE LOR
| | | | |
|---|---|---|---|
| 54 | Parlophone MSP 6120 | If I Give My Heart To You/Hallo Darling | 10 |
| 55 | Parlophone MSP 6148 | Every Day Of My Life/And One To Grow On | 12 |

### KENNY LORAN
| | | | |
|---|---|---|---|
| 59 | Capitol CL 15081 | Mama's Little Baby/Magic Star | 30 |

### L'ORANGE MECHANIK
| | | | |
|---|---|---|---|
| 86 | Art Pop POP 44 | Symphony/Intermezzo (Sprechstimme)/Scherzo (p/s) | 15 |

*(see also Times)*

### JON LORD
| | | | |
|---|---|---|---|
| 76 | Purple PUR 131 | Bourée/Aria | 7 |
| 82 | Harvest HAR 5220 | Bach Onto This/Going Home (p/s) | 6 |
| 84 | Safari SAFE60 | The Country Diary Of An Edwardian Lady (main theme)/Love Theme (p/s) | 8 |
| 71 | Purple TPSA 7501 | GEMINI SUITE (LP, textured gatefold sleeve) | 70 |
| 74 | Purple TPSA 7513 | WINDOWS (LP, gatefold sleeve) | 20 |
| 76 | Purple TPSA 7516 | SARABANDE (LP, die-cut sleeve) | 15 |

*(see also Artwoods, Deep Purple, [Paice] Ashton & Lord, Wizard's Convention, Episode Six, Leading Figures, Whitesnake, Cozy Powell)*

### TONY LORD
| | | | |
|---|---|---|---|
| 66 | Planet PLF 102 | World's Champion/It Makes Me Sad | 25 |

### JERRY LORDAN
| | | | |
|---|---|---|---|
| 59 | Parlophone R 4588 | I'll Stay Single/Can We Kiss | 8 |
| 60 | Parlophone R 4627 | Who Could Be Bluer?/Do I Worry? | 10 |
| 60 | Parlophone R 4653 | Sing Like An Angel/Ev'ry Time | 12 |
| 60 | Parlophone R 4695 | Ring, Write Or Call/I've Still Got You | 12 |
| 61 | Parlophone R 4748 | You Came A Long Way From St. Louis/Let's Try Again | 15 |
| 62 | Parlophone R 4903 | One Good Solid 24 Carat Reason/Second Hand Dress | 20 |
| 70 | CBS 5057 | The Old Man And The Sea/Harlequin Melodies | 30 |
| 61 | Parlophone PMC 1133 | ALL MY OWN WORK (LP, mono) | 50 |
| 61 | Parlophone PCS 3014 | ALL MY OWN WORK (LP, stereo) | 75 |

*(see also Lee & Jay Elvin)*

### LORD BEGINNER
| | | | |
|---|---|---|---|
| 60s | Melodisc CAL 1 | Victory Test Match - Calypso/Sergeant Brown (reissue) | 10 |

*(see also Lord Kitchener)*

### LORD BRISCO(E)
| | | | |
|---|---|---|---|
| 64 | Rio R42 | Fabulous Eyes/What You See | 20 |
| 64 | Black Swan WI 447 | Spiritual Mambo/BABA BROOKS: Fly Right | 25 |
| 64 | Black Swan WI 450 | My Love Has Come/BABA BROOKS: Sweet Eileen | 25 |
| 64 | Black Swan WI 454 | Trojan/I Am The Least | 12 |
| 64 | Island WI 131 | Praise For I/Tell You The Story | 15 |
| 65 | Island WI 187 | Jonah (The Master)/Mr. Cleveland | 15 |

### LORD BRYNNER & SHEIKS
| | | | |
|---|---|---|---|
| 66 | Island WI 266 | Congo War/Teach Me To Ska | 40 |

*(see also Roland Alphonso)*

### LORD BUCKLEY
| | | | |
|---|---|---|---|
| 62 | Fontana 688 010ZL | IN CONCERT (LP) | 20 |
| 67 | Fontana TL 5396 | BLOWING HIS MIND (AND YOURS, TOO) (LP) | 20 |

### LORD CHARLES & HIS BAND
| | | | |
|---|---|---|---|
| 70s | Sound Of Jamaica JA 1 | Jamaican Bits And Pieces/JA Island Soul | 8 |

### LORD COMIC
| | | | |
|---|---|---|---|
| 70 | Bamboo BAM 66 | Rhythm Rebellion/ROY RICHARDS: Reggae Children | 50 |
| 70 | Pressure Beat PR 5507 | Jack Of My Trade/CYNTHIA RICHARDS: United We Stand | 70 |

*(see also Sir Lord Comic)*

### LORD CREATOR
| | | | |
|---|---|---|---|
| 62 | Island WI 001 | Independant [sic] Jamaica Calypso/Remember (B-side is actually Remember Your Mother And Father) | 20 |
| 63 | Kalypso XX 24 | Peeping Tom/Second Hand Piano | 25 |
| 64 | Port-O-Jam PJ 4005 | Rhythm Of The Blues/Simple Things | 12 |
| 64 | Port-O-Jam PJ 4119 | Jamaica's Anniversary/Mother's Love | 22 |
| 64 | National Calypso NC 2001 | Drive With Care/Sweet Jamaica | 20 |
| 65 | Blue Beat BB 292 | Evening News/Good For Creator | 45 |
| 65 | Black Swan WI 463 | Wicked Lady/MAYTALS: My Little Ruby | 25 |
| 66 | Doctor Bird DB 1029 | Obeah Wedding/BERTRAM ENNIS COMBO: Part Two | 10 |
| 67 | Jump Up JU 503 | Jamaica Jump Up/Laziest Man | 25 |
| 67 | Jump Up JU 524 | Big Bamboo/Marjorie And Harry | 25 |
| 76 | Island WIP 6344 | Big Pussy Sally/UPSETTERS: Big Pussy Dub | 6 |

*(see also Kentrick Patrick, Fabulous Flames)*

## LORD CRISTO
| | | | |
|---|---|---|---|
| 67 | Jump Up JU 515 | Dumb Boy And The Parrot/General Hospital | 35 |
| 67 | Jump Up JU 517 | Election War Zone/Bad Luck Man | 35 |

## LORD FLEA & HIS CALYPSONIANS
| | | | |
|---|---|---|---|
| 57 | Capitol CL 14704 | The Naughty Little Flea/Shake Shake Senora | 5 |

## LORD KITCHENER
| | | | |
|---|---|---|---|
| 59 | Melodisc MEL 1498 | Black Puddin'/Piccadilly Folk | 7 |
| 59 | Melodisc MEL 1538 | If You're Brown/Come Back In The Morning | 7 |
| 60 | Melodisc MEL 1577 | Jamaica Turkey/Edna What You Want | 7 |
| 63 | Melodisc CAL 2 | Kitch/Rebound Wife | 6 |
| 63 | Melodisc CAL 3 | Muriel And The Bug/Nora And The Yankee | 6 |
| 63 | Melodisc CAL 4 | Kitch Take It Easy/Redhead | 6 |
| 63 | Melodisc CAL 5 | Drink A Rum/Your Wife | 15 |
| 63 | Melodisc CAL 6 | Too Late Kitch/Saxophone Number Two | 6 |
| 63 | Melodisc CAL 7 | Wife And Mother/Mango Tree | 6 |
| 64 | Melodisc CAL 10 | Kitch Mambo Calypso/Ghana | 6 |
| 64 | Melodisc CAL 11 | Life Begins At Forty/Short Skirts | 6 |
| 64 | Melodisc CAL 12 | Romeo/Kitch Calypso Medley | 6 |
| 64 | Melodisc CAL 14 | Federation/Alfonso In Town | 6 |
| 64 | Melodisc CAL 19 | Black Puddin'/Piccadilly Folk | 6 |
| 64 | Melodisc CAL 21 | Come Back In The Morning/If You're Brown | 6 |
| 64 | Melodisc CAL 22 | Jamaica Turkey/Edna What You Want | 6 |
| 64 | Melodisc CAL 23 | Carnival/More Rice | 6 |
| 60s | Jump Up JU 504 | Love In The Cemetery/Jamaica Woman | 15 |
| 60s | Jump Up JU 506 | Road On Carnival Day/Neighbour, Neighbour | 15 |
| 64 | Jump Up JU 511 | Dr. Kitch/Come Back Home Meh Boy | 15 |
| 65 | Jump Up JU 530 | Kitch You So Sweet/Ain't That Fun | 15 |
| 65 | Aladdin WI 612 | Dr. Kitch/Come Back Home Meh Boy (reissue) | 15 |
| 71 | Duke DU 115 | Dr. Kitch/Love In The Cemetary | 10 |
| 55 | Melodisc MLP 500 | KITCH - KING OF CALYPSO (10" LP) | 25 |
| 57 | Melodisc MLP 510 | KING OF CALYPSO VOL. 2 (10" LP) | 25 |
| 60s | Melodisc 12-129 | CALYPSOS TOO HOT TO HANDLE (LP) | 30 |
| 60s | Melodisc 12-130 | CALYPSOS TOO HOT TO HANDLE VOL. 2 (LP) | 30 |
| 60s | Melodisc 12-199 | CALYPSOS TOO HOT TO HANDLE (LP, reissue with extra tracks) | 30 |
| 60s | Melodisc 12-200 | CALYPSOS TOO HOT TO HANDLE VOL. 2 (LP, reissue with extra tracks) | 30 |

*(see also Lord Beginner)*

## LORD KITCHENER/FITZROY COLEMAN BAND
| | | | |
|---|---|---|---|
| 56 | no label | City And United 1956/The Manchester Football Double (78) | 60 |

## LORD LARGE (FEATURING DEAN PARRISH)
| | | | |
|---|---|---|---|
| 06 | Acid Jazz AJX 185S | Left Right & Centre/Sun In The Sands (7", co. sleeve) | 6 |

## LORD LEBBY
| | | | |
|---|---|---|---|
| 58 | Kalypso RL 101 | Dr Kinsey Report/Ethiopia | 15 |
| 58 | Kalypso XX 05 | Sweet Jamaica/Mama Want No Rice No Peas ) | 10 |
| 60 | Starlite ST45 018 | Caldonia/One Kiss For My Baby | 150 |

## LORD MELODY
| | | | |
|---|---|---|---|
| 58 | Melodisc MEL 1440 | The Devil/No, No | 6 |
| 58 | Melodisc MEL 1449 | Robbery/Men Company | 8 |
| 58 | Melodisc MEL 1474 | Do Able/Happy Holiday | 6 |
| 59 | Melodisc MEL 1491 | I Confess/MIGHTY SPARROW: Goaty | 8 |
| 59 | Melodisc MEL 1503 | Tom Dooley/Jealous Woman | 6 |
| 59 | Melodisc MEL 1504 | Romeo/Knock On Any Door | 6 |
| 60 | Kalypso XX 14 | Rock 'N' Roll Calypso/Bo Bo Man | 5 |
| 60s | Melodisc CAL 16 | Happy Holiday/Do Able | 5 |

## LORD NELSON
| | | | |
|---|---|---|---|
| 63 | Stateside SS 189 | I Got An Itch/Problems On My Mind | 12 |
| 64 | Stateside SS 281 | It's Delinquency/Proud West Indian | 15 |
| 68 | Direction 58-3909 | Michael/No Hot Summer | 10 |
| 64 | Stateside SE 1024 | PROUD WEST INDIAN (EP) | 30 |

## LORD POWER
| | | | |
|---|---|---|---|
| 69 | Coxsone CS 7079 | Temptation/AL & VIBRATORS: Change Everything | 80 |

## LORD RIGBY
| | | | |
|---|---|---|---|
| 60s | Kalypso XX 29 | The Milkman/Old Veterans | 6 |
| 64 | National Calypso NC 1001 | Carnival Jamiacia/Music Teacher | 20 |

## LORD ROCKINGHAM'S XI
| | | | |
|---|---|---|---|
| 58 | Decca F 11024 | The Squelch/Fried Onions | 10 |
| 59 | Decca F 11139 | Ra-Ra Rockingham/Farewell To Rockingham | 8 |
| 62 | Decca F 11426 | Newcastle Twist/Rockingham Twist | 8 |
| 58 | Decca DFE 6555 | OH BOY! (EP) | 25 |
| 68 | Columbia S(C)X 6291 | THE RETURN OF LORD ROCKINGHAM'S XI (LP, mono/stereo) | 25 |

*(see also Robinson Crew, Harry Robinson)*

## LORD ROSE
| | | | |
|---|---|---|---|
| 60s | Kalypso XX 25 | Independent Jamaica/Twistin' Uncle | 40 |

## LORDS
| | | | |
|---|---|---|---|
| 67 | Columbia DB 8121 | Don't Mince Matters/No One Knows | 140 |
| 68 | Columbia DB 8367 | Gloryland/Gypsy Boy | 18 |

## LORDS OF RAP
| | | | |
|---|---|---|---|
| 92 | Mad Dog MADDOG001 | STIX 'N' STONES (EP) | 15 |

MINT VALUE £

## LORD SASSAFROST
82　Star Light SDLP 911　　HORSE MAN CONNECTION (LP) ............................................................... 20

## LORD SITAR
68　Columbia SX/SCX 6256　　LORD SITAR (LP) ........................................................................ 40

## LORD SPOON
70　Escort ERT 839　　Woman A Love In The Night Time/World On A Wheel ............................ 15

## LORD TANAMO
60　Kalypso XX 20　　Blues Have Got Me Down/Sweet Dreaming .......................................... 20
64　Rio R 21　　I Had A Dream/OSBOURNE GRAHAM: Be There .......................................... 12
64　Ska Beat JB 177　　Night Food Ska/My Business ............................................................. 35
65　Ska Beat JB 217　　Mattie Rag/BABA BROOKS BAND: Mattie Rag ...................................... 25
65　Ska Beat JB 224　　I'm In The Mood For Ska/You Never Know ...................................... 150
66　Ska Beat JB 243　　Mother's Love/Downtown Gal ........................................................... 30
60s　Caribou CRC 3　　I Love You Truly/If You Were Only Mine ...................................... 150
70　Bamboo BAM 45　　Rainy Night In Georgia/KEN PACKER: When You're Gone ................... 20
71　Banana BA 319　　Keep On Moving/JACKIE MITTOO: Totaly [sic] Together ................... 125

## LORELEI
74　CBS 2048　　S.T.O.P. (Stop)/I'll Never Let You Down ........................................ 15

## SOPHIA LOREN
58　Philips PB 857　　Love Song From "Houseboat"/Bing! Bang! Bong! .............................. 6
*(see also Peter Sellers & Sophia Loren)*

## LORENZO
69　Harry J HE 6687　　Saturday Vocal Night/Instro ............................................................ 10
69　Beacon BEA 134　　I Ain't Afraid/Beggar .................................................................... 12
71　New Beat NB 094　　I Will Never Let You Down/This Magic Moment .................................. 5
*(see also Laurel Aitken)*

## LORI & CHAMELEONS
78　Zoo CAGE 006　　Touch/Love On The Ganges (p/s) ...................................................... 5
*(see also Teardrop Explodes, Bill Drummond)*

## GARY & JOHN LORRAINE
65　Pye 7N 15836　　I'm Not To Blame/Alone Again ........................................................ 10

## MYRNA LORRIE
55　London HLU 8187　　Underway/I'm Your Man, I'm Your Gal (B-side with Buddy DeVal) ........... 25
56　London HLU 8294　　Life's Changing Scene/Listen To My Heartstrings ............................ 25

## LORRIES
79　Redball RR 016　　The Night/Steal You Anyway/Pushover/Idiot Dances (p/s) ................... 6

## DICK LORY
56　London HLD 8348　　Cool It Baby/Ball Room Baby ......................................................... 400
56　London HLD 8348　　Cool It Baby/Ball Room Baby (78) .................................................... 50
61　London HLG 9284　　My Last Date/Broken Hearted ........................................................ 30
62　Liberty LIB 55415　　Handsome Guy/The Pain Is Here ..................................................... 10
63　Liberty LIB 55529　　Welcome Home Again/I Got Over You .............................................. 10

## LOS DOURADOS
70　EMI Regal/Starline SRS 5018 INTRODUCING LOS DOURADOS (LP) ................................... 15

## JOE LOSS (& HIS ORCHESTRA)
66　HMV POP 1500　　Thunderbirds Theme/"The Avengers" Theme ...................................... 15
66　HMV POP 1517　　The England World Cup March/Auld Lang Syne (March) ....................... 10

## LOST
94　Tenth Planet TP 009　　LOST IN ACTION (LP, with free 7") .................................................. 20

## LOST CHERREES
83　Riot RIOT 3　　NO FIGHTING NO WAR (EP) ............................................................ 10
85　Mortarhate MORT 12　　UNWANTED CHILDREN (12" EP, with inner) .................................... 10
84　Fight Back FIGHT 6　　ALL PART OF GROWING UP (LP, with lyric inner) ............................ 15

## LOST DOG
71　Phoenix SNIX 143　　Latch Key Child/One More Time ..................................................... 60

## LOST FAMOUS
82　Silent SR6703　　Anywhere Else/A Warning ................................................................ 30

## LOST JOCKEY
82　Operation Twilight OPT 11　Professor Slack/Rise And Fall/Animal/Behaviour And Crude Din (10" p/s) ........... 10

## LOT 39 (STRANGERS)
60s　Eyemark EMS 1004　　I'll Get Over You/I Still Love You ................................................ 12

## LOTHAR & THE HAND PEOPLE
69　Capitol CL 15610　　Sdrawkcab (Backwards)/Today Is Only Yesterday's Tomorrow .............. 20
69　Capitol E-ST 247　　SPACE HYMN (LP) ...................................................................... 60

## DENNIS LOTIS
54　Decca F 10287　　Such A Night/Cuddle Me (with Ted Heath Music & Johnston Brothers)....... 12
54　Decca F 10392　　Honey Love/Manhattan Mambo (with Ted Heath Music) ....................... 12
55　Decca F 10469　　Face Of An Angel, Heart Of A Devil/The Golden Ring ........................... 7
55　Decca F 10471　　Chain Reaction/Go, Go, Go (with Ted Heath Music) ............................. 7
68　Polydor 56266　　Funny One/One Man's Life ................................................................ 10
68　Polydor 56298　　Celebration/Why Do They Have To Fall In Love ............................... 10
68　Polydor 56346　　One Woman Man/The Finger Points At you ...................................... 10
57　Nixa NPL 18002　　HOW ABOUT YOU (LP) .................................................................. 15
58　Columbia 33SX 1089　　BIDIN' MY TIME (LP) .................................................................. 15
*(see also Johnstone Brothers)*

### PETER LOTIS
60  Ember EMB S 110          Doo-Dah/You're Singing Our Love Song To Somebody Else (with p/s) ............................ 6

### LOTUS CRUISE
83  Armbury ARM 603          Billy's Got A Gun/Tonight ................................................................................................. 50

### LOTUS EATERS
85  Arista FS 5              It Hurts/Evidence//The Soul In Sparks/Church At Llanbadrig (double pack) ................. 5
*(see also Wild Swans, Care)*

### BONNIE LOU
53  Parlophone MSP 6021      Seven Lonely Days/Dancin' With Someone ...................................................... 50
53  Parlophone MSP 6036      Hand-Me-Down Heart/Scrap Of Paper ........................................................... 50
53  Parlophone MSP 6048      Tennessee Wig Walk/Just Out Of Reach .......................................................... 50
53  Parlophone MSP 6051      Pa-Paya Mama/Since You Said Goodbye ....................................................... 40
54  Parlophone MSP 6072      The Texas Polka/No Heart At All ................................................................... 30
54  Parlophone MSP 6095      Don't Stop Kissing Me Goodnight/The Welcome Mat .................................... 30
54  Parlophone MSP 6108      No One/Huckleberry Pie ................................................................................ 30
54  Parlophone MSP 6117      Blue Tennessee Rain/Wait For Me, Darling .................................................... 30
54  Parlophone MSP 6132      Two Step - Side Step/Please Don't Laugh When I Cry .................................... 30
55  Parlophone MSP 6151      Tennessee Mambo/Train Whistle Blues .......................................................... 40
55  Parlophone MSP 6157      Tweedle Dee/The Finger Of Suspicion Points At You .................................... 40
55  Parlophone MSP 6173      Drop Me A Line/Old Faithful And True Love ................................................. 25
55  Parlophone MSP 6178      The Barnyard Hop/Tell The World .................................................................. 20
55  Parlophone MSP 6188      Dancin' In My Socks/Daddy-O ....................................................................... 40
56  Parlophone MSP 6223      Darlin' Why/Miss The Love (That I've Been Dreaming Of) ............................ 20
56  Parlophone MSP 6234      Bo Weevil (A Country Song)/Chaperon ......................................................... 20
56  Parlophone MSP 6253      Lonesome Lover/Little Miss Bobby Sox ......................................................... 25
56  Parlophone R 4215        No Rock 'N' Roll Tonight/One Track Love ...................................................... 25
57  Parlophone R 4350        Teenage Wedding/Runnin' Away ................................................................... 25
58  Parlophone DP 545        I'm Available/Waiting In Vain (export issue) ................................................. 20

### BONNIE LOU & RUSTY YORK
58  Parlophone R 4409        Let The School Bell Ring Ding-A-Ling/La Dee Dah ....................................... 80
58  Parlophone R 4409        Let The School Bell Ring Ding-A-Ling/La Dee Dah (78) ............................... 30

### BUBBA LOU & THE HIGHBALLS
81  Stiff BUY 114            Love All Over The Place/Over You (Unissued) ................................................. 25
81  Silent SSH3              Love All Over The Place/Over You .................................................................. 10

### LOU & KEVIN
78  Bushays BFM 103          Reunited/Reunited Stepping Out (12") ............................................................. 10
*(see also Rusty York)*

### LOUDER ANIMAL GROUP
80  Ears Pop POP 701         Pip Pop/Six Magnificent Cathedrals (p/s) ...................................................... 10
80  Ears Pop POP 702F        The Fossil Record (1-sided flexi on cardboard with 2 posters & inserts in poly bag) ....... 12

### JOHN D. LOUDERMILK
62  RCA RCA 1323             Angela Jones/Road Hog .................................................................................. 10
62  RCA RD 27248/SF 5123     THE LANGUAGE OF LOVE (LP) ...................................................................... 20
62  RCA Victor RD/SF 7515    TWELVE SIDES OF JOHN D. LOUDERMILK (LP) .......................................... 15
67  RCA Victor RD/SF 7890    SINGS A BIZARRE COLLECTION OF SONGS (LP) ....................................... 15
*(see also Johnny Dee)*

### (THE) LOUDWATER TERN
68  Morgan MR 6S             Senorita/I'll Be Where You Are (some demos credit Damon J Hardy and Polly Perkins
                             as artists) ..................................................................................................... 40

### LISA LOUGHEED
87  Ariola 111 713           Run With Us (Remix)/Ain't No Planes ........................................................... 20

### JOE HILL LOUIS
65  Bootleg 502              Heartache Baby/I Feel Like A Million (99 copies only) .................................... 40
67  Advent LP 2803           MEMPHIS BLUES AND BREAKDOWNS (LP) ................................................ 70
74  Polydor 2383 214         BLUE IN THE MORNING (LP) .......................................................................... 30

### LOUISIANA RED
64  Columbia DB 7270         Keep Your Hands Off My Woman/Don't Cry .................................................. 40
64  Sue WI 337               I Done Woke Up/I Had A Feeling ................................................................... 40
64  Columbia 33SX 1612       LOWDOWN BACK PORCH BLUES (LP) ........................................................ 45
72  Atlantic K 40436         SINGS THE BLUES (LP) ................................................................................. 20
72  Carnival 2941 002        THE SEVENTH SON (LP) ................................................................................ 20

### LOUVIN BROTHERS
59  Capitol CL 14989         Knoxville Girl/I Wish It Had Been A Dream ................................................. 20
59  Capitol CL 15078         You're Learning/My Curly Headed Baby ........................................................ 10
56  Capitol EAP1 769         TRAGIC SONGS OF LIFE (EP) ...................................................................... 10
58  Capitol EAP1 910         IRA AND CHARLIE (EP) ................................................................................ 10
59  Capitol EAP1 1106        COUNTRY LOVE BALLADS (EP) .................................................................. 10

### LOVABLES
68  Stateside SS 2108        You're The Cause Of It/Beautiful Idea .......................................................... 25

### ALAN LOVE AND MERLIN
74  CBS 3452                 Too Too Much/Gettin' Involved ...................................................................... 6

### C.P. LOVE
02  Grapevine 2000 G2K 127   Trick Bag/Plenty Of Room For More (reissue) ............................................... 10

### CHRISTOPHER LOVE
69  London HLU 10263         The Curse Goes On/You May Be The Next ................................................... 18

### DARLENE LOVE
63  London HLU 9725          (Today I Met) The Boy I'm Gonna Marry/Playing For Keeps .......................... 40

MINT VALUE £

| | | | |
|---|---|---|---|
| 63 | London HLU 9765 | Wait 'Til My Bobby Gets Home/Take It From Me | 40 |
| 63 | London HLU 9815 | A Fine Fine Boy/Marshmallow World | 50 |
| 69 | London HLU 10244 | Wait 'Til My Bobby Gets Home/(Today I Met) The Boy I'm Gonna Marry | 15 |
| 74 | Warner Bros/Spector K 19011 | Christmas (Baby Please Come Home)/Wait Till My Bobby Comes Home (blue vinyl) | 6 |
| 77 | Phil Spector Intl. 2010 019 | Lord If You're A Woman/Johnny Baby Please Come Home | 20 |
| 77 | Phil Spector Intl. 2010 019 | Lord If You're A Woman/Johnny Baby Please Come Home (12", some copies 1-sided) | 15 |
| 88 | CBS 6529357 | He's Sure The Man I Love (New Version)/Everybody Needs (p/s) | 5 |
| 90 | Warner Brothers W 9535 | Mr Fix-It/K.D. LANG with TAKE SIX: Ridin' The Rails (with p/s) | 5 |
| 90 | Warner Brothers W 9535 | Mr Fix-It/K.D. LANG with TAKE SIX: Ridin' The Rails | 20 |
| 64 | London RE-U 1411 | WAIT TILL MY BOBBY GETS HOME (EP) | 250 |

*(see also Bob B. Soxx & Blue Jeans, Crystals, Phil Spector, Blossoms, Allisons [U.S.], Date With Soul, Cinders)*

## GARFIELD LOVE & JIMMY SPRUILL
| | | | |
|---|---|---|---|
| 69 | Blue Horizon 57-3150 | Next Time You See Me/Part Time Love | 35 |

## GEOFF LOVE ORCHESTRA
| | | | |
|---|---|---|---|
| 61 | Columbia DB 4627 | Coronation Street Theme/Sophia | 6 |
| 62 | Columbia DB 4881 | Steptoe And Son/Over The Backyard Fence | 5 |
| 70 | Columbia DB 8707 | Coronation Street Theme/ALIRIO DIAZ: Aranjuez Mon Amour (Rodgigo) | 5 |
| 74 | EMI EMI 2105 | Match Of The Day/Bless This House | 6 |

*(see also Mandingo)*

## MARY LOVE
| | | | |
|---|---|---|---|
| 65 | King KG 1024 | You Turned My Bitter Into Sweet/I'm In Your Hands | 250 |
| 67 | Stateside SS 2009 | Lay This Burden Down/Think It Over Baby | 75 |
| 67 | Stateside SS 2009 | Lay This Burden Down/Think It Over Baby (DJ copy) | 125 |
| 68 | Stateside SS 2135 | The Hurt Is Just Beginning/If You Change Your Mind | 15 |
| 82 | Kent TOWN 501 | You Turned My Bitter Into Sweet/SWEETHEARTS: This Couldn't Be Me (green vinyl) | 10 |
| 85 | Kent 6T1 | Hey Stoney Face/IKETTES: It's Been So Long/ETTA JAMES: Wallflower | 20 |

## MIKE LOVE
| | | | |
|---|---|---|---|
| 83 | Creole CR 61 | Jingle Bell Rock/Let's Party (p/s) | 8 |

*(see also Beach Boys)*

## NANA LOVE
| | | | |
|---|---|---|---|
| 77 | Golden Age Music Ltd. GAM 01 | When The Heart Decides/Give Me The Chance | 80 |
| 78 | Nestor NES 01 | Chains Of Love/Sahara | 50 |
| 78 | Nestor NES 0201 | DISCO DOCUMENTARY - FULL OF FUNK (LP) | 200 |

## PRESTON LOVE
| | | | |
|---|---|---|---|
| 00s | Beat Goes Public BGPS 009 | Cissy Popcorn/BRENDA GEORGE: I Can't Stand It | 8 |

## RONNIE LOVE
| | | | |
|---|---|---|---|
| 61 | London HLD 9272 | Chills And Fever/Pledging My Love | 50 |
| 78 | Grapevine GRP 108 | Let's Make Love/Nothing To It | 8 |

## WILLIE LOVE/WILLIE NIX
| | | | |
|---|---|---|---|
| 66 | Highway 51 H 700 | THE TWO WILLIES FROM MEMPHIS (LP, 99 copies only) | 75 |

## LOVE (1)
### SINGLES
| | | | |
|---|---|---|---|
| 66 | London HLZ 10053 | My Little Red Book/Hey Joe | 60 |
| 66 | London HLZ 10073 | 7 And 7 Is/No. Fourteen | 60 |
| 67 | Elektra EKSN 45010 | She Comes In Colours/Orange Skies | 30 |
| 67 | Elektra EKSN 45016 | Softly To Me/The Castle | 30 |
| 68 | Elektra EKSN 45024 | Alone Again Or/Bummer In The Summer | 30 |
| 68 | Elektra EKSN 45026 | The Daily Planet/Andmoreagain | 30 |
| 68 | Elektra EKSN 45038 | Laughing Stock/Your Mind And We Belong Together | 30 |
| 70 | Elektra EKSN 45086 | I'm With You/Robert Montgomery | 15 |
| 70 | Harvest HAR 5014 | Stand Out/Doggone | 15 |
| 70 | Harvest HAR 5030 | The Everlasting First/Keep On Shining | 15 |
| 70 | Elektra 2101 019 | Alone Again Or/Bummer In The Summer (reissue, red label) | 10 |
| 73 | Elektra K 12113 | Alone Again Or/Andmoreagain | 6 |
| 75 | RSO 2090 151 | Time Is Like A River/You Said You Would | 6 |

### ALBUMS : ORIGINAL ALBUMS
| | | | |
|---|---|---|---|
| 66 | Elek. EKL 4001/EKS 74001 | LOVE (LP, gold label, U.K disc in U.S. sleeve) | 150 |
| 67 | Elek. EKL 4005/EKS 74005 | DA CAPO (LP, 1st pressing, mono/stereo, orange label with 'Manufactured in England by Elektra Records (U.K.) Ltd' at the bottom of labels in U.S. sleeves) | 120 |
| 67 | Elek. EKL 4005/EKS 74005 | DA CAPO (LP, 2nd pressing with 'Manufactured in Gt Britain' and 'Polydor Records Ltd' at the bottom of labels in either US or fully laminated UK sleeves) | 120 |
| 67 | Elek. EKL 4013 | FOREVER CHANGES (LP, mono orange label) | 200 |
| 67 | Elek. EKS 74013 | FOREVER CHANGES (LP, stereo orange label) | 150 |
| 69 | Elektra EKL 4049 | FOUR SAIL (LP, orange label, mono, existence unconfirmed) | 70 |
| 69 | Elektra EKS 74049 | FOUR SAIL (LP, orange label, stereo) | 70 |
| 70 | Harvest SHDW 3/4 | OUT HERE (2-LP, gatefold sleeve) | 50 |
| 71 | Harvest SHVL 787 | FALSE START (LP, gatefold sleeve) | 70 |
| 71 | Elektra 2469 009 | LOVE REVISITED (LP, gatefold sleeve) | 18 |
| 73 | Elektra K 32002 | LOVE MASTERS (LP) | 18 |
| 74 | RSO 2394 145 | REEL TO REAL (LP) | 15 |

### ALBUMS : REPRESSINGS
| | | | |
|---|---|---|---|
| 67 | Elek. EKL 4001/EKS 74001 | LOVE (LP, orange label, with U.K. or U.S. sleeve) | 60 |
| 72 | Elektra K 42068 | LOVE (LP, 'butterfly' label) | 25 |
| 71 | Elektra EKS 74005 | DA CAPO (LP, 'butterfly' label) | 18 |
| 72 | Elektra K 42011 | DA CAPO (LP, 'butterfly' label) | 15 |
| 72 | Elektra K 42015 | FOREVER CHANGES (LP, 'butterfly' label) | 20 |

| | | | |
|---|---|---|---|
| 72 | Elektra K 42030 | FOUR SAIL (LP, 'butterfly' label) ...................................................... | 15 |

(see also Arthur Lee)

## LOVE (2)
| | | | |
|---|---|---|---|
| 90 | Fierce FRIGHT 036 | Welsh Girl (1-sided, p/s in bag, hand-finished labels, mail-order only) .................. | 20 |

## LOVE AFFAIR
| | | | |
|---|---|---|---|
| 67 | Decca F 12558 | She Smiled Sweetly/Satisfaction Guaranteed ........................................ | 70 |
| 67 | CBS 3125 | Everlasting Love/Gone Are The Songs Of Yesterday ................................... | 6 |
| 68 | CBS 3366 | Rainbow Valley/Someone Like Me (in p/s, says 'Someone Like Us' on p/s) .......... | 20 |
| 68 | CBS 3366 | Rainbow Valley/Someone Like Us ................................................... | 8 |
| 68 | CBS 3674 | A Day Without Love/I'm Happy ..................................................... | 6 |
| 69 | CBS 3994 | One Road/Let Me Know ............................................................ | 8 |
| 69 | CBS 4300 | Bringing On Back The Good Times/Another Day ....................................... | 8 |
| 69 | CBS 4631 | Baby I Know/Accept Me For What I Am .............................................. | 10 |
| 70 | CBS 4780 | Lincoln County/Sea Of Tranquility ................................................. | 10 |
| 70 | Pye 7N 45218 | Let Me Dance/Love's Looking Out At You ............................................ | 8 |
| 71 | Parlophone R 5887 | Wake Me I Am Dreaming/That's My Home ............................................ | 12 |
| 71 | Parlophone R 5918 | Help (Get Me Some Help)/Long Way Home ........................................... | 12 |
| 72 | CBS 5017 | Speak Of Peace Speak Of Joy/Brings My Whole Life Tumbling Down ................... | 10 |
| 73 | CBS 33967 | Everlasting Love/Bringing On Back The Good Times (p/s, 'Hall Of Fame Hits' series) ...... | 5 |
| 77 | Creole CR 146 | Private Lives/Let A Little Love Come In ............................................. | 6 |
| 68 | CBS 63416 | THE EVERLASTING LOVE AFFAIR (LP, mono/stereo) ................................... | 30 |
| 70 | CBS 64109 | NEW DAY (LP) ...................................................................... | 30 |

(see also Ellis, Steve Ellis, Elastic Band, Widowmaker, Morgan, Phillip Goodhand-Tait, English Rose, Rainbow Ffolly)

## LOVE AMBASSADEUX
| | | | |
|---|---|---|---|
| 85 | Rumpo 12002 | Black Mischief/Driftwood/Oyster Syndrome (12") .................................... | 10 |

## LOVE & UNITY
| | | | |
|---|---|---|---|
| 79 | Studio 16 WE 0014 | Can't Let You Go/Dub Version (12") ................................................ | 30 |
| 80 | Studio 16 (no. Cat. No.) | Put It On/(feat Ranking Bogart)/Dub ............................................... | 35 |
| 80 | Studio 16 WE N1 | Just Don't Care/Cut From The Master Tape (12") .................................... | 25 |
| 80 | Studio 16 WEA 347 | I Adore You/CAPTAIN DESMOND : Lover In Dance (12") .............................. | 25 |

## LOVE AND WAR
| | | | |
|---|---|---|---|
| 80s | SRT SRT9KS 2323 | Touch Of Class (p/s) ............................................................... | 100 |

## LOVE CHILDREN
| | | | |
|---|---|---|---|
| 69 | Deram DM 268 | Easy Squeezy/Every Little Step ..................................................... | 15 |
| 70 | Deram DM 303 | Paper Chase/My Turkey Snuffed It ................................................. | 20 |

## LOVE COMMITTEE
| | | | |
|---|---|---|---|
| 76 | Ariola AA 105 | Can't Win For Losing/Love Wins Every Time ......................................... | 10 |

## LOVE CONNECTION
| | | | |
|---|---|---|---|
| 77 | Strong Like Sampson SLS01 | It's My House/Fall In Love (12") ................................................... | 20 |

## LOVECUT D.B.
| | | | |
|---|---|---|---|
| 91 | Suburbs Of Hell SOH 009EP | Heartspin/Heartspin (Dripping Clock Mix)/(Marisco Disco Mix)/(Porn Cable Mix) (12", p/s) .............................................................................. | 10 |
| 92 | Suburbs Of Hell SOH 011EP | JOURNEY TO THE CENTRE OF LOVE EP (12") ........................................ | 10 |

(see also Sarah Cracknell, St. Etienne)

## LOVE DIMENSION
| | | | |
|---|---|---|---|
| 79 | Black Bear BLA 2010 | You Stepped Into My Life/The Game ................................................ | 15 |

## LOVE GENERATION (JAMAICA)
| | | | |
|---|---|---|---|
| 73 | Grape GR 3046 | Money Raper/HEPTONES: The Magnificent Heptones 3 In One .......................... | 12 |
| 73 | Grape GR 3041 | Warrika Hill/Battlefield (Third And Fourth Generation) ............................... | 12 |

## LOVE GENERATION (U.S.)
| | | | |
|---|---|---|---|
| 67 | Liberty LBF 15018 | She Touched Me/The Love In Me .................................................... | 10 |
| 68 | Liberty LBL/LBS 83121E | LOVE GENERATION (LP) ............................................................. | 25 |

## JOY LOVEJOY
| | | | |
|---|---|---|---|
| 72 | Chess 6145 010 | In Orbit/Uh! Hum (paper label/moulded label) ...................................... | 30 |

## LOVEJOYS
| | | | |
|---|---|---|---|
| 80s | Solid Groove SG 016 | Stranger/Let Me Rock You (12") .................................................... | 20 |

## LOVELACE GREEN
| | | | |
|---|---|---|---|
| 69 | Concord CON 003 | Sister George/Pauper Millionaire ................................................... | 20 |

## LOVELITES
| | | | |
|---|---|---|---|
| 78 | Grapevine GRP 107 | Get It Off My Conscience/Oh, What A Day ........................................... | 10 |

## LOVELY BODIES
| | | | |
|---|---|---|---|
| 81 | Shark Hits LB 1 | Swelter In The Shelter/Come On Too Strong (p/s) .................................... | 30 |

## LOVE PARADE
| | | | |
|---|---|---|---|
| 90 | Turntable Friend TURN 03 | GUILT CHEST (EP) .................................................................. | 25 |

## JOHNNY LOVER
| | | | |
|---|---|---|---|
| 70 | Amalgamated AMG 871 | Pumpkin Eater/Version ............................................................. | 20 |
| 70 | Amalgamated AMG 873 | Two Edged Sword/Version .......................................................... | 35 |

(see also Little Johnny Jones, Heptones)

## LOVERS
| | | | |
|---|---|---|---|
| 58 | Vogue Pop V 9111 | Let's Elope/I Wanna Be Loved ...................................................... | 500 |
| 58 | Vogue Pop V 9111 | Let's Elope/I Wanna Be Loved (78) ................................................. | 150 |

## LOVERS DUB
| | | | |
|---|---|---|---|
| 80 | Venture | CUT 7 (LP) (actually by Eargasm) ................................................... | 40 |

(see also Tradition)

## LOVE SCULPTURE
| | | | |
|---|---|---|---|
| 68 | Parlophone R 5664 | River To Another Day/Brand New Woman ............................................ | 20 |
| 68 | Parlophone R 5731 | Wang-Dang-Doodle/The Stumble .................................................... | 20 |

# Eddie LOVETTE

| 68 | Parlophone R 5744 | Sabre Dance/Think Of Love ............................................................................... 5 |
| 69 | Parlophone R 5807 | Seagull/Farandole ......................................................................................... 15 |
| 70 | Parlophone R 5831 | In The Land Of The Few/People People ......................................................... 20 |
| 68 | Parlophone PMC 7059 | BLUES HELPING (LP, 1st pressing, yellow/black label, mono) ..................... 80 |
| 68 | Parlophone PCS 7059 | BLUES HELPING (LP, 1st pressing, yellow/black label, stereo) ................... 50 |
| 69 | Parlophone PCS 7090 | FORMS AND FEELINGS (LP, 1st pressing, yellow/black label)................... 100 |
| 70 | Parlophone PCS 7059 | BLUES HELPING (LP, 2nd pressing, silver/black label) ................................ 25 |
| 70 | Parlophone PCS 7090 | FORMS AND FEELINGS (LP, 2nd pressing, silver/black label) ...................... 25 |

*(see also Human Beans)*

## EDDIE LOVETTE
| 69 | Big Shot BI 519 | You're My Girl/Let Them Say ........................................................................ 15 |
| 70 | London HLU 10298 | Boomerang/Together..................................................................................... 5 |
| 70 | London HLJ 10311 | Too Experienced/Little Blue Bird ................................................................. 10 |
| 70 | London HA-J 8413 | TOO EXPERIENCED (LP, unissued) .................................................................. 0 |

## LENE LOVICH
| 76 | Polydor 2058 812 | I Saw Mommy Kissing Santa Claus/The Christmas Song (Merry Christmas To You)/ Happy Christmas (p/s)................................................................................... 40 |
| 78 | Stiff BUYJ 32 | I Think We're Alone Now (Japanese)/Lucky Number (mail-order promo only) ............ 25 |
| 78 | Stiff BUY 32 PLUG | I Think We're Alone Now/Lucky Number ("plug" copy on label. p/s) ........... 10 |
| 78 | Stiff BUY 32 | I Think We're Alone Now/Lucky Number (p/s) ............................................... 5 |
| 78 | Stiff BUY 35 | Home/Lucky Number (unreleased, test pressings only) ............................ 100 |
| 79 | Stiff BUY 46 DJ | Say When (1-sided promo, black vinyl) ......................................................... 7 |

## LOVIN'
| 67 | Page One POF 035 | Keep On Believing/I'm In Command.............................................................. 35 |
| 67 | Page One POF 041 | All You've Got/Do It Again ............................................................................ 75 |

*(see also Nerve)*

## LOVIN' SPOONFUL
| 65 | Pye International 7N 25327 | Do You Believe In Magic?/On The Road Again ............................................. 12 |
| 66 | Pye International 7N 25344 | You Didn't Have To Be So Nice/My Gal ......................................................... 15 |
| 66 | Pye Int. 7N 25361 | Daydream/Night Owl Blues............................................................................ 5 |
| 66 | Kama Sutra KAS 200 | Summer In The City/Bald Headed Lena .......................................................... 8 |
| 66 | Kama Sutra KAS 201 | Rain On The Roof/Warm Baby......................................................................... 7 |
| 67 | Kama Sutra KAS 204 | Nashville Cats/Full Measure ........................................................................... 7 |
| 67 | Kama Sutra KAS 207 | Darling Be Home Soon/Darlin' Companion ................................................. 12 |
| 67 | Kama Sutra KAS 208 | Six O'Clock/The Finale .................................................................................. 10 |
| 67 | Kama Sutra KAS 210 | She Is Still A Mystery/Only Pretty, What A Pity ............................................. 8 |
| 67 | Kama Sutra KAS 211 | Money/Close Your Eyes................................................................................... 8 |
| 68 | Kama Sutra KAS 213 | Never Going Back/Forever ............................................................................ 12 |
| 66 | Kama Sutra KEP 300 | DID YOU EVER HAVE TO MAKE UP YOUR MIND (EP) ..................................... 20 |
| 66 | Kama Sutra KEP 301 | JUG BAND MUSIC (EP)................................................................................... 20 |
| 66 | Kama Sutra KEP 302 | SUMMER IN THE CITY (EP)............................................................................ 20 |
| 67 | Kama Sutra KEP 303 | DAY BLUES (EP)............................................................................................. 20 |
| 67 | Kama Sutra KEP 304 | NASHVILLE CATS (EP).................................................................................... 20 |
| 67 | Kama Sutra KEP 305 | LOVIN' YOU (EP) ........................................................................................... 25 |
| 67 | Kama Sutra KEP 306 | SOMETHING IN THE NIGHT (EP).................................................................... 30 |
| 65 | Pye Intl. NPL 28069 | DO YOU BELIEVE IN MAGIC? (LP) .................................................................. 35 |
| 66 | Pye Intl. NPL 28078 | DAYDREAM (LP) ............................................................................................ 25 |
| 67 | Kama Sutra KLP 401 | HUMS OF THE LOVIN' SPOONFUL (LP) .......................................................... 35 |
| 67 | Kama Sutra KLP 402 | YOU'RE A BIG BOY NOW (LP, soundtrack) .................................................... 20 |
| 68 | Kama Sutra KLP 404 | EVERYTHING PLAYING (LP) ........................................................................... 18 |
| 68 | Kama Sutra K(S)LP 405 | THE BEST OF THE LOVIN' SPOONFUL VOL. 2 (LP) ......................................... 15 |
| 69 | Kama Sutra 602 009 | REVELATION: REVOLUTION '69 (LP) ............................................................. 15 |

*(see also John Sebastian, Mugwumps, Zalman Yanovsky, Even Dozen Jug Band)*

## LOVING AWARENESS
| 76 | More Love ML 001 | LOVING AWARENESS (LP, gatefold sleeve with 2 posters)............................ 15 |

*(see also Glencoe, Skip Bifferty, Ian Dury)*

## LOVING KIND
| 66 | Piccadilly 7N 35299 | Accidental Love/Nothing Can Change This Love............................................ 15 |
| 66 | Piccadilly 7N 35318 | I Love The Things You Do/Treat Me Nice....................................................... 18 |
| 66 | Piccadilly 7N 35342 | Ain't That Peculiar/With Rhyme And Reason................................................ 25 |

*(see also Freddie Lennon)*

## LOW
| 96 | Vernon Yard YARD 24 | Over The Ocean/Violence ............................................................................. 10 |
| 96 | Vernon Yard YARD 22 | FINALLY... (EP) .............................................................................................. 20 |
| 98 | Tugboat TUGS 001 | Joan Of Arc/Long Long Long .......................................................................... 6 |
| 01 | Tugboat TUGLP 027 | THINGS WE LOST IN THE FIRE (2-LP, 4th side etched with lyrics) ................. 20 |
| 04 | Rough Trade RTRADCDX 195 | A LIFETIME OF TEMPORARY RELIEF (3-CD and DVD box set) ........................ 20 |
| 05 | Rough Trade RTRADELP 206 | THE GREAT DESTROYER (2-LP) ...................................................................... 18 |

## BRUCE LOW
| 56 | HMV JO 464 | Just Walking In The Rain/Cindy Oh Cindy (export issue) ............................. 20 |

## LOW NUMBERS
| 79 | Warner Brothers K 17493 | Keep In Touch/Nine All Out (p/s)................................................................... 25 |

## LOW PROFYLE
| 80 | Ellie Jay EJSP 9434 | Hangin' Around/Substitute (p/s) ................................................................... 50 |

## LOWBITES
| 70 | Black Swan BW 1403 | I Got It/I Got It (Version) ................................................................................ 6 |
| 80 | Black Joy DH 800 | Can I Go With You?/BOBBY DODSON & TRINITY: Having My Baby (12")...................... 15 |

## DENNIS LOWE
| | | | |
|---|---|---|---|
| 70 | Downtown DT 465 | What's Your Name/MUSIC DOCTORS: Mr Locabe | 20 |
| 70 | Downtown DT 468 | Stand Up For The Sound/OWEN & DENNIS: Old Man Trouble | 20 |

## EARL LOWE
| | | | |
|---|---|---|---|
| 75 | Tafari WL 708 | Jah Can Count On I/Bongo Nyah (12") | 70 |

## JEZ LOWE
| | | | |
|---|---|---|---|
| 80 | Fellside FE 034 | JEZ LOWE (LP, textured sleeve, light green label, large 'Rams Horn' logo) | 15 |
| 83 | Fellside FE 034 | THE OLD DURHAM ROAD (LP) | 15 |
| 85 | Fellisde FE 049 | GALLOWAYS (LP, with lyric insert) | 15 |

## JIM LOWE
| | | | |
|---|---|---|---|
| 55 | London HLD 8171 | Close The Door/Nueva Laredo (gold label print) | 40 |
| 56 | London HLD 8276 | Blue Suede Shoes/Maybellene (silver label print) | 100 |
| 56 | London HLD 8276 | Blue Suede Shoes/Maybellene (silver label print) (78) | 20 |
| 56 | London HLD 8288 | Love Is The $64,000 Dollar Question/Rene La Rue (gold label print) | 80 |
| 56 | London HLD 8317 | The Green Door/The Little Man In Chinatown (as Jim Lowe & High Fives, gold label print) | 50 |
| 56 | London HLD 8317 | The Green Door/The Little Man In Chinatown (as Jim Lowe & High Fives, later silver print label) | 25 |
| 57 | London HLD 8368 | I Feel The Beat/By You, By You, By You (gold label print) | 50 |
| 57 | London HLD 8368 | I Feel The Beat/By You, By You, By You (later silver print label) | 30 |
| 57 | London HLD 8431 | Four Walls/Talkin' To The Blues | 25 |
| 58 | London HLD 8538 | Roc-A-Chicka/The Bright Light (with Billy Vaughan's Orchestra) | 125 |
| 60 | London HLD 9043 | He'll Have To Go/(This Life Is Just A) Dress Rehearsal | 6 |
| 65 | United Artists UP 1096 | Mr Moses/Make Your Back Strong | 5 |
| 58 | London HA-D 2108 | SONGS THEY SING BEHIND THE GREEN DOOR (LP) | 30 |
| 59 | London HA-D 2146 | WICKED WOMEN (LP) | 20 |

*(see also John Barry Seven)*

## NICK LOWE
| | | | |
|---|---|---|---|
| 76 | Stiff BUY 1 | So It Goes/Heart Of The City (promo, 'plug' copy) | 40 |
| 76 | Stiff BUY 1 | So It Goes/Heart Of The City, (push-out centre) | 15 |
| 77 | Stiff LAST 1-12 | Bowi EP (Born A Woman//Marie Provost/Endless Sleep, 12" promo, 50 only) | 100 |
| 77 | Stiff BUY 21 | Halfway To Paradise/I Don't Want The Night To End | 6 |
| 78 | Radar ADA 1 | I Love The Sound Of Breaking Glass/They Called It Rock | 5 |
| 78 | Radar ADA 43 | Little HItler/Cruel To Be Kind | 5 |
| 79 | Radar ADA 43 | Cruel To Be Kind/Endless Grey Ribbon | 5 |
| 78 | Radar ADA 26 | American Squirm/What's So Funny Bout (Peace, Love And Understanding) | 5 |
| 90 | Reprise W 9821 | All Men Are Liars/Gai Gin Man | 5 |

## MUNDELL LOWE QUARTET
| | | | |
|---|---|---|---|
| 56 | London American LTZ U 15020 | MUNDELL LOWE QUARTET (LP) | 15 |

## LOWER LEVELS
| | | | |
|---|---|---|---|
| 81 | Pushover 1 | Get It/So Bloody Lazy (p/s) | 20 |

## LOWLIFE
| | | | |
|---|---|---|---|
| 88 | LOLIF DEMO 1 | THE DEMOS (LP, white label test pressings only, hand-written white sleeve) | 18 |

## LOW/PIANO MAGIC/TRANSIENT WAVES
| | | | |
|---|---|---|---|
| 98 | Rocket Girl RGIRL 4 | Sleep At The Bottom/TRANSIENT WAVES: Green Acres (p/s) | 6 |

## LOWRELL
| | | | |
|---|---|---|---|
| 79 | AVI AVISL 108 | Mellow Mellow Rich On (Four Mixes) (12") | 10 |

## PHILIP LOWRIE
| | | | |
|---|---|---|---|
| 63 | Ember EMB S 179 | I Might Have Known (Before)/I Might Have Known (After) | 10 |

## ART LOWRY
| | | | |
|---|---|---|---|
| 54 | Columbia SCMC 1 | The Curse Of An Aching Heart/Heart Of My Heart (export issue) | 10 |

## HENRY LOWTHER BAND
| | | | |
|---|---|---|---|
| 70 | Deram SML 1070 | CHILD SONG (LP) | 175 |

*(see also Manfred Mann, John Mayall & Bluesbreakers, Keef Hartley Band, Ricotti & Albuquerque)*

## MARK LOYD
| | | | |
|---|---|---|---|
| 65 | Parlophone R 5277 | I Keep Thinking About You/Will It Be The Same | 10 |
| 65 | Parlophone R 5332 | Everybody Tries/She Said No | 60 |
| 66 | Parlophone R 5423 | When Evening Falls/When I'm Gonna Find Her | 200 |
| 66 | Parlophone R 5423 | When Evening Falls/When I'm Gonna Find Her (DJ copy) | 300 |

## L7
| | | | |
|---|---|---|---|
| 92 | Slash L30780 | BRICKS ARE HEAVY (LP, green marbled vinyl) | 20 |

## LTG EXCHANGE
| | | | |
|---|---|---|---|
| 76 | Atlantic K10824 | Huddle/You'll Never Learn (About Love) | 8 |

## JEREMY LUBBOCK
| | | | |
|---|---|---|---|
| 58 | Parlophone R 4399 | Catch A Falling Star/The Man Who Invented Love | 5 |
| 58 | Parlophone R 4421 | Lemon Twist/Tonight | 10 |
| 58 | Parlophone R 4473 | Odd Man Out/Too Bad You're Not Around | 5 |
| 58 | Parlophone GEP 8745 | JUST FOR THE FUN OF IT (EP) | 10 |

## LUCAS (& MIKE COTTON SOUND)
| | | | |
|---|---|---|---|
| 66 | Polydor 56114 | I Saw Pity In The Face Of A Friend/Dance Children Dance (solo) | 20 |
| 67 | Pye 7N 17313 | Step Out Of Line/Ain't Love Good, Ain't Love Proud | 50 |
| 68 | MGM MGM 1398 | Soul Serenade/We Got A Thing Going Baby | 45 |
| 68 | MGM MGM 1427 | Jack And The Beanstalk/Mother-In-Law | 30 |

*(see also Mike Cotton Sound, Artwoods)*

## BUDDY LUCAS BAND
| | | | |
|---|---|---|---|
| 60 | Pye International 7N 25045 | I Want To Know/Deacon John | 20 |

MINT VALUE £

## LUCAS AND THE DYNAMOS
| | | | |
|---|---|---|---|
| 91 | SRTS 91 S2904 | Rock And Roll Is Good For The Soul/Blood Shot/My Gal/Baby Baby | 15 |

## MATT LUCAS
| | | | |
|---|---|---|---|
| 11 | Inferno 3246 | Shake It (1-sided, blue vinyl) | 5 |
| 11 | Made In Detroit MID 1 | You Better Go Go (1-sided) | 5 |
| 12 | Inferno HEAT 1002 | Gimme Some/Shake it | 5 |

## TREVOR LUCAS
| | | | |
|---|---|---|---|
| 66 | Reality RE 505 | Waltzing Matilda/It's On | 20 |
| 66 | Reality RY 1002 | OVERLANDER (LP) | 275 |

*(see also Eclection, Fotheringay, Fairport Convention, Bronco, Sandy Denny)*

## JON LUCIEN
| | | | |
|---|---|---|---|
| 74 | RCA ALP1-0493 | MINDS EYE (LP) | 30 |

## LUCIENNE
| | | | |
|---|---|---|---|
| 80 | Pan 101 | Caribbean/This Boy (p/s) | 8 |

## LUCIFER (1)
| | | | |
|---|---|---|---|
| 71 | Lucifer L 001 | Don't Care/Hypnosis | 15 |
| 72 | Lucifer L 003/004 | Fuck You/Bad | 8 |
| 72 | Lucifer L 005/006 | Prick/Want It | 8 |
| 72 | Lucifer L 005/006/L 003/004 | Prick/Want It/Fuck You/Bad (double pack, black box set) | 40 |
| 73 | Lucifer L007 | Mr Jack/Mr Jack | 50 |
| 72 | Lucifer LLP 1 | BIG GUN (LP, private pressing, with poster/inserts, sold via Oz mag) | 100 |
| 72 | Lucifer LLP 1 | BIG GUN (LP, private pressing, without poster/inserts, sold via Oz mag) | 70 |
| 72 | Lucifer LLP 2 | EXIT (LP, private pressing, with poster, sold via Oz magazine) | 150 |
| 72 | Lucifer LLP 2 | EXIT (LP, private pressing, without poster, sold via Oz magazine) | 70 |

## LUCIFER (2)
| | | | |
|---|---|---|---|
| 75 | EMI 2281 | House For Sale/My Dream World | 5 |

## LUCIFER'S FRIEND
| | | | |
|---|---|---|---|
| 71 | Philips 6003 092 | Ride The Sky/Horla | 15 |
| 71 | Philips 6305 068 | LUCIFER'S FRIEND (LP) | 250 |

*(see also John Lawton, Uriah Heep)*

## THE LUCK OF EDEN HALL
| | | | |
|---|---|---|---|
| 11 | winkle 03 | She Comes In Colours/Never My Love/Chrysalide/The Ottoman Girl (folded p/s, green vinyl, insert) | 0 |

## LUCY SHOW
| | | | |
|---|---|---|---|
| 83 | Shout XS 007 | Leonardo Da Vinci/Kill The Beast (p/s) | 5 |
| 84 | Piggy Bank BANK 999 | Electric Dreams/History Part 1 (p/s) | 7 |
| 85 | A&M AMY 261 | Ephemeral/White Space (12", p/s) | 20 |

## TOM LUCY
| | | | |
|---|---|---|---|
| 82 | Bridgehouse BHS 15 | Paris, France/Man Found Dead In Graveyard (no p/s) | 6 |

*(see also Wasted Youth)*

## LUCY (1)
| | | | |
|---|---|---|---|
| 69 | Major Minor MM667 | Georgie/With Him | 8 |

## LUCY (2)
| | | | |
|---|---|---|---|
| 77 | Lightning BCS 008 | Really Got Me Goin'/Oy (export only p/s) | 15 |
| 77 | Lightning BCS 008 | Really Got Me Goin'/Oy (no p/s) | 10 |
| 78 | Lightning GIL 516 | Never Never/Feel So Good (with export p/s) | 100 |
| 78 | Lightning GIL 516 | Never Never/Feel So Good (without export p/s) | 30 |

*(see also Def Leppard)*

## LUDDITES
| | | | |
|---|---|---|---|
| 83 | Xcentric Noise SECOND 1 | STRENGTH OF YOUR CRY (EP, black foldout p/s) | 15 |
| 83 | Xcentric Noise SECOND 1 | STRENGTH OF YOUR CRY (EP, pink foldout p/s) | 10 |

## LUDLOWS
| | | | |
|---|---|---|---|
| 61 | Pye NEP 24252 | THE SEA AROUND US (EP) | 20 |
| 66 | Pye NPL 18150 | THE WIND AND THE SEA (LP) | 18 |

*(see also Jim McCann)*

## LUDUS
| | | | |
|---|---|---|---|
| 81 | New Hormones ORG 8 | My Cherry Is In Sherry/Anatomy Is Not Destiny (p/s) | 7 |
| 81 | New Hormones ORG 12 | Mother's Hour/Patient (p/s, with poster) | 8 |
| 81 | New Hormones ORG 16 | THE SEDUCTION (2 x 12" EP, each in p/s; whole package in poly bag) | 12 |
| 82 | New Hormones ORG 20 | DANGER CAME SMILING (LP, insert) | 18 |

## LUGWORM
| | | | |
|---|---|---|---|
| 97 | Guided Missile GUIDE 11 | Rococo Negro/BIS: Pop Song (p/s) | 5 |

## LUKE & BLAKE
| | | | |
|---|---|---|---|
| 66 | CBS 202467 | Just You/Wandering Man | 8 |

## ROBIN LUKE
| | | | |
|---|---|---|---|
| 58 | London HLD 8676 | Susie Darlin'/Living's Loving You | 12 |
| 58 | London HLD 8771 | Chicka Chicka Honey/My Girl | 30 |
| 58 | London HLD 8771 | Chicka Chicka Honey/My Girl (78) | 20 |
| 59 | London RED 1222 | ROBIN LUKE (EP) | 50 |

## LULU (& LUVVERS)
| | | | |
|---|---|---|---|
| 64 | Decca F 11884 | Shout/Forget Me Baby (as Lulu & Luvers) | 6 |
| 64 | Decca F 11965 | Can't Hear You No More/I Am In Love | 20 |
| 64 | Decca F 12017 | Here Comes The Night/That's Really Some Good | 15 |
| 65 | Decca F 12128 | Satisfied/Surprise Surprise (as Lulu & Luvers) | 18 |
| 65 | Decca F 12169 | Leave A Little Love/He Don't Want Your Love Anymore | 6 |
| 65 | Decca F 12214 | Try To Understand/Not In This Whole World | 8 |
| 65 | Decca F 12254 | Tell Me Like It Is/Stop Fooling Around | 20 |

| | | | |
|---|---|---|---|
| 66 | Decca F 12326 | Call Me/After You | 7 |
| 66 | Decca F 12491 | What A Wonderful Feeling/Tossin' And Turnin' | 12 |
| 67 | Columbia DB 8169 | The Boat That I Row/Dreary Days And Nights | 8 |
| 67 | Columbia DB 8221 | Let's Pretend/To Sir With Love | 10 |
| 67 | Columbia DB 8295 | Love Loves To Love/You And I | 12 |
| 68 | Columbia DB 8358 | Me, The Peaceful Heart/Lookout | 5 |
| 68 | Columbia DB 8425 | Boy/Sad Memories | 6 |
| 68 | Columbia DB 8500 | I'm A Tiger/Without Him | 5 |
| 69 | Columbia DB 8550 | Boom Bang-A-Bang/March! | 5 |
| 69 | Atco 226 008 | Oh Me, Oh My (I'm A Fool For You Baby)/Sweep Around Your Own Backyard | 6 |
| 71 | Atco 2091049 | Move To My Rhythm/Got To Believe In Love | 8 |
| 65 | Decca DFE 8597 | LULU (EP) | 35 |
| 65 | Decca LK 4719 | SOMETHING TO SHOUT ABOUT (LP) | 50 |
| 67 | Ace Of Clubs ACL 1232 | LULU! (LP) | 20 |
| 67 | Fontana (S)TL 5446 | TO SIR, WITH LOVE (LP, soundtrack, with Ron Grainer & Mindbenders) | 35 |
| 67 | Columbia S(C)X 6201 | LOVE LOVES TO LOVE LULU (LP, John Paul Jones arrangements) | 30 |
| 69 | Columbia S(C)X 6365 | LULU'S ALBUM (LP) | 25 |
| 69 | Atco 228 031 | NEW ROUTES (LP) | 15 |
| 70 | Atco 2400017 | MELODY FAIR (LP) | 15 |

(see also Luvvers)

## LULU BELLE & SCOTTY
| | | | |
|---|---|---|---|
| 65 | London HA-B 8277 | SWEETHEART STILL (LP) | 15 |

## BOB LUMAN
| | | | |
|---|---|---|---|
| 60 | Warner Bros WB 12 | Dreamy Doll/Buttercup | 25 |
| 60 | Warner Bros WB 28 | Why, Why, Bye, Bye/Oh, Lonesome Me | 10 |
| 61 | Warner Bros WB 37 | The Great Snow Man/The Pig Latin Song | 10 |
| 61 | Warner Bros WB 49 | Private Eye/You Turned Down The Lights | 0 |
| 62 | Warner Bros WB 60 | Louisiana Man/Rocks Of Reno (unissued) | 12 |
| 62 | Warner Bros WB 75 | Hey Joe/The Fool | 10 |
| 64 | Hickory 45-1238 | The File/Bigger Men Than I | 20 |
| 61 | Warner Bros WEP 6046 | LET'S THINK ABOUT LIVIN' (EP, mono) | 20 |
| 61 | Warner Bros WSEP 2046 | LET'S THINK ABOUT LIVIN' (EP, stereo) | 30 |
| 62 | Warner Bros WEP 6055 | LET'S THINK ABOUT LIVIN' NO. 2 (EP, mono) | 20 |
| 62 | Warner Bros WSEP 2055 | LET'S THINK ABOUT LIVIN' NO. 2 (EP, stereo) | 20 |
| 62 | Warner Bros WEP 6102 | LET'S THINK ABOUT LIVIN' NO. 3 (EP, mono) | 20 |
| 62 | Warner Bros WSEP 2102 | LET'S THINK ABOUT LIVIN' NO. 3 (EP, stereo) | 20 |
| 60 | Warner Bros WM 4025 | LET'S THINK ABOUT LIVIN' (LP, mono) | 25 |
| 60 | Warner Bros WS 8025 | LET'S THINK ABOUT LIVIN' (LP, stereo) | 20 |
| 64 | Hickory LPM 124 | LIVIN' LOVIN' SOUNDS (LP) | 20 |

(see also Sue Thompson & Bob Luman)

## BOB LUMAN/BOBBY LORD
| | | | |
|---|---|---|---|
| 64 | Hickory LPM 121 | CAN'T TAKE THE COUNTRY FROM THE BOYS (LP, 1 side each) | 15 |

## RUFUS LUMLEY
| | | | |
|---|---|---|---|
| 66 | Stateside SS 516 | I'm Standing/Let's Hide Away (Me And You) | 200 |
| 66 | Stateside SS 516 | I'm Standing/Let's Hide Away (Me And You) (DJ copy) | 400 |
| 78 | EMI International INT 556 | I'm Standing/Let's Hide Away (Me And You) (reissue) | 15 |

## LUNA
| | | | |
|---|---|---|---|
| 95 | Beggars Banquet BBQ 59 | Hedgehog/No Regrets/23 Minutes In Brussels | 5 |
| 97 | Beggars Banquet BBQ 319 | Bobby Peru/Dance With Me/Bob Le Flambeur (white vinyl) | 5 |
| 95 | Beggars Banquet BBQLP 178 | PENTHOUSE (LP) | 20 |
| 97 | Beggars Banquet BBQLP 194 | PUP TENT (LP) | 20 |
| 99 | Beggars Banquet BBQLP 209 | THE DAY OF OUR NIGHTS (LP, white vinyl) | 20 |

(see also Galaxie 500)

## LUNA C
| | | | |
|---|---|---|---|
| 93 | Knifeforce KF 001 | THE LUNA C PROJECT EP (12") | 40 |
| 93 | Knifeforce KF 002 | LUNA C PROJECT 2 - MISSION OF MADNESS (12") | 40 |
| 93 | Knifeforce KF 012 | Death Of A Psychopath/Bass Drum Jungle Music (12") | 10 |
| 94 | Knifeforce KF 025 | Piano Progression (Double Whopper Mix)/Onward (Extra Pepperami Mix) (12") | 10 |

## LUNAR TWO
| | | | |
|---|---|---|---|
| 60s | Spot JWS 551 | Get It Take It/Don't Ever Leave Me | 20 |

## LUNATIC FRINGE
| | | | |
|---|---|---|---|
| 82 | Resurrection | Keep In Touch | 8 |
| 84 | COR 1 | CRINGE WITH THE FRINGE (EP) | 15 |

## LYDIA LUNCH
| | | | |
|---|---|---|---|
| 91 | UFO UFOPF 1 | Spooky (mono)/Spooky (stereo) (no p/s, promo only) | 6 |
| 93 | Clawfist X-PIG 19 | Unearthly Delights/Busted (p/s) | 8 |
| 80 | Celluoid CEL 2 6561 | QUEEN OF SIAM (LP) | 25 |
| 82 | Situation 2 SITU 6 | 13.13 (LP, with inner sleeve) | 20 |
| 84 | Doublevision DVR 5 | IN LIMBO (LP, red vinyl with inner sleeve) | 20 |
| 86 | Widowspeak SWP 01/07 | THE INTIMATE DIARIES OF THE SEXUALLY INSANE (cassette, box set with book, signed) | 25 |
| 87 | Widowspeak WSP 8 | HYSTERIE (2-LP, with inners and poster) | 20 |

(see also Eight-Eyed Spy, Roland S. Howard, No Trend)

## ART LUND
| | | | |
|---|---|---|---|
| 57 | Vogue Coral LVA 9056 | THIS IS ART (LP) | 20 |

## BRAD LUNDY
| | | | |
|---|---|---|---|
| 73 | Pyramid PYR 7006 | I Could Never Have Another (After Loving You)/It Ain't Always What You Do | 12 |

MINT VALUE £

**TED LUNE**
60   Philips PB 1068          Mr Custer/Time Machine ............................................................. 6
*(see also Michael Medwin 8 Army Game Cast)*

**LUNG LEG**
97   Versuvius POMPLP 007     MAID TO MINX (LP)............................................................. 15

**LARRY LUREX**
73   EMI EMI 2030           I Can Hear Music/Goin' Back (demo) ....................................... 300
73   EMI EMI 2030           I Can Hear Music/Goin' Back (press-out centre; beware of solid-centered
                               counterfeits) .................................................................... 200

*(see also Queen)*

**LURKERS**
77   Beggars Banquet BEG 1     Free Admission Single: Shadow/Love Story (p/s, black vinyl)........... 10
77   Beggars Banquet BEG 1     Free Admission Single: Shadow/Love Story (p/s, reissue, red, blue or white vinyl) ....... 12
77   Beggars Banquet BEG 2     Freak Show/Mass Media Believer (p/s).................................... 10
78   Beggars Banquet BEG 6     Ain't Got A Clue/Ooh Ooh I Love You (p/s, 15,000 with gold flexidisc, 'Chaos Brothers
                               Fulham Fallout Firty Free' [BEG 61/2]) ................................... 6
78   Beggars Banquet BEG 6     Ain't Got A Clue/Ooh Ooh I Love You (p/s)............................... 5
78   Beggars Banquet BEG 6     Ain't Got A Clue/Ooh Ooh I Love You (reissue, different p/s, with clear vinyl picture
                               flexidisc) ........................................................................ 5
78   Beggars Banquet BEG 14    Just Thirteen/Countdown ................................................... 5
79   Beggars Banquet BACK 1    Shadow/Love Story//Freak Show/Mass Media Believer (reissue double pack) ............ 5
79   Beggars Banquet BEG 28    New Guitar In Town/Little Ole Wine Drinker Me ....................... 5
79   Beggars Banquet BACK 3    I Don't Need To Tell Her/Pills//Just Thirteen/Countdown (double pack) ............... 5
82   Clay CLAY 17             Drag You Out/Heroin ....................................................... 5
83   Clay CLAY 21             Frankenstein Again/One Man's Meat ..................................... 5
78   Beggars Banquet BEGA 2    FULHAM FALLOUT (LP, gatefold sleeve, some with picture disc flexi 'Chaos Brothers
                               Fulham Fallout Firty Free' [BEG 6 ½] & stickered sleeve) ........... 20

*(see also Fulham Furies, Rowdies)*

**LUSH**
89   4AD JAD 911            SCAR (mini-LP) .............................................................. 15
92   4AD CAD D 2002       SPOOKY (2x10" LP)............................................................ 25
94   4AD CAD 2002         SPOOKY (LP)................................................................... 20
90   4AD CAD 0017         GALA (LP)...................................................................... 25
94   4AD CAD 4011         SPLIT (LP)...................................................................... 35
96   4AD CAD 6004         LOVELIFE (LP, clear vinyl) ................................................. 35

**DON LUSHER BAND**
55   Decca F 10560         Rock 'n' Roll/On With The Don .......................................... 20
56   Decca F 10740         Fast And Furious/Let's Do It ............................................. 8
67   CBS 62883             FROM LUSHER WITH LOVE (LP)............................................. 15

**LUSTMØRD**
81   Sterile SR 3            LUSTMØRD (LP, 1st pressing, white cover with 2 postcards) ......... 60
81   Sterile SR3             LUSTMØRD (LP, 2nd pressing, grey cover) .............................. 35
86   Side Effects SER 07     PARADISE DISOWNED (LP).................................................... 20

**NELLIE LUTCHER (& HER RHYTHM)**
54   Brunswick 05352       Blues In The Night/Breezin' Along With The Breeze .................. 10
55   Brunswick 05437       It's Been Said/Please Come Back........................................ 7
55   Brunswick 05497       Whose Honey Are You?/If I Didn't Love You Like I Do ............... 8
60   Capitol CL 15106      My Mother's Eyes/The Heart Of A Clown .............................. 6
60   Capitol EAP 20066     REAL GONE (EP) .............................................................. 15
56   Philips BBE 12045     NELLIE LUTCHER (EP) ....................................................... 15
51   Capitol LC 6506       REAL GONE! (10" LP) ........................................................ 30
57   London HA-U 2036     OUR NEW NELLIE (LP)........................................................ 25

**LUTHER & LITTLE EVA**
57   Parlophone R 4292     Love Is Strange/Ain't Got No Home ................................... 400
57   Parlophone R 4292     Love Is Strange/Ain't Got No Home (78) .............................. 100

**LUV BUG**
86   Roxy!-Ritz TEASE 2     You Can Count On Me/You Can't Have It (p/s) ...................... 7

**LUV MACHINE**
71   Polydor 2058 080      Witches Wand/In The Early Hours ...................................... 30
71   Polydor 2460 102      LUV MACHINE (LP)............................................................ 300
06   Rise Above Relics RARLP 001 TURNS YOU ON (2-LP) ................................................. 20

**LUVVERS**
66   Parlophone R 5459     The House On The Hill/Most Unlovely.................................. 70
*(see also Lulu)*

**MICK LUVZIT**
66   Decca F 12421         Long Time Between Lovers/Though I Still Love You ................. 10

**GARY LUX**
85   Global LUX 2           Children Of The World/Movies (p/s) .................................. 5

**LUXURY**
91   Spare Beat SBRR 001    LUXURY EP 1 (12") .......................................................... 15
92   Spare Beat SBRR 003    The Silencer/You And Me (12") ......................................... 15

**L-VOAG**
79   Sesame Songs MOVE 1   MOVE (EP, p/s with handmade labels & insert) ..................... 30
81   Axis No. 9             THE WAY OUT (LP, with booklet & poster) ........................... 40
*(see also Homosexuals)*

**LYADRIVE**
84   Bridge BR 003         Anytime/White Dress (no p/s)........................................... 30

## LYDS
| | | | |
|---|---|---|---|
| 96 | Dig The Fuzz DIG 014 | Fly Away With Me/Seperations (p/s) | 15 |

## ARTHUR LYMAN GROUP
| | | | |
|---|---|---|---|
| 61 | Vogue V 9183 | Yellow Bird/Havah Magila | 6 |
| 59 | Vogue VA 160142 | TABOO VOL. 1 (LP, mono) | 15 |
| 59 | Vogue SAV 8002 | TABOO VOL. 1 (LP, stereo) | 18 |
| 61 | Vogue VA 160174 | TABOO VOL. 2 (LP, also stereo SAV 8003) | 15 |

## FRANKIE LYMON (& TEENAGERS)
| | | | |
|---|---|---|---|
| 56 | Columbia SCM 5265 | Why Do Fools Fall In Love?/Please Be Mine (as Teenagers featuring Frankie Lymon) | 60 |
| 56 | Columbia SCM 5285 | I Want You To Be My Girl/I'm Not A Know It All | 50 |
| 56 | Columbia DB 3819 | Who Can Explain?/I Promise To Remember | 50 |
| 56 | Columbia DB 3858 | Share/The A.B.C.'s Of Love | 50 |
| 57 | Columbia DB 3878 | I'm Not A Juvenile Delinquent/Baby, Baby | 30 |
| 57 | Columbia DB 3910 | Teenage Love/Paper Castles | 40 |
| 57 | Columbia DB 3942 | Miracle In The Rain/Out In The Cold Again | 40 |
| 57 | Columbia DB 3983 | Goody Goody/Creation Of Love | 20 |
| 57 | Columbia DB 4028 | My Girl/So Goes My Love | 25 |
| 58 | Columbia DB 4073 | Thumb Thumb/Footsteps (solo) | 30 |
| 58 | Columbia DB 4134 | Mama Don't Allow It/Portable On My Shoulder (solo) | 20 |
| 59 | Columbia DB 4245 | Melinda/The Only Way To Love (solo) | 20 |
| 59 | Columbia DB 4295 | Up Jumped A Rabbit/No Matter What You've Done (solo) | 25 |
| 60 | Columbia DB 4499 | Little Bitty Pretty One/Creation Of Love (solo) | 25 |
| 66 | King KG 1042 | Why Do Fools Fall In Love?/I'm Not A Juvenile Delinquent | 6 |
| 57 | Columbia SEG 7662 | TEENAGE ROCK (EP) | 30 |
| 57 | Columbia SEG 7694 | THE TEENAGERS FEATURING FRANKIE LYMON (EP) | 35 |
| 57 | Columbia SEG 7734 | FRANKIE LYMON AND THE TEENAGERS (EP) | 30 |
| 58 | Columbia 33S 1127 | FRANKIE LYMON IN LONDON (10" LP, solo) | 50 |
| 58 | Columbia 33S 1134 | ROCKIN' WITH FRANKIE LYMON (10" LP, solo) | 300 |

## LEWIS LYMON & TEENCHORDS
| | | | |
|---|---|---|---|
| 58 | Oriole 45-CB 1419 | Too Young/Your Last Chance | 500 |
| 58 | Oriole CB 1419 | Too Young/Your Last Chance (78) | 100 |

## DERMOTT LYNCH
| | | | |
|---|---|---|---|
| 68 | Blue Cat BS 101 | Hot Shot/I've Got Your Number | 100 |
| 68 | Blue Cat BS 122 | I Got Everything/Echo | 200 |
| 68 | Doctor Bird DB 1115 | Adults Only/Cool It | 50 |

*(see also Trevor, Carl Dawkins, Joe White)*

## E D LYNCH
| | | | |
|---|---|---|---|
| 66 | Fontana TF688 | Sad Songs/Shoe Of True Love | 15 |

## JOE LYNCH
| | | | |
|---|---|---|---|
| 69 | Spectrum SP 107 | King Child/Johnny Appleseed | 5 |

## KENNY LYNCH
| | | | |
|---|---|---|---|
| 60 | HMV POP 751 | Mountain Of Love/Why Do You Treat Me This Way? | 10 |
| 60 | HMV POP 786 | Slowcoach/You Make Love So Well | 8 |
| 61 | HMV POP 841 | So/Love Me | 6 |
| 61 | HMV POP 900 | The Story Behind My Tears/Steady Kind | 6 |
| 61 | HMV POP 985 | There's Never Been A Girl/Doll Face | 6 |
| 62 | HMV POP 1005 | It Would Take A Miracle/Strolling Blues | 6 |
| 62 | HMV POP 1057 | Puff/Happy That's Me | 15 |
| 62 | HMV POP 1090 | Up On The Roof/Jump On Your Broomstick | 10 |
| 63 | HMV POP 1136 | Misery/Shut The Door | 10 |
| 63 | HMV POP 1165 | You Can Never Stop Me Loving You/Crazy Crazes | 5 |
| 63 | HMV POP 1229 | For You (There's Not A Thing I Wouldn't Do)/With Somebody | 5 |
| 63 | HMV POP 1260 | Shake And Scream/Harlem Library | 5 |
| 64 | HMV POP 1280 | Stand By Me/Baby It's True | 5 |
| 64 | HMV POP 1321 | That's What Little Girls Are Made For/What Am I To You? | 6 |
| 64 | HMV POP 1367 | My Own Two Feet/So Much To Love You For | 40 |
| 65 | HMV POP 1430 | I'll Stay By You/For Loving You Baby | 7 |
| 65 | HMV POP 1476 | Nothing But The Real Thing/Don't Ask Me To Stop Loving You | 6 |
| 65 | HMV POP 1496 | Get Out Of My Way/One Look At You | 10 |
| 66 | HMV POP 1534 | The World I Used To Know/Come On Come On | 7 |
| 67 | HMV POP 1577 | I Just Wanna Love You/It's Too Late | 15 |
| 67 | HMV POP 1604 | Movin' Away/Could I Count On You | 150 |
| 68 | Columbia DB 8329 | Mister Moonlight/The Other Side Of Dreamland | 15 |
| 68 | Columbia DB 8498 | Along Comes Love/Sweet Situation | 15 |
| 69 | Columbia DB 8599 | The Drifter/Did I Stay Too Long? | 30 |
| 70 | Columbia DB 8703 | In Old Kentucky/Loving You Is Sweeter Than Ever | 8 |
| 63 | HMV 7EG 8820 | HEY GIRL (EP) | 12 |
| 64 | HMV 7EG 8855 | KENNY LYNCH (EP) | 12 |
| 65 | HMV 7EG 8881 | WHAT AM I TO YOU (EP) | 12 |
| 63 | HMV CLP 1635 | UP ON THE ROOF (LP, mono) | 45 |
| 63 | HMV CSD 1489 | UP ON THE ROOF (LP, stereo) | 50 |

## LEE LYNCH (& BLUE ANGELS)
| | | | |
|---|---|---|---|
| 66 | Decca F 12375 | You Won't See Me/You Know There's Me (as Lee Lynch & Blue Angels) | 10 |
| 69 | Ember EMB S 262 | Stay Awhile/Bad Time To Stop Loving Me (p/s) | 10 |
| 70 | Ember EMB S 271 | Sweet Woman/Can't Take My Eyes Off You (p/s) | 10 |
| 70 | Ember EMB S 282 | Joe Poor Loves Daphne Elizabeth Rich/It's Love (p/s) | 10 |
| 67 | Pye 7N 17363 | I'll Hold You In My Heart/Looking Through My Teardrops | 10 |

MINT VALUE £

**LINDA LYNDELL**
| | | | |
|---|---|---|---|
| 68 | Stax 601 041 | Bring Your Love Back To Me/Here I Am | 50 |

**BARBARA LYNN**
| | | | |
|---|---|---|---|
| 64 | London HLW 9918 | Oh! Baby (We Got A Good Thing Goin')/Unfair | 40 |
| 65 | Immediate IM 011 | You Can't Buy My Love/That's What A Friend Will Do | 45 |
| 66 | London HLU 10094 | You Left The Water Running/Until I'm Free | 35 |
| 67 | Sue WI 4028 | Letter To Mommy And Daddy/Second Fiddle Girl | 50 |
| 67 | Sue WI 4038 | You'll Lose A Good Thing/Lonely Heartaches | 55 |
| 71 | Atlantic 2091 133 | Take Your Love And Run/(Until Then) I'll Suffer | 25 |
| 75 | Oval OVAL 1006 | Letter To Mommy And Daddy/You'll Lose A Good Thing | 10 |
| 67 | Sue ILP 949 | THE BARBARA LYNN STORY (LP) | 200 |

**BOBBI LYNN**
| | | | |
|---|---|---|---|
| 68 | Stateside SS 2088 | Earthquake/Opportunity Street | 50 |
| 68 | Stateside SS 2088 | Earthquake/Opportunity Street (DJ copy) | 75 |
| 71 | Bell BLL 1168 | Earthquake/Opportunity Street (reissue) | 10 |

**JESSE LYNN DEAN**
| | | | |
|---|---|---|---|
| 79 | Creole CR 176 | Do It/My Boyfriend's Back In Town (p/s) | 20 |

*(see also the Wasps)*

**DONNA LYNN**
| | | | |
|---|---|---|---|
| 64 | Capitol CL 15359 | Silly Girl/There Goes The Boy I Love With Mary | 6 |

**KARI LYNN**
| | | | |
|---|---|---|---|
| 61 | Oriole CB 1632 | Yo Yo/Summer Day | 15 |
| 61 | Oriole CB 1644 | You've Got To See Mamma Every Night/Lonesome And Sorry | 15 |

**PATTI LYNN**
| | | | |
|---|---|---|---|
| 62 | Fontana H 370 | I See It All Now/Someone Else's Valentine | 15 |
| 62 | Fontana H 391 | Johnny Angel/Tonight You Belong To Me | 15 |
| 62 | Fontana 267 247 TF | Tell Me Telstar/Big Big Love | 20 |
| 62 | Fontana TFE 17392 | PATTI (EP) | 40 |

**TAM(M)I LYNN**
| | | | |
|---|---|---|---|
| 71 | Mojo 209 2012 | That's Understanding/Never No More | 5 |
| 66 | Atlantic AT 4071 | I'm Gonna Run Away From You/The Boy Next Door | 70 |
| 66 | Atlantic AT 4071 | I'm Gonna Run Away From You/The Boy Next Door (DJ Copy) | 100 |
| 71 | Mojo 2092 001 | I'm Gonna Run Away From You/The Boy Next Door (reissue) | 10 |
| 71 | Mojo 2092 012 | That's Understanding/Never No More | 6 |
| 75 | Contempo CS 9026 | I'm Gonna Run Away From You/The Boy Next Door (2nd reissue) | 6 |
| 71 | Mojo 2916 007 | LOVE IS HERE AND NOW YOU'RE GONE (LP) | 25 |

**VERA LYNN**
| | | | |
|---|---|---|---|
| 52 | Decca F 9927 | Auf Wiederseh'n, Sweetheart/From The Time You Say Goodbye | 10 |
| 54 | Decca F 10372 | My Son, My Son/Our Heaven On Earth (with Frank Weir & His Saxophone) | 15 |

*(see also Johnstone Brothers, Frank Weir & His Orchestra)*

**GLORIA LYNNE**
| | | | |
|---|---|---|---|
| 64 | London HLY 9846 | I Wish You Love/Through A Long And Sleeping Night | 8 |
| 64 | London HLY 9888 | I Should Care/Indian Love Call | 8 |
| 69 | Fontana TF 1017 | Problem Child/I've Got To Be Someone | 6 |
| 59 | Top Rank JKP 2024 | MEET GLORIA LYNNE (EP, with Wild Bill Davis) | 20 |
| 60 | Top Rank BUY 031 | LONELY AND SENTIMENTAL (LP) | 25 |
| 64 | London HA-Y 8112 | AT THE LAS VEGAS THUNDERBIRD (LP, with Herman Foster Trio) | 15 |
| 65 | Fontana TL 5315 | INTIMATE MOMENTS (LP) | 15 |
| 72 | Mojo 2916 016 | HAPPY AND IN LOVE (LP) | 25 |

**SUE LYNNE**
| | | | |
|---|---|---|---|
| 68 | RCA Victor RCA 1724 | Reach For The Moon/All Alone | 10 |
| 69 | RCA Victor RCA 1822 | You/Don't Pity Me | 150 |
| 69 | RCA Victor RCA 1822 | You/Don't Pity Me (DJ copy) | 200 |
| 69 | RCA Victor RCA 1874 | Baby Baby Baby/You Lose Again | 7 |

**PHIL LYNOTT**
| | | | |
|---|---|---|---|
| 80 | Vertigo SOLO 2 | King's Call/Ode To A Black Man (p/s) | 5 |
| 81 | Vertigo SOLO 3 | Yellow Pearl/Girls (p/s, clear vinyl) | 5 |
| 85 | Vertigo SOLO 5 | Old Town/Beat Of The Drum (p/s) | 6 |
| 85 | Polydor POSPD 777 | 19/19 (Dub Version)//THIN LIZZY: Whiskey In The Jar (live) (double pack, 2nd disc 1-sided) | 8 |
| 80 | Vertigo PHIL 1 | SOLO IN SOHO (LP, picture disc, die-cut sleeve) | 15 |

*(see also Thin Lizzy, Gary Moore & Phil Lynott, John Sykes, Rockers)*

**JACKIE LYNTON**
| | | | |
|---|---|---|---|
| 61 | Piccadilly 7N 35012 | Over The Rainbow/High In The Sky | 6 |
| 62 | Piccadilly 7N 35055 | Don't Take Away Your Love/Wishful Thinking | 8 |
| 62 | Piccadilly 7N 35064 | All Of Me/I'd Steal | 7 |
| 63 | Piccadilly 7N 35107 | I Believe/The Girl In The Wood | 7 |
| 63 | Piccadilly 7N 35140 | Jeannie With The Light Brown Hair/Teddy Bear's Picnic | 7 |
| 63 | Piccadilly 7N 35156 | I'm Talkin' About You/Lawdy Miss Clawdy | 6 |
| 64 | Piccadilly 7N 35177 | Little Child/Never A Mention | 5 |
| 64 | Piccadilly 7N 35190 | Laura/Ebb Tide | 5 |
| 65 | Decca F 12052 | Three Blind Mice/Corrina Corrine | 6 |
| 67 | Columbia DB 8097 | He'll Have To Go/Only You | 10 |
| 67 | Columbia DB 8180 | Decision/Sporting Life | 10 |
| 67 | Columbia DB 8224 | Answer Me/I Never Loved A Girl Like You | 25 |
| 79 | Thumb TR003 | Dan (The Hedgehog Song)/Farting With The Famous | 8 |

*(see also Savoy Brown Blues Band)*

## LYNX
| | | | |
|---|---|---|---|
| 78 | ST Products SRTS/78/CUS 112 | See The Light/C.I.A. (no p/s, 500 only) | 250 |

## LYNYRD SKYNYRD
| | | | |
|---|---|---|---|
| 74 | MCA MCA 136 | Don't Ask Me No Questions/Take Your Time | 5 |
| 74 | MCA MCA 160 | Sweet Home Alabama/Take Your Time | 5 |
| 75 | MCA MCA 199 | Saturday Night Special/Made In The Shade | 5 |
| 76 | MCA MCA 229 | Double Trouble/Roll Gypsy Roll | 5 |
| 76 | MCA MCA 251 | Free Bird/Sweet Home Alabama/Double Trouble (p/s) | 8 |
| 76 | MCA MCA 275 | Free Bird (Edit)/Gimme Three Steps (p/s) | 8 |
| 74 | MCA MCG 3502 | PRONOUNCED LEH-NERD SKIN-NERD (LP, gatefold sleeve) | 18 |
| 77 | MCA MCG 3525 | STREET SURVIVORS (LP, gatefold sleeve with tour dates on inner sleeve) | 15 |

## BARBARA LYON
| | | | |
|---|---|---|---|
| 55 | Columbia SCM 5186 | I Love To Dance With You/Yes You Are | 10 |
| 55 | Columbia SCM 5207 | Whisper/Where You Are | 10 |
| 56 | Columbia SCM 5232 | Band Of Gold/Such A Day | 10 |
| 56 | Columbia SCM 5276 | Puppy Love/The Birds And The Bees | 8 |
| 56 | Columbia DB 3826 | It's Better In The Dark/A Heart Without A Sweetheart | 6 |
| 56 | Columbia DB 3865 | Falling In Love/Letter To A Soldier | 15 |
| 57 | Columbia DB 3931 | C'est La Vie/Fire Down Below | 5 |
| 57 | Columbia DB 4026 | Thanks For The Loan Of A Dream/Third Finger - Left Hand | 5 |
| 58 | Columbia DB 4137 | Red Was The Moon/Ring On A Ribbon | 40 |
| 60 | Triumph RGM 1027 | My Charlie/Tell Me | 5 |
| 56 | Columbia SEG 7640 | MY FOUR FRIENDS (EP) | 15 |

## RICHARD LYON
| | | | |
|---|---|---|---|
| 59 | Fontana H 206 | All My Own/Private Eye | 22 |

## SUE LYON
| | | | |
|---|---|---|---|
| 62 | MGM 1159 | Lolita Ya Ya/LEROY HOLMES : Main Theme From Lolita | 10 |

*(See also Leroy Holmes)*

## LYONS & MALONE
| | | | |
|---|---|---|---|
| 69 | Jay Boy BOY 9 | Doctor Gentle/She's Alright | 60 |

## LYRICS
| | | | |
|---|---|---|---|
| 67 | Coxsone CS 7003 | A Get It/KEN PARKER: How Strong | 75 |
| 68 | Coxsone CS 7067 | Music Like Dirt/TONETTES: I Give It To You | 150 |
| 70 | Randy's RAN 504 | Give Thanks And Praises/TOMMY McCOOK: Get Ready | 15 |
| 71 | Randy's RAN 511 | Give Thanks/RANDY'S ALL STARS: Give - Version | 15 |

*(see also Randy's All Stars, Viceroys, Jackie Mittoo, Fred Locks)*

## LARS LYSTEDT SEXTET
| | | | |
|---|---|---|---|
| 64 | Realm REP 4004 | LARS LYSTEDT SEXTET (EP) | 10 |

## JIMMY LYTELL
| | | | |
|---|---|---|---|
| 59 | London HL 8873 | Hot Cargo/A Blues Serenade | 10 |

## JOHNNY LYTLE
| | | | |
|---|---|---|---|
| 68 | Minit MLF 11006 | Gonna Get That Boat (Parts 1 & 2) | 15 |

## HUMPHREY LYTTELTON (& HIS BAND)
### SINGLES
| | | | |
|---|---|---|---|
| 51 | Saturn EGX 105 | When The Saints Go Marching In/Careless Love (78, picture disc) | 60 |
| 53 | Parlophone MSP 6001 | Out Of The Gallion/The Old Grey Mare | 10 |
| 53 | Parlophone MSP 6023 | Muskrat Ramble/Mamzelle Josephine (as Lyttelton Paseo Band, B-side with George Brown) | 5 |
| 53 | Parlophone MSP 6033 | Maryland, My Maryland/Blue For Waterloo | 10 |
| 53 | Parlophone MSP 6034 | Shake It And Break It/Jail Break | 10 |
| 54 | Parlophone MSP 6076 | East Coast Trot/Breeze | 5 |
| 54 | Parlophone MSP 6093 | Just Once For All Time/Joshua, Fit The Battle Of Jericho | 5 |
| 54 | Parlophone MSP 6097 | Mainly Traditional/Oh! Dad (with 'Melody Maker' All Stars) | 5 |
| 54 | Parlophone MSP 6128 | Mezzy's Tune/Jelly Bean Blues | 8 |
| 56 | Tempo A 10 | When The Saints Go Marching In/Careless Love | 10 |
| 57 | Parlophone R 4333 | Early Call (Bermondsey Bounce)/Creole Serenade | 20 |
| 58 | Parlophone CMSP 41 | Bad Penny Blues/Baby Doll (export issue) | 5 |
| 58 | Decca F 11058 | La Paloma/Bodega | 8 |
| 59 | Parlophone R 4519 | Saturday Jump/The Bear Steps Out | |

### EPs
| | | | |
|---|---|---|---|
| 55 | Tempo EXA 1 | HUMPHREY LYTTELTON & HIS BAND (EP) | 10 |

### ALBUMS : LPS
| | | | |
|---|---|---|---|
| 53 | Parlophone PMD 1006 | JAZZ CONCERT (10" LP) | 30 |
| 54 | Parlophone PMC 1012 | HUMPH AT THE CONWAY (LP) | 30 |
| 55 | Parlophone PMD 1032 | JAZZ AT THE ROYAL FESTIVAL HALL (10" LP) | 20 |
| 56 | Parlophone PMD 1035 | JAZZ SESSION WITH HUMPH (10" LP) | 15 |
| 56 | Parlophone PMD 1044 | HUMPH SWINGS OUT (10" LP) | 25 |
| 57 | Parlophone PMD 1049 | HERE'S HUMPH (10" LP) | 15 |
| 58 | Parlophone PMD 1052 | KATH MEETS HUMPH (10" LP, with Kathy Stobart) | 20 |
| 58 | Parlophone PMC 1070 | HUMPH IN PERSPECTIVE (LP) | 20 |
| 58 | Decca LK 4276 | I PLAY AS I PLEASE (LP) | 70 |
| 59 | Parlophone PMC 1110 | TRIPLE EXPOSURE (LP) | 20 |
| 54 | Esquire 32-007 | HUMPHREY LYTTELTON AND HIS BAND (LP) | 20 |
| 60 | Columbia 33SX 1239 | BLUES IN THE NIGHT (LP) | 20 |
| 60 | Columbia 33SX 1305 | HUMPH PLAYS STANDARDS (LP) | 30 |
| 60 | Columbia 33SX 1364 | HUMPH MEETS CAB (LP) | 20 |
| 61 | Columbia 33SX 3382 | HUMPH RETURNS TO THE CONWAY (LP) | 18 |

**62  Columbia 33SX 1484**  LATE NIGHT FINAL (LP) ......................................................... MINT VALUE £
...................................................................................................................................... 18
*(see also Shirley Abicair, Sidney Bechet, George Brown, Buck Clayton, Helen Shapiro, Radiohead)o*

## MABEL
**78  Sonet SON 2147**  Boom Boom/FBI On The Nail (p/s) .................................................. 6

## MOMS MABLEY
**69  Mercury MF 1127**  Abraham, Martin And John/Sunny ............................................... 12
**71  Mercury 6052 109**  That's Pops/I Surrender Dear ..................................................... 6

## WILLIE MABON
**64  Sue WI 320**  Got To Have Some/Why Did It Happen To Me......................................... 50
**65  Sue WI 331**  Just Got Some/That's No Big Thing ..................................................... 50
**65  Sue WI 382**  I'm The Fixer/Some More ................................................................... 50

## MABRAK
**78  Different GET A101**  DRUM TALK (mixed by King Tubby) (LP, cover laminated front and back) .................. 150

## DEBBIE MAC
**80  Active ACT 1**  Hots For You/Words (promo only) ....................................................... 8

## SPENCER MAC
**70  Penny Farthing PEN 723**  Blues Up In Down Town/Ka Ka Kabya Mow Mow .......................... 100
**70  Penny Farthing PEN 742**  Commuter/Better By You - Better By Me ................................... 60

## MACABRE
**87  Vinyl Solution SOL 18**  GRIM REALITY (LP, with insert) ....................................... 18
**89  Vinyl Solution SOL 020**  GLOOM (LP) ................................................................ 15

## GLO MACARI
**65  Piccadilly 7N 35218**  He Knows I Love Him Too Much/I've Lost You ............................. 15
**71  Columbia DB 8821**  Looking For Love/People Like You ......................................... 15

## NEIL MACARTHUR
**69  Deram DM 225**  She's Not There/World Of Glass .......................................................... 25
**69  Deram DM 262**  Don't Try To Explain/Without Her......................................................... 15
**69  Deram DM 275**  It's Not Easy/12.29 .......................................................................... 15
*(see also Colin Blunstone, Zombies)*

## MACARTHUR PARK
**70  Columbia DB 8683**  Taffeta Rose/Sammy ........................................................... 12
**71  Philips 6006 086**  Lottie Lottie/Love Is Coming ............................................... 6
*(see also Shadows)*

## MACATTACK
**86  Baad! Records 12HIP1AZ**  ART OF DRUMS (12" EP)..................................................... 15

## DAVID MACBETH
**59  Pye Nixa 7N 15231**  Mr. Blue/Here's A Heart .................................................... 7
**60  Pye 7N 15250**  Tell Her From Me/Livin' Dangerously...................................................... 5
**62  Piccadilly 7N 35072**  Have I Told You Lately That I Love You/A Brother Like You .................... 6
**63  Piccadilly 7N 35092**  A Very Good Year For Girls/Broken Hearts.................................. 5

## MACC LADS
**89  Renegade RS 1**  Jingle Bells/Even Uglier Women (p/s) ..................................................... 5
**90  FM Revolver VHF 42**  Barrels Round/Jingle Bells (p/s)........................................... 5
**86  Hectic House HHS 1**  EH UP! MACC LADS (EP) ...................................................... 8
**85  FM Revolver FMLP 56**  BEER AND SEX AND CHIPS'N'GRAVY (LP, white vinyl) .................... 15
**88  FM Revolver WKFMLP 115**  LIVE AT LEEDS (LP, blue vinyl)....................................... 15

## MACCABEES
**06  Promise PROM 001**  X-Ray/Lego........................................................................... 15
**09  Fiction 2703065**  WALL OF ARMS (LP) ........................................................... 18

## EWAN MACCOLL
**58  Topic 10T 26**  BARRACK ROOM BALLADS (10" LP) ......................................................... 20
**58  Topic 10T 36**  BOLD SPORTSMEN ALL (10" LP, with A.L. Lloyd)........................................... 20
**58  Topic 10T 50**  STILL I LOVE HIM (10" LP with booklet, with Isla Cameron)............................... 20
**60  Topic 12T 41**  STREETS OF SONG (LP, with Dominic Behan, with booklet and original blue label)........ 15
**62  Topic 12T 79**  THE JACOBITE REBELLIONS (LP, with original blue label) ................................ 15
**64  Topic 12T 103**  ENGLISH AND SCOTTISH FOLK BALLADS (LP, with A.L. Lloyd, initial pressing with blue label & booklet) ... 15
**64  Topic 12T 103**  ENGLISH AND SCOTTISH FOLK BALLADS (LP, with A.L. Lloyd)................................ 15
**67  Topic 12T 130**  BUNDOOK BALLADS (LP, originally with blue label) ..................................... 15
**67  Argo ZFB 12**  SOLO FLIGHT (LP; reissued 1972)........................................................... 15
**67  Xtra 1052**  BLOW BOYS BLOW - SONGS OF THE SEA (LP, with A.L. Lloyd) ................................. 15
**68  Argo (Z)DA 85**  THE WANTON MUSE (LP, with booklet) .................................................... 15
*(see also A.L. Lloyd)*

## EWAN MACCOLL & PEGGY SEEGER (& CHARLES PARKER)
**57  Topic 10T 13**  SHUTTLE AND CAGE (10" LP)
**61  Topic 12T 16**  CHORUS FROM THE GALLOWS (LP, original pressing with blue label, insert) ............... 20
**64  Topic 12T 104**  STEAM WHISTLE BALLADS (LP, blue label)............................................... 15
**64  Topic 12T 104**  STEAM WHISTLE BALLADS (LP, later reissue with booklet)................................ 15
**65  Argo RG 474**  THE BALLAD OF JOHN AXON (LP, by Ewan MacColl & Charles Parker) ........................ 18
**67  Topic 12T 147**  THE MANCHESTER ANGEL (LP, original pressing with blue label)......................... 18

| 67 | Argo DA 140 | THE BIG HEWER - A RADIO BALLAD BY EWAN MacCOLL, PEGGY SEEGER, CHARLES PARKER (LP, documentary with music) .......... 20 |
|---|---|---|
| 67 | Argo (Z)DA 66 | LONG HARVEST 1 (LP) .......... 15 |
| 67 | Argo (Z)DA 67 | LONG HARVEST 2 (LP) .......... 15 |
| 67 | Argo (Z)DA 68 | LONG HARVEST 3 (LP) .......... 15 |
| 67 | Argo (Z)DA 69 | LONG HARVEST 4 (LP) .......... 15 |
| 67 | Argo RG 502 | SINGING THE FISHING (LP, with Charles Parker) .......... 25 |
| 67 | Argo DA 142 | SINGING THE FISHING (LP, reissue, with Charles Parker) .......... 18 |
| 60s | XTRA 1054 | SCOTS BALLADS (LP) .......... 20 |
| 60s | Folkways FW 8958 | SONGS OF ROBERT BURNS (LP) .......... 30 |
| 70 | Argo DA 133 | THE TRAVELLING PEOPLE (LP, with Charles Parker) .......... 15 |
| 71 | Argo DA 136 | ON THE EDGE (LP) .......... 15 |

*(see also Peggy Seeger, A.L. Lloyd, Isla Cameron)*

## KIRSTY MACCOLL
| 79 | Stiff BUY 47 | They Don't Know/Motor On (yellow label, 'plug copy' promo, p/s) .......... 15 |
|---|---|---|
| 79 | Stiff BUY 47 | They Don't Know/Motor On (yellow label, push-out centre p/s) .......... 7 |
| 79 | Stiff PBUY 47 | They Don't Know/Motor On (picture disc) .......... 10 |
| 79 | Stiff BUY 57 | You Caught Me Out/Boys (with Boomtown Rats, unreleased, demos only) .......... 50 |
| 81 | Polydor POSP 225 | Keep Your Hands Off My Baby/I Don't Need You (p/s) .......... 7 |
| 81 | Polydor POSP 368 | You Still Believe In Me/Queen Of The High Teas (p/s) .......... 15 |
| 83 | Stiff BUY DJ 190 | Terry/Quietly Alone (Grey promo. "A" label) .......... 5 |
| 83 | Stiff BUY DJ 190 | Terry/Quietly Alone (Pink promo. "A" label) .......... 15 |
| 84 | Stiff BUY 216 | A New England/Patrick (Kirsty close-up p/s) .......... 5 |
| 84 | Stiff BUY 216 | A New England/Patrick (British flag p/s) .......... 10 |
| 85 | Polydor SEPLP 95825 791 | KIRSTY MACCOLL (LP) .......... 15 |

*(see also Drug Addix)*

## FINN MACCUILL
| 79 | Radio Edinburgh REL 460 | SINK YE - SWIM YE (LP) .......... 200 |
|---|---|---|

## GALT MACDERMOT
| 73 | Decca SKLR 5164 | TWO GENTLEMEN OF VERONA (LP) .......... 30 |
|---|---|---|

## GAVIN MACDONALD
| 72 | Regal Zono. SLRZ 1027 | LINES (LP, red/silver label) .......... 25 |
|---|---|---|

*(see also Country Joe & Fish)*

## MACEO & ALL THE KING'S MEN
| 72 | Pye International 7N 25571 | Got To Get 'Cha/Thank You For Letting Me Be Myself Again (Part 1) .......... 18 |
|---|---|---|
| 72 | Mojo 2916 017 | FUNKY MUSIC MACHINE (LP) .......... 30 |
| 75 | Contempo CRM 114 | FUNKY MUSIC MACHINE (LP, reissue) .......... 15 |

*(see also Maceo & The Macks, James Brown)*

## BIG MACEO
| 62 | RCA RCX 203 | KINGS OF THE BLUES (EP) .......... 10 |
|---|---|---|

## MACEO & THE MACKS
| 87 | Urban URB 1 | Cross The Tracks (We Better Go Back)/Soul Power (printed die-cut sleeve) .......... 8 |
|---|---|---|
| 87 | Urban URBX 1 | Cross The Tracks (We Better Go Back) (Extended Version)/Party Part 1/ Soul Power (12", printed die-cut sleeve) .......... 15 |
| 74 | Polydor 2391 122 | US (LP) .......... 30 |

*(see also Maceo & All The King's Men, James Brown)*

## TEO MACERO
| 57 | Esquire 32-113 | TEO (LP) .......... 30 |
|---|---|---|

## MACEYS WINDOW
| 72 | Parlophone R 5893 | It's Getting Harder/Pray For Sister Sunshine .......... 60 |
|---|---|---|

## CIARAN MAC GOWAN
| 80 | Good Vibrations MAC 1 | Little Susi/London Trip (p/s) .......... 6 |
|---|---|---|

## SHANE MACGOWAN & THE POPES
| 97 | ZTT MACG003P | MORE SONGS ABOUT DRINKING AND THINKING (10" EP, p/s) .......... 15 |
|---|---|---|

*(see also Pogues, Nick Cave & Shane MacGowan)*

## MACHINE MEN
| 71 | AXE 1 | Counting Time/Young Blood .......... 15 |
|---|---|---|

## MACHINE (1)
| 67 | Granta GR 7STD | Stupidity/Please Stay (private pressing) .......... 40 |
|---|---|---|

## MACHINE (2)
| 69 | Polydor 56760 | Spooky's Day Off/Nobody Wants You .......... 18 |
|---|---|---|

*(see also Swinging Soul Machine)*

## MACHINE (3)
| 78 | Plastic SRTS/78/CUS/198 | Bored With The City/Brown Eyed Girl (100 only, no p/s) .......... 275 |
|---|---|---|

## MACHINES
| 78 | Wax EAR 1 | True Life/Everything's Technical/You Better Hear/Evening Radio (stamped p/s, white labels) .......... 150 |
|---|---|---|
| 96 | Gecko 5 | True Life/Everything's Technical/You Better Hear/Evening Radio (reissue, pink or orange vinyl) .......... 8 |

## ALURA MACK
| 50s | Poydras 84 | Everybody's Man Is Mine/Monkey Blues .......... 8 |
|---|---|---|

## FREDDY MACK
| 67 | Rayrik TPMLP 143 | LIVE AT TOFT CLUB FOLKSTONE (LP, as Freddy Mack Show, 99 copies only) .......... 300 |
|---|---|---|

## JOHNNY MACK
| 70 | Columbia Blue Beat DB 116 | Reggae All Night Long/A Million Marvellous Feelings .......... 12 |
|---|---|---|

## LONNIE MACK
| 63 | Stateside SS 207 | Memphis/Down In The Dumps .......... 25 |
|---|---|---|
| 63 | Stateside SS 226 | Wham!/Susie-Q .......... 25 |

# MACK SISTERS

| | | | |
|---|---|---|---|
| 64 | Stateside SS 312 | Lonnie On The Move/Say Something Nice To Me | 18 |
| 65 | Stateside SS 393 | Sa-Ba-Hoola/Chickin' Pickin' | 20 |
| 67 | President PT 127 | Where There's A Will/Baby What's Wrong? | 7 |
| 67 | President PT 142 | Save Your Money/Snow On The Mountain | 7 |
| 68 | President PT 198 | Soul Express/I Found A Love | 10 |
| 69 | Elektra EKSN 45044 | Memphis/Why (Edited Version) | 10 |
| 69 | Elektra EKSN 45060 | Save Your Money/In The Band | 8 |
| 71 | Elektra EK 45715 | Lay It Down/She Even Woke Me Up To Say Goodbye | 6 |
| 67 | President PTL 1004 | THE WHAM OF THAT MEMPHIS MAN (LP) | 30 |
| 69 | Elektra EKL 4040 | GLAD I'M IN THE BAND (LP, orange label, also stereo EKS 74040) | 30 |
| 69 | Elektra EKS 74050 | WHATEVER'S RIGHT (LP, orange label) | 30 |

## MACK SISTERS
| | | | |
|---|---|---|---|
| 56 | London HLU 8331 | Long Range Love/Stop What You're Doing | 60 |

## WARNER MACK
| | | | |
|---|---|---|---|
| 58 | Brunswick 05728 | Roc-A-Chicka/Since I Lost You (with Anita Kerr Quartet) | 200 |
| 58 | Brunswick 05728 | Roc-A-Chicka/Since I Lost You (with Anita Kerr Quartet) (78) | 50 |
| 58 | Decca | Roc-A-Chicka/Since I Lost You (export issue, with Anita Kerr Quartet) | 60 |

## ANDY MACKAY
| | | | |
|---|---|---|---|
| 75 | Island WIP 6243 | Wild Weekend/Walking The Whippet (in promo p/s) | 6 |

*(see also Roxy Music, Rock Follies)*

## DUNCAN MACKAY
| | | | |
|---|---|---|---|
| 81 | Edge 14 | Sirius II Mark II/In The Pink (no p/s) | 10 |

## MAHNA MACKAY
| | | | |
|---|---|---|---|
| 69 | Parlophone R 5808 | Mah Na Mah Na/Daydream | 6 |

## RABBIT MACKAY
| | | | |
|---|---|---|---|
| 68 | MCA MU 1041 | Hard Time Woman/Candy | 8 |
| 68 | MCA MUPS 351 | BUG CLOTH (LP) | 15 |

## GISELE MACKENZIE
| | | | |
|---|---|---|---|
| 55 | HMV 7M 318 | Hard To Get/Boston Fancy | 8 |

## MACKENZIE JET COMBO
| | | | |
|---|---|---|---|
| 70 | Torpedo TOR 18 | Milkman's Theme/Capadulah Recipe | 8 |

## JUDY MACKENZIE
| | | | |
|---|---|---|---|
| 70 | Key KL 005 | JUDY (LP) | 22 |
| 71 | Key KL 009 | PEACE AND LOVE AND FREEDOM (LP, with poster) | 22 |

## MACKENZIES
| | | | |
|---|---|---|---|
| 86 | Ron Johnson ZRON 9 | New Breed/Dog's Breakfast (7" p/s) | 6 |

## MACKERAL
| | | | |
|---|---|---|---|
| 66 | Columbia DB 8013 | Funny Fish/This Is Mine | 5 |
| 68 | Columbia DB 8388 | Trying Again/White Man's Burden | 5 |

## KEN MACKINTOSH (& HIS ORCHESTRA)
| | | | |
|---|---|---|---|
| 56 | HMV 7M 343 | Creeping Tom/Lovers In The Dark | 5 |
| 56 | HMV 7M 359 | Start Walking/Curtain Call | 5 |
| 56 | HMV 7M 379 | Blues In The Night/Come Next Spring (B-side with Kenny Bardell) | 5 |
| 56 | HMV 7M 403 | Sleepwalker/The Berkeley Hunt | 5 |
| 56 | HMV 7M 417 | Dizzy Fingers/The Policeman's Holiday | 5 |
| 56 | HMV POP 270 | Soft Summer Breeze/Highway Patrol | 5 |
| 57 | HMV POP 287 | The Buccaneers/Regimental Rock | 5 |
| 57 | HMV POP 300 | Apple-Jack/Slow Walk | 5 |
| 57 | HMV POP 327 | Almost Paradise/Rock Man Rock | 15 |
| 57 | HMV POP 358 | Poni Tail/Keep It Movin' | 10 |
| 57 | HMV POP 396 | Marching Along To The Blues/Six-Five Blues | 8 |
| 57 | HMV POP 426 | Raunchy/Mojo | 10 |
| 58 | HMV POP 441 | The Stroll/The Swingin' Shepherd Blues | 8 |
| 56 | HMV 7EG 8170 | TEENAGER'S SPECIAL (EP) | 15 |

## PETE MACLAINE & CLAN
| | | | |
|---|---|---|---|
| 63 | Decca F 11699 | Yes I Do/U.S. Mail | 10 |

## DOUGIE MACLEAN
| | | | |
|---|---|---|---|
| 88 | Dunkeld DUN 008 | REAL ESTATE (LP) | 20 |

## JOHN MACLEOD SOUND
| | | | |
|---|---|---|---|
| 67 | Spectrum SP 12 | Russian Roulette/West Wind | 6 |
| 60s | Transatlantic TRASP 12 | Russian Roulette/West Wind | 6 |

## JOHN MACLEOD'S FIRST XI
| | | | |
|---|---|---|---|
| 66 | Fontana TF 696 | Don't Shoot The Ref/Tomato Crisps | 7 |

## ANGUS MACLISE
| | | | |
|---|---|---|---|
| 87 | Fierce FRIGHT 010 | Trance (1-sided, with 'Dopechoc' & badge) | 10 |

## PATRICK MACNEE & HONOR BLACKMAN
| | | | |
|---|---|---|---|
| 64 | Decca F 11843 | Kinky Boots/Let's Keep It Friendly | 35 |

*(see also Honor Blackman)*

## MADELINE MACNEIL
| | | | |
|---|---|---|---|
| 69 | Skyline DD 103 | PATCHWORK (LP) | 30 |

## UNCLE DAVE MACON
| | | | |
|---|---|---|---|
| 63 | RCA RCX 7112 | UNCLE DAVE MACON NO. 1 (EP) | 15 |
| 63 | RCA RCX 7113 | UNCLE DAVE MACON NO. 2 (EP) | 15 |

## JOSH MACRAE
| | | | |
|---|---|---|---|
| 60 | Top Rank JAR 290 | Talkin' Army Blues/Talkin' Guitar Blues | 6 |

## MADAME DRACULA
| | | | |
|---|---|---|---|
| 73 | Sunbeam SB 004 | Big Ten/Version | 50 |

*(see also Girlie)*

**JOHNNY MADARA**
57  HMV POP 389 — Be My Girl/Lovesick ............................................................................ 10

**OSIBERT MADDO**
84  Sunsplash SNS 003 — King In The Ring/PAPA SAN: Ghetto Life (12") ...................................... 100

**MAD DOG (1)**
74  Chappell LPC 1053 — POP SOUNDS (LP, library edition) ................................................. 40

**MAD DOG (2)**
85  Brainy CUTN 1 — Sheriff (p/s) ........................................................................ 50

**JOHNNY MADDOX (& HIS ORCHESTRA)**
55  London MSD 1503/1504 — Nickelodeon Tango/Solitude (unissued, demos only) ........................ 30
55  London HL 8134 — The Crazy Otto - Medley/Humoresque ................................................ 15
55  London HLD 8203 — Do, Do, Do/When You Wore A Tulip (And I Wore A Big Red Rose) .................... 15
56  London HLD 8277 — Hop Scotch Boogie/Hands Off ...................................................... 25
56  London HLD 8347 — Heart And Soul/Dixieland Band ................................................... 20
58  London HLD 8540 — Yellow Dog Blues/Sugar Train ..................................................... 15
59  London HLD 8826 — The Hurdy Gurdy Song/Old Fashioned Love .......................................... 10
55  London RE-P 1020 — PRESENTING JOHNNY MADDOX AND THE RHYTHMASTERS (EP) ............................ 12
55  London RE-P 1040 — PRESENTING JOHNNY MADDOX AND THE RHYTHMASTERS NO. 2 (EP) ..................... 12
58  London RE-D 1150 — HONKY TONK JAZZ (EP) ........................................................... 10

**ROSE MADDOX**
59  Capitol CL 15023 — Gambler's Love/What Makes Me Hang Around ....................................... 10

**MADE IN BRITAIN**
91  White MIB001 — Break The Crunch/Mellow Infection (12") ............................................ 60

**MADE IN ENGLAND (1)**
81  Gargoyle GARG 1 — Dance Of The Warriors/The Quest (p/s) ............................................ 50

**MADE IN ENGLAND (2)**
86  Red Bus RBUS 2208 — Prospects/Stay Sharp (A-side with Ray Dorset, p/s) ............................. 6

*(see also Ray Dorset)*

**MADE IN SHEFFIELD**
67  Fontana TF 871 — Amelia Jane/Right Satisfied ..................................................... 30

*(see also Joe Cocker, Grease Band, Chris Stainton)*

**MADE IN SWEDEN**
69  Sonet SLP 71 — MADE IN SWEDEN (LP) ................................................................ 40
69  Sonet SLP 2504 — SNAKES IN A HOLE (LP) ............................................................ 30
70  Sonet SLP 2506 — LIVE AT THE GOLDEN CIRCLE (LP) ................................................... 35
70  Sonet SLP 2512 — MADE IN ENGLAND (LP) ............................................................. 45
71  Sonet SNTF 621 — MAD RIVER (LP) ................................................................... 30

**MAD HATTERS**
76  Epic EPC 4151 — The Humphrey Song/Loving You Ain't Easy ............................................ 6
76  Epic EPC 460 — Love Potion No. 9/Loser ............................................................. 8

**BETTY MADIGAN**
54  MGM SP 1109 — Always You/That Was My Heart You Heard! .............................................. 5
55  MGM SP 1119 — And So I Walked Home/Be A Little Darlin' ............................................. 5
55  MGM SP 1131 — Salute/The Wheels Of Love ............................................................ 5
55  MGM SP 1137 — I Had A Heart/Wonderful Words ........................................................ 5
55  MGM SP 1138 — Teddy Bear/Strangers ................................................................. 5
69  MGM MGM 1482 — I'm Gonna Make You Love Me/Goodnight ................................................ 5

**MAD JOCKS & ENGLISHMEN**
80  Wild Dog DOGLP 18 — TONGUE IN CHEEK (LP) .......................................................... 18
80s Wild Dog DOGLP 50 — THUD & BLUNDER (LP) .......................................................... 18

**MAD LADS (JAMAICA)**
69  Coxsone CS 7099 — Losing You/WINSTON JARRETT: Peck Up A Pagan .................................... 150

**MAD LADS (U.S.)**
85  Champion CHAMP 3 — You Blew It/Trying To Forget About You (with Crossfire Band) ................... 5
65  Atlantic AT 4051 — Don't Have To Shop Around/Tear Maker .......................................... 18
66  Atlantic AT 4083 — I Want Someone/Nothing Can Break Through ...................................... 18
66  Atlantic 584 038 — Sugar Sugar/Get Out Of My Life Woman .......................................... 25

**MADNESS**
**SINGLES**
79  2-Tone TT 3 — The Prince/Madness (paper label, company sleeve) .................................... 20
79  2-Tone TT 3 — The Prince/Madness (second pressing, silver label, company sleeve) ................... 5
79  2-Tone TT 3 — The Prince/Madness (later blue plastic label, company sleeve) ....................... 45
79  Stiff BUY IT 56 — One Step Beyond/Mistakes/Nutty Theme (12", p/s) ................................. 15
79  Stiff MAD 1 — Don't Quote Me On That/Swan Lake (12", promo only, 500 copies) ..................... 50
80  Stiff BUY 84 — Baggy Trousers/The Business (p/s, blue labels instead of green, Mike Barson not credited as songwriter) ....................................................................... 75
81  Stiff BUY IT 112 — Grey Day/Baggy Trousers/Take It Or Leave It/Un Paso Adelante (12", p/s, white or yellow labels) ........................................................................... 20
81  Stiff BUY 112 — Grey Day/Memories (p/s, rare edition with legs instead of feet on label) ........... 15
82  Stiff BUY 153 — Driving In My Car/Animal Farm (poster p/s) ........................................ 20
82  Stiff GRAB 1 — THE MADNESS PACK (6 x 7" in clear plastic folder) ................................. 12
84  Stiff PBUY 196 — Michael Caine/If You Think There's Something (picture disc) ...................... 12
84  Stiff BUY 201 — One Better Day/Guns (poster p/s) .................................................. 5
85  Zarjazz JAZZ SD5 — Yesterday's Men/All I Knew (square picture disc)//Yesterday's Men (Harmonica Mix)/It Must Be Love (live) (double pack, gold PVC wallet) ................................... 12
85  Zarjazz JAZZF 7 — Uncle Sam/Please Don't Go ('flag bag' edition) .................................. 20
85  Zarjazz JAZZY 7 — Uncle Sam/Please Don't Go/Insanity Over Christmas (picture disc) ................ 18

MINT VALUE £

| Year | Label/Cat no | Description | Value |
|---|---|---|---|
| 86 | Zarjazz JAZZ B9-12 | (Waiting For) The Ghost-Train/Maybe In Another Life/Seven Year Scratch (12", p/s with 8-page booklet) | 10 |
| 86 | Zarjazz JAZZS 9 | (Waiting For) The Ghost Train/Maybe In Another Life (square picture disc) | 45 |
| 86 | Strange Fruit SFPS 0007 | THE PEEL SESSIONS (12" p/s, brown label) | 10 |
| 86 | 80s | Sweetest Girl/Jenny (A Portrait Of) (picture disc, stickered PVC sleeve) | 18 |
| 87 | Virgin VS 876 | Our House/Walking With Mr. Wheeze | 15 |
| 88 | Virgin VSX 1054 | I Pronounce You/4BF/Patience/11th Hour (as The Madness, box with badge, 2 cards & sticker) | 15 |
| 88 | Virgin VS 1078 | What's That/Be Good Boy (p/s) | 8 |
| 88 | Virgin VS 1078 | What's That/Be Good Boy (p/s) | 8 |
| 88 | Virgin VST 1078 | What's That/Be Good Boy/Flashings (12", p/s) | 10 |
| 88 | Virgin VSJ 1078 | What's That/Flashings ('Jig' disc, 1st of 2 interlocking shaped picture discs) | 30 |
| 88 | Virgin VSS 1078 | What's That/Be Good Boy 'Saw' disc, 2nd of 2 interlocking shaped picture discs) | 30 |
| 89 | 2-Tone TTP1 | THE SPECIALS: Rudi, A Message To You/Ghost Town//SELECTER: On My Radio/MADNESS: One Step Beyond (promo, 40 only) | 150 |
| 92 | Go! Discs GOD 93 | The Harder They Come/Tomorrow's Just Another Day/Take It Or Leave It (p/s, blue labels) | 8 |
| 99 | Virgin VSLH 1737 | Love Struck/We Are Love (Jukebox issue) | 10 |
| 99 | Virgin VSLH 1740 | Johnny The Horse/I Was The One (Jukebox issue) | 12 |
| 05 | V2 VVR55033247 | Shame And Scandal/Shame And Scandal (Dub Mix) p/s, 2500 only) | 6 |

## ALBUMS

| Year | Label/Cat no | Description | Value |
|---|---|---|---|
| 79 | Stiff SEEZ 17 | ONE STEP BEYOND (LP, first pressing, sleeve lists 'Bed & Breakfast' not 'Bed & Breakfast Man') | 15 |
| 80 | Stiff SEEZ 29 | ABSOLUTELY (LP, first pressing with slightly different front cover image) | 15 |
| 82 | M.I.S. (no cat. no) | THIRTY MINUTES OF CULTURE (fan club cassette) | 25 |
| 84 | Stiff PSEEZ 53 | KEEP MOVING (LP, picture disc, U.S. running order) | 15 |
| 85 | Zarjazz JZLP1 | MAD NOT MAD (LP, withdrawn edition, alternative sleeve omitting gold on front) | 75 |
| 86 | M.I.S. (no cat. no) | SONGS FROM AROUND THE PLONET (fan club cassette, live compilation) | 35 |
| 90 | Virgin VVIP 107 | IT'S MADNESS (LP, 1000 copies) | 35 |
| 90 | Virgin TPAK 8 | ONE STEP BEYOND/ABSOLUTELY/RISE & FALL (3-CD box set, picture discs) | 70 |
| 92 | Virgin 463 166 | DIVINE (Digital compact cassette) | 50 |
| 92 | Virgon MDV 2692 | DIVINE (Mini disc) | 20 |
| 92 | Go! Discs 828 367-1 | MADSTOCK (LP, with picture inner sleeve) | 20 |
| 94 | Simply Vinyl SVLP 309 | DIVINE (LP, Simply Vinyl reissue) | 20 |
| 99 | Virgin MADBOX 2 | THE LOT (6-CD box set of first 6 studio albums) | 15 |
| 09 | Lucky 7 003SE | THE LIBERTY OF NORTON FOLGATE (LP, 3-CD box set including poster, membership card, rule book, letter & badge) | 40 |

## FLEXIDISCS

| Year | Label/Cat no | Description | Value |
|---|---|---|---|
| 81 | Lyntone LYN 10208 | Take It or Leave It (free with Take It Or Leave It magazine) | 10 |
| 81 | Lyn. LYN 10353/EVENT 2 | Event - The Madness (with Event magazine) | 10 |
| 82 | Lyntone LYN 11546 | My Girl (Ballad) (hard vinyl test pressing of Flexipop free flexi) | 200 |
| 82 | Lyntone LYN 10719 | Carols On 45 (fan club disc) | 10 |
| 84 | Lyntone LYN 15280/1 | Insanity Over Christmas/Visit To Castle Dracstein (fan club disc) | 10 |
| 85 | Lyntone LYN 16981 | Merry Christmas: Samantha (live)/Mad Not Mad (live) | 10 |
| 85 | Lyntone LYN 16676 | From Us ... To You (Mad Not Mad tour disc, with tour programme) | 18 |
| 86 | Lyntone LYN 18251 | Last Christmas With Madness:Ghost Train (The Demo)/The Final Goodbye (fan club disc) | 20 |

*(see also Argonauts, Fink Brothers)*

# MADONNA

## SINGLES : SIRE SINGLES

| Year | Label/Cat no | Description | Value |
|---|---|---|---|
| 82 | Sire W 9899 | Everybody/Everybody (Dub Version) (WEA sleeve, no p/s) | 175 |
| 82 | Sire W 9899T | Everybody/Everybody (Dub Version) (12", WEA sleeve, no p/s) | 125 |
| 83 | Sire W 9522 | Lucky Star (Edit)/I Know It ('sunglasses' p/s with no Jellybean credit on label) | 1000 |
| 83 | Sire W 9522T | Lucky Star (Full Length Version)/I Know It (12", 'sunglasses' p/s; | 50 |
| 83 | Sire W 9522TV | Lucky Star (U.S Remix)/I Know It (12", stickered plain white die-cut sleeve) | 35 |
| 83 | Sire W 9405 | Holiday (Edit)/Think Of Me ('train' p/s) | 6 |
| 84 | Sire W 9522 | Lucky Star (Edit)/I Know It (reissue, 'bangles & stars' Jellybean credit on label, p/s) | 5 |
| 84 | Sire W 9522T | Lucky Star (Full Length Version)/I Know It (12" reissue, stickered 'TV screen' p/s) | 10 |
| 84 | Sire W 9522T | Lucky Star (Full Length Version)/I Know It (12" reissue, stickered 'TV screen' p/s, with poster) | 30 |
| 84 | Sire W 9260 | Borderline (Edit)/Physical Attraction (p/s, large 'A' on paper A-side label) | 5 |
| 84 | Sire W 9260F | Borderline (Edit)/Physical Attraction//Holiday (Edit)/Think Of Me ('map' p/s, double pack with European p/s, copies of "Holiday", shrinkwrapped & stickered: beware of counterfeits with less than Mint picture sleeves) | 100 |
| 84 | Sire W 9210T | Like A Virgin (U.S. Dance Remix)/Stay (12", p/s, with poster & sticker) | 35 |
| 85 | Sire W 9083 | Material Girl/Pretender (p/s) | 5 |
| 85 | Sire W 9083T | Material Girl (Jellybean Dance Mix)/Pretender (12", with poster p/s) | 35 |
| 85 | Sire WA6323 | Crazy For You/Sammy Hagar "I'll Fall In Love Again" (7" Madonna shaped picture Disc in stickered PVC sleeve. No p/s.) | 50 |
| 85 | Sire WA6323 | Crazy For You/Sammy Hagar "I'll Fall In Love Again" (Uncut 7" Picture disc on 10" vinyl in PVC sleeve. No p/s) | 800 |
| 85 | Sire W 8934P | Into The Groove/Shoo-Be-Doo (heart-shaped picture disc with 2 stickers) | 40 |
| 85 | Sire W 8934P | Into The Groove/Shoo-Be-Doo (12" uncut heart-shaped picture disc, very few copies) | 1000 |
| 85 | Sire W 8934T | Into The Groove/Everybody/Shoo-Be-Doo (12", p/s, with poster) | 25 |
| 85 | Sire W 9405T | Holiday (Full Length Version 6.08)/Think Of Me (12", 'cross earring' p/s reissue) | 15 |
| 85 | Sire W 9405P | Holiday (Full Length Version 6.08)/Think Of Me (12", picture disc) | 30 |
| 85 | Sire W 8881P | Angel (Edit)/Burning Up (shaped pic disc, with cardboard plinth) | 45 |
| 85 | SireW8881P | Angel (Edit)/Burning Up (shaped pic disc) | 35 |
| 85 | Sire W8881P | Angel (Edit)/Burning Up (Uncut 7" pic disc on 12" vinyl in PVC sleeve, no p/s) | 1000 |
| 85 | Sire A6585 | Gambler/Black 'n' Blue:Nature Of The Beach (7" p/s) | 7 |
| 85 | Sire QA6585 | Gambler/Black 'n' Blue:Nature Of The Beach (7" foldout poster p/s) | 30 |

| 85 | Sire TA6585 | Gambler (Extended Dance Mix)/(Instrumental Remix) Black 'n' Blue: Nature Of The Beach (12" p/s) .................................................................................................... 20 |
|----|-------------|------|
| 85 | Sire W 8848TF | Dress You Up (12" Formal Mix)/(Casual Instrumental)/I Know It (12", foldout p/s with Virgin Tour Video Advert on back) ............................................................................ 35 |
| 85 | Sire W 8848P | Dress You Up/I Know It ('Xmas tree star'-shaped picture disc) .................................... 35 |
| 85 | Sire W 8848P | Dress You Up (Uncut 7" picture disc on 12" vinyl, no p/s) ........................................ 750 |
| 86 | Sire W 9560P | Borderline/Physical Attraction (Madonna-shaped picture disc in pvc sleeve no p/s) ..... 50 |
| 86 | Sire W 9560P | Borderline/Physical Attraction (Uncut 7" picture disc on 12" vinyl,pvc sleeve no p/s) ................................................................................................................ 1000 |
| 86 | Sire W 8717T(W) | Live To Tell (LP Version)/(Edit)/(Instrumental) (12", p/s, with poster) ........................ 20 |
| 86 | Sire W8636T | Papa Don't Preach(Extended Version)/(LP Vesion) Ain't No Big Deal (12" with poster in stickered p/s) ................................................................................................... 20 |
| 86 | Sire W 8636T(W) | Papa Don't Preach (Extended Version)/Papa Don't Preach (LP Version)/ Ain't No Big Deal (12", p/s, initially with free poster) ......................................................................... 15 |
| 86 | Sire W 8636TP | Papa Don't Preach (Extended Remix)/Ain't No Big Deal (LP Version)/ Papa Don't Preach (LP version) (12", picture disc.................................................................... 20 |
| 86 | Sire W 8550TP | True Blue (Extended Dance Version)/Holiday (Full Length Version) (12" picture disc)....20 |
| 86 | Sire W 8480TP | Open Your Heart (Extended Version)/Open Your Heart (Dub Mix)/ Lucky Star (Full Length Version) (12", picture disc) .............................................................................. 10 |
| 87 | Sire W 8378TP | La Isla Bonita (Extended Remix)/(Extended Instrumental) (12", picture disc)................ 20 |
| 87 | Sire W 8341TX | Who's That Girl (Extended Version)/Who's That Girl (Dub Mix)/ White Heat (12" Remix) (12", p/s) .............................................................................................................. 20 |
| 87 | Sire W 8341TP | Who's That Girl (Extended Version)/White Heat (12", picture disc; beware of original decaying PVC sleeves) ....................................................................................... 40 |
| 87 | Sire W 8224 | Causing A Commotion (Silver Screen Single Mix)/Jimmy Jimmy (withdrawn p/s, with sticker stating 'Free personality poster W 8224W', most destroyed when withdrawn in favour of 'badge' insert, no poster) ............................................................ 100 |
| 87 | Sire W 8224 | Causing A Commotion (Silver Screen Single Mix)/Jimmy Jimmy (p/s, with badge shrinkwrapped to p/s)........................................................................................ 60 |
| 87 | Sire W 8224TP | Causing A Commotion (Silver Screen Single Mix)/Causing A Commotion (Movie House Mix)/ Jimmy Jimmy (Fade) (12", picture disc)................................................................ 15 |
| 87 | Sire W 8115TW | The Look Of Love/Love Don't Live Here Anymore/I Know It (12", p/s & poster) ........... 15 |
| 87 | Sire W 8115TP | The Look Of Love/Love Don't Live Here Anymore/I Know It (12", picture disc) ............. 20 |
| 89 | Sire 925 681-2 | Papa Don't Preach (7" Version)/(12" Version)/Pretender (Video)(5" CD-Video p/s) ..... 40 |
| 89 | Sire 7539TX | Like A Prayer (12" Dance Mix)/(Churchapella Mix)/(7"Remix Edit) (12", p/s) ............ 10 |
| 89 | Sire 7539TP | Like A Prayer (12" Extended Remix)/12" Club Version)/ Act Of Contrition (12", picture disc)................................................................................................................ 15 |
| 89 | Sire 7539CD | Like A Prayer/(12" Extended Remix)/(12" Club Version)/Act Of Contrition (3" Gatefold CD) ......................................................................................................................... 12 |
| 89 | Sire W 2948X | Express Yourself (7" Remix)/The Look Of Love (LP) (poster p/s) ............................. 25 |
| 89 | Sire W 2948C | Express Yourself (7" Remix)/The Look Of Love (LP) ('jeans zipper' p/s)...................... 40 |
| 89 | Sire W 2948CX | Express Yourself (Non-Stop Express Mix)/(Stop + Go Dubs) (cassette) ...................... 20 |
| 89 | Sire W 2948CX | Express Yourself/(Non-Stop Express Mix)/(Stop + Go Dubs) (12", 'nude' picture disc)...15 |
| 89 | Sire W 2883TP | Cherish (Extended Version)/(7" Version)/Supernatural (12") ...................................... 10 |
| 89 | Sire W 2668P | Dear Jessie/Till Death Do Us Part (picture disc) ....................................................... 12 |
| 89 | Sire W 2668TW | Dear Jessie/Till Death Do Us Part/Holiday (12" Version) (12", poster p/s) .................. 12 |
| 89 | Sire 2268CDX | Dear Jessie/Till Death Do Us Part/Holiday (12" Version) (CD, picture disc) .............. 125 |
| 89 | Sire 925 681-2 | Papa Don't Preach (7" Version)/(12" Version)/Pretender (LP Version)/ Papa Don't Preach (CD Video) ....................................................................................................... 35 |
| 90 | Sire W 9851P | Vogue/Keep It Together (Single Remix) (picture disc)............................................... 12 |
| 90 | Sire W 9851TW | Vogue (12" Version)/Keep It Together (12" Remix) (12", p/s, with 'Face of the 80s' poster) ..................................................................................................................... 15 |
| 90 | Sire W 9851TX | Vogue (12" Version)/Vogue (Strike-A-Pose Dub) (12", p/s, with 'X-rated' 30" x 20" poster) ..................................................................................................................... 20 |
| 90 | Sire W 9851TP | Vogue (12" Version)/Keep It Together (12" Remix) (12", picture disc) ........................ 20 |
| 90 | Sire W 9789TP | Hanky Panky (Bare Bottom 12" Mix)/(Bare Bones Single Mix)/More (LP Version) (12", picture disc with gatefold insert & foldout poster) ................................................... 20 |
| 90 | Sire W 9000TP | Justify My Love (William Orbit Remix)/Justify My Love/Express Yourself (Shep's 'Spressin' Himself Remix) (12", picture disc with insert) ....................................... 10 |
| 91 | Sire W 0008P | Crazy For You (Remix)/Keep It Together (Single Remix) (shaped picture disc with plinth & insert) .................................................................................................... 15 |
| 91 | Sire W0024 | Rescue Me/Spotlight (7" p/s) ..................................................................................... 5 |
| 91 | Sire W0024TW | Rescue (Titanic Mix)/(Houseboat Mix)/(Titanic Mix) (12" with free poster, p/s) ........... 10 |
| 91 | Sire W 0037TP | Holiday/True Blue (12", clear vinyl picture disc with insert in PVC sleeve) .................. 15 |

## SINGLES : MAVERICK SINGLES

| 92 | Maverick W 0138TP | Erotica (Album Version 5.12)/Erotica (Instrumental 5.12)/Erotica (Radio Edit 4.31) (12", picture disc with gold insert, withdrawn, 138 only) ........................................... 2500 |
|----|-------------------|------|
| 92 | Maverick W 0138TW | Erotica (Album Version 5.12)/Erotica (Instrumental 5.12)/Erotica (Radio Edit 4.31) (12", Free Poster, p/s) ......................................................................................... 10 |
| 92 | Maverick W 0146TP | Deeper And Deeper (Shep's Classic 12")/(Shep's Deep Makeover Mix)/ (Shep's Deep Beats)/(David's Klub Mix)/(David's Deep Mix)/(Shep's Deeper Dub) (12", picture disc) 15 |
| 93 | Maverick W0154TW | Bad Girl (Edit)/Erotica (William Orbit 12")/Erotica (William Orbit Dub)/ Erotica (Madonna's In My Jeep Mix) (12", Free Poster, p/s) ......................................... 10 |
| 93 | Maverick W 0168P | Fever (Edit)/Fever (Radio Edit Remix) (picture disc with numbered insert) .................. 10 |
| 93 | Maverick W0168T | Fever (Hot Sweat 12")/(Extended 12")/(Shep's Remedy Dub)/(Murk Boys Miami Mix)/(Murk Boys Deep South Mix)/(Oscar G's Dope Dub) (12" stickered, p/s) ............. 10 |
| 94 | Maverick W 0268P | Secret (Edit)/Let Down Your Guard (Rough Mix Edit) (picture disc w/insert) .............. 12 |
| 95 | Warner Bros W0285TX | Bedtime Story (Junior's Sound Factory Mix)/(Junior's Sound Factory Dub/ (Orbital Mix)/Junior's Wet Dream Mix) (12" Glitter Holographic Sleeve) ............................... 15 |

## SINGLES : OTHER SINGLES

| 92 | Receiver RRSP 1007 | Shine A Light/On The Ground (picture disc, withdrawn) .............................................. 12 |
|----|--------------------|------|
| 92 | Reciever RRSPT 1007 | Shine A Light/On The Ground/Little Boy (12", picture disc) ......................................... 15 |

## ALBUMS

| 85 | Sire WX 20P | LIKE A VIRGIN (LP, picture disc in die-cut sleeve)........................................................ 50 |
|----|-------------|------|
| 86 | Sire WX 54 | TRUE BLUE (LP, with tour poster)............................................................................... 15 |

## MADONNA & MISSY (ELLIOTT)

| | | | |
|---|---|---|---|
| 87 | Sire WX 76 | YOU CAN DANCE (LP, with poster & gold 'obi') | 15 |
| 90 | Sire 7599 264932 | ROYAL BOX (box set with "Immaculate Collection" CD in satin digipak, video, poster & postcards) | 75 |
| 94 | Sire 9362 45767 1 | BEDTIME STORIES (LP) | 15 |
| 95 | Sire 9362 46100-1 | SOMETHING TO REMEMBER (LP) | 35 |
| 04 | Sire 9362 46847-1 | RAY OF LIGHT (Reissue, 2xLP with inner sleeve 180 gram deluxe vinyl, stickered) | 40 |
| 06 | Sire 9362 494601 | CONFESSIONS ON A DANCE FLOOR (2-LP, gatefold, pink vinyl) | 20 |

**PROMOS**

| | | | |
|---|---|---|---|
| 85 | Sire SAM 251 | Into The Groove (Edit) Holiday (Edit) (12" white label, die-cut sleeve, stickered | 100 |
| 87 | Sire SAM 412 | Spotlight (Dub)/Holiday (Dub)/Over And Over (Dub)/Into The Groove (Dub) 12" white label, die-cut WEA sleeve, no p/s | 50 |
| 89 | Sire SAM 641 | Keep It Together (12" Remix)/(Dub)/(Extended Remix)/(12" Mix) / (Bonus Beats)/(Instrumental) (12") | 15 |
| 90 | Sire SAM 659 | Vogue (12" Version)/Vogue (Strike A Pose Dub) (12") | 15 |
| 90 | Sire SAM 738 | Justify My Love (Remix) (One-sided 12" die-cut sleeve, p/s) | 15 |
| 91 | Sire SAM 800 | Holiday (Edit) (CD) | 15 |
| 92 | Sire SAM 1103 | Erotica (Album Version) (12") | 50 |
| 92 | Sire SAM 1118 | Deeper And Deeper (Edit)/Shep's Deep Makeover Mix)/Shep's Classic 12") David's Klub Mix)/David's Love Dub)/David's Deeper Dub) 12" white label no p/s | 25 |
| 93 | Sire SAM 1131 | Fever (Hot Sweat 12" Mix)/(Shep's Remedy Dub)/(Dub One)/(Dub Two)/ (Bugged Out Bonzai Mix)/(Peggy's Nightclub Mix)/(Radio Edit)/(Murk Boys Miami Mix)/(Murk Boys Deep South Mix)/(Album Version)/(Oscar G's Dope Dub)/(Back To The Dub One)/(Back To The Dub Two) (2x12") | 50 |
| 94 | Warner Bros SAM 1526 | Bedtime Story (Junior's Sound Factory Mix)/(Mixes) (12") | 15 |
| 94 | Warner Bros SAM 1653 | Human Nature: The Remixes/(Mixes) (12", stickered title sleeve) | 15 |
| 95 | Warner Bros SAM 1526 | Bedtime Story (Junior's Sound Factory Mix)/(Junior's Sound Factory Dub)/ (Orbital Mix)/Junior's Wet Dream Mix)/Junior's Wet Dream Dub) (12") | 15 |
| 95 | Warner Bros W 0285 CDDJ2 | Bedtime Story (Junior's Singles Mix) (CD in standard p/s) | 25 |
| 96 | Sire SAM 1880 | Love Don't Live Here Anymore (Mark!s It's A Girl Dub)/(Mark!s It's A Boy Dub)/ (Mark!s Full On Vocal) (12") | 15 |
| 96 | Warner Bros SAM 1982 | Don't Cry For Me Argentina (Miami Mix)/(Mixes) (12", title sleeve) | 10 |
| 98 | Warner Bros 3331000037 | Drowned World/Substitute For Love (BT & Sasha's Bucklodge Ashram Remix)/ Sky Fits Heaven (Sasha Remix)/Substitute For Love (Victor Calderone Remix Edit) (12") | 20 |
| 98 | Sire SAM 3173 | Frozen (Extended Club Mix)/(Stereo MC's Mix)/(Meltdown Mix - Long Version) (12" no p/s) | 10 |
| 98 | Warner Bros SAM 3247 | Ray Of Light (Sasha's Ultra Violet Mix)/(William Orbit's Liquid Mix) (12") | 15 |
| 98 | Warner Bros SAM 3248 | Ray Of Light (Calderone Club Mix)/(Album Version) (12" no p/s) | 15 |
| 98 | Warner Bros SAM 3268 | Ray Of Light (Sasha's Twilo Mix)/(Victor Calderone Drum Mix) (12") | 15 |
| 98 | Warner Bros SAM 3269 | Ray Of Light (Sasha's Strip Down Mix)/(Orbit's Ultra Violet Mix) (12") | 15 |
| 98 | Maverick W0444 LC | Ray Of Light/Has To Be (jukebox promo) | 15 |
| 98 | Maverick W 0453 LC | Drowned World/Substitute For Love//Sky Fits Heaven (promo only) | 8 |
| 99 | Maverick W 495 LC | Beautiful Stranger/Calderone Radio Mix) (Juke box promo) | 10 |
| 00 | Maverick W 519 LC | American Pie (Album Version)/(Richard 'Humpty' Vission Radio Mix) (jukebox promo | 10 |
| 00 | Warner Bros PRO 6584 | Music (mixes) (12" doublepack, title-stickered sleeve) | 25 |
| 01 | Warner Bros MADZ 01 | What It Feels Like For A Girl (Perfecto Mix)/(Above & Beyond Remix) (12" stickered white label, A4 press release, die-cut sleeve no p/s) | 25 |
| 01 | Warner Bros | GHV2 (CD, slimline jewel case, 'collage' insert) | 25 |
| 01 | Warner Bros SAM 00586 | GHV2 (CD, 10" x 10" gatefold p/s) | 50 |
| 02 | Warner Bros SAM 00721 | Die Another Day (Dirty Vegas Main Mix)/(mixes) (12" double pack, stickered title sleeve) | 15 |
| 03 | Warner Bros SAM 00824 | Hollywood (Oakenfold 12" Full Remix)/Jacques Lu Cont Thin White Duck Mix) /Album Version/(Deepsky Home Sweet Home Vocal Remix) (12") | 10 |

**PROMOS : ALBUM PROMO**

| | | | |
|---|---|---|---|
| 89 | Sire MER 0120 | LIKE A PRAYER (Box set in 10" x 7" x 1" box, includes CD, sealed cassette, press Release, badge, slides Rolling Stone re-print, 2 photos) | 200 |

## MADONNA & MISSY (ELLIOTT)

| | | | |
|---|---|---|---|
| 03 | Maverick RRCG 0301 | Into The Hollywood Groove/Hollywood (Jack Lu Cont's Thin White Dick Mix) (GAP in-store promo) | 25 |

## MAD PROFESSOR

| | | | |
|---|---|---|---|
| 82 | Ariwa ARILP 001 | DUB ME CRAZY (LP) | 20 |
| 82 | Ariwa ARIL 002 | BEYOND THE REALMS OF DUB (LP) | 20 |
| 83 | Ariwa ARILP 005 | THE AFRICAN CONNECTION - DUB ME CRAZY PART 3 (LP) | 25 |
| 83 | Ariwa ARILP 011 | ESCAPE TO THE ASYLUM OF DUB (LP) | 20 |
| 85 | Ariwa ARILP 025 | CARIBBEAN TASTE OF TECHNOLOGY GONE CRAZY (LP) | 25 |
| 85 | Ariwa ARILP 021 | DUB ME CRAZY - VOLUME 5 (LP) | 15 |
| 86 | Ariwa ARILP 030 | SCHIZOPHRENIC DUB ME CRAZY VOL. 6 (LP) | 15 |
| 93 | Ariwa ARILP 095 | BLACK LIBERATION DUB (LP) | 15 |

## MAD PROFESSOR & JAH SHAKA

| | | | |
|---|---|---|---|
| 96 | Ariwa AEILP 116 | NEW DECADE OF DUB (LP) | 25 |

## MADRIGAL

| | | | |
|---|---|---|---|
| 71 | Decca F13110 | Blue Eyes In Paradise/Wendy | 20 |
| 72 | Sovereign SOV 1071 | Time Of The Season/Tapestry | 20 |
| 73 | Madrigal MAD 100 | BENEATH THE GREENWOOD TREE (LP, private pressing) | 60 |

## MAD RIVER

| | | | |
|---|---|---|---|
| 69 | Capitol (S)T 2985 | MAD RIVER (LP) | 125 |
| 85 | Edsel ED 140 | MAD RIVER (LP, reissue) | 15 |

## JOHNNY MAESTRO

| | | | |
|---|---|---|---|
| 61 | HMV POP 875 | What A Surprise/The Warning Voice | 25 |
| 61 | HMV POP 909 | Mr. Happiness/Test Of Love | 25 |
| 64 | United Artists UP 1004 | Before I Love Her/Fifty Million Heartbeats | 25 |
| 71 | Buddah 2011 061 | Rain Came/Never Knew This Kind Of Hurt Before | 10 |

(see also Crests, Brooklyn Bridge)

## MAGAZINE
| 78 | Virgin VS 200 | Shot By Both Sides/My Mind Ain't So Open (card p/s) | 8 |
| 78 | Virgin VS 200 | Shot By Both Sides/My Mind Ain't So Open (paper p/s) | 5 |
| 78 | Virgin VS 207 | Touch And Go/Goldfinger (p/s) | 5 |
| 78 | Virgin VS 237 | I Love You You Big Dummy/Give Me Everything | 6 |
| 78 | Virgin VS 237 | Give Me Everything/I Love You You Big Dummy | 5 |
| 79 | Virgin VS 219 | Rhythm Of Cruelty/TV Baby | 5 |
| 78 | Virgin V2100 | REAL LIFE (LP, original blue labels) | 15 |
| 79 | Virgin V2121 | SECONDHAND DAYLIGHT (LP, gatefold) | 15 |
| 80 | Virgin V2156 | THE CORRECT USE OF SOAP (LP) | 15 |
| 80 | Virgin V 2184 | PLAY (LP) | 15 |
| 81 | Virgin V2200 | MAGIC, MURDER AND THE WEATHER (LP) | 15 |
| 82 | Virgin VM 1 | AFTER THE FACT (LP) | 15 |

*(see also Buzzcocks)*

## MAGENTA
| 78 | Cottage COT 821 | CANTERBURY MOON (LP, with insert) | 40 |
| 80 | Little Stan LSP 811 | RECOLLECTIONS (2-LP, gatefold sleeve with insert) | 35 |
| 81 | Little Stan LSP 831 | WOT'S NEXT THEN (LP, with insert) | 25 |

## MAGGIE
| 68 | Columbia DB 8389 | L. David Sloane/Too Young To Get Married | 6 |

## MAGIC CARPET
| 72 | Mushroom 200 MR 20 | MAGIC CARPET (LP, white/brown labels) | 175 |
| 95 | Magic Carpet MC 1001 LP | MAGIC CARPET (LP, reissue) | 25 |

*(see also Clem Alford)*

## MAGIC CHRISTIANS
| 69 | Major Minor MM 673 | If You Want It/Nuts | 12 |
| 69 | Major Minor MM 673 | Come And Get It/Nuts (2nd pressing with correct title) | 20 |
| 70 | Major Minor SMLP 71 | THE MAGIC CHRISTIANS (LP) | 40 |

*(see also Trevor Burton, Gary Wright, Denny Laine, Steve Gibbons)*

## MAGIC LANTERNS
| 66 | CBS 202094 | Excuse Me Baby/Greedy Girl | 7 |
| 66 | CBS 202250 | Rumplestiltskin/I Stumbled | 40 |
| 67 | CBS 202459 | Knight In Rusty Armour/Simple Things | 10 |
| 67 | CBS 202637 | Auntie Grizelda/Time Will Tell (If I'm A Loser) | 10 |
| 67 | CBS 2750 | We'll Meet Again/What Else Can It Be But Love? | 10 |
| 68 | Camp 602 007 | Shame Shame/Baby I Gotta Go Now | 10 |
| 69 | Camp 602 009 | Melt All Your Troubles Away/Bossa Nova 1940 - Hello You Lovers | 6 |
| 70 | Polydor 2038 058 | One Night Stand/Frisco Annie | 5 |
| 73 | Polydor 2058 322 | Stand For Our Rights/Pa Bradley | 5 |
| 67 | CBS (S)BPG 62935 | LIT UP WITH THE MAGIC LANTERNS (LP) | 40 |

## MAGIC MICHAEL
| 80 | Atomic MAGIC 1 | Millionaire/My Friend And I (p/s) | 5 |

*(see also Damned, Captain Sensible)*

## MAGIC MIXTURE
| 68 | Saga STFID 2125 | THIS IS MAGIC MIXTURE (LP, black/silver labels) | 150 |

## MAGIC MUSCLE
| 88 | Five Hours Back TOCK 009 | THE PIPE, THE ROAR, THE GRID (LP, with booklet) | 18 |
| 89 | One Big Guitar OBGLP 9005 | 100 MILES BELOW (LP) | 15 |
| 91 | Woronzow WOO 17 | GULP! (LP) | 20 |

*(see also Keith Christmas, Hawkwind, High Tide, Twink)*

## MAGIC MUSHROOM BAND
| 86 | Pagan PM 003 | THE POLITICS OF ECSTASY (LP, 100 with A1 poster) | 50 |
| 86 | Pagan PM 003 | THE POLITICS OF ECSTASY (LP, 500 with A3 insert) | 25 |
| 87 | Aftermath AFT 3 | BOMSHAMKAR (LP) | 15 |
| 91 | Fungus FUN 005 | SPACED OUT (LP, foldout sleeve with A4 booklet) | 15 |

## MAGIC NIGHT
| 74 | Pye International 7N 25643 | Baby You Belong To Me/Lost And Lonely Boy | 8 |
| 75 | Pye 7N 25698 | If You And I Had Never Met/(version) | 10 |

## MAGIC NOTES
| 60 | Blue Beat BB 9 | Album Of Memory/Why Did You Leave Me | 12 |
| 61 | Blue Beat BB 51 | Rosabel/I'm Not Worthy | 12 |

## THE MAGIC NUMBERS
| 05 | Heavenly HVNLP53 | MAGIC NUMBERS (2-LP with free 1-sided 7" HVBLP53X) | 18 |

## MAGIC SAM
| 69 | Python PEN 701 | Twenty One Days In Jail/Easy Baby (99 copies only) | 45 |
| 69 | Rooster 707 | MEAN MISTREATER (EP) | 20 |
| 70 | Blue Horizon 7-63223 | MAGIC SAM: 1937-1969 (LP) | 100 |
| 70 | Delmark DS 615 | WEST SIDE SOUL (LP, blue label) | 30 |
| 71 | Delmark DS 620 | BLACK MAGIC (LP, blue label) | 35 |

## MAGIC VALLEY
| 69 | Penny Farthing PEN 701 | Taking The Heart Out Of Love/Uptight Basil | 10 |

*(see also Pete Dello, Honeybus)*

## MAGICIAN
| 79 | Hobo | MAGICIAN (LP) | 40 |

## MAGICIANS
| 66 | Decca F 12361 | Wet Your Whistle/Take The A Train | 5 |
| 66 | Decca F 12374 | The Liars/Poggy Goes Pop | 6 |

| | | | |
|---|---|---|---|
| 67 | Decca F 12602 | The Tarzan March/What A Day For A Metamorphosis | 10 |
| 68 | MCA MU 1046 | Painting On Wood/Slow Motion | 40 |

## MAGISTRATES
| | | | |
|---|---|---|---|
| 68 | MGM MGM 1437 | After The Fox/Tear Down The Walls (with Jean Hillary) | 15 |
| 68 | MGM MGM 1425 | Here Comes The Judge/Girl | 10 |
| 68 | MGM MGM 1437 | After The Fox/Tear Down The Walls (with Jean Hillary) | 12 |

*(see also Jane Hillery)*

## MAGITS
| | | | |
|---|---|---|---|
| 79 | Outer H. SRTS/79/CUS/401 | Fragmented/Disconnected/Disjointed/Detached (p/s, with 3 page magazine insert) | 140 |
| 79 | Outer H. SRTS/79/CUS/401 | Fragmented/Disconnected/Disjointed/Detached (p/s, without 3 page magazine insert) | 100 |

*(see also Rudimentary Peni)*

## MAGMA
| | | | |
|---|---|---|---|
| 74 | A&M AMS 7119 | Mekanik Machine/Mekanik Machine (Version) | 20 |
| 70 | Philips 6359 051/2 | MAGMA (2-LP) | 70 |
| 71 | Philips 6397 031 | 1001 CENTIGRADE (LP) | 40 |
| 74 | A&M AMLH 64397 | MEKANIK DESTRUCTIW KOMMANDOH (LP, gatefold sleeve, lyric insert) | 40 |
| 74 | A&M AMLH 68260 | KOHN TARKOSZ (LP) | 20 |

## MAGNA CARTA
| | | | |
|---|---|---|---|
| 69 | Fontana TF 1060 | Romeo Jack/7 O'Clock Man | 20 |
| 69 | Mercury MF 1096 | Mid-Winter/Spinning Wheels Of Time | 20 |
| 70 | Vertigo 6059 013 | Airport Song/Elizabethan | 10 |
| 71 | Vertigo 6059 043 | Time For The Leaving/Wayfarin' | 8 |
| 72 | Vertigo 6059 073 | All My Life/Falkland Green | 12 |
| 73 | Vertigo 6059 092 | Give Me Luv/Song Of Evening | 10 |
| 70s | London Borough of Camden | When You're Young (charity issue for ROSPA) | 5 |
| 69 | Mercury MCL 20166 S | MAGNA CARTA (LP, laminated sleeve, black/silver labels) | 200 |
| 70 | Vertigo 6360 003 | SEASONS (LP, 1st pressing, gatefold sleeve, large swirl label, "Vertigo" at base of label) | 120 |
| 70 | Vertigo 6360 003 | SEASONS (LP, 2nd pressing, gatefold sleeve, small swirl label, "Vertigo" beneath swirl above centre hole) | 50 |
| 71 | Vertigo 6360 040 | SONGS FROM WASTIES ORCHARD (LP, multifold sleeve, large swirl label) | 150 |
| 72 | Vertigo 6360 068 | IN CONCERT (LP, gatefold sleeve, small swirl label) | 18 |
| 73 | Vertigo 6360 093 | LORD OF THE AGES (LP, 1st pressing, side 1 matrix, 1 (crossed out 2) Y//1 1 1 1 1, gatefold sleeve, lyric insert, spaceship label) | 15 |
| 74 | Vertigo 6360 003 | SEASONS (LP, 3rd pressing, 'spaceship label') | 15 |

## MAGNET
| | | | |
|---|---|---|---|
| 69 | CBS 4472 | Let Me Stay/Mr Guy Fawkes | 30 |
| 70 | CBS 4844 | Something To Remember Me By/Everything | 6 |

## MAGNETICS
| | | | |
|---|---|---|---|
| 00 | Grapevine 2000 G2K 104 | The Look On Your Face/You Were Made For Love (with Johnny McKinney) | 10 |
| 02 | Grapevine 2000 G2K 130 | When I'm With My Baby/Count The Days | 10 |
| 02 | Grapevine 2000 G2K 34-119 | I'll Keep Holding On/Jackie Baby | 10 |

## MAGNETS
| | | | |
|---|---|---|---|
| 79 | Hurricane FIRE 1 | Who's The Fool (Me Or You)/Best (with insert, round white cut-out sheet) | 25 |

## MAGNIFICENT
| | | | |
|---|---|---|---|
| 88 | Link LINKLP 027 | HIT AND RUN (LP) | 20 |

## MAGNIFICENT MEN
| | | | |
|---|---|---|---|
| 66 | Capitol CL 15462 | Peace Of Mind/All Your Lovin's Gone To My Head | 30 |
| 68 | Capitol CL 15530 | Sweet Soul Medley Parts 1 & 2 | 10 |
| 68 | Capitol CL 15570 | Save The Country/So Much Love Waiting | 6 |

## MAGNIFICENT MERCURY BROTHERS
| | | | |
|---|---|---|---|
| 74 | Transatlantic BIG 532 | New Girl In School/What About Us | 8 |
| 74 | Transatlantic BIG 536 | Why Do Fools Fall In Love/(I'm Not A) Juvenile Delinquent | 8 |

*(see also Decameron)*

## MAGNOG
| | | | |
|---|---|---|---|
| 90s | Enraptured RAPT 4508 | Mist Waves Riding The Hills/Moving Ahead Again/Ghost States (p/s) | 6 |

## MAGNUM
| | | | |
|---|---|---|---|
| 75 | CBS S CBS 2959 | Sweets For My Sweet/Movin' On (no p/s) | 45 |
| 79 | Jet JET 155 | Changes/Lonesome Star (silver p/s, with sew-on patch) | 5 |
| 81 | Jet JET 7007 | Black Nights (possibly promo only) | 12 |
| 88 | Polydor POSPG 920 | Start Talking Love/C'est La Vie (gatefold pop-up p/s) | 5 |
| 78 | Jet JETLP 210 | KINGDOM OF MADNESS (LP, original 'king' sleeve) | 25 |
| 83 | FM WKFMPD 111 | THE ELEVENTH HOUR (LP, picture disc) | 15 |
| 85 | FM WKFM LP 34 | ON A STORYTELLER'S NIGHT (LP, with bonus single) | 15 |
| 85 | FM WKFM G/C LP 34 | ON A STORYTELLER'S NIGHT (LP, gold or clear vinyl, with poster) | 15 |
| 85 | FM WKFM PD 34 | ON A STORYTELLER'S NIGHT (LP, picture disc, with poster) | 18 |
| 87 | FM Revolver WKFMHP 106 | MIRADOR (LP, blue vinyl, gatefold sleeve, poster and Blue vinyl 12" (12HP106) | 15 |
| 88 | Polydor POLDP 5221 | WINGS OF HEAVEN (LP, picture disc with extra track, die-cut sleeve) | 12 |
| 88 | FM Revolver WKFMPD 119T | MAGNUM II (LP, reissue, picture disc) | 15 |
| 90 | FM Revolver WKFMBX 145 | FOUNDATION (6-LP box set) | 45 |

## TEDDY MAGNUS
| | | | |
|---|---|---|---|
| 71 | Green Door GD 4008 | Flying Machine/VERSION BOYS: Machine Version | 5 |

## MAGOO
| | | | |
|---|---|---|---|
| 95 | Noisebox NBX 013 | MUDSHARK EP: Tom, Lou And Me/Elsie's Skinny Arms/Hop Your Mouth (orange vinyl, numbered p/s, 500 only) | 10 |
| 98 | Fierce Panda NING 47 | Black Sabbath/MOGWAI: Sweet Leaf (p/s) | 7 |

## MAGPIES
| | | | |
|---|---|---|---|
| 68 | Doctor Bird DB 1129 | Lulu/Must I Be Lonely | 18 |

| | | | |
|---|---|---|---|
| 68 | Doctor Bird DB 1132 | Blue Boy/I Guess I'm Crazy | 18 |

**MAG SPIES/MAGAZINE SPIES/MAGSPIES**

| | | | |
|---|---|---|---|
| 79 | Dance Fools Dance GLITCH 1 | LIFEBLOOD (12" EP, 2 tracks by Mag Spies/2 by Obtainers) | 400 |

*(see also The Cure)*

**ALEX MAGUIRE**

| | | | |
|---|---|---|---|
| 87 | Incus INCUS 52 | LIVE AT OSCARS (LP) | 35 |

**MAGUS**

| | | | |
|---|---|---|---|
| 80 | Northern Sound NSR 200 | BREEZIN' AWAY (LP, private pressing) | 50 |

*(see also Blue Epitaph)*

**TAJ MAHAL**

| | | | |
|---|---|---|---|
| 68 | Direction 58-3547 | Everybody's Got To Change Sometime/Statesboro Blues | 12 |
| 69 | Direction 58-4044 | Ee Zee Rider/You Don't Miss Your Water | 12 |
| 70 | Direction 58-4586 | Give Your Woman What She Wants/Further On Down The Road | 8 |
| 71 | CBS 7413 | Diving Duck Blues/Fishin' Blues | 10 |
| 67 | Direction 8-63279 | TAJ MAHAL (LP) | 30 |
| 69 | Direction 8-63397 | THE NATCH'L BLUES (LP) | 30 |
| 69 | Direction 8-66226 | GIANT STEP/DE OLE FOLKS AT HOME (2-LP) | 25 |
| 71 | CBS 66288 | THE REAL THING (2-LP) | 18 |

**MAHAVISHNU ORCHESTRA**

| | | | |
|---|---|---|---|
| 75 | CBS 3007 | Can't Stand Your Funk/Eternity's Breath Part 1 | 6 |
| 72 | CBS 64717 | THE INNER MOUNTING FLAME (LP, with insert) | 15 |
| 74 | CBS CQ 31996 | BIRDS OF FIRE (LP, quadrophonic) | 20 |

*(see also John McLaughlin)*

**MITCH MAHON & EDITIONS**

| | | | |
|---|---|---|---|
| 69 | Pye 7N 17844 | You've Got What I Need/I've Thrown Our Love Away | 5 |

**SKIP MAHONEY & CASUALS**

| | | | |
|---|---|---|---|
| 80 | Underworld UND 1 | Janice/Don't Stop Me Now | 10 |
| 76 | Contempo CLP 539 | LAND OF LOVE (LP) | 20 |

**MAIL**

| | | | |
|---|---|---|---|
| 71 | Parlophone R 5916 | Omnibus/Life Goes On | 25 |

**MAIN**

| | | | |
|---|---|---|---|
| 96 | Beggars Banquet HERTZ 16LP | Hz (2-LP) | 25 |

**MAIN ATTRACTION**

| | | | |
|---|---|---|---|
| 72 | Pye 7N45186 | Oh Girl/Telephone Line | 10 |

**MAIN ATTRACTIONS**

| | | | |
|---|---|---|---|
| 77 | Solid Sound SS 001 | Love/Doug's Love (with Augustus Pablo) | 20 |

**MAIN INGREDIENT**

| | | | |
|---|---|---|---|
| 77 | Power Exchange PX 265 | Everything Man/Reggae Disco | 6 |
| 74 | RCA APBO 0205 | Just Don't Want To Be Lonely/Goodbye My Love | 5 |
| 74 | RCA APBO 0305 | Happiness Is Just Around The Bend/Why Can't We All Unite | 5 |

**MAINFRAME**

| | | | |
|---|---|---|---|
| 84 | YYY | INTO TROUBLE WITH THE NOISE OF ART (12", 7-track EP) | 10 |

**MAINHORSE**

| | | | |
|---|---|---|---|
| 71 | Polydor 2383 049 | MAINHORSE (LP) | 45 |

**MIKE MAINIERI**

| | | | |
|---|---|---|---|
| 69 | Solid State USS 7006 | INSIGHT (LP) | 30 |

**MAINLAND**

| | | | |
|---|---|---|---|
| 79 | Christy ACML 0200 | EXPOSURE (LP) | 15 |

**MAINLINER**

| | | | |
|---|---|---|---|
| 03 | Remorse LP 01 | MELLOW OUT (LP, red vinyl) | 15 |

*(see also Acid Mothers Temple)*

**JULIE MAIRS & CHRIS STOWELL**

| | | | |
|---|---|---|---|
| 77 | Cottage COT 211 | SOFT SEA BLUE (LP) | 25 |

**MAISON ROUGE**

| | | | |
|---|---|---|---|
| 85 | Red Barn RBR 0001 | Questions (p/s) | 5 |

**MAJAMOOD**

| | | | |
|---|---|---|---|
| 66 | Doc. Bird/W.I.R.L. DB 1052 | Two Hundred Million Red Ants/Faces Amassed | 30 |

**MAJESTERIANS**

| | | | |
|---|---|---|---|
| 81 | Daddy Kool DKR 125 | So Many Times/Flute On Fire (12") | 20 |

**MAJESTIC CHOIR AND SOUL STIRRERS**

| | | | |
|---|---|---|---|
| 69 | Chess CRS 8101 | Why Am I Treated So Bad/We Can All Walk A Little Prouder | 15 |

**MAJESTICS**

| | | | |
|---|---|---|---|
| 73 | Cube BUG 34 | Living It All Again/She Troubles My Mind | 25 |

**MAJOR**

| | | | |
|---|---|---|---|
| 78 | North Star NS 104 | MAJOR EP | 50 |

**MAJOR ACCIDENT**

| | | | |
|---|---|---|---|
| 82 | M. Melodies MAME 1001 | Warboots/Terrorist Gang (unissued, test pressings only) | 40 |
| 83 | Step Forward SF 23 | Mr. Nobody/That's You (p/s) | 12 |
| 83 | Flicknife FLS 016 | Fight To Win/Free Man (p/s) | 15 |
| 83 | Flicknife FLS 023 | Leaders Of Tomorrow/Dayo/Breakaway (p/s) | 12 |
| 84 | Flicknife FLS 026 | Respectable/Man On The Wall (p/s) | 12 |
| 83 | Step Forward SFLP 9 | MASSACRED MELODIES (LP) | 30 |
| 84 | Syndicate SYNLP 9 | TORTURED TUNES LIVE (LP) | 25 |
| 85 | Flicknife SHARP 027 | PNEUMATIC PNEUROSIS (LP) | 25 |

*(see also Accident)*

MINT VALUE £

## MAJOR B LASER
80 Charly CYS 1064 — Next To You/Rock On Bolan (p/s) ............................................................ 8

## MAJORETTES
63 Lyntone LYN 982 — White Levi's (flexidisc) ............................................................ 15

## MAJOR FORCE
94 Mo' Wax MW 082LP — Return Of The Original Artform/(Mixes) (5 x 12" box set) ........................ 25

## MAJORINE
69 Pyramid 6069 — Loving Shrine/I Live ............................................................ 20

## MAJORITY
| 65 | Decca F 12186 | Pretty Little Girl/I Don't Wanna Be Hurt No More ........................ 20 |
| 65 | Decca F 12271 | A Little Bit Of Sunlight/Shut 'Em Down In London Town ............ 25 |
| 66 | Decca F 12313 | We Kiss In A Shadow/Ring The Bells ........................................ 15 |
| 66 | Decca F 12453 | Simplified/One Third ........................................................ 100 |
| 66 | Decca F 12504 | To Make Me A Man/Tears Won't Help ...................................... 15 |
| 67 | Decca F 12573 | I Hear A Rhapsody/Wait By The Fire ...................................... 20 |
| 67 | Decca F 12638 | Running Away With My Baby/Let The Joybells Ring ...................... 20 |
| 68 | Decca F 12727 | All Our Christmases/People .................................................. 25 |

## MAJORS (1)
| 62 | London HLP 9602 | A Wonderful Dream/Time Will Tell ...................................... 15 |
| 62 | London HLP 9627 | She's A Troublemaker/A Little Bit Now ................................ 15 |
| 63 | London HLP 9693 | What In The World/Tra La La ............................................ 15 |
| 64 | Liberty LBF 66009 | Ooh Wee Baby/I'll Be There .......................................... 30 |
| 63 | London RE-P 1358 | MEET THE MAJORS (EP) ................................................ 40 |
| 63 | London HA-P 8068 | MEET THE MAJORS (LP) ................................................ 50 |

## MAJORS (2)
77 Magnet MAG 79 — It Only Happens/One Sided Love Affair .................................. 20

## MAJOR SURGERY
77 Next 104 — NEXT CUT (LP) ............................................................ 15

## MAJOR TOM
76 Satril SAT 113 — Spaceman Boy/Spaceman Boy (Instrumental) .......................... 25

## MAKADOPOLOUS
| 60 | Palette PG 9005 | Never On Sunday/Yasou (p/s) .......................................... 8 |
| 60 | Palette PG 9005 | Never On Sunday/Yasou .................................................. 5 |

## PETER MAKANA & HIS RHYTHM BOYS
| 58 | Oriole CB 1445 | Baboon Shepherd (with Black Duke)/Black John ...................... 5 |
| 58 | Oriole CB 1446 | Cool Mood/Sweet Baby .................................................... 5 |

## CARMEN MAKI
69 CBS 4298 — (Sometime I Feel Like) A Lonely Baby/Anata Ga Hoshii ............ 10

## MAKIN' TIME
| 85 | Countdown VAIN 1 | Here Is My Number/Nothing Else (p/s) ................................ 8 |
| 85 | Countdown VAIN 2 | Feels Like It's Love/Honey (Fast Version) ............................ 8 |
| 86 | Countdown VAIN 5 | Pump It Up/Walk A Thin Line (p/s) .................................... 5 |
| 85 | Countdown DOWN 1 | RHYTHM 'N' SOUL (LP) ................................................ 8 |
| 86 | Ready To Eat READY 1 | NO LUMPS OF FAT OR GRISTLE GUARANTEED (LP) .............. 15 |
| 87 | Re-Elect/President ELECT 1 | TIME, TROUBLE AND MONEY (LP) .......................... 18 |

(see also Charlatans)

## MAKKA BEES
77 Congo CO 1 — Nation Fiddler/Fire ........................................................ 20

## MAL & PRIMITIVES
65 Pye 7N 15915 — Every Minute Of Every Day/Pretty Little Face ...................... 80

(see also Primitives, Mal Ryder & Spirits)

## MALA
| 05 | DMZ DMZ 003 | Da Wrath Souljahz Vip Mix/LOEFAH: Twisup Vip (12") .............. 25 |
| 06 | DMZ DMZ 010 | Left Leg Out/Vlue Notez (12") ............................................ 20 |
| 07 | DMZ DMZ 011 | Bury Da Bwoy/Hunter (12") ................................................ 25 |
| 07 | DMZ DMZ 012 | Lean Forward/Learn (12") .................................................. 30 |

## MALAGON SISTERS & CHA CHA RHYTHM BOYS
59 Pye International 7N 25008 — In A Little Spanish Town/Lessons In Cha-Cha-Cha .......... 5

## CARL MALCOLM
| 75 | Black Wax WAX 7 | Miss Wire Waist/SKIN, FLESH & BONES: Wire Dub .................. 10 |
| 77 | Grove Music GMDM 1 | Repatriation (feat. Ranking Trevor)/Take A Tip From Me (feat. Ranking Trevor) (12") ... 40 |

## CARLOS MALCOLM & AFRO CARIBS
65 Island WI 173 — Bonanza Ska/Papa Luiga .................................................. 20

## HUGH MALCOLM
| 68 | Amalgamated AMG 827 | Good Time Rock/LYNN TAITT & JETS: Sleepy Ludy .............. 50 |
| 68 | Amalgamated AMG 829 | Mortgage/CANNONBALL BRYAN TRIO: Man About Town .......... 50 |

## MALIBU
78 Cleverly Bros CBSP 1000 100 — Skateboarding/Billy .......................................... 20

## MALLARD
| 77 | Virgin VS 168 | Harvest/Green Coyote ...................................................... 7 |
| 76 | Virgin V 2045 | MALLARD (LP) .............................................................. 15 |

(see also Captain Beefheart & His Magic Band)

## MALLET
80 Rox ROX 014 — C C Rider/Route 66 ........................................................ 25

## SIW MALMKVIST
59 Oriole CB 1486 — Sermonette/The Preacher .................................................. 20

| | | | |
|---|---|---|---|
| 61 | Parlophone R 4765 | Wedding Cake/Red Roses And Little White Lies | 6 |
| 64 | Columbia DB 7411 | Sole Sole Sole/Sabato Sera (as Siw Malmkvist & Umberto Marcato) | 5 |
| 68 | Atlantic 584 229 | The Man Who Took The Valise Off The Floor Of Grand Central Station/Sadie The Cleaning Lady | 6 |

**MALO**

| 72 | Warner Bros. K16155 | Suavecito/Nena | 10 |
|---|---|---|---|

**CINDY MALONE**

| 61 | RCA RCA 1254 | Weird Beard/Young Marriage | 8 |
|---|---|---|---|

**WIL MALONE**

| 70 | Fontana STL 5541 | WIL MALONE (LP) | 1500 |
|---|---|---|---|
| 10 | Morgan Bluetown BT 5005 | WIL MALONE (LP, reissue, 750 only with signed certificate) | 35 |

(see also Barnaby Rudge, Motherlight, Wilson Malone Voiceband)

**WILSON MALONE VOICEBAND**

| 68 | Morgan MR 112P | FUNNY SAD MUSIC (LP) | 40 |
|---|---|---|---|

(see also Motherlight, Wil Malone)

**MALPRACTICE**

| 80 | SRTS/80/CUS 762 | It's OK/Wish You Would/Don't Take It Out | 30 |
|---|---|---|---|

**RICHARD MALTBY**

| 56 | HMV 7M 393 | Man With The Golden Arm Theme/Heart Of Paris | 5 |
|---|---|---|---|
| 61 | Columbia DB 4606 | The Rat Race/Walkie Talkie | 8 |

**MAMA LAPATO**

| 82 | Bead Records BEAD 20 | MAMA LAPATO (LP) | 20 |
|---|---|---|---|

**MAMA LION**

| 72 | Philips 6078002 | Ain't Too Proud To Beg/Mr. Invitation | 6 |
|---|---|---|---|
| 72 | Philips 6369 153 | MAMA LION (LP) | 15 |

**MAMAS & PAPAS**

| | | | |
|---|---|---|---|
| 66 | RCA Victor RCA 1503 | California Dreamin'/Somebody Groovy | 8 |
| 66 | RCA Victor RCA 1516 | Monday, Monday/Got A Feelin' | 5 |
| 66 | RCA Victor RCA 1533 | I Saw Her Again/Even If I Could | 6 |
| 66 | RCA Victor RCA 1551 | Look Through My Window/Once There Was I Time I Thought | 5 |
| 67 | RCA Victor RCA 1564 | Words Of Love/I Can't Wait | 7 |
| 67 | RCA Victor RCA 1576 | Dedicated To The One I Love/Free Advice | 5 |
| 67 | RCA Victor RCA 1613 | Creeque Alley/No Salt On Her Tail | 6 |
| 67 | RCA Victor RCA 1630 | Straight Shooter/12.30/Young Girls Are Coming To The Canyon | 6 |
| 67 | RCA Victor RCA 1649 | Glad To Be Unhappy/Hey Girl | 7 |
| 68 | RCA Victor RCA 1710 | Safe In My Garden/Too Late | 7 |
| 68 | RCA Victor RCA 1726 | Dream A Little Dream Of Me/Midnight Voyage (as Mama Cass and the Mamas & Papas) | 6 |
| 68 | RCA Victor RCA 1744 | For The Love Of Ivy/Strange Young Girls | 8 |
| 66 | RCA Victor RD 7803 | IF YOU CAN BELIEVE YOUR EYES AND EARS (LP) | 20 |
| 66 | RCA Victor RD/SF 7834 | CASS, JOHN, MICHELLE, DENNY (LP) | 20 |
| 67 | RCA Victor RD/SF 7880 | DELIVER (LP) | 20 |
| 68 | RCA Victor RD/SF 7960 | THE PAPAS AND THE MAMAS (LP) | 15 |
| 68 | Stateside (S)SL 5002 | THE MAMAS AND THE PAPAS GOLDEN ERA VOL. 2 (LP) | 20 |
| 70 | Probe SPB 1013/14 | A GATHERING OF FLOWERS (2-LP) | 15 |
| 71 | Probe SPB 1048 | PEOPLE LIKE US (LP) | 15 |
| 78 | St. Michael MO 101225 | CALIFORNIA DREAMIN' (LP, exclusive to Marks & Spencer) | 15 |

(see also Mama Cass [Elliot], John Phillips, Michelle Phillips, Scott McKenzie, Barry McGuire, Mugwumps, Big Three [U.S], Spanky & Our Gang)

**MAMA'S BOYS**

| 83 | Spartan 12SP 6 | Too Little Of You To Love/Freedom Fighters (12", p/s, with free "Official Bootleg" LP) | 10 |
|---|---|---|---|
| 84 | Spartan SP 11 | Midnight Promises (p/s) | 5 |
| 85 | Jive HIP 24 | POWER AND PASSION (LP, with 12" interview picture disc) | 12 |

**MAMA'S PRIDE**

| 75 | Atlantic K 10709 | Blue Mist/Missouri Skyline | 6 |
|---|---|---|---|

**MAMMATH**

| 84 | Neat NEAT 42 | Rock Me/Rough 'N' Ready (p/s) | 7 |
|---|---|---|---|

**MAMMOTH**

| 89 | Jive MOTHX 4 | All The Days/Fatman/Bet You Wish (12", picture disc, PVC sleeve, withdrawn) | 20 |
|---|---|---|---|

(see also John McCoy, Gillan, Samson, Tiger, Nicky Moore Band, Hackensack)

**BATTI MAMZELLE**

| 74 | Fly 17 | I SEE THE LIGHT (LP) | 20 |
|---|---|---|---|

**MAN**

| | | | |
|---|---|---|---|
| 69 | Pye 7N 17684 | Sudden Life/Love | 35 |
| 71 | Liberty LBF 15448 | Daughter Of The Fireplace/Country Girl | 18 |
| 74 | United Artists UP 35643 | Don't Go Away (possibly unissued) | 15 |
| 74 | United Artists UP 35703 | Taking The Easy Way Out Again/California Silks And Satins | 6 |
| 74 | United Artists UP 35739 | Day And Night/A Hard Way To Live | 5 |
| 76 | MCA MCA 236 | Out Of Your Head/I'm A Love Taker | 5 |
| 69 | Pye N(S)PL 18275 | REVELATION (LP, mono, original pressing with sky blue label with black at top) | 100 |
| 69 | Pye N(S)PL 18275 | REVELATION (LP, stereo, original pressing with sky blue label with black at top) | 80 |
| 69 | Dawn DNLS 3003 | 2 OZS OF PLASTIC WITH A HOLE IN THE MIDDLE (LP, orange label, gatefold sleeve) | 50 |
| 69 | Dawn DNLS 3003 | 2 OZ'S OF PLASTIC WITH A HOLE IN THE MIDDLE (LP, later pressings with lilac then pink 'sun' labels, gatefold sleeve) | 20 |
| 70 | Liberty LBG 83464 | MAN (LP, gatefold textured sleeve) | 40 |
| 72 | United Artists UAS 29236 | DO YOU LIKE IT HERE NOW (ARE YOU SETTLING IN ALRIGHT?) (LP) | 40 |
| 72 | United Artists USP 100 | LIVE AT THE PADGET ROOMS, PENARTH (LP) | 30 |
| 72 | United Artists UAG 29417 | BE GOOD TO YOURSELF AT LEAST ONCE A DAY (LP, fold out 'map' in gatefold sleeve with 'family tree' inner) | 45 |
| 73 | United Artists UDX 205/6 | CHRISTMAS AT THE PATTI (LP, 2 x 10", with other artists) | 22 |

## T. MAN & T. BONES

| | | | |
|---|---|---|---|
| 73 | Utd Artists UAD 60053/4 | BACK INTO THE FUTURE (2-LP, gatefold sleeve, some stickered) | MINT VALUE £ 20 |
| 74 | United Artists UAG 29631 | RHINOS WINOS AND LUNATICS (LP, laminated gatefold) | 15 |
| 74 | United Artists UAG 29675 | SLOW MOTION (LP, lyric inner sleeve) | 15 |
| 75 | United Artists UAG 29872 | MAXIMUM DARKNESS (LP, gatefold sleeve, with poster) | 15 |
| 77 | MCA MCF 2815 | ALL'S WELL THAT ENDS WELL (LP, initial batch with History Of Man booklet) | 20 |

*(see also Bystanders, Eyes Of Blue, Ancient Grease, Big Sleep, Clive John, Alkatraz, Help Yourself, Deke Leonard, Neutrons, Gary Pickford-Hopkins & Friends, Wild Turkey)*

## T. MAN & T. BONES

| | | | |
|---|---|---|---|
| 72 | Sioux SI 007 | True Born African (actually by Winston Jarrett & Righteous Flames)/Tropical Chief | 35 |

## MAN UPSTAIRS

| | | | |
|---|---|---|---|
| 82 | Clock House CH 0502 | Summa/The Gospel According To Mark (p/s) | 15 |
| 85 | Sideline SIDE 1 | Sad In My Heart/Country Boy (p/s) | 15 |
| 85 | Sideline 1SIDE12 | CONSUMERS EP (12", p/s) | 40 |

## (STEPHEN STILLS') MANASSAS

| | | | |
|---|---|---|---|
| 72 | Atlantic K 60021 | MANASSAS (2-LP, with 2 inner sleeves & lyric poster) | 25 |
| 73 | Atlantic K 40440 | DOWN THE ROAD (LP, with inner sleeve) | 18 |

*(see also Stephen Stills, Crosby Stills & Nash, Flying Burrito Brothers)*

## MANASSEH

| | | | |
|---|---|---|---|
| 77 | Genesis 12 | MANASSEH (LP, with insert) | 20 |

## JUNIOR MANCE

| | | | |
|---|---|---|---|
| 60 | HMV CLP 1342 | JUNIOR (LP) | 25 |
| 71 | Atlantic 2400 028 | WITH A LOTTA HELP FROM MY FRIENDS (LP) | 20 |

## STEVE MANCHA/J.J. BARNES

| | | | |
|---|---|---|---|
| 69 | Stax SXATS 1012 | RARE STAMPS (LP) | 60 |

*(see also J.J. Barnes)*

## MANCHESTER CITY F.C.

| | | | |
|---|---|---|---|
| 72 | RCA 2200 | Boys In Blue/Funky City | 6 |

## MANCHESTER MEKON

| | | | |
|---|---|---|---|
| 79 | Newmarket NEW 102 | No Forgetting/Have A Go-Go/Jonathan Livingstone Seafood (hand-painted p/s with insert, 1,000 only) | 25 |

## MICKY MANCHESTER

| | | | |
|---|---|---|---|
| 75 | Rainbow RBW 2001 | Have You Seen Your Daughter, Mrs Jones?/Chamberlain Said | 10 |

## MANCHESTER MOB

| | | | |
|---|---|---|---|
| 67 | Parlophone R 5552 | Bony Maronie At The Hop/Afro Asian | 40 |

*(see also Graham Gouldman, High Society, 10cc, Friday Browne)*

## MANCHESTER UNITED F.C.

| | | | |
|---|---|---|---|
| 78 | Jet 775 | Just One Of Those Teams/Na Na Hey Hey Kiss Him Goodbye (As Manchester United Supporters Club) | 6 |
| 81 | Goldspinners GOLD 1 | Manchester United/Tribute To The Fans (as Manchester United) | 6 |
| 86 | Columbia DB 9107 | We All Follow Man. United/They're The Best/Southbound Glory Glory Man. United (as Manchester United Football Team) | 6 |

## MANCHESTER UNITED FOOTBALL SQUAD

| | | | |
|---|---|---|---|
| 76 | Decca F 13633 | Manchester United/MARTIN BUCHAN: Old Trafford Blues | 8 |
| 79 | RCA MAN 1 | Onward Sexton's Soldiers/Come On You Reds (red vinyl) | 8 |
| 94 | PolyGram TV MANUP 12 | Come On You Reds/(Instrumental) (12" picture disc, with insert) | 15 |

*(see also Status Quo)*

## MANCHESTERS

| | | | |
|---|---|---|---|
| 66 | Ember | TRIBUTE TO THE BEATLES (LP) | 20 |

## MANCHESTER'S PLAYBOYS

| | | | |
|---|---|---|---|
| 66 | Fontana TF 745 | I Feel So Good/I Close My Eyes | 150 |

## MANCINI & FOX

| | | | |
|---|---|---|---|
| 72 | Polydor 2066 170 | Light Song/The Colours Are Still There | 8 |

## HENRY MANCINI & HIS ORCHESTRA

| | | | |
|---|---|---|---|
| 59 | RCA RCA 1134 | Peter Gunn Theme/The Brothers Go To Mother's | 10 |
| 61 | RCA RCA 1256 | Moon River/Breakfast At Tiffanys | 5 |
| 62 | RCA RCA 1285 | Experiment In Terror/Tooty Twist | 10 |
| 62 | RCA RCA 1312 | Man Of The World Theme/Fluter's Ball | 6 |
| 64 | RCA RCA 1431 | Dear Heart/A Shot In The Dark | 5 |
| 68 | RCA RCA 1689 | Wait Until Dark/Norma De Guadalajara | 5 |
| 70 | RCA RCA 1934 | Z-Theme/Midnight Cowboy | 5 |
| 57 | Brunswick LAT 8162 | ROCK, PRETTY BABY (LP, soundtrack, with Rod McKuen) | 80 |

## DAVID MANCUSO

| | | | |
|---|---|---|---|
| 99 | Nuphonic NUX 136 | DAVID MANCUSO PRESENTS THE LOFT (4-LP) | 35 |

## MANDALABAND

| | | | |
|---|---|---|---|
| 75 | Chrysalis CHR 1095 | MANDALABAND (LP) | 20 |
| 78 | Chrysalis CHR 1181 | THE EYE OF WENDOR: PROPHECIES (LP, with booklet) | 20 |

## MANDARIN KRAZE

| | | | |
|---|---|---|---|
| 70 | Carnaby CNS 4008 | How Long Does It Take/Magazine Cottage | 25 |

## HARVEY MANDEL

| | | | |
|---|---|---|---|
| 74 | Janus 6146 024 | Uno Ino/Shangrenade | 6 |
| 68 | Philips SBL 7873 | CRISTO REDENTOR (LP) | 45 |
| 69 | Philips SBL 7904 | RIGHTEOUS (LP) | 20 |
| 70 | Philips SBL 7915 | GAMES GUITARS PLAY (LP) | 15 |
| 71 | Dawn DNLS 3015 | BABY BATTER (LP) | 40 |
| 71 | Philips 6336 009 | CRISTO REDENTOR (LP, reissue) | 15 |
| 72 | London SH-O 8426 | GET OFF IN CHICAGO (LP) | 15 |
| 72 | Janus 6310 210 | THE SNAKE (LP) | 15 |

*(see also Canned Heat, Dewey Terry)*

## RICHARD MANDEL
69   London HL 10256 — Loneliness/Young And Warm And Wonderful .......... 12

## MANDIBLE RUMPUS
79   Mayhem HEM 1 — Whats My Line/Shadows And Passions (p/s) .......... 12

## MANDINGO
73   EMI EMI 2014 — Medicine Man/Black Rite .......... 15
73   EMI 2062 — Fever Pitch/The Cheetah .......... 10
73   EMI EMC 3010 — MANDINGO 1: SACRIFICE (LP) .......... 15
73   Studio Two TWO 400 — MANDINGO 2: PRIMEVAL RHYTHM OF LIFE (LP) .......... 40
73   Studio Two Q4TWO 400 — MANDINGO 2: PRIMEVAL RHYTHM OF LIFE (LP, quadrophonic) .......... 40
75   EMI EMC 3038 — MANDINGO 3: STORY OF SURVIVAL (LP) .......... 30
77   EMI EMC 3217 — MANDINGO 4: SAVAGE RITE (LP) .......... 25
(see also Geoff Love)

## MANDRAGORA
89   SAB 01 — OVER THE MOON (LP, 1st pressing with white label/cream sleeve) .......... 50
89   Babbleon Bab 1 — OVER THE MOON (LP, 2nd pressing with blue label/yellow/blue/white/cream sleeve) . 30
95   Mystic Stones RUNE 14 — TEMPLE BALL (LP) .......... 15
93   Mystic Stones RUNE 13 — EARTHDANCE (LP) .......... 15
91   Resonance 33-9133 — HEAD FIRST (LP) .......... 20

## MANDRAKE
60   Philips PB 1093 — Mandrake/The Witch's Twist .......... 10
61   Philips BF 1153 — Thank Goodness It's Friday/Queen Of Sheba .......... 7

## MANDRAKE MEMORIAL
69   RCA SF 8028 — MEDIUM (LP) .......... 125
70   RCA/Poppy PYS 11003 — PUZZLE (LP) .......... 140

## MANDRAKE PADDLE STEAMERS
69   Parlophone R 5780 — Strange Walking Man/Steam .......... 130
88   Bam Caruso NRIC 033 — Strange Walking Man/Steam (reissue, gatefold p/s) .......... 12
(see also Liverpool Echo)

## MANDRILL
72   Polydor 2391 030 — MANDRILL IS (LP, gatefold) .......... 20
73   Polydor 2391 061 — COMPOSITE TRUTH (LP) .......... 15
73   Polydor 2391 092 — JUST OUTSIDE OF TOWN (LP) .......... 15

## MANDY (SMITH)
87   PWL PWLP 1 — I Just Can't Wait/Instrumental/You're Never Alone (12" picture disc) .......... 10

## MANEATERS
82   Editions EG EGO 8 — Nine To Five/SUZI PINNS: Jerusalem (withdrawn 'Adam & Toyah' p/s) .......... 100
82   Editions EG EGO 8 — Nine To Five/SUZI PINNS: Jerusalem (title p/s) .......... 5
(see also Adam & The Ants)

## MAN FRIDAY & JIVE JUNIOR
83   Malaco MAL 011 — Picking Up Sounds/Picking Up Sounds (Radio Mix) (p/s, features John Deacon) .......... 20
83   Malaco MAL 1211 — Picking Up Sounds (Extended)/Picking Up Sounds (Radio Mix) (12", p/s, features John Deacon) .......... 35
(see also Queen)

## MAN FROM DELMONTE
87   Ugly Man UGLY 3 — Drive Drive Drive (22 And Still In Love With You)/Sun Serious (p/s) .......... 25
87   Ugly Man UGLY 5 — Water In My Eyes/Bored By You (p/s) .......... 12
87   Ugly Man UGLY 5T — Water In My Eyes/Bored By You/The Country (12", p/s) .......... 18
88   Ugly Man UGLY 7 — (Will Nobody Save) Louise/Good Things In Life (p/s) .......... 10
88   Ugly Man UGLY 7T — (Will Nobody Save) Louise/Good Things In Life/Like A Millionaire (12", p/s) .......... 25
89   Bop Cassettes BIP 502 — WAITING FOR ANN (12" EP) .......... 15

## MANGO GREEN
70   Ackee ACK 109 — Birds Of A Feather/Run Down .......... 15

## MANHATTANS
65   Sue WI 384 — I Wanna Be (Your Everything)/Searchin' For My Baby .......... 50
66   Carnival CAR 100 — Baby I Need You/Teach Me (The Philly Dog) .......... 20
66   Carnival CAR 101 — That New Girl/Can I .......... 20
74   CBS 2117 — Soul Train/I'm Not A Run Around .......... 6
73   London SHB 8449 — A MILLION TO ONE (LP) .......... 30

## MANIAC
85   Rentaracket Recordings RKT 1 — KILLING FOR PLEASURE EP (p/s, with booklet) .......... 6

## MANIACS
77   United Artists UP 36327 — Chelsea 1977/Ain't No Legend (p/s) .......... 20
77   United Artists UP 36327 — Chelsea 1977/Ain't No Legend (p/s, green labels, demo versions different mixes) .......... 30
(see also Rings, Physicals)

## MANIAX
66   White Label WLR 101/102 — Out Of Reach/The Devil's Home .......... 20

## MANIC JABS
81   Waldo's MS 009 — Autophagus/The Injuns Are Comin'/Thing Wild (p/s) .......... 10

## MANIC STREET PREACHERS
SINGLES
88   SBS SBS 002 — Suicide Alley/Tennessee (I Get Low) (hand-made p/s with press-cuttings glued to plain card cover) .......... 750
88   SBS SBS 002 — Suicide Alley/Tennessee (I Get Low) (blue p/s, 200 only) .......... 400
88   SBS SBS 002 — Suicide Alley/Tennessee (I Get Low) (no p/s, 100 only) .......... 200
90   Hopelessly Devoted 1 — UK Channel Boredom/LAURENS: I Don't Know What The Trouble Is (p/s flexidisc, free with Hopelessly Devoted fanzine; later repressed) .......... 60

MINT VALUE £

| 90 | Hopelessly Devoted 1 | UK Channel Boredom/LAURENS: I Don't Know What The Trouble Is (p/s flexidisc, without Hopelessly Devoted fanzine; later repressed) | 45 |
|---|---|---|---|
| 90 | Damaged Goods YUBB 4 | NEW ART RIOT EP: New Art Riot/Strip It Down/ Last Exit On Yesterday/Teenage 20/20 (12", white label, 100 copies, plain sleeves rubber stamped with "Made In Wales") | 35 |
| 90 | Damaged Goods YUBB 4 | NEW ART RIOT EP: New Art Riot/Strip It Down/Last Exit On Yesterday/Teenage 20/20 (12" EP, p/s, 1st 1,000 black & white label) | 20 |
| 90 | Damaged Goods YUBB 4 | NEW ART RIOT EP: New Art Riot/Strip It Down/Last Exit On Yesterday/Teenage 20/20 (12" EP, p/s, 2nd 1,000 on black-on-yellow labels) | 15 |
| 91 | Damaged Goods YUBB 004P | NEW ART RIOT EP: New Art Riot/Strip It Down/Last Exit On Yesterday/Teenage 20/20 (12" EP, p/s, later pressing on red, orange & silver & green labels) | 10 |
| | | NEW ART RIOT EP: New Art Riot/Strip It Down/Last Exit On Yesterday/Teenage 20/20 (12" EP, p/s, reissue on pink vinyl) | 25 |
| 91 | Heavenly HVN 812 | Motown Junk/Sorrow 16/We Her Majesty's Prisoners (12", withdrawn p/s) | 35 |
| 91 | Heavenly HVN 8CD | Motown Junk/Sorrow 16/We Her Majesty's Prisoners (CD, withdrawn sleeve) | 80 |
| 91 | Heavenly HVN 10 | You Love Us/Spectators Of Suicide (p/s) | 15 |
| 91 | Heavenly HVN 1012 | You Love Us/Spectators Of Suicide/Starlover/Strip It Down (live) (12", p/s) | 20 |
| 91 | Heavenly HVN 10CD | You Love Us/Spectators Of Suicide/Starlover/Strip It Down (live) (CD) | 25 |
| 91 | Columbia 657337 6 | Stay Beautiful/R.P. McMurphy/Soul Contamination (12", p/s) | 10 |
| 91 | Columbia 657337 8 | Stay Beautiful/R.P. McMurphy/Soul Contamination (12", stickered poster p/s) | 10 |
| 91 | Columbia 657582 6 | Repeat (U.K.)/Love's Sweet Exile/Democracy Coma (12", p/s) | 12 |
| 91 | Columbia 657582 8 | Repeat/Democracy Coma/Love's Sweet Exile/Stay Beautiful (live) (12", gatefold, stickered p/s) | 12 |
| 91 | Caff CAFF 15 | FEMININE IS BEAUTIFUL: Repeat After Me/New Art Riot (p/s, 500 only) | 200 |
| 92 | Columbia 657724 6 | You Love Us/A Vision Of Dead Desire/It's So Easy (live) (12" gatefold p/s) | 10 |
| 92 | Columbia 657873 7 | Slash'N'Burn/Motown Junk (p/s) | 6 |
| 92 | Columbia 657873 6 | Slash'N'Burn/Motown Junk/Ain't Goin' Down (12", with print, stickered p/s) | 12 |
| 92 | Columbia 658083 7 | Motorcycle Emptiness/Bored Out Of My Mind | 6 |
| 92 | Columbia 658083 6 | Motorcycle Emptiness/Bored Out Of My Mind/Under My Wheels (12") | 15 |
| 92 | Columbia 658083 6 | Motorcycle Emptiness/Bored Out Of My Mind/Under My Wheels (12", picture disc, stickered PVC sleeve) | 18 |
| 92 | Damaged Goods YUBB 4CD | New Art Riot/Strip It Down/Last Exit On Yesterday/Teenage 20/20 (CD, picture disc, reissue, 3,000 only) | 10 |
| 92 | Columbia 658382 7 | Theme From MASH EP (Suicide Is Painless)/FATIMA MANSIONS: Everything I Do (I Do It For You) (p/s) | 6 |
| 93 | Columbia 6597277 | Roses In The Hospital/Us Against You/Donkeys (red vinyl, p/s) | 8 |
| 94 | Epic 660447-7 | Faster/P.C.P. | 6 |
| 07 | Columbia 8697075597 | Underdogs (1-sided, p/s) | 20 |
| 11 | Heavenly HVN 8 | Motown Junk/Sorrow 16 (reissue, 1000 only, p/s) | 10 |

## ALBUMS

| 92 | Epic 471060 1 | GENERATION TERRORISTS (2-LP) | 30 |
|---|---|---|---|
| 92 | Columbia 471060 0 | GENERATION TERRORISTS (2-LP, picture discs, inner sleeves, 5,000 only) | 40 |
| 92 | Columbia 471060 9 | GENERATION TERRORISTS (CD, picture disc, 5,000 only) | 40 |
| 93 | Columbia 474064 1 | GOLD AGAINST THE SOUL (LP, inner sleeve, in custom carrier-bag) | 15 |
| 94 | Epic 4774421 0 | THE HOLY BIBLE (LP, picture disc) | 30 |
| 94 | Epic 4774219 | THE HOLY BIBLE (CD, picture disc) | 20 |
| 96 | Epic 483930 | EVERYTHING MUST GO (LP) | 30 |
| 98 | Epic 4917031 | THIS IS MY TRUTH TELL ME YOURS (LP) | 30 |
| 03 | Sony 5123861 | LIPSTICK TRACES (3 x LP, 1,000 only with tactile sleeve) | 45 |

## PROMOS

| 91 | Heavenly HVN 10P | You Love Us (Radio Edit) (promo-only, some with stickered p/s, 1-sided white label, 500 only) | 30 |
|---|---|---|---|
| 93 | Columbia/Damont XPS 272 | Symphony Of Tourette (1-sided, white label, no p/s) | 70 |
| 94 | Columbia | DONE AND DUSTED (12", Chemical Brothers Remixes) | 20 |
| 96 | Columbia XPR 3043 | A Design For Life (Stealth Sonic Orchestra Remix)/(Instrumental) (12") | 20 |
| 96 | Columbia XPR 3049 | Kevin Carter (Stealth Sonic Orchestra Remix) (12", white label, 1-sided, stickered card sleeve, 30 only) | 30 |
| 96 | Columbia XPR 3094 | Australia (Lionrock Remix) (12", white label, 1-sided, stickered card sleeve, 20 only) | 60 |
| 97 | Columbia MANIC 1-6CD | SIX SINGLES FROM GENERATION TERRORISTS (6-CD box set) | 90 |
| 99 | Epic XPR 3320 | Tsunami (Cornelius Remix)/(Electron Ray Tube Mix by Stereolab) (12", p/s, sealed with sticker, promo only) | 10 |

## MANICURED NOISE

| 80 | Pre PRE 003 | Metronome/Moscow (die-cut p/s with postcard) | 5 |
|---|---|---|---|
| 80 | Pre PRE 006 | Faith/Free Time (p/s) | 6 |

*(see also Weatherman & Friends)*

## MANISH BOYS

| 65 | Parlophone R 5250 | I Pity The Fool/Take My Tip | 1000 |
|---|---|---|---|
| 65 | Parlophone R 5250 | I Pity The Fool/Take My Tip (Demo copy) | 500 |

*(see also David Bowie)*

## MANISH BOYS/DAVY JONES & LOWER THIRD

| 79 | EMI 2925 | I Pity The Fool/Take My Tip/DAVY JONES You've Got A Habit Of Leaving/Baby Loves That Way (Demo copy p/s) | |
|---|---|---|---|
| 79 | EMI EMI 2925 | I Pity The Fool/Take My Tip/DAVY JONES & LOWER THIRD: You've Got A Habit Of Leaving/Baby Loves That Way (p/s) | 20 |
| 82 | Charly CYM 1 | I Pity The Fool/Take My Tip/DAVY JONES & LOWER THIRD: You've Got A Habit Of Leaving/Baby Loves That Way (10", p/s, reissue) | 10 |

*(see also David Bowie, Davy Jones, Davie Jones & King Bees)*

## MANITOBA (1)

| 71 | RCA 2055 | Come On Down To My Boat/Dead End Street | 10 |
|---|---|---|---|

## MANITOBA (2)

| 01 | Leaf BAY 16V | STOP BREAKING MY HEART (LP) | 20 |
|---|---|---|---|
| 03 | Leaf BAY 26V | UP IN FLAMES (LP) | 20 |
| 03 | Leaf BAY 26VX | UP IN FLAMES (LP, clear vinyl) | 20 |

*(see also Caribou)*

**MANIX**
| | | | |
|---|---|---|---|
| 94 | Reinforced RIVET 1275 | Intelligent Hoodlums EP (2x12") | 12 |

**EARLE MANKEY**
| | | | |
|---|---|---|---|
| 78 | Bronze BRO 53 | Mau Mau/Crazy | 15 |

**MANKIND**
| | | | |
|---|---|---|---|
| 78 | Pinnacle PIN 71-12 | Dr. Who/Time Traveller (12", p/s, blue vinyl) | 10 |
| 78 | Motor Records MTR 001/12 | Dr. Who/Time Traveller (12", p/s, blue vinyl, p/s) | 12 |

**SYDNEY MANKIND**
| | | | |
|---|---|---|---|
| 82 | Musical Ambassador MAPD 001 | The Truth/EDI FITZROY: Chant It To The Rhythm (12") | 40 |

**ABEL MANN**
| | | | |
|---|---|---|---|
| 70 | Trend TNY 51 | The Sun In The Morning/It's So Easy | 7 |

**BARRY MANN**
| | | | |
|---|---|---|---|
| 61 | HMV POP 911 | Who Put The Bomp (In The Bomp Bomp)/Love True Love | 20 |
| 61 | HMV POP 949 | Little Miss U.S.A./Find Another Fool | 20 |
| 62 | HMV POP 1084 | Hey Baby I'm Dancin'/Like I Don't Love You | 15 |
| 63 | HMV POP 1108 | Bless You/Teenage Has Been | 15 |
| 64 | Colpix PX 776 | Talk To Me Baby/Amy | 15 |
| 66 | Capitol CL 15463 | Angelica/Looking At Tomorrow | 15 |
| 68 | Capitol CL 15538 | The Young Electric Psychedelic Hippy Flippy Folk And Funky Philosophic Turned On Groovy 12 String Band/Take Your Love | 10 |
| 63 | HMV CLP 1559 | WHO PUT THE BOMP IN THE BOMP BOMP BOMP? (LP) | 125 |
| 72 | CBS 64805 | LAY IT ALL OUT (LP, gatefold) | 15 |

**CARL MANN**
| | | | |
|---|---|---|---|
| 59 | London HLS 8935 | Mona Lisa/Foolish One | 50 |
| 59 | London HLS 9006 | Pretend/Rockin' Love | 35 |
| 59 | London HLS 9006 | Pretend/Rockin' Love (78) | 30 |
| 60 | London HLS 9170 | South Of The Border/I'm Comin' Home | 25 |
| 60 | London HA-S 2277 | LIKE MANN - CARL MANN SINGS (LP) | 250 |

**GARY MANN ORCHESTRA**
| | | | |
|---|---|---|---|
| 73 | Penny Farthing PEN 820 | The Original 'Big Match' Theme/Newscoop (The Original 'Grandstand' Theme) | 12 |

**GLORIA MANN**
| | | | |
|---|---|---|---|
| 56 | Brunswick 05569 | Why Do Fools Fall In Love/Partners For Life | 20 |
| 56 | Brunswick 05610 | It Happened Again/My Secret Sin | 10 |

**HERBIE MANN**
| | | | |
|---|---|---|---|
| 66 | Atlantic 584 058 | Love Theme (From 'Is Paris Burning')/Happy Brass | 7 |
| 66 | Atlantic 584 052 | Philly Dog/DAVE PIKE: Sunny | 10 |
| 68 | A&M AMS 719 | Unchain My Heart/Glory Of Love | 10 |
| 67 | Atlantic 584112 | The Beat Goes On/Free For All | 10 |
| 69 | Atlantic 584 297 | Memphis Underground/New Orleans | 6 |
| 72 | Atlantic K 10179 | Philly Dog/Memphis Underground/It's A Funky Thing | 15 |
| 75 | Atlantic K 10580 | Hijack/Orient Express | 15 |
| 75 | Atlantic SAM 26 | Hijack (Disco Cut)/Bertha Boogie Part 1 (12", "Disco Special Cut" on label) | 60 |
| 58 | Fontana TFL 5013 | SALUTE TO THE FLUTE (LP) | 15 |
| 60 | Top Rank 25/015 | FLUTE FOR ETERNITY (10" LP, with Buddy Collette) | 20 |
| 63 | London HA-K/SH-K 8043 | RIGHT NOW (LP) | 20 |
| 64 | Atlantic ATL 5008 | HERBIE MANN AT NEWPORT (LP) | 15 |
| 65 | Atlantic ATL/SAL 5035 | THE ROAR OF THE GREASE PAINT (LP) | 20 |
| 66 | CBS (S)BPG 62585 | LATIN MANN (LP) | 20 |
| 66 | Atlantic ATL/SAL 5038 | STANDING OVATION AT NEWPORT (LP) | 15 |
| 66 | Atlantic 587/588 003 | MONDAY NIGHT AT THE VILLAGE GATE (LP) | 15 |
| 66 | Atlantic 587/588 028 | NIRVANA (LP, with Bill Evans) | 15 |

**LORIE MANN**
| | | | |
|---|---|---|---|
| 59 | Top Rank JAR 116 | A Penny A Kiss, A Penny A Hug/Dream Lover | 6 |
| 59 | Top Rank JAR 148 | Just Keep It Up/You Made Me Care | 8 |
| 59 | Top Rank JAR 237 | So Many Ways/I Wonder | 7 |
| 61 | Pye Int. 7N 25069 | Happy Feet/The Busker | 6 |

**MANFRED MANN**
| | | | |
|---|---|---|---|
| 63 | HMV POP 1189 | Why Should We Not/Brother Jack | 30 |
| 63 | HMV POP 1225 | Cock-A-Hoop/Now You're Needing Me | 20 |
| 64 | HMV POP 1252 | 5-4-3-2-1/Without You | 8 |
| 64 | HMV POP 1282 | Hubble Bubble (Toil And Trouble)/I'm Your Kingpin | 8 |
| 64 | HMV POP 1320 | Do Wah Diddy Diddy/What You Gonna Do? | 5 |
| 64 | HMV POP 1346 | Sha La La/John Hardy | 6 |
| 65 | HMV POP 1413 | Oh No Not My Baby/What Am I Doing Wrong | 6 |
| 65 | HMV POP 1466 | If You Gotta Go, Go Now/Stay Around | 6 |
| 66 | HMV POP 1541 | You Gave Me Somebody To Love/Poison Ivy | 10 |
| 65 | HMV 7TEA 2124 | There's No Living Without Your Loving/Tired Of Trying, Bored With Lying, Scared Of Dying (demo-only EP sampler) | 30 |
| 66 | Fontana TF 730 | Just Like A Woman/I Wanna Be Rich | 6 |
| 66 | Fontana TF 757 | Semi-Detached, Suburban Mr. James/Morning After The Party | 5 |
| 67 | Fontana TF 812 | Ha! Ha! Said The Clown/Feeling So Good (in p/s) | 8 |
| 67 | Fontana TF 828 | Sweet Pea/One Way | 10 |
| 67 | Fontana TF 862 | So Long, Dad/Funniest Gig | 7 |
| 68 | Fontana TF 908 | Up The Junction/Sleepy Hollow (in p/s) | 18 |
| 68 | Fontana TF 908 | Up The Junction/Sleepy Hollow | 5 |
| 68 | Fontana TF 943 | My Name Is Jack/There Is A Man | 5 |
| 68 | Fontana TF 985 | Fox On The Run/Too Many People | 5 |

# MANFRED MANN & MIKE HUG(G)

| | | | |
|---|---|---|---|
| 69 | Fontana TF 1013 | Ragamuffin Man/A 'B' Side | 8 |
| 64 | HMV 7EG 8848 | MANFRED MANN'S COCK-A-HOOP WITH 54321 (EP) | 25 |
| 65 | HMV 7EG 8876 | GROOVIN' WITH MANFRED MANN (EP) | 25 |
| 65 | HMV 7EG 8908 | THE ONE IN THE MIDDLE (EP) | 20 |
| 65 | HMV 7EG 8922 | NO LIVING WITHOUT LOVING (EP) | 10 |
| 66 | HMV 7EG 8942 | MACHINES (EP) | 18 |
| 66 | HMV 7EG 8949 | INSTRUMENTAL ASYLUM (EP, with Jack Bruce) | 25 |
| 66 | HMV 7EG 8962 | AS WAS (EP) | 25 |
| 66 | Fontana TE 17483 | INSTRUMENTAL ASSASSINATION (EP) | 25 |
| 64 | HMV CLP 1731 | THE FIVE FACES OF MANFRED MANN (LP) | 12 |
| 64 | Odeon PCLP 1731 | THE FIVE FACES OF MANFRED MANN (LP, export issue gold/red odeon sticker on cover) | 60 |
| 65 | HMV CLP 1911 | MANN MADE (LP, mono) | 90 |
| 65 | HMV CSD 1628 | MANN MADE (LP, stereo) | 30 |
| 66 | HMV CLP 3559 | MANN MADE HITS (LP) | 40 |
| 66 | Fontana TL 5377 | AS IS (LP, 'alcove' cover, mono) | 35 |
| 66 | Fontana (S)TL 5377 | AS IS (LP, 'alcove' cover, stereo) | 20 |
| 66 | Fontana (S)TL 5377 | AS IS (LP, 'locomotive' cover, mono/stereo) | 30 |
| 67 | HMV CLP 3594 | SOUL OF MANN (LP, mono) | 60 |
| 67 | HMV CSD 3594 | SOUL OF MANN (LP, stereo) | 50 |
| 68 | Fontana (S)TL 5460 | UP THE JUNCTION - ORIGINAL SOUNDTRACK RECORDING (LP) | 70 |
| 68 | Fontana SFL 13003 | WHAT A MANN (LP) | 50 |
| 68 | Fontana TL 5470 | MIGHTY GARVEY! (LP, mono) | 20 |
| 68 | Fontana (S)TL 5470 | MIGHTY GARVEY! (LP, stereo) | 25 |
| 70 | Fontana 6852 005 | UP THE JUNCTION - ORIGINAL SOUNDTRACK RECORDING (LP, reissue) | 15 |

*(see also Paul Jones, Blues Band, Mike Hugg, Henry Lowther, Mike D'Abo, McGuinness Flint, Jack Bruce, Coulson & Dean, Lyn Dobson, Paddy Klaus & Gibson)*

## MANFRED MANN & MIKE HUG(G)

| | | | |
|---|---|---|---|
| 71 | Ski SKI 1 | Ski 'Full-Of-Fitness' Theme/Baby Jane (in p/s) | 15 |
| 71 | Ski SKI 1 | Ski 'Full-Of-Fitness' Theme/Baby Jane | 7 |
| 71 | Michelin MIC+01 | The Michelin Theme (Go Radial, Go Michelin) (1-sided, gatefold p/s) | 15 |

## MANFRED MANN'S CHAPTER III

| | | | |
|---|---|---|---|
| 70 | Vertigo 6059 012 | Happy Being Me/Devil Woman | 10 |
| 69 | Vertigo VO 3 | MANFRED MANN CHAPTER III (LP, 1st pressing, "Manfred Mann Chapter Three" and VO 3 847 902 VTY" in large type on B side, gatefold sleeve, large swirl label) | 150 |
| 70 | Vertigo VO 3 | MANFRED MANN CHAPTER III (LP, 2nd pressing, "Manfred Mann Chapter Three" and VO 3 847 902 VTY" in smaller type on B side, gatefold sleeve, large swirl label) | 100 |
| 70 | Vertigo VO 3 847 902 VTY | MANFRED MANN CHAPTER III (LP, 3rd pressing, without 'A Philips Record Product' text, gatefold sleeve, large swirl label) | 60 |
| 70 | Vertigo 6360 012 | MANFRED MANN CHAPTER III VOL. 2 (LP, gatefold sleeve, large swirl label) | 150 |

## MANFRED MANN'S EARTH BAND

| | | | |
|---|---|---|---|
| 71 | Philips 6006 122 | Living Without You/Tribute (as Manfred Mann) | 6 |
| 71 | Philips 6006 159 | Mrs Henry/Prayer (as Manfred Mann) | 6 |
| 72 | Philips 6006 251 | Meat/Glorified Magnified (as Earth Band) | 6 |
| 73 | Vertigo 6059 078 | Get Your Rocks Off/Sadjoy (as Earth Band) | 7 |
| 71 | Philips 6308 062 | STEPPING SIDEWAYS (LP, unissued) | 0 |
| 72 | Philips 6308 086 | MANFRED MANN'S EARTH BAND (LP, black/silver labels) | 40 |
| 72 | Philips 6308 125 | GLORIFIED MAGNIFIED (LP, gatefold sleeve, 1st pressing, black/silver labels) | 50 |
| 72 | Philips 6308 086 | GLORIFIED MAGNIFIED (LP, gatefold sleeve, 2nd pressing, blue/silver labels) | 20 |
| 73 | Vertigo 6360 087 | MESSIN' (LP, die cut gatefold sleeve, 'spaceship' label) | 25 |
| 73 | Bronze ILPS 9265 | SOLAR FIRE (LP, gatefold sleeve, lyric inner sleeve, Island label credit) | 20 |
| 74 | Bronze ILPS 9306 | THE GOOD EARTH (LP, lyric inner sleeve with uncut corner, Island label credit) | 20 |
| 75 | Bronze ILPS 9337 | NIGHTINGALES AND BOMBERS (LP, 1st pressing with Island matrix numbers ILPS 9337 A-2U/B-2U, "MELYS I.B.C" etched into dead wax) | 20 |

*(see also Australian Playboys, Trifle, AC/DC, Thin Lizzy, Alan Parsons Project, Jeff Wayne)*

## ROBERTO MANN ORCHESTRA

| | | | |
|---|---|---|---|
| 68 | Decca F13904 | Love Theme From Witchfinder General/Both Sides Now | 30 |
| 69 | Deram DM 249 | Theme From The Film "Baby Love" (Guai Guai)/Serenade To Summertime | 6 |

## SHADOW MANN

| | | | |
|---|---|---|---|
| 69 | Roulette RO 504 | Come Live With Me/One By One | 12 |

## SHELLY MANNE

| | | | |
|---|---|---|---|
| 68 | Atlantic 584 180 | Daktari/Out On A Limb | 12 |
| 54 | Vogue LDE 072 | SHELLY MANNE AND HIS MEN VOL. 1 (10" LP) | 15 |
| 55 | Contemporary LDC 143 | SHELLY MANNE VOL. 2 (10" LP, with Andre Previn & Leroy Vinegar) | 15 |
| 56 | Contemporary LDC 190 | SHELLY MANNE, SHORTY ROGERS AND JIMMY GIUFFRE - THE THREE (10" LP) | 15 |
| 56 | Contemporary LDC 192 | SHELLY MANNE AND RUSS FREEMAN (10" LP) | 15 |
| 56 | Contemporary LAC 12075 | SHELLY MANNE AND HIS FRIENDS (LP, with Andre Previn & Leroy Vinegar) | 15 |
| 62 | Contemporary LAC12315 | CHECKMATE (LP) | 15 |

*(see also Gerry Mulligan & Shelly Manne, Shorty Rogers & His Orchestra)*

## MANNIN FOLK

| | | | |
|---|---|---|---|
| 76 | Kelly MAN 2 | KING OF THE SEA (LP) | 35 |
| 70s | Kelly KEP 1 | MANNIN FOLK SING (LP) | 20 |

## LINDA MANNING

| | | | |
|---|---|---|---|
| 66 | King KG 1039 | Buy Me Something Pretty, Joey/Downtown Lonely Girl Blues | 7 |

## MARTY MANNING & CHEETAHS

| | | | |
|---|---|---|---|
| 67 | CBS 2721 | Tarzan March/Sunny | 10 |

## EDDIE MANNION

| | | | |
|---|---|---|---|
| 60 | HMV POP 804 | Just Driftin'/Quiet Girl | 50 |

**CAROL MANNS**
79   SRTS 79 CUS 425         You Me And The Boogie/Seagulls .................................................................... 20

**MAN ON THE MOON**
69   Philips 88457 DE         MAN ON THE MOON (EP, spoken word, 2-part tri-foldout p/s with insert, 'historic souvenir' available via News Of The World newspaper)........................................ 10

**WINGY MANONE ORCHESTRA**
57   Brunswick 05655         Party Doll/Real Gone ..................................................................................... 20

**MAN...OR ASTROMAN**
96   One Louder LOUDER 12    EXPERIMENTAL ZERO (LP, yellow vinyl, with poster) ...................................... 15
94   One Louder LOUDER 4     YOUR WEIGHT ON THE MOON (10 LP", pink, silver or luminous vinyl) .............. 15
95   Clawfist XPIG 28        WELCOME TO THE SONIC SPACE AGE EP (p/s) ................................................ 10
95   One Louder LOUDER 8     INTRAVENOUS TELEVISION CONTINUUM (LP) ................................................. 15

**MANOWAR**
87   Atlantic B 9463         Blow Your Speakers/Violence And Bloodshed (p/s) ............................................. 5
83   Music For Nations MFN 6  INTO GLORY RIDE (LP, with inner) ............................................................... 20
84   Music For Nations MFN 19 HAIL TO ENGLAND (LP, inner) .................................................................... 20
07   SPV 85601              GODS OF WAR (3-LP) ................................................................................... 20
*(see also Orson Welles)*

**MAN PARRISH**
82   Polydor POLD 5101       MAN PARRISH (LP) ...................................................................................... 15

**JOE MANSANO**
69   Blue Cat BS 150         Life On Reggae Planet/RECO & RHYTHM ACES: Z.Z. Beat ............................... 50
72   Sioux SI 022            The Trial Of Pama Dice/JACKIE ROWLAND: Lonely Man .................................. 20
70   Trojan TBL 106          BRIXTON CAT (LP)....................................................................................... 50
*(see also Joe The Boss, Joe's Allstars, Dice The Boss)*

**TONY MANSELL**
54   Parlophone MSP 6130     The High And The Mighty/Hold My Hand (with Johnny Dankworth Orchestra) .............. 8
56   Parlophone MSP 6222     Zambesi (Sweet African)/11th Hour Melody (with Johnny Dankworth Orchestra) ......... 8
58   Parlophone R 4471       Impossible/Who Are They To Say ................................................................... 5
*(see also Johnny Dankworth)*

**JAYNE MANSFIELD**
67   London HL 10147         As The Clouds Drift By/Suey (with Jimi Hendrix, demos more common, £35) ............. 50
62   World Record Club TP 262 JAYNE MANSFIELD IN LAS VEGAS (LP) ....................................................... 60
*(see also Jimi Hendrix)*

**KEITH MANSFIELD ORCHESTRA**
68   CBS 3895               Beautiful/Soul Thing .................................................................................... 20
72   2066 170               Beautiful/The Colours Are Still There ............................................................... 8
68   CBS 63426              ALL YOU NEED IS KEITH MANSFIELD (LP) .................................................... 40
70   CBS 70073              LOOT (LP, soundtrack, with Steve Ellis) ........................................................... 40

**MANSFIELD ORGANISATION**
67   President PT131         Daddy Russian Stoned/Ol' Nick ...................................................................... 20

**CHARLES MANSON**
80   Come Org. WDC 883008   LIE (cassette) ............................................................................................ 50
86   Fierce FRIGHT 006      Rise/Sick City (p/s, 1 side etched, handwritten labels) ......................................... 20
88   Fierce FRIGHT 012      It's Comin' Down Fast (Helter Skelter) (p/s, 1 side etched, hand-made labels) ............ 20
86   Fierce FRIGHT 001      LOVE AND TERROR CULT (LP) ................................................................... 30

**EDDY MANSON**
55   HMV 7M 325             Oh! No!/The Lovers........................................................................................ 8

**JEANE MANSON**
79   CBS S CBS 7222         I've Already Seen It In Your Eyes/J'ai Deja Vu Ca Dans Tes Yeux ........................ 15

**MARILYN MANSON**
97   Interscope INVP 95541   The Horrible People/The Not So Beautiful People (10" picture disc) ........................ 12
97   Interscope INVP 95552   Tourniquet/(remix) (10" picture disc) ............................................................. 12
98   Nothing INVP 95610      The Dope Show/The Dope Show (10" picture disc, same track on both sides) ........... 12
00   Nothing/Universe 4974581 Disposable Teens/Five To One/Diamonds & Pollen (12" picture disc, PVC sleeve.)........ 10
01   Universal 4974911       The Fight Song/(Slipknot Remix)/(Love Song Remix) (12" picture disc, stickered sleeve) ................................................................................................................ 10
                            ........................................................................................................................ 5
03   Universal 9807728       Mobscene/Paranoiac (poster p/s) ................................................................... 10
03   Universal 9810794       This Is The New Shit/(Goldfrapp Version) (10" picture disc) ............................... 10
12   FRY 509                No Reflection (Edit)/No Reflection (Album Version) (white vinyl, p/s) ...................... 18
95   Simply Vinyl SVLP 208   SMELLS LIKE CHILDREN (LP, 180 gm vinyl) .................................................. 20
98   Simply Vinyl SVLP 195   MECHANICAL ANIMALS (2-LP, 180 gm vinyl) ................................................ 45
99   Interscope ADV 490 394-2 MECHANICAL ANIMALS (CD, promo, numbered, card sleeve, with comic, PVC slipcase) ............................................................................................................... 25
02   Simply Vinyl SVLP 055   ANTICHRIST SUPERSTAR (2-LP, 180 gm vinyl, gatefold sleeve) ....................... 70
04   Interscope 9864285      LEST WE FORGET - THE BEST OF (2-LP) ................................................... ...

**MANSUN**
95   Polygram no cat. no.    Take It Easy Chicken (Demo)/Naked Twister/Drastic Sturgeon (cassette, promo only, with title inlay).......................................................................................................... 20
95   Sci Fi Hi Fi MANSON 1   Take It Easy Chicken/Take It Easy Chicken (as Manson, same track both sides, die-cut sleeve, 500 only; promos with "Manson Promo" on label £30) ....................................... 15
99   Fan club MANSUN 001     Taxloss/Everyone Must Win (live) (fanclub-only release) ....................................... 18
97   Parlophone CPCS 7387    ATTACK OF THE GREY LANTERN (2-LP, gatefold sleeve, with inners and poster).......... 40
98   EMI 749672314           SIX (2-LP, gatefold, inners) .......................................................................... 40
00   Parlophone 724352778218  LITTLE KIX (2-LP) ...................................................................................... 30

**JOHN MANTELL**
65   CBS 201783             Remember Child/I'll See You Around ............................................................... 10

MINT VALUE £

## MIKE MANTLER
75  Watt WATT 3                         133/4 (LP, with Carla Bley; with insert) ......................................... 20
*(see also Carla Bley, Jazz Composers Orchestra)*

## BOB MANTON
81  Mainstreet MS 101                    No Trees In Brixton Prison/Brixton Walkabout (p/s) ............................. 8
*(see also Purple Hearts)*

## MANUELLA
65  Decca F 22275                        The Nitty Gritty/Two Shadows ...................................................... 150

## MANUFACTURED ROMANCE
81  Fresh FRESH 16                       The Time Of My Life/Room To Breathe (various coloured p/s) ................ 5

## MANYANA
80  Modello AVR 1938                     LIVE CARROTS (LP, cat. no MHR 101 on sleeve) .............................. 15

## PHIL MANZANERA (& 801)
76  Island ILPS 9444                     801 LIVE (LP) ............................................................................ 15
*(see also Roxy Music, Quiet Sun)*

## RAY MANZAREK
74  Mercury SRM 1703                     THE WHOLE THING STARTED WITH ROCK'N'ROLL (LP) ................. 15
*(see also Doors, Philip Glass)*

## MAP OF AFRICA
05  Whatever We Want WEWW  Black Skin Blue Eyed Boys (12") ................................................ 30
    004

## THOMAS MAPFUMO
86  Earthworks EMW 5506                  GWINDINGWI RINE SHUMBA (LP, insert) .................................... 25

## MAPLEOAK
70  Decca F 13008                        Son Of A Gun/Hurt Me So Much...................................................... 20
71  Decca SKL 5085                       MAPLEOAK (LP, blue/silver label, boxed logo) .............................. 250

## LUCILLE MAPP
57  Columbia DB 3916                     Mangos/On Treasure Island ......................................................... 10
57  Columbia DB 3949                     Jamie Boy/Moonlight In Vermont ................................................. 5
58  Columbia DB 4040                     I'm Available/Lovin' Ya, Lovin' Ya, Lovin' Ya .............................. 5
58  Columbia DB 4071                     Love Is/The Early Birdie ............................................................. 5
59  Columbia DB 4168                     Remember When/I'm A Dreamer, Aren't We All? ........................... 5
    Columbia DB 4261                     Chinchilla/Follow Me ................................................................. 15

## TOMMY MARA
55  MGM SP 1128                          Pledging My Love/Honey Bunch..................................................... 10
58  Felsted AF 109                       Where The Blues Of The Night/What Makes You So Lonely ............ 10
59  Felsted AF 116                       You Don't Know/Marie .............................................................. 5
59  Felsted AF 123                       Until I Hear From You/Now Is The Hour ..................................... 5
58  Felsted GEP 1003                     PRESENTING TOMMY MARA (EP) ........................................... 12

## MARABAR CAVES
85  Tiki MBAR 1                          Sally's Place Crew/Seeds That Never Grew ................................. 10

## (JOSEPH) MARAIS & MIRANDA
53  Columbia SCM 5025                    Old Johnnie Goggabie/The Zulu Warrior.................................... 5
59  Fontana H 225                        I-Ha-She/The Queen Bee (as Marais & Miranda) ) ........................ 5

## MARATHONS
61  Pye International 7N 25088           Peanut Butter/Down In New Orleans ........................................ 20
61  Vogue V 9185                         Peanut Butter/Talkin' Trash ...................................................... 20

## MARAUDERS
63  Decca F 11695                        That's What I Want/Hey What D'ya Say........................................ 15
63  Decca F 11748                        Always On My Mind/Heart Full Of Tears .................................... 15
64  Decca F 11836                        Lucille/Little Egypt .................................................................. 15
65  Fontana TF 609                       Baby I Wanna Be Loved/Somebody Told My Girl ....................... 20
*(see also Danny Davis)*

## MARBLE STAIRCASE
83  Whaam! WHAAM 11                      Still Dreaming/Dark Ages (p/s) .................................................. 12

## MARBLES
68  Polydor 56272                        Only One Woman/The Light Of a Burning Candle ........................ 5
69  Polydor 56310                        The Walls Fell Down/Love You..................................................... 7
70  Polydor 56378                        Breaking Up Is Hard To Do/I Can't See Nobody .......................... 6
*(see also Graham Bonnet, Fut)*

## MARBOO
76  EMI 2424                             What About Love?/I Remember Sunday Morning ........................... 12

## MARC & MAMBAS
82  Some Bizzare BZS 512                 Fun City/Sleaze (Take It, Shake It)/Taking It And Shaking It (12", p/s, fan club issue,
                                         mail-order only)....................................................................... 20
82  Some Bizzare BZS 15                  Big Louise/Empty Eyes (unreleased, artwork only) ........................ 0
82  Some Bizzare BZS 1512               Big Louise/Empty Eyes/The Dirt Behind The Neon (Sleaze Revisited) (12", unreleased,
                                         artwork only)............................................................................ 0
83  Some Bizzare BZS 19                  Black Heart/Your Aura (p/s, with postcard insert) ........................ 0
83  Some Bizzare BZSDJ 21                Torment/You'll Never See On Sunday (promo) .............................. 7
84  Gutterhearts GH 1                    BITE BLACK AND BLUES - RAOUL & THE RUINED LIVE (LP, fan club issue) ...... 30
*(see also Soft Cell, Marc Almond)*

## LYDIA MARCELLE
66  Sue WI 4025                          Another Kind Of Fellow/I've Never Been Hurt Like This Before ......... 80

## MUZZY MARCELLINO
56  London HLU 8355                      Mary Lou/MR. FORD & MR. GOON-BONES: Ain't She Sweet ......... 25

## MARCELS
| 61 | Pye International 7N 25073 | Blue Moon/Goodbye To Love | 8 |
| 61 | Pye International 7N 25083 | Summertime/Teeter Totter Love | 10 |
| 61 | Pye International 7N 25105 | You Are My Sunshine/Find Another Fool | 10 |
| 61 | Pye International 7N 25114 | Heartaches/My Love For You | 10 |
| 62 | Pye International 7N 25124 | My Melancholy Baby/Really Need Your Love | 10 |
| 63 | Pye International 7N 25201 | I Wanna Be The Leader/Give Me Back Your Love | 30 |
| 61 | Pye Intl. NPL 28016 | BLUE MOON (LP) | 40 |

*(see also Tommy Regan)*

## GLORIA MARCH
| 58 | London HLB 8568 | Baby Of Mine/Nippon Wishing Well | 25 |

## HAL MARCH
| 58 | London HLD 8534 | Hear Me Good/One Dozen Roses | 25 |

## JO MARCH
| 58 | London HLR 8696 | Dormi, Dormi, Dormi (Sleep, Sleep, Sleep)/Fare Thee Well, Oh Honey | 8 |
| 58 | London HLR 8763 | The Virgin Mary Had One Son/I, Said The Donkey | 5 |

## (LITTLE) PEGGY MARCH
| 63 | RCA RCA 1338 | I Will Follow Him/Wind Up Doll (as Little Peggy March) | 10 |
| 63 | RCA RCA 1350 | My Teenage Castle/I Wish I Were A Princess (as Little Peggy March) | 10 |
| 63 | RCA RCA 1362 | Hello Heartache, Goodbye Love/Boy Crazy (as Little Peggy March) | 10 |
| 64 | RCA RCA 1426 | Watch What You Do With My Baby/Can't Stop (Peggy March) | 10 |
| 65 | RCA RCA 1472 | Let Her Go/Your Girl | 10 |
| 68 | RCA RCA 1687 | If You Loved Me/Thinking Through My Tears | 30 |
| 68 | RCA RCA 1687 | If You Loved Me/Thinking Through My Tears (DJ copy) | 60 |
| 68 | RCA RCA 1752 | I've Been Here Before/Time And Time Again | 7 |
| 69 | RCA RCA 1809 | What Am I Going To Do Without You/Lilac Skies | 7 |

## BOBBY MARCHAN
| 68 | Atlantic 584 155 | Get Down With It/Half A Mind | 12 |
| 69 | Action ACT 4533 | Ain't No Reason For Girls To Be Lonely Parts 1 & 2 | 20 |

*(see also Huey 'Piano' Smith & Clowns)*

## VICTOR MARCHESE
| 53 | MGM SP 1018 | Fandango/Flamingo | 5 |

## MARCH HARE
| 68 | Chapter One CH 101 | Cry My Heart/With My Eyes Closed | 20 |
| 69 | Deram DM 258 | I Could Make It There With You/Have We Got News For You | 30 |

*(see also Gary & Stu, Koobas)*

## MARCHING GIRLS
| 81 | Pop:Aural POP 011 | True Love/First In Line (p/s) | 45 |

## MARCH VIOLETS
| 82 | Merciful Release MR 013 | Religious As Hell/Fodder/Children On Stun/Bon Bon Babies (p/s) | 20 |
| 83 | Merciful Release MR 017 | Grooving In Green/Stream (p/s) | 8 |

## MARCIA & JEFF
| 68 | Studio One SO 2047 | Words/SHARKS: How Could I Live | 150 |

## MARCO
| 74 | Torpedo 31 | Do Me Bump/Bump On | 12 |
| 75 | Torpedo 33 | I'm Coming Home/Instrumental Version | 20 |

## MARCUS
| 76 | United Artists UAS 30000 | MARCUS (LP) | 15 |

## MARCY JO
| 63 | Stateside SS 235 | Lover's Medley : The More I See You/When I Fall In Love/When You Wore A Tulip | 8 |

*(see also Eddie Rambeau)*

## JANIE MARDEN
| 55 | Decca F 10600 | Soldier Boy/Hard To Get | 10 |
| 55 | Decca F 10605 | I'll Come When You Call/Thank You For The Waltz (with Frank Weir & His Saxophone) | 8 |
| 55 | Decca F 10673 | You Are My Love/A Teen Age Prayer | 8 |
| 56 | Decca F 10765 | Allegheny Moon/Magic Melody | 8 |
| 63 | Piccadilly 7N 35128 | Make The Night A Little Longer/Walk Alone | 10 |
| 65 | Decca F 12101 | They Long To Be Close To You/This Empty Place | 15 |
| 65 | Decca F 12155 | You Really Didn't Mean It/Only The One You Love | 10 |

## MARDEN HILL
| 86 | él GPO 18 | Curtain/Let's Make Shane & MacKenzie (p/s) | 10 |
| 87 | él GPO 30 | Robe/Hangman (p/s) | 8 |

## MARDI GRAS
| 71 | Bell BLL 1270 | Girl I've Got News For You/If I Can't Have You | 10 |

## ARIF MARDIN
| 68 | Atlantic 584201 | Lullaby From "Rosemary's Baby"/The Blue Bull | 6 |
| 69 | Atlantic 584 295 | Glass Onion/How Can I Be Sure | 8 |
| 73 | Atlantic K10309 | Theme From Brother Sun, Sister Moon/Yester Year | 10 |

## ERNIE MARESCA
| 62 | London HLU 9531 | Shout Shout Knock Yourself (Out) /Crying Like A Baby Over You | 15 |
| 62 | London HLU 9579 | Mary Jane/Down On The Beach | 30 |
| 63 | London HLU 9720 | Love Express/Lorelei | 22 |
| 64 | London HLU 9834 | Rovin' Kind/Please Be Fair | 15 |
| 65 | London HLU 10008 | It's Their World/I Can't Dance | 10 |
| 66 | Stateside SS 560 | Rockin' Boulevard Street/Am I Better Off Than Them | 25 |

## MARGAH MAN
| 93 | Margah MMTB1 | Funky Bumpkin (12") | 18 |

MINT VALUE £

## MARGARET AND ANGLE
72   Zella JHLPS 128          KNOCK GOD UP (LP) ................................................................ 75

## MARGO
69   Deram DM 274          The Spark That Lights The Flame/Left Over Love ............................... 20

## MARGO & MARVETTES
64   Parlophone R 5154          Say You Will/Cherry Pie ................................................... 18
64   Parlophone R 5227          Copper Kettle/So Fine ..................................................... 15
67   Piccadilly 7N 35387          Seven Letters/That's How Love Goes ...................................... 15
67   Pye 7N 17423          When Love Slips Away/I'll Be Home (When You Call) ...................... 15
67   Pye 7N 17423          When Love Slips Away/I'll Be Home (When You Call) (DJ copy) ........... 50
*(see also Liza Dulittle)*                                                                                75

## MARGUERITA
64   Black Swan WI 431          Woman Come/ERIC MORRIS: Number One ................................ 30

## VERA MARIA
69   NEMS 56-4043          Martha My Dear/Goodbye Yesterday ..................................... 10

## MARIANNE
68   Columbia DB 8420          As For Marionettes/You Know My Name ................................ 18
68   Columbia DB 8456          You Had Better Change Your Evil Ways/Like A See Saw ................. 25

## MARIANNE & MIKE
64   Vocalion V 9218          As He Once Was Mine/MARIANNE: Go On ................................. 8
64   Vocalion V 9225          You're The Only One/One Good Turn Deserves Another ................. 8
*(see also Friday Brown. These records do not feature Mick Jagger or Marianne Faithfull)*

## CHARLIE MARIANO
56   London LTZN15031          CHARLIE MARIANO QUARTET (LP) ...................................... 70

## A.C. MARIAS
81   Dome DOM 451          Drop/So (black die cut distressed sleeve) ........................... 15

## ANNE MARIE
65   Fontana TF 523          Runaround/There Must Be A Reason .................................. 10

## MARIE CELESTE
71   Private pressing          AND THEN PERHAPS (LP) ........................................... 400

## TEENA MARIE
81   Tamla Motown 12TMG 1251  Portuguese Love/The Ballad Of Cradle Rob And Me (12") ............... 10

## MARIETTA
82   Polydor POSP 305          You're Only Lonely/Making Up My Mind (p/s, with Rick Parfitt & Andy Bown) ...... 6
82   Polydor POSP 483          Do You Wanna Dance/Only In Your Eyes (p/s, with Rick Parfitt & Andy Bown) ...... 6
*(see also Status Quo)*

## MARILLION
82   EMI EMI 5351          Market Square Heroes/Three Boats Down From The Candy (p/s) ............ 5
82   EMI 12 EMIP 5351          Market Square Heroes/Three Boats Down From The Candy/Grendel (12", picture disc, 3,000 only) ................................................. 25
83   EMI EMI 5362          He Knows, You Know/Charting The Single (p/s, originally with blue plastic label & paper sleeve) ................................................... 5
83   EMI 12 EMIP 5362          He Knows, You Know/Charting The Single/He Knows, You Know (Full Length Version) (12", picture disc, unreleased) .......................... 5
83   EMI EMI 5393          Garden Party/Margaret (live) (p/s) ................................. 0
83   EMI EMIP 5393          Garden Party/Margaret (live) ('jester'-shaped picture disc) ......... 5
83   EMI 12 EMIS 5393          Garden Party (Extended Version)/Charting The Single (live)/ Margaret (Extended Live Version) (12", p/s with poster) ............................ 15
84   EMI 12 MARILP 1          Punch And Judy/Market Square Heroes (New Version)/ Three Boats Down From The Candy (New Version) (12", picture disc) ........................ 10
84   EMI MARIL 2          Assassing/Cinderella Search (p/s) ................................... 5
84   EMI 12 MARIL 2          Assassing (Full Length Version)/Cinderella Search (Full Length Version) (12", p/s) ...... 15
84   EMI 12 MARILP 2          Assassing (Full Length Version)/Cinderella Search (Full Length Version) (12", picture disc) ................................................ 10
85   EMI 12 MARILP 3          Kayleigh (Alternative Mix)/Kayleigh (Extended Version)/ Lady Nina (Extended Version) (12", picture disc) ................................ 10
85   EMI 12 MARILP 4          Lavender (Remix)/Freaks/Lavender (12", picture disc) ................ 12
85   EMI 12 MARILP 5          Heart Of Lothian (Full Length Version)/Chelsea Monday (live)/ Heart Of Lothian (7" Version) (12", picture disc) ............................... 10
87   EMI 12MARILP 7          Sugar Mice (Extended Version)/(Album Version)/Tux On (12", picture disc) ...... 12
88   EMI MARLIP 9          Freaks (live)/Kayleigh (live) (Uncut 'jester'-shaped picture disc) ...... 10
84   EMI EMCP 3429          SCRIPT FOR A JESTER'S TEAR (LP, picture disc) ...................... 50
84   EMI MRLP 1          FUGAZI (LP, picture disc) ........................................... 20
85   EMI JESTP 1          REAL TO REEL (LP, picture disc) ..................................... 18
85   EMI MRLP 2          MISPLACED CHILDHOOD (LP, picture disc) ............................. 18
95   EMI EMD 1079          AFRAID OF SUNLIGHT (LP, inner) ..................................... 15
97   EMI LPCENT 25          MISPLACED CHILDHOOD (LP, reissue, EMI 100 Centenary, stickered sleeve) ...... 100
*(see also Chemical Alice)*                                                              100

## MARINA & THE DIAMONDS
09   Neon Gold GOLD 004          CROWN JEWELS (EP, 200 only) ....................................... 30
09   679 Recordings 679L168          Mogwli's Road/Space And The Woods (200 only, in envelope, numbered and signed).. 40
10   679 Recordings 679L173X          I Am Not A Robot/I Am Not A Robot (Clock Opera Remix) (p/s, signed edition) ...... 15
10   679 Recordings 679L17OX          Hollywood/Hollywood (Gonzales Remix) (signed edition) ............... 15

## MARINE GIRLS
82   In Phaze COD 2          On My Mind/The Lure Of The Rockpools (p/s, with insert) ............. 15
82   Cherry Red CHERRY 40          On My Mind/The Lure Of The Rockpools (reissue, different p/s) ....... 5
80   private release          A DAY BY THE SEA (cassette, 50 copies only) ........................ 50
81   In Phaze Tapes 002          BEACH PARTY (cassette, with photocopied drawings, game & handmade sleeve) ...... 40
81   Whaam!/In Phaze COD 1          BEACH PARTY (LP, black & white sleeve & labels, with 2 inserts) ....... 15

| | | |
|---|---|---:|
| 83 | Cherry Red BRED 44 | LAZY WAYS (LP) .......... 18 |

*(see also Tracey Thorn, Everything But The Girl, Jane)*

## MARINERS
| | | |
|---|---|---:|
| 55 | London HLA 8201 | I Love You Fair Dinkum/(At The) Steamboat River Ball .......... 10 |

## MARION (FINLAND)
| | | |
|---|---|---:|
| 73 | Columbia DB 8987 | Tom Tom Tom/My Son John .......... 15 |

## MARIONETTES (1)
| | | |
|---|---|---:|
| 65 | Decca F 12056 | Whirlpool Of Love/Nobody But You .......... 10 |
| 65 | Parlophone R 5300 | Was It Me?/Under The Boardwalk .......... 10 |
| 65 | Parlophone R 5356 | Raining It's Pouring/Pick Up Your Feet (withdrawn) .......... 12 |
| 65 | Parlophone R 5374 | At The End Of The Day/Pick Up Your Feet .......... 5 |
| 66 | Parlophone R 5416 | Like A Man/Tonight It's Going To Storm .......... 15 |

*(see also Rag Dolls [U.K.], Katie Kissoon, Mac Kissoon)*

## MARIONETTES (2)
| | | |
|---|---|---:|
| 90 | Maze Music DSMBC | AVE DEMENTIA (LP) .......... 20 |

## MARK & JOHN
| | | |
|---|---|---:|
| 64 | Decca F 12044 | Walk Right Back/Karen .......... 6 |

## JON MARK
| | | |
|---|---|---:|
| 65 | Brunswick 5952 | Paris Bells/Little Town Girl .......... 12 |
| 69 | Philips BF 1772 | All Neat In Black Stockings/Run To Me .......... 10 |

*(see also Johnny Almond Music Machine, John Mayall, Mark-Almond)*

## LOUISA MARK
| | | |
|---|---|---:|
| 75 | Safari SF 1109 | All My Loving/Sitting By The Wayside .......... 10 |
| 77 | Trojan TRO 9005 | Keep It Like It Is/TROJANS: Fatty Bum Bum Gone To Jail .......... 15 |
| 78 | Bushays BFM 100 | Even Though You're Gone/Gone Clear (12") .......... 10 |
| 79 | Bushays BFM 107 | Six Street Six/Instrumental (12") .......... 12 |
| 79 | Safari SF1105 | Caught You In A Lie/Caught Dubbing .......... 15 |
| 79 | Robot RRS 2 | Six Street Six/Version .......... 8 |
| 81 | Bushays BFM LP 101 | BREAKOUT (LP) .......... 35 |

## MARK-ALMOND
| | | |
|---|---|---:|
| 71 | Harvest HAR 5044 | The City/The Ghetto .......... 12 |
| 71 | Harvest SHSP 4011 | MARK-ALMOND (LP, no EMI logo on label) .......... 25 |
| 73 | Harvest SHVL 809 | RISING (LP, EMI logo on label) .......... 20 |

*(see also Johnny Almond Music Machine, Jon Mark, John Mayall)*

## MARKETTS
| | | |
|---|---|---:|
| 62 | Liberty LIB 55401 | Surfer's Stomp/Start (as Mar-kets) .......... 15 |
| 62 | Liberty LIB 55443 | Balboa Blue/Stompede .......... 15 |
| 64 | Warner Bros WB 120 | Out Of Limits/Bella Delana .......... 25 |
| 64 | Warner Bros WB 130 | Vanishing Point/Borealis .......... 20 |
| 66 | Warner Bros WB 5696 | The Batman Theme/Richie's Theme (with p/s) .......... 40 |
| 66 | Warner Bros WB 5696 | The Batman Theme/Richie's Theme .......... 20 |
| 67 | Warner Bros WB 5847 | Tarzan's March/Stirrin' Up Some Soul .......... 40 |
| 67 | Warner Bros WB 5847 | Tarzan's March/Stirrin' Up Some Soul (DJ copy) .......... 50 |
| 63 | Warner Bros WM 8140 | THE MARKETTS TAKE TO WHEELS (LP) .......... 50 |
| 64 | Warner Bros WM 8147 | OUT OF LIMITS (LP) .......... 40 |
| 66 | Warner Bros W 1642 | BATMAN (LP) .......... 50 |

## MAR-KEYS
| | | |
|---|---|---:|
| 61 | London HLK 9399 | Last Night/Night Before .......... 20 |
| 61 | London HLK 9449 | Morning After/Diana .......... 15 |
| 62 | London HLK 9510 | Foxy/One Degree North .......... 15 |
| 66 | Atlantic AT 4079 | Philly Dog/Honey Pot .......... 15 |
| 67 | Atlantic 584 074 | Last Night/Night Before .......... 8 |
| 69 | Stax STAX 132 | Black/Jive Man .......... 5 |
| 62 | London HA-K 8011 | DO THE POP-EYE (LP) .......... 50 |
| 66 | Atlantic 587/588 024 | THE GREAT MEMPHIS SOUND (LP) .......... 20 |
| 68 | Atlantic 587/588 135 | MELLOW JELLY (LP) .......... 20 |
| 69 | Stax SXATS 1021 | DAMNIFIKNOW! (LP) .......... 20 |

*(see also Booker T. & M.G.'s)*

## MARK FIVE
| | | |
|---|---|---:|
| 64 | Fontana TF 513 | Baby What's Wrong/Tango .......... 65 |

*(see also Nazareth)*

## MARK FOUR
| | | |
|---|---|---:|
| 64 | Mercury MF 815 | Rock Around The Clock/Slow Down .......... 30 |
| 64 | Mercury MF 825 | Try It Baby/Crazy Country Hop .......... 65 |
| 65 | Decca F 12204 | Hurt Me If You Will/I'm Leaving .......... 70 |
| 66 | Fontana TF 664 | Work All Day (Sleep All Night)/Going Down Fast .......... 100 |
| 85 | Bam-Caruso OPRA 037 | LIVE AT THE BEAT SCENE CLUB (EP, promo, 500 only) .......... 12 |

*(see also Creation)*

## PIGMEAT MARKHAM
| | | |
|---|---|---:|
| 68 | Chess CRS 8077 | Here Comes The Judge/The Trial .......... 12 |
| 68 | Chess CRS 8085 | Sock It To 'Em Judge/The Hip Judge .......... 15 |

## MARK II
| | | |
|---|---|---:|
| 60 | Columbia DB 4549 | Night Theme/Confusion .......... 10 |

## MARK IV
| | | |
|---|---|---:|
| 59 | Mercury AMT 1025 | Aah-Oo-Gah/I Got A Wife .......... 5 |
| 59 | Mercury AMT 1045 | Move Over Rover/Dante's Inferno .......... 5 |
| 59 | Mercury AMT 1060 | Ring, Ring, Ring Those Bells/Mairzy Doats .......... 5 |

MINT VALUE £

## MARKSMEN
| | | | |
|---|---|---|---|
| 63 | Parlophone R 5075 | Smersh/Orbit Three | 20 |

*(see also Mark Rogers & Marksmen, Houston Wells & Marksmen)*

## MARLEY MARL
| | | | |
|---|---|---|---|
| 87 | MCA 1135 | He Cuts So Fresh/FINESSE & SYNQUIS: Bass Game (p/s, moulded silver label) | 40 |
| 87 | MCA 1135 | He Cuts So Fresh/FINESSE & SYNQUIS: Bass Game (p/s, paper label) | 50 |

## MIKE MARLAN
| | | | |
|---|---|---|---|
| 73 | Bronze ILPS 9221 | FAIR WARNING (LP, gatefold sleeve, label with Island credit) | 20 |

## BOB MARLEY/WAILERS
### SINGLES
| | | | |
|---|---|---|---|
| 63 | Island WI 088 | Judge Not/Do You Still Love Me (as Robert Marley) | 300 |
| 63 | Island WI 128 | ERNEST RANGLIN: Exodus/R. MARLEY: One Cup Of Coffee | 300 |
| 65 | Island WI 188 | It Hurts To Be Alone/Mr. Talkative | 90 |
| 65 | Island WI 206 | Play Boy/Your Love | 100 |
| 65 | Island WI 211 | Hoot Nanny Hoot (actually by Peter Tosh & Wailers)/ BOB MARLEY: Do You Remember (actually with Wailers) | 125 |
| 65 | Island WI 212 | Hooligan/Maga Dog (B-side actually by Peter Tosh & Wailers) | 70 |
| 65 | Island WI 215 | Shame And Scandal (as Peter Touch [Tosh] & Wailers)/The Jerk | 40 |
| 65 | Island WI 216 | Donna/Don't Ever Leave Me | 60 |
| 65 | Island WI 254 | What's New Pussycat/Where Will I Find | 60 |
| 65 | Ska Beat JB 186 | Simmer Down/I Don't Need Your Love | 75 |
| 65 | Ska Beat JB 211 | Lonesome Feelings/There She Goes | 70 |
| 65 | Ska Beat JB 226 | I Made A Mistake/SOUL BROTHERS: Train To Skaville | 45 |
| 66 | Ska Beat JB 228 | Love And Affection/Teenager In Love | 70 |
| 66 | Ska Beat JB 230 | And I Love Her/Do It Right | 70 |
| 66 | Ska Beat JB 249 | Lonesome Tracks/Zimmerman | 60 |
| 66 | Island WI 260 | Jumbie Jamboree/SKATALITES: Independent Anniversary Ska (I Should Have Known Better) | 80 |
| 66 | Island WI 268 | Put It On/Love Won't Be Mine | 30 |
| 66 | Island WI 3001 | He Who Feels It Knows It/Sunday Morning | 90 |
| 66 | Island WI 3009 | Let Him Go (Rude Boy Get Bail)/Sinner Man (B-side matrix: WI-3009B+) | 70 |
| 66 | Island WI 3009 | Let Him Go (Rude Boy Get Bail)/The Masher (actually by Beverley's All Stars or Soul Brothers) (B-side matrix: WI-3009 B+2) | 70 |
| 66 | Rio R 116 | Dancing Shoes/Don't Look Back | 35 |
| 66 | Doctor Bird DB 1013 | Rude Boy/ROLANDO AL & SOUL BROTHERS: Ringo's Theme (This Boy) | 90 |
| 66 | Doctor Bird DB 1021 | Good Good Rudie (Jailhouse)/CITY SLICKERS: Oceans II | 60 |
| 66 | Doctor Bird DB 1039 | Rasta Put It On/ROLAND AL & SOUL BROTHERS: Ska With Ringo | 100 |
| 67 | Island WI 3035 | Baby I Need You (credited to Ken Boothe)/KEN BOOTHE: I Don't Want To See You Cry | 100 |
| 67 | Island WI 3042 | I Am The Toughest (by Peter Touch [Tosh] & Wailers)/ MARCIA GRIFFITHS: No Faith | 70 |
| 67 | Island WI 3043 | Bend Down Low/Freedom Time | 70 |
| 67 | Coxsone CS 7021 | Oh My Darling/HAMLINS: Trying To Keep A Good Man Down | 90 |
| 67 | Doctor Bird DB 1091 | Nice Time/Hypocrite | 65 |
| 67 | Studio One SO 2010 | Have Faith In The Lord (with Heavenly Sisters; actually by Peter Austin)/ JOE HIGGS: Dinah | 40 |
| 67 | Studio One SO 2024 | I Stand Predominate/NORMA FRAZER: Come By Here | 250 |
| 68 | Fab FAB 34 | Pound Get A Blow/Funeral (white label only) | 150 |
| 68 | Fab FAB 36 | Thank You Lord/Mellow Mood (white label only) | 170 |
| 68 | Fab FAB 37 | Nice Time/Hypocrites (white label only) | 80 |
| 68 | Fab FAB 41 | Burial/Bus Them Shut (existence unconfirmed) | 0 |
| 68 | Trojan TR 617 | Stir It Up/This Train | 45 |
| 70 | Bamboo BAM 55 | Jailhouse (Good Rudy)/JOHN HOLT: A Stranger In Love | 40 |

*(Credited to Wailers unless stated.)*
| | | | |
|---|---|---|---|
| 70 | Trojan TR 7759 | Soul Shake Down Party/BEVERLY'S ALLSTARS: Version | 30 |
| 70 | Escort ERT 842 | Run For Cover/To The Rescue | 70 |
| 70 | Unity UN 562 | Duppy Conqueror/UPSETTERS: Duppy Conqueror (Version) | 40 |
| 70 | Jackpot JP 730 | Mr Chatterbox (as Wailing Wailers)/DOREEN SHAEFFER: Walk Thru' This World | 35 |
| 70 | Upsetter US 340 | My Cup (solo)/LEE PERRY & WAILERS: Son Of Thunder | 35 |
| 70 | Upsetter US 342 | Version Of Cup (solo)/UPSETTERS: Dreamland | 45 |
| 70 | Upsetter US 348 | Doppy Conqueror (song actually titled "Duppy Conqueror" but plays Runaway Child by Dave Barker)/UPSETTERS: Justice | 20 |
| 70 | Upsetter US 349 | UPSETTERS: Upsetting Station (actually plays "Dig Your Grave" by Bob Marley & Wailers/UPSETTERS: Justice (Instrumental) | 40 |
| 71 | Upsetter US 354 | Mr. Brown/UPSETTERS: Dracula | 35 |
| 71 | Upsetter US 356 | Kaya/UPSETTERS: Version | 35 |
| 71 | Upsetter US 357 | Small Axe/All In One | 20 |
| 71 | Upsetter US 368 | Picture On The Wall (as Rass Dawkins & Wailers)/UPSETTERS: Version | 22 |
| 71 | Upsetter US 369 | More Axe (as Bob Marley)/UPSETTERS: Axe Man | 25 |
| 71 | Upsetter US 371 | Dreamland (as Wailers)/UPSETTERS: Version | 25 |
| 71 | Upsetter US 372 | More Axe (as Bob Marley, different version)/UPSETTERS: Axe Man | 25 |
| 71 | Bullet BU 464 | Soultown/Let The Sun Shine On Me | 45 |
| 71 | Bullet BU 493 | Lick Samba/Samba | 40 |
| 71 | Punch PH 69 | Small Axe/DAVE BARKER: What A Confusion | 45 |
| 71 | Punch PH 77 | Down Presser (as Wailers)/JUNIOR BYLES: Got The Tip | 40 |
| 71 | Summit SUM 8526 | Stop The Train/Caution (as Wailers) | 35 |
| 71 | Green Door GD 4005 | Trench Town Rock/Grooving Kingston 12 | 25 |
| 72 | Green Door GD 4022 | Lively Yourself Up/TOMMY McCOOK: Lively | 25 |
| 72 | Green Door GD 4025 | Guava Jelly/Redder Than Red | 20 |
| 72 | Upsetter US 392 | Keep On Moving/African Herbsman | 25 |
| 72 | CBS 8114 | Reggae On Broadway/Oh Lord, I Got To Get There (as Wailers) | 25 |

| | | | |
|---|---|---|---|
| 73 | Blue Mountain BM 1021 | Baby Baby We've Got A Date/Stop That Train | 15 |
| 73 | Punch PH 101 | Screw Face/Face Man | 20 |
| 73 | Punch PH 102 | Lively Up Yourself/TOMMY McCOOK: Version | 20 |
| 73 | Supreme SUP 216 | I Like It Like This (as Bob Marley)/BUNNY GALE: Am Sorry | 45 |
| 73 | Island WIP 6164 | Concrete Jungle/Reincarnated Soul | 10 |
| 73 | Island WIP 6167 | Get Up, Stand Up/Slave Driver (as Wailers) | 8 |
| 73 | Island IDJ 2 | I Shot The Sheriff/Pass It On/Duppy Conqueror (promo only) | 30 |
| 74 | Trojan TR 7911 | Soul Shake Down Party/Caution | 8 |
| 74 | Trojan TR 7926 | Mr Brown/Version | 10 |
| 75 | Island WIP 6212 | So Jah Seh/Natty Dread | 5 |
| 76 | Island WIP 6478 | Stir It Up/Rat Race (withdrawn, demos only) | 15 |
| 77 | Island WIP 6390 | Exodus/Exodus (dub) | 5 |
| 77 | Island WIP 6402 | Waiting In Vain/Roots | 5 |
| 77 | Island WIP 6402 1DJ | Promotional Advert For "Exodus" (handwritten label, same track both sides, with Marley commentary) | 30 |
| 77 | Island WIP 6410 | Jamming/Punky Reggae Party (p/s) | 5 |
| 78 | Island WIP 6420 | Is This Love?/Crisis (Version) (p/s) | 5 |
| 78 | Island WIP 6440 | Satisfy My Soul/Smile Jamaica (p/s) | 5 |
| 80 | Island/Tuff Gong WIP 6641 | Three Little Birds/Every Need Got An Ego To Feed (A label demo in die cut Tuff Gong sleeve) | 10 |
| 84 | Daddy Kool DK 12101 | Rainbow Country (Vocal)/Rainbow Country (Dub)/PABLO & UPSETTERS: Lama Lava (12", p/s) | 15 |
| 84 | Daddy Kool DK 12102 | Natural Mystic/Natural Mystic Rhythm (12", p/s) | 15 |
| 84 | Island 12ISPX 169 | One Love/One Love (Dub Version) (p/s) | 7 |
| 84 | Island 12ISPP 169 | One Love/One Love (Dub Version) (12", picture disc) | 12 |
| 80s | Island 12 BMRM 1 | Get Up Stand Up/Get Up Stand Up (live) ('Rasta' p/s, promo only) | 8 |
| 99 | Columbia XPR 2533 | Turn Your Lights Down Low (with Lauryn Hill)/(original version) (die-cut p/s, promo only) | 8 |
| 03 | Trojan/Sanctuary TJITV005 | LEE PERRY: Disco Devil/BOB MARLEY & WU CHU: Keep On Moving (12" reissue) | 30 |

**ALBUMS**

| | | | |
|---|---|---|---|
| 71 | Upsetter/Trojan TBL 126 | SOUL REBELS (LP) | 100 |
| 71 | Trojan TBL 126 | SOUL REBELS (reissue) | 50 |
| 71 | Trojan TTL 66A/B | SOUL REVOLUTION (LP, white label, test pressing only) | 125 |
| 72 | Island ILPS 9241 | CATCH A FIRE (original 'pink rim' label, 'zippo lighter' sleeve) | 150 |
| 73 | Island ILPS 9256 | BURNIN' (original label, gatefold sleeve with photos on inner) | 20 |
| 73 | Trojan TRLS 62 | AFRICAN HERBSMAN (original issue with "12 Neasden Lane" address and rough orange/white paper labels) | 40 |
| 73 | BBC TS 133425/6 | POP SPECTACULAR IN CONCERT (LP, in buff sleeve with printed sheets) | 300 |
| 73 | Black Power PW2 | WAILERS (LP, no title, no sleeve, pink label) | 50 |
| 74 | Trojan TRLS 89 | RASTA REVOLUTION (reissue of TBL 126 with 2 extra tracks) | 25 |
| 75 | Island ISS 3 | BOB MARLEY & THE WAILERS RADIO SAMPLER (with photos & press release, promo only) | 40 |
| 75 | Island ISS 3 | BOB MARLEY & THE WAILERS RADIO SAMPLER (promo only) | 20 |
| 77 | BBC | ROCK GOES TO COLLEGE IN CONCERT (LP, re-issue of BBC TS 133425/6) | 80 |
| 79 | Island ILPS 9542 | SURVIVAL (LP) | 15 |
| 83 | Island PILPS 97690 | CONFRONTATION (picture disc) | 25 |
| 84 | Island BMSP 100 | THE BOX SET (All 9 Island albums in presentation box - 10,000 only) | 125 |
| 84 | Island PBMW 1 | LEGEND - THE BEST OF BOB MARLEY (picture disc) | 15 |
| 87 | Receiver RRPL 106 | SOUL REBELS (LP, reissue) | 20 |

*(see also Peter Tosh, Rita Marley, Ernest Ranglin, Interns, Skatalites, Rass Dawkins & Wailers, Family Man, Norma Frazer)*

**RITA MARLEY**

| | | | |
|---|---|---|---|
| 65 | Island WI-226 | One More Chance (as Rita and Soulettes)/SKALITES: Dick Tracey | 80 |
| 67 | Rio R 108 | Pied Piper/It's Alright | 90 |
| 67 | Island WI 3052 | Come To Me/SOUL BOYS: Blood Pressure | 150 |

*(see also Soulettes, Soul Brothers)*

**LAURA MARLING**

| | | | |
|---|---|---|---|
| 07 | Way Out West WOW 003 | LONDON TOWN EP (500 only) | 60 |
| 07 | Virgin VS 1956 | MY MANIC AND I EP (with separate promotional booklet) | 50 |
| 07 | Virgin VS 1956 | MY MANIC AND I EP (signed with booklet) | 35 |
| 07 | Virgin VS 1956 | MY MANIC AND I EP (unsigned with booklet) | 15 |
| 08 | Virgin VS 1964 | Ghosts/Man Sings About Romance | 12 |
| 08 | Virgin VS 1973 | Cross Your Fingers/I'm A Fly | 10 |
| 08 | Virgin VS 1979 | Night Terror/Alpha Shallows | 20 |
| 09 | Virgin VS 2004 | Goodbye England (Covered In Snow) (1-sided) | 12 |
| 10 | Third Man TMR 044 | Blues Run The Game/The Needle And The Damage Done (US pressing but 100 shipped over and sold in UK, 3 colour vinyl, signed) | 120 |
| 11 | Virgin – 5099967838073 | Sophia/Rest In Bed (demo) | 12 |
| 13 | Universal/Talenthouse | The Beast (1-sided, Secret Seven, 100 only) | 100 |
| 08 | Virgin V 3040 | ALAS I CANNOT SWIM (LP, with bonus DVD) | 70 |
| 10 | Diverse DIV 028LP | I SPEAK BECAUSE I CAN (LP, gatefold) | 18 |
| 11 | Virgin CDVX 3091 | A CREATURE I DON'T KNOW (Box set, picture disc LP, CD, DVD, postcard, slide viewer and booklet) | 40 |

**MICKI MARLO**

| | | | |
|---|---|---|---|
| 55 | Capitol CL 14271 | Prize Of Gold/Foolish Notion | 15 |
| 57 | London HL 8481 | That's Right/What You've Done To Me (B-side with Paul Anka) | 25 |

*(see also Paul Anka)*

**MARLON**

| | | | |
|---|---|---|---|
| 74 | Purple PUR 120 | Let's Go To The Disco/Broken Man | 7 |

*(see also Roger Glover, Ray Fenwick)*

**ROBERT MARLOW**

| | | | |
|---|---|---|---|
| 83 | Reset 7REST 1 | Pictures Of Dorian Grey/The Tale Of Dorian Grey (p/s) | 5 |

| | | | MINT VALUE £ |
|---|---|---|---|
| 83 | Reset 12REST 1 | Pictures Of Dorian Grey/The Tale Of Dorian Grey (12", p/s) | 10 |
| 83 | Reset 7REST 3 | I Just Want To Dance/No Heart (p/s) | 5 |
| 83 | Reset 12REST 3 | I Just Want To Dance/No Heart (12", p/s) | 10 |
| 84 | Reset 12REST 4 | Claudette/This Happy World (12", p/s) | 10 |
| 85 | Reset 7REST 6 | Calling All Destroyers/In Retrospect (p/s) | 10 |
| 85 | Reset 12REST 6 | Calling All Destroyers/In Retrosepct (12", p/s, existence unconfirmed) | 0 |

*(see also Vince Clarke, Erasure)*

## MARION MARLOWE

| | | | |
|---|---|---|---|
| 56 | London HLA 8306 | The Hands Of Time/Ring, Phone, Ring (withdrawn) | 100 |
| 56 | London HLA 8306 | The Hands Of Time/Ring, Phone, Ring (78) | 50 |

## MARMALADE

| | | | |
|---|---|---|---|
| 66 | CBS 202340 | It's All Leading Up To Saturday Night/Wait A Minute Baby | 20 |
| 67 | CBS 202643 | Can't Stop Now/There Ain't No Use In Hangin' On | 25 |
| 67 | CBS 2948 | I See The Rain/Laughing Man | 25 |
| 67 | CBS 3088 | Man In A Shop/Cry (The Shoob Doroorie Song) | 15 |
| 68 | CBS 3412 | Lovin' Things/Hey Joe | 6 |
| 68 | CBS 3708 | Wait For Me Mary-Anne/Mess Around | 6 |
| 68 | CBS 3892 | Ob-La-Di, Ob-La-Da/Chains | 12 |
| 69 | CBS 4287 | Baby Make It Soon/Time Is On My Side | 5 |
| 69 | CBS 4615 | Butterfly/I Shall Be Released | 6 |
| 69 | Decca F12982 | Reflections Of My Life/Rollin' My Thing | 6 |
| 70 | Decca F13035 | Rainbow/The Ballad Of Cherry Flavar | 5 |
| 71 | Decca F13135 | My Little One/Is Your Life Your Own? | 6 |
| 71 | Decca F13214 | Cousin Norman/Lonely Man | 5 |
| 72 | Decca F13297 | Radancer/Sarah/Just One Woman | 5 |
| 71 | Decca F13251 | Back On The Road/Love Is Hard To Re-Arrange | 6 |
| 76 | Target TGT 105 | Falling Apart At The Seams/Fly Fly Fly | 5 |
| 68 | CBS 63414 | THERE'S A LOT OF IT ABOUT (LP) | 6 |
| 70 | CBS PR 36 | THE BEST OF THE MARMALADE (LP) | 20 |
| 70 | Decca LK 5047 | REFLECTIONS OF MARMALADE (LP, mono) | 15 |
| 70 | Decca SKL 5047 | REFLECTIONS OF THE MARMALADE (LP, stereo) | 30 |
| 71 | Decca SKL 5111 | SONGS (LP) | 15 |
| | | | 20 |

*(see also Dean Ford [& Gaylords], Gaylords, Junior Campbell, Chris McClure Section)*

## LORENZO MARQUES

| | | | |
|---|---|---|---|
| 82 | Siren S82 CUS 1321 | Wardrobes/Lorenzo Marques | 10 |

## MARQUIS DE SADE

| | | | |
|---|---|---|---|
| 81 | Xpose XP-02 | Somewhere Up In The Mountain/Black Angel (p/s with insert) | 200 |
| 82 | Out Of Town HOOT 8 | Crystal Grieff/Vampire Affair (p/s) | 5 |

## MARQUIS OF KENSINGTON

| | | | |
|---|---|---|---|
| 67 | Immediate IM 052 | Changing Of The Guard/Reverse Thrust | 30 |

## HANK MARR

| | | | |
|---|---|---|---|
| 60 | Blue Beat BB 26 | Tonk Game/Hob-Nobbin | 15 |

## RANDY MARR

| | | | |
|---|---|---|---|
| 70 | Warner Bros WB 6115 | I Wonder Who's Kissing Her Now/1941 | 6 |

## MARRAKESH

| | | | |
|---|---|---|---|
| 73 | Bell 1325 | The Prodigal Son Returns/Let Me Down Easy | 8 |
| 73 | Bell 1315 | I Don't Wanna Say Goodnight/Stone | 7 |

## MARRATXI

| | | | |
|---|---|---|---|
| 79 | Clubland SJP 901 | Rock With Me/Swedish Lady | 150 |

## RICARDO MARRERO

| | | | |
|---|---|---|---|
| 09 | Jazzman JMANLP 027 | A TASTE (LP, reissue as Ricardo Marrero And The Group) | 30 |

## MARRIAGE

| | | | |
|---|---|---|---|
| 71 | Decca F13178 | Ever Find Yourself Running/She Follows The Band | 6 |

## A MARRIAGE OF CONVENIENCE

| | | | |
|---|---|---|---|
| 85 | Stranglers Info Service SIS2 | My Young Dreams/Two Sides To Every Story (no p/s, fan club issue) | 5 |

*(see also Stranglers)*

## STEVE MARRIOTT

| | | | |
|---|---|---|---|
| 63 | Decca F 11619 | Give Her My Regards/Imaginary Love | 200 |
| 76 | A&M AMS 7230 | Star In My Life/Midnight Rollin' | 8 |
| 85 | Aura AUS 145 | Wha'cha Gonna Do About It/All Shook Up | 8 |
| 76 | A&M AMLH 64572 | MARRIOTT (LP) | 25 |

*(see also Small Faces, Humble Pie, Spectrum, Pollcats)*

## MARS

| | | | |
|---|---|---|---|
| 86 | Windowspeak WSP 10 | 78 (LP) | 20 |

## MARS FENWICK BAND

| | | | |
|---|---|---|---|
| 86 | President PT 556 | Fire In The City/A Lover Not A Fighter | 5 |

*(see Ray Fenwick)*

## JOHNNY MARS

| | | | |
|---|---|---|---|
| 81 | Ace NS 73 | Born Under A Bad Sign/Horses And Places/Mighty Mars (p/s, withdrawn) | 5 |
| 72 | Polydor 2460 168 | BLUES FROM MARS (LP) | 15 |

## BERYL MARSDEN

| | | | |
|---|---|---|---|
| 63 | Decca F 11707 | I Know (You Don't Love Me No More)/I Only Care About You | 15 |
| 64 | Decca F 11819 | When The Lovelight Starts Shining Through His Eyes/ Love Is Going To Happen To Me | 20 |
| 65 | Columbia DB 7718 | Who You Gonna Hurt?/Gonna Make Him My Baby | 35 |
| 65 | Columbia DB 7797 | Music Talk/Break-A-Way | 30 |
| 66 | Columbia DB 7888 | What's She Got/Let's Go Somewhere | 35 |

*(see also Shotgun Express, She Trinity)*

## GERRY MARSDEN
| 67 | CBS 2784 | Please Let Them Be/I'm Not Blue | 10 |
|----|----------|---------------------------------|-----|
| 67 | CBS 2946 | Gilbert Green/What Makes Me Love You | 15 |
| 68 | CBS 3575 | Liverpool/Charlie Girl (as Gerry Marsden & Derek Nimmo) | 10 |
| 68 | NEMS 56-3831 | In The Year Of April/Every Day | 10 |
| 69 | NEMS 56-4229 | Every Little Minute/In Days Of Old | 6 |
| 71 | Decca F 13172 | I've Got My Ukelele/What A Day | 6 |
| 72 | Phoenix NIX 129 | Amo Credo/Come Break Bread | 5 |
| 76 | DJM DJS 10708 | My Home Town/Lovely Lady (p/s) | 10 |
| 74 | DJM DJS 314 | They Don't Make Them Like That Any More/Can't You Hear The Song | 6 |
| 76 | DJM DJS 10708 | My Home Town/Lovely Lady | 6 |

(see also Gerry & Pacemakers)

## LYNNE MARSDEN
| 84 | Derelict DRL1 | Cocktails For Two/Firefly | 10 |
|----|---------------|--------------------------|-----|

## BRENDA MARSH
| 68 | Mercury MF 1044 | Cross Town Bus/Close | 7 |
|----|-----------------|----------------------|----|

## PETER MARSH
| 81 | Polydor POSP 210 | You Say You Wanna Love Me/I Won't Let You Go | 15 |
|----|------------------|---------------------------------------------|-----|

## STEVIE MARSH
| 59 | Decca F 11181 | If You Were The Only Boy In The World/Leave Me Alone | 6 |
|----|---------------|------------------------------------------------------|----|
| 60 | Decca F 11209 | You Don't Have To Tell Me (I Know)/Wish | 6 |
| 60 | Decca F 11244 | A Girl In Love/Over And Done With | 6 |
| 62 | Ember EMB S 139 | I Shouldn't Be Kissing You/Time And Time Again | 8 |

## WARNE MARSH
| 57 | London LTZ-P 15080 | JAZZ OF TWO CITIES (LP) | 30 |
|----|--------------------|-------------------------|-----|

## WAYNE MARSH
| 70 | Wave LP 6 | RELEASE RECORD SEND TAPE (LP) | 35 |
|----|-----------|-------------------------------|-----|
| 75 | Wave LP 10 | JAZZ FROM THE EAST VILLAGE (LP) | 30 |

## CHUCK MASHALL & TWIST STARS
| 62 | Brunswick STA 3062 | TWIST TO SONGS EVERYBODY KNOWS (LP) | 15 |
|----|--------------------|-------------------------------------|-----|

## GARY MARSHALL
| 61 | Parlophone R 4758 | One Twitchy Baby/Ev'ry Chance I Get | 12 |
|----|-------------------|-------------------------------------|-----|
| 60 | Parlophone R 4636 | Oh You Beautiful Doll/Large As Life | 6 |

## JACK MARSHALL ORCHESTRA & CHORUS
| 58 | Capitol CL 14888 | Thunder Road Chase/Finger Poppin' | 5 |
|----|------------------|-----------------------------------|----|

## JOY MARSHALL
| 64 | Decca F 11863 | When You Hold Me Tight /Rain On Snow | 12 |
|----|---------------|--------------------------------------|-----|
| 65 | Decca F12189 | Heartache Hurry On By/He's For Me | 40 |
| 65 | Decca F 12222 | My Love Come Home/When A Girl Really Loves You | 12 |
| 66 | Decca F 12422 | The More I See You/Taste Of Honey | 20 |
| 68 | Toast 512 | And I'll Find You/I'm So Glad You're Back | 15 |
| 65 | Decca LK 4678 | WHO SAYS THEY DON'T WRITE GOOD SONGS ANY MORE? (LP) | 25 |

## LARRY MARSHALL
| 67 | Blue Beat BB 374 | Move Your Feet/Find A New Baby | 70 |
|----|------------------|--------------------------------|-----|
| 67 | Blue Beat BB 380 | Suspicion/Broken Heart | 175 |
| 67 | Doctor Bird DB 1008 | Snake In The Grass/ROLAND ALPHONSO: V.C. 10 | 125 |
| 68 | Caltone TONE 126 | No One To Give Me Love/PHIL PRATT: Safe Travel | 175 |
| 70 | Bamboo BAM 22 | Girl Of My Dreams/SOUND DIMENSON: Give It Away | 30 |
| 70 | Bamboo BAM 52 | Man From Galilee/Give It Away (as Larry Marshall & Enid Cumberland) | 30 |
| 70 | Bamboo BAM 61 | Let's Make It Up/BURNING SPEAR: Free | 30 |
| 70 | Banana BA 300 | Stay A Little Longer/MAYTALS: He'll Provide | 20 |
| 71 | Banana BA 364 | Maga Dog/OSSIE ROBINSON: Economical Heatwave | 20 |
| 73 | Pama PM 873 | True Believer/FLAMES: Water Your Garden | 6 |
| 75 | Ocean OC 004 | Can't You Understand/KING TUBBY : Locks Of Dub | 18 |
| 75 | Black & White CP 4326 | I Admire You/KING TUBBY: Watergate Rock | 10 |
| 79 | Yard International YI 103 | Birdsong/She's Gone (12") | 15 |

(see also Larry & Alvin, Irving Brown, Fitzroy D. Long, Kingston Pete & Buster's Allstars, Max Romeo, Jackie Mittoo)

## WAYNE MARSHALL
| 85 | Jah Tubbys JT 013 | Give Me The Mix/Mike In My Hand (12", with the Offbeat Posse) | 75 |
|----|-------------------|--------------------------------------------------------------|-----|

## WILLIE MARSHALL
| 70 | Torpedo TOR 20 | Loosen Up Strong Man/Strong Man | 10 |
|----|----------------|---------------------------------|-----|

## MARSHMALLOW WAY
| 69 | United Artists UP 35031 | C'mon Kitty Kitty/Michigan Mints | 8 |
|----|-------------------------|----------------------------------|----|

## MARSHMELLOW HIGHWAY
| 68 | London HLR 10204 | I Don't Wanna Live This Way/Loving You Makes Everything Alright | 18 |
|----|------------------|----------------------------------------------------------------|-----|

## MARSUPILAMI
| 70 | Transatlantic TRA 213 | MARSUPILAMI (LP, white/lilac label, 't' logo) | 200 |
|----|-----------------------|-----------------------------------------------|------|
| 71 | Transatlantic TRA 230 | ARENA (LP, white/lilac label, 't' logo) | 200 |

## LENA MARTELL
| 67 | Pye 7N 17276 | The Pop Group Song/Reflections | 10 |
|----|--------------|--------------------------------|-----|

## PIERA MARTELL
| 74 | CBS S CBS 2293 | My Ship Of Love/Mein Ruf Nach Dir | 12 |
|----|----------------|-----------------------------------|-----|

## RAY MARTELL
| 70 | Joe JRS 3 | She Caught The Train/PAMA DICE: Tea House From Emperor Rosko | 100 |
|----|-----------|-------------------------------------------------------------|------|
| 70 | Attack ATT 8015 | Loving Lover/Cora | 6 |
| 70 | Doctor Bird DB 1503 | This Little Light/Lover | 6 |
| 70 | Trojan TR 7787 | This Little Light/Lover | 6 |

MINT VALUE £

| | | | |
|---|---|---|---|
| 72 | Sioux SI 012 | She Caught The Train/JOE'S ALLSTARS: Tony B.'s Theme | 12 |
| 73 | Rays RA 1 | Working For My Love/King Fuzz - Downtown Rock | 12 |
| 73 | Rays RA 2 | Lover/Dub | 8 |
| 73 | Rays RA 3 | I Wish You Luck/Version | 8 |
| 73 | Rays RA 4 | Angelina/Angelina Part 2 | 8 |
| 77 | Rays RA 077 | Falling In Love/Everlasting Love | 8 |

## MARTELLS
| | | | |
|---|---|---|---|
| 66 | Decca F 12463 | Time To Say Goodnight/The Cherry Song | 40 |

## MARTHA (REEVES) & VANDELLAS
| | | | |
|---|---|---|---|
| 63 | Oriole CBA 1814 | I'll Have To Let Him Go/My Baby Won't Come Back | 450 |
| 63 | Oriole CBA 1819 | Come And Get These Memories/Jealous Lover | 275 |
| 63 | Stateside SS 228 | Heatwave/A Love Like Yours (Don't Come Knockin' Every Day) | 50 |
| 63 | Stateside SS 228 | Heatwave/A Love Like Yours (Don't Come Knockin' Every Day) (DJ copy) | 150 |
| 64 | Stateside SS 250 | Quicksand/Darling, I Hum Our Song | 55 |
| 64 | Stateside SS 250 | Quicksand/Darling, I Hum Our Song (DJ copy) | 125 |
| 64 | Stateside SS 272 | Live Wire/Old Love (Let's Try It Again) | 60 |
| 64 | Stateside SS 272 | Live Wire/Old Love (Let's Try It Again) (DJ copy) | 100 |
| 64 | Stateside SS 305 | In My Lonely Room/A Tear For The Girl | 80 |
| 64 | Stateside SS 305 | In My Lonely Room/A Tear For The Girl (DJ copy) | 150 |
| 64 | Stateside SS 345 | Dancing In The Street/There He Is (At My Door) | 20 |
| 64 | Stateside SS 345 | Dancing In The Street/There He Is (At My Door) (DJ copy) | 125 |
| 65 | Stateside SS 383 | Wild One/Dancing Slow | 50 |
| 65 | Stateside SS 383 | Wild One/Dancing Slow (DJ copy) | 200 |
| 65 | Tamla Motown TMG 502 | Nowhere To Run/Motoring | 25 |
| 65 | Tamla Motown TMG 502 | Nowhere To Run/Motoring (DJ copy) | 120 |
| 65 | Tamla Motown TMG 530 | You've Been In Love Too Long/Love (Makes Me Do Foolish Things) | 35 |
| 65 | Tamla Motown TMG 530 | You've Been In Love Too Long/Love (Makes Me Do Foolish Things) (DJ copy) | 100 |
| 66 | Tamla Motown TMG 549 | My Baby Loves Me/Never Leave Your Baby's Side | 40 |
| 66 | Tamla Motown TMG 549 | My Baby Loves Me/Never Leave Your Baby's Side (DJ copy) | 120 |
| 66 | Tamla Motown TMG 567 | What Am I Going To Do Without Your Love/Go Ahead And Laugh | 35 |
| 66 | Tamla Motown TMG 567 | What Am I Going To Do Without Your Love/Go Ahead And Laugh (DJ copy) | 100 |
| 66 | Tamla Motown TMG 582 | I'm Ready For Love/He Doesn't Love Her Anymore | 20 |
| 66 | Tamla Motown TMG 582 | I'm Ready For Love/He Doesn't Love Her Anymore (DJ copy) | 50 |
| 67 | Tamla Motown TMG 599 | Jimmy Mack/Third Finger, Left Hand | 12 |
| 67 | Tamla Motown TMG 621 | Love Bug Leave My Heart Alone/One Way Out | 35 |
| 67 | Tamla Motown TMG 621 | Love Bug Leave My Heart Alone/One Way Out (DJ copy) | 75 |
| 68 | Tamla Motown TMG 636 | Honey Chile/Show Me The Way | 18 |
| 68 | Tamla Motown TMG 657 | I Promise To Wait, My Love/Forget Me Not | 18 |
| 68 | Tamla Motown TMG 669 | I Can't Dance To That Music You're Playing/I Tried | 25 |
| 69 | Tamla Motown TMG 684 | Dancing In The Street/Quicksand | 7 |
| 69 | Tamla Motown TMG 694 | Nowhere To Run/Live Wire | 7 |
| 71 | Tamla Motown TMG 762 | Forget Me Not/I Gotta Let You Go | 7 |
| 71 | Tamla Motown TMG 794 | Bless You/Hope I Don't Get My Heart Broke | 7 |
| 72 | Tamla Motown TMG 599 | Jimmy Mack/Third Finger, Left Hand (reissue) | 6 |
| 73 | Tamla Motown TMG 843 | No One There/(I've Given You) The Best Years Of My Life | 75 |
| 73 | Tamla Motown TMG 843 | No One There/(I've Given You) The Best Years Of My Life (DJ Copy) | 150 |
| 65 | Tamla Motown TME 2009 | MARTHA AND THE VANDELLAS (EP) | 120 |
| 66 | Tamla Motown TME 2017 | HITTIN' (EP) | 150 |
| 63 | Oriole PS 40052 | COME AND GET THESE MEMORIES (LP) | 400 |
| 65 | Tamla Motown TML 11005 | HEATWAVE (LP) | 55 |
| 65 | Tamla Motown TML 11013 | DANCE PARTY (LP) | 65 |
| 67 | Tamla Motown TML 11040 | GREATEST HITS (LP, original with flipback sleeve, mono) | 25 |
| 67 | Tamla Motown (S)TML 11040 | GREATEST HITS (LP, original with flipback sleeve, stereo) | 30 |
| 67 | Tamla Motown (S)TML 11040 | GREATEST HITS (LP, re-pressing non-flipback sleeve) | 15 |
| 67 | Tamla Motown TML 11051 | WATCH OUT! (LP, mono) | 40 |
| 67 | Tamla Motown STML 11051 | WATCH OUT! (LP, stereo) | 45 |
| 68 | Tamla Motown TML 11078 | RIDIN' HIGH (LP, mono) | 25 |
| 68 | Tamla Motown STML 11078 | RIDIN' HIGH (LP, stereo) | 30 |
| 69 | Tamla Motown (S)TML 11099 | DANCING IN THE STREET (LP, mono/stereo) | 25 |
| 70 | Tamla Motown TML 11134 | SUGAR N' SPICE (LP, mono) | 25 |
| 70 | Tamla Motown STML 11134 | SUGAR N' SPICE (LP, stereo) | 20 |
| 70 | Tamla Motown STML 11166 | NATURAL RESOURCES (LP) | 22 |
| 72 | Tamla Motown STML 11204 | BLACK MAGIC (LP) | 30 |

## MARTIAN SCHOOLGIRLS
| | | | |
|---|---|---|---|
| 79 | Red Planet RPR 1 | Life In The 1980's/Lonely Nights (p/s) | 10 |

## MARTIN
| | | | |
|---|---|---|---|
| 68 | Coxsone CS 7056 | I Second That Emotion (actually by Martin Riley)/ROY TOMLINSON: I Stand For I | 150 |

## ALAN MARTIN
| | | | |
|---|---|---|---|
| 63 | Rio R 3 | The Party/Indeed | 8 |
| 63 | Rio R 6 | You Came Late/Dreaming | 8 |
| 63 | Rio R 9 | Secretly/Fame And Fortune | 8 |
| 63 | Rio R 10 | Mother Brother/Tell Me | 8 |
| 65 | Rio R 66 | Must Know I Love You/VIC BROWN'S COMBO: Rio Special | 12 |
| 65 | Rio R 67 | Sweet Rosemarie/HONEY DUCKERS: Banjo Man | 8 |
| 65 | Rio R 68 | Why Must I Cry/Shirley I Love You | 8 |
| 65 | Rio R 74 | Since I Married Dorothy/You Promised Me | 8 |

| | | | |
|---|---|---|---|
| 65 | Venus VE 1 | Cry Myself To Shame/Baby Don't Go | 10 |
| 66 | Rio R 94 | Days Are Lonely/My Baby | 15 |
| 66 | Rio R 96 | Rome Wasn't Built In A Day/I'm Hurt | 15 |

**MARTIN & DERRICK**

| 61 | Blue Beat BB 48 | Times Are Going/I Love You Baby (with Cavaliers Combo) | 15 |
|---|---|---|---|
| 62 | Island WI 024 | Come On/MONTY & CYCLONES: Organisation | 20 |

*(see also Derrick Morgan)*

**MARTIN & FINLEY**

| 73 | Tamla Motown TMG 867 | It's Another Sunday/Best Friends (withdrawn, demo only) | 250 |
|---|---|---|---|

**BARRY MARTIN**

| 61 | RCA RCA 1234 | Little Lonely One/Are You Sure | 5 |
|---|---|---|---|

**BOBBI MARTIN**

| 64 | Coral Q 72477 | Don't Forget I Still Love You/On The Outside (Lookin' In) | 5 |
|---|---|---|---|
| 65 | Coral Q 72478 | I Can't Stop Thinking About You/Million Thanks To You | 6 |

**CHRIS MARTIN**

| 59 | HMV POP 664 | Lonely Street/Swing A Little Lover | 10 |
|---|---|---|---|
| 60 | HMV POP 692 | Point Of No Return/I Don't Regret A Thing | 6 |

**DAVE MARTIN**

| 64 | Port-O-Jam PJ 4112 | Let Them Fight/OSSIE IRVING SIX: Why I Love You | 18 |
|---|---|---|---|
| 64 | Port-O-Jam PJ 4115 | All My Dreams/Take Your Belongings | 18 |

**DEAN MARTIN**

**SINGLES**

| 54 | Capitol CL 14123 | Hey Brother, Pour The Wine/I'd Cry Like A Baby (green label) | 15 |
|---|---|---|---|
| 54 | Capitol CL 14123 | Hey Brother, Pour The Wine/I'd Cry Like A Baby (purple label) | 10 |
| 54 | Capitol CL 14138 | Sway/Pretty As A Picture | 40 |
| 54 | Capitol CL 14150 | How Do You Speak To An Angel?/Ev'ry Street's A Boulevard In Old New York (with Jerry Lewis) | 5 |
| 54 | Capitol CL 14170 | The Peddlar Man (Ten I Loved)/Try Again | 5 |
| 54 | Capitol CL 14180 | One More Time/If I Could Sing Like Bing | 5 |

*(see also Frank Sinatra)*

**DEREK MARTIN**

| 64 | Sue WI 308 | Daddy Rolling Stone/Don't Put Me Down Like This (credited as Derak Martin) | 100 |
|---|---|---|---|
| 65 | Columbia DB 7694 | You Better Go/You Know | 40 |
| 68 | Stax 601 039 | Soul Power/Sly Girl | 30 |

**DON MARTIN & DANDY (& SUPERBOYS)**

| 67 | Giant GN 6 | Got A Feelin'/CONNECTIONS: At The Junction | 25 |
|---|---|---|---|
| 68 | Giant GN 24 | Keep On Fighting/Rock Steady Boogie (with Superboys) | 25 |

*(see also Dandy & Superboys)*

**GEORGE MARTIN & HIS ORCHESTRA**

| 64 | Parlophone R 5135 | I Saw Her Standing There/All My Loving | 12 |
|---|---|---|---|
| 64 | Parlophone R 5166 | And I Love Her/Ringo's Theme (This Boy) | 12 |
| 65 | Parlophone R 5222 | All Quiet On The Mersey Front/Out Of The Picture | 15 |
| 65 | Parlophone R 5256 | I Feel Fine/The Niagara Theme | 10 |
| 65 | Parlophone R 5375 | Yesterday/Another Girl | 15 |
| 66 | United Artists UP 1154 | By George! - It's The David Frost Theme/Double Scotch | 20 |
| 66 | United Artists UP 1165 | Love In The Open Air/Theme From "The Family Way" | 20 |
| 67 | United Artists UP 1194 | Theme One/Elephants And Castles | 10 |
| 72 | United Artists UP 35423 | Pulp - Theme/Pulp - Love Theme | 35 |
| 65 | Parlophone GEP 8930 | MUSIC FROM "A HARD DAY'S NIGHT" (EP) | 18 |
| 64 | Parlophone PMC 1227 | OFF THE BEATLE TRACK (LP, mono) | 20 |
| 64 | Parlophone PCS 3057 | OFF THE BEATLE TRACK (LP, stereo) | 12 |
| 65 | Parlophone TA-PMC 1227 | OFF THE BEATLE TRACK (reel-to-reel, mono only) | 20 |
| 65 | Columbia SX 1775 | PLAYS HELP! (LP, mono) | 20 |
| 65 | Studio Two TWO 102 | PLAYS HELP! (LP, stereo) | 20 |
| 66 | United Artists (S)ULP 1157 | INSTRUMENTALLY SALUTES THE BEATLES GIRLS (LP) | 30 |
| 66 | Studio Two TWO 141 | AND I LOVE HER (LP) | 20 |
| 67 | Decca LK 4847 | THE FAMILY WAY (LP, mono, soundtrack) | 70 |
| 67 | Decca SKL 4847 | THE FAMILY WAY (LP, stereo, soundtrack) | 90 |
| 68 | United Artists (S)ULP 1196 | BRITISH MAID (LP) | 25 |
| 70 | Sunset SLS 50182 | BY GEORGE! (LP) | 20 |
| 73 | United Artists UAS 29475 | LIVE AND LET DIE (LP, soundtrack, gatefold sleeve) | 25 |
| 74 | Polydor Super 2383 304 | BEATLES TO BOND AND BACH (LP) | 15 |
| 78 | St. Michael IMP 105 | BEATLES TO BOND AND BACH (LP, exclusive to Marks & Spencer) | 20 |

*(see also Beatles, Ray Cathode)*

**GRADY MARTIN & THE SLEWFOOT FIVE**

| 56 | Brunswick 05535 | Nashville/Don't Take Your Love From Me | 15 |
|---|---|---|---|

**HONEYBOY MARTIN**

| 67 | Caltone TONE 103 | Dreader Than Dread (and the Voices)/DANDY: In The Mood | 50 |
|---|---|---|---|
| 70 | Gas GAS 123 | Unchained Melody/SAMMY JONES: You're My Girl | 10 |
| 72 | Sioux SI 011 | Unchained Melody/SAMMY JONES: You're My Girl (reissue) | 8 |
| 72 | Harry J HJ 6643 | Have You Ever Seen The Rain/Spanish Harlem | 5 |

*(see also Lynn Tait & Jets)*

**JACKI MARTIN**

| 64 | Fontana TF 487 | Will You/Till He Tells Me | 12 |
|---|---|---|---|

**JANIS MARTIN**

| 60 | Palette PG 9000 | Here Today And Gone Tomorrow Love/Hard Times Ahead | 25 |
|---|---|---|---|
| 80 | RCA PE 9494 | JANIS MARTIN (EP) | 10 |
| 80 | RCA PL 43153 | THE COMPLETE RCA JANIS MARTIN (2-LP) | 25 |

MINT VALUE £

## JEAN MARTIN
| 63 | Decca F 11751 | Ain't Gonna Kiss Ya/Three Times Three Is Love | 10 |
| 64 | Decca F 11897 | Save The Last Dance For Me/Will You Still Love Me Tomorrow | 10 |

## JERRY MARTIN
| 63 | London HLU 9692 | Shake-A Take-A/Exchange Student | 15 |

## KERRY MARTIN
| 58 | Parlophone R 4449 | Stroll Me/Cold Hands, Warm Heart | 12 |

## LUCIA MARTIN
| 62 | Parlophone R 4915 | Big Jim/Star From Heaven | 12 |

## MARK MARTIN
| 67 | Page One POF 020 | Extraordinary Girl/Love Could Be Like Hell | 6 |

## MARY MARTIN
| 64 | London HLR 9938 | A Spoonful Of Sugar/Feed The Birds | 5 |

## MILES MARTIN FOLK GROUP
| 71 | Amber | MILES MARTIN FOLK GROUP (LP, private pressing) | 70 |

## MILLICENT MARTIN
| 58 | Columbia DB 4171 | Our Language Of Love/Seriously | 5 |
| 63 | Parlophone R5033 | Get Lost My Love/Gravy Waltz | 15 |
| 63 | Parlophone R 4998 | That Was The Week That Was/Gotta Lotta Lovin' (with David Frost) | 5 |
| 64 | Parlophone R 5096 | In The Summer Of His Years/If I Can Help Somebody | 5 |
| 64 | Parlophone R 5120 | Suspicion/Nothing But The Best | 5 |
| 59 | Columbia 33SX 1145 | MILLICENT (LP) | 150 |
| 64 | Philips BL 7591 | MR & MRS (LP) | 25 |

(see also David Frost)

## PATRICK D. MARTIN
| 79 | Deram DMR 432 | I Like Electric Motors/Time (p/s) | 5 |
| 80 | Deram DM 433 | Lucy 'Lectric/I Like Electric Motors/Mutant (p/s) | 10 |

## PAUL MARTIN
| 67 | Sue WI 4041 | Snake In The Grass/I've Got A New Love | 70 |

## RAY MARTIN (& HIS) CONCERT ORCHESTRA
| 53 | Columbia SCM 5001 | Blue Tango/Belle Of The Ball | 8 |
| 53 | Columbia SCM 5002 | The Marching Strings/The Waltzing Cat | 8 |
| 53 | Columbia SCM 5063 | Swedish Rhapsody/Hi-Lili Hi-Lo | 7 |
| 56 | Columbia SCM 5264 | The Carousel Waltz/Port Au Prince | 7 |

(see also Ray Burns)

## RICKY MARTIN & TYME MACHINE
| 68 | Olga OLE 4 | Something Else/Blue Suede Shoes | 15 |

## RODGE MARTIN
| 67 | Polydor 56725 | When She Touches Me/Lovin' Machine | 10 |

## RON MARTIN & JUBILEE STOMPERS
| 68 | Doctor Bird DB 1151 | Give Your Love To Me/I Cry My Heart | 20 |

## RUPIE MARTIN('S ALLSTARS)
| 69 | Ackee ACK 101 | The Arena/Naturally | 60 |
| 70 | Torpedo TOR 24 | Last Flight/Super Lotus | 30 |
| 70 | Torpedo TOR 26 | Musical Container (Parts 1 & 2) | 40 |
| 70 | Punch PH 43 | Death In The Arena (actually by Rupie Martin All Stars)/ MAN COMETH: Julia Caesar (actually by Charlie Ace) | 30 |

## SETH MARTIN
| 68 | Page One POF 073 | Another Day Goes By/Look At Me | 15 |
| 69 | Page One POF 134 | What A Lovely Way To Spend Forever/Mystery Lady | 5 |

## SHANE MARTIN
| 68 | CBS 2894 | You're So Young/I Need You | 275 |
| 68 | CBS 2894 | You're So Young/I Need You (DJ copy) | 350 |

## TONY MARTIN
| 53 | HMV 7M 105 | Tenement Symphony (both sides) | 7 |
| 56 | HMV 7M 414 | Walk Hand In Hand/Flamenco Love | 8 |
| 56 | HMV 7MC 41 | Walk Hand In Hand/Flamenco Love (export issue) | 8 |
| 65 | Stateside SS 394 | Talkin' To Your Picture/Our Rhapsody | 120 |
| 65 | Tamla Motown TMG 537 | The Bigger Your Heart Is (The Harder You'll Fall)/The Two Of Us | 220 |
| 65 | Tamla Motown TMG 537 | The Bigger Your Heart Is (The Harder You'll Fall)/The Two Of Us (DJ copy) | 300 |

(see also Gogi Grant)

## TRADE MARTIN
| 63 | London HL 9662 | Hula Hula Dancin' Doll/Something In The Wind | 15 |

## VINCE MARTIN
| 56 | London HL 8340 | Cindy Oh Cindy/Only If You Praise The Lord | 8 |
| 59 | HMV POP 594 | Old Grey Goose (Aunt Rhodie)/Goodnight, Irene | 8 |

(see also Tarriers)

## MARTIN & THE BROWNSHIRTS
| 78 | Lightning GIL 507 | Taxi Driver/Boring | 40 |

## WINK MARTINDALE
| 59 | London HLD 8962 | Deck Of Cards/Now You Know How It Feels (tri centre) | 10 |

## TONY MARTINEZ QUINTET
| 54 | HMV 7M 264 | Cucusa Tune Mambo/Bernie's Tune Mambo | 5 |

## AL MARTINO
| 54 | Capitol CL 14128 | Wanted/There'll Be No Teardrops Tonight (Green label, tri centre) | 10 |
| 54 | Capitol CL 14128 | Wanted/There'll Be No Teardrops Tonight (Purple label, tri centre) | 5 |

| 54 | Capitol CL 14148 | On And On (In Love With You)/Give Me Something To Go With The Wine (Green label, tri centre) .................................................................................................. 10 |
|----|------------------|-------------|
| 54 | Capitol CL 14148 | On And On (In Love With You)/Give Me Something To Go With The Wine (Purple label, tri centre) .................................................................................................. 5 |
| 54 | Capitol CL 14163 | The Story Of Tina/Destiny (No One Can Change) (Green label, tri centre) ........... 10 |
| 54 | Capitol CL 14163 | The Story Of Tina/Destiny (No One Can Change) (Purple label, tri centre) ........... 5 |
| 54 | Capitol CL 14192 | I Still Believe/When? ............................................................................................. 5 |
| 54 | Capitol CL 14202 | Not As A Stranger/No One But You ........................................................................ 5 |
| 55 | Capitol CL 14224 | Don't Go To Strangers/Say It Again ....................................................................... 5 |
| 55 | Capitol CL 14284 | The Snowy, Snowy Mountains/Love Is Eternal ..................................................... 5 |
| 55 | Capitol CL 14343 | The Man From Laramie/To Please My Lady ........................................................... 10 |
| 55 | Capitol CL 14379 | Come Close To Me/Small Talk ............................................................................... 5 |

*(Originally issued with triangular centres; round-centre reissues are worth around half these values.)*

| 67 | Capitol 15516 | More Than The Eye Can See/Red Is Red .................................................................. 20 |
| 61 | Capitol EAP 1.20153 | TO PLEASE MY LADY (EP) ....................................................................................... 10 |

## MARTINS
| 65 | Studio 66 KEP 113/4 | MARTINS EP (no p/s) ............................................................................................. 50 |

## MARTIN'S MAGIC SOUNDS
| 67 | Deram DM 141 | Mon Amour, Mon Amour/Midem Melody ............................................................ 6 |

## JOHN MARTYN
| 71 | Island WIP 6116 | May You Never/Just Now ....................................................................................... 20 |
|----|-----------------|-------------|
| 77 | Island WIP 6385 | Over The Hill/Head And Heart ............................................................................... 6 |
| 78 | Island WIP 6414 | Dancing/Dealer (Version) ....................................................................................... 6 |
| 78 | Island WIP | Dancing/Dealer (Version) (promo) ........................................................................ 8 |
| 80 | Island WIP 6547 | Johnny Too Bad/Johnny Too Bad (Version) .......................................................... 6 |
| 81 | Island IPR 2046 | Johnny Too Bad (Extended Dub Version)/Big Muff (Extended Mix) (12", promo) .... 10 |
| 82 | WEA K 259987-7 | Gun Money (US Remix)/Hiss On the Tape (live) ................................................... 6 |
| 86 | Island CID 265 | Classic John Martyn: Angeline/Tight Connection To My Heart (Has Anybody Seen My Love)/May You Never/Solid Air/Glistening Glyndebourne (CD, foldout sleeve) ........... 15 |
| 67 | Island ILP 952 | LONDON CONVERSATION (LP, 1st pressing, with black & orange 'circle' logo) ........... 350 |
| 69 | Island ILP 952 | LONDON CONVERSATION (LP, 2nd pressing, pink label, white 'i' logo) ................... 70 |
| 69 | Island ILP 952 | LONDON CONVERSATION (LP, 3rd pressing, 'pink rim' label, 'palm tree' logo) ........... 25 |
| 68 | Island ILP 991 | THE TUMBLER (LP, 1st pressing, with black 'circle' logo, mono) ........................... 250 |
| 68 | Island ILPS 9091 | THE TUMBLER (LP, 1st pressing, with black 'circle' logo, stereo) .......................... 40 |
| 70 | Island ILPS 9091 | THE TUMBLER (LP, 2nd pressing, 'pink rim' label, 'palm tree' logo, fully laminated sleeve) ................................................................................................................. 20 |
| 71 | Island ILPS 9167 | BLESS THE WEATHER (LP, 'pink rim' label, 'palm tree' logo) ............................... 30 |
| 73 | Island ILPS 9226 | SOLID AIR (LP, gatefold sleeve with lyric sheet 'pink rim' label, 'palm tree' logo) ........... 40 |
| 73 | Island ILPS 9253 | INSIDE OUT (LP, gatefold sleeve with inner, 'pink rim' label, 'palm tree' logo) ........... 20 |
| 74 | Island ILPS 9296 | SUNDAY'S CHILD (LP, with lyric inner sleeve, 'palm tree' label) ........................... 15 |
| 75 | Island ILPS 9343 | LIVE AT LEEDS (LP, mail-order, 10,000 only, numbered & some signed) ............. 30 |
| 77 | Island ILPS 9492 | ONE WORLD (LP, inner) ......................................................................................... 20 |

## JOHN & BEVERLEY MARTYN
| 70 | Island WIP 6076 | John The Baptist/The Ocean ................................................................................. 12 |
|----|-----------------|-------------|
| 70 | Island ILPS 9113 | STORMBRINGER (LP, 1st pressing, pink label with 'i' logo) ................................. 100 |
| 70 | Island ILPS 9113 | STORMBRINGER (LP, 2nd pressing, 'pink rim' label, 'palm tree' logo) ................. 15 |
| 70 | Island ILPS 9133 | THE ROAD TO RUIN (LP, 'pink rim' label, 'palm tree' logo) ................................. 25 |

*(see also Beverley)*

## KID MARTYN
| 62 | 77 77LA 12/20 | IN NEW ORLEANS WITH KID SHEIK'S BAND (LP) ................................................... 15 |

## MARVELETTES
| 61 | Fontana H 355 | Please Mr Postman/So Long Baby ........................................................................ 55 |
|----|---------------|-------------|
| 62 | Fontana H 386 | Twistin' Postman/I Want A Guy ............................................................................ 70 |
| 62 | Oriole CBA 1764 | Beechwood 4-5789/Someday Someway ............................................................... 155 |
| 63 | Oriole CBA 1817 | Locking Up My Heart/Forever ............................................................................... 400 |
| 64 | Stateside SS 251 | As Long As I Know He's Mine/Little Girl Blue ...................................................... 60 |
| 64 | Stateside SS 251 | As Long As I Know He's Mine/Little Girl Blue (DJ copy) ...................................... 90 |
| 64 | Stateside SS 273 | He's A Good Guy (Yes He Is)/Goddess Of Love ..................................................... 60 |
| 64 | Stateside SS 273 | He's A Good Guy (Yes He Is)/Goddess Of Love (DJ copy) ..................................... 100 |
| 64 | Stateside SS 334 | You're My Remedy/A Little Bit Of Sympathy, A Little Bit Of Love ...................... 45 |
| 64 | Stateside SS 334 | You're My Remedy/A Little Bit Of Sympathy, A Little Bit Of Love (DJ copy) ....... 100 |
| 65 | Stateside SS 369 | Too Many Fish In The Sea/Need For Love ............................................................. 40 |
| 65 | Stateside SS 369 | Too Many Fish In The Sea/Need For Love (DJ copy) ............................................. 125 |
| 65 | Tamla Motown TMG 518 | I'll Keep Holding On/No Time For Tears .............................................................. 120 |
| 65 | Tamla Motown TMG 518 | I'll Keep Holding On/No Time For Tears (DJ copy) .............................................. 400 |
| 65 | Tamla Motown TMG 535 | Danger Heartbreak Dead Ahead/Your Cheating Ways ........................................ 50 |
| 65 | Tamla Motown TMG 535 | Danger Heartbreak Dead Ahead/Your Cheating Ways (DJ copy) ......................... 150 |
| 66 | Tamla Motown TMG 546 | Don't Mess With Bill/Anything You Wanna Do ................................................... 45 |
| 66 | Tamla Motown TMG 546 | Don't Mess With Bill/Anything You Wanna Do (DJ copy) ................................... 85 |
| 66 | Tamla Motown TMG 562 | You're The One/Paper Boy ................................................................................... 45 |
| 66 | Tamla Motown TMG 562 | You're The One/Paper Boy (DJ copy) ................................................................... 75 |
| 67 | Tamla Motown TMG 594 | The Hunter Gets Captured By The Game/I Think I Can Change You .................... 30 |
| 67 | Tamla Motown TMG 594 | The Hunter Gets Captured By The Game/I Think I Can Change You (DJ copy) ...... 60 |
| 67 | Tamla Motown TMG 609 | When You're Young And In Love/The Day You Take One, You Have To Take The Other .. 15 |
| 68 | Tamla Motown TMG 639 | My Baby Must Be A Magician/I Need Someone .................................................... 22 |
| 68 | Tamla Motown TMG 659 | Here I Am Baby/Keep Off, No Trespassing ........................................................... 25 |
| 69 | Tamla Motown TMG 701 | Reachin' For Something I Can't Have/Destination Anywhere .............................. 15 |
| 73 | Tamla Motown TMG 860 | Reachin' For Something I Can't Have/Here I Am Baby ......................................... 10 |
| 73 | Tamla Motown TMG 860 | Reachin' For Something I Can't Have/Here I Am Baby (DJ copy, plays "My Baby Must Be A Magician") ................................................................................................... 100 |

# MARVELOWS

| | | | |
|---|---|---|---|
| 75 | Tamla Motown TMG 1000 | Finders Keepers, Losers Weepers/KIM WESTON: Do Like I Do | 100 |
| 65 | Tamla Motown TME 2003 | THE MARVELETTES (EP) | 100 |
| 65 | Tamla Motown TML 11008 | THE MARVELLOUS MARVELETTES (LP) | 110 |
| 67 | Tamla Motown TML 11052 | THE MARVELETTES (LP, mono) | 250 |
| 67 | Tamla Motown STML 11052 | THE MARVELETTES (LP, stereo) | 50 |
| 69 | Tamla Motown (S)TML 11090 | SOPHISTICATED SOUL (LP, mono/stereo) | 55 |
| | | | 40 |
| 70 | Tamla Motown STML 11145 | IN FULL BLOOM (LP) | 30 |
| 71 | Tamla Motown STML 11177 | THE RETURN OF THE MARVELETTES (LP, unissued) | 0 |

## MARVELOWS
| | | | |
|---|---|---|---|
| 65 | HMV POP 1433 | I Do/My Heart | 30 |
| 65 | HMV POP 1433 | I Do/My Heart (DJ Copy) | 40 |

## MARVELS (JAMAICA)
| | | | |
|---|---|---|---|
| 62 | Dice CC 8 | Come To The Wedding/Angelo | 10 |
| 63 | Blue Beat BB 191 | Sonia/The More We Are Together | 12 |
| 64 | Blue Beat BB 221 | Millie/Saturday | 20 |
| 70 | Pama PM 813 | Love One Another/Falling Rain | 8 |
| 70 | Pama PM 817 | Don't Let Him Take Your Love From Me/A Little Smile | 5 |
| 70 | Gas GAS 138 | Sail Away/Fight A Broke | 5 |
| 70 | Gas GAS 139 | Someday We'll Be Together/MOHAWKS: The Rhythm | 15 |
| 71 | Pama PM 819 | Oh Lord Why Lord/NEVILLE HINDS: Love Letter | 12 |
| 71 | Pama Supreme PS 338 | Rocksteady/ Be My Baby | 5 |
| 71 | New Beat NB 081 | Co Co/Hey Girl Don't Bother Me | 30 |
| 72 | Pama PM 832 | Do You Know You Have To Cry/Love Power | 5 |
| 72 | Pama Supreme PS 348 | What A Hurricane/If You Love Her | 5 |

## MARVELS (U.K.)
| | | | |
|---|---|---|---|
| 68 | Columbia DB 8341 | Keep On Searching/Heartache | 120 |

## MARVELS FIVE
| | | | |
|---|---|---|---|
| 65 | HMV POP 1423 | Bye Bye Baby Bunting/In Front Of Her House | 7 |
| 65 | HMV POP 1452 | Don't Play That Song/(You Lied) I Forgive | 15 |

## MARVETTE
| | | | |
|---|---|---|---|
| 68 | Amalgamated AMG 804 | Tit For Tat (actually by Lyn Taitt & Jets)/You Take So Long To Know | 50 |
| 68 | Sacred Sound SS 001 | We Are Not Divided/He Is So Real To Me | 8 |
| 68 | Sacred Sound SS 002 | We Shall Have A Grand Time/Let The Power Fall On Me | 8 |
| 68 | Sacred Sound SS 003 | I Was Once Lost In Sin/What A Wonderful Thing | 8 |
| 68 | Tabernacle TS 1001 | I Want A Revival/Tell It | 15 |
| 68 | Tabernacle TS 1003 | Sweet Jesus/When I Look Back | 7 |
| 60s | Coxsone TLP 1002 | IT'S REVIVAL TIME (LP) | 60 |

## MARVIN & FARRAR
| | | | |
|---|---|---|---|
| 73 | EMI EMI 2044 | Music Makes My Day/Skin Deep (with Olivia Newton-John) | 10 |
| 75 | EMI EMI 2335 | Small And Lonely Light/Galadriel (Spirit Of Starlight) | 7 |
| 73 | EMI EMA 755 | HANK MARVIN AND JOHN FARRAR (LP, with Olivia Newton-John on recorder) | 20 |

*(see also Shadows, Hank Marvin, Marvin Welch & Farrar)*

## MARVIN & JOHNNY
| | | | |
|---|---|---|---|
| 57 | Vogue V 9074 | Yak Yak/Pretty Eyes | 300 |
| 57 | Vogue V 9074 | Yak Yak/Pretty Eyes (78) | 75 |
| 58 | Vogue V 9099 | Smack, Smack/You're In My Heart | 300 |
| 58 | Vogue V 9099 | Smack, Smack/You're In My Heart (78) | 75 |
| 65 | Black Swan WI 467 | Cherry Pie/Ain't That Right | 20 |

## BRETT MARVIN & THUNDERBOLTS
| | | | |
|---|---|---|---|
| 70 | Sonet SNTF 616 | BRETT MARVIN AND THE THUNDERBOLTS (LP) | 15 |
| 71 | Sonet SNTF 619 | 12 INCHES OF BRETT MARVIN & THE THUNDERBOLTS (LP) | 20 |

*(see also Jona Lewie)*

## HANK (B.) MARVIN
| | | | |
|---|---|---|---|
| 68 | Columbia DB 8326 | London's Not Too Far/SHADOWS: Running Out Of World | 15 |
| 69 | Columbia DB 8552 | Goodnight Dick/Wahine | 8 |
| 69 | Columbia DB 8601 | Sacha/Sunday For Seven Days | 8 |
| 69 | Columbia DB 8628 | Midnight Cowboy/SHADOWS: Slaughter On Tenth Avenue | 12 |
| 70 | Columbia DB 8693 | Break Another Dawn/Would You Believe It? (demo-only, unissued B-side) | 100 |
| 70 | Columbia DB 8693 | Break Another Dawn/Morning Star | 10 |
| 69 | Columbia SCX 6352 | HANK MARVIN (LP, blue/black label, mono) | 35 |
| 69 | Columbia SCX 6352 | HANK MARVIN (LP, blue/black label, stereo) | 30 |

*(see also Shadows, Marvin & Farrar, Marvin Welch & Farrar, Bruce Welch, Cliff Richard, Spaghetti Junction, Jean-Michel Jarre)*

## JOEL MARVIN
| | | | |
|---|---|---|---|
| 70 | Explosion EX 2028 | Too Late/Each Day (both actually by Gregory Isaacs) | 15 |

*(see also Gregory Isaacs)*

## MARVIN, WELCH & FARRAR
| | | | |
|---|---|---|---|
| 71 | Regal Zonophone RZ 3030 | Faithful/Mr. Sun | 5 |
| 71 | Regal Zonophone RZ 3035 | Lady Of The Morning/Tiny Robin | 5 |
| 72 | Regal Zonophone RZ 3048 | Marmaduke/Strike A Light | 5 |
| 72 | Regal Zono. Q4SRZA 8504 | SECOND OPINION (LP, quadrophonic) | 25 |

*(see also Shadows, Marvin & Farrar, Bruce Welch [& Hank Marvin])*

## GROUCHO MARX
| | | | |
|---|---|---|---|
| 72 | A&M AMS 7057 | Show Me A Rose/Lydia The Tattooed Lady | 7 |

*(see also Jimmy Durante, Jerry Colonna & Groucho Marx)*

## MARZ
| | | | |
|---|---|---|---|
| 80 | Frozen Owl SRR 0023 | Lady Of The Night/On The Road To Freedom/Daydreamer (p/s, with badge) | 90 |

## MARZIPAN
70   Trend 6099 007      My Kind Of Music/Sweet Water Mary ........................................................ 10

## MASAI (1)
74   Contempo CS 2007      Across The Track (We Better Go Back) (Parts 1 & 2) ........................... 30

## MASAI (2)
82   Turbo TURB 01      Stranger To Myself/Lightning (p/s) ............................................. 8

## MASCOTS
63   Pye International 7N 25189      Hey Little Angel/Once Upon A Love ........................................ 20

## HUGH MASEKELA
68   Uni UN 504      Grazing In The Grass/Bajabula Bonke ................................... 10
69   Uni UN 510      I Haven't Slept/Where Has All The Grass Gone? ...................... 6
68   Uni UNL(S) 101      ALIVE AND WELL AT THE WHISKEY (LP) ............................ 20
69   Fontana SFL 13056      HUGH MASEKELA (LP) ....................................................... 20
71   Rare Earth SRE 3002      HUGH MASEKELA AND THE UNION OF SOUTH AFRICA (LP) ... 25
72   Blue Thumb ICD 3      HOME IS WHERE THE MUSIC IS (LP) ................................. 30

## MASHMAKAN
70   CBS S 5170      As The Years Go By/Days When We Are Free .................... 15
74   Youngblood YB1063      Dance A Little Step/One Night Stand ............................... 6

## MASKED PHANTOM
66   Parlophone R 5437      These Clogs Are Made For Walking/Fried Scampi ............... 7

## MASKMAN & AGENTS
69   Direction 58-4059      One Eye Open/Y'awll .................................................... 10

## MASON
73   Dawn DNS 1040      Fading/It's Alright ........................................................ 5
74   Antic K 11505      Follow Me/Peacefully ................................................... 8
73   Dawn DNLS 3050      MASON (LP, export issue, do finished copies exist?) ........... 20

## BARBARA MASON
65   London HL 9977      Yes, I'm Ready/Keep Him ........................................... 40
65   London HL 9977      Yes, I'm Ready/Keep Him (DJ copy) ........................... 75
68   Direction 58-3382      Oh How It Hurts/Ain't Got Nobody ............................ 50
69   Action ACT 4542      Slipping Away/Half A Love ...................................... 25
72   Buddah 2011 133      Bed And Board/Yes It's You ........................................ 10
73   Buddah 2011 154      Give Me Your Love/You Can Be With The One You Don't Love ... 7
75   Buddah BDS 425      From His Woman To You/When You Wake Up In Georgia ... 6
69   Action ACLP 6002      OH HOW IT HURTS (LP) ......................................... 75
75   Buddah BDLP 4027      TRANSITION (LP) ............................................... 20
75   Buddah BDLP 4032      LOVE'S THING (LP) ............................................... 20

## BARRY MASON
66   Decca F 12401      Misty Morning Eyes/Take Your Time ........................ 10
66   Deram DM 104      Over The Hills And Far Away/A Collection Of Recollections ... 45
67   MGM MGM 1356      Rowbottom Square/American Girl ........................... 12
69   Decca F 12895      I'm In Love With You, Pom Pom/Mister D.J. Play Me A Sad Song ... 7
70   MCA MK 5034      When You Do What You're Doing/Oh Baby ............... 6
70   MCA MKS 5054      High Time/You Put Your Tears Away/Monte Carlo ....... 6
75   Magnet MAG 40      Without You/Waiting In The Wings ........................ 5

*(see also Sounds Of Les & Barry)*

## BILL MASON BAND
79   Kingsway KMS 903      Out On The Streets/Mr. G (p/s) ............................ 15

## DAVE MASON
68   Island WIP 6032      Just For You/Little Woman ................................... 12
70   Harvest HAR 5017      World In Changes/Can't Stop Worrying, Can't Stop Lovin' ... 5
70   Harvest HAR 5024      Only You Know And I Know/Sad And Deep As You .... 5
70   Harvest SHTC 251      ALONE TOGETHER (LP, gatefold sleeve with 'gimmick' die cut, ' Gramophone Co' on label rim, no EMI logo, both matrix numbers end in -1 as well as crossed out matrix numbers SHVL 778 A-1/B-1) ... 45
72   Blue Thumb ILPS 9203      HEAD KEEPER (LP) ......................................... 15

*(see also Hellions, Revolution, Traffic, Fox, Jaguars)*

## DAVE MASON & CASS ELLIOT
71   Probe PRO 513      Something To Make You Happy/Next To You (as Mason & Cass, special sleeve) ... 6
71   Probe SPBA 6259      DAVE MASON AND CASS ELLIOT (LP, gatefold sleeve, pink label) ... 15

*(see also Dave Mason, Mama Cass [Elliot])*

## GLEN MASON
56   Parlophone MSP 6240      Hot Diggity (Dog Ziggity Boom)/Baby Girl Of Mine ... 8
56   Parlophone R 4203      Love, Love, Love/Glendora ................................. 8
56   Parlophone R 4244      The Green Door/Why Must You Go, Go, Go ......... 8
57   Parlophone R 4271      Don't Forbid Me/Amore ................................. 6
57   Parlophone R 4291      Round And Round/Walking And Whistling ......... 6
57   Parlophone R 4334      Crying My Heart Out For You/Why Don't They Understand ... 5
57   Parlophone R 4357      By My Side/By The Fireside ............................ 5
58   Parlophone R 4390      What A Beautiful Combination/I'm Alone Because I Love You ... 7
58   Parlophone R 4415      I May Never Pass This Way Again/A Moment Ago ... 6
58   Parlophone R 4451      I Know Where I'm Going/Autumn Souvenir ......... 6
58   Parlophone R 4485      The End/Fall In Love ................................... 5
59   Parlophone R 4562      The Battle Of New Orleans/I Don't Know ......... 8
60   Parlophone R 4626      You Got What It Takes/If There's Someone ....... 6
60   Parlophone R 4723      That's What I Want!/I Like It When It Rains ...... 6
61   Parlophone R 4834      Don't Move/Shadrack .................................. 6
62   Parlophone R 4900      St. Louis Blues/That's Life ........................... 6

MINT VALUE £

**HARVEY MASON**
| | | | |
|---|---|---|---|
| 77 | Arista ARIST 12188 | Till You Take My Love/What's Going On (12") | 10 |
| 81 | Arista 399 | How's It Feel/On And On | 5 |

**MARLIN MASON**
| | | | |
|---|---|---|---|
| 56 | Vogue Coral Q 72168 | Don't Throw My Love Away/The Mystery Of Love | 10 |

**NICK MASON (& RICK FENN)**
| | | | |
|---|---|---|---|
| 85 | Harvest HAR 5238 | Lie For A Lie/And The Address (with Rick Fenn, p/s) | 5 |

*(see also Pink Floyd, 10cc)*

**SPENCER MASON**
| | | | |
|---|---|---|---|
| 67 | Parlophone R 5555 | Flugel In Carnaby Street/Albuferia | 10 |

**MASONICS**
| | | | |
|---|---|---|---|
| 91 | Hangman HANG 43 UP | MASONICS (LP) | 20 |

*(see also Milkshakes)*

**MASQUERADERS**
| | | | |
|---|---|---|---|
| 68 | Bell BLL 1032 | I Ain't Got To Love Nobody Else/I Got It | 10 |
| 70 | Now! NOW 1001 | Love Peace And Understanding/Tell Me You Love Me | 10 |
| 05 | Grapevine 2000 G2K 157 | That's The Same Thing/How Big Is Big (reissue) | 8 |

*(see also Lester Tipton)*

**MASS**
| | | | |
|---|---|---|---|
| 80 | 4AD AD 14 | You And I/Cabbage (with poster insert in die-cut sleeve) | 25 |
| 80 | 4AD AD 14 | You And I/Cabbage (in die-cut sleeve) | 12 |
| 81 | 4AD CAD 107 | LABOUR OF LOVE (LP, with inner sleeve) | 15 |

*(see also Models, Rema-Rema, Wolfgang Press)*

**MASSIEL**
| | | | |
|---|---|---|---|
| 68 | Philips BF 1667 | La La La/He Gives Me Love (La La La) | 7 |

**MASSIVE ATTACK**
| | | | |
|---|---|---|---|
| 88 | Massive Attack MASS 001 | Any Love/Any Love (Bonus)Any Love (Instrumental)/Any Love (Acapella) (12", stickered plain black die-cut sleeve) | 12 |
| 91 | Wild Bunch WBRT 2 | Unfinished Sympathy/Instrumental (12", p/s, as MASSIVE) | 15 |
| 91 | Wild Bunch WBRR 2 | Unfinished Sympathy (Nellee Hooper 12" Mix)/ (Nellee Hooper Instrumental Mix)/(Original) (12", p/s) | 15 |
| 91 | Wild Bunch WBRR 3 | Safe From Harm (7" Version)/(Original)/(Perfecto Mix) (12", p/s) | 10 |
| 91 | Wild Bunch WBRR 3 | Safe From Harm (Perfecto Mix)/(Just A Dub)/(Instrumental) (12") | 10 |
| 92 | Wild Bunch WBRT 4 | MASSIVE ATTACK EP (Hymn Of The Big Wheel (Nellee Hooper Mix)/Home Of The Whale/Be Thankful (Paul Oakenfold Mix)/Any Love (Larry Heard Mix) (12") | 10 |
| 95 | Wild Bunch WBRT 7 | Karmacoma: (Portishead Experience)/(The Napoli Trip)/U.N.K.L.E. Situation)/(Blacksmith Daydreaming) (12") | 10 |
| 98 | Wild Bunch WBRLH 9 | Teardrop/Euro Zero Zero (jukebox issue) | 15 |
| 98 | Circa MASBOX 2 | SINGLES 90/98 (11 x 12" singles in numbered heat sensitive box) | 80 |
| 09 | Vinyl Factory VF 006 | SPLITTING THE ATOM EP (12", numbered p/s. 180 gram vinyl, 1000 only) | 35 |
| 11 | Vinyl Factory | Four Walls/Paradise Circus (12" as Massive Attack V Burial, silk-screened glitter sleeve, 1000 only) | 100 |
| 91 | Wild Bunch WBRLP1 | BLUE LINES (LP, as Massive) | 20 |
| 94 | Wild Bunch WBRLP2 | PROTECTION (LP) | 20 |
| 96 | Wild Bunch WBRLP3 | NO PROTECTION (LP) | 30 |
| 98 | Wild Bunch WBRLP4 | MEZZANINE (2-LP) | 40 |
| 03 | Virgin V2967 | 100th WINDOW (3-LP, gatefold) | 30 |

**MASSIVE DREAD**
| | | | |
|---|---|---|---|
| 79 | His Majesty HM 1001 | MASSIVE DREAD (LP) | 30 |

**MASTER SINGERS**
| | | | |
|---|---|---|---|
| 66 | Parlophone R 5428 | The Highway Code/Rumbletum Song | 5 |
| 66 | Parlophone R 5523 | Weather Forecast/Roadilore | 5 |

**MASTERFLEET**
| | | | |
|---|---|---|---|
| 73 | Sussex LPSX 5 | HIGH ON THE SEA (LP) | 25 |

**MASTERMINDS**
| | | | |
|---|---|---|---|
| 65 | Immediate IM 005 | She Belongs To Me/Taken My Love | 40 |

*(see also Badfinger)*

**MASTERPLAN**
| | | | |
|---|---|---|---|
| 78 | Satril SAT 136 | Love Crazy (Theme From 'Carry On Emmanuel')/Since I've Been Away From My Love (p/s) | 10 |

**CARL MASTERS**
| | | | |
|---|---|---|---|
| 72 | Big Shot BI 604 | Va Va Voom/GOD SONS: Rebel | 15 |

*(see also Max Romeo, Dennis Alcapone)*

**SAMMY MASTERS**
| | | | |
|---|---|---|---|
| 60 | Warner Bros WB 10 | Rockin' Red Wing/Lonely Weekend | 25 |
| 60 | Warner Bros WB 10 | Rockin' Red Wing/Lonely Weekend (78) | 100 |
| 65 | London HLR 9949 | I Fought The Law (And The Law Won)/Big Man Cried | 15 |

**VALERIE MASTERS**
| | | | |
|---|---|---|---|
| 58 | Fontana H 132 | Sharing/The Secret Of Happiness | 6 |
| 58 | Fontana H 145 | (Well-a, Well-a) Ding-Dong/Merci Beaucoup | 6 |
| 59 | Fontana H 175 | Dreams End At Dawn/Wonder | 6 |
| 59 | Fontana H 195 | Jack O' Diamonds/Say When | 6 |
| 59 | Fontana H 224 | If There Are Stars In My Eyes/Just Squeeze Me | 6 |
| 60 | Fontana H 238 | Oh, Gee/No One Understands | 6 |
| 60 | Fontana H 253 | Banjo Boy/Cow Cow Boogie | 6 |
| 60 | Fontana H 268 | Sweeter As The Day Goes By/Fools Fall In Love | 6 |
| 61 | Fontana H 293 | Too Late For Tears/I Got Rhythm | 6 |
| 62 | Fontana H 367 | African Waltz/All Night Long | 8 |
| 63 | HMV POP 1125 | The End Of The World/Sometime Kind Of Love | 10 |

| | | | |
|---|---|---|---|
| 64 | Columbia DB 7426 | Christmas Calling/He Didn't Fool Me | 50 |
| 65 | Polydor 56056 | It's Up To You/Next Train Out | 30 |
| 66 | Polydor 56135 | Don't Ever Go/Say Hello | 30 |

## MASTER'S APPRENTICES
| | | | |
|---|---|---|---|
| 71 | Regal Zonophone RZ 3031 | I'm Your Satisfier/Because I Love You | 35 |
| 71 | Regal Zono. SLRZ 1016 | MASTER'S APPRENTICES (LP, red/silver labels with no EMI logo) | 300 |
| 71 | Regal Zono. SLRZ 1022 | A TOAST TO PANAMA RED (LP, red/silver label with EMI logo) | 250 |

## MASTERS AT WORK
| | | | |
|---|---|---|---|
| 96 | Talkin' Loud 578795-1 | NUYORICAN SOUL (6-LP box set) | 30 |

## MASTERS OF REALITY
| | | | |
|---|---|---|---|
| 88 | Def American DEFA 1 | The Candy Song/The Blue Garden | 10 |
| 88 | Def American 838 474-1 | THE MASTERS OF REALITY (LP) | 20 |

## MASTERSTROKE
| | | | |
|---|---|---|---|
| 80s | DTS DTS 043 | Prisoner Of Love/Burning Heart (no p/s) | 75 |

## MASTERSWITCH
| | | | |
|---|---|---|---|
| 78 | Epic S EPC 6259 | Action Replay/Mass Media Meditation (no p/s) | 25 |

## MASTODON
| | | | |
|---|---|---|---|
| 11 | Warner Bros./Reprise 527517-7 | Just Got Paid/ZZ TOP: Just Got Paid (yellow vinyl, jukebox centre) | 6 |
| 12 | Roadrunner 5439 19780 0 | A Commotion/FEIST: Black Tongue | 8 |

## SUE MASUMA
| | | | |
|---|---|---|---|
| 83 | Dreams DR11/S83 CUS 1903 | Pain & Pleasure/Fallout Shelter (p/s) | 12 |

## MATADOR
| | | | |
|---|---|---|---|
| 71 | Big Shot BI 594 | Nyah Festival (actually "What Am I Living For" by Derrick Morgan)/Brixton Serenade | 12 |

## MATADORS
| | | | |
|---|---|---|---|
| 69 | Crab CRAB 27 | Death A Come (actually by Lloyd Robinson)/The Sword (actually "Zylon" by Lloyd Tyrell [Charmers]) | 20 |
| 70 | Camel CA 45 | Dark Of The Sun (actually by Jackie Mittoo)/Dreader Than Dread | 30 |
| 71 | Green Door GD 4017 | I'm Sorry (actually by Tony Brevett)/JOE WHITE: I'm Sorry Version | 10 |

*(see also Emotions, Little Roys, Ethiopians)*

## MATATA (AIR-FIESTA)
| | | | |
|---|---|---|---|
| 72 | President PT 380 | Wanna Do My Thing/Wild River | 20 |
| 73 | President PT 406 | I Feel Funky/I Want You | 20 |
| 74 | President PT 417 | Return To You/Something In Mind (as Matata) | 20 |
| 75 | President PT 438 | Good Good Understanding/Gimme Some Lovin' (as Matata) | 20 |
| 72 | President PTLS 1052 | MATATA: AIR FIESTA (LP) | 40 |
| 75 | President PTLS 1057 | INDEPENDENCE (LP) | 80 |

## MATAYO
| | | | |
|---|---|---|---|
| 75 | RAK RAK 222 | Matayo/I Like Rock 'N' Roll | 20 |

## MATCHBOX (1)
| | | | |
|---|---|---|---|
| 69 | Polydor 56327 | Run Much Faster/Every Little Thing She Does | 150 |

## MATCHBOX (2)
| | | | |
|---|---|---|---|
| 71 | Rak 113 | Don't Shut Me Out/Rod | 15 |

## MATCHBOX (3)
| | | | |
|---|---|---|---|
| 78 | Raw | Rock Rollin' Boogie/Troublesome Bay (p/s) | 15 |
| 79 | Magnet MAG 155 | Rockabilly Rebel/I Don't Wanna Boogie Alone (p/s) | 5 |
| 81 | Dawn DNS 1104 | Rock 'N' Roll Bank/Born To R 'N' R | 12 |

*(see also Cyclone)*

## MATCHING MOLE
| | | | |
|---|---|---|---|
| 72 | CBS 8101 | O Caroline/Signed Curtain | 22 |
| 72 | CBS 64850 | MATCHING MOLE (LP) | 45 |
| 72 | CBS 65260 | MATCHING MOLE'S LITTLE RED RECORD (LP, with inner sleeve) | 50 |
| 79 | CBS 32105 | MATCHING MOLE (LP, reissue) | 15 |

*(see also Robert Wyatt, Soft Machine, Caravan, Hatfield & The North)*

## MATCHMAKERS
| | | | |
|---|---|---|---|
| 71 | Chapter One | BUBBLEGUM A GO GO (LP) | 25 |

*(see also Mark Wirtz, Philwit & Pegasus, Fickle Finger)*

## MATHAMATIQUES MODERNES
| | | | |
|---|---|---|---|
| 82 | Celluoid ILPS 9690 | MATHAMATIQUES MODERN (LP) | 20 |

## MATHETAI
| | | | |
|---|---|---|---|
| 77 | Cavs CAV 017 | KNOWING (LP) | 50 |

## JODI MATHIS
| | | | |
|---|---|---|---|
| 75 | Capitol CL 15827 | Mama/Don't You Care Anymore | 10 |
| 75 | Capitol CL 15827 | Mama/Don't You Care Anymore (DJ Copy) | 20 |

## MATIC 16
| | | | |
|---|---|---|---|
| 82 | Music Hive (No cat. No) | Jahovah/Ten Man (12") | 45 |
| 82 | Regent RGTDS 1001 | No Money Today/Matic Rock (12") | 40 |

## MATRIX RISE
| | | | |
|---|---|---|---|
| 92 | Mutant 12 MUTATE 6 | D.O.Y.L.E. Factor/Reality (12") | 25 |
| 92 | Mutant 12 MUTATE 8 | Moments Of Pleasure/The Preacher (12") | 40 |

## AL MATTHEWS
| | | | |
|---|---|---|---|
| 75 | CBS 3429 | Fool/Don't Run From My Love | 8 |
| 78 | Electric Co 23 | Run To You/People Are People | 15 |

## IAN MATTHEWS
| | | | |
|---|---|---|---|
| 71 | Vertigo 6059041 | Hearts/Little Knows | 12 |
| 73 | Elektra K 12111 | These Days/Same Old Man | 7 |

MINT VALUE £

| 71 | Vertigo 6360 034 | IF YOU SAW THRO' MY EYES (LP, 1st pressing textured gatefold sleeve, large swirl label) .................................................................................................................... 150 |
| 71 | Vertigo 6360 034 | IF YOU SAW THRO' MY EYES (LP, 2nd LP textured gatefold sleeve, small swirl label) ..... 40 |
| 72 | Vertigo 6360 056 | TIGERS WILL SURVIVE (LP, textured gatefold sleeve, small swirl label) ........................ 150 |
| 73 | Elektra K 42144 | VALLEY HI (LP, textured gatefold sleeve, 'butterfly' label) .......................................... 30 |
| 74 | Elektra K 42160 | SOME DAYS YOU EAT THE BEAR, SOME DAYS THE BEAR EATS YOU (LP) ........................ 20 |
| 74 | Mooncrest CREST 18 | JOURNEYS FROM GOSPEL OAK (LP) .............................................................................. 20 |
| 76 | CBS 81316 | GO FOR BROKE (LP) ....................................................................................................... 18 |

*(see also Pyramid, Fairport Convention, Matthews Southern Comfort, Plainsong, Hi-Fi)*

## JOE MATTHEWS
| 68 | Sue WI 4046 | Sorry Ain't Good Enough/You Better Mend Your Ways ................................................ 90 |
| 98 | Wigan Casino 202 | She's My Beauty Queen/JACKIE BEAVERS: I Need My Baby (p/s, reissue) .................... 8 |

## MILT MATTHEWS
| 75 | London HLF 10479 | All These Changes/When Kids Rule The World ............................................................... 8 |

## RANDY MATTHEWS
| 70s | Myrrh MXX 1035 | NOW DO YOU UNDERSTAND (LP, gatefold sleeve)........................................................ 25 |

## TOBIN MATTHEWS
| 63 | Warner Brothers WB 117 | Can't Stop Talking About You/When You Came Along...................................................... 6 |

## WINSTON MATTHEWS
| 71 | Banana BA 329 | Sun Is Shining/INN KEEPERS: My Friend (B-side actually "The Pressure Is On" by Purpleites) ................................................................................................................... 18 |

## MATTHEWS SOUTHERN COMFORT
| 70 | Uni UNS 513 | Colorado Springs Eternal/The Struggle ...................................................................... 12 |
| 70 | Uni UNS 521 | Ballad Of Obray Ramsey/Parting ................................................................................. 7 |
| 70 | Uni UNS 526 | Woodstock/Scion ......................................................................................................... 5 |
| 70 | Uni UNLS 108 | MATTHEWS SOUTHERN COMFORT (LP, gatefold, lyric insert, yellow swirl label) ......... 40 |
| 70 | Uni UNLS 112 | SECOND SPRING (LP, textured sleeve, lyric insert, yellow swirl label).......................... 30 |
| 70 | Uni MKPS 2015 | LATER THAT SAME YEAR... (LP, red/pink 'dogbone' label) ............................................ 20 |

*(see also Ian Matthews, Marc Ellington, Southern Comfort)*

## MATTHIAS
| 74 | Decca F13545 | Deep Down Under/I Hear A Song .................................................................................. 12 |

## MATUMBI
| 73 | G.G. GG 4540 | Brother Louie Parts 1 & 2 ............................................................................................. 10 |
| 77 | Matumbi Music Corp. MA004 | Music In The Air/Guide Us (12") .................................................................................. 40 |
| 78 | Matumbi Music MR 86 | After Tonight/Take It From Me (12") ............................................................................ 30 |
| 78 | EMI SHSP 4090 | SEVEN SEALS (LP, red/black label with inner, some on green vinyl) ............................. 15 |
| 80 | Extinguish MR 007 | DUB PLANET ORBIT 1 (LP) .......................................................................................... 200 |

## HARVEY MATUSOW'S JEWS HARP BAND
| 69 | Head HDS 4004 | Afghan Red/Wet Socks ................................................................................................... 8 |
| 69 | Head HDLS 6001 | WAR BETWEEN THE FATS & THE THINS (LP) ............................................................... 40 |

## MAUDS
| 67 | Mercury MF 1000 | Hold On/C'mon And Move ............................................................................................ 10 |
| 67 | Philips BL 7791 | HEY, LOOK ME OVER (LP) ............................................................................................. 25 |

## SUSAN MAUGHAN
| 61 | Philips BF 1216 | Mama Do The Twist/Blue Night In Yokohama ............................................................ 10 |
| 62 | Philips BF 1236 | Baby Doll Twist/Some Of These Days .......................................................................... 10 |
| 62 | Philips 326 533BF | I've Got To Learn To Forget/I Didn't Mean What I Said .............................................. 10 |
| 62 | Philips 326 544BF | Bobby's Girl/Come A Little Closer ................................................................................ 10 |
| 63 | Philips 326 562BF | Hand A Handkerchief To Helen/I'm A Lonely One Too ................................................. 6 |
| 63 | Philips 326 586BF | She's New To You/Don't Get Carried Away .................................................................... 6 |
| 63 | Philips BF 1266 | The Verdict Is Guilty/Bachelor Girl .............................................................................. 6 |
| 64 | Philips BF 1301 | Hey Lover/Stop Your Foolin' ......................................................................................... 5 |
| 64 | Philips BF 1336 | Kiss Me Sailor/Call On Me ............................................................................................ 6 |
| 64 | Philips BF 1363 | Little Things Mean A Lot/That Other Place .................................................................. 12 |
| 64 | Philips BF 1382 | Make Him Mine/South American Joe ........................................................................... 6 |
| 65 | Philips BF 1399 | You Can Never Get Away From You/Don't Be Afraid ..................................................... 6 |
| 65 | Philips BF 1417 | When She Walks Away/Come Along Down And See ....................................................... 6 |
| 65 | Philips BF 1445 | Poor Boy/Your Girl ........................................................................................................ 6 |
| 66 | Philips BF 1495 | Come And Get Me/Don't Love Him Too Much ............................................................... 6 |
| 66 | Philips BF 1518 | Where The Bullets Fly/I'll Never Stop Loving You .......................................................... 5 |
| 67 | Philips BF 1564 | Don't Go Home (My Little Darlin')/Somebody To Love ................................................. 6 |
| 68 | Philips PF 1679 | I Remember Loving You/Why Don't You Say You Love Me ............................................. 8 |
| 68 | Philips BF 1713 | Cable Car For Two/Off My Mind ................................................................................... 5 |
| 69 | Philips BF 1824 | We Really Go Together/I'll Never Forget You ............................................................... 5 |
| 62 | Philips BBE 12525 | HI, I'M SUSAN MAUGHAN AND I SING (EP) ................................................................. 10 |
| 63 | Philips BBE 12549 | FOUR BEAUX AND A BELLE (EP) .................................................................................. 10 |
| 62 | Philips 433 621 BE | EFFERVESCENT MISS MAUGHAN (EP) ......................................................................... 10 |
| 63 | Philips 433 641 BE | MORE OF MAUGHAN (EP) ........................................................................................... 10 |
| 63 | Philips 632 300 BL | I WANNA BE BOBBY'S GIRL BUT ... (LP) ...................................................................... 25 |
| 64 | Philips BL 7577 | SWINGIN' SUSAN (LP) .................................................................................................. 20 |
| 65 | Philips BL 7637 | SENTIMENTAL SUSAN (LP) .......................................................................................... 20 |

## MAU-MAUS
| 82 | Pax PAX 6 | SOCIETY'S REJECTS (EP, black or blue sleeve) ............................................................. 15 |
| 82 | Pax PAX 8 | No Concern/Clampdown/Why Do We Suffer (p/s)........................................................ 15 |
| 83 | Pax/Paragon PAX 12 | FACTS OF WAR (EP) ..................................................................................................... 15 |
| 85 | Rebellion REBEL 701 | TEAR DOWN THE WALLS (EP) ...................................................................................... 15 |
| 85 | Rebellion REBEL 1202 | NOWHERE TO RUN (12" EP) ........................................................................................ 15 |
| 83 | Pax PAX 16 | LIVE AT THE MARPLES (LP)........................................................................................... 20 |

| | | |
|---|---|---:|
| 84 | Pax PAX 20 | RUNNING WITH THE PACK (LP) ........................................ 25 |
| 85 | Rebellion REBLP01 | FEAR NO EVIL (LP) .................................................. 15 |

**MAUREENY WISHFULL**
| | | |
|---|---|---:|
| 68 | Moonshine WO 2388 | THE MAUREENY WISHFULL ALBUM (LP, 300 copies, beware of counterfeits) ............ 100 |

*(see also Jimmy Page, Big Jim Sullivan, John Williams)*

**MAURICE & MAC**
| | | |
|---|---|---:|
| 68 | Chess CRS 8074 | You Left The Water Running/You're The One .................................... 12 |
| 68 | Chess CRS 8081 | Why Don't You Try Me/Lean On Me ............................................ 12 |

*(see also Radiants)*

**JOHN MAUS**
| | | |
|---|---|---:|
| 11 | Upset The Rhythm UTR049 | WE MUST BECOME THE PITILESS CENSORS OF OURSELVES (LP, blue vinyl with CD, 100 only) ........................... 30 |
| 11 | Upset The Rhythm UTR049 | WE MUST BECOME THE PITILESS CENSORS OF OURSELVES (LP, clear vinyl with CD) ...... 20 |

**MAWAMBA DUB**
| | | |
|---|---|---:|
| 78 | Warrior DRLP 1001 | MAWANDA DUB (LP) ............................................... 60 |

*(see also Dennis Bovell, Alton Ellis)*

**MAX**
| | | |
|---|---|---:|
| 74 | Caroline C1506 | MAX (LP, black Virgin inner, black/red 'Twin' label, artist is Max Handley) ............... 20 |

**MAX & ELAINE**
| | | |
|---|---|---:|
| 73 | Ackee ACK 516 | I'm Leaving/Version ................................................... 5 |

*(see also Max Romeo)*

**MAX & GREGORY**
| | | |
|---|---|---:|
| 73 | Ackee ACK 525 | My Jamaican Collie/Push It Down, Rub It Up .................................. 7 |

*(see also Max Romeo)*

**MAX GROUP**
| | | |
|---|---|---:|
| 69 | Fab FAB 110 | Abraham Vision/My Heart Was Breaking ...................................... 5 |

**MAX HEADROOM & CARPARKS**
| | | |
|---|---|---:|
| 80 | Parlophone R 6034 | Don't Panic/Rhythm And Bluebeat (p/s) ...................................... 6 |
| 82 | Bandwagon B001 | Soldier (no p/s) ..................................................... 20 |

**PAT MAX AND THE SPECIALISTS**
| | | |
|---|---|---:|
| 68 | Pye 7N 17470 | Too Much/Girl From New Orleans ........................................... 12 |

**SMILEY MAXEDON & HIS OKAW VALLEY BOYS**
| | | |
|---|---|---:|
| 54 | Columbia SCMC 3 | Crazy To Care/In The Window Of My Heart (export issue) ......................... 15 |

**JOE S. MAXEY**
| | | |
|---|---|---:|
| 73 | Action ACT 4607 | Sign Of The Crab/May The Best Man Win (actually plays Packers' "Hole In The Wall"/ "Go Ahead On") ......................... 20 |

**MAXI**
| | | |
|---|---|---:|
| 73 | Decca F 13394 | Do I Dream/Here Today And Gone Tomorrow .................................... 6 |

**MAXIE (ROMEO) & GLEN**
| | | |
|---|---|---:|
| 71 | G.G. GG 4520 | Jordan River (actually by Max Romeo & Glen Adams)/ GLEN ADAMS: Version Two ....... 10 |

*(see also Max Romeo, Ethiopians)*

**MAXIMILIAN**
| | | |
|---|---|---:|
| 61 | London HLX 9356 | The Snake/The Wanderer ................................................ 35 |

**MAXIMO PARK**
| | | |
|---|---|---:|
| 03 | Billingham Records | Graffiti/Going Missing (red vinyl, 500 only, p/s) ............................... 35 |
| 04 | Warp 7WAP 183 | The Coast Is Always Changing/The Night I Lost My Head (500 only, p/s) .............. 15 |
| 05 | Warp 7WAP 190 | Going Missing (1-sided 7" other side etched) ................................. 6 |

**MAXIM'S TRASH**
| | | |
|---|---|---:|
| 79 | Gimp GIMP 1 | Disco Girls/Blu Shoes (plastic p/s & inner, hand-stamped white labels, tracks actually recorded in 1975) ......................... 40 |

*(see also Sunset Boys, Captain Sensible, Johnny Moped)*

**MAXIMUM BAND**
| | | |
|---|---|---:|
| 68 | Fab FAB 51 | Cupid/Hold Me Tight .................................................. 12 |

**MAXIMUM BREED**
| | | |
|---|---|---:|
| 69 | Revolution REV 1 | Sitting In The Park/You've Got It .......................................... 5 |

**MAXIMUM JOY**
| | | |
|---|---|---:|
| 81 | Y 11 | Stretch/Silent Street (p/s) .............................................. 20 |
| 81 | Y Y 11 | Stretch/Silent Street (12", p/s) .......................................... 20 |
| 82 | Y Records Y 15 | White And Green Place/Building Bridges ..................................... 5 |
| 82 | Y Y 15 | White And Green Place/Building Bridges (12", p/s) ............................. 20 |
| 82 | Y 28 | STATION MXJY (LP) ................................................... 25 |

**ERNEST MAXIN**
| | | |
|---|---|---:|
| 59 | Top Rank JAR 267 | On The Beach/Take A Giant Step ........................................... 6 |
| 60 | Top Rank JAR 335 | Conspiracy Of Hearts/No Orchids For My Lady ................................. 6 |

**MAXINE**
| | | |
|---|---|---:|
| 70 | Smash SMA 2301 | My Boy Lollipop/Everybody Needs Love ...................................... 10 |

**BRIAN MAXINE**
| | | |
|---|---|---:|
| 72 | EMI Starline SRS 5140 | BRIAN MAXINE SINGS (LP) .............................................. 40 |
| 75 | Columbia SCX 6575 | RIBBON OF STAINLESS STEEL (LP) ........................................ 30 |

*(see also Fairport Convention)*

**HOLLY MAXWELL**
| | | |
|---|---|---:|
| 69 | Buddah 201 056 | Suffer/No-One Else ................................................... 10 |

**BRIAN MAY**
| | | |
|---|---|---:|
| 83 | EMI EMI 5436 | Starfleet (Single Version)/Son Of Starfleet (p/s) .............................. 15 |
| 91 | Parlophone RDJ 6304 | Driven By You (Edited Version)/(Pollarded Version)/(Special Version)/(Proper Version) (promo only, no stars on p/s) ......................... 70 |

MINT VALUE £

| 92 | Parlophone CDRS 6320 | Too Much Love Will Kill You (Album Version)/I'm Scared (Single Version)/Too Much Love Will Kill You (Guitar Version)/Driven By You (New Version) (CD, red circular gatefold card p/s) | |
| 92 | Parlophone RDJ 6329 | Back To The Light (Radio Version)/Nothin' But Blue (Guitar Version) (promo only, p/s) | 50 |
| 93 | Parlophone 0 7777 80400 19 | BACK TO THE LIGHT (LP, textured sleeve) | 15 |
| 98 | EMI 4949731 | ANOTHER WORLD (LP, picture disc, with inner sleeve) | 15 |

*(see also Queen, MC Spy-D & 'Friends', Eddie Howell, Holly Johnson, D-Rok, Ian & Belinda, Cozy Powell, Black Sabbath)*

## DERRICK MAY
| 90s | R&S TMT 2 | INNOVATOR (2xCD) | 25 |

## MARY MAY
| 63 | Fontana 267266TF | Our Day Will Come/But I Know Now | |
| 64 | Fontana TF 440 | Anyone Who Had A Heart/They Say It's Wonderful | 8 |
| | | | 10 |

## JOHN MAYALL (& BLUESBREAKERS)
### SINGLES
| 64 | Decca F 11900 | Crawling Up A Hill/Mr. James (as John Mayall & Blues Breakers) | 50 |
| 65 | Decca F 12120 | Crocodile Walk/Blues City Shakedown | 45 |
| 65 | Immediate IM 012 | I'm Your Witchdoctor/Telephone Blues | 60 |
| 66 | Purdah 45-3502 | Lonely Years/Bernard Jenkins (as John Mayall & Eric Clapton, 500 copies only) | 450 |
| 66 | Decca F 12490 | Parchman Farm (solo)/Key To Love (B-side with Bluesbreakers) | 30 |
| 66 | Decca F 12506 | Looking Back/So Many Roads (as John Mayall's Bluesbreakers & Peter Green) | 18 |
| 67 | Decca F 12545 | Sitting In The Rain/Out Of Reach (as John Mayall's Bluesbreakers) | 15 |
| 67 | Decca F 12588 | Curly/Rubber Duck (as Bluesbreakers) | 12 |
| 67 | Decca F 12621 | Double Trouble/It Hurts Me Too (as John Mayall's Bluesbreakers) | 20 |
| 67 | Immediate IM 051 | I'm Your Witchdoctor/Telephone Blues (reissue, as John Mayall with Eric Clapton) | 30 |
| 67 | Decca F 12684 | Suspicions (Parts 1 & 2) (as John Mayall's Bluesbreakers) | 15 |
| 68 | Decca F 12732 | Picture On The Wall/Jenny (as John Mayall) | 12 |
| 68 | Decca F 12792 | No Reply/She's Too Young (as John Mayall's Bluesbreakers) | 12 |
| 68 | Decca F 12846 | The Bear/2401 | 10 |
| 69 | Polydor 56544 | Don't Waste My Time/Don't Pick A Flower | 12 |
| 70 | Polydor 2066 021 | Thinking Of My Woman/Plan Your Revolution | 12 |
| 76 | Decca F12120 | Crocodile Walk/Blues City Shakedown (reissue, with boxed Decca logo, uninverted label matrix numbers, double A side) | 15 |

### EPs
| 67 | Decca DFE-R 8673 | THE BLUESBREAKERS WITH PAUL BUTTERFIELD (EP) | 60 |

### ALBUMS
| 65 | Decca LK 4680 | PLAYS JOHN MAYALL - LIVE AT KLOOKS KLEEK! | 120 |
| 66 | Decca LK 4804 | BLUES BREAKERS WITH ERIC CLAPTON (original label, mono, "Beano" cover) | 150 |
| 67 | Decca LK/SKL 4853 | A HARD ROAD (as John Mayall & Bluesbreakers) | 50 |
| 67 | Decca LK 4890 | CRUSADE (Mono, as John Mayall & Bluesbreakers) | 50 |
| 67 | Decca SKL 4890 | CRUSADE (Stereo, as John Mayall & Bluesbreakers) | 30 |
| 67 | Ace of Clubs ACL/SCL 1243 | THE BLUES ALONE (LP, "A Hard Road" on back cover) | 30 |
| 68 | Decca LK/SKL 4918 | THE DIARY OF A BAND VOL. 1 | 30 |
| 68 | Decca LK/SKL 4919 | THE DIARY OF A BAND VOL. 2 | 30 |
| 68 | Decca LK/SKL 4945 | BARE WIRES (gatefold sleeve, as John Mayall & Blues Breakers) | 30 |
| 68 | Decca LK/SKL 4972 | BLUES FROM LAUREL CANYON (LP, unboxed logo, gatefold sleeve) | 40 |

*(The Decca LPs listed above were originally issued with unboxed Decca label logos.)*

| 69 | Polydor 583 571 | THE TURNING POINT | 20 |
| 69 | Decca LK/SKL 5010 | LOOKING BACK (gatefold sleeve) | 25 |
| 70s | Decca LK 4804 | BLUES BREAKERS WITH ERIC CLAPTON (reissue, original label, stereo) | 40 |
| 71 | Decca LK 4804 | BLUES BREAKERS WITH ERIC CLAPTON (reissue, boxed logo, mono) | 20 |
| 71 | Decca SKL 4804 | BLUES BREAKERS WITH ERIC CLAPTON (reissue, boxed logo, stereo) | 15 |
| 70 | Polydor 583 580 | EMPTY ROOMS (with lyric insert) | 15 |
| 71 | Polydor 2657 005 | BACK TO THE ROOTS (2-LP) | 30 |
| 71 | Polydor 2483 016 | BEYOND THE TURNING POINT | 15 |
| 71 | Decca SKL 5086 | THRU THE YEARS | 25 |
| 71 | Polydor 2425 085 | MEMORIES | 15 |
| 72 | Polydor 2425 103 | JAZZ-BLUES FUSION | 15 |

*(see also Paul Butterfield, Eric Clapton, Jack Bruce, Peter Green, McGuinness Flint, Johnny Almond Music Machine, Alan Skidmore, Mick Taylor, Dick Heckstall-Smith, Keef Hartley, Paul Williams, Ray Warleigh, Colosseum, Henry Lowther, Jon Mark, Aynsley Dun)*

## MAYBERRY MOVEMENT
| 06 | Kent 6T 21 | I See Him Making Love To You/THE DEVONNES: Doin' The Gittin' Up | 20 |

## MAY BLITZ
| 70 | Vertigo 6360 007 | MAY BLITZ (LP, gatefold sleeve, large swirl label) | 350 |
| 71 | Vertigo 6360 037 | THE 2ND OF MAY (LP, gatefold sleeve, swirl label) | 450 |

*(see also Jeff Beck, Boxer, Sounds Inc.)*

## MAYDAY
| 80 | Reddingtons R.R. DAN 2 | Day After Day/Love In The Spaceage (p/s) | 20 |

## JOHN MAYER (GROUP)
| 66 | Columbia DB 8037 | Acka Raga (as John Mayer's I-J-7)/Gana (as John Mayer & Joe Harriott Quintet) | 15 |
| 60s | National Petrol W 1 | Music For People Who Go Your Own Way Themes 1 & 2 (p/s, with Frank Cordell) | 10 |
| 67 | Columbia SX 6122 | INDO-JAZZ FUSIONS (LP) | 35 |
| 69 | Sonet SNTF 603 | ETUDES (LP, as John Mayer Indo-Jazz Fusions) | 15 |

*(see also Joe Harriott & John Mayer, Radha Krishna)*

## NATHANIEL MAYER & FABULOUS TWILIGHTS
| 62 | HMV POP 1041 | Village Of Love/I Want A Woman | 50 |

## CURTIS MAYFIELD
| 70 | Buddah 2011 055 | (Don't Worry) If There's A Hell Below We're All Going To Go (Edit)/ The Makings Of You | 8 |

| | | | |
|---|---|---|---|
| 71 | Buddah 2011 080 | Move On Up/Give It Up/Beautiful Brother Of Mine (maxi-single) | 10 |
| 71 | Buddah 2011 101 | We Got To Have Peace/People Get Ready | 6 |
| 72 | Buddah 2011 119 | Keep On Keepin' On/Stone Junkie | 6 |
| 72 | Buddah 2011 141 | Freddie's Dead (Theme From "Superfly")/Underground | 6 |
| 72 | Buddah 2011 156 | Superfly/Give Me Your Love (Love Song) | 8 |
| 73 | Buddah 2011 187 | Back To The World (edit)/The Other Side Of Town | 6 |
| 74 | Buddah BDS 402 | Kung Fu/Right On For The Darkness | 6 |
| 74 | Buddah BDS 410 | Move On Up/Give It Up | 8 |
| 75 | Buddah BDS 426 | Mother's Son/Love Me Right In The Pocket | 6 |
| 71 | Buddah 2318 015 | CURTIS (LP, gatefold sleeve) | 25 |
| 71 | Buddah 2659 004 | CURTIS/LIVE (2-LP) | 20 |
| 72 | Buddah 2318 045 | ROOTS (LP, gatefold sleeve) | 18 |
| 72 | Buddah 2318 065 | SUPERFLY (LP, soundtrack, gatefold sleeve) | 15 |
| 73 | Buddah 2318 091 | CURTIS IN CHICAGO (LP, TV soundtrack, gatefold sleeve, with Impressions, Jerry Butler, Gene Chandler & Leroy Hutson) | 15 |
| 74 | Buddah BDLP 2001 | CURTIS/LIVE (2-LP, reissue) | 18 |
| 74 | Buddah BDLP 4010 | CLAUDINE (LP, soundtrack, with Gladys Knight) | 15 |

*(see also Impressions)*

## PERCY MAYFIELD
| | | | |
|---|---|---|---|
| 63 | HMV POP 1185 | The River's Invitation/Baby Please | 10 |
| 76 | Speciality SPE 5007 | Please Send Me Someone To Love/The River's Invitation | 6 |
| 67 | HMV CLP/CSD 3572 | MY JUG AND I (LP) | 40 |

## MAYFIELD'S MULE
| | | | |
|---|---|---|---|
| 69 | Parlophone R 5817 | Double Dealing Woman/(Drinking My) Moonshine (in p/s) | 30 |
| 69 | Parlophone R 5817 | Double Dealing Woman/(Drinking My) Moonshine | 15 |
| 70 | Parlophone R 5843 | I See A River/"Queen" Of Rock'n'Roll | 15 |
| 70 | Parlophone R 5858 | We Go Rollin'/My Way Of Living | 10 |

*(see also Elastic Band, Sweet, Amen Corner, Andy Scott)*

## MAYFLY
| | | | |
|---|---|---|---|
| 73 | Bumble GE 121 | It's Elusive/Orphan Girl | 10 |

## JUDY MAYHAN
| | | | |
|---|---|---|---|
| 71 | Atlantic 2466006 | MOMENTS (LP) | 15 |

## MAYHEM
| | | | |
|---|---|---|---|
| 82 | Riot City RIOT 13 | GENTLE MURDER EP | 10 |
| 83 | Riot City RIOT 24 | PULLING PUPPETS STRINGS EP | 15 |
| 85 | Vigilante VIG 1 | Bloodrush/Addictive Risk (p/s, lyric insert) | 10 |
| 85 | Vigilante VIG 1T | Bloodrush/Addictive Risk/I Defy (12", p/s) | 15 |
| 96 | Black Metal BMR 002 | Freezing Moon/Carnage (12", picture disc) | 20 |
| 97 | Misanthropy HH 666 | Ancient Skin/Necrolust (CD single in printed PVC sleeve, hand numbered insert, gig freebie, 500 only, beware of bootleg 7" singles of this) | 40 |
| 97 | Misanthropy Amazon 012 | WOLF'S LAIR ABYSS (LP) | 40 |
| 97 | Misanthropy AMAZON CPD 012 | WOLF'S LAIR ABYSS (LP, picture disc) | 50 |

## JENNY MAYNARD
| | | | |
|---|---|---|---|
| 68 | Inter-zel DR 001 | He Gives Me Love/Something Here In My Heart | 5 |

## (TOOTS &) THE MAYTALS
| | | | |
|---|---|---|---|
| 63 | Blue Beat BB 176 | Hallelujah/Helping Ages Past | 20 |
| 64 | Blue Beat BB 215 | He Is Real/Domino | 20 |
| 64 | Blue Beat BB 220 | Pain In My Belly/BUSTER'S ALL STARS: City Riot | 100 |
| 64 | Blue Beat BB 231 | Dog War/RECO & CREATORS: I'll Be Home | 70 |
| 64 | Blue Beat BB 245 | Little Slea (song actually "Little Flea")/Don't Talk (song actually Pain In My Belly) (both sides miscredited as V. Maytals) | 25 |
| 64 | Blue Beat BB 254 | Sweet Love/PRINCE BUSTER: Wings Of A Dove | 35 |
| 64 | Blue Beat BB 255 | Judgement Day/Goodbye Jane | 20 |
| 64 | Blue Beat BB 270 | You've Got Me Spinning/Lovely Walking | 40 |
| 64 | R&B JB 130 | Hurry Up/Love Divide | 20 |
| 64 | R&B JB 141 | Another Chance/FRANKIE ANDERSON: Always On A Sunday | 20 |
| 64 | R&B JB 153 | Give Me Your Love/He Will Provide | 20 |
| 64 | R&B JB 164 | Hello Honey/ROLAND ALPHONSO: Crime Wave | 50 |
| 64 | R&B JB 174 | Christmas Feelings/Let's Kiss | 50 |
| 65 | Blue Beat BB 281 | Looking Down The Street/PRINCE BUSTER: Blues Market | 50 |
| 65 | Blue Beat BB 299 | Light Of The World/Lovely Walking | 30 |
| 65 | Blue Beat BB 306 | Ska War (song actually "Treating Me Bad")/SKATALITES: Perhaps | 90 |
| 65 | Ska Beat JB 202 | Let's Jump/Joy And Jean | 25 |
| 65 | Island WI 200 | Never You Change/What's On Your Mind | 25 |
| 65 | Island WI 213 | My New Name/It's No Use | 25 |
| 65 | Black Swan WI 464 | John James/THEO BECKFORD: Sailing On | 40 |
| 66 | Doctor Bird DB 1019 | If You Act This Way/SIR LORD COMIC & HIS COWBOYS: Ska-ing West | 40 |
| 66 | Doctor Bird DB 1038 | Bam Bam/So Mad In Love (with Byron Lee and the Dragoniares) | 35 |
| 68 | Pyramid PYR 6030 | 54-46, That's My Number/ROLAND ALPHONSO: Dreamland | 30 |
| 68 | Pyramid PYR 6043 | Struggle/ROLAND ALPHONSO: Stream Of Life | 45 |
| 68 | Pyramid PYR 6048 | Just Tell Me/Reborn | 20 |
| 68 | Pyramid PYR 6050 | Bim Today, Bam Tomorrow/Hold On | 25 |
| 68 | Pyramid PYR 6052 | We Shall Overcome/DESMOND DEKKER & ACES: Fu Manchu | 100 |
| 68 | Pyramid PYR 6055 | Schooldays/Big Man | 20 |
| 68 | Pyramid PYR 6056 | Ben Johnson Day/MAYTALS: Ain't Got No Tip | 100 |
| 68 | Pyramid PYR 6057 | Do The Reggay/BEVERLEY'S ALLSTARS: Motoring | 40 |
| 68 | Pyramid PYR 6064 | Scare Him/In My Heart | 20 |
| 69 | Pyramid PYR 6066 | Don't Trouble Trouble/BEVERLEY'S ALLSTARS: Double Action | 20 |

Rare Record Price Guide 2018

| | | | MINT VALUE £ |
|---|---|---|---|
| 69 | Pyramid PYR 6070 | Aldina/Hold On | 30 |
| 69 | Pyramid PYR 6073 | Pressure Drop/BEVERLEY'S ALLSTARS: Express | 30 |
| 69 | Pyramid PYR 6074 | Sweet And Dandy/Oh Yeah | 20 |
| 69 | Trojan TR 7709 | Pressure Drop/BEVERLEY'S ALLSTARS: Smoke Screen | 25 |
| 69 | Nu Beat NB 031 | My Testimony/JOHNSON BOYS: One Dollar Of Soul (actually by Ethiopians) | 20 |
| 69 | Trojan TR 7711 | Monkey Man/Night And Day | 25 |
| 70 | Trojan TR 7726 | Sweet And Dandy/54-46, That's My Number | 16 |
| 70 | Trojan TR 7741 | Bla Bla Bla/Reborn | 15 |
| 70 | Trojan TR 7757 | Water Melon/She's My Scorcher | 15 |
| 70 | Trojan TR 7786 | Doctor Lester/Sun, Moon And Star | 18 |
| 70 | Summit SUM 8510 | Peeping Tom/BEVERLEY'S ALLSTARS: Version | 15 |
| 71 | Trojan TR 7808 | 54-46 Was My Number/BEVERLEY'S ALLSTARS: 54-46 Instrumental | 15 |
| 71 | Trojan TR 7849 | Johnny Cool Man/BEVERLEY's ALLSTARS: Version | 20 |
| 71 | Summit SUM 8513 | Monkey Girl/BEVERLEY'S ALLSTARS: Version | 8 |
| 71 | Summit SUM 8520 | One Eye Enos/BEVERLEY'S ALLSTARS: Enos Version | 20 |
| 71 | Summit SUM 8527 | It's You/BEVERLEY'S ALLSTARS: Version | 10 |
| 71 | Summit SUM 8529 | Walk With Love/BEVERLEY'S ALLSTARS: Version | 10 |
| 71 | Summit SUM 8533 | Never You Change/BEVERLEY'S ALLSTARS: Version | 10 |
| 72 | Attack ATT 8042 | It Was Written Down/Sweet And Dandy | 10 |
| 72 | Summit SUM 8536 | Thy Kingdom Come/BEVERLEY'S ALLSTARS: Version | 10 |
| 72 | Summit SUM 8537 | It Must Be True Love/BEVERLEY'S ALLSTARS: Version | 10 |
| 72 | Blue Mountain BM 1020 | Christmas Song/I Can't Believe | 10 |
| 72 | Dynamic DYN 438 | Redemption Song | 10 |
| 72 | Trojan TR 7865 | Louie Louie/Pressure Drop '72 | 10 |
| 73 | Dragon DRA 1007 | Sit Right Down/Screwface Underground/Pomps & Pride (as Toots & Maytals) | 20 |
| 73 | Dragon DRA 1013 | Country Road/Funky Kingston (as Toots & Maytals) | 8 |
| 73 | Dragon DRA 1016 | In The Dark/Sailing On (as Toots & Maytals) | 30 |
| 74 | Dragon DRA 1021 | Fever/It Was Written Down | 7 |
| 74 | Dragon DRA 1024 | Time Tough/Time Tough Version | 7 |
| 74 | Dragon DRA 1026 | Sailing On/If You Act This Way (as Toots & Maytals) | 7 |
| 80 | Island 1EP 11 DJ | Pressure Drop (1-sided promo) | 20 |
| 80 | Island 1EP 11 | Pressure Drop/54 46 Was My Number/Stick It Up Mister/Time Tough EP | 12 |
| 11 | Beverlys THB 7008 | Do The Boogaloo/Bim Today Bam Tomorrow | 15 |
| 13 | Island WI 3162 | Monkey Man/She's My Scorcher | 8 |
| 64 | Ska Beat JBL 1113 | PRESENTING THE MAYTALS (NEVER GROW OLD) (LP) | 300 |
| 66 | Doctor Bird DLM 5003 | THE SENSATIONAL MAYTALS (LP) | 300 |
| 70 | Trojan TBL 107 | MONKEY MAN (LP, laminated front cover) | 50 |
| 73 | Trojan TRLS 65 | FROM THE ROOTS (LP) | 35 |
| 73 | Dragon DRLS 5002 | FUNKY KINGSTON (LP) | 15 |
| 74 | Dragon DRLS 5004 | IN THE DARK (LP) | 25 |
| 74 | Prince Buster PB 11 | ORIGINAL GOLDEN OLDIES VOLUME 3 (LP) | 20 |
| 77 | State ETAT16 | TOOTS PRESENTS THE MAYTALS (LP) | 15 |

(see also Vikings, Flames, Philip James & Blues Busters, Don Drummond, Stranger, Lord Creator, Larry Marshall, Derrick Morgan, Brentwood Road Allstars, Roland Alphonso, Charmers)

## MAYTONES

| 68 | Blue Cat BS 149 | Billy Goat/Call You Up | 100 |
|---|---|---|---|
| 69 | Blue Cat BS 152 | Loving Reggae/Musical Beat | 60 |
| 69 | Blue Cat BS 166 | Copper Girl/Love | 80 |
| 69 | Blue Cat BS 173 | We Nah Tek You Lick/Dig Away De Money | 80 |
| 69 | Camel CA 27 | Sentimental Reason/Lover Girl | 30 |
| 69 | Songbird SB 1009 | I've Been Loving You/Memphis Reggae | 10 |
| 70 | Punch PH 35 | Serious Love/CHARLIE ACE: Musical Combination | 10 |
| 70 | Explosion EX 2012 | Funny Man/G.G. ALLSTARS: Champion | 20 |
| 70 | Explosion EX 2013 | Sentimental Reason/Lover Girl | 7 |
| 70 | Explosion EX 2014 | Barrabus/G.G. ALLSTARS: Barrabus Part 2 (B-side actually "This Kind Of Life") | 60 |
| 70 | Explosion EX 2027 | Cecelia (actually by Keeling Beckford)/Chariot Without Horse (B-side actually "Willie My Darling") | 10 |
| 70 | Explosion EX 2033 | Another Festival/Happy Time | 10 |
| 70 | Bullet BU 446 | I Don't Like To Interfere/Preaching Love | 8 |
| 70 | Camel CA 47 | Black And White/GLORIA'S ALLSTARS: Jumbo Jet | 15 |
| 70 | Camel CA 49 | Since You Left/GLORIA'S ALL STARS: Bird Wing | 20 |
| 71 | Duke DU 116 | Babylon A Fall/TONY KING: Version Buggy | 15 |
| 71 | Camel CA 61 | Judas (actually by Gladstone Anderson & Followers)/Mi Nah Tek | 15 |
| 71 | Camel CA 63 | Cleanliness/Sister Hold On | 20 |
| 71 | G.G. GG 4508 | Cleanliness/G.G. ALL STARS: Cleanliness Version 2 | 10 |
| 71 | G.G. GG 4511 | Let The Version Play/Lonely Nights | 10 |
| 71 | G.G. GG 4522 | Black And White/TREVOR BROWN: Mr. Brown | 10 |
| 71 | G.G. GG 4525 | Bongo Man Rise/ROY & BIM: Remember | 10 |
| 72 | G.G. GG 4530 | Donkey Face/G.G. ALL STARS: Donkey Face - Version | 10 |
| 72 | G.G. GG 4531 | As Long As You Love Me (Side One)/As Long As You Love Me (Side Two) | 10 |
| 72 | Attack ATT 8029 | Hands And Feet/LLOYD & CAREY: Scorpion | 10 |
| 72 | Grape GR 3028 | If Loving You Was Wrong/FLOWERS & ALVIN: In De Pum Pum | 10 |
| 72 | Pama PM 846 | I'm Feeling Lonely/G.G. ALLSTARS: Version | 10 |
| 72 | Explosion EX 2076 | Brown Girl/SHORTY PERRY: Half-Way-Tree Rock | 10 |
| 73 | Pama PM 871 | All Over The World People Are Changing/Changing World (Dubwise) | 8 |
| 73 | Bread BR 1114 | All Over The World People Are Changing/Changing World (Dubwise) | 5 |
| 73 | Bullet BU 528 | People Get Funny/G.G. ALL STARS: Version | 7 |
| 77 | GG's GG 021 | Money Trouble (with I Roy)/GG'S ALL STARS: Dub Part Two (12") | 20 |
| 82 | Burning Sounds BS 1052 | BEST OF (LP) | 15 |

*(see also Vern & Alvin, Vern & Son, Roland Alphonso, G.G. Rhythm Section, Cynthia Richards, Max Romeo, Charlie Ace, Dennis Alcapone)*

## MAZE (U.K.)
| 66 | Reaction 591 009 | Hello Stranger/Telephone | 100 |
| 67 | MGM MGM 1368 | Catari Catari/Easy Street | 40 |

*(see also M.I. Five, Deep Purple, Paice, Ashton & Lord)*

## MAZZY STAR
| 93 | Rough Trade Singles Club 45 | Five String Serenade/Under My Car (p/s) | 10 |
| | rev 19 | | |
| 94 | Capitol 10CL720 | Fade Into You/Five String Serenade/Under My Car/ Bells Ring (Acoustic) (10" p/s) | 30 |
| 96 | Capitol CL 781 | FLOWERS IN DECEMBER (EP, blue vinyl) | 15 |
| 90 | Rough Trade ROUGH 158 | SHE HANGS BRIGHTLY (LP) | 60 |
| 93 | Capitol EST2206 | SO TONIGHT THAT I MIGHT SEE (LP) | 70 |
| 96 | Capitol 8272241 | AMONG MY SWAN (LP) | 50 |

## M.B.C. BAND AND CHICHIRI QUEENS
| 73 | Ng Omo MBC 002 | Angwazi Kawiri-Kawiri | 20 |
| 74 | Ng Omo MWLP 1 | KOKOLIKO KU MALAWI (LP) | 50 |

## M.B.P. MIX
| 69 | Major Minor MM66 | Light My Fire/There's A Baby | 30 |

## MC FYRE
| 88 | DTI MAC 3 | It's My Rhythm/Kold Rockin' The Crowd (12") | 40 |

## MCALMONT AND BUTLER
| 95 | Hut HUTLP 32 | THE SOUND OF...MCALMONT AND BUTLER (LP, inner) | 20 |

*(see also Bernard Butler, Suede)*

## WINSTON MCANUFF
| 79 | Third World | I Love Jah/FREDDIE McGREGOR : Massachusetts (12") | 30 |

## JACKIE MCAULEY
| 71 | Dawn DNS 1011 | Turning Green/It's Alright | 8 |
| 72 | Dawn DNS 1020 | Rocking Shoes/One Fine Day | 7 |
| 71 | Dawn DNLS 3023 | JACKIE McAULEY (LP, gatefold sleeve) | 150 |

*(see also Them, Belfast Gypsies, Trader Horne, Freaks Of Nature)*

## MCAULEY SCHENKER GROUP
| 90 | EMI EMPD 127 | Anytime/What We Need/Anytime (Edit) (uncut picture disc) | 30 |

*(see also Group, Grand Prix)*

## GERRY MCAVOY
| 79 | Bridgehouse BHS 004 | Street Talk/Many Rivers To Cross (p/s) | 10 |

## JOHNNY MCBEE
| 63 | Airborne NBP 0001 | Nothing But Love/Rose-A-Lee | 80 |

## CECIL MCBEE
| 79 | Inner City IC3023 | MUSIC FROM THE SOURCE (LP) | 15 |

## NICKO MCBRAIN
| 91 | EMI NICKO 1 | Rhythm Of The Beast/Beehive Boogie (p/s) | 8 |
| 91 | EMI NICKOPD 1 | Rhythm Of The Beast/McBrain Damage Interview (shaped picture disc with insert & plinth) | 15 |

*(see also Iron Maiden, Streetwalkers, Pat Travers)*

## DAN MCCAFFERTY
| 75 | Mountain TOP 1 | Out Of Time/Cinnamon Girl | 6 |
| 75 | Mountain TOP 5 | Watcha Gonna Do About It/Nightingale | 5 |
| 75 | Mountain DAN 1 | Stay With Me Baby/Out Of Time/Watcha Gonna Do About It (p/s) | 7 |
| 79 | Mountain TOP 47 DJ | Watcha Gonna Do About It/(7.30 maxi version)/Boots Of Spanish Leather (12" promo) | 10 |

*(see also Nazareth, Sensational Alex Harvey Band, Mitchell/Coe Mysteries, Roger Glover)*

## JERRY MCCAIN
| 69 | Python 02 | Homogenised Love/728 Texas (99 copies only) | 50 |

## CASH MCCALL
| 63 | Ember EMB S 173 | Anytime/From The Very First Rose | 10 |
| 65 | Ember EMB S 204 | Many Are The Words (I've Left Unspoken)/Buenos Noches | 12 |
| 67 | Chess CRS 8056 | It's Wonderful (To Be In Love)/Let's Try It Over | 20 |

## DARRELL MCCALL
| 61 | Capitol CL 15196 | My Kind Of Lovin'/Beyond Imagination | 8 |
| 63 | Philips 304 002 BF | Dear One/I've Been Known | 10 |
| 63 | Philips BF 1259 | Hud/No Place To Hide | 7 |

## TOUSSAINT MCCALL
| 67 | Pye International 7N 25420 | Nothing Takes The Place Of You/Shimmy | 30 |
| 72 | Mojo 2092 035 | Nothing Takes The Place Of You/Shimmy (reissue) | 5 |

## NOEL MCCALLA
| 80 | Direction 58-8731 | Beggin'/Ain't That Peculiar/One More Heartache/Shake Me, Wake Me | 5 |

## DAVID MCCALLUM
| 66 | Capitol CL 15439 | Communication/My Carousel | 12 |
| 66 | Capitol CL 15474 | In The Garden Under The Tree/The House On Breckenridge Lane | 5 |
| 66 | Capitol (S)T 2432 | MUSIC ... A PART OF ME (LP) | 25 |
| 66 | Capitol (S)T 2498 | MUSIC ... A BIT MORE OF ME (LP) | 15 |

## ALISON MCCALLUM
| 75 | RCA 2608 | Love Grows Cold/Lunatic Love (Part 2) | 5 |

## MCCALMANS
| 70 | CBS 564145 | TURN AGAIN (LP) | 35 |
| 73 | One Up OU 2161 | McCALMANS' FOLK (LP) | 15 |

MINT VALUE £

### JIM McCANN
| | | | |
|---|---|---|---|
| 72 | Polydor 2489 053 | McCANNED! (LP) | 40 |

*(see also Ludlows)*

### LES McCANN (LTD)
| | | | |
|---|---|---|---|
| 60 | Vogue V 2417 | Fish This Week/Vakushna (as Les McCann Ltd) | 5 |
| 67 | Mercury MF 973 | All/Bucket O'Grease | 5 |
| 69 | Atlantic 584 284 | With These Hands/Burnin' Coal | 15 |
| 60s | Fontana 688 150ZL | THE WAILERS! (with Gerald Wilson Orchestra) | 10 |

### DON McCARLOS
| | | | |
|---|---|---|---|
| 80 | Negus Roots NERT 003 | I Don't Care/I Love Jah (12") | 45 |

### McCARTHY
| | | | |
|---|---|---|---|
| 86 | Wall Of Salmon MAC 001 | In Purgatory/The Comrade Era/Something Wrong Somewhere (foldover p/s in poly bag, white labels) | 25 |
| 86 | Pink PINKY 12 | Red Sleeping Beauty/From The Damned (stickered p/s) | 8 |
| 87 | Pink PINKY 17 | Frans Hals/The Fall (p/s) | 5 |
| 87 | September SEPT 1 | The Well Of Loneliness/Antiamericancretin/Unfortunately (p/s) | 6 |
| 88 | September SEPTT 4 | This Nelson Rockefeller (p/s) | 10 |

*(see also Stereolab)*

### KEITH McCARTHY
| | | | |
|---|---|---|---|
| 67 | Coxsone CS 7014 | Everybody Rude Now/BASES: Beware | 30 |

### LYN & GRAHAM McCARTHY
| | | | |
|---|---|---|---|
| 65 | Columbia DB 7584 | Seven Doves/Out After Ale | 6 |
| 66 | Columbia DB 7921 | I Can't Help But Wonder/There's Got To Be Love | 6 |
| 66 | Columbia DB 8087 | The Turkey's Trial/Bitter Withy | 6 |
| 68 | Columbia DB 8422 | I Think It's Going To Rain/Once I Was | 6 |
| 68 | RCA RCA 1759 | Scarborough Fair - Canticle/Wild Berries | 5 |

### MARY McCARTHY
| | | | |
|---|---|---|---|
| 67 | CBS 2832 | The Folk I Love/You Know He Did | 100 |
| 67 | CBS 2987 | Happy Days And Lonely Night/Easy Kind Of Love | 70 |

### CECIL McCARTNEY
| | | | |
|---|---|---|---|
| 68 | Columbia DB 8474 | Hey Aleuthia I Want You/Liquid Blue | 25 |
| 69 | Columbia DB 8595 | Orange And Green/Cloudy | 15 |
| 68 | Columbia S(C)X 6283 | OM (LP, first pressing with blue/black label with "Sold in UK..." text) | 150 |
| 68 | Columbia S(C)X 6283 | OM (LP, second pressing with black/silver label, boxed logo) | 40 |

### LINDA McCARTNEY
| | | | |
|---|---|---|---|
| 98 | Parlophone 4979101 | WILD PRAIRIE (LP) | 40 |

*(see also Suzy & The Red Stripes)*

### PAUL McCARTNEY/WINGS
**SINGLES**
| | | | |
|---|---|---|---|
| 71 | Apple R 5889 | Another Day/Oh Woman, Oh Why | 12 |
| 71 | Apple R 5914 | The Back Seat Of My Car/Heart Of The Country (as Paul & Linda McCartney) | 12 |
| 72 | Apple R 5932 | Love Is Strange/I Am Your Singer (unreleased) | 1500 |
| 72 | Apple R 5936 | Give Ireland Back To The Irish/(Version) (as Wings, yellow 'Wings' die-cut sl.) | 12 |
| 72 | Apple R 5949 | Mary Had A Little Lamb/Little Woman Love (p/s) | 10 |
| 72 | Apple R 5973 | Hi Hi Hi/C Moon | 6 |
| 73 | Apple R 5985 | My Love/The Mess (as McCartney's Wings, demos and early retail copies shipped in a plain red sleeve) | 20 |
| 73 | Apple R 5985 | My Love/The Mess (credited to Paul McCartney/Wings) | 5 |
| 73 | Apple R 5987 | Live And Let Die/I Lie Around | 6 |
| 73 | Apple R 5993 | Helen Wheels/Country Dreamer | 5 |
| 74 | Apple R 5996 | Jet/Let Me Roll It | 6 |
| 74 | Apple R 5997 | Band On The Run/Zoo Gang | 10 |
| 74 | Apple R 5999 | Juniors Farm/Sally G | 8 |
| 75 | Capitol R 6006 | Listen To What The Man Said/Love In Song (p/s) | 7 |
| 75 | Capitol R 6008 | Letting Go/You Gave Me The Answer | 8 |
| 75 | Capitol R 6010 | Venus And Mars; Rock Show/Magneto And Titanium Man | 8 |
| 76 | Parlophone R 6015 | Let 'Em In/Beware My Love | 5 |
| 78 | Parlophone R 6018 | Mull Of Kintyre/Girls School (yellow juke box 'Best selling British single ever' p/s) | 60 |
| 78 | Parlophone R 6020 | I've Had Enough/Deliver Your Children (p/s, as Wings) | 10 |
| 79 | Parlophone R6026 | Old Siam Sir/Spin It On (die-cut p/s) | 5 |
| 80 | Parlophone 12R 6039 | Temporary Secretary/Secret Friend (12", p/s) | 35 |
| 82 | Parlophone R 6054 | Ebony And Ivory/Rainclouds (unreleased sepia-toned 'studio photo' p/s; beware of clever counterfeits) | 50 |
| 82 | Epic A 11-2729 | The Girl Is Mine (with Michael Jackson)/MICHAEL JACKSON: Can't Get Outta The Rain (picture disc) | 30 |
| 82 | Parlophone R 6057 | Tug Of War/Get It (p/s) | 5 |
| 84 | Parlophone 12RP 6080 | No More Lonely Nights (Extended Version)/Silly Love Songs/ No More Lonely Nights (Ballad) (12", picture disc) | 20 |
| 84 | Parlophone RP 6086 | We All Stand Together/We All Stand Together (Humming Version) (with Frog Chorus, shaped picture disc, in printed PVC sleeve) | 18 |
| 85 | Parlophone RP 6118 | Spies Like Us/My Carnival (shaped picture disc) | 15 |
| 85 | Parlophone 12RP 6118 | Spies Like Us (Party Mix)/Spies Like Us (Alternative Mix)/Spies Like Us (DJ Version)/ My Carnival (Party Mix) (12", picture disc) | 20 |
| 86 | Parlophone 10R 6133 | Press/It's Not True/Press (Video Edit) (10", circular foldout p/s) | 12 |
| 86 | Parlophone R 6133 | Press (video edit)/It's Not True (p/s) | 10 |
| 86 | Parlophone R 6145 | Pretty Little Head/Write Away (p/s) | 5 |
| 86 | Parlophone R 6148/ R 6018 | Only Love Remains/Tough On A Tightrope//Mull Of Kintyre/Girls' School (p/s, stickered double pack in PVC sleeve, no p/s on R 6018) | 8 |
| 87 | A&M FREE 21 | Long Tall Sally (live)/I Saw Her Standing There (live) (p/s, free with "The Prince's Trust 10th Anniversary Birthday Party" LP [AMA 3906]) | 6 |

| 89 | Parlophone 12RS 6235 | Figure Of Eight/Ou Est Le Soliel? (12" etched vinyl) ............................ 25 |
|----|----------------------|---------------------------------------------------------------------------------|
| 89 | Parlophone RX 6223 | This One/The Long And Winding Road (p/s, envelope pack with 6 postcards) ...... 12 |
| 89 | Parlophone R 6238 | Party Party (1 side etched, p/s) .................................................. 10 |
| 90 | Parlophone R 6271 | Birthday Boy/Good Day Sunshine .................................................... 5 |
| 92 | Parlophone R 6330 | Hope Of Deliverance/Long Leather Coat (p/s) ....................................... 5 |
| 97 | Parlophone RP 6472 | The World Tonight/Used To Be Bad (Picture disc) ................................... 6 |
| 97 | Parlophone RP 6489 | Beautiful Night/Love Come Tumbling Down (picture disc) ............................ 10 |
| 99 | Parlophone R 6257 | No Other Baby/Brown Eyed Handsome Man .............................................. 5 |
| 01 | Parlophone R 6567 | From A Lover To A Friend/Riding Into Jaipur (p/s) ................................. 6 |
| 04 | Parlophone R6649 | Tropic Island Hum/We All Stand Together (p/s, yellow vinyl) ....................... 6 |
| 05 | Parlophone R 6673 | Fine Line/Growing Up Falling Down (p/s, plus art print) ........................... 6 |
| 05 | Parlophone R 6678 | Jenny Wren/Summer Of '59 (red vinyl, p/s) ......................................... 7 |
| 05 | GRA2010 | Really Love You/Lalula (1-side etched, McCartney remixes by TWIN FREAKS 2,500 only) ........................................................................... 20 |
| 07 | HearMusic 88072306219 | Ever Present Past/House Of Wax (live) (p/s) ....................................... 6 |
| 13 | MPL/Universal | Maybe I'm Amazed - Short Version (mono)/Album Version (mono)//Maybe I'm Amazed - Short Version (stereo)/Album Version (stereo) (12" die cut sleeve) ............... 15 |

## ALBUMS

| 70 | Apple PCS 7102 | McCARTNEY (LP, gatefold sleeve) ................................................. 50 |
|----|----------------|----------------------------------------------------------------------------------|
| 70 | Apple TA 7102 | McCARTNEY (reel-to-reel tape, jewel case, mono) ................................. 120 |
| 70 | Apple TD-PCS 7102 | McCARTNEY (reel-to-reel tape, jewel case, stereo) .............................. 50 |
| 70 | Parlophone PPCS 7102 | McCARTNEY (LP, export edition, black/silver label, 'Parlophone' and 'EMI' boxed logos) ......................................................................... 200 |
| 71 | Apple PAS 10003 | RAM (LP, laminated gatefold sleeve) ............................................. 40 |
| 71 | Apple PCS 7142 | WILD LIFE (LP, sleeve with 'sniped' spine edges, yellow inner) .................. 60 |
| 73 | Apple PCTC 251 | RED ROSE SPEEDWAY (LP, laminated gatefold sleeve, with booklet and poster) ...... 100 |
| 73 | Apple PCTC 251 | RED ROSE SPEEDWAY (LP, gatefold sleeve, with booklet and poster) ................ 70 |
| 73 | Apple PCTS 251 | RED ROSE SPEEDWAY (LP, gatefold sleeve, without booklet and poster) ............. 25 |
| 73 | Apple PAS 10007 | BAND ON THE RUN (LP, with lyric inner sleeve & poster) .......................... 40 |
| 73 | Apple PAS 10007 | BAND ON THE RUN (LP, export edition, Apple logo on textured label above catalogue number, circle indent on label, etched not stamped matrix ZYEX-929-3/ZYEX-930-3, 'BLAIR' etched onto dead wax) ................................................. 60 |
| 75 | Capitol PCTC 254 | VENUS AND MARS (LP, gatefold sleeve, inner sleeve, 2 posters & stickers) ........ 50 |
| 76 | MPL PCSP 720 | WINGS OVER AMERICA (3-LP, with poster) .......................................... 35 |
| 79 | Parlophone PCTC 257 | BACK TO THE EGG (LP, with inner) .............................................. 30 |
| 80 | Parlophone PCTC 258 | MCCARTNEY II (LP, with inner) ................................................. 20 |
| 80 | Parlophone CHAT 1 | MCCARTNEY INTERVIEW (LP) ....................................................... 30 |
| 84 | Fame FA 413100-1 | McCARTNEY (LP, gatefold sleeve) ................................................ 15 |
| 84 | Nimbus PAS 10007 | BAND ON THE RUN (LP, with 'Nimbus' sticker) .................................... 200 |
| 89 | Parlophone PCSDX 106 | FLOWERS IN THE DIRT (LP, World Tour pack with outer folder, 'Part' 7" single, poster, familty tree, sticker, postcards & tour itinary) .......................... 40 |
| 90 | Parlophone PCST 7346 | TRIPPING THE LIVE FANTASTIC (3-LP in slip sleeve with inners and 12" x 12" booklet) .. 40 |
| 91 | EMI PAUL 1 | LIVERPOOL ORATORIO (2-LP, box set with booklet) ..................................... 20 |
| | | (With Carl Davis and others. McCartney does not play on this record which is his first classical composition in collaboration with Carl Davis) |
| 93 | Parlophone PCSD 125 | OFF THE GROUND (LP, gatefold) .................................................. 40 |
| 93 | Parlophone PCSD 147 | PAUL IS LIVE (2 x LP) .......................................................... 50 |
| 97 | Parlophone PCSD 171 | FLAMING PIE (LP, gatefold) ..................................................... 60 |
| 99 | Parlophone 5223511 | RUN DEVIL RUN (LP, gatefold) ................................................... 60 |
| 99 | Parlophone 5232291 | RUN DEVIL RUN (8 x 7", box set with booklet) ................................... 70 |
| 99 | EMI Classics 5568971 | WORKING CLASSICAL (2 x LP, gatefold) ......................................... 25 |
| 99 | Parlophone 4991761 | BAND ON THE RUN (2 x LP, gatefold, 25th Anniversary) ........................... 30 |
| 01 | Parlophone 5355101 | DRIVING RAIN (2 x LP) .......................................................... 40 |
| 01 | Parlophone 5328501 | WINGSPAN (4 x LP, gatefold) .................................................... 35 |
| 05 | Parlophone 3383452 | CHAOS AND CREATION IN THE BACKYARD (LP, gatefold with 4 art prints) ............. 40 |
| 12 | Universal 088072335981 | KISSES ON THE BOTTOM (LP) .................................................... 20 |
| 12 | MPL HRM 33451-01 | RAM (2-LP reissue) ............................................................. 20 |

## PROMOS : PROMO SINGLES

| 71 | Apple R 5889 | Another Day/Oh Woman, Oh Why (demo) ............................................. 70 |
|----|--------------|---------------------------------------------------------------------------------|
| 71 | Apple R5914 | The Back Seat Of My Car/Heart Of The Country (demo) ............................. 50 |
| 73 | Apple R5993 | Helen Wheels/Country Dreamer (demo) ............................................. 40 |
| 74 | EMI R 5997 | Band On The Run (Edited Version)/(Full Version) (demo) .......................... 150 |
| 74 | Apple R 5999 | Junior's Farm (Edited Version)/Junior's Farm (Full Version) (demo) .............. 100 |
| 75 | Apple R 5999 | Sally G/Junior's Farm (reversed sides, demo) .................................... 150 |
| 75 | Capitol R 6010 | Venus And Mars; Rock Show/Magneto And Titanium Man (demo) ..................... 30 |
| 76 | Parlophone R 6015 | Let 'Em In (Edited Version)/Let 'Em In (Full Version) (demo) ................... 55 |
| 76 | Parlophone R 6014 | Silly Love Songs (Edited Version)/Silly Love Songs (Full Version) (demo) ....... 50 |
| 77 | MPL Publishing MPL 1 | We've Moved! (music publishing sampler with excerpts by Wings, Peggy Lee, Gene Vincent, Frank Sinatra, etc.; with press pack and insert) ....................... 350 |
| 77 | MPL Publishing MPL 1 | We've Moved! (music publishing sampler with excerpts by Wings, Peggy Lee, Gene Vincent, Frank Sinatra, etc.; without press pack and insert) .................... 250 |
| 77 | Capitol R 6018 | Mull Of Kintyre (Edited Version)/Girls' School (Edited Version) (demo) ......... 50 |
| 78 | Parlophone R 6019 | With A Little Luck (Edited Version)/Backwards Traveller-Cuff Link (demo) ........ 40 |
| 80 | Parlophone R 6037DJ | Waterfalls (3.22) (edit)/Check My Machine (demo) ............................. 40 |
| 80 | Parlophone R 6039A | Temporary Secretary (1-sided demo, no p/s) .................................... 80 |
| 84 | Parlophone 12RDJ 6080T | No More Lonely Nights (Mole Mix) (12", 1-sided, plain white numbered sleeve with plain white inner sleeve & insert, 250 only; beware of counterfeits with scratched [not stamped] matrix) ......................................................... 250 |
| 84 | Parlophone 12R(DJ) 6080 | No More Lonely Nights (Extended Version)/Silly Love Songs/No More Lonely Nights (Ballad) (12", promo, blue 'Give My Regards To Broad Street' label, black die-cut sleeve) ..................................................................... 50 |
| 85 | Parlophone RDJ 6118 | Spies Like Us (DJ Version 3.46)/My Carnival (demo, white printed die-cut sleeve) ........ 35 |

MINT VALUE £

| 88 | Parlophone PMBOX 11-19 | ALL THE BEST! ('Special Edition') (9 x 7" box set, in black die-cut sleeves, with signed 7" print; with genuine signatures) .......... 200 |
| 88 | Parlophone PMBOX 11-19 | ALL THE BEST! ('Special Edition') (9 x 7" box set, in black die-cut sleeves, with signed 7" print) .......... 75 |
| 89 | Parl. 12R LOVE 6223 | This One (Lovejoy's Remix) (12", 1-sided, plain label, black die-cut sleeve) .......... 35 |
| 89 | Parlophone GOOD 1 | Good Sign (6.51)/Good Sign (Groove Mix) (7.22) (12", black die-cut sleeve) .......... 45 |
| 89 | Parlophone RDJ 6235 | Figure Of Eight (Edited Version 3.59)/Ou Est Le Soleil? (Edited Version 3.57) (demo, standard p/s) .......... 30 |
| 89 | Parlophone RDJ 6238 | Party (Remix By Bruce Forest)/Party (different remix) (12", some listed as 'Party Party', with insert) .......... 40 |
| 89 | Parlophone RDJ 6238 | Party (Remix By Bruce Forest)/Party (different remix) (12") .......... 30 |
| 89 | Parlophone R 6213 | My Brave Face/Flying To My Home (promo in retro Parlophone sleeve) .......... 20 |
| 90 | Parlophone 12 SOL 1 | Où Est Le Soleil? (Tub Dub Mix)/Où Est Le Soleil? (Instrumental Mix) (12", black die-cut stickered sleeve, with insert) .......... 40 |
| 90 | Parlophone 12 SOL 1 | Où Est Le Soleil? (Tub Dub Mix)/Où Est Le Soleil? (Instrumental Mix) (12", black die-cut stickered sleeve, some without insert) .......... 20 |
| 90 | Parlophone R 6271 | Birthday Boy/Good Day Sunshine (promo in repro Parlophone sleeve) .......... 30 |
| 90 | Parlophone R 6278 | All My Trials/C Moon (promo in repro Parlophone sleeve) .......... 20 |
| 93 | Parlophone CDRDJ 6338 | C'mon People (Radio Edit)/C'mon People (CD) .......... 30 |
| 93 | Parlophone CDRS 6347 | Biker Like An Icon/Things We Said Today/Mean Woman Blues/ Midnight Special (CD, unissued) .......... 0 |
| 93 | Parlophone CDRDJ 6347 | Biker Like An Icon/Things We Said Today/Mean Woman Blues/ Midnight Special (CD, no inlay, jewel case with large sticker; beware of counterfeits with thicker blurred label print & smaller sticker on case) .......... 70 |
| 93 | Parlophone 12 DELIVDJ 1 | Deliverance/Deliverance (Dub Mix) (12", green label, plain black die-cut sleeve) .......... 20 |
| 99 | Parlophone RDR03 | Run Devil Run/Blue Jean Bop (mock 50's Parlophone label/sleeve) .......... 30 |
| 00 | Hydra FREE 02 | Free Now (as Liverpool Sound Collage, 1-sided, p/s) .......... 25 |
| 01 | WINDJ 002 | Silly Love Songs (Loop Da Loop Mix)/Coming Up (Linus Loves Mix) (12" 50 copies) ..... 150 |
| 03 | Parlophone TEMPSEC 01 | Temporary Secretary (Re-edited by Audioslave) (12", 1-sided) .......... 20 |

**PROMOS : PROMO ALBUMS**

| 79 | Parlophone PCTCP 257 | BACK TO THE EGG (LP, as Wings, MPL in-house picture disc; die-cut sleeve, matrix numbers YEX 987-2 & YEX 988-4 or -1; beware counterfeits) .......... 950 |
| 79 | Parlophone PCTC 257 | BACK TO THE EGG (LP, box set with badge, booklet, sticker, postcard & 5 cigarette cards; with or without T-shirt; beware of counterfeits with blurred printing) .......... 300 |
| 79 | Capitol (no cat. no.) | MPL PRESENTS (6-LP, box set, hand-numbered, 25 only) .......... 700 |
| 93 | Parlophone CDPMCOLDJ 1 | PAUL McCARTNEY COLLECTION (CD, 18-track sampler) .......... 25 |

(see also Beatles, Country Hams, Percy 'Thrills' Thrillington, Fireman, Mike McGear, Suzy & The Red Stripes, George Martin, Spirit Of Play, Ferry Aid, Michael Jackson)

## CAROLINE MCCAUSLAND
| 60s | Happy Face MMLP 1022 | SONGS FOR GALA (LP) .......... 40 |

## DAVE MCCLAREN
| 71 | Big BG 323 | Love Is What I Bring (actually by Dave Barker & Uniques)/ RUPIE EDWARDS ALL STARS: Love Version (with U Roy Junior) .......... 18 |

## DELBERT MCCLINTON
| 62 | Decca F 11541 | Hully Gully/Baby Heartbreak .......... 12 |

## CHRIS MCCLURE (SECTION)
| 66 | Decca F 12346 | The Dying Swan/The Land Of The Golden Tree .......... 10 |
| 68 | Polydor 56227 | Hazy People/I'm Just A Country Boy .......... 12 |
| 68 | Polydor 56259 | Answer To Everything/Meditation .......... 15 |
| 69 | RCA RCA 1849 | Our Song Of Love/Weather Vane .......... 7 |
| 69 | CBS 7646 | You're Only Passing Time/Sing Our Song (as Chris McClure Section) .......... 8 |

(see also Marmalade)

## BRIAN MCCOLLOM FOLK GROUP
| 66 | Pye 7N 17198 | This Dusty Road/Henry Joy McCracken .......... 6 |

## TOMMY MCCOOK (& SUPERSONICS)
| 63 | Island WI 102 | Adam's Apple/MAYTALS: Every Time (B-side actually by Tonettes) .......... 25 |
| 63 | Island WI 118 | Below Zero/LEE PERRY: Never Get Weary .......... 40 |
| 63 | Island WI 124 | Junior Jive/HORACE SEATON: Power .......... 25 |
| 64 | R&B JB 139 | Sampson/ROY & ANNETTE: My Arms Are Waiting .......... 50 |
| 64 | R&B JB 163 | Bridge View/NAOMI & CO: What Can I Do (B-side actually by Naomi & Clive) .......... 45 |
| 64 | Port-O-Jam PJ 4001 | Exodus (& His Group)/LEE PERRY: Help The Weak .......... 40 |
| 64 | Port-O-Jam PJ 4003 | Jam Rock/LEE PERRY: Band Minded People .......... 40 |
| 64 | Port-O-Jam PJ 4010 | Road Bloack/LEE PERRY: Chatty Chatty Woman .......... 40 |
| 64 | Black Swan WI 422 | Two For One/LASCELLES PERKINS: I Don't Know .......... 70 |
| 65 | Island WI 232 | Rocket Ship/JUSTIN HINDS & DOMINOES: Turn Them Back .......... 25 |
| 66 | Rio R 100 | Jerk Time (with Supersonics)/UNIQUES: The Journey .......... 50 |
| 66 | Rio R 101 | Out Of Space (with Supersonics)/UNIQUES: Do Me Good .......... 70 |
| 66 | Rio R 103 | Ska Jam/Smooth Sailing (with Supersonics) .......... 100 |
| 66 | Rio R 104 | Riverton City/HEPTONES: Gunmen Coming To Town .......... 100 |
| 66 | Doctor Bird DB 1028 | More Love/SILVERTONES: True Confession .......... 40 |
| 66 | Doctor Bird DB 1032 | Naked City (with Supersonics)/NORMA FRASER: Heartaches .......... 40 |
| 66 | Doctor Bird DB 1047 | Spanish Eyes (with Lynn Taitt)/STRANGER & HORTENSE: Loving Wine .......... 30 |
| 66 | Doctor Bird DB 1051 | A Little Bit Of Heaven (& His Band)/LLOYD WILLIAMS: Sad World .......... 30 |
| 66 | Doctor Bird DB 1053 | Indian Love Call (with Supersonics)/OWEN & LEON: How Would You Feel .......... 25 |
| 66 | Doctor Bird DB 1056 | Danger Man (with Supersonics)/ERIC MORRIS: If I Didn't Love You .......... 40 |
| 66 | Doctor Bird DB 1061 | What Now/Don't Stay Away .......... 70 |
| 67 | Doctor Bird DB 1058 | Jam Session (with Supersonics)/LLOYD & GLEN: Jezebel .......... 45 |
| 67 | Island WI 3047 | One Two Three Kick/TREASURE ISLE BOYS: What A Fool (B-side actually by Silvertones) .......... 50 |
| 67 | Island WI 3049 | Saboo (with Supersonics)/MOVING BROTHERS: Darling I Love You .......... 40 |
| 67 | Treasure Isle TI 7017 | Persian Cat/JUSTIN HINDS: Once A Man .......... 20 |
| 67 | Treasure Isle TI 7018 | Saboo (with Supersonics)/MOVING BROTHERS: Darling I Love You (reissue) .......... 25 |

| | | | |
|---|---|---|---|
| 67 | Treasure Isle TI 7020 | Shadow Of Your Smile/SILVERTONES: Cool Down | 25 |
| 68 | Treasure Isle TI 7027 | Soul For Sale/SILVERTONES: In The Midnight Hour | 20 |
| 68 | Treasure Isle TI 7032 | Venus/Music Is My Occupation (with Supersonics) | 20 |
| 68 | Treasure Isle TI 7039 | Our Man Flint (with Supersonics)/SILVERTONES: Old Man River | 50 |
| 68 | Treasure Isle TI 7042 | Moving (with Supersonics)/SILVERTONES: Slow And Easy | 50 |
| 68 | Doctor Bird DB 1135 | Mad Mad World/Wonderful World (with Lloyd Williams) | 30 |
| 68 | Unity UN 501 | Last Flight To Reggie (Reggae) City (with Stranger Cole)/Watch Dem Go | 25 |
| 69 | Trojan TR 642 | Breaking Up/Party Time (with Supersonics) (both actually by Alton Ellis) | 20 |
| 69 | Trojan TR 652 | Third Figure/You Should've Known Better | 20 |
| 69 | Trojan TR 657 | When The Saints Go Marching In/SOUL OFROUS: Ease Me Up Officer (B-side actually by Righteous Flames) | 40 |
| 69 | Trojan TR 671 | Moonshot/PHYLLIS DILLON: The Right Shot | 20 |
| 69 | Trojan TR 686 | Tribute To Rameses/PHYLLIS DILLON: Lipstick On Your Collar | 25 |
| 69 | Trojan TR 7706 | Black Coffee (with Supersonics)/VIC TAYLOR: Heartaches | 20 |
| 69 | Unity UN 506 | The Avengers/LAUREL AITKEN: Donkey Man | 25 |
| 69 | Unity UN 534 | Dream Boat/Tommy's Dream | 25 |
| 69 | Unity UN 535 | Peanut Vendor/100,000 Tons Of Rock | 40 |
| 70 | Duke DU 76 | The Rooster (with Supersonics) (actually by Jeff Barnes)/ PHYLLIS DILLON: Walk Through This World | 10 |
| 70 | Duke DU 77 | Open Jaw (with Supersonics)/JOHN HOLT: The Working Kind | 10 |
| 70 | Duke DU 78 | Key To The City (with Supersonics)/DOROTHY REID: Give It To Me | 10 |
| 71 | Treasure Isle TI 7058 | My Best Dress/PHYLISS DILLON: One Life To Live | 20 |
| 71 | Treasure Isle TI 7061 | Testify Version/JOHN HOLT: Let's Build Our Dreams | 20 |
| 71 | Treasure Isle TI 7065 | Black River/JOHN HOLT: Sister Big Stuff | 18 |
| 71 | Treasure Isle TI 7066 | Paragon's Medley Version/JOHN HOLT: Paragon's Medley | 15 |
| 71 | Treasure Isle TI 7070 | Midnight Confession Version/PHYLLIS DILLON: Midnight Confession | 20 |
| 71 | Big Shot BI 585 | Psalm Nine To Keep In Mind (with Observers)/Psalm Nine (Version) | 40 |
| 71 | Spinning Wheel SW 109 | Crying Everynight (with Supersonics) (actually by Stranger Cole)/ HERMAN MARQUIS: Tom's Version | |
| 71 | Spinning Wheel SW 110 | Stupid Doctor (with Supersonics)/ROB WALKER: Grooving In Style (B-side actually by Ken Parker) | 125 |
| 73 | Technique TE 927 | Rub It Down/Rub It Down (Version) (as Tommy McCook Stars) | 6 |
| 73 | G.G. GG 4539 | Bad Cow Skank (with Bobby Ellis)/ GLADSTONE ANDERSON: Drummer Roach | 5 |
| 75 | Vulcan VUL 1002 | Kojak/Cannon (with Aggrovators) | 5 |
| 79 | Grove Music GMDM 26 | Sensimena/TONY TUFF: You Wrong (12") | 20 |
| 13 | Trojan THB 7025 | Michelle/The Lesson | 7 |
| 70 | Trojan TBL 111 | GREATER JAMAICA (MOONWALK REGGAE) (LP, actually by various artists) | 30 |
| 74 | Attack ATLP 1007 | TOMMY McCOOK (LP) | 35 |
| 75 | Trojan HRLP 706 | COOKIN' (LP) | 20 |
| 77 | Third World TWS 920 | HOT LAVA (LP) | 30 |
| 77 | Justice JUS LP 07 | INSTRUMENTAL (LP) | 45 |

*(see also Denis Alcapone, Dave Barker, Dennis Brown, Shenley Duffas, Dennis & Lizzy, Dobby Dobson, Dynamics, Alton Ellis, Ethiopians, Eagles, Emotions, Herman, Heptones, Jamaicans, Hopeton Lewis, Lloyd & Glen, Lloyd & Groovers, Bob Marley, Maytals, Melodians, Mellodites, Millions, Paragons, Hugh Roy, Karl Walker Allstars)*

## TOMMY McCOOK & GLEN BROWN
| | | | |
|---|---|---|---|
| 76 | Groundation GROL 10 | HORNY DUB (LP, white label) | 300 |

## TOMMY McCOOK & BOBBY ELLIS
| | | | |
|---|---|---|---|
| 75 | Grove Music GMLP 002 | BLAZING HORNS (LP) | 50 |

## JASON McCORD
| | | | |
|---|---|---|---|
| 65 | Pye 7N 15925 | It Was A Very Good Year/Song Of The Pine Tree | 35 |

## McCORMICK BROTHERS
| | | | |
|---|---|---|---|
| 63 | Polydor NH 66986 | Red Hen Boogie/Blue Grass Express | 50 |
| 66 | Hickory LPE 1509 | AUTHENTIC BLUEGRASS HITS (EP) | 22 |

## GEORGE McCORMICK
| | | | |
|---|---|---|---|
| 55 | MGM SPC 6 | Don't Fix Up The Doghouse/Gold Wedding Band (export issue) | 18 |

## BUDD McCOY
| | | | |
|---|---|---|---|
| 58 | RCA RCA 1106 | Hiawatha/The Midnight Ride Of Paul Revere | 5 |

## CHARLIE McCOY
| | | | |
|---|---|---|---|
| 75 | Monument MNT 5103 | Stone Fox Chase/Honestly I Love You | 6 |

## CLYDE McCOY
| | | | |
|---|---|---|---|
| 57 | Mercury MEP 9513 | DANCING TO THE BLUES (EP) | 15 |

## JOE McCOY
| | | | |
|---|---|---|---|
| 59 | Collector JDL 81 | One In A Hundred/One More Greasing | 30 |

## (JOHN) McCOY
| | | | |
|---|---|---|---|
| 83 | Legacy LGY 9 | Oh Well! (Edit)/Because You Lied (p/s) | 5 |

*(see also Gillan, Samson, Mammoth, Zzebra, Split Knee Loons)*

## VIOLA McCOY
| | | | |
|---|---|---|---|
| 50s | Ristic LP 27 | VIOLA McCOY 1923-1927 (10" LP) | 40 |

## N McCOY & ALBIANS
| | | | |
|---|---|---|---|
| 78 | K&K K001 | The People/Talk To The People (12") | 70 |

*(see also Albians)*

## McCOYS
| | | | |
|---|---|---|---|
| 65 | Immediate IM 001 | Hang On Sloopy/I Can't Explain It | 8 |
| 65 | Immediate IM 021 | Fever/Sorrow | 12 |
| 66 | Immediate IM 028 | Don't Worry Mother, Your Son's Heart Is Pure/Ko-Ko | 10 |
| 66 | Immediate IM 029 | Up And Down/If You Tell A Lie | 10 |
| 66 | Immediate IM 034 | Runaway/Come On Let's Go | 10 |
| 66 | Immediate IM 037 | (You Make Me Feel) So Good/Every Day I Have To Cry | 10 |
| 67 | Immediate IM 046 | I Got To Go Back/Dynamite | 15 |

# Jimmy McCRACKLIN

| | | | MINT VALUE £ |
|---|---|---|---|
| 67 | London HLZ 10154 | Say Those Magic Words/I Wonder If She Remembers Me | 25 |
| 68 | Mercury MF 1067 | Jesse Brady/Resurrection | 8 |
| 69 | Immediate IM 076 | Hang On Sloopy/This Is Where We Came In | 5 |
| 66 | Immediate IMEP 002 | HITS VOL. 1 (EP) | 40 |
| 66 | Immediate IMEP 003 | HITS VOL. 2 (EP) | 40 |
| 65 | Immediate IMLP 001 | HANG ON SLOOPY (LP) | 55 |
| 68 | Mercury (S)MCL 20128 | THE INFINITE McCOYS (LP) | 40 |
| 71 | Joy JOYS 196 | HANG ON SLOOPY (LP, reissue) | 15 |

*(see also Rick Derringer)*

## JIMMY MCCRACKLIN

| | | | |
|---|---|---|---|
| 58 | London HLM 8598 | The Walk/I'm To Blame (as Jimmy McCracklin & His Band) | 50 |
| 58 | London HL 7035 | The Walk/I'm To Blame (export issue, as Jimmy McCracklin & His Band) | 15 |
| 62 | Top Rank JAR 617 | Just Got To Know/The Drag | 25 |
| 65 | R&B MRB 5001 | I Got Eyes For You/I'm Gonna Tell Your Mother | 25 |
| 66 | Outasite 45 120 | Christmas Time (Parts 1 & 2) (99 copies only) | 40 |
| 65 | Liberty LIB 66094 | Every Night, Every Day/Can't Raise Me | 10 |
| 66 | Liberty LIB 66129 | Think/Steppin' Up In Class | 10 |
| 68 | Minit MLF 11003 | How Do You Like Your Love/Get Together | 10 |
| 68 | Minit MLF 11009 | Pretty Little Sweet Thing/A And I | 10 |
| 65 | Vocalion VEP 170160 | JIMMY McCRACKLIN (EP) | 100 |
| 68 | Minit MLL/MLS 40003 | A PIECE OF JIMMY McCRACKLIN (LP) | 40 |

## GWEN MCCRAE

| | | | |
|---|---|---|---|
| 74 | President PT 416 | It's Worth The Hurt/90% Of Me Is You | 10 |
| 82 | Atlantic FLAM 1 | Keep The Fire Burning/Funky Sensation | 10 |
| 82 | Atlantic FLAM 1T | Keep The Fire Burning/Funky Sensation (12") | 20 |

## DANNY MCCULLOCH

| | | | |
|---|---|---|---|
| 69 | Capitol CL 15607 | Blackbird/Time Of Man | 8 |
| 70 | Pye Intl./Festival 7N 25514 | Colour Of The Sunset/Smokeless Zone | 8 |
| 69 | Capitol E-(S)T 174 | WINGS OF A MAN (LP, black/silver label with boxed logo) | 40 |

*(see also Animals)*

## IAN MCCULLOCH

| | | | |
|---|---|---|---|
| 64 | Decca F11855 | Come On Home/Down By The River | 50 |

## ED MCCURDY

| | | | |
|---|---|---|---|
| 66 | Bounty BY 6017 | BLOOD BOOZE N BONES (LP) | 20 |
| 60s | Elektra ELK 110 | WHEN DALLIANCE WAS IN FLOWER AND MAIDENS LOST THEIR HEADS (LP, with insert) | 40 |
| 60s | Elektra ELK 140 | WHEN DALLIANCE WAS IN FLOWER VOL 2 (LP) | 40 |

## GEORGE MCCURN

| | | | |
|---|---|---|---|
| 63 | London HLH 9705 | I'm Just A Country Boy/In My Little Corner Of The World | 10 |

## LUKE MCDANIEL

| | | | |
|---|---|---|---|
| 55 | Parlophone CMSP 29 | The Automobile Song/I Can't Steal Another's Bride (export issue) | 40 |

## MAISIE MCDANIEL

| | | | |
|---|---|---|---|
| 63 | Fontana TE 17397 | MEET MAISIE McDANIEL! (EP, with The Hunters) | 10 |
| 63 | Fontana TE 17398 | COUNTRY STYLE (EP, with The Hunters) | 12 |

*(see also Hunters)*

## EUGENE MCDANIELS

| | | | |
|---|---|---|---|
| 71 | Atlantic 2465 022 | OUTLAW (LP) | 30 |

## GENE MCDANIELS

| | | | |
|---|---|---|---|
| 61 | London HLG 9319 | A Hundred Pounds Of Clay/Take A Chance On Love | 10 |
| 61 | London HLG 9396 | A Tear/She's Come Back | 10 |
| 61 | London HLG 9448 | Tower Of Strength/Secret | 15 |
| 62 | Liberty LIB 55405 | Chip Chip/Another Tear Falls | 10 |
| 62 | Liberty LIB 55480 | Point Of No Return/Warmer Than A Whisper | 10 |
| 63 | Liberty LIB 55510 | Spanish Lace/Somebody's Waiting | 15 |
| 63 | Liberty LIB 55541 | The Puzzle/Cry Baby Cry | 6 |
| 63 | Liberty LIB 55597 | It's A Lonely Town/False Friends | 6 |
| 63 | Liberty LIB 10130 | Anyone Else/New Love In Old Mexico | 30 |
| 64 | Liberty LIB 55723 | In Times Like These/Make Me A Present Of You | 8 |
| 65 | Liberty LIB 55752 | (There Goes The) Forgotten Man | 15 |
| 65 | Liberty LIB 55805 | Walk With A Winner/A Miracle | 45 |
| 65 | Liberty LIB 55805 | Walk With A Winner/A Miracle (DJ copy) | 100 |
| 61 | London REG 1298 | GENE McDANIELS (EP) | 250 |
| 62 | Liberty LEP 2054 | A CHANGE OF MOOD (EP) | 40 |
| 61 | London HA-G 2384 | A HUNDRED POUNDS OF CLAY (LP, mono) | 40 |
| 61 | London SAH-G 6184 | A HUNDRED POUNDS OF CLAY (LP, stereo) | 60 |
| 62 | Liberty LBY 1003 | ... SOMETIMES I'M HAPPY (LP) | 80 |
| 62 | Liberty LBY 1021 | TOWER OF STRENGTH (LP) | 40 |
| 63 | Liberty (S)LBY 1128 | SPANISH LACE (LP) | 40 |
| 63 | Liberty LBY 1179 | THE WONDERFUL WORLD OF GENE McDANIELS (LP) | 40 |
| 68 | Sunset SLS 50017E | FACTS OF LIFE (LP) | 15 |

## BILL MCDAVID

| | | | |
|---|---|---|---|
| 61 | Starlite ST45 63 | Kiss Me For Christmas/Little Shepherd Boy | 8 |

## CHAS MCDEVITT (SKIFFLE GROUP)

| | | | |
|---|---|---|---|
| 57 | Oriole CB 1352 | Freight Train (with Nancy Whiskey)/The Cotton Song | 10 |
| 57 | Oriole CB 1357 | It Takes A Worried Man/The House Of The Rising Sun | 10 |
| 57 | Oriole CB 1371 | Green Back Dollar (with Nancy Whiskey)/I'm Satisfied | 10 |
| 57 | Oriole CB 1386 | Face In The Rain (with Nancy Whiskey)/Sporting Life (with Tony Kohn) | 10 |
| 57 | Oriole CB 1395 | Sing, Sing, Sing/My Old Man | 10 |

| | | | |
|---|---|---|---|
| 58 | Oriole CB 1403 | Johnny-O (with Nancy Whiskey)/Bad Man Stack-O-Lee | 10 |
| 58 | Oriole CB 1405 | Across The Bridge (with Shirley Douglas)/Deep Down | 10 |
| 58 | Oriole CB 1457 | Real Love (with Shirley Douglas)/Juke-Box Jumble | 15 |
| 59 | Oriole CB 1511 | Teenage Letter (with Shirley Douglas)/SHIRLEY DOUGLAS: Sad Little Girl | 10 |
| 60 | Top Rank JAR 338 | Dream Talk/Forever (with Shirley Douglas) | 10 |
| 61 | HMV POP 845 | One Love/Can It Be Love (with Shirley Douglas) | 5 |
| 61 | HMV POP 928 | Mommy Out De Light/I've Got A Thing About You (with Shirley Douglas) | 5 |
| 62 | HMV POP 999 | Happy Family/Throwing Pebbles In A Pool (with Shirley Douglas) | 5 |
| 65 | Columbia DB 7595 | The Most Of What Is Least/Don't Blame Me (with Shirley Douglas) | 5 |
| 68 | Fontana TF 957 | City Smoke/One Man Band | 5 |
| 57 | Oriole EP 7002 | CHAS AND NANCY (EP, with Nancy Whiskey) | 20 |
| 57 | Oriole MG 10018 | THE INTOXICATING MISS WHISKEY (10" LP, with Nancy Whiskey) | 30 |
| 65 | Columbia 33SX 1738 | SIXTEEN BIG FOLK HITS (LP, with Shirley Douglas) | 15 |

*(see also Nancy Whiskey, Coffee Bar Skifflers)*

### (COUNTRY) JOE MCDONALD

| | | | |
|---|---|---|---|
| 71 | Vanguard 6076 252 | Hold On It's Coming Parts 1 & 2 | 6 |
| 71 | Vanguard 6359 004 | TONIGHT I'M SINGING JUST FOR YOU (LP) | 15 |
| 71 | Sonet SNTF 622 | QUIET DAYS IN CLICHY (LP, soundtrack) | 15 |
| 71 | Vanguard VSD 79314 | HOLD ON - IT'S COMING (LP) | 15 |
| 71 | Vanguard VSD 79315 | WAR WAR WAR (LP) | 15 |

*(see also Country Joe & The Fish)*

### LARRY MCDONALD & DENZIL LAING

| | | | |
|---|---|---|---|
| 71 | Clandisc CLA 228 | Name Of The Game/FABULOUS FLAMES: Holly Version | 10 |

### RITCHIE MCDONALD & GLEN BROWN

| | | | |
|---|---|---|---|
| 72 | Duke DU 141 | Boat To Progress/Boat To Progress - Version | 10 |

### SHELAGH MCDONALD

| | | | |
|---|---|---|---|
| 70 | B&C CAS 1019 | THE SHELAGH McDONALD ALBUM (LP, textured sleeve) | 200 |
| 71 | B&C CAS 1043 | STAR GAZER (LP, with inner sleeve) | 200 |

*(see also Keith Christmas)*

### SKEETS MCDONALD

| | | | |
|---|---|---|---|
| 56 | Capitol CL 14566 | Fallen Angel/It'll Take Me A Long, Long Time | 8 |
| 59 | Capitol EAP1 1040 | GOING STEADY WITH THE BLUES (EP) | 40 |

### TESFA MCDONALD

| | | | |
|---|---|---|---|
| 72 | Dynamic DYN 455 | Life Is The Highest/Recarnate (Re-Incarnate) (actually by Bobby Ellis and Tommy McCook) | 30 |

### MCDONALD & GILES

| | | | |
|---|---|---|---|
| 70 | Island ILPS 9126 | McDONALD AND GILES (LP, 1st pressing, pink label, with 'i' logo) | 150 |
| 70 | Island ILPS 9126 | McDONALD AND GILES (LP, 2nd pressing, 'pink rim' label, 'palm tree' logo) | 30 |
| 70 | Polydor 2302 070 | McDONALD AND GILES (LP) | 15 |

*(see also King Crimson; Giles, Giles & Fripp)*

### ROSE MCDOWALL

| | | | |
|---|---|---|---|
| 88 | Rio Digital 7RDS 3 | Don't Fear The Reaper/Crystal Days (p/s) | 5 |

*(see also Strawberry Switchblade, Ornamental, Psychic TV, Current 93, Death In June)*

### (MISSISSIPPI) FRED MCDOWELL

| | | | |
|---|---|---|---|
| 66 | Bounty BY 6022 | MY HOME IS IN THE DELTA (LP) | 45 |
| 66 | Fontana 688 806 ZL | MISSISSIPPI DELTA BLUES (LP) | 40 |
| 69 | CBS 63735 | LONG WAY FROM HOME (LP) | 30 |
| 69 | Polydor 236 278 | GOING DOWN SOUTH (LP) | 30 |
| 70 | Capitol E-ST 409 | I DO NOT PLAY NO ROCK & ROLL (LP) | 25 |
| 70 | Transatlantic TRA 194 | LONDON 1 (LP) | 18 |
| 71 | Transatlantic TRA 203 | LONDON 2 (LP) | 18 |
| 71 | Revival RVS 1001 | EIGHT YEARS RAMBLIN' (LP, with Johnny Woods) | 18 |
| 74 | Xtra XTRA 1136 | MISSISSIPPI FRED McDOWELL 1904-1972 (LP) | 15 |

### FRED & ANNIE MAE MCDOWELL

| | | | |
|---|---|---|---|
| 64 | Polydor 236 570 | GOING DOWN SOUTH (LP) | 18 |

### BROTHER JACK MCDUFF

| | | | |
|---|---|---|---|
| 64 | Stateside SS 275 | Sanctified Samba/Whistle While You Work | 10 |
| 64 | Stateside SS 302 | Rock Candy/Real Good 'Un | 12 |
| 64 | Stateside SS 328 | Carpetbaggers (Main Theme)/The Pink Panther (Theme) | 10 |
| 66 | Atlantic 584 036 | Down In The Valley/A Change Is Gonna Come | 10 |
| 64 | Stateside SL 10060 | BROTHER JACK McDUFF LIVE! (LP) | 20 |
| 64 | Stateside SL 10101 | THE DYNAMIC JACK McDUFF (LP, as Brother Jack McDuff Quartet) | 20 |
| 65 | Stateside SL 10121 | BROTHER JACK McDUFF QUARTET LIVE! AT THE JAZZ WORKSHOP (LP) | 20 |
| 65 | Stateside SL 10142 | PRELUDE (LP) | 20 |
| 66 | Stateside SL 10165 | THE CONCERT McDUFF (LP) | 18 |
| 66 | Atlantic 587 030 | A CHANGE IS GONNA COME (LP) | 20 |
| 67 | Transatlantic PR 7404 | SILK AND SOUL (LP) | 15 |
| 67 | Transatlantic PR 7476 | WALK ON BY (LP) | 15 |
| 68 | Transatlantic PR 7286 | AT THE JAZZ WORKSHOP (LP) | 15 |
| 68 | Transatlantic ATRA 5056 | DYNAMIC JACK McDUFF (LP) | 15 |

*(see also Roland Kirk, Kenny Burrell, Jimmy Witherspoon)*

### JOHNNY MCEVOY

| | | | |
|---|---|---|---|
| 67 | Pye 17375 | Funny Man/Was It You | 6 |
| 73 | Hawk HALPX 112 | JOHNNY McEVOY (LP) | 15 |
| 74 | Hawk HALPX 117 | SOUNDS LIKE JOHNNY McEVOY (LP) | 20 |

*(see also Rambler)*

### BOB MCFADDEN & DOR

| | | | |
|---|---|---|---|
| 59 | Coral Q 72378 | The Mummy/The Beat Generation (tri centre) | 20 |

Rare Record Price Guide 2018

| | | | MINT VALUE £ |
|---|---|---|---|
| 59 | Coral Q 72378 | The Mummy/The Beat Generation (round centre) | 10 |

*(see also Rod McKuen)*

## MC5

| | | | |
|---|---|---|---|
| 69 | Elektra EKSN 45056 | Kick Out The Jams/Motor City Is Burning | |
| 69 | Elektra EKSN 45067 | Ramblin' Rose/Borderline | 50 |
| 69 | Elektra EKL 4042 | KICK OUT THE JAMS (LP, orange label, gatefold sleeve, mono) | 35 |
| 69 | Elektra EKS 74042 | KICK OUT THE JAMS (LP, orange label, gatefold sleeve, stereo) | 200 |
| 70 | Atlantic 2400 016 | BACK IN THE U.S.A. (LP) | 100 |
| 71 | Atlantic 2400 135 | HIGH TIME (LP) | 100 |
| 77 | Atlantic K50346 | BACK IN THE USA (LP, reissue) | 80 |
| 77 | Elektra K42027 | KICK OUT THE JAMS (LP, reissue with 'Brothers & Sisters' edit) | 25 |
| | | | 30 |

*(see also Wayne Kramer, Destroy All Monsters, Rob Tyner & Hot Rods)*

## MIKE MCGEAR

| | | | |
|---|---|---|---|
| 72 | Island WIP 6131 | Woman/Kill | 15 |
| 74 | Warner Bros K 16446 | Leave It/Sweet Baby (p/s) | 12 |
| 74 | Warner Bros K 16446 | Leave It/Sweet Baby | 8 |
| 75 | Warner Bros K 16520 | Sea Breezes/Givin' Grease A Ride | 8 |
| 75 | Warner Bros K 16573 | Dance The Do/Norton | 10 |
| 75 | Warner Bros K 16658 | Simply Love You/What Do We Really Know (in p/s) | 15 |
| 75 | Warner Bros K 16658 | Simply Love You/What Do We Really Know | 8 |
| 76 | EMI EMI 2485 | Doing Nothing All Day/A To Z | 6 |
| 80 | Carrere CAR 144 | All The Whales In The Ocean/I Juz Want What You Got - Money! (in p/s) | 30 |
| 80 | Carrere CAR 144 | All The Whales In The Ocean/I Juz Want What You Got - Money! | 15 |
| 81 | Conn SRTS/81/CUS 1112 | No Lardidar/God Save The Gracious Queen (in p/s) | 55 |
| 81 | Conn SRTS/81/CUS 1112 | No Lardidar/God Save The Gracious Queen | 35 |
| 72 | Island ILPS 9191 | WOMAN (LP, gatefold, pink rim palm tree label) | 50 |
| 74 | Warner Bros K 56051 | McGEAR (LP, gatefold sleeve with folded lyric insert) | 25 |
| 74 | Warner Bros KMG 1 | McGEAR'S LIMITED EDITION (7-track white label sampler & press kit) | 45 |
| 80s | Centre Labs | McGEAR (LP, 6-track reissue, 500 only, numbered & signed) | 60 |

*(see also Grimms, Scaffold, McGough & McGear, Paul McCartney)*

## BROWNIE MCGHEE

| | | | |
|---|---|---|---|
| 63 | Columbia SEG 8226 | BLUES ON PARADE NO. 1 (EP) | 20 |
| 60s | Xtra 1021 | BROWNIE McGHEE (LP) | 20 |

## BROWNIE MCGHEE & DAVE LEE

| | | | |
|---|---|---|---|
| 57 | Pye Jazz NJE 1060 | THE BLUEST (EP) | 22 |

*(see also Sonny Terry & Brownie McGhee)*

## DONNA MCGHEE

| | | | |
|---|---|---|---|
| 78 | Anchor ANC 1061 | Do As I Do/Mr Blindman | 25 |
| 78 | Anchor ANCT 1061 | Do As I Do/Mr Blindman (12") | 30 |
| 78 | Anchor ANCL 2027 | MAKE IT LAST FOREVER (LP) | 70 |

## HOWARD MCGHEE

| | | | |
|---|---|---|---|
| 61 | Parlophone PMC 1811 | DUSTY BLUE (LP, black/gold label) | 70 |
| 61 | Fontana FJL906 | THE SHARP EDGE (LP) | 40 |

*(see also Scaffold, Adrian Henri, Mike McGear, Jimi Hendrix, Grimms)*

## (ROGER) MCGOUGH & (MIKE) MCGEAR

| | | | |
|---|---|---|---|
| 68 | Parlophone PMC/PCS 7047 | McGOUGH AND McGEAR (LP, with phasing on "So Much"; black/yellow label with "Sold in U.K..." text) | 275 |
| 89 | Parlophone PCS 7332 | McGOUGH AND McGEAR (LP, stereo reissue with inner sleeve, without phasing on "So Much") | 15 |

## ROGER MCGOUGH & BRIAN PATTEN

| | | | |
|---|---|---|---|
| 75 | Argo ZPL 1190 | READ THEIR OWN VERSE - BRITISH POETS OF OUR TIME (LP) | 25 |

## MAUREEN MCGOVERN

| | | | |
|---|---|---|---|
| 73 | Pye Intl. 7N 25603 | The Morning After/Midnight Storm (p/s) | 8 |

## CHRIS MCGREGOR('S BROTHERHOOD OF BREATH)

| | | | |
|---|---|---|---|
| 68 | Polydor 184 137 | VERY URGENT (LP, as Chris McGregor Group) | 80 |
| 68 | Polydor 583 072 | UP TO EARTH (LP, unreleased, test pressings only) | 150 |
| 71 | RCA Neon NE 2 | CHRIS McGREGOR'S BROTHERHOOD OF BREATH (LP, gatefold sleeve) | 70 |
| 72 | RCA SF 8260 | BROTHERHOOD (LP, gatefold sleeve, as Chris McGregor's Brotherhood Of Breath) | 70 |
| 74 | Ogun OG 100 | LIVE, WILLISAU (LP) | 20 |
| 77 | Ogun OG 521 | IN HIS OWN TIME (LP) | 20 |
| 78 | Ogun OG 524 | PROCESSION (LP) | 20 |

*(see also Brotherhood Of Breath, Tunji)*

## FREDDIE MCGREGOR

| | | | |
|---|---|---|---|
| 73 | Fab FAB 261 | Wise Words/NEW ESTABLISHMENT: Version | 20 |
| 79 | Observer OBS 903 | Run Come Rally (12") | 40 |
| 81 | Yashemabeth YM01 | Wine Of Violence/Once A Man (12") | 15 |
| 81 | JB JBD 030 | Leave Yah/20 Miles Blackstar Liner/U BROWN: Step It Up (12", blue/yellow vinyl) | 40 |
| 83 | Intense INT 007 | Jumping Jack/Pretty Woman (12") | 12 |
| 84 | Real Authentic Sound RAS 7008 | Across The Border/Version (12") | 30 |
| 96 | Blacker Dread BDTL 05 | Mr. Pressure Man/CLIVE HYLTON: Babylon Keep On Knocking (12") | 35 |
| 79 | Jackal JALP 7000 | FREDDIE McGREGOR (LP) | 15 |

*(see also Soul Brothers, Young Freddie)*

## JIMMY MCGRIFF

| | | | |
|---|---|---|---|
| 64 | Sue WI 303 | All About My Girl/M.G. Blues | 40 |
| 64 | Sue WI 310 | Last Minute (Parts 1 & 2) | 40 |
| 64 | Sue WI 317 | I've Got A Woman (Parts 1 & 2) | 40 |
| 64 | Sue WI 333 | 'Round Midnight/Lonely Avenue | 40 |
| 66 | United Artists UP 1170 | See See Rider/Hallelujah | 20 |

| 70 | United Artists UP 35025 | The Worm/What's That.................................................................. 30 |
|---|---|---|
| 64 | Sue ILP 907 | I'VE GOT A WOMAN (LP) ............................................................. 100 |
| 64 | Sue ILP 908 | GOSPEL TIME (LP)..................................................................... 100 |
| 65 | London HA-C 8247 | BLUES FOR MISTER JIMMY (LP) ...................................................... 60 |
| 66 | London HA-C 8242 | AT THE APOLLO (LP) .................................................................. 75 |
| 66 | United Artists (S)ULP 1158 | A BAG FULL OF SOUL (LP) ............................................................ 30 |
| 68 | United Artists (S)ULP 1170 | THE BIG BAND (LP) .................................................................... 25 |
| 72 | Groove Merchant GM 503 | GROOVE GREASE (LP) ................................................................ 15 |
| 74 | People PLEO 14 | FLY DUDE (LP)......................................................................... 15 |
| 74 | People PLEO 19 | LET'S STAY TOGETHER (LP) .......................................................... 15 |
| 74 | People PLEO 23 | IF YOU'RE READY COME GO WITH ME (LP) ......................................... 15 |

### BILL MCGUFFIE (TRIO)

| 53 | Parlophone MSP 6040 | Concerto For Boogie/Begin The Beguine (as Bill McGuffie Trio) .................... 7 |
|---|---|---|
| 67 | Philips BF 1550 | Fugue For Thought (from the film 'Dalek Invasion Earth 2150AD')/ Fair's Fair .... 25 |
| 55 | Philips BBR 8054 | JAZZ WITH McGUFFIE (LP) ........................................................... 15 |
| 56 | Philips BBR 8087 | McGUFFIE MAGIC (LP) ................................................................ 20 |
| 56 | Philips BBL 7072 | MORE JAZZ WITH McGUFFIE (LP) ................................................... 20 |
| 58 | Philips BBL 7261 | CONTINENTAL TOUR (LP) ............................................................ 20 |

### ROGER MCGUINN

| 74 | CBS 2649 | Peace On You/Without You ............................................................ 6 |
|---|---|---|
| 77 | CBS 5231 | American Girl/Russian Hill ............................................................. 6 |

*(see also Byrds)*

### MCGUINNESS FLINT

| 70 | Capitol EA-ST 22625 | McGUINNESS FLINT (LP, gatefold sleeve) .......................................... 20 |
|---|---|---|
| 71 | Capitol ST 22794 | HAPPY BIRTHDAY, RUTHY BABY (LP) ................................................ 15 |

*(see also Manfred Mann, Blues Band, John Mayall, Coulson Dean McGuinness Flint, Gallagher & Lyle, Paladin)*

### BARRY MCGUIRE

| 66 | RCA Victor RCA 1525 | Cloudy Summer Afternoon/You've Got To Hide Your Love Away (B-side with Mamas & Papas) .................................................................................. 15 |
|---|---|---|
| 65 | RCA Victor RD 7751 | SINGS EVE OF DESTRUCTION (LP) .................................................... 30 |
| 70s | Sparrow BIRD 105 | C'MON ALONG (LP) .................................................................... 15 |

*(see also Mamas & Papas)*

### MCGUIRE SISTERS

| 54 | Vogue Coral Q 2028 | Lonesome Polecat/Muskrat Ramble .................................................. 15 |
|---|---|---|
| 55 | Vogue Coral Q 72050 | Sincerely/No More ..................................................................... 10 |
| 55 | Vogue Coral Q 72052 | Melody Of Love/Open Up Your Heart ................................................ 10 |
| 55 | Vogue Coral Q 72082 | Something's Gotta Give/It May Sound Silly .......................................... 10 |
| 55 | Vogue Coral Q 72108 | Christmas Alphabet/He ................................................................ 10 |
| 56 | Vogue Coral Q 72117 | Young And Foolish/Doesn't Anybody Love Me? ..................................... 10 |
| 56 | Vogue Coral Q 72145 | Missing/Be Good To Me (Baby, Baby) ............................................... 10 |
| 56 | Vogue Coral Q 72161 | Delilah Jones/Picnic ................................................................... 10 |
| 56 | Vogue Coral Q 72188 | Weary Blues/In The Alps .............................................................. 10 |
| 56 | Vogue Coral Q 72201 | My Baby's Got Such Lovin' Ways/Endless ........................................... 10 |
| 56 | Vogue Coral Q 72209 | Tip Toe Through The Tulips With Me/Do You Remember When? .................. 10 |
| 56 | Vogue Coral Q 72216 | Goodnight My Love, Pleasant Dreams/Mommy ..................................... 10 |
| 57 | Vogue Coral Q 72238 | Heart/Sometimes I'm Happy .......................................................... 10 |
| 57 | Vogue Coral Q 72249 | Kid Stuff/Without Him ................................................................ 10 |
| 57 | Vogue Coral Q 72265 | Rock Bottom/Beginning To Miss You ................................................ 10 |
| 57 | Vogue Coral Q 72272 | He's Got Time/Interlude ............................................................... 10 |
| 57 | Vogue Coral Q 72296 | Forgive Me/Kiss Them For Me ........................................................ 10 |
| 58 | Coral Q 72305 | Sugartime/Banana Split ................................................................ 6 |
| 58 | Coral Q 72327 | Ding Dong/Since You Went Away To School ......................................... 5 |
| 58 | Coral Q 72334 | Volare/Do You Love Me Like You Kiss Me? .......................................... 5 |
| 59 | Coral Q 72356 | May You Always/Achoo-Cha-Cha ..................................................... 6 |
| 59 | Coral Q 72370 | Peace/Summer Dreams................................................................. 8 |
| 59 | Coral Q 72379 | Red River Valley/Compromise ......................................................... 6 |
| 60 | Coral Q 72387 | Lovers' Lullaby/Livin' Dangerously.................................................... 5 |
| 60 | Coral Q 72399 | The Unforgiven Theme (The Need For Love)/I Give Thanks ....................... 5 |
| 60 | Coral Q 72406 | Nine O'Clock/The Last Dance ......................................................... 5 |
| 60 | Coral Q 72415 | I Don't Know Why/To Be Loved ....................................................... 6 |
| 61 | Coral Q 72427 | Really Neat/Just For Old Time's Sake ................................................ 10 |
| 61 | Coral Q 72435 | Will There Be Space In The Spaceship/Tears On My Pillow ....................... 10 |
| 61 | Coral Q 72446 | I Can Dream Can't I/Old Devil Moon.................................................. 5 |
| 62 | Coral Q 72452 | Sugartime Twist/More Hearts Are Broken That Way................................ 6 |
| 58 | Coral FEP 2001 | THE McGUIRE SISTERS (EP) ......................................................... 10 |
| 58 | Coral FEP 2006 | VOLARE (EP) ........................................................................... 10 |
| 59 | Coral FEP 2033 | MAY YOU ALWAYS (EP) ............................................................... 20 |
| 56 | Vogue Coral LVA 9024 | DO YOU REMEMBER WHEN? (LP) .................................................. 15 |
| 57 | Vogue Coral LVA 9072 | CHILDREN'S HOLIDAY (LP)........................................................... 20 |
| 58 | Coral LVA 9073 | TEENAGE PARTY (LP) ................................................................. 15 |
| 58 | Coral LVA 9082 | WHILE THE LIGHTS ARE LOW (LP) .................................................. 15 |
| 59 | Coral LVA 9115 | MAY YOU ALWAYS (LP) ............................................................... 15 |

### KEN MCINTIRE

| 60 | Esquire 32-133 | LOOKING AHEAD (LP, with Eric Dolphy) ............................................ 60 |
|---|---|---|

### DAVID MCIVOR

| 69 | Warner Bros WB8002 | Closing My Eyes/Love That Burns .................................................... 30 |
|---|---|---|

### FREDDIE MCKAY

| 71 | Banana BA 348 | Picture On The Wall/SOUND DIMENSION: Version .................................. 25 |
|---|---|---|
| 71 | Banana BA 353 | Sweet You, Sour You/High School Dance ............................................ 18 |

MINT VALUE £

| | | | |
|---|---|---|---|
| 71 | Banana BA 358 | High School Dance/SOUND DIMENSION: High School Version | 20 |
| 71 | Moodisc HM 110 | Old Joe/Too Much Fire | 12 |
| 72 | Banana BA 370 | Drunken Sailor/SOUND DIMENSION: Version | 50 |
| 73 | Bullet BU 525 | Go On This Way/SANTIC ALL STARS: Santic Dub | 15 |
| 73 | Dragon DRA 1012 | Our Rendezvous/Black Beauty | 15 |
| 73 | Atra ATRA 003 | I'm A Freeman/SWEET HARMONY: Santic Special | 12 |
| 73 | Grape GR 3060 | Our Rendezvous/SOUL DYMAMITES: Version | 12 |
| 74 | Dragon DRA 1022 | Dream My Life Over/YOUTH STARS: Version | 5 |
| 78 | Art & Craft ACD 004 | A Love Like Mine/Version (12") | 12 |
| 81 | Greensleeves GRED 46 | Another Weekend/EARL SIXTEEN: Live Together (12") | 30 |
| 82 | Greensleeves GRED 84 | Roots Man Skanking/TOYAN: Version (12") | 12 |
| 82 | Live & Love LLDIS 2014 | In Times Of Trouble/Version (12") | 30 |
| 71 | Banana BALPS 01 | PICTURE ON THE WALL (LP) | 45 |
| 73 | Attack ATLP 1013 | PICTURE ON THE WALL (LP, reissue) | 15 |
| 78 | GG GG 009 | BEST OF (LP) | 35 |
| 79 | Plant PLAN 10003 | CREATION (LP) | 40 |
| 85 | Move MVLP 6 | TRIBAL INNA YARD (LP) | 80 |

*(see also Lizzy)*

**SCOTT MCKAY**
| | | | |
|---|---|---|---|
| 67 | Columbia DB 8147 | I Can't Make Your Way/Take A Giant Step | 40 |

**SCOTTY MCKAY**
| | | | |
|---|---|---|---|
| 64 | London HLU 9885 | Cold Cold Heart/What You Wanna | 10 |

**TONY MCKAY**
| | | | |
|---|---|---|---|
| 66 | Polydor BM 56513 | Nobody's Perfect/Detroit | 8 |

**LONETTE MCKEE**
| | | | |
|---|---|---|---|
| 75 | Sussex SXX 4 | Save It/Do It To Me | 15 |

**VAL MCKENNA**
| | | | |
|---|---|---|---|
| 65 | Piccadilly 7N 35237 | Baby Do It/I Believe In Love | 15 |
| 65 | Piccadilly 7N 35256 | Mixed Up Shook Up Girl/Now That You've Made Up Your Mind | 25 |
| 66 | Piccadilly 7N 35286 | I Can't Believe What You Say/Don't Hesitate | 15 |
| 69 | Spark SRL 1005 | House For Sale/I'll Be Satisfied | 10 |
| 69 | Spark SRL 1023 | It's All In My Imagination/Sweet Sweet Lovin' | 7 |
| 70 | Spark SRL 1038 | Love Feeling/It's All In My Imagination (silver label) | 25 |

**MCKENNA MENDELSON MAINLINE**
| | | | |
|---|---|---|---|
| 69 | Liberty LBF 15235 | You Better Watch Out/She's Alright | 6 |
| 69 | Liberty LBF 15276 | Don't Give Me No Goose For Christmas/Beltmaker | 6 |
| 69 | Liberty LBS 83251 | STINK (LP) | 50 |

**CANDY MCKENZIE**
| | | | |
|---|---|---|---|
| 10 | Trojan THB 7003 | Breakfast In Bed/Ice Cream | 18 |
| 11 | Upsetter TBL 210 | LEE PERRY PRESENTS (LP) | 25 |

**MERLENE MCKENZIE**
| | | | |
|---|---|---|---|
| 68 | Double D DD 106 | Left Me For Another/BOBBY AITKEN & CARIBBEATS: Cell Block Eleven | 20 |

**SCOTT MCKENZIE**
| | | | |
|---|---|---|---|
| 67 | CBS 2816 | San Francisco (Be Sure To Wear Some Flowers In Your Hair)/What's The Difference | 5 |
| 67 | Capitol CL 15509 | Look In Your Eyes/All I Want Is You | 20 |
| 67 | CBS 3009 | Like An Old-Time Movie/What's The Difference Chapter II | 7 |
| 68 | CBS 3393 | Holy Man/What's The Difference (Chapter 3) | 6 |
| 67 | CBS (S)BPG 63157 | THE VOICE OF SCOTT McKENZIE (LP) | 15 |
| 70 | A&M AMLS 999 | STAINED GLASS MORNING (LP) | 18 |

*(see also Mamas & Papas)*

**TOMMY MCKENZIE**
| | | | |
|---|---|---|---|
| 68 | Pama PM 720 | Fiddlesticks/Please Stay | 35 |
| 71 | Pama Supreme PS 327 | Eastern Promise/Fiddlesticks (as Tommy McKenzie Orchestra) | 10 |

**MCKENZIE, DOUG & BOB**
| | | | |
|---|---|---|---|
| 82 | Mercury HOSER 1 | Take Off/Elron McKenzie (p/s) | 20 |

*(see also Rush)*

**MCKENZIE & GARDINER**
| | | | |
|---|---|---|---|
| 83 | The Sound Of London TSOLL 501 | From Time/From TIme (Version) (12") | 80 |

**LESLIE MCKEOWN**
| | | | |
|---|---|---|---|
| 79 | Ego Trip EGOS 7 | Shall I Do It (One More Number One)/Do It All Again (p/s) | 7 |
| 79 | Ego Trip EGO 001 | ALL WASHED UP (LP, gatefold, with poster) | 20 |

**MCKINLEYS**
| | | | |
|---|---|---|---|
| 64 | Columbia DB 7230 | Someone Cares For Me/A Million Miles Away | 20 |
| 64 | Columbia DB 7310 | When He Comes Along/Then I'll Know It's Love | 10 |
| 64 | Parlophone R 5211 | Sweet And Tender Romance/That Lonely Feeling | 12 |
| 65 | Columbia DB 7583 | Give Him My Love/Once More | 15 |

**ROD MCKUEN**
| | | | |
|---|---|---|---|
| 57 | London HLU 8390 | Happy Is A Boy Named Me/Jaydee | 15 |
| 60 | Brunswick 05828 | Two Brothers/Time After Time | 5 |
| 64 | Capitol CL 15348 | The World I Used To Know/Someplace Green | 5 |
| 66 | Ember EMB 223 | Soldiers Who Want To Be Heroes/Wayfarin' Stranger | 5 |
| 68 | RCA Victor RCA 1734 | Cat Named Sloopy/Where Are We Now | 5 |
| 71 | Buena Vista DF 482 | Pastures Green/Theme From Scandalous John/Train To Quivira (p/s) | 5 |

*(see also Bob McFadden & Dor, Mike Redway, Mike Sarne, Henri Mancini)*

**HAL MCKUSICK SEXTET/QUINTET**
| | | | |
|---|---|---|---|
| 57 | Vogue Coral Q 72258 | Kelly And Me (as Sextet)/When I Fall In Love (as Quintet) | 6 |

**IAN MCLAGAN**
79  Mercury MER1          La De Da/Hold On (p/s) .................................................................. 5
*(see also Faces, Small Faces)*

**TOMMY MCLAIN**
66  London HL 10065       Sweet Dreams/I Need You So ........................................................ 8
66  London HL 10091       Think It Over/I Can't Take No More .............................................. 8

**(MAHAVISHNU) JOHN MCLAUGHLIN**
69  Marmalade 608 007     EXTRAPOLATION (LP) ............................................................... 200
70  Polydor 02343 012     EXTRAPOLATION (LP, reissue) ...................................................... 25
71  Douglas DGL 65075     DEVOTION (LP, gatefold sleeve) .................................................. 15
71  Douglas DGL 69014     MY GOAL'S BEYOND (LP, as Mahavishnu John McLaughlin, gatefold sleeve) ....... 15

**JACKIE MCLEAN QUINTET**
55  Esquire 32-041        LIGHTS OUT (LP) ..................................................................... 30
56  Esquire 32-111        JACKIE'S PALS (LP) ................................................................. 50
*(see also Lifetime, Tony Williams [Lifetime], Mahavishnu Orchestra, John Surman, Santana)*

**NANA MCLEAN**
71  Banana BA 355         A Little Love/SOUND DIMENSION: Heavy Beat ................................... 40

**PHIL MCLEAN**
61  Top Rank JAR 597      Small Sad Sam/Chicken .............................................................. 6
62  Top Rank JAR 613      Big Mouth Bill/Come With Us ....................................................... 5

**CRAIG MCLEARIE**
79  Wealden WS 187        WARP FACTOR (LP) .................................................................. 125

**GERALD MCLEASH**
71  G.G. GG 4516          False Reaper/G.G. ALL STARS: Reaping Version .............................. 25

**LARIS MCLENNON**
67  CBM 04                Confusion/Turn Me Loose ........................................................... 15

**ENOS MCLEOD**
68  Blue Cat BS 135       You Can Never Get Away/ENOS & SHEILA: La La La Bamba .................. 200
83  Stewmac SB 003        BY THE LOOK IN YOUR EYES (LP) ................................................. 50
96  Pressure Sounds PSLP 008  THE GENIUS OF ENOS (LP) ................................................... 20
*(see also Enos & Sheila)*

**SEAN MCLEOD**
69  Aurora 4594           Living Without You/Love Songs From Another Planet .......................... 30

**VINCENT MCLEOD**
69  Jackpot JP 711        Too Late/SIR COLLINS: Late Night .............................................. 12

**OSCAR MCLOLLIE & HIS HONEYJUMPERS**
55  London HL 8130        Take Your Shoes Off, Pop/Love Me Tonight .................................. 250
55  London HL 8130        Take Your Shoes Off, Pop/Love Me Tonight (78) ............................. 40

**EDDIE MCLOYD**
75  Brunswick BR 27       Once You Fall In Love/Baby Get Down .......................................... 10

**BOBBY MCLURE**
66  Chess CRS 8048        Peak Of Love/You Got Me Baby .................................................. 45
66  Chess CRS 8048        Peak Of Love/You Got Me Baby (DJ copy) ..................................... 75
75  Island USA 006        You Bring Out The Love In Me/SURVIVAL KIT: Daybreak ..................... 20
*(see also Fontella Bass)*

**MCLUSKY**
02  Too Pure PURE124S     To Hell With Good Intentions (7" EP) .......................................... 10
02  Too Pure PURE 117LP   MCLUSKY DO DALLAS (LP) ....................................................... 25
02  Too Pure PURE 117LP   MCLUSKY DO DALLAS (LP, orange or white vinyl) ........................... 20
03  Too Pure PURE 132LP   MY PAIN AND SADNESS IS MORE SAD AND PAINFUL THAN YOURS (LP, vinyl reissue of CD release) ... 30
04  Too Pure PURE 154LP   THE DIFFERENCE BETWEEN YOU AND ME IS THAT I'M NOT ON FIRE (LP, with poster) ... 35

**MCLYNNS**
70  CBS 63836             OLD MARKET ST. (LP) .............................................................. 50

**ROSS MCMANUS**
64  HMV POP 1279          Patsy Girl/I'm The Greatest ..................................................... 10
66  HMV POP 1543          Stop Your Playing Around/Girlie Girlie ........................................ 10
67  Decca F 12618         Can't Take My Eyes Off Of You/If I Were A Rich Man .......................... 6
72  Rediffusion ZS 122    THE LEAVING OF LIVERPOOL (LP) ................................................. 12
*(see also Day Costello)*

**MC MELLO**
89  Republic LICT007      Bizzie Rhymin'/Comin' Correct/Wize (EP) ...................................... 12
92  Funki Dreds PA6640    Gone Crazy/Talk Dem Way/Firm Stance (EP) ................................... 20
94  Natural Response MELLO 1  I Hear Voices/Live At Portland (promo only) ............................. 18
90  Republic 4353ILE      THOUGHTS RELEASED (LP) ....................................................... 15

**MARGARET MCMILLEN**
65  Decca F 12272         You Can't Be True Dear/The Love Of My Man .................................. 6

**JAMES VINCENT MCMORROW**
11  Believe BLVDIG 07     We Don't Eat/Higher Love (500 only, hand numbered) .......................... 8

**IAN MCNABB**
91  Way Cool WAY 147      Great Dreams Of Heaven/That's Why I Believe ................................ 8

**BARBARA MCNAIR**
66  Tamla Motown TMG 544  You're Gonna Love My Baby/The Touch Of Time .............................. 350
66  Tamla Motown TMG 544  You're Gonna Love My Baby/The Touch Of Time (DJ copy) .................. 400
59  Coral FEP 2021        FRONT ROW CENTRE VOL. 1 (EP) ............................................... 40
64  Warner Bros WEP 6129  I ENJOY BEING A GIRL (EP) .................................................... 40
*(see also Billy Williams & Barbara McNair)*

## HAROLD McNAIR

| | | | |
|---|---|---|---|
| 68 | RCA Victor RCA 1742 | The Hipster/Indecision | 80 |
| 65 | Island ILP 926 | AFFECTIONATE FINK (LP, with Ornette Coleman's Sidemen) | 500 |
| 68 | RCA SF 7969 | HAROLD McNAIR (LP, 1st pressing, black RCA red dot label) | 300 |
| 68 | RCA SF7969 | HAROLD McNAIR (LP, 2nd pressing, orange label) | 150 |
| 70 | RCA Intl. INTS 1096 | FLUTE AND NUT (LP) | 50 |
| 70 | B&C CAS 1016 | THE FENCE (LP, gatefold with pink envelope containing balloon) | 80 |
| 70 | B&C CAS 1016 | THE FENCE (LP, gatefold with pink envelope without balloon) | 40 |
| 72 | B&C CAS 1045 | HAROLD McNAIR (LP) | 70 |

*(see also Ginger Baker's Airforce)*

## CHARLIE McNAIR'S JAZZ BAND

| | | | |
|---|---|---|---|
| 60 | Waverly SLP 504 | Big House Blues/Fish Man | 6 |

## JOHN McNALLY

| | | | |
|---|---|---|---|
| 69 | CBS 4517 | Mary In The Morning/My Love Forgive Me | 5 |

## TREVOR McNAUGHTON

| | | | |
|---|---|---|---|
| 72 | Hillcrest HCT 5 | No Sins At All/No Sins At All Version | 5 |

*(see also The Melodians)*

## BIG JAY MCNEELY

| | | | |
|---|---|---|---|
| 59 | Top Rank JAR 169 | There Is Something On Your Mind/...Back...Shack...Track ('vocal: Little Sonny') | 40 |
| 65 | Sue WI 373 | There Is Something On Your Mind/...Back...Shack...Track ('vocal: Little Sonny') (reissue) | 20 |
| 64 | Warner Bros WM 8143 | BIG JAY'S PARTY (LP) | 30 |

## AARON MCNEIL

| | | | |
|---|---|---|---|
| 73 | Action ACT 4619 | Soul Of A Black Man/Reap What You Sow | 12 |

## DAVID MCNEIL

| | | | |
|---|---|---|---|
| 68 | President PT 212 | Don't Let Your Chance Go By/Space Plane | 40 |

## PAUL MCNEILL

| | | | |
|---|---|---|---|
| 66 | Decca LK 4803 | TRADITIONALLY AT THE TROUBADOUR (LP) | 40 |

## PAUL MCNEILL & LINDA PETERS

| | | | |
|---|---|---|---|
| 68 | MGM MGM 1408 | You Ain't Goin' Nowhere/I'll Show You How To Sing | 6 |

*(see also Linda Peters, Richard & Linda Thompson)*

## RONNIE MCNEIR

| | | | |
|---|---|---|---|
| 75 | London HLA 10494 | Wendy Is Gone/Give Me A Sign | 10 |

## MCPEAKE FAMILY/FOLK GROUP

| | | | |
|---|---|---|---|
| 60s | Topic | IRISH TRADITIONAL FOLK SONGS AND MUSIC (LP, blue label) | 30 |
| 60s | Topic 12T 87 | THE McPEAKE FAMILY (LP) | 20 |
| 64 | Fontana TL 5214 | IRISH FOLK! (LP, as McPeake Family) | 20 |
| 65 | Fontana TL 5358 | AT HOME WITH THE McPEAKES (LP) | 20 |
| 67 | Fontana TL 5433 | PLEASANT AND DELIGHTFUL (LP, as McPeake Family) | 20 |
| 69 | Evolution Z 1002 | WELCOME HOME (LP, as McPeake Folk Group) | 40 |

## CLYDE MCPHATTER

### SINGLES

| | | | |
|---|---|---|---|
| 56 | London HLE 8250 | Seven Days/I'm Not Worthy Of You | 400 |
| 56 | London HLE 8250 | Seven Days/I'm Not Worthy Of You (78) | 30 |
| 56 | London HL 7006 | Seven Days/I'm Not Worthy Of You (export issue) | 125 |
| 56 | London HLE 8293 | Treasure Of Love/When You're Sincere (gold label lettering) | 150 |
| 56 | London HLE 8293 | Treasure Of Love/When You're Sincere (silver label lettering) | 60 |
| 57 | London HLE 8462 | Just To Hold My Hand/No Matter What (triangular centre) | 150 |
| 57 | London HLE 8462 | Just To Hold My Hand/No Matter What (78) | 20 |
| 57 | London HLE 8476 | Long Lonely Nights/Heartaches (triangular centre) | 100 |
| 57 | London HLE 8476 | Long Lonely Nights/Heartaches (triangular centre) (78) | 20 |
| 57 | London HLE 8525 | Rock And Cry/You'll Be There (triangular centre) | 90 |
| 57 | London HLE 8525 | Rock And Cry/You'll Be There (later round centre) | 40 |
| 57 | London HLE 8525 | Rock And Cry/You'll Be There (78) | 20 |
| 58 | London HLE 8707 | Come What May/Let Me Know (triangular centre) | 60 |
| 58 | London HLE 8707 | Come What May/Let Me Know (78) | 25 |
| 58 | London HLE 8755 | A Lover's Question/I Can't Stand Up Alone (triangular centre) | 30 |
| 58 | London HLE 8755 | A Lover's Question/I Can't Stand Up Alone (78) | 20 |
| 59 | MGM MGM 1014 | I Told Myself A Lie/(I'm Afraid) The Masquerade Is Over | 20 |
| 59 | London HLE 8878 | Lovey Dovey/My Island Of Dreams (triangular centre) | 30 |
| 59 | London HLE 8878 | Lovey Dovey/My Island Of Dreams (78) | 25 |
| 59 | London HLE 8906 | Since You've Been Gone/Try Try Baby (triangular centre) | 40 |
| 59 | London HLE 8906 | Since You've Been Gone/Try Try Baby (78) | 30 |
| 59 | MGM MGM 1040 | Twice As Nice/Where Did I Make My Mistake | 18 |
| 59 | London HLE 9000 | You Went Back On Your Word/There You Go | 40 |
| 59 | London HLE 9000 | You Went Back On Your Word/There You Go (78) | 40 |
| 59 | MGM MGM 1048 | Bless You/Let's Try Again | 18 |
| 60 | London HLE 9079 | Just Give Me A Ring/Don't Dog Me | 45 |
| 60 | MGM MGM 1061 | Think Me A Kiss/When The Right Time Comes Along | 18 |
| 60 | Mercury AMT 1108 | I Ain't Givin' Up Nothin' (If I Can't Get Something)/Ta Ta | 15 |
| 60 | Mercury AMT 1120 | You're For Me/I Just Want To Love You | 18 |
| 61 | Mercury AMT 1136 | Tomorrow Is A-Comin'/I'll Love You Till The Cows Come Home | 40 |
| 62 | Mercury AMT 1174 | Lover Please/Let's Forget About The Past | 20 |
| 62 | Mercury AMT 1181 | Little Bitty Pretty One/Next To Me | 20 |
| 66 | Stateside SS 487 | Everybody's Somebody's Fool/I Belong To You | 18 |
| 66 | Stateside SS 567 | A Shot Of Rhythm And Blues/I'm Not Going To Work Today | 30 |
| 67 | Stateside SS 592 | Lavender Lace/Sweet And Innocent | 20 |
| 68 | Deram DM 202 | Only A Fool/Thank You Love | 25 |

| 69 | Deram DM 223 | Baby I Could Be So Good At Loving You/Baby You've Got It | 25 |
| 69 | Pama PM 775 | A Shot Of Rhythm And Blues/I'm Not Going To Work Today (reissue) | 12 |
| 69 | B&C CB 106 | Denver/Tell Me | 12 |

**EPs**

| 59 | London RE-E 1202 | CLYDE McPHATTER | 250 |
| 60 | London RE-E 1240 | CLYDE McPHATTER NO. 2 (unissued) | 0 |
| 59 | MGM MGM-EP 705 | TWICE AS NICE | 60 |
| 60 | MGM MGM-EP 739 | THIS IS NOT GOODBYE | 60 |

**ALBUMS**

| 63 | Mercury MMC 14120 | LOVER PLEASE | 100 |
| 64 | Atlantic ATL 5001 | THE BEST OF CLYDE McPHATTER | 90 |
| 71 | MCA MUPS 418 | WELCOME HOME | 20 |
| 73 | Atlantic K 30033 | A TRIBUTE TO CLYDE McPHATTER | 20 |

*(see also Drifters, Jackie Wilson, Dominoes, Billy Ward & Dominoes, Jackie Wilson/Clyde McPhatter)*

**TONY (T.S.) McPHEE**

| 66 | Purdah 45-3501 | Someone To Love Me/Ain't Gonna Cry No Mo' (as T.S. McPhee) | 200 |
| 83 | TS 001 | Time Of Action/Born To Be With You (sold at gigs) | 10 |
| 68 | Liberty LBL/LBS 83190 | ME AND THE DEVIL (LP) | 60 |
| 71 | Sunset SLS 50209 | THE SAME THING ON THEIR MINDS (LP, with Jo-Ann Kelly) | 30 |
| 73 | World Wide Artists WWA 1 | THE TWO SIDES OF TONY (T.S.) McPHEE (LP, with insert) | 25 |

*(see also Groundhogs, Champion Jack Dupree, Jo-Ann Kelly, John Dummer Blues Band, Hapshash & Coloured Coat, Herbal Mixture)*

**CHARLES McPHERSON**

| 65 | Stateside SL 10151 | BEBOP REVISITED (LP) | 15 |

**GILLIAN McPHERSON**

| 71 | RCA Victor RCA 2089 | It's My Own Way/Is Somebody In Tune With My Song | 5 |
| 71 | RCA Victor SF 8220 | POETS AND PAINTERS AND PERFORMERS OF THE BLUES (LP) | 60 |

**HERB McQUAY**

| 75 | Bell 1398 | Runnin' Away From You/Storm Clouds | 18 |

**KEVIN McQUINN**

| 62 | Top Rank JAR 598 | Every Step Of The Way/Keep Me On Your Mind | 10 |

**RON McQUINN**

| 77 | Decca F13693 | Look At Love Bleed/Banshee | 20 |

**CARMEN McRAE**

| 57 | Brunswick 05652 | Whatever Lola Wants (Lola Gets)/Ooh (What 'Cha Doin' To Me) (with Dave Lambert Quartet) | 10 |
| 59 | London HLR 8837 | Play For Keeps/Which Way Is Love | 5 |
| 57 | London RE-N 1094 | LONDON'S GIRL FRIENDS (EP) | 15 |
| 56 | Brunswick LAT 8133 | TORCHY (LP) | 15 |

*(see also Sammy Davis Jnr.)*

**IAN McSHANE**

| 62 | Columbia DB 4932 | Harry Brown/The Tinker | 6 |

**MC SPY-D & 'FRIENDS'**

| 95 | Parlophone 12RDJ 6404 | The Amazing Spider-Man (Solution Mix)/(Solution Chilled Mix)/(B&J White Trouser Mix) (12", no p/s, promo only) | 25 |

*(see also Brian May)*

**BLIND WILLIE McTELL**

| 66 | Transatlantic PR 1040 | LAST SESSION (LP) | 35 |
| 67 | Storyville 670 816 | BLIND WILLIE McTELL 1940 (LP) | 22 |
| 60s | Roots RL 324 | BLIND WILLIE McTELL 1929-1935 (LP) | 20 |
| 73 | Atlantic K 40400 | ATLANTA TWELVE STRING GUITAR (LP) | 18 |

**RALPH McTELL**

| 69 | Big T BIG 125 | Summer Comes Along/Girl On A Bicycle | 8 |
| 70 | Big T BIG 131 | Kew Gardens/Father Forgive Them | 8 |
| 70 | Big T BIG 134 | Spiral Staircase/Terminus | 8 |
| 68 | Transatlantic TRA 165 | 8 FRAMES A SECOND (LP, white/lilac label with 't' logo) | 39 |
| 69 | Transatlantic TRA 177 | SPIRAL STAIRCASE (LP, laminated sleeve, with insert) | 25 |
| 69 | Transatlantic TRA 209 | MY SIDE OF YOUR WINDOW (LP, textured sleeve) | 20 |
| 70 | Transatlantic TRA 227 | REVISITED (LP) | 20 |

**MCTELLS**

| 87 | Frank TRUFFAUT 303 | Jesse Man Rae/If Only/Rotten/M.T.B. (p/s in bag) | 10 |

**RAY McVAY SOUND**

| 65 | Pye 7N 15777 | Raunchy/Revenge (Promo copies have "Macvay" spelling) | 45 |
| 65 | Pye 7N 15816 | Kinda Kinky/Kinkdom Come | 50 |
| 66 | Parlophone R 5460 | Genesis/House Of Clowns (as Ray MacVay Band) | 10 |
| 69 | Mercury MF 1121 | Destination Moon/Mexican Scavenger | 10 |
| 71 | Philips 6006 083 | They Call Me Mr. Tibbs (as Ray McVay & Orchestra) | 25 |

**CHRISTINE MCVIE**

| 84 | Warner Bros W 9372PT | Got A Hold On Me/Who's Dreaming This Dream (12", picture disc) | 10 |

*(see also Christine Perfect, Fleetwood Mac, Chicken Shack)*

**CARL McVOY**

| 58 | London HLU 8617 | Tootsie/You Are My Sunshine | 200 |
| 58 | London HLU 8617 | Tootsie/You Are My Sunshine (78) | 40 |

**DAVID MCWILLIAMS**

| 66 | CBS 202348 | God And My Country/Blue Eyes | 10 |
| 67 | Major Minor MM 533 | Harlem Lady/The Days Of Pearley Spencer (some copies later 'flipped') | 15 |
| 68 | Major Minor MM 561 | This Side Of Heaven/Mister Satisfied | 8 |
| 69 | Major Minor MM 592 | The Stranger/Follow Me | 10 |

MINT VALUE £

| 69 | Major Minor MM 616 | Oh Mama Are You My Friend?/I Love Susie In The Summer | 8 |
| 71 | Parlophone R 5886 | Days Of Pearly Spencer/Harlem Lady (reissue) | 6 |
| 67 | Major Minor MMLP 2 | SINGING SONGS BY DAVID McWILLIAMS (LP, laminated sleeve, also stereo SMLP 2) | 15 |
| 67 | Major Minor MMLP 10 | DAVID McWILLIAMS VOL. 2 (LP, laminated front cover, also stereo SMLP 10) | 15 |
| 68 | Major Minor MMLP 11 | VOLUME III (LP, also stereo SMLP 11) | 15 |
| 69 | Major Minor MCP 5026 | THE DAYS OF DAVID McWILLIAMS (LP) | 15 |
| 72 | Dawn DNLS 3039 | LORD OFFALY (LP, textured gatefold sleeve) | 20 |
| 73 | Dawn DNLS 3047 | THE BEGGAR AND THE PRIEST (LP) | 20 |
| 74 | Dawn DNLS 3059 | LIVING'S JUST A STATE OF MIND (LP) | 18 |

**M.D.C.**
| 83 | Crass 121984/5 | MULTI DEATH CORPORATION (EP) | 12 |

**VAUGHN MEADER**
| 63 | MGM MGM 1239 | No Hiding Place/The Elephant Song | 6 |

**MEADOW SWEET**
| 73 | Sunday SUN 1 | Behind You/Dreams In Colour | 40 |

**MEAN MACHINE**
| 76 | Chrysalis CHS 2089 | Boogie To The Drummer/Running With The Rat Pack | 10 |
*(see also Brian Bennett)*

**ME & THEM**
| 64 | Pye 7N 15596 | Feels So Good/I Think I'm Gonna Kill Myself | 18 |
| 64 | Pye 7N 15631 | Everything I Do Is Wrong/Show You Mean It Too | 15 |
| 64 | Pye 7N 15683 | Get Away/Tell Me Why | 15 |

**MEANIES**
| 79 | Vendetta VD 002 | Waiting For You/It's True (p/s) | 100 |

**MEANSTREAK**
| 81 | Meanstreak MS1 | (Time I) Played It Right/You Took The Fire/I Know (p/s) | 50 |

**MEAN STREET**
| 77 | Vortex/NEMS NES 115 | Bunch Of Stiffs/WASPS: Can't Wait 'Til '78 (p/s) | 18 |

**MEAN STREET DEALERS**
| 79 | Graduate GRAD 5 | Japanese Motorbikes/Tight Skirts (p/s) | 20 |
| 79 | Mean St. Dealers MSD 001 | BENT NEEDLES (LP) | 25 |
| 79 | Graduate GRADLP 1 | BENT NEEDLES (LP, reissue) | 18 |
*(see also Tea & Sympathy)*

**MEANWHILE BACK IN COMMUNIST RUSSIA...**
| 00 | Jitter JTR 1SP | No Cigar/Morning After Pill (p/s, 300 only) | 7 |

**MEASLES**
| 65 | Columbia DB 7531 | Casting My Spell/Bye Birdie Fly | 40 |
| 65 | Columbia DB 7673 | Night People/Dog Rough Dan | 25 |
| 66 | Columbia DB 7875 | Kicks/No Baby At All | 35 |
| 66 | Columbia DB 8029 | Walkin' In/Looking For Love | 25 |

**MEAT LOAF**
| 75 | Ode ODS 66304 | Clap Your Hands, Stamp Your Feet/Stand By Me (withdrawn) | 25 |
| 79 | Epic S EPC 12-7018 | Bat Out Of Hell/Heaven Can Wait (12", p/s, red vinyl) | 10 |
| 82 | Epic EPC 11 82419 | BAT OUT OF HELL (LP, picture disc) | 15 |
*(see also Stoney & Meat Loaf, Rocky Horror Show)*

**MEAT WHIPLASH**
| 85 | Creation CRE 020 | Don't Slip Up/Here It Comes (foldaround p/s in poly bag; 1st pressing has photo of band by fence) | 20 |
| 85 | Creation CRE 020 | Don't Slip Up/Here It Comes (foldaround p/s in poly bag; 2nd pressing has photo of band in field) | 8 |
*(see also Jesus & Mary Chain)*

**MECHANICAL HORSETROUGH**
| 70s | Kap KAPS 96 | Dogshit On Your Shoes/Jeremy Germoline/Horsetrough Hoedown (p/s) | 5 |
| 75 | Sonet SON 2068 | When Santa Lost His Trousers/The Ballad Of Big Bruce | 5 |

**MECHANICAL HEARTS**
| 91 | Mechanartz 017 | Precious Time/Pay The Driver | 60 |

**MECKENBURG ZINC**
| 70 | Orange OAS 205 | Hard Working Woman/I'd Like To Help You | 5 |

**MEDDY EVILS**
| 65 | Pye 7N 15941 | Find Somebody To Love/A Place Called Love | 125 |
| 66 | Pye 7N 17091 | It's All For You/Ma's Place | 160 |
*(see also Stu James and the Mojos, the Quik)*

**MEDIA (1)**
| 79 | Takeaway TA 001 | TV Kids/Don't Sit Back/Just For You/Rose And Crown (500 only, p/s) | 60 |

**MEDIA (2)**
| 80 | Brain Booster Music 4 | Back On The Beach Again/South Coast City Rockers (p/s) | 5 |

**MEDIATORS**
| 69 | Coxsone CS 7101 | Darling, There I Stand/PRINCE CHARLIE: Hit And Run | 100 |
| 70 | Supreme SUP 210 | When You Go To A Party (actually by Meditators)/ RUPIE EDWARDS ALLSTARS: Stop The Party | 15 |
*(see also Meditators)*

**MEDICINE HEAD**
| 69 | Dandelion S 4661 | His Guiding Hand/This Love Of Old | 20 |
| 70 | Dandelion S 5075 | Coast To Coast/All For Tomorrow | 12 |
| 71 | Dandelion DAN 7003 | (And The) Pictures In The Sky/Natural Sight (also listed as K 19002) (in p/s) | 10 |
| 72 | Dandelion 2001 276 | Kum On The Land | 6 |
| 72 | Dandelion 2001 325 | Only To Do What Is True/Sittin' In The Sun | 6 |
| 72 | Dandelion 2001 383 | How Does It Feel/Morning Light | 6 |

| | | | |
|---|---|---|---|
| 69 | Dandelion 63757 | NEW BOTTLES, OLD MEDICINE (LP) | 60 |
| 71 | Dandelion DAN 8005 | HEAVY ON THE DRUM (LP, gatefold sleeve, 1st pressing with lyric insert with DAN 8005 on sleeve, label and matrix) | 125 |
| 71 | Dandelion DAN 8005 | HEAVY ON THE DRUM (LP, gatefold sleeve, later pressing listed as K 49005; without lyric insert) | 50 |
| 71 | Dandelion 2310 166 | DARK SIDE OF THE MOON (LP, with insert) | 35 |
| 73 | Polydor 2310 248 | ONE & ONE IS ONE (LP, fold-out sleeve) | 15 |
| 74 | Polydor 2383 272 | THRU' A FIVE (LP) | 15 |

(see also Ashton Gardner & Dyke, British Lions)

## MEDITATIONS (1)

| | | | |
|---|---|---|---|
| 68 | Liberty LBF 15045 | Transcendental Meditation/Beautiful Experience | 7 |

## MEDITATIONS (2)

| | | | |
|---|---|---|---|
| 78 | Island IPR 2022 | Life Is Not Easy/Much Smarter (12") | 10 |
| 70s | GG's GG 097 | Justice/Version (12") | 25 |
| 80 | JB JBD21 | Vanity Lover/Part 2 (12") | 15 |
| 81 | Kingdom KV 8020 12 | Stranger In Love/Unity (12") | 15 |
| 77 | United Artists UAS30178 | MESSAGE FROM THE MEDITATIONS (LP) | 20 |
| 78 | Third World TWS 929 | WAKE UP! (LP) | 25 |
| 79 | Tad's TRDLP 101579 | GUIDANCE (LP) | 25 |
| 83 | Greensleeves GREL52 | NO MORE FRIEND (LP) | 15 |

## MEDITATORS

| | | | |
|---|---|---|---|
| 69 | Bullet BU 403 | Duba Duba/CECIL NICKY THOMAS: Running Alone | 20 |
| 69 | Success RE 901 | Look Who Bust A Style/RUPIE EDWARDS ALL STARS: Look Who Bust A Style | 35 |
| 70 | Big BG 302 | When You Go To A Party/Good Morning Mother Cuba | 20 |
| 71 | Big BG 305 | Music Alone Shall Live/RUPIE EDWARDS AND ALL STARS: Music Alone - Version | 20 |
| 73 | Pyramid PYR 7010 | Great Messiah/Nana Nana | 12 |
| 73 | Smash SMA 2331 | Things Not Easy/BONGO HERMAN & BINGY BUNNY: Ration | 10 |

(see also Busty Brown, Pat Satchmo)

## MEDIUM

| | | | |
|---|---|---|---|
| 68 | CBS 3404 | Edward Never Lies/Colours Of The Rainbow | 40 |

## MEDIUM MEDIUM

| | | | |
|---|---|---|---|
| 80 | APT SAP-01 | Them Or Me/Freeze (p/s) | 7 |
| 81 | Cherry Red CHEER 18 | Hungry, So Angry/Nadsat Dream (p/s) | 7 |
| 81 | Cherry Red BRED 19 | THE GLITTERHOUSE (LP) | 15 |

## MEDIUM WAVE

| | | | |
|---|---|---|---|
| 69 | Ember EMB 5265 | Walk In The Sunshine/Looking Towards The Sky (p/s) | 15 |

## BILL MEDLEY

| | | | |
|---|---|---|---|
| 67 | Verve VS 564 | That Lucky Old Sun/My Darling Clementine | 5 |
| 68 | MGM MGM 1418 | I Can't Make It Alone/One Day Girl | 6 |
| 68 | MGM MGM 1432 | Brown Eyed Woman/Let The Good Times Roll | 6 |
| 68 | MGM MGM 1456 | Peace Brother Peace/Winter Won't Come This Year | 5 |
| 69 | MGM MGM 1475 | This Is A Love Song/Something's So Wrong | 5 |
| 69 | MGM MGM 1491 | Someone Is Standing Outside/Reaching Back | 5 |
| 71 | A&M AMS 898 | You've Lost That Lovin' Feelin'/We've Only Just Begun | 5 |
| 69 | MGM MGM-C(S) 8091 | BILL MEDLEY 100% (LP) | 20 |

(see also Righteous Brothers, Garnet Mimms)

## JOE MEDLIN

| | | | |
|---|---|---|---|
| 59 | Mercury AMT 1032 | I Kneel At Your Throne/Out Of Sight, Out Of Mind | 25 |

## KEITH MEEHAN

| | | | |
|---|---|---|---|
| 69 | Marmalade 598 016 | Darkness Of My Life/TONY MEEHAN: Hooker Street | 30 |

## TONY MEEHAN

| | | | |
|---|---|---|---|
| 64 | Decca F 11801 | Song Of Mexico/Kings Go Fifth | 6 |

(see also Shadows, Jet Harris & Tony Meehan, Keith Meehan, John Paul Jones)

## JOE MEEK ORCHESTRA

| | | | |
|---|---|---|---|
| 63 | Decca F 11796 | The Kennedy March/The Theme Of Freedom | 30 |

(see also Blue Men)

## CARL MEEKS

| | | | |
|---|---|---|---|
| 89 | Greensleeves GREL 132 | JACKMANDORA (LP) | 20 |

## MEET JESUS MUSIC

| | | | |
|---|---|---|---|
| 72 | Echo ECH 002 | MEET JESUS MUSIC (LP) | 20 |

## MEGADETH

| | | | |
|---|---|---|---|
| 87 | Capitol CL 476 | Wake Up Dead/Black Friday (live) (p/s) | 10 |
| 87 | Capitol CLP 476 | Wake Up Dead/Black Friday (live) (skull-shaped picture disc with insert) | 18 |
| 87 | Capitol 12CL 476 | Wake Up Dead/Black Friday (live)/Devil's Island (live)/Wake Up Dead/Black Friday (live) (12", p/s, allegedly shrink-wrapped with 7" picture disc) | 25 |
| 87 | Capitol 12CL 476 | Wake Up Dead/Black Friday (live)/Devil's Island (live)/Wake Up Dead/Black Friday (live) (12", p/s) | 15 |
| 87 | Capitol 12CL 476 | Wake Up Dead/Black Friday (Tommy Vance Show)/Devil's Island (Tommy Vance Show) (12", stickered p/s, with 'Deth' certificate) | 15 |
| 88 | Capitol CL 480 | Anarchy In The U.K./Liar (p/s) | 10 |
| 88 | Capitol CLP 480 | Anarchy In The U.K./Liar (U.K.-shaped picture disc) | 15 |
| 88 | Capitol CL 489 | Mary Jane/Hook In Mouth | 6 |
| 88 | Capitol CLP 489 | Mary Jane/Hook In Mouth (picture disc) | 12 |
| 90 | Capitol CLP 588 | Holy Wars/The Punishment Due (poster p/s) | 5 |
| 90 | SBK SBKPD 4 | No More Mr. Nice Guy/DEAD ON: "Different Breed" (chair-shaped pic disc) | 15 |
| 90 | SBK 12 SBKP 4 | No More Mr. Nice Guy/DEAD ON: "Different Breed"/(DANGEROUS TOYS: Demon Bell [The Ballad Of Horace Pinker] (12", poster p/s) | 10 |
| 91 | Capitol CLS 604 | Hangar 18 (MJ 12 Edit)/The Conjuring (live) (p/s, shrinkwrapped with patch) | 15 |
| 91 | Capitol CLPD 604 | Hangar 18 (MJ 12 Edit)/The Conjuring (live) (Vic-shaped picture disc) | 20 |

| 92 | Capitol 12CLS 662 | Symphony Of Destruction/Breakpoint/Go To Hell (12", p/s, clear vinyl with giant autographed poster) | 20 |
|---|---|---|---|
| 92 | Capitol CLP 669 | Skin O' My Teeth (LP Version)/Holy Wars... The Punishment Due (The General Schwarzkopf Mix) (poster p/s, board game) | 6 |
| 92 | Capitol CLP 669 | Skin O' My Teeth (LP Version)/Holy Wars... The Punishment Due (The General Schwarzkopf Mix)/High Speed Dirt (live)/The Passes (Mustaine Remarks On Game) (10" bronze Megadeth box with passes & game rules) | 20 |
| 92 | Capitol CL 669 | Symphony Of Destruction/Skin O' My Teeth (yellow vinyl, p/s) | 12 |
| 92 | Capitol CL 669 | Symphony Of Destruction/Skin O' My Teeth (picture disc and card in PVC sleeve) | 10 |
| 94 | Capitol CL 730 | Train Of Consequences/Crown Of Worms (clear vinyl with sticker) | 6 |
| 88 | M. For Nations MFN 46P | KILLING IS MY BUSINESS ... AND BUSINESS IS GOOD (LP, picture disc with insert) | 20 |
| 88 | Capitol ESTP 2022 | PEACE SELLS ... BUT WHO'S BUYING? (LP, picture disc with insert) | 20 |
| 88 | Capitol ESTP 2053 | SO FAR, SO GOOD ... SO WHAT (LP, picture disc with insert) | 25 |
| 90 | Capitol ESTPD 2132 | RUST IN PEACE (LP, picture disc, die cut sleeve) | 30 |
| 94 | Capitol ESTPD 2244 | YOUTHANASIA (LP, picture disc) | 25 |
| 94 | Capitol ESTPD 2244 | YOUTHANASIA (LP, gatefold sleeve, blue vinyl) | 35 |
| 95 | Capitol CDESTS 2244 | YOUTHANASIA/HIDDEN TREASURES (2-CD, card sleeve, 2,000 only) | 25 |
| 07 | EMI 50995 13187 28 | WARCHEST ('ammo' box set with 4 CD's, DVD and booklet) | 35 |

## MEGATON
| 71 | Deram DM-R 331 | Out Of Your Own Little World/Niagara | 30 |
|---|---|---|---|
| 81 | Hot Metal HMM 69 | Aluminium Lady/Diehard (p/s) | 80 |
| 71 | Deram SML-R 1086 | MEGATON (LP, white/red label with small logo) | 1000 |

## MEGATONS (JAMAICA)
| 70 | Downtown DT 464 | Take It Easy/Funk The Beat | 15 |
|---|---|---|---|
| 70 | Downtown DT 469 | Militant Man/MUSIC DOCTORS: Reggae Jeggae Version | 15 |

*(see also Revelation)*

## MEGATONS (U.S.)
| 65 | Sue WI 325 | Shimmy Shimmy Walk (Parts 1 & 2) | 40 |
|---|---|---|---|

*(see also Billy Lee Riley)*

## MEGATRONS
| 59 | Top Rank JAR 146 | Velvet Waters/The Merry Piper | 6 |
|---|---|---|---|
| 59 | Top Rank JAR 236 | Tootie Flootie/Whispering Winds | 6 |

## GEORGE MEGGIE
| 72 | Bullet BU 504 | Hard To Believe/MAX ROMEO: Softie | 7 |
|---|---|---|---|
| 72 | Punch PH 112 | People Like People/MAX ROMEO: Softie | 7 |

## MEKONS
| 78 | Fast Products FAST 1 | Never Been In A Riot/32 Weeks/Heart And Soul | 20 |
|---|---|---|---|
| 78 | Fast Products FAST 7 | Where Were You?/I'll Have To Dance Then (On My Own) (p/s) | 10 |
| 80 | Virgon VS300 | Work All Week/Unknown Wrecks | 5 |
| 80 | Red Rhino RED 7 | Snow/Another One | 5 |
| 80 | Virgin SV 101 | Teeth/Guardian//Kill/Stay Cool (double pack, gatefold p/s) | 5 |
| 82 | CNT CNT 1 | This Sporting Life (6.12)/Frustration (6.21)/(mystery live track) (12", p/s) | 10 |
| 82 | CNT CNT 008 | This Sporting Life/Fight The Cuts (p/s) | 10 |
| 79 | Virgin V2143 | THE QUALITY OF MERCY IS NOT STRNEN (LP) | 20 |
| 82 | CNT CNT 009 | THE MEKONS STORY (LP) | 18 |

*(see also Batfish Boys, Ut)*

## MEL & DAVE
| 70 | Upsetter US 330 | Spinning Wheel/Version | 40 |
|---|---|---|---|

## MEL & TIM
| 70 | Concord CON 004 | Backfield In Motion/Do Right Baby (pink label design) | 6 |
|---|---|---|---|
| 70 | Concord CON 004 | Backfield In Motion/Do Right Baby (multi design) | 6 |
| 70 | Concord CON 004 | Backfield In Motion/Do Right Baby (egg design) | 6 |
| 73 | Stax 2025 125 | Starting All Over Again/It Hurts To Want You So Bad | 8 |
| 73 | Stax 2025 171 | What's Your Name/Free For All | 8 |
| 73 | Stax 2325 090 | STARTING ALL OVER AGAIN (LP) | 25 |

## MELANIE
| 68 | Buddah 2011 033 | Alexander Beetle/Christopher Robin/Animal Crackers (p/s) | 6 |
|---|---|---|---|
| 69 | Buddah 201 063 | Tuning My Guitar/Beautiful People (withdrawn, demos may exist) | 10 |

## TERRY MELCHER
| 68 | Rex R 11039 | Indian Lake/Be My Girl | 8 |
|---|---|---|---|
| 74 | Reprise K 54016 | TERRY MELCHER (LP) | 20 |

*(see also Terry Day, The Rip Chords, Freeway)*

## GIL MELLE (QUINTET)
| 55 | Vogue LDE 141 | GIL MELLE QUINTET (10" LP) | 15 |
|---|---|---|---|

## SUSAN MELLEN
| 75 | MAM MAMAS 1014 | THE MELLEN BIRD (LP, with insert) | 30 |
|---|---|---|---|

## MELLODITIES
| 64 | R&B JB 179 | Vacation/TOMMY McCOOK: Music Is My Occupation | 45 |
|---|---|---|---|

## MELLO & MELLOTONES
| 72 | Summit SUM 8538 | Haile Selasie/Old Man River | 10 |
|---|---|---|---|

*(see also Mellotones)*

## MELL(O)TONES
| 68 | Amalgamated AMG 812 | Fat Girl In Red/VERSATILES: Trust The Book | 20 |
|---|---|---|---|
| 68 | Amalgamated AMG 817 | Feel Good (actually maybe by Bleechers)/Soulful Mood (actually by Tommy McCook & Supersonics) | 30 |
| 68 | Doctor Bird DB 1136 | None Such/VAL BENNETT: Popeye On The Shore | 20 |
| 68 | Trojan TR 612 | Uncle Charlie/What A Botheration | 25 |
| 68 | Pyramid PYR 6060 | Let's Join Together/BEVERLEY'S ALLSTARS: I Don't Know | 50 |
| 69 | Camel CA 18 | Facts Of Life/TERMITES: I'll Be Waiting | 35 |

| 70 | Escort ERT 844 | Work It/SOUL MAN: Good Lover | 10 |

*(see also Sexy Girls)*

## MELLOW CANDLE

| 68 | SNB 55-3645 | Feeling High/Tea With The Sun | 100 |
| 72 | Deram DM 357 | Dan The Wing/Silversong (with promotional p/s) | 500 |
| 72 | Deram DM 357 | Dan The Wing/Silversong | 80 |
| 72 | Deram SDL 7 | SWADDLING SONGS (LP) | 2000 |
| 11 | Rise Above Relics RARLP007 | SWADDLING SONGS PLUS (Box set, 2-LP, white vinyl, 2 x 7" booklet) | 40 |

*(see also Alison O'Donnell)*

## MELLOW CATS WITH COUNT OSSIE & WARRICKAS

| 61 | Blue Beat BB 68 | Rock A Man Soul/MONTO & CYCLONES: Lazy Lou (B-side actually by Monty [Alexander] & Cyclones) | 25 |

*(see also Melo Cats)*

## MELLOW FRUITFULNESS

| 67 | Columbia S(C)X 6242 | MEDITATION (LP, mono/stereo) | 15 |

## MELLOW LARKS

| 60 | Blue Beat BB 16 | Time To Pray (Alleluia)/Love You Baby | 20 |
| 61 | Blue Beat BB 38 | No More Wedding/Lite Of My Life | 20 |

*(see also Basil Gabbidon)*

## MELLOW ROSE

| 80 | Studio 16 WE 0018 | Toom Much Heaven/Strike (12", with Vin Gordon) | 25 |
| 80 | Studio 16 WE 348 | Imitation Love/SGT. PEPPER: Dub A Rub Ina Imitation Way (12") | 25 |

## MELLOW SOUNDS

| 70 | Axe AXE 1 | Turn It Down/A Night Of Fear | 50 |

## GEORGE MELLY (& MICK MULLIGAN BAND)

| 51 | Tempo A 96 | Rock Island Line/Send Me To The 'Lectric Chair (78, as The George Melly Trio) | 10 |
| 55 | Decca F 10457 | Frankie And Johnny/I'm Down In The Dumps | 5 |
| 56 | Tempo A 144 | Jenny's Ball/Muddy Water | 5 |
| 56 | Tempo A 147 | Death Letter/Cemetery Blues | 5 |
| 61 | Columbia SEG 8093 | THE PSYCHOLOGICAL SIGNIFICANCE OF ANIMAL SYMBOLISM IN AMERICAN NEGRO FOLK MUSIC AND ALL THAT JAZZ (EP) | 10 |

*(see also Mick Mulligan Band)*

## MELO CATS

| 61 | Blue Beat BB 54 | Another Moses/ROLAND ALPHONSO & ALLEY CATS: Hully Gully Rock | 20 |

*(see also Mellow Cats)*

## MELODIANS

| 66 | Island WI 3014 | Lay It On/Meet Me | 40 |
| 67 | Coxsone CS 7004 | I Should Have Made It Up/JOE HIGGS: Neighbour Neighbour | 150 |
| 67 | Treasure Isle TI 7006 | You Don't Need Me/I Will Get Along | 30 |
| 67 | Treasure Isle TI 7022 | You Have Caught Me/I Know Just How She Feels | 50 |
| 67 | Treasure Isle TI 7023 | Last Train To Expo. '67/TOMMY McCOOK & SUPERSONICS: Expo | 25 |
| 68 | Treasure Isle TI 7028 | Come On, Little Girl/TOMMY McCOOK & SUPERSONICS: Got Your Soul | 30 |
| 68 | Doctor Bird DB 1125 | Little Nut Tree/You Are My Only Love | 25 |
| 68 | Doctor Bird DB 1139 | Swing And Dine/I Could Be King | 60 |
| 68 | Masters Time MT 004 | Let's Join Hands Together/My Last Word | 30 |
| 68 | Fab FAB 61 | Sweet Rose/It Comes And Goes | 40 |
| 69 | Gas GAS 108 | Ring Of Gold/You've Got It | 20 |
| 69 | Gas GAS 116 | Personally Speaking/LLOYD ROBINSON: Trouble Trouble | 45 |
| 69 | Crab CRAB 15 | When There Is You/UNIQUES: My Woman's Love | 45 |
| 69 | Trojan TR 660 | Everybody Bawlin'/TOMMY McCOOK: Kilowatt | 12 |
| 69 | Trojan TR 695 | Sweet Sensation/It's My Delight | 12 |
| 70 | Trojan TR 7720 | A Day Seems So Long/BEVERLEY'S ALLSTARS: Project | 12 |
| 70 | Trojan TR 7764 | Say Darling Say/Come Rock It To Me | 12 |
| 70 | High Note HS 044 | Love Is A Good Thing/No Nola | 12 |
| 70 | Summit SUM 8505 | Walking In The Rain/Rivers Of Babylon | 12 |
| 70 | Summit SUM 8508 | Rivers Of Babylon/BEVERLEY'S ALL STARS: Babylon Version | 12 |
| 71 | Duke DU 128 | The Sensational Melodians (Parts 1 & 2) | 12 |
| 71 | Summit SUM 8512 | It Took A Miracle/BEVERLEY'S ALLSTARS: Miraculous Version | 12 |
| 71 | Summit SUM 8522 | Come Ethiopians, Come/BEVERLEY'S ALLSTARS: Version Two | 12 |
| 71 | Summit SUM 8532 | My Love, My Life/My Love, My Life - Version | 12 |
| 72 | Summit SUM 8534 | The Time Has Come/BEVERLEY'S ALL STARS: McIntosh (B-side actually "No Sins At All" by Melodians) | 12 |
| 72 | Bullet BU 496 | Tropical Land/HUGH ROY & SLIM SMITH: Love I Bring | 12 |
| 72 | Duke DU 130 | The Mighty Melodians (Adapted) (Parts 1 & 2) | 8 |
| 72 | Attack ATT 8025 | This Beautiful Land/MELODIOUS RHYTHMS: Version | 8 |
| 72 | Attack ATT 8031 | Without You (What Would I Do)/DYNAMITES: Instrumental | 6 |
| 72 | Punch PH 111 | Round And Round/UPSETTERS: Round Version | 15 |
| 73 | Randy's RAN 530 | Passion Love/Love Makes The World Go Round | 6 |
| 78 | Sky Note SKYLP18 | PRE MEDITATION (LP) | 30 |

*(see also Gentiles, Tony Brevett, Brent Dowe, Jaylads, Trevor McNaughton, Gaylads, Joe Grinne)*

## MELODY

| 11 | Soul People SWSP 15 | Love Makes A Woman/Selfish One | 6 |

## BOBBY MELODY

| 69 | Duke DU 20 | The Break/BAND OF MERCY AND THE SALVATION: Suffering Stink | 175 |
| 79 | Hit Run HIT DD5 | Anger & Strife (ft. Jah Lion)/JAH LION: Johnnie Walker (12") | 30 |
| 82 | Negus Roots NERT012 | True True Loving/I'm Gonna Keep On Trying (12") | 20 |

## JOHNNY MELODY

| 68 | Pyramid PYR 6041 | You Treating Me Bad/ROLAND ALPHONSO: Peace And Love | 40 |

MINT VALUE £

| | | |
|---|---|---|
| 67 | Pyramid PYR 6023 | Govern Your Mouth (actually by George Dekker)/ROLAND ALPHONSO: Peace And Love ............ 30 |

*(see also Lloyd & Johnny Melody under 'L', Lloyd Terrell)*

## RICKY MELODY
| | | |
|---|---|---|
| 88 | Wolrd Enterprise WED 61 | What An Act/Version (12") ............ 80 |

## MELODY ENCHANTERS
| | | |
|---|---|---|
| 63 | Island WI 049 | Enchanter's Ball/I'll Be True ............ 20 |
| 63 | R&B JB 117 | Gone Gone/Blueberry Hill ............ 18 |

## MELODY FAIR
| | | |
|---|---|---|
| 68 | Decca F 12801 | Something Happened To Me/Sittin', Watchin', Waitin' ............ 6 |

## MELO'S MARITIME
| | | |
|---|---|---|
| 67 | Philips BF 1602 | Blow The Man Up/Maneater ............ 5 |

## KANSAS CITY MELROSE/CASINO SIMPSON
| | | |
|---|---|---|
| 72 | Chicago Piano 12-001 | KANSAS CITY MELROSE/CASINO SIMPSON (LP) ............ 15 |

## MONIQUE MELSEN
| | | |
|---|---|---|
| 71 | Decca F 23170 | The Love Beat/Pomme Pomme Pomme ............ 12 |

## JOE MELSON
| | | |
|---|---|---|
| 61 | Polydor NH 66959 | Oh Yeah!/What's The Use I Still Love You ............ 30 |
| 61 | Polydor NH 66961 | Hey Mister Cupid/No One Really Cares ............ 25 |
| 64 | Hickory 45-1229 | Stay Away From Her/His Girl ............ 5 |

## MELTATIONS
| | | |
|---|---|---|
| 87 | Meltations MEL 701 | 32 Sweet Teeth/I'll Take It As A Compliment (p/s) ............ 80 |

## MELTING BEAR
| | | |
|---|---|---|
| 85 | Beggars Banquet BEG 144 | It Makes No Difference/Nature's Way/Sea Song (unreleased, white label test pressings only) ............ 6 |

*(see also Icicle Works)*

## MELTON CONSTABLE
| | | |
|---|---|---|
| 70s | SIS private pressing | MELTON CONSTABLE (LP) ............ 150 |

## HAROLD MELVIN & BLUE NOTES
| | | |
|---|---|---|
| 72 | CBS 8496 | If You Don't Know Me By Now/Let Me Into Your World ............ 5 |
| 75 | Route RT 06 | Get Out/You May Not Love Me ............ 8 |
| 79 | Source SRC 102 | Prayin/Your Love Is Taking Me On A Journey ............ 8 |

## MELVINS
| | | |
|---|---|---|
| 90 | Tupelo TUPEP 10 | Sweet Young Thing Ain't Sweet No More/STEEL POLE BATH TUB: I Dreamed I Dream (12", p/s, green vinyl, 600 only) ............ 20 |
| 89 | Tupelo TUPL 7 | OZMA (LP) ............ 25 |
| 91 | Tupelo TUP LP 26 | BULLHEAD (LP) ............ 25 |

## MEMBERS
| | | |
|---|---|---|
| 78 | Stiff/One Off OFF 3 | Solitary Confinement/Rat Up A Drainpipe (p/s) ............ 15 |
| 79 | Virgin VS 242 | The Sound Of The Suburbs/Handling The Big Jets (clear vinyl, window p/s) ............ 6 |
| 79 | Virgin VS 292 | Killing Time/G.L.C. (die-cut washing machine p/s) ............ 5 |
| 80 | Virgin VS 352 | Flying Again/Disco Oui Oui//Live In A Lift/Rat Up A Drainpipe (double pack, gatefold p/s) ............ 5 |
| 83 | Albion ION1050 | Working Girl/The Family (square coloured vinyl, p/s) ............ 8 |

## MEMBRANES
| | | |
|---|---|---|
| 80 | Vinyl Drip VD 005 | Fashionable Junkies/Almost China (flexi in p/s) ............ 10 |
| 81 | Vinyl Drip VD 007 | Muscles/All Roads Lead To Norway/Entertaining Friends ............ 5 |

## MEMO
| | | |
|---|---|---|
| 74 | Decca F13539 | Kick A Tin Can/Attilah ............ 8 |

## MEMORIES
| | | |
|---|---|---|
| 74 | Rex R 11091 | Lay It On Me/Did Ya Get It ............ 20 |

## MEMOS
| | | |
|---|---|---|
| 59 | Parlophone R 4616 | The Biddy Leg/My Type Of Girl ............ 60 |

## MEMPHIS BEND
| | | |
|---|---|---|
| 73 | United Artists UP 35571 | Louisiana Hoedown/Right String Baby But The Wrong Yo Yo ............ 10 |
| 76 | United Artists UP 36132 | Ubangi Stomp/Tennessee ............ 8 |

## MEMPHIS HORNS
| | | |
|---|---|---|
| 71 | Atlantic 2091 080 | Woolly Bully/I Can't Turn You Loose ............ 10 |
| 77 | RCA PB 0836 | Get Up And Dance/Don't Abuse It ............ 6 |
| 71 | Mojo 2466 010 | THE MEMPHIS HORNS (LP) ............ 25 |

## MEMPHIS JUG BAND
| | | |
|---|---|---|
| 55 | HMV 7EG 8073 | MEMPHIS JUG BAND (EP, withdrawn) ............ 30 |

## MEMPHIS MINNIE
| | | |
|---|---|---|
| 64 | Heritage H 103 | MEMPHIS MINNIE (EP) ............ 75 |
| 69 | Limited Edition (no cat. no.) | MEMPHIS MINNIE 1934-1936 (LP) ............ 40 |
| 69 | Limited Edition (no cat. no.) | MEMPHIS MINNIE 1934-1941 (LP) ............ 40 |
| 69 | Sunflower ET 1400 | MEMPHIS MINNIE 1941-1949 (LP, 99 copies only) ............ 50 |

## MEMPHIS SLIM
| | | |
|---|---|---|
| 60 | Collector JDN 102 | Pinetop's Blues/How Long ............ 25 |
| 62 | Storyville A 45055 | Big City Girl/El Capitan (p/s) ............ 15 |
| 61 | Collector JEN 5 | GOING TO KANSAS CITY (EP) ............ 30 |
| 62 | Storyville SEP 385 | STORYVILLE BLUES ANTHOLOGY VOL. 5 - BOOGIE WOOGIE AND THE BLUES (EP) ............ 22 |
| 63 | Vocalion VEP 170155 | MEMPHIS SLIM AND LITTLE RICHARD (EP) ............ 80 |
| 63 | Summit LSE 2041 | WORLD'S FOREMOST BLUES SINGERS (EP) ............ 12 |
| 61 | Collector JGN 1004 | MEMPHIS SLIM U.S.A. (LP) ............ 45 |
| 61 | Collector JGN 1005 | MEMPHIS SLIM U.S.A. (VOL. 2) (LP) ............ 45 |
| 62 | Bluesville BV 1018 | JUST BLUES (LP) ............ 30 |
| 62 | Storyville SLP 118 | MEMPHIS SLIM (LP) ............ 22 |

| | | | |
|---|---|---|---|
| 62 | Storyville SLP 138 | THIS IS A GOOD TIME TO WRITE A SONG (LP) | 22 |
| 62 | Fontana 688 302 ZL | NO STRAIN (LP) | 25 |
| 63 | United Artists ULP 1042 | BROKEN SOUL BLUES (LP) | 30 |
| 64 | Storyville SLP 118 | TRAVELLIN' WITH THE BLUES (LP) | 22 |
| 64 | Xtra XTRA 1008 | MEMPHIS SLIM (LP) | 18 |
| 64 | Fontana 688 701 | ALONE WITH MY FRIENDS (LP) | 30 |
| 65 | Fontana TL 5254 | CLAP YOUR HANDS (LP) | 25 |
| 65 | Melodisc MLPS 12-149 | FATTENIN' FROGS FOR SNAKES (LP) | 25 |
| 66 | Fontana 688 315 ZL | FRISCO BAY BLUES (LP) | 30 |
| 67 | Polydor 623 211 | PINETOP'S BLUES (LP) | 18 |
| 68 | Polydor 623 263 | BLUESINGLY YOURS (LP, with Mickey Baker) | 18 |
| 68 | Xtra XTRA 5060 | ALL KINDS OF BLUES (LP) | 15 |
| 69 | Xtra XTRA 1085 | CHICAGO BLUES (LP) | 15 |
| 72 | Barclay 920 214 | BLUE MEMPHIS (LP, with Peter Green) | 75 |
| 72 | Barclay 920 332-3 | OLD TIMES, NEW TIMES (2-LP) | 18 |

*(see also Washboard Sam, Ivory Joe Hunter, Otis Spann)*

## MEMPHIS THREE
| | | | |
|---|---|---|---|
| 68 | Page One POF 070 | Wild Thing/She's A Yum Yum | 7 |

## MEN
| | | | |
|---|---|---|---|
| 79 | Virgin VS 269 | I Don't Depend On You/Cruel (p/s) | 15 |
| 79 | Virgin VS 269-12 | I Don't Depend On You/Cruel (12", p/s) | 20 |

*(see also Human League)*

## MENACE
| | | | |
|---|---|---|---|
| 77 | Illegal IL 004 | Screwed Up/Insane Society (p/s) | 15 |
| 77 | Illegal IL 004 | Screwed Up/Insane Society (12", p/s) | 20 |
| 77 | Small Wonder SMALL 5 | G.L.C./I'm Civilized (p/s) | 15 |
| 78 | Illegal IL 008 | I Need Nothing/Electrocutioner (p/s) | 15 |
| 79 | Small Wonder SMALL 16 | Final Vinyl: Last Year's Youth/Carry No Banners (p/s) | 8 |
| 82 | Fresh FRESH 14 | The Young Ones/Tomorrow's World/Live For Today (p/s) | 15 |
| 86 | Razor RAZ 18 | GLC - RIP (LP) | 25 |

*(see also Aces, Vermilion & Aces)*

## MENACE
| | | | |
|---|---|---|---|
| 01 | Plastica DPFT 004 | Reap What You Sow (12") | 15 |

## MENACE MAKES 3
| | | | |
|---|---|---|---|
| 92 | Danse City DC 1203 | Pure Hysteria (Give Me A Mother Mix)/Do You Feel What I'm Feeling? (Matrix Rise Remix)(12") | 50 |

## CARLOS MENDES
| | | | |
|---|---|---|---|
| 72 | Pye International 7N 25581 | Shadows/Glow-Worm | 8 |

## MENDES PREY
| | | | |
|---|---|---|---|
| 83 | MP AM 076 | On To The Borderline/Runnin' For You (p/s) | 20 |
| 86 | Wag WAG 2 | Wonderland/Can You Believe It (p/s) | 25 |
| 86 | Wag 12 WAG 2 | Wonderland/Can You Believe It (12", p/s) | 25 |

## ENOCH & CHRISTY MENSAH
| | | | |
|---|---|---|---|
| 60 | Melodisc M 1569 | Rebecca/Dakuku Dum | 5 |

## E.T. MENSAH & HIS TEMPO'S BAND
| | | | |
|---|---|---|---|
| 58 | Decca WAL 1001 | A SATURDAY NIGHT (10" LP) | 20 |
| 58 | Decca WAL 1002 | MORE MENSAH (10" LP) | 20 |
| 59 | Decca WAPS 27 | MENSAH's AFRICAN RHYTHMS (LP) | 35 |

## MENTAL
| | | | |
|---|---|---|---|
| 79 | Kamikaze Pig RAM 1 | God For A Day/18/Kill The Bill/Off The Rails (600 only, p/s) | 80 |

## MENTATZ
| | | | |
|---|---|---|---|
| 81 | Naff N 001 | Never Trust A Russian/Dead To The World (p/s) | 5 |

## MIKE MERCADO
| | | | |
|---|---|---|---|
| 67 | Parlophone 5589 | Hey Mister Monk It's Page Nine/Popcorn | 15 |

## MARY MAE MERCER
| | | | |
|---|---|---|---|
| 65 | Decca DFE 8599 | MARY MAE MERCER (EP) | 50 |

## SANDY MERCER
| | | | |
|---|---|---|---|
| 79 | H&L 6105091 | Now That You're In (What Cha Gonna Do About It)/Work Your Body (Work That Body) | 8 |

## MICKEY MERCIAN
| | | | |
|---|---|---|---|
| 84 | Unity Sound UN 029 | Ride The Rhythm/Go Anywhere (12") | 25 |

## FREDDIE MERCURY
| | | | |
|---|---|---|---|
| 84 | CBS WA 4735 | Love Kills/GEORGIO MORODER: Rotwang's Party (picture disc) | 30 |
| 85 | CBS DA 6019 | I Was Born To Love You/Stop All The Fighting//Love Kills (Extended)/ Stop All The Fighting (Extended) (double pack) | 15 |
| 85 | CBS A 6413 | Made In Heaven (Remix 3.59)/She Blows Hot And Cold (p/s) | 5 |
| 85 | CBS WA 6413 | Made In Heaven (Remix)/She Blows Hot And Cold (shaped picture disc) | 30 |
| 85 | CBS WA 6413 | Made In Heaven (Remix)/She Blows Hot And Cold (uncut shaped picture disc) | 500 |
| 85 | CBS A 6725 | Love Me Like There's No Tomorrow/Let's Turn It On (p/s) | 30 |
| 85 | CBS TA 6725 | Love Me Like There's No Tomorrow (Extended Version)/Let's Turn It On (Extended Version) (12", p/s) | 25 |
| 85 | CBS DTA 6725 | Love Me Like There's No Tomorrow (Extended Version)/Let's Turn It On (Extended Version)//Living On My Own (Extended 6.38)/My Love Is Dangerous (Extended 6.25) (12" double pack, shrinkwrapped with sticker) | 50 |
| 85 | CBS TA 6725 | Love Me Like There's No Tomorrow (Extended Version)/Let's Turn It On (Extended Version) (12", promo, white card sleeve, with sticker) | 50 |
| 86 | EMI EMI 5559 | Time (From The Musical)/Time (Instrumental) (p/s, with inner sleeve) | 5 |
| 87 | Parlophone RP 6151 | The Great Pretender/Exercises In Free Love (Mercury Vocal) (shaped picture disc) | 30 |
| 87 | Parlophone RP 6151 | The Great Pretender/Exercises In Free Love (Mercury Vocal) (shaped picture disc, with unfolded or folded plinth) | 60 |

# MERCURY REV

| | | | |
|---|---|---|---|
| 87 | Parlophone RP 6151 | The Great Pretender/Exercises In Free Love (Mercury Vocal) (shaped picture disc, with unfolded or folded plinth) | 40 |
| 87 | Parlophone RP 6151 | The Great Pretender/Exercises In Free Love (Mercury Vocal) (uncut shaped picture disc) | 350 |
| 87 | Parlophone 10R 6151 | The Great Pretender (Extended Version)/(7" Version)/Exercises In Free Love (7" Version) (10", 1-sided, printed white label, plain black die-cut sleeve, promo only) | 25 |
| 87 | Polydor POSP 887 | Barcelona/Exercises In Free Love (Caballé Vocal) (with Montserrat Caballé, with gatefold p/s) | 6 |
| 87 | Polydor POSPP 887 | Barcelona (7" Version)/Exercises In Free Love (Caballé Vocal) (7" Version)/ Barcelona (Extended Version) (12", picture disc) | 30 |
| 87 | Polydor POCD 887 | Barcelona/Exercises In Free Love (Version 2) (Caballé Vocal)/ Barcelona (Extended) (CD, autographed card p/s, promo only) | 300 |
| 87 | Polydor PO 23 DJ | The Golden Boy (with Montserrat Caballé) (radio edit) (1-sided DJ sampler, p/s, with sticker) | 100 |
| 88 | Polydor POSPX 23 | The Golden Boy/The Fallen Priest/The Golden Boy (Instrumental) (12", p/s) | 20 |
| 88 | Polydor PZCD234 | The Golden Boy/The Fallen Priest/The Golden Boy (Instrumental) (CD) | 35 |
| 88 | Polydor PO 29 | How Can I Go On/Overture Piccante (with Montserrat Caballe) (p/s) | 15 |
| 88 | Polydor POSX 29 | How Can I Go On/Overture Piccante (with Montserrat Caballe) (picture disc) | 45 |
| 89 | Polydor PZ 29 | How Can I Go On/Guide Me Home/Overture Piccante (12", p/s) | 25 |
| 89 | Polydor PZCD 29 | How Can I Go On/Guide Me Home/Overture Piccante (CD, picture disc) | 35 |
| 88 | Polydor CD 3 125 211 | The Golden Boy/La Japanese/Barcelona (CD promo, unreleased p/s, jewel case) | 100 |
| 89 | Polydor 0805 548-2 | Ensueno/Barcelona (Edit 4.24)/Exercises In Free Love/Barcelona (Extended Version 7.02)/Barcelona (Video) (CD Video) | 40 |
| 89 | Polydor 0805 580-2 | The Fallen Priest/The Golden Boy (Album Version)/The Golden Boy (Instrumental Version)/The Golden Boy (Video) (CD Video) | 40 |
| 92 | Polydor PO 234 | How Can I Go On/The Golden Boy (yellow p/s) | 7 |
| 92 | Parlophone R 6331 | In My Defence/Love Kills (Wolf Euro Mix) (p/s) | 6 |
| 06 | Parlophone KILLS 001 | Love Kills (Glimmer Mix)/(Pixel 82 Mix)/I Was Born To Love You (George Demure Mix) (12" promo) | 15 |
| 06 | Parlophone KILLS 003 | Living On My Own (mixes) (12" promo) | 15 |
| 85 | CBS CD 86312 | MR. BAD GUY (CD, with 3 extended mixes; beware of counterfeits) | 25 |
| 94 | Parlophone 7234 8 2814 10 | FREDDIE MERCURY REMIXES (LP, unreleased ) | 150 |
| 97 | EMI LPCENT 10 | THE FREDDIE MERCURY ALBUM (LP, reissue, EMI Centenary, stickered sleeve) | 20 |
| 00 | Parlophone FMRARE001 | THE SOLO COLLECTION (10 CD & 2 DVD box set) | 80 |

*(see also Queen, Larry Lurex, Eddie Howell, Billy Squier)*

## MERCURY REV

| | | | |
|---|---|---|---|
| 91 | Mint Film MINT 5 | Car Wash Hair/Coney Island Cyclone (4 track demo) (200 copies only, p/s) | 15 |
| 93 | Beggars Banquet BBQ 5 T | The Hum Is Coming From Her (as Mercury Theremin Sextet)/So There (as Mercury Rev Orchestra with Robert Creely) (10", p/s) | 8 |
| 91 | Mint Film MINTLP 4 | YERSELF IS STEAM (LP, with bonus LP 'Lego My Ego') | 20 |
| 93 | Beggars Banquet BBQLP 140 | BOCES (LP, clear red vinyl) | 20 |
| 95 | Beggars Banquet BBQLP 176 | SEE YOU ON THE OTHER SIDE (LP) | 20 |
| 95 | Beggars Banquet BBQLP 176 P | SEE YOU ON THE OTHER SIDE (LP, picture disc) | 30 |
| 98 | V2 VVR 1002771 | DESERTERS SONGS (LP) | 30 |
| 01 | V2 175218 | ALL IS DREAM (LP) | 20 |
| 05 | Virgin VVR1029231 | THE SECRET MIGRATION (LP) | 15 |
| 08 | V2 VVR1051271 | SNOWFLAKE MIDNIGHT (2-LP) | 18 |

*(see also Harmony Rockets)*

## MERCY

| | | | |
|---|---|---|---|
| 69 | London HLZ 10273 | Love (Can Make You Happy)/Fireball | 20 |

## MERCYFUL FATE

| | | | |
|---|---|---|---|
| 83 | Music For Nations MFN 10 | MELISSA (LP, inner) | 15 |
| 84 | Music For Nations MFN 28 | DON'T BREAK THE OATH (LP, inner) | 15 |

## BURGESS MEREDITH

| | | | |
|---|---|---|---|
| 63 | Colpix PX 690 | Home In The Meadow/No Goodbye | 5 |

## MIKEY MERICAN

| | | | |
|---|---|---|---|
| 85 | Hands & Hearts HHDD 007 | Family Affair/Family Dub (12") | 20 |
| 86 | Unity UN 024 | Control The Dance/Version/Automatic/Version (12") | 20 |
| 86 | Unity UN 029 | Ride The Rhythm/Version/Go Anywhere/Version (12") | 20 |
| 86 | Regal RG 001 | Rub A Dub Party/Money Lover (12", as Mikey Merica) | 15 |

## TRUMAN MERIT

| | | | |
|---|---|---|---|
| 93 | Spurt 3 | ALIEN BOOGIE (LP and free 7") | 18 |

## LOTTIE MERLE

| | | | |
|---|---|---|---|
| 72 | Flyright 001 | Howling In The Moonlight/Catfish | 10 |

## MERLIN Q

| | | | |
|---|---|---|---|
| 69 | Pye 7N 17828 | The Secret/Love's Beautiful | 25 |

## RAY MERRELL

| | | | |
|---|---|---|---|
| 60 | Ember EMB S 113 | Why Did You Leave Me?/Teenage Love (p/s) | 10 |
| 60s | Aral PS 115 | Battle Of Waterloo/Not Any More (p/s) | 10 |
| 70 | Jay Boy BOY 22 | Tears Of Joy/Searchin' (withdrawn) (Beware of bootlegs!) | 200 |
| 70 | Jay Boy BOY 22 | Tears Of Joy/Searchin' (withdrawn) (Beware of bootlegs!) (DJ copy) | 350 |

## TONY MERRICK

| | | | |
|---|---|---|---|
| 66 | Columbia DB 7913 | Lady Jane/Michelle | 10 |
| 66 | Columbia DB 7995 | Wake Up/It's For You | 6 |

## BOB MERRILL

| | | | |
|---|---|---|---|
| 58 | Columbia DB 4086 | Nairobi/Jump When I Say Frog | 15 |

## BUDDY MERRILL

| | | | |
|---|---|---|---|
| 66 | Vocalion VN 9261 | Sweet September/Sherk | 12 |

## HELEN MERRILL

| | | | |
|---|---|---|---|
| 58 | Mercury MMB 12000 | THE NEARNESS OF YOU (LP, features Bill Evans) | 40 |

## MERRITTS
70  Hot Rod HR 113      I Don't Want To (Part 1)/HOT ROD ALL STARS: Version ........... 30

## MERRY MAKER
76  Western Kingston WK 505   Untouchable Special/Straight To Music City Head ........ 10

## MERRYMEN
66  Doctor Bird DB 1004    Big Bamboo/Island Woman ........... 15
69  Trojan TR 7707    Little Drummer Boy/Mary's Boy Child ........... 10
71  Duke DU 113    Big Bamboo/King Ja-Ja (both sides actually with Emille Straker)........... 12
68  Island ILP 984    CARIBBEAN TREASURE CHEST (LP) ........... 30

*(see also Soul Brothers)*

## JASON MERRYWEATHER
69  Crystal CR 001    My Summer Love/Abigail ........... 10

*(see also Ricky Valance)*

## MERSEYBEATS
63  Fontana TF 412    It's Love That Really Counts/The Fortune Teller ........... 12
64  Fontana TF 431    I Think Of You/Mister Moonlight ........... 5
64  Fontana TF 459    Don't Turn Around/Really Mystified ........... 6
64  Fontana TF 482    Wishin' And Hopin'/Milkman ........... 5
64  Fontana TF 504    Last Night/See Me Back ........... 10
65  Fontana TF 568    Don't Let It Happen To Us/It Would Take A Long Long Time ........... 10
65  Fontana TF 607    I Love You, Yes I Do/Good Good Lovin' ........... 8
65  Fontana TF 645    I Stand Accused/All My Life ........... 10
69  Fontana TF 1025    I Think Of You/Wishin' And Hopin' (p/s) ........... 10
81  Tudor CHEM 001    This Is Merseybeat (both sides) (p/s) ........... 6
64  Fontana TE 17422    ON STAGE (EP) ........... 25
64  Fontana TE 17423    I THINK OF YOU (EP) ........... 25
64  Fontana TE 17432    THE MERSEYBEATS (EP) ........... 25
64  Fontana TL 5210    THE MERSEYBEATS (LP) ........... 60
69  Wing WL 1163    THE MERSEYBEATS (LP) ........... 15

*(see also Merseys, Rockin' Horse, Tony Crane, Kirkbys, Quotations, Johnny Gustavson)*

## MERSEYBOYS
64  Ace Of Clubs ACL 1169   15 GREAT SONGS BY JOHN, PAUL AND GEORGE (LP) ........... 20

## MERSEYS
66  Fontana TF 694    Sorrow/Some Other Day ........... 6
66  Fontana TF 732    So Sad About Us/Love Will Continue ........... 15
66  Fontana TF 776    Rhythm Of Love/Is It Love? ........... 10
67  Fontana TF 845    The Cat/Change Of Heart ........... 25
68  Fontana TF 916    Penny In My Pocket/I Hope You're Happy ........... 10
68  Fontana TF 955    Lovely Loretta/Dreaming ........... 15
73  Philips 6006 258    Sorrow/MERSEYBEATS: I Think Of You ........... 5

*(see also Merseybeats, Crackers)*

## WIM MERTENS
87  Factory FACT 190c    EDUCES ME (cassette, in bespoke box with insert) ........... 200

## MERTON PARKAS
79  Beggars Banquet BEG 22   You Need Wheels/I Don't Want To Know You (coloured p/s with patch) ........... 10
79  Beggars Banquet BEG 22   You Need Wheels/I Don't Want To Know You (coloured p/s) ........... 7
79  Beggars Banquet BEG 25   Plastic Smile/The Man With The Disguise (p/s) ........... 6
79  Beggars Banquet BEG 30   Give It To Me Now/Gi' It (p/s) ........... 7
80  Beggars Banquet BEG 43   Put Me In The Picture/In The Midnight Hour (p/s) ........... 7
83  Well Suspect BLAM 002   Flat 19/Band Of Gold (p/s) ........... 10
80s Beggars Banquet BEG 22   You Need Wheels/I Don't Want To Know You (reissue, with silver Moulded label, black & white p/s) ........... 7
79  Beggars Banquet BEGA 11   FACE IN THE CROWD (LP) ........... 18

*(see also Style Council)*

## MESCALINE UNITED
92  R&S RS 92019    We Have Arrived (Aphex Twin QQT Reconstruction Mix)/We Have Arrived (Aphex Twin TTQ Reconstruction Mix) (limited issue 12", also known as "PCP Remixed" plain paper sleeve) ........... 70

## MESS
82  Reasonable MEP 1    Tried And Tested/I'm Falling ........... 12

## MESSAGE (1)
70  Doctor Bird DB 1503    Rum-Bum-A-Loo/Drummer Boy ........... 125
72  Reggae REG 3004    Wrestling/Tricia ........... 60

*(see also Boris Gardner)*

## MESSAGE (2)
75  Decca SKL-R 5213    MESSAGE (LP, blue/silver label) ........... 25

## MESSAGE (3)
81  Is It Original...? ISIT1    Empty Promise/War Of The Music ........... 100

## RICKY MESSENGER & SEMI PROFESSIONALS
80s Kim 019    Now Is The Time For Jah/Mr. Richman (12") ........... 20

## MESSENGERS
64  Columbia DB 7344    I'm Stealin' Back/This Little Light Of Mine ........... 10
65  Columbia DB 7495    When Did You Leave Heaven/More Pretty Girls Than One ........... 8

## MESSENGERS (JAMAICA)
73  Attack ATT 8057    Crowded City/Thula Thula ........... 5
73  Bread BR 1116    Cherry Baby/B.B. SEATON: Summertime ........... 10
73  Mirto MIR 100    Is It Because I'm Black/Just Like A Shelter ........... 12

MINT VALUE £

## MESSENGERS OF THE CROSS
| | | |
|---|---|---|
| 69 | Emblem JDR 21 | MESSENGERS OF THE CROSS (LP) ............................................................ 20 |

## METABOLIST
| | | |
|---|---|---|
| 79 | Drömm DRO 1 | Drömm/Slaves/Eulam's Beat (p/s, rough screen-printed & folded p/s) .................... 20 |
| 79 | Drömm DRO 1 | Drömm/Slaves/Eulam's Beat (p/s, smooth printed & stapled p/s) ....................... 10 |
| 80 | Drömm DRO 3 | Identity/Tizhoznam (p/s) ........................................................................... 15 |
| 79 | Drömm NCN | GOATMANAUT (cassette) ......................................................................... 50 |
| 80 | Drömm DRO 2 | HANSTEN KLORK (LP) ............................................................................. 20 |
| 81 | Cassetteking CK2 | STAGMANAUT! (cassette) ........................................................................ 50 |

## METAL BOYS
| | | |
|---|---|---|
| 79 | Rough Trade RT 016 | Sweet Marilyn/Fugue For A Darkening Island (p/s) ......................................... 8 |

*(see also Metal Urbain)*

## METALLICA
### SINGLES
| | | |
|---|---|---|
| 84 | Music For Nations 12 KUT 105 | Jump In The Fire/Seek And Destroy (live)/Phantom Lord (live) (12", p/s, initial pressing with beige labels) ........................................................................ 25 |
| 84 | Music For Nations 12 KUT 105 | Jump In The Fire/Seek And Destroy (live)/Phantom Lord (live) (12", p/s, later pressing with red/yellow labels) ............................................................................... 20 |
| 84 | Music For Nations CV12 KUT 105 | Jump In The Fire/Seek And Destroy (live)/Phantom Lord (live) (12", red vinyl, p/s) ...... 25 |
| 84 | Music For Nations 12 KUT 105XP | Jump In The Fire/Seek And Destroy (live)/Phantom Lord (live) (12", stickered sleeve with sew-on patch) ................................................................................. 30 |
| 84 | Music For Nations 12 KUT 112 | Creeping Death/Am I Evil?/Blitzkrieg (12", p/s, initial pressing with beige label) .......... 20 |
| 84 | Music For Nations 12 KUT 112 | Creeping Death/Am I Evil?/Blitzkrieg (12", p/s, later pressing with red/yellow labels).. 18 |
| 84 | Music For Nations CV12 KUT 112 | Creeping Death/Am I Evil?/Blitzkrieg (12", p/s, blue vinyl, red/yellow or 'Special Anniversary Edition' labels) ..................................................................... 35 |
| 84 | Music For Nations GV12 KUT 112 | Creeping Death/Am I Evil?/Blitzkrieg (12", no p/s, 'Anniversary Gold Edition', gold vinyl, 3000 only; mispressing with 1 side gold, 1 side black vinyl) ......................... 80 |
| 84 | Music For Nations GV12 KUT 112 | Creeping Death/Am I Evil?/Blitzkrieg (12", no p/s, 'Anniversary Gold Edition', gold vinyl, 3000 only) ................................................................................... 70 |
| 84 | Music For Nations P12 KUT 112 | Creeping Death/Am I Evil?/Blitzkrieg (12", picture disc, initially without barcode) ....... 30 |
| 84 | Music For Nations CD12 KUT 112 | Creeping Death/Am I Evil?/Blitzkrieg Jump In The Fire/ Seek And Destroy (live)/ Phantom Lord (live) (CD) ......................................................................... 60 |
| 86 | Music For Nations PKUT 105 | Jump In The Fire/Phantom Lord (live) (shaped picture disc, initial pressing without barcode) ................................................................................................ 25 |
| 86 | Music For Nations PKUT 105 | Jump In The Fire/Phantom Lord (live) (shaped picture disc, later pressing with barcode) ................................................................................................ 20 |
| 86 | Music For Nations PKUT 105 | Jump In The Fire/Phantom Lord (live) (uncut picture disc) ............................... 150 |
| 87 | Vertigo METAL 112 | $5.98 EP - GARAGE DAYS RE-REVISITED: Helpless/Crash Course In Brain Surgery/The Small Hours/Last Caress - Green Hell (medley) (12" p/s, later copies add "The Wait") .. 35 |
| 88 | Vertigo METAL 212 | Harvester Of Sorrow/Breadfan/The Prince (12", p/s, some with 'skull' label) ........... 18 |
| 89 | Vertigo METAL 312 | Jump In The Fire/Seek And Destroy (live)/Phantom Lord (live) (12", p/s, reissue) ......... 10 |
| 89 | Vertigo METAL 412 | Creeping Death/Am I Evil?/Blitzkrieg (12", p/s, reissue) ................................... 10 |
| 89 | Vertigo 842-219-2 | Creeping Death/Am I Evil?/Blitzkrieg/Jump In The Fire/ Seek And Destroy (live)/ Phantom Lord (live) (CD) ......................................................................... 50 |
| 89 | Vertigo METAP 5 | One/Seek And Destroy (live) (card p/s, some stickered, with rolled poster) ........... 15 |
| 89 | Vertigo METPD 510 | One/Seek And Destroy (live) (10", picture disc with card) ............................... 30 |
| 89 | Vertigo METAL 5 | One/Seek And Destroy (live) (silver/black labels, paper p/s) ............................. 10 |
| 89 | Vertigo METAL 512 | One (Demo Version)/For Whom The Bell Tolls (live)/Welcome Home (Sanitarium) (live) (12", p/s initial pressing with white labels) ........................................ 12 |
| 89 | Vertigo METAL 512 | One (Demo Version)/For Whom The Bell Tolls (live)/Welcome Home (Sanitarium) (live) (12", p/s later pressing with yellow labels) ....................................... 10 |
| 89 | Vertigo METAL 512 | One (Demo Version)/For Whom The Bell Tolls (live)/Welcome Home (Sanitarium) (live) (12", p/s mis-labelled as "Seek And Destroy" [live]) ............................ 10 |
| 89 | Vertigo METG 512 | One (Demo Version)/For Whom The Bell Tolls (live)/Welcome Home (Sanitarium) (live) (12", gatefold p/s, with booklet, mispressed with B-side label on both sides) ...... 20 |
| 90 | Vertigo 875 487 1 | THE GOOD, THE BAD AND THE LIVE - THE 6½ YEARS ANNIVERSARY COLLECTION (6 x 12", with live 4-track EP [METAL 612]) ...................................................... 80 |
| 91 | Vertigo METAL 7 | Enter Sandman/Stone Cold Crazy (p/s) ....................................................... 8 |
| 91 | Vertigo METAL 7 | Enter Sandman/Stone Cold Crazy (picture disc in p/s, stickered) ....................... 15 |
| 91 | Vertigo METBX 712 | Enter Sandman/Stone Cold Crazy/Enter Sandman (Demo) (12", box with 4 photo prints) ................................................................................................ 30 |
| 91 | Vertigo METCD 7 | Enter Sandman/Stone Cold Crazy/Enter Sandman (Demo) (CD, picture disc in box with room for 3 more CDs) ............................................................................... 30 |
| 92 | Vertigo METAL 10 | Nothing Else Matters/Enter Sandman (live) (p/s, black & white label) ................ 10 |
| 92 | Vertigo METCL 10 | Nothing Else Matters - Live At Wembley 20/4/92: Enter Sandman/ Sad But True/ Nothing Else Matters (CD) ....................................................................... 25 |
| 93 | Vertigo METAL 11 | Sad But True/Nothing Else Matters (p/s, stickered, no labels) ........................... 6 |
| 93 | Vertigo METAL 1112 | Sad But True/Nothing Else Matters (Elevator Version)/Creeping Death (live)/ Sad But True (Demo) (12" picture disc with insert) ................................................. 20 |
| 96 | Vertigo METJB 12 | Until It Sleeps/Until It Sleeps (jukebox issue, no p/s) ...................................... 10 |
| 97 | Vertigo METJB 13 | Hero Of The Day/Hero Of The Day (jukebox issue, no p/s) ............................... 8 |
| 97 | Vertigo METJB 15 | The Memory Remains/For Whom The Bell Tolls (Haven't Heard It Yet Remix) (Jukebox issue no p/s) ....................................................................................... 18 |
| 03 | Columbia GABBA 1 | 53rd & 3rd/Outsider (by GREEN DAY)/I Wanna Be Sedated (by OFFSPRING) (blue vinyl, stickered p/s withdrawn single) .................................................... 300 |
| 03 | Vertigo 9865411 | St. Anger/We're A Happy Family ................................................................... 6 |
| 90s | Vertigo METJB 19 | Whiskey In The Jar/Turn The Page (Jukebox issue no p/s) ............................... 6 |
| 10 | Vertigo 00602527391100 | Frantic (UNKLE Remix)/BLACK SABBATH: Paranoid (Alternative Vocal Version (12", 1000 only)) ........................................................................................... 20 |

### ALBUMS
| | | |
|---|---|---|
| 83 | Music For Nations MFN 7 | KILL 'EM ALL (LP, 1st issue with beige labels) ............................................. 35 |

| 83 | Music For Nations MFN 7 | KILL 'EM ALL (LP, later pressing with red/yellow]) | 30 |
|---|---|---|---|
| 84 | M. For Nations MFNCD 7 | KILL 'EM ALL (CD) | 30 |
| 84 | Music For Nations MFN 27 | RIDE THE LIGHTNING (LP, with inner sleeve, initial pressing with beige labels & without barcode) | 25 |
| 84 | M. For Nations MFN 27P | RIDE THE LIGHTNING (CD) | 25 |
| 86 | Music For Nations MFN 60 | MASTER OF PUPPETS (LP, with inner sleeve & insert) | 20 |
| 86 | Music For Nations MFN 60 | MASTER OF PUPPETS (LP, mispressing, Side 1 label on both sides) | 30 |
| 86 | Music For Nations MFN 60P | MASTER OF PUPPETS (LP, picture disc, initially without barcode) | 25 |
| 86 | Music For Nations MFN 60P | MASTER OF PUPPETS (LP, picture disc, with barcode) | 25 |
| 86 | M. For Nations MFNCD 60 | MASTER OF PUPPETS (CD) | 30 |
| 86 | Music For Nations MFN 27P | RIDE THE LIGHTNING (LP, picture disc, initial pressing with no barcode) | 30 |
| 86 | Music For Nations MFN 27P | RIDE THE LIGHTNING (LP, picture disc, with barcode) | 20 |
| 86 | Music For Nations MFN 7P | KILL 'EM ALL (LP reissue, picture disc, lacking picture on 1 side, initially lacking barcode) | 25 |
| 86 | Music For Nations MFN 7P | KILL 'EM ALL (LP reissue, picture disc, with picture on 1 side and barcode) | 22 |
| 87 | Music For Nations MFN 7DM | KILL 'EM ALL (2-LP, 'direct metal mastered' reissue, gatefold sleeve) | 35 |
| 87 | Music For Nations MFN 60DM | MASTER OF PUPPETS (2-LP, 'direct metal mastered' reissue, gatefold sleeve with poster) | 30 |
| 87 | Music For Nations MFN 27DM | RIDE THE LIGHTNING (2-LP, 'direct metal mastered' reissue, gatefold sleeve with insert) | 30 |
| 88 | Vertigo VERH 61 | ...AND JUSTICE FOR ALL (2-LP) | 18 |
| 89 | Vertigo 838-140-1 | RIDE THE LIGHTNING (LP, reissue, mispressing, Side 1 lists Master Of Puppets tracks) | 20 |
| 91 | Vertigo 510 022-1 | METALLICA (2-LP) | 40 |
| 91 | Vertigo MECAN 1/510-022-0 | THE METALLICAN (CD, gold disc in metal 'paint can' with video & T-shirt; 35,000 only) | 100 |
| 93 | Vertigo 518-725-0 | LIVE SHIT, BINGE & PURGE (3-CD box set with 3 videos & 72-page book) | 80 |
| 96 | Ekektra 532618 | LOAD (2-LP, gatefold) | 30 |
| 97 | Elektra 536409 | RELOAD (2-LP, gatefold, stickered sleeve with inners) | 30 |
| 98 | Vertigo 538 351-1 | GARAGE INC. (3-LP, gatefold, inners) | 25 |
| 08 | Vertigo 00602517737310 | DEATH MAGNETIC (Box set, 5x12") | 40 |
| 08 | Vertigo 00602517800502 | DEATH MAGNETIC (LP, coffin-shaped box set, CD, DVD, T-shirt, guitar picks, flag, poster and credit card) | 75 |
| 08 | Universal 0600753085271 | KILL 'EM ALL (2-LP, reissue, gatefold with obi) | 20 |
| 08 | Universal 0600753085240 | RIDE THE LIGHTNING (2-LP, reissue, gatefold with obi) | 25 |
| 08 | Universal 0600753101162 | MASTER OF PUPPETS (2-LP, reissue, gatefold with obi) | 25 |

**PROMOS**

| 88 | Vertigo METDJ 2 | Harvester Of Sorrow/Harvester Of Sorrow (unique p/s) | 60 |
|---|---|---|---|
| 88 | Vertigo MET CD 100 | THE WHIPLASH SAMPLER (CD) | 70 |
| 89 | Vertigo METDJ 5 | One/One (Edit) (unique blue cover, plus insert) | 90 |
| 89 | Vertigo METDJ 512 | One (Demo Version)/For Whom The Bell Tolls (live)/Welcome Home (Sanitarium) (live) (12", unissued, promo-only p/s) | 70 |
| 91 | Vertigo METAL 7 | Enter Sandman/Stone Cold Crazy (jukebox promo) | 10 |
| 91 | Vertigo METDJ 7 | Enter Sandman (Radio Edit)/Stone Cold Crazy (p/s B-side actually silent) | 15 |
| 91 | Vertigo METDJ8 | The Unforgiven (edit)/Killing Time (p/s) | 25 |
| 96 | Mercury MM CJ-1 | MANDATORY METALLICA (CD, 7-track sampler) | 30 |
| 96 | Vertigo MET INT 1 | LOAD - THE INTERVIEW (CD, with cue booklet) | 50 |
| 97 | Vertigo MMCJ-2 | MANDATORY METALLICA 2 (2-CD, 17-track sampler) | 35 |
| 03 | Vertigo FRANTICDJ 1 | Frantic (12" promo) | 15 |

**METAL MIRROR**

| 80 | M&M MM 001 | Rock 'N Roll Ain't Never Gonna Leave Us/English Booze (in p/s) | 80 |
|---|---|---|---|
| 80 | M&M MM 001 | Rock 'N Roll Ain't Never Gonna Leave Us/English Booze | 50 |

**METAL URBAIN**

| 77 | Rough Trade RT 001 | Paris Maquis/Cle De Contact (p/s) | 15 |
|---|---|---|---|
| 78 | Radar ADA 20 | Hysterie Connective/Pas Poubelle | 12 |

**METAPHORCE**

| 95 | Ill Gotten Gains FDN004 | Recipes For Disaster/Behind Enemy Lines (12") | 14 |
|---|---|---|---|

**METEORS (1)**

| 64 | Polydor NH 52263 | Get A Load Of This/Ruby Ann | 10 |
|---|---|---|---|

**METEORS (2)**

| 79 | EMI EMI 2987 | It's Only You/Blitzkreig (p/s) | 8 |
|---|---|---|---|
| 79 | EMI EMI 5000 | My Balls Ache/Action (p/s) | 5 |

**METEORS (3)**

| 81 | Ace SWT 65 | METEOR MADNESS (10" EP, white label test pressings only, custom p/s) | 250 |
|---|---|---|---|
| 81 | Ace SW 65 | METEOR MADNESS (EP, on blue vinyl) | 25 |
| 81 | Ace SW 65 | METEOR MADNESS (EP) | 15 |
| 81 | Lost Souls LOST 101 | The Crazed/Attack Of The Zorch Men (p/s) | 12 |
| 81 | Chiswick CHIS 147 | Radioactive Kid/Graveyard Stomp (p/s) | 12 |
| 81 | Ace NS 74 | Radioactive Kid/Graveyard Stomp (p/s, reissue, black vinyl) | 8 |
| 81 | Ace NS 74 | Radioactive Kid/Graveyard Stomp (p/s, reissue, some clear or blue vinyl) | 10 |
| 82 | I.D. EYE 1 | Johnny Remember Me/Fear Of The Dark/Wreckin' Crew (p/s) | 8 |
| 82 | WXYZ ABCD 5 | Mutant Rock/The Hills Have Eyes (p/s) | 10 |
| 84 | Mad Pig PORK 1 | I'm Just A Dog/Electro Rock (p/s) | 6 |
| 85 | Mad Pig PORK 2 | Fire, Fire/Little Red Riding Hood (p/s) | 10 |
| 85 | Mad Pig PORK 2T | Fire, Fire/Little Red Riding Hood/Stampede (King Ray Bat Scalator In The Dark Mix) (12", p/s) | 10 |
| 85 | Mad Pig PORK 3 | Bad Moon Rising/Rhythm Of The Bell (p/s) | 10 |
| 86 | I.D. EYET 10 | MUTANT ROCK (12" EP, green or blue vinyl) | 12 |
| 86 | Anagram ANA 31 | Surf City/The Edge (p/s) | 10 |
| 86 | Anagram 12ANA 31 | Surf City (Has Beens From Outer Space Mix)/The Edge/Johnny's Here (12", p/s) | 15 |
| 87 | Anagram ANA 35 | Go Buddy Go/You Crack Me Up (p/s) | 7 |

| Year | Label/Cat. No. | Title | MINT VALUE £ |
|---|---|---|---|
| 81 | Ace MAD 1 | THE METEORS MEET SCREAMIN' LORD SUTCH (mini-LP, 1 side each, 1,000 only, stickered cartoon print on plain card sleeve) | 100 |
| 81 | Lost Soul LOSTLP 3001 | IN HEAVEN (LP) | 20 |
| 86 | Big Beat WIKA 47 | TEENAGERS FROM OUTER SPACE (LP) | 20 |
| 86 | Anagram GRAM 27 | SEWERTIME BLUES (LP) | 18 |
| 87 | Dojo LP56P | NIGHT OF THE WEREWOLF (LP, picture disc) | 15 |

(see also Tall Boys, Clapham South Escalators, [Screamin'] Lord Sutch, Deadbeats)

## METERS

| Year | Label/Cat. No. | Title | MINT VALUE £ |
|---|---|---|---|
| 69 | Stateside SS 2140 | Sophisticated Cissy/Sehorn's Farm | 12 |
| 70 | Direction 58-4751 | Look-Ka-Py-Py/This Is My Last Affair | 12 |
| 74 | Reprise K 14367 | People Say/Africa | 6 |
| 75 | Reprise K 14405 | Fire On The Bayou/They All Ask'd For You | 6 |
| 72 | Reprise K 44242 | CABBAGE ALLEY (LP) | 20 |
| 74 | Reprise K 54027 | REJUVENATION (LP) | 20 |
| 74 | Island ILPS 9250 | CISSY STRUT (LP) | 20 |
| 75 | Reprise K 54044 | FIRE ON THE BAYOU (LP) | 30 |
| 76 | Reprise K 54076 | BEST OF THE METERS (LP) | 15 |
| 76 | Reprise K 54078 | TRICK BAG (LP) | 18 |

## METGUMBNERBONE

| Year | Label/Cat. No. | Title | MINT VALUE £ |
|---|---|---|---|
| 83 | Aeon (No Cat. No.) | COPS OF MATTER (cassette) | 40 |
| 83 | Amission REV 13:15 | LIGELIAHORN (LP, 500 only, with insert) | 70 |
| 84 | Private cassette | FOR THE RAVEN (cassette) | 40 |

## METHOD ACTORS

| Year | Label/Cat. No. | Title | MINT VALUE £ |
|---|---|---|---|
| 80 | Armageddon AS 6 | The Method/Can't Act (p/s) | 7 |
| 81 | Armageddon AS 11 | Round World/Eye (p/s) | 7 |

## METHODS

| Year | Label/Cat. No. | Title | MINT VALUE £ |
|---|---|---|---|
| 70 | DJM DJS 225 | Chasing The Sun/And That Is Life | 15 |

## PETER METRO

| Year | Label/Cat. No. | Title | MINT VALUE £ |
|---|---|---|---|
| 82 | Greensleeves GRED 97 | Warn Them Teach Them (with Squiddly Ranking)/Carribean Connection (12") | 10 |

## METRO TRINITY

| Year | Label/Cat. No. | Title | MINT VALUE £ |
|---|---|---|---|
| 87 | Cafeteria CAFF 1 | DIE YOUNG EP (12") | 60 |

## METRO GLIDER

| Year | Label/Cat. No. | Title | MINT VALUE £ |
|---|---|---|---|
| 80 | Racket RKT 1 | Do It Right/Consequences | 20 |

## METROPAK

| Year | Label/Cat. No. | Title | MINT VALUE £ |
|---|---|---|---|
| 80 | Metropak PAK 001 | You're A Rebel/OK Let's Go/Run Run Run (numbered p/s) | 6 |
| 80 | Metropak PAK 002 | Here's Looking At You/Walking (foldout card p/s) | 5 |

## METROPHASE

| Year | Label/Cat. No. | Title | MINT VALUE £ |
|---|---|---|---|
| 79 | Neo London MS 01 | In Black/Neo Beauty/Cold Rebellion (photocopied p/s with lyric insert) | 8 |
| 79 | Neo London MS 02 | New Age/Frames Of Life (foldout p/s, stamped white labels) | 8 |
| 81 | Fresh FRESH 6 | In Black/Neo Beauty/Cold Rebellion (reissue, better quality p/s with insert) | 6 |

(see also Swell Maps)

## METROPOLITAN POLICE BAND

| Year | Label/Cat. No. | Title | MINT VALUE £ |
|---|---|---|---|
| 66 | Columbia DB 8095 | Thunderbirds March/P.C. ALEXANDER MORGAN: Sussex By The Sea | 8 |

## METROTONE

| Year | Label/Cat. No. | Title | MINT VALUE £ |
|---|---|---|---|
| 97 | Wurlitzer Jukebox WJ 40 | Kiss Me Awake/Byddant Fel Y Ser/Four Continuous Tones (p/s, 1,000 only) | 5 |
| 98 | Earworm WORM 21 | THE LESS YOU HAVE THE MORE YOU ARE (LP, 4 copies only on black vinyl) | 25 |

## METROZ

| Year | Label/Cat. No. | Title | MINT VALUE £ |
|---|---|---|---|
| 80 | Plastic Speech PLAS 2 | Video Veto/Cybonette (p/s) | 5 |

## PAUL METSERS

| Year | Label/Cat. No. | Title | MINT VALUE £ |
|---|---|---|---|
| 81 | Highway SHY 7014 | CAUTION TO THE WIND (LP) | 18 |

## MEW

| Year | Label/Cat. No. | Title | MINT VALUE £ |
|---|---|---|---|
| 02 | Epic 672854 7 | Am I Wry? No/Like Paper Cuts | 10 |

## MEXICANO

| Year | Label/Cat. No. | Title | MINT VALUE £ |
|---|---|---|---|
| 75 | Angen ANG 111 | Cut Throat/Gorilla In Manilla | 5 |

## MEXICANS

| Year | Label/Cat. No. | Title | MINT VALUE £ |
|---|---|---|---|
| 68 | Pye 7N 17613 | Alexander Higginbottom/Julie | 12 |
| 68 | Pye 7N 17657 | Without Your Love | 12 |

## MEXICO RED

| Year | Label/Cat. No. | Title | MINT VALUE £ |
|---|---|---|---|
| 88 | Hummingbird | Eternal Flame/Follow Me To Heaven (p/s, insert) | 80 |

## ANTHONY MEYNELL

| Year | Label/Cat. No. | Title | MINT VALUE £ |
|---|---|---|---|
| 82 | Hi-Lo LO 01 | HITS FROM 3000 YEARS AGO (LP, purple sleeve) | 15 |

(see also Squire)

## LEE MEZA

| Year | Label/Cat. No. | Title | MINT VALUE £ |
|---|---|---|---|
| 67 | Stateside SS 589 | If It Happens/One Good Thing Leads To Another | 30 |

## M-G-M SINGING STRINGS

| Year | Label/Cat. No. | Title | MINT VALUE £ |
|---|---|---|---|
| 66 | MGM 1307 | Lara's Theme From "Dr Zhivago"/The Old And The New | 6 |

## M-G-M STUDIO ORCHESTRA

| Year | Label/Cat. No. | Title | MINT VALUE £ |
|---|---|---|---|
| 55 | MGM SP 1144 | Rock Around The Clock/"Blackboard Jungle" Love Theme | 25 |

## MIAMI

| Year | Label/Cat. No. | Title | MINT VALUE £ |
|---|---|---|---|
| 74 | Jay Boy BOY 81 | Party Freaks/(Part 2) | 5 |
| 75 | Jay Boy BOY 86 | Hey Y'all We're Miami/Chicken Yellow | 5 |
| 75 | Jay Boy BOY 96 | Funk It Up/Freak On Down My Way | 5 |
| 76 | Jay Boy BOY 111 | Kill That Roach/Mr Notorious | 5 |

## MIAOW

| Year | Label/Cat. No. | Title | MINT VALUE £ |
|---|---|---|---|
| 85 | Venus VENUS 1 | Belle Vue/Fate (p/s) | 6 |
| 86 | Venus VENUST 1 | Belle Vue/Fate/Grocer's Devil Daughter (12", p/s) | 10 |
| 87 | Factory FAC 189 | Break The Code/Stolen Ears (p/s) | 10 |

**MICHA**
65  Pye 7N 15982     Protest Singer/Serpent ......................................................................................................8

**GEORGE MICHAEL**
87  Epic 460000 9     FAITH (CD, extra tracks, picture disc, PVC box) ................................................18

*(see also High, Elton John, Queen)*

**RAS MICHAEL & THE SONS OF NEGUS**
75  Grounnation GRD 2037     None A Jah Children/Glory Dawn ................................................................18
74  Trojan TRLS 118     NYAHBINGHI (LP) ..............................................................................................20
75  Trojan TRSL 113     DADAWAH (PEACE & LOVE) (LP) ..................................................................45
75  Vulcan VUL 005     RASTAFARI (LP) ................................................................................................25
75  Grounation GROL 505     RASTAFARI (LP) ................................................................................................25
76  Trojan TRLS 203     TRIBUTE TO THE EMPEROR RASTAFORI (LP) ..............................................15

**MICHAEL SCHENKER GROUP**
82  Chysalis PCHR 1393     ASSAULT ATTACK (LP, picture disc) ..............................................................18
83  Chysalis CHRP 1441     BUILT TO DESTROY (LP, picture disc, U.S. remixes) ....................................18

*(see also McAuley Schenker Group, Scorpions, UFO, Cozy Powell, Graham Bonnet, Alex Harvey Band)*

**CODY MICHAELS**
79  Grapevine GRP 121     7 Days - 52 Weeks/VIRTUE ORCHESTRA: Don't Look Back (Instrumental)........................8

**MARILYN MICHAELS**
60  RCA RCA 1208     Tell Tommy I Miss Him/Everyone Was There But You ..................................10

**MICHIGAN RAG**
72  Blue Horizon 2096 009     Don't Run Away/She's Looking Good ..........................................................20

**MICHIGANS**
63  Vogue V 9207     Intermission Riff/Tea For Two..........................................................................15

**MICKEY & LUDELLA**
95  Vinyl Japan ASKLP 52     BEDLAM A GO GO (LP) ....................................................................................30

*(see also Milkshakes, Billy Childish, Del Monas, Thee Headcoatees)*

**MICKEY (BAKER) & KITTY (NOBLE)**
60  London HLE 9054     Buttercup/My Reverie ......................................................................................35

**MICKEY (BAKER) & SYLVIA**
57  HMV POP 331     Love Is Strange/I'm Going Home ................................................................100
57  HMV POP 331     Love Is Strange/I'm Going Home (78) ..........................................................30
58  RCA RCA 1064     Rock And Stroll Room/Bewildered ................................................................50
58  RCA RCA 1064     Rock And Stroll Room/Bewildered (78) ........................................................30
60  RCA RCA 1206     Sweeter As The Day Goes By/Mommy Out De Light ......................................15
65  RCA Victor RCA 1487     Love Is Strange/Dearest ..................................................................................15
65  RCA Camden CDN 5133     LOVE IS STRANGE (LP) ..................................................................................200

*(see also Mickey Baker, Sylvia [Robbins])*

**MICKEY FINN**
64  Blue Beat BB 203     Tom Hark/Please Love Me (as 'Mickey Finn & the Blue Men') ......................25
64  Oriole CB 1927     Pills/Hush Your Mouth (as 'Mickey Finn & the Blue Men') ..........................80
64  Oriole CB 1940     Reelin' & A'Rockin'/I Still Want You (as 'Mickey Finn') ................................50
65  Columbia DB 7510     The Sporting Life/Night Comes Down (as 'The Mickey Finn')........................100
66  Polydor 56719     I Do Love You/If I Had You Baby (as 'The Mickey Finn') ............................100
67  Direction 58-3086     Garden Of My Mind/Time To Start Loving You (as 'The Mickey Finn') ........200
95  Noiseburger 3     Ain't Necessarily So/God Bless The Child (foldaround p/s in poly bag, 1,000 only, 1st 500 signed) ..........8
95  Noiseburger 3     Ain't Necessarily So/God Bless The Child (foldaround p/s in poly bag, 1,000 only)..........5

**BOBBY "BOBCATS" MICKLEBURGH**
55  Esquire EP 40     MICKLEBURGH'S BOBCATS (EP) ....................................................................10
56  Esquire EP 73     MICKLEBURGH'S BOBCATS (EP) ....................................................................10

**MICROBE**
69  CBS 4158     Groovy Baby/MICROBOP ENSEMBLE: Your Turn Now ......................................5

**MICRODISNEY**
82  Kabuki KAMD 2     Hello Rascals/The Helicopter Of The Holy Ghost (p/s) ..................................6
83  Kabuki KAMD 4     Pink Skinned Man/Fiction Land (p/s) ..............................................................5
88  Virgin V2505     39 MINUTES (LP) ............................................................................................18
84  Rough Trade ROUGH 75     EVERYBODY IS FANTASTIC (LP)....................................................................15
84  Rough Trade RTM 155     WE HATE YOU SOUTH AFRICAN BASTARDS (LP) ........................................20

**MICRON**
88  White SG045     Eastenders Rap (12") ......................................................................................10

*(see Rebel MC)*

**STEPHAN MICUS**
76  Caroline C 1517     ARCHAIN CONCERTS (LP) ................................................................................15

**MIDAS MOULD**
72  Columbia DB 8868     Information Emily/Love Sweet Love ..............................................................15

**MIDAS (1)**
70  Solar SL003     I've Seen A New Life/Visit The Sun ..............................................................40

**MIDAS (2)**
83  Small Run SRR 0008     Can't Stop Loving You/Power In The Sky (p/s with insert) ..........................200

**MAX MIDDLETON & ROBERT AWWAI**
79  Harvest SHSP 4103     ANOTHER SLEEPER (LP) ..................................................................................18

**TONY MIDDLETON**
65  London HLR 9983     My Little Red Book (as Burt Bacharach Orchestra with Tony Middleton)/BURT BACHARACH ORCHESTRA: What's New Pussycat ..........30
66  Polydor BM 56704     To The Ends Of The Earth/Don't Ever Leave Me ........................................350
66  Polydor BM 56704     To The Ends Of The Earth/Don't Ever Leave Me (DJ copy) ..........................500

MINT VALUE £

| 78 | Grapevine GRP 115 | Paris Blues/Out Of This World | 10 |
|---|---|---|---|

*(see also Willows, Burt Bacharach)*

**MIDLAKE**

| 05 | Bella Union BELLAV85 | Balloon Maker/Mornings Will Be Kind | 6 |
|---|---|---|---|
| 06 | Bella Union BELAV 128 | Head Home/Roscoe | 8 |
| 10 | Is It Balearic? IIBR 002 | Roscoe (Beyond The Wizard Sleeve Re:animation) (12", B-side contains 5 silent tracks) | 15 |
| 08 | Bella Union BELLAV 117 | THE TRIALS OF VAN OCCUPANTHER (LP) | 40 |
| 10 | Bella Union BELLACD224SP | THE COURAGE OF OTHERS (2-LP) | 25 |
| 10 | Bella Union CD02245P | THE COURAGE OF OTHERS (Box set, 2-LP, DVD, CD & 32 page booklet) | 50 |

*(see also John Grant)*

**MIDNIGHT**

| 78 | Ariola ATTA 514DJ | Don't Bother To Knock/Keep Walking By (DJ Copy, p/s) | 80 |
|---|---|---|---|
| 78 | Ariola ATTA 514 | Don't Bother To Knock/Keep Walking By (p/s) | 75 |

**MIDNIGHT CRUISER**

| 77 | It IT 2 | Rich Bitch/Striker (p/s) | 10 |
|---|---|---|---|

**MIDNIGHT RAGS**

| 80 | Ace ACE 005 | Public Enemy/Alcatraz/Mamma Said (p/s) | 8 |
|---|---|---|---|
| 80 | Velvet Moon VM 1 | The Cars That Ate New York/Oscar Automobile (p/s, withdrawn) | 8 |

*(see also Paul Roland, Weird Strings)*

**MIDNIGHT SHIFT**

| 66 | Decca F 12487 | Saturday Jump/Living Fast | 30 |
|---|---|---|---|

**MIDNIGHT SUN**

| 71 | MCA MKPS 2019 | MIDNIGHT SUN (LP, red/pink 'dogbone' label) | 60 |
|---|---|---|---|
| 72 | MCA MKPS 2024 | WALKING CIRCLES (LP, black/blue hexagon label) | 60 |

**MIDNIGHTERS**

| 55 | Parlophone DP 422 | Annie Had A Baby/THUNDERBIRDS: Pledging My Love (78, export issue) | 10 |
|---|---|---|---|

*(see also Hank Ballard)*

**MIDNIGHTS**

| 66 | Ember EMB S 220 | (Won'tcha) Show Me Around/Only Two Can Play | 18 |
|---|---|---|---|
| 63 | MEP 101/MN 1/EAG-EP-134 | MIDNIGHTS (EP, private pressing) | 130 |

**MI5**

| 80 | Public PUB 002 | Alright On The Night/Television Screen Heroes/Don't Make Waves (p/s) | 7 |
|---|---|---|---|

**M.I. FIVE**

| 66 | Parlophone R 5486 | You'll Never Stop Me Loving You/Only Time Will Tell | 150 |
|---|---|---|---|

*(see also Deep Purple)*

**MIGHT OF COINCIDENCE**

| 72 | Entropia BM 0001 | WHY COULDN'T PEOPLE WAIT (LP) | 100 |
|---|---|---|---|

**MIGHTY ABIJANS**

| 80 | No 1 Rock | Untamed(vocal & DJ Cut)/Dubwise (12") | 10 |
|---|---|---|---|

**MIGHTY AVENGERS (JAMAICA)**

| 66 | Rymska RA 101 | Scatter Shot (actually by Byron Lee & Dragonaires)/BYRON LEE: Like You Do (B-side actually "No One" by Techniques) | 30 |
|---|---|---|---|

**MIGHTY AVENGERS (U.K.)**

| 64 | Decca F 11891 | Hide Your Pride/Hey Senorita | 18 |
|---|---|---|---|
| 64 | Decca F 11962 | So Much In Love/Sometime They Say | 25 |
| 65 | Decca F 12085 | Blue Turns To Grey/I'm Lost Without You | 25 |
| 65 | Decca F 12198 | (Walkin' Thru The) Sleepy City/Sir Edward And Lady Jane | 35 |

*(see also Andrew Oldham)*

**MIGHTY BABY**

| 71 | Blue Horizon 2096 003 | Devil's Whisper/Virgin Spring | 80 |
|---|---|---|---|
| 69 | Head HDLS 6002 | MIGHTY BABY (LP, gatefold sleeve, yellow label) | 400 |
| 71 | Blue Horizon 2931 001 | A JUG OF LOVE (LP, with lyric insert) | 650 |
| 71 | Blue Horizon 2931 001 | A JUG OF LOVE (LP) | 400 |
| 84 | Psycho PSYCHO 31 | EGYPTIAN TOMB (LP, reissue of "Mighty Baby" in different sleeve) | 30 |

*(see also Action, Robin Scott, Habibiyya, Keith Christmas, Gary Farr, Stone's Masonry, Andy Roberts)*

**THEE MIGHTY CAESARS**

| 86 | Empire LWC 604 | Ten Bears Of The Comanches/Baby What's Wrong (p/s) | 15 |
|---|---|---|---|
| 86 | Media Burn MB 5 | Little By Little/The Swag/What You've Got/Cyclonic (12", p/s) | 25 |
| 88 | Swag SWG 001 | She's Just Fifteen Years Old/The Swag (flexi in p/s with Pandora's Box fanzine) | 18 |
| 95 | Toe Rag RAG 1A | Billy B Childish/Dolli Bambi (Free single as FRAT SHACK, p/s) | 8 |
| 85 | Milkshakes NER - 0 | S.T. (LP) | 40 |
| 86 | Milkshakes APOLL - 0 | THEE CAESARS OF TRASH (LP) | 20 |
| 86 | Milkshakes PLAT - 0 | ACROPOLIS NOW (LP) | 35 |
| 86 | Big Beat WIK45 | BEWARE OF THE IDES OF MARCH (LP) | 30 |
| 87 | Hangman HANG 3 UP | DON'T GIVE ANY DINNER TO HENRY CHINASKI (LP) | 50 |
| 87 | Hangman HANG 7 UP | PUNK ROCK SHOWCASE (LP) | 60 |
| 87 | Big Beat WIK 60 | LIVE IN ROME (LP) | 20 |
| 87 | Ambassador AMBAS 2 | WISE BLOOD (LP, colour sleeve) | 30 |
| 89 | Hangman HANG 26 UP | WISE BLOOD (LP, reissue, black and silver sleeve) | 20 |

*(see also Milkshakes, Prisoners, Billy Childish, Thee Headcoats)*

**MIGHTY DIAMONDS**

| 75 | Black Wax WAX13 | I Need A Roof/Joe Joe Dub | 15 |
|---|---|---|---|
| 75 | Virgin VS 137 | Have Mercy/Them Never Love Poor Marcus | 8 |
| 75 | Locks LOX 10 | Back Weh (You No Mafia)/Mafia Dub | 8 |
| 77 | JAMA JAMA 014 | Hey Girl/Fade Away (12") | 20 |
| 79 | Virgin Frontline FLS 122 12 | Bodyguard/One Brother Short (12", p/s) | 10 |
| 80 | Greensleeves GRED 45 | Gates Of Zion/SLY AND ROBBIE - Zion In Dub (12", green vinyl) | 40 |

| | | | |
|---|---|---|---|
| 76 | Virgin V 2052 | RIGHT TIME (LP) | 20 |
| 77 | Virgin V 2078 | ICE ON FIRE (LP) | 15 |
| 79 | Virgin Frontline FLD 6001 | DEEPER ROOTS (LP, with bonus dub LP) | 15 |
| 80 | Mobiliser SRE 31 | LEADER OF THE BLACK COUNTRY (LP) | 20 |

## MIGHTY DOUGLAS

| | | | |
|---|---|---|---|
| 60s | Jump Up JU 501 | Laziest Man/Dance Me Lover | 8 |
| 60s | Jump Up JU 508 | Teacher Teacher/Split Me In Two | 8 |
| 60s | Jump Up JU 509 | Ugliness/My Wicked Boy Child | 8 |

## MIGHTY 'EM

| | | | |
|---|---|---|---|
| 73 | Decca FR 13446 | Jekyll And Hyde/What A Way To Go | 35 |

## MIGHTY ETHNICZ

| | | | |
|---|---|---|---|
| 88 | Good Times EB20 | Freestyle/B Style (12") | 40 |

## MIGHTY FLEA & MICKEY BAKER

| | | | |
|---|---|---|---|
| 72 | Polydor 2058 328 | Bloodshot Eyes/Charley Stone | 6 |
| 73 | Polydor 2460 185 | LET THE GOOD TIMES ROLL (LP) | 22 |

## MIGHTY FLYERS

| | | | |
|---|---|---|---|
| 74 | Myrrh MYR 1016 | LOW FLYING ANGELS (LP, with insert) | 20 |

*(see also Mick Abrahams)*

## MIGHTY HARD

| | | | |
|---|---|---|---|
| 70 | Pye 7N 17878 | Save The Life Of My Child/House Of The Rising Sun | 30 |

## MIGHTY MAYTONES

| | | | |
|---|---|---|---|
| 76 | Mango MAN 1010 | Madness/Madness Version | 6 |
| 78 | GG's GG 029 | Searching In Disco (with Trinity)/Madness In Disco (with U Brown) (12") | 20 |
| 76 | Burning Sounds BS 1002 | MADNESS (LP) | 25 |
| 78 | Burning Sounds BS 1022 | BOAT TO ZION (LP) | 25 |

*(see also Maytones)*

## MIGHTY MEN

| | | | |
|---|---|---|---|
| 62 | Salvo SLO 1804 | No Way Out/You Too Much (99 copies only) | 30 |

## MIGHTY MIGHTY

| | | | |
|---|---|---|---|
| 86 | Girlie GAY 1 | Everybody Knows The Monkey/You're On My Mind (foldover p/s, poly bag) | 10 |
| 86 | Girlie GAY 1 | Everybody Knows The Monkey/You're On My Mind (standard p/s) | 5 |
| 87 | Sha La La Ba Ba Ba Ba Ba 001 | Throwaway (Throwaway Version)/CLOUDS: Jenny Nowhere (p/s, flexi) | 10 |
| 87 | Sha La La Ba Ba Ba Ba Ba 001 | Throwaway (Throwaway Version)/CLOUDS: Jenny Nowhere (p/s, flexi, with Baby Honey Fanzine 1) | 20 |

## MIGHTY MO

| | | | |
|---|---|---|---|
| 72 | Columbia DB 8851 | Ape Call/Heavy Bear | 10 |

## MIGHTY POWER

| | | | |
|---|---|---|---|
| 67 | Jump Up JU 513 | You're Wasting Your Time/Smart Barbarian | 8 |

## MIGHTY SAM

| | | | |
|---|---|---|---|
| 66 | Stateside SS 534 | Sweet Dreams/Good Humor Man | 15 |
| 66 | Stateside SS 544 | Fannie Mae/Badmouthin' | 15 |
| 68 | Stateside SS 2076 | When She Touches Me/Just Like Old Times | 25 |
| 70 | Soul City SC 115 | Papa True Love/I Need A Lot Of Lovin' | 85 |
| 70 | Soul City SCM 004 | MIGHTY SOUL (LP) | 15 |

## MIGHTY SPARROW

| | | | |
|---|---|---|---|
| 60 | Kalypso XX 22 | Mr. Herbert/Simpson | 6 |
| 64 | Jump Up JU 523 | Village Ram/Pull Pistle Gang | 10 |
| 68 | NEMS 56-3558 | Mr. Walker/Carnival In '68 | 6 |
| 69 | Fab FAB 116 | Mr. Walker/Jane | 6 |
| 70 | Fab FAB 147 | I Don't Wanna Lose You/The Truth | 10 |
| 60 | Kalypso XXEP 1 | THIS IS SPARROW (EP) | 10 |
| 60 | Kalypso XXEP 2 | MAN, DIG THIS SPARROW (EP) | 10 |
| 60 | Kalypso XXEP 3 | A PARTY WITH SPARROW (EP) | 10 |
| 61 | Kalypso XXEP 4 | THIS IS THE SPARROW AGAIN (EP) | 10 |
| 61 | Kalypso XXEP 5 | GREETINGS FROM SPARROW (EP) | 10 |
| 62 | Kalypso XXEP 6 | SPARROW THE CONQUEROR (EP) | 30 |
| 63 | Island ILP 902 | THE SLAVE (LP) | 15 |
| 66 | RCA RD 7516 | SPARROW COME BACK (LP) | 25 |
| 68 | Melodisc MLPWI 12-146 | CALYPSO CARNIVAL (LP) | 30 |
| 68 | Melodisc MLPWI 12-148 | MR WALKER (LP) | 15 |
| 72 | Trojan TRL49 | HOTTER THAN EVER (LP) | |

*(see also King , Lord Melody)*

## MIGHTY VIKINGS

| | | | |
|---|---|---|---|
| 67 | Island WI 3060 | Do Re Mi/The Sound Of Music | 35 |
| 67 | Island WI 3074 | Rockitty Fockitty/Give Me Back My Gal (both actually with Sammy Ismay) | 35 |

## MIGIL FIVE

| | | | |
|---|---|---|---|
| 65 | Pye 7N 15757 | Just Behind The Rainbow/Seven Lonely Days | 7 |
| 65 | Pye 7N 15874 | One Hundred Years/I'm In Love Again | 8 |
| 66 | Pye 7N 17023 | Pencil And Paper/Nevertheless (I'm In Love With You) | 5 |
| 67 | Columbia DB 8196 | Together/Superstition | 20 |
| 68 | Jay Boy BOY 4 | If I Had My Way/Somebody's Stolen The Moon | 6 |
| 64 | Pye NEP 24191 | MEET THE MIGIL FIVE (EP) | 15 |
| 64 | Pye NPL 18093 | MOCKING BIRD HILL (LP) | 30 |

*(see also Migil Four, Mike Felix)*

## MIGIL FOUR

| | | | |
|---|---|---|---|
| 63 | Pye 7N 15572 | Maybe/Can't I? | 7 |

*(see also Migil Five)*

## MIKA
| 07 | Universal Island 172 108-4 | Grace Kelly/Satellite | 5 |

## MIKE & MODIFIERS
| 62 | Oriole CB 1775 | I Found Myself A Brand New Baby/It's Too Bad | 800 |

## MIKE STUART SPAN
| 66 | Columbia DB 8066 | Come On Over To Our Place/Still Nights | 100 |
| 67 | Columbia DB 8206 | Dear/Invitation | 100 |
| 68 | Jewel JL 01 | Children Of Tomorrow/Concerto Of Thoughts | 80 |
| 68 | Fontana TF 959 | You Can Understand Me/Baubles And Bangles | 500 |
| 93 | 117 CPAT 1171 | EXSPANSIONS: Second Production/Rescue Me/Remember The Times/World In My Head (EP) | 25 |
| 95 | Tenth Planet TP 014 | TIMESPAN (LP, gatefold sleeve, numbered, 1,000 copies only) | 15 |

*(see also Leviathan, High Defenders, Tony's Defenders, High Broom)*  25

## MIKI
| 69 | RCA RCA 1782 | Dear Auntie Mary/A Piece Of Heaven | 7 |
| 69 | RCA RCA 1844 | Knight In White Armour/It's Easy To Say | 8 |

*(see also Miki Anthony)*

## BOBBY MILANO
| 55 | Capitol CL 14252 | A King Or A Slave/If You Cared | 10 |
| 55 | Capitol CL 14309 | If Tears Could Bring You Back/Make Me A Present Of You | 10 |

## MILBURN
| 03 | Private Pressing | Along Comes Mary (Disc only, no p/s) | 5 |

## AMOS MILBURN
| 57 | Vogue V 9064 | Every Day Of The Week/Girl Of My Dreams (triangular centre) | 150 |
| 57 | Vogue V 9064 | Every Day Of The Week/Girl Of My Dreams (round centre) | 40 |
| 57 | Vogue V 9069 | Rum And Coca Cola/Soft Pillow (triangular centre) | 150 |
| 57 | Vogue V 9069 | Rum And Coca Cola/Soft Pillow (triangular centre) (78) | 85 |
| 57 | Vogue V 9080 | Thinking Of You Baby/If I Could Be With You (One Hour Tonight) (triangular centre) | 150 |
| 57 | Vogue V 9080 | Thinking Of You Baby/If I Could Be With You (One Hour Tonight) (78) | 35 |
| 60 | Vogue V 9163 | One Scotch, One Bourbon, One Beer/Bad, Bad Whiskey | 100 |
| 57 | Vogue VE 1-70102 | ROCK AND ROLL (EP) | 250 |

## AMOS MILBURN JNR
| 63 | London HLU 9795 | Gloria/Look At Me Fool | 20 |

## MILDRED AND THE MICE
| 09 | Third Man TMR 003 | I Like My Mice (Dead)/Spider Bite (100 only, luminous vinyl) | 40 |

## PERCY MILEM
| 66 | Stateside SS 566 | Crying Baby, Baby, Baby/Call On Me | 100 |
| 66 | Stateside SS 566 | Crying Baby, Baby, Baby/Call On Me (DJ copy) | 150 |

## ARTHUR MILES
| 90 | Ffrr 148 | Trippin On Your Love/Helping Hand | 12 |

## BUDDY MILES (EXPRESS)
| 68 | Mercury MF 1065 | Train (Parts 1 & 2) | 10 |
| 69 | Mercury 20137 SMCL | EXPRESSWAY TO YOUR SKULL (LP) | 20 |
| 69 | Mercury 20163 SMCL | ELECTRIC CHURCH (LP) | 20 |
| 70 | Mercury 6338 016 | THEM CHANGES (LP) | 15 |
| 71 | Mercury 6338 028 | WE GOT TO LIVE TOGETHER (LP) | 15 |

*(see also Electric Flag, Jimi Hendrix, Carlos Santana & Buddy Miles)*

## DICK & SUE MILES
| 79 | Sweet Folk & Country SFA 106 | THE DUNMOW FLITCH (LP) | 18 |

## GARRY MILES
| 60 | London HLG 9155 | Look For A Star/Afraid Of Love | 10 |
| 60 | London REG 1264 | LOOK FOR A STAR (EP) | 20 |

## JOHN MILES
| 70 | Orange OAS 508 | Why Don't You Love Me?/If I Could See Through | 20 |
| 71 | Decca F 13196 | Jose/You Make It So Hard | 5 |
| 72 | Orange OAS 207 | Come Away Melinda/Walking With My Head Held High | 5 |
| 72 | Orange OAS 208 | Yesterday (Was Just The Beginning)/Road To Freedom | 5 |
| 73 | Orange OAS 209 | Hard Road/You're Telling Me Lies | 5 |
| 73 | Orange OAS 211 | Jacqueline/Keep On Tryin' | 5 |
| 73 | Orange OAS 213 | One Minute Every Hour/Hollywood Queen | 5 |
| 74 | Orange OAS 220 | Fright Of My Life/Good Time Woman | 5 |
| 74 | Orange OAS 223 | What's On Your Mind/Rock'n'Roll Band | 5 |
| 74 | Orange OAS 224 | What's On Your Mind/To Be Grateful | 5 |
| 78 | Decca FR 13757 | No Hard Feelings/Nice Man Jack | 6 |
| 79 | Decca FR 13827 | I Can't Keep A Man Down/Sweet Lorraine | 6 |

*(see also Influence)*

## LENNY MILES
| 61 | Top Rank JAR 546 | Don't Believe Him Donna/Invisible | 30 |

## LIZZIE MILES
| 56 | HMV 7EG 8178 | THE BLUES THEY SANG (EP, 1 side by Billy Young, both with Jelly Roll Morton) | 20 |

## SARAH MILES
| 65 | Fontana TF 552 | Where Am I/Here Of All Places | 5 |

## MILITAIRES
| 66 | Airborne 0009 | I Need You/Maybe | 15 |

## MILITANT BARRY
| 77 | Conflict COND 2000 | Idi Amin Blood Up/Free Black People (12", die-cut p/s) | 15 |

| | | | |
|---|---|---|---|
| 78 | Conflict COND 2003 | Ambition/Can't Stop Me (12")............................................................................................ | 15 |
| 79 | Vista Sounds STLP 1012 | GREEN VALLEY (LP)...................................................................................................... | 20 |

## MILK & COOKIES
| | | | |
|---|---|---|---|
| 75 | Island WIP.6222 | Little Lost And Innocent/Good Friends (as Milk 'n' Cookies) ..................................... | 12 |

## MILK FROM CHELTENHAM
| | | | |
|---|---|---|---|
| 83 | Its War Boys £3 | TRIPTYCH OF POISONERS (LP, silkscreened sleeve red or blue vinyl) ......................... | 50 |

## MILKSHAKES
| | | | |
|---|---|---|---|
| 82 | Havasong BILK-O | Please Don't Tell My Baby/It's You (p/s) ..................................................................... | 25 |
| 83 | Upright UP 6 | Soldiers Of Love/Shimmy Shimmy (p/s)........................................................................ | 12 |
| 84 | Big Beat NS 94 | Brand New Cadillac/Commanche/Jezebel/Jaguar And Thunderbird (p/s) .................. | 12 |
| 84 | Big Beat SW 105 | Ambassadors Of Love/No More/Gringles And Groyles Again/ Remarkable (p/s) ......... | 12 |
| 86 | Empire UXF 228 | Let Me Love You/She Tells Me She Loves Me (p/s) ....................................................... | 15 |
| 83 | Big Beat NED 4 | 14 RHYTHM AND BEAT GREATS (LP, red, lilac and blue sleeves)................................. | 20 |
| 83 | Upright UPLP 1 | AFTER SCHOOL SESSION (LP, laminated sleeve) .......................................................... | 20 |
| 84 | Milkshake GARB-O | THEE KNIGHTS OF TRASH (LP)....................................................................................... | 30 |
| 84 | Milkshake HARP-O | NOTHING CAN STOP THESE MEN (LP) ........................................................................... | 20 |
| 84 | Big Beat WIK 22 | SHOWCASE (LP)............................................................................................................ | 25 |
| 85 | Big Beat WIK 30 | THEY CAME, THEY SAW, THEY CONQUERED (LP) ......................................................... | 20 |
| 86 | Media Burn MB 6 | THE 107 TAPES (2-LP).................................................................................................... | 25 |
| 86 | Milkshake MILK-O | TALKING 'BOUT MILKSHAKES (LP, with poster)........................................................... | 30 |
| 86 | Milkshake MILK-O | TALKING 'BOUT MILKSHAKES (LP, without poster) ..................................................... | 20 |
| 87 | Hangman HANG 11 UP | LIVE FROM CHATHAM (LP) ............................................................................................ | 18 |
| 87 | Hangman HANG 1 UP | REVENGE - TRASH FROM THE VAULT (THE LEGENDARY MISSING 9th ALBUM) (LP)....... | 25 |
| 92 | Vinyl Japan ASKLP 10 | STILL TALKING 'BOUT (LP)............................................................................................. | 25 |
| 05 | Damaged Goods DAMGOOD 249LP | IN GERMANY (LP) ......................................................................................................... | 15 |

*(see also Prisoners/Milkshakes, Pop Rivits, Len Bright Combo, Billy Childish, Thee Headcoats, Mickey & Ludella, Masonics)*

## MILK TEETH
| | | | |
|---|---|---|---|
| 74 | Bead Records BEAD 1 | A TOUCH OF THE SUN (LP) ............................................................................................ | 150 |

## MILLENIUM
| | | | |
|---|---|---|---|
| 84 | Guardian GRC 2163 | MILLENIUM (LP) ........................................................................................................... | 20 |

## MILLER
| | | | |
|---|---|---|---|
| 65 | Oak RGJ 190 | Baby I've Got News For You/The Girl With The Castle.................................................. | 300 |
| 65 | Columbia DB 7735 | Baby I Got News For You/The Girl With The Castle ...................................................... | 400 |

*(see also Big Boy Pete, Peter Jay & Jaywalkers, Pete Miller, News)*

## BETTY MILLER
| | | | |
|---|---|---|---|
| 59 | Top Rank JAR 115 | Pearly Gates/Old Time Religion ................................................................................... | 6 |
| 59 | Top Rank JAR 127 | Jack O' Diamonds/(It Took) One Kiss ........................................................................... | 8 |

## BOB MILLER & MILLERMEN
| | | | |
|---|---|---|---|
| 57 | Columbia DB 4017 | The Scamp/The Sack Line (as Bob Miller Music)......................................................... | 6 |
| 58 | Columbia DB 4140 | Square Bash/Muchacha (as Bob Miller Music)............................................................ | 5 |
| 59 | Fontana H 181 | Dig This!/The Poacher ................................................................................................. | 10 |
| 59 | Fontana H 192 | Little Dipper/The Keel Row .......................................................................................... | 5 |
| 59 | Fontana H 228 | In The Mood/Joey's Song ............................................................................................. | 5 |
| 60 | Fontana H 236 | The Busker's Tune/My Guy's Come Back ...................................................................... | 5 |
| 60 | Fontana H 245 | 77 Sunset Strip/Manhunt ............................................................................................. | 10 |
| 60 | Fontana H 284 | Night Theme/Last Date ................................................................................................ | 10 |
| 61 | Parlophone R 4779 | Trouble Shooter/Hootin' ............................................................................................. | 7 |
| 61 | Parlophone R 4854 | The "Oliver" Twist/That's It ......................................................................................... | 10 |
| 65 | Mercury MF 947 | Uptown And Downtown/Carnaby Street Parade ......................................................... | 10 |
| 65 | Polydor 56005 | 6-5 Special/Dick Van Dyke Theme .............................................................................. | 8 |
| 66 | Columbia DB 7877 | Get Smart/Bony's Blues (as Bob Miller & His Millermen)........................................... | 8 |
| 72 | Spiral DIT 3 | Doin' The Slosh/Sloshing Around ................................................................................ | 8 |

## BOBBIE MILLER
| | | | |
|---|---|---|---|
| 65 | Decca F 12064 | What A Guy/You Went Away......................................................................................... | 40 |
| 65 | Decca F 12252 | Every Beat Of My Heart/Tomorrow .............................................................................. | 15 |
| 66 | Decca F 12354 | Everywhere I Go/IAN STEWART & RAILROADERS: Stu-Ball ........................................... | 80 |

*(see also Mongrels, Rolling Stones)*

## BRANKO MILLER
| | | | |
|---|---|---|---|
| 68 | CBS 3955 | Candy/Today Is Better Than Yesterday (Branko Miler on demos) ................................ | 8 |

## CHUCK MILLER
| | | | |
|---|---|---|---|
| 56 | Capitol CL 14543 | Rogue River Valley/No Baby Like You .......................................................................... | 15 |
| 57 | Mercury 7MT 153 | The Auctioneer/Me Head's In De Barrel ...................................................................... | 20 |
| 58 | Mercury 7MT 215 | Down The Road A-Piece/Mad About Her Blues ........................................................... | 100 |
| 59 | Mercury AMT 1026 | The Auctioneer/Baby Doll ........................................................................................... | 5 |
| 60 | Mercury ZEP 10058 | GOING GOING GONE (EP).............................................................................................. | 50 |

## COUNT PRINCE (MILLER)
| | | | |
|---|---|---|---|
| 70 | Downtown DT 460 | I'm Gonna Keep On Trying/Girl I Need You (as Count Prince) ...................................... | 5 |
| 70 | MCA MK 5042 | Mule Train/Lucille (p/s) ............................................................................................... | 5 |

*(see also Jimmy James & The Vagabonds)*

## FRANKIE MILLER
| | | | |
|---|---|---|---|
| 59 | Melodisc MEL 1519 | True Blue/Black Land Farmer ...................................................................................... | 15 |
| 59 | Melodisc MEL 1529 | Poppin' Johnnie/Family Man ....................................................................................... | 15 |
| 60 | Melodisc MEL 1552 | Rain, Rain/Baby Rocked Her Dolly .............................................................................. | 15 |
| 62 | Top Rank JKP 3013 | COUNTRY MUSIC (EP) ................................................................................................... | 20 |
| 64 | Ember CW 107 | THE TRUE COUNTRY STYLE OF FRANKIE MILLER (LP) ................................................... | 20 |

## GARY MILLER
| | | | |
|---|---|---|---|
| 64 | Pye 7N 15698 | Aqua Marina/Stingray .................................................................................................. | 12 |

MINT VALUE £

### GLEN MILLER
| | | | |
|---|---|---|---|
| 67 | Doctor Bird DB 1089 | Where Is The Love/Funky Broadway | 300 |
| 68 | Doctor Bird DB 1128 | Rocksteady Party/Book Of Memories | 40 |

### JACOB MILLER
| | | | |
|---|---|---|---|
| 75 | Sound Tracs SK5 | Dock Of The Bay/Version | 8 |
| 76 | Neville King NK 02 | Tired Fe Lick Weed In A Bush/Chillum In A Gully | 12 |
| 78 | Hawkeye HD 009 | Each One Teach One/Matthews Lane Dub/TETRACK: Let's Get It Together/Black ArtsDub (12") | 40 |
| 82 | Greensleeves GREL 166 | WHO SAY JAH NO DREAD (LP) | 15 |

### JAMES MILLER
| | | | |
|---|---|---|---|
| 70 | Trojan TR 7804 | You Got To Me/2001 | 12 |

### JIMMY MILLER & (NEW) BARBECUES
| | | | |
|---|---|---|---|
| 57 | Columbia DB 4006 | Sizzlin' Hot/Free Wheelin' Baby (as Jimmy Miller & Barbecues) | 60 |
| 58 | Columbia DB 4081 | Jelly Baby/Cry, Baby, Cry (as Jimmy Miller & New Barbecues) | 60 |
| 58 | Columbia DB 4081 | Jelly Baby/Cry, Baby, Cry (as Jimmy Miller & New Barbecues) (78) | 30 |

*(see also Station Skiffle Group)*

### JODY MILLER
| | | | |
|---|---|---|---|
| 64 | Capitol CL 15335 | He Walks Like A Man/Looking At The World Through A Tear | 5 |
| 64 | Capitol CL 15356 | The Fever/In My Room | 15 |
| 65 | Capitol CL 15393 | Queen Of The House/The Greatest Actor | 5 |
| 65 | Capitol CL 15404 | Silver Threads And Golden Needles/Melody For Robin | 6 |
| 65 | Capitol CL 15415 | Home Of The Brave/This Is The Life | 15 |
| 66 | Capitol CL 15482 | If You Were A Carpenter/Let Me Walk With You | 5 |
| 65 | Capitol T 2416 | HOME OF THE BRAVE (LP, mono) | 20 |
| 65 | Capitol (S) T 2416 | HOME OF THE BRAVE (LP, stereo) | 20 |
| 66 | Capitol T 2446 | JODY MILLER SINGS THE GREAT HITS OF BUCK OWENS (LP, mono) | 20 |
| 66 | Capitol (S) T 2446 | JODY MILLER SINGS THE GREAT HITS OF BUCK OWENS (LP, stereo) | 25 |

### KENNY MILLER
| | | | |
|---|---|---|---|
| 65 | Stateside SS 405 | Restless/Take My Tip | 150 |

### MITCH MILLER
| | | | |
|---|---|---|---|
| 60 | Philips PB 1146 | The Guns Of Navarone/Alouette March | 6 |
| 62 | CBS AAG 118 | The Longest Day (Vocal Version)/The Longest Day (Instrumental Version) | 6 |
| 63 | CBS AAG 158 | The Great Escape March/It's A Darn Good Thing | 7 |

### MRS MILLER
| | | | |
|---|---|---|---|
| 69 | Jackpot JP 707 | Feel It/LYN BECKFORD: Kiss Me Quick (actually by Keeling Beckford) | 7 |

*(see also Lloyd Terrell)*

### NED MILLER
| | | | |
|---|---|---|---|
| 63 | Capitol EAP1 20492 | NED MILLER (EP) | 15 |
| 63 | London RE 1382 | NED MILLER (EP) | 15 |
| 63 | London HA 8072 | FROM A JACK TO A KING (LP) | 15 |

### PAULETTE MILLER
| | | | |
|---|---|---|---|
| 79 | Rocerks PR 157 | Woman In Love/In Love Dub (12") | 20 |

### PETE MILLER
| | | | |
|---|---|---|---|
| 97 | Tenth Planet TP 030 | SUMMERLAND (LP, numbered, 1000 only) | 15 |

*(see also Miller, Big Boy Pete)*

### RUSS MILLER
| | | | |
|---|---|---|---|
| 57 | HMV POP 391 | I Sit In My Window/Wait For Me, My Love | 50 |

### STEPHEN MILLER & LOL COXHILL
| | | | |
|---|---|---|---|
| 73 | Caroline C 1503 | COXHILL MILLER (LP, black/white/red 'Twin' label) | 25 |
| 74 | Caroline C 1507 | THE STORY SO FAR ... OH REALLY? (LP) | 30 |

*(see also Lol Coxhill)*

### STEVE MILLER BAND
| | | | |
|---|---|---|---|
| 68 | Capitol CL 15539 | Sittin' In Circles/Roll With It | 15 |
| 68 | Capitol CL 15564 | Living In The U.S.A./Quicksilver Girl | 15 |
| 69 | Capitol CL 15604 | My Dark Hour/Song For Our Ancestors | 15 |
| 69 | Capitol CL 15618 | Little Girl/Don't Let Nobody Turn You Around | 7 |
| 70 | Capitol CL 15656 | Going To The Country/Never Kill Another Man | 6 |
| 72 | Capitol CL 15712 | My Dark Hour/The Gangster Is Back/Song For Our Ancestors (33rpm) | 5 |
| 73 | Capitol CL 15765 | The Joker/Something To Believe In | 5 |
| 74 | Capitol CL 15786 | Living In The U.S.A./Kow Kow Calqulator | 5 |
| 68 | Capitol (S)T 2920 | CHILDREN OF THE FUTURE (LP, 'rainbow rim' label) | 50 |
| 69 | Capitol (S)T 2984 | SAILOR (LP, 'rainbow rim' label) | 40 |
| 69 | Capitol E-ST 184 | BRAVE NEW WORLD (LP, mono) | 40 |
| 70 | Capitol E-ST 184 | BRAVE NEW WORLD (LP, stereo) | 60 |
| 70 | Capitol E-ST 331 | YOUR SAVING GRACE (LP) | 40 |
| 77 | Mercury 9286 455 | BOOK OF DREAMS (LP) | 20 |

*(see also Boz Scaggs)*

### SUZI MILLER
| | | | |
|---|---|---|---|
| 54 | Decca F 10389 | Happy Days And Lonely Nights/Tell Me, Tell Me (with Johnston Brothers) | 20 |
| 54 | Decca F 10423 | Two Step, Side Step (with Johnston Brothers)/ Hang My Heart On A Christmas Tree (with Keynotes) | 10 |
| 55 | Decca F 10475 | Tweedlee-Dee (with Johnston Brothers)/That's All I Want From You | 15 |
| 55 | Decca F 10512 | Dance With Me Henry (Wallflower) (with Johnston Brothers)/ Butterfingers (with Marilyn Sisters) | 15 |
| 55 | Decca F 10593 | The Banjo's Back In Town/Go On By | 15 |
| 56 | Decca F 10677 | Ay-Ay-Senores/Reckless | 10 |
| 56 | Decca F 10722 | Get Up! Get Up! (You Sleepy Head)/The Key To My Heart | 7 |
| 57 | Decca F 10848 | I Love My Baby/The Money Tree | 5 |

*(see also Johnston Brothers)*
**MILLER'S THUMB**

| | | | |
|---|---|---|---|
| 76 | Tradition TSC 3 | SITTING ON THE RIGHT SIDE (LP, 100 copies only) | 20 |

**MILLIE (SMALL)**

| | | | |
|---|---|---|---|
| 63 | Fontana TF 425 | Don't You Know/Until You're Mine | 10 |
| 64 | Fontana TF 449 | My Boy Lollipop/Something's Gotta Be Done | 6 |
| 64 | Fontana TF 479 | Sweet William/Oh Henry | 7 |
| 64 | Fontana TF 502 | I Love The Way You Love/Bring It On Home To Me | 8 |
| 64 | Cadbury's BNVT 01F | The Bournvita Song/Three Nights A Week (p/s) | 25 |
| 65 | Fontana TF 515 | I've Fallen In Love With A Snowman/What Am I Living For | 10 |
| 65 | Fontana TF 529 | See You Later Alligator/Chilly Kisses | 12 |
| 65 | Fontana TF 591 | My Street/It's Too Late | 10 |
| 65 | Fontana TF 617 | Bloodshot Eyes/Tongue Tied | 18 |
| 65 | Brit WI 1002 | My Street/A Mixed Up, Fickle, Moody, Self-Centred, Spoiled Kind Of Boy | 15 |
| 66 | Fontana TF 740 | Killer Joe/Carry Go Bring Come (as Millie Small) | 8 |
| 67 | Fontana TF 796 | Chicken Feed/Wings Of A Dove (as Millie Small) | 8 |
| 67 | Island WIP 6021 | You Better Forget/I Am In Love | 10 |
| 68 | Fontana TF 948 | When I Dance With You/Hey Mr. Love | 10 |
| 69 | Decca F 12948 | Readin' Writin' Arithmetic/I Want You Never To Stop | 12 |
| 70 | Pyramid PYR 6080 | My Love And I/Tell Me About Yourself | 10 |
| 70 | Trojan TR 7744 | Enoch Power/Mayfair | 15 |
| 70 | President PT 306 | We're All In A Zoo/Piccaninny Man | 10 |
| 70 | Trojan TR 7801 | Honey Hush/Sunday Morning | 10 |
| 61 | Blue Beat BBEP 302 | MILLIE (EP, with Little Roy & Owen Gray; with sleeve) | 140 |
| 61 | Blue Beat BBEP 302 | MILLIE (EP, with Little Roy & Owen Gray; without sleeve) | 20 |
| 64 | Fontana TE 17425 | MY BOY LOLLIPOP (EP) | 50 |
| 66 | Island IEP 705 | MILLIE AND HER BOYFRIENDS (EP) | 40 |
| 64 | Fontana TL 5220 | MORE MILLIE (LP, mono) | 40 |
| 64 | Fontana (S)TL 5220 | MORE MILLIE (LP, stereo) | 50 |
| 65 | Fontana TL 5276 | MILLIE SINGS FATS DOMINO (LP) | 60 |
| 67 | Island ILP 953 | THE BEST OF MILLIE SMALL (LP) | 50 |
| 69 | Trojan TTL 17 | MILLIE AND HER BOYFRIENDS (LP) | 20 |
| 69 | Trojan TTL 49 | THE BEST OF MILLIE SMALL (LP, reissue) | 15 |
| 70 | Trojan TBL 108 | TIME WILL TELL (LP) | 15 |

*(see also Jackie & Millie, Roy & Millie, Owen & Millie)*
**SPIKE MILLIGAN**

| | | | |
|---|---|---|---|
| 58 | Parlophone R 4406 | Wish I Knew/Will I Find My Love Today? | 12 |
| 61 | Parlophone R 4839 | I'm Walking Out With A Mountain/The Sewers Of The Strand | 8 |
| 62 | Parlophone R 4891 | Wormwood Scrubs Tango/Postman's Knock | 8 |
| 69 | Parlophone R 5771 | The Q.5 Piano Tune/Ning, Nang, Nong | 10 |
| 61 | Parlophone PMC 1148 | MILLIGAN PRESERVED (LP, mono) | 15 |
| 61 | Parlophone PCS 18 | MILLIGAN PRESERVED (LP, stereo) | 20 |

*(see also Famous Eccles)*
**MARY MILLINGTON**

| | | | |
|---|---|---|---|
| 99 | Trunk/Bonk B 01 | COME PLAY ME (EP) | 60 |

**SIR EUGENE MILLINGTON-DRAKE**

| | | | |
|---|---|---|---|
| 65 | Decca LK 4659 | MIXED GRILL (LP) | 60 |

**JEB MILLION**

| | | | |
|---|---|---|---|
| 86 | WEA YZ 82 | Speed Up My Heartbeat/Who Sent You (p/s) | 6 |
| 86 | WEA YZ 82T | Speed Up My Heartbeat (Extended Mix)/Speed Up My Heartbeat/ Who Sent You (12", p/s) | 12 |

**MILLIONAIRES (IRELAND)**

| | | | |
|---|---|---|---|
| 66 | Decca F 12468 | Wishing Well/Chatterbox | 100 |

**MILLIONAIRES (U.S.)**

| | | | |
|---|---|---|---|
| 67 | Mercury 6052301 | Never For Me/If I Had You Babe (paper labels) | 35 |
| 67 | Mercury 6052301 | Never For Me/If I Had You Babe (plastic labels) | 15 |

**MILLIONS**

| | | | |
|---|---|---|---|
| 73 | Duke DU 154 | Murmuring/TOMMY McCOOK & BOBBY ELLIS: Murmuring - Version | 10 |
| 73 | Downtown DT 516 | Love Of Jah Jah Children/Jah Jah Version | 30 |

**BARBARA MILLS**

| | | | |
|---|---|---|---|
| 65 | Hickory 45-1323 | Queen Of Fools/Make It Last, Take Your Time | 400 |
| 65 | Hickory 45-1323 | Queen Of Fools/Make It Last, Take Your Time (DJ copy) | 500 |
| 65 | Hickory 45-1392 | Try/Let's Make A Memory | 15 |
| 75 | London HLE 10491 | Queen Of Fools/Make It Last, Take Your Time (reissue) | 10 |
| 79 | Inferno HEAT 9 | Queen Of Fools/Make It Last, Take Your Time (reissue) | 8 |

**BETTY LOU MILLS**

| | | | |
|---|---|---|---|
| 60s | Shal SHAL 1 | Where Is My Star/Rock Him | 30 |
| 60 | Pilgrim JLPS 101 | EVERYWHERE I LOOK (LP) | 25 |

**GARRY MILLS**

| | | | |
|---|---|---|---|
| 59 | Top Rank JAR 119 | Hey Baby (You're Pretty)/You Alone | 20 |
| 59 | Top Rank JAR 219 | Seven Little Girls Sitting In The Back Seat/The Night You Became 17 | 8 |
| 59 | Oriole CB 1529 | Living Lord/Big Story Breaking | 8 |
| 59 | Oriole CB 1530 | I Am The Great I Am/Rhythm In Religion | 7 |
| 60 | Top Rank JAR 301 | Running Bear/Teen Angel | 7 |
| 60 | Top Rank JAR 336 | Look For A Star/Footsteps | 8 |
| 60 | Top Rank JAR 393 | Comin' Down With Love/I'm Gonna Find Out | 10 |
| 60 | Top Rank JAR 500 | Top Teen Baby/Don't Cheat Me Again (in p/s) | 10 |
| 60 | Top Rank JAR 500 | Top Teen Baby/Don't Cheat Me Again | 5 |

MINT VALUE £

| 61 | Top Rank JAR 542 | Who's Gonna Take You Home Tonight?/Christina | 5 |
| 61 | Decca F 11358 | I'll Step Down/Your Way Is My Way | 5 |
| 61 | Decca F 11383 | Bless You/Footprints In The Sand | 5 |
| 61 | Decca F 11415 | Treasure Island/Sad Little Girl | 5 |
| 62 | Decca F 11471 | Never Believed In Love/Save A Dream For Me | 5 |
| 61 | Top Rank JKP 3001 | LOOK FOR A STAR (EP) | 15 |

*(see also Gary & Ariels)*

**HAYLEY MILLS**

| 61 | Decca F 21396 | Let's Get Together/Cobbler Cobbler | 6 |
| 62 | Decca F 21442 | Jeepers Creepers/Johnny Jingo | 5 |
| 62 | Decca LK 4426 | LET'S GET TOGETHER (LP) | 15 |

**HAYLEY MILLS & EDDIE HODGES**

| 63 | HMV POP 1179 | Flitterin'/Beautiful Beulah | 7 |

*(see also Eddie Hodges)*

**JEFF MILLS**

| 61 | Ember EMB S 133 | Daddy's Home/TIMMY REYNOLDS: Lullaby Of Love | 70 |

**RUDY MILLS**

| 67 | Island WI 3092 | A Long Story/BOBBY ELLIS: Now We Know (actually. with Desmond Miles Seven) | 40 |
| 68 | Island WI 3136 | I'm Trapped/BOBBY ELLIS & CRYSTALLITES: Dollar A Head | 45 |
| 69 | Big Shot BI 509 | John Jones/A Place Called Happiness | 45 |
| 69 | Explosion EX 2007 | Lemi Li/Goody Goody | 70 |
| 69 | Crab CRAB 20 | Tears On My Pillow/I'm Trapped | 20 |
| 69 | Crab CRAB 24 | A Heavy Load/Wholesale Love | 20 |
| 69 | Pama SECO 12 | REGGAE HITS (LP) | 150 |

**STEPHANIE MILLS**

| 74 | Paramount PARA 3050 | I Knew It Was Love/The Passion And The Pain | 6 |
| 76 | Tamla Motown TMG 1020 | This Empty Place/I See You For The First Time (unissued) | 50 |
| 76 | Tamla Motown STML 12017 | FOR THE FIRST TIME (LP) | 20 |

**MILLS BROTHERS**

| 54 | Brunswick 05325 | How Blue?/Why Do I Keep Lovin' You? | 7 |
| 55 | Brunswick 05439 | Smack Dab In The Middle/Opus One | 7 |
| 55 | Brunswick 05488 | That's All I Ask Of You/Suddenly There's A Valley | 7 |
| 55 | Brunswick 05487 | Mi Muchacha (Little Girl)/Gum Drop | 7 |
| 56 | Brunswick 05606 | That's Right/Don't Get Caught | 10 |
| 58 | London HLD 8553 | Get A Job/I Found A Million Dollar Baby | 8 |
| 60 | London HLD 9169 | I Got You/Highways Are Happy Ways | 8 |

**MILLWALL F.C.**

| 72 | Decca F1 3350 | Millwall/The Ballad Of Harry Cripps | 8 |

**RONNIE MILSAP**

| 66 | Pye International 7N 25392 | Ain't No Soul (Left In These Old Shoes)/Another Branch From The Same Old Tree | 60 |
| 66 | Pye International 7N 25392 | Ain't No Soul (Left In These Old Shoes)/Another Branch From The Same Old Tree (DJ copy) | 100 |
| 69 | Pye International 7N 25490 | Denver/Nothing Is As Good As It Used To Be | 6 |
| 72 | Wand WN 26 | Ain't No Soul (Left In These Old Shoes)/Another Branch From The Same Old Tree (reissue) | 10 |

**RONNIE MILSAP/ROSCOE ROBINSON**

| 66 | Pye Intl. NEP 44078 | SOUL SENSATIONS (EP) | 50 |

**NATHAN MILSTEIN**

| 62 | Columbia SAX 2518 | VIVALDI: FOUR CONCERTI (LP, stereo, turquoise/silver label) | 500 |
| 63 | Columbia SAX 2563 | MUSIC OF OLD RUSSIA (LP, stereo, red label) | 450 |
| 65 | Columbia SAX 5254 | MOZART VIOLIN CONCERTOS (LP, stereo, red label) | 100 |
| 66 | Columbia SAX 5275 | PROKOFIEV: THE TWO CONCERTOS FOR VIOLIN & ORCHESTRA (LP, stereo, red label) | 350 |
| 66 | Columbia SAX 5285 | BACH: TWO VIOLIN CONCERTOS/VIVALDI: TWO VIOLIN CONCERTOS (LP, Stereo) | 400 |

**JOHNNY MILTON & CONDORS**

| 61 | Oriole CB 1588 | Charleston Cocktail (medley) (as Johnny Milton Band) | 5 |
| 64 | Decca F 11862 | A Girl Named Sue/Somethin' Else (as Johnny Milton & Condors) | 8 |
| 64 | Fontana TF 488 | Cry Baby/Hurt | 6 |

*(see also Symbols)*

**MILVA**

| 63 | Oriole CB 1899 | I Can't Believe You're Leaving Me/Loneliness Of Autumn | 8 |
| 64 | Oriole CB 1952 | I'll Set My Love To Music/Come Sempre | 8 |
| 67 | Major Minor MM 510 | Love Is A Feeling/Seasons Of Love | 6 |

**MILWAUKEE COASTERS**

| 68 | Pama PM 733 | Treat Me Nice/Sick And Tired (Oh Babe) | 5 |
| 68 | Pama PMLP 2 | WEST COAST ROCK'N'ROLL 1968 (LP) | 15 |

**ILHAN MIMAROGLU**

| 69 | Turnabout TV34177S | ELECTRONIC MUSIC III (LP) | 20 |

**GARNET MIMMS (& ENCHANTERS)**

| 63 | United Artists UP 1033 | Cry Baby/Don't Change Your Heart (with Enchanters) | 25 |
| 63 | United Artists UP 1038 | Baby Don't You Weep/For Your Precious Love (with Enchanters) | 20 |
| 64 | United Artists UP 1048 | Tell Me Baby/Anytime You Want Me (with Enchanters) | 25 |
| 65 | United Artists UP 1090 | It Was Easier To Hurt Her/So Close | 30 |
| 66 | United Artists UP 1130 | I'll Take Good Care Of You/Looking For You | 100 |
| 66 | United Artists UP 1130 | I'll Take Good Care Of You/Looking For You (DJ copy) | 200 |
| 66 | United Artists UP 1147 | It's Been Such A Long Way Home/Thinkin' | 20 |
| 66 | United Artists UP 1153 | My Baby/It Won't Hurt Half As Much | 25 |
| 66 | United Artists UP 1172 | All About Love/The Truth Hurts | 20 |
| 67 | United Artists UP 1181 | Roll With The Punches/Only Your Love | 25 |

| 67 | United Artists UP 1186 | As Long As I Have You/Yesterday | 40 |
| 68 | Verve VS 569 | I Can Hear My Baby Crying/Stop And Think It Over | 20 |
| 68 | Verve VS 569 | I Can Hear My Baby Crying/BILL MEDLEY: That Lucky Old Sun (mispress) | 10 |
| 68 | Verve VS 574 | We Can Find That Love/Can You Top This | 35 |
| 76 | United Artists REM 403 | REMEMBER GARNET MIMMS (EP) | 10 |
| 63 | United Artists ULP 1067 | CRY BABY AND 11 OTHER HITS (LP, with Enchanters) | 125 |
| 66 | United Artists (S)ULP 1145 | WARM AND SOULFUL (LP) | 70 |
| 67 | United Artists (S)ULP 1174 | LIVE (LP, as Garnet Mimms & Senate) | 60 |

## MIND OVER MATTER
| 70 | Haflex HF 01 | Sunrise/Enter The Dragon | 40 |

## MINDBENDERS
| 66 | Fontana TF 644 | A Groovy Kind Of Love/Love Is Good | 5 |
| 66 | Fontana TF 697 | Can't Live With You, Can't Live Without You/One Fine Day | 8 |
| 66 | Fontana TF 731 | Ashes To Ashes/You Don't Know About Love | 7 |
| 66 | Fontana TF 780 | I Want Her, She Wants Me/The Morning After | 18 |
| 67 | Fontana TF 806 | We'll Talk About It Tomorrow/Far Across Town | 8 |
| 67 | Fontana TF 869 | The Letter/My New Day And Age | 10 |
| 67 | Fontana TF 877 | Schoolgirl/Coming Back | 40 |
| 68 | Fontana TF 910 | Blessed Are The Lonely/Yellow Brick Road | 20 |
| 68 | Fontana TF 961 | Uncle Joe, The Ice Cream Man/The Man Who Loved Trees | 15 |
| 69 | Fontana H 1026 | A Groovy Kind Of Love/Ashes To Ashes (p/s) | 7 |
| 66 | Fontana TL 5324 | THE MINDBENDERS (LP, mono) | 45 |
| 66 | Fontana (S)TL 5324 | THE MINDBENDERS (LP, stereo) | 55 |
| 67 | Fontana (S)TL 5403 | WITH WOMAN IN MIND (LP) | 60 |

*(see also Wayne Fontana & Mindbenders, Hotlegs, Lulu)*

## SAL MINEO
| 57 | Philips JK 1024 | Start Movin' (In My Direction)/Love Affair (jukebox issue) | 20 |
| 58 | Fontana H 118 | Little Pigeon/Cuttin' In | 20 |
| 58 | Fontana H 135 | Seven Steps To Love/A Couple Of Crazy Kids | 10 |
| 58 | Fontana TFL 5004 | SAL (LP) | 30 |

## CORINA MINETTE
| 60 | HMV POP 752 | He'll Have To Stay/TOMMY THOMAS ORCHESTRA: Young At Cha Cha | 5 |

## SEXTON MING
| 90 | Hangman HANG 36 UP | BIRDS WITH TEETH (LP) | 15 |
| 98 | Hangman's Daughter HANG 018OP | 6 MORE MILES TO THE GRAVEYARD (LP) | 18 |

*(see also Billy Childish etc.etc. etc.)*

## SEXTON MING (& HIS DIAMOND GUSSETS)
| 96 | D. Goods DAMGOOD 71 | I'm In Love With Danny Edwards/Break His Spirit/Son Of Tractor Nits (p/s) | 8 |

## CHARLES/CHARLIE MINGUS
| 56 | Vogue LDE 178 | CHARLIE MINGUS PRESENTS JAZZ WORKSHOP VOL. 2 (10" LP) | 20 |
| 59 | Parlophone PMC 1092 | EAST COASTING (LP) | 25 |
| 59 | Philips BBL 7352 | MINGUS AH HUM (LP) | 35 |
| 60 | London Jazz LTZ-K 15194 | BLUES AND ROOTS (LP, also stereo SAH-K 6087) | 30 |
| 62 | Atlantic SD 8005 | CHARLES MINGUS PRESENTS CHARLES MINGUS (LP, U.K. issue of U.S. LP) | 30 |
| 62 | United Artists ULP 1004 | JAZZ PORTRAITS (LP) | 25 |
| 62 | London HA-K/SH-K 8007 | OH YEAH (LP, by Charlie Mingus & Jazz Group) | 35 |
| 63 | RCA RD/SF 7514 | TIJUANA MOODS (LP) | 30 |
| 63 | Vocalion LAE 543 | CHAZZ (LP) | 30 |
| 64 | HMV CLP 1694 | THE BLACK SAINT AND THE SINNER LADY (LP) | 30 |
| 65 | United Artists ULP 1068 | TOWN HALL CONCERT (LP) | 30 |
| 65 | Vocalion LAEF/SEAF 591 | CHARLIE MINGUS QUINTET WITH MAX ROACH (LP) | 30 |
| 65 | HMV CLP 1742 | MINGUS, MINGUS, MINGUS (LP, also stereo CSD 1545) | 35 |
| 65 | HMV CLP 1796 | MINGUS PLAYS PIANO (LP) | 30 |
| 65 | Atlantic ATL/SAL 5019 | TONIGHT AT NOON (LP) | 30 |
| 66 | Realm RM 211 | JAZZ COMPOSERS WORKSHOP (NO. 1) (LP) | 30 |
| 66 | CBS (S)BPG 62261 | MINGUS DYNASTY (LP) | 30 |
| 68 | Atlantic 587131 | PITHECANTTHROPUS ERECTUS (LP) | 30 |

## MINIM
| 67 | Polydor 582 011 | WRAPPED IN A UNION JACK (LP) | 22 |

## MINISTRY
| 92 | Sire W 0096 | Jesus Built My Hotrod/T.V. Song (p/s) | 10 |

## MINISTRY OF SOUND
| 66 | Decca F 12449 | White Collar Worker/Back Seat Driver | 40 |

## MINNY POPS
| 81 | Factory FAC 31 | MINNY POPS EP: Dolphin Spurt/Goddess | 10 |
| 82 | Factory FAC 57 | Secret Story/Island | 15 |

## KYLIE MINOGUE
### SINGLES
| 89 | PWL PWLT 35R | Hand On Your Heart (Heartache Mix)/Hand On Your Heart (Dub mix) Just Wanna Love You (12", with stickered p/s) | 30 |
| 89 | PWL PWLT 42R | Wouldn't Change A Thing (Espagna Mix)/Wouldn't Change A Thing (7" Mix)/ It's No Secret (Extended) (12", stickered p/s) | 20 |
| 91 | PWL PWLP 72 | What Do I Have To Do (New Mix)/What Do I Have To Do (Instrumental) (stickered p/s, with postcards) | 15 |
| 91 | PWL PWLT 72R | What Do I Have To Do (Between The Sheets Mix) (12", withdrawn, no p/s) | 100 |
| 91 | PWL PWL P81 | Shocked (DNA 7" Mix)/Shocked (Harding & Curnow 7" Mix) (picture disc) | 15 |
| 91 | PWL PWLT204R | Word Is Out (Summer Breeze Remix) (1-sided 12" Limited Edition with etched Kylie autograph on other side, p/s) | 20 |

MINT VALUE £

| | | | |
|---|---|---|---|
| 97 | DeCon. 7432 1517257 | Some Kind Of Bliss/Love Takes Over Me (numbered limited edition 7", die-cut p/s) | 25 |

## ALBUMS

| | | | |
|---|---|---|---|
| 88 | PWL HFD 4 | KYLIE (DAT) | 150 |
| 90 | PWL HFL 18 | RHYTHM OF LOVE (LP, gold leaf sleeve, 100 only) | 80 |
| 98 | 30DeCon. 74321 58715 1 | MIXES (3xLP, inner sleeves, pink silhouette Kylie outer p/s) | 20 |

## PROMOS

| | | | |
|---|---|---|---|
| 88 | PWL (no cat. no.) | Made In Heaven (3:26) PWL 1-track in-house promo cassette, custom PWL logo inlay typled/stickered, 1 only) | 30 |
| 90 | PWL PWLT 56R | Better The Devil You Know (KC Cohen 'US' Remix) (1-sided 12" promo, withdrawn, die-cut sleeve, 50 only) | 30 |
| 91 | PWL PWLT 72R | What Do I Have To Do (Between The Sheets Mix) (1-sided 12" promo, withdrawn die-cut sleeve) | 30 |
| 91 | PWL ZR-A1 | Keep On Pumpin' It (12" white label issued under pseudonym of 'Angel K', includes Angelic Remix' & 'Astral Flight Mix', handwritten/stamped labels, Some with 'I Guess I Like It' titles. Die-cut sleeve) | 30 |
| 91 | PWL (no cat. no.) | I Guess I Like It Like That (12" 1-sided white label issued under pseudonym of 'Angel K', includes 'Extended/Album Version', 200 only) | 20 |
| 91 | PWL ANGEL-2 | Do You Dare (12" white label issued under pseudonym of 'Angel K', includes NRG Mix' & 'New Rave Mix', handwritten labels, die-cut sleeve, 100 only) | 20 |
| 92 | PWL PWLT 227 | Finer Feelings (Brothers In Rhythm 12" Mix)/Closer (Pleasure Mix) ('Black Diamond' limited promo 12", black diamond label, die cut sleeve) | 10 |
| 92 | PWL PWLT 257 | Celebration (Have A Party Mix)/Let's Get To It (Album Version) ('Black Diamond' limited promo 12", Christmas "leaving PWL" promo p/s, black Diamond label) | 25 |
| 94 | DeCon. 21 227477 JB | Confide In Me (Radio Mix)/(Truth Mix) (7" jukebox issue, no p/s) | 10 |
| 94 | DeCon. 21 246577 JB | Put Yourself In My Place (Radio Mix)/(All Star Mix) (7" jukebox issue, no p/s) | 15 |
| 94 | DeCon. 21 293617 JB | Where Is The Feeling? (BIR Bish Bosh Mix Edit)/(BIR Dolphin Mix) (7" jukebox issue, no p/s) | 10 |
| 95 | DeConstruction FEEL2 | Where Is The Feeling? (BIR Dolphin Mix)/(Morales Club Mix) (12", die-cut sleeve, limited quantities) | 30 |
| 95 | DeConstruction FEEL3 | Where Is The Feeling? (Da Klubb Feelin' Mix)/(Aphroheadz Powerlite Mix)/(Three Rad Vid Clash Mix) (12", promo, no p/s, 200 only) | 25 |
| 95 | DeConstruction FEELING1 | Where Is The Feeling? (UK 7" Edit) (UK export to Japan promo 1-track CD, unique Custom p/s) | 25 |
| 95 | Deconstruction TIME1 | Time Will Pass You By (Paul Masterson's 'Wand Silver Screen Remix') (1-sided 12" White Label, handwritten labels, unreleased mix, withdrawn, 20 only) | 40 |
| 97 | DeConstruction DID2 | Did It Again (Trouser Enthusiasts' Goddess of Contortion Mix)/(Razor N Go Mix) (12" promo, custom Deconstruction die-cut sleeve, limited to 500 only) | 20 |
| 97 | DeCon. 21 535707 JB | Did It Again (Radio Edit)/Tears (7" jukebox issue, no p/s) | 20 |
| 98 | DeCon. 21 570137 JB | Breathe (Radio Edit)/(Tee's Radio Edit) (7" jukebox issue, no p/s) | 20 |
| 98 | DeConstruction TOOFAR 1 | Too Far (Brothers In Rhythm Mix)/(Junior Vasquez Remix) (12", promo, no p/s) | 25 |
| 98 | Arthrob ART021TJ | GBI (Sharp Boys Deee-Liteful Dub)/(Album Version)/(Kylie-Pella) (with Towa Tei) (UK promo 12" part 1, custom Arthrob sleeve) | 15 |
| 98 | Arthrob ART021TJX | GBI (Rekut/DJ Krust Mix)/(Ebony Boogie Down Mix)/Bold Line (not Kylie) (with Towa Tei) (UK promo 12" part 2, custom Arthrob sleeve) | 15 |
| 00 | Parlophone BUTTERFLO1A | Butterfly (Sandstorm Dub) (12" 1-sided DJ white label, butterfly logo stamped die cut paper sleeve) | 40 |
| 00 | Parlophone 12MIND 1 | Spinning Around (Messy Boyz Remix) (12" 1-sided promo featuring unreleased mix, die cut sleeve, Handwritten label, 10 only) | 40 |
| 00 | Parlophone SHARP DJ 1 | Spinning Around (Sharp Vocal Mix)/Spinning Around (Sharp Double Dub) (12" Pink Promo DJ Vinyl, die-cut sleeve, 100 only) | 40 |
| 00 | Parlophone 12RDJ 6551 | Please Stay (Metro Mix)/Please Stay (7th District Club Flava Mix)/ Please Stay (7th District Club Dub) (12" promo, p/s, with inner sleeve) | 20 |
| 01 | Parlophone RLH6562 | Can't Get You Out Of My Head/Boy (7" jukebox issue, no p/s) NOTE: Clear 7" jukebox pressings carrying this 'RLH6562' catalogue number with 'Can't Get Blue Monday out Of my Head' as the B-side are unofficial bootlegs) | 7 |
| 01 | Parlophone 12RDJY 6562 | Can't Get Out Of My Head (Superchumbo Todo Mamado Mix)/ Can't Get Out Of My Head (Superchumbo Leadhead Dub)/(Superchumbo Voltapella Mix) (12" promo issued under the pseudonym of 'Special K', die-cut sleeve) | 7 |
| 04 | Parlophone RDJ6633 | Red Blooded Woman (Promo 1-sided clear 7" vinyl featuring otherwise unreleased 'Play Paul Radio Edit', 50 only) | 30 |
| 04 | Parlophone (no cat. no) | Chocolate (Violanti's Remix) (1-sided 12" white label, unreleased remix, Withdrawn, hand-written label) | 30 |
| 94 | DeConstruction KM 100 | KYLIE MINOGUE (CD, promo, gatefold sl. in lilac slipcase with silver lettering) | 50 |
| 97 | DeConstruction KYLIE 1 | IMPOSSIBLE PRINCESS (CD, promo, with insert, withdrawn, some with Press Release from 'Hall Or Nothing' explaining about the withdrawal of the CD and title due to Princess Diana's death) | 25 |
| 00 | Parlophone LIGHTX 001 | LIGHT YEARS (LP Promo, unique blue outer 'Kylie' logo sleeve, inner picture sleeve, does not include 'Kids' or 'Password', 100 only) | 30 |
| 00 | Parlophone LIGHTX 002 | LIGHT YEARS (LP Promo, unique blue outer 'Kylie' logo sleeve, inner picture sleeve, includes 'Kids' but not 'Password', 100 only) | 30 |
| 00 | BMG HITS1 | HITS+ (CD promo, original withdrawn artwork, card slip case, withdrawn at Kylie's request when she disliked the picture used, most copies incinerated, less than 5 copies exist) | 40 |

## MINORBOPS

| | | | |
|---|---|---|---|
| 58 | Vogue V 9110 | Need You Tonight/Want You For My Own | 800 |
| 58 | Vogue V 9110 | Need You Tonight/Want You For My Own (78) | 250 |

## MINOR THREAT

| | | | |
|---|---|---|---|
| 85 | Discord DISCORD 15 | Salad Days/Stumped/Good Guys (p/s) | 18 |

## MINSTRELS

| | | | |
|---|---|---|---|
| 67 | Studio One SO 2036 | People Get Ready/HAMLINS: Everyone's Got To Be There | 200 |
| 68 | Studio One SO 2050 | Miss Highty Tighty/WESTMORELITES: Let Me Be Yours Until Tomorrow | 90 |

## MINT

| | | | |
|---|---|---|---|
| 69 | Tangerine 014 | Luv/Simone | 20 |
| 73 | Pye 7N.45299 | I'll Meet You Halfway/Three Score And Ten | 6 |

## MINT JULEPS

| | | | |
|---|---|---|---|
| 87 | Stiff BUY DJ 264 | Docklands/Under Pressure (12" test pressing of last Stiff single for 20 years) | 30 |

## DEREK MINTER
| | | | |
|---|---|---|---|
| 60 | Sound Stories EP 304 | STARS OF SPEED (EP) | 10 |

## MINTS
| | | | |
|---|---|---|---|
| 57 | London HLP 8423 | Night Air/KEN COPELAND: Pledge Of Love | 40 |

## MINUCCI
| | | | |
|---|---|---|---|
| 56 | Vogue Coral LVA 9015 | GINA LOLLO BRIGIDA PRESENTS MUSIC OF GINO BY MINUCCI (LP, photo of Gina on cover) | 15 |

## MINUTE MEN
| | | | |
|---|---|---|---|
| 61 | Capitol CL 15206 | Yankee Diddle/Blue Pearl | 6 |

## MINUTEMEN
| | | | |
|---|---|---|---|
| 83 | SST SST 002 | PARANOID TIME (8-track EP) | 18 |
| 85 | Homestead REFLEX-L | TOUR SPIEL (EP, live 4-track) | 10 |

## MIRACLE MILE
| | | | |
|---|---|---|---|
| 86 | Miracle MIR 001 | Bless This Ship/Breaking Down The Barriers (p/s) | 35 |

## (SMOKEY ROBINSON &) MIRACLES
| | | | |
|---|---|---|---|
| 61 | London HL 9276 | Shop Around/Who's Lovin' You | 60 |
| 61 | London HL 9366 | Ain't It Baby/The Only One I Love | 100 |
| 62 | Fontana H 384 | What's So Good About Goodbye/I've Been So Good To You | 200 |
| 63 | Oriole CBA 1795 | You've Really Got A Hold On Me/Happy Landing | 120 |
| 63 | Oriole CBA 1863 | Mickey's Monkey/Whatever Makes You Happy | 80 |
| 64 | Stateside SS 263 | I Gotta Dance To Keep From Crying/Such Is Love, Such Is Life | 55 |
| 64 | Stateside SS 282 | The Man In You/Heartbreak Road | 40 |
| 64 | Stateside SS 324 | I Like It Like That/You're So Fine And Sweet | 45 |
| 64 | Stateside SS 353 | That's What Love Is Made Of/Would I Love You | 35 |
| 65 | Stateside SS 377 | Come On Do The Jerk/Baby Don't You Go | 45 |

*(Credited to The Miracles.)*

| | | | |
|---|---|---|---|
| 65 | Tamla Motown TMG 503 | Ooo Baby Baby/All That's Good | 40 |
| 65 | Tamla Motown TMG 522 | The Tracks Of My Tears/A Fork In The Road | 45 |
| 65 | Tamla Motown TMG 540 | My Girl Has Gone/Since You Won My Heart | 40 |
| 66 | Tamla Motown TMG 547 | Going To A Go-Go/Choosey Beggar | 25 |
| 66 | Tamla Motown TMG 569 | Whole Lotta Shakin' In My Heart/Oh Be My Love | 45 |
| 66 | Tamla Motown TMG 584 | (Come 'Round Here) I'm The One You Need/Save Me | 25 |

*(All of the singles listed above are credited to The Miracles.)*

| | | | |
|---|---|---|---|
| 67 | Tamla Motown TMG 598 | The Love I Saw In You Was Just A Mirage/Swept For You Baby | 25 |
| 67 | Tamla Motown TMG 614 | More Love/Swept For You Baby | 25 |
| 67 | Tamla Motown TMG 614 | More Love/Come Spy With Me (withdrawn B-side) | 80 |
| 67 | Tamla Motown TMG 631 | I Second That Emotion/You Must Be Love | 12 |
| 68 | Tamla Motown TMG 648 | If You Can Want/When The Words From Your Heart Get Caught Up In Your Throat | 15 |
| 68 | Tamla Motown TMG 661 | Yester-Love/Much Better Off | 15 |
| 68 | Tamla Motown TMG 673 | Special Occasion/Give Her Up | 15 |
| 69 | Tamla Motown TMG 687 | Baby, Baby Don't Cry/Your Mother's Only Daughter | 15 |
| 69 | Tamla Motown TMG 696 | The Tracks Of My Tears/Come On Do The Jerk | 7 |
| 70 | Tamla Motown TMG 745 | The Tears Of A Clown/You Must Be Love (with withdrawn B-side) | 40 |
| 70 | Tamla Motown TMG 745 | The Tears Of A Clown/Who's Gonna Take The Blame | 6 |
| 71 | Tamla Motown TMG 761 | (Come Round Here) I'm The One You Need/We Can Make It, We Can | 6 |
| 71 | Tamla Motown TMG 774 | I Don't Blame You At All/That Girl | 6 |
| 72 | Tamla Motown TMG 811 | My Girl Has Gone/Crazy 'Bout The La-La-La | 6 |
| 73 | Tamla Motown TMG 853 | Going To A Go-Go/Whole Lotta Shakin' In My Heart/Yester-Love | 6 |
| 76 | Tamla Motown TMG 1023 | Nightlife/The Miracle Workers: Overture (as The Miracles) | 6 |
| 87 | Motown ZB 41147 D | Just To See Her/Te Quiero Como Si No Hubiera Um Manana//Being With You/ What's In Your Life For Me? (solo, double pack) | 6 |
| 61 | London RE 1295 | SHOP AROUND (EP, as The Miracles) | 200 |
| 63 | Oriole PS 40044 | HI! WE'RE THE MIRACLES (EP) | 250 |
| 64 | Stateside SL 10099 | THE FABULOUS MIRACLES (LP) | 140 |
| 65 | Tamla Motown TML 11003 | I LIKE IT LIKE THAT (LP) | 80 |
| 66 | Tamla Motown TML 11024 | GOIN' TO A GO-GO (LP, as Smokey Robinson & The Miracles, mono) | 45 |
| 66 | Tamla Motown TML 11024 | GOIN' TO A GO-GO (LP, as Smokey Robinson & The Miracles, stereo) | 55 |
| 66 | Tamla Motown TML 11031 | THE MIRACLES FROM THE BEGINNING (LP, mono) | 50 |
| 66 | Tamla Motown STML 11031 | THE MIRACLES FROM THE BEGINNING (LP, stereo) | 50 |
| 67 | Tamla Motown TML 11044 | AWAY WE A-GO-GO (LP, mono) | 50 |
| 67 | Tamla Motown STML 11044 | AWAY WE A-GO-GO (LP, stereo) | 65 |
| 68 | Tamla Motown TML 11067 | MAKE IT HAPPEN (LP, mono) | 30 |
| 68 | Tamla Motown STML 11067 | MAKE IT HAPPEN (LP, stereo) | 35 |
| 68 | Tamla Motown (S)TML 11072 | GREATEST HITS (LP, mono/stereo) | 20 |
| 69 | Tamla Motown (S)TML 11089 | SPECIAL OCCASION (LP, mono/stereo) | 25 |
| 69 | Tamla Motown (S)TML 11107 | SMOKEY ROBINSON & THE MIRACLES LIVE! (LP, mono/stereo) | 25 |
| 70 | Tamla Motown (S)TML 11129 | TIME OUT FOR SMOKEY ROBINSON & THE MIRACLES (LP) | 18 |
| 70 | TamlaMotown STML 11151 | FOUR IN BLUE (LP) | 25 |
| 70 | Tamla Motown STML 11163 | WHAT LOVE HAS JOINED TOGETHER (LP, unissued) | 0 |
| 71 | Tamla Motown STML 11172 | POCKETFUL OF MIRACLES (LP) | 20 |

## MIRAGE
| | | | |
|---|---|---|---|
| 65 | CBS 201772 | It's In Her Kiss/What Ye Gonna Do 'Bout It | 20 |
| 65 | CBS 202007 | Go Away/Just A Face | 20 |
| 66 | Philips BF 1534 | Tomorrow Never Knows/You Can't Be Serious | 50 |
| 67 | Philips BF 1554 | Hold On/Can You Hear Me | 50 |
| 67 | Philips BF 1571 | The Wedding Of Ramona Blair/Lazy Man | 80 |

# MIRETTES

| | | | |
|---|---|---|---|
| 68 | Page One POF 078 | Mystery Lady/Chicago Cottage | 12 |
| 68 | Page One POF 111 | Carolyn/World Goes On Around You | 12 |

*(see also Yellow Payges, Caleb, Jawbone, Spencer Davis Group, Portobello Explosion)*

## MIRETTES

| | | | |
|---|---|---|---|
| 68 | Uni UN 501 | In The Midnight Hour/To Love Somebody | 5 |
| 68 | Uni UN 505 | The Real Thing/Take Me For A Little While | 5 |
| 69 | MCA Soul Bag BAG 8 | Whirlpool/Ain't You Trying To Cross Over | 8 |
| 72 | Jay Boy BOY 65 | Now That I've Found You Baby/He's Alright With Me | 8 |
| 69 | MCA MUP(S) 344 | IN THE MIDNIGHT HOUR (LP) | 20 |

*(see also Ikettes)*

## MIRK

| | | | |
|---|---|---|---|
| 79 | Mother Earth MUM 1205 | MODDANS BOWER (LP) | 80 |
| 82 | Spring Thyme SPR 1009 | TAK A DRAM AFOR YE GO (LP) | 25 |

## MIRKWOOD

| | | | |
|---|---|---|---|
| 71 | Flams Ltd PR 1067 | MIRKWOOD (LP) | 1000 |
| 93 | Tenth Planet TP 003 | MIRKWOOD (LP, reissue, numbered with insert, 500 only) | 30 |

## MIRO

| | | | |
|---|---|---|---|
| 90 | Sacret Heart SH 30008 | GREETINGS FROM GOLBORNE ROAD EP (hand-made and signed p/s) | 20 |

## STEVE MIRO & EYES

| | | | |
|---|---|---|---|
| 78 | Object Music OM 03 | Up And About/Smiling In Reverse (p/s) | 6 |
| 79 | Object Music OM 10 | Dreams Of Desire/Queens Of The Sea (p/s) | 5 |
| 80 | Object Music OBF 008 | RUDE INTRUSIONS (LP) | 15 |
| 81 | Object Music OBJ 015 | SECOND SENTENCE (LP) | 15 |
| 84 | Glaze GZLP101 | TRILEMNA (LP) | 15 |

*(see also Eyes, Noyes Bros)*

## MIRROR

| | | | |
|---|---|---|---|
| 68 | Philips BF 1666 | Gingerbread Man/Faster Than Light | 60 |

## MIRRORS

| | | | |
|---|---|---|---|
| 78 | Lightning GIL 503 | Cure For Cancer/Nice Vice (p/s) | 15 |
| 79 | Lightning GIL 540 | Dark Glasses/999 (p/s) | 25 |

## MISBELIEVED ONES

| | | | |
|---|---|---|---|
| 71 | Croft CR 1 | Sudddenly It Rains/Doctor Death | 70 |

## MISBELIEVERS

| | | | |
|---|---|---|---|
| 71 | Plumett PL01 | High In The Sky/Devil You | 35 |

## MISFITS (U.K.)

| | | | |
|---|---|---|---|
| 66 | A.S.C.C. PRI 101 | You Won't See Me/Hanging Around (Aberdeen Students Charities Campaign) | 10 |

*(see also Complex)*

## MISFITS (U.S.)

| | | | |
|---|---|---|---|
| 81 | Plan 9/Cherry Red PLP 9 | BEWARE (12" EP) | 120 |

## MISSING PRESUMED DEAD

| | | | |
|---|---|---|---|
| 79 | Sequel PART 2 | Say It With Flowers/Double Life/Driving Home/Family Tree (p/s) | 5 |

## MISSING SCIENTISTS

| | | | |
|---|---|---|---|
| 80 | Rough Trade RT 057 | Big City, Bright Lights/Discotheque X (p/s) | 20 |

*(see also Television Personalities, Slaughter)*

## MISSION

| | | | |
|---|---|---|---|
| 86 | Mercury MYSG 1 | Stay With Me/Blood Brother (autographed, gatefold p/s) | 8 |
| 87 | Mercury MYTHP3 | Severina/Tomorrow Never Knows (poster p/s) | 7 |
| 87 | Phonogram MYTHB 2 | IV: Wasteland/Shelter From The Storm (Live)/Serpent's Kiss (Live)/1969 (Live) (doublepack, in box, with insert and photo's) | 12 |
| 80s | Flexi FLEX 1 | Crazy (1-track flexidisc) | 12 |
| 90 | Mercury MYTH 11 | Hands Across The Ocean/Amelia/Love (p/s) | 5 |
| 01 | Playground PGND 001 | Evangeline/Anyone But You//Melt/Swoon (Reprise) (doublepack, pink & blue vinyl, gatefold p/s) | 8 |
| 02 | Playground PGND003 | Shine Like The Stars/Never Let Me Down/Spider And The Fly (In The Ointment)/ Never (2 x 7" on green and white vinyl, gatefold p/s) | 8 |

*(see also Sisters Of Mercy, Dead Or Alive, Pauline Murray, Artery, Red Lorry Yellow Lorry, Expelaires, Knopov's Political Package)*

## MISSION BELLES

| | | | |
|---|---|---|---|
| 65 | Decca F 12154 | Sincerely/When A Girl Really Loves You | 10 |

## MISSISSIPPI

| | | | |
|---|---|---|---|
| 70 | Fox FOX 1 | Mr. Union Railway Man/Main Street | 100 |

## MISS JANE

| | | | |
|---|---|---|---|
| 68 | Pama PM 704 | Bad Mind People/My Heart Is Aching (B-side act. "Witch Doctor" by Coolers) | 15 |

## MISS KATE

| | | | |
|---|---|---|---|
| 79 | TJM TJM 10 | Ebony Eyes/I Love You | 20 |

## MISSPENT YOUTH

| | | | |
|---|---|---|---|
| 79 | Big Bear BB20 | Betcha Won't Dance/Birmingham Boys (p/s) | 20 |

## MISS X (JOYCE BLAIR)

| | | | |
|---|---|---|---|
| 63 | Ember EMB S 175 | Christine/S-E-X | 10 |

## MISTA CHARGE

| | | | |
|---|---|---|---|
| 76 | Target TGT 112 | Show Me What You're Made Of/Down On Arcturas | 5 |

## MISTAKEN IDENTITY

| | | | |
|---|---|---|---|
| 85 | RAM 17CHP 7010 | The Answer/The Answer (Club Version) (12") | 25 |

## MISTAKES

| | | | |
|---|---|---|---|
| 81 | Twist And Shout TN5 | Radiation/16 Pins (insert p/s) | 15 |

## MR. MOST

| | | | |
|---|---|---|---|
| 69 | Downtown DT 408 | Push Wood/Reggae Train | 12 |

## MISTER VERSATILE

| | | |
|---|---|---|
| 69 | Jackpot JP 701 | Apple Blossom/LITTLE BOY BLUE: Dark End Of The Street (act. by Pat Kelly) ................20 |
| 69 | Jackpot JP 702 | Devil's Disciples/ERROL DUNKLEY: Having A Party .................................................8 |

*(see also Lester Sterling)*

## MISTY IN ROOTS

| | | |
|---|---|---|
| 78 | People Unite SJP 781 | ....................................................................................................12 |
| 78 | People Unite SJP 789 | Six One Penny/(DJ Cut) ....................................................................15 |
| 79 | People Unite PU 001 | Oh Wicked Man/Version ...................................................................15 |
| 80 | People Unite PU 002 | See Them A Come/How Long Jah (12", p/s) ......................................25 |
| 80 | People Unite PU 004 | Rich Man/Salvation (12", p/s) ..........................................................12 |
| 81 | People Unite PU 006 | Zapatta/Viva Zapatta ......................................................................10 |
| 81 | People Unite PU 003 | Wandering Wanderer/Cry Out For Peace (12") .................................20 |
| 83 | People Unite PU103S | Peace And Love/BallOut (12") ...........................................................8 |
| 83 | People Unite PU103 | Poor And Needy/Follow Fashion .......................................................25 |
| 86 | People Unite PU 007 | Poor And Needy/Follow Fashion (12") ..............................................15 |
| 88 | People Unite PUM 3 | Own Them Control Them/Own Them Control Them (Version) .............12 |
| 79 | People Unite PU 003 | Together/Together In Dub (12") ........................................................25 |
| 82 | People Unite PU 101 ALB | LIVE AT THE COUNTER EUROVISION '79 (LP) ................................15 |
| 83 | People Unite PU 102 | WISE AND FOOLISH (LP) ..................................................................25 |
| 85 | People Unite PU 105 | EARTH (LP) .......................................................................................20 |
| | | MUSI-O-TUNYA (LP) .........................................................................20 |

## MISTY MEADOWS

| | | |
|---|---|---|
| 70 | Rhone RH 002 | Visions/We See The Sun .................................................................150 |

## MISTY (1)

| | | |
|---|---|---|
| 70 | Parlophone R5852 | Hot Cinnamon/Cascades ..................................................................80 |

## MISTY (2)

| | | |
|---|---|---|
| 77 | Cottage COT 511 | MISTY (LP) ........................................................................................18 |

## MISUNDERSTOOD

| | | |
|---|---|---|
| 66 | Fontana TF 777 | I Can Take You To The Sun/Who Do You Love ...................................80 |
| 69 | Fontana TF 998 | Children Of The Sun/I Unseen (small centre hole) ............................70 |
| 69 | Fontana TF 998 | Children Of The Sun/I Unseen (large centre hole) ............................50 |
| 69 | Fontana TF 1028 | You're Tuff Enough/Little Red Rooster (as Misunderstood featuring Glenn "Fernando" Campbell, in p/s) ...................................................60 |
| 69 | Fontana TF 1028 | You're Tuff Enough/Little Red Rooster (as Misunderstood featuring Glenn "Fernando" Campbell) ...........................................................35 |
| 69 | Fontana TF 1041 | Never Had A Girl (Like You Before)/Golden Glass (as Misunderstood featuring Glenn "Fernando" Campbell) .............................................45 |
| 81 | Cherry Red CHERRY 22 | Children Of The Sun/Who Do You Love/I'll Take You To The Sun (p/s) ......7 |
| 82 | Cherry Red B RED 32 | BEFORE THE DREAM FADED (LP, with inner) .....................................20 |

## BLUE MITCHELL

| | | |
|---|---|---|
| 69 | Blue Note BST 84300 | COLLISION IN BLACK (LP) ..................................................................20 |
| 73 | Mainstream MSL 1015 | THE LAST TANGO = BLUES (LP) .........................................................18 |

## CHAD MITCHELL

| | | |
|---|---|---|
| 62 | London HLR 9509 | Lizzie Borden/Super Skier ..................................................................7 |

## DENNY MITCHELL SOUNDSATIONS

| | | |
|---|---|---|
| 64 | Decca F 11848 | I've Been Crying/For Your Love .........................................................25 |

*(see also Preachers, Moon's Train)*

## GROVER MITCHELL

| | | |
|---|---|---|
| 68 | London HLU 10221 | Turned On/Blue Over You ..................................................................18 |
| 76 | Vanguard VS 5003 | What Hurts/Super Hero .....................................................................40 |

## GUY MITCHELL

### SINGLES : SINGLES & EPS

| | | |
|---|---|---|
| 53 | Columbia SCM 5018 | ....................................................................................................15 |
| 53 | Columbia SCM 5022 | Feet Up (Pat Him On The Po-Po)/Jenny Kissed Me ...........................15 |
| 53 | Columbia SCM 5032 | Cause I Love Ya, That's A-Why/Train Of Love (both with Mindy Carson) ....15 |
| 53 | Columbia SCM 5037 | She Wears Red Feathers/Why Should I Go Home? .............................15 |
| 56 | Philips JK 1001 | Pretty Little Black-Eyed Susie/MITCH MILLER HORNS: Horn Belt Boogie ...20 |
| 57 | Philips JK 1005 | Singing The Blues/Crazy With Love (jukebox issue) ..........................10 |
| 57 | Philips JK 1015 | Knee Deep In The Blues/Take Me Back Baby (jukebox issue) ............10 |
| 57 | Philips JK 1023 | Rock-A-Billy/Got A Feeling (jukebox issue) ......................................10 |
| 57 | Philips JK 1027 | Sweet Stuff/In The Middle Of A Dark, Dark Night (jukebox issue) .....10 |
| 58 | Philips PB 766 | Call Rosie On The Phone/Cure For The Blues (jukebox issue) ...........10 |
| 58 | Philips PB 798 | C'mon Let's Go/The Unbeliever .........................................................8 |
| 58 | Philips PB 830 | Wond'rin' And Worryin'/If Ya Don't Like It, Don't Knock It .................6 |
| 58 | Philips PB 858 | Hangin' Around/Honey Brown Eyes ..................................................10 |
| 58 | Philips PB 885 | Let It Shine, Let It Shine/Butterfly Doll .............................................10 |
| 59 | Philips PB 915 | My Heart Cries For You (2nd Version)/Till We're Engaged ..................7 |
| 59 | Philips PB 964 | Alias Jesse James/Pride O' Dixie .......................................................7 |
| 63 | Pye International 7N 25179 | Heartaches By The Number/Two (with triangular centre) ................12 |
| 63 | Pye International 7N 25185 | Go, Tiger, Go/If You Ever Go Away (unreleased) ...............................0 |
| 66 | CBS 202238 | Have I Told You Lately That I Love You/Blue Violet ............................5 |
| 54 | Columbia SEG 7513 | Singing The Blues/Rock-A-Billy ..........................................................5 |
| 55 | Columbia SEG 7598 | PRETTY LITTLE BLACK EYED SUSIE (EP, plain sleeve) ........................10 |
| | | JENNY KISSED ME (plain sleeve) ......................................................10 |

## JONI MITCHELL

| | | |
|---|---|---|
| 68 | Reprise RS 20694 | ....................................................................................................15 |
| 69 | Reprise RS 23402 | Night In The City/I Had A King ..........................................................12 |
| 70 | Reprise RS 20906 | Chelsea Morning/Both Sides Now .......................................................5 |
| 72 | Asylum AYM 511 | Big Yellow Taxi/Woodstock ................................................................8 |
| 83 | Geffen DA 3122 | You Turn Me On, I'm A Radio/Urge For Going .....................................8 |
| | | Chinese Cafe/Ladies Man (double pack, with bonus interview 7") ......20 |

# McKINLEY 'SOUL' MITCHELL

| 68 | Reprise RSLP 6293 | JONI MITCHELL (LP, gatefold sleeve, 'steamboat' label) | 50 |
|---|---|---|---|
| 69 | Reprise RSLP 6341 | CLOUDS (LP, textured single sleeve, 'steamboat' label) | 45 |
| 69 | Reprise RSLP 6341 | CLOUDS (LP, 2nd pressing, stickered U.S. gatefold sleeve, 'steamboat' label) | 15 |
| 70 | Reprise RSLP 6376 | LADIES OF THE CANYON (LP, gatefold sleeve, 'steamboat' label) | 30 |
| 71 | Reprise K 44128 | BLUE (LP, gatefold sleeve, with blue inner sleeve) | 30 |
| 71 | Reprise K 44128 | BLUE (LP, gatefold sleeve) | 15 |
| 73 | Asylum SYLA 8753 | FOR THE ROSES (LP, gatefold sleeve) | 15 |
| 74 | Asylum SYLA 8756 | COURT AND SPARK (LP, gatefold sleeve) | 20 |
| 75 | Asylum SYLA 8763 | THE HISSING OF SUMMER LAWNS (LP) | 18 |
| 75 | Asylum SYSP 902 | MILES OF AISLES (2-LP, gatefold sleeve with inner flap) | 20 |
| 70s | Asylum K 53053 | HEJIRA (LP, gatefold sleeve) | 15 |
| 82 | Asylum/Nimbus K 53018 | THE HISSING OF SUMMER LAWNS (LP, audiophile pressing, mail order issue) | 60 |

## McKINLEY 'SOUL' MITCHELL

| 68 | President PT 125 | The Town I Live In/No Love Like Your Love | 10 |
|---|---|---|---|
| 68 | President PTL 1005 | McKINLEY 'SOUL' MITCHELL (LP) | 40 |

## PHILIP MITCHELL

| 71 | Jay Boy BOY 37 | I'm Gonna Build California From All Over The World/ The World Needs More People Like You | 30 |
|---|---|---|---|
| 71 | Jay Boy BOY 37 | I'm Gonna Build California From All Over The World/ The World Needs More People Like You (DJ copy) | 50 |
| 72 | Jay Boy BOY 57 | Free For All/Flower Child | 10 |
| 72 | Jay Boy BOY 57 | Free For All/Flower Child (DJ copy) | 10 |
| 74 | London HLU 10444 | Ain't No Love In My Life/Turning Over The Ground | 40 |

## RED MITCHELL

| 62 | London LZ-N1 4017 | HAPPY MINORS (10" LP) | 15 |
|---|---|---|---|

## RONNIE MITCHELL

| 60 | London HLU 9220 | How Many Times/The Only Love | 8 |
|---|---|---|---|

## SINX MITCHELL

| 64 | Hickory 45-1248 | This Weird Sensation/Love Is All I'm Asking For | 20 |
|---|---|---|---|

*(see also Crickets, Earl Sinks)*

## VALERIE MITCHELL

| 65 | Oak RGJ 160 | There Goes My Heart Again/If I Didn't Love You (p/s) | 60 |
|---|---|---|---|
| 65 | HMV POP 1422 | Bitter Tears/Forbidden | 6 |
| 65 | HMV POP 1462 | There Goes My Heart Again/If I Didn't Love You | 6 |
| 65 | HMV POP 1490 | Go My Way/Green Eyes | 6 |
| 66 | HMV POP 1509 | Play With Me/Never Let It Be Said | 8 |
| 66 | HMV POP 1529 | You Can Go/The Windmill Girls | 10 |
| 67 | Columbia DB 8186 | Love Can Be The Sweetest Thing/I'm Sorry | 8 |
| 67 | Columbia DB 8265 | Sunshine/You Belong To Me | 6 |

## WARREN MITCHELL

| 67 | CBS 2824 | The Writing On The Wall/Her Heart's In the Right Place (p/s) | 5 |
|---|---|---|---|

## WILLIE MITCHELL

| 64 | London HLU 9926 | 20-75/Secret Home | 20 |
|---|---|---|---|
| 64 | London HLU 9926 | 20-75/Secret Home (DJ Copy) | 40 |
| 65 | London HLU 10004 | Everything Is Gonna Be Alright/That Driving Beat (Boxed logo) | 15 |
| 65 | London HLU 10004 | Everything Is Gonna Be Alright/That Driving Beat | 20 |
| 65 | London HLU 10004 | Everything Is Gonna Be Alright/That Driving Beat (DJ copy) | 50 |
| 66 | London HLU 10039 | Bad Eye/Sugar T. | 10 |
| 66 | London HLU 10085 | Mercy/Sticks And Stones | 10 |
| 68 | London HLU 10186 | Soul Serenade/Buster Browne | 10 |
| 68 | London HLU 10215 | Prayer Meetin'/Rum Daddy | 8 |
| 68 | London HLU 10224 | Up Hard/Beale Street Mood | 10 |
| 70 | London HLU 10313 | Robbin's Nest/Six To Go | 8 |
| 73 | London HLU 10407 | Last Tango In Paris/Six To Go | 6 |
| 74 | London HLU 10545 | The Champion (2 parts) (DJ copy) | 30 |
| 74 | London HLU 10545 | The Champion (2 parts) | 5 |
| 67 | London HA-U 8319 | THE HIT SOUND OF WILLIE MITCHELL (LP) | 30 |
| 68 | London HA-U/SH-U 8365 | SOUL SERENADE (LP) | 20 |
| 68 | London HA-U/SH-U 8368 | LIVE (LP) | 20 |
| 69 | London HA-U/SH-U 8372 | SOLID SOUL (LP) | 20 |
| 70 | London HA-U/SH-U 8388 | ON TOP (LP) | 20 |
| 70 | London HA-U/SH-U 8408 | SOUL BAG (LP) | 20 |

## MITCHELL/COE MYSTERIES

| 80 | RCA PL 25297 | EXILED (LP, with inner sleeve, with gatefold sleeve) | 15 |
|---|---|---|---|

*(see also Colin Blunstone, Lesley Duncan, Dan McCafferty, Francis Rossi & Berni Frost, Ray Russell, Joe Jammer, Complex, Monsoon)*

## ROBERT MITCHUM

| 57 | Capitol CL 14701 | What Is This Generation Coming To?/Mama Looka Boo Boo | 5 |
|---|---|---|---|
| 62 | Capitol CL 15251 | The Ballad Of Thunder Road/My Honey's Lovin' Arms | 5 |
| 67 | Monument MON 1007 | Little Ole Wine Drinker Me/Walker's Woods | 5 |
| 55 | Brunswick OE 9197 | RACHEL AND THE STRANGER (EP) | 10 |

## MITHRANDIR

| 82 | New Leaf SVC 570 | Dreamers Of Fortune/After Tomorrow (p/s) | 50 |
|---|---|---|---|
| 82 | New Leaf SVC 01 | MAGICK EP (p/s) | 75 |

## JACKIE MITTOO

| 66 | Island WI 293 | Killer Diller (as Jackie Mitto & Soul Brothers)/PATRICK HYTTON: Oh Lady | 150 |
|---|---|---|---|
| 67 | Rio R 114 | Home Made/ETHIOPIANS: I'm Gonna Take Over Now | 150 |
| 67 | Rio R 123 | Got My Buglaoo/ETHIOPIANS: What To Do | 70 |
| 67 | Coxsone CS 7002 | Somebody Help Me/GAYLADS & SOUL VENDORS: The Sound Of Silence | 125 |

| | | |
|---|---|---|
| 67 | Coxsone CS 7009 | Ba Ba Boom/SLIM SMITH & FREEDOM SINGERS: Mercy Mercy ........................... 100 |
| 67 | Coxsone CS 7019 | Ram Jam/SUMMERTAIRES: You're Gonna Leave ................................................ 40 |
| 67 | Coxsone CS 7026 | Something Stupid/LYRICS: Money Lover ........................................................ 50 |
| 68 | Coxsone CS 7040 | Norwegian Wood/GAYLADS: Most Peculiar Man ........................................... 50 |
| 68 | Coxsone CS 7042 | Sure Shot/OCTAVES: The Bottle ................................................................... 200 |
| 68 | Coxsone CS 7046 | Man Pon Spot/BOP & BELTONES: Not For A Moment ................................... 50 |
| 68 | Coxsone CS 7050 | Napoleon Solo/CANNON BALL BRYAN: You're My Everything ...................... 60 |
| 68 | Coxsone CS 7070 | Songbird/JAMAICAN ACTIONS: Catch The Quinella ..................................... 80 |
| 68 | Coxsone CS 7075 | Mission Impossible/HEPTONES: Giddy Up (B-side actually by Actions) ......... 80 |
| 68 | Studio One SO 2043 | Put It One/SOUL VENDORS: Chinese Chicken .............................................. 30 |
| 68 | Studio One SO 2056 | Race Track/BASES: I Don't Mind .................................................................. 40 |
| 69 | Studio One SO 2082 | Hi-Jack/TREVOR CLARKE: Sufferer ............................................................... 40 |
| 69 | Doctor Bird DB 1177 | Dark Of The Sun/MATADOR ALL STARS: Bridge View .................................. 60 |
| 69 | Bamboo BAM 6 | Our Thing (with Sound Dimension)/C. MARSHALL: Tra La La Sweet '69 ......... 60 |
| 69 | Bamboo BAM 15 | Clean Up/Spring Time (as Jackie Mittoo & Sound Dimension) ..................... 40 |
| 70 | Bamboo BAM 17 | Dark Of The Moon/Moon Walk (as Jackie Mittoo & Sound Dimension) ....... 40 |
| 70 | Bamboo BAM 20 | Gold Dust/SUPERTONES: Real Gone Loser ................................................... 40 |
| 70 | Bamboo BAM 31 | Can I Change My Mind/BRENTFORD ALLSTARS: Early Duckling ................... 40 |
| 70 | Bamboo BAM 38 | Baby Why/ETHIOPIANS: You'll Want To Come Back ..................................... 40 |
| 70 | Bamboo BAM 51 | Dancing Groove/BLACK & GEORGE: Peanut Butter ..................................... 50 |
| 70 | Banana BA 315 | Holly Holy/LARRY MARSHALL: I've Got To Make It ....................................... 20 |
| 71 | Banana BA 320 | Peenie Wallie/ROY RICHARDS: Can't Go On .................................................. 20 |
| 72 | London HLU 10357 | Wishbone/Soul Bird (as Jackie Mittoo - The Reggae Beat) ............................ 7 |
| 79 | Justice DIS 001 | Disco Jack/Disco Dub (12") ........................................................................ 35 |
| 80 | Rite Sound RTA 06 | Mystic World/Version (12") ......................................................................... 20 |
| 81 | Black Roots BR20 | These Eyes/Wall Street/Thriller The Killer (12", p/s) ................................... 30 |
| 67 | Coxsone CSL 8009 | IN LONDON (LP) ........................................................................................ 150 |
| 68 | Coxsone CSL 8014 | EVENING TIME (LP, with Soul Vendors) ...................................................... 150 |
| 69 | Coxsone CSL 8020 | KEEP ON DANCING (LP) ............................................................................. 150 |
| 70 | Bamboo BDLP 209 | NOW (LP) .................................................................................................... 80 |
| 72 | London SHU 8436 | WISHBONE (LP) ........................................................................................... 25 |
| 78 | Third World TWS 931 | IN COLD BLOOD (LP) .................................................................................. 35 |
| 79 | Third World TWS 501 | KEYBOARD KING (LP) .................................................................................. 30 |

*(see also Lord Tanamo, Jamaican Actions, Matadors, Jackie Opel, Soul Vendors, Winston Francis, Donna & Freedom Singers, Skatalites)*

## MIX BLOOD
| | | |
|---|---|---|
| 80 | Creole CR 201 | Last Train To Skaville/Move And Move (p/s) ................................................ 10 |

## MIXED BAG
| | | |
|---|---|---|
| 69 | Decca F 12880 | Potiphar (with Ramases III Orchestra)/Million Dollar Bash ............................ 6 |
| 69 | Decca F 12907 | Round And Round/Have You Ever Been In Love .............................................. 6 |

## MIXED FEELINGS
| | | |
|---|---|---|
| 73 | Scotty SCO 2 | Make Me Jump/Stop .................................................................................... 20 |

## MIXMAN
| | | |
|---|---|---|
| 90 | Citizen Kane 12KANE 2 | Bright Child (Manmix)/Bright Child (Dancemix) (12", p/s) ........................... 15 |

## MIXRACE & PRO-TON-ISOSPACE
| | | |
|---|---|---|
| 94 | Stronghold STRONG 3 | The Endless Skies (Hyper-On-Experience Remix)/True Jungle (Brown & Dangerman Remix)/The Endless Skies/True Jungle (12") ............................................... 20 |

## MIXTURE
| | | |
|---|---|---|
| 65 | Fontana TF 640 | One By One/Monkey Jazz .............................................................................. 10 |
| 69 | Parlophone R 5755 | Sad Old Song/Never Trust In Tomorrow .......................................................... 7 |

## MIXTURES
| | | |
|---|---|---|
| 71 | Polydor 205813 | Never Be Untrue/She's Gone Away ............................................................... 20 |

## BILLY MIZE
| | | |
|---|---|---|
| 60 | Top rank JAR 391 | Little Coco Palm/The Windward Isle ............................................................... 7 |

## HANK MIZELL
| | | |
|---|---|---|
| 76 | Charly CEP 115 | HANK MIZELL (EP) ....................................................................................... 10 |

## VIC MIZZY, HIS ORCHESTRA & CHORUS
| | | |
|---|---|---|
| 65 | RCA RCA 1440 | Addams Family Main Theme/Kentucky James Main Theme ........................... 20 |

## M.J.6
| | | |
|---|---|---|
| 60 | Decca F 11212 | Tracy's Theme/Private Eye .............................................................................. 6 |

## MO & STEVE
| | | |
|---|---|---|
| 66 | Pye 7N 17175 | Oh What A Day It's Going To Be/Reach Out For Your Lovin' Touch ................... 5 |

## MO2VATION
| | | |
|---|---|---|
| 93 | No Noise NNDJ 008 | Lowdown & Funky/That Ruff Track (with L Double, 12") ................................ 15 |
| 93 | Pure Noise DASH 3 | THE RHYTHM RIDE EP (12") ........................................................................ 10 |

## MO2VATION & APEX
| | | |
|---|---|---|
| 92 | Hypno Genesis HG 002 | ANIMATION EP (12") .................................................................................... 25 |

## MOB (1)
| | | |
|---|---|---|
| 68 | Mercury MF 1026 | Disappear/I Wish You Would Leave Me Alone ............................................... 15 |
| 71 | Polydor 2001 127 | I Dig Everything About You/Love's Got A Hold On Me .................................... 20 |
| 71 | Polydor 2001 169 | Give It To Me/I'd Like To See More Of You .................................................... 10 |
| 71 | Polydor 2001 200 | Money/Once A Man Twice A Child ................................................................... 5 |
| 73 | MGM 2006 278 | Tear The House Down/One Way Ticket To Nowhere ........................................ 5 |
| 74 | UK USA 4 | Give It To Me/I'd LIke To See More Of You ...................................................... 8 |
| 75 | Private Stock PVT 32 | I Can't Stop This Love Song/Hot Music ........................................................... 8 |
| 71 | Polydor 2344 001 | MOB (LP) ..................................................................................................... 15 |

## MOB (2)
| | | |
|---|---|---|
| 80 | Kalida AKB 1/2 | Send Me To Coventry/Mobbed (p/s) ............................................................... 8 |

MINT VALUE £

## MOB (3)

| 80 | All The Madmen MAD 1 | Youth/Crying Again (p/s) | 40 |
|----|----|----|----|
| 80 | All The Madmen MAD 002 | Witch Hunt/Shuffling Souls/What's Going On (EP, handwritten white labels with sticker & foldout, stapled, gatefold p/s) | 12 |
| 82 | Crass 321984/7 | No Doves Fly Here/I Hear You Laughing (foldout p/s) | 12 |
| 83 | All The Madmen MAD 6 | The Mirror Breaks/Stay (screen-printed p/s, with lyric insert) | 10 |
| 83 | Cause For Concern CFC 2 | LIVE AT THE LMC (LP, with the APOSTLES) | 30 |
| 83 | All The Madmen MAD 4 | LET THE TRIBE INCREASE (LP, with lyric poster) | 25 |
| 86 | All The Madmen MAD 13 | CRYING AGAIN (EP) | 30 |
| 80s | All/Madmen MADPACK 1 | MAD PACK 1 (3 x 7" in 12" pack) | 25 |

## HANK MOBLEY

| 56 | Esquire 32-029 | MOBLEY'S MESSAGE (LP) | 70 |
|----|----|----|----|

## JOHN MOBLEY

| 62 | Stateside SS 136 | Tunnel Of Love/Work Out | 15 |
|----|----|----|----|

## MOBSTER

| 80 | Ensign ENY 41 | The Mobster Shuffle/Simmer Down (p/s) | 6 |
|----|----|----|----|
| 81 | Ensign ENY 209 | Perfect Man/Trinidad (p/s) | 5 |

## MOBY

| 99 | Mute STUMM 172 | PLAY (2-LP, inner, 500 only) | 60 |
|----|----|----|----|
| 02 | Mute STUMM 202 | 18 (2-LP, gatefold) | 35 |

## MOBY DICK

| 82 | Ebony EBON 5 | Nothing To Fear/Can't Have My Body Tonight | 20 |
|----|----|----|----|

## MOBY GRAPE

| 67 | CBS 2953 | Omaha/Hey Grandma | 20 |
|----|----|----|----|
| 68 | CBS 3555 | Can't Be So Bad/Murder In My Heart For The Judge | 15 |
| 69 | CBS 3945 | Trucking Man/Ooh Mama Ooh | 8 |
| 67 | CBS (S)BPG 63090 | MOBY GRAPE (LP) | 60 |
| 68 | CBS 63271 | WOW (LP, mono & stereo) | 40 |
| 69 | CBS 63430 | 69 (LP, mono & stereo) | 40 |
| 69 | CBS 63698 | TRULY FINE CITIZEN (LP, stereo) | 40 |
| 69 | CBS 63430 | TRULY FINE CITIZEN (LP, mono) | 60 |
| 71 | Reprise K 44152 | 20 GRANITE CREEK (LP) | 15 |
| 74 | CBS 64743 | GREAT GRAPE (LP) | 15 |

## MOCCA-SIN & THE TP'S

| 78 | Alaska ALA 2013 | Cherokee Dance/The Raindance | 10 |
|----|----|----|----|

## MOCEDADES

| 73 | Bell BELL 1303 | Touch The Wind/Eres Tu | 6 |
|----|----|----|----|

## MOCKINGBIRDS

| 65 | Columbia DB 7480 | That's How It's Gonna Stay/I Never Should Have Kissed You | 50 |
|----|----|----|----|
| 65 | Columbia DB 7565 | I Can Feel We're Parting/The Flight Of The Mockingbird | 50 |
| 65 | Immediate IM 015 | You Stole My Love/Skit Skat | 150 |
| 66 | Decca F 12434 | One By One/Lovingly Yours | 60 |
| 66 | Decca F 12510 | How To Find A Lover/My Story | 50 |

*(see also 10cc, Graham Gouldman, Whirlwinds, Doctor Father, Hotlegs, Godley & Creme)*

## M.O.D.

| 79 | Vertigo 6059 233 | M.O.D./M.O.D. (2) (p/s, allegedly mispressed on 2-Tone label) | 30 |
|----|----|----|----|
| 79 | Vertigo 6059 233 | M.O.D./M.O.D. (2) (p/s) | 7 |

*(see also David Essex)*

## MOD '79

| 79 | Casino Classics CC 13 | Green Onions/High On Your Love | 5 |
|----|----|----|----|

## MODE

| 66 | Private pressing | THE MODE (EP, white labels, no p/s) | 400 |
|----|----|----|----|

## MODEL MANIA

| 79 | Boob MM1 A/MM 1AA | No Pride Slow Suicide/Epic Cowboy (250 with handmade stamped label) | 100 |
|----|----|----|----|
| 79 | Boob MM1 A/MM 1AA | No Pride Slow Suicide/Epic Cowboy (750 with black labels) | 75 |

## MODELS

| 77 | Step Forward SF 3 | Freeze/Man Of The Year (p/s, 1st pressing with The Models and The Freeze on labels) | 20 |
|----|----|----|----|
| 77 | Step Forward SF-3 | Freeze/Man Of The Year (p/s, 2nd pressing with Models and Freeze on labels) | 15 |

*(see also Adam & The Ants, Mass, Rema Rema, Wolfgang Press)*

## MODERATES

| 81 | Hyped BMRB 53 | Emile/For What It's Worth (not released in p/s) | 10 |
|----|----|----|----|
| 80 | Open Eye OEEP 1001 | FETISHES (12" EP) | 12 |

## MODERN ART

| 84 | Color Disc COLORS 1 | Dreams To Live/Beautiful Truth (p/s) | 25 |
|----|----|----|----|
| 86 | Color Disc COLORS 5 | Penny Valentine/One Way Ticket (1-sided, clear vinyl flexidisc, 1,000 only) | 12 |
| 87 | Color Disc COLOR 3 | STEREOLAND (LP, hand-stencilled with insert, 300 only) | 60 |
| 94 | Acme 8007 LP | ALL ABOARD THE MIND TRAIN (LP, 500 only, numbered) | 18 |

## MODERN ENGLISH

| 79 | Limp LMP 2 | Drowning Man/Silent World (p/s) | 20 |
|----|----|----|----|
| 80 | 4AD AD 6 | Swans On Glass/Incident (p/s) | 8 |
| 80 | 4AD AD 15 | Gathering Dust/Tranquility Of A Summer Moment (p/s) | 8 |
| 81 | 4AD AD 110 | Smiles And Laughter/Mesh And Lace (p/s) | 5 |
| 82 | 4AD AD 212 | I Melt With You/The Prize | 5 |
| 83 | 4AD AD 309 | Someone's Calling (Remix)/Life In The Gladhouse (Remix) | 5 |
| 81 | 4AD CAD 105 | MESH AND LACE (LP) | 15 |

*(see also This Mortal Coil)*

## MODERN EON
| | | | |
|---|---|---|---|
| 80 | Modern Eon EON 001 | PIECES (EP) | 20 |
| 80 | Inevitable INEV 3 | Euthenics/Waiting For The Cavalry (p/s) | 5 |
| 81 | Dinsales 2 | Euthenics/Choreography/Waiting For The Cavalry/The Real Hymn (12", white label LP sampler) | 20 |
| 81 | Dindisc DIN 31 | Child's Play/Visionary | 5 |

## MODERN FOLK QUARTET (M.F.Q.)
| | | | |
|---|---|---|---|
| 64 | Warner Bros WB 147 | The Love Of A Clown/If You All Think | 25 |
| 66 | RCA RCA 1514 | Night Time Girl/Lifetime (as M.F.Q.) | 30 |
| 63 | Warner Bros WM/WS 8135 | THE MODERN FOLK QUARTET (LP) | 20 |
| 85 | Off Beat WIK 55 | MOONLIGHT SERENADE (LP) | 15 |

## MODERN JAZZ QUARTET (M.J.Q.)
| | | | |
|---|---|---|---|
| 55 | Esquire 20-069 | MODERN JAZZ QUARTET (10" LP) | 15 |
| 55 | Esquire 20-038 | MODERN JAZZ QUARTET VOL. 2 (10" LP) | 15 |
| 55 | Esquire 20-090 | THE CLASSICAL PERFORMANCES OF... (10" LP) | 15 |
| 57 | London Jazz LTZK 15022 | FONTESSA (LP, also stereo SAH-K 6031) | 15 |
| 59 | London Jazz LTZ-K 15140 | PLAYS ONE NEVER KNOWS (LP, also stereo SAH-K 6029) | 15 |
| 59 | London Jazz LTZK 15181 | ODDS AGAINST TOMORROW (LP) | 20 |
| 60 | London Jazz LTZ-K 15193 | PYRAMID (LP, also stereo SAH-K 6086) | 15 |
| 61 | London Jazz LTZ-K 15207 | THIRD STREAM MUSIC (LP, with Beaux Arts String Quartet & Jimmy Giuffre Three) | 15 |
| 63 | London HA-K/SH-K 8016 | LONELY WOMAN (LP) | 15 |
| 68 | Apple APCOR 4 | UNDER THE JASMINE TREE (LP, mono) | 50 |
| 68 | Apple SAPCOR 4 | UNDER THE JASMINE TREE (LP, stereo) | 35 |
| 69 | Apple SAPCOR 10 | SPACE (LP, gatefold sleeve, dark green label, black inner) | 50 |
| 70s | Apple SAPCOR 10 | SPACE (LP, later pressing, light green label, single sleeve, white 'Apple' inner) | 75 |
| 93 | Apple SAPCOR 4 | UNDER THE JASMINE TREE (LP, reissue, gatefold sleeve with inner) | 20 |
| 93 | Apple SAPCOR 10 | SPACE (LP, reissue) | 20 |

*(see also John Lewis, Milt Jackson, Sonny Rollins)*

## MODERN JAZZ SEXTET
| | | | |
|---|---|---|---|
| 56 | Columbia Clef 33CX 10048 | MODERN JAZZ SEXTET (LP) | 20 |

## MODERNAIRES (U.K.)
| | | | |
|---|---|---|---|
| 80 | Illuminated ILL 2 | Life In Our Times/Barbed Up (p/s) | 5 |
| 81 | Illuminated ILL 4 | We Did It Again/And Again (p/s, red vinyl) | 5 |

## MODERNAIRES (U.S.)
| | | | |
|---|---|---|---|
| 54 | Vogue Coral Q 2024 | Teach Me Tonight/Mood Indigo (with Georgie Auld) | 5 |
| 54 | Vogue Coral Q 2035 | New Juke Box Saturday Night/Bugle Call Rag | 5 |
| 55 | Vogue Coral Q 72069 | Birds And Puppies And Tropical Fish/Mine! Mine! Mine! | 5 |
| 55 | Vogue Coral Q 72084 | Wine, Women And Gold/Sluefoot (with Bob Crosby Bob Cats) | 5 |
| 55 | Vogue Coral Q 72112 | At My Front Door/Alright, Okay, You Win | 5 |

*(see also Four Guys, Bing Crosby)*

## MODEST MOUSE
| | | | |
|---|---|---|---|
| 00 | Matador OLE 4501 | MOON AND ANTARTICA (2-LP) | 30 |

## MO-DETTES
| | | | |
|---|---|---|---|
| 79 | Mode/Rough Trade MODE 1 | White Mice/Masochistic Opposite (pink [card or paper] or white p/s) | 6 |
| 80 | Deram DET 2 | Deep Park Creeping/Two Can Play | 5 |
| 80 | Deram DET-R-1/MODE 11/2 | Paint It Black/Bitta Truth (with free flexidisc "Twist And Shout" & insert, black & white or blue & white p/s) | 6 |
| 81 | Deram DET 3 | Tonight/Waltz In Blue Minor (p/s, fold-out sleeve with postcards of each band member) | 5 |
| 81 | Human HUM 10 | White Mice/Kray Twins (live) (p/s) | 7 |
| 80 | Deram SML 1120 | THE STORY SO FAR (LP, with insert & free colour sticker) | 15 |

## MODIFIES
| | | | |
|---|---|---|---|
| 70 | Punch PH 45 | Bye Bye Happyness/Sufferation We Must Bear | 12 |

## MODS (1)
| | | | |
|---|---|---|---|
| 64 | RCA RCA 1399 | Something On My Mind/You're Making Me Blue | 25 |

## MODS (2)
| | | | |
|---|---|---|---|
| 80 | Bootlegged Records 007 | LOST TOUCH (LP; sold only in Portobello Market, London) | 25 |

## MODULATIONS
| | | | |
|---|---|---|---|
| 74 | Buddah BDS 406 | I Can't Fight Your Love/Your Love Has Locked Me Up (DJ Copy) | 30 |
| 74 | Buddah BDS 406 | I Can't Fight Your Love/Your Love Has Locked Me Up | 15 |
| 70s | Buddah | THE MODULATIONS (LP) | 40 |

## PETER MOESSER'S MUSIC
| | | | |
|---|---|---|---|
| 70 | Stateside SS 2182 | Hello/Bye Bye (withdrawn) | 7 |

## MOFFAT ALL STARS
| | | | |
|---|---|---|---|
| 70 | Jackpot JP 719 | Riot/IMPERSONATORS: Girls And Boys | 50 |

## LEROY MOFFATT
| | | | |
|---|---|---|---|
| 74 | Atra AR 20 | What It Takes/I Love You Darling | 20 |

## MOGUL THRASH
| | | | |
|---|---|---|---|
| 70 | RCA RCA 2030 | Sleeping In The Kitchen/St. Peter | 15 |
| 71 | RCA SF 8156 | MOGUL THRASH (LP) | 150 |

*(see also Colosseum, Eclection, King Crimson)*

## MOGWAI
| | | | |
|---|---|---|---|
| 96 | Rock Action RAR 01 | Tuner/Lower (p/s, 500 only) | 70 |
| 96 | Ché CHE 59 | 4 TRACK 3 BAND TOUR EP (with Urusei Yatsura & Backwater, p/s, 50 only) | 40 |
| 96 | Ché CHE 61 | Angels Vs Aliens/DWEEB: Buzzsong (p/s, 1st 500 on green vinyl) | 12 |
| 96 | Ché CHE 61 | Angels Vs Aliens/DWEEB: Buzzsong | 6 |
| 96 | Love Train PUBE 014 | Summer/Ithica 27/9 (p/s, 1,500 only, inserts) | 20 |

MINT VALUE £

| 97 | Wurlitzer Jukebox WJ 22 | New Paths To Helicon (Parts 1 & 2) (foldover p/s in polythene bag, 2 inserts, only) | 1,000 |
|---|---|---|---|
| 97 | Flotsam/Jetsam SHAG13.04 | Stereo Dee/PH FAMILY: Club Beatroot Part 4 (p/s, 400 only) | 15 |
| 98 | Chemikal Underground CHEM 026 | NO EDUCATION = NO FUTURE (FUCK THE CURFEW) EP (12") | 15 |
| 99 | Chemikal CHEM 036 | EP (12") | 10 |
| 01 | Rock Action ROCKACT 10 | My Father My King (1-sided 12") | 15 |
| 11 | Rock Action ROCKACT 59 | San Pedro/George Square Thatcher Death Party (Session Version) | 15 |
| 97 | Chemikal U'gnd CHEM 818LP | YOUNG TEAM (2xLP) | 5 |
| 98 | Eye Q EYEUKLP 019 | KICKING A DEAD PIG (2-LP) | 50 |
| 99 | Chemikal Underground CMEM 033 | COME ON DIE YOUNG (2xLP) | 18 |
| 01 | Southpaw PAWLP1 | ROCK ACTION (LP) | 30 |
| 03 | Pias PIASX 035LP | HAPPY SONGS FOR HAPPY PEOPLE (LP, silvered sleeve) | 18 |
| 05 | Pias PIAS051LP | GOVERNMENT COMMISSIONS : BBC SESSIONS 1996-2003 (2-LP) | 20 |
| 06 | Pias PIAS X067DLP | ZIDANE (2-LP) | 25 |
| 07 | Pias PIASX062DLP | MR BEAST (2-LP, one sided etched) | 18 |
| 08 | Wall Of Sound WOS 040DLP | THE HAWK IS HOWLING (2-LP) | 20 |
| 10 | Rock Action ROCKACT 48 | SPECIAL MOVES (3-LP, CD, DVD and signed poster) | 50 |

(see also Magoo)

## ESSRA MOHAWK

| 75 | Mooncrest CREST 24 | ESSRA MOHAWK (LP, with insert) | 15 |
|---|---|---|---|
| 77 | Private Stock PVLP 1016 | ESSRA (LP) | 15 |

## MOHAWKS

| 68 | Pama PM 309 | The Clock/Version | 35 |
|---|---|---|---|
| 68 | Pama PM 719 | The Champ/Sound Of The Witchdoctors (blue label) | 30 |
| 68 | Pama PM 719 | The Champ/Sound Of The Witchdoctors (purple label) | 20 |
| 68 | Pama PM 739 | Baby Hold On (Parts 1 & 2) | 20 |
| 68 | Pama PM 751 | Sweet Soul Music/Hip Jigger | 20 |
| 68 | Pama PM 757 | Mony Mony/Pepsi | 70 |
| 69 | Pama PM 758 | Ride Your Pony/Western Promise | 25 |
| 69 | Pama PM 798 | Skinhead Shuffle/RICO: Red Cow | 40 |
| 70 | Supreme SUP 205 | Wicked Lady/For Our Liberty | 15 |
| 70 | Pama PM 796 | Landscape/Number 1 | 25 |
| 70 | Supreme SUP 204 | Let It Be/Looking Back | 15 |
| 70 | Supreme SUP 205 | For Our Liberty/Wicked Lady | 10 |
| 70 | Supreme SUP 207 | Give Me Some/(Instrumental) | 50 |
| 70 | Supreme SUP 208 | Funky Funky/Funky Funky (instrumental) | 12 |
| 72 | Supreme PS 362 | Storm/And I Love Her | 40 |
| 73 | Supreme PS 376 | The Champ/Cherry Pink | 40 |
| 70s | Star PTP 1011 | Whiter Shade Of Pale/My One Desire | 15 |
| 68 | Pama PMLP 5 | THE CHAMP (LP) | 200 |

(see also Sid & Joe & Mohawks)

## LOUIS MOHOLO

| 78 | Ogun OG 520 | SPIRITS REJOICE (LP) | 30 |
|---|---|---|---|

## MOIST

| 95 | Chrysalis 12CHSS 5019 | SILVER (12" EP, clear vinyl) | 10 |
|---|---|---|---|

## MOJAVE 3

| 95 | 4AD CAD 5013 | ASK ME TOMORROW (LP) | 50 |
|---|---|---|---|
| 98 | 4AD CAD 8018 | OUT OF TUNE (LP) | 50 |
| 00 | 4AD CAD 2K05 | EXCUSES FOR TRAVELLERS (LP) | 30 |
| 03 | 4AD CAD 2309 LP | SPOON & RAFTER (LP) | 25 |
| 06 | 4AD CAD 2604 | PUZZLES LIKE YOU (LP) | 20 |

(see also Slowdive)

## MOJO HANNAH

| 72 | Kingdom KV 8004 | St. Jeremy/You'll Be Alright | 25 |
|---|---|---|---|
| 73 | Kingdom KV 8008 | Six Days On The Road/Moon Dog's Gonna Howl Tonight | 5 |
| 73 | Kingdom KVL 9001 | SIX DAYS ON THE ROAD (LP, orange label) | 35 |

## MOJO MEN

| 65 | Pye International 7N 25336 | Dance With Me/Loneliest Boy In Town | 30 |
|---|---|---|---|
| 66 | Reprise RS 20486 | Hanky Panky/She's My Baby | 30 |
| 67 | Reprise RS 20539 | Sit Down I Think I Love You/Don't Leave Me Crying Like Before | 20 |
| 67 | Reprise RS 20580 | Me About You/When You're In Love | 15 |

## MOJOS

| 63 | Decca F 11732 | They Say/Forever | 15 |
|---|---|---|---|
| 64 | Decca F 11853 | Everything's Alright/Give Your Lovin' To Me | 8 |
| 64 | Decca F 11918 | Why Not Tonight/Don;t Do It Any More | 8 |
| 64 | Decca F 11959 | Seven Daffodils/Nothin' At All | 10 |
| 65 | Decca F 12127 | Comin' On To Cry/That's The Way It Goes | 15 |
| 67 | Decca F 12557 | Goodbye Dolly Gray/I Just Can't Let Her Go | 25 |
| 68 | Liberty LBF 15097 | Until My Baby Comes Home/Seven Park Avenue | 60 |
| 64 | Decca DFE 8591 | THE MOJOS (EP) | 70 |

(see also Stu James & Mojos, Faron's Flamingos)

## MOLDY PEACHES

| 01 | Rough Trade RTRADES 016 | Who's Got The Crack?/NYC's Like A Graveyard (p/s) | 10 |
|---|---|---|---|
| 01 | Rough Trade RTRADELP 014 | THE MOLDY PEACHES (LP) | 50 |

## MOLES

| 68 | Parlophone R 5743 | We Are The Moles (Parts 1 & 2) | 30 |
|---|---|---|---|

## MOLESTERS
| | | | |
|---|---|---|---|
| 79 | Small Wonder SMALL 14 | Disco Love/Commuter Man (p/s) | 5 |
| 79 | Small Wonder SMALL 18 | End Of Civilisation/Girl Behind The Curtain (p/s) | 5 |

## MOLOKO
| | | | |
|---|---|---|---|
| 95 | Echo ECHLP 7 | DO YOU LIKE MY TIGHT SWEATER (2-LP) | 20 |
| 98 | Echo ECHLP 21 | I AM NOT A DOCTOR (2-LP, triple gatefold) | 30 |

## MO-L-RANA
| | | | |
|---|---|---|---|
| 73 | Polydor 2121-158 | So Mt Daddy Says/Alone | 6 |

## MOMENT
| | | | |
|---|---|---|---|
| 85 | Diamond DIA 004 | In This Town/Just Once | 6 |
| 85 | Diamond DIA 008 | One, Two, They Fly/Karl's New Haircut | 5 |
| 80s | Tenth Floor | Poor Mr. Diamond (Parts 1 & 2) | 10 |
| 89 | Big Stuff | Ready To Fall (promo only) | 8 |

## MOMENTS (1)
| | | | |
|---|---|---|---|
| 63 | London HLN 9656 | Walk Right In/Walk Right In (Instrumental) | 12 |

## MOMENTS (2)
| | | | |
|---|---|---|---|
| 76 | All Platinum 6146313 | Nine Times | 8 |

## MOMUS
| | | | |
|---|---|---|---|
| 86 | Él GPO 9T | Nicky/Don't Leave/See A Friend In Tears (12") | 15 |
| 87 | Creation CRE 037 T | Murderers, The Hope Of Women (12", p/s) | 12 |
| 86 | el ACME 2 | CIRCUS MAXIMUS (LP) | 15 |
| 88 | Creation CRELP 036 | TENDER PERVERT (LP, with free 7") | 15 |
| 90 | Creation CRELP 052 | DON'T STOP THE NIGHT (LP) | 15 |
| 91 | Creation CRELP 097 | HIPPOPOTAMOMUS (LP, with "Michelin Man" track & Michelin Man style inlay, withdrawn) | 15 |

*(see also Happy Family)*

## MONACO (1)
| | | | |
|---|---|---|---|
| 78 | Firebird/Pinnacle PIN 64 | Earthy/God Only Knows | 8 |

## STEPHEN MONAHAN
| | | | |
|---|---|---|---|
| 67 | London HLR 10145 | City Of Windsor/Lost People | 12 |

## MONARCHS
| | | | |
|---|---|---|---|
| 64 | London HLU 9862 | Look Homeward Angel/What's Made You Change Your Mind | 30 |

## GRACHAN MONCUR III
| | | | |
|---|---|---|---|
| 74 | JCOA/Virgin J2003 | ECHOES OF PRAYER (LP) | 25 |

## JULIE MONDAY
| | | | |
|---|---|---|---|
| 66 | London HLU 10080 | Come Share The Good Times With Me/Time Is Running Out For Me | 8 |

## MONDO KANE
| | | | |
|---|---|---|---|
| 86 | Lisson DOLEQ 2 | New York Afternoon (mixes)/Manhattan Morning (12", p/s) | 10 |

*(see also Georgie Fame)*

## MONEY (1)
| | | | |
|---|---|---|---|
| 69 | Major Minor MM 571 | Welcome Me Love/Breaking Her Heart | 8 |
| 69 | Major Minor MM 620 | Come Laughing Home/Power Of The Rainbow | 8 |

## MONEY (2)
| | | | |
|---|---|---|---|
| 79 | Gull GULL 64 | Aren't We All Searching/Where Have All The Dancers Gone | 8 |
| 80 | Hobo HOS 011 | FAST WORLD (EP, p/s) | 80 |
| 79 | Gull GULP 1031 | FIRST INVESTMENT (LP) | 18 |

## MONEY JANGLE
| | | | |
|---|---|---|---|
| 72 | President PT 362 | Home/Away Away | 20 |

## MONEY PIT
| | | | |
|---|---|---|---|
| 97 | Bluepose | Smile It's Sugar/Strange And Silent Staircase (P/S) | 10 |

## ZOOT MONEY('S BIG ROLL BAND)
| | | | |
|---|---|---|---|
| 64 | Decca F 11954 | The Uncle Willie/Zoot's Suit (solo) | 50 |
| 65 | Columbia DB 7518 | Good/Bring It Home To Me | 40 |
| 65 | Columbia DB 7600 | Please Stay/You Know You'll Cry | 35 |
| 65 | Columbia DB 7697 | Something Is Worrying Me/Stubborn Kind Of Fellow | 30 |
| 65 | Columbia DB 7768 | The Many Faces Of Love/Jump Back (as Paul Williams & Zoot Money Band) | 30 |
| 66 | Columbia DB 7876 | Let's Run For Cover/Self-Discipline | 30 |
| 66 | Columbia DB 7975 | Big Time Operator/Zoot's Sermon | 20 |
| 66 | Columbia DB 8090 | The Star Of The Show (The La La Song)/The Mound Moves | 35 |
| 67 | Columbia DB 8172 | Nick Knack/I Really Learnt How To Cry | 15 |
| 70 | Polydor 2058 020 | No One But You/Prisoner | 8 |
| 80 | Magic Moon/MPL MACH 3 | Your Feet's Too Big/Ain't Nothin' Shakin' But The Bacon (solo) | 12 |
| 80 | Magic Moon/MPL MACH 6 | The Two Of Us/Ain't Nothin' Shakin' But The Bacon (solo) | 30 |
| 66 | Columbia SEG 8519 | BIG TIME OPERATOR (EP) | 200 |
| 66 | Columbia S(C)X 6075 | ZOOT! - LIVE AT KLOOK'S KLEEK (LP, mono) | 100 |
| 66 | Columbia S(C)X 6075 | ZOOT! - LIVE AT KLOOK'S KLEEK (LP, stereo) | 120 |
| 65 | Columbia 33SX 1734 | IT SHOULD'VE BEEN ME (LP) | 150 |
| 68 | Direction 8-63231 | TRANSITION (LP) | 100 |
| 70 | Polydor 2482 019 | ZOOT MONEY (LP) | 80 |

*(see also Paul Williams & Big Roll Band, Dantalian's Chariot, Eric Burdon & Animals, Grimms, Centipede, Ellis, Johnny Almond Music Machine)*

## MONGOLFIER BROS
| | | | |
|---|---|---|---|
| 84 | Incurable | I Know/Things That Go Bump | 20 |

## MONGREL
| | | | |
|---|---|---|---|
| 73 | Polydor 2058 318 | Lonely Street/Sing A Little Song | 5 |
| 73 | Polydor 2058 347 | Last Night/Twist Her Hand | 5 |
| 73 | Polydor 2383 182 | GET YOUR TEETH INTO THIS (LP) | 25 |

*(see also Wizzard)*

MINT VALUE £

## MONGRELS
| | | | |
|---|---|---|---|
| 64 | Decca F 12003 | I Long To Hear/Everywhere | 30 |
| 65 | Decca F 12086 | My Love For You/Stewball | 30 |

*(see also Bobbie Miller)*

## MONITORS (1)
| | | | |
|---|---|---|---|
| 69 | T. Motown TML 11108 | GREETINGS WE'RE THE MONITORS (LP, mono) | 100 |
| 69 | T. Motown STML 11108 | GREETINGS WE'RE THE MONITORS (LP, stereo) | 90 |

## MONITORS (2)
| | | | |
|---|---|---|---|
| 79 | Monitor MON 1 | Telegram/Compulsory Fun (p/s) | 5 |

## MONK BOUGHT LUNCH
| | | | |
|---|---|---|---|
| 91 | Own Label | Love And Hate/Paint It White/The Sailor's Tilted Hat (p/s) | 40 |

## THELONIOUS MONK
| | | | |
|---|---|---|---|
| 56 | Vogue EPV 1115 | THELONIOUS MONK (EP) | 10 |
| 55 | Esquire 20-039 | THELONIOUS MONK QUINTET (10" LP) | 20 |
| 55 | Esquire 20-049 | THELONIOUS MONK (10" LP) | 30 |
| 56 | Esquire 20-075 | THELONIOUS MONK PLAYS (10" LP) | 30 |
| 57 | London LTZU 15097 | BRILLIANT CORNERS (LP) | 35 |
| 60 | Esquire 32-109 | THELONIOUS MONK QUINTETS (LP) | 35 |
| 61 | Esquire 32-115 | WORK! (LP, with Art Blakey & Sonny Rollins) | 35 |
| 61 | Esquire 32-119 | MONK'S MOODS (LP) | 35 |
| 61 | Riverside RLP 12-201 | MONK PLAYS ELLINGTON (LP) | 30 |
| 61 | Philips BBL 1510 | THELONIOUS MONK VOL. 1 (LP) | 25 |
| 61 | Riverside RLP 12-226 | BRILLIANT CORNERS (LP) | 25 |
| 61 | Riverside RLP 12-262 | MONK IN ACTION (LP) | 25 |
| 62 | Riverside RLP 12-300 | AT THE TOWN HALL (LP, also stereo RLP 1138) | 25 |
| 62 | Riverside RLP 12-323 | AT THE BLACK HAWK (LP, also stereo RLP 1171) | 25 |
| 62 | Philips BBL 1511 | THELONIOUS MONK VOL. 2 (LP) | 25 |
| 62 | Riverside RLP 12-242 | MONK'S MUSIC (LP) | 25 |
| 63 | CBS (S)BPG 62135 | MONK'S DREAM (LP) | 25 |
| 63 | Riverside RLP 12-235 | THELONIOUS HIMSELF (LP) | 25 |
| 63 | Riverside JLP (9)46 | THELONIOUS MONK AND JOHN COLTRANE (LP) | 25 |
| 64 | Riverside RLP 002 | IN EUROPE (VOL. 1) | 30 |
| 64 | CBS (S)BPG 62173 | CRISS-CROSS | 25 |
| 64 | Blue Note (B)BLP 1510 | THE GENIUS OF MODERN MUSIC (VOL. 1) (LP) | 25 |
| 64 | Blue Note (B)BLP 1511 | THE GENIUS OF MODERN MUSIC (VOL. 2) (LP) | 25 |
| 64 | Riverside RLP 279 | MISTERIOSO (LP) | 25 |
| 64 | CBS (S)BPG 62248 | BIG BAND AND QUARTET IN CONCERT (LP) | 25 |
| 65 | CBS (S)BPG 62391 | IT'S MONK'S TIME (LP) | 25 |
| 65 | Riverside RLP 305 | FIVE BY MONK BY FIVE (LP) | 25 |
| 65 | Riverside RLP 003 | IN EUROPE (VOL. 2) (LP) | 25 |
| 65 | CBS (S)BPG 62497 | MONK (LP) | 20 |
| 65 | Riverside RLP 312 | ALONE IN SAN FRANCISCO (LP) | 20 |
| 65 | Fontana FJL 113 | WAY OUT! (LP) | 20 |
| 65 | Realm RM 52223 | NICA'S TEMPO (LP, with Gigi Gryce) | 20 |
| 65 | CBS (S)BPG 62549 | SOLO (LP) | 20 |
| 65 | Stateside SL 10152 | THE GOLDEN MONK (LP) | 20 |
| 67 | Transatlantic PR7169 | WORK! (LP) | 20 |

*(see also John Coltrane, Sonny Rollins, Art Blakey, Miles Davis)*

## MONKEES
| | | | |
|---|---|---|---|
| 66 | RCA Victor RCA 1560 | I'm A Believer/(I'm Not Your) Stepping Stone | 6 |
| 67 | RCA Victor RCA 1580 | A Little Bit Me, A Little Bit You/The Girl I Knew Somewhere | 6 |
| 67 | RCA Victor RCA 1604 | Alternate Title/Forget That Girl | 6 |
| 67 | RCA Victor RCA 1620 | Pleasant Valley Sunday/Words | 6 |
| 67 | RCA Victor RCA 1645 | Daydream Believer/Goin' Down | 7 |
| 68 | RCA Victor RCA 1673 | Valleri/Tapioca Tundra | 7 |
| 68 | RCA Victor RCA 1706 | D.W. Washburn/It's Nice To Be With You | 6 |
| 69 | RCA RCA 1802 | Teardrop City/Man Without A Dream | 6 |
| 69 | RCA RCA 1824 | Someday Man/Listen To The Band | 10 |
| 69 | RCA RCA 1862 | Daddy's Song/The Porpoise Song | 10 |
| 69 | RCA RCA 1887 | Mommy And Daddy/Good Clean Fun | 10 |
| 70 | RCA RCA 1958 | Oh My My/Love You Better | 10 |
| 74 | Bell BLL 1354 | Monkees Theme/I'm A Believer | 12 |
| 67 | RCA Victor RD 7844 | The MONKEES (LP, mono) | 6 |
| 67 | RCA Victor RD 7868 | MORE OF THE MONKEES (LP, mono) | 20 |
| 67 | RCA Victor SF 7868 | MORE OF THE MONKEES (LP, stereo) | 18 |
| 67 | RCA Victor RD 7886 | HEADQUARTERS (LP, mono) | 20 |
| 67 | RCA Victor SF 7886 | HEADQUARTERS (LP, stereo) | 20 |
| 67 | RCA Victor RD 7886 | HEADQUARTERS (LP, with different 'beard' photo on back, mono) | 22 |
| 67 | RCA Victor SF 7886 | HEADQUARTERS (LP, with different 'beard' photo on back, stereo) | 25 |
| 67 | RCA Victor RD/SF 7912 | PISCES, AQUARIUS, CAPRICORN AND JONES LTD. (LP) | 30 |
| 68 | RCA Victor RD/SF 7948 | THE BIRDS, THE BEES & THE MONKEES (LP) | 22 |

*(The above albums were originally issued with black labels; later orange label copies are worth the same value.)*

| | | | |
|---|---|---|---|
| 69 | RCA RD 8016 | INSTANT REPLAY (LP, mono) | 30 |
| 69 | RCA SF 8016 | INSTANT REPLAY (LP, stereo) | 25 |
| 69 | RCA RD 8051 | HEAD (LP, soundtrack, mono) | 90 |
| 69 | RCA SF 8051 | HEAD (LP, soundtrack, stereo) | 60 |
| 79 | Arista MONK-1 1/2 | MONKEEMANIA (LP) | 20 |
| 89 | Circus BOY 1 | IDOLISED, PLASTICISED, PSYCHOANYLYSED, STERILISED (LP, spoken-word convention issue, white vinyl) | 15 |

| 89 | Circus BOY 1 | IDOLISED, PLASTICISED, PSYCHOANYLYSED, STERILISED (LP, spoken-word convention issue, picture disc) | 18 |

*(see also Micky Dolenz, Davy Jones, Michael Nesmith, Tommy Boyce & Bobby Hart)*

## MONKS (1)
| 74 | Rex R11 095 | Roller Coaster Rock N Roll/it's A Crying Shame | 10 |

## MONKS (2)
| 79 | EMI 2972 | I Ain't Gettin' Any/Inter-City Kitty | 5 |
| 79 | EMI 2999 | Johnny B Rotten/Drugs In My Pocket | 6 |

## MONOCHROME SET
| 79 | Rough Trade RT 005 | Alphaville/He's Frank (p/s) | 10 |
| 79 | Rough Trade RT 019 | Eine Symphonie Des Grauens/Lester Leaps In (1st 1,000 with labels on wrong side with explanatory insert, p/s) | 12 |
| 79 | Rough Trade RT 019 | Eine Symphonie Des Grauens/Lester Leaps In (p/s) | 10 |
| 79 | Rough Trade RT 028 | The Monochrome Set/Mr Bizarro | 10 |
| 79 | Disquo Bleu BL 1 | He's Frank (Slight Return)/Silicon Carne/Fallout (all cuts live) (no p/s) | 8 |
| 82 | Cherry Red CHERRY 51 | Cast A Long Shadow/The Bridge | 6 |
| 83 | Cherry Red CHERRY 60 | Jet Set Junta/Love Goes Down The Drain/Noise (Eine Kleine Symphonie) | 6 |
| 80 | Dindisc DID 4 | STRANGE BOUTIQUE (LP) | 25 |
| 80 | DinDisc DID 8 | LOVE ZOMBIES (LP, with lithograph) | 20 |
| 82 | Cherry Red BRED 34 | ELIGIBLE BACHELORS (LP) | 15 |
| 83 | Cherry Red MRED 47 | VOLUME CONTRAST BRILLIANCE (LP) | 15 |

*(see also Art Attacks)*

## MONOCONICS
| 80 | One Zone 001 | Such A Shame (About You)/Exit Stage Left/Sensible Breakdown (p/s) | 6 |

## MONOGRAMS
| 59 | Parlophone R 4515 | Juke Box Cha Cha/The Greatest Mistake Of My Life | 8 |
| 59 | Parlophone R 4545 | Crystal/Teach Me | 5 |

## MONOLITH
| 78 | None | (I'm Not Your) Stepping Stone/Guns Of Time (no p/s) | 60 |

## MONOPOLY
| 67 | Polydor 56164 | House Of Lords/Magic Carpet | 20 |
| 67 | Polydor 56188 | We're All Going To The Seaside/It Isn't Easy | 6 |
| 70 | Pye 7N 17940 | We Belong Together/Gone Tomorrow | 25 |

## MONOS
| 79 | RCA PB 5178 | Ericafire/Louie | 6 |
| 79 | RCA PB 5206 | U.F.O./Teenage Confessions | 6 |

## MONOTONES (U.K.)
| 64 | Pye 7N 15608 | What Would I Do/Is It Right | 10 |
| 64 | Pye 7N 15640 | It's Great/Anymore | 10 |
| 65 | Pye 7N 15761 | No Waiting/Like A Lover Should | 10 |
| 65 | Pye 7N 15814 | Something's Hurting Me/A Girl Like That | 10 |

## MONOTONES (U.S.)
| 58 | London HLM 8625 | Book Of Love/You Never Loved Me | 40 |
| 58 | London HLM 8625 | Book Of Love/You Never Loved Me (78) | 20 |

## MATT MONRO
| 56 | Decca F 10816 | Ev'rybody Falls In Love With Someone/Out Of Sight, Out Of Mind | 10 |
| 57 | Decca F 10845 | The Garden Of Eden/Love Me Do | 10 |
| 57 | Decca F 10870 | My House Is Your House/The Bean Song | 10 |
| 61 | Ember EMB S 120 | The Ghost Of Your Past/Quite Suddenly | 15 |
| 69 | capitol CL 15603 | On Days Like These/On A Clear Day (You Can See Forever) | 25 |
| 70 | Capitol CL 15643 | We''re Gonna Change The World/You're Closer To Me | 7 |
| 63 | Parlophone GEP 8889 | SINGS THE THEME FROM THE FILM 'FROM RUSSIA FROM LOVE' (EP) | 10 |
| 57 | Decca LF 1276 | BLUE AND SENTIMENTAL (10" LP) | 20 |

*(see also John Barry)*

## BARRY MONROE
| 66 | Polydor 56088 | World Of Broken Hearts/Never Again | 6 |

## BILL MONROE (& HIS BLUE GRASS BOYS)
| 56 | Brunswick 05567 | New John Henry Blues/Put My Little Shoes Away | 15 |

## MARILYN MONROE
| 54 | HMV 7M 232 | The River Of No Return/I'm Gonna File My Claim | 60 |
| 59 | London HLT 8862 | I Wanna Be Loved By You/I'm Thru' With Love | 35 |
| 78 | United Artists UP 36484 | I Wanna Be Loved By You/Running Wild/I'm Thru With Love (gatefold p/s) | 6 |
| 55 | HMV 7EG 8090 | THERE'S NO BUSINESS LIKE SHOW BUSINESS - SOUNDTRACK EXCERPTS (EP, company sleeve) | 25 |
| 59 | London RET 1231 | SOME LIKE IT HOT (EP, soundtrack; first pressing with triangular centre) | 80 |
| 59 | London RET 1231 | SOME LIKE IT HOT (EP, soundtrack; later round centre) | 20 |
| 60 | Philips BBE 12414 | LET'S MAKE LOVE - FILM SOUNDTRACK (EP, with Yves Montand & Frankie Vaughan; mono) | 30 |
| 60 | Philips SBBE 9031 | LET'S MAKE LOVE - FILM SOUNDTRACK (EP, with Yves Montand & Frankie Vaughan; stereo) | 40 |
| 53 | MGM MGM-D 116 | GENTLEMEN PREFER BLONDES (10" LP, soundtrack with other artists) | 75 |
| 59 | London HA-T 2176 | SOME LIKE IT HOT (LP, soundtrack with other artists, mono) | 50 |
| 59 | London SAH-T 6040 | SOME LIKE IT HOT (LP, soundtrack with other artists, stereo) | 60 |
| 60 | Philips BBL 7414 | LET'S MAKE LOVE (LP, soundtrack, with Yves Montand & Frankie Vaughan; mono) | 40 |
| 60 | Philips SBBL 592 | LET'S MAKE LOVE (LP, soundtrack, with Yves Montand & Frankie Vaughan; stereo) | 40 |
| 63 | Stateside S(S)L 10048 | MARILYN (LP, soundtrack, mono) | 30 |
| 63 | Stateside S(S)L 10048 | MARILYN (LP, soundtrack, stereo) | 40 |
| 83 | Liberty UASP 30226 | SOME LIKE IT HOT (LP, picture disc) | 10 |

*(see also Frankie Vaughan)*

MINT VALUE £

## VAUGHN MONROE (& HIS ORCHESTRA)
| 53 | HMV 7M 144 | Less Than Tomorrow (But More Than Yesterday)/Ruby | 10 |
| 54 | HMV 7M 247 | They Were Doin' The Mambo/Mister Sandman | 10 |
| 56 | HMV 7M 332 | Black Denim Trousers And Motorcycle Boots/All By Myself | 20 |
| 57 | HMV POP 354 | Wringle Wrangle/Westward Ho The Wagons! | 7 |
| 59 | RCA RCA 1124 | The Battle Of New Orleans/Hercules | 8 |
| 60 | London HLT 9123 | Ballerina/Love Me Forever | 5 |

## MONSOON (1)
| 71 | Trojan TR 7831 | Hot Honolulu Night/Come Back Jane | 6 |
| 72 | Blue Mountain BM 1006 | Night Of The Fly/Caroline The Wine Was Good | 40 |

## MONSOON (2)
| 81 | Indipop IND 1 | Ever So Lonely/Sunset Over The Ganges/The Mirror Of Your Mind/ Shout! (Till You're Heard) (in plastic sleeve with insert) | 8 |

*(see also Complex)*

## MONSTER MAGNET
| 93 | A&M 580 280-7 | Twin Earth/Nod Scene (live) (stickered p/s, sticker, insert) | 10 |
| 93 | A&M 580 281-1 | Twin Earth/Nod Scene (live)/Medicine (live) (12" 1-sided etched sick, p/s) | 10 |
| 93 | A&M AMYDK 291 | Twin Earth/Nod Scene (live)/Medicine (live) (12" promo) | 10 |
| 95 | A&M AMDJ 7 | Negasonic Teenage Warhead/Eclipse This (12", promo, stickered die-cut black sleeve) | 10 |
| 95 | A&M AMDJ 10 | Dopes To Infinity/I'm Five Years Ahead Of My Time (12" promo) | 10 |
| 95 | A&M 540 315-1 | DOPES TO INFINITY (2-LP) | 40 |
| 98 | A&M 540 908-1 | POWERTRIP (2-LP) | 40 |

## MONTANAS
| 65 | Piccadilly 7N 35262 | All That Is Mine Can Be Yours/How Can I Tell | 12 |
| 66 | Pye 7N 17183 | That's When Happiness Began/Goodbye Little Girl | 50 |
| 67 | Pye 7N 17282 | Ciao Baby/Anyone There | 10 |
| 67 | Pye 7N 17338 | Take My Hand/Top Hat | 10 |
| 67 | Pye 7N 17394 | You've Got To Be Loved/Difference Of Opinion | 20 |
| 68 | Pye 7N 17499 | A Step In The Right Direction/Someday (You'll Be Breaking My Heart Again) | 12 |
| 68 | Pye 7N 17597 | You're Making A Big Mistake/Run To Me | 15 |
| 69 | Pye 7N 17697 | Roundabout/Mystery | 15 |
| 69 | Pye 7N 17729 | Ciao Baby/Someday (You'll Be Breaking My Heart Again) | 6 |
| 70 | MCA MK 5036 | Let's Get A Little Sentimental/Hey Diddle Diddle | 8 |
| 71 | MAM R45 | No Smoke Without Fire/Seaport | 15 |
| 71 | MAM MAMR62 | Suzanne/Your Love Is Growing | 15 |

*(see also Trapeze)*

## MONTANA SEXTET
| 83 | Virgin VS 600 | Who Needs Enemies With A Friend Like You/Friendly Vibes (12") | 15 |

## MONTCLAIRS
| 74 | Contempo CS 2008 | Make Up For Lost Time/How Can One Man Live | 8 |
| 75 | Contempo CS 2036 | Hung Up On Your Love/I Need You More Than Ever | 20 |
| 01 | Grapevine 114 | Hey You Don't Fight It/Never Ending Love | 10 |
| 74 | Contempo CLP 503 | DREAMING OF A SEASON (LP) | 15 |

## LOU MONTE
| 54 | HMV 7M 176 | A Baby Cried/One Moment More | 7 |
| 54 | HMV 7M 190 | Darktown Strutters' Ball/I Know How You Feel | 7 |
| 54 | HMV 7M 249 | Chain Reaction/Vera's Veranda | 7 |

## VINNIE MONTE
| 59 | London HL 8947 | Summer Spree/I'll Walk You Home | 10 |
| 63 | Stateside SS 156 | Joanie Don't Be Angry/Take Good Care Of Her | 18 |

## MONTEGO JOE
| 72 | London HLP 10374 | Stand Up And Be Counted/Glooey (with Seeds Of Life) | 5 |

## MONTEGO MELON
| 68 | Sioux SI 004 | Swan Lake/HONG GANG: Reggae Mento | 15 |

## HUGO MONTENEGRO ORCHESTRA
| 62 | Oriole CB 1765 | Palm Canyon Drive/Dark Eyes | 7 |
| 63 | Oriole CB 1792 | Get Off The Moon/Sherry | 20 |
| 65 | RCA 1462 | Darlin' Jill/Candy's Theme | 6 |
| 68 | RCA Victor RCA 1727 | The Good, The Bad And The Ugly/There's Got To Be A Better Way | 5 |
| 68 | RCA Victor RCA 1771 | Hang 'Em High/Tomorrow's Love | 8 |
| 69 | RCA RCA 1807 | Tony's Theme/Good Vibrations | 5 |
| 65 | RCA Victor RD 7758 | THE MAN FROM U.N.C.L.E. (LP, soundtrack) | 50 |
| 66 | RCA Victor RD 7832 | MORE MUSIC FROM THE MAN FROM U.N.C.L.E. (LP, soundtrack) | 45 |
| 67 | RCA Victor RD/SF 7877 | HURRY SUNDOWN (LP, soundtrack) | 20 |
| 69 | RCA SF 8053 | MOOG POWER (LP) | 20 |
| 69 | Stateside S(S)L 10267 | LADY IN CEMENT (LP, soundtrack) | 40 |
| 70 | Pye Intl. NSPL 28136 | DAWN OF DYLAN (LP) | 15 |

## BOBBY MONTEZ
| 60 | Vogue V 9165 | Holiday In Havana/Jungle Stars | 8 |

## CHRIS MONTEZ
| 63 | London HLU 9764 | My Baby Loves To Dance/In An English Towne | 7 |
| 66 | Pye International 7N 25348 | Call Me/Go 'Head On | 15 |
| 66 | Pye International 7N 25369 | The More I See You/You, I Love You | 5 |
| 66 | Pye International 7N 25381 | There Will Never Be Another You/You Can Hurt The One You Love | 7 |
| 63 | London REU 1392 | LET'S DANCE (EP) | 20 |
| 66 | Pye Intl. NEP 44071 | THE MORE I SEE YOU (EP) | 10 |
| 66 | Pye Intl. NEP 44080 | CHRIS MONTEZ (EP) | 10 |
| 63 | London HA-U 8079 | LET'S DANCE AND HAVE SOME KINDA FUN!!! (LP) | 30 |

## JACK MONTGOMERY
| | | |
|---|---|---|
| 85 | Kent TOWN 102 | Dearly Beloved/MARIE KNIGHT: That's No Way To Treat A Girl ........................ 15 |
| 80s | Soul City 124 | Dearly Beloved/Do You Believe It ........................................................................ 15 |

## LITTLE BROTHER MONTGOMERY
| | | |
|---|---|---|
| 61 | Columbia DB 4595 | Pinetop's Boogie Woogie/Cow Cow Blues ........................................................... 25 |
| 61 | Columbia 33SX 1289 | LITTLE BROTHER MONTGOMERY (LP, with Alexis Korner) ................................... 70 |
| 62 | 77' 77LA 12/21 | LITTLE BROTHER MONTGOMERY/SUNNYLAND SLIM (LP) ................................... 30 |
| 65 | Decca LK 4664 | LITTLE BROTHER MONTGOMERY (LP) .................................................................. 30 |
| 66 | Xtra XTRA 1018 | LITTLE BROTHER MONTGOMERY (LP) .................................................................. 20 |
| 71 | Xtra XTRA 1115 | FARRO ST. JIVE (LP) ........................................................................................... 20 |
| 71 | Saydisc SDR 213 | LITTLE BROTHER MONTGOMERY 1930-1969 (LP) ............................................... 20 |
| 72 | Saydisc SDM 223 | HOME AGAIN (LP) .............................................................................................. 20 |

## MARIAN MONTGOMERY
| | | |
|---|---|---|
| 65 | Capitol CL 15375 | When Sunny Gets Blue/Teach Me Tonight .............................................................. 5 |
| 67 | Reaction 591 018 | Love Makes Two People Sing/Monday Thru Saturday ........................................... 25 |
| 68 | Pye 7N 17533 | Why Say Goodbye/Love Today - Cry Tomorrow ..................................................... 5 |
| 72 | Polydor 2383 159 | MARIAN IN THE MORNING (LP) ......................................................................... 20 |

## ROY MONTGOMERY
| | | |
|---|---|---|
| 97 | Enraptured RAPT 4510 | Trajectory One/Trajectory Two (p/s, 27 in handmade p/s) .................................... 15 |
| 97 | Enraptured RAPT 4510 | Trajectory One/Trajectory Two (p/s, 280 clear vinyl) .............................................. 8 |

## STUART MONTGOMERY
| | | |
|---|---|---|
| 69 | Private pressing | CERTAIN SEA WORDS (LP, with insert) ................................................................ 15 |

## WES MONTGOMERY
| | | |
|---|---|---|
| 60 | Riverside RLP 12-320 | THE INCREDIBLE JAZZ GUITAR OF WES MONTGOMERY (LP, mono) .................... 15 |
| 60 | Riverside RLP 12-320 | THE INCREDIBLE JAZZ GUITAR OF WES MONTGOMERY (LP, stereo) ................... 20 |

## MONTY, DERRICK & PATSY
| | | |
|---|---|---|
| 65 | Blue Beat BB 280 | Stir The Pot/Mercy .............................................................................................. 50 |

*(see also Monty Morris, Derrick Morgan)*

## MONTY (MORRIS) & ROY
| | | |
|---|---|---|
| 61 | Blue Beat BB 61 | In And Out The Window/Tra La La Boogie (with Dumbago's Orchestra) ................. 12 |
| 61 | Blue Beat BB 63 | Sweetie Pie/ROLAND ALPHONSO'S GROUP: Green Door ................................... 18 |

*(see also Monty Morris)*

## MONTY PYTHON('S FLYING CIRCUS)
| | | |
|---|---|---|
| 72 | Charisma CB 192 | Spam Song/The Concert (as Monty Python's Flying Circus, p/s) ............................. 6 |
| 72 | Charisma CB 200 | Eric The Half A Bee/The Yangtse Song (Extended) (as Monty Python with Niel [sic] Innes) ................................................................................................................. 5 |
| 74 | Charisma CB 268 | Lumberjack Song/Spam Song (p/s) ....................................................................... 5 |
| 74 | NME/Charisma SFI 1259 | Monty Python's Tiny Black Round Thing (D.P. Gumby Presents "Election '74"/ The Lumberjack Song) (live flexidisc free with NME) ................................................... 10 |
| 75 | Charisma MP PROMO 1 | In Store Commercial (promo only, jukebox single) ................................................. 5 |
| 79 | Warner Bros K 17495 | Always Look On The Bright Side Of Life/Brian (p/s) .............................................. 15 |
| 80 | Charisma CB 374 | I Like Chinese/I Bet You They Won't Play This Song On The Radio/Finland (p/s) ........... 15 |
| 88 | Warner Bros W 7653 | Always Look On The Bright Side Of Life/Brian (p/s, reissue) .................................. 10 |
| 91 | Virgin PYTH 2 | Galaxy Song/Every Sperm Is Sacred (p/s, reissue) ................................................. 5 |
| 76 | Charisma MP 001 | PYTHON ON SONG (EP, double pack [CBS 268/PY 2]) ........................................ 10 |
| 70 | BBC REB 73M | MONTY PYTHON'S FLYING CIRCUS (LP, mono, mustard label) ........................... 18 |
| 70 | Charisma CAS 1049 | ANOTHER MONTY PYTHON RECORD (LP, inner sleeve, 3 inserts, 'scroll' label) ...... 20 |
| 73 | Charisma CAS 1063 | MONTY PYTHON'S PREVIOUS RECORD (LP, with free flexidisc in p/s, Teach Yourself Heath & inner sleeve) ........................................................................................... 15 |
| 73 | Charisma CAS 1080 | MATCHING TIE AND HANDKERCHIEF (LP, parallel grooves on side 2, die-cut sleeve, 2 inserts) ............................................................................................................... 15 |

*(see also John Cleese, Rutles)*

## MONUMENT
| | | |
|---|---|---|
| 71 | Beacon BEAS 15 | THE FIRST MONUMENT (LP) ............................................................................... 60 |

*(see also Zior)*

## MONUMENTAL
| | | |
|---|---|---|
| 81 | Impact IMP 001 | Boy On The Run/Free (p/s) ................................................................................. 10 |

## MONUMENTUM
| | | |
|---|---|---|
| 95 | Misanthropy AMAZON 007 | IN ABSENTIA CHRISTI (LP) ................................................................................. 20 |

## MOOCHE
| | | |
|---|---|---|
| 69 | Pye 7N 17735 | Hot Smoke And Sasafrass/Seen Through A Light ................................................. 20 |

## MOOD MOSAIC
| | | |
|---|---|---|
| 66 | Columbia DB 7801 | A Touch Of Velvet, A Sting Of Brass/Bond Street P.M. .......................................... 35 |
| 66 | Columbia DB 7801 | A Touch Of Velvet, A Sting Of Brass/Bond Street P.M.(DJ Copy) ........................... 50 |
| 67 | Columbia DB 8149 | Chinese Chequers/The Real Mr. Smith ................................................................. 25 |
| 68 | Parlophone R 5716 | The Yellow Spotted Capricorn/ELMER HOCKETT'S HURDY GURDY: Fantastic Fair ........ 15 |
| 69 | Columbia DB 8618 | A Touch Of Velvet, A Sting Of Brass/Bond Street P.M. (reissue) ........................... 15 |
| 67 | Columbia SX 6153 | MOOD MOSAIC (LP, mono) ................................................................................ 35 |
| 67 | Studio Two TWO 160 | MOOD MOSAIC (LP, stereo) ............................................................................... 25 |

*(see also Mark Wirtz Orchestra & Chorus, Keith West)*

## MOOD OF HAMILTON
| | | |
|---|---|---|
| 67 | Columbia DB 8304 | Why Can't There Be More Love?/King's Message ................................................. 25 |

## MOOD REACTION
| | | |
|---|---|---|
| 69 | Gas 136 | Too Much Loving/Roaring Twenties ...................................................................... 20 |
| 70 | Pama PSP 1007 | LIVE AT THE CUMBERLAND (LP) ......................................................................... 30 |

## MOOD SIX
| | | |
|---|---|---|
| 82 | EMI EMI 5300 | Hanging Around/Mood Music (p/s) ........................................................................ 5 |
| 82 | EMI EMI 5336 | She's Too Far/Venus (unreleased; white label copies exist with p/s) .................... 30 |

| | | | MINT VALUE £ |
|---|---|---|---|
| 85 | Psycho PSYCHO 2001 | Plastic Flowers/It's Your Life (p/s) | 5 |
| 85 | Psycho PSYCHO 4001 | PLASTIC FLOWERS (12" EP) | 10 |

**MOODS**

| 63 | Starlite ST45 098 | Duckwalk/Easy Going | 22 |
|---|---|---|---|

**MOODY**

| 73 | Polydor 2310 285 | THE GENTLE RAIN (LP) | 200 |
|---|---|---|---|

**AMEIL MOODY**

| 69 | Blue Cat BS 143 | Mello Reggae/Lifeline | 20 |
|---|---|---|---|
| 69 | Blue Cat BS 164 | Ratchet Knife/Bend The Tree | 70 |

**MOODY BLUES**

| 64 | Decca F 11971 | Steal Your Heart Away/Loose Your Money (But Don't Loose Your Mind) (as Moodyblues) | 45 |
|---|---|---|---|
| 64 | Decca F 12022 | Go Now!/It's Easy Child | 6 |
| 65 | Decca F 12095 | I Don't Want To Go On Without You/Time Is On My Side | 7 |
| 65 | Decca F 12166 | From The Bottom Of My Heart (I Love You)/And My Baby's Gone | 7 |
| 65 | Decca F 12266 | Everyday/You Don't (All The Time) | 10 |
| 66 | Decca F 12498 | Boulevard De La Madelaine/This Is My House (But Nobody Calls) | 12 |
| 67 | Decca F 12543 | Life's Not Life/He Can't Win (withdrawn) | 60 |
| 67 | Decca F 12607 | Fly Me High/Really Haven't Got The Time | 30 |
| 67 | Decca F 12670 | Love And Beauty/Leave This Man Alone | 20 |
| 67 | Deram DM 161 | Nights In White Satin/Cities (1st issue, darker labels than later copies) | 5 |
| 68 | Deram DM 196 | Voices In The Sky/Doctor Livingstone, I Presume | 10 |
| 68 | Deram DM 213 | Ride My See-Saw/A Simple Game | 8 |
| 69 | Deram DM 247 | Never Comes The Day/So Deep Within You | 7 |
| 69 | Threshold TH 1 | Watching And Waiting/Out And In | 8 |
| 83 | Threshold TH 30 | Blue World/Going Nowhere (p/s, with free T-shirt) | 6 |
| 65 | Decca DFE 8622 | THE MOODY BLUES (EP, original label) | 30 |
| 65 | Decca DFE 8622 | THE MOODY BLUES (EP, reissue with boxed Decca logo) | 10 |
| 65 | Decca LK 4711 | THE MAGNIFICENT MOODIES (LP, unboxed red/silver Decca label logo) | 100 |
| 65 | Decca LK 4711 | THE MAGNIFICENT MOODIES (LP, boxed red/silver Decca label logo) | 20 |
| 67 | Deram DML 707 | DAYS OF FUTURE PASSED (LP, originally with white band on sleeve & 'DSS' labels, mono) | 30 |
| 67 | Deram SML 707 | DAYS OF FUTURE PASSED (LP, originally with white band on sleeve & 'DSS' labels, stereo) | 15 |
| 68 | Deram DML 711 | IN SEARCH OF THE LOST CHORD (LP, gatefold sleeve, mono, 'DSS' label) | 40 |
| 69 | Deram DML 1035 | ON THE THRESHOLD OF A DREAM (LP, gatefold sleeve with stapled booklet, mono. Label is white/brown with large logo) | 30 |
| 69 | Deram SML 1035 | ON THE THRESHOLD OF A DREAM (LP, gatefold sleeve with stapled booklet, stereo) | 20 |
| 69 | Threshold THM 1 | TO OUR CHILDREN'S CHILDREN'S CHILDREN (LP, gatefold, with insert, white/pink label, mono) | 40 |
| 69 | Threshold THS 1 | TO OUR CHILDREN'S CHILDREN'S CHILDREN (LP, gatefold, with insert, white/lilac label, stereo) | 20 |
| 70 | Threshold THS 3 | A QUESTION OF BALANCE (1st pressing, Matrixes 10009P-1W/10010P-1W, 'flap' gatefold sleeve with lyric sheet) | 25 |
| 71 | Threshold THS 5 | EVERY GOOD BOY DESERVES A FAVOUR (LP, gatefold, lyric insert, white/blue label) | 18 |
| 72 | Threshold THS 7 | SEVENTH SOJOURN (LP, gatefold sleeve, lyric insert, white/blue label) | 18 |

*(see also Justin Hayward, Denny Laine, Gerry Levene & Avengers)*

**GEORGE MOODY**

| 65 | Fontana TF 631 | Bring A Little Sunshine (To My Heart)/Santa The Swagman | 6 |
|---|---|---|---|

**JAMES MOODY**

| 55 | Esquire 20-071 | MOODY HI FI (10" LP) | 20 |
|---|---|---|---|

**MOOG MACHINE**

| 69 | CBS 63807 | SWITCHED ON ROCK (LP) | 20 |
|---|---|---|---|

**(THE) MOOG**

| 92 | Delirious DELIS 2 | Rush Hour/Jungle Muffin/Live Forever/Hopelessly Volatile/Subtone (12") | 30 |
|---|---|---|---|
| 92 | Delirious DELIS 4 | THE MOOG REMIX EP: Jungle Muffin (Micky Finn Remix)/Rush Hour (Rotor Remix)/Live Forever (Mercy Remix)/Going Crazy (Justice Remix) (12") | 12 |

**MOOM**

| 95 | Delerium DELEC LP 035 | TOOT (LP) | 15 |
|---|---|---|---|

**MOON**

| 68 | Liberty LBF 15076 | Someday Girl/Mothers And Fathers | 25 |
|---|---|---|---|
| 70 | Liberty LBF 15333 | Pirate/Not To Know | 10 |
| 68 | Liberty LBL/LBS 83146 | WITHOUT EARTH (LP) | 80 |

*(see also Beach Boys)*

**KEITH MOON**

| 75 | Polydor 2058 584 | Don't Worry Baby/Together | 20 |
|---|---|---|---|
| 75 | Polydor 2442 134 | TWO SIDES OF THE MOON (LP) | 30 |

**LARRY MOON**

| 63 | Ember EMB 171 | Tia Juana Ball/Bouquet Of Roses | 20 |
|---|---|---|---|

**PERRY MOON**

| 63 | Sway SW 002 | Nine Five Baby/PLANTES: Water Front | 10 |
|---|---|---|---|

**TERRY MOON**

| 63 | Planetone RC 11 | Moon Man/MIKE ELLIOT: This Love Of Mine | 10 |
|---|---|---|---|

**MOON BOYS**

| 69 | Amalgamated AMG 846 | Apollo 11/PIONEERS: Love Love Everyday | 150 |
|---|---|---|---|

*(see also Hippy Boys)*

**MOONCHILD**

| 75 | Look LKSP 5010 | Hourglass/War Orphan (Brother Of The Day) | 20 |
|---|---|---|---|

**MOONDANCE**
70 A&M AMS 792 — Lazy River/Anna St Claire ...................................................................... 5

**MOONDOG**
54 London REP 1010 — ON THE STREETS OF NEW YORK (EP).............................................. 30
59 Esquire 32-055 — MOONDOG (LP) ................................................................................. 150
69 CBS 63906 — MOONDOG (LP, gatefold sleeve)............................................................... 45

**MOONDOGS (1)**
78 Lyntone LT 002 — Heads I Win/Two's A Crowd (p/s) .................................................... 40

**MOONDOGS (2)**
79 Good Vibrations GOT 10 — She's Nineteen/Ya Don't Do Ya (foldout p/s) ........................ 20
80 Real ARE 13 — Who's Gonna Tell Mary/Overcaring Parents (p/s)................................... 12
81 Real ARE 14 — Talking In The Canteen/Make Her Love Me (p/s, with neckerchief)........... 35
81 Real ARE 14 — Talking In The Canteen/Make Her Love Me/You Said (p/s) ...................... 15
81 Real ARE 16 — Imposter/Baby Snatcher (p/s).............................................................. 15

**ART MOONEY (& HIS ORCHESTRA)**
53 MGM SP 1037 — I Played The Fool/I Just Couldn't Take It, Baby (with Cathy Ryan)........... 10
53 MGM SP 1045 — Baby Don't Do It/Believe In Me (with Cathy Ryan)............................... 10
54 MGM SP 1088 — Oh Boy What Joy We Had/Silhouette D'Amour .................................... 8
55 MGM SP 1134 — No Regrets/Honey Babe ...................................................................... 8
55 MGM SP 1145 — Give Me A Band And My Baby/The Girl I Left Behind Me........................ 8
56 MGM SP 1166 — Memories Of You/I'm Looking Over ...................................................... 8
57 MGM MGM 923 — Rebel Without A Cause Theme/"East Of Eden" Theme ....................... 15
57 MGM MGM 943 — Giant/There's Never Been Anyone Else But You................................. 15
57 MGM MGM 951 — Rock And Roll Tumbleweed/Is There A Teenager In The House (with Ocie Smith) ........ 22

*(see also Ocie Smith, Shorty Long, Cloverleafs, Cathy Ryan)*

**MOONGLOWS**
57 London HLN 8374 — I Knew From The Start/Over And Over Again................................... 700
57 London HLN 8374 — I Knew From The Start/Over And Over Again (78)............................ 70

*(see also Harvey & Moonglows, Etta & Harvey)*

**MOONI**
73 Polydor 2058-367 — Wine Ridden Talks/Nightmare ...................................................... 10

*(see also Mott The Hoople)*

**MOONKYTE**
71 Mother SMOT 1 — COUNT ME OUT (LP, with insert, cover has a die-cut spire) ............... 600

**MOONLIGHTERS (1)**
63 Island WI 043 — Going Out/Hold My Hands .................................................................. 20

**MOONLIGHTERS (2)**
65 Columbia DB 7602 — Come On Home/It's Too Late ....................................................... 10
66 Columbia DB 7910 — We'll See It Through/Too Late To Come Home .............................. 10

**MOONPIE**
74 Philips 6006380 — Going away Today/The Race Keeps Moving On ................................. 10

**MOONQUAKE**
73 London HL 10446 — Remember/This Winter.................................................................. 8

**MOON ROCKS & PRINCE JAZZBO**
78 Bushay's BFM 101 — Unite Jah People/Have No Fear (12") ............................................ 40

**MOONSHADOW**
76 Maxi M003 — Chase Me/Fight Hard .............................................................................. 15

**MICKY MOONSHINE**
74 Decca F 13555 — Baby Blue/Name It You Got It............................................................. 20
74 Decca F 13555 — Baby Blue/Name It You Got It (DJ copy)............................................. 40

**MOONSHINE (1)**
70 KJ Roberts ZDR56312 — Susannah/Garden Of Men........................................................ 60

**MOONSHINE (2)**
76 Moo Records MOO 1 — MOONSHINE EP (EP) ............................................................... 70

**MOONSHINERS**
65 Stateside SL 10137 — THE MOONSHINERS BREAKOUT! (LP) .......................................... 18
67 Page One POLS 004 — HOLD UP (LP) ........................................................................... 22

**MOONSTONES**
65 Parlophone R 5331 — Heaven Fell Last Night/Little Roses .............................................. 6
66 Parlophone R 5497 — Violets Of Dawn/Power Of Decision .............................................. 6
67 Mercury MF 1011 — How Many Times/Louisville ........................................................... 6

**MOON'S TRAIN**
67 MGM MGM 1333 — Deed I Do/It's In My Mind .............................................................. 40

*(see also Denny Mitchell, Preachers)*

**MOONTREKKERS**
61 Parlophone R 4814 — Night Of The Vampire/Melodie D'Amour ...................................... 30
62 Parlophone R 4888 — There's Something At The Bottom Of The Well/Hatashiai................ 30
63 Decca F 11714 — Moondust/The Bogey Man ................................................................. 20

**MICHAEL MOORCOCK('S DEEP FIX)**
80 Flicknife FLS 200 — Dodgem Dude/Star Cruiser (p/s) ..................................................... 5
82 Flicknife EJS P9831 — Brothel In Rosenstrasse/Time Centre (numbered, 500 only, with autographed lyric sheet)........... 30
92 Cyborg (no cat. no.) — The Brothel In Rosenstrasse (cassette only) ................................ 20
75 United Artists UAG 29732 — NEW WORLD'S FAIR (LP, with inner sleeve)........................ 40

*(see also Hawkwind)*

**ALICE MOORE**
50s Poydras MC 66 — Prison Blues/My Man Blues ............................................................. 22

MINT VALUE £

## ANTHONY MOORE
| | | | |
|---|---|---|---|
| 76 | Virgin VS 144 | Catch A Falling Star/Back To The Top | 5 |
| 71 | Polydor 2310 062 | PIECES FROM THE CLOUDLAND BALLROOM (LP) | 60 |
| 72 | Polydor 2310 079 | SECRETS OF THE BLUE BAG (LP) | 40 |
| 76 | Virgin V 2057 | OUT (LP, unissued) | 0 |

## BARBARA MOORE
| | | | |
|---|---|---|---|
| 67 | CBS (S) BPG 62839 | A LITTLE MOORE BARBARA (LP) | 40 |

## BOB MOORE & ORCHESTRA
| | | | |
|---|---|---|---|
| 61 | London HLU 9409 | Mexico/Hot Spot | 5 |

## BOBBY MOORE (& RHYTHM ACES)
| | | | |
|---|---|---|---|
| 66 | Chess CRS 8033 | Searching For My Love/Hey Mr D.J. | 25 |
| 75 | Pye International 7N 25691 | Call Me Your Anything Man/Call Me Your Anything Man (Disco Version) (solo) | 6 |
| 66 | Chess CRL 4521 | SEARCHIN' FOR MY LOVE (LP) | 75 |

## BUTCH MOORE
| | | | |
|---|---|---|---|
| 64 | Piccadilly 7N 35170 | Foolin Time/Too Soon To Know | 10 |
| 64 | Pye 7N 15727 | Down Came The Rain/Bye Bye Till Then | 8 |
| 64 | Piccadilly 7N 35182 | I Missed You/Touch Me | 12 |
| 65 | Pye 7N 15832 | Walking The Streets In The Rain/I Stand Still | 10 |
| 65 | Pye 7N 15910 | Our Love Will Go On/Words | 8 |
| 67 | Pye 7N 17368 | Till Then My Love/The Incredible Miss Brown | 7 |

## CHRISTY MOORE
| | | | |
|---|---|---|---|
| 69 | Mercury 20170 SMCL | PADDY ON THE ROAD (LP) | 400 |
| 75 | Polydor 2383 344 | WHATEVER TICKLES YOUR FANCY (LP) | 25 |
| 76 | Polydor 2383 426 | CHRISTY MOORE (LP) | 25 |
| 70s | WEA WX 286 | VOYAGE (LP) | 15 |

## CURLEY MOORE & THE COOL ONES
| | | | |
|---|---|---|---|
| 71 | Pye 25570 | Funky Yeah/Shelly's Rubber Band | 35 |

## DUDLEY MOORE (TRIO)
| | | | |
|---|---|---|---|
| 61 | Parlophone R 4772 | Strictly For The Birds (solo)/Duddly Dell (B-side as Dudley Moore Trio) | 10 |
| 68 | Decca F 12850 | 30 Is A Dangerous Age, Cynthia/The Real Stuff | 10 |
| 69 | Decca F 12882 | Keep It Up/Gently (as Dudley Moore Trio) | 25 |
| 66 | Decca LK 4788 | GENUINE DUD (LP, as Dudley Moore Trio) | 20 |
| 68 | Decca SKL 4923 | BEDAZZLED (LP, stereo, soundtrack) | 90 |
| 69 | Decca LK/SKL 4976 | THE DUDLEY MOORE TRIO (LP) | 30 |

*(see also Peter Cook & Dudley Moore, Cleo Laine)*

## G T MOORE
| | | | |
|---|---|---|---|
| 74 | B&C CB 236 | I'm Still Waiting/Judgement Day | 8 |

## GARY MOORE
| | | | |
|---|---|---|---|
| 78 | MCA MCA 386 | Back On The Streets/Track Nine (in p/s) | 30 |
| 78 | MCA MCA 386 | Back On The Streets/Track Nine | 5 |
| 79 | MCA MCA 419 | Parisienne Walkways/Fanatical Fascists (p/s) | 8 |
| 79 | MCA MCA 534 | Spanish Guitar/Spanish Guitar (instrumental) (p/s) | 8 |
| 81 | Jet JET 12016 | Nuclear Attack/Don't Let Me Be Misunderstood/Run To Your Mama (12", company sleeve, as Gary Moore & Friends) | 10 |
| 83 | Virgin VSY 564 | Falling In Love With You/Falling In Love With You (Instrumental) (picture disc) | 12 |
| 83 | Virgin VS 564 | Falling In Love With You/(Instrumental) (p/s, with comic) | 6 |
| 84 | 10 TENS 13 | Hold On To Love/Devil In Her Heart (plectrum-shaped picture disc) | 10 |
| 84 | 10 TEN 19 | Shapes Of Things/Blinder (p/s, with patch) | 5 |
| 84 | 10 TENS 19 | Shapes Of Things/Blinder (explosion-shaped picture disc) | 10 |
| 73 | CBS 65527 | GRINDING STONE (LP, as Gary Moore Band) | 20 |
| 78 | MCA MCF 2853 | BACK ON THE STREETS (LP, with inner sleeve) | 18 |
| 81 | Jet JETLP 245 | LIVE AT THE MARQUEE (LP, withdrawn test pressing, white sleeve with Jet Info sticker) | 100 |
| 82 | Virgin V 2245 | CORRIDORS OF POWER (LP, with free live EP [VDJ 34]) | 20 |
| 84 | EMI OVED 206 | VICTIMS OF THE FUTURE (LP, with inner & poster) | 20 |
| 86 | 10 DIXP 16 | RUN FOR COVER (LP, picture disc, die-cut sleeve) | 30 |
| 87 | 10 DIXG 56 | WILD FRONTIER (2-LP, gatefold sleeve) | 20 |

*(see also Granny's Intentions, Dr. Strangely Strange, Skid Row, Thin Lizzy, Gary Moore & Phil Lynott, Eddie Howell, G-Force, Cozy Powell, Jack Bruce, National Head)*

## GARY MOORE & PHIL LYNOTT
| | | | |
|---|---|---|---|
| 85 | 10 TENS 49 | Out In The Fields/Military Man (2 1-sided interlocking shaped picture-disc set, stickered gatefold PVC sleeve) | 15 |
| 85 | 10 TENC 49-12 | Military Man (12", 1-sided, B-side etched with signatures, promo only) | 12 |

## JACKIE MOORE
| | | | |
|---|---|---|---|
| 71 | Jay Boy BOY 35 | Dear John/Here Am I | 5 |
| 71 | Atlantic 2091 054 | Precious Precious/Will Power | 5 |
| 71 | Atlantic 2091 095 | Sometimes It's Got To Rain (In Your Love Life)/Wonderful, Marvellous (with Dixie Flyers) | 5 |
| 74 | Atlantic K 10481 | Both Ends Against The Middle/Willpower | 5 |
| 79 | CBS 7722 | This Time Baby/Let's Go Somewhere And Make Love (paper label) | 5 |

## JACQUELINE MOORE
| | | | |
|---|---|---|---|
| 65 | Decca F 12165 | Queen Of The House/What's Going On Here | 7 |

## JERRY MOORE
| | | | |
|---|---|---|---|
| 69 | Fontana STL 5502 | LIFE IS A CONSTANT JOURNEY HOME (LP) | 40 |

## JOHNNY MOORE (2)
| | | | |
|---|---|---|---|
| 02 | Grapevine 2000 G2K 147 | Yesterday Today And Tomorrow/Come Fly With Me | 8 |
| 03 | Beecool 101 | Can't Live Without Your Love/DOTTIE PEARSON: Hello Baby (promo only) | 8 |

## JOHNNY MOORE (1)
| | | |
|---|---|---|
| 67 | Caltone TONE 101 | Sound And Soul/ROY SHIRLEY: Get On The Ball ........................................................ 40 |
| 69 | Doctor Bird DB 1180 | Big Big Boss/CARL CANNONBALL BRYON: Reggae This Reggae ................................... 60 |

*(see also Cannonball & Johnny Melody, Alton Ellis)*

## MATTHEW MOORE
| | | |
|---|---|---|
| 66 | Capitol CL 15467 | A Face In The Crowd/St. James Infirmary ............................................................... 6 |

## MERRILL E. MOORE
| | | |
|---|---|---|
| 55 | Capitol CL 14369 | Five Foot Two, Eyes Of Blue/Hard Top Race (as Merrill Moore) ........................... 200 |
| 55 | Capitol CL 14369 | Five Foot Two, Eyes Of Blue/Hard Top Race (as Merrill Moore) (78) ...................... 20 |
| 56 | Capitol F 3397 | King Porter Stomp/Rock Island Line (export only) ............................................... 150 |
| 68 | Ember EMB S 253 | Down The Road A-Piece/Buttermilk Baby ............................................................ 15 |
| 69 | B&C CB 100 | Sweet Mama Tree Top Tall/Little Green Apples ...................................................... 8 |
| 70 | Bulldog BD 20 | House Of Blue Lights/Red Light ............................................................................ 8 |
| 67 | Ember EMB 3392 | BELLYFUL OF BLUE-THUNDER (LP) ...................................................................... 40 |

## NICKY MOORE BAND
| | | |
|---|---|---|
| 81 | Street Tunes STS 006 | Year Of The Lie ...................................................................................................... 10 |

*(see also Tiger, Samson, Hackensack, Mammoth)*

## OSCAR MOORE TRIO
| | | |
|---|---|---|
| 55 | London H-APB 1035 | KENYA (10" LP) ...................................................................................................... 20 |

## ROGER MOORE
| | | |
|---|---|---|
| 65 | CBS 202014 | Where Does Love Go/Tomorrow After Tomorrow (in p/s) ....................................... 20 |
| 65 | CBS 202014 | Where Does Love Go/Tomorrow After Tomorrow ................................................... 10 |

## SCOTTY MOORE
| | | |
|---|---|---|
| 64 | Columbia 33SX 1680 | THE GUITAR THAT CHANGED THE WORLD! (LP) ................................................... 60 |

*(see also Elvis Presley)*

## SHELLEY MOORE
| | | |
|---|---|---|
| 55 | Columbia SCM 5197 | In The Wee Small Hours Of The Morning/ When You Lose The One You Love (solo) ........ 5 |

## SHELLEY MOORE (& MOORE SESSIONEERS)
| | | |
|---|---|---|
| 58 | Starlite ST45 002 | You've Tied Me Up/Gone On The Guy .................................................................... 7 |
| 58 | Starlite ST45 003 | Where Is The Bluebird?/Everything Is Gonna Be All Right ..................................... 7 |

## THURSTON MOORE & DON FLEMING
| | | |
|---|---|---|
| 97 | Via Satellite V.SAT 6 | Telstar/E.A.R.: Sputnik ......................................................................................... 8 |

## TIM MOORE
| | | |
|---|---|---|
| 75 | Mooncrest Moon 41 | A Fool Like You/Aviation Man ............................................................................... 12 |

## MELBA MOORE
| | | |
|---|---|---|
| 78 | Buddah BDS 464 | Standing Right Here/Living Free .............................................................................. 8 |
| 86 | Kent 6T 2 | Magic Touch/CHUCK JACKSON: Little By Little ...................................................... 30 |
| 87 | Horace's 001 | Magic Touch/TOMMY HUNT: The Pretty Part Of You ............................................ 20 |
| 03 | Kent TOWN 119 | DEAN PARISH: Broken Bottles And Sticks/MELBA MOORE: Magic Touch ................ 8 |

## ALAN MOORHOUSE ORCHESTRA
| | | |
|---|---|---|
| 66 | Pye 7N 17073 | (The Ballad Of) The Green Berets/London Bridge ................................................... 6 |
| 68 | Page One POF 104 | Stop Press/Chloe ................................................................................................... 7 |
| 70 | Columbia DB 8674 | Haunting Me/Soul Bossa ........................................................................................ 6 |

## BIG MOOSE (WALKER)
| | | |
|---|---|---|
| 68 | Python PKM 1 | Puppy Howl Blues/Rambling Woman (pressed with reversed labels) ....................... 35 |

## MOOSE (1)
| | | |
|---|---|---|
| 70 | Escort ERT 840 | Engine No. 9/KURASS: Do It ................................................................................... 7 |

## MOOSE (2)
| | | |
|---|---|---|
| 92 | Hut HUTLP 5 | XYZ (LP, with free 7") ............................................................................................ 20 |

## MOPEDS
| | | |
|---|---|---|
| 68 | Col. Blue Beat DB 108 | Whiskey And Soda/Do It ......................................................................................... 7 |

*(see also Cindy Starr & Mopeds)*

## MOQUETTES
| | | |
|---|---|---|
| 64 | Columbia DB 7315 | Right String, But The Wrong Yo-Yo/You Came Along .............................................. 50 |

## SANTOS MORADOS
| | | |
|---|---|---|
| 68 | Island WIP 6034 | Tonopah/Anytime .................................................................................................... 6 |

## NONO MORALES & HIS ORCHESTRA
| | | |
|---|---|---|
| 54 | HMV 7MC 5 | Istanbul (Not Constantinople)/Am I Blue (export single) ......................................... 6 |

## MORAL SUPPORT
| | | |
|---|---|---|
| 79 | Round RSR 001 | Just Where It's At Tonight/Sin ................................................................................ 20 |

## MIKE MORAN
| | | |
|---|---|---|
| 70s | Alba TAR 053 | PENNY WHISTLES OF ROBERT LOUIS STEVENSON (LP) ......................................... 20 |

## MOYA MORAY
| | | |
|---|---|---|
| 62 | Piccadilly 7N 35023 | My Heart Will Make A Fool Of Me/You're Running Out Of Kisses ........................... 12 |

## MORBID ANGEL
| | | |
|---|---|---|
| 94 | Earache MOSH 112 | LAIBACH REMIXES EP (God Of Emptiness/Sworn To The Black/Sworn To The Black [Laibach Remix]/God Of Emptiness [Laibach Remix]) (12", p/s) ............................... 30 |
| 89 | Earache MOSH 11 | ALTARS OF MADNESS (LP, pink splattered vinyl, stickered sleeve) .......................... 30 |
| 89 | Earache MOSH 11P | ALTARS OF MADNESS (LP, picture disc) ................................................................ 30 |
| 91 | Earache MOSH 31 | BLESSED ARE THE SICK (LP) .................................................................................. 20 |
| 91 | Earache MOSH 31 | BLESSED ARE THE SICK (LP on 6 x 7" in box with 4 page insert) ............................ 40 |
| 91 | Earache MOSH 48 | ABOMINATIONS OF DESOLATION (LP) .................................................................. 25 |
| 95 | Earache MOSH 134 LP | DOMINATION (LP) ................................................................................................. 20 |

## MORE
| | | |
|---|---|---|
| 80 | Atlantic K 11561 | We Are The Band/Atomic Rock (with p/s) ............................................................... 6 |
| 82 | Atlantic K 11744 | Trickster/Hey Joe (p/s) ......................................................................................... 15 |

## A. MORE

| 80 | Quango HMGS 10 | Judy/Lucia (p/s) | 5 |

*(see also Anthony Moore)*

### MANDY MORE
| 72 | Philips 6006 199 | Come With Me To Jesus/Alone In My Yellow | 25 |
| 73 | Philips 6006 277 | San Francisco 5AM/Coffee Cups | 25 |
| 73 | Philips 6006 343 | Every Mother's Child/Blue Seasons | 25 |
| 75 | Fresh Air 6121 119 | Rose Coloured Window/If I Smiled On Saturday | 25 |
| 72 | Philips 6308109 | BUT THAT IS ME (LP) | 250 |

### MORE MONEY SYSTEM
| 69 | Leeds Permanent Building Society LPB 001 | Do Your Own Thing/Call It Anything (p/s) | 10 |

### MORECAMBE & WISE
| 61 | HMV POP 957 | We're The Guys (Who Drive Your Baby Wild)/Me And My Shadow | 5 |
| 63 | HMV POP 1240 | Boom Oo Yatta Ta Ta/Why Did I Let You Go | 5 |
| 64 | HMV POP 1373 | A-Wassailing/The Happiest Christmas Of All | 5 |
| 66 | HMV POP 1518 | Now That You're Here/That Riviera Touch | 5 |
| 69 | Columbia DB 8646 | Bring Me Sunshine/Just Around The Corner | 5 |

### MORGAN
| 73 | RCA SF 8321 | NOVA SOLIS (LP, with insert) | 40 |

*(see also Mott The Hoople, Love Affair, Humpy Bong)*

### AL MORGAN
| 58 | London HLU 8741 | Jealous Heart/Foolish Tears | 12 |
| 51 | London H-APB 1001 | JEALOUS HEART (10" LP) | 12 |
| 51 | London H-APB 1003 | LITTLE RED BOOK (10" LP) | 12 |

### MORGAN AND THE MARK 7
| 66 | Polydor BM 56083 | I'm Gonna Turn My Life Around/Undercover Man | 35 |

### MORGAN BROTHERS
| 59 | MGM MGM 1007 | Nola/Guiding Star | 5 |
| 59 | MGM MGM 1026 | Kissin' On The Red Light/Milk From The Coconut | 6 |

### CARLTON B MORGAN
| 82 | CNT 0666 | DEVILS MUSIC (LP) | 15 |

### DAVID/DAVY MORGAN
| 65 | Columbia DB 7624 | Tomorrow I'll Be Gone/Ain't Got Much More To See (as Davy Morgan) | 45 |
| 68 | Parlophone R 5692 | True To Life/Dawning (as David Morgan) | 25 |

*(see also Wishful Thinking)*

### DERRICK MORGAN
| 60 | Blue Beat BB 7 | Fat Man/I'm Gonna Leave You | 30 |
| 60 | Blue Beat BB 12 | Don't Cry/I Pray For You (as Derrick Morgan & Ebonies) | 25 |
| 60 | Blue Beat BB 18 | Lover Boy/Oh My! | 25 |
| 61 | Blue Beat BB 31 | Now We Know/Nights Are Lonely (with Trenton Spence Orchestra) | 25 |
| 61 | Blue Beat BB 35 | Leave Earth/Wigger Wee Shuffle (with Clue J. & His Blues Busters) | 25 |
| 61 | Blue Beat BB 62 | Shake A Leg/Golden Rule (as Derrick & Drumbago All Stars) | 25 |
| 62 | Blue Beat BB 76 | Sunday, Monday/Be Still | 25 |
| 62 | Blue Beat BB 82 | Don't You Know Little Girl (actually by Derrick & Basil)/ B. GABBIDON: Hully Gully Miss Molly | 25 |
| 62 | Blue Beat BB 85 | Come On Over/Come Back My Darling (with Buster's Group) | 25 |
| 62 | Blue Beat BB 91 | Headache/OWEN GRAY: Millie Girl | 25 |
| 62 | Blue Beat BB 94 | Meekly Wait/Day In And Day Out (both sides with Yvonne [Sterling]) | 20 |
| 62 | Blue Beat BB 100 | In My Heart/BELL'S GROUP: Kingston 13 | 30 |
| 62 | Blue Beat BB 110 | Are You Going To Marry Me?/Troubles (as Derrick Morgan & Patsy) | 25 |
| 62 | Blue Beat BB 130 | Should Be Ashamed/Marjorie (with Buster's Group) | 20 |
| 62 | Blue Beat BB 141 | Joybells (with Duke Reid Group)/Going Down To Canaan (with Denzil Dennis) | 20 |
| 62 | Island WI 004 | Travel On/Teach Me Baby | 35 |
| 62 | Island WI 006 | The Hop/Tell It To Me | 35 |
| 62 | Island WI 011 | Forward March/Please Don't Talk About Me (B-side actually with Eric Morris) | 25 |
| 62 | Island WI 013 | Cherry Home/See And Blind | 35 |
| 63 | Blue Beat BB 148 | Jezebell/Burnette | 25 |
| 63 | Blue Beat BB 177 | Patricia My Dear/The Girl I Left Behind | 25 |
| 63 | Blue Beat BB 187 | Tears On My Pillow/You Should Have Known | 25 |
| 63 | Blue Beat BB 196 | Telephone/Life Is Tough (B-side actually "Tough Man Tough") | 25 |
| 63 | Island WI 037 | Dorothy/Leave Her Alone | 25 |
| 63 | Island WI 051 | Blazing Fire/DERRICK & PATSY: I'm In A Jam | 25 |
| 63 | Island WI 053 | No Raise, No Praise/Loving Baby | 20 |
| 63 | Island WI 080 | Angel With Blue Eyes/Corner Stone | 25 |
| 63 | Rio R 1 | Blazing Fire/Edmarine | 15 |
| 64 | Black Swan WI 402 | Street Girl/Edmarine | 15 |
| 64 | Black Swan WI 425 | Cherry Pie (actually by Frederick Hibbert)/BOB WALLS: Beware | 20 |
| 64 | Blue Beat BB 233 | Let Them Talk/Sleeping | 20 |
| 64 | Blue Beat BB 239 | Miss Lulu/DERRICK & PALOY: She's So Young (B-side act. by Derrick & Patsy) | 20 |
| 64 | Blue Beat BB 261 | The Soldier Man/BUSTER'S ALL STARS: Jet 707 | 100 |
| 64 | Blue Beat BB 268 | Katy Katy/Call On Me | 18 |
| 65 | Blue Beat BB 276 | Weep No More/I Want A Girl | 18 |
| 65 | Blue Beat BB 283 | Johnny Grave/BUSTER'S ALL STARS: Yeah Yeah | 30 |
| 65 | Blue Beat BB 311 | Throw Them Away/Baby Face | 25 |
| 65 | Blue Beat BB 329 | Sweeter Than Honey/You Never Know (with Prince Buster) | 25 |
| 65 | Ska Beat JB 185 | Heart Of Stone/Let Me Go (with Baba Brooks Group) | 25 |
| 65 | Ska Beat JB 218 | Don't Call Me Daddy/BABA BROOK'S BAND: Girl's Town Ska | 30 |

| 65 | Island WI 193 | Two Of A Kind/I Want A Lover (both actually with Naomi) | 30 |
|----|---------------|---------|----|
| 65 | Island WI 225 | Starvation/I Am A Blackhead Again | 30 |
| 66 | Island WI 277 | It's Alright/I Need Someone (both sides actually with Blenders) | 30 |
| 66 | Island WI 289 | Ameletia (actually by Frank Cosmo)/Don't You Worry (B-side with Patsy Todd) | 20 |
| 66 | Island WI 3010 | Gather Together Now (Jamaican Independence Song)/Soft Hand (actually "So Hard") (both sides actually with Blenders) | 30 |
| 66 | Rio R 122 | Cool Off Rudies/Take It Easy | 25 |
| 67 | Island WI 3079 | Someone (actually Derrick & Pauline Morgan)/Do You Love Me (with Pauline) | 18 |
| 67 | Pyramid PYR 6010 | Tougher Than Tough/ROLAND ALPHONSO: Song For My Father | 25 |
| 67 | Pyramid PYR 6013 | Greedy Gal/SOUL BROTHERS: Marcus Junior | 30 |
| 67 | Pyramid PYR 6014 | Court Dismiss/FREDERICK McCLEAN: Fine Fine Fine | 15 |
| 67 | Pyramid PYR 6019 | Judge Dread In Court/Last Chance | 30 |
| 67 | Pyramid PYR 6021 | Kill Me Dead/Don't Be A Fool | 25 |
| 67 | Pyramid PYR 6024 | No Dice/I Mean It | 25 |
| 67 | Pyramid PYR 6025 | Do The Bang Bang/Revenge | 30 |
| 68 | Island WI 3094 | Conquering Ruler/LLOYD & DEVON: Red Rum Ball | 100 |
| 68 | Island WI 3101 | Gimme Back/VICEROYS: Send Requests | 60 |
| 68 | Island WI 3159 | Hold You Jack/One Morning In May | 40 |
| 68 | Pyramid PYR 6029 | I Am The Ruler/I Mean It | 40 |
| 68 | Pyramid PYR 6039 | Woman A Grumble/Don't Be A Fool | 25 |
| 68 | Pyramid PYR 6040 | Want More/ROLAND ALPHONSO: Goodnight My Love | 25 |
| 68 | Pyramid PYR 6045 | Try Me/I'm Leaving (B-side with Pauline) | 25 |
| 68 | Pyramid PYR 6046 | King For Tonight (with Pauline)/Last Chance | 25 |
| 68 | Pyramid PYR 6053 | Me Naw Give Up/BEVERLEY'S ALLSTARS: Dreadnaught | 50 |
| 68 | Pyramid PYR 6061 | What's Your Grouse/BEVERLEY'S ALLSTARS: I Don't Know | 25 |
| 68 | Pyramid PYR 6063 | Johnny Pram Pram/Don't Say (B-side with Pauline Morgan) | 40 |
| 68 | Amalgamated AMG 824 | I Want To Go Home/JACKIE ROBINSON: Let The Little Girl Dance | 20 |
| 68 | Crab CRAB 3 | River To The Bank/PETER KING: Reggae Limbo | 20 |
| 68 | Trojan TR 626 | Fat Man/VAL BENNETT: South Parkway Rock | 25 |
| 68 | Nu Beat NB 016 | I Love You/JUNIOR SMITH: Searching | 25 |
| 68 | Big Shot BI 506 | Shower Of Rain/VAL BENNETT: It Might As Well Be Spring | 20 |
| 69 | Crab CRAB 8 | Seven Letters/TARTANS: Lonely Heartaches (B-side act. by Clarendonians) | 20 |
| 69 | Crab CRAB 11 | My First Taste Of Love/TARTANS: Dance All Night | 20 |
| 69 | Crab CRAB 18 | Don't Play That Song/How Can I Forget You? | 20 |
| 69 | Crab CRAB 23 | Send Me Some Loving/Come What May | 20 |
| 69 | Crab CRAB 22 | Mek It Tan Deah/Gimme Back | 20 |
| 69 | Crab CRAB 28 | Hard Time/ROY RICHARDS: Death Rides A Horse | 50 |
| 69 | Crab CRAB 30 | Man Pon Spot/What A Thing | 25 |
| 69 | Crab CRAB 32 | Moon Hop/Harris Wheel | 40 |
| 69 | Jackpot JP 700 | Seven Letters/Too Bad | 10 |
| 69 | Unity UN 507 | Belly Woman/PAULETT & LOVERS: Please Stay | 10 |
| 69 | Unity UN 540 | Derrick - Top The Pop/GLEN ADAMS: Capone's Revenge | 20 |
| 70 | Unity UN 546 | Return Of Jack Slade/Fat Man | 20 |
| 70 | Unity UN 569 | The Conquering Ruler/Bedweight | 40 |
| 70 | Crab CRAB 44 | A Night At The Hop/Telephone | 30 |
| 70 | Crab CRAB 51 | I Wish I Was An Apple/The Story | 10 |
| 70 | Crab CRAB 52 | Take A Letter Maria/OWEN GRAY: Just A Little Loving | 10 |
| 70 | Crab CRAB 57 | My Dickie/Brixton Hop | 10 |
| 70 | Crab CRAB 58 | I Can't Stand It No Longer/Beyond The Wall | 10 |
| 70 | Crab CRAB 59 | Endlessly/Who's Making Love | 10 |
| 70 | Crab CRAB 62 | Hurt/Julia | 10 |
| 70 | Pama PM 822 | Love Bug/My Dickie | 10 |
| 71 | Bullet BU 467 | Nobody's Business/Standing By | 10 |
| 71 | Camel CA 84 | I Am Just A Sufferer/We Want To Know | 10 |
| 71 | Crab CRAB 67 | Searching So Long/MORGAN'S ALL STARS: Drums Of Passion | 10 |
| 72 | Grape GR 3032 | Send A Little Rain/DERRICK MORGAN ALL STARS: A Little Rain (Version) | 10 |
| 72 | Jackpot JP 793 | Let Them Talk/Bringing In The Guns | 12 |
| 72 | Jackpot JP 794 | Won't Be This Way/Ain't No Love | 12 |
| 72 | Jackpot JP 797 | Me Naw Run/All Night Long | 12 |
| 72 | Jackpot JP 802 | Festival 10/Festival 10 - Version | 7 |
| 72 | Punch PH 107 | Forward March/Plenty Of One | 7 |
| 72 | Buster PB 60 | Tears On My Pillow/KEITH REID: Worried Over You (actually by Keith & Enid) | 7 |
| 73 | Attack ATT 8048 | Derrick's Big Eleven/My Ding A Ling | 7 |
| 73 | Big Shot BI 617 | Housewives Choice/Don't You Worry (both sides with Hortense Ellis) | 5 |
| 73 | Bread BR 1119 | I Who Have Nothing/I'm Not Home | 5 |
| 73 | Downtown DT 520 | Hey Little Girl/Don't Blame The Man | 5 |
| 73 | Pama Supreme PS 387 | I'll Never Give Up/I Who Have Nothing | 5 |
| 75 | Klik KL 603 | Wet Dreams Part 1/Wet Dreams Part 2 | 5 |
| 63 | Island ILP 903 | FORWARD MARCH (LP) | 250 |
| 69 | Doctor Bird DLMB 5014 | BEST OF DERRICK MORGAN (LP) | 150 |
| 69 | Island ILP 990 | DERRICK MORGAN AND HIS FRIENDS (LP) | 150 |
| 69 | Pama ECO 10 | DERRICK MORGAN IN LONDON (LP) | 100 |
| 69 | Pama PSP 1006 | MOON HOP (LP) | 100 |
| 69 | Trojan TTL 5 | SEVEN LETTERS (LP) | 40 |
| 70 | Trojan TTL 38 | FORWARD MARCH (LP, reissue) | 25 |
| 74 | Magnet MGT 004 | IN THE MOOD (LP) | 90 |

*(see also Roland Alphonso; Frank Cosmo; Copy Cats, Derrick & Lloyd; Derrick, Morris & Patsy; Derrick & Patsy; Derrick & Naomi; Derrick & Paulette; Derrick & Pauline; Morgan's All Stars; Martin & Derrick; Larry Lawrence; Matador, Jackie Robinson)*

MINT VALUE £

## FREDDY MORGAN
| | | | |
|---|---|---|---|
| 59 | London HL 7077 | Side Saddle/64 Rue Blondell (export issue) | 8 |

## GEORGE MORGAN
| | | | |
|---|---|---|---|
| 68 | London HLB 10197 | Barbara/Sad Bird | 5 |
| 57 | Philips BBE 12149 | COUNTRY AND WESTERN SPECTACULAR (EP) | 20 |
| 68 | London HAB 8353 | COUNTRY HITS BY CANDLELIGHT (LP) | 22 |

## MORGAN JAMES DUO
| | | | |
|---|---|---|---|
| 64 | Philips BF 1462 | Sweet Pussycat/Bye Bye Brown Eyes | 7 |
| 64 | Philips BF 1325 | Sometimes I'm Happy/It Ain't Necessarily So | 7 |
| 67 | Philips BF 1630 | If It Comes To That/Tell Me Where Our Love Went Wrong | 7 |
| 68 | Philips BF 1707 | Let's Ride/After The Storm | 7 |
| 66 | Fontana SFL 13071 | AT THE BAR OF MUSIC (LP) | 25 |
| 66 | Philips BL 7702 | SHHHH...TALENT STRIKES AGAIN (LP) | 30 |

## JANE MORGAN (& TROUBADORS)
| | | | |
|---|---|---|---|
| 55 | London HL 8148 | Why - Oh Why/The Heart You Break (May Be Your Own) | 15 |
| 57 | London HLR 8395 | From The First Hello To The Last Goodbye/ Come Home, Come Home, Come Home | 20 |
| 57 | London HLR 8436 | Around The World/It's Not For Me To Say | 10 |
| 57 | London HLR 8468 | Fascination (with Troubadors)/Why Don't They Leave Us Alone | 10 |
| 58 | London HLR 8539 | I'm New At The Game Of Romance/It's Been A Long Long Time (with Troubadors) | 10 |
| 58 | London HLR 8611 | I've Got Bells On My Heart/Only One Love | 15 |
| 58 | London HLR 8649 | Enchanted Island/Once More, My Love, Once More | 10 |
| 58 | London HLR 8751 | The Day The Rains Came/Le Jour Ou La Pluie Viendra | 5 |
| 58 | London HL 7064 | The Day The Rains Came/I May Never Pass This Way Again (export issue) | 10 |
| 59 | London HLR 8810 | If Only I Could Only Live My Life Again/To Love And Be Loved | 5 |
| 59 | London HLR 8925 | With Open Arms/I Can't Begin To Tell You | 5 |
| 67 | Columbia DB 7645 | Maybe/Walking The Streets In The Rain | 15 |
| 67 | HMV POP 1608 | This Is My World Without You/Somebody, Someplace | 10 |
| 57 | London HA-R 2086 | FASCINATION (LP) | 15 |
| 58 | London HA-R 2110 | ALL THE WAY (LP, with Troubadors) | 15 |
| 58 | London HA-R 2133 | SOMETHING OLD, SOMETHING NEW, SOMETHING BORROWED, SOMETHING BLUE (LP) | 15 |
| 61 | London HA-R 2371 | JANE MORGAN TIME (LP) | 15 |

*(see also Troubadors, Roger Williams)*

## JAYE P. MORGAN
| | | | |
|---|---|---|---|
| 55 | HMV 7M 327 | The Longest Walk/Swanee | 15 |
| 56 | HMV 7M 348 | If You Don't Want My Love/Pepper Hot Baby | 25 |
| 56 | HMV 7M 365 | Not One Goodbye/My Bewildered Heart | 10 |
| 56 | Brunswick 05519 | Have You Ever Been Lonely?/Baby Don't Do It | 10 |
| 57 | RCA RCA 1014 | You, You Romeo/Graduation Ring | 8 |
| 59 | MGM MGM 1005 | Are You Lonesome Tonight?/Miss You | 5 |
| 59 | MGM MGM 1021 | (It Took) One Kiss/My Reputation | 5 |
| 59 | MGM MGM 1039 | Somebody Loses, Somebody Wins/Somebody Else Is Taking My Place | 5 |
| 60 | MGM MGM 1093 | I Walk The Line/Wondering Where You Are | 6 |
| 62 | MGM MGM 1182 | Heartache Named Johnny/He Thinks I Still Ache | 6 |
| 62 | MGM MGM 1190 | Brotherhood Of Man/Nobody's Sweetheart | 6 |
| 54 | London RE-P 1013 | JAYE P. SINGS (EP) | 12 |
| 59 | MGM MGM-C 793 | SLOW AND EASY (LP) | 15 |

## JOHN MORGAN
| | | | |
|---|---|---|---|
| 72 | Carnaby 6302 010 | KALEIDOSCOPE (LP, white label with red 'crab' logo) | 100 |
| 70s | SWP 1007 | LIVE AT DURRANT HOUSE (LP, private pressing) | 100 |

*(see also Spirit Of John Morgan)*

## LEE MORGAN
| | | | |
|---|---|---|---|
| 61 | Columbia 33SX 1399 | THE BIRDLAND STORY VOL. 1 (LP) | 20 |
| 62 | Stateside SL 10016 | EXPOOBIDENT (LP) | 30 |

## MACE MORGAN THUNDERBIRDS
| | | | |
|---|---|---|---|
| 63 | Starlite STEP 36 | SHAKE AND SWING (EP) | 60 |

## MARIA MORGAN
| | | | |
|---|---|---|---|
| 75 | President PT 440 | Touch Me Baby/Reaching Out For Your Love | 7 |

## MARY MORGAN
| | | | |
|---|---|---|---|
| 56 | Parlophone MSP 6204 | Jimmy Unknown/You Are My Love | 10 |
| 56 | Parlophone R 4227 | From The Candy Store On The Corner/No-One Was There But You | 10 |
| 57 | Parlophone R 4348 | A Call To Arms/One For Sorrow, Two For Joy | 6 |

## P.C. ALEXANDER MORGAN
| | | | |
|---|---|---|---|
| 66 | Columbia DB 8095 | Sussex By The Sea/METROPOLITAN POLICE BAND: Thunderbirds March | 8 |

## RAY MORGAN
| | | | |
|---|---|---|---|
| 70 | B&C CB 128 | Long And Winding Road/The Sweetest Wine | 5 |

## RUSS MORGAN ORCHESTRA
| | | | |
|---|---|---|---|
| 55 | Brunswick 05464 | Alabamy Bound/SCRANTON 7: The Popcorn Song | 5 |
| 55 | Brunswick 05493 | Dog Face Soldier/Don't Cry Sweetheart | 5 |
| 56 | Brunswick 05537 | The Poor People Of Paris (Poor John)/Silver Moon | 5 |
| 56 | Brunswick 05602 | Lay Down Your Arms/My Best You You | 5 |

## SAMMY MORGAN
| | | | |
|---|---|---|---|
| 70 | Bullet BU 455 | Get Out Of This Land/SYDNEY ALL STARS: Landmark | 10 |
| 70 | Punch PH 57 | Get Out Of This Land/SYDNEY ALL STARS: Landmark | 5 |

## TONY MORGAN
| | | | |
|---|---|---|---|
| 69 | Beacon BEA 115 | Racial Segregation/Racial Segregation (instrumental) | 15 |
| 72 | Beacon BEA 188 | Black Skin Blue Eyed Boys/Why Build A Mountain | 15 |

## MORGAN TWINS
| | | | |
|---|---|---|---|
| 58 | RCA RCA 1083 | T.V. Hop/Let's Get Going | 60 |
| 58 | RCA RCA 1083 | T.V. Hop/Let's Get Going (78) | 20 |

## MORGAN'S ALL STARS
| | | | |
|---|---|---|---|
| 71 | Camel CA 76 | I Love You The Most (actually by Lloyd Clarke)/I Love You The Most - Version | 5 |

*(see also B. Leggs, Derrick Morgan, Marvels)*

## TIM MORGON
| | | | |
|---|---|---|---|
| 72 | MCA MU 1173 | Take A Look Around/For All We Know | 6 |

## (RON PAUL) MORIN & (LUKE P.) WILSON
| | | | |
|---|---|---|---|
| 72 | Sovereign SVNA 7252 | PEACEFUL COMPANY (LP) | 20 |

## JOHNNY MORISETTE
| | | | |
|---|---|---|---|
| 62 | Stateside SS 107 | Meet Me At The Twistin' Place/Any Time Any Day Any Where | 15 |

## ALANIS MORISSETTE
| | | | |
|---|---|---|---|
| 95 | Maverick 9362 45901 | JAGGED LITTLE PILL (LP, German pressing but imported into U.K.) | 50 |
| 12 | Maverick 8122797168 | JAGGED LITTLE PILL (LP, reissue) | 15 |

## MORNIN
| | | | |
|---|---|---|---|
| 69 | CBS 4883 | Cheatin' On You/Let Me Love You | 20 |

## MORNING
| | | | |
|---|---|---|---|
| 70 | Liberty LBS 83463 | MORNING (LP) | 40 |
| 72 | United Artists UAS 29337 | STRUCK LIKE SILVER (LP) | 20 |

## MORNING AFTER
| | | | |
|---|---|---|---|
| 71 | Sky SKYLP 71014 | BLUE BLOOD (LP) | 80 |

## MORNING GLORY
| | | | |
|---|---|---|---|
| 71 | Chapter 1 CHS 148 | Green On The Other Side Of The Mountain/Monday Street | 7 |
| 73 | Island ILPS 9237 | MORNING GLORY (LP, gatefold, pink rim palm tree label) | 30 |

*(see also John Surman)*

## MOROCCAN COCO
| | | | |
|---|---|---|---|
| 83 | SR 001 | Steam Radio/One Day (p/s) | 35 |

## GIORGIO MORODER
| | | | |
|---|---|---|---|
| 66 | Page One POF 003 | Full Stop/Believe Me | 15 |
| 67 | Page One POF 028 | How Much Longer Must I Wait/Bla Bla Diddley | 15 |
| 80 | Polydor POSP 134 | Night Drive/The Apartment | 7 |
| 90s | Cause-N-Effect | I Wanna Rock You (Thee Maddcat Mix)/(Thee DrumDrum Mix) (12", no p/s) | 15 |

*(see also Giorgio)*

## ENNIO MORRICONE ORCHESTRA
| | | | |
|---|---|---|---|
| 67 | RCA Victor RD/SF 7875 | A FISTFUL OF DOLLARS (LP, soundtrack) | 30 |
| 68 | RCA Victor RD 7994 | A FISTFUL OF DOLLARS/FOR A FEW DOLLARS MORE/THE GOOD, THE BAD AND THE UGLY (LP, soundtrack) | 15 |
| 68 | United Artists (S)ULP 1197 | THE GOOD, THE BAD AND THE UGLY (LP, soundtrack) | 15 |
| 69 | United Artists UAS 29005 | A PROFESSIONAL GUN (LP, soundtrack) | 25 |
| 70 | CBS 70067 | LOVE CIRCLE (LP, soundtrack) | 50 |
| 70 | MCA MKPS 2013 | TWO MULES FOR SISTER SARA (LP, soundtrack) | 30 |
| 72 | United Artists UAS 29345 | A FISTFUL OF DYNAMITE (LP, soundtrack) | 40 |

## ERIC MORRIS
| | | | |
|---|---|---|---|
| 61 | Starlite ST45 052 | Search The World/Buster's Shack | 40 |
| 61 | Blue Beat BB 53 | Humpty Dumpty/Corn Bread And Butter (as Eric 'Humpty Dumpty' Morris & Drumbago All Stars; [B-side actually by Drumbago All Stars]) | 20 |
| 62 | Blue Beat BB 74 | My Forty-Five/I've Tried Everybody (as Eric 'Humpty Dumpty' Morris & Drumbago All Stars) | 20 |
| 62 | Blue Beat BB 81 | Sinners Repent And Pray/Now And Forever More (B-side act. by Alton Ellis) | 20 |
| 62 | Blue Beat BB 83 | Money Can't Buy Life (with Buster's Group)/A. ELLIS: True Love | 20 |
| 62 | Blue Beat BB 105 | Pack Up Your Troubles/Oh What A Smile Can Do (with D. Cosmo & Drumbago's All Stars) | 20 |
| 62 | Blue Beat BB 115 | G.I. Lady/Going To The River | 20 |
| 62 | Blue Beat BB 128 | Over The Hills/Lazy Woman (with Buster's Group) | 20 |
| 62 | Blue Beat BB 137 | Miss Peggy's Grandmother/BUSTER'S GROUP: Megaton | 20 |
| 62 | Blue Beat BB 140 | Seven Long Years/For Your Love | 20 |
| 63 | Blue Beat BB 153 | Lonely Blue Boy/PRINCE BUSTER: Oh We | 22 |
| 63 | Blue Beat BB 184 | Sweet Love/BUSTER, DEREK, ERIC: Country Girl | 15 |
| 64 | Blue Beat BB 218 | Love Can Break A Man/Worried People | 20 |
| 64 | Blue Beat BB 273 | Stitch In Time/For Ever | 20 |
| 64 | Black Swan WI 412 | Sampson/BABA BROOKS: Jelly Beans | 30 |
| 64 | Black Swan WI 414 | Solomon Grundie/BABA BROOKS: Key To The City | 40 |
| 64 | Black Swan WI 433 | Supper In The Gutter/Words Of My Mouth | 20 |
| 64 | Black Swan WI 439 | River Come Down/Seek And You'll Find | 20 |
| 64 | Black Swan WI 445 | Home Sweet Home/LESTER STERLING: '64 Special | 25 |
| 64 | Island WI 142 | Penny-Reel/DUKE REID'S GROUP: Darling When (B-side act. Dotty & Bonnie) | 35 |
| 64 | Island WI 147 | Mama No Fret/FRANKIE ANDERSON: Santa Lucia (B-side w/Roland Alphonso) | 20 |
| 64 | Island WI 150 | Drop Your Sword/Catch A Fire (B-side actually by Roland Alphonso) | 25 |
| 64 | Island WI 151 | What A Man Doeth/DUKE REID'S GROUP: Rude Boy (B-side actually by Baba Brooks) | 25 |
| 64 | Port-O-Jam PJ 4006 | Oh My Dear/Lena Belle | 25 |
| 64 | Rio R 39 | Little District/True And Just | 25 |
| 64 | Rio R 48 | Live As A Man/Man Will Rule | 25 |
| 65 | Rio R 72 | By The Sea/I Wasn't Around | 25 |
| 65 | Island WI 177 | Drop Your Sword/Catch A Fire | 25 |
| 65 | Island WI 183 | Love Can Make A Mansion (actually "Love Can Break A Man")/ Ungodly People | 15 |
| 65 | Island WI 185 | Suddenly/Many Long Years | 25 |
| 65 | Island WI 199 | Fast Mouth/The Harder They Come | 18 |
| 65 | Island WI 234 | Children Of Today/BABA BROOKS: Greenfield Ska | 25 |

MINT VALUE £

| | | | |
|---|---|---|---|
| 65 | Blue Beat BB 298 | Those Teardrops/DON DRUMMOND: Ska Town | 50 |
| 66 | Blue Beat BB 349 | I'm The Greatest/BUSTER'S ALL STARS: Picket Line | 60 |
| 60s | Fab BB 30 | Humpty Dumpty (as Eric 'Humpty Dumpty' Morris & Buster All Stars)/ FOLKS BROTHERS: Carolina | 7 |
| 13 | Island WI 3163 | Terrible Mistake/Festival Time | 8 |

*(see also Monty Morris, Byron Lee & Dragonaires, Cool Sticky, Tommy McCook, Zoot Simms, Marguerita, Cool Cats)*

### HELMSLEY MORRIS
| | | | |
|---|---|---|---|
| 67 | Caltone TONE 104 | Love Is Strange/DON D. JUNIOR: Sir Pratt Special | 90 |
| 68 | Pama PM 720 | Stay Loose Mama/You Think I'm A Fool (as Hainsley Morris) | 20 |

### LIBBY MORRIS
| | | | |
|---|---|---|---|
| 56 | Parlophone R 4225 | When Liberace Winked At Me/None Of That Now | 6 |
| 65 | RCA RCA 1499 | One Of Those Songs/The Phoenix Love Theme (Senza Fine) | 5 |
| 67 | Polydor 56206 | Bye, Yum, Pum, Pum/Ballad Of yesterday's Idol | 5 |
| 66 | RCA RD 7789 | AD-LIBBY (LP) | 15 |

### MILTON MORRIS
| | | | |
|---|---|---|---|
| 69 | Upsetter US 318 | No Bread And Butter/UPSETTERS: Soulful I | 12 |

### MONTY MORRIS
| | | | |
|---|---|---|---|
| 67 | Doctor Bird DB 1067 | Play It Cool/BABA BROOKS' BAND: Open The Door | 70 |
| 67 | Doctor Bird DB 1081 | Put On Your Red Dress/BABA BROOKS' BAND: Faberge | 60 |
| 68 | Doctor Bird DB 1162 | Last Laugh/You Really Got A Hold On Me | 60 |
| 68 | Pama PM 721 | Say What You're Saying/Tears In Your Eyes | 40 |
| 68 | Nu Beat NB 007 | True Romance/BUNNY & RUDDY: Rhythm And Soul | 25 |
| 68 | Nu Beat NB 011 | Simple Simon/BUNNY & RUDDY: On The Town | 50 |
| 69 | Doctor Bird DB 1176 | Same Face/A Little Bit Of This (miscredited to Tennors) | 60 |
| 69 | Big Shot BI 513 | Deportation/Say I'm Back | 100 |
| 69 | Camel CA 12 | Can't Get No Peace/UPSETTERS: For A Few Dollars More | 60 |
| 69 | Camel CA 28 | No More Teardrops/Love Me Or Leave Me (as Monty Morris & Maples) | 50 |
| 70 | Unity UN 557 | Do It My Way/Where In The World (Are You Going) | 12 |
| 70 | Explosion EX 2016 | Higher Than The Highest Mountain/G.G. ALL STARS: Musical Shot | 12 |
| 73 | Ackee ACK 527 | I'm Ready To Go/TOMMY McCook: Flower Pot | 7 |
| 10 | Duke THB 7004 | Deep In My Soul/TOMMY MCCOOK: Reggae To Jeggae | 10 |

*(see also Eric Morris, Monty, Derrick & Patsy, Monty & Roy, Alton Ellis)*

### NAGGO MORRIS
| | | | |
|---|---|---|---|
| 79 | Hit Run DD 111 | Jah Will Explain/DOCTOR PABLO: Wicked Feel It (12") | 25 |
| 82 | S & G SG 12 | A True You Na No/Going Places (12") | 50 |
| 82 | S & G SG 23 | False Rasta/Two Time Girl (12") | 70 |
| 82 | Black Roots BR0036A | A True Them No Know/Version/Africa/Version (12") | 30 |

### RICHIE MORRIS
| | | | |
|---|---|---|---|
| 73 | Satril SAT 11 | Zimbabwa/Seasons Change | 8 |

### ROGER MORRIS
| | | | |
|---|---|---|---|
| 72 | Regal Zono. SRZA 8509 | FIRST ALBUM (LP, textured gatefold sleeve, red/silver label) | 500 |

### RUSSELL MORRIS
| | | | |
|---|---|---|---|
| 69 | Decca F 22964 | The Real Thing (Parts I & II)/It's Only A Matter Of Time | 80 |
| 70 | Decca F 23066 | Rachel/Slow Joey | 5 |

### VICTOR MORRIS
| | | | |
|---|---|---|---|
| 68 | Amalgamated AMG 813 | Now I'm Alone/Rise And Fall | 20 |

### MORRIS & MINORS
| | | | |
|---|---|---|---|
| 80 | Round MOR 1 | STATE THE OBVIOUS (EP, p/s in poly bag) | 10 |

### MORRIS & MITCH
| | | | |
|---|---|---|---|
| 57 | Decca F 10900 | Cumberland Gap/I'm Not A Juvenile Delinquent | 10 |
| 57 | Decca F 10929 | What Is A Skiffler?/The Tommy Rot Story | 6 |
| 58 | Decca F 11086 | Highway Patrol/Bird Dog | 6 |
| 68 | Trend TRE 1010 | The Magical Musherishi Tourists/Mister D.J. Man | 15 |
| 58 | Decca DFE 6486 | SIX FIVE NOTHING SPECIAL (EP) | 15 |

### MORRIS FAMILY & GOSPEL JUBILEERS
| | | | |
|---|---|---|---|
| 60 | Top Rank JAR 322 | Wake Up Jonah/He Never Complained | 7 |

### CURLEY JIM MORRISON
| | | | |
|---|---|---|---|
| 61 | Starlite ST45 065 | Air Force Blues/Didn't I Tell You | 50 |

### DOROTHY MORRISON
| | | | |
|---|---|---|---|
| 69 | Elektra EKSN 45070 | All God's Children Got Soul/Put A Little Love In Your Heart | 12 |

### PROFESSOR MORRISON'S LOLLIPOP
| | | | |
|---|---|---|---|
| 68 | London HLU 10228 | You Got The Love/Gypsy Lady | 6 |
| 69 | London HLU 10254 | Oo-Poo-Pah Susie/You Take It | 6 |

### VAN MORRISON
| | | | |
|---|---|---|---|
| 67 | London HLZ 10150 | Brown-Eyed Girl/Goodbye Baby (Baby Goodbye) | 50 |
| 70 | Warner Brothers WB 7383 | Come Running/Crazy Love | 10 |
| 70 | Warner Brothers WB 7434 | Domino/Sweet Jannie | 20 |
| 70 | Warner Brothers WB 7434 | Domino/Sweet Jannie (DJ Copy) | 35 |
| 70 | President PT 328 | Brown-Eyed Girl/Goodbye Baby (Baby Goodbye) (reissue) | 15 |
| 72 | Warner Brothers K 16210 | Jackie Wilson Said/You've Got The Power | 10 |
| 74 | London HLM 10453 | Brown-Eyed Girl/Goodbye Baby (Baby Goodbye) (2nd reissue) | 15 |
| 74 | Warner Brothers K 16392 | Caldonia/What's Up, Crazy Pup | 10 |
| 77 | Warner Brothers K 16939 | The Eternal Kansas City/Joyous Sound (p/s) | 8 |
| 77 | Warner Brothers K 16986 | Joyous Sound/Mechanical Bliss | 6 |
| 79 | Mercury 6001 121 | Bright Side Of The Road/Rolling Hills (p/s) | 5 |
| 89 | Polydor VANCD 2 | Whenever God Shines His Light (7" Version) (with Cliff Richard)/ I'd Love To Write Another Song/Cry For Home/Whenever God Shines His Light (Album Version) (CD) | 6 |
| 68 | London HA-Z 8346 | BLOWIN' YOUR MIND (LP) | 175 |

| 69 | Warner Brothers WS 1768 | ASTRAL WEEKS (LP, laminated front sleeve, flipbacks, orange label) | 250 |
|----|----|----|----|
| 71 | Warner Brothers WS 1768 | ASTRAL WEEKS (LP, green label) | 50 |
| 70 | Warner Brothers WS 1835 | MOONDANCE (LP, orange label) | 175 |
| 70 | Warner Brothers WS 1835 | MOONDANCE (LP, green label) | 20 |
| 71 | Warner Brothers WS 1884 | HIS BAND AND STREET CHOIR (LP, green label) | 35 |
| 71 | President PTLS 1045 | THE BEST OF VAN MORRISON (LP) | 15 |
| 71 | Warner Brothers K 46114 | TUPELO HONEY (LP, gatefold sleeve, green label) | 30 |
| 72 | Warner Brothers K 46172 | SAINT DOMINIC'S PREVIEW (LP, with folded insert, green label) | 35 |
| 73 | Warner Brothers K 46024 | ASTRAL WEEKS (LP, reissue, 'Burbank' label) | 25 |
| 73 | Warner Brothers K 46040 | MOONDANCE (LP, reissue, 'Burbank' label) | 15 |
| 73 | Warner Brothers K 46066 | HIS BAND AND STREET CHOIR (LP, reissue, 'Burbank' label) | 15 |
| 73 | Warner Brothers K 46242 | HARD NOSE THE HIGHWAY (LP, gatefold sleeve, 'Burbank' label) | 15 |
| 74 | London HSM 5008 | T.B. SHEETS (LP, laminated front cover) | 15 |
| 74 | Warner Brothers K 86007 | IT'S TOO LATE TO STOP NOW (2-LP, gatefold sleeve, 'Burbank' label) | 15 |
| 74 | Warner Brothers K 56068 | VEEDON FLEECE (LP, 'Burbank' label) | 20 |
| 77 | Bang 6467 625 | THIS IS WHERE I CAME IN (LP) | 15 |
| 84 | Mercury MERH 54 | A SENSE OF WONDER (LP, white label test pressings with "Crazy Jane On God") | 25 |
| 84 | Mercury MERH 54 | A SENSE OF WONDER (LP, credits but doesn't play "Crazy Jane On God") | 15 |
| 93 | Polydor 519219 | TOO LONG IN EXILE (2-LP) | 30 |
| 95 | Exile 527307 | DAYS LIKE THIS (LP) | 30 |
| 97 | Exile 5371011 | HEALING GAME (LP) | 60 |
| 99 | Simply Vinyl SVLP 253 | BACK ON TOP (LP) | 40 |
| 02 | Polydor 589177-1 | DOWN THE ROAD (2-LP) | 40 |

*(see also Them)*

# MORRISSEY

## SINGLES

| 88 | Parlophone POP 1618 | Suedehead/I Know Very Well How I Got My Name | 6 |
|----|----|----|----|
| 88 | HMV TCPOP 1618 | Suedehead/I Know Very Well How I Got My Name | 20 |
| 88 | HMV TCPOP 1618 | Suedehead/I Know Very Well How I Got My Name/Oh Well, I'll Never Learn (mispressed cassette, plays "Ordinary Boys" instead of I Know Very Well... withdrawn) | 20 |
| 88 | HMV 12 POP 1618 | Suedehead/I Know Very Well How I Got My Name/Hairdresser On Fire (12", 1st pressings in brown p/s) | 20 |
| 88 | HMV CDPOP 1618 | Suedehead/I Know Very Well How I Got My Name/Hairdresser On Fire/ Oh Well, I'll Never Learn (CD) | 25 |
| 88 | HMV POP 1619 | Everyday Is Like Sunday/Disappointed (p/s) | 7 |
| 88 | HMV 12 POP 1619 | Everyday Is Like Sunday/Sister I'm A Poet/Disappointed/ Will Never Marry (12", p/s) | 10 |
| 89 | Parlophone POP 1620 | The Last Of The Famous International Playboys/Lucky Lisp | 5 |
| 89 | HMV 12 POP 1620 | The Last Of The Famous International Playboys/Lucky Lisp/Michaels Bones (12") | 10 |
| 89 | HMV POP 1621 | Interesting Drug/Such A Little Thing Makes Such A Big Difference (p/s) | 5 |
| 89 | HMV 12 POP 1621 | Interesting Drug/Such A Little Thing Makes Such A Big Difference/ Sweet And Tender Hooligan (live) (12", p/s) | 10 |
| 89 | HMV 12 POPS 1621 | Interesting Drug/Such A Little Thing Makes Such A Big Difference (12", p/s, 1 side etched) | 12 |
| 90 | HMV POP 1622 | Ouija Board, Ouija Board/Yes, I Am Blind (p/s) | 6 |
| 90 | HMV POP 1623 | November Spawned A Monster/He Knows I'd Love To See Him (p/s) | 6 |
| 90 | HMV 12 POP 1623 | November Spawned A Monster/Girl Least Likely To/ He Knows I'd Love To See Him (12", p/s) | 10 |
| 90 | HMV POP 1624 | Piccadilly Palare/Get Off The Stage (p/s) | 8 |
| 90 | HMV 12 POP 1624 | Piccadilly Palare/At Amber/Get Off The Stage (12, p/s) | 10 |
| 91 | HMV POP 1625 | Our Frank/Journalists Who Lie (p/s) | 5 |
| 91 | HMV 12 POP 1625 | Our Frank/Journalists Who Lie/Tony The Pony (12", p/s) | 12 |
| 91 | HMV POP 1626 | Sing Your Life/That's Entertainment (p/s) | 6 |
| 91 | HMV POP 1627 | Pregnant For The Last Time/Skin Storm (p/s) | 8 |
| 91 | HMV 12 POP 1627 | Pregnant For The Last Time/Skin Storm/Cosmic Dancer (live)/ Disappointed (live) (12", p/s) | 12 |
| 92 | Parlophone R6243 | You're The One For Me, Fatty/Pashernate Love | 7 |
| 92 | Parlophone 12POP 1630 | You're The One For Me, Fatty/Pashernate Friend/There Speaks A True Friend (12") | 10 |
| 92 | HMV POP 1629 | We Hate It When Our Friends Become Successful/Suedehead (live) | 5 |
| 92 | HMV 12POP 1629 | We Hate It When Our Friends Become Successful/Suedehead/I've Changed My Plea To Guilty/Pregnant For The Last Time (12", p/s) | 12 |
| 92 | HMV CDPOP 1629 | We Hate It When Our Friends Become Successful/Suedehead/I've Changed My Plea To Guilty/Alsatian Cousin (12", p/s) | 10 |
| 92 | EMI CDMOZBX 1 | THE SINGLES COLLECTION 1986-1992 (13 x CD singles set hinged black/purple box with numbered insert) | 90 |
| 92 | Parlophone POP 1631 | Certain People I Know/Jack The Ripper | 8 |
| 92 | Parlophone POP 1631 | Certain People I Know/You've Had Her/Jack The Ripper (12") | 10 |
| 94 | Parlophone R 6372 | The More You Ignore Me, The Closer I Get/Used To Be A Sweet Boy (poster, numbered p/s) | 7 |
| 94 | Parlophone 12R6372 | The More You Ignore Me, The Closer I Get/Used To Be A Sweet Boy/I'd Love To (poster, numbered p/s) | 10 |
| 94 | Parlophone RDJ 6372 | The More You Ignore, Me The Closer I Get/Used To Be A Sweet Boy (yellow p/s) | 12 |
| 94 | Parlophone R6383 | Hold On To Your Friends/Moonriver (numbered p/s) | 8 |
| 94 | Parlophone 12 R6383 | Hold Onto Your Friends/Moonriver (12", gatefold sleeve) | 15 |
| 95 | Parlophone R 6400 | Boxers/Have-A-Go Merchant (p/s) | 8 |
| 95 | Parlophone 12R 6400 | Boxers/Have-A-Go Merchant/Whatever Happens. I Love You (12") | 12 |
| 95 | RCA 74321332947 | Boy Racer/London (Live Version) (p/s) | 10 |
| 95 | Parlophone R6243 | Sunny/Black-Eyed Susan | 10 |
| 95 | RCA Victor LC 0316 | Dagenham Dave/Nobody Loves Us (p/s) | 8 |
| 97 | Island IS 667 | Alma Matters/Heir Apparent (p/s) | 25 |
| 97 | Parlophone 12 IS 667 | Alma Matters/Heir Apparent/I Can Have Both (12") | 25 |
| 97 | Island IS 671 | Roy's Keen/Lost (p/s) | 25 |

MINT VALUE £

| Year | Catalogue | Title | Value |
|---|---|---|---|
| 97 | Island 12 IS 671 | Roy's Keen/Lost/The Edges Are No Longer Paralle (12") | 45 |
| 97 | Island IS 686 | Satan Rejected My Soul/Now I Am A Was (p/s) | 25 |
| 97 | Island 12IS 686 | Satan Rejected My Soul/Now I Am A Was/This Is Not Your Country (12") | 40 |
| 00 | EMI EMI 8872932 | SINGLES 88-91 (10 x CDs, card sleeves) | 40 |
| 01 | EMI EMI 8797452 | SINGLES 91-95 (9 X CDs, card sleeves, in box) | 40 |
| 04 | Attack ATKI002 | Irish Blood, English Heart/It's Hard To Walk Tall When You're Small | 6 |
| 04 | Attack ATKSE008 | Let Me Kiss You/Don't Make Fun Of Daddy's Voice | 6 |
| 04 | Attack ATKSE 011 | I Have Forgiven Jesus/No One Can Hold A Candle To You | 7 |
| 05 | Attack ATKSE015 | Redondo Beach/There Is A Light That Never Goes Out (live) | 5 |
| 06 | Attack ATKSE021 | First Of The Gang To Die/My Life Is A Succession Of People Saying Goodbye | 8 |
| 06 | Attack ATKTW 020 | First Of The Gang To Die (12" 4-track EP) | 10 |
| 06 | Attack ATKSE023 | I Just Want To See The Boy Happy/Speedway | 5 |
| 06 | Attack ATKTW025 | I Just Want To See The Boy Happy/Sweetie-Pie/I Want The One I Can't Have/Speedway/Late Night, Maudlin Street (12" picture disc, 1,000 only) | 10 |
| 06 | Attack ATKSE021 | In The Future When All's Well/Christian Dior | 7 |
| 08 | Decca 20003 | All You Need Is Me/Drive-In Saturday | 5 |
| 08 | Decca F20004 | All You Need Is Me/My Dearest Love | 5 |
| 09 | Decca F20006/Polydor 4781539 | I'm Throwing My Arms Around Paris/Death Of A Disco Dancer ('naked' band inner) | 8 |
| 09 | Polydor 4781877 | Something Is Squeezing My Soul/I Keep Mine Hidden | 5 |
| 12 | EMI/Liberty 10LBF15461 | Suedehead (Mael Mix)/We'll Let You Know (live)/Now My Heart Is Full (live) (picture disc, stickered) | 12 |

## ALBUMS

| Year | Catalogue | Title | Value |
|---|---|---|---|
| 90 | HMV CLP 3788 | BONA DRAG (LP) | 20 |
| 91 | EMI CSD 3789 | KILL UNCLE (LP, gatefold) | 20 |
| 92 | HMV CSD 3790 | YOUR ARSENAL (LP) | 40 |
| 93 | HMV CSD 3791 | BEETHOVEN WAS DEAF (LP) | 25 |
| 94 | Parlophone/EMI PCSD 148 | VAUXHALL AND I (LP, gatefold) | 70 |
| 95 | RCA Victor 74321299531 | SOUTHPAW GRAMMAR (LP, with limited edition booklet) | 70 |
| 95 | RCA 29953 1 | SOUTHPAW GRAMMAR (LP) | 50 |
| 95 | Parlophone PCS 7374 | BONA DRAG (LP, reissue) | 20 |
| 95 | Parlophone PCS 7375 | KILL UNCLE (LP, reissue) | 20 |
| 95 | Parlophone PCS 7376 | VIVA HATE (LP, reissue) | 20 |
| 97 | Island ILPS 8059 | MALADJUSTED (LP) | 40 |
| 97 | EMI EMC 2771 | SUEDEHEAD: THE BEST OF MORRISSEY (2-LP, gatefold) | 50 |
| 97 | Parlophone PCSD 163 | WORLD OF MORRISSEY (LP, classic yellow/black Parlophone label) | 50 |
| 04 | Sanctuary ATKLP 001 | YOU ARE THE QUARRY (LP, 5,000 only) | 20 |
| 06 | Attack ATKLP 016 | RINGLEADER OF THE TORMENTORS (LP, gatefold) | 40 |
| 09 | Polydor/Decca SKL6014/4781581 | YEARS OF REFUSAL (LP) | 20 |
| 10 | Major Minor SMLP70 | BONA DRAG (2-LP, 20th aniversary edition, inners, poster) | 20 |

## PROMOS

| Year | Catalogue | Title | Value |
|---|---|---|---|
| 88 | Factory FA 244+ | I Know Very Well How I Got My Note Wrong (7" promo, as Vincent Gerrard and Stephen Patrick, 1,000 only) | 50 |
| 88 | Factory FACD 244+ | I Know Very Well How I Got My Note Wrong (CD promo, as Vincent Gerrard and Stephen Patrick, 1,000 only) | 40 |
| 88 | HMV 12POP DJ 1618 | Suedehead/I Know Very Well How I Got My Name/Hairdresser On Fire (12" promo) | 25 |
| 88 | HMV 12 POP DJ 1619 | Everyday Is Like A Sunday (12", promo, 1-sided) | 20 |
| 89 | Parlophone POP 1620 | The Last Of The Famous International Playboys/Lucky Lisp (test pressing with different version of Lucky Lisp to official release - matrixes A-1U-1-1/B-1U-1-1 | 200 |
| 89 | HMV 12POP DJ 1620 | The Last Of The Famous International Playboys/Lucky Lisp/Michaels Bones (12" promo) | 20 |
| 89 | EMI SPM 29 | Interesting Drug/Such A Little Thing Makes Such A Big Difference (12" die cut red sleeve, promo) | 15 |
| 89 | EMI SPM 29 | Interesting Drug/etched B side (12", die cut black sleeve, promo) | 60 |
| 90 | HMV (No Cat. No) | November The Second (12" promo, white label 'Dance Mix' destroyed on order of Morrissey, i known copy) | 2000 |
| 90 | Parlophone 12POPDJ 1623 | November Spawned A Monster/He Knows I'd Love To See Him/ Girl Least Likely To (12" promo) | 30 |
| 89 | Parlophone 12POPDJ 1622 | Ouija Board, Ouija Board/Yes, I Am Blind/East West (12" A label promo) | 30 |
| 90 | HMV POPDJ 1624 | Piccadilly Palare/Get Off The Stage (promo, in die-cut HMV sleeve) | 35 |
| 91 | Parlophone POPDJ1625 | Our Frank/Journalists Who Lie (red 'A' label promo in die-cut retro sleeve) | 200 |
| 91 | HMV POP DJ 1626 | Sing Your Life/That's Entertainment (promo, die-cut HMV sleeve) | 35 |
| 91 | HMV POP DJ1627 | Pregnant For The TIme Last/Skin Storm (promo) | 50 |
| 91 | HMV POPDJ1628 | My Love Life/I've Changed My Plea To Guilty ('A' label promo in die cut sleeve) | 80 |
| 92 | HMV POP DJ 1630 | You're The One For Me, Fatty/You're The One For Me, Fatty (10", A-side plays at 45rpm, B-side at 78rpm, die-cut sleeve) | 40 |
| 92 | HMV POP DJ 1629 | We Hate It When Our Friends Become Successful/We Hate It When Our Friends Become Successful (10", A-side plays at 45rpm, B-side at 78rpm, die-cut sleeve) | 40 |
| 92 | HMV POPDJ 1631 | Certain People I Know/Jack The Ripper (die-cut 'Moz' p/s, 300 only) | 175 |
| 93 | Parlophone POPDJ1632 | Jack The Ripper/Sister I'm A Poet (promo in p/s) | 25 |
| 93 | HMV POPDJ 1632 | Jack The Ripper/Sister I'm A Poet (p/s) | 12 |
| 94 | Parlophone RDJ 6372 | The More You Ignore Me The Closer I Get/Used to Be A Sweet Boy ('photographer' sleeve) | 45 |
| 94 | Parlophone CDRDJ 6372 | The More You Ignore, Me The Closer I Get (CD, with '45rpm' logo on disc, withdrawn) | 45 |
| 94 | Parlophone R 6383 | Hold Onto Your Friends/Moonriver (promo in different p/s, 150 only) | 100 |
| 95 | Parlophone RDJ 6400 | Have-A-Go Merchant/Whatever Happens, I Love You (p/s) | 25 |
| 95 | Parlophone CDRDJ 6400 | Have-A-Go Merchant/Whatever Happens, I Love You (CD, 'skinhead' card p/s) | 25 |
| 95 | Parlophone/EMI RDJ 6400 | Have-A-Go Merchant/Whatever Happens, I Love You p/s, promo for unreleased single) | 75 |
| 95 | RCA SOLO 1 | OUTSIDE TOUR SAMPLER (CD promo features Boy Racer) | 60 |
| 04 | Sanctuary (No Cat. No) | YOU ARE THE QUARRY (CD-R interview promo) | 35 |

| | | | |
|---|---|---|---|
| 11 | Stateside SS 2242 | Glamorous Glue (2011 remaster)/VINCE EAGER: The World's Loneliest Man (Retro A label 'Stateside' promo in die-cut 'Stateside' sleeve, 150 only) | 150 |

*(see also Smiths, Durutti Column)*

**DICK MORRISSEY**

| | | | |
|---|---|---|---|
| 61 | 77' LEU 12/8 | HAVE YOU HEARD? (LP) | 350 |
| 61 | Fontana TFL 5149 | IT'S MORRISSEY MAN! (LP) | 400 |
| 67 | Mercury 20093 | HERE AND NOW AND SOUNDING GOOD (LP) | 300 |
| 67 | Mercury 20077MCL | STORM WARNING (LP) | 350 |

*(see also If)*

**MORRISSEY & SIOUXSIE**

| | | | |
|---|---|---|---|
| 94 | Parlphone R 6365 | Interlude/Interlude (Extended) | 8 |
| 94 | Parlophone 12R 6365 | Interlude/Interlude (Extended)/Interlude (Instrumental) (12") | 15 |

**BUDDY MORROW & HIS ORCHESTRA**

| | | | |
|---|---|---|---|
| 53 | HMV 7M 145 | Heap Big Beat/I Can't Get Started | 6 |
| 53 | HMV 7M 151 | I Can't Get Started/Heap Big Beat (reissue) | 6 |
| 53 | HMV 7M 162 | Dragnet/Your Mouth's Got A Hole In It | 8 |
| 54 | HMV 7M 216 | Knock On Wood (with Shaye Cogan)/All Night Long | 10 |
| 60 | RCA RCA 1167 | Staccato's Theme/Scraunchy | 6 |
| 60 | RCA RCX 174 | IMPACT (EP) | 10 |

**ELLA MAE MORSE**

| | | | |
|---|---|---|---|
| 55 | Capitol CL 14223 | Bring Back My Baby To Me/Lovey Dovey | 50 |
| 55 | Capitol CL 14303 | Smack Dab In The Middle/Yes, Yes I Do | 50 |
| 55 | Capitol CL 14332 | Livin', Livin', Livin'/Heart Full Of Hope | 40 |
| 55 | Capitol CL 14341 | Razzle-Dazzle/Ain't That A Shame (with Big Dave & His Music) | 100 |
| 55 | Capitol CL 14341 | Razzle-Dazzle/Ain't That A Shame (with Big Dave & His Music) (78) | 25 |
| 55 | Capitol CL 14362 | Seventeen/Piddily Patter Song (with Big Dave & His Music) | 100 |
| 55 | Capitol CL 14362 | Seventeen/Piddily Patter Song (with Big Dave & His Music) (78) | 25 |
| 55 | Capitol CL 14376 | Birmin'ham/An Occasional Man | 40 |

*(The 45s listed above were originally issued with triangular centres; later round-centres issues are worth around half to two-thirds of these values.)*

| | | | |
|---|---|---|---|
| 56 | Capitol CL 14508 | When Boy Kiss Girl (It's Love)/Sing-Ing-Ing-Ing | 30 |
| 56 | Capitol CL 14572 | Rock And Roll Wedding/Down In Mexico | 40 |
| 56 | Capitol CL 14572 | Rock And Roll Wedding/Down In Mexico (78) | 20 |
| 57 | Capitol CL 14726 | What Good'll It Do Me/Mister Money Maker | 20 |
| 57 | Capitol CL 14760 | I'm Gone/Sway Me | 20 |
| 55 | Capitol EAP1 513 | BARRELHOUSE BOOGIE AND THE BLUES (EP) | 15 |
| 54 | Capitol LC 6687 | BARRELHOUSE BOOGIE AND THE BLUES (10" LP) | 20 |

*(see also 'Tennessee' Ernie Ford)*

**ELLA MAE MORSE & FREDDIE SLACK**

| | | | |
|---|---|---|---|
| 67 | Ember SPE 6605 | ROCKIN' BREW (LP) | 25 |

**MORTA SKULD**

| | | | |
|---|---|---|---|
| 93 | Peaceville CC 4 | Sacrificial Rite/VITAL REMAINS: Amulet Of The Conquering (clear vinyl, p/s) | 15 |
| 93 | Deaf DEAF 11 | DYING REMAINS (LP) | 25 |
| 94 | Deaf DEAF 15 | HUMANITY FADES (LP) | 20 |

**MORTICIANS**

| | | | |
|---|---|---|---|
| 87 | Tin Soldier TIN 1 | FREAK OUT WITH THE MORTICIANS (LP) | 20 |

**MORTIMER**

| | | | |
|---|---|---|---|
| 67 | Philips BF 1664 | Dedicated Music Man/To Understand Someone | 10 |

**AZIE MORTIMER**

| | | | |
|---|---|---|---|
| 60 | London HLX 9237 | Lips/Wrapped Up In A Dream | 100 |

**MIKE MORTON CONGREGATION**

| | | | |
|---|---|---|---|
| 70 | Plexium PXM 19 | Burning Bridges/You Gotta Be Mine | 15 |

**LIONEL MORTON**

| | | | |
|---|---|---|---|
| 67 | Philips BF 1578 | What To Do With Laurie/I'll Just | 7 |
| 67 | Philips BF 1607 | First Love Never Dies/Try Not To Cry | 7 |
| 69 | RCA RCA 1875 | Waterloo Road/Floral Street | 7 |
| 72 | Cube BUG 24 | What A Woman Does/Listen To The Music | 6 |
| 75 | Beeb 011 | Don't Let Life Get You Down/Play Away | 7 |

*(see also Four Pennies)*

**MANDY MORTON (BAND)**

| | | | |
|---|---|---|---|
| 79 | Banshee BANS 791 | Song For Me (Music Prince)/Little Inbetween (with Spriguns) | 15 |
| 80 | Polydor 2382 101 | Ghost Of Christmas Past/Black Nights (p/s) | 6 |
| 78 | Banshee BAN 1011 | MAGIC LADY (LP, with lyric insert, 1,000 only) | 350 |
| 78 | Banshee BAN 1011 | MAGIC LADY (LP, with lyric insert, blue vinyl, 20 only) | 600 |
| 80 | Polydor 2382 101 | SEA OF STORMS (LP, solo, with insert) | 70 |
| 83 | Banshee | VALLEY OF LIGHT (LP, private pressing) | 100 |

**MORWELLS**

| | | | |
|---|---|---|---|
| 75 | Sir Jessus JES 4 | Come On Little Girl/Version '75 | 15 |
| 79 | Attack TACK 5 | Kingston Twelve Tuffie/PRINCE JAMMY: Jammin' For Survival (12") | 12 |
| 79 | Greensleeves GRED 17 | Thief A Dub (12") | 40 |
| 77 | Burning Sounds BS 1006 | CRAB RACE (LP) | 50 |
| 79 | Bushays BFMLP 100 | COOL RUNNING (LP) | 35 |
| 80 | Trojan TRLS 193 | A1 DUB (LP) | 35 |

**MOSAIC**

| | | | |
|---|---|---|---|
| 71 | Parlophone R5928 | Blue Bird/Bird Of Fire | 15 |

**MOSAICS**

| | | | |
|---|---|---|---|
| 66 | Columbia DB 7990 | Let's Go Drag Racing/Now That You're Here | 35 |

MINT VALUE £

**HARRY MOSCO**
80   Samba SA003      Step On/Sexy Dancer (12") ............................................................ 20

**MOSCOVITE FIVE**
82   In Phaze      WINTER WEEKENDS (cassette) .......................................................... 20

**ADRIAN MOSELY**
68   Redcar RC001      Silent Night/Ellusive Face ............................................................. 60

**JOSHUA MOSES**
78   More Cut MCT 6001      Africa Is Our Land/Home (12", die-cut p/s) ...................................... 70

**PABLO MOSES**
75   Treble C CCC 01      I Man A Grasshopper/Grasshopper (Part 2) ...................................... 20
75   Treble C CCC 09      Blood Money/Version ................................................................... 20
76   Lizzard 001      We Should Be In Angola/Dubbing In Angola ..................................... 20
76   Klik KL 625      Give I Fe I Name/Version .............................................................. 25
80   Island 12WIP      Dubbing Is A Must/Revolutionary Step (12") ...................................... 8
82   Island 10WIP 6781      Proverbs Extractions/Music Is My Desire (10") ................................... 25
77   Klik KLP 9026      REVOLUTIONARY DREAM (LP) ........................................................ 35
78   Different GETL 104      REVOLUTIONARY DREAM (LP) ........................................................ 50
             ..................................................................................... 20

**MOSFETS**
82   Sub SUB 1      The Great War/Power Games (p/s) ................................................. 60

**MOSIAH**
79   Big SOLD 6      Rumours Of War/Channel Dub ....................................................... 35

**MOSKOW**
78   Moskow SRS 2103      Man From U.N.C.L.E./White Black (p/s) ............................................. 8
79   Rialto TREB 107      Man From U.N.C.L.E./Too Much Commotion (reissue in different p/s) ...... 5

**MOSQUITOS**
83   Discovery DIX 003      How Could They Know/Somethin Outa Nothin (p/s) ............................... 7

**MOSS**
06   Rise Above RISE7/085 5      MOSS: Maimed & Slaughtered/THE PLAGUE OF GENTLEMEN: Rainbow Demon (test pressings only) ........................................................................... 100
09   Rise Above RISE10/110      TOMBS OF THE BLIND DRUGGED (12" EP) ........................................ 12
08   Rise Above RISELP 108      SUB TEMPULUM (2-LP) ................................................................ 25

**BILL MOSS**
69   Pama PM 765      Sock It To 'Em Soul Brother (Parts 1 & 2) ....................................... 15
70   Pama PM 796      Number One/MOHAWKS: Lanscape ................................................ 20

**BUDDY MOSS**
60s   Kokomo K 1003      GEORGIA BLUES VOLUME 2 (LP) ..................................................... 50

**JENNY MOSS**
63   Columbia DB 7061      Hobbies/Big Boys ....................................................................... 40

**STIRLING MOSS**
60   HMV 7EG 8583      MOTOR RACING WITH STERLING MOSS (EP) ...................................... 10

**TEDDY MOSS/JOSH WHITE**
62   Jazz Collector JEL 5      THE MALE BLUES (EP) ................................................................. 10

**GERRY MORRIS**
72   York SYK 525      Come On Home/Nothing To Declare .............................................. 20
73   York SYK 557      Sunlove/Only The Beginning ........................................................ 30
73   York FYK 415      ONLY THE BEGINNING (LP) ......................................................... 150

**MOST**
79   SRT SRTS/CUS/570      Carefree/In And Out (1,000 only stamped lyric insert) ........................ 60

**ABE MOST OCTET**
55   London RE-P 1028      PRESENTING THE ABE MOST OCTET (EP) .......................................... 20

**MOST DOMINANT**
93   Kold Sweat KSEP210      PUSHED TO DA LIMIT (EP) ........................................................... 15

**MICKIE MOST (& GEAR)**
63   Decca F 11664      Mr. Porter/Yes Indeed I Do .......................................................... 30
63   Columbia DB 7117      The Feminine Look/Shame On You Boy ........................................... 15
63   Columbia DB 7180      Sea Cruise/It's A Little Bit Hot ..................................................... 15
64   Columbia DB 7245      Money Honey/That's Alright (as Mickey Most & Gear) ........................ 20
*(see also Most Brothers)*

**MOST BROTHERS**
57   Decca F 10968      Whistle Bait/I'm Comin' Home ..................................................... 20
58   Decca F 10998      Whole Lotta Woman/Teen Angel ................................................... 20
58   Decca F 11040      Don't Go Home/Dottie ............................................................... 20
*(see also Mickie Most, Alex Murray)*

**MOTHER EARTH**
69   Mercury MF 1081      I Did My Part/Goodnight Melda Grebe The Telephone Company Has Cut Us Off.......... 8
71   Reprise K 14089      Temptation Took Control Of Me/I'll Be Long Gone ............................... 5
68   Mercury SMCL 20143      LIVING WITH THE ANIMALS (LP) ................................................... 25

**MOTHER FREEDOM BAND**
77   All Platinum 6146326      Beautiful Summer Day/Flick Of the Wrist .......................................... 20

**MOTHER LIZA**
83   Vista VSLP 2005      MOTHER LIZA MEETS PAPA TOLLO (TULLO) (LP) ................................ 15

**MOTHER NATURE (1)**
71   B & C CB 166      Orange Days And Purple Nights/Where Did She Go ............................ 12
72   Kingdom KV8003      Once There Was A Time/Clear Blue Sky ........................................... 10

**MOTHER NATURE (2)**
84   Ariwa ARILP 017      A BREATH OF FRESH AIR (LP) ...................................................... 15

## MOTHER NATURES CHILDREN
77   President PT468          Money Back Ride/Rollin Down ............................................................ 10

## MOTHER YOD
97   Prescription DRUG 1     MOTHER YOD (LP, 99 copies only) ................................................... 25

## MOTHERLIGHT
69   Morgan Bluetown BT 5003   BOBAK, JONS, MALONE (LP) ........................................................ 600
88   Morgan Blue Town BT5008   BOBAK, JOHNS, MALONE (LP, reissue) ......................................... 35
*(see also Will Malone [Voice Band], Orange Bicycle)*

## MOTHERLODE
69   Buddah 201 064          When I Die/Hard Life ...................................................................... 6
69   Buddah 2318 043         WHEN I DIE (LP) ............................................................................ 15

## MOTHER'S RUIN
81   Spectra SPC 1           Streetfighters/Leaving You (in p/s) ............................................... 55
81   Spectra SPC 1           Streetfighters/Leaving You ........................................................... 40
82   Spectra SPC 6           Street Lights/Turn A Corner (p/s) ................................................. 20
82   Spectra SPC 7           Say It's Not True/It's Illogical (p/s) ............................................... 35

## MOTHER'S SONS
70   J-Dan JDN 4415          I Want To Tell The World/Underground Man .................................. 6

## MOTHMEN
79   Absurd ABSURD 6         Does It Matter Irene?/Please Let Go (p/s) ...................................... 6
81   Do It DUN 12            Show Me Your House And Car/People People (p/s, deleted after 1 day) ... 8
81   Do It DUNIT 12          Show Me Your House And Car/People People (12", p/s, deleted after 1 day) ... 10
81   Do It DUN 14            Temptation/People People (p/s) ................................................... 5
82   Do It DUN 19            Wadada/As They Are (p/s) ............................................................ 5
80s  On-U-Sound LP 2         PAY ATTENTION (LP) ...................................................................... 15
*(see also Alberto Y Lost Trios Paranoias)*

## MOTHS
69   Deroy                  MOTHS (LP, private pressing in plain white sleeve) ......................... 500

## MOTIFFE
72   Deroy 777              MOTIFFE (LP, private pressing in hand-illustrated white sleeve) ...... 300

## MOTIFS
82   MM1                    Shadow Of Fear/On The Inside ...................................................... 50

## MOTION
79   DD Records DDLP04       MOTION (LP) ................................................................................. 40
*(see also Aswad)*

## MOTION PICTURES
80   STAT 100               Twisted Avenues/Unknown Quantity .............................................. 8

## MOTIONS
66   Pye International 7N 25390   Stop Your Crying/Every Step I Take ........................................... 25

## MOTIVATION
68   Direction 58-3248       Come On Down/Little Man ............................................................. 35

## MOTIVES
80   Romantic RR 0001        King Of The Dub/Lies And Stories .................................................. 15

## FRANK MOTLEY & KING HERBERT
99   Jazzman JM 002          Ya Ya/Ooga Boogaloo (as Frank Motley & The Bridge Crossing) ...... 10
98   Jazzman JMANLP 001      CANADA'S MESSAGE TO THE METERS (THE BEST OF...) (LP) .......... 20

## MOTLEY CREW (1)
68   MJB BEV 429             MOTLEY CREW (EP, hand made sleeve) ........................................ 25

## MOTLEY CREW (2)
80   Cherrys CHERRYS 1       City Girl/Don't Start Me Talkin .................................................... 8

## MÖTLEY CRÜE
84   Elektra E 9756T         Looks That Kill/Piece Of The Action/Live Wire (12", p/s with free tattoo) ... 15
84   Elektra E 9756TP        Looks That Kill/Piece Of The Action/Live Wire (12", picture disc) ...... 20
84   Elektra E 9732T         Too Young To Fall In Love/Take Me To The Top (12", p/s, with poster) ... 15
86   Elektra EKR 16TP        Smokin' In The Boys' Room/Use It Or Lose It (mask-shaped pic disc & sticker) ... 15
86   Elektra EKR 33P         Smokin' In The Boys' Room/Home Sweet Home (2 different interlocking mask-shaped picture disc set) ... 20
86   Elektra EKR 33T         Smokin' In The Boys' Room/Home Sweet Home/Shout At The Devil (12", p/s with poster) ... 20
87   Elektra EKR 59V         Girls, Girls, Girls/Sumthin' For Nuthin' ('X-rated' stickered p/s, 3,000 only) ... 10
87   Elektra EKR 59TP        Girls, Girls, Girls/Sumthin' For Nuthin'/Smokin' In The Boys' Room (12", picture disc) .. 10
88   Elektra EKR 65TB        You're All I Need/Wild Side/Home Sweet Home/Looks That Kill (12", box set with poster, tour pass & patch) ... 10
89   Elektra EKR97P          Dr. Feelgood/Sticky Sweet (shaped picture disc) ......................... 12
89   Elektra EKR 109P        Without You/Lime Wire (Original Leather Mix) (Shaped picture disc) ... 12
83   Elektra 9602 89-1       SHOUT AT THE DEVIL (LP, with bonus 12" picture disc & poster) ...... 18

## MOTORCYCLE RIDE
93   Fierce FRIGHT 060       Union City Blue/Atomic (p/s) ........................................................ 12
*(see also Ride)*

## MOTORDAMN
07   DJB66613               Over The Top (MotorDamn)/Ballroom Blitz (The Damned with Lemmy) ... 10
*(see also Damned, Motorhead)*

## MOTÖRHEAD
76   Stiff BUY 9             Leaving Here/White Line Fever (Unreleased, but included in Stiff box set of first 10 singles and some also sold via mail order) ... 40
77   Stiff BUY 9             Leaving Here/White Line Fever (mispressing, A side plays Neat Neat Neat by THE DAMNED) ... 100
77   Chiswick S 13           Motörhead/City Kids (p/s) ............................................................ 20

| | | | |
|---|---|---|---|
| 77 | Chiswick S 13A | Motörhead/City Kids (12", p/s) | 20 |
| 78 | Bronze BRO 60 | Louie Louie/Tear Ya Down (p/s) | 8 |
| 79 | Bronze BRO 67 | Overkill/Too Late, Too Late (p/s, iwith 'Overkill' badge) | 10 |
| 79 | Bronze BRO 67 | Overkill/Too Late, Too Late (p/s) | 5 |
| 79 | Bronze 12 BRO 67 | Overkill/Too Late, Too Late (12", p/s) | 10 |
| 79 | Bronze BRO 78 | No Class/Like A Nightmare (3 different sleeves) | 50 |
| 79 | Bronze BRO 85 | Bomber/Over The Top (p/s, on blue vinyl) | 10 |
| 79 | Big Beat NS 13 | Motörhead/City Kids (p/s, black, pink, blue, orange or white vinyl) | 7 |
| 80 | Big Beat NSP 13 | Motörhead/City Kids (p/s, black & white picture disc) | 12 |
| 80 | Big Beat NSP 13 | Motörhead/City Kids (p/s, blue & white picture disc) | 15 |
| 80 | Bronze BRO 92 DJ | Leaving Here (live)/Stone Dead Forever (live) (2-track promo for Golden Years EP, no p/s) | 40 |
| 80 | Bronze BRO 106 | Ace Of Spades/DIrty Love (p/s) | 10 |
| 80 | Bronze BROX 106 | Ace Of Spades/Dirty Love (12", 'Xmas' sleeve) | 10 |
| 82 | Bronze BRO 146 | Iron Fist/Remember Me I'm Gone (p/s, blue vinyl) | 12 |
| 82 | Bronze BRO 146 | Iron Fist/Remember Me I'm Gone (p/s, red vinyl) | 6 |
| 82 | Bronze BRO 151 | Stand By Your Man/No Class/Masterplan (p/s, as Lemmy & Wendy O. Williams) | 8 |
| 83 | Bronze BRO 165 | I Got Mine/Turn You Round Again (p/s) | 5 |
| 83 | Bronze BRO 167 | Shine/Hoochie Coochie Man (live) (p/s) | 7 |
| 83 | Bronze BROX 167/BROX 92 | Shine/Hoochie Coochie Man (live)/Don't Need Religion (live)/ THE GOLDEN YEARS (12", p/s, stickered, shrinkwrapped double pack) | 18 |
| 83 | Lyntone LYN 4383 | In Their Own Words/BRONZ: Taken By Storm (flexi free with Kerrang! mag) | 10 |
| 84 | Bronze BRO 185 | Killed By Death/Under The Knife (p/s) | 5 |
| 84 | Bronze BROP 185 | Killed By Death/Under The Knife (logo skull-shaped picture disc) | 20 |
| 84 | Bronze BROX 185 | Killed By Death (Full Length Version)/Under The Knife/Under The Knife (12", stickered p/s, with poster) | 15 |
| 84 | Bronze BROP 185 | Killed By Death/Under The Knife (logo skull-shaped picture disc, mispressing, A side plays Banana Banana and B side plays Bo Diddley Goes East by KING KURT)! | 100 |
| 88 | GWR GWR 15 | Ace Of Spades/Dogs/Traitor (sold at concerts & through fan club, no p/s) | 20 |
| 90 | Epic 656578 0 | The One To Sing The Blues/Dead Man's Hand (shaped picture disc) | 15 |
| 93 | WGAF 101 | Ace Of Spades/Tear Ya Down/Over The Top/Too Late Too Late (12" picture disc) | 10 |
| 80 | Big Beat SWT 61 | BEER DRINKERS EP (12", p/s, blue vinyl) | 10 |
| 80 | Big Beat SWT 61 | BEER DRINKERS EP (12", p/s, pink or orange vinyl) | 15 |
| 80 | Big Beat SWT 61 | BEER DRINKERS EP (12", p/s, brown vinyl) | 40 |
| 81 | Bronze BROX 116 | ST. VALENTINES DAY MASSACRE (10" EP, with Girlschool) | 12 |
| 77 | Chiswick WIK 2 | MOTÖRHEAD (LP, black and silver sleeve with inner, 600 only) | 200 |
| 77 | Chiswick WIK 2 | MOTÖRHEAD (LP, black & white laminated sleeve with inner) | 35 |
| 77 | Chiswick CWK 3008 | MOTÖRHEAD (LP, white vinyl) | 30 |
| 78 | United Artists LBR 1004 | ON PAROLE (LP) | 15 |
| 79 | Bronze BRON 515 | OVERKILL (LP, green vinyl) | 25 |
| 79 | Bronze BRO 523 | BOMBER (LP, 3 different shades of blue vinyl) | 18 |
| 80 | Bronze BRONG 531 | ACE OF SPADES (LP, gold vinyl, stickered sleeve) | 15 |
| 80 | Big Beat WIK 2 | MOTÖRHEAD (LP, reissue, red or clear vinyl with inner sleeve) | 15 |
| 81 | Bronze BRONG 535 | NO SLEEP 'TIL HAMMERSMITH (LP, gold vinyl, stickered sleeve) | 20 |
| 84 | Bronze/Pro MOTOR 1 | NO REMORSE (2-LP, leather sleeve with inners) | 25 |
| 86 | GWR GWRLP 1 | ORGASMATRON (LP, picture disc) | 20 |
| 90 | Castle TFOLP 024 | BOMBER/ACE OF SPADES (2-LP, reissue) | 20 |
| 91 | Epic 467481-0 | 1916 (LP, picture disc, stickered PVC sleeve) | 20 |
| 91 | Epic 467481 9 | 1916 (CD, 'tour' picture disc shrinkwrapped with booklet, stickered case) | 30 |
| 92 | Receiver RRLP 005 | JAILBAT (2-LP) | 20 |
| 93 | Castle CTVLP 125 | ALL THE ACES (2-LP, gatefold) | 20 |
| 93 | Castle/Bronze CTVCD 125 | ALL THE ACES (CD, numbered promo, in box with metal skull, 10 only) | 200 |
| 00 | Metal-Is MISL 002 | THE BEST OF...(3-LP, numbered with insert & bonus exclusive live EP) | 45 |
| 04 | SPV 22325 | INFERNO (2xLP) | 18 |
| 10 | Back To Black 5326582 | ACE OF SPADES (LP, picture disc, reissue, with download card) | 15 |

*(see also Lemmy & Upsetters, Hawkwind, Girlschool, Wild Horses, Young & Moody, Rocking Vickers, Blue Goose, Motordamn, Persian Risk)*

## MOTORWAY

| | | | |
|---|---|---|---|
| 79 | Neat NEAT 01 | All I Wanna Be Is Your Romeo/It's Easy When You're Alone | 10 |

## MOTOWN SOUNDS

| | | | |
|---|---|---|---|
| 79 | Tamla Motown TMG 1143 | Space Dance/Bad Mouthin | 10 |

## MOTT THE HOOPLE

| | | | |
|---|---|---|---|
| 69 | Island WIP 6072 | Rock And Roll Queen/Road To Birmingham | 25 |
| 71 | Island WIP 6105 | Midnight Lady/The Debt (in p/s) | 18 |
| 71 | Island WIP 6105 | Midnight Lady/The Debt | 6 |
| 71 | Island WIP 6112 | Downtown/Home | 10 |
| 74 | CBS 2439 | Foxy Foxy/Trudi's Song (cherry vinyl) | 5 |
| 76 | CBS 3963 | All The Young Dudes/Roll Away The Stone (p/s) | 5 |
| 69 | Island ILPS 9108 | MOTT THE HOOPLE (LP, gatefold sleeve, pink label with white 'i' logo; with "Backsliding Fearlessly" in correct order) | 100 |
| 69 | Island ILPS 9108 | MOTT THE HOOPLE (LP, pink label; mispress with 5 alternate mixes & Road To Birmingham in place of "Backsliding Fearlessly" or one alternative mix with "Road To Birmingham", and "Rock And Roll Queen" correctly credited. This price for each copy) | 90 |
| 70 | Island ILPS 9119 | MAD SHADOWS (LP, pink label with white 'i' logo, gatefold sleeve) | 50 |
| 71 | Island ILPS 9144 | WILD LIFE (LP, gatefold, pink rim palm tree label) | 50 |
| 71 | Island ILPS 9178 | BRAIN CAPERS (LP, pink rim palm tree label & inner sleeve, with mask) | 100 |
| 71 | Island ILPS 9178 | BRAIN CAPERS (LP, pink rim palm tree label & inner sleeve, without mask) | 20 |
| 72 | CBS 65184 | ALL THE YOUNG DUDES (LP, with inner sleeve) | 30 |
| 72 | Island ILPS 9215 | ROCK AND ROLL QUEEN (LP, 'pink rim palm tree' label) | 25 |
| 73 | CBS 69038 | MOTT (LP, die-cut gatefold sleeve with plastic flap, inner sleeve, orange label, stickered) | 40 |

| | | | |
|---|---|---|---|
| 74 | CBS 569062 | THE HOOPLE (LP, with insert) | 40 |
| 80 | Island IRSP 8 | TWO MILES FROM HEAVEN (LP, early copies listing "Moving On" on rear sleeve) | 20 |

(see also Ian Hunter, At Last The 1958 Rock & Roll Show, Morgan, Mick Ronson, British Lions, Luther Grosvenor, Charlie Woolfe)

## KEN MOULE'S LONDON JAZZ CHAMBER GROUP
| | | | |
|---|---|---|---|
| 70 | Ember EMB S 275 | Mae West/Zsa Zsa Gabor (in p/s) | 15 |
| 70 | Ember EMB S 275 | Mae West/Zsa Zsa Gabor | 5 |
| 69 | Ember CJS 823 | ADAM'S RIB SUITE (LP) | 70 |

(see also London Jazz Chamber Group, Ken Moule Seven)

## KEN MOULE SEVEN
| | | | |
|---|---|---|---|
| 57 | Decca LK 4192 | KEN MOULE ARRANGES FOR (LP) | 25 |
| 58 | Decca LK 4261 | JAZZ AT TOAD HALL (LP) | 30 |

(see also London Jazz Chamber Group)

## MOULIN ROUGE
| | | | |
|---|---|---|---|
| 81 | Teesbeat TB3 | Easy/Holding Out (p/s) | 8 |

## MATTIE MOULTRIE
| | | | |
|---|---|---|---|
| 67 | CBS 202547 | That's How Strong My Love Is/The Saddest Story Ever Told | 20 |
| 67 | CBS 202547 | That's How Strong My Love Is/The Saddest Story Ever Told (DJ Copy) | 40 |

## MOUND CITY BLUE BLOWERS
| | | | |
|---|---|---|---|
| 60 | Collector JEL 1 | BLUES BLOWING JAZZ VOL. 1 (EP) | 10 |

## MOUNT KIMBIE
| | | | |
|---|---|---|---|
| 11 | Hotflush CNL 003 | CARBONATED EP (2 x 12") | 15 |
| 13 | Hotflush HF 021 | MAYBES EP (12") | 12 |
| 13 | Beat/Warp WAP 251J | You Took Your Time ()neman Remix) (12") | 30 |

## MOUNT RUSHMORE
| | | | |
|---|---|---|---|
| 68 | Dot DOT 115 | Stone Free/She's No Good To Me | 10 |

## MOUNTAIN
| | | | |
|---|---|---|---|
| 70 | Bell BLL 1112 | Mississippi Queen/The Laird | 15 |
| 70 | Bell BLL 1125 | Sittin' On A Rainbow/To My Friend | 20 |
| 71 | Island WIP 6119 | Roll Over Beethoven/Crossroader | 8 |
| 70 | Bell SBLL 133 | MOUNTAIN CLIMBING! (LP) | 25 |
| 71 | Island ILPS 9148 | NANTUCKET SLEIGHRIDE (LP, 'pink rim palm tree' label) | 20 |
| 71 | Island ILPS 9179 | FLOWERS OF EVIL (LP, 'pink rim palm tree' label) | 15 |

(see also West Bruce & Laing, Leslie West, Jolliver Arkansas)

## MOUNTAIN ASH
| | | | |
|---|---|---|---|
| 75 | Witches Bane LKLP 6036 | THE HERMIT (LP, private pressing with insert) | 200 |

## MOUNTAIN GOATS
| | | | |
|---|---|---|---|
| 02 | 4AD AD 2208 | See America Right/New Chevrolet In Flames (p/s) | 5 |
| 03 | 4AD AD 2306 | Palmcorder Yajna/Butter Teeth (p/s) | 5 |

## MOUNTAIN MEN
| | | | |
|---|---|---|---|
| 65 | Eos CE 717 | Too Many People/Without You | 250 |

## VALERIE MOUNTAIN
| | | | |
|---|---|---|---|
| 61 | Columbia DB 4660 | Go It Alone/Gentle Christ | 5 |
| 62 | Pye 7N 15450 | Some People/Yes You Did | 5 |

(see also Eagles)

## MOURNING AFTER
| | | | |
|---|---|---|---|
| 94 | Detour DR 017 | Doin' Me In/Out For The Count (p/s, 100 blue vinyl) | 6 |

## MOURNING PHASE
| | | | |
|---|---|---|---|
| 71 | Eden | MOURNING PHASE (LP, private pressing) | 200 |
| 91 | Eden EDEN 1 | EDEN (LP, reissue of "Mourning Phase") | 20 |

## MOUSE
| | | | |
|---|---|---|---|
| 73 | Sovereign SOV 122 | We Can Make It/It's Happening To Me And You | 20 |
| 74 | Sovereign SOV 127 | All The Fallen Teen Angels/Just Came Back | 12 |
| 73 | Sovereign SVNA 7262 | LADY KILLER (LP, gatefold sleeve) | 300 |

(see also Ginhouse, Ray Russell Quartet, Running Man)

## MOUSE & TRAPS
| | | | |
|---|---|---|---|
| 68 | President PT 174 | L.O.V.E. Love/Beg Borrow And Steal | 40 |
| 68 | President PT 210 | Sometimes You Just Can't Win/Crying Inside | 20 |

## MOUSEFOLK
| | | | |
|---|---|---|---|
| 80s | Tea Time SURFS UP 03 | Grannie's Cake Crisis/Mrs Marr's Daughter (foldaround p/s, with badge) | 5 |

## MOUSEHOUSE
| | | | |
|---|---|---|---|
| 79 | Fort FORT 001 | Where Young Cats Fear To Tread/When Dave Says He Has He Hasn't | 5 |

## MOUSETRAP
| | | | |
|---|---|---|---|
| 71 | Aurora AU 4324 | Susie/Greenfields | 35 |

## MOUTH
| | | | |
|---|---|---|---|
| 81 | Recreationa Records SPORT 3 | Ooh Ah Yeah/Ooh | 8 |
| 82 | Y Y20 | Who's Hot/Catch A Cab | 8 |

## MOUTH TO MOUTH
| | | | |
|---|---|---|---|
| 79 | Mouth To Mouth MT 1 | Gallery Of Dolls/Life In The Subbterrain (hand stamped labels, no p/s) | 200 |

## MOVE
| | | | |
|---|---|---|---|
| 66 | Deram DM 109 | Night Of Fear/Disturbance | 8 |
| 67 | Deram DM 117 | I Can Hear The Grass Grow/Wave The Flag And Stop The Train | 10 |
| 67 | Regal Zonophone RZ 3001 | Flowers In The Rain/(Here We Go Round) The Lemon Tree | 7 |
| 67 | Regal Zonophone | Cherry Blossom Clinic/Vote For Me (unissued) | 0 |
| 68 | Regal Zonophone RZ 3005 | Fire Brigade/Walk Upon The Water | 7 |
| 68 | Regal Zonophone RZ 3012 | Wild Tiger Woman/Omnibus | 12 |
| 69 | Regal Zonophone RZ 3015 | Blackberry Way/Something | 7 |

MINT VALUE £

| 69 | Regal Zonophone RZ 3021 | Curly/This Time Tomorrow | 7 |
| 70 | Regal Zonophone RZ 3026 | Brontosaurus/Lightnin' Never Strikes Twice | 7 |
| 70 | Fly BUG 2 | When Alice Comes Back To The Farm/What? | 5 |
| 71 | Harvest HAR 5036 | Ella James/No Time (unissued) | 0 |
| 71 | Harvest HAR 5038 | Tonight/Don't Mess Me Up | 5 |
| 71 | Harvest HAR 5043 | Chinatown/Down On The Bay | 5 |
| 72 | MagniFly ECHO 104 | Fire Brigade/I Can Hear The Grass Grow/Night Of Fear | 5 |
| 72 | Harvest HAR 5050 | California Man/Do Ya/Ella James | 5 |
| 74 | Harvest HAR 5086 | Do Ya/No Time | 5 |
| 68 | Regal Zono. TRZ 2001 | SOMETHING ELSE FROM THE MOVE (EP, 33rpm) | 75 |
| 68 | Regal Zono. LRZ 1002 | THE MOVE (LP, mono, red/silver labels with "Sold in the U.K..." text) | 150 |
| 68 | Regal Zono. SLRZ 1002 | THE MOVE (LP, stereo, red/silver labels with "Sold in the U.K..." text) | 100 |
| 68 | Regal Zono. TA-LRZ 1002 | THE MOVE (reel-to-reel, mono only) | 15 |
| 70 | Regal Zono. SLRZ 1012 | SHAZAM (LP, many with pressing flaw on track "Don't Make My Baby Blue" that makes record skip on this track, red/silver label) | 150 |
| 70 | Fly HIFLY 1 | LOOKING ON (LP, white label, 'Fly' logo) | 40 |
| 71 | Harvest SHSP 4013 | MESSAGE FROM THE COUNTRY (LP, with EMI logo on label) | 80 |
| 72 | Fly TOOFA 5/6 | THE MOVE/SHAZAM (2-LP reissue) | 18 |
| 74 | Harvest SHSP 4035 | CALIFORNIA MAN (LP) | 20 |

(see also Roy Wood, ELO, Idle Race, Trevor Burton, Nicky James Movement, Ace Kefford Stand, Grunt Futtock, Rick Price, Uglys, Charlie Wayne)

## MOVEMENT (1)
| 68 | Pye 7N 17443 | Tell Her/Something You've Got | 120 |
| 68 | Target 7N 17443 | Something You've Got/Tell Her (Irish issue) | 120 |
| 68 | Big T BIG 112 | Head For The Sun/Mister Mann | 180 |

## MOVEMENT (2)
| 80 | Ballistic TRIF 2 | No Man Is An Island/JAMDOWN PLAYERS: Levi's Choice (dubwise)/ Togetherness/ Deviate/Consolidate/Progression (12") | 30 |

## MOVERS (1)
| 65 | Ska Beat JB 191 | Jo-Anne/DON DRUMMOND: Don De Lion | 45 |

## MOVERS (2)
| 68 | Capitol CL 15562 | Birmingham/Leave Me Loose | 25 |

## MOVERS (3)
| 60s | Junior Records Ltd JR 109 | Rock Rock/Reggay Rock | 200 |

## MOVIES (2)
| 80 | Gem GEMS 20 | Love Is A Sacrifice/Fat Girl | 6 |

## MOVIE STARS
| 82 | Lansater LG10 | No Time To Kill/Heroes (no p/s) | 30 |

## MOVIETONE
| 94 | Planet PUNK 003 | She Smiled Mandarine Like/Orange Zero (p/s) | 6 |
| 94 | Planet PUNK 009 | Mono Valley/Under The 3000 Foot Red Ceiling (p/s, 1,000 only) | 5 |
| 95 | Planet PUNK 010 | MOVIETONE (LP) | 15 |
| 97 | Domino WIGLP 36 | DAY AND NIGHT (LP) | 20 |
| 00 | Domino WIGLP 79 | THE BLOSSOM FILLED STREETS (LP) | 20 |
| 03 | Domino WIGLP 131 | THE SAND AND THE STARS (LP) | 20 |

## MOVING BROTHERS
| 67 | Island WI 3049 | Darling I Love You/TOMMY McCOOK & SUPERSONICS: Saboo | 30 |
| 67 | Treasure Isle TI 7018 | Darling I Love You/TOMMY McCOOK & SUPERSONICS: Saboo (reissue) | 15 |

## MOVING ENGLAND
| 80 | English ER 001 | Moving Back/Stretching Back (Part 3) | 20 |

## MOVING FINGER
| 68 | Mercury MF 1051 | Jeremy The Lamp/Pain Of My Misfortune | 50 |
| 69 | Mercury MF 1077 | Higher And Higher/Shake And Fingerpop | 70 |
| 73 | Decca F 13406 | So Many People/We're Just As Happy As We Are | 8 |

(see also Anglians)

## MOVING VIOLATION
| 74 | Atlantic 10516 | Spinnin' Top/Wild Goose Chase | 10 |

## JUDY MOWATT
| 73 | Gayfeet GS 207 | Emergency Call/Emergency Call - Version | 8 |
| 75 | Torpedo 52 | Too Good For Me/Cry To Me | 10 |
| 80 | Grove Muzik IPR 2041 | Black Woman (feat. Joy Tulloch)/My My People (12") | 25 |

(see also Jean & Gaytones)

## IRVIN MOWREY
| 79 | Initial IRS 001 | The Queen Of Maybe/Fat City | 6 |

## MOWREY JNR. & WATSON
| 76 | Riverdale RRL 1000 | BUSKER (LP, with insert) | 30 |

## MP'S
| 80 | Moving Plastic WSP 006 | Housewives' Choice/Life On The Dole | 5 |

## MR. BLOE
| 70 | DJM DJS 216 | Groovin' With Mr. Bloe/Sinful | 6 |
| 70 | DJM DJLPS 409 | GROOVIN' WITH MR. BLOE (LP) | 18 |

(see also Harry Pitch)

## MR BROOKS
| 74 | EMI 2168 | The Family Theme/Easy Going | 10 |

## MR. BUNGLE
| 91 | London 828 276-1 | MR BUNGLE (LP, picture disc) | 40 |

## MR. CALYPSON
| 71 | Jump Up JU 40 | Mohammed Ali/SAMSON DE LARK: Undemocratic Rhodesia | 6 |

**MR CHIPPS**
77   Spiral SPF 7014    The Way I Am/Lady Elaine (no p/s) ............................................. 30

**MR CLEAN & SOUL INC**
09   Jazzman JSERATO 001    What's Going On?/Serato Conrol Tone (die-cut sleeve) ..................... 10

**MR. CONCEPT**
85   Cordelia ERICAT 009    NOVEMBER (LP) ......................................................................... 30

**MR. DYNAMITE**
67   Sue WI 4027    Sh'mon/DYNAMITE ORCHESTRA: Sh'mon (Part Two) ...................... 300

**MR. FINGERS**
88   Jack Trax 12 J TRAX 10    SLAM DANCE EP (12") ................................................................ 50
94   Black Market BMI 022 LP    BACK TO LOVE (LP) ................................................................. 35
95   Black Market BMI 024 LP    CLASSIC FINGERS (2xLP) .......................................................... 20

**MR. FLOOD'S PARTY**
71   Ember EMB S 312    Compared To What/Unbreakable Toy ........................................ 20
71   Ember EMB S 312    Compared To What/Unbreakable Toy (DJ copy) ........................ 40
75   Bulldog BD 6    Compared To What/Unbreakable Toy (reissue) .......................... 8
*(see also Mike Corbett & Jay Hirsch)*

**MR. FORD & MR. GOON-BONES**
56   London HLU 8355    Ain't She Sweet/MUZZY MARCELLINO: Mary Lou ........................ 25
*(see also Mr. Goon-Bones & Cavaliers)*

**MR FOUNDATION**
67   Studio One SO 2001    See Them A Come/KEN PARKER: Have A Good Time ..................... 60
67   Studio One SO 2003    All Rudies In Jail (actually by Zoot Sims/HORTENSE & ALTON Easy Squeeze ..... 70
68   Studio One SO 2061    Timo Oh/DUDLEY SIBLEY & PETER AUSTIN: Hole In Your Soul ..... 100
68   Studio One SO 2069    Reggae Rumble/MARCIA GRIFFITHS : You Keep Me On The Move ..... 60
69   Supreme SUP 201    Time To Pray (actually by Lloyd Robinson)/Young Budd (by Leonard Dillon) ..... 20
*(see also Sound Dimension)*

**MR. FOX**
70   Big T BIG 135    Little Woman/Join Us In Our Game ........................................... 8
70   Transatlantic TRA 226    MR FOX (LP) ........................................................................... 75
71   Transatlantic TRA 236    THE GIPSY (LP, gatefold sleeve, plaatic inner with foam opening) ..... 125
75   Transatlantic TRA 303    THE COMPLETE MR FOX (2-LP, reissue of "Mr Fox" & "The Gypsy") ..... 20
*(see also Bob Pegg, Bob & Carol Pegg)*

**MR. MO'S MESSENGERS**
67   Columbia DB 8133    Feelin' Good/The Handyman ................................................... 15

**MISTER MOST**
69   Downtown DT 409    Reggae Train/Pushwood .......................................................... 30

**MR. PINK/MR. BLONDE**
96   Resevoir BP1    Payin' The Price/Death Before Dishonour (12") ......................... 15
97   Resevoir BP2    Jamaica Crime Wave (12") ...................................................... 12

**MR. REJECT**
71   private pressing    MR. REJECT (LP) .................................................................... 40

**MR STONE**
79   Strictly Pre PRE 1    Jah Jah Higher Than I/Unbeliever (12") ................................... 45

**MR. TWISTER & TORNADOS**
63   Starlite ST45 099    Big Twist (Parts 1 & 2) ........................................................... 15

**MU**
74   United Artists UAG 29709    LEMURIAN MUSIC (LP) ..................................................... 35

**MU5**
72   Crystal CR 7015    Mrs Watson/Rain Dance ......................................................... 50

**MUCKY DUCK**
70   Deram DM314    Jefferson/Psycho's On The Run ............................................... 15

**MUD**
67   CBS 203002    Flower Power/You're My Mother (in p/s) ................................... 50
67   CBS 203002    Flower Power/You're My Mother ............................................. 35
68   CBS 3355    Up The Airy Mountain/Latter Days ........................................... 30
69   Philips BF 1775    Shangri-La/House On The Hill ................................................. 20
70   Philips 6006 022    Jumping Jehosaphat/Won't Let It Go ...................................... 20
74   Rak RAK 187    Lonely This Christmas/I Can't Stand It (p/s) .............................. 5
75   Rak RAK 194    The Secrets That You Keep/Still Watching The Clock (p/s) .......... 5
76   Rak RR 6    Tiger Feet/Oh Boy/Dynamite (p/s) ............................................ 5
76   Private Stock PVT 65    Shake It Down/Laugh, Live, Love (p/s) .............................. 5
*(see also Dum)*

**MUDHONEY**
89   Blast First BFFP 46    Halloween/SONIC YOUTH: Touch Me I'm Sick (12", with tour/gig flyer) ..... 10
95   Reprise 9362 458401    MY BROTHER THE COW (LP, with 6-track EP, [PRO S 7492]) ..... 20
*(see also Sonic Youth, Greenriver)*

**MUD HUTTERS**
79   Defensive SRTS/79/CUS 263    INFORMATION EP (paper wrap p/s) ....................... 50
79   Defensive SRTS/79/CUS 496    THE DECLARATION EP (paper wrap p/s) ............... 30
80   Defensive PACT 1    FACTORY FARMING (LP) ..................................................... 30

**MUDIE'S ALL STARS**
70   Moodisc HM 3503    Wha Who Wha - Version/G.G. RUSSELL: Wha Who Wha ........... 15
*(see also I Roy, Eternals, King Cannon, John Holt, Niney, Jolly Boys, Jo Jo Bennett)*

**MUDLARKS**
59   Columbia DB 4331    Waterloo/Mary .................................................................. 6
58   Columbia SEG 7854    THE MUDLARKS! (EP) ....................................................... 15

MINT VALUE £

## MUFF
| 71 | Mother MOT 7 | Hurdy Gurdy/Why Did You Leave Me | 15 |
| 74 | Bell Bell 1380 | Sexy Sexy Lady/Burnin' | 5 |
| 75 | UA UP 3595 | Do The Hand Jive/Discotheque King | 5 |

## MUFFIN
| 72 | Dart ART 2018 | Smokey Blues Away/Acapulco Gold | 6 |

## MUGGINS BLIGHT
| 79 | Look LK/EP 6455 | Mr Somebody/They Go Up! They Go Down!/Malcolm Where's the Talcum? (p/s) | 25 |

## MUGWUMPS
| 64 | Warner Bros WB 144 | I'll Remember Tonight/I Don't Wanna Know | 12 |
| 67 | Warner Bros W 1697 | THE MUGWUMPS - AN HISTORICAL RECORDING (LP) | 35 |
| 70 | Valiant VS 134 | THE MUGWUMPS - AN HISTORICAL RECORDING (LP, reissue) | 18 |

*(see also Mamas & Papas, Mama Cass Elliot, Lovin' Spoonful, Zalman Yanovsky)*

## BOBBY MUIR & BLUEBEATS
| 60 | Blue Beat BB 20 | Baby What You Done Me Wrong/Go Pretty Baby Go (as Blue Beats) | 12 |
| 61 | Blue Beat BB 44 | Honey Please/That's My Girl (as Bobby Kingdom & Blue Beats) | 25 |
| 62 | Blue Beat BB 77 | Brand New Automobile/Spanish Town Twist (as Bobby Kingdom & Blue Beats) | 12 |

## JAMIE MUIR & DEREK BAILEY
| 81 | Incus INCUS 41 | DART DRUG (LP) | 50 |

*(see also Derek Bailey)*

## LINDSAY MUIR'S UNTAMED
| 66 | Planet PLF 113 | Daddy Long Legs/Trust Yourself A Little Bit (initial release with plain white white sleeve) | 250 |
| 66 | Planet PLF 113 | Daddy Long Legs/Trust Yourself A Little Bit (with Planet company sleeve) | 240 |

*(see also Untamed)*

## MULCAYS
| 55 | London HLF 8188 | Harbour Lights/Dipsy Doodle | 20 |
| 54 | London REP 1016 | MERRY CHRISTMAS (EP) | 12 |

## MULDOONS
| 65 | Decca F 12164 | I'm Lost Without You/Come Back Now Baby | 30 |

## MULESKINNERS
| 65 | Fontana TF 527 | Back Door Man/Need Your Lovin' | 200 |
| 65 | Keepoint KEE-EP-7104 | MULESKINNERS (EP, private pressing, no p/s) | 750 |

*(see also Small Faces, Faces)*

## MOON MULLICAN
| 56 | Parlophone MSP 6254 | Seven Nights To Rock/Honolulu Rock-A Roll-A (with Boyd Bennett & His Rockets) | 300 |
| 56 | Parlophone R 4195 | Seven Nights To Rock/Honolulu Rock-A Roll-A (with Boyd Bennett & His Rockets) (78) | 50 |
| 59 | Parlophone GEP 8794 | COUNTRY ROUND UP (EP) | 60 |
| 50s | Parlophone CGEP 13 | MOON MULLICAN (EP, export issue) | 40 |
| 50s | Parlophone CGEP 15 | PIANO BREAKDOWN (EP, export issue, company sleeve) | 20 |

*(see also Boyd Bennett & His Rockets)*

## GERRY MULLIGAN
| 53 | Capitol LC 6621 | THE GERRY MULLIGAN TENTETTE - ROCKER (10" LP) | 15 |
| 53 | Vogue LDE 029 | THE GERRY MULLIGAN QUARTET VOL. 1 (10" LP) | 15 |
| 53 | Vogue LDE 030 | THE GERRY MULLIGAN QUARTET VOL. 2 (10" LP) | 15 |
| 53 | Vogue LDE 031 | THE GERRY MULLIGAN QUARTET VOL. 3 (10" LP) | 15 |
| 54 | Vogue LDE 075 | THE GERRY MULLIGAN QUARTET (10" LP) | 15 |
| 54 | Vogue LDE 083 | THE GERRY MULLIGAN QUARTET VOL. 4 (10" LP) | 15 |
| 54 | Esquire 20-032 | GERRY MULLIGAN ALLSTARS - MULLIGAN'S TOO (10" LP) | 15 |
| 55 | Vogue LDE 156 | GERRY MULLIGAN QUARTET WITH LEE KONITZ (10" LP) | 15 |
| 56 | Esquire 32-014 | GERRY MULLIGAN ALLSTARS (LP) | 15 |
| 56 | Vogue LAE 12006 | THE GERRY MULLIGAN QUARTET (LP) | 15 |
| 56 | Vogue LAE 12015 | THE GERRY MULLIGAN QUARTET - PARIS JAZZ FAIR 1954 (LP) | 15 |
| 56 | Emarcy EJL 101 | PRESENTING THE GERRY MULLIGAN SEXTET (LP) | 15 |
| 57 | Emarcy EJL 1259 | MAINSTREAM OF JAZZ (LP, by Gerry Mulligan Sextet) | 15 |
| 58 | Columbia Clef 33CX 10113 | GERRY MULLIGAN AND PAUL DESMOND QUARTET (LP) | 15 |
| 58 | HMV CLP 1204 | PHIL SUNKEL'S "JAZZ CONCERTO GROSSO" (LP, with Bob Brookmeyer) | 15 |
| 59 | Philips SBBL 552 | WHAT IS THERE TO SAY? (LP, stereo) | 15 |
| 59 | Vogue SEA 5006 | GERRY MULLIGAN SONGBOOK (LP, stereo) | 15 |
| 59 | Vogue SEA 5007 | REUNION WITH CHET BAKER (LP, stereo, as Gerry Mulligan Quartet) | 15 |
| 62 | Riverside RLP 12-247 | MULLIGAN MEETS MONK (LP, with Thelonious Monk) | 15 |

*(see also Gerry Mulligan, Chet Baker, Shelly Manne, Annie Ross)*

## MICK MULLIGAN'S JAZZ BAND
| 57 | Tempo TAP 14 | JAZZ AT THE RAILWAY ARMS (LP, with George Melly) | 50 |
| 59 | Pye Jazz NJL 21 | MEET MICK MULLIGAN (LP) | 20 |
| 59 | Parlophone PMC 1103 | THE SAINTS MEET THE SINNERS (LP, with George Melly & Saints Jazz Band) | 6 |

*(see also George Melly)*

## MULTI STORY
| 83 | Loco LOCO 1010 | Cutting Close/Star Traveller (no p/s) | 10 |

## MUM
| 02 | Fat Cat FATLP 18 | FINALLY WE ARE NO ONE (2 x 10") | 50 |
| 07 | Fat Cat FATLP46 | GO GO SMEAR THE POISON IVY (LP, with bonus 7") | 18 |

## GENE MUMFORD
| 58 | Philips PB 862 | More Than You Know/Please Give Me One More Chance | 8 |

## MUMFORD & SONS
| 08 | Chess Club CC 006 | LEND ME YOUR EYES EP (10", p/s) | 175 |
| 08 | Chess Club CC 009 | LOVE YOUR GROUND EP (10", p/s) | 150 |

| | | | |
|---|---|---|---|
| 09 | Gentlemen Of The Road/ Island 2728222, | Winter Winds/Hold On To What You Believe (p/s, cream coloured vinyl) | 18 |
| 09 | Chess Club CC 015 | The Cave/My Heart Told My Head (Winter Winds) (1-sided 10", gatefold p/s, 300 only, signed) | 100 |
| 09 | Chess Club CC 015 | The Cave/My Heart Told My Head (Winter Winds) (1-sided 10", gatefold p/s, 300 only, unsigned) | 50 |
| 09 | Island 2720975 | Little Lion Man/To Darkness (p/s) | 8 |
| 10 | Universal 27424111 | Roll Away Your Stone/White Blank Page (live) (p/s, green vinyl) | 12 |
| 12 | Gentlemen Of The Road/ Island 3716215 | I Will Wait/I Will Wait (live) (p/s, no'd, 500 only) | 18 |
| 12 | Gentlemen Of The Road/ Island 3723020 | Lover Of The Light/Thistle & Weeds (live) (p/s, 1000 only, no'd) | 15 |
| 13 | Gentlemen Of The Road/ Island 3732348 | Whispers In The Dark/Whispers In The Dark (live) (p/s, no'd 1000 only) | 6 |
| 10 | Chess Club WEDDING 1 | FIRST DANCE EP (tour 10" as The Wedding Band) | 80 |
| 09 | V2 VVR 723601 | SIGH NO MORE (LP) | 15 |

## MUMMIES

| | | | |
|---|---|---|---|
| 89 | Hangman HANG 47 UP | FUCKS C.D.S. ITS...(LP) | 20 |

## MUMMY CALLS

| | | | |
|---|---|---|---|
| 83 | MC 12 | Mary I Swear/Unicorn Jones (p/s) | 10 |

## MUNDANES

| | | | |
|---|---|---|---|
| 79 | Groucho | Groucho Party/Groucho Party (faux 2-Tone sleeve, insert) | 8 |

## HUGH MUNDELL

| | | | |
|---|---|---|---|
| 78 | Greensleeves GRE9 | Let's All Unite/Unity Dub | 15 |
| 79 | Warrior WAR 131 | Stop Them Jah/Push Dawta Push (12") | 30 |
| 80 | J&F 002 | Jah Fire Will Be Burning/King Of Israel (12") | 30 |
| 81 | Greensleeves GRED 54 | Can't Pop No Style/JUNIOR REID: Know Myself (12") | 40 |
| 80 | Mun Rock MMLP 001 | TIME AND PLACE (LP) | 25 |
| 80 | Live And Love LAP 13 | JAH FIRE (LP, with Lacksley Castell and Augustus Pablo) | 40 |
| 82 | Greensleeves GREL 36 | MUNDELL (LP) | 15 |
| 86 | Message GREL 94 | AFRICA MUST BE FREE BY 1983 (LP, reissue) | 15 |
| 88 | Astra 1007 | ARISE (LP) | 15 |

*(see also Ray Dorset, King Earl Boogie Band, Horizon, Made In England, Jigilo Jug Band, P. King, Paul King, P. Rufus King, Russian Roulette)*

## MUNGO JERRY

| | | | |
|---|---|---|---|
| 70 | Dawn DNX 2502 | In The Summertime/Mighty Man/Dust Pneumonia Blues (p/s) | 5 |
| 70 | Pye 7N 2502 | In The Summertime/Mighty Man (jukebox issue) | 8 |
| 71 | Dawn DNX 2505 | Baby Jump/The Man Behind The Piano/Live From Hollywood: Maggie/Midnight Special/Mighty Man (p/s) | 5 |
| 71 | Dawn DNX 2510 | Lady Rose/Have A Whiff On Me/Milk Cow Blues/Little Louis (p/s, withdrawn) | 5 |
| 71 | Dawn DNX 2510 | Lady Rose/She Rowed/Milk Cow Blues/Little Louis (re-pressing with different track, p/s) | 5 |
| 83 | Mach 1 MAGIC 008 | There Goes My Heart Again/Thinking Of You (featuring Ray Dorset & Tarts) | 5 |
| 85 | Orbit TRIP 4 | Sunshine Reggae/Nightlife (reissue of Horizon 45; as Mungo Jerry & Horizon) | 6 |
| 87 | Illegal MUNG 1 | In The Summertime '87/Got A Job (as Mungo Jerry & Brothers Grimm, p/s) | 5 |
| 96 | Fan Club 12/1 | Sugar In The Bowl/In The Summertime (fan club only, white label, autographed) | 5 |
| 70 | Dwn DNLS 3008 | MUNGO JERRY (LP, gatefold sleeve, with 3-D glasses) | 25 |
| 71 | Dawn DNLS 3028 | YOU DON'T HAVE TO BE IN THE ARMY (LP, gatefold sleeve, with lyric insert) | 15 |
| 71 | Dawn DNLS 3020 | ELECTRONICALLY TESTED (LP, gatefold sleeve) | 20 |
| 72 | Dawn DNLS 3041 | BOOT POWER (LP, with 'Dennis The Menace' or 'gun' gatefold sleeve) | 15 |

*(see also Ray Dorset, King Earl Boogie Band, Horizon, Made In England, Jigilo Jug Band, P. King, Paul King, P. Rufus King, Russian Roulette)*

## RAY MUNNINGS

| | | | |
|---|---|---|---|
| 79 | Tammi TAM 102 | It Could Happen To You/Let's Boogie | 20 |
| 79 | Tammi TAM 103 | Funky Nassau/Jump In The Water | 20 |
| 79 | Tammi TAM 103 | Funky Nassau/Jump In The Water (12") | 40 |

## CAROLINE MUNRO

| | | | |
|---|---|---|---|
| 67 | Columbia DB 8189 | Tar And Cement/The Sporting Life | 15 |
| 85 | Numa NU 5 | Pump Me Up/The Picture (p/s) | 6 |
| 85 | Numa NUM 5 | Pump Me Up (Ext. 6.09)/The Picture/Pump Me Up (4.00 7" Version) (12", p/s) | 10 |

*(see also Gary Numan)*

## HAL MUNRO

| | | | |
|---|---|---|---|
| 58 | Embassy WB 284 | Breathless/Wear My Ring Around Your Neck | 5 |
| 59 | Embassy WB 336 | C'mon Everybody/It's Late | 5 |
| 59 | Embassy WB 340 | Dream Lover/Where Were You | 5 |
| 59 | Embassy WB 386 | You Got What It Takes/California Here I Come | 5 |
| 60 | Embassy WB 401 | Good Timin'/I Wanna Go Home | 5 |

*(see also Neville Taylor)*

## SHEILA MUNRO

| | | | |
|---|---|---|---|
| 79 | Munrover SM 1 | Summertime/Vehicle/You Made Me So Very Happy (promo only) | 25 |

## ADRIAN MUNSEY

| | | | |
|---|---|---|---|
| 79 | Virgin VS 266 | C'Est Sheep (Part 1)/C'Est Sheep (Part 2) (p/s) | 6 |

*(see also Sparks)*

## STEPHAN MUNSON & FRIENDS

| | | | |
|---|---|---|---|
| 82 | Rhythmic RMNS 2 | And David Cried/And Dem Bahnhoff (fold-out photocopied p/s) | 8 |

## MURCOF

| | | | |
|---|---|---|---|
| 02 | Leaf BAY 23 | MARTES (2-LP) | 25 |
| 05 | Leaf BAY 47 V | REMEMBRANZA (2-LP) | 20 |

## MURDER INC.

| | | | |
|---|---|---|---|
| 80 | MIL MIL 1 | SOUNDS SO FALSE (EP) | 8 |

*(see also Business)*

## MURDER THE DISTURBED

MINT VALUE £

79 Small Wonder   Walking Corpses The Ultimate System/Small Seventeen (p/s) ........................ 8

### MURGATROYD BAND
71 Decca F 12809   Magpie (Theme From The TV Series)/Twice A Week (p/s) ........................... 40
71 Decca F 13256   Magpie (Theme From The TV Series)/Twice A Week (without p/s) .......... 15
71 Decca F 13256   Magpie (Theme From The TV Series)/Twice A Week (with p/s) ................. 25

*(see also Spencer Davis Group, Ray Fenwick)*

### MURMAIDS
63 Stateside SS 247   Popsicles And Icicles/Comedy And Tragedy ...................................... 20

### MURMURS OF URMA
97 Dolly 001   Coloured Rice/Magic Shop/Vacuum Cleaner/Cloudwatch HQ (P/S) ................ 12
99 Dolly 002   Banoffe Boy Writing To A Friend/Super Vacillation Day Snails Into Fast Food (p/s) ......... 8

### ARTHUR MURPHY
59 Parlophone R 4523   Sixteen Candles/Molly Malone ...................................................... 10

### BRIAN MURPHY
78 Pye 7N 46086   Jogging/THe Great Gnome Robbery ..................................................... 7

### KEITH MURPHY & THE DAZE
68 Polydor 56542   Slightly Reminiscent Of Her/Dirty Old Sam ...................................... 40

### LYLE MURPHY
58 Contemporary LAC 12135   GONE WITH THE WOODWINDS (LP) ..................................... 20

### MARK MURPHY
57 Brunswick 05701   Goodbye Baby Blues/The Right Kind Of Woman................................ 6
58 Capitol CL 14962   Belong To Me/Don't Cry My Love .............................................. 5
60 Capitol CL 15117   Send For Me/Come To Me........................................................ 5
63 Riverside RIF 106901   Stoppin The Clock/Angel Eyes.............................................. 5
63 Riverside RIF 106905   Like Love/Fly Away My Sadness ........................................... 5
63 Riverside RIF 106908   Fly Me To The Moon/Why Don't You Do Right....................... 30
65 Fontana TF 572   High On Windy Hill/Broken Heart............................................... 15
67 Fontana TF 803   (Ain't That) Just Like A Woman/Do You Wonder If I Love You ........... 5
69 Pye 7N 17661   Come Back To Me/Dear Heart ................................................... 5
66 Immediate IMLP/IMSP 004   WHO CAN I TURN TO (LP) .......................................... 25
69 Phoenix PMS 1001   THIS MUST BE EARTH (LP) .................................................. 90
71 Riverside RLP 395   RAH (LP) ............................................................................ 30

### NOEL MURPHY
67 Fontana TL 5450   NYA-A-A-H! (LP)................................................................ 15
73 Village Thing VTS 25   MURF (LP) ..................................................................... 15

### ROISIN MURPHY
05 Echo ECSY 158   SEQUINS EP 1 (12")........................................................... 10
05 Echo ECHLP 63   RUBY BLUE (2-LP, with booklet) ............................................ 40
07 EMI 507 0911   OVERPOWERED (2-LP, promo version on pink/orange vinyl)............... 25

*(see also Moloko)*

### ROSE MURPHY
52 Oriole/Mercury MG 10004   SONGS BY ROSE MURPHY (10" LP) ......................... 20

### MURPHY FEDERATION
81 London Madras LM 1/2   The Fed Up Skank/Slipping Past On The Inside (handmade p/s, cut up wallpaper with artwork on each side stapled together, paper inner sleeve)................. 70

### ALEX MURRAY
60 Decca F 11203   Teen Angel/Paper Doll............................................................ 6
60 Decca F 11225   All On My Own/String Along .................................................... 7
61 Decca F 11345   When You Walked Out/Send For Me .......................................... 7

*(see also Most Brothers)*

### LADY MURRAY
66 Clan 597 002   Mister Abercrombie Taught Me/In My Imagination....................... 8

*(see also Grazina, Mr & Mrs Murray)*

### MARTIN MURRAY
66 Pye 7N 17070   I Know What I Want/Goodbye Baby ....................................... 10

### MICKEY MURRAY
67 Polydor 56738   Shout Bama Lama/Lonely Room ........................................... 10

### MISTER MURRAY
65 Fontana TF 623   Down Came The Rain/Whatever Happened To Music? ............... 8
66 Fontana TF 674   I Drink To Your Memory/I Was A Good Song............................. 6

*(see also Mitch Murray Clan, Mr & Mrs Murray)*

### MITCH MURRAY CLAN
66 Clan 597 001   Skyliner/Cherokee.............................................................. 15

### MR & MRS MURRAY
68 CBS 3633   You're Outa Your Mind/A Little Bit Of You ................................ 6

*(see also Mitch Murray Clan, Lady Murray, Grazina, Mister Murray)*

### RUBY MURRAY
55 Columbia SCM 5162   Softly, Softly/What Could Be More Beautiful......................... 10
55 Columbia SCM 5165   Spring, Spring, Spring/Goin' Co'tin (with Ray Burns, Diana Decker & Ronnie Harris) ....... 5
55 Columbia SCM 5169   If Anyone Finds This, I Love You (with Anne Warren)/Before We Know It .......... 10

*(see also Norman Wisdom & Ruby Murray, Ray Burns, Ronnie Harris, Diana Decker)*

### MURRYS MONKEY
65 Pye &N 15800   Gipsy/I'll Be There ............................................................. 10

### JOHN MURTAUGH
70 Polydor 2482 015   BLUES CURRENT (LP) ....................................................... 20

## MUSE

| | | | |
|---|---|---|---|
| 99 | Mushroom MUSH 50S | Uno/Agitated (p/s, clear vinyl) | 40 |
| 99 | Mushroom MUSH 58S | Cave/Cave (Instrumental Remix) (clear vinyl, p/s) | 35 |
| 99 | Mushroom MUSH 66S | Muscle Museum/Escape (p/s) | 15 |
| 99 | Mushroom MUSH 66S | Muscle Museum/Minimum (clear vinyl, autographed p/s, 1000 only) | 60 |
| 99 | Mushroom MUSH 68S | Sunburn/(Live Acoustic Version) (stickered p/s, clear vinyl) | 18 |
| 00 | Mushroom MUSH 72S | Unintended/Sober (p/s, clear vinyl) | 18 |
| 00 | Mushroom MUSH 84S | Muscle Museum/Sober (The Saint Remix) (p/s) | 12 |
| 01 | Mushroom MUSH 89S | Plug In Baby/Nature 1 (p/s) | 20 |
| 01 | Mushroom MUSH 92S | New Born/Shrinking Universe (p/s, limited issue) | 18 |
| 01 | Mushroom MUSH 96S | Bliss/Hyper Chondriac Music (p/s) | 15 |
| 01 | Mushroom MUSH 96S | Bliss/The Gallery (p/s) | 15 |
| 01 | Mushroom MUSH 97S | Hyper Music/Feeling Good (numbered p/s) | 18 |
| 01 | Mushroom MUSH 104S | Dead Star/In Your World (p/s) | 15 |
| 03 | East West EW 272 | Time is Running Out/The Groove (clear vinyl, p/s) | 15 |
| 03 | East West EW 278 | Hysteria/Eternally Missed (clear vinyl, p/s) | 15 |
| 04 | East West EW 285 | Sing For Absolution/Fury (p/s, clear vinyl) | 12 |
| 04 | Atlantic ATUK 003 | Butterflies And Hurricanes/Butterflies And Hurricanes (Glastonbury 2004) (p/s, clear vinyl) | 10 |
| 06 | Warner Brothers HEL 3003 | Starlight/Supermassive Black Hole (Remix) (picture disc, stickered) | 12 |
| 06 | A & E HEL 3004 | Knights of Cydonia/Assassion (picture disc, stickered) | 18 |
| 07 | Warner Brothers HEL3005 | Invincible/Glorious (picture disc, stickered) | 18 |
| 07 | Warner Brothers HEL3005 | Invincible/Glorious (in static shield bag, this price for unopened) | 30 |
| 07 | Warner Brothers HEL3005 | Invincible/Glorious (in static shield bag, this price for opened) | 15 |
| 10 | Helium 3 WEA 460 | Resistance/Popcorn (picture disc in stickered PVC sleeve) | 12 |
| 98 | Dangerous DREX CDEP 103 | MUSE EP (CD, 999 copies, numbered sticker) | 300 |
| 98 | Dangerous DREX CDEP 104 | MUSCLE MUSEUM EP: Sober/Uno/Unintended/Instant Messenger/Muscle Museum #2/Muscle Museum (CD, 999 copies, numbered sticker) | 175 |
| 00 | Mushroom MUSH 59LP | SHOWBIZ (2-LP, clear vinyl, gatefold sleeve, with inners, numbered) | 150 |
| 01 | Mushroom MUSH 93LP | ORIGIN OF SYMMETRY (2-LP, gatefold sleeve, with lyric inner sleeves, 1500 only) | 100 |
| 03 | East West 5046 68587-1 | ABSOLUTION (2-LP, gatefold sleeve) | 40 |
| 09 | Warner Bros. 825646869664 | THE RESISTANCE (Box set, CD, DVD, USB stick) | 50 |
| 12 | Warner Bros. 2564656876 | THE 2ND LAW (Box set, 2-LP, DVD, CD, book, print and heat sensitive sleeve) | 50 |

## MUSHROOM

| | | | |
|---|---|---|---|
| 73 | Hawk HASP 320 | Devil Among The Tailors/Sun Ni Dhuibir/King Of Ireland's Daughter | 25 |
| 74 | Hawk HASP 340 | Kings And Queens/Met A Friend | 25 |
| 73 | Hawk HALPX 116 | EARLY ONE MORNING (LP, with poster inner) | 700 |
| 73 | Hawk HALPX 116 | EARLY ONE MORNING (LP, without poster inner) | 450 |

*(see also Joe O'Donnell)*

## (THE) MUSIC

| | | | |
|---|---|---|---|
| 01 | Fierce Panda NING 107 | Take The Long Road And Walk It/The Walls Get Smaller (p/s, 1,000 only) | 8 |
| 01 | Fierce Panda NINGT 107 | Take The Long Road And Walk It/The Walls Get Smaller (12", p/s, 250 only) | 18 |

## MUSIC BOX

| | | | |
|---|---|---|---|
| 72 | Westwood MRS 013 | SONGS OF SUNSHINE (LP) | 110 |

## MUSIC DOCTORS

| | | | |
|---|---|---|---|
| 69 | Downtown DT 447 | Music Doctor (Parts 1 & 2) | 20 |
| 71 | Downtown DT480 | The Pliers/Pliers (Version) | 18 |
| 70 | J-Dan JDN 4402 | Electric Shock/KING DENNIS: Black Robin | 20 |
| 70 | J-Dan JDN 4403 | Bush Doctor/Lick Your Stick | 20 |
| 70 | J-Dan JDN 4411 | The Wild Bunch/ISRAELITES: Born To Be Strong | 40 |
| 70 | J-Dan JDN 4414 | In The Summertime/Foundation Track | 15 |
| 70 | J-Dan JDN 4417 | Discretion Version/Doctor Dan, Boy Friday And Friend | 15 |
| 70 | Trojan TBL 117 | REGGAE IN THE SUMMERTIME (LP) | 30 |

*(see also Dennis Lowe, Desmond Riley, Megatons, Prince Of Darkness, Gene Rondo)*

## MUSIC EMPORIUM

| | | | |
|---|---|---|---|
| 83 | Psycho PSYCHO 11 | MUSIC EMPORIUM (LP) | 15 |

## MUSIC EXPLOSION

| | | | |
|---|---|---|---|
| 67 | Stateside SS 2028 | A Little Bit O' Soul/I See The Light | 25 |
| 67 | Stateside SS 2054 | Sunshine Games/Can't Stop Now | 20 |
| 67 | Philips BF 1547 | Little Black Egg/Stay By My Side | 10 |
| 69 | London HLP 10272 | A Little Bit O' Soul/Everybody | 10 |
| 67 | London HA-P/SH-P 8352 | A LITTLE BIT O' SOUL (LP) | 50 |

## MUSIC MACHINE

| | | | |
|---|---|---|---|
| 67 | Pye International 7N 25407 | Talk Talk/Come On In | 50 |
| 67 | Pye International 7N 25414 | The People In Me/Masculine Intuition | 60 |

## MUSIC MOTOR

| | | | |
|---|---|---|---|
| 70 | Deram DM 282 | Happy/Where Am I Going? | 15 |

## MUSIC SPECIALISTS

| | | | |
|---|---|---|---|
| 70 | London HLJ 10309 | Dynamic Pressure/Flip | 7 |

## MUSIC STAND

| | | | |
|---|---|---|---|
| 69 | Fresh FR 003 | Sunbird/Dreamland | 20 |

## MUSIC TAPES

| | | | |
|---|---|---|---|
| 98 | Earworm WORM 32 | The Television Tells Us/Freeing Song By Reindeer (p/s, pop-up sleeve with 2 inserts, 1,500 copies only) | 5 |

## MUSIC THROUGH SIX

| | | | |
|---|---|---|---|
| 68 | Domain D3 | Riff Raff/ROY DOCKER: Mellow Moonlight | 30 |

*(see also Jason Sims & Music Through Six)*

## MUSIC UK
82   Fairview FMR 061               Jose/Unemployment/House With A Red Gate ........................................................ 30

## MUSICA ELETTRONICA VIVA
69   Polydor 583 769               MUSICA ELETTRONICA VIVA (LP) ..................................................................... 100

## MUSICAL DOCTORS
69   Downtown DT 447              Musical Doctor Chaper 1/Musical Doctor Chapter 2 ..................................... 20

## MUSICIANS
66   King KG 1055                    Jaunty Joe/The Chelsea Set ............................................................................... 7

## MUSICOLOGY
91   B12 B1201                        Musicology (12") .................................................................................................. 40
91   B12 B1201                        Musicology (12", clear vinyl) ............................................................................ 100
92   B12 B1204                        Outlook (12") ...................................................................................................... 40
92   B12 B1206                        Hall Of Mirrors (12") .......................................................................................... 15
92   B12 B1206                        Hall Of Mirrors (12" Ltd, yellow vinyl) ............................................................. 40

## MUSIQUE CONCRET
81   United Dairies UD 010        BRINGING UP BABY (LP, blue vinyl, 100 only) ............................................... 120
81   United Dairies UD 010        BRINGING UP BABY (LP, black vinyl, 400 only) ............................................. 100
87   United Dairies UDT 10        BRINGING UP BABY (cassette) ......................................................................... 40

## MUSKETEER GRIPWEED & THIRD TROOP
66   United Artists UP 1196       How I Won The War/Aftermath .......................................................................... 175
66   United Artists UP 1196       How I Won The War/Aftermath (demo copy) ................................................... 100
*(see also John Lennon)*

## MUSKETEERS
69   Philips BF 1773                 Fight/Magnifico ................................................................................................... 6

## MUSKYTEERS
69   Upsetter US 309                Endlessly/Kidd-O ............................................................................................... 35

## MUSLIMGAUZE
83   Hessian 1                        Hammer And Sickle/Fear Of Gadaffi/Nettle Cloth/Baize Tents ................ 15
84   Limited Editions LIMITED 1   HUNTING OUT WITH AN AERIAL EYE (12" 45rpm EP) ................................ 15
83   Product Kinematograph        KABUL (LP, die cut 12" sleeve, some with Facsimile fanzine) ..................... 50
     PKR-1
84   Recloose LOOSE 008           BUDDHIST ON FIRE (LP, some with free Triptych EP and inserts) .............. 50
85   Limited Editions LIMITED 2   BLINDED HORSES (LP) ........................................................................................ 25
86   Limited Editions LIMITED 3   FLAJELATA (LP) ................................................................................................... 20
86   Limited Editions LIMITED 4   HAJJ (LP) ............................................................................................................. 20
87   Limited Editions LIMITED 5   JAZIRAT-UL-ARAB (LP) ..................................................................................... 20
87   Limited Editions LIMITED 6   ABU NIDAL (LP) .................................................................................................. 20
88   Limited Editions LIMITED 7   THE RAPE OF PALESTINE (LP) ......................................................................... 20
*(see also Eg Oblique Graph)*

## CHARLIE MUSSELWHITE BLUES BAND
69   Vanguard SVRL 19012         STONE BLUES (LP) .............................................................................................. 22

## MUSTANG
67   Parlophone R 5579            Why/Here, There And Everywhere ................................................................... 25

## MUSTARD
74   EMI EMI 2165                    Good Time Comin'/I Saw I Heard ..................................................................... 25

## MUS-TWANGS
61   Mercury AMT 1140            Roch Lomond/Marie ......................................................................................... 12

## MUTANTS
77   Rox ROX 002                     Boss Man/Back Yard Boys (p/s) ....................................................................... 15
78   Rox ROX 005                     School Teacher/Hard Time/Lady (p/s, red vinyl) ........................................... 10

## MUTE DRIVERS
80s  Mute Drivers MD 001        MUTE DRIVERS (LP, with insert in handmade painted sleeve, 300 only) ...... 15
*(see also Anonymes)*

## MUTT 'N' JEFF
66   Decca F 12335                  Don't Nag Me Ma/Strolling The Blues ............................................................. 12

## MVP'S
71   Buddah BDS 469                Turnin' My Heartbeat Up/Every Man For Herself ......................................... 30

## M.W.A.B.
83   M.W.A.B. Records              Angus Young/Is Michael Bum An Apple? ........................................................ 15

## MWANAMKE MWFICA
82   African Woman AWLP 101    AFRICAN WOMAN ABROAD (LP) ..................................................................... 80

## MX-80 SOUND
77   Island ILPS 9520               HARD ATTACK (LP, insert) ................................................................................. 30

## MY BLOODY VALENTINE
86   Fever FEV 5X                     No Place To Go/Moonlight (p/s) ....................................................................... 60
86   Fever FEV 5                       GEEK! (12" EP) .................................................................................................... 40
86   Kaleid. Sound KS 101         THE NEW RECORD BY MY BLOODY VALENTINE (12" EP) .............................. 50
87   Lazy LAZY 04                     Sunny Sundae Smile/Paint A Rainbow (p/s) .................................................. 30
87   Lazy LAZY 04T                   Sunny Sundae Smile/Paint A Rainbow/Kiss The Eclipse/ Sylvie's Head (12", p/s) ...... 40
87   Lazy LAZY 07                     Strawberry Wine/Never Say Goodbye/Can I Touch You (12", p/s) .............. 50
88   Creation CRE 055              You Made Me Realise/Slow (die-cut company sleeve) ................................... 25
88   Creation CRE 055T            You Made Me Realise/Slow/Thorn/Cigarette/Drive It All Over Me (12", p/s) ...... 30
88   Creation CRE 061              Feed Me With Your Kiss/Emptiness Inside (plays "I Believe") (die-cut company sleeve) ...... 20
88   Creation CRE 061T            Feed Me With Your Kiss/I Believe/Emptiness Inside/I Need No Trust (12", p/s) ...... 25
89   Creation CRE 085              To Here Knows When/Swallow (p/s) ................................................................ 15
89   Creation CRE 085T            Tremolo/To Here Knows When (12", p/s) ...................................................... 20

| | | | |
|---|---|---|---|
| 89 | Lyntone CAT 067 | Sugar/PACIFIC: December, With The Day (square flexidisc free with The Catalogue magazine, issue 67) | 10 |
| | | | 12 |
| 90 | Creation CRE 073 | Soon/Glider (p/s) | 25 |
| 90 | Creation CRE 073T | GLIDER EP (12", p/s) | 25 |
| 90 | Creation CRE 073X | GLIDER EP (12", remixed by Andy Weatherall, stickered die-cut sleeve) | 20 |
| 87 | Lazy LAZY 08 | ECSTACY (mini-LP, 3,000 only) | 50 |
| 88 | Creation CRELP 040 | ISN'T ANYTHING (LP, first pressing with black label, 3,000 copies with bonus 7" "Instrumental"/"Instrumental" [CRE FRE 4, no p/s] & stickered sleeve) | 60 |
| 88 | Creation CRELP 040 | ISN'T ANYTHING (LP, 2nd pressing, brown label, without bonus 7") | 35 |
| 89 | Lazy LAZY 12 | ECSTACY & WINE (LP, compilation of LAZY 07 & LAZY 08) | 30 |
| 89 | Lazy LAZY 12CD | ECSTACY & WINE (CD) | 25 |
| 91 | Creation CRELP 060 | LOVELESS (LP) | 70 |
| 13 | MBV mbvlp01 | M.B.V (LP, gatefold with CD) | 18 |

(see also Primal Scream, Collapsed Lung, Snowpony, Dinosaur Jr.)

## MY CAPTAINS
| | | | |
|---|---|---|---|
| 81 | 4AD AD 103 | Fall/Converse/History/Nothing (p/s) | 15 |

## MY CHEMICAL ROMANCE
| | | | |
|---|---|---|---|
| 03 | 20:20 TWENTY 7s 003 | Honey, This Mirror Isn't Big Enough For The Two Of Us/This Is The Best Day Ever (p/s) | 50 |
| 04 | 20:20 TWENTY 7s 004 | Headfirst For Halos/Our Lady Of Sorrows (Live) (p/s) | 45 |
| 04 | Reprise W 661 | Thank You For The Venom/Jack The Ripper (Live) (red vinyl, p/s) | 40 |
| 05 | Reprise W 666 | I'm Not Okay (I Promise)/Bury Me In Black (Demo) (red vinyl, p/s) | 7 |
| 06 | Reprise 116796-1 | THE BLACK PARADE (2-LP box set) | 30 |

## MY DEAR WATSON
| | | | |
|---|---|---|---|
| 68 | Parlophone R 5687 | Elusive Face/The Shame Just Drained | 30 |
| 68 | Parlophone R 5737 | Make This Day Last/Stop, Stop, I'll Be There | 30 |
| 70 | DJM DJS 224 | Have You Seen Your Saviour/White Line Road | 10 |

(see also Johnny & Copycats)

## MY DYING BRIDE
| | | | |
|---|---|---|---|
| 90 | Private pressing | Towards The Sinister EP (4 track demo cassette) | 40 |
| 92 | Peaceville VILE 27 | Symphonaire Infernus Et Spera Empyrium Act 1/ Symphonaire Infernus Et Spera Empyrium Act 2 (12", p/s) | 25 |
| 93 | Peaceville VILE 44T | I Am The Bloody Earth/Transcending (Into The Exquisite) (12", p/s) | 20 |
| 93 | Peaceville VILE 37T | The Thrash Of Naked Limbs/Le Cerf Malade/Gather Me Up Forever (12", p/s) | 25 |
| 93 | Unbridled Voyage (No Cat. No) | Unreleased Bitterness: The Bitterness And The Bereavement (1-sided flexidisc, fold-out p/s in poly sleeve, 1150 only) | 20 |
| 94 | Peaceville CC5 | Sexuality Of Bereavement/Crown Of Sympathy (Remix) (p/s) | 25 |
| 92 | Peaceville VILE 30 | AS THE FLOWER WITHERS (LP, gatefold sleeve) | 15 |
| 93 | Peaceville VILE 39 | TURN LOOSE THE SWANS (LP, double) | 35 |
| 94 | Peaceville VILE 45 | THE STORIES EP (box set, 1000 only) | 75 |
| 95 | Peaceville VILE 50 | THE ANGEL AND THE DARK RIVER (LP, picture disc) | 15 |

## TIM MYCROFT
| | | | |
|---|---|---|---|
| 71 | Parlophone R5919 | Shadra/Bournemouth Rock | 15 |

## AMINA CLAUDINE MYERS
| | | | |
|---|---|---|---|
| 80 | Leo LR 100 | SONG FOR MOTHER E (LP) | 20 |
| 80 | Leo LR 103 | AMINA CLAUDINE MYERS SALUTES BESSIE SMITH (LP) | 45 |

## ROWLAND MYERS
| | | | |
|---|---|---|---|
| 75 | MSE MSE 2SSP/P | Give Them A Hand/Pandemonium | 30 |
| 74 | Deroy DER 1063 | JUST FOR THE RECORD (LP, private pressing, also listed as Music Sound Enterprise MSE 1) | 120 |

## MY FRIENDS AND I
| | | | |
|---|---|---|---|
| 69 | Marroo MR 001 | Susan/Wake The Dead | 40 |

## MY KIND OF PEOPLE
| | | | |
|---|---|---|---|
| 70 | CBS 555133 | Somebodys Coming/Nobody Knows Why The Butterfly Died | 25 |

## BILLY MYLES
| | | | |
|---|---|---|---|
| 57 | HMV POP 423 | The Joker (That's What They Call Me)/Honey Bee | 50 |

## MEG MYLES
| | | | |
|---|---|---|---|
| 56 | Capitol CL 14555 | Sing On, Baby/Will You Shed A Tear For Me? | 7 |

## MY LIFE STORY
| | | | |
|---|---|---|---|
| 86 | Think Tank CHAPTER 1 | HOME SWEET ZOO: Boring Dream/Sliding Bookcase (gatefold p/s, 500 only) | 30 |

## MY LORDE SHERIFFE'S COMPLAINTE
| | | | |
|---|---|---|---|
| 79 | Frog FROG 1 | MY LORDE SHERIFFE'S COMPLAINTE (LP, private pressing) | 15 |

## MYND MUZIC
| | | | |
|---|---|---|---|
| 94 | Poor Person Prod. | IMAGINE THIS (LP, handmade sleeve, 500 only) | 20 |

## MYRTELLES
| | | | |
|---|---|---|---|
| 63 | Oriole CB 1805 | Don't Wanna Cry Again/Just Let Me Cry | 40 |

(see also Sue & Sunshine, Sue & Sunny, Stockingtops)

## MYSTERE FIVE'S
| | | | |
|---|---|---|---|
| 80 | Flicknife FLS 001 | No Message/Shake Some Action (p/s) | 5 |
| 81 | Flicknife FLS 202 | Never Say Thank You/Heart Rules The Head (p/s) | 5 |

(see also Wayne County & Electric Chairs)

## MYSTERIES
| | | | |
|---|---|---|---|
| 64 | Decca F 11919 | Give Me Rhythm And Blues/Teardrops | 30 |

## MYSTERIOUS FOOTSTEPS
| | | | |
|---|---|---|---|
| 80 | Yest YET 1 | White Dread/Like They Do In The Movies | 10 |

## WILLIAM MYSTERIOUS
| | | | |
|---|---|---|---|
| 82 | Mezzanine MEZ 1 | Security Of Noise/Alright (p/s, with Fay Fife & Revettes) | 10 |

(see also Rezillos, Revillos)

## MYSTERY GIRLS

MINT VALUE £

| | | | |
|---|---|---|---|
| 79 | Strange HAM 1 | SOUNDS LIKE THE MYSTERY GIRLS EP | 15 |
| 81 | Strange HAM 002 | I'm A Believer/Modern Mystery Pop/Walking Backwards (p/s) | 10 |

## MYSTERY GUESTS

| | | | |
|---|---|---|---|
| 80 | Boys Own/Heater Volume BO 1 | Wurlitzer Junction/The Merry Shark You Are (handmade stickered white labels) | 10 |
| 81 | Boys Own BO 3 | The Sparrow That Ate New York/The Nude (p/s) | 10 |

## MYSTERY JETS

| | | | |
|---|---|---|---|
| 78 | Raw RAW 21 | The Sun Story/A Song For Gene | 7 |

## MYSTERY MAKER

| | | | |
|---|---|---|---|
| 77 | Caves UHC 3 | MYSTERY MAKER (LP, private pressing with booklet) | 120 |

## MYSTIC EMP

| | | | |
|---|---|---|---|
| 80 | His Majesty HMD 006 | Reality/JAH THOMAS: Throw Away Vanity/MYSTIC EMP & JAH THOMAS: Reality Dub (12") | 20 |

## MYSTIC EYES

| | | | |
|---|---|---|---|
| 79 | Greensleeves GRED 11 | Perilous Times (with Trinity)/REVOLUTIONARIES: Roots Man Version (12") | 30 |
| 79 | Warrior WAR 135 | Elaine/MIKEY DREAD: Schoolgirls (12") | 25 |
| 78 | Burning Sounds BS 1033 | MYSTERIOUS (LP) | 45 |

## MYSTIC INSTITUTE

| | | | |
|---|---|---|---|
| 92 | Evolution EVO 06 | CYBERDON EP (12") | 18 |

*(see also Global Communications, Reload, Link)*

## MYSTIC MATT & THE ANTHILL MOB

| | | | |
|---|---|---|---|
| 99 | Love Peace & Unity LOVE 05 | A SHOCK 2 DA SYSTEM EP (12", p/s) | 25 |

*(see also Anthill Mob)*

## MYSTIC MOODS

| | | | |
|---|---|---|---|
| 73 | Warner Bros K 16265 | Cosmic Sea/Awakening | 7 |
| 74 | Warner Bros K 46250 | AWAKENING (LP) | 15 |

## MYSTIC NUMBER NATIONAL BANK

| | | | |
|---|---|---|---|
| 69 | Probe SPB 1001 | THE MYSTIC NUMBER NATIONAL BANK (LP) | 25 |

## MYSTIC RADICS

| | | | |
|---|---|---|---|
| 81 | Water Mount WMT 1 | Nation Wide/Dub Version (12") | 250 |

## MYSTIC TOUCH

| | | | |
|---|---|---|---|
| 75 | Champagne 505 | Get Yourself Together/Pary People | 15 |

## MYSTICS

| | | | |
|---|---|---|---|
| 59 | HMV POP 646 | Hushabye/Adam And Eve | 30 |
| 59 | Top Rank JAR 243 | Don't Take The Stars/So Tenderly | 30 |

## MYSTICS (JAMAICA)

| | | | |
|---|---|---|---|
| 75 | Grounation GRO 2049 | God Bless The Youths/Dub | 5 |

## MYSTREATED

| | | | |
|---|---|---|---|
| 94 | Twist TWIST 15 | SHE'S GONE (EP) | 6 |
| 95 | Twist TWIST 18 | LIVE AT THE BBC (EP) | 6 |
| 96 | Hangman's Daughter KETCH 7 UP | Never Question Why/Take A Look In The Mirror (p/s, 500 only) | 8 |
| 97 | Detour DR 054 | (What's In) Your Mind Today/I'll Be There (p/s) | 10 |
| 98 | Detour DR 060 | Contrasts (I've Got Plenty)/Right Here | 5 |
| 92 | Hangman TWISTBIG 4 | 10 BOSS CUTS (LP) | 20 |
| 94 | Twist TWISTBIG 4 | LOOKING RIGHT THROUGH (LP) | 15 |
| 95 | Twist TWISTBIG 7 | EVERY QUESTIONING WHY (LP) | 15 |
| 96 | Twist TWISTBIG 8 | THIS IS... (LP) | 12 |

## MYTHRA

| | | | |
|---|---|---|---|
| 79 | Guardian GRMA 16 | DEATH & DESTINY: Death And Destiny/Killer/Overload/UFO (EP, no p/s) | 12 |
| 80 | Streetbeat LAMP 2 | Death Or Destiny/Killer/U.F.O. (with p/s) | 90 |
| 80 | Streetbeat LAMP 2 | Death Or Destiny/Killer/U.F.O. | 10 |
| 80 | Streetbeat 12 LAMP 2 | Death Or Destiny/Killer/Overlord/U.F.O. (12", with p/s) | 125 |
| 80 | Streetbeat 12 LAMP 2 | Death Or Destiny/Killer/Overlord/U.F.O. (12") | 20 |

## M ZONE & DJ GOLLUM

| | | | |
|---|---|---|---|
| 97 | UK44 UK44 EP3 | Harmony (Get Me)/Harmony (12") | 12 |

*(see also DJ Gollum)*

# N

## NABAY

| | | | |
|---|---|---|---|
| 80 | Grapevine GRP 143 | Believe It Or Not/Believe It Or Not (Instrumental) | 30 |

## RICKY NADIR

| | | | |
|---|---|---|---|
| 75 | Charisma CB 345 | Birthday Special/Shingle Song | 10 |
| 79 | Charisma CB 339 | The Polaroid/PETER HAMMILL: The Old School Tie | 10 |

*(see also Peter Hammill)*

## MARISSA NADLER

| | | | |
|---|---|---|---|
| 06 | My Kung Fu MYKUNGFU 016 | Diamond Heart/Leather Made Shoes | 6 |

## NADRIAN

| | | | |
|---|---|---|---|
| 71 | Dolphin DO 514 | Something Passing By/You Can't Lose Out | 250 |

## NAFFI

| | | | |
|---|---|---|---|
| 79 | Absurd ABSURD 8 | Slice 1/Slice 2 (as Naafi Sandwich) | 20 |

MINT VALUE £

| | | | |
|---|---|---|---|
| 81 | Naffi Productions RUM 5 | D'ya Hear Me/Freedie's Fever (dub)/The Hutch (dub) | 20 |
| 82 | Ark DOVE 1 | YUM YUM YUM YA (LP) | 25 |

## NAIROBI SISTERS
| | | | |
|---|---|---|---|
| 76 | Jamatel JAL 07 | Promised Land/Version | 35 |

## NAKED CITY
| | | | |
|---|---|---|---|
| 90 | Earache MOSH 28 | TORTURE GARDEN EP (12") | 20 |

## NAKED LUNCH
| | | | |
|---|---|---|---|
| 81 | Ramkup CAC 003 | Rabies/Slipping Again (p/s) | 15 |
| 84 | Plezure PLZS 841 | You Tie Me Down/Laugh Your Mind Away | 10 |

## NAKED TRUTH
| | | | |
|---|---|---|---|
| 70 | Deram DM 287 | Two Little Rooms/Rag Doll Boy | 7 |

## NAME
| | | | |
|---|---|---|---|
| 80 | Din Disc DIN 14 | Forget Art, Let's Dance/Misfits (p/s) | 10 |
| 87 | China WOK 15 | Jesus And The Devil/The Great Depression (p/s) | 8 |

## NAMES
| | | | |
|---|---|---|---|
| 80 | Factory FAC 29 | Nightshift/I Wish I Could Speak Your Language (p/s) | 12 |

## ZBIGNIEW NAMYSLOWSKI MODERN JAZZ QUARTET
| | | | |
|---|---|---|---|
| 64 | Decca LK/SKL 4644 | LOLA (LP) | 175 |

## NANETTE
| | | | |
|---|---|---|---|
| 70 | Columbia DB 8659 | Flying Machine/You're Wasting Your Time | 35 |
| 70 | Columbia DB 8673 | Every Night When I Cry Myself To Sleep/Jamie | 10 |
| 70 | Columbia DB 8733 | Let Me Be The One/To Be Loved | 10 |
| 71 | Columbia DB 8751 | Everybody's Singing Right Now/Could I Forget | 10 |
| 70 | Columbia SCX 6398 | NANETTE (LP) | 30 |

## ED NANGLE
| | | | |
|---|---|---|---|
| 68 | Blue Cat BS 120 | Good Girl/ENFORCERS: Musical Fever | 200 |
| 68 | Coxsone CS 7038 | Whipping The Prince (actually by Ed Nangle & Alton Ellis & Soul Vendors)/HEPTONES: If You Knew | 100 |

## NICK NANTOS & HIS FIREBALLERS
| | | | |
|---|---|---|---|
| 63 | Summit LSE 2042 | GUITARS ON FIRE (EP) | 15 |
| 64 | Summit ATL 4114 | GUITARS ON FIRE (LP) | 15 |

*(see also Bill Haley & Comets)*

## NAOMI
| | | | |
|---|---|---|---|
| 70 | Gayfeet GS 207 | You're Not My Kind/GAYTONES: You're Not My Kind (Version II) | 20 |
| 70 | High Note HS 047 | Natural Woman/GAYTONES: Natural Woman - Version | 20 |

*(see also Derrick Morgan, Tommy McCook)*

## NAPALM DEATH
| | | | |
|---|---|---|---|
| 87 | Strange Fruit SFPS 049 | THE PEEL SESSIONS (12", p/s) | 15 |
| 89 | Rise Above RISE 001 | NAPALM DEATH EP (poster p/s, sold at gigs) | 25 |
| 89 | Earache 7MOSH 14 | Mentally Murdered/Cause And effect (stickered p/s) | 10 |
| 89 | Earache MOSH 014 | MENTALLY MURDERED EP (Rise Above/The Missing Link/Mentally Murdered Walls Of Confinement/Cause And Effect/No Mental Effort) (12", p/s) | 20 |
| 90 | Earache 7MOSH 24L | Suffer The Children/The Kill/Scum/Extremity Retained/Life? (stickered p/s, sticker sheet) | 10 |
| 90 | Earache MOSH 024 | Suffer The Children/Siege Of Power/Harmony Corruption (12", p/s) | 10 |
| 91 | Earache 7MOSH 46 | Mass Appeal Madness/Pride Assassin (p/s) | 10 |
| 91 | Earache MOSH 046 | Mass Appeal Madness/Pride Assassin/Unchallenged Hate/Social Sterility (12", p/s) | 10 |
| 92 | Earache MOSH 65 | THE WORLD KEEPS TURNING EP (12", p/s) | 12 |
| 93 | Earache 7MOSH 92 | Nazi Punks Fuck Off/Aryanisms/Nazi Punks Fuck Off (Live)/Contemptuous (Xtreem Mix) (p/s) | 20 |
| 95 | Earache MOSH 146 | GREED KILLING EP (Greed Kiling/My Own Worst Enemy/Self Betrayal/Finer Truths White Lies/Antibody/All Links Severed/Plague Rages [Live]) (10", p/s) | 15 |
| 96 | Earache 7 MOSH 168 | Food Chains/Upward And Uninterested (demo version)/COALESCE: A Safe Place/Harvest Of Maturity) (p/s, insert, purple vinyl) | 15 |
| 96 | Earache 7 MOSH 168 | Food Chains/Upward And Uninterested (demo version)/COALESCE: A Safe Place/Harvest Of Maturity) (p/s, insert) | 10 |
| 87 | Earache MOSH 3 | SCUM (LP, lyric insert, black/orange, black/green, black red orblack/yellow cover) | 20 |
| 88 | Earache MOSH 8 | FROM ENSLAVEMENT TO OBLITERATION (LP, gatefold sleeve, free 7" EP The Curse [7MOSH 8]) | 35 |
| 90 | Earache MOSH 19/19L | HARMONY CORRUPTION (2-LP, with inserts) | 25 |
| 90 | Earache MOSH 19P | HARMONY CORRUPTION (LP, picture disc) | 20 |
| 91 | Earache MOSH 3 | SCUM (LP, reissue, white and black swirl vinyl, black and gold sleeve, 2000 only) | 18 |
| 92 | Earache MOSH 53 | UTOPIA BANISHED (LP, free 7" EP [MOSH 53L]) | 25 |
| 92 | Earache MOSH8/19/51/67L | BOX SET (4-CD) | 25 |
| 06 | Earache MOSH 003PD | SCUM (LP, 2nd reissue, picture disc, stickered PVC sleeve, 1500 only) | 15 |

## MARTY NAPOLEON
| | | | |
|---|---|---|---|
| 55 | London EZ-NI9001 | NAPOLEON SINGS AND SWINGS (EP) | 15 |

## NAPOLEON XIV
| | | | |
|---|---|---|---|
| 66 | Warner Bros W 1661 | THEY'RE COMING TO TAKE ME AWAY HA-HA-A! (LP) | 40 |

*(see also Jerry Samuels, Kim Fowley)*

## RAYMOND NAPTALI AND ROY RANKING
| | | | |
|---|---|---|---|
| 81 | KG Imperial KG 006 | New Cross Fire/Brixton Incident (12", blue vinyl) | 25 |

## NAPTHALI
| | | | |
|---|---|---|---|
| 91 | Black Legacy BLLP 001 | MENTAL SLAVERY SHOWCASE (LP) | 60 |

## PETER NARDINI
| | | | |
|---|---|---|---|
| 80s | Kettle KS 701 | I Think You're Great/Ma Maw's A Mod (in p/s) | 15 |
| 80s | Kettle KS 701 | I Think You're Great/Ma Maw's A Mod | 8 |

## NARNIA
| | | | |
|---|---|---|---|
| 74 | Myrrh MYR 1007 | NARNIA - ASLAN IS NOT A TAME LION (LP) | 80 |

# Billy NASH

MINT VALUE £

*(see also After The Fire, Pauline Filby)*

## BILLY NASH
| | | | |
|---|---|---|---|
| 61 | Philips PB 1181 | Sunset/Nobody Loves Me Like You (as Billy Nash Combo) | 7 |
| 63 | Philips 370 406 BF | The Madison Step/Madison Rhythm (as Billy Nash Rock Band) | 7 |

## GENE NASH
| | | | |
|---|---|---|---|
| 59 | Capitol CL 15042 | I'm An Eskimo Too/Ja, Ja, Ja (Deutsche Rock 'N Roll) | 5 |

## GRAHAM NASH
| | | | |
|---|---|---|---|
| 71 | Atlantic 2091 096 | Chicago/Simple Man | 6 |
| 71 | Atlantic 2091 135 | Military Madness/I Used To Be A King | 6 |
| 71 | Atlantic 2401 011 | SONGS FOR BEGINNERS (LP) | 18 |

*(see also Hollies, Crosby Stills Nash & Young)*

## JOHNNY NASH
| | | | |
|---|---|---|---|
| 57 | HMV POP 402 | Ladder Of Love/I'll Walk Alone | 10 |
| 58 | HMV POP 435 | Won't You Let Me Share My Love With You?/A Very Special Love | 10 |
| 58 | HMV POP 475 | It's Easy To Say/My Pledge To You | 10 |
| 58 | HMV POP 553 | Almost In Your Arms/Midnight Moonlight | 7 |
| 59 | HMV POP 597 | Walk With Faith In Your Heart/Roots Of Heaven | 7 |
| 59 | HMV POP 620 | As Time Goes By/Voice Of Love | 7 |
| 59 | HMV POP 651 | And The Angels Sing/Baby, Baby, Baby | 7 |
| 59 | HMV POP 673 | Take A Giant Step/Imagination | 6 |
| 60 | HMV POP 746 | A Place In The Sun/Goodbye | 6 |
| 60 | HMV POP 822 | Somebody/Kisses | 6 |
| 62 | Warner Bros WB 65 | Don't Take Away Your Love/Moment Of Weakness | 20 |
| 62 | Warner Bros WB 76 | Ol' Man River/My Dear Little Sweetheart | 30 |
| 63 | Warner Bros WB 93 | Cigareets, Whiskey And Wild, Wild Women/I'm Moving On | 15 |
| 64 | Pye International 7N 25250 | Love Ain't Nothin'/Talk To Me | 60 |
| 65 | Chess CRS 8005 | Strange Feelin'/Rainin' In My Heart | 25 |
| 66 | Pye International 7N 25353 | Let's Move And Groove (Together)/Understanding | 20 |
| 66 | Pye International 7N 25363 | One More Time/Tryin' To Find Her | 20 |
| 68 | Regal Zono. RZ 3010 | Hold Me Tight/Let's Move And Groove Together | 10 |
| 68 | Major Minor MM 586 | You've Got Soul/Don't Cry | 7 |
| 68 | Major Minor MM 603 | Cupid/People In Love | 10 |
| 69 | MGM MGM R 9 | (I'm So) Glad You're My Baby/Stormy | 35 |
| 71 | MAM MAM R 9 | Falling In And Out Of Love/People In Love | 7 |
| 64 | RCA Victor RCX 7163 | PRESENTING JOHNNY NASH (EP) | 100 |
| 59 | HMV CLP 1251 | JOHNNY NASH (LP) | 40 |
| 59 | HMV CLP 1299 | QUIET HOUR WITH JOHNNY NASH (LP) | 25 |
| 60 | HMV CLP 1325 | I GOT RHYTHM (LP, mono) | 30 |
| 60 | HMV CSD 1288 | I GOT RHYTHM (LP, stereo) | 30 |
| 62 | Encore ENC 2005 | LET'S GET LOST (LP) | 15 |
| 69 | Major Minor MMLP/SMLP 47 | YOU GOT SOUL (LP) | 15 |
| 69 | Major Minor MMLP/SMLP 56 | SOUL FOLK (LP) | 15 |
| 69 | Major Minor MMLP/SMLP 63 | PRINCE OF PEACE (LP) | 15 |

## KATE NASH
| | | | |
|---|---|---|---|
| 07 | Moshi Moshi MOMO 4 | Caroline's A Victim/Birds | 6 |
| 06 | Fiction 1755804 | MADE OF BRICKS (LP, pink vinyl) | 50 |

## TONY NASH
| | | | |
|---|---|---|---|
| 70 | Hot Rod HR 110 | Keep On Trying/WINSTON JAMES: Just Can't Do Without Your Love | 40 |

## NASHVILLE FIVE
| | | | |
|---|---|---|---|
| 62 | Decca F 11427 | Stand Up And Say That/Like Nashville | 7 |
| 62 | Decca F 11484 | Some Other Love/Brainwave | 7 |
| 62 | Decca DFE 6706 | LIKE NASHVILLE (EP) | 40 |

## NASHVILLE TEENS
| | | | |
|---|---|---|---|
| 64 | Decca F 11930 | Tobacco Road/I Like It Like That | 8 |
| 64 | Decca F 12000 | Google Eye (some misspelled "Goggle Eye" on label)/T.N.T. | 8 |
| 65 | Decca F 12089 | Find My Way Back Home/Devil-In-Law | 8 |
| 65 | Decca F 12143 | This Little Bird/Whatcha Gonna Do? | 8 |
| 65 | Decca F 12255 | I Know How It Feels To Be Loved/Soon Forgotten | 8 |
| 66 | Decca F 12316 | The Hard Way/Upside Down | 15 |
| 66 | Decca F 12458 | Forbidden Fruit/Revived 45 Time | 25 |
| 66 | Decca F 12542 | That's My Woman/Words | 18 |
| 67 | Decca F 12580 | I'm Coming Home/Searching | 10 |
| 67 | Decca F 12657 | The Biggest Night Of Her Life/Last Minute | 10 |
| 68 | Decca F 12754 | All Along The Watchtower/Sun-Dog | 15 |
| 69 | Major Minor MM 599 | The Lament Of The Cherokee Reservation Indian/Looking For You | 18 |
| 69 | Decca F 12929 | Tobacco Road/All Along The Watchtower | 6 |
| 71 | Parlophone R 5925 | Ella James/Tennessee Woman | 20 |
| 72 | Parlophone R 5961 | You Shouldn't Have Been So Nice/Tell The People (unissued) | 0 |
| 73 | Enterprise ENT S101 | Lawdy Miss Clawdy/Let It Rock/Rocking On The Railroad/Break Up | 7 |
| 77 | Sky 1007 | Tobacco Road/Chips And Peas | 5 |
| 65 | Decca DFE 8600 | THE NASHVILLE TEENS (EP) | 50 |
| 75 | New World NW 6002 | THE NASHVILLE TEENS (LP) | 40 |

*(see also Arizona Swamp Company, Jerry Lee Lewis, Carl Perkins)*

## NASTY FACTS
| | | | |
|---|---|---|---|
| 81 | 5th Column FC 2 | Drive My Car/Gotta Get To You/Crazy 'Bout you (p/s) | 60 |

## NASTY HABIT
| | | | |
|---|---|---|---|
| 92 | Reinforced RIVET 1233 | As Nasty As I Wanna Be (12") | 25 |
| 92 | Reinforced RIVET 1233R | As Nasty As I Wanna Be (Remixes) (12") | 25 |

## NASTY MEDIA
| | | | |
|---|---|---|---|
| 78 | Lightning GIL 542 | Spiked Copy/Winter (p/s) | 20 |

## NATCHBAND
| | | | |
|---|---|---|---|
| 78 | Far In FARS 01 | Cadillac (Made In USA)/Being From The Sky (p/s) | 6 |

## BARRY NATHAN TRIO
| | | | |
|---|---|---|---|
| 80 | EMAL BNT 1 | MORNING SONGRISE (LP) | 50 |

## NATIONAL
| | | | |
|---|---|---|---|
| 05 | Beggars Banquet BBQ 385 | Abel/Warm Singing Whores (p/s) | 10 |
| 07 | Beggars Banquet BBQ 405 | Mistaken For Strangers/Blank Slate (p/s) | 8 |
| 07 | Beggars Banquet BBQ 407 | Apartment Story/Mansion On The Hill (live) (yellow vinyl) | 15 |
| 07 | Beggars Banquet BBQ 408 CDP | EXTRAS EP (tour CD, 1000 only) | 30 |
| 10 | 4AD AD3X50 | Terrible Love/You Were A Kindness (purple vinyl, p/s) | 12 |
| 03 | Brassland HWY 003 | SAD SONGS FOR DIRTY LOVERS (LP) | 40 |
| 05 | Beggars Banquet BBQLP 241 | ALLIGATOR (LP) | 18 |
| 07 | Beggars Banquet BBQLP 252 | BOXER (LP) | 18 |
| 10 | 4AD CAD 3X03X | HIGH VIOLET (2-LP, violet vinyl) | 30 |
| 13 | 4AD CAD 3315 | TROUBLE WILL FIND ME (2-LP, clear vinyl, card inserts box set) | 40 |

## NATIONAL ART HATE WEEK
| | | | |
|---|---|---|---|
| 09 | No Cat no | God Save Marcel Duchamp/Silent Revolt (p/s, mail order only, 350 copies, numbered) | 15 |

## NATIONAL-ELLS
| | | | |
|---|---|---|---|
| 67 | Parlophone R 5609 | Mr. Moon/Dance, Dance | 7 |

## NATIONAL HEAD BAND
| | | | |
|---|---|---|---|
| 71 | Warner Bros K 46094 | ALBERT 1 (LP) | 50 |

*(see also Caravan, Gary Moore, Toe-Fat, Uriah Heep)*

## NATIONAL HEALTH
| | | | |
|---|---|---|---|
| 78 | Affinity AFF 6 | NATIONAL HEALTH (LP) | 20 |
| 78 | Charly CRL 5010 | OF QUEUES AND CURES (LP) | 20 |

*(see also Hatfield & The North)*

## NATIONAL PINION POLE
| | | | |
|---|---|---|---|
| 66 | Planet PLF 111 | Make Your Mark Little Man/I Was The One You Came In With (in Planet sleeve) | 20 |
| 66 | Planet PLF 111 | Make Your Mark Little Man/I Was The One You Came In With | 15 |

## NATIONAL FLAG
| | | | |
|---|---|---|---|
| 75 | Private Pressing | THANK YOU AND GOODNIGHT (LP, insert, 100 only) | 400 |

## NATIVES
| | | | |
|---|---|---|---|
| 84 | Fearless FEAR 2 | Here Is The News/Love In A Day | 20 |

## NATO
| | | | |
|---|---|---|---|
| 81 | DV DVR 1 | Gangland/Tied Down (p/s) | 50 |

## NAT RUS & RANKING GLAD
| | | | |
|---|---|---|---|
| 77 | Nat Rus | Mash It/Come From Africa/Africa (12") | 40 |

## NATURAL ACOUSTIC BAND
| | | | |
|---|---|---|---|
| 73 | RCA RCA 2324 | Echoes/Is It True Blue | 5 |
| 72 | RCA SF 8272 | LEARNING TO LIVE (LP, textured gatefold sleeve) | 35 |
| 72 | RCA SF 8314 | BRANCHING IN (LP, with lyric insert) | 25 |

*(see also Krysia)*

## NATURAL BRIDGE BUNCH
| | | | |
|---|---|---|---|
| 69 | Atlantic 584 231 | Pig Snoots (Parts 1 & 2) | 7 |

## CLIVE NATURAL
| | | | |
|---|---|---|---|
| 77 | WIRL WIRL 1 | Marridge Rekka/No Money (12") | 40 |

## NATURAL FOUR
| | | | |
|---|---|---|---|
| 75 | Curtom 16583 | Love's So Wonderful/What's Happening Here | 15 |
| 75 | Atlantic K 56142 | HEAVEN RIGHT HERE ON EARTH (LP) | 30 |

## NATURAL GAS
| | | | |
|---|---|---|---|
| 76 | Private Stock PVLP 1007 | NATURAL GAS (LP, gatefold sleeve with inner sleeve) | 15 |

*(see also Badfinger, Blue Goose, Humble Pie, Uriah Heep, Quiver)*

## NATURAL IMPULSE
| | | | |
|---|---|---|---|
| 08 | Soul Junction SJ 502 | She Went Away/Time Was Right | 10 |

## THE NATURAL ITES AND THE REALISTICS
| | | | |
|---|---|---|---|
| 83 | CSA 12CSA 501 | Picture On My Wall/Jah Works Mama (12") | 12 |
| 84 | Realistic RR 03 | Black Roses/Gwan Do It (12") | 15 |

## NATURAL MAGIC
| | | | |
|---|---|---|---|
| 75 | Oyster OYR 102 | Strawberry Fields Forever/Isolated Lady | 10 |

*(see also Roger Glover, Eddie Hardin)*

## NATURAL MYSTIC
| | | | |
|---|---|---|---|
| 85 | Starlight SDLP 914 | GROOVE ROCKING (LP) | 15 |

## NATURAL MYSTIQUE
| | | | |
|---|---|---|---|
| 82 | Dune 2AA | Generals/In This Time (p/s) | 60 |

## NATURAL ROOTS
| | | | |
|---|---|---|---|
| 82 | Fasim FS106 | Know Yourself/Ain't Got No Money (12") | 20 |

## NATURAL VIBES
| | | | |
|---|---|---|---|
| 83 | Suffering & Faith SWEET 1 | Sweet Sensation/Version (12") | 30 |
| 82 | Starlight Records SDLP 907 | LIFE HARD IN A YARD (LP) | 35 |

MINT VALUE £

## NATURALITY
69   Ackee ACK 101      The Arena/Natural ................................................................. 50

## NATURALLY
79   Bushays BFM 111      I'll Get By/All I Have Is Written In Your Eyes (12") ......................... 15

## NATURALS (U.K.) (1)
64   Parlophone R 5116      Daisy Chain/That Girl ............................................................. 8
64   Parlophone R 5165      I Should Have Known Better/Didn' I? ........................................ 8
64   Parlophone R 5202      It Was You/Look At Me Now .................................................... 8
65   Parlophone R 5257      Blue Roses/Shame On You ..................................................... 8

*(see also Greatest Show On Earth)*

## NATURALS (U.K.) (2)
80   Refined RR2      STRANGE DAYS (EP, 500 only) ................................................. 30
81   Just For The Records      Six Girls & Alice (fold-out cover) ............................................. 15
82   Logo GO 414      Six Girls & Alice (fold-out cover, reissue) .................................. 8

## NATURALS (U.S.)
55   MGM SP 1123      The Finger Of Suspicion Points At You/You Forgot To Remember ........ 12
57   MGM MGM 939      The Buccaneers/The Ballad Of Sir Lancelot ............................... 8

*(see also Debbie Reynolds)*

## NAUGHTY THOUGHTS
82   Maestro MR 004      All Of Nothing/Weekdays (foldover p/s, some with press release inserts) ........ 30

## FATS NAVARRO
56   London LZ-C 14015      MEMORIAL (LP) ................................................................. 15

## NAVY BLUE
82   AP 572      THE PUSSERS (EP) ............................................................... 15

## JERRY NAYLOR
61   Top Rank JAR 591      Stop Your Crying/You're Thirteen ........................................... 25
67   Stateside SS 2029      Sweet Violets/Temptation Leads Me ........................................ 6
70   CBS 4882      But For Love/Angeline ......................................................... 5

## SHEL NAYLOR
63   Decca F 11776      How Deep Is The Ocean/La Bamba ........................................... 20
64   Decca F 11856      One Fine Day/It's Gonna Happen Soon ...................................... 200

*(see also Lieutenant Pigeon, Stavely Makepeace)*

## NAZARETH
72   Pegasus PGS 2      Dear John/Friends ............................................................. 20
72   Pegasus PGS 2      Dear John/Friends (2nd issue, PEG label, B-side lists 'Occasional Failure') ............ 25
72   Pegasus BCP 3      Dear John/Witchdoctor Woman/Morning Dew (unreleased, promo only, stamped white labels and insert) ........ 50
72   Pegasus PGS 4      Morning Dew/Spinning Top (PEG label) ..................................... 20
72   Pegasus BCP 8      Fool About You/Woke Up This Morning/Morning Dew (unreleased, promo only, handwritten white labels) ........ 50
72   Pegasus PGS 5      If You See My Baby/Hard Living (PEG label) ................................ 20
73   Mooncrest MOON 9      Bad Bad Boy/Hard Living/Spinning Top (in p/s) ........................... 5
74   Mooncrest MOON 22      Shanghai'd In Shanghai/Love, Now You're Gone ......................... 5
74   Mooncrest MOON 37      Love Hurts/Down ............................................................. 5
75   Mooncrest MOON 44      Hair Of The Dog/Too Bad, Too Sad ......................................... 5
75   Mooncrest MOON 47      My White Bicycle/My White Bicycle (A label promo only) ............... 12
75   Mooncrest MOON 47      My White Bicycle/Miss Misery ............................................... 5
76   Mountain PSLP191      I Don't Want To Go On Without You/Waiting For The Man (12" promo) ........ 15
92   Mausoleum 3670010.7      Every Time It Rains/This Flight Tonight (p/s) ................................ 5
78   Mountain TOP 37      Place In Your Heart/Kentucky Fried Blues (mispressing, B-side plays Bee Gees track, company sleeve) ........ 15
79   Mountain NAZ 4      Whatever You Want Babe/Telegram Parts 1, 2 & 3 (p/s, purple vinyl) ........ 10
80   NEMS BSD 1      NAZARETH LIVE (2 x 7", gatefold) ........................................... 6
71   Pegasus PEG 10      NAZARETH (LP, 1st issue, Pegasus picture label, textured matt sleeve) ........ 150
72   Pegasus PEG 10      NAZARETH (LP, 2nd issue, PEG label/glossy sleeve) ...................... 50
72   Pegasus PEG 14      EXERCISES (LP, gatefold sleeve) ............................................. 100
73   Mooncrest CREST 1      RAZAMANAZ (LP) ............................................................. 70
73   Mooncrest CREST 4      LOUD 'N' PROUD (LP) ......................................................... 70
75   Mountain TOPS 103      EXERCISES (LP, reissue) ....................................................... 15
74   Mooncrest CREST 10      NAZARETH (LP, reissue) ...................................................... 15
74   Mooncrest CREST 15      RAMPANT (LP, inner sleeeve, sticker insert) ............................... 70
75   Mountain TOPS 104      RAZAMANAZ (LP, reissue) .................................................... 15
75   Mooncrest CREST 27      HAIR OF THE DOG (LP, with inner) .......................................... 70
76   Mountain TOPS 109      CLOSE ENOUGH FOR ROCK 'N' ROLL (LP) .................................. 40
76   Mountain TOPS 113      PLAY 'N' THE GAME (LP, with inner sleeve) ............................... 30
77   Mountain TOPS 115      EXPECT NO MERCY (LP, with inner sleeve) ................................ 20
79   Mountain TOPS 123      NO MEAN CITY (LP, with inner sleeve) ..................................... 15
85   Sahara SAH 131      LOUD 'N' PROUD (LP, reissue) ............................................... 15

*(see also Dan McCafferty, Mark Five, Sensational Alex Harvey Band, Tandoori Cassette, Billy Rankin)*

## NAZIS AGAINST FASCISM
79   Truth TRUTH 1      Sid Did It (Intelligible)/Sid Did It (Radio Version) (p/s, 2 different issues) ........ 8

*(see also Vibrators)*

## NAZZ
68   Screen Gems SGC 219001      Open My Eyes/Hello It's Me ................................................. 25
69   Screen Gems SGC 219002      Hello It's Me/Crowded ....................................................... 15
69   Screen Gems SGC 219003      Not Wrong Long/Under The Ice .............................................. 10
69   Screen Gems SGC 221001      NAZZ (LP) ...................................................................... 65

*(see also Todd Rundgren)*

## 'N BETWEENS
66   Columbia DB 8080     You Better Run/Evil Witchman (demos credit In-Be-Tweens) .................................... 400

*(see also Slade, Vendors)*

## CHRIS NEAL
71   Fly BUG 15     Blame It All On Eve/All The Time In The World (p/s) ......................................... 6

## JOHNNY NEAL & STARLINERS
65   Pye 7N 15838     And I Will Love You/Walk Baby Walk ................................................................. 80
70   Parlophone R 5870     Put Your Hand In The Hand/Now........................................................................ 7

*(see also Storyteller)*

## RAY NEAL & ALLSTARS
81   Jookboy JOOK 1     Doin The Boogie/Get It On Moe (no p/s) ......................................................... 5

## TOMMY NEAL
68   Vocalion VL 9290     Goin' To A Happening/Tee Ta........................................................................... 50
68   Vocalion VL 9290     Goin' To A Happening/Tee Ta (DJ copy)......................................................... 125

## NEARLY NORMAL
80   Insurrection Now! INA 1     Bedtime/Die Baby Die!(hand-made p/s) ....................................................... 60

## NEAT
80s   Neatbeat LYN 6269     Hormones In Action/Take Your Chances (p/s) ................................................ 50

## NEAT CHANGE
68   Decca F 12809     I Lied To Auntie May/Sandman (in foldout p/s) ........................................... 120
68   Decca F 12809     I Lied To Auntie May/Sandman....................................................................... 60

*(see also Peter Banks, English Rose)*

## NEBULA
03   Sweet Nothing SNLP 026     ATOMIC RITUAL (LP)......................................................................................... 30

## NEBULA II
92   Reinforced RIVET 1232R     X-Plore H-Core/Peace Maker (Remixes) (12") ............................................... 15

## NECESSARIES
81   Sire SRK 3573     BIG SKY (LP) ..................................................................................................... 15
82   Sire SRK 3574     EVENT HORIZON (LP)....................................................................................... 15

*(see also Arthur Russell)*

## NECROMANDUS
90   Reflection MM 09     QUICKSAND DREAM (LP, 500 only) ................................................................. 18

## BERNIE NEE
58   Philips PB 794     Lend Me Your Comb/Medal Of Honour ......................................................... 10

*(see also Bernie Knee)*

## NEED
80   SKITZ 1     Let Them Eat Valium/Seduction (p/s) ............................................................ 30

## NEEDLES (1)
80   Ellie Jay EJSP 9340     Gotta Know You/Jayneski (no p/s) .................................................................. 70

## LOUIS NEEFS
69   Columbia DB 8561     Jennifer Jennings/I Love You .......................................................................... 25

## ELGIN NEELY
65   Vogue V 9240     Four Walls/I Could Be...................................................................................... 12

## NEGATIVE FX
84   Fundamental HOLY 7     NEGATIVE FX (LP) ............................................................................................ 25

## NEGATIVES
78   Look LK/SP 6478     Stakeout (50 copies with p/s) ....................................................................... 200
78   Look LK/SP 6478     Stakeout (no p/s) ............................................................................................ 40
80   Aardvark STEAL 1     Electric Waltz/Money Talks (p/s) ................................................................... 10
81   Aardvark STEAL 3     Scene Of The Crime (p/s).................................................................................. 8

## NEGATIVES IN COLOUR
82   NEG 1     Caught In Possession/Everyman...................................................................... 18

## NEGAZIONE
85   Children Of The Revolution     MUCCHIO SELVAGGIO (split LP with DECLINO)................................................ 75
    GURT 7

## NEGRIL
75   Torpedo TOR 51     I Shot The Sheriff/Negril.................................................................................. 10
75   Klik KLP 9005     NEGRIL (LP) ....................................................................................................... 30

## NEGRO
80   Negro NEG 1     Unite/DJ A HUMBLE I: Unite Tonight ........................................................... 120

## NEGUS DAWTAS
78   Natty Congo NATTY 001     I Speak The Truth/Hail Rastafari (Actually by Ranking Reuben)...................... 20

## NEGUS ROOTS MEETS THE MAD PROFESSOR
83   Negus Roots NERLP 009     DUB ROCKERS VOLUME 2 (LP) ....................................................................... 80

*(see also Lackley Castell)*

## CHRISTOPHER NEIL
72   RAK SRKA 6753     WHERE I BELONG (LP) ..................................................................................... 25

## FRED NEIL
69   Elektra EKSN 45036     Candy Man/The Water Is Wide ........................................................................ 8
69   Capitol CL 15616     Everybody's Talkin'/Badi-Da.......................................................................... 12
67   Elektra EKS 7293     BLEECKER & MACDOUGAL (LP) ...................................................................... 60
70   Capitol E-ST 657     OTHER SIDE OF THIS LIFE (LP) ....................................................................... 35

## DON NEILSON
60   Philips BF 1058     The House Is Haunted/For All We Know ........................................................... 5
62   Piccadilly 7N 35044     Forgotten Dreams/These Things Remain ........................................................ 5
63   Piccadilly 7N 35103     I Will Live My Life For You/How Do You Keep From Crying ............................. 5

MINT VALUE £

## NEKTAR

| | | | |
|---|---|---|---|
| 73 | United Artists NEK 1 | What Ya Gonna Do?/Day In The Life Of A Preacher Pt. One (Edit) (p/s) | 15 |
| 74 | United Artists UP 35706 | Fidgety Queen/Little Boy | 15 |
| 75 | United Artists UP 35853 | Astral Man/Nelly The Elephant | 10 |
| 73 | United Artists UAD 60041/2 | SOUNDS LIKE THIS (2-LP) | 10 |
| 74 | United Artists UAS 29499 | A TAB IN THE OCEAN (LP, gatefold sleeve) | 40 |
| 74 | United Artists UAG 29545 | REMEMBER THE FUTURE (LP, gatefold) | 35 |
| 74 | United Artists UAG 29680 | DOWN TO EARTH (LP, gatefold sleeve) | 35 |
| 76 | Decca SKL-R 5250 | RECYCLED (LP) | 30 |
| | | | 15 |

*(see also Robert Calvert)*

## NELLIE

| | | | |
|---|---|---|---|
| 69 | Gas GAS 126 | I Who Have Nothing/You Send Me | 60 |

## BILL NELSON('S RED NOISE)

| | | | |
|---|---|---|---|
| 71 | Smile LAF 2182/HG 116 | NORTHERN DREAM (LP, 250 only, numbered, in foldover gatefold sleeve with booklet) | 35 |
| 71 | Smile LAF 2182/HG 116 | NORTHERN DREAM (LP, 250 second pressing unnumbered, (reissues on the Butt label, £15) | 20 |
| 78 | Harvest SHSP 4095 | SOUND ON SOUND (LP) | 15 |
| 85 | Cocteau JEAN 1 | PERMANENT FLAME SINGLES BOX (box set of 5 singles) | 10 |
| 85 | Cocteau JEAN 2 | TRIAL BY INTIMACY (THE BOOK OF SPLENDOURS) (4-LP, box set, with book & postcards, initial copies misspelt as "The Book Splendours") | 20 |
| 11 | Esoteric COCDBOX 1002 | THE PRACTICE OF EVERYDAY LIFE (8-CD box set) | 40 |

*(see also A - Austr, Astral Navigations, Gagalactyca, Be-Bop Deluxe)*

## CLARE NELSON

| | | | |
|---|---|---|---|
| 59 | MGM MGM 1025 | The Valley Of Love/You Are My Sunshine | 8 |

## EARL NELSON

| | | | |
|---|---|---|---|
| 59 | London HLW 8950 | No Time To Cry/Come On | 30 |

## OLIVER NELSON

| | | | |
|---|---|---|---|
| 60 | Esquire 32-148 | SCREAMIN THE BLUES (LP, as the Oliver Nelson Sextet) | 50 |
| 63 | Verve VLP 9053 | FULL NELSON (LP) | 15 |
| 68 | HMV CLP 1868 | MORE BLUES AND THE ABSTRACT TRUTH (LP) | 18 |

## OZZIE & HARRIET NELSON

| | | | |
|---|---|---|---|
| 59 | London HA-P 2145 | OZZIE AND HARRIET NELSON (LP) | 30 |

## PETER NELSON

| | | | |
|---|---|---|---|
| 65 | Piccadilly 7N 35278 | Donna/I Want To Be Wanted | 8 |
| 66 | Piccadilly 7N 35314 | Don't Make Promises (You Can't Keep)/No Need To Cry | 7 |
| 72 | Peacock PEA502 | Good Scotch Whiskey/I Am A Ship | 20 |

## RICK(Y) NELSON

### 78s

| | | | |
|---|---|---|---|
| 57 | HMV POP 355 | I'm Walkin'/A Teenager's Romance | 40 |
| 57 | HMV POP 390 | You're My One And Only Love/BARNEY KESSEL: Honey Rock | 40 |
| 57 | London HLP 8499 | Be-Bop Baby/Have I Told You Lately That I Love You | 20 |
| 58 | London HLP 8542 | Stood Up/Waitin' In School | 20 |
| 58 | London HLP 8594 | Believe What You Say/My Bucket's Got A Hole In It | 20 |
| 58 | London HLP 8732 | Someday/I Got A Feeling | 20 |
| 58 | London HLP 8738 | Lonesome Town/My Babe | 20 |
| 59 | London HLP 8817 | It's Late/Never Be Anyone Else But You | 20 |
| 59 | London HLP 8927 | Just A Little Too Much/Sweeter Than You | 25 |
| 60 | London HLP 9021 | I Wanna Be Loved/Mighty Good | 60 |
| 60 | London HLP 9121 | Young Emotions/Right By My Side | 30 |
| 60 | London HLP 9188 | Yes, Sir, That's My Baby/I'm Not Afraid | 60 |

### SINGLES

| | | | |
|---|---|---|---|
| 57 | HMV POP 355 | I'm Walkin'/A Teenager's Romance (gold label lettering) | 150 |
| 57 | HMV POP 355 | I'm Walkin'/A Teenager's Romance (silver label lettering) | 40 |
| 57 | HMV POP 390 | You're My One And Only Love/BARNEY KESSEL: Honey Rock | 50 |
| 57 | London HLP 8499 | Be-Bop Baby/Have I Told You Lately That I Love You | 20 |
| 58 | London HLP 8542 | Stood Up/Waitin' In School | 20 |
| 58 | London HLP 8594 | Believe What You Say/My Bucket's Got A Hole In It | 20 |
| 58 | London HLP 8670 | Poor Little Fool/Don't Leave Me This Way | 5 |
| 58 | London HLP 8732 | Someday/I Got A Feeling | 5 |
| 58 | London HLP 8738 | Lonesome Town/My Babe | 5 |
| 59 | London HLP 8817 | It's Late/Never Be Anyone Else But You (all black or silver-top label) | 8 |
| 59 | London HLP 8894 | Just A Little Too Much/Sweeter Than You (unreleased) | 0 |
| 59 | London HLP 8927 | Just A Little Too Much/Sweeter Than You (triangular centre) | 10 |

*(The 45s listed above were originally issued with triangular centres; later round-centre copies are worth half to two-thirds these values.)*

| | | | |
|---|---|---|---|
| 59 | London HL 7081 | Just A Little Too Much/Sweeter Than You (export issue) | 10 |
| 60 | London HLP 9021 | I Wanna Be Loved/Mighty Good | 10 |
| 60 | London HLP 9121 | Young Emotions/Right By My Side | 5 |
| 60 | London HLP 9188 | Yes, Sir, That's My Baby/I'm Not Afraid | 5 |
| 61 | London HLP 9260 | You Are The Only One/Milk Cow Blues | 20 |
| 61 | London HLP 9260 | You Are The One And Only/Milk Cow Blues (with different label credit) | 15 |
| 61 | London HLP 9347 | Hello Mary Lou Goodbye Heart/Travelin' Man (later copies as "Hello Marylou Goodbye Heart") | 5 |
| 61 | London HLP 9440 | Everlovin'/A Wonder Like You | 6 |

*(The 45s listed above are credited to Ricky Nelson)*

| | | | |
|---|---|---|---|
| 62 | London HLP 9524 | Young World/Summertime | 10 |
| 62 | London HLP 9583 | Teen Age Idol/I've Got My Eyes On You (And I Like What I See) | 10 |
| 63 | London HLP 9648 | It's Up To You/I Need You | 5 |
| 63 | Brunswick 05885 | I Got A Woman/You Don't Love Me Anymore | 5 |

| | | | |
|---|---|---|---|
| 63 | Brunswick 05889 | String Along/Gypsy Woman | 5 |
| 63 | Brunswick 05895 | Fools Rush In/Down Home | 5 |
| 64 | Brunswick 05900 | For You/That's All She Wrote | 5 |
| 64 | Liberty LIB 66004 | Today's Teardrops/Thank You Darling | 5 |
| 64 | Brunswick 05908 | The Very Thought Of You/I Wonder | 5 |
| 64 | Brunswick 05918 | Lonely Corner/There's Nothing I Can Say | 5 |
| 64 | Brunswick 05924 | A Happy Guy/Don't Breathe A Word | 5 |
| 65 | Brunswick 05939 | Come Out Dancin'/Yesterday's Love | 10 |
| 66 | Brunswick 05964 | Louisiana Man/You Just Can't Quit (as Ricky Nelson) | 10 |
| 66 | Liberty LIB 12033 | I Need You/Wonder Like You | 10 |
| 69 | MCA MU 1106 | She Belongs To Me/Promises | 5 |
| 70 | MCA MU 1124 | Red Balloon/I Shall Be Released | 5 |
| 71 | MCA MU 1135 | Life/California (with Stone Canyon Band) | 5 |
| 72 | MCA MU 1147 | Love Minus Zero: No Limit/Gypsy Pilot (with Stone Canyon Band) | 5 |
| 72 | MCA MU 1165 | Garden Party/So Long Mama | 5 |
| 73 | MCA MUS 1181 | Palace Guard/A Flower Opens Gently By Itself | 5 |
| 73 | MCA MUS 1225 | Lifestream/Evil Woman Child | 5 |
| 74 | MCA MCA 126 | Windfall/Legacy (with Stone Canyon Band) | 5 |
| 74 | MCA MCA 144 | One Night Stand/Lifestream (with Stone Canyon Band) | 5 |
| 75 | MCA MCA 198 | Try (Try To Fall In Love)/Louisiana Belle (with Stone Canyon Band) | 5 |
| 77 | Epic S EPC 5821 | You Can't Dance/It's Another Day | 5 |

**EPs**

| | | | |
|---|---|---|---|
| 58 | London RE-P 1141 | RICKY PART 1 | 20 |
| 58 | London RE-P 1142 | RICKY PART 2 | 20 |
| 58 | London RE-P 1143 | RICKY PART 3 | 20 |
| 58 | London RE-P 1144 | RICKY PART 4 | 20 |
| 59 | London RE-P 1168 | RICKY NELSON PART 1 | 20 |
| 59 | London RE-P 1169 | RICKY NELSON PART 2 | 20 |
| 59 | London RE-P 1170 | RICKY NELSON PART 3 | 20 |
| 59 | London RE-P 1200 | RICKY SINGS AGAIN PART 1 | 20 |
| 59 | London RE-P 1201 | RICKY SINGS AGAIN PART 2 | 20 |
| 60 | London RE-P 1238 | I GOT A FEELING | 20 |
| 60 | London RE-P 1249 | RICKY SINGS SPIRITUALS | 20 |
| 61 | London RE-P 1300 | RICKY NELSON PART 4 | 20 |

*(The EPs listed above are credited to Ricky Nelson)*

| | | | |
|---|---|---|---|
| 62 | London RE-P 1339 | IT'S A YOUNG WORLD | 20 |
| 63 | London RE-P 1362 | IT'S UP TO YOU | 30 |
| 63 | Brunswick OE 9502 | ONE BOY TOO LATE | 30 |
| 64 | Liberty LEP 4001 | SINGS FOR YOU | 60 |
| 64 | Liberty LEP 4019 | THAT'S ALL | 60 |
| 65 | Liberty LEP 4028 | I'M IN LOVE AGAIN | 60 |
| 65 | Brunswick OE 9512 | HAPPY GUY | 30 |

**ALBUMS : LPS**

| | | | |
|---|---|---|---|
| 57 | London HA-P 2080 | RICKY | 40 |
| 58 | London HA-P 2119 | RICKY NELSON | 40 |
| 59 | London HA-P 2159 | RICKY SINGS AGAIN | 30 |
| 59 | London HA-P 2206 | SONGS BY RICKY | 30 |
| 60 | London HA-P 2290 | MORE SONGS BY RICKY (gatefold sleeve, mono) | 25 |
| 60 | London SAH-P 6102 | MORE SONGS BY RICKY (gatefold sleeve, stereo) | 30 |
| 61 | London HA-P 2379 | RICK IS 21 (mono) | 25 |
| 61 | London SAH-P 6179 | RICK IS 21 (stereo) | 25 |

*(Credited to Ricky Nelson)*

| | | | |
|---|---|---|---|
| 62 | London HA-P 2445 | ALBUM SEVEN (mono) | 25 |
| 62 | London SAH-P 6236 | ALBUM SEVEN (stereo) | 25 |
| 63 | London HA-P 8066 | IT'S UP TO YOU | 25 |
| 63 | Brunswick LAT 8545 | FOR YOUR SWEET LOVE (mono) | 25 |
| 63 | Brunswick STA 8545 | FOR YOUR SWEET LOVE (stereo) | 30 |
| 64 | Brunswick LAT 8562 | RICKY SINGS "FOR YOU" (mono) | 25 |
| 64 | Brunswick STA 8562 | RICKY SINGS "FOR YOU" (stereo) | 40 |
| 64 | Liberty LBY 3027 | MILLION SELLERS | 25 |
| 64 | Brunswick LAT/STA 8581 | THE VERY THOUGHT OF YOU | 20 |
| 64 | Brunswick LAT/STA 8596 | SPOTLIGHT ON RICK | 20 |
| 65 | Brunswick LAT 8615 | BEST ALWAYS | 20 |
| 65 | Brunswick LAT/STA 8630 | LOVE AND KISSES | 20 |
| 66 | Brunswick LAT/STA 8657 | BRIGHT LIGHTS, COUNTRY MUSIC | 20 |
| 67 | Brunswick LAT/STA 8680 | COUNTRY FEVER | 20 |

**SANDY NELSON**

| | | | |
|---|---|---|---|
| 59 | Top Rank JAR 197 | Teen Beat/Big Jump | 5 |
| 59 | London HLP 9015 | Drum Party/The Big Noise From Winnetka (tri centre) | 12 |
| 59 | London HLP 9015 | Drum Party/The Big Noise From Winnetka (78) | 25 |
| 60 | London HLP 9214 | I'm Walkin'/Bouncy (as Sandy Nelson & His Combo) | 10 |
| 61 | London HLP 9377 | Get With It/Big Noise From The Jungle | 10 |
| 61 | London HLP 9466 | Let There Be Drums/Quite A Beat (as Sandy Nelson On The Drums) | 5 |
| 62 | London HLP 9521 | Drums Are My Beat/My Girl Josephine | 7 |
| 62 | London HLP 9558 | Drummin' Up A Storm/Drum Stomp | 5 |
| 62 | London HLP 9612 | ...And Then There Were Drums/Live It Up | 5 |
| 63 | London HLP 9717 | Ooh Poo Pah Doo/Feel So Good | 5 |
| 64 | Liberty LIB 66060 | Teen Beat '65/Kitty's Theme | 5 |

# Terry NELSON (& FIREBALLS)

| 66 | Liberty LIB 12062 | Hey Joe/Come On Let's Go | 5 |
| 60 | Top Rank JKP 2060 | RUSHING FOR PERCUSSION (EP, 2 tracks by Preston Epps) | 10 |
| 62 | London REP 1337 | LET THERE BE DRUMS (EP) | 10 |
| 63 | London REP 1371 | IN THE MOOD (EP) | 10 |
| 65 | Liberty LEP 4033 | SANDY NELSON PLAYS (EP) | 10 |
| 60 | London HA-P 2260 | TEEN BEAT (LP, mono) | 20 |
| 60 | London SAH-P 6082 | TEEN BEAT (LP, stereo) | 25 |
| 61 | London HA-P 2425 | LET THERE BE DRUMS (LP, mono) | 20 |
| 61 | London SAH-P 6221 | LET THERE BE DRUMS (LP, stereo) | 25 |
| 62 | London HA-P 2446 | DRUMS ARE MY BEAT! (LP, mono) | 20 |
| 62 | London SAH-P 6237 | DRUMS ARE MY BEAT! (LP, stereo) | 25 |
| 62 | London HA-P 8009 | DRUMMIN' UP A STORM (LP, mono) | 20 |
| 62 | London SH-P 8009 | DRUMMIN' UP A STORM (LP, stereo) | 25 |
| 63 | London HA-P/SH-P 8029 | COMPELLING PERCUSSION (LP) | 20 |
| 63 | London HA-P/SH-P 8051 | TEENAGE HOUSE PARTY (LP) | 20 |
| 65 | Liberty LBY 3007 | SANDY NELSON PLAYS (LP) | 20 |
| 65 | Liberty LBY 3035 | LIVE IN LAS VEGAS (LP) | 20 |
| 66 | Liberty LBY 3061 | DRUMS A GO-GO (LP) | 20 |
| 66 | Liberty (S)LBY 3080 | SUPERDRUMS (LP) | 20 |

*(see also Preston Epps)*

## TERRY NELSON (& FIREBALLS)

| 65 | Dice CC 22 | I'll Stand By You/Love On A Saturday Night | 10 |
| 65 | Dice CC 23 | Run Run Baby/Bonita (as Terry Nelson & Fireballs) | 12 |
| 65 | Dice CC 25 | Bulldog Push/Pretty Little Girl (as Terry Nelson & Fireballs) | 12 |
| 65 | Dice CC 27 | Tomorrow Will Soon Be Here/My Blue Eyed Baby | 8 |
| 65 | Blue Beat BB 326 | Help/PRINCE BUSTER: Johnny Dollar | 25 |
| 66 | Halagala HG 11 | Take These Chains From My Heart/Let-Kiss | 6 |
| 67 | Halagala HG 19 | That True Love Must Be Me/Bulldog Walk | 5 |
| 69 | Rude Boy RBH 002 | Woman Whine And Grine/Dem City Girls (actually the FIRE-BALLS) | 20 |

## WILLIE NELSON

| 63 | Liberty LIB 55532 | Half A Man/The Last Letter | 5 |
| 64 | Liberty LIB 55697 | River Boy/Opportunity To Cry | 5 |
| 69 | RCA RCA 1867 | My Own Peculiar Way/Natural To Be Gone | 5 |
| 66 | RCA Victor RD 7749 | COUNTRY WILLIE (LP) | 15 |
| 66 | Liberty (S)LBY 1240 | AND THEN I WROTE (LP) | 15 |
| 69 | RCA RD 7997 | TEXAS IN MY SOUL (LP) | 15 |

## NELSON TRIO (U.K.)

| 57 | Oriole CB 1360 | Tear It Up/Roll The Carpet Up | 5 |

## NELSON TRIO (U.S.)

| 60 | London HLL 9019 | All In Good Time/The Town Crier | 15 |

## NEO MAYA

| 67 | Pye 7N 17371 | I Won't Hurt You/U.F.O. | 75 |

*(see also Episode Six)*

## CHIITRA NEOGY

| 68 | Gemini GMX 5030 | THE PERFUMED GARDEN (LP) | 22 |

## NEON BOYS

| 90 | Overground OVER 11 | TIME (12" EP, 20 test pressings only) | 20 |
| 91 | Overground OVER 19 | That's All I Know (Right Now)/Love Comes In Spurts/High Heeled Wheels/Don't Die/Time (last 2 tracks credited to Richard Hell & Voidoids [Part III]) (12" p/s, 2,000 only, clear vinyl) | 8 |

*(see also Richard Hell, Television)*

## NEON DIOR

| 80 | Diskatron DTRON 1 | Kid At Heart/It's In Her Kiss (p/s) | 10 |

## NEON HEARTS

| 77 | Neon Hearts NEON 1 | Venus Eccentric/Regulations (8" p/s) | 40 |
| 78 | Satril SAT 133 | Answers/Armchair Thriller (p/s) | 15 |
| 79 | Satril SAT 139 | Popular Music/Pretty As A Picture (p/s) | 8 |
| 79 | Satril SATL 4012 | POPULAR MUSIC (LP) | 15 |

## NEON (1)

| 78 | Sensible FAB 3 | Anytime Anyplace Anywhere/Bottles/I'm Only Little | 10 |
| 78 | Radar ADA 27 | Don't Eat Bricks/Hanging Off An O (p/s) | 5 |

## NEON (2)

| 80 | 3D 3D1 | Making Waves/Me I See In You (p/s) | 20 |
| 80 | Carrere 201 | Communication Without Sound/Remote Control | 12 |

## NEON BARBS

| 81 | Ligical Step | Break Your Chains/Adjust To Red (p/s) | 8 |

## NEON TETRA

| 82 | Deeda DD 01 | Tightrope/Night Boat To Amsterdam | 20 |

## NEPTUNE'S EMPIRE

| 71 | Polymax PXX 01 | NEPTUNE'S EMPIRE (LP) | 150 |

## NERO & GLADIATORS

| 61 | Decca F 11329 | Entry Of The Gladiators/Boots | 10 |
| 61 | Decca F 11367 | In The Hall Of The Mountain King/The Trek To Rome | 10 |
| 61 | Decca F 11413 | Czardas/That's A Long Time Ago | 12 |

*(see also Laurie Jay, Gladiators, Screaming Lord Sutch & Savages, State Of Mickey & Tommy)*

## PETER NERO

| 69 | CBS 4277 | Soulful Strut/For Once In My Life | 8 |
| 69 | CBS 4464 | Theme From Picasso Summer/Be In | 6 |

## PAUL NERO (SOUNDS)
68   Liberty LBL 83100                     NERO'S SOUL PARTY (LP) ............................................................................ 25

## NERVE (1)
67   Page One POF 019                      No. 10 Downing Street/Georgie's March .................................................. 12
68   Page One POF 055                      Magic Spectacles/Come The Day ............................................................ 20
68   Page One POF 081                      It Is/Mystery Lady ................................................................................. 18
68   Page One POF 097                      Piece By Piece/Satisfying Kind .............................................................. 15

*(see also Lovin')*

## NERVE (2)
95   Straw B001                            Submarine/Seeds From The Electric Garden (p/s) ....................................... 6

## NERVES (1)
78   Lightning GIL 520                     TV Adverts/Sex Education (p/s) .............................................................. 35

## NERVES (2)
81   Good Vibrations BIG 3                 NOTRE DEMO (LP, official bootleg, foldover sleeve with booklet) ............... 20

## NERVES (3)
94   Inflammable Material BURN             Bits/SUBSTANDARD: Rostock (p/s) ........................................................... 7
     2

## NERVE SENTA
81   Tense Raven FRM 041                   You Turn Me On/Secret Admirer .............................................................. 25

## NERVOUS EATERS
80   Elektra K12481                        Loretta/Get Stuffed ................................................................................. 5

## NERVOUS CHOIR
89   Cathexis CRN 5407                     O'David/Tonight We Start On Witches/Alsatians/Introducing (p/s, with inserts) ........... 7

## NERVOUS NORVUS
56   London HLD 8338                       Ape Call/Wild Dog Of Kentucky (gold label print) ................................... 50
56   London HLD 8338                       Ape Call/Wild Dog Of Kentucky (silver label print) ................................. 20
57   London HLD 8383                       Dig/Bullfrog Hop (gold label print) ....................................................... 60
57   London HLD 8383                       Dig/Bullfrog Hop (silver label print) ..................................................... 30
62   Salvo SLO 1812                        Does A Chinese Chicken Have A Pigtail/ROD BARTON: Dear Old San Francisco ........... 20
85   Big Beat NED 12                       NERVOUS NORVUS (mini-LP) ................................................................... 15

## NERVOUS GERMANS
82   Rondelet ROUND 3000                   These Boots Are Made For Walking/Watch Out............................................ 6

*(see also Razar. Soho Jets)*

## JIM NESBIT
65   Vocalion V 9241                       Tiger In My Tank/I Can't Stand This Living Alone.................................... 25

## SAM NESBIT
75   Right On 103                          Keep On Hustling Baby/Instrumental Version............................................. 6

## MICHAEL NESMITH (& FIRST/SECOND NATIONAL BAND)
70   RCA RCA 2001                          Joanne/The Crippled Lion (with First National Band) ................................ 5
71   RCA RCA 2053                          Silver Moon/Lady Of The Valley (with First National Band)......................... 5
71   RCA RCA 2086                          Nevada Fighter/Here I Am (with First National Band) ................................ 5
70   RCA SF 8136                           MAGNETIC SOUTH (LP, with First National Band) ..................................... 25
71   RCA SF 8209                           NEVADA FIGHTER (LP, with First National Band) ..................................... 25
72   RCA SF 8276                           TANTAMOUNT TO TREASON VOLUME ONE (LP, with Second National Band) ........... 20
73   RCA APL1 0164                         PRETTY MUCH YOUR STANDARD RANCH STASH (LP, solo) ....................... 15
75   Island ILPS 9428                      THE PRISON (LP, boxed with book, unreleased in U.K.) ................................ 0
76   RCA RS 1064                           THE BEST OF MICHAEL NESMITH (LP) ...................................................... 15

*(see also Monkees, Wichita Train Whistle)*

## NESSIE
81   SRTS 81 CUS 1092                      Can I See Her Tomorrow/Tell Her.......................................................... 10

## NEU!
73   United Artists UP 35485               Super/Neuschnee (p/s) ........................................................................... 25
73   United Artists UP 35485               Super/Neuschnee .................................................................................. 20
75   United Artists UP 35874               Isi/After Eight...................................................................................... 20
72   United Artists UAS 29396              NEU (LP, laminated cover) .................................................................... 80
73   United Artists UAS 29500              NEU II (LP, gatefold sleeve) .................................................................. 80
75   United Artists UAS 29782              NEU '75 (LP, gatefold sleeve) ................................................................ 70
10   Gronland LPGRONI                      NEU (LP, gatefold, reissue, white vinyl) ................................................ 15
10   Gronland LPGRONII                     NEU 2 (LP, gatefold, reissue, white vinyl) ............................................. 15
10   Gronland LPGRONIII                    NEU '75 (LP, reissue) ........................................................................... 15

*(see also Kraftwerk, La Dusseldorf)*

## NEU ELECTRIC
79   Synthethesia SGS 207                  SURREAL MODERN MUZIK EP ................................................................. 8

## NEU ELEKTRIKK
79   Synthethesia SGS 107                  Lust Of Berlin/Distractions (p/s, stamped white labels) ........................... 20
80   Synthethesia SYN 1                    COVER GIRL EP ..................................................................................... 10

## NEUROSIS
04   Neurot NR 033                         THE EYE OF EVERY STORM (LP, gatefold, inner, poster, grey marbled vinyl) ......... 30
07   Neurot NR 050                         GIVEN TO THE RISING (LP, gatefold, inner, black/white splattered vinyl) ......... 20

## NEUTRAL MILK HOTEL
95   Fire BLAZE 79                         Everything Is/Snow Song Part 1............................................................. 20
98   Blue Rose BRRC 10237                  Holland, 1945/Engine (picture disc, numbered fold-out poster in polythene bag......... 30

## NEUTRONS
74   United Artists UP 35704               Dance Of The Psychedelic Lounge Lizard/Suzy And The Wonder Boy ............. 5
74   United Artists UAG 29652              BLACK HOLE STAR (LP, with inner sleeve) ............................................. 15
75   United Artists UAG 29726              TALES FROM THE BLUE COCOONS (LP, laminated gatefold sleeve)................ 15

*(see also Clive John, Gentle Giant, Man)*

## NEVER NEVER
88  Candy 001                          Come On Yvonne/Space Blues ................................................................................ 5

## NEVER! NEVER!
87  Round NN001                        Americana/Over The Top ...................................................................................... 5

## NEVILLE (WILLOUGHBY)
72  Explosion EX 2057                  I Love Jamaica/Marry Me Marie ........................................................................... 5
*(see also Whistling Willie)*

## AARON NEVILLE
67  Stateside SS 584                   Tell It Like It Is/Why Worry .................................................................................. 20
67  Stateside SS 584                   Tell It Like It Is/Why Worry (DJ Copy) ................................................................ 40
69  B&C CB 107                         Tell It Like It Is/Why Worry (reissue) .................................................................... 5
91  A&M AMY 835                        Voodoo/Close Your Eyes/Hercules (12") ........................................................... 15
67  Liberty LBY 3089                   LIKE IT 'TIS (LP) .................................................................................................. 50

## ART NEVILLE
76  Specialty SON 5008                 Cha-Dooky-Doo/Zing Zing .................................................................................... 5

## NEW AGE
81  Dining Out TUX 14                  Jane Fonda/Radio Show (p/s) ............................................................................... 5
82  Dining Out TUX 18                  LIVIN FOR NOW (12" EP, p/s) ............................................................................. 15
82  Dining Out TUX 25                  ALL THE MONKEYS AREN'T IN THE ZOO, MARYLOO (LP) ............................... 20

## NEW CULTURE
72  Priory PRY 002                     Seek Out The Sun/Strange ............................................................................... 100

## NEW RECRUITS
82  Dischord DIS 1                     Over The Pillow/The Aufrau Principle/All In An Hour (no p/s) ............................ 20

## NEW YORK NEW YORK
83  Urchin NY 2001                     Roger Wilson Said/Too Drunk To Drive (p/s) ...................................................... 8
85  Beach Culture 2 BC                 I WANNA BE LIKE YOU (12" EP) .......................................................................... 15
85  Izuma IZUMA LP 1                   NEW YORK NEW YORK (LP) ................................................................................ 18
*(see also Higsons. Terry Edwards, Serious Drinking)*

## NEW AGE STEPPERS
80  On-U Sound ONU 1                   Fade Away/LONDON UNDERGROUND: Learn A Language (p/s) ...................... 12
81  Statik 6                           My Love/Love Forever ......................................................................................... 6
81  Statik 612                         My Love/Love Forever (12") ............................................................................... 20
11  For Us FU 047                      Fade Away/Conquer (p/s, 600 only) ................................................................... 5
80  On-U Sound ONULP 1                 NEW AGE STEPPERS (LP) .................................................................................... 25
81  Statik/On U Sound STATLP 2         ACTION BATTLEFIELD (LP) .................................................................................. 25
82  On U Sound ONULP 21                FOUNDATION STEPPERS (LP) .............................................................................. 25

## NEW ASIA
81  Situation 2                        Central Proposition/Here And There Now And Then (p/s) ...................................... 5

## NEW BAD THINGS
95  Lissys LISS 9                      Nesting/I'll Arrest Myself/Like (p/s) .................................................................... 5

## NEWBEATS
64  Hickory 45-1269                    Bread And Butter/Tough Little Buggy (pink or black/blue label) .......................... 7
64  Hickory 45-1282                    Everything's Alright/Pink Dally Rue ................................................................... 10
65  Hickory 45-1290                    Break Away/Hey O Daddy O ............................................................................... 10
65  Hickory 45-1305                    The Birds Are For The Bees/Better Watch Your Step ........................................... 8
65  Hickory 45-1320                    I Can't Hear You No More/Little Child ............................................................... 15
65  Hickory 45-1332                    Run Baby Run/Mean Woolly Willie .................................................................... 30
65  Hickory 45-1332                    Run Baby Run/Mean Woolly Willie (DJ copy) .................................................... 70
66  Hickory 45-1366                    Shake Hands (And Come Out Crying)/Too Sweet To Be Forgotten ..................... 20
66  Hickory 45-1387                    Crying My Heart Out/Short Of Love ................................................................... 40
66  Hickory 45-1387                    Crying My Heart Out/Short Of Love (DJ copy) ................................................... 70
66  Hickory 45-1422                    My Yesterday Love/Patent On Love .................................................................... 10
71  London HLE 10341                   Run Baby Run (Back Into My Arms)/Am I Not My Brother's Keeper ................... 6
65  Hickory LPE 1503                   NEWBEATS (EP) .................................................................................................. 30
65  Hickory LPE 1506                   AIN'T THAT LOVIN' YOU BABY (EP) .................................................................... 30
66  Hickory LPE 1510                   OH! GIRLS GIRLS (EP) ......................................................................................... 30
65  Hickory LPM 120                    BREAD AND BUTTER (LP) .................................................................................... 35
72  London SHE 8428                    RUN BABY RUN (LP) ........................................................................................... 15
*(see also Dean & Mark, Larry Henley)*

## NEW BLOCKADERS
82  Private Pressing                   CHANGEZ LES BLOCKEURS (LP, 100 only, white label A4 sheet as cover) ...... 300
91  Hypnagogia GOG 01                  SYMPHONIE IN X MAJOR (LP, 500 only, numbered) .......................................... 20

## NEWBOY
73  Count Shelly CS007                 Sweet Talk/J ENGLISH: One And Only ................................................................ 20

## NEW BREED
65  Decca F 12295                      Friends And Lovers Forever/Unto Us ................................................................. 75

## MICKEY NEWBURY
72  Elektra K 12047                    An American Trilogy/San Francisco Mabel Joy ..................................................... 6

## NEWBY
65  Pye 7N 15986                       I Can't Grow Peaches On A Cherry Tree/The Children Sleep ................................ 7

## NEWBY & JOHNSON
70  Mercury 6052 027                   I Want To Give You My Everything/Sweet Happiness ......................................... 25

## NEWCASTLE BIG BAND
72  Impulse ISS NBB 106                NEWCASTLE BIG BAND (LP, white labels, 2,000 only) ................................... 150
*(see also Last Exit, Police, Sting, Radio Actors)*

## NEW CENSATION
75  DJM DJS 10371                      First Round Knockout/Everybody's Got A Story ................................................... 8

**NEW COLONY SIX**
66    London HLZ 10033    I Confess/Dawn Is Breaking ............................................................. 75
66    Stateside SS 522    At The River's Edge/I Lie Awake ...................................................... 50
68    Mercury MF 1030    I Will Always Think About You/Hold Me With Your Eyes ............. 12
69    Mercury MF 1086    Things I'd Like To Say/Come And Give Your Love To Me ............. 10

**NEWCOMERS**
72    Stax 2025 063    Pin The Tail On The Donkey/Mannish Boy .................................... 8
75    Stax STXS 2023    Keep An Eye On Your Close Friends/(Instrumental Version) ...... 10

**NEW CUOREY**
73    Taurus TR 101    Vietnam/The Girl I Had .................................................................. 25

**NEW DAWN**
69    private pressing    MAINLINE (LP) ................................................................................ 80

**NEW DEAL STRING BAND**
69    Argo ZDA 104    DOWN IN THE WILLOW (LP, with insert) ..................................... 30

**NEW DECADE**
92    Out Of Romford ROCC 002    Get The Message/ABC Remix (12", stamped white labels) ......... 10
94    Out Of Romford OOR 011    NARROW MINDS (2-LP) ................................................................. 18

**NEW DEPARTURES QUARTET**
60s    Transatlantic TRA 134    THE NEW DEPARTURES QUARTET (LP, with Stan Tracey) ........... 40
*(see also Stan Tracey)*

**MARTIN NEWELL**
80    Off Street OSR 001    Young Jobless/Sylvie In Toytown (p/s) ......................................... 30
80    Liberty BP 392    Young Jobless/Sylvie In Toytown (p/s reissue) ............................. 8
*(see also Gypp, Cleaners From Venus)*

**NEW ENGLAND**
79    Infinity INF 110    P.U.N.K./Shoot (green vinyl, 'lightning' PVC sleeve) .................... 5

**DENNIS NEWEY**
61    Philips PB 1134    Checkpoint/Title Unknown ............................................................ 10
61    Philips PB 1198    Border Patrol/Yes Yes .................................................................... 10
62    Philips 326 588 BF    The Nightriders/The Pied Piper ..................................................... 10

**NEW FACES**
65    Pye 7N 15842    So Small/Blue Mist .......................................................................... 10
65    Pye 7N 15931    Never Gonna Love Again/You'll Be Too Late .................................. 8
66    Pye 7N 17029    Like A Man/Shake Up The Party (Myra) ....................................... 15
67    Pye 7N 17335    Lace Covered Window/The Life That I Lead ................................. 10
68    Decca F 12746    We Can Get There By Candlelight/The Yellow Road ..................... 8
68    Decca F 12862    Someday/Biscuit Coloured Overcoat ............................................ 7
69    Decca F 12933    Carnival Day/Grandfather Dugan .................................................. 7
69    Decca F 12968    There Is An Island In The Sun/Happy The Heart That I Own ......... 7
74    Ember MBS 334    Where Would I Find Another You/Lullaby ..................................... 6

**NEW FORESTERS**
65    Lyntone LYN 932/933    Travel/LIZARDS: My Love Goes On (Sheffield Students Rag record) ...... 30

**NEW FORMULA**
67    Piccadilly 7N 35381    Do It Again A Little Bit Slower/I'm On The Outside Looking In ...... 18
67    Piccadilly 7N 35401    I Want To Go Back There Again/Can't You See That She Loves Me ..... 18
68    Pye 7N 17552    My Baby's Coming Home/Burning In The Background Of My Mind ..... 20
69    Pye 7N 17818    Stay Indoors/Hare Krishna (in export p/s) .................................. 40
69    Pye 7N 17818    Stay Indoors/Hare Krishna ........................................................... 25

**NEW GENERATION**
69    Spark SRL 1000    Sadie And Her Magic Mister Garland/Digger ............................... 15
69    Spark SRL 1007    Smokey Blues Away/She's A Soldier Boy ...................................... 10
70    Spark SRL 1019    Police Is Here/Mister C .................................................................. 15

**NEW HEARTS**
77    CBS 5800    Just Another Teenage Anthem/Blood On The Knife (p/s) ........... 10
78    CBS 6381    Plain Jane/My Young Teacher (p/s) .............................................. 10
*(see also Secret Affair)*

**NEW HERITAGE**
73    Westwood WRS 028    ALL MANNER OF THINGS (LP) ...................................................... 50

**NEW HOPE**
69    London HL 10296    Won't Find Better Than Me/They Call It Love .............................. 18
*(see also Kit Kats)*

**NEW HORIZON**
73    Decca F13463    Hullabaloo/Believe In Yourself ..................................................... 10

**NEW INSPIRATION**
67    Major Minor MM 539    You Made A Fool of Me/M.T. ......................................................... 25
73    Penny Farthing PEN 803    Medicine Man/Is It Really That Hard To Understand .................... 10

**NEW JAZZ GROUP**
56    Tempo EXA 39    MODERN JAZZ SCENE (EP) ........................................................... 50

**NEW JAZZ ORCHESTRA**
65    Decca LK 4690    WESTERN REUNION (LONDON 1965) (LP) ..................................... 80
69    Verve SVLP 9236    DEJEUNER SUR L'HERBE (LP) ....................................................... 250
*(see also Neil Ardley, Nucleus)*

**NEW JERSEY CONNECTION**
82    Nitelife LIFE 1    Love Don't Come Easy/Love Don't Come Easy (Instrumental) ...... 10
82    Nitelife LIFE 1    Love Don't Come Easy/Love Don't Come Easy (Instrumental) (12") ...... 15

**NEW JUMP BAND**
68    Domain D 1    The Only Kind Of Girl/Seven Kinds Of Sweet Lovin' ..................... 25

MINT VALUE £

## NEW LEAF
| | | | |
|---|---|---|---|
| 80 | LEAF 101 | Warning Take Warning/Roots Rock Reggae (no p/s) | 30 |

## ANDY NEWMAN
| | | | |
|---|---|---|---|
| 72 | Track 2406 103 | RAINBOW (LP, gatefold sleeve, black/silver label) | 25 |

*(see also Thunderclap Newman)*

## BRAD NEWMAN
| | | | |
|---|---|---|---|
| 62 | Fontana H 357 | Somebody To Love/This Time It's Love | 15 |
| 62 | Fontana H 369 | Get A Move On/Here And Now And Evermore | 15 |
| 62 | Fontana 267 220TF | Stay By Me/Candy Lips | 10 |
| 62 | Fontana 267 243TF | Point Of No Return/Now I've Lost You | 10 |
| 63 | Fontana 267 273TF | I'll Find You Another Baby/No Man Should Ever Be Alone | 10 |
| 64 | Piccadilly 7N 35174 | Please Don't Cry/Every Hour Of Living | 8 |

## CARLTON NEWMAN
| | | | |
|---|---|---|---|
| 85 | Roots Pool RP 003 | Front Line/EDI FITZROY: Pressure | 20 |

## COLIN NEWMAN
| | | | |
|---|---|---|---|
| 80 | Beggars Banquet BEG 48 | B/Classic Remains/Alone On Piano (p/s) | 5 |
| 81 | Beggars Banquet BEG 52 | Inventory/This Picture (p/s) | 5 |
| 80 | Beggars Banquet BEGA 20 | A-Z (LP) | 15 |
| 81 | 4AD CAD 108 | PROVISIONALLY ENTITLED THE SINGING FISH (LP) | 15 |
| 82 | 4AD CAD 201 | NOT TO (LP) | 15 |

*(see also Wire)*

## DEL NEWMAN SOUND
| | | | |
|---|---|---|---|
| 67 | Columbia SCX 6181 | FLOWER GARDEN (LP) | 20 |

## JIMMY (C.) NEWMAN
| | | | |
|---|---|---|---|
| 57 | London HLD 8460 | A Fallen Star/I Can't Go On This Way | 30 |
| 59 | MGM MGM 1009 | What'cha Gonna Do/So Soon | 15 |
| 59 | MGM MGM 1037 | Grin And Bear It/The Ballad Of Baby Doe | 10 |
| 60 | MGM MGM 1085 | A Lovely Work Of Art/What About Me | 8 |
| 61 | MGM MGM 1112 | Now That You're Gone/Wanting You With Me Tonight | 8 |
| 59 | MGM MGM-EP 706 | GRIN AND BEAR IT - COUNTRY AND WESTERN STYLE (EP) | 30 |

## JOE NEWMAN (SEXTET)
| | | | |
|---|---|---|---|
| 57 | Vogue Coral Q 72244 | Cocktails For Two/Later For The Happenings | 5 |

## MARK NEWMAN
| | | | |
|---|---|---|---|
| 69 | Lestar 712 | MARK NEWMAN (EP) | 30 |

## NANETTE NEWMAN
| | | | |
|---|---|---|---|
| 77 | B&C BCS 0004 | Fun Food Factory/Morris (The Studio Mouse) | 6 |

## PAUL NEWMAN
| | | | |
|---|---|---|---|
| 66 | Mercury MF 969 | Ain't You Got A Heart/Tears On My Pillow | 50 |

## RANDY NEWMAN
| | | | |
|---|---|---|---|
| 68 | Reprise RS 20692 | Love Story/I Think It's Going To Rain Today | 5 |
| 70 | Reprise RS 20945 | Gone Dead Train/JACK NITZSCHE: Harry Flowers | 5 |
| 68 | Reprise R(S)LP 6286 | RANDY NEWMAN CREATES SOMETHING NEW UNDER THE SUN (LP) | 15 |
| 70 | Reprise RSLP 6373 | 12 SONGS (LP) | 15 |

*(see also Harry Nilsson, Tom Petty & Heartbreakers)*

## TOM NEWMAN
| | | | |
|---|---|---|---|
| 75 | Virgin VS120 | Sad Sing/Ali's Got A Broken Bone | 8 |
| 75 | Virgin VS130 | Don't Treat Your Woman Bad/Why Does Love Hurt So Bad | 5 |
| 75 | Virgin VS133 | Sleep/Darling Corey | 6 |
| 75 | Virgin V 2022 | FINE OLD TOM (LP, features Mike Oldfield) | 20 |
| 75 | Virgin V 2042 | LIVE AT THE ARGONAUT (LP, unreleased, test pressings only) | 80 |
| 77 | Decca TXS 123 | FAERIE SYMPHONY (LP, gatefold sleeve) | 30 |
| 88 | Oceandisc | OZYMANDIAS (LP, unissued, 20 test pressings only in proof sleeve) | 30 |

*(see also Jade Warrior, July, Mike Oldfield)*

## TONY NEWMAN
| | | | |
|---|---|---|---|
| 68 | Decca F 12795 | Soul Thing/Let The Good Times Roll | 30 |
| 70 | Decca F 13041 | Soul Thing/Let The Good Times Roll (reissue) | 10 |

*(see also Sounds Incorporated, Flying Machine, Pinkerton['s Assorted Colours], May Blitz, Three Man Army)*

## THE NEW MASTERSOUNDS
| | | | |
|---|---|---|---|
| 00 | Blow It Hard BIH 017 | One Note Brown/Burnt Black | 20 |

## NEW MATH
| | | | |
|---|---|---|---|
| 79 | Reliable Gum 002 | Die Trying/Angela (original issue, p/s) | 20 |
| 79 | CBS 7916 | Die Trying/Angela (p/s, reissue) | 8 |

## NEWMENS
| | | | |
|---|---|---|---|
| 72 | Parlophone R5941 | Start My Life Again/A Million Tears | 10 |

## NEW MODEL
| | | | |
|---|---|---|---|
| 83 | Mr. Clean MERC 001 | Chilean Warning/The World Thru Our Eyes/Totalitarian Terror (p/s, in 7" x 10" folder) | 10 |
| 83 | Mr. Clean MERC 001 | Chilean Warning/The World Thru Our Eyes/Totalitarian Terror (p/s) | 6 |

## NEW MODEL SOLDIER
| | | | |
|---|---|---|---|
| 81 | Bunny Rabbit Catch The Man<br>BUN 001 | DANCE THE DEATH OF A THOUSAND CUTS EP | 200 |

## NEW MONITORS
| | | | |
|---|---|---|---|
| 72 | Buddah 2011 118 | Fence Around Your Heart/Have You Seen Her | 30 |

## PETER NEWNHAM
| | | | |
|---|---|---|---|
| 77 | B & C BCS 011 | Rudi/Outside My Window (100 only) | 150 |

## NEW ORDER (1)
| | | | |
|---|---|---|---|
| 81 | Come Org WDC 883011 | BRADFORD RED LIGHT DISTRICT (cassette) | 50 |
| 81 | Come Org. CARA12 | BRADFORD RED LIGHT DISTRICT (LP) | 110 |

*(see also Come)*

## NEW ORDER (2)

| | | | |
|---|---|---|---|
| 81 | Factory FAC 33 | Ceremony/In A Lonely Place (p/s) | 15 |
| 81 | Factory FAC 33T | Ceremony/In A Lonely Place (12") | 12 |
| 81 | Factory FAC 3312 | Ceremony (Re-recording)/In A Lonely Place (Extended) (12", cream & blue p/s) | 12 |
| 81 | Factory FAC 53 | Procession/Everything's Gone Green (9 different coloured sleeves : black, brown, red, orange, yellow, green, aquamarine, blue and purple on a grey background) | 10 |
| 81 | Factory Benelux FBNL 8 | Everything's Gone Green/Mesh/Cries & Whispers (12", yellow sleeve) | 12 |
| 81 | Factory FAC 51B | Rocking Carol/Ode To Joy (flexidisc, given away at Hacienda, 4,000 only) | 30 |
| 82 | Factory FAC 63 | Temptation/Hurt (p/s) | 10 |
| 82 | Factory FAC 63 | Temptation/Hurt (12", p/s) | 10 |
| 83 | Factory FAC 7312 | Blue Monday/The Beach (12", first pressing, die-cut sleeve, silver insert) | 20 |
| 82 | Factory FAC7312 | Blue Monday/The Beach (12", second pressing, die-cut sleeve, black insert) | 12 |
| 83 | Factory FAC 93 | Confusion (Edit)/Confusion (Edit) (p/s, DJ promo only) | 20 |
| 84 | Factory FAC 103 | Thieves Like Us (Edit)/Lonesome Tonight (Edit) (p/s, DJ promo only) | 15 |
| 88 | Factory FAC 73RD | Blue Monday 1988/Blue Monday (Dub mix) (12", p/s, DJ promo only) | 10 |
| 88 | Factory FACDV 73R | Blue Monday 1988 (12 Inch)/Blue Monday 1988 (7 Inch)/Beach Buggy/Blue Monday 1988 (Video) (CD Video) | 50 |
| 88 | Factory FACDV 183 | True Faith (Remix 12 Inch)/Evil Dust/True Faith (7 Inch) (CD Video)/True Faith (CD Video) | 40 |
| 89 | Factory FAC 263DJ | Round & Round (Ben Grosse Mix)/(12" Mix)/(Detroit Mix) (12", p/s, DJ only) | 12 |
| 89 | Factory FAC 273/7 | Run 2 (Edit)/MTO (Edit) (DJ promo only, 500 pressed) | 10 |
| 11 | Rhino FAC 33 | Ceremony (Original Version)/In A Lonely Place (12" Version)//Ceremony (Heart & Soul Rehearsal Version)/In A Lonely Place (Unreleased Rehearsal Version) (12") | 25 |
| 81 | Factory FACT 50 | MOVEMENT (LP) | 20 |
| 83 | Factory FACT 75 | POWER CORRUPTION & LIES (LP, die cut sleeve) | 15 |
| 85 | Factory FACT 100 | LOW-LIFE (LP, rice paper outer sleeve) | 18 |
| 86 | Factory FACT 150SP | BROTHERHOOD (LP, limited metallic sleeve) | 20 |
| 86 | Factory FACD 150SP | BROTHERHOOD (CD with 'State Of The Nation' & metallic booklet) | 25 |
| 87 | Factory FACT 200 | SUBSTANCE (LP, 2 inners) | 20 |
| 87 | Factory FACT 200 | THE GATEFOLD SUBSTANCE (LP, numbered gatefold sleeve, 1,000 only) | 30 |
| 87 | Factory FACT 200c | SUBSTANCE (cassette, 200 only in box set with insert) | 20 |
| 93 | London 8284131 | REPUBLIC (LP) | 25 |
| 95 | London 8286571 | (THE REST OF) NEW ORDER (2-LP) | 20 |
| 94 | London 8285801 | BEST OF (2-LP, with inner sleeve) | 30 |
| 01 | London 8573896211 | GET READY (LP) | 35 |
| 05 | London 2564622021 | WAITING FOR THE SIREN'S CALL (2-LP) | 30 |
| 15 | Mute BXSTUMM 390 | MUSIC COMPLETE (8 x 12", coloured vinyl, boxed set, signed) | 100 |
| 15 | Mute BXSTUMM 390 | MUSIC COMPLETE (8 x 12", coloured vinyl, boxed set, unsigned) | 60 |

*(see also Joy Division, Electronic)*

## NEW ORLEANS BOOTBLACKS

| | | | |
|---|---|---|---|
| 54 | Columbia SCM 5090 | Flat Foot/Mad Dog | 8 |

## NEW OVERLANDERS

| | | | |
|---|---|---|---|
| 69 | RCA 1861 | Thought Back/These Are Not My People | 6 |
| 70 | RCA 1953 | Unchained Melody/Memories | 6 |

## NEW RACE

| | | | |
|---|---|---|---|
| 83 | Statik STAT LP 16 | THE FIRST & THE LAST (LP) | 25 |

## NEW RELIGION

| | | | |
|---|---|---|---|
| 72 | Bamboo BAM 70 | In The Black Caribbean/Black Is Black | 50 |
| 73 | Ackee ACK 526 | Walk Away Renee/What's It All About | 8 |

## NEWS FROM BABEL

| | | | |
|---|---|---|---|
| 86 | Recommended RE 6116 | NEWS FROM BABEL (LP, hand-screened sleeve) | 25 |
| 85 | ReR 6116 RE 6116 | WORK RESUMED ON THE TOWER (LP) | 25 |

## NEWS (1)

| | | | |
|---|---|---|---|
| 66 | Decca F 12356 | The Entertainer/I Count The Tears | 18 |
| 66 | Decca F 12477 | This Is The Moment (from the TV series "Adam Adamant")/Ya Ya Da Da | 12 |

*(see also Patto, Glenn Hughes, Finders Keepers, Miller, Big Boy Pete)*

## NEWS (2)

| | | | |
|---|---|---|---|
| 78 | GENTS WIB 001 | Get Out Of My Bed/Tearing Away (1st pressing without 'Gents' name or sticker) | 8 |

## NEW SETTLERS

| | | | |
|---|---|---|---|
| 74 | York YR 218 | She Didn't Forget Her Shoes/Lifelight | 12 |

## NEWSFLASH

| | | | |
|---|---|---|---|
| 89 | Newsflash NF 002 | Touch Me/Finding Out The Hard Way/White Beat (12" p/s) | 40 |
| 90 | Newsflash 001 | Nobodies Home/Mundane Me And You (p/s) | 50 |

## JOANNA NEWSOM

| | | | |
|---|---|---|---|
| 05 | Drag City DC 303 | YS (2-LP, gatefold, booklet) | 20 |

## BOBBY NEWSOME

| | | | |
|---|---|---|---|
| 72 | Mojo 2093 018 | Jody Come And Get Your Shoes/Post Office | 10 |

## WAYNE NEWTON

| | | | |
|---|---|---|---|
| 73 | Chelsea 2005 001 | May The Road Rise To Meet You/While We're Still Young | 6 |

## OLIVIA NEWTON-JOHN

| | | | |
|---|---|---|---|
| 66 | Decca F 12396 | Till You Say You'll Be Mine/For Ever | 350 |
| 71 | Pye International 7N 25543 | If Not For You/The Biggest Clown | 6 |
| 80 | Jet JET 10-185 | Xanadu/Fool Country (10" pink vinyl, die-cut p/s, with ELO) | 12 |
| 78 | EMI EMAP 789 | TOTALLY HOT (LP, picture disc) | 20 |

*(see also Toomorrow, Marvin & Farrar)*

## NEWTOWN NEUROTICS

| | | | |
|---|---|---|---|
| 79 | No Wonder A 45 | Hypocrite/You Said No (no p/s, with insert & sticker) | 80 |
| 79 | No Wonder A 45 | Hypocrite/You Said No | 20 |

| 80 | No Wonder NOW 4 | When The Oil Runs Out/Oh No (p/s) | 40 |
| 82 | CNT 4/No Wonder NOW 56 | Kick Out The Tories!/Mindless Violence! (p/s) | 15 |
| 82 | CNT CNT 010 | Licensing Hours/No Sanctuary (p/s) | 18 |
| 83 | Razor RZS 107 | Blitzkrieg Bop/Hypocrite (New Version)/I Remember You (p/s) | 12 |
| 84 | No Wonder NOW 6T | Suzi/Fools (p/s) | 12 |
| 83 | Razor RAZ 6 | BEGGARS CAN BE CHOOSERS (LP) | 20 |

## NEW TRENDS
| 67 | Columbia SX 6245 | THE NEW TRENDS (LP) | 20 |

## NEW VICTORY BAND
| 78 | Topic 12TS 382 | ONE MORE DANCE AND THEN (LP) | 15 |

## NEW WALK
| 83 | Web WEB 22 | Pressure Point/Shape Of Things To Come (p/s) | 12 |

## NEW WANDERERS
| 79 | Grapevine GRP 144 | This Man In Love/Adam And Eve | 15 |
| 79 | Grapevine GRP 144 | This Man In Love/Adam And Eve (DJ Copy) | 30 |

## NEW WORLD
| 83 | Slipped Discs HD 106 | I Talk To My Car (Some copies have New crossed out) | 60 |

## NEW YORK DOLLS
| 73 | Mercury 6052 402 | Jet Boy/Vietnamese Baby | 20 |
| 74 | Mercury 6052 615 | Stranded In The Jungle/Who Are The Mystery Girls | 10 |
| 77 | Mercury 6160 008 | Jet Boy/Babylon/Who Are The Mystery Girls | 10 |
| 73 | Mercury 6338 270 | NEW YORK DOLLS (LP, laminated front and black sleeve) | 60 |
| 74 | Mercury 6338 498 | TOO MUCH TOO SOON (LP) | 40 |
| 77 | Mercury 9286.996/7 | NEW YORK DOLLS (LP) | 20 |

*(see also Johnny Thunders, Heartbreakers, Sylvain Sylvain, Idols)*

## NEW YORK PUBLIC LIBRARY
| 66 | Columbia DB 7948 | I Ain't Gonna Eat Out My Heart Anymore/Rejected | 25 |
| 68 | MCA MU 1025 | Gotta Get Away/Time Wastin' | 15 |
| 68 | MCA MU 1045 | Love Me Two Times/Which Way To Go | 10 |
| 72 | B & C CB 176 | Whei Ling Ty Luu/Boozy Queen | 8 |

## NEW YORK ROCK ENSEMBLE
| 71 | CBS 5292 | Running Down The Highway/Law And Order | 15 |

## NEXT BAND
| 78 | Gannet SRTS/79/CUS 159 | FOUR BY THREE EP (p/s) | 60 |

## NEXUS 21
| 89 | Blue Chip BLUE C34R | (Still) Life Keeps Moving Remix (12") | 10 |
| 89 | Blue Chip BLUE C34T | (Still) Life Keeps Moving (12") | 10 |
| 91 | Network NWKT 35 | I Know We Can Make It (12", white label) | 10 |
| 89 | Blue Chip BLUE TEC. 2 | THE RHYTHM OF LIFE (LP) | 15 |

## NIADEM'S GHOST
| 86 | Hibination HIDE 001 | IN SHELTERED WINDS (LP) | 25 |

*(see also IQ)*

## NIANATTY
| 81 | S&G SG 13 | One Love Stylee/DESMOND RHYTHM SECTION: One Love (12") | 60 |

## NICE
| 67 | Immediate IM 059 | The Thoughts Of Emerlist Davjack/Angel Of Death | 15 |
| 68 | Immediate IM 068 | America/The Diamond Hard Blue Apples Of The Moon (pink label, in p/s) | 20 |
| 68 | Immediate IM 068 | America/The Diamond Hard Blue Apples Of The Moon (pink label) | 10 |
| 68 | Immediate IM 072 | Brandenburger/Happy Freuds | 10 |
| 69 | Immediate AS 4 | She Belongs To Me/She Belongs To Me ('single sampler', promo) | 20 |
| 70 | Charisma CB 132 | Country Pie/One Of Those People | 6 |
| 70s | Immediate IM 068 | America/The Diamond Hard Blue Apples Of The Moon (white label, reissue in p/s) | 6 |
| 67 | Immediate AS 2 | ALBUM SAMPLER - THE THOUGHTS OF EMERLIST DAVJACK (1-sided LP, promo only) | 60 |
| 67 | Immediate IMLP 016 | THE THOUGHTS OF EMERLIST DAVJACK (LP, mono) | 70 |
| 67 | Immediate IMSP 016 | THE THOUGHTS OF EMERLIST DAVJACK (LP, stereo) | 50 |
| 68 | Immediate IMSP 020 | ARS LONGA VITA BREVIS (LP, laminated front, flipbacks, pink label, "Sold in U.K..." text) | 40 |
| 69 | Immediate IMSP 026 | THE NICE (LP, gatefold sleeve) | 30 |
| 70 | Charisma CAS 1014 | FIVE BRIDGES (LP, pink label, gatefold sleeve) | 20 |
| 71 | Charisma CAS 1030 | ELEGY (LP, gatefold sleeve pink 'scroll' label) | 20 |
| 72 | Charisma CS1 | AUTUMN '67 AND SPRING '68 (LP) | 30 |

*(see also Keith Emerson, Emerson Lake & Palmer, Jackson Heights, Habits, Brian Davison, Refugee, Attack, Jet, P.P. Arnold)*

## NICK NICELY
| 80 | Voxette VOX 1001 | D.C.T. Dreams/Treeline (p/s, reissue copies £4) | 20 |
| 81 | EMI EMI 5256 | Hillyfields (1892)/49 Cigars (p/s) | 15 |
| 12 | Fruits De Mer Crustacean 27 | Hilly Fields (1982)/Hilly Fields (The Mourning) (p/s, 300 on dark red and 300 on grey vinyl) | 8 |
| 04 | Tenth Planet TP 059 | PSYCHOTROPIA (LP, 1000 copies only) | 20 |

## ALBERT NICHOLAS
| 56 | Tempo A 129 | How Long Blues (with Al Fairweather)/Rose Room (with Lise West) | 10 |

## PAUL NICHOLAS
| 68 | Polydor 56285 | Where Do I Go/Here Comes The Clown | 5 |
| 69 | Polydor 56322 | Who Can I Turn To/Sing A Sad Song For Sammy | 5 |
| 70 | Polydor 56374 | Freedom City/Run Shaker Life (with p/s) | 100 |
| 70 | Polydor 56374 | Freedom City/Run Shaker Life | 70 |
| 71 | Polydor 2058 086 | The World Is Beautiful/Lamplighter | 45 |

*(see also Oscar, Paul Dean)*

## BILLY NICHOLLS

| | | | |
|---|---|---|---:|
| 68 | Immediate IM 063 | Would You Believe/Daytime Girl (features Small Faces) | 70 |
| 73 | Track 2094 109 | Forever's No Time At All/This Song Is Green (with Pete Townshend) | 20 |
| 74 | GM GMS 018 | White Lightning/Daytime Girl | 20 |
| 68 | Immediate IMCP 009 | WOULD YOU BELIEVE (LP, withdrawn) | 5000 |
| 98 | Tenth Planet TP 042 | WOULD YOU BELIEVE (LP, reissue, with insert) | 45 |
| 99 | South West SELP 003 | SNAPSHOT (LP) | 25 |
| 07 | Castle CMQLP 1523 | WOULD YOU BELIEVE (2-LP, reissue, black or green vinyl) | 40 |

## PENNY NICHOLS

| | | | |
|---|---|---|---:|
| 68 | Pye int 7N 2451 | Look Around Rock/Farina | 35 |

## ROSEMARY NICHOLS

| | | | |
|---|---|---|---:|
| 70 | Gemini GMS 013 | Once Upon A Time/Baby | 10 |

## ROGER NICHOLSON

| | | | |
|---|---|---|---:|
| 72 | Trailer LER 3034 | NONSUCH FOR DULCIMER (LP, red label) | 20 |

## VIVIAN NICHOLSON

| | | | |
|---|---|---|---:|
| 79 | SRTS 79414 | Spend Spend Spend/You're Number One | 50 |

## NICKELSON

| | | | |
|---|---|---|---:|
| 72 | Decca F13328 | Sitting On A Fence/Oh How Much | 8 |

## NICKY AND THE DOTS

| | | | |
|---|---|---|---:|
| 78 | Small Wonder SMALL 12 | Never Been So Stuck/Linoleum Walk (p/s) | 15 |

## NICO

| | | | |
|---|---|---|---:|
| 65 | Immediate IM 003 | I'm Not Sayin'/The Last Mile (early copies in blue/white "immediate" sleeves) | 90 |
| 65 | Immediate IM 003 | I'm Not Sayin'/The Last Mile (in standard black/white "immediate" sleeves) | 80 |
| 81 | Flicknife FLS 206 | Vegas/Saeta (p/s) | 8 |
| 82 | Immediate IMS 003 | I'm Not Saying/The Last Mile (p/s, reissue) | 25 |
| 82 | Half 1?2 1 | Procession/All Tomorrow's Parties (p/s) | 5 |
| 83 | Aura AUS 137 | Heroes/One More Chance (p/s) | 5 |
| 85 | Beggars Banquet BEG 139 | My Funny Valentine/My Heart Is Empty (p/s, as Nico and the Faction) | 5 |
| 88 | Strange Fruit SFPS 064 | PEEL SESSIONS (12", p/s) | 15 |
| 10 | Elektra 8122797856 | Frozen Warnings/No One Is There (die-cut sleeve, 750 only) | 8 |
| 68 | Elektra EKL 4029 | THE MARBLE INDEX (LP, orange label, mono) | 100 |
| 68 | Elektra EKS 74029 | THE MARBLE INDEX (LP, orange label, stereo) | 80 |
| 71 | Reprise RSLP 6424 | DESERT SHORE (LP, with John Cale) | 50 |
| 71 | Reprise K 44102 | DESERT SHORE (LP, with John Cale, 2nd pressing) | 25 |
| 71 | MGM Select 2353 025 | CHELSEA GIRL (LP) | 50 |
| 74 | Island ILPS 9311 | THE END (LP) | 40 |
| 81 | Aura AUL 715 | DRAMA OF EXILE (LP, colour cover) | 18 |
| 85 | Island ILPS 9311 | THE END (LP, reissue, blue label) | 18 |
| 86 | Polydor 2353 025 | CHELSEA GIRL (LP, reissue) | 15 |

*(see also John Cale, Velvet Underground, Ayers Cale Nico & Eno)*

## NICODEMUS

| | | | |
|---|---|---|---:|
| 81 | Cha Cha CHAD 44 | Gunman Connection/It Have To Ram (12") | 20 |
| 81 | Greensleeves GRED 75 | BONE CONNECTION/LEROY SMART: All My Love (12") | 15 |
| 82 | Cha Cha CHALP 011 | GUNMAN CONNECTION (LP) | 40 |
| 82 | Black Joy DHLP 2003 | DANCE HALL STYLE (LP) | 50 |

## JIMMY NICOL (& SHUBDUBS)

| | | | |
|---|---|---|---:|
| 64 | Pye 7N 15623 | Humpty Dumpty/Night Train | 25 |
| 64 | Pye 7N 15666 | Husky/Don't Come Back (solo) | 18 |
| 64 | Pye 7N 15699 | Baby Please Don't Go/Shub Dubbery (possibly unissued) | 20 |

*(see also Sound Of Jimmy Nicol, Georgie Fame)*

## NICOLETTE

| | | | |
|---|---|---|---:|
| 89 | Shut Up & Dance SUAD 14 | Waking Up (12") | 10 |

## WATT NICOLL

| | | | |
|---|---|---|---:|
| 71 | Xtra XTRA 1122 | NICE TO BE NICE (LP, laminated front cover) | 15 |

## NICRA

| | | | |
|---|---|---|---:|
| 77 | Ogun OG 010 | LISTEN/HEAR (LP) | 18 |

*(see also Keith Tippett)*

## NIDDY GRIDDY BAND

| | | | |
|---|---|---|---:|
| 68 | Pye 7N 17461 | Dinny Girgy/Summertime | 6 |

## NIEMEN

| | | | |
|---|---|---|---:|
| 72 | CBS 564896 | STRANGE IS THIS WORLD (LP, orange/black label) | 25 |

## STEVE NIEVE

| | | | |
|---|---|---|---:|
| 80 | Comb 1 | OUTLINE ON A HAIRDO (EP) | 20 |

## NIGGER KOJAK

| | | | |
|---|---|---|---:|
| 83 | Nigger Kojak NKLP 002 | ROCK JACK KOJAK (LP) | 15 |

## NIGGY HOI!

| | | | |
|---|---|---|---:|
| 80s | Deli K1Z | Theme From Niggy Hoi!/Titanium Kedi (p/s) | 8 |

## NIGHT DOCTOR

| | | | |
|---|---|---|---:|
| 81 | Race Records RB DIS 001 | Romancin'/Menelik (12") | 35 |

## NIGHTAIR

| | | | |
|---|---|---|---:|
| 76 | SRTY 79 CUS 410 | NIGHTAIR (LP) | 15 |

## NIGHTBIRDS

| | | | |
|---|---|---|---:|
| 59 | Oriole CB 1490 | Cat On A Hot Tin Roof/The Square | 12 |

## NIGHTBLOOMS

| | | | |
|---|---|---|---:|
| 90 | Fierce FRIGHT 041 | Crystal Eyes/Never Dream At All (p/s) | 10 |

MINT VALUE £

### NIGHTCHILL
| | | |
|---|---|---|
| 13 | Kent CITY 031 | I Don't Play Games/ROMEO & JULIET : You Got What It Takes (reissue) ........................ 8 |

### NIGHTCRAWLERS
| | | |
|---|---|---|
| 67 | London HLR 10109 | The Little Black Egg/You're Running Wild ........................ 60 |

### NIGHTIME FLYER (1)
| | | |
|---|---|---|
| 69 | Pye 7N 17739 | Talk To Me/Spinning Wheel........................ 6 |
| 69 | Pye 7N 17798 | Don't Push Me Baby/Thru' Loving You........................ 7 |
| 71 | Pye 7N 45046 | Love On Borrowed Time/It's A Hurtin' Thing ........................ 6 |

### NIGHTIME FLYER (2)
| | | |
|---|---|---|
| 81 | Red Eye EYE 2 | Out With A Vengeance/Heavy Metal Rules (p/s) ........................ 20 |
| 03 | Phoenix NWOBHM 7007 | Out With A Vengeance/Heavy Metal Rules (yellow vinyl reissue, numbered, 250 copies, 7.5 inch sleeve)........................ 10 |

### TUNDE NIGHTINGALE & HIS HIGHLIFE BOYS
| | | |
|---|---|---|
| 68 | Melodisc MLPAS 12-142 | THE BIRDS THAT SINGS ALL THE NIGHT (LP) ........................ 15 |

### NIGHTINGALES
| | | |
|---|---|---|
| 81 | Cherry Red CHERRY 34 | Use Your Loaf/Inside Out /Under The Lash (p/s)........................ 5 |
| 81 | Rough Trade/Vindaloo RT 075/UGH 4 | Idiot Strength/Seconds ........................ 8 |
| 83 | Cherry Red CHERRY 56 | Urban Ospreys/Cakehole ........................ 5 |

### NIGHTMARE
| | | |
|---|---|---|
| 79 | PVK PV 30 | Great Balls Of Fire/Witch Woman (p/s) ........................ 10 |
| 83 | PVK PV 119 | I Wanna Be Shot/Ruth Ellis (P/S) ........................ 6 |

### NIGHTMARES IN WAX
| | | |
|---|---|---|
| 79 | Inevitable INEV 0002 | BIRTH OF A NATION (EP, with wraparound p/s) ........................ 20 |
| 84 | KY KY 9 | Black Leather/Shangri-La (12", 'horror' p/s) ........................ 18 |
| 85 | KY KY 9 1/2 | Black Leather/Shangri-La/Girls Song (12", different p/s, 3,000 only)........................ 20 |

*(see also Dead Or Alive)*

### NIGHTMARES ON WAX
| | | |
|---|---|---|
| 91 | Warp WARPLP4 | A WORD OF SCIENCE (THE 1st & FINAL CHAPTER) (LP) ........................ 20 |
| 95 | Warp WARPLP 36 | SMOKERS DELIGHT (2-LP) ........................ 40 |
| 99 | Warp WARPLP 61 | CARBOOT SOUL (2-LP) ........................ 30 |
| 06 | Warp WARPLP 133 | IN A SPACE OUTTA SOUND (2-LP) ........................ 25 |

### NIGHT MOVES
| | | |
|---|---|---|
| 83 | GC GCT 2 | Transdance (New York Disco Mix)/Transdance (UK Disco Mix)/Nightdrive (12") .......... 30 |
| 84 | GC/MCA GCT 1001 | Transdance (Robot Rock) (UK Club Mix)/You Can Take My Love/Beat This/Nightdrive (12", p/s)........................ 20 |

### NIGHT PILOTS
| | | |
|---|---|---|
| 79 | Christy CML 0107 | Dancing With Myself/Open Top Sports Car........................ 10 |

### NIGHTRIDER
| | | |
|---|---|---|
| 79 | Wessex WEX 272 | DIGITAL TECHNIQUES EP: Gruesome Girls/Stay Clean/Happy Day (p/s) ........................ 35 |

### NIGHTRIDERS (1)
| | | |
|---|---|---|
| 66 | Polydor BM 56066 | Love Me Right Now/Your Friend (withdrawn)........................ 120 |
| 66 | Polydor BM 56066 | Love Me Right Now/Your Friend (promo copy) ........................ 85 |
| 66 | Polydor BM 56116 | It's Only The Dog/Your Friend ........................ 60 |
| 79 | Stardust STR 1001 | I Saw Her With Another Guy/London Town (picture insert)........................ 25 |

*(see also Mike Sheridan & Nightriders, Mike Sheridan's Lot, Idle Race)*

### NIGHTRIDERS (2)
| | | |
|---|---|---|
| 79 | Stardust STR 1001 | I Saw Her With Another Guy/London Town (picture insert) ........................ 25 |

### NIGHTSHIFT (1)
| | | |
|---|---|---|
| 65 | Piccadilly 7N 35243 | Corrine Corrina/Lavender Tree ........................ 15 |
| 65 | Piccadilly 7N 35264 | That's My Story/Stormy Monday Blues ........................ 18 |

### NIGHTSHIFT (2)
| | | |
|---|---|---|
| 79 | Zum 9 | Jet Set/Bad Dreams........................ 6 |

### NIGHT-TIMERS
| | | |
|---|---|---|
| 65 | Parlophone R 5355 | The Music Played On/Yield Not To Temptation (featuring Herbie Goins)........................ 70 |

*(see also Herbie Goins & Night-Timers, Ronnie Jones)*

### NIGHTWING
| | | |
|---|---|---|
| 80 | Ovation OVS 1209 | Barrel Of Pain/Nightwing (p/s)........................ 10 |
| 84 | Gull GULS 75 | Treading Water/Call Your Name (p/s)........................ 6 |
| 84 | Gull GULS 7512 | Treading Water/Call Your Name/Barrel Of Pain (12", red vinyl, p/s) ........................ 10 |
| 84 | Gull GULS 77 | Night Of Mystery/Dressed To Kill (p/s) ........................ 10 |
| 84 | Gull GULS 7712 | Night Of Mystery/Dressed To Kill (12", p/s) ........................ 12 |
| 85 | Gull GULS 80 | Strangers Are Welcome/Games To Play//The Devil Walks Behind You/ Cell 151 (double pack, gatefold p/s) ........................ 5 |
| 83 | Gull PGULP 1038 | STAND UP AND BE COUNTED (LP, picture disc)........................ 15 |

*(see also Alec Johnson Band, Nutz)*

### NIGHTWISH
| | | |
|---|---|---|
| 04 | Back On Black BOBV 003 DPD | ANGELS FALL FIRST (2-LP picture discs, stickered bag)........................ 20 |
| 04 | Back On Black BOBV 004 DPD | OCEANBORN (2-LP picture discs, stickered bag)........................ 20 |
| 04 | Back On Black BOBV 007 DPD | OVER THE HILLS AND FAR AWAY (2-LP picture discs, stickered bag)........................ 20 |
| 04 | Back On Black BOBV 006 DPD | WISHMASTER (2-LP picture discs, stickered bag) ........................ 20 |
| 04 | Back On Black BOBV 008 DPD | CENTURY CHILD (2-LP picture discs, stickered bag) ........................ 20 |
| 05 | Back On Black BOBV 035 DPD | ONCE (2-LP picture discs, stickered bag) ........................ 20 |

## NIGHTWRITERS
88  Jack Trax JTX 19    Let The Music Use You (Club Mix)/(Radio Mix)/(Dub Mix) (12") ................................. 20

## NIHILIST SPASM BAND
85  United Dairies UD 016    1X - X = X (LP) ................................................................. 20

## BILL NILES
67  Decca F 12661    Pashionella Grundy/Bric-A-Bric Man ............................................. 15

## WILLY NILLY
84  Ad Hoc AH 1    On The Spur Of The Moment/Half A Job (p/s, with 'time-table' insert) ...................... 45

*(see also Randy Newman, Ringo Starr, Cher)*

## (HARRY) NILSSON
| | | |
|---|---|---|
| 67 | RCA Victor RCA 1632 | You Can't Do That/Ten Little Indians ................................ 5 |
| 68 | RCA Victor RCA 1675 | One/Sister Marie ................................................ 5 |
| 68 | RCA RCA 1707 | Everybody's Talkin'/Don't Leave Me .............................. 5 |
| 68 | RCA RCA 1764 | Mournin' Glory Story/Rainmaker ................................. 6 |
| 69 | RCA RCA 1864 | Maybe/The Puppy Song .......................................... 5 |
| 69 | RCA RCA 1876 | Everybody's Talkin'/One ........................................ 5 |
| 72 | RCA RCA 2266 | You're Breaking My Heart/Spaceman (possibly withdrawn, Demo stamped copy) ........ 12 |
| 68 | RCA Victor RD/SF 7928 | PANDEMONIUM SHADOW SHOW (LP, mono) ........................ 18 |
| 68 | RCA Victor RD/SF 7928 | PANDEMONIUM SHADOW SHOW (LP, stereo) ....................... 15 |
| 68 | RCA RD/SF 7973 | AERIAL BALLET (LP, mono) ...................................... 18 |
| 68 | RCA RD/SF 7973 | AERIAL BALLET (LP, stereo) ..................................... 15 |
| 69 | RCA SF 8010 | SKIDOO (LP, soundtrack) ........................................ 20 |
| 69 | RCA SF 8046 | HARRY (LP) ..................................................... 15 |
| 74 | Rapple/RCA APL1-0220 | SON OF DRACULA (LP, soundtrack, with Ringo Starr, fold-out sleeve) ......... 15 |
| 80 | RCA 6302 022 | FLASH HARRY (LP, first pressing, those with 'barcode' are repressings) .......... 30 |

## NILSSON TWINS
57  Capitol CL 14698    Rain On My Window/I Dance When I Walk ..................................... 5

## NIMBO
| | | |
|---|---|---|
| 71 | Pye 7N 450097 | Maisie Jones/Forget Her ........................................ 8 |
| 72 | Pye 7N 45174 | When The Swallows Fly/Noticeingly By ............................ 15 |

## LEONARD NIMOY
| | | |
|---|---|---|
| 68 | Dot (S)LPD 511 | MR. SPOCK PRESENTS MUSIC FROM OUTER SPACE (LP) ................ 25 |
| 72 | Rediffusion ZS 156 | MUSIC FROM OUTER SPACE (LP, reissue of DOT (S) LPD 511) ............ 20 |

## NINA
69  CBS 4681    Do You Know How Christmas Trees Are Grown?/The More Things Change ................... 12

## NINE BELOW ZERO
| | | |
|---|---|---|
| 80 | M&L ML 1 | EP ............................................................ 10 |
| 81 | A&M AMS 8127 | Ain't Comin' Back/Liquor Lover (p/s) ............................. 5 |
| 81 | A&M AMS 8110 | Three Times Enough/Doghouse (p/s, yellow vinyl) .................. 5 |

## NINE DAYS WONDER
71  Harvest SHSP 4014    NINE DAYS WONDER (LP, textured sleeve, EMI logo on label) ...................... 100

*(see also Gnidralog)*

## NINE INCH NAILS
| | | |
|---|---|---|
| 90 | Island 12IS 482 | Down On It (Skin)/Terrible Lie (Sympathetic Mix)/Down On It (Shred)/Down On It (Singe)/Terrible Lie (Empathetic Mix)/Down On It (Demo) (12", numbered limited edition) ........ 20 |
| 91 | Island IS 484 | Head Like A Hole/Head Like A Hole (Copper Mix) (p/s) ............... 5 |
| 91 | Island 10ISP 484 | Head Like A Hole (Slate)/Head Like A Hole (Copper) (10", poster p/s) .......... 8 |
| 91 | Island 12IS 484 | Head Like A Hole (Slate)/Head Like A Hole (Copper)/Head Like A Hole (Opal) (12", ps) . 10 |
| 91 | Island ISDJ 484 | Head Like A Hole (Radio Edit) (promo, stickered p/s, same track both sides) ......... 20 |
| 91 | Island ISDJ 508 | Sin (Radio Edit)/(same) (promo only, stickered p/s) .................. 12 |
| 91 | Island 9IS 508 | Sin (Long)/Sin (Dub)/Get Down Make Love (9", p/s) ................. 10 |
| 92 | Island IS 552DJ | Wish (Radio Edit) (1-sided, stickered plain sleeve, promo only) ........ 12 |
| 92 | Island IS 552 | Physical (You're So)/Suck ....................................... 15 |
| 94 | Island IS 592 | March Of The Pigs/A Violent Fluid (p/s, etched disc) ............... 5 |
| 94 | Island 9IS 592 | March Of The Pigs/A Violent Fluid/All The Pigs, All Lined Up/Underneath The Skin (9",numbered p/s) ............. 12 |
| 94 | Island 12IS 596 | Closer (Deviation)/Closer (Further Away)/Closer (6.26)/Closer (Precursor)/Closer (Internal) (12", p/s) ........... 10 |
| 94 | Island 12ISX 596 | Closer to God/March Of The Fuckheads/Heresy (Blind)/Memorabilia (12", p/s) .......... 10 |
| 91 | Island ILPS 9973 | PRETTY HATE MACHINE (LP) ..................................... 18 |
| 92 | Interscope ILPM 8004 | BROKEN (1-sided 6 track mini LP with free 7" "Physical [your'e so]' / 'Suck') ......... 30 |
| 92 | Island ILPM 8005 | FIXED (remix mini LP) .......................................... 20 |
| 94 | Island ILPSD 8012 | THE DOWNWARD SPIRAL (double LP, gatefold sleeve) ................ 18 |
| 99 | Island ILPST 8091 | THE FRAGILE (3-LP, inners, booklet) ............................. 30 |

## 999
| | | |
|---|---|---|
| 77 | Labritain LAB 999 | I'm Alive/Quite Disappointing (p/s) .............................. 15 |
| 77 | United Artists UP 36299 | Nasty Nasty/No Pity (p/s, green vinyl) ............................ 10 |
| 77 | United Artists UP 36299 | Nasty Nasty/No Pity (p/s, black vinyl) ............................ 5 |
| 77 | United Artists FREE 7 | Nasty Nasty/No Pity (78rpm promo, 50 copies only) ................. 200 |
| 78 | United Artists UP 36399 | Emergency/My Street Stinks (p/s) ................................ 5 |
| 78 | United Artists UP 36376 | Me And My Desire/Crazy (p/s) ................................... 5 |
| 78 | United Artists UP 36435 | Feelin' Alright With The Crew/Titanic (My Over) Reaction (p/s) ........ 5 |
| 78 | United Artists UP 36467 | Homicide/Soldier (p/s, green vinyl) .............................. 5 |
| 79 | Radar ADA 46 | Found Out Too Late/Lie, Lie, Lie (p/s) ............................ 5 |
| 79 | United Artists UP 36519 | I'm Alive/Quite Disappointing (reissue, different p/s) ............... 5 |
| 81 | Albion ION 1011 | Obsessed/Change/Lie, Lie, Lie (live) (p/s, with laminated sleeve, shrinkwrapped with patch) ........ 6 |

MINT VALUE £

| | | | |
|---|---|---|---|
| 81 | Albion ION 1017 | Li'l Red Riding Hood/Waiting For Your Number To Be Called/I Ain't Gonna Tell Ya (live) (p/s, with stencil; shrinkwrapped) | 6 |
| 81 | Albion ION 1023 | Indian Reservation/So Greedy (Remixed)/Taboo (Remix) (p/s, clear vinyl, with sticker) | 5 |
| 78 | United Artists UAG 30199 | 999 (LP, with inner sleeve) | 15 |
| 78 | United Artists UAG 30209 | SEPARATES (LP, with inner sleeve) | 15 |
| 90 | Link LINK LP 125 | CELLBLOCK TAPES (LP) | 15 |

*(see also Kilburn & High Roads)*

**SADIE NINE**

| | | | |
|---|---|---|---|
| 81 | Precious AVE 3 | If You Take A Morning From My Life/Kiss Me Not Him | 6 |

**9.30 FLY**

| | | | |
|---|---|---|---|
| 72 | Ember NR 5062 | 9.30 FLY (LP, textured gatefold sleeve) | 250 |

**9LAZY9**

| | | | |
|---|---|---|---|
| 94 | Ninja Tune ZEN 9 | PARADISE BLOWN (2-LP) | 18 |

**NINESENSE**

| | | | |
|---|---|---|---|
| 76 | Ogun OG 900 | OH! FOR THE EDGE (LP) | 30 |
| 77 | Ogun OG 910 | HAPPY DAZE (LP) | 30 |

*(see also Elton Dean, Julie Tippetts, Keith Tippett, Mark Charig, Harold Beckett, Alan Skidmore)*

**1984 (1)**

| | | | |
|---|---|---|---|
| 69 | Big T BIG 117 | This Little Boy/Rosalyn | 12 |
| 69 | Big T BIG 120 | Got To Have Your Love/Here We Are | 8 |
| 71 | Decca F23159 | Little Girl/Laramee | 12 |

**1984 (2)**

| | | | |
|---|---|---|---|
| 79 | LaVista | Music Press/She's A Razor (stamped plain die cut sleeve) | 60 |

**1919**

| | | | |
|---|---|---|---|
| 82 | Red Rhino RED 22 | Repulsion/Tear Down These Walls (p/s) | 6 |
| 82 | Red Rhino RED 22 | Repulsion/Tear Down These Walls (white hand-written labels, 500 only) | 25 |
| 83 | Abstract 12 ABS 017 | Cry Wolf/Dream/Storm (12", p/s) | 18 |
| 83 | Red Rhino REDLP 25 | MACHINE (LP) | 15 |

**1910 FRUITGUM CO.**

| | | | |
|---|---|---|---|
| 68 | Pye Intl. N(S)PL 28115 | SIMON SAYS (LP) | 15 |
| 69 | Buddah 203 014 | GOODY GOODY GUMDROPS (LP) | 15 |
| 70 | Buddah 2359 006 | HARD RIDE (LP) | 20 |

**1910 FRUITGUM CO./LEMON PIPERS**

| | | | |
|---|---|---|---|
| 68 | Pye Intl. NEP 44091 | PRESENTING... (EP, 1 side each) | 10 |

**90 DEGREES**

| | | | |
|---|---|---|---|
| 79 | Virgin VS 311 | No Doctor/Fantasy Woman (p/s) | 8 |

**NINEY (& DESTROYERS/OBSERVERS)**

| | | | |
|---|---|---|---|
| 70 | Amalgamated AMG 856 | Niney Special/Danger Zone | |
| 70 | Pressure Beat PR 5501 | Honey No Money/INSPIRATIONS: This Message To You | 35 |
| 71 | Big BG 317 | You Must Believe/You Must Believe Version | 12 |
| 71 | Big Shot BI 568 | Blood And Fire/Mud And Water | 15 |
| 71 | Big Shot BI 586 | Message To The Ungodly/Message To The Ungodly - Version | 20 |
| 71 | Supreme SUP 214 | You Must Believe Me/RUPIE EDWARDS ALLSTARS: Funk The Funk | 12 |
| 71 | Gas GAS 167 | Blood And Fire/ROLAND ALPHONSO: 33 66 | 12 |
| 71 | Moodisc HME 111 | People Let Love Shine/MUDIES ALL STARS: Too Much | 25 |
| 72 | Big Shot BI 607 | Hiding By The Riverside/The Red Sea | 6 |
| 72 | Big Shot BI 609 | Beg In The Gutter/Beg In The Gutter Version | 5 |
| 72 | Big Shot BI 610 | Everyday Music (by The Observers)/Observing The Avenue | 6 |
| 72 | Bullet BU 503 | Aily And Ailaloo (& Max)/Version | 5 |
| 72 | Downtown DT 494 | Get Out My Life/Get Out My Life - Version (with the Observers) | 5 |
| 72 | Downtown DT 495 | Hi Diddle/Hi Diddle - Version | 5 |
| 88 | Trojan TRLS 263 | BLOOD & FIRE (LP) | 15 |
| 05 | Auralux LUXXLP 009 | SUFFERATION (2-LP) | 25 |

*(see also Niney's All Stars, Observers)*

**NINEY'S ALL STARS**

| | | | |
|---|---|---|---|
| 70 | Unity UN 563 | Skankee/Skankee - Version | 10 |

*(see also Niney, Observers)*

**NING**

| | | | |
|---|---|---|---|
| 71 | Decca F 23114 | Machine/More Ning | 25 |

**NINO & EBBTIDES**

| | | | |
|---|---|---|---|
| 61 | Top Rank JAR 572 | Those Oldies But Goodies/Don't Run Away | 15 |

**9TH CREATION**

| | | | |
|---|---|---|---|
| 75 | Pye 12138 | FALLING IN LOVE (LP) | 20 |

**NIPPLE ERECTORS**

| | | | |
|---|---|---|---|
| 78 | Soho SH 1/2 | King Of The Bop/Nervous Wreck (with glossy p/s) | 40 |
| 78 | Soho SH 1/2 | King Of The Bop/Nervous Wreck (later matt p/s) | 20 |

*(see also Nips, Pogues)*

**NIPS**

| | | | |
|---|---|---|---|
| 78 | Soho SH 4 | All The Time In The World/Private Eyes (foldover p/s) | 40 |
| 80 | Soho SH 9 | Gabrielle/Vengeance | 30 |
| 80 | Soho SH 9 | Gabrielle/Vengeance (tour copy with 'licensed to cool' stamp) | 30 |
| 80 | Chiswick CHIS 119 | Gabrielle/Vengeance (reissue, p/s) | 15 |
| 81 | Test Pressing TP 5 | Happy Song/Nobody To Love (p/s) | 50 |
| 80 | Soho HOHO 1 | ONLY AT THE END OF THE BEGINNING (LP, with insert, white labels) | 35 |

*(see also Nipple Erectors, Pogues)*

**NIRVANA (U.K.)**

| | | | |
|---|---|---|---|
| 67 | Island WIP 6016 | Tiny Goddess/I Believe In Magic | 30 |

| 67 | Island WIP 6020 | Pentecost Hotel/Feelin' Shattered | 25 |
|---|---|---|---|
| 68 | Island WIP 6029 | Rainbow Chaser/Flashbulb | 25 |
| 68 | Island WIP 6038 | Girl In The Park/C Side In Ocho Rios | 25 |
| 68 | Island WIP 6045 | All Of Us (The Touchables)/Trapeze | 15 |
| 69 | Island WIP 6052 | Wings Of Love/Requiem To John Coltrane | 25 |
| 69 | Island WIP 6057 | Oh! What A Performance/Darling Darlene | 30 |
| 70 | Pye International 7N 25525 | The World Is Cold Without You/Christopher Lucifer | 20 |
| 71 | Vertigo 6059 035 | The Saddest Day Of My Life/(I Wanna Go) Home | 25 |
| 71 | Philips 6006 127 | Pentecost Hotel/Lazy Day Drift | 12 |
| 72 | Philips 6006 166 | Stadium/Please Believe Me | 12 |
| 76 | Bradleys BRAD 7602 | Two Of A Kind/Before Midnight | 6 |
| 76 | Island WIP 6180 | Rainbow Chaser/Tiny Goddess (p/s) | 10 |
| 78 | Pepper UP 36461 | Love Is/Pascale | 5 |
| 79 | Pepper UP 36538 | Restless Wind/Thank You And Goodnight | 5 |
| 81 | Zilch ZILCH 8 | The Picture Of Dorian Gray/No It Isn't | 6 |
| 82 | Zilch ZILCH 15 | Black And White Or Colour/Tall Trees And Mansions | 5 |
| 88 | Bam Caruso OPRA 45 | Black Flower/WIMPLE WINCH: Save My Soul (jukebox issue, die-cut sleeve) | 8 |
| 68 | Island ILP 959 | THE STORY OF SIMON SIMOPATH (LP, mono, pink label, black/orange circle logo) | 300 |
| 68 | Island ILPS 9059 | THE STORY OF SIMON SIMOPATH (LP, stereo, pink label, black/orange circle logo) | 400 |
| 68 | Island ILPS 9087 | ALL OF US (LP, pink label, black/orange circle logo) | 250 |
| 70 | Pye Intl. NSPL 28132 | DEDICATED TO MARKOS III (LP) | 250 |
| 71 | Vertigo 6360 031 | LOCAL ANAESTHETIC (LP, gatefold sleeve, swirl label) | 300 |
| 72 | Philips 6308 089 | SONGS OF LOVE AND PRAISE (LP) | 150 |
| 87 | Bam-Caruso KIRI 061 | BLACK FLOWER (LP) | 20 |

*(see also Patrick Campbell-Lyons, Ray Singer, Pica, Hat & Tie, Informants)*

## NIRVANA (U.S.)

| 89 | Tupelo TUP EP8 | Blew/Love Buzz/Been A Son/Stain (12", p/s) | 40 |
|---|---|---|---|
| 89 | Tupelo TUP CD8 | Blew/Love Buzz/Been A Son/Stain (CD) | 30 |
| 90 | Tupelo TUP 25 | Sliver/Dive (gatefold p/s, green vinyl only, 2,000 pressed) | 25 |
| 91 | Tupelo TUP EP25 | Sliver/Dive/About A Girl (live)/Dive (12", p/s) | 10 |
| 91 | Tupelo TUP EP25 | Sliver/Dive/About A Girl (live)/Dive (12", repressing, blue vinyl, p/s) | 20 |
| 91 | Geffen DGCT 5 | Smells Like Teen Spirit (Edit)/Even In His Youth/Even In His Youth (12", p/s) | 15 |
| 91 | Geffen DGCS 5 | Smells Like Teen Spirit (Edit)/Drain You (p/s) | 8 |
| 91 | Geffen DGCTP 5 | Smells Like Teen Spirit (Edit)/Drain You (LP Version)/Aneurysm (12", picture disc, die-cut p/s) | 15 |
| 92 | Geffen DGCS 7 | Come As You Are/Endless Nameless (silver labels) | 20 |
| 92 | Geffen DGCTP 7 | Come As You Are/Endless Nameless/School (Live) | 35 |
| 92 | Geffen DGCTP 7 | Come As You Are/Endless, Nameless/School (live) (12", picture disc, die-cut p/s) | 20 |
| 92 | Geffen DGCS 9 | Lithium/Been A Son (live) | 7 |
| 92 | Geffen DGCTP 9 | Lithium/Been A Son (live)/Curmudgeon (12", picture disc, die-cut p/s) | 20 |
| 92 | Geffen GFS 34 | In Bloom/Sliver (live)/Polly (live) (p/s) | 15 |
| 92 | Geffen DGCTP 34 | In Bloom/Sliver (live)/Polly (live) (12", picture disc, die-cut p/s) | 40 |
| 93 | Touch & Go TG 83 | Oh, The Guilt/JESUS LIZARD: Puss (p/s, blue vinyl, with poster) | 20 |
| 93 | Touch & Go TG 83 | Oh, The Guilt/JESUS LIZARD: Puss (p/s, blue vinyl, without poster) | 15 |
| 93 | Geffen GFS 54 | Heart Shaped Box/Marigold | 15 |
| 93 | Geffen GFST 54 | Heart Shaped Box/Milk It/Marigold (12" p/s) | 6 |
| 93 | Geffen GF 566 | All Apologies/Rape Me/MV | 12 |
| 93 | Geffen GFST 66 | All Apologies/Rape Me/MV (12", p/s with 2 art prints) | 20 |
| 94 | Geffen (no cat. no.) | Penny Royal Tea (Scott Litt Mix)/Where Did You Sleep Last Night (live) (unreleased, 10 test pressings only) | 600 |
| 94 | Geffen NIRPRO (no cat. no.) | Penny Royal Tea (Scott Litt Mix) (CD, 1-track, no inlay, promo only) | 600 |
| 95 | Geffen GED 24901 | SINGLES (6 x CD box set) | 25 |
| 11 | DGC B0015411-01 | HOARMOANING (12", brown vinyl) | 25 |
| 89 | Tupelo TUP LP 6 | BLEACH (LP, 300 on white vinyl) | 175 |
| 89 | Tupelo TUP LP 6 | BLEACH (LP, 2,000 on green vinyl) | 50 |
| 89 | Tupelo TUP LP 6 | BLEACH (LP, black vinyl) | 20 |
| 91 | Geffen DGC 24425 | NEVERMIND (LP, with inner sleeve) | 20 |
| 92 | Geffen GEF 24504 | INCESTICIDE (LP, inner) | 15 |
| 93 | Geffen GEF 24536 | IN UTERO (LP) | 25 |
| 94 | Geffen GED 24727 | UNPLUGGED IN NEW YORK (LP, white vinyl with inner sleeve) | 35 |
| 96 | Geffen GEF 25105 | FROM THE MUDDY BANKS OF THE WISHKAH (2-LP) | 25 |
| 02 | Sub Pop 9878700341 | BLEACH (LP, reissue, 13 tracks, white marbled vinyl) | 15 |
| 02 | Sub Pop 9878400341 | BLEACH (LP, reissue, 11 tracks, white vinyl) | 15 |
| 09 | Simply Vinyl SVLP 0038 | NEVERMIND (LP, reissue) | 50 |
| 11 | Geffen/Back To Black 602527779041 | NEVERMIND (4 x LP, gatefold sleeve) | 40 |
| 11 | Geffen/Back To Black 602527779041 | NEVERMIND (4 x picture disc, gatefold sleeve) | 80 |

*(see also Foo Fighters)*

## NITE-LITERS

| 72 | RCA 2214 | K-Jee/Tanga Boo Gonk (Night Lighters on label) | 5 |
|---|---|---|---|
| 72 | RCA SF 8282 | INSTRUMENTAL DIRECTIONS (LP) | 20 |

## NITE PEOPLE

| 66 | Fontana TF 747 | Sweet Tasting Wine/Nobody But You | 25 |
|---|---|---|---|
| 67 | Fontana TF 808 | Trying To Find Another Man/Stay As Sweet As You Are | 20 |
| 67 | Fontana TF 885 | Summertime Blues/In The Springtime | 60 |
| 68 | Fontana TF 919 | Morning Sun/Where You There | 50 |
| 69 | Page One POF 149 | Love, Love, Love/Hot Smoke And Sassafras (with insert) | 25 |
| 69 | Page One POF 149 | Love, Love, Love/Hot Smoke And Sassafras | 15 |
| 69 | Page One POF 159 | Is This A Dream/Cream Tea | 25 |

# NITE ROCKERS

| | | | MINT VALUE £ |
|---|---|---|---|
| 70 | Page One POF 174 | Season Of The Rain/P.M. | 20 |
| 69 | Page One POLS 025 | P.M. (LP) | 600 |

*(see also Banana Bunch)*

## NITE ROCKERS
| | | | |
|---|---|---|---|
| 58 | RCA RCA 1079 | Nite Rock (Lonely Train)/Oh! Baby | 50 |
| 58 | RCA RCA 1079 | Nite Rock (Lonely Train)/Oh! Baby (78) | 30 |

## NITESHADES
| | | | |
|---|---|---|---|
| 65 | CBS 201763 | Be My Guest/I Must Reveal | 18 |
| 65 | CBS 201817 | Fell So Fast/I'm Not Gonna Worry | 12 |

## NITS
| | | | |
|---|---|---|---|
| 79 | CBS 8049 | Tutti Raqazzi/Harrow Accident | 8 |

## NITTY GRITTY
| | | | |
|---|---|---|---|
| 85 | Greensleeves GRED 187 | Hog In A Minty/Run Down The World | 12 |
| 86 | Greensleeves GRED 195 | Man In A House/Version/False Alarm/Version (12") | 15 |
| 86 | Greensleeves GREL 93 | TURBO CHARGED (LP) | 18 |

## NITTY GRITTY DIRT BAND
| | | | |
|---|---|---|---|
| 67 | Liberty LIB 55948 | Buy Me For The Rain/Candy Man | 10 |
| 68 | Liberty LBF 15099 | Collegiana/End Of Your Line | 10 |
| 69 | Liberty LBF 15275 | Some of Shelly's Blues/Yukon Railway | 6 |
| 70 | Liberty LBF 15358 | Rave On/The Cure | 6 |
| 68 | Liberty LBL/LBS 83122 | PURE DIRT (LP) | 30 |
| 69 | Liberty LBL/LBS 83286 | DEAD AND ALIVE (LP) | 25 |
| 71 | Liberty LBG 83345 | UNCLE CHARLIE AND HIS DOG TEDDY (LP, gatefold sleeve) | 20 |
| 72 | United Artists UAS 29284 | ALL THE GOOD TIMES (LP) | 15 |
| 74 | United Artists USD 307/8 | STARS AND STRIPES FOREVER (2-LP) | 18 |

*(see also Kaleidoscope, Chris Darlow)*

## NITZER EBB
| | | | |
|---|---|---|---|
| 85 | Own label | BASIC PAIN PROCEDURE (EP, cassette, given away at gig) | 20 |

## JACK NITZSCHE
| | | | |
|---|---|---|---|
| 63 | Reprise R 20202 | The Lonely Surfer/Song For A Summer Night | 30 |
| 63 | Reprise R 20337 | Night Walker/Green Grass Of Texas | 15 |
| 78 | MCA MCA 366 | Hard Workin' Man (featuring Captain Beefheart)/Coke Machine | 15 |
| 74 | Warner Bros K 41211 | ST GILES CRIPPLEGATE (LP) | 20 |

*(see also Date With Soul, Mick Jagger, Captain Beefheart, Randy Newman, Crazy Horse)*

## NIVENS
| | | | |
|---|---|---|---|
| 89 | Woosh WOOSH 5 | Yesterday/I Hope You'll Always Be My Friend (p/s) | 5 |

## NIX
| | | | |
|---|---|---|---|
| 82 | Electric Bubblegum EB 102 | Requiem For Mr. Spock/Hoots Mon (no p/s) | 40 |

## NIX-NOMADS
| | | | |
|---|---|---|---|
| 64 | HMV POP 1354 | You're Nobody (Till Somebody Loves You)/She'll Be Sweeter Than You (demos miscredited to Nix-Nomands) | 60 |

## MEL NIXON
| | | | |
|---|---|---|---|
| 72 | Parlophone R5958 | Pillars Of Straw/Ev'ry Little Beat Of Your Heart | 6 |
| 75 | Alaska ALA 26 | Every Beat Of Your Heart/ASTRA NOVA ORCHESTRA: Soul Sleeper | 6 |

## NKENGAS
| | | | |
|---|---|---|---|
| 73 | Orbitone OT 005 | DESTRUCTION (LP) | 100 |
| 73 | Orbitone OT 006 | NKENGAS IN LONDON (LP) | 30 |

## NMONIC
| | | | |
|---|---|---|---|
| 00 | YNR YNR002 | REQUIEM (EP) | 12 |

## NO DEPOSIT
| | | | |
|---|---|---|---|
| 79 | None | NO RETURN (LP, die cut white sleeve, hand stamped, hand numbered, lyric insert) | 100 |

## NO DOUBT
| | | | |
|---|---|---|---|
| 96 | INTERSCOPE INSP 95515 | Don't Speak/Greener Pastures (picture disc - p/s) | 5 |

## NO SUPPORT/LIMPS
| | | | |
|---|---|---|---|
| 79 | Matchbox Classics MC 1 | OPPOSITE SIDES EP (Split 7" with 2 tracks by Limps and 2 tracks by No Support, p/s) | 20 |
| 79 | Matchbox Classics MC 2 | ANOTHER MATCHBOX CLASSIC? (Split EP, 2 tracks by Limps and 2 by No Support, with folded p/s) | 40 |
| 79 | Matchbox Classics MC 2 | ANOTHER MATCHBOX CLASSIC? (Split EP, 2 tracks by Limps and 2 by No Support, without folded p/s, just die-cut stamped sleeve) | 15 |

## RAB NOAKES
| | | | |
|---|---|---|---|
| 78 | Ring O' 2017 115 | Waiting Here For You/Restless (in p/s) | 18 |
| 78 | Ring O' 2017 115 | Waiting Here For You/Restless | 12 |
| 78 | Ring O' 2017 117 | I Won't Let You Down/Long After Dark (unreleased) | 0 |
| 70 | Decca SKL 5061 | DO YOU SEE THE LIGHTS (LP) | 40 |
| 72 | A&M AMLS 68119 | RAB NOAKES (LP, with Stealers Wheel) | 25 |
| 75 | Warner Bros. K56114 | NEVER TOO LATE (LP) | 15 |

## NOBELMEN
| | | | |
|---|---|---|---|
| 59 | Top Rank JAR 155 | Thunder Wagon/Dragon Walk | 20 |

## BARRY NOBLE
| | | | |
|---|---|---|---|
| 68 | Columbia DB 8438 | I've Got My Eyes On You/I've Always Wanted You | 5 |

## KEITH NOBLE & RADO KLOSE
| | | | |
|---|---|---|---|
| 70 | Eden EDEN LP 14 | MR COMPROMISE (LP,, private pressing, handmade sleeve) | 500 |

## PATSY ANN NOBLE
| | | | |
|---|---|---|---|
| 61 | HMV POP 980 | Good Looking Boy/The Guy Who Can Mend A Broken Heart | 25 |
| 63 | Columbia DB 4956 | Don't You Ever Change Your Mind/Sour Grapes | 15 |
| 63 | Columbia DB 7008 | Heartbreak Avenue/I'm Nobody's Baby | 15 |
| 63 | Columbia DB 7060 | I Was Only Foolin' Myself/Ordinary Love | 10 |

| | | | |
|---|---|---|---|
| 63 | Columbia DB 7088 | Accidents Will Happen/He Tells Me With His Eyes | 15 |
| 63 | Columbia DB 7148 | It's Better To Cry Today/Don't Tell Him I Told You | 10 |
| 64 | Columbia DB 7258 | I Did Nothing Wrong/Better Late Than Never | 10 |
| 64 | Columbia DB 7318 | Private Property/Crack In The Door | 10 |
| 64 | Columbia DB 7386 | Tied Up With Mary/Green Eyed People | 10 |
| 65 | Columbia DB 7472 | Then You Can Tell Me Goodbye/If You Wanna Be More Than Friends | 10 |
| 65 | Polydor BM 56054 | He Who Rides A Tiger/City Of Night | 30 |

*(see also Trisha Noble)*

**TRISHA NOBLE**
| 67 | MGM MGM 1371 | Live For Life/The New Is Rarely Patchka | 20 |

*(see also Patsy Ann Noble)*

**WOODROW NOBLE**
| 79 | Baby Mother HIT DD10 | Reggae A The Best (Feat. Prince Hammer)/Strike The Hammer Wild (12") | 30 |

**NOBLE KIND**
| 86 | TNK 001 | Back In The Race/Where's Christopher? | 15 |

**CLIFF NOBLES (& CO.)**
| 68 | Direction 58-3518 | The Horse/Love Is Alright | 5 |
| 68 | Direction 58-3738 | Judge Baby, I'm Back/Horse Fever (solo) | 5 |
| 69 | Direction 58-4205 | Switch It On/Burning Desire | 5 |
| 68 | Direction 8-63477 | THE HORSE (LP) | 25 |

**NO CHOICE**
| 83 | Riot City RIOT 20 | SADIST DREAM (EP) | 10 |

**NO COVER**
| 82 | Guardian GRC 136 | 200 Voices/Seen Too Much | 50 |

**NOCTURNAL EMISSIONS**
| 81 | Sterile ION 2 | FRUITING BODY (LP) | 50 |
| 84 | Sterile SR 6 | NO SACRIFICE (12", p/s, 2,000 only) | 12 |
| 84 | CFC LP 2 | CHAOS - LIVE AT THE RITZY (LP) | 20 |
| 84 | Illuminated JAMS LP 33 | VIRAL SHEDDING (LP) | 20 |
| 84 | Sterile EMISS 001 | TISSUE OF LIES (LP, 1st batch numbered) | 50 |
| 84 | Sterile EMISS 001 | TISSUE OF LIES (LP, later pressing in blue sleeve) | 25 |
| 84 | Sterile SR 4 | DROWNING IN A SEA OF BLISS (LP) | 50 |
| 84 | Sterile SR 5 | BEFEHLSNOTSTAND (LP) | 25 |
| 85 | Sterile SR 7 | SONGS OF LOVE AND REVOLUTION (LP) | 15 |
| 86 | Sterile SR 9 | SHAKE THOSE CHAINS, RATTLE THOSE CAGES (LP) | 15 |
| 87 | Earthly Delights EARTH 02 | THE WORLD IS MY WOMB (LP) | 20 |
| 88 | Earhtly Delights EARTH 04 | SPIRITFLESH (LP) | 20 |
| 89 | Earthly Delights EARTH 05 | BEYOND LOGIC (LP, 250 signed) | 25 |
| 89 | Earthly Delights EARTH 05 | BEYOND LOGIC (LP) | 18 |
| 90 | Earthly Delights EARTH 06 | MOUTH OF THE BABES (LP) | 30 |
| 93 | Earthly Delights EARTH 08 | THE QUICKENING (LP, 250 signed) | 25 |
| 93 | Earthly Delights EARTH 08 | THE QUICKENING (LP) | 18 |

*(see also Caroline K)*

**NOCTURNES (1)**
| 55 | MGM SP 1120 | Whodat? (Buck Dance)/Hey Punchinello | 10 |
| 55 | MGM SP 1148 | Birmin'ham/Toodle-oo Igaloo | 10 |

**NOCTURNES (2)**
| 64 | Solar SRP 102 | Trioka/Rawhide | 15 |

**NOCTURNES (3)**
| 67 | Columbia DB 8158 | Wish You Would Show Me Your Mind/I Do, I Do | 10 |
| 67 | Columbia DB 8219 | Why (Am I Treated So Bad?)/Save The Last Dance For Me | 10 |
| 68 | Columbia DB 8332 | A New Man/Suddenly Free | 15 |
| 68 | Columbia DB 8453 | Carpet Man/Look At Me | 40 |
| 68 | Columbia DB 8493 | Montage/Fairground Man | 30 |
| 68 | Columbia S(C)X 6223 | THE NOCTURNES (LP) | 30 |
| 68 | Columbia S(C)X 6315 | WANTED LIVE (LP) | 30 |

*(see also Lyn Paul)*

**NOCTURNS**
| 64 | Decca F 12002 | Carryin' On/Three Cool Cats | 10 |

**NOCTURNUS**
| 92 | Earache MOSH 55 | THRESHOLDS (LP) | 20 |

**PROFESSOR ERNEST NODE & HIS MUG & JUG BAND**
| 67 | Columbia DB 8100 | The Egg Plant That Ate Chicago/I'm In The Doghouse | 7 |

**NODENS ICTUS**
| 87 | (No cat no) | THE GROVE OF SELVES (Cassette LP) | 50 |

*(see also Ozric Tentacles)*

**DICK NOEL**
| 56 | London HLH 8295 | (The Same Thing Happens With) The Birds And The Bees/Birth Of The Blues | 20 |

*(see also Nick Nobel)*

**NOEL & THE FIREBALLS**
| 70 | Pama PM 807 | Confussion (sic)/We Got To Have Loving | 15 |
| 70 | Pama PM 808 | Can't Turn You Loose/Skinny Legs | 15 |

**NO FAITH**
| 81 | No Faith NF 001 | Double Trouble/Only The Good Die Young (p/s, private pressing) | 120 |

**JACKY NOGUEZ**
| 60 | Pye Int. 7N.25063 | Hover On Sunday/Chanson Du Jan Gadeiro | 6 |

## NOIR

| | | | |
|---|---|---|---|
| **NOIR** | | | |
| 71 | Dawn DNLS 3029 | WE HAD TO LET YOU HAVE IT (LP, with insert) | 90 |
| **NOISE** | | | |
| 79 | Rok ROK IX/X | Criminal/BLUE MOVIES: Mary Jane | 15 |
| **NOISE FACTORY** | | | |
| 92 | 3rd Party 3RD#01 | MY MIND EP (12") | 20 |
| 92 | 3rd Party 3RD#02 | THE FIRE EP (12") | 50 |
| 92 | 3rd Party 3RD#03 | ALIENATION EP (12") | 25 |
| 92 | 3rd Party 3RD#04 | The CAPSULE EP (12") | 20 |
| 93 | 3rd Party 3RD#07 | A NEW SOMETHING EP (12") | 20 |
| **NOISE TOYS** | | | |
| 79 | Anti Pop AP 1 | Pocket Money/ARTHUR 2 STROKE: The Wundersea World Of Jacques Cousteau (p/s) | 7 |
| **NOIZ BOIZ** | | | |
| 81 | Caveman CMR 03 | Noiz Boiz/Flashback (p/s) | 30 |
| **NO KIDDING** | | | |
| 74 | Wave | NO KIDDING (LP) | 15 |
| **DENNIS NOLAN** | | | |
| 90 | Blakamix BLKM 003 | Pillow Talk/Killer Thriller (12") | 15 |
| **JOE NOLAN & HIS BAND** | | | |
| 69 | Jolly JY 013 | Cool It With Reggae/Reggae With Me | 150 |
| 69 | Jolly JY 016 | Confidential/Poison Reggae | 40 |
| *(see also Bonnie Frankson)* | | | |
| **TERRY NOLAND** | | | |
| 58 | Coral Q 72311 | Oh Baby! Look At Me/Puppy Love | 80 |
| 58 | Coral Q 72311 | Oh Baby! Look At Me/Puppy Love (78) | 25 |
| **PIERRE NOLES** | | | |
| 63 | Oriole CB 1791 | Jacqueline/Marilyn | 7 |
| **NAZ NOMAD & NIGHTMARES** | | | |
| 84 | Big Beat NS 93 | I Had Too Much To Dream (Last Night)/Cold Turkey (p/s) | 5 |
| 84 | Big Beat WIK 21 | GIVE DADDY THE KNIFE CINDY (LP, purple vinyl) | 20 |
| *(see also Damned)* | | | |
| **NOMADS (1)** | | | |
| 65 | Grampian NAN 1008 | I'm Coming Home/Hey Little Girl | 70 |
| **NOMADS (2)** | | | |
| 70 | Pye 7N 17906 | The Singer Sang His Song/Lovin' Him | 6 |
| **NO-MAN** | | | |
| 90s | Hidden Art HA4 | Colours/Colours Remodelled (7", promo, fold-out cover, 8 page press sheet) | 30 |
| 90 | Probe Plus PP27T | COLOURS (EP) (12") | 35 |
| 91 | One Little Indian 57TP12 | DAYS IN THE TREES EP (12") | 20 |
| 92 | One Little Indian 63TP12 | OCEAN SONG EP (12") | 20 |
| 91 | One Little Indian TPLP 47M | LOVESIGHS - AN ENTERTAINMENT (LP) | 20 |
| 93 | One Little Indian 83TP12 | ONLY BABY EP (12") | 20 |
| 93 | One Little Indian TPLP57 | LOVEBLOWS AND LOVECRIES (CD) | 25 |
| 93 | One Little Indian TPLP 057 | LOVEBLOWS & LOVECRIES - A CONFESSION (LP) | 40 |
| 94 | One Little Indian TPLP 067 | FLOWERMOUTH (2-LP) | 50 |
| *(see also Porcupine Tree, Japan)* | | | |
| **NO MAN IS AN ISLAND** | | | |
| 89 | Plastic Head | The Girl From Missouri/Forest Almost Burning/Night Sky Sweet Earth/The Ballet Beast (uncredited) (12") | 60 |
| *(see also No-Man, Porcupine Tree, Japan)* | | | |
| **NOMEANSNO** | | | |
| 89 | Alternative Tentacles VIRUS 77 | WRONG (LP, insert) | 15 |
| **KLAUS NOMI** | | | |
| 81 | RCA RCALP 6026 | KLAUS NOMI (LP) | 15 |
| 82 | RCA PL 70229 | SIMPLE MAN (LP) | 15 |
| **NON** | | | |
| 80 | Mute MUTE 7 | I Can't Look Straight/SMEGMA: Flash Cards (p/s, with 2 centre holes) | 20 |
| 81 | Mute MUTE 015 | NON EP (Rise/Out Out Out/Romance Fatal Dentro Deun Auto) (12", p/s) | 15 |
| 00 | Mute MUTE 250 | Solitude/Receive The Flame (p/s, two centre holes, A-side plays at 45 rpm, B-side has closed grooves and plays at any speed, 700 copies only) | 10 |
| *(see also Boyd Rice)* | | | |
| **NO NAMES** | | | |
| 65 | Polydor NH 59080 | All Because Of You/She Is Mine | 40 |
| **NONE SO BLIND** | | | |
| 83 | Beat Trouser PANT 01 | The Virus/My Favourite Eyes | 6 |
| **NOOKIE** | | | |
| 92 | Absolute 2 ABS 005DJ | THE LOVE IS EP (12", p/s) | 10 |
| 92 | Reflective REFLECT 003 | ACCOUSTIC ASSAULT SQUAD EP (12") | 40 |
| 93 | Reinforced RIVET 1239 | RETURN OF NOOKIE EP (12", p/s) | 20 |
| 94 | Reinforced RIVET 1255 | Give A Little Love/Give A Little Love (Manix Mix)/ Livin' Inside A Dream/T-Three (12") | 15 |
| 94 | Reinforced RIVET 1268 | Only You/Celebrate Life (12") | 10 |
| 95 | Reinforced RIVET LP 05 | THE SOUND OF MUSIC (2xLP) | 40 |
| **NOONDAY UNDERGROUND** | | | |
| 03 | Setana SET 120 | I'll Walk Right On (Paul Weller on vocals)/The Light Brigade (Cut Copy Remix) | 6 |
| 00 | Guided Missile GUIDE 45LP | SELF ASSEMBLY (LP) | 15 |

**PETER NOONE**
| | | | |
|---|---|---|---|
| 70 | RAK 106 | Lady Barbara/Don't Just Stand There | 5 |
| 71 | RAK 114 | Oh You Pretty Thing/Together Forever (first pressing with incorrect song title) | 7 |
| 71 | RAK 114 | Oh You Pretty Things/Together Forever (second pressing with correct song title) | 6 |
| 71 | RAK 121 | Walnut Whirl/Right On Mother | 6 |
| 72 | RAK 129 | Shoo Be Doo Ah/Because You're There | 6 |
| 72 | RAK 136 | Should I/Each And Every Minute | 6 |
| 76 | Bus Stop BUS 1034 | We Don't Need The Money/Love Don't Change | 7 |
| 77 | Bus Stop BUS 1057 | Goodbye Sam Hello Samantha/Can I Put My Song In Your Heart | 7 |

**NO OTHER NAME**
| | | | |
|---|---|---|---|
| 79 | Daylight LD 500 | DEATH INTO LIFE (LP, with insert) | 25 |

**NO QUARTER**
| | | | |
|---|---|---|---|
| 83 | Reel REEL 1 | Survivors/Time And Space/Racing For Home (12", foldout p/s) | 40 |
| 83 | Bonzo Bear | BIRDS OF PREY EP (12") | 30 |

**NORA/BUNNY**
| | | | |
|---|---|---|---|
| 72 | Tropical AL 0015 | Butterfly/TROPICAL ALL STARS: Fly Version | 6 |

**NORBITON SURFERS**
| | | | |
|---|---|---|---|
| 80 | Hut S/80/CUS 700 | Ivor The Engine/My Ego Dies (DIY p/s) | 20 |

**KEN NORDINE**
| | | | |
|---|---|---|---|
| 57 | London RE-D 1091 | KEN NORDINE READS (EP, with Billy Vaughn Orchestra) | 10 |
| 59 | London Jazz EZ-D 19040 | WORD JAZZ (EP) | 10 |
| 67 | Philips BL 7785 | COLOURS (LP) | 25 |

*(see also Billy Vaughn & His Orchestra)*

**NORFOLK & JOY**
| | | | |
|---|---|---|---|
| 79 | Dara MPA 031 | SCOTSOUNDS (LP) | 30 |

**NO RIGHT TURN**
| | | | |
|---|---|---|---|
| 83 | Chelful CHL 001 | NO (LP) | 25 |

**NORMA & TONY**
| | | | |
|---|---|---|---|
| 69 | (No Cat. No.) | YOU ARE ALWAYS WELCOME AT OUR HOUSE (LP, private pressing, 100 only) | 80 |

**NORMAL**
| | | | |
|---|---|---|---|
| 78 | Mute MUTE 001 | Warm Leatherette/T.V.O.D (p/s) | 15 |
| 11 | Mute MUTE 001 | Warm Leatherette/T.V.O.D (p/s, reissue, white vinyl, 500 only) | 7 |

*(see also Robert Rental)*

**NORMAN CONQUEST**
| | | | |
|---|---|---|---|
| 67 | MGM MGM 1376 | Two People/Upside Down | 120 |

*(see also Factory, Peter & Wolves, John Pantry)*

**NORMAN & HOOLIGANS**
| | | | |
|---|---|---|---|
| 77 | President PT 461 | I'm A Punk/Re-Entry | 20 |

**NORMAN & INVADERS**
| | | | |
|---|---|---|---|
| 64 | United Artists UP 1031 | Stacey/Our Wedding Day | 12 |
| 64 | United Artists UP 1058 | Our Wedding Day/Stacey (reissue) | 6 |
| 65 | United Artists UP 1077 | Night Train To Surbiton/Likely Lads | 12 |

**LARRY NORMAN**
| | | | |
|---|---|---|---|
| 81 | Solid Rock CS 103A | I Feel Like Dying/Alwyn Wall - Hold On | 12 |
| 76 | Solid Rock ROCKY 1 | IN ANOTHER LAND (LP, gatefold sleeve) | 15 |

**MONTY NORMAN**
| | | | |
|---|---|---|---|
| 55 | HMV 7M 349 | The Shifting, Whispering Sands/Bonnie Blue Gal | 8 |
| 57 | HMV POP 281 | The Garden Of Eden/Priscilla | 8 |
| 63 | United Artists UEP 1010 | EXCERPTS FROM DR.NO - FILM SOUNDTRACK (EP) | 20 |
| 63 | United Artists ULP 1097 | DOCTOR NO (LP, soundtrack, mono) | 50 |
| 63 | United Artists (S)ULP 1097 | DOCTOR NO (LP, soundtrack, stereo) | 100 |

**OLIVER NORMAN**
| | | | |
|---|---|---|---|
| 67 | Polydor 56176 | Down In The Basement/Drowning In My Own Despair | 60 |
| 68 | Polydor 56247 | People People/You'll Find It Will Come | 6 |

**NORMIL HAWAIIANS**
| | | | |
|---|---|---|---|
| 80 | Dining Out TUX 13 | The Beat Goes On/Ventilation (p/s) | 8 |
| 81 | Illuminated ILL 7 | Still Obedient/Should You Forget? (p/s) | 8 |
| 81 | Red Rhino RED 8 | GALA FAILED (12" EP, p/s) | 10 |
| 82 | Illuminated JAMS 23 | MORE WEALTH THAN MONEY (2-LP) | 30 |
| 84 | Illuminated JAMS 28 | WHAT'S GOING ON? (LP) | 30 |

**NORTH BANK**
| | | | |
|---|---|---|---|
| 72 | Polydor 2058225 | Arsenal We're On Your Side/Half Time | 5 |

**ROY NORTH**
| | | | |
|---|---|---|---|
| 63 | Oak RGJ 107 | Blues In Three/Blues In Five | 50 |

**NORTH STARS**
| | | | |
|---|---|---|---|
| 65 | Fontana TF 581 | For My True Love/Nothing But The Best | 10 |
| 66 | Fontana TF 726 | She's So Far Out She's In/Eeenie Meenie Minee Mo | 30 |

**TOM NORTHCOTT**
| | | | |
|---|---|---|---|
| 68 | Warner Bros WB 7160 | 1941/Other Times | 12 |

**NORTHERN LIGHT**
| | | | |
|---|---|---|---|
| 75 | CBS 3370 | Minnesota/Minnesota (DJ Version) | 25 |

**NORTHERN LIGHTS**
| | | | |
|---|---|---|---|
| 66 | United Artists UP 1123 | No Time/Time To Move Along | 50 |
| 66 | United Artists UP 1161 | Through Darkness, Light/Baby Those Are The Rules | 50 |

*(see also Hooten[anny] Singers, Abba)*

## NORTHERN PICTURE LIBRARY

MINT VALUE £

| | | | |
|---|---|---|---|
| 93 | Vinyl Japan TASK 6 | Love Song For The Dead Che/The Way That Stars Die (12", p/s) | 15 |
| 94 | Vinyl Japan TASK 25 | BLUE DISSOLVE EP (12", p/s) | 15 |
| 94 | Sarah SARAH 95 | Last September's Farewell Kiss/Signs (p/s, insert) | 18 |
| 94 | Sarah SARAH 94 | Paris/Norfolk Windmills (p/s, insert) | 18 |
| 93 | Vinyl Japan ASKLP 23 | ALASKA (LP) | 20 |

## NORTHERN JAZZ ORCHESTRA

| | | | |
|---|---|---|---|
| 79 | SRTY 79 CUS 410 | THAT'S THE ONE (LP) | 15 |

## NORTHWIND

| | | | |
|---|---|---|---|
| 71 | Regal Zono. SLRZ 1020 | SISTER, BROTHER, LOVER (LP) | 350 |

(see also Elastic Band)

## NORWICH CITY FOOTBALL CLUB

| | | | |
|---|---|---|---|
| 82 | NCP NCFC 1 | Something To Shout About/Supporters - Canary Celebration | 7 |

## NOSEBLEEDS

| | | | |
|---|---|---|---|
| 77 | Rabid TOSH 12 | Ain't Bin To No Music School/Fascist Pigs (p/s) | 30 |

(see also Durutti Column, Ed Banger, Blue Orchids)

## NO SECURITY

| | | | |
|---|---|---|---|
| 89 | Peaceville VILE 11 | BURY THE DEBT NOT THE DEAD (split LP with DOOM) | 18 |

## NO SPORTS

| | | | |
|---|---|---|---|
| 90 | Unicorn PHZA-6 | Stay Rude Say Rebel/Tour De France/Love Song/Girl (Tango) (12", p/s) | 12 |
| 87 | Unicorn PHZ 49 | KING SKA (LP) | 15 |

## NOSTROMO

| | | | |
|---|---|---|---|
| 79 | Bronze BRO 12BRO80 | Alien/Around The World In 60 Seconds (12", 'Alien' p/s) | 15 |
| 79 | Bronze BRO 80 | Alien/Around The World In 60 Seconds ('Alien' p/s) | 7 |

## NO SWEAT (1)

| | | | |
|---|---|---|---|
| 79 | Rip Off RIP 4 | Start All Over Again/You Should Be So Lucky (p/s) | 30 |

(see also Clive Culbertson)

## NO SWEAT (2)

| | | | |
|---|---|---|---|
| 78 | Eel Pie EPS 002 | Work On Her/Gimme Some Action | 6 |

## NOTATIONS (U.K.)

| | | | |
|---|---|---|---|
| 72 | Chapter One SCH 174 | Need Your Love/Just Nothing Left To Give | 25 |

## NOTATIONS (U.S.)

| | | | |
|---|---|---|---|
| 76 | Curtom K 16696 | Think Before You Stop/I'm Losing | 5 |
| 76 | Curtom K 56212 | NOTATIONS (LP) | 30 |

## FREDDIE NOTES & RUDIES

| | | | |
|---|---|---|---|
| 69 | Downtown DT 427 | I Don't Wanna Lose That Girl/Train From Vietnam | 20 |
| 69 | Grape GR 3010 | Guns Of Navarone/Yester-Me, Yester-You | 50 |
| 69 | Grape GR 3011 | Babylon Girl/Girl I've Got A Date | 15 |
| 69 | Trojan TR 7713 | Shanghai/Rome Wasn't Built In A Day | 15 |
| 70 | Bullet BU 421 | The Feeling Is Fine/Girl You're Killing Me | 12 |
| 70 | Trojan TR 7724 | Rocco/Don't Tell Your Mama | 20 |
| 70 | Trojan TR 7734 | Down On The Farm/Easy Street | 30 |
| 70 | Trojan TR 7791 | Montego Bay/RUDIES: Blue Mountain | 10 |
| 70 | Trojan TR 7810 | Walk A Mile In My Shoes/JOHNNY ARTHEY ORCHESTRA: Reggae Rouser | 6 |
| 70 | Duke DU 63 | The Bull/River Ben Come Up | 75 |
| 70 | Duke DU 68 | Chicken Inn/Chicken Scratch | 15 |
| 70 | B&C CB 125 | It Came Out The Sky/Well Oh Well (p/s) | 6 |
| 70 | Trojan TBL 109 | UNITY (LP) | 25 |
| 70 | Trojan TBL 152 | MONTEGO BAY (LP) | 20 |

## NOTHINGS

| | | | |
|---|---|---|---|
| 65 | CBS 201779 | At Times Like This/Love So Sweet | 15 |

## NOTSENSIBLES

| | | | |
|---|---|---|---|
| 79 | Redball RR 02 | (I'm In Love With) Margaret Thatcher/Little Boxes/Gary Bushell's Band Of The Week (p/s) | 30 |
| 80 | Bent SMALL BENT 5 | Death To Disco/Coronation Street Hustle/Lying On The Sofa (p/s) | 25 |
| 80 | Snotty Snail NELCOL 1 | (I'm In Love With) Margaret Thatcher/Little Boxes/Gary Bushell's Band Of The Week (p/s, reissue) | 12 |
| 80 | Snotty Snail NELCOL 3 | I Thought You Were Dead/I Make A Balls Of Everything I Do/Teenage Revolution (p/s) | 12 |
| 81 | Snotty Snail NELCOL 6 | I Am The Bishop/The Telephone Rings Again (p/s) | 10 |
| 80 | Bent BIGBENT 6 | INSTANT CLASSICS (LP) | 50 |
| 80 | Snotty Snail SSLP 1 | INSTANT CLASSICS (LP, reissue) | 30 |

## NOTTINGHAM JAZZ ORCHESTRA

| | | | |
|---|---|---|---|
| 71 | Swift SP 55 | FESITVAL SUITE (LP) | 50 |

## NOTTS ALLIANCE

| | | | |
|---|---|---|---|
| 72 | Tradition TSR 011 | THE CHEERFUL 'ORN (LP, with Roy Harris) | 15 |

## NOUVELLE VAGUE

| | | | |
|---|---|---|---|
| 95 | Peacefrog PFG 051 | NOUVELLE VAGUE (LP, inner) | 30 |
| 06 | Peacefrog PFG 079 | BANDE A PART (LP, poster) | 20 |

## NOVA LOCAL

| | | | |
|---|---|---|---|
| 69 | MCA MUPS 377 | NOVA 1 (LP) | 40 |

## PAUL NOVA

| | | | |
|---|---|---|---|
| 82 | Exhibit 1 EX 001 | Julie Ann/Video Age | 60 |
| 83 | Exhibit 1 EX 002 | Famous Boys/Home Sweet Home | 60 |
| 85 | Exhibit 1 EX 004 | FANTASY AND FEELING EP | 60 |
| 84 | Exhibit 1 EX 003 | TREES WITHOUT LEAVES (LP) | 200 |

## NOVAK
| | | | |
|---|---|---|---|
| 97 | Enraptured WORM 2 | Silver Seas/Schmaltz (p/s in outer hand-sewn cloth sleeve with embroidered "Hand-knitted by Novak" label, 200 only, each different) | 15 |
| 97 | Enraptured WORM 2 | Silver Seas/Schmaltz (p/s, 800 only) | 8 |
| 97 | Kitty Kitty CHOOSY 007 | Rapunzel/Almost Chinook (hand crayoned p/s, 1,000 only) | 8 |

## NOVAS
| | | | |
|---|---|---|---|
| 63 | RCA RCA 1360 | Push A Little Harder/Oh, Gee Baby! | 30 |
| 65 | London HLU 9940 | The Crusher/Take 7 | 30 |

## KAREN NOVOTNY X
| | | | |
|---|---|---|---|
| 10 | Great Pop Supplement GPS 66 | UNTITLED EP (300 only) | 10 |

## NOW GENERATION
| | | | |
|---|---|---|---|
| 73 | Green Door GD 4055 | Alone Again, Naturally/MIND-BODY-SOUL: My Part (Version) | 5 |
| 73 | Pyramid PYR 7007 | Baby Don't Do It/You'll Never Know | 5 |
| 74 | Trojan TRLS 78 | FOR THE GOOD TIMES (LP) | 20 |

*(see also I Roy, B.B. Seaton, Audley Rollins)*

## NOW (1)
| | | | |
|---|---|---|---|
| 69 | NEMS 56-4125 | Marcia/The Hands On My Clock Stand Still | 35 |
| 73 | President PT 401 | I Wanna Be Free/People Are Standing | 12 |

## NOW (2)
| | | | |
|---|---|---|---|
| 77 | Ultimate ULT 401 | Development Corporations/Why (p/s) | 20 |
| 77 | Ultimate ULT 401 | Development Corporations/Why (p/s, blue vinyl) | 40 |
| 79 | Raw RAW 31 | Into The 1980s/Nine O'Clock (p/s, 800 only) | 40 |

## NO WAY
| | | | |
|---|---|---|---|
| 78 | Our Own IS/NW/1035 | Breaking Point/TV Pox/30 Seconds (p/s) | 100 |

## NOYES BROTHERS
| | | | |
|---|---|---|---|
| 80 | Object Music OBJ 009/010 | SHEEP FROM GOATS (2-LP) | 25 |

*(see also Steve Miro & Eyes, Spherical Objects)*

## NOY'S BAND
| | | | |
|---|---|---|---|
| 74 | Dawn 1075 | Love Potion Number 9/Eldorado | 10 |

*(see also Jan Dukes De Grey)*

## NOYS OF US
| | | | |
|---|---|---|---|
| 60s | KPS KPS 502 | He's Alright Jill/What Can I Do | 30 |

## NQB
| | | | |
|---|---|---|---|
| 72 | Epic S EPC 2151 | Long Long Weekend/Free The People | 6 |

## N.R.B.Q. (NEW RHYTHM & BLUES QUINTET)
| | | | |
|---|---|---|---|
| 69 | CBS 4290 | Stomp/I Didn't Know Myself | 5 |
| 69 | CBS 4501 | C'mon Everybody/Rocket Number 9 | 5 |
| 69 | CBS 63653 | N.R.B.Q. (LP) | 20 |

*(see also Carl Perkins)*

## N.S.U.
| | | | |
|---|---|---|---|
| 69 | Stable SLE 8002 | TURN ON OR TURN ME DOWN (LP) | 200 |

## GUITAR NUBBIT
| | | | |
|---|---|---|---|
| 64 | Bootleg 501 | Georgia Chain Gang/Hard Road (99 copies only) | 45 |
| 60s | XX MIN 705 | GUITAR NUBBIT (EP) | 20 |

## NUCHA
| | | | |
|---|---|---|---|
| 90 | CBS 655885 7 | Together/Ha Sempre Alguem | 5 |

## NUCLEAR ASSAULT
| | | | |
|---|---|---|---|
| 88 | Under One Flag 12 FLAG 107 | GOOD TIMES, BAD TIMES (12" EP) | 10 |
| 88 | Under One Flag FLAG 21P | SURVIVE (LP, picture disc) | 15 |
| 88 | Under One Flag FLAG 21 | SURVIVE (LP) | 15 |
| 89 | Under One Flag FLAG 35 | HANDLE WITH CARE (LP) | 15 |

## NUCLEAR SOCKETTS
| | | | |
|---|---|---|---|
| 81 | Subversive SUB 001 | HONOUR BEFORE GLORY (EP, folded p/s, 33rpm) | 25 |
| 81 | Subversive SUB 002 | Play Loud/Shadow On The Map | 25 |
| 82 | None | Riot Squad (magazine flexi-disc with fold out picture insert) | 20 |

## (IAN CARR'S) NUCLEUS
| | | | |
|---|---|---|---|
| 70 | Vertigo 6360 008 | ELASTIC ROCK (LP, die cut gatefold sleeve, large swirl label) | 175 |
| 70 | Vertigo 6360 008 | ELASTIC ROCK (LP, die cut gatefold sleeve, later 'spaceship' label) | 30 |
| 71 | Vertigo 6360 027 | WE'LL TALK ABOUT IT LATER (LP, die cut gatefold sleeve, large swirl label) | 175 |
| 71 | Vertigo 6360 027 | WE'LL TALK ABOUT IT LATER (LP, die cut gatefold sleeve, 'spaceship' label) | 20 |
| 71 | Vertigo 6360 039 | SOLAR PLEXUS (LP, as Ian Carr's Nucleus, 1st pressing, Matrix side 1, 6360076 1Y//1 1 1 3 Side 2, 6360076 2Y//1 1 1 3, gatefold sleeve, large swirl label) | 200 |
| 72 | Vertigo 6360 076 | BELLADONNA (LP, as Ian Carr, 1st pressing, Matrix side 1, 6360076 1Y//1 1 1 3 Side 2, 6360076 2Y//1 1 1 3, gatefold sleeve, swirl label) | 200 |
| 73 | Vertigo 6360 039 | SOLAR PLEXUS (LP, as Ian Carr's Nucleus, 2nd pressing, gatefold sleeve, small swirl label) | 70 |
| 74 | Vertigo 6360 076 | BELLADONNA (LP, as Ian Carr, 2nd pressing, Matrix side 1, 6360076 1Y//1 1 1 4 Side 2, 6360076 2Y//1 1 1 5, gatefold sleeve, swirl label) | 80 |
| 73 | Vertigo 6360 091 | LABYRINTH (LP, 'spaceship' label, any with swirl are Italian pressings!) | 60 |
| 73 | Vertigo 6360 100 | ROOTS (LP, 'spaceship' label) | 35 |
| 74 | Vertigo 6360 110 | UNDER THE SUN (LP, 'spaceship' label) | 25 |
| 75 | Vertigo 6360 076 | BELLADONNA (LP, as Ian Carr, gatefold sleeve, 'spaceship' label) | 30 |
| 75 | Vertigo 6360 119 | SNAKE HIPS ETCETERA (LP, laminated sleeve, 'spaceship' label) | 25 |
| 75 | Vertigo 6360 124 | ALLEY CAT (LP, 'spaceship' label) | 25 |
| 76 | Vertigo 6360 039 | SOLAR PLEXUS (LP, as Ian Carr's Nucleus, 3rd pressing gatefold sleeve, 'spaceship' label) | 20 |
| 76 | Vertigo 9286 019 | DIRECT HITS (LP, 'spaceship' label) | 35 |
| 77 | Capitol EST 11771 | IN FLAGRANTI DELICTO (LP) | 20 |

MINT VALUE £

| 79 | Capitol E-ST 11916 | OUT OF THE LONG DARK (LP) ................................................................ 15 |
| 80 | Mood 24000 | AWAKENING (LP) ................................................................................... 15 |
| 89 | BGO LP 47 | ELASTIC ROCK (LP, reissue) .................................................................... 15 |

*(see also Don Rendell & Ian Carr Quintet, Neil Ardley, Centipede, Michael Garrick, New Jazz Orchestra, Linda Hoyle)*

## TED NUGENT (& AMBOY DUKES)

| 74 | Discreet K 19200 | Sweet Revenge/Ain't It The Truth (as Ted Nugent & Amboy Dukes) ............... 8 |
| 75 | Epic S EPC 3900 | Stormtroopin'/Hey Baby (some in p/s, orange label) .................................. 5 |
| 76 | Epic S EPC 4796 | Dog Eat Dog/Love You So I Told You A Lie ............................................... 5 |
| 77 | Epic S EPC 5482 | Cat Scratch Fever/A Thousand Nights ..................................................... 5 |
| 78 | Epic S EPC 9545 | Homebound/Death By Misadventure (p/s) ............................................... 5 |
| 75 | Discreet K 59203 | CALL OF THE WILD (LP) ......................................................................... 15 |

*(see also [American] Amboy Dukes)*

## NUGGETS

| 55 | Capitol CL 14216 | Quirl Up In My Arms/So Help Me, I Love You ........................................... 12 |
| 55 | Capitol CL 14267 | Shtiggy Boom/Anxious Heart ................................................................ 12 |

## GARY NUMAN

### SINGLES

| 79 | Beggars Banquet BEG 23 | Cars/Asylum (p/s,orange plastic labels) .................................................. 6 |
| 79 | Beggars Banquet BEG 23 | Cars/Asylum (p/s, 'mispressed' on dark red vinyl) .................................... 10 |
| 79 | Beggars Banquet BEG 29 | Complex/Bombers (live) (p/s, 'mispressed' on dark red vinyl) .................... 18 |
| 80 | Beggars Banquet BEG 35 | We Are Glass/Trois Gymnopedies (First Movement) (p/s, custom factory pressings on green and yellow vinyl) ................................................................ 500 |
| 80 | Beggars Banquet BEG 35 | We Are Glass/Trois Gymnopedies (1st Movement) (p/s, 'mispressed' on dark red vinyl) ................................................................................................ 12 |
| 80 | Beggars Banquet BEG 46 | I Die, You Die/Down In The Park (Piano Version) (p/s, dark red vinyl 'mispress')........... 8 |
| 80 | Beggars Banquet BEG 46 | I Die, You Die/Down In The Park (Piano Version) (p/s, mispressing, plays Remember I Was Vapour & "On Broadway" [SAM 126]) ............................................... 22 |
| 81 | Beggars Banquet BEG 62 | She's Got Claws/I Sing Rain (p/s, mispressing, plays Dollar's Hand Held In Black And White) ................................................................................................ 60 |
| 82 | Beggars Banquet BEG 77 | We Take Mystery (To Bed)/The Image Is (mispressed sleeve, no writing) ....... 35 |
| 83 | Beggars Banquet BEG 95P | Warriors/My Car Slides (aeroplane-shaped picture disc) ........................... 12 |
| 83 | Beggars Banquet BEG 95P | Warriors/My Car Slides (Uncut, aeroplane-shaped picture disc) ................. 400 |
| 84 | Beggars Banquet TUB 1 | This Is My Life (unissued promo for "THE PLAN LP", 300 white label test pressings only) ................................................................................................. 100 |
| 85 | Numa NUP 9 | Your Fascination/We Need It (mispressed picture disc with pictures on the wrong side) ................................................................................................. 18 |
| 85 | Numa NU PROMO 1002 | WHITE NOISE (12" 4-track sampler Beserker/We Are Glass/Cars/Are "Friends" Electric?) .......................................................................................... 30 |
| 85 | Numa NUM 7 | THE LIVE EP (12", p/s, custom factory pressing on multicoloured vinyl) ...... 200 |
| 85 | Numa NUM 13 | Miracles (Extended)/The Fear (Extended) (12" mispressed sleeve: no red writing) ....... 30 |
| 86 | Numa NUMX 16 | This Is Love/Survival//Call Out The Dogs (Extended)/No Shelter/This Ship Comes Apart (12", p/s, stickered double pack, shrinkwrapped) ............................ 10 |
| 86 | Numa NUP 17 | I Can't Stop/Faces (Uncut, aeroplane-shaped picture disc) ...................... 100 |
| 86 | Numa NUM 17 DJ | I Can't Stop (Special Club Mix) (12" 1-sided DJ promo) ............................. 10 |
| 87 | Beggars Banquet BEG 199T | Cars Extended E Reg Model/Are Friends Electric?/Cars (E Reg Model)/Cars (Motorway Mix) (12" yellow/green/silver labels, export copies p/s) ......................... 25 |
| 88 | I.R.S. ILSP 1003 | New Anger/I Don't Believe (poster p/s) .................................................. 5 |
| 88 | I.R.S. ILSPD 1004 | America/Respect (live) (mispressed picture disc, 'Gary' picture both sides) ...... 45 |
| 91 | I.R.S. NUMAN 1 | Heart/Icehouse (p/s, black vinyl)............................................................ 6 |
| 91 | Numa NUM 22 | Emotion/In A Glasshouse (p/s) ............................................................... 5 |
| 92 | Numa NU 23 | The Skin Game/Dark Mountain (p/s)........................................................ 5 |
| 92 | Numa NU 24DJ | Machine & Soul/Machine & Soul (fan club issue, white label, mail-order only) ........ 8 |
| 93 | Beggars Banquet BEG 264T | Cars (Multivalve)/Cars (Endurance Model)/Cars (Top Gear Model) (12", black vinyl, promo only) .......................................................................................... 12 |
| 93 | Beggars Banquet BEG 264 | Cars ('93 Sprint)/Cars (Top Gear) (poster p/s) ......................................... 6 |
| 93 | Beggars Banquet BEG 246L | Cars ('93 Sprint)/Cars (Endurance) (Uncut McLaren F1-shaped picture disc) ............... 175 |
| 93 | Beggars Banquet | Cars ('93 Sprint)/(Multivalve)/(Classic)/(Endurance)/(Top Gear)/('E' Reg Version) (CD, withdrawn, Extended 'E' Reg Model replaces Motorway Mix)........... 30 |
| 93 | Beggars Banquet BEG 264CD | Cars '93 Sprint)/(Multivalve)/(Classic)/(Endurance)/(Top Gear)/(Motorway Mix)/'E' Reg Model) (CD, Autosports Awards issue, 300 only) ................................ 40 |
| 94 | Salvation SACD 1 | THE RADIAL PAIR (CD EP, fan club issue, mail order only)........................... 25 |
| 94 | Numa NUM 26 | A Question Of Faith (12", withdrawn, black labels with blue print) ................ 25 |
| 94 | Numa NU 26 | A Question Of Faith/Whisper Of Truth (fan club issue, white label, mail-order only) .... 25 |
| 96 | The Record Label SPIND 6 | Radio (with N.R.G.)/Radio (extended mix) (CD, withdrawn) ....................... 150 |

### ALBUMS

| 80 | Beggars Banquet BEGA 19 | TELEKON (LP, dark red vinyl 'mispressing', with stickered sleeve.; with bonus single SAM 126 "Remember I Was Vapour [live]"/"On Broadway" [Live]).................. 20 |
| 80 | Beggars Banquet BEGA 19 | TELEKON (LP, dark red vinyl 'mispressing', with stickered sleeve) ............... 15 |
| 84 | B. Banquet BEGA 55P | THE PLAN (LP, picture disc) .................................................................. 15 |
| 84 | Numa NUP 4 | BESERKER (Uncut picture disc) ............................................................ 375 |
| 84 | Numa NUMA 1001 | BESERKER (LP, mispressing, plays Imagination's GOLD on side 2) ................. 80 |
| 86 | Numa NUMAP 1003 | THE FURY (LP, mispress picture disc, "Your Fascination" 12" photo on A-side with lyric insert) ................................................................................................ 25 |
| 86 | Numa GNFCDA 1 | IMAGES 1 & 2 (2-LP, fan club issue with photo inserts, mail-order only, initial signed copies) ................................................................................................ 20 |
| 87 | Numa GNFCDA 2 | IMAGES 3 & 4 (2-LP, fan club issue with photo inserts, mail-order only, initial signed copies) ................................................................................................ 20 |
| 87 | Numa GNFCDA 3 | IMAGES 5 & 6 (2-LP, fan club issue with photo inserts, mail-order only, initial signed copies) ................................................................................................ 20 |
| 87 | Numa GNF CDA 4 | IMAGES 7 & 8 (2-LP, fan club issue with photo inserts, mail-order only, initial signed copies) ................................................................................................ 20 |
| 89 | Numa GNF CDA 5 | IMAGES 9 & 10 (2-LP, fan club issue with photo inserts, mail-order only, initial signed copies) ................................................................................................ 20 |

| | | | |
|---|---|---|---|
| 88 | I.R.S. ILPPD 035 | METAL RHYTHM (LP, picture disc) | 12 |
| 88 | Beggars Banquet BBL 47 | WARRIORS (LP, 'Lowdown' reissue, white lettering on sleeve) | 35 |
| 91 | Numa NUMACD 1001 | BERSERKER (CD, fan club issue, mail order only, blue text on CD & inlay) | 25 |
| 94 | Numa NUMA 1010 | DREAM CORROSION (3-LP, autographed gatefold sleeve; copies bought at HMV with signed 10" x 8" photo) | 20 |
| 94 | Numa NUMA 1011 | SACRIFICE (LP, with lyric sheet, stickered sleeve & bonus single: The Seed Of A Lie [5.26]/"The Seed Of A Lie [7.07]") | 40 |
| 96 | Polygram TV 531 149-2 | PREMIER HITS (CD, mispressing, plays Mark Knogfler's Golden Heart) | 40 |
| 98 | Eagle EAGBX025 | THE NUMA YEARS (5-CD set of Beserker, The Fury, Strange Charm, Machine and Soul Sacrifice.) | 40 |
| 03 | Jagged Halo JHLP 5 | HYBRID (2-LP, numbered gatefold sleeve) | 30 |
| 06 | Mortal Records LP001 | JAGGED (1,000 only, white vinyl, first 250 copies hand signed, numbered and sold via offical Gary Numan website) | 45 |
| 06 | Mortal Records LP001 | JAGGED (LP, 1,000 only, white vinyl) | 25 |
| 08 | OTB LP1 | PURE (LP, 300 pressed in purple/red/clear vinyl (100 of each). Final 2 tracks pressed on separate yellow vinyl 7) | 35 |
| 08 | OTB LP2 | EXILE (LP, 300 copies, turquoise/white/orange vinyl (100 of each). | 30 |
| 08 | Beggars Banquet BBQCD 2057 | REPLICAS REDUX (2-CD with additional 6 track of mixes and versions CD in card sleeve (GNCD 2008) | 25 |
| 08 | VIN 180 LP 001 | THE PLEASURE PRINCIPLE (LP, reissue) | 15 |
| | *(LP, 180 gram vinyl, numbered with 8" x 6" print)* | | |
| 09 | Beggars Banquet BBQCD 2063 | THE PLEASURE PRINCIPLE (2-CD 30th Anniversary set, initial copies with bonus CD THE LIVE EP's (BBQCD 2070) | 25 |
| 10 | Vinyl 180 VIN180LP027 | 1978/79 (4-LP box set, 500 copies comprising of Tubeway Army/Replicas/The Pleasure Principle and The Plan only for those who had bought earlier reissues of Replicas and The Pleasure Principle) | 90 |
| 11 | Vinyl 180 VIN180LP038 | 1980/81 (5-LP box set, Telekon 2-LPs, and Living Ornaments 3-LPs)) | 60 |
| 11 | Vinyl 180 VIN180LP037 | TELEKON (2-LP reissue in gatefold sleeve) | 25 |
| 13 | Mortal MORTAL LP 14 | SPLINTER (2-LP, first issue with limited edition 12" x 12" signed print sold via official Gary Numan website) | 30 |

*(see also Tubeway Army, Paul Gardiner, Dramatis, Claire Hamill, Radio Heart, Nicky Robson, Paper Toys, Caroline Munro, Generator, Bauhaus, Bill Sharpe, Sharpe & Numan, Battles)*

## NUMBER NINE BREAD STREET
| | | | |
|---|---|---|---|
| 67 | Holy Ground HG 112/1109 | NUMBER NINE BREAD STREET (LP, 250 copies only) | 400 |

## NUMBERS
| | | | |
|---|---|---|---|
| 79 | Blasto SRTS 79/CUS/358 | ROCK STARS (EP, with insert) | 50 |
| 80s | Homegrown HG 701 | Here Today/Put 'Em All To Shame/Another Day/Tear You Down (photocopied or green & white sleeve; with poster) | 10 |
| 80s | Homegrown HG 701 | Here Today/Put 'Em All To Shame/Another Day/Tear You Down (photocopied or green & white sleeve; without poster) | 10 |

## NUMSKULLZ
| | | | |
|---|---|---|---|
| 96 | High Noon NUM003 | Enough Of That (12") | 12 |
| 98 | Hombre MEX003 | Signs Of The End/The Difference (12") | 10 |
| 98 | Hombre MEX005 | THE UNEXPECTED (EP) | 10 |
| 00 | Hombre MEX 018 | AD INFINITUM (LP) | 15 |

## NU NOTES
| | | | |
|---|---|---|---|
| 63 | HMV POP 1232 | Hall Of Mirrors/Fury | 20 |
| 64 | HMV POP 1311 | Kathy/Sunset | 20 |

*(see also Russ Sainty & Nu Notes)*

## NUNS
| | | | |
|---|---|---|---|
| 81 | Butt FUN 2 | Wild/Suicide Child (p/s) | 15 |
| 81 | Butt ALSO 001 | THE NUNS (LP) | 15 |

## NURSE WITH WOUND
| | | | |
|---|---|---|---|
| 83 | L.A.Y.L.A.H. LAY 3 | GYLLENSKÖLD, GEIJERSTAM AND I AT RYDBERG'S (12" EP) | 40 |
| 84 | L.A.Y.L.A.H. LAY 7 | BRAINED BY FALLING MASONRY (12" EP) | 12 |
| 86 | Torso 33016 | SPIRAL INSANA (12" EP) | 12 |
| 87 | Crystal/Wisewound WW 01 | Crank/TERMITE QUEEN: Wisecrack (numbered plain black sleeve with printed band, 500 only) | 20 |
| 88 | Yangki 002 | FAITH'S FAVOURITES EP: Swamp Rat (with Current 93)/Ballad Of The Pale Girl (12", laminated p/s) | 30 |
| 88 | Idle Hole MIRROR 003 | Cooloorta Moon/Great Empty Space (12", p/s) | 20 |
| 90 | Harbinger 001 | The Burial Of The Stoned Sardine/CURRENT 93: No Hiding From The Blackbird | 15 |
| 90 | United Dairies UD 031 | SORESUCKER EP: I Am The Poison/Journey Through Cheese (12", p/s, 2,000 only) | 20 |
| 90 | Shock SX 004 | Sinister Senile: Human Human Human/Psychedelic Underground (45/33rpm, 1,000 only) | 25 |
| 92 | Clawfist 12 | Steel Dream March Of The Metal Men/The Dadda's Intoxication ('singles club' release, 33rpm, foldover p/s in poly bag, 1,400 only) | 15 |
| 93 | Clawfist 20 | CRUMB DUCK (10" EP, shared with Stereolab, 37 with handmade p/s (Gain/Sadier only) | 100 |
| 93 | Clawfist 20 | CRUMB DUCK (10" EP, shared with Stereolab, 1450 regular without handmade p/s) | 20 |
| 93 | World Serpent WS 7003 | Alien (1-sided, company sleeve 1,000 only) | 25 |
| 95 | WN 001 | ALICE THE GOON (1-sided 12", p/s, 500 only) | 75 |
| 04 | United Durtro – UNITED DURTRO/JNANA 1974 | HAVING FUN WITH THE PRINCE OF DARKNESS (7", p/s, insert, signed by Stapleton, also 'stamped' with image of Stapleton, UK edition of 40 copies) | 70 |
| 79 | United Dairies UD 01 | CHANCE MEETING ON A DISSECTING TABLE OF A SEWING MACHINE AND AN UMBRELLA (LP, 500 only, originals have hand-painted numbers; beware of bootlegs with printed numbers) | 200 |
| 80 | United Dairies UD 03 | TO THE QUIET MEN FROM A TINY GIRL (LP, numbered, 500 only, originals have hand-painted numbers; beware of bootlegs with printed numbers) | 150 |
| 80 | United Dairies UD 04 | MERZBILD SCHWET (LP, numbered, 500 only, originals have hand-painted numbers; beware of bootlegs with printed numbers) | 150 |
| 81 | United Dairies UD 08 | INSECT AND INDIVIDUAL SILENCED (LP, 1,000 only) | 80 |
| 83 | Mi Mort MI MORT iii | GYLLENSKÖLD, GEIJERSTAM & FRIENDS, LIVE AT BAR MALDOROR (LP, some with insert) | 40 |
| 83 | Third Mind TMR 03 | OSTRANENIE 1913 (LP, 3,000 only) | 60 |

| 85 | L.A.Y.L.A.H. LAY 15 | THE SYLVIE AND BABS HI-FI COMPANION (LP, gatefold sleeve) | 25 |
| 85 | United Dairies UD 110 | DRUNK WITH THE OLD MAN OF THE MOUNTAINS (LP) | 25 |
| 85 | United Dairies UD 012 | HOMOTOPY TO MARIE (LP, 5,000 only) | 35 |
| 86 | United Dairies UD 019 | AUTOMATING VOL. 1 (LP, 3,000 only) | 30 |
| 86 | United Dairies UD 020 | A MISSING SENSE (LP, 1 side only; other side by Organum; 2,000 only) | 30 |
| 87 | United Dairies UD 025 | DRUNK WITH THE OLD MAN OF THE MOUNTAINS (LP, reissue, handmade custom sleeve, with insert, signed, 100 only) | 150 |
| 88 | United Dairies UD 027 | ALAS THE MADONNA DOES NOT FUNCTION (mini-LP, 45/33rpm, 3,000 only) | 25 |
| 88 | Idle Hole MIRROR ONE | SOLILOQUY FOR LILITH (3-LP box set, 5,000 only) | 80 |
| 88 | Idle Hole MIRROR 1C | SOLILOQUY FOR LILITH PTS 5/6 (LP, with insert) | 25 |
| 89 | Idle Hole MIRROR TWO | PRESENTS THE SISTERS OF PATAPHYSICS (LP, 1,000 only) | 25 |
| 89 | United Dairies UD 030 | AUTOMATING VOL. II (LP) | 20 |
| 89 | United Dairies UD 032 | A SUCKED ORANGE (LP, with full colour insert) | 35 |
| 89 | United Dairies UD 032 | A SUCKED ORANGE (LP) | 30 |
| 89 | Yangki 003 | LUMBS SISTER (LP) | 30 |
| 90 | United Dairies UD 134 | PSILOTRIPITAKA (3-LP [UD 01, 03 & 04], with bonus LP "Registered Nurse" [UD 00], 1,000 only, in leather bag) | 400 |
| 90 | United Dairies UD 134 | PSILOTRIPITAKA (3-LP [UD 01, 03 & 04], with bonus LP "Registered Nurse" [UD 00], 1,000 only) | 150 |
| 90 | United Dairies UD 134CD | PSILOTRIPITAKA (3-CD [UD 01, 03 & 04], with bonus CD "Registered Nurse" [UD 00CD], 1,000 only, 30 in 'leather bondage bag') | 400 |
| 90 | United Dairies UD 134CD | PSILOTRIPITAKA (3-CD [UD 01, 03 & 04], with bonus CD "Registered Nurse" [UD 00CD], 1,000 only)) | 60 |
| 90 | L.A.Y.L.A.H. LAY 30 | BRAINED/GYLLENSKÖLD (LP, withdrawn) | 35 |
| 91 | United Dairies UD 038 | CREAKINESS (LP, with Spasm) | 20 |
| 91 | United Dairies UD 09 | THE 150 MURDEROUS PASSIONS (LP) | 30 |
| 91 | United Dairies UD 09CD | THE 150 MURDEROUS PASSIONS (CD, sealed in black plastic, 500 only) | 30 |
| 93 | United Dairies UD 059 | CRUMB DUCK (LP, shared with Stereolab, reissue of Clawfist EP, 50 copies on pink vinyl) | 50 |
| 93 | United Dairies UD 059 | CRUMB DUCK (LP, shared with Stereolab, reissue of Clawfist EP, 500 on fluorescent yellow vinyl) | 25 |
| 94 | United Dairies UD 043 | SECOND PIRATE SESSION - ROCK'N'ROLL STATION - SPECIAL EDITION (LP, red vinyl, 500 only) | 20 |
| 99 | United Dairies UD 056 | AN AWKWARD PAUSE (2-LP, translucent grey vinyl, 500 only, 1 side not available on CD) | 40 |
| 00 | United Dairies UD 081 | ALICE THE GOON (1-sided reissue, 800 copies) | 50 |
| 02 | United Durtro UD 102 | MAN WITH THE WOMAN FACE (LP, ltd. edition clear vinyl, poly sleeve, 2 inserts) | 15 |
| 00s | United Dairies UDX 092 | SOLILOQUY FOR LILITH (3-CD box set) | 30 |
| 07 | United Dairies UD 08.C | INSECT AND INDIVIDUAL SILENCED (CD, 120 copies numbered with "insect") | 90 |
| 09 | United Dirter DPROMOCD 72 | THE SURVEILLANCE LOUNGE/THE MEMORY SURFACE (3-CD) | 30 |

(see also Current 93, Organum/New Blockaders, Diana Rogerson, Sol Invictus, Steven Stapleton & David Tibet, Tibet & Stapleton, Whitehouse)

## NU-SOUND EXPRESS LTD.
| 72 | Pye Int'l 7N 25580 | One More Time Y'all/A Rose For A Lady | 20 |

## NUTHIN' FANCY
| 80s | Dynamic Cat DC 1001 | Looking For A Good Time/Too Much Rock'n'Roll (p/s) | 250 |

(see also Terraplane, Thunder)

## NU TORNADOS
| 58 | London HLU 8756 | Philadelphia U .S.A./Magic Record | 10 |

## NUTRONS
| 60s | Melodisc M 1593 | The Very Best Things/Stop For The Music | 15 |

## NUTSHELL
| 77 | Myrrh MYR 1056 | FLYAWAY (LP, inner) | 18 |
| 75 | Myrrh MYR 1029 | IN YOUR EYES (LP, lyric inner sleeve) | 20 |

## MAY'F NUTTER
| 66 | Vocalion VL 9282 | Head Shrinker/Don't Know What To Do | 15 |
| 73 | London HLL 10414 | I Don't Care/Hitch Hike Nightmare | 6 |

## NUTTY SQUIRRELS
| 59 | Pye Int. 7N.25044 | Uh! Oh! (Pts. 1 & 2) | 7 |

## NUTZ
| 75 | A&M AMLS 68306 | NUTZ TOO (LP) | 15 |

(see also Rage, Nightwing)

## NYAH FEARTIES
| 86 | Nya DOPLP 001 | A TASTY HEIDFUL (LP) | 25 |

## NYAH SHUFFLE
| 70 | Grape GR 3021 | Sting Ray/Paradise | 20 |
| 70 | Grape GR 3019 | Boot Lace/Honey Won't You Stay? | 20 |

## NYAM NYAM
| 81 | Vital VTL 004 | When We Can't Make Laughter Stay/Knowledge (Chapter II) | 10 |

## JUDY NYLON
| 82 | On-U-Sound LP 16 | PAL JUDY (LP) | 15 |

(see also John Cale, Snatch)

## NYLONS
| 82 | Attic NYLON 1 | A Million Ways/Up On The Roof (p/s) | 8 |

## MICHAEL NYMAN
| 76 | Obscure OBS 6 | DECAY MUSIC (LP) | 25 |
| 89 | VRL VEBN55 | THE NYMAN GREENAWAY SOUNDTRACKS (4-LP box set, booklet) | 40 |

## NYMONIC
| 00 | Y N R YNR02 | REQIEM (EP) | 18 |

## LAURA NYRO

| 67 | Verve Forecast VS 1502 | Wedding Bell Blues/Stoney End | 15 |
|---|---|---|---|
| 68 | CBS 3604 | Eli's Coming/Sweet Blindness | 8 |
| 68 | CBS 4031 | Once It Was Alright Now (Farmer Joe)/Woman's Blues | 7 |
| 69 | CBS 4719 | Time And Love/The Man Who Sends Me Home | 7 |
| 68 | CBS 63346 | ELI AND THE THIRTEENTH CONFESSION (LP, gatefold sleeve, orange label) | 40 |
| 69 | CBS 63510 | NEW YORK TENDABERRY (LP, orange label) | 20 |
| 69 | Verve Forecast SVLP 6022 | THE FIRST SONGS (LP) | 15 |
| 70 | CBS 64157 | CHRISTMAS AND THE BEADS OF SWEAT (LP, orange label) | 15 |
| 71 | CBS S 64770 | GONNA TAKE A MIRACLE (LP, with Labelle) | 20 |

## O

## OAK

| 71 | Topic 12TS 212 | WELCOME TO OUR FAIR (LP) | 55 |
|---|---|---|---|

*(see also Peta Webb)*

## OAK TREE

| 70 | President PT 316 | The Sun It Always Shone/My Baby Don't Cry | 6 |
|---|---|---|---|

## OAKENSHIELD

| 82 | Acorn OAK 001 | ACROSS THE NARROW SEAS (LP) | 18 |
|---|---|---|---|
| 85 | Acorn OAK 002 | AGAINST THE GRAIN (LP, with insert) | 18 |

## OASIS

### SINGLES

| 94 | Creation CRE 176 | Supersonic/Take Me Away (p/s) | 18 |
|---|---|---|---|
| 94 | Creation CRE 182 | Shakermaker/D'Yer Wanna Be A Spaceman? (p/s) | 18 |
| 94 | Creation CRE 185 | Live Forever/Up In The Sky (Acoustic) (jukebox issue, large centre hole) | 20 |
| 94 | Creation CRE 185 | Live Forever/Up In The Sky (Acoustic) (numbered foldover p/s in stickered poly bag) | 15 |
| 94 | Creation CRE 195 | Whatever/(It's Good) To Be Free (no'd foldover p/s in stickered poly bag) | 18 |
| 95 | Creation CRE 212 | Roll With It/It's Better People | 5 |
| 95 | Creation CRE 215 | Wonderwall/Round Are Way (wraparound p/s) | 15 |
| 95 | Creation CRE 204 | Some Might Say/Talk Tonight | 5 |
| 96 | Creation CRE 221 | Don't Look Back In Anger/Step Out (p/s, with poly outer) | 10 |
| 97 | Creation CRE 256 | D'You Know What I Mean/Stay Young | 5 |
| 97 | Creation CRE 278 | Stand By Me/I Got The Fever (gatefold p/s) | 7 |
| 97 | Creation CRE 292 | All Around The World/The Fame (numbered p/s) | 5 |
| 00 | Big Brother RKID 001 | Go Let It Out/Let's All Make Believe | 5 |
| 02 | Big Brother RKID 24 | Stop Crying Your Heart Out/Thank You For The Good Times | 5 |
| 02 | Big Brother RKID 23 | The Hindu Times/Just Getting Older (p/s, limited edition) | 6 |
| 02 | Big Brother RKID 26 | Little By Little/She Is Love | 8 |
| 03 | Big Brother RKID 27 | Songbird/(You've Got) The Heart Of A Star | 8 |
| 05 | Big Brother RKID 29 | Lyla/Eyeball Ticker | 5 |
| 05 | Big Brother RKID 31 | The Importance Of Being Idle/Pass Me Down The WIne | 6 |
| 06 | Big Brother RKID37 | Stop The Clocks EP (2 x 7", stickers, numbered) | 12 |
| 08 | Big Brother RKID55 | I'm Outta TIme/To Be Where There's Life (Neon Neon Remix) | 5 |
| 08 | Big Brother RKID55X | I'm Outta Time (remix)/The Shock Of The Lightning (The Jagz Kooner Remix) | 5 |

### ALBUMS

| 94 | Creation CRELP 169 | DEFINITELY MAYBE (2-LP, gatefold sleeve) | 50 |
|---|---|---|---|
| 95 | Creation CRELP 189 | (WHAT'S THE STORY) MORNING GLORY? (2-LP, multifold sleeve) | 50 |
| 97 | Creation CRELP 219 | BE HERE NOW (2-LP, gatefold) | 30 |
| 98 | Creation CRELP 241 | THE MASTERPLAN (3-LP) | 60 |
| 00 | Big Brother RKID LP005 | FAMILIAR TO MILLIONS (3-LP) | 70 |
| 00 | Big Brother RKID LP002 | STANDING ON THE SHOULDER OF GIANTS | 20 |
| 02 | Big Brother RKID LP25 | HEATHEN CHEMISTRY (2-LP, booklet) | 30 |
| 05 | Big Brother RKID LP30X | DON'T BELIEVE THE TRUTH (LP, numbered art print) | 30 |
| 06 | Big Brother RKID LP36 | STOP THE CLOCKS (3-LP box-set) | 50 |
| 09 | Big Brother RKIDBOX 58 | LP BOX SET (8-LP, numbered, 1,500 only) | 300 |

### PROMOS : PROMOS: SINGLES

| 93 | Creation CTP 8 | Columbia (Demo) (12", 1-sided, white label, 510 pressed) | 200 |
|---|---|---|---|
| 94 | Creation CRE 176TP | Supersonic/Take Me Away/I Will Believe (Live) (12", company sleeve) | 40 |
| 94 | Creation CRE 182TP | Shakermaker/D'Yer Wanna Be A Spaceman?/Alive (8 Track Demo) (12") | 60 |
| 94 | Creation CRE 185TP | Live Forever/Up In The Sky (Acoustic)/Cloudburst (12") | 70 |
| 94 | Creation CTP 190TP | I Am The Walrus (Live At Glasgow Cathouse June '94) (12", 250 only, co. sl.) | 250 |
| 94 | Creation CTP 190CL | Cigarettes & Alcohol (12", 1-sided) | 75 |
| 94 | Creation CTP 190CL | Cigarettes & Alcohol/I Am The Walrus (live Glasgow Cathouse June '94)/ Fade Away (12", 300 only) | 75 |
| 94 | Creation CRE 195TP | Whatever (12", 1-sided, 560 only) | 75 |
| 94 | Creation CTP 195 | (It's Good) To Be Free (12", 1-sided, 360 only) | 50 |
| 94 | Creation CREDM 001 | DEFINITELY MAYBE (4 x 7" box set, in silver cigarette-pack-shaped plastic box, with booklet & interview CD) | 25 |
| 95 | Creation CCD 169 | Slide Away (CD, 1-track Brits Awards issue, 1,000 only; beware of counterfeits) | 30 |
| 95 | Creation CCD 204 | Some Might Say (CD, 1-track, 350 only) | 60 |
| 95 | Creation CREMG 001 | (WHAT'S THE STORY) MORNING GLORY? (4 x 7" box set, in gold cigarette-pack-shaped plastic box, with booklet & interview CD) | 25 |
| 95 | Creation CTP 204 | Acquiesce (12", 1-sided, 570 only) | 80 |

MINT VALUE £

| | | | |
|---|---|---|---|
| 95 | Creation CCD 204P | Acquiesce (CD, 1-track, 300 only) | 60 |
| 95 | Creation CTP 212 | Roll With It (12", 1-sided) | 40 |
| 95 | Creation CTP 215 | Round Are Way (12", 1-sided, 843 only) | 60 |
| 96 | Creation CTP 221X | Cum On Feel The Noize/Champagne Supernova (Lynchmob Beats Mix) (12", 1,203 pressed, plain die-cut sleeve; beware of counterfeits) | 40 |
| 96 | Creation CCD 221 | Cum On Feel The Noize (CD, pic. disc, 1-track, with football motif, no inlay, 500 only) | 60 |
| 97 | Creation CTP 256 | D'You Know What I Mean?/Heroes (12") | 30 |
| 97 | Creation CTP 278 | Stand By Me/I Got The Fever (12") | 35 |
| 97 | Creation CTP 282 | All Around The World/Street Fighting Man (12", black die-cut sleeve) | 25 |
| 97 | Creation (no cat. no.) | VOX BOX (9-CD, wooden guitar-amp-shaped box set in outer box, with booklets from "Silver" & "Gold" CD box sets; contains commerical issues of "Supersonic" through to "Don't Look Back In Anger"; in house giveaway only) | 500 |
| 98 | Creation CCD 241 | Acquiesce/Talk Tonight/Rockin' Chair/The Masterplan (CD sampler) | 25 |
| 98 | Creation CRELP 241P | THE MASTERPLAN SAMPLER (Acquiesce/Underneath The Sky/ I Am The Walrus/The Masterplan) (12" sampler) | 25 |
| 00 | Creation CTP 327 | Go Let It Out (12", 1-track, 1-sided, p/s) | 25 |
| 00 | Big Brother FITB 001 | Fuckin' In The Bushes (12", 1-sided, white label) | 40 |
| 00 | Big Brother RKID 004TP | Sunday Morning Call (12", 1-sided, flipback laminated p/s) | 25 |
| 00 | Big Brother RKID 03TP | Who Feels Love? (12", 1-sided, laminated p/s) | 25 |
| 01 | Own label OASIS 10 | 10 YEARS OF NOISE & CONFUSION (Columbia/Rock & Roll Star (Live)/ Acquiesce/ Fuckin' In The Bushes) (10", promo-only, custom labels, die-cut sleeve, 200 only, with press release) | 35 |
| 01 | Own label OASIS 10 | 10 YEARS OF NOISE & CONFUSION (Columbia/Rock & Roll Star (Live)/ Acquiesce/ Fuckin' In The Bushes) (10", promo-only, custom labels, die-cut sleeve, 200 only, without press release) | 30 |
| 02 | Big Brother RKID 23TP | The Hindu Times (Spike Mix) (12", promo-only, custom logo sleeve, 250 only) | 25 |
| 02 | Big Brother RKID 24TP | Stop Crying Your Heart Out (Spike Mix) (12", custom sleeve, 250 only) | 20 |
| 02 | Big Brother RKID 25TPX | Hung In A Bad Place (12", 1-track, 1-sided, custom mauve/pink or brown sleeve) | 30 |
| 02 | Big Brother RKID26TPX | My Generation (12" 1-sided promo with Union Jack Sleeve. 800 only) | 35 |
| 02 | Big Brother RKID27TP | Columbia (Live)/(You've Got) The Heart Of A Star (12", custom sleeve) | 30 |
| 02 | Big Brother (No cat. no) | Songbird (Demo) (CD-R promo, 25 only) | 200 |
| 05 | Big Brother RKID28TPX | Can You See It Now? I Can See It Now (12" 1-sided white label promo 50 only) | 200 |
| 05 | Big Brother RKID29TP | Lyla (12" 1-sided promo. 770 only) | 25 |
| 05 | Big Brother RKID31TP | Turn Up The Sun (12" 1-sided promo in card sleeve and inner sleeve. 1,120 only) | 35 |
| 05 | Big Brother RKID32TP | Mucky Fingers (12" 1-sided promo in double p/s. 950 copies) | 30 |
| 05 | Big Brother RKID1 NIL | Meaning Of Soul (CD-R promo) | 150 |
| 05 | Big Brother (No cat. no) | Cast No Shadow (UNKLE Beachhead Mix) (CD-R promo) | 30 |
| 06 | Big Brother RKIDSCD35TP | Champagne Supernova (Lynchmob Beats Mix) (12", promo-only) | 20 |
| 06 | Big Brother RKIDSCD35P | Champagne Supernova (Lynchmob Beats Mix) (CD-R, promo-only) | 200 |
| 06 | Big Brother RKIDSCD37P1 | Acquiesce | 10 |
| 06 | Big Brother RKIDSCD37P2 | The Masterplan | 10 |
| 07 | Big Brother RKID39TP | Lord Don't Slow Me Down (12", promo-only) | 40 |
| 07 | Big Brother RKIDSCD39P | Lord Don't Slow Me Down (CD-R, promo) | 40 |

PROMOS : PROMOS: ALBUMS

| | | | |
|---|---|---|---|
| 94 | Creation CRECD 169P | DEFINITELY MAYBE (CD) | 50 |
| 95 | Creation CRECD 189P | (WHAT'S THE STORY) MORNING GLORY? (CD, with "Step Out", black card p/s, withdrawn, beware of counterfeits) | 45 |
| 95 | Creation CRECD 189P | (WHAT'S THE STORY) MORNING GLORY? (CD, without "Step Out", black card p/s) | 30 |
| 95 | Creation C-CRE 189P | (WHAT'S THE STORY) MORNING GLORY? (cassette, with "Step Out", card p/s, withdrawn) | 25 |
| 97 | Creation (no cat. no.) | BE HERE NOW (LP, mail-order 12" box set, with The Making Of Be Here Now booklet, 1,000 only) | 70 |
| 97 | Creation (no cat. no.) | BE HERE NOW (CD, mail-order 12" box set, with The Making Of Be Here Now booklet, 1,000 only) | 50 |
| 97 | Creation CCD 219 | BE HERE NOW (CD, black card sleeve, in custom picture sleeve) | 30 |
| 97 | Creation CCD 219 | BE HERE NOW (CD, black card sleeve, not in custom picture sleeve) | 25 |
| 98 | | THE MASTERPLAN (CD, slimline case, p/s) | 35 |
| 98 | Creation CRELX 241 | THE MASTERPLAN (mail-order 7 x 10" single box set) | 70 |

*(see also Beady Eye. Noel Gallagher And HIgh Flying Birds)*

## OBERON
| | | | |
|---|---|---|---|
| 71 | Acorn (no cat. no.) | A MIDSUMMER NIGHT'S DREAM (LP, private pressing) | 1000 |

## OBITUARY
| | | | |
|---|---|---|---|
| 89 | Roadracer RO 9489 | SLOWLY WE ROT (LP) | 18 |
| 90 | Roadracer RO 9370 | CAUSE OF DEATH (LP) | 15 |

## MICHAEL O'BRIEN
| | | | |
|---|---|---|---|
| 79 | Stiff BUY 50 | Made In Germany/The Queen Likes Pop (p/s) | 5 |

## DERMOT O'BRIEN
| | | | |
|---|---|---|---|
| 66 | Envoy ENV 016 | The Merry Plough Boy/Off To Dublin/In The Green/Come Down the Mountain Katie Daly | 8 |

## JIMMY O'BRYANT
| | | | |
|---|---|---|---|
| 60 | Heritage RE-101 | FAMOUS ORIGINAL WASHBOARD BAND, VOL. 1 (99 copies only) (EP) | 20 |
| 60 | Heritage RE-106 | FAMOUS ORIGINAL WASHBOARD BAND, VOL. 2 (99 copies only) (EP) | 20 |

## OBSCURE BY DEGREES
| | | | |
|---|---|---|---|
| 81 | Ka KA 10 | I'm Dying/A Woman Like You (p/s) | 40 |

## OBSERVERS ALL STARS & KING TUBBY
| | | | |
|---|---|---|---|
| 75 | Attack ATLP 017 | DUBBING WITH THE OBSERVER (LP) | 45 |

## OBSERVERS (1)
| | | | |
|---|---|---|---|
| 71 | Big Shot BI 575 | Brimstone And Fire/Lightning And Thunder | 20 |
| 71 | Big Shot BI 588 | Keep Pushing/Hot Tip | 10 |
| 72 | Big Shot BI 610 | Everyday Music/NINEY: Observing The Av | 10 |
| 72 | Songbird SB 1083 | International Pum/Reggaematic | 5 |

*(see also Niney)*

**OBSERVERS (2)**
80  ST ST2          This Age/Suicide (p/s) ........................................................................... 8

**OBSESSION**
82  Wilde Bros SRTS 82 CUS   Clockwork Man/Hava Naglia ................................................................ 50
     1344

**OBTAINERS**
79  Dance Fools Dance (No cat.  Yeh Yeh Yeh/Pussy Wussy/MAG-SPYS: Lifeblood/Bombs (stickered plain sleeve, 100
     no.)                  only) ............................................................................................. 400

*(see also Cure)*

**OBX**
81  Cara CARA 002        Sailplane/Breakdown And Cry ............................................................... 20

**OCCASIONALLY DAVID**
79  Oven Ready OD 77901    TWIST AND SHOUT (EP)........................................................................ 20
80  Oven Ready OD 1/98002  I Can't Get Used To Losing You (So I'm Coming Back)/Will You Miss Me Tonight?
                       (foldout p/s) .................................................................................... 20

**OCCASIONAL WORD ENSEMBLE**
69  Dandelion 63753      THE YEAR OF THE GREAT LEAP SIDEWAYS (LP) ....................................... 40

**OCCULT CHEMISTRY**
80  Bikini Girl (no. cat. no.)   Water Earth Fire Air (Rough Version) (5" clear flexidisc in stamped envelope with
                       Bikini Girl magazine) ......................................................................... 15
81  Dining Out TUX 4      Water Earth Fire Air/Fire Air Water Earth (handmade p/s)........................... 15

*(see also Twilight Zonerz)*

**OCCULT PUNK BAND**
78  Gaslight GAS 001      Happy With My Life/Black Mass (no p/s, 200 only).................................... 15

**OCEAN**
71  Kama Sutra 2013027    No Other Woman/Deep Enough For Me...................................................... 6

**OCEAN COLOUR SCENE**
90  !Phffft WAVE 1P       One Of These Days/Talk On (p/s, promo only) ......................................... 10
90  !Phffft WAVE 1        One Of These Days/Talk On (12", p/s, promo only)................................... 12
96  MCA OCS 2          You've Got It Bad (Full Length Demo Version)/Mona Lisa Eyes (featuring Jimmy Miller)
                       (p/s, mail-order only) ........................................................................ 8
96  MCA MCA 60008      MOSELEY SHOALS (2-LP, inners, stickered sleeve) .................................... 40
97  MCA MCD 60034      B-SIDES, SEASIDES AND FREE RIDES (2-LP, with lyric booklet) .................... 18
97  MCA MCA 60048      MARCHIN' ALREADY (2-LP, with booklet)................................................ 30
99  Island 546 671-1      ONE FROM THE MODERN (2-LP) ......................................................... 20
01  Island 548 686-1      MECHANICAL WONDER (LP) ............................................................... 18
03  Sanctuary SANLP 160    NORTH ATLANTIC DRIFT (LP) ............................................................. 25

*(see also Boys, Fanatics, Echo Base)*

**HUMPHREY OCEAN**
78  Stiff BUY 29          Whoops A Daisy/Davy Crockett (p/s, blue, black, red, green, white and clear vinyl
                       pressed, p/s) .................................................................................... 7

**OCEANS**
82  Record Shack SHACK 129  Pacific Dreams/Pacific Dreams (Instrumental) (12", white label, stickered or stamped
                       label) ......................................................................................... 150

**PHIL OCHS**
66  Elektra EKSN 45002    I Ain't Marching Any More/That Was The President ................................ 15
68  A&M AMS 716         Outside Of A Small Circle Of Friends/Miranda ........................................ 8
65  Elektra EKL 269       ALL THE NEWS THAT'S FIT TO SING (LP, 'guitar player' label, UK record in US sleeve) .... 30
65  Elektra EKL 287       I AIN'T MARCHIN' ANYMORE (LP)........................................................ 30
66  Elektra EKL 310       PHIL OCHS IN CONCERT (LP, gold label) ............................................... 30
67  A&M AML(S) 913      PLEASURES OF THE HARBOR (LP)........................................................ 25
68  A&M AMLS 919       TAPE FROM CALIFORNIA (LP).............................................................. 25
69  A&M AMLS 934       REHEARSALS FOR RETIREMENT (LP)...................................................... 25
70  A&M AMLS 973       GREATEST HITS (LP) ......................................................................... 18

**GENE OCTOBER**
84  Slipped Discs SPLAT 001  Don't Quit/Burning Sound (p/s) ............................................................ 5
83  Illegal ILS 0034       Suffering In The Land/Suffering Love (p/s)............................................... 5

*(see also Chelsea)*

**JOHNNY OCTOBER**
59  Capitol CL 15070      Growin' Prettier/Young And In Love ...................................................... 15
60  Capitol CL 15121      So Mean/There'll Always Be A Feeling................................................... 15

**OCTODRED**
95  Acid Fever MDMA 9501   BIG FOOT EP (12") ........................................................................... 40
95  Acid Fever MDMA 9502   DOUBLE DIPPED EP (12") ................................................................... 15
96  Acid Fever MDMA 9601   TECHNOLOGICAL ILLUSION VOL. 1 EP (12") .......................................... 30
96  Acid Fever MDMA 9603   TECHNOLOGICAL ILLUSIONS VOL. 2 EP (12") ......................................... 25
96  Acid Fever MDMA 9606   UNTITLED EP (12").......................................................................... 40
96  Acid Fever MDMA 9608   PSYCHIK MONK EP (12").................................................................... 30

**OCTOPUS**
69  Penny Farthing PEN 705  Laugh At The Poor Man/Girl Friend ...................................................... 20
70  Penny Farthing PEN 716  The River/Thief ................................................................................ 20
73  Mooncrest MOON 7     Hey Na Na/Future Feelings................................................................... 6
70  Penny Farthing PELS 508  RESTLESS NIGHT (LP, gatefold sleeve, red/black label) ........................... 600
96  Essex ESSEX 1013LP    RESTLESS NIGHT (LP, reissue, gatefold sleeve)....................................... 20

*(see also Cortinas)*

**MARTIN O'CUTHBERT**
78  SRTS/78/CUS-114 Esoteric  B.E.M.S (Bug Eyed Monsters)/Fragments Of A Possessed Ego (1st pressing, 1000
     EEE 1                  copies, push-out centre, folded b/w sleeve with SRTS cat no) ...................... 20

# Ray O'DANIEL

| | | | |
|---|---|---|---|
| 78 | SRTS/78/CUS-114 Esoteric EEE 1 | B.E.M.S (Bug Eyed Monsters)/Fragments Of A Possessed Ego (2nd pressing, 1000 copies, push-out centre, folded b/w sleeve with EEE1 cat no) | 10 |
| 78 | Esoteric EE 2 | Serene Machines/Space Shall Weave Our Destiny | 8 |
| 83 | Martoc 001 | FOR ALIEN EARS (LP) | 30 |

## RAY O'DANIEL
| | | | |
|---|---|---|---|
| 62 | Longhorn BLH 0001 | What Goes Up Always Comes Down/You're The Only Love For Me | 8 |

## ANITA O'DAY
| | | | |
|---|---|---|---|
| 56 | HMV POP 245 | You're The Top/Honeysuckle Rose | |
| 60 | HMV POP 821 | Tea For Two/Sweet Georgia Brown | 12 |
| 56 | HMV CLP 1085 | ANITA (LP) | 5 |
| 56 | Columbia Clef 33C 9020 | ANITA O'DAY COLLATES (10" LP) | 15 |
| 57 | Columbia Clef 33CX 10068 | AN EVENING WITH ANITA O'DAY (LP) | 15 |
| 58 | Columbia Clef 33CX 10125 | ANITA SINGS THE MOST (LP) | 15 |

## PAT O'DAY
| | | | |
|---|---|---|---|
| 55 | MGM SP 1129 | Earth Angel (Will You Be Mine?)/A Rusty Old Halo | 25 |
| 55 | MGM SP 1142 | Soldier Boy/Annie Oakley | 15 |
| 60 | Pye International 7N 25048 | I'll Build A Stairway To Your Paradise/No One Understands | 6 |

## ODD BAND
| | | | |
|---|---|---|---|
| 82 | Gyro GY 010 | Xmas On The Dole/Christmas Dub | 10 |

## ODD
| | | | |
|---|---|---|---|
| 84 | OK OK 007 | Last Time I Saw You/Look Into My Eyes (p/s) | 15 |

## BILL ODDIE
| | | | |
|---|---|---|---|
| 64 | Parlophone R 5153 | Nothing Better To Do/Traffic Island | 5 |
| 65 | Parlophone R 5346 | Knitting Song/Ain't Got Rhythm | 5 |
| 66 | Parlophone R 5433 | I Can't Get Through/Because She Is My Love | 15 |
| 69 | Decca F 12903 | We Love Jimmy Young/Irish Get Out (as Bill Oddie & Average Mothers) | 5 |
| 70 | Dandelion S 4786 | On Ilkla Moor Baht'at/Harry Krishna | 5 |

*(see also Ricky Livid)*

## ODD NUMBERS
| | | | |
|---|---|---|---|
| 95 | Detour DR 032 | The Easy Life/Clubbin' (A Jazz Odyssey) (p/s, coloured vinyl) | 5 |

## ODDS
| | | | |
|---|---|---|---|
| 80 | Double R RED 001 | Saturday Night/Not Another Love Song (p/s) | 15 |
| 81 | JSO EAT 1 | Yesterday Man/So You Think (p/s) | 25 |
| 81 | JSO EAT 7 | Dread In My Bed/Spare Rib (with press release) | 10 |

## ODDSOCKS
| | | | |
|---|---|---|---|
| 75 | Sweet Folk & C. SFA 030 | MEN OF THE MOMENT (LP) | 20 |

*(see also Bevis Frond)*

## ANN ODELL
| | | | |
|---|---|---|---|
| 73 | DJM DJS 10280 | Swing Song/Everything's Fine Sunshine | 6 |
| 73 | DJM DJLPS 434 | A LITTLE TASTE (LP, gatefold) | 30 |

*(see also Chopyn, Blue Mink, CMU)*

## DOYE O'DELL
| | | | |
|---|---|---|---|
| 57 | London HAP-B 1073 | DOYE (10" LP) | 12 |

## MAC ODELL
| | | | |
|---|---|---|---|
| 54 | Parlophone CMSP 25 | The Stone Was Rolled Away/Heaven-Bound Gospel Train (export issue) | 8 |

## RONNIE O'DELL & HIS ORCHESTRA
| | | | |
|---|---|---|---|
| 57 | London HLD 8439 | Melody Of Napoli/Struttin' Down Jane Street | 10 |

## ODEONS
| | | | |
|---|---|---|---|
| 80 | Ellie Jay EJSP 9480 | Maybe Today/5.30 Anthem (p/s) | 25 |

## ODIN'S PEOPLE
| | | | |
|---|---|---|---|
| 67 | Major Minor MM 501 | From A Distance/I Need You | 10 |
| 67 | Major Minor MM 505 | Tommy Jones/I Need Your Hand In Mine | 10 |

## JOE ODOM
| | | | |
|---|---|---|---|
| 69 | Capitol CL 15600 | Big Love/It's In Your Power | 15 |

## AL O'DONNELL
| | | | |
|---|---|---|---|
| 72 | Trailer LER 2073 | AL O'DONNELL (LP, red label) | 20 |

## ALISON O' DONNELL
| | | | |
|---|---|---|---|
| 08 | Fruits De Mer CRUSTACIAN 03 | Day Is Done/Frozen Warnings (p/s. coloured vinyl 300 only) | 25 |

*(see also Mellow Candle)*

## JOE O'DONNELL
| | | | |
|---|---|---|---|
| 77 | Polydor 2383 465 | GAODHAL'S VISION (LP) | 22 |

*(see also East of Eden, Mushroom, Rory Gallagher, Jade Warrior)*

## ROCK O'DOODLE
| | | | |
|---|---|---|---|
| 73 | Decca F 13450 | Queen Of Rock & Roll/Woman | 10 |

*(see also Patrick Campbell-Lyons)*

## ODYSSEY (U.K.)
| | | | |
|---|---|---|---|
| 66 | Strike JH 312 | How Long Is Time/Beware | 35 |

*(see also Sons Of Fred)*

## ODYSSEY (U.S.)
| | | | |
|---|---|---|---|
| 73 | Mowest MWS 7002 | ODYSSEY (LP) | 75 |

## OEDIPUS COMPLEX
| | | | |
|---|---|---|---|
| 69 | Phillips BF 1771 | Up Down Round & Round/Empty Highways | 40 |

## OF MONTREAL
| | | | |
|---|---|---|---|
| 01 | Jonathon Whisky 16 | Inside A Room Full Of Treasures, A Black Pygmi Horse's Head Pops Up Like A Periscope/LATE B.P. HELIUM: Song For Marie/Alright Yeah (P/s, 250 only) | 10 |
| 03 | Track & Field LANE 18 | Jennifer Louise/There Is Nothing Wrong With Hating Rock Critics (p/s) | 8 |

| | | | |
|---|---|---|---|
| 02 | Track & Field HEAT 10 LP | ALDHILS ARBORETURN (LP) | 20 |

**OFFICERS & GENTLEMEN**

| | | | |
|---|---|---|---|
| 84 | Gap GAP 001 | That's Life And Love/Noise (no p/s) | 50 |

**OFFICIAL SECRETS**

| | | | |
|---|---|---|---|
| 81 | Round RR1 | Fooling My Heart/Paradise Time (p/s) | 40 |

**OFFSIDE**

| | | | |
|---|---|---|---|
| 70 | Pye Intl. 25534 | Match Of The Day/Small Deal (p/s) | 15 |

**OFFSPRING (1)**

| | | | |
|---|---|---|---|
| 84 | Offspring Records OP001/ SRT4K5169 | One More Night/Nota Sad Song (this is how it is typed on B-side label) | 30 |

**OFO**

| | | | |
|---|---|---|---|
| 74 | Decca F13496 | Let's Go Where The Action Is/The Book | 10 |

**OFO THE BLACK COMPANY**

| | | | |
|---|---|---|---|
| 72 | London FL12261 | Allah Wakbarr/Beautiful Daddy | 75 |

**JAMES O'GWYNN**

| | | | |
|---|---|---|---|
| 59 | Mercury AMT 1052 | How Can I Think Of Tomorrow/Were You Ever A Stranger | 10 |

**JOHN O'HARA**

| | | | |
|---|---|---|---|
| 72 | Spark SRL 1075 | Hand Me Down Man/I Am The Candidate For Love | 12 |
| 77 | President PT 465 | Starsky And Hutch/Sister Rae | 5 |

**O'HARA'S PLAYBOYS**

| | | | |
|---|---|---|---|
| 66 | Fontana TF 763 | Start All Over/I've Been Wondering | 6 |
| 67 | Fontana TF 793 | Spicks And Specks/One Fine Lady | 8 |
| 67 | Fontana TF 872 | Ballad Of The Soon Departed/Tell Me Why | 50 |
| 67 | Fontana TF 893 | Island In The Sun/Harry | 6 |
| 68 | Fontana TF 924 | In The Shelter Of My Heart/Goodnight Mr. Nightfall | 6 |
| 68 | Fontana TF 974 | I Started A Joke/Show Me | 10 |
| 68 | Fontana (S)TL 5461 | GET READY (LP) | 50 |

**OHIO EXPRESS**

| | | | |
|---|---|---|---|
| 68 | Pye Intl. TH25439 | Yummy Yummy Yummy/Zigzag | 5 |
| 68 | Pye Intl. 7N 25469 | Down At Lulu's/She's Not Coming Home | 6 |
| 69 | Pye Intl. NSPL 28117 | OHIO EXPRESS (LP) | 20 |
| 69 | Buddah 203 015 | CHEWY CHEWY (LP) | 15 |

*(see also Joey Vine)*

**OHIO KNOX**

| | | | |
|---|---|---|---|
| 71 | Reprise RSLP 6435 | OHIO KNOX (LP, gatefold sleeve) | 20 |

*(see also Fifth Avenue Band)*

**OHIO PLAYERS**

| | | | |
|---|---|---|---|
| 69 | Capitol CL 15587 | Here Today And Gone Tomorrow/Bad Bargain | 10 |

**OHM**

| | | | |
|---|---|---|---|
| 79 | OHM 001 | Kanon/Airship To Bali (no p/s) | 8 |
| 79 | Ohm 003 | Whale Song/Ohm Sweet Ohn (no p/s, as Overhead Music) | 7 |

**OHR MUSIK**

| | | | |
|---|---|---|---|
| 97 | Prescription DRUG 2 | OHR MUSIK (LP, 99 copies only) | 20 |

*(see also Spiral Sky)*

**OI POLLOI**

| | | | |
|---|---|---|---|
| 86 | EDR 5 | RESIST THE ATOMIC MESSAGE (EP) | 10 |
| 88 | Words Of Warning WOW 5 | OUTRAGE (EP) | 10 |
| 89 | Words Of Warning WOW 17 | OMNICIDE (EP) | 12 |
| 87 | Oi! OIR 011 | UNITE AND WIN (LP, with lyric sheet) | 15 |

**OIL CITY SHEIKS**

| | | | |
|---|---|---|---|
| 79 | United Artists UP 36514 | Don't Take But A Few Minutes/Blues Jam (p/s) | 7 |

*(see also Dr. Feelgood, Lew Lewis)*

**O'JAYS**

| | | | |
|---|---|---|---|
| 65 | Liberty LIB 66102 | Lipstick Traces/Think It Over Baby | 40 |
| 65 | Liberty LIB 66102 | Lipstick Traces/Think It Over Baby (DJ copy) | 80 |
| 66 | Liberty LIB 66197 | Stand In For Love/Friday Night | 20 |
| 67 | Stateside SS 2073 | I'll Be Sweeter Tomorrow/I Dig Your Act | 50 |
| 67 | Stateside SS 2073 | I'll Be Sweeter Tomorrow/I Dig Your Act (DJ copy) | 100 |
| 68 | Bell BLL 1020 | Look Over Your Shoulder/I'm So Glad I Found You | 30 |
| 68 | Bell BLL 1020 | Look Over Your Shoulder/I'm So Glad I Found You (DJ copy) | 50 |
| 68 | Bell BLL 1033 | The Choice/Going Going Gone | 15 |
| 70 | Now! NOW 1002 | Don't You Know A True Love/That's Alright | 8 |
| 72 | United Artists UP 35337 | Working On Your Case/Hold On | 15 |
| 73 | CBS 1181 | Love Train/Who Am I? | 6 |
| 73 | Mojo 2092 052 | I Dig Your Act/I'll Be Sweeter Tomorrow (reissue) | 8 |

**O'KAYSIONS**

| | | | |
|---|---|---|---|
| 68 | Stateside SS 2126 | Girl Watcher/Deal Me In | 25 |
| 68 | Stateside SS 2126 | Girl Watcher/Deal Me In (DJ copy) | 50 |

**JOHNNY O'KEEFE (& DEE JAYS)**

| | | | |
|---|---|---|---|
| 58 | Coral Q 72330 | Shake Baby Shake/Real Wild Child (as Johnny O'Keefe & Dee Jays) | 150 |
| 58 | Coral Q 72330 | Shake Baby Shake/Real Wild Child (as Johnny O'Keefe & Dee Jays) (78) | 60 |
| 60s | Zodiac ZR 0016 | Sing/Tell The Blues So Long | 10 |

**(ROGER) EARL OKIN**

| | | | |
|---|---|---|---|
| 67 | Parlophone R 5644 | Yellow Petals/I Can't Face The Animals (as Roger Earl Okin) | 6 |
| 69 | CBS 4495 | Stop And You'll Become Aware/You're Not There At All (as Earl Okin) | 22 |

**OLA (& JANGLERS)**

| | | | |
|---|---|---|---|
| 67 | Decca F 12646 | I Can Wait/Eeny Meeny Miney Moe | 15 |

# Babatunde OLATUNJI

| | | | |
|---|---|---|---:|
| 68 | Big T BIG 108 | What A Way To Die/That's Why I Cry (solo) | 15 |
| 69 | Sonet SON 2004 | Let's Dance/Bird, Bird | 10 |

## BABATUNDE OLATUNJI
| | | | |
|---|---|---|---:|
| 73 | Paramount PARA 3038 | Soul Makossa (Parts 1 & 2) | 10 |
| 73 | Paramount SPFL 289 | SOUL MAKOSSA (LP) | 15 |

## OLD SCHOOL TIE
| | | | |
|---|---|---|---:|
| 80 | Modello MHMS 195 | Gambler/Oscar (p/s) | 10 |

## OLDEST PROFESSION
| | | | |
|---|---|---|---:|
| 72 | Midas Private Pressing | THE OLDEST PROFESSION (LP) | 150 |

## MIKE OLDFIELD
### SINGLES
| | | | |
|---|---|---|---:|
| 74 | Virgin VS 101 | Mike Oldfield's Single ("Tubular Bells" Theme)/ Froggy Went A-Courtin' (in p/s) | 10 |
| 75 | Virgin VS 117 | Don Alfonso (with David Bedford)/In Dulci Jubilo (For Maureen) | 5 |
| 76 | Virgin VS 163 | Portsmouth/Speak (Tho' You Only Say Farewell) (Roger Dean or blue/red label; reissued in brown wraparound p/s) | 5 |
| 79 | Virgin VS 245 | Guilty/Excerpt From Incantations (p/s, red/green or white/blue label) | 5 |
| 79 | Virgin VS 317 | Blue Peter/Woodhenge (p/s, sudden or 'refined' ending (A7 matrix)) | 5 |
| 85 | Virgin VSD 836 | Pictures In The Dark/Legend/Moonlight Shadow/Rite Of Man (double pack in PVC gatefold stickered p/s) | 8 |
| 86 | Virgin VSS 863 | Shine (with Jon Anderson)/The Path (uncut picture disc) | 200 |
| 86 | Virgin VSS 863 | Shine (with Jon Anderson)/The Path (shaped picture disc) | 10 |

### ALBUMS
| | | | |
|---|---|---|---:|
| 73 | Virgin V 2001 | TUBULAR BELLS (LP, gloss laminate sleeve with "130 Notting Hill Gate" address, White/black 'Twin' label) | 40 |
| 74 | Virgin QV 2001 | TUBULAR BELLS (LP, quadrophonic, with model plane noise at the end of side 2, stickered sleeve) | 20 |
| 74 | Virgin V2013 | HERGEST RIDGE (LP, A-1U/B-1U matrixes, poor pressing and many returned, most other "girl/dragon" pressings £5) | 15 |
| 75 | Virgin QVQS 2043 | OMMADAWN (LP, quadrophonic, stickered sleeve) | 18 |
| 75 | Virgin VD 2502 | V (2-LP, compilation, includes long version of 'Don Alfonso') | 20 |
| 76 | Virgin QV 2043 | OMMADAWN (LP, different quadrophonic mix, stickered sleeve) | 18 |
| 76 | Virgin VBOX 1 | BOXED (4-LP box set, with booklet) | 20 |
| 78 | Virgin VDT 101 | INCANTATIONS (2-LP, some with 7" red vinyl of Julie Covington, & poster) | 30 |
| 78 | Virgin VP 2001 | TUBULAR BELLS (LP, picture disc, die-cut sleeve, stereo remix of 1976 Boxed quadrophonic mix; with or without model plane noise) | 15 |
| 79 | Virgin V 2141 | PLATINUM (LP, with inner sleeve & 'Sally'; matrix reads "V 2141 B1" or B2, 30,000 copies, withdrawn) | 20 |
| 79 | Tellydisc TELLY 4 | IMPRESSIONS (LP, mail-order only) | 20 |
| 84 | Virgin V 2328 | THE KILLING FIELDS (LP, with 20 page film booklet) | 15 |
| 97 | Virgin LPCENT 18 | TUBULAR BELLS (LP, coloured Dean label, audiophile pressing) | 20 |
| 01 | Simply Vinyl SVLP 322 | OMMADAWN (LP, Audiophile pressing on 180g vinyl, with 2 stickers) | 15 |

### PROMOS
| | | | |
|---|---|---|---:|
| 74 | Virgin VS 112 | Hergest Ridge (1-sided white label) | 100 |
| 75 | Virgin VDJ 1 | Extract from The Orchestral Tubular Bells/Extract from The Orchestral Tubular Bells | 40 |
| 75 | Virgin VS 117 | Don Alfonso ('A' label) | 15 |
| 75 | Virgin VDJ 9 | An Extract From Ommadawn Part 1/An Extract From Ommadawn Part 2 (On Horseback) (12") | 50 |
| 75 | Virgin VS 131 | In Dulci Jubilo/On Horseback ('A' label) | 5 |
| 76 | Virgin VS 163 | Portsmouth/Speak (Tho' You Only Say Farewell) (Roger Dean label) | 5 |
| 77 | Virgin VS 167 | The William Tell Overture/Argiers (blue Virgin 'A' label) | 8 |
| 79 | Virgin VSDJ 317 | Blue Peter (1-sided) | 20 |
| 85 | Virgin SWALLOW 1 | Etude/Moonlight Shadow/Portsmouth/In Dulci Jubilo (p/s, promo-only for "The Complete Mike Oldfield") | 30 |
| 87 | Virgin CDEP 6 | Islands/When The Night's On Fire/The Wind Chimes(Part One)/ Islands (Extended Version) (white gatefold stickered card p/s) | 20 |
| 92 | WEA SAM 1094 | OLDFIELD V THE ORB: Sentinel (Total Overhaul/Sentinel Nobel Prize Mix/ Sentinel Orbular Bells/Sentinel 7" Mix (12") | 15 |
| 92 | WEA SAM 1150 | SENTINEL RESTRUCTURE MIXES: Satoshi Tomii Interpretation/ Global Lust Mix/ TranceMix/Tubular Beats (12", title stickered red sleeve) | 15 |
| 92 | WEA SAM 1470 | A SHOT OF MOONSHINE: Jungle Mix (Featuring Rankin' Sean & Peter Lee)/ A Shot Of Moonshine (Jungle Instrumental)/A Shot of Moonshine (Solution Hoedown Mix) (12", lists artist as MOT2) | 12 |
| 92 | WEA YZ 708CDDJ | Tattoo (stickered p/s) | 12 |
| 76 | Virgin QVQS 2043 | OMMADAWN (LP, unreleased different quadrophonic mix, promo stickered sleeve) | 30 |
| 76 | Virgin V BOX 1 | COLLABORATIONS (LP, green/yellow label in stamped white sleeve) | 20 |
| 79 | (no cat. no.) | THE SPACE MOVIE (4 x 1-sided acetates of unreleased LP containing music from soundtrack to the 'Space Movie' video; includes Orchestral Hergest Ridge, Orchestral Tubular Bells, Incantations, Ommadawn and Portsmouth, some extracts otherwise released) | 400 |
| 92 | WEA WX 2002 | TUBULAR BELLS 2 (LP, stickered sleeve) | 15 |
| 94 | WEA SAM 1477 | THE SONGS OF DISTANT EARTH (CD in film can, with 2 inserts) | 100 |
| 98 | WEA 3331000043 | TUBULAR BELLS III (CD, in card sleeve, with bag, TB III tag, press releases and premiere concert details) | 30 |
| 99 | WEA (no cat. no.) | MILLENNIUM BELL (CD-R, some tracks with different samples to released album) | 10 |
| 99 | WEA (no cat. no.) | MILLENNIUM BELL (CD-R) | 10 |

*(see also Sallyangie, David Bedford, Kevin Ayers & Whole World, Pekka, Tom Newman)*

## OLD GOLD
| | | | |
|---|---|---|---:|
| 70 | Trend TNT 56 | It's Goodbye/Teachers Of Electricity | 30 |

## ANDREW OLDHAM (ORCHESTRA)
| | | | |
|---|---|---|---:|
| 64 | Decca F 11878 | 365 Rolling Stones/Oh I Do Like To See Me On The 'B' Side | 30 |
| 64 | Decca F 11987 | We Don't All Wear D'Same Size Boots/Right Of Way | 30 |
| 64 | Ace Of Clubs ACL 1180 | 16 HIP HITS (LP) | 40 |

| 64 | Decca LK 4636 | LIONEL BART'S MAGGIE MAY (LP) | 40 |
| 66 | Decca LK/SKL 4796 | THE ROLLING STONES SONGBOOK (LP) | 100 |

(see also Aranbee Pop Symphony, Rolling Stones, Cleo, Bo & Peep, Jeannie & Her Redheads, Gulliver's Travels, Mighty Avengers, John Paul Jones)

## WILL OLDHAM
| 97 | Domino WIGLP 39 | JOYA (LP, insert) | 15 |
| 00 | Domino WIGLP 74 | GUARAPERO (LOST BLUES 2) (2-LP) | 20 |

(see also Bonnie 'Prince' Billy, Palace Brothers)

## TONY O'LEARY AND THE CAPITOL
| 71 | Dolphin DOS61 | She Meant Everything/Whole World Shaking | 6 |

## JOHNNY OLENN & HIS BAND
| 57 | London HLU 8388 | I Ain't Gonna Cry No More/My Idea Of Love | 250 |
| 57 | London HLU 8388 | I Ain't Gonna Cry No More/My Idea Of Love (78) | 60 |
| 59 | Mercury AMT 1050 | Born Reckless/You Lovable You (as Johnny Olenn & Blockbusters) | 150 |

## O-LEVEL
| 78 | Psycho PSYCHO 2 | East Sheen/Pseudo Punk ('map' p/s) | 175 |
| 78 | Psycho PSYCHO 2 | East Sheen/Pseudo Punk ('schoolboy' p/s) | 150 |
| 70 | Psycho PSYCHO 1 | East Sheen/Pseudo Punk ('collage' p/s) | 175 |
| 78 | Kings Road KR 002 | THE MALCOLM EP (photocopied wraparound p/s) | 150 |
| 78 | Kings Road KR 002 | THE MALCOLM EP (printed p/s) | 40 |

(see also Teenage Filmstars, Times, Television Personalities)

## OLIVE BRANCH
| 68 | Wren WRE 1044 | WREN (EP) | 15 |

## JOHNNY OLIVER
| 56 | MGM SP 1165 | Chain Gang/These Hands | 25 |
| 60 | Mercury AMT 1095 | What A Kiss Won't Do/That's All I'm Living For | 12 |

## OLIVER & TWISTERS
| 64 | Pye Intl. NPL 28018 | LOOK WHO'S TWISTIN' (LP) | 15 |

## OLIVER (1)
| 69 | CBS 4435 | Good Morning Starshine/Can't You See | 5 |
| 70 | Crewe CRW 1 | Jean/Good Morning Starshine (Arrangement) (p/s) | 5 |

## OLIVER (2)
| 74 | Oliv OL 1 | STANDING STONE (LP, private pressing, withdrawn blue sleeve) | 1000 |
| 74 | Oliv OL 1 | STANDING STONE (LP, private pressing, withdrawn, later green sleeve) | 800 |
| 92 | Tenth Planet TP 001 | STANDING STONE (LP, reissue, numbered, 500 only) | 20 |

## OLLIE & NIGHTINGALES
| 69 | Stax STAX 109 | You're Leaving Me/Showered With Love | 12 |

## NIGEL OLSSONS DRUM ORCHESTRA & CHORUS
| 71 | DJM DJS 239 | Natures Way/Natures Way | 10 |
| 72 | DJM DJS 266 | Alabama/Sunshine Looks Like Rain | 10 |
| 71 | DJM DJLP 5 | NIGEL OLSSON'S DRUM ORCHESTRA AND CHORUS (LP, with poster) | 25 |

(see also Elton John, Hookfoot, Plastic Penny)

## OLYMPICS
| 58 | HMV POP 528 | Western Movies/Well! | 12 |
| 58 | HMV POP 564 | (I Wanna) Dance With The Teacher/Everybody Needs Love | 20 |
| 59 | Columbia DB 4346 | Private Eye/(Baby) Hully Gully | 25 |
| 60 | Vogue Pop V 9174 | I Wish I Could Shimmy Like My Sister Kate/Workin' Hard | 15 |
| 61 | Vogue Pop V 9181 | Dance With A Dolly/Dodge City | 25 |
| 61 | Vogue Pop V 9184 | Little Pedro/CAPPY LEWIS: Bullfight | 15 |
| 62 | Vogue Pop V 9196 | The Twist/Everybody Likes To Cha Cha Cha | 20 |
| 62 | Vogue Pop V 9198 | The Stomp/Mash Them 'Taters | 25 |
| 62 | Vogue Pop V 9204 | Baby It's Hot/The Scotch | 40 |
| 64 | Sue WI 348 | The Bounce/Fireworks | 15 |
| 65 | Warner Bros WB 157 | Good Lovin'/Olympic Shuffle | 20 |
| 66 | Fontana TF 678 | We Go Together (Pretty Baby)/Secret Agents | 20 |
| 66 | Fontana TF 778 | Baby, Do The Philly Dog/Western Movies | 20 |
| 69 | Action ACT 4539 | Baby, Do The Philly Dog/Mine Exclusively | 40 |
| 70 | Action ACT 4556 | I'll Do A Little Bit More/Same Old Thing | 10 |
| 71 | Jay Boy BOY 27 | Hully Gully/Big Boy Pete | 12 |
| 72 | Jay Boy BOY 56 | Baby, Do The Philly Dog/Secret Agents | 10 |
| 72 | Jay Boy BOY 74 | I'll Do A Little Bit More/Same Old Thing (reissue) | 100 |
| 61 | Vocalion VAH 8059 | DANCE BY THE LIGHT OF THE MOON (LP) | 0 |
| 67 | London HA-M 8327 | SOMETHING OLD, SOMETHING NEW (LP, unissued) | 60 |
| 67 | Fontana TL 5407 | SOMETHING OLD, SOMETHING NEW (LP) | 20 |
| 72 | Jay Boy JSX 2008 | THE OLYMPICS (LP) | |

(see also Cappy Lewis)

## PATRICK O'MAGICK
| 74 | Chrysalis CHS 2041 | You're A Winner/The Proposal | 5 |

(see also Patrick Campbell-Lyons)

## OMEGA RED STAR
| 69 | Decca LK/SKL 4974 | OMEGA RED STAR (LP, unboxed Decca on label) | 180 |

## OMEGA TRIBE
| 82 | Crass 221984/10 | ANGRY SONGS (EP) | 15 |
| 84 | Corpus Christi CHRIST ITS12 | It's A Hard Life/Young John | 6 |
| 83 | Corpus Christi CHRIST 05 | NO LOVE LOST (LP, inner) | 20 |
| 00 | Rugger Bugger SEEP 018LP | MAKE TEA NOT WAR (LP, printed inner sleeve) | 15 |

(see also Pete Fender)

## OMEGA (1)
| | | |
|---|---|---|
| 75 | Decca SKL-R 5219 | HALL OF FLOATERS IN THE SKY (LP) .................... 20 |
| 76 | Decca SKL-R 5243 | TIME ROBBER (LP) .................... 20 |

## OMEGA (2)
| | | |
|---|---|---|
| 85 | Rock Machine MACH 1 | THE PROPHET (LP) .................... 35 |

## OMEN
| | | |
|---|---|---|
| 69 | Ackee ACK 102 | Don't Leave Me Never/No More .................... 20 |

## OMEN SEARCHER
| | | |
|---|---|---|
| 82 | OCS 001 | Too Much/Teacher Of Sin (p/s) .................... 50 |
| 82 | OCS 002 | Teacher Of Sin/Too Much (p/s) .................... 50 |

## OMENKA BROTHERS
| | | |
|---|---|---|
| 77 | Ashiko | MR CROOKED CHIAUOTU (LP) .................... 35 |

## OMNI TRIO
| | | |
|---|---|---|
| 93 | Moving Shadow SHADOW 36 | RENEGADE SNARES VOL 3 (EP) .................... 18 |

## OMNIA OPERA
| | | |
|---|---|---|
| 93 | Delerium DELEC LP 011 | OMNIA OPERA (LP) .................... 60 |
| 97 | Delerium DELECLP 044 | RED SHIFT (LP) .................... 20 |

## ON A FRIDAY
| | | |
|---|---|---|
| 86 | OAF (no cat no) | ON A FRIDAY (11-track demo cassette) .................... 300 |
| 88 | (No label or cat no) | Happy Song/To Be A Brilliant Light/Sinking Ship (cassette) .................... 250 |
| 90 | (No label or cat no) | THE GREAT SHINDIG (Cassette, 15 tracks, as SHINDIG) .................... 250 |
| 91 | (No label or cat no) | What Is That You Say?/Stop Whispering (Demo)/Give It Up (Cassette, 3 known different cover inlays) .................... 250 |
| 91 | (No label or cat no) | I Can't (Demo)/Nothing Touches Me/Thinking About You (EP Version)/Phillipa Chicken/You (Demo) (Cassette, known as "Manic hedgehog" demos) .................... 250 |

*(see also Radiohead)*

## ONDIOLINE BAND
| | | |
|---|---|---|
| 66 | London HL 10022 | Last Bicycle To Brussels/Lovers Of Cologne .................... 6 |

## ONE
| | | |
|---|---|---|
| 69 | Fontana STL 5539 | ONE (LP, gatefold sleeve, black/silver label) .................... 225 |

## ONE & ONE
| | | |
|---|---|---|
| 64 | Decca F 11948 | I'll Give You Lovin'/It's Me .................... 15 |

*(see also Ivy League, Flowerpot Men)*

## ONE EYED JACKS (1)
| | | |
|---|---|---|
| 65 | Ember EMBS 206 | For Us There'll Be No Tomorrow/Soul Chart .................... 8 |

## ONE EYED JACKS (2)
| | | |
|---|---|---|
| 78 | Pennine PSS 154 | TAKE AWAY (LP, in "One Eyed Jacks" brown paper carrier bag) .................... 25 |
| 78 | Pennine PSS 154 | TAKE AWAY (LP) .................... 20 |

## ONE GANG LOGIC
| | | |
|---|---|---|
| 79 | Stark 1 | Alienate/Queue Here/Repeat Action/Who Killed Sex (numbered p/s) .................... 15 |

## ONE HIT WONDERS
| | | |
|---|---|---|
| 72 | CBS 7760 | Hey Hey Jump Now/Goodbye .................... 18 |

## 101'ERS
| | | |
|---|---|---|
| 76 | Chiswick (N)S 3 | Keys To Your Heart/5 Star Rock & Rock Petrol (with p/s) .................... 30 |
| 76 | Chiswick (N)S 3 | Keys To Your Heart/5 Star Rock & Rock Petrol .................... 10 |
| 79 | Big Beat NS 3 | Keys To Your Heart/5 Star Rock & Rock Petrol (reissue, with p/s) .................... 10 |
| 79 | Big Beat NS 3 | Keys To Your Heart/5 Star Rock & Rock Petrol .................... 8 |
| 80 | Big Beat NS 63 | Sweet Revenge/Rabies (From The Dogs Of Love) (p/s) .................... 5 |
| 81 | Andalucia AND 101 | ELGIN AVENUE BREAKDOWN (LP, gatefold flip back sleeve with booklet) .................... 40 |
| 81 | Andalucia AND 101 | ELGIN AVENUE BREAKDOWN (LP, without booklet) .................... 25 |

*(see also Clash, Alvaro, Aquila)*

## 100% PROOF
| | | |
|---|---|---|
| 80 | Smile SR 929 | NEW WAY OF LIVIN' (EP) .................... 25 |
| 81 | Myrrh MYR 1107 | 100% PROOF (LP, with insert) .................... 50 |

## 100% PURE POISON
| | | |
|---|---|---|
| 74 | EMI Untl. 501 | You Keep Coming Back/(And When I Said) I Love You .................... 20 |
| 77 | EMI Intl. INS 3001 | COMING RIGHT AT YOU (LP) .................... 150 |

## ONE IN A MILLION
| | | |
|---|---|---|
| 67 | CBS 202513 | Use Your Imagination/Hold On .................... 250 |
| 67 | MGM MGM 1370 | Fredereek Hernando/Double Sight .................... 1000 |

*(see also Thunderclap Newman)*

## ONE MILLION FUZZTONE GUITARS
| | | |
|---|---|---|
| 82 | Monsters In Orbit TVEYE 3 | Heaven/Annuese (foldover p/s, at least 2 different designs) .................... 6 |

## 1 SYNTAX 1
| | | |
|---|---|---|
| 84 | Proteus PRT 101 | Negatives/Feel No Touch (p/s) .................... 25 |

## ONE HAND CLAPPING
| | | |
|---|---|---|
| 79 | Curve Of The Earth COTE 001 | The Rich Get Rich/Running Down Creek (poster p/s) .................... 7 |

## MATTY O'NEIL
| | | |
|---|---|---|
| 54 | London L 1037 | Don't Sell Daddy Any More Whiskey/Little Rusty (gold label, tri-centre) .................... 30 |
| 54 | London L 1037 | Don't Sell Daddy Any More Whiskey/Little Rusty (silver label, tri-centre) .................... 15 |
| 54 | London L 1037 | Don't Sell Daddy Any More Whiskey/Little Rusty (silver top, round centre) .................... 10 |

## ONE TAKES
| | | |
|---|---|---|
| 80 | No Choice NC 001 | Accident/Street Kid/Backdoor Dump/Eviction Orders (p/s) .................... 20 |

## 1,000 MEXICANS
| | | |
|---|---|---|
| 83 | Whaam! WHAAM 12 | The Art Of Love/News For You (p/s, 1,500 only) .................... 6 |

## 1,000 VIOLINS

| | | | |
|---|---|---|---|
| 85 | Dreamworld DREAM 2 | Halcyon Days/I Remember When Everybody Used To Ride Bikes ... Now We All Drive Cars (12", p/s, 1,000 only) | 20 |
| 86 | Dreamworld DREAM 8 | Please Don't Sandblast My House/Time I Broke Down (p/s, 2,000 only) | 12 |
| 86 | Dreamworld DREAM 8T | Please Don't Sandblast My House/You Ungrateful Bastard/Though It Poured The Next Day, I Never Noticed The Rain (12", p/s) | 12 |
| 87 | Dreamworld DREAM 14 | Locked Out Of The Love-In (p/s) | 15 |
| 87 | Report REPX 1 | If I Were A Bullet (Then For Sure I'd Find A Way To Your Heart)/Poet (p/s) | 8 |
| 89 | Immaculate IMMAC 9 | If Only Words (Would Let Me Conquer You)/Orange Sunshine Ride | 6 |
| 89 | Immaculate 12 IMMAC 9 | If Only Words (Would Let Me Conquer You)/Orange Sunshine Ride/I Left My Mind In San Francisco (12", p/s) | 20 |
| 88 | Immaculate IMMACLP 1 | HEY MAN, THAT'S BEAUTIFUL (LP) | 20 |
| 00 | Vinyl Japan ASKLP 119 | LIKE ONE THOUSAND VIOLINS (LP) | 20 |

*(see also Page Boys)*

## ONE TIME SYNCOPATED CODPIECE

| | | | |
|---|---|---|---|
| 70s | Jon Hassell HASLP 1195 | ONCE MORE WITH FEELING (LP, insert) | 100 |

## ONE TWO & THREE

| | | | |
|---|---|---|---|
| 65 | Decca F 12093 | Black Pearl/Bahama Lullaby | 15 |
| 65 | Decca LK 4682 | BLACK PEARLS AND GREEN DIAMONDS (LP) | 200 |

## ONE WAY SYSTEM

| | | | |
|---|---|---|---|
| 82 | Lightbeat WAY 1 | Stab The Judge/Riot Torn City/Me And You (p/s) | 12 |
| 82 | Anagram ANA 1 | Give Us A Future/Just Another Hero (p/s) | 5 |
| 83 | Anagram ANA 5 | Jerusalem/Jackie Was A Junkie (p/s) | 10 |
| 83 | Anagram ANA 9 | Cum On Feel The Noise/Breakin' In (p/s) | 6 |
| 83 | Anagram ANA 14 | This Is The Age/Into Fires (p/s) | 5 |
| 84 | Anagram ANA 19 | Visions Of Angels/Shine Again (p/s) | 5 |
| 83 | Anagram GRAM 003 | ALL SYSTEMS GO (LP, with lyric inner) | 15 |
| 83 | Anagram GRAM 008 | WRITING ON THE WALL (LP, with lyric inner) | 15 |

## ONE WAY TICKET

| | | | |
|---|---|---|---|
| 78 | President PTLS 1069 | TIME IS RIGHT (LP, featuring tracks from "Five Day Rain" LP) | 150 |

*(see also Five Day Rain)*

## ONLOOKERS

| | | | |
|---|---|---|---|
| 82 | Demon D 1012 | You And I/Understand/Julia (p/s) | 18 |

## ONLY ONES

| | | | |
|---|---|---|---|
| 77 | Vengeance VEN 001 | Lovers Of Today/Peter And The Pets (p/s) | 12 |
| 77 | Vengeance VEN 001 | Lovers Of Today/Peter And The Pets (12", with 7" x 7" sticker) | 12 |
| 78 | CBS S CBS 6228 | Another Girl, Another Planet/Special View (p/s) | 15 |
| 78 | CBS S CBS 6576 | Another Girl, Another Planet/As My Wife Says | 10 |
| 78 | CBS S CBS 12-6576 | Another Girl, Another Planet/As My Wife Says (12", p/s) | 12 |
| 79 | CBS S CBS 7086 | You've Got To Pay/This Ain't All (It's Made Out To Be) (p/s) | 6 |
| 79 | CBS S CBS 7285 | Out There In The Night/Lovers Of Today | 5 |
| 79 | CBS S CBS 12-7285 | Out There In The Night/Lovers Of Today/Peter And The Pets (12", p/s, blue vinyl, 2 slight sleeve variations) | 10 |
| 79 | CBS S CBS 7963 | Trouble In The World/Your Chosen Life (withdrawn 'group' black & red p/s) | 350 |
| 79 | CBS S CBS 7963 | Trouble In The World/Your Chosen Life (standard p/s) | 5 |
| 80 | CBS S CBS 8535 | Fools/Castle Built On Sand (p/s, with Pauline Murray) | 5 |
| 83 | Vengeance VEN 002 | Baby's Got A Gun/PETER PERRETT: Silent Night | 5 |
| 78 | CBS 82830 | THE ONLY ONES (LP, orange label, with insert) | 20 |
| 79 | CBS 83451 | EVEN SERPENTS SHINE (LP, embossed sleeve, orange label) | 20 |
| 89 | Strange Fruit SFRLP 102 | PEEL SESSIONS ALBUM (LP) | 15 |

*(see also England's Glory)*

## YOKO ONO

| | | | |
|---|---|---|---|
| 71 | Apple APPLE 38 | Mrs. Lennon/Midsummer New York | 20 |
| 72 | Apple APPLE 41 | Mind Train/Listen, The Snow Is Falling (p/s) | 25 |
| 73 | Apple APPLE 47 | Death Of Samantha/Yang Yang | 20 |
| 73 | Apple APPLE 48 | Run Run Run/Men Men Men | 20 |
| 70 | Apple SAPCOR 17 | YOKO ONO/PLASTIC ONO BAND (LP, with inner sleeve) | 60 |
| 71 | Apple SAPTU 101/2 | FLY (2-LP, laminated gatefold, inner sleeves, poster & postcard) | 70 |
| 73 | Apple SAPDO 1001 | APPROXIMATELY INFINITE UNIVERSE (2-LP, with lyric inner sleeves) | 40 |
| 73 | Apple SAPCOR 26 | FEELING THE SPACE (LP) | 40 |

*(see also John Lennon, Bill Elliott & Elastic Oz Band)*

## ONSLAUGHT (1)

| | | | |
|---|---|---|---|
| 83 | Complete Control TROL 1 | First Strike/State Control/No More (p/s) | 12 |
| 85 | Children Of The Revolution GURT 2 | POWER FROM HELL (LP, with inner) | 20 |

## ONSLAUGHT (2)

| | | | |
|---|---|---|---|
| 85 | 69 Records SRTSK 5375 | My Generation/Angel Of Mercy | 15 |

## ON THE CARDS

| | | | |
|---|---|---|---|
| 84 | OTC 001 | This Is My Home Town/All In Vain | 18 |

## ON THE WATERFRONT

| | | | |
|---|---|---|---|
| 86 | Wizz | The Kids Are Allright/Never Surrender/Far From The Madding Crowd/Mrs. Harrington (12", p/s) | 60 |

## ONYX

| | | | |
|---|---|---|---|
| 68 | Pye 7N 17477 | You've Gotta Be With Me/It's All Put On | 30 |
| 68 | Pye 7N 17622 | My Son John/Step By Step | 30 |
| 69 | Pye 7N 17768 | Tamaris Khan/So Sad Inside | 70 |
| 69 | CBS 4635 | Time Off/Movin' In | 20 |
| 71 | Parlophone R 5888 | Air/Our House | 12 |
| 71 | Parlophone R 5906 | The Next Stop Is Mine/What's That You Say | 12 |

MINT VALUE £

### OO BANG JIGGLY JANG
| | | | |
|---|---|---|---|
| 71 | President PT 356 | Hanging Tree/1000 Leagues | 15 |

### OPAL
| | | | |
|---|---|---|---|
| 85 | One Big Guitar OBG 002T | Northern Line/Empty Bottles/Soul Giver (12") | 15 |
| 87 | Rough Trade RTT 129 | Fell From The Sun/Freight Train/Grains Of Sand (12") | 15 |
| 87 | Rough Trade ROUGH 116 | HAPPY NIGHTMARE BABY (LP) | 20 |
| 89 | Rough Trade ROUGH 128 | EARLY RECORDINGS (LP) | 20 |

(see also Mazzy Star)

### OPAL BUTTERFLY
| | | | |
|---|---|---|---|
| 68 | CBS 3576 | Beautiful Beige/Speak Up | 35 |
| 69 | CBS 3921 | Mary Anne With The Shakey Hand/My Gration Or? | 60 |
| 70 | Polydor 2058 041 | You're A Groupie Girl/Gigging Song | 60 |

(see also Hawkwind, Motorhead, Mott The Hoople)

### JACKIE OPEL
| | | | |
|---|---|---|---|
| 63 | Jump Up JU 512 | TV In Jamaica/Worrell's Captaincy | 25 |
| 64 | Black Swan WI 421 | You're No Good/King Liges | 40 |
| 64 | R&B JB 138 | Stand By Me (as Jackie Opel & Hortense Ellis)/Solid Rock | 50 |
| 64 | R&B JB 160 | Pity The Fool/The Day Will Come | 50 |
| 65 | King KG 1011 | Cry Me A River/Eternal Love | 25 |
| 65 | Island WI 203 | Wipe Those Tears/Don't Take Your Love | 30 |
| 65 | Island WI 209 | Go Whey/Shelter The Storm | 250 |
| 65 | Island WI 227 | Old Rockin' Chair/SKATALITES: Song Of Love (B-side is actually "Ska In Vienna Woods") | 250 |
| 65 | Ska Beat JB 190 | Done With A Friend/More Wood In The Fire | 40 |
| 65 | Ska Beat JB 227 | The Lord Is With Thee/A Little More | 150 |
| 66 | Island WI 264 | A Love To Share/ROLAND ALPHONSO: Devoted To You | 25 |
| 66 | Rio R 117 | I Am What I Am/JACKIE MITTOO & SKATALITES: Devil's Bug | 60 |
| 66 | Rio R120 | I Don't Want Her/SOUL BOYS: Rudie Get Wise | 60 |

(see also Jackie & Doreen, Doreen & Jackie, Hortense & Jackie)

### OPEN
| | | | |
|---|---|---|---|
| 03 | Loog 9813076 | NEVER ENOUGH EP (1,000 only, p/s) | 12 |
| 04 | Loog 9817238 | Close My Eyes/The View (mail order only 12" p/s) | 12 |

### OPEN CASKET
| | | | |
|---|---|---|---|
| 73 | Royal RY1 | Turning To The Sun/She Can Leave Now | 30 |

### OPEN HOUSE
| | | | |
|---|---|---|---|
| 72 | Nest NRS 102A | Mr Sparky/My Song | 40 |

### OPEN MIND
| | | | |
|---|---|---|---|
| 69 | Philips BF 1805 | Magic Potion/Cast A Spell (Demo copy) | 500 |
| 69 | Philips BF 1790 | Horses And Chariots/Before My Time | 100 |
| 69 | Philips BF 1805 | Magic Potion/Cast A Spell | 600 |
| 69 | Philips SBL 7893 | OPEN MIND (LP, laminated sleeve, black/silver label) | 1000 |
| 86 | Antar ANTAR 2 | OPEN MIND (LP, reissue) | 20 |

(see also Drag Set)

### OPEN ROAD
| | | | |
|---|---|---|---|
| 72 | Greenwich GSS 102 | Swamp Fever/Lost And Found | 12 |
| 71 | Greenwich GSLP 1001 | WINDY DAZE (LP, gatefold sleeve) | 50 |

(see also Warm Sounds, Denny Gerrard, Donovan)

### OPEN BOOK
| | | | |
|---|---|---|---|
| 87 | HAG 002 | Pension Day/I'm Incomplete | 8 |

### OPERA
| | | | |
|---|---|---|---|
| 79 | Bead records BEAD 13 | OPERA (LP) | 25 |

### OPETH
| | | | |
|---|---|---|---|
| 01 | Music For Nations MFSN 264 | BLACKWATER PARK (2xLP) | 35 |
| 02 | Peaceville DLPVILE 78 | STILL LIFE (2-LP, 1000 only) | 40 |
| 03 | Music For Nations MFSN 297 | DAMNATION (LP) | 45 |
| 10 | Peaceville VILLELP78 | STILL LIFE (2-LP, reissue, 2000 only) | 30 |

### OPPO
| | | | |
|---|---|---|---|
| 76 | EMI 2541 | Miracles (A Mini Epic)/The Flame | 5 |

### OPPRESSED
| | | | |
|---|---|---|---|
| 83 | Oppressed OPPO 1 | Work Together/Victims (p/s) | 20 |
| 83 | Firm NICK 1 | NEVER SAY DIE (EP) | 18 |
| 84 | Oppressed OPLP 1 | OI! OI! MUSIC (LP) | 20 |
| 85 | Skinhead CREW 1 | FATAL BLOW (LP) | 20 |
| 88 | OIR 12 | DEAD AND BURIED (LP) | 15 |

(see also Rude Boys (2))

### OPTIMISTS
| | | | |
|---|---|---|---|
| 81 | Armageddon AS 018 | Mull Of Kintyre/The Plumbers Song (p/s) | 18 |

### OPUS
| | | | |
|---|---|---|---|
| 70 | Columbia DB 8675 | Baby, Come On/Angela Grey | 15 |

### ORA
| | | | |
|---|---|---|---|
| 69 | Tangerine OPLOP 0025 | ORA (LP) | 350 |

(see also Byzantium, Movies)

### ORAL EXCITERS
| | | | |
|---|---|---|---|
| 79 | Three Elms TE 001 | It's A Holiday/Tonight (p/s, 500 only) | 60 |

### ORAL SEX
| | | | |
|---|---|---|---|
| 82 | Conquest Quest 6 | ORAL SEX (LP) | 20 |

**DAPHNE ORAM**
62   HMV 7EG8762                          LISTEN, MOVE AND DANCE 3 - ELECTRONIC SOUND PATTERNS (EP) ............................ 30

**O RANG**
94   Echo ECHLP 2                          HEARD OF INSTINCT (LP) ...................................................................................... 30
97   Echo ECHLP 10                         FIELDS AND WAVES (LP) ..................................................................................... 40

**ORANGE ALABASTER MUSHROOM**
98   Earworm WORM 36                       The Slug/Ethel Tripped A Mean Gloss (p/s, with sticker)........................................ 8

**ORANGE BICYCLE**
67   Columbia DB 8259                      Hyacinth Threads/Amy Peate ........................................................................... 35
67   Columbia DB 8311                      Laura's Garden/Lavender Girl ........................................................................... 25
68   Columbia DB 8352                      Early Pearly Morning/Go With Goldie ............................................................... 20
68   Columbia DB 8413                      Jenskadajka/Nicely .......................................................................................... 18
68   Columbia DB 8483                      Sing This All Together/Trip On An Orange Bicycle .............................................. 25
69   Parlophone R 5789                     Tonight I'll Be Staying Here With You/Last Cloud Home ..................................... 15
69   Parlophone R 5811                     Carry That Weight/You Never Give Me Your Money/Want To B Side.................... 18
70   Parlophone R 5827                     Take Me To The Pilot/It's Not My World ........................................................... 20
70   Parlophone R 5854                     Jelly On The Bread/Make It Rain ...................................................................... 20
71   Regal Zonophone RZ 3029              Goodbye Stranger/Country Comforts ............................................................... 15
70   Parlophone PCS 7108                   ORANGE BICYCLE (LP, laminated front sleeve, black/silver label) ..................... 250
88   M'n Blue Town MBT 5003               LET'S TAKE A TRIP ON AN ORANGE BICYCLE (LP) .............................................. 15
11   Morgan Bluetown BT 5007              ORANGE BICYCLE (LP, reissue, 500 only, orange vinyl, with numbered certificate)......... 20
*(see also Motherlight)*

**ORANGE BLOSSOM**
74   Westwood WRS 038                      KEEP ON PUSHING (LP) ...................................................................................... 30

**ORANGE DISASTER**
80s  Neuter OD 1                           Something's Got To Give/Out Of The Room/Hiding From Frank ........................... 20
*(see also Varicose Veins)*

**ORANGE GOBLIN**
04   Rise Above RISE7/051                  Some You Win, Some You Lose/White Night Cyanide (p/s) ..................................... 6
00   The Music Cartel TMC 036LP           THE BIG BLACK (LP) ........................................................................................... 20
04   Rise Above RISELP 46                  THIEVING FROM THE HOUSE OF GOD (LP, orange vinyl, 1000 only)...................... 25
07   Mayan MYNLP 058                       HEALING THROUGH FIRE (LP) .............................................................................. 18
12   Back On Black BOBV 289LP             A EULOGY FOR THE DAMNED (LP, gatefold, merchandise insert, clear vinyl) ......... 20

**ORANGE JUICE**
80   Postcard 80-1                         Falling And Laughing/Moscow Olympics/Moscow (foldover p/s in poly bag, with postcard; and with flexidisc "Felicity (live)" [I Wish I Was A Postcard 1], 963 only)...... 200
80   Postcard 80-1                         Falling And Laughing/Moscow Olympics/Moscow (foldover p/s in poly bag, without postcard and without flexidisc, 963 only) ............................................................ 100
80   I Wish I Was A Postcard 1            Felicity (live) (freebie flexidisc, also given away with fanzines) ............................. 12
80   Postcard 80-2                         Blue Boy/Lovesick (hand-coloured p/s in poly bag, blue labels).......................... 35
80   Postcard 80-2                         Blue Boy/Lovesick (yellow labels/cream cover sleeve)........................................ 8
80   Postcard 80-2                         Blue Boy/Lovesick (3rd issue, brown labels in brown company sleeve) ................. 8
80   Postcard 80-6                         Simply Thrilled Honey/Breakfast Time (p/s, with picture insert in poly bag) ......... 40
80   Postcard 80-6                         Simply Thrilled Honey/Breakfast Time (2nd issue, brown labels in brown company sleeve) ............................................................................................................ 8
81   Postcard 81-2                         Poor Old Soul/Poor Old Soul Pt. 2 (die-cut co. sleeve, with postcard) ................. 30
81   Postcard 81-2                         Poor Old Soul/Poor Old Soul Pt. 2 (die-cut co. sleeve, without postcard) .............. 5
81   Postcard 81-6                         Wan Light/You Old Eccentric (unreleased) .......................................................... 0
83   Polydor POSP 547                      Rip It Up/Snake Charmer (p/s, with free live 21/4/79 cassette) ............................ 6
83   Polydor OJ 4                          Flesh Of My Flesh/Lord John White And The Bottleneck Train ............................. 6
84   Polydor OJ 5/JUICE 1                  Bridge/Out For The Count (stickered p/s, with free flexidisc Poor Old Soul [live]) .......... 6
84   Polydor OJ 6/OJC 6                    What Presence?!/A Place In My Heart (Dub) (p/s, with free cassette The Felicity Flexi Session: The Formative Years) ....................................................................................... 6
82   Polydor POLS 1057                     YOU CAN'T HIDE YOUR LOVE FOREVER (LP, inner).............................................. 18
92   Postcard DUBH 922                     OSTRICH CHURCHYARD (LP, 1,000 with bonus 10" "Irritation Disc" [922TEN]).......... 20
10   Domino REWIGCD38X                     ...COALS TO NEWCASTLE (7-CD box set) ........................................................... 30
*(see also Edwyn Collins, Paul Quinn & Edwyn Collins, Fun Four, Josef K)*

**ORANGE MACHINE**
68   Pye 7N 17559                          Three Jolly Little Dwarfs/Real Life Permanent Dream ...................................... 200
69   Pye 7N 17680                          You Can All Join In/Dr. Crippen's Waiting Room ............................................... 175
*(see also Danny Hughes)*

**ORANGE PEEL**
71   Reflection HRS 5                      I Got No Time/Searching For A Place To Hide..................................................... 25

**ORANGE SEAWEED**
68   Pye 7N 17515                          Stay Awhile/Pictures In The Sky ...................................................................... 70
*(see also Fadin' Colours)*

**ORB**
**SINGLES**
89   Wau! Mr Modo MWS 010T                KISS (12" EP, 949 only, die-cut company sleeve)................................................ 15
90   Wau! Mr Modo MWS 017T                A Huge Ever Growing Pulsating Brain That Rules From The Centre Of The Ultraworld: Loving You (Orbital Mix)/(Bucket And Spade Mix)/Why Is 6 Scared of 7? (12" p/s, B-side matrix states 'MWS 016T') ............................................................................. 15
90   Big Life BLR 270T                     A Huge Ever-Growing Pulsating Brain That Rules From The Centre Of The Ultraworld : Loving You (edited)/(Bucket And Spade Mix)/(Why Is 6 Scared of 7?) (12" p/s, 8,000 only, B-side matrix 'MWS 016T') ............................................................................ 10

**ALBUMS**
91   Big Life BLRDLP 5                     THE ORB'S ADVENTURES BEYOND THE UNDERWORLD (2-LP, with inner sleeve, 'classical pressing' sticker on sleeve)............................................................................ 20
91   Big Life BLRLP 14                     THE ORB AUBREY MIXES: THE ULTRAWORLD EXCURSIONS (LP, with inner sleeve, deleted on day of release)..................................................................................... 15

# ORBIDÖIG

| 93 | Island ILPSQ 8022 | LIVE 93 (4-LP) | 20 |
| 95 | Island ILPSD 8037 | ORBUS TERRARUM (2-LP) | 20 |
| 97 | ILPSD 8055 | OBLIVION (2-LP) | 18 |
| 92 | Big Life BLRLA 18 | U.F.ORB (2xLP, 12" and 2 art prints in unopened blue plastic cover) | 30 |

**PROMOS**

| 90 | Wau! Mr Modo MWS 017T | A Huge Ever-Growing Pulsating Remix/From One Ear To Another/Why Is 6 Scared Of 7? (12", white label, 100 only) | 20 |
| 90 | Wau! Mr Modo MWS 017R | A Huge Ever-Growing Pulsating Brain That Rules From The Centre Of The Ultraworld (Orbital Dance Mix)/(Orbital Radio Mix)/(Aubrey Mix Mk II) (12", stamped white label, 1,000 only) | 15 |
| 90 | Big Life ORB PROMO 2 | Little Fluffy Clouds (Dance Mk 1)/Into The Fourth Dimension/Little Fluffy Clouds (Ambient Mk 1) (12") | 10 |
| 91 | Big Life ORB PICTURE 3 | Perpetual Dawn: Ultrabass II (12", 1-sided picture disc, mispressing, plays "Towers Of Dub (Ambient)", 400 pressed but 300 allegedly destroyed) | 15 |

*(see also System 7, KLF, Jah Wobble, Apollo XI, Space)*

## ORBIDÖIG

| 81 | Situation 2 SIT 15 | Nocturnal Operation/Down Periscope (p/s) | 25 |

*(see also Sensational Creed)*

## ROY ORBISON

**SINGLES**

| 60 | London HLU 9149 | Only The Lonely (Know How I Feel)/Here Comes That Song Again | 6 |
| 60 | London HLU 9149 | Only The Lonely (Know How I Feel)/Here Comes That Song Again (78) | 400 |
| 60 | London HLU 9207 | Blue Angel/Today's Teardrops | 10 |
| 61 | London HLU 9307 | I'm Hurtin'/I Can't Stop Loving You | 10 |
| 61 | London HLU 7108 | I'm Hurtin'/I Can't Stop Loving You (export issue) | 15 |
| 61 | London HLU 9342 | Runnin' Scared/Love Hurts | 7 |
| 61 | London HLU 9405 | Cryin'/Candy Man | 5 |
| 62 | London HLU 9511 | Dream Baby/The Actress | 5 |
| 62 | London HLU 9561 | The Crowd/Mama | 5 |
| 62 | London HLU 9607 | Workin' For The Man/Leah | 5 |
| 63 | London HLU 9676 | In Dreams/Shahdaroba | 5 |
| 64 | Ember EMB S 197 | Rock House/You're My Baby | 20 |
| 64 | Ember EMB S 200 | This Kind Of Love/I Never Knew (in p/s) | 20 |
| 64 | Ember EMB S 200 | This Kind Of Love/I Never Knew | 8 |
| 65 | Ember EMB S 209 | Sweet And Easy To Love/You're Gonna Cry (in p/s) | 15 |
| 65 | Ember EMB S 209 | Sweet And Easy To Love/You're Gonna Cry | 5 |
| 68 | London HLU 10176 | Born To Be Loved By You/Shy Away | 10 |
| 68 | London HLU 10206 | Walk On/Flowers | 5 |
| 68 | London HLU 10222 | Heartache/Sugar Man | 5 |

**EPs**

| 57 | London RE-S 1089 | HILLBILLY ROCK (orange p/s, mauve/silver label, triangular centre) | 150 |
| 57 | London RE-S 1089 | HILLBILLY ROCK (orange p/s, mauve/silver label, round centre) | 100 |
| 60 | London RE-U 1274 | ONLY THE LONELY | 25 |
| 63 | London RE-S 1089 | HILLBILLY ROCK (re-pressing, yellow p/s, silver-top, round centre) | 80 |
| 63 | London RE-U 1354 | ROY ORBISON | 20 |

*(Later pressings are on London Monument label as were later pressings of RE-U 1274 and RE-U 1354)*

| 63 | London RE-U 1373 | IN DREAMS | 10 |
| 64 | Ember EP 4546 | SWEET AND EASY TO LOVE | 40 |
| 64 | Ember EP 4563 | TRYIN' TO GET TO YOU | 40 |
| 64 | London RE-U 1435 | IT'S OVER | 10 |
| 64 | London RE-U 1437 | OH PRETTY WOMAN | 10 |
| 65 | London RE-U 1439 | ROY ORBISON'S STAGE SHOW HITS | 10 |
| 65 | Ember EP 4570 | DEVIL DOLL | 40 |
| 65 | London RE-U 1440 | LOVE HURTS | 10 |

## ALBUMS : LONDON LPS

| 61 | London HA-U 2342 | LONELY AND BLUE | 20 |
| 62 | London HA-U 2437 | CRYIN' (mono) | 20 |
| 62 | London SAH-U 6229 | CRYIN' (stereo) | 25 |
| 63 | London HA-U 8108 | IN DREAMS (mono) | 25 |
| 63 | London SH-U 8108 | IN DREAMS (stereo) | 25 |
| 64 | London HA-U 8207 | OH, PRETTY WOMAN | 15 |
| 65 | London HA-U 8252 | THERE IS ONLY ONE ROY ORBISON (mono) | 15 |
| 65 | London SH-U 8252 | THERE IS ONLY ONE ROY ORBISON (stereo) | 20 |
| 66 | London HA-U 8279 | THE ORBISON WAY (mono) | 15 |
| 66 | London SH-U 8279 | THE ORBISON WAY (stereo) | 20 |
| 66 | London HA-U 8297 | THE CLASSIC ROY ORBISON (mono) | |

*(The London LPs listed above were originally issued with plum labels [mono] or blue labels [stereo]. Later copies were re-pressed with black labels [mono] or plum labels [stereo] with a boxed London logo)*

| 66 | London HA-U 8297 | THE CLASSIC ROY ORBISON (black label mono) | 15 |
| 66 | London SH-U 8297 | THE CLASSIC ROY ORBISON (blue label stereo) | 15 |
| 67 | London HA-U 8318 | SINGS DON GIBSON (black label mono) | 15 |
| 67 | London SH-U 8318 | SINGS DON GIBSON (blue label stereo) | 15 |
| 68 | London HA-U/SH-U 8357 | CRY SOFTLY, LONELY ONE | 15 |
| 70 | London HA-U 8406 | THE BIG "O" (mono) | 15 |

## ALBUMS : OTHER ALBUMS

| 64 | Ember NR 5013 | THE EXCITING SOUNDS OF ROY ORBISON (original copies list 'Great Newport Street' address on cover; reissued 1972) | 25 |
| 64 | Ember NR 5013 | THE EXCITING SOUNDS OF ROY ORBISON (reissued 1972) | 15 |
| 65 | Ember FA 2005 | ROY ORBISON AND OTHERS (with 4 tracks by Orbison) | 15 |

*(see also Traveling Wilburys)*

## ORBIT FIVE
| | | |
|---|---|---|
| 68 | Decca F 12799 | I Wanna Go To Heaven/Walking (in p/s) ...................................... 25 |
| 68 | Decca F 12799 | I Wanna Go To Heaven/Walking ............................................... 15 |

## ORBITAL
### SINGLES
| 89 | Oh Zone ZONE 1 | Chime/Deeper (12", p/s) ....................................................... 20 |
|---|---|---|

### ALBUMS
| | | |
|---|---|---|
| 91 | FFRR 828248-1 | ORBITAL (2-LP) ................................................................. 35 |
| 93 | Internal TRULP 2 | ORBITAL 2 (2-LP) .............................................................. 35 |
| 94 | Internal TRULP 5 | SNIVILISATION (2-LP, gatefold sleeve, poster) ............................ 25 |
| 96 | Internal TRULP 10 | IN SIDES (3-LP) ............................................................... 35 |
| 02 | Ffrr 092746190 | WORK 1989-2002 (2-LP) ....................................................... 25 |

### PROMOS
| | | |
|---|---|---|
| 91 | Ffrr FRRDJ 163 | Midnight (Radio Edit)/Choice (Radio Edit) ................................. 5 |
| 91 | Ffrr FRRXDJ 163 | Midnight/Midnight (Sasha Mix)/Choice/Choice Remix (12") ........... 12 |

## ORBITONES
| 73 | Explosion EX 207 | Memories Of Love/SONNY EARLE: In Peace ............................... 5 |
|---|---|---|

## ORCA
| | | |
|---|---|---|
| 92 | Micro Genetic 001 | 9 Lives/Shining Bright (12") ................................................. 20 |
| 92 | Lucky Spin LSR-ORC 1 | DANCES WITH DOLPHINS EP NO. 1 (12", stickered, black die-cut sleeve) ......... 30 |
| 92 | Lucky Spin LSR 002 | My Brothers/The Power (12") ................................................ 30 |
| 93 | Lucky Spin LRS 006 | DANCES WITH DOLPHINS EP NO. 2 (12") ................................ 25 |
| 93 | Lucky Spin LSR 011 | 4AM/Pure Bliss/Jungle Vibes/Pure Bliss (Remix) (100 on red vinyl) .......... 50 |
| 93 | Lucky Spin LSR 011 | 4AM/Pure Bliss/Jungle Vibes/Pure Bliss (Remix) (black vinyl) ............. 30 |
| 93 | Lucky Spin ORCA 6 | BACK TO THE JUNGLE EP (12") .............................................. 12 |
| 94 | Lucky Spin STU 06 | 4AM (Remix 1)/4AM (Remix 2) (12") ....................................... 12 |
| 94 | Lucky Spin LSR 016 | Intalect/Tranquility To Earth (12") .......................................... 12 |

## ORCHESTRA BAOBAB
| 89 | World Circuit WCB 014 | PIRATES CHOICE - LEGENDARY 1982 SESSION (LP) ..................... 25 |
|---|---|---|

## ORCHESTRA DEL ORO
| 62 | Pye Int 7N.25143 | Main Theme From Lolita/Lolita Ya Ya (in PS) ............................. 8 |
|---|---|---|

## ORCHESTRAL MANOEUVRES IN THE DARK (O.M.D.)
| | | |
|---|---|---|
| 79 | Factory FAC 6 | Electricity/Almost (black 'braille' p/s) ...................................... 70 |
| 79 | Din Disc DIN 2 | Electricity (Re-Recorded Version)/Almost (p/s, reissue) ................. 5 |
| 80 | Din Disc DIN 6 | Red Frame-White Light/I Betray My Friends (p/s) ....................... 5 |
| 80 | Din Disc DIN 15-10 | Messages (Extended)/Waiting For The Man/Taking Sides Again (10", p/s) ...... 6 |
| 80 | Din Disc DIN 22-12 | Enola Gay (Extended)/Annex (p/s) ......................................... 6 |
| 84 | Virgin VSS 660 | Locomotion/Her Body In My Soul (uncut train-shaped picture disc) ......... 35 |
| 84 | Virgin VSS 660 | Locomotion/Her Body In My Soul (train-shaped picture disc) ............ 10 |
| 84 | Virgin VSY 727 | Never Turn Away/Wrappup (picture disc) .................................. 10 |
| 85 | Virgin VSY 766-14 | So In Love (Extended)/Concrete Hands (Extended)/Maria Gallant (12" picture disc) ..... 15 |
| 85 | Virgin VS 766 | So In Love/Concrete Hands//Maria Gallante/White Trash (live) (double pack, stickered gatefold p/s) ............ 6 |
| 80 | Din Disc DID 2 | ORCHESTRAL MANOEUVRES IN THE DARK (LP, 12" x 12" grid sleeve, black, blue or grey outer sleeves with orange, pink or red inner) ....................... 25 |
| 80 | Din Disc DID 6 | ORGANISATION (LP, stickered sleeve, with insert & 7": "Introducing Radios"/ Distance Fades Between Us/"Progress"/"Once When I Was Six" [DEP 2]) ................ 15 |
| 91 | Virgin V 2648 | SUGAR TAX (LP, mispressing with extra track "All She Wants Is Everything" instead of "Neon Lights") ....................... 15 |
| 84 | Virgin V 2310 | JUNK CULTURE (LP, stickered sleeve, with free 7": "[Angels Keep Turning] The Wheels Of The Universe" [JUNK 1]) .......... 15 |
| 96 | Virgin V2807 | UNIVERSAL (LP) ............................................................... 80 |

## ORCHIDS (1)
| | | |
|---|---|---|
| 63 | Decca F 11743 | Gonna Make Him Mine/Stay At Home ...................................... 25 |
| 63 | Decca F 11785 | Love Hit Me/Don't Make Me Mad ........................................... 20 |
| 64 | Decca F 11861 | I've Got That Feeling/Larry .................................................. 25 |

*(see also Exceptions)*

## ORCHIDS (2)
| | | |
|---|---|---|
| 88 | Sarah SARAH 002 | I've Got A Habit/Give Me Some Peppermint Freedom/Apologies (foldover p/s with poster, 1,000 only) ............... 100 |
| 88 | Sarah SARAH 011 | UNDERNEATH THE WINDOW, UNDERNEATH THE SINK EP (p/s) ......... 10 |
| 88 | Sha La La BaBaBaBaBa 5 | From This Day/SEA URCHINS: Summertime (flexi, 2,500 only, 1,000 in p/s) ...... 15 |
| 89 | Sarah SARAH 023 | WHAT WILL WE DO NEXT? EP (p/s) ........................................ 12 |
| 90 | Sarah SARAH 029 | Something For The Longing/Farewell Dear Bonnie/On A Sunday (p/s, with inserts) ..... 10 |
| 90 | Caff CAFF 11 | An Ill Wind That Blows/All Those Things (p/s, with insert) ............... 20 |
| 91 | Sarah SARAH 042 | PENETRATION EP (12", p/s with insert) ................................... 12 |
| 92 | Sarah SARAH 66 | Thaumaturgy/I Was Just Dreaming/Between Sleeping And Waking (p/s, insert) ...... 10 |
| 91 | Sarah SARAH 605 | UNHOLY SOUL (LP) ............................................................ 20 |
| 94 | Sarah SARAH 617 | STRIVING FOR THE LAZY PERFECTION (LP) ................................ 40 |
| 95 | Sarah SARAH 611 LP | EPICUREAN: A SOUNDTRACK (2-LP) ........................................ 30 |

## ORE
| 82 | Bandit BR 003 | Your Time Will Come/Yellow River (p/s) ................................. 100 |
|---|---|---|

## CHARLES ORGANAIRE
| | | |
|---|---|---|
| 64 | Blue Beat BB 241 | How Did Moses Cross The Red Sea/You May Not Believe (as Big Charlie) ...... 18 |
| 64 | R&B JB 149 | Little Village/It Happens On A Holiday ..................................... 35 |
| 64 | Rio R 28 | Little Village/It Happens On A Holiday (reissue) ......................... 20 |

MINT VALUE £

## ORGANISATION
| | | | |
|---|---|---|---|
| 70 | RCA SF 8111 | TONE FLOAT (LP) | 300 |

*(see also Kraftwerk)*

## ORGANISERS
| | | | |
|---|---|---|---|
| 66 | Pye 7N 17022 | Lonesome Road/The Organiser | 75 |

## ORGANUM
| | | | |
|---|---|---|---|
| 94 | Aeroplane AR 15 | Gloria (1-sided, numbered p/s, 113 only) | 50 |
| 95 | Aeroplane AR 16 | Lysis (1-sided, 72 only) | 50 |
| 95 | Aeroplane AR 17 | Kanroku (1-sided 12", black outer sleeve, illustrated, stamped, signed and no'd inner sleeve, 111 only) | 60 |
| 95 | Aeroplane AR 19 | Rotor (1-sided, signed, no'd, 83 only, p/s) | 60 |
| 95 | Aeroplane AR 20 | Arc (1-sided, signed, no'd, 85 only, p/s) | 50 |
| 96 | Aeroplane AR 23 | Shovels (1-sided, signed, no'd, 91 only, p/s) | 50 |
| 96 | Aeroplane AR 24 | Raw (1-sided, signed, no'd, 83 only, p/s) | 50 |
| 88 | United Dairies UN 023 | SUBMISSION (LP, 1000 only) | 40 |
| 94 | Aeroplane AR 14 | SPHYX (LP, black picture label, 546 only) | 20 |
| 94 | Aeroplane AR 14 | SPHYX (LP, blue picture label, 509 only, reissue) | 20 |

*(see also David Jackman)*

## ORGANUM/NEW BLOCKADERS
| | | | |
|---|---|---|---|
| 84 | Aeroplane AR 7 | Pulp Parts 1 & 2 (gatefold p/s, 279 only) | 60 |
| 85 | Laylah/Antirecords LAY 19 | IN EXTREMIS (LP) | 20 |
| 88 | Laylah LAY 012 | TOWER OF SILENCE (LP) | 20 |

*(see also Current 93, Nurse With Wound, Eddie Prevost Band, David Jackman, New Blockaders)*

## ORIGINAL CHECKMATES
| | | | |
|---|---|---|---|
| 62 | Pye 7N 15428 | Hot Toddy/Tuxedo Junction | 10 |
| 62 | Pye 7N 15442 | Checkmate Stomp/Begin The Beguine | 15 |
| 63 | Decca F 11688 | Union Pacific/The Spy | 30 |

*(see also Checkmates)*

## ORIGINAL DOWNTOWN SYNCOPATORS
| | | | |
|---|---|---|---|
| 63 | J.R.T. Davies DAVLP 301/2 | THE ORIGINAL DOWNTOWN SYNCOPATORS (10" LP, white labels only) | 10 |

*(see also Ron Geesin)*

## ORIGINAL DYAKS
| | | | |
|---|---|---|---|
| 67 | Columbia DB 8184 | Got To Get A Good Thing Going/Would You Love Me Too | 10 |

## ORIGINAL MIRRORS
| | | | |
|---|---|---|---|
| 79 | Mercury 6007 245 | Could This Be Heaven?Night Of The Angels (p/s) | 5 |

## ORIGINAL NEW ORLEANS RHYTHM KINGS
| | | | |
|---|---|---|---|
| 54 | Columbia SCM 5113 | Golden Leaf Strut/She's Crying For Me | 10 |

## ORIGINALS (1)
| | | | |
|---|---|---|---|
| 62 | Top Rank JAR 600 | Gimme A Little Kiss, Will Ya, Huh/At Times Like This | 35 |

## ORIGINALS (2)
| | | | |
|---|---|---|---|
| 67 | Tamla Motown TMG 592 | Goodnight Irene/Need Your Lovin', Want You Back | 80 |
| 67 | Tamla Motown TMG 592 | Goodnight Irene/Need Your Lovin', Want You Back (DJ copy) | 150 |
| 70 | Tamla Motown TMG 733 | Baby I'm For Real/The Moment Of Truth | 18 |
| 72 | Tamla Motown TMG 822 | God Bless Whoever Sent You/I Like Your Style/Baby I'm For Real | 8 |
| 69 | Tamla Motown TMG 702 | Green Grow The Lilacs/You're The One | 20 |
| 76 | Tamla Motown TMG 1066 | Six Million Dollar Man/Mother Nature's Best (unreleased) | 0 |
| 69 | Tamla Motown TML 11116 | GREEN GROW THE LILACS (LP, mono) | 60 |
| 69 | Tamla Motow STML 11116 | GREEN GROW THE LILACS (LP, stereo) | 55 |

## ORIGINAL SIN
| | | | |
|---|---|---|---|
| 84 | Sin S1N | The Shadow/Salvation (12", p/s, private pressing) | 25 |

## ORIGINAL TORNADOS
| | | | |
|---|---|---|---|
| 75 | SRT SRTS 75350 | Telstar/Red Rocket | 10 |

*(see also Tornados)*

## ORIGINATION
| | | | |
|---|---|---|---|
| 92 | Rudeboy RUDE 001 | Break Down/Bass/R.E.S.P.E.C.T. (12") | 15 |
| 92 | Rudeboy RUDE 002 | Breakdown (Remix)/Breakdown (Original Edit)/ Breaking Out The B-Line/Gimme Ya Luv (12") | 12 |
| 93 | Rudeboy RUDE 005 | Sunrise/Sunrise (Ruff Mix)/Make Ya Wanna Do Right/Out Of This World (12") | 10 |
| 93 | Rudeboy RUDE 006 | Music Takes Control/Signal To Noise/Music Takes Control (Remix) (12') | 10 |
| 94 | Rudeboy RUDE 007 | Shine on '94/Shine On (Unreleased '92 Remix)/ Shine On '94 (Dub Version)/Shine On (Original '92 Mix) (12") | 30 |

## ORIGINELLS 4
| | | | |
|---|---|---|---|
| 64 | Columbia DB 7259 | My Girl/Kathy (as Origenells) | 20 |
| 64 | Columbia DB 7388 | Nights/I Can Make You Mine | 18 |

## ORIGIN UNKNOWN
| | | | |
|---|---|---|---|
| 92 | Ram RAMM 002 | Untitled (6.03)/Untitled (5.01)/Untitled (5.22)/Untitled (6.12) (12", stamped white labels, promo only, not released) | 20 |
| 93 | Ram RAMM 004 | The Touch/Valley Of The Shadows (12") | 10 |
| 93 | Ram RAMM 004R | The Touch (Part 2)/Valley Of The Shadows (Long Dark Remix) (12") | 10 |
| 95 | Ram RAMM 014 | Truly one/Mission control (12") | 12 |
| 90s | Ram RAMM 002 | EASTERN PROMISE EP (12", stamped white label, 4 untitled tracks, promo only) | 120 |
| 96 | Ram RAMM 16 | Valley Of The Shadows (original Mix)/Valley Of The Shadows (Awake '96 Remix) (12") | 10 |

## ORION (1)
| | | | |
|---|---|---|---|
| 84 | Lost Moment LM 02 | Insane In Another World/Storm (p/s) | 15 |

## ORION (2)
| | | | |
|---|---|---|---|
| 87 | Gypsy GYP 001 | JACK ORION (LP) | 30 |

## ORIOR
| | | | |
|---|---|---|---|
| 79 | Crystal Groove 7E 2 | Elevation/Tutankhamen/Quiet Sky (wraparound p/s, insert) | 10 |

## TONY ORLANDO
| | | | |
|---|---|---|---|
| 61 | Fontana H 308 | Halfway To Paradise/Lonely Tomorrows | 20 |
| 61 | Fontana H 330 | Bless You/Am I The Guy | 10 |
| 61 | Fontana H 350 | Happy Times (Are Here To Stay)/Lonely Am I | 10 |
| 62 | Fontana H 366 | Talkin' About You/My Baby's A Stranger | 10 |
| 62 | Columbia DB 4871 | Chills/At The Edge Of Tears | 20 |
| 63 | Columbia DB 4954 | Beautiful Dreamer/The Loneliest | 25 |
| 63 | Columbia DB 4991 | Shirley/Joanie | 8 |
| 64 | Columbia DB 7288 | Tell Me What Can I Do/She Doesn't Know It | 10 |
| 63 | Columbia SEG 8238 | BLESS YOU (EP) | 40 |
| 63 | Fontana TFL 5167 | BLESS YOU (LP, mono) | 50 |
| 63 | Fontana STFL 582 | BLESS YOU (LP, stereo) | 60 |

## ORLANDO (1)
| | | | |
|---|---|---|---|
| 69 | NEMS 56-4159 | Am I The Same Guy/Poor Little Me | 100 |

## ORLONS
| | | | |
|---|---|---|---|
| 62 | Columbia DB 4865 | The Wah Watusi/Holiday Hill | 35 |
| 62 | Cameo Parkway C 231 | Don't Hang Up/The Conservative | 25 |
| 63 | Cameo Parkway C 243 | South Street/Them Terrible Boots | 20 |
| 63 | Cameo Parkway C 257 | Not Me/My Best Friend | 15 |
| 63 | Cameo Parkway C 273 | Crossfire/It's No Big Thing | 15 |
| 63 | Cameo Parkway C 287 | Bon Doo Wah/Don't Throw Your Love Away | 20 |
| 63 | Cameo Parkway C 295 | Shimmy Shimmy/Everything Nice | 15 |
| 64 | Cameo Parkway C 319 | Rules Of Love/Heartbreak Hotel | 15 |
| 64 | Cameo Parkway C 332 | Knock Knock (Who's There)/Goin' Places | 15 |
| 66 | Planet PLF 117 | Spinnin' Top/Anyone Who Had A Heart | 150 |
| 72 | Mojo 2092 029 | Spinnin' Top/Anyone Who Had A Heart (reissue) | 15 |
| 62 | Cameo Parkway C 1033 | ALL THE HITS (LP) | 60 |
| 63 | Cameo Parkway C 1061 | BIGGEST HITS (LP) | 60 |
| 78 | London HA-U 8504 | CAMEO PARKWAY SESSIONS (LP) | 30 |

*(see also Rosetta Hightower)*

## ORNAMENTAL
| | | | |
|---|---|---|---|
| 88 | One Little Indian 18TP 7 | Crystal Nights/Yonilingaphonics (p/s) | 5 |

*(see also Sugarcubes, Rose McDowall)*

## OROONIES
| | | | |
|---|---|---|---|
| 91 | Demi Monde DMLP 1027 | OF HOOF AND HORN (LP) | 18 |

## ORPHAN (1)
| | | | |
|---|---|---|---|
| 80 | Orphan Records ORP-1 | Little Mother/I Don't Want To Go (To Work Tomorrow), stamped inner sleeve and insert p/s | 20 |

## ORPHAN (2)
| | | | |
|---|---|---|---|
| 85 | Swoop RTLS 013 | Nervous/Little England (p/s) | 15 |

## ORPHEUS
| | | | |
|---|---|---|---|
| 66 | Red Bird RB 10-041 | My Life/Music Minus Orpheus | 40 |
| 68 | MGM MGM 1413 | I've Never Seen Love Like This/Lesley's World | 12 |
| 68 | MGM MGM C(S) 8072 | ORPHEUS (LP) | 25 |

## RIZ ORTOLANI
| | | | |
|---|---|---|---|
| 71 | United Artists UP 35278 | The Hunting Party/CAROL CARMICHAEL: Where's Poppa? | 8 |

## BETH ORTON
| | | | |
|---|---|---|---|
| 96 | Heavenly HVN 56 | I Wish I Never Saw The Sunshine (p/s, 1-sided limited edition, 500 only) | 20 |
| 96 | Heavenly HVNLP 17 | TRAILER PARK (LP, 100 copies only) | 50 |
| 99 | Heavenly HVNLP 22 | CENTRAL RESERVATION (2-LP, gatefold sleeve, 1000 copies only) | 30 |
| 02 | Heavenly HVNLP 37 | DAYBREAKER (LP) | 20 |
| 12 | Anti 7118-1 | SUGARING SEASON (LP & CD) | 15 |

*(see also Spill)*

## EILEEN OSBORNE
| | | | |
|---|---|---|---|
| 75 | Seagull SG1 | SINGING SHORES (LP) | 15 |

## MIKE OSBORNE
| | | | |
|---|---|---|---|
| 71 | Turtle TUR 300 | OUTBACK (LP) | 60 |
| 73 | Cadillac SGC 1002 | ORIGINAL (LP, as Mike Osborne & Stan Tracey) | 20 |
| 75 | Ogun OG 300 | BORDER CROSSING (LP) | 15 |
| 76 | Ogun OG 700 | ALL NIGHT LONG (LP) | 20 |
| 77 | Ogun OG 210 | TANDEM - LIVE AT BRACKNELL FESTIVAL (LP, with Stan Tracey) | 18 |
| 77 | Ogun OG 810 | MARCEL'S MUSE (LP) | 25 |

*(see also Stan Tracey)*

## OZZY OSBOURNE
| | | | |
|---|---|---|---|
| 80 | Jet JET 197 | Crazy Train/You Looking At Me Looking At You (p/s) | 6 |
| 80 | Jet JET 7003 | Mr. Crowley (live)/You Said It All (live) (p/s) | 8 |
| 80 | Jet JET 12003 | Mr. Crowley (live)/You Said It All (live)/Suicide Solution (live) (12", p/s) | 10 |
| 80 | Jet JETP 12003 | Mr. Crowley (live)/You Said It All (live)/Suicide Solution (live) (12", picture disc) | 15 |
| 81 | Jet JET 7017 | Over The Mountain/I Don't Know (p/s) | 5 |
| 82 | Jet JET 7030 | Symptom Of The Universe/N.I.B. (p/s) | 6 |
| 82 | Jet JETP 7030 | Symptom Of The Universe/N.I.B. (picture disc) | 10 |
| 83 | Epic TA 3915 | Bark At The Moon/One Up The B-Side (12", p/s, silver vinyl) | 15 |
| 83 | Epic WA 3915 | Bark At The Moon/One Up The B-Side (12", picture disc, unreleased) | 0 |
| 84 | Epic WA 4452 | So Tired/Bark At The Moon (live)/Waiting For Darkness/Suicide Solution/Paranoid (live) (12", p/s, gold vinyl) | 12 |
| 86 | Epic A 6859 | Shot In The Dark/Rock'n'Roll Rebel (p/s, with signature card) | 6 |
| 86 | Epic QA 6859 | Shot In The Dark/Rock'n'Roll Rebel (poster p/s) | 8 |
| 86 | Epic A 7311 | The Ultimate Sin/Lightning Strikes (p/s, with free patch) | 5 |

# Johnny OSBOURNE (& SENSATIONS)

| 91 | Epic 657 4406 | No More Tears (extended version)/S.I.N./Party With The Animals (12" pic. disc).......... 12 |
|----|---------------|------------------------------------------------------------------------------|
| 86 | Epic EPC 11-26404 | THE ULTIMATE SIN (LP, picture disc) ................................................ 20 |

*(see also Black Sabbath)*

## JOHNNY OSBOURNE (& SENSATIONS)

| 70 | Big Shot BI 549 | See And Blind (solo)/THE TECHNIQUES: Scar Face .............................. 30 |
|----|-----------------|--------------------------------------------------------------|
| 72 | Techniques TE 916 | See And Blind/TECHNIQUES ALL STARS: Rema Skank ........................ 30 |
| 80 | Jammys JM 002 | Long Long Life/HIGH MUNDELL: Walk With Jah (12") ...................... 15 |
| 80 | Cha Cha CHAD 27 | Kiss Somebody/Version (12") ............................................ 30 |
| 80 | Black Joy DH 810 | Purify Your Heart/Politician (blue vinyl) ................................ 30 |
| 80 | Greensleeves GRED 34 | Fally Ranking/Trench Town School (12") ................................ 30 |
| 81 | Greensleeves GRED 50 | Back Off (with PAPA TULLO).Dub (12") ................................ 35 |
| 81 | Cha Cha CHAD 31 | Nightfall/Dub Fall (12") .................................................. 20 |
| 81 | Greensleeves GRED 60 | Trying To Turn Me On/Turn On Dub (12") ............................ 15 |
| 81 | Simba LION 1 | 13 Dead (Nothing Said)/Black Lion Band Murder (12") .................. 25 |
| 81 | Simba SIM 002 | Don't Bite The Hand (with ASWAD)/Dub (10") ........................ 25 |
| 82 | Oak Sounds OSD 006 | Yo Yo/ECHO MINOTT : Man In Love (12") ............................ 15 |
| 86 | Greensleeves GRED 208 | Dub Plate Playing/COCOA TEA: Cocoa Tea Medley (12") ................ 40 |
| 89 | Live & Love LLD 119 | Chain Grabber/Watch Them A Watch (12", with PAPPA SAN) .......... 15 |
| 70 | Trojan TTL29 | COME BACK DARLING (LP) ............................................ 40 |
| 73 | Big Shot BILP 103 | READY OR NOT (LP) .................................................... 75 |
| 80 | Greensleeves GREL 12 | FALLY LOVER (LP, red vinyl) .......................................... 30 |
| 80 | Jammy's JAM 1000 | FOLLY RANKING (LP) .................................................. 30 |
| 81 | Cha Cha CHALP 010 | IN NAH DISCO STYLE (LP) ............................................ 40 |
| 81 | Black Joy DHLP 2001 | WARRIOR (LP) ........................................................ 20 |
| 82 | Arrival ALP 002 | YO YO (LP) ............................................................ 15 |
| 82 | Greensleeves GREL 38 | NEVER STOP FIGHTING (LP) ........................................ 15 |
| 84 | Selection SELP 01 | REALITY (LP) .......................................................... 25 |

## BOB OSBURN

| 64 | London HLD 9869 | Bound To Happen/Think Of Me ...................................... 15 |
|----|-----------------|--------------------------------------------------------------|

## OSCAR BICYCLE

| 68 | CBS 3237 | On A Quiet Night/The Room Revolves Around Me .................... 60 |
|----|----------|--------------------------------------------------------------|

## OSCAR (1)

| 66 | Reaction 591 003 | Club Of Lights/Waking Up ............................................ 60 |
|----|------------------|--------------------------------------------------------------|
| 66 | Reaction 591 006 | Join My Gang/Days Gone By ........................................ 40 |
| 67 | Reaction 591 012 | Over The Wall We Go/Every Day Of My Life .......................... 40 |
| 67 | Reaction 591 016 | Holiday/Give Her All She Wants .................................... 30 |
| 68 | Polydor 56257 | Open Up The Skies/Wild Ones........................................ 30 |

*(see also Paul Dean, Paul Nicholas)*

## OSCAR (2)

| 74 | Buk BULP 2001 | OSCAR (LP) .......................................................... 15 |
|----|---------------|--------------------------------------------------------------|

## OSCILLATORS

| 79 | Warren Records WAR-SEP-465 | Leonard Cheshire/Fast Breeder Reactor (fold-out p/s, with or without 'group' drawing, 1000 only) ...................................................... 60 |
|----|-----|------|
| 80 | Yawn SRTS/80/CUS693 | Marilyn Brown/E-Boat (fold out p/s) .................................. 20 |

## PETER OSGOOD

| 70 | Penny Farthing PEN 715 | Chelsea/Stamford Bridge ............................................ 10 |
|----|------------------------|--------------------------------------------------------------|

## OSIBISA

| 71 | Smooke 001 | Black Ant/Kotoko .................................................... 20 |
|----|------------|--------------------------------------------------------------|
| 71 | MCA MDKS 8001 | OSIBISA (LP, gatefold, purple/red 'dogbone' label) .................... 30 |
| 71 | MCA MDKS 8005 | WOYAYA (LP, gatefold, black/blue/white hexagon label) .............. 20 |
| 72 | MCA MDKS 8007 | HEADS (LP, gatefold, black/blue/white label) ........................ 20 |
| 73 | Buddah 2318 087 | SUPER FLY T.N.T. (LP, soundtrack).................................. 15 |

*(see also Del Richardson)*

## OSMOSIS

| 70 | RCA VICTOR LPS 4369 | OSMOSIS (LP)........................................................ 20 |
|----|---------------------|--------------------------------------------------------------|

## OSMOND BROTHERS

| 63 | MGM MGM 1208 | Be My Little Baby Bumble Bee/I Wouldn't Know .................... 15 |
|----|--------------|--------------------------------------------------------------|
| 63 | MGM MGM 1245 | Travels Of Jamie McPheeters/Aura Lee .............................. 12 |
| 63 | MGM MGM-C 1011 | NEW SOUND OF THE BROTHERS (LP) .............................. 30 |

## OSSIE & SWEET BOYS

| 67 | Polydor 56167 | Nothing Takes The Place Of You/Brixton Boo-Ga-Loo................ 15 |
|----|---------------|--------------------------------------------------------------|

## OSSIE & UPSETTERS

| 66 | Doctor Bird DB 1018 | Turn Me On/True Love .............................................. 30 |
|----|---------------------|--------------------------------------------------------------|

*(see also Upsetters, Desmond Dekkar)*

## AL OSTER

| 60s | Dominion LP 1321 | ECHO OF THE YUKON (LP)............................................ 20 |
|-----|------------------|--------------------------------------------------------------|

## OSU

| 83 | Shaka XAKA 2 | Light Up My Fire/Merry Go Round (p/s) .............................. 10 |
|----|--------------|--------------------------------------------------------------|

## GILBERT O'SULLIVAN

| 71 | Columbia DB 8779 | I Wish I Could Cry/Mr Moody's Garden .............................. 8 |
|----|------------------|--------------------------------------------------------------|

*(see also Gilbert)*

## PETER O'SULLIVAN

| 76 | Charisma CAS 1160 | PETER O'SULLIVAN TALKS TURF (LP) ................................ 15 |
|----|-------------------|--------------------------------------------------------------|

## RAMON OTANO

| 64 | Jump Up/Island JU 250 | Fiesta En La Joya/Mambo Trinidad ................................ 10 |
|----|-----------------------|--------------------------------------------------------------|

## OTHER BROTHERS

| 69 | Pama PM 785 | Let's Get Together/Little Girl ........................................ 25 |
|----|-------------|--------------------------------------------------------------|

## OTHER SIDE
| | | |
|---|---|---|
| 87 | Casual Sax SRT 8KS 1432 | Is It Any Wonder/Let's Be Perfect (p/s) ...... 40 |

## OTHER TWO (1)
| | | |
|---|---|---|
| 64 | Decca F 11911 | I Wanna Be With You/Grumbling Guitar ...... 12 |
| 65 | RCA RCA 1465 | Don't You Wanna Love Me Baby/Hold Back The Light Of Dawn ...... 10 |
| 66 | RCA RCA 1531 | I'll Never Let You Go/Hot At Night ...... 12 |

*(see also Storyteller, J.J. Jackson)*

## OTHER TWO (2)
| | | |
|---|---|---|
| 93 | London 520028.1 | THE OTHER TWO AND YOU (LP) ...... 20 |

## OTHERS
| | | |
|---|---|---|
| 64 | Fontana TF 501 | Oh Yeah/I'm Taking Her Home ...... 60 |

*(see also Sands, Sundragon)*

## JOHNNY OTIS SHOW
| | | |
|---|---|---|
| 57 | Capitol CL 14794 | Ma (He's Makin' Eyes At Me)/Romance In The Dark ...... 5 |
| 58 | Capitol CL 14817 | Bye Bye Baby (as Johnny Otis Show with Marie Adams)/Good Golly ...... 15 |
| 58 | Capitol CL 14837 | The Light Still Shines In My Window/All I Want Is Your Love (with Marie Adams) ...... 25 |
| 58 | Capitol CL 14854 | Well, Well, Well, Well!/You Just Kissed Me Goodbye (with Mel Williams) ...... 25 |
| 58 | Capitol CL 14875 | Ring-A-Ling/The Johnny Otis Hand Jive ...... 25 |
| 58 | Capitol CL 14875 | Ring-A-Ling/The Johnny Otis Hand Jive (78) ...... 20 |
| 58 | Capitol CL 14941 | Crazy Country Hop/Willie Did The Cha Cha ...... 25 |
| 59 | Capitol CL 15008 | You/My Dear (as Johnny Otis Show with Mel Williams) ...... 18 |
| 59 | Capitol CL 15018 | Castin' My Spell/Telephone Baby (as Johnny Otis Show with Marci Lee) ...... 25 |
| 59 | Capitol CL 15057 | Three Girls Named Molly Doin' The Hully Gully/I'll Do The Same Thing For You ...... 20 |
| 60 | Capitol CL 15112 | Mumblin' Mosie/Hey Baby, Don't You Know? ...... 15 |
| 64 | Ember EMB S 192 | Hand Jive One More Time/Baby I Got News For You ...... 10 |
| 69 | Sonet SON 608 | Country Girl/Signifyin' Monkey ...... 6 |
| 72 | Epic EPC 7896 | The Watts Breakaway/You Can Depend On Me ...... 8 |
| 72 | Epic EPC 8071 | The Watts Breakaway/Willie And The Hand Jive ...... 8 |
| 59 | Capitol EAP1 1134 | THE JOHNNY OTIS SHOW (EP) ...... 25 |
| 65 | Vocalion VEP 170162 | JOHNNY OTIS (EP) ...... 50 |
| 58 | Capitol T 940 | THE JOHNNY OTIS SHOW (LP) ...... 100 |
| 69 | Sonet SNTF 613 | COLD SHOT (LP) ...... 15 |
| 72 | Ember SPE 6604 | FORMIDABLE (LP) ...... 15 |

*(see also Marie Adams)*

## SHUGGIE OTIS
| | | |
|---|---|---|
| 70 | CBS 63996 | HERE COMES SHUGGIE OTIS (LP) ...... 30 |

*(see also Al Kooper & Shuggie Otis)*

## NOIT OTNI & PITS
| | | |
|---|---|---|
| 79 | Automotive AERS 107 | A Heart Can Only Be Broken Once/Moving Target (in p/s) ...... 35 |
| 79 | Automotive AERS 107 | A Heart Can Only Be Broken Once/Moving Target ...... 25 |

## FRAN O TOOLE
| | | |
|---|---|---|
| 74 | Emerald MD 1179 | Clap Your Hands And Stamp Your Feet/Drift Away ...... 10 |

## JOHN OTWAY
| | | |
|---|---|---|
| 72 | County COUN 215 | Gypsy/Misty Mountain (private pressing, County Recording Service, Bracknell on label, with duplicated lyric sheet) ...... 25 |
| 76 | Viking YRS CF 01 | Louisa On A Horse/Beware Of The Flowers (private pressing) ...... 15 |
| 78 | Polydor 2059 001 | Geneve/It's A Long Time Since I Heard Homestead On The Farm (p/s) ...... 5 |
| 78 | Polydor 2059 060 | Baby's In The Club/Julie Julie Julie (p/s) ...... 5 |
| 79 | Polydor 2059 105 | Frightened And Scared (instrumental)/Are You On My Side? (p/s, only 3 copies pressed!) ...... 50 |
| 80 | Stiff BUY 101 | Green Green Grass Of Home/Wednesday Club (p/s) ...... 5 |
| 82 | Empire HAM 3 | In Dreams/You Ain't Seen Nothing Yet (as John Otway Sweat, p/s) ...... 5 |
| 86 | 'Warner Bros' OTWEAY 1 | The New Jerusalem/The Tyger (private pressing) ...... 20 |

## JOHN OTWAY & WILD WILLY BARRETT
| | | |
|---|---|---|
| 73 | Track 2094 111 | Murder Man/If I Did ...... 8 |
| 76 | Track 2094 133 | Louisa On A Horse/Misty Mountain ...... 5 |
| 77 | Polydor 2058 916 | Racing Cars (Jet Spotter Of The Track)/Running From The Law (p/s) ...... 10 |
| 77 | Polydor 2058 951 | Really Free/Beware Of The Flowers (Cos I'm Sure They're Going To Get You Yeh) (p/s) ...... 6 |
| 77 | Polydor 2058 951 | Really Free/Beware Of The Flowers (Cos I'm Sure They're Going To Get You Yeh) (die-cut 'review' sleeve) ...... 5 |
| 82 | Stiff Indie STIN 1 | Headbutts/Live Version Headbutts (p/s) ...... 7 |
| 82 | Empire HAM 5T | 12 STITCH EP (12" EP in polythene bag with jay-card) ...... 15 |
| 87 | VM VMS 6 | The Last Of The Mohicans/Fashion (brown paper bag sleeve) ...... 5 |
| 77 | Extracted EXLP 1 | JOHN OTWAY AND WILD WILLY BARRETT (LP, handmade stickered sleeve) ...... 20 |
| 77 | White label OBL 1 | OTWAY AND BARRETT LIVE AT THE ROUNDHOUSE (private pressing LP, freebie, handwritten labels, plain sleeve, 250 numbered copies only) ...... 35 |

*(see also Wild Willy Barrett)*

## OUCH
| | | |
|---|---|---|
| 92 | Cavell CVLL 1 | I Need You More/Carina ...... 7 |

## OUR PLASTIC DREAM
| | | |
|---|---|---|
| 67 | Go AJ 11411 | A Little Bit Of Shangrila/Encapsulated Marigold ...... 200 |

## OUT
| | | |
|---|---|---|
| 79 | Rabid TOSH 113 | Who Is Innocent/Linda's Just A Statue (p/s) ...... 7 |

## OUTCASTS
| | | |
|---|---|---|
| 78 | It IT 4 | Frustration/Don't Want To Be No Adult/You're A Disease (p/s) ...... 30 |
| 78 | Good Vibrations GOT 3 | Just Another Teenage Rebel/Love Is For Sops (poster p/s, various colours; 'band' p/s) ...... 25 |
| 78 | Good Vibrations GOT 3 | Just Another Teenage Rebel/Love Is For Sops (poster p/s, various colours; 'type' p/s) ...... 25 |
| 79 | Good Vibrations GOT 17 | Self Conscious Over You/Love You For Never (p/s) ...... 15 |
| 81 | GBH GBH 001 | Magnum Force/Gangland Warfare (p/s) ...... 20 |

MINT VALUE £

| 81 | Outcasts Only 0001 | Programme Love/Beating And Screaming (Parts 1 & 2)/Mania (p/s)........................5 |
| 79 | Good Vibrations BIG 1 | SELF CONSCIOUS OVER YOU (LP) ...........................................25 |

## OUTER LIMITS
| 60s | Teldisc TD 154 | Paradise For Two/Don't Ever Change...................................20 |
| 67 | Deram DM 125 | Just One More Chance/Help Me Please...............................30 |
| 68 | Instant IN 001 | Great Train Robbery/Sweet Freedom...................................50 |
| 70s | Snow/Deroy 1049 | (I'm Not) Your Stepping Stone/Great Balls Of Fire.....................500 |

## OUTER LIMITS
| 67 | Elephant LUR 100 | When The Work Is Thru'/5 MAN CARGO: What A Wonderful Feeling (Leeds Students Charity Rag record) ...............................55 |
| 68 | Immediate IM 067 | Great Train Robbery/Sweet Freedom (demo only)......................70 |
| 71 | Decca F 13176 | The Dark Side Of The Moon/Black Boots ...............................10 |

*(see also Christie, Acid Gallery)*

## OUTLAW BLUES BAND
| 69 | Stateside SSL 10290 | BREAKING IN (LP) ...........................................30 |

## OUTLAW POSSE
| 91 | Outlaw OP1 | Sonz Of The Devil (12")...........................................12 |

## OUTLAWS
| 61 | HMV POP 844 | Swingin' Low/Spring Is Near ...........................................15 |
| 61 | HMV POP 877 | Ambush/Indian Brave ...........................................15 |
| 61 | HMV POP 927 | Valley Of The Sioux/Crazy Drums ...................................20 |
| 62 | HMV POP 990 | Ku-pow!/Last Stage West ...........................................20 |
| 62 | HMV POP 1074 | Sioux Serenade/Fort Knox ...........................................20 |
| 63 | HMV POP 1124 | The Return Of The Outlaws/Texan Spiritual ..........................20 |
| 63 | HMV POP 1195 | That Set The Wild West Free/Hobo ...................................20 |
| 63 | HMV POP 1241 | Law And Order/Do-Da-Day...........................................20 |
| 64 | HMV POP 1277 | Keep-A-Knockin'/Shake With Me ...................................20 |
| 61 | HMV CLP 1489 | DREAM OF THE WEST (LP, mauve label, gold print)....................40 |
| 61 | HMV CLP 1489 | DREAM OF THE WEST (LP, later black label)..........................80 |

*(see also Mike Berry, Bobbie Graham, Chaps, Rally Rounders, Houston Wells [& Marksmen])*

## OUT OF DARKNESS
| 70 | Key KL 006 | OUT OF DARKNESS (LP, laminated front sleeve)......................200 |

## OUT OF ORDER
| 81 | Daviton SPEP 120 | OUT OF CONTROL (EP, export copy, 500 only)........................40 |

## OUTPATIENTS
| 80 | KIK 1 | Life On Earth/Home Is Where The Heart Is (with p/s).................50 |
| 80 | KIK 1 | Life On Earth/Home Is Where The Heart Is (without p/s)..............30 |

## OUTRAGE
| 70 | Kama Sutra 618 027 | The Letter/The Way I See It...........................................5 |

## OUTRIDERS
| 74 | Dart ART 20149 | The Telegram Song/Love You More Than Any Other ..................8 |

## OUTSIDERS (U.K.)
| 78 | Xciting Plastic | Vital Hours/Take Up (unissued)...........................................0 |

*(see also Second Layer, Sound)*

## OUTSIDERS (U.K. 1)
| 65 | Decca F 12213 | Keep On Doing It/Songs We Sang Last Summer ........................35 |

*(see also Bunch Of Fives, Junior's Eyes, Tickle)*

## OUTSIDERS (U.K. 2)
| 77 | Raw Edge RER 002 | ONE TO INFINITY (EP)........................................... |
| 77 | Raw Edge RER 001 | CALLING ON YOUTH (LP, laminated sleeve)..........................25 |
| 78 | Raw Edge RER 003 | CLOSE UP (LP, with insert) ...........................................45 |
|  |  | ...........................................40 |

## OUTSIDERS (U.S.)
| 66 | Capitol CL 15435 | Time Won't Let Me/Was It Really Real?................................ |
| 66 | Capitol CL 15435 | Time Won't Let Me/Was It Really Real? (DJ copy).....................35 |
| 66 | Capitol CL 15450 | Girl In Love/What Makes You So Bad, You Weren't Brought Up That Way ..50 |
| 66 | Capitol CL 15468 | Respectable/Lost In My World ...........................................15 |
| 66 | Capitol CL 15480 | Help Me Girl/You Gotta Look...........................................20 |
| 67 | Capitol CL 15495 | I'll Give You Time/I'm Not Tryin' To Hurt You .........................10 |
|  |  | ...........................................20 |

## OUTSKIRTS OF INFINITY
| 87 | Woronzow WOO 7 | LORD OF THE DARK SKIES (LP) ...................................... |
| 94 | Dark Skies DSKLP 2 | INCIDENT AT PILATUS (2-LP) ...........................................15 |
|  |  | ...........................................18 |

## OUT TO LUNCH
| 76 | Transatlantic BIG 547 | Jeepers Creepers/Everythings Nice........................................6 |

## OVALTINEES
| 83 | BAA 021 | BRITISH JUSTICE EP (p/s) ...........................................80 |

## OVARY LODGE
| 73 | RCA SF 8372 | OVARY LODGE (LP) ...........................................100 |
| 76 | Ogun OG 600 | OVARY LODGE (LP) ...........................................30 |

*(see also Keith Tippett)*

## OVATIONZ
| 81 | Dread At The Controls DCD 005 | Forever Love/Forever Dub (12") ...................................15 |

## OVERCOMERS
| 68 | Bamboo BAM 64 | Stop And Let Me Tell You/Take Courage Soul (unissued: white labels only)..................50 |

## OVERDRIVE
| 81 | Boring Grantham BGR 1 | ON THE RUN (EP) ...........................................80 |

## OVERKILL
| | | |
|---|---|---|
| 80 | Killer EJSP 9357 | Elemental/On My Own ............................................................................ 75 |

## OVERLANDERS
| | | |
|---|---|---|
| 63 | Pye 7N 15544 | Summer Skies And Golden Sands/Call Of The Wild .................................... 12 |
| 63 | Pye 7N 15568 | Movin'/Rainbow ...................................................................................... 7 |
| 66 | Pye NEP 24245 | MICHELLE (EP) ......................................................................................... 25 |
| 66 | Pye NPL 18138 | MICHELLE (LP, laminated front sleeve with flipbacks) .............................. 35 |

*(see also Cuppa T)*

## OVERLOAD
| | | |
|---|---|---|
| 80 | MCA MCA 618 | Into Overload/Follow The Lines (p/s) ...................................................... 10 |
| 81 | MCA MCA 656 | Who Are You/Drift Away .......................................................................... 10 |

## OVERLORD
| | | |
|---|---|---|
| 78 | Airebeat ABT 3 | Lucy/Guardsman/Johnny (p/s) ................................................................. 30 |

## RUNE OVERMAN
| | | |
|---|---|---|
| 63 | Decca F 11605 | Big Bass Boogie/Madison Piano ............................................................... 10 |

## OVERNIGHT PLAYERS
| | | |
|---|---|---|
| 80 | Cha Cha CHALP 008 | BABYLON DESTRUCTION (LP) .................................................................... 35 |

## OVERTAKERS
| | | |
|---|---|---|
| 68 | Amalgamated AMG 803 | That's The Way You Like It/The Big Take-Over .......................................... 50 |
| 68 | Amalgamated AMG 809 | Girl You Ruff/KEITH BLAKE: Woo Oh Oh ................................................... 50 |

## OWEN (GRAY) & DANDY (LIVINGSTONE)
| | | |
|---|---|---|
| 69 | Downtown DT 428 | Lovey Dovey/HERBIE GRAY & RUDIES: Kitty Wait ....................................... 8 |

## OWEN (DA SILVERA) & LEON
| | | |
|---|---|---|
| 64 | Island WI 146 | Nextdoor Neighbour/ROLAND ALPHONSO: Feeling Fine ........................... 25 |
| 64 | Island WI 163 | My Love For You/How Many Times ........................................................... 25 |
| 64 | Island WI 164 | The Fits Is On Me/SKATALITES: Good News .............................................. 25 |
| 64 | Island WI 165 | Running Around/SKATALITES: Around The World ..................................... 30 |
| 65 | Island WI 170 | I Want My Cock/I Am Only Human (DERAK HARRIOTT) (probably withdrawn) ............. 50 |
| 65 | Ska Beat JB 189 | Woman/BABA BROOKS with DON DRUMMOND: Doctor Decker ................ 25 |

*(see also Leon & Owen, Tommy McCook)*

## OWEN (GRAY) & MILLIE
| | | |
|---|---|---|
| 62 | Blue Beat BB 96 | Sit And Cry/Do You Know (with City Slickers Orchestra) ........................... 10 |
| 62 | Island WI 014 | Sugar Plum/OWEN GRAY: Jezebel ........................................................... 15 |

*(see also Owen Gray, Millie, Owen & Leon, Leon & Owen)*

## RAY OWEN('S MOON)
| | | |
|---|---|---|
| 69 | Fontana TF 1045 | Tonight I'll Be Staying Here With You/Down, Don't Bother Me (solo) ......... 6 |
| 71 | Polydor 2058 095 | Hey Sweety/Free Man (as Ray Owen's Moon) ............................................ 7 |
| 71 | Polydor 2066-119 | Try My Love/Talk To Me .......................................................................... 25 |
| 71 | Polydor 2325 061 | RAY OWEN'S MOON (LP, textured sleeve) ................................................ 80 |

*(see also Juicy Lucy)*

## REG OWEN & HIS ORCHESTRA
| | | |
|---|---|---|
| 56 | Parlophone PMD 1045 | SWING ME HIGH (10" LP) ......................................................................... 20 |

## BUCK OWENS (& BUCKAROOS)
| | | |
|---|---|---|
| 59 | Capitol CL 15009 | Everlasting Love/Second Fiddle .............................................................. 10 |
| 60 | Capitol CL 15123 | Above And Beyond/Til These Dreams Come True ....................................... 7 |
| 60 | Capitol CL 15162 | Excuse Me (I Think I've Got A Heartache)/I've Got A Right To Know ............ 7 |
| 61 | Capitol CL 15187 | Foolin' Around/High As The Mountain ...................................................... 5 |
| 62 | Longhorn BLH 0006 | Down On The Corner Of Love/Right After The Dance (estimated that 1000 pressed) ...... 7 |
| 63 | Capitol CL 15321 | Love's Gonna Live Here/Getting Used To Losing You .................................. 5 |
| 64 | Capitol CL 15364 | Together Again/Ain't It Amazin' Gracie (as Buck Owens & Buckaroos) ........ 5 |
| 65 | Capitol CL 15379 | I've Got A Tiger By The Tail/Cryin' Time .................................................... 5 |
| 66 | Capitol CL 15452 | Think Of Me/Heart Of Glass ..................................................................... 5 |
| 67 | Capitol CL 15501 | Sam's Place/Don't Ever Tell Me Goodbye (as Buck Owens & Buckaroos)...... 5 |
| 63 | Capitol EAP1 1550 | FOOLIN' AROUND (EP) ............................................................................. 10 |
| 65 | Capitol EAP1 20602 | ACT NATURALLY (EP) ............................................................................... 10 |

## DONNIE OWENS
| | | |
|---|---|---|
| 58 | London HLU 8747 | Need You/If I'm Wrong............................................................................ 25 |
| 59 | London HLW 8897 | Ask Me Anything/Between Midnight And Dawn (unissued) ........................ 0 |

## JAMIE OWENS
| | | |
|---|---|---|
| 73 | Light LS 7012 | LAUGHTER IN YOUR SOUL (LP) ................................................................ 15 |

## OWL
| | | |
|---|---|---|
| 68 | United Artists UP 2240 | Run To The Sun/Shades Of Blue And Green Water Flies .............................. 20 |

## O.W.L.
| | | |
|---|---|---|
| 70s | Shebazz SHE 002 | Shady Tree/4TH STREET ORCHESTRA: Sun Hot .......................................... 8 |

## TONY OXLEY (QUARTET)
| | | |
|---|---|---|
| 69 | CBS 52664 | THE BAPTISED TRAVELLER (LP) ............................................................... 120 |
| 70 | CBS 64071 | 4 COMPOSITIONS FOR SEXTET (LP, with Derek Bailey) ............................ 125 |
| 71 | RCA SF 8215 | ICHNOS (LP) ........................................................................................... 90 |
| 70s | Incus INCUS 8 | TONY OXLEY (LP, with Derek Bailey, et al.) ............................................. 100 |
| 70s | Incus INCUS 18 | FEBRUARY PAPERS (LP) ........................................................................... 40 |
| 80s | Bead BEAD 25 | THE GLIDER & THE GRINDER (LP) ............................................................. 30 |

*(see also Derek Bailey, Howard Riley)o*

## TONY OXLEY, WOLFGANG FUCHS, PHILIPP WACHSMANN & HUGH METCALFE
| | | |
|---|---|---|
| 87 | Bead Records BEAD 25 | THE GLIDER AND THE GRINDER (LP) ......................................................... 20 |

## OXYM
| | | |
|---|---|---|
| 80 | Cargo CRS 003 | Music Power/Mind Key (p/s)..................................................................... 40 |

MINT VALUE £

## OYSTER BAND
| | | | |
|---|---|---|---|
| 86 | Cooking Vinyl FRY 001 | Hal-an-Tow/Ashes To Ashes (p/s) | 6 |
| 89 | Cooking Vinyl FRYX 012 | Love Vigilantes/Polish Plain/I Fought The Law (Live)/Between The Wars (Live) (10", pink vinyl, poster sleeve) | 10 |
| 82 | Pukka YOP 01 | ENGLISH ROCK 'N' ROLL, 1800-1850 (LP) | 30 |
| 85 | Pukka YOP 04 | LIE BACK AND THINK OF ENGLAND (LP) | 30 |
| 85 | Pukka YOP 07 | LIBERTY HALL (LP) | 30 |

## OYSTER CEILIDH BAND
| | | | |
|---|---|---|---|
| 80 | Dingles DIN 309 | JACK'S ALIVE (LP) | 20 |

## OZARKS
| | | | |
|---|---|---|---|
| 63 | Vocalion V 9210 | Who Stole My Bird Dog/Any Waltz | 30 |

## OZO
| | | | |
|---|---|---|---|
| 76 | DJM DJS 628 | Listen To The Buddah/Kites | 6 |
| 77 | DJM DJT 10764 | Anambra (Edited Version)/Anambra (12") | 35 |
| 82 | Sphinx SPS 1201 | Anambra River (Tranquil Rivers From The Floating Crystal City Of Budatan Shire Of Western Heaven)/Skintight (No Room To Move Up) (12") | 15 |
| 76 | DJM DJF 20488 | LISTEN TO THE BUDDHA (LP) | 40 |

## OZRIC TENTACLES
| | | | |
|---|---|---|---|
| 91 | Dovetail DOVEST 3 | Sploosh!/Live Throbbe (12" P/s) | 10 |
| 89 | Demi-Monde DMLP 1017 | PUNGENT EFFULGENT (LP) | 18 |
| 90 | Dovetail Records DOVE LP1 | ERPLAND (2-LP) | 25 |
| 91 | Dovetail DOVE LP 3 | STRANGETUDE (LP) | 15 |
| 92 | Black Adder OZT 01 | MUCK KICKER (LP) | 20 |
| 93 | Dovetail DOVELP6 | JURASSIC SHIFT (LP) | 15 |
| 94 | Dovetail DOVE LP7 | ARBORESCENE (2-LP) | 25 |
| 94 | Dovetail DOVEBOX 1 | VITAMIN ENHANCED (6-CD box set) | 30 |

*(see also Oroonies)*

## AUGUSTUS PABLO
| | | | |
|---|---|---|---|
| 71 | Big Shot BI 578 | The Mood/HERMAN CHIN-LOY: New Love | 40 |
| 71 | Big Shot BI 579 | East Of The River Nile/HERMAN CHIN-LOY: East Of River Nile Version (B-side actually by Aquarians) | 40 |
| 71 | Creole CR 1004 | 405 (actually "The Mood" by Tommy McCook)/Duck It Up (actually "Confidential Version" by Charmers) | 25 |
| 71 | Ackee ACK 134 | Still Yet/AQUARIANS: Version | 20 |
| 71 | Ackee ACK 138 | Snowball And Pudding/AQUARIANS: Version | 20 |
| 71 | Duke DU 122 | Reggae In The Fields/TOMMY McCOOK: Love Brother | 40 |
| 73 | Randy's RAN 536 | Bedroom Mazurka (as Augustus Pablo & Fay)/Melodica Version | 30 |
| 73 | Atra ATRA 011 | Lover's Mood/Lover's Rock | 25 |
| 74 | Tropical AL 025 | Too Late/Dub Organiser | 15 |
| 74 | Tropical AL 035 | Tales Of Pablo/BOOTHE STARS: Tales Dub | 15 |
| 74 | Sydna DL1276 | Pablo's Mercy/Version | 20 |
| 75 | Fay Music FM 603 | Fort Augustus Rock/Augustus In Kingston | 20 |
| 75 | Island WIP 6226 | King Tubby Meets The Rockers Uptown/Baby I Love You So | 25 |
| 75 | Island 12 WIP 6226 | King Tubby Meets The Rockers Uptown/JACOB MILLER: Baby I Love You So (12") | 30 |
| 75 | Treble C CCC06 | Liberation/Dubbing Pablo | 15 |
| 75 | Treble C CCC014 | Don Drummond/Thunderbolt Lady | 15 |
| 77 | Hawkeye HE 005 | East Of The River Nile/East Africa | 15 |
| 77 | Solid Sound SS1 | Doug's Love/Version | 15 |
| 78 | Rough Trade RT 002 | Pablo Meets Mr. Bassie/Mr. Bassie Special (with Rockers All Stars) (with colour sticker) | 10 |
| 77 | EJI 011 | No Entry/BIG YOUTH: Strictly Rockers (12") | 40 |
| 79 | Rockers APD 5 | Power Of The Trinity/West Abyssinia Dub (12") | 30 |
| 79 | Rockers APD 6 | Twin Seal/Dub/NORRIS REID: Entrance To Jah World (12") | 25 |
| 79 | Rockers AP 1023 | Crucial Burial/ROCKERS ALL STARS: Pope Paul Feel It/Sound Of Redemption - Scientist In Dub (12") | 30 |
| 79 | Rockers AB1 | Israel In Harmony/HUGH MUNDELL: Feeling Alright/Dub (12") | 35 |
| 80 | Rockers APD 7 | Hot Milk/Dub/Robin Bay Step/Dub (12") | 25 |
| 74 | Tropical TROPS 101 | THIS IS AUGUSTO PABLO (LP) | 45 |
| 75 | Trojan TRLS 115 | ITAL DUB (LP, original issue with "12 Neasden Lane" address on sleeve and rough orange/white paper labels) | 30 |
| 75 | Nationwide NW 03 | THRILLER (LP) | 30 |
| 78 | Greensleeves GREL 98 | AFRICA MUST BE FREE BY 83 DUB (LP) | 20 |
| 79 | Greensleeves GREL 8 | ORIGINAL ROCKERS (LP) | 25 |
| 79 | Atra ATRALP 1003 | LEGENDS (LP) | 20 |
| 80 | Echo STLP 1002 | THRILLER (LP, reissue) | 15 |
| 86 | Greensleeves GREL 90 | RISING SUN (LP) | 18 |
| 86 | Trojan TRLS 115 | ITAL DUB (LP, reissue, blue/white label) | 15 |
| 89 | Yard RLP 001 | KING TUBBYS MEETS THE ROCKERS UPTOWN (LP, reissue) | 25 |
| 91 | Greensleeves GREL 145 | ROCKERS INTERNATIONAL (LP) | 20 |
| 92 | Greensleeves GREL 168 | ROCKERS INTERNATIONAL II (LP) | 15 |

*(see also Mickey Lee, I Roy)*

## PACESETTERS
| | | | |
|---|---|---|---|
| 70 | Saga BC 101 | Cool Coffee/Israelites | 12 |

| 70 | Escort ERT 829 | Bits And Pieces/Nimrod Leap | 8 |
| 74 | Saga SAGA 8154 | REGGAE MEETS POP (LP) | 25 |

## PACIFIC DRIFT
| 70 | Deram DM 304 | Water Woman/Yes You Do | 20 |
| 70 | Deram Nova DN 13 | FEELIN' FREE (LP, mono, blue/silver labels) | 250 |
| 70 | Deram Nova SDN 13 | FEELIN' FREE (LP, stereo, red/silver labels) | 175 |

*(see also Wimple Winch, Just Four Men)*

## PACIFIC EARDRUM
| 78 | Charisma CAS 1136 | BEYOND PANIC (LP) | 20 |

## PACIFIC GAS & ELECTRIC (P.G. & E.)
| 70 | CBS 5039 | Are You Ready?/Staggolee | 6 |
| 70 | CBS 5204 | Father Come On Home/Elvira | 5 |
| 69 | B&C CAS 1003 | GET IT ON (LP) | 50 |
| 69 | CBS 63822 | PACIFIC GAS & ELECTRIC (LP, orange label) | 20 |
| 70 | CBS 64026 | ARE YOU READY (LP, orange label) | 20 |
| 71 | CBS 64295 | HARD BURN (LP, orange label) | 20 |

## PACIFIC SOUND
| 71 | M&M FMSS 10012 | Tribute To Jimi/Thick Fog | 30 |

*(see also Theatre Of Hate, Spear Of Destiny, Senate)*

## PACK (1)
| 65 | Columbia DB 7702 | Do You Believe In Magic?/Things Bring Me Down | 40 |

## PACK (2)
| 79 | SS PAK 1 | Brave New Soldiers/Heathen (p/s, 2,500 only) | 18 |
| 79 | Rough Trade RT 025 | King Of Kings/Number 12 (p/s) | 10 |
| 80 | SS SS 1N2/SS 2N1 | KIRK BRANDON AND THE PACK OF LIES (EP, with printed inner sleeve) | 12 |

## PACKABEATS
| 61 | Parlophone R 4729 | Gypsy Beat/Big Man | 15 |
| 62 | Pye 7N 15480 | Evening In Paris/The Traitors | 20 |
| 63 | Pye 7N 15549 | Dream Lover/Packabeat | 20 |

## PACKERS
| 66 | Pye International 7N 25343 | Hole In The Wall/Go 'Head On | 20 |
| 69 | Soul City SC 111 | Hole In The Wall/Go 'Head On (reissue) | 15 |
| 70 | Soul City SCM 003 | HOLE IN THE WALL (LP) | 25 |

## PAC-KEYS
| 68 | Speciality SPE 1003 | Stone Fox/Diggin' | 20 |

## PAD ANTHONY
| 87 | Jammys JAM 7 | Gotta Be Strong/Version//You Gonna Be Late/Version (12") | 25 |

## BERNARD PADDEN
| 83 | Dancing Sideways DS6X6 | Mass Movement/Career Advice (p/s) | 15 |

## PADDY, KLAUS & GIBSON
| 65 | Pye 7N 15906 | I Wanna Know/I Tried | 20 |
| 66 | Pye 7N 17060 | No Good Without You Baby/Rejected | 50 |
| 66 | Pye 7N 17112 | Teresa/Quick Before They Catch Us | 40 |

*(see also Manfred Mann, Big Three, Rory Storm & Hurricanes, Kingsize Taylor)*

## PAGAN BEAU
| 82 | RVNIC Records AMO 24 | Odd Man Out/Natures Daughter (p/s) | 15 |

## PAGAN BO
| 78 | Planet ICLP 01 | TRADITIONAL BARD AND THE FUTURE INEVITABLE (LP) | 175 |

## BILLY PAGE
| 65 | London HLU 10006 | It's Pop/American Girl | 12 |

## CHRIS PAGE
| 66 | Cameo Parkway CP 751 | Wait And See/Mine Mine Mine | 12 |

## CLEO PAGE
| 79 | JSP 4502 | I Love To Eat It - Hamburger/Goodie Train | 15 |
| 79 | JSP JSP 1003 | LEAVING MISSISSIPPI (LP) | 15 |

## PAGE FIVE
| 66 | Parlophone R 5426 | Let Sleeping Dogs Lie/I Know All About Her | 35 |

## HOT LIPS PAGE & HIS ORCHESTRA
| 55 | Parlophone MSP 6172 | Ain't Nothing Wrong With That Boy/The Cadillac Song | 20 |

## JIMMY PAGE
| 65 | Fontana TF 533 | She Just Satisfies/Keep Moving (promo sticker on label) | 750 |
| 65 | Fontana TF 533 | She Just Satisfies/Keep Moving | 650 |
| 88 | Geffen GEF 41 | Wasting My Time/Writes Of Winter (p/s, withdrawn) | 8 |
| 91 | Fontana TF 533 | She Just Satisifies/Keep Moving (reissue as part of Fontana box set) | 15 |
| 12 | Jimmypage.com JPRLP0002 | LUCIFER RISING (AND OTHER SOUNDTRACKS) (LP, 93 signed) | 100 |
| 12 | Jimmypage.com JPRLP0002 | LUCIFER RISING (AND OTHER SOUNDTRACKS) (LP, 418 copies, these unsigned) | 60 |

*(see also Led Zeppelin, Page & Plant, Firm, Yardbirds, Paul, Carter-Lewis & Southerners, Neil Christian & Crusaders, Bobby Graham, Robert Plant, Honeydrippers, Cartoone, Maureeny Wishfull, Coverdale-Page)*

## MALLY PAGE
| 66 | Pye 7N 17105 | The Life And Soul Of The Party/You Can Be Wrong About Boys | 6 |

## PAGE & PLANT
| 95 | Fontana PPCDJ 3 | Kashmir (CD promo, withdrawn) | 30 |
| 98 | Mercury ADV 1998 | Walking Into Clarksdale (CD promo, card sleeve) | 40 |
| 94 | Fontana PP ID 1 | NO QUARTER UNLEDDED (CD, radio-promo only, with 'question' booklet) | 50 |
| 98 | Mercury ADV 982 | TBA (CD, advance promo for WALKING INTO CLARKSDALE) | 30 |
| 98 | Mercury PPTIC 1 | WALKING INTO CLARKSDALE AN INTERVIEW (CD radio promo) | 30 |
| 98 | Mercury 558 025 1 | WALKING INTO CLARKSDALE (LP) | 25 |

*(see also Jimmy Page, Robert Plant)*

## PAGE BOYS (U.K.)
83   Whaam! WHAAM 10   You're My Kind Of Girl/In Love With You (p/s, 1,000 only) ............................ 20

*(see also 1,000 Violins)*

## PAGEBOYS (U.S.)
65   London HLU 9948   When I Meet A Girl Like You/I Have Love ...................................................... 10

## PAGE ONE & THE OBSERVERS
76   Carib Gems CGLP 004   OBSERVATION OF LIFE DUB (LP) ............................................................ 40

## LARRY PAGE (ORCHESTRA)
57   Columbia DB 3965   Cool Shake/Start Movin' (In My Direction) .......................................... 20
58   Columbia DB 4012   That'll Be The Day/Please Don't Blame Me ......................................... 18
58   Columbia DB 4080   Under Control/This Is My Life ............................................................ 18
59   Saga SAG 45-2902   Big Blon' Baby/I Vibrate .................................................................. 20
60   Saga SAG 45-2903   How'm I Doing, Hey Hey/Throw All Your Lovin' My Way ...................... 10
60   Saga SAG 45-2904   Little Old Fashioned You/Marylin ........................................................ 7
66   Decca F 12320   Waltzing To Jazz/Jo Jo (as Larry Page Orchestra) ................................. 5
66   Decca F 12368   Peyton Place Theme/Leanda's Theme (as Larry Page Orchestra) ............. 5
68   Page One POF 068   Take Five/Michelle ........................................................................... 5
68   Page One POF 096   Hey Jude/Those Were The Days (as Larry Page Orchestra) .................... 5
69   Page One POF 125   Wichita Lineman/Scarboro Fair ......................................................... 6
65   Decca LK 4692   KINKY MUSIC (LP, as Larry Page Orchestra) ....................................... 50
68   Page One POL(S) 002   EXECUTIVE SUITE (LP, as Larry Page Orchestra) ............................. 20

## PAGE TEN
65   Decca F 12248   Boutique/Colour Talk ........................................................................ 18

*(see also Niney)*

## CARLOS PAIAO
81   EMI EMI 5174   Playback (English)/Playback (Portuguese) ........................................... 7

## PAICE, ASHTON & LORD
77   Polydor/Oyster 2391 269   MALICE IN WONDERLAND (LP, with inner sleeve) ..................... 15

*(see also Deep Purple, Jon Lord, Ashton & Lord, Ashton Gardner & Dyke, Elf)*

## MARTY PAICH
57   London LZ-U 14040   MARTY PAICH QUARTET (LP, with Art Pepper) .............................. 30

## HAL PAIGE & WHALERS
60   Melodisc MEL 1553   Going Back To My Home Town/After Hours Blues ......................... 40

## JOEY PAIGE
65   Fontana TF 554   Cause I'm In Love With You/Yeah Yeah Yeah .................................... 20

## ROSALIND PAIGE
55   London HL 8120   When The Saints Go Marching In/Nobody's Sweetheart Now ............ 30
57   MGM MGM 937   Love, Oh Careless Love/That Funny Melody ...................................... 10

## PAIN KILLER
91   Earache MOSH 45   GUTS OF A VIRGIN (LP) ................................................................ 15

## PAIN FAMINE
86   A.V. AVS1   Starvision/Vanity Fayre ................................................................................ 7
86   A.V. AVS 3   The State Of Art/Sunset Lullaby ................................................................... 7

## PAINS OF BEING PURE AT HEART
08   Atomic Beat ABR 003   Kurt Cobain's Cardigan/PARALLELOGRAMS: 1 2 3 Go/Pop The Bubbles (p/s) ............ 45
09   Fortuna Pop! FPOP 84   Young Adult Friction/Ramona (p/s) .......................................... 6
09   Fortuna Pop! FPOP83LP   THE PAINS OF BEING PURE AT HEART (LP) ........................... 15
09   Fortuna Pop! FPOP83LP   THE PAINS OF BEING PURE AT HEART (LP, white/black splatter vinyl) ............ 20

## PAINTBOX
70   Young Blood YB 1013   Get Ready For Love/Can I Get To Know You .............................. 10
71   Young Blood YB 1029   Get Ready For Love/Can I Get To Know You (reissue) ................... 6

*(see also Easybeats, Haffy's Whiskey Sour)*

## PAINTED SHIP
67   Mercury MF 988   Frustration/I Told Those Little White Lies .................................... 130

## PAISLEYS
83   Psycho PSYCHO 7   COSMIC MIND AT PLAY (LP, reissue) ........................................... 20

## PALACE BROTHERS
93   Big Cat ABB 51 S   Ohio Riverboat Song/Drinking Woman (p/s) .................................. 8
94   Domino RUG 21T   AN ARROW THROUGH THE BITCH (12" EP, p/s) .............................. 15
95   Domino RUG 35T   The Mountain/Gulf Shores/(End Of) Travelling/West Palm Beach (12", stickered p/s as Palace) ............ 18
93   Big Cat ABB 50   THERE IS NO ONE WHAT WILL TAKE CARE OF YOU (LP) ..................... 15
94   Domino WIG 14   PALACE BROTHERS (LP) .............................................................. 15
95   Domino WIGLP 21X   VIVA LAST BLUES (LP with 7" (RUG 39) stickered sleeve, as Palace Music) ......... 25
95   Domino WIGLP 21   VIVA LAST BLUES (LP, as Palace Music, without 7") ............................ 20
98   Domino WIGLP 33   LOST BLUES AND OTHER SONGS (2-LP, gatefold, poster) ................... 25
96   Domino WIGLP 24   ARISE THEREFORE (LP) ............................................................... 15

*(see also Bonnie 'Prince' Billy, Will Oldham)*

## PALACE OF LIGHT
86   Bam Caruso OPRA 035   Safer/Bitter Seal ..................................................................... 10

## PALADIN
72   Bronze BRO 3   Sweet Sweet Music/Get On Together ................................................. 10
71   Bronze ILPS 9150   PALADIN (LP, textured sleeve, Island credit on label) ...................... 40
72   Bronze ILPS 9190   CHARGE (LP, gatefold sleeve, Island credit on label) ...................... 50

*(see also Arthur Brown, Glass Menagerie, McGuinness Flint)*

## PALE FOUNTAINS
| | | | |
|---|---|---|---|
| 82 | Operation Twilight OPT 09 | (There's Always) Something On My Mind/Just A Girl (p/s) | 25 |
| 83 | Virgin VS 568 | Palm Of My Hand/(Instrumental)/Love's A Beautiful Place (p/s) | 5 |
| 85 | Virgin VS 737 | Jean's Not Happening/Bicycle Thieves | 5 |
| 85 | Virgin VS 750 | From Across The Kitchen Table/Bicycle Thieves//Thank You/ Just A Girl (double pack) | 5 |
| 84 | Virgin V 2274 | PACIFIC STREET (LP) | 15 |
| 85 | Virgin V 2333 | FROM ACROSS THE KITCHEN TABLE (LP, with inner sleeve) | 15 |

*(see also Shack, Michael Head & Strands)*

## PALE SAINTS
| | | | |
|---|---|---|---|
| 91 | 4AD AD 1009 | Kinky Love/Hair Shoes (demo) (p/s) | 10 |
| 90 | 4AD CAD 0002 | THE COMFORTS OF MADNESS (LP, with 3 postcards) | 30 |
| 92 | 4AD CAD 2004 | IN RIBBONS (LP, with free 7" "A Thousand Stars Burst Open"/A Revelation [RIB 1]) | 20 |
| 94 | 4AD CAD 4014 | SLOW BUILDINGS (LP) | 18 |

## TOM PALEY
| | | | |
|---|---|---|---|
| 76 | Kicking Mule SNKF 119 | HARD LUCK PAPA (LP) | 18 |

*(see also Peggy Seeger)*

## PALEY BROTHERS
| | | | |
|---|---|---|---|
| 78 | Sire SRE 4005 | Come On Let's Go/Magic Power (p/s) | 12 |
| 78 | Sire 6078 613 | Ecstacy/Rendezvous/Hide N' Seek/Come Out And Play (12", p/s) | 12 |

*(see also Ramones)*

## PALI GAP
| | | | |
|---|---|---|---|
| 82 | Sinister SYN 001 | Under The Sun/The Knives Are Out (p/s, with insert) | 20 |

## MORTY PALITZ & ACES
| | | | |
|---|---|---|---|
| 59 | London HLJ 8778 | The Grocer's Cha Cha Cha/Eso Es El Amor (This Is Love) | 8 |

## PALLAS
| | | | |
|---|---|---|---|
| 82 | Granite Wax GWS 1 | Arrive Alive/Stranger (On The Edge Of Time) (two different p/s, with insert) | 50 |
| 82 | Granite Wax GWS 1 | Arrive Alive/Stranger (On The Edge Of Time) (two different p/s, without insert) | 40 |
| 83 | Cool King CK010 | Paris Is Burning/The Hammer Falls (p/s) | 5 |
| 83 | Cool King 12CK010 | Paris Is Burning/The Hammer Falls/Stranger At The Edge Of Time (12", p/s) | 12 |
| 84 | EMI Harvest PLSP1 | Eyes In The Night (Arrive Alive)/East West (picture disc) | 10 |
| 84 | EMI Harvest PLSP1 | Eyes In The Night (Arrive Alive)/East West/Crown Of Thorns (12", p/s) | 10 |
| 84 | EMI Harvest PLS2 | Shock Treatment/March On Atlantis (poster p/s) | 5 |
| 84 | EMI Harvest 12PLS2 | Shock Treatment/March On Atlantis/Heart Attack (12", p/s) | 10 |
| 78 | Sue-i-cide PAL/101 | THE PALLAS EP (stamped plain die-cut sleeve) | 50 |
| 85 | Harvest 12PLS3P | THE KNIGHT MOVES EP (12" picture disc) | 12 |
| 85 | Harvest 12PLS3D | THE KNIGHT MOVES EP (12" + free 7" Mad Machine / Stitch In Time, sealed in plastic sleeve) | 15 |
| 83 | Cool King CKLP002 | ARRIVE ALIVE (LP) | 15 |
| 84 | Harvest SHSP2400 121 | THE SENTINAL (LP, gatefold sleeve, with poster and sticker) | 18 |
| 86 | Harvest SHVL 850 | THE WEDGE (LP + inner sleeve) | 15 |

## PALMA VIOLETS
| | | | |
|---|---|---|---|
| 12 | Rough Trade RTRAD 5655 | Best Of Friends/Last Of The Summer Wine (50 copies with sticker, purple vinyl, signed) | 10 |
| 13 | Rough Trade TRADS 702 | Invasion Of The Tribbles (1-sided other side etched, 2 badges in fold-out sleeve) | 35 |

## EARL PALMER & HIS TEN PIECE ROCKIN' BAND
| | | | |
|---|---|---|---|
| 58 | Capitol CL 14859 | Drum Village (Parts 1 & 2) | 5 |
| 58 | Capitol EAP1 1026 | SWINGIN' DRUMS (EP) | 10 |

## EDDIE PALMER
| | | | |
|---|---|---|---|
| 57 | Decca F 10873 | The Sky/The Twilight Theme | 8 |

## JERRY PALMER
| | | | |
|---|---|---|---|
| 66 | London 10026 | Walking The Dog/Don't Leave Me Baby | 25 |

## MICHAEL PALMER
| | | | |
|---|---|---|---|
| 84 | Greensleeves GREL 155 | Done With It/Can't Take The Fuss (12") | 15 |
| 84 | Simba SM 08 | Me Nah Run/JACKIE PARRIS: When Your Are Young (12", with Aswad) | 25 |

## MICHAEL PALMER AND JIM BROWN
| | | | |
|---|---|---|---|
| 83 | Greensleeves GRED 131 | Ghetto Dance/JAH THOMAS & ROOTS RADICS: Ghetto Dub (12") | 10 |

## RICK PALMER
| | | | |
|---|---|---|---|
| 59 | London HLL 8900 | You Threw A Heart/My Greatest Wish (unreleased) | 0 |

## ROY PALMER & STATE STREET RAMBLERS
| | | | |
|---|---|---|---|
| 54 | London AL 3518 | A CHICAGO SKIFFLE SESSION (10" LP) | 30 |

## TONY PALMER
| | | | |
|---|---|---|---|
| 77 | Eji E00009 | Jah Shall Conquer/Commissioner (instrumental) (12") | 18 |

## TRISTAN PALMER/PALMA
| | | | |
|---|---|---|---|
| 81 | Greensleeves GRED 66 | Entertainment/JAH THOMAS & TOYAN: Jah Guide (12") | 15 |
| 81 | Art & Craft ACS 011 | Fussing And Fighting (with Ranking Joe)/Version (12") | 18 |
| 82 | Greensleeves GRED 93 | Joker Smoker/PAPA BRUCE: Loafter Smoker (12") | 25 |
| 83 | Greensleeves GRED 126 | No Shot No Fire/BARRY BROWN: Jukes And Watches (12") | 15 |
| 82 | Greensleeves GREL 43 | JOKER SMOKER (LP) | 20 |

## PALMETTO KINGS
| | | | |
|---|---|---|---|
| 60 | Starlite ST45 021 | Ten Rum Bottles/Home Cookin' Mama | 15 |

## CHARLIE PALMIERI
| | | | |
|---|---|---|---|
| 68 | Atlantic 588157 | LATIN BUGALU (LP) | 40 |

## PAN
| | | | |
|---|---|---|---|
| 93 | Big Cat ABB 49 | HANGIN' OUT FOR JUNE (LP) | 15 |

## PANACHE
| | | | |
|---|---|---|---|
| 83 | Mach 1 MAGIC 004 | I Wanna Dance/Crazy For Your Love (with Ray Dorset) | 7 |

*(see also Ray Dorset)*

## PANAMA FRANCIS BLUES BAND
64   Stateside SL 10070    TOUGH TALK!! (LP) ................................................................ 35

## PANAMA LIMITED (JUG BAND)
| 69 | Harvest HAR 5010 | Lady Of Shallot/Future Blues................................................... 30 |
| 70 | Harvest HAR 5022 | Round And Round/Rotting Wooden In A White Collar's Grave ............ 30 |
| 69 | Harvest SHVL 753 | PANAMA LIMITED JUG BAND (LP, laminated gatefold sleeve, "Sold in U.K..." text on 5 lines", no EMI on label) ............................................ 250 |
| 70 | Harvest SHVL 753 | PANAMA LIMITED JUG BAND (LP, laminated gatefold sleeve, 2nd pressing, no "Sold in U.K..." no EMI on label) ................................................... 60 |
| 70 | Harvest SHVL 779 | INDIAN SUMMER (LP, as Panama Limited, gatefold sleeve, no EMI on label).............. 450 |

*(see also Ian (A) Anderson)*

## ALPHONSO PANCHO
79   Attack TACK 3    Love Is A Pleasure/Never Give Up In A Babylon ........................ 20

*(see also Pancho Alphonso)*

## GENE PANCHO
68   Giant GN 21    I Like Sweet Music/Seven Days (with Sandy & Superboys)................. 20

*(see also Gene Rondo)*

## PANDA BEAR
| 10 | Domino RUG 375 | You Can Count On Me/Alsatian Darn ..................................... 5 |
| 10 | Fat Cat 7 FAT 94 | Last Night At The Jetty/Drone ............................................ 5 |

*(see also Animal Collective)*

## PANDEMONIUM
| 67 | CBS 202462 | Season Of The Witch/Today I'm Happy ..................................... 60 |
| 67 | CBS 2664 | No Presents For Me/The Sun Shines From His Eyes........................... 300 |
| 68 | CBS 3451 | Chocolate Buster Dan/Fly With Me Forever................................ 70 |

## PANDIT PRAN NATH
69   Transatlantic TRA 193    EARTH GROOVE (LP)............................................................ 40

## PANDORAS
67   Liberty LIB 55954    (I Could Write A Book) About My Baby/New Day ...................... 18

## PANHANDLE
72   Decca SKL 5105    PANHANDLE (LP, laminated cover, blue/silver label with boxed logo) ......... 30

*(see also Chris Spedding)*

## PANIC IN THE YEAR ZERO
81   Vada ABER 4128    Liberty Caps/Sometimes I Don't Know ................................... 20

## PANIK
77   Rainy City SHOT 1    IT WON'T SELL (EP) ........................................................ 15

## PAN PIPERS
69   Pye 7N 17699    Stop/Money Or Love ........................................................ 125

## PANS PEOPLE
74   Epic SEPC 2606    You Can Really Rock N Roll Me/The Singer Not The Song..................... 8

## PAN SONIC
| 95 | Blast First VBFFP 118 | VAKIO (2-LP, reissue) ..................................................... 25 |
| 97 | Blast First BFFP 132 | KULMA (LP, 2 x 12") ...................................................... 20 |
| 00 | Blast First BFFP 166 | AALTOPIIRI (2-LP, print) .................................................. 20 |
| 04 | Blast first BFFP 180BX | KESTO (4-CD box set).................................................. 30 |

## PANT
79   Redball RR019X    Mother Fo/Modern/No Possessions/Mummy Told You ...................... 25

## GARY PANTER & JAY COTTON
90   Blast First FU 7    ONE HELL SOUNDWICH (LP, picture disc) ................................ 20

## JAN PANTER
| 65 | Oriole CB 1938 | My Two Arms Minus You Equals Tears/Does My Heart Show ............. 25 |
| 65 | CBS 201810 | Let It Be Now/Stand By And Cry ......................................... 20 |
| 66 | Pye 7N 17097 | Scratch My Back/Put Yourself In My Place ............................ 250 |
| 69 | President PT 241 | Si Si Senor/Stella In Lights ........................................... 10 |

## PANTHER BURNS
| 81 | Rough Trade RT 077 | Train Kept A Rollin'/Red Headed Woman (p/s) ......................... 10 |
| 81 | Rough Trade ROUGH 32 | BEHIND THE MAGNOLIA CURTAIN (LP) ................................. 20 |

*(see also Alex Chilton)*

## ROY PANTON
| 63 | Blue Beat BB 182 | Mighty Ruler/Run Old Man ............................................. 30 |
| 64 | Blue Beat BB 219 | Good From The Bad/Hell Gate........................................... 30 |
| 64 | Rio R 19 | Cherita/Seek And You Shall Find......................................... 20 |
| 64 | Rio R 33 | You Don't Know Me/KING EDWARD'S ALLSTARS: Doctor No ............. 35 |
| 64 | Island WI 137 | Goodbye Peggy Darling (actually "Goodbye Peggy" by Stranger Cole)/ BABA BROOKS: Portrait Of My Love......................................... 25 |
| 70 | Harry J HJ 6624 | The Same Old Life/JAYBOYS: Life Version.................................. 8 |

*(see also Roy & Annette, Roy & Millie, Roy & Paulette, Roy & Yvonne, Roy & Duke Allstars, Roy & Patsy, Derrick Harriot, Leon & Owen, Charmers)*

## JOHN PANTRY
| 72 | Philips 6006 250 | Net Of Concern/Words.................................................. 10 |
| 79 | Kingsway KMS 902 | Nothing Is Impossible/Jesus On The Airwaves ......................... 8 |
| 72 | Philips 6308 129 | JOHN PANTRY (LP)...................................................... 40 |
| 73 | Philips 6308 138 | LONG WHITE TRAIL (LP)................................................ 18 |
| 80 | Kingsway KMR 323 | TO STRANGERS AND FRIENDS (LP) ..................................... 15 |
| 80s | Tenth Planet TP 040 | THE UPSIDE DOWN WORLD OF JOHN PANTRY (LP, limited edition, 1,000 only)............ 35 |

*(see also Factory, Peter & Wolves, Norman Conquest, Sounds Around)*

## PANZA DIVISION
82   Panza Traz PTO1    We Will Rock The World/Standing On The Outside......................... 10

## PAPA CHARJAN
82   CF CF 006          DJ Pumping/COURTNEY BARKELY: I Am Alright (12") ........................ 20

## PAPA DOO RUN RUN
75   RCA RCA 2620        Be True To Your School/Disney Girls ............................................... 8

## PAPA MICHIGAN & GENERAL SMILEY
81   Tuff Gong IPR 2035     One Love Jame Down/FREDDIE MCGREGOR: Joggin' (12") ............... 10

## PAPA TULLO
81   Negus Roots NERT 006  Church And State/Righteous Rock (12") ....................................... 15
82   Negus Roots NERLP 004 TULLO AT HOME (LP) ........................................................... 40

## NIKKI PAPAS
59   Parlophone R 4590    49 State Rock/Try Again ................................................................ 40
60   Parlophone R 4652    By The River/Don't Leave Me Alone .............................................. 10

## PAPER BAGS
79   Retread TREAD 1     Joss Bay/Drat! (p/s) ..................................................................... 7

## PAPER BLITZ TISSUE
67   RCA Victor RCA 1652  Boy Meets Girl/Grey Man .......................................................... 500
*(see also Cupid's Inspiration)*

## PAPER BUBBLE
70   Deram DML/SML 1059  SCENERY (LP, white/red label) .................................................. 100
*(see also Dave Cousins)*

## PAPER DOLLS
68   Pye 7N 17456       Something Here In My Heart/All The Time In The World ................... 5
68   Pye 7N 17547       My Life Is In Your Hands/There's Nobody I'd Sooner Love ............... 8
68   Pye 7N 17655       Someday/Any Old Time You're Lonely And Sad .............................. 7
70   RCA RCA 1919       My Boyfriend's Back/Mister Good Time Friday ............................... 7
70   RCA RCA 2007       Remember December/Same Old Story ......................................... 7
68   Pye N(S)PL 18226    PAPER DOLLS HOUSE (LP) ........................................................... 50

## PAPER DRAGON
69   Bell BLL 1054       April Fool/Get Something Going .................................................. 12

## PAPER TISSUE
72   Dresden DR2        Wild Fire/Visions In The NIght .................................................... 50

## PAPERHOUSE
91   Mystic Stones RUNE LP 11 SPONGY COMESTIBLES (LP) .................................................... 20

## PARADE
67   A&M AMS 701       Sunshine Girl/This Old Melody .................................................. 18
67   A&M AMS 720       Radio Song/I Can See Love ........................................................ 15

## VANESSA PARADIS
87   Polydor POSPG 902    Joe Le Taxi/Varvara Pavlovna (poster p/s) ..................................... 6

## PARADISE HAMMER
70   Polydor 2058048     She Is Love/You Got Me In ......................................................... 25
71   Polydor 2058084     1+1=2/To Live ......................................................................... 15

## PARADISE LOST
90   Peaceville VILE 17    LOST PARADISE (LP) .................................................................. 15
91   Peaceville VILE26L    GOTHIC (LP, gatefold, red vinyl) ................................................. 25
91   Peaceville VILE26L    GOTHIC (LP, gatefold) .............................................................. 18
92   Music For Nations MFN 135 SHADES OF GOD (LP) ............................................................. 20
93   Music For Nations MFN 152 ICON (2-LP) ........................................................................ 25
95   Music For Nations MFN 184 DRACONIAN TIMES (2-LP) ...................................................... 35
97   Music For Nations MFN 222 LOST (2-LP) ......................................................................... 25

## PARADISE SQUARE
74   None             NEVER THOUGHT I'D SEE THE DAY (LP, 100 only, hand-drawn covers) ....................... 750

## PARADISE (1)
77   Clubland SJP 775     One Of These Days/You're The One I Need (no p/s, 500 only) ................. 15

## PARADISE (2)
80   Ebony EB 701       PARADISE (LP) ...................................................................... 125
82   Ebony EB 702       WORLD'S MIDNIGHT (LP) ........................................................ 100
83   Priority PLP 1       LOVE IS THE ANSWER (LP) ...................................................... 100

## PARADONS
60   Top Rank JAR 514     Diamonds And Pearls/I Want Love ............................................... 60

## PARADOX VOYEUR
80   Brigade BRIG 001     Deceit/E.D./Choosy (p/s) ........................................................... 15

## PARADOX (1)
68   Polydor 56275       The Wednesday Theme/Ring The Changes .................................. 125
*(see also David Walker)*

## PARAFFIN JACK FLASH LTD
68   Pye NSPL 18252      MOVERS AND GROOVERS (LP) ................................................. 18

## PARAGONS
66   Doctor Bird DB 1060   Happy-Go-Lucky Girl/Love Brings Pain .......................................... 35
67   Island WI 3045      On The Beach/CAROL & TOMMY McCOOK: Sweet And Gentle (B-side actually by
                   Tommy McCook & Supersonics) ................................................ 40
67   Island WI 3067      Talking Love/If I Were You ........................................................ 40
67   Island WI 3093      So Depressed/We Were Meant To Be ......................................... 80
67   Treasure Isle TI 7009   Only A Smile/The Tide Is High ................................................... 25
67   Treasure Isle TI 7011   Mercy, Mercy, Mercy/Riding On A High And Windy Day ................. 25
67   Treasure Isle TI 7013   The Same Song/TOMMY McCOOK & SUPERSONICS: Soul Serenade .......... 30
67   Treasure Isle TI 7025   Wear You To The Ball/You Mean The World To Me ....................... 30
68   Treasure Isle TI 7034   Silver Bird/My Best Girl ........................................................... 25

MINT VALUE £

| | | |
|---|---|---|
| 68 | Island WI 3138 | Memories By The Score/The Number One For Me ........... 30 |
| 69 | Studio One SO 2081 | Have You Ever Been In Love/Change Your Style ........... 50 |
| 69 | Duke DU 7 | Left With A Broken Heart/I've Got To Get Away ........... 80 |
| 69 | Crab 13 | Take Your Hand From My Neck/Equality And Justice ........... 40 |
| 77 | Wildflower WF 523 | Do The Best Thing/Best Thing ........... 15 |
| 80 | Virgin VS 389 | The Tide Is High/U ROY: Tide Is High ........... 12 |
| 12 | Treasure Isle THB 7020 | Joy In My Soul/THE TECHNIQUES: Travelling Man ........... 15 |
| 67 | Doctor Bird DLM 5010 | ON THE BEACH (LP) ........... 250 |
| 81 | Starlight Records SLDLP 909 | NOW (LP) ........... 15 |
| 81 | Island ILPS 9631 | THE PARAGONS (LP) ........... 15 |
| 74 | Horse HRLP 703 | THE PARAGONS WITH ROSALYN SWEAT (LP) ........... 25 |

*(see also John Holt, Lester Sterling)*

## PARALEX
| | | |
|---|---|---|
| 80 | Reddingtons R.R. DAN 4 | White Lightning/Travelling Man/Black Widow, (12", p/s, green vinyl) ........... 50 |

## PARALLELOGRAMS
| | | |
|---|---|---|
| 08 | Atomic Beat ABR 003 | 1 2 3 Go/Pop The Bubbles/PAINS OF BEING PURE AT HEART: Kurt Cobain's Cardigan (p/s) ........... 45 |

## PARAMEDIC SQUAD
| | | |
|---|---|---|
| 81 | Gargoyle GRGL 2 | Movement In Time/For You/Thinking Psychedelia (p/s) ........... 25 |

## PARAMETER
| | | |
|---|---|---|
| 70 | Deroy | GALACTIC RAMBLE (LP, 450 only, 4 page inner) ........... 300 |

## NORRIE PARAMOR & HIS ORCHESTRA
| | | |
|---|---|---|
| 53 | Columbia SCM 5051 | April In Portugal/The Song From Moulin Rouge ........... 8 |
| 54 | Columbia SCM 5126 | Johnny Guitar/Paramambo ........... 8 |
| 54 | Columbia SCM 5136 | The High And The Mighty/Rip Van Twinkle ........... 8 |
| 56 | Columbia SCM 5251 | Theme From Threepenny Opera/Poor John ........... 7 |
| 56 | Columbia DB 3815 | Autumn Concerto/Lullaby Of Birdland ........... 6 |
| 60 | Columbia DB 4419 | Summer Place (Theme)/Half Pint ........... 5 |
| 62 | Columbia DB 4789 | Theme From Z Cars/Them From Ballad Of A Soldier ........... 5 |
| 64 | Columbia DB 7114 | Dream Of Tomorrow/Laramie ........... 7 |
| 65 | Columbia DB 7446 | Dance Of The Warriors/Dragon Dance ........... 6 |
| 68 | Columbia DB 8430 | Soul Coaxing/Autumn In London Town ........... 7 |
| 70 | Polydor 56375 | Randall And Hopkirk (Deceased)/A Summer Palace ........... 65 |

*(see also Harry Gold)*

## PARAMORE
| | | |
|---|---|---|
| 06 | Fueled By Ramen ATUK 037 | Emergency/O'Star (poster sleeve) ........... 15 |
| 07 | Fueled By Ramen ATUK 0279 | Misery Business/My Hero (Electronic Mix) (Clear vinyl, poster sleeve) ........... 10 |
| 07 | Fueled By Ramen AT 0279X | Misery Business (Album Version)/Sunday Bloody Sunday (Bonus Version) ........... 6 |
| 07 | Fueled by Ramen AT 0284 | Hallelujah (Album Version)/Decoy (Bonus Version) (gatefold p/s, poster) ........... 10 |
| 07 | Fueled By Ramen AT 0284X | Hallelujah (Album Version)/(1-sided etched disc, poster sleeve) ........... 6 |
| 07 | Fueled By Ramen AT 0295 | Crush Crush Crush (Album Version)/Misery Business (Live) (stickered p/s, sheet of stickers) ........... 6 |
| 07 | Fueled By Ramen AT 0295X | Crush Crush Crush (Album Version)/For A Pessimist I'm Pretty Optimistic (Live) (blue vinyl, printed PVC sleeve, insert) ........... 10 |

## PARAMOUNT ALL-STARS
| | | |
|---|---|---|
| 50 | Tempo R 20 | Hometown Skiffle (Parts 1 & 2) (78) ........... 20 |

*(see also Blind Blake, Georgia Tom, Papa Charlie Jackson, Blind Lemon Jefferson, Charlie Spand)*

## PARAMOUNT FOUR
| | | |
|---|---|---|
| 09 | Kent 6T 26 | Sorry Ain't The Word/GENE & GARY: Baby Without You ........... 15 |

## PARAMOUNTS
| | | |
|---|---|---|
| 63 | Parlophone R 5093 | Poison Ivy/I Feel Good All Over ........... 12 |
| 64 | Parlophone R 5107 | Little Bitty Pretty One/A Certain Girl ........... 20 |
| 64 | Parlophone R 5155 | I'm The One Who Loves You/It Won't Be Long ........... 25 |
| 64 | Parlophone R 5187 | Bad Blood/Do I ........... 25 |
| 65 | Parlophone R 5272 | Blue Ribbons/Cuttin' In ........... 20 |
| 65 | Parlophone R 5351 | You Never Had It So Good/Don't Ya Like My Love ........... 50 |
| 64 | Parlophone GEP 8908 | THE PARAMOUNTS (EP) ........... 200 |

*(see also Procol Harum)*

## PARANOIA
| | | |
|---|---|---|
| 84 | Rot ASS 8 | Dead Man's Dreams/Man In Black (p/s) ........... 10 |
| 84 | Rot ASS 11 | SHATTERED GLASS (LP) ........... 25 |

## PARANOIDS
| | | |
|---|---|---|
| 79 | Hurricane FIRE 4 | Anticipation/TV Heroes (p/s) ........... 8 |
| 79 | Hurricane FIRE 8 | Stupid Guy/Road To Ruin (p/s) ........... 10 |
| 80 | Hurricane FIRE 14 | The Love Job/Theme From Gravity's Rainbow (p/s) ........... 10 |

## PARCHMENT
| | | |
|---|---|---|
| 73 | Pye 7N 45261 | You Are My Morning/Getting Out Of This Town ........... 5 |
| 72 | Pye 7N 45178 | Light Up The Fire/Let There Be Light (p/s) ........... 5 |
| 73 | Pye 7N 45214 | Where Can I Find You/Working Man ........... 8 |
| 72 | Pye NSPL 18388 | LIGHT UP THE FIRE (LP, textured sleeve with poster insert) ........... 20 |
| 75 | Myrrh MYR 1028 | SHAMBLEJAM (LP) ........... 18 |

## WALTER PARDON
| | | |
|---|---|---|
| 75 | Leader LED 2063 | A PROPER SORT (LP) ........... 20 |

## PAULA PARFITT
| | | |
|---|---|---|
| 69 | Beacon BEA 135 | I'm Gonna Give You Back Your Ring/Love Is Wonderful (Beware of bootlegs! - originals have anti-slip grips around the label) ........... 150 |
| 70 | Up Front UPF4 | Peace Of Mind/Baby You Give Me A Good Song To Sing ........... 10 |

## TINY PARHAM
| | | |
|---|---|---|
| 50s | Audubon AAC | TINY PARHAM (10" LP) ........... 25 |

**PARIS**
| | | |
|---|---|---|
| 72 | Avalanche AV 67312 | I've Lost The Way/Long Time ........ 8 |
| 76 | Thunderbird THE 114 | Circles/Liar ........ 5 |

**BOBBY PARIS**
| | | |
|---|---|---|
| 68 | Polydor 56747 | Per So Nal Ly/Tragedy ........ 80 |
| 69 | Polydor 56762 | Let The Sun Shine In/You ........ 22 |
| 77 | London HLU 10553 | Night Owl/YVONNE BAKER: You Didn't Say A Word ........ 10 |

**PARIS CONNECTION**
| | | |
|---|---|---|
| 73 | Explosion EX 2085 | That Lady/Sonia ........ 20 |

**MICA PARIS**
| | | |
|---|---|---|
| 91 | 4th & Broadway 12BRWDJ207 | A STAND FOR LOVE EP (12" promo p/s. Misspress, plays Prince's vocal version of 'A Stand For Love') ........ 100 |

**PRISCILLA PARIS**
| | | |
|---|---|---|
| 74 | Rak RAK 184 | I Love How You Love Me/Over You ........ 10 |

*(see also Paris Sisters)*

**PARIS SISTERS**
| | | |
|---|---|---|
| 61 | Top Rank JAR 588 | I Love How You Love Me/I'll Be Crying Tomorrow ........ 50 |
| 64 | MGM MGM 1240 | Dream Lover/Lonely Girl ........ 50 |

*(see also Date With Soul, Priscilla Paris)*

**PARIS AND THE ATMOSPHERES**
| | | |
|---|---|---|
| 79 | SRTS/79/CUS-281 | Atmosphere/Deborah And Me (p/s) ........ 10 |

**JOHN PARISH & POLLY JEAN HARVEY**
| | | |
|---|---|---|
| 96 | Island IS 648 | That Was My Veil/Losing Ground (p/s) ........ 12 |
| 96 | Island HEELCD1 | Heela (Promo-only CD, unreleased single) ........ 10 |
| 96 | Island ILPS 8051 | DANCE HALL AT LOUSE POINT (LP) ........ 35 |

**PARISH HALL**
| | | |
|---|---|---|
| 70 | Liberty LBS 83374 | PARISH HALL (LP) ........ 75 |

**SIMON PARK**
| | | |
|---|---|---|
| 74 | EMI EMC 3059 | SOMETHING IN THE AIR (LP) ........ 20 |

**PARKE**
| | | |
|---|---|---|
| 71 | Folk Heritage FHR 018S | PARKE (LP) ........ 80 |
| 72 | Folk Heritage FHR 028 | JOY HEALTH LOVE AND PEACE (LP) ........ 70 |

**ALAN PARKER**
| | | |
|---|---|---|
| 70 | Aristocrat AR 1022 | GUITAR FANTASY (LP) ........ 20 |
| 73 | MCA MUPS 471 | BAND OF ANGELS (LP) ........ 20 |

*(see also Hungry Wolf, Ugly Custard)*

**BENNY PARKER & DYNAMICS**
| | | |
|---|---|---|
| 64 | Decca F 11944 | Boys And Girls/You'll Be On Your Way ........ 45 |

**BILLY PARKER**
| | | |
|---|---|---|
| 63 | Decca F 11668 | Thanks A Lot/Out Of Your Heart ........ 7 |

**BOBBY PARKER**
| | | |
|---|---|---|
| 61 | London HLU 9393 | Watch Your Step/Steal Your Heart Away ........ 60 |
| 64 | Sue WI 340 | Watch Your Step/Steal Your Heart Away (reissue) ........ 55 |
| 69 | Blue Horizon 57-3151 | It's Hard But It's Fair/I Couldn't Quit My Baby ........ 45 |

**BONNIE PARKER & ACME ATTRACTIONS**
| | | |
|---|---|---|
| 81 | Orchid OR 1 | Eve Of Destruction/It's OK ........ 10 |

**CHARLIE PARKER**

ALBUMS
| | | |
|---|---|---|
| 52 | Vogue LDE 004 | CHARLIE PARKER VOLUME ONE (10") ........ 75 |
| 53 | Vogue LDE 016 | CHARLIE PARKER VOLUME TWO (10") ........ 75 |
| 56 | Vogue LAE 12002 | CHARLIE PARKER MEMORIAL ALBUM (gatefold sleeve w/ 2 inserts) ........ 25 |
| 55 | Melodisc MLP 12-105 | BIRD AT ST. NICK'S ........ 30 |
| 55 | Columbia Clef 33CX 10004 | CHARLIE PARKER BIG BAND ........ 40 |
| 56 | Columbia Clef 33C 9026 | BIRD AND DIZ (10", with Dizzy Gillespie) ........ 40 |
| 57 | Columbia Clef 33CX 10081 | APRIL IN PARIS (as Charlie Parker With Strings) ........ 35 |
| 57 | Columbia Clef 33CX 10090 | CHARLIE PARKER PLAYS COLE PORTER ........ 25 |
| 58 | Columbia Clef 33CX 10117 | CHARLIE PARKER JAZZ PERENNIAL ........ 15 |
| 58 | London Jazz LTZ-C 15104 | THE IMMORTAL CHARLIE PARKER VOL. 1 ........ 15 |
| 58 | London Jazz LTZ-C 15105 | THE IMMORTAL CHARLIE PARKER VOL. 2 ........ 15 |
| 58 | London Jazz LTZ-C 15106 | THE IMMORTAL CHARLIE PARKER VOL. 3 ........ 15 |
| 58 | London Jazz LTZ-C 15107 | THE IMMORTAL CHARLIE PARKER VOL. 4 ........ 15 |
| 58 | Mercury MPL 12-105 | BIRD AT NICK'S ........ 15 |
| 60 | Collector JGN 1002 | CHARLIE PARKER IN SWEDEN ........ 30 |

*(see also Dizzy Gillespie & Charlie Parker, Sir Charles Thompson)*

**DAVID PARKER**
| | | |
|---|---|---|
| 71 | Polydor 2460 101 | DAVID PARKER (LP) ........ 50 |

*(see also Andwella's Dream)*

**DEAN PARKER & REDCAPS**
| | | |
|---|---|---|
| 62 | Decca F 11555 | Stormy Evening/Blue Eyes And Golden Hair ........ 45 |

**DYON PARKER**
| | | |
|---|---|---|
| 69 | Marble Arch MAL 787 | OUT ON THE HIGHWAY (LP) ........ 20 |

**EDDIE PARKER**
| | | |
|---|---|---|
| 55 | Columbia SCM 5211 | Far Away From Everybody/Bella Notte ........ 8 |
| 56 | Columbia DB 3804 | Love Me As Though There Were No Tomorrow/Rich In Love ........ 8 |

**EULA PARKER**
| | | |
|---|---|---|
| 58 | Oriole CB 1411 | Silhouettes/Hedgehopper ........ 20 |

*(see also Frank Weir)*

## EVAN PARKER

MINT VALUE £

| | | | |
|---|---|---|---|
| 75 | Incus INCUS 19 | SAXOPHONE SOLOS (LP) | 40 |
| 78 | Incus INCUS 27 | MONOCEROS (LP) | 40 |
| 80 | Incus INCUS 39 | SIX OF ONE (LP) | 30 |
| 86 | Incus INCUS 49 | THE SNAKE DECIDES (LP) | 30 |
| 89 | Cadillac (no cat no) | COLLECTED SOLOS (4 x LP and cassette hand numbered to 200) | 50 |

## EVAN PARKER, DEREK BAILEY, HAN BENNINK
| | | | |
|---|---|---|---|
| 70 | Incus INCUS 1 | THE TOPOGRAPHY OF THE LUNGS (LP) | 150 |

## EVAN PARKER, BARRY GUY & PAUL LYTTON
| | | | |
|---|---|---|---|
| 83 | Incus INCUS 42 | TRACKS (LP) | 40 |

## EVAN PARKER & GEORGE LEWIS
| | | | |
|---|---|---|---|
| 80 | Incus INCUS 35 | FROM SAXOPHONE & TROMBONE (LP) | 40 |

## EVAN PARKER, GEORGE LEWIS, BARRY GUY & PAUL LYTTON
| | | | |
|---|---|---|---|
| 83 | Incus INCUS 45 | HOOK, DRIFT & SHUFFLE (LP) | 50 |

## EVAN PARKER & PAUL LYTTON
| | | | |
|---|---|---|---|
| 72 | Incus INCUS 5 | COLLECTIVE CALLS (URBAN) (TWO MICROPHONES) (LP) | 40 |
| 75 | Incus INCUS 14 | AT THE UNITY THEATRE (LP) | 40 |

*(see also Derek Bailey & Evan Parker, Derek Bailey Evan Parker & Han Bennink)*

## FESS PARKER
| | | | |
|---|---|---|---|
| 57 | Oriole CB 1378 | Wringle Wrangle/Ballad Of John Colter | 10 |

## JIMMY PARKER
| | | | |
|---|---|---|---|
| 62 | Top Rank JAR 608 | We Gonna/No Word From Betty | 10 |

## (LITTLE) JUNIOR PARKER
| | | | |
|---|---|---|---|
| 61 | Vogue V 9179 | Stand By Me/I'll Forget About You (as Little Junior Parker) | 30 |
| 62 | Vogue V 9193 | Mary Jo/Annie Get Your Yo-Yo (as Little Junior Parker) | 30 |
| 66 | Vocalion VP 9256 | These Kind Of Blues (Parts 1 & 2) | 40 |
| 66 | Vocalion VP 9256 | These Kind Of Blues (Parts 1 & 2) (DJ copy) | 60 |
| 66 | Vocalion VP 9275 | Goodbye Little Girl/Walking The Floor Over You | 30 |
| 67 | Mercury SMCL 20097 | LIKE IT IS (LP) | 50 |
| 72 | Groove Merchant GM 502 | BLUE SHADOWS FALLING (LP) | 15 |
| 73 | Groove Merchant GM 2205 | GOOD THINGS DON'T HAPPEN EVERY DAY (LP, with Jimmy McGriff) | 15 |
| 73 | Vogue LDM 30163 | MEMORIAL (LP) | 15 |
| 73 | People PLEO 4 | YOU DON'T HAVE TO BE BLACK TO LOVE THE BLUES (LP) | 20 |

## KEN PARKER
| | | | |
|---|---|---|---|
| 67 | Island WI 3082 | How Could I/SONNY BURKE: Choo Choo Train | 60 |
| 67 | Studio One SO 2001 | See Them A-Come/MR FOUNDATION: Have A Good Time | 40 |
| 68 | Island WI 3096 | Down Low/Sad Mood | 50 |
| 68 | Island WI 3105 | Lonely Man/ERROL DUNKLEY: I Am Going Home | 100 |
| 68 | Giant GN 34 | Change Is Gonna Come/VAL BENNETT: Jumping With Val | 175 |
| 69 | Bamboo BAM 1 | My Whole World Is Falling Down/The Chokin' Kind | 30 |
| 69 | Amalgamated AMG 847 | It's Alright/COBBS: One One | 100 |
| 69 | Amalgamated AMG 853 | Only Yesterday/COBBS: Joe Gibbs Mood | 30 |
| 70 | Duke DU 79 | I Can't Hide/TOMMY McCOOK: Kansas City | 10 |
| 70 | Unity UN 553 | When You Were Mine/CLAREDONIANS: The Angels (song actually "The Angels Listened In") | 8 |
| 71 | Duke Reid DR 2504 | Sugar Pantie (as Ken Parker & Tommy McCook; actually by Andy Capp)/ TOMMY McCOOK: All Afire | 10 |
| 71 | Duke Reid DR 2521 | Jimmy Brown/Version | 8 |
| 71 | Big BG 332 | Ain't Misbehaving/Genuine Love | 8 |
| 72 | Jackpot JP 805 | Guilty/AGGROVATORS: Guilty (Version) | 8 |
| 72 | Pama PM 844 | Shake It Loose/TOMMY McCOOK: Shake It Loose - Version (actually titled "Help Me Make It Through The Night") | 8 |
| 72 | Treasure Isle TI 7073 | Help Me Make It Through The Night/TOMMY McCOOK & ALLSTARS (Version) | 8 |
| 73 | Dragon DRA 1003 | Will The Circle Be Unbroken/DYNAMITES: Instrumental | 8 |
| 73 | Dragon DRA 1015 | Say Wonderful Things/It's True | 8 |
| 74 | Attack ATT 8063 | Kiss An Angel/TOMMY McCOOK: Inez | 8 |
| 74 | Attack ATT 8073 | Count Your Blessings/Count Your Blessings (Version) | 6 |
| 74 | Trojan TRLS 80 | JIMMY BROWN (LP) | 25 |

*(see also Lyrics)*

## LARRY PARKER
| | | | |
|---|---|---|---|
| 80 | Brightheath BRH 1 | Perfect Dreams/Light | 20 |

## LEWIS PARKER
| | | | |
|---|---|---|---|
| 95 | White JED1 | B BOY ANTICS (EP, different recording to Bite It! version - first batch with a black and white sticker, later batch has coloured sticker) | 70 |
| 96 | Bite It! BITEDJ10 | B BOY ANTICS (EP) | 45 |
| 96 | Bite It! BITE11 | Rise/Visions Of Splendour/Sea Freestyle (12") | 25 |
| 95 | White LEWIS1 | Wonderwall (7", 100 only) | 30 |
| 98 | Melankolic SADTDJ3 | Shadows Of Autumn/101 Pianos (12") | 10 |
| 00 | M'lic LEWISTDJ1LC03098 | THE OPTIONS (EP) | 25 |
| 01 | White SADTDJ13 | It's All Happening Now/Schemes/What The Ancients Say (remixes) (EP, 50 copies only) | 20 |
| 03 | Dusty Vinyl DV1JEDI | Mr Parker's Siesta/Blood (12") | 18 |
| 13 | King Underground KU/WODV008 | Fragments Of Glass (10" that came with a small number of THE PUZZLE: EPISODE 2) | 12 |
| 98 | Melankolic SADT4 | MASQUERADES AND SILHOUETTES (LP) | 30 |
| 02 | Melankolic LPSAD14 | IT'S ALL HAPPENING NOW (LP) | 75 |
| 06 | Dusty Vinyl DVJEDI008 | MASQUERADES AND SILHOUETTES INSTRUMENTALS (LP, 200 only with unreleased track) | 50 |
| 13 | King Underground KU/WODV007 | THE PUZZLE EPISODE 2 - THE GLASS CEILING (LP) | 15 |

**RAYMOND PARKER**
66   Sue WI 4024                        Ring Around The Roses/She's Coming Home ...................................... 50

**ROBERT PARKER**
66   Island WI 286                      Barefootin'/Let's Go Baby (Where The Action Is) .............................. 30
66   Island WI 3008                     Happy Feet/The Scratch ....................................................... 20
74   Island USA 001                     Get Ta Steppin'/Get Right On Down ............................................ 8
74   Contemporaries CS 9010             Barefootin'/I Caught You In A Lie ............................................ 10
66   Island ILP 942                     BAREFOOTIN' (LP) ............................................................. 80

*(see also Huey 'Piano' Smith & Clowns)*

**SONNY PARKER**
56   Vogue V 2392                       My Soul's On Fire/Disgusted Blues ........................................... 300
56   Vogue V 2392                       My Soul's On Fire/Disgusted Blues (78) ...................................... 50

*(see also Lionel Hampton)*

**EDDIE PARKER (U.S.)**
79   Grapevine GRP 119                  Love You Baby (Parts 1 & 2) (in p/s) ........................................ 10
79   Grapevine GRP 119                  Love You Baby (Parts 1 & 2) (in p/s) (DJ copy) .............................. 20

**WILLIE PARKER**
67   President PT 171                   You Got Your Finger In My Eye/I Live The Life I Love ........................ 10

**WINFIELD PARKER**
72   Mojo 2093 019                      Stop Her On Sight/I'm On My Way .............................................. 8

**GRAHAM PARKER**
80   Stiff BUY 72                       Stupefaction/Women In Charge (p/s) ........................................... 5
80   Stiff BUY 72                       Stupefaction/Paralysed (p/s) ............................................... 10

**PARKING LOT**
69   Parlophone R 5779                  Carpet Man/World Spinning Sadly ............................................. 45

**PARKINGSON'S LAW**
72   RCA RCA 2291                       Daughter Of Thunder And Lightning/I Need Your Loving And I Can't Let Go .. 8

**JIMMY PARKINSON**
56   Columbia SCM 5236                  The Great Pretender/Hand In Hand ............................................ 30
56   Columbia SCM 5267                  Walk Hand In Hand/Cry Baby .................................................. 10
56   Columbia DB 3808                   Gina/A Lover's Quarrel ....................................................... 8
56   Columbia DB 3833                   In The Middle Of The House/You To Me ......................................... 8
57   Columbia DB 3876                   But You/Together (You And I) ................................................. 6
57   Columbia DB 3912                   Round And Round/Whatever Lola Wants (Lola Gets) .............................. 6
57   Columbia 33S 1109                  SOLO (10" LP) ............................................................... 20

**BERNICE PARKS**
55   Coral Q 72056                      Lovin' Machine/Only Love Me ................................................. 15

**LLOYD PARKS**
70   Harry J. HJ 6603                   Feel A Little Better/I'll Be Your Man ....................................... 15
71   Upsetter US 379                    Mighty Cloud Of Joy/UPSETTERS: Version ...................................... 25
72   Randy's RAN 524                    Stars/Stars - Version ....................................................... 20
74   Fab FAB 273                        Schooldays/Version .......................................................... 15
75   Cactus CT 75                       Mafia/Mafia Version (Dub) ................................................... 40
74   Attack – ATLP 1009                 OFFICIALLY (LP) ............................................................. 20
75   Trojan Records TRLS 109            GIRL IN THE MORNING (LP) .................................................... 30
76   Trojan TRLS 126                    LLOYD PARKS (LP) ............................................................ 15

*(see also L. Sparks)*

**SONNY PARKS**
63   Warner Bros WB 100                 New Boy In Town/Us Kids Have Got To Make Up Our Minds ....................... 10

**VAN DYKE PARKS**
66   MGM MGM 1301                       Number Nine/Do What You Wanta ............................................... 12
69   Warner Bros W(S) 1727              SONG CYCLE (LP) ............................................................. 35

**PARLET**
79   Casablanca CAL 2052                INVASION OF THE BOOTY SNATCHERS (LP) ........................................ 15

*(see also Parliament)*

**PARLIAMENT**
71   Invictus INV 513                   The Silent Boatman/Livin' The Life .......................................... 10
72   Invictus INV 522                   Come In Out Of The Rain/Little Ole Country Boy ............................... 8
75   Casablanca CBX 505                 Up On The Down Stroke/Presence Of A Brain .................................... 8
76   Casablanca CBX 518                 Tear The Roof Off The Sucker (Give Up The Funk)/P. Funk ...................... 5
77   Casablanca CAN 103                 Tear The Roof Off The Sucker (Give Up The Funk)/Dr. Funkenstein/P. Funk ...... 5
78   Casablanca CAN 115                 Bop Gun/I've Been Watching You ............................................... 5
78   Casablanca CAN 136                 Aqua Boogie/Water Sign ....................................................... 5
79   Casablanca CAN 154                 Deep/Flashlight ............................................................. 80
71   Invictus SVT 1004                  OSMIUM (LP) ................................................................. 15
74   Casablanca NBLP 7002               UP ON THE DOWN STROKE (LP) ..................................................

*(see also Parliaments, Funkadelic, Parlet, Bootsy's Rubber Band, P-Funk Allstars)*

**PARLIAMENTS**
67   Track 604 013                      I Wanna Testify/I Can Feel The Ice Melting ................................. 30
69   Track 604 032                      I Wanna Testify/I Can Feel The Ice Melting (reissue) ....................... 20

*(see also Parliament, Funkadelic)*

**PARLOPHONE POPS ORCHESTRA**
56   Parlophone R 4250                  Giddy Up A Ding Dong/(We're Gonna) Rock Around The Clock ................... 15

*(see also Ron Goodwin)*

**PARLOUR BAND**
72   Deram SDL 10                       IS A FRIEND? (LP, laminated gatefold sleeve, white/red label) ............. 500

MINT VALUE £

## CHRIS PARMENTER ORCHESTRA
| 66 | Polydor 56107 | Cul De Sac/Donkey | 20 |

## JACK PARNELL (ORCHESTRA)
| 53 | Parlophone MSP 6009 | Waltzing The Blues/Catherine Wheel (as Jack Parnell Band) | 10 |
| 53 | Parlophone MSP 6031 | Night Train/Hawk Talks (as Jack Parnell & His Music Makers) | 10 |
| 53 | Parlophone MSP 6046 | Cotton Tail/April In Paris | 10 |
| 53 | Parlophone MSP 6054 | Dragnet/Fuller Bounce (as Jack Parnell & His Music Makers) | 10 |
| 54 | Parlophone MSP 6066 | Route 66/The Creep | 10 |
| 54 | Parlophone MSP 6078 | Skin Deep/Devil's Eyes (B-side with Dennis Hale) | 20 |
| 54 | Parlophone MSP 6094 | Knock Out/Blowin' Wild (B-side with Dennis Hale) | 12 |
| 54 | Parlophone MSP 6102 | The Bandit (with Dennis Hale)/Annie's Blues (with Annie Ross) | 18 |
| 54 | Parlophone MSP 6138 | Sky Blue Shirt And Rainbow Tie/Trip To Mars | 10 |
| 58 | Parlophone R 4500 | Topsy/Cha Cha Rock | 10 |
| 59 | HMV POP 630 | Kansas City/The Golden Striker | 8 |
| 60 | Philips PB 1005 | 77 Sunset Strip/Teen Ride | 10 |
| 64 | Decca F 11958 | The Kiss/The Hidden Truth | 8 |
| 55 | Parlophone GEP 8532 | JACK PARNELL AND HIS ORCHESTRA (EP) | 10 |
| 55 | Parlophone GEP 8564 | PARNELL ON PARADE (EP) | 10 |
| 58 | Parlophone GEP 8707 | KICK OFF! (EP) | 10 |
| 52 | Decca LF 1065 | THE JACK PARNELL QUARTET (10" LP) | 10 |
| 58 | Parlophone PMD 1053 | TRIP TO MARS (10" LP) | 80 |

*(see also Dennis Hale)*

## PAROT
| 73 | Royal Blue RB 001 | Wake Up/I've Dreamed Of The Sun (p/s) | 25 |

## CATHERINE PARR
| 65 | Decca F 12210 | You Belong To Me/He's My Guy | 12 |

## JACKIE PARRIS AND BIG YOUTH
| 79 | Book Of Psalms BP 001 | Let Him Try/Really Together (12") | 15 |

## BRIAN PARRISH
| 69 | United Artists UP 35049 | In Good Time (Love Chant)/I Wanna Go To Sleep | 10 |

## DEAN PARRISH
| 66 | Stateside SS 531 | Tell Her/Fall On Me | 60 |
| 66 | Stateside SS 531 | Tell Her/Fall On Me (DJ copy) | 100 |
| 66 | Stateside SS 550 | Turn On Your Lovelight/Determination | 100 |
| 66 | Stateside SS 550 | Turn On Your Lovelight/Determination (DJ copy) | 100 |
| 67 | Stateside SS 580 | Skate (Parts 1 & 2) | 150 |
| 67 | Stateside SS 580 | Skate (Parts 1 & 2) (DJ copy) | 60 |
| 75 | UK USA 2 | I'm On My Way/Watch Out | 100 |
| 75 | UK USA 2 | I'm On My Way/Watch Out (DJ copy) | 10 |
| 03 | Kent TOWN 119 | Broken Bottles And Sticks/MELBA MOORE: Magic Touch | 8 |

## PARRISH & GURVITZ
| 71 | Regal Zono. SRZA 8506 | PARRISH & GURVITZ (LP, textured gatefold sleeve) | 35 |

*(see also Baker Gurvitz Army, Three Man Army)*

## GAYLORD PARRY
| 67 | CBS 2685 | I'm On The Way Up/I'm Coming Home | 10 |

## SAM PARRY
| 73 | Argo ZDA 155 | IF SADNESS COULD SING (LP) | 300 |

## PARSON & SMITH
| 72 | Polydor 2058229 | The Letter/When It Rains | 30 |

## ALAN PARSONS PROJECT
| 77 | Arista AL 7002 | I ROBOT (LP) | 15 |

*(see also Andrew Powell & Philharmonic Orchestra))*

## BILL PARSONS & HIS ORCHESTRA
| 59 | London HL 8798 | The All American Boy/Rubber Dolly | 8 |

## GENE PARSONS
| 74 | Warner Bros K 46257 | KINDLING (LP) | 18 |

*(see also Byrds, Flying Burrito Brothers)*

## GRAM PARSONS
| 73 | Reprise K 14245 | The New Soft Shoe/She | 8 |
| 73 | Reprise K 44228 | GP (LP, gatefold sleeve) | 35 |
| 74 | Reprise K 54018 | GRIEVOUS ANGEL (LP, with Emmylou Harris) | 30 |
| 76 | A&M AMLH 65478 | SLEEPLESS NIGHTS (LP, with Flying Burrito Brothers & Emmylou Harris) | 25 |
| 82 | Sundown SDLP 003 | GRAM PARSONS AND THE FALLEN ANGELS (LP, featuring Emmylou Harris) | 15 |

*(see also Byrds, Flying Burrito Brothers)*

## PARTICULAR PEOPLE
| 68 | Big T BIG 105 | Boys Cry/What's The Matter With Juliet | 6 |

## PARTISANS (1)
| 82 | No Future OI 2 | Police Story/Killing Machine (p/s, with lyric insert) | 12 |
| 82 | No Future OI 12 | 17 Years Of Hell/The Power And The Greed/Bastards In Blue (p/s) | 10 |
| 83 | Cloak & Dagger PART 1 | Blind Ambition/Come Clean (p/s) | 15 |
| 83 | No Future PUNK 4 | PARTISANS (LP) | 22 |
| 84 | Cloak & Dagger PARTLP 1 | THE TIME WAS RIGHT (LP, with inner) | 35 |

## PARTISANS (2)
| 88 | Hotwire HWS 863 | Open Your Eyes/Partisan (p/s) | 8 |

*(see also Blades)*

## PARTNERS IN CRIME
| 84 | Epic A 4803 | Hold On/She's Got Eyes For You (p/s) | 6 |

| 85 | Epic A 5040 | Miracles/What You Gonna Do? (p/s) ........................................................... 6 |
| 85 | Epic A 6170 | Hollywood Dreams/She's Got Eyes For You (p/s) ...................................... 7 |
| 85 | Epic TX 6170 | Hollywood Dreams (Extended)/She's Got Eyes For You (12", p/s) .......... 10 |

*(see also Status Quo)*

### PART ONE
| 82 | Paraworm | FUNERAL PARADE (EP) .................................................................................. 12 |

### DON PARTRIDGE
| 69 | Columbia DB 8617 | Going To Germany/Ask Me Why ................................................................ 6 |

*(see also Accolades)*

### PARTY BOYS
| 87 | Epic 651230 0 | He's Gonna Step On You Again/She's A Mystery (shaped picture disc)............ 12 |

*(see also Status Quo)*

### PARTY DAY
| 83 | Party Day FX 301 | Row The Boat Ashore/Poison (p/s, insert) ................................................ 15 |
| 84 | Party Day FX 302 | The Spider/Flies (p/s) .................................................................................. 8 |
| 85 | Rouska COME 1T | Glasshouse/My Heroine/Let Us Shine/Smile (12", p/s) ........................... 20 |
| 85 | Party Day FXLP 401 | GLASSHOUSE (LP) ........................................................................................ 30 |
| 86 | Party Day PDLP 501 | SIMPLICITY (LP) ............................................................................................ 30 |

### PASADENA ROOF ORCHESTRA
| 78 | CBS CBS 12-637 | Pennies From Heaven/Back In Your Own Back Yard/Pennies From Heaven (10" p/s, 2nd side plays at 78 rpm) ......................................................................................... 15 |

### PASHA
| 69 | Liberty LBF 15199 | Someone Shot The Lollipop Man/Pussy Willow Dragon.................................... 120 |

*(see also Searchers)*

### JOE PASS
| 60s | Fontana 688 137 ZL | CATCH ME (LP) ............................................................................................. 20 |

### PASSAGE
| 78 | Object Music OMO 2 | Love Song/The Competition/Slit Machine/New Kind Of Love (p/s)............... 10 |
| 79 | Object OM 8 | Taking My Time/Clock Paradox/Sixteen Hours/Time Delay (p/s) ............. 6 |

*(see also Contact)*

### PASSENGERS (1)
| 79 | No label or cat. no | Something About You (I Don't Like)/Two Lovers (1st press, hand-written labels) ......... 15 |
| 79 | Blue Inc INC 8 | Something About You (I Don't Like)/Two Lovers (2nd press, no p/s) ...................... 10 |
| 79 | Epic SEPC 7830 | Something About You (I Don't Like)/Two Lovers (3rd press, no p/s) ...................... 5 |
| 79 | Epic EPC 7967 | Two Lovers/Love Fades (no p/s) ............................................................................ 6 |

### PASSENGERS (2)
| 95 | Island IS 625 | Miss Sarajevo/One (live) (7", with poster in 12" card in PVC p/s)................... 10 |
| 96 | Island OST 3 | Your Blue Room (CD, 1-track promo, card sleeve, export issue) ...................... 50 |
| 95 | Island OST 2 | ORIGINAL SOUNDCHAT 1 (2-CD, music & interview disc, fold-out digipaks, with cue sheet, promo only) .......................................................................................... 60 |
| 95 | Island ILPS8043 | ORIGINAL SOUNDTRACKS (LP) ............................................................................. 45 |

*(see also U2, Brian Eno)*

### PASSION BLADES
| 83 | Caprice CAP 1 | Living In A Lighthouse/Dub Version (no p/s) ........................................................ 8 |

### PASSION POLKA
| 82 | Kinetic KR 01 | Obsessions/Juliet (no p/s) ...................................................................................... 40 |

### PASSIONS (1)
| 58 | Capitol CL 14874 | My Aching Heart/Jackie Brown ............................................................................. 75 |

### PASSIONS (2)
| 59 | Top Rank JAR 224 | Just To Be With You/Oh Melancholy Me .............................................................. 60 |
| 60 | Top Rank JAR 313 | I Only Want You/This Is My Love ........................................................................... 70 |

### PASSIONS (3)
| 79 | Soho SH5 | Needles And Pills/Body And Soul .......................................................................... 10 |
| 79 | Fiction FICS 008 | Hunted/Oh No, It's You ......................................................................................... 5 |

### PAST AND PRESENT
| 79 | Rook CUS 423 | FIRST TIME OUT (LP, private pressing)................................................................... 30 |

### PAST SEVEN DAYS
| 86 | 4AD AD 102 | Raindance/So Many Others/Nothing (p/s) ............................................................ 12 |

### PASTELS
| 82 | Whaam! WHAAM 005 | Songs For Children: Heavens Above!/Tea Time Tales (p/s) .......................... 40 |
| 83 | Rough Trade RT 137 | I Wonder Why/Supposed To Understand (p/s) ............................................. 30 |
| 84 | Creation CRE 005 | Something Going On/Stay With Me Till Morning (foldaround p/s in poly bag)............ 25 |
| 84 | Creation CRE 011T | A Million Tears/Baby Honey/Surprise Me (12", p/s) ......................................... 15 |
| 85 | Villa 21 VILLA 3 | Heavens Above!/Tea Time Tales/I Wonder Why (live)/Tea Time Tales (live) (p/s)........... 25 |
| 87 | Glass 050 | Crawl Babies/Empty House ................................................................................... 6 |
| 90 | Overground OVER 06 | Heavens Above!/Tea Time Tales/Something Going On (demo)/ Until Morning Comes (demo) (p/s; 200 clear vinyl) ......................................................................................... 5 |
| 90 | Overground OVER 06 | Heavens Above!/Tea Time Tales/Something Going On (demo)/Until Morning Comes (demo) (p/s; 157 green vinyl) ......................................................................................... 6 |
| 87 | Glass GLAL P021 | UP FOR A BIT WITH THE PASTELS (LP, with inner) ............................................. 20 |
| 89 | Chapter 22 CHAPLP 43 | SITTIN' PRETTY (LP) ..................................................................................... 20 |
| 94 | Domino WIGLP 17 | MOBILE SAFARI (LP, with free 7") ......................................................................... 20 |
| 97 | Domino WIGLP 34 | ILLUMINATION (LP) ................................................................................................ 20 |
| 88 | Creation CRELP 031 | SUCK ON (LP) ............................................................................................... 15 |
| 03 | Geographic GEOG18LP | LAST GREAT WILDERNESS (LP) ..................................................................... 18 |

*(see also Buba & Shop Assistants, Jad Fair, Vaselines)*

### PASTEL SIX
| 63 | London HLU 9651 | The Cinnamon Cinder/Bandido ............................................................................. 20 |

MINT VALUE £

## PASTORAL SYMPHONY
68    President PT 202                Love Machine/Spread A Little Love Around ............................................................. 20

## PAT
71    Gas GAS 158                     Teach Me (actually "Words Of Temptation" by Earl Lawrence)/RHYTHM RULERS: Sea
                                      Breeze (actually by Im & David).......................................................................... 30

## PAT & MARIE
66    Ska Beat JB 234                 I Try Not To Tell You/PAT RHODEN: Don't Blame It On Me............................................. 15
66    Ska Beat JB 235                 You're Really Leaving/PAT RHODEN: Broken Heart ................................................... 15
*(see also Pat Rhoden)*

## PAT & ROXIE
65    Caribou CRC 2                   Sing To Me/Things I Used To Do............................................................................ 10

## PATCHES
72    Warner Bros K 16201             Living In America/Quicksand..................................................................................8
75    Bradley BRAD 7516               Telltale/Chug-A-Lug...............................................................................................5

## PATCHWORK (1)
72    Decca FR 13346                  Laughing Sam (On The Phone)/Afrodisiac............................................................ 40

## PATCHWORK (2)
78    Wasps WSP 1                     JOhanne Of The Zuider Zee (Far Canal)/Nothing Wrong With Women (no p/s) .............. 6

## JOHNNY PATE ORCHESTRA
58    Parlophone 4437                 I'm Stepping Out Of The Picture/Muskeeta ............................................................ 12
73    Probe SPB 1077                  SHAFT IN AFRICA (LP, soundtrack, with Four Tops)................................................. 40

## PAMELA PATERSON
72    Polydor 2001 278                Finally (Theme From 'Gumshoe')/OLYMPIC STUDIO CONCERT ORCHESTRA: Music
                                      From 'Gumshoe' (p/s) ......................................................................................... 20

## PATHETIX
78    No Records NO 001               Aleister Crowley/Don't Touch My Machine/Snuffed It (p/s, with insert) ..................... 30
79    TJM TJM 9                       Love In Decay/Nil Carborundum/What Do You Expect? (with p/s)............................ 200
79    TJM TJM 9                       Love In Decay/Nil Carborundum/What Do You Expect? (without p/s) ....................... 40

## PATHFINDERS (1)
64    Decca F 12038                   I Love You Caroline/Something I Can Always Do ..................................................... 18

## PATHFINDERS (2)
64    Hayton SP 138/139               What Do You Do/What'd I Say (private pressing)..................................................... 20

## PATHFINDERS (3)
65    Parlophone R 5372               Don't You Believe It/Castle Of Love ..................................................................... 20
*(see also [White] Trash, Poets)*

## PATHWAY TO YOUR MIND
68    Major Minor SMLP 19             PREPARING THE MIND AND BODY FOR MEDITATION (LP, spoken word)..................... 25

## PATIENCE & PRUDENCE
56    London HLU 8321                 Tonight You Belong To Me/A Smile And A Ribbon (Gold label) ................................. 30
56    London HLU 8321                 Tonight You Belong To Me/A Smile And A Ribbon (Silver label) ............................... 15
57    London HLU 8369                 Gonna Get Along Without Ya Now/The Money Tree (Gold label)............................. 30
57    London HLU 8369                 Gonna Get Along Without Ya Now/The Money Tree (Silver label)............................ 15
57    London HL 7017                  Gonna Get Along Without Ya Now/The Money Tree (export issue) ......................... 20
57    London HLU 8425                 Dreamer's Bay/We Can't Sing Rhythm And Blues ................................................... 15
57    London HLU 8493                 You Tattletale/Very Nice Is Bali Bali ..................................................................... 15
58    London HLU 8773                 Tom Thumb's Tune/Golly Oh Gee ..........................................................................8
57    London REU 1087                 A SMILE AND A SONG (EP).................................................................................... 40

## SALLY PATIENCE
84    Disc DEL 1                      The Triangle Man/Buried In My Boots (p/s)............................................................ 35

## LEON PATILLO
70s   Maranatha MM 0049              DANCE CHILDREN, DANCE (LP) ............................................................................ 18
70s   Myrrh MYR 1136                 LIVE EXPERIENCE (LP) ......................................................................................... 18

## SANDY & CAROLINE PATON
60    Topic TOP 57                    HUSH LITTLE BABY (EP)......................................................................................... 10
*(see also Beat Brothers, Tony Sheridan & Beat Brothers)*

## BOBBY PATRICK BIG SIX
64    Decca F 11898                   Shake It Easy Baby/Wildwood Days ...................................................................... 40
64    Decca F 12030                   Monkey Time/Sweet Talk Me Baby ....................................................................... 30
64    Decca DFE 8570                  TEENBEAT 3 (FROM STAR CLUB, HAMBURG) (EP)................................................. 120

## DAN PATRICK
67    Stateside SS 2004               Tiger Lee/Call Of The Wild.................................................................................... 10

## KENTRICK PATRICK
63    Island WI 066                   Man To Man/ROLAND ALFONSO: Blockade (B-side actually "Hit And Run").............. 30
63    Island WI 079                   Don't Stay Out Late/Forever And Ever .................................................................. 30
63    Island WI 104                   The End Of The World/Little Princess ................................................................... 25
63    Island WI 119                   Golden Love/Beyond............................................................................................ 40
64    Island WI 132                   Take Me To The Party/I'm Sorry............................................................................ 25
64    Island WI 140                   I Am Wasting Time/RANDY'S GROUP: Royal Charley............................................. 120
*(see also Lord Creator)*

## PATRICK & LLOYD
70    Big Shot BI 550                 Return Of The Pollock/PROPHETS: Concorde ........................................................ 25
*(see also Lloyd & Prophets)*

## PATRIOTS
66    Fontana TF 650                  Prophet/I'll Be There ........................................................................................... 20

## PATRON OF THE ARTS
66    Page One POF 012                The True Patron Of The Arts/Eleanor Rigby (USA release credits it as Queen City Show
                                      Band)................................................................................................................. 50

## PATSY
| 68 | Doctor Bird DB 1113 | A Man Is Two Faced/LENNIE HIBBERT & COUNT OSSIE: Pure Soul | 150 |
| 68 | Doctor Bird DB 1122 | Little Flea/The Retreat Song | 60 |
| 68 | High Note HS012 | We Were Lovers/DELANO STEWART : Give Me A Chance | 35 |

(see also Patsy Todd, Derrick & Patsy, Stranger & Patsy, Emotions)

## PATSY & PEGGY
| 70 | Hot Rod HR 107 | Dog Your Woman/Strictly Invitation | 100 |

## BRIAN PATTEN
| 70 | Caedmon TC 1300 | BRIAN PATTEN (LP) | 20 |
| 76 | Tangent TGS 116 | VANISHING TRICK (LP) | 20 |

(see also Liverpool Scene, Roger McGough & Brian Patten)

## PATTERN PEOPLE
| 68 | MGM MGM 1429 | Love Is A Lover Loving To Be Loved/Take A Walk In The Sunshine | 20 |

## PATTERNS
| 80 | Heater Volume Records HVR 002 | No Violent Pacing/Bishop In The Fridge | 10 |

## PATTERNS IN PERU
| 86 | Vernon YZ 60 | This Is The Night/Playing Games | 25 |
| 86 | Vernon YZ60T | This Is The Night (Extended)/Playing Games/This Is The Night (12" p/s) | 40 |

## BOBBY PATTERSON (& MUSTANGS)
| 68 | Pama PM 735 | Broadway Ain't Funky No More/I Met My Match (with Mustangs) | 15 |
| 68 | Pama PM 743 | The Good Ol' Days/Don't Be So Mean | 20 |
| 68 | Pama PM 754 | Busy Busy Bee/Sweet Taste Of Love (with Mustangs) | 20 |
| 69 | Pama PM 763 | T.C.B. Or T.Y.A./What A Wonderful Night For Love (with Mustangs) | 20 |
| 69 | Pama PM 773 | My Thing Is Your Thing/Keep It In The Family | 20 |
| 72 | Action ACT 4604 | I'm In Love With You/Married Lady | 90 |
| 77 | Contempo 2115 | I Got To Get Over/If He Hadn't Slipped And Got Caught | 20 |
| 72 | Mojo 2092 037 | How Do You Spell Love/She Don't Have To See You | 10 |

## KELLEE PATTERSON
| 76 | Mint CHEW 10 | I'm Gonna Love You Just A Little More Baby/You Are So Beautiful | 60 |
| 95 | Hubbub Records – HUBLP03 | KELLEE (LP, reissue) | 20 |

## MANLEY PATTERSON
| 72 | Pama Supreme PS 337 | I Stayed Away Too Long/Country Boy | 5 |

## MARY-ANNE PATTERSON
| 70 | Joy JOYS 162 | ME (LP) | 300 |

## OTTILIE PATTERSON
| 55 | Decca F 10472 | I Hate A Man Like You/Reckless Blues (with Chris Barber's Jazz Band) | 10 |
| 55 | Decca F 10621 | Weeping Willow Blues/Nobody Knows You When You're Down And Out | 10 |
| 57 | Pye 7N 15109 | Kay-Cee Rider/I Love You Baby | 10 |
| 58 | Pye Jazz 7NJ 2015 | Jailhouse Blues/Beale Street Blues | 10 |
| 58 | Pye Jazz 7NJ 2025 | Trombone Cholly/Lawdy, Lawdy Blues | 10 |
| 61 | Columbia DB 4760 | Blueberry Hill/I'm Crazy 'Bout My Baby | 12 |
| 62 | Columbia DB 4834 | I Hate Myself/Come On Baby | 10 |
| 63 | Columbia DB 7140 | Jealous Heart/Won't Be Long | 10 |
| 63 | Columbia DB 7208 | Baby Please Don't Go/I Feel So Good (with Sonny Boy Williamson) | 50 |
| 65 | Columbia DB 7332 | Tell Me Where Is Fancy/Oh Me What Eyes | 10 |
| 69 | Marmalade 598 016 | Spring Song/Sound Of The Door As It Closes | 25 |
| 69 | Marmalade 598 020 | Bitterness Of Death/Spring Song | 12 |
| 56 | Decca DFE 6303 | BLUES (EP) | 10 |
| 56 | Pye Jazz Today NJE 1023 | THAT PATTERSON GIRL VOL. 2 (EP) | 10 |
| 60 | Columbia SEG 7998 | SWINGS THE IRISH (EP) | 15 |
| 59 | Pye NPL 18028 | OTTILIE'S IRISH NIGHT (LP) | 125 |
| 69 | Marmalade 608 011 | 3000 YEARS WITH OTTILIE (LP) | 15 |
| 69 | Polydor 2384 031 | SPRING SONG (LP) | 35 |

(see also Chris Barber)

## ROBERT PATTERSON SINGERS
| 60s | United Artists UAS 29003 | THE SOUL OF GOSPEL (LP) | 25 |
| 65 | Fontana 688 516 ZL | I'M SAVED (LP) | 18 |

## PATTERSONS
| 70 | CBS 5083 | I Can Fly/An Cailin Deas | 15 |
| 69 | CBS M 63532 | AGAIN (LP, mono) | 18 |
| 69 | CBS 63522 | AGAIN (LP, stereo) | 15 |

## PATTERSON'S PEOPLE
| 66 | Mercury MF 913 | Shake Hands With The Devil/Deadly Nightshade | 40 |

## PATTIE
| 69 | Columbia DB 8542 | Gravitation/Let The Music Start | 12 |

## PATTI & PATETTES
| 75 | Dart ART 2053 | Bill/It's My Party | 8 |
| 76 | United Artists UP 36077 | Summer Heartbreak/Too Much | 12 |

## HUBERT PATTISON
| 66 | Pye 7N 17207 | Bare Back Rider/The Baby 1 & 2 Problem | 5 |
| 67 | Fontana TF 859 | My Home's In My Pocket/Saturday Morning Bride | 10 |

## LITTLE JOHN PATTISON
| 64 | Giv-A-Disc LYN 510 | Needles And Pins/All My Loving (flexidisc with Giv-A-Disc booklet) | 10 |

## (MIKE) PATTO
| 66 | Columbia DB 8091 | Can't Stop Talking About My Baby/Love (as Mike Patto) | 100 |
| 74 | Goodear EAR 106 | Sitting In The Park/Get Up And Dig It (as Mike Patto) | 10 |

# Alexander PATTON

| | | | |
|---|---|---|---|
| 70 | Vertigo 6360 016 | PATTO (LP, textured gatefold sleeve, large swirl label) | 300 |
| 71 | Vertigo 6360 032 | HOLD YOUR FIRE (LP, 3-flap gatefold, small swirl label) | 500 |
| 72 | Island ILPS 9210 | ROLL 'EM SMOKE 'EM PUT ANOTHER LINE OUT (LP, pink rim/palm tree label) | 60 |

*(see also Bo Street Runners, Breakaways, Boxer, News, Chicago Line, Timebox, Felder's Orioles, Steve York, Centipede, Grimms, Spooky Tooth, V.I.P.s)*

## ALEXANDER PATTON
| | | | |
|---|---|---|---|
| 66 | Capitol CL 15461 | A Lil Lovin' Sometimes/No More Dreams | 250 |
| 66 | Capitol CL 15461 | A Lil Lovin' Sometimes/No More Dreams (DJ copy) | 350 |

## CHARLIE PATTON
| | | | |
|---|---|---|---|
| 50s | Heritage REU 4 | CHARLIE PATTON (EP, 99 only) | 60 |

## JOHN PATTON
| | | | |
|---|---|---|---|
| 64 | Blue Note 45-1889 | I'll Never Be Free/Along Came John | 8 |

## PATTY & EMBLEMS
| | | | |
|---|---|---|---|
| 64 | Stateside SS 322 | Mixed Up Shook Up Girl/Ordinary Guy | 50 |
| 64 | Stateside SS 322 | Mixed Up Shook Up Girl/Ordinary Guy (DJ copy) | 100 |

## PATTY FLABBIE'S COUGHED ENGINE
| | | | |
|---|---|---|---|
| 69 | Stateside SS 2136 | Billy's Got A Goat/Tin Can Eater | 6 |

## PAUL
| | | | |
|---|---|---|---|
| 65 | Polydor BM 56045 | Will You Follow Me/Head Death | 80 |

*(see also Jimmy Page)*

## ANDREW PAUL
| | | | |
|---|---|---|---|
| 85 | Fashion FAD 038 | Hustle Them A Hustle/Bad Boys (12") | 25 |
| 85 | Y&D YDD 0126 | Under Me Sensima/Can't Take It No Longer (12", with the Offbeat Posse) | 30 |

## BILLY PAUL
| | | | |
|---|---|---|---|
| 73 | Epic EPC 65456 | EBONY WOMAN (LP) | 15 |
| 74 | Phil. Intl. PIR 65861 | WAR OF THE GODS (LP, gatefold sleeve) | 15 |

## BUNNY PAUL
| | | | |
|---|---|---|---|
| 54 | Columbia SCM 5102 | New Love/You'll Never Leave My Side | 10 |
| 54 | Columbia SCM 5112 | Such A Night/I'm Gonna Have Some Fun | 20 |
| 54 | Columbia SCM 5131 | Lovey Dovey/Answer The Call | 20 |
| 54 | Columbia SCM 5151 | You Came A Long Way From St. Louis/You Are Always In My Heart | 12 |
| 55 | Capitol CL 14279 | Please Have Mercy (On A Fool)/These Are The Things We'll Share | 12 |
| 55 | Capitol CL 14304 | Leave My Heart Alone/Two Castanets | 12 |
| 55 | Capitol CL 14368 | Song Of The Dreamer/For The Very First Time | 10 |

## DARLENE PAUL
| | | | |
|---|---|---|---|
| 64 | Capitol CL 15344 | Act Like Nothing Happened/Little Bit Of Heaven | 30 |

## DEREK PAUL
| | | | |
|---|---|---|---|
| 73 | Youngblood YB 1006 | Drugtaker/Riverboat | 8 |

## DON PAUL
| | | | |
|---|---|---|---|
| 68 | RCA 1666 | Wise/Ways Of The World | 12 |

## EUGENE PAUL
| | | | |
|---|---|---|---|
| 70 | Pama Supreme PS 303 | Don't Let The Tears Fall/Another Saturday Night | 6 |
| 70 | Pama Supreme PS 305 | I Found A Man In My Bed/So Many Things | 6 |
| 71 | Pama Supreme PS 317 | Farewell My Darling/Whole Lot Of Woman | 6 |
| 71 | Pama Supreme PS 329 | Somebody's Changing My Sweet Baby's Mind/Hard Minded Neighbour | 6 |
| 72 | Pama PM 838 | Beautiful Sunday/Take Care Son | 6 |
| 72 | Pama Supreme PS 357 | I'll Take You There/Beautiful Baby | 6 |
| 73 | Pama Supreme PS 382 | Power To All Our Friends/RANNY WILLIAMS ALLSTARS: Wicked And Dreadful | 7 |

## EUGENE PAUL & PILOTS
| | | | |
|---|---|---|---|
| 70 | Torpedo TOR 17 | Sugar Dumpling/I May Dwell | 15 |

## FRANKIE PAUL
| | | | |
|---|---|---|---|
| 85 | Greensleeves GRED 189 | Fools Fighting/Fighting Dub (12") | 12 |
| 85 | Tonos TON 007 | Shining Star/If I Am Wrong (12") | 30 |

## JASON PAUL
| | | | |
|---|---|---|---|
| 69 | Pye 7N 17710 | Shine A Little Light Into My Room/Paradise Pudding | 20 |

*(see also Svensk)*

## JOHN E. PAUL
| | | | |
|---|---|---|---|
| 67 | Decca F 12685 | Prince Of Players/I Wanna Know (DJ copy with curved Decca logo inverted matrix) | 200 |
| 67 | Decca F 12685 | Prince Of Players/I Wanna Know (Boxed Decca logo, inverted matrix) | 100 |
| 67 | Decca F 12685 | Prince Of Players/I Wanna Know (Matrix number 41387 correct way up) | 20 |

## LES PAUL (& MARY FORD)
| | | | |
|---|---|---|---|
| 54 | Capitol CL 14185 | Mandolino/Whither Thou Goest | 8 |
| 55 | Capitol CL 14212 | Mister Sandman/That's What I Like | 15 |
| 55 | Capitol CL 14233 | Someday Sweetheart/Song In Blue | 8 |
| 55 | Capitol CL 14300 | No Letter Today/Genuine Love | 8 |
| 55 | Capitol CL 14342 | Goodbye My Love/Hummingbird | 8 |
| 56 | Capitol CL 14502 | Alabamy Bound/Texas Lady | 8 |

## LYN PAUL
| | | | |
|---|---|---|---|
| 74 | Polydor 2058 472 | Sail The Summer Winds/Lay Me Down (with John Barry) | 7 |
| 75 | Polydor 2383 340 | GIVE ME LOVE (LP) | 15 |

*(see also Nocturnes)*

## RIM D. PAUL
| | | | |
|---|---|---|---|
| 68 | Philips BF 1737 | Thousand Hours/Downstairs To Meet Her | 5 |

## SHELLEY PAUL
| | | | |
|---|---|---|---|
| 69 | Jay Boy BOY 10 | Clowns Are Coming In/Take Me To Your Heart | 6 |

## PAULA & JETLINERS
| | | | |
|---|---|---|---|
| 66 | Rainbow RAI 102 | The Great Pretender/The Legend Of The Man From U.N.C.L.E. | 15 |

| | | |
|---|---|---|
| 66 | Rainbow RAi 105 | I Know Someday/Something On My Mind (B-side with Carols) ..........................8 |

## PAUL & LINDA
| | | |
|---|---|---|
| 69 | Page One POF 140 | You're Taking My Bag/When I Hear Your Name ..........................10 |

## PAUL & PAULA
| | | |
|---|---|---|
| 63 | Philips 304 016 BF | Young Lovers/Ba-hey-be..........................5 |
| 63 | Philips BF 1256 | First Quarrel/School Is Thru..........................5 |
| 63 | Philips BF 1269 | Something Old, Something New/Flipped Over You..........................5 |
| 63 | Philips BF 1281 | First Day Back At School/A Perfect Pair..........................5 |
| 64 | Philips BF 1380 | No Other Baby/Too Dark To See..........................7 |
| 63 | Philips BBE 12639 | YOUNG LOVERS (EP)..........................20 |
| 63 | Philips 652 026BL | SING FOR YOUNG LOVERS (LP)..........................25 |
| 63 | Philips BL 7573 | WE GO TOGETHER (LP)..........................25 |
| 63 | Philips BL 7587 | HOLIDAY FOR TEENS (LP)..........................20 |

## PAUL AND RITCHIE & CRYING SHAMES
| | | |
|---|---|---|
| 66 | Decca F 12483 | September In The Rain/Come On Back (more common demos are worth, £80) ..........120 |

*(see also Cryin' Shames, Gary Walker & Rain)*

## PAULETTE (WILLIAMS)
| | | |
|---|---|---|
| 68 | Major Minor MM 565 | One Love In My Heart/Must We Say Goodbye..........................6 |
| 73 | Summit SUM 8543 | Every Day Is The Same Kind Of Thing/ SHORTY PERRY: The Sweat Of Your Brow..........6 |

*(see also Paulette & Gee)*

## PAULETTE & DELROY
| | | |
|---|---|---|
| 63 | Island WI 120 | Little Lover/Lovin' Baby..........................30 |

*(see also Paulette, Paulette & Gee)*

## PAULETTE & GEE
| | | |
|---|---|---|
| 70 | G.G. GG 4506 | Hold On Tight/G.G. ALL STARS: Tight Version..........................8 |

*(see also Paulette, Sister, Winston Wright)*

## PAULETTE SISTERS
| | | |
|---|---|---|
| 55 | Capitol CL 14294 | Dream Boat/Leave My Honey Be..........................12 |
| 55 | Capitol CL 14310 | Ring-A-Dang-A-Doo/Lonely One..........................12 |
| 55 | Capitol CL 14347 | You Win Again/Mama, El Baion..........................12 |

## PAULINE (& BROWN SUGAR)
| | | |
|---|---|---|
| 80 | Studio WE 706 | I Am So Proud/NATTY LOCKS: Studio 16 Workshop (12")..........................25 |
| 80 | Isis 1 | Lion, Me And My Dread/Revelation Side (12")..........................40 |

*(see also Brown Sugar)*

## PAUL'S DISCIPLES
| | | |
|---|---|---|
| 65 | Decca F 12081 | See That My Grave Is Kept Clean/Sixteen Tons..........................35 |

## PAUL'S TROUBLES
| | | |
|---|---|---|
| 67 | Ember EMB S 233 | You'll Find Out/You've Got Something..........................25 |

## PAUPERS
| | | |
|---|---|---|
| 68 | Verve Forecast VS 1514 | Think I Care/White Song..........................15 |
| 69 | Verve Forecast VS 1520 | Southdown Road/Numbers..........................15 |
| 68 | Verve Forecast (S)VLP 6017 | ELLIS ISLAND (LP, mono/stereo)..........................30 |

*(see also Lighthouse)*

## PAVEMENT
| | | |
|---|---|---|
| 92 | Big Cat ABB 35S | Trigger Cut/Sue Me Jack/So Stark (You're A Skyscraper) (p/s)..........................6 |
| 94 | Big Cat ABB 55S | Cut Your Hair/Camera/Stare (p/s)..........................6 |
| 94 | Big Cat UK ABB 55T | Cut Your Hair/Camera/Stare (uncredited track) (12")..........................10 |
| 94 | Big Cat ABB 70T | Gold Soundz/Kneeling Bus/Strings Of Nashville/Exit Theory (12")..........................6 |
| 95 | Big Cat ABB 86S | Rattled By La Rush/False Skorpion/Easily Fooled (p/s)..........................5 |
| 95 | Big Cat ABB 77S | Range Life/Raft Coolin By Sound (p/s)..........................10 |
| 95 | Big Cat ABB 91S | Father To A Sister Of Thought/Kris Kraft/Mussle Rock Is A Horse In Transition (p/s)........6 |
| 96 | Big Cat ABB 110 S | Give It A Day/Gangsters & Pranksters/Saganaw/I Love Perth (p/s)..........................12 |
| 92 | Big Cat ABB 38P | WATERY, DOMESTIC (12" EP, picture disc, stickered poly sleeve)..........................10 |
| 91 | Big Cat ABB 34 | SLANTED AND ENCHANTED (LP, with lyric sheet)..........................25 |
| 93 | Big Cat ABB 40 | WESTING (BY MUSKET AND SEXTANT) (LP)..........................20 |
| 94 | Big Cat ABB 56L | CROOKED RAIN CROOKED RAIN (LP, with inner sleeve, some with free 7": "Haunt You Down"/"Jam Kids")..........................30 |
| 95 | Big Cat LC 5661 | WOWEE ZOWEE (2-LP, 3-sided, 1 side etched gatefold cover)..........................20 |
| 97 | Domino WIGLP 31 | BRIGHTEN THE CORNERS (LP)..........................20 |
| 99 | Domino WIGLP 66 | TERROR TWILIGHT (LP)..........................15 |

*(see also Stephen Malkmus)*

## PAX EXTERNAL
| | | |
|---|---|---|
| 71 | Decca F 13167 | A Second Chance Mr. Jones/You See Him As Your Brother..........................6 |

## GARY PAXTON
| | | |
|---|---|---|
| 62 | Liberty LIB 55485 | Stop Twistin' Baby/Alley Oop Was A Two Dab Man..........................15 |

*(see also Skip & Flip)*

## TOM PAXTON
| | | |
|---|---|---|
| 66 | Elektra EKSN 45001 | The Last Thing On My Mind/Goin' To The Zoo..........................20 |
| 66 | Elektra EKSN 45003 | One Time And One Time Only/Bottle Of Wine..........................5 |
| 67 | Elektra EKSN 45006 | Leaving London/All The Way Home..........................5 |
| 69 | Elektra EKSN 45021 | Jennifer's Rabbit/The Marvellous Toy..........................5 |
| 69 | Elektra EKSN 45064 | Crazy John/The Things I Notice Now..........................5 |
| 69 | Elektra EKSN 45049 | Victoria Dines Alone/Clarissa Jones..........................20 |
| 67 | Elektra EPK 802 | TOM PAXTON (EP)..........................20 |
| 66 | Elektra EKL 298/EKS 7298 | AIN'T THAT NEWS (LP, U.K. pressing in U.S. sleeve)..........................20 |

## DAVEY PAYNE & MEDIUM WAVE
| | | |
|---|---|---|
| 69 | Ember EMB S 265 | Walk In The Sunshine/Looking Towards The Sky (p/s)..........................30 |

| | | | MINT VALUE £ |
|---|---|---|---|

**DAVEY PAYNE**
79   Stiff HORN 1     Saxophone Man/Foggy Day (p/s) ................................................................7

*(see also Kilburn & The High Roads, Ian Dury & The Blockheads)*

**FREDA PAYNE**
| 62 | HMV POP 1091 | He Who Laughs Last (Desafinado)/Slightly Out Of Tune | 15 |
| 70 | Invictus INV 502 | Band Of Gold/ The Easiest Way To Fall | 5 |
| 70 | Invictus INV 505 | Deeper And Deeper/Unhooked Generation | 5 |
| 71 | Invictus INV 509 | Cherish What Is Dear To You (While It's Near To You)/ The World Don't Owe You A Thing | 5 |
| 71 | Invictus INV 512 | Rock Me In The Cradle (Of Your Lovin' Arms)/ Now Is The Time To Say Goodbye | 5 |
| 71 | Invictus INV 515 | Bring Home The Boys/Odds And Ends | 5 |
| 71 | Invictus INV 518 | You've Got To Love Somebody/Mama's Gone | 5 |
| 72 | Invictus INV 520 | You Brought Me Joy/Suddenly It's Yesterday | 6 |
| 72 | Invictus INV 526 | Unhooked Generation/Come Back | 6 |
| 73 | Invictus INV 529 | I Shall Not Be Moved/Thru' The Memory Of My Mind | 5 |
| 73 | Invictus INV 533 | Band Of Gold/The Easiest Way To Fall (reissue, withdrawn) | 30 |
| 75 | ABC ABC 4087 | You/Lost In Love | 5 |

**JACKIE PAYNE**
77   Barak 4     I Found Myself/Instrumental ................................................................15

**JOHN PAYNTER**
70   Universal Editions LYN 2351   HEAR AND NOW (EP) ................................................................50

**LOLA PAYOLA**
81   Epic EPC 1499     Schoolgirl Song/I Got Married To A Man From Space (p/s) ................................25

**LAWRENCE PAYTON**
| 74 | ABC 4021 | Tell Me You Love Me/Instrumental (DJ Copy) | 30 |
| 74 | ABC 4021 | Tell Me You Love Me/Instrumental | 20 |

*(see also the Four Tops)*

**PAZ**
79   Magnus 2     PAZ AT CHICHESTER (LP) ................................................................25

*(see also Lol Coxhill)*

**P BROTHERS**
| 01 | White (Heavy Bronx) PBHB 01 | HEAVY BRONX EXPERIENCE VOL. 1 (EP) | 40 |
| 01 | White (Heavy Bronx) PBHB 002 | HEAVY BRONX EXPERIENCE VOL. 2 (EP) | 20 |

**PC LTD**
69   Fontana TF 1032     Sunny Was A Fool/Here We Come ................................................................6

**DAVE PEABODY**
73   Village Thing VTS 22     PEABODY HOTEL (LP, with insert) ................................................................50

**PEACE**
| 12 | Deadly People | Follow Baby/Li'l Echo (picture disc, 500 only, 20 signed by band) | 12 |
| 12 | Deadly People 88725473021 | DELICIOUS EP (12" white vinyl, 300 only) | 20 |
| 13 | Columbia 8883706487 | California Daze (1-sided RSD picture disc) | 8 |

**DAVE PEACE QUARTET**
69   Saga FID 2155     GOOD MORNING MR. BLUES (LP) ................................................................15

*(see also Birmingham)*

**PEACEMAKERS**
| 65 | Herald ELR 1070 | PEACEMAKERS EP | 15 |
| 65 | Herald ELR 1079 | PEACEMAKERS EP (repressing) | 15 |

**PEACHES**
| 02 | Kitty Yo XLLP 163 | TEACHES OF PEACHES (LP as 5x12") | 30 |
| 03 | Kitty Yo XLLP 171 | FATHERFUCKER (2-LP, pink vinyl) | 18 |
| 11 | XL Recordings XLLP 163 | TEACHES OF PEACHES (2-LP, reissue, pink vinyl) | 20 |

**PEACHES & HERB**
| 67 | CBS 202509 | Let's Fall In Love/We're In This Thing Together | 30 |
| 67 | CBS 202509 | Let's Fall In Love/We're In This Thing Together (DJ copy) | 40 |
| 67 | CBS 2711 | Close Your Eyes/I Will Watch Over You | 8 |
| 67 | CBS 2866 | For Your Love/I Need Your Love So Desperately | 25 |
| 67 | CBS 2866 | For Your Love/I Need Your Love So Desperately (DJ copy) | 40 |
| 67 | Direction 58-3096 | Love Is Strange/Two Little Kids | 10 |
| 68 | Direction 58-3415 | Let It Be Me/I Need Your Love So Desperately | 10 |
| 68 | Direction 58-3548 | United/Thank You | 8 |
| 68 | Direction 58-3829 | Let's Make A Promise/Me And You | 10 |
| 69 | Direction 58-4085 | When He Touches Me/Thank You | 7 |
| 70 | Direction 58-4909 | Satisfy My Hunger/It's Just A Game, Love | 8 |
| 70 | Direction 58-5249 | Soothe Me With Your Love/We're So Much In Love | 8 |
| 71 | CBS 5249 | Soothe Me With Your Love/We're So Much In Love (reissue) | 6 |
| 77 | Epic EPC 4903 | Soothe Me With Your Love/Satisy My Hunger (coloured vinyl) | 6 |

**PEACOCK**
71   Famous FAM 109     Sun Was In Your Eyes/Just A Lonely Man ................................................................20

**ANNETTE PEACOCK**
| 72 | RCA SF 8255 | I'M THE ONE (LP) | 22 |
| 79 | Aura | LIVE IN PARIS (LP) | 18 |

**ANNETTE PEACOCK & PAUL BLEY**
73   Freedom 2383 105     DUAL UNITY (LP) ................................................................50

*(see also Paul Bley, Bley-Peacock Synthesiser Show, Annette Peacock)*

**ROGER PEACOCK**
65   Columbia DB7764     Everybody's Talking About My Baby/Times Have Changed ................................20

## TREVOR PEACOCK
| | | | |
|---|---|---|---|
| 61 | Decca F 11414 | I Didn't Figure On Him To Come Back/Can I Walk You Home | 22 |

## PEAK FOLK
| | | | |
|---|---|---|---|
| 76 | Folk Heritage FHR 082 | THE PEAK FOLK (LP) | 40 |

## PEANUT
| | | | |
|---|---|---|---|
| 65 | Pye 7N 15901 | Thank Goodness For The Rain/I'm Not Sad | 10 |
| 65 | Pye 7N 15963 | Home Of The Brave/I Wanna Hear It Again | 30 |
| 66 | Columbia DB 8032 | I'm Waiting For The Day/Someone's Gonna Be Sorry | 22 |
| 67 | Columbia DB 8104 | I Didn't Love Him Anyway/Come Tomorrow | 20 |

*(see also Katie Kissoon, Ragdolls U.K.)*

## PEANUT BUTTER CONSPIRACY
| | | | |
|---|---|---|---|
| 67 | CBS 2981 | It's A Happening Thing/Twice Is Life | 15 |
| 68 | CBS 3543 | Turn On A Friend/Captain Sandwich | 10 |
| 69 | London HLH 10290 | Back In L.A./Have A Little Faith | 10 |
| 68 | CBS 63277 | THE GREAT CONSPIRACY (LP) | 40 |

## PEANUTS
| | | | |
|---|---|---|---|
| 71 | Philips 6006087 | Goldendays/Headin Straight For You | 10 |

## BOB PEARCE BLUES BAND
| | | | |
|---|---|---|---|
| 74 | Westwood WRS 040 | LET'S GET DRUNK AGAIN (LP) | 18 |

*(see also Brother Bung)*

## PEARL JAM
| | | | |
|---|---|---|---|
| 92 | Epic 657 572-7 | Alive/Once (white/red vinyl p/s) | 12 |
| 92 | Epic 657 572-6 | Alive/Once/Wash (12", poster p/s) | 10 |
| 92 | Epic 657 867-7 | Even Flow/Oceans (p/s) | 5 |
| 92 | Epic 657 857-8 | Even Flow/Dirty Frank/Oceans (12", white vinyl, p/s) | 15 |
| 92 | Epic 658 258-7 | Jeremy/Alive (live) (white vinyl, p/s) | 10 |
| 92 | Epic 658 258-6 | Jeremy/Alive (live)/Footsteps (12", picture disc, with card insert) | 25 |
| 92 | Epic 658 258-2 | Jeremy/Yellow Ledbetter/Alive (live) (CD, picture disc) | 15 |
| 93 | Epic 660 020-6 | Daughter/Blood (Live)/Yellow Ledbetter (Live) (12", ltd. ed. poster sleeve) | 15 |
| 93 | Epic 659 795-6 | Go Alone/Elderly Woman Behind The Counter In A Small Town (Acoustic) (12", with free cassette [plays 'Animal' (Live)]) | 12 |
| 93 | Epic 660 020-7 | Daughter/Blood (live) (red vinyl p/s) | 5 |
| 94 | Epic 660 441-7 | Dissident/Rearviewmirror (live) (stickered poster p/s) | 5 |
| 00 | Epic 669 374 7 | Nothing As It seems/Insignificance (blue vinyl, p/s) | 12 |
| 00 | Epic 669628 7 | Light Years/Soon Forget (live) (clear sleeve, insert, numbered) | 10 |
| 91 | Epic 468884 | TEN (LP) | 20 |
| 92 | Epic 468 884-0 | TEN (LP, printed plastic sleeve, insert, picture disc) | 30 |
| 94 | Epic 477861-1 | VITALOGY (LP, embossed gatefold sleeve, booklet) | 25 |
| 96 | Epic 484448-1 | NO CODE (LP, multi fold gatefold sleeve, inners, 9 photo cards) | 70 |
| 98 | Epic 489365-1 | YIELD (LP, die-cut sleeve, inner sleeve) | 25 |
| 98 | Epic 429859-1 | LIVE ON TWO LEGS (2-LP, stickered gatefold sleeve with inner sleeves) | 40 |
| 00 | Sony E263665 | BINAURAL (2 x LP, 3-part fold out sleeve with booklet) | 20 |
| 02 | Epic 510000-1 | RIOT ACT (2-LP, gatefold sleeve, inner sleeves) | 80 |

*(see also Temple Of The Dog)*

## PEARLS BEFORE SWINE
| | | | |
|---|---|---|---|
| 68 | Fontana STL 5503 | BALAKLAVA (LP) | 45 |
| 68 | Fontana STL 5505 | ONE NATION UNDERGROUND (LP) | 40 |
| 69 | Reprise RSLP 6364 | THESE THINGS TOO (LP) | 20 |
| 70 | Reprise RSLP 6405 | THE USE OF ASHES (LP) | 30 |
| 71 | Reprise RSLP 6442 | CITY OF GOLD (LP) | 20 |
| 71 | Reprise RSLP 6467 | BEAUTIFUL LIES YOU COULD LIVE (LP) | 15 |

## PEARLS (1)
| | | | |
|---|---|---|---|
| 72 | Bell BELL 1217 | Third Finger, Left Hand/Little Lady Love Me | 5 |
| 72 | Bell 1372 | Wizard Of Love/Playing Around | 6 |
| 72 | Bell BELL 1254 | You Came, You Saw, You Conquered/Sing Out To Me | 5 |
| 74 | Bell BELL 1352 | Guilty/I'll Say It Over Again | 5 |
| 74 | Bell 1394 | Doctor Love/Pass It On | 6 |

*(see also Bud Ashton)*

## PEARLS (2)
| | | | |
|---|---|---|---|
| 75 | Private Stock PVT39 | The Cheater/I'm Gonna Steal Your Heart Away | 8 |

## BUSTER PEARSON BAND
| | | | |
|---|---|---|---|
| 73 | Action ACT 4612 | Big Funky/Pretty Woman | 15 |
| 75 | K&B 5516 | Take It Easy/Instrumental | 6 |

## DUKE PEARSON
| | | | |
|---|---|---|---|
| 68 | Polydor 583 723 | ANGEL EYES (LP) | 100 |

## JOHNNY PEARSON
| | | | |
|---|---|---|---|
| 62 | Oriole CB 1721 | Doh La La/Johnny's Tune | 7 |
| 62 | Parlophone R 4977 | Theme From The L-Shaped Room Part 1/Part 2 | 7 |
| 66 | Columbia DB 7851 | Rat Catcher's Theme/Weaver's Green Theme | 20 |
| 73 | BBC RESL 6 | Spy Trap/Playgirl (with Quator) | 10 |
| 70 | Aristocrat AR 103 | SOUNDS EXTRAVAGANZA (LP) | 20 |

*(see also John Barry Seven)*

## JOSH T PEARSON
| | | | |
|---|---|---|---|
| 06 | Bella Union BELLA SPECIAL 1 | I'm So Lonesome I Could Cry/DIRTY THREE: Doris (split 7" white marbled vinyl) | 12 |

## RONNIE PEARSON
| | | | |
|---|---|---|---|
| 58 | HMV POP 489 | Flippin' Over You/Teen-Age Fancy | 700 |
| 58 | HMV POP 489 | Flippin' Over You/Teen-Age Fancy (78) | 150 |

## PEASANTS

MINT VALUE £

| | | | |
|---|---|---|---|
| 65 | Columbia DB 7642 | Got Some Lovin' For You Baby/Let's Get Together | 160 |

### PEBBLES & BAMM BAMM / FLINTSTONES
| | | | |
|---|---|---|---|
| 65 | Pye Int. 7N.25332 | Daddy (mono)/The World Is Full Of Joys (For Girls And Boys) | 7 |

### PEBBLES (1)
| | | | |
|---|---|---|---|
| 68 | Major Minor MM 574 | 40 Miles Inside Your Heart/Get Around | 15 |
| 69 | Decca F 22944 | Incredible George/Playing Chess | 15 |
| 70 | Deram DM 305 | Stand Up And Be Counted/May In The Morning | 8 |
| 71 | Parlophone R 5900 | Goodnight Ma/Sadness Of A Summer's Afternoon | 8 |
| 71 | Parlophone R 5921 | First Time Loving/Party | 8 |

### PEBBLES (2)
| | | | |
|---|---|---|---|
| 77 | Arakwak AR01 | Positive Vibrations/Cosmic Idrens | 15 |

### PEDDLERS
| | | | |
|---|---|---|---|
| 64 | Philips BF 1375 | Let The Sunshine In/True Girl | 8 |
| 65 | Philips BF 1404 | Whatever Happened To The Good Times/Song For The Blues | 6 |
| 65 | Philips BF 1455 | Over The Rainbow/You Must Be Having Me On | 6 |
| 66 | Philips BF 1506 | Adam's Apple/Anybody's Fool | 6 |
| 66 | Philips BF 1530 | I've Got To Hold On/Gassin' | 6 |
| 67 | Philips BF 1557 | What'll I Do/Delicious Lady | 8 |
| 67 | CBS 2947 | Irresistable You/Murray's Mood | 8 |
| 67 | CBS 3055 | You're The Reason I'm Living/Nine Miles High | 8 |
| 68 | CBS 3333 | Handel With Care/Horse's Collar | 8 |
| 68 | CBS 3734 | Comin' Home Baby/Empty Club Blues | 25 |
| 68 | CBS 4050 | That's Life/Wasting My Time | 8 |
| 69 | CBS 4449 | Birth/Steel Mill | 8 |
| 69 | CBS 4720 | Girlie/P.S I Love You | 8 |
| 70 | Phillips 6006034 | Tell The World We're Not In/Rainy Day In London | 6 |
| 73 | Philips 6006 283 | Sing Me An Old Song/It's So Easy | 20 |
| 74 | EMI 2106 | Is There Anyone Out There/Just A Thought Ago | 30 |
| 66 | Philips BE 12954 | SWINGING SCENE (EP) | 8 |
| 67 | Philips (S)BL 7768 | LIVE AT THE PICKWICK (LP, flipback sleeve) | 15 |
| 67 | CBS (S)BPG 63183 | FREE WHEELERS (LP) | 15 |
| 72 | Philips 6308 102 | SUITE LONDON (LP) | 40 |

### PEDESTRIANS
| | | | |
|---|---|---|---|
| 81 | Metropolis MET 1 | Commuter Fantasy/1984 | 8 |

### MIKE PEDICIN QUINTET
| | | | |
|---|---|---|---|
| 62 | HMV POP 1001 | When Cats Come Twistin' In/Gotta Twist | 15 |

### BOBBY PEDRICK
| | | | |
|---|---|---|---|
| 58 | London HLX 8740 | White Bucks And Saddle Shoes/Stranded | 25 |

### ANN PEEBLES
| | | | |
|---|---|---|---|
| 70 | London HLU 10322 | Part Time Love/I Still Love You | 5 |
| 71 | London HLU 10328 | I Pity The Fool/Heartaches, Heartaches | 8 |
| 71 | London HLU 10346 | Slipped, Tripped And Fell In Love/99 lbs | 12 |
| 72 | London HLU 10361 | Breaking Up Somebody's Home/Troubles, Heartaches And Sadness | 5 |
| 72 | London HLU 10385 | Somebody's On Your Case/I've Been There Before | 5 |
| 73 | London HLU 10405 | I'm Gonna Tear Your Playhouse Down/One Way Street | 5 |
| 73 | London HLU 10428 | I Can't Stand The Rain/I've Been There Before | 5 |
| 74 | EMI 2106 | (You Keep Me) Hangin' On/Run Run Run | 5 |
| 75 | London HLU 10484 | Beware/You Got To Feed The Fire | 5 |
| 75 | London HLU 10508 | Come On Mama/I'm Leaving You | 5 |
| 72 | London SHU 8434 | STRAIGHT FROM THE HEART (LP) | 20 |
| 74 | London SHU 8468 | I CAN'T STAND THE RAIN (LP) | 20 |

### PAUL PEEK
| | | | |
|---|---|---|---|
| 61 | Pye International 7N 25102 | Brother In Law/Through The Teenage Years | 20 |
| 66 | CBS 202073 | Pin The Tail On The Donkey/Rockin' Pneumonia | 12 |

*(see also Gene Vincent & Blue Caps)*

### DAVID PEEL (& LOWER EAST SIDE)
| | | | |
|---|---|---|---|
| 68 | Elektra EKL 4032 | HAVE A MARIJUANA (LP, red label, mono) | 40 |
| 68 | Elektra EKS 74032 | HAVE A MARIJUANA (LP, red label, stereo) | 25 |
| 70 | Elektra 2401 001 | AMERICAN REVOLUTION (LP) | 20 |

### PEELERS
| | | | |
|---|---|---|---|
| 72 | Polydor Folk Mill 2460 165 | BANISHED MISFORTUNE (LP) | 150 |

### PEELS
| | | | |
|---|---|---|---|
| 66 | Stateside SS 513 | Juanita Banana/Fun | 8 |
| 66 | Audio Fidelity AFSP 527 | Scrooey Mooey/Time Marches On | 30 |

### PEENUTS
| | | | |
|---|---|---|---|
| 67 | Ember EMB S 242 | The Theme For "The Monkees"/The World's Been Good To Me Tonight (in p/s) | 20 |
| 67 | Ember EMB S 242 | The Theme For "The Monkees"/The World's Been Good To Me Tonight | 10 |

### PEEPERS
| | | | |
|---|---|---|---|
| 72 | Bumble GE102 | Ayeo/A Heavy Drinking Ego Shrinking | 20 |

### PEEPS
| | | | |
|---|---|---|---|
| 65 | Philips BF 1421 | Now Is The Time/Got Plenty Of Love | 15 |
| 65 | Philips BF 1443 | What Can I Say?/Don't Talk About Love | 15 |
| 66 | Philips BF 1478 | Gotta Get A Move On/I Told You Before | 60 |
| 66 | Philips BF 1509 | Tra La La/Loser Wins | 10 |

*(see also Martin Cure & Peeps, Sabres, Rainbows)*

**PEEP SHOW**
| 67 | Polydor 56196 | Your Servant, Stephen/Mazy | 90 |
| 68 | Polydor 52226 | Esprit De Corps/Mino In A Mix Up | 15 |

**BEV PEGG (AND FRIENDS)**
| 75 | Beaujangle DB 0006 | AWAY FROM THE SAND (LP, 50 copies only) | 200 |

*(see also Bev Pegg, Dave Cartwright, Brindley Brae)*

**BEV PEGG (& HIS GOIN' NOWHERE BAND)**
| 78 | Beaujangle DB 0007 | NOSTALGIA IS A THING OF THE PAST (LP, private pressing, with booklet, 50 only; as Bev Pegg & His Goin' Nowhere Band) | 150 |
| 80 | Beaujangle DB 0008 | THE FOUNDRY DITTY AND THE INDUSTRIAL AIR (LP, private pressing, 500 only, 150 destroyed so only 350 out there...) | 45 |

*(see also David Cartwright, Brindley Brae)*

**BOB PEGG**
| 74 | Transatlantic TRA 280 | THE SHIPBUILDER (LP, with Nick Strutt, credited to Bob Pegg) | 18 |
| 75 | Transatlantic TRA 299 | ANCIENT MAPS (LP, with lyric insert) | 20 |

**BOB & CAROL PEGG**
| 71 | Trailer LER 3016 | HE CAME FROM THE MOUNTAIN (LP, red label, as Carole Pegg) | 35 |
| 72 | Galliard GAL 4017 | AND NOW IT IS SO EARLY - THE SONGS OF SYDNEY CARTER (LP) | 25 |

*(see also Carol Pegg, Carolanne Pegg, Mr. Fox)*

**BOB PEGG & NICK STRUTT**
| 73 | Transatlantic TRA 265 | BOB PEGG & NICK STRUTT (LP) | 25 |

**CAROL(ANNE) PEGG**
| 73 | Transatlantic TRA 226 | CAROLANNE PEGG (LP, gatefold sleeve) | 80 |

*(see also Bob & Carol Pegg)*

**PEGGY**
| 70 | Trojan TR 7752 | All Kinds Of Everything Part 1/CARL LEVEY: Instrumental Version | 6 |
| 70 | Hot Rod HR 103 | I Shall Follow The Star/CARL LEVEY: Gifted At The Top | 20 |

**PEGGY & JIMMY**
| 70 | Hot Rod HR 101 | Pum Pum Lover/CARL LEVY: Remember Easter Monday | 8 |

**PEGGY'S LEG**
| 73 | Bunch BAN 2001 | GRINILLA (LP, with insert) | 400 |

*(see also Skid Row, Jimi Slevin)*

**PEKKA**
| 75 | Virgin V 2036 | B THE MAGPIE (LP as Pekka Pohjolo) | 20 |
| 77 | Virgin V 2084 | THE MATHEMATICIANS AIR DISPLAY (LP, features Mike Oldfield) | 15 |

**PEKO AND NAKA**
| 77 | The Label TLR 002 | Ageso Na Omae/Yamete (p/s) | 10 |

**DAVE PELL OCTET**
| 54 | London RE-P 1008 | IRVING BERLIN GALLERY VOL. 1 (EP) | 10 |
| 55 | London RE-P 1018 | RODGERS AND HART (EP) | 10 |
| 54 | London H-APB 1034 | RODGERS AND HART GALLERY (10" LP) | 15 |

**LANA PELLAY**
| 86 | Sublime LIMET 101 | Pistol In My Pocket/Dirty Harry Version (12", p/s) | 12 |

**PELOTON**
| 00 | Chemikal Underground CHEM 040 | THE GREAT EASTERN (LP) | 20 |

**JACK PENATE**
| 06 | Young Turks YT 001 | Second Minute Or Hour/Got My Favourite... (die-cut p/s with colour numbered Polaroid photo initialled by artist, PVC bag, 1,000 only) | 8 |

**PENCILS**
| 83 | Next 705 | Pictures Of Paris/Steal Your Love | 8 |

**TRACY PENDARVIS**
| 60 | London HLS 9059 | A Thousand Guitars/Is It Too Late | 25 |
| 60 | London HLS 9213 | Is It Me/South Bound Line | 15 |

**MIKE PENDER**
| 86 | Sierra FED 23 | It's Over/Brothers And Sisters (p/s) | 6 |

*(see also The Searchers)*

**PENDLEFOLK**
| 70 | Folk Heritage FHR 007 | PENDLEFOLK (LP) | 18 |

**PENDRAGON**
| 87 | Awareness AWS 101 | Red Shoes/Searching/Contact (p/s) | 5 |
| 89 | Toff PENDS 7S | Saved By You/Lady Luck (p/s) | 5 |

**PENELOPES FRIEND**
| 87 | MTG MTG 1 | THE GAP EP (12") | 40 |

**PENETRATION**
| 77 | Virgin VS 192 | Don't Dictate/Money Talks (p/s, blue label) | 9 |
| 78 | Virgin VS 213 | Firing Squad/Never (p/s) | 8 |
| 78 | Virgin VS 226 | Life's A Gamble/V.I.P. (p/s) | 5 |
| 79 | Virgin VS 257 | Danger Signs/Stone Heroes (live) (p/s) | 5 |
| 79 | Virgin VS 268 | Come Into The Open/Lifeline (p/s) | 5 |
| 08 | Damaged Goods DAMGOOD 17-7 | Our World/Sea Song (red vinyl) | 15 |
| 78 | Virgin V 2109 | MOVING TARGETS (LP, 15,000 on luminous vinyl) | 15 |

**PENETRATIONS**
| 80 | Kik KIK 5 | Coming To You/Cheap Thrills | 100 |

**JIM PENFOLD & THE HOLLYWOOD KILLERS**
| 76 | Rollerball ROLL 1 | Hot Hazy Days/Unknown Person (no p/s) | 15 |

*(see also Hollywood Killers)*

| | | | MINT VALUE £ |
|---|---|---|---|

**BOB PENFOLD**
78   A C Wall ACW 01 — Free/Mother Natures Child ....................................................... 12

**PENGUINS**
55   London HL 8114 — Earth Angel/Hey Senorita (gold label print, triangular centre) .............. 1500
55   London HL 8114 — Earth Angel/Hey Senorita (large centre hole, export issue) ............... 350
55   London HL 8114 — Earth Angel/Hey Senorita (78) ....................................................... 60

**BOBBY PENN**
10   Kent Select City 019 — Without Your Love/LARRY BANKS: Ooh It Hurts Me ....................... 8

**DAWN PENN**
66   Rio R 113 — Long Days Short Night/Are You There (label lists 'Dawn Tenn') .................... 60
67   Studio One SO 2030 — You Don't Love Me/SOUL VENDORS: Portobello Road ...................... 50
68   Island WI 3097 — I'll Never Let You Go/MARK BROWN: Brown Low Special ..................... 45
*(see also Max Romeo, Viceroys)*

**TONY PENN**
62   Starlite ST45 083 — That's What I Like/I Won't Cry Anymore ....................................... 30

**LEONARD PENNARIO**
54   Capitol CL 14173 — Midnight On The Cliffs/Dream Rhapsody (with Les Baxter Orchestra) ....... 10
*(see also Les Baxter)*

**PENNSYLVANIA SIXPENCE**
67   Pye 7N 17326 — Love Of The Common People/Midweek Excursion ................................. 8

**PENNY**
61   Piccadilly 7N 35009 — Who Does He Think He Is/Sparks ............................................... 8
62   Piccadilly 7N 35045 — Shall I Take My Heart And Go/What'd I Do? ................................... 8

**PENNY CANDLES**
89   Red Eye RED 04 — THE TAJ MAHAL EP (12" p/s) ...................................................... 20

**GEORGE A. PENNY**
68   Trojan TR 625 — Win Your Love/VAL BENNETT: All In The Game .................................. 12

**HANK PENNY**
56   Parlophone MSP 6202 — Bloodshot Eyes/Wham! Bam! Thank You Ma'am ......................... 100

**PENNY LANE**
70   CBS 4903 — Heartbreak House/He's Got A Hold Of My Heart ...................................... 5

**PENNY PEEPS**
68   Liberty LBF 15053 — Little Man With A Stick/Model Village ......................................... 300
68   Liberty LBF 15114 — I See The Morning/Curly, The Knight Of The Road ............................ 40

**PENNY WAGER**
72   Folk Heritage FHR 0256 — LIGHT OF OTHER DAYS (LP) .............................................. 75

**PENNY ARCADE**
70   Pye 7N.17943 — The Two Of Us/Don't Need You Anymore ......................................... 20

**PENNYWORTH**
69   CBS 4573 — Malena Malena/Who Are You? ........................................................... 12

**CHARLES PENROSE**
57   Columbia SEG 7743 — THE ADVENTURE OF THE LAUGHING POLICEMAN (EP) .................... 10

**PENTAD**
65   Parlophone R 5288 — Silver Dagger/Nothing But Love ............................................... 25
65   Parlophone R 5368 — Don't Throw It All Away/Too Many Ways ..................................... 20
66   Parlophone R 5424 — Something Other People Call Love/It Better Be Me .......................... 25

**PENTAGONS**
61   London HLU 9333 — To Be Loved Forever/Down At The Beach ................................... 100

**PENTAGRAM**
87   Napalm FLAME 006 — DAY OF RECKONING (LP) ......................................................
92   Peaceville — 1972-1979 (LP) ........................................................................... 45
93   Peaceville VILE 38 — RELENTLESS (LP, reissue of US self-titled debut) ............................ 15
93   Peaceville VILE 40 — DAY OF RECKONING (LP, reissue) ............................................ 30
94   Peaceville VILE 42 — BE FOREWARNED (2-LP, insert) ............................................... 25
                50

**PENTANGLE**
68   Big T BIG 109 — Travellin' Song/Mirage (in title die-cut sleeve) ................................... 10
68   Big T BIG 109 — Travellin' Song/Mirage ..............................................................
69   Big T BIG 124 — Once I Had A Sweetheart/I Saw An Angel ......................................... 6
70   Big T BIG 128 — Light Flight/Cold Mountain ......................................................... 20
73   Big T BIG 567 — Light Flight/Market Song/The Time Has Come ................................... 6
68   Transatlantic TRA 162 — THE PENTANGLE (LP, laminated sleeve) .................................. 6
68   Transatlantic TRA 178 — SWEET CHILD (2-LP) ....................................................... 50
69   Transatlantic TRA 205 — BASKET OF LIGHT (LP, gatefold sleeve) .................................. 50
70   Transatlantic TRA 228 — CRUEL SISTER (LP, gatefold sleeve) ..................................... 30
71   Transatlantic TRA 240 — REFLECTION (LP, gatefold sleeve with inner sleeve) .................... 25
72   Reprise K 44197 — SOLOMON'S SEAL (LP, with lyric insert) ...................................... 20
85   Spindrift SPIN 111 — OPEN THE DOOR (LP) ......................................................... 60
                20
*(see also Bert Jansch, John Renbourn, Duffy's Nucleus)*

**PENTHOUSE**
71   Penny Farthing PEN 765 — 40 Days Of Rain/I'm Nobody's Fool .................................. 12

**PENWYKE**
70   Cannon CN 11 — Time To Let Go/No One Cares (p/s) .............................................. 20

**PEOPLE BAND**
70   Transatlantic TRA 214 — THE PEOPLE BAND (LP, with Charlie Watts) ............................ 75
*(see also Charlie Watts, Battered Ornaments)*

### PEOPLE (1)
| 69 | Capitol CL 15553 | I Love You/Somebody Tell Me My Name | 22 |
|----|------------------|--------------------------------------|----|
| 69 | Capitol CL 15599 | Ulla/Turnin' Me In | 22 |
| 70 | RCA RCA 2028 | I Am (The Preacher)/September's Son | 10 |
| 71 | Deram DM 346 | In Ancient Times/Glastonbury | 45 |
| 70 | Paramount SPFL 261 | THERE ARE PEOPLE AND THERE ARE PEOPLE (LP) | 25 |

### PEOPLE (2)
| 81 | Race RB 003 | Musical Man/Sons & Daughters | 10 |
|----|-------------|-------------------------------|----|

### PEPPELKADE 14
| 88 | Top Shelf CAV 031 | TIME FLIES EP (12") | 40 |
|----|-------------------|---------------------|----|

### PEPPER
| 68 | Pye 7N 17569 | We'll Make It Together/(Look Out) I'm On The Way Down | 10 |
|----|--------------|-------------------------------------------------------|----|

### ART PEPPER
| 54 | Vogue LDE 067 | ART PEPPER QUARTET (10" LP) | 50 |
|----|---------------|-----------------------------|----|
| 57 | London HLZ V 14038 | ART PEPPER QUARTET (10" LP) | 50 |
| 60 | Contemporary LAC 12229 | MODERN JAZZ CLASSICS (LP, as Art Pepper Eleven) | 25 |

*(see also Chet Baker)*

### JIM PEPPER
| 71 | Atlantic 2400 149 | PEPPER'S POW WOW (LP) | 25 |
|----|-------------------|------------------------|----|

### KEN PEPPER
| 61 | Top Rank JAR 535 | Just A Little At A Time/I Get The Blues When It Rains | 7 |
|----|------------------|-------------------------------------------------------|---|

### RED PEPPER
| 73 | Phoenix SN1X 145 | I'm Gonna Sit Right Down And Write Myself A Letter/I See A Land | 20 |
|----|------------------|------------------------------------------------------------------|----|

### DANNY PEPPERMINT (& JUMPING JACKS)
| 61 | London HLL 9478 | The Peppermint Twist/Somebody Else Is Taking My Place (with Jumping Jacks) | 5 |
|----|-----------------|-----------------------------------------------------------------------------|---|
| 62 | London HLL 9516 | One More Time/La Dee Dah | 5 |
| 62 | London HLL 9614 | Maybe Tomorrow (But Not Today)/Passing Parade | 5 |
| 62 | London HA-L 2438 | TWIST WITH DANNY PEPPERMINT (LP) | 20 |

### PEPPERMINT CIRCUS
| 67 | Olga OLE 007 | All The King's Horses/It Didn't Take Long | 10 |
|----|--------------|--------------------------------------------|----|
| 68 | Polydor 56288 | I Won't Be There/Keeping My Head Above Water | 6 |
| 69 | Polydor 56312 | Please Be Patient/Take My Love | 6 |
| 70 | A&M AMS 765 | One Thing Could Lead To Another/It's So Easy | 6 |

### PEPPERMINT RAINBOW
| 68 | MCA MU 1034 | Walking In Different Circles/Pink Lemonade | 12 |
|----|-------------|---------------------------------------------|----|
| 69 | MCA MU 1076 | Will You Be Staying After Sunday/And I'll Be There | 20 |
| 69 | MCA MU 1091 | Don't Wake Up In The Morning, Michael/Rosemary | 10 |

### PEPPERMINT TROLLEY COMPANY
| 68 | Dot DOT 110 | Baby You Come Rolling 'Cross My Mind/Nine O'Clock Business Man | 10 |
|----|-------------|-----------------------------------------------------------------|----|

### PEPPI
| 62 | Decca F 11520 | Stories/When I Think Of You | 5 |
|----|---------------|------------------------------|---|
| 63 | Decca F 11638 | Can You Waddle/I Never Danced Before | 10 |
| 64 | Decca F 11991 | Pistol Packin' Mama/Roll On Baby | 5 |
| 64 | Fontana TF 446 | So Used To Loving You/Don't Trust My Friend | 8 |
| 65 | Decca F 12055 | The Skip/Do The Skip | 8 |

### ARMANDO PERAZA
| 68 | Fontana STL 5525 | WILD THING (LP) | 25 |
|----|------------------|------------------|----|

### PERCELLS
| 63 | HMV POP 1154 | What Are Boys Made Of?/Cheek To Cheek | 20 |
|----|--------------|----------------------------------------|----|

### LANCE PERCIVAL
| 63 | Parlophone R 507 | The Beetroot Song/Dancing In The Streets Tonight | 5 |
|----|------------------|---------------------------------------------------|---|
| 65 | Parlophone R 5335 | Shame And Scandal In The Family/There's Another One Behind | 5 |

### NORMAN PERCIVAL
| 67 | United Artists UP 1197 | Theme From "Billion Dollar Brain"/Shades Of Green | 5 |
|----|------------------------|----------------------------------------------------|---|

### PERCY PAVILION
| 84 | Dead Good Dolly P. DMS 2 | Gower Power/You're An Extra Baby (p/s) | 5 |
|----|---------------------------|-----------------------------------------|---|

*(see also Captain Sensible)*

### PEREGRINE
| 72 | Westwood WRS 016 | SONGS OF MINE (LP) | 100 |
|----|------------------|---------------------|-----|

### RAY PEREIRA
| 70 | Baf BAF 5 | Don't Mess With Cupid/CATS: Falling In Love | 8 |
|----|-----------|----------------------------------------------|---|
| 70 | Baf BAF 6 | On Broadway/Hey Chick | 30 |

### PERERIN
| 80 | Gwerin SYWM 215 | HAUL AR YR EIRA (LP, with insert) | 180 |
|----|-----------------|------------------------------------|-----|
| 81 | SYWM 230 | TEITHGAN (LP) | 120 |

### PERE UBU
| 79 | Chrysalis CHS 2372 | The Fabulous Sequel (Have Shoes Will Walk)/Humour Me (live)/ The Book Is On The Table (p/s) | 8 |
|----|--------------------|----------------------------------------------------------------------------------------------|---|
| 80 | Rough Trade RT 049 | Final Solution/My Dark Ages (p/s) | 8 |
| 81 | Rough Trade RT 066 | Not Happy/Lonesome Cowboy Dave (p/s) | 8 |
| 78 | Radar RDR 1 | DATAPANIK IN THE YEAR ZERO (12" EP) | 15 |
| 78 | Blank BLANK 001 | THE MODERN DANCE (LP) | 35 |
| 78 | Chrysalis CHR 1207 | DUB HOUSING (LP) | 25 |
| 79 | Rough Trade ROUGHUS 20 | NEW PICNIC TIME (LP) | 15 |
| 80 | Rough Trade ROUGH 14 | THE ART OF WALKING (LP, original with "Miles" & "Arabia") | 18 |
| 81 | Rough Trade ROUGH 22 | THE MODERN DANCE (LP, reissue) | 20 |
| 81 | Rough Trade ROUGH 23 | 390° OF SIMULATED STEREO - UBU LIVE: VOLUME 1 (LP) | 15 |

MINT VALUE £

| 85 | Rough Trade ROUGHUS 14 | DUB HOUSING (LP, reissue) | 15 |
| 85 | Rough Trade ROUGH 83 | TERMINAL TOWER (LP, gatefold sleeve) | 15 |
| 88 | Fontana SFLP 5 | THE TENEMENT YEAR (LP) | 15 |

*(see also David Thomas)*

## CHRISTINE PERFECT

| 69 | Blue Horizon 57-3165 | When You Say/No Road Is The Right Road | 35 |
| 70 | Blue Horizon 57-3172 | I'm Too Far Gone (To Turn Around)/Close To Me | 35 |
| 70 | Blue Horizon 7-63860 | CHRISTINE PERFECT (LP) | 100 |
| 82 | CBS 32198 | CHRISTINE PERFECT (LP, reissue) | 15 |

*(see also Christine McVie, Fleetwood Mac, Illusive Dream, Chicken Shack, Rick Hayward)*

## PERFECT DISASTER
| 87 | Glass GLALP 027 | PERFECT DISASTER (LP) | 30 |

## PERFECT END
| 81 | Hellfire HELL 1 | Sweet Dreams/Natural Causes/Puppets | 15 |

## PERFECT PEOPLE
| 69 | MCA MU 1079 | House In The Country/Polyanna | 15 |

## PERFECTION
| 70 | Stem ST 001 | Ride High/Magic Meadow (p/s) | 80 |

## PERFECTORS
| 80 | Active ACT 4 | YT50295ID/Tiny Radios (p/s) | 100 |

## PERFORMANCE (1)
| 73 | Polydor 2058 324 | Funny Little Things/Rejoice | 6 |

## PERFORMANCE (2)
| 86 | Clay CLAY 47 | Wish I Was Free Again/Free Again | 8 |

## PERFORMERS
| 69 | Action ACT 4552 | I Can't Stop You/L.A. Stomp | 22 |

## PERFORMING FERRET BAND
| 80 | Dead Hippy DHR3 | Brow Beaton/Hoo-Shar/Disco One (EP, p/s) | 20 |
| 81 | Pig PIG 1 | PERFORMING FERRET BAND (LP) | 35 |

## PERIDOTS
| 81 | Optional Goods OG 1 | Open Season/Calm (p/s) | 20 |

## PERISHERS
| 68 | Fontana TF 965 | How Does It Feel/Bye Bye Baby | 40 |

*(see also Seftones)*

## CARL PERKINS
### 78s
| 56 | London HLU 8271 | Blue Suede Shoes/Honey Don't | 30 |
| 57 | London HLS 8408 | Matchbox/Your True Love | 40 |
| 57 | London HLS 8527 | Glad All Over/Forever Yours | 50 |
| 58 | London HLS 8608 | Lend Me Your Comb/That's Right | 60 |
| 59 | Philips PB 983 | I Don't See Me In Your Eyes Anymore/One Ticket To Loneliness | 70 |

### SINGLES
| 56 | London HLU 8271 | Blue Suede Shoes/Honey Don't | 175 |
| 57 | London HLS 8408 | Matchbox/Your True Love | 175 |
| 57 | London HLS8527 | Glad All Over/Forever Yours | 70 |
| 58 | London HLS 8608 | Lend Me Your Comb/That's Right | 70 |
| 59 | Philips PB 983 | I Don't See Me In Your Eyes Anymore/One Ticket To Loneliness | 20 |
| 61 | Philips PB 1179 | Anyway The Wind Blows/The Unhappy Girls | 15 |
| 64 | Brunswick 05905 | Help Me Find My Baby/I Wouldn't Have You | 15 |
| 64 | Brunswick 05909 | Big Bad Blues/Lonely Heart (with Nashville Teens) | 15 |
| 64 | Brunswick 05923 | The Monkey Shine/Let My Baby Be | 15 |
| 67 | Stateside SS 599 | A Country Boy's Dream/If I Could Come Back | 15 |
| 68 | London HLP 7125 | A Country Boy's Dream/Shine Shine Shine (export issue) | 15 |
| 68 | Spark SRL 1009 | Lake County, Cotton Country/It's You | 10 |
| 68 | London HLS 10192 | Blue Suede Shoes/Matchbox | 10 |
| 69 | CBS 3932 | Restless/11.43 | 10 |
| 70 | CBS 4991 | All Mama's Children/Step Aside (with N.R.B.Q.) | 6 |
| 77 | Mercury ELV 15 | The E.P. Express/Big Bad Blues (p/s) | 5 |

### ALBUMS
| 59 | London HA-S 2202 | THE DANCE ALBUM OF CARL PERKINS (plum label, flipback sleeve) | 150 |
| 59 | London HA-S 2202 | THE DANCE ALBUM OF CARL PERKINS (plum label, non-flipback sleeve) | 50 |
| 66 | Ember NR 5038 | SUNSTROKE (shared with Jerry Lee Lewis) | 20 |
| 66 | CBS Realm 52305 | WHOLE LOTTA CARL PERKINS (original pressing with boxed square logo) | 50 |
| 66 | CBS Realm 52305 | WHOLE LOTTA CARL PERKINS | 25 |
| 68 | CBS 63309 | KING OF ROCK | 15 |
| 68 | London HA-P/SH-P 8366 | COUNTRY BOY'S DREAM | 20 |
| 82 | Sun BOX 101 | THE SUN YEARS (3-LP, box set with booklet) | 20 |

*(see also N.R.B.Q.)*

## JOE PERKINS
| 72 | Mojo 2092 047 | Wrapped Up In Your Love/Looking For A Woman | 8 |

## LASCELLES PERKINS
| 61 | Blue Beat BB 41 | Creation/Lonely Robin | 20 |
| 63 | Island WI 038 | Tango Lips (with Yvonne)/DENNIS SINDREY: Rub Up (B-side actually plays "Jamaica's Song") | 25 |
| 64 | R&B JB 175 | I Am So Grateful/When I Survey | 20 |
| 70 | Escort ES 814 | Please Stay/MATADORS: Voyage From The Moon | 20 |
| 71 | Banana BA 317 | Tell It All Brothers/SOUND DIMENSION: Polkadots | 15 |

*(see also Tommy McCook)*
## POLLY PERKINS
| | | | |
|---|---|---|---|
| 63 | Decca F 11583 | I Reckon You (as Polly Perkins & Bill)/The Girls Are At It Again | 10 |
| 63 | Oriole CB 1869 | Sweet As Honey/I've Gotta Tell You | 10 |
| 63 | Oriole CB 1929 | Young Lover/You Too Can Be A Beatle | 10 |
| 63 | Oriole CB 1979 | Faling In Love Again/I Went By Your House Today | 10 |
| 73 | Chapter One CMS 1018 | LIBERATED WOMAN (LP) | 25 |

*(see also Academy)*
## TONY PERKINS
| | | | |
|---|---|---|---|
| 58 | RCA RCA 1018 | Moonlight Swim/First Romance | 12 |

## KATIE PERKS
| | | | |
|---|---|---|---|
| 83 | Plastichead PLAS 001 | Small/Cold Stone (p/s) | 8 |

## PERMANENTS
| | | | |
|---|---|---|---|
| 63 | London HLU 9803 | Oh Dear, What Can The Matter Be/Let Me Be Baby | 12 |

## JEAN-JACQUES PERREY
| | | | |
|---|---|---|---|
| 72 | Vanguard VAN 1005 | Gossipo Perpetuo/Moog Indigo | 10 |
| 73 | Vanguard VAN 1008 | Minuet Of The Robots/Porcupine Rock | 10 |
| 71 | Vanguard VSD 6525 | KALEIDOSCOPIC VIBRATIONS - SPOTLIGHT ON THE MOOG (LP, 'kaleidoscope' sleeve, with Gershon Kingsley) | 18 |
| 72 | Vanguard VSD 6549 | MOOG INDIGO (LP, title sleeve) | 25 |
| 73 | Vanguard VSD 79222 | THE IN SOUND FROM WAY OUT! (LP, green/black 'starburst' sleeve, with Gershon Kingsley) | 20 |
| 73 | Vanguard VSD 79286 | THE AMAZING NEW ELECTRONIC POP SOUND OF... (LP) | 15 |
| 74 | Vanguard DPS 2051 | THE BEST OF THE MOOG (2-LP) | 18 |

## PAT PERRIN
| | | | |
|---|---|---|---|
| 68 | Island WI 3115 | Over You/LLOYD TERRELL: Lost Without You | 25 |

## PERRI'S
| | | | |
|---|---|---|---|
| 59 | Oriole CB 1481 | Jerri-Lee/Ballad Of A Happy Heart | 15 |

## BARBARA PERRY
| | | | |
|---|---|---|---|
| 70 | Pama PM 795 | Say You Need Me/Unloved | 15 |
| 10 | Kent CITY 015 | A Man Is A Mean Thing/GLADYS BRUCE: I've Got A Feeling For You Baby | 7 |

## JEFF PERRY
| | | | |
|---|---|---|---|
| 76 | Arista ARIST 51 | Love Don't Come No Stronger/I've Got To See You Right Away | 40 |

## LEE 'SCRATCH' PERRY (& UPSETTERS)
| | | | |
|---|---|---|---|
| 63 | R&B JB 102 | Prince In The Black/Don't Copy | 50 |
| 63 | R&B JB 104 | Old For New/Prince And Duke | 50 |
| 63 | R&B JB 106 | Mad Head/Man And Wife | 50 |
| 63 | R&B JB 135 | Royalty/Can't Be Wrong | 50 |
| 63 | Island WI 118 | Never Get Weary/TOMMY McCOOK: Below Zero | 40 |
| 64 | Port-O-Jam PJ 4001 | Help The Weak/TOMMY McCOOK: Exodus | 40 |
| 64 | Port-O-Jam PJ 4003 | Bad Minded People/TOMMY McCOOK & HIS GROUP: Jam Rock | 50 |
| 64 | Port-O-Jam PJ 4010 | Chatty Chatty Woman/TOMMY McCOOK & HIS GROUP: Road Block | 70 |
| 65 | Island WI 210 | Please Don't Go/Bye, St. Peter (both sides with Soulettes) | 40 |
| 65 | Island WI 223 | Country Girl/Strange Country (as Upsetters; both act. by Ossie & Upsetters) | 30 |
| 65 | Ska Beat JB 201 | Roast Duck/Hand To Hand, Man To Man | 45 |
| 65 | Ska Beat JB 203 | Trail And Crosses/Jon Tom | 50 |
| 65 | Ska Beat JB 212 | Wishes Of The Wicked/Hold Down | 60 |
| 65 | Ska Beat JB 215 | Open Up/ROLAND ALPHONSO: Twin Double | 50 |
| 66 | Ska Beat JB 251 | The Woodman/Give Me Justice | 70 |
| 66 | Island WI 259 | Just Keep It Up/ROLAND ALPHONSO: James Bond | 150 |
| 66 | Island WI 292 | Doctor Dick (as King Perry)/SOUL BROTHERS: Magic Star | 40 |
| 66 | Island WI 298 | Rub And Squeeze (as King Perry & Soulettes)/SOUL BROTHERS: Here Comes The Minx | 40 |
| 67 | Doctor Bird DB 1073 | Run For Cover/Something You've Got (as Lee 'King' Perry & Sensations) | 45 |
| 67 | Doctor Bird DB 1098 | Whop Whop Man/Wind-Up Doll (with Dynamites) | 50 |
| 68 | Amalgamated AMG 808 | The Upsetter/Thank You Baby | 60 |
| 68 | Doctor Bird DB 1146 | People Funny Boy/BURT WALTERS: Blowing In The Wind | 35 |
| 68 | Trojan TR 629 | Sentence (as Danny & Lee)/LEE PERRY: You Crummy | 40 |
| 68 | Trojan TR 644 | Uncle Desmond/Bronco (with Upsetters) | 20 |
| 69 | Upsetter US 303 | People Funny Fi True/UPSETTERS: Ten To Twelve | 35 |
| 69 | Upsetter US 324 | Yakety Yak/Tackio (with Upsetters) | 35 |
| 70 | Upsetter US 325 | Kill Them All/Soul Walk (with Upsetters) | 25 |
| 71 | Bullet BU 461 | All Combine Pts 1& 2 (as Lee Perry & Upsetters) | 20 |
| 72 | Upsetter US 385 | French Connection (with Upsetters)/UPSETTERS: Version | 20 |
| 72 | Upsetter US 389 | Back Biter (with Dennis Alcapone)/UPSETTERS: Version | 20 |
| 73 | Upsetter US 397 | Jungle Lion/Freakout Skank | 100 |
| 73 | Upsetter US 398 | Cow Thief Skank (actually by Lee Perry & Charlie Ace)/Seven And Three Quarters Skank | 18 |
| 73 | Bread BR 1111 | Station Underground/CARLTON & SHOES: Better Days | 75 |
| 73 | Downtown DT 513 | Bucky Skank/Mid East Rock | 25 |
| 73 | Jackpot JP 812 | Justice To The People/UPSETTERS: Version | 20 |
| 74 | Dip DL 5037 | Dub A Pum Pum (with Silvertones)/Version | 10 |
| 74 | Dip DL 5060 | Dreader Locks (& Junior Byles)/Militant Rock | 20 |
| 76 | Island WIP 6370 | Dreadlocks In Moonlight/Cut Throat | 6 |
| 79 | Black Art BH 001 | Reggae Music (actually by Hugo Blackwood)/DOC ALIMANTADO: Rastaman Train (12") | 35 |
| 03 | Trojan/Sanctuary TJITV005 | Disco Devil/BOB MARLEY & WU CHU: Keep On Moving (12" reissue) | 30 |
| 71 | Trojan Records TBL 166 | AFRICA'S BLOOD (LP) | 25 |
| 73 | RHINO 8002 | CLOAK & DAGGER (LP, as Scratch The Upsetter) | 70 |
| 75 | Cactus CTLP 112 | REVOLUTION DUB (LP) | 100 |

MINT VALUE £

| 75 | DIP DLPD 6002 | KUNG FU MEETS THE DRAGON (LP, as The Mighty Upsetter) | 100 |
| 79 | Island ILPS 9583 | SCRATCH ON THE WIRE (LP) | 18 |
| 83 | Seven Leaves SLLP5 | MEGATON DUB 2 (LP) | 20 |
| 85 | Trojan PERRY 1 | UPSETTER BOX SET (3-LP) | 40 |
| 88 | Trojan TRLS 254 | GIVE ME POWER (LP, as Lee Perry & Friends) | 15 |
| 89 | Trojan PERRY 2 | OPEN THE GATE (3-LP as Lee Perry & Friends) | 30 |
| 95 | Trojan Records TBL 166 | AFRICA'S BLOOD (LP, reissue, blue/white labels) | 15 |
| 95 | Justice League JJLP5000 | KUNG FU MEETS THE DRAGON (LP, reissue, various coloured vinyl) | 20 |
| 98 | Pressure Sounds PSLP19 | PRODUCED & DIRECTED BY UPSETTER (2-LP) | 20 |
| 99 | Pressure Sounds PSLP32 | DIVINE MADNESS DEFINITELY (2-LP) | 25 |
| 05 | Trojan TJBX 244 | I AM THE UPSETTER (8 x 7" box set) | 35 |
| 70s | Jet Star PTLP 1023 | THE BEST OF (LP) | 30 |

*(see also Upsetters, Defenders, Roland Alphonso, Bob Marley/Wailers, King Scratch, Punchers, Roy Shirley, Pioneers, Desmond Dekker)*

## MARK PERRY
| 80 | NB NB 7 | You Cry Your Tears/Music Death? (with Dennis Burns, p/s in poly bag) | 7 |
| 80 | Deptford Fun City DFC 12 | Whole World's Down On Me/I Live - He Dies (p/s) | 7 |
| 80 | Deptford Fun City DLP 06 | SNAPPY TURNS (LP) | 25 |

*(see also Alternative TV)*

## SHORT(L)Y PERRY
| 72 | Attack ATT 8043 | Musical Goat/WINSTON GRENNON & J. JACKSON: Stinging Dub | 8 |
| 72 | Explosion EX 2067 | Sprinkle Some Water/FLOWERS & ALVIN: Howdy And Tenky | 7 |
| 72 | Bullet BU 512 | Sprinkle Some Water/FLOWERS & ALVIN: Howdy And Tenky | 7 |
| 73 | Bullet BU 529 | Yama Skank/U ROY JUNIOR: Doctor Run Come Quick | 10 |
| 73 | Downtown DT 517 | Dedicated To Illiteracy/G.G. ALL STARS: Illiteracy Dub | 7 |
| 73 | Grape GR 3052 | Abusing And Assaulting (by Flowers & Alvin)/Food Control | 7 |
| 73 | Green Door GD 4043 | President Mash Up The Resident/President Mash Up The Resident Part Two | 10 |

*(see also Shorty, Cornell Campbell, Maytones, Paulette Williams)*

## STEVE PERRY
| 60 | HMV POP 745 | Step By Step/Because They're Young | 15 |
| 62 | Decca F 11462 | Ginny Come Lately/Two Of A Kind | 10 |
| 62 | Decca F 11526 | Young And In Love/Let It Come True | 6 |
| 63 | Decca F 11656 | Find Me A Girl/My Dad | 6 |
| 64 | Decca F 11895 | Crooked Little Man/Day Dreams | 6 |

## PERRY SISTERS
| 59 | Brunswick 05802 | Fabian/Willie Boy | 25 |

## PERSIAN FLOWERS
| 84 | Fourth Dimension FDS 02 | Somebody Else's Sin/Summer Of Love (1000 only, p/s) | 7 |

*(see also Wasted Youth)*

## PERSIAN RISK
| 81 | SRT SRTS/81/CUS/1146 | Calling For You/Chasing The Dragon (p/s) | 140 |
| 83 | Neat NEAT 24 | Ridin' High/Hurt You (p/s) | 18 |
| 86 | Metal Masters METALLP 2 | RISE UP (LP) | 18 |

*(see also Motorhead)*

## PERSIANS
| 69 | Pama PM 772 | I Only Have Eyes For You/The Sun Gotta Shine In Your Heart | 12 |
| 72 | Capitol CL 15726 | Baby Come Back Home/I Want To Go Home | 8 |

## PERSIMMON'S PECULIAR SHADES
| 68 | Major Minor MM 554 | Watchmaker/Coplington | 40 |

## PERSONALITIES
| 65 | Dice CC 30 | I Remember/Suffering | 15 |
| 65 | Ska Beat JB 222 | Hey Little Girl/Teardrops | 30 |
| 66 | Blue Beat BB 354 | Push It Down/BUSTER'S ALL STARS: Blues Market | 50 |

## PERSONS UNKNOWN
| 81 | Po 1 | Addiction/Addiction (p/s) | 25 |

## PERSUADERS!
| 93 | Detour DR 001 | Finished Forever/In The Night (p/s, 300 only) | 20 |
| 94 | Detour DR 011 | Waiting For The Nowhere Express/Girl/The Paperchase (p/s, 100 on red vinyl) | 8 |
| 94 | Detour DR 011 | Waiting For The Nowhere Express/Girl/The Paperchase (p/s) | 5 |

## PERSUADERS (U.S.)
| 72 | Atlantic K 40370 | THE THIN LINE BETWEEN LOVE AND HATE (LP) | 20 |
| 73 | Atlantic K 40476 | THE PERSUADERS (LP) | 15 |

## PERSUASIONS
| 65 | Columbia DB 7560 | I'll Go Crazy/Try Me | 30 |
| 65 | Columbia DB 7700 | Big Brother/Deep Down Love | 30 |
| 66 | Columbia DB 7859 | La, La, La, La, La/Opportunity | 30 |

## PERSUASIONS (U.S.)
| 69 | Minit MLF 11017 | Party In The Woods/It's Better To Have Loved And Lost | 20 |
| 73 | MCA MUS 1222 | Good Old Acappella/You Must Believe Me | 7 |
| 70 | Straight STS 1062 | A CAPPELLA (LP) | 40 |
| 72 | Island ILPS 9201 | STREET CORNER SYMPHONY (LP) | 20 |

## MORRIS PERT
| 75 | Chantry ABM 21 | LUMINOS/CHROMOSPHERE/4 JAPANESE VERSES (LP) | 40 |
| 80 | Chantry CHT 001 | LUMINOS/CHROMOSPHERE/4 JAPANESE VERSES (LP, reissue) | 30 |
| 82 | Chantry CHT 007 | BOOK OF LOVE/FRAGMENTI I/ULTIMATE DECAY (LP) | 30 |

## JON PERTWEE
| 72 | Purple PUR 111 | Who Is The Doctor/Pure Mystery | 20 |
| 85 | Safari DOCTOR 1 | Who Is The Doctor/Doctor Blood Donor (p/s) | 6 |

| | | |
|---|---|---|
| 62 | Phillips BBL 7558 | SONGS FOR VULGAR BOATMEN (LP) ........................................ 20 |

*(see also Rupert Hine, Derek Roy, BBC Radiophonic Workshop)o*

## PERUVIAN HIPSTERS
| | | |
|---|---|---|
| 88 | Hip HIP 001 | Tony Hadley/It Doesn't Happen Everyday (p/s) ........................ 35 |

## PESKY GEE!
| | | |
|---|---|---|
| 69 | Pye 7N 17708 | Where Is My Mind/A Place Of Heart Break ........................ 50 |
| 69 | Pye N(S)PL 18293 | EXCLAMATION MARK (LP, textured sleeve) ........................ 200 |

*(see also Black Widow, Agony Bag)*

## PEST
| | | |
|---|---|---|
| 03 | Ninja Tune ZEN 74 | NECESSARY MEASURES (2-LP) ........................ 20 |

## PETALS
| | | |
|---|---|---|
| 63 | Decca F 11650 | Let's Do The Tamoure/Look At Me ........................ 8 |

## PETARDS
| | | |
|---|---|---|
| 69 | Liberty LBF 15206 | Misty Island/Tartarex ........................ 60 |

## PETER
| | | |
|---|---|---|
| 70 | Sonet SON 2012 | Peace/Values ........................ 15 |

## PETER & ALEX
| | | |
|---|---|---|
| 70 | Carnaby 4018 | Big Beat/On The Loose ........................ 7 |

## PETER & GORDON
| | | |
|---|---|---|
| 65 | Columbia DB 7729 | Baby I'm Yours/When The Black Of Your Eyes Turns To Grey ........ 5 |
| 66 | Columbia DB 7834 | Woman/Wrong From The Start ........................ 5 |
| 66 | Columbia DB 7951 | Don't Pity Me/To Show I Love You ........................ 5 |
| 66 | Columbia DB 8003 | Lady Godiva/Morning's Calling ........................ 5 |
| 66 | Columbia DB 8075 | Knight In Rusty Armour/The Flower Lady ........................ 5 |
| 67 | Columbia DB 8159 | Sunday For Tea/Start Trying Someone Else ........................ 5 |
| 67 | Columbia DB 8198 | The Jokers/Red, Cream And Velvet ........................ 20 |
| 68 | Columbia DB 8398 | I Feel Like Going Out/The Quest For The Holy Grail ........ 20 |
| 68 | Columbia DB 8451 | You've Had Better Times/Sipping My Wine ........................ 8 |
| 69 | Columbia DB 8585 | I Can Remember (Not Too Long Ago)/Hard Time, Rainy Day ........ 10 |
| 64 | Columbia SEG 8348 | NOBODY I KNOW (EP) ........................ 15 |
| 64 | Columbia 33SX 1630 | PETER AND GORDON (LP, mono) ........................ 20 |
| 64 | Columbia SCX 3518 | PETER AND GORDON (LP, stereo) ........................ 25 |
| 64 | Columbia 33SX 1660 | IN TOUCH WITH PETER AND GORDON (LP, mono) ........ 25 |
| 64 | Columbia SCN 3532 | IN TOUCH WITH PETER AND GORDON (LP, stereo) ........ 25 |
| 65 | Columbia 33SX 1761 | HURTIN 'N' LOVIN' (LP, mono) ........................ 20 |
| 65 | Columbia SCX 3565 | HURTIN 'N' LOVIN' (LP, stereo) ........................ 25 |
| 66 | Columbia SX 6045 | PETER AND GORDON (LP, mono) ........................ 20 |
| 66 | Columbia SCX 6045 | PETER AND GORDON (LP, stereo) ........................ 25 |
| 66 | Columbia SX 6097 | SOMEWHERE... (LP, mono) ........................ 20 |
| 66 | Columbia SCX 6097 | SOMEWHERE... (LP, stereo) ........................ 25 |
| 65 | Columbia SCXC 25 | I GO TO PIECES (LP, export issue) ........................ 20 |
| 66 | Columbia SCXC 29 | WOMAN (LP, export issue) ........................ 20 |
| 66 | Columbia SCXC 33 | LADY GODIVA (LP, export issue) ........................ 25 |

*(see also Gordon Waller)*

## PETER & HEADLINES
| | | |
|---|---|---|
| 64 | Decca F 11980 | Don't Cry Little Girl/It Was Love ........................ 15 |
| 64 | Decca F 12035 | Tears And Kisses/I've Got My Reasons ........................ 15 |

*(see also Count Downe & Zeros)*

## PETER & MARY
| | | |
|---|---|---|
| 54 | Columbia SCMC 6 | Crazy Mix Up Song/What Shall We Do With The Lonesome Lover (export issue) ........ 6 |

*(see also Peter Lind Hayes)*

## PETER & PAUL
| | | |
|---|---|---|
| 66 | Blue Beat BB 364 | Hosana/Schoolgirl ........................ 20 |

## PETER & PERSUADERS
| | | |
|---|---|---|
| 65 | Oak RGJ 197 | The Wanderer/Wine Glass Rock/Oh My Soul/Cross My Heart (EP) ........ 50 |

## PETER & TEST TUBE BABIES
| | | |
|---|---|---|
| 81 | No Future OI 4 | Banned From The Pubs/Moped Lads/Peacehaven Wild Lads (p/s) ........ 10 |
| 82 | No Future OI 15 | Run Like Hell/Up Yer Bum (p/s) ........................ 8 |
| 83 | Trapper EARS 1 | Zombie Creeping Flesh/No Invitation/Smash And Grab (p/s) ........ 6 |
| 83 | Trapper EARS 2 | The Jinx/Trapper Ain't Got A Bird (p/s) ........................ 6 |
| 82 | No Future Punk 3 | PISSED AND PROUD (LP) ........................ 15 |
| 83 | Trapper THIN 1 | MATING SOUNDS OF SOUTH AMERICAN FROGS (LP, with lyric inner) ........ 15 |
| 87 | Dojo LP 49 | SOBERPHOBIA (LP) ........................ 15 |

## PETER & WOLVES
| | | |
|---|---|---|
| 67 | MGM MGM 1352 | Little Girl Lost And Found/Is Me ........................ 35 |
| 68 | MGM MGM 1374 | Lanternlight/Break Up-Break Down ........................ 30 |
| 68 | MGM MGM 1397 | Julie/Birthday ........................ 20 |
| 68 | MGM MGM 1452 | Woman On My Mind/Old & The New ........................ 35 |
| 70 | UPC UPC 104 | Something In The Way She Moves/The Lady And Me ........ 10 |

*(see also Factory, Norman Conquest, John Pantry, Sounds Around)*

## PETER B'S
| | | |
|---|---|---|
| 66 | Columbia DB 7862 | If You Wanna Be Happy/Jodrell Blues ........................ 70 |

*(see also Tony Colton, Peter Bardens, Peter Green, Cheynes, Shotgun Express)*

## PETER, PAUL & MARY
| | | |
|---|---|---|
| 63 | Warner Bros WB 95 | Puff/Pretty Mary ........................ 6 |
| 63 | Warner Bros WB 104 | Blowing In The Wind/Flora ........................ 5 |
| 64 | Warner Bros WB 142 | The Times They Are A-Changin'/Blue ........................ 5 |

# PETER'S FACES

*(see also Mary Travers)*

### PETER'S FACES
| | | | |
|---|---|---|---|
| 64 | Piccadilly 7N 35178 | Why Did You Bring Him To The Dance/She's In Love | 10 |
| 64 | Piccadilly 7N 35196 | Try A Little Love My Friend/I Don't Care | 10 |
| 64 | Piccadilly 7N 35205 | Just Like Romeo And Juliet/Wait | 25 |
| 65 | Piccadilly 7N 35225 | De-Boom-Lay-Boom/Suzie Q | 10 |

*(see also Flowerpot Men, White Plains)*

### GORDON PETERS
| | | | |
|---|---|---|---|
| 61 | Embassy 45 WB 482 | Take Five/Take Good Care Of My Baby | 10 |

### JANICE PETERS & PLAYBOYS
| | | | |
|---|---|---|---|
| 58 | Columbia DB 4222 | This Little Girl's Gone Rockin'/Kiss Cha Cha | 30 |
| 59 | Columbia DB 4276 | A Girl Likes/You're The One | 30 |

### JO PETERS
| | | | |
|---|---|---|---|
| 61 | Pye 7N 15350 | I Love The Long Light Evenings/I May Be Wrong | 6 |
| 62 | Pye 7N 15413 | When Opportunity Knocks/Never Cheat Your Sweetheart | 7 |

### JOHNNY PETERS
| | | | |
|---|---|---|---|
| 65 | Decca F 12172 | When You Ask About Love/People Say | 25 |

### LENNIE PETERS
| | | | |
|---|---|---|---|
| 63 | Oriole CB 1887 | And My Heart Cried/For A Lifetime | 7 |
| 64 | Oriole CB 1956 | Let The Tears Begin/Love Me, Love Me (Love Me, Love Me) | 7 |

### LINDA PETERS
| | | | |
|---|---|---|---|
| 70 | Warlock Music WMM 101/2 | WARLOCK MUSIC SAMPLER (LP, sampler, 7 tracks by Elton John) | 1000 |

*(see also Paul McNeill & Linda Peters, Richard & Linda Thompson)*

### MARK PETERS & SILHOUETTES
| | | | |
|---|---|---|---|
| 63 | Oriole CB 1836 | Fragile (Handle With Care)/Janie | 30 |
| 64 | Oriole CB 1909 | Cindy's Gonna Cry/Show Her | 30 |
| 64 | Piccadilly 7N 35207 | Don't Cry For Me/I Told You So | 15 |

### PETER'S PRIVATE ARMY
| | | | |
|---|---|---|---|
| 83 | Spartan SP 9 | The Gaol Song (Hip For The Day)/Bounce Back | 7 |

### SCOTT PETERS
| | | | |
|---|---|---|---|
| 61 | Pye 7N 15343 | Kookie Talk/Game Of Love | 7 |
| 61 | Pye 7N 15363 | Bobbie Allen/It's The Natural Thing To Do | 6 |
| 61 | Columbia DB 8244 | Go Tell The World/More And More | 6 |

### WENDY PETERS
| | | | |
|---|---|---|---|
| 68 | Saga OPP 1 | Morning Dew/I Don't Understand | 18 |

### JENNY PETERS
| | | | |
|---|---|---|---|
| 79 | Redball RR008 | JENNY PETERS (EP) | 12 |

### CLIVE PETERSEN
| | | | |
|---|---|---|---|
| 61 | Columbia DB 4687 | For Every Boy/If No One Tells You | 15 |

### PAUL PETERSEN
| | | | |
|---|---|---|---|
| 62 | Pye International 7N 25153 | Keep Your Love Locked/Be Everything To Anyone You Love | 7 |
| 62 | Pye International 7N 25163 | Lollipops And Roses/Please Mr Sun | 10 |
| 63 | Pye International 7N 25173 | My Dad/Little Boy Sad | 10 |
| 63 | Pye International 7N 25196 | Amy/Goody Goody | 10 |
| 68 | Tamla Motown TMG 670 | A Little Bit For Sandy/Your Love's Got Me Burnin' Alive | 8 |

### PAUL PETERSEN & SHELLEY FABARES
| | | | |
|---|---|---|---|
| 62 | Pye International 7N 25133 | She Can't Find Her Keys/Very Unlikely | 10 |

*(see also Shelley Fabares)*

### BOBBY PETERSON (QUINTET)
| | | | |
|---|---|---|---|
| 59 | Top Rank JAR 232 | The Hunch/Love You Pretty Baby (as Bobby Peterson Quintet) | 15 |
| 64 | Sue WI 342 | Rockin' Charlie (Parts 1 & 2) (solo) | 30 |
| 65 | Sue WI 346 | Piano Rock/One Day (solo) | 30 |

### RAY PETERSON
| | | | |
|---|---|---|---|
| 59 | RCA RCA 1131 | The Wonder Of You/I'm Gone | 8 |
| 59 | RCA RCA 1154 | Shirley Purley/Come And Get It | 12 |
| 60 | RCA RCA 1175 | Answer Me/Goodnight My Love, Pleasant Dreams | 15 |
| 60 | RCA RCA 1195 | Tell Laura I Love Her/Wedding Day | 10 |
| 60 | London HLX 9246 | Corrine, Corrina/Be My Girl | 10 |
| 61 | London HLX 9332 | Sweet Little Kathy/You Didn't Care | 10 |
| 61 | London HLX 9379 | Missing You/You Thrill Me | 10 |
| 62 | London HLX 9489 | I Could Have Loved You So Well/Why Don't You Write Me | 15 |
| 62 | London HLX 9569 | You Didn't Care/You Know Me Much Too Well | 8 |
| 63 | London HLX 9746 | Without Love/Give Us Your Blessing | 8 |
| 64 | MGM MGM 1249 | Oh No/If You Were Here | 5 |
| 64 | MGM MGM 1258 | Across The Street/When I Stop Dreaming | 5 |
| 65 | MGM MGM 1273 | House Without Windows/Wish I Could Say No To You | 5 |
| 65 | MGM MGM 1288 | I'm Only Human/One Lonesome Rose | 7 |
| 66 | MGM MGM 1303 | Everybody/Love Hurts | 5 |
| 61 | London REX 1293 | CORRINE CORRINA (EP) | 25 |

### PETER, SUE & MARC & PFURI, GORPS & KNIRL
| | | | |
|---|---|---|---|
| 79 | EMI EMI 2940 | Second Hand Company/Troedler & Co. | 6 |

### PET HATE
| | | | |
|---|---|---|---|
| 83 | FM 12VHF 2 | Roll Away The Stone/Caught/Playing With My Heart (12", p/s) | 12 |

*(see also Silverwing)*

### PETITES
| | | | |
|---|---|---|---|
| 60 | Philips PB 1035 | Get Your Daddy's Car Tonight/Sun Showers | 10 |

## PETR & PAVEL
| | | | |
|---|---|---|---|
| 68 | Page One POF 112 | Laska/Wencelas Square............................................................. | 6 |

## PETS
| | | | |
|---|---|---|---|
| 58 | London HL 8652 | Cha-Hua-Hua/Cha-Kow-Ski....................................................... | 15 |
| 59 | Pye International 7N 25004 | (You Wandered) Beyond The Sea/Wow-ee!!! ............................ | 10 |

## PET SHOP BOYS
### SINGLES
| | | | |
|---|---|---|---|
| 84 | Epic A 4292 | West End Girls/Pet Shop Boys (p/s) ......................................... | 20 |
| 84 | Epic TA 4292 | West End Girls (Extended)/Pet Shop Boys (12", p/s) ............... | 30 |
| 85 | Parlophone R 6097 | Opportunities (Let's Make Lots of Money)/In The Night (matrix: A-3-1-2) (1st mix, white p/s) ............................ | 12 |
| 85 | Parlophone 12R 6097 | Opportunities (Let's Make Lots of Money) (Dance Mix)/In The Night (Extended) (12", white p/s) ............................ | 20 |
| 85 | Parlophone 12RA 6097 | Opportunities (Let's Make Lots of Money) (Version Latina)/(Dub For Money Remix)/In The Night (Extended Mix) (12", large picture labels, die-cut p/s) ......... | 40 |
| 85 | Parlophone 12R 6097 | Opportunities (Let's Make Lots of Money) (Dance Mix)/In The Night (Extended) (12", p/s, mispressing, B-side plays "Opportunities [Dub For Money] Remix") ................ | 30 |
| 85 | Parlophone 12R 6097 | Opportunities (Let's Make Lots of Money) (Dance Mix)/ In The Night (Extended) (12", p/s, 2nd mispressing, A-side plays "Opportunities [Version Latina]") ............ | 30 |
| 85 | Parlophone 10R 6115 | West End Girls (Untitled Mix)/A Man Could Get Arrested (4.09 Mix)/ West End Girls (7" Mix) (10", round foldout p/s; sealed with sticker) ......................... | 60 |
| 86 | Parlophone 12RA 6115 | West End Girls (Shep Pettibone Mastermix)/West End Dub/A Man Could Get Arrested (4.09 Mix) (12", black/blue/red p/s, standard labels) ............. | 10 |
| 86 | Parlophone 12RA 6115 | West End Girls (Shep Pettibone Mastermix)/West End Dub/A Man Could Get Arrested (4.09 Mix) (12", same as above with 6" yellow circle on sleeve) ............. | 10 |
| 86 | Parlophone 12RA 6115 | West End Girls (Shep Pettibone Mastermix)/West End Dub/A Man Could Get Arrested (4.09 Mix) (12", stickered black/blue/red p/s with 6" die-cut hole & 6" yellow picture labels) ............. | 10 |
| 86 | Parlophone 10R 6116 | Love Comes Quickly (Dance Mix)/That's My Impression (Disco Mix) (10", PVC sleeve with poster) ......................... | 60 |
| 86 | Parlophone 12R 6116 | Love Comes Quickly (Dance Mix)/That's My Impression (Disco Mix) (12", large picture labels, die-cut white sleeve) ......................... | 10 |
| 86 | Parlophone RD 6140 | Suburbia/Paninaro/Love Comes Quickly (Shep Pettibone Remix)/Jack The Lad/ Suburbia Part Two (double pack, gatefold p/s) ............ | 6 |
| 88 | Parlophone CDR 6177 | Heart (Disco Mix)/I Get Excited (You Get Excited Too)/Heart (Dance Mix)............ | 8 |
| 93 | Parlophone R 6348 | Can You Forgive Her? (7" Version)/Hey Headmaster (red or blue vinyl, factory custom pressing, p/s) ......................... | 600 |
| 97 | Parlophone Fan Club | It Doesn't Often Snow At Christmas (CD, fan club issue, in sealed silver bubble wrap) | 125 |
| 06 | Parlophone R6708 | Minimal/In Private (clear vinyl, p/s) ......................... | 5 |
| 06 | Parlophone R6723 | Numb/Party Song (p/s) ......................... | 5 |
| 10 | Parlophone R 6810 | Love Life/A Powerful Friend (Jukebox centre, blue parlophone sleeve, 1000 only)........ | 12 |
| 12 | Parlophone R 6879 | Leaving/Leaving (Demo) (signed p/s) ............ | 20 |
| 12 | Parlophone 12R 6879 | Leaving (Lost Her Remix)/(Happy Sad Remix)/Happy Hour Remix) (12" signed p/s) ..... | 20 |

### ALBUMS
| | | | |
|---|---|---|---|
| 87 | Parlophone CDPCSDX 104 | ACTUALLY (CD, with U.S. import "Always On My Mind" CD single) ............ | 25 |
| 88 | Parlophone PCSX 7325 | INTROSPECTIVE (LP, 3 x clear vinyl 12" factory custom pressing, with wraparound paper strip, 10 copies only) ......................... | 800 |
| 88 | Parlophone PCSX 7325 | INTROSPECTIVE (LP, 3 x black vinyl 12", with picture labels & wraparound paper obi strip) ......................... | 15 |
| 93 | Parlophone PCSD 143 | VERY (LP) ......................... | 25 |
| 93 | Parlophone CDPSDX 143 | VERY (CD, with 6-track bonus CD "Relentless" in foldout 'bubble' wallet) ............ | 15 |
| 96 | Parlophone PCSD 170 | BILINGUAL (LP) ......................... | 20 |
| 00 | Parlophone 724352185719 | NIGHTLIFE (LP) ......................... | 25 |
| 02 | Parlophone 0 724358146 | DISCO 3 (3-LP) ......................... | 50 |
| 03 | Parlophone 5938841 | POPART - THE HITS (3-LP) ......................... | 50 |
| 09 | Vinyl Factory | YES (11 x 12" in smoked perspex box with gold-plated 'tick' on cover, with art print, signed and numbered by both band members, 300 only) ............ | 500 |

### PROMOS
| | | | |
|---|---|---|---|
| 84 | Epic A4292 | West End Girls/Pet Shop Boys (p/s, 'A' label promo) ............ | 30 |
| 85 | Parlophone R 12R 6097 | Opportunities (Let's Make Lots of Money)/In The Night (12", "photocopy" sl.) ......... | 30 |
| 86 | Parlophone R 6116 | Love Comes Quickly (1-sided, p/s) ............ | 40 |
| 86 | Parlophone 12R 6129 | Opportunities (Let's Make Lots of Money) (7.18 Shep Pettibone Mastermix)/ Opportunities (4.27 Reprise)/Opportunities (6.44 Original Dance Mix)/Was That What It Was (12", autographed black die-cut sleeve, with press release) ......... | 35 |
| 86 | Parlophone 12R 6129 | Opportunities (Let's Make Lots of Money) (7.18 Shep Pettibone Mastermix)/ Opportunities (4.27 Reprise)/Opportunities (6.44 Original Dance Mix)/Was That What It Was (12", autographed black die-cut sleeve, without press release) ......... | 35 |
| 88 | Parlophone 12RDJ 6198 | Left To My Own Devices (The Disco Mix)/Left To My Own Devices/ The Sound Of The Atom Splitting (12", unique title sleeve) ............ | 12 |
| 89 | Parlophone CDPCSD 113 | BEHAVIOUR (CD, commercial issue, different inlay, in white monogrammed pouch, with full-album cassette & chronology) ......................... | 50 |
| 91 | Parlophone MFB 1 | Music For Boys (12", 3 untitled mixes, hand-stamped white label) ............ | 25 |
| 91 | Parlophone 12MFBX 1 | Music For Boys (12", 2 untitled mixes, white label) ............ | 12 |
| 92 | Parlophone CDRX 6332 | Go West (7" Version)/West End Girls (Sacha Mix)/Forever/Go West (Extended Dance Mix) (cassette, title sleeve) ............ | 150 |
| 93 | Parlophone 12RXDJ 6348 | Can You Forgive Her? (MK Remix)/(MK Bicycle Dub)/I Want To Wake Up (Johnny Marr 1993 Remix)/(Johnny Marr Groove Mix) (12") ............ | 10 |
| 93 | Abbey Road | COMPILED EP (CD-R, Abbey Road title sleeve; autographed by The Boys, 20 only)...... | 800 |
| 94 | Parlophone 12RDJ 6386 | Yesterday When I Was Mad (Jam & Spoon Mix)/(Junior Vasquez Factory Dub)/(Junior Vasquez Fabulous Dub)/Junior Vasquez Body Dub)/(Coconut 12" Mix)/(RAF Zone Mix)/(RAF Dub Zone)/Euroboy/Some Speculation (12", double pack unique p/s)........ | 15 |
| 96 | Parlophone 12RDJD 6431 | Before (Classic Paradise Mix)/(Afrodisiac Mix)/(Hedboys Mix)/ (Dub)/(Extended Mix) (2 x 12", blue 'penis' p/s) ............ | 25 |
| 96 | Parlophone 12RJD 6431 | Before (Underground Mix)/(Bonus Dub)/(Underground Instrumental)/(Bonus Beats) (12", red 'penis' p/s) ............ | 25 |

MINT VALUE £

| | | | |
|---|---|---|---|
| 97 | Parlophone 12 BARDJ 2 | The Truck Driver & His Mate/Before (Love To Infinity Classic Paradise Mix) (12", 'two knobs' p/s, 150 copies) | 150 |
| 97 | Parlophone 12RDJ 6460 | A Red Letter Day (Trouser Enthusiasts Autoerotic Decapitation Mix)/(Trouser Enthusiasts Congo Dongo Dubstramental) (12") | 10 |
| 97 | Parlophone 12BOYDJ 101 | The Boy Who Couldn't Keep His Clothes On (Main Vocal)/(INT... Club Mix)/(Banji Girlfriend Beats)/(On Stage At Twilo)/(Radio Edit) (12", die-cut sleeve) | 60 |
| 99 | Parlophone (no cat. no.) | NIGHTLIFE (10" x 10" box in PVC slip case, contains interview CD, music CD, book, EPK & 3 photographs) | 50 |
| 01 | 10th Planet/PSBP/RUG | FIVE TITLES FROM CLOSER TO HEAVEN: Positive Role Model/Friendly Fire/Shameless/K-Hole/For All Of Us (CD-R, title sleeve, all sung by Neil Tennant) | 150 |
| 06 | Parlophone FUNDA001 | Fundamentalism Part 1 (12", promo) | 15 |
| 06 | Parlophone FUNDA002 | Fundamentalism Part 2 (12", promo) | 15 |
| 06 | Parlophone PSB002 | Psychological (1-sided 12" no Pet Shop Boys credit on label) | 15 |
| 06 | Parlophone REMIXES01 | Psychological (Ewan Pearson Mixes) (12" promo) | 25 |
| 06 | Parlophone 0094634979721 | I'm With Stupid Remixes (CD, 6-track promo, card p/s) | 25 |
| 06 | Parlophone STUPID002 | I'm With Stupid Remixes 1 (12" promo) | 15 |
| 06 | Parlophone STUPID001 | I'm With Stupid Remixes 2 (12" promo) | 15 |
| 06 | Parlophone STUPID003 | I'm With Stupid Remixes 3 (12" promo) | 15 |
| 06 | Parlophone 0094637114421 | Minimal Remixes (CD, 10-track, promo card p/s) | 25 |
| 06 | Parlophone PRIVATE001 | In Private (Tomcraft Mixes) (12" promo) | 20 |
| 93 | Parlophone DF 118 | RELENTLESS (3 x 12", on pink/yellow/blue vinyl) | 60 |
| 96 | Parlophone BILING 1 | BILINGUAL (A4 yellow box set, including "A Taste Of Bilingual" CD: (Discoteca/Electricity/A Red Letter Day/It Always Comes As A Surprise/Se A Vida E) (with 2 photos & inset in transparent PVC box) | 50 |
| 96 | Parlophone PSBCDDJ 1 | BILINGUAL (A4 pale blue launch party promo box set including "A Taste Of Bilingual" CD [Before/Se A Vida E], & album cassette, unique inlay) | 200 |
| 01 | Really Useful Group | CLOSER TO HEAVEN (CD-R, title sleeve; 19 tracks, all sung by Neil Tennant) | 250 |
| 07 | Parlophone DISCO004 | DISCO 4 ALBUM SAMPLER (12" 4-tracks) | 20 |
| 07 | Parlophone (no cat. No.) | DISCO FOUR (Promo CD-R, 5-track album sampler and press sheet, 30 copies) | 40 |

*(see also Eighth Wonder, Dusty Springfield, Electronic, Ian Wright)*

**PEPPER POT**
| | | | |
|---|---|---|---|
| 73 | Jumbo JB 034 | Lift Up Your Shirt/Ride The Pony | 12 |

**MARY PETTI**
| | | | |
|---|---|---|---|
| 61 | RCA RCA 1239 | Hey! Lawdy Lawdy/Gee, But It Hurts | 40 |

**PETTICOATS**
| | | | |
|---|---|---|---|
| 80 | Bla Bla Bla 01 | Normal/Allergy/I'm Free (with insert) | 20 |

**FRANK PETTY TRIO**
| | | | |
|---|---|---|---|
| 53 | MGM SP 1010 | St. Louis Blues (Boogie Woogie)/Somebody Stole My Girl | 20 |
| 53 | MGM SP 1033 | Side By Side/Who's Sorry Now | 7 |
| 53 | MGM SP 1038 | Sugar/Sioux City Sue | 7 |
| 53 | MGM SP 1053 | Sweet Jenny Lee/Yes Sir That's My Baby | 6 |
| 54 | MGM SP 1092 | Loch Lomond/Pino Pantaloni | 6 |
| 54 | MGM SP 1112 | Mr Pogo/Sunday | 6 |

**NORMAN PETTY TRIO**
| | | | |
|---|---|---|---|
| 54 | HMV 7M 274 | Mood Indigo/Petty's Little Polka | 10 |

**TOM PETTY (& HEARTBREAKERS)**
| | | | |
|---|---|---|---|
| 77 | Shelter WIP 6377 | American Girl/Wild One Forever (some in p/s) | 5 |
| 76 | Shelter ISA 5014 | TOM PETTY AND THE HEARTBREAKERS (LP) | 15 |
| 76 | Shelter 1DJ 24A | OFFICIAL LIVE BOOTLEG (LP, with Heartbreakers, 1-sided 5-track, promo only) | 20 |
| 78 | Shelter ISA 5017 | YOU'RE GONNA GET IT! (LP) | 15 |
| 79 | MCA MCF 3044 | DAMN THE TORPEDOS (LP) | 15 |
| 89 | MCA Records MCG 6034 | FULL MOON FEVER (LP) | 20 |
| 94 | Warner Bros. Records 9362 45759-1 | WILDFLOWERS (2-LP) | 60 |
| 99 | Warner Bros. Records 9362-47294-1 | ECHO (2-LP) | 70 |

*(see also Randy Newman, Traveling Wilburys, k.d. lang & Roy Orbison)*

**P.F.M.**
| | | | |
|---|---|---|---|
| 73 | Manticore K 43502 | PHOTOS OF GHOSTS (LP, laminated gatefold sleeve) | 25 |
| 74 | Manticore K 53502 | THE WORLD BECAME THE WORLD (LP, die-cut sleeve with inner) | 20 |
| 74 | Manticore K 53506 | COOK (LP) | 15 |

**P45**
| | | | |
|---|---|---|---|
| 80 | Jet 190 | Right Direction/B.I.N.Y.C. | 15 |

**PHANTOM**
| | | | |
|---|---|---|---|
| 78 | Cool Ghoul COOL 1 | Lazy Fascist/Power Dub | 6 |

*(see also Tom Robinson, Blazing Sons)*

**PHANTOM BAND**
| | | | |
|---|---|---|---|
| 71 | Polydor 2058-176 | Loop-Di-Love/Funkin' About | 30 |
| 72 | Polydor 2058-290 | Silhouettes/Drummitt | 15 |

**PHANTOM CHORDS**
| | | | |
|---|---|---|---|
| 92 | Camden Town GNAR 003 | Town Without Pity/She's A Bad Motorcycle (p/s, 2,000 only) | 8 |

*(see also Damned)*

**PHANTOMS**
| | | | |
|---|---|---|---|
| 61 | Palette PG 9014 | Phantom Guitar/Cachina | 20 |
| 60s | Arc ARC | GREAT GUITAR HITS (LP) | 20 |

**PHARAOHS**
| | | | |
|---|---|---|---|
| 58 | Decca DFE 6522 | THE PHARAOHS (EP) | 500 |

**PHARCYDE**
| | | | |
|---|---|---|---|
| 92 | East West 7567-92222-1 | BIZARRE RIDE II THE PHARCYDE (LP, European edition, 2-LP set is USA) | 20 |
| 95 | Go! Beat 828 736-1 | LABCABINCALIFORNIA (2-LP, red and blue vinyl, free 12") | 25 |

**RORY PHARE**
88   Parlophone RP 1   Laughing Inside/Laughing Inside (actually by Roy Harper; p/s, promo only)....................7
*(see also Roy Harper)*

**PHASE 4**
66   Decca F 12327   What Do You Say About That/Think I'll Sit Down And Cry (1st issue) .............................25
66   Fab FAB 1   What Do You Say About That/I'm Gonna Sit Down And Cry (2nd issue) ........................20
67   Fab FAB 6   Man Am I Worried?/Listen To The Blues.........................................................................50

**PHASE 5**
70   Polydor 2058 063   Star Trek/Enterprise ...................................................................................................30

**PHASE 3**
71   Mushroom SMR 5   Walkin' Free/Bill Bailey .................................................................................................10

**PHATES**
79   Personal Propaganda PROP 4MODACOM: Cool Jerk/Tears Of A Dog (hand-made labels and p/s, 500 only) ...... 20

**PHEETUS**
78   Ric Rac RRS 002   Nomads/Blind Man (no p/s, 200 only)..............................................................................35

**JAMES PHELPS**
72   Paramount PARA 3019   Check Yourself/My Lover's Prayer ................................................................................12

**PHENOMENA**
85   Bronze BRO 193   Dance With The Devil/Hell On Wings (p/s) ......................................................................7
85   Bronze BROX 193   Dance With The Devil (MIdnight Mix)/Hell On Wings (12", p/s with poster) ............... 10
*(see also Trapeze, Whitesnake, Cozy Powell, Black Sabbath, Thin Lizzy, Budgie, A-Ha)*

**PHEON BEAR**
73   Pye 7N 45232   War Against War/87th Precinct .....................................................................................25

**PHIL & FLINTSTONES**
64   Bedrock PR 5371   Love Potion No. 9/Honey Don't (private pressing) .......................................................80

**PHI LIFE CYPHER**
98   Compressed Knowledge CK001   Baddest Man/Da Shinn/Rap 'N' Bullshit/Forever (12") .............................................12
02   Jazz Fudge JFR 030   The Chosen Few EP (with Taskforce)............................................................................20

**PHILIP & HIS FOETUS VIBRATIONS**
82   Self Immol. WOMB KX 07   Tell Me, What Is The Bane Of Your Life/Mother I've Killed The Cat (p/s) .................25
*(see also You've Got Foetus On Your Breath, Foetus Äœber Frisco, Foetus Under Glass, Scraping Foetus Off The Wheel)*

**LOUIS PHILIPPE**
86   él GPO 15   Like Nobody Do/Twangy Twangy (p/s) ...........................................................................6
87   el GPO 23T   YOU MARY YOU (12" EP, p/s) .....................................................................................12
88   él ACME 15   IVORY TOWER (LP) .......................................................................................................20
89   el ACME 23   AN APPOINTMENT WITH VENUS (LP) ........................................................................30
89   él ACME 36   YURI GAGARIN (LP) ....................................................................................................20

**BRENDAN PHILIPS**
66   Mercury MF 896   Is It Worth A Try/When She's Kissing Me .......................................................................25

**NOEL PHILIPS**
71   CBS 7036   Eternal Loner/Snowman ...............................................................................................10
71   CBS 7415   If You Could Believe In Me/Such Is The Meaning Of Your Love.......................................10

**TONY PHILIPS & THE HAYSEEDS**
66   CBS 202337   Shropshire Lad/Situation Vacant ...................................................................................12

**PHILL MOST CHILL**
06   Diggers With Gratitude DWG BE INTELLEGENT (EP, 100 only) .......................................300
   001
11   Diggers With Gratitude DWG ALL CUTS RECORDED RAW (LP)........................................35
   008
11   Diggers With Gratitude DWG ALL CUTS RECORDED RAW (LP, 25 copies only, alternative pressing, white stickered
   008   cover)................................................................................................................................350
11   Diggers With Gratitude DWG ALL CUTS RECORDED RAW (LP, coloured vinyl, alternative pressing EP and 7") .......... 100
   008

**ANTHONY PHILLIPS**
79   Arista SPART 1085/AFLP 1   SIDES (LP, 1st 500 copies sealed with free LP "Private Parts & Pieces") ......................20
*(see also Genesis)*

**BARRE PHILLIPS**
69   Music Man SMLS 601   UNACCOMPANIED BARRE (LP)...................................................................................100

**CONFREY PHILLIPS (TRIO)**
56   Columbia SCM 5223   Love And Marriage/The Others I Like ..............................................................................5
57   Decca F 10835   Am I Going Out Of My Mind?/Afterglow .........................................................................5
57   Decca F 10866   Shotgun Rock 'n' Roll/Hokey-Kokey Rock 'n' Roll (as Confrey Phillips Trio) .................20

**EDDY/EDWIN PHILLIPS**
76   Charisma CB 283   Limbo Jimbo/Change My Ways (as Eddy Phillips) ............................................................5
*(see also Creation, Mark Four, Spectrum)*

**(LITTLE) ESTHER (PHILLIPS)**
62   Stateside SS 140   Release Me/Don't Feel Rained On ..................................................................................25
63   Ember EMB S 174   Am I That Easy To Forget/I Really Don't Want To Know (as Little Esther Phillips) ...........15
65   Sue WI 395   The Chains/Feel Like I Wanna Cry (as Esther Philips)......................................................40
65   Atlantic AT 4028   And I Love Him/Shangri-La ............................................................................................18
65   Atlantic AT 4048   Let Me Know When It's Over/I Saw Me .........................................................................15
66   Atlantic AT 4077   I Could Have Told You/Just Say Goodbye ......................................................................80
66   Atlantic AT 4077   I Could Have Told You/Just Say Goodbye (DJ Copy) ......................................................100
66   Ember EMBS 221   Release Me/Be Honest With Me (as Little Esther Phillips) ............................................12
66   Atlantic 584 013   When A Woman Loves A Man/Ups And Downs ............................................................15
67   Atlantic 584 062   Somebody Else Is Taking My Place/When Love Comes To The Human Race .................10
67   Atlantic 584 103   And I Love Him/Shangri-La (reissue) ...............................................................................8

## Flip PHILLIPS

MINT VALUE £

| 67 | Atlantic 584 126 | I'm Sorry/Cheater Man ........ 15 |
|---|---|---|
| 69 | Roulette RO 505 | Too Late To Worry, Too Blue To Cry/I'm In The Mood For Love (Moody's Mood For Love) |
| 69 | Roulette RO 508 | Tonight I'll Be Staying Here With You/Sweet Dreams ........ 8 |
| 72 | Atlantic K 10168 | Catch Me I'm Falling/Release Me ........ 6 |
| 72 | Kudu KUS 4000 | Home Is Where The Hatred Is/Til My Back Ain't Got No Bone ........ 18 |
| 73 | Kudu KUS 4002 | I've Never Found A Man/Cherry Red ........ 20 |
| 75 | Kudu 925 | What A Difference A Day Made/Turn Around, Look At Me ........ 15 |
| 63 | Ember CW 103 | REFLECTIONS OF GREAT COUNTRY AND WESTERN STANDARDS (LP) ........ 5 |
| 65 | Atlantic ATL 5030 | AND I LOVE HIM (LP) ........ 50 |
| 67 | Atlantic 587/588 010 | ESTHER PHILLIPS SINGS (LP) ........ 50 |
| 72 | Kudu KUL 2 | FROM A WHISPER TO A SCREAM (LP) ........ 30 |

## FLIP PHILLIPS
| 56 | Columbia/Clef 33C 9003 | FLIP PHILLIPS QUARTET (10" LP) ........ 12 |

## GLENN PHILLIPS
| 75 | Caroline C 1519 | LOST AT SEA (LP) ........ 20 |

## GREGORY PHILLIPS
| 63 | Pye 7N 15546 | Angie/Please Believe Me ........ 12 |
| 64 | Pye 7N 15593 | Everybody Knows/Closer To Me (with Remo Four) ........ 8 |
| 64 | Pye 7N 15633 | Don't Bother Me/Make Sure That You're Mine ........ 8 |
| 65 | Immediate IM 004 | Down In The Boondocks/That's The One ........ 30 |
*(see also Remo Four)*

## JOHN PHILLIPS
| 70 | Stateside SS 8046 | Mississippi/April Anne ........ 6 |
| 70 | Stateside-Dunhill SSL 5027 | JOHN PHILLIPS: THE WOLFKING OF L.A. (LP) ........ 35 |
*(see also Mamas & Papas)*

## LESLIE PHILLIPS
| 59 | Parlophone R 4610 | The Navy Lark/The Disc ........ 7 |
| 62 | Parlophone R 4912 | Jolly Old Spring/I Must Resist Temptation ........ 6 |
| 69 | Columbia DB 8562 | The Man Most Likely To/Marigold ........ 6 |

## MICHELLE PHILLIPS
| 76 | A&M AMS 7250 | No Love Today/Aloha Louie ........ 7 |
| 77 | A&M AMS 7340 | Victim Of Romance/Lady Of Fantasy ........ 15 |
| 77 | A&M AMLS 64651 | VICTIM OF ROMANCE (LP) ........ 30 |
*(see also Mamas & Papas)*

## NOEL PHILLIPS
| 80 | Jammys JM001 | Youth Man/Living In The Ghetto (12") ........ 25 |

## PHIL PHILLIPS & TWILIGHTS
| 59 | Mercury AMT 1059 | Sea Of Love/Juella ........ 35 |
| 60 | Mercury AMT 1072 | Take This Heart/Verdi Mae ........ 30 |
| 60 | Mercury AMT 1093 | Your True Love Once More/What Will I Tell My Heart ........ 30 |
| 61 | Mercury AMT 1139 | I Love To Love You/No One Else But You ........ 30 |

## SHAWN PHILLIPS
| 65 | Columbia DB 7611 | Hey Nelly Nelly/Solitude ........ 12 |
| 65 | Columbia DB 7699 | Doesn't Anybody Know My Name?/Nobody Listens ........ 12 |
| 65 | Columbia DB 7789 | Little Tin Soldier/London Town ........ 8 |
| 66 | Columbia DB 7956 | Summer Came/Storm ........ 8 |
| 67 | Parlophone R 5606 | Stargazer/Woman Mine ........ 80 |
| 70 | A&M AMS 819 | Christmas Song/Lovely Lady ........ 6 |
| 65 | Columbia 33SX 1748 | I'M A LONER (LP) ........ 140 |
| 66 | Columbia S(C)X 6006 | SHAWN (LP) ........ 250 |
| 70 | A&M AMLS 978 | CONTRIBUTION (LP) ........ 18 |
| 71 | A&M AMLS 2006 | SECOND CONTRIBUTION (LP, with insert) ........ 18 |
| 72 | A&M AMLS 64324 | COLLABORATION (LP) ........ 18 |

## SID PHILLIPS BAND
| 56 | HMV POP 269 | Farewell Blues (Rock 'N' Roll Style)/It Goes Like This ........ 6 |

## STU PHILLIPS
| 58 | London HL 8673 | The Champlain And St. Lawrence Line/The Priest Who Slept 100 Years ........ 10 |
| 60 | Pye International 7N 25062 | Strangers When We Meet/BOB MERSEY ORCHESTRA: Song Of India ........ 6 |
| 67 | RCA RCA 1601 | Angel Of Love/The Great El Tigre ........ 5 |
| 69 | Pye Intl. NEP 44001 | STU PHILLIPS (EP) ........ 12 |

## TEDDY PHILLIPS & HIS ORCHESTRA
| 54 | Parlophone CMSP 4 | Down Boy/Meet "Miss Pippin" (export issue) ........ 12 |
| 54 | Parlophone CMSP 12 | The Old Red Barn/JIMMY BLUE CREW: The Old Shoe Cobbler (export issue) ........ 8 |
| 54 | Parlophone CMSP 28 | Life Is Like A Slice Of Cake/One-Sided Love Affair (export issue) ........ 12 |

## TOM PHILLIPS/GAVIN BRYERS/FRED ORTON
| 78 | Obscure OBS 9 | IRMA - AN OPERA (LP) ........ 20 |

## WARREN PHILLIPS & THE ROCKETS
| 69 | Decca (S)PA 43 | THE WORLD OF ROCK 'N' ROLL (LP) ........ 15 |
*(see also Foghat)*

## WOOLF PHILLIPS & HIS ORCHESTRA
| 54 | Decca F 10416 | Count Your Blessings Instead Of Sheep/Your Heart, My Heart (B-side with Dennis Morley - Vocal) ........ 6 |

## PHILLY DOG
| 74 | Penny Farthing PEN 581 | You Got The Gun/Hijack ........ 10 |

## PHILOSOPHERS
| 69 | Pye 7N 17740 | The Lovedene Girls/I Believe Forever ........ 25 |

## VINCE PHILPOTT & DRAGS
64 Decca F 11997     The Cramp/Eenie Meenie Miny Mo ...................................................................................... 15

## PHILWIT & PEGASUS
70 Chapter One CHR 130     And She Came - Final Thought/Pauper's Son ..................................................................... 8
70 Chapter One CHR 131     And I Try/Pauper's Son ...................................................................................................... 8
70 Chapter One CHR 137     The Elephant Song/Pseudo Phoney Mixed Up Croney ...................................................... 40
70 Chapter One CHSR 805     PHILWIT AND PEGASUS (LP) ............................................................................................ 40

*(see also Mark Wirtz)*

## PAT PHOENIX
62 HMV POP 1030     The Rovers Chorus/Coronation Street Monologue ............................................................ 12

## PHOENIX (1)
69 President PT 246     Tour De France/Time To Go .............................................................................................. 5

## PHOENIX (2)
81 Rising PR 433032     PHOENIX RISING EP (Lonely Attack/The Minstrel/Understanding/Phoenix Rising 'Av An 'Am) (12" EP) ...... 35

## PHOENIX (3)
00 Source 7243 8 488531 1     UNITED (LP) ...................................................................................................................... 40
04 Source SOUR LP 095     ALPHABETICAL (LP) .......................................................................................................... 35
09 V2 VVR703394     WOLFGANG AMEDUES PHOENIX (LP, white vinyl) ............................................................ 20

## PHONADS
81 SRT S81 CUS 1024     Talk To Me/You And Me (plain stickered sleeve) .............................................................. 50

## PHOTOGRAPHED BY LIGHTNING
86 Fierce FRIGHT 008     Sleep's Terminator/Winter Trees (foldaround p/s, hand-coloured labels) ........................ 30

## PHOTOGRAPHS
79 Do Not Bend AERS 106     Second Best/Seas/Here I Go Again (no p/s) ...................................................................... 20

## PHUTURE PHANTASY
88 Low Fat Vinyl LFV 1     SLAM (12") ....................................................................................................................... 15

## PHUTURE PRIMITIVE
93 Knifeforce KF 006     Full Metal Jacket/Twinkle (12") ....................................................................................... 30
94 Knifeforce KF 026     Lift Me Up/Infect Me (12") ............................................................................................... 15

## PHYSICALS
79 Big Beat NS 58     Be Like Me/Pain In Love (p/s) .......................................................................................... 6

*(see also Maniacs)*

## PAUL PIACENTINI
85 Acting School Again ASA 01     OUT OF MY BOX (mini-LP) ............................................................................................... 40

## PIANO MAGIC
96 i IRE 1071     Wrong French/Non-Fiction/General Electric With Fairylights (12", p/s) ............................ 10
97 i IRE 2031     Wintersport/Cross Country/Angel Pie/Magic Tree/Magnetic North (12", p/s) ................. 10
97 Wurlitzer Jukebox WJ 26     For Engineers A/For Engineers AA (p/s) ............................................................................ 7
98 Lissy's LISS 32     Music For Rolex/MATMOS: The Soldering Social (p/s) ...................................................... 6
98 Debut DEBT 001SP     French Mittens/Icebreaker: Melody For Nato (p/s) ........................................................... 8
98 Bad Jazz BEBOP 9     Music For Annahbird/Music For Wasps/Me At 19 (p/s) .................................................... 8
98 Piao! PIAO! 12     The Fun Of The Century/The Sharpest Knife In The Drawer/Industrial Cutie/I Am The Sub-Librarian (12", p/s) ...... 12
99 Rocket Girl RGIRL 12     There's No Need For Us To Be Alone/The Canadian Brought Us Snow (p/s) ...................... 5
00 Morr MUSIC 008     Panic Amigo - Piano Magic Remixed (12" EP) .................................................................. 10

## PIANO RED
53 HMV 7M 108     Rockin' With Red/Red's Boogie ....................................................................................... 100
64 RCA RCX 7138     RHYTHM AND BLUES VOL. 2 (EP) .................................................................................... 15

*(see also Dr. Feelgood [U.S.])*

## PICA
70 Polydor 2058 056     Take The Barriers Down/Insurance Man ........................................................................... 10
71 Philips 6006 129     Rainbow Chaser/Ad Lib .................................................................................................... 100

*(see also Nirvana [UK])*

## PICADILLY LINE
67 CBS 2785     At The Third Stroke/How Could You Say You're Leaving Me ............................................. 30
67 CBS 2958     Emily Small (The Huge World Thereof)/Gone Gone Gone .................................................. 25
68 CBS 3595     Yellow Rainbow/Evenings With Corrina ............................................................................ 30
68 CBS 3595     Yellow Rainbow/I Know, She Believes (reissue with different B-side) ................................ 25
68 CBS 3743     Evenings With Corrina/My Best Friend .............................................................................. 20
67 CBS (S)BPG 63129     THE HUGE WORLD OF EMILY SMALL (LP, laminated front sleeve) .................................... 350
67 CBS (S)BPG 63129     THE HUGE WORLD OF EMILY SMALL (LP, laminated front sleeve, promo insert) ........... 400

*(see also Edwards Hand)*

## PIC & BILL
67 Page One POF 024     All I Want Is You/It's Not You ........................................................................................... 10
67 Page One POF 037     This Is It/Nobody But My Baby ......................................................................................... 10
68 Page One POF 052     Sad World Without You/Just A Tear ................................................................................. 10

## PICARDY
68 Statside SIDE 8004     Montage/How Sweet It Is .................................................................................................. 5

## PIERO PICCIONI
67 Fontana TF 898     Main Theme From 'The Tenth Victim'/Part 2 (mono) ....................................................... 12

## PICK A POW
93 Sunjam SR 0014     Time Hard/RICK WAYNE: Our Younger Years (12") ......................................................... 40
94 Sunjam SR 0015     Wicked People/Only You (12") .......................................................................................... 25

## BUSTER PICKENS
60s Heritage HLP 1008     TEXAS PIANO (LP, 99 only) .............................................................................................. 60

### J.B. PICKERS
| | | | |
|---|---|---|---:|
| 71 | London HLU 10334 | Super Soul Sounds/KIM & DAVE: Nobody Knows | 15 |

### BOBBY (BORIS) PICKETT & CRYPT-KICKERS
| | | | |
|---|---|---|---:|
| 62 | London HLU 9597 | Monster Mash/Monsters' Mash Party | 10 |
| 73 | London HLU 10436 | Me And My Mummy/Monster Holiday | 7 |
| 73 | London ZGU 133 | MONSTER MASH (LP) | 20 |

### DAN PICKETT
| | | | |
|---|---|---|---:|
| 60s | XX MIN 710 | DAN PICKETT (EP) | 15 |

### KENNY PICKETT
| | | | |
|---|---|---|---:|
| 80 | F Beat PRO 2 | Got A Gun/Same | 15 |

*(see also The Creation)*

### NICK PICKETT
| | | | |
|---|---|---|---:|
| 72 | Warner Bros K 14156 | America/Lady Luck | 6 |
| 72 | Reprise K 44172 | SILVERSLEEVES (LP) | 30 |

*(see also John Dummer Blues Band)*

### WILSON PICKETT
| | | | |
|---|---|---|---:|
| 63 | Liberty LIB 10115 | It's Too Late/I'm Gonna Love You | 30 |
| 65 | Atlantic AT 4036 | In The Midnight Hour/I'm Not Tired | 20 |
| 65 | MGM MGM 1286 | Let Me Be Your Boy/My Heart Belongs To You | 50 |
| 65 | MGM MGM 1286 | Let Me Be Your Boy/My Heart Belongs To You (DJ copy) | 100 |
| 65 | Atlantic AT 4052 | Don't Fight It/It's All Over | 12 |
| 66 | Atlantic AT 4072 | 634-5789/That's A Man's Way | 12 |
| 66 | Atlantic 584 023 | 99 And A Half (Won't Do)/Danger Zone | 12 |
| 66 | Atlantic 584 039 | Land Of 1000 Dances/You're So Fine | 10 |
| 66 | Atlantic 584 066 | Mustang Sally/Three Time Loser | 10 |
| 67 | Atlantic 584 101 | Everybody Needs Somebody To Love/Nothing You Can Do | 10 |
| 67 | Atlantic 584 107 | New Orleans/Soul Dance III | 10 |
| 67 | London HLU 10146 | Billy The Kid/I Don't Want No Part-Time Love (with Falcons) | 10 |
| 67 | Atlantic 584 130 | Funky Broadway/I'm Sorry About That | 10 |
| 67 | Atlantic 584 142 | Stag-O-Lee/I'm In Love | 10 |
| 68 | Atlantic 584 150 | In The Midnight Hour/Danger Zone | 7 |
| 68 | Atlantic 584 173 | That Kind Of Love/I've Come A Long Way | 8 |
| 68 | Atlantic 584 183 | She's Looking Good/We've Got To Have Love | 10 |
| 68 | Atlantic 584 203 | I'm A Midnight Mover/Deborah | 5 |
| 68 | Atlantic 584 221 | I Found A True Love/For Better Or Worse | 5 |
| 69 | Atlantic 584 236 | Hey Jude/Night Owl | 8 |
| 69 | Atlantic 584 261 | Mini-Skirt Minnie/Back In Your Arms | 10 |
| 69 | Atlantic 584 281 | Hey Joe/Born To Be Wild | 5 |
| 70 | Atlantic 584 313 | You Keep Me Hangin' On/Now You See Me, Now You Don't | 8 |
| 70 | Atlantic 2091 005 | Sugar, Sugar/Cole, Cooke And Redding | 5 |
| 70 | Atlantic 2091 032 | (Get Me Back On Time) Engine No. 9/International Playboy | 5 |
| 71 | Atlantic 2091 086 | Fire And Water/Don't Let The Green Grass Fool You | 5 |
| 71 | Atlantic 2091 124 | Don't Knock My Love (Parts 1 & 2) | 5 |
| 72 | Atlantic K 10166 | Don't Let The Green Grass Fool You/Covering The Same Old Ground | 5 |
| 72 | President PT 319 | If You Need Me/I'm Gonna Love You | 5 |
| 73 | President PT 322 | I Can't Stop/Down To My Last Heartbreak | 5 |
| 65 | Atlantic ATL 5037 | IN THE MIDNIGHT HOUR (LP) | 50 |
| 66 | Atlantic 587/588 029 | THE EXCITING WILSON PICKETT (LP) | 20 |
| 66 | Atlantic 587 032 | IN THE MIDNIGHT HOUR (LP, reissue) | 20 |
| 67 | Atlantic 587/588 057 | THE WICKED PICKETT (LP) | 20 |
| 67 | Atlantic 587/588 080 | THE SOUND OF WILSON PICKETT (LP) | 20 |
| 68 | Atlantic 587/588 092 | THE BEST OF WILSON PICKETT (LP) | 20 |
| 68 | Atlantic 587/588 107 | I'M IN LOVE (LP) | 20 |
| 68 | Atlantic 587/588 111 | MIDNIGHT MOVER (LP) | 20 |
| 69 | Atlantic 588 170 | HEY JUDE (LP) | 20 |
| 70 | Atlantic 2465 002 | RIGHT ON (LP) | 15 |
| 70 | Joy JOYS 181 | IF YOU NEED ME (LP) | 15 |
| 71 | Atlantic 2400 026 | ENGINE NO. 9 - IN PHILADELPHIA (LP) | 15 |

*(see also Falcons)*

### GARY PICKFORD-HOPKINS & FRIENDS
| | | | |
|---|---|---|---:|
| 83 | Spartan SP 143 | Why? (The Song)/Why? (The Story) (p/s) | 8 |
| 83 | Spartan SP 143T | Why? (The Song)/Why? (The Story) (12", p/s) | 10 |

*(see also Deke Leonard, Man, Andy Fairweather-Low, Alan Ross, Big Sleep, Eyes Of Blue, Wild Turkey)*

### PICKWICKS
| | | | |
|---|---|---|---:|
| 64 | Decca F 11901 | Apple Blossom Time/I Don't Wanna Tell You Again | 18 |
| 64 | Decca F 11957 | You're Old Enough/Hello Lady | 15 |
| 65 | Warner Bros WB 151 | Little By Little/I Took My Baby Home | 100 |

### PICNIC BOYS
| | | | |
|---|---|---|---:|
| 82 | Challet BEAN 001 | White Hotel/Dawn Patrol (p/s) | 20 |

### PICTURE BOOK
| | | | |
|---|---|---|---:|
| 84 | Crystal 2 | Laughing In My Hand/Reflex Action (with insert) | 70 |

### PICTURE FRAME SEDUCTION
| | | | |
|---|---|---|---:|
| 84 | SOSO 33 | I'm Good Enough For Me/Sabotage The Classes/Fur Queue | 40 |
| 87 | PFS 2 | Try With A Little Help From My Friends/And Entertainment USA | 40 |
| 85 | Rot PFS 1 | HAND OF THE RIDER (LP) | 40 |

### PICTURE POSTCARD
| | | | |
|---|---|---|---:|
| 70 | Polydor 2058 106 | Give A Little Love To Someone/Another Day Another Dollar | 8 |

### PICTURES LIKE THIS
83   TW HIT 112              A Night's Vendetta/Defeat (p/s) .................................................. 251

### RANDY PIE AND FAMILY
72   Atlantic K10248         Queen Of Dreams/Train Goe On .................................................. 10

### PIED PIPERS (1)
54   Parlophone CMSP 21      Kissin' Drive Rock/Please Understand (export issue) ................... 15

### PIED PIPERS (2)
66   Columbia DB 7883        Ragamuffin/Fat Marie ............................................................... 30

### JEFFREY LEE PIERCE
85   Statik STATLP 25        WILDWEED (LP, with free 7" PROMO 2) .................................... 20
85   Statik STATLP 25        WILDWEED (LP) ........................................................................ 15
(see also Gun Club)

### WEBB PIERCE
50s  Decca BM 311368         We'll Find A Way/Any Old Time (export issue)........................... 30
55   Decca BM 31172          Teen Age Boogie/I'm Really Glad You Hurt Me (export) ........... 150
56   Brunswick 05630         Teenage Boogie/Any Old Time ............................................... 150
57   Brunswick 05682         Bye, Bye Love/Honky Tonk Song............................................ 40
59   Brunswick 05809         I Ain't Never/Shanghaied ....................................................... 20
60   Brunswick 05820         No Love Have I/Whirlpool Of Love .......................................... 10
60   Brunswick 05842         Drifting Texas Sand/All I Need Is You ..................................... 10
56   Brunswick OE 9253       WEBB PIERCE PT. 1 (EP) .......................................................... 10
56   Brunswick OE 9254       WEBB PIERCE PT. 2 (EP) .......................................................... 10
56   Brunswick OE 9255       WEBB PIERCE PT. 3 (EP) .......................................................... 10
62   Ember EMB 4520          COUNTRY AND WESTERN FAVOURITES VOL. 1 (EP) ................ 10
59   Parlophone GEP 8792     COUNTRY ROUND UP (EP) ...................................................... 20
55   Brunswick LA 8716       THE WONDERING BOY (10" LP) ................................................ 30
60   Brunswick LAT 8324      WEBB! (LP) ............................................................................. 15
65   Brunswick LAT 8540      HIDEAWAY HEART (LP) ........................................................... 15
65   Brunswick LAT 8551      CROSS COUNTRY (LP) ............................................................. 15
(see also Red Sovine & Webb Pierce)

### PIERCES
07   Lizard King 102X        Sticks And Stones/Turn On Billie ............................................ 20

### CLIVE PIG & THE HOPEFUL CHINAMEN
79   Pinnacle PIN 21         Happy Birthday Sweet Sixteen/Our Movement (p/s).................. 10
(see also Trixie's Big Red Motorbike)

### PIGEON DETECTIVES
06   Dance To The Radio DTTR 08   I'm Not Sorry/I'm Always Right (p/s) ................................ 8

### PIGEON FLYERS
68   Columbia DB 8449        The Heaven We Shared Together/Keep On Sayin' ..................... 8

### PIGS
77   Bristol Recorder NBR 01   Youthenasia/They Say/Psychopath/National Front (p/s) ......... 10

### PIGSTY HILL LIGHT ORCHESTRA
72   Village Thing VTS 8     PIGGERY JOKERY (LP) ............................................................. 20

### DAVE PIKE
63   Starlite ST45 094       Melvalita/Ginha - Bossa Nova ................................................... 5
66   Atlantic 584 052        Sunny/HERBIE MANN: Philly Dog ........................................... 15
66   Atlantic 588 005        JAZZ FOR THE JET SET (LP) ..................................................... 25

### RAY PILGRIM (& BEATMEN)
60   Oriole CB 1557          Baby Doll/Gambler's Guitar (solo) ......................................... 15
61   Oriole CB 1616          Little Miss Makebelieve/Granada (solo) .................................... 8
62   Oriole CB 1710          Red Red Roses/There's Always Me (solo) ............................... 10
64   Embassy WB 645          Kissin' Cousins (with Beatmen)/ JAYBIRDS: Some Day We're Gonna Love Again........ 5
(see also Bud Ashton, Jaybirds, Typhoons)

### PILGRIM FATHERS
69   Tangerine 009           Love And The World Will Love/Come A Day ............................... 7

### TONY PILLEY
79   Barclay Towers BT2      Off The Hook/Mummy & Daddy (p/s, with poster) .................... 15
79   Barclay Towers BT2      Off The Hook/Mummy & Daddy (p/s, without poster).................. 8

### PILOT
74   EMI 2217                Magic/Just Let Me Be............................................................... 5
74   EMI 2255                January/Never Give Up .............................................................. 5

### PILTDOWN MEN
62   Capitol CL 15245        A Pretty Girl Is Like A Melody/Big Lizzard .............................. 20
61   Capitol EAP1 20155      GOODNIGHT MRS. FLINTSTONE (EP).................................... 15

### SIR HUBERT PIMM
55   London HL 8155          Goodnight And Cheerio/Honky Tonk Train Blues ..................... 50
55   London RE-U 1032        PIMM'S PARTY (EP, with Ellen Sutton) .................................. 20
(see also Duke & Duchess)

### MICHAEL PINDER
76   Threshold TH 23         Carry On/I only Want To Be With You ...................................... 25

### PINEAPPLE CHUNKS
65   Mercury MF 922          Drive My Car/Dream About....................................................... 15

### PINEAPPLE THIEF
00   Obtuse OBT 001          Shertbert Gods/Perpetual Flying Objects (wraparound p/s in poly bag) ......... 25

### PINEWOOD STUDIO ORCHESTRA
59   Top Rank JAR 112        Sapphire/Tiger Bay.................................................................... 6
62   Parlophone R 4906       The Waltz Of The Toreadors/Picture Parade ............................. 6

MINT VALUE £

## PINEWOOD TOM/TOM TALL
| | | | |
|---|---|---|---|
| 59 | Jazz Collector JEL 5 | THE MALE BLUES VOLUME 4 (EP) | 18 |

## 'PING PING' & AL VERLANE
| | | | |
|---|---|---|---|
| 60 | Oriole CB 1589 | Sucu Sucu/Maria Della Montagna | 8 |

## RICHARD PINHAS
| | | | |
|---|---|---|---|
| 80 | Pulse 500 | West Side/Houston 69 (p/s) | 5 |

## PINK AND BLACK
| | | | |
|---|---|---|---|
| 85 | Illuminated ILL4912 | Sometimes I Wish (Dramadance U.S.A. Mix)/Sometimes I Wish (Radio)/Miss Fortune (12", p/s) | 12 |

## PINK ELEPHANT
| | | | |
|---|---|---|---|
| 72 | Pye 7N 45143 | Down In The Valley/I'm Living In This World Just For You | 15 |

## PINK FAIRIES
| | | | |
|---|---|---|---|
| 76 | Stiff BUY 2 | Between The Lines/Spoiling For A Fight (promo 'plug' copy) | 15 |
| 71 | Polydor 2058 089 | The Snake/Do It | 25 |
| 72 | Polydor 2059 302 | Well Well Well/Hold On | 25 |
| 76 | Stiff BUY 2 | Between The Lines/Spoiling For A Fight (p/s) | 10 |
| 71 | Polydor 2383 045 | NEVERNEVERLAND (LP, printed PVC outer & gatefold card inner, in yellow bag with photos & notes) | 250 |
| 71 | Polydor 2383 045 | NEVERNEVERLAND (LP, printed PVC outer & gatefold card inner, pink vinyl & "pink plastic" in text on rear sleeve, around 100 pressed) | 500 |
| 71 | Polydor 2383 045 | NEVERNEVERLAND (LP, black vinyl, standard sleeve) | 50 |
| 72 | Polydor 2383 132 | WHAT A BUNCH OF SWEETIES (LP) | 30 |
| 73 | Polydor 2383 212 | KINGS OF OBLIVION (LP, with poster) | 50 |
| 75 | Polydor 2384 071 | FLASHBACK (LP) | 18 |
| 87 | Demon FIEND 105 | KILL EM AND EAT EM (LP) | 15 |

*(see also Twink, Larry Wallis, Deviants, Lightning Raiders, Shagrat)*

## PINK FLOYD
### SINGLES
| | | | |
|---|---|---|---|
| 67 | Columbia DB 8156 | Arnold Layne/Candy And A Currant Bun | 80 |
| 67 | Columbia DB 8214 | See Emily Play/Scarecrow | 60 |
| 67 | Columbia DB 8310 | Apples And Oranges/Paintbox | 125 |
| 68 | Columbia DB 8401 | It Would Be So Nice/Julia Dream | 90 |
| 68 | Columbia DB 8511 | Point Me At The Sky/Careful With That Axe, Eugene | 100 |
| 79 | Harvest HAR 5194 | Another Brick In The Wall (Part 2)/One Of My Turns (initial pressing, plain B-side label without 'window' picture) | 8 |
| 81 | Harvest HAR 5217 | Money (Edit)/Let There Be More Light (unreleased, die-cut sleeve) | 0 |
| 81 | Harvest 12HAR 5217 | Money (Full Length)/Let There Be More Light (12", unreleased) | 0 |
| 82 | Harvest HAR 5222 | When The Tigers Broke Free/Bring The Boys Back Home (gatefold p/s) | 10 |
| 82 | Harvest HAR 5222 | When The Tigers Broke Free/Bring The Boys Back Home (standard p/s) | 8 |
| 83 | Harvest HAR 5224 | Not Now John/The Hero's Return | 7 |
| 87 | EMI EMDJ 26 | Learning To Fly (Edited Version)/One Slip (Edited Version)/Terminal Frost (no p/s, mispressing without "One Slip", 50 on black vinyl) | 20 |
| 87 | EMI EMDJ 26 | Learning To Fly (Edited Version)/One Slip (Edited Version)/Terminal Frost (no p/s, mispressing without "One Slip", 1,000 only on pink vinyl) | 15 |
| 87 | EMI EM 34 | On The Turning Away (Album)/Run Like Hell (Live Version) (p/s) | 5 |
| 87 | EMI EMP 34 | On The Turning Away (Album)/Run Like Hell (Live Version) (p/s, pink vinyl, 1000 only) | 10 |
| 87 | EMI 12EMP 34 | On The Turning Away (Album)/Run Like Hell (Live Version)/On The Turning Away (Live Version) (12", poster p/s) | 12 |
| 87 | EMI 12EMP 34 | On The Turning Away (Album)/Run Like Hell (Live Version)/On The Turning Away (Live Version) | 12 |
| 88 | EMI EMG 52 | One Slip/Terminal Frost (pink vinyl, gatefold p/s with ticket application) | 12 |
| 88 | EMI 12EMP 52 | One Slip/Terminal Frost/The Dogs Of War (live) (12", poster p/s) | 10 |
| 94 | EMI EM 309 | Take It Back (Edit)/Astronomy Domine (live) (jukebox issue, black vinyl) | 8 |
| 94 | EMI EM 309 | Take It Back (Edit) /Astronomy Domine (Live) (p/s) | 7 |
| 94 | EMI EM 309 | Take It Back (Edit)/Astronomy Domine (Live) (red vinyl, p/s) | 10 |
| 94 | EMI EM 342 | High Hopes (Radio Edit)/Keep Talking (Radio Edit) (clear vinyl, poster p/s) | 12 |
| 94 | EMI 12EM 342 | High Hopes (Album Version)/Keep Talking (Album Version)/One Of These Days (live) (12", 1-sided, laser-etched blue vinyl, p/s in outer gtefold p/s with 7 postcards) | 20 |
| 13 | Columbia DB 8214 | See Emily Play/Scarecrow (p/s, reissue, pink vinyl, poster) | 15 |

### ALBUMS
| | | | |
|---|---|---|---|
| 67 | Columbia SX 6157 | THE PIPER AT THE GATES OF DAWN (LP, 1st pressing, mono, blue/black label, with "Sold in the U.K..." text. first known matrixes XAX 3419 - 2 G1/XAX 3420 - 1 G1) | 800 |
| 67 | Columbia SCX 6157 | THE PIPER AT THE GATES OF DAWN (LP, 1st pressing, stereo, blue/black label, with "Sold in the U.K..." text, first known matrixes YAX 3419 - 1G1/YAX 3420 - 1-G1) | 500 |

*(Second pressings have "File Under Pop" on the right of the flipback; first pressings do not have this. Second pressing worth half to a third less)*

| | | | |
|---|---|---|---|
| 68 | Columbia SX 6258 | A SAUCERFUL OF SECRETS (LP, 1st pressing, mono, blue/black label, "Sold in U.K..." text, Gilmour spelt 'Gilmore' on label and sleeve, earliest matrixes XAX 3633-1 G1/XAX 3634-1 G1) | 600 |
| 68 | Columbia SCX 6258 | A SAUCERFUL OF SECRETS (LP, 1st pressing, stereo, blue/black label, "Sold in U.K..." text, earliest matrixes YAX 3633-1 G1/YAX 3634-1 R1) | 400 |
| 69 | Columbia SCX 6346 | SOUNDTRACK FROM THE FILM 'MORE' (LP, laminated flipback sleeve, 'couple facing west' photo on green-tinted rear sleeve. Ist pressing with black/silver label, boxed logo and "Sold in UK..." text) | 70 |
| 69 | Harvest SHDW 1/2 | UMMAGUMMA (2-LP, 1st pressing, without EMI logo, laminated gatefold sleeve with 'London' spelt as 'Londen' with Ernest J Day & Co' printing credit) | 100 |
| 69 | Harvest SHDW 1/2 | UMMAGUMMA (2-LP, 2nd pressing with EMI logo and 'The Gramophone Co Ltd' label text, laminated gatefold sleeve) | 40 |
| 69 | Harvest SHDW 1/2 | UMMAGUMMA (2-LP, 3rd pressing, with EMI logo and 'EMI Records' label text, laminated gatefold sleeve) | 30 |
| 70 | Columbia SCX 6157 | THE PIPER AT THE GATES OF DAWN (LP, re-pressing, laminated sleeve, silver & black label with boxed EMI logo) | 80 |
| 69 | Columbia SX 6258 | A SAUCERFUL OF SECRETS (LP, 2nd pressing, mono, silver & black label, one EMI box at top) | 80 |

| Year | Catalogue | Description | Value |
|---|---|---|---|
| 70 | Columbia SCX 6258 | A SAUCERFUL OF SECRETS (LP, 2nd pressing, stereo, silver & black label, one EMI box at top) | 50 |
| 70s | Columbia SCX 6346 | SOUNDTRACK FROM THE FILM 'MORE' (LP, laminated non-flipback sleeve, 'couple facing west' photo on black-tinted rear sleeve) | 45 |
| 70s | Columbia SCX 6346 | SOUNDTRACK FROM THE FILM 'MORE' (LP, laminated non-flipback sleeve, 'couple facing east' photo on black-tinted rear sleeve) | 50 |
| 70 | MGM 2315 002 | ZABRISKIE POINT (LP, soundtrack, with Jerry Garcia/Kaleidoscope, et al.) | 30 |
| 70 | Harvest SHVL 781 | ATOM HEART MOTHER (LP, 1st pressing, gatefold sleeve, no EMI logo) | 90 |

*(First pressing Harvest LPs of UMMAGUMMA and ATOM HEART MOTHER have "The Gramophone..." text on label rim and "Harvest" on the left side of the label; second pressings have "The Gramophone..." text with a boxed EMI logo above "Harvest")*

| Year | Catalogue | Description | Value |
|---|---|---|---|
| 71 | Harvest SHVL 795 | MEDDLE (LP, textured inside/outside gatefold sleeve) | 50 |
| 71 | Harvest SHVL 795 | ATOM HEART MOTHER (LP, 2nd pressing with EMI logo, 'The Gramophone Co' label text, gatefold sleeve, matrixes SHVL 781 A-4 RD 2/SHVL 781 B-3 AO 1) | 35 |
| 71 | Harvest SHVL 795 | MEDDLE (LP, textured outside gatefold sleeve) | 20 |
| 71 | Starline SRS 5071 | RELICS (LP, white textured sleeve) | 15 |
| 72 | Harvest SHSP 4020 | OBSCURED BY CLOUDS (LP, rounded sleeve, EMI logo on label) | 50 |
| 74 | Harvest SHVL 781 | ATOM HEART MOTHER (LP, 3rd pressing with EMI logo, 'EMI Records Ltd' label text, gatefold sleeve) | 30 |
| 73 | Harvest SHVL 804 | THE DARK SIDE OF THE MOON (LP, first pressing, solid light blue triangle label, black inner, 2 posters & 2 stickers, gatefold sleeve, only one side opening) | 1000 |
| 73 | Harvest SHVL 804 | THE DARK SIDE OF THE MOON (LP, blue & black label, gatefold sleeve with black inner, 2 posters & 2 stickers, with stickered sleeve) | 35 |
| 73 | Harvest SHVL 804 | THE DARK SIDE OF THE MOON (LP, blue & black label, gatefold sleeve with black inner, 2 posters & 2 stickers, without stickered sleeve) | 25 |
| 73 | Harvest Q4 SHVL 804 | THE DARK SIDE OF THE MOON (LP, quadrophonic, gatefold sleeve, no inserts) | 40 |
| 70s | Harvest SHVL 804 | THE DARK SIDE OF THE MOON (LP, repressing, blue & silver label, gatefold sleeve with black inner, 2 posters & 2 stickers) | 35 |
| 73 | Harvest Q4 SHVL 781 | ATOM HEART MOTHER (LP, quadrophonic, gatefold sleeve, with 'quadrophonic' logo on front sleeve) | 35 |
| 73 | Harvest Q4 SHVL 781 | ATOM HEART MOTHER (LP, quadrophonic, gatefold sleeve, without 'quadrophonic' logo on front sleeve, logo is inside) | 25 |
| 73 | Harvest SHDW 403 | A NICE PAIR (2-LP, gatefold sleeve, with 2 inner sleeves; early copies with 'Mr Phang' dentist cover) | 40 |
| 73 | Harvest SHDW 403 | A NICE PAIR (2-LP, gatefold sleeve, with 2 inner sleeves) | 20 |
| 75 | Harvest SHVL 814 | WISH YOU WERE HERE (LP, with inner sleeve, postcard & black cellophane wraparound with sticker, sealed) | 400 |
| 75 | Harvest SHVL 814 | WISH YOU WERE HERE (LP, with inner sleeve, postcard & black cellophane wraparound with sticker, unsealed) | 50 |
| 76 | Harvest Q4 SHVL 814 | WISH YOU WERE HERE (LP, quadrophonic, with inner sleeve) | 75 |
| 70s | Harvest SHVL 814 | WISH YOU WERE HERE (LP, audiophile edition, Nimbus supercut sold through Hi-Fi Today magazine) | 500 |
| 77 | Harvest SHVL 815 | ANIMALS (LP, 1st pressing, picture labels, non-barcode gatefold sleeve printed by 'Garrod & Lofthouse', with card inner with rounded edges, large thumb notch at top and catalogue number on bottom right of inner, Matrix numbers: SHVL 815 A-2U/B-2U) | 100 |
| 77 | Harvest SHVL 815 | ANIMALS (LP, contract pressing, no EMI stamper at 3 o clock) | 150 |
| 77 | Harvest SHVL 815 | ANIMALS (LP, gatefold, later pressing, gloss or matt sleeve, inner) | 20 |
| 79 | Harvest SHDW 4111/4112 | THE WALL (2-LP, First press, MATRIXES: SHSP 4111 A-2U/B-3U/SHSP 4112 A-1U/B-5U: TML-M/TML-X/TML-M/TML-M stamped into dead wax. Creamy coloured sleeve, bricks do not align right to bottom of sleeve, inner surface of sleeve is heavyweight card and creamy in colour, 8th brick states "produced by David Gilmour" then "written by Roger Waters". 9th brick "words and music Roger Waters except "Young Lust", "Comfortably Numb"" etc. Inner sleeve has rounded edges and thumb notch along top edge. "SHDW 4111/1" in bottom right corner. Gatefold sleeve with 'static transparent "title" sticker) | 80 |
| 79 | Harvest SHDW 4111/4112 | THE WALL (2-LP, later pressings, lighter inner card browner in colour,. Inside gatefold on right hand side 9th brick "Bob Ezrin, Roger Waters", 10th brick: no text, then Pink Floyd, names of the band. Square inner sleeve - usually - with OC-15863411/SHSP4111/2 catalogue numbers. Gatefold sleeve) | 20 |
| 79 | Harvest PF 11 | THE FIRST XI (11-LP set, original sleeves, plus exclusive "Dark Side Of The Moon" & "Wish You Were Here" picture discs, 1,000 only) | 200 |
| 83 | Fame FA 3163 | A SAUCERFUL OF SECRETS (LP, reissue) | 20 |
| 83 | Fame FA 3065 | THE PIPER AT THE GATES OF DAWN (LP, reissue) | 20 |
| 83 | Harvest SHPF 1983 | THE FINAL CUT (LP, gatefold sleeve with title sticker) | 20 |
| 85 | Harvest SHVL 804 | DARK SIDE OF THE MOON (LP, reissue, gatefold sleeve, 2 posters and stickers 'barcode' on sleeve) | 20 |
| 85 | Harvest SHVL 815 | ANIMALS (LP, repressing, 'barcode' on sleeve) | 15 |
| 87 | EMI EMD 1003 | A MOMENTARY LAPSE OF REASON (LP, gatefold sleeve with inner) | 20 |
| 88 | EMI EQ 5009 | DELICATE SOUND OF THUNDER (2-LP, gatefold, 2 inners) | 20 |
| 93 | EMI CDDSOM 20 | THE DARK SIDE OF THE MOON (CD, 20th anniversary box set with booklet & 5 art cards) | 18 |
| 92 | EMI CDS 7805572 | SHINE ON (9-CD box set, with book and postcards) | 90 |
| 94 | EMI EMD 1055 | THE DIVISION BELL (LP, gatefold sleeve, with inner) | 70 |
| 95 | EMI EMD 578 | PULSE (4-LP box set in slipcase with hardback book) | 150 |
| 97 | EMI 859 857-1 | THE PIPER AT THE GATES OF DAWN (LP, reissue, gatefold sleeve with inner, mono) | 25 |
| 97 | EMI LPCENT 11 | THE DARK SIDE OF THE MOON (LP, reissue, EMI 100 Centenary, stickered sleeve) | 30 |
| 97 | EMI EMD 1115 | WISH YOU WERE HERE (LP, reissue, 'magnifying glass' cover) | 25 |
| 97 | EMI SIGMA 630 | '97 VINYL COLLECTION (7-LP set, die-cut box, includes "The Piper At The Gates Of Dawn" [EMD 1110], "The Wall" [EMD 1111], "Atom Heart Mother" [EMD 1112], "Relics" [EMD 1113], "The Dark Side Of The Moon" [EMD 1114], "Wish You Were Here" [EMD 1115], each in | 150 |
| 97 | EMI EMD 1133 | RELICS (LP, gatefold with poster) | 40 |
| 01 | EMI 724353611118 | ECHOES (4-LP box set) | 75 |
| 03 | EMI 5821361 | DARK SIDE OF THE MOON (LP, gatefold sleeve, 30th anniversary edition) | 25 |
| 11 | EMI 029 8801 | WISH YOU WERE HERE (LP, reissue, poster and postcard) | 18 |

## ALBUMS : EXPORT LPS

| Year | Catalogue | Description | Value |
|---|---|---|---|
| 67 | Odeon PSCX 6157 | THE PIPER AT THE GATES OF DAWN (LP, stereo, UK sleeve with gold 'Odeon' sticker over Columbia logo on rear, 'The Gramophone Co Ltd' label text on rim and 'Made in Gt. Britain' on black/silver label) | 2000 |

| | | | |
|---|---|---|---|
| 68 | Odeon PSCX 6258 | A SAUCERFUL OF SECRETS (LP, Stereo, UK sleeve with gold 'Odeon' sticker over 'Columbia logo on rear of sleeve, black/silver Odeon label) | 1000 |
| 69 | Odeon PSCX 6346 | MORE (LP, UK sleeve with gold 'Odeon' sticker over Columbia logo on rear of sleeve, black/silver Odeon label) | 800 |

**PROMOS**

| | | | |
|---|---|---|---|
| 67 | Columbia DB 8156 | Arnold Layne/Candy And A Currant Bun (demo copy in promo-only p/s) | 1500 |
| 67 | Columbia DB 8214 | See Emily Play/Scarecrow (demo copy in promo-only p/s) | 1500 |
| 67 | Columbia DB 8310 | Apples And Oranges/Paintbox (demo copy in promo-only p/s) | 1500 |
| 68 | Columbia DB 8401 | It Would Be So Nice (1-sided demo) | 1000 |
| 68 | Columbia DB 8511 | Point Me At The Sky/Careful With That Axe, Eugene (demo, with newsletter) | 900 |
| 68 | Columbia DB 8511 | Point Me At The Sky/Careful With That Axe, Eugene (demo, with postcard) | 750 |
| 69 | Emidisc no cat. no. | The Narrow Way (acetate, different version, 1 copy only) | 2000 |
| 81 | Harvest HAR 5217 | Money (1-sided pink vinyl promo in p/s, 200 only) | 100 |
| 81 | Harvest HAR 5217 | Money (Edited Version) (1-sided, pink vinyl, 200 only) | 40 |
| 81 | Harvest HAR 5217 | Money (Edited Version) (1-sided, pink vinyl, mispressing with "Let There Be More Light" label on B-side) | 50 |
| 83 | Harvest HARDJ 5224 | Not Now John/The Hero's Return (I & II) | 30 |
| 87 | EMI EMDJ 34 | On The Turning Away (edit)/On The Turning Away (album) (stickered p/s) | 10 |
| 88 | EMI 12PF 1 | Delicate Sound Of Thunder Sampler: Another Brick In The Wall Part 2/ One Of These Days/Run Like Hell (12", black & pink sleeve) | 20 |
| 88 | EMI PSLP 1026 | Pink Floyd In Europe '88: Money/Shine On/Another Brick In The Wall Part 2/ One Slip/On The Turning Away/Learning To Fly (12", with "Another Brick...Part 1" miscredit on rear p/s) | 20 |

*(see also Syd Barrett, Roger Waters, David Gilmour, Rick Wright, Nick Mason, Joker's Wild, Ron Geesin)*

**PINK INDUSTRY**

| | | | |
|---|---|---|---|
| 82 | Zulu ZULU 1 | Is This The End?/47/Don't Let Go/Final Cry (12", p/s) | 10 |
| 85 | Zulu ZULU RA 8 | What I Wouldn't Give/Bound By Silence (p/s) | 10 |
| 87 | Cathexis CRL 16 | Don't Let Go/Ticket To Heaven/Empty Beach (Remix) (12", p/s) | 15 |
| 83 | Zulu ZULU 2 | LOW TECHNOLOGY (LP) | 15 |
| 83 | Zulu ZULU 4 | WHO TOLD YOU - YOU WERE NAKED (LP) | 15 |
| 85 | Zulu ZULU 7 | NEW BEGINNINGS (LP) | 20 |
| 88 | Cathexis CRL 18 | PINK INDUSTRY (LP) | 20 |

*(see also Pink Military, Big In Japan)*

**PINK MILITARY**

| | | | |
|---|---|---|---|
| 80 | Eric's ERIC'S 005 | Did You See Her/Everyday (p/s) | 7 |
| 80 | Virgin/Eric's ERIC'S 004 | DO ANIMALS BELIEVE IN GOD? (LP) | 15 |

*(see also Pink Industry, Big In Japan)*

**PINK PEOPLE**

| | | | |
|---|---|---|---|
| 64 | Philips BF 1355 | Psychologically Unsound/Cow Catcher | 50 |
| 64 | Philips BF 1356 | Indian Hate Call/I Dreamt I Dwelt In Marble Halls | 20 |

*(see also Four Squares)*

**PINK RHYTHM**

| | | | |
|---|---|---|---|
| 85 | Beggars Banquet BEG 136T | Can't Get Enough Of Your Love/Can't Get Enough Of Your Dub (12", p/s) | 15 |
| 85 | Beggars Banquet BEG 149T | India/Trust Me/More And More/India (Instrumental) (12", p/s) | 15 |

**PINKERTON'S ('ASSORTED' COLOURS)**

| | | | |
|---|---|---|---|
| 65 | Decca F 12307 | Mirror Mirror/She Don't Care (as Pinkerton's 'Assorted' Colours) | 8 |
| 66 | Decca F 12377 | Don't Stop Loving Me Baby/Will Ya? (as Pinkerton's 'Assorted' Colours) | 15 |
| 66 | Decca F 12493 | Magic Rocking Horse/It Ain't Right (as Pinkerton's Colours) | 35 |
| 67 | Pye 7N 17327 | Mum And Dad/On A Street Car (as Pinkerton's Colours) | 18 |
| 67 | Pye 7N 17414 | There's Nobody I'd Sooner Love/Look At Me (as Pinkerton's) | 40 |
| 68 | Pye 7N 17574 | Kentucky Woman/Behind The Mirror (as Pinkerton's) | 18 |

*(see also Flying Machine, Liberators, Tony Newman)*

**PINKOES**

| | | | |
|---|---|---|---|
| 79 | Popular POP1 | INTO THE RED (EP) | 12 |

**PINKY (& FELLAS)**

| | | | |
|---|---|---|---|
| 65 | Polydor BM 56009 | All Cried Out/Back Where I Belong | 10 |
| 68 | Decca F 12748 | Manchester And Liverpool/Come Back Again (as Pinky & Fellas) | 5 |
| 69 | Polydor BM 56338 | Let The Music Start/Oh, A Beautiful Day (as Pinky & Fellas) | 5 |

**PINKY & PERKY**

| | | | |
|---|---|---|---|
| 63 | Columbia 33SX 1550 | PINKY & PERKY'S MELODYMASTER (LP) | 20 |

**PINNACLE**

| | | | |
|---|---|---|---|
| 74 | Stag HP 125 | ASSASSIN (LP, laminated sleeve, black/silver label) | 150 |

**DELROY PINNOCK**

| | | | |
|---|---|---|---|
| 81 | SG 5 | Babylon Walls/MIKEY RANKS : I Want To Be | 70 |

**GERALDO PINO**

| | | | |
|---|---|---|---|
| 05 | Soundway SNDWLP005 | AFRO SOCO SOUL LIVE (LP, reissue, 1000 only) | 20 |
| 05 | Soundway SNDWLP006 | LET'S HAVE A PARTY (LP, reissue, 1000 only) | 20 |

**PINPOINT**

| | | | |
|---|---|---|---|
| 79 | Albion CEL 8 | Richmond/Love Substiture (p/s) | 25 |
| 80 | Albion ION 102 | Waking Up To Morning/Floods And Trickles (fold-out poster p/s, lyric insert and die-cut Albion sleeve) | 10 |
| 80 | Albion ALB103 | THIRD STATE (LP, with free 12") | 20 |

**PIONEERS**

| | | | |
|---|---|---|---|
| 66 | Rio R 102 | Good Nannie/Doreen Girl | 40 |
| 66 | Rio R 106 | Too Late/Give Up | 40 |
| 68 | Blue Cat BS 100 | Shake It Up/Rudies Are The Greatest | 60 |
| 68 | Blue Cat BS 103 | Give It To Me/LEADERS: Someday Someway | 50 |
| 68 | Blue Cat BS 105 | Whip Them/Having A Bawl | 60 |
| 68 | Blue Cat BS 139 | Reggae Beat/Miss Eva | 125 |

| | | | |
|---|---|---|---|
| 68 | Caltone TONE 119 | I Love No Other Girl/MILTON BOOTHE: I Used To Be A Fool | 70 |
| 68 | Amalgamated AMG 811 | Give Me A Little Loving/This Is Soul (B-side actually by Lyn Tait & Jets) | 18 |
| 68 | Amalgamated AMG 814 | Long Shot/Dip And Fall Back | 30 |
| 68 | Amalgamated AMG 821 | Jackpot/CREATORS: Kimble (B-side actually by Lee Perry) | 30 |
| 68 | Amalgamated AMG 823 | No Dope Me Pony/LORD SALMONS: Great - Great In '68 | 45 |
| 68 | Amalgamated AMG 826 | Tickle Me For Days/VERSATILES: The Time Has Come | 25 |
| 68 | Amalgamated AMG 828 | Catch The Beat/SIR GIBB'S ALLSTARS: Jana (B-side actually Immortals' "Jane Anne") | 30 |
| 68 | Amalgamated AMG 830 | Sweet Dreams/DON DRUMMOND JUNIOR: Caterpillar Rock | 20 |
| 68 | Pyramid PYR 6062 | Easy Come, Easy Go/BEVERLEY'S ALLSTARS: Only A Smile (B-side actually by Lyn Tait & Jets) | 55 |
| 69 | Pyramid PYR 6065 | Pee Pee Cluck Cluck/BEVERLEY'S ALLSTARS: Exclusively | 15 |
| 69 | Amalgamated AMG 833 | Don't You Know/Me Naw Go A Believe | 40 |
| 69 | Amalgamated AMG 835 | Mama Look Deh/BLENDERS: Decimal Currency | 35 |
| 69 | Amalgamated AMG 840 | Who The Cap Fits/I'm Moving On | 60 |
| 69 | Amalgamated AMG 850 | Alli Button/HIPPY BOYS: Death Rides | 100 |
| 69 | Trojan TR 672 | Long Shot Kick The Bucket/RICO: Jumping The Gun | 25 |
| 69 | Trojan TR 685 | Black Bud/Too Late | 25 |
| 69 | Trojan TR 698 | Poor Rameses/BEVERLEY'S ALLSTARS: In Orbit | 20 |
| 70 | Trojan TR 7781 | Money Day/BEVERLEY ALL STARS: Ska Ba Do | 20 |
| 70 | Trojan TR 7795 | I Need Your Sweet Inspiration/Everything Nice | 15 |
| 71 | Summit SUM 8511 | Starvation/BEVERLEY'S ALLSTARS: Version | 15 |
| 72 | Summit SUM 8535 | Story Book Children/SIDNEY, GEORGE AND JACKIE: Gorgeous, Marvellous | 15 |
| 74 | Trojan TR 7923 | Honey Bee/Hot Blooded Man | 25 |
| 76 | Mercury 6198061 | Feel The Rhythm Of You and I/Version | 8 |
| 77 | Mercury 6007147 | My Good Friend James/Secrets Of You | 125 |
| 78 | Trojan 9043 | Riot In A Notting Hill/Ahuma | 12 |
| 78 | Ice GUY 14 | My Good Friend James/Secrets Of You (reissue) | 100 |
| 11 | Doctor Bird THB 7007 | Easy Come Easy Go/DERRICK MORGAN AND DESMOND DEKKER: Mercy Mercy | 15 |
| 13 | Trojan THB 7026 | Mettle/BEVERLY'S ALL STARS: Hook, Line And Sinker | 8 |
| 68 | Amalgam. AMGLP 2003 | GREETINGS FROM THE PIONEERS (LP) | 100 |
| 70 | Trojan TBL 103 | LONGSHOT (LP) | 35 |
| 70 | Trojan TBL 139 | BATTLE OF THE GIANTS (LP) | 35 |
| 71 | Trojan TRL 24 | YEAH! (LP) | 15 |
| 74 | Trojan TRLS 64 | FREEDOM FEELING (LP) | 15 |
| 74 | Trojan TRLS 98 | I'M GONNA KNOCK ON YOUR DOOR (LP) | 18 |
| 76 | Mercury 9286172 | FEEL THE RHYTHM (LP) | 25 |
| 78 | Trojan TRLS 156 | PUSHER MAN (LP) | 25 |
| 79 | Trojan TRLS 172 | GREATEST HITS (LP) | 18 |

*(see also Sir Gibbs, Rebels [Jamaica], Jackey Robinson, Moonboys, Sidney George & Jackie)*

## PIPE DREAM
| | | | |
|---|---|---|---|
| 70 | Penny Farthing PEN 710 | If You Do What You Gotta Do/Here We Go Again | 5 |

## PIPES OF PAN (1)
| | | | |
|---|---|---|---|
| 67 | Page One POF 038 | Monday Morning Rain/Monday Morning Rain (Instrumental Mix) | 20 |

## PIPES OF PAN (2)
| | | | |
|---|---|---|---|
| 71 | Rolling Stones COC 49100 | BRIAN JONES PLAYS WITH THE PIPES OF PAN AT JOUJOUKA (LP, gatefold sleeve with foldout insert; front cover with misprinted title) | 100 |
| 71 | Rolling Stones COC 49100 | BRIAN JONES PRESENTS THE PIPES OF PAN AT JOUJOUKA (LP, gatefold sleeve with foldout insert; "Presents" sticker on misprinted cover) | 90 |
| 71 | Rolling Stones COC 49100 | BRIAN JONES PRESENTS THE PIPES OF PAN AT JOUJOUKA (LP, gatefold sleeve with foldout insert; corrected title on front cover) | 80 |

*(see also Rolling Stones)*

## PIPETTES
| | | | |
|---|---|---|---|
| 04 | No label or cat no | In The Bleak Midwinter (CD, gig freebie, 200 only) | 25 |
| 05 | Unpopular UNPOP 6 | I Like A Boy In Uniform/It Hurts To See You Dance So Well (hand-numbered p/s, insert, 500 only) | 25 |
| 05 | Transgressive TRANS 005 | ABC/Judy/Simon Says (white vinyl, p/s, 500 only) | 10 |
| 05 | Total Gaylord TGR 008 | Judy/It Hurts To See You Dance So Well/KFC (pink vinyl) | 7 |
| 06 | Memphis Industries MI 071S1 | Pull Shapes/Guess Who Ran Off With The Milkman (white vinyl, p/s) | 6 |

*(see also Gwenno)*

## PIPP
| | | | |
|---|---|---|---|
| 70 | Decca F 23030 | Otaki/Which Way Did She Go | 12 |

## PIPS
| | | | |
|---|---|---|---|
| 61 | Top Rank JAR 574 | Every Beat Of My Heart/Room In Your Heart | 45 |

*(see also Gladys Knight & Pips)*

## PIRATES
| | | | |
|---|---|---|---|
| 64 | HMV POP 1250 | My Babe/Casting My Spell | 40 |
| 66 | Polydor BM 56712 | Shades Of Blue/Can't Understand | 20 |
| 77 | Warner Bros K 17002 | Sweet Love On My Mind/You Don't Own Me (p/s) | 15 |
| 78 | Warner Bros K 17113 | All In It Together/Dr. Feelgood (p/s) | 10 |
| 78 | Warner Bros K 17231 | Shakin' All Over/Saturday Night Shoot Out | 5 |

*(see also Johnny Kidd & Pirates, [Billy J. Kramer &] Dakotas)*

## PISCES
| | | | |
|---|---|---|---|
| 71 | Trailer LER 2025 | PISCES (LP) | 30 |

## JAY JAY PISTOLET
| | | | |
|---|---|---|---|
| 08 | Chess Club CC0001 | We Are Free/Holly (p/s) | 12 |

## PISTONS
| | | | |
|---|---|---|---|
| 81 | Humdrum ZIT 1 | Solitary Reality/Hyper Active (p/s and insert) | 70 |

## HARRY PITCH
| | | | |
|---|---|---|---|
| 68 | MOR MR 101P | HARMONICA JEWEL BOX (LP) | 20 |

# PITCHSHIFTER

*(see also Mr. Bloe)* ━━━━━━━━━━━━━━━━━━━━━━━━━━━━━━━ MINT VALUE £

**PITCHSHIFTER**
92   Earache MOSH 66          SUBMIT EP (12") ...................................................................................10

**PITMAN**
02   Son HM001               Phone Pitman/Pitman Sez...........................................................................15

**GENE PITNEY**
SINGLES
61   London HL 9270          (I Wanna) Love My Life Away/I Laughed So Hard I Cried ...............................10
61   HMV POP 933             Every Breath I Take/Mr Moon, Mr Cupid & I .................................................10
61   United Artists POP 952  Town Without Pity/Air Mail Special .............................................................30
62   United Artists POP 1018 The Man Who Shot Liberty Valance/Take It Like A Man ...............................10
62   United Artists UP 1005  If I Didn't Have A Dime/Only Love Can Break A Heart ...................................10
63   United Artists UP 1012  Half Heaven, Half Heartache/Tower Tall ......................................................5
63   United Artists UP 1021  Mecca/Teardrop By Teardrop ......................................................................5
63   United Artists UP 1030  True Love Never Runs Smooth/Donna Means Heartbreak ............................8
63   United Artists UP 1035  Twenty Four Hours From Tulsa/Lonely Night Dreams (blue or black label)........5
64   United Artists UP 1045  That Girl Belongs To Yesterday/Who Needs It? ............................................5
64   United Artists UP 1055  I'm Gonna Find Myself A Girl/Lips Are Redder On You .................................7
64   United Artists UP 1063  It Hurts To Be In Love/Hawaii ...................................................................10
64   Stateside SS 358        I'm Gonna Be Strong/Aladdin's Lamp ..........................................................7
64   Stateside SS 365        It Hurts To Be In Love (reissue) .................................................................6
65   Stateside SS 390        I Must Be Seeing Things/Save Your Love .....................................................5
65   Stateside SS 420        Lookin' Thru The Eyes Of Love/Last Chance To Turn Around .......................5
65   Stateside SS 471        Princess In Rags/Amore Mio .....................................................................5
66   Stateside SS 490        Backstage/In Love Again ...........................................................................5
66   Stateside SS 518        Nobody Needs Your Love/Dream World .......................................................5
66   Stateside SS 558        Just One Smile/The Boss's Daughter...........................................................5
67   Stateside SS 597        (In The) Cold Light Of Day/Flower Girl ......................................................5
67   Stateside SS 2060       Something's Gotten Hold Of My Heart/Building Up My Dream World ............8
67   Stateside SS 2060       Something's Gotten Hold Of My Heart/Where Did The Magic Go (withdrawn) ......20
68   Stateside SS 2103       Somewhere In The Country/Lonely Drifter ..................................................5
68   Stateside SS 2118       Love Grows/Conquistador ........................................................................5
68   Stateside SS 2131       Yours Until Tomorrow/She's A Heartbreaker ...............................................5
68   Stateside SS 2131       Yours Until Tomorrow/She's A Heartbreaker (DJ copy) ...............................15
69   Stateside SS 2142       Maria Elena/The French Horn ..................................................................30
70   Stateside SS 2177       Shady Lady/Billy, You're My Friend............................................................6
71   Pye International 7N 25564  Run Run Road Runner/Rain Maker............................................................5
72   Pye International 7N 25579  I Just Can't Help Myself/Beautiful Sounds ...............................................10
75   Bronze BRO 63           Train Of Thought/I'll Still Be In Love With You (A label demo).......................7
EPs
63   HMV 7EG 8832            TOWN WITHOUT PITY ................................................................................20
64   United Artists UEP 1001 TWENTY FOUR HOURS FROM TULSA .............................................................20
64   United Artists UEP 1002 THAT GIRL BELONGS TO YESTERDAY ...........................................................10
65   Stateside SE 1032       GENE ITALIANO ........................................................................................10
66   Stateside SE 1036       GENE PITNEY SINGS JUST FOR YOU ...........................................................10

ALBUMS : LPS
62   HMV CLP 1566            THE MANY SIDES OF GENE PITNEY .............................................................30
63   United Artists ULP 1028 ONLY LOVE CAN BREAK A HEART (mono)......................................................30
63   United Artists (S)ULP 1028 ONLY LOVE CAN BREAK A HEART (stereo) ...................................................20
63   United Artists ULP 1043 GENE PITNEY SINGS JUST FOR YOU ...........................................................30
64   United Artists ULP 1061 BLUE GENE ...............................................................................................20
64   United Artists ULP 1064 GENE PITNEY MEETS THE FAIR YOUNG LADIES OF FOLKLAND .......................20
64   United Artists ULP 1073 GENE PITNEY'S BIG SIXTEEN .....................................................................20
65   Stateside SL 10120      I'M GONNA BE STRONG ............................................................................15
65   Stateside SL 10132      GENE PITNEY'S MORE BIG SIXTEEN (VOL. 2) .............................................15
65   Stateside SL 10147      GEORGE JONES AND GENE PITNEY (with George Jones)................................15
65   Stateside SL 10148      LOOKING THRU THE EYES OF LOVE .............................................................15
65   Stateside SL 10156      SINGS THE GREAT SONGS OF OUR TIME ....................................................15
66   Stateside SL 10173      IT'S COUNTRY TIME AGAIN (with George Jones) ........................................15
*(see also Marc Almond & Gene Pitney, George Jones)*

**TERRY PITTS JAZZ BAND**
61   Oriole CB 1621          A Drop Of The Hard Stuff/Show Me The Way To Go Home ..............................6

**PIXIES**
89   4AD BAD 904             THIS MONKEY'S GONE TO HEAVEN EP (12")..................................................10
89   4AD BAD 909             HERE COMES YOUR MAN EP (12", p/s) .........................................................10
90   4AD AD 0014             Dig For Fire/Velvety (p/s) .........................................................................10
90   4AD BAD 0014            DIG FOR FIRE EP (12", p/s) .........................................................................8
89   4AD PIX ONE             DOOLITTLE SAMPLER: Debaser/Wave Of Mutilation/I Bleed/Gouge Away (12",
                             1-sided, title sleeve, promo only) ...........................................................10
89   4AD PIX 2               Into The White/Wave Of Mutilation (U.K. Surf) (12", 1-sided, promo only)........15
90   4AD PIX 3               EXTRACTS FROM BOSSANOVA: Allison/Rock Music/Down To The Well/The Happening
                             (12", 1-sided, promo only).......................................................................10
91   4AD PIX 4               EXTRACTS FROM TROMPE LE MONDE: U-Mass/Letter To Memphis/Subbacultcha (10",
                             same track both sides, promo only)...........................................................15
87   4AD MAD 709             COME ON PILGRIM (mini-LP) .....................................................................15
88   4AD CAD 803             SURFER ROSA (LP, with inner) ...................................................................20
89   4AD CAD 905             DOOLITTLE (LP, with lyric booklet & postcard, in carrier bag)........................20
89   4AD CAD 905             DOOLITTLE (LP, with lyric booklet & postcard) ...........................................35
90   4AD CAD 0010            BOSSANOVA (LP, with booklet) ..................................................................25
                                                                                                                 20

| 90 | 4AD CAD 1014 | TROMPE LE MONDE (LP) | 20 |
| 97 | 4AD DADD 7011 | DEATH TO THE PIXIES (4-10" LP, box set) | 50 |
| 02 | Cooking Vinyl COOK 234 | PIXIES - THE PURPLE TAPE (LP, inner) | 18 |
| 11 | 4AD CAD 2406 | WAVE OF MUTILATION: THE BEST OF (2-LP, orange vinyl) | 20 |
| 14 | Pixies PM006DLPR | INDIE CINDY (2-12", free 7" and download card) | 18 |

*(see also Breeders, Frank Black)*

## PIXIES THREE
| 63 | Mercury AMT 1214 | Birthday Party/Our Love | 25 |

## PLACEBO
| 95 | Fierce Panda NING 13 | Bruise Pristine/SOUP: M.E.L.T.D.O.W.N. (foldover p/s, 1500 only) | 35 |
| 96 | Deceptive BLUFF 024 | Come Home/Drowning By Numbers (p/s) | 12 |
| 96 | Elevator FLOOR 001 | 36 degrees/Dark globe (p/s) | 10 |
| 96 | Hut FLOOR 3 | Teenage Angst/Hug Bubble/Been Smoking Too Long (part 1 0f 2, p/s) | 6 |
| 96 | Hut FLOOR 4 | Nancy Boy (Sex Mix)/Slackerbitch (p/s) | 6 |
| 97 | Hut FLOOR 5 | Bruise Pristine/(One Punch Remix) (p/s) | 10 |
| 98 | Elevator FLOORLH 6 | Pure Morning/Leeloo (jukebox issue) | 8 |
| 98 | Elevator FLOORLH 7 | You Don't Care About Us/20th Century Boy (jukebox issue) | 12 |
| 99 | Hut FLOOR TP 10 | Without You I'm Nothing (with David Bowie) (UNKLE Remix)/(Flexirol Mix)/(Brothers In Rhythm Club Mix) (12" promo, 500 only, stickered die-cut sleeve) | 15 |
| 03 | Virgin 7432547480743 | Special Needs/English Summer Rain (p/s) | 10 |
| 04 | Virgin 724381618776 | Twenty Years/Detox 5 | 10 |
| 96 | Hut LPFLOORY 2 | PLACEBO (LP) | 60 |
| 98 | Elevator FLOORLP 8 | WITHOUT YOU I'M NOTHING (LP, gatefold) | 80 |
| 00 | Elevator FLOORLP 13 | BLACK MARKET MUSIC (LP, gatefold) | 45 |
| 03 | Elevator FLOORLP 17 | SLEEPING WI TH GHOSTS (LP, gatefold) | 45 |
| 10 | Elevator FLOORLP 23 | COVERS (LP, reissue, 1000 only) | 45 |
| 04 | Elevator FLOORLP 23 | ONCE MORE WITH FEELING (2-LP) | 60 |
| 06 | Elevator LPFLOOR 26 | MEDS (LP, gatefold) | 50 |
| 09 | Dreambrother BATTLE01BS | BATTLE FOR THE SUN (2-LP, 2-DVD box set) | 40 |

## PLAGUE (1)
| 68 | Decca F 12730 | Looking For The Sun/Here Today, Gone Tomorrow | 250 |
| 11 | Decca F 12730 | Looking For The Sun/Here Today, Gone Tomorrow (reissue) | 8 |

## PLAGUE (2)
| 79 | Psycho P2615 | In Love/Wimpey Bar Song (silk screened fold-out cover) | 50 |
| 79 | Psycho P 2615 | In Love/Wimpey Bar Song (2nd pressing, printed sleeve, pink vinyl) | 25 |
| 80 | Evolution EV 4 | Out With Me All Night/Er/Don't Want To Be Like Jimmy | 50 |

## PLAID
| 92 | GPR GENP(X) 7 | Scoobs In Columbia (remixes) (12", custom sleeve) | 30 |
| 94 | Clear CLR 409 | ANDROID (12" EP, p/s, clear vinyl) | 20 |
| 94 | Clear CLR 409 | ANDROID (12" EP, p/s, black vinyl) | 15 |
| 95 | Rumble RUMBLE 01 | MIND OVER RHYTHM MEET THE MEN FROM PLAID (3 x 10" in p/s) | 15 |
| 92 | Black Dog Prods. LP 1 | MBUKI MVUKI (LP) | 80 |
| 97 | Warp WARLP54 | NOT FOR THREES (2-LP) | 25 |
| 99 | Warp WARLP63 | REST PROOF CLOCKWORK (2-LP) | 20 |
| 00 | Warp WARPLP74 | TRAINER (3-LP) | 20 |
| 01 | Warp WARLP84 | DOUBLE FIGURE (2-LP) | 20 |
| 03 | Warp WARPLP114 | SPOKES (LP) | 20 |

*(see also Black Dog)*

## PLAINSONG
| 72 | Elektra K 12976 | Even The Guiding Light/Yoko Man/Call The Tune | 7 |
| 72 | Elektra K 42120 | IN SEARCH OF AMELIA EARHART (LP, gatefold sleeve with lyric insert) | 25 |
| 73 | Elektra K 42136 | PLAINSONG II (LP, white label, promo only) | 120 |

*(see also Andy Roberts, Ian Matthews)*

## PLANET EARTH
| 78 | Pye NSPL 18556 | PLANET EARTH (LP) | 25 |

## PLANET GONG
| 77 | Affinity AF 5101 | Opium For The People/Poet For Sale (p/s) | 8 |
| 78 | Charly CYX 202 | Opium For The People/Stoned Innocent Frankenstein (10", p/s) | 18 |
| 78 | Charly CRM 2000 | FLOATING ANARCHY - LIVE 1977 (LP) | 18 |

*(see also Daevid Allen, Gong)*

## PLANET P PROJECT
| 83 | Geffen A3205 | Why Me/Only You And Me (p/s) | 6 |
| 85 | MCA MCSP311 | PINK WORLD (2LP, gatefold sleeve) | 18 |

*(see also Tony Carey, Rainbow)*

## PLANETS (1)
| 60 | Palette PG 9008 | Like Party/Ippy Yippy Beatnik (only this value if in p/s) | 25 |
| 60 | Palette PG 9008 | Like Party/Ippy Yippy Beatnik (no p/s) | 10 |

## PLANETS (2)
| 60 | HMV POP 818 | Chunky/Screwball | 20 |
| 61 | HMV POP 832 | Jam Roll/Delaney's Theme | 25 |
| 61 | HMV POP 895 | Jungle Street/The Grasshopper | 25 |

## PLANETS (3)
| 73 | Bullet BU 528 | People Get Funny/DOCBIRD ALL STARS : Funny Version | 10 |

## ROBERT PLANT
| 67 | CBS 202656 | Our Song/Laughin', Cryin', Laughin' | 350 |
| 67 | CBS 202656 | Our Song/Laughin' Cryin' Laughin' ('A' label demo) | 300 |
| 67 | CBS 202858 | Long Time Coming/I've Got A Secret | 300 |
| 67 | CBS 202858 | Long Time Coming/I've Got A Secret ('A' label demo) | 250 |

MINT VALUE £

| Year | Label/Cat No | Title | Value |
|---|---|---|---|
| 82 | Swan Song SSK 19429T | Burning Down One Side/Far Post (12", p/s) | 10 |
| 82 | Swan Song SAM154 | PICTURES AT ELEVEN (LP, promo interview disc with cue sheet) | 18 |
| 82 | Es Paranza SAM 169 | THE PRINCIPLE OF MOVEMENTS (LP, promo interview disc with cue sheet) | 18 |
| 88 | Es Paranza PR 2244 | NON STOP GO! (LP, two disc set interview promo for NOW AND ZEN album) | 15 |
| 90 | Es Paranza WX 339X | MANIC NIRVANA (LP, gatefold, numbered, picture inner bag) | 18 |
| 93 | Fontana 514 867-1 | FATE OF NATIONS (LP) | 70 |
| 02 | Mercury 063094-1 | DREAMLAND (2xLP, numbered) | 100 |
| 05 | Sanctuary SANLP 356 | MIGHTY REARRANGER (LP) | 45 |

*(see also Led Zeppelin, Listen, Jimmy Page, Robert Plant & The Strange Sensation, Page & Plant, Honeydrippers)*

## PLASMATICS

| Year | Label/Cat No | Title | Value |
|---|---|---|---|
| 80 | Stiff BUY 76 | Butcher Baby/Tight Black Pants (splatter vinyl, p/s) | 5 |
| 80 | Stiff BUY 76 | Butcher Baby/Tight Black Pants (black vinyl, p/s) | 8 |
| 80 | Stiff BUY 91 | Monkey Suit/Squirm (splatter vinyl, p/s) | 5 |
| 80 | Stiff SEEZ 24 | NEW HOPE FOR THE WRETCHED (LP, splatter vinyl) | 20 |

## PLASTIC BERTRAND

| Year | Label/Cat No | Title | Value |
|---|---|---|---|
| 78 | Sire 9103258 | AN 1 (LP, gatefold) | 20 |

## PLASTIC GANGSTERS

| Year | Label/Cat No | Title | Value |
|---|---|---|---|
| 83 | Secret SHH 144 | Plastic Gangster/Sretsgnag Citsalp (7", 12", no p/s on 12" stamped p/s on 7", unissued, 10 DJ copies only) | 250 |
| 11 | Secret SHH 144 | Plastic Gangster (I Could Be So Good For You)/Sretsgnag Citsalp (reissue, on red, white or blue vinyl) | 7 |

*(see also 4 Skins)*

## PLASTIC PENNY

| Year | Label/Cat No | Title | Value |
|---|---|---|---|
| 67 | Page One POF 051 | Everything I Am/No Pleasure Without Pain My Love | 5 |
| 68 | Page One POF 062 | Nobody Knows It/Just Happy To Be With You | 10 |
| 68 | Page One POF 079 | Your Way To Tell Me Go/Baby You're Not To Blame | 20 |
| 69 | Page One POF 107 | Hound Dog/Currency | 20 |
| 69 | Page One POF 146 | She Does/Genevieve | 20 |
| 68 | Page One POL(S) 005 | TWO SIDES OF THE PENNY (LP, laminated front sleeve, flipbacks) | 100 |
| 69 | Page One POLS 014 | CURRENCY (LP, laminated front sleeve, flipbacks) | 140 |
| 70 | Page One POLS 611 | HEADS YOU WIN, TAILS I LOSE (LP) | 65 |

*(see also Universals, Circles, Brian Keith, Mick Grabham)*

## PLASTIC PEOPLE

| Year | Label/Cat No | Title | Value |
|---|---|---|---|
| 79 | Rising Son RS1 | Demolition/XTRAVERTS: Police State (multi coloured vinyl) | 60 |

## PLASTIC SANDWICHES

| Year | Label/Cat No | Title | Value |
|---|---|---|---|
| 81 | Ellie Jay EJSP 9746 | Bayonets And Colours/Parties At War (p/s is two separate 7" pieces of paper) | 20 |

## PLASTICS

| Year | Label/Cat No | Title | Value |
|---|---|---|---|
| 79 | Rough Trade RT 030 | Robot/Copy | 8 |

## PLASTIKMAN

| Year | Label/Cat No | Title | Value |
|---|---|---|---|
| 94 | Nova Mute L NO MU 37 | MUSIK (2-LP, with bonus 1-sided etched 12") | 20 |
| 95 | Nova Mute NOMU22LP | SHEET ONE (2-LP) | 20 |
| 03 | Nova Mute NOMULP 100LP | CLOSER (3-LP) | 25 |

## PLATFORM SIX

| Year | Label/Cat No | Title | Value |
|---|---|---|---|
| 65 | Piccadilly 7N 35255 | Money Will Not Mean A Thing/Girl Down Town | 70 |

## EDDIE PLATT

| Year | Label/Cat No | Title | Value |
|---|---|---|---|
| 58 | Columbia DB 4101 | Tequila/Pop Corn | 25 |

## PLATTERS

### 78s

| Year | Label/Cat No | Title | Value |
|---|---|---|---|
| 59 | Mercury AMT 1039 | Enchanted/The Sound And The Fury | 20 |
| 59 | Mercury AMT 1053 | Remember When/Love Of A Lifetime (featuring Tony Williams) | 30 |
| 60 | Mercury AMT 1081 | Harbour Lights/(By The) Sleepy Lagoon | 40 |

### SINGLES

| Year | Label/Cat No | Title | Value |
|---|---|---|---|
| 56 | Mercury MT 117 | The Great Pretender/Only You (And You Alone) (export issue) | 40 |
| 58 | Mercury 7MT 197 | Helpless/Indiff'rent | 30 |
| 58 | Mercury 7MT 205 | Don't Let Go/Are You Sincere? | 30 |
| 58 | Mercury 7MT 214 | Twilight Time/Out Of My Mind | 10 |
| 58 | Mercury 7MT 227 | You're Making A Mistake (featuring Tony Williams)/My Old Flame | 20 |
| 58 | Mercury AMT 1001 | I Wish/It's Raining Outside | 18 |
| 58 | Mercury AMT 1016 | Smoke Gets In Your Eyes/No Matter What You Are | 5 |
| 59 | Mercury AMT 1039 | Enchanted/The Sound And The Fury | 6 |
| 59 | Mercury AMT 1053 | Remember When/Love Of A Lifetime (featuring Tony Williams) | 10 |
| 59 | Mercury AMT 1066 | My Blue Heaven/Wish It Were Me | 6 |
| 60 | Mercury AMT 1076 | My Secret/What Does It Matter | 5 |
| 60 | Mercury AMT 1081 | Harbour Lights/(By The) Sleepy Lagoon | 5 |
| 60 | Mercury AMT 1098 | Ebb Tide/(I'll Be With You In) Apple Blossom Time (featuring Tony Williams) | 5 |
| 60 | Mercury AMT 1106 | Red Sails In The Sunset/Sad River (featuring Tony Williams) | 5 |
| 60 | Mercury AMT 1118 | To Each His Own/Down The River Of Golden Dreams | 5 |
| 61 | Mercury AMT 1128 | If I Didn't Care/True Lover | 5 |
| 61 | Mercury AMT 1154 | I'll Never Smile Again/You Don't Say | 5 |
| 62 | Ember JBS 701 | Only You/Tell The World | 80 |
| 66 | Stateside SS 511 | I Love You 1000 Times/Hear No Evil, Speak No Evil, See No Evil | 25 |
| 66 | Stateside SS 568 | I'll Be Home/(You've Got) The Magic Touch | 12 |
| 67 | Stateside SS 2007 | With This Ring/If I Had A Love | 25 |
| 67 | Stateside SS 2042 | Washed Ashore (On A Lonely Island In The Sea)/What Name Shall I Give You My Love | 25 |
| 67 | Stateside SS 2042 | Washed Ashore (On A Lonely Island In The Sea)/What Name Shall I Give You My Love (DJ copy) | 60 |
| 67 | Stateside SS 2067 | Sweet Sweet Lovin'/Sonata | 20 |
| 67 | Stateside SS 2067 | Sweet Sweet Lovin'/Sonata (DJ copy) | 60 |

| 69 | Stateside SS 2150 | With This Ring/If I Had A Love (reissue)..................................................................8 |
|----|-------------------|------------------------------------------------------------------------------------|
| 71 | Pye Intl. 7N 25559 | Sweet Sweet Lovin'/Going Back To Detroit..........................................................15 |
| 71 | Pye Intl. 7N 25569 | With This Ring/I Washed Ashore (On A Lonely Island In The Sea) ..........................8 |
| 87 | Kent 6T3 | SAMMY AMBROSE: Welcome To Dreamsville/PLATTERS: Not My Girl......................25 |

**EPs**

| 56 | Mercury MEP 9504 | THE FABULOUS PLATTERS ...............................................................................10 |
|----|------------------|------------------------------------------------------------------------------------|
| 57 | Mercury MEP 9514 | THE FABULOUS PLATTERS VOL. II .....................................................................10 |
| 57 | Mercury MEP 9524 | THE FABULOUS PLATTERS VOL. III ....................................................................12 |
| 58 | Mercury MEP 9526 | THE FLYING PLATTERS VOL. I...........................................................................15 |
| 58 | Mercury MEP 9528 | THE FLYING PLATTERS VOL. II..........................................................................15 |
| 58 | Mercury MEP 9537 | THE PLATTERS ...............................................................................................15 |
| 59 | Mercury ZEP 10000 | PICK OF THE PLATTERS NO. 1..........................................................................10 |
| 59 | Mercury ZEP 10008 | PICK OF THE PLATTERS NO. 2..........................................................................10 |
| 59 | Mercury ZEP 10025 | PICK OF THE PLATTERS NO. 3..........................................................................10 |
| 59 | Mercury ZEP 10031 | PICK OF THE PLATTERS NO. 4..........................................................................10 |
| 59 | Mercury ZEP 10042 | PICK OF THE PLATTERS NO. 5..........................................................................10 |
| 60 | Mercury ZEP 10056 | PICK OF THE PLATTERS NO. 6..........................................................................10 |
| 60 | Mercury ZEP 10070 | PICK OF THE PLATTERS NO. 7..........................................................................10 |
| 61 | Mercury ZEP 10112 | HARBOUR LIGHTS ........................................................................................10 |
| 62 | Mercury ZEP 10126 | THE PLATTERS ON A PLATTER .........................................................................15 |

**ALBUMS : LPS**

| 57 | Mercury MPL 6504 | THE PLATTERS ...............................................................................................35 |
|----|------------------|------------------------------------------------------------------------------------|
| 57 | Mercury MPL 6511 | THE PLATTERS VOL. 2 .....................................................................................30 |
| 58 | Mercury MPL 6528 | THE FLYING PLATTERS.....................................................................................30 |
| 58 | Parlophone PMD 1058 | THE PLATTERS (10")...................................................................................200 |
| 59 | Mercury MMC 14009 | AROUND THE WORLD WITH THE FLYING PLATTERS............................................15 |
| 59 | Mercury MMC 14010 | THE PLATTERS ON PARADE .............................................................................15 |
| 59 | Mercury MMC 14014 | REMEMBER WHEN? .......................................................................................15 |
| 60 | Mercury MMC 14045 | REFLECTIONS.................................................................................................15 |
| 61 | Mercury MMC 14072 | LIFE IS JUST A BOWL OF CHERRIES ..................................................................15 |
| 67 | Stateside S(S)L 10208 | GOING BACK TO DETROIT.............................................................................15 |

*(see also Buck Ram's Ramrocks, Linda Hayes)*

**PLAY**

| 82 | Survival SUR 12 008 | CHASING THE SUN EP (12", p/s) .......................................................................10 |
|----|---------------------|------------------------------------------------------------------------------------|
| 85 | Survival SUR B1 | RED MOVIES (LP)............................................................................................20 |
| 84 | Survival SUR 12 022 | IN MY MIND EP (12", p/s) ...............................................................................10 |

**PLAYBOYS (JAMAICA)**

| 71 | Tropical AL 007 | Change Change/TROPICAL ALL STARS: Version 2...............................................5 |
|----|-----------------|------------------------------------------------------------------------------------|

**PLAYBOYS (U.S.)**

| 58 | London HLU 8681 | Over The Weekend/Double Talk ......................................................................40 |
|----|-----------------|------------------------------------------------------------------------------------|

**PLAYBOYS (U.S.)**

| 69 | Capitol CL 15621 | Let's Get Back To Rock And Roll/Homemade Cookin' .........................................6 |
|----|------------------|------------------------------------------------------------------------------------|

*(see also Rad Bryan)*

**PLAY DEAD**

| 81 | Fresh FRESH 29 | Poison Takes A Hold/Introduction (p/s)..............................................................7 |
|----|----------------|------------------------------------------------------------------------------------|
| 81 | Fresh FRESH 38 | T.V. Eye/Final Epitaph (p/s).............................................................................7 |

**PLAYERS**

| 63 | Oriole CB 1861 | Mockingbird/Bizet As It May ..........................................................................25 |
|----|----------------|------------------------------------------------------------------------------------|

**PLAYGIRLS (JAMAICA)**

| 65 | Black Swan WI 456 | Looks Are Deceiving/BABA BROOKS: Dreadnaught...........................................45 |
|----|-------------------|------------------------------------------------------------------------------------|

**PLAYGIRLS (U.S.)**

| 59 | RCA RCA 1133 | Hey Sport/Young Love Swings The World .........................................................15 |
|----|--------------|------------------------------------------------------------------------------------|

**PLAYGROUND**

| 67 | MGM MGM 1351 | At The Zoo/Yellow Balloon .............................................................................20 |
|----|--------------|------------------------------------------------------------------------------------|
| 69 | NEMS 56-4019 | I Could Be So Good/The Girl Behind The Smile ................................................10 |
| 69 | NEMS 56-4442 | Things I Do For You/Lazy Days ........................................................................10 |

**PLAYGROUP**

| 82 | On U Sound BRED 28 | EPIC SOUND BATTLES CHAPTER ONE (LP)........................................................15 |
|----|--------------------|------------------------------------------------------------------------------------|

**PLAYING AT TRAINS**

| 87 | Idea IDT 001 | A World Without Love/Just Around The Mountain/Playing At Trains/A Japanese Intervention (12" p/s) .....................................................................................85 |
|----|--------------|------------------------------------------------------------------------------------|

*(see also Waving At Trains)*

**PLAYMATES**

| 57 | Columbia DB 3941 | Pretty Woman/Barefoot Girl .........................................................................10 |
|----|------------------|------------------------------------------------------------------------------------|
| 57 | Columbia DB 4033 | Island Girl/Darling, It's Wonderful..................................................................10 |
| 58 | Columbia DB 4084 | Jo-Ann/You Can't Stop Me From Dreaming......................................................10 |
| 58 | Columbia DB 4127 | Let's Be Lovers/Give Me Another Chance ........................................................10 |
| 58 | Columbia DB 4224 | Beep Beep/Your Love...................................................................................8 |
| 59 | Columbia DB 4288 | Star Love/The Thing-A-Ma-Jig ........................................................................5 |
| 60 | Columbia DB 4551 | Wait For Me/Eyes Of An Angel .......................................................................7 |
| 58 | Columbia SEG 7864 | AT PLAY WITH THE PLAYMATES (EP)................................................................10 |
| 59 | Columbia SEG 7949 | PARTY PLAYMATES NO. 1 (EP)........................................................................10 |
| 59 | Columbia SEG 7966 | PARTY PLAYMATES NO. 2 (EP)........................................................................10 |

**PLAYMATES (IRELAND)**

| 70 | Emerald MD 1150 | Don't Fight It/Jodi ........................................................................................10 |
|----|-----------------|------------------------------------------------------------------------------------|

**PLAYTHINGS**

| 70 | Pye 7N 45212 | Stop What You're Doing To Me/Sad (light blue label) ........................................6 |
|----|--------------|------------------------------------------------------------------------------------|

| | | | MINT VALUE £ |
|---|---|---|---|

**Bobby PLEASE** (continued)

| 70 | Pye 7N 45212 | Stop What You're Doing To Me/Sad | 10 |
| 73 | Pye 7N 45399 | Surrounded By A Ray Of Sunshine/Dance The Night Away | 5 |

**BOBBY PLEASE**

| 57 | London HLB 8507 | Your Driver's Licence, Please/Heartache Street (unissued, 2x 1-sided demos - price is for BOTH demos together) | 100 |
| 57 | London HLB 8507 | Your Driver's Licence, Please/Heartache Street (78) | 40 |

**PLEASERS**

| 77 | Solid Gold SGR 104 | You Know What I'm Thinking Girl/Hello Little Girl | 8 |
| 77 | Arista ARIST 21 | Girl I Know/Don't Go Breaking My Heart (p/s) | 5 |
| 77 | Arista ARIST 152 | You Keep Tellin' Lies/I'm In Love/Who Are You (p/s, silver label) | 5 |
| 77 | Arista ARIST 152 | You Keep Tellin' Lies/I'm In Love/Who Are You (p/s, blue label) | 10 |
| 78 | Arista ARIST 180 | The Kids Are Alright/Stay With Me (p/s) | 12 |

**PLEASURE BEACH**

| 90s | Acid Jazz AJX 124S | Rollercoaster/Smells Like Teen Spirit (p/s) | 6 |

**PLEASURE CELL**

| 86 | (No label) ANG 1 | New Age/Common Ground | 25 |

**PLEASURE FAIR**

| 68 | Uni UN 500 | Morning Glory Blues/Fade Out Fade In | 12 |
| 67 | Uni UNL(S) 100 | PLEASURE FAIR (LP) | 25 |

*(see also Bread)*

**PLEASURE GARDEN**

| 68 | Sound For Industry SFI 31H/ 32H | Permissive Paradise/EMPEROR ROSKO & JONATHAN KING: Young London (flexidisc, art sleeve with small booklet) | 100 |

*(see also Iveys)*

**PLEASURES**

| 65 | Sue WI 357 | Music City/If I Had A Little Money | 45 |

**PLEBS**

| 64 | Decca F 12006 | Bad Blood/Babe I'm Gonna Leave You | 80 |
| 60s | Oak | THE PLEBS (LP, 1-sided, private pressing) | 1000 |

**PLEXUS**

| 78 | Look LKLP 6175 | PLEXUS (LP) | 65 |
| 79 | Hill & Dale HD004 | LIFE UP THE CREEK (LP) | 55 |

**PLINTH**

| 10 | Smalls Lighthouse SL 05 | MUSIC FOR SMALLS LIGHTHOUSE (CD-R in box with book, 150 only) | 25 |
| 13 | Clay Pipe 08 | MUSIC FOR SMALLS LIGHTHOUSE (LP, numbered, 500 only) | 15 |
| 14 | Kit (No cat no) | WINTERSONGS (LP, lino cut sleeve, vinyl repressing, 200 only) | 15 |

**PLONE**

| 99 | Warp WARPLP64 | FOR BEGINNER PIANO (LP) | 15 |

**PLUGS**

| 79 | Cathedral CATH 1 | Too Late/UFO/Sally (gatefold p/s) | 20 |
| 80 | Pop 1 | CRACKIN' UP EP | 12 |
| 81 | Plugpop GRGL 782 | Indoor Shopping Centre/High Society | 10 |

**JEAN PLUM**

| 76 | London HLU 10514 | Look At The Boy/Back At You | 10 |

**JON PLUM**

| 69 | SNB 55-3971 | Alice/Sunshine | 20 |
| 69 | SNB 55-4317 | You Keep Changing Your Mind/An Apple Falls | 15 |

**PLUM & YOUTH**

| 80s | Checkmount CHK 1 | I Got You Babe/Got To Be Moving On (p/s, withdrawn) | 15 |

*(see also Cozy Powell, Rainbow, Big Bertha)*

**PLUMMERS**

| 64 | Blue Beat BB 260 | Johnny/Little Stars (actually by Plamers) | 22 |

**PLUMMET AIRLINES**

| 76 | Stiff BUY 8 | Silver Shirt/This Is The World (p/s, push-out centre) | 8 |

**PLUNDER**

| 08 | Lolarox ROX 1 | Hellion Castle/I Spy On Love (p/s, booklet, 200 only) | 5 |

**PLUS**

| 70 | Probe SPB 1009 | SEVEN DEADLY SINS (LP, laminated front sleeve, flipbacks) | 120 |

**PLUTO**

| 71 | Dawn DNS 1017 | Rag A Bone Joe/Stealing My Thunder | 20 |
| 72 | Dawn DNS 1026 | I Really Want It/Something That You Loved | 30 |
| 71 | Dawn DNLS 3030 | PLUTO (LP, laminated sleeve, lilac label) | 250 |
| 89 | See For Miles SEE 265 | PLUTO...PLUS (LP, reissue) | 25 |

*(see also Dry Ice, Foundations)*

**PLUTOS PEOPLE**

| 78 | Jay Lee JL 6 | Little Lady/It's Up To You (no p/s) | 15 |

**NICK PLYTAS**

| 79 | Do It DUN 5 | Johnny Runaway/Your Dream Is A Daydream (p/s) | 5 |

**PNEUMONIA (1)**

| 68 | Oak RGJ 625 | I Can See Your Face | 500 |

**PNEUMONIA (2)**

| 79 | Plastic PLAS 001 | Exhibition/Coming Attack/U.K. DECAY: U.K. Decay/Carcrash (folded p/s) | 25 |

**POACHER**

| 79 | RK 1022 | Star Love/Question Of Trust | 5 |

**POCKETS**

| 77 | CBS 5780 | Come Go With Me/Pt. 2 | 8 |

## POEME ELECTRONIQUE
| | | | |
|---|---|---|---|
| 82 | Carrere CAR 228 | The Echoes Fade/V.O.I.C.E. (p/s) | 200 |

## POEMSO
| | | | |
|---|---|---|---|
| 81 | Polka DOT 1 | ACHIEVING UNITY (EP, initially with booklet) | 10 |

*(see also Strawberry Switchblade)*

## POET & ONE MAN BAND
| | | | |
|---|---|---|---|
| 69 | Verve Forecast SVLP 6012 | THE POET AND THE ONE MAN BAND (LP, laminated front sleeve, flipbacks) | 100 |

*(see also Tony Colton, Nicky Hopkins, Heads Hands & Feet)*

## POETS
| | | | |
|---|---|---|---|
| 64 | Decca F 11995 | Now We're Thru/There Are Some | 20 |
| 65 | Decca F 12074 | That's The Way It's Got To Be/I'll Cry With The Moon | 50 |
| 65 | Decca F 12195 | I Am So Blue/I Love Her Still | 60 |
| 65 | Immediate IM 006 | Call Again/Some Things I Can't Forget | 100 |
| 66 | Immediate IM 024 | Baby Don't You Do It/I'll Come Home | 100 |
| 67 | Decca F 12569 | Wooden Spoon/In Your Tower | 450 |
| 71 | Strike Cola SC 1 | Heyla Hola/Fun Buggy | 50 |
| 88 | Bam Caruso OPRA 088 | I Love Her Still/GHOST: Time Is My Enemy (company sleeve, promo only) | 12 |

*(see also Pathfinders, [White] Trash, Blue)*

## POETS (IRELAND)
| | | | |
|---|---|---|---|
| 68 | Pye 7N 17668 | Locked In A Room/Alone Am I | 240 |
| 68 | Target 7N 17668 | Locked In A Room/Alone Am I (Irish issue, different label) | 240 |

## POGUE MAHONE
| | | | |
|---|---|---|---|
| 84 | Pogue Mahone PM 1 | Dark Streets Of London/The Band Played Waltzing Mathilda | 10 |
| 84 | Pogue Mahone PM 1 | Dark Streets Of London/The Band Played Waltzing Mathilda (white label tour copy with 'harp' stamp, 237 only) | 50 |

*(see also Pogues)*

## POGUES
| | | | |
|---|---|---|---|
| 84 | Stiff BUY DJ 212 | The Irish Rover/DUBLINERS: Rare Old Mountain Dew (promo, dirty verse taken out for airplay) | 15 |
| 84 | Stiff BUY 207 | Dark Streets Of London/The Band Played Waltzing Mathilda (reissue of Pogue Mahone) | 10 |
| 84 | Stiff BUY 212 | Boys From The County Hell/Repeal Of The Licensing Laws (green-tinted p/s) | 10 |
| 84 | Stiff BUY 212 | Boys From The County Hell/Repeal Of The Licensing Laws (A-label promos in blue-tinted p/s) | 15 |
| 84 | Stiff BUY 207/BUY 212 | Dark Streets Of London/The Band Played Waltzing Mathilda//Boys From The County Hell/Repeal Of The Licensing Laws (shrinkwrapped double pack) | 20 |
| 85 | Stiff BUY220 | A Pair Of Brown Eyes/Whiskey You're The Devil (sealed and stickered with free copy of Boys From The County Hell 7") | 30 |
| 85 | Stiff DBUY 220 | A Pair Of Brown Eyes/Whiskey You're The Devil (picture disc) | 15 |
| 85 | Stiff BUYIT 220 | A Pair Of Brown Eyes/Whiskey You're The Devil/Muirshin Durkin (12", p/s) | 15 |
| 85 | Stiff BUY 212/BUY 220 | Boys From The County Hell/Repeal Of The Licensing Laws//A Pair Of Brown Eyes/Whiskey You're The Devil (shrinkwrapped double pack) | 15 |
| 85 | Stiff BUY 224 | Sally MacLennane/Wild Rover (wraparound poster p/s, green vinyl) | 10 |
| 85 | Stiff BUY 224 | Sally MacLennane/Wild Rover (wraparound poster p/s) | 7 |
| 85 | Stiff BUY 224 | Sally MacLennane/Wild Rover (standard p/s) | 6 |
| 85 | Stiff PBUY 229 | Dirty Old Town/A Pistol For Paddy Garcia (picture disc) | 10 |
| 85 | Stiff BUYIT 229 | Dirty Old Town/A Pistol For Paddy Garcia/The Parting Glass (12", with poster & stickered p/s) | 20 |
| 85 | Stiff BUYIT 229 | Dirty Old Town/A Pistol For Paddy Garcia/The Parting Glass (12", without poster & stickered p/s) | 15 |
| 85 | Stiff MAIL 3 | Dirty Old Town (live)/Sally MacLennane (live)/(interview) (12", mail-order) | 12 |
| 87 | Stiff/Hell BLOOD 1 | The Good, The Bad & The Ugly/Rake At The Gates Of Hell (unreleased) | 0 |
| 87 | Stiff/Hell BLOODY 1 | The Good, The Bad & The Ugly/Rake At The Gates Of Hell (12", unreleased) | 0 |
| 85 | Stiff SEEZ 58 | RUM SODOMY & THE LASH (LP) | 15 |

*(see also Pogue Mahone, Nips, Nipple Erectors, Radiators From Space, Shane MacGowan & the Popes)*

## POINDEXTER BROTHERS
| | | | |
|---|---|---|---|
| 66 | Verve VS 550 | (Git Your) Backfield In Motion/(Grandma) Give That Girl Some Slack | 20 |

## POINT
| | | | |
|---|---|---|---|
| 80 | Pendulum PT 001 | My Mind/Mr. Benson | 8 |
| 81 | Pendulum PT 002 | Metropolis/After Seven | 8 |

## POINT BLANK MCS
| | | | |
|---|---|---|---|
| 92 | Kold Sweat KS120 | Planting Semtex/Revenge Of The Ghetto Child (12") | 12 |

## POINTED STICKS
| | | | |
|---|---|---|---|
| 79 | Stiff BUY 59 | Out Of Luck/What Do You Want Me To Do/Somebody's Mom ("Plug Copy on label, p/s) | 10 |
| 79 | Stiff BUY 59 | Out Of Luck/What Do You Want Me To Do/Somebody's Mom (p/s) | 9 |
| 79 | Stiff BUY 59 | Out Of Luck/What Do You Want Me To Do/Somebody's Mom (12", p/s) | 10 |

## POINTS PROVEN
| | | | |
|---|---|---|---|
| 92 | Payday PD002 | Pass The Mic/Noisy Music Part 2/Funky Rhymes, Funky Style (EP) | 12 |

## POISON GIRLS
| | | | |
|---|---|---|---|
| 79 | Small Wonder WEENY 4 | HEX (12" EP, with lyric insert) | 15 |
| 80 | Crass 421984/9 | HEX (12", reissue) | 10 |
| 80 | Crass/Xntrix 421984/1 | Persons Unknown/CRASS: Bloody Revolutions (folded 21" x 14" poster p/s) | 10 |
| 81 | Crass 421984/10 | Pretty Polly/Bully Boys (live) (square red or clear flexidisc free with In The City fanzine, with magazine) | 10 |
| 81 | Crass 421984/8 | All Systems Go/Promenade Immortelle/Dirty Work (p/s with lyrics) | 5 |
| 83 | Illuminated ILL 23 | One Good Reason/Cinnamon Gardens (p/s) | 5 |
| 83 | Illuminated ILL 25 | Are You Happy Now?/Cream Dream (p/s) | 5 |
| 80 | Crass 421984/2 | CHAPPAQUIDICK (LP, thin stapled gatefold sleeve with free flexidisc "Statement" [421984/7]) | 15 |
| 81 | XENTRIX XN2003 | TOTAL EXPOSURE (LP, gold LP with outer poly bag) | 20 |

MINT VALUE £

| | | | |
|---|---|---|---|
| 81 | XENTRIX XN 2003 | WHERE'S THE PLEASURE? (LP, lyric insert) | 15 |
| 85 | XENTRIX XN 2208 | SONGS OF PRAISE (LP) | 15 |

*(see also Crass)*

### POISON IDEA
| | | | |
|---|---|---|---|
| 89 | In Your Face FACE 06 | IAN MACKAYE (EP) | 15 |
| 91 | Vinyl Solution VS 29 | Plastic Bomb/We Got The Beat/Harder They Come/Lawdy Miss Clawdy (double pack, p/s) | 8 |
| 91 | Vinyl Solution VS325 | Punish Me/Mario The Cop (p/s, purple vinyl) | 8 |
| 93 | Dirtier Promotions 7DPROMS 11 | Feel The Darkness (Remix)/Feel The Darkness (Remix) (foldover p/s in poly bag, same track both sides free with Fear & Loathing fanzine) | 8 |
| 90 | Vinyl Solution SOL 025 | FEEL THE DARNESS (LP, inner) | 15 |
| 92 | Vinyl Solution SOL 033 | BLANK BLACKOUT VACANT (LP, inner, poster and free 7" [FART 4]) | 20 |

### POISON IVY
| | | | |
|---|---|---|---|
| 64 | Granta GR 7EP 1011 | CLINGING MEMORIES (EP) | 110 |

### POISONED ELECTRIC HEAD
| | | | |
|---|---|---|---|
| 89 | Dead Fly ACAD 002 | Cap Of Flies/Trickeroo (p/s) | 10 |

### POLECATS
| | | | |
|---|---|---|---|
| 81 | Nervous NER 001 | Rockabilly Guy/Chicken Shack (p/s) | 6 |
| 81 | Mercury POLE 3 | Jeepster/Marie Celeste | 5 |
| 81 | Mercury POLE 1 | John I'm Only Dancing/Big Green Car (p/s) | 5 |

### POLES
| | | | |
|---|---|---|---|
| 88 | Warm WARM 1 | Letters To Send/Grow Old | 8 |

### ROLO POLEY
| | | | |
|---|---|---|---|
| 69 | Jackpot JP 704 | Zapatoo The Tiger/Music House (both sides actually by Lester Sterling) | 45 |

### POLICE
| | | | |
|---|---|---|---|
| 77 | Illegal IL 001 | Fall Out/Nothing Achieving (black & white p/s, red & black label, various designs) | 10 |
| 78 | A&M AMS 7348 | Roxanne/Peanuts (2.52) ('telephone' p/s, typed matrix no., 'All Rights ...' on top half of label) | 5 |
| 78 | A&M AMS 7348 | Roxanne/Peanuts (12", 'telephone' p/s) | 15 |
| 78 | A&M AMS 7381 | Can't Stand Losing You/Dead End Job (glossy p/s, original issue, label credited to 'Police', rarer black vinyl) | 10 |
| 78 | A&M AMS 7381 | Can't Stand Losing You/Dead End Job (glossy p/s, original issue, label credited to 'Police', mid-blue vinyl) | 7 |
| 78 | A&M AMS 7402 | So Lonely/Time This Time (p/s, miscredited flip, label credited to 'Police') | 5 |
| 79 | A&M AMS 7348 | Roxanne/Peanuts (3.54) (reissue, 'group' p/s, handwritten matrix number, blue vinyl) | 6 |
| 79 | A&M AMS 7348 | Roxanne/Peanuts (2.52) (reissue, 'group' p/s, typed matrix number, blue) | 6 |
| 79 | A&M AMSP 7348 | Roxanne/Peanuts (12", reissue, 'group' p/s) | 10 |
| 79 | A&M AMS 7381 | Can't Stand Losing You/Dead End Job (reissue, label credited to 'The Police'; dark blue or light blue vinyl) | 10 |
| 79 | A&M AMS 7381 | Can't Stand Losing You/Dead End Job (p/s, reissue, red, yellow, green or white vinyl) | 10 |
| 79 | A&M AMS 7381 | Can't Stand Losing You/Dead End Job (p/s, mispressed B-side, plays "No Time This Time") | 20 |
| 79 | AMSP 7474 | Message In A Bottle (Test pressing of unreleased 12") | 700 |
| 79 | Illegal IL 001 | Fall Out/Nothing Achieving (reissue, various label designs, green/black p/s) | 5 |
| 79 | Illegal IL 001 | Fall Out/Nothing Achieving (reissue, various label designs, purple/blue p/s) | 15 |
| 79 | Illegal IL 001 | Fall Out/Nothing Achieving (reissue, various label designs, black & orange p/s) | 30 |
| 80 | A&M AMPP 6001 | POLICE PACK (6 x 7" printed foldout PVC pack [AMS 7348, 7381, 7402, 7474 & 7494] & "The Bed's Too Big Without You"/"Truth Hits Everybody" [AMPP 6001/E]; on blue vinyl with 6 inserts) | 25 |
| 80 | A&M SAMP 5 | SIX-TRACK RADIO SAMPLER (custom p/s, promo radio sampler) | 15 |
| 80 | A&M AMS 7564 | Don't Stand So Close To Me/Friends (poster p/s) | 7 |
| 81 | A&M AMS 8194 | Spirits (In The Material World)/Low Life (poster p/s, with badge) | 8 |
| 83 | A&M AM 117 | Every Breath You Take/Murder By Numbers (p/s, with free badge) | 5 |
| 83 | A&M AM 117/AM 01 | Every Breath You Take/Murder By Numbers//Truth Hits Everybody/ Man In A Suitcase (double pack, gatefold) | 30 |
| 83 | A&M AMSP 117 | Every Breath You Take/Murder By Numbers (picture disc) | 10 |
| 83 | A&M AMP 127 | Wrapped Around Your Finger/Someone To Talk To (Andy Summers or Stewart Copeland picture disc, 1,000 each) | 10 |
| 78 | A&M AMLH 68502 | OUTLANDOS D'AMOUR (LP, blue vinyl) | 25 |

*(see also Sting, Radio Actors, Zoot Money's Big Roll Band, Last Exit, Newcastle Big Band, Eberhard Schoener)*

### POLIPHONY
| | | | |
|---|---|---|---|
| 73 | Zella JHLPS 136 | POLIPHONY (LP, private pressing) | 150 |

### POLITICIANS (1)
| | | | |
|---|---|---|---|
| 72 | Hot Wax HWX 114 | Love Machine/Free Your Mind | 15 |
| 72 | Hot Wax SHW 5007 | THE POLITICIANS FEATURING MCKINLEY JACKSON (LP) | 30 |

### POLITICIANS (2)
| | | | |
|---|---|---|---|
| 79 | Political PEP 1 | EP: Street Signs/Time Is Tight/Go Away/Fly With Me (p/s, 500 only) | 100 |

### FRANK POLK
| | | | |
|---|---|---|---|
| 65 | Capitol CL 15389 | Trying To Keep Up With The Joneses/Welcome Home, Baby | 60 |
| 65 | Capitol CL 15389 | Trying To Keep Up With The Joneses/Welcome Home, Baby (DJ copy) | 125 |

### RAY POLLARD
| | | | |
|---|---|---|---|
| 65 | United Artists UP 1111 | The Drifter/Let Him Go (And Let Me Love You) | 200 |
| 65 | United Artists UP 1111 | The Drifter/Let Him Go (And Let Me Love You) (DJ Copy) | 300 |
| 66 | United Artists UP 1133 | It's A Sad Thing/All The Things You Are | 100 |
| 66 | United Artists UP 1133 | It's A Sad Thing/All The Things You Are (DJ Copy) | 200 |

*(see also Wanderers)*

### POLLCATS
| | | | |
|---|---|---|---|
| 90 | Community Charge AXT 1 | Poll Tax Blues/Poll Tax Blues (same track both sides, p/s) | 10 |

*(see also Steve Marriott)*

### POLYGON WINDOW
| | | | |
|---|---|---|---|
| 93 | Warp WARP 33 | QUOTH (12" EP, clear vinyl) | 18 |

| 92 | Warp WARP LP 7 | SURFING ON SINE WAVES (2-LP) | 40 |
| 92 | Warp WARP LP 7LTD | SURFING ON SINE WAVES (LP, clear vinyl) | 60 |

*(see also Aphex Twin)*

## POLYPHEMUS

| 93 | BB 212 | Masses Of Tiny Dots/Fire Breathing Annabella (p/s) | 10 |
| 95 | Beggars Banquet BBQ 57CD | Stonecutter (p/s) | 8 |
| 95 | Acme AC 8010LP | SCRAPBOOK OF MADNESS (LP, reissue with insert, 500 only) | 18 |
| 95 | Acme AC 8016LP | STONEHOUSE (LP, gatefold sleeve, 700 only) | 18 |

## POLYPHONIC SPREE

| 02 | 679 679LO14 | ORCHESTRAL: Light And Day/Soldier Girl (p/s, 500 only) | 12 |
| 02 | Good Records 679L011TLP | BEGINNING STAGES OF (2-LP) | 20 |

## POMPHEY

| 72 | Green Door GD 4029 | Jamaica Skank/JOHNNY MOORE: Bing Comes To Town | 10 |

## PONI-TAILS

| 58 | HMV POP 516 | Born Too Late/Come On Joey, Dance With Me (as Pony-Tails) | 10 |
| 58 | HMV POP 558 | Close Friends/Seven Minutes In Heaven | 10 |
| 59 | HMV POP 596 | Early To Bed/Father Time | 10 |
| 59 | HMV POP 644 | Moody/Oom Pah Polka | 10 |
| 59 | HMV POP 663 | I'll Be Seeing You/I'll Keep Tryin' | 15 |
| 58 | HMV 7EG 8427 | THE PONI-TAILS (EP) | 125 |

## JEAN-LUC PONTY

| 69 | Liberty LBL/LBS 83262 | ELECTRIC CONNECTION (LP) | 20 |
| 70 | Liberty LBL/LBS 83375 | KING KONG (LP) | 20 |

*(see also Frank Zappa)*

## PONY

| 73 | Pye 7N 25663 | It's Gonna Be So Easy/Til I Met You | 25 |

## POODLES

| 75 | Priivate Stock PVT 9 | Chicago Box Car (Boston Back)/Love And Sorrow (no p/s) | 5 |

## POOGY

| 74 | EMI EMI 2136 | She Looked Me In The Eye (I Gave Her My Life)/Morris And His Turtle | 8 |

## POOH

| 72 | CBS 7930 | I'll Close The Door Behind Me/The Suitcase | 20 |

## POOH STICKS

| 88 | Fierce FRIGHT 011 | On Tape (p/s, 1-sided, etched) | 40 |
| 88 | Fierce FRIGHT 011 | On Tape (p/s, with unetched B-side) | 35 |
| 88 | Fierce FRIGHT 021 | 1-2-3 Red Light (p/s, 1-sided) | 20 |
| 88 | Fierce FRIGHT 023 | Heartbreak (1-sided, etched B-side, hand-coloured promo p/s, with insert) | 40 |
| 88 | Fierce FRIGHT 021-025 | FIERCE BOX SET (5 x 1-sided etched discs, hand-coloured labels, with insert) | 50 |
| 88 | Fierce FRIGHT 028 | HEROES AND VILLAINS (LP, with inner) | 18 |
| 89 | Fierce FRIGHT 034 | Dying For It (p/s, sold at U.L.U. gig, 300 only, signed) | 25 |
| 89 | Fierce FRIGHT 034 | Dying For It (p/s, sold at U.L.U. gig, 300 only, unsigned) | 15 |
| 89 | Fierce FRIGHT 034 | Dying For It (1-sided, different p/s to above) | 15 |
| 89 | Woosh WOOSH 007/WOOSH 6 | Hard On Love (yellow flexi with Pooh Sticks fanzine)//GROOVE FARM: Heaven Is Blue/ESMERALDA'S KITE: Vampire girl (red flexi) (with Woosh fanzine 3) | 12 |
| 92 | Fierce/BMG FRIGHT 42 | Million Seller (1-sided) | 6 |
| 89 | 53rd & 3rd AGAMC 5 | ORGASM (LP, pink vinyl with insert for export) | 25 |
| 89 | Fierce FRIGHT 025 | THE POOH STICKS (mini-LP, with inner, black & white sleeve, 1-sided, side 2 etched) | 20 |
| 89 | Fierce FRIGHT 035 | TRADE MARK OF QUALITY (LP, mail-order only, plain stickered sleeve with insert, numbered) | 18 |

*(see also Dumb Angels)*

## BRIAN POOLE

| 66 | Decca F 12402 | Hey Girl/Please Be Mine | 10 |
| 66 | CBS 202349 | Everything I Touch Turns To Tears/I Need Her Tonight | 22 |
| 67 | CBS 202661 | That Reminds Me Baby/Tomorrow Never Comes | 6 |
| 67 | CBS 3005 | Just How Loud/The Other Side Of The Sky | 20 |
| 69 | President PT 239 | Send Her To Me/Pretty In The City (as Brian Poole & Seychelles) | 5 |
| 69 | President PT 264 | What Do Women Most Desire/Treat Her Like A Woman (with Seychelles) | 5 |
| 75 | Pinnacle P 8407 | Satisfied/Red Leather (with Carousel) | 6 |
| 83 | Outlook OUT 100K | Do You Love Me/Twist And Shout/Time And Tide (with Tramline) | 6 |

*(see also Brian Poole & Tremeloes)*

## BRIAN POOLE & TREMELOES

| 62 | Decca F 11455 | Twist Little Sister/Lost Love (some with 'Trimiloes' on label) | 15 |
| 62 | Decca F 11515 | That Ain't Right/Blue | 12 |
| 63 | Decca F 11567 | A Very Good Year For Girls/Meet Me Where We Used Meet | 10 |
| 63 | Decca F 11616 | Keep On Dancing/Run Back Home | 10 |
| 63 | Decca F 11694 | Twist And Shout/We Know | 6 |
| 63 | Decca F 11739 | Do You Love Me/Why Can't You Love Me | 5 |
| 63 | Decca F 11771 | I Can Dance/Are You Loving Me At All | 6 |
| 64 | Decca F 11823 | Candy Man/I Wish I Could Dance | 6 |
| 64 | Decca F 11951 | Twelve Steps To Love/Don't Cry | 6 |
| 65 | Decca F 12124 | After A While/You Know | 6 |
| 65 | Decca F 12197 | I Want Candy/Love Me Baby | 10 |
| 65 | Decca F 12274 | Good Lovin'/Could It Be You | 6 |
| 64 | Decca DFE 8566 | BRIAN POOLE AND THE TREMELOES (EP) | 15 |
| 65 | Decca DFE 8610 | BRIAN POOLE AND THE TREMELOES (EP) | 15 |
| 63 | Ace of Clubs ACL 1146 | BIG BIG HITS OF '62 (LP) | 15 |
| 63 | Decca LK 4550 | TWIST AND SHOUT WITH BRIAN POOLE AND THE TREMELOES (LP) | 25 |
| 65 | Decca LK 4685 | IT'S ABOUT TIME (LP) | 25 |

# Lou & LAURA POOLE

*(see also Brian Poole, Tremeloes)*

**LOU & LAURA POOLE**
72　Jay Boy BOY 63　　　　Only You And I Know/Look At Me ................................................................. 15

**POOR SOULS**
65　Decca F 12183　　　　When My Baby Cries/My Baby She's Not There ............................................. 25
66　Alp ALP 595 004　　　Love Me/Please Don't Change Your Mind..................................................... 50

**POOR THINGS**
66　CBS 202431　　　　　We Trust In A Better Way Of Life/Danny Boy .............................................. 50

**POORBOYS**
82　Ace SW 81　　　　　　MOVE BABY MOVE EP (p/s) ............................................................................ 8

**GROOVY JOE POOVEY**
70　Injun 100　　　　　　Ten Long Fingers On The 88 Keys/Thrill Of Love ........................................ 15
71　Injun 101　　　　　　Move Around/BILL REEDER: Till I Waltz Again With You ........................... 15
81　President PR 497　　　Lightning From The Sky/You Are My Sunshine ............................................ 10

**IGGY POP**
77　RCA PB 9093　　　　　China Girl/Baby ................................................................................................ 5
77　RCA PB 9160　　　　　Success/The Passenger .................................................................................... 5
77　RCA PB 9160　　　　　Some Weird Sin/The Passenger ...................................................................... 5
78　RCA PB 9213　　　　　I Got A Right/Sixteen (some in b/w picture sleeve) .................................... 10
78　Radar ADA 4　　　　　Kill City (with James Williamson)/I Got Nothin' (p/s) ................................. 5
79　Arista ARIST 255　　　I'm Bored/African Man ................................................................................... 5
79　Arista ARIST 274　　　Five Foot One/Pretty Flamingo ...................................................................... 5
80　Arista ARIST 327　　　Loco Mosquito/Take Care Of Me (p/s) ......................................................... 5
81　Arista ARIST 407　　　Bang Bang/Sea Of Love .................................................................................. 5
73　CBS 65586　　　　　　RAW POWER (LP, with inner, orange label, as Iggy & Stooges) ............... 40
78　Radar RAD 2　　　　　KILL CITY (LP, as Iggy Pop & James Williamson).................................... 15
77　RCA PL12275　　　　　THE IDIOT (LP, 1st pressing, orange labels) ............................................... 30
77　RCA PL12488　　　　　LUST FOR LIFE (LP, 1st pressing, orange label) ......................................... 25
77　RCA PL 12796　　　　TV EYE - 1977 LIVE (LP) ................................................................................. 15
79　Arista SPART 1092　　NEW VALUES (LP) ............................................................................................ 15
81　RCA Int. INTS 5172　　THE IDIOT (LP, reissue, green labels) ......................................................... 15
81　RCA Int. INTS 5114　　LUST FOR LIFE (LP, reissue, green labels) ................................................. 15
93　Virgin VUSLP 64　　　AMERICAN CAESAR (2-LP) ............................................................................ 25
96　Virgin VUSLP 102　　　NAUGHTY LITTLE DOGGIE (LP) .................................................................... 25
*(see also Stooges)*

**POP WILL EAT ITSELF**
86　Desperate SRT 1　　　THE POPPIES SAY GRRrrr! (EP in stamped brown paper bag, stamped white labels)...... 20
87　Chapter 22 LCHAP 16　Beaver Patrol/Bubbles (p/s, pink vinyl, autographed)............................... 5

**POPCORNS**
63　Columbia DB 4968　　Zero Zero/Chinese Twist................................................................................ 15

**TIM POPE**
84　Fiction FICS 21　　　　I Want To Be A Tree/The Double Crossing Of Two Faced Fred (p/s) ........ 15
84　Fiction FICSX 21　　　I Want To Be A Tree/(Elephant) Song/The Double Crossing Of Two Faced Fred (12",
　　　　　　　　　　　　p/s) ................................................................................................................... 25
*(see also Cure)*

**POP GROUP**
79　Radar ADA 29　　　　She Is Beyond Good And Evil/3.38 (p/s) ..................................................... 10
79　Radar ADA 1229　　　She Is Beyond Good And Evil/3.38 (12", p/s) ............................................. 20
79　Rough Trade RT 023　We Are All Prostitutes/Amnesty International Report On British Army Torture Of Irish
　　　　　　　　　　　　Prisoners (p/s) .............................................................................................. 18
80　Rough Trade RT 039/ Y Y1　Where There's A Will There's A Way/SLITS: In The Beginning There Was Rhythm (p/s). 12
79　Radar RAD 20　　　　Y (LP, with foldout colour poster) ................................................................ 50
80　Rough Trade ROUGH 9　FOR HOW MUCH LONGER DO WE TOLERATE MASS MURDER? (LP, with 4 black-and-
　　　　　　　　　　　　white posters)................................................................................................. 40
80　Y/Rough Trade ROUGH 12　WE ARE TIME (LP, plain black sleeve)......................................................... 20
*(see also Slits)*

**ANDRE POPP**
74　Polydor 2383 278　　　MY MOVIE DREAMS (LP) ................................................................................ 15

**FRANK POPP ENSEMBLE**
01　Blow Up BU026　　　　Hip Teens Don't Wear Blue Jeans/The Catwalk ......................................... 30
03　Expansion SCEX 7　　Breakaway/You've Been Gone Too Long ......................................................... 5

**POPPIES**
66　Columbia DB 7879　　Lullaby Of Love/I Wonder Why ..................................................................... 30

**KEITH POPPIN**
73　Randy's RAN 531　　　Kick The Bucket/I'm A Man Of My Word ...................................................... 6
75　Sunshot SS001　　　　Envious/Fed Up ............................................................................................... 8
76　Sunshot SS004　　　　Who Are You/Dub Heavier Than Lead .......................................................... 15
76　Sunshot SS006　　　　It's Too Late/Part 2 ......................................................................................... 8
76　Sunshot SS012　　　　Someday Girl/Version ..................................................................................... 8
76　Mango 1002　　　　　Time Slipping Away/King Tubby's Time ...................................................... 12
79　JB Music JBD 006　　　Hold Not Thy Peace/Birdie (12").................................................................. 50

**POPPY FAMILY**
69　Decca F 22976　　　　Which Way You Going Billy/Endless Sleep .................................................... 8
70　Decca F13092　　　　That's Where It Went Wrong/Shadows On The Wall.................................. 10
71　Decca F 13132　　　　I Was Wondering/Where Evil Grows............................................................. 6

**POPPYHEADS**
88　Sha La La Ba Ba Ba Ba 4　POSTCARD FOR FLOSSY (EP, 1-sided flexidisc, p/s in poly bag) ................ 10

| 88 | Sarah SARAH 006 | Cremation Town/Pictures You Weave/Dreamboat (foldaround p/s with large poster in poly bag) .................... 40 |

## POP RIVETS
| 79 | M.T. Sounds HEP 001 | BACK FROM NOWHERE (EP, no p/s) .................... 30 |
| 79 | M.T. Sounds HEP 002 | BACK FROM NOWHERE (EP, split single with SULPHATE, no p/s) .................... 30 |
| 79 | Hypocrite JIM 1 | FUN IN THE U.K. (EP, no p/s, double pack) .................... 30 |
| 02 | (No label) HAD 1 | Kray Twins/BUFFS: All My Feelings Denied (no p/s, 450 free with Chatham's Burning fanzine) .................... 25 |
| 02 | (No label) HAD 01 | Kray Twins/BUFFS: All MY Feelings Denied (no p/s, without Chatham's Burning fanzine) .................... 10 |
| 79 | Hypocrite HIP 007 | THE POP RIVETS GREATEST HITS (LP, printed sleeve, stamped white labels) .................... 50 |
| 79 | Hypocrite HIP 007 | THE POP RIVETS GREATEST HITS (LP, title sleeve with Pop Rivets printed repeatedly across white sleeve, stamped white labels, 50 only) .................... 100 |
| 79 | Hypocrite HIP-O | EMPTY SOUNDS FROM ANARCHY RANCH (LP, coloured back, stamped labels) .................... 25 |
| 80 | Hypocrite HIP 007 | THE POP RIVETS GREATEST HITS (LP, screen printed sleeve, 2 inserts, 50 only) .................... 150 |
| 89 | Hangman HANG 27 UP | ORIGINAL FIRST ALBUM!!! (LP) .................... 20 |
| 90 | Hangman HANG 35 UP | LIVE IN GERMANY '79 (LP) .................... 15 |
| 90s | Damaged Goods DAMGOOD 142 | CHATHAM'S BURNING (LP, brown vinyl) .................... 20 |

*(see also Milkshakes)*

## POPSICLES
| 65 | Vocalion VH 9243 | I Don't Want To Be Your Baby Anymore/Baby I Miss You .................... 50 |

*(see also Ellie Greenwich, Raindrops)*

## POPTICIANS
| 84 | Off The Kerb DAD 1 | Mobile Home/Spare Pear .................... 5 |

## POP TOPS
| 72 | A&M AMS 7001 | Suzanne Suzanne/Oh Lord Why Lord .................... 15 |
| 69 | Major MInor MM 594 | That Woman/The Man I m Today (Adagio Cardinal) .................... 10 |

## POPULAR 5
| 68 | Minit MLF 11011 | I'm A Lovemaker/Little Bitty Pretty One .................... 15 |

## POPULAR MECHANICS
| 87 | Ark DOVE 5 | INSECT CULTURE (LP) .................... 50 |

## POP WORKSHOP
| 68 | Page One POF 091 | Fairyland/When My Little Girl Is Happy .................... 30 |
| 69 | Page One POF 129 | Punch And Judy Man/Love Is A One Way Highway .................... 10 |

## PORCUPINE TREE
| 92 | Delerium DELEC EP 010 | VOYAGE 34 (12" EP) .................... 50 |
| 90 | Private (No Cat. No.) | LOVE, DEATH AND MUSSOLINI (EP, 10 copies, plain black cassette with 3 page booklet) .................... 400 |
| 92 | Delerium DELEC EP 007 | VOYAGE 34 (Astralasia Remix) (12" EP) .................... 25 |
| 92 | Delerium DELECD EP 010 | VOYAGE 34 (CD EP, first 100 with blue not green artwork) .................... 60 |
| 94 | Delerium DELEC EP 032 | Stars Die/Moonloop (12", p/s) .................... 15 |
| 96 | Delerium DELEC EP 049 | WAITING (EP 12") .................... 25 |
| 98 | Chromatic CHR 003 | METANOIA (EP, 2 x 10", 1,000 only) .................... 60 |
| 99 | K-Scope/Snapper SMAS 103 | Piano Lessons/Oceans Have No Memory (p/s, 1,000 copies) .................... 18 |
| 99 | K-Scope/Snapper SMAS 107 | Stranger By The Minute/Hallogallo (p/s, 1,000 only) .................... 18 |
| 99 | K-Scope/Snapper SMAS 110 | Pure Narcotic/Nine Cats - Acoustic (p/s) .................... 15 |
| 00 | K-Scope/Snapper SMAS 120 | Shesmovedon/Novak (p/s, 1000 only) .................... 12 |
| 00 | K-Scope/Snapper SMAS 7111 | 4 Chords That Made A Million/Orchidia (p/s, 1,000 only) .................... 15 |
| 01 | Delerium (No Cat. No.) | TRANSMISSION IV - MOONLOOP EP (Free to Transmission Subscribers, 500 only) .................... 80 |
| 89 | Delerium DELC 0002 | TARQUIN'S SEAWEED FARM (cassette, 1st issue, around 50 only) .................... 300 |
| 92 | Delerium DELEC 008 | ON THE SUNDAY OF LIFE (2-LP, gatefold sleeve, 1,000 only) .................... 80 |
| 92 | Delerium DELEC CD 008 | ON THE SUNDAY OF LIFE (CD) .................... 25 |
| 93 | Delerium DELEC 020 | UP THE DOWNSTAIR (LP) .................... 60 |
| 94 | Delerium DELEC PROMO CASS 5 | SPIRAL CIRCUS (cassette give away free with Transmission newsletter) .................... 150 |
| 94 | Magic Gnome MG 4299325 | YELLOW HEADGROW DREAMSCAPE (CD, 2,500 only) .................... 100 |
| 95 | Delerium DELECLP 028 | THE SKY MOVES SIDEWAYS (LP, 2,000 on blue vinyl with poster) .................... 60 |
| 96 | Delerium DELECLP 045 | SIGNIFY (double LP, gatefold sleeve) .................... 60 |
| 97 | Chromatic CHR 002 | SPIRAL CIRCUS (LP, 500 only) .................... 150 |
| 99 | Gates Of Dawn GOD 005 | YELLOW HEDGEROW DREAMSCAPE (2-LP reissue, gold vinyl) .................... 40 |
| 01 | K-Scope/Snapper SMACD840 | RECORDINGS (CD, numbered slipcase, 20,000 only) .................... 50 |
| 05 | Gates Of Dawn GOD 009 | DEADWING (2-LP, black vinyl with poster) .................... 70 |
| 06 | Delerium DELECLP999 | MOONLOOP (LP, 500 black vinyl in screen printed blue vinyl bag) .................... 50 |
| 06 | Delerium DELECLP 999 | MOONLOOP (LP, 99 clear vinyl in screen printed blue vinyl bag) .................... 50 |
| 06 | Delerium DELECLP 999 | MOONLOOP (LP, 500 white vinyl in screen printed blue vinyl bag) .................... 30 |
| 06 | Gates Of Dawn GOD 011 | STUPID DREAM (2-LP, black/grey 'marbled' vinyl) .................... 70 |
| 08 | Kscope KSCOPE 802 | UP THE DOWNSTAIR (2-LP, reissue) .................... 20 |
| 07 | Tonefloat TF40 | FEAR OF A BLANK PLANET (2-LP, gatefold) .................... 20 |
| 07 | Tonefloat TF40 | FEAR OF A BLANK PLANET (2-LP, 1000 only special edition with poster, booklet and slipcase) .................... 40 |

*(see also No Man, Steve Wilson)*

## PORK DUKES
| 77 | Wood WOOD 9 | Bend And Flush/Throbbing Gristle (p/s) .................... 10 |
| 77 | Wood BRANCH 9 | Making Bacon/Tight Pussy (12", p/s, yellow vinyl) .................... 12 |
| 78 | Wood Standard WOOD 56 | Telephone Masturbator/Melody Makers (p/s) .................... 10 |
| 94 | Damaged Goods FNARR8 | THE FILTHY NASTY PORK DUKES EP .................... 6 |
| 78 | Wood PORK 001 | THE PORK DUKES (LP, pink vinyl with warning sticker & postcard) .................... 25 |
| 80 | Wood PORK 002 | PIG OUT OF HELL (LP) .................... 25 |

MINT VALUE £

## PORNO CASSETTES
82    Heresy Records DOC 1    You're Face, A Fucking Disgrace/Dead End Yobs.................................... 150

## PORNO FOR PYROS
93    Warner Bros. 9362 45228-1    PORNO FOR PYROS (LP) ............................................................... 20

## DAVID PORTER
70    Stax STAX 155    One Part - Two Parts/Can't I See You When I Want To ........................... 8
70    Stax SXATS 1034    GRITTY, GROOVY AND GETTIN' IT (LP) ........................................ 15
71    Stax STX 1030    VICTIM OF THE JOKE (LP) ........................................................... 20
71    Stax 2362 006    INTO A REAL THING (LP) ............................................................. 15

## NOLAN PORTER
72    Probe PRO 580    If I Could Only Be Sure/Work It Out In The Morning ........................... 75
72    Probe PRO 580    If I Could Only Be Sure/Work It Out In The Morning (DJ copy) ............ 100
72    Probe SPB 1067    NOLAN (LP) .............................................................................. 25

## ROBIE PORTER
66    MGM 1306    Here In My Arms/I've Often Wondered ............................................... 6
66    MGM 1313    Either Way I Lose/That's The Way Love Goes..................................... 20

## PORTER CUNNINGHAM
72    Folk Heritage FHR 027    OBSERVATIONS (LP)................................................ 100

## PORTION CONTROL
82    In Phaze POR CON 006    Surface And Be Seen/Spinola (Blotch)/Terror Leads To Better Days/Simple As ABC/
     Monstrous Bulk/He Is A Barbarian (12" p/s, with plastic outer sleeve) ...................... 40
83    Illuminated ILL 2612    Raise The Pulse/Collapse/Bite My Head ................................... 8
83    Illuminated ILL 2612    Raise The Pulse/Collapse/Bite My Head (12", p/s) .................. 10
85    Rhythmic/Havoc 7RMIC 7    The Great Divide/Totall Recall (p/s)................................... 5
85    Rhythmic/Havoc 12RMICX 7    The Great Divide (Julian Mendelsohn Remix)/Divided/Bolt It Down (12", p/s) ............ 12
81    In Phaze PORCON 002    DINING ON THE FLESH (cassette box set with free flexi 7") ........ 70
81    In Phaze PORCON 002    GAINING MOMENTUM (cassette) ............................................ 40
82    In Phaze CP 007    I STAGGERED MENTALLY (LP) ....................................................... 50
82    In Phase NCN    WITH MIXED EMOTION (cassette) ...................................................... 40
82    Third Mind TMT 07    SHOT IN THE BELLY (cassette) ................................................ 40
83    In Phaze EZ 2    HIT THE PULSE (mini-LP, 45/33rpm)................................................. 18
84    Illuminated JAMS 44    STEP FORWARD (LP)............................................................ 12
85    In Phaze PHA 5    SIMULATE SENSUAL (LP, clear vinyl, PVC sleeve with insert) ............... 20

## PORTISHEAD
94    Go Beat GODX 120    Glory Box/Toy Box/Scorn/Sheared Box (12", p/s)..................... 12
11    XL XLT 557    Chase The Tear/Doldrums Reimagine (12", signed)................................. 30
94    Go Beat 828 522    DUMMY (LP, inner)................................................................ 30
97    Go Beat 314 539189-1    PORTISHEAD (2-LP)............................................................ 30
97    Go Beat 539189-1    PORTISHEAD (LP, gloss sleeve)................................................... 30
98    Go Beat 559 424-1    ROSELAND NYC LIVE (2-LP, with poster)..................................... 20
99    Simply Vinyl SVLP 115    PORTISHEAD (2-LP, reissue).............................................. 18
00    Simply Vinyl SVLP 162    DUMMY (LP, reissue)........................................................ 18
08    Island 1766390    THIRD (2-LP, etched 12", print, with USB stick, numbered) ................. 25
*(see also Jimi Entley Sound, Beak>)*

## PORTOBELLO EXPLOSION
69    Carnaby CNS 4001    We Can Fly/Hot Smoke And Sasafrass (label credits Portebello Explosion)................... 30
*(see also Mirage, Jawbone, Spencer Davis Group)*

## PORTRAIT
71    Pye 7N 45043    Tokaido Lines/Cuddle Me Closer ....................................................... 6

## PORTRAIT OF DAN TRACY
94    Direct Lite 726    Silly Girl/I Know Where Syd Barrett Lives/Remember Bridget Riley A Picture Of Dorian
     Grey (p/s)........................................................................................ 10

## PORTSMOUTH FOOTBALL PLAYERS
70s   Solent SS 046    Sing Along With Pompey/Pompey City With A Heart.............................. 8

## PORTSMOUTH SINFONIA
81    Springtime WIP 6736    Classical Muddly/Hallelujah Chorus ...................................... 5
73    Transatlantic TRA 275    PLAY THE POPULAR CLASSICS (LP) ...................................... 35
74    Transatlantic TRA 285    HALLELUJAH (LP) ........................................................... 25
79    Philips 9109 231    20 CLASSIC ROCK CLASSICS (LP) ............................................. 30

## PORTWAY PEDLARS
84    Greenwich Village GVR 229    IN GREENWOOD SHADES (LP)........................................ 15

## SANDY POSEY
66    MGM MGM 1321    Born A Woman/Caution To The Wind ............................................... 5
66    MGM MGM 1330    Single Girl/Blue Is My Best Colour ............................................... 6
67    MGM MGM 1335    What A Woman In Love Won't Do/Shattered ..................................... 8
67    MGM MGM 1342    I Take It Back/The Boy I Love .................................................... 8
67    MGM MGM 1364    Are You Never Coming Home/I Can Show You How To Live ..................... 8
67    MGM MGM-C(S) 8035    BORN A WOMAN (LP) ...................................................... 30
67    MGM MGM-C(S) 8042    SINGLE GIRL (LP) .......................................................... 25
68    MGM MGM-C(S) 8051    SANDY POSEY (LP) ......................................................... 25
68    MGM MGM-C 8060    THE BEST OF SANDY POSEY (LP, original with blue label) ............... 20
68    MGM MGM-C(S) 8073    LOOKING AT YOU (LP)...................................................... 25

## POSH
81    Marathon RUN 1    Letter To Linda/Racey Tracey (p/s)............................................... 10

## POSITIVE SIGNALS
80    Yob YOB 001    Media Man/Only For A Day/STRAND: Here Today Gone Tomorrow/Changing World
     (split EP, p/s)....................................................................................... 15

## POSSESSED
| | | | |
|---|---|---|---|
| 86 | Under One Flag FLAG 3 | BEYOND THE GATES (LP) | 15 |
| 87 | Under One Flag M FLAG 16 | THE EYES OF HORROR EP (12", p/s) | 15 |

## HOWIE POST & SWIFTIES
| | | | |
|---|---|---|---|
| 63 | Fontana TF 421 | Tom Swift/The Elephant | 10 |

## POST MORTEM
| | | | |
|---|---|---|---|
| 83 | Regime FM 006 | BETER OFF DEAD (EP) | 25 |

## ADRIENNE POSTER/POSTA
| | | | |
|---|---|---|---|
| 63 | Oriole CB 1890 | Only Fifteen/There's Nothing You Can Do About That | 30 |
| 63 | Decca F 11797 | Only Fifteen/There's Nothing You Can Do About That (reissue) | 20 |
| 64 | Decca F 11864 | Shang A Doo Lang/When A Girl Really Loves You | 25 |
| 65 | Decca F 12079 | He Doesn't Love Me/The Way You Do The Things You Do | 25 |
| 65 | Decca F 12181 | The Winds That Blow/Back Street Girl | 25 |
| 66 | Decca F 12329 | Something Beautiful/So Glad You're Mine | 35 |
| 66 | Decca F 12455 | They Long To Be Close To You/How Can I Hurt You (as Adrienne Posta) | 20 |
| 73 | DJM DJS 286 | Dog Song/Express Yourself | 12 |

## POTATOES
| | | | |
|---|---|---|---|
| 66 | Fontana TF 756 | The Bend/Bend Ahead | 7 |

## POTENTIAL BAD BOY
| | | | |
|---|---|---|---|
| 06 | Sublogic/Ninety-Two Retro SLVR 001/9T2RX | Everyday Child (1-sided 12", 100 only, stamped and hand-numbered labels) | 40 |

## POTENTIAL THREAT
| | | | |
|---|---|---|---|
| 82 | Out Of Town HOOT 7 | WHAT'S SO GREAT BRITAIN! (EP) | 30 |
| 84 | Children Of The Revolution COR 6 | Brainwashed/Turn A Blind Eye/A Cry For Help/Conflict (p/s) | 15 |
| 80s | Mortarhate MORT 24 | DEMAND AN ALTERNATIVE (LP) | 30 |

## KEITH POTGER
| | | | |
|---|---|---|---|
| 69 | Mercury MF 1073 | The World Would Never Turn Again/Santa Marie (in p/s) | 8 |
| 69 | Mercury MF 1073 | The World Would Never Turn Again/Santa Marie | 6 |

*(see also Seekers, Judith Durham)*

## POTLIQUOR
| | | | |
|---|---|---|---|
| 72 | Janus 6146 011 | Cheer/Chatanooga | 8 |
| 70 | Dawn DNLS 3016 | FIRST TASTE (LP, withdrawn) | 90 |
| 72 | Janus 6310 202 | LEVEE BLUES (LP) | 30 |

## PHIL POTTER
| | | | |
|---|---|---|---|
| 76 | Genesis GEN 10 | MY SONG IS LOVE UNKNOWN (LP) | 20 |
| 79 | Dove DOVE 61 | THE RESTORER (LP) | 15 |

## POTTERS
| | | | |
|---|---|---|---|
| 72 | Trent JT 100 | We'll Be With You/Theme For A Team | 20 |

## POTTING SHEDS
| | | | |
|---|---|---|---|
| 90 | Mad Cat BSE 002 | Second Best/Shape Out | 15 |
| 92 | Mad Cat BSE 005 | GOLDFISH MEMORY EP (12") | 15 |

## POUND HOUNDS
| | | | |
|---|---|---|---|
| 55 | Brunswick 05484 | Home Sweet Home/MELLOMEN: Lady | 5 |

*(see also Peggy Lee)*

## POUND OF FLESH
| | | | |
|---|---|---|---|
| 75 | Creole CR 106 | Funky March/Part 2 | 10 |

## ALLEN POUND'S GET RICH
| | | | |
|---|---|---|---|
| 66 | Parlophone R 5532 | Searchin' In The Wilderness/Hey You (rare stock copy) | 1000 |
| 66 | Parlophone R 5532 | Searchin' In The Wilderness/Hey You (more common demo) | 600 |

## FRANCK POURCEL
| | | | |
|---|---|---|---|
| 59 | HMV POP 622 | Only You/Rainy Night In Paris | 8 |

## BUD POWELL (TRIO)
| | | | |
|---|---|---|---|
| 55 | Vogue EPV 1030 | BUD POWELL TRIO (EP) | 15 |
| 55 | Vogue EPV 1033 | BUD POWELL'S MODERNISTS (EP) | 15 |
| 55 | Vogue EPV 1036 | BUD POWELL TRIO (EP) | 15 |
| 55 | Columbia Clef SEB 10013 | BUD POWELL (EP) | 15 |
| 57 | Columbia Clef SEB 10074 | GENIUS OF BUD POWELL (EP) | 15 |
| 58 | Columbia Clef SEB 10094 | GENIUS OF BUD POWELL NO. 2 (EP) | 15 |
| 52 | Vogue LDE 010 | THE BUD POWELL TRIO (10" LP) | 20 |
| 54 | Vogue LDE 053 | JAZZ AT THE MASSEY HALL VOL. 2 (10" LP) | 20 |
| 56 | Columbia Clef 33C 9016 | BUD POWELL TRIO (10" LP) | 25 |
| 57 | Columbia Clef 33CX 10069 | JAZZ ORIGINAL (LP) | 30 |
| 58 | Columbia Clef 33CX 10123 | BLUES FOR BUD (LP) | 30 |
| 59 | HMV CLP 1294 | THE LONELY ONE (LP) | 30 |
| 63 | Vogue LAE 558 | THE BUD POWELL TRIO (LP) | 15 |
| 63 | Columbia 33SX 1575 | THE BUD POWELL TRIO FEATURING MAX ROACH (LP) | 25 |
| 64 | Fontana FJL 903 | HOT HOUSE (LP) | 25 |
| 68 | Fontana SFJL 901 | BLUES FOR BOUFFEMONT (LP) | 25 |

## COZY POWELL
| | | | |
|---|---|---|---|
| 73 | Rak RAK 164 | Dance With The Devil/And Then There Was Skin (export copy, European diff p/s) | 10 |
| 73 | Rak 4C 006 94962 | Dance With The Devil/And Then There Was Skin (export issue, p/s, RAK 164 in run out groove, blue or yellow vinyl) | 20 |
| 73 | Rak 4C 006 94962 | Dance With The Devil/And Then There Was Skin (export issue, p/s, RAK 164 in run out groove) | 10 |

*(see also Rainbow, Young Blood, Big Bertha, Ace Kefford Stand, Bedlam, Phenomena, Black Sabbath, Jeff Beck, Whitesnake, Michael Schenker Group, Donovan, Gary Moore, Young & Moody, Brian May, Chick Churchill, Graham Bonnet, Forcefield, Emerson Lake & Powell, Jack Bruce, Plum & Youth, Suzi Quatro)*

MINT VALUE £

## JANE POWELL

| | | |
|---|---|---|
| 54 | Capitol LC 6665 | THREE SAILORS AND A GIRL (10" LP) ........................ 20 |
| 57 | HMV CLP 1131 | JANE POWELL (LP) ............................................. 20 |

*(see also Marilyn Monroe)*

## JIMMY POWELL (& DIMENSIONS)

| | | |
|---|---|---|
| 62 | Decca F 11447 | Sugar Babe (Parts 1 & 2) (solo) .............................. 15 |
| 62 | Decca F 11544 | Tom Hark/Dance Her By Me (solo) ........................... 15 |
| 63 | Decca F 11570 | Remember Them/Everyone But You (solo) .................. 10 |
| 64 | Pye 7N 15663 | That's Alright/I'm Looking For A Woman .................... 8 |
| 64 | Pye 7N 15735 | Sugar Babe/I've Been Watching You (as Jimmy Powell & 5 Dimensions) .. 60 |
| 66 | Strike JH 309 | I Can Go Down/Love Me Right ................................ 20 |
| 67 | Decca F 12664 | Unexpected Mirrors/Time Mends Broken Hearts (with Dimensions) .. 15 |
| 68 | Decca F 12751 | I Just Can't Get Over You/Real Cool (with Dimensions) ..... 10 |
| 68 | Decca F 12793 | Sugar Baby (Parts 1 & 2) ...................................... 20 |

## JUDITH POWELL

| | | |
|---|---|---|
| 67 | RCA RCA 1569 | Greener Days/No Goodbyes .................................... 6 |

## KEITH POWELL (& VALETS)

| | | |
|---|---|---|
| 63 | Columbia DB 7116 | The Answer Is No!/Come On And Join The Party (with Valets) .. 15 |
| 64 | Columbia DB 7229 | Tore Up/You Better Let Him Go (with Valets) .............. 25 |
| 64 | Columbia DB 7366 | I Should Know Better (But I Don't)/Too Much Monkey Business (with Valets) .. 35 |
| 65 | Piccadilly 7N 35235 | People Get Ready/Paradise ................................... 15 |
| 65 | Piccadilly 7N 35249 | Come Home Baby/Beyond The Hill ........................... 15 |
| 66 | Piccadilly 7N 35275 | Goodbye Girl/It Was Easier To Hurt Her .................... 15 |
| 66 | Piccadilly 7N 35300 | Victory/Some People Only .................................... 15 |
| 66 | Piccadilly 7N 35353 | It Keeps Rainin'/Song of The Moon .......................... 20 |

*(see also Move, Carl Wayne & Vikings)*

## KEITH (POWELL) & BILLIE (DAVIES)

| | | |
|---|---|---|
| 66 | Piccadilly 7N 35288 | When You Move, You Lose/Tastes Sour, Don't It? (as Keith & Billie) .. 15 |
| 66 | Piccadilly 7N 35321 | You Don't Know Like I Know/Two Little People ............ 15 |
| 66 | Piccadilly 7N 35340 | Swingin' Tight/That's Really Some Good .................... 15 |

*(see also Keith Powell, Billie Davis)*

## MARILYN POWELL

| | | |
|---|---|---|
| 64 | Fontana TF 448 | All My Loving/After The Party ................................ 7 |
| 65 | Fontana TF 526 | Please Go Away/Where Did I Go Wrong ..................... 40 |
| 65 | Fontana TF 557 | As Long As You Come Back To Me/Go Away ................. 5 |
| 65 | Fontana TF 687 | Showdown/Came The Day ...................................... 5 |
| 68 | CBS 2331 | Something To Hold On To/Kiss Me Again .................... 5 |
| 69 | CBS 4440 | Have Another Dream On Me/Afraid To Love You ........... 5 |

## POWER

| | | |
|---|---|---|
| 82 | Malaco MAL1 | Groovin'/Instrumental ......................................... 8 |

## POWER CUT/CASH CREW

| | | |
|---|---|---|
| 88 | Vinyl Lab VL 004T | Mission Impossible/Microphone Maniac (12") .............. 15 |

## DUFFY POWER

| | | |
|---|---|---|
| 59 | Fontana H 194 | Dream Lover/That's My Little Suzie .......................... 15 |
| 59 | Fontana H 214 | Kissin' Time/Ain't She Sweet ................................. 15 |
| 59 | Fontana H 230 | Starry-Eyed/Prettier Than You ............................... 15 |
| 60 | Fontana H 279 | Whole Lotta Shakin' Goin' On/If I Can Dream .............. 30 |
| 61 | Fontana H 302 | I've Got Nobody/When We're Walking Close ............... 15 |
| 61 | Fontana H 344 | No Other Love/What Now ..................................... 12 |
| 63 | Parlophone R 4992 | It Ain't Necessarily So/If I Get Lucky Someday ............ 12 |
| 63 | Parlophone R 5024 | I Saw Her Standing There (with Graham Bond Quartet)/Farewell Baby .. 40 |
| 63 | Parlophone R 5059 | Hey Girl/Woman Made Trouble ............................... 15 |
| 64 | Parlophone R 5111 | Parchman Farm/Tired, Broke And Busted (with Paramounts) .. 40 |
| 64 | Parlophone R 5169 | Where Am I?/I Don't Care ..................................... 40 |
| 67 | Parlophone R 5631 | Davy O'Brien (Leave That Baby Alone)/July Tree .......... 30 |
| 70 | CBS 5176 | Hell Hound/Hummingbird ..................................... 15 |
| 71 | Epic EPC 7139 | Hummingbird/Hell Hound (reissue) .......................... 6 |
| 73 | GSF GSZ 6 | River/Little Soldiers ........................................... 5 |
| 73 | GSF GSZ 8 | Liberation/Song About Jesus ................................. 5 |
| 71 | Transatlantic TRA 229 | INNOVATIONS (LP) ............................................ 50 |
| 73 | GSF GS 502 | DUFFY POWER (LP) ............................................ 20 |
| 73 | Spark SRLM 2005 | DUFFY POWER (LP) ............................................ 20 |
| 76 | Buk BULP 2010 | POWERHOUSE (LP, revised reissue of GSF GS 502) ....... 15 |

*(see also Alexis Korner, John McLaughlin, Jack Bruce, Graham Bond, Duffy's Nucleus)*

## POWER CUT CREW

| | | |
|---|---|---|
| 88 | PowerCut PC001 | Power Cut 1/African Beats (12") .............................. 30 |

## POWERHOUSE

| | | |
|---|---|---|
| 66 | Decca F 12471 | Chain Gang/Can You Hear Me? ............................... 20 |
| 66 | Decca F 12507 | Raindrops/La Bamba ........................................... 10 |

## POWERLINE

| | | |
|---|---|---|
| 81 | Elite DAZZ 09 | Step One/POWERLINE: Watching You (12") .................. 50 |
| 81 | Elite DAZZ 7 | Journey (6.54)/Double Journey (13.05) (12", stickered die cut sleeve) .. 25 |
| 83 | PLR PLR 1-7 | Watching You (Vocal)/Watching You (Instrumental) ....... 30 |
| 83 | PLR 1-12 | Watching You (Vocal)/Watching You (Instrumental) (12") .. 60 |
| 83 | PLR 2-7 | You The Girl (Vocal)/You The Girl (Instrumental) ......... 30 |
| 83 | PLR 2-12 | You The Girl (Vocal)/You The Girl (Instrumental) (12") ... 75 |

## POWERPACK

| | | |
|---|---|---|
| 66 | CBS 202335 | It Hurts Me So/What You Gonna Do ......................... 50 |

MINT VALUE £

| | | | |
|---|---|---|---|
| 67 | CBS 202551 | I'll Be Anything For You/The Lost Summer | 20 |
| 69 | Polydor 56319 | Hannibal Brooks/Juliet Simkins | 8 |
| 70 | Polydor 2001 077 | Oh Calcutta/Soul Searchin' | 20 |
| 69 | Polydor 583 057 | SOUL CURE (LP) | 60 |

*(see also Procol Harum, Emperor Rosko & Power Pack)*

## POWERPILL
| | | | |
|---|---|---|---|
| 92 | ffrreedom TAB 110 | Pac-Man (Original Edit)/Pac-Man (Mickey Finn's Yum Yum Edit) | 25 |
| 92 | ffrreedom TABX 110 | PAC MAN EP: Powerpill Mix/Ghost Mix/Choci's Hi Score Mix/Mickey Finn's Yum Yum Mix (12", limited edition yellow vinyl) | 30 |
| 92 | ffrreedom TABX 110 | PAC MAN EP: Powerpill Mix/Ghost Mix/Choci's Hi Score Mix/Mickey Finn's Yum Yum Mix (12") | 20 |

*(see also Aphex Twin)*

## JETT POWERS
| | | | |
|---|---|---|---|
| 70 | Liberty LBS 83320 | CALIFORNIA LICENCE (LP) | 40 |

*(see also P.J. Proby)*

## JOEY POWERS
| | | | |
|---|---|---|---|
| 63 | Stateside SS 236 | Midnight Mary/Where Do You Want The World Delivered | 10 |

## POWERS OF BLUE
| | | | |
|---|---|---|---|
| 67 | CBS 62953 | FLIP OUT! (LP) | 20 |

## P.P. & PRIMES
| | | | |
|---|---|---|---|
| 96 | Nice (no cat. no.) | Understanding/STEVIE'S BUZZ (i.e. Buzzcocks): Autumn Stone (promo only) | 10 |

*(see also Primal Scream, P.P. Arnold)*

## PEREZ 'PREZ' PRADO & HIS ORCHESTRA
| | | | |
|---|---|---|---|
| 55 | HMV 7M 295 | Cherry Pink And Apple Blossom White/Maria Elena | 10 |
| 58 | RCA RD 27102 | DILO (LP) | 15 |
| 60 | RCA RD 27046 | LATIN SATIN (LP) | 15 |
| 64 | Parlophone PMC 1226 | A CAT IN LATIN (LP) | 15 |
| 74 | Contour 2870 385 | NOW (LP) | 15 |

## PRAG VEC
| | | | |
|---|---|---|---|
| 78 | Spec SP 001 | Wolf/Cigarettes/Existential/Bits! (p/s) | 12 |
| 79 | Spec SP 002 | Expert/The Follower! (p/s) | 10 |
| 81 | Spec RESPECT 1 | NO COWBOYS (LP, with insert) | 22 |

*(see also Foetus etc.)*

## PRAISE
| | | | |
|---|---|---|---|
| 76 | No Seven 001 | BLESSED QUIETNESS (LP) | 40 |

## PRAISE SPACE ELECTRIC
| | | | |
|---|---|---|---|
| 91 | Pop God PGTT 005 | PRAISE SPACE ELECTRIC (LP) | 15 |
| 94 | Delerium DELEC LP 015 | LEAVING DEMONS (LP) | 20 |

## PRAM
| | | | |
|---|---|---|---|
| 93 | Too Pure PURE 17 | IRON LUNG EP (12", red vinyl) | 10 |
| 92 | Howl WAIL 001 | GASH (LP) | 15 |
| 93 | Too Pure PURE 26 | THE STARS ARE SO BIG THE EARTH IS SO SMALL...STAY AS YOU ARE (LP, lyric inner) | 30 |
| 95 | Too Pure PURE 46 | SARGASSO SEA (LP, lyric inner) | 20 |
| 98 | Domino WIGLP 49 | NORTH POLE RADIO STATION (LP) | 30 |
| 00 | Domino WIGLP 80 | THE MUSEUM OF IMAGINARY ANIMALS (LP, lyric inner) | 30 |
| 01 | Too Pure PURE 41 | HELIUM (LP) | 15 |
| 03 | Domino WIGLP 120 | DARK ISLAND (LP) | 15 |

## PRAMS (1)
| | | | |
|---|---|---|---|
| 81 | Product/Ltd. Edition TAKE 2/4 | Me/Modern Men/TV PRODUCT: Nowhere's Safe/Jumping Off Walls (foldout p/s) | 20 |

## PRAMS (2)
| | | | |
|---|---|---|---|
| 85 | Classic Quotes CLASS 1 | Black Sheep/Classic Quotes (p/s) | 6 |

## PRATS
| | | | |
|---|---|---|---|
| 80 | Rough Trade RT 042 | 1990's POP EP (p/s) | 10 |

## ANDY PRATT
| | | | |
|---|---|---|---|
| 73 | Epic SEPC 1846 | Give It All To Music/Deer Song | 8 |
| 69 | Polydor 2489 003 | RECORDS ARE LIKE LIFE (LP) | 25 |

## GRAHAM & EILEEN PRATT
| | | | |
|---|---|---|---|
| 78 | Cottage Records | CLEAR AIR OF THE DAY (LP) | 20 |
| 80 | Dingle's DIN 308 | TO FRIEND & FOE (LP) | 20 |
| 81 | Dingle's DIN | BANDSTAND (LP) | 18 |
| 85 | Plant Life PLR 068 | HEIROGLYPHICS (LP, insert) | 15 |

## PHIL PRATT
| | | | |
|---|---|---|---|
| 69 | Jolly JY 008 | Sweet Song For My Baby/THRILLERS: I'm Restless | 200 |
| 78 | Burning Sounds BS 1019 | STAR WARS DUB (LP) | 40 |

*(see also Charlie Ace, Larry Marshall, Don Drummond)*

## PHIL PRATT ALL STARS
| | | | |
|---|---|---|---|
| 70 | Jackpot JP 748 | Cut Throat/KEN BOOTHE: You Left The Water Running | 30 |
| 71 | Punch PH 94 | Winey Winey (actually "Kingstonians Medley" by Kingstonians)/There Is A Place (actually by Barrington Spence) | 30 |

*(see also Dennis Alcapone, Horace Andy, Dennis Brown, Ken Boothe, Erroll Dunkley, John Holt, Delroy Wilson)*

## PRAYING MANTIS
| | | | |
|---|---|---|---|
| 79 | Ripper/Harvest HAR 5201 | THE SOUNDHOUSE TAPES PART 2: Captured City/Johnny Cool (p/s) | 60 |
| 79 | Ripper/Harvest 12HAR 5201 | THE SOUNDHOUSE TAPES PART 2 (12") | 15 |
| 80 | Gem GEMS 36 | Praying Mantis/High Roller (p/s, with transfer) | 20 |
| 80 | Gem GEMS 36 | Praying Mantis/High Roller (p/s) | 18 |
| 81 | Arista ARIST 397 | All Day And All Of The Night/Beads Of Ebony (p/s) | 12 |
| 81 | Arista ARIST 478 | Cheated/Thirty Pieces Of Silver/Flirting With Suicide/Panic In The Streets (2x7", gatefold sleeve) | 8 |

| | | MINT VALUE £ |
|---|---|---|
| 82 | Jet JET 7026 | Tell Me The Nightmare's Wrong/A Question Of Time/Turn The Tables (p/s) ............... 20 |
| 81 | Arista SPART 1153 | TIME TELLS NO LIES (LP, with inner sleeve) .............................................. 25 |

*(see also Stratus, Grand Prix, Uriah Heep)*

## PREACHERS
| 65 | Columbia DB 7680 | Hole In My Soul/Too Old In The Head....................................... 100 |
|---|---|---|

*(see also Herd, Denny Mitchel & Soundsations, Moon's Train)*

## PRECIOUS LITTLE
| 80 | Rock On ROR 2 | Give It To Me Now/Clean Living Boy (p/s)................................ 20 |
|---|---|---|

## PRECISIONS
| 67 | Track 604 014 | If This Is Love (I'd Rather Be Lonely)/You'll Soon Be Gone............ 40 |
|---|---|---|
| 79 | Grapevine GRP 129 | Such Misery/A Lovers Plea ......................................... 10 |

## PREDATOR (1)
| 78 | Bust! SOL 2 | Punk Man/Paperboy Song (with insert)................................ 60 |
|---|---|---|

## PREDATOR (2)
| 85 | CTM C 001 | Don't Stop/Shotdown (in p/s) .................................... 80 |
|---|---|---|
| 85 | CTM C 001 | Don't Stop/Shotdown ............................................ 30 |

## PREDATORS
| 83 | Ears And Eyes EER 012 | SOCIAL DECAY (LP) ............................................. 40 |
|---|---|---|

## PREDATUR
| 82 | Quicksilver QUICK 5 | Take A Walk/Seen You Here (p/s)................................ 75 |
|---|---|---|

## PREFAB SPROUT
| 82 | Candle CANDLE 1 | Lions In My Own Garden (Exit Someone)/Radio Love ........... 25 |
|---|---|---|

## PREFECTS (1)
| 79 | Rough Trade TR 040 | Going Through The Motions/Things In General (no p/s) ...... 10 |
|---|---|---|

## PREFECTS (2)
| 82 | Variety BBY 402 | Love Is All Around/I Saw The Night.......................... 6 |
|---|---|---|

## PREFUSE 73
| 03 | Warp WARPLP 105 | ONE WORD EXTINGUISHER (2-LP) .............................. 20 |
|---|---|---|

## PREGNANT INSOMNIA
| 67 | Direction 58-3132 | Wallpaper/You Intrigue Me ................................ 50 |
|---|---|---|

## PRELUDE (1)
| 72 | Crotchet CME 18A/B | PRELUDE (LP, private pressing) ........................... 70 |
|---|---|---|
| 73 | Dawn DNLS 3052 | HOW LONG IS FOREVER (LP, textured gatefold sleeve)....... 20 |

## PRELUDE (2)
| 72 | Decca F13292 | Edge Of The Sea/Looking For Indians....................... 10 |
|---|---|---|

## PRELUDE (3)
| 83 | Black Crow CROS 1 | Freedom/Prelude .......................................... 10 |
|---|---|---|

## PREMIERS (U.K.)
| 64 | Silver Phoenix 1002 | Tears, Tears/Bye Bye Johnny.............................. 45 |
|---|---|---|

## PREMIERS (U.S.)
| 64 | Warner Bros WB 134 | Farmer John/Duffy's Blues ............................... 15 |
|---|---|---|
| 64 | Warner Bros W 1565 | FARMER JOHN "LIVE" (LP) ................................. 60 |

## PREMO & HOPETON
| 67 | Rio R 139 | Your Safekeep/Loving And Kind............................. 20 |
|---|---|---|
| 68 | Pama PM 753 | Peace On Earth/SCHOOL BOYS: Love Is A Message (as Premo & Joesph)........... 300 |

## YVONNE PRENOSILOVA
| 65 | Pye 7N 15775 | When My Baby Cries/Come On Home ..................... 35 |
|---|---|---|

## PRESENCE(1)
| 79 | SRTS.79/CUS 296 | No Reason/I Care For You (no p/s)........................ 20 |
|---|---|---|

## PRESENCE (2)
| 76 | NC SLCW 1031 | PRESENCE (LP)............................................ 35 |
|---|---|---|

## PRESENCE (3)
| 91 | Reality LOL 1 | In Wonder/Soft (p/s, withdrawn) ......................... 5 |
|---|---|---|

*(see also Cure)*

## PRESIDENTS (1)
| 64 | Decca F 11826 | Candy Man/Let The Sunshine In........................... 50 |
|---|---|---|

## ELVIS PRESLEY
### 78S : HMV 78S
| 56 | HMV POP 182 | Heartbreak Hotel/I Was The One .......................... 20 |
|---|---|---|
| 56 | HMV POP 213 | Blue Suede Shoes/Tutti Frutti............................ 20 |
| 56 | HMV POP 235 | I Want You, I Need You, I Love You/My Baby Left Me ....... 25 |
| 56 | HMV POP 253 | Love Me Tender/Anyway You Want Me (That's How I Will Be)... 25 |
| 56 | HMV POP 272 | Blue Moon/I Don't Care If The Sun Don't Shine ........... 20 |
| 57 | HMV POP 295 | Mystery Train/Love Me ................................... 30 |
| 57 | HMV POP 305 | Rip It Up/Baby, Let's Play House ........................ 40 |
| 57 | HMV POP 330 | Too Much/Playing For Keeps .............................. 40 |
| 57 | HMV POP 378 | Paralyzed/When My Blue Moon Turns To Gold Again ......... 30 |
| 57 | HMV POP 408 | Tryin' To Get To You/Lawdy, Miss Clawdy ................. 30 |
| 58 | HMV POP 428 | I'm Left, You're Right, She's Gone/How Do You Think I Feel? ... 40 |

### 78S : RCA 78S
| 57 | RCA RCA 1025 | Santa Bring My Baby Back (To Me)/Santa Claus Is Back In Town ... 25 |
|---|---|---|
| 58 | RCA RCA 1043 | Don't/I Beg Of You .................................... 25 |
| 58 | RCA RCA 1058 | Wear My Ring Around Your Neck/Doncha' Think It's Time.... 30 |
| 58 | RCA RCA 1070 | Hard Headed Woman/Don't Ask Me Why ..................... 30 |
| 58 | RCA RCA 1081 | King Creole/Dixieland Rock ............................. 30 |
| 58 | RCA RCA 1088 | All Shook Up/Heartbreak Hotel .......................... 100 |

| 58 | RCA RCA 1095 | Hound Dog/Blue Suede Shoes | 100 |
|---|---|---|---|
| 59 | RCA RCA 1100 | One Night/I Got Stung | 60 |
| 59 | RCA RCA 1113 | (Now And Then There's) A Fool Such As I/I Need Your Love Tonight | 60 |
| 59 | RCA RCA 1136 | A Big Hunk O' Love/My Wish Came True | 100 |
| 60 | RCA RCA 1187 | Stuck On You/Fame And Fortune | 500 |
| 60 | RCA RCA 1194 | A Mess Of Blues/The Girl Of My Best Friend | 750 |

## SINGLES : HMV 45S :PURPLE LABEL/SILVER PRINT

| 56 | HMV 7M 385 | Heartbreak Hotel/I Was The One | 175 |
|---|---|---|---|
| 56 | HMV 7M 405 | Blue Suede Shoes/Tutti Frutti | 250 |
| 56 | HMV 7M 424 | I Want You, I Need You, I Love You/My Baby Left Me | 150 |
| 56 | HMV POP 249 | Hound Dog/Don't Be Cruel | 100 |
| 56 | HMV POP 253 | Love Me Tender/Anyway You Want Me (That's How I Will Be) | 100 |
| 56 | HMV POP 272 | Blue Moon/I Don't Care If The Sun Don't Shine | 100 |
| 57 | HMV POP 295 | Mystery Train/Love Me | 150 |
| 57 | HMV POP 305 | Rip It Up/Baby, Let's Play House | 150 |
| 57 | HMV POP 330 | Too Much/Playing For Keeps | 150 |
| 57 | HMV POP 359 | All Shook Up/That's When Your Heartaches Begin ('removable/replaceable' centre) | 125 |
| 57 | HMV POP 359 | All Shook Up/That's When Your Heartaches Begin (solid centre) | 50 |
| 57 | HMV POP 378 | Paralyzed/When My Blue Moon Turns To Gold Again | 50 |
| 57 | HMV POP 408 | Tryin' To Get To You/Lawdy, Miss Clawdy | 50 |
| 58 | HMV POP 428 | I'm Left, You're Right, She's Gone/How Do You Think I Feel? | 50 |

## SINGLES : HMV 45S: PURPLE LABEL/GOLD PRINT

| 56 | HMV 7M 385 | Heartbreak Hotel/I Was The One ('removable/replaceable' centre) | 300 |
|---|---|---|---|
| 56 | HMV 7M 385 | Heartbreak Hotel/I Was The One (solid centre) | 200 |
| 56 | HMV 7M 405 | Blue Suede Shoes/Tutti Frutti | 300 |
| 56 | HMV 7M 424 | I Want You, I Need You, I Love You/My Baby Left Me ('removable/replaceable centre) | 300 |
| 56 | HMV 7M 424 | I Want You, I Need You, I Love You/My Baby Left Me ('solid centre) | 200 |
| 56 | HMV POP 249 | Hound Dog/Don't Be Cruel | 150 |
| 56 | HMV POP 253 | Love Me Tender/Anyway You Want Me (That's How I Will Be) | 150 |
| 56 | HMV POP 272 | Blue Moon/I Don't Care If The Sun Don't Shine ('removable/replaceable' centre) | 200 |
| 56 | HMV POP 272 | Blue Moon/I Don't Care If The Sun Don't Shine (solid centre) | 150 |
| 57 | HMV POP 295 | Mystery Train/Love Me ('removable/replaceable' centre) | 350 |
| 57 | HMV POP 295 | Mystery Train/Love Me (solid centre) | 200 |
| 57 | HMV 7MC 42 | Mystery Train/I Forgot To Remember To Forget (U.K. issue of export single, gold label print only, smooth edge to labels) | 300 |
| 57 | HMV POP 305 | Rip It Up/Baby, Let's Play House ('removable/replaceable' centre) | 300 |
| 57 | HMV POP 305 | Rip It Up/Baby, Let's Play House (solid centre) | 200 |
| 57 | HMV POP 330 | Too Much/Playing For Keeps | 120 |
| 57 | HMV POP 359 | All Shook Up/That's When Your Heartaches Begin (push-out centre) | 150 |
| 57 | HMV POP 359 | All Shook Up/That's When Your Heartaches Begin (solid centre) | 100 |
| 57 | HMV POP 378 | Paralyzed/When My Blue Moon Turns To Gold Again | 100 |

## SINGLES : ORIGINAL RCA 45S: BLACK LABELS

| 57 | RCA RCA 1013 | (Let Me Be Your) Teddy Bear/Loving You | 20 |
|---|---|---|---|
| 57 | RCA RCA 1020 | Party/Got A Lot O' Livin' To Do | 20 |
| 57 | RCA RCA 1025 | Santa Bring My Baby Back (To Me)/Santa Claus Is Back In Town | 20 |
| 58 | RCA RCA 1028 | Jailhouse Rock/Treat Me Nice | 15 |
| 58 | RCA RCA 1043 | Don't/I Beg Of You | 15 |
| 58 | RCA RCA 1058 | Wear My Ring Around Your Neck/Doncha' Think It's Time | 15 |
| 58 | RCA RCA 1070 | Hard Headed Woman/Don't Ask Me Why | 15 |
| 58 | RCA RCA 1081 | King Creole/Dixieland Rock | 15 |
| 58 | RCA RCA 1088 | All Shook Up/Heartbreak Hotel | 50 |
| 58 | RCA RCA 1095 | Hound Dog/Blue Suede Shoes | 50 |
| 59 | RCA RCA 1100 | One Night/I Got Stung | 15 |
| 59 | RCA RCA 1113 | (Now And Then There's) A Fool Such As I/I Need Your Love Tonight | 15 |
| 59 | RCA RCA 1136 | A Big Hunk O' Love/My Wish Came True | 15 |

*(The above 45s were issued with a triangular centre, round-centre re-pressings are worth half to two-thirds these values. RCA Victor re-pressings are on a par with Triangular centre prices)*

| 60 | RCA RCA 1187 | Stuck On You/Fame And Fortune | 5 |
|---|---|---|---|
| 60 | RCA RCA 1194 | A Mess Of Blues/The Girl Of My Best Friend | 5 |
| 60 | RCA RCA 1207 | It's Now Or Never (O Sole Mio)/Make Me Know It | 5 |
| 61 | RCA RCA 1216 | Are You Lonesome Tonight?/I Gotta Know | 5 |
| 61 | RCA RCA 1226 | Wooden Heart/Tonight Is So Right For Love | 5 |
| 61 | RCA RCA 1227 | Surrender (Torna A Surriento)/Lonely Man | 5 |
| 61 | RCA RCA 1244 | Wild In The Country/I Feel So Bad | 5 |
| 61 | RCA RCA 1258 | (Marie's The Name) His Latest Flame/Little Sister | 5 |
| 61 | RCA RCA 1270 | Rock-A-Hula Baby/Can't Help Falling In Love | 5 |
| 62 | RCA RCA 1280 | Good Luck Charm/Anything That's Part Of You | 5 |
| 62 | RCA RCA 1303 | She's Not You/Just Tell Him Jim Said Hello | 5 |
| 62 | RCA RCA 1320 | Return To Sender/Where Do You Come From | 5 |

## SINGLES : ORIGINAL RCA VICTOR 45S: BLACK LABELS

| 62 | RCA Victor RCA 1280 | Good Luck Charm/Anything That's Part Of You | 5 |
|---|---|---|---|
| 62 | RCA Victor RCA 1303 | She's Not You/Just Tell Her Jim Said Hello | 6 |
| 62 | RCA Victor RCA 1320 | Return To Sender/Where Do You Come From | 6 |
| 63 | RCA Victor RCA 1337 | One Broken Heart For Sale/They Remind Me Too Much Of You | 8 |
| 63 | RCA Victor RCA 1355 | (You're The) Devil In Disguise/Please Don't Drag That String Around | 5 |
| 63 | RCA Victor RCA 1374 | Bossa Nova Baby/Witchcraft | 6 |
| 62 | RCA Victor RCA 1375 | Kiss Me Quick/Something Blue | 6 |
| 64 | RCA Victor RCA 1390 | Viva Las Vegas/What'd I Say | 8 |

| | | | |
|---|---|---|---|
| 64 | RCA Victor RCA 1404 | Kissin' Cousins/It Hurts Me | 6 |
| 64 | RCA Victor RCA 1411 | Such A Night/Never Ending | 7 |
| 64 | RCA Victor RCA 1422 | Ain't That Loving You Baby/Ask Me | 6 |
| 64 | RCA Victor RCA 1430 | Blue Christmas/White Christmas | 8 |
| 65 | RCA Victor RCA 1443 | Do The Clam/You'll Be Gone | 7 |
| 66 | RCA Victor RCA 1509 | Frankie And Johnny/Please Don't Stop Loving Me | 15 |
| 66 | RCA Victor RCA 1526 | Love Letters/Come What May | 7 |
| 66 | RCA Victor RCA 1545 | All That I Am/Spinout | 10 |
| 66 | RCA Victor RCA 1557 | If Every Day Was Like Christmas/How Would You Like To Be? | 8 |
| 67 | RCA Victor RCA 1565 | Indescribably Blue/Fools Fall In Love | 20 |
| 67 | RCA Victor RCA 1593 | The Love Machine/You Gotta Stop | 15 |
| 67 | RCA Victor RCA 1616 | Long-Legged Girl (With The Short Dress On)/That's Someone You Never Forget | 20 |
| 67 | RCA Victor RCA 1628 | Judy/There's Always Me | 40 |
| 67 | RCA Victor RCA 1642 | Big Boss Man/You Don't Know Me | 20 |
| 68 | RCA Victor RCA 1663 | Guitar Man/Hi-Heel Sneakers | 10 |
| 68 | RCA Victor RCA 1688 | U.S. Male/Stay Away | 15 |
| 68 | RCA Victor RCA 1714 | Your Time Hasn't Come Yet Baby/Let Yourself Go | 15 |
| 68 | RCA Victor RCA 1747 | You'll Never Walk Alone/We Call On Him | 30 |
| 68 | RCA Victor RCA 1768 | A Little Less Conversation/Almost In Love | 25 |

## SINGLES : ORIGINAL RCA VICTOR ORANGE LABEL 45S

| | | | |
|---|---|---|---|
| 69 | RCA Victor RCA 1795 | If I Can Dream/Memories | 10 |
| 69 | RCA Victor RCA 1831 | In The Ghetto/Any Day Now | 6 |
| 69 | RCA Victor RCA 1869 | Clean Up Your Own Backyard/The Fair's Moving On | 6 |
| 69 | RCA Victor RCA 1900 | Suspicious Minds/You'll Think Of Me (p/s) | 10 |
| 70 | RCA Victor RCA 1916 | Don't Cry Daddy/Rubberneckin' (p/s) | 15 |
| 70 | RCA Victor RCA 1949 | Kentucky Rain/My Little Friend (p/s) | 10 |
| 70 | RCA Victor RCA 1999 | I've Lost You/The Next Step Is Love | 6 |
| 71 | RCA Victor RCA 2060 | There Goes My Everything/I Really Don't Want To Know (p/s) | 10 |
| 71 | RCA Victor RCA 2084 | Rags To Riches/Where Did They Go, Lord (p/s) | 10 |
| 71 | RCA Victor RCA 2125 | I'm Leavin'/Heart Of Rome | 6 |
| 71 | RCA Victor RCA 2158 | I Just Can't Help Believin'/How The Web Was Woven | 6 |
| 72 | RCA Victor RCA 2188 | Until It's Time For You To Go/We Can Make The Morning (p/s) | 10 |
| 72 | RCA Victor RCA 2229 | American Trilogy/The First Time Ever I Saw Your Face | 10 |
| 72 | RCA Victor RCA 2267 | Burning Love/It's A Matter Of Time | 8 |
| 72 | RCA Victor RCA 2304 | Always On My Mind/Separate Ways | 7 |
| 73 | RCA Victor RCA 2359 | Polk Salad Annie/See See Rider | 7 |
| 73 | RCA Victor RCA 2393 | Fool/Steamroller Blues | 7 |
| 73 | RCA Victor RCA 2435 | Raised On Rock/For Ol' Times Sake | 7 |
| 74 | RCA Victor APBO 0196 | Take Good Care Of Her/I've Got A Thing About You Baby (solid centre; most copies as U.S. imports with large centre hole in U.S. p/s) | 200 |
| 74 | RCA Victor APBO 0280 | If You Talk In Your Sleep/Help Me | 10 |
| 74 | RCA Victor RCA 2458 | My Boy/Loving Arms | 5 |
| 74 | RCA Victor PB 10074 | Promised Land/It's Midnight (1st pressing) | 5 |
| 74 | RCA Victor PB 10074 | Promised Land/It's Midnight And I Miss You (2nd pressing with correct B-side title) | 15 |
| 75 | RCA Victor RCA 2562 | T-R-O-U-B-L-E/Mr. Songman | 5 |
| 76 | RCA Victor RCA 2674 | Hurt/For The Heart | 10 |

## SINGLES : OTHER RCA 45S

| | | | |
|---|---|---|---|
| 83 | RCA RCAP 1028 | Jailhouse Rock/The Elvis Medley (with "Hound Dog" credit on B-side) (reissue, picture disc) | 15 |
| 83 | RCA RCA 369 | I Can Help/The Lady Loves Me (p/s) | 5 |
| 83 | RCA RCAP 369 | I Can Help/If Every Day Was Like Christmas/The Lady Loves Me (10", picture disc in clear plastic sleeve) | 15 |
| 84 | RCA RCA 405 | Green Green Grass Of Home/Release Me (And Let Me Love Again)/ Solitaire (p/s, with poster) | 20 |
| 84 | RCA RCA 405 | Green Green Grass Of Home/Release Me (And Let Me Love Again)/ Solitaire (p/s) | 5 |
| 84 | RCA RCA 459 | The Last Farewell/It's Easy for You (p/s) | 5 |
| 84 | RCA RCAT 459 | The Last Farewell/It's Easy for You (10", p/s) | 10 |
| 85 | RCA RCA 476 | The Elvis Medley/Blue Suede Shoes (p/s) | 5 |
| 85 | RCA PB 49943 | Always On My Mind (Alternate Version)/Tomorrow Night (p/s) | 5 |
| 87 | RCA ARON 1 | Bossa Nova Baby/Ain't That Loving You Baby (p/s) | 5 |
| 87 | RCA ARONT 1 | Bossa Nova Baby/Ain't That Loving You Baby (12", p/s) | 15 |
| 87 | RCA ARON 2 | Love Me Tender/If I Can Dream (p/s) | 5 |
| 87 | RCA ARONT 2 | Love Me Tender/If I Can Dream (p/s) (12", p/s) | 10 |
| 88 | RCA PB 49177 | Are You Lonesome Tonight/Reconsider Baby (p/s) | 5 |
| 88 | RCA PB 49177 | Are You Lonesome Tonight/Reconsider Baby (12", p/s) | 10 |
| 88 | RCA PB 49473 | Mean Woman Blues/I Beg Of Of You (p/s) | 10 |
| 88 | RCA PT 49474 | Mean Woman Blues/I Beg Of Of You (12", p/s) | 20 |
| 88 | RCA PB 49545 | Stuck On You/Any Way You Want Me (p/s) | 5 |
| 88 | RCA PT 49546 | Stuck On You/Any Way You Want Me (12", p/s) | 10 |
| 88 | RCA PB 49943 | Always On My Mind/Tomorrow Night (p/s) | 10 |
| 88 | RCA PT 49944 | Always On My Mind/Tomorrow Night (12", p/s) | 10 |
| 90 | RCA TCB 1 | (Now And Then There's) A Fool Such As I (Take 3)/Danny (promo only) | 12 |
| 04 | BMG 82876 619211 | That's All Right/Blue Moon Of Kentucky (10", brown die-cut sleeve, with 'Sun' labels) | 15 |

## SINGLES : OTHER SINGLES AND FLEXIDISCS

| | | | |
|---|---|---|---|
| 57 | Weekend Mail (no cat. no.) | THE TRUTH ABOUT ME (1-sided 6" 78 rpm, mail-order only, in mailer) | 40 |
| 57 | Weekend Mail (no cat. no.) | THE TRUTH ABOUT ME (1-sided 6" 78 rpm, mail-order only, not in mailer) | 25 |
| 77 | RCA Victor 2694-2709 | GOLD 16 SERIES (16 x p/s 7" in foldout cardboard carrier) | 30 |
| 79 | RCA LB 1 | The Wonder Of You/Noel Edmonds Introduces Record Year (Lever Brothers premium) | 20 |

## SINGLES : RCA VICTOR 45S: BLACK LABEL REISSUES

| 64 | RCA Victor RCA 1020 | Party/Got A Lot O' Livin' To Do ..................................................... 10 |
|----|---------------------|---|
| 64 | RCA Victor RCA 1025 | Santa Bring My Baby Back (To Me)/Santa Claus Is Back In Town ............ 15 |
| 64 | RCA Victor RCA 1028 | Jailhouse Rock/Treat Me Nice ...................................................... 15 |
| 64 | RCA Victor RCA 1043 | Don't/I Beg Of You ................................................................... 15 |
| 64 | RCA Victor RCA 1058 | Wear My Ring Around Your Neck/Doncha' Think It's Time.................... 10 |
| 64 | RCA Victor RCA 1070 | Hard Headed Woman/Don't Ask Me Why ....................................... 15 |
| 64 | RCA Victor RCA 1081 | King Creole/Dixieland Rock ......................................................... 15 |
| 64 | RCA Victor RCA 1088 | All Shook Up/Heartbreak Hotel .................................................... 15 |
| 64 | RCA Victor RCA 1095 | Hound Dog/Blue Suede Shoes ...................................................... 10 |
| 64 | RCA Victor RCA 1100 | One Night/I Got Stung............................................................... 10 |
| 64 | RCA Victor RCA 1113 | (Now And Then There's) A Fool Such As I/I Need Your Love Tonight........ 10 |
| 64 | RCA Victor RCA 1136 | A Big Hunk O' Love/My Wish Came True ......................................... 10 |
| 64 | RCA Victor RCA 1187 | Stuck On You/Fame And Fortune .................................................. 10 |
| 64 | RCA Victor RCA 1194 | A Mess Of Blues/The Girl Of My Best Friend ..................................... 8 |
| 64 | RCA Victor RCA 1207 | It's Now Or Never (O Sole Mio)/Make Me Know It .............................. 15 |
| 64 | RCA Victor RCA 1216 | Are You Lonesome Tonight?/I Gotta Know...................................... 8 |
| 64 | RCA Victor RCA 1226 | Wooden Heart/Tonight Is So Right For Love ..................................... 8 |
| 64 | RCA Victor RCA 1227 | Surrender (Torna A Surriento)/Lonely Man ...................................... 8 |
| 64 | RCA Victor RCA 1244 | Wild In The Country/I Feel So Bad ................................................. 6 |
| 64 | RCA Victor RCA 1258 | (Marie's The Name) His Latest Flame/Little Sister .............................. 6 |
| 64 | RCA Victor RCA 1270 | Rock-A-Hula Baby/Can't Help Falling In Love .................................... 7 |

## SINGLES : RCA VICTOR 45S: ORANGE LABEL REISSUES

| 69 | RCA Victor RCA 1088 | All Shook Up/Heartbreak Hotel .................................................... 15 |
|----|---------------------|---|
| 69 | RCA Victor RCA 1095 | Hound Dog/Blue Suede Shoes ...................................................... 15 |
| 69 | RCA Victor RCA 1207 | It's Now Or Never (O Sole Mio)/Make Me Know It .............................. 15 |
| 69 | RCA Victor RCA 1216 | Are You Lonesome Tonight?/I Gotta Know...................................... 15 |
| 69 | RCA Victor RCA 1226 | Wooden Heart/Tonight Is So Right For Love ..................................... 30 |
| 69 | RCA Victor RCA 1688 | U.S. Male/Stay Away ................................................................. 100 |
| 71 | RCA MAXI 2104 | Heartbreak Hotel/Hound Dog/Don't Be Cruel ('Maximillion' sleeve) ........ 10 |
| 71 | RCA MAXI 2153 | Jailhouse Rock/Are You Lonesome Tonight?/(Let Me Be Your)Teddy Bear/ Steadfast, Loyal And True ('Maximillion' sleeve) ................................. 10 |
| 75 | RCA MAXI 2601 | Blue Moon/You're A Heartbreaker/I'm Left, You're Right, She's Gone ('Maximillion' sleeve) ............................................................... 20 |

## SINGLES : RETROSPECTIVE RCA BLUE LABEL 45S

| 78 | RCA PB 9265 | Don't Be Cruel/Hound Dog (p/s)..................................................... 5 |
|----|-------------|---|
| 78 | RCA PB 9334 | Old Shep/Paralysed (p/s) ............................................................. 5 |
| 80 | RCA RCA 4 | It's Only Love/Beyond The Reef (p/s) ............................................... 5 |
| 80 | RCA RCA 16 | Santa Claus Is Back In Town/I Believe (p/s) ....................................... 5 |
| 81 | RCA RCA 43 | Guitar Man/Faded Love (with matt U.K. p/s [cat. no. RCA 43]) .............. 50 |
| 81 | RCA RCA 43 | Guitar Man/Faded Love (with glossy U.S. p/s [cat. no. PB 12158]) ........... 5 |
| 82 | RCA RCA 196 | Are You Lonesome Tonight? (Laughing Version)/From A Jack To A King (p/s) ........ 6 |

## SINGLES : SINGLES BOX SET

| 77 | RCA (no cat. no.) | PRESLEY GOLD - 16 NUMBER ONES (16 x 7", each in p/s, black box set)........................ 40 |
|----|-------------------|---|

## EXPORT SINGLES : HMV EXPORT 45S

| 57 | HMV 7MC 42 | Mystery Train/I Forgot To Remember To Forget (gold label print, serrated edge to labels).............................................................. 300 |
|----|------------|---|
| 57 | HMV 7MC 45 | I Want You, I Need You, I Love You/My Baby Left Me (gold label print) ......... 200 |
| 57 | HMV 7MC 50 | Hound Dog/Don't Be Cruel (gold label print) ................................... 150 |
| 57 | HMV JO 465 | Love Me Tender/Anyway You Want Me (That's How I'll Be) (gold label print) ............. 150 |
| 57 | HMV JO 466 | Too Much/Playing For Keeps (gold label print) ................................. 200 |
| 57 | HMV JO 473 | All Shook Up/That's When Your Heartaches Begin (gold label print)........... 150 |

## EPS : EP BOXED SETS

| 82 | RCA EP 1 | THE EP COLLECTION (11-EP box set, reissues, with booklet)........................... 35 |
|----|----------|---|
| 83 | RCA EP 2 | THE EP COLLECTION VOL. 2 (11-EP box set, reissues, with booklet)................... 50 |

## EPS : HMV EPS

| 57 | HMV 7EG 8199 | LOVE ME TENDER (soundtrack, round centre)........................................ 70 |
|----|--------------|---|
| 57 | HMV 7EG 8199 | LOVE ME TENDER (soundtrack, removeable centre) ............................. 100 |
| 57 | HMV 7EG 8256 | GOOD ROCKIN' TONIGHT (round centre only)........................................ 200 |

## EPS : ORIGINAL RCA EPS : ROUND CENTRES

| 60 | RCA RCX 190 | SUCH A NIGHT ........................................................................ 25 |
|----|-------------|---|
| 62 | RCA RCX 211 | FOLLOW THAT DREAM (soundtrack) ................................................. 10 |
| 62 | RCA RCX 211 | FOLLOW THAT DREAM (mispressing, 2nd side features Jim Reeves)............. 100 |
| 62 | RCA RCX 7109 | KID GALAHAD (soundtrack) ......................................................... 10 |
| 64 | RCA Victor RCX 7141 | LOVE IN LAS VEGAS (soundtrack)..................................................... 20 |
| 64 | RCA Victor RCX 7142 | ELVIS FOR YOU VOL. 1 ................................................................. 50 |
| 64 | RCA Victor RCX 7143 | ELVIS FOR YOU VOL. 2 ................................................................. 50 |
| 64 | RCA Victor RCX 135 | ELVIS IN TENDER MOOD ............................................................. 20 |
| 65 | RCA Victor RCX 7173 | TICKLE ME (soundtrack) .............................................................. 35 |
| 65 | RCA Victor RCX 7174 | TICKLE ME VOL. 2 (soundtrack)....................................................... 35 |
| 67 | RCA Victor RCX 7187 | EASY COME, EASY GO (soundtrack) ................................................. 40 |

## EPS : RCA EPS : ROUND CENTRE REPRESSINGS

| 60s | RCA RCX 101 | PEACE IN THE VALLEY ................................................................. 20 |
|-----|-------------|---|
| 60s | RCA RCX 104 | ELVIS PRESLEY ........................................................................ 15 |
| 60s | RCA RCX 106 | JAILHOUSE ROCK (soundtrack) ...................................................... 15 |
| 60s | RCA RCX 117 | KING CREOLE VOL. 1 (soundtrack) .................................................. 15 |
| 60s | RCA RCX 118 | KING CREOLE VOL. 2 (soundtrack) .................................................. 10 |

| | | | MINT VALUE £ |
|---|---|---|---|
| 60s | RCA RCX 121 | ELVIS SINGS CHRISTMAS SONGS (gatefold p/s) | 60 |
| 60s | RCA RCX 131 | ELVIS SAILS (interview record) | 25 |
| 60s | RCA RCX 135 | ELVIS IN TENDER MOOD | 20 |
| 60s | RCA RCX 1045 | A TOUCH OF GOLD | 25 |
| 60s | RCA RCX 175 | STRICTLY ELVIS | 20 |
| 60s | RCA RCX 1048 | A TOUCH OF GOLD VOL. 2 | 35 |

### EPS : RCA EPS: TRIANGULAR CENTRES

| | | | |
|---|---|---|---|
| 57 | RCA RCX 101 | PEACE IN THE VALLEY | 30 |
| 57 | RCA RCX 104 | ELVIS PRESLEY | 40 |
| 58 | RCA RCX 106 | JAILHOUSE ROCK (soundtrack) | 40 |
| 58 | RCA RCX 117 | KING CREOLE VOL. 1 (soundtrack, black label, cream or white rear p/s) | 30 |
| 58 | RCA RCX 118 | KING CREOLE VOL. 2 (soundtrack, cream or white rear sleeve) | 30 |
| 58 | RCA RCX 121 | ELVIS SINGS CHRISTMAS SONGS (1st issue, single sleeve) | 60 |
| 58 | RCA RCX 131 | ELVIS SAILS (interview record, sleeve laminated front & back) | 40 |
| 59 | RCA RCX 135 | ELVIS IN TENDER MOOD (with red print on rear sleeve) | 40 |

*(Originally issued with laminated front and back sleeves; later copies with front-only laminate are worth three quarters of these values.)*

| | | | |
|---|---|---|---|
| 59 | RCA RCX 1045 | A TOUCH OF GOLD (laminated front sleeve only) | 50 |
| 59 | RCA RCX 175 | STRICTLY ELVIS | 40 |
| 60 | RCA RCX 1048 | A TOUCH OF GOLD VOL. 2 | 80 |

### EPS : RCA VICTOR EPS: BLACK LABEL RE-PRESSINGS

| | | | |
|---|---|---|---|
| 64 | RCA Victor RCX 101 | PEACE IN THE VALLEY | 15 |
| 64 | RCA Victor RCX 104 | ELVIS PRESLEY | 15 |
| 64 | RCA Victor RCX 106 | JAILHOUSE ROCK (soundtrack) | 15 |
| 64 | RCA Victor RCX 117 | KING CREOLE VOL. 1 (soundtrack) | 15 |
| 64 | RCA Victor RCX 118 | KING CREOLE VOL. 2 (soundtrack) | 15 |
| 64 | RCA Victor RCX 121 | ELVIS SINGS CHRISTMAS SONGS (single p/s) | 30 |
| 64 | RCA Victor RCX 131 | ELVIS SAILS (interview record) | 25 |
| 64 | RCA Victor RCX 1045 | A TOUCH OF GOLD | 15 |
| 64 | RCA Victor RCX 175 | STRICTLY ELVIS | 15 |
| 64 | RCA Victor RCX 1048 | A TOUCH OF GOLD VOL. 2 | 25 |
| 64 | RCA Victor RCX 190 | SUCH A NIGHT | 10 |
| 64 | RCA Victor RCX 211 | FOLLOW THAT DREAM (soundtrack) | 10 |
| 64 | RCA Victor RCX 7106 | KID GALAHAD (soundtrack) | 10 |

### EPS : RCA VICTOR EPS: ORANGE LABEL RE-PRESSINGS

| | | | |
|---|---|---|---|
| 69 | RCA Victor RCX 101 | PEACE IN THE VALLEY (push-out centre) | 10 |
| 69 | RCA Victor RCX 104 | ELVIS PRESLEY (push-out centre) | 12 |
| 69 | RCA Victor RCX 106 | JAILHOUSE ROCK (soundtrack, solid centre) | 10 |
| 69 | RCA Victor RCX 117 | KING CREOLE VOL. 1 (soundtrack, push-out centre) | 15 |
| 69 | RCA Victor RCX 118 | KING CREOLE VOL. 2 (soundtrack, push-out centre) | 10 |
| 69 | RCA Victor RCX 131 | ELVIS SAILS (interview record, push-out or solid centre) | 10 |
| 69 | RCA Victor RCX 135 | ELVIS IN TENDER MOOD (push-out or solid centre, with different take of "Lover Doll") | 10 |
| 69 | RCA Victor RCX 1045 | A TOUCH OF GOLD (push-out centre) | 15 |
| 69 | RCA Victor RCX 1045 | A TOUCH OF GOLD (solid centre) | 10 |
| 69 | RCA Victor RCX 175 | STRICTLY ELVIS (push-out or solid centre) | 10 |
| 69 | RCA Victor RCX 1048 | A TOUCH OF GOLD VOL. 2 (push-out centre) | 15 |
| 69 | RCA Victor RCX 1048 | A TOUCH OF GOLD VOL. 2 (solid centre) | 10 |
| 69 | RCA Victor RCX 190 | SUCH A NIGHT (push-out centre) | 10 |

### ALBUMS : CDS

| | | | |
|---|---|---|---|
| 84 | RCA PD 89061/2/3 | THE LEGEND (3-CD, gold box set, with booklet, numbered, 5,000 only) | 60 |
| 84 | RCA PD 89061/2/3 | THE LEGEND (3-CD, silver box set, 5,000 only, with booklet, numbered) | 60 |

### ALBUMS : LPS: 'LARGE' ORANGE RCA VICTOR STEREO RE-PRESSINGS

| | | | |
|---|---|---|---|
| 72 | RCA Victor SF 8232 | ELVIS FOR EVERYONE ('blue shirt'/'TV Special' sleeve) | 40 |

### ALBUMS : LPS: 'SMALL' ORANGE RCA VICTOR MONO RE-PRESSINGS

| | | | |
|---|---|---|---|
| 69 | RCA Victor RD 27052 | ELVIS' CHRISTMAS ALBUM | 40 |
| 69 | RCA Victor RD 27088 | KING CREOLE (soundtrack) | 30 |
| 69 | RCA Victor RD 27120 | ELVIS | 30 |
| 69 | RCA Victor RD 27128 | A DATE WITH ELVIS | 30 |
| 69 | RCA Victor RD 27159 | ELVIS' GOLDEN RECORDS VOL. 2 | 30 |
| 69 | RCA Victor RD 27171 | ELVIS IS BACK! (gatefold sleeve) | 30 |
| 69 | RCA Victor RD 27192 | G.I. BLUES (soundtrack) | 30 |
| 69 | RCA Victor RD 27211 | HIS HAND IN MINE | 15 |
| 69 | RCA Victor RD 27224 | SOMETHING FOR EVERYBODY | 30 |
| 69 | RCA Victor RD 27238 | BLUE HAWAII (soundtrack) | 30 |
| 69 | RCA Victor RD 7528 | ROCK 'N' ROLL NO. 2 | 30 |
| 69 | RCA Victor RD 7630 | ELVIS' GOLDEN RECORDS VOL. 3 | 30 |
| 69 | RCA Victor RD 7723 | FLAMING STAR AND SUMMER KISSES (soundtrack, orange label) | 400 |
| 69 | RCA Victor RD 7810 | PARADISE, HAWAIIAN STYLE (soundtrack) | 20 |
| 69 | RCA Victor RD 7867 | HOW GREAT THOU ART | 20 |
| 69 | RCA Victor RD 7917 | CLAMBAKE (soundtrack) | 30 |
| 69 | RCA Victor RD 7924 | ELVIS' GOLD RECORDS VOLUME 4 | 15 |
| 69 | RCA Victor RD 7957 | SPEEDWAY (soundtrack, with Nancy Sinatra) | 20 |

### ALBUMS : LPS: BLACK/RED SPOT RCA VICTOR RE-PRESSINGS

| | | | |
|---|---|---|---|
| 64 | RCA Victor RD 7528 | ROCK 'N' ROLL NO. 2 (reissue of HMV LP, mono) | 18 |
| 64 | RCA Victor SF 7528 | ROCK 'N' ROLL NO. 2 (reissue of HMV LP, stereo) | 25 |

### ALBUMS : LPS: BLACK/SILVER SPOT RCA VICTOR RE-PRESSINGS

| | | | |
|---|---|---|---|
| 64 | RCA Victor RC 24001 | LOVING YOU (10" LP, mono only) | 60 |

| 64 | RCA Victor RD 27052 | ELVIS' CHRISTMAS ALBUM (laminated front & back covers, no pictures on back cover, mono only) | 60 |
| 64 | RCA Victor RD 7528 | ROCK 'N' ROLL NO. 2 (reissue of HMV LP, mono) | 18 |
| 64 | RCA Victor SF 7528 | ROCK 'N' ROLL NO. 2 (reissue of HMV LP, stereo) | 25 |
| 64 | RCA Victor RD 27088 | KING CREOLE (soundtrack, mono only) | 30 |
| 64 | RCA Victor RD 27120 | ELVIS (mono only) | 35 |
| 64 | RCA Victor RD 27128 | A DATE WITH ELVIS (mono only) | 20 |
| 64 | RCA Victor RD 27159 | ELVIS' GOLDEN RECORDS VOL. 2 (mono only) | 15 |
| 64 | RCA Victor RD 27171 | ELVIS IS BACK! (gatefold sleeve, mono) | 30 |
| 64 | RCA Victor SF 5060 | ELVIS IS BACK! (gatefold sleeve, stereo) | 40 |
| 64 | RCA Victor RD 27192 | G.I. BLUES (soundtrack, mono) | 15 |
| 64 | RCA Victor SF 5078 | G.I. BLUES (soundtrack, stereo) | 30 |
| 64 | RCA Victor RD 27211 | HIS HAND IN MINE (mono) | 25 |
| 64 | RCA Victor SF 5094 | HIS HAND IN MINE (stereo) | 30 |
| 64 | RCA Victor RD 27224 | SOMETHING FOR EVERYBODY (mono) | 18 |
| 64 | RCA Victor SF 5106 | SOMETHING FOR EVERYBODY (stereo) | 30 |
| 64 | RCA Victor RD 27238 | BLUE HAWAII (soundtrack, mono) | 18 |
| 64 | RCA Victor SF 5115 | BLUE HAWAII (soundtrack, stereo) | 25 |
| 64 | RCA Victor RD 27265 | POT LUCK (mono) | 15 |
| 64 | RCA Victor SF 5135 | POT LUCK (stereo) | 30 |

## ALBUMS : LPS: GREEN RCA INTERNATIONAL ISSUES
| 72 | RCA Intl. INTS 1414 | BURNING LOVE AND HITS FROM HIS MOVIES (U.K. disc in U.K. sleeve) | 30 |

## ALBUMS : LPS: HMV ISSUES
| 56 | HMV CLP 1093 | ROCK 'N' ROLL | 500 |
| 57 | HMV CLP 1105 | ROCK 'N' ROLL NO. 2 | 700 |
| 57 | HMV DLP 1159 | THE BEST OF ELVIS (10") | 200 |

## ALBUMS : LPS: ORIGINAL BLACK/RED SPOT RCA VICTOR ISSUES
| 64 | RCA Victor RD 7630 | ELVIS' GOLDEN RECORDS VOL. 3 (mono) | 20 |
| 64 | RCA Victor SF 7630 | ELVIS' GOLDEN RECORDS VOL. 3 (stereo) | 30 |
| 64 | RCA Victor RD 7645 | KISSIN' COUSINS (soundtrack, mono) | 18 |
| 64 | RCA Victor SF 7645 | KISSIN' COUSINS (soundtrack, stereo) | 30 |
| 64 | RCA Victor RD 7678 | ROUSTABOUT (soundtrack, mono) | 15 |
| 64 | RCA Victor SF 7678 | ROUSTABOUT (soundtrack, stereo) | 25 |
| 65 | RCA Victor RD 7714 | GIRL HAPPY (soundtrack, mono) | 20 |
| 65 | RCA Victor SF 7714 | GIRL HAPPY (soundtrack, stereo) | 30 |
| 65 | RCA Victor RD 7723 | FLAMING STAR AND SUMMER KISSES (soundtrack, mono only, black label) | 50 |
| 65 | RCA Victor RD/SF 7752 | ELVIS FOR EVERYONE (mono, 'orange shirt' sleeve) | 35 |
| 65 | RCA Victor SF 7752 | ELVIS FOR EVERYONE (stereo, 'orange shirt' sleeve) | 45 |
| 65 | RCA Victor RD 7767 | HAREM HOLIDAY (soundtrack, mono) | 20 |
| 65 | RCA Victor SF 7767 | HAREM HOLIDAY (soundtrack, stereo) | 25 |
| 66 | RCA Victor RD 7793 | FRANKIE AND JOHNNY (soundtrack, mono) | 20 |
| 66 | RCA Victor SF 7793 | FRANKIE AND JOHNNY (soundtrack, stereo) | 30 |
| 66 | RCA Victor RD 7810 | PARADISE, HAWAIIAN STYLE (soundtrack, mono) | 20 |
| 66 | RCA Victor SF 7810 | PARADISE, HAWAIIAN STYLE (soundtrack, stereo) | 30 |
| 66 | RCA Victor RD 7820 | CALIFORNIA HOLIDAY (soundtrack, mono) | 20 |
| 66 | RCA Victor SF 7820 | CALIFORNIA HOLIDAY (soundtrack, stereo) | 30 |
| 67 | RCA Victor RD 7867 | HOW GREAT THOU ART (mono) | 25 |
| 67 | RCA Victor SF 7867 | HOW GREAT THOU ART (stereo) | 35 |
| 67 | RCA Victor RD 7892 | DOUBLE TROUBLE (soundtrack, mono) | 15 |
| 67 | RCA Victor SF 7892 | DOUBLE TROUBLE (soundtrack, stereo) | 20 |
| 68 | RCA Victor RD 7917 | CLAMBAKE (soundtrack, black/red dot labels, mono) | 20 |
| 68 | RCA Victor SF 7917 | CLAMBAKE (soundtrack, black/red dot labels, stereo) | 25 |
| 68 | RCA Victor RD 7924 | ELVIS' GOLD RECORDS VOLUME 4 (with "Never Ending" listed on sleeve instead of "Love Letters"; mono) | 30 |
| 68 | RCA Victor SF 7924 | ELVIS' GOLD RECORDS VOLUME 4 (with "Never Ending" listed on sleeve instead of "Love Letters"; stereo) | 40 |
| 68 | RCA Victor RD 7924 | ELVIS' GOLD RECORDS VOLUME 4 (corrected sleeve, mono) | 25 |
| 68 | RCA Victor SF 7924 | ELVIS' GOLD RECORDS VOLUME 4 (corrected sleeve, stereo) | 25 |
| 68 | RCA Victor RD 7957 | SPEEDWAY (soundtrack, with Nancy Sinatra, mono) | 30 |
| 68 | RCA Victor SF 7957 | SPEEDWAY (soundtrack, with Nancy Sinatra, stereo) | 25 |

## ALBUMS : LPS: ORIGINAL BLACK/SILVER SPOT RCA ISSUES
| 57 | RCA RC 24001 | LOVING YOU (10", soundtrack) | 75 |
| 57 | RCA RD 27052 | ELVIS' CHRISTMAS ALBUM (laminated front & back covers with 4 pictures on back cover) | 100 |
| 58 | RCA RD 27088 | KING CREOLE (soundtrack) | 40 |
| 59 | RCA RD 27120 | ELVIS | 75 |
| 59 | RCA RD 27128 | A DATE WITH ELVIS | 60 |
| 60 | RCA RD 27159 | ELVIS' GOLDEN RECORDS VOL. 2 | 30 |
| 60 | RCA RD 27171 | ELVIS IS BACK! (gatefold sleeve, mono) | 40 |
| 60 | RCA SF 5060 | ELVIS IS BACK! (gatefold sleeve, stereo) | 60 |
| 60 | RCA RD 27192 | G.I. BLUES (soundtrack, mono) | 18 |
| 60 | RCA SF 5078 | G.I. BLUES (soundtrack, stereo) | 25 |
| 61 | RCA RD 27211 | HIS HAND IN MINE (mono) | 25 |
| 61 | RCA SF 5094 | HIS HAND IN MINE (stereo) | 45 |
| 61 | RCA RD 27224 | SOMETHING FOR EVERYBODY (mono) | 20 |
| 61 | RCA SF 5106 | SOMETHING FOR EVERYBODY (stereo) | 35 |
| 61 | RCA RD 27238 | BLUE HAWAII (soundtrack, mono) | 15 |
| 61 | RCA SF 5115 | BLUE HAWAII (soundtrack, stereo) | 20 |
| 62 | RCA RD 27265 | POT LUCK (mono) | 20 |

| | | | MINT VALUE £ |
|---|---|---|---|
| 62 | RCA SF 5135 | POT LUCK (stereo) | 30 |

## ALBUMS : LPS: ORIGINAL BLACK/SILVER SPOT RCA VICTOR ISSUES

| | | | |
|---|---|---|---|
| 63 | RCA Victor RD 7534 | GIRLS! GIRLS! GIRLS! (soundtrack, mono) | 15 |
| 63 | RCA Victor SF 7534 | GIRLS! GIRLS! GIRLS! (soundtrack, stereo) | 35 |
| 63 | RCA Victor RD 7565 | IT HAPPENED AT THE WORLD'S FAIR (soundtrack, mono) | 18 |
| 63 | RCA Victor SF 7565 | IT HAPPENED AT THE WORLD'S FAIR (soundtrack, stereo) | 35 |
| 63 | RCA Victor RD 7609 | FUN IN ACAPULCO (soundtrack, mono) | 20 |
| 63 | RCA Victor SF 7609 | FUN IN ACAPULCO (soundtrack, stereo) | 35 |

## ALBUMS : LPS: ORIGINAL ORANGE RCA VICTOR ISSUES

| | | | |
|---|---|---|---|
| 69 | RCA Victor RD 8011 | ELVIS ("TV Special" Soundtrack) | 15 |
| 69 | RCA Victor RD 8029 | FROM ELVIS IN MEMPHIS (mono) | 15 |
| 70 | RCA Victor SF 8080/1 | FROM MEMPHIS TO VEGAS - FROM VEGAS TO MEMPHIS (2-LP, with 2 x 10" x 8" photos, glossy cover) | 30 |
| 70 | RCA Victor SF 8080/1 | FROM MEMPHIS TO VEGAS - FROM VEGAS TO MEMPHIS (2-LP, with 2 x 10" x 8" photos, matt cover) | 25 |
| 70 | RCA SF 8128 | ON STAGE, FEBRUARY 1970 (with 30" x 20" colour poster; glossy cover) | 15 |
| 70 | RCA LPM 6401 | WORLDWIDE 50 GOLD AWARD HITS VOL. 1 - A TOUCH OF GOLD (4-LP, box set with 20-page photo book) | 30 |
| 71 | RCA LPM 6402 | THE OTHER SIDES - WORLDWIDE 50 GOLD AWARD HITS VOL. 2 (4-LP, box with material patch & colour portrait) | 30 |
| 71 | RCA Victor SF 8162 | THAT'S THE WAY IT IS (glossy cover) | 15 |
| 71 | RCA Victor SF 8172 | I'M 10,000 YEARS OLD - ELVIS COUNTRY (with colour print, glossy cover) | 15 |
| 71 | RCA Victor SF 8221 | ELVIS SINGS THE WONDERFUL WORLD OF CHRISTMAS | 15 |
| 72 | RCA Victor SF 8266 | ELVIS NOW | 15 |
| 72 | RCA Victor SF 8275 | HE TOUCHED ME | 15 |
| 73 | RCA Victor SF 8378 | ELVIS (with "Fool" sticker, must be UK disc and UK cover!) | 40 |
| 73 | RCA DPS 2040 | ALOHA FROM HAWAII VIA SATELLITE (2-LP) | 20 |
| 73 | RCA APL1 0388 | RAISED ON ROCK/FOR OL' TIMES SAKE (U.K. disc in U.K. sleeve) | 150 |
| 74 | RCA APL1 0475 | GOOD TIMES (back cover credits "Loving Arms" or "Lovin' Arms") | 18 |
| 74 | RCA APL1 0606 | ELVIS AS RECORDED ON STAGE IN MEMPHIS | 15 |
| 74 | RCA LPL1 7527 | HITS OF THE 70s | 15 |
| 75 | RCA APL1 0873 | PROMISED LAND | 15 |
| 75 | RCA APM1 0818 | HAVING FUN WITH ELVIS ON STAGE | 20 |
| 75 | RCA RS 1011 | TODAY | 18 |
| 76 | RCA RS 1060 | FROM ELVIS PRESLEY BOULEVARD, MEMPHIS, TENNESSEE | 15 |
| 77 | RCA PL 12274 | WELCOME TO MY WORLD | 15 |
| 80 | RCA CPL8 3699 | ELVIS ARON PRESLEY (8-LP, box set) | 50 |
| 83 | RCA RCALPP 9020 | JAILHOUSE ROCK/LOVE IN LAS VEGAS (picture disc) | 12 |
| 84 | RCA PLP 89287 | I CAN HELP (picture disc) | 12 |
| 84 | RCA PL 85172 | A GOLDEN CELEBRATION (6-LP box set with inserts) | 30 |

## ALBUMS : LPS: SILVER SPOT/'RED SEAL' RCA ISSUES

| | | | |
|---|---|---|---|
| 58 | RCA RB 16069 | ELVIS' GOLDEN RECORDS (maroon 'silver spot' label, gatefold sleeve with stapled-in 4-page photo booklet) | 100 |
| 60 | RCA RB 16069 | ELVIS' GOLDEN RECORDS ('Red Seal'/'silver spot' label, gatefold sleeve with stapled-in 2-page photo booklet) | 30 |
| 63 | RCA RB 16069 | ELVIS' GOLDEN RECORDS ('Red Seal'/'black spot' label, no booklet, gatefold sleeve) | 20 |
| 67 | RCA RB 16069 | ELVIS' GOLDEN RECORDS ('Red Seal'/'black spot' label, no booklet, single sleeve) | 18 |

## ALBUMS : OTHER LPS

| | | | |
|---|---|---|---|
| 71 | Camden CDS 1088 | YOU'LL NEVER WALK ALONE (LP, withdrawn) | 150 |
| 78 | St. Michael IMP 113 | ELVIS (exclusive to Marks & Spencer) | 60 |
| 78 | St. Michael IMPD 204 | THE WONDERFUL WORLD OF ELVIS PRESLEY (2-LP, via Marks & Spencer) | 30 |
| 79 | Hammer HMR 6002 | THE KING SPEAKS (green sleeve) | 30 |
| 84 | Imperial Records DR 1124 | AMERICAN TRILOGY (3-LP, box set) | 25 |
| 85 | Sunday 1 | ELVIS: THE GOLDEN ALBUM (LP, available via Sunday Times magazine) | 20 |
| 86 | RCA AREP 1 | ACUFF-ROSE PRESENTS ELVIS (promo-only, 300 copies) | 150 |

## ALBUMS : CASTLE REISSUES

| | | | |
|---|---|---|---|
| 00 | Castle Music/BMG ELVIS 102 | THAT'S THE WAY IT IS (5-LP) | 45 |
| 99 | Castle Music/BMG ELVIS 100P | ARTIST OF THE CENTURY (box set, 5 x picture disc LPs & booklet, numbered) | 40 |
| 99 | Castle Music/BMG ELVIS 100 | ARTIST OF THE CENTUY (5-LP box set & booklet, numbered) | 40 |
| 99 | Castle Music/BMG ELVIS 100R | ARTIST OF THE CENTURY (box set, 5-LP red vinyl & booklet, numbered) | 50 |
| 99 | Castle Music/BMG ELVIS 100X | ARTIST OF THE CENTURY (box set, 5-LP, blue vinyl & booklet, numbered, HMV exclusive) | 50 |
| 99 | Castle Music/BMG ELVIS 101X | THE SUN SINGLES COLLECTION (6 x 7" box set, yellow vinyl, numbered HMV exclusive) | 35 |
| 99 | Castle Music/BMG ELVIS 101 | THE SUN SINGLES COLLECTION (6 x 7" box set with poster, numbered) | 35 |
| 00 | Castle Music/BMG ELVIS 103 | THE UK NO. 1 SINGLES COLLECTION (17 x 7" box set with booklet) | 50 |
| 00 | Castle Music/BMG ELVIS 103X | THE UK NO. 1 SINGLES COLLECTION (17 x 7" box set with booklet, coloured vinyl) | 75 |
| 00 | Castle Music/BMG ELVIS 104X | PEACE IN THE VALLEY (5-LP box set, with bonus 10" EP) | 40 |
| 00 | Castle Music/BMG ELVIS 104 | PEACE IN THE VALLEY (5-LP box set) | 30 |
| 01 | Castle Music/BMG ELVIS 105 | THE INTERNATIONAL EP COLLECTION (11 x 7" EP box set with insert) | 30 |
| 01 | Castle Music/BMG ELVIS 106 | G.I. BLUES (LP, with bonus EP) | 15 |
| 01 | Castle Music/BMG ELVIS 108 | LIVE IN LAS VEGAS (5-LP box set) | 60 |
| 01 | Castle Music/BMG ELVIS 107 | BLUE HAWAII (LP, with bonus EP) | 15 |
| 02 | Castle Music/BMG ELVIS 111 | JAILHOUSE ROCK (LP, with bonus EP) | 15 |
| 02 | Castle Music/BMG ELVIS 112 | KING CREOLE (LP, with bonus EP) | 15 |
| 02 | Castle Music/BMG ELVIS 113 | TICKLE ME (LP, with bonus EP) | 25 |
| 02 | Castle Music/BMG ELVIS 110 | LOVING YOU (LP, with bonus EP) | 15 |

*(see also Jordanaires, Scotty Moore, Bill Black's Combo)*

## REG PRESLEY
| | | | |
|---|---|---|---|
| 69 | Page One POF 131 | Lucinda Lee/Wichita Lineman | 8 |
| 73 | CBS 1478 | 'S Down To You Marianne/Hey Little Girl | 5 |

*(see also Troggs, Suzi Quatro)*

## PRESSGANG
| | | | |
|---|---|---|---|
| 89 | Vox Pop VOX 022 | ROGUES (LP) | 15 |

## RAY PRESSLEY
| | | | |
|---|---|---|---|
| 62 | Longhorn BLH 0002 | Living, Learning, Trying To Forget/Half A Love (estimated that around 1000 pressed) | 15 |

## PRESSURE
| | | | |
|---|---|---|---|
| 82 | SRT/Macca SPLIFF 1/S82CUS 1394 | Fool To Yourself/Dub To Yourself (no p/s) | 8 |

## PRESSURE 28
| | | | |
|---|---|---|---|
| 82 | Helen Of Oi! HOO 01 | Get Ready/Up Yours | 8 |

## PRESSURE GROUP
| | | | |
|---|---|---|---|
| 87 | Poltroon POL 001 | ONLY GOD IS PERFECT (EP, 300 only) | 60 |

## PRESSURE POINT
| | | | |
|---|---|---|---|
| 82 | Pressure Point PP 001 | Big Deal/Straight To The Point (p/s) | 15 |

## PRESSURE STOPS
| | | | |
|---|---|---|---|
| 80 | Airplay PLAY 1 | Crash Wanderer/Shirts | 12 |

## PRESTIGE BLUES SWINGERS
| | | | |
|---|---|---|---|
| 59 | Esquire 32-082 | BLUES GROOVE (Tiny Grimes & Coleman Hawkins as Prestige Blues Swingers (LP) | 20 |
| 60 | Esquire 32-110 | OUTSKIRTS OF TOWN (LP) | 20 |

## BILLY PRESTON
| | | | |
|---|---|---|---|
| 66 | Sue WI 4012 | Billy's Bag/Don't Let The Sun Catch You Cryin' | 25 |
| 66 | Capitol CL 15458 | In The Midnight Hour/Advice | 25 |
| 66 | Capitol CL 15458 | In The Midnight Hour/Advice (DJ copy) | 50 |
| 66 | Capitol CL 15471 | Sunny/Let The Music Play | 15 |
| 69 | President PT 263 | Billy's Bag/Don't Let The Sun Catch You Crying (reissue) | 10 |
| 69 | President PT 263 | Billy's Bag/Goldfinger (different B-side) | 15 |
| 69 | Apple APPLE 12 | That's The Way God Planned It/What About You (p/s) | 10 |
| 69 | Apple APPLE 19 | Everything's Alright/I Want To Thank You | 20 |
| 70 | Apple APPLE 21 | All That I've Got/As I Get Older (some in p/s) | 25 |
| 70 | Apple APPLE 21 | All That I've Got/As I Get Older (some in p/s) | 8 |
| 70 | President PT 298 | If I Had A Hammer/Ferry 'Cross The Mersey | 5 |
| 70 | Soul City SC 107 | Greazee (Parts 1 & 2) | 20 |
| 70 | Soul City SC 107 | Greazee (Parts 1 & 2) (DJ Copy) | 100 |
| 67 | Capitol (S)T 2532 | THE WILDEST ORGAN IN TOWN (LP) | 35 |
| 67 | Sue ILP 935 | THE MOST EXCITING ORGAN EVER (LP) | 60 |
| 69 | President PTLS 1034 | APPLE OF THEIR EYE (LP) | 20 |
| 69 | Apple SAPCOR 9 | THAT'S THE WAY GOD PLANNED IT (LP) | 30 |
| 70 | Apple SAPCOR 14 | ENCOURAGING WORDS (LP) | 60 |
| 70 | Soul City SCM 002 | GREAZEE SOUL (LP) | 30 |
| 70 | Joy JOYS 174 | GOSPEL IN MY SOUL (LP) | 20 |
| 91 | Apple SAPCOR 9 | THAT'S THE WAY GOD PLANNED IT (LP, gatefold sleeve, with bonus 12" [SAPCOR 92]) | 20 |
| 93 | Apple SAPCOR 14 | ENCOURAGING WORDS (LP, gatefold sleeve with bonus 12" [SAPCOR 142]) | 20 |

*(see also Beatles)*

## EARL PRESTON
| | | | |
|---|---|---|---|
| 63 | Fontana TF 406 | I Know Something/Watch Your Step (as Earl Preston & T.T.'s) | 20 |
| 64 | Fontana TF 481 | Raindrops/That's For Sure (as Earl Preston & Realms) | 20 |

*(see also Realm)*

## JOHNNY PRESTON
| | | | |
|---|---|---|---|
| 60 | Mercury AMT 1079 | Running Bear/My Heart Knows | 5 |
| 60 | Mercury AMT 1079 | Running Bear/My Heart Knows (78) | 40 |
| 60 | Mercury AMT 1092 | Cradle Of Love/City Of Tears (some in p/s) | 20 |
| 60 | Mercury AMT 1092 | Cradle Of Love/City Of Tears (no p/s) | 5 |
| 60 | Mercury AMT 1104 | Feel So Fine/I'm Starting To Go Steady | 8 |
| 60 | Mercury AMT 1114 | Charming Billy/Up In The Air | 8 |
| 61 | Mercury AMT 1129 | Leave My Kitten Alone/Do What You Did | 20 |
| 61 | Mercury AMT 1145 | Big Chief Heartbreak/Madre De Dios (Mother Of God) | 20 |
| 61 | Mercury AMT 1164 | New Baby For Christmas/Rock And Roll Guitar | 25 |
| 61 | Mercury AMT 1167 | Free Me/Kissing Tree | 25 |
| 60 | Mercury ZEP 10078 | RUNNING BEAR (EP) | 35 |
| 60 | Mercury ZEP 10098 | RING TAIL TOOTER (EP) | 35 |
| 61 | Mercury ZEP 10116 | TOKEN OF LOVE (EP) | 40 |
| 60 | Mercury MMC 14051 | JOHNNY PRESTON - RUNNING BEAR (LP) | 50 |

## MIKE PRESTON
| | | | |
|---|---|---|---|
| 58 | Decca F 11053 | A House, A Car And A Wedding Ring/My Lucky Love | 6 |
| 58 | Decca F 11087 | Why, Why, Why/Whispering Grass | 6 |
| 59 | Decca F 11120 | Dirty Old Town/In Surabaya | 8 |
| 59 | Decca F 11167 | Mr. Blue/Just Ask Your Heart | 5 |
| 60 | Decca F 11222 | A Girl Like You/Too Old | 5 |
| 60 | Decca F 11255 | I'd Do Anything/Where Is Love? | 5 |
| 60 | Decca F 11287 | Togetherness/Farewell My Love | 5 |
| 61 | Decca F 11335 | Marry Me/Girl Without A Heart | 5 |
| 61 | Decca F 11366 | It's All Happening/Just As I Am | 5 |
| 62 | Decca F 11493 | It's A Sin To Tell A Lie/Careless Love | 5 |
| 63 | Decca F 11613 | Punish Her/From The Very First Rose | 5 |

MINT VALUE £

| 64 | Decca F 11810 | No Strings/Nobody Told Me | 5 |
| 66 | Emerald MD1028 | Our Love Will Go On/Forgive Me | 10 |

## PRETTY BOY FLOYD & GEMS
| 79 | Rip Off RIP OFF 1 | Spread The Word Around/Hold Tight (p/s) | 15 |
| 79 | Rip Off RIP 10 | Sharon/The Instigator (p/s) | 20 |

## PRETTY THINGS
| 64 | Fontana TF 469 | Rosalyn/Big Boss Man | 15 |
| 64 | Fontana TF 503 | Don't Bring Me Down/We'll Be Together | 12 |
| 65 | Fontana TF 537 | Honey I Need/I Can Never Say | 12 |
| 65 | Fontana TF 585 | Cry To Me/Get A Buzz | 20 |
| 65 | Fontana TF 647 | Midnight To Six Man/Can't Stand The Pain | 22 |
| 66 | Fontana TF 688 | Come See Me/£.s.d. | 35 |
| 66 | Fontana TF 722 | A House In The Country/Me Needing You | 25 |
| 66 | Fontana TF 773 | Progress/Buzz The Jerk | 30 |
| 67 | Fontana TF 829 | Children/My Time | 20 |
| 67 | Columbia DB 8300 | Defecting Grey/Mr. Evasion | 100 |
| 68 | Columbia DB 8353 | Talkin' About The Good Times/Walking Through My Dreams | 80 |
| 68 | Columbia DB 8494 | Private Sorrow/Balloon Burning | 40 |
| 69 | Fontana TF 1024 | Rosalyn/Don't Bring Me Down (p/s) | 15 |
| 70 | Harvest HAR 5016 | The Good Mr. Square/Blue Serge Blues | 12 |
| 70 | Harvest HAR 5031 | October 26/Cold Stone | 10 |
| 71 | Harvest HAR 5037 | Stone-Hearted Mama/Summertime/Circus Mind | 10 |
| 72 | Warner Bros K 16225 | Over The Moon/Havana Bound | 5 |
| 12 | Fruits De Mer Crustacean 29 | Honey I Need (live)/I Can Never Say (Demo) (p/s, 500 dark red transluscent, 500 white and 200 black vinyl) | 8 |
| 12 | Fruits De Mer Crustacean 31 | S.F. SORROW LIVE IN LONDON EP (gatefold p/s, poster, white, black or maroon vinyl) | 7 |
| 64 | Fontana TE 17434 | THE PRETTY THINGS (EP) | 60 |
| 65 | Fontana TE 17442 | RAININ' IN MY HEART (EP) | 70 |
| 66 | Fontana TE 17472 | ON FILM (EP) | 150 |
| 65 | Fontana TL 5239 | THE PRETTY THINGS (LP) | 150 |
| 65 | Fontana TL 5280 | GET THE PICTURE (LP) | 200 |
| 67 | Wing WL 1164 | BEST OF THE PRETTY THINGS (LP) | 35 |
| 67 | Fontana (S)TL 5425 | EMOTIONS (LP, mono/stereo) | 150 |
| 67 | Wing WL 1167 | THE PRETTY THINGS (LP, reissue) | 40 |
| 68 | Columbia SX 6306 | S.F. SORROW (LP, gatefold sleeve, blue/black label, mono) | 700 |
| 68 | Columbia SCX 6306 | S.F. SORROW (LP, gatefold sleeve, blue/black label, stereo) | 400 |
| 70 | Columbia SCX 6306 | S.F. SORROW (LP, gatefold sleeve; silver/black label re-pressing, stereo) | 50 |
| 70 | Harvest SHVL 774 | PARACHUTE (LP, gatefold sleeve) | 125 |
| 70 | Fontana Special SFL 13140 | EMOTIONS (LP, reissue) | 20 |
| 72 | Warner Bros K 46190 | FREEWAY MADNESS (LP, gatefold sleeve) | 18 |
| 75 | Harvest SHDW 406 | S.F. SORROW/PARACHUTE (2-LP) | 40 |
| 78 | Butt Nott DO1 | ELECTRIC BANANA THE SEVEN TIES (LP) | 15 |
| 77 | Harvest SHSM 2022 | SINGLES A'S & B'S (LP) | 20 |
| 89 | Edsel XED236 | S.F. SORROW (LP, reissue, gatefold) | 20 |

*(see also Electric Banana, Twink, Viv Prince, Sunshine, Fenmen, Kate, Zac Zolar & Electric Banana)*

## EDDIE PREVOST BAND
| 78 | Matchless MR 1 | LIVE VOLUME 1 (LP, private pressing) | 15 |

*(see also Amm, Organum)*

## JOEL PREVOST
| 78 | CBS SCBS 6300 | Somewhere Sometime/Il Y Aura Toujours Des Violons | 10 |

## ALAN PRICE (SET)
| 65 | Decca F 12217 | Any Day Now (My Wild Beautiful Baby)/Never Be Sick On Sunday | 12 |
| 66 | Decca F 12367 | I Put A Spell On You/Iechyd-Da | 7 |
| 66 | Decca F 12518 | Willow Weep For Me/Yours Until Tomorrow | 6 |
| 67 | Decca F 12691 | Shame/Don't Do That Again | 6 |
| 68 | Decca F 12774 | When I Was A Cowboy/Tappy Turquoise (export issue) | 8 |
| 68 | Decca F 12808 | Love Story/My Old Kentucky Home | 20 |
| 69 | Deram DM 263 | Trimdon Grange Explosion/Falling In Love Again | 5 |
| 70 | Decca F 13017 | Sunshine And Rain (The Name Of The Game)/ Is There Anybody Out There? (solo) | 6 |
| 67 | Decca DFE 8677 | THE AMAZING ALAN PRICE (EP) | 30 |
| 66 | Decca LK 4839 | THE PRICE TO PLAY (LP, laminate front cover, flipbacks) | 30 |
| 67 | Decca LK/SKL 4907 | A PRICE ON HIS HEAD (LP, laminated front cover) | 25 |

*(see also Animals, Paul Williams Set, Johnny Almond Music Machine, Dave Greenslade)*

## KENNY PRICE
| 66 | Stateside SS 554 | Walking On New Grass/Wasting My Time | 6 |

## LLOYD PRICE
| 57 | London HL 8438 | Just Because/Why (triangular centre) | 150 |
| 57 | London HL 8438 | Just Because/Why (round centre) | 80 |
| 57 | London HL 8438 | Just Because/Why (78) | 20 |
| 59 | HMV POP 580 | Stagger Lee/You Need Love | 15 |
| 59 | HMV POP 580 | Stagger Lee/You Need Love (78) | 25 |
| 59 | HMV POP 598 | Where Were You (On Our Wedding Day)?/Is It Really Love? | 12 |
| 59 | HMV POP 598 | Where Were You (On Our Wedding Day)?/Is It Really Love? (78) | 25 |
| 59 | HMV POP 626 | Personality/Have You Ever Had The Blues? | 10 |
| 59 | HMV POP 626 | Personality/Have You Ever Had The Blues? (78) | 25 |
| 59 | HMV POP 650 | I'm Gonna Get Married/Three Little Pigs | 10 |
| 59 | HMV POP 650 | I'm Gonna Get Married/Three Little Pigs (78) | 60 |
| 59 | HMV POP 672 | Won't 'Cha Come Home/Come Into My Heart | 10 |
| 60 | HMV POP 712 | Lady Luck/Never Let Me Go | 15 |

| 60 | HMV POP 712 | Lady Luck/Never Let Me Go (78) | 30 |
| 60 | HMV POP 741 | For Love/No If's - No And's | 10 |
| 60 | HMV POP 772 | Question/If I Look A Little Blue (as Lloyd Price Orchestra) | 10 |
| 60 | HMV POP 772 | Question/If I Look A Little Blue (as Lloyd Price Orchestra) (78) | 40 |
| 60 | HMV POP 799 | Just Call Me (And I'll Understand)/Who Coulda' Told You (They Lied) | 10 |
| 61 | HMV POP 826 | Know What You're Doin'/That's Why Tears Come And Go (as Lloyd Price Orchestra) | 10 |
| 61 | HMV POP 926 | Boo Hoo/I Made You Cry | 10 |
| 62 | HMV POP 983 | Be A Leader/'Nother Fairy Tale | 10 |
| 62 | HMV POP 1100 | Under Your Spell, Again/Happy Birthday Mama | 10 |
| 63 | Liberty LIB 10127 | Misty/Cry On | 10 |
| 72 | President PT 321 | Ready For Betty/Beat In Trinidad | 10 |
| 73 | GSF GSZ 5 | Love Music/Just For Baby | 10 |
| 73 | GSF GSZ 11 | Trying To Slip Away/They Get Down | 10 |
| 59 | HMV 7EG 8538 | THE EXCITING LLOYD PRICE (EP, mono) | 50 |
| 59 | HMV GES 5784 | THE EXCITING LLOYD PRICE (EP, stereo) | 70 |
| 59 | HMV CLP 1285 | THE EXCITING LLOYD PRICE (LP) | 60 |
| 59 | HMV CLP 1314 | MR. PERSONALITY (LP) | 60 |
| 60 | London HA-U 2213 | LLOYD PRICE (LP) | 60 |
| 60 | HMV CLP 1361 | MR. PERSONALITY SINGS THE BLUES (LP) | 50 |
| 60 | HMV CLP 1393 | THE FANTASTIC LLOYD PRICE (LP, mono) | 40 |
| 60 | HMV CSD 1323 | THE FANTASTIC LLOYD PRICE (LP, stereo) | 50 |
| 62 | HMV CLP 1519 | COOKIN' (LP, mono) | 25 |
| 62 | HMV CSD 1413 | COOKIN' (LP, stereo) | 30 |
| 63 | Encore ENC 2004 | PRICE SINGS THE MILLION DOLLAR SELLERS (LP) | 15 |
| 69 | Major Minor SMLP 57 | LLOYD PRICE NOW (LP) | 20 |

**RAY PRICE**

| 57 | Philips BBE 12137 | RAY PRICE (EP) | 25 |

*(see also Cherry Wainer)*

**(ROCKIN') RED PRICE**

| 56 | Decca F 10822 | Rocky Mountain Gal/Rock O' The North (as Red Price & His Rockin' Rhythm) | 15 |
| 57 | Woodbine | Woodbine Rock (78, with picture on label, promo only) | 40 |
| 57 | Woodbine | Woodbine Rock (78, without picture on label, promo only) | 15 |
| 58 | Pye 7N 15169 | Weekend/The Sneeze | 20 |
| 58 | Pye 7N 15169 | Weekend/The Sneeze (78) | 25 |
| 60 | Pye 7N 15262 | Wow!/My Baby's Door | 10 |
| 61 | Parlophone R 4789 | Theme From "Danger Man"/Blackjack (as Red Price Combo) | 30 |

**RED PRICE & BLUE BEATS**

| 64 | Blue Beat BB 209 | Blue Beats Over (The White Cliffs Of Dover)/Kiss The Baby (When You Grow Too Old To Dream) | 10 |

**RICK PRICE**

| 70 | Gemini GMS 012 | Davey Has No Dad/Bitter Sweet | 10 |
| 71 | Gemini GMS 017 | Top Ten Record/Beautiful Sally | 10 |
| 71 | Gemini GME 1017 | TALKING TO THE FLOWERS (LP, laminated front sleeve) | 40 |

*(see also Move, Sheridan-Price, Sight & Sound)*

**RIKKI PRICE**

| 58 | Fontana H 162 | Tom Dooley/(It Looks Like Rain In) Cherry Blossom Lane | 6 |
| 59 | Fontana H 171 | Honey, Honey/The Very Thought Of You | 8 |
| 59 | Fontana H 217 | Mr. Blue/Man On My Trail | 6 |
| 62 | Fontana H 371 | You're For Real/When You Pass By | 6 |
| 58 | Fontana TFE 17100 | RIKKI PRICE (EP) | 20 |

*(see also Sheridan-Price)*

**SAMMY PRICE**

| 63 | Storyville A 45 068 | Boogieing With Big Sid/133 Street Boogie (with p/s) | 30 |
| 63 | Storyville A 45 068 | Boogieing With Big Sid/133 Street Boogie | 20 |
| 57 | Columbia SEG 7679 | ORIGINAL SAMMY BLUES (EP) | 20 |
| 58 | Vogue EPV 1146 | SAMMY PRICE (EP) | 60 |
| 58 | Vogue EPV 1151 | SAMMY PRICE'S BLUESICIANS (EP) | 60 |
| 58 | Vogue LAE 12027 | SWINGIN' PARIS STYLE (LP) | 40 |
| 62 | London Jazz LTZ-R 15240 | THE BLUES AIN'T NOTHIN' (LP, mono) | 30 |
| 62 | London Jazz SAH-R 6234 | THE BLUES AIN'T NOTHIN' (LP, stereo) | 40 |

*(see also Sister Rosetta Tharpe)*

**VINCENT PRICE**

| 77 | EMI EMI 2659 | The Monster Mash/The Bard's Own Recipe | 10 |
| 59 | Columbia 33SX 1141 | VINCENT PRICE (LP) | 45 |

**PRIDE**

| 85 | Pride P.R.T. 001 | What's Love/No Emotion (p/s) | 25 |

**DICKIE PRIDE**

| 59 | Columbia DB 4283 | Slippin' 'N' Slidin'/Don't Make Me Love You | 36 |
| 59 | Columbia DB 4296 | Fabulous Cure/Midnight Oil | 30 |
| 59 | Columbia DB 4340 | Frantic/Primrose Lane | 20 |
| 60 | Columbia DB 4403 | Betty, Betty (Go Steady With Me)/No John | 20 |
| 60 | Columbia DB 4451 | You're Singin' Our Love Song To Somebody Else/Bye Bye Blackbird | 10 |
| 59 | Columbia SEG 7937 | SHEIK OF SHAKE (EP) | 250 |
| 61 | Columbia 33SX 1307 | PRIDE WITHOUT PREJUDICE (LP, mono) | 60 |
| 61 | Columbia SCX 3369 | PRIDE WITHOUT PREJUDICE (LP, stereo) | 70 |

*(see also Guvners)*

**LOUIS PRIMA (& HIS ORCHESTRA)**

| 56 | Capitol CL 14669 | 5 Months, 2 Weeks, 2 Days/Banana Split For My Baby | 20 |

| 58 | Capitol CL 14821 | Buona Sera/Beep! Beep! | 15 |
|----|------------------|------------------------|-----|
| 60 | London HLD 9230 | Ol' Man Moses (with Sam Butera's Witnesses)/Wonderland By Night | 10 |
| 64 | Prima PR 1001 | Fee Fie Foo Part 1/Fee Fie Foo Part 2 | 6 |
| 59 | Capitol EAP1 1132 | STRICTLY PRIMA (EP) | 10 |
| 58 | Capitol T 908 | THE WILDEST SHOW AT TAHOE (LP) | 20 |
| 57 | Capitol T 755 | THE WILDEST (LP) | 30 |
| 58 | Capitol T 836 | THE CALL OF THE WILDEST (LP) | 20 |

*(see also Sam Butera's Witnesses)*

## LOUIS PRIMA & KEELY SMITH
| 54 | Columbia SCM 5092 | Take A Little Walk Around The Block/LOUIS PRIMA: Oh! Cumari | 6 |
|----|-------------------|------------------------------------------------------------|-----|
| 59 | Capitol T 1160 | HEY BOY! HEY GIRL! (LP) | 25 |

*(see also Keely Smith)*

## PRIMAL SCREAM
| 85 | Creation CRE 017 | All Fall Down/It Happens (foldaround p/s in poly bag) | 25 |
|----|------------------|------------------------------------------------------|-----|
| 86 | Creation CRE 026 | Crystal Crescent/Velocity Girl (p/s) | 18 |
| 86 | Creation CRE 026T | Crystal Crescent/Velocity Girl/Spirea X (12", p/s) | 12 |
| 87 | Elevation ACID 3 | Gentle Tuesday/Black Star Carnival (p/s) | 5 |
| 87 | Elevation ACID 5 | Imperial/Star Fruit Surf Rider (p/s) | 8 |
| 87 | Elevation ACID 5T | Imperial/Star Fruit Surf Rider/So Sad About Us/Imperial (demo) (12", in poster p/s with 'special price' sticker) | 10 |
| 89 | Creation CRE 067 | Ivy Ivy Ivy/You're Just Too Dark To Care | 5 |
| 87 | Elevation ELV 2 | SONIC FLOWER GROOVE (LP) | 15 |
| 89 | Creation CRELP 054 | PRIMAL SCREAM (LP, with bonus 45 "Split Wide Open 1"/ Lone Star Girl 1 [CREFRE 6, no p/s]) | 20 |
| 91 | Creation CRELP 076 | SCREAMADELICA (2-LP) | 30 |
| 94 | Creation CRELP 146 | GIVE OUT BUT DON'T GIVE UP (2-LP, inners) | 25 |
| 97 | Creation CREL 7224 | ECHO DEK (5 x 7", box set) | 18 |
| 98 | Creation CRELP 178 | VANISHING POINT (2-LP, gatefold) | 40 |
| 99 | Sony/Creation 88697811063 | SCREAMADELICA (2-LP, reissue, red vinyl, numbered) | 35 |
| 00 | Creation CRELP 239 | EXTERMINATOR (EXTMNTR) (2-LP) | 40 |
| 02 | Columbia 508923 | EVIL HEAT (2-LP) | 18 |
| 03 | Columbia 5136031 | DIRTY HITS (3-LP) | 25 |
| 06 | Columbia 82876831651 | RIOT CITY BLUES (2-LP) | 18 |
| 08 | B-Unique BUN 142 LP | BEAUTIFUL FUTURE (Box set, LP, poster, booklet) | 40 |

*(see also Jesus & Mary Chain, Revolving Paint Dream, P.P. & Primes, Death In Vegas)*

## PRIMARY
| 83 | Goldfish 002 | Radio Silence/Responding (p/s) | 7 |
|----|--------------|--------------------------------|-----|

## PRIME MOVERS
| 89 | Cyanide CND 001 | SINS OF THE FOURFATHERS (LP) | 25 |
|----|-----------------|------------------------------|-----|

## PRIME RHYME MASTERS
| 91 | Kold Sweat KS115 | You Need Discipline/To Kill A Mockingbird (12") | 15 |
|----|------------------|------------------------------------------------|-----|

## PRIME-MATES
| 69 | Action ACT 4530 | Hot Tamales (Versions 1 & 2) | 30 |
|----|-----------------|------------------------------|-----|

## PRIMETTES
| 68 | Ember EMBS 3398 | LOOKING BACK WITH THE PRIMETTES AND EDDIE FLOYD (LP, 1 side each) | 40 |
|----|-----------------|-----------------------------------------------------------------|-----|
| 73 | Windmill WMD 192 | THE ROOTS OF DIANA ROSS AND EDDIE FLOYD (LP, reissue) | 15 |

*(see also Supremes, Eddie Floyd)*

## PRIMITIVE MAN
| 71 | Decca F13188 | Animal Love/Major Barmy From The Army | 30 |
|----|--------------|---------------------------------------|-----|

## PRIMITIVES
| 64 | Pye 7N 15721 | Help Me/Let Them Tell | 220 |
|----|--------------|-----------------------|------|
| 65 | Pye 7N 15755 | You Said/How Do You Feel | 250 |

*(see also Mal & Primitives)*

## PRIMITIVES
| 86 | Head HEAD 010 | Thru The Flowers/Across My Shoulder/Lazy/She Don't Need You (12", unreleased, white label test pressings only) | 30 |
|----|---------------|--------------------------------------------------------------------------------------------------------------|-----|
| 86 | Lazy LAZY 01 | Thru The Flowers/Across My Shoulder/She Don't Need You/Lazy (12", p/s) | 10 |
| 86 | Lazy LAZY 02 | Really Stupid/We Found A Way To The Sun (p/s) | 5 |
| 86 | Lazy LAZY 03 | Stop Killing Me/Buzz Buzz Buzz (p/s, with postcard, sleeves printed back-to-front; with badge) | 5 |
| 87 | Lazy LAZY 05 | Ocean Blue/Shadow (2,000 only, given away free at London Astoria gig) | 6 |

## PRIMROSE
| 69 | NEMS 56-4129 | Just For You/Nine Till Five | 25 |
|----|--------------|-----------------------------|-----|

## PRIMROSE CIRCUS
| 70 | President PT 314 | P.S. Call Me Lulu/In My Mind | 10 |
|----|------------------|------------------------------|-----|

## PRIMUS
| 90 | Caroline CAROLLP 10 | FRIZZLE FRY (LP) | 20 |
|----|---------------------|------------------|-----|

## PRINCE
### SINGLES
| 79 | Warner Bros K 17537 | I Wanna Be Your Lover/Just As Long As We're Together | 5 |
|----|---------------------|------------------------------------------------------|-----|
| 79 | Warner Bros K 17537T | I Wanna Be Your Lover/Just As Long As We're Together (12", company sleeve) | 15 |
| 80 | Warner Bros K 17590 | Sexy Dancer/Bambi (die-cut company sleeve) | 25 |
| 80 | Warner Bros K 17590T | Sexy Dancer (Remix)/Bambi (12", die-cut company sleeve) | 50 |
| 81 | Warner Bros K 17768 | Do It All Night/Head (die-cut company sleeve) | 25 |
| 81 | Warner Bros K 17768T | Do It All Night/Head (12", die-cut company sleeve) | 60 |
| 81 | Warner Bros K 17819 | Gotta Stop (Messin' About)/Uptown (p/s) | 60 |
| 81 | Warner Bros K 17819 | Gotta Stop (Messin' About)/I Wanna Be Your Lover (p/s) | 60 |
| 81 | Warner Bros LV 47 | Gotta Stop (Messin' About)/Uptown/Head (12", stickered p/s) | 60 |

| 81 | Warner Bros LV 47 | Gotta Stop (Messin' About)/I Wanna Be Your Lover/Head (12", stickered, colour p/s) .. 60 |
|----|------------------|---------|
| 81 | Warner Bros K 17866 | Controversy/When You Were Mine (p/s) .................................................................. 20 |
| 81 | Warner Bros K 17866T | Controversy/When You Were Mine (12", p/s) ........................................................... 30 |
| 82 | Warner Bros K 17922 | Let's Work/Ronnie, Talk To Russia (p/s) .................................................................. 40 |
| 82 | Warner Bros K 17922T | Let's Work (Extended)/Ronnie, Talk To Russia (12", p/s) ......................................... 40 |
| 83 | Warner Bros W 9896 | 1999/How Come U Don't Call Me Anymore (paper labels, p/s, with free cassette mini-album in card p/s: "1999 (Edit)"/"Uptown"/"Controvesy"/"Dirty Minds"/"Sexuality") 40 |
| 83 | Warner Bros W 9896 | 1999/How Come U Don't Call Me Anymore (paper labels, p/s).................................. 8 |
| 83 | Warner Bros W 9688 | Little Red Corvette/Lady Cab Driver (p/s) .............................................................. 10 |
| 83 | Warner Bros W 9688T | Little Red Corvette (Full Length Version)/Automatic/International Lover (12", stickered p/s, with poster insert)......................................................................... 40 |
| 83 | Warner Bros W 9688T | Little Red Corvette (Full Length Version)/Automatic/International Lover (12", stickered p/s)........................................................................................................ 12 |
| 83 | Warner Bros W 9688T | Little Red Corvette (Full Length Version)/Automatic/International Lover (12", 'negative image' p/s)............................................................................................ 20 |
| 83 | Warner Bros W 9436 | Little Red Corvette/Horny Toad (poster calendar p/s) ........................................... 55 |
| 83 | Warner Bros W 9436 | Little Red Corvette/Horny Toad (standard p/s) ...................................................... 40 |
| 83 | Warner Bros W 9436T | Little Red Corvette (Full Length Version)/Horny Toad/D.M.S.R. (12", p/s) ............... 15 |
| 83 | Warner Bros W 9436T | Little Red Corvette (Full Length Version)/Horny Toad/D.M.S.R. (12", p/s, with spiral-bound calendar)................................................................................................... 85 |
| 83 | Warner Bros W 9436T | Little Red Corvette (Full Length Version)/Horny Toad/D.M.S.R. (12", p/s, with poster).. 75 |
| 84 | Warner Bros W 9286T | When Doves Cry/17 Days//1999/D.M.S.R. (12", stickered shrinkwrapped double pack)...................................................................................................................... 20 |
| 84 | Warner Bros W 9174P | Purple Rain/God (motorbike-shaped picture disc) ................................................. 50 |
| 84 | Warner Bros W 9174T | Purple Rain/God (instrumental)/God (12", p/s, initial pressing with poster).............. 15 |
| 84 | Warner Bros W 9121TE | I Would Die 4 U (U.S. Remix)/Another Lonely Christmas (U.S. Remix) (12", p/s) .......... 20 |
| 85 | Paisley Park W 9052P | Paisley Park/She's Always In My Hair (shaped picture disc) .................................... 25 |
| 85 | Paisley Park W 9052T | Paisley Park/She's Always In My Hair/Paisley Park (Remix) (12", mispressing with repeated 2nd track "She's Always In My Hair")............................................................ 25 |
| 86 | Paisley Park W 8751P | Kiss/Love Or Money (shaped picture disc with plinth) ........................................... 30 |
| 86 | Paisley Park W 8751T | Kiss (Extended)/Love Or Money (12", p/s, with poster) .......................................... 15 |
| 86 | Paisley Park W 8711TE | Mountains (Ext.)/Alexa De Paris (10", white vinyl in PVC sleeve) ........................... 20 |
| 86 | Paisley Park W 8711T | Mountains (Extended 9.56)/Alexa De Paris (12", p/s, with poster) ........................... 20 |
| 86 | Paisley Park W 8586F | Girls And Boys (Edit)/Under The Cherry Moon//She's Always In My Hair/ 17 Days (double pack, gatefold p/s).................................................................................... 15 |
| 86 | Paisley Park W 8586P | Girls And Boys (Edit)/Under The Cherry Moon (shaped picture disc) ....................... 40 |
| 86 | Paisley Park W 8586T | Girls And Boys/Under The Cherry Moon/Erotic City (12", p/s, with poster advertising London gigs)........................................................................................................ 18 |
| 86 | Paisley Park W 8521W | Anotherloverholenyohead/I Wanna Be Your Lover (paper or plastic labels, poster p/s)........................................................................................................................ 12 |
| 86 | Paisley Park W 8521T | Anotherloverholenyohead (Extended)/I Wanna Be Your Lover (12", p/s)................... 10 |
| 87 | Paisley Park W 8399TP | Sign O' The Times (Extended)/La La La He He Hee (Extended) (12", picture disc) .......... 10 |
| 87 | Paisley Park W 8334W | If I Was Your Girlfriend/Shockadelica (poster p/s) ................................................. 8 |
| 87 | Paisley Park W 8334E | If I Was Your Girlfriend/Shockadelica (peach vinyl, PVC cover, with postcards & stickers)...................................................................................................................... 15 |
| 87 | Paisley Park W 8334TP | If I Was Your Girlfriend/Shockadelica (Extended) (12", picture disc) ....................... 12 |
| 87 | Paisley Park W 8288TP | I Could Never Take The Place Of Your Man/Hot Thing (Remixed Edit)/ Hot Thing (Extended) (12", picture disc)........................................................................................ 15 |
| 88 | Paisley Park W 7745 | I Wish U Heaven (Edit)/Scarlet Pussy (Edit) (poster p/s)........................................... 5 |
| 88 | Paisley Park W 8751TP | Kiss/Love Or Money (shaped picture disc, 're-promoted' edition with longer, extended version of B-side & without plinth)........................................................ 10 |

## ALBUMS

| 83 | Warner Bros 923 809-1 | 1999 (LP, original issue, single disc) .................................................................... 18 |
|----|----------------------|---------|
| 83 | Warner Bros. 92 3720-1 | 1999 (2-LP)...................................................................................................... 20 |
| 84 | Warner Bros 925 110-1 | PURPLE RAIN - MUSIC FROM THE MOTION PICTURE (LP, purple vinyl with poster) ....... 25 |
| 86 | Paisley Park WX 39P | PARADE - MUSIC FROM "UNDER THE CHERRY MOON" (LP, pic. disc, die-cut sleeve) ..... 35 |
| 89 | Paisley Park 925 978-2 | BATMAN (CD, picture disc in 'Bat' tin with booklet)............................................... 15 |
| 92 | Warner Bros. 9362-45037-1 | LOVE SYMBOL (2-LP) ....................................................................................... 40 |
| 94 | Warners 936245793-1 | BLACK ALBUM (LP, title sticker) ........................................................................ 35 |
| 94 | Warner Bros. 9362 45700-1 | COME (LP).......................................................................................................... 50 |
| 95 | NPG 6103-1 | EXODUS (LP, as NPG) ........................................................................................ 15 |
| 95 | Warner Bros. 9362-45999-1 | THE GOLD EXPERIENCE (2-LP) ........................................................................... 50 |
| 96 | NPG EMI CDEMO 1102 | EMANCIPATION (3-CD, as ß) .............................................................................. 25 |
| 98 | NPG BCT 9871 | CRYSTAL BALL (4-CD, import only, as ß) ............................................................... 40 |
| 99 | Arista 07822 14624 1 | RAVE UN2 THE JOY FANTASTIC (2-LP)................................................................... 40 |

## PROMOS

| 81 | Warner Bros SAM 172 | Dance Music Sex Romance/Dance Music Sex Romance (12", p/s, promo only) .......... 100 |
|----|--------------------|---------|
| 84 | Warner Bros | Purple Rain (promo only p/s, purple vinyl) ........................................................... 60 |
| 84 | Warner Bros SAM 230 | I Would Die 4 U/I would Die 4 U .......................................................................... 30 |
| 91 | Warner Brothers SAM 888 | Gett Off (Urge Single Edit) (1-sided promo)........................................................... 15 |
| 92 | Paisley Park W 0113 | Thunder (DJ Edit) (1-sided promo only white label, stickered company sleeve)......... 15 |
| 95 | NPG 61225 | Get Wild (Money Maker Radio Mix) (CD, as NPG, radio programmer's picture disc)....... 45 |
| 95 | NPG 61047 | Get Wild/Beautiful Girl (no p/s, as NPG) ............................................................... 6 |
| 96 | NPG 60667 | Lovesign/MARGIE COX: Standing At The altar (no p/s, as ß) ................................... 10 |
| 96 | NPG 60600 | Lovesign (Radio Edit Mix)/(1-800 New Funk Version)/(The Storyboard Video Mix) (12", as ß, most with title sticker)........................................................................ 35 |
| 96 | NPG 60605 | Lovesign (Radio Edit Mix)/(1-800 New Funk Version)/(The Storyboard Video Mix) (CD, as ß)............................................................................................................... 30 |
| 04 | Urban CK92560LP | MUSICOLOGY (2-LP, promo) .............................................................................. 50 |

## PRINCE ALLAH

| 78 | Freedom Sounds FSD 020 | Bucket Bottom/FULL WOOD: Stop And Think Me Over (12") ................................... 25 |
|----|------------------------|---------|

## PRINCE BROTHERS

| | | | |
|---|---|---|---|
| 77 | Carib Gems CG 010 | Ram Jam/REVOLUTIONARIES: Version To Jam | 6 |

## PRINCE BUSTER (& ALL STARS)

| | | | |
|---|---|---|---|
| 61 | Starlite ST45 052 | Buster's Shack (as Buster's Group)/ERIC MORRIS: Search The World | 30 |
| 62 | Blue Beat BB 101 | My Sound That Goes Around/They Got To Go (with Torchlighters) | 18 |
| 62 | Blue Beat BB 116 | Independence Song (with Bluebeats)/RICO & BLUEBEATS: August 1962 | 25 |
| 62 | Blue Beat BB 133 | Time Longer Than Rope/Fake King (with Voice Of The People) | 25 |
| 62 | Blue Beat BB 138 | One Hand Washes The Other/Cowboy Comes To Town | 30 |
| 63 | Blue Beat BB 150 | Run Man Run/Danny, Dane And Lorraine | 25 |
| 63 | Blue Beat BB 158 | Open Up, Bartender/Enjoy It (B-side actually "Enjoy Yourself") | 25 |
| 63 | Blue Beat BB 162 | Money/SCHOOL BOYS: Little Boy Blue | 40 |
| 63 | Blue Beat BB 163 | King, Duke, Sir/I See Them In My Sight | 30 |
| 63 | Blue Beat BB 167 | The Ten Commandments (with All Stars)/Buster's Welcome | 20 |
| 63 | Blue Beat BB 170 | Madness/PRINCE BUSTER ALL STARS: Toothache | 20 |
| 63 | Blue Beat BB 173 | Burning Creation/PRINCE BUSTER ALL STARS: Boop | 30 |
| 63 | Blue Beat BB 180 | Three More Rivers To Cross/RAYMOND HARPER & PRINCE BUSTER ALL STARS: African Blood | 25 |
| 63 | Blue Beat BB 186 | Fowl Thief/Remember Me | 60 |
| 63 | Blue Beat BB 189 | Watch It Blackhead/Hello My Dear | 25 |
| 63 | Blue Beat BB 192 | Rollin' Stone (with Charmers)/RICO & HIS BLUES BAND: This Day | 30 |
| 63 | Blue Beat BB 197 | Window Shopping/Sodom And Gomorrah | 35 |
| 63 | Blue Beat BB 199 | Spider And Fly/Three Blind Mice | 30 |
| 63 | Blue Beat BB 200 | Wash All Your Troubles Away/RICO & BLUE BEATS: Soul Of Africa | 20 |
| 63 | Dice CC 6 | They Got To Come/These Are The Times (with Voice Of The People) | 15 |
| 63 | Dice CC 11 | Blackhead Chinaman/You Ask (I Had A Girl) | 18 |
| 63 | Dice CC 18 | World Peace/The Lion Roars (as Prince Buster & Hazel) | 15 |
| 64 | Stateside SS 335 | 30 Pieces Of Silver/Everybody Ska | 25 |
| 64 | Blue Beat BB 210 | Wash All Your Troubles Away/RICO & BLUE BEATS: Soul Of Africa (p/s reissue) | 90 |
| 64 | Blue Beat BB 211 | Bluebeat Spirit/Beggars Are No Choosers | 35 |
| 64 | Blue Beat BB 216 | You're Mine/Tongue Will Tell | 35 |
| 64 | Blue Beat BB 225 | Three Blind Mice/I Know | 35 |
| 64 | Blue Beat BB 232 | Sheep On Top (song actually titled "She Pon Top")/Midnight | 45 |
| 64 | Blue Beat BB 234 | She Loves You/Healing | 60 |
| 64 | Blue Beat BB 243 | Jealous/Buster's Ska | 35 |
| 64 | Blue Beat BB 248 | Thirty Pieces Of Silver/The National Dance | 35 |
| 64 | Blue Beat BB 254 | Wings Of A Dove/MAYTALLS: Sweet Love | 35 |
| 64 | Blue Beat BB 262 | Old Lady/Dayo Ska | 35 |
| 64 | Blue Beat BB 271 | No Knowledge In College/In The Middle Of The Night | 45 |
| 64 | Blue Beat BB 274 | I May Never Love You Again/Hey Little Girl | 35 |
| 65 | Blue Beat BB 278 | Blood Pressure/Islam | 150 |
| 65 | Blue Beat BB 281 | Blues Market/MAYTALS: Looking Down The Street | 50 |
| 65 | Blue Beat BB 282 | Big Fight/Red Dress | 35 |
| 65 | Blue Beat BB 293 | Agua Fumar/Long Winter (with Charmers) | 40 |
| 65 | Blue Beat BB 302 | Ling Ting Tong/Walk Along | 100 |
| 65 | Blue Beat BB 307 | Bonanza/Wonderful Life | 30 |
| 65 | Blue Beat BB 309 | Here Comes The Bride (with Patsy Todd, as Jamaica's Greatest)/ BUSTER'S ALLSTARS: Burkes' Law | 40 |
| 65 | Blue Beat BB 313 | Everybody Yeah Yeah (as Jamaica's Greatest)/ BUSTER'S ALLSTARS: Gun The Man Down | 50 |
| 65 | Blue Beat BB 314 | Float Like A Butterfly/Haunted Room | 50 |
| 65 | Blue Beat BB 316 | Sugar Pop/Feel Up (as Prince & Jamaica's Greatest) | 40 |
| 65 | Blue Beat BB 317 | Come Home/I Thank You (as Jamaica's Greatest) | 45 |
| 65 | Blue Beat BB 321 | My Girl/BUSTER'S ALL STARS: The Fugitive | 50 |
| 65 | Blue Beat BB 324 | Al Capone/One Step Beyond (as Prince Buster's Allstars) (blue label) | 15 |
| 65 | Blue Beat BB 324 | Al Capone/One Step Beyond (as Prince Buster's Allstars) (other label colours) | 15 |
| 65 | Blue Beat BB 328 | Ambition/BUSTER'S ALL STARS: Ryging | 30 |
| 65 | Blue Beat BB 330 | Rum And Coca Cola/I Love Her | 100 |
| 65 | Blue Beat BB 334 | The Ten Commandments/BUSTER'S ALL STARS: Sting Like A Bee (reissue) | 15 |
| 65 | Blue Beat BB 335 | Respect/BUSTER'S ALL STARS: Virginia (B-side actually Dance Jamaica by Val Bennett & Prince Buster's All Stars) | 45 |
| 66 | Blue Beat BB 338 | Big Fight (Prince Buster Versus Duke Reid)/Adios, Senorita | 40 |
| 66 | Blue Beat BB 339 | Under Arrest (But Officer)/PRINCE BUSTER'S ALLSTARS: Say Boss Man | 40 |
| 66 | Blue Beat BB 343 | Prince Of Peace/Don't Throw Stones | 100 |
| 66 | Blue Beat BB 352 | Day Of Light (song actually "Dayo")/It's Too Late | 25 |
| 66 | Blue Beat BB 355 | Sunshine With My Girl/Girl Answer Your Name | 120 |
| 66 | Blue Beat BB 357 | I Won't Let You Cry/Hard Man Fe Dead | 80 |
| 66 | Blue Beat BB 359 | The Prophet (actually "Feel The Spirit" with Slim Smith)/ BUSTER'S ALL STARS: Lion Of Judah | 100 |
| 66 | Blue Beat BB 362 | To Be Loved/BUSTER'S ALLSTARS: Set Me Free | 30 |
| 66 | Rainbow RAI 107 | Your Turn (Sad Song)/If You Leave Me (with Allstars) | 25 |
| 67 | Blue Beat BB 370 | Shanty Town (Get Scanty)/BUSTER'S ALL STARS: Duppy | 30 |
| 67 | Blue Beat BB 373 | Knock On Wood/And I Love Her | 50 |
| 67 | Blue Beat BB 377 | Dark End Of The Street/Love Oh Love | 45 |
| 67 | Blue Beat BB 378 | Drunkard's Psalm (Wise Man)/7 Wonders Of The World (as Prince Buster All Stars) | 175 |
| 67 | Blue Beat BB 382 | Sit And Wonder (with His All Stars)/ROLAND ALFONSO: Sunrise In Kingston | 60 |
| 67 | Blue Beat BB 383 | Sharing You/You'll Be Lonely On The Blue Train (as Prince Buster's Allstars; A-side actually by Prince Buster, B-side actually by Rico's Band) | 30 |
| 67 | Blue Beat BB 384 | Take It Easy/Why Must I Cry (2nd issue, B-side actually by Hopeton Lewis) | 20 |
| 67 | Blue Beat BB 387 | Judge Dread (Judge Four Hundred Years)/FITZROY CAMPBELL & PRINCE BUSTER ALL STARS: Waiting For My Rude Girl | 25 |
| 67 | Blue Beat BB 388 | Dance Cleopatra/All In My Mind | 100 |

| 67 | Blue Beat BB 390 | Soul Serenade/Too Hot | 30 |
|----|------------------|-----------------------|-----|
| 67 | Blue Beat BB 391 | Land Of Imagination/The Appeal (B-side actually "The Barrister Appeal") | 30 |
| 67 | Blue Beat BB 393 | Johnny Dollar/Rude Boys Rude | 45 |
| 67 | Blue Beat BB 395 | This Gun's For Hire/Yes, Daddy | 30 |
| 67 | Blue Beat BB 397 | Quit Place/Rude Boys Rude | 40 |
| 67 | Blue Beat BB 400 | All In My Mind/Judge Dread Dance (The Pardon) | 30 |
| 67 | Blue Beat BB 402 | Vagabond/PRINCE BUSTER ALL STARS: Come Get Me | 30 |
| 67 | Philips BF 1552 | The Ten Commandments/Don't Make Me Cry | 15 |
| 67 | Fab FAB 10 | Shakin' Up Orange Street/Black Girl (with Allstars) | 30 |
| 67 | Fab FAB 11 | Johnny Cool (Parts 1 & 2) (with Allstars) | 30 |
| 67 | Fab FAB 16 | Bye Bye Baby/Human (with Allstars) | 30 |
| 67 | Fab FAB 25 | Train To Girls Town/Give Love A Try (with Allstars) | 40 |
| 67 | Fab FAB 26 | Going To The River (as Prince Buster & Allstars)/ PRINCE BUSTER'S ALLSTARS: Julie On My Mind | 30 |
| 68 | Fab FAB 31 | Kings Of Old (My Ancestors)/Sweet Inspiration (with Allstars) | 45 |
| 68 | Fab FAB 35 | Try A Little Tenderness/All My Loving (with Allstars) | 300 |
| 68 | Fab FAB 36 | The Glory Of Love/Another Sad Nite | 30 |
| 68 | Fab FAB 37 | This Is A Hold Up/Julie On My Mind (with Allstars) | 30 |
| 68 | Fab FAB 38 | Free Love (with Allstars)/DALTONS: All Over The World | 18 |
| 68 | Fab FAB 40 | Rough Rider (with Allstars)/PRINCE BUSTER: 127 Orange Street (B-side actually by Prince Buster Allstars) | 20 |
| 68 | Fab FAB 41 | Shepherd Beng Beng (with Teddy King)/TENNORS: Ride Your Donkey | 20 |
| 68 | Fab FAB 47 | Going To Ethiopia (as Prince Buster & Allstars)/ PRINCE BUSTER ALLSTARS: Shakin' Up Orange Street | 20 |
| 68 | Fab FAB 49 | Glory Of Love/WAILERS: Mellow Mood (possibly white labels only) | 100 |
| 68 | Fab FAB 56 | Intensified Dirt/Don't You Know I Love You (with Allstars) | 35 |
| 68 | Fab FAB 57 | Green Green Grass Of Home (as Prince Buster's Allstars; actually by Prince Buster & Allstars)/SOUL MAKERS: Girls Like You | 20 |
| 68 | Fab FAB 58 | We Shall Overcome/Keep The Faith (as Prince Buster's Allstars; actually by Prince Buster & Allstars) | 15 |
| 68 | Fab FAB 64 | Cool Stroker/It's You I Love (B-side actually by Little Roy) | 40 |
| 68 | Fab FAB 80 | Hypocrite/New Dance (B-side actually by Little Roy) | 20 |
| 68 | Fab FAB 81 | Whine And Grind/The Scorcher (with Allstars) | 80 |
| 69 | Unity UN 522 | 30 Pieces Of Silver/Everybody Ska (reissue) | 20 |
| 69 | Fab FAB 82 | Dr. Rodney (Black Power)/Taxation | 35 |
| 69 | Fab FAB 92 | Pharaoh House Crash/Ob-La-Di, Ob-La-Da | 20 |
| 69 | Fab FAB 93 | Ob-La-Di, Ob-La-Da/Wreck A Pum Pum | 15 |
| 69 | Fab FAB 94 | Hey Jude/Django Fever | 35 |
| 69 | Fab FAB 102 | Black Soul/CALEDONIANS: Oh Baby (B-side actually by Claredonians) | 15 |
| 69 | Fab FAB 108 | Whine And Grind/The Scorcher (with Allstars) (reissue) | 20 |
| 69 | Fab FAB 118 | Bull Buck/ROLAND ALPHONSO: One Heart | 15 |
| 69 | Fab FAB 119 | Let Her Go/Tie The Donkey's Tail | 15 |
| 69 | Fab FAB 122 | Stand Up/Happy Reggae (with Allstars) | 15 |
| 70 | Fab FAB 127 | Young Gifted And Black/PRINCE BUSTER'S ALLSTARS: The Rebel | 15 |
| 70 | Fab FAB 131 | That's All/The Preaching (B-side actually titled "The Preacher") | 15 |
| 70 | Fab FAB 132 | Ganja Plant/Creation | 30 |
| 70 | Fab FAB 140 | Hit Me Back/Give Peace A Chance | 15 |
| 70 | Fab FAB 150 | Big Five/Musical College | 8 |
| 70 | Prince Buster PB 1 | Big Five/Musical College (reissue) | 8 |
| 70 | Prince Buster PB 2 | Rat Trap/Black Organ (B-side with Allstars but actually by Ansell Collins & Prince Buster's Allstars) | 10 |
| 71 | Fab FAB 162 | Baby Version (with Jan Fender)/Holly | 8 |
| 71 | Fab FAB 176 | Police Trim Rasta (with Allstars)/Smooth (B-side actually by Ansell Collins & Prince Buster Allstars) | 10 |
| 71 | Prince Buster PB 4 | Fishey/More Fishey | 7 |
| 71 | Prince Buster PB 7 | I Wish Your Picture Was You/PRINCE BUSTER ALLSTARS: It Mash Up - Version (B-side actually by Dennis Alcapone) | 8 |
| 71 | Prince Buster PB 8 | Sons Of Zion (actually by Dennis Alcapone)/ANSELL COLLINS: Short Circuit | 8 |
| 71 | Prince Buster PB 9 | My Happiness/Human (with Allstars) | 7 |
| 71 | Prince Buster PB10 | Still/Version | 10 |
| 72 | Prince Buster PB 14 | Big Sister Stuff/Satta Massagana (with Allstars) | 12 |
| 72 | Prince Buster PB 15 | Protection/Cool Operator (with Allstars) | 8 |
| 72 | Prince Buster PB 16 | I Stand Accused/My Heart is Gone (with Allstars) | 7 |
| 72 | Prince Buster PB 19 | Four In One Medley/Drums Drums (as Prince Buster & Allstars, B-side actually by Prince Buster Allstars) | 7 |
| 72 | Prince Buster PB20 | They Got To Come/Time Longer Than Rope | 20 |
| 72 | Prince Buster PB24 | Giant/Science | 20 |
| 72 | Prince Buster PB 32 | Still/Sister Big Stuff (with Allstars) | 7 |
| 72 | Prince Buster PB 36 | South Of The Border/South Of The Border (Version) (with Allstars) | 7 |
| 72 | Fab FAB 36 | South Of The Border/South Of The Border (Version) (with Allstars) | 7 |
| 72 | Prince Buster PB 47 | Baldhead Pum Pum/Giver Her (with Allstars) | 12 |
| 79 | Blue Beat DDBB 324 | Al Capone/One Step Beyond (12", p/s) | 10 |
| 79 | Blue Beat DDBB 334 | THREE OF THE BEST (12" EP, p/s) | 150 |
| 63 | Blue Beat BBLP 802 | I FEEL THE SPIRIT (LP) | 150 |
| 65 | Blue Beat BBLP 805 | SKA-LIP-SOUL (LP, with His All Stars) | 150 |
| 65 | Blue Beat BBLP 806 | IT'S BURKE'S LAW - JAMAICA SKA EXPLOSION! (LP, as Prince Buster All Stars; 2 different sleeves, laminated plain and unlaminated 'explosion') | 300 |
| 67 | Blue Beat BBLP 807 | WHAT A HARD MAN FE DEAD - PRINCE BUSTER SINGS FOR THE PEOPLE (LP, with Baba Brooks) | 350 |
| 67 | Blue Beat BBLP 808 | ON TOUR (LP) | 150 |
| 67 | Blue Beat BBLP 809 | JUDGE DREAD (LP) | 125 |
| 67 | Blue Beat BBLP 820 | SHE WAS A ROUGH RIDER (LP) | 100 |

| 68 | Fab BBLP 820 | SHE WAS A ROUGH RIDER (LP, reissue on Fab label) | 30 |
|---|---|---|---|
| 68 | Fab BBLP 821 | WRECK A PUM PUM (LP) | 45 |
| 69 | Fab BBLP 822 | THE OUTLAW (LP, title listed as "Queen Of The Outlaws" on disc) | 120 |
| 70 | Fab MS 1 | FABULOUS GREATEST HITS (LP, original issue with 'West Brothers Printers' credit on rear of sleeve) | 30 |
| 70 | Fab MS 2 | I FEEL THE SPIRIT (LP) | 60 |
| 70 | Fab MS 6 | TUTTI FRUTTI (LP) | 45 |
| 72 | Melodisc MLP 12-156 | SISTER BIG STUFF (LP) | 50 |
| 72 | Melodisc MLP 12-157 | BIG FIVE (LP) | 30 |
| 73 | Prince Buster PB 9 | ORIGINAL GOLDEN OLDIES VOLUME 1 (LP) | 20 |
| 70s | Fab MS 7 | THE MESSAGE DUBWISE (LP) | 70 |
| 80 | Fab MS1 | FABULOUS GREATEST HITS (LP, reissue) | 15 |

*(see also Buster's Allstars, Buster's Group, Dennis Alcapone, Jim Dakota, Hortense Ellis, Heptones, Eric Morris, Schoolboys, Protegue, Vietnam All Stars)*

**PRINCE CHARLIE**

| 69 | Coxsone CS 7101 | Hit And Run/MEDIATORS: Darling, There I Stand | 100 |
|---|---|---|---|

**PRINCE FAR I**

| 78 | Virgin Front Line FLS 112 | No More War/Version | 10 |
|---|---|---|---|
| 82 | On-U Sound DP 1 | Virgin/Danger (10") | 15 |
| 83 | Pre PRE 11-12 | 83 Struggle (with ASHANTIE ROY)/KONGO ASHANTIE ROY/Weeping Wailing (12") | 25 |
| 75 | Carib Gems CGLP 1002 | PSALMS FOR I (LP) | 30 |
| 78 | Virgin Front Line FL 1013 | MESSAGE FROM THE KING (LP) | 20 |
| 78 | Virgin Front Line FL 1021 | LONG LIFE (LP) | 20 |
| 79 | Trojan TRLS 175 | FREE FROM SIN (LP) | 20 |
| 79 | Virgin Front Line FLX 4002 | CRY TUFF DUB ENCOUNTER PART 2 (LP) | 40 |
| 79 | Hit Run APLP 9006 | DUB TO AFRICA (LP, as Prince Far I & The Arabs) | 50 |
| 79 | Trojan Records TRLS 175 | FREE FROM SIN (LP) | 15 |
| 80 | Daddy Kool DKLP 15 | CRY TUFF DUB ENCOUNTER CHAPTER III (LP, as Prince Far I & the Arabs) | 25 |
| 80 | Trojan TRLS 205 | CRY TUFF DUB ENCOUNTER CHAPTER IV (LP) | 25 |
| 80 | Trojan Records TRLS 190 | JAMAICAN HEROES (LP) | 15 |
| 80 | Pre PRE XF 3 | SHOWCASE IN A SUITCASE (LP) | 50 |
| 80 | Pre PRE X 7 | LIVITY (LP) | 25 |
| 81 | Trojan TRLS 204 | VOICE OF THUNDER (LP) | 15 |
| 84 | Kingdom KVL 9016 | UMKHONTO WE SIZWE (LP) | 15 |

*(see also Arabs)*

**PRINCE HAMMER**

| 77 | Baby Mother HIT DD 11 | Them Must Fall/Ball Of Fire (12") | 30 |
|---|---|---|---|
| 78 | Hit Run HIT DP 15 | Ten Thousand Lions/North London Thing (Carry The Swing) (12") | 60 |
| 83 | Saab (No catalogue number) | Warika Hill/Africa Dance Hall (12") | 45 |
| 78 | Virgin Frontline FL1004 | BIBLE (LP) | 30 |
| 79 | Hit Run APLP 9007 | WORLD WAR DUB PART 1 (LP) | 90 |
| 79 | Miss Pat Walker PW1 | ROOTS ME ROOTS (LP) | 60 |

**PRINCE HAROLD**

| 66 | Mercury MF 952 | Forget About Me/Baby You've Got Me | 15 |
|---|---|---|---|

**PRINCE HERON**

| 79 | Jah Lion JBDC 806 | Wip The Wicked Man/Kingston Rock (12", with Jah Brokie) | 15 |
|---|---|---|---|

**PRINCE JAMMY**

| 79 | Trojan TRLS 174 | KAMIKAZI DUB (LP) | 25 |
|---|---|---|---|
| 82 | Greensleeves GREL 29 | DESTROYS THE INVADERS (LP) | 25 |
| 83 | CSA Records – CSLP 10 | OSBOURNE IN DUB (LP) | 15 |
| 86 | Greensleeves Records GREL 92 | COMPUTERISED DUB (LP) | 25 |
| 96 | Trojan TRLS 174 | KAMAKAZI DUB (LP, reissue) | 15 |

**PRINCE JAZZBO**

| 73 | Count Shelley CS 025 | Wise Shepherd (with Linval Carthy)/ EARL GEORGE: Gonna Give Her All The Love I've Got | 10 |
|---|---|---|---|
| 74 | Cactus CT 31 | Concubine Donkey/Part 2 | 8 |
| 74 | Count Shelley CS 057 | Step Forward Youth/Black Is Power | 8 |
| 73 | Grape GR 3047 | Free From Chains/LLOYD & PATSY: Papa Do It Sweet | 8 |
| 73 | Techniques TE 921 | Mr. Harry Skank/GLEN BROWN: Telavid Drums | 8 |
| 74 | Ackee ACK 532 | Kick Boy Face/Version | 8 |
| 74 | Dip DL 5036 | Penny Reel/Good Things | 8 |
| 75 | ABI AB 001 | Bag A Wolf/Version | 8 |
| 76 | Attack ATT 8122 | The Wormer/The Great Pablo | 10 |
| 76 | Third World TWLP 109 | KICK BOY FACE (LP) | 30 |
| 76 | Black Wax WAXLP 1 | NATTY PASSING THRU' (LP) | 150 |

*(see also Earl George)*

**PRINCE JAZZBO & I ROY**

| 78 | Live & Love LAP 003 | STEP FORWARD YOUTH (LP) | 25 |
|---|---|---|---|

**PRINCE LASHA ENSEMBLE**

| 66 | CBS SBPG 62409 | INSIGHT (LP) | 30 |
|---|---|---|---|

**PRINCE OF DARKNESS**

| 69 | Downtown DT 441 | Burial Of Long Shot/MUSIC DOCTORS: Burial Of Long Shot | 25 |
|---|---|---|---|
| 69 | Downtown DT 448 | Meeting Over Yonder/MUSIC DOCTORS: Ghost Rider | 25 |
| 71 | Downtown DT 467 | Sound Of Today/MUSIC DOCTORS: Red Red Wine Version | 50 |

**PRINCE PATO EXPEDITION**

| 70s | Beacon BEAS 18 | FIREBIRD (LP) | 30 |
|---|---|---|---|

**PRINCE & PRINCESS**

| 65 | Aladdin WI 609 | Ready Steady Go/Take Me Serious | 25 |
|---|---|---|---|

## PRINCE SISTERS
55  Decca 45-F1050          A Rusty Old Halo/Love Love Beautiful Love ...................................................... 8

## PRINCE TALLIS & THE CHALLIS
72  Upsetter US 383         Who Feels It/THE UPSETTERS: He Who Feels It (Chapter 2)....................... 20

## VIV PRINCE
66  Columbia DB 7960        Light Of The Charge Brigade/Minuet For Ringo ........................................ 30
*(see also Pretty Things, Bunch Of Fives, Kate, Vamp, Chicago Line)*

## PRINCE WILLIAMS
73  Atra ATRA 004           Action Wood Part 1/Action Wood Part 2 ................................................... 8

## PRINCESS
86  Supreme CDSU 1          PRINCESS (CD)...................................................................................... 60

## PRINCESS BALOU
81  PB YYS 11               Making Love To You/Making Love To You (Part II) (p/s) ......................... 10

## PRINCESS & SWINEHERD
68  Oak RGJ 633             PRINCESS AND THE SWINEHERD (LP, plain black sleeve) ...................... 100

## PRINCESS TINYMEAT
84  Rough Trade RTT 160     Sloblands/The Fairest Of Them All (12", some with sticker) ............... 15
87  Rough Trade ROUGH 108   HERSTORY (LP) ..................................................................................... 20
*(see laso Virgin Prunes, Daniel Figgis)*

## PRINCIPAL EDWARDS MAGIC THEATRE
69  Dandelion S 4405        Ballad Of The Big Girl Now/Lament For The Earth ............................. 10
73  Deram DM 391            Captain Lifeboy/Nothing ...................................................................... 5
73  Deram DM 398            Weekdaze/Whizzmore Kid ..................................................................... 15
69  Dandelion 63752         SOUNDTRACK (LP, gatefold sleeve) ....................................................... 60
71  Dandelion DAN 8002      THE ASOMOTO RUNNING BAND (LP, gatefold sleeve) ....................... 40
74  Deram SML 1108          ROUND ONE (LP, white/red label with small logo) ............................ 35

## MADDY PRIOR
78  Chrysalis CHS 2232      Baggy Pants/Woman In The Wings ......................................................... 6
80  EMI EMI 5903            Wake Up England/Paradise (p/s, as Maddy Prior Band)....................... 6
82  Plant Life PLRS 001     Face To Face/Half Listening (p/s, as Maddy Prior Band) ................... 6
83  RCA/Spindrift RCA 379   Deep In The Darkest Night/Western Movies (p/s) ............................... 6
85  Making Waves SURF 108   Stookie/Incidental Music From Stookie (p/s)..................................... 6
85  Making Waves SURF 109   Deep In The Darkest Night/Western Movies (p/s, reissue) ............... 6
*(see also Steelye Span,Tim Hart & Maddy Prior)*

## PRIORITY
79  Brimstone BRS 1         Visions Of Miranda Grey/Escape (p/s) ................................................. 30

## PRIORY PARK
78  Wild Dog DOGLP 16       TRY FOR THE SUN (LP) ......................................................................... 40

## PRISONERS
83  Big Beat NS 90          Hurricane/Tomorrow (She Said) (p/s) ................................................. 12
86  Countdown VAIN 4        Whenever I'm Gone/Promised Land (p/s) ............................................ 7
86  Countdown 12 VAIN 4    Whenever I'm Gone/Promised Land/Gravedigger (12" p/s) ................ 8
97  Deceptive BLUFF 043     Shine On Me/Judgement Song (p/s) ..................................................... 7
84  Big Beat SW 98          ELECTRIC FIT (EP)................................................................................ 12
82  Own Up OWN UP U2        A TASTE OF PINK (LP).......................................................................... 30
83  Big Beat WIK 19         THE WISERMISERDEMELZA (LP)........................................................... 15
85  Own Up OWN UP U2        A TASTE OF PINK (LP, reissue in pink sleeve on pink vinyl)............... 30
85  Own Up OWN UP U3        THE LAST FOURFATHERS (LP) ............................................................. 20
86  Countdown DOWN 2        IN FROM THE COLD (LP) ...................................................................... 20
89  Hangman HANG 23 UP      RARE AND UNISSUED (LP) ................................................................... 25
91  Cyanide CND 2           RARE AND UNISSUED (LP, reissue) ...................................................... 20
*(see also James Taylor Quartet)*

## PRISONERS/MILKSHAKES
86  Empire MIC 001          THE LAST NIGHT AT THE MIC CLUB (LP, live, 1 side each) ............... 18
86  Media Burn MB 17        THEE MILKSHAKES VS. THE PRISONERS (LP, live, 1 side each) ........ 18
*(see also Milkshakes)*

## PRIVATE DICKS
79  Heartbeat PULSE 6       She Said So/Private Dicks (p/s)........................................................... 20

## PRIVATE LIFE
72  Realm RM 3              Put Her Down/Chasing Dragons ......................................................... 400

## PRIVATE PARTY
87  IMW 1201                Puppet Capers/Tennants Super Mix (12") ........................................... 10

## PRIVATE SECTOR
78  TJM TJM 8               Just Just (Wanna) Stay Free/Things Get Worse (p/s) ......................... 20

## PRIVATE VIEW
84  New 7NL 100             Fashion Changeling/Walls (p/s)........................................................... 25

## PRIVATE EYE
83  Spider SPY 001          Water Under The Bridge/I Cry For You (no p/s)................................. 35

## PRIVATES
82  Dune DUNE 1             Ashamed To Be White/Takes Your Breath Away (p/s) ......................... 7

## P.J. PROBY
62  Liberty LIB 55367       Try To Forget Her/There Stands The One ........................................... 10
64  Decca F 11904           Hold Me/The Tips Of My Fingers .......................................................... 5
64  Decca F 11967           Together/Sweet And Tender Romance ................................................... 5
64  Liberty LIB 10182       Somewhere/Just Like Him .................................................................... 5
65  Liberty LIB 10188       I Apologise/What's On Your Mind ......................................................... 5
65  Liberty LIB 10206       Let The Water Run Down/I Don't Want To Hear It Anymore ............. 10

| 65 | Liberty LIB 10215 | That Means A Lot/My Prayer | MINT VALUE £ 10 |
|----|-------------------|----------------------------|--------|
| 65 | Liberty LIB 10218 | Maria/She Cried | 5 |
| 66 | Liberty LIB 10223 | You've Come Back/It Ain't Necessarily So | 5 |
| 66 | Liberty LIB 10236 | To Make A Big Man Cry/Wicked Woman | 10 |
| 66 | Fab FAB 2 | You've Got Me Cryin'/I Need Love (in die-cut p/s) | 20 |
| 66 | Fab FAB 2 | You've Got Me Cryin'/I Need Love | 7 |
| 66 | Liberty LIB 10250 | I Can't Make It Alone/Sweet Summer Wine | 12 |
| 67 | Liberty LIB 55936 | Nicki Hoeky/Good Things Are Coming My Way | 15 |
| 67 | Liberty LIB 55974 | You Can't Come Home Again/Work With Me Annie | 15 |
| 67 | Liberty LIB 55974 | You Can't Come Home Again/Work With Me Annie (DJ Copy) | 30 |
| 68 | Liberty LBF 15046 | It's Your Day Today/I Apologise Baby | 10 |
| 68 | Liberty LBF 15046 | It's Your Day Today/I Apologise Baby (DJ Copy) | 30 |
| 68 | Liberty LBF 15085 | What's Wrong With My World/Why Baby Why | 7 |
| 68 | Liberty LBF 15152 | The Day That Lorraine Came Down/Mery Hoppkins Never Had Days Like These (B-side features Led Zeppelin) | 15 |
| 69 | Liberty LBF 15245 | Hanging From Your Loving Tree/Empty Bottles | 15 |
| 70 | Liberty LBF 15280 | Today I Killed A Man/It's Too Good To Last | 10 |
| 70 | Liberty LBF 15386 | It's Goodbye/Gift Of Love | 10 |
| 70s | Rooster ROO 101 | You've Got It All (with Polly Brown)/Starting All Over Again | 20 |
| 72 | Columbia DB 8874 | We'll Meet Again/Clown Shoes | 10 |
| 73 | Ember EMB S 328 | Put Your Head On My Shoulder/Momma Married A Preacher | 7 |
| 74 | Seven Sun SSUN 13 | The Champ (Parts 1 & 2) | 8 |
| 81 | Rooster RONS 101 | You've Got It All/Starting All Over Again (with Polly Brown) | 5 |
| 64 | Liberty LEP 2192 | P. J. PROBY (EP) | 15 |
| 65 | Liberty LEP 2229 | SOMEWHERE (EP) | 15 |
| 65 | Liberty LEP 2239 | CHRISTMAS WITH P. J. (EP) | 15 |
| 66 | Liberty LEP 2251 | P. J.'s HITS (EP) | 20 |
| 67 | Liberty LEP 2267 | PROBY AGAIN (EP) | 30 |
| 65 | Liberty LBY 1235 | I AM P. J. PROBY (LP) | 20 |
| 65 | Liberty LBY 1264 | P. J. PROBY (LP) | 20 |
| 66 | Liberty LBY 1291 | P. J. PROBY IN TOWN (LP) | 20 |
| 67 | Liberty LBY 1361 | ENIGMA (LP) | 15 |
| 67 | Liberty LBL/LBS 83045 | PHENOMENON (LP) | 15 |
| 68 | Liberty LBL/LBS 83087 | BELIEVE IT OR NOT (LP) | 15 |
| 69 | Liberty LBS 83219E | THREE WEEK HERO (LP, featuring Led Zeppelin on "Jim's Blues") | 60 |
| 73 | Ember NR 5069 | I'M YOURS (LP) | 15 |
| 78 | Astoria 1 | ELVIS (LP, sold at theatres) | 15 |

*(see also Jett Powers, Marc Almond)*

## PROCESSION

| 68 | Mercury MF 1053 | Every American Citizen/Essentially Susan (p/s) | 10 |
|----|-----------------|------------------------------------------------|-----|
| 68 | Mercury MF 1070 | One Day In Every Week/Wigwam City | 10 |
| 69 | Mercury SMCL 20132 | PROCESSION (LP) | 30 |

## PROCOL HARUM

| 67 | Deram DM 126 | A Whiter Shade Of Pale/Lime Street Blues (1st issue with darker labels) | 5 |
|----|--------------|--------------------------------------------------------------------------|-----|
| 67 | Regal Zonophone RZ 3003 | Homburg/Good Captain Clack | 5 |
| 68 | Regal Zonophone RZ 3007 | Quite Rightly So/In The Wee Small Hours Of Sixpence | 8 |
| 69 | Regal Zonophone RZ 3019 | A Salty Dog/Long Gone Geek | 10 |
| 72 | Fly Magni Fly ECHO 101 | A Whiter Shade Of Pale/A Salty Dog/Homburg (p/s) | 5 |
| 72 | Chrysalis CHS 2003 | Conquistador/Luskus Delph (PS) | 6 |
| 79 | RCA LB 6 | A Whiter Shade Of Pale/Noel Edmonds Introduces Record Year (Lever Brothers premium) | 5 |
| 67 | Regal Zono. LRZ 1001 | PROCOL HARUM (LP, laminated front sleeve, flipbacks, blue/silver label) | 100 |
| 68 | Regal Zono. LRZ 1004 | SHINE ON BRIGHTLY (LP, mono), laminated front sleeve, blue/silver label) | 150 |
| 67 | Regal Zono. SLRZ 1004 | SHINE ON BRIGHTLY (LP, stereo), laminated front sleeve, red/silver label) | 70 |
| 69 | Regal Zono. SLRZ 1009 | A SALTY DOG (LP, laminated sleeve, red/silver label) | 50 |
| 70 | Regal Zono. SLRZ 1014 | HOME (LP, with lyric sheet) | 50 |
| 71 | Chrysalis ILPS 9158 | BROKEN BARRICADES (LP, gatefold sleeve, first pressing with a small white "i" at the top of the label) | 15 |
| 73 | Chrysalis CHR 1037 | GRAND HOTEL (LP, gatefold sleeve, booklet, green label) | 25 |

*(see also Paramounts, Legend, Matthew Fisher, Robin Trower, Matthew Ellis, Freedom, Mick Grabham, Power Pack)*

## JUDD PROCTOR

| 61 | Parlophone R 4769 | Rio Grande/Plainsman | |
|----|-------------------|----------------------|-----|
| 61 | Parlophone R 4809 | Palamino/Nola | 10 |
| 61 | Parlophone R 4841 | Speakeasy/Clearway | 10 |
| 62 | Parlophone R 4885 | The Turk/Mad | 10 |
| 62 | Parlophone R 4920 | Backfire/It's Bluesy | 10 |
| 64 | Parlophone R 5126 | Better Late/Boots | 10 |
| 68 | Morgan MR 103P | GUITARS GALORE (LP) | 10 |
| 70s | Gemini GMX 5004 | GUITARS GALORE (LP, reissue) | 40 |

*see also Ray Ellington* 25

## MIKE PROCTOR

| 67 | Columbia DB 8254 | Mr. Commuter/Sunday, Sunday, Sunday | 225 |
|----|------------------|-------------------------------------|-----|

## PRODIGAL

| 82 | D Records D7 | Prodigal Son/Bye Bye Baby | 12 |
|----|--------------|---------------------------|-----|

## PRODIGY

| 91 | XL XLT 17 | WHAT EVIL LURKS EP (What Evil Lurks/We Gonna Rock/Android/ Everybody In The Place) (12", company sleeve) | 30 |
|----|-----------|---------------------------------------------------------------------------------------------------------|-----|
| 91 | XL XLS 21 | Charly/Charly (Original Mix) | 10 |
| 91 | XL XLS 26 | Everybody In The Place (Fairground Edit)/G-Force (Energy Flow) | 8 |
| 92 | XL XLS 30 | Fire (Edit)/Jericho (Original Version) | 8 |

| 92 | XL XLS 35 | Out Of Space/Ruff In The Jungle Bizness (Uplifting Vibes Remix) ...... 8 |
| 93 | XL XLS 39 | Wind It Up (Rewound)/We Are The Ruffest ...... 8 |
| 93 | XL EB 1 | EARTHBOUND 1 : One Love (original Mix)/Full Throttle (original Mix) (12") ...... 50 |
| 95 | XL SC 1 | SCIENIDE (12", white label, 500 hand-stamped promos only) ...... 50 |
| 96 | XL XL70CDPR | Firestarter Sampler (CD picture disc, promo only) ...... 12 |
| 05 | XL XLT 213 | Spitfire (05 Version)Spitfire (Future Funk Squad's "Dogfight" Remix/Spitfire (Nightbreed Remix) (12" stickered p/s, with 2 stickers, 2000 only) ...... 25 |
| 05 | XL XLS 213 CDE | Spitfire (05 Version)/Spitfire (Nightbreed Remix)/Spitfire (Future Funk Squad's "Dogfight" Remix) (CD stickered digipak 500 only) ...... 30 |
| 92 | XL XLLP 110 | THE PRODIGY EXPERIENCE (2-LP) ...... 30 |
| 94 | XL XLLP 114 | MUSIC FOR THE JILTED GENERATION (LP) ...... 30 |
| 97 | XL XLLP 121 | THE FAT OF THE LAND (2xLP) ...... 30 |
| 04 | XL XLLP 183 | ALWAYS OUTNUMBERED, NEVER OUTGUNNED (3-LP) ...... 25 |
| 09 | Take Me To The Hospital HOSPLP001 | INVADERS MUST DIE (2-LP) ...... 20 |
| 09 | Take Me To The Hospital HOSPBOX001 | INVADERS MUST DIE (Box set, CD/DVD/5x7") ...... 30 |

## PRODUCERS
| 80 | Magic Moon MACH 1.S | On The Beach/Goin' Steady (die cut sleeve) ...... 20 |

## PRODUCT OF REASON
| 83 | Tenuous Lynx LYNX 1 | Man Of Your Dreams/These Days ...... 15 |

## PROFESSIONALS
| 80 | Virgin VS 353 | Just Another Dream/Action Man (p/s) ...... 5 |
| 80 | Virgin VS 376 | 1-2-3/White Light White Heat/Baby I Don't Care (p/s, with giant foldout poster in stickered PVC sleeve) ...... 5 |
| 80 | Virgin VS 376 | 1-2-3/White Light White Heat/Baby I Don't Care (p/s, signed by Cook & Jones) ...... 15 |
| 81 | Virgin VS 426 | Join The Professionals/Has Anybody Got An Alibi? (gatefold p/s) ...... 7 |
| 81 | Virgin V 2220 | I DIDN'T SEE IT COMING (LP) ...... 15 |

*(see also Sex Pistols, Greedies, Lightning Raiders, Steve Jones)*

## PROFESSOR LONGHAIR
| 65 | Sue WI 397 | Baby Let Me Hold Your Hand/Looka' No Hair ...... 40 |
| 78 | Harvest HAR 5154 | Mess Around/Tipitina ...... 15 |
| 72 | Speakeasy 10-78 | NEW ORLEANS 88 (10" LP) ...... 45 |
| 72 | Atlantic K 40402 | NEW ORLEANS PIANO (LP) ...... 30 |
| 78 | Harvest SHSP 4086 | LIVE ON THE QUEEN MARY (LP) ...... 30 |
| 80 | Sonet SNTF 830 | CRAWFISH SIESTA (LP) ...... 15 |
| 83 | Stateside SSL 6004 | LIVE ON THE QUEEN MARY (LP, reissue) ...... 18 |
| 81 | JSP 1025 | THE LONDON CONCERT (LP) ...... 15 |

## FRANK PROFFITT
| 66 | Topic 12T 162 | NORTH CAROLINA SONGS AND BALLADS (LP) ...... 20 |

## PROFIL
| 80 | CBS S CBS 8574 | Hey Music Man/Jour De Chance (p/s) ...... 10 |

## PROFILE (1)
| 65 | Mercury MF 875 | Haven't They Got Better Things To Do/Touch Of Your Hand ...... 12 |
| 65 | Mercury MF 981 | Got To Find A Way/Don't Say Goodbye ...... 12 |
| 69 | Philips BF 1757 | Politician Man/Where Is Love ...... 8 |

*(see also Karl Stuart & Profiles, Voice)*

## PROFILE (2)
| 74 | Surrey International SIT 5006 | I Like It Like That/Easy Come Easy Go ...... 8 |

## PROLES
| 79 | Rock Against Racism RAR 1 | Stereo Love/Thought Crime/CONDEMNED: Soldier Boys/ Endless Revolution (p/s) ...... 45 |
| 79 | Small Wonder SMALL 23 | Softground/SMK (p/s) ...... 6 |

## PROLETARIAT
| 85 | Homestead HMS 037 | Marketplace/Death Of a Headon (p/s) ...... 8 |

## PROMISE
| 69 | NEMS 56-4129 | Just For You/Nine To Five ...... 100 |

## PROPAGANDA
| 85 | ZTT 12 ZTAS 2 | Das Testaments Des Mabuse/Femme Fatale/The 9th Life (Of Dr. Mabuse) (12", white p/s, title sticker reads "13th Life New Mix") ...... 15 |
| 85 | ZTT P ZTAS 8 | Duel/Jewel (Rough Cut) (ZTT logo-shaped picture disc) ...... 10 |
| 85 | ZTT PROP 1 | Bejewelled (12", 1-sided, white label, stickered title sleeve, promo only) ...... 12 |

*(see also Act, Ralph Dorper, Claudia Brucken)*

## PROPERTY
| 70 | Staple ST01 | My Mind Sleeps/Calling You (some with p/s) ...... 150 |

## PROPHECY OF DOOM
| 89 | Prophecy SRT 9KS 2178 | Calculated Mind Rape/Hybrid Thought (p/s) ...... 10 |
| 90 | Deaf DEAF 02 | ACKNOWLEDGE THE CONFUSION MASTER (LP, insert) ...... 20 |
| 90 | Strange Fruit SFPS 079 | PEEL SESSIONS EP (12", p/s) ...... 15 |

## PROPHET
| 74 | UK UK 64 | Have Love Will Travel/Blues In B Sharp ...... 30 |

## MICHAEL PROPHET
| 79 | Grove GMDM 17 | Turn Me Loose/Praise You Jah Jah (12") ...... 20 |
| 79 | Grove GMDM 25 | Warn Them Jah/Don't Interfere (12") ...... 20 |
| 80 | Greensleeves GRED 44 | Help Them Please/WAILING SOULS : See Baba Joe ...... 25 |
| 80 | Island/Grove Music 12WIP 6583 | Fight to The Top (Discomix)/Love And Unity/Mash Down Rome (12") ...... 20 |
| 80 | Love Linch LL 002 | True Born African (with Soul Syndicate)/RANKING TOYAN: What A Bam Bam (12") ...... 30 |
| 80 | Love Linch LL 012 | Struggle/80s Struggle (12", some on blue vinyl) ...... 15 |
| 80s | WLN WLN 003 | Rock Me Baby/Don't Throw Stone (12") ...... 20 |

MINT VALUE £

| | | | |
|---|---|---|---|
| 81 | Greensleeves GRED 59 | Gunman/Cassandra (12") | 15 |
| 82 | Greensleeves GRED 72 | Here Comes The Bride/MYSTIC EYES: Bring The Kuchie Come | 20 |
| 82 | Greensleeves GRED 87 | Boom Him Up Now/Trouble Nobody (12") | 15 |
| 82 | Greensleeveves GRED 104 | Just Talking/Thru Me (with Papa Dimes) (12") | 15 |
| 90 | Living Room LM 043 | Hypocrites/Version (12", with Daddy Freddy) | 12 |
| 90 | Passion PE 6 | Your Love (Michael Prophet Version)/Your Love (Ricky Tuff Version)/Acapella Version (12") | 10 |
| 80 | Island ILPS 9606 | SERIOUS REASONING (LP) | 25 |
| 81 | Greensleeves GRED 104 | MICHAEL PROPHET (LP) | 15 |

## ORVAL PROPHET
| | | | |
|---|---|---|---|
| 63 | London HLL 9729 | Run Run Run/My Lois And Me | 10 |

## REX PROPHET
| | | | |
|---|---|---|---|
| 55 | Brunswick OE 9144 | CANADIAN PLOWBOY (EP) | 10 |

## PROPHETS
| | | | |
|---|---|---|---|
| 78 | Grove Music GMDM 12 | Give Thanks And Praise/Till I Kiss You (12") | 30 |
| 79 | Grove Music GMDM 4 | Blessed Are The Meek (feat Trinity)/TOMMY MCCOOK: Stepping High (12") | 25 |

## PROPHETS (JAMAICA)
| | | | |
|---|---|---|---|
| 70 | Big Shot BI 554 | Crystal Blue Persuasion (Parts 1 & 2) | 15 |
| 70 | Big Shot BI 555 | Tumble Time (Parts 1 & 2) | 20 |
| 70 | Big Shot BI 557 | Revenge Of Eastwood Version One/Version Two | 40 |
| 70 | Jackpot JP 712 | Let's Fall In Love/Purple Moon | 30 |

*(see also Lloyd & Prophets, Claudette, Lloyd & Claudette, Patrick & Lloyd)*

## PROPHETS (U.S.)
| | | | |
|---|---|---|---|
| 69 | Mercury MF 1097 | I Got The Fever/Soul Control | 30 |
| 69 | Mercury MF 1097 | I Got The Fever/Soul Control (DJ copy) | 50 |

*(see also Creation [U.S.])*

## PROPHETS OF DOOM
| | | | |
|---|---|---|---|
| 80 | Nonchalent N1 | Apathy/1984 (1000 only, no p/s) | 8 |

## PROS & CONS
| | | | |
|---|---|---|---|
| 66 | CBS 202341 | Bend It/No Time | 7 |

## PROTECTORS
| | | | |
|---|---|---|---|
| 73 | Live Wire SON 4004 | Loretta/Jump The Sidewalk | 15 |

## PROTEGUE (& PRINCE BUSTER'S ALL STARS)
| | | | |
|---|---|---|---|
| 67 | Blue Beat BB 398 | Foul Dance/PRINCE BUSTER'S ALL STARS: This Is It | 30 |

## PROTEX
| | | | |
|---|---|---|---|
| 78 | Good Vibrations GOT 6 | Don't Ring Me Up/(Just Want) Your Attention/Listening In (wraparound p/s) | 20 |
| 79 | Rough Trade GOT 1 | Don't Ring Me Up/(Just Want) Your Attention/Listening In (reissue, 1st pressing, text above telephone p/s) | 10 |
| 79 | Rough Trade GOT 1 | Don't Ring Me Up/(Just Want) Your Attention/Listening In (reissue, 2nd pressing, text above telephone p/s) | 8 |
| 79 | Polydor 2059 124 | I Can't Cope/Popularity (p/s) | 12 |
| 79 | Polydor 2059 167 | I Can Only Dream/Heartache (p/s) | 15 |
| 80 | Polydor 2059 245 | A Place In Your Heart/Jeepster (p/s) | 15 |
| 01 | Good Vibrations BIG 4 | LISTENING IN (LP) | 18 |

## BRIAN PROTHEROE
| | | | |
|---|---|---|---|
| 74 | Chrysalis CHS 2043 | Pinball/Money Love | 5 |

## PROTON
| | | | |
|---|---|---|---|
| 80 | Ballistic 12BP 264 | We're Funkin'/Make Your Move (Instrumental Version) | 20 |

## PROTOS
| | | | |
|---|---|---|---|
| 82 | Airship AP 391 | ONE DAY A NEW HORIZON (LP) | 140 |

## PROUDFOOT
| | | | |
|---|---|---|---|
| 73 | Jam 33 | Giant/Wanderer | 7 |

## PROVIDENCE
| | | | |
|---|---|---|---|
| 73 | Threshold TH 14 | Fantasy Fugue/Island Of Light | 5 |
| 72 | Threshold THS 9 | EVER SENSE THE DAWN (LP, gatefold sleeve with insert) | 30 |

## PROWLER (1)
| | | | |
|---|---|---|---|
| 73 | Parlophone R 5986 | Pale Green (Hnmmmm) Driving Man/Jaywick Cowboy | 30 |

## PROWLER (2)
| | | | |
|---|---|---|---|
| 83 | Pirate SS 226 S8 | Forgotten Angels/Don't Let Go (p/s) | 80 |
| 85 | SRT SRT5KS/368 | Alcatraz/So Lonely (p/s) | 70 |

## PRUDES
| | | | |
|---|---|---|---|
| 89 | Yo Yo PRU 1 | P.S. I'm Leaving/Lighthouse Keeper's Daughter (p/s, white vinyl) | 5 |

## PRUNES
| | | | |
|---|---|---|---|
| 70 | Songbird SB 1023 | Come A Little Closer/Come A Little Closer Version II | 8 |

*(see also Eric Donaldson, West Indians)*

## SNOOKY PRYOR
| | | | |
|---|---|---|---|
| 70 | Flyright LP 100 | SNOOKY PRYOR (LP) | 15 |

## RED PRYSOCK
| | | | |
|---|---|---|---|
| 59 | Mercury AMT 1028 | Chop Suey/Margie | 20 |
| 58 | Mercury MPL 6535 | THE BEAT (LP) | 50 |
| 58 | Mercury MPL 6550 | FRUIT BOOTS (LP) | 40 |
| 56 | Mercury MPT 7517 | JUMP RED JUMP (10" LP) | 40 |

## PSEUDO EXISTORS
| | | | |
|---|---|---|---|
| 80 | Dead Good DEAD 2 | Pseudo Existence/Coming Up For Air/New Modern Warfare (rubber-stamped folded p/s, pink/white label) | 60 |
| 80 | Dead Good DEAD 2 | Pseudo Existence/Coming Up For Air/New Modern Warfare (rubber-stamped folded p/s, later red/black label & stamped white sleeve) | 35 |

**P.S. PERSONAL**
83  New World NEW 1      Shoot Me Down/Shoot Me Down (no p/s) ...........................................25

**PSYCHE**
82  Burning World         Never Laugh/Psyche (p/s) .............................................................6

**PSYCHEDELIC FURS**
79  Epic EPC 8005         We Love You/Pulse (green, pink or orange p/s) ...........................5
81  CBS A 1166            Dumb Waiters/Dash (1st 5,000 with playable p/s)........................5
*(see also Unwanted)*

**PSYCHEOUT**
00  Discord DISCORD 002   BOOM EP (12") ..........................................................................15
00  Discord DISCORD 003   WARP EP (12") (12") ..................................................................60
00  Discord DISCORD 004   TRAIN TRAX EP (12"). ................................................................15
00  Discord DISCORD 005   SURGE EP (12"). .......................................................................10

**PSYCHIC PHENOMENA**
97  Lowlife LOW05         THE WHOLE CIRCUMFERENCE (12", EP) .......................................25

**PSYCHIC TV**
82  Some Bizzare PTV 1    Just Drifting/Breakthrough (p/s) ...............................................10
82  Some Bizzare PTV 1T   Just Drifting/Just Drifting (Midnight) (12", p/s)........................15
84  Temple TOPY 001       Unclean/Mirrors (12", p/s) .........................................................10
86  Temple TOPYS 009      Godstar/Godstar (BJ Mix)/Discopravity/Yes It's The B Side (double pack, gatefold p/s) ..8
86  Temple TOPIC 009      Godstar/Godstar (California Mix) (12", picture disc) ..................15
86  Temple TOPYD 023      Good Vibrations/Interzone/Roman P/Hex-Sex/Godstar (Ugly Mix)/Je T'Aime (double pack, gatefold p/s) ...........................................................................6
86  Temple TOPYT 023      Roman P (Fireball Mix)/Interzone/Good Vibrations (Kundalini Mix)/Hex-Sex (Voodoo Mix) (12", p/s) ...................................................................................10
88  Temple TOPY 037       Tune In (Turn On To Thee Acide House) (12", p/s, as (Psychic TV/Jack The Tab) ...........10
88  DC DC 23              Superman/Jack The Tab (12", p/s, no artist credit on label) .........15
89  Temple TOPY 048       Love, War, Riot/Eve Of Destruction (Vocoder Mixes) (12", p/s, including sticker) ..........10
82  Some Bizzare PSY 1    FORCE THE HAND OF CHANCE (LP, with bonus LP & double-sided poster, featuring Marc Almond) ...................................................................................40
83  CBS 25737             DREAMS LESS SWEET (LP, with inner sleeve, some with free 12" EP [XPR 1251])...........30
83  CBS 25737             DREAMS LESS SWEET (LP, with inner sleeve) ...............................25
84  Temple TOPY 003       PAGAN DAY (LP, picture disc, 999 copies) ..................................40
84  Gramm GRAMM 23        THOSE WHO DO NOT (2-LP, 5000 copies) .....................................30
85  Temple TOPY 004       THEMES 2 (LP) .........................................................................15
85  Temple TOPY 008       THEMES 3 (LP) .........................................................................15
85  Temple TOPIC 010      MOUTH OF THE NIGHT (LP, picture disc) .....................................18
86  Temple TOPIC 009      GODSTAR (LP, with picture disc) ...............................................15
87  Temple TOPY 029       LIVE IN GOTTINGEN (LP) ...........................................................15
88  Temple TOPY 031       PSYCHIC TV (LP, picture disc) ...................................................15
88  Temple TOPY 032       ALBUM 10 (LP, picture disc) .......................................................15
88  Temple TOPY 038       ALLEGORY AND SELF (LP, blue vinyl) ..........................................15
89  Temple TOPY 047       LIVE AT THE PYRAMID NYC (LP, picture disc) .............................12

**PSYCHO'S MUM**
89  Woronzow W 011        A SIBILANT SIN (LP, with insert) ................................................15

**PSYCOMETRIC**
97  Acid Fever MDMA 9701  Piano Dreams/Funk Bits/The Kaison Ogle/DJ CYCLONE: Spare Parts/Meltdown/Chaos (12") ..........................................................................................12

**PSYKYK VOLTS**
79  Ellie Jay EJPS 9262   Totally Useless/Horror Story No. 5 (p/s) .....................................20
79  MHG GHM 109           Totally Useless/Horror Story No. 5 ............................................35

**PSYLONS**
86  E Type ETYPE 1        The Mockery Of Decline/Clear Sky .............................................10
87  Iron Lung IL 001      All The Things We Need (12", p/s) .............................................15
90  Unsigned UN 001       No Choice/Surf Song (p/s) ..........................................................8

**PTOLOMY PSYCON**
71  Hollick and Taylor HT/IPS 1306    LOOSE CAPACITOR (10" LP, 50 only, silkscreened front sleeve, printed back)..............800

**PUBLIC ENEMY**
88  Def Jam 652 833-0     Don't Believe The Hype/Prophets Of Rage (p/s, with patch) .........5
88  Def Jam 653 089-7     Night Of The Living Baseheads/Terminator X To The Edge Of Panic (p/s, badge pack) .....5
13  Slamjamz/Talenthouse  Harder Than You Think (1-sided, Secret Seven, 100 only) ...........50
88  Def Jam 462415-1      IT TAKES A NATION OF MILLIONS TO HOLD US BACK (LP, inner) ......20
90  Def Jam 466281        FEAR OF A BLACK PLANET (LP, inner) ...........................................15
91  Def Jam 468751        APOCALYPSE 91 (2-LP, gatefold, inners) ......................................20

**PUBLIC FOOT THE ROMAN**
73  Sovereign SVNA 7259   PUBLIC FOOT THE ROMAN (LP, gatefold sleeve)...........................100
*(see also Movies)*

**PUBLIC IMAGE LTD (PIL)**
78  Virgin VS 228         Public Image/The Cowboy Song (foldout 'newspaper' p/s) ...........20
79  Virgin VS 29912       Memories/Another (12", p/s) .....................................................10
79  Virgin VS 274-12      Death Disco/And No Bird Do Sing (1/2 Mix)/Death Disco Megamix (12", p/s, 5,000 only) ...................................................................................15
81  Virgin VS 397-12      Flowers Of Romance (Exended Version)/Home Is Where The Heart Is (12", p/s)...........12
86  Virgin VSD 855        Home/Round/Rise (Rise Instrumental) (double pack) ..................6
87  Virgin VS 988         Seattle/Selfish Rubbish (box set with 7", badge, postcard & sew-on patch) ..........6
78  Virgin V2114          FIRST ISSUE (LP. 1st pressing, with colour inner sleeve and PiL on both labels) .............25
79  Virgin V2114          FIRST ISSUE (LP, repressing with plain white inner sleeve) ..........15
79  Virgin METAL 1        METAL BOX (LP, 3 x 12" with circular paper dividers & inner sheet in round tin) ..........80

# PUBLIC DISGRACE

| | | | |
|---|---|---|---|
| 79 | Virgin VD 2512 | SECOND EDITION (standard issue, of Metal Box, 2-LP, gatefold) | 20 |
| 92 | Virgin V 2681 | THAT WHAT IS NOT (LP) | 15 |

*(see also Sex Pistols, Jah Wobble, Don Letts & Jah Wobble, Vivien Goldman, Cowboys International)*

## PUBLIC DISGRACE
| | | | |
|---|---|---|---|
| 82 | Probe Plus PP2 | TOXTETH EP | 6 |

## PUBLIC ZONE
| | | | |
|---|---|---|---|
| 77 | Logo GO 104 | Naive/Innocence (p/s) | 6 |

## GARY PUCKETT (& UNION GAP)
| | | | |
|---|---|---|---|
| 68 | CBS 3365 | Young Girl/I'm Losing You (as Union Gap featuring Gary Puckett) | 5 |
| 68 | CBS 3551 | Lady Willpower/Daylight Stranger | 5 |
| 68 | CBS 3714 | Over You/If The Day Would Come | 7 |
| 69 | CBS 4122 | Don't Give In To Him/Could I | 7 |
| 69 | CBS 4505 | This Girl Is A Woman Now/His Other Woman | 8 |
| 68 | CBS (S) 63342 | YOUNG GIRL (LP) | 20 |
| 68 | CBS (S) 63429 | INCREDIBLE (LP) | 20 |
| 70 | CBS 63794 | THE NEW GARY PUCKETT AND THE UNION GAP ALBUM (LP) | 20 |

## PUDDING
| | | | |
|---|---|---|---|
| 67 | Decca F 12603 | The Magic Bus/It's Too Late | 70 |

## TITO PUENTE
| | | | |
|---|---|---|---|
| 57 | RCA RD 27002 | LET'S CHA-CHA WITH PUENTE (LP) | 15 |
| 58 | RCA SF 5008 | MUCHO PUENTE (LP) | 15 |

## PUFFIN CLUB
| | | | |
|---|---|---|---|
| 81 | Big Nob NOB 001 | Great Western Revival/Feel So Low/Anhedonia/Set A Table (no p/s, 50 only) | 15 |

## DUDU PUKWANA
| | | | |
|---|---|---|---|
| 74 | Caroline C1504 | IN THE TOWNSHIPS (LP, as Dudu Pukwana & Spear) | 20 |
| 81 | Jika ZL 1 | SOUNDS ZILA (LP) | 15 |
| 83 | Jika ZL 2 | LIFE IN BRACKNELL & WILLISAU (LP, featuring Dinise Saul) | 25 |
| 86 | Jika ZL 3 | ZILA 86 (LP) | 15 |

## LEROY PULLENS
| | | | |
|---|---|---|---|
| 66 | London HLR 10056 | I'm A Nut/Knee Deep | 12 |
| 77 | MCA 315 | I'm A Nut/Knee Deep (Reissue) | 5 |

## VERNE PULLENS
| | | | |
|---|---|---|---|
| 72 | Injun 107 | Mama Don't Allow No Boppin'/Bop Crazy Baby | 15 |
| 72 | Injun 111 | Bop Crazy Baby/Would You Be Happy | 15 |

## PULLOVERS
| | | | |
|---|---|---|---|
| 80 | Supermusic SUP 24/LYN 8613/4 | Peter Pan Pill/Spare Part Surgery (p/s, some with kidney donor card) | 20 |

## PULP
### SINGLES
| | | | |
|---|---|---|---|
| 83 | Red Rhino RED 32 | My Lighthouse (Remix)/Looking For Life (p/s) | 70 |
| 83 | Red Rhino RED 37 | Everybody's Problem/There Was (p/s) | 50 |
| 85 | Fire BLAZE 5 | Little Girl (With Blue Eyes)/Simultaneous/Blue Glow/The Will To Power (12", p/s) | 25 |
| 85 | Fire BLAZE 5 | Little Girl (With Blue Eyes)/Simultaneous/Blue GLow/The Will To Power, 12" promo) | 40 |
| 86 | Fire BLAZE 10 | Dogs Are Everywhere/The Mark Of The Devil/97 Lovers/Aborigine/ Goodnight (12", p/s) | 25 |
| 87 | Fire BLAZE 17 | They Suffocate At Night (Edited Version)/Tunnel (Cut Up Version) (p/s) | 12 |
| 87 | Fire BLAZE 17T | They Suffocate At Night (Uncut Version)/Tunnel (Full Length Version) (12", p/s) | 15 |
| 87 | Fore BLAZE 21T | Masters Of The Universe (Sanitised Vresion)/Manon/Silence (12", promo) | 25 |
| 87 | Fire BLAZE 21T | Masters Of The Universe (Sanitised Version)/Manon/Silence (12", p/s) | 20 |
| 90 | Fire BLAZE 44T | Is This House?/This House Is Condemned (12" promo, 1-sided) | 25 |
| 90 | Fire BLAZE 44T | My Legendary Girlfriend/Is This House?/This House Is Condemned (12", p/s) | 10 |
| 91 | Fire BLAZE 51T | Countdown/Death Goes To The Disco/Countdown (Radio Edit) (12", p/s) | 10 |
| 92 | Gift GIF 1 | O.U. (Gone Gone)/Space/O.U. (Gone Gone) (Radio Edit) 12" promo & press sheet) | 20 |
| 92 | Caff CAFF 17 | My Legendary Girlfriend/Sickly Grin/Back In L.A. (foldover p/s with insert in poly bag, 500 only) | 80 |
| 92 | GIF 3 | Babies/Styloroc (Nites Of Suburbia)/Sheffield : Sex City (12" promo with press sheet) | 40 |
| 92 | Gift GIF 3 | Babies/Styloroc (Nites Of Suburbia)/Sheffield: Sex City (12", p/s) | 15 |
| 93 | Gift 7GIF6 | Razzmatazz/Inside Susan/59 Lyndhurst Grove (p/s) | 15 |
| 93 | Gidt GIF 6 | Razzmatazz/Inside Susan : A Story In 3 Songs (Stacks/Inside Susan/59 Lyndhurst Grove) (12" promo with press sheet) | 30 |
| 93 | gift GIF6 | Razzmatazz/Stacks/Inside Susan/59 Lyndhurst Grove (12" p/s) | 10 |
| 93 | Island IS 567 | Lipgloss/You're A Nightmare (p/s) | 8 |
| 94 | Island IS 595 | THE SISTERS EP (gatefold, numbered) | 12 |
| 94 | Island 12IS 595 | THE SISTERS EP (12", p/s with print) | 10 |
| 95 | Island 12 IS 613 | Common People/Underwear/Common People (Motiv8 Mix/Common People (Vocoda Mix) (12") | 12 |
| 96 | Island ISC 613 | Common People/Underwear (reissue, yellow vinyl) | 30 |
| 96 | Island ISC 620 | Sorted For E's And Whizz/Miss-Shapes (reissue, blue vinyl) | 12 |
| 96 | Island ISC 632 | Something Changed/Mile End (pink vinyl) | 12 |
| 96 | Island ISC 567 | Lipgloss/You're A Nightmare (p/s, reissue, red vinyl) | 8 |
| 96 | Island ISC 574 | Do You Remember The First Time/Street Lites (reissue, brown vinyl, p/s) | 10 |
| 96 | Island ISC 595 | THE SISTERS EP (p/s, reissue, white vinyl) | 10 |
| 96 | Island ISC 623 | Disco 2000/Ansaphone (orange vinyl) | 18 |
| 96 | Island 12 IS 623 | Disco 2000 (7" Mix)/Ansaphone/Disco 2000 (Motiv & Gimp Dub)/Disco 2000 (Motiv & Discoid Mix) (12" p/s) | 12 |
| 96 | Island 12 IS 620 | Mis-Shapes/Sorted For E's & Wiz/P.T.A. (Parent Teacher Association)/Common People (Live At Glastonbury (12". p/s) | 10 |

### ALBUMS
| | | | |
|---|---|---|---|
| 84 | Red Rhino REDLP 29 | IT (mini-LP) | 40 |

| | | | |
|---|---|---|---|
| 87 | Fire FIRELP 5 | FREAKS (LP) | 20 |
| 92 | Fire FIRE 11026 | SEPARATIONS (LP) | 30 |
| 93 | Island ILPM 2076 | INTRO (LP) | 30 |
| 93 | Fire FIRELP 5 | FREAKS (LP, reissue, barcode on rear of sleeve) | 15 |
| 94 | Island ILPS 8025 | HIS 'N' HERS (LP) | 50 |
| 94 | Fire FIRE LP 36 | MASTERS OF THE UNIVERSE (PULP ON FIRE 1985-86) | 20 |
| 95 | Island ILPS 8041 | DIFFERENT CLASS (LP, die-cut sleeve with 6 inserts) | 80 |
| 95 | Island ILPS 8041 | DIFFERENT CLASS (LP, with 1 insert) | 50 |
| 96 | Nectar NTMLP 521 | COUNTDOWN 1992-1983 (LP) | 20 |
| 98 | Island ILPSD 8066 | THIS IS HARDCORE (2 x LP, gatefold, with insert) | 60 |
| 99 | Cooking Vinyl COOK CD 178 | PULPED 93-92 (4-CD box set with booklet) | 30 |
| 00 | Simply Vinyl SVLP 166 | DIFFERENT CLASS (LP, reissue 180gm vinyl) | 20 |
| 01 | Island ILPS 8110 | WE LOVE LIFE (LP) | 50 |
| 12 | Fire FV223E | IT (mini-LP, reissue) | 18 |

*(see also Jarvis Cocker, Relaxed Muscle)*

**PULP MUSIC**

| | | | |
|---|---|---|---|
| 79 | Pulp Music PB 1 | Low Flying Aircraft/Something Just Behind My Back/So Lo (blank labels, some numbered up to 2,000 & signed, with handmade sleeve) | 25 |
| 79 | Pulp Music PB 1 | Low Flying Aircraft/Something Just Behind My Back/So Lo (blank labels, some numbered up to 2,000 & signed) | 20 |

**PULSALLAMA**

| | | | |
|---|---|---|---|
| 82 | Y Y25 | The Devil Lives In My Husband's Body/Ungawa Pt. II (p/s) | 5 |
| 83 | Y Y103 | Oui Oui (A Canadian In Paris)/Pulsallama On The Rag p/s) | 5 |

**PULSAR**

| | | | |
|---|---|---|---|
| 76 | Decca SKL-R 5228 | POLLEN (LP) | 20 |
| 77 | Decca TXS 119 | STRANDS OF THE FUTURE (LP, gatefold sleeve) | 25 |

**PULSE (1)**

| | | | |
|---|---|---|---|
| 70 | Major Minor SMLP 64 | PULSE (LP) | 60 |

**PULSE (2)**

| | | | |
|---|---|---|---|
| 82 | Tomato OK 1 | Trouble With John/Red Day In Dallas | 40 |

**PULSEBEAT**

| | | | |
|---|---|---|---|
| 83 | A Love Bite ALB 1 | Ride A White Swan/(Have) No Regrets | 6 |

**PUMPHOUSE GANG**

| | | | |
|---|---|---|---|
| 77 | Kitsch FAD 1 | Motorcity Fantasy/Cocaine (p/s) | 7 |
| 79 | Splash SP 001 | Spotlight/Lights Out (no p/s) | 15 |
| 80 | Splash SP 101 | Judy Turn Out The Light/A Girl Like You | 12 |

*(see also Slush)*

**PUNCHERS**

| | | | |
|---|---|---|---|
| 70 | Punch PH 46 | Sons Of Thunder (actually by Lee Perry & The Upsetters)/ Only If You Understand | 25 |

**PUNCHIN' JUDY**

| | | | |
|---|---|---|---|
| 73 | Transatlantic TRA 272 | PUNCHIN' JUDY (LP, laminated front sleeve) | 20 |

*(see also Downliner Sect)*

**PUNCTURE**

| | | | |
|---|---|---|---|
| 77 | Small Wonder SMALL 1 | Mucky Pup/Can't Rock'n'Roll (p/s) | 20 |

**PUNCTURED TOUGH GUY**

| | | | |
|---|---|---|---|
| 85 | Xcentric Noise NINIH 1 | ACID RAINS EP | 18 |

**PUNISHMENT OF LUXURY**

| | | | |
|---|---|---|---|
| 78 | Small Wonder SMALL 8 | Puppet Life/The Demon (p/s) | 8 |
| 79 | United Artists UP 36507 | Engine Of Excess/Jellyfish (p/s) | 6 |
| 79 | United Artists UP 36537 | Secrets/Brainbomb (p/s) | 6 |
| 80 | United Artists BP 317 | Laughing Academy/Baby Don't Jump (p/s) | 8 |
| 79 | United Artists UAG 30258 | LAUGHING ACADEMY (LP, with inner sleeve) | 15 |

**PUNKETTES**

| | | | |
|---|---|---|---|
| 77 | Response SR 511 | Going Out Wiv A Punk/Polythene | 5 |

**PUPILS**

| | | | |
|---|---|---|---|
| 66 | Wing WL 1150 | A TRIBUTE TO THE ROLLING STONES (LP) | 40 |
| 69 | Fontana SFL 13087 | A TRIBUTE TO THE ROLLING STONES (LP, reissue) | 15 |

*(see also Eyes)*

**PUPPETS**

| | | | |
|---|---|---|---|
| 63 | Pye 7N 15556 | Poison Ivy/Everybody's Talking | 50 |
| 64 | Pye 7N 15625 | Shake With Me/Three Boys Looking For Love (existence unconfirmed) | 0 |
| 64 | Pye 7N 15634 | Baby Don't Cry/Shake With Me | 60 |

**DANNY PURCHES**

| | | | |
|---|---|---|---|
| 55 | Columbia SCM 5183 | Mama/Just One More Time | 8 |

**(BERNARD) PRETTY PURDEY**

| | | | |
|---|---|---|---|
| 68 | Direction 58-3301 | Funky Donkey/Caravan | 10 |
| 68 | Direction 58-3628 | Soul Clappin'/Blow Your Lid | 10 |
| 71 | Philips 6073 708 | Good Livin' Good Lovin'/Day Dreaming | 6 |
| 68 | Direction 8-63290 | SOUL DRUMS (LP) | 40 |
| 71 | Philips 6369 421 | SOUL IS ... (LP) | 20 |

**PURE EVIL**

| | | | |
|---|---|---|---|
| 73 | Hybrid HB20 | Never Trust A Woman/I See You Now | 30 |

**PURE GOLD**

| | | | |
|---|---|---|---|
| 69 | President PT 250 | Fairground/You've Gotta Give It Time | 10 |

**PURE HELL**

| | | | |
|---|---|---|---|
| 78 | Golden Sphinx GSX 002 | These Boots Are Made For Walking/No Rules (p/s) | 20 |

MINT VALUE £

**PURE LOVE & PLEASURE**
70   Stateside SSL 5026          A RECORD OF PURE LOVE AND PLEASURE (LP)................................... 30

**PURE PRODUCT**
79   Streets Ahead SA2           Rejection/Sugar Plum (p/s) ............................................................... 6

**PURE REASON REVOLUTION**
04   Poptones MC50896            Apprentice Of The Universe/Nimos & Tambos (p/s) .......................... 5

**PURESSENCE**
92   Damn Loud 2DM01             PETROL SKIN (EP, 1,000 only)............................................................ 30
93   Damn Loud 2DM02             OFFSHORE (EP, 1,000 only) ............................................................... 35
96   Island ILPS 8946            PURESSENCE (LP) ............................................................................. 30
98   Island ILPS 8064            ONLY FOREVER (LP) .......................................................................... 25

**PURGE**
69   Corn CP 101                 The Mayor Of Simpleton Hall/The Knave (p/s) .............................. 200
69   Corn CP 101                 The Mayor Of Simpleton Hall/The Knave (without p/s) .................... 90

**JAMES & BOBBY PURIFY**
66   Stateside SS 547            I'm Your Puppet/So Many Reasons.................................................. 20
67   Stateside SS 595            Wish You Didn't Have To Go/You Can't Keep A Good Man Down ..... 15
67   Stateside SS 2016           Shake A Tail Feather/Goodness Gracious........................................ 25
67   Stateside SS 2039           I Take What I Want/Sixteen Tons ................................................... 12
67   Stateside SS 2049           Let Love Come Between Us/I Don't Want To Have To Wait ............. 25
68   Stateside SS 2093           Do Unto Me/Everybody Needs Somebody ....................................... 20
68   Bell BLL 1008               I Can't Remember/I Was Born To Lose Out ..................................... 10
68   Bell BLL 1024               Help Yourself To All My Lovin'/Last Piece Of Love ........................ 10
69   Bell BLL 1043               Untie Me/We're Finally Gonna Make It ............................................ 8
69   Bell BLL 1056               Let Love Come Between Us/Shake A Tail Feather ........................... 10
69   Bell BLL 1067               Do Unto Me/Wish You Didn't Have To Go.......................................... 8
72   Mojo 2092 056               I'm Your Puppet/Wish You Didn't Have To Go .................................. 8
67   Stateside SL 10206          JAMES AND BOBBY PURIFY (LP)..................................................... 60
67   Bell MBLL/SBLL 101          THE PURE SOUND OF THE PURIFYS (LP) ........................................ 40

**PURITAN GUITARS**
80   Riverside Records           £100 In 15 Minutes/Making It (p/s, stamped white labels) ............ 20

**PURITY RING**
11   Transparent TP 027          Ungirthed/Lofticries (p/s, 300 only) ............................................ 15

**ALTON PURNELL**
70   Dixie DIX 4                 TRAVELLING LIGHT (LP) ................................................................. 30

**PURPLE ALGAE**
95   Poor Person Prod. PPPR 7    ADRIFT ON A SEA OF SOUND (LP, handmade sleeve & 2 inserts, no'd, 500 only) ........... 15

**PURPLE GANG**
67   Big T BIG 101               Granny Takes A Trip/Bootleg Whisky .............................................. 15
68   Big T BIG 111               Kiss Me Goodnight Sally Green/Auntie Monica ............................... 7
68   Transatlantic TRA 174       THE PURPLE GANG STRIKES (LP) .................................................. 60

**PURPLE HAZE**
85   S.R.S. SRS 6                Hear It On The Radio (p/s)............................................................. 55

**PURPLE HEARTS**
79   Fiction FICS 003            Millions Like Us/Beat That! (p/s) ................................................. 10
79   Fiction FICS 007            Frustration/Extraordinary Sensations (p/s)................................... 10
80   Fiction FICS 9              Jimmy/What Am I Gonna Do (p/s) .................................................. 10
80   Safari SAFE 30              My Life's A Jigsaw/The Guy Who Made Her A Star/Just To Please You (in foldout jigsaw p/s) .......... 12
80   Safari SAFE 30              My Life's A Jigsaw/The Guy Who Made Her A Star/Just To Please You ......... 8
82   Road Runner RR 1            Plane Crash/Scooby Doo/Gun Of Life (p/s) .................................... 12
86   UNICORN PHZ3                Friends Again/Head On Collision Time (p/s) .................................... 8
80   Fiction FIX 002/2383 568    BEAT THAT! (LP).......................................................................... 20
     *(see also Bob Manton, Rage)*

**PURPLE WINE**
71   NBR (No cat no)             PURPLE WINE (LP, plain white cover)............................................ 300
71   The Mental Health Council   It's My Mind/I'm Lonely/Friends (p/s)........................................... 100

**PURPLEMAN & PAPPA TULLO**
83   Vista Sounds VSLP 4024      PURPLEMAN SAVES PAPPA TOLLO IN A DANCEHALL (LP)................... 40

**PURSON**
12   Rise Above B007929F6W       Rocking Horse/Twos And Ones (p/s, 1st press, black vinyl, 250 only)......... 8
12   Rise Above B007929F6W       Rocking Horse/Twos And Ones (p/s, 1st press, clear vinyl, 100 only) ..... 12
12   Rise Above B007929F6W       Rocking Horse/Twos And Ones (p/s, 1st press, purple vinyl, 250 only)..... 8
13   Rise Above RISE7/173        The Contract/Blueprints Of The Dream (p/s, 200 on black vinyl)......... 10
13   Rise Above RISE7/173        The Contract/Blueprints Of The Dream (p/s, 100 on black vinyl)......... 15
13   Rise Above RISELP 152       THE CIRCLE & THE BLUE DOOR (LP, 'die hard' edition, 180 gram vinyl, A2 poster, patch and die-cut gatefold sleeve, 100 only) ........... 30

**PURSUIT OF COLOUR**
84   Colour                      LOVE PLAYS EGO: Can't Let You Go/Radomontade (b/w, p/s allegedly 50 copies only) ........... 200

**PUSSY (1)**
69   Morgan Bluetown BT 5002     PUSSY PLAYS (LP)..................................................................... 1500
09   Morgan Bluetown BT 5002     PUSSY PLAYS (LP, reissue by Secret Records/Record Collector, 350 only with signed and numbered laminated insert) ........... 35
     *(see also Angel Pavement, Fortes Mentum)*

**PUSSY (2)**
72   Deram DM 368                Feline Woman/Ska Child ............................................................... 35
     *(see also Jerusalem. Gillan, Deep Purple)*

## PUSSYFOOT
| | | | |
|---|---|---|---|
| 66 | Decca F 12474 | Freeloader/Things That Still Remind Me | 25 |
| 67 | Decca F 12561 | Mr Hyde/Hasty Words | 30 |
| 67 | Pye 7N 17395 | Dee Dee Do Your Dance/Big Brown Eyes | 30 |
| 68 | Pye 7N 17520 | Good Times/Till You Don't Want Me Anymore | 25 |

*(see also Rare Breed)*

## PUSSY GALORE
| | | | |
|---|---|---|---|
| 87 | Vinyl Drip SUK 001 | GROOVY HATE FUCK (LP) | 20 |
| 87 | Product Inc. 33PROD 19 | RIGHT NOW (LP) | 18 |
| 89 | Product INCLP 1 | DIAL M FOR MOTHERFUCKER (LP) | 18 |
| 90 | Rough Trade ROUGH 149 | HISTORIA DE LA MUSICA ROCK (LP) | 18 |

*(see also Jon Spencer Blues Explosion)*

## ASHA PUTHLI
| | | | |
|---|---|---|---|
| 76 | CBS 4623 | The Devil Is Loose/Space Talk | 10 |
| 73 | CBS 65804 | ASHA PUTHLI (LP) | 20 |
| 75 | CBS 80978 | SHE LOVES TO HEAR THE MUSIC (LP) | 15 |
| 76 | CBS 81443 | THE DEVIL IS LOOSE (LP) | 30 |

## PUTNEY BRIDGE
| | | | |
|---|---|---|---|
| 71 | Chapter One CH 145 | Take A Ride/Road To Purity | 10 |

## PUZZLE
| | | | |
|---|---|---|---|
| 69 | Stateside SS 2146 | Hey Medusa/Make The Children Happy | 25 |
| 72 | Jam JAM 1 | Houla/Do You Feel The Pain | 40 |
| 69 | Stateside SSL 10285 | PUZZLE (LP) | 50 |

## PVC 2
| | | | |
|---|---|---|---|
| 77 | Zoom ZUM 2 | Put You In The Picture/Pain/Deranged, Demented and Free (p/s) | 12 |

*(see also Midge Ure, Zones)o*

## PYLON
| | | | |
|---|---|---|---|
| 80 | Armageddon ARM 1 | Cool/Dub/Driving School/Danger!! (10") | 10 |

## PYLONS
| | | | |
|---|---|---|---|
| 80 | Hi Voltage HVVS 701 | Marvel World/Spoof (p/s) | 30 |

## NATASHA PYNE
| | | | |
|---|---|---|---|
| 66 | Polydor 56713 | It's All In Your Head/I'm A Dreamer | 15 |

## PYRAMID
| | | | |
|---|---|---|---|
| 67 | Deram DM 111 | Summer Of Last Year/Summer Evening | 50 |

*(see also Fairport Convention, Ian Matthews)*

## PYRAMIDS (JAMAICA)
| | | | |
|---|---|---|---|
| 67 | President PT 161 | Train Tour To Rainbow City/John Chewey | 20 |
| 68 | President PT 177 | Wedding In Peyton Place/Girls Girls Girls | 10 |
| 68 | President PT 195 | All Change On The Bakerloo Line/Playing Games | 10 |
| 68 | President PT 206 | Mexican Moonlight/Mule | 10 |
| 68 | President PT 225 | Tisko My Darling/Movement All Around | 10 |
| 69 | President PT 243 | Do-Re-Mi/I'm Outnumbered | 10 |
| 69 | President PT 274 | I'm A Man/Dragon Fly | 10 |
| 69 | Doctor Bird DB 1307 | Stay With Him/Chicken Mary | 20 |
| 70 | Duke DU 80 | Geronimo/Feel Alright | 10 |
| 70 | Trojan TR 7755 | Feel Alright/Telstar | 12 |
| 70 | Trojan TR 7770 | To Sir With Love/Reggae Shuffle | 12 |
| 71 | Trojan TR 7803 | All For You/All For You Version | 12 |
| 71 | Creole CR 1003 | Mosquito Bite/Mother's Bath | 12 |
| 68 | President PTL 1021 | THE PYRAMIDS (LP) | 70 |

*(see also Equals, Little Grants & Eddie, Seven Letters, Bruce Ruffin)*

## PYRAMIDS (U.S.)
| | | | |
|---|---|---|---|
| 64 | London HLU 9847 | Penetration/Here Comes Marsha | 50 |

## PYTHAGORAS THEOREM
| | | | |
|---|---|---|---|
| 70 | Pye 7N 17924 | Give A Damn/London Bridge | 12 |
| 70 | Pye 7N 17990 | Our House/Free Like Me | 7 |

## PYTHON LEE JACKSON
| | | | |
|---|---|---|---|
| 76 | Young Blood YB 1077 | The Blues/Cloud Nine | 10 |
| 80 | Young Blood YB 0089 | In A Broken Dream/The Blues | 6 |
| 80 | Young Blood YEP 89 | In A Broken Dream (mono)/In A Broken Dream (stereo)/The Blues/ Cloud Nine (EP, "Kelly Girl" Employment Agency advert on p/s) | 10 |

*(see also Rod Stewart)*

## Q
| | | | |
|---|---|---|---|
| 82 | Cocteau COC 6 | Playback/Music's Gone (p/s) | 15 |

## Q.A.X.
| | | | |
|---|---|---|---|
| 82 | Vinyl Beat VB 001 | Heart Alone/Does Me Good (p/s) | 15 |
| 82 | Vinyl Beat VB 002 | Lightning Touch/Unconfirmed (p/s) | 15 |
| 82 | Vinyl Beat VB003 | Gimme Your Love/The Heat Of Love (p/s) | 8 |

## Q-CHASTIC
| | | | |
|---|---|---|---|
| 92 | Rephlex 002EP | Q-CHASTIC EP (double pack, existence unconfirmed) | 200 |

*(see also Aphex Twin)*

## Q8
| | | |
|---|---|---|
| 78 | Flame FLM 018 | Superband/Give A Little Love .................................................................................. 10 |

## Q.LAZZARUS
| | | |
|---|---|---|
| 91 | All Nations ANRS 001 | Goodby Horses/White Lines (p/s) ............................................................................ 100 |
| 91 | All Nations 12ANRS 001 | Goodby Horses/Goodby Horses (7" version)/White Lines (12", p/s) ................ 150 |

## QPR
| | | |
|---|---|---|
| 67 | Eyemark EMS 1008 | QPR The Greatest/Supporters Support Us ............................................................ 45 |

## Q-PROJECT
| | | |
|---|---|---|
| 92 | QTIP 001 | FREESTYLE FANATIC EP (12", stamped white label, 4 untitled tracks) .................. 39 |
| 93 | Legend LEG 001 | Return Of Q Project/Champion Sound/Night Moves (12") ................................. 20 |

## QRUUX ADU XA
| | | |
|---|---|---|
| 82 | Shooting Star STAR 007 | Shakin' All Over/Robotics (p/s, as K.A.D.) .......................................................... 15 |

## QT'S
| | | |
|---|---|---|
| 79 | SRT SRTS/79/CUS 429 | SAVAGE IN THE CITY EP .......................................................................................... 35 |

## QUAD
| | | |
|---|---|---|
| 97 | Acme AC 8020LP | QUAD (LP, clear vinyl in printed clear PVC cover) .............................................. 30 |
| 97 | Prescription DRUG 3 | QUAD (LP, 99 copies only, handmade sleeve with colour photo, mail-order only) ........ 50 |

*(see also Sun Dial)*

## QUADROPHONICS
| | | |
|---|---|---|
| 75 | Contempo 2054 | Betcha If You Check It Out/Prove My Love To You .......................................... 10 |

## QUADS
| | | |
|---|---|---|
| 79 | Big Bear BB 23 | There Must Be Thousands/You Gotta Jive ............................................................ 6 |
| 79 | Big Bear BB25 | There's Never Been A Night/Take It ...................................................................... 5 |
| 80s | Big Bear BB29 | UFO/Astronaut's Journey (p/s) ............................................................................ 10 |

## CHRISTINE QUAITE
| | | |
|---|---|---|
| 62 | Oriole CB 1739 | Guilty Eyes/Oh My! ............................................................................................. 20 |
| 62 | Oriole CB 1772 | Your Nose Is Gonna Grow/Our Last Chance ..................................................... 15 |
| 63 | Oriole CB 1845 | Mister Heartache/Whisper Wonderful Words .................................................. 15 |
| 63 | Oriole CB 1876 | In The Middle Of The Floor/Tell Me Mama ....................................................... 60 |
| 63 | Oriole CB 1921 | I Believe In Love/Here She Comes ..................................................................... 20 |
| 64 | Oriole CB 1945 | Mister Stuck Up/Will You Be The Same Tomorrow ......................................... 15 |
| 65 | Stateside SS 435 | If You've Got A Heart/So Near So Far .................................................................. 20 |
| 66 | Stateside SS 482 | Long After Tonight Is All Over/I'm Hoping ........................................................ 50 |
| 66 | Stateside SS 482 | Long After Tonight Is All Over/I'm Hoping (DJ copy) ...................................... 100 |

## QUAKER CITY BOYS
| | | |
|---|---|---|
| 59 | London HLU 8796 | Teasin'/Won't Y' Come Out, Mary Ann ............................................................. 15 |

## QUAKERS
| | | |
|---|---|---|
| 65 | Oriole CB 1992 | I'm Ready/Down The Road A Piece ................................................................... 150 |
| 65 | Studio 36 KSP 109/110 | She's Alright/Talk To Me (only 50 pressed) ..................................................... 600 |

## QUALITY DRIVEL
| | | |
|---|---|---|
| 81 | No Cure WHOOP 1 | SUBLIMINAL CUTS EP (p/s) ................................................................................. 35 |

## QUANDO QUANGO
| | | |
|---|---|---|
| 84 | Factory FAC 102 | Atom Rock (p/s) ................................................................................................... 6 |
| 85 | Factory FAC 137 | Genius/This Feeling (p/s) ...................................................................................... 6 |
| 85 | Factory FACT 110 | PIGS & BATTLESHIPS (LP) .................................................................................... 18 |

## QUANTIC
| | | |
|---|---|---|
| 00 | Breakin' Bread BNB 002 | We Got Soul/Fresh Rhythm ................................................................................ |
| 01 | Tru Thoughts TRU 014 | Life In The Rain/Common Knowledge/Time Is The Enemy (12") ................... 25 |
| 01 | Tru Thoughts TRU LP 016 | THE 5TH EXOTIC (2xLP) ...................................................................................... 15 |
| 02 | Tru Thoughts TRU LP 034 | APRICOT MORNING (2xLP) ................................................................................. 40 |

## QUANTIC SOUL ORCHESTRA
| | | |
|---|---|---|
| 01 | Tru Thoughts TRU7 018 | Super 8 (Part 1)/Super 8 (Part 2) ...................................................................... 30 |
| 02 | Tru Thoughts TRU7 023 | Assassin (Part 1)/Assassin (Part 2) ................................................................... 12 |
| 03 | Tru Thoughts TRU7 051 | Pushin' On/Pushin' On My Thing .......................................................................... 5 |
| 03 | Tru Thoughts TRU7 055 | Babarabatiri/The Conspirator ............................................................................... 8 |
| 03 | Tru Thoughts TRU LP 029 | STAMPEDE (LP) .................................................................................................... 10 |
| 07 | Tru Thoughts TRULP 139 | TROPIDELICO (LP) ............................................................................................... 20 |

## QUARRY
| | | |
|---|---|---|
| 87 | QP QP 001 | Just Another Day/Promised Land ...................................................................... 25 |

## QUARRY MEN
| | | |
|---|---|---|
| 58 | 'P.F. Phillips Kensington' | That'll Be The Day/In Spite Of All The Danger (78 rpm shellac acetate, handwritten labels, 1 copy only, owned by Paul McCartney) .............. 200000 |
| 81 | 'Percy Philips, Kensington' | That'll Be The Day/In Spite Of All The Danger (78rpm, private pressing reproduction of 1958 demo disc, repro Parlophone co. sleeve, 25 only) .............. 10000 |
| 81 | 'Percy Philips, Kensington' | That'll Be The Day/In Spite Of All The Danger (45rpm, private pressing reproduction of 1958 demo disc, repro Parlophone co. sleeve, 25 only) .............. 10000 |

*(see also Beatles, Trad Grads)*

## QUARTER NOTES
| | | |
|---|---|---|
| 57 | Parlophone R 4365 | My Fantasy/Ten Minutes To Midnight ............................................................... 15 |

## JOE QUARTERMAN & FREE SOUL
| | | |
|---|---|---|
| 73 | GSF GSZ 3 | So Much Trouble In My Mind (Parts 1 & 2) .......................................................... 5 |
| 74 | GSF GSZ 12 | Thanks Dad Parts 1 & 2 ......................................................................................... 5 |
| 73 | GSF GS 504 | JOE QUARTERMAN & FREE SOUL (LP) ............................................................... 30 |

## QUARTET
| | | |
|---|---|---|
| 69 | Decca F12974 | Now/Will My Lady Come ........................................................................................ 8 |
| 70 | Decca F13072 | Mama Where Did You Fail/Joseph ...................................................................... 10 |

## QUARTZ (1)
| | | | |
|---|---|---|---|
| 77 | Blyth Jex School | Witch Queen/Social Values (gatefold p/s) | 7 |

## QUARTZ (2)
| | | | |
|---|---|---|---|
| 77 | Jet UP 36290 | Sugar Rain/Street Fighting Lady/Mainline Riders | 15 |
| 77 | Jet UP 36317 | Street Fighting Lady/Mainline Riders | 12 |
| 80 | Reddingtons R.R. DAN 1 | Nantucket Sleighride/Wildfire (p/s, white or blue vinyl) | 10 |
| 80 | Reddingtons R.R. DAN 1 | Nantucket Sleighride/Wildfire (p/s, black vinyl) | 5 |
| 80 | Jet SJET 189 | Street Fighting Lady/Mainline Riders (p/s, reissue, demos £15) | 8 |
| 80 | Logo GOT 387 | Satan's Serenade/Bloody Fool/Roll Over Beethoven (live) (12", p/s, blue vinyl) | 20 |
| 80 | Logo GOT 387 | Satan's Serenade/Bloody Fool/Roll Over Beethoven (live) (12", p/s, red vinyl) | 15 |
| 80 | MCA MCA 642 | Stoking The Fires Of Hell/Circles (p/s) | 10 |
| 80 | Logo MOGO 4007 | LIVE QUARTZ (12" EP) | 12 |
| 81 | MCA MCA 661 | Stand Up And Fight/Charlie Snow (p/s) | 12 |
| 83 | Heavy Metal HEAVY 17 | Tell Me Why/Streetwalker (p/s) | 7 |
| 77 | Jet UAG 30081 | QUARTZ (LP, with inner sleeve) | 50 |
| 79 | Jet JETLP 233 | DELETED (LP, in sealed brown paper bag with insert. Reissue of 1st LP) | 18 |
| 80 | Reddingtons R.R. REDD 001 | QUARTZ LIVE - COUNT DRACULA (LP, in b&w 'live' sleeve) | 15 |
| 80 | MCA MCF 3080 | STAND UP AND FIGHT (LP, with lyric insert) | 15 |
| 83 | Heavy Metal HMRPD 9 | AGAINST ALL ODDS (LP, picture disc) | 20 |

*(see also Black Sabbath, Copperfield, Bandy Legs)*

## QUASAR
| | | | |
|---|---|---|---|
| 82 | Q QUA 1 | FIRE IN THE SKY (LP, with insert) | 20 |

*(see also Solstice)*

## QUASI
| | | | |
|---|---|---|---|
| 98 | Domino WIGLP 55 | FEATURING "BIRDS" (LP) | 20 |
| 99 | Domino WIGLP 69 | FIELD STUDIES (LP) | 20 |
| 01 | Domino WIGLP 97 | THE SWORD OF GOD (2-LP) | 18 |

## QUATERMASS (1)
| | | | |
|---|---|---|---|
| 70 | Harvest SVHL 775 | QUATERMASS (LP, gatefold sleeve, no EMI logo on label) | 250 |
| 75 | Harvest SHSM 2002 | QUATERMASS (LP, reissue, different sleeve) | 30 |

*(see also Ian Gillan Band, Episode Six, Hard Stuff)*

## QUATERMASS (2)
| | | | |
|---|---|---|---|
| 97 | Metropolitan MM 027 | The Judgement (12", no p/s) | 15 |

## QUATOR
| | | | |
|---|---|---|---|
| 72 | BBC RESL 6 | Spy Trap/Playgirl | 30 |

## QUATRAIN
| | | | |
|---|---|---|---|
| 69 | Polydor 583 743 | QUATRAIN (LP) | 60 |

## SUZI QUATRO
| | | | |
|---|---|---|---|
| 72 | Rak RAK 134 | Rolling Stone/Brain Confusion (For All The Lonely People) | 30 |
| 73 | Rak PSR 355 | Primitive Love/Shakin' All Over (promo only) | 30 |
| 75 | Rak RAK 200 | I Bit Off More Than I Could Chew/Red Hot Rosie | 5 |
| 75 | Rak RAK 215 | I May Be Too Young/Don't Mess Around | 5 |
| 75 | Rak RAK 256 | Roxy Roller/I'll Grow On You | 5 |
| 78 | Rak RAK 285 | Stumblin' In/Stranger With You (with Chris Norman) (2 different p/s) | 5 |
| 79 | Rak RAK 299 | She's In Love With You/Space Cadets (p/s) | 5 |
| 87 | Hackenbacker HACK 101 | Am I Dreaming/Who Needs Chairs/Will You Take This Woman (only available at pantomime show) | 10 |
| 73 | SRAK 505 | SUZI QUATRO (LP) | 20 |
| 74 | RAK SRAK 509 | QUATRO (LP) | 15 |

## QUBISM
| | | | |
|---|---|---|---|
| 94 | em:t 2294 | QUBISM (CD, digipak) | 50 |

## QUE BONO
| | | | |
|---|---|---|---|
| 81 | Naked BARE 1 | Making Noise/Emelia | 15 |

## QUEEN
### SINGLES
| | | | |
|---|---|---|---|
| 73 | EMI EMI 2036 | Keep Yourself Alive/Son And Daughter | 40 |
| 74 | EMI EMI 2121 | Seven Seas Of Rhye/See What A Fool I've Been | 5 |
| 74 | EMI EMI 2229 | Killer Queen/Flick Of The Wrist | 5 |
| 75 | EMI EMI 2256 | Now I'm Here/Lily Of The Valley | 5 |
| 75 | EMI EMI 2375 | Bohemian Rhapsody/I'm In Love With My Car (p/s; beware counterfeits with 'computer-scanned' logo) | 35 |
| 76 | EMI EMI 2565 | Somebody To Love/White Man (p/s, beware of counterfeit sleeves) | 10 |
| 77 | EMI EMI 2593 | Tie Your Mother Down/You And I | 8 |
| 77 | EMI EMI 2623 | QUEEN'S FIRST EP: Good Old Fashioned Lover Boy/Death On Two Legs/ Tenement Funster/White Queen (As It Began) (p/s) | 10 |
| 77 | EMI EMI 2708 | We Are The Champions/We Will Rock You (p/s) | 8 |
| 78 | EMI EMI 2575 | Spread Your Wings/Sheer Heart Attack (p/s) | 6 |
| 78 | EMI EMI 2870 | Bicycle Race/Fat Bottomed Girls (p/s) | 6 |
| 78 | EMI EMI 2870 | Bicycle Race/Fat Bottomed Girls (different p/s for export to Belgium) | 200 |
| 79 | EMI EMI 2910 | Don't Stop Me Now/In Only Seven Days (p/s) | 6 |
| 79 | EMI EMI 2959 | Love Of My Life (live)/Now I'm Here (live) | 20 |
| 79 | EMI EMI 5001 | Crazy Little Thing Called Love/We Will Rock You (live) (p/s) | 5 |
| 80 | EMI EMI 5022 | Save Me/Let Me Entertain You (live) (p/s) | 5 |
| 80 | EMI EMI 5076 | Play The Game/A Human Body (p/s, beige label with red 'EMI' logo or white label with large black 'Queen' logo) | 6 |
| 80 | EMI EMI 5102 | Another One Bites The Dust/Dragon Attack (p/s) | 8 |
| 82 | EMI EMI 5293 | Body Language/Life Is Real (Song For Lennon) (p/s) | 6 |
| 82 | EMI EMI 5316 | Las Palabras De Amor (The Words Of Love)/Cool Cat (p/s) | 6 |
| 82 | EMI EMI 5325 | Backchat/Staying Power (p/s) | 10 |

| | | | |
|---|---|---|---|
| 82 | EMI 12EMI 5325 | Backchat (Extended)/Staying Power (12", p/s) | 20 |
| 84 | EMI 12QUEEN 1 | Radio Ga Ga (Ext. Version)/Radio Ga Ga (Instrumental)/I Go Crazy (12", p/s) | 10 |
| 84 | EMI QUEEN 2 | I Want To Break Free (Remix)/Machines (Back To Humans) ('Freddie' p/s, gold lettering) | 10 |
| 84 | EMI QUEEN 2 | I Want To Break Free (Remix)/Machines (Back To Humans) ('Freddie' p/s, white lettering) | 8 |
| 84 | EMI QUEEN 2 | I Want To Break Free (Remix)/Machines (Back To Humans) ('Brian', p/s, with gold lettering) | 12 |
| 84 | EMI QUEEN 2 | I Want To Break Free (Remix)/Machines (Back To Humans) ('Roger' p/s, with gold lettering) | 15 |
| 84 | EMI QUEEN 2 | I Want To Break Free (Remix)/Machines (Back To Humans) ('John' p/s, with gold lettering) | 18 |
| 84 | EMI 12QUEEN 2 | I Want To Break Free (Extended Remix)/Machines (Back To Humans) (12", p/s, with red background with gold lettering) | 20 |
| 84 | EMI 12QUEEN 2 | I Want To Break Free (Extended Remix)/Machines (Back To Humans) (12", p/s, with red background with black lettering) | 12 |
| 84 | EMI 12QUEEN 2 | I Want To Break Free (Extended Remix)/Machines (Back To Humans) (12", p/s, with white background) | 10 |
| 84 | EMI QUEEN 3 | It's A Hard Life/Is This The World We Created...? (p/s) | 6 |
| 84 | EMI QUEEN 3 | It's A Hard Life/Is This The World We Created...? ('Roger Taylor' overprinted photo p/s) | 20 |
| 84 | EMI 12QUEEN 3 | It's A Hard Life (Extended)/It's A Hard Life/ Is This The World We Created...? (12") | 25 |
| 84 | EMI 12QUEENP 3 | It's A Hard Life/Is This The World We Created...? (12", picture disc) | 20 |
| 84 | EMI QUEEN 4 | Hammer To Fall (Edit)/Tear It Up ('live' p/s, withdrawn) | 100 |
| 84 | EMI QUEEN 4 | Hammer To Fall (Edit)/Tear It Up (red p/s) | 6 |
| 84 | EMI 12 QUEEN 4 | Hammer To Fall (The Headbangers Mix)/Tear It Up (12", 'live' p/s, withdrawn) | 120 |
| 84 | EMI 12 QUEEN 4 | Hammer To Fall (The Headbangers Mix)/Tear It Up (12", red p/s) | 12 |
| 84 | EMI QUEEN 5 | Man On The Prowl/Keep Passing The Open Windows (unreleased, white label test pressings only) | 150 |
| 84 | EMI QUEEN 5 | Thank God It's Christmas/Man On The Prowl/ Keep Passing The Open Windows (p/s) | 8 |
| 84 | EMI 12QUEEN 5 | Thank God It's Christmas/Man On The Prowl (Extended Version)/ Keep Passing The Open Windows (Extended Version) (12", p/s) | 10 |
| 84 | EMI G 45 1 | You're My Best Friend/Killer Queen (re-issue, Golden 45's series) | 20 |
| 85 | EMI QUEEN 6 | One Vision (7" Mix)/Blurred Vision (p/s, with red lyric inner sleeve) | 7 |
| 85 | EMI QUEEN 6 | One Vision (7" Mix)/Blurred Vision (p/s) | 5 |
| 85 | EMI 12QUEEN 6 | One Vision (Extended Vision)/Blurred Vision (12", p/s, with red lyric inner sleeve) | 12 |
| 85 | EMI 12QUEEN 6 | One Vision (Extended Vision)/Blurred Vision (12", p/s) | 10 |
| 85 | EMI 12QUEEN 6 | One Vision (Extended Vision)/Blurred Vision (12", printed PVC sleeve & red inner) | 20 |
| 86 | EMI 12QUEEN 7 | A Kind Of Magic (Ext. Version)/A Dozen Red Roses For My Darling (12", p/s) | 12 |
| 86 | EMI 12QUEENP7 | A Kind Of Magic (Extended Version)/Don't Lose Your Head (Instrumental Version) (12", picture disc) | 35 |
| 86 | EMI QUEEN 8 | Friends Will Be Friends/Seven Seas Of Rhye (p/s) | 6 |
| 86 | EMI QUEEN P8 | Friends Will Be Friends/Seven Seas Of Rhye (picture disc) | 40 |
| 86 | EMI 12QUEEN 8 | Friends Will Be Friends (Extended Version)/Friends Will Be Friends (7" Version)/Seven Seas Of Rhye (12", p/s) | 10 |
| 86 | EMI QUEEN 9 | Who Wants To Live Forever/Killer Queen (p/s) | 8 |
| 86 | EMI 12QUEEN 9 | Who Wants To Live Forever (7" Version)/(Album Version)/Killer Queen/ Who Wants To Live Forever (Piano Version) (12", p/s) | 15 |
| 89 | Parlophone 12QUEEN 10 | I Want It All (Single Version)/Hang On In There/ I Want It All (Album Version) (12", p/s) | 12 |
| 89 | Parlophone CDQUEEN 10 | I Want It All (Album Version)/Hang On In There/I Want It All (Single Version) (CD, picture disc) | 20 |
| 89 | Parlophone QUEEN PD 11 | Breakthru' (7" Mix)/Stealin' (shaped picture disc, 12" PVC sleeve with insert) | 20 |
| 89 | Parlophone QUEEN PD 11 | Breakthru' (7" Mix)/Stealin' (uncut picture disc, 12" PVC sleeve with insert) | 150 |
| 89 | Parlophone CD QUEEN 11 | Breakthru' (12" Version)/Stealin'/Breakthru' (7" Mix) (CD) | 25 |
| 89 | Parlophone QUEEN 12 | The Invisible Man/Hijack My Heart (black vinyl, p/s) | 5 |
| 89 | Parlophone QUEEN X12 | The Invisible Man/Hijack My Heart (clear vinyl, p/s) | 12 |
| 89 | Parlophone 12QUEEN 12 | The Invisible Man (12" Version)/(7" Version)/Hijack My Heart (12", p/s) | 12 |
| 89 | Parlophone 12QUEENX12 | The Invisible Man (12" Version)/The Invisible Man (7" Version)/ Hijack My Heart (12", clear vinyl, PVC sleeve with insert) | 20 |
| 89 | Parlophone CD QUEEN 12 | The Invisible Man (12" Version)/Hijack My Heart/ The Invisible Man (Single Version) (CD) | 30 |
| 89 | Parlophone QUEEN 14 | Scandal/My Life Has Been Saved (p/s) | 8 |
| 89 | Parlophone QUEEN P14 | Scandal/My Life Has Been Saved (poster p/s) | 20 |
| 89 | Parlophone 12QUEEN 14 | Scandal (12" Version)/Scandal (7" Version)/My Life Has Been Saved (12", p/s) | 10 |
| 89 | Parlophone 12QUEENS 14 | Scandal (12" Version)/My Life Has Been Saved/Scandal (7" Version)/ (12", p/s, 1-sided, B-side etched with group's signatures) | 20 |
| 89 | Parlophone CD QUEEN 14 | Scandal (12" Version)/My Life Has Been Saved/Scandal (7" Version) (CD) | 25 |
| 89 | Parlophone QUEEN 15 | The Miracle/Stone Cold Crazy (live) (p/s) | 8 |
| 89 | Parlophone QUEEN H15 | The Miracle/Stone Cold Crazy (live) (orange hologram p/s) | 15 |
| 89 | Parlophone QUEEN H15 | The Miracle/Stone Cold Crazy (live) (proof sleeve with negative hologram p/s) | 300 |
| 89 | Parlophone 12QUEEN 15 | The Miracle/Stone Cold Crazy (live)/My Melancholy Blues (live) (12", yellow p/s) | 15 |
| 89 | Parlophone 12QUEENP 15 | The Miracle/Stone Cold Crazy (live)/My Melancholy Blues (live) (12", turquoise p/s with insert print) | 18 |
| 89 | Parlophone QUEENCD 15 | The Miracle/Stone Cold Crazy (live)/My Melancholy Blues (live) (CD) | 30 |
| 91 | Parlophone QUEEN 16 | Innuendo/Bijou (p/s) | 6 |
| 91 | Parl. 12QUEEN PD16 | Innuendo (Explosive Version)/Under Pressure/Bijou (12", picture disc, PVC sleeve with insert) | 20 |
| 91 | Parlophone QUEEN 17 | I'm Going Slightly Mad/The Hitman (p/s) | 5 |
| 91 | Parlophone QUEEN PD 17 | I'm Going Slightly Mad/The Hitman (shaped picture disc with insert) | 20 |
| 91 | Parlophone QUEEN PD 17 | I'm Going Slightly Mad/The Hitman (uncut picture disc with insert) | 125 |
| 91 | Parlophone 12QUEENG 17 | I'm Going Slightly Mad/The Hitman/Lost Opportunity (12", gatefold p/s) | 15 |
| 91 | Parlophone 12QUEEN PD18 | Headlong/All God's People/Mad The Swine (12", clear vinyl picture disc, with insert in PVC sleeve) | 15 |
| 91 | Parlophone QUEEN 19 | The Show Must Go On/Keep Yourself Alive (p/s) | 5 |

| | | | |
|---|---|---|---|
| 91 | Parlophone 12QUEENSG 19 | The Show Must Go On/Keep Yourself Alive/Queen Talks (12", 1-sided, B-side etched with group's signatures, gatefold p/s) | 18 |
| 91 | Parlophone QUEEN 19/20 | The Show Must Go On/Bohemian Rhapsody (unissued, no p/s) | 500 |
| 91 | Parlophone QUEEN 20 | Bomemian Rhapsody/These Are The Days Of Our Lives (reissue, p/s) | 5 |
| 95 | Parlophone QUEENLH 24 | Let Me Live/Fat Bottomed Girls (Jukebox 45, black vinyl no p/s) | 15 |
| 96 | Parlophone QUEEN 23 | Too Much Love Will Kill You/We Will Rock You/We Are The Champions (p/s, pink vinyl) | 8 |
| 97 | parlophone QUEENLH 26 | No-One But You/We Will Rock You (Original 1977 version) (unreleased) | 20 |
| 97 | Parlophone QUEEN 26 | No-One But You (Only The Good Die Young)/Princes Of The Universe/ We Will Rock You (Rick Rubin 'Ruined' Remix)/Gimme The Prize (Instrumental 'Eye' Remix) (Unissued 7") | 150 |
| 97 | Parlophone QUEENPD 27 | No-One But You (Only The Good Die Young)/We Will Rock You (Rick Rubin 'Ruined' Remix)/Tie Your Mother Down/Gimme The Prize (Instrumental 'Eye' Remix) (picture disc) | 6 |
| 98 | Parlophone QUEEN PD28 | Under Pressure (picture disc) | 8 |
| 11 | Island | Stormtroopers In Stilettos/Stone Cold Crazy/Keep Yourself Alive (numbered picture disc in PVC sleeve, 2000 only) | 15 |

## SINGLES : 3" CD SINGLES

| | | | |
|---|---|---|---|
| 80s | Parlophone | QUEEN : THE 3" SINGLES (gatefold wallet, card insert) | 150 |

## ALBUMS

| | | | |
|---|---|---|---|
| 73 | EMI EMC 3006 | QUEEN (LP, 1st pressing with "KIP-HUGGYPOO KISSY" hand-etched into run out groove on side 1, laminated cover) | 40 |
| 74 | EMI EMA 767 | QUEEN II (LP, laminated gatefold sleeve, lyric inner version) | 40 |
| 74 | EMI EMC 3061 | SHEER HEART ATTACK (LP, laminated sleeve, inner lyric sleeve) | 40 |
| 75 | EMI EMTC 103 | A NIGHT AT THE OPERA (LP, 1st pressing, embossed gatefold sleeve with cut corner inner, YAX 5063/4-2 "BLAIRS" in run-off) | 60 |
| 75 | EMI EMTC 103 | A NIGHT AT THE OPERA (LP, later pressings, embossed gatefold sleeve with 'shaped' inner sleeve) | 25 |
| 76 | EMI EMTC 104 | A DAY AT THE RACES (LP, gatefold, inner sleeve) | 40 |
| 77 | EMI EMA 784 | NEWS OF THE WORLD (LP, gatefold with lyric inner sleeve) | 35 |
| 78 | EMI EMA 788 | JAZZ (LP, gatefold sleeve with attached poster, inner sleeve has band shot on olne side and track listing on the other) | 40 |
| 80 | EMI EMA 795 | THE GAME (LP, inner sleeve) | 15 |
| 81 | EMI EMTV30 | GREATEST HITS (LP) | 15 |
| 81 | EMI EMTV 30 | GREATEST HITS (LP, mispress, side 2 plays "Anne Murray's Greatest Hits") | 30 |
| 85 | EMI QB 1 | THE COMPLETE WORKS (14-LP box set including "Complete Vision" LP of non-LP tracks, 2 booklets & map, numbered; 600 autographed) | 1000 |
| 85 | EMI QB 1 | THE COMPLETE WORKS (14-LP box set including "Complete Vision" LP of non-LP tracks, 2 booklets & map, numbered) | 125 |
| 86 | EMI EU 3509 | A KIND OF MAGIC ('Princes Of The Universe' proof sleeve; unreleased) | 500 |
| 89 | Band Of Joy BOJLP 001 | QUEEN AT THE BEEB (LP) | 20 |
| 91 | Parlophone PCSD 115 | INNUENDO (LP, inner) | 30 |
| 91 | Parlophone PMTV 2 | GREATEST HITS 2 (2-LP, embossed gatefold sleeve) | 25 |
| 92 | Parlophone PCSP 725 | LIVE AT WEMBLEY (2-LP, gatefold sleeve) | 25 |
| 92 | Parlophone CDQTEL 0001 | BOX OF TRIX (CD, box set, with video, book, poster, T-shirt, patch & badge) | 60 |
| 92 | Parlophone CQTEL 0001 | BOX OF TRIX (cassette, box set, with video, book, poster, T-shirt, patch & badge) | 50 |
| 95 | Parlophone 724383608812 | MADE IN HEAVEN (LP, stickered gatefold sleeve with inserts, ivory vinyl) | 60 |
| 95 | Parlophone QUEEN BOX 20 | ULTIMATE QUEEN (20 x CD set, in numbered glazed box and numbered cardboard outer box, with Freddie hologram and 2 booklets) | 450 |
| 97 | EMI LPCENT 25 | A NIGHT AT THE OPERA (LP, reissue, EMI 100 Centenary, stickered sleeve) | 30 |
| 99 | Parlophone 7243 5 23452 1 1 | GREATEST HITS III (2-LP with inners) | 40 |
| 05 | Parlophone 724386321114 | QUEEN ON FIRE (3-LP box set) | 60 |
| 09 | EMI 686644-1 | ABSOLUTE GREATEST (3-LP box set) | 70 |

## PROMOS

| | | | |
|---|---|---|---|
| 73 | EMI 2036 | Keep Yourself Alive/Son And Daughter (demo copy, different mix of A side to that later released) | 150 |
| 73 | EMI (no cat. no.) | QUEEN (LP, white label, EMI conference custom issue, die-cut sleeve, with outer envelope) | 500 |
| 73 | EMI (no cat. no.) | QUEEN (LP, white label, EMI conference custom issue, die-cut sleeve, without outer envelope) | 400 |
| 74 | EMI 2121 | Seven Seas Of Rhye/See What A Fool I've Been (demo) | 20 |
| 77 | EMI SP SLP 241 A1U | We Will Rock You/We Are The Champions/Spread Your Wings (12", 1-sided) | 400 |
| 77 | EMI (no cat. no.) | NEWS OF THE WORLD (LP, box set, with factory sample sticker, 5 photos, bio, badge & demo copy of "We Are The Champions"/"We Will Rock You", 50 only) | 500 |
| 78 | EMI EMI 2375 | Bohemian Rhapsody/I'm In Love With My Car (EMI 'Queen's Award For Export' in-house edition, blue vinyl, Queen crest label, hand-numbered, purple p/s., with invites, matches, pen, ticket, menu, outer card sleeve, scarf & EMI goblets in card box) | 5000 |
| 78 | EMI EMI 2375 | Bohemian Rhapsody/I'm In Love With My Car (EMI 'Queen's Award For Export' in-house edition, blue vinyl, Queen crest label, hand-numbered, purple p/s., with outer 'EMI International' carrying envelope) | 3800 |
| 78 | EMI EMI 2375 | Bohemian Rhapsody/I'm In Love With My Car (EMI 'Queen's Award For Export' in-house edition, blue vinyl, Queen crest label, hand-numbered, purple p/s. | 3500 |

*(The blue vinyl 'Bohemian Rhapsody' was limited to 200 numbered copies)*

| | | | |
|---|---|---|---|
| 84 | EMI QUEEN 1 | Radio Ga Ga (Edit)/I Go Crazy ('video shoot' p/s, unreleased, proofs only) | 450 |
| 84 | EMI QUEENDJ 5 | Man On The Prowl/Thank God It's Christmas | 150 |
| 84 | Flexi Ltd. (no cat. no.) | Excerpts From Their New Album 'The Works' (flexidisc sampler, p/s) | 15 |
| 86 | (no label or cat. no.) | A Message From Queen (cassette, 1st Fan Club Convention issue) | 20 |
| 86 | Parlophone EMCDV 2 | THE HIGHLANDER SELECTION (CD Video, 50 only) | 400 |
| 86 | EMI/Channel 4 QUEEN 7 | NETWORK QUEEN ('A Kind Of Magic' 7" housed in promotional fold-out sleeve that opens up to depict illustrated band playing to audience. 50 made to promote TV advertising for July 1986 Wembley Stadium concerts) | 800 |
| 89 | Flexi Ltd. (no cat. no.) | A Message From Queen (flexidisc, 4th Fan Club Convention issue) | 25 |
| 89 | Parlophone QUEEN 10 | I Want It All/Hang On In There (p/s in promo gatefold p/s, press release, B&W photo) | 25 |
| 91 | Parlophone (no cat. no.) | A SAMPLE OF MAGIC (CD, segued excerpts from "Greatest Hits 2") | 60 |
| 91 | EMI QUEEN DJ 16 | Innuendo/Innuendo (12" promo, p/s) | 20 |

# QUEENS OF THE STONE AGE

| 91 | Parlophone (no cat. no.) | HINTS OF INNUENDO (cassette, edits/out-takes sampler for "Innuendo") | 30 |
|----|--------------------------|----------------------------------------------------------------------|-----|
| 91 | EMI | INNUENDO (Promo boxed set with CD, cassette, calendar, folder, bio & photos) | 60 |
| 91 | Parlophone (no cat. no.) | EIGHT GOOD REASONS TO BUY GREATEST HITS 2 (cassette, segued excerpts) | 30 |
| 94 | EMI CD DIG 1 | DIGITAL MASTER SAMPLER (CD, picture disc) | 45 |
| 95 | EMI QUEEN DJ95 | Bohemian Rhapsody/I'm In Love With My Car (purple vinyl, hand numbered, p/s, Fan Club Convention issue, 2,000 only) | 150 |
| 95 | Parlophone QUEENDJ 22 | A Winter's Tale/Thank God It's Christmas (jukebox issue, plain white sleeve, with jukebox strip) | 10 |
| 95 | Parlophone CDD JUKE | Heaven For Everyone (single version) | 10 |
| 95 | Parlophone QUEENLHDJ 21 | Heaven For Everyone (Album Version)/Heaven For Everyone (Single Version) (jukebox issue, plain white sleeve, with poster, fold-out card & jukebox strip) | 20 |
| 96 | Parlophone QUEENDJ 23 | Too Much Love Will Kill You/We Are The Champions (jukebox issue, plain white sleeve, with jukebox strip) | 10 |
| 96 | Parlophone VIRGIN 1 | Heaven For Everyone/Heaven For Everyone (12", white label, Virgin Radio 'Queen Day' competition prize, black 'Queen crest' p/s with handwritten details; mispressing with same tracks both sides, unreleased) | 0 |
| 96 | Parlophone VIRGIN 2 | Heaven For Everyone (12", 1-sided, white labels, Virgin Radio 'Queen Day' competition prize, 'Queen crest' p/s w/ handwritten details, 15 copies only) | 750 |
| 96 | Parlophone VIRGIN 3 | A Winter's Tale (12", 1-sided, white labels, Virgin Radio 'Queen Day' competition prize, 'Queen crest' p/s with handwritten details, 15 only) | 750 |
| 96 | Parlophone VIRGIN 4 | Mother Love (12", 1-sided, white labels, Virgin Radio 'Queen Day' competition prize, 'Queen crest' p/s with handwritten details, 15 only) | 750 |
| 96 | Parlophone VIRGIN 5 | Let Me Live (12", 1-sided, white labels, Virgin Radio 'Queen Day' competition prize, 'Queen crest' p/s with handwritten details, 15 only) | 750 |
| 96 | Parlophone VIRGIN 6 | You Don't Fool Me (12", 1-sided, white labels, Virgin Radio 'Queen Day' competition prize, 'Queen crest' p/s with handwritten details, 15 only) | 750 |
| 96 | Parlophone VIRGIN 7 | It's A Beautiful Day (12", 1-sided, white labels, Virgin Radio 'Queen Day' competition prize, 'Queen crest' p/s with handwritten details, 15 only) | 750 |
| 96 | Parlophone VIRGIN 8 | I Was Born To Love You (12", 1-sided, white labels, Virgin Radio 'Queen Day' competition prize, 'Queen crest' p/s with handwritten details, 15 only) | 750 |
| 97 | Parlophone CDQT 1 | QUEEN ROCKS (CD, Brian May interview) | 75 |
| 99 | EMI QUEENWL 28 | Under Pressure (Remixes) (with David Bowie) (12", white label, unreleased mix, promo only) | 30 |

## MISPRESSINGS

| 75 | EMI EMI 2378 | Bohemian Rhapsody/I'm In Love With My Car (2nd issue, with incorrect cat. no.) | 12 |
|----|--------------|----------------------------------------------------------------------------------|-----|
| 78 | EMI EMI 2870 | Bicycle Race/Fat Bottomed Girls (p/s, B-side plays Crystal Gayle's 3 O'Clock In The Morning or Dollar track) | 10 |
| 79 | EMI EMI 2975 | CLIFF RICHARD: We Don't Talk Anymore/Count Me Out (A-side plays "Bohemian Rhapsody") | 12 |
| 79 | EMI EMI 5001 | Crazy Little Thing Called Love/We Will Rock You (live) (p/s, both sides play "We Will Rock You") | 15 |
| 80 | EMI EMI 5076 | Play The Game/A Human Body (p/s, both sides play "A Human Body") | 12 |
| 86 | Parlophone RP 5452 | BEATLES: Paperback Writer/Rain (picture disc, A-side plays Friends Will Be Friends) | 75 |

*(see also Freddie Mercury, Brian May, Roger Taylor, Larry Lurex, Cross, Immortals, Hilary Hilary, Eddie Howell, Man Friday & Jive Junior)*

## QUEENS OF THE STONE AGE

| 00 | Interscope 497 387-7 | The Lost Art Of Keeping A Secret/Ode To Clarrisa (p/s) | 10 |
|----|----------------------|--------------------------------------------------------|-----|
| 02 | Interscope 497 812-7 | No One Knows/Tension Head (Live From The Mean Fiddler) (p/s, grey vinyl) | 15 |
| 03 | Interscope 9810506 | First It Giveth/The Most Exalted Potentate Of Love (red vinyl, p/s) | 6 |
| 05 | Interscope 988 354-2 | In My Head/I Think I Lost My Headache (picture disc) | 6 |
| 05 | No label FUNMACHINE1 | The Fun Machine Took A Shit And Died/Commentary (white label, signed) | 20 |
| 07 | Interscope 1753953 | Make It Wit Chu (Acoustic)/White Wedding (p/s, with sticker) | 5 |
| 07 | Interscope 1753954 | Make It Wit Chu (edit)/Needles In The Camel's Eye (with Bobby Gillespie, p/s, with sticker) | 5 |
| 11 | Rekords REK 004 | How To Handle A Rope (A Lesson In The Lariat)/Avon (p/s, 1000 only, numbered) | 12 |
| 98 | Roadrunner RR 8674-2 | QUEENS OF THE STONE AGE (2-LP) | 25 |
| 00 | Interscope 490 683-1 | X (LP, gatefold sleeve) | 40 |
| 02 | Interscope 493435-1 | SONGS FOR THE DEAF (2 x LP, gatefold) | 60 |
| 03 | Interscope 493 436-2 | SONGS FOR THE DEAF (2-CD tour edition) | 30 |
| 11 | Music On Vinyl MOVLP 250 | LULLABIES TO PARADISE (2-LP, one side etched) | 20 |
| 11 | Music On Vinyl MOVLP 250 | LULLABIES TO PARADISE (2-LP, red vinyl, one side etched) | 25 |
| 13 | Matador OLE 1048-1 | ...LIKE CLOCKWORK (2-LP, blue sleeve) | 20 |
| 13 | Matador OLE 1048-1 | ...LIKE CLOCKWORK (LP, black artwork, 800 only) | 30 |
| 13 | Matador OLE 1040-0 | ...LIKE CLOCKWORK (2-LP, red sleeve, 180 gram edition, booklet) | 25 |

## QUEENSRYCHE

| 86 | EMI America EAD 22 | Gonna Get Close To You/Prophecy//Queen Of The Reich (live)/Deliverance (live) (double pack) | 6 |
|----|--------------------|---------------------------------------------------------------------------------------------|-----|
| 94 | EMI MTL 1081 | PROMISED LAND (LP, clear vinyl) | 20 |

## QUEERS

| 90 | Shakin Street YEAH HUP 010 | GROW UP (LP) | 30 |
|----|-----------------------------|--------------|-----|

## QUEL DOMAGE

| 84 | Xcentric Noise SEVENTH 1 | Bright Lights/Music For Serious And Solemn Occasions/Amendment (p/s) | 7 |
|----|--------------------------|----------------------------------------------------------------------|-----|

## ? & THE MYSTERIANS

| 66 | Cameo Parkway C 428 | 96 Tears/Midnight Hour | 40 |
|----|---------------------|------------------------|-----|
| 66 | Cameo Parkway C 441 | I Need Somebody/'8' Teen | 45 |
| 67 | Cameo Parkway C 467 | Can't Get Enough Of You, Baby/Smokes | 30 |
| 67 | Cameo Parkway C 479 | Girl (You Captivate Me)/Got To | 25 |
| 67 | Cameo Parkway C 496 | Do Something To Me/Love Me Baby | 25 |
| 76 | London HLU 10534 | 96 Tears/'8' Teen | 10 |

## QUESTIONS (1)

| 68 | Decca F 22740 | We Got Love/Something Wonderful | 35 |
|----|---------------|---------------------------------|-----|

## QUESTIONS (2)

| 76 | Look LK SP 6059 | Sixty Nine/Mumbling Mosey | 8 |
|----|-----------------|---------------------------|-----|

## TOMMY QUICKLY (& REMO FOUR)

| | | | |
|---|---|---|---|
| 63 | Piccadilly 7N 35137 | Tip Of My Tongue/Heaven Only Knows (solo) | 30 |
| 63 | Piccadilly 7N 35151 | Kiss Me Now/No Other Love | 8 |
| 64 | Piccadilly 7N 35167 | Prove It/Haven't You Noticed | 6 |
| 64 | Piccadilly 7N 35183 | You Might As Well Forget Him/It's As Simple As That | 6 |
| 64 | Pye 7N 15708 | The Wild Side Of Life/Forget The Other Guy | 6 |
| 64 | Pye 7N 15748 | Humpty Dumpty/I'll Go Crazy | 8 |

*(see also Remo Four)*

## QUICKSAND

| | | | |
|---|---|---|---|
| 70 | Carnaby CNS 4015 | Passing By/Cobblestones | 15 |
| 73 | Dawn DNS 1046 | Time To Live/Empty Street, Empty Heart | 10 |
| 73 | Dawn DNLS 3056 | HOME IS WHERE I BELONG (LP, gatefold sleeve, pink 'sun' label) | 120 |

*(see also Man)*

## QUICKSILVER MESSENGER SERVICE

| | | | |
|---|---|---|---|
| 76 | Capitol CL 15859 | Gypsy Lights/Witches' Moon | 5 |
| 68 | Capitol (S)T 2904 | QUICKSILVER MESSENGER SERVICE (LP, black label with rainbow rim) | 40 |
| 69 | Capitol E-(S)T 120 | HAPPY TRAILS (LP) | 25 |
| 70 | Capitol E-ST 391 | SHADY GROVE (LP) | 18 |
| 70 | Capitol EA-ST 498 | JUST FOR LOVE (LP) | 20 |
| 71 | Capitol EA-ST 630 | WHAT ABOUT ME? (LP) | 15 |
| 72 | Capitol E-SW 819 | QUICKSILVER (LP) | 15 |
| 83 | Psycho PSYCHO 10 | MAIDEN OF THE CANCER MOON (2-LP) | 40 |

*(see also Dino Valenti, Nicky Hopkins)*

## QUIET FIVE

| | | | |
|---|---|---|---|
| 65 | Parlophone R 5273 | When The Morning Sun Dries The Dew/Tomorrow I'll Be Gone (in p/s) | 20 |
| 65 | Parlophone R 5273 | When The Morning Sun Dries The Dew/Tomorrow I'll Be Gone | 10 |
| 65 | Parlophone R 5302 | Honeysuckle Rose/Let's Talk It Over | 8 |
| 66 | Parlophone R 5421 | Homeward Bound/Ain't It Funny What Some Lovin' Can Do | 18 |
| 66 | Parlophone R 5470 | I Am Waiting/What About The Time For Me | 10 |
| 67 | CBS 202586 | Goodnight Sleep Tight/Just For Tonight | 6 |

*(see also Kris Ife, Richard Barnes)*

## QUIET SUN

| | | | |
|---|---|---|---|
| 75 | Island HELP 19 | MAINSTREAM (LP, black label with pink 'i' label) | 20 |

*(see also Phil Manzanera, Roxy Music)*

## QUIET WORLD

| | | | |
|---|---|---|---|
| 69 | Dawn DNS 1001 | Miss Whittington/There Is A Mountain (as Quiet World Of Lea & John) | 40 |
| 70 | Dawn DNS 1005 | Children Of The World/Love Is Walking | 40 |
| 70 | Pye 7N 45005 | Rest Comfortably/Gemima | 12 |
| 71 | Pye 7N 45074 | Visitor/Sam | 10 |
| 70 | Dawn DNLS 3007 | THE ROAD (LP) | 200 |

*(see also Steve Hackett, Genesis)*

## QUIK

| | | | |
|---|---|---|---|
| 67 | Deram DM 121 | Love Is A Beautiful Thing/Bert's Apple Crumble | 150 |
| 67 | Deram DM 139 | King Of The World/My Girl | 50 |
| 67 | Deram DM 155 | I Can't Sleep/Soul Full Of Sorrow | 70 |
| 98 | Klooks Kleek 60 | Bert's Apple Crumble/THE SONICS: The Witch (re-issue) | 10 |

*(see also Meddy Evils)*

## QUILL (1)

| | | | |
|---|---|---|---|
| 79 | Kite KR 10 | LIVE (LP) | 15 |

## QUILL (2)

| | | | |
|---|---|---|---|
| 80 | Kite KRS 10A | Love In A Jar/Time (no p/s) | 18 |

## QUILLER

| | | | |
|---|---|---|---|
| 75 | BBC RESL 25 | Quiller/General Direction | 7 |

## QUINCEHARMON

| | | | |
|---|---|---|---|
| 71 | Columbia DB 8772 | Suddenly The Whole World Is Mine/Strange Feeling | 15 |
| 71 | Columbia DB 8798 | On The Buses/Don't Tell Me It's Over | 10 |
| 72 | Columbia DB8929 | Sunshine City/Mr Sun | 8 |

## PAUL QUINCHETTE

| | | | |
|---|---|---|---|
| 57 | Esquire 32-057 | ON THE SUNNY SIDE (LP) | 40 |

## QUINCICASM

| | | | |
|---|---|---|---|
| 73 | Saydisc SDL 249 | QUINCICASM (LP) | 50 |

## MIKE QUINN

| | | | |
|---|---|---|---|
| 66 | Fontana TF 761 | Someone's Slipping Into My Mind/I Know What You Know | 7 |
| 69 | CBS 4506 | Apple Pie/There's A Time | 6 |
| 69 | Jay Boy BOY 7 | Toothbrush Nell/Fairy Cakes | 5 |

## PAUL QUINN

| | | | |
|---|---|---|---|
| 92 | Postcard DUBH 921 | THE PHANTOMS AND THE ARCHETYPES (LP) | 40 |

## PAUL QUINN & EDWYN COLLINS

| | | | |
|---|---|---|---|
| 84 | Swamplands SWP 1 | Pale Blue Eyes (Edited Version)/Burro (p/s) | 5 |
| 84 | Swamplands SWX 1 | Pale Blue Eyes/Pale Blues Eyes (Western)/Burro (12", original pressing with 'film' p/s, inner sleeve & yellow obi) | 10 |

*(see also Edwyn Collins, Orange Juice)*

## QUINTESSENCE

| | | | |
|---|---|---|---|
| 70 | Island WIP 6075 | Notting Hill Gate/Move Into The Light | 7 |
| 71 | Neon NE 1003 | Sweet Jesus/You Never Stay The Same (in p/s) | 15 |
| 71 | Neon NE 1003 | Sweet Jesus/You Never Stay The Same | 6 |
| 69 | Island ILPS 9110 | IN BLISSFUL COMPANY (LP, gatefold, pink label with white 'i' logo, booklet) | 90 |
| 70 | Island ILPS 9128 | QUINTESSENCE (LP, tri-fold sleeve, pink label with white 'i' logo) | 80 |

MINT VALUE £

| | | | |
|---|---|---|---|
| 71 | Island ILPS 9143 | DIVE DEEP (LP, inner sleeve, pink rim palm tree label) | 60 |
| 72 | RCA SF 8273 | SELF (LP) | 20 |
| 72 | RCA SF 8317 | INDWELLER (LP) | 15 |

*(see also Kala)*

## QUINTET MODERNE
| | | | |
|---|---|---|---|
| 87 | Bead Records BEAD 26 | IKKUNAN TAKANA (LP) | 20 |

## QUINTET OF HOT CLUB OF FRANCE
| | | | |
|---|---|---|---|
| 53 | Decca LF 1139 | SWING FROM PARIS (10" LP) | 15 |

## QUINTET OF THE YEAR
| | | | |
|---|---|---|---|
| 54 | Vogue L.D.E. 087 | JAZZ AT THE MASSAY HALL VOL. 3 (10" LP) | 18 |

## QUIRE
| | | | |
|---|---|---|---|
| 72 | Polydor 2058 297 | Strange One/Half Way Up The Hill | 7 |

## QUIREBOYS
| | | | |
|---|---|---|---|
| 90 | Parlophone RPD 6248 | I Don't Love You Anymore/Mayfair (Original Version) (uncut shaped picture disc) | 10 |

*(see also Wildhearts)*

## DARYL QUIST
| | | | |
|---|---|---|---|
| 63 | Pye 7N 15538 | Thanks To You/Keep Moving (in p/s) | 10 |
| 63 | Pye 7N 15538 | Thanks To You/Keep Moving | 5 |
| 63 | Pye 7N 15563 | Goodbye To Love/All Through The Night | 5 |
| 64 | Pye 7N 15605 | True To You/Above And Beyond | 5 |
| 64 | Pye 7N 15656 | See The Funny Little Clown/When She Comes To You | 5 |
| 65 | Decca F 12058 | Put Away Your Teardrops/Across The Street (Is A Million Miles Away) | 5 |

## QUIVER
| | | | |
|---|---|---|---|
| 72 | Warner Bros K 16165 | Green Tree/I Might Stumble | 6 |
| 71 | Warner Bros K 46089 | QUIVER (LP) | 30 |

*(see also Bridget St. John, Natural Gas, Sutherland Brothers, Village)*

## QUODLING'S DELIGHT
| | | | |
|---|---|---|---|
| 76 | Fanfare FR 2179 | AMONG THE LEAVES SO GREEN (LP) | 25 |

## QUOTATIONS (U.K.)
| | | | |
|---|---|---|---|
| 64 | Decca F 11907 | Alright Baby/Love You All Over Again | 25 |
| 68 | CBS 3716 | Cool It/Mark Of Her Head | 35 |
| 69 | CBS 4378 | Hello Memories/Pretend | 10 |

*(see also Fleur De Lys, Johnny B. Great, Johnny Gustafson, Merseybeats, Johnny Goodison)*

## QUOTATIONS (U.S.)
| | | | |
|---|---|---|---|
| 61 | HMV POP 975 | Imagination/Ala-Men-Sy | 60 |

## QUOTING MARX
| | | | |
|---|---|---|---|
| 77 | Full Stop PUNC 28 | Opening And Closing/66 And 99 | 12 |

# R

## RAAW
| | | | |
|---|---|---|---|
| 78 | Tempus TEM 111 | Lili Twil/Just A Little Different (p/s) | 15 |

## RABBI JOSEPH GORDAN
| | | | |
|---|---|---|---|
| 85 | Bam Caruso Intl. NRICO 30 | Competition/Belief In Him (large centre hole, plain beige sleeve) | 10 |

*(see also Julian Cope)*

## RABBIT
| | | | |
|---|---|---|---|
| 73 | Island WIP6161 | Broken Arrows/Blues My Guitar | 5 |
| 73 | Island ILPS 9238 | BROKEN ARROWS (LP, gatefold sleeve, pink rim palm tree label) | 18 |
| 74 | Island ILPS 9289 | DARK SALOON (LP) | 15 |

*(see also Free; Kossoff, Kirke, Tetsu & Rabbit)*

## RABBITS
| | | | |
|---|---|---|---|
| 79 | Stortbeat BEAT 4 | Kitchen Parties/Tonight (numbered p/s, 1000 only) | 15 |

## RABID
| | | | |
|---|---|---|---|
| 82 | Fallout FALL 007 | BLOODY ROAD TO GLORY (EP, with poster) | 10 |

## MICHAEL RABIN
| | | | |
|---|---|---|---|
| 58 | Columbia 33CX 1597 | MENDELSSOHN VIOLIN CONCERTO (LP) | 300 |
| 59 | Capitol SP 8506 | MOSAICS (LP, stereo) | 700 |
| 60 | Capitol SP 8510 | THE MAGIC BOW (LP, stereo) | 450 |
| 60 | Capitol SP 8534 | PAGANINI: CONCERTO NO 1 IN D MAJOR/WIENIAWSKI: CONCERTO NO.2 IN D MAJOR (LP, stereo) | 300 |

## MIKE RABIN (& DEMONS)
| | | | |
|---|---|---|---|
| 64 | Columbia DB 7350 | Head Over Heels/Leaving You (as Mike Rabin & Demons) | 70 |
| 65 | Polydor BM 56007 | If I Were You/What Do You Do | 25 |

## STEVE RACE
| | | | |
|---|---|---|---|
| 61 | Parlophone R 4808 | Crosstrap/Stop Look Listen | 10 |

## RACE FANS
| | | | |
|---|---|---|---|
| 68 | Trojan TR 610 | Bookie Man/UNIQUES: More Love | 40 |
| 68 | Trojan TR 637 | Time Marches On/SILVERTONES: Party Night | 40 |

## YANK RACHELL TENNESSEE JUG BUSTERS
| | | | |
|---|---|---|---|
| 64 | '77' LA 12-23 | MANDOLIN BLUES (LP) | 30 |

## RACONTEURS
| | | | |
|---|---|---|---|
| 08 | XL XLS 227 | Steady As She Goes/Store Bought Bones (1st issue, 1,000 only, p/s Jack White to right of cover) | 8 |

| 08 | XL XLS 385 | Many Shades Of Black/Many Shades Of Black (B-side features Adele)............................5 |
| 06 | XL XLLP 196X | BROKEN BOY SOLDIERS (LP) ............................................................................20 |
| 08 | XL XLLP 359 | CONSOLERS OF THE LONELY (2-LP) .................................................................25 |

*(see also White Stripes)*

## RADAR
| 83 | House Of Wax WAX 1 | Leave Her Alone/Reach For The Sky (p/s) ..........................................................10 |

## JIMMY RADCLIFFE
| 65 | Stateside SS 374 | Long After Tonight Is Over/What I Want I Can Never Have...............................35 |
| 65 | Stateside SS 374 | Long After Tonight Is Over/What I Want I Can Never Have (DJ copy) ...........150 |
| 73 | Pye International 7N 25614 | Long After Tonight Is Over/What I Want I Can Never Have (reissue) ..............5 |
| 77 | DJM DJS 10772 | Long After Tonight Is Over/What I Want I Can Never Have (2nd reissue) (P/S) (Promo)...5 |

*(see also Steve Karmen Big Band)*

## RADGE
| 79 | Radge RAD 100 | ABSOLUTELY...EP ..............................................................................................8 |

## RADHA KRISHNA
| 71 | Columbia SCX 6462 | RADHA KRISHNA (LP, composed & directed by John Mayer) ..........................45 |

*(see also John Mayer)*

## RADHA KRISHNA TEMPLE (LONDON)
| 69 | Apple APPLE 15 | Hare Krishna Mantra/Prayer To The Spiritual Masters (p/s, as Radha Krishna Temple [London], with insert) ...........................................................30 |
| 69 | Apple APPLE 15 | Hare Krishna Mantra/Prayer To The Spiritual Masters (p/s, as Radha Krishna Temple [London], without insert) ......................................................20 |
| 69 | Apple APPLE 15 | Hare Krishna Mantra/Prayer To The Spiritual Masters (no p/s, as Radha Krishna Temple [London]) .................................................................6 |
| 70 | Apple APPLE 25 | Govinda/Govinda Jai Jai (p/s) .........................................................................30 |
| 70 | Apple APPLE 25 | Govinda/Govinda Jai Jai (in company sleeve) ................................................12 |
| 70 | Apple APPLE 25 | Govinda/Govinda Jai Jai .....................................................................................5 |
| 71 | Apple SAPCOR 18 | THE RADHA KRISHNA TEMPLE (LP, gatefold sleeve, with insert)...............50 |
| 71 | Apple SAPCOR 18 | THE RADHA KRISHNA TEMPLE (LP, gatefold sleeve, without insert) ..........40 |
| 93 | Apple SAPCOR 18 | THE RADHA KRISHNA TEMPLE (LP, reissue, gatefold sleeve with inner)........15 |

## RADIANTS
| 64 | Chess CRS 8002 | Voice Your Choice/If I Only Had You ...............................................................40 |
| 64 | Chess CRS 8002 | Voice Your Choice/If I Only Had You (DJ copy) ..............................................60 |
| 68 | Chess CRS 8073 | Hold On/I'm Glad I'm The Loser .......................................................................20 |
| 68 | Chess CRS 8073 | Hold On/I'm Glad I'm The Loser (DJ copy).......................................................50 |

*(see also Maurice & Mac, Caston & Majors)*

## RADIATION
| 80 | Martin's Mart 1X | Johnny/Last Day (no p/s)...................................................................................15 |

## RADIATORS (FROM SPACE)
| 77 | Chiswick S 10 | Television Screen/Love Detective (p/s, original issue has laminate sleeve) ...................10 |
| 77 | Chiswick NS 19 | Enemies/Psychotic Reaction (p/s) .....................................................................5 |
| 78 | Chiswick NS 24 | Prison Bars/(Why Can't I Be A) Teenager In Love (unreleased, promo only white label in stamped white sleeve & loose printed labels)...........................40 |
| 78 | Chiswick NS 29 | Million Dollar Hero (In A Five And Ten Cent Store)Blitzin At The Ritz (as the Radiators) ..5 |
| 79 | Chiswick NS 45 | Walkin' Home Alone Again/Try And Stop Me/The Hucklebuck (unreleased; white label test pressings exist with loose labels; as Radiators) ..........................40 |
| 79 | Chiswick CHIS 115 | Kitty Ricketts/Ballad Of The Faithful Departed (company sleeve)....................8 |
| 81 | Chiswick CHIS 144 | Song Of The Faithful Departed/They're Looting In The Town ......................10 |
| 77 | Chiswick WIK 4 | TV TUBE HEART (LP) .........................................................................................20 |

*(see also Pogues)*

## RADICAL DANCE FACTION
| 80 | Earth Zone EZ 001 | BORDERLAND CASES (LP, 1st pressing with white picture sleeve) ...............20 |
| 80 | Earth Zone EZ 001 | BORDERLAND CASES (LP, 2nd pressing with black picture sleeve) ..............15 |
| 81 | Earth Zone EZ 003 | WATERLAND (LP).............................................................................................15 |
| 91 | Zone EZ3V | WASTELAND EARTH (LP)...................................................................................15 |
| 95 | Inna State 004DS4A | RAGAMUFFIN STATEMENT (LP)..........................................................................35 |

## RADICALS
| 84 | Bluetrac BTR 003 | Rum Tree/Racids In Dub (12") ........................................................................50 |

## MARK RADICE
| 72 | Paramount PARA 3024 | Hey My Love/Your Love Is Like Fire................................................................8 |
| 72 | Paramount PARA 3025 | New Day/Take Me To The Park .......................................................................6 |

## RADIO DEPT
| 02 | Rex REKD 30S | Liebling/We Would Fall Against The Tide (die-cut Rex sleeve)........................15 |
| 04 | Rex REKD 41S | Why Don't You Talk About It?/I Don't Need Love, I've Got My Band (p/s)..................15 |
| 04 | XL XLS 196 | Where Damage Isn't Already Done/You And Me Then?/Peace Of Mind ............12 |
| 04 | XL XLS 203 | Ewan/Slottet/The Things That Went Wrong (p/s) .........................................12 |
| 04 | XL XLLP 177 | LESSER MATTERS (LP) .......................................................................................50 |

## RADIOACTIVE
| 77 | Beeb BEEB 021 | Ten Years After/All Time Needletime Loser (no p/s)........................................30 |

## RADIO ACTORS
| 79 | Charly CYS 1058 | Nuclear Waste/Digital Love (p/s, reissue of Fast Breeder & Radio Actors single, 2 slightly different label designs)........................................................................20 |
| 79 | DB DBS 5 | Nuclear Waste/Digital Love (different p/s, 2nd reissue) ...................................5 |

*(see also Fast Breeder & Radio Actors, Sting, Newcastle Big Band, Police, Gilli Smyth, Inner City Unit, Steve Hillage, Sphynx)*

## RADIO BIRDMAN
| 78 | Sire 6078 617 | What Gives/Anglo Girl Desire.........................................................................20 |
| 78 | Sire 9103 332 | RADIOS APPEAR (LP, with inner sleeve) .........................................................35 |

## RADIO CITY
| 80 | Media Wave MW 001 | Love And A Picture/She's A Radio (p/s) .....................................................200 |

## RADIO DOOM

| 79 | Private Pressing | RADIO DOOM (LP, white sleeve 250 only) | 50 |

## RADIOHEAD

### SINGLES

| 92 | Parlophone TCR 6312 | DRILL EP (Prove Yourself/Stupid Car/You/Thinking About You) (cassette, 3,000 only) | 40 |
| 92 | Parlophone 12R 6312 | DRILL EP (Prove Yourself/Stupid Car/You/Thinking About You) (12", p/s, 3,000 only) | 80 |
| 92 | Parlophone CDR 6312 | DRILL EP (Prove Yourself/Stupid Car/You/Thinking About You) (CD, 3,000 only) | 80 |
| 92 | Parlophone 12R 6078 | Creep/Lurgee/Inside My Head/Million $ Question (12", p/s, 6,000 only) | 25 |
| 93 | Parlophone 12R 6333 | Anyone Can Play Guitar/Faithless, The Wonder Boy/Coke Babies (12", p/s) | 15 |
| 93 | Parlophone 12R 6345 | Pop Is Dead/Banana Co. (Acoustic)/Creep (live)/Ripcord (live) (12", g/fold p/s) | 20 |
| 93 | Parlophone RS 6359 | Creep/Yes I Am/Blow Out (Remix)/Inside My Head (live) (p/s, clear vinyl) | 20 |
| 93 | Parlophone 12RG 6359 | U.S. LIVE EP (Creep [Acoustic KROQ]/You [live]/Vegetable [live]/Killer Cars [live]) (12", numbered gatefold p/s) | 15 |
| 94 | Parlophone 12R 6394 | My Iron Lung/Punchdrunk Lovesick Singalong/The Trickster/ Lewis (Mistreated) (12", numbered p/s) | 15 |
| 95 | Parlophone 12R 6405 | Planet Telex/(remixes)/High & Dry (12", limited edition, numbered p/s) | 12 |
| 95 | Parlophone 8 83115 2 | The Bends/My Iron Lung (Live At Forum)/Bones (Live At Forum) (CD, for export to Ireland, slimline jewel case) | 35 |
| 95 | Parlophone 8 83115 2 | The Bends/My Iron Lung (Live At Forum)/Bones (Live At Forum) (CD, for export to Ireland, mispressed with "Planet Telex" instead of "The Bends" slimline jewel case) | 40 |
| 96 | Parlophone R 6419 | Street Spirit (Fade Out)/Bishop's Robes (die-cut p/s, white vinyl) | 18 |
| 96 | Parlophone R 6419LH | Street Spirit (Fade Out)/Bishop's Robes (jukebox issue, black vinyl) | 10 |
| 97 | Parlophone NODATA 01 | Paranoid Android/Polyethelene (Parts 1 & 2) (blue vinyl, die-cut p/s) | 12 |
| 97 | Parlophone NODATALH 03 | Karma Police (Album Version)/Lull (jukebox issue, black vinyl) | 10 |
| 97 | Parlophone 12NODATA 03 | Karma Police/Meeting Up The Aisle/Climbing Up The Walls (Zero 7 Mix) (12", p/s) | 15 |
| 97 | Parlophone NODATALH 04 | No Surprises/Palo Alto (jukebox issue, black vinyl) | 8 |
| 97 | Parlophone NODATALH 04 | No Surprises/How I Made My Millions (jukebox 7") | 8 |
| 98 | Parlophone 12NODATA 04 | No Surprises/Palo Alto (12", p/s) | 20 |
| 01 | Parlophone 12FHEIT 45102 | Pyramid Song/Fast Track/The Amazing Sounds Of Orgy (12", p/s) | 10 |
| 08 | XL XLS 326 | Jigsaw Falling into Place/Videotape (live) (p/s) | 5 |
| 08 | XL XLS 350 | Nude/4 Minute Warning (p/s) | 5 |
| 11 | XL TICK 02 | Supercollider/The Butcher (12" p/s, 2000 only, some with reversed labels) | 12 |
| 12 | Young Turks YT 077 | Bloom (Jamie XX Rework Pt. 3) (1-sided 12") | 40 |

### ALBUMS

| 93 | Parlophone PCS 7360 | PABLO HONEY (LP) | 40 |
| 95 | Parlophone PCS 7372 | THE BENDS (LP, inner) | 40 |
| 97 | Parlophone NODATA 02 | OK COMPUTER (2-LP) | 50 |
| 00 | Parlophone LPKIDA | KID A (2xLP 10") | 40 |
| 01 | Parlophone LPFHEIT 45101 | AMNESIAC (2xLP, 10") | 18 |
| 01 | Parlophone 12FHEIT 45104 | I MIGHT BE WRONG (mini-LP) | 20 |
| 03 | Parlophone 5848052 | HAIL TO THE THIEF (CD, limited issue, with foldout map) | 30 |
| 03 | Parlophone 724358454314 | HAIL TO THE THIEF (2xLP) | 25 |
| 07 | Parlophone 5.09995E+12 | RADIOHEAD (Mail-order 4GB shaped USB stick, bespoke box, 7 albums as WAV files) | 95 |
| 07 | Xurbia Xendless Ltd X X001 | IN RAINBOWS (box set, 2 x CD, 2-LP, 2xbooklets in presentation case) | 60 |
| 07 | XL Recordings XLLP 324 | IN RAINBOWS (LP) | 20 |
| 08 | Parlophone 5099921b 210716 | THE BEST OF (4-LP) | 50 |
| 09 | Parlophone 584 5431 | HAIL TO THE THIEF (2xLP, reissue, 180gm vinyl) | 20 |
| 11 | Ticker Tape/XL TICK 001S | THE KING OF LIMBS (2-10" clear vinyl LPs, with CD, newspaper, acid tab sheet, mail order only in sealed plastic bag) | 40 |
| 11 | Ticker Tape TICK001LP | THE KING OF LIMBS (LP, reissue) | 18 |
| 11 | Ticker Tape TICK 010 | TKOL RMX 1234567 (Box set, 7 x 12") | 80 |

### PROMOS

| 93 | EMI (no cat no) | Nothing Touches Me/Prove Yourself/I Can't (3-track internal EMI cassette) | 300 |
| 92 | Parlophone 12 R 6312 | DRILL EP (White label promo in die cut sleeve) | 80 |
| 92 | Parlophone 12RDJ 6078 | Creep/Lurgee/Inside My Head/Million Dollar Question (12", die-cut sleeve) | 40 |
| 92 | Parlophone CDRDJ 6078 | Creep (Radio Version)/Lurgee/Inside My Head/Million Dollar Question (CD) | 30 |
| 93 | Parlophone CDRDJ 6345 | Pop Is Dead/Banana Co. (live)/Creep (live)/Ripcord (live) (CD) | 40 |
| 93 | Parlophone CDRDJ 6359 | Creep (CD, picture disc) | 25 |
| 93 | Parlophone 12RDJ 6369 | Ripcord/Prove Yourself/Faithless, The Wonderboy/Stop Whispering (Album Version) (12", p/s) | 40 |
| 93 | Parlophone 12RDJ 6333 | Anyone Can Play Guitar/Faithless, The Wonder Boy/Coke Babies (12", die-cut sleeve) | 20 |
| 93 | Parlophone (no cat. No.) | Stop Whispering (U.S. Version - Chris Sheldon Remix)/Creep (Acoustic)/Pop Is Dead/ Inside My Head (Live) (CD) | 30 |
| 94 | Parlophone (no cat. no.) | PLANET TELEX: LFO & Hexidecimal mixes (12") | 12 |
| 94 | Parlophone 12RSDJ 6394 | My Iron Lung/Lozenge Of Love/The Trickster/Punchdrunk Lovesick Singalong (12", die-cut red sleeve) | 18 |
| 94 | Parlophone 12RSDJ 6394 | My Iron Lung/Lozenge Of Love/The Trickster/Punchdrunk Lovesick Singalong (12", die-cut blue sleeve) | 18 |
| 94 | Parlophone 12RSDJ 6394 | My Iron Lung/Lewis (Mistreated)/Permanent Daylight/You Never Wash Up After Yourself (12" die-cut red sleeve) | 15 |
| 94 | Parlophone 12RSDJ 6394 | My Iron Lung/Lewis (Mistreated)/Permanent Daylight/You Never Wash Up After Yourself (12" die-cut blue sleeve) | 15 |
| 95 | Parlophone 12RDJ 6405 | CLUB MIX DJ: PLANET TELEX (Album version)/Hexidecimal Mix)/L.F.O DJ Mix)/ Trashed Mix) (12") | 12 |
| 95 | Parlophone 12RDJ 6411 | Fake Plastic Trees/India Rubber/How Can You Be Sure? (12", die-cut sleeve) | 18 |
| 95 | Parlophone 12RDJ 6145 | Just/Planet Telex/Killer Cars (12", die-cut sleeve) | 12 |
| 95 | Parlophone 12RDJ 6145 | Just/Planet Telex (Karma Sun Ra Mix)Killer Cars (Mogadon Version) (12") | 15 |
| 95 | Parlophone RHEAD US 1 | JUST FOR COLLEGE: India Rubber/Maquiladora/How Can I Be Sure?/Just (CD) | 70 |
| 96 | Parlophone 12RDJ 6419 | Street Spirit (Fade Out)/Talk Show Host/Bishop's Robes (12", promo-only) | 18 |
| 97 | EMI (no cat no.) | Airbag (1-track Abbey Road CD-R with mini bio and title sleeve) | 15 |
| 98 | Parlophone 12DATADJO3 | Climbing Up The Walls (Zero 7 Mix)/(Fila Brazilia Mix) (1-sided 12", 200 only) | 40 |

| | | | |
|---|---|---|---|
| 00 | Parlophone 12KIDA 6 | Idioteque (12", white label test pressing, p/s) | 18 |
| 01 | Parlophone AMNESIAC 01 | 4 SONGS FROM AMNESIAC: Pyramid Song/I Might Be Wrong/Packt Like Sardines In A Crushed Tin Box/Dollars & Cents (CD, card sleeve) | 30 |
| 03 | Parlophone 12RDJWL 6623 | SKTTERBRAIN (Four Tet Mix)/REMYXOMOTOSIS (Super Collider Mix) (12", 100 only) | 35 |
| 97 | Parlophone 724385522925 | OK COMPUTER (Stickered jewel case, printed disc, mispressing plays Deep Purple's 'The Collection') | 40 |
| 97 | Parlophone (no cat. no.) | OK COMPUTER (Cassette, in customized jiffy bag) | 35 |
| 97 | Parlophone (no cat. no.) | OK COMPUTER (promo Aiwa personal stereo, glued-in cassette, two stickers) | 120 |
| 97 | Parlophone CDPP 005 | OK COMPUTER (CD, numbered title sleeve) | 35 |
| 97 | Parlophone NODATA 02 | OK COMPUTER (EPK, with CD & video in polystyrene case in jiffy bag) | 70 |
| 01 | Parlophone AMNESIAC 02 | AMNESIAC (CD, in facsmile library book, with press release & inserts) | 25 |

*(see also Headless Chickens, On A Friday, Thom Yorke, Jonny Greenwood, Atoms For Peace)*

## RADIO HEART
| | | | |
|---|---|---|---|
| 87 | GFM GFMG 109 | Radio Heart/Radio Heart (Instrumental) (Uncut picture disc) | 150 |
| 87 | GFM GFMX 112 | London Times/Rumous (Uncut picture disc) | 150 |
| 87 | NBR NBRL 1 | RADIO HEART (LP, withdrawn) | 15 |

*(see also Gary Numan)*

## RADIO MOSCOW
| | | | |
|---|---|---|---|
| 87 | Status RM 100 | Hand Of Freedom (p/s) | 8 |
| 91 | Status RMLP 103 | WORLD SERVICE (LP) | 15 |
| 92 | Status RMLP 104 | GET A NEW LIFE (LP) | 15 |

## RADIO 9
| | | | |
|---|---|---|---|
| 90s | Enraptured RAPT 1031 | Motorik/Fluid/Moving In Two Directions/Pianosong (10", 9 only) | 15 |

## RADIOPHONIC WORKSHOP
| | | | |
|---|---|---|---|
| 73 | BBC RESL 13 | Moonbase 3/World Of Dr. Who | 20 |

*(see also BBC Radiophonic Workshop)*

## RADIO RADIO
| | | | |
|---|---|---|---|
| 83 | Radio RAD 101 | Calling/Signed With A Star | 20 |

## RADIO STARS
| | | | |
|---|---|---|---|
| 77 | Chiswic S9 | Dirty Pictures/Sail Away (1st pressing with laminated sleeve, 1000 only) | 7 |
| 77 | Chiswick SW 17 | STOP IT EP | 6 |
| 78 | Chiswick CWK 3001 | HOLIDAY ALBUM (LP, with inner sleeve) | 15 |

*(see also John's Children, Andy Ellison, Trevor White)*

## RADIUM
| | | | |
|---|---|---|---|
| 81 | Isotope 731 | THROUGH THE SMOKE (EP) | 125 |

## RAELET(T)S
| | | | |
|---|---|---|---|
| 67 | HMV POP 1591 | One Hurt Deserves Another/One Room Paradise (as Raelets) | 30 |
| 71 | Tangerine 6121 002 | Bad Water/That Goes To Show You | 5 |
| 71 | Tangerine 6121 003 | Here I Go Again/Leave My Man (Woman) Alone | 5 |

*(see also Ray Charles, Clydie King, Merry Clayton)*

## RAG DOLLS (U.K.)
| | | | |
|---|---|---|---|
| 67 | Columbia DB 8289 | Never Had So Much Loving/Any Little Bit | 10 |
| 68 | Columbia DB 8378 | My Old Man's A Groovy Old Man/They Didn't Believe Me | 10 |

*(see also Marionettes, Peanut, Katie Kissoon, Mac Kissoon)*

## RAG DOLLS (U.S.)
| | | | |
|---|---|---|---|
| 64 | Cameo Parkway P 921 | Society Girl/Ragen (with Caliente Combo) | 35 |
| 65 | Stateside SS 398 | Dusty/Hey Hoagy | 40 |

## RAG RUBY RED
| | | | |
|---|---|---|---|
| 84 | Rag RAG 001 | Phantoms Of Fame/Sweet Banana | 60 |

*(see also Level 42)*

## RAGAMUFFIN
| | | | |
|---|---|---|---|
| 72 | Decca F13312 | Can I Have My Money Back/Fresh As A Daisy | 12 |

## RAGE AGAINST THE MACHINE
| | | | |
|---|---|---|---|
| 93 | Epic 658 492-6 | Killing In The Name/Clear The Lane/Darkness Of Greed (12" white vinyl, p/s) | 18 |
| 93 | Epic 659 258-6 | Bullet In The Head (Remix)/Bullet In The Head/(Album Version) Settle For Nothing (live) (12" picture disc, p/s) | 10 |
| 93 | Epic 658 492-7 | Killing In The Name/Clear The Lane/Darkness Of Greed (white vinyl, p/s) | 12 |
| 96 | Epic 663 152-7 | Bulls On Parade/Hadda Be Playing On The Jukebox (red vinyl) | 8 |
| 92 | Epic EPC 72224 | RAGE AGAINST THE MACHINE (LP) | 20 |
| 92 | Epic 47 22240 | RAGE AGAINST THE MACHINE (LP, red vinyl, 12", tour edition) | 70 |
| 96 | Epic 481026 | EVIL EMPIRE (LP) | 25 |

## RAGE (1)
| | | | |
|---|---|---|---|
| 80 | Carrere CAR 159 | Money/Thank That Woman (p/s) | 8 |
| 80 | Carrere CAR 159CT | Money/Thank That Woman (10", red vinyl, stickered clear sleeve) | 12 |
| 81 | Carrere CAR 182 | Out Of Control/Double Dealer (p/s) | 5 |
| 81 | Carrere CAR 182CT | Out Of Control (Extended Version)/Double Dealer (12", yellow vinyl, PVC sleeve) | 15 |
| 83 | Carrere CAR 304 | Cry From A Hill (p/s) | 10 |

*(see also Nutz)*

## RAGE (2)
| | | | |
|---|---|---|---|
| 86 | Diamond RAGE 1 | Looking For You/Come On Now (p/s) | 20 |
| 86 | Diamond RAGE 112 | Looking For You/Come On Now/Great Balls Of Fire/Hallelujah I Love Her So (12", unissued, test pressings only) | 25 |

*(see also Case, Long Tall Shorty, Purple Hearts, Chords)*

## RAGGAMUFFINS
| | | | |
|---|---|---|---|
| 67 | London HLU 10134 | Four Days Of Rain/It Wasn't Happening At All | 15 |

## RAGGED HEROES
| | | | |
|---|---|---|---|
| 83 | Celtic CM 013 | ANNUAL (LP) | 25 |

MINT VALUE £

**RAGGED TROUSERS**
75   EMI 2300                    Mountain Child/Maybe I'm In Love ....................................................... 15

**RAGING STORMS**
62   London HLU 9556             The Dribble/Hound Dog .................................................................. 25

**LOU RAGLAND**
73   Warner Bros K 16312         Since You Said You'd Be Mine/I Didn't Mean To Love You ............. 30

**RAGPICKERS**
59   Saga SAG 45-2906            Fifi/Cat On A Cool Tin Roof (p/s) ....................................................... 5
*(see also Bert Weedon)*

**RAIDER OF THE LOST DUB**
81   Island ILPS 9705            RAIDERS OF THE LOST DUB (LP) (withdrawn due to legal action) ......... 40

**RAIDERS**
70   CBS 4801                    Just Seventeen/Sorceress With Blue Eyes.................................... 10
70   CBS 5015                    Gone Movin' On/Interlude (to Be Forgotten) ............................. 10
71   CBS 7474                    Birds Of A Feather/The Turkey ...................................................... 6
72   CBS 7808                    Country Wing/It's Hard Getting Up Today..................................... 6
72   CBS 8428                    Song Seller/A Simple Song............................................................ 10
*(see also Paul Revere)*

**RAINBEAUS**
60   Vogue V 9161               That's All I'm Asking Of You/Maybe It's Wrong........................ 150

**(RITCHIE BLACKMORE'S) RAINBOW**
74   Oyster OYR 103             Man On The Silver Mountain/Snake Charmer (as Ritchie Blackmore's Rainbow) ........... 8
77   Polydor 2066 845           Kill The King (live)/Man On The Silver Mountain (live)/Mistreated (live) (p/s) .............. 5
78   Polydor 2066 913           Long Live Rock'n'Roll/Sensitive To Light (p/s) ................................ 5
78   Polydor 2066 968           L.A. Connection/Lady Of The Lake (p/s, initial pressing on red vinyl) ................ 10
83   Polydor POSPP 631          Street Of Dreams/Anybody There? (picture disc, 2000 only)................ 20
83   Polydor POSPP 654          Can't Let You Go/All Night Long (live) (guitar-shaped picture disc)............... 15
75   Oyster OYA 2001            RITCHIE BLACKMORE'S RAINBOW (LP, gatefold sleeve, as Ritchie Blackmore's Rainbow) ......... 40
76   Polydor 2490 137           RAINBOW RISING (LP, gatefold)................................................... 15
77   Polydor 2808 010 010       RAINBOW ON STAGE (LP, music & interview disc, with insert, promo only) .......... 100
79   Polydor POLD 5023          DOWN TO EARTH (LP, clear vinyl, with inner sleeve) .................... 18
78   Polydor POLD 5002          LONG LIVE ROCK 'N' ROLL (LP, gatefold sleeve, insert) ............... 15
83   Polydor POLD 5116          BENT OUT OF SHAPE (LP) ............................................................ 15
*(see also Deep Purple, Elf, Dio, Graham Bonnet, Cozy Powell, Roger Glover, Wild Horses, Tony Carey)*

**CHRIS RAINBOW**
81   EMI 5215-6                 Body Music/Girl In Collision (p/s)................................................. 8
81   EMI 12EMI 5215             Body Music/Girl In Collision (12", p/s) ...................................... 15

**RAINBOW FAMILY**
72   President PT 375           Travellin' Lady/My Father ........................................................... 60

**RAINBOW FFOLLY**
68   Parlophone R 5701          Go Girl/Drive My Car................................................................. 60
67   Parlophone PMC/PCS 7050    SALLIES FFORTH (LP, laminated front, flipbacks, black/yellow label, "Sold in U.K..." text)............................................................................... 750
*(see also Love Affair)*

**RAINBOW PEOPLE**
68   Pye 7N 17582               Walk'll Do You Good/Dream Time ............................................. 15
68   Pye 7N 17624               The Sailing Song/Rainbows .......................................................... 15
69   Pye 7N 17759               Living In A Dream World/Happy To See You Again ..................... 30

**RAINBOWS**
69   CBS 3995                   Rainbows/Nobody But You ......................................................... 20
69   CBS 4568                   New Day Dawning/Days And Nights............................................ 40
*(see also Peeps, Martin Cure & Peeps)*

**RAINCHECKS**
64   Solar SRP 104              Something About You/You're My Angel....................................... 20
65   R&B MRB 5002               How Are You Boy/Bye Bye Baby .................................................. 40

**RAINCOATS**
95   Rough Trade R4047          Don't Be Mean/Vicious/I Keep Walking (p/s) ................................ 6
79   Rough Trade RT 013         Adventures Close to Home/In Love/Fairytale In The Supermarket................ 20
82   Rough Trade TR 093         Running Away/No Ones Little Girl ............................................... 20
83   Rough Trade RTT 153        Animal Rhapsody/Honey Mad Woman/No-Ones Little Girl (12")............. 18
94   Blast First BFFP99         EXTENDED PLAY 10" EP) ............................................................ 10
79   Rough Trade ROUGH 3        THE RAINCOATS (LP, with lyric booklet) ..................................... 35
81   Rough Trade ROUGH 13       ODYSHAPE (LP)............................................................................ 35
83   Rough Trade ROUGH 66       MOVING (LP)................................................................................ 20
*(see also Slits)*

**RAINDANCE**
87   Raindance X1S 121          RAINDANCE (LP)........................................................................... 40

**RAINDROPS (U.K.)**
59   Parlophone R 4559          Italian Style/Along Came Jones ................................................. 10
60   Oriole CB 1544             Let's Make A Foursome/If I Had My Life To Live Over .................... 5
60   Oriole CB 1555             Banjo Boy/Crazy Rhythm.............................................................. 5
61   Oriole CB 1595             Will You Love Me Tomorrow/Raindrops ..................................... 10
62   Oriole CB 1707             Paintin' The Town With Teardrops/A Letter From Anne ................ 5
67   CBS 202669                 Foolman/Got To Find A Reason (credited to Raindrops '67) .......... 10
*(see also Jackie & Raindrops, Jackie Lee, Jacky, Emma Rede, Vince Hill)*

**RAINDROPS (U.S.)**
63   London HL 9718             What A Guy/It's So Wonderful ................................................... 25

| | | | |
|---|---|---|---|
| 63 | London HL 9769 | The Kind Of Boy You Can't Forget/Even Though You Can't Dance | 30 |
| 64 | London HL 9825 | That Boy John/Hanky Panky | 20 |
| 64 | Fontana TF 463 | The Book Of Love/I Won't Cry | 25 |
| 64 | London RE 1415 | WHAT A GUY (EP) | 125 |
| 64 | London HA 8140 | THE RAINDROPS (LP) | 125 |

*(see also Ellie Greenwich, Popsicles)*

**CLAIRE RAINE**
| | | | |
|---|---|---|---|
| 68 | Jolly JY 010 | La-La-La/I Want You | 20 |

**LORRY RAINE**
| | | | |
|---|---|---|---|
| 54 | London HL 8043 | You Broke My Broken Heart/I'm In Love With A Guy | 25 |
| 55 | London HL 8132 | Love Me Tonight/What Would I Do | 40 |

**MA RAINEY**
| | | | |
|---|---|---|---|
| 53 | London AL 3502 | MA RAINEY VOLUME 1 (10" LP) | 25 |
| 55 | London AL 3538 | MA RAINEY VOLUME 2 (10" LP) | 25 |
| 56 | London AL 3558 | MA RAINEY VOLUME 3 (10" LP) | 25 |
| 50s | Ristic LP 13 | MA RAINEY (10" LP) | 25 |
| 50s | Ristic LP 19 | MA RAINEY (10" LP) | 25 |
| 62 | Riverside RL 12-108 | MA RAINEY SINGS THE BLUES (LP) | 20 |
| 64 | Riverside RLP 8807 | MOTHER OF THE BLUES (LP, gatefold sleeve with booklet) | 20 |

**MA RAINEY & IDA COX**
| | | | |
|---|---|---|---|
| 60 | Jazz Collector JEL 12 | THE FEMALE BLUES VOL. 1 (EP) | 10 |

*(see also Ida Cox, Tommy Ladnier)*

**MA RAINEY & PAPA CHARLIE JACKSON**
| | | | |
|---|---|---|---|
| 50s | Poydras 11 | Ma And Papa Poorhouse Blues/Big Feeling Blues | 15 |

**RAIN PARADE**
| | | | |
|---|---|---|---|
| 83 | Enigma BOB 4/LYN 15263 | Sad Eyes Kill (3.16) (hard vinyl white label test pressing) | 12 |

**RAIN TREE CROW**
| | | | |
|---|---|---|---|
| 91 | Virgin V2659 | RAIN TREE CROW (LP) | 20 |

**MARVIN RAINWATER**
| | | | |
|---|---|---|---|
| 55 | MGM SP 1150 | Tennessee Houn' Dog Yodel/Albino (Pink-Eyed) Stallion | 50 |
| 56 | MGM MGM 929 | What Am I Supposed To Do/Why Did You Have To Go And Leave Me | 25 |
| 57 | MGM MGM 961 | Gonna Find Me A Bluebird/So You Think You've Got | 15 |
| 58 | MGM MGM 974 | Whole Lotta Woman/Baby, Don't Go | 6 |
| 58 | MGM MGM 980 | I Dig You Baby/Two Fools In Love (B-side with Sister Patty) | 6 |
| 58 | MGM MGM 988 | Dance Me Daddy/Because I'm A Dreamer (B-side with Sister Patty) | 6 |
| 59 | MGM MGM 1030 | Half-Breed/A Song Of New Love | 5 |
| 60 | MGM MGM 1052 | Nothin' Needs Nothin' (Like I Need You)/The Valley Of The Moon | 10 |
| 61 | London HLU 9447 | Boo Hoo/I Can't Forget | 80 |
| 58 | MGM MGM-EP 647 | MEET MARVIN RAINWATER (EP) | 15 |
| 58 | MGM MGM-EP 662 | WHOLE LOTTA MARVIN (EP) | 15 |
| 59 | MGM MGM-EP 685 | MARVIN RAINWATER SINGS (EP) | 15 |
| 63 | Ember EMB 4521 | COUNTRY AND WESTERN FAVOURITES VOL. 2 (EP) | 15 |
| 58 | MGM MGM-D 152 | SONGS BY MARVIN RAINWATER (10" LP) | 60 |

*(see also Connie Francis & Marvin Rainwater)*

**RAINY DAY**
| | | | |
|---|---|---|---|
| 84 | EMI EMI 5472 | Painting Pictures/Welche Farbe Hat Der Sonnenschein (p/s) | 12 |
| 84 | Rough Trade ROUGH 70 | RAINY DAY (LP) | 25 |

**RAINY DAZE**
| | | | |
|---|---|---|---|
| 67 | CBS 3200 | What Do You Think/Autumn Leaves | 18 |
| 67 | Polydor 56731 | That Acapulco Gold/In My Mind Lives A Forest | 20 |
| 68 | Polydor 56737 | Blood Of Oblivion/Stop Sign | 20 |
| 68 | CBS 56731 | THAT ACAPULCO GOLD (LP, unissued in U.K.) | 0 |

**RAISINS**
| | | | |
|---|---|---|---|
| 68 | Major Major MM 540 | Ain't That Lovin' You Baby/Stranger Things Have Happened | 15 |
| 69 | Major Minor MM 602 | I Thank You/Don't Leave Me Like This | 8 |
| 68 | Major Minor MMLP 20 | THE RAISINS (LP, also stereo SMLP 20) | 30 |

*(see also Coloured Raisins)*

**RAKES**
| | | | |
|---|---|---|---|
| 04 | Trash Aesthetics TA 702 | 22 Grand Job/Something Clicked And I Fell Off The Edge (Pink vinyl, insert and Fold-out sleeve. 480 only) | 18 |
| 05 | V2 VVR1032761 | CAPTURE/RELEASE (LP) | 18 |
| 07 | V2 VVR1041851 | TEN NEW MESSAGES (LP) | 20 |

**RALFI**
| | | | |
|---|---|---|---|
| 75 | Island USA 005 | Wonderful Things/The Gambler | 15 |

**DON RALKE ORCHESTRA**
| | | | |
|---|---|---|---|
| 59 | Vogue V 9152 | Maverick/Travellin' West | 5 |
| 60 | Warner Bros. WM 4007/ WS8007 | BUT YOU NEVER HEARD GERSHWIN WITH BONGOS (LP) | 10 |

**RALLY ROUNDERS**
| | | | |
|---|---|---|---|
| 64 | Lyntone LYN 573/574 | Bike Beat Part 1/Bike Beat Part 2 (actually by the Outlaws) (p/s, flexidisc) | 50 |

*(see also Outlaws)*

**RALPH & PONYTAILS**
| | | | |
|---|---|---|---|
| 80 | Pony Tunes RATP 1 | James Bond/James Bond (Different Version) (p/s) | 5 |

**BUCK RAM'S RAMROCKS**
| | | | |
|---|---|---|---|
| 63 | London HLU 9677 | Benfica/Odd Man Theme | 15 |

*(see also Little Richard, Platters)*

**RAMA**
| | | | |
|---|---|---|---|
| 69 | Polydor 56328 | God Created Love/Memory Of Love | 6 |

MINT VALUE £

## RAMA (4TH STREET ORCHESTRA)
| | | | |
|---|---|---|---|
| 77 | Rama RM 001 | AH WHO SHE? GO-DEH! (LP) | 60 |
| 77 | Rama RM 004 | (SCIENTIFIC) HIGHER RANKING DUB (LP) | 150 |
| 77 | Rama RMLP 005 | YUH LEARN! (LP) | 90 |

(see also Dennis Bowell, Matumbi)

## RAMASES
| | | | |
|---|---|---|---|
| 71 | Philips 6113 001 | Ballroom/Muddy Water | |
| 71 | Philips 6113 003 | Jesus Come Back/Hello Mister | 20 |
| 71 | Vertigo 6360 046 | SPACE HYMNS (LP, foldout poster sleeve, small swirl label) | 10 |
| 71 | Vertigo 6360 046 | SPACE HYMNS (LP, foldout sleeve, later 'spaceship' label) | 300 |
| 75 | Vertigo 6360 115 | GLASS TOP COFFIN (LP, die-cut gatefold sleeve, 'spaceship' label) | 70 |
| | | | 45 |

(see also 10cc, Ramases & Seleka, Ramases & Selket)

## RAMASES & SELEKA
| | | | |
|---|---|---|---|
| 70 | Major Minor MM 704 | Love You/Gold Is The Ring | 50 |

(see also Ramases)

## RAMASES & SELKET
| | | | |
|---|---|---|---|
| 68 | CBS 3717 | Crazy One/Mind's Eye | 80 |

(see also Ramases)

## RAMATAM
| | | | |
|---|---|---|---|
| 72 | Atlantic K 40415 | RAMATAM (LP) | 15 |

(see also Iron Butterfly)

## EDDIE RAMBEAU
| | | | |
|---|---|---|---|
| 62 | Stateside SS 116 | Summertime Guy/Last Night Was My Last Night | 10 |
| 64 | Stateside SS 301 | Come Closer/She's Smilin' At Me | 8 |
| 65 | Stateside SS 448 | My Name Is Mud/I Just Need Your Love | 8 |
| 66 | Stateside SS 486 | The Train/Yesterday's Newspapers | 8 |
| 66 | Stateside SS 501 | I'm The Sky/I Just Need Your Love | 7 |
| 66 | Stateside SS 561 | The Clock/If I Were You | 7 |

(see also Marcy Jo & Eddie Rambeau)

## RAMBLER
| | | | |
|---|---|---|---|
| 66 | Pye 7N 17164 | Love Minus Zero No Limit/An Bonnan Bui | 7 |

(see also Johnny McEvoy)

## RAMBLERS
| | | | |
|---|---|---|---|
| 63 | Decca F 11775 | Dodge City/Just For Chicks | 40 |

## RAMBLERS TWO
| | | | |
|---|---|---|---|
| 65 | Pye 7N 15989 | Today Is The Highway/The Mountains And The Sea | 5 |

## RAMBLETTES
| | | | |
|---|---|---|---|
| 65 | Brunswick 05932 | Thinking Of You/On Back Street (DJ Copy) | 35 |
| 65 | Brunswick 05932 | Thinking Of You/On Back Street | 20 |

## SID RAMIN
| | | | |
|---|---|---|---|
| 70 | CBS 4813 | Stiletto/Sugar In The Rain | 20 |
| 69 | CBS 70062 | STILETTO (LP, soundtrack) | 30 |

## LOUIE RAMIREZ
| | | | |
|---|---|---|---|
| 67 | Mercury 20113 | IN THE HEART OF SPANISH HARLEM (LP) | 20 |

## RAM JAM BAND
| | | | |
|---|---|---|---|
| 65 | Columbia DB 7621 | Shake Shake Senora/Akinla | 25 |

(see also Geno Washington & Ram Jam Band, Ram John Holder, Ram Holder Brothers)

## RAMLEH
| | | | |
|---|---|---|---|
| 83 | Broken Flag BF V4 | THE HAND OF GLORY (EP, p/s) | 30 |
| 91 | Shock SX 013 | Slammers/Black Moby Dick (p/s, numbered, 500 only) | 8 |
| 92 | Dying Earth DE 003 | Loser Patrol/Tracers (p/s, numbered, 500 only, 1st 30 in red sleeve) | 15 |
| 92 | Dying Earth DE 003 | Loser Patrol/Tracers (p/s, numbered, 500 only) | 8 |
| 93 | Dying Earth DE 007 | Say Fuck/Slackjaw (wraparound p/s, numbered, 500 only) | 8 |
| 94 | Format Supremacy 1 Of EACH | Welcome/Pristine Womankind (cardboard p/s, 500 only) | 8 |
| 82 | Broken Flag BF 01 | 31/5/1962 - 1982 (cassette) | 70 |
| 83 | Broken Flag BF V2 | A RETURN TO SLAVERY (LP, with Libertarian Recordings) | 30 |
| 83 | Broken Flag BF 07 | LIVE McCARTHY (cassette) | 50 |
| 83 | Broken Flag BF 20 | LIVE NEW FORCE (cassette) | 50 |
| 83 | Broken Flag BF 24 | LIVE PHENOL (cassette) | 50 |
| 83 | Broken Flag BF 25 | LIVE PROSSNECK (cassette) | 50 |
| 83 | Broken Flag BF 28 | LIVE AT MORDEN TOWER (cassette) | 50 |
| 84 | Broken Flag BF 37 | 104 WEEKS (cassette) | 40 |
| 84 | Broken Flag BF 38 | AS I HAVE WON (cassette) | 40 |
| 85 | Broken Flag BF 40 | AWAKE! (6 cassettes in lockable steel box with booklet) | 400 |
| 87 | Broken Flag BF 59 | HOLE IN THE HEART (cassette) | 40 |
| 94 | Broken Flag BF 75 | SOUNDCHECK CHANGLING (cassette) | 20 |
| 95 | Broken Flag BF 77 | AIRBORNE BABEL (cassette) | 20 |
| 95 | Broken Flag BF 80 | ELITE GYMNASTICS/LIVE 1983 (cassette) | 20 |

(see also Skullflower)

## RAMMALAMMA
| | | | |
|---|---|---|---|
| 75 | Private Stock PVT 10 | Roll It Over/Can't You Feel It | 5 |

## RAMMSTEIN
| | | | |
|---|---|---|---|
| 09 | Pilgrim/Spinefarm/Universal 2718498 | Pussy (p/s, limited edition) | 10 |

## RAMON & CRYSTALITES
| | | | |
|---|---|---|---|
| 71 | Songbird SB 1053 | Golden Chickens/Stranger Version | 25 |

## DEE DEE RAMONE
97   Blackout BLK 5000-7        I Am Seeing UFOs (featuring Joey Ramone)/Bad Horoscope (2,500 copies only) ............ 8

## DEE DEE RAMONE & ICLC
94   World Service/Rough Trade  I HATE FREAKS LIKE YOU (LP, with inner)................................................................. 15
     RTD 157.1757.1

*(see also Ramones)*

## RAMONES
| | | | |
|---|---|---|---|
| 76 | Sire 6078 601 | Blitzkrieg Bop/Havana Affair (in rare p/s) ................................................ 200 |
| 76 | Sire 6078 601 | Blitzkrieg Bop/Havana Affair .............................................................. 12 |
| 77 | Sire 6078 603 | I Remember You/California Sun (live)/I Don't Wanna Walk Around With You (live) (p/s)................................................................................................ 45 |
| 77 | Sire RAM 001 (6078 606) | Sheena Is A Punk Rocker/Commando/I Don't Care (12", with T-shirt offer on perforated centre of numbered p/s, 12,000 only) ....................................... 20 |
| 77 | Sire RAM 001 (6078 606) | Sheena Is A Punk Rocker/Commando/I Don't Care (12", without T-shirt offer on perforated centre of numbered p/s, 12,000 only) ....................................... 10 |
| 77 | Sire 6078 607 | Swallow My Pride/Pinhead/Let's Dance (live) (p/s) ..................................... 20 |
| 77 | Sire 6078 611 | Rockaway Beach/Teenage Lobotomy/Beat On The Brat (p/s) ....................... 20 |
| 77 | Sire 6078 611 | Rockaway Beach/Teenage Lobotomy/Beat On The Brat (12", p/s, with poster) ............ 30 |
| 77 | Sire 6078 611 | Rockaway Beach/Teenage Lobotomy/Beat On The Brat (12", p/s, without poster) ....... 12 |
| 78 | Sire 6078 615 | Do You Wanna Dance?/It's A Long Way Back To Germany/Cretin Hop (p/s) ............. 18 |
| 78 | Sire (no cat. no.) | Questioningly/Don't Come Close/Sedated/I Just Want To Have Something To Do (with p/s, promo only, with spoken intros by Joey Ramone) .................. 45 |
| 78 | Sire (no cat. no.) | Questioningly/Don't Come Close/Sedated/I Just Want To Have Something To Do (without p/s, promo only, with spoken intros by Joey Ramone) ................ 15 |
| 78 | Sire SRE 1031 | Don't Come Close/I Don't Want You (p/s, yellow vinyl) ............................... 15 |
| 78 | Sire SRE 1031 | Don't Come Close/I Don't Want You (p/s) ............................................... 5 |
| 78 | Sire SRE 1031 | Don't Come Close/I Don't Want You (12", p/s, yellow or red vinyl, red vinyl lacks p/s).. 10 |
| 79 | Sire SIR 4009 | She's The One/I Wanna Be Sedated (p/s) ............................................... 15 |
| 79 | Sire SIR 4021 | Rock'n'Roll High School/Rockaway Beach (live)/Sheena Is A Punk Rocker (live) (p/s)...... 7 |
| 80 | Sire SIR 4037 | Do You Remember Rock'n'Roll Radio/I Want You Around (p/s)........................ 5 |
| 80 | RSO RSO 70 (2090 512) | I Wanna Be Sedated/The Return Of Jackie And Judy (p/s) ......................... 18 |
| 80 | Sire SREP 1 | MELTDOWN WITH THE RAMONES: I Just Want To Have Something To Do/ Here Today Gone Tomorrow/I Wanna Be Your Boyfriend/Questioningly (EP) .................. 15 |
| 80 | Sire SIR 4031 | Baby I Love You/High RIsk Insurance .................................................... 5 |
| 81 | Sire SIR 4051 | We Want The Airwaves/You Sound LIke You're Sick (p/s) .............................. 6 |
| 81 | Sire SIR 4052 | She's A Sensation/All Quiet On The Eastern Front (no p/s) ........................... 8 |
| 83 | Sire W 9606 | Time Has Come Today/Psycho Therapy (p/s) ........................................... 15 |
| 83 | Sire W 9606T | Time Has Come Today/Sheena Is A Punk Rocker/Teenage Lobotomy/ Rock'n'Roll Radio (12", p/s) ................................................................. 20 |
| 85 | Beggars Banquet BEG 128 | Howling At The Moon/Chasing The Night (p/s)....................................... 5 |
| 85 | Beggars Banquet BEG 128D | Howling At The Moon//Smash You/ Chasing The Night/Street Fighting Man (double pack, gatefold sleeve).......................................................... 8 |
| 85 | Beggars Banquet BEG 140 | Bonzo Goes To Bitburg/Go Home Ann (p/s)......................................... 7 |
| 86 | Beggars Banquet BEG 157 | Somebody Put Something In My Drink/Something To Believe In (p/s) ............. 5 |
| 86 | Beggars Banquet BEG 157T | Somebody Put Something In My Drink/(You) Can't Say Anything Nice/ Something To Believe In (12", p/s, with promo poster)................................ 15 |
| 86 | Beggars Banquet BEG 167 | Crummy Stuff/She Belongs To Me (p/s) ............................................... 7 |
| 86 | Beggars Banquet BEG 167T | Crummy Stuff/Something To Believe In/I Don't Want To Live This Life (12", p/s)........... 12 |
| 87 | Beggars Banquet BEG 198 | Real Cool Time/Life Goes On (p/s)..................................................... 5 |
| 87 | Beggars Banquet BEG 201 | I Wanna Live/Merry Christmas (I Don't Want To Fight Tonight) (p/s)................. 5 |
| 89 | Chrysalis CHS 3423 | Pet Semetary/All Screwed Up (p/s) .................................................... 5 |
| 92 | Chrysalis CHS 3917 | Poison Heart/Censorshit (p/s) ......................................................... 5 |
| 92 | Chrysalis 0946 3 23917 66 | Poison Heart/Chinese Rocks/Sheena Is A Punk Rocker (live)/ Rockaway Beach (live) (12", yellow vinyl, p/s) .......................................... 10 |
| 76 | Sire 9103 253 | RAMONES (LP, with insert) ............................................................. 40 |
| 77 | Sire 9103 254 | RAMONES LEAVE HOME (LP, with "Carbona Not Glue" with inner sleeve) ............ 20 |
| 77 | Sire 9103 255 | ROCKET TO RUSSIA (LP, with inner sleeve)............................................ 20 |
| 78 | Sire SRK 6063 | ROAD TO RUIN (LP, yellow vinyl, inner) ............................................... 20 |
| 79 | Sire SRK 6077 | END OF THE CENTURY (LP, inner)...................................................... 20 |
| 79 | Sire SRK2 6074 | IT'S ALIVE (2-LP) ....................................................................... 20 |
| 81 | Sire SRK 3571 | PLEASANT DREAMS (LP) ................................................................ 20 |
| 85 | Beggars Banquet BEGA 59 | TOO TOUGH TO DIE (LP) ............................................................... 15 |
| 86 | Beggars Banquet BEGA 70 | ANIMAL BOY (LP, picture inner sleeve and poster)................................. 15 |
| 90 | Beggar's Banquet | END OF THE DECADE (6 x 12" singles, box set with t-shirt, postcards & poster, 2,500 copies only)................................................................. 50 |
| 91 | Chysalis CHR 1901 | LOCO LIVE (LP, inner)................................................................... 15 |
| 92 | Chrysalis 094632196019 | MONDO BIZARRO (LP)................................................................... 20 |
| 93 | Chrysalis CHR 6052 | ACID EATERS (LP)........................................................................ 15 |
| 95 | Chrysalis 724383413614 | ADIOS AMIGOS (LP) ..................................................................... 30 |

*(see also Paley Brothers & Ramones, Holly & Joey, Dee Dee Ramone)*

## MICHEL RAMOS
55   London DEP 95013   PLAYING THE CLASSICS (EP, export) ........................................................... 20

## RAMP
77   ABC/Blue Thumb BT 6028   COME INTO KNOWLEDGE (LP) ............................................................ 40

## RAMPENT
80   FMR 030 S80 CUS 804   Back Street Walker/Livin In The Past/Fight Back/No Friend Of Mine ................. 100

## RAM RAM GO GO SOUND
69   Halagala HG 26   Pep 77/USA Outcry ................................................................................. 15

## RAMRODS
65   United Artists UP 1113   Overdrive/Stalker.................................................................................. 15

## RAMRODS (U.S.)
| | | | |
|---|---|---|---|
| 61 | London HLU 9282 | Riders In The Sky/Zig Zag | 6 |
| 61 | London HLU 9355 | Loch Lomond Rock/Take Me Back To My Boots And Saddle | 20 |
| 61 | London RE-U 1292 | RIDERS IN THE SKY (EP) | 70 |

## BILL RAMSEY
| | | | |
|---|---|---|---|
| 62 | Polydor NH 66812 | Go Man Go/Rocking Mountain | 12 |

## LEE RAMSEY
| | | | |
|---|---|---|---|
| 96 | Real Deal RD 001 | RISE TO SHINE (EP) | 12 |
| 96 | Real Deal RD002 | RD STYLE (EP) | 10 |

## ANDREW RANCE
| | | | |
|---|---|---|---|
| 79 | Trash TRA 1001 | It Really Shouldn't Matter/Cold (no p/s) | 14 |

## RANCHERS
| | | | |
|---|---|---|---|
| 65 | Cavern Sound IMSTL 2 | An American Sailor At The Cavern/Sidetracked | 25 |

## RANCID
| | | | |
|---|---|---|---|
| 95 | Out Of Step WOOS 8 S | Time Bomb/The War's End/Blast 'Em (p/s) | 6 |
| 96 | Epitaph 86464-7 | Ruby Soho/That's Entertainment/Disorder And Disarray (p/s) | 6 |
| 98 | Epitaph 1005-7 | Bloodclot/Endrine/Stop (p/s) | 6 |
| 98 | Epitaph 1009-7 | Hooligans/Cash, Culture and Violence (Bass Drop Mix)/Things to Come (Dance hall Mix) (p/s) | 6 |
| 00 | Epitaph 1040-7 | Let Me Go/Ben Zanotto/Dead And Fone (p/s) | 6 |
| 03 | Warner Brothers W 618 | Fall Back Down/Killing Zone (p/s) | 5 |

## RANDALL AND ANDY C.
| | | | |
|---|---|---|---|
| 94 | Ram RAMM 11 | Sound Control/Feel It (12") | 15 |

*(see also Andy C)*

## ELLIOTT RANDALL
| | | | |
|---|---|---|---|
| 71 | Polydor 2489 004 | RANDALL'S ISLAND (LP) | 20 |

## FREDDY RANDALL & HIS BAND
| | | | |
|---|---|---|---|
| 58 | Parlophone GEP 8715 | CHICAGO JAZZ (EP) | 10 |
| 58 | Parlophone PMD 1046 | DR JAZZ (LP) | 20 |

## ALAN RANDALL
| | | | |
|---|---|---|---|
| 68 | Electratone S1002 | The Meditating Hindoo Man/Why Don't Women Like Me | 15 |
| 68 | Electratone s1002 | The Meditating Hindoo Man/Why Don't Women Like Me | 8 |

## TEDDY RANDAZZO (& DAZZLERS)
| | | | |
|---|---|---|---|
| 59 | HMV POP 578 | It's Magic/Richer Than I | 10 |
| 60 | HMV POP 806 | Journey To Love/Misery | 10 |
| 61 | HMV POP 866 | Happy Ending/But You Broke My Heart | 10 |
| 61 | HMV POP 925 | Let The Sunshine In/Broken Bell | 10 |
| 62 | HMV POP 1067 | Dance To The Locomotion/Cottonfields (as Teddy Randazzo & Dazzlers) | 15 |
| 63 | HMV POP 1119 | Echoes/It Wasn't A Dream | 5 |
| 63 | Pye International 7N 25181 | Big Wide World/Be Sure, My Love | 10 |
| 62 | HMV CLP 1527 | JOURNEY TO LOVE (LP, mono) | 35 |
| 62 | HMV CSD 1421 | JOURNEY TO LOVE (LP, stereo) | 40 |
| 63 | HMV CLP 1601 | TEDDY RANDAZZO TWISTS (LP, with Dazzlers) | 90 |

*(see also Three Chuckles)*

## LYNNE RANDELL
| | | | |
|---|---|---|---|
| 67 | CBS 2847 | Ciao Baby/Stranger In My Arms (DJ Copy) | 250 |
| 67 | CBS 2847 | Ciao Baby/Stranger In My Arms | 200 |
| 67 | CBS 2927 | That's A Hoe Down/I Need You Boy | 30 |

## RAN-DELLS
| | | | |
|---|---|---|---|
| 63 | London HLU 9760 | The Martian Hop/Forgive Me Darling (I Have Lied) | 25 |

## BARBARA RANDOLPH
| | | | |
|---|---|---|---|
| 67 | Tamla Motown TMG 628 | I Got A Feelin'/You Got Me Hurtin' All Over | 65 |
| 67 | Tamla Motown TMG 628 | I Got A Feelin'/You Got Me Hurtin' All Over (DJ copy) | 100 |
| 71 | Tamla Motown TMG 788 | I Got A Feelin'/You Got Me Hurtin' All Over (reissue) | 10 |
| 79 | Tamla Motown TMG 1133 | Can I Get A Witness/You Got Me Hurtin' All Over/I Got A Feeling | 15 |

## BOOTS RANDOLPH
| | | | |
|---|---|---|---|
| 62 | London HLU 9567 | Bluebird Of Happiness/Keep A Light In Your Window Tonight | 6 |
| 63 | London HLU 9685 | Yakety Sax/I Really Don't Want To Know | 6 |
| 63 | London RE-U 1365 | THE YAKETY SAX OF BOOTS RANDOLPH (EP) | 10 |

## CHARLES RANDOLPH GREAN SOUND
| | | | |
|---|---|---|---|
| 69 | London HLD 10283 | Quintin's Theme/Number One At The Blue Whale | 6 |

## RANDOM HOLD
| | | | |
|---|---|---|---|
| 79 | Polydor POSP 85 | Etceteraville/Precarious Timbers | 5 |

## RANDY
| | | | |
|---|---|---|---|
| 96 | Rugger Bugger SEEP 20 | THE REST IS SILENCE (LP, printed inner sleeve) | 25 |
| 99 | Rugger Bugger SEEP 026 | YOU CAN'T KEEP A GOOD BAND DOWN (LP, gatefold) | 25 |

## RANDY & RAINBOWS
| | | | |
|---|---|---|---|
| 63 | Stateside SS 214 | Denise/Come Back | 50 |

## RANDY'S ALLSTARS
| | | | |
|---|---|---|---|
| 70 | Randy's RAN 500 | I'm The One, You're The One/End Us | 12 |
| 70 | Randy's RAN 501 | Pepper Pot (act. with Count Machuki)/Same Thing (B-side actually by Gaylads) | 70 |
| 70 | Randy's RAN 502 | Dixie/Five Cents (B-side actually "A Lover's Question" by Winston Samuels) | 7 |
| 70 | Randy's RAN 505 | Emperor Waltz/War | 10 |
| 70 | Randy's RAN 506 | Blue Danube Waltz/Together (B-side actually by Delroy Wilson) | 8 |
| 70 | Randy's RAN 507 | Bridge Over Troubled Water (actually by Lyrics)/Waterfall | 5 |
| 71 | Explosion EX 2052 | Hold On Girl (actually by Lyrics)/Hold On Girl (Version) | 5 |

*(see also Impact Allstars, Lyrics, Dave Barker, Ethiopians, Jimmy London)*

### RANEE & RAJ
| | | |
|---|---|---|
| 68 | Fontana TF 920 | Feel Like A Clown/Rainbow Land ......... 20 |
| 68 | Fontana TF 941 | Don't Tell Me I Must Go/Razor Edge ......... 20 |

### SUE RANEY
| | | |
|---|---|---|
| 57 | Capitol CL 14757 | The Careless Years/What's The Good Word, Mr. Bluebird ......... 6 |
| 57 | Capitol CL 14792 | Please Hurry Home/Don't Take My Happiness ......... 6 |
| 58 | Capitol T 964 | WHEN YOUR LOVER HAS GONE (LP) ......... 15 |

### WAYNE RANEY (STRING BAND)
| | | |
|---|---|---|
| 54 | Parlophone CSMP 20 | Adam/The Roosters Are Crowing (export issue) ......... 25 |
| 55 | Parlophone DP 413 | Mama (Don't You Remember When You Were Young)/Trying To Live Without You (78, export issue) ......... 8 |
| 58 | Parlophone GEP 8746 | COUNTRY AND WESTERN (EP) ......... 30 |

### RANGLERS
| | | |
|---|---|---|
| 68 | Trend TRE 1007 | You Never Said Goodbye/Step Down ......... 60 |

### ERNEST RANGLIN
| | | |
|---|---|---|
| 62 | Island WI 015 | Harmonica Twist/Mitty Gritty (as Ernest Ranglin Orchestra) ......... 40 |
| 63 | Island WI 128 | Exodus/ROBERT MARLEY: One Cup Of Coffee ......... 300 |
| 66 | Black Swan IEP 704 | ERNEST RANGLIN & THE G.B.'s (EP, with p/s) ......... 180 |
| 66 | Black Swan IEP 704 | ERNEST RANGLIN & THE G.B.'s (EP) ......... 50 |
| 64 | Island ILP 909 | WRANGLIN' (LP) ......... 150 |
| 64 | Island ILP 915 | REFLECTIONS (LP) ......... 150 |
| 60s | Vista Sounds | FROM KINGSTON J.A. TO MIAMI U.S.A. (LP) ......... 25 |

*(see also Owen Gray, Graham Bond)*

### KATNYA RANIERI
| | | |
|---|---|---|
| 60 | MGM 1088 | The Torch/Kaniya ......... 6 |
| 60 | MGM MGM 1094 | Never On Sunday/La Mia Felicita ......... 5 |

### MASSIMO RANIERI
| | | |
|---|---|---|
| 71 | CBS 7207 | Goodbye My Love/The Sun Shining Down On Me ......... 12 |

### BILLY RANKIN
| | | |
|---|---|---|
| 83 | A&M AM 172 | Baby Come Back/Part Of The Scenery (p/s) ......... 6 |

*(see also Nazareth)*

### KENNY RANKIN
| | | |
|---|---|---|
| 60 | Brunswick 05845 | As Sure As You're Born/Teasin' Heart ......... 8 |
| 70 | Mercury MF1128 | Peaceful/The Dolphin ......... 15 |
| 73 | Atlantic K 10275 | Comin' Down/Stringman ......... 5 |
| 74 | Little David | Carfish/Silver Morning ......... 8 |

### ROY RANKIN AND RAYMOND NAPTALI
| | | |
|---|---|---|
| 81 | KG Imperial KG 004 | Go Deh In A Late Night Blues/Late Night Session/Babylon Policy/Peaceful Something (12", green vinyl) ......... 25 |
| 81 | KG Imperial KG 007 | African Daughter/Disc Jockey In A 81 Style (12") ......... 15 |
| 82 | CF CFLP 001 | LATE NIGHT SESSION (LP) ......... 50 |

### RANKING ANN
| | | |
|---|---|---|
| 82 | Ariwa ARIL 002 | A SLICE OF ENGLISH TOAST (LP) ......... 20 |
| 82 | Ariwa ARILP 010 | SOMETHING FISHY GOING ON (LP) ......... 20 |

### RANKING DREAD
| | | |
|---|---|---|
| 78 | Greensleeves GRE10 | Dub Sister Dub It/Nine Months Belly ......... 10 |
| 80 | Art & Craft ACD 005 | DISCO EP SHOWCASE: Honda Accord/Joe Grine Girl/Baby Mother/Nice Up The Lawn (12") ......... 15 |
| 80 | Art & Craft AC006 | DISCO EP SHOWCASE: My Liza/Same Thing/Hard Times Leave My Life/Jah Walk Through Galilee (12" green vinyl) ......... 20 |
| 81 | Greensleeves GRED 65 | Fattie Boom Boom/SLY & ROBBIE : Dub Boom (12") ......... 12 |
| 82 | Greensleeves GRED 82 | Shut Me Mouth/Shut Up Shut Up (Dub Version) ......... 25 |
| 82 | Greensleeves GRED 96 | My Mammy/Mammy Mammy (12") ......... 15 |
| 76 | Burning Sounds BS 1025 | GIRLS FIESTA (LP) ......... 25 |
| 79 | Burning Sounds BS 1037 | KUNTA KINTE ROOTS (LP) ......... 25 |
| 80 | Freedom Sounds FSLP 001 | LOTS OF LOVING (LP) ......... 25 |
| 82 | Silver Camel SCLP 002 | RANKING DREAD IN DUB (LP) ......... 20 |

### RANKING JOE
| | | |
|---|---|---|
| 80 | Art & Craft ACD 005 | DISCO EP SHOWCASE (12") ......... 12 |
| 78 | Greensleeves GREL 2 | WEAKHEART FADEAWAY (LP) ......... 30 |
| 79 | Student NWLP 009 | ROUND THE WORLD (LP) ......... 60 |
| 80 | Greensleeves GREL 16 | SATURDAY NIGHT JAMDOWN STYLE (LP) ......... 20 |
| 81 | Copasetic COPLPS 003 | DISCO SKATE (LP, blue or black vinyl) ......... 20 |

### PETER RANKING AND GENERAL LUCKY
| | | |
|---|---|---|
| 82 | Greensleeves GRED 98 | Beverly Black/Walk And Talk (12") ......... 15 |

### RANKING ROCKER
| | | |
|---|---|---|
| 80 | Disco Mix DM 01 | Give Jah The Glory/Jah Words Of Wisdom/Out Of The Ghetto/Songs Of Jah (Disco Mix) (12") ......... 20 |

### RANKING TREVOR
| | | |
|---|---|---|
| 78 | Virgin Frontline FL1015 | IN FINE STYLE (LP) ......... 20 |

### RANKING TREVOR AND TRINITY
| | | |
|---|---|---|
| 78 | Cha Cha CHALP 001 | THREE PIECE CHICKEN AND CHIPS (LP) ......... 30 |

### RANKING SUPERSTAR
| | | |
|---|---|---|
| 80 | Lord Koos KLP 1 | REPATRIATION TIME (LP) ......... 45 |

### RANSOME HEAD
| | | |
|---|---|---|
| 71 | York SYK 506 | Sing/Wide Wide River ......... 30 |

### PETER RANSOME
| | | |
|---|---|---|
| 72 | York FYK 402 | PETER RANSOME (LP, blue/silver label) ......... 25 |

MINT VALUE £

### RAOUL & RUINED
84   Gutter Hearts GH 1      BITE BACK + BLUES (LP, fan-club only issue) ............................................. 50

*(see also Marc Almond)*

### RAPED
78   Parole KNIT 1      PRETTY PAEDOPHILES (EP) ................................................................ 20
78   Parole PURL 1      Cheap Night Out/Foreplay Playground (p/s, with ad sheet) ........................... 12
84   Iguana PILLAGED 1      PHILES AND SMILES (LP, official bootleg, with booklet) ............................... 50

*(see also Cuddly Toys)*

### RAPEMAN
88   Fierce FRIGHT 031      Hated Chinee/Marmoset (p/s) ....................................................... 15

*(see also Big Black)*

### RAPHAEL
67   Hispa Vox HXS 303      Please Speak To Me Of Love/While I Live ............................................. 8
68   Columbia DB 8471      Ave Maria (Listen To Me)/Goin' Out Of My Head ..................................... 6

### JOHNNY RAPHAEL
58   Vogue V 9104      We're Only Young Once/The Lonely Road To Nowhere ................................ 50
58   Vogue V 9104      We're Only Young Once/The Lonely Road To Nowhere (78) ......................... 25

### RAPID DANCE
82   Resolute RO 1      Fragments Of Youth/Hidden So Well (p/s) ........................................... 15

### RAPIERS (1)
60s   Ilford Sound ILF 272      The Phantom Stage/Valencia ....................................................... 20

### RAPIERS (2)
86   Off Beat NS 112A      The Closing Theme/Still I Cry ....................................................... 10
83   Red Door RA 001      THE RAPIERS VOL. 1 (EP) .......................................................... 18
84   Twang RA 002      THE RAPIERS VOL. 2 (EP) .......................................................... 12
85   Twang RA 003      THE RAPIERS VOL. 3 (EP) .......................................................... 12
86   Twang RA 004      THE RAPIERS VOL. 4 (EP) .......................................................... 12
91   Fury DEP 3018      THE RETURN OF THE RAPIERS (EP) ................................................ 10
85   Off Beat WIK 40      STRAIGHT TO THE POINT (LP) ..................................................... 18
87   Off Beat WIK 67      1961 (LP) ......................................................................... 18

### BRIAN RAPKIN & KELVIN JONES
70s   MSR      DREAMS OF THE BEAST (LP) ...................................................... 20

### RARE AMBER
69   Polydor BM 56309      Malfunction Of The Engine/Blind Love ............................................. 30
69   Polydor 583 046      RARE AMBER (LP) ................................................................ 250

### RARE BIRD
70   Charisma CB 120      Sympathy/Devil's High Concern (in p/s) ............................................ 15
70   Charisma CB 138      What You Want To Know/Hammerhead .............................................. 10
72   Charisma CB 179      Sympathy/Devil's High Concern/What Do You Want To Know/Hammerhead (p/s) ....... 10
73   Polydor 2058 402      Virgina/Lonely Street ............................................................... 5
74   Polydor 2058 471      Body And Soul/Redman .............................................................. 5
74   Polydor SH 1041/2      Diamonds/BARCLAY JAMES HARVEST: Negative Earth (flexi, with Sounds)............. 10
69   Charisma CAS 1005      RARE BIRD (LP, laminated front sleeve, pink 'scroll label) ......................... 100
70   Charisma CAS 1011      AS YOUR MIND FLIES BY (LP, textured gatefold, pink 'scroll' label) ................. 75
72   Polydor 2442 101      EPIC FOREST (LP & poster, with bonus EP "Roadside Welcome"/Four Grey Walls/ "You're Lost" [2814 011], p/s)................................................... 110
72   Polydor 2442 101      EPIC FOREST (LP, gatefold with free EP but no poster)............................... 60
72   Polydor 2442 101      EPIC FOREST (LP with no poster or free EP) ......................................... 30
73   Polydor 2383 211      SOMEBODY'S WATCHING (LP, gatefold sleeve) ....................................... 20

*(see also Fruit Machine)*

### RARE BREED
66   Strike JH 316      Beg, Borrow And Steal/Jeri's Theme ................................................ 30

*(see also Ohio Express)*

### RARE EARTH
70   Rare Earth RES 114      (I Know) I'm Losing You/When Joanie Smiles......................................... 7
71   Rare Earth RES 104      Hey Big Brother/Under God's Light .................................................. 8
71   Rare Earth RES 102      I Just Want To Celebrate/The Seed .................................................. 6
70   Tamla Motown TMG 742      Get Ready/Magic Key ............................................................... 20
70   Tamla Motown STML 11165      GET READY (LP) .................................................................... 20
71   Tamla Motown STML 11180      ECOLOGY (LP) ..................................................................... 20
71   Rare Earth SREA 4001      ONE WORLD (LP, textured gatefold sleeve) .......................................... 18

### RARE PLEASURE
76   DJM DJS 10738      Let Me Down Easy/Let Me Down Easy (Long Version) (Promo p/s) ................... 10
76   DJM DJS 10738      Let Me Down Easy/Let Me Down Easy (Long Version)................................. 7

### HERMAN RAREBELL
81   Harvest HAR 5215      I'll Say Goodbye/Junk Funk ........................................................ 10

### RARE MOODS
86   AGR AGR 5      I've Got Love/Closer To Your Love (p/s) ............................................. 20
86   AGR AGR T5      I've Got Love/Closer To Your Love (12") ............................................ 50

### RASCALS (1)
68   Atlantic 584 182      A Beautiful Morning/Rainy Day ...................................................... 8
68   Atlantic 584 210      People Got To Be Free/My World ..................................................... 8
69   Atlantic 584 255      Heaven/Baby I'm Blue ............................................................... 8
69   Atlantic 584 274      See/Away Away ...................................................................... 8
69   Atlantic 584 292      Carry Me Back/Real Thing ........................................................... 7
70   Atlantic 584 307      Hold On/I Believe ................................................................... 8
70   Atlantic 2091 029      Glory, Glory/You Don't Know ........................................................ 6
71   CBS 7363      Love Me/Happy Song ................................................................ 6

|    |                          |                                                                           |     |
|----|--------------------------|---------------------------------------------------------------------------|-----|
| 71 | CBS 7672                 | Lucky Day/Love Letter                                                     | 6   |
| 68 | Atlantic 587/588 098     | ONCE UPON A DREAM (LP)                                                    | 18  |
| 71 | CBS S 64406              | PEACEFUL WORLD (2xLP)                                                     | 18  |

(see also Young Rascals)

### RASCALS (2)
| 81 | Flexible FR 001 | UP TO MISCHIEF (sleeve back to front, no spine) | 80 |

### RENATO RASCEL
| 60 | RCA RCA 1177 | Romantica/TEDDY RENO - Libero | 5 |

(see also Royal Rasses)

### (EMPRESS) RASHEDA
| 87 | Jah Shaka 862           | Psalms 61 (Hear My Cry)/BLACK STEEL AND JAH SHAKA: Hear My Dub (12") | 12 |
| 92 | Rasheda Lioness RLM 001 | Only Jah Worthy/Give Jah Praise (12")                               | 20 |
| 95 | Roots Music RRLP 011    | HAIL H.I.M (LP)                                                     | 25 |

### RASI
| 83 | Yard Beat TB 001 | Jah Spoke To I/You Wan Tan Style | 25 |

### RAS I
| 96 | Conscious Sounds DNC 1204 | Bad Boys/BUSH CHEMISTS: Dub//Exploitation/Bush Chemists: Dub (12") | 12 |

### RAS IMRU
| 80 | Jah Shaka KMD001 | Marshall/SHAKA RYDIM SECTION : Warrior Style (12") | 60 |

### RAS MIDAS
| 77 | Black Swan WIP 6371 | Kude A Bamba/Congo Dub                                        | 10 |
| 79 | Tribesman TM 24     | Natty Dread Surprise/Good Old Days Original (with I-Roy) (12") | 60 |
| 79 | Warrior WAR 138     | Can't Stop Rasta Now/Rain And Fire (12")                      | 20 |

### RAS NATURAL
| 03 | Unity Sound US006 | Roar Like A Lion/Lion Chant/Version (10") | 20 |

### RASPBERRY PIRATES
| 68 | Atlantic 584 230 | Looky Looky My Cookie's Gone/Good Morning Baby | 8 |

### RASTAFARI
| 73 | Satril SAT8 | Funky City/In The Garden | 50 |

### THE RAT & THE WHALE
| 80 | Rewind REWIND 5 | Wheels On Fire/Wheels On Fire (Long Version) (p/s) | 5 |

(see also Alternative TV, Rat Scabies)

### RATCHELL
| 72 | MCA MUPS 455 | RATCHELL (LP) | 15 |

### RATIO
| 70 | Big Chief BC 102 | Let There Be Peace In The World/Pharaoh's Walk | 7 |

### RATIONAL ANTHEM
| 86 | Radio Humberside/HLS 001 | THE NORTHERN TRAWL (LP) | 50 |

### ARMAN RATIP
| 70 | Columbia SCX 6532     | INTRODUCING THE ARMAN RATIP TRIO (LP)       | 100 |
| 73 | Regal Zono. SLRZ 1038 | THE SPY FROM ISTANBUL (LP, gatefold sleeve) | 120 |

### RATS (1)
| 64 | Oak RGJ 145     | Spoonful (1-sided, with foldout p/s)                                                                   | 400 |
| 64 | Oak RGJ 145     | Spoonful (1-sided)                                                                                     | 250 |
| 65 | Columbia DB 7483 | Spoonful/I've Got My Eyes On You Baby                                                                 | 120 |
| 65 | Columbia DB 7607 | I Gotta See My Baby Everyday/Headin' Back (To New Orleans)                                            | 90  |
| 95 | Tenth Planet TP | THE RISE AND FALL OF BERNIE GRIPPLESTONE & THE SPIDERS FROM HULL (LP, gatefold sleeve, 1,000 only)     | 15  |

(see also Beat Boys, Mark Peters)

### RATS (2)
| 64 | Oriole CB 1967 | Parchman Farm/Every Day I Have The Blues | 100 |
| 65 | CBS 201740     | Sack Of Woe/Gimme That Wine           | 100 |

### RATS (3)
| 74 | MAM MAM 113          | Don't Let Go/Dragon Child            | 8  |
| 74 | Goodear Records EAR. 101 | Turtle Dove/Oxford Donna (with p/s)  | 40 |
| 74 | Goodear EAR 101      | Turtle Dove/Oxford Donna (without p/s) | 15 |
| 74 | Goodear EARLH 5003   | FIRST (LP)                           | 18 |

(see also World of Oz)

### RATTLES
| 63 | Philips BF 1277   | The Stomp/Zip A Dee Doo Dah                        | 20  |
| 64 | Decca F 11873     | Bye Bye Johnny/Roll Over Beethoven                 | 25  |
| 64 | Decca F 11936     | Tell Me What I Can Do/Sunbeam At The Sky           | 25  |
| 65 | Fontana TF 618    | Come On And Sing/Candy To Me                       | 25  |
| 66 | Fontana TF 724    | Say All Right/Love Of My Life                      | 6   |
| 70 | Decca F 23058     | The Witch/Geraldine                                | 15  |
| 71 | Decca F 23119     | You Can't Have Sunshine Everyday/Where Is The Friend | 15 |
| 71 | Decca FR 13243    | The Devil's On The Loose/I Know You Don't Know     | 20  |
| 73 | Decca FR 13390    | Devils Son/What Do I Care                          | 125 |
| 64 | Decca DFE 8568    | TEENBEAT FROM THE STAR CLUB HAMBURG (EP)           | 100 |
| 64 | Philips BL 7614   | TWIST AT THE STAR CLUB HAMBURG (LP)                | 30  |
| 67 | Mercury MG 1127   | GREATEST HITS (LP)                                 | 30  |
| 71 | Decca SKL-R 5088  | THE RATTLES (LP)                                   |     |

(see also Wonderland )

### RATTLING THRONTONS
| 80 | Beat Street BEAT 1 | RATTLING THRONTONS EP | 15 |

### CHRIS RAVEL & RAVERS
| 63 | Decca F 11696 | I Do/Don't You Dig This Kind Of Beat | 20 |

*(see also Chris Andrews)*

## RAVEN
| | | | |
|---|---|---|---|
| 80 | Neat NEAT 06 | Don't Need Your Money/Wiped Out (p/s) | 8 |
| 81 | Neat NEAT 11 | Hard Ride/Crazy World (p/s) | 6 |
| 82 | Neat NEAT 1512 | CRASH BANG WALLOP (Crash Bang Wallop/Firepower/Run Them Down/Rock Hard) (12" EP, mauve splattered vinyl) | 15 |
| 86 | WEA A 9453 | Gimme Some Lovin' (no p/s) | 8 |
| 83 | Neat NEATP1001 | ROCK UNTIL YOU DROP (reissue picture disc LP) | 15 |

## JON RAVEN
| | | | |
|---|---|---|---|
| 70s | Broadside | HARVEST (LP, with book) | 15 |
| 71 | Argo ZFB 29 | KATE OF COALBROOKDALE (LP, as Jon & Mike Raven with Jean Ward) | 100 |
| 73 | Trailer LER 2083 | SONGS OF A CHANGING WORLD (LP, with Nic Jones & Tony Rose, red label with insert) | 25 |
| 76 | Broadside BRO 117 | HARVEST (LP) | 50 |
| 81 | Dingles DIN 319 | REGAL SLIP (LP) | 30 |

*(see also Halliard, Black Country Three, John Kirkpatrick)*

## MICHAEL RAVEN AND JOAN MILLS
| | | | |
|---|---|---|---|
| 70 | Roman Head RH 021 | A COLLECTION OF FOLKSONGS AND GUITAR MUSIC (LP, 99 copies only) | 80 |
| 72 | Folk Heritage FHR 047 | DEATH AND THE LADY (LP) | 250 |
| 74 | Folk Heritage FHR 053 | THE JOLLY MACHINE (LP) | 50 |

## MIKE RAVEN
| | | | |
|---|---|---|---|
| 66 | Xtra 1046 | GUITAR MAGIC (LP) | 30 |

## PAUL RAVEN (1)
| | | | |
|---|---|---|---|
| 61 | Parlophone R 4812 | Walk On Boy/All Grown Up | 8 |
| 61 | Parlophone R 4842 | Tower Of Strength/Livin' The Blues | 8 |

## PAUL RAVEN (2)
| | | | |
|---|---|---|---|
| 68 | MCA MU 1024 | Musical Man/Wait For Me | 15 |
| 68 | MCA MU1035 | Soul Thing/We'll Go Where The World Can't | 12 |

*(see also Rubber Bucket)*

## SIMON RAVEN
| | | | |
|---|---|---|---|
| 66 | Piccadilly 7N 35301 | I Wonder If She Remembers Me/Sea Of Love | 60 |

## RAVENS ROCK GROUP
| | | | |
|---|---|---|---|
| 61 | Pye International 7N 25077 | The Ghoul Friend/Career Girl | 20 |

## RAVENS (2)
| | | | |
|---|---|---|---|
| 63 | Oriole CB 1910 | I Just Wanna Hear You Say/Send Me A Letter | 30 |

## RAVE ONS
| | | | |
|---|---|---|---|
| 60s | Sounds Good MT 103 | She's A Spoon/Keep Wrong | 120 |

## RAVERS
| | | | |
|---|---|---|---|
| 69 | Upsetter US 312 | Babam Bam/UPSETTERS: Medical Operation | 125 |

## RAW DEAL (1)
| | | | |
|---|---|---|---|
| 78 | Honky Tonk HTEP 44 | Struck Down By Your Love/Rocky Rollin Road/Taking My Time/They're Red Hot (p/s) | 12 |

## RAW DEAL (2)
| | | | |
|---|---|---|---|
| 81 | White Witch WIT 701 | Out Of My Head/In The Mood (no p/s) | 50 |
| 81 | Neat NEAT 12 | Lonewolf/Take The Sky (p/s) | 10 |

## RAW DEAL (3)
| | | | |
|---|---|---|---|
| 95 | Mental Disorder MAD 666 | THE LEGENDARY RAW DEAL (10" LP) | 12 |

## PETER RAWES
| | | | |
|---|---|---|---|
| 87 | Official OFFA 5 | Why Should I Ask Her To Stay?/Theme From Shark/Theme From Forever (with Jet Harris) (p/s) | 6 |

*(see also Jet Harris)*

## LOU RAWLS
| | | | |
|---|---|---|---|
| 65 | Capitol CL 15398 | Three O'Clock In The Morning/Nothing Really Feels The Same | 10 |
| 66 | Capitol CL 15465 | Love Is A Hurtin' Thing/Memory Lane | 10 |
| 67 | Capitol CL 15488 | You Can Bring Me All Your Heartaches/A Woman Who's A Woman | 15 |
| 67 | Capitol CL 15499 | Dead End Street/Yes It Hurts Doesn't It | 20 |
| 67 | Capitol CL 15507 | Show Business/When Loves Goes Wrong | 25 |
| 67 | Capitol CL 15515 | Hard To Get Thing Called Love/(How Do You Say) I Don't Love You Anymore | 10 |
| 67 | Capitol CL 15522 | Little Drummer Boy/Child With A Toy | 8 |
| 68 | Capitol CL 15533 | My Ancestors/Evil Woman | 8 |
| 68 | Capitol CL 15548 | You're Good For Me/Soul Serenade | 10 |
| 68 | Capitol CL 15560 | Down Here On The Ground/I'm Satisfied | 8 |
| 69 | Capitol CL 15583 | It's You/Sweet Charity | 8 |
| 69 | Capitol CL 15611 | Your Good Thing (Is About To End)/Season Of The Witch | 8 |
| 70 | Capitol CL 15630 | You've Made Me So Very Happy/Let's Burn Down The Cornfield | 5 |
| 74 | Bell BELL 1390 | She's Gone/Hourglass | 5 |
| 63 | Capitol EAP-1 20646 | LOST AND LOOKIN' (EP) | 50 |
| 65 | Capitol T 1824 | BLACK AND BLUE (LP) | 25 |
| 66 | Capitol (S)T 2459 | LIVE (LP) | 20 |
| 67 | Capitol (S)T 2566 | SOULIN' (LP) | 25 |
| 67 | Capitol (S)T 2632 | CARRYIN' ON! (LP) | 20 |
| 68 | Capitol (S)T 2864 | FEELIN' GOOD (LP) | 30 |
| 69 | Capitol ST 2927 | YOU'RE GOOD FOR ME (LP) | 20 |
| 69 | Capitol E-ST 215 | THE WAY IT WAS THE WAY IT IS (LP) | 20 |

## RAW MATERIAL
| | | | |
|---|---|---|---|
| 69 | Evolution E 2441 | Time And Illusion/Bobo's Party | 60 |
| 69 | Evolution E 2445 | Hi There Hallelujah/Days Of The Fighting Cock | 50 |
| 70 | Evolution E 24495 | Travelling Man (Part 1)/Part 2 | 50 |
| 71 | RCA Neon NE 1002 | Ride On Pony/Religion | 50 |

| 70 | Evolution Z 1006 | RAW MATERIAL (LP) | 1000 |
| 71 | RCA Neon NE 8 | TIME IS (LP, gatefold sleeve) | 1000 |

*(see also Deep Feelings, Shoot)*

**ANNITA RAY**

| 62 | MGM 1177 | Wouldn't It Be Lovely/I'm In Love With Jim | 6 |

**DANNY RAY**

| 76 | Doctor DR 01 | REVOLUTION ROCK (LP) | 30 |

**DANNY RAY & FALCONS**

| 70 | MCA MK 5037 | Scorpion/I Love You Girl | 10 |

**DIANE RAY**

| 63 | Mercury AMT 1209 | Please Don't Talk To The Lifeguard/That's All I Want From You | 22 |

**FROGGIE RAY**

| 71 | Big BG 313 | Uncle Charlie/Party Version | 8 |
| 71 | Big BG 314 | Half Moon/RUPIE EDWARDS ALL STARS: Full Moon | 7 |

**JAMES RAY**

| 62 | Pye International 7N 25126 | If You Gotta Make A Fool Of Somebody/It's Been A Drag | 25 |
| 62 | Pye International 7N 25147 | Itty Bitty Pieces/You Remember The Face | 20 |

**JOHNNIE RAY**

| 53 | Columbia SCM 5015 | Walkin' My Baby Back Home/The Lady Drinks Champagne (B-side with the Four Lads) | 20 |
| 53 | Columbia SCM 5033 | Ma Says, Pa Says/A Full Time Job (with Doris Day) | 20 |
| 53 | Columbia SCM 5041 | Whiskey And Gin/Tell The Lady I Said Goodbye | 20 |
| 53 | Columbia SCM 5074 | Please Don't Talk About Me When I'm Gone/Coffee And Cigarettes (B-side with the Four Lads) | 10 |
| 54 | Columbia SCM 5111 | Nobody's Sweetheart/I Can't Escape From You | 10 |
| 54 | Columbia SCM 5122 | She Didn't Say Nothin' At All/I'm Just A Shadow Of Myself | 10 |
| 57 | Philips JK 1004 | You Don't Owe Me A Thing/Look Homeward, Angel (jukebox issue) | 10 |
| 57 | Philips JK 1011 | So Long/I Miss You So (jukebox issue) | 10 |
| 57 | Philips JK 1016 | Yes, Tonight, Josephine/No Wedding Today (jukebox issue) | 10 |
| 57 | Philips JK 1025 | Build Your Love (On A Strong Foundation)/Street Of Memories (jukebox issue) | 10 |
| 57 | Philips JK 1026 | Up Above My Head, I Hear Music On The Air/Good Evening Friends/Memories (with Frankie Laine, jukebox issue only) | 10 |
| 57 | Philips JK 1033 | Pink Sweater Angel/Texas Tambourine (jukebox issue) | 30 |
| 58 | Philips PB 785 | Miss Me Just A Little/Soliloquy Of A Fool | 5 |
| 58 | Philips PB 808 | Strollin' Girl/Plant A Little Seed | 5 |
| 58 | Philips PB 829 | Lonely For A Letter/Endlessly | 5 |
| 58 | Philips PB 849 | No Regrets/Up Until Now | 5 |
| 58 | Philips PB 884 | What More Can I Say/You're The One Who Knows | 5 |
| 59 | Philips PB 901 | When's Your Birthday, Baby/One Man's Love Song Is Another Man's Blues | 5 |
| 59 | Philips PB 918 | Call Me Yours/Here And Now | 5 |
| 59 | Philips PB 952 | You're All That I Live For/I'll Never Fall In Love Again | 6 |
| 59 | Philips PB 952 | You're All That I Live For/I'll Never Fall In Love Again (78) | 20 |
| 60 | Philips PB 990 | When It's Springtime In The Rockies/Wagon Wheels | 6 |
| 60 | Philips PB 1025 | Before You/I'll Make You Mine | 6 |
| 60 | Philips PB 1047 | Tell Me/Don't Leave Me Now | 5 |
| 60 | London HLA 9216 | In The Heart Of A Fool/Let's Forget It Now | 5 |
| 61 | Philips PB 1126 | An Ordinary Couple/Cool Water | 5 |
| 62 | London HLG 9484 | I Believe (with Timi Yuro)/TIMI YURO: Smile | 15 |
| 63 | Brunswick 05884 | Lookout Chatanooga/After My Laughter Came Tears | 5 |
| 69 | Pye 7N 17691 | Wise To The Ways Of The World/Since I Lost You Baby | 5 |
| 69 | Pye 7N 17760 | Long And Lonely Nights/Brokenhearted Me, Evilhearted You | 5 |
| 76 | EPIC MEPC 4533 | Cry/The Little White Cloud That Cried | 5 |

*(see also Frankie Laine & Johnnie Ray, Timi Yuro)*

**RICARDO RAY**

| 68 | Roulette RO 501 | Nitty Gritty/Mony Mony | 20 |

**WADE RAY**

| 63 | London HL 9700 | Burning Desire/Two Red Red Lips | 8 |

**RAY & COLLUNEY**

| 71 | Westwood WRS 001 | TYRANTS OF ENGLAND (LP) | 40 |

**RAY & HIS COURT**

| 00 | Jazzman JM 014 | Soul Freedom/RAY & HIS FAMILY: Cookie Crumbs | 5 |

**CHRIS(TINE) RAYBURN**

| 63 | Parlophone R 5098 | Slow Loving Woman/Same Old Places | 10 |
| 64 | Parlophone R 5144 | I've Paid My Last Tear/You Forgot To Say When | 10 |
| 66 | Parlophone R 5422 | I Wanna Be In Love Again/Another Night Alone | 10 |
| 68 | Music Factory CUB 2 | One Way Ticket/Photograph Of Love | 10 |
| 69 | Pye 7N 17679 | Skip A Rope/Starlight (as Christine Rayburn) | 10 |
| 66 | Parlophone PCS7001 | CHRIS RAYBURN (LP) | 25 |

**MARGIE RAYBURN**

| 56 | Capitol CL 14532 | The Wedding Song/That's The Chance I've Got To Take | 10 |
| 57 | London HLU 8515 | I'm Available/If You Were | 25 |
| 58 | London HLU 8648 | I Would/Alright, But It Won't Be Easy | 18 |

**CLYDE RAY**

| 57 | Columbia DB 3875 | Follow Me/Steady As A Rock | 10 |
| 58 | Columbia DB 4106 | Locked In The Arms Of Love/I'm Not Afraid Anymore | 10 |

**ANTHONY RAYE**

| 80 | Grapevine GRP 147 | Give Me One More Chance/Hold On To What You've Got | 8 |

**SOL RAYE**

| 63 | Oriole CB 1855 | Dear Michelle/I Love You Because | 10 |

MINT VALUE £

| | | |
|---|---|---|
| 67 | Deram DM 154 | While I'm Here/To Be With You ........................................... 12 |

**BILLY RAYMOND**

| | | |
|---|---|---|
| 58 | HMV POP 503 | Making Love/I Would ........................................... 5 |
| 58 | HMV POP 526 | One In Particular/Seven Daughters ........................................... 5 |
| 59 | HMV POP 614 | Charlie Is Their Darling/Loch Lomond ........................................... 5 |

**DANNY RAYMOND**

| | | |
|---|---|---|
| 71 | Big Shot BI 587 | Sister Big Stuff/BOY FRIDAY: Free Man ........................................... 20 |

**LEE RAYMOND WITH COSTELLO SISTERS**

| | | |
|---|---|---|
| 55 | Brunswick 05438 | Foolishly Yours/Baby Darling ........................................... 10 |

**MARK RAYMOND & CROWD**

| | | |
|---|---|---|
| 64 | Columbia DB 7308 | Girls/Remember Me To Julie ........................................... 15 |

**TONY RAYMOND**

| | | |
|---|---|---|
| 59 | Fontana H 213 | Broken-Hearted Melody/This Earth Is Mine ........................................... 8 |
| 62 | Oriole CB 1708 | Handful Of Songs/She'll Have To Go ........................................... 8 |
| 62 | Oriole CB 1777 | The Infant King/Because Of You ........................................... 6 |

**IVOR RAYMONDE & HIS ORCHESTRA**

| | | |
|---|---|---|
| 65 | Mercury MF 866 | Feelin' Fruggy/Grotty ........................................... 12 |

**JULIE RAYNE**

| | | |
|---|---|---|
| 59 | HMV POP 665 | Waltz Me Around/Love Where Can You Be? ........................................... 10 |
| 60 | HMV POP 785 | Bim Bam Bom/One More Time ........................................... 10 |
| 61 | HMV POP 868 | Green With Envy Purple With Passion/My First Romance ........................................... 10 |
| 63 | Windsor WPS 123 | Faithfully/Free To Love ........................................... 10 |
| 64 | Windsor WPS 128 | You Can't Come Back/Straight To Your Arms ........................................... 10 |

**LISA RAYNE**

| | | |
|---|---|---|
| 65 | Fontana TF 563 | Don't Ever Change/It Had To Be You ........................................... 10 |

**MARTIN RAYNOR & SECRETS**

| | | |
|---|---|---|
| 65 | Columbia DB 7563 | Candy To Me/You're A Wonderful One ........................................... 60 |

*(see also Secrets, Simon's Secrets, Clifford T. Ward)*

**MIKE RAYNOR & THE CONDORS**

| | | |
|---|---|---|
| 67 | Decca F22690 | Is She A Woman NOw/My Shy Serenade (export p/s) ........................................... 40 |

**RAYS**

| | | |
|---|---|---|
| 57 | London HLU 8505 | Silhouettes/Daddy Cool ........................................... 25 |

**RAZAR**

| | | |
|---|---|---|
| 78 | Polydor 2058 983 | Ascension Day/Ain't No Mystery (company sleeve) ........................................... 35 |
| 78 | Charisma CB 320 | Idle Rich/One Room Doom (p/s) ........................................... 10 |

*(see also Third World War, Soho Jets, Nervous Germans)*

**RAZBERRY HOLIDAY BAND**

| | | |
|---|---|---|
| 89 | Caleche LIS 001 | Hangover Square/Promise ........................................... 20 |

**RAZORCUTS**

| | | |
|---|---|---|
| 86 | Subway Org. SUBWAY 5 | Big Pink Cake/I'll Still Be There (foldover p/s with insert, poly bag, 2,000 only) ........... 18 |
| 86 | Subway Org. SUBWAY 8 | Sorry To Embarrass You/Summer In Your Heart (p/s, with insert, 2,000 only) ............... 15 |
| 87 | Sha La La BaBaBaBaBa 02 | Sad Kaleidoscope/TALULAH GOSH: I Told You So (flexidisc p/s, 2,500 only) ................. 10 |
| 80s | Caff CAFF 10 | Sometimes I Worry About You/For Always/Sorry To Embarrass You/ Music From The Big Pink (foldaround p/s with insert, 500 only) ........................................... 20 |
| 88 | Creation CRELP 026 | STORYTELLER (LP) ........................................... 25 |
| 89 | Creation CRELP 045 | THE WORLD KEEPS TURNING (LP) ........................................... 20 |

*(see also Cinematics, Red Chair Fadeaway)*

**RAZORLIGHT**

| | | |
|---|---|---|
| 04 | Vertigo 986 710-1 | UP ALL NIGHT (LP, with free 7") ........................................... 18 |
| 06 | Vertigo 17010901 | RAZORLIGHT (LP) ........................................... 20 |
| 09 | Vertigo 17050004 | SLIPWAY FIRES (LP) ........................................... 18 |

**RAZOR'S EDGE**

| | | |
|---|---|---|
| 66 | Stateside SS 532 | Let's Call It A Day, Girl/April ........................................... 15 |

**RAZZY**

| | | |
|---|---|---|
| 74 | MCA 2006437 | I Hate Hate/Singing Other Peoples Songs ........................................... 8 |

**CHRIS REA**

| | | |
|---|---|---|
| 74 | Magnet MAG 10 | So Much Love/Born To Lose (no p/s) ........................................... 25 |

**REACTA**

| | | |
|---|---|---|
| 79 | Battery Operated WAC 1 | Stop The World/SUS (p/s) ........................................... 100 |

*(see also Television Personalities)*

**REACTION (1)**

| | | |
|---|---|---|
| 68 | President PT 208 | That Man/Falling In Love With You ........................................... 12 |

**REACTION (2)**

| | | |
|---|---|---|
| 70 | Columbia Blue Beat DB 119 | Oh Me, Oh My/RECO: It's Love ........................................... 12 |
| 70 | Attack ATT 8022 | You Yes You/CIMARONS: Be There ........................................... 15 |

*(see also Ezz Reco, Joe Higgs)*

**REACTION (3)**

| | | |
|---|---|---|
| 78 | Island WIP 6437 | I Can't Resist/I Am A Case (p/s) ........................................... 20 |

*(see also Talk Talk, Mark Hollis)*

**REACTION (4)**

| | | |
|---|---|---|
| 87 | Waterloo Sunset RUSS 105 | Make Up Your Mind/Four By Four ........................................... 25 |

**PAT READER**

| | | |
|---|---|---|
| 60 | Triumph RGM 1024 | Ricky/Dear Daddy ........................................... 60 |
| 62 | Piccadilly 7N 35077 | Cha Cha On The Moon/May Your Heart Stay Young Forever ........................................... 30 |
| 63 | Oriole CB 1903 | Helpless/Lover's Lane ........................................... 30 |

**BERTICE READING**

| | | |
|---|---|---|
| 55 | Parlophone R 4057 | Songs From "Jazz Train" Parts 1 & 2 (with Edric Connor) ........................................... 6 |

| 57 | Decca F 10965 | No Flowers By Request/September In The Rain | 15 |
| 58 | Parlophone R 4462 | Rock Baby Rock/It's A Boy | 60 |
| 58 | Parlophone R 4487 | My Big Best Shoes/No More In Life | 10 |

**READY STEADY GO**
78  Storm SR 027 — I Want You Little DArlin/Rocerbilly Blues (no p/s) .......... 5

**REAL MACABRE**
85  Push 2 — White Horses/The Call (p/s) .......... 7

**REALISTS**
78  Stiff OFF 4 — I've Got A Heart/Living in The City (p/s) .......... 6
81  Eccentric YUR 1 — Wonderland/Glad To Be Alive (1000 only, p/s) .......... 7

**REALITY FROM DREAM**
75  (no label) CP 109 — REALITY FROM DREAM (LP, private pressing) .......... 140

**REALITY (1)**
67  Birchwood BW 01 — Simple Skies/Ran Into The Forest .......... 150

**REALITY (2)**
82  Subversive SUB — BLIND TO THE TRUTH (EP, foldout sleeve and insert) .......... 10
84  Fight Back FIGHT 3 — WHO KILLED THE GOLDEN GOOSE? (EP) .......... 10

**REALITY CONTROL**
83  Volume VOL 7 — THE REPRODUCTION OF HATE EP .......... 8

**REAL KIDS**
78  Bronze BRO 54 — All Kindsa Girls/Common At Noon (p/s) .......... 8
78  Bronze BRON 509 — REAL KIDS (LP) .......... 22

**REALLY FREE**
78  Sya RFSM 002 — New Day Dawning/Thank You Jesus .......... 10

**REALLY 3RDS**
81  EJSP 9610 — Everyday Everywhere/Daptapper (no p/s) .......... 35

**REALM**
66  CBS 202044 — Hard Time Loving You/Certain Kind Of Girl .......... 35
*(see also Earl Preston & Realms)*

**REAL MCCOY**
| 67 | Fontana TF 794 | Show Me How You Milk A Cow/I Paid For My Laughs | 8 |
| 68 | Target 7N 17669 | Quick Joey Small/Happiness Is Love | 20 |
| 68 | Pye 7N 17618 | I Get So Excited/Somebody's Taken Maria Away | 8 |
| 69 | Pye 7N 17669 | Quick Joey Small/Happiness Is Love | 8 |
| 69 | Pye 7N 17704 | Round The Gum Tree/I Will | 8 |
| 69 | Pye 7N 17772 | Gitarzan/Anytime You Need Me | 8 |
| 69 | Pye 7N 17850 | Many The Memories/She's Different, She's Beautiful | 8 |
| 71 | CBS 7065 | I'll Give You Things/Baby, Go Home | 8 |
| 70 | Marble Arch MAL 1251 | THIS IS THE REAL McCOY (LP) | 20 |
*(see also Tony Colton)*

**REALMS**
70s  Summertime BUSS 11 — Happiness Is Your Name/Happiest Dread .......... 10

**REAL THING**
72  Bell BLL 1232 — Vicious Circles Parts 1 & 2 .......... 5
81  Calibre CAB 109 — I Believe In You/You're My Number One .......... 30
81  Calibre CABL 109 — I Believe In You (Extended Version)/You're My Number One (12") .......... 30
*(see also Chants)*

**REASONS**
78  Island WIP 6467 — Hard Day At The Office/Baby Bright Eyes (p/s) .......... 30

**REBEL**
81  Bridge House BHS 2 — Rocka Shocka/Drift Away (p/s) .......... 12
86  Flying Pig REBS 1 — Valentino/Lonely Traveller (p/s, with free single) .......... 12

**REBEL CHRISTENING**
85  Clay 12 CLAY 44 — TRIBAL EYE (12" EP, p/s) .......... 12

**REBEL ROUSERS**
68  Fontana TF 973 — Should I?/As I Look .......... 200
*(see also Cliff Bennett & Rebel Rousers, Soul Sounds)*

**REBELS**
78  Rigid IS REB 1029 — Suicide/The Leader Of The Rebellion .......... 250

**REBELS & ALLIES**
79  Brixton Sound BS01234 — BROKEN HEART (LP) .......... 20

**REBELS (JAMAICA)**
70  Bullet BU 440 — Nice Grind/SIDNEY ALL STARS: Nice Grind - Version .......... 10
70  Trojan TR 7779 — It's All In The Game/Easy Come .......... 12
76  Black Wax WAX 16 — Rhodesia/Version .......... 20
*(see also The Pioneers)*

**REBELS (U.K.)**
67  Page One POF 017 — Hard To Love You/Call Me .......... 40

**REBOUNDS**
64  Fontana TF 461 — Help Me/The World Is Mine .......... 25

**REBS**
58  Capitol CL 14932 — Bunky/Renegade .......... 15

**RECKLESS**
92  Pulse-8 12LOSE 24 — Time To Make The Floor Burn (The Reckless Hypermix)/Take Me (Ruff Mix)/Take Me (Uplifting Piano Mix) (12", p/s) .......... 25

## RECO

| | | | |
|---|---|---|---|
| 69 | Downtown DT 417 | Quando Quando/Reg 'A' Jeg (as Reco & Rudies) | 25 |
| 69 | Jackpot JP 710 | Memory Of Don Drummond/THE TOBIES: Resting | 15 |
| 69 | Treasure Isle TI 7052 | The Lion Speaks/ANDY CAPP: Pop A Top | 10 |
| 69 | Pama ECO 14 | RECO IN REGGAE LAND (LP) | 120 |

*(see also Reaction, Don Reco, Rico Rodriguez, Father Sketto, Joe Monsano, Slim Smith, Laurel Aitken)*

## DON RECO

| | | | |
|---|---|---|---|
| 71 | Big Shot BI 597 | Waterloo Rock/LLOYD'S ALL STARS: Walls Soul | 20 |

*(see also Reco)*

## EZZ RECO & LAUNCHERS

| | | | |
|---|---|---|---|
| 64 | Columbia DB 7217 | King Of Kings/Blue Beat Dance | 12 |
| 64 | Columbia DB 7222 | Little Girl/The Bluest Beat | 7 |
| 64 | Columbia DB 7290 | Please Come Back/At A Party | 7 |
| 64 | Columbia SEG 8326 | JAMAICAN BLUE BEAT (EP) | 30 |

*(see also Reaction)*

## RECORD PLAYERS

| | | | |
|---|---|---|---|
| 80 | Wreckord WRECK 002 | Give An Inch/Squirming In The Vermin By The Bonny Banks Of Clyde/ 67/Parasite (p/s) | 6 |

## RECRUITS

| | | | |
|---|---|---|---|
| 89 | SRT 9KS 1994 RE 2 | See My Face/Dream Heaven Scene (p/s) | 20 |

## RECTIFY

| | | | |
|---|---|---|---|
| 88 | Taffcore TAFF 001 | 20TH CENTURY EP (foldout p/s) | 10 |

## RED ALERT (1)

| | | | |
|---|---|---|---|
| 69 | Total TL3 | Witch Woman/Sabra | 50 |

## RED ALERT (2)

| | | | |
|---|---|---|---|
| 80 | Guardian GM-RA/B 61 | BORDER GUARDS (EP) | 250 |
| 82 | No Future OI 5 | In Britain/Screaming At The Nation/Murder Missile (p/s) | 10 |
| 82 | No Future OI 33 | Take No Prisoners/Empire Of Crime/Sell Out (p/s) | 10 |
| 83 | No Future OI 20 | City Invasion/Negative Reaction (p/s) | 8 |
| 83 | No Future OI 27 | THERE'S A GUITAR BURNING (12" EP) | 15 |
| 83 | No Future PUNK 5 | WE'VE GOT THE POWER (LP) | 15 |

## RED ALERT (3)

| | | | |
|---|---|---|---|
| 82 | Steel City AJS7R | Run To Ground/Wild You (no p/s) | 10 |

## RED ALLIGATOR

| | | | |
|---|---|---|---|
| 69 | Youngblood YB1004 | Real Cool/Slow Down | 18 |

*(see also Jimmy Powell)*

## RED BALUNE

| | | | |
|---|---|---|---|
| 78 | MCCB 001 | Capitalist Kid/Spider In Love (p/s) | 12 |

## DANNY RED

| | | | |
|---|---|---|---|
| 93 | Abba Jahnoi AJ 001 | Jah Is Here/Version (12") | 18 |

## RED FLY

| | | | |
|---|---|---|---|
| 70 | Red Fly RF 01 | Colour It Black/Scream It Out | 30 |

## RED STRIPE

| | | | |
|---|---|---|---|
| 80 | Snotty Snail NELCOL 4 | Inside Of Pain/Wogs Go Home/Trois Vielles Sacs Assises Lisant (hand stamped sleeve and insert) | 100 |

## RED (1)

| | | | |
|---|---|---|---|
| 77 | Electric WOT EP 1 | RIDER IN THE SKY EP (p/s) | 10 |

## RED (2)

| | | | |
|---|---|---|---|
| 83 | Jigsaw SAW 2 | RED (LP, private pressing) | 25 |

## RED BEANS & RICE

| | | | |
|---|---|---|---|
| 80 | Chiswick CHIS 124 | That Driving Beat/Throw It In The Grass | 10 |

## REDBONE

| | | | |
|---|---|---|---|
| 70 | CBS 5061 | Crazy Cajun Cakewalk Band/Night Come Down | 5 |
| 70 | CBS 5326 | Maggie/New Blue Sermonette | 6 |
| 70 | CBS 64069 | REDBONE (LP) | 15 |
| 70 | CBS 64198 | POTLATCH (LP) | 15 |
| 72 | Epic EQ 30815 | MESSAGE FROM A DRUM (LP, quadraphonic) | 20 |

## REDCAPS

| | | | |
|---|---|---|---|
| 63 | Decca F 11716 | Shout/Little Things You Do | 20 |
| 63 | Decca F 11789 | Talkin' 'Bout You/Come On Girl | 10 |
| 64 | Decca F 11903 | Mighty Fine Girl/Funny Things | 10 |

## REDCELL

| | | | |
|---|---|---|---|
| 92 | B12 B1205 | REDCELL EP (12") | 25 |
| 92 | B12 B1205 | REDCELL EP (12", purple vinyl) | 80 |
| 92 | B12 B1207 | RETREAT FROM UNPLEASANT REALITIES EP (12") | 40 |
| 92 | B12 B1207 | RETREAT FROM UNPLEASANT REALITIES EP (12", blue vinyl) | 60 |
| 92 | B12 B1207 | RETREAT FROM UNPLEASANT REALITIES EP (12", red vinyl) | 60 |
| 93 | B12 B1208 | INTERIM OUTERIM EP(12") | 15 |
| 93 | B12 B1208 | INTERIM OUTERIM EP (12", white vinyl) | 60 |
| 96 | B12 B1215 | Untitled (12", White label promo) | 60 |

## RED CHAIR FADEAWAY

| | | | |
|---|---|---|---|
| 89 | Cosmic Eng. M. CTA 103 | Let It Happen/Myra/Dragonfly/Grasshopper (12", p/s, 500 only) | 15 |
| 90 | Cosmic Eng. M. CTA 105 | Mr Jones/Chimney Pots/Faraway Lights/Out Of The Grey (12", p/s, 450 only) | 15 |
| 91 | Waterbomb SPLAT 002 | Never Remember/FUDGE: Girlwish (flexi, p/s) | 12 |
| 91 | Tangerine MM 10 | CURIOUSER AND CURIOUSER (LP, foldaround sleeve with booklet, no'd) | 20 |

*(see also Razorcuts)*

## RED CRAYOLA

| | | | |
|---|---|---|---|
| 78 | Radar SAM 88 | Pink Stainless Tail/13TH FLOOR ELEVATORS She Lives (In A Time Of Her Own) (promo) | 15 |

| | | | |
|---|---|---|---|
| 78 | Radar ADA 22 | Wives In Orbit/Yik Yak (p/s, red vinyl) | 7 |
| 78 | Radar RAD 12 | THE PARABLES OF ARABLE LAND (LP, stickered sleeve) | 15 |

**FREDDIE REDD**

| | | | |
|---|---|---|---|
| 58 | Nixa NJL 19 | GET HAPPY (LP) | 200 |

**GENE REDD & GLOBETROTTERS**

| | | | |
|---|---|---|---|
| 59 | Parlophone R 4584 | Red River Valley Rock/Kentucky Home Rock | 15 |

**OTIS REDDING**

**SINGLES : SINGLES AND LPS**

| | | | |
|---|---|---|---|
| 64 | London HLK 9833 | Pain In My Heart/Something Is Worrying Me | 25 |
| 64 | London HLK 9876 | Come To Me/Don't Leave Me This Way | 25 |
| 65 | Atlantic AT 4024 | Mr Pitiful/That's How Strong My Love Is | 25 |
| 65 | Sue WI 362 | Shout Bamalama/Fat Girl | 30 |
| 65 | Atlantic AT 4029 | I've Been Loving You Too Long/Winter Wonderland (unissued, demos only) | 75 |
| 65 | Atlantic AT 4039 | Respect/I've Been Loving You Too Long | 18 |
| 65 | Atlantic AT 4050 | My Girl/Down In The Valley | 15 |
| 66 | Atlantic AT 4080 | (I Can't Get No) Satisfaction/Any Ole Way | 12 |
| 66 | Atlantic 584 019 | My Lover's Prayer/Don't Mess With Cupid | 12 |
| 66 | Atlantic 584 030 | I Can't Turn You Loose/Just One More Day | 10 |
| 66 | Atlantic 584 049 | Fa-Fa-Fa-Fa-Fa (Sad Song)/Good To Me | 10 |
| 67 | Atlantic 584 070 | Try A Little Tenderness/I'm Sick Y'all | 10 |
| 67 | Atlantic 584 091 | Respect/These Arms Of Mine | 8 |
| 67 | Atlantic 584 092 | My Girl/Mr Pitiful | 8 |
| 67 | Stax 601 005 | Day Tripper/Shake (dark blue labels) | 10 |
| 67 | Stax 601 007 | Let Me Come On Home/I Love You More Than Words Can Say (dark blue labels) | 10 |
| 67 | Stax 601 011 | Shake (live)/634-5789 (live) | 10 |
| 67 | Stax 601 017 | The Glory Of Love/I'm Coming Home | 8 |
| 67 | Stax 601 027 | (I Can't Get No) Satisfaction/I've Been Loving You Too Long | 8 |
| 68 | Stax 601 031 | (Sittin' On) The Dock Of The Bay/My Sweet Lorene | 8 |
| 68 | Stax 601 040 | The Happy Song/Open The Door | 8 |
| 68 | Pye International 7N 25463 | She's All Right/Gama Lama | 10 |
| 68 | Atlantic 584 199 | Hard To Handle/Amen | 8 |
| 68 | Atlantic 584 220 | Champagne And Wine/I've Got Dreams To Remember | 10 |
| 68 | Atlantic 584 234 | Papa's Got A Brand New Bag/Direct Me | 8 |
| 69 | Atlantic 584 249 | A Lover's Question/You Made A Man Out Of Me | 10 |
| 69 | Atco 226 001 | Love Man/That's How Strong My Love Is | 10 |
| 69 | Atco 226 002 | Free Me/Higher And Higher | 8 |
| 69 | Evolution E 2442 | She's All Right/Tuff Enuff | 15 |
| 70 | Atco 226 012 | Look At That Girl/That's A Good Idea | 12 |
| 70 | Atco 2091 020 | Wonderful World/Security | 8 |
| 71 | Atlantic 2091 062 | I've Been Loving You Too Long/Try A Little Tenderness | 5 |
| 71 | Atlantic 2091 112 | (Sittin' On) The Dock Of The Bay/Respect/Mr Pitiful (reissue) | 5 |
| 72 | Atlantic K 10206 | White Christmas/Merry Christmas, Baby | 5 |
| 05 | Atco 002 | Loving By The Pound/BENNY TROY: I Wanna Give You Tomorrow (promo, 500 only) | 10 |
| 08 | Kent Select CITY 008 | Loving By The Pound/BARBARA AND THE BROWNS: I'm Gonna Start A War | 5 |
| 66 | Sue IEP 710 | EARLY OTIS REDDING (EP) | 100 |
| 65 | Atlantic ATL 5029 | THE GREAT OTIS REDDING SINGS SOUL BALLADS (LP) | 50 |
| 66 | Atlantic ATL 5041 | OTIS BLUE: OTIS REDDING SINGS SOUL (LP) | 40 |
| 66 | Atlantic 587 011 | THE SOUL ALBUM (LP) | 30 |
| 66 | Atlantic 587 035 | THE GREAT OTIS REDDING SINGS SOUL BALLADS (LP, reissue) | 20 |
| 66 | Atlantic 587/588 036 | OTIS BLUE: OTIS REDDING SINGS SOUL (LP, reissue, mono/stereo) | 20 |
| 67 | Atlantic 587/588 050 | COMPLETE AND UNBELIEVABLE: THE OTIS REDDING DICTIONARY OF SOUL (LP) | 25 |
| 67 | Atlantic 587 042 | PAIN IN MY HEART (LP) | 25 |
| 67 | Stax VOLT 418 | THE HISTORY OF OTIS REDDING (LP) | 25 |
| 68 | Stax 589 016 | OTIS REDDING IN EUROPE (LP) | 20 |
| 68 | Stax 230 001/231 001 | THE DOCK OF THE BAY (LP) | 20 |
| 68 | Atlantic 587/588 113 | THE IMMORTAL OTIS REDDING (LP) | 25 |
| 68 | Atlantic 587/588 148 | OTIS REDDING AT THE WHISKEY A GO GO, LOS ANGELES (LP) | 20 |
| 69 | Atco 228 025 | LOVE MAN (LP) | 25 |
| 70 | Atlantic 2464 003 | REMEMBERING (LP) | 18 |
| 71 | Atco 2400 018 | TELL THE TRUTH (LP) | 18 |
| 71 | Reprise K 40430 | LIVE AT THE MONTEREY INTERNATIONAL POP FESTIVAL ( LP, shared with Jimi Hendrix) | 30 |

**OTIS REDDING & CARLA THOMAS**

| | | | |
|---|---|---|---|
| 67 | Stax 601 012 | Tramp/Oooh Carla, Oooh Otis (with Carla Thomas) | 8 |
| 67 | Stax 601 021 | Knock On Wood/Let Me Be Good To You | 8 |
| 68 | Stax 601 033 | Lovey Dovey/New Year's Resolution | 8 |
| 67 | Stax 589 007 | THE KING AND QUEEN OF SOUL | 30 |

*(see also Carla Thomas)*

**RED DIRT**

| | | | |
|---|---|---|---|
| 70 | Fontana STL 5540 | RED DIRT (LP) | 1750 |
| 10 | Morgan Bluetown BT 5004 | RED DIRT (LP, reissue, 500 only, with signed and numbered certificate) | 25 |

**RED DRAGON**

| | | | |
|---|---|---|---|
| 86 | Redman Intl. RED 4 | Ease Off/ADMIRAL TIBET: New Tactics (12") | 20 |

**EMMA REDE**

| | | | |
|---|---|---|---|
| 67 | Columbia DB 8136 | Just Like A Man/I Gotta Be With You | 20 |

*(see also Jacky, Jackie Lee, Jackie & Raindrops, Raindrops)*

**TEDDY REDELL**

| | | | |
|---|---|---|---|
| 60 | London HLK 9140 | Judy/Can't You See | 60 |

MINT VALUE £

## REDGEE SEEBOE
74   Bug 38                                   Please Don't Bring Your Sister/Daphnies Brains ..........................................15

## VANESSA REDGRAVE
64   Topic STOP 111                           Hanging On A Tree/Where Have All The Flowers Gone (in title sleeve) ...........6

## MICHAEL REDGRAVE & JULIET MILLS
61   Parlophone R 4804                        No My Darling Daughter/Blimp's Blues ....................................................7

## RED HARVEST
87   Quiet QS 019                             Murder/Fifty Years/Burning Party (p/s) .................................................20

## RED HAWKES
66   ALP 595001                               Friday Night/Lonely Boy ..................................................................50
*(see also Mark Five, Nazareth)*

## REDHEAD
73   UK UK R 38                               We Ran And We Ran/Lookin' For You .......................................................8

## RED HERRING
87   Crystal 717                              Albert Road/Harbour Lights ...............................................................30

## RED HOT
91   Robin Hood RH 005                        Letter To My Baby/Version (12") ..........................................................15

## RED HOT & BLUE
85   Northwood NOR 1                          RED HOT & BLUE (LP) ......................................................................25

## RED HOT CHILI PEPPERS
85   EMI America EA 205                        Hollywood (Africa)/Never Mind (p/s) ...................................................10
85   EMI America 12EA 205                      Hollywood (Africa) (Remix)/Hollywood (Africa) (Dub Mix)/Never Mind (12", p/s) ........12
89   EMI 12MT 70                               KNOCK ME DOWN EP (12", p/s) ..........................................................15
89   EMI 12MT 75                               Higher Ground/Catholic Schoolgirls Rule (p/s) ........................................10
90   EMI 12MTX 85                              TASTE THE PAIN EP (12", push-out sleeve with inner) .................................12
90   EMI 10MTX 85                              TASTE THE PAIN EP (square disc, numbered).............................................12
90   EMI 12MTG 88                              Higher Ground/Catholic Schoolgirls Rule/None As Weird As Me (12", gatefold sleeve).15
90   EMI 12MTPD 88                             Higher Ground/Catholic Schoolgirls Rule/None As Weird As Me (12", picture disc,
                                               card insert)....................................................................12
99   Warner Bros. 9362 47386-1                 CALIFORNICATION (2-LP) ..................................................................30
06   Warner Bros 9362499961                    STADIUM ARCADIUM (4xLP box set with foil outer & 2 booklets) ...........60
06   Warner Bros 9362443911                    STADIUM ARCADIUM (4xLP, standard edition) ..............................20
*(see also Atoms For Peace)*

## RED HOUSE PAINTERS
94   4AD BAD 4004                              Shock Me/Sundays And Holidays/Three-Legged Cat/Shock Me (12", p/s) ..........40
92   4AD CAD 2014                              DOWN COLOURFUL HILL (LP)................................................................80
93   4AD DAD 3008                              RED HOUSE PAINTERS (2-LP, inner sleeves)..............................................80
93   4AD CAD 3016                              RED HOUSE PAINTERS (LP, different release from DAD 3008) ...................60
95   4A DADD 5005                              OCEAN BEACH (LP, 2 x 10" with inner sleeves) .........................................60

## RED LETTERS
79   Burning Bing CPS 025                      SACRED VOICES EP: Sacred Voices/Shot In The Dark/Science Has The Answer (folded
                                               p/s) .........................................................................120

## RED LIGHTS
78   Free Range PF 5                           Never Wanna Leave/Seventeen (p/s) .....................................................70

## RED LINE EXPLOSION
71   Penny Farthing PEN 753                    Sweet Talking Mother/Evil Woman .........................................................8

## RED LONDON
83   Razor RZS 105                             Sten Guns In Sunderland/This Is England/Soul Train/Revolution Times (p/s) ...........12
84   Razor RAZ 10                              THIS IS ENGLAND (LP).....................................................................30

## RED LORRY, YELLOW LORRY
82   Red Rhino RED 20                          Beating My Head/I'm Still Waiting (p/s) .................................................10
83   Red Rhino RED 28                          Take It All/Happy (p/s) .....................................................................5
83   Red Rhino ED 39                           He's Red/See The Fire (p/s) ................................................................7

## RED MEAT
72   Worsley WR 1                              She/My Mind Sleeps On (p/s) .............................................................50

## RED MONEY
90   PF&G PFG 001                              MY ERSTWHILE COMPANION EP .........................................................15

## RED ONION JAZZ BABIES
60   Collector JE 19                           RED ONION JAZZ BABIES (EP) ............................................................10

## JEAN REDPATH
66   Bounty BY 6004                            LOVE LILT AND LAUGHTER (LP) ..........................................................20

## RED PYJAMAS
88   Ride SRT 8KS1750                          Hands Off, Hands On, Lucinda Loves You/Lets Get Happy (p/s)..........................6

## RED RAGE
80   Flicknife FLS 203                         Total Control/I Give You This (p/s) .....................................................40

## RED RIVER BAND
70   Banana BA 35                              I'm Gonna Use What I've Got/Shame Shame........................................8

## REDS
79   A&M AMS 7454                              Whatcha' Doin' To Me/Not You (p/s, green vinyl) ......................................5

## REDSKINS
82   CNT CNT 007                               Lev Bronstein/The Peasant Army (p/s) ..................................................25
83   CNT CNT 016                               Lean On Me!/Unionize! (p/s) ..............................................................7

## RED SQUARES
67   Columbia DB 8160                          Mountain's High/Pity Me ..................................................................20
67   Columbia DB 8257                          True Love Story/Lollipop ..................................................................12

### RED STAR BELGRADE
82  Stage Coach MAIL 36          Mad Dogs And Englishmen/Barricades (p/s) .................................................. 5

### RED TELEVISION
71  Brecht Times                 RED TELEVISION (LP, private pressing with insert)................................ 120

### REDUCERS
78  Vibes XP 1/VR 001            Things Go Wrong/We Are Normal (p/s)........................................................ 50
79  Vibes VR 003                 Man With A Gun/Vengeance/Can't Stop Now (p/s)................................... 50
80  EMI EMI 5028                 Airways/Waiting For No One (p/s) ............................................................ 10

### MIKE REDWAY
64  Oriole CB 1948               Many People/It's So Funny I Could Cry ...................................................... 8
65  CBS 201755                   Darling Take Me Back/That's The Way Love Goes ...................................... 5
65  CBS 202017                   Magic Rocking Chair/When You Go .......................................................... 8
66  CBS 202092                   One Day/Let Me Be The Someone ............................................................ 5
67  Deram DM 124                 Have No Fear, Bond Is Here (Casino Royale)/My Poem For You.................. 10
67  Deram DM 157                 Don't Speak Of Me/Sometimes I Remember ............................................ 5
69  RCA 1873                     Through The Eyes Of Love/Love Me ........................................................ 6

*(see also Rod McKuen, Typhoons, Bud Ashton)*

### REDWOOD
79  SRT SRTS/79/CUS 582          Give The Indian Back His Land/Rock Of Ages (500 only, this price for 300 in p/s and insert) ................................................................................................ 35
79  SRT SRTS/79/CUS 582          Give The Indian Back His Land/Rock Of Ages (500 only, this price for 200 with no p/s) . 15

### REDWOODS
62  Columbia DB 4859             Please Mr Scientist/Where You Used To Be ............................................. 25

### DIZZY REECE QUINTET
56  Tempo A 140                  Chorus/Basie Line ................................................................................. 10
58  Tempo EXA 84                 A VARIATION ON MONK (EP) ................................................................ 200
59  Tempo EXA 86                 NOWHERE TO GO (EP, featuring Tubby Hayes) ...................................... 200
59  Tempo EXA 89                 ON THE SCENE (EP) .............................................................................. 100
55  Tempo LAP 3                  A NEW STAR... (10" LP) ....................................................................... 250
57  Tempo TAP 9                  PROGRESS REPORT (LP) ....................................................................... 600
58  Esquire 32 185               ASIA MINOR (LP) .................................................................................. 100
84  Jasmine JASM 2013            PROGRESS REPORT (LP, reissue) ............................................................ 20

*(see also Victor Feldman, Ronnie Scott)*

### BOBBY REED
    Shrine 114                   Caldonia Brown/Baby Don't Leave Me ..................................................... 6

### CHUCK REED
57  Brunswick 05646              Whispering Heart/Another Love Has Ended .............................................. 15
58  Columbia DB 4113             No School Tomorrow/Let's Put Our Hearts Together................................ 30
62  Stateside SS 108             Just Plain Hurt/Talking No Trash ............................................................ 15

### DEAN REED
59  Capitol CL 14986             The Search/Annabelle ........................................................................... 10
59  Capitol CL 15030             I Kissed A Queen/A Pair Of Scissors (And A Pot Of Glue)......................... 10

### DENNY REED
61  London HLK 9274              A Teenager Feels It Too/Hot Water ........................................................ 18

### JERRY REED
58  Capitol CL 14851             Bessie Baby/Too Young To Be Blue ...................................................... 300
58  Capitol CL 14851             Bessie Baby/Too Young To Be Blue (78) .................................................. 50
69  RCA RCA 1798                 Oh What A Woman/Claw ......................................................................... 5
70  RCA RCA 2025                 Georgia Sunshine/Singing '69 ................................................................. 5
71  RCA RCA 2063                 Amos Moses/The Preacher And The Bear................................................. 5
69  RCA SF 8006                  ALABAMA WILD MAN (LP) ..................................................................... 18

### JIMMY REED
60  Top Rank JAR 333             Baby What You Want Me To Do/Caress Me Baby...................................... 20
60  Top Rank JAR 394             Found Love/Where Can You Be .............................................................. 20
60  Top Rank JAR 533             Hush-Hush/Going By The River .............................................................. 20
63  Stateside SS 205             Shame Shame Shame/Let's Get Together ................................................. 22
64  Stateside SS 330             Shame Shame Shame/Let's Get Together (reissue)..................................... 12
66  Sue WI 4004                  Odds And Ends/Going By The River Pt. II (B-side actually Pt. I) ................. 40
67  HMV POP 1579                 Two Ways To Skin A Cat/Got Nowhere To Go........................................... 40
64  Stateside SE 1016            BLUES OF JIMMY REED (EP) ................................................................... 30
64  Stateside SE 1026            I'M JIMMY REED (EP) ........................................................................... 30
62  Stateside SL 10012           JIMMY REED AT CARNEGIE HALL (LP) ..................................................... 20
64  Stateside SL 10055           JUST JIMMY REED (LP) ......................................................................... 30
64  Stateside SL 10069           SINGS THE BEST OF THE BLUES (LP) ...................................................... 20
64  Stateside SL 10086           PLAYS 12-STRING GUITAR BLUES (LP) .................................................... 20
64  Stateside SL 10091           THE BOSS MAN OF THE BLUES (LP) ........................................................ 30
65  Fontana 688 514 ZL           THINGS AIN'T WHAT THEY USED TO BE (LP) ........................................... 20
67  HMV CLP/CSD 3611             THE NEW JIMMY REED (LP) ................................................................... 20
68  Stateside S(S)L 10221        SOULIN' (LP) ....................................................................................... 35
69  Action ACLP 6011             DOWN IN VIRGINIA (LP) ........................................................................ 60

### JOE REED
71  Dawn DNS 1012                Ain't That A Shame/Follow Me ............................................................... 6

### LES REED
66  Fontana TF 765               Good King Went Ridiculous/Valley Of Kings ............................................. 6
67  Deram DM 128                 Imogene/Pay Off .................................................................................. 10
69  Deram DM 244                 Don't Linger With Your Finger On The Trigger/Big Drum .......................... 10

*(see also Sounds of Les & Barry)*

MINT VALUE £

## LOU REED

| | | | |
|---|---|---|---|
| 72 | RCA RCA 2240 | Walk And Talk It/Wild Child | 10 |
| 72 | RCA RCA 2303 | Walk On The Wild Side/Perfect Day | 6 |
| 73 | RCA RCA 2318 | Vicious/Satellite Of Love | 6 |
| 73 | MGM 2006 283 | I'm Waiting For The Man/Run Run Run/Candy Says (with Velvet Underground) | 10 |
| 74 | RCA APBO 0221 | Caroline Says (Parts 1 & 2) | 5 |
| 74 | RCA APBO 0238 | Sweet Jane/Lady Day | 5 |
| 74 | RCA RCA 2467 | Sally Can't Dance/Ennui | 5 |
| 76 | RCA RCA 2666 | Charley's Girl/Nowhere At All | 5 |
| 72 | RCA SF 8281 | LOU REED (LP, laminated sleeve, orange label) | 40 |
| 72 | RCA LSP 4807 | TRANSFORMER (LP, 1st pressing, laminated sleeve) | 70 |
| 73 | RCA LSP 4807 | TRANSFORMER (LP, 2nd pressing, non-laminated sleeve) | 15 |
| 73 | RCA RS 1002 | BERLIN (LP, orange label with insert) | 20 |
| 75 | RCA CPL 2 1101 | METAL MACHINE MUSIC (2-LP, U.S. import with U.K. sticker) | 35 |
| 78 | Arista SPART 1045 | STREET HASSLE (LP, insert) | 15 |

*(see also Velvet Underground)*

## LULA REED

| | | | |
|---|---|---|---|
| 55 | Parlophone CMSP 34 | Troubles On Your Mind/Bump On A Log (export issue) | 60 |
| 55 | Parlophone DP 408 | Troubles On Your Mind/Bump On A Log (78, export issue) | 15 |

## LULA REED & SYL JOHNSON

| | | | |
|---|---|---|---|
| 63 | Ember EMB EP 4535 | RHYTHM & BLUES BLUE BEAT STYLE (EP) | 70 |

## LULA REED & FREDDIE KING

| | | | |
|---|---|---|---|
| 63 | Ember EMB 4536 | LULA REED AND FREDDIE KING (EP) | 60 |

*(see also Freddie King)*

## OLIVER REED

| | | | |
|---|---|---|---|
| 61 | Decca F 11390 | The Wild One/Lonely For A Girl | 15 |
| 62 | Piccadilly 7N 35037 | Sometimes/Ecstasy | 10 |

## TAWNY REED

| | | | |
|---|---|---|---|
| 65 | Pye 7N 15935 | Needle In A Haystack/I've Got A Feeling | 50 |
| 66 | Pye 7N 17078 | You Can't Take It Away/My Heart Cries | 30 |

## VIVIEN REED

| | | | |
|---|---|---|---|
| 68 | Direction 58-3574 | I Wanna Be Free/Yours Until Tomorrow | 8 |
| 71 | Epic 7387 | I Feel The Earth MOve/Don't Close The Door On Me | 6 |

## WINSTON REED

| | | | |
|---|---|---|---|
| 72 | Pama Supreme PS 365 | Breakfast In Bed/RANNY WILLIAMS: Guitar Shuffle | 7 |
| 73 | Pama PM 863 | Big Eight/RANNY WILLIAMS & CLASSICS: Big Eight - Version | 7 |

## WINSTON REEDY

| | | | |
|---|---|---|---|
| 82 | SG SG 17 | Daughter Of Zion/Zion Dub (12") | 30 |
| 83 | Carousel 12CAR 48 | Dim The Light/Shower Of Rain (12") | 20 |
| 84 | Dep DEP 21 | Ambition/Romantic Girl (12") | 15 |

## VALA REEGAN & VALARONS

| | | | |
|---|---|---|---|
| 66 | Atlantic 584 009 | Fireman/Living In The Past | 250 |
| 66 | Atlantic 584 009 | Fireman/Living In The Past (DJ copy) | 300 |

## REELS

| | | | |
|---|---|---|---|
| 79 | Back Door 003 | Prefab Hearts/Spot The Ridge | 8 |

## JUSTYN REES

| | | | |
|---|---|---|---|
| 70 | Breakthrough HP 102 | DOWN MY ROAD (LP) | 35 |

## TONY REES & COTTAGERS

| | | | |
|---|---|---|---|
| 75 | Sonet SON 2059 | Viva El Fulham/Rainbow | 7 |

## DELLA REESE

| | | | |
|---|---|---|---|
| 57 | London HL 7024 | I Cried For You (Now It's Your Turn To Cry Over Me)/And That Reminds Me (export issue) | 10 |
| 58 | London HLJ 8687 | You Gotta Love Everybody/I Wish | 10 |
| 59 | London HLJ 8814 | Sermonette/Dreams End At Dawn | 10 |
| 59 | RCA RCA 1160 | Not One Minute More/Soldier Won't You Marry Me | 7 |
| 62 | RCA 1306 | Blow Out The Sun/I Love You So Much It Hurts | 6 |
| 66 | HMV POP 1553 | It Was A Very Good Year/Solitary Woman | 30 |
| 68 | Stateside SS 2128 | It Was A Very Good Year/I Had To Know My Way Around | 20 |
| 72 | Avco Embassy 6105 010 | If It Feels Good, Do It/Good Lovin' (Makes It Right) (paper label) | 10 |
| 74 | People PEO 106 | Who Is She And What Is She To You/If Loving You Is Wrong | 6 |
| 59 | London LTZ-J 15163 | THE HISTORY OF THE BLUES (LP) | 30 |
| 60 | RCA RD 27167/SF 5057 | DELLA (LP) | 15 |
| 61 | RCA RD 27208/SF 5091 | DELLA DELLA CHA-CHA-CHA (LP) | 18 |
| 62 | RCA RD 27234/SF 5112 | SPECIAL DELIVERY (LP) | 20 |
| 63 | RCA Victor RD/SF 7508 | ON STAGE (LP) | 15 |
| 68 | Stateside SL 10261 | I GOTTA BE ME...THIS TRIP OUT (LP) | 35 |
| 74 | People PLEO 7 | LET ME IN YOUR LIFE (LP) | 30 |

## TONY REESE

| | | | |
|---|---|---|---|
| 59 | London HLJ 8987 | Just About This Time Tomorrow/Lesson In Love | 20 |

## DEL REEVES

| | | | |
|---|---|---|---|
| 65 | United Artists UP 1092 | Girl On The Billboard/Eyes Don't Come Crying To Me | 7 |
| 66 | United Artists UP 1122 | Women Do Funny Things To Me/My Half Of Our Past | 7 |
| 66 | United Artists UP 1145 | Gettin' Any Feed For Your Chickens/Plain As The Tears On My Face | 7 |

## EDDIE REEVES

| | | | |
|---|---|---|---|
| 62 | London HL 9548 | Cry Baby/Talk Talk | 20 |

## JIM REEVES
### 78s

| | | | |
|---|---|---|---|
| 59 | RCA RCA 1144 | Partners/I'm Beginning To Forget You | 30 |
| 60 | RCA RCA 1168 | He'll Have To Go/In A Mansion Stands My Love | 40 |

### SINGLES

| | | | |
|---|---|---|---|
| 54 | London HL 8014 | Bimbo/Gipsy Heart | 100 |
| 54 | London HL 8030 | Mexican Joe/I Could Cry (with Circle O Ranch Boys) | 100 |
| 54 | London HL 8055 | Butterfly Love/It's Hard To Love Just One (with String Band) | 100 |
| 54 | London HL 8064 | Echo Bonita/Then I'll Stop Loving You (with Louisiana Hayride Band) | 100 |
| 54 | London HL 8105 | Padre Of Old San Antone/Mother Went A-Walkin' | 60 |
| 55 | London HL 8118 | Penny Candy/I'll Follow You (with Louisiana Hayride Band) | 60 |
| 55 | London HLU 8185 | Tahiti/Give Me One More Kiss | 60 |
| 55 | London HL 8159 | Drinking Tequila/Red-Eyed And Rowdy | 100 |

*(The 45s listed above were issued with gold label print on black labels.)*

| | | | |
|---|---|---|---|
| 56 | London HLU 8351 | The Wilder Your Heart Beats, The Sweeter You Love/ Where Does A Broken Heart Go | 50 |
| 57 | RCA RCA 1005 | Four Walls/I Know And You Know | 10 |
| 58 | RCA RCA 1074 | Blue Boy/Theme Of Love | 10 |
| 59 | RCA RCA 1144 | Partners/I'm Beginning To Forget You (triangular or round centre) | 10 |

### EPs

| | | | |
|---|---|---|---|
| 54 | London RE-P 1015 | THE BIMBO BOY (EP) | 40 |
| 55 | London RE-P 1033 | THE BIMBO BOY VOL. 2 (EP) | 40 |

## REFARENDUM

| | | | |
|---|---|---|---|
| 69 | RCA 1834 | Love (Can Make You Happy)/Valley Of Love | 8 |
| 70 | RCA 1973 | Lost and Found/Please Help Somebody | 20 |

## REFLECTION

| | | | |
|---|---|---|---|
| 68 | Reflection RS 6001 | Brave New Day/Lord I Believe (p/s) | 60 |
| 68 | Reflection RL 3015 | THE PRESENT TENSE: SONGS OF SYDNEY CARTER (LP) | 18 |

*(see also Sounds Of Salvation)*

## REFLECTIONS A.O.B.

| | | | |
|---|---|---|---|
| 86 | Keep KEEP 1 12 | ONLY IN MY DREAMS EP (12") | 40 |

## REFLECTIONS (U.K.)

| | | | |
|---|---|---|---|
| 74 | Purple PUR 124 | Love And Affection/No More | 10 |
| 75 | Purple PUR 127 | Moon Power/Little Star | 10 |

## REFLECTIONS (U.S.)

| | | | |
|---|---|---|---|
| 64 | Stateside SS 294 | (Just Like) Romeo & Juliet/Can't You Tell By The Look In My Eyes | 60 |
| 64 | Stateside SS 294 | (Just Like) Romeo & Juliet/Can't You Tell By The Look In My Eyes (DJ copy) | 100 |
| 65 | Stateside SS 406 | Poor Man's Son/Comin' At You | 30 |
| 74 | Tamla Motown TMG 907 | (Just Like) Romeo & Juliet/Can't You Tell By The Look In My Eyes (reissue) | 15 |
| 77 | ABC ABC 4181 | Like Adam And Eve/AUGUST & DENEEN: We Go Together | 15 |
| 65 | Stateside SE 1034 | POOR MAN'S SON (EP) | 125 |

*(see also The High and Mighty)*

## REFUGEE

| | | | |
|---|---|---|---|
| 74 | Charisma CAS 1087 | REFUGEE (LP, with lyric inner sleeve, large 'Mad Hatter' label) | 20 |

*(see also Nice, Yes)*

## REGAL DEWY

| | | | |
|---|---|---|---|
| 78 | RCA XB 1032 | Love Music/Where Would I Be Without Me | 8 |

## NORRIS REGAL

| | | | |
|---|---|---|---|
| 83 | Sirion SRN 001 | Struggle/Version (12") | 40 |

## REGAL ZONE

| | | | |
|---|---|---|---|
| 81 | XS XS 1 | FACTORY GIRL EP | 10 |

## JOAN REGAN

| | | | |
|---|---|---|---|
| 54 | Decca F 10362 | Wait For Me, Darling (with Johnston Brothers)/Two Kinds Of Tears (gold lettering) | 20 |
| 54 | Decca F 10362 | Wait For Me, Darling (with Johnston Brothers)/Two Kinds Of Tears (silver lettering) | 8 |
| 54 | Decca F 10373 | If I Give My Heart To You/Faded Flowers | 8 |
| 54 | Decca F 10397 | This Ole House/Can This Be Love? | 8 |
| 55 | Decca F 10432 | Prize Of Gold/When You're In Love | 8 |
| 55 | Decca F 10474 | Open Up Your Heart And Let The Love In (with Rusty Regan)/ If You Learn To Love Each Other | 8 |
| 55 | Decca F 10505 | Danger! Heartbreak Ahead/Don't Be Afraid Of Love | 8 |
| 55 | Decca F 10521 | Just Say You Love Her/Nobody Danced With Me | 8 |
| 55 | Decca F 10598 | The Shepherd Boy/The Rose And The Flame | 8 |
| 56 | Decca F 10659 | Love And Marriage/Cross Of Gold (Croce Di Oro) | 8 |
| 56 | Decca F 10757 | Sweet Heartaches/Second Fiddle (with Ted Heath) | 7 |
| 57 | Decca F 10871 | Nearer To Me/Cross My Ever-Loving Heart | 6 |
| 58 | HMV POP 555 | Love Like Ours/Take Me In Your Arms | 6 |
| 60 | Pye Nixa 7N 15238 | Happy Anniversary/So Close To My Heart | 5 |
| 60 | Pye 7N 15278 | Papa Loves Mama/When You Know Somebody Loves You | 5 |
| 60 | Pye 7N 15303 | Must Be Santa/Will Santa Come To Shanty Town | 5 |
| 60 | Pye 7N 15259 | If Only You'd Be Mine/O Dio Mio | 5 |
| 60 | Pye 7N 15310 | One Of The Lucky Ones/My Thanks to You | 15 |
| 66 | CBS 202100 | Don't Talk To Me About Love/I'm No Toy | 20 |
| 66 | CBS 202100 | Don't Talk To Me About Love/I'm No Toy (DJ copy) | 30 |
| 67 | CBS 2657 | No-One Beside Me/A Love So Fine | 20 |
| 54 | Decca LF 1182 | THE GIRL NEXT DOOR (10" LP) | 40 |
| 56 | Decca LK 4153 | JUST JOAN (LP) | 100 |

## RUSS REGAN

| | | | |
|---|---|---|---|
| 59 | Capitol CL 15084 | Adults Only/Just The Two Of Us | 10 |

## TOMMY REGAN
| 64 | Colpix PX 725 | I'll Never Stop Loving You/This Time I'm Losing You (DJ Copy) | 125 |
| 64 | Colpix PX 725 | I'll Never Stop Loving You/This Time I'm Losing You | 100 |

*(see also Marcels)*

## REGENTS (U.K.) (1)
| 63 | Oriole CB 1912 | Bye Bye Johnny/Come Along | 40 |

*(see also Buddy Britten)*

## REGENTS (U.K.) (2)
| 66 | CBS 202247 | Words/Worryin' Kind | 45 |

## REGENTS (U.K.) (3)
| 79 | Rialto TREB 111 | 7 Teen (Uncensored Version)/Hole In The Heart (p/s) | 6 |

## REGENTS (U.S.)
| 61 | Columbia DB 4666 | Barbara Ann/I'm So Lonely | 30 |
| 61 | Columbia DB 4694 | Runaround/Laura My Darling | 28 |

## REGGAE BOYS
| 69 | Amalgamated AMG 841 | Me No Born Ya/The Wicked Must Survive | 35 |
| 69 | Amalgamated AMG 843 | The Reggae Train/Dolly House On Fire | 35 |
| 69 | Gas GAS 135 | Ba Ba/GLEN ADAMS: Power Cut | 60 |
| 69 | Unity UN 530 | What You Gonna Do/HEDLEY BENNETT: Hot Coffee | 70 |
| 70 | Bullet BU 431 | Pupa Live On Eye Top/Give Me Faith | 35 |
| 70 | Gas GAS 122 | Phrases/Give Me Faith | 50 |
| 70 | Upsetter US 339 | Hurry Up/Upsetters: The Thanks We Get | 35 |
| 70 | Pressure Beat PR 5503 | Walk By Day, Fly By Night/JOE GIBBS & DESTROYERS: Unknown Tongue | 20 |

*(see also Glen Adams, Alva Lewis, Upsetters)*

## REGGAE GEORGE
| 83 | Greensleeves GRED 114 | You'll Never Know/We Still Survive (12") | 15 |

## REGGAE GIRLS
| 69 | Nu Beat NB024 | Rescue Me/SOULMATES: Unity Is Strength | 60 |

## REGGAE REGULAR
| 77 | Greensleeves GRE 001 | Where Is Jah?/Jah Is Here | 8 |
| 78 | Greensleeves GRE 004 | The Black Star Liner/It's Coming | 6 |
| 78 | Greensleeves GRED 2 | The Black Star Liner/Where Is Jah? (12") | 12 |
| 84 | Greensleeves GREL 64 | GHETTO ROCK (LP) | 30 |

## REGGAE STRINGS
| 73 | Trojan TRLS 54 | REGGAE STRINGS (LP) | 20 |

*(see also Horace Faith)*

## ELIS REGINA
| 69 | Philis BF 1812 | Zazueiro/Corrioa De Jangada | 50 |
| 69 | Philips SBL 7905 | ELIS REGINA IN LONDON (LP) | 100 |

## REGULARS
| 81 | Soundoff SOFFLP 001 | I & I (LP, with band name on gold sticker on front of sleeve) | 30 |

## LOU REICHNER BAND
| 80 | ESR Records S/80/CUS 733 | Photograph/I Sit And Stare/The End Of The World/Out On The Streets (also listed as ESR 4, 300 only, with insert) | 50 |
| 80 | ESR Records S/80/CUS 733 | Photograph/I Sit And Stare/The End Of The World/Out On The Streets (also listed as ESR 4, 300 only, without insert) | 20 |

## AL REID
| 69 | Blue Cat BS 161 | Vietcong/MAX ROMEO: Me Want Man | 50 |
| 69 | Blue Cat BS 163 | Darling/MAX ROMEO: It's Not The Way | 50 |

## ALTYMAN REID
| 72 | Green Door GD 4026 | A Sugar/A Sugar Part Two (with Roy Shirley) | 7 |

*(see also Roy Shirley)*

## CARLTON REID
| 66 | Ska Beat JB 254 | Funny/Turn On The Lights | 25 |
| 69 | Blue Cat BS 162 | Leave Me To Cry/Warning | 125 |

## DENNIS REID
| 77 | Greensleeves GRE 6 | Land Of The Rising Sun/DENNIS REID & REVOLUTIONARIES: Rising Sun Version | 8 |

## DUKE REID (& HIS GROUP)
| 60 | Blue Beat BB 24 | Duke's Cookies (with His Group)/JIVING JUNIORS: I Wanna Love | 20 |
| 62 | Blue Beat BB 119 | Twelve Minutes To Go (actually by Don Drummond)/ HORTENSE ELLIS: Midnight Train | 30 |
| 63 | Duke DK 1002 | Pink Lane Shuffle (with His Group)/LAUREL AITKEN: Low Down Dirty Girl | 20 |
| 67 | Master's Time MT 003 | Religious Service At Bond Street Gospel Hall/Religious Service At Bond Street Gospel Hall (Continued) | 15 |
| 67 | Trojan TR 001 | Judge Sympathy (actually by Freedom Singers & Duke Reid All Stars)/ROLAND ALPHONSO: Never To Be Mine | 50 |
| 60s | Doctor Bird DB 1028 | True Confessions/TOMMY McCCOOK : More Love | 35 |
| 72 | Duke Reid DR 2522 | Hurt Parts 1 & 2 (actually by Eagles [Jamaica]) | 15 |
| 69 | Trojan TTL 8 | GOLDEN HITS (LP) | 20 |

*(see also Chuck & Darby, Derrick Morris, Stranger)*

## LEYROY REID
| 68 | Blue Cat BS 125 | The Fiddler/LOVELETTES: Shook | 40 |
| 68 | Blue Cat BS 127 | Great Surprise/TEN(N)ORS: Khaki | 30 |

*(see also Nehemiah Reed)*

## MARC REID
| 66 | CBS 202244 | For No One/Lonely City Blues | 15 |
| 67 | CBS 202581 | Magic Book/My World Turns Around | 18 |
| 67 | CBS 2950 | We Should Live Together/Sale By Auction | 15 |

## NEHEMIAH REID('S ALL STARS)
| | | | |
|---|---|---|---|
| 68 | Island WI 3102 | Family War/Give Me That Love | 40 |
| 70 | Hot Shot HS 03 | Hot Pepper/Seawave (as Nehemiah Reid's All Stars) | 40 |
| 70s | Torpedo TOR 23 | Mafia/H.E.L.L. 5 (as Nehemiah Reid's All Stars) | 20 |

*(see also Leyroy Reid, Cynthia Richards)*

## NORVELLE REID
| | | | |
|---|---|---|---|
| 57 | Brunswick 05725 | All The Way/The World Won't End (export issue) | 5 |

## P. REID
| | | | |
|---|---|---|---|
| 65 | Ska Beat JB 197 | Redeemed/Goodbye World | 18 |

## TERRY REID (& JAYWALKERS)
| | | | |
|---|---|---|---|
| 67 | Columbia DB 8166 | The Hand Don't Fit The Glove/This Time (as Terry Reid & Jaywalkers) | 12 |
| 68 | Columbia DB 8409 | Better By Far/Fires Alive | 20 |
| 69 | Columbia PSRS 323 | Superlungs (promo only, as "Terry Reid Is Superlungs") | 25 |
| 76 | ABC 4137 | Oooh Baby/Brave Awakening | 5 |
| 79 | Capitol CL 16071 | Ain't No Shadow/Bowangi | 5 |
| 69 | Columbia SCX 6370 | TERRY REID (LP, laminated front, flipbacks) | 50 |
| 73 | Atlantic K 40340 | RIVER (LP, gatefold sleeve) | 20 |
| 76 | ABC ABCL 5162 | SEED OF MEMORY (LP) | 18 |

*(see also Peter Jay & Jaywalkers)*

## REIGN
| | | | |
|---|---|---|---|
| 70 | Regal Zonophone RZ 3028 | Line Of Least Resistance/Natural Lovin' Man | 90 |

*(see also Yardbirds, Keith Relf, Renaissance, Armageddon, Illusion)*

## REINCARNATE
| | | | |
|---|---|---|---|
| 82 | Zipp REIN 001 | Take It Or Leave It/Metal In Disguise | 70 |

## REINDEER SECTION
| | | | |
|---|---|---|---|
| 01 | Bright Star BSR 14V | Y'ALL GET SCARED NOW, YA HEAR! (LP) | 20 |
| 02 | Bright Star BSR 19V | SON OF EVIL REINDEER (LP) | 20 |

*(see also Arab Strap, Belle & Sebastian, Snow Patrol, Mogwai, Teenage Fanclub, Idlewild)*

## JOE REISMAN ORCHESTRA
| | | | |
|---|---|---|---|
| 56 | HMV 7M 364 | Robin Hood/His Name Was Judas | 5 |
| 60 | Columbia DB 4553 | The World Of Suzi Wong (Theme)/Melodie D'Amour | 5 |
| 61 | Pye International 7N 25087 | The Guns Of Navarone/Yassu | 5 |

## REIVERS
| | | | |
|---|---|---|---|
| 59 | Top Rank JAR 244 | Wee Magic Stane/The Wreck Of The John B | 6 |
| 60 | Top Rank JAR 283 | Down In The Mines (Dark As Dungeon)/Govan Is A Busy Place | 6 |

## LOU REIZNER
| | | | |
|---|---|---|---|
| 69 | Phillips | On Days Like This/Get A Bloomin' Move On | 15 |

## REJECTS
| | | | |
|---|---|---|---|
| 85 | FM VHF 7 | Back To The Start/Leave It (FM label house sleeve) | 10 |
| 84 | Heavy Metal HMR 22 | QUIET STORM (LP) | 15 |

*(see also Cockney Rejects)*

## REJOICE!
| | | | |
|---|---|---|---|
| 69 | Stateside SS 8010 | November Snow/Quick Draw Man | 5 |
| 69 | Stateside S(S)L 5009 | REJOICE! (LP) | 20 |

## BOB RELF
| | | | |
|---|---|---|---|
| 75 | Black Magic BM 101 | Blowin' My Mind To Pieces/PAULA RUSSELL: Blowin' My Mind To Pieces | 5 |

*(see also Bob & Earl)*

## JANE RELF
| | | | |
|---|---|---|---|
| 71 | Decca F 13231 | Without A Song From You/Make My Time Pass By | 30 |
| | Findus Frozen Foods SD/DS/ 7001 | Gone Fishing/Gordon Jackson - Hints From The Findus Kitchen (P/S) | 10 |

*(see also Renaissance, Gordon Jackson)*

## KEITH RELF
| | | | |
|---|---|---|---|
| 66 | Columbia DB 7920 | Mr. Zero/Knowing | 70 |
| 66 | Columbia DB 8084 | Shapes In My Mind/Blue Sands | 100 |

*(see also Yardbirds, Jim McCarty, Renaissance, Reign, Together, Armageddon)*

## RELICT/THE CLIENTELE
| | | | |
|---|---|---|---|
| 01 | Johnny Kane KANE 004 | Held In Glass/(I Can't Seem) To Make You Mine | 5 |

*(see also Clientele)*

## RELIGIOUS OVERDOSE
| | | | |
|---|---|---|---|
| 80 | Glass GLASS 004 | Control Addicts/25 Minutes (p/s with green label) | 5 |

## RELOAD
| | | | |
|---|---|---|---|
| 92 | Evolution EVO 01 | RELOAD EP (12", plain sleeve) | 20 |
| 92 | Evolution EVO 02 | AUTO RELOAD EP (12", with E 621) | 30 |
| 92 | Evolution EVO 03 | RELOAD EP (12", 1-side credited to E 621) | 40 |
| 93 | Infonet INF 13 | AUTO RELOAD EP VOLUME 2 (12", p/s) | 10 |
| 93 | Infonet INF 04LP | A COLLECTION OF SHORT STORIES (2-LP, with colour booklet) | 50 |
| 93 | Infonet INF 04LP | A COLLECTION OF SHORT STORIES (2-LP) | 40 |

*(see also Global Communications, Link, Mystic Institute)*

## RELUCTANT STEREOTYPES
| | | | |
|---|---|---|---|
| 79 | Oval 1013 | LULL EP (p/s) | 7 |

## R.E.M.
**SINGLES**
| | | | |
|---|---|---|---|
| 83 | I.R.S. PFSX 1026 | Talk About The Passion/Shaking Through/Carnival Of Sorts (Box Cars)/ 1,000,000 (12", p/s) | 15 |
| 84 | I.R.S. IRS 105 | S. Central Rain (I'm Sorry)/King Of The Road (p/s) | 8 |
| 84 | I.R.S. IRSX 105 | S. Central Rain (I'm Sorry)/Voice Of Harold/Pale Blue Eyes (12", p/s) | 12 |

MINT VALUE £

| | | | |
|---|---|---|---|
| 84 | I.R.S. IRSX 107 | (Don't Go Back To) Rockville/Wolves/9 - 9 (Live Version)/ Gardening At Night (live) (12", p/s) | |
| 85 | I.R.S. IRM 102 | Can't Get There From Here/Bandwagon (p/s) | 10 |
| 85 | I.R.S. IRM 105 | Wendell Gee/Crazy (p/s) | 6 |
| 85 | I.R.S. IRMD 105 | Wendell Gee/Crazy//Ages Of You/Burning Down (double pack) | 6 |
| 86 | I.R.S. DIRM 128 | Superman/White Tornado/Femme Fatale (CD, unissued) | 8 |
| 87 | I.R.S. IRM 145 | It's The End Of The World As We Know It (And I Feel Fine) (2.59 edit)/ This One Goes Out (live) (p/s, gold or metallic blue label) | 0 |
| 87 | I.R.S. IRM 146 | The One I Love/Last Date (bronze label, glossy p/s; silver label, matt p/s) | 8 |
| 88 | I.R.S. DIRM 161 | Finest Worksong (LP Version)/Time After Time, Etc. (live)/ It's The End Of The World As We Know It (And I Feel Fine) (CD, numbered stencilled 7" box, 5,000 only) | 8 |
| 88 | I.R.S. IRM161 | Finest Worksong/Time After Time Etc live (p/s) | 15 |
| 88 | I.R.S. IRMT161 | Finest Worksong Lengthy Club Mix/Other Mix/Time After Time Etc medley (12", p/s) | 8 |
| 92 | I.R.S. DIRM 180 | It's The End Of The World As We Know It (And I Feel Fine)/Radio Free Europe (Hib-Tone Version) (gold or silver labels, p/s, with Album version of 'Radio Free Europe') | 10 |

**SINGLES : WARNER BROS SINGLES**

| | | | |
|---|---|---|---|
| 89 | Warner Bros W 2833W | Stand/Pop Song '89 (Acoustic) (stencil die-cut p/s) | 10 |
| 89 | Warner Bros W 2960B | Orange Crush/Ghost Riders ('The Green Package' box set with poster) | 8 |
| 95 | Warner Bros W0281X | Crush With Eyeliner (p/s, orange vinyl + calendar) | 5 |
| 95 | Warner Bros W0290X | Strange Currencies/Strange Currencies Instrumental (p/s, Dayglo yellow/green vinyl + pin badge) | 6 |
| 08 | Warner Bros. W807 | Man Sized Wreath/Living Well Jesus Dog (clear vinyl, PVC stickered sleeve) | 5 |
| 11 | Warners 527426-1 | THREE (Record Store Day box of 3 x 7") | 12 |

**ALBUMS**

| | | | |
|---|---|---|---|
| 83 | IRS SP70604 | MURMUR (LP) | 20 |
| 90 | IRS 46588-2 | THE COLLECTION (5-CD box set) | 40 |
| 91 | Warner Bros. WX404 | OUT OF TIME (LP, with free 7") | 25 |
| 91 | Warner Bros. WX404 | OUT OF TIME (LP) | 18 |
| 92 | Warner Bros. WX488 | AUTOMATIC FOR THE PEOPLE (LP, inner) | 20 |
| 94 | Warners 9362-45740-1 | MONSTER (LP) | 25 |
| 96 | Warners 9362-463210-1 | NEW ADVENTURES IN HI-FI (2-LP, gatefold) | 50 |
| 98 | Warners 9362-47112-1 | UP (2-LP) | 45 |
| 03 | Warners 9362 48381-1 | IN TIME: THE BEST OF REM 1988-2003 (2-LP) | 70 |
| 04 | Warners 9362 48894-1 | AROUND THE SUN (2-LP) | 30 |
| 11 | Warners 9362-49626-9 | COLLAPSE INTO NOW (LP) | 15 |

**PROMOS**

| | | | |
|---|---|---|---|
| 83 | I.R.S. PFP 1017 | Radio Free Europe/There She Goes Again (p/s) | 40 |
| 83 | I.R.S. PFP 1026 | Talk About The Passion/Talk About The Passion (plain sleeve, promo only) | 10 |
| 88 | I.R.S. WIRM(T) 161 DL | Finest Worksong (Lengthy Club Mix)/Finest Worksong (Other Mix)/Time After Time Etc. (12" in 'media' p/s) | 15 |
| 92 | I.R.S. CDREM 92 | THE ALTERNATIVE RADIO SAMPLER (CD, 7-track promo, includes unreleased version of 'Gardening At Night') | 50 |
| 92 | Warner Bros REM 1 | SAMPLER FROM THE BEST OF REM (CD, Brit Awards nomination issue) | 25 |
| 03 | Warners PR 04359 | THE BEST OF REM - IN TIME 1980-2003 (promo box set containing 18 1-track CDs each housed in individual card sleeve in flip top box) | 40 |

**FLEXIDISCS : FLEXIDISCS & OTHER RELEASES**

| | | | |
|---|---|---|---|
| 85 | Bucketfull Of Brains BOB 5 | Tighten Up (hard vinyl test pressing, 50 only) | 50 |
| 92 | Lyntone BOB 32 | Academy Fight Song (live)/COAL PORTERS: Watching Blue Grass Burn (p/s, free with Bucketfull Of Brains magazine, double issue 39/40) | 10 |
| 92 | Lyntone BOB 32 | Academy Fight Song (live)/COAL PORTERS: Watching Blue Grass Burn (white label test pressing) | 20 |

*(see also Syd Straw)*

**REMA-REMA**

| | | | |
|---|---|---|---|
| 80 | 4AD BAD 5 | WHEEL IN THE ROSES: Feedback Song/Rema-Ream/Instrumental/Fond Affections (12" EP, original pressing with blue labels) | 20 |
| 80 | 4AD BAD 5 | WHEEL IN THE ROSES: Feedback Song/Rema-Ream/Instrumental/Fond Affections (12" EP) | 15 |

*(see also Adam & The Ants, Mass, Models, Wolfgang Press)*

**REMEMBER THIS**

| | | | |
|---|---|---|---|
| 75 | Penny Farthing PEN 862 | Rock' N' Roll Revival/Over And Over Again | 6 |

**REMO FOUR**

| | | | |
|---|---|---|---|
| 64 | Piccadilly 7N 35175 | I Wish I Could Shimmy Like My Sister Kate/Peter Gunn | 25 |
| 64 | Piccadilly 7N 35186 | Sally Go Round The Roses/I Know A Girl | 25 |
| 67 | Fontana TF 787 | Live Like A Lady/Sing Hallelujah | 70 |

*(see also Tommy Quickly, Johnny Sandon, Gregory Phillips, Ashton Gardner & Dyke, Mike Hurst, George Harrison)*

**RENAISSANCE (U.K.)**

| | | | |
|---|---|---|---|
| 70 | Island WIP 6079 | Island/The Sea | 15 |
| 75 | Warner Bros. K 17177 | Northern Lights/Opening Out | 5 |
| 78 | Sire SRE 1022 | Northern Lights/Opening Out (picture disc, export issue) | 15 |
| 79 | Sire SIR 4019 | Jekyll And Hyde/Forever Changing (withdrawn) | 15 |
| 69 | Island ILPS 9114 | RENAISSANCE (LP, gatefold, pink label with white 'i' logo) | 30 |
| 71 | Island HELP 27 | ILLUSION (LP, withdrawn, export only, black labeil with pink 'i' logo) | 50 |

*(see also Jim McCarty, Keith Relf, Jane Relf, Yardbirds, Rupert's People, Reign)*

**RENAISSANCE (U.S.)**

| | | | |
|---|---|---|---|
| 68 | Polydor BM 56736 | Mary Jane (Get Off The Devil's Merry-Go-Round)/Daytime Lovers | 35 |

**RENAULTS**

| | | | |
|---|---|---|---|
| 60 | Warner Bros WB 11 | Meloncolie/Stella | 7 |

**DIANE RENAY**

| | | | |
|---|---|---|---|
| 64 | Stateside SS 270 | Navy Blue/Unbelievable Guy | 15 |
| 64 | Stateside SS 290 | Kiss Me Sailor/Soft Spoken Guy | 15 |

| | | | |
|---|---|---|---|
| 64 | MGM MGM 1262 | Watch Out Sally/Billy Blue Eyes | 25 |
| 65 | MGM MGM 1274 | Troublemaker/I Had A Dream | 25 |

*(see also Laura Greene)*

## JOHN RENBOURN

| | | | |
|---|---|---|---|
| 65 | Transatlantic TRA 135 | JOHN RENBOURN (LP) | 40 |
| 66 | Transatlantic TRA 149 | ANOTHER MONDAY (LP) | 30 |
| 68 | Transatlantic TRA 167 | SIR JOHN ALOT OF MERRIE ENGLANDE'S MUSICK THYNGE AND YE GREENE KNIGHT (LP) | 30 |
| 70 | Transatlantic TRA 224 | THE LADY AND THE UNICORN (LP) | 20 |
| 72 | Transatlantic TRA 247 | FARO ANNIE (LP) | 30 |
| 76 | Transatlantic TRA 336 | THE HERMIT (LP) | 15 |
| 73 | Transatlantic TRASAM 28 | SO CLEAR - THE JOHN RENBOURN SAMPLER VOL. 2 (LP) | 15 |

*(see also Pentangle, Bert Jansch & John Renbourn, Steve Tilston, Dorris Henderson)*

## JOHN RENBOURN'S SHIP OF FOOLS

| | | | |
|---|---|---|---|
| 88 | Run River 009 | SHIP OF FOOLS (LP) | 20 |

## DON RENDELL

| | | | |
|---|---|---|---|
| 55 | Tempo A 108 | Muskrat Ramble/Thames Walk | 30 |
| 55 | Tempo A 110 | You Stepped Out Of A Dream/Slow Boat To China (78, as Don Rendell Quartet) | 10 |
| 55 | Tempo A 112 | Didn't We/Dance Of The Ooblies (78, as Don Rendell Sextet) | 10 |
| 55 | Tempo A 114 | From This Moment On/Blow Mr. Dexter (78, as Don Rendell Quartet) | 10 |
| 55 | Tempo EXA 11 | DON RENDELL QUARTET (EP) | 100 |
| 55 | Tempo EXA 12 | DON RENDELL SEXTET (EP) | 100 |
| 55 | Tempo EXA 16 | DON RENDELL SEXTET/DAMIAN ROBINSON TRIO (EP, 2 tracks each) | 50 |
| 55 | Tempo EXA 20 | DON RENDELL QUINTET (EP) | 60 |
| 57 | Pye Jazz NJE 1044 | DON RENDELL JAZZ SIX (EP) | 40 |
| 58 | Decca DFE 6501 | PACKET OF BLUES (EP, as Don Rendell Jazz Six) | 30 |
| 54 | Decca LK 4087 | JAZZ AT THE FESTIVAL HALL (LP) | 70 |
| 54 | Vogue LDE 050 | MUSIC IN THE MAKING (10" LP) | 100 |
| 55 | Vogue LDE 144 | DON RENDELL IN PARIS (10" LP, with Bobby Jaspa) | 100 |
| 55 | Tempo LAP 1 | MEET DON RENDELL (10" LP) | 1000 |
| 56 | Nixa NJL 4 | TENORAMA (LP) | 300 |
| 57 | Nixa Jazz Today NJL 7 | DON RENDELL PRESENTS THE JAZZ SIX (LP) | 200 |
| 58 | Decca LK 4265 | PLAYTIME (LP, as Don Rendell Jazz 6) | 100 |
| 62 | Jazzland JLP 51 | ROARIN' (LP, as Don Rendell New Jazz Quintet [with Graham Bond]) | 250 |
| 72 | Columbia SCX 6491 | SPACEWALK (LP, as Don Rendell Quintet) | 150 |

*(see also Frank Horrox)*

## DON RENDELL & IAN CARR QUINTET

| | | | |
|---|---|---|---|
| 65 | Columbia 33SX 1733 | SHADES OF BLUE (LP) | 1000 |
| 66 | Columbia S(C)X 6064 | DUSK FIRE (LP, first pressing with blue label) | 800 |
| 68 | Columbia S(C)X 6064 | DUSK FIRE (LP, reissue, silver/black Columbia label with EMI box logo) | 350 |
| 68 | Columbia S(C)X 6214 | PHASE III (LP) | 400 |
| 69 | Columbia S(C)X 6316 | LIVE (LP) | 300 |
| 69 | Columbia SCX 6368 | CHANGE IS (LP) | 400 |
| 10 | Stamford STAMLP1006 | LIVE AT THE UNION (2-LP) | 20 |

*(see also Neil Ardley, Nucleus)*

## DON RENDELL QUARTET/JOE HARRIOT QUARTET

| | | | |
|---|---|---|---|
| 57 | MGM MGM-EP 615 | JAZZ BRITANNIA (EP, 2 tracks each) | 60 |

*(see also Joe Harriott)*

## DON RENDES

| | | | |
|---|---|---|---|
| 76 | Neville King NK 3 | Beware/Dun Beware | 10 |

## RENDESVIEW

| | | | |
|---|---|---|---|
| 71 | Philron SP0019 | It Shouldn't Have Happened/I'll Give You Love | 100 |

## RENE & HIS ALLIGATORS

| | | | |
|---|---|---|---|
| 66 | Decca F 22324 | She Broke My Heart/I Can Wait | 18 |

## GOOGIE RENE COMBO

| | | | |
|---|---|---|---|
| 60 | London HLY 9056 | Forever/Ez-zee | 20 |
| 66 | Atlantic AT 4076 | Smokey Joe's La La/Needing You | 30 |
| 66 | Atlantic 584 015 | Chica-Boo/Mercy Mercy (Too Much For The Soul) | 10 |

## HENRI RENE

| | | | |
|---|---|---|---|
| 55 | HMV 7M 308 | Enchantment/Crystal Chandelier (with Hugo Winterhalter Orchestra) | 7 |
| 59 | London HLP 8960 | La Shabla (The Shovel)/Destiny (with His Orchestra & Chorus) | 7 |

## RENE & RENE

| | | | |
|---|---|---|---|
| 65 | HMV POP 1468 | Chantilly Lace/I'm Not The Only One | 10 |
| 67 | Island WIP 6001 | Loving You Could Hurt Me So Much/Little Diamonds | 8 |

## RENEGADE (1)

| | | | |
|---|---|---|---|
| 73 | Parlophone R 5981 | Loving And Forgiving/never Let Me Go | 20 |
| 74 | Dawn DNS 1067 | A Little Rock 'N' Roll/My Revolution | 25 |

## RENEGADE (2)

| | | | |
|---|---|---|---|
| 80 | White Witch WIT 1 | LONELY ROAD (12" EP, with insert) | 100 |

## RENEGADES

| | | | |
|---|---|---|---|
| 66 | Polydor BM 56508 | Cadillac/Every Minute Of The Day | 30 |
| 66 | President PT 106 | Thirteen Women/Walking Down The Street | 200 |
| 67 | Parlophone R 5592 | Take A Message/Second Thoughts | 25 |
| 68 | Columbia DB 8383 | No Man's Land/Sugar Loaf Mountain | 25 |

## RENIA

| | | | |
|---|---|---|---|
| 73 | Transatlantic TRA 261 | FIRST OFFENDERS (LP) | 30 |

## DON RENNIE

| | | | |
|---|---|---|---|
| 56 | Parlophone MSP 6218 | To Love, To Love Is Wonderful/One Girl - One Boy | 7 |

## Don RENO & RED SMILEY

| 56 | Parlophone MSP 6237 | Who Are We?/Can You Find It In Your Heart? | 7 |

### DON RENO & RED SMILEY
| 58 | Parlophone GEP 8777 | COUNTRY AND WESTERN (EP) | 30 |

### GERRY RENO
| 62 | Decca F 11477 | Don't Ever Change/What Would You Do | 8 |
| 62 | Decca F 11516 | Who's Fooling You/Three Deadly Sins | 8 |
| 63 | Decca F 11774 | It Only Happens In The Movies/One Lonely Guy | 15 |

### GINETTE RENO
| 69 | Decca F 22972 | Don't Let Me Be Misunderstood/Everything That I Am | 8 |

### PAUL RENO
| 63 | Oriole CB 1872 | Lonely Little Girl/Angela | 10 |

### CHRIS RENSHAW & THE KEEPERS
| 73 | Pye 7N 45285 | Banksie (A Tribute To Gordon Banks)/National (Health) Anthem (p/s) | 6 |

### ROBERT RENTAL
| 78 | Regular ER 102 | Paralysis/A.C.C. (photocopied black & white foldover p/s) | 30 |
| 78 | Company/Regular RECO 2 | Paralysis/A.C.C. (reissue, card gatefold p/s) | 20 |
| 80 | Mute MUTE 010 | On Location/Double Heart (p/s) | 15 |
| 79 | Industrial IR 0007 | THE BRIDGE (LP, with Thomas Leer) | 40 |
| 80 | Rough Trade ROUGH 17 | ROBERT RENTAL AND THE NORMAL (LP, 1-sided, plain red sleeve) | 25 |
| (see also Thomas Leer) | | | |

### REPARATA & DELRONS
| 65 | Stateside SS 382 | Whenever A Teenager Cries/He's My Guy | 30 |
| 65 | Stateside SS 414 | Tommy/Momma Don't Allow | 25 |
| 68 | Bell BLL 1002 | Captain Of Your Ship/Toom Toom (Is A Little Boy) | 15 |
| 68 | RCA Victor RCA 1691 | I Can Hear The Rain/Always Waitin' | 30 |
| 68 | Bell BLL 1014 | Saturday Night Didn't Happen/Panic | 50 |
| 68 | Bell BLL 1014 | Saturday Night Didn't Happen/Panic (DJ copy) | 60 |
| 68 | Bell BLL 1021 | Weather Forecast/You Can't Change A Young Boy's Mind | 20 |
| 72 | Dart ART 2057 | Your Life Is Gone/Octopus Garden (credited to Reparata) | 10 |
| 76 | Polydor 2058 688 | Jesabee Lancer (The Belly Dancer)/We Need You | 7 |
| 72 | Avco 6467 250 | ROCK AND ROLL REVOLUTION (LP) | 40 |

### REPLACEMENTS
| 86 | Sire W 8727 | Swingin' Party/Left Of The Dial | 8 |
| 86 | Sire W 8679 | Kiss Me On The Bus/Little Mascara (p/s) | 8 |
| 87 | Sire W 8297 | Alex Chilton/Election day (p/s) | 20 |
| 87 | Sire W8297 | THE REPLACEMENTS EP | 15 |
| 84 | Zippo ZONG 002 | LET IT BE (LP) | 15 |
| 85 | Sire 925330 | TIM (LP) | 15 |
| 87 | Sire 925557 | PLEASED TO MEET ME (LP) | 20 |
| 89 | What Goes On ON 20 | STINK (mini-LP) | 18 |

### REPORTERS (1)
| 81 | GW1 | Scoop/NBZ (p/s) | 40 |

### REPORTERS (2)
| 81 | Cloggtown CLOGGTOWN 1 | Office Staff/Cinema/Lady Luck (p/s) | 20 |

### REPTILE RANCH
| 87 | Z Block Z-1 | Don't Give The Lifeguard A Second Chance: WTB/Lifeguard (fold over p/s, 1000 only) | 10 |

### REPULSION
| 89 | Necrosis NECRO 0002 | HORRIFIED (LP) | 30 |

### REQUIEM
| 80 | Sacrificial SAC 001 | Angel Of Sin/Sacrificial Wanderer (no p/s) | 80 |

### RESCUE COMPANY NO 1
| 71 | RAK 122 | Life's Too Short/Then I Think About You | 10 |
| 72 | Jam JAM 14 | I Want To Save You/Amanda | 15 |
| 72 | Jam JAM 27 | I Stand Alone/You Shouldn't Have Been So Nice | 15 |
| 73 | Jam JAM 45 | It's Only Words/Look Out | 25 |
| 74 | DJM DJS 309 | Esmerelda/As Long As You Want Me | 10 |

### RESERVE
| 88 | Sha La La Ba Ba Ba-Ba Ba 006 | Wherever You Go/SIDDELEYS: The Sun Slid Down/Behind The Tower (flexidisc, foldover p/s) | 10 |

### RESIDENTS
| 80 | Pre PRE 009 | THE COMMERCIAL SINGLE (p/s) | 6 |
| 84 | Korova KOW 36 | It's A Man's Man's Man's World/I'll Go Crazy (p/s, 5,000 only) | 5 |
| 79 | Virgin VR 3 | NIBBLES (LP, stickered sleeve, 5,000 only) | 15 |
| 80 | Pre PRE X2 | THE COMMERCIAL ALBUM (LP, 5,000 only, with incorrect song order) | 15 |

### RESISTANCE
| 81 | Fontana KIT 1 | Survival Kit/Big Flame (p/s) | 6 |

### RESISTANCE 77
| 82 | Riot City RIOT 18 | NOWHERE TO PLAY (EP) | 18 |
| 84 | Resistance RESIST 1 | You Reds/Young And Wrong (p/s) | 5 |
| 84 | Rot ASS 6 | Vive The Resistance | 20 |
| 84 | Rot ASS 14 | THOROUGHBRED MEN (LP) | 80 |

### RESISTORS
| 80 | Break SMASH 1 | For Jeanie/Takeaway Love/End Of The Line (p/s) | 10 |
| 83 | DT 027 | That's It/Steal My Love | 25 |

### REST
| 79 | Shooting Star SSR 1 | Carnival/Small Town Rockers | 7 |
| 80 | Shooting Star SSR 2 | Raga/My House (screen printed p/s) | 10 |

**RESTFULL ONES**
70   Grade One GR 1 — Turn To The Sun/She's MIne ....................................................................50

**JOHNNY RESTIVO**
59   RCA RCA 1143 — The Shape I'm In/Ya Ya (with triangular centre) ..............................30
59   RCA RCA 1143 — The Shape I'm In/Ya Ya (later round centre pressing) ....................15
59   RCA RCA 1159 — I Like Girls/Dear Someone ..............................................................15
59   RCA RCA 1159 — I Like Girls/Dear Someone (78) ......................................................20
60   Ember EMB S 135 — Look Here Now/Sweet Sweet Lovin' ..........................................15

**RESTRICTED HOURS**
79   Stevenage (no cat. no.) — Getting Things Done/Still Living Out The Car Crash/SYNDICATE: One Way Or Another/I Want To Be Somebody (white label, foldover p/s) ................12

*(see also Astronauts)*

**RETREADS**
81   Eddi Osmo EO 101 — Would You Listen Girl/One After 909/You Said You Knew (p/s, with mini-poster insert) ...............60

**RETREAT FROM MOSCOW**
80   Wicker Monkey WM 001/ — To The Night/Perception (p/s) ..................................15
     MHMS 169/EJSP 9328

**REVELATION (JAMAICA)**
70   Trojan TR 7727 — Suffering/MEGATONS: Crazy Elephant ..........................................7

**REVELATION (1)**
78   Write Sounds WTS 1003 — With You Boy/Dub You ..................................................10
78   Write Sounds WTS 1003 — Jah Feelings/With You Boy (12") ....................................18
78   Write Sounds WTS 1004 — Jah Feelings/Dub Feelings ............................................10
81   Kingdom KV 8013 — Tonight/Fussin' And Fightin' ....................................................6
81   Kingdom KV 8013-12 — Tonight/Fussin' And Fightin' (12") ....................................10
78   Burning Sounds BS 1030 — BOOK OF REVELATION (LP) ..........................................25
79   Burning Vibrations BV 1007 — VARIATION ON A THEM (LP) ....................................20

**REVELATION (2)**
80   Handshake HANDS 1 — Feel It/When I Fall In Love ..................................................8

**REVELATION (3)**
91   Rise Above RISE 6 — SALVATIONS ANSWER (LP, stickered sleeve) ..........................30

**REVELLERS**
66   Columbia DB 8093 — Believe, Believe/Love Is The Greatest Thing ............................7
67   Spin SP2002 — Yasmin/When I Needed A Neighbour ................................................12
67   Spin LP 1703 — REVELLERS AGAIN (LP) ..................................................................35

**REVELLS**
71   CBS 7050 — Mind Party/Indian Ropeman ..............................................................50

**DIGGER REVELL'S DENVERMEN**
63   Decca F 11657 — Surfside/Lisa Marie ......................................................................20

**REVELS**
59   Top Rank JAR 235 — Midnight Stroll/Talking To My Heart ......................................40

**REVENGE (1)**
78   Loony LOO 2 — We're Not Gonna Take It/Pornography (glossy p/s, counterfeits have matt sleeve, and lack ridge around label) ................200
76   Normal QS 000 — Go Away/Game ..........................................................................12
78   Loony LOO 1 — Our Generation/I Love Her Way (counterfeits lack ridge around label) ..........450
70s  Blood CUS 614 — Don't Tell Me Lies/Gimme The Good Times ................................10

**REVERB**
94   Ochre OCH 001 — Pedal/Swift (Foldover p/s in poly bag) ......................................10

**PAUL REVERE & THE RAIDERS (FEATURING MARK LINDSAY)**
61   Top Rank JAR 557 — Like Long Hair/Sharon ............................................................20
65   Sue WI 344 — Like Long Hair/Sharon (reissue) ......................................................30
65   CBS 202003 — Steppin' Out/Blue Fox ....................................................................10
66   CBS 202027 — Just Like Me/B F D R F Blues ..........................................................20
66   CBS 202205 — Kicks/Shake It Up ..........................................................................15
66   CBS 202253 — Hungry/There She Goes ..................................................................10
66   CBS 202411 — The Great Airplane Strike/In My Community ....................................12
67   CBS 202502 — Good Thing/Undecided Man ............................................................12
67   CBS 202610 — Ups And Downs/Leslie ....................................................................10
67   CBS 2737 — Him Or Me - What's It Gonna Be?/The Legend Of Paul Revere ..........10
67   CBS 2919 — I Had A Dream/Upon Your Leaving ......................................................6
67   CBS 3186 — Mo'reen/Oh! To Be A Man ..................................................................10
68   CBS 3310 — Too Much Talk/Happening '68 (featuring Mark Lindsay) ....................20
68   CBS 3586 — Don't Take It So Hard/Observation From Flight 285 (featuring Mark Lindsay) ......8
68   CBS 3757 — Cinderella Sunshine/Theme From It's Happening (featuring Mark Lindsay) ......6
69   CBS 4025 — Mr. Sun, Mr. Moon/With You (featuring Mark Lindsay) ......................6
69   CBS 4260 — Let Me/I Don't Know (featuring Mark Lindsay) ....................................7
69   CBS 4504 — We Gotta All Get Up Together/Frankfurt Side Street (featuring Mark Lindsay) ......6
76   Jay Boy BOY 108 — Ain't Nothin' Wrong/ou're Really Sayin' Something ..................7
66   CBS (S)BPG 62406 — JUST LIKE US (LP) ................................................................25
66   CBS (S)BPG 62797 — MIDNIGHT RIDE (LP) ............................................................25
67   CBS (S)BPG 62963 — GOOD THING (LP) ..................................................................20
68   CBS (S)BPG 63095 — REVOLUTION (LP) ..................................................................20
69   CBS 63265 — GOIN' TO MEMPHIS (LP, mono/stereo) ..............................................20
69   CBS 63649 — HARD 'N' HEAVY (LP) ......................................................................20

*(see also Mark Lindsay, Raiders)*

MINT VALUE £

## REVEREND W AWDRY
| | | | |
|---|---|---|---|
| 57 | Chiltern C1000 | Edwards Day Out/Edward And John (not in printed picture company sleeve) | 10 |
| 67 | Chiltern C1000 | Edwards Day Out/Edward And John (in printed picture company sleeve) | 20 |

## REVIEW
| | | | |
|---|---|---|---|
| 80s | All The Madmen REV 1 | England's Glory (stapled gatefold p/s with lyric insert) | 10 |

## REVILLOS
| | | | |
|---|---|---|---|
| 79 | Snatzo/Dindisc DIN 1 | Where's The Boy For Me/The Fiend (p/s) | 5 |
| 79 | Snatzo/Dindisc DIN 5 | Motor Bike Beat/No Such Luck (p/s) | 5 |
| 80 | Snatzo/Dindisc DINZ 16 | Scuba Scuba/Scuba Boy Bop (p/s) | 5 |
| 80 | Snatzo/Dindisc DINZ 20 | Hungry For Love/Voodoo 2 (p/s, label also lists SP 703) | 5 |
| 82 | Superville SV 1001 | She's Fallen In Love With A Monster Man/Mind Bending Cutie Doll (p/s) | 10 |
| 82 | Superville SV 2001 | Bongo Brain/Hip City - You Were Meant For Me (p/s) | 6 |
| 82 | Aura AUS 135 | Tell Him/Graveyard Groove (p/s) | 6 |
| 83 | EMI RVL 1 | Bitten By A Love Bug/Cat Call | 5 |
| 84 | EMI RVL 2 | Midnight/Z-X-7 (p/s) | 5 |
| 96 | Damaged Goods DAMGOOD 93 | Jack The Ripper/A Yeah Yeah Yeah Yeah/Meet The Revillos (pink vinyl, p/s) | 7 |
| 80 | Snatzo/Dindisc DID X 3 | REV UP (LP, green or pink titles) | 20 |
| 82 | Superville SV 4001 | ATTACK! (LP, withdrawn) | 40 |

*(see also Rezillos)*

## REVOLUTION
| | | | |
|---|---|---|---|
| 66 | Piccadilly 7N 35289 | Hallelujah/Shades Of Blue | 65 |

*(see also Hellions, Luther Grosvenor, Traffic, Dave Mason & Cass Elliot, Spirit)*

## (THE) REVOLUTIONARIES
| | | | |
|---|---|---|---|
| 77 | Sky Note SKY DD 002 | Afro Rock Part 1/Afro Rock Part 2 (12") | 40 |
| 77 | Sky Note SKY 1002 | El Bamba | 20 |
| 78 | Island IPR 2024 | Headache/Bellyache/Toothache/Headache (12") | 30 |
| 78 | Ballistic FORCE 2003 | FATAL DUB (12" EP) | 20 |
| 75 | Love LOV 01 | GUN COURT DUB (LP) | 40 |
| 76 | Trenchtown TRELP 001 | REVOLUTIONARY DUB (LP, with the We The People Band) | 60 |
| 78 | Hawkeye HALP 001 | DREAD AT THE CONTROLS (LP) | 40 |
| 78 | Cha Cha CHALP 002 | REACTION IN DUB (LP) | 35 |
| 78 | Cha Cha CHALP 005 | JONKANOO DUB (LP) | 30 |
| 79 | Burning Vibrations BV 1002 | DUTCH MAN DUB (LP) | 30 |
| 79 | Burning Vibrations BV 1004 | GREEN BAY DUB (LP) | 50 |
| 79 | Burning Vibrations BV 1010 | BURNING DUB (LP) | 30 |
| 79 | Trojan TRLS 169 | OUTLAW DUB (LP) | 25 |
| 80 | Manzie DRS LP 002 | KING'S DUB (LP) | 25 |
| 82 | Cha Cha CHALP 014 | REVIVAL (LP) | 40 |
| 07 | Pressure Sounds PSLP 55 | DRUM SOUND: MORE GEMS FROM THE CHANNEL ONE DUB ROOM 1974-1980 (2-LP) | 20 |

## REVOLUTIONARY ARMY OF INFANT JESUS
| | | | |
|---|---|---|---|
| 87 | Probe Plus PROBE 12 | THE GIFT OF TEARS (LP) | 40 |

## REVOLUTIONARY BLUES BAND
| | | | |
|---|---|---|---|
| 70 | MCA MUP(S) 402 | REVOLUTIONARY BLUES BAND (LP) | 20 |

## REVOLUTIONARY CORPS OF TEENAGE JESUS VS SUICIDE
| | | | |
|---|---|---|---|
| 96 | Creeping Bent BENT 005 | FRANKIE TEARDROP EP (Frankie Teardrop [126 b.p.m.]/U.S.A. '95/Frankie Teardrop [114 b.p.m.]/Womb 17) (12", p/s, 1,000 only) | 10 |

*(see also Suicide, Future Pilot A.KA.)*

## REVOLVER (1)
| | | | |
|---|---|---|---|
| 69 | Young BLood YB 1006 | Frisco Annie/Imaginations | 20 |

## REVOLVER (2)
| | | | |
|---|---|---|---|
| 78 | Rockburgh ROCS 203 | Silently Screaming/On The Run (p/s) | 15 |
| 79 | Rox ROX 10 | One And One Is Two/Nobody I Know | 8 |

## REVOLVING PAINT DREAM
| | | | |
|---|---|---|---|
| 84 | Creation CRE 002 | Flowers In The Sky/In The Afternoon (foldaround p/s in poly bag) | 20 |

*(see also Laughing Apple, Primal Scream)*

## REVULSION
| | | | |
|---|---|---|---|
| 85 | Radical Change RC 7 | Ever Get The Feeling Of Utter... (12") | 20 |

## KIMBERLEY REW
| | | | |
|---|---|---|---|
| 80 | Armageddon AS 004 | Stomping All Over The World/Nothing's Going To Change In Your Life/Fighting Someone's War (p/s) | 5 |
| 81 | Armageddon AS 012 | My Baby Does Her Hairdo Long/Fishing (p/s, with dB's) | 5 |

*(see also Soft Boys, Waves)*

## REX (MORRIS) & MINORS
| | | | |
|---|---|---|---|
| 60 | Triumph RGM 1023 | Chicken Sax/Snake Eyes | 50 |

## ROBERTA REX
| | | | |
|---|---|---|---|
| 68 | Fontana TF 967 | Joey/I Can Feel It | 6 |

## ALVINO REY
| | | | |
|---|---|---|---|
| 61 | London HLD 9431 | Original Mama Blues/Steel Guitar Rag | 10 |
| 62 | London HA-D 2414 | ALVINO REY'S GREATEST HITS (LP) | 20 |

## CHICO REY & JET BAND
| | | | |
|---|---|---|---|
| 70 | Pye 7N 17899 | Stiletto/Midnight In Mexico | 40 |

## LITTLE BOBBY REY & HIS BAND
| | | | |
|---|---|---|---|
| 60 | Top Rank JAR 525 | Rockin' "J" Bells/Dance Of The New Year | 8 |

## REYNARD
| | | | |
|---|---|---|---|
| 76 | Pilgrim/Grapevine GRA 102 | FRESH FROM THE EARTH (LP) | 40 |

## DEBBIE REYNOLDS
| | | | |
|---|---|---|---|
| 55 | MGM SP 1127 | Carolina In The Morning/Never Mind The Noise In The Market (B-side as Debbie Reynolds' Naturals) | 10 |
| 56 | MGM SP 1155 | (Love Is) The Tender Trap/Canoodlin' Rag | 8 |
| 58 | MGM MGM-EP 670 | DEBBIE REYNOLDS (EP) | 15 |
| 59 | MGM MGM-EP 694 | DELIGHTFUL DEBBIE REYNOLDS (EP) | 10 |
| 60 | MGM MGM-EP 725 | FROM DEBBIE WITH LOVE (EP) | 10 |
| 59 | London HA-D 2200 | DEBBIE (LP, mono) | 20 |
| 59 | London SAH-D 6051 | DEBBIE (LP, stereo) | 25 |

*(see also Naturals [U.S.])*

## DONN REYNOLDS
| | | | |
|---|---|---|---|
| 58 | MGM MGM 996 | Blue Eyes Crying In The Rain/Bella Belinda | 6 |
| 58 | Pye 7N 15122 | Swing Low Sweet Chariot/Ramona | 6 |
| 59 | Pye NEP 24098 | THE DONN REYNOLDS SONGBAG (EP) | 10 |

## ELI REYNOLDS
| | | | |
|---|---|---|---|
| 70 | Punch PH 37 | Mr Car Man/Chiney Man | 15 |

## JODY REYNOLDS
| | | | |
|---|---|---|---|
| 58 | London HL 8651 | Endless Sleep/Tight Capris | 25 |

## TIMMY REYNOLDS
| | | | |
|---|---|---|---|
| 62 | Ember EMB S 133 | Lullaby Of Love/JEFF MILLS: Daddy's Home | 70 |

## REZILLOS
| | | | |
|---|---|---|---|
| 77 | Sensible FAB 1 | Can't Stand My Baby/I Wanna Be Your Man (p/s, 15,000, 5,000 numbered) | 15 |
| 77 | Sensible FAB 1 | Can't Stand My Baby/I Wanna Be Your Man (p/s, 15,000, 10,000 unnumbered) | 10 |
| 77 | Sensible FAB 2 | Flying Saucer Attack/(My Baby Does) Good Sculptures (p/s, unissued) | 0 |
| 77 | Sire 6078 612 | Flying Saucer Attack/(My Baby Does) Good Sculptures (p/s) | 12 |
| 78 | Sire 6198 215 | Cold Wars/William Mysterious Overture (unissued, rare picture sleeve) | 150 |
| 78 | Sire SIR 4001 | Top Of The Pops/20,000 Rezillos Under The Sea (p/s) | 8 |
| 78 | Sire SIR 4008 | Destination Venus/Mystery Action (p/s) | 6 |
| 79 | Sire SIR 4014 | Cold Wars (live)/Flying Saucer Attack (live)/Twist & Shout (live) (p/s) | 12 |
| 79 | Sensible FAB 1 (Mark 2) | Can't Stand My Baby/I Wanna Be Your Man (reissue, new p/s, run out groove reads "Come Back John Lennon") | 7 |
| 79 | Sensible FAB 1 (Mark 2) | Can't Stand My Baby/I Wanna Be Your Man (reissue, p/s, mispressing, B-side plays "(My Baby Does) Good Sculptures (live)", run-off groove reads "De-sire-able product?", 4,000 only) | 6 |
| 78 | Sire K 56530 | CAN'T STAND THE REZILLOS (LP, with inner sleeve & postcard insert) | 30 |
| 78 | Sire SRK 6069 | MISSION ACCOMPLISHED ... BUT THE BEAT GOES ON (LP, live) | 18 |

*(see also Revillos, Shake, Jo Callis, William Mysterious)*

## RHABSTALLION
| | | | |
|---|---|---|---|
| 81 | Rhab RHAB 001 | Day To Day/Breadline (p/s, with badge) | 30 |
| 81 | Rhab RHAB 001 | Day To Day/Breadline (p/s) | 20 |

## RHINOCEROS
| | | | |
|---|---|---|---|
| 69 | Elektra EKSN 45051 | Apricot Brandy/I Don't Want To Discuss It | 10 |
| 69 | Elektra EKSN 45058 | I Will Serenade You/Belbuekul | 7 |
| 70 | Elektra EKSN 45080 | Back Door/In A Little Room | 6 |
| 70 | Elektra 2101 009 | Old Age/Let's Party | 6 |
| 69 | Elektra EKL 4030 | RHINOCEROS (LP, orange label, also stereo EKS 74030) | 20 |
| 69 | Elektra EKL 4056 | SATIN CHICKENS (LP, also stereo EKS 74056) | 20 |
| 70 | Elektra 2469 006 | BETTER TIMES ARE COMING (LP, gatefold sleeve) | 15 |

## RHODA WITH THE SPECIAL A.K.A.
| | | | |
|---|---|---|---|
| 82 | 2-Tone CHS TT 18 | The Boiler/Theme From The Boiler (paper labels) | 8 |
| 82 | 2-Tone CHS 7718 | The Boiler/Theme From The Boiler (plastic labels) | 5 |
| 82 | 2-Tone CHS TT 1218 | The Boiler/Theme From The Boiler (12", p/s existence unconfirmed) | 20 |

*(see also Special A.K.A.)*

## JAN RHODE & HIS COOL CATS
| | | | |
|---|---|---|---|
| 60 | Qualiton Offbeat PSP 7128 | Come Back Baby/So Shy | 8 |

## PAT RHODEN
| | | | |
|---|---|---|---|
| 65 | Ska Beat JB 195 | Jezebel/You Can Hold My Hand | 20 |
| 66 | Blue Beat BB 360 | Send Your Love/Make Believe | 15 |
| 68 | Trojan TR 606 | Woman Is Greedy/Endlessly | 10 |
| 70 | Pama PM 811 | Maybe The Next Time/Got To See You | 8 |
| 70 | Pama Supreme PS 298 | Do What You Gotta Do/Crying Won't Help You | 8 |
| 70 | Mary Lyn ML 101 | Time Is Tight/MILTON & DENZIL: I Like It Like That | 20 |
| 73 | Pama Supreme PS 378 | Out Of Time/Put A Little Rain Into My Life | 8 |

*(see also Pat Riden, Pat & Marie, Denzil & Pat)*

## EMITT RHODES
| | | | |
|---|---|---|---|
| 71 | Probe PRO 520 | Fresh As A Daisy/You Take The Dark Out Of The Night | 5 |
| 71 | Probe PRO 529 | With My Face On The Floor/Somebody Made For Me | 5 |
| 71 | A&M AMS 865 | You're A Very Lovely Woman/Till The Day After | 5 |
| 72 | Probe PRO 565 | Tame The Lion/Golden Child Of God | 5 |
| 71 | Probe SPBA 6256 | EMITT RHODES (LP, gatefold sleeve) | 15 |
| 71 | A&M AMLS 64254 | AMERICAN DREAM (LP) | 15 |

## TODD RHODES ORCHESTRA
| | | | |
|---|---|---|---|
| 55 | Parlophone MSP 6171 | Specks/Silver Sunset | 30 |

## RHODESIANS
| | | | |
|---|---|---|---|
| 80 | Period PER 001 | Clock!!!/Postmortem (p/s) | 15 |

## RHUBARB RHUBARB
| | | | |
|---|---|---|---|
| 68 | President PT 229 | Rainmaker/Moneylender | 160 |

## GRUFF RHYS

| | | | |
|---|---|---|---|
| 11 | Ovni OVNI 006 | Y Baban Bach/Y Baban Back (instrumental) (tour 7", 300 only) | 10 |
| 04 | Placid Casual PLC10LP | YR ATAL GENHEDLAETH (LP) | 25 |
| 11 | Ovni OVNI 003 | HOTEL SHAMPOO (LP) | 20 |
| 14 | Turnstile TS008LP | AMERICAN INTERIOR (LP, 12", CD, print, box set) | 40 |

*(see also Super Furry Animals)*

## RHYTHM HAWKS
| | | | |
|---|---|---|---|
| 79 | Redball RR 011 | ZODIAC EP | 25 |

## RHYTHM METHODISTS
| | | | |
|---|---|---|---|
| 81 | Methodisques MD 1 | Don't Rely On Me/Cooler Relations (hand-made p/s) | 12 |

## RHYTHM ACES
| | | | |
|---|---|---|---|
| 61 | Starlite ST45 061 | A Thousand Teardrops/Wherever You May Go | 20 |
| 61 | Starlite ST45 066 | Please Don't Go Away/Oh My Darling | 20 |
| 62 | Blue Beat BB 134 | I'll Be There/DON DRUMMOND: Dewdrops | 20 |
| 62 | Island WI 032 | C-H-R-I-S-T-M-A-S/TOP GRANT: A Christmas Drink | 18 |

## RHYTHM & BLUES INC.
| | | | |
|---|---|---|---|
| 65 | Fontana TF 524 | Louie Louie/Honey Don't | 75 |

## RHYTHM CATS
| | | | |
|---|---|---|---|
| 79 | Tyger TYG 3 | ROCK WITH THE RHYTHM CATS EP (1,000 only) | 8 |

## RHYTHMETTES
| | | | |
|---|---|---|---|
| 59 | Coral Q 72358 | Page From The Future/I'll Be With You In Apple Blossom Time | 10 |

## RHYTHM FORCE
| | | | |
|---|---|---|---|
| 72 | Tropical AL 0013 | Satta Call/Satta Version | 6 |

## RHYTHM KINGS
| | | | |
|---|---|---|---|
| 63 | Vocalion POP V 9212 | Blue Soul/Exotic | 30 |

## RHYTHM OF LIFE
| | | | |
|---|---|---|---|
| 81 | Rational RATE 6 | Soon/Summertime (p/s; label also lists Rhythm RHYTHM 1) | 10 |
| 82 | Rational RATE 7 | Uncle Sam/Portrait Of The Heart (p/s; label also lists Rhythm RHYTHM 2) | 15 |

*(see also Josef K, Paul Haig)*

## RHYTHM RULERS
| | | | |
|---|---|---|---|
| 70 | Bullet BU 447 | Second Pressure/Sammy Dead | 20 |
| 70 | Trojan TBL 132 | MUDIES MOODS (LP) | 20 |

*(see also Lloyd Jones, U Roy Junior, Matadors, Winston Groovy, Pat, Winston Wright)*

## RIBS
| | | | |
|---|---|---|---|
| 78 | Aerco AERS 101 | Man With No Brain/Long Time Coming (p/s) | 25 |

## RICARDOS
| | | | |
|---|---|---|---|
| 95 | Raucous RAUC 023 | RIVERSIDE ROCKABILLY EP | 10 |
| 96 | Raucous RAUC 026 | Slinky/Sinful Woman/Let Me In | 8 |

## BOYD RICE & FRIENDS
| | | | |
|---|---|---|---|
| 81 | Mute STUMM 4 | BOYD RICE (LP) | 15 |
| 90 | New European BADVC 1969 | MUSIC, MARTINIS AND MISANTHROPY (LP, with inner sleeve) | 25 |

*(see also Non, Death In June, Current 93)*

## MACK RICE
| | | | |
|---|---|---|---|
| 69 | Atlantic 584 250 | Love's A Mother Brother/Coal Man | 12 |

## TIM RICE & WEBBER GROUP
| | | | |
|---|---|---|---|
| 69 | RCA RCA 1895 | Come Back Richard (Your Country Needs You)/Roll On Over The Atlantic | 8 |
| 74 | Chrysalis CHS 2059 | Not Fade Away/Nothing Different (Nothing Altered, Nothing Changed) | 5 |

*(see also Tales Of Justine)*

## MANDY RICE-DAVIES
| | | | |
|---|---|---|---|
| 64 | Ember EMB 4537 | MANDY (EP) | 30 |

## BOB RICH
| | | | |
|---|---|---|---|
| 70 | Mother MOT 1 | Christas In My Pants/My Woman | 8 |
| 73 | Mother MOT 5 | Filthy Rich/Navy Blue Blues | 10 |

## BOBBY RICH
| | | | |
|---|---|---|---|
| 03 | Grapevine G2K 45 139 | There's A Girl Somewhere For Me/I Can't Help Myself | 7 |

## BUDDY RICH
| | | | |
|---|---|---|---|
| 67 | Fontana TF836 | Norwegian Wood (This Bird Has Flown)/Monitor Theme | 20 |

## CHARLIE RICH
| | | | |
|---|---|---|---|
| 60 | London HLU 9107 | Lonely Weekends/Everything I Do Is Wrong | 50 |
| 62 | London HLS 9482 | Just A Little Bit Sweet/It's Too Late | 40 |
| 65 | RCA RCA 1433 | Too Many Teardrops/It's All Over Now | 10 |
| 65 | Philips BF 1432 | Mohair Sam/I Washed My Hands In Muddy Water | 10 |
| 67 | London HLU 10104 | Love Is After Me/Pass On By (silver-top label) | 15 |
| 67 | London HLU 10104 | Love Is After Me/Pass On By (later boxed logo label) | 10 |
| 67 | London HLU 10104 | Love Is After Me/Pass On By (DJ copy) | 70 |
| 69 | Mercury MF 1109 | Mohair Sam/I Washed My Hands In Muddy Water (reissue) | 10 |
| 65 | RCA RD 7719 | THAT'S RICH (LP) | 40 |

## DAVE RICH
| | | | |
|---|---|---|---|
| 58 | RCA RCA 1092 | Burn On Love Fire/City Lights | 15 |
| 66 | Polydor BM 56113 | Last Two People On Earth/I Just Wanna Dance | 6 |

## JOHNNY RICH
| | | | |
|---|---|---|---|
| 64 | Mercury MF 836 | Dream On/Together | 6 |

## LEWIS RICH
| | | | |
|---|---|---|---|
| 66 | Parlophone R 5434 | I Don't Want To Hear It Anymore/Shedding Tears | 15 |

## SKETTO RICH
| | | | |
|---|---|---|---|
| 70 | Pama PM 806 | Hound Dog/Black Girl | 7 |

71   Big Shot BI 596          Know Your Friend/Know Your Friend - Version ..................................................5

*(see Buddy & Sketto, Ruddy & Sketto, Father Sketto, Owen Gray)*

## TONY RICH
66   Piccadilly 7N 35291      Save Your Love/Don't Mention Your Name................................................10
66   Piccadilly 7N 35323      It's All Up To You Now/See Saw .............................................................15

*(see also Tony Sheveton)*

## RICHARD
69   Parlophone R 5754        A Little Bit/Take Me............................................................................15

## CLIFF RICHARD (& DRIFTERS/SHADOWS)
### 78s
58   Columbia DB 4178         Move It!/Schoolboy Crush........................................................................35
58   Columbia DB 4203         High Class Baby/My Feet Hit The Ground .............................................30
59   Columbia DB 4249         Livin' Lovin' Doll/Steady With You ........................................................80
59   Columbia DB 4290         Mean Streak/Never Mind ......................................................................80
59   Columbia DB 4306         Living Doll/Apron Strings .....................................................................40

*(The above 78s were credited to Cliff Richard & Drifters)*

59   Columbia DB 4351         Travellin' Light/Dynamite (as Cliff Richard & Shadows)...........................45
60   Columbia DB 4398         A Voice In The Wilderness/Don't Be Mad At Me (credited to Cliff Richard & Shadows) ........................................................................................100

### SINGLES : COLUMBIA
58   Columbia DB 4178         Move It!/Schoolboy Crush (green label) ................................................25
58   Columbia DB 4178         Move It!/Schoolboy Crush (later pressing with black label) ...................15
58   Columbia DB 4203         High Class Baby/My Feet Hit The Ground (green label) .........................25
58   Columbia DB 4203         High Class Baby/My Feet Hit The Ground (later pressing with black label) ...15
59   Columbia DB 4249         Livin' Lovin' Doll/Steady With You (green label) ...................................40
59   Columbia DB 4249         Livin' Lovin' Doll/Steady With You (later pressing with black label)..........15
59   Columbia DB 4290         Mean Streak/Never Mind (green label) .................................................20
59   Columbia DB 4290         Mean Streak/Never Mind (later pressing with black label) ......................8
59   Columbia DB 4306         Living Doll/Apron Strings (green label) ................................................15
59   Columbia DB 4306         Living Doll/Apron Strings (later pressing with black label) ...................15
59   Columbia DB 4351         Travellin' Light/Dynamite .....................................................................5
60   Columbia DB 4398         A Voice In The Wilderness/Don't Be Mad At Me .....................................5
60   Columbia DB 4431         Fall In Love With You/Willie And The Hand Jive ...................................5
60   Columbia DB 4479         Please Don't Tease/Where Is My Heart ................................................5
60   Columbia DB 4506         Nine Times Out Of Ten/Thinking Of Our Love ......................................6
60   Columbia DB 4547         I Love You/"D" In Love .......................................................................5
61   Columbia DB 4593         Theme For A Dream/Mumblin' Mosie ..................................................5
61   Columbia DB 4667         A Girl Like You/Now's The Time To Fall In Love ...................................5
61   Columbia DB 4716         When The Girl In Your Arms Is The Girl In Your Heart/ Got A Funny Feeling (solo)...........5
62   Columbia DB 4761         The Young Ones/We Say Yeah (green label).........................................5
62   Columbia DB 4761         The Young Ones/We Say Yeah (later black label) .................................7
62   Columbia DB 4828         I'm Lookin' Out The Window/Do You Want To Dance?...........................5
62   Columbia DB 4886         It'll Be Me/Since I Lost You .................................................................6

*(The above 45s were originally green labels; later black label copies are worth at least twice the listed values)*

62   Columbia DB 4950         The Next Time/Bachelor Boy ...............................................................5
63   Columbia DB 4977         Summer Holiday/Dancing Shoes ..........................................................5
63   Columbia DB 7034         Lucky Lips/I Wonder............................................................................5
63   Columbia DB 7089         It's All In The Game/Your Eyes Tell On You (solo) ................................5
63   Columbia DB 7150         Don't Talk To Him/Say You're Mine.....................................................5
64   Columbia DB 7203         I'm The Lonely One/Watch What You Do With My Baby .........................5
64   Columbia DB 7272         Constantly (solo)/True True Lovin' ......................................................5
64   Columbia DB 7305         On The Beach/A Matter Of Moments ...................................................5
64   Columbia DB 7372         The Twelfth Of Never/I'm Afraid To Go Home (solo) ............................5
64   Columbia DB 7420         I Could Easily Fall (In Love With You)/I'm In Love With You ..................5

*(The above singles credited to Cliff Richard & Shadows unless otherwise stated, those listed below are Cliff Richard solo unless otherwise stated)*

64   Columbia DB 7435         This Was My Special Day/I'm Feeling Oh So Lovely (withdrawn, credited to Cliff Richard, Audrey Bayley, Joan Palethorpe & Faye Fisher) ..................20
65   Columbia DB 7496         The Minute You're Gone/Just Another Guy .........................................5
65   Columbia DB 7596         On My Word/Just A Little Bit Too Late .................................................6
65   Columbia DB 7660         The Time In Between/Look Before You Love (as Cliff Richard & Shadows) .......6
65   Columbia DB 7745         Wind Me Up (Let Me Go)/The Night.....................................................5
66   Columbia DB 7866         Blue Turns To Grey/Somebody Loses (as Cliff Richard & Shadows)...........6
66   Columbia DB 7968         Visions/What Would I Do (For The Love Of A Girl?) ..............................6
66   Columbia DB 8017         Time Drags By/La La La Song (as Cliff Richard & Shadows) ...................7
66   Columbia DB 8094         In The Country/Finders Keepers (as Cliff Richard & Shadows)................7
66   Columbia PSRS 304        Finders Keepers (promo only, 1-sided, with spoken intro by Simon Dee) ...30
67   Columbia DB 8150         It's All Over/Why Wasn't I Born Rich?..................................................5
67   Columbia DB 8210         I'll Come Runnin'/I Get The Feelin' .....................................................7
67   Columbia DB 8245         The Day I Met Marie/Our Story Book ...................................................5
67   Columbia DB 8293         All My Love/Sweet Little Jesus Boy ......................................................5
68   Columbia DB 8376         Congratulations/High 'N' Dry...............................................................5
68   Columbia DB 8437         I'll Love You Forever Today/Girl, You'll Be A Woman Soon ....................8
68   Columbia DB 8476         Marianne/Mr Nice ..............................................................................5
68   Columbia DB 8503         Don't Forget To Catch Me/What's More (I Don't Need Her) ..................5
69   Columbia DB 8548         Good Times (Better Times)/Occasional Rain ........................................7
69   Columbia DB 8581         Big Ship/She's Leaving You .................................................................7
69   Columbia DB 8615         Throw Down A Line (as Cliff & Hank)/Reflections ................................5
69   Columbia DB 8641         With The Eyes Of A Child/So Long ......................................................7

| 70 | Columbia DB 8657 | Joy Of Living (as Cliff & Hank)/CLIFF RICHARD: Leave My Woman Alone/ HANK MARVIN: Boogatoo ........ 8 |
| 70 | Columbia DB 8685 | Goodbye Sam, Hello Samantha/You Never Can Tell ........ 5 |
| 70 | Columbia DB 8708 | I Ain't Got Time Anymore/Monday Comes Too Soon ........ 7 |
| 71 | Columbia DB 8747 | Sunny Honey Girl/Don't Move Away (with Olivia Newton-John)/ I Was Only Fooling Myself ........ 7 |
| 71 | Columbia DB 8774 | Silvery Rain/Annabella Umbrella/Time Flies ........ 8 |
| 71 | Columbia DB 8797 | Flying Machine/Pigeon ........ 10 |
| 71 | Columbia DB 8836 | Sing A Song Of Freedom/A Thousand Conversations ........ 6 |
| 72 | Columbia DB 8864 | Jesus/Mister Cloud ........ 8 |
| 72 | Columbia DB 8917 | Living In Harmony/Empty Chairs ........ 5 |
| 72 | Columbia DB 8957 | Brand New Song/The Old Accordion ........ 6 |

## SINGLES : EMI SINGLES

| 73 | EMI EMI 2022 | Help It Along/Tomorrow Rising/The Days Of Love/Ashes To Ashes (in p/s) ........ 6 |
| 74 | EMI PSR 368 | Nothing To Remind Me/The Learning (promo only) ........ 40 |
| 75 | EMI EMI 2344 | Honky Tonk Angel/(Wouldn't You Know It) Got Myself A Girl (withdrawn) ........ 15 |
| 78 | EMI EMI 2730 | Yes! He Lives/Good On The Sally Army ........ 5 |
| 78 | EMI EMI 2885 | Can't Take The Hurt Anymore/Needing A Friend (p/s) ........ 5 |
| 79 | EMI EMI 2920 | Green Light/Imagine Love (in p/s) ........ 5 |
| 79 | EMI EMI 2975 | We Don't Talk Anymore/Count Me Out (p/s, mispress, A-side plays Queen's "Bohemian Rhapsody") ........ 12 |
| 84 | EMI 5457 | Ocean Deep/Baby You're Dynamite (p/s) ........ 20 |

## EXPORT SINGLES

| 61 | Columbia DC 756 | Gee Whiz It's You/I Cannot Find A True Love ........ 5 |
| 63 | Columbia DC 758 | What'd I Say/Blue Moon ........ 150 |
| 65 | Columbia DC 762 | Angel/Razzle Dazzle ........ 50 |

## EPs

| 59 | Columbia SEG 7895 | SERIOUS CHARGE (soundtrack) ........ 30 |
| 59 | Columbia SEG 7903 | CLIFF NO. 1 (mono) ........ 25 |
| 59 | Columbia ESG 7754 | CLIFF NO. 1 (stereo) ........ 30 |
| 59 | Columbia SEG 7910 | CLIFF NO. 2 (mono) ........ 20 |
| 59 | Columbia ESG 7769 | CLIFF NO. 2 (stereo) ........ 25 |
| 59 | Columbia SEG 7971 | EXPRESSO BONGO (soundtrack, mono) ........ 20 |
| 59 | Columbia ESG 7783 | EXPRESSO BONGO (soundtrack, stereo) ........ 30 |
| 60 | Columbia SEG 7979 | CLIFF SINGS NO. 1 (mono) ........ 25 |
| 60 | Columbia ESG 7788 | CLIFF SINGS NO. 1 (stereo) ........ 30 |
| 60 | Columbia SEG 7987 | CLIFF SINGS NO. 2 (mono) ........ 25 |
| 60 | Columbia ESG 7794 | CLIFF SINGS NO. 2 (stereo) ........ 30 |
| 60 | Columbia SEG 8005 | CLIFF SINGS NO. 3 (mono) ........ 25 |
| 60 | Columbia ESG 7808 | CLIFF SINGS NO. 3 (stereo) ........ 30 |
| 60 | Columbia SEG 8021 | CLIFF SINGS NO. 4 (mono) ........ 20 |
| 60 | Columbia ESG 7816 | CLIFF SINGS NO. 4 (stereo) ........ 30 |
| 60 | Columbia SEG 8050 | CLIFF'S SILVER DISCS ........ 20 |
| 60 | Columbia SEG 8065 | ME AND MY SHADOWS NO. 1 (mono) ........ 25 |
| 60 | Columbia ESG 7837 | ME AND MY SHADOWS NO. 1 (stereo) ........ 30 |
| 61 | Columbia SEG 8071 | ME AND MY SHADOWS NO. 2 (mono) ........ 25 |
| 61 | Columbia ESG 7481 | ME AND MY SHADOWS NO. 2 (stereo) ........ 30 |
| 61 | Columbia SEG 8078 | ME AND MY SHADOWS NO. 3 (mono) ........ 25 |
| 61 | Columbia ESG 7843 | ME AND MY SHADOWS NO. 3 (stereo) ........ 30 |
| 61 | Columbia SEG 8105 | LISTEN TO CLIFF NO. 1 (mono) ........ 25 |
| 61 | Columbia ESG 7858 | LISTEN TO CLIFF NO. 1 (stereo) ........ 30 |
| 61 | Columbia SEG 8119 | DREAM (mono) ........ 15 |
| 61 | Columbia ESG 7867 | DREAM (stereo) ........ 20 |
| 61 | Columbia SEG 8126 | LISTEN TO CLIFF NO. 2 (mono) ........ 15 |
| 61 | Columbia ESG 7870 | LISTEN TO CLIFF NO. 2 (stereo) ........ 20 |
| 62 | Columbia SEG 8133 | CLIFF'S HIT PARADE ........ 20 |
| 62 | Columbia SEG 8151 | CLIFF RICHARD ........ 20 |
| 62 | Columbia SEG 8159 | HITS FROM 'THE YOUNG ONES' ........ 20 |
| 62 | Columbia SEG 8168 | CLIFF RICHARD NO. 2 ........ 20 |

*(The above EPs were originally issued with turquoise labels, later blue/black label copies are worth two-thirds these values.)*

| 62 | Columbia SEG 8203 | CLIFF'S HITS ........ 20 |
| 63 | Columbia SEG 8228 | TIME FOR CLIFF AND THE SHADOWS (mono) ........ 20 |
| 63 | Columbia ESG 7887 | TIME FOR CLIFF AND THE SHADOWS (stereo, turquoise label) ........ 20 |
| 63 | Columbia ESG 7887 | TIME FOR CLIFF AND THE SHADOWS (stereo, blue/black label) ........ 20 |
| 63 | Columbia SEG 8246 | HOLIDAY CARNIVAL (mono) ........ 15 |
| 63 | Columbia ESG 7892 | HOLIDAY CARNIVAL (stereo) ........ 20 |
| 63 | Columbia SEG 8250 | HITS FROM 'SUMMER HOLIDAY' (mono) ........ 15 |
| 63 | Columbia ESG 7896 | HITS FROM 'SUMMER HOLIDAY' (stereo) ........ 20 |
| 63 | Columbia SEG 8263 | MORE HITS FROM 'SUMMER HOLIDAY' (mono) ........ 15 |
| 63 | Columbia ESG 7898 | MORE HITS FROM 'SUMMER HOLIDAY' (stereo) ........ 20 |
| 63 | Columbia SEG 8269 | CLIFF'S LUCKY LIPS ........ 20 |
| 63 | Columbia SEG 8272 | LOVE SONGS (mono) ........ 20 |
| 63 | Columbia ESG 7900 | LOVE SONGS (stereo) ........ 20 |
| 64 | Columbia SEG 8290 | WHEN IN FRANCE ........ 20 |
| 64 | Columbia SEG 8299 | CLIFF SINGS 'DON'T TALK TO HIM' ........ 15 |
| 64 | Columbia SEG 8320 | CLIFF'S PALLADIUM SUCCESSES ........ 15 |
| 64 | Columbia SEG 8338 | WONDERFUL LIFE (mono) ........ 10 |
| 64 | Columbia ESG 7902 | WONDERFUL LIFE (stereo) ........ 15 |
| 64 | Columbia SEG 8347 | A FOREVER KIND OF LOVE ........ 15 |

| 64 | Columbia SEG 8354 | WONDERFUL LIFE NO. 2 (mono) | 12 |
|---|---|---|---|
| 64 | Columbia ESG 7903 | WONDERFUL LIFE NO. 2 (stereo) | 15 |
| 64 | Columbia SEG 8376 | HITS FROM 'WONDERFUL LIFE' (mono) | 12 |
| 64 | Columbia ESG 7906 | HITS FROM 'WONDERFUL LIFE' (stereo) | 15 |
| 65 | Columbia SEG 8384 | WHY DON'T THEY UNDERSTAND? | 15 |
| 65 | Columbia SEG 8395 | CLIFF'S HITS FROM 'ALADDIN AND HIS WONDERFUL LAMP' | 10 |
| 65 | Columbia SEG 8405 | LOOK IN MY EYES, MARIA | 15 |
| 65 | Columbia SEG 8444 | ANGEL | 15 |
| 65 | Columbia SEG 8450 | TAKE FOUR | 15 |
| 66 | Columbia SEG 8474 | WIND ME UP | 15 |
| 66 | Columbia SEG 8478 | HITS FROM 'WHEN IN ROME' | 15 |
| 66 | Columbia SEG 8488 | LOVE IS FOREVER | 15 |
| 66 | Columbia SEG 8510 | THUNDERBIRDS ARE GO! (3 tracks by Cliff & Shadows, 1 solo) | 50 |
| 66 | Columbia SEG 8517 | LA LA LA LA LA (1 track by Bruce Welch & Hank Marvin) | 20 |
| 67 | Columbia SEG 8527 | CINDERELLA | 40 |
| 67 | Columbia SEG 8533 | CAROL SINGERS | 15 |
| 68 | Columbia SEG 8540 | CONGRATULATIONS | 15 |

## ALBUMS : COLUMBIA LPS

| 59 | Columbia 33SX 1147 | CLIFF (green labels) | 50 |
|---|---|---|---|
| 59 | Columbia 33SX 1147 | CLIFF (later blue/black labels) | 20 |
| 59 | Columbia 33SX 1192 | CLIFF SINGS (green labels) | 50 |
| 59 | Columbia 33SX 1192 | CLIFF SINGS (later blue/black labels) | 20 |
| 60 | Columbia 33SX 1261 | ME AND MY SHADOWS (mono) | 20 |
| 60 | Columbia SCX 3330 | ME AND MY SHADOWS (stereo) | 30 |
| 61 | Columbia 33SX 1320 | LISTEN TO CLIFF! (mono) | 20 |
| 61 | Columbia SCX 3375 | LISTEN TO CLIFF! (stereo) | 30 |
| 61 | Columbia 33SX 1368 | 21 TODAY (mono) | 20 |
| 61 | Columbia SCX 3409 | 21 TODAY (stereo) | 30 |
| 61 | Columbia SCX 3397 | THE YOUNG ONES (soundtrack with inner, stereo) | 15 |
| 62 | Columbia 33SX 1431 | 32 MINUTES AND 17 SECONDS WITH... (mono) | 20 |
| 62 | Columbia SCX 3436 | 32 MINUTES AND 17 SECONDS WITH... | 25 |
| 63 | Columbia SCX 3488 | WHEN IN SPAIN (stereo) | 15 |
| 64 | Columbia SCX 3522 | ALADDIN AND HIS WONDERFUL LAMP (with stage cast, gatefold sleeve, stereo) | 15 |
| 65 | Columbia SX 1709 | CLIFF RICHARD (mono) | 25 |
| 65 | Columbia SCX 3546 | CLIFF RICHARD (stereo) | 20 |
| 65 | Columbia SX 1762 | WHEN IN ROME | 15 |
| 65 | Columbia SX 1769 | LOVE IS FOREVER (also stereo SCX 3569) | 15 |
| 66 | Columbia SX 6039 | KINDA LATIN (mono) | 20 |
| 66 | Columbia SCX 6039 | KINDA LATIN (stereo) | 20 |
| 66 | Columbia SX 6079 | FINDERS KEEPERS (soundtrack, with inner sleeve, mono) | 15 |
| 66 | Columbia SCX 6079 | FINDERS KEEPERS (soundtrack, with inner sleeve, stereo) | 15 |
| 67 | Columbia S(C)X 6103 | CINDERELLA (with stage cast) | 15 |
| 67 | Columbia S(C)X 6133 | DON'T STOP ME NOW | 30 |
| 67 | Columbia JSX 6167 | GOOD NEWS (export issue) | 20 |
| 68 | Columbia S(C)X 6244 | CLIFF IN JAPAN (blue/black labels) | 20 |
| 68 | Columbia S(C)X 6262 | TWO A PENNY (blue/black labels) | 20 |
| 68 | Columbia S(C)X 6262 | TWO A PENNY (later pressing with white/black labels) | 15 |
| 68 | Columbia SX 6282 | ESTABLISHED 1958 (gatefold sleeve, half tracks by Shadows, mono) | 15 |
| 69 | Columbia SX 6357 | SINCERELY CLIFF RICHARD (mono) | 15 |
| 70 | Columbia SCX 6408 | ABOUT THAT MAN (4 songs plus narration) | 15 |
| 70 | Columbia SCX 6435 | TRACKS 'N' GROOVES | 15 |
| 70 | Columbia SCX 6443 | HIS LAND (documentary soundtrack, with Cliff Barrows) | 15 |

## ALBUMS : EMI LPS

| 73 | EMI EMC 3016 | TAKE ME HIGH (soundtrack, with poster) | 15 |
|---|---|---|---|

## ALBUMS : OTHER LPS

| 63 | Elstree Extra Range | SUMMER HOLIDAY (2-LP, full soundtrack recording, 80 copies only) | 250 |
|---|---|---|---|
| 64 | Elstree Extra Range | WONDERFUL LIFE (2-LP, full soundtrack recording, 150 copies only) | 150 |
| 64 | World Record Club (S)T 643 | HOW WONDERFUL TO KNOW (stereo) | 15 |
| 64 | EMI Regal SREG 1120 | ME AND MY SHADOWS (export issue) | 40 |
| 69 | World R. Club STP 1051 | CLIFF RICHARD | 20 |

## FLEXIDISCS : FLEXIDISCS & OTHER RELEASES

| 98 | Cruisin' The 50's CASB 007 | Breathless/Lawdy Miss Clawdy (10" 78, p/s, with 6 inserts) | 30 |
|---|---|---|---|

*(see also Drifters [U.K.], Shadows, Olivia Newton-John, Sheila Walsh, Elton John, Phil Everly, Grazina)*

## WENDY RICHARD & DIANA BERRY

| 63 | Decca F 11680 | We Had A Dream/Keep 'Em Looking Around | 15 |
|---|---|---|---|

*(see also Mike Sarne)*

## RICHARD & GLEN

| 72 | Duke DU 141 | Boat To Progress (Parts 1 & 2) | 15 |
|---|---|---|---|

## RICHARD & YOUNG LIONS

| 66 | Philips BF 1520 | Open Up Your Door/Once Upon Your Smile | 50 |
|---|---|---|---|

## RICHARD BROTHERS

| 63 | Island WI 060 | I Need A Girl/Desperate Lover | 15 |
|---|---|---|---|
| 63 | Island WI 109 | I Shall Wear A Crown/BABA BROOKS: Robin Hood | 20 |

*(see also Joe White)*

## CYNTHIA RICHARDS

| 69 | Clandisc CLA 203 | Foolish Fool/KING STITT: On The Street | 25 |
|---|---|---|---|
| 70 | Clandisc CLA 210 | Conversation/DYNAMITES: Conversation Version II | 20 |
| 70 | Clandisc CLA 216 | Can't Wait/Promises | 12 |

| 70 | Clandisc CLA 220 | Foolish Fool/CLANCY & STITT: Dance Beat | 12 |
| 71 | Clandisc CLA 229 | Stand By Your Man (actually by Merlene Webber)/DYNAMITES: Version 2 | 10 |
| 71 | Big Shot BI 581 | I'm Moving On/HIPPY BOYS: I'm Moving On - Version | 10 |
| 71 | Escort ERT 861 | Love & Unity/MAYTONES: Wah Noh Dead | 7 |
| 71 | G.G. GG 4528 | Place In My Heart/You've Got A Friend (act. Irving [Brown] & Cynthia Richards) | 8 |
| 72 | Pama Supreme PS 366 | Mr Postman/SKIN, FLESH AND BONES: Version | 10 |
| 73 | Attack ATT 8047 | Aily I/REID'S ALL STARS: Aily I - Version | 6 |
| 70 | Trojan TBL 123 | FOOLISH FOOL (LP, actually Clancy Eccles productions compilation) | 50 |

*(see also Bobby Aitken, Lord Comic, Sir Lord Comic)*

## JOHNNY RICHARDS
| 59 | Esquire 32-076 | THE RITES OF DIABLO (LP) | 25 |

## KEITH RICHARDS
| 79 | Rolling Stones RSR 102 | Run Rudolph Run/The Harder They Come (p/s) | 15 |
| 86 | Arista ARIST 678P | Jumping Jack Flash/Integrity (with Aretha Franklin) (shaped pic disc & plinth) | 12 |
| 88 | Virgin VS 1125 | Take It So Hard/I Could Have Stood You Up (p/s) | 5 |
| 89 | Virgin VS 1179 | Make No Mistake (Edit)/It Means A Lot (p/s) | 6 |
| 88 | Virgin KEITH 1234 | Make No Mistake/Locked Away/Struggle/Big Enough (4 x 1-sided 7", "Talk Is Cheap" sampler box set, promo only) | 90 |
| 88 | Virgin 2-91047 A/B/C | TALK IS CHEAP (3 x 3" CDs in tin) | 40 |
| 92 | Virgin VUSLP 59 | MAIN OFFENDER (LP) | 50 |

*(see also Rolling Stones, Aranbee Pop Symphony Orchestra, Dirty Strangers, Screamin' Jay Hawkins)*

## LISA RICHARDS
| 65 | Vocalion VP 9244 | Mean Old World/Take A Chance | 55 |
| 65 | Vocalion VP 9244 | Mean Old World/Take A Chance (DJ copy) | 70 |

## LLOYD RICHARDS
| 64 | Port-O-Jam PJ 4004 | Be Good/I Need You | 25 |

## ROY RICHARDS
| 66 | Doctor Bird DB 1012 | Contact/Maureen | 20 |
| 66 | Island WI 297 | Green Collie/MARCIA GRIFFITHS: You No Good | 30 |
| 66 | Island WI 283 | Double Trouble/FITSY & FREDDY: Why Did You Do It | 25 |
| 66 | Island WI 299 | Western Standard Time/(JA) EAGLES: What An Agony | 35 |
| 66 | Island WI 3000 | South Viet Nam/You Must Be Sorry (Vocal) | 25 |
| 67 | Island WI 3027 | Rub-A-Dub/SHARKS: Baby Come Home | 25 |
| 67 | Tabernacle TS 1000 | When I see Jesus/My Savior Come | 25 |
| 67 | Island WI 3037 | Hopeful Village Ska/DELROY WILSON: Ungrateful Baby | 35 |
| 67 | Island WI 3050 | Port-O-Jam/DELROY WILSON: Get Ready | 45 |
| 67 | Studio One SO 2020 | Hanky Panky/ALTON ELLIS: I Am Still In Love | 50 |

*(see also Roland Alphonso, Lord Comic, Soul Vendors, Jackie Mittoo, Derrick Morgan, Righteous Flames)*

## RUSTY RICHARDS
| 60 | Top Rank JAR 297 | Middle Hand Road/Golden Moon (China Night) | 7 |

## TRUDY RICHARDS
| 57 | Capitol CL 14728 | Wishbone/Hangin' Around | 10 |
| 57 | Capitol CL 14744 | Weaker Than Wise/I Want A Big Butter And Egg Man | 6 |
| 58 | Capitol CL 14857 | Somebody Just Like You/The Night When Love Was Born | 6 |
| 57 | Capitol T 838 | CRAZY IN LOVE (LP) | 15 |

## VIC RICHARDS
| 67 | Polydor 56163 | Jonathan Whatsit/Goodbye | 70 |

## WINSTON RICHARDS
| 67 | Rio R 124 | Studio Blitz/Don't Up | 20 |

## DEL RICHARDSON
| 73 | MCA MUPS 491 | PIECES OF A JIGSAW (LP, black/silver label) | 100 |

*(see also Osibisa, Sundae Times)*

## JOE 'GROUNDHOG' RICHARDSON
| 69 | Major Minor MM 632 | Take It Off/Blues To Take It Off | 15 |

## MARK RICHARDSON
| 65 | Stateside SS 440 | Baby, I'm Sorry/Blanket Fair | 7 |
| 65 | Stateside SS 467 | See It My Way/Think | 7 |

## RICH FEVER
| 70 | Parlophone R5869 | Everything's Moving/King Of All The Kingdoms | 15 |
| 71 | Parlophone R 5894 | Song Of A Sad Man/Island Dreams | 12 |

## RICH GYPSY
| 80 | Splash SP 016 | What Hit Me (no p/s) | 25 |

## TONY RICHIE
| 68 | Beacon BEA 114 | Anybody At The Party Seen Jenny/You Can't Win | 40 |

## RICH KIDS
| 78 | EMI EMI 2738 | Rich Kids/Empty Words (red vinyl, laminated p/s with EMI 2738 06599) | 5 |
| 78 | EMI EMI 2803 | Marching Men/Here Comes The Nice (p/s) | 6 |
| 78 | EMI 2848 | Ghosts Of Princes Towers/Only Arsenic (company sleeve) | 6 |
| 78 | EMI EMC 3263 | GHOSTS OF PRINCES IN TOWERS (LP) | 15 |

*(see also Sex Pistols, Ultravox, Spectres, Visage)*

## JONATHAN RICHMAN & MODERN LOVERS
| 84 | Rough Trade RT152 | That Summer Music/This Kind of Music (p/s) | 5 |
| 75 | United Artists UP 36006 | Road Runner/It Will Stand | 7 |
| 77 | Beserkley BZZ 1 | Road Runner (Once)/Road Runner (Twice) (p/s) | 5 |
| 77 | Beserkley BSERK 9 | ROCK 'N' ROLL WITH THE MODERN LOVERS (LP) | 20 |
| 77 | Beserkley BSERK 2 | JONATHAN RICHMAN AND THE MODERN LOVERS (LP) | 25 |
| 77 | Beserkley BSERK 12 | MODERN LOVERS LIVE (LP) | 15 |
| 77 | Beserkley BSERK 17 | BACK IN YOUR LIFE (LP) | 18 |

| 81 | Mohawk LBOM 1 | ORIGINAL (LP) ................................................................ 20 |
|----|---------------|--------------------------------------------------|
| 84 | Rough Trade ROUGH 52 | JONATHAN SINGS (LP) ........................................ 15 |
| 85 | Rough Trade ROUGH 72 | ROCKIN' & ROMANCE (LP) .................................. 15 |
| 86 | Rough Trade ROUGH 92 | IT'S TIME FOR (LP) .............................................. 20 |
| 88 | Demon FIEND 106 | MODERN LOVERS 88 (LP) .................................... 15 |
| 89 | Special Delivery SPD 1024 | JONATHAN RICHMAN (LP) .............................. 15 |
| 90 | Special Delivery SPD 1037 | JONATHAN GOES COUNTRY (LP) .................. 15 |
| 90 | Castle ESDLP 128 | 23 GREAT RECORDINGS BY (2-LP) ...................... 18 |

## RICH MIX
| 83 | Satril 12 SAT 509 | I Got The Love/Version (12") ................................ 15 |
|----|------------------|--------------------------------------|

## RICHMOND
| 73 | Dart ART 2008 | Candy Dora/Willow Farm ............................................ 12 |
|----|---------------|--------------------------------------|
| 73 | Dart ART 2025 | Frightened/Breakfast ................................................ 8 |
| 73 | Dart ART 2031 | Raise Your Heads To The Wind/All I Really Need ........ 5 |
| 74 | Dart ART 2044 | Peaches/Work For My Baby ...................................... 10 |
| 73 | Dart ARTS 65371 | FRIGHTENED (LP, textured sleeve, lyric insert) ........ 30 |

## BEN RICHMOND
| 63 | Piccadilly 7N 35092 | Blue Bird/Bells All Started Ringing ...................... 6 |
|----|---------------------|--------------------------------------|
| 63 | Piccadilly 7N 35132 | You Gotta Have Love/I Don't Care ...................... 6 |

## FIONA RICHMOND
| 73 | Raymond PR 112 | FRANKLY FIONA (LP) .............................................. 50 |
|----|----------------|--------------------------------------|

## JANET RICHMOND
| 60 | Top Rank JAR 288 | You Got What It Takes/Not One Minute More .......... 10 |
|----|------------------|--------------------------------------|
| 60 | Top Rank JAR 378 | June Bride/My One And Only Love .......................... 7 |
| 61 | Top Rank JAR 536 | Senora/I Need You .................................................. 10 |

## RICH PICKINGS
| 69 | Cresta CR 1 | Time To Leave/Mind In Motion .................................. 200 |
|----|-------------|--------------------------------------|
| 73 | Taylor Made TM 11 | Jump To It/My Heroes Back (not sure if this is same group as above) ...... 20 |

## RICHUS FLAMES
| 67 | Fab FAB 17 | Need To Be Loved/I Am Going Home ........................ 50 |
|----|------------|--------------------------------------|

*(see also Righteous Flames)*

## RICK & KEENS
| 61 | Mercury AMT 1150 | Peanuts/I'll Be Home .............................................. 50 |
|----|------------------|--------------------------------------|

## RICK & SANDY
| 65 | Decca F 12196 | Lost My Girl/I Can't Help It .................................... 35 |
|----|---------------|--------------------------------------|
| 65 | Decca F 12311 | Creation/In A 100 Years From Now ........................ 25 |

## BERESFORD RICKETTS
| 60 | Starlite ST45 025 | Cherry Baby/I Want To Know .................................. 30 |
|----|-------------------|--------------------------------------|
| 60 | Starlite ST45 029 | Baby Baby/When I Woke Up .................................... 30 |
| 61 | Starlite ST45 048 | Hold Me Tight/Dream Girl (as Ricketts & Rowe) ...... 30 |
| 62 | Starlite ST45 079 | I'm Going To Cry/Waiting For Me .......................... 30 |
| 62 | Blue Beat BB 107 | You Better Be Going/I've Been Walking (as Beresford Ricketts & Blue Beats) .. 22 |
| 63 | Dice CC 12 | Oh Jean/Rivers Of Tears (as Lauren Aitken's Group) .. 20 |
| 66 | Blue Beat BB 350 | Jailer Bring Me Water/Careless Love ...................... 22 |

## RICKY & THE MUTATIONS
| 83 | Cool Ghoul COOL 003 | Thatcher Rap (12") ............................................ 25 |
|----|---------------------|--------------------------------------|

## RICKY BAILEY
| 78 | K&B KB 5525 | Proud Mary/Proud Man .......................................... 6 |
|----|-------------|--------------------------------------|

## RICO (RODRIGUEZ)
| 61 | Blue Beat BB 56 | Luke Lane Shuffle (as Rico Rodrigues & Buster's All Stars)/ BUSTER'S GROUP: Little Honey ...................... 25 |
|----|-----------------|--------------------------------------|
| 62 | Island WI 022 | Rico Special (as Emanuel Rodrigues Orchestra; some copies may credit Reco & His Happy Orchestra)/BUNNY & SKITTER: A Little Mashin' ...... 35 |
| 62 | Planetone RC 1 | London Here I Come/Midnight In Ethiopia .............. 25 |
| 62 | Planetone RC 4 | Planet Rock/You Win .............................................. 20 |
| 62 | Planetone RC 5 | Youth Boogie/Western Serenade (as Rico's Combo) .. 20 |
| 67 | Fab FAB 12 | Jingle Bells/Silent Night (with His Boys) .................. 10 |
| 68 | Pama PM 706 | Soul Man/It's Not Unusual (as Reco Rodriguez) ...... 15 |
| 68 | Pama PM 715 | Tender Foot Ska/Memories (as Reco Rodriguez) ...... 20 |
| 69 | Blue Cat BS 160 | The Bullet/Rhythm In (as Reco Rodriguez & His Rhythm Aces) .. 25 |
| 69 | Doctor Bird DB 1302 | Baby Face (as Reco & Rudies)/RUDIES: News .......... 25 |
| 69 | Bullet BU 407 | Tribute To Don Drummond/Japanese Invasion (as Rico Rodriquez) .. 60 |
| 71 | Duke DU 96 | Surprise Package (as Rico & Satch)/PETE JOHNSON: I'm Sorry .... 20 |
| 77 | Island WIP 6399 | Africa/Afro-Dub .................................................... 15 |
| 78 | Island IPR 2002 | Dial Africa/Dub (12") ............................................ 25 |
| 79 | Island IPR 2016 | Take 5/Sound Check (12") ...................................... 20 |
| 70s | Island IPR 2006 | Ska-Wars/Ramble (12") .......................................... 25 |
| 80 | Island IPR 2030 | Children Of Sanchez/You Really Got Me/Midnight In Ethiopia (12") .. 30 |
| 80 | 2-Tone CHS TT 15 | Sea Cruise/Carolina .............................................. 20 |
| 82 | 2-Tone CHS TT 19 | Jungle Music/Rasta Call You (paper label, 2-Tone sleeve, with Special A.K.A.) .... 25 |
| 82 | 2-Tone CHS TT 1219 | Jungle Music/Rasta Call You/Easter Island (12", p/s, with Special A.K.A.) .. 20 |
| 69 | Trojan TTL 12 | BLOW YOUR HORN (LP, as Rico & Rudies) .............. 35 |
| 78 | Island ILPS 9485 | MAN FROM WARREIKA (LP) .................................... 30 |
| 78 | Ghetto Rockers PRE 1 | WARREIKA DUB (LP, white label, white sleeve, beware of bootlegs) .. 80 |
| 81 | 2 Tone CHR TT 5005 | THAT MAN IS FORWARD (LP) ................................ 35 |
| 82 | 2 Tone CHR TT5006 | JAMA RICO (LP) .................................................... 50 |
| 00 | Simply Vinyl SVLP 187 | MAN FROM WAREIKA (LP, reissue) ...................... 18 |

*(see also Special A.K.A., Reco, Andy Capp, Don Reco, Prince Buster, Pioneers, Stranger)*

MINT VALUE £

### RICOCHET
| | | | |
|---|---|---|---|
| 80 | Heavy Rock HER 1 | Midas Light/Off The Rails (p/s) | 150 |

### RICOCHET KLASHNEKOFF
| | | | |
|---|---|---|---|
| 02 | Y n R YNR09 | Daggo Mentality/Jankrowville (12") | 12 |

### RICOTTI & ALBUQUERQUE
| | | | |
|---|---|---|---|
| 71 | Pegasus PEG 2 | FIRST WIND (LP) | 50 |

(see also Frank Ricotti, Henry Lowther)

### FRANK RICOTTI QUARTET
| | | | |
|---|---|---|---|
| 69 | CBS 52668 | OUR POINT OF VIEW (LP) | 40 |

(see also Ricotti & Albuquerque, Chris Spedding)

### NELSON RIDDLE ORCHESTRA
| | | | |
|---|---|---|---|
| 55 | Capitol CL 14241 | Vera Cruz/You Won't Forget Me | 6 |
| 55 | Capitol CL 14262 | The Pendulum Song/Brother John | 6 |
| 56 | Capitol CL 14510 | Robin Hood/In Old Lisbon (Lisboa Antigua) | 6 |
| 63 | Capitol CL 15253 | Route 66 Theme/Lolita Ya Ya | 5 |
| 63 | Capitol CL 15309 | Supercar/The Dick Van Dyke Theme | 8 |
| 66 | Stateside SS 517 | Batman Theme (from the T.V. series)/Nelson's Riddler | 8 |
| 59 | Capitol EAP 1034 | JOHNNY CONCHO (EP) | 6 |
| 62 | MGM MGM-C 896 | LOLITA (LP, soundtrack) | 25 |
| 64 | Reprise R 2021 | ROBIN AND THE SEVEN HOODS (LP, soundtrack) | 20 |
| 66 | Stateside S(S)L 10179 | BATMAN (LP, TV soundtrack) | 50 |

### RIDDLERS
| | | | |
|---|---|---|---|
| 66 | Polydor BM 56716 | Batman Theme/Weegie Walk | 30 |

### RIDE
| | | | |
|---|---|---|---|
| 92 | Creation CRE 150P | Twisterella/Going Blank Again (promo) | 15 |
| 89 | Creation CRE 072T | RIDE EP (12") | 15 |
| 90 | Creation CRE 075T | PLAY EP (12") | 12 |
| 90 | Creation CRE 087T | FALL EP (12") | 12 |
| 91 | No Label | Like A Snowflake (7" sold at London ULU gig 19/12/91) | 20 |
| 91 | Creation CRE 100T | TODAY FOREVER EP (12" p/s) | 12 |
| 92 | Creation CRE 123T | Leave Them All Behind/Chrome Waves/Grasshopper (12", p/s) | 10 |
| 92 | Creation CRE 150T | Twisterella/Going Blank Again/Howard Hughes/Stampede (12") | 10 |
| 94 | Creation CRE 155TC | Birdman/Rolling Thunder No. 2/Let's Get Lost/Don't Let It Die (12", clear vinyl) | 10 |
| 94 | Creation CRE 184T | HOW DOES IT FEEL TO FEEL EP (12", p/s) | 10 |
| 94 | Creation CRE 189T | I DON'T KNOW WHERE IT COMES FROM EP (12", p/s) | 10 |
| 94 | Creation CRE 199T | BLACK NITE CRASH EP (12", p/s) | 10 |
| 90 | Creation CRELP 074 | NOWHERE (LP, inner) | 30 |
| 92 | Creation CRELP 124 | GOING BLANK AGAIN (2-LP) | 40 |
| 94 | Creation CRELP 147 | CARNIVAL OF LIGHT (2-LP, gatefold sleeve, lyric insert) | 50 |
| 96 | Creation CRELP 180 | TARANTULA (LP) | 40 |
| 01 | Ignition IGN LP 14 | OX4: THE BEST OF (2-LP) | 25 |
| 15 | Ride RIDEMSC02LPX | NOWHERE (2-LP, reissue, gatefold, white/marbled vinyl, numbered) | 20 |
| 15 | Ride Music RIDEMSC06LP | OX4: THE BEST OF (2-LP, reissue, red vinyl) | 18 |

(see also Motorcycle Ride)

### PAT RIDEN & BROTHER LLOYD'S ALL STARS
| | | | |
|---|---|---|---|
| 69 | Mercury MF 1072 | I Need Help/Let The Red Wine Flow (actually by Pat Rhoden) | 6 |

(see also Pat Rhoden)

### JACKIE RIDING & IMESON SOUND
| | | | |
|---|---|---|---|
| 66 | Fab FAB 4 | Don't Wanna Leave/The Wave | 8 |

### RIDJ XYLON
| | | | |
|---|---|---|---|
| 95 | Roots Man Pro RMP 001 | Black Consciousness/War Rumour Of War//NAPHTALI: Satan Disciples/Conscious Dub/Satan War Dub (12") | 50 |

### RIFF
| | | | |
|---|---|---|---|
| 64 | Blue Beat BB 242 | Oh What A Feeling/Primitive Man | 70 |

### RIFF-RAFF
| | | | |
|---|---|---|---|
| 73 | RCA RCA 2396 | Copper Kettle/You Must Be Joking | 5 |
| 73 | RCA SF 8351 | RIFF-RAFF (LP, with booklet) | 45 |
| 73 | RCA SF 8351 | RIFF-RAFF (LP, without booklet) | 25 |
| 74 | RCA LPL1 5023 | ORIGINAL MAN (LP) | 30 |

### RIFF RAFF
| | | | |
|---|---|---|---|
| 78 | Chiswick SW 34 | I WANNA BE A COSMONAUT (EP) | 12 |
| 79 | Albion DEL 6 | Barking Park Lane/RUAN O' LOCHLAINN: Sweet Narcissis | 15 |
| 80 | Geezer GZ 2 | Kitten/Fantocide (p/s) | 8 |
| 80 | Geezer GZ 3 | Little Girls Know/She Don't Matter (p/s) | 10 |
| 80 | Geezer GZ 4 | New Home Town/Richard (p/s) | 6 |
| 80 | Geezer GZ 3 | Every Girl/You Shaped House (p/s) | 10 |

### RIFKIN
| | | | |
|---|---|---|---|
| 68 | Page One POF 071 | Continental Hesitation/We're Not Those People Any More | 60 |

### THE RIFLES
| | | | |
|---|---|---|---|
| 05 | Blow Up BU 029 | Peace And Quiet/Breakdown (die-cut Blow Up sleeve) | 8 |
| 05 | Xtra Mile XMR 007 | When I'm Alone/ Holiday In The Sun (p/s) | 7 |
| 06 | Red Ink 82876 85972 1 | NO LOVE LOST (LP) | 25 |

### JOHN L RIGBY & THE ALWOODLEY JETS
| | | | |
|---|---|---|---|
| 77 | Petal PTL 020 | HEAVEN CAN'T WAIT EP | 10 |
| 77 | Petal PTL 020 | Sleepwalkin/4/12 (500 only, no p/s) | 15 |
| 77 | Petal PTL 020 | Sleepwalkin/4/12 (500 only, only a small number in this p/s) | 50 |

## BRAM RIGG SET
| | | | |
|---|---|---|---|
| 67 | Stateside SS 2020 | Take The Time Be Yourself/I Can Only Give You Everything | 60 |

## DIANA RIGG
| | | | |
|---|---|---|---|
| 72 | RCA RCA 2178 | Forget Yesterday/Sentimental Journey | 20 |
| 02 | Harkit HRKLP | DIANA RIGG SINGS (LP, test pressings only) | 50 |

## JACKIE RIGGS
| | | | |
|---|---|---|---|
| 56 | London HLF 8244 | The Great Pretender/His Gold Will Melt | 40 |

## RIGHT IDEA
| | | | |
|---|---|---|---|
| 70 | Wastelands WL003 | Memories/Strike Back | 25 |

## RIGHTEOUS BROTHERS
| | | | |
|---|---|---|---|
| 63 | London HL 9743 | Little Latin Lupe Lu/I'm So Lonely | 12 |
| 63 | London HL 9814 | My Babe/Fee-Fi-Fidily-I-Oh | 10 |
| 64 | London HL 9975 | You've Lost That Lovin' Feelin'/There's A Woman | 5 |
| 65 | London HL 9975 | Unchained Melody/Hung On You | 6 |
| 65 | London HL 10066 | Just Once In My Life/The Blues | 6 |
| 65 | Pye International 7N 25297 | Bring Your Love To Me/Try And Find Another Man | 8 |
| 65 | Pye International 7N 25304 | Something's Got A Hold On Me/Night Owl | 7 |
| 65 | Pye Int. 7N 25323 | Let The Good Times Roll/B Flat Blues | 6 |
| 65 | London HL 10011 | Ebb Tide/(I Love You) For Sentimental Reasons | 10 |
| 65 | London HL 9962 | Just Once In My Life/The Blues (withdrawn) | 25 |
| 66 | Pye International 7N 25358 | Georgia On My Mind/My Tears Will Go Away | 7 |
| 66 | Verve VS 535 | (You're My) Soul And Inspiration/B Side-Blues | 7 |
| 66 | Verve VS 537 | He/He Will Break Your Heart | 6 |
| 66 | Sue WI 4018 | You Can Have Her/Justine | 20 |
| 66 | London HL 10086 | The White Cliffs Of Dover/Baby She's Mine | 7 |
| 66 | Verve VS 547 | Island In The Sun/What Now My Love | 8 |
| 67 | Verve VS 560 | Standing In The Middle Of No Place/Been So Nice | 12 |
| 77 | Phil Spector Int'l 2010 022 | You've Lost That Lovin' Feelin'/RIGHTEOUS BROTHERS BAND: Rat Race (ins't) | 5 |
| 65 | Pye Intl. NEP 44043 | THE RIGHTEOUS BROTHERS (EP) | 15 |
| 66 | Verve VEP 5024 | SOUL AND INSPIRATION (EP) | 15 |
| 66 | Verve VEP 5025 | THE RIGHTEOUS BROTHERS (EP, reissue) | 10 |
| 65 | Pye Intl. NPL 28056 | SOME BLUE-EYED SOUL (LP) | 20 |
| 65 | London HA-U 8226 | YOU'VE LOST THAT LOVIN' FEELIN' (LP) | 20 |
| 65 | Pye Intl. NPL 28059 | RIGHT NOW! (LP) | 18 |
| 65 | London HA 8245 | JUST ONCE IN MY LIFE (LP) | 15 |
| 66 | London HA 8278 | BACK TO BACK (LP) | 15 |
| 66 | Verve (S)VLP 9131 | SOUL AND INSPIRATION (LP) | 15 |
| 66 | Sue ILP 937 | IN ACTION! (LP) | 40 |
| 68 | Verve (S)VLP 9190 | SOULED OUT (LP) | 15 |
| 67 | Verve VLP 9168 | SAYIN SOMETHIN' (LP) | 15 |

*(see also Bill Medley, Bobby Hatfield)*

## RIGHTEOUS FLAMES
| | | | |
|---|---|---|---|
| 67 | Fab FAB 18 | Gimme Some Sign Girl/Let's Go To The Dance (B-side act. by Prince Buster) | 150 |
| 67 | Fab FAB 30 | When A Girl Loves A Boy | 60 |
| 68 | Coxsone CS 7061 | You Don't Know/ROY RICHARDS & SOUL VENDORS: Summertime | 450 |
| 71 | High Note HS 052 | Run To The Rock/GAYTONES: Run To The Rock Version | 20 |
| 71 | Nu Beat NB 083 | Love And Emotion/Version | 20 |
| 73 | RCA Victor RCA 2353 | Let The Music Play/True Born African | 10 |
| 75 | Grounation GRO 2026 | Revolution/Version | 10 |

*(see also Richus Flames, Alton Ellis, Flames, Soul Vendors)*

## RIGHTEOUS HOMES (FLAMES)
| | | | |
|---|---|---|---|
| 68 | Coxsone CS 7049 | I Was Born To Be Loved/NORMA FRAZER: Heartaches | 60 |
| 68 | Blue Cat BS 112 | Seven Letters (actually by Winston Jarrett)/SOUL VENDORS: To Sir With Love | 100 |

## RIGHTEOUS SOULS
| | | | |
|---|---|---|---|
| 71 | Supreme SUP 217 | Mount Zion/ECCLE & NEVILL: All Over | 10 |

## RIGHTEOUS TWINS
| | | | |
|---|---|---|---|
| 69 | Blue Cat BS 174 | If I Could Hear My Master/Satan Can't Prevail | 40 |

## RIGOR MORTIS
| | | | |
|---|---|---|---|
| 73 | Track 2094 107 | Made In Japan/Hound Dog | 8 |
| 73 | Track 2406 106 | RIGOR MORTIS SETS IN (LP, gatefold, inner sleeve) | 20 |

*(see John Entwistle, Who)*

## RIKKI & CUFFLINKS
| | | | |
|---|---|---|---|
| 79 | Different HAVE 17 | Nervous Breakdown/Steamin' On | 5 |

## RIKKI & THE LAST DAYS OF EARTH
| | | | |
|---|---|---|---|
| 77 | (own label) | Oundle 29/5/77 (1-sided) (Tracks are City Of The Damned/Dorian Grey) | 60 |
| 77 | DJM DJS 10814 | City Of The Damned/Victimized (p/s) | 10 |
| 78 | DJM DJS 10822 | Loaded/Street Fighting Man//City Of The Damned/Victimized (double pack) | 7 |

## J RILEY
| | | | |
|---|---|---|---|
| 68 | Coxsone CS 7051 | Great 68 Train/You Should Have Known | 250 |

## RILEY ALL STARS
| | | | |
|---|---|---|---|
| 76 | Concrete Jungle CJDPLP | CONCRETE JUNGLE DUB (LP, 300 pressed) | 400 |

## BILLY LEE RILEY
| | | | |
|---|---|---|---|
| 65 | King KG 1015 | I've Been Searchin'/Everybody's Twistin' | 8 |
| 69 | Stax STAX 120 | Going Back To Memphis/Family Portrait | 10 |
| 72 | CBS 8182 | I Got A Thing About You Baby/You Don't Love Me A.K.A Shimmy Shimmy Walk | 7 |

*(see also Megatons)*

MINT VALUE £

## BOB RILEY
58  MGM MGM 977  The Midnight Line/Wanda Jean ........................................................................ 50

## DESMOND RILEY
69  Downtown DT 432  Tear Them/GEORGE LEE & RUDIES: Chaka Ground ...................................... 50
69  Downtown DT 435  Tears On My Pillow/RUDIES: Man Pon Spot ................................................ 20
69  Downtown DT 436  If I Had Wings/AUDREY: You'll Lose A Good Thing ..................................... 100
69  Downtown DT 438  Out Your Fire/No Return .............................................................................. 40
69  Downtown DT 450  Skinhead, A Message To You/MUSIC DOCTORS: Going Strong ............... 125
69  Downtown DT 454  If I Had Wings/AUDREY: You'll Lose A Good Thing (reissue) .................... 20

## HOWARD RILEY (TRIO)
68  Opportunity CP 2499  DISCUSSIONS (LP with insert, as Howard Riley Trio) ........................... 800
69  CBS 52669  ANGLE (LP) .................................................................................................... 50
70  CBS 64077  THE DAY WILL COME (LP) .............................................................................. 60
71  Turtle TUR 301  FLIGHT (LP, gatefold sleeve) ...................................................................... 150
76  Incus INCUS 13  SYNOPSIS (LP, as Howard Riley Trio with Tony Oxley & Barry Guy) ........ 100
79  Spotlite  THE OTHER SIDE (LP) .................................................................................... 15
89  Falcon 1  SOLO 74 (cassette LP) .................................................................................. 40
(see also Colosseum)

## JIMI/JIMMY RILEY
71  Supreme SUP 217  Mount Zion (actually by Jimi Riley & Stranger Cole)/ ECCLE & NEVIL: All Over ............. 10
75  Dip DL 5067  Ram Goat Liver/OMAR & MARSHA PERRY: Ram Goat Dub .................... 10
76  Upsetter UP 101  Give Me A Love/UPSETTERS: Give Me A Dub ........................................... 15
79  Attack TACK 1  Give Thanks And Praise/Feeling Is Believing (12") ................................. 20
78  Burning Sounds BS 1011  SHOWCASE (LP) ........................................................................................... 25
78  Burning Sounds BS 1029  MAJORITY RULE (LP) .................................................................................... 25
79  Trojan TRLS 167  TELL THE YOUTHS THE TRUTH (LP) ............................................................ 20
(see also Martin Riley, Sensations, Uniques)

## MARTIN RILEY
69  Gas GAS 114  Walking Proud/LLOYD CHARMERS: Why Baby ....................................... 50
69  Punch PH 7  Trying To Be Free/I've Got It Bad ............................................................. 15
70  Camel CA 53  Catch This Sound/Suspense ...................................................................... 15
70  Escort ES 823  It Grows (actually "It's Growing")/We Had A Good Thing Going .............. 20
71  Camel CA 77  When Will We Be Paid/WILLIE FRANCIS: He's Got The Whole World In His Hands ......... 8
(see also Slim Smith, Slickers)

## TERRY RILEY
71  CBS 64259  CHURCH OF ANTHRAX (LP, with John Cale) .............................................. 20
71  CBS 64564  A RAINBOW IN CURVED AIR (LP) ................................................................ 20
71  CBS 64665  IN "C" (LP) ..................................................................................................... 20
72  Shandar 83501/2  PERSIAN SURGERY DERVISHES (2-LP) ....................................................... 40
(see also John Cale)

## WINSTON RILEY
73  Techniques TE 922  Woman Don't You Go Astray/Travelling Man .......................................... 15
(see also Techniques)

## RILEY'S ALLSTARS
71  Banana BA 343  Glory Of Love (actually "Mystic Blue" by Hugh Hendricks & Buccaneers)/We'll Cry
Together - Version ......................................................................................... 15
(see also Bobby Davis, Techniques)

## RIMBARA
85  Cordelia  ON DRY LAND (LP, with free 7", 400 copies only) ................................... 30

## RIMINGTON
73  Man MAM 95  In The Grip Of The Mullah/Dragon Child ................................................ 20

## RIMSHOTS (1)
81  Spectro SPEC 101  At Night/Little Boys And Little Girls ....................................................... 15

## RIMSHOTS (2)
82  Respond RESP 3  Sweet Talk/What's The Matter Baby (p/s) ............................................... 6

## RINGS
77  Chiswick S 14  I Wanna Be Free/Automobile (p/s) .......................................................... 12
(see also Maniacs, Twink)

## RINGS & THINGS
68  Fontana TF 987  Strange Things Are Happening/To Me: To Me: To Me ........................... 200

## RINKY DINKS
58  London HLE 8679  Early In The Morning/Now We're One (as Rinky-Dinks featuring Bobby Darin) ........... 25
59  London HLE 8793  Mighty Mighty Man/You're Mine (as Bobby Darin with Rinky Dinks) ............. 30
(see also Bobby Darin)

## BOBBY RIO (U.S.)
63  Stateside SS 211  Don Diddley/I Got You ............................................................................... 25

## BOBBY RIO (& REVELLES)
65  Pye 7N 15790  Boy Meets Girl/Don't Break My Heart And Run Away ........................... 60
65  Pye 7N 15897  Everything In The Garden/When Love Was Young .................................. 50
65  Pye 7N 15958  Value For Love/I'm Not Made Of Clay .................................................... 50
66  Piccadilly 7N 35303  Ask The Lonely/Be Lonely Little Girl (solo) ............................................ 25
66  Piccadilly 7N 35337  Angelica/Lovin' You (solo) ......................................................................... 12

## RIO GRANDE
71  RCA SF 8208  RIO GRANDE (LP) ......................................................................................... 15

## RIO GRANDES
66  Pyramid PYR 6001  Soldiers Take Over/Moses ......................................................................... 15

## RIOT CLONE
| | | | |
|---|---|---|---|
| 82 | Riot Clone RC 001 | THERE'S NO GOVERNMENT LIKE NO GOVERNMENT (EP) | 15 |
| 82 | Riot Clone RC 002 | DESTROY THE MYTH OF MUSICAL DESTRUCTION (EP) | 12 |

## RIOTOUS BROTHERS
| | | | |
|---|---|---|---|
| 80 | Riotous RI 001 | Vicki's Dancing/Operation Zero/Emotional Cripple (p/s) | 12 |

## RIOT ROCKERS
| | | | |
|---|---|---|---|
| 76 | Box BOX 23A | Cast Iron Arm/Be Bop A Lula/Mystery Train/Mess Of Blues (no p/s) | 60 |
| 78 | Raw RAW 11 | Tennessee Saturday Night/Some Kinda Earthquake (with 'fast' version of A side) | 20 |
| 78 | Raw RAW 11 | Tennessee Saturday Night/Some Kinda Earthquake (with 'slow' version of A side) | 15 |

## RIOTS
| | | | |
|---|---|---|---|
| 65 | Island WI 176 | Telling Lies/Don't Leave Me (actually by Techniques) | 40 |
| 65 | Island WI 195 | You Don't Know (actually by Techniques)/DON DRUMMOND & DRUMBAGO: Treasure Island | 40 |
| 65 | Island WI 197 | I Am In Love/When You're Wrong (actually by Techniques) | 40 |
| 65 | Island WI 247 | Yeah Yeah/BABA BROOKS: Virginia Ska | 40 |

*(see also Techniques)*

## RIOT SQUAD & MATUMBI
| | | | |
|---|---|---|---|
| 82 | Extinguish EXT 004 | Why Do You Make Me Wait/Paraphrase (12") | 20 |

## RIOT SQUAD (1)
| | | | |
|---|---|---|---|
| 65 | Pye 7N 15752 | Any Time/Jump | 50 |
| 65 | Pye 7N 15817 | I Wanna Talk About My Baby/Gonna Make You Mine | 60 |
| 65 | Pye 7N 15869 | Nevertheless/Not A Great Talker | 60 |
| 66 | Pye 7N 17041 | Cry Cry Cry/How Is It Done | 50 |
| 66 | Pye 7N 17092 | I Take It We're Through/Working Man | 175 |
| 66 | Pye 7N 17130 | It's Never Too Late To Forgive/Try To Realise | 50 |
| 67 | Pye 7N 17237 | Gotta Be A First Time/Bitter Sweet Love | 60 |

*(see also Graham Bonney, Jimi Hendrix Experience, Blue Aces)*

## RIOT SQUAD (2)
| | | | |
|---|---|---|---|
| 82 | Rondelet ROUND 23 | Fuck The Tories/Civil Destruction (p/s) | 8 |
| 82 | Rondelet ROUND 25 | Riot In The City/Religion (p/s) | 8 |
| 83 | Rot ASS 1 | DON'T BE DENIED (EP) | 20 |
| 83 | Rot ASS 2 | I'm OK Fuck You/In The Future/Friday Night (p/s) | 15 |
| 84 | Rot ASS 13 | NO POTENTIAL THREAT (LP, with free single [ASS3], stickered sleeve) | 18 |

## RIP CHORDS
| | | | |
|---|---|---|---|
| 78 | Cells SELL 1 | Ringing In The Streets/Music's Peace Artist/Television Television (p/s) | 18 |

## RIP CHORDS (U.S.)
| | | | |
|---|---|---|---|
| 63 | CBS AAG 143 | Here I Stand/Karen | 20 |
| 63 | CBS AAG 162 | Gone/She Thinks I Still Care | 20 |
| 64 | CBS AAG 181 | Hey Little Cobra/The Queen | 30 |
| 64 | CBS AAG 202 | Three Window Coupe/Hot Rod USA | 35 |
| 64 | CBS BPG 62228 | HEY LITTLE COBRA (LP) | 100 |

*(see also Terry Day, Terry Melcher, Bruce Johnston)*

## RIPCORD
| | | | |
|---|---|---|---|
| 89 | Raging Records RAGE 2 | HARVEST HARDCORE (EP, foldout sleeve) | 15 |
| 86 | Raging RAGE 1 | DAMAGE IS DONE (Flexi) | 10 |
| 87 | Manic Ears ACHE 005 | DEFIANCE OF POWER (LP, with insert) | 20 |
| 88 | Raging RAGE 001 | POETIC JUSTICE (LP, with inner) | 15 |

## MINNIE RIPERTON
| | | | |
|---|---|---|---|
| 74 | Epic SEPC 80426 | PERFECT ANGEL (LP) | 15 |
| 75 | Epic EPC 69142 | ADVENTURES IN PARADISE (LP) | 15 |

## RIPLEY WAYFARERS
| | | | |
|---|---|---|---|
| 71 | Tradition TSR 006 | CHIPS AND BROWN SAUCE (LP, 500 only with front-laminated dark green and white flipback sleeve, title in blue) | 30 |
| 73 | Tradition TSR 006 | CHIPS AND BROWN SAUCE (LP, reissue, plain green sleeve, title in black) | 15 |

## RIP 'N' LAW
| | | | |
|---|---|---|---|
| 71 | Crab CRAB 64 | In The Ghetto/Something Sweet | 30 |

## RIPPERS
| | | | |
|---|---|---|---|
| 68 | Saga | HONESTLY (LP) | 29 |

## RIP RIG & PANIC
| | | | |
|---|---|---|---|
| 81 | Virgin VZZ13 | GOD (2x12") | 15 |

## RISAN
| | | | |
|---|---|---|---|
| 82 | Saffron | Eastern Palace/Part 2 | 30 |

## RISING FIRE
| | | | |
|---|---|---|---|
| 81 | Cha Cha CHAD 45 | You Lied/Free Blackman (12") | 20 |

## RISING HEAT
| | | | |
|---|---|---|---|
| 73 | Firestone FS 02 | My Magic Thimble/Evolution | 25 |
| 75 | Newbury N32 | Drop The Act/Follow Me Home | 40 |

## RISING MOON
| | | | |
|---|---|---|---|
| 74 | Theatre Projects | RISING MOON (LP) | 30 |

## RISING SONS (U.K.)
| | | | |
|---|---|---|---|
| 68 | Pye 7N 17554 | Hold Me Just A Little While Longer/Fountain Of Love | 10 |

## RISING SONS (U.S.)
| | | | |
|---|---|---|---|
| 65 | Stateside SS 426 | You're My Girl/Try To Be A Man | 35 |

## RISING SUNS
| | | | |
|---|---|---|---|
| 72 | Polydor 2121 49 | Shay Laka Day/Happy Song | 7 |

## RISK (1)
| | | | |
|---|---|---|---|
| 79 | Redball RR 023 | Blazing Lights/Yesterday's Youth (no p/s) | 8 |

## RISK (2)

MINT VALUE £

| | | | |
|---|---|---|---|
| 85 | Big Idea FAB 2 | Forget The Girl/Know The Truth (p/s) | 5 |

## RITA
| | | | |
|---|---|---|---|
| 69 | Major Minor MM 653 | Erotica/Sexologie | 15 |

## RITA (ALSTON)
| | | | |
|---|---|---|---|
| 69 | Jackpot JP 718 | Love Making/NAT COLE: My Love | 20 |

*(see also Rita Alston)*

## RITA & TIARAS
| | | | |
|---|---|---|---|
| 79 | Destiny DS 1002 | Gone With The Wind Is My Love/Wild Times (with p/s) | 5 |
| 79 | Destiny DS 1002 | Gone With The Wind Is My Love/Wild Times | 5 |
| 79 | Destiny DS 1002 | Gone With The Wind Is My Love/Wild Times (DJ copy with p/s) | 18 |
| 09 | Kent CITY 009 | Gone With The Wind Is My Love/DORE STRINGS: Gone With The Wind Is My Love | 8 |

## TEX RITTER
| | | | |
|---|---|---|---|
| 55 | Capitol CL 14335 | Marshal Of Wichita/September Song | 5 |

## BOB RITTERBUSH
| | | | |
|---|---|---|---|
| 59 | Top Rank JAR 118 | I Wish That You Were Mine/Darling Corey | 7 |

## RITUAL (1)
| | | | |
|---|---|---|---|
| 82 | Red Flame RF 712 | Mind Disease/Nine | 8 |

## RITUAL (2)
| | | | |
|---|---|---|---|
| 90 | Romany RMY VI | Into The Night/Burning | 10 |

## RITZ
| | | | |
|---|---|---|---|
| 74 | Dawn DNS 1070 | Jenny Gentle/Why Love | 20 |

*(see also Paul Ryder & The Time Machine)*

## RIVAL SCHOOLS
| | | | |
|---|---|---|---|
| 02 | Island 548936 | UNITED BY FATE (LP) | 20 |
| 13 | Shop Radio Cast 022 | FOUND (LP, green vinyl, UK pressing sold via band website) | 20 |

## RIVALS (1)
| | | | |
|---|---|---|---|
| 74 | Decca F 13509 | Speedway/Hoskins Still Rides | 10 |

## RIVALS (2)
| | | | |
|---|---|---|---|
| 78 | Sound On Sound SOS 100 | Skateboarding In The UK/Top Of The Pops | 35 |

## RIVALS (3)
| | | | |
|---|---|---|---|
| 80 | Ace ACE 007 | Future Rights/Flowers (p/s) | 100 |
| 80 | Oakwood/Ace ACE 011 | Here Comes The Night/Both Sides (p/s) | 40 |

## RIVAL SAVAGES
| | | | |
|---|---|---|---|
| 80 | Savage VC 1968 | Get Some/Garden Of The Damned (fold-out p/s, dust sleeve stapled) | 20 |

## HECTOR RIVERA
| | | | |
|---|---|---|---|
| 67 | Polydor 65728 | At The Party/Do It To Me | 60 |

## RIVERBANK
| | | | |
|---|---|---|---|
| 71 | Horse HOSS 2 | Summer Is The Season/Riding My Bicycle | 5 |

## BLUE RIVERS & MAROONS
| | | | |
|---|---|---|---|
| 67 | Columbia Blue Beat DB 103 | Witchcraft Man/Searching For You Baby | 30 |
| 68 | Spectrum SP 105 | Take It Or Leave It/I've Been Pushed Around | 10 |
| 68 | Columbia S(C)X 6192 | BLUE BEAT IN MY SOUL (LP) | 65 |

## CLIFF RIVERS
| | | | |
|---|---|---|---|
| 63 | London HLU 9739 | True Lips/Marsha | 40 |

## DANNY RIVERS
| | | | |
|---|---|---|---|
| 60 | Top Rank JAR 408 | Hawk/I Got | 30 |
| 60 | Decca F 11294 | Can't You Hear My Heart/I'm Waiting For Tomorrow | 25 |
| 61 | Decca F 11357 | Once Upon A Time/My Baby's Gone Away (with Alexander Combo) | 40 |
| 64 | Decca F 11865 | There Will Never Be Anyone Else/I Don't Think You Know How I Feel | 20 |
| 62 | HMV POP 1000 | We're Gonna Dance/Movin' In (as Danny Rivers & River Men) | 50 |

## DEEK RIVERS
| | | | |
|---|---|---|---|
| 62 | Oriole CB 1735 | One Kiss/Outsider | 25 |

## JOHNNY RIVERS
| | | | |
|---|---|---|---|
| 61 | Pye Intl. 7n 25118 | Blue Skies/That Someone Should Be Me | 10 |
| 64 | Liberty LIB 66032 | Memphis/It Won't Happen With Me | 10 |
| 64 | Liberty LIB 66056 | Maybellene/Walk Myself n Home | 10 |
| 64 | Liberty LIB 66075 | Mountain Of Love/Moody River | 12 |
| 65 | Liberty LIB 66087 | Midnight Special/Cupid | 10 |
| 65 | Liberty LIB 66112 | The Seventh Son/Un-Square Dance | 8 |
| 65 | Liberty LIB 12021 | He Don't Love You Like I Love You/Where Have All The Flowers Gone | 7 |
| 66 | Liberty LIB 12023 | Secret Agent Man/Tom Dooley | 7 |
| 66 | Liberty LIB 66144 | Under Your Spell Again/Long Time Man | 15 |
| 66 | Liberty LIB 66175 | I Washed My Hands In Muddy Water/Roogalator | 7 |
| 66 | Liberty LIB 66205 | Poor Side Of Town/A Man Can Cry | 15 |
| 67 | Liberty LIB 66227 | Baby I Need Your Loving/Getting Ready For Tommorow | 12 |
| 68 | Liberty LIB 15078 | Look To Your Soul/Something Strange | 10 |
| 68 | Liberty LBF 15163 | Right Relations/A Better Life | 7 |
| 69 | Liberty LBF 15241 | Muddy River/Resurrection | 7 |
| 66 | Liberty LEP 4049 | MORE JOHNNY RIVERS (EP) | 15 |
| 64 | Liberty LBY 3031 | AT THE WHISKY A GO-GO (LP) | 15 |
| 65 | Liberty LBY 3036 | HERE WE A GO-GO AGAIN (LP) | 15 |
| 65 | Liberty LBY 3064 | RIVERS ROCKS THE FOLK (LP) | 15 |
| 68 | Liberty LBS 83040 | REWIND (LP) | 12 |

## MAVIS RIVERS
| | | | |
|---|---|---|---|
| 60 | Capitol CL 15120 | So Rare/Longing, Longing, Longing | 5 |
| 63 | Reprise RS 20115 | Slightly Out Of Tune/Footsteps Of A Fool | 15 |

## ROYD RIVERS & CLIFF AUNGIER
| | | | |
|---|---|---|---|
| 65 | Decca LK 4696 | WANDERIN' (LP) | 35 |

*(see also Cliff Aungier)*

## TONY RIVERS & THE CASTAWAYS
| | | | |
|---|---|---|---|
| 63 | Columbia DB 7135 | Shake Shake Shake/Row Row Row | 20 |
| 64 | Columbia DB 7224 | I Love The Way You Walk/I Love You | 15 |
| 64 | Columbia DB 7336 | Life's Too Short/Tell On Me | 15 |
| 65 | Columbia DB 7448 | She/Till We Get Home | 15 |
| 65 | Columbia DB 7536 | Come Back/What To Do | 15 |
| 66 | Columbia DB 7971 | God Only Knows/Charade | 20 |
| 66 | Parlophone R 5400 | Nowhere Man/The Girl From New York City | 25 |
| 66 | Immediate IM 027 | Girl Don't Tell Me/The Girl From Salt Lake City | 50 |
| 68 | Polydor 56245 | I Can Guarantee Your Love/Pantomime | 12 |

*(see also Capability Brown, Grapefruit, Harmony Grass, Senators, Sugarbeats)*

## RIVIERA
| | | | |
|---|---|---|---|
| 69 | Pye 7N 17712 | Baby Won't Leave Me Alone/The Love Story | 5 |

## RIVIERAS
| | | | |
|---|---|---|---|
| 60 | HMV POP 773 | Blessing Of Love/Moonlight Cocktails | 120 |

## RIVIERAS (U.S.)
| | | | |
|---|---|---|---|
| 64 | Pye International 7N 25237 | California Sun/H B Goose Step | 45 |

## RIVINGTONS
| | | | |
|---|---|---|---|
| 62 | Liberty LIB 55427 | Papa Oom Mow Mow/Deep Water | 50 |
| 63 | Liberty LIB 55553 | The Bird's The Word/I'm Losing My Grip | 60 |
| 66 | CBS 202088 | Rose Growing In The Ruins/Tend To Business | 40 |

## RIVVITS
| | | | |
|---|---|---|---|
| 79 | Alien AUX 1 | Saturday Night At The Dance/Girl Next Door (p/s, with flexi) | 10 |
| 79 | Alien | Alright On The Night (1-sided 5" flexi) | 5 |
| 79 | Alien ALIX 002 | Never/Boy Meets Girl | 5 |

## R N B SPITFIRES
| | | | |
|---|---|---|---|
| 82 | Mrs K GRC 143 | Honeymaker/I Ain't Him (p/s) | 8 |

## FREDDIE ROACH
| | | | |
|---|---|---|---|
| 67 | Transatlantic PR 7490 | THE SOUL BOOK (LP) | 15 |

## MAX ROACH
| | | | |
|---|---|---|---|
| 60 | Mercury MMC 14054 | QUIET AS IT'S KEPT (LP) | 20 |
| 62 | HMV CLP 1522 | PERC 'N' BITTER SUITE (LP) | 15 |

## MAX ROACH (& CLIFFORD BROWN GROUP)
| | | | |
|---|---|---|---|
| 58 | Emarcy ERE 1572 | MAX ROACH AND CLIFFORD BROWN (EP, withdrawn) | 12 |
| 55 | Vogue LDE 117 | MAX ROACH & CLIFFORD BROWN IN CONCERT VOL. 1 (10" LP) | 15 |
| 55 | Vogue LDE 128 | MAX ROACH & CLIFFORD BROWN IN CONCERT VOL. 2 (10" LP) | 15 |
| 58 | Emarcy EJL 1282 | JAZZ IN THREE-QUARTER TIME (LP) | 15 |
| 59 | Emarcy MMB 12005 | MAX ROACH, NEWPORT (LP, by Max Roach) | 15 |
| 59 | Emarcy MMB 12009 | THE MAX ROACH FOUR PLUS FOUR (LP, by Max Roach) | 15 |

*(see also Clifford Brown)*

## ROAD
| | | | |
|---|---|---|---|
| 73 | Rare Earth SRE 3006 | ROAD (LP) | 50 |

*(see also Noel Redding)*

## ROADRUNNERS
| | | | |
|---|---|---|---|
| 65 | Cavern Sound 2BSNL 7 | PANTOMANIA (EP, with tracks by Chris Edwards & Clive Wood) | 35 |

## ROADSTER
| | | | |
|---|---|---|---|
| 81 | Mayhem SRTS 81 | Fantasy/45 MPH (p/s) | 30 |

## ROADSTERS
| | | | |
|---|---|---|---|
| 64 | Stateside SS 293 | Joy Ride/Drag | 40 |

## ROAMING DOG
| | | | |
|---|---|---|---|
| 72 | Perfect PF 01 | Sign Your Name/Eclipse | 50 |

## ROARING SIXTIES
| | | | |
|---|---|---|---|
| 66 | Marmalade 598 001 | We Love The Pirates/I'm Leaving Town | 40 |

*(see also Ivy League)*

## ROBAN'S SKIFFLE GROUP
| | | | |
|---|---|---|---|
| 61 | Storyville A45 062 | Careless Love/Frankie And Johnny (with p/s) | 35 |
| 61 | Storyville A45 062 | Careless Love/Frankie And Johnny | 18 |

## E.G. ROBB
| | | | |
|---|---|---|---|
| 63 | Columbia DB 7100 | Stage To Cimarron/Jezebel | 15 |

## MARTY ROBBINS
### SINGLES
| | | | |
|---|---|---|---|
| 57 | Philips JK 1019 | A White Sport Coat (And A Pink Carnation)/Grown-Up Tears (jukebox issue) | 15 |
| 57 | Philips PB 741 | Please Don't Blame Me/Teen-Age Dream | 10 |
| 58 | Fontana H 128 | Stairway Of Love/Just Married | 8 |
| 58 | Fontana H 150 | Sittin' In A Tree House/She Was Only Seventeen | 8 |
| 59 | Fontana H 184 | The Hanging Tree (from film)/The Blues Country Style | 7 |
| 59 | Fontana H 212 | Cap And Gown/Last Night About This Time | 7 |
| 60 | Fontana H 270 | Ballad Of The Alamo/Five Brothers (in p/s) | 10 |

*(see also Jordanaires)*

## MEL ROBBINS
| | | | |
|---|---|---|---|
| 59 | London HLM 8966 | Save It/To Know You (initially pressing with triangular centre) | 300 |
| 59 | London HLM 8966 | Save It/To Know You (later round centre) | 100 |
| 59 | London HLM 8966 | Save It/To Know You (78) | 40 |

MINT VALUE £

## SYLVIA ROBBINS
| 60 | London HLJ 9118 | Frankie And Johnny/Come Home | 35 |

*(see also Mickey & Sylvia)*

## ROBERT & REMOULDS
| 79 | Black & White BW 1 | X No. 1/Do Eyes Ever Meet? (p/s) | 60 |

## ANDY ROBERTS
| 73 | Elektra K 12109 | Baby Baby/All Around My Grandmother's Floor | 5 |
| 70 | RCA SF 8086 | HOME GROWN (LP, laminated front sleeve, lyric insert) | 80 |
| 71 | Charisma CAS 1034 | HOME GROWN (LP, reissue, different sleeve) | 15 |
| 71 | B&C | HOME GROWN (LP, reissue) | 20 |
| 71 | Pegasus PEG 5 | NINA AND THE DREAM TREE (LP) | 20 |
| 73 | Elektra K 42139 | URBAN COWBOY (LP, with insert, 'butterfly' label) | 80 |
| 73 | Elektra K 42151 | ANDY ROBERTS AND THE GREAT STAMPEDE (LP, gatefold sleeve) | 15 |

*(see also Clayton Squares, Liverpool Scene, Everyone, Plainsong, Mighty Baby)*

## BOB ROBERTS
| 70 | Explosion EX 2021 | Stick By Me/TOMMY McCOOK: The Designer | 7 |

## BOB ROBERTS (U.K.)
| 81 | Solent SS 054 | BREEZE FOR A BARGEMAN (LP) | 15 |

## HUGH ROBERTS
| 70 | Explosion EX 2041 | California Dreaming/One Woman (both sides actually by Lloyd Charmers) | 12 |

## J. ROBERTS
| 70 | Bamboo BAM 30 | Someday We'll Be Together/SOUND DIMENSION: Everyday People | 20 |

## JOHN ROBERTS
| 68 | Sue WI 4042 | Sockin' 1, 2, 3, 4/Sophisticated Funk | 50 |
| 68 | Action ACT 4511 | I'll Forget You/Be My Baby | 40 |

## KEITH ROBERTS
| 72 | Trailer LER 3031 | PIER OF THE REALM (LP, red label) | 15 |

## KENNY ROBERTS (1)
| 57 | Brunswick 05638 | I'm Looking For The Bully Of The Town/Broken Teenage Heart | 12 |

## KENNY ROBERTS (2)
| 66 | Pye 7N 17054 | Run Like The Devil/Where Goes My Heart | 25 |
| 65 | Pye 7N 15882 | Say, Do You Mean It/Since My Love Has Gone | 15 |

*(see also Kenny Damon)*

## KIM ROBERTS
| 64 | Decca F 11813 | I'll Prove It/For Loving Me This Way | 65 |

## PADDY ROBERTS
| 62 | Decca F 11552 | Merry Christmas You Suckers/Got 'n' Idea | 6 |

## RENEE ROBERTS
| 62 | Oriole CB 1731 | I Want To Love You/Aching Heart | 10 |

## ROCKY ROBERTS
| 67 | Durium DRL 50026 | SABATO SERA (LP) | 30 |

## STEVE ROBERTS
| 80s | EXPLP 2002 | DO YOU KNOW WHO I AM (LP) | 15 |

*(see also U.K.Subs)*

## DON ROBERTSON
| 50 | London L 629 | Gamblin' Fever/On The Hudson Bay Line (78, with Lou) | 8 |
| 56 | Capitol CL 14575 | The Happy Whistler/You're Free To Go (B-side with Lou Dinning) | 12 |
| 56 | Capitol CL 14629 | Every Day That I Live (with Lou Dinning)/You | 5 |
| 59 | Capitol CL 15088 | Fine Day/The Merry Men | 5 |

## JIM ROBERTSON
| 55 | MGM SPC 7 | Pride Of My Heart/Walkin' And Talkin' With The Lord (export issue) | 15 |

## DAVE ROBIN
| 65 | Eyemark EMS 1003 | You I Don't Want To Share/Life's Too Short | 6 |

## EDE ROBIN
| 75 | Crystal CR 7023 | There Must Be A Love Somewhere/Soul Over Easy | 8 |

## RICHIE ROBIN
| 60 | Top Rank JAR 262 | Strange Dream/GERRY GRANAHAN: It Hurts | 15 |

## TINA ROBIN
| 57 | Vogue Coral Q 72284 | Over Somebody Else's Shoulder/Lady Fair | 10 |
| 57 | Vogue Coral Q 72294 | Never In A Million Years/Ça C'est L'Amour | 10 |
| 58 | Coral Q 72309 | Everyday/Believe Me ) | 20 |
| 58 | Coral Q 72323 | No School Tomorrow/Sugar Blues | 20 |
| 62 | Mercury AMT 1199 | Why Did You Go/Get Out Of My Life | 5 |

## ROGER ROBIN
| 95 | Saxon SHF 004 | Do Right/Tell Me (12") | 20 |
| 98 | Saxon SAX 065 | Unity/Mix 2//My Medication/Version (12") | 15 |

## ROBIN HOODS
| 65 | Mercury MF 865 | Wait For The Dawn/Love You So | 10 |

## ROBINS
| 60 | Vogue V 9168 | Cherry Lips/Out Of The Picture | 100 |
| 60 | Vogue V 9173 | Just Like That/Whole Lot Imagination | 100 |

*(see also H.B. Barnum)*

## JIMMY ROBINS
| 68 | President PT 118 | I Can't Please You/I Made It Over | 150 |

## ALVIN ROBINSON
| 64 | Pye International 7N 25248 | Something You Got/Searchin' | 25 |

| | | | |
|---|---|---|---|
| 64 | Red Bird RB 10010 | Down Home Girl/Fever | 30 |
| 66 | Strike JH 307 | You Brought My Heart Right Down To My Knees/Whatever You Had | 20 |

**ANDY ROBINSON**
| | | | |
|---|---|---|---|
| 68 | Philips SBL 7887 | PATTERNS OF REALITY (LP, laminated sleeve, black/silver label) | 30 |

**BROTHER CLEOPHUS ROBINSON**
| | | | |
|---|---|---|---|
| 57 | Vogue EPV 1196 | BROTHER CLEOPHUS ROBINSON (EP) | 25 |

**ROBINSON CREW**
| | | | |
|---|---|---|---|
| 63 | Decca F 11706 | Taxi (Theme From TV Series)/Stormalong | 7 |

*(see also Lord Rockingham's XI)*

**DAVE ROBINSON**
| | | | |
|---|---|---|---|
| 79 | Bushays BFM 124 | Ruby & Diamond (feat. Jah Thomas/Dub (12") | 20 |

**EDDIE ROBINSON**
| | | | |
|---|---|---|---|
| 71 | Ember EMB S 301 | Hey Blackman Parts 1 & 2 | 5 |
| 74 | Myrrh MYR 1013 | REFLECTIONS OF THE MAN INSIDE (LP) | 15 |

**FLOYD ROBINSON**
| | | | |
|---|---|---|---|
| 59 | RCA RCA 1146 | Makin' Love/My Girl (initially with triangular centre) | 7 |
| 59 | RCA RCA 1146 | Makin' Love/My Girl (later round centre) | 5 |
| 60 | RCA RCA 1179 | I Believe In Love/Tattletale | 8 |
| 60 | RCA RD 27166 | FLOYD ROBINSON (LP) | 40 |

**FREDDY ROBINSON**
| | | | |
|---|---|---|---|
| 72 | Stax 2325 085 | AT THE DRIVE-IN (LP) | 18 |

**HARRY ROBINSON**
| | | | |
|---|---|---|---|
| 60 | Top Rank JAR 325 | The Skirl/Wimoweh (as Harry Robinson "String Sound") | 5 |
| 61 | Decca F 11319 | Heavy Date/Sentimental Journey (as Harry Robinson's XV) | 5 |

*(see also Lord Rockingham's XI)*

**JACKEY ROBINSON**
| | | | |
|---|---|---|---|
| 70 | Punch PH 50 | Heart Made Of Stone (actually by Jackie Bernard)/BOB TAYLOR: I May Never See My Baby Anymore | 20 |

*(see also Jackie Robinson, Pioneers)*

**JACKIE ROBINSON**
| | | | |
|---|---|---|---|
| 68 | Amalgamated AMG 819 | Over And Over/Woman Of Samaria | 30 |
| 68 | Amalgamated AMG 824 | Let The Little Girl Dance/DERRICK MORGAN: I Want To Go Home | 30 |
| 74 | Harry J. HJ 6695 | My Love For You/R.D. Livingstone: Smokey Mountains | 5 |

**JIM ROBINSON NEW ORLEANS BAND**
| | | | |
|---|---|---|---|
| 61 | Riverside RLP 369 | NEW ORLEANS: THE LIVING LEGENDS (LP) | 15 |
| 64 | Riverside RLP 393 | PLAYS SPIRITUAL AND BLUES (LP) | 15 |

**J.P. ROBINSON**
| | | | |
|---|---|---|---|
| 72 | Atlantic K 10149 | George Jackson/Wall To Wall Love | 10 |
| 72 | Atlantic K 10209 | What Can I Tell Her/Please Accept My Call | 15 |

**LLOYD ROBINSON**
| | | | |
|---|---|---|---|
| 62 | Blue Beat BB 122 | Give Me A Chance/When You Walk | 20 |
| 63 | Blue Beat BB 159 | I Need Your Love/You Told Me | 30 |
| 69 | Duke DU 5 | Cuss Cuss/Lavender Blue | 200 |
| 70 | Camel CA 41 | The Worm/NEVILLE HYNES: Afro (actually by Neville Hinds) | 40 |
| 72 | Green Door GD 4028 | I Can't Forget/LLOYD AND THE NOW GENERATION: I Can't Forget - Version | 6 |
| 77 | Cactus CT 109 | Rocky Road/Version | 20 |
| 04 | Trojan TJGSE014 | Cuss Cuss/KING CANNON: Soul Special (reissue) | 15 |

*(see also Lloyd Clarke, Lloyd Charmers, Harry J. Allstars, Matadors, Melodians)*

**M. ROBINSON**
| | | | |
|---|---|---|---|
| 64 | Port-O-Jam PJ 4114 | Who Are You/Follow You | 15 |

**MARTEL ROBINSON**
| | | | |
|---|---|---|---|
| 75 | Arrow AR 006 | Sunny Soil/Sunny | 15 |

**PAUL ROBINSON**
| | | | |
|---|---|---|---|
| 83 | King City KCD 006 | Come On Sister/Instrumental (12") | 80 |

**ROSCO ROBINSON**
| | | | |
|---|---|---|---|
| 66 | Pye International 7N 25385 | That's Enough/One More Time | 50 |
| 66 | Pye International 7N 25385 | That's Enough/One More Time (DJ copy) | 100 |
| 72 | Wand WN 27 | That's Enough/One More Time (reissue) | 10 |
| 73 | Contempo C 16 | We're Losing It Baby/We Got A Good Thing Going | 8 |

**SANDRA ROBINSON**
| | | | |
|---|---|---|---|
| 85 | Trojan TROT 9079 | Sensi For Sale (Part 1)/TUFF TONES: Boogie Mix (Part 2)/SANDRA ROBINSON & TUFF TONES: Depression/DAN AMBRASSA: Life's Riddle/TUFF TONES: Boogie Mix (12") | 20 |

**SUGAR CHILE ROBINSON**
| | | | |
|---|---|---|---|
| 53 | Capitol LC 6586 | CAPITOL PRESENTS SUGAR CHILE ROBINSON (10" LP) | 40 |

**TOM ROBINSON (BAND)**
| | | | |
|---|---|---|---|
| 75 | Chebel SRT/CUS 015 | GLAD TO BE GAY (EP, as Bradford Gay Liberation Front, no p/s) | 250 |
| 79 | Deviant Wrecords DEVIATE 1 | A Dyke's Gotta Do (What A Dyke's Gotta Do)/NOEL GREIG: Stand Together (All You Gay Women All You Gay Men) (die cut sleeve with sticker) | 20 |
| 79 | EMI EMI 2946 | All Right All Night/Black Angel (withdrawn, demo-only) | 8 |

*(see also Cafe Society, Phantom, Billy Karloff [& Extremes])*

**ROBIN WANTS REVENGE**
| | | | |
|---|---|---|---|
| 90 | Jungle Jam JJR 102 | ROBIN WANTS REVENGE EP (12") | 40 |

**CARSON ROBISON (& HIS PLEASANT VALLEY BOYS)**
| | | | |
|---|---|---|---|
| 53 | MGM SP 1004 | Lady Round The Lady/Pokeberry Promenade | 10 |
| 53 | MGM SP 1024 | Square Dance Jitterbug/Keep On Circlin' 'Round | 18 |

**RALPH ROBLES**
| | | | |
|---|---|---|---|
| 69 | London HA/SH 8385 | TAKING OVER (LP) | 20 |

MINT VALUE £

## JEREMY ROBSON
| | | |
|---|---|---|
| 63 | Columbia SEG 8244 | BLUES FOR THE LONELY (EP, with Michael Garrick and Shake Keane) .......................... 100 |

## NICKY ROBSON
| | | |
|---|---|---|
| 80 | Scratch SCR 006 | Stars/Eye To Eye (p/s)................................................................. 20 |
| 80 | Scratch SCRT 006 | Stars (Extended)/Eye To Eye (12")....................................................... 45 |

*(see also Gary Numan)*

## ROCAMARS
| | | |
|---|---|---|
| 65 | King KG 1031 | All In Black Woman/Give Me Time ................................................. 20 |

## TONY ROCCO
| | | |
|---|---|---|
| 62 | Parlophone R 4886 | Stalemate/Keep A Walking............................................. 15 |
| 62 | Parlophone R 4946 | Competition/Torture ................................................. 15 |

## HARRY ROCHE CONSTELLATION
| | | |
|---|---|---|
| 67 | CBS 202653 | Casino Royale/In The Pad Of The Mountain King............................. 10 |
| 67 | CBS SBPG 63013 | CASINO ROYALE (LP) ............................................. 35 |
| 71 | Studio Two TWO 340 | SPINDRIFT (LP) .................................................. 20 |
| 73 | Pye Intl. NSPL 41024 | SPIRAL (LP, laminated sleeve) ................................... 30 |
| 73 | Pye QUAD 1022 | SOMETIMES (LP, quadrophonic) ................................... 20 |

## JACKIE ROCHELLE
| | | |
|---|---|---|
| 68 | Olga OLE 011 | Till The End/Grown Up Games .................................................. 5 |

## DICKIE ROCK & MIAMI SHOWBAND
| | | |
|---|---|---|
| 63 | Piccadilly 7N 35154 | Boys/There's Always Me ......................................................... 5 |
| 64 | Piccadilly 7N 35202 | From The Candy Store/Twenty Flight Rock ................................... 7 |
| 64 | Pye 7N 15729 | Just For Old Times Sake/Me Not You ....................................... 7 |
| 65 | Pye 7N 15750 | Round And Around/Little Baby ............................................. 7 |
| 65 | Pye 7N 15855 | Every Step Of The Way/Rock And Roll Music ............................ 7 |
| 65 | Pye 7N 17063 | Come Back To Stay/Can't Make Up My Mind (p/s)........................ 7 |

## JOHNNY ROCK
| | | |
|---|---|---|
| 55 | Vogue VE170112 | JOHNNY ROCK (EP)........................................................... 40 |

## PETE ROCK & C.L. SMOOTH
| | | |
|---|---|---|
| 92 | Elektra EKT 105 | MECCA AND THE SOUL BROTHER (2-LP) .............................. 25 |
| 94 | Elektra 7559-61661-1 | THE MAIN INGREDIENT (2-LP) .................................... 18 |

## ROCKABILLY REBS
| | | |
|---|---|---|
| 79 | SRTS 79 CUS 524 | ROCKABILLY REBS (EP, no p/s) ...................................... 100 |

## ROCK-A-TEENS
| | | |
|---|---|---|
| 59 | Columbia DB 4361 | Woo-Hoo/Untrue ............................................................ 40 |

## ROCK BROTHERS
| | | |
|---|---|---|
| 56 | Parlophone MSP 6201 | Dungaree Doll/Livin' It Up ............................................. 90 |
| 56 | Parlophone R 4119 | Dungaree Doll/Livin' It Up (78) ....................................... 30 |

## ROCK CANDY
| | | |
|---|---|---|
| 71 | MCA MK 5069 | Remember/Don't Put Me Down................................................ 6 |

## ROCKERS ALL STARS
| | | |
|---|---|---|
| 78 | Rough Trade RT 002 | Pablo Meets Mr. Bassie/Mr. Bassie Special (basically, Augustus Pablo) ............ 10 |

## ROCKERS HI-FI
| | | |
|---|---|---|
| 96 | Different Drummer 12 G 001 | GOING UNDER (THE KRUDER & DORFMEISTER SESSIONS EP) (12" p/s)........................ 12 |

## ROCKERS (1)
| | | |
|---|---|---|
| 59 | Oriole CB 1501 | Get Cracking/Counter Melody.................................................. 10 |

## ROCKERS (2)
| | | |
|---|---|---|
| 83 | CBS TA 3929 | We Are The Boys (Who Make All The Noise) (Extended Version)/Rockin' On Stage (12", p/s)............................................. 12 |
| 83 | CBS A 3929 | We Are The Boys (Who Make All The Noise)/Rockin' On Stage (p/s)........................ 8 |

*(see also Phil Lynott, Roy Wood, Status Quo)*

## ROCKET 88
| | | |
|---|---|---|
| 81 | Atlantic K 50776 | ROCKET 88 (LP) ....................................................... 20 |

*(see also Charlie Watts, Alexis Korner, Jack Bruce, Dick Heckstall-Smith)*

## ROCKET FROM THE CRYPT
| | | |
|---|---|---|
| 93 | Southern Studios PUS 007 | Glazed/Pressures/Cut It Loose (white label test pressing, 5-10 copies only) ................ 30 |
| 95 | Elemental ELM 32S | Born in 69/Ciao Patsy (p/s)................................................. 8 |
| 96 | Elemental ELM 33S | Young Livers/Burning Army Men (p/s)................................... 8 |
| 96 | Dinked 1 | Used/Lose Your Clown (in-store giveaway)............................ 20 |
| 98 | Elemental ELM 48S | Lipstick/Hot Heart (p/s)............................................... 6 |
| 98 | Elemental ELM 49S | Break It Up/Turkish Revenge (p/s)................................... 6 |
| 95 | Elemental ELM 27LP | HOT CHARITY (LP) .................................................. 15 |
| 08 | One Little Indian ELM 50DMM | ROCKET FROM THE CRYPT (LP, 1000 only)........................... 18 |
| 08 | One Little indian ELM34DMM | SCREAM DRACULA SCREAM! (LP) ...................................... 20 |

## ROCKETS
| | | |
|---|---|---|
| 60 | Philips PB 982 | Gibraltar Rock/Walkin' Home .......................................... 20 |
| 60 | Philips PB 982 | Gibraltar Rock/Walkin' Home (78) .................................... 40 |
| 61 | Zodiac ZR 0010 | Warrior/Countdown ...................................................... 22 |

## ROCKIN' BERRIES
| | | |
|---|---|---|
| 63 | Decca F 11698 | Wah Wah Wah Woo/Rockin' Berry Stomp ............................. 25 |
| 63 | Decca F 11760 | Itty Bitty Pieces/The Twitch ............................................ 20 |
| 64 | Piccadilly 7N 35197 | I Didn't Mean To Hurt You/You'd Better Come Home .................... 10 |
| 64 | Piccadilly 7N 35203 | He's In Town/Flashback ................................................. 6 |
| 65 | Piccadilly 7N 35217 | What The World's Come Over You/You Don't Know What To Do ............ 6 |
| 65 | Piccadilly 7N 35236 | Poor Man's Son/Follow Me ............................................. 6 |

| | | | |
|---|---|---|---|
| 65 | Piccadilly 7N 35254 | You're My Girl/Brother Bill | 10 |
| 65 | Piccadilly 7N 35270 | The Water Is Over My Head/Doesn't Time Fly | 10 |
| 66 | Piccadilly 7N 35304 | I Could Make You Fall In Love/Land Of Love | 5 |
| 66 | Piccadilly 7N 35327 | Midnight Mary/Money Grows On Trees | 5 |
| 67 | Piccadilly 7N 35373 | Sometimes/Needs To Be | 6 |
| 67 | Piccadilly 7N 35400 | Smile/Breakfast At Sam's | 6 |
| 67 | Pye 7N 17411 | Dawn (Go Away)/She's Not Like Any Girl | 6 |
| 68 | Pye 7N 17519 | When I Reach The Top/Pain | 10 |
| 68 | Pye 7N 17589 | Mr. Blue/Land Of Love | 10 |
| 73 | Satril SAT 9 | Day To Day/Big Louie's Birthday | 10 |
| 74 | Pye 7N 45394 | Rock-A-Bye Nursery Rhyme/Long Time Ago | 5 |
| 75 | Pye 7N 45439 | Black Gold/Eve | 5 |
| 75 | Satril SAT 101 | Lonely Summertime/Send Me No Letters | 6 |
| 65 | Piccadilly NEP 34039 | I DIDN'T MEAN TO HURT YOU (EP) | 35 |
| 65 | Piccadilly NEP 34043 | NEW FROM THE BERRIES (EP) | 35 |
| 65 | Piccadilly NEP 34045 | HAPPY TO BE BLUE (EP) | 50 |
| 78 | Hollick & Taylor HT EPS 1561 | 5 FROM THE BERRIES (EP) | 15 |
| 64 | Piccadilly NPL 38013 | IN TOWN (LP) | 40 |
| 65 | Piccadilly NPL 38022 | LIFE IS JUST A BOWL OF BERRIES (LP) | 40 |

*(see also Jefferson)*

## ROCKIN' DEVILS
| | | | |
|---|---|---|---|
| 79 | Hit Stuff HS 004 | Apache/Bony Moronie/Give Me Muddy Water/Rumplestiltskin (no p/s) | 10 |
| 75 | Hot Stuff HSL 001 | BRING BACK ROCK'N' ROLL (LP) | 20 |
| 75 | Hot Stuff HSL 003 | WITH A LITTLE HELP FROM OUR FRIEND (LP) | 20 |

## ROCKIN' FOO
| | | | |
|---|---|---|---|
| 70 | Stateside SS 2168 | Rochester River/Stranger In The Attic | 6 |
| 70 | Stateside SSL 10303 | ROCKIN' FOO (LP) | 22 |

## ROCKIN' HENRI & HAYSEEDS
| | | | |
|---|---|---|---|
| 63 | Decca F 11700 | Sally/Sweet Adeline | 7 |

## ROCKIN' HORSE
| | | | |
|---|---|---|---|
| 71 | Philips 6006 156 | The Biggest Gossip In Town/You Say | 12 |
| 72 | Philips 6006 200 | Julian The Hooligan/Stayed Out Late Last Night | 12 |
| 71 | Philips 6308 075 | YES IT IS (LP, laminated sleve, black/silver label) | 150 |

*(see also Jimmy Campbell, 23rd Turnoff, Kirkbys, Merseys)*

## ROCKIN' RAMRODS
| | | | |
|---|---|---|---|
| 66 | Polydor BM 56512 | Don't Fool With Fu Manchu/Tears Melt The Stone | 25 |

## ROCKIN' REBELS
| | | | |
|---|---|---|---|
| 63 | Stateside SS 162 | Wild Weekend/Wild Weekend Cha Cha | 22 |
| 63 | Stateside SS 187 | Rockin' Crickets/Hully Gully Rock (both sides actually by Hot-Toddys) | 20 |

*(see also Hot-Toddys)*

## ROCKIN' R'S
| | | | |
|---|---|---|---|
| 59 | London HL 8872 | The Beat/Crazy Baby | 40 |
| 59 | London HL 8872 | The Beat/Crazy Baby (78) | 30 |

## ROCKIN' SAINTS
| | | | |
|---|---|---|---|
| 60 | Brunswick 05843 | Cheat On Me, Baby/Half And Half | 100 |

## ROCKIN' SHADES
| | | | |
|---|---|---|---|
| 79 | SRTS 79 CUS 404 | LIVE AT CAISTER EP | 20 |
| 79 | Magnum MF EP 002 | LIVE AT CAISTER EP | 12 |

## ROCKIN' STRINGS
| | | | |
|---|---|---|---|
| 59 | Columbia DB 4349 | Red Sail In The Sunset/Autumn Leaves | 5 |

## ROCKIN' VICKERS
| | | | |
|---|---|---|---|
| 64 | Decca F 11993 | I Go Ape/Someone Like You (as Rocking Vickers) | 40 |
| 66 | CBS 202051 | It's Alright/Stay By Me | 55 |
| 66 | CBS 202241 | Dandy/I Don't Need Your Kind | 40 |

*(see also Motorhead)*

## ROCKING DEVILS
| | | | |
|---|---|---|---|
| 75 | Hot Stuff HSL 002 | THAT OLD ROCK MUSIC'S HERE TO STAY (LP, most copies signed on front cover) | 25 |
| 79 | Hot Stuff HS 007 | GOT THEM BLUES (EP, red vinyl) | 20 |

## ROCKING HORSE
| | | | |
|---|---|---|---|
| 71 | Camel CA 75 | Running Back Home/SOUL SYNDICATE BAND: Running Back - Version | 6 |
| 72 | Randy's RAN 522 | Hard Time/Change Your Ways | 8 |
| 73 | Randy's RAN 535 | I'm So Fed Up/I'm So Fed Up - Version | 5 |
| 74 | Pyramid PYR 7009 | New Situation/New Version | 8 |
| 74 | Sydna SYD 5026 | Be Thankful/Thankful Dub | 8 |

## ROCKING RICHARD AND WHISTLING VIC TEMPLAR
| | | | |
|---|---|---|---|
| 87 | Hangman HANG 14 UP | PRESENT: TEA AND BACCY (LP) | 15 |

## ROCKITS
| | | | |
|---|---|---|---|
| 73 | Mowest MW 3012 | Livin' Without You/Love My Love | 6 |
| 74 | Mowest MW 3016 | Gimme True Love/I'm Losing You | 8 |

## ROCK MACHINE
| | | | |
|---|---|---|---|
| 73 | T.I.M. | THEMES (LP) | 60 |

*(see also Ugly Custard)*

## ROCK'N'ROLL REVIVAL SHOW
| | | | |
|---|---|---|---|
| 68 | Decca F 12752 | Midnight Train/Oh Boy (both sides featuring Tommy Bishop) | 5 |

*(see also Tommy Bishop's Ricochets)*

## ROCK-OLGA
| | | | |
|---|---|---|---|
| 60 | Ember EMB S 105 | Red Sails In The Sunset/My Dixieland Doll (in p/s) | 10 |

MINT VALUE £

| 60 | Ember EMB S 105 | Red Sails In The Sunset/My Dixieland Doll | 5 |

## ROCKS
| 88 | GOTELOAN GLP A1 88 TR | Human Music/Freedom | 15 |

## ROCKSLIDE
| 75 | Reward MAG 004 | Jump Bump Boogaloo/Roller Coaster | 8 |

## ROCKSTAR
| 76 | MCA MCA 265 | Mummy/Over The Hill | 15 |

## ROCKSTEADYS
| 67 | Giant GN 2 | Squeeze And Freeze/JUNIOR SMITH: I'm A Good Boy | 15 |

## ROCKSTONES
| 70 | Trojan TR 7762 | A.B.C. Reggae/BEVERLEY'S ALLSTARS: Be Yours | 20 |
| 70 | Summit SUM 8501 | Everything Is Beautiful/BEVERLEY'S ALLSTARS: Give Up | 10 |

*(see also Gaylads)*

## ROCK WORKSHOP
| 70 | CBS 5046 | You To Lose/Born In The City | 6 |
| 71 | CBS 7252 | Very Last Time/Light Is Light | 5 |
| 70 | CBS 64075 | ROCK WORKSHOP (LP, orange label) | 40 |
| 71 | CBS 64394 | THE VERY LAST TIME (LP, gatefold sleeve, orange label) | 40 |

*(see also Bob Downes, Alex Harvey)*

## ROCKY FELLERS
| 63 | Stateside SS 175 | Killer Joe/Lonely Treardrops | 20 |
| 63 | Stateside SS 212 | Like The Big Guys Do/Great Big World | 18 |
| 63 | Pye International 7N 25225 | Ching A Ling Baby/Hey Little Donkey | 22 |

## ROCKY HORROR SHOW
| 75 | Ode ODS 66305 | Science Fiction Double Feature/Time Warp | 8 |
| 87 | Ode RHVX 1 | ROCKY HORROR BOX SET (4-LP box, with inserts, numbered) | 20 |
| 87 | Ode RHBXLP 1 | ROCKY HORROR BOX SET (4-LP box, with different inserts to above) | 20 |
| 90 | Ode RHBXCD 1 | THE ROCKY HORROR PICTURE ALBUMS (15th ANNIVERSARY) (4-CD, with booklet) | 40 |

*(see also Tim Curry, Meat Loaf, Original Soundtracks)*

## ROCOCO
| 73 | Deram DM 375 | Ultrastar/Wildfire | 10 |
| 76 | Mountain TOP 9 | Follow That Car/Lucinda | 6 |

## ROD & CAROLYN
| 63 | Pye 7N 15519 | How Can You Tell/What About The Teardrops | 6 |
| 63 | Pye 7N 15565 | Bye-Bye My Lover/To Be Alone | 6 |
| 64 | Pye 7N 15629 | Young Love/Talk To Me | 6 |
| 64 | Pye 7N 15706 | Love Is Where You Are/I've Got You On My Mind | 6 |

## GENE RODDENBERRY
| 76 | CBS 4692 | Star Trek Theme/Star Trek Philosophy | 12 |

## RODD-KEN & CAVALIERS
| 60 | Triumph RGM 1001 | Magic Wheel/Happy Valley | 40 |

*(see also Blue Men)*

## RODDY RADIATION & THE TEARJERKERS
| 80 | Dodgy Demo Co | NOTHING LASTS FOREVER EP | 25 |
| 82 | Chiswick DICE 15 | Desire/Western Song (p/s) | 5 |

*(see also Specials)*

## TIM RODDY
| 82 | Tiara 001 | Frankly Fiona/Don't Turn The Light Out On Me | 8 |

## CLODA(GH) RODGERS
| 62 | Decca F 11534 | Believe Me I'm No Fool/End Of The Line | 10 |
| 63 | Decca F 11607 | Sometime Kind Of Love/I See More Of Him | 10 |
| 63 | Decca F 11667 | To Give My Love To You/I Only Live To Love You | 10 |
| 64 | Decca F 11812 | Mister Heartache/Time | 10 |
| 65 | Columbia DB 7468 | Wanting You/Johnny Come Home | 8 |
| 66 | Columbia DB 7926 | Every Day Is Just The Same/You'll Come A Running | 7 |
| 66 | Columbia DB 8038 | Stormy Weather/Lonely Room | 8 |
| 68 | RCA 1684 | Room Full Of Roses/Play The Drame To The End | 20 |
| 68 | RCA 1748 | Rhythm Of Love/River Of Tears | 8 |
| 69 | RCA 1891 | Biljo/Spider | 8 |
| 69 | RCA SF 8033 / RD 8033 | CLODAGH RODGERS (LP) | 20 |
| 69 | RCA SF 8071 | MIDNIGHT CLODAGH (LP) | 20 |
| 71 | RCA SF 8180 | RODGERS AND HEART (LP) | 20 |

## EILEEN RODGERS
| 58 | Fontana H 136 | Careful, Careful/I'm Alone Because I Love You | 12 |
| 58 | Fontana H 156 | Treasure Of Your Love/Little Bit Bluer | 12 |
| 61 | London HLR 9271 | Sailor (Your Home Is The Sea)/Wait Till Tomorrow | 15 |

## JEAN RODGERS
| 65 | Columbia DB 7637 | Take What I Have/Baby What You Gonna Do? | 6 |

## JIMMIE RODGERS (THE BLUE YODELLER)
| 58 | HMV 7EG 8163 | JIMMIE RODGERS (EP) | 19 |
| 60 | RCA RCX 1058 | LEGENDARY JIMMIE RODGERS (EP) | 10 |
| 59 | RCA RD 27110 | TRAIN WHISTLE BLUES (LP) | 15 |
| 59 | RCA RD 27138 | NEVER NO MO' BLUES (JIMMIE RODGERS MEMORIAL ALBUM) (LP) | 15 |
| 61 | RCA RD 27203 | MY ROUGH AND ROWDY WAYS (LP) | 15 |
| 61 | RCA RD 27241 | JIMMIE THE KID (LP) | 15 |
| 62 | RCA RD 7505 | COUNTRY MUSIC HALL OF FAME (LP) | 15 |
| 63 | RCA RD 7562 | THE SHORT BUT BRILLIANT LIFE OF JIMMIE RODGERS (LP) | 15 |

| | | | |
|---|---|---|---|
| 64 | RCA RD 7644 | MY TIME AIN'T LONG (LP) | 15 |

## JIMMIE RODGERS
| | | | |
|---|---|---|---|
| 57 | Columbia DB 3986 | Honeycomb/Their Hearts Were Full Of Spring (as Jimmy Rodgers) | 10 |
| 57 | Columbia DB 4052 | Kisses Sweeter Than Wine/Better Loved You'll Never Be | 8 |
| 58 | Columbia DB 4078 | Oh-Oh, I'm Falling In Love Again/The Long Hot Summer | 8 |
| 58 | Columbia DB 4130 | Secretly/Make Me A Miracle | 7 |
| 58 | Columbia DB 4175 | Are You Really Mine/The Wizard | 5 |
| 58 | Columbia DB 4206 | Woman From Liberia/Girl In The Wood | 5 |
| 58 | Columbia 33SX 1082 | JIMMIE RODGERS (LP) | 25 |
| 58 | Columbia 33SX 1097 | THE NUMBER ONE BALLADS (LP) | 25 |

## RODIGAN V WILLIAMS
| | | | |
|---|---|---|---|
| 79 | Exclusive/Ethnic Fight EFLP 60-11-13 | ROCKERS ARENA (LP) | 50 |

## RODNEY & BRUNETTES
| | | | |
|---|---|---|---|
| 79 | London/Bomp HLZ 10574 | NEW YORK BLONDES featuring MADAME X: Little GTO/Holocaust On Sunset Boulevard(no p/s) | 12 |

*(see also Blondie, Debbie Harry)*

## RODNEY P (AKA RODDIE ROK)
| | | | |
|---|---|---|---|
| 01 | Riddim Killah RK001 | Murderer Style/Friction (12") | 10 |
| 04 | Riddim Killah RKP04LP | THE FUTURE (LP- Limited White Vinyl) | 20 |

*(see also London Posse)*

## RODS
| | | | |
|---|---|---|---|
| 79 | Rods ROD 1 | Like A Mirror/Hear I Am | 10 |

## TOMMY ROE (& ROEMANS)
| | | | |
|---|---|---|---|
| 62 | HMV POP 1060 | Sheila/Save Your Kisses | 7 |
| 62 | HMV POP 1092 | Susie Darlin'/Piddle De Pat | 8 |
| 63 | HMV POP 1117 | Gonna Take A Chance/Don't Cry Donna | 5 |
| 63 | HMV POP 1138 | The Folk Singer/Count On Me | 6 |
| 63 | HMV POP 1174 | Kiss And Run/What Makes The Blues (Want To Pick On Me) | 6 |
| 63 | HMV POP 1207 | Everybody/There's A Great Day A-Coming | 5 |
| 63 | HMV POP 1259 | Come On/There Will Be Better Years | 6 |
| 64 | HMV POP 1290 | Be A Good Little Girl/Carol | 6 |
| 64 | HMV POP 1364 | Little Miss Heartache/You Might As Well Forget Him | 10 |
| 65 | HMV POP 1368 | Diane From Manchester Square/Part Girl | 8 |
| 65 | HMV POP 1469 | Doesn't Anybody Know My Name/I'm A Rambler, I'm A Gambler | 8 |
| 66 | HMV POP 1539 | Sweet Pea/Much More Love | 8 |
| 69 | Stateside SS 2143 | Dizzy/The You I Need | 5 |
| 69 | Stateside SS 2152 | Heather Honey/Money Is My Pay | 8 |
| 63 | HMV CLP 1614 | SHEILA (LP) | 25 |
| 64 | HMV CLP 1704 | EVERYBODY LIKES TOMMY ROE (LP) | 20 |
| 65 | HMV CLP 1860 | BALLADS AND BEAT (LP) | 20 |
| 69 | Stateside S(S)L 10282 | DIZZY (LP) | 15 |

## CE CE ROGERS
| | | | |
|---|---|---|---|
| 89 | WEA A 8852T | Forever (12" Extended Mix)/Forever (Club Mix)/Someday (12" Extended Mix) (12", no p/s) | 10 |

## DANE ROGERS & NU BEATS
| | | | |
|---|---|---|---|
| 64 | Pye 7N 15621 | Mary Jane/Jeanette | 10 |

## DEAN ROGERS
| | | | |
|---|---|---|---|
| 60 | Parlophone R 4732 | End Of Time (as Dean Rogers & Hi-Fi's)/Keep The Miracle Going | 10 |
| 61 | Parlophone R 4835 | Timber/High In A Misty Sky | 20 |

*(see also Sydney James)*

## ERIC ROGERS
| | | | |
|---|---|---|---|
| 63 | Decca F 11585 | The Iron Maiden/Fly-Wheel | 7 |

## JULIE ROGERS
| | | | |
|---|---|---|---|
| 68 | Philips BF 1727 | Tar And Cement/The Muffin Man | 5 |
| 65 | Mercury 20048 (S)MCL | THE SOUND OF JULIE (LP, mono/stereo) | 20 |
| 66 | Mercury 20086 (S)MCL | CONTRASTS (LP, mono/stereo) | 20 |

## LINCOLN ROGERS
| | | | |
|---|---|---|---|
| 73 | Phoenix NIX 137 | Let Love Come Between Us/She Looked At Me With Love | 15 |

## LYNNE ROGERS
| | | | |
|---|---|---|---|
| 65 | RCA RCA 1479 | Sometimes/I Shouldn't Care | 7 |

## MARK ROGERS & MARKSMEN
| | | | |
|---|---|---|---|
| 63 | Parlophone R 5045 | Bubble Pop/Hold It! | 25 |

*(see also Marksmen, Mark Wirtz)*

## PAUL ROGERS
| | | | |
|---|---|---|---|
| 61 | HMV POP 872 | Four An' Twenty Thousand Kisses/Free To Love | 10 |
| 63 | HMV POP 1121 | Always/Joanie Don't Be Angry | 10 |

## PAULINE ROGERS
| | | | |
|---|---|---|---|
| 54 | Columbia SCM 5106 | Spinnin' The Blues/But Good | 20 |

## PIERCE ROGERS & OVERLANDERS
| | | | |
|---|---|---|---|
| 61 | Parlophone R 4838 | Do You Still Love Me?/That Someone | 12 |

## SHORTY ROGERS & HIS ORCHESTRA
| | | | |
|---|---|---|---|
| 52 | Capitol LC 6549 | MODERN SOUNDS (10" LP, as Shorty Rogers & His Giants) | 15 |
| 54 | HMV DLP 1030 | COOL AND CRAZY (10" LP, featuring Giants) | 15 |
| 54 | HMV DLP 1058 | EIGHT SHORTY ROGERS' NUMBERS (10" LP) | 15 |
| 56 | Contemporary LDC 190 | SHELLY MANNE, SHORTY ROGERS AND JIMMY GIUFFRE - THE THREE (10" LP, with Shelly Manne & Jimmy Giuffre) | 18 |

*(see also Boots Brown, Bud Shank, Shelly Manne, Jimmy Giuffre)*

MINT VALUE £

## SIDNEY ROGERS
| | | | |
|---|---|---|---|
| 73 | Techniques TE 923 | Don't Throw Stones/Toughness | 8 |
| 78 | Ethnic Fight FTDD 4448 | I Don't Want To End Up In Slavery/Mary And Bobby (12") | 60 |
| 74 | Ethnic Fight – ETH 2214S | MIRACLE WORKER (LP) | 30 |
| 75 | Ethnic EF 2222S | TIPPIN' IN (LP) | 80 |

## TIMMIE ROGERS
| | | | |
|---|---|---|---|
| 57 | London HLU 8510 | Back To School Again/I've Got A Dog Who Loves Me | 60 |
| 57 | London HLU 8510 | Back To School Again/I've Got A Dog Who Loves Me (78) | 20 |
| 58 | London HLU 8601 | Take Me To Your Leader/Fla-Ga-La-Pa | 60 |
| 58 | London HLU 8601 | Take Me To Your Leader/Fla-Ga-La-Pa (78) | 20 |

## TRACY ROGERS
| | | | |
|---|---|---|---|
| 65 | Polydor 56029 | How Love Used To Be/When I Realise | 7 |
| 65 | Polydor 56037 | Love Story/I Remember When I Loved You (p/s) | 10 |
| 66 | Polydor 56077 | Baby/Through Thick And Thin | 25 |
| 67 | Polydor 56197 | Back With You Baby/In The Morning | 12 |

## VERN ROGERS & HI-FI'S
| | | | |
|---|---|---|---|
| 62 | Oriole CB 1785 | That Ain't Right/Be Everything To Anyone You Love | 20 |
| 63 | Oriole CB 1826 | He's New To You/Can't Complain | 15 |
| 63 | Oriole CB 1885 | I Will/One Way Love Affair | 20 |
| 63 | Oriole CB 1923 | Anna/Pride | 15 |

## DIANA ROGERSON
| | | | |
|---|---|---|---|
| 85 | United Dairies UD 017 | THE INEVITABLE CHRYSTAL BELLE SCRODD RECORD (LP) | 25 |
| 86 | United Dairies UD 021 | CHRYSTAL BELLE SCRODD: BELLE DE JOUR (LP) | 25 |

*(see also Nurse With Wound)*

## ROG & PIP
| | | | |
|---|---|---|---|
| 14 | Rise Above Relics RARLP 013 | OUR REVOLUTION (LP) | 25 |

## ROGUES (U.K.)
| | | | |
|---|---|---|---|
| 67 | Decca F 12718 | Memories Of Missy/And You Let Her Pass By | 30 |

## ROGUES (U.S.)
| | | | |
|---|---|---|---|
| 65 | CBS 201731 | Everyday/Rogers Reef | 20 |

*(see also Terry Day, Terry Melcher, Bruce Johnston)*

## CHRIS ROHMANN
| | | | |
|---|---|---|---|
| 73 | RCA Victor SF 8364 | THE MAN I AM TODAY (LP) | 22 |

## ROKES
| | | | |
|---|---|---|---|
| 67 | RCA RCA 1587 | Let's Live For Today/Ride On | 30 |
| 67 | RCA RCA 1646 | Hold My Hand/Regency Sue | 50 |
| 68 | RCA RCA 1694 | When The Wind Arises/The Works Of Bartholemew | 70 |

## ROKKA
| | | | |
|---|---|---|---|
| 80 | Rock Trax RT 01 | Come Back/Touch & Go | 10 |

## CHERRY ROLAND
| | | | |
|---|---|---|---|
| 63 | Decca F 11579 | Handy Sandy/Stay As I Am | 12 |
| 63 | Decca F 11648 | What A Guy/Just For Fun | 12 |

*(see also Cherry Rowland)*

## PAUL ROLAND
| | | | |
|---|---|---|---|
| 82 | Aristocrat ARC 1389 | Doctor Strange/Madelaine (p/s) | 8 |
| 83 | Aftermath AEP 12011 | Blades Of Battenburg (Remix)/Captain Blood/Puppet Master/Cavalier (12", p/s) | 10 |
| 86 | Aftermath AEP 12013 | Gabrielle/Berlin/Sword & Sorcery (p/s) | 8 |
| 86 | Imaginary MIRAGE 002 | Demon In A Glass Case/In The Opium Den (oversized p/s) | 7 |
| 87 | Bam Caruso PABL 094 | Alice's House/Go Down You Murderers/Happy Families/Jumbee (demo) (p/s) | 8 |
| 80 | Ace ACE 013 | THE WEREWOLF OF LONDON (LP) | 18 |

*(see also Weird Strings, Midnight Rags, Beau Brummel)*

## WALTER ROLAND/GEORGIA SLIM
| | | | |
|---|---|---|---|
| 59 | Jazz Collector JEL 2 | THE MALE BLUES VOL. 1 (EP) | 22 |

## BARRY ROLFE
| | | | |
|---|---|---|---|
| 73 | Philips 6006 331 | Look The Business/Molly Molly | 30 |
| 73 | Philips 6006 348 | Beam Me Aboard, Mr. Spock/Boadecia | 8 |
| 74 | Philips 6006 381 | Going Up/Johnny Bo Jangle | 6 |

## ROLFE, GIFFORD & ANDREW MULLINS
| | | | |
|---|---|---|---|
| 72 | Look REM 104 | Tutankamun/Sad Eyes | 10 |

## PETER ROLFE
| | | | |
|---|---|---|---|
| 66 | Strike JH 314 | London/In The Middle Of Town | 20 |

## ROLLERBALL
| | | | |
|---|---|---|---|
| 79 | ABC ABC 1 | Teach Me To Rock & Roll/I'm So Lonely (no p/s) | 5 |
| 79 | ABC MBC 2 | Let's Go To America/She's A loner (no p/s) | 5 |

## ROLLERS (1)
| | | | |
|---|---|---|---|
| 61 | London HLG 9340 | Continental Walk/I Want You So | 18 |

## ROLLERS (2)
| | | | |
|---|---|---|---|
| 79 | Arista 259 | Turn On The Radio/Washington's Birthday (p/s) | 6 |

## ROLLING STONES
### SINGLES : DECCA SINGLES
| | | | |
|---|---|---|---|
| 63 | Decca F 11675 | Come On/I Want To Be Loved (demo copies £350) | 50 |
| 63 | Decca F 11742 | Fortune Teller/Poison Ivy (solid centre, withdrawn) | 1500 |
| 63 | Decca F 11764 | I Wanna Be Your Man/Stones (B-side mis-spelled) | 35 |
| 63 | Decca F 11764 | I Wanna Be Your Man/Stoned | 20 |
| 64 | No Cat. No. | We Were Falling In Love (EMI disc acetate, unreleased single) | 1000 |
| 64 | Decca F 11845 | Not Fade Away/Little By Little | 12 |

| | | | |
|---|---|---|---|
| 64 | Decca F 11934 | It's All Over Now/Good Times, Bad Times | 12 |
| 64 | Decca F 12014 | Little Red Rooster/Off The Hook | 12 |

*(The above singles were originally issued with "Recording first published..." text and wide label lettering.)*

| | | | |
|---|---|---|---|
| 65 | Decca F 12104 | The Last Time/Play With Fire | 15 |
| 65 | Decca F 12220 | (I Can't Get No) Satisfaction/The Spider And The Fly | 15 |
| 65 | Decca F 12263 | Get Off Of My Cloud/The Singer Not The Song | 15 |
| 66 | Decca F 12331 | 19th Nervous Breakdown/As Tears Go By | 10 |
| 66 | Decca F 12395 | Paint It, Black/Long Long While | 15 |

*(The above singles were originally issued with a round Decca logo; later boxed-logo pressings are worth £4 each.)*

| | | | |
|---|---|---|---|
| 66 | Decca F 12497 | Have You Seen Your Mother, Baby, Standing In The Shadow?/ Who's Driving Your Plane | 15 |
| 67 | Decca F 12546 | Let's Spend The Night Together/Ruby Tuesday | 12 |
| 67 | Decca F 12654 | We Love You/Dandelion | 15 |
| 68 | Decca F 12782 | Jumping Jack Flash/Child Of The Moon | 15 |
| 69 | Decca F 12952 | Honky Tonk Women/You Can't Always Get What You Want (in demo-only p/s) | 70 |
| 69 | Decca F 12952 | Honky Tonk Women/You Can't Always Get What You Want | 12 |
| 71 | Decca F 13195 | Street Fighting Man/Surprise Surprise/Everybody Needs Somebody To Love (33rpm maxi-single) | 10 |
| 71 | Decca F 13203 | Street Fighting Man/Surprise Surprise (jukebox edition) | 30 |
| 73 | Decca F 13404 | Sad Day/You Can't Always Get What You Want | 20 |
| 74 | Decca F 13517 | Paint It Black/It's All Over Now (release cancelled, demo-only) | 220 |
| 75 | Decca F 13584 | I Don't Know Why I Love You (credited to either 'Jagger/Richard/Taylor'/Try A Little Harder | 20 |
| 75 | Decca F 13584 | I Don't Know Why I Love You (credited Stevie Wonder')/Try A Little Harder | 15 |
| 75 | Decca F 13597 | Out Of Time/Jiving Sister Fanny | 8 |
| 76 | Decca F 13635 | Honky Tonk Women/Sympathy For The Devil | 8 |
| 70s | Decca F 11934 | It's All Over Now/Good Times, Bad Times (repressing, with stereo mix on A-side, [ZXDR instead of XDR matrix no.] boxed Decca logo) | 8 |
| 87 | Decca F 102 | Jumping Jack Flash/Child Of The Moon (p/s, reissue) | 8 |
| 87 | Decca FX 102 | Jumping Jack Flash/Child Of The Moon/Sympathy For The Devil (12", p/s, reissue) | 20 |

## SINGLES : ROLLING STONES LABEL SINGLES

| | | | |
|---|---|---|---|
| 71 | Rolling Stones RS 19100 | Brown Sugar/Bitch/Let It Rock (in p/s) | 50 |
| 71 | Rolling Stones RS 19100 | Brown Sugar/Bitch/Let It Rock | 7 |
| 74 | Rolling Stones RS 19114 | It's Only Rock 'N' Roll/Through The Lonely Nights | 6 |
| 78 | R. Stones 12EMI 2802 | Miss You (8.26)/Faraway Eyes (12", p/s, pink vinyl) | 12 |
| 81 | Rolling Stones | Beast Of Burden/Everything Is Turning Gold (unreleased) | 0 |
| 82 | Rolling Stones RSR 111 | Time Is On My Side (live)/Twenty Flight Rock (live) (p/s) | 5 |
| 82 | Rolling Stones 12RSR 111 | Time Is On My Side (live)/Twenty Flight Rock (live)/ Under My Thumb (live) (12", p/s) | 10 |
| 84 | Rolling Stones RSR 114 | She Was Hot/I Think I'm Going Mad (p/s) | 5 |
| 84 | Rolling Stones RSR 114 | She Was Hot/I Think I'm Going Mad (yellow paper label, p/s) | 5 |
| 84 | Rolling Stones RSRP 114 | She Was Hot/I Think I'm Going Mad (shaped picture disc) | 10 |
| 84 | Rolling Stones SUGAR 1 | Brown Sugar/Bitch (p/s, reissue) | 5 |
| 93 | Rolling Stone RS LH 1 | Brown Sugar/Start Me Up (jukebox issue, no p/s) | 15 |
| 93 | Rolling Stone ORDER LH 1 | Gimme Shelter (Live Version)/NEW MODEL ARMY FEATURING TOM JONES: Gimme Shelter (jukebox issue, no p/s) | 15 |

## SINGLES : CBS SINGLES

| | | | |
|---|---|---|---|
| 86 | CBS QA 6864 | Harlem Shuffle/Had It With You (poster p/s) | 5 |
| 86 | CBS QTA 6864 | Harlem Shuffle (N.Y. Mix)/(London Mix)/Had It With You (12", p/s) | 10 |
| 86 | CBS A 7160 | One Hit (To The Body)/Fight (p/s) | 5 |
| 89 | CBS 655 193-7 | Mixed Emotions/Fancyman Blues (p/s) | 8 |
| 89 | CBS 655 193-2 | Mixed Emotions (7" Version)/Mixed Emotions (Chris Kimsey's 12")/ Fancyman Blues (CD, picture disc, card sleeve) | 10 |
| 89 | CBS 655 193-5 | Mixed Emotions (7" Version)/Fancyman Blues/Tumbling Dice/Miss You (CD, picture disc, in circular tin with 'tongue' logo sticker) | 35 |
| 89 | CBS 655 214-2 | Mixed Emotions (7" Version)/Fancyman Blues/Shattered/Waiting On A Friend (CD, picture disc, in circular tin with 'tongue' logo sticker) | 35 |
| 89 | CBS 655 422-7 | Rock And A Hard Place/Cook Cook Blues (p/s) | 5 |
| 89 | CBS 655 422-2 | Rock And A Hard Place (7" Version)/(Dance Mix)/(Bonus Beats Mix)/ Cook Cook Blues (CD, picture disc, card sleeve) | 15 |
| 89 | CBS 655 448-2 | Rock And A Hard Place (7" Version)/Cook Cook Blues/It's Only Rock'n'Roll (But I Like It)/Rocks Off (3rd CD, picture disc, 7" box set with poster) | 25 |
| 90 | CBS 656 065-7 | Almost Hear You Sigh/Wish I'd Never Met You (p/s) | 8 |
| 90 | CBS 656 065-5 | Almost Hear You Sigh/Miss You/Waiting On A Friend/Wish I'd Never Met You (CD, in tin with 'Urban Jungle' sticker) | 30 |
| 90 | CBS 656 065-2 | Almost Hear You Sigh/Beast Of Burden/Angie/Fool To Cry (CD, gold disc) | 25 |
| 90 | CBS 656 1227 | Terrifying/Rock And A Hard Place (p/s) | 8 |
| 91 | CBS 656 756-7 | Highwire/2000 Light Years Away (p/s) | 8 |
| 91 | CBS 656 892-6 | Ruby Tuesday/Play With Fire (live)/You Can't Always Get What You Want (live)/Rock And A Hard Place (live) (12", p/s) | 10 |

## SINGLES : VIRGIN SINGLES

| | | | |
|---|---|---|---|
| 94 | Virgin VS 1503 | Love Is Strong/The Storm (numbered p/s, 7,000 only) | 10 |
| 94 | Virgin VCS 1503 | Love Is Strong/The Storm (injection moulded jukebox copy) | 12 |
| 94 | Virgin VS 1518 | You Got Me Rocking/Jump On Top Of Me (numbered p/s, 7,000 only) | 10 |
| 94 | Virgin VS 1524 | Out Of Tears/I'm Gonna Drive (numbered p/s, 7,000 only) | 10 |
| 94 | Virgin VSCDG 1524 | Out Of Tears (Don Was Edit)/I'm Gonna Drive/So Young/The Storm/ Jump On Top Of Me (CD, digipak, numbered, 4,000 only, withdrawn) | 250 |
| 94 | Virgin VSP 1539 | I Go Wild/I Go Wild (live) (numbered picture disc) | 20 |
| 96 | Virgin VS 1578 | Wild Horses/Tumbling Dice/Gimme Shelter (unreleased) | 0 |
| 96 | Virgin VSCDT 1578 | Wild Horses/Tumbling Dice/Gimme Shelter (CD, unreleased) | 0 |
| 97 | Virgin VST 1653 | Anybody Seen My Baby? (LP Edit)/(Soul Solution Remix)/(Bonus Roll) (12", p/s) | 15 |
| 97 | Virgin VS 1653 | Anybody Seen My Baby? (LP Edit)/(Soul Solution Remix Edit) (numbered picture disc, p/s, 7,500 only) | 15 |

Rare Record Price Guide 2018

MINT VALUE £

| | | | |
|---|---|---|---|
| 98 | Virgin VS 1667 | Saint Of Me/Anyway You Look At It (7" picture disc) | 10 |
| 98 | Virgin VSY 1667 | Saint Of Me (Radio Edit)/Anyway You Look At It (picture disc) | 10 |
| 98 | Virgin VSLH 1667 | Saint Of Me/Radio Edit/Anyway You Look At It (injection moulded jukebox labels) | 8 |
| 98 | Virgin VSTTDT 1667 | Saint Of Me (remixes)/Anybody Seen My Baby? (remixes) (12", double pack, stickered p/s) | 15 |
| 98 | Virgin VSTX 1667 | Saint Of Me (remixes)/Anybody Seen My Baby? (remixes) (12", double pack, stickered p/s) | 15 |
| 98 | Virgin VSY 1700 | Out Of Control (Album Radio Edit)/In Hand With Fluke Radio Edit (p/s) | 10 |
| 98 | Virgin VSY 1700 | Out Of Control (Album Radio Edit)/(In Hand With Fluke Radio Edit) | 10 |
| 02 | Virgin VS 1838 | Don't Stop (Edit)/New Rock Remix (red vinyl, numbered p/s) | 12 |
| 05 | Virgin VS 1905 | Streets Of Love/Rough Justice (red vinyl, p/s) | 10 |
| 05 | Virgin VS 1907 | Rain Fall Down (Will i Am Remix)/(Ashley Beedle's Heavy Vocal Re-Edit) (7", p/s) | 10 |
| 06 | Virgin VS 1914 | Biggest Mistake/Hand Of Fate (red vinyl, p/s) | 10 |

## SINGLES : OTHER SINGLES

| | | | |
|---|---|---|---|
| 72 | Sound For Industry 107 | Mick Jagger Introduces 'Exile On Main Street' (flexidisc free with NME) | 15 |
| 74 | Atlantic K 19107 | Brown Sugar/Happy/Rocks Off (unissued) | 150 |
| 02 | Virgin VS1838 | Don't Stop/New Rock Remix (Limited edition red vinyl, numbered) | 12 |
| 03 | Abkco 0602498106136 | Sympathy For The Devil (Neptune's Radio Edit)/Original Version (p/s) | 8 |
| 10 | Universal 273 547-7 | Plundered My Soul/All Down The Line (p/s) | 10 |
| 11 | Universal 0602527643410 | Brown Sugar/Bitch/Let It Rock (Live At Leeds 13th March 1971) (p/s) | 7 |
| 12 | Universal 3723278 | Doom And Gloom (Jeff Bhasker Mix) (10" 1-sided, other side etched, 1500 only) | 10 |

## SINGLES : SINGLES BOX SETS

| | | | |
|---|---|---|---|
| 80 | Decca STONE 1-12 | SINGLE STONES (12-single box set) | 60 |
| 80 | Decca BROWSE 1 | SINGLE STONES (in-store, 3 x 12-single box set [STONE 1-12], with poster & badge, also available via mail-order) | 150 |

## EXPORT SINGLES

| | | | |
|---|---|---|---|
| 63 | Decca AT 15005 | I Wanna Be Your Man/Stoned | 150 |
| 64 | Decca AT 15006 | Not Fade Away/Little By Little | 150 |
| 64 | Decca AT 15032 | Come On/Tell Me (You're Coming Back) | 150 |
| 64 | Decca AT 15035 | Empty Heart/Around And Around | 175 |
| 65 | Decca AT 15039 | Time Is On My Side/Congratulations | 175 |
| 65 | Decca AT 15040 | Little Red Rooster/Off The Hook | 110 |
| 65 | Decca AT 15043 | (I Can't Get No) Satisfaction/The Under Assistant West Coast Promotional Man (p/s) | 150 |
| 65 | Decca F 12104 | The Last Time/Play With Fire (with Dutch or Scandinavian p/s) | 85 |
| 65 | Decca F 12220 | (I Can't Get No) Satisfaction/The Under Assistant West Coast Promotional Man (with p/s) | 75 |
| 65 | Decca F 12220 | (I Can't Get No) Satisfaction/The Under Assistant West Coast Promotional Man | 30 |
| 65 | Decca F 22180 | Heart Of Stone/What A Shame (in p/s) | 140 |
| 65 | Decca F 22180 | Heart Of Stone/What A Shame | 100 |
| 65 | Decca F 22265 | Get Off My Cloud/I'm Free | 30 |
| 65 | Decca F 22265 | Get Off My Cloud/I'm Free (in p/s) | 75 |
| 66 | Decca F 12395 | Paint It, Black/Long Long While (p/s) | 50 |
| 66 | Decca F 12331 | 19th Nervous Breakdown/As Tears Go By (with Dutch p/s) | 50 |
| 67 | Decca F 12546 | Let's Spend The Night Together/Ruby Tuesday (p/s) | 50 |
| 67 | Decca F 12654 | We Love You/Dandelion (p/s) | 50 |
| 67 | Decca F 22706 | 2,000 Light Years From Home/She's A Rainbow | 50 |
| 68 | Decca F 22825 | Street Fighting Man (remix)/No Expectations (in p/s) | 50 |
| 68 | Decca F 22825 | Street Fighting Man (remix)/No Expectations | 30 |
| 69 | Decca F 12952 | Honky Tonk Women/You Can't Always Get What You Want (p/s) | 50 |
| 71 | Decca F 13195 | Street Fighting Man/Surprise Surprise/Everybody Needs Somebody To Love (33rpm maxi-single, p/s) | 40 |
| 71 | Decca F 13126 | Little Queenie/Love In Vain (in p/s) | 55 |
| 71 | Decca F 13126 | Little Queenie/Love In Vain | 20 |
| 71 | Decca F 13204 | Street Fighting Man/Everybody Needs Somebody To Love | 20 |
| 71 | Decca F 13204 | Street Fighting Man/Everybody Needs Somebody To Love (in p/s) | 40 |

## EPs

| | | | |
|---|---|---|---|
| 64 | Decca DFE 8560 | THE ROLLING STONES (with unboxed Decca logo) | 40 |
| 64 | Decca DFE 8560 | THE ROLLING STONES (later boxed Decca logo) | 12 |
| 64 | Decca DFE 8590 | FIVE BY FIVE (with unboxed Decca logo) | 40 |
| 64 | Decca DFE 8590 | FIVE BY FIVE (later boxed Decca logo) | 12 |
| 65 | Decca DFE 8620 | GOT LIVE IF YOU WANT IT! (with unboxed Decca logo) | 40 |
| 65 | Decca DFE 8620 | GOT LIVE IF YOU WANT IT! (later boxed Decca logo) | 12 |
| 83 | Decca DFEX 8560 | THE ROLLING STONES (12", reissue) | 12 |
| 83 | Decca DFEX 8590 | FIVE BY FIVE (12", reissue) | 12 |
| 83 | Decca DFEX 8620 | GOT LIVE IF YOU WANT IT (12", reissue) | 12 |

## EPS : EXPORT EPS

| | | | |
|---|---|---|---|
| 64 | Decca SDE 7260 | ROLLING STONES | 125 |
| 64 | Decca SDE 7501 | THE ROLLING STONES VOLUME 2 | 125 |
| 65 | Decca SDE 8620 | GOT LIVE IF YOU WANT IT! (red label, some with yellow titles on p/s) | 125 |
| 65 | Decca SDE 7502 | GOT LIVE IF YOU WANT IT! | 125 |
| 65 | Decca SDE 7503 | ROLLING STONES (with "Out Of Our Heads [U.K. version]" sleeve) | 125 |

## ALBUMS : DECCA ALBUMS

| | | | |
|---|---|---|---|
| 64 | Decca LK 4605 | ROLLING STONES (1st pressing, plays 2.52 version of "Tell Me"; Side 2 matrix: XARL 6272-1A) | 1000 |
| 64 | Decca LK 4605 | ROLLING STONES (2nd pressing, plays 4.06 version of "Tell Me"; sleeves list "Mona") | 350 |
| 64 | Decca LK 4605 | ROLLING STONES (2nd pressing, plays 4.06 version of "Tell Me"; more common, with sleeves that list "I Need You, Baby") | 200 |
| 65 | Decca LK 4661 | ROLLING STONES NO. 2 | 200 |
| 65 | Decca LK 4661 | ROLLING STONES NO. 2 (with 'blind man' text pasted over on rear sleeve) | 250 |

| | | | |
|---|---|---|---|
| 65 | Decca LK 4733 | OUT OF OUR HEADS (mono) | 120 |
| 65 | Decca SKL 4733 | OUT OF OUR HEADS (stereo) | 150 |

*(The above LPs were simultaneously pressed with both flipback and non-flipback sleeves. Values are the same.)*

| | | | |
|---|---|---|---|
| 66 | Decca LK 4786 | AFTERMATH (mono) | 125 |
| 66 | Decca SKL 4786 | AFTERMATH (stereo) | 150 |
| 66 | Decca LK 4786 | AFTERMATH (mono, front cover title has purple shadow) | 250 |
| 66 | Decca SKL 4786 | AFTERMATH (stereo, front cover title is shadowed) | 200 |
| 66 | Decca TXL 101 | BIG HITS (HIGH TIDE AND GREEN GRASS) (1st pressing, gatefold sleeve, with stapled 12" x 12" picture booklet, mono) | 100 |
| 66 | Decca TXS 101 | BIG HITS (HIGH TIDE AND GREEN GRASS) (1st pressing, gatefold sleeve, with stapled 12" x 12" picture booklet, stereo) | 100 |
| 66 | Decca TXL/TXS 101 | COULD YOU WALK ON THE WATER (unreleased, proof sleeves exist) | 0 |
| 67 | Decca TXS 101 | BIG HITS (HIGH TIDE AND GREEN GRASS) (2nd pressing, gatefold sleeve, without booklet, stereo) | 50 |
| 67 | Decca TXL 101 | BIG HITS (HIGH TIDE AND GREEN GRASS) (2nd pressing, gatefold sleeve, without booklet, mono) | 30 |
| 70s | Decca TXS 101 | BIG HITS (HIGH TIDE AND GREEN GRASS) (2nd pressing, gatefold sleeve, later issue with foldout insert & later Decca logo, stereo only) | 15 |
| 67 | Decca LK 4852 | BETWEEN THE BUTTONS (mono) | 150 |
| 67 | Decca SKL 4852 | BETWEEN THE BUTTONS (stereo) | 125 |
| 67 | Decca TXL 103 | THEIR SATANIC MAJESTIES REQUEST (3-D gatefold sleeve with red inner, mono) | 200 |
| 67 | Decca TXS 103 | THEIR SATANIC MAJESTIES REQUEST (3-D gatefold sleeve with red inner, stereo) | 150 |
| 68 | Decca LK 4955 | BEGGARS BANQUET (gatefold sleeve, with Stones Decca label insert, mono) | 200 |
| 68 | Decca SKL 4955 | BEGGARS BANQUET (gatefold sleeve, with Stones Decca label insert, stereo) | 150 |
| 69 | Decca LK 5019 | THROUGH THE PAST, DARKLY (BIG HITS VOL. 2) (octagonal gatefold sleeve, mono) | 80 |
| 69 | Decca SKL 5019 | THROUGH THE PAST, DARKLY (BIG HITS VOL. 2) (octagonal gatefold sleeve, stereo) | 65 |
| 69 | Decca LK 5025 | LET IT BLEED (mono, red inner, with poster, with stickered sleeve) | 400 |
| 69 | Decca LK 5025 | LET IT BLEED (mono, red inner, with poster, without stickered sleeve) | 100 |
| 69 | Decca SKL 5025 | LET IT BLEED (stereo, blue inner, with poster, with stickered sleeve) | 200 |
| 69 | Decca SKL 5025 | LET IT BLEED (stereo, blue inner, with poster, without stickered sleeve) | 60 |
| 69 | Decca TXL/TXS 103 | THEIR SATANIC MAJESTIES REQUEST (2nd pressing, gatefold sleeve with red inner, stereo, stereo disc in stickered mono sleeve) | 60 |

*All of the above LPs were originally issued with Decca labels with a large-print logo without a box surrounding it; later pressings with smaller print & boxed logo are worth around two-thirds the value.*

| | | | |
|---|---|---|---|
| 69 | Decca TXL/TXS 103 | THEIR SATANIC MAJESTIES REQUEST (2nd pressing, gatefold sleeve with red inner, mono) | 50 |
| 70 | Decca SKL 5065 | GET YER YA-YA'S OUT! (1st pressing with fully laminated sleeve front and back, with "sleeve printed in England" XZAL 10076 1W/XZAL 10077 1W) | 80 |
| 70 | Decca SKL 5065 | GET YER YA-YA'S OUT! (2nd pressing with laminated front sleeve front and un-laminated rear sleeve with "sleeve printed in England by Clout & Baker Ltd." ) | 20 |
| 70s | Decca SKL 4733 | OUT OF OUR HEADS (2nd pressing, light green sleeve, box Decca logo) | 30 |
| 71 | Decca SKL 5025 | LET IT BLEED (LP, reissue, stereo only, no mono/stereo indicator hole on rear sleeve, poster and inner sleeve, boxed logo on label) | 50 |
| 71 | Decca SKL 5084 | STONE AGE | 20 |
| 71 | Decca NPS2 | THEIR SATANIC MAJESTIES REQUEST (LP, gatefold, stereo reissue, boxed Decca logo) | 25 |
| 73 | Decca SKL 5165 | GOLDEN B-SIDES (unreleased, test pressings only) | 1000 |
| 73 | Decca SKL 5173 | NO STONE UNTURNED | 20 |

*(Except where noted, the above Decca LPs were originally issued with dark blue labels & laminated sleeves; later copies are worth two-thirds the value.)*

| | | | |
|---|---|---|---|
| 75 | Decca (no cat. no.) | THE HISTORY OF THE ROLLING STONES (3-LP box set; 3x12" pink label test pressings exist, no sleeves, matrices read: ZAL 12996/7, ZAL 12998/9 & ZAL 13000/1; release cancelled in favour of "Rolled Gold" 2-LP set) | 1000 |
| 75 | Decca SKL 5212 | METAMORPHOSIS (dark blue label, matt sleeve) | 20 |
| 75 | Decca TXS 103 | THEIR SATANIC MAJESTIES REQUEST (3rd pressing, 3-D matt gatefold sleeve, stereo only) | 25 |
| 75 | Decca ROST 3/4 | LIVE STONES (2-LP compilation, pink label test pressings only, follow-up to "Rolled Gold", unreleased) | 500 |
| 80 | Decca TAB 1 | SOLID ROCK (LP) | 20 |
| 83 | Decca ROLL 1 | THE FIRST EIGHT STUDIO ALBUMS (8-LP set, with 192-page book; wraparound card box, each LP has star printed on rear sleeve) | 250 |

## ALBUMS : EXPORT LPS

| | | | |
|---|---|---|---|
| 64 | London LL 3402 | 12 X 5 (LP, for export with 'Congratulations' mis-print on rear of sleeve) | 300 |
| 65 | Decca SKL 4725 | OUT OF OUR HEADS (with U.S. track listing & cover design, unboxed Decca label logo, stereo, withdrawn) | 250 |
| 65 | Decca LK 4725 | OUT OF OUR HEADS (export, LP, with U.S. track listing & cover design, unboxed Decca label logo, mono, withdrawn) | 200 |
| 66 | Decca LK 4838 | HAVE YOU SEEN YOUR MOTHER, LIVE (export LP, laminated sleeve & unboxed Decca label logo, mono) | 200 |
| 66 | Decca SKL 4838 | HAVE YOU SEEN YOUR MOTHER, LIVE (export LP, laminated sleeve & unboxed Decca label logo, stereo) | 250 |
| 67 | Decca LK 4888 | FLOWERS (export LP, mono, laminated sleeve, unboxed Decca label logo) | 400 |
| 67 | Decca SKL 4888 | FLOWERS (export LP, stereo, laminated sleeve, unboxed Decca label logo) | 250 |
| 70 | Decca SKL 4786 | AFTERMATH (export LP, white label, black print, supposedly for export) | 20 |
| 70 | Decca SKL 5065 | GET YER YA-YA'S OUT! (export LP, white label, black print, supposedly for export) | 20 |
| 70 | Decca TXS 103 | THEIR SATANIC MAJESTIES REQUEST (export LP, gatefold sleeve, white label, black print, supposedly for export) | 25 |
| 72 | Decca LK/SKL 4838 | HAVE YOU SEEN YOUR MOTHER, LIVE (export LP, later pressing, boxed logo, laminated sleeve) | 80 |
| 72 | Decca LK/SKL 4888 | FLOWERS (export LP, later pressing, laminated sleeve, boxed Decca label logo) | 100 |

## ALBUMS : ROLLING STONES LABEL LPS

| | | | |
|---|---|---|---|
| 71 | Rolling Stones COC 59100 | STICKY FINGERS ('big' zip sleeve with insert) | 80 |
| 71 | Rolling Stones COC 59100 | STICKY FINGERS (zip sleeve with insert) | 40 |
| 72 | Rolling Stones COC 69100 | EXILE ON MAIN STREET (2-LP, gatefold, with inners, postcard inserts) | 150 |
| 72 | Rolling Stones COC 69100 | EXILE ON MAIN STREET (2-LP, with inners, without postcard inserts) | 40 |
| 73 | Rolling Stones COC 59101 | GOAT'S HEAD SOUP (gatefold sleeve, with 2 inserts) | 40 |

| | | | MINT VALUE £ |
|---|---|---|---|
| 74 | Rolling Stones COC 59103 | IT'S ONLY ROCK 'N' ROLL (LP) | 20 |
| 76 | Rolling Stones COC 59106 | BLACK AND BLUE (LP, gatefold) | 20 |
| 78 | Rolling Stones CUN 39108 | SOME GIRLS (LP, die cut sleeve with uncensored inner sleeve, featuring Farrah Fawcett, Raquel Welch, Judy Garland and Marilyn Monroe) | 35 |
| 78 | Rolling Stones CUN 39108 | SOME GIRLS (LP, die cut sleeve with censored inner cover, it is believed that those with the red 'Some Girls' title is the rarest with blue, green and yellow being more common) | 15 |
| 80 | Rolling Stones CUN 39111 | EMOTIONAL RESCUE (LP with poster) | 15 |
| 81 | Rolling Stones CUN 39114 | TATTOO YOU (LP) | 20 |
| 82 | Rolling Stones CUN 39115 | STILL LIFE (AMERICAN CONCERT 1981) (LP) | 20 |
| 82 | R. Stones CUNP 39115 | STILL LIFE (AMERICAN CONCERT 1981) (LP, picture disc, mispressed with wrong tracks) | 15 |
| 82 | R. Stones CUNP 39115 | STILL LIFE (AMERICAN CONCERT 1981) (LP, picture disc) | 140 |
| 83 | Rolling Stones 1A 0641654361 | UNDERCOVER (LP) | 25 |
| 84 | Rolling Stones 450196 | EXILE ON MAIN STREET (2-LP, reissue in single sleeve) | 18 |
| 91 | Rolling Stones 4681351 | FLASHPOINT (LP, stickered sleeve. 12 page booklet) | 20 |

## ALBUMS : OTHER ALBUMS

| | | | |
|---|---|---|---|
| 77 | CBS 450 208 | LOVE YOU LIVE (2-LP) | 20 |
| 83 | R. Digest GROLA 119 | THE GREAT YEARS (4-LP, box set) | 25 |
| 86 | CBS 86321 | DIRTY WORK (LP, with inner) | 25 |
| 89 | CBS 465752 | STEEL WHEELS (LP) | 25 |
| 89 | ABKCO 820900-1 | ROLLING STONES SINGLES COLLECTION/LONDON YEARS (4-LP set) | 15 |
| 89 | CBS 466 918 2 | COLLECTION 1971-1989 (15-CD box set, with bonus CD, 'Collector's Edition') | 45 |
| 91 | Sony 468 135-9/468 135-2 | FLASHPOINT/INTERVIEW 1990 (2-CD pack, shrinkwrapped with tongue logo sticker, numbered) | 130 |
| 94 | Virgin V2750 | VOODOO LOUNGE (2-LP) | 40 |
| 95 | Virgin V 2801 | STRIPPED (2-LP with inner sleeves) | 50 |
| 97 | Virgin V2840 | BRIDGES TO BABYLON (2-LP, with inner sleeves) | 50 |
| 02 | Virgin CDVDXX2964 | FORTY LICKS (Ltd edition CD box set) | 50 |
| 10 | Eagle Rock ERELP 815 | LADIES AND GENTLEMEN (2-LP) | 35 |
| 13 | Eagle Vision ERDVLP 079 | SWEET SUMMER SUN (3-LP, DVD foldout sleeve with inners) | 40 |

## PROMOS : PROMO SINGLES

| | | | |
|---|---|---|---|
| 76 | Rolling Stones RS 19121 DJ | Fool To Cry/Crazy Mama (7" promo, mono mix, edited down to 3.59, no 'phased' electric piano intro) | 100 |
| 83 | R. Stones RSR 112 (DJ) | Let's Spend The Night Together (live)/Start Me Up (live) | 20 |
| 91 | CBS A 026/B 027 | Highwire/Sympathy For The Devil (live) (12") | 15 |
| 93 | EMI ORDERLH 1 | Gimme Shelter (live) (1-sided jukebox issue) | 20 |
| 93 | Virgin STONES 1 | JUMP BACK (EP) | 25 |
| 98 | Virgin VSTDJ 1667 | Saint Of Me (Deep Dish Grunge Garage Remix) (Part 1)/(Part 2)/ (Grunge Garage Dub)/(Rolling Dub)/Anyone Seen My Baby? (Armand's Rolling Steelo Mix)/Anyone Seen My Baby? (Bonus Roll) (12" double pack, stickered sleeve) | 20 |
| 98 | Virgin VSTDJ 1700 | Out Of Control (In Hand With Fluke)/(In Hand Full Version)/ (Bi-Polar's Fat Controller Mix)/(Bi-Polar At The Controls) (12") | 10 |
| 98 | Virgin VSP 1700 | Out Of Control (Bi-Polar At The Controls)/(Bi-Polar Outer Version) (withdrawn brown label) | 30 |
| 98 | Virgin VSTDDJ 1700 | Out Of Control (In Hand With Fluke Instrumental)/(In Hand Full Version)/ Bi-Polar's Fat Controller Mix)/(Bi-Polar At The Controls) (12") | 10 |
| 98 | Virgin VSP 1700 | Out Of Control (Bi-Polar At The Controls)/(Bi-Polar Outer Version) (withdrawn silver label) | 15 |
| 00s | Virgin DEVIL 666 | Sympathy For The Devil (Fatboy Slim Remix)/(Neptunes Remix)//(Full Phat Remix)/ (Original Version) (2x12", with press sheet) | 20 |

## PROMOS : PROMO LPS

| | | | |
|---|---|---|---|
| 67 | Decca TXL/TXS 103 | THEIR SATANIC MAJESTIES REQUEST (LP, padded silk sleeve) | 2500 |
| 69 | Decca RSM. 1 | PROMOTIONAL ALBUM (LP, U.K. disc in U.S. sleeve [lists RSD-1], 200 copies pressed [100 each for U.K. & U.S.], U.K. issues include a letter from Decca) | 2000 |
| 86 | CBS SAMP 1103 | STONES ON CD - A RADIO SAMPLER (CD, poly sleeve) | 200 |
| 89 | CBS (no catalogue no.) | STEEL WHEELS - THE ALBUM OF THE TOUR (box set, with LP, CD, cassette and "Terrifying" 12", European tour dates & sticker) | 150 |
| 89 | CBS SAMPC 1347 | SAY AHHH! (LP, promo-only compilation) | 200 |
| 95 | Virgin IVDG 2801 | STRIPPED (2-CD, interview disc & album, fold-out digipak) | 40 |
| 97 | Virgin (no catalogue no.) | BRIDGES TO BABYLON (CD in promo press box, with "Anybody Seen My Baby?" promo CD, press release, bottle opener, notebook and sheet of stamps, 200 only) | 150 |
| 97 | Virgin IVDG 2840 | BRIDGES TO BABYLON INTERVIEW (2-CD, interview disc & album, fold-out digipak) | 30 |
| 97 | Virgin CDVDJ 2840 | BRIDGES TO BABYLON (CD, with spoken word intros, 200 only) | 70 |
| 99 | Virgin CDIDJ 2880 | NO SECURITY (3-CD [2 interview discs], foldout digipak) | 45 |
| 90s | Virgin CDVDY 2964 | FORTY LICKS (CD) | 45 |

*(see also Mick Jagger, Keith Richards, Pipes Of Pan, Bill Wyman, Charlie Watts, Andrew Oldham, Bobbie Miller)*

## AUDLEY ROLLINS

| | | | |
|---|---|---|---|
| 72 | Explosion EX 2062 | Repatriation/HUGH ROY JUNIOR: Repatriation - Version | 10 |
| 73 | Attack ATT 8060 | Without You In My World/It's Flowing (actually "It's Growing") | 10 |
| 73 | Harry J HJ 6654 | What's Your Name/NOW GENERATION: What's Your Name - Version | 6 |

*(see also A. Boyne)*

## (HENRY) ROLLINS BAND

| | | | |
|---|---|---|---|
| 91 | Vinyl Solution VS 30 | Let There Be Rock/Carry Me Down (12", p/s, as Henry Rollins & Hard-Ons) | 25 |
| 94 | Imago 7432323057 | LIAR (EP, poster p/s) | 12 |

## BIRD ROLLINS

| | | | |
|---|---|---|---|
| 72 | Mojo 2092 049 | Love Man From Carolina/She Needs Loving All The Time | 10 |

## SONNY ROLLINS

| | | | |
|---|---|---|---|
| 56 | Esquire 20-050 | SONNY ROLLINS QUARTET (10" LP) | 65 |
| 57 | Esquire 20-080 | SONNY ROLLINS QUINTET (10" LP) | 50 |
| 57 | Esquire 32-025 | SONNY ROLLINS PLUS FOUR (LP) | 50 |

| 57 | Esquire 32-035 | PERSPECTIVES (LP, with Modern Jazz Quartet) | 50 |
| 58 | Esquire 32-038 | WORKTIME (LP) | 70 |
| 58 | Esquire 32-045 | SAXOPHONE COLOSSUS (LP, as Sonny Rollins Four) | 150 |
| 58 | Contemporary LAC 12118 | WAY OUT WEST (LP) | 50 |
| 58 | Esquire 32-058 | TENOR MADNESS (LP) | 50 |
| 59 | Esquire 32-075 | ROLLINS PLAYS FOR BIRD (LP) | 50 |
| 59 | Esquire 32-085 | TOUR-DE-FORCE (LP) | 40 |
| 59 | MGM MGM-C 776 | SONNY ROLLINS AND THE BIG BRASS (LP) | 20 |
| 60 | Contemporary SCA 5013 | SONNY ROLLINS AND THE CONTEMPORARY LEADERS (LP, stereo only) | 20 |
| 61 | Riverside RLP 12-241 | THE SOUND OF SONNY (LP) | 25 |
| 62 | Riverside RLP 12-258 | FREEDOM SUITE (LP) | 25 |
| 62 | Esquire 32-155 | MOVIN' OUT (LP) | 50 |
| 62 | RCA RD/SF 7504 | THE BRIDGE (LP) | 15 |
| 63 | Esquire 32-175 | SONNY BOY (LP) | 30 |
| 63 | RCA RD/SF 7524 | WHAT'S NEW (LP) | 20 |
| 63 | RCA RD/SF 7546 | OUR MAN IN JAZZ (LP) | 20 |
| 64 | RCA RD/SF 7593 | SONNY MEETS HAWK (LP, with Coleman Hawkins) | 20 |
| 64 | RCA RD/SF 7626 | SONNY ROLLINS & CO. (LP) | 20 |
| 65 | RCA RD 7670 | NOW'S THE TIME (LP) | 20 |
| 65 | Fontana FJL 124 | BLOW! (LP) | 25 |
| 66 | HMV CLP 1915 | ROLLINS ON IMPULSE (LP) | 25 |
| 66 | Stateside SL 10164 | SAXOPHONE COLOSSUS (LP, reissue) | 15 |
| 67 | RCA RD/SF 7736 | STANDARD SONNY ROLLINS (LP) | 15 |
| 67 | HMV CLP/CSD 3529 | SONNY PLAYS ALFIE (LP) | 15 |
| 67 | HMV CLP/CSD 3610 | EAST BROADWAY RUNDOWN (LP) | 15 |

*(see also Modern Jazz Quartet, Thelonious Monk, Clifford Brown, Coleman Hawkins)*

## ROLL MOVEMENT
| 67 | Go AJ 11410 | I'm Out On My Own/Just One Thing | 35 |

## ROLL-UPS
| 80 | Bridgehouse BHS 6 | Blackmail/Hold On (p/s) | 15 |
| 79 | Bridgehouse BHLP 004 | LOW DIVES FOR HIGHBALLS (LP) | 25 |

## GLORIA ROMA
| 64 | Decca F 12001 | It Hurts Me So/I Didn't Know What Time It Was | 8 |

## DICK ROMAN
| 59 | MGM MGM 1004 | Party Girl/My Greatest Mistake | 5 |
| 65 | London HLU 10007 | The Truth Hurts/What Good Does It Do Me | 5 |

## ROMAN INDEX
| 81 | 123 Se 15V | Revolution/Burn Those Books (p/s) | 20 |

## MIMI ROMAN
| 61 | Warner Bros WB 55 | Johnny Will/Let It Be Me | 8 |

## MURRAY ROMAN
| 69 | Track 613 007 | YOU CAN'T BEAT PEOPLE UP AND HAVE THEM SAY I LOVE YOU (LP) | 20 |
| 69 | Track 613 015 | A BLIND MAN'S MOVIE (LP) | 20 |

## SANDY ROMAN
| 66 | Columbia DB 7931 | Dale Anne/Home Is Where The Heart Is | 5 |

## TONY ROMAN
| 67 | Stateside SS 2022 | Shadows On A Foggy Day/Maggie | 7 |

## LYN ROMAN
| 67 | Stateside SS2069 | The Penthouse/Born To Lose | 12 |

## MAX ROMEO
| 68 | Island WI 3104 | Put Me In The Mood/My One Girl | 50 |
| 68 | Island WI 3111 | Walk Into The Room/DAWN PENN: I'll Get You | 50 |
| 68 | Island WI 3124 | Twelfth Of Never (actually by Pat Kelly)/VAL BENNETT: Caledonia | 50 |
| 68 | Unity UN 503 | Wet Dream/She's But A Little Girl | 10 |
| 69 | Blue Cat BS 161 | We Want Man/AL REID: Vietcong | 40 |
| 69 | Blue Cat BS 163 | It's Not The Way/AL REID: Darling | 50 |
| 69 | Nu Beat NB 022 | Blowing In The Wind/LARRY MARSHALL: Money Girl | 25 |
| 69 | Trojan TR 656 | Sweet Chariot/Far Far Away (with Hippy Boys) | 20 |
| 69 | Unity UN 507 | Belly Woman (actually by Derrick Morgan)/PAULETT & LOVERS: Please Stay | 10 |
| 69 | Unity UN 511 | Twelfth Of Never (actually by Pat Kelly)/TARTONS: Solid As A Rock (actually by Tartans) | 15 |
| 69 | Unity UN 516 | Wine Her Goosie/KING CANNON: Fire Ball | 18 |
| 69 | Unity UN 532 | Mini-Skirt Vision/Far Far Away | 25 |
| 70 | Unity UN 544 | Melting Pot/HIPPY BOYS: Death Rides A Horse | 40 |
| 70 | Unity UN 545 | Clap Clap (with Hippy Boys)/Death Rides A Horse | 40 |
| 70 | Unity UN 547 | What A Cute Man/Buy You A Rainbow | 35 |
| 70 | Unity UN 560 | Fish In The Pot/Feel It | 20 |
| 71 | Bullet BU 478 | Mother Oh Mother/Dreams Of Passion (actually "Judgement Rock" by Charlie Ace) | 10 |
| 71 | Pama Supreme PS 328 | Ginal Ship/UPSETTERS: Version 2 | 15 |
| 71 | Pama Supreme PS 306 | Let The Power Fall On I/The Raid | 10 |
| 71 | Pama Supreme PS 318 | Don't You Weep/Weeping (Version) | 10 |
| 71 | Punch PH 73 | Chie Chie Bud/Version | 10 |
| 71 | Unity UN 571 | Macabee (Version)/SOUL SYNDICATE: Music Book | 10 |
| 71 | Camel CA 66 | Black Equality/Suffering | 20 |
| 71 | Camel CA 82 | The Coming Of Jah/Watch And Pray | 6 |
| 71 | Prince Buster PB 11 | Words Sounds And Power/Version | 12 |
| 72 | Camel CA 85 | Rasta Bandwagon/When Jah Speaks | 6 |
| 72 | Camel CA 86 | Public Enemy Number One/How Long Must We Wait | 35 |

MINT VALUE £

| | | | |
|---|---|---|---|
| 72 | Big BG 334 | Are You Sure/RUPIE EDWARDS ALL STARS: Are You Sure - Version | 6 |
| 72 | Dynamic DYN 444 | We Love America/SOUL RHYTHM: We Love Jamaica Version | 6 |
| 72 | G.G. GG 4535 | Is It Really Over?/MAYTONES: Born To Be Loved | 6 |
| 72 | High Note Hs 058 | Pray For Me (with Gaytones)/GAYTONES: Pray For Me - Version | 8 |
| 72 | Pama PM 836 | Wet Dream/("Bang Bang Lulu" by Lloyd Tyrell)/("Birth Control" by Lloyd Tyrell)/ Sex Education by Classics) (Maxi-Single) | 5 |
| 72 | Pama Supreme PS 345 | Pray For Me/Version | 5 |
| 72 | Pama Supreme PS 359 | Are You Sure/CARL MASTERS: Va-Va-Voom | 5 |
| 72 | Prince Buster PB 11 | River Jordan/Words Sound And Power | 8 |
| 73 | Dragon DRA 1028 | No Joshua No/JOSHUA'S ALL STARS: No Joshua No (Version) | 5 |
| 73 | Magnet MA 032 | Murder In The Place/Version | 7 |
| 73 | Magnet MA 032 | I Woke Up In Love/Version | 5 |
| 73 | Pama PM 875 | Pussy Watchman/You Are My Sunshine | 5 |
| 73 | Pama Supreme PS 383 | Hide Away/SOUL SYNDICATE: Sweet And Gentle | 5 |
| 73 | Pama Supreme PS 385 | Everyman Aught To Know/Version | 5 |
| 73 | Unity UN 572 | Rent Crisis/Version | 7 |
| 74 | Ackee ACK 529 | Sixpence/Eating Competition | 5 |
| 75 | Tropical Sound Tracs TST 107 | Big Jack/Cross Over The Bridge/Please Help Me, I'm Falling | 5 |
| 76 | Island WIP 6305 | One Step Forward/One Step Dub | 10 |
| 76 | Island WIP 6330 | Chase The Devil/UPSETTERS FEAT. PRINCE JAZZBO: Croaking Lizard | 40 |
| 76 | Mango MAN 1014 | Fire Fe The Vatican/JAH LLOYD: Leggo | 7 |
| 69 | Pama PMLP 11 | A DREAM (LP) | 60 |
| 71 | Pama PMP 2010 | LET THE POWER FALL (LP) | 50 |
| 75 | Count Shelly CSLP 06 | EVERY MAN OUGHT TO KNOW (LP) | 60 |
| 76 | Island ILPS 9392 | WAR INA BABYLON (LP) | 30 |
| 76 | Tropical TSL 1000 | REVELATION TIME (LP) | 60 |
| 78 | Mango MLPS 9503 | RECONSTRUCTION (LP, blue rim) | 30 |
| 95 | Jah Shaka SHAKA 951 | OUR RIGHTS (LP) | 15 |

*(see also Max & Elaine, Maxie & Glen, Henry & Lisa, Dennis Alcapone, George Meggie, David Isaacs)*

## VICTOR ROMEO
| | | | |
|---|---|---|---|
| 80 | Local LR 3 | Slacks And Sovereigns/DETONATORS: Working Dub (12") | 6 |

*(see also Detonators)*

## ROMEO Z
| | | | |
|---|---|---|---|
| 66 | CBS 202645 | Come Back Baby/Since My Baby Said Goodbye | 30 |

## ROMEO & EMOTIONS
| | | | |
|---|---|---|---|
| 67 | Caltone TONE 106 | Don't Want To Let You Go/I Can't Do No More | 80 |

## CHAN ROMERO
| | | | |
|---|---|---|---|
| 59 | Columbia DB 4341 | The Hippy Hippy Shake/If I Had A Way | 100 |
| 60 | Columbia DB 4405 | My Little Ruby/I Don't Care Now | 200 |

## ROMFORD STOMPERS
| | | | |
|---|---|---|---|
| 81 | Rott ROTT 1 | Dead Girls/MARY & KEN: Happy (stamped labels in stamped paper die-cut sleeve) | 20 |

## ROMI & JAZZ
| | | | |
|---|---|---|---|
| 90 | Chrysalis CHSR 123545 | One Love One World (Feel The Rhythm Mix)/One Love One World (Unity '90 Mix)/ Love Crime (Sunrise Mix) (12", p/s) | 12 |

## RON AND MEL
| | | | |
|---|---|---|---|
| 65 | Columbia DB 7469 | In A Shabby Little Hut/I See Your Face | 6 |

## RONALD & LLOYD
| | | | |
|---|---|---|---|
| 74 | Magnet MG 042 | Back In My Arms/HEPTONES: Drifting Away | 12 |

## RONALD & RUBY
| | | | |
|---|---|---|---|
| 58 | RCA RCA 1053 | Lollipop/Fickle Baby | 10 |

## TERRY RONALD
| | | | |
|---|---|---|---|
| 91 | MCA 1569 | What The Child Needs/Overnight Dub | 8 |

## RONDELLS
| | | | |
|---|---|---|---|
| 58 | London HLU 8716 | Good Good/Dreamy (with Ned Jr.) | 60 |
| 58 | London HLU 8716 | Good Good/Dreamy (with Ned Jr.) (78) | 40 |

## RONDELS
| | | | |
|---|---|---|---|
| 61 | London HLU 9404 | Back Beat No. 1/Shades Of Green | 20 |

## DON RONDO
| | | | |
|---|---|---|---|
| 57 | London HLJ 8466 | White Silver Sands/Stars Fell On Alabama | 8 |
| 58 | London HLJ 8567 | What A Shame/Made For Each Other | 10 |
| 58 | London HLJ 8610 | I've Got Bells On My Heart/School Dance | 8 |
| 58 | London HLJ 8641 | Blonde Bombshell/Her Hair Was Yellow | 6 |

## GENE RONDO
| | | | |
|---|---|---|---|
| 68 | Giant GN 39 | Ben Nevis/Grey Lies | 15 |
| 68 | Jolly JY 004 | Mary, Mary/Baby, Baby | 10 |
| 69 | Downtown DT 422 | A Lover's Question/HERBIE GRAY & RUDIES: Blue Moon | 20 |
| 69 | Downtown DT 431 | Sentimental Reasons/Then You Can Tell Me Goodbye | 20 |
| 70 | Downtown DT 459 | Spreading Peace/MUSIC DOCTORS: Guitar Riff | 7 |
| 72 | Downtown DT 490 | Wanna Be Like Daddy/STUDIO SOUND: A Little More | 10 |
| 72 | Count Shelly CS 005 | Happy Birthday Sweet Sixteen/Meditation | 5 |
| 73 | Magnet MA 001 | Prisoner Of Love/How Many Times Girl | 5 |
| 73 | Magnet MA 006 | Each Moments/If You Do Want Me | 5 |
| 73 | Magnet MA 028 | Oh Sweet Africa/This Is Love | 8 |
| 73 | Magnet MA 035 | Valley Of Tears/He'll Break Your Heart | 5 |
| 85 | Roots Pool RP002 | No One But You/SUGAR MINOTT: Children Of Africa | 15 |

*(see also Gene Pancho)*

## RONETTES
| | | | |
|---|---|---|---|
| 63 | London HLU 9793 | Be My Baby/Tedesco And Pitman | 10 |

| 64 | London HLU 9826 | Baby I Love You/Miss Joan And Mr Sam ........................................................ 10 |
|----|------------------|---|
| 64 | London HLU 9905 | (The Best Part Of) Breakin' Up/Big Red .......................................................... 20 |
| 64 | London HLU 9922 | Do I Love You?/When I Saw You .................................................................... 20 |
| 64 | London HLU 9931 | (Walking) In The Rain/How Does It Feel? ......................................................... 18 |
| 65 | London HLU 9952 | Born To Be Together/Blues For Baby ............................................................... 20 |
| 65 | London HLU 9976 | Is This What I Get For Loving You?/You Baby .................................................... 30 |
| 66 | London HLU 10087 | I Can Hear Music/When I Saw You (withdrawn) .............................................. 100 |
| 69 | London HLU 10240 | Be My Baby/Baby I Love You ........................................................................ 8 |
| 69 | A&M AMS 748 | You Came, You Saw, You Conquered/I Can Hear Music .................................... 8 |
| 75 | Phil Spector Intl. 2010 009 | I'm A Woman In Love/When I Saw You ............................................................ 10 |
| 77 | Phil Spector Intl. 2010 017 | I Wonder/Walking In The Rain ...................................................................... 10 |
| 64 | London HA-U 8212 | PRESENTING THE FABULOUS RONETTES FEATURING VERONICA (LP, original pressing on plum label) ........................................................................................ 100 |
| 64 | London HA-U 8212 | PRESENTING THE FABULOUS RONETTES FEATURING VERONICA (LP, later pressing on black label) ................................................................................................. 50 |
| 65 | Colpix PXL 486 | THE RONETTES (LP) ..................................................................................... 80 |

*(see also Ronnie Spector, Joey Dee & Starlighters)*

### RONNIE & DEL AIRES
| 64 | Coral Q 72473 | Drag/Wigglin' 'N' Wobblin' ........................................................................... 35 |
|----|---|---|

### RONNIE & HI-LITES
| 62 | Pye International 7N 25140 | I Wish That We Were Married/Twistin' And Kissin' ......................................... 30 |

### RONNIE & RAINBOWS
| 61 | London HL 9345 | Loose Ends/Sombrero .................................................................................. 25 |

### RONNIE & ROY
| 59 | Capitol CL 15028 | Big Fat Sally/Here I Am .............................................................................. 150 |

### RONNO
| 71 | Vertigo 6059 029 | Fourth Hour Of My Sleep/Powers Of Darkness .............................................. 65 |

*(see also Mick Ronson)*

### RONNY
| 64 | Decca F 21908 | Oh! My Darling Caroline/Lu La Lu ................................................................ 10 |

### RONNY & THE DAYTONAS
| 64 | Stateside SS 333 | G.T.O./Hot Rod Baby .................................................................................. 25 |
| 64 | Stateside SS 367 | California Bound/Hey Little Girl .................................................................... 25 |
| 65 | Stateside SS 391 | Bucket T/Little Rail Job ............................................................................... 30 |
| 65 | Stateside SS 432 | Beach Boy/No Wheels ................................................................................ 30 |
| 66 | Stateside SS 484 | Sandy/Sandy (Instrumental) ........................................................................ 20 |

*(see also Buzz & Bucky)*

### MICK RONSON
| 74 | RCA APBO 0212 | Love Me Tender/Only After Dark ................................................................... 6 |
| 74 | RCA 11474 XSP | Love Me Tender/Slaughter On 10th Avenue (1-sided red or black interview flexidisc, included in press kits) ................................................................................... 15 |
| 74 | RCA LPBO 5022 | Slaughter On 10th Avenue/Leave My Heart Alone ........................................... 6 |
| 75 | RCA RCA 2482 | Billy Porter/Seven Days ................................................................................ 6 |
| 74 | RCA Victor APL1-0353 | SLAUGHTER ON 10th AVENUE (LP) ............................................................. 15 |
| 74 | RCA APL1-0681 | PLAY DON'T WORRY (LP, laminated gatefold sleeve) ...................................... 15 |
| 94 | Epic EPC 474742 1 | HEAVEN AND HULL (LP, picture disc) ........................................................... 15 |

*(see also Ronno, David Bowie, Mott The Hoople, Slaughter & The Dogs, Ian Hunter)*

### RONYSAN
| 88 | 2 Man MAN 1 | I Take Pictures Of You/In The Valley Of The Larne .......................................... 5 |

### ROOGALATOR
| 76 | Stiff BUY 3 | WITH THE ROOGALATOR: All Aboard/Cincinnati Fatback (p/s, push-out centre) ........... 8 |
| 76 | Stiff BUY 3 | WITH THE ROOGALATOR: All Aboard/Cincinnati Fatback (p/s, 2nd pressing solid centre) ...................................................................................................... 6 |
| 78 | Do It DUN 2 | Zero Hero/Sweet Mama Kundalini (p/s) .......................................................... 5 |

### ROOM 10
| 65 | Decca F 12249 | I Love My Love/Going Back .......................................................................... 15 |

### ROOM 13
| 82 | Woronzow W 002 | Murder Mystery/Need Some Dub (12", p/s) .................................................... 25 |

*(see also Bevis Frond)*

### ROOM FOR HUMANS
| 81 | Bandit BR 001 | Telephone Telephone/Girl Friend ................................................................. 35 |

### ROOM (1)
| 70 | Deram SML 1073 | PRE-FLIGHT (LP, non-laminated sleeve, white/red label) ............................ 1200 |

### ROOM (2)
| 80 | Box BOX 001 | Motion/Waiting Room (p/s) ........................................................................... 6 |
| 81 | Box BOX 003 | In Sickness And Health/Bated Breath (p/s) ...................................................... 5 |

### MARY ROOS
| 72 | CBS 7959 | Wake Me Early In The Morning/When You're Singing (Don't Forget) ................... 6 |

### ROOSEVELT SINGERS
| 73 | Sioux SI 025 | Heavy Reggae/HONG GANG: Smoking Wild .................................................. 20 |

### ROOT BOYS
| 70 | Columbia Blue Beat DB 115 | Please Don't Stop The Wedding/Your Love, Your Love ................................... 10 |

### ROOTS & JENNY JACKSON
| 70 | Beacon BEA 164 | Save Me/If I Didn't Love You ........................................................................ 40 |

*(see also (Root and) Jenny Jackson)*

### ROOTS MANUVA
| 95 | Sound Of Money SNM006 | Next Typa Motion/Raw Uncut (12") ............................................................... 25 |
| 99 | Big Dada BD009 | Juggle Tings Proper/Strange Behaviour (12") ................................................. 12 |

## ROOTS MANUVA/MC SKEME

| | | | | |
|---|---|---|---|---|
| 01 | Big Dada BD022/7 | Witness (1 Hope)/(Walworth Rockers Dub) | | 20 |
| 05 | Big Dada BD073P | Colossal Insight (Royskopp remix) | | 6 |
| 99 | Big Dada BD010 | BRAND NEW SECOND HAND (LP) | | 25 |
| 01 | Big Dada BDLP032 | RUN COME SAVE ME (LP) | | 20 |
| 02 | Big Dada BDLP040 | DUB COME SAVE ME (LP) | | 20 |
| 05 | Big Dada BD 072 | AWFULLY DEEP (LP) | | 15 |

*(see also IQ Procedure)*

## ROOTS MANUVA/MC SKEME
| 96 | Wayward AHP01 | Fever/Herbman Hustling/Life's Funny (12") | 12 |
|---|---|---|---|

## ROOTS MANUVA/SKITZ
| 96 | Ronin RDP5 | Where My Mind Is At/Blessed Be The Manner/Fuck Being Polite (12") | 12 |
|---|---|---|---|

## ROOTS RADICS
| 84 | Kingdom KV 8032 | Earsay/I'm Not A King | 10 |
|---|---|---|---|
| 79 | Form BB1004 | OUTERNATIONAL RIDDIM (LP, with Revolutionaries) | 30 |
| 82 | Cha Cha CHALP 012 | RADICFATION (LP) | 25 |
| 82 | Solid Groove SGL 102 | RADICAL DUB SESSION (LP) | 30 |

## ROOTS (1)
| 78 | Greensleeves GRE 7 | Mash Down/Solja Man Skank | 20 |
|---|---|---|---|

## ROOTS (2)
| 94 | Geffen GEF 24708 | DO YOU WANT MORE?!!!??! (2-LP) | 20 |
|---|---|---|---|

## GEORGE ROPER & PIPEDREAM
| 70s | Goldspinners GOLD 1 | Manchester United/Tribute To The Fans | 5 |
|---|---|---|---|

## RO RO
| 70 | Parlophone R 5920 | Here I Go Again/What You Gonna Do | 20 |
|---|---|---|---|
| 72 | Regal Zonophone RZ 3056 | Goin' Round My Head/Down On The Road | 10 |
| 73 | Regal Zonophone RZ 3076 | Blackbird/Feel It Coming | 10 |
| 72 | Regal Zono. SRZA 8510 | MEET AT THE WATER (LP, textured gatefold sleeve, red/silver label) | 250 |

## ROSARIES
| 92 | Sarah SARAH 623 | FOREVER EP (p/s, insert) | 10 |
|---|---|---|---|

## ANDY ROSE
| 58 | London HLU 8761 | Lov-A Lov-A Love/Just Young | 25 |
|---|---|---|---|

## DAVID ROSE ORCHESTRA
| 53 | MGM SP 1009 | Harlem Nocturne (with Woody Herman)/Vanessa | 5 |
|---|---|---|---|
| 56 | MGM SP 1181 | Forbidden Planet/The Portuguese Washerwomen | 5 |
| 60 | MGM MGM 1110 | Bonanza/Gloria's Theme From Butterfield 8 | 5 |
| 62 | MGM MGM 1158 | The Stripper/Ebb Tide | 5 |

*(see also Woody Herman)*

## DUSTY ROSE
| 55 | London HLU 8162 | The Birds And The Bees/It Makes Me So Mad | 50 |
|---|---|---|---|
| 57 | London RE-U 1078 | COUNTRY SONGS (EP) | 40 |

## JOHNNY ROSE
| 60 | Capitol CL 15166 | Linda Lee/The Last One To Know | 18 |
|---|---|---|---|

## MICHAEL ROSE
| 79 | Attack TACK 7 | Born Free (with JAMMY)/DAD BROWN: Stand & Look (12") | 30 |
|---|---|---|---|

## TIM ROSE
| 67 | CBS 202631 | Morning Dew/You're Slipping Away From Me | 8 |
|---|---|---|---|
| 68 | CBS 3277 | I Got A Loneliness/Long Time Man | 30 |
| 68 | CBS 3478 | I Guess It's Over/Hello Sunshine | 6 |
| 68 | CBS 3598 | Long-Haired Boy/Looking At A Baby | 6 |
| 69 | CBS 4209 | Roanoke/Baby You Turn Me On | 6 |
| 70 | CBS 2631 | Morning Dew/You're Slipping Away From Me (reissue) | 6 |
| 70 | Capitol CL 15664 | I've Gotta Get A Message To You/Ode To An Old Ball | 5 |
| 74 | Dawn DN51085 | You've Got To Hide Your Love Away/If I Were A Carpenter | 8 |
| 67 | CBS (S)BPG 63168 | TIM ROSE (LP) | 30 |
| 69 | CBS 63636 | THROUGH ROSE COLOURED GLASSES (LP) | 30 |
| 71 | Capitol ST 22673 | LOVE - A KIND OF HATE STORY (LP) | 30 |
| 74 | Dawn DNLS 3062 | TIM ROSE (LP) | 18 |

## TONY ROSE
| 70 | Trailer LER 2013 | YOUNG HUNTING (LP) | 15 |
|---|---|---|---|
| 72 | Trailer LER 2024 | UNDER THE GREENWOOD TREE (LP) | 15 |

## ROSE GARDEN
| 68 | Atlantic 584 163 | Next Plane To London/Flower Town | 10 |
|---|---|---|---|

## ROSEHIPS
| 87 | Subway Organisation SUBWAY 10 | Room In Your Heart/Thrilled To Bits/Dead End (foldaround p/s with insert in poly bag) | 10 |
|---|---|---|---|
| 87 | Subway Organisation SUBWAY 10T | Room In Your Heart/Middle Of Next Week/Thrilled To Bits/So Naive/ Just Another Girl/Dead End (12", p/s) | 12 |
| 87 | Subway Organisation SUBWAY 16 | I Shouldn't Have To Say/Loophole/Wastin' My Time/All Mine/ Sad As Sunday (p/s, with insert) | 8 |
| 87 | Subway Organisation SUBWAY 16T | I Shouldn't Have To Say/Loophole/Wastin' My Time/All Mine/ Sad As Sunday (12", p/s with insert) | 12 |
| 88 | Sweet William BILLY 001 | Ask Johnny Dee/FAT TULIPS: You Opened My Eyes (33rpm flexi, p/s w/insert) | 12 |

## ROSEMARY'S CHILDREN
| 86 | él GPO 012 | Southern Fields/Whatever Happened To Alice | 12 |
|---|---|---|---|
| 87 | Cherry Red MRED 077 | KINGS AND PRINCES EP (12", p/s) | 12 |

## LEONARD ROSENMAN ORCHESTRA
| 57 | London HA-P 2040 | A TRIBUTE TO JAMES DEAN (LP) | 20 |
|---|---|---|---|

## ROSE OF AVALANCHE
| | | | |
|---|---|---|---|
| 86 | Fire BLAZE 14 | Velveteen/Who Cares (p/s) | 6 |
| 89 | Avalanche AVE4T | A PEACE INSIDE (LP) | 20 |

## ROSE OF VICTORY
| | | | |
|---|---|---|---|
| 83 | No Future OI 24 | Suffragette City/Overdrive (p/s) | 12 |

*(see also Blitz)*

## ROSES ARE RED
| | | | |
|---|---|---|---|
| 79 | Posthumous Petal PET 1 | Can't Understand/Your Love Is Like A Ballistic Missile (p/s) | 60 |

## ROSE TATTOO
| | | | |
|---|---|---|---|
| 78 | Carrere CAL 125 | Bad Boy For Love/Tramp (p/s) | 6 |
| 78 | Epic EPC 9411 | Rock 'N' Roll Outlaw/One Of The Boys (p/s) | 5 |
| 80 | Repeal PRS 2724 | Release Legalise/COL PATERSON: Bong On Aussie (500 only) | 40 |
| 81 | Mirage PR 405 | Rock 'N' Roll Is King/Sidewalk Sally (12", promo only) | 10 |
| 81 | Carrere CAR 220 | Assault And Battery/Astra Wally//One Of The Boys/Manzil Madness (double pack, gatefold p/s) | 5 |
| 82 | Albert Productions AP 854 | We Can't Be Beaten/Fightin' Sons | 5 |
| 82 | Albert Productions AP 898 | Branded/Dead Set | 5 |
| 82 | Albert Productions AP 1007 | It's Gonna Work Itself Out/Sydney Girls | 5 |

## ROSEWATER
| | | | |
|---|---|---|---|
| 71 | Lost Dog L 001 | Sally Anne/Mind Your Head | 15 |

## ROSIE (& ORIGINALS)
| | | | |
|---|---|---|---|
| 61 | London HLU 9266 | Angel Baby/Give Me Love (as Rosie & Originals) | 30 |
| 61 | Coral Q 72426 | Lonely Blue Nights/We'll Have A Chance | 40 |

## ROSKO
| | | | |
|---|---|---|---|
| 70 | Trojan TR 7758 | Al Capone/Kaiser Bill | 10 |
| 70 | Philips 6009 070 | Grab The Rabbit/Mohammed Ben Ali | 15 |

*(see also Emperor Rosko & Power Pack)*

## EMPEROR ROSKO & POWER PACK
| | | | |
|---|---|---|---|
| 69 | Polydor 56316 | Opposite Lock Parts 1 & 2 | 10 |
| 71 | B&C CB 148 | The Customs Man/Take It In Your Stride | 12 |

*(see also Rosko, Power Pack, Pleasure Garden)*

## FRANK ROSOLINO SEXTET
| | | | |
|---|---|---|---|
| 54 | Capitol KC 65001 | That Old Black Magic/Yo Yo | 5 |

## ANNIE ROSS
| | | | |
|---|---|---|---|
| 55 | Decca F 10514 | Mama (He Treats Your Daughter Mean)/The Fish | 12 |
| 55 | Decca F 10637 | I Want You To Be My Baby (with Tony Crombie)/TONY CROMBIE & HIS ORCHESTRA: Three Little Words | 6 |
| 56 | Decca F 10680 | Cry Me A River/Only You | 10 |
| 63 | Ember EMB S 182 | Bye Bye Blues/A Lot Of Livin' To Do | 10 |
| 72 | Columbia DB 8912 | Straight On Till Morning/God Bless The Child | 10 |
| 57 | Pye Jazz NJE 1035 | NOCTURNE FOR VOCALIST (EP) | 60 |
| 54 | Esquire EP 1 | WITH THE TEACHO WILTSHIRE GROUP (EP) | 40 |
| 58 | Pieces Of Eight PEP 604 | WITH THE TONY CROMBIE FOURTET (EP) | 12 |
| 64 | Transatlantic TRAEP 112 | GO TO THE WALL (EP) | 15 |
| 57 | Nixa Jazz NJT 504 | ANNIE BY CANDLELIGHT (10" LP) | 125 |
| 59 | Vogue LAE 12203 | ANNIE ROSS (LP, with Gerry Mulligan Quintet) | 60 |
| 60 | Vogue LAE 12233 | A GASSER (LP, with Zoot Sims) | 60 |
| 63 | Ember NR 5008 | A HANDFULL OF SONGS (LP) | 75 |
| 63 | Transatlantic TRA 107 | LOGUERRHYTHMS (LP) | 60 |
| 65 | Golden Guinea GGL 0316 | ANNIE BY CANDLELIGHT (LP, reissue) | 50 |
| 66 | Xtra XTRA 1049 | ANNIE ROSS WITH THE TONY KINSEY QUINTET (LP) | 60 |
| 71 | Decca SKL 5099 | YOU AND ME BABY (LP) | 20 |

*(see also Tony Crombie, Dave Lambert, Gerry Mulligan, Zoot Sims, Jack Parnell, Art Blakey, Quincy Jones)*

## DAVID ROSS
| | | | |
|---|---|---|---|
| 58 | Oriole CB 1416 | Pit-A-Patter Boom Boom/Everybody's Got A Girl But Tino (as Dave Ross) | 6 |

## DIANA ROSS
| | | | |
|---|---|---|---|
| 70 | Tamla Motown TMG 743 | Reach Out And Touch (Somebody's Hand)/Dark Side Of The World | 6 |
| 70 | Tamla Motown TMG 751 | Ain't No Mountain High Enough/Can't It Wait Until Tomorrow | 6 |
| 71 | Tamla Motown TMG 768 | Remember Me/How About You | 6 |
| 71 | Tamla Motown TMG 781 | I'm Still Waiting/Reach Out I'll Be There | 6 |
| 71 | Tamla Motown TMG 792 | Surrender/I'm A Winner (green/white demo, stereo, has YTMG on label and etched into dead wax)) | 15 |
| 71 | Tamla Motown TMG 792 | Surrender/I'm A Winner (mono) | 6 |
| 71 | Tamla Motown TMG 792 | Surrender/I'm A Winner (stereo) | 10 |

*(see also Supremes)*

## DOCTOR (ISAIAH) ROSS
| | | | |
|---|---|---|---|
| 66 | Blue Horizon LP 1 | THE FLYING EAGLE (LP, 99 copies only) | 1500 |
| 66 | Xtra XTRA 1038 | DOCTOR ROSS (LP, reissue of "The Flying Eagle") | 40 |
| 66 | Bounty BY 6020 | CALL THE DOCTOR (LP) | 60 |
| 72 | Polydor 2460 169 | LIVE AT MONTREUX (LP) | 30 |
| 75 | Big Bear BEAR 2 | THE HARMONICA BOSS (LP) | 25 |

## ERROL ROSS
| | | | |
|---|---|---|---|
| 80 | Carrere CAR 149 | Round And Round In Circles/Reggae Music Of Today (p/s) | 6 |

## GENE ROSS
| | | | |
|---|---|---|---|
| 58 | Parlophone R 4434 | Endless Sleep/The Only One | 25 |

## JACK ROSS
| | | | |
|---|---|---|---|
| 62 | London HLD 9534 | Cinderella/Margarita | 6 |

MINT VALUE £

## JACKIE ROSS
| 64 | Pye International 7N 25259 | Selfish One/Everything But Love ........................................................ | 60 |
| 64 | Pye International 7N 25259 | Selfish One/Everything But Love (DJ copy) .................................... | 100 |
| 64 | Chess CRS 8003 | Jerk And Twine/New Lover ................................................................ | 40 |
| 64 | Chess CRS 8003 | Jerk And Twine/New Lover (DJ copy) ............................................ | 70 |

## JOAN ROSS
| 70 | Crab CRAB 61 | Band Of Gold/HAMMERS: Midnight Sunshine ................................ | 20 |

*(see also T.T. Ross)*

## JOE E. ROSS
| 64 | Columbia 335X1710 | LOVE SONGS FROM A COP (LP) ........................................................ | 18 |

## RONNIE ROSS
| 58 | Parlophone PMC 1079 | DOUBLE EVENT (LP) ........................................................................ | 125 |
| 61 | Ember EMB 3323 | STOMPIN' WITH (LP) ...................................................................... | 100 |
| 65 | Ember FA 2023 | THE SWINGIN' SOUNDS OF THE JAZZ MAKERS (LP, with Allan Ganley) ... | 70 |
| 69 | Fontana SFJL 915 | CLEOPATRA'S NEEDLE (LP) .............................................................. | 250 |

*(see also Bill Le Sage)*

## SONNY ROSS
| 71 | Mojo 2093 001 | Alakazam/The Piper Must Be Paid ................................................ | 10 |

## SPENCER ROSS
| 60 | Philips PB 992 | Tracy's Theme/Thanksgiving Day Parade .................................... | 6 |
| 60 | London HLX 9141 | Theme Of A Lonely Evening/Bobby's Blues .................................. | 7 |

## T.T. ROSS (JOAN ROSS)
| 75 | Dip DL 5079 | Single Girl/Funny What Love Can Do ............................................ | 5 |
| 76 | Dip DL 5104 | Last Date/I Am Sorry .................................................................... | 5 |
| 76 | Lucky LY 6000 | No Charge/When I Was A Little Girl .............................................. | 5 |
| 76 | Lucky LY 6014 | Baby Why/TOUGH GANG: Part 2 .................................................. | 5 |
| 76 | Lucky LY 6017 | Misty Blue/Version ........................................................................ | 5 |
| 76 | House Of Eve 001 | Let The World Go Away/Part 2 .................................................... | 5 |
| 76 | House Of Eve 002 | Piece Of My Heart/Part 2 .............................................................. | 5 |
| 77 | Lovers Rock CJ 622 | I Will/I Will Dub .............................................................................. | 5 |

## JOHN ROSSALL
| 75 | Bell 1411 | I Was Only Dreaming/Every Night And Every Day ...................... | 6 |
| 75 | Bell 1428 | You'll Never know/Don't Beleive A Word .................................... | 6 |

## LEON ROSSELSON
| 62 | Topic TOP 77 | SONGS FOR CITY SQUARES (EP) .................................................... | 15 |
| 70 | Acorn CF 206 | SONGS FOR SCEPTICAL CIRCLES (EP) .......................................... | 20 |
| 66 | BOUNTY BY 6029 | SONGS FOR SCEPTICAL CIRCLES (LP) .......................................... | 100 |
| 71 | Trailer LER 3015 | THE WORD IS HUGGA MUGGA CHUGGA HUMBUGGA BOOM CHIT (LP, with Roy Bailey & Martin Carthy) .... | 20 |
| 75 | Acorn CF 249 | PALACES OF GOLD (LP) .................................................................. | 18 |
| 75 | Acorn CF 251 | THAT'S NOT THE WAY IT'S GOT TO BE (LP, with Roy Bailey) ........ | 18 |

*(see also Three City Four, Roy Bailey)*

## NITA ROSSI
| 65 | Piccadilly 7N 35258 | Every Little Day Now/Untrue Unfaithful ...................................... | 40 |
| 66 | Piccadilly 7N 35307 | Here I Go Again/Something To Give .............................................. | 40 |
| 66 | Piccadilly 7N 35307 | Here I Go Again/Something To Give (DJ copy) ............................ | 70 |
| 66 | Piccadilly 7N 35354 | The Daddy Christmas Song/Our Love Was Meant To Be .............. | 8 |
| 67 | Piccadilly 7N 35384 | Misty Blue/Come Around ................................................................ | 12 |

*(see also Status Quo, Bernie Frost, Boz Frost, Mickey Jupp, Mitchell/Coe Mysteries, Tokyo Olympics)*

## JOHN HENRY ROSTILL
| 71 | Columbia DB 8794 | Funny Old World/Green Apples ...................................................... | 30 |

*(see also Shadows)*

## STEVE ROSTRON
| 74 | Sweet Folk & Country SFA 009 | NO STRANGER'S FACE (LP) .............................................................. | 30 |

## VINCENT ROSWELL
| 82 | Water Mount MW 001 | Apple Of My Eye/Going To A Dance (12") .................................... | 100 |

## NINO ROTA
| 72 | Paramount PARA 3023 | Love Theme Form "The Godfather"/The Godfather Waltz .......... | 6 |

## ROTARY CONNECTION
| 68 | Chess CRS 8072 | Soul Man/Ruby Tuesday .................................................................. | 6 |
| 69 | Chess CRS 8103 | The Weight/Respect ...................................................................... | 6 |
| 70 | Chess CRS 8106 | Want You To Know/Memory Band ................................................ | 10 |
| 68 | Chess CRL 4538 | ROTARY CONNECTION (LP) ............................................................ | 15 |
| 69 | Chess CRL(S) 4547 | ALADDIN (LP) .................................................................................. | 15 |
| 69 | Chess CRLS 4551 | SONGS (LP) ...................................................................................... | 15 |

## ROTATION
| 70 | Polydor 2041-037 | Ra-Ta-Ta/Rotation .......................................................................... | 15 |

## ROTEN ROSEN
| 87 | Virgin VS 1031 | Itsy Bitsy Teenie Weenie Honolulu-Strand Bikini (German Version) Itsy Bitsy Teenie Weenie Honolulu-Strand Bikini (English Version) (p/s) .... | 100 |
| 87 | Virgin VST 1031 | Itsy Bitsy Teenie Weenie Honolulu-Strand Bikini (German Version) Itsy Bitsy Teenie Weenie Honolulu-Strand Bikini (English Version)/Agent X (12", p/s) .... | 150 |

## DAVID LEE ROTH
| 86 | Warner Bros W 8656P | Yankee Rose/Shy Boy (pin-up shaped picture disc) ...................... | 10 |

*(see also Van Halen)*

## ROTHCHILDS
| 66 | Decca F 12411 | You've Made Your Choice/It's Love .............................................. | 10 |

| 66 | Decca F 12488 | Artificial City/I Let Her Go | 15 |

**LINDA ROTHWELL**

| 73 | Chapter One SCH 180 | Write Me A Letter/Tell Me | 8 |

**ROTOVATORS**

| 78 | Rotovator SRTS/78/CUS 143 | Meat/East Coast Resort (hand folder and stapled p/s) | 8 |

**ROOTS TRUNKS AND BRANCHES**

| 79 | Splendor Heights WJWX 1945/2 | Just The Way You Are/Chicken Disco (12") | 20 |

**ROTTEN TO THE CORE**

| 73 | Pye 7N 45257 | Don't Let Me Wait Too Long/Let's Do It One More TIme | 10 |

**ROUGE**

| 78 | SRT SRTSCUS 78104 | Have You Seen Gene/Hard To Rock N Roll (no p/s) | 75 |

**ROUGH DIAMOND**

| 90 | Bedrock BR 1 | Woman's Touch (p/s) | 12 |

**ROUGH ELEMENT**

| 92 | UAR UAR120020 | The Elements/Breaking The Silence/Unbound Rage (remix) (EP) | 50 |
| 94 | UAR 003 | Reflex Reaction/Criminal Behaviour (12") | 15 |

**ROUGH JUSTICE (1)**

| 79 | Croft | Black Knight (A Gothic Legend)/White Dove (200 only no p/s but all come with insert) | 35 |

**ROUGH JUSTICE (2)**

| 80s | Rough Justice RJ 001 | MILLION TO ONE (EP, p/s) | 200 |

**ROUGH RIDERS**

| 69 | Jay Boy BOY 13 | Boss/President House | 30 |
| 74 | Rare Earth RES 118 | Hot California Beach/Do You See Me | 20 |

**ROULETTES**

| 62 | Pye 7N 15467 | Hully Gully Slip 'N' Slide/La Bamba | 15 |
| 63 | Parlophone R 5072 | Soon You'll Be Leaving Me/Tell Tale Tit | 15 |
| 64 | Parlophone R 5110 | Bad Time/Can You Go | 20 |
| 64 | Parlophone R 5148 | I'll Remember Tonight/You Don't Love Me | 15 |
| 64 | Parlophone R 5218 | Stubborn Kind Of Fellow/Somebody | 25 |
| 65 | Parlophone R 5278 | I Hope He Breaks Your Heart/Find Out The Truth | 15 |
| 65 | Parlophone R 5382 | The Long Cigarette/Junk | 25 |
| 66 | Parlophone R 5419 | The Tracks Of My Tears/Jackpot | 20 |
| 66 | Oak RGJ 205 | I Can't Stop (1-sided, with p/s) | 250 |
| 66 | Oak RGJ 206 | I Can't Stop (1-sided) | 150 |
| 66 | Parlophone R 5461 | I Can't Stop/Yesterday, Today And Tomorrow | 20 |
| 67 | Fontana TF 822 | Rhyme Boy, Rhyme/Airport People | 40 |
| 67 | Fontana TF 876 | Help Me To Help Myself/To A Taxi Driver | 20 |
| 65 | Parlophone PMC 1257 | STAKES AND CHIPS (LP, laminated front cover, flipbacks, black/yellow label with "Sold in the U.K..." text) | 500 |

*(see also Adam Faith, Unit 4 + 2, Argent)*

**ROUND ROBIN**

| 64 | London HLU 9908 | Kick That Little Foot Sally Ann/Slauson Party | 20 |
| 64 | London HLU 9908 | Kick That Little Foot Sally Ann/Slauson Party (DJ copy) | 50 |

**ROUNDTABLE**

| 69 | Jay Boy BOY 18 | Saturday Gigue/Scarborough Fair | 20 |
| 69 | Jay Boy JSL 2 | SPINNING WHEEL (LP) | 40 |

**CHARLIE ROUSE QUINTET**

| 60 | Riverside/Jazzland JLP19 | TAKIN' CARE OF BUSINESS (LP) | 15 |

**ROUTERS**

| 62 | Warner Bros WB 77 | Let's Go (Pony)/Mashy | 10 |
| 63 | Warner Bros WB 91 | Make It Snappy/Half Time | 10 |
| 63 | Warner Bros WB 97 | Stingray/Snap Happy | 10 |
| 63 | Warner Bros WB 108 | Big Band/A Ooga | 12 |
| 64 | Warner Bros WB 139 | Stamp And Shake/Ah Ya | 12 |
| 73 | Warner Bros K 16156 | Let's Go/Mashy (reissue) | 5 |
| 63 | Warner Bros WM/WS 8126 | LET'S GO! WITH THE ROUTERS (LP, features Scott Walker) | 40 |
| 64 | Warner Bros WM/WS 8144 | PLAY 1963'S GREAT INSTRUMENTALS (LP) | 25 |
| 65 | Warner Bros WM/WS 8162 | CHARGE! (LP) | 20 |

*(see also Scott Walker)*

**ROVERS**

| 55 | Capitol CL 14283 | Ichi-Bon Tami, Dachi/Why Oh-h (Why Do You Lie To Me?) | 500 |
| 55 | Capitol CL 14283 | Ichi-Bon Tami, Dachi/Why Oh-h (Why Do You Lie To Me?) (78) | 90 |

**ROVING KIND**

| 65 | Decca F 12264 | Ain't It True/Don't Tell Me The Time | 8 |
| 66 | Decca F 12381 | Lies A Million/How Many Times | 7 |

**ROWAN BROTHERS**

| 72 | CBS 1125 | All Together/Lady Of Laughter | 20 |

**ROWDIES**

| 78 | Birds Nest BN 109 | A.C.A.B. (All Coppers Are Bastards)/Negative Malfunction/Free Zone | 50 |
| 79 | Teenage Depression TD 1/2 | She's No Angel/Had Me A Real Good Time (p/s, different line-up) | 8 |

*(see also Boys, Lurkers, Steve Sharp & Cleancuts)*

**KEITH ROWE**

| 77 | Black Swan BS6 | Groovy Situation/Groovy Dub (12") | 12 |
| 77 | Black Swan BS 6 | Groovy Situation/Groovy Dub | 20 |
| 81 | Seven Leaves SLD 02 | Groovy Situation/Groovy Dub | 15 |

## NORMIE ROWE
| | | | |
|---|---|---|---|
| 66 | Polydor 56132 | It's Not Easy/Mary Mary | 15 |
| 66 | Polydor 56144 | Ain't Nobody Home/Ooh La La | 6 |
| 67 | Polydor 56159 | Going Home/I Don't Care (Just Take Me There) (in p/s) | 10 |
| 67 | Polydor 56159 | Going Home/I Don't Care (Just Take Me There) | 5 |
| 67 | Polydor 56169 | But I Know/Sunshine Secret | 10 |

## MAJOR ROWELY
| | | | |
|---|---|---|---|
| 65 | Stateside SS 438 | There's A Riot Going On/Do It The Right Way | 15 |

## JEFF ROWENA FIVE
| | | | |
|---|---|---|---|
| 63 | Oriole CB 1797 | Dance Baby Dance/Love Me once Again | 10 |

## CHERRY ROWLAND
| | | | |
|---|---|---|---|
| 63 | Fontana TF 420 | Nobody But Me/Boys | 12 |
| 74 | Decca F 13491 | Here Is Where The Love Is/I Can Give You Back Yourself | 6 |

*(see also Cherry Roland)*

## JACKIE ROWLAND
| | | | |
|---|---|---|---|
| 72 | Sioux SI 015 | Indian Reservation/JUNIOR SMITH: I'm In A Dancing Mood | 15 |
| 72 | Sioux SI 022 | Lonely Man/JOE MANSANO: The Trial Of Pama Dice | 20 |

*(see also Joe Higgs)*

## STEVE ROWLAND
| | | | |
|---|---|---|---|
| 67 | Fontana TF 844 | So Sad/I See Red | 40 |

*(see also Family Dogg)*

## JOHN ROWLES
| | | | |
|---|---|---|---|
| 68 | MCA MUP 335 | JOHN ROWLES (LP) | 15 |

## ROX
| | | | |
|---|---|---|---|
| 82 | Teenteeze ROX 100 | HOT LOVE IN THE CITY (Hot Love In The City/Do Ya Feel Like Lovin'/Love Ya Like A Diamond (EP) | 25 |
| 83 | Music For Nations MFN 11 | VIOLENT BREED (LP, with innersleeve) | 15 |

## ROXY MUSIC
| | | | |
|---|---|---|---|
| 86 | E.G. EGOX 26 | Love Is The Drug/Let's Stick Together (12", p/s, promo only) | 10 |
| 72 | Island ILPS 9200 | ROXY MUSIC (LP, 1st pressing, Matrixes ILPS 9200 A-1U GM 1/ILPS 9200 B-1U GR 1, matt gatefold sleeve with Basing Street London W11 address, pink rim palm tree label) | 35 |
| 72 | Island ILPS 9200 | ROXY MUSIC (LP, 2nd pressing, Matrixes ILPS 9200 A-2U MR 1/ILPS 9200 B-3U GM 1, laminated gatefold sleeve with Basing Street London W11 address, pink rim palm tree label) | 20 |
| 73 | Island ILPS 9232 | FOR YOUR PLEASURE (LP, 1st pressing, Matrixes ILPS 9232 A-1 LA 1/ILPS 9232 B-1 GDG 1, laminated gatefold sleeve with Basing Street London W11 address , pink rim/palm tree label) | 30 |
| 73 | Island ILPS 9252 | STRANDED (LP, gatefold, pink rim, palm tree label) | 20 |
| 74 | Island ILPS 9303 | COUNTRY LIFE (LP, inner, pink rim palm tree label) | 20 |
| 75 | Island ILPS 9344 | SIREN (LP) | 15 |
| 81 | Polydor/E.G. EGBS 001 | THE FIRST SEVEN ALBUMS (7-LP box set plus insert) | 80 |

*(see also Brian Eno, Bryan Ferry, Andy Mackay, Phil Manzanera, Dumbelles, Fripp & Eno)*

## ALVIN ROY & THE SARATOGA JAZZ BAND
| | | | |
|---|---|---|---|
| 61 | Interdisc INT 45001 | Yogi/Broken Promises | 5 |

## D ROY BAND
| | | | |
|---|---|---|---|
| 70s | D Roy MFLP 1001 | ORTHODOX DUB (white label LP in stamped, plain white sleeve) | 150 |

## DEREK ROY
| | | | |
|---|---|---|---|
| 57 | Oriole CB 1415 | Derek Roy's All-Star Party (with Bob Monkhouse, Richard Murdoch, Jon Pertwee, Ted Ray & others) | 8 |

*(see also Jon Pertwee)*

## HUGH ROY/U ROY
| | | | |
|---|---|---|---|
| 70 | Supreme SUP 211 | Double Attack/Puzzle | 20 |
| 70 | Explosion EX 2040 | Whisper A Little Prayer (actually by Audley Rollins)/ Rain A Fall (actually by Melanie) | 15 |
| 70 | Punch PH 34 | Scandal/Son Of The Wise | 15 |
| 70 | Duke Reid DR 2509 | Wake The Town/Big Boy And Teacher | 20 |
| 70 | Duke Reid DR 2510 | Rule The Nation/NORA DEAN: Ay Ay Ay Ay | 30 |
| 70 | Duke Reid DR 2513 | Wear You To The Ball (with John Holt)/EARL LINDO: The Ball | 25 |
| 70 | Duke Reid DR 2514 | You'll Never Get Away/TOMMY McCOOK QUINTET: Rock Away | 25 |
| 70 | Duke Reid DR 2515 | Version Galore/TOMMY McCOOK: Nehru | 30 |
| 71 | Duke Reid DR 2516 | Testify/TOMMY McCOOK: Super Soul | 25 |
| 71 | Duke Reid DR 2517 | Tom Drunk (with Hopeton Lewis)/TOMMY McCOOK: Wailing | 12 |
| 71 | Duke Reid DR 2518 | True True/On The Beach | 12 |
| 71 | Duke Reid DR 2519 | Flashing My Whip/Do It Right | 18 |
| 71 | Treasure Isle TI 7059 | Drive Her Home (Parts 1 & 2) (with Hopeton Lewis) | 15 |
| 71 | Treasure Isle TI 7062 | Behold/Way Back Home (with Tommy McCook) | 12 |
| 71 | Treasure Isle TI 7064 | Everybody Bawlin'/Ain't That Loving You | 15 |
| 71 | Upsetter US 375 | Earthquake/Suspicious Minds | 20 |
| 71 | Duke DU 105 | Love I Tender/JOYA LANDIS: When The Lights Are Low | 15 |
| 71 | Duke Reid DR 2517 | Tom Drunk/Wailing (as U Roy, B-side actually by Tommy McCook) | 15 |
| 72 | G.G. GG 4532 | Way Down South/BILLY DYCE: Be My Guest | 15 |
| 72 | Duke DU 137 | Live It Up/DENNIS BROWN: Baby Don't Do It | 15 |
| 72 | Jackpot JP 806 | Two Ton Gulleto/Version | 15 |
| 72 | Dynamic DYN 448 | Festival Wise/Festival Wise Part 2 | 15 |
| 72 | Banana BA 367 | Keep On Running/LARRY'S ALL STARS: Version | 15 |
| 72 | Grape GR 3026 | On Top The Peak/TYPHOON ALLSTARS: Race Attack | 15 |
| 72 | Pama PM 835 | Way Down South/BILLY DYCE: Be My Guest | 15 |
| 72 | Punch PH 104 | Nannyscrank (title actually "Nanny Skank")/PITTSBURG ALLSTARS: Scank Version | 15 |
| 72 | Green Door GD 4034 | Hudson Affair/KEITH HUDSON: Hot Stick - Version | 18 |
| 72 | Trojan TR 7884 | Hat Trick/Wet Vision | 10 |

| 73 | Green Door GD 4052 | King Tubby's Special/Here Come The Heartaches | 12 |
| 73 | Gayfeet GS 210 | Hard Feeling/Regular Style | 12 |
| 73 | Duke DU 157 | Higher The Mountain/OLD BOYS INC.: Version | 8 |
| 73 | Harry J. HJ 6651 | Treasure Isle Skank/Words Of Wisdom | 12 |
| 73 | Lord Koos KOO 25 | Call On I (with D. Wilson)/DJ Special | 8 |
| 75 | Virgin VS 138 | Runaway Girl/Chalice In The Palace | 6 |
| 76 | Soulfood SF 001 | High Priest/London City Rock | 15 |
| 71 | Trojan TBL 161 | VERSION GALORE (LP, as U Roy) | 30 |
| 74 | Attack ATLP 1006 | U ROY (LP, as U Roy) | 25 |
| 75 | Virgin V2048 | DREAD IN A BABYLON (LP) | 20 |
| 76 | Virgin V 2059 | NATTY REBEL (LP) | 20 |
| 77 | Virgin V2092 | RASTA AMBASSADOR (LP) | 20 |
| 78 | Virgin Frontline FL 1023 | JAH SON OF AFRICA (LP, red vinyl) | 20 |
| 79 | Virgin Frontline FLX 4004 | WITH WORDS OF WISDOM (LP) | 20 |

*(see also Jeff Barnes, Melodians, Delroy Wilson)*

## HUGH ROY JUNIOR

| 71 | Big BG 329 | Papacito/RUPIE EDWARDS: I'm Gonna Live Some Life | 12 |
| 71 | Supreme SUP 211 | Double Attack/MURPHY'S ALL STARS: Puzzle | 12 |
| 72 | Ashanti ASH 405 | King Of The Road/ROOSEVELT ALL STARS: Version | 8 |
| 72 | Jackpot JP 806 | Two Ton Guletto/Version | 8 |

## I ROY

| 71 | Moodisc MU 3509 | Musical Pleasure/JO JO BENNETT: Hot Pop | 15 |
| 71 | Moodisc MU 3510 | Heart Don't Leap (as I. Roy & Dennis Walks)/ DENNIS WALKS & MUDIE'S ALLSTARS: Snow Bird | 15 |
| 71 | Moodisc MU 3512 | Let Me Tell You Boy (with Ebony Sisters)/MUDIE'S ALLSTARS: Version | 15 |
| 71 | Moodisc HM 104 | The Drifter (with Dennis Walks)/JO JO BENNETT: Snowbird | 18 |
| 72 | Green Door GD 4030 | Hot Bomb (with Jumpers)/JUMPERS: The Bomb | 12 |
| 72 | Soferno B SOF 001 | No Money/Version | 10 |
| 72 | Green Door GD 4044 | Make Love/STAGE: Tic Toc Bill | 10 |
| 73 | Pyramid PYR 7001 | Tip From The Prince/Fat Beef Skank | 20 |
| 73 | Attack ATT 8050 | Space Flight/JERRY LEWIS: Burning Wire | 20 |
| 73 | Downtown DT 503 | Blackman's Time/High Jacking | 30 |
| 73 | Downtown DT 519 | Clapper's Tail/Live And Learn | 25 |
| 73 | Duke DU 156 | Buck And The Preacher/PETE WESTON ALLSTARS: Preacher - Version | 12 |
| 73 | Smash SMA 2337 | The Magnificent Seven/Leggo Beast | 12 |
| 73 | Smash SMA 2338 | Rose Of Sheron/Slip Out | 15 |
| 73 | Techniques TE 926 | Pauper And The King/GREGORY ISAACS: Loving Pauper | 15 |
| 73 | Techniques TE 930 | Monkey Fashion/Medley Mood | 10 |
| 73 | Ackee ACK 503 | Great Great Great (with Ken Parker)/RUPIE EDWARDS ALLSTARS: Version | 22 |
| 73 | Ackee ACK 510 | Sound Education/AUGUSTUS PABLO: Cinderella In Black | 25 |
| 73 | Harry J HJ-6655 | Musical Drum Sound/NOW GENERATION: Musical Drum - Version | 20 |
| 73 | Pama PM 854 | Cowtown Skank/AUGUSTUS PABLO: Cowtown Skank Version | 20 |
| 73 | Dip DL73 5006 | Don't Get Weary Joe Frazier/Don't Get Weary | 15 |
| 74 | Atra ATRA 017 | Yah Ma Ride/SWEET HARMONY: Mexican Rockin' | 12 |
| 74 | Ashanti ASH 412 | Mood For Love (Parts 1 & 2) | 12 |
| 75 | Bullet BU 551 | Step Right Up/ANDY'S ALLSTARS: Banjo Serenade | 8 |
| 75 | Lucky DL 5098 | I Man Time/Version | 12 |
| 75 | Third World TW 015 | Mr Benwood Dick/Mad Mad Hatter | 8 |
| 75 | Third World TW 85 | New York City/CORNELL CAMPBELL: Blessed Are They | 8 |
| 75 | Student STU 1001 | Jazz Bo Have Fe Run/Version | 12 |
| 76 | Dip DL 5107 | Padlock/Lock And Key (copies also exist with Lucky label) | 10 |
| 77 | ATA ATA 1005 | Roots Man/Observer Mix | 10 |
| 77 | Observer OB 002 | Jamaican Girl/River Jordan/ OBSERVER IN FINE STYLE: First Cut/Second Cut (12", p/s) | 25 |
| 78 | Jungle Beat JBDC 805 | Troubles/I Man (12" with FREDDY CLARKE) | 80 |
| 78 | GG's GG 011 | Natty Get Ready/Version | 6 |
| 79 | Virgin Front Line FLS 124 12 | Fire In A Wire/Hill And Gully (12") | 15 |
| 70s | Nationwide NW 005 | Tea Pot/Tea Cup | 12 |
| 73 | Trojan TRLS 63 | PRESENTING I ROY (LP, original issue with "12 Neasden Lane" address and rough orange/white paper labels) | 40 |
| 74 | Trojan TRLS 71 | HELL AND SORROW (LP, original issue with "12 Neasden Lane" address and rough orange/white paper labels) | 30 |
| 74 | Trojan TRLS 91 | THE MANY MOODS OF I ROY (LP, original issue with "12 Neasden Lane" address and rough orange/white paper labels) | 30 |
| 75 | Grounation GROL 504 | TRUTH & RIGHTS (LP) | 25 |
| 76 | Caroline CA 2011 | CRISIS TIME (LP) | 25 |
| 76 | Klik 9020 | DREAD BALDHEAD (LP) | 45 |
| 77 | Justice JUS LP 08 | CAN'T CONQUER RASTA (LP) | 30 |
| 77 | Virgin V 2075 | MUSICAL SHARK ATTACK (LP) | 20 |
| 77 | Virgin Frontline VF 1001 | HEART OF A LION (LP) | 20 |
| 78 | Virgin Frontline FL 1028 | TEN COMANDMENTS (LP) | 15 |
| 78 | Third World TWS 930 | THE GODFATHER (LP) | 20 |
| 79 | Virgin Frontline FLD 6002 | THE GENERAL (LP, with free dub LP SPIDER'S WEB) | 30 |
| 79 | Virgin Frontline FL 1033 | WORLD ON FIRE (LP) | 15 |
| 79 | Virgin Front Line FLX 4001 | CANCER DUB (LP) | 20 |
| 97 | Blood & Fire BAFLP 016 | DON'T CHECK WITH ME NO LIGHTWEIGHT STUFF (1972-75) (LP) | 20 |

*(see also Keith Hudson & I Roy)*

## LEE ROY
| 65 | Island WI 251 | Oh Ee Baby/My Loving Baby Come Back | 20 |

## MAD ROY
| 70 | Banana BA 324 | Nanny Version (actually by Dennis Alcapone)/BIGGER D: Freedom Version | 25 |

MINT VALUE £

| | | | |
|---|---|---|---|
| 71 | Banana BA 326 | Home Version (actually by Dennis Alcapone)/SOUND DIMENSION: One Time | 20 |
| 71 | Banana BA 327 | Universal Love/ROLAND ALPHONSO: Shelly Belly | 20 |
| 71 | Banana BA 328 | Duppy Serenade/Sunshine Version (both sides actually by Dennis Alcapone) | 20 |

**ROY REDMOND**

| | | | |
|---|---|---|---|
| 67 | Warner Bros WB 2075 | Good Day Sunshine/That Old Time Feeling | 20 |

**U ROY JUNIOR**

| | | | |
|---|---|---|---|
| 72 | Big BG 313 | Uncle Charlie/Socialise | 20 |
| 72 | Duke Reid DR 2520 | Rock To The Beat/Love Is Not A Gamble (both actually by Dennis Alcapone) | 12 |
| 72 | Attack ATT 8030 | This Is A Pepper (as U Roy Junior)/JOHN HOLT: Justice | 12 |
| 72 | Sioux SI 024 | The Wedding (as U Roy Junior)/LLOYD'S ALL STARS: Buttercup | 8 |
| 73 | Randy's RAN 532 | Froggie (as U Roy Junior)/RHYTHM RULERS: Version | 10 |
| 73 | Techniques TE 928 | Aunt Kereba (as U Roy Junior)/DON RECO: Waterloo Rock (B-side actually by Reco Rodriquez) | 12 |

*(see also Hugh Roy, Dennis Alcapone, Sir Harry, Shorty Perry, Heptones, Herman Chin-Loy)*

**BILLY JOE ROYAL**

| | | | |
|---|---|---|---|
| 62 | Oriole CB 1751 | Never In A Hundred Years/We Haven't A Moment To Lose | 20 |
| 65 | CBS 201802 | Down In The Boondocks/Oh! What A Night | 15 |
| 65 | CBS 201983 | You Make Me Feel Like A Man/I've Got To Be Somebody | 6 |
| 65 | CBS 202009 | I Knew You When/Steal Away | 6 |
| 66 | CBS 202052 | It's A Good Time/Don't Wait Up For Me Mama | 6 |
| 66 | CBS 202087 | Heart's Desire/Everybody's Gotta Cry | 40 |
| 66 | CBS 202087 | Heart's Desire/Everybody's Gotta Cry (DJ copy) | 75 |
| 66 | CBS 202400 | High On A Hilltop/I'm Gonna Get Right Tonight | 6 |
| 66 | Atlantic 584 002 | Never In A Hundred Years/We Haven't A Moment To Lose (reissue) | 7 |
| 67 | CBS 202548 | Yo Yo/We Tried | 10 |
| 67 | CBS 3044 | Hush/Watching From The Bandstand | 8 |
| 68 | CBS 3644 | Storybook Children/Just Between Me And You | 8 |
| 68 | CBS 3858 | Gabriel/Movies In My Mind | 7 |
| 69 | CBS 4470 | Cherry Hill Park/Helping Hand | 7 |
| 71 | CBS 7302 | Tulsa/Pick Up The Pieces | 7 |
| 72 | CBS 7727 | We Go Back/Colorado Rain | 7 |
| 66 | CBS BPG 62590 | INTRODUCING BILLY JOE ROYAL (LP) | 20 |

**BOBBY ROYAL**

| | | | |
|---|---|---|---|
| 63 | HMV POP 1253 | Big Big Star/Little Word Of Love | 12 |
| 65 | Decca F 12097 | Within My Lonely Heart/When I Found You | 10 |

**ROYAL HOLIDAYS**

| | | | |
|---|---|---|---|
| 58 | London HLU 8722 | Margaret/I'm Sorry (I Did You Wrong) | 70 |
| 58 | London HLU 8722 | Margaret/I'm Sorry (I Did You Wrong) (78) | 20 |

**ROBBIE ROYAL**

| | | | |
|---|---|---|---|
| 65 | Mercury MF 923 | Only Me/I Don't Need You | 8 |
| 65 | Decca F 12097 | Within My Lonely Heart/When I Found You | 6 |

**ROYAL BLOOD**

| | | | |
|---|---|---|---|
| 13 | Black Mammoth BMR 001 | Out Of The Black/Come One Over (p/s, 500 only) | 40 |
| 14 | Warners WEA 493 | Come On Over/You Want Me | 10 |
| 14 | Warner Brothers 825646278541 | ROYAL BLOOD (LP, white vinyl, 800 only sold via Rough Trade) | 50 |
| 14 | Black Mammoth 8256462785541 | ROYAL BLOOD (LP, signed, 500 copies) | 50 |
| 14 | Black Mammoth 8256462785541 | ROYAL BLOOD (LP, repressing, 100 only, numbered) | 20 |

**ROYAL BLUES**

| | | | |
|---|---|---|---|
| 69 | Pye 7N 17670 | Mountain Of Love/Wishful Thinking | 6 |
| 69 | Pye 7N 17732 | Mendocino/Hi-Lili Hi-Lo | 5 |
| 69 | Pye 7N 17769 | Proud Mary/Sunny Girl Friend | 6 |
| 69 | Pye 7N 17847 | High As A Mountain/Wildwood Flower | 5 |

**ROYALETTES**

| | | | |
|---|---|---|---|
| 65 | MGM MGM 1272 | Poor Boy/Watch What Happens | 15 |
| 65 | MGM MGM 1279 | It's Gonna Take A Miracle/Out Of Sight Out Of Mind | 25 |
| 65 | MGM MGM 1279 | It's Gonna Take A Miracle/Out Of Sight Out Of Mind (DJ copy) | 55 |
| 65 | MGM MGM 1292 | I Want To Meet Him/Never Again | 18 |
| 66 | MGM MGM 1302 | You Bring Me Down/Only When You're Lonely | 20 |
| 66 | MGM MGM 1324 | It's A Big Mistake/I Want To Meet Him | 15 |
| 68 | Big T BIG 106 | River Of Tears/Something Wonderful | 15 |
| 66 | MGM MGM-C 8028 | THE ELEGANT SOUND OF THE ROYALETTES (LP) | 100 |

**ROYAL FAMILY & THE POOR**

| | | | |
|---|---|---|---|
| 82 | Factory FAC 43 | ART-DREAM DOMINATION EP (12", p/s) | 15 |
| 84 | Factory FACT 95 | THE PROJECT - PHASE 1 OF THE TEMPLE OF THE 13TH TRIBE (LP, with booklet) | 20 |
| 87 | Gaia PHASE 3 | IN THE SEA OF E (LP) | 15 |

**JAMES ROYAL (& HAWKS)**

| | | | |
|---|---|---|---|
| 65 | Parlophone R 5290 | She's About A Mover/Black Cloud (as James Royal & Hawks) | 25 |
| 65 | Parlophone R 5383 | Work Song/I Can't Stand It | 35 |
| 67 | CBS 202525 | Call My Name/When It Comes To My Baby | 20 |
| 67 | CBS 2739 | It's All In The Game/Green Days | 7 |
| 68 | CBS 2959 | Take Me Like I Am/Sitting In The Station | 5 |
| 68 | CBS 3232 | I Can't Stand It/Little Bit Of Rain (DJ copy) | 125 |
| 68 | CBS 3232 | I Can't Stand It/Little Bit Of Rain | 60 |
| 68 | CBS 3450 | Hey Little Boy/Thru' The Love (DJ Copy) | 60 |
| 68 | CBS 3450 | Hey Little Boy/Thru' The Love | 30 |
| 68 | CBS 3624 | A Woman Called Sorrow/Fire | 20 |

| 69 | CBS 3797 | Time Hangs On My Mind/Anna-Lee | 6 |
| 69 | CBS 3915 | House Of Jack/Which Way To Nowhere | 30 |
| 69 | CBS 4139 | I've Something Bad On My Mind/She's Independent | 6 |
| 69 | CBS 4181 | That Kind Of Girl/Will You Be Staying After Sunday | 6 |
| 69 | CBS 4463 | Send Out Love/I've Lost You | 30 |
| 70 | CBS 5032 | And Soon The Darkness/I'm Going Home | 6 |
| 70 | Carnaby CNS 4021 | Carolina/Big Heat On The Loose | 6 |
| 71 | Carnaby 6151 002 | Carolina/A Woman Called Sorrow | 8 |
| 72 | Carnaby 6151 006 | Two Of Us/Who Are We (with Liz Christian) | 5 |
| 69 | CBS 63780 | CALL MY NAME (LP) | 30 |
| 70 | Carnaby CNLS 6008 | ONE WAY (LP) | 50 |
| 72 | Carnaby 6302 011 | THE LIGHT AND SHADE OF JAMES ROYAL (LP) | 40 |

## ROYAL RASSES
| 76 | Neville King NK 01 | Love The Way It Should Be/Bud The Way It Should Be | 10 |
| 77 | Neville King NK 4 | Kingston 11/Dub Up Kingston | 10 |
| 79 | Ballistic 12 315 | You Gotta Have Love (Jah Love)/Humanity (Love The Way It Should Be)/They Know Not Jah (12", clear vinyl) | 12 |
| 79 | Warrior BP 327 | Royal Rasses - Aint' Nobody Here But Me/Kingston 11 (Ghetto Rock) (12") | 15 |
| 79 | Ballistic PRE 1 | GOD SENT DUB (white label/plain sleeve) (LP) | 40 |
| 79 | Warrior WARLP 2002 | HARDER NA RASS! (LP) | 40 |
| 80 | Ballistic LBR 1031 | HARDER NA RASS! (LP) | 20 |

## ROYAL ROCKERS
| 60 | Top Rank JAR 326 | Jet II/Swinging Mambo | 20 |

## ROYALS
| 64 | Blue Beat BB 259 | Save Mama/Out De Fire | 30 |
| 68 | Amalgamated AMG 831 | Never See Come See/CANNONBALL BRYAN TRIO: Jumping Jack | 45 |
| 69 | Trojan TR 662 | Pick Out Me Eye/Think You Too Bad | 60 |
| 69 | Duke DU 29 | Never Gonna Give You Up/Don't Mix Me Up | 20 |
| 73 | Dip DL 5016 | Promised Land/Every Jamaican Is A Rebel | 6 |
| 79 | Warrior WAR 143 | Rising Sun/It's Real (Gone Sweet) | 15 |
| 77 | Magnum DEAD 1004 | PICK UP THE PIECES (LP) | 25 |
| 78 | Balistic UAS 30189 | TEN YEARS AFTER (LP) | 30 |
| 78 | Ballistic UAG 30206 | ISRAEL BE WISE (LP) | 20 |
| 81 | Kingdom KVLP 9006 | MOVING ON (LP) | 20 |

## ROYAL TEENS
| 58 | HMV POP 454 | Short Shorts/Planet Rock | 30 |
| 58 | HMV POP 454 | Short Shorts/Planet Rock (78) | 20 |
| 59 | Capitol CL 15068 | Little Cricket/Believe Me | 30 |

## ROYALTONES
| 58 | London HLJ 8744 | Poor Boy/Wail! | 15 |
| 58 | London HLJ 8744 | Poor Boy/Wail! (78) | 20 |
| 61 | London HLU 9296 | Flamingo Express/Tacos | 15 |
| 64 | Stateside SS 309 | Our Faded Love/Holy Smokes | 10 |

## ROYAL TRUX
| 95 | Hut 12790 | LIVE IN DENVER EP (10" promo) | 12 |
| 93 | Domino WIGLP 6 | CATS & DOGS (LP) | 15 |
| 95 | Hut HUTLP 23 | THANK YOU (LP, purple vinyl) | 15 |
| 97 | Domino WIGLP 40 | SINGLES, LIVES, UNRELEASED (3-LP box set) | 18 |
| 98 | Domino WIGLP 45 | ACCELERATOR (LP) | 18 |
| 99 | Domino WIGLP 68 | VETERANS OF DISORDER (LP) | 15 |

## ROYALTY
| 69 | CBS 4181 | That Kind Of Girl/Will You Be Staying After Sunday | 50 |
| 69 | CBS 4498 | Let's Ride/I Need Your Love | 60 |

## ROY & ANNETTE
| 63 | R&B JB 107 | My Baby/Go Your Ways | 20 |
*(see also Tommy McCook, Lester Sterling)*

## ROY & DUKE ALL STARS
| 68 | Blue Cat BS 113 | Pretty Blue Eyes Parts 1 & 2 | 40 |
| 68 | Blue Cat BS 117 | The Train Parts 1 & 2 | 40 |
*(see also Roy Panton)*

## ROY & ENID
| 68 | Coxsone CS 7063 | Rocking Time/RALPH BLAKE: High Blood Pressure | 100 |
| 68 | Coxsone CS 7069 | He'll Have To Go/CARLTON & SHOES: Love Is A Treasure | 120 |
| 69 | Coxsone CS 7088 | Reggae For Days/SOUND DIMENSION: Holy Moses | 50 |
*(see also Little Roys)*

## (LITTLE) ROY & JOY
| 73 | Camel CA 107 | Rainy Weather/THE DEN BROTHERS: Version | 8 |

## ROY (PANTON) & MILLIE
| 62 | Island WI 005 | We'll Meet/ROLAND ALPHONSO: Back Beat (B-side act. with City Slickers) | 25 |
| 63 | Island WI 050 | This World/Never Say Goodbye | 20 |
| 63 | Island WI 090 | There'll Come A Day/I Don't Want You | 20 |
| 63 | Blue Beat BB 154 | Over And Over/I'll Go (with Prince Buster All Stars) | 20 |
| 64 | Black Swan WI 409 | Cherry I Love You/You're The Only One | 30 |
| 64 | Black Swan WI 410 | Oh Merna/DON DRUMMOND: Dog War Bossa Nova | 30 |
| 64 | Black Swan WI 427 | Oh Shirley/Marie | 25 |
*(see also Roy Panton, Millie [Small])*

## ROY (RICHARDS) & PAULETTE
| 63 | Island WI 067 | Have You Seen My Baby/Since You're Gone | 25 |

MINT VALUE £

## ROY (PANTON) & YVONNE (HARRISON)
| | | | |
|---|---|---|---|
| 64 | Blue Beat BB 258 | Little Girl/No More | 20 |
| 64 | Black Swan WI 436 | Two Roads/Join Together | 20 |

*(see also Roy Panton)*

## ROY (PANTON) & PATSY
| | | | |
|---|---|---|---|
| 62 | Blue Beat BB 118 | My Happy Home/In Your Arms Dear (with Hersang & His Combo) | 25 |

*(see also Roy Panton)*

## EARL ROYCE & OLYMPICS
| | | | |
|---|---|---|---|
| 64 | Columbia DB 7433 | Que Sera Sera/I Really Do | 25 |
| 65 | Parlophone R 5261 | Guess Things Happen That Way/Sure To Fall (In Love With You) | 25 |

## ROY'S BOYS
| | | | |
|---|---|---|---|
| 64 | Columbia DB 7425 | Do Wah Diddy Diddy-I'm Into Something Good-I Want To Hold Your Hand/ Oh! Pretty Woman-Have I The Right?-It's All Over Now | 7 |

## ROYSTON
| | | | |
|---|---|---|---|
| 79 | Tuzmadoner TUZMADONER 001 | Snake's Song/Gerald's Eyes//DIFFERENT EYES: Uncomfortable/Snake's Song (stapled photocopied cover, rubber-stamped labels) | 100 |

## LITA ROZA
| | | | |
|---|---|---|---|
| 53 | Decca F 75082 | (How Much Is) That Doggie In The Window/Tell Me We'll Meet Again (export issue) | 20 |
| 54 | Decca F 10240 | Changing Partners/Just A Dream Or Two Ago (B-side with Stargazers) | 10 |
| 54 | Decca F 10269 | Bell Bottom Blues (with Johnston Brothers)/Make Love To Me (both with Ted Heath Orchestra) | 10 |
| 54 | Decca F 10277 | Young At Heart/Secret Love | 10 |
| 54 | Decca F 10393 | Call Off The Wedding/The "Mama-Doll" Song | 10 |
| 55 | Decca F 10427 | Heartbeat/Leave Me Alone | 10 |
| 55 | Decca F 10431 | Let Me Go, Lover!/Make Yourself Comfortable | 10 |
| 55 | Decca F 10479 | Tomorrow/Foolishly | 8 |
| 55 | Decca F 10536 | Two Hearts, Two Kisses (Make One Love)/Keep Me In Mind | 8 |
| 55 | Decca F 10541 | The Man In The Raincoat/Today And Ev'ry Day | 8 |
| 55 | Decca F 10611 | Hey There/Hernando's Hideaway | 8 |
| 56 | Decca F 10679 | Jimmy Unknown/The Rose Tattoo | 8 |
| 56 | Decca F 10728 | Too Young To Go Steady/You're Not Alone | 7 |
| 56 | Decca F 10761 | No Time For Tears/But Love Me (Love But Me) | 7 |
| 56 | Decca F 10792 | Innismore/The Last Waltz | 7 |
| 56 | Decca F 10830 | Hey! Jealous Lover/Julie | 7 |
| 57 | Decca F 10861 | Lucky Lips/Tears Don't Care Who Cries Them | 7 |
| 57 | Decca F 10884 | Tonight My Heart She Is Crying/Five Oranges, Four Apples | 7 |
| 58 | Pye Nixa 7N 15149 | Hillside In Scotland/Sorry, Sorry, Sorry | 5 |
| 58 | Pye Nixa 7N 15155 | Nel Blu Dipinto Di Blu (Volare)/It's A Boy | 5 |
| 59 | Pye Nixa 7N 15204 | Allentown Jail/Once In A While | 5 |
| 63 | Ember EMB S 168 | Mama (He Treats Your Daughter Mean)/(He's My) Dreamboat (as Lisa Rosa) | 30 |
| 65 | Columbia DB 7689 | Keep Watch Over Him/Stranger Things Have Happened | 8 |
| 57 | Decca DFE 6386 | LITA ROZA SELECTION (EP) | 30 |
| 57 | Decca DFE 6399 | LITA ROZA (EP) | 20 |
| 58 | Decca DFE 6443 | BETWEEN THE DEVIL AND THE DEEP BLUE SEA NO. 1 (EP) | 20 |
| 54 | Decca LF 1187 | PRESENTING LITA ROZA (10" LP) | 80 |
| 56 | Decca LF 1243 | LISTENING IN THE AFTER HOURS (10" LP) | 100 |
| 57 | Decca LK 4171 | LOVE IS THE ANSWER (LP) | 100 |
| 57 | Decca LK 4218 | BETWEEN THE DEVIL AND THE DEEP BLUE SEA (LP) | 90 |
| 58 | Pye Nixa NPL 18020 | ME ON A CAROUSEL (LP, mono) | 60 |
| 58 | Pye Nixa NSPL 83003 | ME ON A CAROUSEL (LP, stereo) | 80 |
| 60 | Pye NPL 18047 | DRINKA LITA ROZA DAY (LP) | 50 |
| 64 | Ember NR 5009 | LOVE SONGS FOR NIGHT PEOPLE (LP) | 25 |

*(see also Stargazers, Johnston Brothers)*

## ROZAA & WINE
| | | | |
|---|---|---|---|
| 76 | Right On! 104 | Disco Boogie Woman/Disco Boogie Woman Part 2 | 20 |

*(see also David & Rozaa)*

## RT & B
| | | | |
|---|---|---|---|
| 79 | Splendor Heights SH 1 | Forward/Join Them (12") | 20 |

## MISTER JACK RUANE ESQUIRE
| | | | |
|---|---|---|---|
| 68 | Pye 7N 17529 | Everybody Wants To Go To Heaven/Just For Fun | 7 |

## RUB-A-DUBS WITH DANDY
| | | | |
|---|---|---|---|
| 65 | Blue Beat BB 304 | Without Love/I Know | 25 |

*(see also Dandy)*

## RUBAIYATS
| | | | |
|---|---|---|---|
| 68 | Action ACT 4516 | Omar Khayam/Tomorrow | 40 |

## GIDEON JAH RUBBAAL
| | | | |
|---|---|---|---|
| 77 | Greensleeves GRE 003 | Love Rasta/GIDEON JAH RUBBAAL ALL STARS: Rasta Version | 8 |

## RUBBER BAND
| | | | |
|---|---|---|---|
| 73 | Youngblood YB 1052 | Moonwalker/Wichita | 6 |
| 69 | Major Minor SMCP 5045 | CREAM SONGBOOK (LP) | 20 |
| 69 | Major Minor SMCP 5048 | HENDRIX SONGBOOK (LP) | 20 |

## RUBBER BOOTZ
| | | | |
|---|---|---|---|
| 67 | Deram DM 134 | Joy Ride/Chicano | 30 |

## RUBBER BUCKET
| | | | |
|---|---|---|---|
| 69 | MCA MK 5006 | We're All Living In One Place/Take Me Away | 10 |

*(see also Paul Raven)*

## JOHNNY RUBBISH
| | | | |
|---|---|---|---|
| 78 | United Artists UP 36405 | Living In NW3 4JR/Other Side (p/s) | 10 |

## RUBIN
| 75 | MCA MU 196 | You've Been Away/Baby, You're My Everything .................................................. 10 |
|----|-----------|------|
| 75 | MCA MU 196 | You've Been Away/Baby, You're My Everything (DJ copy) ................................ 20 |

## RUBY
| 74 | Chrysalis CHR 1061 | RED CRYSTAL FANTASIES (LP, textured sleeve, green label) ........................... 20 |
|----|-----------|------|

*(see also Procol Harum)*

## RUBY & GLORIA
| 71 | Big Shot BI 583 | Worried Over You/Worried Over You - Version ................................................ 8 |
|----|-----------|------|
| 71 | Black Swan BW 1409 | Talk To Me Baby/LLOYD'S ALL STARS: Talk To Me Baby - Version ................ 8 |

## RUBY & ROMANTICS
| 63 | London HLR 9679 | Our Day Will Come/Moonlight And Music .......................................................... 10 |
|----|-----------|------|
| 63 | London HLR 9734 | My Summer Love/Sweet Love And Sweet Forgiveness ..................................... 10 |
| 63 | London HLR 9771 | Hey There Lonely Boy/Not A Moment Too Soon .............................................. 10 |
| 63 | London HLR 9801 | Young Wings Can Fly/Day Dreaming ................................................................. 10 |
| 64 | London HLR 9881 | Our Everlasting Love/Much Better Off Than I've Ever Been ............................ 15 |
| 64 | London HLR 9916 | Baby Come Home/Every Day's A Holiday .......................................................... 15 |
| 64 | London HLR 9935 | When You're Young And In Love/I Cry Alone .................................................... 15 |
| 65 | London HLR 9972 | Your Baby Doesn't Love You Anymore/We'll Meet Again ................................ 15 |
| 69 | A&M AMS 750 | Hurting Each Other/Baby I Could Be So Good At Loving You .......................... 15 |
| 63 | London RE-R 1389 | OUR DAY WILL COME (EP) .................................................................................. 35 |
| 64 | London RE-R 1427 | HEY THERE LONELY BOY (EP) ............................................................................. 40 |
| 63 | London HA-R 8078 | OUR DAY WILL COME (LP) ................................................................................. 40 |
| 66 | London HA-R 8282 | GREATEST HITS (LP) ........................................................................................... 30 |

*(see also Danny Davis Orchestra)*

## RUDDY & SKETTO
| 62 | Dice CC 2 | Please Enid/ABC Boogie .................................................................................... 12 |
|----|-----------|------|
| 62 | Dice CC 7 | Little Schoolgirl/Hush Baby ............................................................................... 10 |
| 63 | Dice CC16 | Hold The Fire/Good Morning Mr Jones ............................................................ 15 |
| 71 | Supreme SUP 218 | Every Night/Ethiopia .......................................................................................... 8 |

*(see also Sketto Rich)*

## RUD(D)Y (GRANT) & SKETTO (RICH)
| 62 | Dice CC 5 | Summer Is Just Around The Corner/Nothing Like Time (as Ruddy & Sketto & Reco's All Stars) ................................................................................................. 25 |
|----|-----------|------|
| 62 | Dice CC 7 | Little Schoolgirl/Hush Baby (as Ruddy & Sketto & Baron Twist & His Knights) .... 25 |
| 62 | Dice CC 10 | Mr Postman/Christmas Blues (as Rudy & Sketto with Laurel's Group) .......... 25 |
| 63 | Dice CC 16 | Hold The Fire/Good Morning Mr Jones ............................................................ 25 |
| 63 | Dice CC 19 | Never Set You Free/Brothers And Sisters ........................................................ 20 |
| 63 | Blue Beat BB 198 | Was It Me/Minna Don't Deceive Me .................................................................. 20 |
| 64 | Blue Beat BB 208 | Show Me The Way To Go Home/Let Me Dream ................................................ 20 |
| 64 | Blue Beat BB 230 | Ten Thousand Miles From Home/I Need Someone (as Ruddy & Sketto) ........ 25 |
| 64 | Blue Beat BB 252 | I Love You/If Only Tomorrow ............................................................................. 25 |
| 65 | Blue Beat BB 297 | See What You Done/Heart's Desire (as Ruddy & Sketto) ................................ 20 |
| 65 | Blue Beat BB 310 | Oh Dolly/You're Mine (as Ruddy & Sketto) ..................................................... 20 |

*(see also Ruddy & Sketto)*

## RUDE AND DEADLY
| 95 | Unity UNITY 002 | Lightnin' and Tundra/Mash Dem Down (12") ................................................... 40 |
|----|-----------|------|
| 95 | No Smoking SMOKE 7 | Give Me A Dub/Murder De boy (12", as Rude And Deadly Vs. The Dogz) ....... 15 |
| 97 | Smokers Inc SINC 1200 | Give Me A Dubplate (97 Remix) (12", 1-sided, stamped white labels) ........... 15 |
| 97 | Smokers Inc SINC 1200 | Give Me A Dubplate (97 Remix)/Give Me A Dubplate (Original Mix) (12") ..... 15 |

## RUDE ASS TINKER
| 90s | Deathchant DEATH 30 | Imperial Break/Silk Ties (12", limited issue) .................................................. 18 |
|-----|-----------|------|

*(see also Mu-Ziq, Tusken Raiders, U-Ziq)*

## RUDE BOYS (1)
| 67 | Island WI 3088 | Rock Steady Massachusetts/Going Home .......................................................... 30 |
|----|-----------|------|

## RUDE BOYS (2)
| 89 | Ska SKAT 002 | RUDE BOY SHUFFLE EP (12") ............................................................................. 15 |
|----|-----------|------|

*(see also Oppressed)*

## RUDI
| 78 | Good Vibrations GOT 1 | Big Time/Number 1 (folded p/s, 3,000 only, push-put centre) ...................... 30 |
|----|-----------|------|
| 79 | Good Vibrations GOT 1 | Big Time/No. 1 (reissue p/s) ............................................................................. 10 |
| 79 | Good Vibrations GOT 12 | I Spy/Genuine Reply/Sometimes/Ripped In Two (p/s) ................................... 30 |
| 81 | Jamming! CREATE 1 | When I Was Dead/The Pressure's On (p/s) ........................................................ 5 |
| 82 | Jamming! CREATE 3 | Crimson/14 Steps (p/s) ...................................................................................... 5 |

## RUDIES (FANATICS)
| 68 | Blue Cat BS 107 | The 7-11 Go To The Go Go Club (Parts 1 & 2) ................................................ 120 |
|----|-----------|------|
| 68 | Blue Cat BS 109 | Cupid/RECO'S ALLSTARS: Wise Message ......................................................... 40 |
| 68 | Nu Beat NB 001 | Train To Vietnam/Skaville To Rainbow City ..................................................... 35 |
| 68 | Nu Beat NB 005 | Engine 59/My Girl ............................................................................................... 35 |
| 68 | Fab FAB 46 | I Wanna Go Home/La Mer ................................................................................. 20 |
| 68 | Fab FAB 70 | Give Me The Rights/I Do Love You (as Rudies Fanatics) ................................. 25 |
| 68 | Fab FAB 71 | Mighty Meaty/Go (as Rudies Fanatics) ............................................................ 25 |
| 69 | Doctor Bird DB 1301 | Sin Thing/What's Your Name ............................................................................. 25 |
| 69 | Doctor Bird DB 1302 | Boss Sound/RECO & RUDIES: Peace ................................................................. 30 |
| 69 | Fab FAB 104 | Brixton Rocket/Rudie's Joy .............................................................................. 250 |
| 70 | Pama PM 789 | Give Peace A Chance/She ................................................................................... 15 |
| 70 | Trojan TR 7798 | Patches/Split ....................................................................................................... 10 |
| 70 | Grape GA 3016 | Henry The Great/Black Scorcher ....................................................................... 45 |
| 71 | Spinning Wheel SW 106 | My Sweet Lord/Devil's Lead Soup .................................................................... 45 |

# RUDIMENTAL

*(see also Freddie Notes, Sonny, Binns & Rudies, Rico, Dandy, Owen & Dandy, Downtown All Stars, Desmond Riley)*

## RUDIMENTAL
| | | | |
|---|---|---|---|
| 13 | The Vinyl Factory VF 084 | HOME (3-LP) | 60 |

## RUDIMENTARY PENI
| | | | |
|---|---|---|---|
| 81 | Outer Himalayan SRTS 81 CUS 1097 | RUDIMENTARY PENI (EP, A4 foldout p/s with booklet) | 30 |
| 81 | Outer Himalayan BOOBOO 1 | RUDIMENTARY PENI (EP, later 14" x 7" sleeve) | 20 |
| 82 | Crass 221984/2T | FARCE EP (Test pressing mispressed on 12" vinyl) | 200 |
| 82 | Crass 211984/2 | FARCE (EP, initial pressing in 21" x 14" foldout black & white p/s) | 20 |
| 97 | Outer Himalayan BOOB 006 | ECHOES OF ANGUISH (12", EP) | 12 |
| 83 | Corpus Christi CHRIST ITS 6 | DEATH CHURCH (LP, fold put poster sleeve) | 30 |
| 87 | Corpup Christi CHRIST IT'S 15 | THE EPS OF RP (LP) | 25 |
| 89 | Corpus Christi BOOBOO 2 | CACOPHONY (LP, with booklet) | 20 |

*(see also Magits)*

## RUEFREX
| | | | |
|---|---|---|---|
| 80 | Good Vibrations GOT 8 | One By One/Cross The Line/Don't Panic (foldover p/s, 2 different designs) | 15 |
| 83 | Kabuki KAR 7 | Capital Letters/April Fool (p/s) | 5 |

## RAY RUFF & CHECKMATES
| | | | |
|---|---|---|---|
| 64 | London HLU 9889 | I Took A Liking To You/A Fool Again | 15 |

## RUFF WITH THE SMOOTH
| | | | |
|---|---|---|---|
| 93 | Basement BRSS 023 | Art Of Intelligence/Sounds Superior (12") | 15 |
| 94 | Basement BRSS 037 | Twisted Girl/Who's Loving Me (12") | 10 |

*(see also Jack Smooth)*

## RUFFIANS
| | | | |
|---|---|---|---|
| 71 | Banana BA 359 | Room Full Of Tears (actually by Sensations)/Black Soul (actually "Black And White - Version" by Riley's Allstars) | 20 |

*(see also Al Brown, Sensations)*

## BRUCE RUFFIN
| | | | |
|---|---|---|---|
| 69 | Songbird SB 1002 | Long About Now/Come See About Me (as Bruce Ruffin & Temptations) | 30 |
| 69 | Trojan TR 7704 | Dry Up Your Tears/BEVERLEY'S ALLSTARS: One Way Street | 30 |
| 70 | Trojan TR 7737 | I'm The One/Who's Gonna Be Your Man? | 12 |
| 70 | Trojan TR 7776 | Cecelia/BEVERLEY ALL STARS: Stand Up | 10 |
| 70 | Summit SUM 8509 | O-o-h Child/Bitterness Of Life | 15 |
| 71 | Summit SUM 8516 | Candida/Are You Ready | 15 |
| 71 | Trojan TR 7814 | Rain/THE PYRAMIDS: Geronimo (B-side actually by Pyramids) | 8 |
| 71 | Trojan TR 7814 | Rain/THE PYRAMIDS: Off Limits (B-side actually by Aquarians) | 8 |
| 71 | Trojan TR 7832 | One Big Happy Family (Parts 1 & 2) | 5 |
| 72 | Trojan TRM 9000 | Songs Of Peace/You Are The Best/We Can Make It | 12 |
| 72 | Rhino RNO 101 | Mad About You/Save The People | 6 |
| 73 | Rhino RNO 114 | Tickle Me/I Like Everything About You | 6 |
| 71 | Trojan TRL 23 | RAIN (LP) | 35 |

*(see also Bruce Downer)*

## DAVID RUFFIN
| | | | |
|---|---|---|---|
| 69 | Tamla Motown TMG 689 | My Whole World Ended (The Moment You Left Me)/ I've Got To Find Myself A Brand New Baby | 20 |
| 69 | Tamla Motown TMG 711 | I've Lost Everything I've Ever Loved/We'll Have A Good Thing Going On | 15 |
| 76 | Tamla Motown TMG 1022 | Heavy Love/Me And Rock And Roll Are Here To Stay | 6 |
| 69 | T. Motown (S)TML 11118 | MY WHOLE WORLD ENDED (LP, mono/stereo) | 20 |
| 70 | T. Motown (S)TML 11139 | FEELIN' GOOD (LP) | 30 |
| 73 | Tamla Motown STML 11228 | DAVID RUFFIN (LP) | 20 |

*(see also Temptations)*

## JIMMY RUFFIN
| | | | |
|---|---|---|---|
| 66 | Tamla Motown TMG 577 | What Becomes Of The Broken-Hearted?/Baby I've Got It | 18 |
| 66 | Tamla Motown TMG 577 | What Becomes Of The Broken-Hearted?/Baby I've Got It (DJ copy) | 85 |
| 67 | Tamla Motown TMG 593 | I've Passed This Way Before/Tomorrow's Tears | 20 |
| 67 | Tamla Motown TMG 593 | I've Passed This Way Before/Tomorrow's Tears (DJ copy) | 20 |
| 67 | Tamla Motown TMG 603 | Gonna Give Her All The Love I Got/World So Wide, Nowhere To Hide (DJ copy) | 60 |
| 67 | Tamla Motown TMG 603 | Gonna Give Her All The Love I Got/World So Wide, Nowhere To Hide | 50 |
| 67 | Tamla Motown TMG 617 | Don't You Miss Me A Little Bit Baby/I Want Her Love | 15 |
| 67 | Tamla Motown TMG 617 | Don't You Miss Me A Little Bit Baby/I Want Her Love (DJ copy) | 40 |
| 68 | Tamla Motown TMG 649 | I'll Say Forever My Love/Everybody Needs Love | 15 |
| 68 | Tamla Motown TMG 649 | I'll Say Forever My Love/Everybody Needs Love (DJ copy) | 45 |
| 68 | Tamla Motown TMG 664 | Don't Let Him Take Your Love From Me/Lonely Lonely Man Am I | 18 |
| 68 | Tamla Motown TMG 664 | Don't Let Him Take Your Love From Me/Lonely Lonely Man Am I (DJ copy) | 30 |
| 69 | Tamla Motown TMG 703 | I've Passed This Way Before/Tomorrow's Tears | 7 |
| 70 | Tamla Motown TMG 726 | Farewell Is A Lonely Sound/If You Let Me, I Know I Can | 6 |
| 70 | Tamla Motown TMG 740 | I'll Say Forever My Love/Everybody Needs Love | 6 |
| 70 | Tamla Motown TMG 753 | It's Wonderful (To Be Loved By You)/Maria (You Were The Only One) | 6 |
| 71 | Tamla Motown TMG 767 | Let's Say Goodbye Tomorrow/Living In A world I Created For Myself | 7 |
| 71 | Tamla Motown TMG 784 | On The Way Out (On The Way In)/Honey Come Back | 12 |
| 67 | T. Motown TML 11048 | THE JIMMY RUFFIN WAY (LP, mono) | 40 |
| 67 | Tamla Motown STML 11048 | THE JIMMY RUFFIN WAY (LP, stereo) | 45 |
| 69 | Tamla Motown TML 11106 | RUFF 'N' READY (LP, mono) | 35 |
| 69 | T. Motown STML 11106 | RUFF 'N' READY (LP, stereo) | 30 |
| 70 | Tamla Motown STML 11161 | JIMMY RUFFIN ... FOREVER (LP) | 15 |
| 73 | Polydor 2383 240 | JIMMY RUFFIN (LP) | 15 |

## JIMMY & DAVID RUFFIN
| | | | |
|---|---|---|---|
| 71 | Tamla Motown STML 11176 | I AM NOT MY BROTHER'S KEEPER (LP) | 25 |

*(see also David Ruffin, Temptations)*

**RUFFNECK**
93   Represent REPREC 1      Radford(You Get Me)/You And Me (12") .................................................. 12

**RUFIGE CRU**
92   Reinforced RIVET 1220     Krisp Biscuit (Power)/Killa Muffin (The Band Dog Mix) (12", die-cut title sleeve with tracks and artist mispelt) ........................................................... 15
92   Reinforced RIVET 1224     Darkrider/Believe/Menace/Jim Skreech (12", p/s) ............................... 30
93   Reinforced RIVET 1244     Terminator II Remix/Fabio's Ghost (The Edit)/ Ghosts Of My Life/High Rollerz Ghostin' Out (12", promo only) ......................................................... 25

**RUFIGE KRU**
07   Exit EXIT 010        Is This Real/Is This Real (I'm Not Sure Remix) (12", p/s, yellow vinyl, poster) ............... 25

**RUGBYS**
69   Polydor 56781        You And I/Stay With Me ............................................................ 45
70   Polydor 56789        Wendegahl The Warlock/Light ..................................................... 20

**PETE RUGOLO (& DIAMONDS)**
60   Warner Bros WM 4001     BEHIND BRIGITTE BARDOT - COOL SOUNDS FROM HER HOT SCENES (LP, gatefold, also stereo WS 8001) ................................................................. 25

*(see also Diamonds)*

**RULERS**
66   Rio R 105         Don't Be A Rude Boy/Be Good ..................................................... 25
66   Rio R 107         Copasetic/Too Late .............................................................. 30
67   Rio R 132         Wrong 'em Boyo/Why Don't You Change ............................................. 40
67   Rio R 135         Well Covered/CARL DAWKINS: Help Time ............................................ 20
67   Rio R 138         Be Mine/CARL DAWKINS: Hot And Sticky ............................................ 20
69   Trojan TR 696        Got To Be Free/Situation ......................................................... 25

**RUMBLE**
70   Warner Bros WB 8011     Rich Man, Poor Man/Let Me Down ................................................... 30

**RUMBLERS**
63   London HLD 9684      Boss/I Don't Need You No More ..................................................... 20
65   King KG 1021        Soulful Jerk/Hey Did A Da Da ...................................................... 60
63   London RE-D 1396      BOSSOUNDS (EP) ................................................................. 100
63   London HA-D 8081      BOSSOUNDS (LP, mono) ............................................................ 90
63   London SH-D 8081      BOSSOUNDS (LP, stereo) .......................................................... 100

**RUMOUR**
79   Stiff RUM 1         Frozen Years/All Fall Down (promo in promo p/s) ..................................... 6
79   Stiff BUY 43         Frozen Years/All Fall Down (p/s) .................................................... 5
79   Stiff BUY 45 DJ       Emotional Traffic/Hard Enough To Show (1-sided promo, black vinyl) .................. 10
79   Stiff BUY 45 DJ       Emotional Traffic/Hard Enough To Show (1-sided promo, blue vinyl) ................... 7

*(see also Graham Parker)*

**RUMPLESTILTSKIN**
70   Bell BLL 1101        Squadron Leader Johnson/Rumplestiltskin .......................................... 20
71   Bell BLL 1157        Wimoweh/Through My Looking Glass ................................................. 6
70   Bell SBLL 130        RUMPLESTILTSKIN (LP, gatefold sleeve) ............................................. 60

*(see also Clem Cattini)*

**RUN DMC**
86   Profile LOXPD 104      Walk This Way/Walk This Way (instrumental)/My Adidas (12" picture disc) ............. 10
84   4th & Broadway BRLP 506   RUN DMC (LP) .................................................................... 15

**RUN 229**
80   MM JR 7040S        Soho/Dance/In This Day And Age .................................................... 40

**RUNAWAYS**
76   Mercury 6167 392      Cherry Bomb/Blackmail ............................................................ 15
77   Mercury 6167 493      Queens Of Noise/Born To Be Bad ................................................... 10
77   Mercury 6167 587      School Days/Wasted (p/s) .......................................................... 12
79   Cherry Red CHERRY 8    Right Now/Black Leather (p/s) ...................................................... 12
76   Mercury 9100 029      THE RUNAWAYS (LP, with gatefold sleeve & lyric sheet; U.S. pressing, with cat. no. SRM 1 1090, in U.K. sleeve) .......................................................... 20
77   Mercury 9100 032      QUEENS OF NOISE (LP, with lyric sheet) ............................................ 18
77   Mercury 9100 046      LIVE IN JAPAN (LP) ............................................................... 15
77   Mercury 9100 047      WAITIN' FOR THE NIGHT (LP) ....................................................... 15
79   Cherry Red ARED 38     AND NOW ... THE RUNAWAYS (LP, 1,000 copies each in yellow, red, blue & orange vinyl, numbered) ................................................................ 25

*(see also Joan Jett, Lita Ford & Ozzy Osbourne)o*

**TODD RUNDGREN**
72   Bearsville K 15502      I Saw The Light/Marlene ............................................................ 6

*(see also Utopia)*

**RUNESTAFF**
85   FM VHF 5          Road To Ruin/Last Chances (p/s) ................................................... 10
85   FM VHF 17         Do It!/Runestaff (no p/s) ........................................................... 6
85   Heavy Metal HMRLP 26    RUNESTAFF (LP) ................................................................. 15

**RUNNER**
79   Acrobat BAT 2        Run For Your Life/Gone Too Long ..................................................... 8
79   Acrobat ACRO1       RUNNER (LP, with inner) ........................................................... 15

**RUNNERS**
74   Ariel AR 11         Choose Me/Come Out Fighting ..................................................... 15

**RUNNING DOGS (1)**
80   Shooting Star SSR 1     Present Tense/Click Click Propaganda (no p/s) ....................................... 7

**RUNNING DOGS (2)**
80   Shattered 1.5        EP (p/s) ......................................................................... 10

MINT VALUE £

## RUNNING MAN

| | | | |
|---|---|---|---|
| 72 | RCA Neon NE 11 | THE RUNNING MAN (LP) | 750 |

*(see also Ray Russell Quartet, Rock Workshop)*

## RUNRIG

| | | | |
|---|---|---|---|
| 83 | Ridge RRS 003 | Loch Lomond/Tuireadh Iain Ruaida (p/s) | 15 |
| 84 | Simple SIM 4 | Dance Called America/Na H Uain A's T-Earrach (p/s) | 30 |
| 84 | Simple 12 SIM 4 | Dance Called America/Na H Uain A's T-Earrach/Ribhinn (12", p/s) | 20 |
| 84 | Simple SIM 8 | Skye/Hey Mandu (p/s) | 15 |
| 86 | Ridge RRS 006 | The Work Song/This Time Of Year (p/s) | 10 |
| 86 | Ridge RRS 007 | Alba/Worker For The Wind (p/s) | 12 |
| 88 | Chrysalis CHS 3284 | Protect And Survive/Hearts Of Olden Glory (live) (p/s) | 6 |
| 88 | Chrysalis CHS 12 3284 | Protect And Survive/Hearts Of Olden Glory (live)/Protect And Survive (live) (12", p/s) | 10 |
| 89 | Chrysalis CHS 3404 | News From Heaven/Chi Mi'n Tir (p/s) | 5 |
| 89 | Chrysalis CHS 12T 3404 | News From Heaven/Chi Mi'n Tir/The Times They Are A'Changing (12", picture disc) | 20 |
| 89 | Chrysalis CHS 3451 | Every River/This Time Of Year (p/s) | 6 |
| 90 | Chrysalis CHSCD 1235941 | CAPTURE THE HEART EP: Stepping Down The Glory Road/Satellite Flood/Harvest Moon/The Apple Came Down (12", p/s) | 15 |
| 90 | Chrysalis CHS 38051 | Flower Of The West/Ravenscraig/Ch Mi'n Greamhradh (p/s) | 5 |
| 91 | Chrysalis CHS 123805 | FLOWER OF THE WEST EP (12", numbered box set, with poster, discography & sticker) | 10 |
| 93 | Chrysalis CHSS 3952 | Wonderful/April Come She Will (limited edition blue vinyl) | 5 |
| 78 | Neptune NA 105 | RUNRIG PLAY GAELIC (LP) | 20 |
| 79 | Ridge RR 001 | THE HIGHLAND CONNECTION (LP) | 15 |
| 81 | Ridge RR 002 | RECOVERY (LP, with inner) | 20 |

## RUNS

| | | | |
|---|---|---|---|
| 80 | Carrere CAR 139 | Bun In The Oven/(Censored)(no p/s) | 20 |

## RUNT

| | | | |
|---|---|---|---|
| 71 | Bearsville K 44505 | RUNT (LP) | 15 |
| 71 | Bearsville K 44506 | RUNT - THE BALLAD OF TODD RUNDGREN (LP) | 15 |

*(see also Todd Rundgren, Utopia, Nazz)*

## R.U.1.2.

| | | | |
|---|---|---|---|
| 78 | SRTS/78/CUS 131 | She's Gone/Purely Physical/Teenage Girl (p/s) | 20 |

## RUPERT'S PEOPLE

| | | | |
|---|---|---|---|
| 67 | Columbia DB 8226 | Reflections Of Charles Brown/Hold On | 75 |

*(this is the Fleur-De-Lys, they do not appear on the other 2 singles)*

| | | | |
|---|---|---|---|
| 67 | Columbia DB 8278 | A Prologue To A Magic World/Dream In My Mind | 100 |
| 68 | Columbia DB 8362 | I Can Show You/I've Got The Love | 120 |

*(see also Renaissance, Fleur-De-Lys, Gun, Sweet Feeling)*

## RUPIE AND SIDY

| | | | |
|---|---|---|---|
| 70 | Success RE 910 | Return Of Herbert Spliffington/RUPIE EDWARDS ALL STARS: Young, Gifted And Black | 25 |

## RUSH (AUSTRALIA)

| | | | |
|---|---|---|---|
| 67 | Decca F 12614 | Happy/Once Again | 20 |
| 67 | Decca F 12635 | Make Mine Music/Enjoy It | 20 |

## RUSH (CANADA)

| | | | |
|---|---|---|---|
| 77 | Mercury RUSH 7 | Closer To The Heart/Bastille Day/Temples Of Syrinx (metallic blue label) | 18 |
| 77 | Mercury RUSH 7 | Closer To The Heart/Bastille Day/Temples Of Syrinx (beige label) | 8 |
| 78 | Mercury RUSH 12 | Closer To The Heart/Anthem/Bastille Day/Temples Of Syrinx (12", p/s) | 10 |
| 80 | Mercury RADIO 7 | Spirit Of Radio/The Trees (p/s) | 10 |
| 80 | Mercury RADIO 12 | Spirit Of Radio/The Trees/Working Man (12", p/s) | 10 |
| 81 | Mercury VITAL 7 | Vital Signs/In The Mood (p/s) | 8 |
| 81 | Mercury EXIT 7 | Tom Sawyer (live)/A Passage To Bangkok (live) (p/s) | 6 |
| 81 | Mercury RUSH 1 | Closer To The Heart (live)/The Trees (live) (p/s) | 5 |
| 82 | Mercury RUSH 8 | New World Man/Vital Signs (live) (p/s) | 5 |
| 82 | Mercury RUSH 812 | New World Man/Vital Signs (live)/Freewill (live) (12", p/s) | 15 |
| 82 | Mercury RUSH P9 | Subdivisions/Red Barchetta (live) (picture disc) | 10 |
| 82 | Mercury RUSH 10 PD | Countdown/New World Man (shaped picture disc) | 15 |
| 82 | Mercury RUSH 1012 | Countdown/New World Man/Spirit Of Radio (live)/Interview Excerpts (12", p/s) | 10 |
| 84 | Vertigo RUSH 11 | The Body Electric/The Analog Kid (p/s) | 5 |
| 84 | Vertigo RUSH 1110 | The Body Electric/The Analog Kid/Distant Early Warning (10", p/s, red vinyl) | 12 |
| 84 | Vertigo RUSH 1112 | The Body Electric/The Analog Kid/Distant Early Warning (12", p/s) | 50 |
| 74 | Mercury 9100011 | RUSH (LP, gatefold) | 30 |
| 75 | Mercury 9100 013 | FLY BY NIGHT (LP, gatefold) | 30 |
| 75 | Mercury 9100 018 | CARESS OF STEEL (LP, gatefold) | 30 |
| 76 | Mercury 9100 039 | 2112 (LP) | 30 |
| 78 | Mercury 9100 059 | HEMISPHERES (LP, gatefold sleeve) | 30 |
| 78 | Mercury 9100 059 | HEMISPHERES (LP, mispressing, both sides play Side 1) | 50 |
| 80 | Mercury 9100 071 | PERMANENT WAVES (LP, with newspaper and lyric inner) | 20 |
| 81 | Mercury 6337 160 | MOVING PICTURES (LP) | 30 |
| 85 | Vertigo VERHP 31 | POWER WINDOWS (LP, picture disc, with discography on sleeve) | 20 |
| 91 | Atlantic 756782293-1 | ROLL THE BONES (LP) | 25 |
| 93 | Anthem 7567 82528-1 | COUNTERPARTS (LP) | 60 |
| 04 | Atlantic 7567 83728 1 | FEEDBACK (LP) | 30 |

*(see also McKenzie Doug & Bob, Max Webster Band)*

## ED RUSH

| | | | |
|---|---|---|---|
| 92 | Primavera PRIM 001 | Edrush/Fat Girl (12", as Edrush) | 20 |
| 92 | ER 007 | I Wanna Stay In The Jungle/5AM/Touch Me/Keep On (12") | 20 |
| 92 | PSY 001 | Look What They've Done/What If My Heart Stops?/Look What They've Done (Dub Mix) (12") | 20 |
| | No U-Turn NUT 002 | Bludclot Artattack/Bludclot Artattack (Dark Mix) (12") | 20 |
| | Jet Star XCT 001 | Selecta/Selecta (Remix) (12") | 30 |

## MERRILEE RUSH & TURNABOUTS
| | | | |
|---|---|---|---|
| 68 | Bell BLL 1013 | Angel Of The Morning/Reap What You Sow | 6 |
| 68 | Bell BLL 1026 | That Kind Of Woman/Sunshine And Roses | 6 |
| 69 | Bell BLL 1041 | Reach Out I'll Be There/Love Street | 10 |
| 68 | Bell MBLL/SBLL 109 | MERRILEE RUSH (LP) | 25 |

## OTIS RUSH
| | | | |
|---|---|---|---|
| 66 | Vocalion V-P 9260 | Homework/I Have To Laugh | 75 |
| 66 | Vocalion V-P 9260 | Homework/I Have To Laugh (DJ copy) | 125 |
| 69 | Blue Horizon 57-3159 | All Your Love/Double Trouble | 25 |
| 68 | Blue Horizon 7-63222 | THIS ONE'S A GOOD UN (LP) | 90 |
| 69 | Atlantic 588 188 | MOURNING IN THE MORNING (LP) | 40 |
| 70s | Atlantic K 40495 | MOURNING IN THE MORNING (LP, reissue) | 15 |
| 70 | Python KM 3 | GROANING THE BLUES (LP) | 50 |
| 76 | Delmark DS 63? | COLD DAY IN HELL (LP) | 25 |

## TOM RUSH
| | | | |
|---|---|---|---|
| 67 | Elektra EKSN 45004 | Who Do You Love/On The Road Again | 8 |
| 67 | Elektra EKSN 45015 | On The Road Again/Love's Made A Fool Of You | 8 |
| 68 | Elektra EKSN 45025 | No Regrets/Shadow Dream Song | 7 |
| 68 | Elektra EKSN 45032 | Something In The Way She Moves/Rockport Sunday | 8 |
| 66 | Xtra XTRA 5024 | BLUES, SONGS & BALLADS (LP) | 30 |
| 66 | Xtra XTRA 5053 | I GOT A MIND TO RAMBLE (LP) | 30 |
| 67 | Elektra EKL 308 | TAKE A LITTLE WALK WITH ME (LP, also stereo EKS 7308) | 30 |
| 68 | Elektra EKL 4018 | THE CIRCLE GAME (also stereo EKS 74018) (LP, 1st issue black 'Elektra' on red label) | 25 |
| 69 | Elektra EKL 4062 | CLASSIC RUSH (LP, red label, also stereo EKS 74062) | 20 |

## JIMMY RUSHING (WITH ADA MOORE & BUCK CLAYTON)
| | | | |
|---|---|---|---|
| 55 | Vanguard PPT 12002 | SINGS THE BLUES (10" LP) | 30 |
| 57 | Vanguard PPT 12016 | SHOWCASE (10" LP) | 30 |
| 57 | Philips BBL 7105 | CAT MEETS CHICK (LP, with Ada Moore & Buck Clayton) | 15 |
| 57 | Philips BBL 7166 | THE JAZZ ODYSSEY OF JAMES RUSHING ESQ (LP, with Buck Clayton) | 15 |
| 58 | Vanguard PPL 11008 | IF THIS AIN'T THE BLUES (LP) | 15 |

*(see also Count Basie, Dave Brubeck)*

## JIMMY RUSHING/CHAMPION JACK DUPREE
| | | | |
|---|---|---|---|
| 64 | Ember CJS 800 | TWO SHADES OF BLUE (LP, 1 side each) | 30 |

*(see also Champion Jack Dupree)*

## BARBARA RUSKIN
| | | | |
|---|---|---|---|
| 65 | Piccadilly 7N 35224 | Halfway To Paradise/I Can't Believe In Miracles | 10 |
| 65 | Piccadilly 7N 35246 | You Can't Blame A Girl For Trying/No More To Fall | 12 |
| 66 | Piccadilly 7N 35274 | Well How Does It Feel/Wishing Your Life Away | 40 |
| 66 | Piccadilly 7N 35296 | Song Without End/Love Came Too Late | 10 |
| 66 | Piccadilly 7N 35328 | Light Of Love/At Times Like These Mama | 10 |
| 67 | Parlophone R 5571 | Take It Easy/Sunshowers | 10 |
| 67 | Parlophone R 5593 | Euston Station/Hear That Telephone | 10 |
| 67 | Parlophone R 5642 | Come Into My Arms Again/Just A Little While Longer | 10 |
| 68 | Parlophone R 5685 | Is This Another Way/The Night Of The Spanish Tightrope Walker | 5 |
| 68 | President PT 217 | Pawnbroker Pawnbroker/Almost | 25 |
| 69 | President PT 238 | Gentlemen Please/24th Of July | 6 |
| 69 | President PT 261 | Hail Love/Lady Of Leisure | 6 |
| 70 | President PT 280 | A Little Bit Of This (And A Little Bit Of That)/Where Are We | 6 |
| 70 | President PT 315 | For The First Time In My Life/Merry-Go-Round | 6 |
| 71 | President PT 350 | (I Wanna Be) Your Teddy Bear/It Really Doesn't Matter | 6 |

## ROGER RUSKIN SPEAR
| | | | |
|---|---|---|---|
| 74 | United Artists UP 35683 | On Her Doorstep Last Night/Frank The Ripper | 12 |
| 74 | United Artists UP 35721 | I Love To Bumpity Bump/When Yuba Plays The Rhumba On The Tuba Down In Cuba | 20 |
| 71 | United Artists UP 35221 | REBEL TROUSER: Trouser Freak/Trouser Press/Release Me/Drop Out (EP, without p/s) | 10 |
| 71 | United Artists UP 35221 | REBEL TROUSER: Trouser Freak/Trouser Press/Release Me/Drop Out (EP, with p/s) | 20 |
| 74 | United Artists UAS 29508 | UNUSUAL (LP) | 20 |

*(see also Bonzo Dog Doo-Dah Band, Topo D. Bill)*

## EDDIE RUSS
| | | | |
|---|---|---|---|
| 76 | Impact IMP 5 | Zaius/See The Light/Tea Leaves (12") | 150 |

## LONNIE RUSS
| | | | |
|---|---|---|---|
| 62 | Fontana 267263 TF | Something Old Something New/My Wife Can't Cook | 7 |

## THANE RUSSAL (& THREE)
| | | | |
|---|---|---|---|
| 66 | CBS 202049 | Security/Your Love Is Burning Me (in p/s) | 300 |
| 66 | CBS 202049 | Security/Your Love Is Burning Me | 150 |
| 66 | CBS 202403 | Drop Everything And Run/I Need You (solo) | 150 |

## RUSSANT
| | | | |
|---|---|---|---|
| 82 | Mach 1 MAGIC 003 | It Happened Then/Synthamation (no p/s) | 10 |

## CHARLOTTE RUSSE
| | | | |
|---|---|---|---|
| 68 | Fontana BF1683 | Anyway The Wind Blows/High On A Roof Top | 25 |

## ROLAND RUSSEL
| | | | |
|---|---|---|---|
| 68 | Nu Beat NB 019 | Rhythm Hips/RHYTHM FLAMES: Deltone Special | 40 |

## ANDY RUSSELL
| | | | |
|---|---|---|---|
| 58 | RCA RCA 1076 | Seven Daughters/A Certain Smile | 6 |

## ARTHUR RUSSELL
| | | | |
|---|---|---|---|
| 86 | Rough Trade RT RTT184 | Let's Go Swimming (Coastal Dub)/(Gulf Stream Dub)/(Puppy Surf Dub) (12" p/s) | 20 |
| 87 | Rough Trade ROUGH 114 | WORLD OF ECHO (LP) | 20 |
| 04 | Soul Jazz SJRLP 083 | THE WORLD OF ARTHUR RUSSELL (3-LP, original 2004 pressing) | 20 |

MINT VALUE £

| 10 | Rough Trade RTRADLP 161 | CALLING OUT OF CONTEXT (2-LP) | 18 |

*(see also Dinosaur L, Necessaries)*

## BOBBY RUSSELL
| 68 | Bell BLL 1019 | Dusty/I Made You This Way | 6 |
| 68 | Bell BLL 1034 | 1432 Franklin Pike Circle Hero/Let's Talk About It | 6 |
| 69 | Bell BLL 1050 | Carlie/Ain't Society Great? | 6 |
| 71 | United Artists UP 35283 | Saturday Morning Confusion/Little Ole Song About Love | 5 |

## CONNIE RUSSELL
| 54 | Capitol CL 14171 | No One But You/One Arabian Night | 10 |
| 54 | Capitol CL 14197 | Love Me/Papa's Puttin' The Pressure On | 10 |
| 55 | Capitol CL 14214 | Foggy Night In San Francisco/This Is My Love | 10 |
| 55 | Capitol CL 14236 | Ayuh, Ayuh/I'm Making Believe | 15 |
| 55 | Capitol CL 14246 | Snow Dreams/Green Fire | 6 |
| 55 | Capitol CL 14268 | Farewell, Farewell/The Magnificent Matador | 6 |
| 57 | Capitol CL 14676 | All Of You/This Is My Love | 6 |

## DAVE RUSSELL
| 66 | Columbia DB 7828 | When I Grow Too Old To Dream/All The Tears In The World | 5 |

*(see also Dave & Diamonds)*

## DEVON RUSSELL
| 82 | Ethnic ETH 2237 | Come A Me Girl/Gully Banking | 20 |
| 91 | CS Sweetest CSLP 2 | DARKER THAN BLUE (LP) | 18 |

## DOROTHY RUSSELL
| 71 | Duke Reid DR 2524 | You're The One I Love/Version | 20 |

## GEORGE RUSSELL
| 71 | Flying Dutchman FD10124 | ELECTRONIC SONATA FOR SOULS (LP) | 20 |

## JANE RUSSELL
| 53 | Columbia SCM 5043 | Please Do It Again/Two Sleepy People (B-side with Bob Lowery) | 15 |
| 56 | Capitol CL 14590 | If You Wanna See Mamie Tonight/Keep Your Eyes On The Hands | 10 |
| 59 | MGM MGM-EP 702 | JANE RUSSELL (EP) | 40 |

## JANET RUSSELL
| 88 | Harbourtown HAR 003 | GATHERING THE FRAGMENTS (LP) | 20 |

## JOHN RUSSELL/RICHARD COLDMAN
| 79 | Incus INCUS 31 | HOME COOKING/GUITAR SOLOS (LP, 1 side each) | 35 |

## JOHNNY RUSSELL
| 60 | MGM MGM 1074 | Lonesome Boy/Baby Won't You Tell Me So | 10 |

## KEITH RUSSELL
| 65 | Piccadilly 7N 35235 | People Get Ready/Paradise | 10 |

## KIT RUSSELL
| 73 | Deram DM 399 | Peppers Last Stand/Shuffle Back | 15 |

## LEON RUSSELL
| 65 | Dot DS 16771 | Everybody's Talkin' 'Bout The Young/It's Alright With Me | 8 |

*(see also Asylum Choir)*

## RAY RUSSELL QUARTET
| 68 | CBS Realm 52586 | TURN CIRCLE (LP) | 60 |
| 69 | CBS Realm 52663 | DRAGON HILL (LP) | 60 |
| 71 | RCA SF 8214 | JUNE 11TH 1971 (LP) | 40 |
| 71 | CBS 64271 | RITES AND RITUALS (LP) | 45 |
| 73 | Black Lion BLP 12100 | SECRET ASYLUM (LP, gatefold) | 30 |

*(see also Running Man, Chopyn)*

## ROSALIND RUSSELL & EDITH ADAMS
| 55 | Brunswick 05406 | Ohio/Little Bit Of Love | 5 |

## IAN RUSSELL
| 70 | Lucky LU 112 | Love Locked Out/The Worm Song | 10 |

## RUSSIAN ROULETTE
| 84 | Red Bus RBUS 86 | Come Into My Room/Lyin' Again (p/s) | 5 |

*(see also Paul King, Mungo Jerry)*

## CHARLIE RUSSO
| 63 | Stateside SS 165 | Preacherman/Teresa | 8 |

## WILLIAM RUSSO
| 63 | Columbia 33SX 1508 | RUSSO IN LONDON (LP) | 20 |
| 66 | Columbia 33SX 1758 | STONEHENGE (LP, with the London Jazz Orchestra) | 35 |

## RUSTIKS
| 64 | Decca F 11960 | What A Memory Can Do/Hello Anne | 10 |
| 65 | Decca F 12059 | I'm Not The Loving Kind/Can't You See | 10 |

## RUSTLERS
| 61 | Pye 7N 15398 | High Strung/Matter Of Who | 12 |

## RUSTY & DOUG (KERSHAW)
| 59 | Oriole CB 1510 | Hey Mae!/Why Don't You Love Me | 100 |
| 59 | Oriole CB 1510 | Hey Mae!/Why Don't You Love Me (78) | 30 |
| 9 | London HL 8972 | I Like You (Like This)/Dancing Shoes | 30 |
|  | London HL 8972 | I Like You (Like This)/Dancing Shoes (78) | 30 |
|  | Polydor NH 66970 | Hey Mae!/Sweet Thing | 20 |
|  | ontana 267 238 TF | Cajun Joe (The Ballad Of The Bayou)/Sweet Sweet Girl To Me | 15 |

*(Doug Kershaw)*

## HARNESS
|  | EMB S 283 | Ain't Gonna Get Married/Goodbye (in p/s) | 10 |
|  | EMB S 283 | Ain't Gonna Get Married/Goodbye | 5 |

I went into the dining room and pulled a bottle of gin and a couple of tonics out of the sideboard. He'd need a drink when he heard what I had to say.

Then I realized he'd never make it. From Earls Court it would take him at least half an hour to reach us at Maida Vale and he'd probably get no further than Marble Arch.

I filled my glass out of the virtually bottomless bottle of scotch and tried to work out a plan of action.

The first step was to get hold of someone like myself who retained his awareness of the past switch-backs. Somewhere else there must be others trapped in their little 15-minute cages who were also wondering desperately how to get out. I could start by phoning everyone I knew and then going on at random through the phonebook. But what could we do if we did find each other? In fact there was nothing to do except sit tight and wait for it all to wear off. At least I knew I wasn't looping my loop. Once these billows or whatever they were had burnt themselves out we'd be able to get off the round-about.

Until then I had an unlimited supply of whisky waiting for me in the half-empty bottle standing on the sink, though of course there was one snag: I'd never be able to get drunk.

I was musing round some of the other possibilities available and wondering how to get a permanent record of what was going on when an idea hit me.

I got out the phone-directory and looked up the number of KBC-TV, Channel 9.

A girl at reception answered the phone. After haggling with her for a couple of minutes I persuaded her to put me through to one of the producers.

'Hullo,' I said. 'Is the jackpot question in tonight's programme known to any members of the studio audience?'

'No, of course not.'

'I see. As a matter of interest, do you yourself know it?'

'No,' he said. 'All the questions tonight are known only to our senior programme producer and M. Phillipe Soisson of Savoy Hotels Limited. They're a closely guarded secret.'

'Thanks,' I said. 'If you've got a piece of paper handy I'll give you the jackpot question. "List the complete menu at the Guildhall Coronation Banquet in July 1953."'

There were muttered consultations, and a second voice came through.

'Who's that speaking?'

'Mr H.R. Bartley, 129b Sutton Court Road, N.W. –'

Before I could finish I found myself back in the lounge.

The jump-back had caught me. But instead of being stretched out on the sofa I was standing up, leaning on one elbow against the mantelpiece, looking down at the newspaper.

'The scotch. You brought it in a couple of minutes ago. It was on the table.'

'You've been dreaming,' she said gently. She leant forward and started watching the play.

I went into the pantry and found the bottle. As I filled a tumbler I noticed the clock over the kitchen sink. 9.07. An hour slow, now that I thought about it. But my wristwatch said 9.05, and always ran perfectly. And the clock on the mantelpiece in the lounge also said 9.05.

Before I really started worrying I had to make sure.

Mullvaney, our neighbour in the flat above, opened his door when I knocked.

'Hello, Bartley. Corkscrew?'

'No, no,' I told him. 'What's the right time? Our clocks are going crazy.'

He glanced at his wrist. 'Nearly ten past.'

'Nine or ten?'

He looked at his watch again. 'Nine, should be. What's up?'

'I don't know whether I'm losing my –' I started to say. Then I stopped.

Mullvaney eyed me curiously. Over his shoulder I heard a wave of studio applause, broken by the creamy, unctuous voice of the giveaway compère.

'How long's that programme been on?' I asked him.

'About twenty minutes. Aren't you watching?'

'No,' I said, adding casually, 'Is anything wrong with your set?'

He shook his head. 'Nothing. Why?'

'Mine's chasing its tail. Anyway, thanks.'

'OK,' he said. He watched me go down the stairs and shrugged as he shut his door.

I went into the hall, picked up the phone and dialled.

'Hello, Tom?' Tom Farnold works the desk next to mine at the office. 'Tom, Harry here. What time do you make it?'

'Time the liberals were back.'

'No, seriously.'

'Let's see. Twelve past nine. By the way, did you find those pickles I left for you in the safe?'

'Yeah, thanks. Listen, Tom,' I went on, 'the goddamdest things are happening here. We were watching Diller's play on Channel 2 when –'

'I'm watching it now. Hurry it up.'

'You are? Well, how do you explain this repetition business? And the way the clocks are stuck between 9 and 9.15?'

Tom laughed. 'I don't know,' he said. 'I suggest you go outside and give the house a shake.'

I reached out for the glass I had with me on the hall table, wondering how to explain to –

The next moment I found myself back on the sofa. I was holding the newspaper and looking at 17 down. A part of my mind was thinking about antique clocks.

I pulled myself out of it and glanced across at Helen. She was sitting quietly with her needle basket. The all too familiar play was repeating itself and by the clock on the mantelpiece it was still just after 9.

I went back into the hall and dialled Tom again, trying not to stampede myself. In some way, I hadn't begun to understand how, a section of time was spinning round in a circle, with myself in the centre.

'Tom,' I asked quickly as soon as he picked up the phone. 'Did I call you five minutes ago?'

'Who's that again?'

'Harry here. Harry Bartley. Sorry, Tom.' I paused and rephrased the question, trying to make it sound intelligible. 'Tom, did you phone me up about five minutes ago? We've had a little trouble with the line here.'

'No,' he told me. 'Wasn't me. By the way, did you get those pickles I left in the safe?'

'Thanks a lot,' I said, beginning to panic. 'Are you watching the play, Tom?'

'Yes. I think I'll get back to it. See you.'

I went into the kitchen and had a long close look at myself in the mirror. A crack across it dropped one side of my face three inches below the other, but apart from that I couldn't see anything that added up to a psychosis. My eyes seemed steady, pulse was in the low seventies, no tics or clammy traumatic sweat. Everything around me seemed much too solid and authentic for a dream.

I waited for a minute and then went back to the lounge and sat down. Helen was watching the play.

I leant forward and turned the knob round. The picture dimmed and swayed off.

'Harry, I'm watching that! Don't switch it off.'

I went over to her. 'Poppet,' I said, holding my voice together. 'Listen to me, please. Very carefully. It's important.'

She frowned, put her sewing down and took my hands.

'For some reason, I don't know why, we seem to be in a sort of circular time trap, just going round and round. You're not aware of it, and I can't find anyone else who is either.'

Helen stared at me in amazement. 'Harry,' she started, 'what are you –'

'Helen!' I insisted, gripping her shoulders. 'Listen! For the last two hours a section of time about 15 minutes long has been repeating itself. The clocks are stuck between 9 and 9.15. That play you're watching has –'

'Harry, darling.' She looked at me and smiled helplessly. 'You are silly. Now turn it on again.'

I gave up.

*     *     *

As I switched the set on I ran through all the other channels ) if anything had changed.

The panel stared at their pot, the fat woman won her sports car, farmer ranted. On Channel 1, the old BBC service which put out a c of hours on alternate evenings, two newspaper men were interview scientific pundit who appeared on popular educational programmes.

'What effect these dense eruptions of gas will have so far it's impossi to tell. However, there's certainly no cause for any alarm. These billow have mass, and I think we can expect a lot of strange optical effects as the light leaving the sun is deflected by them gravitationally.'

He started playing with a set of coloured celluloid balls running on concentric metal rings, and fiddled with a ripple tank mounted against a mirror on the table.

One of the newsmen asked: 'What about the relationship between light and time? If I remember my relativity they're tied up together pretty closely. Are you sure we won't all need to add another hand to our clocks and watches?'

The pundit smiled. 'I think we'll be able to get along without that. Time is extremely complicated, but I can assure you the clocks won't suddenly start running backwards or sideways.'

I listened to him until Helen began to remonstrate. I switched the play on for her and went off into the hall. The fool didn't know what he was talking about. What I couldn't understand was why I was the only person who realized what was going on. If I could get Tom over I might just be able to convince him.

I picked up the phone and glanced at my watch.

9.13. By the time I got through to Tom the next changeover would be due. Somehow I didn't like the idea of being picked up and flung to the sofa, however painless it might be. I put the phone down and went into the lounge.

The jump-back was smoother than I expected. I wasn't conscious of anything, not even the slightest tremor. A phrase was stuck in my mind: Olden Times.

The newspaper was back on my lap, folded around the crossword. I looked through the clues.

17 down: Told by antique clocks? 5, 5.

I must have solved it subconsciously.

I remembered that I'd intended to phone Tom.

'Hullo, Tom?' I asked when I got through. 'Harry here.'

'Did you get those pickles I left in the safe?'

'Yes, thanks a lot. Tom, could you come round tonight? Sorry to ask you this late, but it's fairly urgent.'

'Yes, of course,' he said. 'What's the trouble?'

'I'll tell you when you get here. As soon as you can?'

'Sure. I'll leave right away. Is Helen all right?'

'Yes, she's fine. Thanks again.'

My eyes were focused clearly on the crossword puzzle, and before I pulled them away and started thinking over my call to the studio I noticed something that nearly dropped me into the grate.

17 down had been filled in.

I picked up the paper and showed it to Helen.

'Did you do this clue? 17 down?'

'No,' she said. 'I never even look at the crossword.'

The clock on the mantelpiece caught my eye, and I forgot about the studio and playing tricks with other people's time.

9.03.

The merry-go-round was closing in. I thought the jump-back had come sooner than I expected. At least two minutes earlier, somewhere around 9.13.

And not only was the repetition interval getting shorter, but as the arc edged inwards on itself it was uncovering the real time stream running below it, the stream in which the other I, unknown to myself here, had solved the clue, stood up, walked over to the mantelpiece and filled in 17 down.

I sat down on the sofa, watching the clock carefully.

For the first time that evening Helen was thumbing over the pages of a magazine. The work basket was tucked away on the bottom shelf of the bookcase.

'Do you want this on any longer?' she asked me. 'It's not very good.'

I turned to the panel game. The three professors and the chorus girl were still playing around with their pot.

On Channel 1 the pundit was sitting at the table with his models.

'. . . alarm. The billows have mass, and I think we can expect a lot of strange optical effects as the light –'

I switched it off.

The next jump-back came at 9.11. Somewhere I'd left the mantelpiece, gone back to the sofa and lit a cigarette.

It was 9.04. Helen had opened the verandah windows and was looking out into the street.

The set was on again so I pulled the plug out at the main. I threw the cigarette into the fire; not having seen myself light it, made it taste like someone else's.

'Harry, like to go out for a stroll?' Helen suggested. 'It'll be rather nice in the park.'

Each successive jump-back gave us a new departure point. If now I bundled her outside and got her down to the end of the road, at the next jump we'd both be back in the lounge again, but probably have decided to drive to the pub instead.

'Harry?'

'What, sorry?'

'Are you asleep, angel? Like to go for a walk? It'll wake you up.'

'All right,' I said. 'Go and get your coat.'

'Will you be warm enough like that?'

She went off into the bedroom

I walked round the lounge and convinced myself that I was awake. The shadows, the solid feel of the chairs, the definition was much too fine for a dream.

It was 9.08. Normally Helen would take ten minutes to put on her coat.

The jump-back came almost immediately.

It was 9.06.

I was still on the sofa and Helen was bending down and picking up her work basket.

This time, at last, the set was off.

'Have you got any money on you?' Helen asked.

I felt in my pocket automatically. 'Yes. How much do you want?'

Helen looked at me. 'Well, what do you usually pay for the drinks? We'll only have a couple.'

'We're going to the pub, are we?'

'Darling, are you all right?' She came over to me. 'You look all strangled. Is that shirt too tight?'

'Helen,' I said, getting up. 'I've got to try to explain something to you. I don't know why it's happening, it's something to do with these billows of gas the sun's releasing.'

Helen was watching me with her mouth open.

'Harry,' she started to say nervously. 'What's the matter?'

'I'm quite all right,' I assured her. 'It's just that everything is happening very rapidly and I don't think there's much time left.'

I kept on glancing at the clock and Helen followed my eyes to it and went over to the mantelpiece. Watching me she moved it round and I heard the pendulum jangle.

'No, no,' I shouted. I grabbed it and pushed it back against the wall.

We jumped back to 9.07.

Helen was in the bedroom. I had exactly a minute left.

'Harry,' she called. 'Darling, do you want to, or don't you?'

I was by the lounge window, muttering something.

I was out of touch with what my real self was doing in the normal time channel. The Helen talking to me now was a phantom.

It was I, not Helen and everybody else, who was riding the merry-go-round.

Jump.

9.07-15.

Helen was standing in the doorway.

'. . . down to the . . . the . . .' I was saying.

Helen watched me, frozen. A fraction of a minute left.

I started to walk over to her.

to walk over to her

ver to her

er

I came out of it like a man catapulted from a revolving door. I was stretched out flat on the sofa, a hard aching pain running from the top of my head down past my right ear into my neck.

I looked at the time. 9.45. I could hear Helen moving around in the dining room. I lay there, steadying the room round me, and in a few minutes she came in carrying a tray and a couple of glasses.

'How do you feel?' she asked, making up an alka-seltzer.

I let it fizzle down and drank it.

'What happened?' I asked. 'Did I collapse?'

'Not exactly. You were watching the play. I thought you looked rather seedy so I suggested we go out for a drink. You went into a sort of convulsion.'

I stood up slowly and rubbed my neck. 'God, I didn't dream all that! I couldn't have done.'

'What was it about?'

'A sort of crazy merry-go-round –' The pain grabbed at my neck when I spoke. I went over to the set and switched it on. 'Hard to explain coherently. Time was –' I flinched as the pain bit in again.

'Sit down and rest,' Helen said. 'I'll come and join you. Like a drink?'

'Thanks. A big scotch.'

I looked at the set. On Channel 1 there was a breakdown sign, a cabaret on 2, a flood-lit stadium on 5, and a variety show on 9. No sign anywhere of either Diller's play or the panel game.

Helen brought the drink in and sat down on the sofa with me.

'It started off when we were watching the play,' I explained, massaging my neck.

'Sh, don't bother now. Just relax.'

I put my head on Helen's shoulder and looked up at the ceiling, listening to the sound coming from the variety show. I thought back through each turn of the round-about, wondering whether I could have dreamt it all.

Ten minutes later Helen said, 'Well, I didn't think much of that. And they're doing an encore. Good heavens.'

'Who are?' I asked. I watched the light from the screen flicker across her face.

'That team of acrobats. The something Brothers. One of them even slipped. How do you feel?'

'Fine.' I turned my head round and looked at the screen.

Three or four acrobats with huge v-torsos and skin briefs were doing simple handstands on to each other's arms. They finished the act and went into a more involved routine, throwing around a girl in leopard skin panties. The applause was deafening. I thought they were moderately good.

Two of them began to give what seemed to be a demonstration of dynamic tension, straining against each other like a pair of catatonic bulls, their necks and legs locked, until one of them was levered slowly off the ground.

'Why do they keep on doing that?' Helen said. 'They've done it twice already.'

'I don't think they have,' I said. 'This is a slightly different act.'

The pivot man tremored, one of his huge banks of muscles collapsed, and the whole act toppled and then sprung apart.

'They slipped there the last time,' Helen said.

'No, no,' I pointed out quickly. 'That one was a headstand. Here they were stretched out horizontally.'

'You weren't watching,' Helen told me. She leant forward. 'Well, what are they playing at? They're repeating the whole thing for the third time.'

It was an entirely new act to me, but I didn't try to argue.

I sat up and looked at the clock.

10.05.

'Darling,' I said, putting my arm round her. 'Hold tight.'

'What do you mean?'

'This is the merry-go-round. And you're driving.'

**· 1956**

# THE CONCENTRATION CITY

Noon talk on Millionth Street:

'Sorry, these are the West Millions. You want 9775335th East.'

'Dollar five a cubic foot? Sell!'

'Take a westbound express to 495th Avenue, cross over to a Redline elevator and go up a thousand levels to Plaza Terminal. Carry on south from there and you'll find it between 568th Avenue and 422nd Street.'

'There's a cave-in down at KEN County! Fifty blocks by twenty by thirty levels.'

'Listen to this – "PYROMANIACS STAGE MASS BREAKOUT! FIRE POLICE CORDON BAY COUNTY!"'

'It's a beautiful counter. Detects up to .005 per cent monoxide. Cost me three hundred dollars.'

'Have you seen those new intercity sleepers? They take only ten minutes to go up 3,000 levels!'

'Ninety cents a foot? Buy!'

'You say the idea came to you in a dream?' the voice snapped. 'You're sure no one else gave it to you.'

'No,' M. said. A couple of feet away from him a spot-lamp threw a cone of dirty yellow light into his face. He dropped his eyes from the glare and waited as the sergeant paced over to his desk, tapped his fingers on the edge and swung round on him again.

'You talked it over with your friends?'

'Only the first theory,' M. explained. 'About the possibility of flight.'

'But you told me the other theory was more important. Why keep it from them?'

M. hesitated. Outside somewhere a trolley shunted and clanged along the elevated. 'I was afraid they wouldn't understand what I meant.'

The sergeant laughed. 'Do you mean they would have thought you really were insane?'

M. shifted uncomfortably on the stool. Its seat was only six inches off the floor and his thighs felt like slabs of inflamed rubber. After three hours of cross-questioning logic had faded. 'The concept was a little abstract. There weren't any words for it.'

The sergeant shook his head. 'I'm glad to hear you say it.' He sat

23

down on the desk, watched M. for a moment and then went over to him.

'Now look,' he said confidentially. 'It's getting late. Do you still think both theories are reasonable?'

M. looked up. 'Aren't they?'

The sergeant turned to the man watching in the shadows by the window. 'We're wasting our time,' he snapped. 'I'll hand him over to Psycho. You've seen enough, haven't you, Doctor?'

The surgeon stared at his hands. He had taken no part in the interrogation, as if bored by the sergeant's method of approach.

'There's something I want to find out,' he said. 'Leave me alone with him for half an hour.'

When the sergeant had gone the surgeon sat down behind the desk and stared out of the window, listening to the dull hum of air through the ventilator shaft which rose out of the street below the station. A few roof lights were still burning and two hundred yards away a single policeman patrolled the iron catwalk running above the street, his boots ringing across the darkness.

M. sat on the stool, elbows between his knees, trying to edge a little life back into his legs.

Eventually the surgeon glanced down at the charge sheet.

```
Name.................  Franz M.
Age..................  20.
Occupation...........  Student.
Address..............  3599719 West 783rd St, Level
                       549-7705-45 KNI (Local).
Charge...............  Vagrancy.
```

'Tell me about this dream,' he said, idly flexing a steel rule between his hands as he looked across at M.

'I think you've heard everything, sir,' M. said.

'In detail.'

M. shifted uneasily. 'There wasn't much to it, and what I do remember isn't too clear now.'

The surgeon yawned. M. waited and then started to recite what he had already repeated twenty times.

'I was suspended in the air above a flat stretch of open ground, something like the floor of an enormous arena. My arms were out at my sides, and I was looking down, floating –'

'Hold on,' the surgeon interrupted. 'Are you sure you weren't swimming?'

'No,' M. said. 'I'm certain I wasn't. All around me there was free space. That was the most important part about it. There were no walls. Nothing but emptiness. That's all I remember.'

The surgeon ran his finger along the edge of the rule.

'Go on.'

'Well, the dream gave me the idea of building a flying machine. One of my friends helped me construct it.'

The surgeon nodded. Almost absently he picked up the charge sheet and crushed it with a single motion of his hand.

'Don't be absurd, Franz!' Gregson remonstrated. They took their places in the chemistry cafeteria queue. 'It's against the laws of hydrodynamics. Where would you get your buoyancy?'

'Suppose you had a rigid fabric vane,' Franz explained as they shuffled past the hatchways. 'Say ten feet across, like one of those composition wall sections, with hand grips on the ventral surface. And then you jumped down from the gallery at the Coliseum Stadium. What would happen?'

'You'd make a hole in the floor. Why?'

'No, seriously.'

'If it was large enough and held together you'd swoop down like a paper dart.'

'Glide,' Franz said. 'Right.' Thirty levels above them one of the intercity expresses roared over, rattling the tables and cutlery in the cafeteria. Franz waited until they reached a table and sat forward, his food forgotten.

'And say you attached a propulsive unit, such as a battery-driven ventilator fan, or one of those rockets they use on the Sleepers. With enough thrust to overcome your weight. What then?'

Gregson shrugged. 'If you could control the thing, you'd, you'd . . .' He frowned at Franz. 'What's the word? You're always using it.'

'Fly.'

'Basically, Matheson, the machine is simple,' Sanger, the physics lector, commented as they entered the science library. 'An elementary application of the Venturi Principle. But what's the point of it? A trapeze would serve its purpose equally well, and be far less dangerous. In the first place consider the enormous clearances it would require. I hardly think the traffic authorities will look upon it with any favour.'

'I know it wouldn't be practical here,' Franz admitted. 'But in a large open area it should be.'

'Allowed. I suggest you immediately negotiate with the Arena Garden on Level 347–25,' the lector said whimsically. 'I'm sure they'll be glad to hear about your scheme.'

Franz smiled politely. 'That wouldn't be large enough. I was really thinking of an area of totally free space. In three dimensions, as it were.'

Sanger looked at Franz curiously. 'Free space? Isn't that a contradiction in terms? Space is a dollar a cubic foot.' He scratched his nose. 'Have you begun to construct this machine yet?'

'No,' Franz said.

'In that event I should try to forget all about it. Remember, Matheson, the task of science is to consolidate existing knowledge, to systematize and reinterpret the discoveries of the past, not to chase wild dreams into the future.'

He nodded and disappeared among the dusty shelves.

Gregson was waiting on the steps.

'Well?' he asked.

'Let's try it out this afternoon,' Franz said. 'We'll cut Text 5 Pharmacology. I know those Fleming readings backwards. I'll ask Dr McGhee for a couple of passes.'

They left the library and walked down the narrow, dimly-lit alley which ran behind the huge new civil engineering laboratories. Over seventy-five per cent of the student enrolment was in the architectural and engineering faculties, a meagre two per cent in pure sciences. Consequently the physics and chemistry libraries were housed in the oldest quarter of the university, in two virtually condemned galvanized hutments which once contained the now closed philosophy school.

At the end of the alley they entered the university plaza and started to climb the iron stairway leading to the next level a hundred feet above. Halfway up a white-helmeted F.P. checked them cursorily with his detector and waved them past.

'What did Sanger think?' Gregson asked as they stepped up into 637th Street and walked across to the suburban elevator station.

'He's no use at all,' Franz said. 'He didn't even begin to understand what I was talking about.'

Gregson laughed ruefully. 'I don't know whether I do.'

Franz took a ticket from the automat and mounted the down platform. An elevator dropped slowly towards him, its bell jangling.

'Wait until this afternoon,' he called back. 'You're really going to see something.'

The floor manager at the Coliseum initialled the two passes.

'Students, eh? All right.' He jerked a thumb at the long package Franz and Gregson were carrying. 'What have you got there?'

'It's a device for measuring air velocities,' Franz told him.

The manager grunted and released the stile.

Out in the centre of the empty arena Franz undid the package and they assembled the model. It had a broad fan-like wing of wire and paper, a narrow strutted fuselage and a high curving tail.

Franz picked it up and launched it into the air. The model glided for twenty feet and then slithered to a stop across the sawdust.

'Seems to be stable,' Franz said. 'We'll tow it first.'

He pulled a reel of twine from his pocket and tied one end to the nose. As they ran forward the model lifted gracefully into the air and followed them around the stadium, ten feet off the floor.

'Let's try the rockets now,' Franz said. He adjusted the wing and tail settings and fitted three firework display rockets into a wire bracket mounted above the wing.

The stadium was four hundred feet in diameter and had a roof two hundred and fifty feet high. They carried the model over to one side and Franz lit the tapers.

There was a burst of flame and the model accelerated across the floor, two feet in the air, a bright trail of coloured smoke spitting out behind it. Its wings rocked gently from side to side. Suddenly the tail burst into flames. The model lifted steeply and looped up towards the roof, stalled just before it hit one of the pilot lights and dived down into the sawdust.

They ran across to it and stamped out the glowing cinders. 'Franz!' Gregson shouted. 'It's incredible! It actually works.'

Franz kicked the shattered fuselage. 'Of course it works,' he said impatiently. 'But as Sanger said, what's the point of it?'

'The point? It flies! Isn't that enough?'

'No. I want one big enough to hold me.'

'Franz, slow down. Be reasonable. Where could you fly it?'

'I don't know,' Franz said fiercely. 'But there must be somewhere!'

The floor manager and two assistants, carrying fire extinguishers, ran across the stadium to them.

'Did you hide the matches?' Franz asked quickly. 'They'll lynch us if they think we're Pyros.'

Three afternoons later Franz took the elevator up 150 levels to 677–98, where the Precinct Estate Office had its bureau.

'There's a big development between 493 and 554 in the next sector,' one of the clerks told him. 'I don't know whether that's any good to you. Sixty blocks by twenty by fifteen levels.'

'Nothing bigger?' Franz queried.

The clerk looked up. 'Bigger? No. *What* are you looking for – a slight case of agoraphobia?'

Franz straightened the maps spread across the counter. 'I wanted to find an area of more or less continuous development. Two or three hundred blocks long.'

The clerk shook his head and went back to his ledger. 'Didn't you go to engineering school?' he asked scornfully. 'The City won't take it. One hundred blocks is the maximum.'

Franz thanked him and left.

A south-bound express took him to the development in two hours. He left the car at the detour point and walked the three hundred yards to the end of the level.

The street, a seedy but busy thoroughfare of garment shops and small business premises running through the huge ten-mile-thick B.I.R. Industrial Cube, ended abruptly in a tangle of ripped girders and concrete. A steel rail had been erected along the edge and Franz looked down over it into the cavity, three miles long, a mile wide and twelve hundred feet deep, which thousands of engineers and demolition workers were tearing out of the matrix of the City.

Eight hundred feet below him unending lines of trucks and railcars carried away the rubble and debris, and clouds of dust swirled up into the arc-lights blazing down from the roof. As he watched, a chain of explosions ripped along the wall on his left and the whole face slipped and fell slowly towards the floor, revealing a perfect cross-section through fifteen levels of the City.

Franz had seen big developments before, and his own parents had died in the historic QUA County cave-in ten years earlier, when three master-pillars had sheared and two hundred levels of the City had abruptly sunk ten thousand feet, squashing half a million people like flies in a concertina, but the enormous gulf of emptiness still stunned his imagination.

All around him, standing and sitting on the jutting terraces of girders, a silent throng stared down.

'They say they're going to build gardens and parks for us,' an elderly man at Franz's elbow remarked in a patient voice. 'I even heard they might be able to get a tree. It'll be the only tree in the whole county.'

A man in a frayed sweat-shirt spat over the rail. 'That's what they always say. At a dollar a foot promises are all they can waste space on.'

Below them a woman who had been looking out into the air started to simper nervously. Two bystanders took her by the arms and tried to lead her away. The woman began to thresh about and an F.P. came over and pulled her away roughly.

'Poor fool,' the man in the sweat-shirt commented. 'She probably lived out there somewhere. They gave her ninety cents a foot when they took it away from her. She doesn't know yet she'll have to pay a dollar ten to get it back. Now they're going to start charging five cents an hour just to sit up here and watch.'

Franz looked out over the railing for a couple of hours and then bought a postcard from one of the vendors and walked back to the elevator.

He called in to see Gregson before returning to the student dormitory. The Gregsons lived in the West millions on 985th Avenue, in a top three-room flat right under the roof. Franz had known them since his parents' death, but Gregson's mother still regarded him with a mixture of sympathy and suspicion. As she let him in with her customary smile of welcome he noticed her glancing at the detector mounted in the hall.

Gregson was in his room, happily cutting out frames of paper and pasting them on to a great rickety construction that vaguely resembled Franz's model.

'Hullo, Franz. What was it like?'

Franz shrugged. 'Just a development. Worth seeing.'

Gregson pointed to his construction. 'Do you think we can try it out there?'

'We could do.' Franz sat down on the bed. He picked up a paper dart lying beside him and tossed it out of the window. It swam into the street, lazed down in a wide spiral and vanished into the open mouth of the ventilator shaft.

'When are you going to build another model?' Gregson asked.

'I'm not.'

Gregson looked up. 'Why? You've proved your theory.'

'That's not what I'm after.'

'I don't get you, Franz. What are you after?'

'Free space.'

'Free?' Gregson repeated.

Franz nodded. 'In both senses.'

Gregson shook his head sadly and snipped out another paper panel. 'Franz, you're mad.'

Franz stood up. 'Take this room,' he said. 'It's twenty feet by fifteen by ten. Extend its dimensions infinitely. What do you find?'

'A development.'

'*Infinitely!*'

'Non-functional space.'

'Well?' Franz asked patiently.

'The concept's absurd.'

'Why?'

'Because it couldn't exist.'

Franz pounded his forehead in despair. '*Why* couldn't it?'

Gregson gestured with the scissors. 'It's self-contradictory. Like the statement "I am lying". Just a verbal freak. Interesting theoretically, but it's pointless to press it for meaning.' He tossed the scissors on to the table. 'And anyway, do you know how much free space would cost?'

Franz went over to the bookshelf and pulled out one of the volumes. 'Let's have a look at your street atlas.' He turned to the index. 'This gives a thousand levels. KNI County, one hundred thousand cubic miles, population 30 million.'

Gregson nodded.

Franz closed the atlas. 'Two hundred and fifty counties, including KNI, together form the 493rd Sector, and an association of 1,500 adjacent sectors comprise the 298th Local Union.' He broke off and looked at Gregson. 'As a matter of interest, ever heard of it?'

Gregson shook his head. 'No. How did –'

Franz slapped the atlas on to the table. 'Roughly $4 \times 10^{15}$ cubic Great-Miles.' He leaned on the window-ledge. 'Now tell me: what lies beyond the 298th Local Union?'

'Other unions, I suppose,' Gregson said. 'I don't see your difficulty.'

'And beyond those?'

'Farther ones. Why not?'

'For ever?' Franz pressed.

'Well, as far as for ever is.'

'The great street directory in the old Treasury Library on 247th Street is the largest in the county,' Franz said. 'I went down there this morning. It occupies three complete levels. Millions of volumes. But it doesn't extend beyond the 598th Local Union. No one there had any idea what lay farther out. Why not?'

'Why should they?' Gregson asked. 'Franz, what are you driving at?'

Franz walked across to the door. 'Come down to the Bio-History Museum. I'll show you.'

The birds perched on humps of rock or waddled about the sandy paths between the water pools.

'"Archaeopteryx",' Franz read off one of the cage indicators. The bird, lean and mildewed, uttered a painful croak when he fed a handful of beans to it.

'Some of these birds have the remnants of a pectoral girdle,' Franz said. 'Minute fragments of bone embedded in the tissues around their rib cages.'

'Wings?'

'Dr McGhee thinks so.'

They walked out between the lines of cages.

'When does he think they were flying?'

'Before the Foundation,' Franz said. 'Three million years ago.'

When they were outside the museum they started down 859th Avenue. Halfway down the street a dense crowd had gathered and people were packed into the windows and balconies above the elevated, watching a squad of Fire Police break their way into a house.

The bulkheads at either end of the block had been closed and heavy steel traps sealed off the stairways from the levels above and below. The ventilator and exhaust shafts were silent and already the air was stale and soupy.

'Pyros,' Gregson murmured. 'We should have brought our masks.'

'It's only a scare,' Franz said. He pointed to the monoxide detectors which were out everywhere, their long snouts sucking at the air. The dial needles stood safely at zero. 'Let's wait in the restaurant opposite.'

They edged their way over to the restaurant, sat down in the window and ordered coffee. This, like everything else on the menu, was cold. All cooking appliances were thermostated to a maximum 95°F., and only in the more expensive restaurants and hotels was it possible to obtain food that was at most tepid.

Below them in the street a lot of shouting went up. The Fire Police seemed unable to penetrate beyond the ground floor of the house and had started to baton back the crowd. An electric winch was wheeled up and bolted to the girders running below the kerb, and half a dozen heavy steel grabs were carried into the house and hooked round the walls.

Gregson laughed. 'The owners are going to be surprised when they get home.'

Franz was watching the house. It was a narrow shabby dwelling sandwiched between a large wholesale furniture store and a new supermarket.

An old sign running across the front had been painted over and evidently the ownership had recently changed. The present tenants had made a half-hearted attempt to convert the ground floor room into a cheap stand-up diner. The Fire Police appeared to be doing their best to wreck everything, and pies and smashed crockery were strewn all over the pavement.

The noise died away and everyone waited as the winch began to revolve. The hawsers wound in and tautened, and the front wall of the house staggered outwards in rigid jerky movements.

Suddenly there was a yell from the crowd.

Franz raised his arm. 'Up there! Look!'

On the fourth floor a man and woman had come to the window and were looking down helplessly. The man lifted the woman on to the ledge and she crawled out and clung to one of the waste pipes. Bottles were lobbed up at them and bounced down among the police. A wide crack split the house from top to bottom and the floor on which the man was standing dropped and catapulted him backwards out of sight. Then one of the lintels in the first floor snapped and the entire house tipped over and collapsed.

Franz and Gregson stood up, almost knocking over the table.

The crowd surged forward through the cordon. When the dust had settled there was nothing left but a heap of masonry and twisted beams. Embedded in this was the battered figure of the man. Almost smothered by the dust he moved slowly, trying to free himself with one hand, and the crowd started roaring again as one of the grabs wound in and dragged him down under the rubble.

The manager of the restaurant pushed past Franz and leant out of the window, his eyes fixed on the dial of a portable detector. Its needle, like all the others, pointed to zero.

A dozen hoses were playing on the remains of the house and after a few minutes the crowd shifted and began to thin out.

The manager switched off the detector and left the window, nodding to Franz. 'Damn Pyros. You can relax now, boys.'

Franz pointed at the detector. 'Your dial was dead. There wasn't a trace of monoxide anywhere here. How do you know they were Pyros?'

'Don't worry, we know.' He smiled obliquely. 'We don't want that sort of element in this neighbourhood.'

Franz shrugged and sat down. 'I suppose that's one way of getting rid of them.'

The manager eyed Franz. 'That's right, boy. This is a good dollar five neighbourhood.' He smirked to himself. 'Maybe a dollar six now everybody knows about our safety record.'

'Careful, Franz,' Gregson warned him when the manager had gone. 'He may be right. Pyromaniacs do take over small cafés and food bars.'

Franz stirred his coffee. 'Dr McGhee estimates that at least fifteen per cent of the City's population are submerged Pyros. He's convinced the number's growing and that eventually the whole City will flame-out.'

He pushed away his coffee. 'How much money have you got?'

'On me?'

'Altogether.'

'About thirty dollars.'

'I've saved fifteen,' Franz said. 'Forty-five dollars; that should be enough for three or four weeks.'

'Where?' Gregson asked.

'On a Supersleeper.'

'Super –!' Gregson broke off, alarmed. 'Three or four weeks! What do you mean?'

'There's only one way to find out,' Franz explained calmly. 'I can't just sit here thinking. Somewhere there's free space and I'll ride the Sleeper until I find it. Will you lend me your thirty dollars?'

'But Franz –'

'If I don't find anything within a couple of weeks I'll change tracks and come back.'

'But the ticket will cost . . .' Gregson searched '. . . billions. Forty-five dollars won't even get you out of the Sector.'

'That's just for coffee and sandwiches,' Franz said. 'The ticket will be free.' He looked up from the table. 'You know . . .'

Gregson shook his head doubtfully. 'Can you try that on the Supersleepers?'

'Why not? If they query it I'll say I'm going back the long way round. Greg, will you?'

'I don't know if I should.' Gregson played helplessly with his coffee. 'Franz, how can there be free space? How?'

'That's what I'm going to find out,' Franz said. 'Think of it as my first physics practical.'

Passenger distances on the transport system were measured point to point by the application of $a = \sqrt{b^2 + c^2 + d^2}$. The actual itinerary taken was the passenger's responsibility, and as long as he remained within the system he could choose any route he liked. Tickets were checked only at the station exits, where necessary surcharges were collected by an inspector. If the passenger was unable to pay the surcharge – ten cents a mile – he was sent back to his original destination.

Franz and Gregson entered the station on 984th Street and went over to the large console where tickets were automatically dispensed. Franz put in a penny and pressed the destination button marked 984. The machine rumbled, coughed out a ticket, and the change slot gave him back his coin.

'Well, Greg, goodbye,' Franz said as they moved towards the barrier. 'I'll see you in about two weeks. They're covering me down at the dormitory. Tell Sanger I'm on Fire Duty.'

'What if you don't get back, Franz?' Gregson asked. 'Suppose they take you off the Sleeper?'

'How can they? I've got my ticket.'

'And if you do find free space? Will you come back then?'

'If I can.'

Franz patted Gregson on the shoulder reassuringly, waved and disappeared among the commuters.

He took the local Suburban Green to the district junction in the next county. The Green Line train travelled at an interrupted 70 m.p.h. and the ride took two and a half hours.

At the junction he changed to an express elevator which lifted him out of the sector in ninety minutes, at 400 m.p.h. Another fifty minutes in a Through-Sector Special brought him to the Mainline Terminus which served the Union.

There he bought a coffee and gathered his determination together. Supersleepers ran east and west, halting at this and every tenth station. The next arrived in seventy-two hours time, westbound.

The Mainline Terminus was the largest station Franz had seen, a mile-long cavern thirty levels in depth. Hundreds of elevator shafts sank through the station and the maze of platforms, escalators, restaurants, hotels and theatres seemed like an exaggerated replica of the City itself.

Getting his bearings from one of the information booths, Franz made his way up an escalator to Tier 15, where the Supersleepers berthed. Running the length of the station were two steel vacuum tunnels each three hundred feet in diameter, supported at thirty-four intervals by huge concrete buttresses.

Franz walked along the platform and stopped by the telescopic gangway that plunged into one of the airlocks. Two hundred and seventy degrees true, he thought, gazing up at the curving underbelly of the tunnel. It must come out somewhere. He had forty-five dollars in his pocket, sufficient coffee and sandwich money to last him three weeks, six if he needed it, time anyway to find the City's end.

He passed the next three days nursing cups of coffee in any of the thirty cafeterias in the station, reading discarded newspapers and sleeping in the local Red trains which ran four-hour journeys round the nearest sector.

When at last the Supersleeper came in he joined the small group of Fire Police and municipal officials waiting by the gangway, and followed them into the train. There were two cars; a sleeper which no one used, and a day coach.

Franz took an inconspicuous corner seat near one of the indicator panels in the day coach, and pulled out his notebook ready to make his first entry.

*1st Day: West 270°. Union 4,350.*

'Coming out for a drink?' a Fire Captain across the aisle asked. 'We have a ten-minute break here.'

'No thanks,' Franz said. 'I'll hold your seat for you.'

Dollar five a cubic foot. Free space, he knew, would bring the price down. There was no need to leave the train or make too many inquiries. All he had to do was borrow a paper and watch the market averages.

*2nd Day: West 270°. Union 7,550.*

'They're slowly cutting down on these Sleepers,' someone told him. 'Everyone sits in the day coach. Look at this one. Seats sixty, and only four people in it. There's no need to move around. People are staying where they are. In a few years there'll be nothing left but the suburban services.'

*97 cents.*

At an average of a dollar a cubic foot, Franz calculated idly, it's so far worth about $4 \times 10^{27}$.

'Going on to the next stop, are you? Well, goodbye, young fellow.'

Few of the passengers stayed on the Sleeper for more than three or four hours. By the end of the second day Franz's back and neck ached from the constant acceleration. He managed to take a little exercise walking up and down the narrow corridor in the deserted sleeping coach, but had to spend most of his time strapped to his seat as the train began its long braking runs into the next station.

*3rd Day: West 270°. Federation 657.*

'Interesting, but how could you demonstrate it?'

'It's just an odd idea of mine,' Franz said, screwing up the sketch and dropping it in the disposal chute. 'Hasn't any real application.'

'Curious, but it rings a bell somewhere.'

Franz sat up. 'Do you mean you've seen machines like this? In a newspaper or a book?'

'No, no. In a dream.'

Every half day's run the pilot signed the log, the crew handed over to their opposites on an Eastbound sleeper, crossed the platform and started back for home.

*125 cents.*

$8 \times 10^{28}$.

*4th Day: West 270°. Federation 1,225.*

'Dollar a cubic foot. You in the estate business?'

'Starting up,' Franz said easily. 'I'm hoping to open a new office of my own.'

He played cards, bought coffee and rolls from the dispenser in the washroom, watched the indicator panel and listened to the talk around him.

'Believe me, a time will come when each union, each sector, almost I might say, each street and avenue will have achieved complete local independence. Equipped with its own power services, aerators, reservoirs, farm laboratories ...'

The car bore.

$6 \times 10^{75}$.

*5th Day: West 270°. 17th Greater Federation.*

At a kiosk on the station Franz bought a clip of razor blades and glanced at the brochure put out by the local chamber of commerce.

'12,000 levels, 98 cents a foot, unique Elm Drive, fire safety records unequalled ...'

He went back to the train, shaved, and counted the thirty dollars left. He was now ninety-five million Great-Miles from the suburban station on 984th Street and he knew he could not delay his return much longer. Next time he would save up a couple of thousand.

$7 \times 10^{127}$.

*7th Day: West 270°. 212th Metropolitan Empire.*

Franz peered at the indicator.

'Aren't we stopping here?' he asked a man three seats away. 'I wanted to find out the market average.'

'Varies. Anything from fifty cents a –'

'Fifty!' Franz shot back, jumping up. 'When's the next stop? I've got to get off!'

'Not here, son.' He put out a restraining hand. 'This is Night Town. You in real estate?'

Franz nodded, holding himself back. 'I thought ...'

'Relax.' He came and sat opposite Franz. 'It's just one big slum. Dead areas. In places it goes as low as five cents. There are no services, no power.'

It took them two days to pass through.

'City Authority are starting to seal it off,' the man told him. 'Huge blocks. It's the only thing they can do. What happens to the people inside I hate to think.' He chewed on a sandwich. 'Strange, but there are a lot of these black areas. You don't hear about them, but they're growing. Starts in a back street in some ordinary dollar neighbourhood; a bottleneck in the sewage disposal system, not enough ash cans, and before you know it – a million cubic miles have gone back to jungle. They try a relief scheme, pump in a little cyanide, and then – brick it up. Once they do that they're closed for good.'

Franz nodded, listening to the dull humming air.

'Eventually there'll be nothing left but these black areas. The City will be one huge cemetery!'

*10th Day: East 90°. 755th Greater Metropolitan –*

'Wait!' Franz leapt out of his seat and stared at the indicator panel.

'What's the matter?' someone opposite asked.

'East!' Franz shouted. He banged the panel sharply with his hand but the lights held. 'Has this train changed direction?'

'No, it's eastbound,' another of the passengers told him. 'Are you on the wrong train?'

'It should be heading west,' Franz insisted. 'It has been for the last ten days.'

'Ten days!' the man exclaimed. 'Have you been on this sleeper for ten days?'

Franz went forward and found the car attendant. 'Which way is this train going? West?'

The attendant shook his head. 'East, sir. It's always been going east.'

'You're crazy,' Franz snapped. 'I want to see the pilot's log.'

'I'm afraid that isn't possible. May I see your ticket, sir?'

'Listen,' Franz said weakly, all the accumulated frustration of the last twenty years mounting inside him. 'I've been on this . . .'

He stopped and went back to his seat.

The five other passengers watched him carefully.

'Ten days,' one of them was still repeating in an awed voice.

Two minutes later someone came and asked Franz for his ticket.

'And of course it was completely in order,' the police surgeon commented. 'Strangely enough there's no regulation to prevent anyone else doing the same thing. I used to go for free rides myself when I was younger, though I never tried anything like your journey.'

He went back to the desk. 'We'll drop the charge,' he said. 'You're not a vagrant in any indictable sense, and the transport authorities can do nothing against you. How this curvature was built into the system they can't explain, it seems to be some inherent feature of the City itself. Now about yourself. Are you going to continue this search?'

'I want to build a flying machine,' M. said carefully. 'There must be free space somewhere. I don't know . . . perhaps on the lower levels.'

The surgeon stood up. 'I'll see the sergeant and get him to hand you over to one of our psychiatrists. He'll be able to help you with your dreams!'

The surgeon hesitated before opening the door. 'Look,' he began to explain, 'you can't get out of time, can you? Subjectively it's a plastic dimension, but whatever you do to yourself you'll never be able to stop that clock' – he pointed to the one on the desk – 'or make it run backwards. In exactly the same way you can't get out of the City.'

'The analogy doesn't hold,' M. said. He gestured at the walls around them and the lights in the street outside. 'All this was built by us. The question nobody can answer is: what was here before we built it?'

'It's always been here,' the surgeon said. 'Not these particular bricks and girders, but others before them. You accept that time has no beginning and no end. The City is as old as time and continuous with it.'

'The first bricks were laid by someone,' M. insisted. 'There was the Foundation.'

'A myth. Only the scientists believe in that, and even they don't try to make too much of it. Most of them privately admit that the Foundation Stone is nothing more than a superstition. We pay it lip service out of convenience, and because it gives us a sense of tradition. Obviously there can't have been a first brick. If there was, how can you explain who laid it and, even more difficult, where they came from?'

'There must be free space somewhere,' M. said doggedly. 'The City must have bounds.'

'*Why?*' the surgeon asked. 'It can't be floating in the middle of nowhere. Or is that what you're trying to believe?'

M. sank back limply. 'No.'

The surgeon watched M. silently for a few minutes and paced back to the desk. 'This peculiar fixation of yours puzzles me. You're caught between what the psychiatrists call paradoxical faces. I suppose you haven't misinterpreted something you've heard about the Wall?'

M. looked up. 'Which wall?'

The surgeon nodded to himself. 'Some advanced opinion maintains that there's a wall around the City, through which it's impossible to penetrate. I don't pretend to understand the theory myself. It's far too abstract and sophisticated. Anyway I suspect they've confused this Wall with the bricked-up black areas you passed through on the Sleeper. I prefer the accepted view that the City stretches out in all directions without limits.'

He went over to the door. 'Wait here, and I'll see about getting you a probationary release. Don't worry, the psychiatrists will straighten everything out for you.'

When the surgeon had left M. stared at the floor, too exhausted to feel relieved. He stood up and stretched himself, walking unsteadily round the room.

Outside the last pilot lights were going out and the patrolman on the catwalk under the roof was using his torch. A police car roared down one of the avenues crossing the street, its rails screaming. Three lights snapped on along the street and then one by one went off again.

M. wondered why Gregson hadn't come down to the station. Then the calendar on the desk riveted his attention. The date exposed on the fly leaf was 12 August. That was the day he had started off on his journey – exactly three weeks ago.

*Today!*

\* \* \*

Take a westbound Green to 298th Street, cross over at the intersection and get a Red elevator up to Level 237. Walk down to the station on Route 175, change to a 438 suburban and go down to 795th Street. Take a Blue line to the Plaza, get off at 4th and 275th, turn left at the roundabout and –
    You're back where you first started from.
    $Hell $\times$ $10^n$.

**1957**

# VENUS SMILES

Low notes on a high afternoon.

As we drove away after the unveiling my secretary said, 'Mr Hamilton, I suppose you realize what a fool you've made of yourself?'

'Don't sound so prim,' I told her. 'How was I to know Lorraine Drexel would produce something like that?'

'Five thousand dollars,' she said reflectively. 'It's nothing but a piece of old scrap iron. And the noise! Didn't you look at her sketches? What's the Fine Arts Committee for?'

My secretaries have always talked to me like this, and just then I could understand why. I stopped the car under the trees at the end of the square and looked back. The chairs had been cleared away and already a small crowd had gathered around the statue, staring up at it curiously. A couple of tourists were banging one of the struts, and the thin metal skeleton shuddered weakly. Despite this, a monotonous and high-pitched wailing sounded from the statue across the pleasant morning air, grating the teeth of passers-by.

'Raymond Mayo is having it dismantled this afternoon,' I said. 'If it hasn't already been done for us. I wonder where Miss Drexel is?'

'Don't worry, you won't see her in Vermilion Sands again. I bet she's halfway to Red Beach by now.'

I patted Carol on the shoulder. 'Relax. You looked beautiful in your new skirt. The Medicis probably felt like this about Michelangelo. Who are we to judge?'

'*You* are,' she said. 'You were on the committee, weren't you?'

'Darling,' I explained patiently. 'Sonic sculpture is the thing. You're trying to fight a battle the public lost thirty years ago.'

We drove back to my office in a thin silence. Carol was annoyed because she had been forced to sit beside me on the platform when the audience began to heckle my speech at the unveiling, but even so the morning had been disastrous on every count. What might be perfectly acceptable at Expo 75 or the Venice Biennale was all too obviously passé at Vermilion Sands.

When we had decided to commission a sonic sculpture for the square in the centre of Vermilion Sands, Raymond Mayo and I had agreed that we should patronize a local artist. There were dozens of professional sculptors in Vermilion Sands, but only three had deigned to present themselves before the committee. The first two we saw were large, bearded men with enormous fists and impossible schemes – one for a hundred-foot-high vibrating aluminium pylon, and the other for a vast booming family group that involved over fifteen tons of basalt mounted on a megalithic step-pyramid. Each had taken an hour to be argued out of the committee room.

The third was a woman: Lorraine Drexel. This elegant and autocratic creature in a cartwheel hat, with her eyes like black orchids, was a sometime model and intimate of Giacometti and John Cage. Wearing a blue crêpe de Chine dress ornamented with lace serpents and other art nouveau emblems, she sat before us like some fugitive Salome from the world of Aubrey Beardsley. Her immense eyes regarded us with an almost hypnotic calm, as if she had discovered that very moment some unique quality in these two amiable dilettantes of the Fine Arts Committee.

She had lived in Vermilion Sands for only three months, arriving via Berlin, Calcutta and the Chicago New Arts Centre. Most of her sculpture to date had been scored for various Tantric and Hindu hymns, and I remembered her brief affair with a world-famous pop-singer, later killed in a car crash, who had been an enthusiastic devotee of the sitar. At the time, however, we had given no thought to the whining quarter-tones of this infernal instrument, so grating on the Western ear. She had shown us an album of her sculptures, interesting chromium constructions that compared favourably with the run of illustrations in the latest art magazines. Within half an hour we had drawn up a contract.

I saw the statue for the first time that afternoon thirty seconds before I started my speech to the specially selected assembly of Vermilion Sands notables. Why none of us had bothered to look at it beforehand I fail to understand. The title printed on the invitation cards – 'Sound and Quantum: Generative Synthesis 3' – had seemed a little odd, and the general shape of the shrouded statue even more suspicious. I was expecting a stylized human figure but the structure under the acoustic drapes had the proportions of a medium-sized radar aerial. However, Lorraine Drexel sat beside me on the stand, her bland eyes surveying the crowd below. A dream-like smile gave her the look of a tamed Mona Lisa.

What we saw after Raymond Mayo pulled the tape I tried not to think about. With its pedestal the statue was twelve feet high. Three spindly metal legs, ornamented with spikes and crosspieces, reached up from the plinth to a triangular apex. Clamped on to this was a jagged structure that at first sight seemed to be an old Buick radiator grille. It had been bent into a rough U five feet across, and the two arms jutted out horizontally, a single row of sonic cores, each about a foot long, poking up like the teeth of an enormous comb. Welded on apparently at random all over the statue were twenty or thirty filigree vanes.

That was all. The whole structure of scratched chromium had a blighted look like a derelict antenna. Startled a little by the first shrill whoops emitted by the statue, I began my speech and was about halfway through when I noticed that Lorraine Drexel had left her seat beside me. People in the audience were beginning to stand up and cover their ears, shouting to Raymond to replace the acoustic drape. A hat sailed through the air over my head and landed neatly on one of the sonic cores. The statue was now giving out an intermittent high-pitched whine, a sitar-like caterwauling that seemed to pull apart the sutures of my skull. Responding to the boos and protests, it suddenly began to whoop erratically, the horn-like sounds confusing the traffic on the far side of the square.

As the audience began to leave their seats *en masse* I stuttered inaudibly to the end of my speech, the wailing of the statue interrupted by shouts and jeers. Then Carol tugged me sharply by the arm, her eyes flashing. Raymond Mayo pointed with a nervous hand.

The three of us were alone on the platform, the rows of overturned chairs reaching across the square. Standing twenty yards from the statue, which had now begun to whimper plaintively, was Lorraine Drexel. I expected to see a look of fury and outrage on her face, but instead her unmoving eyes showed the calm and implacable contempt of a grieving widow insulted at her husband's funeral. As we waited awkwardly, watching the wind carry away the torn programme cards, she turned on a diamond heel and walked across the square.

No one else wanted anything to do with the statue, so I was finally presented with it. Lorraine Drexel left Vermilion Sands the day it was dismantled. Raymond spoke briefly to her on the telephone before she went. I presumed she would be rather unpleasant and didn't bother to listen in on the extension.

'Well?' I asked. 'Does she want it back?'

'No.' Raymond seemed slightly preoccupied. 'She said it belonged to us.'

'You and me?'

'Everybody.' Raymond helped himself to the decanter of scotch on the veranda table. 'Then she started laughing.'

'Good. What at?'

'I don't know. She just said that we'd grow to like it.'

There was nowhere else to put the statue so I planted it out in the garden. Without the stone pedestal it was only six feet high. Shielded by the shrubbery, it had quietened down and now emitted a pleasant melodic harmony, its soft rondos warbling across the afternoon heat. The sitar-like twangs, which the statue had broadcast in the square like some pathetic love-call from Lorraine Drexel to her dead lover, had vanished completely, almost as if the statue had been rescored. I had been so stampeded by the disastrous unveiling that I had had little chance to see it and I thought it looked a lot better in the garden than it had done in Vermilion Sands, the chromium struts and abstract shapes standing out against the desert like something in a vodka advertisement. After a few days I could almost ignore it.

A week or so later we were out on the terrace after lunch, lounging back in the deck chairs. I was nearly asleep when Carol said, 'Mr Hamilton, I think it's moving.'

'What's moving?'

Carol was sitting up, head cocked to one side. 'The statue. It looks different.'

I focused my eyes on the statue twenty feet away. The radiator grille at the top had canted around slightly but the three stems still seemed more or less upright.

'The rain last night must have softened the ground,' I said. I listened to the quiet melodies carried on the warm eddies of air, and then lay back drowsily. I heard Carol light a cigarette with four matches and walk across the veranda.

When I woke in an hour's time she was sitting straight up in the deck chair, a frown creasing her forehead.

'Swallowed a bee?' I asked. 'You look worried.'

Then something caught my eye.

I watched the statue for a moment. 'You're right. It is moving.'

Carol nodded. The statue's shape had altered perceptibly. The grille had spread into an open gondola whose sonic cores seemed to feel at the sky, and the three stem-pieces were wider apart. All the angles seemed different.

'I thought you'd notice it eventually,' Carol said as we walked over to it. 'What's it made of?'

'Wrought iron – I think. There must be a lot of copper or lead in it. The heat is making it sag.'

'Then why is it sagging upwards instead of down?'

I touched one of the shoulder struts. It was springing elastically as the air moved across the vanes and went on vibrating against my palm. I gripped it in both hands and tried to keep it rigid. A low but discernible pulse pumped steadily against me.

I backed away from it, wiping the flaking chrome off my hands. The Mozartian harmonies had gone, and the statue was now producing a series of low Mahler-like chords. As Carol stood there in her bare feet I remembered that the height specification we had given to Lorraine Drexel had been exactly two metres. But the statue was a good three feet higher than Carol, the gondola at least six or seven across. The spars and struts looked thicker and stronger.

'Carol,' I said. 'Get me a file, would you? There are some in the garage.'

She came back with two files and a hacksaw.

'Are you going to cut it down?' she asked hopefully.

'Darling, this is an original Drexel.' I took one of the files. 'I just want to convince myself that I'm going insane.'

I started cutting a series of small notches all over the statue, making sure they were exactly the width of the file apart. The metal was soft and worked easily; on the surface there was a lot of rust but underneath it had a bright sappy glint.

'All right,' I said when I had finished. 'Let's go and have a drink.'

We sat on the veranda and waited. I fixed my eyes on the statue and could have sworn that it didn't move. But when we went back an hour later the gondola had swung right round again, hanging down over us like an immense metal mouth.

There was no need to check the notch intervals against the file. They were all at least double the original distance apart.

'Mr Hamilton,' Carol said. 'Look at this.'

She pointed to one of the spikes. Poking through the outer scale of chrome were a series of sharp little nipples. One or two were already beginning to hollow themselves. Unmistakably they were incipient sonic cores.

Carefully I examined the rest of the statue. All over it new shoots of metal were coming through: arches, barbs, sharp double helixes, twisting the original statue into a thicker and more elaborate construction. A medley of half-familiar sounds, fragments of a dozen overtures and symphonies, murmured all over it. The statue was well over twelve feet high. I felt one of the heavy struts and the pulse was stronger, beating steadily through the metal, as if it was thrusting itself on to the sound of its own music.

Carol was watching me with a pinched and worried look.

'Take it easy,' I said. 'It's only growing.'

We went back to the veranda and watched.

By six o'clock that evening it was the size of a small tree. A spirited simultaneous rendering of Brahms's *Academic Festival Overture* and Rachmaninov's First Piano Concerto trumpeted across the garden.

'The strangest thing about it,' Raymond said the next morning, raising his voice above the din, 'is that it's still a Drexel.'

'Still a piece of sculpture, you mean?'

'More than that. Take any section of it and you'll find the original motifs being repeated. Each vane, each helix has all the authentic Drexel mannerisms, almost as if she herself were shaping it. Admittedly, this penchant for the late Romantic composers is a little out of keeping with all that sitar twanging, but that's rather a good thing, if you ask me. You can probably expect to hear some Beethoven any moment now – the Pastoral Symphony, I would guess.'

'Not to mention all five piano concertos – played at once,' I said sourly. Raymond's loquacious delight in this musical monster out in the garden annoyed me. I closed the veranda windows, wishing that he himself had installed the statue in the living room of his downtown apartment. 'I take it that it won't go on growing for ever?'

Carol handed Raymond another scotch. 'What do you think we ought to do?'

Raymond shrugged. 'Why worry?' he said airily. 'When it starts tearing the house down cut it back. Thank God we had it dismantled. If this had happened in Vermilion Sands . . .'

Carol touched my arm. 'Mr Hamilton, perhaps that's what Lorraine Drexel expected. She wanted it to start spreading all over the town, the music driving everyone crazy –'

'Careful,' I warned her. 'You're running away with yourself. As Raymond says, we can chop it up any time we want to and melt the whole thing down.'

'Why don't you, then?'

'I want to see how far it'll go,' I said. In fact my motives were more mixed. Clearly, before she left, Lorraine Drexel had set some perverse jinx at work within the statue, a bizarre revenge on us all for deriding her handiwork. As Raymond had said, the present babel of symphonic music had no connection with the melancholy cries the statue had first emitted. Had those forlorn chords been intended to be a requiem for her dead lover – or even, conceivably, the beckoning calls of a still unsurrendered heart? Whatever her motives, they had now vanished into this strange travesty lying across my garden.

I watched the statue reaching slowly across the lawn. It had collapsed under its own weight and lay on its side in a huge angular spiral, twenty feet long and about fifteen feet high, like the skeleton of a futuristic whale. Fragments of the *Nutcracker Suite* and Mendelssohn's 'Italian' Symphony sounded from it, overlaid by sudden blaring excerpts from the closing movements of Grieg's Piano Concerto. The selection of these hack classics seemed deliberately designed to get on my nerves.

I had been up with the statue most of the night. After Carol went to bed I drove my car on to the strip of lawn next to the house and turned on the headlamps. The statue stood out almost luminously in the darkness, booming away to itself, more and more of the sonic cores budding out in the yellow glare of the lights. Gradually it lost its original shape; the toothed grille enveloped itself and then put out new struts and barbs that spiralled upwards, each throwing off secondary and tertiary shoots in its turn. Shortly after midnight it began to lean and then suddenly toppled over.

By now its movement was corkscrew. The plinth had been carried into the air and hung somewhere in the middle of the tangle, revolving slowly, and the main foci of activity were at either end. The growth rate was accelerating. We watched a new shoot emerge. As one of the struts curved round a small knob poked through the flaking chrome. Within a minute it grew into a spur an inch long, thickened, began to curve and five minutes later had developed into a full-throated sonic core twelve inches long.

Raymond pointed to two of my neighbours standing on the roofs of their houses a hundred yards away, alerted by the music carried across to them. 'You'll soon have everyone in Vermilion Sands out here. If I were you, I'd throw an acoustic drape over it.'

'If I could find one the size of a tennis court. It's time we did something, anyway. See if you can trace Lorraine Drexel. I'm going to find out what makes this statue go.'

Using the hacksaw, I cut off a two-foot limb and handed it to Dr Blackett, an eccentric but amiable neighbour who sometimes dabbled in sculpture himself. We walked back to the comparative quiet of the veranda. The single sonic core emitted a few random notes, fragments from a quartet by Webern.

'What do you make of it?'

'Remarkable,' Blackett said. He bent the bar between his hands. 'Almost plastic.' He looked back at the statue. 'Definite circumnutation there. Probably phototropic as well. Hmm, almost like a plant.'

'Is it alive?'

Blackett laughed. 'My dear Hamilton, of course not. How can it be?'

'Well, where is it getting its new material? From the ground?'

'From the air. I don't know yet, but I imagine it's rapidly synthesizing an allotropic form of ferrous oxide. In other words, a purely physical rearrangement of the constituents of rust.' Blackett stroked his heavy brush moustache and stared at the statue with a dream-like eye. 'Musically, it's rather curious – an appalling conglomeration of almost every bad note ever composed. Somewhere the statue must have suffered some severe sonic trauma. It's behaving as if it had been left for a week in a railroad shunting yard. Any idea what happened?'

'Not really.' I avoided his glance as we walked back to the statue. It seemed to sense us coming and began to trumpet out the opening bars of Elgar's 'Pomp and Circumstance' march. Deliberately breaking step, I said to Blackett: 'So in fact all I have to do to silence the thing is chop it up into two-foot lengths?'

'If it worries you. However, it would be interesting to leave it, assuming you can stand the noise. There's absolutely no danger of it going on indefinitely.' He reached up and felt one of the spars. 'Still firm, but I'd say it was almost there. It will soon start getting pulpy like an over-ripe fruit and begin to shred off and disintegrate, playing itself out, one hopes, with Mozart's *Requiem* and the finale of the *Götterdämmerung*.' He smiled at me, showing his strange teeth. 'Die, if you prefer it.'

However, he had reckoned completely without Lorraine Drexel.

At six o'clock the next morning I was woken by the noise. The statue was now fifty feet long and crossing the flower beds on either side of the garden. It sounded as if a complete orchestra were performing some Mad Hatter's symphony out in the centre of the lawn. At the far end, by the rockery, the sonic cores were still working their way through the Romantic catalogue, a babel of Mendelssohn, Schubert and Grieg, but near the veranda the cores were beginning to emit the jarring and syncopated rhythms of Stravinsky and Stockhausen.

I woke Carol and we ate a nervous breakfast.

'Mr Hamilton!' she shouted. 'You've got to stop it!' The nearest tendrils were only five feet from the glass doors of the veranda. The largest limbs were over three inches in diameter and the pulse thudded through them like water under pressure in a fire hose.

When the first police cars cruised past down the road I went into the garage and found the hacksaw.

The metal was soft and the blade sank through it quickly. I left the pieces I cut off in a heap to one side, random notes sounding out into the air. Separated from the main body of the statue, the fragments were almost inactive, as Dr Blackett had stated. By two o'clock that afternoon I had cut back about half the statue and got it down to manageable proportions.

'That should hold it,' I said to Carol. I walked round and lopped off a few of the noisier spars. 'Tomorrow I'll finish it off altogether.'

I wasn't in the least surprised when Raymond called and said that there was no trace anywhere of Lorraine Drexel.

At two o'clock that night I woke as a window burst across the floor of my bedroom. A huge metal helix hovered like a claw through the fractured pane, its sonic core screaming down at me.

A half-moon was up, throwing a thin grey light over the garden. The statue had sprung back and was twice as large as it had been at its peak the previous morning. It lay all over the garden in a tangled mesh, like the skeleton of a crushed building. Already the advance tendrils had reached the bedroom windows, while others had climbed over the garage and were sprouting downwards through the roof, tearing away the galvanized metal sheets.

All over the statue thousands of sonic cores gleamed in the light thrown down from the window. At last in unison, they hymned out the finale of Bruckner's *Apocalyptic Symphony.*

I went into Carol's bedroom, fortunately on the other side of the house, and made her promise to stay in bed. Then I telephoned Raymond Mayo. He came around within an hour, an oxyacetylene torch and cylinders he had begged from a local contractor in the back seat of his car.

The statue was growing almost as fast as we could cut it back, but by the time the first light came up at a quarter to six we had beaten it.

Dr Blackett watched us slice through the last fragments of the statue. 'There's a section down in the rockery that might just be audible. I think it would be worth saving.'

I wiped the rust-stained sweat from my face and shook my head. 'No. I'm sorry, but believe me, once is enough.'

Blackett nodded in sympathy, and stared gloomily across the heaps of scrap iron which were all that remained of the statue.

Carol, looking a little stunned by everything, was pouring coffee and brandy. As we slumped back in two of the deck chairs, arms and faces black with rust and metal filings, I reflected wryly that no one could accuse the Fine Arts Committee of not devoting itself wholeheartedly to its projects.

I went off on a final tour of the garden, collecting the section Blackett had mentioned, then guided in the local contractor who had arrived with his truck. It took him and his two men an hour to load the scrap – an estimated ton and a half – into the vehicle.

'What do I do with it?' he asked as he climbed into the cab. 'Take it to the museum?'

'No!' I almost screamed. 'Get rid of it. Bury it somewhere, or better still, have it melted down. As soon as possible.'

When they had gone Blackett and I walked around the garden together. It looked as if a shrapnel shell had exploded over it. Huge divots were strewn all over the place, and what grass had not been ripped up by the statue had been trampled away by us. Iron filings lay on the lawn like dust, a faint ripple of lost notes carried away on the steepening sunlight.

Blackett bent down and scooped up a handful of grains. 'Dragon's teeth. You'll look out of the window tomorrow and see the B Minor Mass coming up.' He let it run out between his fingers. 'However, I suppose that's the end of it.'

He couldn't have been more wrong.

Lorraine Drexel sued us. She must have come across the newspaper reports and realized her opportunity. I don't know where she had been hiding, but her lawyers materialized quickly enough, waving the original contract and pointing to the clause in which we guaranteed to protect the statue from any damage that might be done to it by vandals, livestock or other public nuisance. Her main accusation concerned the damage we had done to her reputation – if we had decided not to exhibit the statue we should have supervised its removal to some place of safekeeping, not openly dismembered it and then sold off the fragments to a scrap dealer. This deliberate affront had, her lawyers insisted, cost her commissions to a total of at least fifty thousand dollars.

At the preliminary hearings we soon realized that, absurdly, our one big difficulty was going to be proving to anyone who had not been there that the statue had actually started growing. With luck we managed to get several postponements, and Raymond and I tried to trace what we could of the statue. All we found were three small struts, now completely inert, rusting in the sand on the edge of one of the junkyards in Red Beach. Apparently taking me at my word, the contractor had shipped the rest of the statue to a steel mill to be melted down.

Our only case now rested on what amounted to a plea of self-defence.

Raymond and myself testified that the statue had started to grow, and then Blackett delivered a long homily to the judge on what he believed to be the musical shortcomings of the statue. The judge, a crusty and short-tempered old man of the hanging school, immediately decided that we were trying to pull his leg. We were finished from the start.

The final judgment was not delivered until ten months after we had first unveiled the statue in the centre of Vermilion Sands, and the verdict, when it came, was no surprise.

Lorraine Drexel was awarded thirty thousand dollars.

'It looks as if we should have taken the pylon after, all,' I said to Carol as we left the courtroom. 'Even the step-pyramid would have been less trouble.'

Raymond joined us and we went out on to the balcony at the end of the corridor for some air.

'Never mind,' Carol said bravely. 'At least it's all over with.'

I looked out over the rooftops of Vermilion Sands, thinking about the thirty thousand dollars and wondering whether we would have to pay it ourselves.

The court building was a new one and by an unpleasant irony ours had been the first case to be heard there. Much of the floor and plasterwork had still to be completed, and the balcony was untiled. I was standing on an exposed steel crossbeam; one or two floors down someone must have been driving a rivet into one of the girders, and the beam under my feet vibrated soothingly.

Then I noticed that there were no sounds of riveting going on anywhere, and that the movement under my feet was not so much a vibration as a low rhythmic pulse.

I bent down and pressed my hands against the beam. Raymond and Carol watched me curiously. 'Mr Hamilton, what is it?' Carol asked when I stood up.

'Raymond,' I said. 'How long ago did they first start on this building? The steel framework, anyway.'

'Four months, I think. Why?'

'Four.' I nodded slowly. 'Tell me, how long would you say it took any random piece of scrap iron to be reprocessed through a steel mill and get back into circulation?'

'Years, if it lay around in the wrong junkyards.'

'But if it had actually arrived at the steel mill?'

'A month or so. Less.'

I started to laugh, pointing to the girder. 'Feel that! Go on, feel it!'

Frowning at me, they knelt down and pressed their hands to the girder. Then Raymond looked up at me sharply.

I stopped laughing. 'Did you feel it?'

'Feel it?' Raymond repeated. 'I can *hear* it. Lorraine Drexel – the statue. It's here!'

Carol was patting the girder and listening to it. 'I think it's humming,' she said, puzzled. 'It sounds like the statue.'

When I started to laugh again Raymond held my arm. 'Snap out of it, the whole building will be singing soon!'

'I know,' I said weakly. 'And it won't be just this building either.' I took Carol by the arm. 'Come on, let's see if it's started.'

We went up to the top floor. The plasterers were about to move in and there were trestles and laths all over the place. The walls were still bare brick, girders at fifteen-foot intervals between them.

We didn't have to look very far.

Jutting out from one of the steel joists below the roof was a long metal helix, hollowing itself slowly into a delicate sonic core. Without moving, we counted a dozen others. A faint twanging sound came from them, like early arrivals at a rehearsal of some vast orchestra of sitar-players, seated on every plain and hilltop of the earth. I remembered when we had last heard the music, as Lorraine Drexel sat beside me at the unveiling in Vermilion Sands. The statue had made its call to her dead lover, and now the refrain was to be taken up again.

'An authentic Drexel,' I said. 'All the mannerisms. Nothing much to look at yet, but wait till it really gets going.'

Raymond wandered round, his mouth open. 'It'll tear the building apart. Just think of the noise.'

Carol was staring up at one of the shoots. 'Mr Hamilton, you said they'd melted it all down.'

'They did, angel. So it got back into circulation, touching off all the other metal it came into contact with. Lorraine Drexel's statue is here, in this building, in a dozen other buildings, in ships and planes and a million new automobiles. Even if it's only one screw or ball-bearing, that'll be enough to trigger the rest off.'

'They'll stop it,' Carol said.

'They might,' I admitted. 'But it'll probably get back again somehow. A few pieces always will.' I put my arm round her waist and began to dance to the strange abstracted music, for some reason as beautiful now as Lorraine Drexel's wistful eyes. 'Did you say it was all over? Carol, it's only just beginning. The whole world will be singing.'

**· 1957**

# MANHOLE 69

For the first few days all went well.

'Keep away from windows and don't think about it,' Dr Neill told them. 'As far as you're concerned it was just another compulsion. At eleven thirty or twelve go down to the gym and throw a ball around, play some table-tennis. At two they're running a film for you in the Neurology theatre. Read the papers for a couple of hours, put on some records. I'll be down at six. By seven you'll be in a manic swing.'

'Any chance of a sudden blackout, Doctor?' Avery asked.

'Absolutely none,' Neill said. 'If you get tired, rest, of course. That's the one thing you'll probably have a little difficulty getting used to. Remember, you're still using only 3,500 calories, so your kinetic level – and you'll notice this most by day – will be about a third lower. You'll have to take things easier, make allowances. Most of these have been programmed in for you, but start learning to play chess, focus that inner eye.'

Gorrell leaned forward. 'Doctor,' he asked, 'if we want to, can we look out of the windows?'

Dr Neill smiled. 'Don't worry,' he said. 'The wires are cut. You couldn't go to sleep now if you tried.'

Neill waited until the three men had left the lecture room on their way back to the Recreation Wing and then stepped down from the dais and shut the door. He was a short, broad-shouldered man in his fifties, with a sharp, impatient mouth and small features. He swung a chair out of the front row and straddled it deftly.

'Well?' he asked.

Morley was sitting on one of the desks against the back wall, playing aimlessly with a pencil. At thirty he was the youngest member of the team working under Neill at the Clinic, but for some reason Neill liked to talk to him.

He saw Neill was waiting for an answer and shrugged.

'Everything seems to be all right,' he said. 'Surgical convalescence is over. Cardiac rhythms and EEG are normal. I saw the X-rays this morning and everything has sealed beautifully.'

Neill watched him quizzically. 'You don't sound as if you approve.'

Morley laughed and stood up. 'Of course I do.' He walked down the aisle between the desks, white coat unbuttoned, hands sunk deep in his pockets. 'No, so far you've vindicated yourself on every point. The party's only just beginning, but the guests are in damn good shape. No doubt about it. I thought three weeks was a little early to bring them out of hypnosis, but you'll probably be right there as well. Tonight is the first one they take on their own. Let's see how they are tomorrow morning.'

'What are you secretly expecting?' Neill asked wryly. 'Massive feedback from the medulla?'

'No,' Morley said. 'There again the psychometric tests have shown absolutely nothing coming up at all. Not a single trauma.' He stared at the blackboard and then looked round at Neill. 'Yes, as a cautious estimate I'd say you've succeeded.'

Neill leaned forward on his elbows. He flexed his jaw muscles. 'I think I've more than succeeded. Blocking the medullary synapses has eliminated a lot of material I thought would still be there – the minor quirks and complexes, the petty aggressive phobias, the bad change in the psychic bank. Most of them have gone, or at least they don't show in the tests. However, they're the side targets, and thanks to you, John, and to everyone else in the team, we've hit a bull's eye on the main one.'

Morley murmured something, but Neill ran on in his clipped voice. 'None of you realize it yet, but this is as big an advance as the step the first ichthyoid took out of the protozoic sea 300 million years ago. At last we've freed the mind, raised it out of that archaic sump called sleep, its nightly retreat into the medulla. With virtually one cut of the scalpel we've added twenty years to those men's lives.'

'I only hope they know what to do with them,' Morley commented.

'Come, John,' Neill snapped back. 'That's not an argument. What they do with the time is their responsibility anyway. They'll make the most of it, just as we've always made the most, eventually, of any opportunity given us. It's too early to think about it yet, but visualize the universal application of our technique. For the first time Man will be living a full twenty-four hour day, not spending a third of it as an invalid, snoring his way through an eight-hour peepshow of infantile erotica.'

Tired, Neill broke off and rubbed his eyes. 'What's worrying you?'

Morley made a small, helpless gesture with one hand. 'I'm not sure, it's just that I . . .' He played with the plastic brain mounted on a stand next to the blackboard. Reflected in one of the frontal whorls was a distorted image of Neill, with a twisted chinless face and vast domed cranium. Sitting alone among the desks in the empty lecture room he looked like an insane genius patiently waiting to take an examination no one could set him.

Morley turned the model with his finger, watched the image blur and dissolve. Whatever his doubts, Neill was probably the last person to understand them.

'I know all you've done is close off a few of the loops in the hypothalamus, and I realize the results are going to be spectacular. You'll probably precipitate the greatest social and economic revolution since the Fall. But for some reason I can't get that story of Chekov's out of my mind – the one about the man who accepts a million-rouble bet that he can't shut himself up alone for ten years. He tries to, nothing goes wrong, but one minute before the time is up he deliberately steps out of his room. Of course, he's insane.'

'So?'

'I don't know. I've been thinking about it all week.'

Neill let out a light snort. 'I suppose you're trying to say that sleep is some sort of communal activity and that these three men are now isolated, exiled from the group unconscious, the dark oceanic dream. Is that it?'

'Maybe.'

'Nonsense, John. The further we hold back the unconscious the better. We're reclaiming some of the marshland. Physiologically sleep is nothing more than an inconvenient symptom of cerebral anoxaemia. It's not *that* you're afraid of missing, it's the dream. You want to hold on to your front-row seat at the peepshow.'

'No,' Morley said mildly. Sometimes Neill's aggressiveness surprised him; it was almost as if he regarded sleep itself as secretly discreditable, a concealed vice. 'What I really mean is that for better or worse Lang, Gorrell and Avery are now stuck with themselves. They're never going to be able to get away, not even for a couple of minutes, let alone eight hours. How much of yourself can you stand? Maybe you need eight hours off a day just to get over the shock of being yourself. Remember, you and I aren't always going to be around, feeding them with tests and films. What will happen if they get fed up with themselves?'

'They won't,' Neill said. He stood up, suddenly bored by Morley's questions. 'The total tempo of their lives will be lower than ours, these stresses and tensions won't begin to crystallize. We'll soon seem like a lot of manic-depressives to them, running round like dervishes half the day, then collapsing into a stupor the other half.'

He moved towards the door and reached out to the light switch. 'Well, I'll see you at six o'clock.'

They left the lecture room and started down the corridor together.

'What are you doing now?' Morley asked.

Neill laughed. 'What do you think?' he said. 'I'm going to get a good night's sleep.'

A little after midnight Avery and Gorrell were playing table-tennis in the floodlit gymnasium. They were competent players, and passed the ball backwards and forwards with a minimum of effort. Both felt strong and alert; Avery was sweating slightly, but this was due to the arc-lights blazing down from the roof – maintaining, for safety's sake, an illusion of continuous day – rather than to any excessive exertion of his own. The oldest of the three volunteers, a tall and somewhat detached figure, with a lean, closed face, he made no attempt to talk to Gorrell and concentrated on adjusting himself to the period ahead. He knew he would find no trace of fatigue, but as he played he carefully checked his respiratory rhythms and muscle tonus, and kept one eye on the clock.

Gorrell, a jaunty, self-composed man, was also subdued. Between strokes he glanced cautiously round the gymnasium, noting the hangar-like walls, the broad, polished floor, the shuttered skylights in the roof. Now and then, without realizing it, he fingered the circular trepan scar at the back of his head.

Out in the centre of the gymnasium a couple of armchairs and a sofa had been drawn up round a gramophone, and here Lang was playing chess with Morley, doing his section of night duty. Lang hunched forward over the chessboard. Wiry-haired and aggressive, with a sharp nose and mouth, he watched the pieces closely. He had played regularly against Morley since he arrived at the Clinic four months earlier, and the two were almost equally matched, with perhaps a slight edge to Morley. But tonight Lang had opened with a new attack and after ten moves had completed his development and begun to split Morley's defence. His mind felt clear and precise, focused sharply on the game in front of him, though only that morning had he finally left the cloudy limbo of post-hypnosis through which he and the two others had drifted for three weeks like lobotomized phantoms.

Behind him, along one wall of the gymnasium, were the offices housing the control unit. Over his shoulder he saw a face peering at him through the circular observation window in one of the doors. Here, at constant alert, a group of orderlies and interns sat around waiting by their emergency trollies. (The end door, into a small ward containing three cots, was kept carefully locked.) After a few moments the face withdrew. Lang smiled at the elaborate machinery watching over him. His transference on to Neill had been positive and he had absolute faith in the success of the experiment. Neill had assured him that, at worst, the sudden accumulation of metabolites in his bloodstream might induce a mild torpor, but his brain would be unimpaired.

'Nerve fibre, Robert,' Neill had told him time and again, 'never fatigues. The brain cannot tire.'

While he waited for Morley to move he checked the time from the clock mounted against the wall. Twelve twenty. Morley yawned, his face drawn under the grey skin. He looked tired and drab. He slumped down into the armchair, face in one hand. Lang reflected how frail and primitive those who slept would soon seem, their minds sinking off each evening under the load of accumulating toxins, the edge of their awareness worn and frayed. Suddenly he realized that at that very moment Neill himself was asleep. A curiously disconcerting vision of Neill, huddled in a rumpled bed two floors above, his blood-sugar low, and his mind drifting, rose before him.

Lang laughed at his own conceit, and Morley retrieved the rook he had just moved.

'I must be going blind. What am I doing?'

'No,' Lang said. He started to laugh again. 'I've just discovered I'm awake.'

Morley smiled. 'We'll have to put that down as one of the sayings of the week.' He replaced the rook, sat up and looked across at the table-tennis pair. Gorrell had hit a fast backhand low over the net and Avery was running after the ball.

'They seem to be okay. How about you?'

'Right on top of myself,' Lang said. His eyes flicked up and down the board and he moved before Morley caught his breath back.

Usually they went right through into the end-game, but tonight Morley had to concede on the twentieth move.

'Good,' he said encouragingly. 'You'll be able to take on Neill soon. Like another?'

'No. Actually the game bores me. I can see that's going to be a problem.'

'You'll face it. Give yourself time to find your legs.'

Lang pulled one of the Bach albums out of its rack in the record cabinet. He put a Brandenburg Concerto on the turntable and lowered the sapphire. As the rich, contrapuntal patterns chimed out he sat back, listening intently to the music.

Morley thought: Absurd. How fast can you run? Three weeks ago you were strictly a hep-cat.

The next few hours passed rapidly.

At one thirty they went up to the Surgery, where Morley and one of the interns gave them a quick physical, checking their renal clearances, heart rate and reflexes.

Dressed again, they went into the empty cafeteria for a snack and sat on the stools, arguing what to call this new fifth meal. Avery suggested 'Midfood', Morley 'Munch'.

At two they took their places in the Neurology theatre, and spent a couple of hours watching films of the hypno-drills of the past three weeks.

When the programme ended they started down for the gymnasium, the night almost over. They were still relaxed and cheerful; Gorrell led the way, playfully teasing Lang over some of the episodes in the films, mimicking his trance-like walk.

'Eyes shut, mouth open,' he demonstrated, swerving into Lang, who jumped nimbly out of his way. 'Look at you; you're doing it even now. Believe me, Lang, you're not awake, you're somnambulating.' He called back to Morley, 'Agreed, Doctor?'

Morley swallowed a yawn. 'Well, if he is, that makes two of us.' He followed them along the corridor, doing his best to stay awake, feeling as if he, and not the three men in front of him, had been without sleep for the last three weeks.

Though the Clinic was quiet, at Neill's orders all lights along the corridors and down the stairway had been left on. Ahead of them two orderlies checked that windows they passed were safely screened and doors were shut. Nowhere was there a single darkened alcove or shadow-trap.

Neill had insisted on this, reluctantly acknowledging a possible reflex association between darkness and sleep: 'Let's admit it. In all but a few organisms the association *is* strong enough to be a reflex. The higher mammals depend for their survival on a highly acute sensory apparatus, combined with a varying ability to store and classify information. Plunge them into darkness, cut off the flow of visual data to the cortex, and they're paralysed. Sleep is a defence reflex. It lowers the metabolic rate, conserves energy, increases the organism's survival-potential by merging it into its habitat . . .'

On the landing halfway down the staircase was a wide, shuttered window that by day opened out on to the parkscape behind the Clinic. As he passed it Gorrell stopped. He went over, released the blind, then unlatched the shutter.

Still holding it closed, he turned to Morley, watching from the flight above.

'Taboo, Doctor?' he asked.

Morley looked at each of the three men in turn. Gorrell was calm and unperturbed, apparently satisfying nothing more sinister than an idle whim. Lang sat on the rail, watching curiously with an expression of clinical disinterest. Only Avery seemed slightly anxious, his thin face wan and pinched. Morley had an irrelevant thought: four a.m. shadow – they'll need to shave twice a day. Then: why isn't Neill here? He knew they'd make for a window as soon as they got the chance.

He noticed Lang giving him an amused smile and shrugged, trying to disguise his uneasiness.

'Go ahead, if you want to. As Neill said, the wires are cut.'

Gorrell threw back the shutter, and they clustered round the window and stared out into the night. Below, pewter-grey lawns stretched towards the pines and low hills in the distance. A couple of miles away on their left a neon sign winked and beckoned.

Neither Gorrell nor Lang noticed any reaction, and their interest began to flag within a few moments. Avery felt a sudden lift under the heart, then controlled himself. His eyes began to sift the darkness; the sky was clear and cloudless, and through the stars he picked out the narrow, milky traverse of the galactic rim. He watched it silently, letting the wind cool the sweat on his face and neck.

Morley stepped over to the window and leaned his elbows on the sill next to Avery. Out of the corner of his eye he carefully waited for any motor tremor – a fluttering eyelid, accelerated breathing – that would signal a reflex discharging. He remembered Neill's warning: 'In Man sleep is largely volitional, and the reflex is conditioned by habit. But just because we've cut out the hypothalamic loops regulating the flow of consciousness doesn't mean the reflex won't discharge down some other pathway. However, sooner or later we'll have to take the risk and give them a glimpse of the dark side of the sun.'

Morley was musing on this when something nudged his shoulder.

'Doctor,' he heard Lang say. 'Doctor Morley.'

He pulled himself together with a start. He was alone at the window. Gorrell and Avery were halfway down the next flight of stairs.

'What's up?' Morley asked quickly.

'Nothing,' Lang assured him. 'We're just going back to the gym.' He looked closely at Morley. 'Are you all right?'

Morley rubbed his face. 'God, I must have been asleep.' He glanced at his watch. Four twenty. They had been at the window for over fifteen minutes. All he could remember was leaning on the sill. 'And I was worried about *you*.'

Everybody was amused, Gorrell particularly. 'Doctor,' he drawled, 'if you're interested I can recommend you to a good narcotomist.'

After five o'clock they felt a gradual ebb of tonus from their arm and leg muscles. Renal clearances were falling and breakdown products were slowly clogging their tissues. Their palms felt damp and numb, the soles of their feet like pads of sponge rubber. The sensation was vaguely unsettling, allied to no feelings of mental fatigue.

The numbness spread. Avery noticed it stretching the skin over his cheekbones, pulling at his temples and giving him a slight frontal migraine. He doggedly turned the pages of a magazine, his hands like lumps of putty.

Then Neill came down, and they began to revive. Neill looked fresh and spruce, bouncing on the tips of his toes.

'How's the night shift going?' he asked briskly, walking round each one of them in turn, smiling as he sized them up. 'Feel all right?'

'Not too bad, Doctor,' Gorrell told him. 'A slight case of insomnia.'

Neill roared, slapped him on the shoulder and led the way up to the Surgery laboratory.

At nine, shaved and in fresh clothes, they assembled in the lecture room. They felt cool and alert again. The peripheral numbness and slight head torpor had gone as soon as the detoxication drips had been plugged in, and Neill told them that within a week their kidneys would have enlarged sufficiently to cope on their own.

All morning and most of the afternoon they worked on a series of IQ, associative and performance tests. Neill kept them hard at it, steering swerving blips of light around a cathode screen, juggling with intricate numerical and geometric sequences, elaborating word-chains.

He seemed more than satisfied with the results.

'Shorter access times, deeper memory traces,' he pointed out to Morley when the three men had gone off at five for the rest period. 'Barrels of prime psychic marrow.' He gestured at the test cards spread out across the desk in his office. 'And you were worried about the Unconscious.

Look at those Rorschachs of Lang's. Believe me, John, I'll soon have him reminiscing about his foetal experiences.'

Morley nodded, his first doubts fading.

Over the next two weeks either he or Neill was with the men continuously, sitting out under the floodlights in the centre of the gymnasium, assessing their assimilation of the eight extra hours, carefully watching for any symptoms of withdrawal. Neill carried everyone along, from one programme phase to the next, through the test periods, across the long hours of the interminable nights, his powerful ego injecting enthusiasm into every member of the unit.

Privately, Morley worried about the increasing emotional overlay apparent in the relationship between Neill and the three men. He was afraid they were becoming conditioned to identify Neill with the experiment. (Ring the meal bell and the subject salivates; but suddenly stop ringing the bell after a long period of conditioning and it temporarily loses the ability to feed itself. The hiatus barely harms a dog, but it might trigger disaster in an already oversensitized psyche.)

Neill was fully alert to this. At the end of the first two weeks, when he caught a bad head cold after sitting up all night and decided to spend the next day in bed, he called Morley into his office.

'The transference is getting much too positive. It needs to be eased off a little.'

'I agree,' Morley said. 'But how?'

'Tell them I'll be asleep for forty-eight hours,' Neill said. He picked up a stack of reports, plates and test cards and bundled them under one arm. 'I've deliberately overdosed myself with sedative to get some rest. I'm worn to a shadow, full fatigue syndrome, load-cells screaming. Lay it on.'

'Couldn't that be rather drastic?' Morley asked. 'They'll hate you for it.'

But Neill only smiled and went off to requisition an office near his bedroom.

That night Morley was on duty in the gymnasium from ten p.m. to six a.m. As usual he first checked that the orderlies were ready with their emergency trollies, read through the log left by the previous supervisor, one of the senior interns, and then went over to the circle of chairs. He sat back on the sofa next to Lang and leafed through a magazine, watching the three men carefully. In the glare of the arc-lights their lean faces had a sallow, cyanosed look. The senior intern had warned him that Avery and Gorrell might overtire themselves at table-tennis, but by eleven p.m. they stopped playing and settled down in the armchairs. They read desultorily and made two trips up to the cafeteria, escorted each time by one of the orderlies. Morley told them about Neill, but surprisingly none of them made any comment.

Midnight came slowly. Avery read, his long body hunched up in an armchair. Gorrell played chess against himself.

Morley dozed.

Lang felt restless. The gymnasium's silence and absence of movement oppressed him. He switched on the gramophone and played through a Brandenburg, analysing its theme-trains. Then he ran a word-association test on himself, turning the pages of a book and using the top right-hand corner words as the control list.

Morley leaned over. 'Anything come up?' he asked.

'A few interesting responses.' Lang found a note-pad and jotted something down. 'I'll show them to Neill in the morning – or whenever he wakes up.' He gazed up pensively at the arc-lights. 'I was just speculating. What do you think the next step forward will be?'

'Forward where?' Morley asked.

Lang gestured expansively. 'I mean up the evolutionary slope. Three hundred million years ago we became air-breathers and left the seas behind. Now we've taken the next logical step forward and eliminated sleep. What's next?'

Morley shook his head. 'The two steps aren't analogous. Anyway, in point of fact you haven't left the primeval sea behind. You're still carrying a private replica of it around as your bloodstream. All you did was encapsulate a necessary piece of the physical environment in order to escape it.'

Lang nodded. 'I was thinking of something else. Tell me, has it ever occurred to you how completely death-orientated the psyche is?'

Morley smiled. 'Now and then,' he said, wondering where this led.

'It's curious,' Lang went on reflectively. 'The pleasure-pain principle, the whole survival-compulsion apparatus of sex, the Super-Ego's obsession with tomorrow – most of the time the psyche can't see farther than its own tombstone. Now why has it got this strange fixation? For one very obvious reason.' He tapped the air with his forefinger. 'Because every night it's given a pretty convincing reminder of the fate in store for it.'

'You mean the black hole,' Morley suggested wryly. 'Sleep?'

'Exactly. It's simply a pseudo-death. Of course, you're not aware of it, but it must be terrifying.' He frowned. 'I don't think even Neill realizes that, far from being restful, sleep is a genuinely traumatic experience.'

So that's it, Morley thought. The great father analyst has been caught napping on his own couch. He tried to decide which were worse – patients who knew a lot of psychiatry, or those who only knew a little.

'Eliminate sleep,' Lang was saying, 'and you also eliminate all the fear and defence mechanisms erected round it. Then, at last, the psyche has a chance to orientate towards something more valid.'

'Such as . . . ?' Morley asked.

'I don't know. Perhaps . . . Self?'

'Interesting,' Morley commented. It was three ten a.m. He decided to spend the next hour going through Lang's latest test cards.

He waited a discretionary five minutes, then stood up and walked over to the surgery office.

Lang hooked an arm across the back of the sofa and watched the orderly room door.

'What's Morley playing at?' he asked. 'Have either of you seen him anywhere?'

Avery lowered his magazine. 'Didn't he go off into the orderly room?'

'Ten minutes ago,' Lang said. 'He hasn't looked in since. There's supposed to be someone on duty with us continuously. Where is he?'

Gorrell, playing solitaire chess, looked up from his board. 'Perhaps these late nights are getting him down. You'd better wake him before Neill finds out. He's probably fallen asleep over a batch of your test cards.'

Lang laughed and settled down on the sofa. Gorrell reached out to the gramophone, took a record out of the rack and slid it on to the turntable.

As the gramophone began to hum Lang noticed how silent and deserted the gymnasium seemed. The Clinic was always quiet, but even at night a residual ebb and flow of sound – a chair dragging in the orderly room, a generator charging under one of the theatres – eddied through and kept it alive.

Now the air was flat and motionless. Lang listened carefully. The whole place had the dead, echoless feel of an abandoned building.

He stood up and strolled over to the orderly room. He knew Neill discouraged casual conversation with the control crew, but Morley's absence puzzled him.

He reached the door and peered through the window to see if Morley was inside.

The room was empty.

The light was on. Two emergency trollies stood in their usual place against the wall near the door, a third was in the middle of the floor, a pack of playing cards strewn across its deck, but the group of three or four interns had gone.

Lang hesitated, reached down to open the door, and found it had been locked.

He tried the handle again, then called out over his shoulder:

'Avery. There's nobody in here.'

'Try next door. They're probably being briefed for tomorrow.'

Lang stepped over to the surgery office. The light was off but he could see the white enamelled desk and the big programme charts round the wall. There was no one inside.

Avery and Gorrell were watching him.

'Are they in there?' Avery asked.

'No.' Lang turned the handle. 'The door's locked.'

Gorrell switched off the gramophone and he and Avery came over. They tried the two doors again.

'They're here somewhere,' Avery said. 'There must be at least one person on duty.' He pointed to the end door. 'What about that one?'

'Locked,' Lang said. '69 always has been. I think it leads down to the basement.'

'Let's try Neill's office,' Gorrell suggested. 'If they aren't in there we'll stroll through to Reception and try to leave. This must be some trick of Neill's.'

There was no window in the door to Neill's office. Gorrell knocked, waited, knocked again more loudly.

Lang tried the handle, then knelt down. 'The light's off,' he reported.

Avery turned and looked round at the two remaining doors out of the gymnasium, both in the far wall, one leading up to the cafeteria and the Neurology wing, the other into the car park at the rear of the Clinic.

'Didn't Neill hint that he might try something like this on us?' he asked. 'To see whether we can go through a night on our own.'

'But Neill's asleep,' Lang objected. 'He'll be in bed for a couple of days. Unless . . .'

Gorrell jerked his head in the direction of the chairs. 'Come on. He and Morley are probably watching us now.'

They went back to their seats.

Gorrell dragged the chess stool over to the sofa and set up the pieces. Avery and Lang stretched out in armchairs and opened magazines, turning the pages deliberately. Above them the banks of arc-lights threw their wide cones of light down into the silence.

The only noise was the slow left-right, left-right motion of the clock.

Three fifteen a.m.

*The shift was imperceptible. At first a slight change of perspective, a fading and regrouping of outlines. Somewhere a focus slipped, a shadow swung slowly across a wall, its angles breaking and lengthening. The motion was fluid, a procession of infinitesimals, but gradually its total direction emerged.*

*The gymnasium was shrinking. Inch by inch, the walls were moving inwards, encroaching across the periphery of the floor. As they shrank towards each other their features altered: the rows of skylights below the ceiling blurred and faded, the power cable running along the base of the wall merged into the skirting board, the square baffles of the air vents vanished into the grey distemper.*

*Above, like the undersurface of an enormous lift, the ceiling sank towards the floor . . .*

Gorrell leaned his elbows on the chessboard, face sunk in his hands. He had locked himself in a perpetual check, but he continued to shuttle the pieces in and out of one of the corner squares, now and then gazing into the air for inspiration, while his eyes roved up and down the walls around him.

Somewhere, he knew, Neill was watching him.

He moved, looked up and followed the wall opposite him down to the far corner, alert for the telltale signs of a retractable panel. For some while he had been trying to discover Neill's spy-hole, but without any success. The walls were blank and featureless; he had twice covered every square foot of the two facing him, and apart from the three doors there appeared to be no fault or aperture of even the most minute size anywhere on their surface.

After a while his left eye began to throb painfully, and he pushed away the chessboard and lay back. Above him a line of fluorescent tubes hung down from the ceiling, mounted in checkered plastic brackets that diffused the light. He was about to comment on his search for the spy-hole to Avery and Lang when he realized that any one of them could conceal a microphone.

He decided to stretch his legs, stood up and sauntered off across the floor. After sitting over the chessboard for half an hour he felt cramped and restless, and would have enjoyed tossing a ball up and down, or flexing his muscles on a rowing machine. But annoyingly no recreational facilities, apart from the three armchairs and the gramophone, had been provided.

He reached the end wall and wandered round, listening for any sound from the adjacent rooms. He was beginning to resent Neill spying on him and the entire keyhole conspiracy, and he noted with relief that it was a quarter past three: in under three hours it would all be over.

*The gymnasium closed in. Now less than half its original size, its walls bare and windowless, it was a vast, shrinking box. The sides slid into each other, merging along an abstract hairline, like planes severing in a multi-dimensional flux. Only the clock and a single door remained . . .*

Lang had discovered where the microphone was hidden.

He sat forward in his chair, cracking his knuckles until Gorrell returned, then rose and offered him his seat. Avery was in the other armchair, feet up on the gramophone.

'Sit down for a bit,' Lang said. 'I feel like a stroll.'

Gorrell lowered himself into the chair. 'I'll ask Neill if we can have a ping-pong table in here. It should help pass the time and give us some exercise.'

'A good idea,' Lang agreed. 'If we can get the table through the door. I doubt if there's enough room in here, even if we moved the chairs right up against the wall.'

He walked off across the floor, surreptitiously peering through the orderly room window. The light was on, but there was still no one inside.

He ambled over to the gramophone and paced up and down near it for a few moments. Suddenly he swung round and caught his foot under the flex leading to the wall socket.

The plug fell out on to the floor. Lang left it where it lay, went over and sat down on the arm of Gorrell's chair.

'I've just disconnected the microphone,' he confided.

Gorrell looked round carefully. 'Where was it?'

Lang pointed. 'Inside the gramophone.' He laughed softly. 'I thought I'd pull Neill's leg. He'll be wild when he realizes he can't hear us.'

'Why do you think it was in the gramophone?' Gorrell asked.

'What better place? Besides, it couldn't be anywhere else. Apart from in there.' He gestured at the light bowl suspended from the centre of the ceiling. 'It's empty except for the two bulbs. The gramophone is the obvious place. I had a feeling it was there, but I wasn't sure until I noticed we had a gramophone, but no records.'

Gorrell nodded sagely.

Lang moved away, chuckling to himself.

Above the door of Room 69 the clock ticked on at three fifteen.

*The motion was accelerating. What had once been the gymnasium was now a small room, seven feet wide, a tight, almost perfect cube. The walls plunged inwards, along colliding diagonals, only a few feet from their final focus . . .*

Avery noticed Gorrell and Lang pacing around his chair. 'Either of you want to sit down yet?' he asked.

They shook their heads. Avery rested for a few minutes and then climbed out of the chair and stretched himself.

'Quarter past three,' he remarked, pressing his hands against the ceiling. 'This is getting to be a long night.'

He leaned back to let Gorrell pass him, and then started to follow the others round the narrow space between the armchair and the walls.

'I don't know how Neill expects us to stay awake in this hole for twenty-four hours a day,' he went on. 'Why haven't we got a television set in here? Even a radio would be something.'

They sidled round the chair together, Gorrell, followed by Avery, with Lang completing the circle, their shoulders beginning to hunch, their heads down as they watched the floor, their feet falling into the slow, leaden rhythm of the clock.

*This, then, was the manhole: a narrow, vertical cubicle, a few feet wide, six deep. Above, a solitary, dusty bulb gleamed down from a steel grille. As if crumbling under the impetus of their own momentum, the surface of the walls had coarsened, the texture was that of stone, streaked and pitted . . .*

Gorrell bent down to loosen one of his shoelaces and Avery bumped into him sharply, knocking his shoulder against the wall.

'All right?' he asked, taking Gorrell's arm. 'This place is a little overcrowded. I can't understand why Neill ever put us in here.'

He leaned against the wall, head bowed to prevent it from touching the ceiling, and gazed about thoughtfully.

Lang stood squeezed into the corner next to him, shifting his weight from one foot to the other.

Gorrell squatted down on his heels below them.

'What's the time?' he asked.

'I'd say about three fifteen,' Lang offered. 'More or less.'

'Lang,' Avery asked, 'where's the ventilator here?'

Lang peered up and down the walls and across the small square of ceiling. 'There must be one somewhere.' Gorrell stood up and they shuffled about, examining the floor between their feet.

'There may be a vent in the light grille,' Gorrell suggested. He reached up and slipped his fingers through the cage, running them behind the bulb.

'Nothing there. Odd. I should have thought we'd use the air in here within half an hour.'

'Easily,' Avery said. 'You know, there's something –'

Just then Lang broke in. He gripped Avery's elbow.

'Avery,' he asked. 'Tell me. How did we get here?'

'What do you mean, get here? We're on Neill's team.'

Lang cut him off. 'I know that.' He pointed at the floor. 'I mean, in here.'

Gorrell shook his head. 'Lang, relax. How do you think? Through the door.'

Lang looked squarely at Gorrell, then at Avery.

'What door?' he asked calmly.

Gorrell and Avery hesitated, then swung round to look at each wall in turn, scanning it from floor to ceiling. Avery ran his hands over the heavy masonry, then knelt down and felt the floor, digging his fingers at the rough stone slabs. Gorrell crouched beside him, scrabbling at the thin seams of dirt.

Lang backed out of their way into a corner, and watched them impassively. His face was calm and motionless, but in his left temple a single vein fluttered insanely.

When they finally stood up, staring at each other unsteadily, he flung himself between them at the opposite wall.

'Neill! Neill!' he shouted. He pounded angrily on the wall with his fists. 'Neill! Neill!'

Above him the light began to fade.

Morley closed the door of the surgery office behind him and went over to the desk. Though it was three fifteen a.m., Neill was probably awake, working on the latest material in the office next to his bedroom. Fortunately that afternoon's test cards, freshly marked by one of the interns, had only just reached his in-tray.

Morley picked out Lang's folder and started to sort through the cards. He suspected that Lang's responses to some of the key words and suggestion triggers lying disguised in the question forms might throw illuminating sidelights on to the real motives behind his equation of sleep and death.

The communicating door to the orderly room opened and an intern looked in.

'Do you want me to take over in the gym, Doctor?'

Morley waved him away. 'Don't bother. I'm going back in a moment.'

He selected the cards he wanted and began to initial his withdrawals. Glad to get away from the glare of the arc-lights, he delayed his return as long as he could, and it was three twenty-five a.m. when he finally left the office and stepped back into the gymnasium.

The men were sitting where he had left them. Lang watched him approach, head propped comfortably on a cushion. Avery was slouched down in his armchair, nose in a magazine, while Gorrell hunched over the chessboard, hidden behind the sofa.

'Anybody feel like coffee?' Morley called out, deciding they needed some exercise.

None of them looked up or answered. Morley felt a flicker of annoyance, particularly at Lang, who was staring past him at the clock.

Then he saw something that made him stop.

Lying on the polished floor ten feet from the sofa was a chess piece. He went over and picked it up. The piece was the black king. He wondered how Gorrell could be playing chess with one of the two essential pieces of the game missing when he noticed three more pieces lying on the floor near by.

His eyes moved to where Gorrell was sitting.

Scattered over the floor below the chair and sofa was the rest of the set. Gorrell was slumped over the stool. One of his elbows had slipped and the arm dangled between his knees, knuckles resting on the floor. The other hand supported his face. Dead eyes peered down at his feet.

Morley ran over to him, shouting: 'Lang! Avery! Get the orderlies!'

He reached Gorrell and pulled him back off the stool.

'Lang!' he called again.

Lang was still staring at the clock, his body in the stiff, unreal posture of a waxworks dummy.

Morley let Gorrell loll back on to the sofa, leaned over and glanced at Lang's face.

He crossed to Avery, stretched out behind the magazine, and jerked his shoulder. Avery's head bobbed stiffly. The magazine slipped and fell from his hands, leaving his fingers curled in front of his face.

Morley stepped over Avery's legs to the gramophone. He switched it on, gripped the volume control and swung it round to full amplitude.

Above the orderly room door an alarm bell shrilled out through the silence.

*       *       *

'Weren't you with them?' Neill asked sharply.

'No,' Morley admitted. They were standing by the door of the emergency ward. Two orderlies had just dismantled the electro-therapy unit and
were wheeling the console away on a trolley. Outside in the gymnasium
a quiet, urgent traffic of nurses and interns moved past. All but a single
bank of arc-lights had been switched off, and the gymnasium seemed like
a deserted stage at the end of a performance.

'I slipped into the office to pick up a few test cards,' he explained. 'I
wasn't gone more than ten minutes.'

'You were supposed to watch them continuously,' Neill snapped. 'Not
wander off by yourself whenever you felt like it. What do you think we
had the gym and this entire circus set up for?'

It was a little after five thirty a.m. After working hopelessly on the three
men for a couple of hours, he was close to exhaustion. He looked down at
them, lying inertly in their cots, canvas sheets buckled up to their chins.
They had barely changed, but their eyes were open and unblinking, and
their faces had the empty, reflexless look of psychic zero.

An intern bent over Lang, thumbing a hypodermic. Morley stared at
the floor. 'I think they would have gone anyway.'

'How can you say that?' Neill clamped his lips together. He felt
frustrated and impotent. He knew Morley was probably right – the
three men were in terminal withdrawal, unresponsive to either insulin
or electrotherapy, and a vice-tight catatonic seizure didn't close in
out of nowhere – but as always refused to admit anything without
absolute proof.

He led the way into his office and shut the door.

'Sit down.' He pulled a chair out for Morley and prowled off round
the room, slamming a fist into his palm.

'All right, John. What is it?'

Morley picked up one of the test cards lying on the desk, balanced it
on a corner and spun it between his fingers. Phrases swam through his
mind, tentative and uncertain, like blind fish.

'What do you want me to say?' he asked. 'Reactivation of the infantile
imago? A regression into the great, slumbering womb? Or to put it more
simply still – just a fit of pique?'

'Go on.'

Morley shrugged. 'Continual consciousness is more than the brain can
stand. Any signal repeated often enough eventually loses its meaning.
Try saying the word "sleep" fifty times. After a point the brain's self-
awareness dulls. It's no longer able to grasp who or why it is, and it
rides adrift.'

'What do we do then?'

'Nothing. Short of re-scoring all the way down to Lumbar 1. The central
nervous system can't stand narcotomy.'

Neill shook his head. 'You're lost,' he said curtly. 'Juggling with
generalities isn't going to bring those men back. First, we've got to find

out what happened to them, what they actually felt and saw.'

Morley frowned dubiously. 'That jungle is marked "private". Even if you do, is a psychotic's withdrawal drama going to make any sense?'

'Of course it will. However insane it seems to us, it was real enough to them. If we know the ceiling fell in or the whole gym filled with ice-cream or turned into a maze, we've got something to work on.' He sat down on the desk. 'Do you remember that story of Chekov's you told me about?'

'"The Bet"? Yes.'

'I read it last night. Curious. It's a lot nearer what you're really trying to say than you know.' He gazed round the office. 'This room in which the man is penned for ten years symbolizes the mind driven to the furthest limits of self-awareness ... Something very similar happened to Avery, Gorrell and Lang. They must have reached a stage beyond which they could no longer contain the idea of their own identity. But far from being unable to grasp the idea, I'd say that they were conscious of nothing else. Like the man in the spherical mirror, who can only see a single gigantic eye staring back at him.'

'So you think their withdrawal is a straightforward escape from the eye, the overwhelming ego?'

'Not escape,' Neill corrected. 'The psychotic never escapes from anything. He's much more sensible. He merely readjusts reality to suit himself. Quite a trick to learn, too. The room in Chekov's story gives me an idea as to how they might have re-adjusted. Their particular equivalent of this room was the gym. I'm beginning to realize it was a mistake to put them in there – all those lights blazing down, the huge floor, high walls. They merely exaggerate the sensation of overload. In fact the gym might easily have become an external projection of their own egos.'

Neill drummed his fingers on the desk. 'My guess is that at this moment they're either striding around in there the size of hundred-foot giants, or else they've cut it down to their own dimensions. More probably that. They've just pulled the gym in on themselves.'

Morley grinned bleakly. 'So all we've got to do now is pump them full of honey and apomorphine and coax them out. Suppose they refuse?'

'They won't,' Neill said. 'You'll see.'

There was a rap on the door. An intern stuck his head through.

'Lang's coming out of it, Doctor. He's calling for you.'

Neill bounded out.

Morley followed him into the ward.

Lang was lying in his cot, body motionless under the canvas sheet. His lips were parted slightly. No sound came from them but Morley, bending over next to Neill, could see his hyoid bone vibrating in spasms.

'He's very faint,' the intern warned.

Neill pulled up a chair and sat down next to the cot. He made a visible effort of concentration, flexing his shoulders. He bent his head close to Lang's and listened.

Five minutes later it came through again.

Lang's lips quivered. His body arched under the sheet, straining at the buckles, and then subsided.

'Neill . . . Neill,' he whispered. The sounds, thin and strangled, seemed to be coming from the bottom of a well. 'Neill . . . Neill . . . Neill . . .'

Neill stroked his forehead with a small, neat hand.

'Yes, Bobby,' he said gently. His voice was feather-soft, caressing. 'I'm here, Bobby. You can come out now.'

**· 1957**

# TRACK 12

'Guess again,' Sheringham said.

Maxted clipped on the headphones, carefully settled them over his ears. He concentrated as the disc began to spin, trying to catch some echo of identity.

The sound was a rapid metallic rustling, like iron filings splashing through a funnel. It ran for ten seconds, repeated itself a dozen times, then ended abruptly in a string of blips.

'Well?' Sheringham asked. 'What is it?'

Maxted pulled off his headphones, rubbed one of his ears. He had been listening to the records for hours and his ears felt bruised and numb.

'Could be anything. An ice-cube melting?'

Sheringham shook his head, his little beard wagging.

Maxted shrugged. 'A couple of galaxies colliding?'

'No. Sound waves don't travel through space. I'll give you a clue. It's one of those *proverbial* sounds.' He seemed to be enjoying the catechism.

Maxted lit a cigarette, threw the match onto the laboratory bench. The head melted a tiny pool of wax, froze and left a shallow black scar. He watched it pleasurably, conscious of Sheringham fidgeting beside him.

He pumped his brains for an obscene simile. 'What about a fly –'

'Time's up,' Sheringham cut in. '*A pin dropping.*' He took the 3-inch disc off the player, angled it into its sleeve.

'In actual fall, that is, not impact. We used a fifty-foot shaft and eight microphones. I thought you'd get that one.'

He reached for the last record, a 12-inch LP, but Maxted stood up before he got it to the turntable. Through the french windows he could see the patio, a table, glasses and decanter gleaming in the darkness. Sheringham and his infantile games suddenly irritated him; he felt impatient with himself for tolerating the man so long.

'Let's get some air,' he said brusquely, shouldering past one of the amplifier rigs. 'My ears feel like gongs.'

'By all means,' Sheringham agreed promptly. He placed the record carefully on the turntable and switched off the player. 'I want to save this one until later anyway.'

They went out into the warm evening air. Sheringham turned on the Japanese lanterns and they stretched back in the wicker chairs under the open sky.

'I hope you weren't too bored,' Sheringham said as he handled the decanter. 'Microsonics is a fascinating hobby, but I'm afraid I may have let it become an obsession.'

Maxted grunted non-committally. 'Some of the records are interesting,' he admitted. 'They have a sort of crazy novelty value, like blown-up photographs of moths' faces and razor blades. Despite what you claim, though, I can't believe microsonics will ever become a scientific tool. It's just an elaborate laboratory toy.'

Sheringham shook his head. 'You're completely wrong, of course. Remember the cell division series I played first of all? Amplified 100,000 times animal cell division sounds like a lot of girders and steel sheets being ripped apart – how did you put it? – a car smash in slow motion. On the other hand, plant cell division is an electronic poem, all soft chords and bubbling tones. Now there you have a perfect illustration of how microsonics can reveal the distinction between the animal and plant kingdoms.'

'Seems a damned roundabout way of doing it,' Maxted commented, helping himself to soda. 'You might as well calculate the speed of your car from the apparent motion of the stars. Possible, but it's easier to look at the speedometer.'

Sheringham nodded, watching Maxted closely across the table. His interest in the conversation appeared to have exhausted itself, and the two men sat silently with their glasses. Strangely, the hostility between them, of so many years' standing, now became less veiled, the contrast of personality, manner and physique more pronounced. Maxted, a tall fleshy man with a coarse handsome face, lounged back almost horizontally in his chair, thinking about Susan Sheringham. She was at the Turnbulls' party, and but for the fact that it was no longer discreet of him to be seen at the Turnbulls' – for the all-too-familiar reason – he would have passed the evening with her, rather than with her grotesque little husband.

He surveyed Sheringham with as much detachment as he could muster, wondering whether this prim unattractive man, with his pedantry and in-bred academic humour, had any redeeming qualities whatever. None, certainly, at a casual glance, though it required some courage and pride to have invited him round that evening. His motives, however, would be typically eccentric.

The pretext, Maxted reflected, had been slight enough – Sheringham, professor of biochemistry at the university, maintained a lavish home laboratory; Maxted, a run-down athlete with a bad degree, acted as torpedo-man for a company manufacturing electron microscopes; a visit, Sheringham had suggested over the phone, might be to the profit of both.

Of course, nothing of this had in fact been mentioned. But nor, as yet, had he referred to Susan, the real subject of the evening's charade. Maxted speculated upon the possible routes Sheringham might take towards the inevitable confrontation scene; not for him the nervous circular pacing, the well-thumbed photostat, or the tug at the shoulder. There was a vicious adolescent streak running through Sheringham –

Maxted broke out of his reverie abruptly. The air in the patio had become suddenly cooler, almost as if a powerful refrigerating unit had been switched on. A rash of goose-flesh raced up his thighs and down the back of his neck, and he reached forward and finished what was left of his whisky.

'Cold out here,' he commented.

Sheringham glanced at his watch. 'Is it?' he said. There was a hint of indecision in his voice; for a moment he seemed to be waiting for a signal. Then he pulled himself together and, with an odd half-smile, said: 'Time for the last record.'

'What do you mean?' Maxted asked.

'Don't move,' Sheringham said. He stood up. 'I'll put it on.' He pointed to a loudspeaker screwed to the wall above Maxted's head, grinned and ducked out.

Shivering uncomfortably, Maxted peered up into the silent evening sky, hoping that the vertical current of cold air that had sliced down into the patio would soon dissipate itself.

A low noise crackled from the speaker, multiplied by a circle of other speakers which he noticed for the first time had been slung among the trellis-work around the patio.

Shaking his head sadly at Sheringham's antics, he decided to help himself to more whisky. As he stretched across the table he swayed and rolled back uncontrollably into his chair. His stomach seemed to be full of mercury, ice-cold and enormously heavy. He pushed himself forward again, trying to reach the glass, and knocked it across the table. His brain began to fade, and he leaned his elbows helplessly on the glass edge of the table and felt his head fall onto his wrists.

When he looked up again Sheringham was standing in front of him, smiling sympathetically.

'Not too good, eh?' he said.

Breathing with difficulty, Maxted managed to lean back. He tried to speak to Sheringham, but he could no longer remember any words. His heart switchbacked, and he grimaced at the pain.

'Don't worry,' Sheringham assured him. 'The fibrillation is only a side effect. Disconcerting, perhaps, but it will soon pass.'

He strolled leisurely around the patio, scrutinizing Maxted from several angles. Evidently satisfied, he sat down on the table. He picked up the siphon and swirled the contents about. 'Chromium cyanate. Inhibits the coenzyme system controlling the body's fluid balances, floods hydroxyl ions into the bloodstream. In brief, you drown. Really drown, that is, not merely suffocate as you would if you were immersed in an external bath. However, I mustn't distract you.'

He inclined his head at the speakers. Being fed into the patio was a curiously muffled spongy noise, like elastic waves lapping in a latex sea. The rhythms were huge and ungainly, overlaid by the deep leaden wheezing of a gigantic bellows. Barely audible at first, the sounds rose until they filled the patio and shut out the few traffic noises along the highway.

'Fantastic, isn't it?' Sheringham said. Twirling the siphon by its neck he stepped over Maxted's legs and adjusted the tone control under one of the speaker boxes. He looked blithe and spruce, almost ten years younger. 'These are 30-second repeats, 400 microsens, amplification one thousand. I admit I've edited the track a little, but it's still remarkable how repulsive a beautiful sound can become. You'll never guess what this was.'

Maxted stirred sluggishly. The lake of mercury in his stomach was as cold and bottomless as an oceanic trench, and his arms and legs had become enormous, like the bloated appendages of a drowned giant. He could just see Sheringham bobbing about in front of him, and hear the slow beating of the sea in the distance. Nearer now, it pounded with a dull insistent rhythm, the great waves ballooning and bursting like bubbles in a lava sea.

'I'll tell you, Maxted, it took me a year to get that recording,' Sheringham was saying. He straddled Maxted, gesturing with the siphon. 'A year. Do you know how ugly a year can be?' For a moment he paused, then tore himself from the memory. 'Last Saturday, just after midnight, you and Susan were lying back in this same chair. You know, Maxted, there are audio-probes everywhere here. Slim as pencils, with a six-inch focus. I had four in that headrest alone.' He added, as a footnote: 'The wind is your own breathing, fairly heavy at the time, if I remember; your interlocked pulses produced the thunder effect.'

Maxted drifted in a wash of sound.

Some while later Sheringham's face filled his eyes, beard wagging, mouth working wildly.

'Maxted! You've only two more guesses, so for God's sake concentrate,' he shouted irritably, his voice almost lost among the thunder rolling from the sea. 'Come on, man, what is it? Maxted!' he bellowed. He leapt for the nearest loudspeaker and drove up the volume. The sound boomed out of the patio, reverberating into the night.

Maxted had almost gone now, his fading identity a small featureless island nearly eroded by the waves beating across it.

Sheringham knelt down and shouted into his ear.

'Maxted, can you hear the sea? Do you know where you're drowning?'

A succession of gigantic flaccid waves, each more lumbering and enveloping than the last, rode down upon them.

'In a kiss!' Sheringham screamed. 'A kiss!'

The island slipped and slid away into the molten shelf of the sea.

**·1958**

# · THE WAITING GROUNDS

Whether Henry Tallis, my predecessor at Murak Radio Observatory, knew about the Waiting Grounds I can't say. On the whole it seems obvious he must have done, and that the three weeks he spent handing the station over to me – a job which could easily have been done in three days – were merely to give him sufficient time to decide whether or not to tell me about them. Certainly he never did, and the implied judgment against me is one I haven't yet faced up to.

I remember that on the first evening after my arrival at Murak he asked me a question I've been puzzling over ever since.

We were up on the lounge deck of the observatory, looking out at the sand-reefs and fossil cones of the volcano jungle glowing in the false dusk, the great 250-foot steel bowl of the telescope humming faintly in the air above us.

'Tell me, Quaine,' Tallis suddenly asked, 'where would you like to be when the world ends?'

'I haven't really thought about it,' I admitted. 'Is there any urgency?'

'Urgency?' Tallis smiled at me thinly, his eyes amiable but assessing me shrewdly. 'Wait until you've been here a little longer.'

He had almost finished his last tour at the observatory and I assumed he was referring to the desolation around us which he, after fifteen years, was leaving thanklessly to my entire care. Later, of course, I realized how wrong I was, just as I misjudged the whole of Tallis's closed, complex personality.

He was a lean, ascetic-looking man of about fifty, withheld and moody, as I discovered the moment I debarked from the freighter flying me in to Murak – instead of greeting me at the ramp he sat in the half-track a hundred yards away at the edge of the port, watching silently through dark glasses as I heaved my suitcases across the burning, lava-thick sunlight, legs weary after the massive deceleration, stumbling in the unfamiliar gravity.

The gesture seemed characteristic. Tallis's manner was aloof and sardonic; everything he said had the same deliberately ambiguous overtones, that air of private mystery recluses and extreme introjects assume as a defence. Not that Tallis was in any way pathological – no one could spend fifteen years, even with six-monthly leaves, virtually alone on a remote planetary clinker like Murak without developing a few curious mannerisms. In fact, as I all too soon realized, what was really remarkable about Tallis was the degree to which he had preserved his sanity, not surrendered it.

He listened keenly to the latest news from Earth.

'The first pilotless launchings to Proxima Centauri are scheduled for 2250 ... the UN Assembly at Lake Success have just declared themselves a sovereign state ... V-R Day celebrations are to be discontinued – you must have heard it all on the radiocasts.'

'I haven't got a radio here,' Tallis said. 'Apart from the one up there, and that's tuned to the big spiral networks in Andromeda. On Murak we listen only to the important news.'

I nearly retorted that by the time it reached Murak the news, however important, would be a million years old, but on that first evening I was preoccupied with adjusting myself to an unfamiliar planetary environment – notably a denser atmosphere, slightly higher (1.2 E) gravity, vicious temperature swings from –30° to +160° – and programming new routines to fit myself into Murak's 18-hour day.

Above all, there was the prospect of two years of near-absolute isolation.

Ten miles from Murak Reef, the planet's only settlement, the observatory was sited among the first hills marking the northern edge of the inert volcano jungle which spread southward to Murak's equator. It consisted of the giant telescope and a straggling nexus of twenty or thirty asbestos domes which housed the automatic data processing and tracking units, generator and refrigerating plant, and a miscellany of replacement and vehicle stores, workshops and ancillary equipment.

The observatory was self-sufficient as regards electric power and water. On the near-by slopes farms of solar batteries had been planted out in quarter-mile strips, the thousands of cells winking in the sunlight like a field of diamonds, sucking power from the sun to drive the generator dynamos. On another slope, its huge mouth permanently locked into the rock face, a mobile water synthesizer slowly bored its way through the desert crust, mining out oxygen and hydrogen combined into the surface minerals.

'You'll have plenty of spare time on your hands,' the Deputy Director of the Astrographic Institute on Ceres had warned me when I initialled the contract. 'There's a certain amount of routine maintenance, checking the power feeds to the reflector traverses and the processing units, but otherwise you won't need to touch the telescope. A big digital does the heavy thinking, tapes all the data down in 2000-hour schedules. You fly the cans out with you when you go on leave.'

'So apart from shovelling the sand off the doorstep there's virtually nothing for me to do?' I'd commented.

'That's what you're being paid for. Probably not as much as you deserve. Two years will seem a long time, even with three leave intervals. But don't worry about going crazy. You aren't alone on Murak. You'll just be bored. £2000 worth, to be exact. However, you say you have a thesis to write. And you never know, you may like it there. Tallis, the observer you're taking over from, went out in '03 for two years like yourself, and stayed fifteen. He'll show you the ropes. Pleasant fellow, by all accounts, a little whimsical, probably try to pull your leg.'

Tallis drove me down to the settlement the first morning to collect my heavy vacuum baggage that had travelled spacehold.

'Murak Reef,' he pointed out as the old '95 Chrysler half-track churned through the thick luminous ash silted over the metal road. We crossed a system of ancient lava lakes, flat grey disks half a mile wide, their hard crusts blistered and pocked by the countless meteor showers that had driven into Murak during the past million years. In the distance a group of long flat-roofed sheds and three high ore elevators separated themselves from the landscape.

'I suppose they warned you. One supplies depot, a radio terminal and the minerals concession. Latest reliable estimates put the total population at seven.'

I stared out at the surrounding desert floor, cracked and tiered by the heat swings into what looked like huge plates of rusted iron, and at the massed cones of the volcano jungle yellowing in the sand haze. It was 4 o'clock local time – early morning – but the temperature was already over 80°. We drove with windows shuttered, sun curtain down, refrigerating unit pumping noisily.

'Must be fun on Saturday night,' I commented. 'Isn't there anything else?'

'Just the thermal storms, and a mean noon temperature of 160°.'

'In the shade?'

Tallis laughed. 'Shade? You must have a sense of humour. There isn't any shade on Murak. Don't ever forget it. Half an hour before noon the temperature starts to go up two degrees a minute. If you're caught out in it you'll be putting a match to your own pyre.'

Murak Reef was a dust hole. In the sheds backing onto the depot the huge ore crushers and conveyors of the extraction plants clanked and slammed. Tallis introduced me to the agent, a morose old man called Pickford, and to two young engineers taking the wraps off a new grader. No one made any attempt at small talk. We nodded briefly, loaded my luggage onto the half-track and left.

'A taciturn bunch,' I said. 'What are they mining?'

'Tantalum, Columbium, the Rare Earths. A heartbreaking job, the concentrations are barely workable. They're tempted to Murak by fabulous commission rates, but they're lucky if they can even fill their norms.'

'You can't be sorry you're leaving. What made you stay here fifteen years?'

'It would take me fifteen years to tell you,' Tallis rejoined. 'I like the empty hills and the dead lakes.'

I murmured some comment, and aware that I wasn't satisfied he suddenly scooped a handful of grey sand off the seat, held it up and let it sift away through his fingers. 'Prime archezoic loam. Pure bedrock. Spit on it and anything might happen. Perhaps you'll understand me if I say I've been waiting for it to rain.'

'Will it?'

Tallis nodded. 'In about two million years, so someone who came here told me.'

He said it with complete seriousness.

During the next few days, as we checked the stores and equipment inventories and ran over the installation together, I began to wonder if Tallis had lost his sense of time. Most men left to themselves for an indefinite period develop some occupational interest: chess or an insoluble dream-game or merely a compulsive wood-whittling. But Tallis, as far as I could see, did nothing. The cabin, a three-storey drum built round a central refrigerating column, was spartan and comfortless. Tallis's only recreation seemed to be staring out at the volcano jungle. This was an almost obsessive activity – all evening and most of the afternoon he would sit up on the lounge deck, gazing out at the hundreds of extinct cones visible from the observatory, their colours running the spectrum from red to violet as the day swung round into night.

The first indication of what Tallis was watching for came about a week before he was due to leave. He had crated up his few possessions and we were clearing out one of the small storage domes near the telescope. In the darkness at the back, draped across a pile of old fans, track links and beer coolers, were two pedal-powered refrigerator suits, enormous unwieldy sacks equipped with chest pylons and hand-operated cycle gears.

'Do you ever have to use these?' I asked Tallis, glumly visualizing what a generator failure could mean.

He shook his head. 'They were left behind by a survey team which did some work out in the volcanoes. There's an entire camp lying around in these sheds, in case you ever feel like a weekend on safari.'

Tallis was by the door. I moved my flashlight away and was about to switch it off when something flickered up at me from the floor. I stepped over the debris, searched about and found a small circular aluminium chest, about two feet across by a foot deep. Mounted on the back was a battery pack, thermostat and temperature selector. It was a typical relic of an expensively mounted expedition, probably a cocktail cabinet or hat box. Embossed in heavy gold lettering on the lid were the initials 'C.F.N.'

Tallis came over from the door.

'What's this?' he asked sharply, adding his flash to mine.

I would have left the case where it lay, but there was something in Tallis's voice, a distinct inflection of annoyance, that made me pick it up and shoulder past into the sunlight.

I cleaned off the dust, Tallis at my shoulder. Keying open the vacuum seals I sprung back the lid. Inside was a small tape recorder, spool racks and a telescopic boom mike that cantilevered three feet up into the air, hovering a few inches from my mouth. It was a magnificent piece of equipment, a single-order job hand-made by a specialist, worth at least £500 apart from the case.

'Beautifully tooled,' I remarked to Tallis. I tipped the platform and watched it spring gently. 'The air bath is still intact.'

I ran my fingers over the range indicator and the selective six-channel reading head. It was even fitted with a sonic trip, a useful device which could be set to trigger at anything from a fly's foot-fall to a walking crane's.

The trip had been set; I wondered what might have strayed across it when I saw that someone had anticipated me. The tape between the spools had been ripped out, so roughly that one spool had been torn off its bearings. The rack was empty, and the two frayed tabs hooked to the spool axles were the only pieces of tape left.

'Somebody was in a hurry,' I said aloud. I depressed the lid and polished the initials with my fingertips. 'This must have belonged to one of the members of the survey. C. F. N. Do you want to send it on to him?'

Tallis watched me pensively. 'No. I'm afraid the two members of the team died here. Just over a year ago.'

He told me about the incident. Two Cambridge geologists had negotiated through the Institute for Tallis's help in establishing a camp ten miles out in the volcano jungle, where they intended to work for a year, analysing the planet's core materials. The cost of bringing a vehicle to Murak was prohibitive, so Tallis had transported all the equipment to the camp site and set it up for them.

'I arranged to visit them once a month with power packs, water and supplies. The first time everything seemed all right. They were both over sixty, but standing up well to the heat. The camp and laboratory were running smoothly, and they had a small transmitter they could have used in an emergency.

'I saw them three times altogether. On my fourth visit they had vanished. I estimated that they'd been missing for about a week. Nothing was wrong. The transmitter was working, and there was plenty of water and power. I assumed they'd gone out collecting samples, lost themselves and died quickly in the first noon high.'

'You never found the bodies?'

'No. I searched for them, but in the volcano jungle the contours of the valley floors shift from hour to hour. I notified the Institute and two months later an inspector flew in from Ceres and drove out to the site with me. He certified the deaths, told me to dismantle the camp and store it here. There were a few personal things, but I've heard nothing from any friends or relatives.'

'Tragic,' I commented. I closed the tape recorder and carried it into the shed. We walked back to the cabin. It was an hour to noon, and the parabolic sun bumper over the roof was a bowl of liquid fire.

I said to Tallis: 'What on earth were they hoping to catch in the volcano jungle? The sonic trip was set.'

'Was it?' Tallis shrugged. 'What are you suggesting?'

'Nothing. It's just curious. I'm surprised there wasn't more of an investigation.'

'Why? To start with, the fare from Ceres is £800, over £3000 from Earth. They were working privately. Why should anyone waste time and money doubting the obvious?'

I wanted to press Tallis for detail, but his last remark seemed to close the episode. We ate a silent lunch, then went out on a tour of the solar farms, replacing burnt-out thermo-couples. I was left with a vanished tape, two deaths, and a silent teasing suspicion that linked them neatly together.

Over the next days I began to watch Tallis more closely, waiting for another clue to the enigma growing around him.

I did learn one thing that astonished me.

I had asked him about his plans for the future; these were indefinite – he said something vague about a holiday, nothing he anticipated with any eagerness, and sounded as if he had given no thought whatever to his retirement. Over the last few days, as his departure time drew closer, the entire focus of his mind became fixed upon the volcano jungle; from dawn until late into the night he sat quietly in his chair, staring out at the ghostless panorama of disintegrating cones, adrift in some private time sea.

'When are you coming back?' I asked with an attempt at playfulness, curious why he was leaving Murak at all.

He took the question seriously. 'I'm afraid I won't be. Fifteen years is long enough, just about the limit of time one can spend continuously in a single place. After that one gets institutionalized –'

'Continuously?' I broke in. 'You've had your leaves?'

'No, I didn't bother. I was busy here.'

'Fifteen years!' I shouted. 'Good God, why? In this of all places! And what do you mean, "busy"? You're just sitting here, waiting for nothing. What are you supposed to be watching for, anyway?'

Tallis smiled evasively, started to say something and then thought better of it.

The question pressed round him. What *was* he waiting for? Were the geologists still alive? Was he expecting them to return, or make some signal? As I watched him pace about the cabin on his last morning I was convinced there was something he couldn't quite bring himself to tell me. Almost melodramatically he watched out over the desert, delaying his departure until the thirty-minute take-off siren hooted from the port. As we climbed into the half-track I fully expected the glowing spectres of the two geologists to come looming out of the volcano jungle, uttering cries of murder and revenge.

He shook my hand carefully before he went aboard. 'You've got my address all right? You're quite sure?' For some reason, which confused my cruder suspicions, he had made a special point of ensuring that both I and the Institute would be able to contact him.

'Don't worry,' I said. 'I'll let you know if it rains.'

He looked at me sombrely. 'Don't wait too long.' His eyes strayed past my head towards the southern horizon, through the sand-haze to the endless sea of cones. He added: 'Two million years is a long time.'

I took his arm as we walked to the ramp. 'Tallis,' I asked quietly, 'what are you watching for? There's something, isn't there?'

He pulled away from me, collected himself. 'What?' he said shortly, looking at his wristwatch.

'You've been trying to tell me all week,' I insisted. 'Come on, man.'

He shook his head abruptly, muttered something about the heat and stepped quickly through the lock.

I started to shout after him: 'Those two geologists are out there ... !' but the five-minute siren shattered the air and by the time it stopped Tallis had disappeared down the companionway and crewmen were shackling on the launching gantry and sealing the cargo and passenger locks.

I stood at the edge of the port as the ship cleared its take-off check, annoyed with myself for waiting until the last impossible moment to press Tallis for an explanation. Half an hour later he was gone.

Over the next few days Tallis began to slide slowly into the back of my mind. I gradually settled into the observatory, picked out new routines to keep time continuously on the move. Mayer, the metallurgist down at the mine, came over to the cabin most evenings to play chess and forget his pitifully low extraction rates. He was a big, muscular fellow of thirty-five who loathed Murak's climate, geology and bad company, a little crude but the sort of tonic I needed after an overdose of Tallis.

Mayer had met Tallis only once, and had never heard about the deaths of the two geologists.

'Damned fools, what were they looking for? Nothing to do with geology, Murak hasn't got one.'

Pickford, the old agent down at the depot, was the only person on Murak who remembered the two men, but time had garbled his memories.

'Salesmen, they were,' he told me, blowing into his pipe. 'Tallis did the heavy work for them. Should never have come here, trying to sell all those books.'

'Books?'

'Cases full. Bibles, if I recall.'

'Textbooks,' I suggested. 'Did you see them?'

'Sure I did,' he said, puttering to himself. 'Guinea moroccos.' He jerked his head sharply. 'You won't sell them here, I told them.'

It sounded exactly like a dry piece of academic humour. I could see Tallis and the two scientists pulling Pickford's leg, passing off their reference library as a set of commercial samples.

I suppose the whole episode would eventually have faded, but Tallis's charts kept my interest going. There were about twenty of them, half million aerials of the volcano jungle within a fifteen-mile radius of the observatory. One of them was marked with what I assumed to be the camp site of the geologists and alternative routes to and from the observatory. The camp was just over ten miles away, across terrain that was rough but not over-difficult for a tracked car.

I still suspected I was getting myself wound up over nothing. A meaningless approach arrow on the charts, the faintest suggestion of a cryptic 'X', and I should have been off like a rocket after a geldspar mine or two mysterious graves. I was almost sure that Tallis had not been responsible, either by negligence or design, for the deaths of the two men, but that still left a number of unanswered questions.

The next clear day I checked over the half-track, strapped a flare pistol into my knee holster and set off, warning Pickford to listen out for a mayday call on the Chrysler's transmitter.

It was just after dawn when I gunned the half-track out of the observatory compound and headed up the slope between two battery farms, following the route mapped out on the charts. Behind me the telescope swung slowly on its bogies, tirelessly sweeping its great steel ear through the Cepheid talk. The temperature was in the low seventies, comfortably cool for Murak, the sky a fresh cerise, broken by lanes of indigo that threw vivid violet lights on the drifts of grey ash on the higher slopes of the volcano jungle.

The observatory soon fell behind, obscured by the exhaust dust. I passed the water synthesizer, safely pointed at ten thousand tons of silicon hydrate, and within twenty minutes reached the nearest cone, a white broad-backed giant two hundred feet high, and drove round it into the first valley. Fifty feet across at their summits, the volcanoes jostled together like a herd of enormous elephants, separated by narrow dust-filled valleys, sometimes no more than a hundred yards apart, here and there giving way to the flat mile-long deck of a fossil lava lake. Wherever possible the route took advantage of these, and I soon picked up the tracks left by the Chrysler on its trips a year earlier.

I reached the site in three hours. What was left of the camp stood on a beach overlooking one of the lakes, a dismal collection of fuel cylinders, empty cold stores and water tanks sinking under the tides of dust washed up by the low thermal winds. On the far side of the lake the violet-capped cones of the volcanoes ranged southwards. Behind, a crescent of sharp cliffs cut off half the sky.

I walked round the site, looking for some trace of the two geologists. A battered tin field-desk lay on its side, green paint blistered and scratched. I turned it over and pulled out its drawers, finding nothing except a charred notebook and a telephone, the receiver melted solidly into its cradle.

Tallis had done his job too well.

The temperature was over 100° by the time I climbed back into the half-track and a couple of miles ahead I had to stop as the cooling unit was draining power from the spark plugs and stalling the engine. The outside temperature was 130°, the sky a roaring shield, reflected in the slopes around me so that they seemed to stream with molten wax. I sealed all the shutters and changed into neutral, even then having to race the ancient engine to provide enough current for the cooler. I sat there for over an hour in the dim gloom of the dashboard, ears deadened by the engine roar, right foot cramping, cursing Tallis and the two geologists.

That evening I unfurled some crisp new vellum, flexed my slide rule and determined to start work on my thesis.

One afternoon, two or three months later, as we turned the board between chess games, Mayer remarked: 'I saw Pickford this morning. He told me he had some samples to show you.'

'TV tapes?'

'Bibles, I thought he said.'

I looked in on Pickford the next time I was down at the settlement. He was hovering about in the shadows behind the counter, white suit dirty and unpressed.

He puffed smoke at me. 'Those salesmen,' he explained. 'You were inquiring about. I told you they were selling Bibles.'

I nodded. 'Well?'

'I kept some.'

I put out my cigarette. 'Can I see them?'

He gestured me round the counter with his pipe. 'In the back.'

I followed him between the shelves, loaded with fans, radios and TV-scopes, all outdated models imported years earlier to satisfy the boom planet Murak had never become.

'There it is,' Pickford said. Standing against the back wall of the depot was a three-by-three wooden crate, taped with metal bands. Pickford ferreted about for a wrench. 'Thought you might like to buy some.'

'How long has it been here?'

'About a year. Tallis forgot to collect it. Only found it last week.'

Doubtful, I thought: more likely he was simply waiting for Tallis to be safely out of the way. I watched while he prised off the lid. Inside was a tough brown wrapping paper. Pickford broke the seals and folded the sides back carefully, revealing a layer of black morocco-bound volumes.

I pulled out one of them and held the heavily ribbed spine up to the light.

It was a Bible, as Pickford had promised. Below it were a dozen others.

'You're right,' I said. Pickford pulled up a radiogram and sat down, watching me.

I looked at the Bible again. It was in mint condition, the King James Authorized Version. The marbling inside the endboards was unmarked. A publisher's ticket slipped out onto the floor, and I realized that the copy had hardly come from a private library.

The bindings varied slightly. The next volume I pulled out was a copy of the Vulgate.

'How many crates did they have altogether?' I asked Pickford.

'Bibles? Fourteen, fifteen with this one. They ordered them all after they got here. This was the last one.' He pulled out another volume and handed it to me. 'Good condition, eh?'

It was a Koran.

I started lifting the volumes out and got Pickford to help me sort them on the shelves. When we counted them up there were ninety in all: thirty-five Holy Bibles (twenty-four Authorized Versions and eleven Vulgates), fifteen copies of the Koran, five of the Talmud, ten of the Bhagavat Gita and twenty-five of the Upanishads.

I took one of each and gave Pickford a £10 note.

'Any time you want some more,' he called after me. 'Maybe I can arrange a discount.' He was chuckling to himself, highly pleased with the deal, one up on the salesmen.

When Mayer called round that evening he noticed the six volumes on my desk.

'Pickford's samples,' I explained. I told him how I had found the crate at the depot and that it had been ordered by the geologists after their arrival. 'According to Pickford they ordered a total of fifteen crates. All Bibles.'

'He's senile.'

'No. His memory is good. There were certainly other crates because this one was sealed and he knew it contained Bibles.'

'Damned funny. Maybe they were salesmen.'

'Whatever they were they certainly weren't geologists. Why did Tallis say they were? Anyway, why didn't he ever mention that they had ordered all these Bibles?'

'Perhaps he'd forgotten.'

'Fifteen crates? Fifteen crates of Bibles? Heavens above, what did they do with them?'

Mayer shrugged. He went over to the window. 'Do you want me to radio Ceres?'

'Not yet. It still doesn't add up to anything.'

'There might be a reward. Probably a big one. God, I could go home!'

'Relax. First we've got to find out what these so-called geologists were doing here, why they ordered this fantastic supply of Bibles. One thing: whatever it was, I swear Tallis knew about it. Originally I thought they

might have discovered a geldspar mine and been double-crossed by Tallis
– that sonic trip was suspicious. Or else that they'd deliberately faked their
own deaths so that they could spend a couple of years working the mine,
using Tallis as their supply source. But all these Bibles mean we must start
thinking in completely different categories.'

Round the clock for three days, with only short breaks for sleep hunched
in the Chrysler's driving seat, I systematically swept the volcano jungle,
winding slowly through the labyrinth of valleys, climbing to the crest
of every cone, carefully checking every exposed quartz vein, every rift
or gulley that might hide what I was convinced was waiting for me.

Mayer deputized at the observatory, driving over every afternoon. He
helped me recondition an old diesel generator in one of the storage domes
and we lashed it on to the back of the half-track to power the cabin heater
needed for the −30° nights and the three big spotlights fixed on the roof,
providing a 360° traverse. I made two trips with a full cargo of fuel out
to the camp site, dumped them there and made it my base.

Across the thick glue-like sand of the volcano jungle, we calculated, a
man of sixty could walk at a maximum of one mile an hour, and spend
at most two hours in 70° or above sunlight. That meant that whatever
there was to find would be within twelve square miles of the camp site,
three square miles if we included a return journey.

I searched the volcanoes as exactingly as I could, marking each cone
and the adjacent valleys on the charts as I covered them, at a steady five
miles an hour, the great engine of the Chrysler roaring ceaselessly, from
noon, when the valleys filled with fire and seemed to run with lava again,
round to midnight, when the huge cones became enormous mountains of
bone, sombre graveyards presided over by the fantastic colonnades and
hanging galleries of the sand reefs, suspended from the lake rims like
inverted cathedrals.

I forced the Chrysler on, swinging the bumpers to uproot any suspicious
crag or boulder that might hide a mine shaft, ramming through huge drifts
of fine white sand that rose in soft clouds around the half-track like the
dust of powdered silk.

I found nothing. The reefs and valleys were deserted, the volcano slopes
untracked, craters empty, their shallow floors littered with meteor debris,
rock sulphur and cosmic dust.

I decided to give up just before dawn on the fourth morning, after waking
from a couple of hours of cramped and restless sleep.

'I'm coming in now,' I reported to Mayer over the transmitter. 'There's
nothing out here. I'll collect what fuel there is left from the site and see
you for breakfast.'

Dawn had just come up as I reached the site. I loaded the fuel cans
back onto the half-track, switched off the spotlights and took what
I knew would be my last look round. I sat down at the field desk
and watched the sun arching upward through the cones across the

lake. Scooping a handful of ash off the desk, I scrutinized it sadly for geldspar.

'Prime archezoic loam,' I said, repeating Tallis's words aloud to the dead lake. I was about to spit on it, more in anger than in hope, when some of the tumblers in my mind started to click.

About five miles from the far edge of the lake, silhouetted against the sunrise over the volcanoes, was a long 100-foot-high escarpment of hard slate-blue rock that lifted out of the desert bed and ran for about two miles in a low clean sweep across the horizon, disappearing among the cones in the south-west. Its outlines were sharp and well defined, suggesting that its materials pre-dated the planet's volcanic period. The escarpment sat squarely across the desert, gaunt and rigid, and looked as if it had been there since Murak's beginning, while the soft ashy cones and grey hillocks around it had known only the planet's end.

It was no more than an uninformed guess, but suddenly I would have bet my entire two years' salary that the rocks of the escarpment were archezoic. It was about three miles outside the area I had been combing, just visible from the observatory.

The vision of a geldspar mine returned sharply!

The lake took me nearly halfway there. I raced the Chrysler across it at forty, wasted thirty minutes picking a route through an elaborate sand reef, and then entered a long steeply walled valley which led directly towards the escarpment.

A mile away I saw that the escarpment was not, as it first seemed, a narrow continuous ridge, but a circular horizontal table. A curious feature was the almost perfect flatness of the table top, as if it had been deliberately levelled by a giant sword. Its sides were unusually symmetrical; they sloped at exactly the same angle, about 35°, and formed a single cliff unbroken by fissures or crevices.

I reached the table in an hour, parked the half-track at its foot and looked up at the great rounded flank of dull blue rock sloping away from me, rising like an island out of the grey sea of the desert floor.

I changed down into bottom gear and floored the accelerator. Steering the Chrysler obliquely across the slope to minimize the angle of ascent, I roared slowly up the side, tracks skating and racing, swinging the half-track around like a frantic pendulum.

Scaling the crest, I levelled off and looked out over a plateau about two miles in diameter, bare except for a light blue carpet of cosmic dust.

In the centre of the plateau, at least a mile across, was an enormous metallic lake, heat ripples spiralling upwards from its dark smooth surface.

I edged the half-track forward, head out of the side window, watching carefully, holding down the speed that picked up too easily. There were no meteorites or rock fragments lying about; presumably the lake surface cooled and set at night, to melt and extend itself as the temperature rose the next day.

Although the roof seemed hard as steel I stopped about 300 yards from the edge, cut the engine and climbed up onto the cabin.

The shift of perspective was slight but sufficient. The lake vanished, and I realized I was looking down at a shallow basin, about half a mile wide, scooped out of the roof.

I swung back into the cab and slammed in the accelerator. The basin, like the table top, was a perfect circle, sloping smoothly to the floor about one hundred feet below its rim, in imitation of a volcanic crater.

I braked the half-track at the edge and jumped out.

Four hundred yards away, in the basin's centre, five gigantic rectangular slabs of stone reared up from a vast pentagonal base.

This, then, was the secret Tallis had kept from me.

The basin was empty, the air warmer, strangely silent after three days of the Chrysler's engine roaring inside my head.

I lowered myself over the edge and began to walk down the slope towards the great monument in the centre of the basin. For the first time since my arrival on Murak I was unable to see the desert and the brilliant colours of the volcano jungle. I had strayed into a pale blue world, as pure and exact as a geometric equation, composed of the curving floor, the pentagonal base and the five stone rectangles towering up into the sky like the temple of some abstract religion.

It took me nearly three minutes to reach the monument. Behind me, on the sky-line, the half-track's engine steamed faintly. I went up to the base stone, which was a yard thick and must have weighed over a thousand tons, and placed my palms on its surface. It was still cool, the thin blue grain closely packed. Like the megaliths standing on it, the pentagon was unornamented and geometrically perfect.

I heaved myself up and approached the nearest megalith. The shadows around me were enormous parallelograms, their angles shrinking as the sun blazed up into the sky. I walked slowly round into the centre of the group, dimly aware that neither Tallis nor the two geologists could have carved the megaliths and raised them onto the pentagon, when I saw that the entire inner surface of the nearest megalith was covered by row upon row of finely chiselled hieroglyphs.

Swinging round, I ran my hands across its surface. Large patches had crumbled away, leaving a faint indecipherable tracery, but most of the surface was intact, packed solidly with pictographic symbols and intricate cuneiform glyphics that ran down it in narrow columns.

I stepped over to the next megalith. Here again, the inner face was covered with tens of thousands of minute carved symbols, the rows separated by finely cut dividing rules that fell the full fifty-foot height of the megalith.

There were at least a dozen languages, all in alphabets I had never seen before, strings of meaningless ciphers among which I could pick odd

cross-hatched symbols that seemed to be numerals, and peculiar serpentine forms that might have represented human figures in stylized poses.

Suddenly my eye caught:

| | | |
|---|---|---|
| CYR*RK VII | A*PHA LEP**IS | *D 1317 |

Below was another, damaged but legible.

| | | |
|---|---|---|
| AMEN*TEK LC*V | *LPHA LE*ORIS | AD 13** |

There were blanks among the letters, where time had flaked away
minute grains of the stone.

My eyes raced down the column. There were a score more entries:

| | | |
|---|---|---|
| PONT*AR*H*CV | ALPH* L*PORIS | A* *318 |
| MYR*K LV* | A**HA LEPORI* | AD 13*6 |
| KYR** XII | ALPH* LEP*RIS | AD 1*19 |
| .................... | .................... | .................... |
| .................... | .................... | .................... |

The list of names, all from Alpha Leporis, continued down the column.
I followed it to the base, where the names ended three inches from the
bottom, then moved along the surface, across rows of hieroglyphs, and
picked up the list three or four columns later.

| | | |
|---|---|---|
| M*MARYK XX*V | A*PHA LEPORI* | AD 1389 |
| CYRARK IX | ALPHA *EPORIS | AD 1390 |
| .................... | .................... | .................... |

I went over to the megalith on my left and began to examine the
inscriptions carefully.

Here the entries read:

| | | |
|---|---|---|
| MINYS-259 | DELT* ARGUS | AD 1874 |
| TYLNYS-413 | DELTA ARGUS | *D 1874 |
| .................... | .................... | .................... |

There were fewer blanks; to the right of the face the entries were more
recent, the lettering sharper. In all there were five distinct languages, four
of them, including Earth's, translations of the first entry running down
the left-hand margin of each column.

The third and fourth megaliths recorded entries from Gamma Grus and
Beta Trianguli. They followed the same pattern, their surfaces divided into
eighteen-inch-wide columns, each of which contained five rows of entries,
the four hieroglyphic languages followed by Earth's, recording the same
minimal data in the same terse formula: Name – Place – Date

I had looked at four of the megaliths. The fifth stood with its back to the sun, its inner face hidden.

I walked over to it, crossing the oblique panels of shadow withdrawing to their sources, curious as to what fabulous catalogue of names I should find.

*The fifth megalith was blank.*

My eyes raced across its huge unbroken surface, marked only by the quarter-inch-deep grooves of the dividing rules some thoughtful master mason from the stars had chiselled to tabulate the entries from Earth that had never come.

I returned to the other megaliths and for half an hour read at random, arms outstretched involuntarily across the great inscription panels, fingertips tracing the convolutions of the hieroglyphs, seeking among the thousands of signatures some clue to the identity and purpose of the four stellar races.

| | | |
|---|---|---|
| COPT*C LEAGUE MILV | BETA TRIANGULI | *D 1723 |
| ISARI* LEAGUE *VII | BETA *RIANGULI | AD 1724 |
| | | |
| MAR-5-GO | GAMMA GRUS | AD 1959 |
| VEN-7-GO | GAMMA GRUS | AD 1960 |
| | | |
| TETRARK XII | ALPHA LEPORIS | AD 2095 |

Dynasties recurred again and again, Cyrark's, Minys-'s, -Go's, separated by twenty- or thirty-year intervals that appeared to be generations. Before AD 1200 all entries were illegible. This represented something over half the total. The surfaces of the megaliths were almost completely covered, and initially I assumed that the first entries had been made roughly 2200 years earlier, shortly after the birth of Christ. However, the frequency of the entries increased algebraically: in the 15th century there were one or two a year, by the 20th century there were five or six, and by the present year the number varied from twenty entries from Delta Argus to over thirty-five from Alpha Leporis.

The last of these, at the extreme right corner of the megalith, was:

| | | |
|---|---|---|
| CYRARK CCCXXIV | ALPHA LEPORIS | AD 2218 |

The letters were freshly incised, perhaps no more than a day old, even a few hours. Below, a free space of two feet reached to the floor.

Breaking off my scrutiny, I jumped down from the base stone and carefully searched the surrounding basin, sweeping the light dust carpet for vehicle or foot marks, the remains of implements or scaffolding.

But the basin was empty, the dust untouched except for the single file of prints leading down from the half-track.

I was sweating uncomfortably, and the thermo-alarm strapped to my wrist rang, warning me that the air temperature was 85°, ninety minutes to noon. I re-set it to 100°, took a last look round the five megaliths, and then made my way back to the half-track.

Heat waves raced and glimmered round the rim of the basin, and the sky was a dark inflamed red, mottled by the thermal pressure fields massing overhead like storm clouds. I jogged along at a half run, in a hurry to contact Mayer. Without his confirmation the authorities on Ceres would treat my report as the fantasy of a sand-happy lunatic. In addition, I wanted him to bring his camera; we could develop the reels within half an hour and radio a dozen stills as indisputable proof.

More important, I wanted someone to share the discovery, provide me with at least some cover in numbers. The frequency of entries on the megaliths, and the virtual absence of any further space – unless the reverse sides were used, which seemed unlikely – suggested a climax was soon to be reached, probably the climax for which Tallis had been waiting. Hundreds of entries had been made during his fifteen years on Murak; watching all day from the observatory he must have seen every landing.

As I swung into the half-track the emergency light on the transceiver above the windscreen was pulsing insistently. I switched to audio and Mayer's voice snapped into my ear.

'Quaine? Is that you? Where the hell are you, man? I nearly put out a mayday for you!'

He was at the camp site. Calling in from the observatory when I failed to arrive, he assumed I had broken down and abandoned the half-track, and had come out searching for me.

I picked him up at the camp site half an hour later, retroversed the tracks in a squealing circle of dust and kicked off again at full throttle. Mayer pressed me all the way back but I told him nothing, driving the Chrysler hard across the lake, paralleling the two previous sets of tracks and throwing up a huge cloud of dust 150 feet into the air. It was now over 95°, and the ash hills in the valley at the end of the lake were beginning to look angry and boiled.

Eager to get Mayer down into the basin, and with my mind spinning like a disintegrating flywheel, it was only as the half-track roared up the table slope that I felt a first chilling pang of fear. Through the windscreen I hesitantly scanned the tilting sky. Soon after reaching the basin we would have to shut down for an hour, two of us crammed together in the fume-filled cabin, deafened by the engine, sitting targets with the periscope blinded by the glare.

The centre of the plateau was a pulsing blur, as the air trapped in the basin throbbed upward into the sun. I drove straight towards it, Mayer stiffening in his seat. A hundred yards from the basin's edge the air suddenly cleared and we could see the tops of the megaliths. Mayer leapt up and swung out of the door onto the running board as I cut the engine and slammed the half-track to a halt by the rim. We jumped down, grabbing flare pistols and shouting to each other, slid into the basin and sprinted through the boiling air to the megaliths looming up in the centre.

I half-expected to find a reception party waiting for us, but the megaliths were deserted. I reached the pentagon fifty yards ahead of Mayer, climbed up and waited for him, gulping in the molten sunlight.

I helped him up and led him over to one of the megaliths, picked a column and began to read out the entries. Then I took him round the others, recapitulating everything I had discovered, pointing out the blank tablet reserved for Earth.

Mayer listened, broke away and wandered off, staring up dully at the megaliths.

'Quaine, you've really found something,' he muttered softly. 'Crazy, must be some sort of temple.'

I followed him round, wiping the sweat off my face and shielding my eyes from the glare reflected off the great slabs.

'Look at them, Mayer! They've been coming here for ten thousand years! Do you know what this means?'

Mayer tentatively reached out and touched one of the megaliths. '"Argive League XXV ... Beta Tri-"' he read out. 'There are others, then. God Almighty. What do you think they look like?'

'What does it matter? Listen. They must have levelled this plateau themselves, scooped out the basin and cut these tablets from the living rock. Can you even imagine the tools they used?'

We crouched in the narrow rectangle of shadow in the lee of the sunward megalith. The temperature climbed, forty-five minutes to noon, 105°

'What is all this, though?' Mayer asked. 'Their burial ground?'

'Unlikely. Why leave a tablet for Earth? If they've been able to learn our language they'd know the gesture was pointless. Anyway, elaborate burial customs are a sure sign of decadence, and there's something here that suggests the exact opposite. I'm convinced they expect that some time in the future we'll take an active part in whatever is celebrated here.'

'Maybe, but what? Think in new categories, remember?' Mayer squinted up at the megaliths. 'This could be anything from an ethnological bill of lading to the guest list at an all-time cosmic house party.'

He noticed something, frowned, then suddenly wrenched away from me. He leapt to his feet, pressed his hands against the surface of the slab behind us and ran his eyes carefully over the grain.

'What's worrying you?' I asked.

'Shut up!' he snapped. He scratched his thumbnail at the surface, trying to dislodge a few grains. 'What are you talking about, Quaine, these slabs aren't made of stone!'

He slipped out his jack knife, sprung the blade and stabbed viciously at the megalith, slashing a two-foot-long groove across the inscriptions.

I stood up and tried to restrain him but he shouldered me away and ran his finger down the groove, collecting a few fragments.

He turned on me angrily. 'Do you know what this is? *Tantalum oxide!* Pure ninety-nine per cent paygold. No wonder our extraction rates are fantastically small. I couldn't understand it, but these people –' he jerked his thumb furiously at the megaliths '– have damn well milked the planet dry to build these crazy things!'

It was 115°. The air was beginning to turn yellow and we were breathing in short exhausted pants.

'Let's get back to the truck,' I temporized. Mayer was losing control, carried away by his rage. With his big burly shoulders hunched in anger, staring up blindly at the five great megaliths, face contorted by the heat, he looked like an insane sub-man pinned in the time trophy of a galactic super-hunter.

He was ranting away as we stumbled through the dust towards the half-track.

'What do you want to do?' I shouted. 'Cut them down and put them through your ore crushers?'

Mayer stopped, the blue dust swirling about his legs. The air was humming as the basin floor expanded in the heart. The half-track was only fifty yards away, its refrigerated cabin a cool haven.

Mayer was watching me, nodding slowly. 'It could be done. Ten tons of Hy-Dyne planted round those slabs would crack them into small enough pieces for a tractor to handle. We could store them out at the observatory, then sneak them later into my refining tanks.'

I walked on, shaking my head with a thin grin. The heat was hitting Mayer, welling up all the irrational bitterness of a year's frustration. 'It's an idea. Why don't you get in touch with Gamma Grus? Maybe they'll give you the lease.'

'I'm serious, Quaine,' Mayer called after me. 'In a couple of years we'd be rich men.'

'You're crazy!' I shouted back at him. 'The sun's boiling your brains.'

I began to scale the slope up to the rim. The next hour in the cabin was going to be difficult, cooped up with a maniac eager to tear the stars apart. The butt of the flare pistol swinging on my knee caught my eye; a poor weapon, though, against Mayer's physique.

I had climbed almost up to the rim when I heard his feet thudding through the dust. I started to turn round just as he was on me, swinging a tremendous blow that struck me on the back of the head. I fell, watched him close in and then stood up, my skull exploding, and grappled with him. We stumbled over each other for a moment, the walls of the basin diving around us like a switchback, and then he knocked my hands away and smashed a heavy right cross into my face.

I fell on my back, stunned by the pain; the blow seemed to have loosened my jaw and damaged all the bones on the left side of my face. I managed to sit up and saw Mayer running past. He reached one hand to the rim, pulled himself up and lurched over to the half-track.

I dragged the flare pistol out of its holster, snapped back the bolt and trained it at Mayer. He was thirty yards away, turning the nearside door handle. I held the butt with both hands and fired as he opened the door. He looked round at the sharp detonation and watched the silver shell soar swiftly through the air towards him, ready to duck.

The shell missed him by three feet and exploded against the cabin roof. There was a brilliant flash of light that resolved itself a fraction of a second later into a fireball of incandescent magnesium vapour ten feet in diameter. This slowly faded to reveal the entire driving cabin, bonnet and forward side-panels of the half-track burning strongly with a loud, heavy crackling. Out of this maelstrom suddenly plunged the figure of Mayer, moving with violent speed, blackened arms across his face. He tripped over the rim, catapulted down into the dust and rolled for about twenty yards before he finally lay still, a shapeless bundle of smoking rags.

I looked numbly at my wristwatch. It was ten minutes to noon. The temperature was 130°. I pulled myself to my feet and trudged slowly up the slope towards the half-track, head thudding like a volcano, uncertain whether I would be strong enough to lift myself out of the basin.

When I was ten feet from the rim I could see that the windscreen of the half-track had melted and was dripping like treacle onto the dashboard.

I dropped the flare pistol and turned round.

It was five minutes to noon. Around me, on all sides, enormous sheets of fire were cascading slowly from the sky, passing straight through the floor of the basin, and then rising again in an inverted torrent. The megaliths were no longer visible, screened by curtains of brilliant light, but I groped forward, following the slope, searching for what shade would still be among them.

Twenty yards farther on I saw that the sun was directly overhead. It expanded until the disc was as wide as the basin, and then lowered itself to about ten feet above my head, a thousand rivers of fire streaming across its surface in all directions. There was a terrifying roaring and barking noise, overlaid by a dull, massive pounding as all the volcanoes in the volcano jungle began to erupt again. I walked on, in a dream, shuffling slowly, eyes closed to shut out the furnace around me. Then I discovered that I was sitting on the floor of the basin, which started to spin, setting up a high-pitched screaming.

*A strange vision swept like a flame through my mind.*

*For aeons I plunged, spiralling weightlessly through a thousand whirling vortexes, swirled and buffeted down chasmic eddies, splayed out across the disintegrating matrix of the continuum, a dreamless ghost in flight from the cosmic* Now. *Then a million motes of light prickled the darkness above me, illuminating enormous curving causeways of time and space veering out past the stars to the rim of the galaxy. My dimensions shrank to a metaphysical extension of astral zero, I was propelled upward to the stars. Aisles of light broke and splintered around me, I passed Aldebaran, soared over Betelgeuse and Vega, zoomed past Antares, finally halted a hundred light years above the crown of Canopus.*

*Epochs drifted. Time massed on gigantic fronts, colliding like crippled universes. Abruptly, the infinite worlds of tomorrow unfolded before me – ten thousand years, a hundred thousand, unnumbered millennia raced past me in a blur of light, an iridescent cataract of stars and nebulae, interlaced by flashing trajectories of flight and exploration.*

*I entered deep time.*

Deep Time: 1,000,000 mega-years. I saw the Milky Way, a wheeling carousel of fire, and Earth's remote descendants, countless races inhabiting every stellar system in the galaxy. The dark intervals between the stars were a continuously flickering field of light, a gigantic phosphorescent ocean, filled with the vibrating pulses of electromagnetic communication pathways.

To cross the enormous voids between the stars they have progressively slowed their physiological time, first ten, then a hundred-fold, so accelerating stellar and galactic time. Space has become alive with transient swarms of comets and meteors, the constellations have begun to dislocate and shift, the slow majestic rotation of the universe itself is at last visible.

Deep Time: 10,000,000 mega-years. Now they have left the Milky Way, which has started to fragment and dissolve. To reach the island galaxies they have further slowed their time schemes by a factor of 10,000, and can thus communicate with each other across vast inter-galactic distances in a subjective period of only a few years. Continuously expanding into deep space, they have extended their physiological dependence upon electronic memory banks which store the atomic and molecular patterns within their bodies, transmit them outward at the speed of light, and later re-assemble them.

Deep Time: 100,000,000 mega-years. They have spread now to all the neighbouring galaxies, swallowing thousands of nebulae. Their time schemes have decelerated a million-fold, they have become the only permanent forms in an ever-changing world. In a single instant of their lives a star emerges and dies, a sub-universe is born, a score of planetary life-systems evolve and vanish. Around them the universe sparkles and flickers with myriad points of light, as untold numbers of constellations appear and fade.

Now, too, they have finally shed their organic forms and are composed of radiating electromagnetic fields, the primary energy substratum of the universe, complex networks of multiple dimensions, alive with the constant tremor of the sentient messages they carry, bearing the life-ways of the race.

To power these fields, they have harnessed entire galaxies riding the wave-fronts of the stellar explosions out towards the terminal helixes of the universe.

Deep Time: 1,000,000,000 mega-years. They are beginning to dictate the form and dimensions of the universe. To girdle the distances which circumscribe the cosmos they have reduced their time period to 0.00000001 of its previous phase. The great galaxies and spiral nebulae which once seemed to live for eternity are now of such brief duration that they are no longer visible. The universe is now almost filled by the great vibrating mantle of ideation, a vast shimmering harp which has completely translated itself into pure wave form, independent of any generating source.

As the universe pulses slowly, its own energy vortices flexing and dilating, so the force-fields of the ideation mantle flex and dilate in sympathy, growing like an embryo within the womb of the cosmos, a child which will soon fill and consume its parent.

Deep Time: 10,000,000,000 mega-years. The ideation-field has now swallowed the cosmos, substituted its own dynamic, its own spatial and temporal dimensions. All primary time and energy fields have been engulfed. Seeking the final extension of itself within its own bounds the mantle has reduced its time period to an almost infinitesimal $0.00000000 \ldots n$ of its previous interval. Time has virtually ceased to exist, the ideation-field is nearly stationary, infinitely slow eddies of sentience undulating outward across its mantles.

Ultimately it achieves the final predicates of time and space, eternity and infinity, and slows to absolute zero. Then with a cataclysmic eruption it disintegrates, no longer able to contain itself. Its vast energy patterns begin to collapse, the whole system twists and thrashes in its mortal agony, thrusting outwards huge cataracts of fragmenting energy. In parallel, time emerges.

Out of this debris the first proto-galactic fields are formed, coalescing to give the galaxies and nebulae, the stars encircled by their planetary bodies. Among these, from the elemental seas, based on the carbon atom, emerge the first living forms.

So the cycle renews itself . . .

*The stars swam, their patterns shifting through a dozen constellations, novas flooded the darkness like blinding arcs, revealing the familiar profiles of the Milky Way, the constellations Orion, Coma Berenices, Cygnus.*

*Lowering my eyes from the storm-tossed sky, I saw the five megaliths. I was back on Murak. Around me the basin was filled with a great concourse of silent figures, ranged upward along the darkened slopes, shoulder to shoulder in endless ranks, like spectators in a spectral arena.*

*Beside me a voice spoke, and it seemed to have told me everything I had witnessed of the great cosmic round.*

*Just before I sank into unconsciousness for the last time I tried to ask the question ever present in my drifting mind, but it answered before I spoke, the star-littered sky, the five megaliths and the watching multitude spinning and swirling away into a dream as it said*

*'Meanwhile we wait here, at the threshold of time and space, celebrating the identity and kinship of the particles within our bodies with those of the sun and the stars of our brief private times with the vast periods of the galaxies, with the total unifying time of the cosmos . . .'*

I woke lying face downward in the cool evening sand, shadows beginning to fill the basin, the thermal winds blowing a crisp refreshing breeze across my head and back. Below, the megaliths rose up into the thin blue air, their lower halves cut by the shadow-line of the sinking sun. I lay quietly, stirring my legs and arms tentatively, conscious of the gigantic rifts that had driven through my mind. After a few minutes I pulled myself to my feet and gazed round at the slopes curving away from me, the memory of the insane vision vivid in my mind.

The vast concourse that had filled the basin, the dream of the cosmic cycle, the voice of my interlocutor – were still real to me, a world in parallel I had just stepped from, and the door to which hung somewhere in the air around me.

Had I dreamed everything, assembling the entire fantasy in my mind as I lay raving in the noon heat, saved by some thermodynamic freak of the basin's architecture?

I held my thermo-alarm up to the fading light, checking the maximum and minimum levels. The maximum read 162°. Yet I had survived! I felt relaxed, restored, almost rejuvenated. My hands and face were unburnt – a temperature of over 160° would have boiled the flesh off my bones, left my skin a blackened crisp.

Over my shoulder I noticed the half-track standing on the rim. I ran towards it, for the first time remembering Mayer's death. I felt my cheek-bones, testing my jaw muscles. Surprisingly Mayer's heavy punches had left no bruise.

*Mayer's body had gone!* A single line of footsteps led down from the half-track to the megaliths, but otherwise the carpet of light blue dust was untouched. Mayer's prints, all marks of our scuffle, had vanished.

I quickly scaled the rim and reached the half-track, peering under the chassis and between the tracks. I flung open the cabin door, found the compartment empty.

*The windscreen was intact.* The paintwork on the door and bonnet was unmarked, the metal trim around the windows unscratched. I dropped to my knees, vainly searched for any flakes of magnesium ash. On my knee the flare pistol lodged securely in its holster, a primed star shell in the breach.

I left the Chrysler, jumped down into the basin and ran over to the megaliths. For an hour I paced round them, trying to resolve the countless questions that jammed my mind.

Just before I left I went over to the fifth tablet. I looked up at the top left corner, wondering whether I should have qualified for its first entry had I died that afternoon.

A single row of letters, filled with shadow by the falling light, stood out clearly.

I stepped back and craned up at them. There were the symbols of the four alien languages, and then, proudly against the stars:

CHARLES FOSTER NELSON  EARTH                              AD 2217

*'Tell me, Quaine, where would you like to be when the world ends?'*
In the seven years since Tallis first asked me this question I must have re-examined it a thousand times. Somehow it seems the key to all the extraordinary events that have happened on Murak, with their limitless implications for the people of Earth (to me a satisfactory answer contains an acceptable statement of one's philosophy and beliefs, an adequate discharge of the one moral debt we owe ourselves and the universe).

Not that the world is about to 'end'. The implication is rather that it has already ended and regenerated itself an infinite number of times, and that the only remaining question is what to do with ourselves in the meantime. The four stellar races who built the megaliths chose to come to Murak. What exactly they are waiting for here I can't be certain. A cosmic redeemer, perhaps, the first sight of the vast mantle of ideation I glimpsed in my vision. Recalling the period of two million years Tallis cited for life to appear on Murak it may be that the next cosmic cycle will receive its impetus here, and that we are advance spectators, five kings come to attend the genesis of a super-species which will soon outstrip us.

That there are others here, invisible and sustained by preternatural forces, is without doubt. Apart from the impossibility of surviving a Murak noon, I certainly didn't remove Mayer's body from the basin and arrange to have him electrocuted by one of the data-processing units at the observatory. Nor did I conceive the vision of the cosmic cycle myself.

It looks as if the two geologists stumbled upon the Waiting Grounds, somehow divined their significance, and then let Tallis in on their discovery. Perhaps they disagreed, as Mayer and I did, and Nelson may have been forced to kill his companion, to die himself a year later in the course of his vigil.

Like Tallis I shall wait here if necessary for fifteen years. I go out to the Grounds once a week and watch them from the observatory the rest of the time. So far I have seen nothing, although two or three hundred more names have been added to the tablets. However, I am certain that whatever we are waiting for will soon arrive. When I get tired or impatient, as I sometimes do, I remind myself that they have been coming to Murak and waiting here, generation upon generation, for 10,000 years.

Whatever it is, it must be worth waiting for.

**1959**

# NOW: ZERO

You ask: how did I discover this insane and fantastic power? Like Dr Faust, was it bestowed upon me by the Devil himself, in exchange for the deed to my soul? Did I, perhaps, acquire it with some strange talismanic object – idol's eyepiece or monkey's paw – unearthed in an ancient chest or bequeathed by a dying mariner? Or, again, did I stumble upon it myself while researching into the obscenities of the Eleusinian Mysteries and the Black Mass, suddenly perceiving its full horror and magnitude through clouds of sulphurous smoke and incense?

None of these. In fact, the power revealed itself to me quite accidentally, during the commonplaces of the everyday round, appearing unobtrusively at my fingertips like a talent for embroidery. Indeed, its appearance was so unheralded, so gradual, that at first I failed to recognize it at all.

But again you ask: why should I tell you this, describe the incredible and hitherto unsuspected sources of my power, freely catalogue the names of my victims, the date and exact manner of their quietus? Am I so mad as to be positively eager for justice – arraignment, the black cap, and the hangman leaping on to my shoulders like Quasimodo, ringing the deathbell from my throat?

No, (consummate irony!) it is the strange nature of my power that I have nothing to fear from broadcasting its secret to all who will listen. I am the power's servant, and in describing it now I still serve it, carrying it faithfully, as you shall see, to its final conclusion.

However, to begin.

Rankin, my immediate superior at the Everlasting Insurance company, became the hapless instrument of the fate which was first to reveal the power to me.

I loathed Rankin. He was bumptious and assertive, innately vulgar, and owed his position solely to an unpleasant cunning and his persistent refusal to recommend me to the directorate for promotion. He had consolidated his position as department manager by marrying a daughter of one of the directors (a dismal harridan, I may add) and was consequently unassailable. Our relationship was based on mutual contempt, but whereas I was prepared to accept my role, confident that my own qualities would ultimately recommend themselves to the directors, Rankin deliberately took advantage of his seniority, seizing every opportunity to offend and denigrate me.

He would systematically undermine my authority over the secretarial staff, who were tacitly under my control, by appointing others at random to the position. He would give me long-term projects of little significance to work on, so segregating me from the rest of the office. Above all, he sought to antagonize me by his personal mannerisms. He would sing, hum, sit uninvited on my desk as he made small talk with the typists, then call me into his office and keep me waiting pointlessly at his shoulder as he read silently through an entire file.

Although I controlled myself, my abomination of Rankin grew remorselessly. I would leave the office seething with anger at his viciousness, sit in the train home with my newspaper opened but my eyes blinded by rage. My evenings and weekends would be ruined, wastelands of anger and futile bitterness.

Inevitably, thoughts of revenge grew, particularly as I suspected that Rankin was passing unfavourable reports of my work to the directors. Satisfactory revenge, however, was hard to achieve. Finally I decided upon a course I despised, driven to it by desperation: the anonymous letter – not to the directors, for the source would have been too easily discovered, but to Rankin and his wife.

My first letters, the familiar indictments of infidelity, I never posted. They seemed naïve, inadequate, too obviously the handiwork of a paranoiac with a grudge. I locked them away in a small steel box, later re-drafted them, striking out the staler crudities and trying to substitute something more subtle, a hint of perversion and obscenity, that would plunge deeper barbs of suspicion into the reader's mind.

It was while composing the letter to Mrs Rankin, itemizing in an old notebook the more despicable of her husband's qualities, that I discovered the curious relief afforded by the exercise of composition, by the formal statement, in the minatory language of the anonymous letter (which is, certainly, a specialized branch of literature, with its own classical rules and permitted devices) of the viciousness and depravity of the letter's subject and the terrifying nemesis awaiting him. Of course, this catharsis is familiar to those regularly able to recount unpleasant experiences to priest, friend or wife, but to me, who lived a solitary, friendless life, its discovery was especially poignant.

Over the next few days I made a point each evening on my return home of writing out a short indictment of Rankin's iniquities, analysing his motives, and even anticipating the slights and abuses of the next day. These I would cast in the form of narrative, allowing myself a fair degree of licence, introducing imaginary situations and dialogues that served to highlight Rankin's atrocious behaviour and my own stoical forbearance.

The compensation was welcome, for simultaneously Rankin's campaign against me increased. He became openly abusive, criticized my work before junior members of the staff, even threatened to report me to the directors. One afternoon he drove me to such a frenzy that I barely restrained myself from assaulting him. I hurried home, unlocked my writing box and sought relief in my diaries. I wrote page after page, re-enacting in my narrative the day's events, then reaching forward to our final collision the following morning, culminating in an accident that intervened to save me from dismissal.

My last lines were:

*. . . Shortly after 2 o'clock the next afternoon, spying from his usual position on the 7th floor stairway for any employees returning late from lunch, Rankin suddenly lost his balance, toppled over the rail and fell to his death in the entrance hall below.*

As I wrote this fictitious scene it seemed scant justice, but little did I realize that a weapon of enormous power had been placed gently between my fingers.

Coming back to the office after lunch the next day I was surprised to find a small crowd gathered outside the entrance, a police car and ambulance pulled up by the kerb. As I pushed forward up the steps, several policemen emerged from the building clearing the way for two orderlies carrying a stretcher across which a sheet had been drawn, revealing the outlines of a human form. The face was concealed, and I gathered from conversation around me that someone had died. Two of the directors appeared, their faces shocked and drawn.

'Who is it?' I asked one of the office boys who were hanging around breathlessly.

'Mr Rankin,' he whispered. He pointed up the stairwell. 'He slipped over the railing on the 7th floor, fell straight down, completely smashed one of those big tiles outside the lift . . .'

He gabbled on, but I turned away, numbed and shaken by the sheer physical violence that hung in the air. The ambulance drove off, the crowd dispersed, the directors returned, exchanging expressions of grief and astonishment with other members of the staff, the janitors took away their mops and buckets, leaving behind them a damp red patch and the shattered tile.

Within an hour I had recovered. Sitting in front of Rankin's empty office, watching the typists hover helplessly around his desk, apparently unconvinced that their master would never return, my heart began to warm and sing. I became transformed, a load which had threatened to break me had been removed from my back, my mind relaxed, the tensions and bitterness dissipated. Rankin had gone, finally and irrevocably. The era of injustice had ended.

I contributed generously to the memorial fund which made the rounds of the office; I attended the funeral, gloating inwardly as the coffin was bundled into the sod, joining fulsomely in the expressions of regret. I readied myself to occupy Rankin's desk, my rightful inheritance.

My surprise a few days later can easily be imagined when Carter, a younger man of far less experience and generally accepted as my junior, was promoted to fill Rankin's place. At first I was merely baffled, quite unable to grasp the tortuous logic that could so offend all laws of precedence and merit. I assumed that Rankin had done his work of denigrating me only too well.

However, I accepted the rebuff, offered Carter my loyalty and assisted his reorganization of the office.

Superficially these changes were minor. But later I realized that they were far more calculating than at first seemed, and transferred the bulk of power within the office to Carter's hands, leaving me with the routine work, the files of which never left the department or passed to the directors. I saw too that over the previous year Carter had been carefully familiarizing himself with all aspects of my job and was taking credit for work I had done during Rankin's tenure of office.

Finally I challenged Carter openly, but far from being evasive he simply emphasized my subordinate role. From then on he ignored my attempts at a rapprochement and did all he could to antagonize me.

The final insult came when Jacobson joined the office to fill Carter's former place and was officially designated Carter's deputy.

That evening I brought down the steel box in which I kept record of Rankin's persecutions and began to describe all that I was beginning to suffer at the hands of Carter.

During a pause the last entry in the Rankin diary caught my eye:

> *. . . Rankin suddenly lost his balance, toppled over the rail and fell to his death in the entrance hall below.*

The words seemed to be alive, they had strangely vibrant overtones. Not only were they a remarkably accurate forecast of Rankin's fate, but they had a distinctly magnetic and compulsive power that separated them sharply from the rest of the entries. Somewhere within my mind a voice, vast and sombre, slowly intoned them.

On a sudden impulse I turned the page, found a clean sheet and wrote:

> *The next afternoon Carter died in a street accident outside the office.*

What childish game was I playing? I was forced to smile at myself, as primitive and irrational as a Haitian witch doctor transfixing a clay image of his enemy.

\*     \*     \*

I was sitting in the office the following day when the squeal of tyres in the street below riveted me to my chair. Traffic stopped abruptly and there was a sudden hubbub followed by silence. Only Carter's office overlooked the street; he had gone out half an hour earlier so we pressed past his desk and leaned out through the window.

A car had skidded sharply across the pavement and a group of ten or a dozen men were lifting it carefully back on to the roadway. It was undamaged but what appeared to be oil was leaking sluggishly into the gutter. Then we saw the body of a man outstretched beneath the car, his arms and head twisted awkwardly.

The colour of his suit was oddly familiar.

Two minutes later we knew it was Carter.

That night I destroyed my notebook and all records I had made about Rankin's behaviour. Was it coincidence, or in some way had I willed his death, and in the same way Carter's? Impossible – no conceivable connection could exist between the diaries and the two deaths, the pencil marks on the sheets of paper were arbitrary curved lines of graphite, representing ideas which existed only in my mind.

But the solution to my doubts and speculations was too obvious to be avoided.

I locked the door, turned a fresh page of the notebook and cast round for a suitable subject. I picked up my evening paper. A young man had just been reprieved from the death penalty for the murder of an old woman. His face stared from a photograph coarse, glowering, conscienceless.

I wrote:

*Frank Taylor died the next day in Pentonville Prison.*

The scandal created by Taylor's death almost brought about the resignations of both the Home Secretary and the Prison Commissioners. During the next few days violent charges were levelled in all directions by the newspapers, and it finally transpired that Taylor had been brutally beaten to death by his warders. I carefully read the evidence and findings of the tribunal of enquiry when they were published, hoping that they might throw some light on the extraordinary and malevolent agency which linked the statements in my diaries with the inevitable deaths on the subsequent day.

However, as I feared, they suggested nothing. Meanwhile I sat quietly in my office, automatically carrying out my work, obeying Jacobson's instructions without comment, my mind elsewhere, trying to grasp the identity and import of the power bestowed on me.

Still unconvinced, I decided on a final test, in which I would give precisely detailed instructions, to rule out once and for all any possibility of coincidence.

Conveniently, Jacobson offered himself as my subject.

So, the door locked securely behind me, I wrote with trembling fingers, fearful lest the pencil wrench itself from me and plunge into my heart.

*Jacobson died at 2.43 P.M. the next day after slashing his wrists with a razor blade in the second cubicle from the left in the men's washroom on the third floor.*

I sealed the notebook into an envelope, locked it into the box and lay awake through a sleepless night, the words echoing in my ears, glowing before my eyes like jewels of Hell.

After Jacobson's death – exactly according to my instructions – the staff of the department were given a week's holiday (in part to keep them away from curious newspapermen, who were beginning to scent a story, and also because the directors believed that Jacobson had been morbidly influenced by the deaths of Rankin and Carter). During those seven days I chafed impatiently to return to work. My whole attitude to the power had undergone a considerable change. Having to my own satisfaction verified its existence, if not its source, my mind turned again towards the future. Gaining confidence, I realized that if I had been bequeathed the power it was my obligation to restrain any fears and make use of it. I reminded myself that I might be merely the tool of some greater force.

*Alternatively, was the diary no more than a mirror which revealed the future, was I in some fantastic way twenty-four hours ahead of time when I described the deaths, simply a recorder of events that had already taken place?*

These questions exercised my mind ceaselessly.

On my return to work I found that many members of the staff had resigned, their places being filled only with difficulty, news of the three deaths, particularly Jacobson's suicide, having reached the newspapers. The directors' appreciation of those senior members of the staff who remained with the firm I was able to turn to good account in consolidating my position. At last I took over command of the department – but this was no more than my due, and my eyes were now set upon a directorship.

All too literally, I would step into dead men's shoes.

Briefly, my strategy was to precipitate a crisis in the affairs of the firm which would force the board to appoint new executive directors from the ranks of the department managers. I therefore waited until a week before the next meeting of the board, and then wrote out four slips of paper, one for each of the executive directors. Once a director I should be in a position to propel myself rapidly to the chairmanship of the board, by appointing my own candidates to vacancies as they successively appeared. As chairman I should automatically find a seat on the board of the parent company, there to repeat the process, with whatever variations necessary. As soon as real power came within my orbit my rise to absolute national, and ultimately global, supremacy would be swift and irreversible.

If this seems naïvely ambitious, remember that I had as yet failed to appreciate the real dimensions and purpose of the power, and still thought in the categories of my own narrow world and background.

A week later, as the sentences on the four directors simultaneously expired, I sat calmly in my office, reflecting upon the brevity of human life, waiting for the inevitable summons to the board. Understandably, the news of their deaths, in a succession of car accidents, brought general consternation upon the office, of which I was able to take advantage by retaining the only cool head.

To my amazement the next day I, with the rest of the staff, received a month's pay in lieu of notice. Completely flabbergasted – at first I feared that I had been discovered – I protested volubly to the chairman, but was assured that although everything I had done was deeply appreciated, the firm was nonetheless no longer able to support itself as a viable unit and was going into enforced liquidation.

A farce indeed! So a grotesque justice had been done. As I left the office for the last time that morning I realized that in future I must use my power ruthlessly. Hesitation, the exercise of scruple, the calculation of niceties – these merely made me all the more vulnerable to the inconstancies and barbarities of fate. Henceforth I would be brutal, merciless, bold. Also, I must not delay. The power might wane, leave me defenceless, even less fortunately placed than before it revealed itself.

My first task was to establish the power's limits. During the next week I carried out a series of experiments to assess its capacity, working my way progressively up the scale of assassination.

It happened that my lodgings were positioned some two or three hundred feet below one of the principal airlanes into the city. For years I had suffered the nerve-shattering roar of airliners flying in overhead at two-minute intervals, shaking the walls and ceiling, destroying thought. I took down my notebooks. Here was a convenient opportunity to couple research with redress.

You wonder did I feel no qualms of conscience for the 75 victims who hurtled to their deaths across the evening sky twenty-four hours later, no sympathy for their relatives, no doubts as to the wisdom of wielding my power indiscriminately?

I answer: No! Far from being indiscriminate I was carrying out an experiment vital to the furtherance of my power.

I decided on a bolder course. I had been born in Stretchford, a mean industrial slum that had done its best to cripple my spirit and body. At last it could justify itself by testing the efficacy of the power over a wide area.

In my notebook I wrote the short flat statement:

*Every inhabitant of Stretchford died at noon the next day.*

Early the following morning I went out and bought a radio, sat by it patiently all day, waiting for the inevitable interruption of the afternoon programmes by the first horrified reports of the vast Midland holocaust.

Nothing, however, was reported! I was astonished, the orientations of my mind disrupted, its very sanity threatened. Had my power dissipated itself, vanishing as quickly and unexpectedly as it had appeared?

Or were the authorities deliberately suppressing all mention of the cataclysm, fearful of national hysteria?

I immediately took the train to Stretchford.

At the station I tactfully made inquiries, was assured that the city was firmly in existence. Were my informants, though, part of the government's conspiracy of silence, was it aware that a monstrous agency was at work, and was somehow hoping to trap it?

But the city was inviolate, its streets filled with traffic, the smoke of countless factories drifting across the blackened rooftops.

I returned late that evening, only to find my landlady importuning me for my rent. I managed to postpone her demands for a day, promptly unlocked my diary and passed sentence upon her, praying that the power had not entirely deserted me.

The sweet relief I experienced the next morning when she was discovered at the foot of the basement staircase, claimed by a sudden stroke, can well be imagined.

*So my power still existed!*

During the succeeding weeks its principal features disclosed themselves. First, I discovered that it operated only within the bounds of feasibility. Theoretically the simultaneous deaths of the entire population of Stretchford might have been effected by the coincident explosions of several hydrogen bombs, but as this event was itself apparently impossible (hollow, indeed, are the boastings of our militarist leaders) the command was never carried out.

Secondly, the power entirely confined itself to the passage of the sentence of death. I attempted to control or forecast the motions of the stock market, the results of horse races, the behaviour of my employers at my new job – all to no avail.

As for the sources of the power, these never revealed themselves. I could only conclude that I was merely the agent, the willing clerk, of some macabre nemesis struck like an arc between the point of my pencil and the vellum of my diaries.

Sometimes it seemed to me that the brief entries I made were cross-sections through the narrative of some vast book of the dead existing in another dimension, and that as I made them my handwriting overlapped that of a greater scribe's along the narrow pencilled line where our respective planes of time crossed each other, instantly drawing from the eternal banks of death a final statement of account on to some victim within the tangible world around me.

The diaries I kept securely sealed within a large steel safe and all entries were made with the utmost care and secrecy, to prevent any suspicion linking me with the mounting catalogue of deaths and disasters. The majority of these were effected solely for purposes of experiment and brought me little or no personal gain.

It was therefore all the more surprising when I discovered that the police had begun to keep me under sporadic observation.

I first noticed this when I saw my landlady's successor in surreptitious conversation with the local constable, pointing up the stairs to my room and making head-tapping motions, presumably to indicate my telepathic and mesmeric talents. Later, a man whom I can now identify as a plainclothes detective stopped me in the street on some flimsy pretext and started a wandering conversation about the weather, obviously designed to elicit information.

No charges were ever laid against me, but subsequently my employers also began to watch me in a curious manner. I therefore assumed that the possession of the power had invested me with a distinct and visible aura, and it was this that stimulated curiosity.

As this aura became detectable by greater and greater numbers of people – it would be noticed in bus queues and cafés – and the first oblique, and for some puzzling reason, amused references to it were made openly by members of the public, I knew that the power's period of utility was ending. No longer would I be able to exercise it without fear of detection. I should have to destroy the diary, sell the safe which so long had held its secret, probably even refrain from ever thinking about the power lest this alone generate the aura.

To be forced to lose the power, when I was only on the threshold of its potential, seemed a cruel turn of fate. For reasons which still remained closed to me, I had managed to penetrate behind the veil of commonplaces and familiarity which masks the inner world of the timeless and the preternatural. Must the power, and the vision it revealed, be lost forever?

This question ran through my mind as I looked for the last time through my diary. It was almost full now, and I reflected that it formed one of the most extraordinary texts, if unpublished, in the history of literature. Here, indeed, was established the primacy of the pen over the sword!

Savouring this thought, I suddenly had an inspiration of remarkable force and brilliance. I had stumbled upon an ingenious but simple method of preserving the power in its most impersonal and lethal form without having to wield it myself and itemize my victims' names.

This was my scheme: I would write and have published an apparently fictional story in conventional narrative in which I would describe, with complete frankness, my discovery of the power and its subsequent history. I would detail precisely the names of my victims, the mode of their deaths, the growth of my diary and the succession of experiments I carried out. I would be scrupulously honest, holding nothing back whatsoever. In conclusion I would tell of my decision to abandon the power and publish a full and dispassionate account of all that had happened.

Accordingly, after a considerable labour, the story was written and published in a magazine of wide circulation.

You show surprise? I agree; as such I should merely have been signing my own death warrant in indelible ink and delivering myself straight to the gallows. However, I omitted a single feature of the story: its denouement, or surprise ending, the twist in its tail. Like all respectable stories, this one too had its twist, indeed one so violent as to throw the earth itself out of its orbit. This was precisely what it was designed to do.

For the twist in this story was that it contained my last command to the power, my final sentence of death.

Upon whom? Who else, but upon the story's reader!

Ingenious, certainly, you willingly admit. As long as issues of the magazine remain in circulation (and their proximity to victims of this extraordinary plague guarantees that) the power will continue its task of annihilation. Its author alone will remain unmolested, for no court will hear evidence at second hand, and who will live to give it at first hand?

But where, you ask, was the story published, fearful that you may inadvertently buy the magazine and read it.

I answer: Here! It is the story that lies before you now. Savour it well, its finish is your own. As you read these last few lines you will be overwhelmed by horror and revulsion, then by fear and panic. Your heart seizes, its pulse falling . . . your mind clouds . . . your life ebbs . . . you are sinking, within a few seconds you will join eternity . . . three . . . two . . . one . . .

Now!

Zero.

**1959**

# THE SOUND-SWEEP

## ONE

By midnight Madame Gioconda's headache had become intense. All day the derelict walls and ceiling of the sound stage had reverberated with the endless din of traffic accelerating across the mid-town flyover which arched fifty feet above the studio's roof, a frenzied hypermanic babel of jostling horns, shrilling tyres, plunging brakes and engines that hammered down the empty corridors and stairways to the sound stage on the second floor, making the faded air feel leaden and angry.

Exhausting but at least impersonal, these sounds Madame Gioconda could bear. At dusk, however, when the flyover quietened, they were overlaid by the mysterious clapping of her phantoms, the sourceless applause that rustled down on to the stage from the darkness around her. At first a few scattered ripples from the front rows, it soon spread to the entire auditorium, mounting to a tumultuous ovation in which she suddenly detected a note of sarcasm, a single shout of derision that drove a spear of pain through her forehead, followed by an uproar of boos and catcalls that filled the tortured air, driving her away towards her couch where she lay gasping helplessly until Mangon arrived at midnight, hurrying on to the stage with his sonovac.

Understanding her, he first concentrated on sweeping the walls and ceiling clean, draining away the heavy depressing under-layer of traffic noises. Carefully he ran the long snout of the sonovac over the ancient scenic flats (relics of her previous roles at the Metropolitan Opera House) which screened in Madame Gioconda's make-shift home – the great collapsing Byzantine bed (*Othello*) mounted against the microphone turret; the huge framed mirrors with their peeling silver-screen (*Orpheus*) stacked in one corner by the bandstand; the stove (*Trovatore*) set up on the programme director's podium; the gilt-trimmed dressing table and wardrobe (*Figaro*) stuffed with newspaper and magazine cuttings. He swept them methodically, moving the sonovac's nozzle in long strokes, drawing out the dead residues of sound that had accumulated during the day.

By the time he finished the air was clear again, the atmosphere lightened, its overtones of fatigue and irritation dissipated. Gradually Madame Gioconda recovered. Sitting up weakly, she smiled wanly at

Mangon. Mangon grinned back encouragingly, slipped the kettle on to the stove for Russian tea, sweetened by the usual phenobarbitone chaser, switched off the sonovac and indicated to her that he was going outside to empty it.

Down in the alley behind the studio he clipped the sonovac on to the intake manifold of the sound truck. The vacuum drained in a few seconds, but he waited a discretionary two or three minutes before returning, keeping up the pretence that Madame Gioconda's phantom audience was real. Of course the cylinder was always empty, containing only the usual daily detritus – the sounds of a door slam, a partition collapsing somewhere or the kettle whistling, a grunt or two, and later, when the headaches began, Madame Gioconda's pitiful moanings. The riotous applause, which would have lifted the roof off the Met, let alone a small radio station, the jeers and hoots of derision were, he knew, quite imaginary, figments of Madame Gioconda's world of fantasy, phantoms from the past of a once great *prima donna* who had been dropped by her public and had retreated into her imagination, each evening conjuring up a blissful dream of being once again applauded by a full house at the Metropolitan, a dream that guilt and resentment turned sour by midnight, inverting it into a nightmare of fiasco and failure.

Why she should torment herself was difficult to understand, but at least the nightmare kept Madame Gioconda just this side of sanity and Mangon, who revered and loved Madame Gioconda, would have been the last person in the world to disillusion her. Each evening, when he finished his calls for the day, he would drive his sound truck all the way over from the West Side to the abandoned radio station under the flyover at the deserted end of F Street, go through the pretence of sweeping Madame Gioconda's apartment on the stage of studio 2, charging no fee, make tea and listen to her reminiscences and plans for revenge, then see her asleep and tiptoe out, a wry but pleased smile on his youthful face.

He had been calling on Madame Gioconda for nearly a year, but what his precise role was in relation to her he had not yet decided. Oddly enough, although he was more or less indispensable now to the effective operation of her fantasy world she showed little personal interest or affection for Mangon, but he assumed that this indifference was merely part of the autocratic personality of a world-famous *prima donna*, particularly one very conscious of the tradition, now alas meaningless, Melba – Callas – Gioconda. To serve at all was the privilege. In time, perhaps, Madame Gioconda might accord him some sign of favour.

Without him, certainly, her prognosis would have been poor. Lately the headaches had become more menacing, as she insisted that the applause was growing stormier, the boos and catcalls more vicious. Whatever the psychic mechanism generating the fantasy system, Mangon realized that ultimately she would need him at the studio all day, holding back the enveloping tides of nightmare and insanity with sham passes of the sonovac. Then, perhaps, when the dream crumbled, he would regret having helped her to delude herself. With luck though she might achieve her ambition of making a comeback. She had told him something of her scheme – a serpentine mixture of blackmail and bribery – and privately Mangon hoped to launch a plot of his own to return her to popularity. By now she had unfortunately reached the point where success alone could save her from disaster.

She was sitting up when he returned, propped back on an enormous gold *lamé* cushion, the single lamp at the foot of the couch throwing a semicircle of light on to the great flats which divided the sound stage from the auditorium. These were all from her last operatic role – *The Medium* – and represented a complete interior of the old spiritualist's seance chamber, the one coherent feature in Madame Gioconda's present existence. Surrounded by fragments from a dozen roles, even Madame Gioconda herself, Mangon reflected, seemed compounded of several separate identities. A tall regal figure, with full shapely shoulders and massive rib-cage, she had a large handsome face topped by a magnificent coiffure of rich blue-black hair – the exact prototype of the classical diva. She must have been almost fifty, yet her soft creamy complexion and small features were those of a child. The eyes, however, belied her. Large and watchful, slashed with mascara, they regarded the world around her balefully, narrowing even as Mangon approached. Her teeth too were bad, stained by tobacco and cheap cocaine. When she was roused, and her full violet lips curled with rage, revealing the blackened hulks of her dentures and the acid flickering tongue, her mouth looked like a very vent of hell. Altogether she was a formidable woman.

As Mangon brought her tea she heaved herself up and made room for him by her feet among the debris of beads, loose diary pages, horoscopes and jewelled address books that littered the couch. Mangon sat down, surreptitiously noting the time (his first calls were at 9.30 the next morning and loss of sleep deadened his acute hearing), and prepared himself to listen to her for half an hour.

Suddenly she flinched, shrank back into the cushion and gestured agitatedly in the direction of the darkened bandstand.

'They're still clapping!' she shrieked. 'For God's sake sweep them away, they're driving me insane. Oooohh . . .' she rasped theatrically, 'over there, quickly . . . !'

Mangon leapt to his feet. He hurried over to the bandstand and carefully focused his ears on the tiers of seats and plywood music stands. They were all immaculately clean, well below the threshold at which embedded sounds began to radiate detectable echoes. He turned to the corner walls and ceiling. Listening very carefully he could just hear seven muted pads, the dull echoes of his footsteps across the floor. They faded and vanished, followed by a low threshing noise like blurred radio static – in fact Madame Gioconda's present tantrum. Mangon could almost distinguish the individual words, but repetition muffled them.

Madame Gioconda was still writhing about on the couch, evidently not to be easily placated, so Mangon climbed down off the stage and made his way through the auditorium to where he had left his sonovac by the door. The power lead was outside in the truck but he was sure Madame Gioconda would fail to notice.

For five minutes he worked away industriously, pretending to sweep the bandstand again, then put down the sonovac and returned to the couch.

Madame Gioconda emerged from the cushion, sounded the air carefully with two or three slow turns of the head, and smiled at him.

'Thank you, Mangon,' she said silkily, her eyes watching him thoughtfully. 'You've saved me again from my assassins. They've become so cunning recently, they can even hide from you.'

Mangon smiled ruefully to himself at this last remark. So he had been a little too perfunctory earlier on; Madame Gioconda was keeping him up to the mark.

However, she seemed genuinely grateful. 'Mangon, my dear,' she reflected as she remade her face in the mirror of an enormous compact, painting on magnificent green eyes like a cobra's, 'what would I do without you? How can I ever repay you for looking after me?'

The questions, whatever their sinister undertones (had he detected them, Mangon would have been deeply shocked) were purely rhetorical, and all their conversations for that matter entirely one-sided. For Mangon was a mute. From the age of three, when his mother had savagely punched him in the throat to stop him crying, he had been stone dumb, his vocal cords irreparably damaged. In all their endless exchanges of midnight confidences, Mangon had contributed not a single spoken word.

His muteness, naturally, was part of the attraction he felt for Madame Gioconda. Both of them in a sense had lost their voices, he to a cruel mother, she to a fickle and unfaithful public. This bound them together, gave them a shared sense of life's injustice, though Mangon, like all innocents, viewed his misfortune without rancour. Both, too, were social outcasts. Rescued from his degenerate parents when he was four, Mangon had been brought up in a succession of state institutions, a solitary wounded child. His one talent had been his remarkable auditory powers, and at fourteen he was apprenticed to the Metropolitan Sonic Disposal Service. Regarded as little better than garbage collectors, the sound-sweeps were an outcast group of illiterates, mutes (the city authorities preferred these – their discretion could be relied upon) and social cripples who lived in a chain of isolated shacks on the edge of an old explosives plant in the sand dunes to the north of the city which served as the sonic dump.

Mangon had made no friends among the sound-sweeps, and Madame Gioconda was the first person in his life with whom he had been intimately involved. Apart from the pleasure of being able to help her, a considerable factor in Mangon's devotion was that until her decline she had represented (as to all mutes) the most painful possible reminder of his own voiceless condition, and that now he could at last come to terms with years of unconscious resentment.

This soon done, he devoted himself wholeheartedly to serving Madame Gioconda.

Inhaling moodily on a black cigarette clamped into a long jade holder, she was outlining her plans for a comeback. These had been maturing for several months and involved nothing less than persuading Hector LeGrande, chairman-in-chief of Video City, the huge corporation that transmitted a dozen TV and radio channels, into providing her with a complete series of television spectaculars. Built around Madame Gioconda and lavishly dressed and orchestrated, they would spearhead the international revival of classical opera that was her unfading dream.

'La Scala, Covent Garden, the Met – what are they now?' she demanded angrily. 'Bowling alleys! Can you believe, Mangon, that in those immortal theatres where I created my Tosca, my Butterfly, my Brünnhilde, they now have –' she spat out a gust of smoke '– beer and skittles!'

Mangon shook his head sympathetically. He pulled a pencil from his breast-pocket and on the wrist-pad stitched to his left sleeve wrote:

*Mr LeGrande?*

Madame Gioconda read the note, let it fall to the floor.

'Hector? Those lawyers poison him. He's surrounded by them, I think they steal all my telegrams to him. Of course Hector had a complete breakdown on the spectaculars. Imagine, Mangon, what a scoop for him, a sensation! 'The great Gioconda will appear on television!' Not just some moronic bubblegum girl, but the Gioconda in person.'

Exhausted by this vision Madame Gioconda sank back into her cushion, blowing smoke limply through the holder.

Mangon wrote:

*Contract?*

Madame Gioconda frowned at the note, then pierced it with the glowing end of her cigarette.

'I am having a new contract drawn up. Not for the mere 300,000 I was prepared to take at first, not even 500,000. For each show I shall now demand precisely *one million* dollars. Nothing less! Hector will have to pay for ignoring me. Anyway, think of the publicity value of such a figure. Only a star could think of such vulgar extravagance. If he's short of cash he can sack all those lawyers. Or devalue the dollar, I don't mind.'

Madame Gioconda hooted with pleasure at the prospect. Mangon nodded, then scribbled another message.

*Be practical.*

Madame Gioconda ground out her cigarette. 'You think I'm raving, don't you, Mangon? "Fantastic dreams, million-dollar contracts, poor old fool." But let me assure you that Hector will be only too eager to sign the contract. And I don't intend to rely solely on his good judgement as an impresario.' She smirked archly to herself.

*What else?*

Madame Gioconda peered round the darkened stage, then lowered her eyes.

'You see, Mangon, Hector and I are very old friends. You know what I mean, of course?' She waited for Mangon, who had swept out a thousand honeymoon hotel suites, to nod and then continued: 'How well I remember that first season at Bayreuth, when Hector and I . . .'

Mangon stared unhappily at his feet as Madame Gioconda outlined this latest venture into blackmail. Certainly she and LeGrande had been intimate friends – the cuttings scattered around the stage testified frankly to this. In fact, were it not for the small monthly cheque which LeGrande sent Madame Gioconda she would long previously have disintegrated. To turn on him and threaten ancient scandal (LeGrande was shortly to enter politics) was not only grotesque but extremely dangerous, for LeGrande was ruthless and unsentimental. Years earlier he had used Madame Gioconda as a stepping-stone, reaping all the publicity he could from their affair, then abruptly kicking her away.

Mangon fretted. A solution to her predicament was hard to find. Brought about through no fault of her own, Madame Gioconda's decline was all the harder to bear. Since the introduction a few years earlier of ultrasonic music, the human voice – indeed, audible music of any type – had gone completely out of fashion. Ultrasonic music, employing a vastly greater range of octaves, chords and chromatic scales than are audible by the human ear, provided a direct neural link between the sound stream and the auditory lobes, generating an apparently sourceless sensation of harmony, rhythm, cadence and melody uncontaminated by the noise and vibration of audible music. The re-scoring of the classical repertoire allowed the ultrasonic audience the best of both worlds. The majestic rhythms of Beethoven, the popular melodies of Tchaikovsky, the complex fugal elaborations of Bach, the abstract images of Schoenberg – all these were raised in frequency above the threshold of conscious audibility. Not only did they become inaudible, but the original works were re-scored for the much wider range of the ultrasonic orchestra, became richer in texture, more profound in theme, more sensitive, tender or lyrical as the ultrasonic arranger chose.

The first casualty in this change-over was the human voice. This alone of all instruments could not be re-scored, because its sounds were produced by non-mechanical means which the neurophonic engineer could never hope, or bother, to duplicate.

The earliest ultrasonic recordings had met with resistance, even ridicule. Radio programmes consisting of nothing but silence interrupted at half-hour intervals by commercial breaks seemed absurd. But gradually the public discovered that the silence was golden, that after leaving the radio switched to an ultrasonic channel for an hour or so a pleasant atmosphere of rhythm and melody seemed to generate itself spontaneously around them. When an announcer suddenly stated that an ultrasonic version of Mozart's Jupiter Symphony or Tchaikovsky's Pathétique had just been played the listener identified the real source.

A second advantage of ultrasonic music was that its frequencies were so high they left no resonating residues in solid structures, and consequently there was no need to call in the sound-sweep. After an audible performance of most symphonic music, walls and furniture throbbed for days with disintegrating residues that made the air seem leaden and tumid, an entire room virtually uninhabitable.

An immediate result was the swift collapse of all but a few symphony orchestras and opera companies. Concert halls and opera houses closed overnight. In the age of noise the tranquillizing balms of silence began to be rediscovered.

But the final triumph of ultrasonic music had come with a second development – the short-playing record, spinning at 900 r.p.m., which condensed the 45 minutes of a Beethoven symphony to 20 seconds of playing time, the three hours of a Wagner opera to little more than two minutes. Compact and cheap, SP records sacrificed nothing to brevity. One 30-second SP record delivered as much neurophonic pleasure as a natural length recording, but with deeper penetration, greater total impact.

Ultrasonic SP records swept all others off the market. Sonic LP records became museum pieces – only a crank would choose to listen to an audible full-length version of *Siegfried* or the *Barber of Seville* when he could have both wrapped up inaudibly inside the same five-minute package *and* appreciate their full musical value.

The heyday of Madame Gioconda was over. Unceremoniously left on the shelf, she had managed to survive for a few months vocalizing on radio commercials. Soon these too went ultrasonic. In a despairing act of revenge she bought out the radio station which fired her and made her home on one of the sound stages. Over the years the station became derelict and forgotten, its windows smashed, neon portico collapsing, aerials rusting. The huge eight-lane flyover built across it sealed it conclusively into the past.

Now Madame Gioconda proposed to win her way back at stiletto-point.

Mangon watched her impassively as she ranted on nastily in a cloud of purple cigarette smoke, a large seedy witch. The phenobarbitone was making her drowsy and her threats and ultimatums were becoming disjointed.

'. . . memoirs too, don't forget, Hector. Frank exposure, no holds barred. I mean . . . damn, have to get a ghost. Hotel de Paris at Monte, lots of pictures. Oh yes, I kept the photographs.' She grubbed about on the couch, came up with a crumpled soap coupon and a supermarket pay slip. 'Wait till those lawyers see them. Hector –' Suddenly she broke off, stared glassily at Mangon and sagged back.

Mangon waited until she was finally asleep, stood up and peered closely at her. She looked forlorn and desperate. He watched her reverently for a moment, then tiptoed to the rheostat mounted on the control panel behind the couch, damped down the lamp at Madame Gioconda's feet and left the stage.

He sealed the auditorium doors behind him, made his way down to the foyer and stepped out, sad but at the same time oddly exhilarated, into the cool midnight air. At last he accepted that he would have to act swiftly if he was to save Madame Gioconda.

## TWO

Driving his sound truck into the city shortly after nine the next morning, Mangon decided to postpone his first call – the weird Neo-Corbusier Episcopalian Oratory sandwiched among the office blocks in the downtown financial sector – and instead turned west on Mainway and across the park towards the white-faced apartment batteries which reared up above the trees and lakes along the north side.

The Oratory was a difficult and laborious job that would take him three hours of concentrated effort. The Dean had recently imported some rare thirteenth-century pediments from the Church of St Francis at Assisi, beautiful sonic matrices rich with seven centuries of Gregorian chant, overlaid by the timeless tolling of the Angelus. Mounted into the altar they emanated an atmosphere resonant with litany and devotion, a mellow, deeply textured hymn that silently evoked the most sublime images of prayer and meditation.

But at 50,000 dollars each they also represented a terrifying hazard to the clumsy sound-sweep. Only two years earlier the entire north transept of Rheims Cathedral, rose window intact, purchased for a record 1,000,000 dollars and re-erected in the new Cathedral of St Joseph at San Diego, had been drained of its priceless heritage of tonal inlays by a squad of illiterate sound-sweeps who had misread their instructions and accidentally swept the wrong wall.

Even the most conscientious sound-sweep was limited by his skill, and Mangon, with his auditory super-sensitivity, was greatly in demand for his ability to sweep selectively, draining from the walls of the Oratory all extraneous and discordant noises – coughing, crying, the clatter of coins and mumble of prayer – leaving behind the chorales and liturgical chants which enhanced their devotional overtones. His skill alone would lengthen the life of the Assisi pediments by twenty years; without him they would soon become contaminated by the miscellaneous traffic of the congregation. Consequently he had no fears that the Dean would complain if he failed to appear as usual that morning.

Halfway along the north side of the park he swung off into the forecourt of a huge forty-storey apartment block, a glittering white cliff ribbed by jutting balconies. Most of the apartments were Superlux duplexes occupied by showbusiness people. No one was about, but as Mangon entered the hallway, sonovac in one hand, the marble walls and columns buzzed softly with the echoing chatter of guests leaving parties four or five hours earlier.

In the elevator the residues were clearer – confident male tones, the sharp wheedling of querulous wives, soft negatives of amatory blondes, punctuated by countless repetitions of 'dahling'. Mangon ignored the echoes, which were almost inaudible, a dim insect hum. He grinned to himself as he rode up to the penthouse apartment; if Madame Gioconda had known his destination she would have strangled him on the spot.

Ray Alto, doyen of the ultrasonic composers and the man more than any other responsible for Madame Gioconda's decline, was one of Mangon's regular calls. Usually Mangon swept his apartment once a week, calling at three in the afternoon. Today, however, he wanted to make sure of finding Alto before he left for Video City, where he was a director of programme music.

The houseboy let him in. He crossed the hall and made his way down the black glass staircase into the sunken lounge. Wide studio windows revealed an elegant panorama of park and mid-town skyscrapers.

A white-slacked young man sitting on one of the long slab sofas – Paul Merrill, Alto's arranger – waved him back.

'Mangon, hold on to your dive breaks. I'm really on reheat this morning.' He twirled the ultrasonic trumpet he was playing, a tangle of stops and valves from which half a dozen leads trailed off across the cushions to a cathode tube and tone generator at the other end of the sofa.

Mangon sat down quietly and Merrill clamped the mouthpiece to his lips. Watching the ray tube intently, where he could check the shape of the ultrasonic notes, he launched into a brisk allegretto sequence, then quickened and flicked out a series of brilliant arpeggios, stripping off high P and Q notes that danced across the cathode screen like frantic eels, fantastic glissandos that raced up twenty octaves in as many seconds, each note distinct and symmetrically exact, tripping off the tone generator in turn so that escalators of electronic chords interweaved the original scale, a multi-channel melodic stream that crowded the cathode screen with exquisite, flickering patterns. The whole thing was inaudible, but the air around Mangon felt vibrant and accelerated, charged with gaiety and sparkle, and he applauded generously when Merrill threw off a final dashing riff.

'*Flight of the Bumble Bee*,' Merrill told him. He tossed the trumpet aside and switched off the cathode tube. He lay back and savoured the glistening air for a moment. 'Well, how are things?'

Just then the door from one of the bedrooms opened and Ray Alto appeared, a tall, thoughtful man of about forty, with thinning blonde hair, wearing pale sunglasses over cool eyes.

'Hello, Mangon,' he said, running a hand over Mangon's head. 'You're early today. Full programme?' Mangon nodded. 'Don't let it get you down.' Alto picked a dictaphone off one of the end tables, carried it over to an armchair. 'Noise, noise, noise – the greatest single disease-vector of civilization. The whole world's rotting with it, yet all they can afford is a few people like Mangon fooling around with sonovacs. It's hard to believe that only a few years ago people completely failed to realize that sound left any residues.'

'Are we any better?' Merrill asked. 'This month's *Transonics* claims that eventually unswept sonic resonances will build up to a critical point where they'll literally start shaking buildings apart. The entire city will come down like Jericho.'

'Babel,' Alto corrected. 'Okay, now, let's shut up. We'll be gone soon, Mangon. Buy him a drink, would you, Paul.'

Merrill brought Mangon a coke from the bar, then wandered off. Alto flipped on the dictaphone, began to speak steadily into it. 'Memo 7: Betty, when does the copyright on Stravinsky lapse? Memo 8: Betty, file melody for projected nocturne: L, L sharp, BB, Y flat, Q, VT, L, L sharp. Memo 9: Paul, the bottom three octaves of the ultra-tuba are within the audible spectrum of the canine ear – congrats on that SP of the *Anvil Chorus* last night; about three million dogs thought the roof had fallen in on them. Memo 10: Betty –' He broke off, put down the microphone. 'Mangon, you look worried.'

Mangon, who had been lost in reverie, pulled himself together and shook his head.

'Working too hard?' Alto pressed. He scrutinized Mangon suspiciously. 'Are you still sitting up all night with that Gioconda woman?'

Embarrassed, Mangon lowered his eyes. His relationship with Alto was, obliquely, almost as close as that with Madame Gioconda. Although Alto was brusque and often irritable with Mangon, he took a sincere interest in his welfare. Possibly Mangon's muteness reminded him of the misanthropic motives behind his hatred of noise, made him feel indirectly responsible for the act of violence Mangon's mother had committed. Also, one artist to another, he respected Mangon's phenomenal auditory sensitivity.

'She'll exhaust you, Mangon, believe me.' Alto knew how much the personal contact meant to Mangon and hesitated to be over-critical. 'There's nothing you can do for her. Offering her sympathy merely fans her hopes for a come-back. She hasn't a chance.'

Mangon frowned, wrote quickly on his wrist-pad:

*She WILL sing again!*

Alto read the note pensively. Then, in a harder voice, he said: 'She's using you for her own purposes, Mangon. At present you satisfy one whim of hers – the neurotic headaches and fantasy applause. God forbid what the next whim might be.'

*She is a great artist.*

'She *was*,' Alto pointed out. 'No more, though, sad as it is. I'm afraid that the times change.'

Annoyed by this, Mangon gritted his teeth and tore off another sheet.

*Entertainment, perhaps. Art, No!*

Alto accepted the rebuke silently; he reproved himself as much as Mangon did for selling out to Video City. In his four years there his output of original ultrasonic music consisted of little more than one nearly finished symphony – aptly titled *Opus Zero* – shortly to receive its first performance, a few nocturnes and one quartet. Most of his energies went into programme music, prestige numbers for spectaculars and a mass of straight transcriptions of the classical repertoire. The last he particularly despised, fit work for Paul Merrill, but not for a responsible composer.

He added the sheet to the two in his left hand and asked: 'Have you ever heard Madame Gioconda sing?'

Mangon's answer came back scornfully:

*No! But you have. Please describe.*

Alto laughed shortly, tore up his sheets and walked across to the window.

'All right, Mangon, you've made your point. You're carrying a torch for art, doing your duty to one of the few perfect things the world has ever produced. I hope you're equal to the responsibility. La Gioconda might be quite a handful. Do you know that at one time the doors of Covent Garden, La Scala *and* the Met were closed to her? They said Callas had temperament, but she was a girl guide compared with Gioconda. Tell me, how is she? Eating enough?'

Mangon held up his coke bottle.

'Snow? That's tough. But how does she afford it?' He glanced at his watch. 'Dammit, I've got to leave. Clean this place out thoroughly, will you. It gives me a headache just listening to myself think.'

He started to pick up the dictaphone but Mangon was scribbling rapidly on his pad.

*Give Madame Gioconda a job.*

Alto read the note, then gave it back to Mangon, puzzled. 'Where? In this apartment?' Mangon shook his head. 'Do you mean at V.C.? *Singing?*' When Mangon began to nod vigorously he looked up at the ceiling with a despairing groan. 'For heaven's sake, Mangon, the last vocalist sang at Video City over ten years ago. No audience would stand for it. If I even suggested such an idea they'd tear my contract into a thousand pieces.' He shuddered, only half-playfully. 'I don't know about you, Mangon, but I've got my ulcer to support.'

He made his way to the staircase, but Mangon intercepted him, pencil flashing across the wrist-pad.

*Please. Madame Gioconda will start blackmail soon. She is desperate.*
*Must sing again. Could arrange make-believe programme in research studios. Closed circuit.*

Alto folded the note carefully, left the dictaphone on the staircase and walked slowly back to the window.

'This blackmail. Are you absolutely sure? Who, though, do you know?' Mangon nodded, but looked away. 'Okay, I won't press you. LeGrande, probably, eh?' Mangon turned round in surprise, then gave an elaborate parody of a shrug.

'Hector LeGrande. Obvious guess. But there are no secrets there, it's all on open file. I suppose she's just threatening to make enough of an exhibition of herself to block his governorship.' Alto pursed his lips. He loathed LeGrande, not merely for having bribed him into a way of life he could never renounce, but also because, once having exploited his weakness, LeGrande never hesitated to remind Alto of it, treating him and his music with contempt. If Madame Gioconda's blackmail had the slightest hope of success he would have been only too happy, but he knew LeGrande would destroy her, probably take Mangon too.

Suddenly he felt a paradoxical sense of loyalty for Madame Gioconda. He looked at Mangon, waiting patiently, big spaniel eyes wide with hope.

'The idea of a closed circuit programme is insane. Even if we went to all the trouble of staging it she wouldn't be satisfied. She doesn't want to sing, she wants to be a *star*. It's the trappings of stardom she misses – the cheering galleries, the piles of bouquets, the green room parties. I could arrange a half-hour session on closed circuit with some trainee technicians – a few straight selections from *Tosca* and *Butterfly*, say, with even a sonic piano accompaniment, I'd be glad to play it myself – but I can't provide the gossip columns and theatre reviews. What would happen when she found out?'

*She wants to SING.*

Alto reached out and patted Mangon on the shoulder. 'Good for you. All right, then, I'll think about it. God knows how we'd arrange it. We'd have to tell her that she'll be making a surprise guest appearance on one of the big shows – that'll explain the absence of any programme announcement and we'll be able to keep her in an isolated studio. Stress the importance of surprise, to prevent her from contacting the newspapers . . . Where are you going?'

Mangon reached the staircase, picked up the dictaphone and returned to Alto with it. He grinned happily, his jaw working wildly as he struggled to speak. Strangled sounds quavered in his throat.

Touched, Alto turned away from him and sat down. 'Okay, Mangon,' he snapped brusquely, 'you can get on with your job. Remember, I haven't promised anything.' He flicked on the dictaphone, then began: 'Memo 11: Ray . . .'

## THREE

It was just after four o'clock when Mangon braked the sound truck in the alley behind the derelict station. Overhead the traffic hammered along the flyover, dinning down on to the cobbled walls. He had been trying to finish his rounds early enough to bring Madame Gioconda the big news before her headaches began. He had swept out the Oratory in an hour, whirled through a couple of movie theatres, the Museum of Abstract Art, and a dozen private calls in half his usual time, driven by his almost overwhelming joy at having won a promise of help from Ray Alto.

He ran through the foyer, already fumbling at his wrist-pad. For the first time in many years he really regretted his muteness, his inability to tell Madame Gioconda orally of his triumph that morning.

Studio 2 was in darkness, the rows of seats and litter of old programmes and ice-cream cartons reflected dimly in the single light masked by the tall flats. His feet slipped in some shattered plaster fallen from the ceiling and he was out of breath when he clambered up on to the stage and swung round the nearest flat.

Madame Gioconda had gone!

The stage was deserted, the couch a rumpled mess, a clutter of cold saucepans on the stove. The wardrobe door was open, dresses wrenched outwards off their hangers.

For a moment Mangon panicked, unable to visualize why she should have left, immediately assuming that she had discovered his plot with Alto.

Then he realized that never before had he visited the studio until midnight at the earliest, and that Madame Gioconda had merely gone out to the supermarket. He smiled at his own stupidity and sat down on the couch to wait for her, sighing with relief.

As vivid as if they had been daubed in letters ten feet deep, the words leapt out from the walls, nearly deafening him with their force.

*'You grotesque old witch, you must be insane! You ever threaten me again
and I'll have you destroyed! LISTEN, you pathetic –'*

Mangon spun round helplessly, trying to screen his ears. The words
must have been hurled out in a paroxysm of abuse, they were only an hour
old, vicious sonic scars slashed across the immaculately swept walls.

His first thought was to rush out for the sonovac and sweep the walls
clear before Madame Gioconda returned. Then it dawned on him that
she had already heard the original of the echoes – in the background he
could just detect the muffled rhythms and intonations of her voice.

All too exactly, he could identify the man's voice.

He had heard it many times before, raging in the same ruthless tirades,
when deputizing for one of the sound-sweeps, he had swept out the main
boardroom at Video City.

Hector LeGrande! So Madame Gioconda had been more desperate than
he thought.

The bottom drawer of the dressing table lay on the floor, its contents
upended. Propped against the mirror was an old silver portrait frame,
dull and verdigrised, some cotton wool and a tin of cleansing fluid next
to it. The photograph was one of LeGrande, taken twenty years earlier.
She must have known LeGrande was coming and had searched out the
old portrait, probably regretting the threat of blackmail.

But the sentiment had not been shared.

Mangon walked round the stage, his heart knotting with rage, filling
his ears with LeGrande's taunts. He picked up the portrait, pressed it
between his palms, and suddenly smashed it across the edge of the
dressing table.

*'Mangon!'*

The cry riveted him to the air. He dropped what was left of the frame,
saw Madame Gioconda step quietly from behind one of the flats.

'Mangon, please,' she protested gently. 'You frighten me.' She sidled
past him towards the bed, dismantling an enormous purple hat. 'And do
clean up all that glass, or I shall cut my feet.'

She spoke drowsily and moved in a relaxed, sluggish way that Mangon
first assumed indicated acute shock. Then she drew from her handbag six
white vials and lined them up carefully on the bedside table. These were
her favourite confectionery – so LeGrande had sweetened the pill with
another cheque. Mangon began to scoop the glass together with his feet,
at the same time trying to collect his wits. The sounds of LeGrande's abuse
dinned the air, and he broke away and ran off to fetch the sonovac.

Madame Gioconda was sitting on the edge of the bed when he returned,
dreamily dusting a small bottle of bourbon which had followed the cocaine
vials out of the handbag. She hummed to herself melodically and stroked
one of the feathers in her hat.

'Mangon,' she called when he had almost finished. 'Come here.'

Mangon put down the sonovac and went across to her.

She looked up at him, her eyes suddenly very steady. 'Mangon, why

did you break Hector's picture?' She held up a piece of the frame.
'Tell me.'

Mangon hesitated, then scribbled on his pad:

*I am sorry. I adore you very much. He said such foul things to you.*

Madame Gioconda glanced at the note, then gazed back thoughtfully
at Mangon. 'Were you hiding here when Hector came?'

Mangon shook his head categorically. He started to write on his pad
but Madame Gioconda restrained him.

'That's all right, dear. I thought not.' She looked around the stage for a
moment, listening carefully. 'Mangon, when you came in could you hear
what Mr LeGrande said?'

Mangon nodded. His eyes flickered to the obscene phrases on the walls
and he began to frown. He still felt LeGrande's presence and his attempt
to humiliate Madame Gioconda.

Madame Gioconda pointed around them. 'And you can actually hear
what he said even now? How remarkable. Mangon, you have a won-
drous talent.'

*I am sorry you have to suffer so much.*

Madame Gioconda smiled at this. 'We all have our crosses to bear. I have
a feeling you may be able to lighten mine considerably.' She patted the bed
beside her. 'Do sit down, you must be tired.' When he was settled she went
on, 'I'm very interested, Mangon. Do you mean you can distinguish entire
phrases and sentences in the sounds you sweep? You can hear complete
conversations hours after they have taken place?'

Something about Madame Gioconda's curiosity made Mangon hesitate.
His talent, so far as he knew, was unique, and he was not so naïve as to fail
to appreciate its potentialities. It had developed in his late adolescence and
so far he had resisted any temptation to abuse it. He had never revealed
the talent to anyone, knowing that if he did his days as a sound-sweeper
would be over.

Madame Gioconda was watching him, an expectant smile on her lips.
Her thoughts, of course, were solely of revenge. Mangon listened again
to the walls, focused on the abuse screaming out into the air.

*Not complete conversations. Long fragments, up to twenty syllables.
Depending on resonances and matrix. Tell no one. I will help you have
revenge on LeGrande.*

Madame Gioconda squeezed Mangon's hand. She was about to reach
for the bourbon bottle when Mangon suddenly remembered the point
of his visit. He leapt off the bed and started frantically scribbling on his
wrist-pad.

He tore off the first sheet and pressed it into her startled hands, then filled three more, describing his encounter with the musical director at V.C., the latter's interest in Madame Gioconda and the conditional promise to arrange her guest appearance. In view of LeGrande's hostility he stressed the need for absolute secrecy.

He waited happily while Madame Gioconda read quickly through the notes, tracing out Mangon's child-like script with a long scarlet fingernail. When she finished he nodded his head rapidly and gestured triumphantly in the air.

Bemused, Madame Gioconda gazed uncomprehendingly at the notes. Then she reached out and pulled Mangon to her, taking his big faun-like head in her jewelled hands and pressing it to her lap.

'My dear child, how much I need you. You must never leave me now.'

As she stroked Mangon's hair her eyes roved questingly around the walls.

The miracle happened shortly before eleven o'clock the next morning.

After breakfast, sprawled across Madame Gioconda's bed with her scrapbooks, an old gramophone salvaged by Mangon from one of the studios playing operatic selections, they had decided to drive out to the stockades – the sound-sweeps left for the city at nine and they would be able to examine the sonic dumps unmolested. Having spent so much time with Madame Gioconda and immersed himself so deeply in her world, Mangon was eager now to introduce Madame Gioconda to his. The stockades, bleak though they might be, were all he had to show her.

For Mangon, Madame Gioconda had now become the entire universe, a source of certainty and wonder as potent as the sun. Behind him his past life fell away like the discarded chrysalis of a brilliant butterfly, the grey years of his childhood at the orphanage dissolving into the magical kaleidoscope that revolved around him. As she talked and murmured affectionately to him, the drab flats and props in the studio seemed as brightly coloured and meaningful as the landscape of a mescalin fantasy, the air tingling with a thousand vivid echoes of her voice.

They set off down F Street at ten, soon left behind the dingy warehouses and abandoned tenements that had enclosed Madame Gioconda for so long. Squeezed together in the driving-cab of the sound truck they looked an incongruous pair – the gangling Mangon, in zip-fronted yellow plastic jacket and yellow peaked cap, at the wheel, dwarfed by the vast flamboyant Madame Gioconda, wearing a parrot-green cartwheel hat and veil, her huge creamy breast glittering with pearls, gold stars and jewelled crescents, a small selection of the orders that had showered upon her in her heyday.

She had breakfasted well, on one of the vials and a tooth-glass of bourbon. As they left the city she gazed out amiably at the fields stretching away from the highway, and trilled out a light recitative from *Figaro*.

Mangon listened to her happily, glad to see her in such good form. Determined to spend every possible minute with Madame Gioconda, he had decided to abandon his calls for the day, if not for the next week and month. With her he at last felt completely secure. The pressure of her hand and the warm swell of her shoulder made him feel confident and invigorated, all the more proud that he was able to help her back to fame.

He tapped on the windshield as they swung off the highway on to the narrow dirt track that led towards the stockades. Here and there among the dunes they could see the low ruined outbuildings of the old explosives plant, the white galvanized iron roof of one of the sound-sweep's cabins. Desolate and unfrequented, the dunes ran on for miles. They passed the remains of a gateway that had collapsed to one side of the road; originally a continuous fence ringed the stockade, but no one had any reason for wanting to penetrate it. A place of strange echoes and festering silences, overhung by a gloomy miasma of a million compacted sounds, it remained remote and haunted, the graveyard of countless private babels.

The first of the sonic dumps appeared two or three hundred yards away on their right. This was reserved for aircraft sounds swept from the city's streets and municipal buildings, and was a tightly packed collection of sound-absorbent baffles covering several acres. The baffles were slightly larger than those in the other stockades; twenty feet high and fifteen wide, each supported by heavy wooden props, they faced each other in a random labyrinth of alleyways, like a store lot of advertisement hoardings. Only the top two or three feet were visible above the dunes, but the charged air hit Mangon like a hammer, a pounding niagara of airliners blaring down the glideway, the piercing whistle of jets jockeying at take-off, the ceaseless mind-sapping roar that hangs like a vast umbrella over any metropolitan complex.

All around, odd sounds shaken loose from the stockades were beginning to reach them. Over the entire area, fed from the dumps below, hung an unbroken phonic high, invisible but nonetheless as tangible and menacing as an enormous black thundercloud. Occasionally, when super-saturation was reached after one of the summer holiday periods, the sonic pressure fields would split and discharge, venting back into the stockades a nightmarish cataract of noise, raining on to the sound-sweeps not only the howling of cats and dogs, but the multi-lunged tumult of cars, express trains, fairgrounds and aircraft, the cacophonic *musique concrète* of civilization.

To Mangon the sounds reaching them, though scaled higher in the register, were still distinct, but Madame Gioconda could hear nothing and felt only an overpowering sense of depression and irritation. The air seemed to grate and rasp. Mangon noticed her beginning to frown and hold her hand to her forehead. He wound up his window and indicated to her to do the same. He switched on the sonovac mounted under the dashboard and let it drain the discordancies out of the sealed cabin.

Madame Gioconda relaxed in the sudden blissful silence. A little further on, when they passed another stockade set closer to the road, she turned to Mangon and began to say something to him.

Suddenly she jerked violently in alarm, her hat toppling. Her voice had frozen! Her mouth and lips moved frantically, but no sounds emerged. For a moment she was paralysed. Clutching her throat desperately, she filled her lungs and screamed.

A faint squeak piped out of her cavernous throat, and Mangon swung round in alarm to see her gibbering apoplectically, pointing helplessly to her throat.

He stared at her bewildered, then doubled over the wheel in a convulsion of silent laughter, slapping his thigh and thumping the dashboard. He pointed to the sonovac, then reached down and turned up the volume.

'. . . aaauuuoooh,' Madame Gioconda heard herself groan. She grasped her hat and secured it. 'Mangon, what a dirty trick, you should have warned me.'

Mangon grinned. The discordant sounds coming from the stockades began to fill the cabin again, and he turned down the volume. Gleefully, he scribbled on his wrist-pad:

*Now you know what it is like!*

Madame Gioconda opened her mouth to reply, then stopped in time, hiccuped and took his arm affectionately.

## FOUR

Mangon slowed down as they approached a side road. Two hundred yards away on their left a small pink-washed cabin stood on a dune overlooking one of the stockades. They drove up to it, turned into a circular concrete apron below the cabin and backed up against one of the unloading bays, a battery of red-painted hydrants equipped with manifold gauges and release pipes running off into the stockade. This was only twenty feet away at its nearest point, a forest of door-shaped baffles facing each other in winding corridors, like a set from a surrealist film.

As she climbed down from the truck Madame Gioconda expected the same massive wave of depression and overload that she had felt from the stockade of aircraft noises, but instead the air seemed brittle and frenetic, darting with sudden flashes of tension and exhilaration.

As they walked up to the cabin Mangon explained:

*Party noises – company for me.*

The twenty or thirty baffles nearest the cabin he reserved for those screening him from the miscellaneous chatter that filled the rest of the stockade. When he woke in the mornings he would listen to the laughter and small talk, enjoy the gossip and wisecracks as much as if he had been at the parties himself.

The cabin was a single room with a large window overlooking the stockade, well insulated from the hubbub below. Madame Gioconda showed only a cursory interest in Mangon's meagre belongings, and after a few general remarks came to the point and went over to the window. She opened it slightly, listened experimentally to the stream of atmospheric shifts that crowded past her.

She pointed to the cabin on the far side of the stockade. 'Mangon, whose is that?'

*Gallagher's. My partner. He sweeps City Hall, University, V.C., big mansions on 5th and A. Working now.*

Madame Gioconda nodded and surveyed the stockade with interest. 'How fascinating. It's like a zoo. All that talk, talk, talk. And *you* can hear it all.' She snapped back her bracelets with swift decisive flicks of the wrist.

Mangon sat down on the bed. The cabin seemed small and dingy, and he was saddened by Madame Gioconda's disinterest. Having brought her all the way out to the dumps he wondered how he was going to keep her amused. Fortunately the stockade intrigued her. When she suggested a stroll through it he was only too glad to oblige.

Down at the unloading bay he demonstrated how he emptied the tanker, clipping the exhaust leads to the hydrant, regulating the pressure through the manifold and then pumping the sound away into the stockade.

Most of the stockade was in a continuous state of uproar, sounding something like a crowd in a football stadium, and as he led her out among the baffles he picked their way carefully through the quieter aisles. Around them voices chattered and whined fretfully, fragments of conversation drifted aimlessly over the air. Somewhere a woman pleaded in thin nervous tones, a man grumbled to himself, another swore angrily, a baby bellowed. Behind it all was the steady background murmur of countless TV programmes, the easy patter of announcers, the endless monotones of race-track commentators, the shrieking audiences of quiz shows, all pitched an octave up the scale so that they sounded an eerie parody of themselves.

A shot rang out in the next aisle, followed by screams and shouting. Although she heard nothing, the pressure pulse made Madame Gioconda stop.

'Mangon, wait. Don't be in so much of a hurry. Tell me what they're saying.'

Mangon selected a baffle and listened carefully. The sounds appeared to come from an apartment over a launderette. A battery of washing machines chuntered to themselves, a cash register slammed interminably, there was a dim almost sub-threshold echo of 60-cycle hum from an SP record-player.

He shook his head, waved Madame Gioconda on.

'Mangon, what did they *say*?' she pestered him. He stopped again, sharpened his ears and waited. This time he was more lucky, an over-emotional female voice was gasping '. . . but if he finds you here he'll kill you, he'll kill us both, what shall we do . . .' He started to scribble down this outpouring, Madame Gioconda craning breathlessly over his shoulder, then recognized its source and screwed up the note.

'Mangon, for heaven's sake, what was it? Don't throw it away! Tell me!' She tried to climb under the wooden superstructure of the baffle to recover the note, but Mangon restrained her and quickly scribbled another message.

*Adam and Eve. Sorry.*

'What, the film? Oh, how ridiculous! Well, come on, try again.'

Eager to make amends, Mangon picked the next baffle, one of a group serving the staff married quarters of the University. Always a difficult job to keep clean, he struck paydirt almost at once.

'. . . my God, there's Bartok all over the place, that damned Steiner woman, I'll swear she's sleeping with her . . .'

Mangon took it all down, passing the sheets to Madame Gioconda as soon as he covered them. Squinting hard at his crabbed handwriting, she gobbled them eagerly, disappointed when, after half a dozen, he lost the thread and stopped.

'Go on, Mangon, what's the matter?' She let the notes fall to the ground. 'Difficult, isn't it. We'll have to teach you shorthand.'

They reached the baffles Mangon had just filled from the previous day's rounds. Listening carefully he heard Paul Merrill's voice: '. . . month's *Transonics* claims that . . . the entire city will come down like Jericho.'

He wondered if he could persuade Madame Gioconda to wait for fifteen minutes, when he would be able to repeat a few carefully edited fragments from Alto's promise to arrange her guest appearance, but she seemed eager to move deeper into the stockade.

'You said your friend Gallagher sweeps out Video City, Mangon. Where would that be?'

Hector LeGrande. Of course, Mangon realized, why had he been so obtuse. This was the chance to pay the man back.

He pointed to an area a few aisles away. They climbed between the baffles, Mangon helping Madame Gioconda over the beams and props, steering her full skirt and wide hat brim away from splinters and rusted metalwork.

*          *          *

The task of finding LeGrande was simple. Even before the baffles were in sight Mangon could hear the hard, unyielding bite of the tycoon's voice, dominating every other sound from the Video City area. Gallagher in fact swept only the senior dozen or so executive suites at V.C., chiefly to relieve their occupants of the distasteful echoes of LeGrande's voice.

Mangon steered their way among these, searching for LeGrande's master suite, where anything of a really confidential nature took place.

There were about twenty baffles, throwing off an unending chorus of 'Yes, H.L.', 'Thanks, H.L.', 'Brilliant, H.L.' Two or three seemed strangely quiet, and he drew Madame Gioconda over to them.

This was LeGrande with his personal secretary and PA. He took out his pencil and focused carefully.

'... of Third National Bank, transfer two million to private holding and threaten claim for stock depreciation ... redraft escape clauses, including non-liability purchase benefits ...'

Madame Gioconda tapped his arm but he gestured her away. Most of the baffle appeared to be taken up by dubious financial dealings, but nothing that would really hurt LeGrande if revealed.

Then he heard –

'... Bermuda Hilton. Private Island, with anchorage, have the beach cleaned up, last time the water was full of fish ... I don't care, poison them, hang some nets out ... Imogene will fly in from Idlewild as Mrs Edna Burgess, warn Customs to stay away ...'

'... call Cartiers, something for the Contessa, 17 carats say, ceiling of ten thousand. No, make it eight thousand ...'

'... hat-check girl at the Tropicabana. Usual dossier ...'

Mangon scribbled furiously, but LeGrande was speaking at rapid dictation speed and he could get down only a few fragments. Madame Gioconda barely deciphered his handwriting, and became more and more frustrated as her appetite was whetted. Finally she flung away the notes in a fury of exasperation.

'This is absurd, you're missing everything!' she cried. She pounded on one of the baffles, then broke down and began to sob angrily. 'Oh God, God, *God*, how ridiculous! Help me, I'm going insane ...'

Mangon hurried across to her, put his arms round her shoulders to support her. She pushed him away irritably, railing at herself to discharge her impatience. 'It's useless, Mangon, it's stupid of me, I was a fool –'

'*STOP!*'

The cry split the air like the blade of a guillotine.

They both straightened, stared at each other blankly. Mangon put his fingers slowly to his lips, then reached out tremulously and put his hands in Madame Gioconda's. Somewhere within him a tremendous tension had begun to dissolve.

'Stop,' he said again in a rough but quiet voice. 'Don't cry. I'll help you.'

Madame Gioconda gaped at him with amazement. Then she let out a tremendous whoop of triumph.

'Mangon, you can talk! You've got your voice back! It's absolutely astounding! Say something, quickly, for heaven's sake!'

Mangon felt his mouth again, ran his fingers rapidly over his throat. He began to tremble with excitement, his face brightened, he jumped up and down like a child.

'I can talk,' he repeated wonderingly. His voice was gruff, then seesawed into a treble. 'I can talk,' he said louder, controlling its pitch. 'I can talk, I can talk, *I can talk!*' He flung his head back, let out an ear-shattering shout. 'I CAN TALK! HEAR ME!' He ripped the wrist-pad off his sleeve, hurled it away over the baffles.

Madame Gioconda backed away, laughing agreeably. 'We can hear you, Mangon. Dear me, how sweet.' She watched Mangon thoughtfully as he cavorted happily in the narrow interval between the aisles. 'Now don't tire yourself out or you'll lose it again.'

Mangon danced over to her, seized her shoulders and squeezed them tightly. He suddenly realized that he knew no diminutive or Christian name for her.

'Madame Gioconda,' he said earnestly, stumbling over the syllables, the words that were so simple yet so enormously complex to pronounce. 'You gave me back my voice. Anything you want –' He broke off, stuttering happily, laughing through his tears. Suddenly he buried his head in her shoulder, exhausted by his discovery, and cried gratefully, 'It's a *wonderful* voice.'

Madame Gioconda steadied him maternally. 'Yes, Mangon,' she said, her eyes on the discarded notes lying in the dust. 'You've got a wonderful voice, all right.' *Sotto voce*, she added: 'But your hearing is even more wonderful.'

Paul Merrill switched off the SP player, sat down on the arm of the sofa and watched Mangon quizzically.

'Strange. You know, my guess is that it was psychosomatic.'

Mangon grinned. 'Psychosemantic,' he repeated, garbling the word half-deliberately. 'Clever. You can do amazing things with words. They help to crystallize the truth.'

Merrill groaned playfully. 'God, you sit there, you drink your coke, you philosophize. Don't you realize you're supposed to stand quietly in a corner, positively dumb with gratitude? Now you're even ramming your puns down my throat. Never mind, tell me again how it happened.'

'Once a pun a time –' Mangon ducked the magazine Merrill flung at him, let out a loud 'Olé!'

For the last two weeks he had been *en fête*.

Every day he and Madame Gioconda followed the same routine; after breakfast at the studio they drove out to the stockade, spent two or three hours compiling their confidential file on LeGrande, lunched at the cabin

and then drove back to the city, Mangon going off on his rounds while
Madame Gioconda slept until he returned shortly before midnight. For
Mangon their existence was idyllic; not only was he rediscovering himself
in terms of the complex spectra and patterns of speech – a completely new
category of existence – but at the same time his relationship with Madame
Gioconda revealed areas of sympathy, affection and understanding that he
had never previously seen. If he sometimes felt that he was too preoccupied
with his side of their relationship and the extraordinary benefits it had
brought him, at least Madame Gioconda had been equally well served.
Her headaches and mysterious phantoms had gone, she had cleaned
up the studio and begun to salvage a little dignity and self-confidence,
which made her single-minded sense of ambition seem less obsessive.
Psychologically, she needed Mangon less now than he needed her, and
he was sensible to restrain his high spirits and give her plenty of attention.
During the first week Mangon's incessant chatter had been rather wearing,
and once, on their way to the stockade, she had switched on the sonovac
in the driving-cab and left Mangon mouthing silently at the air like a
stranded fish. He had taken the hint.

'What about the sound-sweeping?' Merrill asked. 'Will you give it up?'

Mangon shrugged. 'It's my talent, but living at the stockade, let in at
back doors, cleaning up the verbal garbage – it's a degraded job. I want
to help Madame Gioconda. She will need a secretary when she starts to
go on tour.'

Merrill shook his head warily. 'You're awfully sure there's going to be
a sonic revival, Mangon. Every sign is against it.'

'They have not heard Madame Gioconda sing. Believe me, I know
the power and wonder of the human voice. Ultrasonic music is great
for atmosphere, but it has no content. It can't express ideas, only
emotions.'

'What happened to that closed circuit programme you and Ray were
going to put on for her?'

'It – fell through,' Mangon lied. The circuits Madame Gioconda would
perform on would be open to the world. He had told them nothing of the
visits to the stockade, of his power to read the baffles, of the accumulating
file on LeGrande. Soon Madame Gioconda would strike.

Above them in the hallway a door slammed, someone stormed through
into the apartment in a tempest, kicking a chair against a wall. It was Alto.
He raced down the staircase into the lounge, jaw tense, fingers flexing
angrily.

'Paul, don't interrupt me until I've finished,' he snapped, racing past
without looking at them. 'You'll be out of a job but I warn you, if
you don't back me up one hundred per cent I'll shoot you. That goes
for you too, Mangon, I need you in on this.' He whirled over to the
window, bolted out the traffic noises below, then swung back and
watched them steadily, feet planted firmly in the carpet. For the first

time in the three years Mangon had known him he looked aggressive and confident.

'Headline,' he announced. 'The Gioconda is to sing again! Incredible and terrifying though the prospect may seem, exactly two weeks from now the live, uncensored voice of the Gioconda will go out coast to coast on all three V.C. radio channels. Surprised, Mangon? It's no secret, they're printing the bills right now. Eight-thirty to nine-thirty, right up on the peak, even if they have to give the time away.'

Merrill sat forward. 'Bully for her. If LeGrande wants to drive the whole ship into the ground, why worry?'

Alto punched the sofa viciously. 'Because you and I are going to be on board! Didn't you hear me? Eight-thirty, a fortnight today! *We* have a programme on then. Well, guess who our guest star is?'

Merrill struggled to make sense of this. 'Wait a minute, Ray. You mean she's actually going to appear – she's going to *sing* – in the middle of *Opus Zero*?' Alto nodded grimly. Merrill threw up his hands and slumped back. 'It's crazy, she can't. Who says she will?'

'Who do you think? The great LeGrande.' Alto turned to Mangon. 'She must have raked up some real dirt to frighten him into this. I can hardly believe it.'

'But why on *Opus Zero*?' Merrill pressed. 'Let's switch the première to the week after.'

'Paul, you're missing the point. Let me fill you in. Sometime yesterday Madame Gioconda paid a private call on LeGrande. Something she told him persuaded him that it would be absolutely wonderful for her to have a whole hour to herself on one of the feature music programmes, singing a few old-fashioned songs from the old-fashioned shows, with a full-scale ultrasonic backing. Eager to give her a completely free hand he even asked her which of the regular programmes she'd like. Well, as the last show she appeared on ten years ago was cancelled to make way for Ray Alto's *Total Symphony* you can guess which one she picked.'

Merrill nodded. 'It all fits together. We're broadcasting from the concert studio. A single ultrasonic symphony, no station breaks, not even a commentary. Your first world première in three years. There'll be a big invited audience. White tie, something like the old days. Revenge is sweet.' He shook his head sadly. 'Hell, all that work.'

Alto snapped: 'Don't worry, it won't be wasted. Why should we pay the bill for LeGrande? This symphony is the one piece of serious music I've written since I joined V.C. and it isn't going to be ruined.' He went over to Mangon, sat down next to him. 'This afternoon I went down to the rehearsal studios. They'd found an ancient sonic grand somewhere and one of the old-timers was accompanying her. Mangon, it's ten years since she sang last. If she'd practised for two or three hours a day she might have preserved her voice, but you sweep her radio station, you know she hasn't sung a note. She's an old woman now. What time alone hasn't done to her, cocaine and self-pity have.' He paused, watching Mangon searchingly. 'I hate to say it, Mangon, but it sounded like a cat being strangled.'

*You lie*, Mangon thought icily. *You are simply so ignorant, your taste in music is so debased, that you are unable to recognize real genius when you see it.* He looked at Alto with contempt, sorry for the man, with his absurd silent symphonies. He felt like shouting: *I know what silence is! The voice of the Gioconda is a stream of gold, molten and pure, she will find it again as I found mine.* However, something about Alto's manner warned him to wait.

He said: 'I understand.' Then: 'What do you want me to do?'

Alto patted him on the shoulder. 'Good boy. Believe me, you'll be helping her in the long run. What I propose will save all of us from looking foolish. We've got to stand up to LeGrande, even if it means a one-way ticket out of V.C. Okay, Paul?' Merrill nodded firmly and he went on: 'Orchestra will continue as scheduled. According to the programme Madame Gioconda will be singing to an accompaniment by *Opus Zero*, but that means nothing and there'll be no connection at any point. In fact she won't turn up until the night itself. She'll stand well down-stage on a special platform, and the only microphone will be an aerial about twenty feet diagonally above her. It will be live – *but her voice will never reach it.* Because you, Mangon, will be in the cue-box directly in front of her, with the most powerful sonovac we can lay our hands on. As soon as she opens her mouth you'll let her have it. She'll be at least ten feet away from you so she'll hear herself and won't suspect what is happening.'

'What about the audience?' Merrill asked.

'They'll be listening to my symphony, enjoying a neurophonic experience of sufficient beauty and power, I hope, to distract them from the sight of a blowzy *prima donna* gesturing to herself in a cocaine fog. They'll probably think she's conducting. Remember, they may be expecting her to sing but how many people still know what the word really means? Most of them will assume it's ultrasonic.'

'And LeGrande?'

'He'll be in Bermuda. Business conference.'

## FIVE

Madame Gioconda was sitting before her dressing-table mirror, painting on a face like a Hallowe'en mask. Beside her the gramophone played scratchy sonic selections from *Traviata*. The stage was still a disorganized jumble, but there was now an air of purpose about it.

Making his way through the flats, Mangon walked up to her quietly and kissed her bare shoulder. She stood up with a flourish, an enormous monument of a woman in a magnificent black silk dress sparkling with thousands of sequins.

'Thank you, Mangon,' she sang out when he complimented her. She swirled off to a hat-box on the bed, pulled out a huge peacock feather and stabbed it into her hair.

Mangon had come round at six, several hours before usual; over the past two days he had felt increasingly uneasy. He was convinced that Alto was in error, and yet logic was firmly on his side. Could Madame Gioconda's voice have preserved itself? Her spoken voice, unless she was being particularly sweet, was harsh and uneven, recently even more so. He assumed that with only a week to her performance nervousness was making her irritable.

Again she was going out, as she had done almost every night. With whom, she never explained; probably to the theatre restaurants, to renew contacts with agents and managers. He would have liked to go with her, but he felt out of place on this plane of Madame Gioconda's existence.

'Mangon, I won't be back until very late,' she warned him. 'You look rather tired and pasty. You'd better go home and get some sleep.'

Mangon noticed he was still wearing his yellow peaked cap. Unconsciously he must already have known he would not be spending the night there.

'Do you want to go to the stockade tomorrow?' he asked.

'Hmmmh . . . I don't think so. It gives me rather a headache. Let's leave it for a day or two.'

She turned on him with a tremendous smile, her eyes glittering with sudden affection.

'Goodbye, Mangon, it's been wonderful to see you.' She bent down and pressed her cheek maternally to his, engulfing him in a heady wave of powder and perfume. In an instant all his doubts and worries evaporated, he looked forward to seeing her the next day, certain that they would spend the future together.

For half an hour after she had gone he wandered around the deserted sound stage, going through his memories. Then he made his way out to the alley and drove back to the stockade.

As the day of Madame Gioconda's performance drew closer Mangon's anxieties mounted. Twice he had been down to the concert studio at Video City, had rehearsed with Alto his entry beneath the stage to the cue-box, a small compartment off the corridor used by the electronics engineers. They had checked the power points, borrowed a sonovac from the services section – a heavy duty model used for shielding VIPs and commentators at airports – and mounted its nozzle in the cue-hood.

Alto stood on the platform erected for Madame Gioconda, shouted at the top of his voice at Merrill sitting in the third row of the stalls.

'Hear anything?' he called afterwards.

Merrill shook his head. 'Nothing, no vibration at all.'

Down below Mangon flicked the release toggle, vented a long-drawn-out 'Fiivvveeee! . . . Foouuurrr! . . . Thrreeeee! . . . Twooooo! . . . Onnneeee . . . !'

'Good enough,' Alto decided. Chicago-style, they hid the sonovac in a triple-bass case, stored it in Alto's office.

'Do you want to hear her sing, Mangon?' Alto asked. 'She should be rehearsing now.'

Mangon hesitated, then declined.

'It's tragic that she's unable to realize the truth herself,' Alto commented. 'Her mind must be fixed fifteen or twenty years in the past, when she sang her greatest roles at La Scala. That's the voice she hears, the voice she'll probably always hear.'

Mangon pondered this. Once he tried to ask Madame Gioconda how her practice sessions were going, but she was moving into a different zone and answered with some grandiose remark. He was seeing less and less of her, whenever he visited the station she was either about to go out or else tired and eager to be rid of him. Their trips to the stockade had ceased. All this he accepted as inevitable; after the performance, he assured himself, after her triumph, she would come back to him.

He noticed, however, that he was beginning to stutter.

On the final afternoon, a few hours before the performance that evening, Mangon drove down to F Street for what was to be the last time. He had not seen Madame Gioconda the previous day and he wanted to be with her and give her any encouragement she needed.

As he turned into the alley he was surprised to see two large removal vans parked outside the station entrance. Four or five men were carrying out pieces of furniture and the great scenic flats from the sound stage.

Mangon ran over to them. One of the vans was full; he recognized all Madame Gioconda's possessions – the rococo wardrobe and dressing table, the couch, the huge Desdemona bed, up-ended and wrapped in corrugated paper – as he looked at it he felt that a section of himself had been torn from him and rammed away callously. In the bright daylight the peeling threadbare flats had lost all illusion of reality; with them Mangon's whole relationship with Madame Gioconda seemed to have been dismantled.

The last of the workmen came out with a gold cushion under his arm, tossed it into the second van. The foreman sealed the doors and waved on the driver.

'W . . . wh . . . where are you going?' Mangon asked him urgently.

The foreman looked him up and down. 'You're the sweeper, are you?' He jerked a thumb towards the station. 'The old girl said there was a message for you in there. Couldn't see one myself.'

Mangon left him and ran into the foyer and up the stairway towards Studio 2. The removers had torn down the blinds and a grey light was flooding into the dusty auditorium. Without the flats the stage looked exposed and derelict.

He raced down the aisle, wondering why Madame Gioconda had decided to leave without telling him.

The stage had been stripped. The music stands had been kicked over, the stove lay on its side with two or three old pans around it, underfoot there was a miscellaneous litter of paper, ash and empty vials.

Mangon searched around for the message, probably pinned to one of the partitions.

Then he heard it screaming at him from the walls, violent and concise.

*'GO AWAY YOU UGLY CHILD! NEVER TRY TO SEE ME AGAIN!'*

He shrank back, involuntarily tried to shout as the walls seemed to fall in on him, but his throat had frozen.

As he entered the corridor below the stage shortly before eight-twenty, Mangon could hear the sounds of the audience arriving and making their way to their seats. The studio was almost full, a hubbub of well-heeled chatter. Lights flashed on and off in the corridor, and oblique atmospheric shifts cut through the air as the players on the stage tuned their instruments.

Mangon slid past the technicians manning the neurophonic rigs which supplied the orchestra, trying to make the enormous triple-bass case as inconspicuous as possible. They were all busy checking the relays and circuits, and he reached the cue-box and slipped through the door unnoticed.

The box was almost in darkness, a few rays of coloured light filtering through the pink and white petals of the chrysanthemums stacked over the hood. He bolted the door, then opened the case, lifted out the sonovac and clipped the snout into the canister. Leaning forward, with his hands he pushed a small aperture among the flowers.

Directly in front of him he could see a velvet-lined platform, equipped with a white metal rail to the centre of which a large floral ribbon had been tied. Beyond was the orchestra, disposed in a semicircle, each of the twenty members sitting at a small box-like desk on which rested his instrument, tone generator and cathode tube. They were all present, and the light reflected from the ray screens threw a vivid phosphorescent glow on to the silver wall behind them.

Mangon propped the nozzle of the sonovac into the aperture, bent down, plugged in the lead and switched on.

Just before eight-twenty-five someone stepped across the platform and paused in front of the cue-hood. Mangon crouched back, watching the patent leather shoes and black trousers move near the nozzle.

'Mangon!' he heard Alto snap. He craned forward, saw Alto eyeing him. Mangon waved to him and Alto nodded slowly, at the same time smiling to someone in the audience, then turned on his heel and took his place in the orchestra.

At eight-thirty a sequence of red and green lights signalled the start of the programme. The audience quietened, waiting while an announcer in an off-stage booth introduced the programme.

A compère appeared on stage, standing behind the cue-hood, and addressed the audience. Mangon sat quietly on the small wooden seat fastened to the wall, staring blankly at the canister of the sonovac. There was a round of applause, and a steady green light shone downwards through the flowers. The air in the cue-box began to sweeten, a cool motionless breeze eddied vertically around him as a rhythmic ultrasonic pressure wave pulsed past. It relaxed the confined dimensions of the box, with a strange mesmeric echo that held his attention. Somewhere in his mind he realized that the symphony had started, but he was too distracted to pull himself together and listen to it consciously.

Suddenly, through the gap between the flowers and the sonovac nozzle, he saw a large white mass shifting about on the platform. He slipped off the seat and peered up.

Madame Gioconda had taken her place on the platform. Seen from below she seemed enormous, a towering cataract of glistening white satin that swept down to her feet. Her arms were folded loosely in front of her, fingers flashing with blue and white stones. He could only just glimpse her face, the terrifying witch-like mask turned in profile as she waited for some off-stage signal.

Mangon mobilized himself, slid his hand down to the trigger of the sonovac. He waited, feeling the steady subliminal music of Alto's symphony swell massively within him, its tempo accelerating. Presumably Madame Gioconda's arranger was waiting for a climax at which to introduce her first aria.

Abruptly Madame Gioconda looked forward at the audience and took a short step to the rail. Her hands parted and opened palms upward, her head moved back, her bare shoulders swelled.

The wave front pulsing through the cue-box stopped, then soared off in a continuous unbroken crescendo. At the same time Madame Gioconda thrust her head out, her throat muscles contracted powerfully.

As the sound burst from her throat Mangon's finger locked rigidly against the trigger guard. An instant later, before he could think, a shattering blast of sound ripped through his ears, followed by a slightly higher note that appeared to strike a hidden ridge half-way along its path, wavered slightly, then recovered and sped on, like an express train crossing lines.

Mangon listened to her numbly, hands gripping the barrel of the sonovac. The voice exploded in his brain, flooding every nexus of cells with its violence. It was grotesque, an insane parody of a classical soprano. Harmony, purity, cadence had gone. Rough and cracked, it jerked sharply from one high note to a lower, its breath intervals uncontrolled, sudden precipices of gasping silence which plunged through the volcanic torrent, dividing it into a loosely connected sequence of *bravura* passages.

He barely recognized what she was singing: the Toreador song from *Carmen*. Why she had picked this he could not imagine. Unable to reach its higher notes she fell back on the swinging rhythm of the refrain, hammering out the rolling phrases with tosses of her head. After a dozen bars her pace slackened, she slipped into an extempore humming, then broke out of this into a final climactic assault.

Appalled, Mangon watched as two or three members of the orchestra stood up and disappeared into the wings. The others had stopped playing, were switching off their instruments and conferring with each other. The audience was obviously restive; Mangon could hear individual voices in the intervals when Madame Gioconda refilled her lungs.

Behind him someone hammered on the door. Startled, Mangon nearly tripped across the sonovac. Then he bent down and wrenched the plug out of its socket. Snapping open the two catches beneath the chassis of the sonovac, he pulled off the canister to reveal the valves, amplifier and generator. He slipped his fingers carefully through the leads and coils, seized them as firmly as he could and ripped them out with a single motion. Tearing his nails, he stripped the printed circuit off the bottom of the chassis and crushed it between his hands.

Satisfied, he dropped the sonovac to the floor, listened for a moment to the caterwauling above, which was now being drowned by the mounting vocal opposition of the audience, then unlatched the door.

Paul Merrill, his bow tie askew, burst in. He gaped blankly at Mangon, at the blood dripping from his fingers and the smashed sonovac on the floor.

He seized Mangon by the shoulders, shook him roughly. 'Mangon, are you crazy? What are you trying to do?'

Mangon attempted to say something, but his voice had died. He pulled himself away from Merrill, pushed past into the corridor.

Merrill shouted after him. 'Mangon, help me fix this! Where are you going?' He got down on his knees, started trying to piece the sonovac together.

From the wings Mangon briefly watched the scene on the stage.

Madame Gioconda was still singing, her voice completely inaudible in the uproar from the auditorium. Half the audience were on their feet, shouting towards the stage and apparently remonstrating with the studio officials. All but a few members of the orchestra had left their instruments, these sitting on their desks and watching Madame Gioconda in amazement.

The programme director, Alto and one of the compères stood in front of her, banging on the rail and trying to attract her attention. But Madame Gioconda failed to notice them. Head back, eyes on the brilliant ceiling lights, hands gesturing majestically, she soared along the private causeways of sound that poured unrelentingly from her throat, a great white angel of discord on her homeward flight.

Mangon watched her sadly, then slipped away through the stage-hands pressing around him. As he left the theatre by the stage door a small crowd was gathering by the main entrance. He flicked away the blood from his fingers, then bound his handkerchief round them.

He walked down the side street to where the sound truck was parked, climbed into the cab and sat still for a few minutes looking out at the bright evening lights in the bars and shopfronts.

Opening the dashboard locker, he hunted through it and pulled out an old wrist-pad, clipped it into his sleeve.

In his ears the sounds of Madame Gioconda singing echoed like an insane banshee.

He switched on the sonovac under the dashboard, turned it full on, then started the engine and drove off into the night.

**1960**

# ·ZONE OF TERROR

Larsen had been waiting all day for Bayliss, the psychologist who lived in the next chalet, to pay the call he had promised on the previous evening. Characteristically, Bayliss had made no precise arrangements as regards time; a tall, moody man with an off-hand manner, he had merely gestured vaguely with his hypodermic and mumbled something about the following day: he would look in, probably. Larsen knew damned well he would look in, the case was too interesting to miss. In an oblique way it meant as much to Bayliss as it did to himself.

Except that it was Larsen who had to do the worrying – by three that afternoon Bayliss had still not materialized. What was he doing except sitting in his white-walled, air-conditioned lounge, playing Bartok quartets on the stereogram? Meanwhile Larsen had nothing to do but roam around the chalet, slamming impatiently from one room to the next like a tiger with an anxiety neurosis, and cook up a quick lunch (coffee and three amphetamines, from a private cache Bayliss as yet only dimly suspected. God, he needed the stimulants after those massive barbiturate shots Bayliss had pumped into him after the attack). He tried to settle down with Kretschmer's *An Analysis of Psychotic Time*, a heavy tome, full of graphs and tabular material, which Bayliss had insisted he read, asserting that it filled in necessary background to the case. Larsen had spent a couple of hours on it, but so far he had got no further than the preface to the third edition.

Periodically he went over to the window and peered through the plastic blind for any signs of movement in the next chalet. Beyond, the desert lay in the sunlight like an enormous bone, against which the aztec-red fins of Bayliss's Pontiac flared like the tail feathers of a flamboyant phoenix. The remaining three chalets were empty; the complex was operated by the electronics company for which he and Bayliss worked as a sort of 're-creational' centre for senior executives and tired 'think-men'. The desert site had been chosen for its hypotensive virtues, its supposed equivalence to psychic zero. Two or three days of leisurely reading, of watching the motionless horizon, and tension and anxiety thresholds rose to more useful levels.

However, two days there, Larsen reflected, and he had very nearly gone mad. It was lucky Bayliss had been around with his hypodermic. Though the man was certainly casual when it came to supervising his patients; he left them to their own resources. In fact, looking back, he – Larsen – had been responsible for just about all the diagnosis. Bayliss had done little more than thumb his hypo, toss Kretschmer into his lap, and offer some cogitating asides.

Perhaps he was waiting for something?

Larsen tried to decide whether to phone Bayliss on some pretext; his number – O, on the internal system – was almost too inviting. Then he heard a door clatter outside, and saw the tall, angular figure of the psychologist crossing the concrete apron between the chalets, head bowed pensively in the sharp sunlight.

Where's his case, Larsen thought, almost disappointed. Don't tell me he's putting on the barbiturate brakes. Maybe he'll try hypnosis. Masses of post-hypnotic suggestions, in the middle of shaving I'll suddenly stand on my head.

He let Bayliss in, fidgeting around him as they went into the lounge.

'Where the hell have you been?' he asked. 'Do you realize it's nearly four?'

Bayliss sat down at the miniature executive desk in the middle of the lounge and looked round critically, a ploy Larsen resented but never managed to anticipate.

'Of course I realize it. I'm fully wired for time. How have you felt today?' He pointed to the straight-backed chair placed in the interviewee's position. 'Sit down and try to relax.'

Larsen gestured irritably. 'How can I relax while I'm just hanging around here, waiting for the next bomb to go off?' He began his analysis of the past twenty-four hours, a task he enjoyed, larding the case history with liberal doses of speculative commentary.

'Actually, last night was easier. I think I'm entering a new zone. Everything's beginning to stabilize, I'm not looking over my shoulder all the time. I've left the inside doors open, and before I enter a room I deliberately anticipate it, try to extrapolate its depth and dimensions so that it doesn't *surprise* me – before I used to open a door and just dive through like a man stepping into an empty lift shaft.'

Larsen paced up and down, cracking his knuckles. Eyes half closed, Bayliss watched him. 'I'm pretty sure there won't be another attack,' Larsen continued. 'In fact, the best thing is probably for me to get straight back to the plant. After all, there's no point in sitting around here indefinitely. I feel more or less completely okay.'

Bayliss nodded. 'In that case, then, why are you so jumpy?'

Exasperated, Larsen clenched his fists. He could almost hear the artery thudding in his temple. 'I'm *not* jumpy! For God's sake, Bayliss, I thought the advanced view was that psychiatrist and patient shared the illness together, forgot their own identities and took equal responsibility. You're trying to evade –'

'I am not,' Bayliss cut in firmly. 'I accept complete responsibility for you. That's why I want you to stay here until you've come to terms with this thing.'

Larsen snorted. '"Thing"! Now you're trying to make it sound like something out of a horror film. All I had was a simple hallucination. And I'm not even completely convinced it was that.' He pointed through the window. 'Suddenly opening the garage door in that bright sunlight – it might have been a shadow.'

'You described it pretty exactly,' Bayliss commented. 'Colour of the hair, moustache, the clothes he wore.'

'Back projection. The detail in dreams is authentic too.' Larsen moved the chair out of the way and leaned forwards across the desk. 'Another thing. I don't feel you're being entirely frank.'

Their eyes levelled. Bayliss studied Larsen carefully for a moment, noticing his widely dilated pupils.

'Well?' Larsen pressed.

Bayliss buttoned his jacket and walked across to the door. 'I'll call in tomorrow. Meanwhile try to unwind yourself a little. I'm not trying to alarm you, Larsen, but this problem may be rather more complicated than you imagine.' He nodded, then slipped out before Larsen could reply.

Larsen stepped over to the window and through the blind watched the psychologist disappear into his chalet. Disturbed for a moment, the sunlight again settled itself heavily over everything. A few minutes later the sounds of one of the Bartok quartets whined fretfully across the apron.

Larsen went back to the desk and sat down, elbows thrust forward aggressively. Bayliss irritated him, with his neurotic music and inaccurate diagnoses. He felt tempted to climb straight into his car and drive back to the plant. Strictly speaking, though, the psychologist outranked Larsen, and probably had executive authority over him while he was at the chalet, particularly as the five days he had spent there were on the company's time.

He gazed round the silent lounge, tracing the cool horizontal shadows that dappled the walls, listening to the low soothing hum of the air-conditioner. His argument with Bayliss had refreshed him and he felt composed and confident. Yet residues of tension and uneasiness still existed, and he found it difficult to keep his eyes off the open doors to the bedroom and kitchen.

He had arrived at the chalet five days earlier, exhausted and over-wrought, on the verge of a total nervous collapse. For three months he had been working without a break on programming the complex circuitry of a huge brain simulator which the company's Advanced Designs Division were building for one of the major psychiatric foundations. This was a complete electronic replica of the central nervous system, each spinal level represented by a single computer, other computers holding memory banks in which sleep, tension, aggression and other psychic functions were coded and stored, building blocks that could be played into the CNS simulator to construct models of dissociation states and withdrawal syndromes – any psychic complex on demand.

The design teams working on the simulator had been watched vigilantly by Bayliss and his assistants, and the weekly tests had revealed the mounting load of fatigue that Larsen was carrying. Finally Bayliss had pulled him off the project and sent him out to the desert for two or three days' recuperation.

Larsen had been glad to get away. For the first two days he had lounged aimlessly around the deserted chalets, pleasantly fuddled by the barbiturates Bayliss prescribed, gazing out across the white deck of the desert floor, going to bed by eight and sleeping until noon. Every morning the caretaker had driven in from the town near by to clean up and leave the groceries and menu slips, but Larsen never saw her. He was only too glad to be alone. Deliberately seeing no one, allowing the natural rhythms of his mind to re-establish themselves, he knew he would soon recover.

In fact, however, the first person he had seen had stepped up to him straight out of a nightmare.

Larsen still looked back on the encounter with a shudder.

After lunch on his third day at the chalet he had decided to drive out into the desert and examine an old quartz mine in one of the canyons. This was a two-hour trip and he had made up a thermos of iced martini. The garage was adjacent to the chalet, set back from the kitchen side entrance, and fitted with a roll steel door that lifted vertically and curved up under the roof.

Larsen had locked the chalet behind him, then raised the garage door and driven his car out on to the apron. Going back for the thermos which he had left on the bench at the rear of the garage, he had noticed a full can of petrol in the shadows against one corner. For a moment he paused, adding up his mileage, and decided to take the can with him. He carried it over to the car, then turned round to close the garage door.

The roll had failed to retreat completely when he had first raised it, and reached down to the level of his chin. Putting his weight on the handle, Larsen managed to move it down a few inches, but the inertia was too much for him. The sunlight reflected in the steel panels was dazzling his eyes. Pressing his palms under the door, he jerked it upwards slightly to gain more momentum on the downward swing.

The space was small, no more than six inches, but it was just enough for him to see into the darkened garage.

Hiding in the shadows against the back wall near the bench was the indistinct but nonetheless unmistakable figure of a man. He stood motionless, arms loosely at his sides, watching Larsen. He wore a light cream suit – covered by patches of shadow that gave him a curious fragmentary look – a neat blue sports-shirt and two-tone shoes. He was stockily built, with a thick brush moustache, a plump face, and eyes that stared steadily at Larsen but somehow seemed to be focused beyond him.

Still holding the door with both hands, Larsen gaped at the man. Not only was there no means by which he could have entered the garage – there were no windows or side doors – but there was something aggressive about his stance.

Larsen was about to call to him when the man moved forward and stepped straight out of the shadows towards him.

Aghast, Larsen backed away. The dark patches across the man's suit were not shadows at all, but the outline of the work bench directly behind him.

The man's body and clothes were transparent.

Galvanized into life, Larsen seized the garage door and hurled it down. He snapped the bolt in and jammed it closed with both hands, knees pressed against it.

Half paralysed by cramp and barely breathing, his suit soaked with sweat, he was still holding the door down when Bayliss drove up thirty minutes later.

Larsen drummed his fingers irritably on the desk, stood up and went into the kitchen. Cut off from the barbiturates they had been intended to counteract, the three amphetamines had begun to make him feel restless and overstimulated. He switched the coffee percolator on and then off, prowled back to the lounge and sat down on the sofa with the copy of Kretschmer.

He read a few pages, increasingly impatient. What light Kretschmer threw on his problem was hard to see; most of the case histories described deep schizos and irreversible paranoids. His own problem was much more superficial, a momentary aberration due to overloading. Why wouldn't Bayliss see this? For some reason he seemed to be unconsciously wishing for a major crisis, probably because he, the psychologist, secretly wanted to become the patient.

Larsen tossed the book aside and looked out through the window at the desert. Suddenly the chalet seemed dark and cramped, a claustrophobic focus of suppressed aggressions. He stood up, strode over to the door and stepped out into the clear open air.

Grouped in a loose semicircle, the chalets seemed to shrink towards the ground as he strolled to the rim of the concrete apron a hundred yards away. The mountains behind loomed up enormously. It was late afternoon, on the edge of dusk, and the sky was a vivid vibrant blue, the deepening colours of the desert floor overlaid by the huge lanes of shadow that reached from the mountains against the sunline. Larsen looked back at the chalets. There was no sign of movement, other than a faint discordant echo of the atonal music Bayliss was playing. The whole scene seemed suddenly unreal.

Reflecting on this, Larsen felt something shift inside his mind. The sensation was undefined, like an expected cue that had failed to materialize, a forgotten intention. He tried to recall it, unable to remember whether he had switched on the coffee percolator.

He walked back to the chalets, noticing that he had left the kitchen door open. As he passed the lounge window on his way to close it he glanced in.

A man was sitting on the sofa, legs crossed, face hidden by the volume of Kretschmer. For a moment Larsen assumed that Bayliss had called in to see him, and walked on, deciding to make coffee for them both. Then he noticed that the stereogram was still playing in Bayliss's chalet.

Picking his steps carefully, he moved back to the lounge window. The man's face was still hidden, but a single glance confirmed that the visitor was not Bayliss. He was wearing the same cream suit Larsen had seen two days earlier, the same two-tone shoes. But this time the man was no hallucination; his hands and clothes were solid and palpable. He shifted about on the sofa, denting one of the cushions, and turned a page of the book, flexing the spine between his hands.

Pulse thickening, Larsen braced himself against the window-ledge. Something about the man, his posture, the way he held his hands, convinced him that he had seen him before their fragmentary encounter in the garage.

Then the man lowered the book and threw it on to the seat beside him. He sat back and looked through the window, his focus only a few inches from Larsen's face.

Mesmerized, Larsen stared back at him. He recognized the man without doubt, the pudgy face, the nervous eyes, the too thick moustache. Now at last he could see him clearly and realized he knew him only too well, better than anyone else on Earth.

The man was himself.

Bayliss clipped the hypodermic into his valise, and placed it on the lid of the stereogram.

'Hallucination is the wrong term altogether,' he told Larsen, who was lying stretched out on Bayliss's sofa, sipping weakly at a glass of hot whisky. 'Stop using it. A psychoretinal image of remarkable strength and duration, but not an hallucination.'

Larsen gestured feebly. He had stumbled into Bayliss's chalet an hour earlier, literally beside himself with fright. Bayliss had calmed him down, then dragged him back across the apron to the lounge window and made him accept that his double was gone. Bayliss was not in the least surprised at the identity of the phantom, and this worried Larsen almost as much as the actual hallucination. What else was Bayliss hiding up his sleeve?

'I'm surprised you didn't realize it sooner yourself,' Bayliss remarked. 'Your description of the man in the garage was so obvious – the same cream suit, the same shoes and shirt, let alone the exact physical similarity, even down to your moustache.'

Recovering a little, Larsen sat up. He smoothed down his cream gabardine suit and brushed the dust off his brown-and-white shoes. 'Thanks for warning me. All you've got to do now is tell me who he is.'

Bayliss sat down in one of the chairs. 'What do you mean, who he is? He's you, of course.'

'I know that, but why, where does he come from? God, I must be going insane.'

Bayliss snapped his fingers. 'No you're not. Pull yourself together. This is a purely functional disorder, like double vision or amnesia; nothing more serious. If it was, I'd have pulled you out of here long ago. Perhaps I should have done that anyway, but I think we can find a safe way out of the maze you're in.'

He took a notebook out of his breast pocket. 'Let's have a look at what we've got. Now, two features stand out. First, the phantom is yourself. There's no doubt about that; he's an exact replica of you. More important, though, he is you as you are now, your exact contemporary in time, unidealized and unmutilated. He isn't the shining hero of the super-ego, or the haggard grey-beard of the death wish. He is simply a photographic double. Displace one eyeball with your finger and you'll see a double of me. Your double is no more unusual, with the exception that the displacement is not in space but in time. You see, the second thing I noticed about your garbled description of this phantom was that, not only was he a photographic double, but he was doing exactly what you yourself had been doing a few minutes previously. The man in the garage was standing by the workbench, just where you stood when you were wondering whether to take the can of petrol. Again, the man reading in the armchair was merely repeating exactly what you had been doing with the same book five minutes earlier. He even stared out of the window as you say you did before going out for a stroll.'

Larsen nodded, sipping his whisky. 'You're suggesting that the hallucination was a mental flashback?'

'Precisely. The stream of retinal images reaching the optic lobe is nothing more than a film strip. Every image is stored away, thousands of reels, a hundred thousand hours of running time. Usually flashbacks are deliberate, when we consciously select a few blurry stills from the film library, a childhood scene, the image of our neighbourhood streets we carry around with us all day near the surface of consciousness. But upset the projector slightly – overstrain could do it – jolt it back a few hundred frames, and you'll superimpose a completely irrelevant strip of already exposed film, in your case a glimpse of yourself sitting on the sofa. It's the apparent irrelevancy that is so frightening.'

Larsen gestured with his glass. 'Wait a minute, though. When I was sitting on the sofa reading Kretschmer I didn't actually see myself, any more than I can see myself now. So where did the superimposed images come from?'

Bayliss put away his notebook. 'Don't take the analogy of the film strip too literally. You may not see yourself sitting on that sofa, but your awareness of being there is just as powerful as any visual corroboration. It's the stream of tactile, positional and psychic images that form the real data store. Very little extrapolation is needed to transpose the observer's eye a few yards to the other side of a room. Purely visual memories are never completely accurate anyway.'

'How do you explain why the man I saw in the garage was transparent?'

'Quite simply. The process was only just beginning, the intensity of the image was weak. The one you saw this afternoon was much stronger. I cut you off barbiturates deliberately, knowing full well that those stimulants you were taking on the sly would set off something if they were allowed to operate unopposed.'

He went over to Larsen, took his glass and refilled it from the decanter. 'But let's think of the future. The most interesting aspect of all this is the light it throws on one of the oldest archetypes of the human psyche – the ghost – and the whole supernatural army of phantoms, witches, demons and so on. Are they all, in fact, nothing more than psychoretinal flashbacks, transposed images of the observer himself, jolted on to the retinal screen by fear, bereavement, religious obsession? The most notable thing about the majority of ghosts is how prosaically equipped they are, compared with the elaborate literary productions of the great mystics and dreamers. The nebulous white sheet is probably the observer's own nightgown. It's an interesting field for speculation. For example, take the most famous ghost in literature and reflect how much more sense Hamlet makes if you realize that the ghost of his murdered father is really Hamlet himself.'

'All right, all right,' Larsen cut in irritably. 'But how does this help me?'

Bayliss broke off his reflective up-and-down patrol of the floor and fixed an eye on Larsen. 'I'm coming to that. There are two methods of dealing with this disfunction of yours. The classical technique is to pump you full of tranquillizers and confine you to a bed for a year or so. Gradually your mind would knit together. Long job, boring for you and everybody else. The alternative method is, frankly, experimental, but I think it might work. I mentioned the phenomenon of the ghost because it's an interesting fact that although there have been tens of thousands of recorded cases of people being pursued by ghosts, and a few of the ghosts themselves being pursued, there have been no cases of ghost and observer actually meeting of their own volition. Tell me, what would have happened if, when you saw your double this afternoon, you had gone straight into the lounge and spoken to him?'

Larsen shuddered. 'Obviously nothing, if your theory holds. I wouldn't like to test it.'

'That's just what you're going to do. Don't panic. The next time you see a double sitting in a chair reading Kretschmer, go up and speak to him. If he doesn't reply sit down in the chair yourself. That's all you have to do.'

Larsen jumped up, gesticulating. 'For heaven's sake, Bayliss, are you crazy? Do you know what it's like to suddenly see yourself? All you want to do is run.'

'I realize that, but it's the worst thing you can do. Why whenever anyone grapples with a ghost does it always vanish instantly? Because forcibly occupying the same physical co-ordinates as the double jolts the psychic projector on to a single channel again. The two separate streams of retinal images coincide and fuse. You've got to try, Larsen. It may be quite an effort, but you'll cure yourself once and for all.'

Larsen shook his head stubbornly. 'The idea's insane.' To himself he added: I'd rather shoot the thing. Then he remembered the .38 in his suitcase, and the presence of the weapon gave him a stronger sense of security than all Bayliss's drugs and advice. The revolver was a simple symbol of aggression, and even if the phantom was only an intruder in his own mind, it gave that portion which still remained intact greater confidence, enough possibly to dissipate the double's power.

Eyes half closed with fatigue, he listened to Bayliss. Half an hour later he went back to his chalet, found the revolver and hid it under a magazine in the letterbox outside the front door. It was too conspicuous to carry and anyway might fire accidentally and injure him. Outside the front door it would be safely hidden and yet easily accessible, ready to mete out a little old-fashioned punishment to any double dealer trying to get into the game.

Two days later, with unexpected vengeance, the opportunity came.

Bayliss had driven into town to buy a new stylus for the stereogram, leaving Larsen to prepare lunch for them while he was away. Larsen pretended to resent the chore, but secretly he was glad of something to do. He was tired of hanging around the chalets while Bayliss watched him as if he were an experimental animal, eagerly waiting for the next crisis. With luck this might never come, if only to spite Bayliss, who had been having everything too much his own way.

After laying the table in Bayliss's kitchenette and getting plenty of ice ready for the martinis (alcohol was just the thing, Larsen readily decided, a wonderful CNS depressant) he went back to his chalet and put on a clean shirt. On an impulse he decided to change his shoes and suit as well, and fished out the blue office serge and black oxfords he had worn on his way out to the desert. Not only were the associations of the cream suit and sports shoes unpleasant, but a complete change of costume might well forestall the double's reappearance, provide a fresh psychic image of himself powerful enough to suppress any wandering versions. Looking at himself in the mirror, he decided to carry the principle even farther. He switched on his shaver and cut away his moustache. Then he thinned out his hair and plastered it back smoothly across his scalp.

The transformation was effective. When Bayliss climbed out of his car and walked into the lounge he almost failed to recognize Larsen. He flinched back at the sight of the sleek-haired, dark-suited figure who stepped from behind the kitchen door.

'What the hell are you playing at?' he snapped at Larsen. 'This is no time for practical jokes.' He surveyed Larsen critically. 'You look like a cheap detective.'

Larsen guffawed. The incident put him in high spirits, and after several martinis he began to feel extremely buoyant. He talked away rapidly through the meal. Strangely, though, Bayliss seemed eager to get rid of him; he realized why shortly after he returned to his chalet. His pulse had quickened. He found himself prowling around nervously; his brain felt overactive and accelerated. The martinis had only been partly responsible for his elation. Now that they were wearing off he began to see the real agent – a stimulant Bayliss had given him in the hope of precipitating another crisis.

Larsen stood by the window, staring out angrily at Bayliss's chalet. The psychologist's utter lack of scruple outraged him. His fingers fretted nervously across the blind. Suddenly he felt like kicking the whole place down and speeding off. With its plywood-thin walls and match-box furniture the chalet was nothing more than a cardboard asylum. Everything that had happened there, the breakdowns and his nightmarish phantoms, had probably been schemed up by Bayliss deliberately.

Larsen noticed that the stimulant seemed to be extremely powerful. The take-off was sustained and unbroken. He tried hopelessly to relax, went into the bedroom and kicked his suitcase around, lit two cigarettes without realizing it.

Finally, unable to contain himself any longer, he slammed the front door back and stormed out across the apron, determined to have everything out with Bayliss and demand an immediate sedative.

Bayliss's lounge was empty. Larsen plunged through into the kitchen and bedroom, discovered to his annoyance that Bayliss was having a shower. He hung around in the lounge for a few moments, then decided to wait in his chalet.

Head down, he crossed the bright sunlight at a fast stride, and was only a few steps from the darkened doorway when he noticed that a man in a blue suit was standing there watching him.

Heart leaping, Larsen shrank back, recognizing the double even before he had completely accepted the change of costume, the smooth-shaven face with its altered planes. The man hovered indecisively, flexing his fingers, and appeared to be on the verge of stepping down into the sunlight.

Larsen was about ten feet from him, directly in line with Bayliss's door. He backed away, at the same time swinging to his left to the lee of the garage. There he stopped and pulled himself together. The double was still hesitating in the doorway, longer, he was sure, than he himself had done. Larsen looked at the face, repulsed, not so much by the absolute accuracy of the image, but by a strange, almost luminous pastiness that gave the double's features the waxy sheen of a corpse. It was this unpleasant gloss that held Larsen back – the double was an arm's length from the letterbox holding the .38, and nothing could have induced Larsen to approach it.

He decided to enter the chalet and watch the double from behind. Rather than use the kitchen door, which gave access to the lounge on the double's immediate right, he turned to circle the garage and climb in through the bedroom window on the far side.

He was picking his way through a dump of old mortar and barbed wire behind the garage when he heard a voice call out:

'Larsen, you idiot, what do you think you're doing?'

It was Bayliss, leaning out of his bathroom window. Larsen stumbled, found his balance and waved Bayliss back angrily. Bayliss merely shook his head and leaned farther out, drying his neck with a towel.

Larsen retraced his steps, signalling to Bayliss to keep quiet. He was crossing the space between the garage wall and the near corner of Bayliss's chalet when out of the side of his eye he noticed a dark-suited figure standing with its back to him a few yards from the garage door.

The double had moved! Larsen stopped, Bayliss forgotten, and watched the double warily. He was poised on the balls of his feet, as Larsen had been only a minute or so earlier, elbows up, hands waving defensively. His eyes were hidden, but he appeared to be looking at the front door of Larsen's chalet.

Automatically, Larsen's eyes also moved to the doorway.

The original blue-suited figure still stood there, staring out into the sunlight.

There was not one double now, but two.

For a moment Larsen stared helplessly at the two figures, standing on either side of the apron like half-animated dummies in a waxworks tableau.

The figure with its back to him swung on one heel and began to stalk rapidly towards him. He gazed sightlessly at Larsen, the sunlight exposing his face. With a jolt of horror Larsen recognized for the first time the perfect similarity of the double – the same plump cheeks, the same mole by the right nostril, the white upper lip with the same small razor cut where the moustache had been shaved away. Above all he recognized the man's state of shock, the nervous lips, the tension around the neck and facial muscles, the utter exhaustion just below the surface of the mask.

His voice strangled, Larsen turned and bolted.

He stopped running about two hundred yards out in the desert beyond the edge of the apron. Gasping for breath, he dropped to one knee behind a narrow sandstone outcropping and looked back at the chalets. The second double was making his way around the garage, climbing through the tangle of old wire. The other was crossing the space between the chalets. Oblivious of them both, Bayliss was struggling with the bathroom window, forcing it back so that he could see out into the desert.

Trying to steady himself, Larsen wiped his face on his jacket sleeve. So Bayliss had been right, although he had never anticipated that more than one image could be seen during any single attack. But in fact Larsen had spawned two in close succession, each at a critical phase during the last five minutes. Wondering whether to wait for the images to fade, Larsen remembered the revolver in the letterbox. However irrational, it seemed his only hope. With it he would be able to test the ultimate validity of the doubles.

The outcropping ran diagonally to the edge of the apron. Crouching forwards, he scurried along it, pausing at intervals to follow the scene. The two doubles were still holding their positions, though Bayliss had closed his window and disappeared.

Larsen reached the edge of the apron, which was built on a shallow table about a foot off the desert floor, and moved along its rim to where an old fifty-gallon drum gave him a vantage point. To reach the revolver he decided to go round the far side of Bayliss's chalet, where he would find his own doorway unguarded except for the double watching by the garage.

He was about to step forward when something made him look over his shoulder.

Running straight towards him along the outcropping, head down, hands almost touching the ground, was an enormous ratlike creature. Every ten or fifteen yards it paused for a moment, and looked out at the chalets, and Larsen caught a glimpse of its face, insane and terrified, another replica of his own.

'Larsen! Larsen!'

Bayliss stood by the chalet, waving out at the desert.

Larsen glanced back at the phantom hurtling towards him, now only thirty feet away, then jumped up and lurched helplessly across to Bayliss.

Bayliss caught him firmly with his hands. 'Larsen, what's the matter with you? Are you having an attack?'

Larsen gestured at the figures around him. 'Stop them, Bayliss, for God's sake,' he gasped. 'I can't get away from them.'

Bayliss shook him roughly. 'You can see *more* than one? Where are they? Show me.'

Larsen pointed at the two figures hovering luminously near the chalet, then waved limply in the direction of the desert. 'By the garage, and over there along the wall. There's another hiding along that ridge.'

Bayliss seized him by the arm. 'Come on, man, you've got to face up to them, it's no use running.' He tried to drag Larsen towards the garage, but Larsen slipped down on to the concrete.

'I can't, Bayliss, believe me. There's a gun in my letterbox. Get it for me. It's the only way.'

Bayliss hesitated, looking down at Larsen. 'All right. Try to hold on.'

Larsen pointed to the far corner of Bayliss's chalet. 'I'll wait over there for you.'

As Bayliss ran off he hobbled towards the corner. Halfway there he tripped across the remains of a ladder lying on the ground and twisted his right ankle between two of the rungs.

Clasping his foot, he sat down just as Bayliss appeared between the chalets, the revolver in his hand. He looked around for Larsen, who cleared his throat to call him.

Before he could open his mouth he saw the double who had followed him along the ridge leap up from behind the drum and stumble up to Bayliss across the concrete floor. He was dishevelled and exhausted, jacket almost off his shoulders, the tie knot under one ear. The image was still pursuing him, dogging his footsteps like an obsessed shadow.

Larsen tried to call to Bayliss again, but something he saw choked the voice in his throat.

Bayliss was looking at his double.

Larsen stood up, feeling a sudden premonition of terror. He tried to wave to Bayliss, but the latter was watching the double intently as it pointed to the figures near by, nodding to it in apparent agreement.

'Bayliss!'

The shot drowned his cry. Bayliss had fired somewhere between the garages, and the echo of the shot bounded among the chalets. The double was still beside him, pointing in all directions. Bayliss raised the revolver and fired again. The sound slammed across the concrete, making Larsen feel stunned and sick.

Now Bayliss too was seeing simultaneous images, not of himself but of Larsen, on whom his mind had been focusing for the past weeks. A repetition of Larsen stumbling over to him and pointing at the phantoms was being repeated in Bayliss's mind, at the exact moment when he had returned with the revolver and was searching for a target.

Larsen started to crawl away, trying to reach the corner. A third shot roared through the air, the flash reflected in the bathroom window.

He had almost reached the corner when he heard Bayliss shout. Leaning one hand against the wall, he looked back.

Mouth open, Bayliss was staring wildly at him, the revolver clenched like a bomb in his hand. Beside him the blue-suited figure stood quietly, straightening its tie. At last Bayliss had realized he could see two images of Larsen, one beside him, the other twenty feet away against the chalet.

But how was he to know which was the real Larsen?

Staring at Larsen, he seemed unable to decide.

Then the double by his shoulder raised one arm and pointed at Larsen, towards the corner wall to which he himself had pointed a minute earlier.

Larsen tried to shout, then hurled himself at the wall and pulled himself along it. Behind him Bayliss's feet came thudding across the concrete.

He heard only the first of the three shots.

**· 1960**

# · CHRONOPOLIS

His trial had been fixed for the next day. Exactly when, of course, neither Newman nor anyone else knew. Probably it would be during the afternoon, when the principals concerned – judge, jury and prosecutor – managed to converge on the same courtroom at the same time. With luck his defence attorney might also appear at the right moment, though the case was such an open and shut one that Newman hardly expected him to bother – besides, transport to and from the old penal complex was notoriously difficult, involved endless waiting in the grimy depot below the prison walls.

Newman had passed the time usefully. Luckily, his cell faced south and sunlight traversed it for most of the day. He divided its arc into ten equal segments, the effective daylight hours, marking the intervals with a wedge of mortar prised from the window ledge. Each segment he further subdivided into twelve smaller units.

Immediately he had a working timepiece, accurate to within virtually a minute (the final subdivision into fifths he made mentally). The sweep of white notches, curving down one wall, across the floor and metal bedstead, and up the other wall, would have been recognizable to anyone who stood with his back to the window, but no one ever did. Anyway, the guards were too stupid to understand, and the sundial had given Newman a tremendous advantage over them. Most of the time, when he wasn't recalibrating the dial, he would press against the grille, keeping an eye on the orderly room.

'Brocken!' he would shout out at 7.15, as the shadow line hit the first interval. 'Morning inspection! On your feet, man!' The sergeant would come stumbling out of his bunk in a sweat, cursing the other warders as the reveille bell split the air.

Later, Newman sang out the other events on the daily roster: roll-call, cell fatigues, breakfast, exercise and so on round to the evening roll just before dusk. Brocken regularly won the block merit for the best-run cell deck and he relied on Newman to programme the day for him, anticipate the next item on the roster and warn him if anything went on for too long – in some of the other blocks fatigues were usually over in three minutes while breakfast or exercise could go on for hours, none of the warders knowing when to stop, the prisoners insisting that they had only just begun.

Brocken never inquired how Newman organized everything so exactly;

once or twice a week, when it rained or was overcast, Newman would be strangely silent, and the resulting confusion reminded the sergeant forcefully of the merits of co-operation. Newman was kept in cell privileges and all the cigarettes he needed. It was a shame that a date for the trial had finally been named.

Newman, too, was sorry. Most of his research so far had been inconclusive. Primarily his problem was that, given a northward-facing cell for the bulk of his sentence, the task of estimating the time might become impossible. The inclination of the shadows in the exercise yards or across the towers and walls provided too blunt a reading. Calibration would have to be visual; an optical instrument would soon be discovered.

What he needed was an internal timepiece, an unconsciously operating psychic mechanism regulated, say, by his pulse or respiratory rhythms. He had tried to train his time sense, running an elaborate series of tests to estimate its minimum in-built error, and this had been disappointingly large. The chances of conditioning an accurate reflex seemed slim.

However, unless he could tell the exact time at any given moment, he knew he would go mad.

His obsession, which now faced him with a charge of murder, had revealed itself innocently enough.

As a child, like all children, he had noticed the occasional ancient clock tower, bearing the same white circle with its twelve intervals. In the seedier areas of the city the round characteristic dials often hung over cheap jewellery stores, rusting and derelict.

'Just signs,' his mother explained. 'They don't mean anything, like stars or rings.'

Pointless embellishment, he had thought.

Once, in an old furniture shop, they had seen a clock with hands, upside down in a box full of fire-irons and miscellaneous rubbish.

'Eleven and twelve,' he had pointed out. 'What does it mean?'

His mother had hurried him away, reminding herself never to visit that street again. Time Police were still supposed to be around, watching for any outbreak. 'Nothing,' she told him sharply. 'It's all finished.' To herself she added experimentally: Five and twelve. Five *to* twelve. Yes.

Time unfolded at its usual sluggish, half-confused pace. They lived in a ramshackle house in one of the amorphous suburbs, a zone of endless afternoons. Sometimes he went to school, until he was ten spent most of his time with his mother queueing outside the closed food stores. In the evenings he would play with the neighbourhood gang around the abandoned railway station, punting a home-made flat car along the overgrown tracks, or break into one of the unoccupied houses and set up a temporary command post.

He was in no hurry to grow up; the adult world was unsynchronized and ambitionless. After his mother died he spent long days in the attic, going through her trunks and old clothes, playing with the bric-à-brac of hats and beads, trying to recover something of her personality.

In the bottom compartment of her jewellery case he came across a small flat gold-cased object, equipped with a wrist strap. The dial had no hands but the twelve-numbered face intrigued him and he fastened it to his wrist.

His father choked over his soup when he saw it that evening.

'Conrad, my God! Where in heaven did you get that?'

'In Mamma's bead box. Can't I keep it?'

'No. Conrad, give it to me! Sorry, son.' Thoughtfully: 'Let's see, you're fourteen. Look, Conrad, I'll explain it all in a couple of years.'

With the impetus provided by this new taboo there was no need to wait for his father's revelations. Full knowledge came soon. The older boys knew the whole story, but strangely enough it was disappointingly dull.

'Is that all?' he kept saying. 'I don't get it. Why worry so much about clocks? We have calendars, don't we?'

Suspecting more, he scoured the streets, carefully inspecting every derelict clock for a clue to the real secret. Most of the faces had been mutilated, hands and numerals torn off, the circle of minute intervals stripped away, leaving a shadow of fading rust. Distributed apparently at random all over the city, above stores, banks and public buildings, their real purpose was hard to discover. Sure enough, they measured the progress of time through twelve arbitrary intervals, but this seemed barely adequate grounds for outlawing them. After all, a whole variety of timers were in general use: in kitchens, factories, hospitals, wherever a fixed period of time was needed. His father had one by his bed at night. Sealed into the standard small black box, and driven by miniature batteries, it emitted a high penetrating whistle shortly before breakfast the next morning, woke him if he overslept. A clock was no more than a calibrated timer, in many ways less useful, as it provided you with a steady stream of irrelevant information. What if it was half past three, as the old reckoning put it, if you weren't planning to start or finish anything then?

Making his questions sound as naïve as possible, he conducted a long, careful poll. Under fifty no one appeared to know anything at all about the historical background, and even the older people were beginning to forget. He also noticed that the less educated they were the more they were willing to talk, indicating that manual and lower-class workers had played no part in the revolution and consequently had no guilt-charged memories to repress. Old Mr Crichton, the plumber who lived in the basement apartment; reminisced without any prompting, but nothing he said threw any light on the problem.

'Sure, there were thousands of clocks then, millions of them, everybody had one. Watches we called them, strapped to the wrist, you had to screw them up every day.'

'But what did you *do* with them, Mr Crichton?' Conrad pressed.

'Well, you just – looked at them, and you knew what time it was. One o'clock, or two, or half past seven – that was when I'd go off to work.'

'But you go off to work now when you've had breakfast. And if you're late the timer rings.'

Crichton shook his head. 'I can't explain it to you, lad. You ask your father.'

But Mr Newman was hardly more helpful. The explanation promised for Conrad's sixteenth birthday never materialized. When his questions persisted Mr Newman tired of side-stepping, shut him up with an abrupt: 'Just stop thinking about it, do you understand? You'll get yourself and the rest of us into a lot of trouble.'

Stacey, the young English teacher, had a wry sense of humour, liked to shock the boys by taking up unorthodox positions on marriage or economics. Conrad wrote an essay describing an imaginary society completely preoccupied with elaborate rituals revolving around a minute by minute observance of the passage of time.

Stacey refused to play, however, gave him a non-committal beta plus, after class quietly asked Conrad what had prompted the fantasy. At first Conrad tried to back away, then finally came out with the question that contained the central riddle.

'Why is it against the law to have a clock?'

Stacey tossed a piece of chalk from one hand to the other.

'Is it against the law?'

Conrad nodded. 'There's an old notice in the police station offering a bounty of one hundred pounds for every clock or wristwatch brought in. I saw it yesterday. The sergeant said it was still in force.'

Stacey raised his eyebrows mockingly. 'You'll make a million. Thinking of going into business?'

Conrad ignored this. 'It's against the law to have a gun because you might shoot someone. But how can you hurt anybody with a clock?'

'Isn't it obvious? You can time him, know exactly how long it takes him to do something.'

'Well?'

'Then you can make him do it faster.'

At seventeen, on a sudden impulse, he built his first clock. Already his preoccupation with time was giving him a marked lead over his class-mates. One or two were more intelligent, others more conscientious, but Conrad's ability to organize his leisure and homework periods allowed him to make the most of his talents. When the others were lounging around the railway yard on their way home Conrad had already completed half his prep, allocating his time according to its various demands.

As soon as he finished he would go up to the attic playroom, now his workshop. Here, in the old wardrobes and trunks, he made his first experimental constructions: calibrated candles, crude sundials, sand-glasses, an elaborate clockwork contraption developing about half a horse power that drove its hands progressively faster and faster in an unintentional parody of Conrad's obsession.

His first serious clock was water-powered, a slowly leaking tank holding a wooden float that drove the hands as it sank downwards. Simple but accurate, it satisfied Conrad for several months while he carried out his ever-widening search for a real clock mechanism. He soon discovered that although there were innumerable table clocks, gold pocket watches and timepieces of every variety rusting in junk shops and in the back drawers of most homes, none of them contained their mechanisms. These, together with the hands, and sometimes the digits, had always been removed. His own attempts to build an escapement that would regulate the motion of the ordinary clockwork motor met with no success; everything he had heard about clock movements confirmed that they were precision instruments of exact design and construction. To satisfy his secret ambition – a portable timepiece, if possible an actual wristwatch – he would have to find one, somewhere, in working order.

Finally, from an unexpected source, a watch came to him. One afternoon in a cinema an elderly man sitting next to Conrad had a sudden heart attack. Conrad and two members of the audience carried him out to the manager's office. Holding one of his arms, Conrad noticed in the dim aisle light a glint of metal inside the sleeve. Quickly he felt the wrist with his fingers, identified the unmistakable lens-shaped disc of a wristwatch.

As he carried it home its tick seemed as loud as a death-knell. He clamped his hand around it, expecting everyone in the street to point accusingly at him, the Time Police to swoop down and seize him.

In the attic he took it out and examined it breathlessly, smothering it in a cushion whenever he heard his father shift about in the bedroom below. Later he realized that its noise was almost inaudible. The watch was of the same pattern as his mother's, though with a yellow and not a red face. The gold case was scratched and peeling, but the movement seemed to be in perfect condition. He prised off the rear plate, watched the frenzied flickering world of miniature cogs and wheels for hours, spellbound. Frightened of breaking the main spring, he kept the watch only half wound, packed away carefully in cotton wool.

In taking the watch from its owner he had not, in fact, been motivated by theft; his first impulse had been to hide the watch before the doctor discovered it feeling for the man's pulse. But once the watch was in his possession he abandoned any thought of tracing the owner and returning it.

That others were still wearing watches hardly surprised him. The water clock had demonstrated that a calibrated timepiece added another dimension to life, organized its energies, gave the countless activities of everyday existence a yardstick of significance. Conrad spent hours in the attic gazing at the small yellow dial, watching its minute hand revolve slowly, its hour hand press on imperceptibly, a compass charting his passage through the future. Without it he felt rudderless, adrift in a grey purposeless limbo of timeless events. His father began to seem idle and stupid, sitting around vacantly with no idea when anything was going to happen.

Soon he was wearing the watch all day. He stitched together a slim cotton sleeve, fitted with a narrow flap below which he could see the face. He timed everything – the length of classes, football games, meal breaks, the hours of daylight and darkness, sleep and waking. He amused himself endlessly by baffling his friends with demonstrations of this private sixth sense, anticipating the frequency of their heartbeats, the hourly newscasts on the radio, boiling a series of identically consistent eggs without the aid of a timer.

Then he gave himself away.

Stacey, shrewder than any of the others, discovered that he was wearing a watch. Conrad had noticed that Stacey's English classes lasted exactly forty-five minutes, let himself slide into the habit of tidying his desk a minute before Stacey's timer pipped up. Once or twice he noticed Stacey looking at him curiously, but he could not resist the temptation to impress Stacey by always being the first one to make for the door.

One day he had stacked his books and clipped away his pen when Stacey pointedly asked him to read out a précis he had done. Conrad knew the timer would pip out in less than ten seconds, and decided to sit tight and wait for the usual stampede to save him the trouble.

Stacey stepped down from the dais, waiting patiently. One or two boys turned around and frowned at Conrad, who was counting away the closing seconds.

Then, amazed, he realized that the timer had failed to sound! Panicking, he first thought his watch had broken, just restrained himself in time from looking at it.

'In a hurry, Newman?' Stacey asked dryly. He sauntered down the aisle to Conrad, smiling sardonically. Baffled, and face reddening with embarrassment, Conrad fumbled open his exercise book, read out the précis. A few minutes later, without waiting for the timer, Stacey dismissed the class.

'Newman,' he called out. 'Here a moment.'

He rummaged behind the rostrum as Conrad approached. 'What happened then?' he asked. 'Forget to wind up your watch this morning?'

Conrad said nothing. Stacey took out the timer, switched off the silencer and listened to the pip that buzzed out.

'Where did you get it from? Your parents? Don't worry, the Time Police were disbanded years ago.'

Conrad examined Stacey's face carefully. 'It was my mother's,' he lied. 'I found it among her things.' Stacey held out his hand and Conrad nervously unstrapped the watch and handed it to him.

Stacey slipped it half out of its sleeve, glanced briefly at the yellow face. 'Your mother, you say? Hmh.'

'Are you going to report me?' Conrad asked.

'What, and waste some over-worked psychiatrist's time even further?'

'Isn't it breaking the law to wear a watch?'

'Well, you're not exactly the greatest living menace to public security.' Stacey started for the door, gesturing Conrad with him. He handed the watch back. 'Cancel whatever you're doing on Saturday afternoon. You and I are taking a trip.'

'Where?' Conrad asked.

'Back into the past,' Stacey said lightly. 'To Chronopolis, the Time City.'

Stacey had hired a car, a huge battered mastodon of chromium and fins. He waved jauntily to Conrad as he picked him up outside the public library.

'Climb into the turret,' he called out. He pointed to the bulging briefcase Conrad slung on to the seat between them. 'Have you had a look at those yet?'

Conrad nodded. As they moved off around the deserted square he opened the briefcase and pulled out a thick bundle of road maps. 'I've just worked out that the city covers over 500 square miles. I'd never realized it was so big. Where is everybody?'

Stacey laughed. They crossed the main street, cut down into a long tree-lined avenue of semi-detached houses. Half of them were empty, windows wrecked and roofs sagging. Even the inhabited houses had a makeshift appearance, crude water towers on home-made scaffolding lashed to their chimneys, piles of logs dumped in over-grown front gardens.

'Thirty million people once lived in this city,' Stacey remarked. 'Now the population is little more than two, and still declining. Those of us left hang on in what were once the distal suburbs, so that the city today is effectively an enormous ring, five miles in width, encircling a vast dead centre forty or fifty miles in diameter.'

They wove in and out of various back roads, past a small factory still running although work was supposed to end at noon, finally picked up a long, straight boulevard that carried them steadily westwards. Conrad traced their progress across successive maps. They were nearing the edge of the annulus Stacey had described. On the map it was overprinted in green so that the central interior appeared a flat, uncharted grey, a massive *terra incognita*.

They passed the last of the small shopping thoroughfares he remembered, a frontier post of mean terraced houses, dismal streets spanned by massive steel viaducts. Stacey pointed up at one as they drove below it. 'Part of the elaborate railway system that once existed, an enormous network of stations and junctions that carried fifteen million people into a dozen great terminals every day.'

For half an hour they drove on, Conrad hunched against the window, Stacey watching him in the driving mirror. Gradually, the landscape began to change. The houses were taller, with coloured roofs, the sidewalks were railed off and fitted with pedestrian lights and turnstiles. They had entered the inner suburbs, completely deserted streets with multi-level supermarkets, towering cinemas and department stores.

Chin in one hand, Conrad stared out silently. Lacking any means of transport he had never ventured into the uninhabited interior of the city, like the other children always headed in the opposite direction for the open country. Here the streets had died twenty or thirty years earlier; plate-glass shopfronts had slipped and smashed into the roadway, old neon signs, window frames and overhead wires hung down from every cornice, trailing a ragged webwork of disintegrating metal across the pavements. Stacey drove slowly, avoiding the occasional bus or truck abandoned in the middle of the road, its tyres peeling off their rims.

Conrad craned up at the empty windows, into the narrow alleys and side-streets, but nowhere felt any sensation of fear or anticipation. These streets were merely derelict, as unhaunted as a half-empty dustbin.

One suburban centre gave way to another, to long intervening stretches of congested ribbon developments. Mile by mile, the architecture altered its character; buildings were larger, ten- or fifteen-storey blocks, clad in facing materials of green and blue tiles, glass or copper sheathing. They were moving forward in time rather than, as Conrad had expected, back into the past of a fossil city.

Stacey worked the car through a nexus of side-streets towards a six-lane expressway that rose on tall concrete buttresses above the roof-tops. They found a side road that circled up to it, levelled out and then picked up speed sharply, spinning along one of the clear centre lanes.

Conrad craned forward. In the distance, two or three miles away, the tall rectilinear outlines of enormous apartment blocks reared up thirty or forty storeys high, hundreds of them lined shoulder to shoulder in apparently endless ranks, like giant dominoes.

'We're entering the central dormitories here,' Stacey told him. On either side buildings overtopped the motorway, the congestion mounting so that some of them had been built right up against the concrete palisades.

In a few minutes they passed between the first of the apartment batteries, the thousands of identical living units with their slanting balconies shearing up into the sky, the glass in-falls of the aluminium curtain walling speckling in the sunlight. The smaller houses and shops of the outer suburbs had vanished. There was no room on the ground level. In the narrow intervals between the blocks there were small concrete gardens, shopping complexes, ramps banking down into huge underground car parks.

And on all sides there were the clocks. Conrad noticed them immediately, at every street corner, over every archway, three-quarters of the way up the sides of buildings, covering every conceivable angle of approach.

Most of them were too high off the ground to be reached by anything
less than a fireman's ladder and still retained their hands. All registered
the same time: 12.01.

Conrad looked at his wristwatch, noted that it was just 2.45 p.m.

'They were driven by a master clock,' Stacey told him. 'When that
stopped they all seized at the same moment. One minute after midnight,
thirty-seven years ago.'

The afternoon had darkened, as the high cliffs cut off the sunlight,
the sky a succession of narrow vertical intervals opening and closing
around them. Down on the canyon floor it was dismal and oppressive,
a wilderness of concrete and frosted glass. The expressway divided and
pressed on westwards. After a few more miles the apartment blocks gave
way to the first office buildings in the central zone. These were even taller,
sixty or seventy storeys high, linked by spiralling ramps and causeways.
The expressway was fifty feet off the ground yet the first floors of the
office blocks were level with it, mounted on massive stilts that straddled
the glass-enclosed entrance bays of lifts and escalators. The streets were
wide but featureless. The sidewalks of parallel roadways merged below the
buildings, forming a continuous concrete apron. Here and there were the
remains of cigarette kiosks, rusting stairways up to restaurants and arcades
built on platforms thirty feet in the air.

Conrad, however, was looking only at the clocks. Never had he
visualized so many, in places so dense that they obscured each other.
Their faces were multi-coloured: red, blue, yellow, green. Most of them
carried four or five hands. Although the master hands had stopped at a
minute past twelve, the subsidiary hands had halted at varying positions,
apparently dictated by their colour.

'What were the extra hands for?' he asked Stacey. 'And the different
colours?'

'Time zones. Depending on your professional category and the consumer-
shifts allowed. Hold on, though, we're almost there.'

They left the expressway and swung off down a ramp that fed them into
the north-east corner of a wide open plaza, eight hundred yards long and
half as wide, down the centre of which had once been laid a continuous
strip of lawn, now rank and overgrown. The plaza was empty, a sudden
block of free space bounded by tall glass-faced cliffs that seemed to carry
the sky.

Stacey parked, and he and Conrad climbed out and stretched themselves. Together they strolled across the wide pavement towards the strip
of waist-high vegetation. Looking down the vistas receding from the plaza
Conrad grasped fully for the first time the vast perspectives of the city, the
massive geometric jungle of buildings.

Stacey put one foot up on the balustrade running around the lawn
bed, pointed to the far end of the plaza, where Conrad saw a low-lying
huddle of buildings of unusual architectural style, nineteenth-century
perpendicular, stained by the atmosphere and badly holed by a number

of explosions. Again, however, his attention was held by the clock face built into a tall concrete tower just behind the older buildings. This was the largest clock dial he had ever seen, at least a hundred feet across, huge black hands halted at a minute past twelve. The dial was white, the first they had seen, but on wide semicircular shoulders built out off the tower below the main face were a dozen smaller faces, no more than twenty feet in diameter, running the full spectrum of colours. Each had five hands, the inferior three halted at random.

'Fifty years ago,' Stacey explained, gesturing at the ruins below the tower, 'that collection of ancient buildings was one of the world's greatest legislative assemblies.' He gazed at it quietly for a few moments, then turned to Conrad. 'Enjoy the ride?'

Conrad nodded fervently. 'It's impressive, all right. The people who lived here must have been giants. What's really remarkable is that it looks as if they left only yesterday. Why don't we go back?'

'Well, apart from the fact that there aren't enough of us now, even if there were we couldn't control it. In its hey-day this city was a fantastically complex social organism. The communications problems are difficult to imagine merely by looking at these blank façades. It's the tragedy of this city that there appeared to be only one way to solve them.'

'Did they solve them?'

'Oh, yes, certainly. But they left themselves out of the equation. Think of the problems, though. Transporting fifteen million office workers to and from the centre every day, routeing in an endless stream of cars, buses, trains, helicopters, linking every office, almost every desk, with a videophone, every apartment with television, radio, power, water, feeding and entertaining this enormous number of people, guarding them with ancillary services, police, fire squads, medical units – it all hinged on one factor.'

Stacey threw a fist out at the great tower clock. 'Time! Only by synchronizing every activity, every footstep forward or backward, every meal, bus-halt and telephone call, could the organism support itself. Like the cells in your body, which proliferate into mortal cancers if allowed to grow in freedom, every individual here had to subserve the overriding needs of the city or fatal bottlenecks threw it into total chaos. You and I can turn on the tap any hour of the day or night, because we have our own private water cisterns, but what would happen here if everybody washed the breakfast dishes within the same ten minutes?'

They began to walk slowly down the plaza towards the clock tower. 'Fifty years ago, when the population was only ten million, they could just provide for a potential peak capacity, but even then a strike in one essential service paralysed most of the others; it took workers two or three hours to reach their offices, as long again to queue for lunch and get home. As the population climbed the first serious attempts were made to stagger hours; workers in certain areas started the day an hour earlier or later than those in others. Their railway passes and car number plates were coloured accordingly, and if they tried to travel outside the permitted periods they were turned back. Soon the practice spread; you could only switch on your washing machine at a given hour, post a letter or take a bath at a specific period.'

'Sounds feasible,' Conrad commented, his interest mounting. 'But how did they enforce all this?'

'By a system of coloured passes, coloured money, an elaborate set of schedules published every day like the TV or radio programmes. And, of course, by all the thousands of clocks you can see around you here. The subsidiary hands marked out the number of minutes remaining in any activity period for people in the clock's colour category.'

Stacey stopped, pointed to a blue-faced clock mounted on one of the buildings overlooking the plaza. 'Let's say, for example, that a lower-grade executive leaving his office at the allotted time, 12 o'clock, wants to have lunch, change a library book, buy some aspirin, and telephone his wife. Like all executives, his identity zone is blue. He takes out his schedule for the week, or looks down the blue-time columns in the newspaper, and notes that his lunch period for that day is 12.15 to 12.30. He has fifteen minutes to kill. Right, he then checks the library. Time code for today is given as 3, that's the third hand on the clock. He looks at the nearest blue clock, the third hand says 37 minutes past – he has 23 minutes, ample time, to reach the library. He starts down the street, but finds at the first intersection that the pedestrian lights are only shining red and green and he can't get across. The area's been temporarily zoned off for lower-grade women office workers – red, and manuals – greens.'

'What would happen if he ignored the lights?' Conrad asked.

'Nothing immediately, but all blue clocks in the zoned area would have returned to zero, and no shops or the library would serve him, unless he happened to have red or green currency and a forged set of library tickets. Anyway, the penalties were too high to make the risk worthwhile, and the whole system was evolved for his convenience, no one else's. So, unable to reach the library, he decides on the chemist. The time code for the chemist is 5, the fifth, smallest hand. It reads 54 minutes past: he has six minutes to find a chemist and make his purchase. This done, he still has five minutes before lunch, decides to phone his wife. Checking the phone code he sees that no period has been provided for private calls that day – or the next. He'll just have to wait until he sees her that evening.'

'What if he did phone?'

'He wouldn't be able to get his money in the coin box, and even then, his wife, assuming she is a secretary, would be in a red time zone and no longer in her office for that day – hence the prohibition on phone calls. It all meshed perfectly. Your time programme told you when you could switch on your TV set and when to switch off. All electric appliances were fused, and if you strayed outside the programmed periods you'd have a hefty fine and repair bill to meet. The viewer's economic status obviously determined the choice of programme, and vice versa, so there was no question of coercion. Each day's programme listed your permitted activities: you could go to the hairdresser's, cinema, bank, cocktail bar, at stated times, and if you went then you were sure of being served quickly and efficiently.'

They had almost reached the far end of the plaza. Facing them on its tower was the enormous clock face, dominating its constellation of twelve motionless attendants.

'There were a dozen socio-economic categories: blue for executives, gold for professional classes, yellow for military and government officials – incidentally, it's odd your parents ever got hold of that wristwatch, none of your family ever worked for the government – green for manual workers and so on. But, naturally, subtle subdivisions were possible. The lower-grade executive I mentioned left his office at 12, but a senior executive, with exactly the same time codes, would leave at 11.45, have an extra fifteen minutes, would find the streets clear before the lunch-hour rush of clerical workers.'

Stacey pointed up at the tower. 'This was the Big Clock, the master from which all others were regulated. Central Time Control, a sort of Ministry of Time, gradually took over the old parliamentary buildings as their legislative functions diminished. The programmers were, effectively, the city's absolute rulers.'

As Stacey continued Conrad gazed up at the battery of timepieces, poised helplessly at 12.01. Somehow time itself seemed to have been suspended, around him the great office buildings hung in a neutral interval between yesterday and tomorrow. If one could only start the master clock the entire city would probably slide into gear and come to life, in an instant be repeopled with its dynamic jostling millions.

They began to walk back towards the car. Conrad looked over his shoulder at the clock face, its gigantic arms upright on the silent hour.

'Why did it stop?' he asked.

Stacey looked at him curiously. 'Haven't I made it fairly plain?'

'What do you mean?' Conrad pulled his eyes off the scores of clocks lining the plaza, frowned at Stacey.

'Can you imagine what life was like for all but a few of the thirty million people here?'

Conrad shrugged. Blue and yellow clocks, he noticed, outnumbered all others; obviously the major governmental agencies had operated from the plaza area. 'Highly organized but better than the sort of life we lead,' he replied finally, more interested in the sights around him. 'I'd rather have the telephone for one hour a day than not at all. Scarcities are always rationed, aren't they?'

'But this was a way of life in which everything was scarce. Don't you think there's a point beyond which human dignity is surrendered?'

Conrad snorted. 'There seems to be plenty of dignity here. Look at these buildings, they'll stand for a thousand years. Try comparing them with my father. Anyway, think of the beauty of the system, engineered as precisely as a watch.'

'That's all it was,' Stacey commanded dourly. 'The old metaphor of the cog in the wheel was never more true than here. The full sum of your existence was printed for you in the newspaper columns, mailed to you once a month from the Ministry of Time.'

Conrad was looking off in some other direction and Stacey pressed on in a slightly louder voice. 'Eventually, of course, revolt came. It's interesting that in any industrial society there is usually one social revolution each century, and that successive revolutions receive their impetus from progressively higher social levels. In the eighteenth century it was the urban proletariat, in the nineteenth the artisan classes, in this revolt the white collar office worker, living in his tiny so-called modern flat, supporting through credit pyramids an economic system that denied him all freedom of will or personality, chained him to a thousand clocks . . .' He broke off. 'What's the matter?'

Conrad was staring down one of the side streets. He hesitated, then asked in a casual voice: 'How were these clocks driven? Electrically?'

'Most of them. A few mechanically. Why?'

'I just wondered . . . how they kept them all going.' He dawdled at Stacey's heels, checking the time from his wristwatch and glancing to his left. There were twenty or thirty clocks hanging from the buildings along the side street, indistinguishable from those he had seen all afternoon.

*Except for the fact that one of them was working!*

It was mounted in the centre of a black glass portico over an entrance-way fifty yards down the right-hand side, about eighteen inches in diameter, with a faded blue face. Unlike the others its hands registered 3.15, the correct time. Conrad had nearly mentioned this apparent coincidence to Stacey when he had suddenly seen the minute hand move on an interval. Without doubt someone had restarted the clock; even if it had been running off an inexhaustible battery, after thirty-seven years it could never have displayed such accuracy.

He hung behind Stacey, who was saying: 'Every revolution has its symbol of oppression . . .'

The clock was almost out of view. Conrad was about to bend down and tie his shoelace when he saw the minute hand jerk downwards, tilt slightly from the horizontal.

He followed Stacey towards the car, no longer bothering to listen to him. Ten yards from it he turned and broke away, ran swiftly across the roadway towards the nearest building.

'Newman!' he heard Stacey shout. 'Come back!' He reached the pavement, ran between the great concrete pillars carrying the building. He paused for a moment behind an elevator shaft, saw Stacey climbing hurriedly into the car. The engine coughed and roared out, and Conrad sprinted on below the building into a rear alley that led back to the side-street. Behind him he heard the car accelerating, a door slam as it picked up speed.

When he entered the side-street the car came swinging off the plaza thirty yards behind him. Stacey swerved off the roadway, bumped up on to the pavement and gunned the car towards Conrad, throwing on the brakes in savage lurches, blasting the horn in an attempt to frighten him. Conrad side-stepped out of its way, almost falling over the bonnet, hurled himself up a narrow stairway leading to the first floor and raced up the steps to a short landing that ended in tall glass doors. Through them he could see a wide balcony that ringed the building. A fire-escape crisscrossed upwards to the roof, giving way on the fifth floor to a cafeteria that spanned the street to the office building opposite.

Below he heard Stacey's feet running across the pavement. The glass doors were locked. He pulled a fire-extinguisher from its bracket, tossed the heavy cylinder against the centre of the plate. The glass slipped and crashed to the tiled floor in a sudden cascade, splashing down the steps. Conrad stepped through on to the balcony, began to climb the stairway. He had reached the third floor when he saw Stacey below, craning upwards. Hand over hand, Conrad pulled himself up the next two flights, swung over a bolted metal turnstile into the open court of the cafeteria. Tables and chairs lay about on their sides, mixed up with the splintered remains of desks thrown down from the upper floors.

The doors into the covered restaurant were open, a large pool of water lying across the floor. Conrad splashed through it, went over to a window and peered down past an old plastic plant into the street. Stacey seemed to have given up. Conrad crossed the rear of the restaurant, straddled the counter and climbed through a window on to the open terrace running across the street. Beyond the rail he could see into the plaza, the double line of tyre marks curving into the street below.

He had almost crossed to the opposite balcony when a shot roared out into the air. There was a sharp tinkle of falling glass and the sound of the explosion boomed away among the empty canyons.

For a few seconds he panicked. He flinched back from the exposed rail, his ear drums numbed, looking up at the great rectangular masses towering above him on either side, the endless tiers of windows like the faceted eyes of gigantic insects. So Stacey had been armed, almost certainly was a member of the Time Police!

On his hands and knees Conrad scurried along the terrace, slid through the turnstiles and headed for a half-open window on the balcony.

Climbing through, he quickly lost himself in the building.

He finally took up a position in a corner office on the sixth floor, the cafeteria just below him to the right, the stairway up which he had escaped directly opposite.

All afternoon Stacey drove up and down the adjacent streets, sometimes free-wheeling silently with the engine off, at others blazing through at speed. Twice he fired into the air, stopping the car afterwards to call out, his words lost among the echoes rolling from one street to the next. Often he drove along the pavements, swerved about below the buildings as if he expected to flush Conrad from behind one of the banks of escalators.

Finally he appeared to drive off for good, and Conrad turned his attention to the clock in the portico. It had moved on to 6.45, almost exactly the time given by his own watch. Conrad reset this to what he assumed was the correct time, then sat back and waited for whoever had wound it to appear. Around him the thirty or forty other clocks he could see remained stationary at 12.01.

For five minutes he left his vigil, scooped some water off the pool in the cafeteria, suppressed his hunger and shortly after midnight fell asleep in a corner behind the desk.

He woke the next morning to bright sunlight flooding into the office. Standing up, he dusted his clothes, turned around to find a small grey-haired man in a patched tweed suit surveying him with sharp eyes. Slung in the crook of his arm was a large black-barrelled weapon, its hammers menacingly cocked.

The man put down a steel ruler he had evidently tapped against a cabinet, waited for Conrad to collect himself.

'What are you doing here?' he asked in a testy voice. Conrad noticed his pockets were bulging with angular objects that weighed down the sides of his jacket.

'I . . . er . . .' Conrad searched for something to say. Something about the old man convinced him that this was the clock-winder. Suddenly he decided he had nothing to lose by being frank, and blurted out: 'I saw the clock working. Down there on the left. I want to help wind them all up again.'

The old man watched him shrewdly. He had an alert bird-like face, twin folds under his chin like a cockerel's.

'How do you propose to do that?' he asked.

Stuck by this one, Conrad said lamely: 'I'd find a key somewhere.'

The old man frowned. 'One key? That wouldn't do much good.' He seemed to be relaxing slowly, shook his pockets with a dull chink.

For a few moments neither of them said anything. Then Conrad had an inspiration, bared his wrist. 'I have a watch,' he said. 'It's 7.45.'

'Let me see.' The old man stepped forward, briskly took Conrad's wrist, examined the yellow dial. 'Movado Supermatic,' he said to himself. 'CTC issue.' He stepped back, lowering the shotgun, seemed to be summing Conrad up. 'Good,' he remarked at last. 'Let's see. You probably need some breakfast.'

They made their way out of the building, began to walk quickly down the street.

'People sometimes come here,' the old man said. 'Sightseers and police. I watched your escape yesterday, you were lucky not to be killed.' They swerved left and right across the empty streets, the old man darting between the stairways and buttresses. As he walked he held his hands stiffly to his sides, preventing his pockets from swinging. Glancing into them, Conrad saw that they were full of keys, large and rusty, of every design and combination.

'I presume that was your father's watch,' the old man remarked.

'Grandfather's,' Conrad corrected. He remembered Stacey's lecture, and added: 'He was killed in the plaza.'

The old man frowned sympathetically, for a moment held Conrad's arm.

They stopped below a building, indistinguishable from the others nearby, at one time a bank. The old man looked carefully around him, eyeing the high cliff walls on all sides, then led the way up a stationary escalator.

His quarters were on the second floor, beyond a maze of steel grilles and strongdoors, a stove and a hammock slung in the centre of a large workshop. Lying about on thirty or forty desks in what had once been a typing pool, was an enormous collection of clocks, all being simultaneously repaired. Tall cabinets surrounded them, loaded with thousands of spare parts in neatly labelled correspondence trays – escapements, ratchets, cogwheels, barely recognizable through the rust.

The old man led Conrad over to a wall chart, pointed to the total listed against a column of dates. 'Look at this. There are now 278 running continuously. Believe me, I'm glad you've come. It takes me half my time to keep them wound.'

He made breakfast for Conrad, told him something about himself. His name was Marshall. Once he had worked in Central Time Control as a programmer, had survived the revolt and the Time Police, ten years later returned to the city. At the beginning of each month he cycled out to one of the perimeter towns to cash his pension and collect supplies. The rest of the time he spent winding the steadily increasing number of functioning clocks and searching for others he could dismantle and repair.

'All these years in the rain hasn't done them any good,' he explained, 'and there's nothing I can do with the electrical ones.'

Conrad wandered off among the desks, gingerly feeling the dismembered timepieces that lay around like the nerve cells of some vast unimaginable robot. He felt exhilarated and yet at the same time curiously calm, like a man who has staked his whole life on the turn of a wheel and is waiting for it to spin.

'How can you make sure that they all tell the same time?' he asked Marshall, wondering why the question seemed so important.

Marshall gestured irritably. 'I can't, but what does it matter? There is no such thing as a perfectly accurate clock. The nearest you can get is one that has stopped. Although you never know when, it *is* absolutely accurate twice a day.'

Conrad went over to the window, pointed to the great clock visible in an interval between the rooftops. 'If only we could start that, and run all the others off it.'

'Impossible. The entire mechanism was dynamited. Only the chimer is intact. Anyway, the wiring of the electrically driven clocks perished years ago. It would take an army of engineers to recondition them.'

Conrad nodded, looked at the scoreboard again. He noticed that Marshall appeared to have lost his way through the years – the completion dates he listed were seven and a half years out. Idly, Conrad reflected on the significance of this irony, but decided not to mention it to Marshall.

For three months Conrad lived with the old man, following him on foot as he cycled about on his rounds, carrying the ladder and the satchel full of keys with which Marshall wound up the clocks, helping him to dismantle recoverable ones and carry them back to the workshop. All day, and often through half the night, they worked together, repairing the movements, restarting the clocks and returning them to their original positions.

All the while, however, Conrad's mind was fixed upon the great clock in its tower dominating the plaza. Once a day he managed to sneak off and make his way into the ruined Time buildings. As Marshall had said, neither the clock nor its twelve satellites would ever run again. The movement house looked like the engine-room of a sunken ship, a rusting tangle of rotors and drive wheels exploded into contorted shapes. Every week he would climb the long stairway up to the topmost platform two hundred feet above, look out through the bell tower at the flat roofs of the office blocks stretching away to the horizon. The hammers rested against their trips in long ranks just below him. Once he kicked one of the treble trips playfully, sent a dull chime out across the plaza.

The sound drove strange echoes into his mind.

Slowly he began to repair the chimer mechanism, rewiring the hammers and the pulley systems, trailing fresh wire up the great height of the tower, dismantling the winches in the movement room below and renovating their clutches.

He and Marshall never discussed their self-appointed tasks. Like animals obeying an instinct they worked tirelessly, barely aware of their own motives. When Conrad told him one day that he intended to leave and continue the work in another sector of the city, Marshall agreed immediately, gave Conrad as many tools as he could spare and bade him goodbye.

Six months later, almost to the day, the sounds of the great clock chimed out across the rooftops of the city, marking the hours, the half-hours and the quarter-hours, steadily tolling the progress of the day. Thirty miles away, in the towns forming the perimeter of the city, people stopped in the streets and in doorways, listening to the dim haunted echoes reflected through the long aisles of apartment blocks on the far horizon, involuntarily counting the slow final sequences that told the hour. Older people whispered to each other: 'Four o'clock, or was it five? They have started the clock again. It seems strange after these years.'

And all through the day they would pause as the quarter and half hours reached across the miles to them, a voice from their childhoods reminding them of the ordered world of the past. They began to reset their timers by the chimes, at night before they slept they would listen to the long count of midnight, wake to hear them again in the thin clear air of the morning.

Some went down to the police station and asked if they could have their watches and clocks back again.

After sentence, twenty years for the murder of Stacey, five for fourteen offences under the Time Laws, to run concurrently, Newman was led away to the holding cells in the basement of the court. He had expected the sentence and made no comment when invited by the judge. After waiting trial for a year the afternoon in the courtroom was nothing more than a momentary intermission.

He made no attempt to defend himself against the charge of killing Stacey, partly to shield Marshall, who would be able to continue their work unmolested, and partly because he felt indirectly responsible for the policeman's death. Stacey's body, skull fractured by a twenty- or thirty-storey fall, had been discovered in the back seat of his car in a basement garage not far from the plaza. Presumably Marshall had discovered him prowling around and dealt with him single-handed. Newman recalled that one day Marshall had disappeared altogether and had been curiously irritable for the rest of the week.

The last time he had seen the old man had been during the three days before the police arrived. Each morning as the chimes boomed out across the plaza Newman had seen his tiny figure striding briskly down the plaza towards him, waving up energetically at the tower, bareheaded and unafraid.

Now Newman was faced with the problem of how to devise a clock that would chart his way through the coming twenty years. His fears increased when he was taken the next day to the cell block which housed the long-term prisoners – passing his cell on the way to meet the superintendent he noticed that his window looked out on to a small shaft. He pumped his brains desperately as he stood to attention during the superintendent's homilies, wondering how he could retain his sanity. Short of counting the seconds, each one of the 86,400 in every day, he saw no possible means of assessing the time.

Locked into his cell, he sat limply on the narrow bed, too tired to unpack his small bundle of possessions. A moment's inspection confirmed the uselessness of the shaft. A powerful light mounted halfway up masked the sunlight that slipped through a steel grille fifty feet above.

He stretched himself out on the bed and examined the ceiling. A lamp was recessed into its centre, but a second, surprisingly, appeared to have been fitted to the cell. This was on the wall, a few feet above his head. He could see the curving bowl of the protective case, some ten inches in diameter.

He was wondering whether this could be a reading light when he realized that there was no switch.

Swinging round, he sat up and examined it, then leapt to his feet in astonishment.

*It was a clock!* He pressed his hands against the bowl, reading the circle of numerals, noting the inclination of the hands. 4.53, near enough the present time. Not simply a clock, but one in running order! Was this some sort of macabre joke, or a misguided attempt at rehabilitation?

His pounding on the door brought a warder.

'What's all the noise about? The clock? What's the matter with it?' He unlocked the door and barged in, pushing Newman back.

'Nothing. But why is it here? They're against the law.'

'Oh, is that what's worrying you.' The warder shrugged. 'Well, you see, the rules are a little different in here. You lads have got a lot of time ahead of you, it'd be cruel not to let you know where you stood. You know how to work it, do you? Good.' He slammed the door, bolted it fast, smiled at Newman through the cage. 'It's a long day here, son, as you'll be finding out, that'll help you get through it.'

Gleefully, Newman lay on the bed, his head on a rolled blanket at its foot, staring up at the clock. It appeared to be in perfect order, electrically driven, moving in rigid half-minute jerks. For an hour after the warder left he watched it without a break, then began to tidy up his cell, glancing over his shoulder every few minutes to reassure himself that it was still there, still running efficiently. The irony of the situation, the total inversion of justice, delighted him, even though it would cost him twenty years of his life.

He was still chuckling over the absurdity of it all two weeks later when for the first time he noticed the clock's insanely irritating tick . . .

· **1960**

# THE VOICES OF TIME

## ONE

Later Powers often thought of Whitby, and the strange grooves the biologist had cut, apparently at random, all over the floor of the empty swimming pool. An inch deep and twenty feet long, interlocking to form an elaborate ideogram like a Chinese character, they had taken him all summer to complete, and he had obviously thought about little else, working away tirelessly through the long desert afternoons. Powers had watched him from his office window at the far end of the Neurology wing, carefully marking out his pegs and string, carrying away the cement chips in a small canvas bucket. After Whitby's suicide no one had bothered about the grooves, but Powers often borrowed the supervisor's key and let himself into the disused pool, and would look down at the labyrinth of mouldering gulleys, half-filled with water leaking in from the chlorinator, an enigma now past any solution.

Initially, however, Powers was too preoccupied with completing his work at the Clinic and planning his own final withdrawal. After the first frantic weeks of panic he had managed to accept an uneasy compromise that allowed him to view his predicament with the detached fatalism he had previously reserved for his patients. Fortunately he was moving down the physical and mental gradients simultaneously – lethargy and inertia blunted his anxieties, a slackening metabolism made it necessary to concentrate to produce a connected thought-train. In fact, the lengthening intervals of dreamless sleep were almost restful. He found himself beginning to look forward to them, and made no effort to wake earlier than was essential.

At first he had kept an alarm clock by his bed, tried to compress as much activity as he could into the narrowing hours of consciousness, sorting out his library, driving over to Whitby's laboratory every morning to examine the latest batch of X-ray plates, every minute and hour rationed like the last drops of water in a canteen.

Anderson, fortunately, had unwittingly made him realize the pointlessness of this course.

After Powers had resigned from the Clinic he still continued to drive in once a week for his check-up, now little more than a formality. On what turned out to be the last occasion Anderson had perfunctorily taken his blood-count, noting Powers' slacker facial muscles, fading pupil reflexes and unshaven cheeks.

He smiled sympathetically at Powers across the desk, wondering what to say to him. Once he had put on a show of encouragement with the more intelligent patients, even tried to provide some sort of explanation. But Powers was too difficult to reach – neurosurgeon extraordinary, a man always out on the periphery, only at ease working with unfamiliar materials. To himself he thought: *I'm sorry, Robert. What can I say – 'Even the sun is growing cooler' –?* He watched Powers drum his fingers restlessly on the enamel desk top, his eyes glancing at the spinal level charts hung around the office. Despite his unkempt appearance – he had been wearing the same unironed shirt and dirty white plimsolls a week ago – Powers looked composed and self-possessed, like a Conradian beachcomber more or less reconciled to his own weaknesses.

'What are you doing with yourself, Robert?' he asked. 'Are you still going over to Whitby's lab?'

'As much as I can. It takes me half an hour to cross the lake, and I keep on sleeping through the alarm clock. I may leave my place and move in there permanently.'

Anderson frowned. 'Is there much point? As far as I could make out Whitby's work was pretty speculative –' He broke off, realizing the implied criticism of Powers' own disastrous work at the Clinic, but Powers seemed to ignore this, was examining the pattern of shadows on the ceiling. 'Anyway, wouldn't it be better to stay where you are, among your own things, read through Toynbee and Spengler again?'

Powers laughed shortly. 'That's the last thing I want to do. I want to *forget* Toynbee and Spengler, not try to remember them. In fact, Paul, I'd like to forget everything. I don't know whether I've got enough time, though. How much can you forget in three months?'

'Everything, I suppose, if you want to. But don't try to race the clock.'

Powers nodded quietly, repeating this last remark to himself. Racing the clock was exactly what he had been doing. As he stood up and said goodbye to Anderson he suddenly decided to throw away his alarm clock, escape from his futile obsession with time. To remind himself he unfastened his wristwatch and scrambled the setting, then slipped it into his pocket. Making his way out to the car park he reflected on the freedom this simple act gave him. He would explore the lateral byways now, the side doors, as it were, in the corridors of time. Three months could be an eternity.

He picked his car out of the line and strolled over to it, shielding his eyes from the heavy sunlight beating down across the parabolic sweep of the lecture theatre roof. He was about to climb in when he saw that someone had traced with a finger across the dust caked over the windshield:

96,688,365,498,721

Looking over his shoulder, he recognized the white Packard parked next to him, peered inside and saw a lean-faced young man with blond sun-bleached hair and a high cerebrotonic forehead watching him behind dark glasses. Sitting beside him at the wheel was a raven-haired girl whom he had often seen around the psychology department. She had intelligent but somehow rather oblique eyes, and Powers remembered that the younger doctors called her 'the girl from Mars'.

'Hello, Kaldren,' Powers said to the young man. 'Still following me around?'

Kaldren nodded. 'Most of the time, doctor.' He sized Powers up shrewdly. 'We haven't seen very much of you recently, as a matter of fact. Anderson said you'd resigned, and we noticed your laboratory was closed.'

Powers shrugged. 'I felt I needed a rest. As you'll understand, there's a good deal that needs re-thinking.'

Kaldren frowned half-mockingly. 'Sorry to hear that, doctor. But don't let these temporary setbacks depress you.' He noticed the girl watching Powers with interest. 'Coma's a fan of yours. I gave her your papers from *American Journal of Psychiatry*, and she's read through the whole file.'

The girl smiled pleasantly at Powers, for a moment dispelling the hostility between the two men. When Powers nodded to her she leaned across Kaldren and said: 'Actually I've just finished Noguchi's autobiography – the great Japanese doctor who discovered the spirochaete. Somehow you remind me of him – there's so much of yourself in all the patients you worked on.'

Powers smiled wanly at her, then his eyes turned and locked involuntarily on Kaldren's. They stared at each other sombrely for a moment, and a small tic in Kaldren's right cheek began to flicker irritatingly. He flexed his facial muscles, after a few seconds mastered it with an effort, obviously annoyed that Powers should have witnessed this brief embarrassment.

'How did the clinic go today?' Powers asked. 'Have you had any more . . . headaches?'

Kaldren's mouth snapped shut, he looked suddenly irritable. 'Whose care am I in, doctor? Yours or Anderson's? Is that the sort of question you should be asking now?'

Powers gestured deprecatingly. 'Perhaps not.' He cleared his throat; the heat was ebbing the blood from his head and he felt tired and eager to get away from them. He turned towards his car, then realized that Kaldren would probably follow, either try to crowd him into the ditch or block the road and make Powers sit in his dust all the way back to the lake. Kaldren was capable of any madness.

'Well, I've got to go and collect something,' he said, adding in a firmer voice: 'Get in touch with me, though, if you can't reach Anderson.'

He waved and walked off behind the line of cars. From the reflection in the windows he could see Kaldren looking back and watching him closely.

He entered the Neurology wing, paused thankfully in the cool foyer, nodding to the two nurses and the armed guard at the reception desk. For some reason the terminals sleeping in the adjacent dormitory block attracted hordes of would-be sightseers, most of them cranks with some magical anti-narcoma remedy, or merely the idly curious, but a good number of quite normal people, many of whom had travelled thousands of miles, impelled towards the Clinic by some strange instinct, like animals migrating to a preview of their racial graveyards.

He walked along the corridor to the supervisor's office overlooking the recreation deck, borrowed the key and made his way out through the tennis courts and callisthenics rigs to the enclosed swimming pool at the far end. It had been disused for months, and only Powers' visits kept the lock free. Stepping through, he closed it behind him and walked past the peeling wooden stands to the deep end.

Putting a foot up on the diving board, he looked down at Whitby's ideogram. Damp leaves and bits of paper obscured it, but the outlines were just distinguishable. It covered almost the entire floor of the pool and at first glance appeared to represent a huge solar disc, with four radiating diamond-shaped arms, a crude Jungian mandala.

Wondering what had prompted Whitby to carve the device before his death, Powers noticed something moving through the debris in the centre of the disc. A black, horny-shelled animal about a foot long was nosing about in the slush, heaving itself on tired legs. Its shell was articulated, and vaguely resembled an armadillo's. Reaching the edge of the disc, it stopped and hesitated, then slowly backed away into the centre again, apparently unwilling or unable to cross the narrow groove.

Powers looked around, then stepped into one of the changing stalls and pulled a small wooden clothes locker off its rusty wall bracket. Carrying it under one arm, he climbed down the chromium ladder into the pool and walked carefully across the slithery floor towards the animal. As he approached it sidled away from him, but he trapped it easily, using the lid to lever it into the box.

The animal was heavy, at least the weight of a brick. Powers tapped its massive olive-black carapace with his knuckle, noting the triangular warty head jutting out below its rim like a turtle's, the thickened pads beneath the first digits of the pentadactyl forelimbs.

He watched the three-lidded eyes blinking at him anxiously from the bottom of the box.

'Expecting some really hot weather?' he murmured. 'That lead umbrella you're carrying around should keep you cool.'

He closed the lid, climbed out of the pool and made his way back to the supervisor's office, then carried the box out to his car.

'. . . Kaldren continues to reproach me (Powers wrote in his diary). For some reason he seems unwilling to accept his isolation, is elaborating a series of private rituals to replace the missing hours of sleep. Perhaps

*I should tell him of my own approaching zero, but he'd probably regard this as the final unbearable insult, that I should have in excess what he so desperately yearns for. God knows what might happen. Fortunately the nightmarish visions appear to have receded for the time being . . .'*

Pushing the diary away, Powers leaned forward across the desk and stared out through the window at the white floor of the lake bed stretching towards the hills along the horizon. Three miles away, on the far shore, he could see the circular bowl of the radio-telescope revolving slowly in the clear afternoon air, as Kaldren tirelessly trapped the sky, sluicing in millions of cubic parsecs of sterile ether, like the nomads who trapped the sea along the shores of the Persian Gulf.

Behind him the air-conditioner murmured quietly, cooling the pale blue walls half-hidden in the dim light. Outside the air was bright and oppressive, the heat waves rippling up from the clumps of gold-tinted cacti below the Clinic blurring the sharp terraces of the twenty-storey Neurology block. There, in the silent dormitories behind the sealed shutters, the terminals slept their long dreamless sleep. There were now over 500 of them in the Clinic, the vanguard of a vast somnambulist army massing for its last march. Only five years had elapsed since the first narcoma syndrome had been recognized, but already huge government hospitals in the east were being readied for intakes in the thousands, as more and more cases came to light.

Powers felt suddenly tired, and glanced at his wrist, wondering how long he had to 8 o'clock, his bedtime for the next week or so. Already he missed the dusk, soon would wake to his last dawn.

His watch was in his hip-pocket. He remembered his decision not to use his timepieces, and sat back and stared at the bookshelves beside the desk. There were rows of green-covered AEC publications he had removed from Whitby's library, papers in which the biologist described his work out in the Pacific after the H-tests. Many of them Powers knew almost by heart, read a hundred times in an effort to grasp Whitby's last conclusions. Toynbee would certainly be easier to forget.

His eyes dimmed momentarily, as the tall black wall in the rear of his mind cast its great shadow over his brain. He reached for the diary, thinking of the girl in Kaldren's car – Coma he had called her, another of his insane jokes – and her reference to Noguchi. Actually the comparison should have been made with Whitby, not himself; the monsters in the lab were nothing more than fragmented mirrors of Whitby's mind, like the grotesque radio-shielded frog he had found that morning in the swimming pool.

Thinking of the girl Coma, and the heartening smile she had given him, he wrote:

*Woke 6-33 am. Last session with Anderson. He made it plain he's seen*

*enough of me, and from now on I'm better alone. To sleep 8-00? (these
countdowns terrify me.)*

He paused, then added:

*Goodbye, Eniwetok.*

## TWO

He saw the girl again the next day at Whitby's laboratory. He had driven
over after breakfast with the new specimen, eager to get it into a vivarium
before it died. The only previous armoured mutant he had come across
had nearly broken his neck. Speeding along the lake road a month or
so earlier he had struck it with the offside front wheel, expecting the
small creature to flatten instantly. Instead its hard lead-packed shell had
remained rigid, even though the organism within it had been pulped, had
flung the car heavily into the ditch. He had gone back for the shell,
later weighed it at the laboratory, found it contained over 600 grammes
of lead.

Quite a number of plants and animals were building up heavy metals
as radiological shields. In the hills behind the beach house a couple of
old-time prospectors were renovating the derelict gold-panning equipment abandoned over eighty years ago. They had noticed the bright
yellow tints of the cacti, run an analysis and found that the plants were
assimilating gold in extractable quantities, although the soil concentrations
were unworkable. Oak Ridge was at last paying a dividend!!

Waking that morning just after 6-45 – ten minutes later than the
previous day (he had switched on the radio, heard one of the regular
morning programmes as he climbed out of bed) – he had eaten a light
unwanted breakfast, then spent an hour packing away some of the books in
his library, crating them up and taping on address labels to his brother.

He reached Whitby's laboratory half an hour later. This was housed in a
100-foot-wide geodesic dome built beside his chalet on the west shore of
the lake about a mile from Kaldren's summer house. The chalet had been
closed after Whitby's suicide, and many of the experimental plants and
animals had died before Powers had managed to receive permission to
use the laboratory.

As he turned into the driveway he saw the girl standing on the apex of
the yellow-ribbed dome, her slim figure silhouetted against the sky. She
waved to him, then began to step down across the glass polyhedrons and
jumped nimbly into the driveway beside the car.

'Hello,' she said, giving him a welcoming smile. 'I came over to see
your zoo. Kaldren said you wouldn't let me in if he came so I made him
stay behind.'

She waited for Powers to say something while he searched for his keys, then volunteered: 'If you like, I can wash your shirt.'

Powers grinned at her, peered down ruefully at his dust-stained sleeves. 'Not a bad idea. I thought I was beginning to look a little uncared-for.' He unlocked the door, took Coma's arm. 'I don't know why Kaldren told you that – he's welcome here any time he likes.'

'What have you got in there?' Coma asked, pointing at the wooden box he was carrying as they walked between the gear-laden benches.

'A distant cousin of ours I found. Interesting little chap. I'll introduce you in a moment.'

Sliding partitions divided the dome into four chambers. Two of them were storerooms, filled with spare tanks, apparatus, cartons of animal food and test rigs. They crossed the third section, almost filled by a powerful X-ray projector, a giant 250 amp G.E. Maxitron, angled on to a revolving table, concrete shielding blocks lying around ready for use like huge building bricks.

The fourth chamber contained Powers' zoo, the vivaria jammed together along the benches and in the sinks, big coloured cardboard charts and memos pinned on to the draught hoods above them, a tangle of rubber tubing and power leads trailing across the floor. As they walked past the lines of tanks dim forms shifted behind the frosted glass, and at the far end of the aisle there was a sudden scurrying in a large cage by Powers' desk.

Putting the box down on his chair, he picked a packet of peanuts off the desk and went over to the cage. A small black-haired chimpanzee wearing a dented jet pilot's helmet swarmed deftly up the bars to him, chirped happily and then jumped down to a miniature control panel against the rear wall of the cage. Rapidly it flicked a series of buttons and toggles, and a succession of coloured lights lit up like a juke box and jangled out a two-second blast of music.

'Good boy,' Powers said encouragingly, patting the chimp's back and shovelling the peanuts into its hands. 'You're getting much too clever for that one, aren't you?'

The chimp tossed the peanuts into the back of its throat with the smooth, easy motions of a conjuror, jabbering at Powers in a sing-song voice.

Coma laughed and took some of the nuts from Powers. 'He's sweet. I think he's talking to you.'

Powers nodded. 'Quite right, he is. Actually he's got a two-hundred-word vocabulary, but his voice box scrambles it all up.' He opened a small refrigerator by the desk, took out half a packet of sliced bread and passed a couple of pieces to the chimp. It picked an electric toaster off the floor and placed it in the middle of a low wobbling table in the centre of the cage, whipped the pieces into the slots. Powers pressed a tab on the switchboard beside the cage and the toaster began to crackle softly.

'He's one of the brightest we've had here, about as intelligent as a five-year-old child, though much more self-sufficient in a lot of ways.' The two pieces of toast jumped out of their slots and the chimp caught them neatly, nonchalantly patting its helmet each time, then ambled off into a small ramshackle kennel and relaxed back with one arm out of a window, sliding the toast into its mouth.

'He built that house himself,' Powers went on, switching off the toaster. 'Not a bad effort, really.' He pointed to a yellow polythene bucket by the front door of the kennel, from which a battered-looking geranium protruded. 'Tends that plant, cleans up the cage, pours out an endless stream of wisecracks. Pleasant fellow all round.'

Coma was smiling broadly to herself. 'Why the space helmet, though?'

Powers hesitated. 'Oh, it – er – it's for his own protection. Sometimes he gets rather bad headaches. His predecessors all –' He broke off and turned away. 'Let's have a look at some of the other inmates.'

He moved down the line of tanks, beckoning Coma with him. 'We'll start at the beginning.' He lifted the glass lid off one of the tanks, and Coma peered down into a shallow bath of water, where a small round organism with slender tendrils was nestling in a rockery of shells and pebbles.

'Sea anemone. Or was. Simple coelenterate with an open-ended body cavity.' He pointed down to a thickened ridge of tissue around the base. 'It's sealed up the cavity, converted the channel into a rudimentary notochord, first plant ever to develop a nervous system. Later the tendrils will knot themselves into a ganglion, but already they're sensitive to colour. Look.' He borrowed the violet handkerchief in Coma's breast-pocket, spread it across the tank. The tendrils flexed and stiffened, began to weave slowly, as if they were trying to focus.

'The strange thing is that they're completely insensitive to white light. Normally the tendrils register shifting pressure gradients, like the tympanic diaphragms in your ears. Now it's almost as if they can *hear* primary colours, suggests it's re-adapting itself for a non-aquatic existence in a static world of violent colour contrasts.'

Coma shook her head, puzzled. 'Why, though?'

'Hold on a moment. Let me put you in the picture first.' They moved along the bench to a series of drum-shaped cages made of wire mosquito netting. Above the first was a large white cardboard screen bearing a blown-up microphoto of a tall pagoda-like chain, topped by the legend: 'Drosophila: 15 röntgens/min.'

Powers tapped a small perspex window in the drum. 'Fruitfly. Its huge chromosomes make it a useful test vehicle.' He bent down, pointed to a grey V-shaped honeycomb suspended from the roof. A few flies emerged from entrances, moving about busily. 'Usually it's solitary, a nomadic scavenger. Now it forms itself into well-knit social groups, has begun to secrete a thin sweet lymph something like honey.'

'What's this?' Coma asked, touching the screen.

'Diagram of a key gene in the operation.' He traced a spray of arrows

leading from a link in the chain. The arrows were labelled: 'Lymph gland' and subdivided 'sphincter muscles, epithelium, templates.'

'It's rather like the perforated sheet music of a player-piano,' Powers commented, 'or a computer punch tape. Knock out one link with an X-ray beam, lose a characteristic, change the score.'

Coma was peering through the window of the next cage and pulling an unpleasant face. Over her shoulder Powers saw she was watching an enormous spider-like insect, as big as a hand, its dark hairy legs as thick as fingers. The compound eyes had been built up so that they resembled giant rubies.

'He looks unfriendly,' she said. 'What's that sort of rope ladder he's spinning?' As she moved a finger to her mouth the spider came to life, retreated into the cage and began spewing out a complex skein of interlinked grey thread which it slung in long loops from the roof of the cage.

'A web,' Powers told her. 'Except that it consists of nervous tissue. The ladders form an external neural plexus, an inflatable brain as it were, that he can pump up to whatever size the situation calls for. A sensible arrangement, really, far better than our own.'

Coma backed away. 'Gruesome. I wouldn't like to go into his parlour.'

'Oh, he's not as frightening as he looks. Those huge eyes staring at you are blind. Or, rather, their optical sensitivity has shifted down the band, the retinas will only register gamma radiation. Your wristwatch has luminous hands. When you moved it across the window he started thinking. World War IV should really bring him into his element.'

They strolled back to Powers' desk. He put a coffee pan over a bunsen and pushed a chair across to Coma. Then he opened the box, lifted out the armoured frog and put it down on a sheet of blotting paper.

'Recognize him? Your old childhood friend, the common frog. He's built himself quite a solid little air-raid shelter.' He carried the animal across to a sink, turned on the tap and let the water play softly over its shell. Wiping his hands on his shirt, he came back to the desk.

Coma brushed her long hair off her forehead, watched him curiously. 'Well, what's the secret?'

Powers lit a cigarette. 'There's no secret. Teratologists have been breeding monsters for years. Have you ever heard of the "silent pair"?'

She shook her head.

Powers stared moodily at the cigarette for a moment, riding the kick the first one of the day always gave him. 'The so-called "silent pair" is one of modern genetics' oldest problems, the apparently baffling mystery of the two inactive genes which occur in a small percentage of all living organisms, and appear to have no intelligible role in their structure or development. For a long while now biologists have been trying to activate them, but the difficulty is partly in identifying the silent genes in the fertilized germ cells of parents known to contain them, and partly in focusing a narrow enough X-ray beam which will do no damage to the

remainder of the chromosome. However, after about ten years' work Dr Whitby successfully developed a whole-body irradiation technique based on his observation of radiobiological damage at Eniwetok.'

Powers paused for a moment. 'He had noticed that there appeared to be more biological damage after the tests – that is, a greater transport of energy – than could be accounted for by direct radiation. What was happening was that the protein lattices in the genes were building up energy in the way that any vibrating membrane accumulates energy when it resonates – you remember the analogy of the bridge collapsing under the soldiers marching in step – and it occurred to him that if he could first identify the critical resonance frequency of the lattices in any particular silent gene he could then radiate the entire living organism, and not simply its germ cells, with a low field that would act selectively on the silent gene and cause no damage to the remainder of the chromosomes, whose lattices would resonate critically only at other specific frequencies.'

Powers gestured around the laboratory with his cigarette. 'You see some of the fruits of this "resonance transfer" technique around you.'

Coma nodded. 'They've had their silent genes activated?'

'Yes, all of them. These are only a few of the thousands of specimens who have passed through here, and as you've seen, the results are pretty dramatic.'

He reached up and pulled across a section of the sun curtain. They were sitting just under the lip of the dome, and the mounting sunlight had begun to irritate him.

In the comparative darkness Coma noticed a stroboscope winking slowly in one of the tanks at the end of the bench behind her. She stood up and went over to it, examining a tall sunflower with a thickened stem and greatly enlarged receptacle. Packed around the flower, so that only its head protruded, was a chimney of grey-white stones, neatly cemented together and labelled:

Cretaceous Chalk: 60,000,000 years

Beside it on the bench were three other chimneys, these labelled 'Devonian Sandstone: 290,000,000 years', 'Asphalt: 20 years', 'Polyvinyl-chloride: 6 months'.

'Can you see those moist white discs on the sepals,' Powers pointed out. 'In some way they regulate the plant's metabolism. It literally *sees* time. The older the surrounding environment, the more sluggish its metabolism. With the asphalt chimney it will complete its annual cycle in a week, with the PVC one in a couple of hours.'

'Sees time,' Coma repeated, wonderingly. She looked up at Powers, chewing her lower lip reflectively. 'It's fantastic. Are these the creatures of the future, doctor?'

'I don't know,' Powers admitted. 'But if they are their world must be a monstrous surrealist one.'

## THREE

He went back to the desk, pulled two cups from a drawer and poured out the coffee, switching off the bunsen. 'Some people have speculated that organisms possessing the silent pair of genes are the forerunners of a massive move up the evolutionary slope, that the silent genes are a sort of code, a divine message that we inferior organisms are carrying for our more highly developed descendants. It may well be true – perhaps we've broken the code too soon.'

'Why do you say that?'

'Well, as Whitby's death indicates, the experiments in this laboratory have all come to a rather unhappy conclusion. Without exception the organisms we've irradiated have entered a final phase of totally disorganized growth, producing dozens of specialized sensory organs whose function we can't even guess. The results are catastrophic – the anemone will literally explode, the Drosophila cannibalize themselves, and so on. Whether the future implicit in these plants and animals is ever intended to take place, or whether we're merely extrapolating – I don't know. Sometimes I think, though, that the new sensory organs developed are parodies of their real intentions. The specimens you've seen today are all in an early stage of their secondary growth cycles. Later on they begin to look distinctly bizarre.'

Coma nodded. 'A zoo isn't complete without its keeper,' she commented. 'What about Man?'

Powers shrugged. 'About one in every 100,000 – the usual average – contain the silent pair. You might have them – or I. No one has volunteered yet to undergo whole-body irradiation. Apart from the fact that it would be classified as suicide, if the experiments here are any guide the experience would be savage and violent.'

He sipped at the thin coffee, feeling tired and somehow bored. Recapitulating the laboratory's work had exhausted him.

The girl leaned forward. 'You look awfully pale,' she said solicitously. 'Don't you sleep well?'

Powers managed a brief smile. 'Too well,' he admitted. 'It's no longer a problem with me.'

'I wish I could say that about Kaldren. I don't think he sleeps anywhere near enough. I hear him pacing around all night.' She added: 'Still, I suppose it's better than being a terminal. Tell me, doctor, wouldn't it be worth trying this radiation technique on the sleepers at the Clinic? It might wake them up before the end. A few of them must possess the silent genes.'

'They *all* do,' Powers told her. 'The two phenomena are very closely linked, as a matter of fact.' He stopped, fatigue dulling his brain, and wondered whether to ask the girl to leave. Then he climbed off the desk and reached behind it, picked up a tape-recorder.

Switching it on, he zeroed the tape and adjusted the speaker volume.

'Whitby and I often talked this over. Towards the end I took it all down. He was a great biologist, so let's hear it in his own words. It's absolutely the heart of the matter.'

He flipped the table on, adding: 'I've played it over to myself a thousand times, so I'm afraid the quality is poor.'

An older man's voice, sharp and slightly irritable, sounded out above a low buzz of distortion, but Coma could hear it clearly.

WHITBY: . . . for heaven's sake, Robert, look at those FAO statistics. Despite an annual increase of five per cent in acreage sown over the past fifteen years, world wheat crops have continued to decline by a factor of about two per cent. The same story repeats itself *ad nauseam*. Cereals and root crops, dairy yields, ruminant fertility – are all down. Couple these with a mass of parallel symptoms, anything you care to pick from altered migratory routes to longer hibernation periods, and the overall pattern is incontrovertible.

POWERS: Population figures for Europe and North America show no decline, though.

WHITBY: Of course not, as I keep pointing out. It will take a century for such a fractional drop in fertility to have any effect in areas where extensive birth control provides an artificial reservoir. One must look at the countries of the Far East, and particularly at those where infant mortality has remained at a steady level. The population of Sumatra, for example, has declined by over fifteen per cent in the last twenty years. A fabulous decline! Do you realize that only two or three decades ago the Neo-Malthusians were talking about a 'world population explosion'? In fact, it's an implosion. Another factor is –

Here the tape had been cut and edited, and Whitby's voice, less querulous this time, picked up again.

. . . just as a matter of interest, tell me something: how long do you sleep each night?

POWERS: I don't know exactly; about eight hours, I suppose.

WHITBY: The proverbial eight hours. Ask anyone and they say automatically 'eight hours'. As a matter of fact you sleep about ten and a half hours, like the majority of people. I've timed you on a number of occasions. I myself sleep eleven. Yet thirty years ago people did indeed sleep eight hours, and a century before that they slept six or seven. In Vasari's *Lives* one reads of Michelangelo sleeping for only four or five hours, painting all day at the age of eighty and then working through the night over his anatomy table with a candle strapped to his forehead. Now he's regarded as a prodigy, but it was unremarkable then. How do you think the ancients, from Plato to Shakespeare, Aristotle to Aquinas, were able to cram so much work into their lives? Simply because they had an extra six or seven hours every day. Of course, a second disadvantage under which we labour is a lowered basal metabolic rate – another factor no one will explain.

POWERS: I suppose you could take the view that the lengthened sleep interval is a compensation device, a sort of mass neurotic attempt to escape from the terrifying pressures of urban life in the late twentieth century.

WHITBY: You could, but you'd be wrong. It's simply a matter of biochemistry. The ribonucleic acid templates which unravel the protein chains in all living organisms are wearing out, the dies inscribing the protoplasmic signature have become blunted. After all, they've been running now for over a thousand million years. It's time to re-tool. Just as an individual organism's life span is finite, or the life of a yeast colony or a given species, so the life of an entire biological kingdom is of fixed duration. It's always been assumed that the evolutionary slope reaches forever upwards, but in fact the peak has already been reached, and the pathway now leads downwards to the common biological grave. It's a despairing and at present unacceptable vision of the future, but it's the only one. Five thousand centuries from now our descendants, instead of being multi-brained star-men, will probably be naked prognathous idiots with hair on their foreheads, grunting their way through the remains of this Clinic like Neolithic men caught in a macabre inversion of time. Believe me, I pity them, as I pity myself. My total failure, my absolute lack of any moral or biological right to existence, is implicit in every cell of my body . . .

The tape ended, the spool ran free and stopped. Powers closed the machine, then massaged his face. Coma sat quietly, watching him and listening to the chimp playing with a box of puzzle dice.

'As far as Whitby could tell,' Powers said, 'the silent genes represent a last desperate effort of the biological kingdom to keep its head above the rising waters. Its total life period is determined by the amount of radiation emitted by the sun, and once this reaches a certain point the sure-death line has been passed and extinction is inevitable. To compensate for this, alarms have been built in which alter the form of the organism and adapt it to living in a hotter radiological climate. Soft-skinned organisms develop hard shells, these contain heavy metals as radiation screens. New organs of perception are developed too. According to Whitby, though, it's all wasted effort in the long run – but sometimes I wonder.'

He smiled at Coma and shrugged. 'Well, let's talk about something else. How long have you known Kaldren?'

'About three weeks. Feels like ten thousand years.'

'How do you find him now? We've been rather out of touch lately.'

Coma grinned. 'I don't seem to see very much of him either. He makes me sleep all the time. Kaldren has many strange talents, but he lives just for himself. You mean a lot to him, doctor. In fact, you're my one serious rival.'

'I thought he couldn't stand the sight of me.'

'Oh, that's just a sort of surface symptom. He really thinks of you continually. That's why we spend all our time following you around.' She eyed Powers shrewdly. 'I think he feels guilty about something.'

'Guilty?' Powers exclaimed. '*He* does? I thought I was supposed to be the guilty one.'

'Why?' she pressed. She hesitated, then said: 'You carried out some experimental surgical technique on him, didn't you?'

'Yes,' Powers admitted. 'It wasn't altogether a success, like so much of what I seem to be involved with. If Kaldren feels guilty, I suppose it's because he feels he must take some of the responsibility.'

He looked down at the girl, her intelligent eyes watching him closely. 'For one or two reasons it may be necessary for you to know. You said Kaldren paced around all night and didn't get enough sleep. Actually he doesn't get any sleep at all.'

The girl nodded. 'You ...' She made a snapping gesture with her fingers.

'... narcotomized him,' Powers completed. 'Surgically speaking, it was a great success, one might well share a Nobel for it. Normally the hypothalamus regulates the period of sleep, raising the threshold of consciousness in order to relax the venous capillaries in the brain and drain them of accumulating toxins. However, by sealing off some of the control loops the subject is unable to receive the sleep cue, and the capillaries drain while he remains conscious. All he feels is a temporary lethargy, but this passes within three or four hours. Physically speaking, Kaldren has had another twenty years added to his life. But the psyche seems to need sleep for its own private reasons, and consequently Kaldren has periodic storms that tear him apart. The whole thing was a tragic blunder.'

Coma frowned pensively. 'I guessed as much. Your papers in the neurosurgery journals referred to the patient as K. A touch of pure Kafka that came all too true.'

'I may leave here for good, Coma,' Powers said. 'Make sure that Kaldren goes to his clinics. Some of the deep scar tissue will need to be cleaned away.'

'I'll try. Sometimes I feel I'm just another of his insane terminal documents.'

'What are those?'

'Haven't you heard? Kaldren's collection of final statements about *homo sapiens*. The complete works of Freud, Beethoven's blind quartets, transcripts of the Nuremberg trials, an automatic novel, and so on.' She broke off. 'What's that you're drawing?'

'Where?'

She pointed to the desk blotter, and Powers looked down and realized he had been unconsciously sketching an elaborate doodle, Whitby's four-armed sun. 'It's nothing,' he said. Somehow, though, it had a strangely compelling force.

Coma stood up to leave. 'You must come and see us, doctor. Kaldren has so much he wants to show you. He's just got hold of an old copy of the last signals sent back by the Mercury Seven twenty years ago when they reached the moon, and can't think about anything else. You remember the strange messages they recorded before they died, full of poetic ramblings about the white gardens. Now that I think about it they behaved rather like the plants in your zoo here.'

She put her hands in her pockets, then pulled something out. 'By the way, Kaldren asked me to give you this.'

It was an old index card from the observatory library. In the centre had been typed the number:

96,688,365,498,720

'It's going to take a long time to reach zero at this rate,' Powers remarked dryly. 'I'll have quite a collection when we're finished.'

After she had left he chucked the card into the waste bin and sat down at the desk, staring for an hour at the ideogram on the blotter.

Halfway back to his beach house the lake road forked to the left through a narrow saddle that ran between the hills to an abandoned Air Force weapons range on one of the remoter salt lakes. At the nearer end were a number of small bunkers and camera towers, one or two metal shacks and a low-roofed storage hangar. The white hills encircled the whole area, shutting it off from the world outside, and Powers liked to wander on foot down the gunnery aisles that had been marked down the two-mile length of the lake towards the concrete sight-screens at the far end. The abstract patterns made him feel like an ant on a bone-white chess-board, the rectangular screens at one end and the towers and bunkers at the other like opposing pieces.

His session with Coma had made Powers feel suddenly dissatisfied with the way he was spending his last months. *Goodbye, Eniwetok*, he had written, but in fact systematically forgetting everything was exactly the same as remembering it, a cataloguing in reverse, sorting out all the books in the mental library and putting them back in their right places upside down.

Powers climbed one of the camera towers, leaned on the rail and looked out along the aisles towards the sight-screens. Ricocheting shells and rockets had chipped away large pieces of the circular concrete bands that ringed the target bulls, but the outlines of the huge 100-yard-wide discs, alternately painted blue and red, were still visible.

For half an hour he stared quietly at them, formless ideas shifting through his mind. Then, without thinking, he abruptly left the rail and climbed down the companionway. The storage hangar was fifty yards away. He walked quickly across to it, stepped into the cool shadows and peered around the rusting electric trolleys and empty flare drums. At the far end, behind a pile of lumber and bales of wire, were a stack of unopened cement bags, a mound of dirty sand and an old mixer.

Half an hour later he had backed the Buick into the hangar and hooked the cement mixer, charged with sand, cement and water scavenged from the drums lying around outside, on to the rear bumper, then loaded a dozen more bags into the car's trunk and rear seat. Finally he selected a few straight lengths of timber, jammed them through the window and set off across the lake towards the central target bull.

For the next two hours he worked away steadily in the centre of the great blue disc, mixing up the cement by hand, carrying it across to the crude wooden forms he had lashed together from the timber, smoothing it down so that it formed a six-inch high wall around the perimeter of the bull. He worked without pause, stirring the cement with a tyre lever, scooping it out with a hub-cap prised off one of the wheels.

By the time he finished and drove off, leaving his equipment where it stood, he had completed a thirty-foot-long section of wall.

## FOUR

*June 7: Conscious, for the first time, of the brevity of each day. As long as I was awake for over twelve hours I still orientated my time around the meridian, morning and afternoon set their old rhythms. Now, with just over eleven hours of consciousness left, they form a continuous interval, like a length of tape-measure. I can see exactly how much is left on the spool and can do little to affect the rate at which it unwinds. Spend the time slowly packing away the library; the crates are too heavy to move and lie where they are filled.*
*Cell count down to 400,000.*
*Woke 8-10. To sleep 7-15. (Appear to have lost my watch without realizing it, had to drive into town to buy another.)*

*June 14: 9½ hours. Time races, flashing past like an expressway. However, the last week of a holiday always goes faster than the first. At the present rate there should be about 4–5 weeks left. This morning I tried to visualize what the last week or so – the final, 3, 2, 1, out – would be like, had a sudden chilling attack of pure fear, unlike anything I've ever felt before. Took me half an hour to steady myself for an intravenous.*
*Kaldren pursues me like my luminescent shadow, chalked up on the gateway '96,688,365,498,702'. Should confuse the mail man.*
*Woke 9-05. To sleep 6-36.*

*June 19: 8¾ hours. Anderson rang up this morning. I nearly put the phone down on him, but managed to go through the pretence of making the final arrangements. He congratulated me on my stoicism, even used the word 'heroic'. Don't feel it. Despair erodes everything – courage, hope, self-discipline, all the better qualities. It's so damned difficult to sustain that impersonal attitude of passive acceptance implicit in the scientific tradition. I try to think of Galileo before the Inquisition, Freud surmounting the endless pain of his jaw cancer surgery.*

*Met Kaldren down town, had a long discussion about the Mercury Seven. He's convinced that they refused to leave the moon deliberately, after the 'reception party' waiting for them had put them in the cosmic picture. They were told by the mysterious emissaries from Orion that the exploration of deep space was pointless, that they were too late as the life of the universe is now virtually over!!! According to K. there are Air Force generals who take this nonsense seriously, but I suspect it's simply an obscure attempt on K.'s part to console me.*

*Must have the phone disconnected. Some contractor keeps calling me up about payment for 50 bags of cement he claims I collected ten days ago. Says he helped me load them on to a truck himself. I did drive Whitby's pick-up into town but only to get some lead screening. What does he think I'd do with all that cement? Just the sort of irritating thing you don't expect to hang over your final exit. (Moral: don't try too hard to forget Eniwetok.)*

*Woke 9-40. To sleep 4-15.*

*June 25: 7½ hours. Kaldren was snooping around the lab again today. Phoned me there, when I answered a recorded voice he'd rigged up rambled out a long string of numbers, like an insane super-Tim. These practical jokes of his get rather wearing. Fairly soon I'll have to go over and come to terms with him, much as I hate the prospect. Anyway, Miss Mars is a pleasure to look at.*

*One meal is enough now, topped up with a glucose shot. Sleep is still 'black', completely unrefreshing. Last night I took a 16 mm. film of the first three hours, screened it this morning at the lab. The first true horror movie, I looked like a half-animated corpse.*

*Woke 10-25. To sleep 3-45.*

*July 3: 5¾ hours. Little done today. Deepening lethargy, dragged myself over to the lab, nearly left the road twice. Concentrated enough to feed the zoo and get the log up to date. Read through the operating manuals Whitby left for the last time, decided on a delivery rate of 40 röntgens/min., target distance of 350 cm. Everything is ready now.*

*Woke 11-05. To sleep 3-15.*

Powers stretched, shifted his head slowly across the pillow, focusing on the shadows cast on to the ceiling by the blind. Then he looked down at his feet, saw Kaldren sitting on the end of the bed, watching him quietly.

'Hello, doctor,' he said, putting out his cigarette. 'Late night? You look tired.'

Powers heaved himself on to one elbow, glanced at his watch. It was just after eleven. For a moment his brain blurred, and he swung his legs around and sat on the edge of the bed, elbows on his knees, massaging some life into his face.

He noticed that the room was full of smoke. 'What are you doing here?' he asked Kaldren.

'I came over to invite you to lunch.' He indicated the bedside phone. 'Your line was dead so I drove round. Hope you don't mind me climbing in. Rang the bell for about half an hour. I'm surprised you didn't hear it.'

Powers nodded, then stood up and tried to smooth the creases out of his cotton slacks. He had gone to sleep without changing for over a week, and they were damp and stale.

As he started for the bathroom door Kaldren pointed to the camera tripod on the other side of the bed. 'What's this? Going into the blue movie business, doctor?'

Powers surveyed him dimly for a moment, glanced at the tripod without replying and then noticed his open diary on the bedside table. Wondering whether Kaldren had read the last entries, he went back and picked it up, then stepped into the bathroom and closed the door behind him.

From the mirror cabinet he took out a syringe and an ampoule, after the shot leaned against the door waiting for the stimulant to pick up.

Kaldren was in the lounge when he returned to him, reading the labels on the crates lying about in the centre of the floor.

'Okay, then,' Powers told him, 'I'll join you for lunch.' He examined Kaldren carefully. He looked more subdued than usual, there was an air almost of deference about him.

'Good,' Kaldren said. 'By the way, are you leaving?'

'Does it matter?' Powers asked curtly. 'I thought you were in Anderson's care?'

Kaldren shrugged. 'Please yourself. Come round at about twelve,' he suggested, adding pointedly: 'That'll give you time to clean up and change. What's that all over your shirt? Looks like lime.'

Powers peered down, brushed at the white streaks. After Kaldren had left he threw the clothes away, took a shower and unpacked a clean suit from one of the trunks.

Until his liaison with Coma, Kaldren lived alone in the old abstract summer house on the north shore of the lake. This was a seven-storey folly originally built by an eccentric millionaire mathematician in the form of a spiralling concrete ribbon that wound around itself like an insane serpent, serving walls, floors and ceilings. Only Kaldren had solved the building, a geometric model of $\sqrt{-1}$, and consequently he had been able to take it off the agents' hands at a comparatively low rent. In the evenings Powers had often watched him from the laboratory, striding restlessly from one level to the next, swinging through the labyrinth of inclines and terraces to the roof-top, where his lean angular figure stood out like a gallows against the sky, his lonely eyes sifting out radio lanes for the next day's trapping.

Powers noticed him there when he drove up at noon, poised on a ledge 150 feet above, head raised theatrically to the sky.

'Kaldren!' he shouted up suddenly into the silent air, half-hoping he might be jolted into losing his footing.

Kaldren broke out of his reverie and glanced down into the court. Grinning obliquely, he waved his right arm in a slow semi-circle.

'Come up,' he called, then turned back to the sky.

Powers leaned against the car. Once, a few months previously, he had accepted the same invitation, stepped through the entrance and within three minutes lost himself helplessly in a second-floor cul-de-sac. Kaldren had taken half an hour to find him.

Powers waited while Kaldren swung down from his eyrie, vaulting through the wells and stairways, then rode up in the elevator with him to the penthouse suite.

They carried their cocktails through into a wide glass-roofed studio, the huge white ribbon of concrete uncoiling around them like toothpaste squeezed from an enormous tube. On the staged levels running parallel and across them rested pieces of grey abstract furniture, giant photographs on angled screens, carefully labelled exhibits laid out on low tables, all dominated by twenty-foot-high black letters on the rear wall which spelt out the single vast word:

# YOU

Kaldren pointed to it. 'What you might call the supraliminal approach.' He gestured Powers in conspiratorially, finishing his drink in a gulp. 'This is *my* laboratory, doctor,' he said with a note of pride. 'Much more significant than yours, believe me.'

Powers smiled wryly to himself and examined the first exhibit, an old EEG tape traversed by a series of faded inky wriggles. It was labelled: 'Einstein, A.; Alpha Waves, 1922.'

He followed Kaldren around, sipping slowly at his drink, enjoying the brief feeling of alertness the amphetamine provided. Within two hours it would fade, leave his brain feeling like a block of blotting paper.

Kaldren chattered away, explaining the significance of the so-called Terminal Documents. 'They're end-prints, Powers, final statements, the products of total fragmentation. When I've got enough together I'll build a new world for myself out of them.' He picked a thick paper-bound volume off one of the tables, riffled through its pages. 'Association tests of the Nuremberg Twelve. I have to include these . . .'

Powers strolled on absently without listening. Over in the corner were what appeared to be three ticker-tape machines, lengths of tape hanging from their mouths. He wondered whether Kaldren was misguided enough to be playing the stock market, which had been declining slowly for twenty years.

'Powers,' he heard Kaldren say. 'I was telling you about the Mercury Seven.' He pointed to a collection of typewritten sheets tacked to a screen. 'These are transcripts of their final signals radioed back from the recording monitors.'

Powers examined the sheets cursorily, read a line at random.

'. . . BLUE . . . PEOPLE . . . RE-CYCLE . . . ORION . . . TELEMETERS . . .'

Powers nodded noncommittally. 'Interesting. What are the ticker tapes for over there?'

Kaldren grinned. 'I've been waiting for months for you to ask me that. Have a look.'

Powers went over and picked up one of the tapes. The machine was labelled: 'Auriga 225-G. Interval: 69 hours.'

The tape read:

    96,688,365,498,695
    96,688,365,498,694
    96,688,365,498,693
    96,688,365,498,692

Powers dropped the tape. 'Looks rather familiar. What does the sequence represent?'

Kaldren shrugged. 'No one knows.'

'What do you mean? It must replicate something.'

'Yes, it does. A diminishing mathematical progression. A countdown, if you like.'

Powers picked up the tape on the right, tabbed: 'Aries 44R951. Interval: 49 days.'

Here the sequence ran:

    876,567,988,347,779,877,654,434
    876,567,988,347,779,877,654,433
    876,567,988,347,779,877,654,432

Powers looked round. 'How long does it take each signal to come through?'

'Only a few seconds. They're tremendously compressed laterally, of course. A computer at the observatory breaks them down. They were first picked up at Jodrell Bank about twenty years ago. Nobody bothers to listen to them now.'

Powers turned to the last tape.

6,554
6,553
6,552
6,551

'Nearing the end of its run,' he commented. He glanced at the label on the hood, which read: 'Unidentified radio source, Canes Venatici. Interval: 97 weeks.'

He showed the tape to Kaldren. 'Soon be over.'

Kaldren shook his head. He lifted a heavy directory-sized volume off a table, cradled it in his hands. His face had suddenly become sombre and haunted. 'I doubt it,' he said. 'Those are only the last four digits. The whole number contains over 50 million.'

He handed the volume to Powers, who turned to the title page. 'Master Sequence of Serial Signal received by Jodrell Bank Radio-Observatory, University of Manchester, England, 0012-59 hours, 21-5-72. Source: NGC 9743, Canes Venatici.' He thumbed the thick stack of closely printed pages, millions of numerals, as Kaldren had said, running up and down across a thousand consecutive pages.

Powers shook his head, picked up the tape again and stared at it thoughtfully.

'The computer only breaks down the last four digits,' Kaldren explained. 'The whole series comes over in each 15-second-long package, but it took IBM more than two years to unscramble one of them.'

'Amazing,' Powers commented. 'But what is it?'

'A countdown, as you can see. NGC 9743, somewhere in Canes Venatici. The big spirals there are breaking up, and they're saying goodbye. God knows who they think we are but they're letting us know all the same, beaming it out on the hydrogen line for everyone in the universe to hear.' He paused. 'Some people have put other interpretations on them, but there's one piece of evidence that rules out everything else.'

'Which is?'

Kaldren pointed to the last tape from Canes Venatici. 'Simply that it's been estimated that by the time this series reaches zero the universe will have just ended.'

Powers fingered the tape reflectively. 'Thoughtful of them to let us know what the real time is,' he remarked.

'I agree, it is,' Kaldren said quietly. 'Applying the inverse square law that signal source is broadcasting at a strength of about three million megawatts raised to the hundredth power. About the size of the entire Local Group. Thoughtful is the word.'

Suddenly he gripped Powers' arm, held it tightly and peered into his eyes closely, his throat working with emotion.

'You're not alone, Powers, don't think you are. These are the voices of

time, and they're all saying goodbye to you. Think of yourself in a wider
context. Every particle in your body, every grain of sand, every galaxy
carries the same signature. As you've just said, you know what the time
is now, so what does the rest matter? There's no need to go on looking
at the clock.'

Powers took his hand, squeezed it firmly. 'Thanks, Kaldren. I'm glad
you understand.' He walked over to the window, looked down across the
white lake. The tension between himself and Kaldren had dissipated, he
felt that all his obligations to him had at last been met. Now he wanted
to leave as quickly as possible, forget him as he had forgotten the faces
of the countless other patients whose exposed brains had passed between
his fingers.

He went back to the ticker machines, tore the tapes from their slots
and stuffed them into his pockets. 'I'll take these along to remind myself.
Say goodbye to Coma for me, will you.'

He moved towards the door, when he reached it looked back to see
Kaldren standing in the shadow of the three giant letters on the far wall,
his eyes staring listlessly at his feet.

As Powers drove away he noticed that Kaldren had gone up on to
the roof, watched him in the driving mirror waving slowly until the car
disappeared around a bend.

## FIVE

The outer circle was now almost complete. A narrow segment, an arc
about ten feet long, was missing, but otherwise the low perimeter wall ran
continuously six inches off the concrete floor around the outer lane of the
target bull, enclosing the huge rebus within it. Three concentric circles, the
largest a hundred yards in diameter, separated from each other by ten-foot
intervals, formed the rim of the device, divided into four segments by the
arms of an enormous cross radiating from its centre, where a small round
platform had been built a foot above the ground.

Powers worked swiftly, pouring sand and cement into the mixer, tipping
in water until a rough paste formed, then carried it across to the wooden
forms and tamped the mixture down into the narrow channel.

Within ten minutes he had finished, quickly dismantled the forms
before the cement had set and slung the timbers into the back seat of
the car. Dusting his hands on his trousers, he went over to the mixer and
pushed it fifty yards away into the long shadow of the surrounding hills.

Without pausing to survey the gigantic cipher on which he had laboured
patiently for so many afternoons, he climbed into the car and drove off on
a wake of bone-white dust, splitting the pools of indigo shadow.

He reached the laboratory at three o'clock, jumped from the car as it
lurched back on its brakes. Inside the entrance he first switched on the

lights, then hurried round, pulling the sun curtains down and shackling them to the floor slots, effectively turning the dome into a steel tent.

In their tanks behind him the plants and animals stirred quietly, responding to the sudden flood of cold fluorescent light. Only the chimpanzee ignored him. It sat on the floor of its cage, neurotically jamming the puzzle dice into the polythene bucket, exploding in bursts of sudden rage when the pieces refused to fit.

Powers went over to it, noticing the shattered glass fibre reinforcing panels bursting from the dented helmet. Already the chimp's face and forehead were bleeding from self-inflicted blows. Powers picked up the remains of the geranium that had been hurled through the bars, attracted the chimp's attention with it, then tossed a black pellet he had taken from a capsule in the desk drawer. The chimp caught it with a quick flick of the wrist, for a few seconds juggled the pellet with a couple of dice as it concentrated on the puzzle, then pulled it out of the air and swallowed it in a gulp.

Without waiting, Powers slipped off his jacket and stepped towards the X-ray theatre. He pulled back the high sliding doors to reveal the long glassy metallic snout of the Maxitron, then started to stack the lead screening shields against the rear wall.

A few minutes later the generator hummed into life.

*The anemone stirred. Basking in the warm subliminal sea of radiation rising around it, prompted by countless pelagic memories, it reached tentatively across the tank, groping blindly towards the dim uterine sun. Its tendrils flexed, the thousands of dormant neural cells in their tips regrouping and multiplying, each harnessing the unlocked energies of its nucleus. Chains forged themselves, lattices tiered upwards into multi-faceted lenses, focused slowly on the vivid spectral outlines of the sounds dancing like phosphorescent waves around the darkened chamber of the dome.*

*Gradually an image formed, revealing an enormous black fountain that poured an endless stream of brilliant light over the circle of benches and tanks. Beside it a figure moved, adjusting the flow through its mouth. As it stepped across the floor its feet threw off vivid bursts of colour, its hands racing along the benches conjured up a dazzling chiaroscuro, balls of blue and violet light that exploded fleetingly in the darkness like miniature star-shells.*

*Photons murmured. Steadily, as it watched the glimmering screen of sounds around it, the anemone continued to expand. Its ganglia linked, heeding a new source of stimuli from the delicate diaphragms in the crown of its notochord. The silent outlines of the laboratory began to echo softly, waves of muted sound fell from the arc lights and echoed off the benches and furniture below. Etched in sound, their angular forms resonated with sharp persistent overtones. The plastic-ribbed chairs were a buzz of staccato discords, the square-sided desk a continuous double-featured tone.*

*Ignoring these sounds once they had been perceived, the anemone turned to the ceiling, which reverberated like a shield in the sounds pouring steadily from the fluorescent tubes. Streaming through a narrow skylight, its voice clear and strong, interweaved by numberless overtones, the sun sang . . .*

It was a few minutes before dawn when Powers left the laboratory and stepped into his car. Behind him the great dome lay silently in the darkness, the thin shadows of the white moonlit hills falling across its surface. Powers freewheeled the car down the long curving drive to the lake road below, listening to the tyres cutting across the blue gravel, then let out the clutch and accelerated the engine.

As he drove along, the limestone hills half hidden in the darkness on his left, he gradually became aware that, although no longer looking at the hills, he was still in some oblique way conscious of their forms and outlines in the back of his mind. The sensation was undefined but none the less certain, a strange almost visual impression that emanated most strongly from the deep clefts and ravines dividing one cliff face from the next. For a few minutes Powers let it play upon him, without trying to identify it, a dozen strange images moving across his brain.

The road swung up around a group of chalets built on to the lake shore, taking the car right under the lee of the hills, and Powers suddenly felt the massive weight of the escarpment rising up into the dark sky like a cliff of luminous chalk, and realized the identity of the impression now registering powerfully within his mind. Not only could he see the escarpment, but he was aware of its enormous age, felt distinctly the countless millions of years since it had first reared out of the magma of the earth's crust. The ragged crests three hundred feet above him, the dark gulleys and fissures, the smooth boulders by the roadside at the foot of the cliff, all carried a distinct image of themselves across to him, a thousand voices that together told of the total time that had elapsed in the life of the escarpment, a psychic picture defined and clear as the visual image brought to him by his eyes.

Involuntarily, Powers had slowed the car, and turning his eyes away from the hill face he felt a second wave of time sweep across the first. The image was broader but of shorter perspectives, radiating from the wide disc of the salt lake, breaking over the ancient limestone cliffs like shallow rollers dashing against a towering headland.

Closing his eyes, Powers lay back and steered the car along the interval between the two time fronts, feeling the images deepen and strengthen within his mind. The vast age of the landscape, the inaudible chorus of voices resonating from the lake and from the white hills, seemed to carry him back through time, down endless corridors to the first thresholds of the world.

He turned the car off the road along the track leading towards the target range. On either side of the culvert the cliff faces boomed and echoed with vast impenetrable time fields, like enormous opposed magnets. As he finally emerged between them on to the flat surface of the lake it seemed to Powers that he could feel the separate identity of each sand-grain and salt crystal calling to him from the surrounding ring of hills.

He parked the car beside the mandala and walked slowly towards the outer concrete rim curving away into the shadows. Above him he could hear the stars, a million cosmic voices that crowded the sky from one horizon to the next, a true canopy of time. Like jostling radio beacons, their long aisles interlocking at countless angles, they plunged into the sky from the narrowest recesses of space. He saw the dim red disc of Sirius, heard its ancient voice, untold millions of years old, dwarfed by the huge spiral nebulae in Andromeda, a gigantic carousel of vanished universes, their voices almost as old as the cosmos itself. To Powers the sky seemed an endless babel, the time-song of a thousand galaxies overlaying each other in his mind. As he moved slowly towards the centre of the mandala he craned up at the glittering traverse of the Milky Way, searching the confusion of clamouring nebulae and constellations.

Stepping into the inner circle of the mandala, a few yards from the platform at its centre, he realized that the tumult was beginning to fade, and that a single stronger voice had emerged and was dominating the others. He climbed on to the platform, raised his eyes to the darkened sky, moving through the constellations to the island galaxies beyond them, hearing the thin archaic voices reaching to him across the millennia. In his pockets he felt the paper tapes, and turned to find the distant diadem of Canes Venatici, heard its great voice mounting in his mind.

Like an endless river, so broad that its banks were below the horizons, it flowed steadily towards him, a vast course of time that spread outwards to fill the sky and the universe, enveloping everything within them. Moving slowly, the forward direction of its majestic current almost imperceptible, Powers knew that its source was the source of the cosmos itself. As it passed him, he felt its massive magnetic pull, let himself be drawn into it, borne gently on its powerful back. Quietly it carried him away, and he rotated slowly, facing the direction of the tide. Around him the outlines of the hills and the lake had faded, but the image of the mandala, like a cosmic clock, remained fixed before his eyes, illuminating the broad surface of the stream. Watching it constantly, he felt his body gradually dissolving, its physical dimensions melting into the vast continuum of the current, which bore him out into the centre of the great channel, sweeping him onward, beyond hope but at last at rest, down the broadening reaches of the river of eternity.

As the shadows faded, retreating into the hill slopes, Kaldren stepped out of his car, walked hesitantly towards the concrete rim of the outer circle. Fifty yards away, at the centre, Coma knelt beside Powers' body, her small hands pressed to his dead face. A gust of wind stirred the sand, dislodging a strip of tape that drifted towards Kaldren's feet. He bent down and picked it up, then rolled it carefully in his hands and slipped it into his pocket. The dawn air was cold, and he turned up the collar of his jacket, watching Coma impassively.

'It's six o'clock,' he told her after a few minutes. 'I'll go and get the police. You stay with him.' He paused and then added: 'Don't let them break the clock.'

Coma turned and looked at him. 'Aren't you coming back?'

'I don't know.' Nodding to her, Kaldren swung on his heel.

He reached the lake road, five minutes later parked the car in the drive outside Whitby's laboratory.

The dome was in darkness, all its windows shuttered, but the generator still hummed in the X-ray theatre. Kaldren stepped through the entrance and switched on the lights. In the theatre he touched the grilles of the generator, felt the warm cylinder of the beryllium end-window. The circular target table was revolving slowly, its setting at 1 r.p.m., a steel restraining chair shackled to it hastily. Grouped in a semicircle a few feet away were most of the tanks and cages, piled on top of each other haphazardly. In one of them an enormous squid-like plant had almost managed to climb from its vivarium. Its long translucent tendrils clung to the edges of the tank, but its body had burst into a jellified pool of globular mucilage. In another an enormous spider had trapped itself in its own web, hung helplessly in the centre of a huge three-dimensional maze of phosphorescing thread, twitching spasmodically.

All the experimental plants and animals had died. The chimp lay on its back among the remains of the hutch, the helmet forward over its eyes. Kaldren watched it for a moment, then sat down on the desk and picked up the phone.

While he dialled the number he noticed a film reel lying on the blotter. For a moment he stared at the label, then slid the reel into his pocket beside the tape.

After he had spoken to the police he turned off the lights and went out to the car, drove off slowly down the drive.

When he reached the summer house the early sunlight was breaking across the ribbon-like balconies and terraces. He took the lift to the penthouse, made his way through into the museum. One by one he opened the shutters and let the sunlight play over the exhibits. Then he pulled a chair over to a side window, sat back and stared up at the light pouring through into the room.

Two or three hours later he heard Coma outside, calling up to him. After half an hour she went away, but a little later a second voice appeared and shouted up at Kaldren. He left his chair and closed all the shutters overlooking the front courtyard, and eventually he was left undisturbed.

Kaldren returned to his seat and lay back quietly, his eyes gazing across the lines of exhibits. Half-asleep, periodically he leaned up and adjusted the flow of light through the shutter, thinking to himself, as he would do through the coming months, of Powers and his strange mandala, and of the seven and their journey to the white gardens of the moon, and the blue people who had come from Orion and spoken in poetry to them of ancient beautiful worlds beneath golden suns in the island galaxies, vanished for ever now in the myriad deaths of the cosmos.

· **1960**

# THE LAST WORLD OF MR GODDARD

For no apparent reason, the thunder particularly irritated Mr Goddard. All day, as he moved about his duties as ground floor supervisor, he listened to it booming and rolling in the distance, almost lost amid the noise and traffic of the department store. Twice, on some pretext, he took the lift up to the roof-top cafeteria and carefully scanned the sky, searching the horizons for any sign of storm-cloud or turbulence. As usual, however, the sky was a bland, impassive blue, mottled by a few clumps of leisurely cumuli.

This was what worried Mr Goddard. Leaning on the cafeteria railing he could hear the thunder distinctly, cleaving the air only a thousand feet above his head, the huge claps lumbering past like the colliding wing streams of enormous birds. Intermittently the sounds would stop, to re-start a few minutes later.

Mr Goddard was not the only one to notice them – the people at the tables on the terrace were craning up at the sourceless din, as perplexed as himself. Normally Mr Goddard would have exchanged some pleasantry with them – his elderly grey-haired figure in its old-world herringbone suit had been a byword for kindly concern for over twenty years – but today he hurried past without even looking at them. Down on the ground floor he felt less uneasy, but throughout the afternoon, while he roved among the busy counters, patting the children on the head, he listened to the thunder sounding faintly in the distance, inexplicable and strangely threatening.

At six o'clock he took up his position in the time-keeper's booth, waited impatiently until the final time card had been stamped, then handed over to the night watchman, and the last of the staff had left for home. As he made his way out, pulling on his ancient overcoat and deerstalker, the clear evening air was still stirred by occasional rumblings.

Mr Goddard's house was less than half a mile away, a small two-storey villa surrounded by tall hedges. Superficially dilapidated though still sound, at first glance it was indistinguishable from any other bachelor residence, although anyone entering the short drive would have noticed one unusual feature – all the windows, both upstairs and down, were securely shuttered. Indeed, they had remained shuttered for so long that the ivy growing across the front of the house had matted itself through the wooden slats, here and there pulling apart the rotting wood.

Closer inspection at these points would have revealed, behind the dusty panes, the interlocking diagonals of steel grilles.

Collecting a bottle of milk off the doorstep, Mr Goddard let himself into the kitchen. This was furnished with an armchair and a small couch, and served him as his living room. He busied himself preparing an evening meal. Halfway through, a neighbouring cat, a regular visitor, scratched at the door and was allowed in. They sat at the table together, the cat on its customary cushion up on one of the chairs, watching Mr Goddard with its small, hard eyes.

Shortly before eight o'clock Mr Goddard began his invariable evening routine. Opening the kitchen door, he glanced up and down the side entrance, then locked it behind him, securing both windows and door with a heavy drop bar. He next entered the hall, ushering the cat before him, and began his inspection of the house.

This was done with great care, using the cat as his sixth sense. Mr Goddard watched it carefully, noting its reactions as it wandered softly through the deserted rooms, singing remotely to itself.

The house was completely empty. Upstairs the floorboards were bare, the windows without curtains, lamp bulbs shadeless. Dust gathered in the corners and stained the fraying Victorian wallpaper. All the fireplaces had been bricked up, and the bare stonework above the mantels showed that the chimneys had been solidly filled in.

Once or twice Mr Goddard tested the grilles, which effectively turned the room into a succession of steel cages. Satisfied, he made his way downstairs and went into the front room, noting that nothing was amiss. He steered the cat into the kitchen, poured it a bowl of milk as a reward and slipped back into the hallway, latching the door behind him.

One room he had still not entered – the real lounge. Taking a key from his pocket, Mr Goddard turned the lock and let himself through.

Like the other rooms, this was bare and unfurnished, except for a wooden chair and a large black safe that stood with its back to one wall. The other distinctive feature was a single light bulb of considerable power suspended on an intricate pulley system from the centre of the ceiling.

Buttoning his jacket, Mr Goddard went over to the safe. Massive and ancient, it was approximately three feet wide and deep. Once it had been painted a dark bottle green, but by now most of the paint had peeled, revealing a dull black steel. A huge door, the full width and depth of the safe, was recessed into its face.

Beside the safe was the chair, a celluloid visor slung over its back. Mr Goddard pulled this on, giving himself the look of a refined elderly counterfeiter about to settle down to a hard evening's work. From his key chain he selected a small silver key, and fitted it into the lock. Turning the handle full circle, he drew the caissons back into the door, then pulled steadily with both hands and swung it open.

The safe was without shelves, a single continuous vault. Occupying the entire cavity, separated from the three-inch-thick walls by a narrow interval, was a large black tin document box.

Pausing to regain his breath, Mr Goddard heard a dull rumble of thunder sound through the darkness beyond the shuttered windows. Frowning involuntarily, he suddenly noticed a feathery thudding noise coming from inside the safe. He bent down and was just in time to see a large white moth emerge from the space above the document box, ricocheting erratically off the roof, at each impact sending a dull echo reverberating through the tin walls.

Mr Goddard smiled broadly to himself, as if divining something that had puzzled him all day. Leaning on the safe, he watched the moth circle the light, frantically shaking to pieces its damaged wings. Finally it plunged into one of the walls and fell stunned to the floor. Mr Goddard went over and swept it through the door with his foot, then returned to the safe. Reaching inside, with great care he lifted the document box out by the handles fastened to the centre of the lid.

The box was heavy. It required all Mr Goddard's efforts to steer it out without banging it against the safe, but with long practice he withdrew it in a single motion. He placed it gently on the floor, pulled up the chair and lowered the light until it was a few inches above his head. Releasing a catch below the lid, he tilted it back on its hinges.

Below him, brightly reflected in the light, was what appeared to be an elaborate doll's house. In fact, however, it was a whole complex of miniature buildings, perfectly constructed models with carefully detailed roof-tops and cornices, walls and brickwork so exactly duplicating the original that but for the penumbral figure of Mr Goddard looming out of the darkness they might have passed for real buildings and houses. The doors and windows were exquisitely worked, fitted with minute lattices and panes, each the size of a soap flake. The paving stones, the street furniture, the camber of the roadways, were perfect scale reductions.

The tallest building in the box was about fourteen inches high, containing six storeys. It stood at one corner of a crossroads that traversed the centre of the box, and was obviously a replica of the department store at which Mr Goddard worked. Its interior had been furnished and decorated with as much care as its external façade; through the windows could be seen the successive floors laid out with their miniature merchandise, rolls of carpet on the first, lingerie and women's fashions on the second, furniture on the third. The roof-top cafeteria had been equipped with small metal chairs and tables, set with plates, cutlery and bowls of tiny flowers.

On the corners to the left and right of the store were the bank and supermarket, with the town hall diagonally opposite. Again, these were perfect replicas of their originals: in the drawers behind the counters in the bank were bundles of minuscule banknotes, a glitter of coins like heaps of silver dust. The interior of the supermarket was an exercise in a thousand virtuosities. The stalls were stacked with pyramids of tins and coloured packets almost too small for the eye to distinguish.

Beyond the buildings dominating the crossroads were the lesser shops and premises lining the side-streets – the drapers, a public house, shoeshops and tobacconists. Looking around, the entire town seemed to stretch away into the distance. The walls of the box had been painted so skilfully, with such clever control of perspective, that it was almost impossible to tell where the models ended and the walls intervened. The micro-cosmic world was so perfect in its own right, the illusion of reality so absolute that it appeared to be the town itself, its very dimensions those of reality.

Suddenly, through the warm early morning sunlight, a shadow moved. The glass door of one of the shoeshops opened, a figure stepped out for a moment onto the pavement, glanced up and down the still deserted street, then retreated into the dark recesses of the shop's interior. A middle-aged man in a grey suit and white collar, it was presumably the manager opening the shop in the morning. In agreement with this, a second doorway opened farther down the street; and this time a woman came out of a hairdresser's, and began to wind down the blind. She wore a black skirt and pink plastic smock. As she went back into the salon she waved to someone walking down the street towards the town hall.

More figures emerged from the doorways, strolled along the pavements talking to each other, starting the day's business. Soon the streets were full; the offices over the shops came to life, typists moving in among the desks and filing cabinets. Signs were put up or taken down; calendars moved on. The first customers arrived at the department store and supermarket, ambled past the fresh counter displays. At the town hall clerks sat at their ledgers, in their private offices behind the oak panelling the senior officials had their first cups of tea. Like a well-ordered hive, the town came to life.

High above it all, his gigantic face hidden in the shadows, Mr Goddard quietly watched his lilliputian scene like a discreet aged Gulliver. He sat forward, the green shade shielding his eyes, hands clasped lightly in his lap. Occasionally he would lean over a few inches to catch a closer glimpse of the figures below him, or tilt his head to see into one of the shops or offices. His face showed no emotion, he seemed content to be simply a spectator. Two feet away the hundreds of tiny figures moved about their lives, and a low murmur of street noises crept out into the room.

The tallest of the figures were no more than an inch and a half in height, yet their perfectly formed faces were completely furnished with character and expression. Most of them Mr Goddard knew by sight, many by name. He saw Mrs Hamilton, the lingerie buyer, late for work, hurrying down the alleyway to the staff entrance. Through a window he could see the managing director's office, where Mr Sellings was delivering his usual weekly pep-talk to a trio of department heads. In the streets outside were scores of regular customers Mr Goddard had known intimately for years, buying their groceries, posting their letters, exchanging gossip.

As the scene below him unfolded, Mr Goddard gradually edged nearer the box, taking a particular interest in two or three of the score of separate tableaux. An interesting feature of his vantage point was that by some freak of architecture or perspective it afforded him a multiplicity of perfect angles by which to observe almost every one of the diminutive figures. The high windows of the bank provided him with a view of each of the clerks at their counters; a transom beyond exposed the strongroom, the rows of deposit boxes on their shelves behind the grille, one of the junior cashiers amusing himself by reading the labels. The department store, with its wide floors, he could cover merely by inclining his head. The smaller shops along the streets were just as exposed. Rarely more than two rooms deep, their rear windows and fanlights provided him all the access he needed. Nothing escaped Mr Goddard's scrutiny. In the back alleys he could see the stacked bicycles, the charwomen's mops in their buckets by the basement doors, the dustbins half-filled with refuse.

The first scene to attract Mr Goddard's attention was one involving the stockroom supervisor at the store, Mr Durrant. Casting his eye at random through the bank, Mr Goddard noticed him in the manager's office, leaning across the latter's desk and explaining something earnestly. Usually Durrant would have been a member of the group being harangued by Mr Sellings, and only urgent business could have taken him to the bank. The manager, however, appeared to be doing what he could to get rid of Durrant, avoiding his face and fiddling with some papers. Suddenly Durrant lost his temper. Tie askew, he began to shout angrily. The manager accepted this silently, shaking his head slowly with a bleak smile. Finally Durrant strode to the door, hesitated with a look of bitter reproach, and stalked out.

Leaving the bank, and apparently oblivious of his duties at the store, he walked briskly down the High Street. Stopping at the hairdresser's, he went in and made his way through to a private booth at the back where a large man in a check suit, still wearing a green trilby, was being shaved. Mr Goddard watched their conversation through a skylight above them. The man in the chair, the local bookmaker, lay back silently behind his lather until Durrant finished talking, then with a casual flip of one hand waved him to a seat.

Putting two and two together, Mr Goddard waited with interest for their conversation to be resumed. What he had just seen confirmed suspicions recently prompted by Durrant's distracted manner.

However, just as the bookmaker pulled off the towel and stood up, something more important caught Mr Goddard's eye.

\*       \*       \*

Directly behind the department store was a small cul-de-sac sealed off from the alleyway leading in from the street by high wooden doors. It was piled with old packing cases and miscellaneous refuse, and its far side was formed by the rear wall of the box, a sheer cliff that rose straight up into the distant glare above. The glazed windows of a service lift shaft overlooked the yard, topped on the fifth floor by a small balcony.

It was this balcony that had attracted Mr Goddard's attention. Two men were crouched on it, manipulating a long wooden contraption that Mr Goddard identified as a telescopic ladder. Together they hoisted it into the air, and by pulling on a system of ropes extended it against the wall to a point about fifteen feet above their heads. Satisfied, they lashed the lower end securely to the balcony railings; then one of them mounted the ladder and climbed up to its topmost rung, arms outstretched across the wall, high over the yard below.

*They were trying to escape from the box!* Mr Goddard hunched forward, watching them with astonishment. The top of the ladder was still seven or eight inches from the overhanging rim of the box, thirty or forty feet away from the men on the balcony, but their industry was impressive. He watched them motionlessly while they tightened the guyropes.

Dimly, in the distance, midnight chimed. Mr Goddard looked at his watch, then without a further glance into the box pushed the lamp towards the ceiling and lowered the lid. He stood up and carried the box carefully to the safe, stowed it away, and sealed the door. Switching off the light, he let himself noiselessly out of the room.

The next day at the store Mr Goddard made his usual rounds, dispensing his invariable prescription of friendly chatter and *bonhomie* to sales assistants and customers alike, making full use of the countless trivial insights he had been provided with the previous evening. All the while he kept a constant lookout for Mr Durrant; reluctant to interfere, he was nevertheless afraid that without some drastic re-direction of the man's fortunes his entanglement with the bookmaker would soon end in tragedy.

No one in the stockrooms had seen Durrant all morning, but shortly after 12 o'clock Mr Goddard spotted him hurrying down the street past the main entrance. Durrant stopped, glanced around indecisively, then began to wander through the showcases as he pondered something.

Mr Goddard made his way out, and casually sidled up to Durrant.

'Fine day, isn't it?' he remarked. 'Everybody's starting to think about their holidays.'

Durrant nodded absently, examining a display of alpine equipment in the sports-goods window. 'Are they? Good.'

'You going away, Mr Durrant? South of France again, I suppose.'

'What? No, I don't think we will be this year.' Durrant began to move off, but Mr Goddard caught up with him.

'Sorry to hear that, Mr Durrant. I thought you deserved a good holiday abroad. Nothing the trouble, I hope.' He looked searchingly into Durrant's face. 'If I can help at all, do let me know. I'd be glad to make you a small loan. An old man like me hasn't much use for it.'

Durrant stopped and peered thoughtfully at Mr Goddard. 'That's kind of you, Goddard,' he said at last. 'Very kind.'

Mr Goddard smiled deprecatingly. 'Don't give it a thought. I like to stand by the firm, you know. Forgive me mentioning it, but would fifty be any use to you?'

Durrant's eyes narrowed slightly. 'Yes, it would be a lot of use.' He paused, then asked quietly: 'Are you doing this off your own bat, or did Sellings put you up to it?'

'Put me up to it –?'

Durrant closed the interval between them, and in a harder voice rapped out: 'You must have been following me around for days. You know just about everything about everybody, don't you, Goddard? I've a damn good mind to report you.'

Mr Goddard backed away, wondering how to retrieve the situation. Just then he noticed that they were alone at the showcases. The groups of people who usually milled around the windows were pressing into the alleyway beside the store; there was a lot of shouting in the distance.

'What the hell's going on?' Durrant snapped. He joined the crowd in the alleyway and peered over the heads.

Mr Goddard hurried back into the store. All the assistants were craning over their shoulders and whispering to each other; some had left the counters and were gathering around the service doors at the rear.

Mr Goddard pushed his way through, someone was calling for the police and a woman from the personnel department came down in the freight lift carrying a pair of blankets.

The commissionaire holding the throng back let Mr Goddard past. In the yard outside was a group of fifteen or twenty people, all looking up at the fifth-floor balcony. Tied to the railings was the lower half of a home-made ladder, jutting up into the air at an angle of 45 degrees. The top section, a limb about twelve feet long, had been lashed to the upper end, but the joint had failed, and the section now hung down vertically, swinging slowly from side to side above the heads of the people in the yard.

With an effort Mr Goddard controlled his voice. Someone had covered the two bodies with the blankets, and a man kneeling beside them – presumably a doctor – was shaking his head slowly.

'What I can't understand,' one of the assistant managers was whispering to the commissionaire, 'is where they were trying to climb to. The ladder must have pointed straight up into the air.'

The commissionaire nodded. 'Mr Masterman and Mr Streatfield, too. What would they be building a ladder for, senior men like that?'

Mr Goddard followed the line of the ladder up towards the sky. The rear wall of the yard was only seven or eight feet high, beyond it lay the galvanized iron roof of a bicycle shed and an open car park. The ladder had pointed nowhere, but the compulsion driving the two men had been blind and irresistible.

That evening Mr Goddard made the rounds of his house more perfunctorily than usual, glanced briefly into the empty rooms, closing the doors before the cat had a chance to do more than test the air. He shut it into the kitchen, then hurried off to unlock the safe.

Carrying the box out into the centre of the floor, he unlatched the lid.

As the town came to life below him he scrutinized it carefully, moving up and down the miniature streets, peering through all the windows in turn, fixing the identity and role of as many as possible of the tiny inhabitants. Like a thousand shuttles weaving an infinitely intricate pattern, they threaded through the shops and offices, in and out of countless doorways, every one of them touching a score of others somewhere among the pavements and arcades, adding another stitch to the tapestry of incident and motive ravelling their lives together. Mr Goddard traced each thread, trying to detect any shift in direction, and untoward interlocking of behaviour.

The pattern, he realized, was changing. As yet it was undefined, but slight variations were apparent, subtle shifts in the relationships between the people in the box: rival storekeepers seemed to be on intimate terms, strangers had begun to talk to each other, there was a great deal of unnecessary and purposeless activity.

Mr Goddard searched for a focus, an incident that would unmask the sources of the new pattern. He examined the balcony behind the lift shaft, watching for any further attempts to escape. The ladder had been removed but nothing had been done to replace it. Other potential escape routes – the roof of the cinema, the clock tower of the town hall – revealed no further clues.

One incident alone stood out, puzzling him even more. This was the unique spectacle, in a quiet alcove of the billiards saloon, of Mr Durrant introducing his bank manager to the bookmaker. The trio were still in earnest conversation when he closed the box reluctantly at two o'clock the next morning.

Over the following days Mr Goddard watched the crowds passing through the store, waiting to detect, as it were in the macrocosm, some of the tendencies he had observed in the box. His sixty-fifth birthday, soon due to fall, was a handy topic which provided ready conversational access to the senior members of the staff. Curiously, however, the friendly responses he expected were missing; the exchanges were brief, sometimes almost to the point of rudeness. This he put down to the changed atmosphere in the store since the deaths of the two ladder climbers. At the inquest there had been a confused hysterical outburst by one of the saleswomen, and the coroner had cryptically remarked that it appeared that information was being deliberately withheld. A murmur of agreement had spontaneously swept the entire room, but what exactly he meant no one seemed to know.

Another symptom of this uneasiness was the rash of notices that were handed in. Almost a third of the staff were due to leave, most of them for reasons that were patently little more than excuses. When Mr Goddard probed for the real reasons he discovered that few people were aware of them. The motivation was purely unconscious.

As if to emphasize this intrusion of the irrational, one evening as Mr Goddard was leaving the store he saw the bank manager standing high above the street on the clock tower of the town hall, gazing up into the sky.

During the next week little occurred within the box to clarify the situation. The shifting and regrouping of relationships continued. He saw the bank manager more and more in the company of the book-maker, and realized that he had been completely mistaken in assuming that Durrant was under pressure of his gambling debts – in fact, his role seemed to be that of intermediary between the bookmaker and bank manager, who had at last been persuaded to join them in their scheme.

That some sort of conspiracy was afoot he was sure. At first he assumed that a mass break-out from the box was being planned, but nothing confirmed this. Rather he felt that some obscure compulsion, as yet unidentified to itself, was generating within the minds of those in the box, reflected in the bizarre and unpredictable behaviour of their counterparts in the outside world. Unconscious of their own motives and only half aware of themselves, his fellow employees at the store had begun to resemble the pieces of some enormous puzzle, like disjointed images fixed in the fragments of a shattered mirror. In conclusion he decided on a policy of *laissez-faire*. A few more weeks would certainly reveal the sources of the conspiracy.

Unfortunately, sooner than Mr Goddard anticipated, events moved forward rapidly to a spectacular crisis.

The day of his sixty-fifth birthday, he made his way to the store half an hour later than usual, and on arrival was told that Mr Sellings wished to see him.

Sellings first offered his congratulations, then launched into a recapitulation of Mr Goddard's years of service to the store, and concluded by wishing him as many years again of contented retirement.

It took Mr Goddard several moments to grasp the real significance of this. Nothing had ever been said to him about his retirement, and he had always assumed that he would stay on until, like many members of the staff, he was well into his seventies.

Collecting himself, he said as much to Sellings. 'I haven't exactly been expecting retirement, Mr Sellings. I think there must have been some mistake.'

Sellings stood up, shaking his head with a quick smile. 'No mistake at all, Mr Goddard, I assure you. As a matter of fact the board carefully considered your case yesterday, and we agreed that you well deserve an uninterrupted rest after all these years.'

Mr Goddard frowned. 'But I don't wish to retire, sir. I've made no plans.'

'Well, now's the time to start.' Sellings was on his way to the door, handshake ready. 'Comfortable pension, little house of your own, the world's your oyster.'

Mr Goddard sat tight, thinking quickly. 'Mr Sellings, I'm afraid I can't accept the board's decision. I'm sure, for the sake of the business, I should stay on in my present post.' The smile had gone from Sellings' face; he looked impatient and irritable. 'If you were to ask the floor managers and assistants, not to speak of the customers, they would all insist that I stay on. They would be very shocked at the suggestion of retirement.'

'Would they?' Sellings asked curtly. 'My information is to the contrary. Believe me, your retirement has come at a very lucky time for you, Mr Goddard. I've had a great number of complaints recently that otherwise I should have been obliged to act upon. Promptly and drastically.'

As he left the accounts department for the last time Mr Goddard numbly repeated these words to himself. He found them almost impossible to believe. And yet Sellings was a responsible man who would never take a single opinion on such an important matter. Somehow, though, he was colossally in error.

Or was he? As he made his farewell rounds, half-hoping that the news of his sudden retirement would rally support to him, Mr Goddard realized that Sellings was right. Floor by floor, department by department, counter by counter, he recognized the same inner expression, the same attitude of tacit approval. *They were all glad he was going.* Not one of them showed real regret; a good number slipped away before he could shake hands with them, others merely grunted briefly. Several of the older hands, who had known Mr Goddard for twenty or thirty years, seemed slightly embarrassed, but none of them offered a word of sympathy.

Finally, when one group in the furniture department deliberately turned their backs to avoid speaking to him, Mr Goddard cut short his tour. Stunned and humiliated, he collected his few possessions from his locker and made his way out.

It seemed to take him all day to reach his house. Head down, he walked slowly along the quiet side-streets, oblivious of the passers-by, pathetically trying to absorb this blow to all he had assumed about himself for so many years. His interest in other people was sincere and unaffected, he knew without doubt. Countless times he had gone out of his way to be of help to others, had put endless thought into arriving at the best solutions to their problems. But with what result? He had aroused only contempt, envy and distrust.

On his doorstep the cat waited patiently. Surprised to see him so early it ran forward, purring and rubbing itself against his legs as he latched the gate. But Mr Goddard failed to notice it. Fumbling, he unlocked the kitchen door, closed it automatically behind him. Taking off his coat, he made himself some tea, and without thinking poured a saucer of milk for the cat. He watched it drink, still trying helplessly to understand the antagonism he had aroused in so many people.

Suddenly he pushed his tea away and went to the door. Without bothering to go upstairs he made his way straight into the lounge. Switching on the light, he stared heavily at the safe. Somewhere here, he knew, was the reason for his dismissal that morning. If only his eyes were sharp enough, he would discover it.

Unlocking the safe, he unclasped the door and pulled it back abruptly, wrenching himself slightly against its great inertia. Impatient to open the box he ignored the twinge in his shoulder, reached down and seized the butterfly handles.

As he swung the box out of the safe he realized that its weight was, momentarily, too much for him. Trying to brace himself, he edged one knee under the box and leaned his elbows on the lid, his shoulder against the safe.

The position was awkward, and he could only support it for a few seconds. Heaving again at the box, in an effort to replace it in the safe, he suddenly began to feel dizzy. A small spiral revolved before his eyes, gradually thickening into a deep black whirlpool that filled his head.

Before he could restrain it, the box tore itself from his hands and plunged to the floor with a violent metallic clatter.

Kneeling beside the safe, Mr Goddard slumped back limply against the wall, head lolling onto his chest.

The box lay on its side, just within the circle of light. The impact had forced the catches on the lid, and this was now open; a single narrow beam reflected off the under-surface into the interior of the box.

For a few minutes the room was quiet, except for the laboured uneven sounds of Mr Goddard's breathing. Then, almost imperceptibly, something moved in the interval between the lid and the floor. A small figure stepped tentatively out of the shadow, peered around itself in the full glare of the light, and disappeared again. Ten seconds later three more figures emerged, followed by others. In small groups they spread out across the floor, their tiny legs and arms rippling in the light. Behind them a score more appeared, pressing out in a solid stream, pushing past each other to escape from the box. Soon the circle of light was alive with swarms of the tiny figures, flickering like minnows in a floodlit pool.

In the darkness by the corner, the door creaked sharply. Together, the hundreds of figures froze. Eyes glinting suspiciously, the head of Mr

Goddard's cat swung round into the room. For a moment it paused, assessing the scene before it.

A sharp cry hissed through its teeth. With vicious speed, it bounded forward.

It was several hours later that Mr Goddard pulled himself slowly to his feet. Leaning weakly against the safe, he looked down at the upended safe beneath the bright cone of light. Carefully collecting himself, he rubbed his cheekbones and painfully massaged his chest and shoulders. Then he limped across to the box and steered it back onto its base. Gingerly, he lifted the lid and peered inside.

Abruptly he dropped the lid, glanced around the floor, swinging the light so that it swept the far corners. Then he turned and hurried out into the hall, switched on the light and examined the floor carefully, along the skirting boards and behind the grilles.

Over his shoulder he noticed that the kitchen door was open. He crossed to it and stepped in on tiptoe, eyes ranging between the table and chair legs, behind the broom and coal bucket.

'Sinbad!' Mr Goddard shouted.

Startled, the cat dropped the tiny object between its paws and backed away below the couch.

Mr Goddard bent down. He stared hard at the object for a few seconds, then stood up and leaned against the cupboard, his eyes closing involuntarily.

The cat pounced, its teeth flickering at its paws. It gulped noisily.

'Sinbad,' Mr Goddard said in a quieter voice. He gazed listlessly at the cat, finally stepped over to the door.

'Come outside,' he called to it.

The cat followed him, its tail whipping slowly from side to side. They walked down the pathway to the gate. Mr Goddard looked at his watch. It was 2.45, early afternoon. The houses around him were silent, the sky a distant, pacific blue. Here and there sunlight was reflected off one of the upstairs bay windows, but the street was motionless, its stillness absolute and unbroken.

Mr Goddard gestured the cat onto the pavement and closed the gate behind it.

Together they walked out into an empty world.

**· 1960**

# STUDIO 5, THE STARS

Every evening during the summer at Vermilion Sands the insane poems of my beautiful neighbour drifted across the desert to me from Studio 5, The Stars, the broken skeins of coloured tape unravelling in the sand like the threads of a dismembered web. All night they would flutter around the buttresses below the terrace, entwining themselves through the balcony railings, and by morning, before I swept them away, they would hang across the south face of the villa like a vivid cerise bougainvillaea.

Once, after I had been to Red Beach for three days, I returned to find the entire terrace filled by an enormous cloud of coloured tissues, which burst through the french windows as I opened them and pushed into the lounge, spreading across the furniture and bookcases like the delicate tendrils of some vast and gentle plant. For days afterwards I found fragments of the poems everywhere.

I complained several times, walking the three hundred yards across the dunes to deliver a letter of protest, but no one ever answered the bell. I had only once seen my neighbour, on the day she arrived, driving down the Stars in a huge El Dorado convertible, her long hair swept behind her like the head-dress of a goddess. She had vanished in a glimmer of speed, leaving me with a fleeting image of sudden eyes in an ice-white face.

Why she refused to answer her bell I could never understand, but I noticed that each time I walked across to Studio 5 the sky was full of sand-rays, wheeling and screeching like anguished bats. On the last occasion, as I stood by her black glass front door, deliberately pressing the bell into its socket, a giant sand-ray had fallen out of the sky at my feet.

But this, as I realized later, was the crazy season at Vermilion Sands, when Tony Sapphire heard a sand-ray singing, and I saw the god Pan drive by in a Cadillac.

Who was Aurora Day, I often ask myself now. Sweeping across the placid out-of-season sky like a summer comet, she seems to have appeared in a different role to each of us at the colony along the Stars. To me, at first, she was a beautiful neurotic disguised as a *femme fatale*, but Raymond Mayo saw her as one of Salvador Dali's exploding madonnas, an enigma serenely riding out the apocalypse. To Tony Sapphire and the rest of her followers along the beach she was a reincarnation of Astarte herself, a diamond-eyed time-child thirty centuries old.

I can remember clearly how I found the first of her poems. After dinner one evening I was resting on the terrace – something I did most of the time at Vermilion Sands – when I noticed a streamer lying on the sand below the railing. A few yards away were several others, and for half an hour I watched them being blown lightly across the dunes. A car's headlamps shone in the drive at Studio 5, and I assumed that a new tenant had moved into the villa, which had stood empty for several months.

Finally, out of curiosity, I straddled the rail, jumped down on to the sand and picked up one of the ribbons of pink tissue. It was a fragment about three feet long, the texture of rose petal, so light that it began to flake and dissolve in my fingers.

Holding it up I read: ... COMPARE THEE TO A SUMMER'S DAY, THOU ART MORE LOVELY ...

I let it flutter away into the darkness below the balcony, then bent down and carefully picked up another, disentangling it from one of the buttresses.

Printed along it in the same ornate neo-classical type was: ... SET KEEL TO BREAKERS, FORTH ON THAT GODLY SEA ...

I looked over my shoulder. The light over the desert had gone now, and three hundred yards away my neighbour's villa was lit like a spectral crown. The exposed quartz veins in the sand reefs along the Stars rippled like necklaces in the sweeping headlights of the cars driving into Red Beach.

I glanced at the tape again.

Shakespeare and Ezra Pound? My neighbour had the most curious tastes. My interest fading, I returned to the terrace.

Over the next few days the streamers continued to blow across the dunes, for some reason always starting in the evening, when the lights of the traffic illuminated the lengths of coloured gauze. But to begin with I hardly noticed them – I was then editing *Wave IX*, an avant-garde poetry review, and the studio was full of auto-tapes and old galley proofs. Nor was I particularly surprised to find I had a poetess for my neighbour. Almost all the studios along the Stars are occupied by painters and poets – the majority abstract and non-productive. Most of us were suffering from various degrees of beach fatigue, that chronic malaise which exiles the victim to a limbo of endless sunbathing, dark glasses and afternoon terraces.

Later, however, the streamers drifting across the sand became rather more of a nuisance. When the protest notes achieved nothing I went over to my neighbour's villa with a view to seeing her in person. On this last occasion, after a dying ray had plummeted out of the sky and nearly stung me in its final spasm, I realized that there was little chance of reaching her.

A hunchbacked chauffeur with a club foot and a twisted face like a senile faun's was cleaning the cerise Cadillac in the drive. I went over to him and pointed to the strands of tissue trailing through the first-floor windows and falling on to the desert below.

'These tapes are blowing all over my villa,' I told him. 'Your mistress must have one of her VT sets on open sequence.'

He eyed me across the broad hood of the El Dorado, sat down in the driving seat and took a small flute from the dashboard.

As I walked round to him he began to play some high, irritating chords. I waited until he had finished and asked in a louder voice: 'Do you mind telling her to close the windows?'

He ignored me, his lips pressed moodily to the flute. I bent down and was about to shout into his ear when a gust of wind swirled across one of the dunes just beyond the drive, in an instant whirled over the gravel, flinging up a miniature tornado of dust and ash. This miniature tornado completely enclosed us, blinding my eyes and filling my mouth with grit. Arms shielding my face, I moved away towards the drive, the long streamers whipping around me.

As suddenly as it had started, the squall vanished. The dust stilled and faded, leaving the air as motionless as it had been a few moments previously. I saw that I had backed about thirty yards down the drive, and to my astonishment realized that the Cadillac and chauffeur had disappeared, although the garage door was still open.

My head rang strangely, and I felt irritable and short of breath. I was about to approach the house again, annoyed at having been refused entry and left to suffer the full filthy impact of the dust squall, when I heard the thin piping refrain sound again into the air.

Low, but clear and strangely menacing, it sang in my ears, the planes of sound shifting about me in the air. Looking around for its source, I noticed the dust flicking across the surface of the dunes on either side of the drive.

Without waiting, I turned on my heel and hurried back to my villa.

Angry with myself for having been made such a fool of, and resolved to press some formal complaint, I first went around the terrace, picking up all the strands of tissue and stuffing them into the disposal chute. I climbed below the villa and cut away the tangled masses of streamers.

Cursorily, I read a few of the tapes at random. All printed the same erratic fragments, intact phrases from Shakespeare, Wordsworth, Keats and Eliot. My neighbour's VT set appeared to have a drastic memory fault, and instead of producing a variant on the classical model the selector head was simply regurgitating a dismembered version of the model itself. For a moment I thought seriously of telephoning the IBM agency in Red Beach and asking them to send a repair man round.

That evening, however, I finally spoke to my neighbour in person.

I had gone to sleep at about eleven, and an hour or so later something woke me. A bright moon was at apogee, moving behind strands of pale green cloud that cast a thin light over the desert and the Stars. I stepped out on to the veranda and immediately noticed a curiously luminescent glow moving between the dunes. Like the strange music I had heard from the chauffeur's flute, the glow appeared to be sourceless, but I assumed it was cast by the moon shining through a narrow interval between the clouds.

Then I saw her, appearing for a moment among the dunes, strolling across the midnight sand. She wore a long white gown that billowed out behind her, against which her blue hair drifted loosely in the wind like the tail-fan of a paradise bird. Streamers floated about her feet, and overhead two or three purple rays circled endlessly. She walked on, apparently unaware of them, a single light behind her shining through an upstairs window of her villa.

Belting my dressing gown, I leaned against a pillar and watched her quietly, for the moment forgiving her the streamers and her ill-trained chauffeur. Occasionally she disappeared behind one of the green-shadowed dunes, her head raised slightly, moving from the boulevard towards the sand reefs on the edge of the fossil lake.

She was about a hundred yards from the nearest sand reef, a long inverted gallery of winding groynes and over-hanging grottoes, when something about her straight path and regular unvarying pace made me wonder whether she might in fact be sleepwalking.

I hesitated briefly, watching the rays circling around her head, then jumped over the rail and ran across the sand towards her.

The quartz flints stung at my bare feet, but I managed to reach her just as she neared the edge of the reef. I broke into a walk beside her and touched her elbow.

Three feet above my head the rays spat and whirled in the darkness. The strange luminosity that I had assumed came from the moon seemed rather to emanate from her white gown.

My neighbour was not somnambulating, as I thought, but lost in some deep reverie or dream. Her black eyes stared opaquely in front of her, her slim white-skinned face like a marble mask, motionless and without expression. She looked round at me sightlessly, one hand gesturing me away. Suddenly she stopped and glanced down at her feet, abruptly becoming aware of herself and her midnight walk. Her eyes cleared and she saw the mouth of the sand reef. She stepped back involuntarily, the light radiating from her gown increasing with her alarm.

Overhead the rays soared upwards into the air, their arcs wider now that she was awake.

'Sorry to startle you,' I apologized. 'But you were getting too close to the reef.'

She pulled away from me, her long black eyebrows arching.

'What?' she said uncertainly. 'Who are you?' To herself, as if completing her dream, she murmured sotto voce: 'Oh God, Paris, choose me, not

Minerva –' She broke off and stared at me wildly, her carmine lips fretting. She strode off across the sand, the rays swinging like pendulums through the dim air above her, taking with her the pool of amber light.

I waited until she reached her villa and turned away. Glancing at the ground, I noticed something glitter in the small depression formed by one of her footprints. I bent down, picked up a small jewel, a perfectly cut diamond of a single carat, then saw another in the next footprint. Hurrying forwards, I picked up half-a-dozen of the jewels, and was about to call out after her disappearing figure when I felt something wet in my hand.

Where I had held the jewels in the hollow of my palm now swam a pool of ice-cold dew.

I found out who she was the next day.

After breakfast I was in the bar when I saw the El Dorado turn into the drive. The club-footed chauffeur jumped from the car and hobbled over in his curious swinging gait to the front door. In his black-gloved hand he carried a pink envelope. I let him wait a few minutes, then opened the letter on the step as he went back to the car and sat waiting for me, his engine running.

> *I'm sorry to have been so rude last night. You stepped right into my dream and startled me. Could I make amends by offering you a cocktail? My chauffeur will collect you at noon.*
>
> AURORA DAY

I looked at my watch. It was 11:55. The five minutes, presumably, gave me time to compose myself.

The chauffeur was studying his driving wheel, apparently indifferent to my reaction. Leaving the door open, I stepped inside and put on my beach-jacket. On the way out I slipped a proof copy of *Wave IX* into one of the pockets.

The chauffeur barely waited for me to climb in before moving the big car rapidly down the drive.

'How long are you staying in Vermilion Sands?' I asked, addressing the band of curly russet hair between the peaked cap and black collar.

He said nothing. As we drove along the Stars he suddenly cut out into the oncoming lane and gunned the Cadillac forward in a tremendous burst of speed to overtake a car ahead.

Settling myself, I put the question again and waited for him to reply, then smartly tapped his black serge shoulder.

'Are you deaf, or just rude?'

For a second he took his eyes off the road and glanced back at me. I had a momentary impression of bright red pupils, ribald eyes that regarded me with a mixture of contempt and unconcealed savagery. Out of the side of his mouth came a sudden cackling stream of violent imprecations, a short filthy blast that sent me back into my seat.

*     *     *

He jumped out when we reached Studio 5 and opened the door for me, beckoning me up the black marble steps like an attendant spider ushering a very small fly into a particularly large web.

Once inside the doorway he seemed to disappear. I walked through the softly lit hall towards an interior pool where a fountain played and white carp circled tirelessly. Beyond it, in the lounge, I could see my neighbour reclining on a chaise longue, her white gown spread around her like a fan, the jewels embroidered into it glittering in the fountain light.

As I sat down she regarded me curiously, putting away a slender volume bound in yellow calf which appeared to be a private edition of poems. Scattered across the floor beside her was a miscellaneous array of other volumes, many of which I could identify as recently printed collections and anthologies.

I noticed a few coloured streamers trailing through the curtains by the window, and glanced around to see where she kept her VT set, helping myself to a cocktail off the low table between us.

'Do you read a lot of poetry?' I asked, indicating the volumes around her.

She nodded. 'As much as I can bear to.'

I laughed. 'I know what you mean. I have to read rather more than I want.' I took a copy of *Wave IX* from my pocket and passed it to her. 'Have you come across this one?'

She glanced at the title page, her manner moody and autocratic. I wondered why she had bothered to ask me over. 'Yes, I have. Appalling, isn't it? "Paul Ransom",' she noted. 'Is that you? You're the editor? How interesting.'

She said it with a peculiar inflection, apparently considering some possible course of action. For a moment she watched me reflectively. Her personality seemed totally dissociated, her awareness of me varying abruptly from one level to another, like light-changes in a bad motion picture. However, although her mask-like face remained motionless, I none the less detected a quickening of interest.

'Well, tell me about your work. You must know so much about what is wrong with modern poetry. Why is it all so bad?'

I shrugged. 'I suppose it's principally a matter of inspiration. I used to write a fair amount myself years ago, but the impulse faded as soon as I could afford a VT set. In the old days a poet had to sacrifice himself in order to master his medium. Now that technical mastery is simply a question of pushing a button, selecting metre, rhyme, assonance on a dial, there's no need for sacrifice, no ideal to invent to make the sacrifice worthwhile —'

I broke off. She was watching me in a remarkably alert way, almost as if she were going to swallow me.

Changing the tempo, I said: 'I've read quite a lot of your poetry, too.

Forgive me mentioning it, but I think there's something wrong with your Verse-Transcriber.'

Her face snapped and she looked away from me irritably. 'I haven't got one of those dreadful machines. Heavens above, you don't think *I* would use one?'

'Then where do the tapes come from?' I asked. 'The streamers that drift across every evening. They're covered with fragments of verse.'

Off-handedly, she said: 'Are they? Oh, I didn't know.' She looked down at the volumes scattered about on the floor. 'Although I should be the last person to write verse, I have been forced to recently. Through sheer necessity, you see, to preserve a dying art.'

She had baffled me completely. As far as I could remember, most of the poems on the tapes had already been written.

She glanced up and gave me a vivid smile.

'I'll send you some.'

The first ones arrived the next morning. They were delivered by the chauffeur in the pink Cadillac, neatly printed on quarto vellum and sealed by a floral ribbon. Most of the poems submitted to me come through the post on computer punch-tape, rolled up like automat tickets, and it was certainly a pleasure to receive such elegant manuscripts.

The poems, however, were impossibly bad. There were six in all, two Petrarchan sonnets, an ode and three free-form longer pieces. All were written in the same hectoring tone, at once minatory and obscure, like the oracular deliriums of an insane witch. Their overall import was strangely disturbing, not so much for the content of the poems as for the deranged mind behind them. Aurora Day was obviously living in a private world which she took very seriously indeed. I decided that she was a wealthy neurotic able to over-indulge her private fantasies.

I flipped through the sheets, smelling the musk-like scent that misted up from them. Where had she unearthed this curious style, these archaic mannerisms, the 'arise, earthly seers, and to thy ancient courses pen now thy truest vows'? Mixed up in some of the metaphors were odd echoes of Milton and Virgil. In fact, the whole tone reminded me of the archpriestess in the Aeneid who lets off blistering tirades whenever Aeneas sits down for a moment to relax.

I was still wondering what exactly to do with the poems – promptly on nine the next morning the chauffeur had delivered a second batch – when Tony Sapphire called to help me with the make-up of the next issue. Most of the time he spent at his beach-chalet at Lagoon West, programming an automatic novel, but he put in a day or two each week on *Wave IX*.

I was checking the internal rhyme chains in an IBM sonnet sequence of Xero Paris's as he arrived. While I held the code chart over the sonnets, checking the rhyme lattices, he picked up the sheets of pink quarto on which Aurora's poems were printed.

'Delicious scent,' he commented, fanning the sheets through the air. 'One way to get round an editor.' He started to read the first of the poems, then frowned and put it down.

'Extraordinary. What are they?'

'I'm not altogether sure,' I admitted. 'Echoes in a stone garden.'

Tony read the signature at the bottom of the sheets. '"Aurora Day." A new subscriber, I suppose. She probably thinks *Wave IX* is the *VT Times*. But what is all this – "nor psalms, nor canticles, nor hollow register to praise the queen of night –"?' He shook his head. 'What are they supposed to be?'

I smiled at him. Like most other writers and poets, he had spent so long sitting in front of his VT set that he had forgotten the period when poetry was actually handspun.

'They're poems, of a sort, obviously.'

'Do you mean she wrote these herself?'

I nodded. 'It has been done that way. In fact the method enjoyed quite a vogue for twenty or thirty centuries. Shakespeare tried it, Milton, Keats and Shelley – it worked reasonably well then.'

'But not now,' Tony said. 'Not since the VT set. How can you compete with an IBM heavy-duty logomatic analogue? Look at this one, for heaven's sake. It sounds like T.S. Eliot. She can't be serious.'

'You may be right. Perhaps the girl's pulling my leg.'

'Girl. She's probably sixty and tipples her eau de cologne. Sad. In some insane way they may mean something.'

'Hold on,' I told him. I was pasting down one of the Xero's satirical pastiches of Rupert Brooke and was six lines short. I handed Tony the master tape and he played it into the IBM, set the metre, rhyme scheme, verbal pairs, and then switched on, waited for the tape to chunter out of the delivery head, tore off six lines and passed them back to me. I didn't even need to read them.

For the next two hours we worked hard. At dusk we had completed over one thousand lines and broke off for a well-earned drink. We moved on to the terrace and sat, in the cool evening light, watching the colours melting across the desert, listening to the sand-rays cry in the darkness by Aurora's villa.

'What are all these streamers lying around under here?' Tony asked. He pulled one towards him, caught the strands as they broke in his hand and steered them on to the glass-topped table.

'"– nor canticles, nor hollow register –"' He read the line out, then released the tissue and let it blow away on the wind.

He peered across the shadow-covered dunes at Studio 5. As usual a single light was burning in one of the upper rooms, illuminating the threads unravelling in the sand as they moved towards us.

Tony nodded. 'So that's where she lives.' He picked up another of the streamers that had coiled itself through the railing and was fluttering instantly at his elbow.

'You know, old sport, you're quite literally under siege.'

I was. During the next days a ceaseless bombardment of ever more obscure and bizarre poems reached me, always in two instalments, the first brought by the chauffeur promptly at nine o'clock each morning, the second that evening when the streamers began to blow across the dusk to me. The fragments of Shakespeare and Pound had gone now, and the streamers carried fragmented versions of the poems delivered earlier in the day, almost as if they represented her working drafts. Examining the tapes carefully I realized that, as Aurora Day had said, they were not produced by a VT set. The strands were too delicate to have passed through the spools and high-speed cams of a computer mechanism, and the lettering along them had not been printed but embossed by some process I was unable to identify.

Each day I read the latest offerings, carefully filed them away in the centre drawer of my desk. Finally, when I had a week's production stacked together, I placed them in a return envelope, addressed it 'Aurora Day, Studio 5, The Stars, Vermilion Sands', and penned a tactful rejection note, suggesting that she would feel ultimately more satisfied if her work appeared in another of the wide range of poetry reviews.

That night I had the first of what was to be a series of highly unpleasant dreams.

Making myself some strong coffee the next morning, I waited blearily for my mind to clear. I went on to the terrace, wondering what had prompted the savage nightmare that had plagued me through the night. The dream had been the first of any kind I had had for several years – one of the pleasant features of beach fatigue is a heavy dreamless sleep, and the sudden irruption of a dream-filled night made me wonder whether Aurora Day, and more particularly her insane poems, were beginning to prey on my mind more than I realized.

My headache took a long time to dissipate. I lay back, watching the Day villa, its windows closed and shuttered, awnings retracted, like a sealed crown. Who was she anyway, I asked myself, and what did she really want?

Five minutes later, I saw the Cadillac swing out of the drive and coast down the Stars towards me.

Not another delivery! The woman was tireless. I waited by the front door, met the driver halfway down the steps and took from him a wax-sealed envelope.

'Look,' I said to him confidentially. 'I'd hate to discourage an emerging talent, but I think you might well use any influence you have on your mistress and, you know, generally . . .' I let the idea hang in front of him, and added: 'By the way, all these streamers that keep blowing across here are getting to be a damn nuisance.'

The chauffeur regarded me out of his red-rimmed foxy eyes, his beaked face contorted in a monstrous grin. Shaking his head sadly, he hobbled back to the car.

As he drove off I opened the letter. Inside was a single sheet of paper.

> Mr Ransom,
> Your rejection of my poems astounds me. I seriously advise you to reconsider your decision. This is no trifling matter. I expect to see the poems printed in your next issue.
>
> AURORA DAY

That night I had another insane dream.

The next selection of poems arrived when I was still in bed, trying to massage a little sanity back into my mind. I climbed out of bed and made myself a large Martini, ignoring the envelope jutting through the door like the blade of a paper spear.

When I had steadied myself I slit it open, and scanned the three short poems included.

They were dreadful. Dimly I wondered how to persuade Aurora that the requisite talent was missing. Holding the Martini in one hand and peering at the poems in the other, I ambled on to the terrace and slumped down in one of the chairs.

With a shout I sprang into the air, knocking the glass out of my hand. I had sat down on something large and spongy, the size of a cushion but with uneven bony contours.

Looking down, I saw an enormous dead sand-ray lying in the centre of the seat, its white-tipped sting, still viable, projecting a full inch from its sheath above the cranial crest.

Jaw clamped angrily, I went straight into my study, slapped the three poems into an envelope with a rejection slip and scrawled across it: 'Sorry, entirely unsuitable. Please try other publications.'

Half an hour later I drove down to Vermilion Sands and mailed it myself. As I came back I felt quietly pleased with myself.

That afternoon a colossal boil developed on my right cheek.

Tony Sapphire and Raymond Mayo came round the next morning to commiserate. Both thought I was being pigheaded and pedantic.

'Print one,' Tony told me, sitting down on the foot of the bed.

'I'm damned if I will,' I said. I stared out across the desert at Studio 5. Occasionally a window moved and caught the sunlight but otherwise I had seen nothing of my neighbour.

Tony shrugged. 'All you've got to do is accept one and she'll be satisfied.'

'Are you sure?' I asked cynically. 'This may be only the beginning. For all we know she may have a dozen epics in the bottom of her suitcase.'

Raymond Mayo wandered over to the window beside me, slipped on his dark glasses and scrutinized the villa. I noticed that he looked even more dapper than usual, dark hair smoothed back, profile adjusted for maximum impact.

'I saw her at the "psycho i" last night,' he mused. 'She had a private balcony upon the mezzanine. Quite extraordinary. They had to stop the floor show twice.' He nodded to himself. 'There's something formless and unstated there, reminded me of Dali's "Cosmogonic Venus". Made me realize how absolutely terrifying all women really are. If I were you I'd do whatever I was told.'

I set my jaw, as far as I could, and shook my head dogmatically. 'Go away. You writers are always pouring scorn on editors, but when things get tough who's the first to break? This is the sort of situation I'm prepared to handle, my whole training and discipline tell me instinctively what to do. That crazy neurotic over there is trying to bewitch me. She thinks she can call down a plague of dead rays, boils and nightmares and I'll surrender my conscience.'

Shaking their heads sadly over my obduracy, Tony and Raymond left me to myself.

Two hours later the boil had subsided as mysteriously as it had appeared. I was beginning to wonder why when a pick-up from The Graphis Press in Vermilion Sands delivered the advance five-hundred of the next issue of *Wave IX*.

I carried the cartons into the lounge, then slit off the wrapping, thinking pleasurably of Aurora Day's promise that she would have her poems published in the next issue. She had failed to realize that I had passed the final pages two days beforehand, and that I could hardly have printed her poems even if I had wanted to.

Opening the pages, I turned to the editorial, another in my series of examinations of the present malaise affecting poetry.

However, in place of the usual half-dozen paragraphs of 10-point type I was astounded to see a single line of 24-point, announcing in italic caps:

### A CALL TO GREATNESS!

I broke off, hurriedly peered at the cover to make sure Graphis had sent me advance copies of the right journal, then raced rapidly through the pages.

The first poem I recognized immediately. I had rejected it only two days earlier. The next three I had also seen and rejected, then came a series that were new to me, all signed 'Aurora Day' and taking the place of the poems I had passed in page proof.

The entire issue had been pirated! Not a single one of the original poems remained, and a completely new make-up had been substituted. I ran back into the lounge and opened a dozen copies. They were all the same.

Ten minutes later I had carried the three cartons out to the incinerator, tipped them in and soaked the copies with petrol, then tossed a match into the centre of the pyre. Simultaneously, a few miles away Graphis Press were doing the same to the remainder of the 5,000 imprint. How the misprinting had occurred they could not explain. They searched out the copy, all on Aurora's typed notepaper, but with editorial markings in my handwriting! My own copy had disappeared, and they soon denied they had ever received it.

As the heavy flames beat into the hot sunlight I thought that through the thick brown smoke I could see a sudden burst of activity coming from my neighbour's house. Windows were opening under the awnings, and the hunchbacked figure of the chauffeur was scurrying along the terrace.

Standing on the roof, her white gown billowing around her like an enormous silver fleece, Aurora Day looked down at me.

Whether it was the large quantity of Martini I had drunk that morning, the recent boil on my cheek or the fumes from the burning petrol, I'm not sure, but as I walked back into the house I felt unsteady, and sat down hazily on the top step, closing my eyes as my brain swam.

After a few seconds my head cleared again. Leaning on my knees, I focused my eyes on the blue glass step between my feet. Cut into the surface in neat letters was:

> *Why so pale and wan, fond lover?*
> *Prithee, why so pale?*

Still too weak to more than register an automatic protest against this act of vandalism, I pulled myself to my feet, taking the door key out of my dressing-gown pocket. As I inserted it into the lock I noticed, inscribed into the brass seat of the lock:

> *Turn the key deftly in the oiled wards.*

There were other inscriptions all over the black leather panelling of the door, cut in the same neat script, the lines crossing each other at random, like filigree decoration around a baroque salver.

Closing the door behind me, I walked into the lounge. The walls seemed darker than usual, and I realized that their entire surface was covered with row upon row of finely cut lettering, endless fragments of verse stretching from ceiling to floor.

I picked my glass off the table and raised it to my lips. The blue crystal bowl had been embossed with the same copperplate lines, spiralling down the stem to the base.

*Drink to me only with thine eyes.*

Everything in the lounge was covered with the same fragments – the desk, lampstands and shades, the bookshelves, the keys of the baby grand, even the lip of the record on the stereogram turntable.

Dazed, I raised my hand to my face, in horror saw that the surface of my skin was interlaced by a thousand tattoos, writhing and coiling across my hands and arms like insane serpents.

Dropping my glass, I ran to the mirror over the fireplace, saw my face covered with the same tattooing, a living manuscript in which the ink still ran, the letters running and changing as if the pen still cast them.

*You spotted snakes with double tongue . . .*
*Weaving spiders, come not here.*

I flung myself away from the mirror, ran out on to the terrace, my feet slipping in the piles of coloured streamers which the evening wind was carrying over the balcony, then vaulted down over the railing on to the ground below.

I covered the distance between our villas in a few moments, raced up the darkening drive to the black front door. It opened as my hand reached for the bell, and I plunged through into the crystal hallway.

Aurora Day was waiting for me on the chaise longue by the fountain pool, feeding the ancient white fish that clustered around her. As I stepped across to her she smiled quietly to the fish and whispered to them.

'Aurora!' I cried. 'For heaven's sake, I give in! Take anything you want, anything, but leave me alone!'

For a moment she ignored me and went on quietly feeding the fish. Suddenly a thought of terror plunged through my mind. Were the huge white carp now nestling at her fingers once her lovers?

We sat together in the luminescent dusk, the long shadows playing across the purple landscape of Dali's 'Persistence of Memory' on the wall behind Aurora, the fish circling slowly in the fountain beside us.

She had stated her terms: nothing less than absolute control of the magazine, freedom to impose her own policy, to make her own selection of material. Nothing would be printed without her first approval.

'Don't worry,' she had said lightly. 'Our agreement will apply to one issue only.' Amazingly she showed no wish to publish her own poems – the pirated issue had merely been a device to bring me finally to surrender.

'Do you think one issue will be enough?' I asked, wondering what really she would do with it now.

She looked up at me idly, tracing patterns across the surface of the pool with a green-tipped finger. 'It all depends on you and your companions. When will you come to your senses and become poets again?'

I watched the patterns in the pool. In some miraculous way they remained etched across the surface.

In the hours, like millennia, we had sat together I seemed to have told her everything about myself, yet learned almost nothing about Aurora. One thing alone was clear – her obsession with the art of poetry. In some curious way she regarded herself as personally responsible for the present ebb at which it found itself, but her only remedy seemed completely retrogressive.

'You must come and meet my friends at the colony,' I suggested.

'I will,' she said. 'I hope I can help them. They all have so much to learn.'

I smiled at this. 'I'm afraid you won't find them very sympathetic to that view. Most of them regard themselves as virtuosos. For them the quest for the perfect sonnet ended years ago. The computer produces nothing else.'

Aurora scoffed. 'They're not poets but mere mechanics. Look at these collections of so-called verse. Three poems and sixty pages of operating instructions. Nothing but volts and amps. When I say they have everything to learn, I mean about their own hearts, not about technique; about the soul of music, not its form.'

She paused to stretch herself, her beautiful body uncoiling like a python. She leaned forward and began to speak earnestly. 'Poetry is dead today, not because of these machines, but because poets no longer search for their true inspiration.'

'Which is?'

Aurora shook her head sadly. 'You call yourself a poet and yet you ask me that?'

She stared down at the pool, her eyes listless. For a moment an expression of profound sadness passed across her face, and I realized that she felt some deep sense of guilt or inadequacy, that some failing of her own was responsible for the present malaise. Perhaps it was this sense of inadequacy that made me unafraid of her.

'Have you ever heard the legend of Melander and Corydon?' she asked.

'Vaguely,' I said, casting my mind back. 'Melander was the Muse of Poetry, if I remember. Wasn't Corydon a court poet who killed himself for her?'

'Good,' Aurora told me. 'You're not completely illiterate, after all. Yes, the court poets found that they had lost their inspiration and that their ladies were spurning them for the company of the knights, so they sought out Melander, the Muse, who told them that she had brought this spell upon them because they had taken their art for granted, forgetting the source from whom it really came. They protested that of course they thought of her always – a blatant lie – but she refused to believe them and told them that they would not recover their power until one of them sacrificed his life for her. Naturally none of them would do so, with the exception of a young poet of great talent called Corydon, who loved the goddess and was the only one to retain his power. For the other poets' sake he killed himself . . .'

'. . . to Melander's undying sorrow,' I concluded. 'She was not expecting him to give his life for his art. A beautiful myth,' I agreed. 'But I'm afraid you'll find no Corydons here.'

'I wonder,' Aurora said softly. She stirred the water in the pool, the broken surface throwing a ripple of light across the walls and ceiling. Then I saw that a long series of friezes ran around the lounge depicting the very legend Aurora had been describing. The first panel, on my extreme left, showed the poets and troubadours gathered around the goddess, a tall white-gowned figure whose face bore a remarkable resemblance to Aurora's. As I traced the story through the successive panels the likeness became even more marked, and I assumed that she had sat as Melander for the artist. Had she, in some way, identified herself with the goddess in the myth? In which case, who was her Corydon? – perhaps the artist himself. I searched the panels for the suicidal poet, a slim blond-maned youth whose face, although slightly familiar, I could not identify. However, behind the principal figures in all the scenes I certainly recognized another, her faun-faced chauffeur, here with ass's legs and wild woodwind, representing none other than the attendant Pan.

I had almost detected another likeness among the figures in the friezes when Aurora noticed me searching the panels. She stopped stirring the pool. As the ripples subsided the panels sank again into darkness. For a few seconds Aurora stared at me as if she had forgotten who I was. She appeared to have become tired and withdrawn, as if recapitulating the myth had evoked private memories of pain and fatigue. Simultaneously the hallway and glass-enclosed portico seemed to grow dark and sombre, reflecting her own darkening mood, so dominant was her presence that the air itself paled as she did. Again I felt that her world, into which I had stepped, was completely compounded of illusion.

She was asleep. Around her the room was almost in darkness. The pool lights had faded, the crystal columns that had shone around us were dull and extinguished, like trunks of opaque glass. The only light came from the flower-like jewel between her sleeping breasts.

I stood up and walked softly across to her, looked down at her strange face, its skin smooth and grey, like some pharaonic bride in a basalt dream. Then, beside me at the door I noticed the hunched figure of the chauffeur. His peaked cap hid his face, but the two watchful eyes were fixed on me like small coals.

As we left, hundreds of sleeping sand-rays were dotted about the moonlit floor of the desert. We stepped between them and moved away silently in the Cadillac.

When I reached the villa I went straight into the study, ready to start work on assembling the next issue. During the return ride I had quickly decided on the principal cue-themes and key-images which I would play into the VT sets. All programmed for maximum repetition, within twenty-four hours I would have a folio of moon-sick, muse-mad dithyrambs which would stagger Aurora Day by their heartfelt simplicity and inspiration.

As I entered the study my shoe caught on something sharp. I bent down in the darkness, and found a torn strip of computer circuitry embedded in the white leather flooring.

When I switched on the light I saw that someone had smashed the three VT sets, pounding them to a twisted pulp in a savage excess of violence.

Mine had not been the only targets. Next morning, as I sat at my desk contemplating the three wrecked computers, the telephone rang with news of similar outrages all the way down the Stars. Tony Sapphire's 50-watt IBM had been hammered to pieces, and Raymond Mayo's four new Philco Versomatics had been smashed beyond hope of repair. As far as I could gather, not a single VT set had been left untouched. The previous evening, between the hours of six and midnight, someone had moved rapidly down the Stars, slipped into the studios and apartments and singlemindedly wrecked every VT set.

I had a good idea who. As I climbed out of the Cadillac on my return from Aurora I had noticed two heavy wrenches on the seat beside the chauffeur. However, I decided not to call the police and prefer charges. For one thing, the problem of filling *Wave IX* now looked almost insoluble. When I telephoned Graphis Press I found, more or less as expected, that all Aurora's copy had been mysteriously mislaid.

The problem remained – what would I put in the issue? I couldn't afford to miss an edition or my subscribers would fade away like ghosts.

I telephoned Aurora and pointed this out.

'We should go to press again within a week, otherwise our contract expires and I'll never get another. And reimbursing a year's advance subscriptions would bankrupt me. We've simply got to find some copy. As the new managing editor have you any suggestions?'

Aurora chuckled. 'I suppose you're thinking that I might mysteriously reassemble all those smashed machines?'

'It's an idea,' I agreed, waving at Tony Sapphire who had just called in. 'Otherwise I'm afraid we're never going to get any copy.'

'I can't understand you,' Aurora replied: 'Surely there's one very simple method.'

'Is there? What's that?'

'Write some yourself!'

Before I could protest she burst into a peal of high laughter. 'I gather there are some twenty-three able-bodied versifiers and so-called poets in Vermilion Sands' – this was exactly the number of places broken into the previous evening – 'well, let's see some of them versify.'

'Aurora!' I snapped. 'You can't be serious. Listen, for heaven's sake, this is no joking –'

But she had put the phone down. I turned to Tony Sapphire, then sat back limply and contemplated an intact tape spool I had recovered from one of the sets. 'It looks as if I've had it. Did you hear that – "Write some yourself"?'

'She must be insane,' Tony agreed.

'It's all part of this tragic obsession of hers,' I explained, lowering my voice. 'She genuinely believes she's the Muse of Poetry, returned to earth to re-inspire the dying race of poets. Last night she referred to the myth of Melander and Corydon. I think she's seriously waiting for some young poet to give his life for her.'

Tony nodded. 'She's missing the point, though. Fifty years ago a few people wrote poetry, but no one read it. Now no one writes it either. The VT set merely simplifies the whole process.'

I agreed with him, but of course Tony was somewhat prejudiced there, being one of those people who believed that literature was in essence both unreadable and unwritable. The automatic novel he had been 'writing' was over ten million words long, intended to be one of those gigantic grotesques that tower over the highways of literary history, terrifying the unwary traveller. Unfortunately he had never bothered to get it printed, and the memory drum which carried the electronic coding had been wrecked in the previous night's pogrom.

I was equally annoyed. One of my VT sets had been steadily producing a transliteration of James Joyce's *Ulysses* in terms of a Hellenic Greek setting, a pleasant academic exercise which would have provided an objective test of Joyce's masterpiece by the degree of exactness with which the transliteration matched the original Odyssey. This too had been destroyed.

We watched Studio 5 in the bright morning light. The cerise Cadillac had disappeared somewhere, so presumably Aurora was driving around Vermilion Sands, astounding the café crowds.

I picked up the terrace telephone and sat on the rail. 'I suppose I might as well call everyone up and see what they can do.'

I dialled the first number.

Raymond Mayo said: 'Write some myself? Paul, you're insane.'

Xero Paris said: 'Myself? Of course, Paul, with my toes.'

Fairchild de Mille said: 'It would be rather chic, but . . .'

Kurt Butterworth said, sourly: 'Ever tried to? How?'

Marlene McClintic said: 'Darling, I wouldn't dare. It might develop the wrong muscles or something.'

Sigismund Lutitsch said. 'No, no. Siggy now in new zone. Electronic sculpture, plasma in super-cosmic collisions. Listen –'

Robin Saunders, Macmillan Freebody and Angel Petit said: 'No.'

\*    \*    \*

Tony brought me a drink and I pressed on down the list. 'It's no good,' I said at last. 'No one writes verse any more. Let's face it. After all, do you or I?'

Tony pointed to the notebook. 'There's one name left – we might as well sweep the decks clean before we take off for Red Beach.'

'Tristram Caldwell,' I read. 'That's the shy young fellow with the footballer's build. Something is always wrong with his set. Might as well try him.'

A soft honey-voiced girl answered the phone.

'Tristram?' she purred. 'Er, yes, I think he's here.'

There were sounds of wrestling around on a bed, during which the telephone bounced on the floor a few times, and then Caldwell answered.

'Hello, Ransom, what can I do for you?'

'Tristram,' I said, 'I take it you were paid the usual surprise call last night. Or didn't you notice? How's your VT set?'

'VT set?' he repeated. 'It's fine, just fine.'

'What?' I shouted. 'You mean yours is undamaged? Tristram, pull yourself together and listen to me!' Quickly I explained our problem, but Tristram suddenly began to laugh.

'Well, I think that's just damn funny, don't you? Really rich. I think she's right. Let's get back to the old crafts –'

'Never mind the old crafts,' I told him irritably. 'All I'm interested in is getting some copy together for the next issue. If your set is working we're saved.'

'Well there, wait a minute, Paul. I've been slightly preoccupied recently, haven't had a chance to see the set.'

I waited while he wandered off. From the sounds of his footsteps and an impatient shout of the girl's, to which he replied distantly, it seemed he had gone outside into the yard. A door slammed open somewhere and there was a vague rummaging. A curious place to keep a VT set, I thought. Then there was a loud hammering noise.

Finally Tristram picked up the phone again. 'Sorry, Paul, but it looks as if she paid me a visit too. The set's a total wreck.' He paused while I cursed the air, then said: 'Look, though, is she really serious about the hand-made material? I take it that's what you were calling about?'

'Yes,' I told him. 'Believe me, I'll print anything. It has to get past Aurora, though. Have you got any old copy lying around?'

Tristram chuckled again. 'You know, Paul, old boy, I believe I have. Rather despaired of ever getting it into print but I'm glad now I held on to it. Tell you what, I'll tidy it up and let you have it tomorrow. Few sonnets, a ballad or two, you should find it interesting.'

He was right. Five minutes after I opened his parcel the next morning I knew he was trying to fool us.

'This is the same old thing,' I explained to Tony. 'That cunning Adonis. Look at these assonances and feminine rhymes, the drifting caesura – the unmistakable Caldwell signature, worn tapes on the rectifier circuits and a leaking condenser. I've been having to re-tread these for years to smooth them out. He's got his set there working away after all.'

'What are you going to do?' Tony asked. 'He'll just deny it.'

'Obviously. Anyway, I can use the material. Who cares if the whole issue is by Tristram Caldwell.'

I started to slip the pages into an envelope before taking them round to Aurora, when an idea occurred to me.

'Tony, I've just had another of my brilliancies. The perfect method of curing this witch of her obsession and exacting sweet revenge at the same time. Suppose we play along with Tristram and tell Aurora that these poems were hand-written by him. His style is thoroughly retrograde and his themes are everything Aurora could ask for – listen to these – "Homage to Cleo", "Minerva 231", "Silence becomes Electra". She'll pass them for press, we'll print this weekend and then, lo and behold, we reveal that these poems apparently born out of the burning breast of Tristram Caldwell are nothing more than a collection of cliché-ridden transcripts from a derelict VT set, the worst possible automatic maunderings.'

Tony whooped. 'Tremendous! She'd never live it down. But do you think she'll be taken in?'

'Why not? Haven't you realized that she sincerely expects us all to sit down and produce a series of model classical exercises on "Night and Day", "Summer and Winter", and so on. When only Caldwell produces anything she'll be only too glad to give him her imprimatur. Remember, our agreement only refers to this issue, and the onus is on her. She's got to find material somewhere.'

So we launched our scheme. All afternoon I pestered Tristram, telling him that Aurora had adored his first consignment and was eager to see more. Duly the next day a second batch arrived, all, as luck would have it, in longhand, although remarkably faded for material fresh from his VT set the previous day. However, I was only too glad for anything that would reinforce the illusion. Aurora was more and more pleased, and showed no suspicions whatever. Here and there she made a minor criticism but refused to have anything altered or rewritten.

'But we always rewrite, Aurora,' I told her. 'One can't expect an infallible selection of images. The number of synonyms is too great.' Wondering whether I had gone too far, I added hastily: 'It doesn't matter whether the author is man or robot, the principle is the same.'

'Really?' Aurora said archly. 'However, I think we'll leave these just as Mr Caldwell wrote them.'

I didn't bother to point out the hopeless fallacy in her attitude, and merely collected the initialled manuscripts and hurried home with them. Tony was at my desk, deep in the phone, pumping Tristram for more copy.

He capped the mouthpiece and gestured to me. 'He's playing coy, probably trying to raise us to two cents a thousand. Pretends he's out of material. Is it worth calling his bluff?'

I shook my head. 'Dangerous. If Aurora discovers we're involved in this fraud of Tristram's she might do anything. Let me talk to him.' I took the phone. 'What's the matter, Tristram, production's way down. We need more material, old boy. Shorten the line, why are you wasting tapes with all these alexandrines?'

'Ransom, what the hell are you talking about? I'm not a damned factory, I'm a poet, I write when I have something to say in the only suitable way to say it.'

'Yes, yes,' I rejoined, 'but I have fifty pages to fill and only a few days in which to do it. You've given me about ten so you've just got to keep up the flow. What have you produced today?'

'Well, I'm working on another sonnet, some nice things in it – to Aurora herself, as a matter of fact.'

'Great,' I told him, 'but careful with those vocabulary selectors. Remember the golden rule: the ideal sentence is one word long. What else have you got?'

'What else? Nothing. This is likely to take all week, perhaps all year.'

I nearly swallowed the phone. 'Tristram, what's the matter? For heaven's sake, haven't you paid the power bill or something? Have they cut you off?'

Before I could find out, however, he had rung off.

'One sonnet a day,' I said to Tony. 'Good God, he must be on manual. Crazy idiot, he probably doesn't realize how complicated those circuits are.'

We sat tight and waited. Nothing came the next morning, and nothing the morning after that. Luckily, however, Aurora wasn't in the least surprised; in fact, if anything she was pleased that Tristram's rate of progress was slowing.

'One poem is enough,' she told me, 'a complete statement. Nothing more needs to be said, an interval of eternity closes for ever.'

Reflectively, she straightened the petals of a hyacinth. 'Perhaps he needs a little encouragement,' she decided.

I could see she wanted to meet him.

'Why don't you ask him over for dinner?' I suggested.

She brightened immediately. 'I will.' She picked up the telephone and handed it to me.

As I dialled Tristram's number I felt a sudden pang of envy and disappointment. Around me the friezes told the story of Melander and Corydon, but I was too preoccupied to anticipate the tragedy the next week would bring.

During the days that followed Tristram and Aurora Day were always together. In the morning they would usually drive out to the film sets at Lagoon West, the chauffeur at the wheel of the huge Cadillac. In the evenings, as I sat out alone on the terrace, watching the lights of Studio 5 shine out into the warm darkness, I could hear their fragmented voices carried across the sand, the faint sounds of crystal music.

I would like to think that I resented their relationship, but to be truthful I cared very little after the initial disappointment had worn off. The beach fatigue from which I suffered numbed the senses insidiously, blunting despair and hope alike.

When, three days after their first meeting, Aurora and Tristram suggested that we all go ray-fishing at Lagoon West, I accepted gladly, eager to observe their affair at closer quarters.

As we set off down the Stars there was no hint of what was to come. Tristram and Aurora were together in the Cadillac while Tony Sapphire, Raymond Mayo and I brought up the rear in Tony's Chevrolet. We could see them through the blue rear window of the Cadillac, Tristram reading the sonnet to Aurora which he had just completed. When we climbed out of the cars at Lagoon West and made our way over to the old abstract film sets near the sand reefs, they were walking hand in hand. Tristram in his white beach shoes and suit looked very much like an Edwardian dandy at a boating party.

The chauffeur carried the picnic hampers, and Raymond Mayo and Tony the spear-guns and nets. Down the reefs below we could see the rays nesting by the thousands, scores of double mambas sleek with off-season hibernation.

After we had settled ourselves under the awnings Raymond and Tristram decided on the course and then gathered everyone together. Strung out in a loose line we began to make our way down into one of the reefs, Aurora on Tristram's arm.

'Ever done any ray-fishing?' Tristram asked me as we entered one of the lower galleries.

'Never,' I said. 'I'll just watch this time. I hear you're quite an expert.'

'Well, with luck I won't be killed.' He pointed to the rays clinging to the cornices above us, wheeling up into the sky as we approached, whistling and screeching. In the dim light the white tips of their stings flexed in their sheaths. 'Unless they're really frightened they'll stay well away from you,' he told us. 'The art is to prevent them from becoming frightened, select one and approach it so slowly that it sits staring at you until you're close enough to shoot it.'

Raymond Mayo had found a large purple mamba resting in a narrow crevice about ten yards on our right. He moved up to it quietly, watching the sting protrude from its sheath and weave menacingly, waiting just long enough for it to retract, lulling the ray with a low humming sound. Finally, when he was five feet away, he raised the gun and took careful aim.

'There may seem little to it,' Tristram whispered to Aurora and me, 'but in fact he's completely at the ray's mercy now. If it chose to attack he'd be defenceless.' The bolt snapped from Raymond's gun and struck the ray on its spinal crest, stunning it instantly. Quickly he stepped over and scooped it into the net, where it revived after a few seconds, threshed its black triangular wings helplessly and then lay inertly.

We moved through the groynes and galleries, the sky a narrow winding interval overhead, following the pathways that curved down into the bed of the reef. Now and then the wheeling rays rising out of our way would brush against the reef and drifts of fine sand would cascade over us. Raymond and Tristram shot several more rays, leaving the chauffeur to carry the nets. Gradually our party split into two, Tony and Raymond taking one pathway with the chauffeur, while I stayed with Aurora and Tristram.

As we moved along I noticed that Aurora's face had become less relaxed, her movements slightly more deliberate and controlled. I had the impression she was watching Tristram carefully, glancing sideways at him as she held his arm.

We entered the terminal fornix of the reef, a deep cathedral-like chamber from which a score of galleries spiralled off to surface like the arms of a galaxy. In the darkness around us the thousands of rays hung motionlessly, their phosphorescing stings flexing and retracting like winking stars.

Two hundred feet away, on the far side of the chamber, Raymond Mayo and the chauffeur emerged from one of the galleries. They waited there for a few moments. Suddenly I heard Tony shouting out. Raymond dropped his spear-gun and disappeared into the gallery.

Excusing myself, I ran across the chamber. I found them in the narrow corridor, peering around in the darkness.

'I tell you,' Tony was insisting. 'I heard the damn thing singing.'

'Impossible,' Raymond told him. They argued with each other, then gave up the search for the mysterious song-ray and stepped down into the chamber. As we went I thought I saw the chauffeur replace something in his pocket. With his beaked face and insane eyes, his hunched figure hung about with the nets of writhing rays, he looked like a figure from Hieronymus Bosch.

After exchanging a few words with Raymond and Tony I turned to make my way back to the others, but they had left the chamber. Wondering which of the galleries they had chosen, I stepped a few yards into the mouth of each one, finally saw them on one of the ramps curving away above me.

I was about to retrace my steps and join them when I caught a glimpse of Aurora's face in profile, saw once again her expression of watchful intent. Changing my mind, I moved quietly along the spiral, just below them, the falls of sand masking my footsteps, keeping them in view through the intervals between the overhanging columns.

At one point I was only a few yards from them, and heard Aurora say clearly: 'Isn't there a theory that you can trap rays by singing to them?'

'By mesmerizing them?' Tristram asked. 'Let's try.'

They moved farther away, and Aurora's voice sounded out softly, a low crooning tone. Gradually the sound rose, echoing and re-echoing through the high vaults, the rays stirring in the darkness.

As we neared the surface their numbers grew, and Aurora stopped and guided Tristram towards a narrow sun-filled arena, bounded by hundred-foot walls, open to the sky above.

Unable to see them now, I retreated into the gallery and climbed the inner slope on to the next level, and from there on to the stage above. I made my way to the edge of the gallery, from which I could now easily observe the arena below. As I did so, however, I was aware of an eerie and penetrating noise, at once toneless and all-pervading, which filled the entire reef, like the high-pitched sounds perceived by epileptics before a seizure. Down in the arena Tristram was searching the walls, trying to identify the source of the noise, hands raised to his head. He had taken his eyes off Aurora, who was standing behind him, arms motionless at her sides, palms slightly raised, like an entranced medium.

Fascinated by this curious stance, I was abruptly distracted by a terrified screeching that came from the lower levels of the reef. It was accompanied by a confused leathery flapping, and almost immediately a cloud of flying rays, frantically trying to escape from the reef, burst from the galleries below.

As they turned into the arena, sweeping low over the heads of Tristram and Aurora, they seemed to lose their sense of direction, and within a moment the arena was packed by a swarm of circling rays, all diving about uncertainly.

Screaming in terror at the rays whipping past her face, Aurora emerged from her trance. Tristram had taken off his straw hat and was striking furiously at them, shielding Aurora with his other arm. Together they backed towards a narrow fault in the rear wall of the arena, which provided an escape route into the galleries on the far side. Following this route to the edge of the cliffs above, I was surprised to see the squat figure of the chauffeur, now divested of his nets and gear, peering down at the couple below.

By now the hundreds of rays jostling within the arena almost obscured Tristram and Aurora. She reappeared from the narrow fault, shaking her head desperately. Their escape route was sealed! Quickly Tristram motioned her to her knees, then leapt into the middle of the arena, slapping wildly at the rays with his hat, trying to drive them away from Aurora.

For a few seconds he was successful. Like a cloud of giant hornets the rays wheeled off in disorder. Horrified, I watched them descend upon him again. Before I could shout Tristram had fallen. The rays swooped and hovered over his outstretched body, then swirled away, soaring into the sky, apparently released from the vortex.

Tristram lay face downwards, his blond hair spilled across the sand, arms twisted loosely. I stared at his body, amazed by the swiftness with which he had died, and looked across to Aurora.

She too was watching the body, but with an expression that showed neither pity nor terror. Gathering her skirt in one hand, she turned and slipped away through the fault –

The escape route had been open after all! Astonished, I realized that Aurora had deliberately told Tristram that the route was closed, virtually forcing him to attack the rays.

A minute later she emerged from the mouth of the gallery above. Briefly she peered down into the arena, the black-uniformed chauffeur at her elbow, watching the motionless body of Tristram. Then they hurried away.

Racing after them, I began to shout at the top of my voice, hoping to attract Tony and Raymond Mayo. As I reached the mouth of the reef my voice boomed and echoed into the galleries below. A hundred yards away Aurora and the chauffeur were stepping into the Cadillac. With a roar of exhaust it swung away among the sets, sending up clouds of dust that obscured the enormous abstract patterns.

I ran towards Tony's car. By the time I reached it the Cadillac was half a mile away, burning across the desert like an escaping dragon.

That was the last I saw of Aurora Day. I managed to follow them as far as the highway to Lagoon West, but there, on the open road, the big car left me behind, and ten miles farther on, by the time I reached Lagoon West, I had lost them completely. At one of the gas stations where the highway forks to Vermilion Sands and Red Beach I asked if anyone had seen a cerise Cadillac go by. Two attendants said they had, on the road *towards* me, and although they both swore this, I suppose Aurora's magic must have confused them.

I decided to try her villa and took the fork back to Vermilion Sands, cursing myself for not anticipating what had happened. I, ostensibly a poet, had failed to take another poet's dreams seriously. Aurora had explicitly forecast Tristram's death.

Studio 5, The Stars, was silent and empty. The rays had gone from the drive, and the black glass door was wide open, the remains of a few streamers drifting across the dust that gathered on the floor. The hallway and lounge were in darkness, and only the white carp in the pool provided a glimmer of light. The air was still and unbroken, as if the house had been empty for centuries.

Cursorily I ran my eye round the friezes in the lounge, then saw that I knew all the faces of the figures in the panels. The likenesses were almost photographic. Tristram was Corydon, Aurora Melander, the chauffeur the god Pan. And I saw myself, Tony Sapphire, Raymond Mayo, Fairchild de Mille and the other members of the colony.

Leaving the friezes, I made my way past the pool. It was now evening, and through the open doorway were the distant lights of Vermilion Sands, the headlights sweeping along the Stars reflected in the glass roof-tiles of my villa. A light wind had risen, stirring the streamers, and as I went down the steps a gust of air moved through the house and caught the door, slamming it behind me. The loud report boomed through the house, a concluding statement upon the whole sequence of fantasy and disaster, a final notice of the departure of the enchantress.

As I walked back across the desert and last streamers were moving over the dark sand, I strode firmly through them, trying to reassemble my own reality again. The fragments of Aurora Day's insane poems caught the dying desert light as they dissolved about my feet, the fading debris of a dream.

Reaching the villa, I saw that the lights were on. I raced inside and to my astonishment discovered the blond figure of Tristram stretched out lazily in a chair on the terrace, an ice-filled glass in one hand.

He eyed me genially, winked broadly before I could speak and put a forefinger to his lips.

I stepped over to him. 'Tristram,' I whispered hoarsely. 'I thought you were dead. What on earth happened down there?'

He smiled at me. 'Sorry, Paul, I had a hunch you were watching. Aurora got away, didn't she?'

I nodded. 'Their car was too fast for the Chevrolet. But weren't you hit by one of the rays? I saw you fall, I thought you'd been killed outright.'

'So did Aurora. Neither of you know much about rays, do you? Their stings are passive in the on season, old chap, or nobody would be allowed in there.' He grinned at me. 'Ever hear of the myth of Melander and Corydon?'

I sat down weakly on the seat next to him. In two minutes he explained what had happened. Aurora had told him of the myth, and partly out of sympathy for her, and partly for amusement, he had decided to play out his role. All the while he had been describing the danger and viciousness of the rays he had been egging Aurora on deliberately, and had provided her with a perfect opportunity to stage his sacrificial murder.

'It *was* murder, of course,' I told him. 'Believe me, I saw the glint in her eye. She really wanted you killed.'

Tristram shrugged. 'Don't look so shocked, old boy. After all, poetry is a serious business.'

Raymond and Tony Sapphire knew nothing of what had happened. Tristram had put together a story of how Aurora had suffered a sudden attack of claustrophobia, and rushed off in a frenzy.

'I wonder what Aurora will do now,' Tristram mused. 'Her prophecy's been fulfilled. Perhaps she'll feel more confident of her own beauty. You know, she had a colossal sense of physical inadequacy. Like the original Melander, who was surprised when Corydon killed himself, Aurora confused her art with her own person.'

I nodded. 'I hope she isn't too disappointed when she finds poetry is still being written in the bad old way. That reminds me, I've got twenty-five pages to fill. How's your VT set running?'

'No longer have one. Wrecked it the morning you phoned up. Haven't used the thing for years.'

I sat up. 'Do you mean that those sonnets you've been sending in are all hand-written?'

'Absolutely, old boy. Every single one a soul-grafted gem.'

I lay back groaning. 'God, I was relying on your set to save me. What the hell am I going to do?'

Tristram grinned. 'Start writing it yourself. Remember the prophecy. Perhaps it will come true. After all, Aurora thinks I'm dead.'

I cursed him roundly. 'If it's any help, I wish you were. Do you know what this is going to cost me?'

After he had gone I went into the study and added up what copy I had left, found that there were exactly twenty-three pages to fill. Oddly enough that represented one page for each of the registered poets at Vermilion Sands. Except that none of them, apart from Tristram, was capable of producing a single line.

It was midnight, but the problems facing the magazine would take every minute of the next twenty-four hours, when the final deadline expired. I had almost decided to write something myself when the telephone rang. At first I thought it was Aurora Day – the voice was high and feminine – but it was only Fairchild de Mille.

'What are you doing up so late?' I growled at him. 'Shouldn't you be getting your beauty sleep?'

'Well, I suppose I should, Paul, but do you know a rather incredible thing happened to me this evening. Tell me, are you still looking for original hand-written verse? I started writing something a couple of hours ago, it's not bad really. About Aurora Day, as a matter of fact. I think you'll like it.'

Sitting up, I congratulated him fulsomely, noting down the linage.

Five minutes later the telephone rang again. This time it was Angel Petit. He too had a few hand-written verses I might be interested in. Again, dedicated to Aurora Day.

Within the next half hour the telephone rang a score of times. Every poet in Vermilion Sands seemed to be awake. I heard from Macmillan Freebody, Robin Saunders and the rest of them. All, mysteriously that evening, had suddenly felt the urge to write something original, and in a few minutes had tossed off a couple of stanzas to the memory of Aurora Day.

I was musing over it when I stood up after the last call. It was 12.45, and I should have been tired out, but my brain felt keen and alive, a thousand ideas running through it. A phrase formed itself in my mind. I picked up my pad and wrote it down.

Time seemed to dissolve. Within five minutes I had produced the first piece of verse I had written for over ten years. Behind it a dozen more poems lay just below the surface of my mind, waiting like gold in a loaded vein to be brought out into daylight.

Sleep would wait. I reached for another sheet of paper and then noticed a letter on the desk to the IBM agency in Red Beach, enclosing an order for three new VT sets.

Smiling to myself, I tore it into a dozen pieces.

**1961**

# DEEP END

They always slept during the day. By dawn the last of the townsfolk had gone indoors and the houses would be silent, heat curtains locked across the windows, as the sun rose over the deliquescing salt banks. Most of them were elderly and fell asleep quickly in their darkened chalets, but Granger, with his restless mind and his one lung, often lay awake through the afternoons, while the metal outer walls of the cabin creaked and hummed, trying pointlessly to read through the old log books Holliday had salvaged for him from the crashed space platforms.

By six o'clock the thermal fronts would begin to recede southwards across the kelp flats, and one by one the air-conditioners in the bedrooms switched themselves off. While the town slowly came to life, its windows opening to the cool dusk air, Granger strode down to breakfast at the Neptune Bar, gallantly doffing his sunglasses to left and right at the old couples settling themselves out on their porches, staring at each other across the shadow-filled streets.

Five miles to the north, in the empty hotel at Idle End, Holliday usually rested quietly for another hour, and listened to the coral towers, gleaming in the distance like white pagodas, sing and whistle as the temperature gradients cut through them. Twenty miles away he could see the symmetrical peak of Hamilton, nearest of the Bermuda Islands, rising off the dry ocean floor like a flat-topped mountain, the narrow ring of white beach still visible in the sunset, a scum-line left by the sinking ocean.

That evening he felt even more reluctant than usual to drive down into the town. Not only would Granger be in his private booth at the Neptune, dispensing the same mixture of humour and homily – he was virtually the only person Holliday could talk to, and inevitably he had come to resent his dependence on the older man – but Holliday would have his final interview with the migration officer and make the decision which would determine his entire future.

In a sense the decision had already been made, as Bullen, the migration officer, realized on his trip a month earlier. He did not bother to press Holliday, who had no special skills to offer, no qualities of character or leadership which would be of use on the new worlds. However, Bullen pointed out one small but relevant fact, which Holliday duly noted and thought over in the intervening month.

'Remember, Holliday,' he warned him at the end of the interview in the requisitioned office at the rear of the sheriff's cabin, 'the average age of the settlement is over sixty. In ten years' time you and Granger may well be the only two left here, and if that lung of his goes you'll be on your own.'

He paused to let this prospect sink in, then added quietly: 'All the kids are leaving on the next trip – the Merryweathers' two boys, Tom Juranda (*that lout, good riddance,* Holliday thought to himself, *look out Mars*) – do you realize you'll literally be the only one here under the age of fifty?'

'Katy Summers is staying,' Holliday pointed out quickly, the sudden vision of a white organdy dress and long straw hair giving him courage.

The migration officer had glanced at his application list and nodded grudgingly. 'Yes, but she's just looking after her grandmother. As soon as the old girl dies Katy will be off like a flash. After all, there's nothing to keep her here, is there?'

'No,' Holliday had agreed automatically.

There wasn't now. For a long while he mistakenly believed there was. Katy was his own age, twenty-two, the only person, apart from Granger, who seemed to understand his determination to stay behind and keep watch over a forgotten Earth. But the grandmother died three days after the migration officer left, and the next day Katy had begun to pack. In some insane way Holliday had assumed that she would stay behind, and what worried him was that all his assumptions about himself might be based on equally false premises.

Climbing off the hammock, he went on to the terrace and looked out at the phosphorescent glitter of the trace minerals in the salt banks stretching away from the hotel. His quarters were in the penthouse suite on the tenth floor, the only heat-sealed unit in the building, but its steady settlement into the ocean bed had opened wide cracks in the load walls which would soon reach up to the roof. The ground floor had already disappeared. By the time the next floor went – six months at the outside – he would have been forced to leave the old pleasure resort and return to the town. Inevitably, that would mean sharing a chalet with Granger.

A mile away, an engine droned. Through the dusk Holliday saw the migration officer's helicopter whirling along towards the hotel, the only local landmark, then veer off once Bullen identified the town and circle slowly towards the landing strip.

Eight o'clock, Holliday noted. His interview was at 8.30 the next morning. Bullen would rest the night with the Sheriff, carry out his other duties as graves commissioner and justice of the peace, and then set off after seeing Holliday on the next leg of his journey. For twelve hours Holliday was free, still able to make absolute decisions (or, more accurately, not to make them) but after that he would have committed himself. This was the migration officer's last trip, his final circuit from the deserted cities near St Helena up through the Azores and Bermudas and on to the main Atlantic ferry site at the Canaries. Only two of the big launching platforms were still in navigable orbit – hundreds of others were continuously falling out of the sky – and once they came down Earth was, to all intents, abandoned. From then on the only people likely to be picked up would be a few military communications personnel.

Twice on his way into the town Holliday had to lower the salt-plough fastened to the front bumper of the jeep and ram back the drifts which had melted across the wire roadway during the afternoon. Mutating kelp, their genetic shifts accelerated by the radio-phosphors, reared up into the air on either side of the road like enormous cacti, turning the dark salt-banks into a white lunar garden. But this evidence of the encroaching wilderness only served to strengthen Holliday's need to stay behind on Earth. Most of the nights, when he wasn't arguing with Granger at the Neptune, he would drive around the ocean floor, climbing over the crashed launching platforms, or wander with Katy Summers through the kelp forests. Sometimes he would persuade Granger to come with them, hoping that the older man's expertise – he had originally been a marine biologist – would help to sharpen his own awareness of the bathypelagic flora, but the original sea bed was buried under the endless salt hills and they might as well have been driving about the Sahara.

As he entered the Neptune – a low cream and chromium saloon which abutted the landing strip and had formerly served as a passenger lounge when thousands of migrants from the Southern Hemisphere were being shipped up to the Canaries – Granger called to him and rattled his cane against the window, pointing to the dark outline of the migration officer's helicopter parked on the apron fifty yards away.

'I know,' Holliday said in a bored voice as he went over with his drink. 'Relax, I saw him coming.'

Granger grinned at him. Holliday, with his intent serious face under an unruly thatch of blond hair, and his absolute sense of personal responsibility, always amused him.

'*You* relax,' Granger said, adjusting the shoulder pad under his Hawaiian shirt which disguised his sunken lung. (He had lost it skin-diving thirty years earlier.) '*I'm* not going to fly to Mars next week.'

Holliday stared sombrely into his glass. 'I'm not either.' He looked up at Granger's wry saturnine face, then added sardonically. 'Or didn't you know?'

Granger roared, tapping the window with his cane as if to dismiss the helicopter. 'Seriously, you're not going? You've made up your mind?'

'Wrong. And right. I haven't made up my mind yet – but at the same time I'm not going. You appreciate the distinction?'

'Perfectly, Dr Schopenhauer.' Granger began to grin again. He pushed away his glass. 'You know, Holliday, your trouble is that you take yourself too seriously. You don't realize how ludicrous you are.'

'Ludicrous? Why?' Holliday asked guardedly.

'What does it matter whether you've made up your mind or not? The only thing that counts now is to get together enough courage to head straight for the Canaries and take off into the wide blue yonder. For heaven's sake, what are you staying for? Earth is dead and buried. Past, present and future no longer exist here. Don't you feel any responsibility to your own biological destiny?'

'Spare me that.' Holliday pulled a ration card from his shirt pocket, passed it across to Granger, who was responsible for the stores allocations. 'I need a new pump on the lounge refrigerator. 30-watt Frigidaire. Any left?'

Granger groaned, took the card with a snort of exasperation. 'Good God, man, you're just a Robinson Crusoe in reverse, tinkering about with all these bits of old junk, trying to fit them together. You're the last man on the beach who decides to stay behind after everyone else has left. Maybe you are a poet and dreamer, but don't you realize that those two species are extinct now?'

Holliday stared out at the helicopter on the apron, at the lights of the settlement reflected against the salt hills that encircled the town. Each day they moved a little nearer, already it was difficult to get together a weekly squad to push them back. In ten years' time his position might well be that of a Crusoe. Luckily the big water and kerosene tanks – giant cylinders, the size of gasometers – held enough for fifty years. Without them, of course, he would have had no choice.

'Let's give me a rest,' he said to Granger. 'You're merely trying to find in me a justification for your own enforced stay. Perhaps I am extinct, but I'd rather cling to life here than vanish completely. Anyway, I have a hunch that one day they'll be coming back. Someone's got to stay behind and keep alive a sense of what life here has meant. This isn't an old husk we can throw away when we've finished with it. We were born here. It's the only place we really remember.'

Granger nodded slowly. He was about to speak when a brilliant white arc crossed the darkened window, then soared out of sight, its point of impact with the ground lost behind one of the storage tanks.

Holliday stood up and craned out of the window.

'Must be a launching platform. Looked like a big one, probably one of the Russians'.' A long rolling crump reverberated through the night air, echoing away among the coral towers. Flashes of light flared up briefly. There was a series of smaller explosions, and then a wide diffuse pall of steam fanned out across the north-west.

'Lake Atlantic,' Granger commented. 'Let's drive out there and have a look. It may have uncovered something interesting.'

Half an hour later, a set of Granger's old sample beakers, slides and mounting equipment in the back seat, they set off in the jeep towards the southern tip of Lake Atlantic ten miles away.

It was here that Holliday discovered the fish.

*     *     *

Lake Atlantic, a narrow ribbon of stagnant brine ten miles in length by a mile wide, to the north of the Bermuda Islands, was all that remained of the former Atlantic Ocean, and was, in fact, the sole remnant of the oceans which had once covered two-thirds of the Earth's surface. The frantic mining of the oceans in the previous century to provide oxygen for the atmospheres of the new planets had made their decline swift and irreversible, and with their death had come climatic and other geophysical changes which ensured the extinction of Earth itself. As the oxygen extracted electrolytically from sea-water was compressed and shipped away, the hydrogen released was discharged into the atmosphere. Eventually only a narrow layer of denser, oxygen-containing air was left, little more than a mile in depth, and those people remaining on Earth were forced to retreat into the ocean beds, abandoning the poisoned continental tables.

At the hotel at Idle End, Holliday spent uncounted hours going through the library he had accumulated of magazines and books about the cities of the old Earth, and Granger often described to him his own youth when the seas had been half-full and he had worked as a marine biologist at the University of Miami, a fabulous laboratory unfolding itself for him on the lengthening beaches.

'The seas are our corporate memory,' he often said to Holliday. 'In draining them we deliberately obliterated our own pasts, to a large extent our own self-identities. That's another reason why you should leave. Without the sea, life is insupportable. We become nothing more than the ghosts of memories, blind and homeless, flitting through the dry chambers of a gutted skull.'

They reached the lake within half an hour, worked their way through the swamps which formed its banks. In the dim light the grey salt dunes ran on for miles, their hollows cracked into hexagonal plates, a dense cloud of vapour obscuring the surface of the water. They parked on a low promontory by the edge of the lake and looked up at the great circular shell of the launching platform. This was one of the larger vehicles, almost three hundred yards in diameter, lying upside down in the shallow water, its hull dented and burnt, riven by huge punctures where the power plants had torn themselves loose on impact and exploded off across the lake. A quarter of a mile away, hidden by the blur, they could just see a cluster of rotors pointing up into the sky.

Walking along the bank, the main body of the lake on their right, they moved nearer the platform, tracing out its riveted CCCP markings along the rim. The giant vehicle had cut enormous grooves through the nexus of pools just beyond the tip of the lake, and Granger waded through the warm water, searching for specimens. Here and there were small anemones and starfish, stunted bodies twisted by cancers. Web-like algae draped themselves over his rubber boots, their nuclei beading like jewels in the phosphorescent light. They paused by one of the largest pools, a circular basin 300 feet across, draining slowly as the water poured out through a breach in its side. Granger moved carefully down the deepening bank, forking specimens into the rack of beakers, while Holliday stood on the narrow causeway between the pool and the lake, looking up at the dark overhang of the space platform as it loomed into the darkness above him like the stern of a ship.

He was examining the shattered air-lock of one of the crew domes when he suddenly saw something move across the surface of the deck. For a moment he imagined that he had seen a passenger who had somehow survived the vehicle's crash, then realized that it was merely the reflection in the aluminized skin of a ripple in the pool behind him.

He turned around to see Granger, ten feet below him, up to his knees in the water, staring out carefully across the pool.

'Did you throw something?' Granger asked.

Holliday shook his head. 'No.' Without thinking, he added: 'It must have been a fish jumping.'

'Fish? There isn't a single fish alive on the entire planet. The whole zoological class died out ten years ago. Strange, though.'

Just then the fish jumped again.

For a few moments, standing motionless in the half-light, they watched it together, as its slim silver body leapt frantically out of the tepid shallow water, its short glistening arcs carrying it to and fro across the pool.

'Dog-fish,' Granger muttered. 'Shark family. Highly adaptable – need to be, to have survived here. Damn it, it may well be the only fish still living.'

Holliday moved down the bank, his feet sinking in the oozing mud. 'Isn't the water too salty?'

Granger bent down and scooped up some of the water, sipped it tentatively. 'Saline, but comparatively dilute.' He glanced over his shoulder at the lake. 'Perhaps there's continuous evaporation off the lake surface and local condensation here. A freak distillation couple.' He slapped Holliday on the shoulder. 'Holliday, this should be interesting.'

The dog-fish was leaping frantically towards them, its two-foot body twisting and flicking. Low mud banks were emerging all over the surface of the pool; in only a few places towards the centre was the water more than a foot deep.

Holliday pointed to the breach in the bank fifty yards away, gestured Granger after him and began to run towards it.

Five minutes later they had effectively dammed up the breach. Holliday returned for the jeep and drove it carefully through the winding saddles between the pools. He lowered the ramp and began to force the sides of the fish-pool in towards each other. After two or three hours he had narrowed the diameter from a hundred yards to under sixty, and the depth of the water had increased to over two feet. The dog-fish had ceased to jump and swam smoothly just below the surface, snapping at the countless small plants which had been tumbled into the water by the jeep's ramp. Its slim white body seemed white and unmarked, the small fins trim and powerful.

Granger sat on the bonnet of the jeep, his back against the windshield, watching Holliday with admiration.

'You obviously have hidden reserves,' he said ungrudgingly. 'I didn't think you had it in you.'

Holliday washed his hands in the water, then stepped over the churned mud which formed the boundary of the pool. A few feet behind him the dog-fish veered and lunged.

'I want to keep it alive,' Holliday said matter-of-factly. 'Don't you see, Granger, the fishes stayed behind when the first amphibians emerged from the seas two hundred million years ago, just as you and I, in turn, are staying behind now. In a sense all fish are images of ourselves seen in the sea's mirror.'

He slumped down on the running board. His clothes were soaked and streaked with salt, and he gasped at the damp air. To the west, just above the long bulk of the Florida coastline, rising from the ocean floor like an enormous aircraft carrier, were the first dawn thermal fronts. 'Will it be all right to leave it until this evening?'

Granger climbed into the driving seat. 'Don't worry. Come on, you need a rest.' He pointed up at the overhanging rim of the launching platform. 'That should shade it for a few hours, help to keep the temperature down.'

As they neared the town Granger slowed to wave to the old people retreating from their porches, fixing the shutters on the steel cabins.

'What about your interview with Bullen?' he asked Holliday soberly. 'He'll be waiting for you.'

'Leave here? After last night? It's out of the question.'

Granger shook his head as he parked the car outside the Neptune. 'Aren't you rather over-estimating the importance of one dog-fish? There were millions of them once, the vermin of the sea.'

'You're missing the point,' Holliday said, sinking back into the seat, trying to wipe the salt out of his eyes. 'That fish means that there's still something to be done here. Earth isn't dead and exhausted after all. We can breed new forms of life, a completely new biological kingdom.'

Eyes fixed on this private vision, Holliday sat holding the steering wheel while Granger went into the bar to collect a crate of beer. On his return the migration officer was with him.

Bullen put a foot on the running board, looked into the car. 'Well, how about it, Holliday? I'd like to make an early start. If you're not interested I'll be off. There's a rich new life out there, first step to the stars. Tom Juranda and the Merryweather boys are leaving next week. Do you want to be with them?'

'Sorry,' Holliday said curtly. He pulled the crate of beer into the car and let out the clutch, gunned the jeep away down the empty street in a roar of dust.

Half an hour later, as he stepped out on to the terrace at Idle End, cool and refreshed after his shower, he watched the helicopter roar overhead, its black propeller scudding, then disappear over the kelp flats towards the hull of the wrecked space platform.

'Come on, let's go! What's the matter?'

'Hold it,' Granger said. 'You're getting over-eager. Don't interfere too much, you'll kill the damn thing with kindness. What have you got there?' He pointed to the can Holliday had placed in the dashboard compartment.

'Breadcrumbs.'

Granger sighed, then gently closed the door. 'I'm impressed. I really am. I wish you'd look after me this way. I'm gasping for air too.'

They were five miles from the lake when Holliday leaned forward over the wheel and pointed to the crisp tyre-prints in the soft salt flowing over the road ahead.

'Someone's there already.'

Granger shrugged. 'What of it? They've probably gone to look at the platform.' He chuckled quietly. 'Don't you want to share the New Eden with anyone else? Or just you alone, and a consultant biologist?'

Holliday peered through the windshield. 'Those platforms annoy me, the way they're hurled down as if Earth were a garbage dump. Still, if it wasn't for this one I wouldn't have found the fish.'

They reached the lake and made their way towards the pool, the erratic track of the car ahead winding in and out of the pools. Two hundred yards from the platform it had been parked, blocking the route for Holliday and Granger.

'That's the Merryweathers' car,' Holliday said as they walked around the big stripped-down Buick, slashed with yellow paint and fitted with sirens and pennants. 'The two boys must have come out here.'

Granger pointed. 'One of them's up on the platform.'

The younger brother had climbed on to the rim, was shouting down like an umpire at the antics of two other boys, one his brother, the other Tom Juranda, a tall broad-shouldered youth in a space cadet's jerkin. They were standing at the edge of the fish-pool, stones and salt blocks in their hands, hurling them into the pool.

Leaving Granger, Holliday sprinted on ahead, shouting at the top of his voice. Too preoccupied to hear him, the boys continued to throw their missiles into the pool, while the younger Merryweather egged them on from the platform above. Just before Holliday reached them Tom Juranda ran a few yards along the bank and began to kick the mud-wall into the air, then resumed his target throwing.

'Juranda! Get away from there!' Holliday bellowed. 'Put those stones down!'

He reached Juranda as the youth was about to hurl a brick-sized lump of salt into the pool, seized him by the shoulder and flung him round, knocking the salt out of his hand into a shower of damp crystals, then lunged at the elder Merryweather boy, kicking him away.

The pool had been drained. A deep breach had been cut through the bank and the water had poured out into the surrounding gulleys and pools. Down in the centre of the basin, in a litter of stones and spattered salt, was the crushed but still wriggling body of the dog-fish, twisting itself helplessly in the bare inch of water that remained. Dark red blood poured from wounds in its body, staining the salt.

Holliday hurled himself at Juranda, shook the youth savagely by the shoulders.

'Juranda! Do you realize what you've done, you –' Exhausted, Holliday released him and staggered down into the centre of the pool, kicked away the stones and stood looking at the fish twitching at his feet.

'Sorry, Holliday,' the older Merryweather boy said tentatively behind him. 'We didn't know it was your fish.'

Holliday waved him away, then let his arms fall limply to his sides. He felt numbed and baffled, unable to resolve his anger and frustration.

Tom Juranda began to laugh, and shouted something derisively. Their tension broken, the boys turned and ran off together across the dunes towards their car, yelling and playing catch with each other, mimicking Holliday's outrage.

Granger let them go by, then walked across to the pool, wincing when he saw the empty basin.

'Holliday,' he called. 'Come on.'

Holliday shook his head, staring at the beaten body of the fish.

Granger stepped down the bank to him. Sirens hooted in the distance as the Buick roared off. 'Those damn children.' He took Holliday gently by the arm. 'I'm sorry,' he said quietly. 'But it's not the end of the world.'

Bending down, Holliday reached towards the fish, lying still now, the mud around it slick with blood. His hands hesitated, then retreated.

'Nothing we can do, is there?' he said impersonally.

Granger examined the fish. Apart from the large wound in its side and the flattened skull the skin was intact. 'Why not have it stuffed?' he suggested seriously.

Holliday stared at him incredulously, his face contorting. For a moment he said nothing. Then, almost berserk, he shouted: 'Have it stuffed? Are you crazy? Do you think I want to make a dummy of myself, fill my own head with straw?'

Turning on his heel, he shouldered past Granger and swung himself roughly out of the pool.

**· 1961**

# THE OVERLOADED MAN

Faulkner was slowly going insane.

After breakfast he waited impatiently in the lounge while his wife tidied up in the kitchen. She would be gone within two or three minutes, but for some reason he always found the short wait each morning almost unbearable. As he drew the Venetian blinds and readied the reclining chair on the veranda he listened to Julia moving about efficiently. In the same strict sequence she stacked the cups and plates in the dishwasher, slid the pot roast for that evening's dinner into the auto-cooker and selected the alarm, lowered the air-conditioner, refrigerator and immersion heater settings, switched open the oil storage manifolds for the delivery tanker that afternoon, and retracted her section of the garage door.

Faulkner followed the sequence with admiration, counting off each successive step as the dials clicked and snapped.

You ought to be in B-52's, he thought, or in the control house of a petrochemicals plant. In fact Julia worked in the personnel section at the Clinic, and no doubt spent all day in the same whirl of efficiency, stabbing buttons marked 'Jones', 'Smith', and 'Brown', shunting paraplegics to the left, paranoids to the right.

She stepped into the lounge and came over to him, the standard executive product in brisk black suit and white blouse.

'Aren't you going to the school today?' she asked.

Faulkner shook his head, played with some papers on the desk. 'No, I'm still on creative reflection. Just for this week. Professor Harman thought I'd been taking too many classes and getting stale.'

She nodded, looking at him doubtfully. For three weeks now he had been lying around at home, dozing on the veranda, and she was beginning to get suspicious. Sooner or later, Faulkner realized, she would find out, but by then he hoped to be out of reach. He longed to tell her the truth, that two months ago he had resigned from his job as a lecturer at the Business School and had no intention of ever going back. She'd get a damn big surprise when she discovered they had almost expended his last pay cheque, might even have to put up with only one car. Let her work, he thought, she earns more than I did anyway.

With an effort Faulkner smiled at her. *Get out!* his mind screamed, but she still hovered around him indecisively.

'What about your lunch? There's no —'

'Don't worry about me,' Faulkner cut in quickly, watching the clock. 'I gave up eating six months ago. You have lunch at the Clinic.'

Even talking to her had become an effort. He wished they could communicate by means of notes; had even bought two scribble pads for this purpose. However, he had never quite been able to suggest that she use hers, although he did leave messages around for her, on the pretext that his mind was so intellectually engaged that talking would break up his thought trains.

Oddly enough, the idea of leaving her never seriously occurred to him. Such an escape would prove nothing. Besides, he had an alternative plan.

'You'll be all right?' she asked, still watching him warily.

'Absolutely,' Faulkner told her, maintaining the smile. It felt like a full day's work.

Her kiss was quick and functional, like the automatic peck of some huge bottle-topping machine. The smile was still on his face as she reached the door. When she had gone he let it fade slowly, then found himself breathing again and gradually relaxed, letting the tension drain down through his arms and legs. For a few minutes he wandered blankly around the empty house, then made his way into the lounge again, ready to begin his serious work.

His programme usually followed the same course. First, from the centre drawer of his desk he took a small alarm clock, fitted with a battery and wrist strap. Sitting down on the veranda, he fastened the strap to his wrist, wound and set the clock and placed it on the table next to him, binding his arm to the chair so that there was no danger of dragging the clock onto the floor.

Ready now, he lay back and surveyed the scene in front of him.

Menninger Village, or the 'Bin' as it was known locally, had been built about ten years earlier as a self-contained housing unit for the graduate staff of the Clinic and their families. In all there were some sixty houses in the development, each designed to fit into a particular architectonic niche, preserving its own identity from within and at the same time merging into the organic unity of the whole development. The object of the architects, faced with the task of compressing a great number of small houses into a four-acre site, had been, firstly, to avoid producing a collection of identical hutches, as in most housing estates, and secondly, to provide a showpiece for a major psychiatric foundation which would serve as a model for the corporate living units of the future.

However, as everyone there had found out, living in the Bin was hell on earth. The architects had employed the so-called psycho-modular system – a basic L-design – and this meant that everything under- or overlapped everything else. The whole development was a sprawl of interlocking frosted glass, white rectangles and curves, at first glance exciting and abstract (*Life* magazine had done several glossy photographic treatments of the new 'living trends' suggested by the Village) but to the people

within formless and visually exhausting. Most of the Clinic's senior staff
had soon taken off, and the Village was now rented to anyone who could
be persuaded to live there.

Faulkner gazed out across the veranda, separating from the clutter
of white geometric shapes the eight other houses he could see without
moving his head. On his left, immediately adjacent, were the Penzils,
with the McPhersons on the right; the other six houses were directly
ahead, on the far side of a muddle of interlocking garden areas, abstract
rat-runs divided by waist-high white panelling, glass angle-pieces and
slatted screens.

In the Penzils' garden was a collection of huge alphabet blocks, each
three high, which their two children played with. Often they left messages
out on the grass for Faulkner to read, sometimes obscene, at others merely
gnomic and obscure. This morning's came into the latter category. The
blocks spelled out:

STOP AND GO

Speculating on the total significance of this statement, Faulkner let his
mind relax, his eyes staring blankly at the houses. Gradually their already
obscured outlines began to merge and fade, and the long balconies and
ramps partly hidden by the intervening trees became disembodied forms,
like gigantic geometric units.

Breathing slowly, Faulkner steadily closed his mind, then without any
effort erased his awareness of the identity of the house opposite.

He was now looking at a cubist landscape, a collection of random
white forms below a blue backdrop, across which several powdery green
blurs moved slowly backwards and forwards. Idly, he wondered what
these geometric forms really represented – he knew that only a few
seconds earlier they had constituted an immediately familiar part of
his everyday existence – but however he rearranged them spatially in his
mind, or sought their associations, they still remained a random assembly
of geometric forms.

He had discovered this talent only about three weeks ago. Balefully
eyeing the silent television set in the lounge one Sunday morning, he had
suddenly realized that he had so completely accepted and assimilated the
physical form of the plastic cabinet that he could no longer remember its
function. It had required a considerable mental effort to recover himself
and re-identify it. Out of interest he had tried out the new talent on other
objects, found that it was particularly successful with over-associated ones
such as washing machines, cars and other consumer goods. Stripped of
their accretions of sales slogans and status imperatives, their real claim
to reality was so tenuous that it needed little mental effort to obliterate
them altogether.

The effect was similar to that of mescaline and other hallucinogens,
under whose influence the dents in a cushion became as vivid as the

craters of the moon, the folds in a curtain the ripples in the waves of eternity.

During the following weeks Faulkner had experimented carefully, training his ability to operate the cut-out switches. The process was slow, but gradually he found himself able to eliminate larger and larger groups of objects, the mass-produced furniture in the lounge, the over-enamelled gadgets in the kitchen, his car in the garage – de-identified, it sat in the half-light like an enormous vegetable marrow, flaccid and gleaming; trying to identify it had driven him almost out of his mind. 'What on earth could it *possibly* be?' he had asked himself helplessly, splitting his sides with laughter – and as the facility developed he had dimly perceived that here was an escape route from the intolerable world in which he found himself at the Village.

He had described the facility to Ross Hendricks, who lived a few houses away, also a lecturer at the Business School and Faulkner's only close friend.

'I may actually be stepping out of time,' Faulkner speculated. 'Without a time sense consciousness is difficult to visualize. That is, eliminating the vector of time from the de-identified object frees it from all its everyday cognitive associations. Alternatively, I may have stumbled on a means of repressing the photo-associative centres that normally identify visual objects, in the same way that you can so listen to someone speaking your own language that none of the sounds has any meaning. Everyone's tried this at some time.'

Hendricks had nodded. 'But don't make a career out of it, though.' He eyed Faulkner carefully. 'You can't simply turn a blind eye to the world. The subject-object relationship is not as polar as Descartes' "Cogito ergo sum" suggests. By any degree to which you devalue the external world so you devalue yourself. It seems to me that your real problem is to reverse the process.'

But Hendricks, however sympathetic, was beyond helping Faulkner. Besides, it was pleasant to see the world afresh again, to wallow in an endless panorama of brilliantly coloured images. What did it matter if there was form but no content?

A sharp click woke him abruptly. He sat up with a jolt, fumbling with the alarm clock, which had been set to wake him at 11 o'clock. Looking at it, he saw that it was only 10.55. The alarm had not rung, nor had he received a shock from the battery. Yet the click had been distinct. However, there were so many servos and robots around the house that it could have been anything.

A dark shape moved across the frosted glass panel which formed the side wall of the lounge. Through it, into the narrow drive separating his house from the Penzils', he saw a car draw to a halt and park, a young woman in a blue smock climb out and walk across the gravel. This was Penzil's sister-in-law, a girl of about twenty who had been staying with them for a couple of months. As she disappeared into the house Faulkner quickly unstrapped his wrist and stood up. Opening the veranda doors, he sauntered down into the garden, glancing back over his shoulder.

The girl, Louise (he had never spoken to her), went to sculpture classes in the morning, and on her return regularly took a leisurely shower before going out onto the roof to sunbathe.

Faulkner hung around the bottom of the garden, flipping stones into the pond and pretending to straighten some of the pergola slats, then noticed that the McPhersons' 15-year-old son Harvey was approaching along the other garden.

'Why aren't you at school?' he asked Harvey, a gangling youth with an intelligent ferretlike face under a mop of brown hair.

'I should be,' Harvey told him easily. 'But I convinced Mother I was overtense, and Morrison' – his father – 'said I was ratiocinating too much.' He shrugged. 'Patients here are overpermissive.'

'For once you're right,' Faulkner agreed, watching the shower stall over his shoulder. A pink form moved about, adjusting taps, and there was the sound of water jetting.

'Tell me, Mr Faulkner,' Harvey asked. 'Do you realize that since the death of Einstein in 1955 there hasn't been a single living genius? From Michelangelo, through Shakespeare, Newton, Beethoven, Goethe, Darwin, Freud and Einstein there's always been a living genius. Now for the first time in 500 years we're on our own.'

Faulkner nodded, his eyes engaged. 'I know,' he said. 'I feel damned lonely about it too.'

When the shower was over he grunted to Harvey, wandered back to the veranda, and took up his position again in the chair, the battery lead strapped to his wrist.

Steadily, object by object, he began to switch off the world around him. The houses opposite went first. The white masses of the roofs and balconies he resolved quickly into flat rectangles, the lines of windows into small squares of colour like the grids in a Mondrian abstract. The sky was a blank field of blue. In the distance an aircraft moved across it, engines hammering. Carefully Faulkner repressed the identity of the image, then watched the slim silver dart move slowly away like a vanishing fragment from a cartoon dream.

As he waited for the engines to fade he was conscious of the sourceless click he had heard earlier that morning. It sounded only a few feet away, near the French window on his right, but he was too immersed in the unfolding kaleidoscope to rouse himself.

When the plane had gone he turned his attention to the garden, quickly blotted out the white fencing, the fake pergola, the elliptical disc of the ornamental pool. The pathway reached out to encircle the pool, and when he blanked out his memories of the countless times he had wandered up and down its length it reared up into the air like a terracotta arm holding an enormous silver jewel.

Satisfied that he had obliterated the Village and the garden, Faulkner then began to demolish the house. Here the objects around him were more familiar, highly personalized extensions of himself. He began with the veranda furniture, transforming the tubular chairs and glass-topped table into a trio of involuted green coils, then swung his head slightly and selected the TV set inside the lounge on his right. It clung limply to its identity. Easily he unfocused his mind and reduced the brown plastic box, with its fake wooden veining, to an amorphous blur.

One by one he cleared the bookcase and desk of all associations, the standard lamps and picture frames. Like lumber in some psychological warehouse, they were suspended behind him *in vacuo*, the white armchairs and sofas like blunted rectangular clouds.

Anchored to reality only by the alarm mechanism clamped to his wrist, Faulkner craned his head from left to right, systematically obliterating all traces of meaning from the world around him, reducing everything to its formal visual values.

Gradually these too began to lose their meaning, the abstract masses of colour dissolving, drawing Faulkner after them into a world of pure psychic sensation, where blocks of ideation hung like magnetic fields in a cloud chamber . . .

With a shattering blast, the alarm rang out, the battery driving sharp spurs of pain into Faulkner's forearm. Scalp tingling, he pulled himself back into reality and clawed away the wrist strap, massaging his arm rapidly, then slapped off the alarm.

For a few minutes he sat kneading his wrist, re-identifying all the objects around him, the houses opposite, the gardens, his home, aware that a glass wall had been inserted between them and his own psyche. However carefully he focused his mind on the world outside, a screen still separated them, its opacity thickening imperceptibly.

On other levels as well, bulkheads were shifting into place.

His wife reached home at 6.00, tired out after a busy intake day, annoyed to find Faulkner ambling about in a semistupor, the veranda littered with dirty glasses.

'Well, clean it up!' she snapped when Faulkner vacated his chair for her and prepared to take off upstairs. 'Don't leave the place like this. What's the matter with you? Come on, *connect!*'

Cramming a handful of glasses together, Faulkner mumbled to himself and started for the kitchen, found Julia blocking the way out when he tried to leave. Something was on her mind. She sipped quickly at her martini, then began to throw out probes about the school. He assumed she had rung there on some pretext and had found her suspicions reinforced when she referred in passing to himself.

'Liaison is terrible,' Faulkner told her. 'Take two days off and no one remembers you work there.' By a massive effort of concentration he had managed to avoid looking his wife in the face since she arrived. In fact, they had not exchanged a direct glance for over a week. Hopefully he wondered if this might be getting her down.

Supper was slow agony. The smells of the auto-cooked pot roast had permeated the house all afternoon. Unable to eat more than a few mouthfuls, he had nothing on which to focus his attention. Luckily Julia had a brisk appetite and he could stare at the top of her head as she ate, let his eyes wander around the room when she looked up.

After supper, thankfully, there was television. Dusk blanked out the other houses in the Village, and they sat in the darkness around the set, Julia grumbling at the programmes.

'Why do we watch *every* night?' she asked. 'It's a total time waster.'

Faulkner gestured airily. 'It's an interesting social document.' Slumped down into the wing chair, hands apparently behind his neck, he could press his fingers into his ears, at will blot out the sounds of the programme. 'Don't pay any attention to what they're saying,' he told his wife. 'It makes more sense.' He watched the characters mouthing silently like demented fish. The close-ups in melodramas were particularly hilarious; the more intense the situation the broader was the farce.

Something kicked his knee sharply. He looked up to see his wife bending over him, eyebrows knotted together, mouth working furiously. Fingers still pressed to his ears, Faulkner examined her face with detachment, for a moment speculated whether to complete the process and switch her off as he had switched off the rest of the world earlier that day. When he did he wouldn't bother to set the alarm . . .

'Harry!' he heard his wife bellow.

He sat up with a start, the row from the set backing up his wife's voice.

'What's the matter? I was asleep.'

'You were in a trance, you mean. For God's sake answer when I talk to you. I was saying that I saw Harriet Tizzard this afternoon.' Faulkner groaned and his wife swerved on him. 'I know you can't stand the Tizzards but I've decided we ought to see more of them . . .'

As his wife rattled on, Faulkner eased himself down behind the wings. When she was settled back in her chair he moved his hands up behind his neck. After a few discretionary grunts, he slid his fingers into his ears and blotted out her voice, then lay quietly watching the silent screen.

By 10 o'clock the next morning he was out on the veranda again, alarm strapped to his wrist. For the next hour he lay back enjoying the disembodied forms suspended around him, his mind free of its anxieties. When the alarm woke him at 11.00 he felt refreshed and relaxed. For a few moments he was able to survey the nearby houses with the visual curiosity their architects had intended. Gradually, however, everything began to secrete its poison again, its overlay of nagging associations, and within ten minutes he was looking fretfully at his wristwatch.

When Louise Penzil's car pulled into the drive he disconnected the alarm and sauntered out into the garden, head down to shut out as many of the surrounding houses as possible. As he was idling around the pergola, replacing the slats torn loose by the roses, Harvey McPherson suddenly popped his head over the fence.

'Harvey, are you still around? Don't you ever go to school?'

'Well, I'm on this relaxation course of Mother's,' Harvey explained. 'I find the competitive context of the classroom is –'

'I'm trying to relax too,' Faulkner cut in. 'Let's leave it at that. Why don't you beat it?'

Unruffled, Harvey pressed on. 'Mr Faulkner, I've got a sort of problem in metaphysics that's been bothering me. Maybe you could help. The only absolute in space-time is supposed to be the speed of light. But as a matter of fact any estimate of the speed of light involves the component of time, which is subjectively variable – so, bam, what's left?'

'Girls,' Faulkner said. He glanced over his shoulder at the Penzil house and then turned back moodily to Harvey.

Harvey frowned, trying to straighten his hair. 'What are you talking about?'

'Girls,' Faulkner repeated. 'You know, the weaker sex, the distaff side.'

'Oh, for Pete's sake.' Shaking his head, Harvey walked back to his house, muttering to himself.

That'll shut you up, Faulkner thought. He started to scan the Penzils' house through the slats of the pergola, then suddenly spotted Harry Penzil standing in the centre of his veranda window, frowning out at him.

Quickly Faulkner turned his back and pretended to trim the roses. By the time he managed to work his way indoors he was sweating heavily. Harry Penzil was the sort of man liable to straddle fences and come out leading with a right swing.

Mixing himself a drink in the kitchen, Faulkner brought it out onto the veranda and sat down waiting for his embarrassment to subside before setting the alarm mechanism.

He was listening carefully for any sounds from the Penzils' when he heard a familiar soft metallic click from the house on his right.

Faulkner sat forward, examining the veranda wall. This was a slab of heavy frosted glass, completely opaque, carrying white roof timbers, clipped onto which were slabs of corrugated polythene sheeting. Just beyond the veranda, screening the proximal portions of the adjacent gardens, was a ten-foot-high metal lattice extending about twenty feet down the garden fence and strung with japonica.

Inspecting the lattice carefully, Faulkner suddenly noticed the outline of a square black object on a slender tripod propped up behind the first vertical support just three feet from the open veranda window, the disc of a small glass eye staring at him unblinkingly through one of the horizontal slots.

A camera! Faulkner leapt out of his chair, gaping incredulously at the instrument. For days it had been clicking away at him. God alone knew what glimpses into his private life Harvey had recorded for his own amusement.

Anger boiling, Faulkner strode across to the lattice, prised one of the metal members off the support beam and seized the camera. As he dragged it through the space the tripod fell away with a clatter and he heard someone on the McPhersons' veranda start up out of a chair.

Faulkner wrestled the camera through, snapping off the remote control cord attached to the shutter lever. Opening the camera, he ripped out the film, then put it down on the floor and stamped its face in with the heel of his shoe. Then, ramming the pieces together, he stepped forward and hurled them over the fence towards the far end of the McPhersons' garden.

As he returned to finish his drink the phone rang in the hall.

'Yes, what is it?' he snapped into the receiver.

'Is that you, Harry? Julia here.'

'Who?' Faulkner said, not thinking. 'Oh, yes. Well, how are things?'

'Not too good, by the sound of it.' His wife's voice had become harder. 'I've just had a long talk with Professor Harman. He told me that you resigned from the school two months ago. Harry, what are you playing at? I can hardly believe it.'

'I can hardly believe it either,' Faulkner retorted jocularly. 'It's the best news I've had for years. Thanks for confirming it.'

'Harry!' His wife was shouting now. 'Pull yourself together! If you think I'm going to support you you're very much mistaken. Professor Harman said –'

'That idiot Harman!' Faulkner interrupted. 'Don't you realize he was trying to drive me insane?' As his wife's voice rose to an hysterical squawk he held the receiver away from him, then quietly replaced it in the cradle. After a pause he took it off again and laid it down on the stack of directories.

Outside, the spring morning hung over the Village like a curtain of silence. Here and there a tree stirred in the warm air, or a window opened and caught the sunlight, but otherwise the quiet and stillness were unbroken.

Lying on the veranda, the alarm mechanism discarded on the floor below his chair, Faulkner sank deeper and deeper into his private reverie, into the demolished world of form and colour which hung motionlessly around him. The houses opposite had vanished, their places taken by long white rectangular bands. The garden was a green ramp at the end of which poised the silver ellipse of the pond. The veranda was a transparent cube, in the centre of which he felt himself suspended like an image floating on a sea of ideation. He had obliterated not only the world around him, but his own body, and his limbs and trunk seemed an extension of his mind, disembodied forms whose physical dimensions pressed upon it like a dream's awareness of its own identity.

Some hours later, as he rotated slowly through his reverie, he was aware of a sudden intrusion into his field of vision. Focusing his eyes, with surprise he saw the dark-suited figure of his wife standing in front of him, shouting angrily and gesturing with her handbag.

For a few minutes Faulkner examined the discrete entity she familiarly presented, the proportions of her legs and arms, the planes of her face. Then, without moving, he began to dismantle her mentally, obliterating her literally limb by limb. First he forgot her hands, forever snapping and twisting like frenzied birds, then her arms and shoulders, erasing all his memories of their energy and motion. Finally, as it pressed closer to him, mouth working wildly, he forgot her face, so that it presented nothing more than a blunted wedge of pink-grey dough, deformed by various ridges and grooves, split by apertures that opened and closed like the vents of some curious bellows.

Turning back to the silent dreamscape, he was aware of her jostling insistently behind him. Her presence seemed ugly and formless, a bundle of obtrusive angles.

Then at last they came into brief physical contact. Gesturing her away, he felt her fasten like a dog upon his arm. He tried to shake her off but she clung to him, jerking about in an outpouring of anger.

Her rhythms were sharp and ungainly. To begin with he tried to ignore them; then he began to restrain and smooth her, moulding her angular form into a softer and rounder one.

As he worked away, kneading her like a sculptor shaping clay, he noticed a series of crackling noises, over which a persistent scream was just barely audible. When he finished he let her fall to the floor, a softly squeaking lump of spongy rubber.

Faulkner returned to his reverie, re-assimilating the unaltered landscape. His brush with his wife had reminded him of the one encumbrance that still remained – his own body. Although he had forgotten its identity it none the less felt heavy and warm, vaguely uncomfortable, like a badly made bed to a restless sleeper. What he sought was pure ideation, the undisturbed sensation of psychic being untransmuted by any physical medium. Only thus could he escape the nausea of the external world.

Somewhere in his mind an idea suggested itself. Rising from his chair, he walked out across the veranda, unaware of the physical movements involved, but propelling himself towards the far end of the garden.

Hidden by the rose pergola, he stood for five minutes at the edge of the pond, then stepped into the water. Trousers billowing around his knees, he waded out slowly. When he reached the centre he sat down, pushing the weeds apart, and lay back in the shallow water.

Slowly he felt the puttylike mass of his body dissolving, its temperature growing cooler and less oppressive. Looking out through the surface of the water six inches above his face, he watched the blue disc of the sky, cloudless and undisturbed, expanding to fill his consciousness. At last he had found the perfect background, the only possible field of ideation, an absolute continuum of existence uncontaminated by material excrescences.

Steadily watching it, he waited for the world to dissolve and set him free.

· **1961**

# · MR F. IS MR F.

And baby makes three.

*... Eleven o'clock. Hanson should have reached here by now. Elizabeth!*
*Damn, why does she always move so quietly?*

Climbing down from the window overlooking the road, Freeman ran
back to his bed and jumped in, smoothing the blankets over his knees. As
his wife poked her head around the door he smiled up at her guilelessly,
pretending to read a magazine.

'Everything all right?' she asked, eyeing him shrewdly. She moved her
matronly bulk towards him and began to straighten the bed. Freeman
fidgeted irritably, pushing her away when she tried to lift him off the
pillow on which he was sitting.

'For heaven's sake, Elizabeth, I'm not a child!' he remonstrated, controlling his sing-song voice with difficulty.

'What's happened to Hanson? He was supposed to be here half an
hour ago.'

His wife shook her large handsome head and went over to the window.
The loose cotton dress disguised her figure, but as she reached up to the
bolt Freeman could see the incipient swell of her pregnancy.

'He must have missed his train.' With a single twist of her forearm she
securely fastened the upper bolt, which had taken Freeman ten minutes
to unlatch.

'I thought I could hear it banging,' she said pointedly. 'We don't want
you to catch a cold, do we?'

Freeman waited impatiently for her to leave, glancing at his watch.
When his wife paused at the foot of the bed, surveying him carefully,
he could barely restrain himself from shouting at her.

'I'm getting the baby's clothes together,' she said, adding aloud to
herself, 'which reminds me, you need a new dressing gown. That old
one of yours is losing its shape.'

Freeman pulled the lapels of the dressing gown across each other, as
much to hide his bare chest as to fill out the gown.

'Elizabeth, I've had this for years and it's perfectly good. You're
getting an obsession about renewing everything.' He hesitated, realizing
the tactlessness of this remark – he should be flattered that she was
identifying him with the expected baby. If the strength of the identification was sometimes alarming, this was probably because she was

having her first child at a comparatively late age, in her early forties. Besides, he had been ill and bed-ridden during the past month (and what were *his* unconscious motives?) which only served to reinforce the confusion.

'Elizabeth. I'm sorry. It's been good of you to look after me. Perhaps we should call a doctor.'

*No!* something screamed inside him.

As if hearing this, his wife shook her head in agreement.

'You'll be all right soon. Let nature take its proper course. I don't think you need to see the doctor yet.'

*Yet?*

Freeman listened to her feet disappearing down the carpeted staircase. A few minutes later the sound of the washing machine drummed out from the kitchen.

*Yet!*

Freeman slipped quickly out of bed and went into the bathroom.

The cupboard beside the wash-basin was crammed with drying baby clothes, which Elizabeth had either bought or knitted, then carefully washed and sterilized. On each of the five shelves a large square of gauze covered the neat piles, but he could see that most of the clothes were blue, a few white and none pink.

*I hope Elizabeth is right,* he thought. *If she is it's certainly going to be the world's best-dressed baby. We're supporting an industry single-handed.*

He bent down to the bottom compartment, and from below the tank pulled out a small set of scales. On the shelf immediately above he noticed a large brown garment, a six-year-old's one-piece romper suit. Next to it was a set of vests, outsize, almost big enough to fit Freeman himself. He stripped off his dressing gown and stepped on to the platform. In the mirror behind the door he examined his small hairless body, with its thin shoulders and narrow hips, long coltish legs.

*Six stone nine pounds yesterday.* Averting his eyes from the dial, he listened to the washing machine below, then waited for the pointer to steady.

'Six stone two pounds!'

Fumbling with his dressing gown, Freeman pushed the scales under the tank.

*Six stone two pounds! A drop of seven pounds in twenty-four hours!*

He hurried back into bed, and sat there trembling nervously, fingering for his vanished moustache.

Yet only two months ago he had weighed over eleven stone. Seven pounds in a single day, at this rate –

His mind baulked at the conclusion. Trying to steady his knees, he reached for one of the magazines, turned the pages blindly.

And baby makes two.

\*         \*         \*

He had first become aware of the transformation six weeks earlier, almost immediately after Elizabeth's pregnancy had been confirmed.

Shaving the next morning in the bathroom before going to the office, he discovered that his moustache was thinning. The usually stiff black bristles were soft and flexible, taking on their former ruddy-brown colouring.

His beard, too, was lighter; normally dark and heavy after only a few hours, it yielded before the first few strokes of the razor, leaving his face pink and soft.

Freeman had credited this apparent rejuvenation to the appearance of the baby. He was forty when he married Elizabeth, two or three years her junior, and had assumed unconsciously that he was too old to become a parent, particularly as he had deliberately selected Elizabeth as an ideal mother-substitute, and saw himself as her child rather than as her parental partner. However, now that a child had actually materialized he felt no resentment towards it. Complimenting himself, he decided that he had entered a new phase of maturity and could whole-heartedly throw himself into the role of young parent.

Hence the disappearing moustache, the fading beard, the youthful spring in his step. He crooned:

> 'Just Lizzie and me,
> And baby makes three.'

Behind him, in the mirror, he watched Elizabeth still asleep, her large hips filling the bed. He was glad to see her rest. Contrary to what he had expected, she was even more concerned with him than with the baby, refusing to allow him to prepare his own breakfast. As he brushed his hair, a rich blond growth, sweeping back off his forehead to cover his bald dome, he reflected wryly on the time-honoured saws in the maternity books about the hypersensitivity of expectant fathers – evidently Elizabeth took these counsels seriously.

He tiptoed back into the bedroom and stood by the open window, basking in the crisp early morning air. Downstairs, while he waited for breakfast, he pulled his old tennis racquet out of the hall cupboard, finally woke Elizabeth when one of his practice strokes cracked the glass in the barometer.

To begin with Freeman had revelled in his new-found energy. He took Elizabeth boating, rowing her furiously up and down the river, rediscovering all the physical pleasures he had been too preoccupied to enjoy in his early twenties. He would go shopping with Elizabeth, steering her smoothly along the pavement, carrying all her baby purchases, shoulders back, feeling ten feet tall.

However, it was here that he had his first inkling of what was really happening.

Elizabeth was a large woman, attractive in her way, with broad shoulders and strong hips, and accustomed to wearing high heels. Freeman, a stocky man of medium height, had always been slightly shorter than her, but this had never worried him.

When he found that he barely reached above her shoulder he began to examine himself more closely.

On one of their shopping expeditions (Elizabeth always took Freeman with her, unselfishly asked his opinions, what he preferred, almost as if *he* would be wearing the tiny matinee coats and dresses) a saleswoman unwittingly referred to Elizabeth as his 'mother'. Jolted, Freeman had recognized the obvious disparity between them – the pregnancy was making Elizabeth's face puffy, filling out her neck and shoulders, while his own features were smooth and unlined.

When they reached home he wandered around the lounge and dining room, realized that the furniture and bookshelves seemed larger and more bulky. Upstairs in the bathroom he climbed on the scales for the first time, found that he had lost one stone six pounds in weight.

Undressing that night, he made another curious discovery.

Elizabeth was taking in the seams of his jackets and trousers. She had said nothing to him about this, and when he saw her sewing away over her needle basket he had assumed she was preparing something for the baby.

During the next days his first flush of spring vigour faded. Strange changes were taking place in his body – his skin and hair, his entire musculature, seemed transformed. The planes of his face had altered, the jaw was trimmer, the nose less prominent, cheeks smooth and unblemished.

Examining his mouth in the mirror, he found that most of his old metal fillings had vanished, firm white enamel taking their place.

He continued to go to the office, conscious of the stares of his colleagues around him. The day after he found he could no longer reach the reference books on the shelf behind his desk he stayed at home, feigning an attack of influenza.

Elizabeth seemed to understand completely. Freeman had said nothing to her, afraid that she might be terrified into a miscarriage if she learned the truth. Swathed in his old dressing gown, a woollen scarf around his neck and chest to make his slim figure appear more bulky, he sat on the sofa in the lounge, blankets piled across him, a firm cushion raising him higher off the seat.

Carefully he tried to avoid standing whenever Elizabeth was in the room, and when absolutely necessary circled behind the furniture on tiptoe.

A week later, however, when his feet no longer touched the floor below the dining-room table, he decided to remain in his bed upstairs.

Elizabeth agreed readily. All the while she watched her husband with her bland impassive eyes, quietly readying herself for the baby.

*Damn Hanson*, Freeman thought. At eleven forty-five he had still not appeared. Freeman flipped through the magazine without looking at it, glancing irritably at his watch every few seconds. The strap was now too large for his wrist and twice he had prised additional holes for the clasp.

How to describe his metamorphosis to Hanson he had not decided, plagued as he was by curious doubts. He was not even sure what *was* happening. Certainly he had lost a remarkable amount of weight – up to eight or nine pounds each day – and almost a foot in height, but without any accompanying loss of health. He had, in fact, reverted to the age and physique of a fourteen-year-old schoolboy.

But what was the real explanation? Freeman asked himself. Was the rejuvenation some sort of psychosomatic excess? Although he felt no conscious animosity towards the expected baby, was he in the grip of an insane attempt at retaliation?

It was this possibility, with its logical prospect of padded cells and white-coated guards, that had frightened Freeman into silence. Elizabeth's doctor was brusque and unsympathetic, and almost certainly would regard Freeman as a neurotic malingerer, perpetrating an elaborate charade designed to substitute himself for his own child in his wife's affections.

Also, Freeman knew, there were other motives, obscure and intangible. Frightened of examining them, he began to read the magazine.

It was a schoolchild's comic. Annoyed, Freeman stared at the cover, then looked at the stack of magazines which Elizabeth had ordered from the newsagent that morning. They were all the same.

His wife entered her bedroom on the other side of the landing. Freeman slept alone now in what would eventually be the baby's nursery, partly to give himself enough privacy to think, and also to save him the embarrassment of revealing his shrinking body to his wife.

She came in, carrying a small tray on which were a glass of warm milk and two biscuits. Although he was losing weight, Freeman had the eager appetite of a child. He took the biscuits and ate them hurriedly.

Elizabeth sat on the bed, producing a brochure from the pocket of her apron.

'I want to order the baby's cot,' she told him. 'Would you like to choose one of the designs?'

Freeman waved airily. 'Any of them will do. Pick one that's strong and heavy, something he won't be able to climb out of too easily.'

His wife nodded, watching him pensively. All afternoon she spent ironing and cleaning, moving the piles of dry linen into the cupboards on the landing, disinfecting pails and buckets.

They had decided she would have the baby at home.

*Four and a half stone!*

Freeman gasped at the dial below his feet. During the previous two days he had lost over one stone six pounds, had barely been able to reach up to the handle of the cupboard and open the door. Trying not to look at himself in the mirror, he realized he was now the size of a six-year-old, with a slim chest, slender neck and face. The skirt of the dressing gown trailed across the floor behind him, and only with difficulty could he keep his arms through the voluminous sleeves.

When Elizabeth came up with his breakfast she examined him critically, put the tray down and went out to one of the landing cupboards. She returned with a small sports-shirt and a pair of corduroy shorts.

'Would you like to wear these, dear?' she asked. 'You'll find them more comfortable.'

Reluctant to use his voice, which had degenerated into a piping treble, Freeman shook his head. After she had gone, however, he pulled off the heavy dressing gown and put on the garments.

Suppressing his doubts, he wondered how to reach the doctor without having to go downstairs to the telephone. So far he had managed to avoid raising his wife's suspicions, but now there was no hope of continuing to do so. He barely reached up to her waist. If she saw him standing upright she might well die of shock on the spot.

Fortunately, Elizabeth left him alone. Once, just after lunch, two men arrived in a van from the department store and delivered a blue cot and play-pen, but he pretended to be asleep until they had gone. Despite his anxiety, Freeman easily fell asleep – he had begun to feel tired after lunch – and woke two hours later to find that Elizabeth had made the bed in the cot, swathing the blue blankets and pillow in a plastic sheet.

Below this, shackled to the wooden sides, he could see the white leather straps of a restraining harness.

The next morning Freeman decided to escape. His weight was down to only three stone one pound, and the clothes Elizabeth had given him the previous day were already three sizes too large, the trousers supporting themselves precariously around his slender waist. In the bathroom mirror Freeman stared at the small boy, watching him with wide eyes. Dimly he remembered snapshots of his own childhood.

After breakfast, when Elizabeth was out in the garden, he crept downstairs. Through the window he saw her open the dustbin and push inside his business suit and black leather shoes.

Freeman waited helplessly for a moment, and then hurried back to his room. Striding up the huge steps required more effort than he imagined, and by the time he reached the top flight he was too exhausted to climb on to the bed. Panting, he leaned against it for a few minutes. Even if he reached the hospital, how could he convince anyone there of what had happened without having to call Elizabeth along to identify him?

Fortunately, his intelligence was still intact. Given a pencil and paper he would soon demonstrate his adult mind, a circumstantial knowledge of social affairs that no infant prodigy could ever possess.

His first task was to reach the hospital or, failing that, the local police station. Luckily, all he needed to do was walk along the nearest main thoroughfare – a four-year-old child wandering about on his own would soon be picked up by a constable on duty.

Below, he heard Elizabeth come slowly up the stairs, the laundry basket creaking under her arm. Freeman tried to lift himself on to the bed, but only succeeded in disarranging the sheets. As Elizabeth opened the door he ran around to the far side of the bed and hid his tiny body behind it, resting his chin on the bedspread.

Elizabeth paused, watching his small plump face. For a moment they gazed at each other, Freeman's heart pounding, wondering how she could fail to realize what had happened to him. But she merely smiled and walked through into the bathroom.

Supporting himself on the bedside table, he climbed in, his face away from the bathroom door. On her way out Elizabeth bent down and tucked him up, then slipped out of the room, shutting the door behind her.

The rest of the day Freeman waited for an opportunity to escape, but his wife was busy upstairs, and early that evening, before he could prevent himself, he fell into a deep dreamless sleep.

He woke in a vast white room. Blue light dappled the high walls, along which a line of giant animal figures danced and gambolled. Looking around, he realized that he was still in the nursery. He was wearing a small pair of polka-dot pyjamas (had Elizabeth changed him while he slept?) but they were almost too large for his shrunken arms and legs.

A miniature dressing gown had been laid out across the foot of the bed, a pair of slippers on the floor. Freeman climbed down from the bed and put them on, his balance unsteady. The door was closed, but he pulled a chair over and stood on it, turning the handle with his two small fists.

On the landing he paused, listening carefully. Elizabeth was in the kitchen, humming to herself. One step at a time, Freeman moved down the staircase, watching his wife through the rail. She was standing over the cooker, her broad back almost hiding the machine, warming some milk gruel. Freeman waited until she turned to the sink, then ran across the hall into the lounge and out through the french windows.

The thick soles of his carpet slippers muffled his footsteps, and he broke into a run once he reached the shelter of the front garden. The gate was almost too stiff for him to open, and as he fumbled with the latch a middle-aged woman stopped and peered down at him, frowning at the windows.

Freeman pretended to run back into the house, hoping that Elizabeth had not yet discovered his disappearance. When the woman moved off, he opened the gate, and hurried down the street towards the shopping centre.

He had entered an enormous world. The two-storey houses loomed like canyon walls, the end of the street one hundred yards away below the horizon. The paving stones were massive and uneven, the tall sycamores as distant as the sky. A car came towards him, daylight between its wheels, hesitated and sped on.

He was still fifty yards from the corner when he tripped over one of the pavement stones and was forced to stop. Out of breath, he leaned against a tree, his legs exhausted.

He heard a gate open, and over his shoulder saw Elizabeth glance up and down the street. Quickly he stepped behind the tree, waited until she returned to the house, and then set off again.

Suddenly, sweeping down from the sky, a vast arm lifted him off his feet. Gasping with surprise, he looked up into the face of Mr Symonds, his bank manager.

'You're out early, young man,' Symonds said. He put Freeman down, holding him tightly by one hand. His car was parked in the drive next to them. Leaving the engine running, he began to walk Freeman back down the street. 'Now, let's see, where do you live?'

Freeman tried to pull himself away, jerking his arm furiously, but Symonds hardly noticed his efforts. Elizabeth stepped out of the gate, an apron around her waist, and hurried towards them. Freeman tried to hide between Symonds' legs, felt himself picked up in the bank manager's strong arms and handed to Elizabeth. She held him firmly, his head over her broad shoulder, thanked Symonds and carried him back into the house.

As they crossed the pathway Freeman hung limply, trying to will himself out of existence.

In the nursery he waited for his feet to touch the bed, ready to dive below the blankets, but instead Elizabeth lowered him carefully to the floor, and he discovered he had been placed in the baby's play-pen. He held the rail uncertainly, while Elizabeth bent over and straightened his dressing gown. Then, to Freeman's relief, she turned away.

For five minutes Freeman stood numbly by the rail, outwardly recovering his breath, but at the same time gradually realizing something of which he had been dimly afraid for several days – by an extraordinary inversion of logic, Elizabeth identified him with the baby inside her womb! Far from showing surprise at Freeman's transformation into a three-year-old child, his wife merely accepted this as a natural concomitant of her own pregnancy. In her mind she had externalized the child within her. As Freeman shrank progressively smaller, mirroring the growth of her child, her eyes were fixed on their common focus, and all she could see was the image of her baby.

Still searching for a means of escape, Freeman discovered that he was unable to climb out of the play-pen. The light wooden bars were too strong for his small arms to break, the whole cage too heavy to lift. Exhausting himself, he sat down on the floor, and fiddled nervously with a large coloured ball.

Instead of trying to evade Elizabeth and hide his transformation from her, he realized that he must now attract her attention and force her to recognize his real identity.

Standing up, he began to rock the play-pen from side to side, edging it across to the wall where the sharp corner set up a steady battering.

Elizabeth came out of her bedroom.

'Now, darling, what's all the noise for?' she asked, smiling at him. 'How about a biscuit?' She knelt down by the pen, her face only a few inches from Freeman's.

Screwing up his courage, Freeman looked straight at her, searching the large, unblinking eyes. He took the biscuit, cleared his throat and said carefully: 'I'd nod blor aby.'

Elizabeth ruffled his long blond hair. 'Aren't you, darling? What a sad shame.'

Freeman stamped his foot, then flexed his lips. 'I'd nod blor aby!' he shouted. 'I'd blor usban!'

Laughing to herself, Elizabeth began to empty the wardrobe beside the bed. As Freeman remonstrated with her, struggling helplessly with the strings of consonants, she took out his dinner jacket and overcoat. Then she emptied the chest of drawers, lifting out his shirts and socks, and wrapped them away inside a sheet.

After she had carried everything out she returned and stripped the bed, pushed it back against the wall, putting the baby cot in its place.

Clutching the rail of the play-pen, Freeman watched dumbfounded as the last remnants of his former existence were dispatched below.

'Lisbeg, lep me, I'd –!'

He gave up, searched the floor of the play-pen for something to write with. Summoning his energies, he rocked the cot over to the wall, and in large letters, using the spit which flowed amply from his mouth, wrote:

ELIZABETH HELP ME! I AM NOT A BABY

Banging on the door with his fists, he finally attracted Elizabeth's attention, but when he pointed to the wall the marks had dried. Weeping with frustration, Freeman toddled across the cage and began to retrace the message. Before he had completed more than two or three letters Elizabeth put her arms around his waist and lifted him out.

A single place had been set at the head of the dining-room table, a new high chair beside it. Still trying to form a coherent sentence, Freeman felt himself rammed into the seat, a large bib tied around his neck.

During the meal he watched Elizabeth carefully, hoping to detect in her motionless face some inkling of recognition, even a fleeting awareness that the two-year-old child sitting in front of her was her husband. Freeman played with his food, smearing crude messages on the tray around his dish, but when he pointed at them Elizabeth clapped her hands, apparently joining in his little triumphs, and then wiped the tray clean. Worn out, Freeman let himself be carried upstairs, lay strapped in the cot under the miniature blankets.

Time was against him. By now, he found, he was asleep for the greater portion of each day. For the first hours he felt fresh and alert, but his energy faded rapidly and after each meal an overwhelming lethargy closed his eyes like a sleeping draught. Dimly he was aware that his metamorphosis continued unchecked – when he woke he could sit up only with difficulty. The effort of standing upright on his buckling legs tired him after a few minutes.

His power of speech had vanished. All he could produce were a few grotesque grunts, or an inarticulate babble. Lying on his back with a bottle of hot milk in his mouth, he knew that his one hope was Hanson. Sooner or later he would call in and discover that Freeman had disappeared and all traces of him had been carefully removed.

Propped against a cushion on the carpet in the lounge, Freeman noted that Elizabeth had emptied his desk and taken down his books from the shelves beside the fireplace. To all intents she was now the widowed mother of a twelve-month-old son, parted from her husband since their honeymoon.

Unconsciously she had begun to assume this role. When they went out for their morning walks, Freeman strapped back into the pram, a celluloid rabbit rattling a few inches from his nose and almost driving him insane, they passed many people he had known by sight, and all took it for granted that he was Elizabeth's son. As they bent over the pram, poking him in the stomach and complimenting Elizabeth on his size and precosity, several of them referred to her husband, and Elizabeth replied that he was away on an extended trip. In her mind, obviously, she had already dismissed Freeman, forgetting that he had ever existed.

He realized how wrong he was when they returned from what was to be his last outing.

As they neared home Elizabeth hesitated slightly, jolting the pram, apparently uncertain whether to retrace her steps. Someone shouted at them from the distance, and as Freeman tried to identify the familiar voice Elizabeth bent forwards and pulled the hood over his head.

Struggling to free himself, Freeman recognized the tall figure of Hanson towering over the pram, doffing his hat.

'Mrs Freeman, I've been trying to ring you all week. How are you?'

'Very well, Mr Hanson.' She jerked the pram around, trying to keep it between herself and Hanson. Freeman could see that she was momentarily confused. 'I'm afraid our telephone is out of order.'

Hanson side-stepped around the pram, watching Elizabeth with interest. 'What happened to Charles on Saturday? Have to go off on business?'

Elizabeth nodded. 'He was very sorry, Mr Hanson, but something important came up. He'll be away for some time.'

*She knew,* Freeman said automatically to himself.

Hanson peered under the hood at Freeman. 'Out for a morning stroll, little chap?' To Elizabeth he commented: 'Fine baby there. I always like the angry-looking ones. Your neighbour's?'

Elizabeth shook her head. 'The son of a friend of Charles's. We must be getting along, Mr Hanson.'

'Do call me Robert. See you again soon, eh?'

Elizabeth smiled, her face composed again. 'I'm sure we will, Robert.'

'Good show.' With a roguish grin, Hanson walked off.

*She knew!*

Astounded, Freeman pushed the blankets back as far as he could, watching Hanson's retreating figure. He turned once to wave to Elizabeth, who raised her hand and then steered the pram through the gate.

Freeman tried to sit up, his eyes fixed on Elizabeth, hoping she would see the anger in his face. But she wheeled the pram swiftly into the passageway, unfastened the straps and lifted Freeman out.

As they went up the staircase he looked down over her shoulder at the telephone, saw that the receiver was off its cradle. All along she had known what was happening, had deliberately pretended not to notice his metamorphosis. She had anticipated each stage of the transformation, the comprehensive wardrobe had been purchased well in advance, the succession of smaller and smaller garments, the play-pen and cot, had been ordered for him, not for the baby.

For a moment Freeman wondered whether she was pregnant at all. The facial puffiness, the broadening figure, might well have been illusory. When she told him she was expecting a baby he had never imagined that *he* would be the baby.

Handling him roughly, she bundled Freeman into his cot and secured him under the blankets. Downstairs he could hear her moving about rapidly, apparently preparing for some emergency. Propelled by an uncharacteristic urgency, she was closing the windows and doors. As he listened to her, Freeman noticed how cold he felt. His small body was swaddled like a new-born infant in a mass of shawls, but his bones were like sticks of ice. A curious drowsiness was coming over him, draining away his anger and fear, and the centre of his awareness was shifting from his eyes to his skin. The thin afternoon light stung his eyes, and as they closed he slipped off into a blurring limbo of shallow sleep, the tender surface of his body aching for relief.

Some while later he felt Elizabeth's hands pull away the blankets, and was aware of her carrying him across the hallway. Gradually his memory of the house and his own identity began to fade, and his shrinking body clung helplessly to Elizabeth as she lay on her broad bed.

Hating the naked hair that rasped across his face, he now felt clearly for the first time what he had for so long repressed. Before the end he cried out suddenly with joy and wonder, as he remembered the drowned world of his first childhood.

As the child within her quietened, stirring for the last time, Elizabeth sank back on to the pillow, the birth pains slowly receding. Gradually she felt her strength return, the vast world within her settling and annealing itself. Staring at the darkened ceiling, she lay resting for several hours, now and then adjusting her large figure to fit the unfamiliar contours of the bed.

The next morning she rose for half an hour. The child already seemed less burdensome, and three days later she was able to leave her bed completely, a loose smock hiding what remained of her pregnancy. Immediately she began the last task, clearing away all that remained of the baby's clothing, dismantling the cot and play-pen. The clothing she tied into large parcels, then telephoned a local charity which came and collected them. The pram and cot she sold to the second-hand dealer who drove down the street. Within two days she had erased every trace of her husband, stripping the coloured illustrations from the nursery walls and replacing the spare bed in the centre of the floor.

All that remained was the diminishing knot within her, a small clenching fist. When she could almost no longer feel it Elizabeth went to her jewel box and took off her wedding ring.

On her return from the shopping centre the next morning, Elizabeth noticed someone hailing her from a car parked outside her gate.

'Mrs Freeman!' Hanson jumped out of the car and accosted her gaily. 'It's wonderful to see you looking so well.'

Elizabeth gave him a wide heart-warming smile, her handsome face made more sensual by the tumescence of her features. She was wearing a bright silk dress and all visible traces of the pregnancy had vanished.

'Where's Charles?' Hanson asked. 'Still away?'

Elizabeth's smile broadened, her lips parted across her strong white teeth. Her face was curiously expressionless, her eyes momentarily fixed on some horizon far beyond Hanson's face.

Hanson waited uncertainly for Elizabeth to reply. Then, taking the hint, he leaned back into his car and switched off the engine. He rejoined Elizabeth, holding the gate open for her.

So Elizabeth met her husband. Three hours later the metamorphosis of Charles Freeman reached its climax. In that last second Freeman came to his true beginning, the moment of his conception coinciding with the moment of his extinction, the end of his last birth with the beginning of his first death.

And baby makes one.

**· 1961**

# BILLENNIUM

All day long, and often into the early hours of the morning, the tramp of feet sounded up and down the stairs outside Ward's cubicle. Built into a narrow alcove in a bend of the staircase between the fourth and fifth floors, its plywood walls flexed and creaked with every footstep like the timbers of a rotting windmill. Over a hundred people lived in the top three floors of the old rooming house, and sometimes Ward would lie awake on his narrow bunk until 2 or 3 a.m., mechanically counting the last residents returning from the all-night movies in the stadium half a mile away. Through the window he could hear giant fragments of the amplified dialogue booming among the rooftops. The stadium was never empty. During the day the huge four-sided screen was raised on its davit and athletics meetings or football matches ran continuously. For the people in the houses abutting the stadium the noise must have been unbearable.

Ward, at least, had a certain degree of privacy. Two months earlier, before he came to live on the staircase, he had shared a room with seven others on the ground floor of a house in 755th Street, and the ceaseless press of people jostling past the window had reduced him to a state of exhaustion. The street was always full, an endless clamour of voices and shuffling feet. By 6.30, when he woke, hurrying to take his place in the bathroom queue, the crowds already jammed it from sidewalk to sidewalk, the din punctuated every half minute by the roar of the elevated trains running over the shops on the opposite side of the road. As soon as he saw the advertisement describing the staircase cubicle he had left (like everyone else, he spent most of his spare time scanning the classifieds in the newspapers, moving his lodgings an average of once every two months) despite the higher rental. A cubicle on a staircase would almost certainly be on its own.

However, this had its drawbacks. Most evenings his friends from the library would call in, eager to rest their elbows after the bruising crush of the public reading room. The cubicle was slightly more than four and a half square metres in floor area, half a square metre over the statutory maximum for a single person, the carpenters having taken advantage, illegally, of a recess beside a nearby chimney breast. Consequently Ward had been able to fit a small straight-backed chair into the interval between the bed and the door, so that only one person at a time needed to sit on the bed – in most single cubicles host and guest had to sit side by side on the bed, conversing over their shoulders and changing places periodically to avoid neck-strain.

'You were lucky to find this place,' Rossiter, the most regular visitor, never tired of telling him. He reclined back on the bed, gesturing at the cubicle. 'It's enormous, the perspectives really zoom. I'd be surprised if you haven't got at least five metres here, perhaps six.'

Ward shook his head categorically. Rossiter was his closest friend, but the quest for living space had forged powerful reflexes. 'Just over four and a half, I've measured it carefully. There's no doubt about it.'

Rossiter lifted one eyebrow. 'I'm amazed. It must be the ceiling then.'

Manipulating the ceiling was a favourite trick of unscrupulous land-lords – most assessments of area were made upon the ceiling, out of convenience, and by tilting back the plywood partitions the rated area of a cubicle could be either increased, for the benefit of a prospective tenant (many married couples were thus bamboozled into taking a single cubicle), or decreased temporarily on the visits of the housing inspectors. Ceilings were criss-crossed with pencil marks staking out the rival claims of tenants on opposite sides of a party wall. Someone timid of his rights could be literally squeezed out of existence – in fact, the advertisement 'quiet clientele' was usually a tacit invitation to this sort of piracy.

'The wall does tilt a little,' Ward admitted. 'Actually, it's about four degrees out – I used a plumb-line. But there's still plenty of room on the stairs for people to get by.'

Rossiter grinned. 'Of course, John. I'm just envious, that's all. My room is driving me crazy.' Like everyone, he used the term 'room' to describe his tiny cubicle, a hangover from the days fifty years earlier when people had indeed lived one to a room, sometimes, unbelievably, one to an apartment or house. The microfilms in the architecture catalogues at the library showed scenes of museums, concert halls and other public buildings in what appeared to be everyday settings, often virtually empty, two or three people wandering down an enormous gallery or staircase. Traffic moved freely along the centre of streets, and in the quieter districts sections of sidewalk would be deserted for fifty yards or more.

Now, of course, the older buildings had been torn down and replaced by housing batteries, or converted into apartment blocks. The great banqueting room in the former City Hall had been split horizontally into four decks, each of these cut up into hundreds of cubicles.

As for the streets, traffic had long since ceased to move about them. Apart from a few hours before dawn when only the sidewalks were crowded, every thoroughfare was always packed with a shuffling mob of pedestrians, perforce ignoring the countless 'Keep Left' signs suspended over their heads, wrestling past each other on their way to home and office, their clothes dusty and shapeless. Often 'locks' would occur when a huge crowd at a street junction became immovably jammed. Sometimes these locks would last for days. Two years earlier Ward had been caught in one outside the stadium, for over forty-eight hours was trapped in a gigantic pedestrian jam containing over 20,000 people, fed by the crowds leaving the stadium on one side and those approaching it on the other. An entire square mile of the local neighbourhood had been paralysed, and he vividly remembered the nightmare of swaying helplessly on his feet as the jam shifted and heaved, terrified of losing his balance and being trampled underfoot. When the police had finally sealed off the stadium and dispersed the jam he had gone back to his cubicle and slept for a week, his body blue with bruises.

'I hear they may reduce the allocation to three and a half metres,' Rossiter remarked.

Ward paused to allow a party of tenants from the sixth floor to pass down the staircase, holding the door to prevent it jumping off its latch. 'So they're always saying,' he commented. 'I can remember that rumour ten years ago.'

'It's no rumour,' Rossiter warned him. 'It may well be necessary soon. Thirty million people are packed into this city now, a million increase in just one year. There's been some pretty serious talk at the Housing Department.'

Ward shook his head. 'A drastic revaluation like that is almost impossible to carry out. Every single partition would have to be dismantled and nailed up again, the administrative job alone is so vast it's difficult to visualize. Millions of cubicles to be redesigned and certified, licences to be issued, plus the complete resettlement of every tenant. Most of the buildings put up since the last revaluation are designed around a four-metre modulus – you can't simply take half a metre off the end of each cubicle and then say that makes so many new cubicles. They may be only six inches wide.' He laughed. 'Besides, how can you live in just three and a half metres?'

Rossiter smiled. 'That's the ultimate argument, isn't it? They used it twenty-five years ago at the last revaluation, when the minimum was cut from five to four. It couldn't be done they all said, no one could stand living in only four square metres, it was enough room for a bed and suitcase, but you couldn't open the door to get in.' Rossiter chuckled softly. 'They were all wrong. It was merely decided that from then on all doors would open outwards. Four square metres was here to stay.'

Ward looked at his watch. It was 7.30. 'Time to eat. Let's see if we can get into the food-bar across the road.'

Grumbling at the prospect, Rossiter pulled himself off the bed. They left the cubicle and made their way down the staircase. This was crammed with luggage and packing cases so that only a narrow interval remained around the banister. On the floors below the congestion was worse. Corridors were wide enough to be chopped up into single cubicles, and the air was stale and dead, cardboard walls hung with damp laundry and makeshift larders. Each of the five rooms on the floors contained a dozen tenants, their voices reverberating through the partitions.

People were sitting on the steps above the second floor, using the staircase as an informal lounge, although this was against the fire regulations, women talking to the men queueing in their shirtsleeves outside the washroom, children diving around them. By the time they reached the entrance Ward and Rossiter were having to force their way through the tenants packed together on every landing, loitering around the notice boards or pushing in from the street below.

Taking a breath at the top of the steps, Ward pointed to the food-bar on the other side of the road. It was only thirty yards away, but the throng moving down the street swept past like a river at full tide, crossing them from right to left. The first picture show at the stadium started at 9 o'clock, and people were setting off already to make sure of getting in.

'Can't we go somewhere else?' Rossiter asked, screwing his face up at the prospect of the food-bar. Not only was it packed and take them half an hour to be served, but the food was flat and unappetizing. The journey from the library four blocks away had given him an appetite.

Ward shrugged. 'There's a place on the corner, but I doubt if we can make it.' This was two hundred yards upstream; they would be fighting the crowd all the way.

'Maybe you're right.' Rossiter put his hand on Ward's shoulder. 'You know, John, your trouble is that you never go anywhere, you're too disengaged, you just don't realize how bad everything is getting.'

Ward nodded. Rossiter was right. In the morning, when he set off for the library, the pedestrian traffic was moving with him towards the down-town offices; in the evening, when he came back, it was flowing in the opposite direction. By and large he never altered his routine. Brought up from the age of ten in a municipal hostel, he had gradually lost touch with his father and mother, who lived on the east side of the city and had been unable, or unwilling, to make the journey to see him. Having surrendered his initiative to the dynamics of the city he was reluctant to try to win it back merely for a better cup of coffee. Fortunately his job at the library brought him into contact with a wide range of young people of similar interests. Sooner or later he would marry, find a double cubicle near the library and settle down. If they had enough children (three was the required minimum) they might even one day own a small room of their own.

They stepped out into the pedestrian stream, carried along by it for ten or twenty yards, then quickened their pace and sidestepped through the crowd, slowly tacking across to the other side of the road. There they found the shelter of the shop-fronts, slowly worked their way back to the food-bar, shoulders braced against the countless minor collisions.

'What are the latest population estimates?' Ward asked as they circled a cigarette kiosk, stepping forward whenever a gap presented itself.

Rossiter smiled. 'Sorry, John, I'd like to tell you but you might start a stampede. Besides, you wouldn't believe me.'

Rossiter worked in the Insurance Department at the City Hall, had informal access to the census statistics. For the last ten years these had been classified information, partly because they were felt to be inaccurate, but chiefly because it was feared they might set off a mass attack of claustrophobia. Minor outbreaks had taken place already, and the official line was that world population had reached a plateau, levelling off at 20,000 million. No one believed this for a moment, and Ward assumed that the 3 per cent annual increase maintained since the 1960s was continuing.

How long it could continue was impossible to estimate. Despite the gloomiest prophecies of the Neo-Malthusians, world agriculture had managed to keep pace with the population growth, although intensive cultivation meant that 95 per cent of the population was permanently trapped in vast urban conurbations. The outward growth of cities had at last been checked; in fact, all over the world former suburban areas were being reclaimed for agriculture and population additions were confined within the existing urban ghettos. The countryside, as such, no longer existed. Every single square foot of ground sprouted a crop of one type or other. The one-time fields and meadows of the world were now, in effect, factory floors, as highly mechanized and closed to the public as any industrial area. Economic and ideological rivalries had long since faded before one over-riding quest – the internal colonization of the city.

Reaching the food-bar, they pushed themselves into the entrance and joined the scrum of customers pressing six deep against the counter.

'What is really wrong with the population problem,' Ward confided to Rossiter, 'is that no one has ever tried to tackle it. Fifty years ago short-sighted nationalism and industrial expansion put a premium on a rising population curve, and even now the hidden incentive is to have a large family so that you can gain a little privacy. Single people are penalized simply because there are more of them and they don't fit neatly into double or triple cubicles. But it's the large family with its compact, space-saving logistic that is the real villain.'

Rossiter nodded, edging nearer the counter, ready to shout his order. 'Too true. We all look forward to getting married just so that we can have our six square metres.'

Directly in front of them, two girls turned around and smiled. 'Six square metres,' one of them, a dark-haired girl with a pretty oval face, repeated. 'You sound like the sort of young man I ought to get to know. Going into the real estate business, Henry?'

Rossiter grinned and squeezed her arm. 'Hello, Judith. I'm thinking about it actively. Like to join me in a private venture?'

The girl leaned against him as they reached the counter. 'Well, I might. It would have to be legal, though.'

The other girl, Helen Waring, an assistant at the library, pulled Ward's sleeve. 'Have you heard the latest, John? Judith and I have been kicked out of our room. We're on the street right at this minute.'

'What?' Rossiter cried. They collected their soups and coffee and edged back to the rear of the bar. 'What on earth happened?'

Helen explained: 'You know that little broom cupboard outside our cubicle? Judith and I have been using it as a sort of study hole, going in there to read. It's quiet and restful, if you can get used to not breathing. Well, the old girl found out and kicked up a big fuss, said we were breaking the law and so on. In short, out.' Helen paused. 'Now we've heard she's going to let it as a single.'

Rossiter pounded the counter ledge. 'A broom cupboard? Someone's going to live there? But she'll never get a licence.'

Judith shook her head. 'She's got it already. Her brother works in the Housing Department.'

Ward laughed into his soup. 'But how can she let it? No one will live in a broom cupboard.'

Judith stared at him sombrely. 'You really believe that, John?'

Ward dropped his spoon. 'No, I suppose you're right. People will live anywhere. God, I don't know who I feel more sorry for – you two, or the poor devil who'll be living in that cupboard. What are you going to do?'

'A couple in a place two blocks west are sub-letting half their cubicle to us. They've hung a sheet down the middle and Helen and I'll take turns sleeping on a camp bed. I'm not joking, our room's about two feet wide. I said to Helen that we ought to split up again and sublet one half at twice our rent.'

They had a good laugh over all this. Then Ward said good night to the others and went back to his rooming house.

There he found himself with similar problems.

The manager leaned against the flimsy door, a damp cigar butt revolving around his mouth, an expression of morose boredom on his unshaven face.

'You got four point seven two metres,' he told Ward, who was standing out on the staircase, unable to get into his room. Other tenants pressed by on to the landing, where two women in curlers and dressing gowns were arguing with each other, tugging angrily at the wall of trunks and cases. Occasionally the manager glanced at them irritably. 'Four seven two. I worked it out twice.' He said this as if it ended all possibility of argument.

'Ceiling or floor?' Ward asked.

'Ceiling, whaddya think? How can I measure the floor with all this junk?' He kicked at a crate of books protruding from under the bed.

Ward let this pass. 'There's quite a tilt on the wall,' he pointed out. 'As much as three or four degrees.'

The manager nodded vaguely. 'You're definitely over the four. Way over.' He turned to Ward, who had moved down several steps to allow a man and woman to get past. 'I can rent this as a double.'

'What, only four and a half?' Ward said incredulously. 'How?'

The man who had just passed him leaned over the manager's shoulder and sniffed at the room, taking in every detail in a one-second glance. 'You renting a double here, Louie?'

The manager waved him away and then beckoned Ward into the room, closing the door after him.

'It's a nominal five,' he told Ward. 'New regulation, just came out. Anything over four five is a double now.' He eyed Ward shrewdly. 'Well, whaddya want? It's a good room, there's a lot of space here, feels more like a triple. You got access to the staircase, window slit –' He broke off as Ward slumped down on the bed and started to laugh. 'Whatsa matter? Look, if you want a big room like this you gotta pay for it. I want an extra half rental or you get out.'

Ward wiped his eyes, then stood up wearily and reached for the shelves. 'Relax, I'm on my way. I'm going to live in a broom cupboard. "Access to the staircase" – that's really rich. Tell me, Louie, is there life on Uranus?'

Temporarily, he and Rossiter teamed up to rent a double cubicle in a semi-derelict house a hundred yards from the library. The neighbourhood was seedy and faded, the rooming houses crammed with tenants. Most of them were owned by absentee landlords or by the city corporation, and the managers employed were of the lowest type, mere rent-collectors who cared nothing about the way their tenants divided up the living space, and never ventured beyond the first floors. Bottles and empty cans littered the corridors, and the washrooms looked like sumps. Many of the tenants were old and infirm, sitting about listlessly in their narrow cubicles, wheedling at each other back to back through the thin partitions.

Their double cubicle was on the third floor, at the end of a corridor that ringed the building. Its architecture was impossible to follow, rooms letting off at all angles, and luckily the corridor was a cul de sac. The mounds of cases ended four feet from the end wall and a partition divided off the cubicle, just wide enough for two beds. A high window overlooked the area ways of the buildings opposite.

Possessions loaded on to the shelf above his head, Ward lay back on his bed and moodily surveyed the roof of the library through the afternoon haze.

'It's not bad here,' Rossiter told him, unpacking his case. 'I know there's no real privacy and we'll drive each other insane within a week, but at least we haven't got six other people breathing into our ears two feet away.'

The nearest cubicle, a single, was built into the banks of cases half a dozen steps along the corridor, but the occupant, a man of seventy, was deaf and bed-ridden.

'It's not bad,' Ward echoed reluctantly. 'Now tell me what the latest growth figures are. They might console me.'

Rossiter paused, lowering his voice. 'Four per cent. *Eight hundred million extra people in one year* – just less than half the earth's total population in 1950.'

Ward whistled slowly. 'So they will revalue. What to? Three and a half?'

'Three. From the first of next year.'

'Three square metres!' Ward sat up and looked around him. 'It's unbelievable! The world's going insane, Rossiter. For God's sake, when are they going to do something about it? Do you realize there soon won't be room enough to sit down, let alone lie down?'

Exasperated, he punched the wall beside him, on the second blow knocked in one of the small wooden panels that had been lightly papered over.

'Hey!' Rossiter yelled. 'You're breaking the place down.' He dived across the bed to retrieve the panel, which hung downwards supported by a strip of paper. Ward slipped his hand into the dark interval, carefully drew the panel back on to the bed.

'Who's on the other side?' Rossiter whispered. 'Did they hear?'

Ward peered through the interval, eyes searching the dim light. Suddenly he dropped the panel and seized Rossiter's shoulder, pulled him down on to the bed.

'Henry! Look!'

Directly in front of them, faintly illuminated by a grimy skylight, was a medium-sized room some fifteen feet square, empty except for the dust silted up against the skirting boards. The floor was bare, a few strips of frayed linoleum running across it, the walls covered with a drab floral design. Here and there patches of the paper peeled off and segments of the picture rail had rotted away, but otherwise the room was in habitable condition.

Breathing slowly, Ward closed the open door of the cubicle with his foot, then turned to Rossiter.

'Henry, do you realize what we've found? Do you realize it, man?'

'Shut up. For Pete's sake keep your voice down.' Rossiter examined the room carefully. 'It's fantastic. I'm trying to see whether anyone's used it recently.'

'Of course they haven't,' Ward pointed out. 'It's obvious. There's no door into the room. We're looking through it now. They must have panelled over this door years ago and forgotten about it. Look at that filth everywhere.'

Rossiter was staring into the room, his mind staggered by its vastness.

'You're right,' he murmured. 'Now, when do we move in?'

Panel, by panel, they prised away the lower half of the door and nailed it on to a wooden frame, so that the dummy section could be replaced instantly.

Then, picking an afternoon when the house was half empty and the manager asleep in his basement office, they made their first foray into the room, Ward going in alone while Rossiter kept guard in the cubicle.

For an hour they exchanged places, wandering silently around the dusty room, stretching their arms out to feel its unconfined emptiness, grasping at the sensation of absolute spatial freedom. Although smaller than many of the sub-divided rooms in which they had lived, this room seemed infinitely larger, its walls huge cliffs that soared upward to the skylight.

Finally, two or three days later, they moved in.

For the first week Rossiter slept alone in the room, Ward in the cubicle outside, both there together during the day. Gradually they smuggled in a few items of furniture: two armchairs, a table, a lamp fed from the socket in the cubicle. The furniture was heavy and Victorian; the cheapest available, its size emphasized the emptiness of the room. Pride of place was taken by an enormous mahogany wardrobe, fitted with carved angels and castellated mirrors, which they were forced to dismantle and carry into the house in their suitcases. Towering over them, it reminded Ward of the micro-films of gothic cathedrals, with their massive organ lofts crossing vast naves.

After three weeks they both slept in the room, finding the cubicle unbearably cramped. An imitation Japanese screen divided the room adequately and did nothing to diminish its size. Sitting there in the evenings, surrounded by his books and albums, Ward steadily forgot the city outside. Luckily he reached the library by a back alley and avoided the crowded streets. Rossiter and himself began to seem the only real inhabitants of the world, everyone else a meaningless by-product of their own existence, a random replication of identity which had run out of control.

It was Rossiter who suggested that they ask the two girls to share the room with them.

'They've been kicked out again and may have to split up,' he told Ward, obviously worried that Judith might fall into bad company. 'There's always a rent freeze after a revaluation but all the landlords know about it so they're not re-letting. It's damned difficult to find anywhere.'

Ward nodded, relaxing back around the circular red-wood table. He played with the tassel of the arsenic-green lamp shade, for a moment felt like a Victorian man of letters, leading a spacious, leisurely life among overstuffed furnishings.

'I'm all for it,' he agreed, indicating the empty corners. 'There's plenty of room here. But we'll have to make sure they don't gossip about it.'

After due precautions, they let the two girls into the secret, enjoying their astonishment at finding this private universe.

'We'll put a partition across the middle,' Rossiter explained, 'then take it down each morning. You'll be able to move in within a couple of days. How do you feel?'

'Wonderful!' They goggled at the wardrobe, squinting at the endless reflections in the mirrors.

There was no difficulty getting them in and out of the house. The turnover of tenants was continuous and bills were placed in the mail rack. No one cared who the girls were or noticed their regular calls at the cubicle.

However, half an hour after they arrived neither of them had unpacked her suitcase.

'What's up, Judith?' Ward asked, edging past the girls' beds into the narrow interval between the table and wardrobe.

Judith hesitated, looking from Ward to Rossiter, who sat on the bed, finishing off the plywood partition. 'John, it's just that . . .'

Helen Waring, more matter-of-fact, took over, her fingers straightening the bed-spread. 'What Judith's trying to say is that our position here is a little embarrassing. The partition is –'

Rossiter stood up. 'For heaven's sake, don't worry, Helen,' he assured her, speaking in the loud whisper they had all involuntarily cultivated. 'No funny business, you can trust us. This partition is as solid as a rock.'

The two girls nodded. 'It's not that,' Helen explained, 'but it isn't up all the time. We thought that if an older person were here, say Judith's aunt – she wouldn't take up much room and be no trouble, she's really awfully sweet – we wouldn't need to bother about the partition – except at night,' she added quickly.

Ward glanced at Rossiter, who shrugged and began to scan the floor.

'Well, it's an idea,' Rossiter said. 'John and I know how you feel. Why not?'

'Sure,' Ward agreed. He pointed to the space between the girls' beds and the table. 'One more won't make any difference.'

The girls broke into whoops. Judith went over to Rossiter and kissed him on the cheek. 'Sorry to be a nuisance, Henry.' She smiled at him. 'That's a wonderful partition you've made. You couldn't do another one for Auntie – just a little one? She's very sweet but she is getting on.'

'Of course,' Rossiter said. 'I understand. I've got plenty of wood left over.'

Ward looked at his watch. 'It's seven-thirty, Judith. You'd better get in touch with your aunt. She may not be able to make it tonight.'

Judith buttoned her coat. 'Oh she will,' she assured Ward. 'I'll be back in a jiffy.'

The aunt arrived within five minutes, three heavy suitcases soundly packed.

'It's amazing,' Ward remarked to Rossiter three months later. 'The size of this room still staggers me. It almost gets larger every day.'

Rossiter agreed readily, averting his eyes from one of the girls changing behind the central partition. This they now left in place as dismantling it daily had become tiresome. Besides, the aunt's subsidiary partition was attached to it and she resented the continuous upsets. Ensuring she followed the entrance and exit drills through the camouflaged door and cubicle was difficult enough.

Despite this, detection seemed unlikely. The room had obviously been built as an afterthought into the central well of the house and any noise was masked by the luggage stacked in the surrounding corridor. Directly below was a small dormitory occupied by several elderly women, and Judith's aunt, who visited them socially, swore that no sounds came through the heavy ceiling. Above, the fanlight let out through a dormer window, its lights indistinguishable from the hundred other bulbs in the windows of the house.

Rossiter finished off the new partition he was building and held it upright, fitting it into the slots nailed to the wall between his bed and Ward's. They had agreed that this would provide a little extra privacy.

'No doubt I'll have to do one for Judith and Helen,' he confided to Ward.

Ward adjusted his pillow. They had smuggled the two armchairs back to the furniture shop as they took up too much space. The bed, anyway, was more comfortable. He had never become completely used to the soft upholstery.

'Not a bad idea. What about some shelving around the wall? I've got nowhere to put anything.'

The shelving tidied the room considerably, freeing large areas of the floor. Divided by their partitions, the five beds were in line along the rear wall, facing the mahogany wardrobe. In between was an open space of three or four feet, a further six feet on either side of the wardrobe.

The sight of so much spare space fascinated Ward. When Rossiter mentioned that Helen's mother was ill and badly needed personal care he immediately knew where her cubicle could be placed – at the foot of his bed, between the wardrobe and the side wall.

Helen was overjoyed. 'It's awfully good of you, John,' she told him, 'but would you mind if Mother slept beside me? There's enough space to fit an extra bed in.'

So Rossiter dismantled the partitions and moved them closer together, six beds now in line along the wall, This gave each of them an interval two and a half feet wide, just enough room to squeeze down the side of their beds. Lying back on the extreme right, the shelves two feet above his head, Ward could barely see the wardrobe, but the space in front of him, a clear six feet to the wall ahead, was uninterrupted.

Then Helen's father arrived.

Knocking on the door of the cubicle, Ward smiled at Judith's aunt as she let him in. He helped her swing out the made-up bed which guarded the entrance, then rapped on the wooden panel. A moment later Helen's father, a small, grey-haired man in an undershirt, braces tied to his trousers with string, pulled back the panel.

Ward nodded to him and stepped over the luggage piled around the floor at the foot of the beds. Helen was in her mother's cubicle, helping the old woman to drink her evening broth. Rossiter, perspiring heavily, was on his knees by the mahogany wardrobe, wrenching apart the frame of the central mirror with a jemmy. Pieces of the wardrobe lay on his bed and across the floor.

'We'll have to start taking these out tomorrow,' Rossiter told him. Ward waited for Helen's father to shuffle past and enter his cubicle. He had rigged up a small cardboard door, and locked it behind him with a crude hook of bent wire.

Rossiter watched him, frowning irritably. 'Some people are happy. This wardrobe's a hell of a job. How did we ever decide to buy it?'

Ward sat down on his bed. The partition pressed against his knees and he could hardly move. He looked up when Rossiter was engaged and saw that the dividing line he had marked in pencil was hidden by the encroaching partition. Leaning against the wall, he tried to ease it back again, but Rossiter had apparently nailed the lower edge to the floor.

There was a sharp tap on the outside cubicle door – Judith returning from her office. Ward started to get up and then sat back. 'Mr Waring,' he called softly. It was the old man's duty night.

Waring shuffled to the door of his cubicle and unlocked it fussily, clucking to himself.

'Up and down, up and down,' he muttered. He stumbled over Rossiter's tool-bag and swore loudly, then added meaningly over his shoulder: 'If you ask me there's too many people in here. Down below they've only got six to our seven, and it's the same size room.'

Ward nodded vaguely and stretched back on his narrow bed, trying not to bang his head on the shelving. Waring was not the first to hint that he move out. Judith's aunt had made a similar suggestion two days earlier. Since he had left his job at the library (the small rental he charged the others paid for the little food he needed) he spent most of his time in the room, seeing rather more of the old man than he wanted to, but he had learned to tolerate him.

Settling himself, he noticed that the right-hand spire of the wardrobe, all he had been able to see of it for the past two months, was now dismantled.

It had been a beautiful piece of furniture, in a way symbolizing this whole private world, and the salesman at the store told him there were few like it left. For a moment Ward felt a sudden pang of regret, as he had done as a child when his father, in a moment of exasperation, had taken something away from him and he had known he would never see it again.

Then he pulled himself together. It was a beautiful wardrobe, without doubt, but when it was gone it would make the room seem even larger.

· **1961**

# THE GENTLE ASSASSIN

By noon, when Dr Jamieson arrived in London, all entrances into the city had been sealed since six o'clock that morning. The Cornonation Day crowds had waited in their places along the procession route for almost twenty-four hours, and Green Park was deserted as Dr Jamieson slowly made his way up the sloping grass towards the Underground station below the Ritz. Abandoned haversacks and sleeping bags lay about among the litter under the trees, and twice Dr Jamieson stumbled slightly. By the time he reached the station entrance he was perspiring freely, and sat down on a bench, resting his heavy gun-metal suitcase on the grass.

Directly in front of him was one of the high wooden stands. He could see the backs of the top row of spectators, women in bright summer dresses, men in shirtsleeves, newspapers shielding their heads from the hot sunlight, parties of children singing and waving their Union Jacks. All the way down Piccadilly the office blocks were crammed with people leaning out of windows, and the street was a mass of colour and noise. Now and then bands played in the distance, or an officer in charge of the troops lining the route bellowed an order and re-formed his men.

Dr Jamieson listened with interest to all these sounds, savouring the sun-filled excitement. In his middle sixties, he was a small neat figure with greying hair and alert sensitive eyes. His forehead was broad, with a marked slope, which made his somewhat professorial manner appear more youthful. This was helped by the rakish cut of his grey silk suit, its ultra-narrow lapels fastened by a single embroidered button, heavy braided seams on the sleeves and trousers. As someone emerged from the first-aid marquee at the far end of the stand and walked towards him Dr Jamieson sensed the discrepancy between their attire – the man was wearing a baggy blue suit with huge flapping lapels – and frowned to himself in annoyance. Glancing at his watch, he picked up the suitcase and hurried into the Underground station.

The Coronation procession was expected to leave Westminster Abbey at three o'clock, and the streets through which the cortège would pass had been closed to traffic by the police. As he emerged from the station exit on the north side of Piccadilly, Dr Jamieson looked around carefully at the tall office blocks and hotels, here and there repeating a name to himself as he identified a once-familiar landmark. Edging along behind the crowds packed on to the pavement, the metal suitcase bumping painfully against his knees, he reached the entrance to Bond Street, there deliberated carefully and began to walk to the taxi rank fifty yards away. The people pressing down towards Piccadilly glanced at him curiously, and he was relieved when he climbed into the taxi.

'Hotel Westland,' he told the driver, refusing help with the suitcase.

The man cocked one ear. 'Hotel *where*?'

'Westland,' Dr Jamieson repeated, trying to match the modulations of his voice to the driver's. Everyone around him seemed to speak in the same guttural tones. 'It's in Oxford Street, one hundred and fifty yards east of Marble Arch. I think you'll find there's a temporary entrance in Grosvenor Place.'

The driver nodded, eyeing his elderly passenger warily. As they moved off he leaned back. 'Come to see the Coronation?'

'No,' Dr Jamieson said matter-of-factly. 'I'm here on business. Just for the day.'

'I thought maybe you came to watch the procession. You get a wonderful view from the Westland.'

'So I believe. Of course, I'll watch if I get a chance.'

They swung into Grosvenor Square and Dr Jamieson steered the suitcase back onto the seat, examining the intricate metal clasps to make sure the lid held securely. He peered up at the buildings around him, trying not to let his heart become excited as the memories rolled back. Everything, however, differed completely from his recollections, the overlay of the intervening years distorting the original images without his realizing it. The perspectives of the street, the muddle of unrelated buildings and tangle of overhead wires, the signs that sprouted in profuse variety at the slightest opportunity, all seemed entirely new. The whole city was incredibly antiquated and confused, and he found it hard to believe that he had once lived there.

*Were his other memories equally false?*

He sat forward with surprise, pointing through the open window at the graceful beehive curtain-wall of the American Embassy, answering his question.

The driver noticed his interest, flicked away his cigarette. 'Funny style of place,' he commented. 'Can't understand the Yanks putting up a dump like that.'

'Do you think so?' Dr Jamieson asked. 'Not many people would agree with you.'

The driver laughed. 'You're wrong there, mister. I never heard a good word for it yet.' He shrugged, deciding not to offend his passenger. 'Still, maybe it's just ahead of its time.'

Dr Jamieson smiled thinly at this. 'That's about it,' he said, more to himself than to the driver. 'Let's say about thirty-five years ahead. They'll think very highly of it then.'

His voice had involuntarily become more nasal, and the driver asked: 'You from abroad, sir? New Zealand, maybe?'

'No,' Dr Jamieson said, noticing that the traffic was moving down the left-hand side of the road. 'Not exactly. I haven't been to London for some time, though. But I seem to have picked a good day to come back.'

'You have that, sir. A great day for the young Prince. Or King I should say, rather. King James III, sounds a bit peculiar. But good luck to him, and the new Jack-a-what's-a-name Age.'

'The New Jacobean Age,' Dr Jamieson corrected, laughter softening his face for the first time that day. 'Oh yes, that was it.' Fervently, his hands straying to the metal suitcase, he added *sotto voce*. 'As you say, good luck to it.'

Stepping out at the hotel, he went in through the temporary entrance, pushed among the throng of people in the small rear foyer, the noise from Oxford Street dinning in his ears. After a five-minute wait, he reached the desk, the suitcase pulling wearily at his arm.

'Dr Roger Jamieson,' he told the clerk. 'I have a room reserved on the first floor.' He leaned against the counter as the clerk hunted through the register, listening to the hubbub in the foyer. Most of the people were stout middle-aged women in floral dresses, conversing excitedly on their way to the TV lounge, where the Abbey ceremony would be on at two o'clock. Dr Jamieson ignored them, examining the others in the foyer, telegraph messenger boys, off-duty waiters, members of the catering staff organizing the parties held in the rooms above. Each of their faces he scrutinized carefully, as if expecting to see someone he knew.

The clerk peered shortsightedly at the ledger. 'Was the reservation in your name, sir?'

'Certainly. Room 17, the corner room on the first floor.'

The clerk shook his head doubtfully. 'There must have been some mistake, sir, we have no record of any reservation. You aren't with one of the parties upstairs?'

Controlling his impatience, Dr Jamieson rested the suitcase on the floor, securing it against the desk with his foot. 'I assure you, I made the reservation myself. Explicitly for Room 17. It was some time ago but the manager told me it was completely in order and would not be cancelled whatever happened.'

Leafing through the entries, the clerk ran carefully through the entries marked off that day. Suddenly he pointed to a faded entry at the top of the first page.

'Here we are, sir. I apologize, but the booking had been brought forward from the previous register. "Dr Roger Jamieson, Room 17."' Putting his finger on the date with surprise, he smiled at Dr Jamieson. 'A lucky choice of day, Doctor, your booking was made over two years ago.'

Finally locking the door of his room, Dr Jamieson sat down thankfully on one of the beds, his hands still resting on the metal case. For a few minutes he slowly recovered his breath, kneading the numbed muscles in his right forearm. Then he pulled himself to his feet and began a careful inspection of the room.

One of the larger rooms in the hotel, the two corner windows gave it a unique view over the crowded street below. Venetian blinds screened the windows from the hot sunlight and the hundreds of people in the balconies of the department store opposite. Dr Jamieson first peered into the built-in cupboards, then tested the bathroom window onto the interior well. Satisfied that they were secure, he moved an armchair over to the side window which faced the procession's direction of approach. His view was uninterrupted for several hundred yards, each one of the soldiers and policemen lining the route plainly visible.

A large piece of red bunting, part of a massive floral tribute, ran diagonally across the window, hiding him from the people in the building adjacent, and he could see down clearly into the pavement, where a crowd ten or twelve deep was pressed against the wooden palisades. Lowering the blind so that the bottom vane was only six inches from the ledge, Dr Jamieson sat forward and quietly scanned them.

None seemed to hold his interest, and he glanced fretfully at his watch. It was just before two o'clock, and the young king would have left Buckingham Palace on his way to the Abbey. Many members of the crowd were carrying portable radios, and the din outside slackened off as the commentary from the Abbey began.

Dr Jamieson went over to the bed and pulled out his key-chain. Both locks on the case were combination devices. He switched the key left and right a set number of times, pressed home and lifted the lid.

Lying inside the case, on the lower half of the divided velvet mould, were the dismantled members of a powerful sporting rifle, and a magazine of six shells. The metal butt had been shortened by six inches and canted so that when raised to the shoulder in the firing position the breach and barrel pointed downwards at an angle of 45°, both the sights in line with the eye.

Unclipping the sections, Dr Jamieson expertly assembled the weapon, screwing in the butt and adjusting it to the most comfortable angle. Fitting on the magazine, he snapped back the bolt, then pressed it forward and drove the top shell into the breach.

His back to the window, he stared down at the loaded weapon lying on the bedspread in the dim light, listening to the roistering from the parties farther along the corridor, the uninterrupted roar from the street outside. He seemed suddenly very tired, for once the firmness and resolution in his face faded and he looked like an old weary man, friendless in a hotel room in a strange city where everyone but himself was celebrating. He sat down on the bed beside the rifle, wiping the gun-grease off his hands with his handkerchief, his thoughts apparently far away. When he rose he moved stiffly and looked uncertainly around the room, as if wondering why he was there.

Then he pulled himself together. Quickly he dismantled the rifle, clipped the sections into their hasps and lowered the lid, then placed the case in the bottom drawer of the bureau, adding the key to his chain ring. Locking the door behind him, he made his way out of the hotel, a determined spring in his step.

Two hundred yards down Grosvenor Place, he turned into Hallam Street, a small thoroughfare interspersed with minor art galleries and restaurants. Sunlight played on the striped awnings and the deserted street might have been miles from the crowds along the Coronation route. Dr Jamieson felt his confidence return. Every dozen yards or so he stopped under the awnings and surveyed the empty pavements, listening to the distant TV commentaries from the flats above the shops.

Halfway down the street was a small café with three tables outside. Sitting with his back to the window, Dr Jamieson took out a pair of sunglasses and relaxed in the shade, ordering an iced orange juice from the waitress. He sipped it quietly, his face masked by the dark lenses with their heavy frames. Periodically, prolonged cheers drifted across the roof-tops from Oxford Street, marking the progress of the Abbey ceremony, but otherwise the street was quiet.

Shortly after three o'clock, when the deep droning of an organ on the TV sets announced that the Coronation service had ended, Dr Jamieson heard the sounds of feet approaching on his left. Leaning back under the awning, he saw a young man and girl in a white dress walking hand in hand. As they drew nearer Dr Jamieson removed his glasses to inspect the couple more closely, then quickly replaced them and rested one elbow on the table, masking his face with his hand.

The couple were too immersed in each other to notice Dr Jamieson watching them, although to anyone else his intense nervous excitement would have been obvious. The man was about twenty-eight, dressed in the baggy unpressed clothes Dr Jamieson had found everyone wearing in London, an old tie casually hand-knotted around a soft collar. Two fountain pens protruded from his breast pocket, a concert programme from another, and he had the pleasantly informal appearance of a young university lecturer. His handsome introspective face was topped by a sharply sloping forehead, thinning brown hair brushed back with his fingers. He gazed into the girl's face with patent affection, listening to her light chatter with occasional amused interjections.

Dr Jamieson was also looking at the girl. At first he had stared fixedly at the young man, watching his movements and facial expressions with the oblique wariness of a man seeing himself in a mirror, but his attention soon turned to the girl. A feeling of enormous relief surged through him, and he had to restrain himself from leaping out of his seat. He had been frightened of his memories, but the girl was more, not less beautiful than he had remembered.

Barely nineteen or twenty, she strolled along with her head thrown back, long straw-coloured hair drifting lightly across her softly tanned shoulders. Her mouth was full and alive, her wild eyes watching the young man mischievously.

As they passed the café she was in full flight about something, and the young man cut in: 'Hold on, June, I need a rest. Let's sit down and have a drink, the procession won't reach Marble Arch for half an hour.'

'Poor old chap, am I wearing you out?' They sat at the table next to Dr Jamieson, the girl's bare arm only a few inches away, the fresh scent of her body adding itself to his other recollections. Already a whirlwind of memories reeled in his mind, her neat mobile hands, the way she held her chin and spread her flared white skirt across her thighs. 'Still, I don't really care if I miss the procession. This is *my* day, not his.'

The young man grinned, pretending to get up. 'Really? They've all been misinformed. Just wait here, I'll get the procession diverted.' He held her hand across the table, peered critically at the small diamond on her finger. 'Pretty feeble effort. Who bought that for you?'

The girl kissed it fondly. 'It's as big as the Ritz.' She gave a playful growl. 'H'm, what a man, I'll have to marry him one of these days. Roger, isn't it wonderful about the Prize? Three hundred pounds! You're really rich. A pity the Royal Society don't let you spend it on anything, like the Nobel Prizes. Wait till you get one of those.'

The young man smiled modestly. 'Easy darling, don't build your hopes on that.'

'But of course you will. I'm absolutely sure. After all, you've more or less discovered time travel.'

The young man drummed on the table. 'June, for heaven's sake, get this straight, I have *not* discovered time travel.' He lowered his voice, conscious of Dr Jamieson sitting at the next table, the only other person in the deserted street. 'People will think I'm insane if you go around saying that.'

The girl screwed up her pert nose. 'You have, though, let's face it. I know you don't like the phrase, but once you take away the algebra that's what it boils down to, doesn't it?'

The young man gazed reflectively at the table top, his face, as it grew serious, assuming massive intellectual strength. 'In so far as mathematical concepts have their analogies in the physical universe, yes – but that's an enormous caveat. And even then it's not time travel in the usual sense, though I realize the popular press won't agree when my paper in *Nature* comes out. Anyway, I'm not particularly interested in the time aspect. If I had thirty years to spare it might be worth pursuing, but I've got more important things to do.'

He smiled at the girl, but she leaned forward thoughtfully, taking his hands. 'Roger, I'm not so sure you're right. You say it hasn't any applications in everyday life, but scientists always think that. It's really fantastic, to be able to go backward in time. I mean –'

'Why? We're able to go *forward* in time now, and no one's throwing their hats in the air. The universe itself is just a time machine that from our end of the show seems to be running one way. Or mostly one way. I happened to have noticed that particles in a cyclotron sometimes move in the opposite direction, that's all, arrive at the end of their infinitesimal trips before they've started. That doesn't mean that next week we'll all be able to go back and murder our own grandfathers.'

'What would happen if you did? Seriously?'

The young man laughed. 'I don't know. Frankly, I don't like to think about it. Maybe that's the real reason why I want to keep the work on a theoretical basis. If you extend the problem to its logical conclusion my observations at Harwell must be faulty, because events in the universe obviously take place independently of time, which is just the perspective we put on them. Years from now the problem will probably be known as the Jamieson Paradox, and aspiring mathematicians will be bumping off their grandparents wholesale in the hope of disproving it. We'll have to make sure that all our grandchildren are admirals or archbishops.'

As he spoke Dr Jamieson was watching the girl, every fibre in his body strained to prevent himself from touching her on the arm and speaking to her. The pattern of freckles on her slim forearm, the creases in her dress below her shoulder blades, her minute toenails with their chipped varnish, was each an absolute revelation of his own existence.

He took off his sunglasses and for a moment he and the young man stared straight at each other. The latter seemed embarrassed, realizing the remarkable physiognomical similarity between them, the identical bone structure of their faces, and angled sweep of their foreheads. Fleetingly, Dr Jamieson smiled at him, a feeling of deep, almost paternal affection for the young man coming over him. His naïve earnestness and honesty, his relaxed, gawky charm, were suddenly more important than his intellectual qualities, and Dr Jamieson knew that he felt no jealousy towards him.

He put on his glasses and looked away down the street, his resolve to carry through the next stages of his plan strengthened.

The noise from the streets beyond rose sharply, and the couple leapt to their feet.

'Come on, it's three-thirty!' the young man cried. 'They must be almost here.'

As they ran off the girl paused to straighten her sandal, looking back at the old man in dark glasses who had sat behind her. Dr Jamieson leaned forward, waiting for her to speak, one hand outstretched, but the girl merely looked away and he sank into his chair.

When they reached the first intersection he stood up and hurried back to his hotel.

Locking the door of his room, Dr Jamieson quickly pulled the case from the bureau, assembled the rifle and sat down with it in front of the window. The Coronation procession was already passing, the advance files of marching soldiers and guardsmen, in their ceremonial uniforms, each led by a brass band drumming out martial airs. The crowd roared and cheered, tossing confetti and streamers into the hot sunlight.

Dr Jamieson ignored them and peered below the blind onto the pavement. Carefully he searched the throng, soon picked out the girl in the white dress tip-toeing at the back. She smiled at the people around her and wormed her way towards the front, pulling the young man by the hand. For a few minutes Dr Jamieson followed the girl's every movement, then as the first landaus of the diplomatic corps appeared he began to search the remainder of the crowd, scrutinizing each face carefully, line upon line. From his pocket he withdrew a small plastic envelope; he held it away from his face and broke the seal. There was a hiss of greenish gas and he drew out a large newspaper cutting, yellowed with age, folded to reveal a man's portrait.

Dr Jamieson propped it against the window ledge. The cutting showed a dark-jowled man of about thirty with a thin weasel-like face, obviously a criminal photographed by the police. Under it was the caption: *Anton Remmers.*

Dr Jamieson sat forward intently. The diplomatic corps passed in their carriages, followed by members of the government riding in open cars, waving their silk hats at the crowd. Then came more Horse Guards, and there was a tremendous roar farther down the street as the spectators near Oxford Circus saw the royal coach approaching.

Anxiously, Dr Jamieson looked at his watch. It was three forty-five, and the royal coach was due to pass the hotel in only seven minutes. Around him a tumult of noise made it difficult to concentrate, and the TV sets in the near-by rooms seemed to be at full volume.

Suddenly he clenched the window ledge.

'Remmers!' Directly below, in the entrance to a cigarette kiosk, was a sallow-faced man in a wide-brimmed green hat. He stared at the procession impassively, hands deep in the pockets of a cheap raincoat. Fumbling, Dr Jamieson raised the rifle, resting the barrel on the ledge, watching the man. He made no attempt to press forward into the crowd, and waited by the kiosk, only a few feet from a small arcade that ran back into a side street.

Dr Jamieson began to search the crowd again, the effort draining his face. A gigantic bellow from the crowd deafened him as the gold-plated royal coach hove into view behind a bobbing escort of household cavalry. He tried to see if Remmers looked around at an accomplice, but the man was motionless, hands deep in his pockets.

'Damn you!' Dr Jamieson snarled. 'Where's the other one?' Frantically he pushed away the blind, every ounce of his shrewdness and experience expended as he carried out a dozen split-second character analyses of the people below.

'There were two of them!' he shouted hoarsely to himself. 'There were *two*!'

Fifty yards away, the young king sat back in the golden coach, his robes a blaze of colour in the sunlight. Distracted, Dr Jamieson watched him, then realized abruptly that Remmers had moved. The man was now stepping swiftly around the edge of the crowd, darting about on his lean legs like a distraught tiger. As the crowd surged forward, he pulled a blue thermos flask from his raincoat pocket, with a quick motion unscrewed the cap. The royal coach drew abreast and Remmers transferred the thermos to his right hand, a metal plunger clearly visible in the mouth of the flask.

'*Remmers* had the bomb!' Dr Jamieson gasped, completely disconcerted. Remmers stepped back, extended his right hand low to the ground behind him like a grenadier and then began to throw the bomb forward with a carefully timed swing.

The rifle had been pointed at the man automatically and Dr Jamieson trained the sights on his chest and fired, just before the bomb left his hand. The discharge jolted Dr Jamieson off his feet, the impact tearing at his shoulder, the rifle jangling up into the venetian blind. Remmers slammed back crookedly into the cigarette kiosk, legs lolling, his face like a skull's. The bomb had been knocked out of his hand and was spinning straight up into the air as if tossed by a juggler. It landed on the pavement a few yards away, kicked underfoot as the crowd surged sideways after the royal coach.

Then it exploded.

There was a blinding pulse of expanding air, followed by a tremendous eruption of smoke and hurtling particles. The window facing the street dropped in a single piece and shattered on the floor at Dr Jamieson's feet, driving him back in a blast of glass and torn plastic. He fell across the chair, recovered himself as the shouts outside turned to screams, then dragged himself over to the window and stared out through the stinging air. The crowd was fanning out across the road, people running in all directions, horses rearing under their helmetless riders. Below the window twenty or thirty people lay or sat on the pavement. The royal coach, one wheel missing but otherwise intact, was being dragged away by its team of horses, guardsmen and troops encircling it. Police were swarming down the road towards the hotel, and Dr Jamieson saw someone point up to him and shout.

He looked down at the edge of the pavement, where a girl in a white dress was stretched on her back, her legs twisted strangely. The young man kneeling beside her, his jacket split down the centre of his back, had covered her face with his handkerchief, and a dark stain spread slowly across the tissue.

Voices rose in the corridor outside. He turned away from the window, the rifle still in his hand. On the floor at his feet, unfurled by the blast of the explosion, was the faded newspaper cutting. Numbly, his mouth slack, Dr Jamieson picked it up.

### ASSASSINS ATTEMPT TO MURDER KING JAMES
#### Bomb Kills 27 in Oxford Street
#### Two men shot dead by police

A sentence had been ringed: '. . . one was Anton Remmers, a professional killer believed to have been hired by the second assassin, an older man whose bullet-ridden body the police are unable to identify . . .'

Fists pounded on the door. A voice shouted, then kicked at the handle. Dr Jamieson dropped the cutting, and looked down at the young man kneeling over the girl, holding her dead hands.

As the door ripped back off its hinges he knew who the second unknown assassin was, the man he had returned to kill after thirty-five years. So his attempt to alter past events had been fruitless, by coming back he had merely implicated himself in the original crime, doomed since he first analysed the cyclotron freaks to return and help to kill his young bride. If he had not shot Remmers the assassin would have lobbed the bomb into the centre of the road, and June would have lived. His whole stratagem selflessly devised for the young man's benefit, a free gift to his own younger self, had defeated itself, destroying the very person it had been intended to save.

Hoping to see her again for the last time, and warn the young man to forget her, he ran forward into the roaring police guns.

**1961**

# · THE INSANE ONES

Ten miles outside Alexandria he picked up the coast road that ran across the top of the continent through Tunis and Algiers to the transatlantic tunnel at Casablanca, gunned the Jaguar up to 120 and burned along through the cool night air, letting the brine-filled slipstream cut into his six-day tan. Lolling back against the headrest as the palms flicked by, he almost missed the girl in the white raincoat waving from the steps of the hotel at El Alamein, had only three hundred yards to plunge the car to a halt below the rusting neon sign.

'Tunis?' the girl called out, belting the man's raincoat around her trim waist, long black hair in a Left Bank cut over one shoulder.

'Tunis – Casablanca – Atlantic City,' Gregory shouted back, reaching across to the passenger door. She swung a yellow briefcase behind the seat, settling herself among the magazines and newspapers as they roared off. The headlamps picked out a United World cruiser parked under the palms in the entrance to the war cemetery, and involuntarily Gregory winced and floored the accelerator, eyes clamped to the rear mirror until the road was safely empty.

At 90 he slacked off and looked at the girl, abruptly felt a warning signal sound again. She seemed like any demi-beatnik, with a long melancholy face and grey skin, but something about her rhythms, the slack facial tone and dead eyes and mouth, made him uneasy. Under a flap of the raincoat was a blue-striped gingham skirt, obviously part of a nurse's uniform, out of character, like the rest of her strange gear. As she slid the magazines into the dashboard locker he saw the home-made bandage around the left wrist.

She noticed him watching her and flashed a too-bright smile, then made an effort at small talk.

'Paris *Vogue, Neue Frankfurter,* Tel Aviv *Express* – you've really been moving.' She pulled a pack of Del Montes from the breast pocket of the coat, fumbled unfamiliarly with a large brass lighter. 'First Europe, then Asia, now Africa. You'll run out of continents soon.' Hesitating, she volunteered: 'Carole Sturgeon. Thanks for the lift.'

Gregory nodded, watching the bandage slide around her slim wrist. He wondered which hospital she had sneaked away from. Probably Cairo General, the old-style English uniforms were still worn there. Ten to one the briefcase was packed with some careless salesman's pharmaceutical samples. 'Can I ask where you're going? This is the back end of nowhere.'

The girl shrugged. 'Just following the road. Cairo, Alex, you know –' She added: 'I went to see the pyramids.' She lay back, rolling slightly against his shoulder. 'That was wonderful. They're the oldest things on earth. Remember their boast: *"Before Abraham, I was"*?'

They hit a dip in the road and Gregory's licence swung out under the steering column. The girl peered down and read it. 'Do you mind? It's a long ride to Tunis. "Charles Gregory, MD –"' She stopped, repeating his name to herself uncertainly.

Suddenly she remembered. '*Gregory!* Dr Charles Gregory! Weren't you – Muriel Bortman, the President's daughter, she drowned herself at Key West, you were sentenced –' She broke off, staring nervously at the windshield.

'You've got a long memory,' Gregory said quietly. 'I didn't think anyone remembered.'

'Of course I remember.' She spoke in a whisper. 'They were mad what they did to you.' For the next few minutes she gushed out a long farrago of sympathy, interspersed with disjointed details from her own life. Gregory tried not to listen, clenching the wheel until his knuckles whitened, deliberately forgetting everything as fast as she reminded him.

There was a pause, as he felt it coming, the way it invariably did. 'Tell me, doctor, I hope you forgive me asking, but since the Mental Freedom laws it's difficult to get help, one's got to be so careful – you too, of course . . .' She laughed uneasily. 'What I really mean is –'

Her edginess drained power from Gregory. '– you need psychiatric assistance,' he cut in, pushing the Jaguar up to 95, eyes swinging to the rear mirror again. The road was dead, palms receding endlessly into the night.

The girl choked on her cigarette, the stub between her fingers a damp mess. 'Well, not me,' she said lamely. 'A close friend of mine. She really needs help, believe me, doctor. Her whole feeling for life is gone, nothing seems to mean anything to her any more.'

Brutally, he said: 'Tell her to look at the pyramids.'

But the girl missed the irony, said quickly: 'Oh, she has. I just left her in Cairo. I promised I'd try to find someone for her.' She turned to examine Gregory, put a hand up to her hair. In the blue desert light she reminded him of the madonnas he had seen in the Louvre two days after his release, when he had run from the filthy prison searching for the most beautiful things in the world, the solemn-faced more-than-beautiful 13-year-olds who had posed for Leonardo and the Bellini brothers. 'I thought perhaps you might know someone –?'

He gripped himself and shook his head. 'I don't. For the last three years I've been out of touch. Anyway, it's against the MF laws. Do you know what would happen if they caught me giving psychiatric treatment?'

Numbly the girl stared ahead at the road. Gregory flipped away his cigarette, pressing down on the accelerator as the last three years crowded back, memories he had hoped to repress on his 10,000-mile drive . . . three years at the prison farm near Marseilles, treating scrofulous farm-workers and sailors in the dispensary, even squeezing in a little illicit depth analysis for the corporal of police who couldn't satisfy his wife, three embittered years to accept that he would never practise again the one craft in which he was fully himself. Trick-cyclist or assuager of discontents, whatever his title, the psychiatrist had now passed into history, joining the necromancers, sorcerers and other practitioners of the black sciences.

The Mental Freedom legislation enacted ten years earlier by the ultra-conservative UW government had banned the profession outright and enshrined the individual's freedom to be insane if he wanted to, provided he paid the full civil consequences for any infringements of the law. That was the catch, the hidden object of the MF laws. What had begun as a popular reaction against 'subliminal living' and the uncontrolled extension of techniques of mass manipulation for political and economic ends had quickly developed into a systematic attack on the psychological sciences. Over-permissive courts of law with their condoning of delinquency, pseudo-enlightened penal reformers, 'Victims of society', the psychologist and his patient all came under fierce attack. Discharging their self-hate and anxiety onto a convenient scapegoat, the new rulers, and the great majority electing them, outlawed all forms of psychic control, from the innocent market survey to lobotomy. The mentally ill were on their own, spared pity and consideration, made to pay to the hilt for their failings. The sacred cow of the community was the psychotic, free to wander where he wanted, drooling on the doorsteps, sleeping on sidewalks, and woe betide anyone who tried to help him.

Gregory had made that mistake. Escaping to Europe, first home of psychiatry, in the hope of finding a more tolerant climate, he set up a secret clinic in Paris with six other émigré analysts. For five years they worked undetected, until one of Gregory's patients, a tall ungainly girl with a psychogenic stutter, was revealed to be Muriel Bortman, daughter of the UW President-General. The analysis had failed tragically when the clinic was raided; after her death a lavish show trial (making endless play of electric shock apparatus, movies of insulin coma and the testimony of countless paranoids rounded up in the alleyways) had concluded in a three-year sentence.

Now at last he was out, his savings invested in the Jaguar, fleeing Europe and his memories of the prison for the empty highways of North Africa. He didn't want any more trouble.

'I'd like to help,' he told the girl. 'But the risks are too high. All your friend can do is try to come to terms with herself.'

The girl chewed her lip fretfully. 'I don't think she can. Thanks, anyway, doctor.'

*     *     *

For three hours they sat back silently in the speeding car, until the lights of Tobruk came up ahead, the long curve of the harbour.

'It's 2 A.M.,' Gregory said. 'There's a motel here. I'll pick you up in the morning.'

After they had gone to their rooms he sneaked back to the registry, booked himself into a new chalet. He fell asleep as Carole Sturgeon wandered forlornly up and down the verandas, whispering out his name.

After breakfast he came back from the sea, found a big United World cruiser in the court, orderlies carrying a stretcher out to an ambulance.

A tall Libyan police colonel was leaning against the Jaguar, drumming his leather baton on the windscreen.

'Ah, Dr Gregory. Good morning.' He pointed his baton at the ambulance. 'A profound tragedy, such a beautiful American girl.'

Gregory rooted his feet in the grey sand, with an effort restrained himself from running over to the ambulance and pulling back the sheet. Fortunately the colonel's uniform and thousands of morning and evening cell inspections kept him safely to attention.

'I'm Gregory, yes.' The dust thickened in his throat. 'Is she dead?'

The colonel stroked his neck with the baton. 'Ear to ear. She must have found an old razor blade in the bathroom. About 3 o'clock this morning.' He headed towards Gregory's chalet, gesturing with the baton. Gregory followed him into the half light, stood tentatively by the bed.

'I was asleep then. The clerk will vouch for that.'

'Naturally.' The colonel gazed down at Gregory's possessions spread out across the bedcover, idly poked the black medical bag.

'She asked you for assistance, doctor? With her personal problems?'

'Not directly. She hinted at it, though. She sounded a little mixed up.'

'Poor child.' The colonel lowered his head sympathetically. 'Her father is a first secretary at the Cairo Embassy, something of an autocrat. You Americans are very stern with your children, doctor. A firm hand, yes, but understanding costs nothing. Don't you agree? She was frightened of him, escaped from the American Hospital. My task is to provide an explanation for the authorities. If I had an idea of what was really worrying her . . . no doubt you helped her as best you could?'

Gregory shook his head. 'I gave her no help at all, colonel. In fact, I refused to discuss her problems altogether.' He smiled flatly at the colonel. 'I wouldn't make the same mistake twice, would I?'

The colonel studied Gregory thoughtfully. 'Sensible of you, doctor. But you surprise me. Surely the members of your profession regard themselves as a special calling, answerable to a higher authority. Are these ideals so easy to cast off?'

'I've had a lot of practice.' Gregory began to pack away his things on the bed, bowed to the colonel as he saluted and made his way out into the court.

*      *      *

Half an hour later he was on the Benghasi road, holding the Jaguar at 100, working off his tension and anger in a savage burst of speed. Free for only ten days, already he had got himself involved again, gone through all the agony of having to refuse help to someone desperately needing it, his hands itching to administer relief to the child but held back by the insane penalties. It wasn't only the lunatic legislation but the people enforcing it who ought to be swept away – Bortman and his fellow oligarchs.

He grimaced at the thought of the cold dead-faced Bortman, addressing the World Senate at Lake Success, arguing for increased penalties for the criminal psychopath. The man had stepped straight out of the 14th-century Inquisition, his bureaucratic puritanism masking two real obsessions: dirt and death. Any sane society would have locked Bortman up for ever, or given him a complete brain-lift. Indirectly Bortman was as responsible for the death of Carole Sturgeon as he would have been had he personally handed the razor blade to her.

After Libya, Tunis. He blazed steadily along the coast road, the sea like a molten mirror on the right, avoiding the big towns where possible. Fortunately they weren't so bad as the European cities, psychotics loitering like stray dogs in the uptown parks, wise enough not to shop-lift or cause trouble, but a petty nuisance on the café terraces, knocking on hotel doors at all hours of the night.

At Algiers he spent three days at the Hilton, having a new engine fitted to the car, and hunted up Philip Kalundborg, an old Toronto colleague now working in a WHO children's hospital.

Over their third carafe of burgundy Gregory told him about Carole Sturgeon.

'It's absurd, but I feel guilty about her. Suicide is a highly suggestive act, I reminded her of Muriel Bortman's death. Damn it, Philip, I could have given her the sort of general advice any sensible layman would have offered.'

'Dangerous. Of course you were right,' Philip assured him. 'After the last three years who could argue otherwise?'

Gregory looked out across the terrace at the traffic whirling over the neon-lit cobbles. Beggars sat at their pitches along the sidewalk, whining for sous.

'Philip, you don't know what it's like in Europe now. At least 5 per cent are probably in need of institutional care. Believe me, I'm frightened to go to America. In New York alone they're jumping from the roofs at the rate of ten a day. The world's turning into a madhouse, one half of society gloating righteously over the torments of the other. Most people don't realize which side of the bars they are. It's easier for you. Here the traditions are different.'

Kalundborg nodded. 'True. In the villages up-country it's been standard practice for centuries to blind schizophrenics and exhibit them in a cage.

Injustice is so widespread that you build up an indiscriminate tolerance to every form.'

A tall dark-bearded youth in faded cotton slacks and rope sandals stepped across the terrace and put his hands on their table. His eyes were sunk deep below his forehead, around his lips the brown staining of narcotic poisoning.

'Christian!' Kalundborg snapped angrily. He shrugged hopelessly at Gregory, then turned to the young man with quiet exasperation. 'My dear fellow, this has gone on for too long. I can't help you, there's no point in asking.'

The young man nodded patiently. 'It's Marie,' he explained in a slow roughened voice. 'I can't control her. I'm frightened what she may do to the baby. Postnatal withdrawal, you know –'

'Nonsense! I'm not an idiot, Christian. The baby is nearly three. If Marie is a nervous wreck you've made her so. Believe me, I wouldn't help you if I was allowed to. You must cure yourself or you are finished. Already you have chronic barbiturism. Dr Gregory here will agree with me.'

Gregory nodded. The young man stared blackly at Kalundborg, glanced at Gregory and then shambled off through the tables.

Kalundborg filled his glass. 'They have it all wrong today. They think our job was to further addiction, not cure it. In their pantheon the father-figure is always benevolent.'

'That's invariably been Bortman's line. Psychiatry is ultimately self-indulgent, an encouragement to weakness and lack of will. Admittedly there's no one more single-minded than an obsessional neurotic. Bortman himself is a good example.'

As he entered the tenth-floor bedroom the young man was going through his valise on the bed. For a moment Gregory wondered whether he was a UW spy, perhaps the meeting on the terrace had been an elaborate trap.

'Find what you want?'

Christian finished whipping through the bag, then tossed it irritably onto the floor. He edged restlessly away from Gregory around the bed, his eyes hungrily searching the wardrobe top and lamp brackets.

'Kalundborg was right,' Gregory told him quietly. 'You're wasting your time.'

'The hell with Kalundborg,' Christian snarled softly. 'He's working the wrong levels. Do you think I'm looking for a jazz heaven, doctor? With a wife and child? I'm not that irresponsible. I took a Master's degree in law at Heidelberg.' He wandered off around the room, then stopped to survey Gregory closely.

Gregory began to slide in the drawers. 'Well, get back to your juris-prudence. There are enough ills to weigh in this world.'

'Doctor, I've made a start. Didn't Kalundborg tell you I sued Bortman for murder?' When Gregory seemed puzzled he explained: 'A private civil action, not criminal proceedings. My father killed himself five years ago after Bortman had him thrown out of the Bar Association.'

Gregory picked up his valise off the floor. 'I'm sorry,' he said noncommittally. 'What happened to your suit against Bortman?'

Christian stared out through the window into the dark air. 'It was never entered. Some World Bureau investigators saw me after I started to be a nuisance and suggested I leave the States for ever. So I came to Europe to get my degree. I'm on my way back now. I need the barbiturates to stop myself trying to toss a bomb at Bortman.'

Suddenly he propelled himself across the room, before Gregory could stop him was out on the balcony, jack-knifed over the edge. Gregory dived after him, kicked away his feet and tried to pull him off the ledge. Christian clung to it, shouting into the darkness, the lights from the cars racing in the damp street below. On the sidewalk people looked up.

Christian was doubled up with laughter as they fell back into the room, slumped down on the bed, pointing his finger at Gregory, who was leaning against the wardrobe, gasping in exhausted spasms.

'Big mistake there, doctor. You better get out fast before I tip off the Police Prefect. Stopping a suicide! God, with your record you'd get ten years for that. What a joke!'

Gregory shook him by the shoulders, temper flaring. 'Listen, what are you playing at? What do you want?'

Christian pushed Gregory's hands away and lay back weakly. 'Help me, doctor. I want to kill Bortman, it's all I think about. If I'm not careful I'll really try. Show me how to forget him.' His voice rose desperately. 'Damn, I *hated* my father, I was glad when Bortman threw him out.'

Gregory eyed him thoughtfully, then went over to the window and bolted out the night.

Two months later, at the motel outside Casablanca, Gregory finally burned the last of the analysis notes. Christian, clean-shaven and wearing a neat white tropical suit, a neutral tie, watched from the door as the stack of coded entries gutted out in the ashtray, then carried them into the bathroom and flushed them away.

When Christian had loaded his suitcases into the car Gregory said: 'One thing before we go. A complete analysis can't be effected in two months, let alone two years. It's something you work at all your life. If you have a relapse, come to me, even if I'm in Tahiti, or Shanghai or Archangel.' Gregory paused. 'If they ever find out, you know what will happen?' When Christian nodded quietly he sat down in the chair by the writing table, gazing out through the date palms at the huge domed mouth of the transatlantic tunnel a mile away. For a long time he knew he would be unable to relax. In a curious way he felt that the three years at Marseilles had been wasted, that he was starting a suspended sentence of indefinite length. There had been no satisfaction at the successful treatment, perhaps because he had given in to Christian partly for fear of being incriminated in an attack on Bortman.

'With luck, you should be able to live with yourself now. Try to remember that whatever evils Bortman may perpetrate in the future he's irrelevant to *your* problem. It was the stroke your mother suffered after your father's death that made you realize the guilt you felt subconsciously for hating him, but you conveniently shifted the blame onto Bortman, and by eliminating him you thought you could free yourself. The temptation may occur again.'

Christian nodded, standing motionlessly by the doorway. His face had filled out, his eyes were a placid grey. He looked like any well-groomed UW bureaucrat.

Gregory picked up a newspaper. 'I see Bortman is attacking the American Bar Association as a subversive body, probably planning to have it proscribed. If it succeeds it'll be an irreparable blow to civil liberty.' He looked up thoughtfully at Christian, who showed no reaction. 'Right, let's go. Are you still fixed on getting back to the States?'

'Of course.' Christian climbed into the car, then shook Gregory's hand. Gregory had decided to stay in Africa, find a hospital where he could work and had given Christian the car. 'Marie will wait for me in Algiers until I finish my business.'

'What's that?'

Christian pressed the starter, sent a roar of dust and exhaust across the compound.

'I'm going to kill Bortman,' he said quietly.

Gregory gripped the windscreen. 'You're not serious.'

'You cured me, doctor, and give or take the usual margins I'm completely sane, more than I probably ever will be again. Damn few people in this world are now, so that makes the obligation on me to act rationally even greater. Well, every ounce of logic tells me that someone's got to make the effort to get rid of the grim menagerie running things now, and Bortman looks like a pretty good start. I intend to drive up to Lake Success and take a shot at him.' He shunted the gear change into second, and added, 'Don't try to have me stopped, doctor, because they'll only dig out our long weekend here.'

As he started to take his foot off the clutch Gregory shouted: 'Christian! You'll never get away with it! They'll catch you anyway!' but the car wrenched forward out of his hand.

Gregory ran through the dust after it, stumbling over half-buried stones, realizing helplessly that when they caught Christian and probed down into the past few months they would soon find the real assassin, an exiled doctor with a three-year-grudge.

'Christian!' he yelled, choking on the white ash. 'Christian, you're insane!'

**1962**

# THE GARDEN OF TIME

Towards evening, when the great shadow of the Palladian villa filled the terrace, Count Axel left his library and walked down the wide marble steps among the time flowers. A tall, imperious figure in a black velvet jacket, a gold tie-pin glinting below his George V beard, cane held stiffly in a white-gloved hand, he surveyed the exquisite crystal flowers without emotion, listening to the sounds of his wife's harpsichord, as she played a Mozart rondo in the music room, echo and vibrate through the translucent petals.

The garden of the villa extended for some two hundred yards below the terrace, sloping down to a miniature lake spanned by a white bridge, a slender pavilion on the opposite bank. Axel rarely ventured as far as the lake; most of the time flowers grew in a small grove just below the terrace, sheltered by the high wall which encircled the estate. From the terrace he could see over the wall to the plain beyond, a continuous expanse of open ground that rolled in great swells to the horizon, where it rose slightly before finally dipping from sight. The plain surrounded the house on all sides, its drab emptiness emphasizing the seclusion and mellowed magnificence of the villa. Here, in the garden, the air seemed brighter, the sun warmer, while the plain was always dull and remote.

As was his custom before beginning his evening stroll, Count Axel looked out across the plain to the final rise, where the horizon was illuminated like a distant stage by the fading sun. As the Mozart chimed delicately around him, flowing from his wife's graceful hands, he saw that the advance column of an enormous army was moving slowly over the horizon. At first glance, the long ranks seemed to be progressing in orderly lines, but on closer inspection, it was apparent that, like the obscured detail of a Goya landscape, the army was composed of a vast throng of people, men and women, interspersed with a few soldiers in ragged uniforms, pressing forward in a disorganized tide. Some laboured under heavy loads suspended from crude yokes around their necks, others struggled with cumbersome wooden carts, their hands wrenching at the wheel spokes, a few trudged on alone, but all moved on at the same pace, bowed backs illuminated in the fleeting sun.

The advancing throng was almost too far away to be visible, but even as Axel watched, his expression aloof yet observant, it came perceptibly nearer, the vanguard of an immense rabble appearing from below the horizon. At last, as the daylight began to fade, the front edge of the throng reached the crest of the first swell below the horizon, and Axel turned from the terrace and walked down among the time flowers.

The flowers grew to a height of about six feet, their slender stems, like rods of glass, bearing a dozen leaves, the once transparent fronds frosted by the fossilized veins. At the peak of each stem was the time flower, the size of a goblet, the opaque outer petals enclosing the crystal heart. Their diamond brilliance contained a thousand faces, the crystal seeming to drain the air of its light and motion. As the flowers swayed slightly in the evening air, they glowed like flame-tipped spears.

Many of the stems no longer bore flowers, and Axel examined them all carefully, a note of hope now and then crossing his eyes as he searched for any further buds. Finally he selected a large flower on the stem nearest the wall, removed his gloves and with his strong fingers snapped it off.

As he carried the flower back on to the terrace, it began to sparkle and deliquesce, the light trapped within the core at last released. Gradually the crystal dissolved, only the outer petals remaining intact, and the air around Axel became bright and vivid, charged with slanting rays that flared away into the waning sunlight. Strange shifts momentarily transformed the evening, subtly altering its dimensions of time and space. The darkened portico of the house, its patina of age stripped away, loomed with a curious spectral whiteness as if suddenly remembered in a dream.

Raising his head, Axel peered over the wall again. Only the farthest rim of the horizon was lit by the sun, and the great throng, which before had stretched almost a quarter of the way across the plain, had now receded to the horizon, the entire concourse abruptly flung back in a reversal of time, and appeared to be stationary.

The flower in Axel's hand had shrunk to the size of a glass thimble, the petals contracting around the vanishing core. A faint sparkle flickered from the centre and extinguished itself, and Axel felt the flower melt like an ice-cold bead of dew in his hand.

Dusk closed across the house, sweeping its long shadows over the plain, the horizon merging into the sky. The harpsichord was silent, and the time flowers, no longer reflecting its music, stood motionlessly, like an embalmed forest.

For a few minutes Axel looked down at them, counting the flowers which remained, then greeted his wife as she crossed the terrace, her brocade evening dress rustling over the ornamental tiles.

'What a beautiful evening, Axel.' She spoke feelingly, as if she were thanking her husband personally for the great ornate shadow across the lawn and the dark brilliant air. Her face was serene and intelligent, her hair, swept back behind her head into a jewelled clasp, touched with silver. She wore her dress low across her breast, revealing a long slender neck and high chin. Axel surveyed her with fond pride. He gave her his arm and together they walked down the steps into the garden.

'One of the longest evenings this summer,' Axel confirmed, adding: 'I picked a perfect flower, my dear, a jewel. With luck it should last us for several days.' A frown touched his brow, and he glanced involuntarily at the wall. 'Each time now they seem to come nearer.'

His wife smiled at him encouragingly and held his arm more tightly.

Both of them knew that the time garden was dying.

Three evenings later, as he had estimated (though sooner than he secretly hoped), Count Axel plucked another flower from the time garden.

When he first looked over the wall the approaching rabble filled the distant half of the plain, stretching across the horizon in an unbroken mass. He thought he could hear the low, fragmentary sounds of voices carried across the empty air, a sullen murmur punctuated by cries and shouts, but quickly told himself that he had imagined them. Luckily, his wife was at the harpsichord, and the rich contrapuntal patterns of a Bach fugue cascaded lightly across the terrace, masking any other noises.

Between the house and the horizon the plain was divided into four huge swells, the crest of each one clearly visible in the slanting light. Axel had promised himself that he would never count them, but the number was too small to remain unobserved, particularly when it so obviously marked the progress of the advancing army. By now the forward line had passed the first crest and was well on its way to the second; the main bulk of the throng pressed behind it, hiding the crest and the even vaster concourse spreading from the horizon. Looking to left and right of the central body, Axel could see the apparently limitless extent of the army. What had seemed at first to be the central mass was no more than a minor advance guard, one of many similar arms reaching across the plain. The true centre had not yet emerged, but from the rate of extension Axel estimated that when it finally reached the plain it would completely cover every foot of ground.

Axel searched for any large vehicles or machines, but all was amorphous and uncoordinated as ever. There were no banners or flags, no mascots or pike-bearers. Heads bowed, the multitude pressed on, unaware of the sky.

Suddenly, just before Axel turned away, the forward edge of the throng appeared on top of the second crest, and swarmed down across the plain. What astounded Axel was the incredible distance it had covered while out of sight. The figures were now twice the size, each one clearly within sight.

Quickly, Axel stepped from the terrace, selected a time flower from the garden and tore it from the stem. As it released its compacted light, he returned to the terrace. When the flower had shrunk to a frozen pearl in his palm he looked out at the plain, with relief saw that the army had retreated to the horizon again.

Then he realized that the horizon was much nearer than previously, and that what he assumed to be the horizon was the first crest.

*       *       *

When he joined the Countess on their evening walk he told her nothing of this, but she could see behind his casual unconcern and did what she could to dispel his worry.

Walking down the steps, she pointed to the time garden. 'What a wonderful display, Axel. There are so many flowers still.'

Axel nodded, smiling to himself at his wife's attempt to reassure him. Her use of 'still' had revealed her own unconscious anticipation of the end. In fact a mere dozen flowers remained of the many hundred that had grown in the garden, and several of these were little more than buds – only three or four were fully grown. As they walked down to the lake, the Countess's dress rustling across the cool turf, he tried to decide whether to pick the larger flowers first or leave them to the end. Strictly, it would be better to give the smaller flowers additional time to grow and mature, and this advantage would be lost if he retained the larger flowers to the end, as he wished to do, for the final repulse. However, he realized that it mattered little either way; the garden would soon die and the smaller flowers required far longer than he could give them to accumulate their compressed cores of time. During his entire lifetime he had failed to notice a single evidence of growth among the flowers. The larger blooms had always been mature, and none of the buds had shown the slightest development.

Crossing the lake, he and his wife looked down at their reflections in the still black water. Shielded by the pavilion on one side and the high garden wall on the other, the villa in the distance, Axel felt composed and secure, the plain with its encroaching multitude a nightmare from which he had safely awakened. He put one arm around his wife's smooth waist and pressed her affectionately to his shoulder, realizing that he had not embraced her for several years, though their lives together had been timeless and he could remember as if yesterday when he first brought her to live in the villa.

'Axel,' his wife asked with sudden seriousness, 'before the garden dies . . . may I pick the last flower?'

Understanding her request, he nodded slowly.

One by one over the succeeding evenings, he picked the remaining flowers, leaving a single small bud which grew just below the terrace for his wife. He took the flowers at random, refusing to count or ration them, plucking two or three of the smaller buds at the same time when necessary. The approaching horde had now reached the second and third crests, a vast concourse of labouring humanity that blotted out the horizon. From the terrace Axel could see clearly the shuffling, straining ranks moving down into the hollow towards the final crest, and occasionally the sounds of their voices carried across to him, interspersed with cries of anger and the cracking of whips. The wooden carts lurched from side to side on tilting wheels, their drivers struggling to control them. As far as Axel could tell, not a single member of the throng was aware of its overall direction. Rather, each one blindly moved forward across the ground directly below the heels of the person in front of him, and the only unity was that of the cumulative compass. Pointlessly, Axel hoped that the true centre, far below the horizon, might be moving in a different direction, and that gradually the multitude would alter course, swing away from the villa and recede from the plain like a turning tide.

On the last evening but one, as he plucked the time flower, the forward edge of the rabble had reached the third crest, and was swarming past it. While he waited for the Countess, Axel looked at the two flowers left, both small buds which would carry them back through only a few minutes of the next evening. The glass stems of the dead flowers reared up stiffly into the air, but the whole garden had lost its bloom.

Axel passed the next morning quietly in his library, sealing the rarer of his manuscripts into the glass-topped cases between the galleries. He walked slowly down the portrait corridor, polishing each of the pictures carefully, then tidied his desk and locked the door behind him. During the afternoon he busied himself in the drawing rooms, unobtrusively assisting his wife as she cleaned their ornaments and straightened the vases and busts.

By evening, as the sun fell behind the house, they were both tired and dusty, and neither had spoken to the other all day. When his wife moved towards the music-room, Axel called her back.

'Tonight we'll pick the flowers together, my dear,' he said to her evenly. 'One for each of us.'

He peered only briefly over the wall. They could hear, less than half a mile away, the great dull roar of the ragged army, the ring of iron and lash, pressing on towards the house.

Quickly, Axel plucked his flower, a bud no bigger than a sapphire. As it flickered softly, the tumult outside momentarily receded, then began to gather again.

Shutting his ears to the clamour, Axel looked around at the villa, counting the six columns in the portico, then gazed out across the lawn at the silver disc of the lake, its bowl reflecting the last evening light, and at the shadows moving between the tall trees, lengthening across the crisp turf. He lingered over the bridge where he and his wife had stood arm in arm for so many summers –

'Axel!'

The tumult outside roared into the air, a thousand voices bellowed only twenty or thirty yards away. A stone flew over the wall and landed among the time flowers, snapping several of the brittle stems. The Countess ran towards him as a further barrage rattled along the wall. Then a heavy tile whirled through the air over their heads and crashed into one of the conservatory windows.

'Axel!' He put his arms around her, straightening his silk cravat when her shoulder brushed it between his lapels.

'Quickly, my dear, the last flower!' He led her down the steps and through the garden. Taking the stem between her jewelled fingers, she snapped it cleanly, then cradled it within her palms.

For a moment the tumult lessened slightly and Axel collected himself. In the vivid light sparkling from the flower he saw his wife's white, frightened eyes. 'Hold it as long as you can, my dear, until the last grain dies.'

Together they stood on the terrace, the Countess clasping the brilliant dying jewel, the air closing in upon them as the voices outside mounted again. The mob was battering at the heavy iron gates, and the whole villa shook with the impact.

While the final glimmer of light sped away, the Countess raised her palms to the air, as if releasing an invisible bird, then in a final access of courage put her hands in her husband's, her smile as radiant as the vanished flower.

'Oh, Axel!' she cried.

Like a sword, the darkness swooped down across them.

Heaving and swearing, the outer edges of the mob reached the knee-high remains of the wall enclosing the ruined estate, hauled their carts over it and along the dry ruts of what once had been an ornate drive. The ruin, formerly a spacious villa, barely interrupted the ceaseless tide of humanity. The lake was empty, fallen trees rotting at its bottom, an old bridge rusting into it. Weeds flourished among the long grass in the lawn, overrunning the ornamental pathways and carved stone screens.

Much of the terrace had crumbled, and the main section of the mob cut straight across the lawn, by-passing the gutted villa, but one or two of the more curious climbed up and searched among the shell. The doors had rotted from their hinges and the floors had fallen through. In the music-room an ancient harpsichord had been chopped into firewood, but a few keys still lay among the dust. All the books had been toppled from the shelves in the library, the canvases had been slashed, and gilt frames littered the floor.

As the main body of the mob reached the house, it began to cross the wall at all points along its length. Jostled together, the people stumbled into the dry lake, swarmed over the terrace and pressed through the house towards the open doors on the north side.

One area alone withstood the endless wave. Just below the terrace, between the wrecked balcony and the wall, was a dense, six-foot-high growth of heavy thorn-bushes. The barbed foliage formed an impenetrable mass, and the people passing stepped around it carefully, noticing the belladonna entwined among the branches. Most of them were too busy finding their footing among the upturned flagstones to look up into the centre of the thornbushes, where two stone statues stood side by side, gazing out over the grounds from their protected vantage point. The larger of the figures was the effigy of a bearded man in a high-collared jacket, a cane under one arm. Beside him was a woman in an elaborate full-skirted dress, her slim, serene face unmarked by the wind and rain. In her left hand she lightly clasped a single rose, the delicately formed petals so thin as to be almost transparent.

As the sun died away behind the house a single ray of light glanced through a shattered cornice and struck the rose, reflected off the whorl of petals on to the statues, lighting up the grey stone so that for a fleeting moment it was indistinguishable from the long-vanished flesh of the statues' originals.

, **1962**

# ·THE THOUSAND DREAMS OF STELLAVISTA

No one ever comes to Vermilion Sands now, and I suppose there are few people who have ever heard of it. But ten years ago, when Fay and I first went to live at 99 Stellavista, just before our marriage broke up, the colony was still remembered as the one-time playground of movie stars, delinquent heiresses and eccentric cosmopolites in those fabulous years before the Recess. Admittedly most of the abstract villas and fake palazzos were empty, their huge gardens overgrown, two-level swimming pools long drained, and the whole place was degenerating like an abandoned amusement park, but there was enough bizarre extravagance in the air to make one realize that the giants had only just departed.

I remember the day we first drove down Stellavista in the property agent's car, and how exhilarated Fay and I were, despite our bogus front of bourgeois respectability. Fay, I think, was even a little awed – one or two of the big names were living on behind the shuttered terraces – and we must have been the easiest prospects the young agent had seen for months.

Presumably this was why he tried to work off the really weird places first. The half dozen we saw to begin with were obviously the old regulars, faithfully paraded in the hope that some unwary client might be staggered into buying one of them, or failing that, temporarily lose all standards of comparison and take the first tolerably conventional pile to come along.

One, just off Stellavista and M, would have shaken even an old-guard surrealist on a heroin swing. Screened from the road by a mass of dusty rhododendrons, it consisted of six aluminium-shelled spheres suspended like the elements of a mobile from an enormous concrete davit. The largest sphere contained the lounge, the others, successively smaller and spiralling upwards into the air, the bedrooms and kitchen. Many of the hull plates had been holed, and the entire slightly tarnished structure hung down into the weeds poking through the cracked concrete court like a collection of forgotten spaceships in a vacant lot.

Stamers, the agent, left us sitting in the car, partly shielded by the rhododendrons. He ran across to the entrance and switched the place on (all the houses in Vermilion Sands, it goes without saying, were psychotropic). There was a dim whirring, and the spheres tipped and began to rotate, brushing against the undergrowth.

Fay sat in the car, staring up in amazement at this awful, beautiful thing, but out of curiosity I got out and walked over to the entrance, the main sphere slowing as I approached, uncertainly steering a course towards me, the smaller ones following.

According to the descriptive brochure, the house had been built eight years earlier for a TV mogul as a weekend retreat. The pedigree was a long one, through two movie starlets, a psychiatrist, an ultrasonic composer (the late Dmitri Shochmann – a notorious madman. I remembered that he had invited a score of guests to his suicide party, but no one had turned up to watch. Chagrined, he bungled the attempt.) and an automobile stylist. With such an overlay of more or less blue-chip responses built into it, the house should have been snapped up within a week, even in Vermilion Sands. To have been on the market for several months, if not years, indicated that the previous tenants had been none too happy there.

Ten feet from me, the main sphere hovered uncertainly, the entrance extending downwards. Stamers stood in the open doorway, smiling encouragingly, but the house seemed nervous of something. As I stepped forward it suddenly jerked away, almost in alarm, the entrance retracting and sending a low shudder through the rest of the spheres.

It's always interesting to watch a psychotropic house try to adjust itself to strangers, particularly those at all guarded or suspicious. The responses vary, a blend of past reactions to negative emotions, the hostility of the previous tenants, a traumatic encounter with a bailiff or burglar (though both these usually stay well away from PT houses; the dangers of an inverting balcony or the sudden deflatus of a corridor are too great). The initial reaction can be a surer indication of a house's true condition than any amount of sales talk about horsepower and moduli of elasticity.

This one was definitely on the defensive. When I climbed on to the entrance Stamers was fiddling desperately with the control console recessed into the wall behind the door, damping the volume down as low as possible. Usually a property agent will select medium/full, trying to heighten the PT responses.

He smiled thinly at me. 'Circuits are a little worn. Nothing serious, we'll replace them on contract. Some of the previous owners were showbusiness people, had an over-simplified view of the full life.

I nodded, walking on to the balcony which ringed the wide sunken lounge. It was a beautiful room all right, with opaque plastex walls and white fluo-glass ceiling, but something terrible had happened there. As it responded to me, the ceiling lifted slightly and the walls grew less opaque, reflecting my perspective-seeking eye. I noticed that curious mottled knots were forming where the room had been strained and healed faultily. Hidden rifts began to distort the sphere, ballooning out one of the alcoves like a bubble of over-extended gum.

Stamers tapped my elbow.

'Lively responses, aren't they, Mr Talbot?' He put his hand on the wall behind us. The plastex swam and whirled like boiling toothpaste, then extruded itself into a small ledge. Stamers sat down on the lip, which quickly expanded to match the contours of his body, providing back and arm rests. 'Sit down and relax, Mr Talbot, let yourself feel at home here.'

The seat cushioned up around me like an enormous white hand, and immediately the walls and ceiling quietened – obviously Stamers's first job was to get his clients off their feet before their restless shuffling could do any damage. Someone living there must have put in a lot of anguished pacing and knuckle-cracking.

'Of course, you're getting nothing but custom-built units here,' Stamers said. 'The vinyl chains in this plastex were hand-crafted literally molecule by molecule.'

I felt the room shift around me. The ceiling was dilating and contracting in steady pulses, an absurdly exaggerated response to our own respiratory rhythms, but the motions were overlayed by sharp transverse spasms, feed-back from some cardiac ailment.

The house was not only frightened of us, it was seriously ill. Somebody, Dmitri Shochmann perhaps, overflowing with self-hate, had committed an appalling injury to himself, and the house was recapitulating its previous response. I was about to ask Stamers if the suicide party had been staged here when he sat up and looked around fretfully.

At the same time my ears started to sing. Mysteriously, the air pressure inside the lounge was building up, gusts of old grit whirling out into the hallway towards the exit.

Stamers was on his feet, the seat telescoping back into the wall.

'Er, Mr Talbot, let's stroll around the garden, give you the feel of –'

He broke off, face creased in alarm. The ceiling was only five feet above our heads, contracting like a huge white bladder.

'– explosive decompression,' Stamers finished automatically, taking my arm. 'I don't understand this,' he muttered as we ran out into the hallway, the air whooshing past us.

I had a shrewd idea what was happening, and sure enough we found Fay peering into the control console, swinging the volume tabs.

Stamers dived past her. We were almost dragged back into the lounge as the ceiling began its outward leg and sucked the air in through the doorway. He reached the emergency panel and switched the house off.

Wide-eyed, he buttoned his shirt. 'That was close, Mrs Talbot, really close.' He gave a light hysterical laugh.

As we walked back to the car, the giant spheres resting among the weeds, he said: 'Well, Mr Talbot, it's a fine property. A remarkable pedigree for a house only eight years old. An exciting challenge, you know, a new dimension in living.'

I gave him a weak smile. 'Maybe, but it's not exactly *us*, is it?'

\*      \*      \*

We had come to Vermilion Sands for two years, while I opened a law office in downtown Red Beach twenty miles away. Apart from the dust, smog and inflationary prices of real estate in Red Beach, a strong motive for coming out to Vermilion Sands was that any number of potential clients were mouldering away there in the old mansions – forgotten movie queens, lonely impresarios and the like, some of the most litigious people in the world. Once installed, I could make my rounds of the bridge tables and dinner parties, tactfully stimulating a little righteous will-paring and contract-breaking.

However, as we drove down Stellavista on our inspection tour I wondered if we'd find anywhere suitable. Rapidly we went through a mock Assyrian ziggurat (the last owner had suffered from St Vitus's Dance, and the whole structure still jittered like a galvanized Tower of Pisa), and a converted submarine pen (here the problem had been alcoholism, we could *feel* the gloom and helplessness come down off those huge damp walls).

Finally Stamers gave up and brought us back to earth. Unfortunately his more conventional properties were little better. The real trouble was that most of Vermilion Sands is composed of early, or primitive-fantastic psychotropic, when the possibilities offered by the new bio-plastic medium rather went to architects' heads. It was some years before a compromise was reached between the one hundred per cent responsive structive and the rigid non-responsive houses of the past. The first PT houses had so many senso-cells distributed over them, echoing every shift of mood and position of the occupants, that living in one was like inhabiting someone else's brain.

Unluckily bioplastics need a lot of exercise or they grow rigid and crack, and many people believe that PT buildings are still given unnecessarily subtle memories and are far too sensitive – there's the apocryphal story of the millionaire of plebian origins who was literally frozen out of a million-dollar mansion he had bought from an aristocratic family. The place had been trained to respond to their habitual rudeness and bad temper, and reacted discordantly when readjusting itself to the millionaire, unintentionally parodying his soft-spoken politeness.

But although the echoes of previous tenants can be intrusive, this naturally has its advantages. Many medium-priced PT homes resonate with the bygone laughter of happy families, the relaxed harmony of a successful marriage. It was something like this that I wanted for Fay and myself. In the previous year our relationship had begun to fade a little, and a really well-integrated house with a healthy set of reflexes – say, those of a prosperous bank president and his devoted spouse – would go a long way towards healing the rifts between us.

Leafing through the brochures when we reached the end of Stellavista I could see that domesticated bank presidents had been in short supply at Vermilion Sands. The pedigrees were either packed with ulcer-ridden, quadri-divorced TV executives, or discreetly blank.

99 Stellavista was in the latter category. As we climbed out of the car and walked up the short drive I searched the pedigree for data on the past tenants, but only the original owner was given: a Miss Emma Slack, psychic orientation unstated.

That it was a woman's house was obvious. Shaped like an enormous orchid, it was set back on a low concrete dais in the centre of a blue gravel court. The white plastex wings, which carried the lounge on one side and the master bedroom on the other, spanned out across the magnolias on the far side of the drive. Between the two wings, on the first floor, was an open terrace around a heart-shaped swimming pool. The terrace ran back to the central bulb, a three-storey segment containing the chauffeur's apartment and a vast two-decker kitchen.

The house seemed to be in good condition. The plastex was unscarred, its thin seams running smoothly to the far rim like the veins of a giant leaf.

Curiously, Stamers was in no hurry to switch on. He pointed to left and right as we made our way up the glass staircase to the terrace, underlining various attractive features, but made no effort to find the control console, and suspected that the house might be a static conversion – a fair number of PT houses are frozen in one or other position at the end of their working lives, and make tolerable static homes.

'It's not bad,' I admitted, looking across the powder-blue water as Stamers piled on the superlatives. Through the glass bottom of the pool the car parked below loomed like a coloured whale asleep on the ocean bed. 'This is the sort of thing, all right. But what about switching it on?'

Stamers stepped around me and headed after Fay. 'You'll want to see the kitchen first, Mr Talbot. There's no hurry, let yourself feel at home here.'

The kitchen was fabulous, banks of gleaming control panels and auto units. Everything was recessed and stylized, blending into the overall colour scheme, complex gadgets folding back into self-sealing cabinets. Boiling an egg there would have taken me a couple of days.

'Quite a plant,' I commented. Fay wandered around in a daze of delight, automatically fingering the chrome. 'Looks as if it's tooled up to produce penicillin.' I tapped the brochure. 'But why so cheap? At twenty-five thousand it's damn nearly being given away.'

Stamers's eyes brightened. He flashed me a broad conspiratorial smile which indicated that this was *my* year, *my* day. Taking me off on a tour of the rumpus room and library, he began to hammer home the merits of the house, extolling his company's thirty-five-year, easy-purchase plan (they wanted anything except cash – there was no money in that) and the beauty and simplicity of the garden (mostly flexible polyurethane perennials).

Finally, apparently convinced that I was sold, he switched the house on.

I didn't know then what it was, but something strange had taken place in that house. Emma Slack had certainly been a woman with a powerful and oblique personality. As I walked slowly around the empty lounge, feeling the walls angle and edge away, doorways widen when I approached, curious echoes stirred through the memories embedded in the house. The responses were undefined, but somehow eerie and unsettling, like being continually watched over one's shoulder, each room adjusting itself to my soft, random footsteps as if they contained the possibility of some explosive burst of passion or temperament.

Inclining my head, I seemed to hear other echoes, delicate and feminine, a graceful swirl of movement reflected in a brief, fluid sweep in one corner, the decorous unfolding of an archway or recess.

Then, abruptly, the mood would invert, and the hollow eeriness return.

Fay touched my arm. 'Howard, it's strange.'

I shrugged. 'Interesting, though. Remember, our own responses will overlay these within a few days.'

Fay shook her head. 'I couldn't stand it, Howard. Mr Stamers must have something normal.'

'Darling, Vermilion Sands is Vermilion Sands. Don't expect to find the suburban norms. People here were individualists.'

I looked down at Fay. Her small oval face, with its childlike mouth and chin, the fringe of blonde hair and pert nose, seemed lost and anxious.

I put my arm around her shoulder. 'Okay, sweetie, you're quite right. Let's find somewhere we can put our feet up and relax. Now, what are we going to say to Stamers?'

Surprisingly, Stamers didn't seem all that disappointed. When I shook my head he put up a token protest but soon gave in and switched off the house.

'I know how Mrs Talbot feels,' he conceded as we went down the staircase. 'Some of these places have got too much personality built into them. Living with someone like Gloria Tremayne isn't too easy.'

I stopped, two steps from the bottom, a curious ripple of recognition running through my mind.

'Gloria Tremayne? I thought the only owner was a Miss Emma Slack.'

Stamers nodded. 'Yes. Gloria Tremayne. Emma Slack was her real name. Don't say I told you, though everybody living around here knows it. We keep it quiet as long as we can. If we said Gloria Tremayne no one would even look at the place.'

'Gloria Tremayne,' Fay repeated, puzzled. 'She was the movie star who shot her husband, wasn't she? He was a famous architect – Howard, weren't you on that case?'

As Fay's voice chattered on I turned and looked up the staircase towards the sun-lounge, my mind casting itself back ten years to one of the most famous trials of the decade, whose course and verdict were as much as anything else to mark the end of a whole generation, and show up the irresponsibilities of the world before the Recess. Even though Gloria Tremayne had been acquitted, everyone knew that she had cold-bloodedly murdered her husband, the architect Miles Vanden Starr. Only the silver-tongued pleading of Daniel Hammett, her defence attorney, assisted by a young man called Howard Talbot, had saved her. I said to Fay, 'Yes, I helped to defend her. It seems a long time ago. Angel, wait in the car. I want to check something.'

Before she could follow me I ran up the staircase on to the terrace and closed the glass double doors behind me. Inert and unresponsive now, the white walls rose into the sky on either side of the pool. The water was motionless, a transparent block of condensed time, through which I could see the drowned images of Fay and Stamers sitting in the car, like an embalmed fragment of my future.

For three weeks, during her trial ten years earlier, I sat only a few feet from Gloria Tremayne, and like everyone else in that crowded courtroom I would never forget her mask-like face, the composed eyes that examined each of the witnesses as they gave their testimony – chauffeur, police surgeon, neighbours who heard the shots – like a brilliant spider arraigned by its victims, never once showing any emotion or response. As they dismembered her web, skein by skein, she sat impassively at its centre, giving Hammett no encouragement, content to repose in the image of herself ('The Ice Face') projected across the globe for the previous fifteen years.

Perhaps in the end this saved her. The jury were unable to outstare the enigma. To be honest, by the last week of the trial I had lost all interest in it. As I steered Hammett through his brief, opening and shutting his red wooden suitcase (the Hammett hallmark, it was an excellent jury distractor) whenever he indicated, my attention was fixed completely on Gloria Tremayne, trying to find some flaw in the mask through which I could glimpse her personality. I suppose that I was just another naive young man who had fallen in love with a myth manufactured by a thousand publicity agents, but for me the sensation was the real thing, and when she was acquitted the world began to revolve again.

That justice had been flouted mattered nothing. Hammett, curiously, believed her innocent. Like many successful lawyers he had based his career on the principle of prosecuting the guilty and defending the innocent – this way he was sure of a sufficiently high proportion of successes to give him a reputation for being brilliant and unbeatable. When he defended Gloria Tremayne most lawyers thought he had been tempted to depart from principle by a fat bribe from her studio, but in fact he volunteered to take the case. Perhaps he, too, was working off a secret infatuation.

Of course, I never saw her again. As soon as her next picture had been safely released her studio dropped her. Later she briefly reappeared on a narcotics charge after a car smash, and then disappeared into a limbo of alcoholics hospitals and psychiatric wards. When she died five years afterwards few newspapers gave her more than a couple of lines.

Below, Stamers sounded the horn. Leisurely I retraced my way through the lounge and bedrooms, scanning the empty floors, running my hands over the smooth plastex walls, bracing myself to feel again the impact of Gloria Tremayne's personality. Blissfully, her presence would be everywhere in the house, a thousand echoes of her distilled into every matrix and senso-cell, each moment of emotion blended into a replica more intimate than anyone, apart from her dead husband, could ever know. The Gloria Tremayne with whom I had become infatuated had ceased to exist, but this house was the shrine that entombed the very signatures of her soul.

To begin with everything went quietly. Fay remonstrated with me, but I promised her a new mink wrap out of the savings we made on the house. Secondly, I was careful to keep the volume down for the first few weeks, so that there would be no clash of feminine wills. A major problem of psychotropic houses is that after several months one has to increase the volume to get the same image of the last owner, and this increases the sensitivity of the memory cells and their rate of contamination. At the same time, magnifying the psychic underlay emphasizes the cruder emotional ground-base. One begins to taste the lees rather than the distilled cream of the previous tenancy. I wanted to savour the quintessence of Gloria Tremayne as long as possible so I deliberately rationed myself, turning the volume down during the day while I was out, then switching on only those rooms in which I sat in the evenings.

Right from the outset I was neglecting Fay. Not only were we both preoccupied with the usual problems of adjustment faced by every married couple moving into a new house – undressing in the master bedroom that first night was a positive honeymoon debut all over again – but I was completely immersed in the exhilarating persona of Gloria Tremayne, exploring every alcove and niche in search of her.

In the evenings I sat in the library, feeling her around me in the stirring walls, hovering nearby as I emptied the packing cases like an attendant succubus. Sipping my scotch while night closed over the dark blue pool, I carefully analysed her personality, deliberately varying my moods to evoke as wide a range of responses. The memory cells in the house were perfectly bonded, never revealing any flaws of character, always reposed and self-controlled. If I leapt out of my chair and switched the stereogram abruptly from Stravinsky to Stan Kenton to the MJQ, the room adjusted its mood and tempo without effort.

And yet how long was it before I discovered that there was another personality present in that house, and began to feel the curious eeriness Fay and I had noticed as soon as Stamers switched the house on? Not for a few weeks, when the house was still responding to my star-struck idealism. While my devotion to the departed spirit of Gloria Tremayne was the dominant mood, the house played itself back accordingly, recapitulating only the more serene aspects of Gloria Tremayne's character.

Soon, however, the mirror was to darken.

It was Fay who broke the spell. She quickly realized that the initial responses were being overlaid by others from a more mellow and, from her point of view, more dangerous quarter of the past. After doing her best to put up with them she made a few guarded attempts to freeze Gloria out, switching the volume controls up and down, selecting the maximum of bass lift – which stressed the masculine responses – and the minimum of alto lift.

One morning I caught her on her knees by the console, poking a screwdriver at the memory drum, apparently in an effort to erase the entire store.

Taking it from her, I locked the unit and hooked the key on to my chain.

'Darling, the mortgage company could sue us for destroying the pedigree. Without it this house would be valueless. What are you try-ing to do?'

Fay dusted her hands on her skirt and stared me straight in the eye, chin jutting.

'I'm trying to restore a little sanity here and if possible, find my own marriage again. I thought it might be in there somewhere.'

I put my arm around her and steered her back towards the kitchen. 'Darling, you're getting over-intuitive again. Just relax, don't try to upset everything.'

'Upset –? Howard, what are you talking about? Haven't I a right to my own husband? I'm sick of sharing him with a homicidal neurotic who died five years ago. It's positively ghoulish!'

I winced as she snapped this out, feeling the walls in the hallway darken and retreat defensively. The air became clouded and frenetic, like a dull storm-filled day.

'Fay, you know your talent for exaggeration . . .' I searched around for the kitchen, momentarily disoriented as the corridor walls shifted and backed. 'You don't know how lucky you –'

I didn't get any further before she interrupted. Within five seconds we were in the middle of a blistering row. Fay threw all caution to the winds, deliberately, I think, in the hope of damaging the house permanently, while I stupidly let a lot of my unconscious resentment towards her come out. Finally she stormed away into her bedroom and I stamped into the shattered lounge and slumped down angrily on the sofa.

*     *     *

Above me the ceiling flexed and quivered, the colour of roof slates, here and there mottled by angry veins that bunched the walls in on each other. The air pressure mounted but I felt too tired to open a window and sat stewing in a pit of black anger.

It must have been then that I recognized the presence of Miles Vanden Starr. All echoes of Gloria Tremayne's personality had vanished, and for the first time since moving in I had recovered my normal perspectives. The mood of anger and resentment in the lounge was remarkably persistent, far longer than expected from what had been little more than a tiff. The walls continued to pulse and knot for over half an hour, long after my own irritation had faded and I was sitting up and examining the room clear-headedly.

The anger, deep and frustrated, was obviously masculine. I assumed, correctly, that the original source had been Vanden Starr, who had designed the house for Gloria Tremayne and lived there for over a year before his death. To have so grooved the memory drum meant that this atmosphere of blind, neurotic hostility had been maintained for most of that time.

As the resentment slowly dispersed I could see that for the time being Fay had succeeded in her object. The serene persona of Gloria Tremayne had vanished. The feminine motif was still there, in a higher and shriller key, but the dominant presence was distinctly Vanden Starr's. This new mood of the house reminded me of the courtroom photographs of him; glowering out of 1950-ish groups with Le Corbusier and Lloyd Wright, stalking about some housing project in Chicago or Tokyo like a petty dictator, heavy-jowled, thyroidal, with large lustreless eyes, and then the Vermilion Sands: 1970 shots of him, fitting into the movie colony like a shark into a goldfish bowl.

However, there was power behind those baleful drives. Cued in by our tantrum, the presence of Vanden Starr had descended upon 99 Stellavista like a thundercloud. At first I tried to recapture the earlier halcyon mood, but this had disappeared and my irritation at losing it only served to inflate the thundercloud. An unfortunate aspect of psychotropic houses is the factor of resonance – diametrically opposed personalities soon stabilize their relationship, the echo inevitably yielding to the new source. But where the personalities are of similar frequency and amplitude they mutually reinforce themselves, each adapting itself for comfort to the personality of the other. All too soon I began to assume the character of Vanden Starr, and my increased exasperation with Fay merely drew from the house a harder front of antagonism.

Later I knew that I was, in fact, treating Fay in exactly the way that Vanden Starr had treated Gloria Tremayne, recapitulating the steps of their tragedy with consequences that were equally disastrous.

Fay recognized the changed mood of the house immediately. 'What's happened to our lodger?' she gibed at dinner the next evening. 'Our beautiful ghost seems to be spurning you. Is the spirit unwilling although the flesh is weak?'

'God knows,' I growled testily. 'I think you've really messed the place up.' I glanced around the dining room for any echo of Gloria Tremayne, but she had gone. Fay went out to the kitchen and I sat over my half-eaten hors d'oeuvres, staring at it blankly, when I felt a curious ripple in the wall behind me, a silver dart of movement that vanished as soon as I looked up. I tried to focus it without success, the first echo of Gloria since our row, but later that evening, when I went into Fay's bedroom after I heard her crying, I noticed it again.

Fay had gone into the bathroom. As I was about to find her I felt the same echo of feminine anguish. It had been prompted by Fay's tears, but like Vanden Starr's mood set off by my own anger, it persisted long after the original cue. I followed it into the corridor as it faded out of the room but it diffused outwards into the ceiling and hung there motionlessly.

Starting to walk down to the lounge, I realized that the house was watching me like a wounded animal.

Two days later came the attack on Fay.

I had just returned home from the office, childishly annoyed with Fay for parking her car on my side of the garage. In the cloakroom I tried to check my anger; the senso-cells had picked up the cue and began to suck the irritation out of me, pouring it back into the air until the walls of the cloakroom darkened and seethed.

I shouted some gratuitous insult at Fay, who was in the lounge. A second later she screamed: 'Howard! Quickly!'

Running towards the lounge, I flung myself at the door, expecting it to retract. Instead, it remained rigid, frame locked in the archway. The entire house seemed grey and strained, the pool outside like a tank of cold lead.

Fay shouted again. I seized the metal handle of the manual control and wrenched the door back.

Fay was almost out of sight, on one of the slab sofas in the centre of the room, buried beneath the sagging canopy of the ceiling which had collapsed on to her. The heavy plastex had flowed together directly above her head, forming a blob a yard in diameter.

Raising the flaccid plastex with my hands, I managed to lift it off Fay, who was spread-eagled into the cushions with only her feet protruding. She wriggled out and flung her arms around me, sobbing noiselessly.

'Howard, this house is insane, I think it's trying to kill me!'

'For heaven's sake, Fay, don't be silly. It was simply a freak accumulation of senso-cells. Your breathing probably set it off.' I patted her shoulder, remembering the child I had married a few years earlier. Smiling to myself, I watched the ceiling retract slowly, the walls grow lighter in tone.

'Howard, can't we leave here?' Fay babbled. 'Let's go and live in a static house. I know it's dull, but what does it matter –?'

'Well,' I said, 'it's not just dull, it's dead. Don't worry, angel, you'll learn to like it here.'

Fay twisted away from me. 'Howard, I can't stay in this house any more. You've been so preoccupied recently, you're completely changed.' She started to cry again, and pointed at the ceiling. 'If I hadn't been lying down, do you realize it would have killed me?'

I dusted the end of the sofa. 'Yes, I can see your heel marks.' Irritation welled up like bile before I could stop it. 'I thought I told you not to stretch out here. This isn't a beach, Fay. You know it annoys me.'

Around us the walls began to mottle and cloud again.

Why did Fay anger me so easily? Was it, as I assumed at the time, unconscious resentment that egged me on, or was I merely a vehicle for the antagonism which had accumulated during Vanden Starr's marriage to Gloria Tremayne and was now venting itself on the hapless couple who followed them to 99 Stellavista? Perhaps I'm over-charitable to myself in assuming the latter, but Fay and I had been tolerably happy during our five years of marriage, and I am sure my nostalgic infatuation for Gloria Tremayne couldn't have so swept me off my feet.

Either way, however, Fay didn't wait for a second attempt. Two days later I came home to find a fresh tape on the kitchen memophone. I switched it on to hear her tell me that she could no longer put up with me, my nagging or 99 Stellavista and was going back east to stay with her sister.

Callously, my first reaction, after the initial twinge of indignation, was sheer relief. I still believed that Fay was responsible for Gloria Tremayne's eclipse and the emergence of Vanden Starr, and that with her gone I would recapture the early days of idyll and romance.

I was only partly right. Gloria Tremayne did return, but not in the role expected. I, who had helped to defend her at her trial, should have known better.

A few days after Fay left I became aware that the house had taken on a separate existence, its coded memories discharging themselves independently of my own behaviour. Often when I returned in the evening, eager to relax over half a decanter of scotch, I would find the ghosts of Miles Vanden Starr and Gloria Tremayne in full flight. Starr's black and menacing personality crowded after the tenuous but increasingly resilient quintessence of his wife. This rapier-like resistance could be observed literally – the walls of the lounge would stiffen and darken in a vortex of anger that converged upon a small zone of lightness hiding in one of the alcoves, as if to obliterate its presence, but at the last moment Gloria's persona would flit nimbly away, leaving the room to seethe and writhe.

Fay had set off this spirit of resistance, and I visualized Gloria Tremayne going through a similar period of living hell. As her personality re-emerged in its new role I watched it carefully, volume at maximum despite the damage the house might do to itself. Once Stamers stopped by and offered to get the circuits checked for me. He had seen the house from the road, flexing and changing colour like an anguished squid. Thanking him, I made up some excuse and declined. Later he told me that I had kicked him out unceremoniously – apparently he hardly recognized me; I was striding around the dark quaking house like a madman in an Elizabethan horror tragedy, oblivious of everything.

Although submerged by the personality of Miles Vanden Starr, I gradually realized that Gloria Tremayne had been deliberately driven out of her mind by him. What had prompted his implacable hostility I can only hazard – perhaps he resented her success, perhaps she had been unfaithful to him. When she finally retaliated and shot him it was, I'm sure, an act of self-defence.

Two months after she went east Fay filed a divorce suit against me. Frantically I telephoned her, explaining that I would be grateful if she postponed the action as the publicity would probably kill my new law office. However, Fay was adamant. What annoyed me most was that she sounded better than she had done for years, really happy again. When I pleaded with her she said she needed the divorce in order to marry again, and then, as a last straw, refused to tell me who the man was.

By the time I slammed the phone down my temper was taking off like a lunar probe. I left the office early and began a tour of the bars in Red Beach, working my way slowly back to Vermilion Sands. I hit 99 Stellavista like a one-man task force, mowing down most of the magnolias in the drive, ramming the car into the garage on the third pass after wrecking both auto-doors.

My keys jammed in the door lock and I finally had to kick my way through one of the glass panels. Raging upstairs on to the darkened terrace I flung my hat and coat into the pool and slammed into the lounge. By 2 a.m., as I mixed myself a nightcap at the bar and put the last act of *Götterdämmerung* on the stereogram, the whole place was really warming up.

On the way to bed I lurched into Fay's room to see what damage I could do to the memories I still retained of her, kicked in a wardrobe and booted the mattress on to the floor, turning the walls literally blue with a salvo of epithets.

Shortly after three o'clock I fell asleep, the house revolving around me like an enormous turntable.

It must have been only four o'clock when I woke, conscious of a curious silence in the darkened room. I was stretched across the bed, one hand around the neck of the decanter, the other holding a dead cigar stub.

The walls were motionless, unstirred by even the residual eddies which drift through a psychotropic house when the occupants are asleep.

Something had altered the normal perspectives of the room. Trying to focus on the grey underswell of the ceiling, I listened for footsteps outside. Sure enough, the corridor wall began to retract. The archway, usually a six-inch wide slit, rose to admit someone. Nothing came through, but the room expanded to accommodate an additional presence, the ceiling ballooning upwards. Astounded, I tried not to move my head, watching the unoccupied pressure zone move quickly across the room towards the bed, its motion shadowed by a small dome in the ceiling.

The pressure zone paused at the foot of the bed and hesitated for a few seconds. But instead of stabilizing, the walls began to vibrate rapidly, quivering with strange uncertain tremors, radiating a sensation of acute urgency and indecision.

Then, abruptly, the room stilled. A second later, as I lifted myself up on one elbow, a violent spasm convulsed the room, buckling the walls and lifting the bed off the floor. The entire house started to shake and writhe. Gripped by this seizure, the bedroom contracted and expanded like the chamber of a dying heart, the ceiling rising and falling.

I steadied myself on the swinging bed and gradually the convulsion died away, the walls realigning. I stood up, wondering what insane crisis this psychotropic *grand mal* duplicated.

The room was in darkness, thin moonlight coming through the trio of small circular vents behind the bed. These were contracting as the walls closed in on each other. Pressing my hands against the ceiling, I felt it push downwards strongly. The edges of the floor were blending into the walls as the room converted itself into a sphere.

The air pressure mounted. I tumbled over to the vents, reached them as they clamped around my fists, air whistling through my fingers. Face against the openings, I gulped in the cool night air, and tried to force apart the locking plastex.

The safety cut-out switch was above the door on the other side of the room. I dived across to it, clambering over the tilting bed, but the flowing plastex had submerged the whole unit.

Head bent to avoid the ceiling, I pulled off my tie, gasping at the thudding air. Trapped in the room, I was suffocating as it duplicated the expiring breaths of Vanden Starr after he had been shot. The tremendous spasm had been his convulsive reaction as the bullet from Gloria Tremayne's gun crashed into his chest.

I fumbled in my pockets for a knife, felt my cigarette lighter, pulled it out and flicked it on. The room was now a grey sphere ten feet in diameter. Thick veins, as broad as my arm, were knotting across its surface, crushing the endboards of the bedstead.

I raised the lighter to the surface of the ceiling, and let it play across the opaque fluoglass. Immediately it began to fizz and bubble. It flared alight and split apart, the two burning lips unzipping in a brilliant discharge of heat.

As the cocoon bisected itself, I could see the twisted mouth of the corridor bending into the room below the sagging outline of the dining room ceiling. Feet skating in the molten plastex, I pulled myself up on to the corridor. The whole house seemed to have been ruptured. Walls were buckled, floors furling at their edges. Water was pouring out of the pool as the unit tipped forwards on the weakened foundations. The glass slabs of the staircase had been shattered, the razor-like teeth jutting from the wall.

I ran into Fay's bedroom, found the cut-out switch and stabbed the sprinkler alarm.

The house was still throbbing, but a moment later it locked and became rigid. I leaned against the dented wall and let the spray pour across my face from the sprinkler jets.

Around me, its wings torn and disarrayed, the house reared up like a tortured flower.

Standing in the trampled flower beds, Stamers gazed at the house, an expression of awe and bewilderment on his face. It was just after six o'clock. The last of the three police cars had driven away, the lieutenant in charge finally conceding defeat. 'Dammit, I can't arrest a house for attempted homicide, can I?' he'd asked me somewhat belligerently. I roared with laughter at this, my initial feelings of shock having given way to an almost hysterical sense of fun.

Stamers found me equally difficult to understand.

'What on earth were you doing in there?' he asked, voice down to a whisper.

'Nothing. I tell you I was fast asleep. And relax. The house can't hear you. It's switched off.'

We wandered across the churned gravel and waded through the water which lay like a black mirror. Stamers shook his head.

'The place must have been insane. If you ask me it needs a psychiatrist to straighten it out.'

'You're right,' I told him. 'In fact, that was exactly my role – to reconstruct the original traumatic situation and release the repressed material.'

'Why joke about it? It tried to kill you.'

'Don't be absurd. The real culprit is Vanden Starr. But as the lieutenant implied, you can't arrest a man who's been dead for ten years. It was the pent-up memory of his death which tried to kill me. Even if Gloria Tremayne was driven to pulling the trigger, Starr pointed the gun. Believe me, I lived out his role for a couple of months. What worries me is that if Fay hadn't had enough good sense to leave she might have been hypnotized by the persona of Gloria Tremayne into killing *me*.'

\*      \*      \*

Much to Stamers's surprise, I decided to stay on at 99 Stellavista. Apart from the fact that I hadn't enough cash to buy another place, the house had certain undeniable memories for me that I didn't want to forsake. Gloria Tremayne was still there, and I was sure that Vanden Starr had at last gone. The kitchen and service units were still functional, and apart from their contorted shapes most of the rooms were habitable. In addition I needed a rest, and nothing is so quiet as a static house.

Of course, in its present form 99 Stellavista can hardly be regarded as a typical static dwelling. Yet, the deformed rooms and twisted corridors have as much personality as any psychotropic house. The PT unit is still working and one day I shall switch it on again. But one thing worries me. The violent spasms which ruptured the house may in some way have damaged Gloria Tremayne's personality. To live with it might well be madness for me, as there's a subtle charm about the house even in its distorted form, like the ambiguous smile of a beautiful but insane woman.

Often I unlock the control console and examine the memory drum. Her personality, whatever it may be, is there. Nothing would be simpler than to erase it. But I can't.

One day soon, whatever the outcome, I know that I shall have to switch the house on again.

**1962**

# THIRTEEN TO CENTAURUS

Abel knew.

Three months earlier, just after his sixteenth birthday, he had guessed, but had been too unsure of himself, too overwhelmed by the logic of his discovery, to mention it to his parents. At times, lying back half asleep in his bunk while his mother crooned one of the old lays to herself, he would deliberately repress the knowledge, but always it came back, nagging at him insistently, forcing him to jettison most of what he had long regarded as the real world.

None of the other children at the Station could help. They were immersed in their games in Playroom, or chewing pencils over their tests and homework.

'Abel, what's the matter?' Zenna Peters called after him as he wandered off to the empty store-room on D-Deck. 'You're looking sad again.'

Abel hesitated, watching Zenna's warm, puzzled smile, then slipped his hands into his pockets and made off, springing down the metal stairway to make sure she didn't follow him. Once she sneaked into the store-room uninvited and he had pulled the light-bulb out of the socket, shattered about three weeks of conditioning. Dr Francis had been furious.

As he hurried along the D-Deck corridor he listened carefully for the doctor, who had recently been keeping an eye on Abel, watching him shrewdly from behind the plastic models in Playroom. Perhaps Abel's mother had told him about the nightmare, when he would wake from a vice of sweating terror, an image of a dull burning disc fixed before his eyes.

*If only Dr Francis could cure him of that dream.*

Every six yards down the corridor he stepped through a bulkhead, and idly touched the heavy control boxes on either side of the doorway. Deliberately unfocusing his mind, Abel identified some of the letters above the switches

M–T—R SC—N

but they scrambled into a blur as soon as he tried to read the entire phrase. Conditioning was too strong. After he trapped her in the store-room Zenna had been able to read a few of the notices, but Dr Francis whisked her away before she could repeat them. Hours later, when she came back, she remembered nothing.

As usual when he entered the store-room, he waited a few seconds before switching on the light, seeing in front of him the small disc of burning light that in his dreams expanded until it filled his brain like a thousand arc lights. It seemed endlessly distant, yet somehow mysteriously potent and magnetic, arousing dormant areas of his mind close to those which responded to his mother's presence.

As the disc began to expand he pressed the switch tab.

To his surprise, the room remained in darkness. He fumbled for the switch, a short cry slipping involuntarily through his lips.

Abruptly, the light went on.

'Hello, Abel,' Dr Francis said easily, right hand pressing the bulb into its socket. 'Quite a shock, that one.' He leaned against a metal crate. 'I thought we'd have a talk together about your essay.' He took an exercise book out of his white plastic suit as Abel sat down stiffly. Despite his dry smile and warm eyes there was something about Dr Francis that always put Abel on his guard.

*Perhaps Dr Francis knew too?*

'The Closed Community,' Dr Francis read out. 'A strange subject for an essay, Abel.'

Abel shrugged. 'It was a free choice. Aren't we really expected to choose something unusual?'

Dr Francis grinned. 'A good answer. But seriously, Abel, why pick a subject like that?'

Abel fingered the seals on his suit. These served no useful purpose, but by blowing through them it was possible to inflate the suit. 'Well, it's a sort of study of life at the Station, how we all get on with each other. What else is there to write about? I don't see that it's so strange.'

'Perhaps not. No reason why you shouldn't write about the Station. All four of the others did too. But you called yours "The Closed Community". The Station isn't closed, Abel, is it?'

'It's closed in the sense that we can't go outside,' Abel explained slowly. 'That's all I meant.'

'Outside,' Dr Francis repeated. 'It's an interesting concept. You must have given the whole subject a lot of thought. When did you first start thinking along these lines?'

'After the dream,' Abel said. Dr Francis had deliberately sidestepped his use of the word 'outside' and he searched for some means of getting to the point. In his pocket he felt the small plumbline he carried around. 'Dr Francis, perhaps you can explain something to me. Why is the Station revolving?'

'Is it?' Dr Francis looked up with interest. 'How do you know?'

Abel reached up and fastened the plumbline to the ceiling stanchion.

'The interval between the ball and the wall is about an eighth of an inch greater at the bottom than at the top. Centrifugal forces are driving it outwards. I calculated that the Station is revolving at about two feet per second.'

Dr Francis nodded thoughtfully. 'That's just about right,' he said matter-of-factly. He stood up. 'Let's take a trip to my office. It looks as if it's time you and I had a serious talk.'

The Station was on four levels. The lower two contained the crew's quarters, two circular decks of cabins which housed the 14 people on board the Station. The senior clan was the Peters, led by Captain Theodore, a big stern man of taciturn disposition who rarely strayed from Control. Abel had never been allowed there, but the Captain's son, Matthew, often described the hushed dome-like cabin filled with luminous dials and flickering lights, the strange humming music.

All the male members of the Peters clan worked in Control – grandfather Peters, a white-haired old man with humorous eyes, had been Captain before Abel was born – and with the Captain's wife and Zenna they constituted the elite of the Station.

However, the Grangers, the clan to which Abel belonged, was in many respects more important, as he had begun to realize. The day-to-day running of the Station, the detailed programming of emergency drills, duty rosters and commissary menus, was the responsibility of Abel's father, Matthias, and without his firm but flexible hand the Bakers, who cleaned the cabins and ran the commissary, would never have known what to do. And it was only the deliberate intermingling in Recreation which his father devised that brought the Peters and Bakers together, or each family would have stayed indefinitely in its own cabins.

Lastly, there was Dr Francis. He didn't belong to any of the three clans. Sometimes Abel asked himself where Dr Francis had come from, but his mind always fogged at a question like that, as the conditioning blocks fell like bulkheads across his thought trains (logic was a dangerous tool at the Station). Dr Francis' energy and vitality, his relaxed good humour – in a way, he was the only person in the Station who ever made any jokes – were out of character with everyone else. Much as he sometimes disliked Dr Francis for snooping around and being a know-all, Abel realized how dreary life in the Station would seem without him.

Dr Francis closed the door of his cabin and gestured Abel into a seat. All the furniture in the Station was bolted to the floor, but Abel noticed that Dr Francis had unscrewed his chair so that he could tilt it backwards. The huge vacuum-proof cylinder of the doctor's sleeping tank jutted from the wall, its massive metal body able to withstand any accident the Station might suffer. Abel hated the thought of sleeping in the cylinder – luckily the entire crew quarters were accident-secure – and wondered why Dr Francis chose to live alone up on A-Deck.

'Tell me, Abel,' Dr Francis began, 'has it ever occurred to you to ask why the Station is here?'

Abel shrugged. 'Well, it's designed to keep us alive, it's our home.'

'Yes, that's true, but obviously it has some other object than just our own survival. Who do you think built the Station in the first place?'

'Our fathers, I suppose, or grandfathers. Or *their* grandfathers.'

'Fair enough. And where were they before they built it?'

Abel struggled with the *reductio ad absurdum*. 'I don't know, they must have been floating around in mid-air!'

Dr Francis joined in the laughter. 'Wonderful thought. Actually it's not that far from the truth. But we can't accept that as it stands.'

The doctor's self-contained office gave Abel an idea. 'Perhaps they came from another Station? An even bigger one?'

Dr Francis nodded encouragingly. 'Brilliant, Abel. A first-class piece of deduction. All right, then, let's assume that. Somewhere away from us, a huge Station exists, perhaps a hundred times bigger than this one, maybe even a thousand. Why not?'

'It's possible,' Abel admitted, accepting the idea with surprising ease.

'Right. Now you remember your course in advanced mechanics – the imaginary planetary system, with the orbiting bodies held together by mutual gravitational attraction? Let's assume further that such a system actually exists. Okay?'

'Here?' Abel said quickly. 'In your cabin?' Then he added 'In your sleeping cylinder?'

Dr Francis sat back. 'Abel, you do come up with some amazing things. An interesting association of ideas. No, it would be too big for that. Try to imagine a planetary system orbiting around a central body of absolutely enormous size, each of the planets a million times larger than the Station.' When Abel nodded, he went on. 'And suppose that the big Station, the one a thousand times larger than this, were attached to one of the planets, and that the people in it decided to go to another planet. So they build a smaller Station, about the size of this one, and send it off through the air. Make sense?'

'In a way.' Strangely, the completely abstract concepts were less remote than he would have expected. Deep in his mind dim memories stirred, interlocking with what he had already guessed about the Station. He gazed steadily at Dr Francis. 'You're saying that's what the Station is doing? That the planetary system exists?'

Dr Francis nodded. 'You'd more or less guessed before I told you. Unconsciously, you've known all about it for several years. A few minutes from now I'm going to remove some of the conditioning blocks, and when you wake up in a couple of hours you'll understand everything. You'll know then that in fact the Station is a space ship, flying from our home planet, Earth, where our grandfathers were born, to another planet millions of miles away, in a distant orbiting system. Our grandfathers always lived on Earth, and we are the first people ever to undertake such a journey. You can be proud that you're here. Your grandfather, who volunteered to come, was a great man, and we've got to do everything to make sure that the Station keeps running.'

Abel nodded quickly. 'When do we get there – the planet we're flying to?'

Dr Francis looked down at his hands, his face growing sombre. 'We'll never get there, Abel. The journey takes too long. This is a multi-generation space vehicle, only our children will land and they'll be old by the time they do. But don't worry, you'll go on thinking of the Station as your only home, and that's deliberate, so that you and your children will be happy here.'

He went over to the TV monitor screen by which he kept in touch with Captain Peters, his fingers playing across the control tabs. Suddenly the screen lit up, a blaze of fierce points of light flared into the cabin, throwing a brilliant phosphorescent glitter across the walls, dappling Abel's hands and suit. He gaped at the huge balls of fire, apparently frozen in the middle of a giant explosion, hanging in vast patterns.

'This is the celestial sphere,' Dr Francis explained. 'The starfield into which the Station is moving.' He touched a bright speck of light in the lower half of the screen. 'Alpha Centauri, the star around which revolves the planet the Station will one day land upon.' He turned to Abel. 'You remember all these terms I'm using, don't you, Abel? None of them seems strange.'

Abel nodded, the wells of his unconscious memory flooding into his mind as Dr Francis spoke. The TV screen blanked and then revealed a new picture. They appeared to be looking down at an enormous top-like structure, the flanks of a metal pylon sloping towards its centre. In the background the starfield rotated slowly in a clockwise direction. 'This is the Station,' Dr Francis explained, 'seen from a camera mounted in the nose boom. All visual checks have to be made indirectly, as the stellar radiation would blind us. Just below the ship you can see a single star, the Sun, from which we set out 50 years ago. It's now almost too distant to be visible, but a deep inherited memory of it is the burning disc you see in your dreams. We've done what we can to erase it, but unconsciously all of us see it too.'

He switched off the set and the brilliant pattern of light swayed and fell back. 'The social engineering built into the ship is far more intricate than the mechanical, Abel. It's three generations since the Station set off, and birth, marriage and birth again have followed exactly as they were designed to. As your father's heir great demands are going to be made on your patience and understanding. Any disunity here would bring disaster. The conditioning programmes are not equipped to give you more than a general outline of the course to follow. Most of it will be left to you.'

'Will you always be here?'

Dr Francis stood up. 'No, Abel, I won't. No one here lives forever. Your father will die, and Captain Peters and myself.' He moved to the door. 'We'll go now to Conditioning. In three hours' time, when you wake up, you'll find yourself a new man.'

Letting himself back into his cabin, Francis leaned wearily against the bulkhead, feeling the heavy rivets with his fingers, here and there flaking away as the metal slowly rusted. When he switched on the TV set he looked tired and dispirited, and gazed absently at the last scene he had shown Abel, the boom camera's view of the ship. He was just about to select another frame when he noticed a dark shadow swing across the surface of the hull.

He leaned forward to examine it, frowning in annoyance as the shadow moved away and faded among the stars. He pressed another tab, and the screen divided into a large chessboard, five frames wide by five deep. The top line showed Control, the main pilot and navigation deck lit by the dim glow of the instrument panels, Captain Peters sitting impassively before the compass screen.

Next, he watched Matthias Granger begin his afternoon inspection of the ship. Most of the passengers seemed reasonably happy, but their faces lacked any lustre. All spent at least 2–3 hours each day bathing in the UV light flooding through the recreation lounge, but the pallor continued, perhaps an unconscious realization that they had been born and were living in what would also be their own tomb. Without the continuous conditioning sessions, and the hypnotic reassurance of the sub-sonic voices, they would long ago have become will-less automatons.

Switching off the set, he prepared to climb into the sleeping cylinder. The airlock was three feet in diameter, waist-high off the floor. The time seal rested at zero, and he moved it forward 12 hours, then set it so that the seal could only be broken from within. He swung the lock out and crawled in over the moulded foam mattress, snapping the door shut behind him.

Lying back in the thin yellow light, he slipped his fingers through the ventilator grille in the rear wall, pressed the unit into its socket and turned it sharply. Somewhere an electric motor throbbed briefly, the end wall of the cylinder swung back slowly like a vault door and bright daylight poured in.

Quickly, Francis climbed out onto a small metal platform that jutted from the upper slope of a huge white asbestos-covered dome. Fifty feet above was the roof of a large hangar. A maze of pipes and cables traversed the surface of the dome, interlacing like the vessels of a giant bloodshot eye, and a narrow stairway led down to the floor below. The entire dome, some 150 feet wide, was revolving slowly. A line of five trucks was drawn up by the stores depot on the far side of the hangar, and a man in a brown uniform waved to him from one of the glass-walled offices.

At the bottom of the ladder he jumped down on to the hangar floor, ignoring the curious stares from the soldiers unloading the stores. Halfway across he craned up at the revolving bulk of the dome. A black perforated sail, 50 feet square, like a fragment of a planetarium, was suspended from the roof over the apex of the dome, a TV camera directly below it, a large metal sphere mounted about five feet from the lens. One of the guy-ropes had snapped and the sail tilted slightly to reveal the catwalk along the centre of the roof.

He pointed this out to a maintenance sergeant warming his hands in one of the ventilator outlets from the dome. 'You'll have to string that back. Some fool was wandering along the catwalk and throwing his shadow straight on to the model. I could see it clearly on the TV screen. Luckily no one spotted it.'

'Okay, Doctor, I'll get it fixed.' He chuckled sourly. 'That would have been a laugh, though. Really give them something to worry about.'

The man's tone annoyed Francis. 'They've got plenty to worry about as it is.'

'I don't know about that, Doctor. Some people here think they have it all ways. Quiet and warm in there, nothing to do except sit back and listen to those hypno-drills.' He looked out bleakly at the abandoned airfield stretching away to the cold tundra beyond the perimeter, and turned up his collar. 'We're the boys back here on Mother Earth who do the work, out in this Godforsaken dump. If you need any more spacecadets, Doctor, remember me.'

Francis managed a smile and stepped into the control office, made his way through the clerks sitting at trestle tables in front of the progress charts. Each carried the name of one of the dome passengers and a tabulated breakdown of progress through the psychometric tests and conditioning programmes. Other charts listed the day's rosters, copies of those posted that morning by Matthias Granger.

Inside Colonel Chalmers' office Francis relaxed back gratefully in the warmth, describing the salient features of his day's observation. 'I wish you could go in there and move around them, Paul,' he concluded. 'It's not the same spying through the TV cameras. You've got to talk to them, measure yourself against people like Granger and Peters.'

'You're right, they're fine men, like all the others. It's a pity they're wasted there.'

'They're not wasted,' Francis insisted. 'Every piece of data will be immensely valuable when the first space ships set out.' He ignored Chalmers' muttered 'If they do' and went on: 'Zenna and Abel worry me a little. It may be necessary to bring forward the date of their marriage. I know it will raise eyebrows, but the girl is as fully mature at 15 as she will be four years from now, and she'll be a settling influence on Abel, stop him from thinking too much.'

Chalmers shook his head doubtfully. 'Sounds a good idea, but a girl of 15 and a boy of 16 –? You'd raise a storm, Roger. Technically they're wards of court, every decency league would be up in arms.'

Francis gestured irritably. 'Need they know? We've really got a problem with Abel, the boy's too clever. He'd more or less worked out for himself that the Station was a space ship, he merely lacked the vocabulary to describe it. Now that we're starting to lift the conditioning blocks he'll want to know everything. It will be a big job to prevent him from smelling a rat, particularly with the slack way this place is being run. Did you see the shadow on the TV screen? We're damn lucky Peters didn't have a heart attack.'

Chalmers nodded. 'I'm getting that tightened up. A few mistakes are bound to happen, Roger. It's damn cold for the control crew working around the dome. Try to remember that the people outside are just as important as those inside.'

'Of course. The real trouble is that the budget is ludicrously out of date. It's only been revised once in 50 years. Perhaps General Short can generate some official interest, get a new deal for us. He sounds like a pretty brisk new broom.' Chalmers pursed his lips doubtfully, but Francis continued 'I don't know whether the tapes are wearing out, but the negative conditioning doesn't hold as well as it used to. We'll probably have to tighten up the programmes. I've made a start by pushing Abel's graduation forward.'

'Yes, I watched you on the screen here. The control boys became quite worked up next door. One or two of them are as keen as you, Roger, they'd been programming ahead for three months. It meant a lot of time wasted for them. I think you ought to check with me before you make a decision like that. The dome isn't your private laboratory.'

Francis accepted the reproof. Lamely, he said 'It was one of those spot decisions, I'm sorry. There was nothing else to do.'

Chalmers gently pressed home his point. 'I'm not so sure. I thought you rather overdid the long-term aspects of the journey. Why go out of your way to tell him he would never reach planet-fall? It only heightens his sense of isolation, makes it that much more difficult if we decide to shorten the journey.'

Francis looked up. 'There's no chance of that, is there?'

Chalmers paused thoughtfully. 'Roger, I really advise you not to get too involved with the project. Keep saying to yourself they're-not-going-to-Alpha-Centauri. They're here on Earth, and if the government decided it they'd be let out tomorrow. I know the courts would have to sanction it but that's a formality. It's 50 years since this project was started and a good number of influential people feel that it's gone on for too long. Ever since the Mars and Moon colonies failed, space programmes have been cut right back. They think the money here is being poured away for the amusement of a few sadistic psychologists.'

'You know that isn't true,' Francis retorted. 'I may have been over-hasty, but on the whole this project has been scrupulously conducted. Without exaggeration, if you did send a dozen people on a multi-generation ship to Alpha Centauri you couldn't do better than duplicate everything that's taken place here, down to the last cough and sneeze. If the information we've obtained had been available the Mars and Moon colonies never would have failed!'

'True. But irrelevant. Don't you understand, when everyone was eager to get into space they were prepared to accept the idea of a small group being sealed into a tank for 100 years, particularly when the original team volunteered. Now, when interest has evaporated, people are beginning to feel that there's something obscene about this human zoo; what began as a grand adventure of the spirit of Columbus, has become a grisly joke. In one sense we've learned too much – the social stratification of the three families is the sort of unwelcome datum that doesn't do the project much good. Another is the complete ease with which we've manipulated them, made them believe anything we've wanted.' Chalmers leaned forward across the desk. 'Confidentially, Roger, General Short has been put in command for one reason only – to close this place down. It may take years, but it's going to be done, I warn you. The important job now is to get those people out of there, not keep them in.'

Francis stared bleakly at Chalmers. 'Do you really believe that?'

'Frankly, Roger, yes. This project should never have been launched. You can't manipulate people the way we're doing – the endless hypno-drills, the forced pairing of children – look at yourself, five minutes ago you were seriously thinking of marrying two teenage children just to stop them using their minds. The whole thing degrades human dignity, all the taboos, the increasing degree of introspection – sometimes Peters and Granger don't speak to anyone for two or three weeks – the way life in the dome has become tenable only by accepting the insane situation as the normal one. I think the reaction against the project is healthy.'

Francis stared out at the dome. A gang of men were loading the so-called 'compressed food' (actually frozen foods with the brand names removed) into the commissary hatchway. Next morning, when Baker and his wife dialled the pre-arranged menu, the supplies would be promptly delivered, apparently from the space-hold. To some people, Francis knew, the project might well seem a complete fraud.

Quietly he said: 'The people who volunteered accepted the sacrifice, and all it involved. How's Short going to get them out? Just open the door and whistle?'

Chalmers smiled, a little wearily. 'He's not a fool, Roger. He's as sincerely concerned about their welfare as you are. Half the crew, particularly the older ones, would go mad within five minutes. But don't be disappointed, the project has more than proved its worth.'

'It won't do that until they "land". If the project ends it will be we who have failed, not them. We can't rationalize by saying it's cruel or unpleasant. We owe it to the 14 people in the dome to keep it going.'

Chalmers watched him shrewdly. '14? You mean 13, don't you, Doctor? Or are you inside the dome too?'

This ship had stopped rotating. Sitting at his desk in Command, planning the next day's fire drill, Abel noticed the sudden absence of movement. All morning, as he walked around the ship – he no longer used the term Station – he had been aware of an inward drag that pulled him towards the wall, as if one leg were shorter than the other.

When he mentioned this to his father the older man merely said: 'Captain Peters is in charge of Control. Always let him worry where the navigation of the ship is concerned.'

This sort of advice now meant nothing to Abel. In the previous two months his mind had attacked everything around him voraciously, probing and analysing, examining every facet of life in the Station. An enormous, once-suppressed vocabulary of abstract terms and relationships lay latent below the surface of his mind, and nothing would stop him applying it.

Over their meal trays in the commissary he grilled Matthew Peters about the ship's flight path, the great parabola which would carry it to Alpha Centauri.

'What about the currents built into the ship?' he asked. 'The rotation was designed to eliminate the magnetic poles set up when the ship was originally constructed. How are you compensating for that?'

Matthew looked puzzled. 'I'm not sure, exactly. Probably the instruments are automatically compensated.' When Abel smiled sceptically he shrugged. 'Anyway, Father knows all about it. There's no doubt we're right on course.'

'We hope,' Abel murmured *sotto voce*. The more Abel asked Matthew about the navigational devices he and his father operated in Control the more obvious it became that they were merely carrying out low-level instrument checks, and that their role was limited to replacing burnt-out pilot lights. Most of the instruments operated automatically, and they might as well have been staring at cabinets full of mattress flock.

What a joke if they were!

Smiling to himself, Abel realized that he had probably stated no more than the truth. It would be unlikely for the navigation to be entrusted to the crew when the slightest human error could throw the space ship irretrievably out of control, send it hurtling into a passing star. The designers of the ship would have sealed the automatic pilots well out of reach, given the crew light supervisory duties that created an illusion of control.

That was the real clue to life aboard the ship. None of their roles could be taken at face value. The day-to-day, minute-to-minute programming carried out by himself and his father was merely a set of variations on a pattern already laid down; the permutations possible were endless, but the fact that he could send Matthew Peters to the commissary at 12 o'clock rather than 12.30 didn't give him any real power over Matthew's life. The master programmes printed by the computers selected the day's menus, safety drills and recreation periods, and a list of names to choose from, but the slight leeway allowed, the extra two or three names supplied, were here in case of illness, not to give Abel any true freedom of choice.

One day, Abel promised himself, he would programme himself out of the conditioning sessions. Shrewdly he guessed that the conditioning still blocked out a great deal of interesting material, that half his mind remained submerged. Something about the ship suggested that there might be more to it than –

'Hello, Abel, you look far away.' Dr Francis sat down next to him. 'What's worrying you?'

'I was just calculating something,' Abel explained quickly. 'Tell me, assuming that each member of the crew consumes about three pounds of non-circulated food each day, roughly half a ton per year, the total cargo must be about 800 tons, and that's not allowing for any supplies after planet-fall. There should be at least 1,500 tons aboard. Quite a weight.'

'Not in absolute terms, Abel. The Station is only a small fraction of the ship. The main reactors, fuel tanks and space holds together weigh over 30,000 tons. They provide the gravitational pull that holds you to the floor.'

Abel shook his head slowly. 'Hardly, Doctor. The attraction must come from the stellar gravitational fields, or the weight of the ship would have to be about $6 \times 10^{20}$ tons.'

Dr Francis watched Abel reflectively, aware that the young man had led him into a simple trap. The figure he had quoted was near enough the Earth's mass. 'These are complex problems, Abel. I wouldn't worry too much about stellar mechanics. Captain Peters has that responsibility.'

'I'm not trying to usurp it,' Abel assured him. 'Merely to extend my own knowledge. Don't you think it might be worth departing from the rules a little? For example, it would be interesting to test the effects of continued isolation. We could select a small group, subject them to artificial stimuli, even seal them off from the rest of the crew and condition them to believe they were back on Earth. It could be a really valuable experiment, Doctor.'

As he waited in the conference room for General Short to finish his opening harangue, Francis repeated the last sentence to himself, wondering idly what Abel, with his limitless enthusiasm, would have made of the circle of defeated faces around the table.

'... regret as much as you do, gentlemen, the need to discontinue the project. However, now that a decision has been made by the Space Department, it is our duty to implement it. Of course, the task won't be an easy one. What we need is a phased withdrawal, a gradual readjustment of the world around the crew that will bring them down to Earth as gently as a parachute.' The General was a brisk, sharp-faced man in his fifties, with burly shoulders but sensitive eyes. He turned to Dr Kersh, who was responsible for the dietary and biometric controls aboard the dome. 'From what you tell me, Doctor, we might not have as much time as we'd like. This boy Abel sounds something of a problem.'

Kersh smiled. 'I was looking in at the commissary, overheard him tell Dr Francis that he wanted to run an experiment on a small group of the crew. An isolation drill, would you believe it. He's estimated that the tractor crews may be isolated for up to two years when the first foraging trips are made.'

Captain Sanger, the engineering officer, added: 'He's also trying to duck his conditioning sessions. He's wearing a couple of foam pads under his earphones, missing about 90 per cent of the subsonics. We spotted it when the EEG tape we record showed no alpha waves. At first we thought it was a break in the cable, but when we checked visually on the screen we saw that he had his eyes open. He wasn't listening.'

Francis drummed on the table. 'It wouldn't have mattered. The sub-sonic was a maths instruction sequence – the four-figure antilog system.'

'A good thing he did miss them,' Kersh said with a laugh. 'Sooner or later he'll work out that the dome is travelling in an elliptical orbit 93 million miles from a dwarf star of the $G_0$ spectral class.'

'What are you doing about this attempt to evade conditioning, Dr Francis?' Short asked. When Francis shrugged vaguely he added: 'I think we ought to regard the matter fairly seriously. From now on we'll be relying on the programming.'

Flatly, Francis said: 'Abel will resume the conditioning. There's no need to do anything. Without the regular daily contact he'll soon feel lost. The sub-sonic voice is composed of his mother's vocal tones; when he no longer hears it he'll lose his orientations, feel completely deserted.'

Short nodded slowly. 'Well, let's hope so.' He addressed Dr Kersh. 'At a rough estimate, Doctor, how long will it take to bring them back? Bearing in mind they'll have to be given complete freedom and that every TV and newspaper network in the world will interview each one a hundred times.'

Kersh chose his words carefully. 'Obviously a matter of years, General. All the conditioning drills will have to be gradually rescored; as a stop-gap measure we may need to introduce a meteor collision . . . guessing, I'd say three to five years. Possibly longer.'

'Fair enough. What would you estimate, Dr Francis?'

Francis fiddled with his blotter, trying to view the question seriously. 'I've no idea. *Bring them back.* What do you really mean, General? Bring what back?' Irritated, he snapped: 'A hundred years.'

Laughter crossed the table, and Short smiled at him, not unamiably.

'That's fifty years more than the original project, Doctor. You can't have been doing a very good job here.'

Francis shook his head. 'You're wrong, General. The original project was to get them to Alpha Centauri. Nothing was said about bringing them *back*.' When the laughter fell away Francis cursed himself for his foolishness; antagonizing the General wouldn't help the people in the dome.

But Short seemed unruffled. 'All right, then, it's obviously going to take some time.' Pointedly, with a glance at Francis he added: 'It's the men and women in the ship we're thinking of, not ourselves; if we need a hundred years we'll take them, not one less. You may be interested to hear that the Space Department chiefs feel about fifteen years will be necessary. At least.' There was a quickening of interest around the table. Francis watched Short with surprise. In fifteen years a lot could happen, there might be another spaceward swing of public opinion.

'The Department recommends that the project continue as before, with whatever budgetary parings we can make – stopping the dome is just a start – and that we condition the crew to believe that a round trip is in progress, that their mission is merely one of reconnaissance, and that they are bringing vital information back to Earth. When they step out of the spaceship they'll be treated as heroes and accept the strangeness of the world around them.' Short looked across the table, waiting for someone to reply. Kersh stared doubtfully at his hands, and Sanger and Chalmers played mechanically with their blotters.

Just before Short continued Francis pulled himself together, realizing that he was faced with his last opportunity to save the project. However much they disagreed with Short, none of the others would try to argue with him.

'I'm afraid that won't do, General,' he said, 'though I appreciate the Department's foresight and your own sympathetic approach. The scheme you've outlined sounds plausible, but it just won't work.' He sat forward, his voice controlled and precise. 'General, ever since they were children these people have been trained to accept that they were a closed group, and would never have contact with anyone else. On the unconscious level, on the level of their functional nervous systems, no one else in the world exists, for them the neuronic basis of reality is isolation. You'll never train them to invert their whole universe, any more than you can train a fish to fly. If you start to tamper with the fundamental patterns of their psyches you'll produce the sort of complete mental block you see when you try to teach a left-handed person to use his right.'

Francis glanced at Dr Kersh, who was nodding in agreement. 'Believe me, General, contrary to what you and the Space Department naturally assume, the people in the dome do *not* want to come out. Given the choice they would prefer to stay there, just as the goldfish prefers to stay in its bowl.'

Short paused before replying, evidently re-assessing Francis. 'You may be right, Doctor,' he admitted. 'But where does that get us? We've got 15 years, perhaps 25 at the outside.'

'There's only one way to do it,' Francis told him. 'Let the project continue, exactly as before, but with one difference. Prevent them from marrying and having children. In 25 years only the present younger generation will still be alive, and a further five years from then they'll all be dead. A life span in the dome is little more than 45 years. At the age of 30 Abel will probably be an old man. When they start to die off no one will care about them any longer.'

There was a full half minute's silence, and then Kersh said: 'It's the best suggestion, General. Humane, and yet faithful both to the original project and the Department's instructions. The absence of children would be only a slight deviation from the conditioned pathway. The basic isolation of the group would be strengthened, rather than diminished, also their realization that they themselves will never see planet-fall. If we drop the pedagogical drills and play down the space flight they will soon become a small close community, little different from any other out-group on the road to extinction.'

Chalmers cut in: 'Another point, General. It would be far easier – and cheaper – to stage, and as the members died off we could progressively close down the ship until finally there might be only a single deck left, perhaps even a few cabins.'

Short stood up and paced over to the window, looking out through the clear glass over the frosted panes at the great dome in the hangar.

'It sounds a dreadful prospect,' he commented. 'Completely insane. As you say, though, it may be the only way out.'

Moving quietly among the trucks parked in the darkened hangar, Francis paused for a moment to look back at the lighted windows of the control deck. Two or three of the night staff sat watch over the line of TV screens, half asleep themselves as they observed the sleeping occupants of the dome.

He ducked out of the shadows and ran across to the dome, climbed the stairway to the entrance point thirty feet above. Opening the external lock, he crawled in and closed it behind him, then unfastened the internal entry hatch and pulled himself out of the sleeping cylinder into the silent cabin.

A single dim light glowed over the TV monitor screen as it revealed the three orderlies in the control deck, lounging back in a haze of cigarette smoke six feet from the camera.

Francis turned up the speaker volume, then tapped the mouthpiece sharply with his knuckle.

Tunic unbuttoned, sleep still shadowing his eyes, Colonel Chalmers leaned forward intently into the screen, the orderlies at his shoulder.

'Believe me, Roger, you're proving nothing. General Short and the

Space Department won't withdraw their decision now that a special bill of enactment has been passed.' When Francis still looked sceptical he added: 'If anything, you're more likely to jeopardize them.'

'I'll take a chance,' Francis said. 'Too many guarantees have been broken in the past. Here I'll be able to keep an eye on things.' He tried to sound cool and unemotional; the cine-cameras would be recording the scene and it was important to establish the right impression. General Short would be only too keen to avoid a scandal. If he decided Francis was unlikely to sabotage the project he would probably leave him in the dome.

Chalmers pulled up a chair, his face earnest, 'Roger, give yourself time to reconsider everything. You may be more of a discordant element than you realize. Remember, nothing would be easier than getting you out – a child could cut his way through the rusty hull with a blunt can-opener.'

'Don't try it,' Francis warned him quietly. 'I'll be moving down to C-Deck, so if you come in after me they'll all know. Believe me, I won't try to interfere with the withdrawal programmes. And I won't arrange any teen-age marriages. But I think the people inside may need me now for more than eight hours a day.'

'Francis!' Chalmers shouted. 'Once you go down there you'll never come out! Don't you realize you're entombing yourself in a situation that's totally unreal? You're deliberately withdrawing into a nightmare, sending yourself off on a non-stop journey to *nowhere!*'

Curtly, before he switched the set off for the last time, Francis replied: 'Not nowhere, Colonel: Alpha Centauri.'

Sitting down thankfully in the narrow bunk in his cabin, Francis rested briefly before setting off for the commissary. All day he had been busy coding the computer punch tapes for Abel, and his eyes ached with the strain of manually stamping each of the thousands of minuscule holes. For eight hours he had sat without a break in the small isolation cell, electrodes clamped to his chest, knees and elbows while Abel measured his cardiac and respiratory rhythms.

The tests bore no relation to the daily programmes Abel now worked out for his father, and Francis was finding it difficult to maintain his patience. Initially Abel had tested his ability to follow a prescribed set of instructions, producing an endless exponential function, then a digital representation of *pi* to a thousand places. Finally Abel had persuaded Francis to cooperate in a more difficult test – the task of producing a totally random sequence. Whenever he unconsciously repeated a simple progression, as he did if he was tired or bored, or a fragment of a larger possible progression, the computer scanning his progress sounded an alarm on the desk and he would have to start afresh. After a few hours the buzzer rasped out every ten seconds, snapping at him like a bad-tempered insect. Francis had finally hobbled over to the door that afternoon, entangling himself in the electrode leads, found to his annoyance that the door was locked (ostensibly to prevent any interruption by a fire patrol), then saw through the small porthole that the computer in the cubicle outside was running unattended.

But when Francis' pounding roused Abel from the far end of the next laboratory he had been almost irritable with the doctor for wanting to discontinue the experiment.

'Damn it, Abel, I've been punching away at these things for three weeks now.' He winced as Abel disconnected him, brusquely tearing off the adhesive tape. 'Trying to produce random sequences isn't all that easy – my sense of reality is beginning to fog.' (Sometimes he wondered if Abel was secretly waiting for this.) 'I think I'm entitled to a vote of thanks.'

'But we arranged for the trial to last three days, Doctor,' Abel pointed out. 'It's only later that the valuable results begin to appear. It's the errors you make that are interesting. The whole experiment is pointless now.'

'Well, it's probably pointless anyway. Some mathematicians used to maintain that a random sequence was impossible to define.'

'But we can assume that it *is* possible,' Abel insisted. 'I was just giving you some practice before we started on the trans-finite numbers.'

Francis baulked here. 'I'm sorry, Abel. Maybe I'm not so fit as I used to be. Anyway, I've got other duties to attend to.'

'But they don't take long, Doctor. There's really nothing for you to do now.'

He was right, as Francis was forced to admit. In the year he had spent in the dome Abel had remarkably streamlined the daily routines, provided himself and Francis with an excess of leisure time, particularly as the latter never went to conditioning (Francis was frightened of the sub-sonic voices – Chalmers and Short would be subtle in their attempts to extricate him, perhaps too subtle).

Life aboard the dome had been more of a drain on him than he anticipated. Chained to the routines of the ship, limited in his recreations and with few intellectual pastimes – there were no books aboard the ship – he found it increasingly difficult to sustain his former good humour, was beginning to sink into the deadening lethargy that had overcome most of the other crew members. Matthias Granger had retreated to his cabin, content to leave the programming to Abel, spent his time playing with a damaged clock, while the two Peters rarely strayed from Control. The three wives were almost completely inert, satisfied to knit and murmur to each other. The days passed indistinguishably. Sometimes Francis told himself wryly he nearly *did* believe that they were en route for Alpha Centauri. That would have been a joke for General Short!

At 6.30 when he went to the commissary for his evening meal, he found that he was a quarter of an hour late.

'Your meal time was changed this afternoon,' Baker told him, lowering the hatchway. 'I got nothing ready for you.'

Francis began to remonstrate but the man was adamant. 'I can't make a special dip into space-hold just because you didn't look at Routine Orders can I, Doctor?'

On the way out Francis met Abel, tried to persuade him to countermand the order. 'You could have warned me, Abel. Damnation, I've been sitting inside your test rig all afternoon.'

'But you went back to your cabin, Doctor,' Abel pointed out smoothly. 'You pass three SRO bulletins on your way from the laboratory. Always look at them at every opportunity, remember. Last-minute changes are liable at any time. I'm afraid you'll have to wait until 10.30 now.'

Francis went back to his cabin, suspecting that the sudden change had been Abel's revenge on him for discontinuing the test. He would have to be more conciliatory with Abel, or the young man could make his life a hell, literally starve him to death. Escape from the dome was impossible now – there was a mandatory 20 year sentence on anyone making an unauthorized entry into the space simulator.

After resting for an hour or so, he left his cabin at 8 o'clock to carry out his duty checks of the pressure seals by the B-Deck Meteor Screen. He always went through the pretence of reading them, enjoying the sense of participation in the space flight which the exercise gave him, deliberately accepting the illusion.

The seals were mounted in the control point set at ten yard intervals along the perimeter corridor, a narrow circular passageway around the main corridor. Alone there, the servos clicking and snapping, he felt at peace within the space vehicle. 'Earth itself is in orbit around the Sun,' he mused as he checked the seals, 'and the whole solar system is travelling at 40 miles a second towards the constellation Lyra. The degree of illusion that exists is a complex question.'

Something cut through his reverie.

The pressure indicator was flickering slightly. The needle wavered between 0.001 and 0.0015 psi. The pressure inside the dome was fractionally above atmospheric, in order that dust might be expelled through untoward cracks (though the main object of the pressure seals was to get the crew safely into the vacuum-proof emergency cylinders in case the dome was damaged and required internal repairs).

For a moment Francis panicked, wondering whether Short had decided to come in after him – the reading, although meaningless, indicated that a breach had opened in the hull. Then the hand moved back to zero, and footsteps sounded along the radial corridor at right angles past the next bulkhead.

Quickly Francis stepped into its shadow. Before his death old Peters had spent a lot of time mysteriously pottering around the corridor, probably secreting a private food cache behind one of the rusting panels.

He leaned forward as the footsteps crossed the corridor.

Abel?

\*     \*     \*

He watched the young man disappear down a stairway, then made his way into the radial corridor, searching the steel-grey sheeting for a retractable panel. Immediately adjacent to the end wall of the corridor, against the outer skin of the dome, was a small fire control booth.

A tuft of slate-white hairs lay on the floor of the booth.

Asbestos fibres!

Francis stepped into the booth, within a few seconds located a loosened panel that had rusted off its rivets. About ten inches by six, it slid back easily. Beyond it was the outer wall of the dome, a hand's breadth away. Here too was a loose plate, held in position by a crudely fashioned hook.

Francis hesitated, then lifted the hook and drew back the panel.

*He was looking straight down into the hangar!*

Below, a line of trucks was disgorging supplies on to the concrete floor under a couple of spotlights, a sergeant shouting orders at the labour squad. To the right was the control deck, Chalmers in his office on the evening shift.

The spy-hole was directly below the stairway, and the overhanging metal steps shielded it from the men in the hangar. The asbestos had been carefully frayed so that it concealed the retractable plate. The wire hook was as badly rusted as the rest of the hull, and Francis estimated that the window had been in use for over 30 or 40 years.

So almost certainly old Peters had regularly looked out through the window, and knew perfectly well that the space ship was a myth. None the less he had stayed aboard, perhaps realizing that the truth would destroy the others, or preferring to be captain of an artificial ship rather than a self-exposed curiosity in the world outside.

Presumably he had passed on the secret. Not to his bleak taciturn son, but to the one other lively mind, one who would keep the secret and make the most of it. For his own reasons he too had decided to stay in the dome, realizing that he would soon be the effective captain, free to pursue his experiments in applied psychology. He might even have failed to grasp that Francis was not a true member of the crew. His confident mastery of the programming, his lapse of interest in Control, his casualness over the safety devices, all meant one thing –

*Abel knew!*

· **1962**

# · PASSPORT TO ETERNITY

It was half past love on New Day in Zenith and the clocks were striking heaven. All over the city the sounds of revelry echoed upwards into the dazzling Martian night, but high on Sunset Ridge, among the mansions of the rich, Margot and Clifford Gorrell faced each other in glum silence.

Frowning, Margot flipped impatiently through the vacation brochure on her lap, then tossed it away with an elaborate gesture of despair.

'But Clifford, why do we have to go to the same place every summer? I'd like to do something interesting for a change. This year the Lovatts are going to the Venus Fashion Festival, and Bobo and Peter Anders have just booked into the fire beaches at Saturn. They'll all have a wonderful time, while we're quietly taking the last boat to nowhere.'

Clifford Gorrell nodded impassively, one hand cupped over the sound control in the arm of his chair. They had been arguing all evening, and Margot's voice threw vivid sparks of irritation across the walls and ceiling. Grey and mottled, they would take days to drain.

'I'm sorry you feel like that, Margot. Where would you like to go?'

Margot shrugged scornfully, staring out at the corona of a million neon signs that illuminated the city below. 'Does it matter?'

'Of course. You arrange the vacation this time.'

Margot hesitated, one eye keenly on her husband. Then she sat forward happily, turning up her fluorescent violet dress until she glowed like an Algolian rayfish.

'Clifford, I've got a wonderful idea! Yesterday I was down in the Colonial Bazaar, thinking about our holiday, when I found a small dream bureau that's just been opened. Something like the Dream Dromes in Neptune City everyone was crazy about two or three years ago, but instead of having to plug into whatever programme happens to be going you have your own dream plays specially designed for you.'

Clifford continued to nod, carefully increasing the volume of the sound-sweeper.

'They have their own studios and send along a team of analysts and writers to interview us and afterwards book a sanatorium anywhere we like for the convalescence. Eve Corbusier and I decided a small party of five or six would be best.'

'Eve Corbusier,' Clifford repeated. He smiled thinly to himself and switched on the book he had been reading. 'I wondered when that Gorgon was going to appear.'

'Eve isn't too bad when you get to know her, darling,' Margot told him. 'Don't start reading yet. She'll think up all sorts of weird ideas for the play.' Her voice trailed off. 'What's the matter?'

'Nothing,' Clifford said wearily. 'It's just that I sometimes wonder if you have any sense of responsibility at all.' As Margot's eyes darkened he went on. 'Do you really think that I, a supreme court justice, could take that sort of vacation, even if I wanted to? Those dream plays are packed with advertising commercials and all sorts of corrupt material.' He shook his head sadly. 'And I told you not to go into the Colonial Bazaar.'

'What are we going to do then?' Margot asked coldly. 'Another honeyMoon?'

'I'll reserve a couple of singles tomorrow. Don't worry, you'll enjoy it.' He clipped the hand microphone into his book and began to scan the pages with it, listening to the small metallic voice.

Margot stood up, the vanes in her hat quivering furiously. 'Clifford!' she snapped, her voice dead and menacing. 'I warn you, I'm not going on another honeyMoon!'

Absently, Clifford said: 'Of course, dear,' his fingers racing over the volume control.

'Clifford!'

Her shout sank to an angry squeak. She stepped over to him, her dress blazing like a dragon, jabbering at him noiselessly, the sounds sucked away through the vents over her head and pumped out across the echoing rooftops of the midnight city.

As he sat back quietly in his private vacuum, the ceiling shaking occasionally when Margot slammed a door upstairs, Clifford looked out over the brilliant diadem of down-town Zenith. In the distance, by the space-port, the ascending arcs of hyperliners flared across the sky while below the countless phosphorescent trajectories of hop-cabs enclosed the bowl of rooflight in a dome of glistening hoops.

Of all the cities of the galaxy, few offered such a wealth of pleasures as Zenith, but to Clifford Gorrell it was as distant and unknown as the first Gomorrah. At 35 he was a thin-faced, prematurely ageing man with receding hair and a remote abstracted expression, and in the dark sombre suit and stiff white dog-collar which were the traditional uniform of the Probate Department's senior administrators he looked like a man who had never taken a holiday in his life.

At that moment Clifford wished he hadn't. He and Margot had never been able to agree about their vacations. Clifford's associates and superiors at the Department, all of them ten or twenty years older than himself, took their pleasures conservatively and expected a young but responsible justice to do the same. Margot grudgingly acknowledged this, but her friends who frequented the chic playtime clinics along the beach at Mira

Mira considered the so-called honeyMoon trips back to Earth derisively old-fashioned, a last desperate resort of the aged and infirm.

And to tell the truth, Clifford realized, they were right. He had never dared to admit to Margot that he too was bored because it would have been more than his peace of mind was worth, but a change might do them good.

He resolved – next year.

Margot lay back among the cushions on the terrace divan, listening to the flamingo trees singing to each other in the morning sunlight. Twenty feet below, in the high-walled garden, a tall muscular young man was playing with a jet-ball. He had a dark olive complexion and swarthy good looks, and oil gleamed across his bare chest and arms. Margot watched with malicious amusement his efforts to entertain her. This was Trantino, Margot's play-boy, who chaperoned her during Clifford's long absences at the Probate Department.

'Hey, Margot! Catch!' He gestured with the jet-ball but Margot turned away, feeling her swim-suit slide pleasantly across her smooth tanned skin. The suit was made of one of the newer bioplastic materials, and its living tissues were still growing, softly adapting themselves to the contours of her body, repairing themselves as the fibres became worn or grimy. Upstairs in her wardrobes the gowns and dresses purred on their hangers like the drowsing inmates of some exquisite arboreal zoo. Sometimes she thought of commissioning her little Mercurian tailor to run up a bioplastic suit for Clifford – a specially designed suit that would begin to constrict one night as he stood on the terrace, the lapels growing tighter and tighter around his neck, the sleeves pinning his arms to his sides, the waist contracting to pitch him over –

'Margot!' Trantino interrupted her reverie, sailed the jet-ball expertly through the air towards her. Annoyed, Margot caught it with one hand and pointed it away, watched it sail over the wall and the roofs beyond.

Trantino came up to her. 'What's the matter?' he asked anxiously. For his part he felt his inability to soothe Margot a reflection on his professional skill. The privileges of his caste had to be guarded jealously. For several centuries now the managerial and technocratic elite had been so preoccupied with the work of government that they relied on the Templars of Aphrodite not merely to guard their wives from any marauding suitors but also to keep them amused and contented. By definition, of course, their relationship was platonic, a pleasant revival of the old chivalrous ideals, but sometimes Trantino regretted that the only tools in his armoury were a handful of poems and empty romantic gestures. The Guild of which he was a novitiate member was an ancient and honoured one, and it wouldn't do if Margot began to pine and Mr Gorrell reported him to the Masters of the Guild.

'Why are you always arguing with Mr Gorrell?' Trantino asked her.

One of the Guild's axioms was 'The husband *is always* right.' Any discord between him and his wife was the responsibility of the play-boy.

Margot ignored Trantino's question. 'Those trees are getting on my nerves,' she complained fractiously. 'Why can't they keep quiet?'

'They're mating,' Trantino told her. He added thoughtfully: 'You should sing to Mr Gorrell.'

Margot stirred lazily as the shoulder straps of the sun-suit unclasped themselves behind her back. 'Tino,' she asked, 'what's the most unpleasant thing I could do to Mr Gorrell?'

'Margot!' Trantino gasped, utterly shocked. He decided that an appeal to sentiment, a method of reconciliation despised by the more proficient members of the Guild, was his only hope. 'Remember, Margot, you will always have me.'

He was about to permit himself a melancholy smile when Margot sat up abruptly.

'Don't look so frightened, you fool! I've just got an idea that should make Mr Gorrell sing to me.'

She straightened the vanes in her hat, waited for the sun-suit to clasp itself discreetly around her, then pushed Trantino aside and stalked off the terrace.

Clifford was browsing among the spools in the library, quietly listening to an old 22nd Century abstract on systems of land tenure in the Trianguli.

'Hello, Margot, feel better now?'

Margot smiled at him coyly. 'Clifford, I'm ashamed of myself. Do forgive me.' She bent down and nuzzled his ear. 'Sometimes I'm very selfish. Have you booked our tickets yet?'

Clifford disengaged her arm and straightened his collar. 'I called the agency, but their bookings have been pretty heavy. They've got a double but no singles. We'll have to wait a few days.'

'No, we won't,' Margot exclaimed brightly. 'Clifford, why don't you and I take the double? Then we can really be together, forget all that ship-board nonsense about never having met before.'

Puzzled, Clifford switched off the player. 'What do you mean?'

Margot explained. 'Look, Clifford, I've been thinking that I ought to spend more time with you than I do at present, really share your work and hobbies. I'm tired of all these play-boys.' She drooped languidly against Clifford, her voice silky and reassuring. 'I want to be with you, Clifford. *Always.*'

Clifford pushed her away. 'Don't be silly, Margot,' he said with an anxious laugh. 'You're being absurd.'

'No, I'm not. After all, Harold Kharkov and his wife haven't got a play-boy and she's very happy.'

Maybe she is, Clifford thought, beginning to panic. Kharkov had once been the powerful and ruthless director of the Department of Justice, now was a third-rate attorney hopelessly trying to eke out a meagre living on the open market, dominated by his wife and forced to spend virtually 24 hours a day with her. For a moment Clifford thought of the days when he had courted Margot, of the long dreadful hours listening to her inane chatter. Trantino's real role was not to chaperone Margot while Clifford was away but while he was at home.

'Margot, be sensible,' he started to say, but she cut him short. 'I've made up my mind, I'm going to tell Trantino to pack his suitcase and go back to the Guild.' She switched on the spool player, selecting the wrong speed, smiling ecstatically as the reading head grated loudly and stripped the coding off the record. 'It's going to be wonderful to share everything with you. Why don't we forget about the vacation this year?'

A facial tic from which Clifford had last suffered at the age of ten began to twitch ominously.

Tony Harcourt, Clifford's personal assistant, came over to the Gorrells' villa immediately after lunch. He was a brisk, polished young man, barely controlling his annoyance at being called back to work on the first day of his vacation. He had carefully booked a sleeper next to Dolores Costane, the most beautiful of the Jovian Heresiarch's vestals, on board a leisure-liner leaving that afternoon for Venus, but instead of enjoying the fruits of weeks of blackmail and intrigue he was having to take part in what seemed a quite uncharacteristic piece of Gorrell whimsy.

He listened in growing bewilderment as Clifford explained.

'We were going to one of our usual resorts on Luna, Tony, but we've decided we need a change. Margot wants a vacation that's different. Something new, exciting, original. So go round all the agencies and bring me their suggestions.'

'All the agencies?' Tony queried. 'Don't you mean just the registered ones?'

'All of them,' Margot told him smugly, relishing every moment of her triumph.

Clifford nodded, and smiled at Margot benignly.

'But there must be 50 or 60 agencies organizing vacations,' Tony protested. 'Only about a dozen of them are accredited. Outside Empyrean Tours and Union-Galactic there'll be absolutely nothing suitable for you.'

'Never mind,' Clifford said blandly. 'We only want an idea of the field. I'm sorry, Tony, but I don't want this all over the Department and I know you'll be discreet.'

Tony groaned. 'It'll take me weeks.'

'Three days,' Clifford told him. 'Margot and I want to leave here by the end of the week.' He looked longingly over his shoulder for the absent Trantino. 'Believe me, Tony, we really need a holiday.'

Fifty-six travel and vacation agencies were listed in the Commercial Directory, Tony discovered when he returned to his office in the top floor of the Justice building in downtown Zenith, all but eight of them alien. The Department had initiated legal proceedings against five, three had closed down, and eight more were fronts for other enterprises.

That left him with forty to visit, spread all over the Upper and Lower Cities and in the Colonial Bazaar, attached to various mercantile, religious and paramilitary organizations, some of them huge concerns with their own police and ecclesiastical forces, others sharing a one-room office and transceiver with a couple of other shoestring firms.

Tony mapped out an itinerary, slipped a flask of Five-Anchor Neptunian Rum into his hip pocket and dialled a helicab.

The first was ARCO PRODUCTIONS INC., a large establishment occupying three levels and a bunker on the fashionable west side of the Upper City. According to the Directory they specialized in hunting and shooting expeditions.

The helicab put him down on the apron outside the entrance. Massive steel columns reached up to a reinforced concrete portico, and the whole place looked less like a travel agency than the last redoubt of some interstellar Seigfreid. As he went in a smart jackbooted guard of janissaries in black and silver uniforms snapped to attention and presented arms.

Everyone inside the building was wearing a uniform, moving about busily at standby alert. A huge broad-shouldered woman with sergeant's stripes handed Tony over to a hard-faced Martian colonel.

'I'm making some inquiries on behalf of a wealthy Terran and his wife,' Tony explained. 'They thought they'd do a little big-game hunting on their vacation this year. I believe you organize expeditions.'

The colonel nodded curtly and led Tony over to a broad map-table. 'Certainly. What exactly have they in mind?'

'Well, nothing really. They hoped you'd make some suggestions.'

'Of course.' The colonel pulled out a memo-tape. 'Have they their own air and land forces?'

Tony shook his head. 'I'm afraid not.'

'I see. Can you tell me whether they will require a single army corps, a combined task force or –'

'No,' Tony said. 'Nothing as big as that.'

'An assault party of brigade strength? I understand. Quieter and less elaborate. All the fashion today.' He switched on the star-map and spread his hands across the glimmering screen of stars and nebulae. 'Now the question of the particular theatre. At present only three of the game reserves have open seasons. Firstly the Procyon system; this includes about 20 different races, some of them still with only atomic technologies. Unfortunately there's been a good deal of dispute recently about declaring Procyon a game reserve, and the Resident of Alschain is trying to have it admitted to the Pan-Galactic Conference. A pity, I feel,' the colonel added, reflectively stroking his steel-grey moustache. 'Procyon always put up a great fight against us and an expedition there was invariably lively.'

Tony nodded sympathetically. 'I hadn't realized they objected.'

The colonel glanced at him sharply. 'Naturally,' he said. He cleared his throat. 'That leaves only the Ketab tribes of Ursa Major, who are having their Millennial Wars, and the Sudor Martines of Orion. They are an entirely new reserve, and your best choice without doubt. The ruling dynasty died out recently, and a war of succession could be conveniently arranged.'

Tony was no longer following the colonel, but he smiled intelligently.

'Now,' the colonel asked, 'what political or spiritual creeds do your friends wish to have invoked?'

Tony frowned. 'I don't think they want any. Are they absolutely necessary?'

The colonel regarded Tony carefully. 'No,' he said slowly. 'It's a question of taste. A purely military operation is perfectly feasible. However, we always advise our clients to invoke some doctrine as a *casus belli*, not only to avoid adverse publicity and any feelings of guilt or remorse, but to lend colour and purpose to the campaign. Each of our field commanders specializes in a particular ideological pogrom, with the exception of General Westerling. Perhaps your friends would prefer him?'

Tony's mind started to work again. 'Schapiro Westerling? The former Director-General of Graves Commission?'

The colonel nodded. 'You know him?'

Tony laughed. 'Know him? I thought I was prosecuting him at the current Nova Trials. I can see that we're well behind with the times.' He pushed back his chair. 'To tell the truth I don't think you've anything suitable for my friends. Thanks all the same.'

The colonel stiffened. One of his hands moved below the desk and a buzzer sounded along the wall.

'However,' Tony added, 'I'd be grateful if you'd send them further details.'

The colonel sat impassively in his chair. Three enormous guards appeared at Tony's elbow, idly swinging energy truncheons.

'Clifford Gorrell, Stellar Probate Division, Department of Justice,' Tony said quickly.

He gave the colonel a brief smile and made his way out, cursing Clifford and walking warily across the thickly piled carpet in case it had been mined.

The next one on his list was the A-Z JOLLY JUBILEE COMPANY, alien and unregistered, head office somewhere out of Betelgeuse. According to the Directory they specialized in 'all-in cultural parties and guaranteed somatic weekends.' Their premises occupied the top two tiers of a hanging garden in the Colonial Bazaar. They sounded harmless enough but Tony was ready for them.

'No,' he said firmly to a lovely Antarean wraith-fern who shyly raised a frond to him as he crossed the terrace. 'Not today.'

Behind the bar a fat man in an asbestos suit was feeding sand to a siliconic fire-fish swimming round in a pressure brazier.

'Damn things,' he grumbled, wiping the sweat off his chin and fiddling aimlessly with the thermostat. 'They gave me a booklet when I got it, but it doesn't say anything about it eating a whole beach every day.' He spaded in another couple of shovels from a low dune of sand heaped on the floor behind him. 'You have to keep them at exactly 5750°K. or they start getting nervous. Can I help you?'

'I thought there was a vacation agency here,' Tony said.

'Sure. I'll call the girls for you.' He pressed a bell.

'Wait a minute,' Tony cut in. 'You advertise something about cultural parties. What exactly are they?'

The fat man chuckled. 'That must be my partner. He's a professor at Vega Tech. Likes to keep the tone up.' He winked at Tony.

Tony sat on one of the stools, looking out over the crazy spiral roof-tops of the Bazaar. A mile away the police patrols circled over the big apartment batteries which marked the perimeter of the Bazaar, keeping their distance.

A tall slim woman appeared from behind the foliage and sauntered across the terrace to him. She was a Canopan slave, hot-housed out of imported germ, a slender green-skinned beauty with moth-like fluttering gills.

The fat man introduced Tony. 'Lucille, take him up to the arbour and give him a run through.'

Tony tried to protest but the pressure brazier was hissing fiercely. The fat man started feeding sand in furiously, the exhaust flames flaring across the terrace.

Quickly, Tony turned and backed up the stairway to the arbour. 'Lucille,' he reminded her firmly, 'this is strictly cultural, remember.'

Half an hour later a dull boom reverberated up from the terrace.

'Poor Jumbo,' Lucille said sadly as a fine rain of sand came down over them.

'Poor Jumbo,' Tony agreed, sitting back and playing with a coil of her hair. Like a soft sinuous snake, it circled around his arm, sleek with blue oil. He drained the flask of Five-Anchor and tossed it lightly over the balustrade. 'Now tell me more about these Canopan prayerbeds . . .'

When, after two days, Tony reported back to the Gorrells he looked hollow-eyed and exhausted, like a man who had been brain-washed by the Wardens.

'What happened to you?' Margot asked anxiously, 'we thought you'd been going round the agencies.'

'Exactly,' Tony said. He slumped down in a sofa and tossed a thick folder across to Clifford. 'Take your pick. You've got about 250 schemes there in complete detail, but I've written out a synopsis which gives one or two principal suggestions from each agency. Most of them are out of the question.'

Clifford unclipped the synopsis and started to read through it.

## (1) ARCO PRODUCTIONS INC. Unregistered. Private subsidiary of Sagittarius Security Police.

Hunting and shooting. Your own war to order. Raiding parties, revolutions, religious crusades. In anything from a small commando squad to a 3,000-ship armada. ARCO provide publicity, mock War Crimes Tribunal, etc. Samples:

(a) Operation Torquemada. 23-day expedition to Bellatrix IV. 20 ship assault corps under Admiral Storm Wengen. Mission: liberation of (imaginary) Terran hostages. Cost: 300,000 credits.

(b) Operation Klingsor. 15-year crusade against Ursa Major. Combined task force of 2,500 ships. Mission: recovery of runic memory dials stolen from client's shrine.

Cost: 500 billion credits (ARCO will arrange lend-lease but this is dabbling in realpolitik).

## (2) ARENA FEATURES INC. Unregistered. Organizers of the Pan-Galactic Tournament held tri-millennially at the Sun Bowl 2-Heliopolis, NGC 3599.

Every conceivable game in the Cosmos is played at the tournament and so formidable is the opposition that a winning contestant can virtually choose his own apotheosis. The challenge round of the Solar Megathlon Group 3 (that is, for any being whose function can be described, however loosely, as living) involves Quantum Jumping, 7-dimensional Maze Ball and Psychokinetic Bridge (pretty tricky against a telepathic Ketos D'Oma). The only Terran ever to win an event was the redoubtable Chippy Yerkes of Altair 5 The Clowns, who introduced the unplayable blank Round Dice. Being a spectator is as exhausting as being a contestant, and you're well advised to substitute.

Cost: 100,000 credits/day.

## (3) AGENCE GENERALE DE TOURISME. Registered. Venus.

Concessionaires for the Colony Beatific on Lake Virgo, the Mandrake Casino Circuit and the Miramar-Trauma Senso-channels. Dream-baths, vu-dromes, endocrine-galas. Darleen Costello is the current Aphrodite and Laurence Mandell makes a versatile Lothario. Plug into these two from 30:30 VST. Room and non-denominational bath at the Gomorrah-Plaza on Mount Venus comes to 1,000 credits a day, but remember to keep out of the Zone. It's just too erotogenous for a Terran.

### (4) TERMINAL TOURS LTD. Unregistered. Earth.

For those who want to get away from it all the *Dream of Osiris*, an astral-rigged, 1,000-foot leisure-liner is now fitting out for the Grand Tour. Round-cosmos cruise, visiting every known race and galaxy.

Cost: Doubles at a flat billion, but it's cheap when you realize that the cruise lasts for ever and you'll never be back.

### (5) SLEEP TRADERS. Unregistered.

A somewhat shadowy group who handle all dealings on the Blue Market, acting as a general clearing house and buying and selling dreams all through the Galaxy.

Sample: Like to try a really new sort of dream? The Set Corrani Priests of Theta Piscium will link you up with the sacred electronic thought-pools in the Desert of Kish. These mercury lakes are their ancestral memory banks. Surgery is necessary but be careful. Too much cortical damage and the archetypes may get restive. In return one of the Set Corrani (polysexual delta-humanoids about the size of a walking dragline) will take over your cerebral functions for a long weekend. All these transactions are done on an exchange basis and SLEEP TRADERS charge nothing for the service. But they obviously get a rake-off, and may pump advertising into the lower medullary centres. Whatever they're selling I wouldn't advise anybody to buy.

### (6) THE AGENCY. Registered. M33 in Andromeda.

The executive authority of the consortium of banking trusts floating Schedule D, the fourth draw of the gigantic PK pyramid lottery sweeping all through the continuum from Sol III out to the island universes. Trance-cells everywhere are now recruiting dream-readers and ESPerceptionists, and there's still time to buy a ticket. There's only one number on all the tickets – the winning one – but don't think that means you'll get away with the kitty. THE AGENCY has just launched UNILIV, the emergency relief fund for victims of Schedule C who lost their deposits and are now committed to paying off impossible debts, some monetary, some moral (if you're unlucky in the draw you may find yourself landed with a guilt complex that would make even a Colonus Rex look sad).

Cost: 1 credit – but with an evaluation in the billions if you have to forfeit.

### (7) ARCTURIAN EXPRESS. Unregistered.

Controls all important track events. The racing calendar this year is a causal and not a temporal one and seems a little obscure, but most of the established classics are taking place.

(a) The Rhinosaur Derby. Held this year at Betelgeuse Springs under the rules of the Federation of Amorphs. First to the light horizon. There's always quite a line-up for this one and any form of vehicle is allowed – rockets, beams, racial migrations, ES thought patterns – but frankly it's a waste of effort. It's not just that by the time you're out of your own sight you're usually out of your mind as well, but the Nils of Rigel, who always enter a strong team, are capable of instantaneous transmission.

(b) The Paraplegic Handicap. Recently instituted by the Protists of Lambda Scorpio. The course measures only 0.00015 mm, but that's a long way to urge an Aldebaran Torpid. They are giant viruses embedded in bauxite mountains, and by varying their pressure differentials it's sometimes possible to tickle them into a little life. K 2 on Regulus IX is holding the big bets, but even so the race is estimated to take about 50,000 years to run.

## (8) NEW FUTURES INC. Unregistered.

Tired of the same dull round? NEW FUTURES will take you right out of this world. In the island universes the continuum is extra-dimensional, and the time channels are controlled by rival cartels. The element of chance apparently plays the time role, and it's all even more confused by the fact that you may be moving around in someone else's extrapolation.

In the tourist translation manual 185 basic tenses are given, and of these 125 are future conditional. No verb conjugates in the present tense, and you can invent and copyright your own irregulars. This may explain why I got the impression at the bureau that they were only half there.

Cost: simultaneously 3,270 and 2,000,000 credits. They refuse to quibble.

## (9) SEVEN SIRENS. Registered. Venus.

A subsidiary of the fashion trust controlling senso-channel Astral Eve.

Ladies, like to win your own beauty contest? Twenty-five of the most beautiful creatures in the Galaxy are waiting to pit their charms against yours, but however divine they may be – and two or three of them, such as the Flamen Zilla Quel-Queen (75–9–25) and the Orthodox Virgin of Altair (76–953–?) certainly will be – they'll stand no chance against you. Your specifications will be defined as the ideal ones.

## (10) GENERAL ENTERPRISES. Registered.

Specialists in culture cycles, world struggles, ethnic trends. Organize vacations as a sideline. A vast undertaking for whom ultimately we all work. Their next venture, epoch-making by all accounts, is starting now, and everybody will be coming along. I was politely but firmly informed that it was no use worrying about the cost. When I asked –

Before Clifford could finish one of the houseboys came up to him.
'Priority Call for you, sir.'
Clifford handed the synopsis to Margot. 'Tell me if you find anything. It looks to me as if we've been wasting Tony's time.'
He left them and went through to his study.
'Ah, Gorrell, there you are.' It was Thornwall Harrison, the attorney

who had taken over Clifford's office. 'Who the hell are all these people trailing in to see you night and day? The place looks like Colonial Night at the Arena Circus. I can't get rid of them.'

'Which people?' Clifford asked. 'What do they want?'

'You apparently,' Thornwall told him. 'Most of them thought I was you. They've been trying to sell me all sorts of crazy vacation schemes. I said you'd already gone on your vacation and I myself never took one. Then one of them pulled a hypodermic on me. There's even an Anti-Cartel agent sleuthing around, wants to see you about block bookings. Thinks you're a racketeer.'

Back in the lounge Margot and Tony were looking out through the terrace windows into the boulevard which ran from the Gorrells' villa to the level below.

A long column of vehicles had pulled up under the trees: trucks, half-tracks, huge Telesenso studio location vans and several sleek white ambulances. The drivers and crew-men were standing about in little groups in the shadows, quietly watching the villa. Two or three radar scanners on the vans were rotating, and as Clifford looked down a convoy of trucks drove up and joined the tail of the column.

'Looks like there's going to be quite a party,' Tony said. 'What are they waiting for?'

'Perhaps they've come for us?' Margot suggested excitedly.

'They're wasting their time if they have,' Clifford told her. He swung round on Tony. 'Did you give our names to any of the agencies?'

Tony hesitated, then nodded. 'I couldn't help it. Some of those outfits wouldn't take no for an answer.'

Clifford clamped his lips and picked the synopsis off the floor. 'Well, Margot, have you decided where you want to go?'

Margot fiddled with the synopsis. 'There are so many to choose from.'

Tony started for the door. 'Well, I'll leave you to it.' He waved a hand at them. 'Have fun.'

'Hold on,' Clifford told him. 'Margot hasn't made up her mind yet.'

'What's the hurry?' Tony asked. He indicated the line of vehicles outside, their crews now climbing into their driving cabs and turrets. 'Take your time. You may bite off more than you can chew.'

'Exactly. So as soon as Margot decides where we're going you can make the final arrangements for us and get rid of that menagerie.'

'But Clifford, give me a chance.'

'Sorry. Now Margot, hurry up.'

Margot flipped through the synopsis, screwing up her mouth. 'It's so difficult, Clifford, I don't really like any of these. I still think the best agency was the little one I found in the Bazaar.'

'No,' Tony groaned, sinking down on a sofa. 'Margot, please, after all the trouble I've gone to.'

'Yes, definitely that one. The dream bureau. What was it called –'

Before she could finish there was a roar of engines starting up in the boulevard. Startled, Clifford saw the column of cars and trucks churn across the gravel towards the villa. Music, throbbing heavily, came down from the room above, and a sick musky odour seeped through the air.

Tony pulled himself off the sofa. 'They must have had this place wired,' he said quickly. 'You'd better call the police. Believe me, some of these people don't waste time arguing.'

Outside three helmeted men in brown uniforms ran past the terrace, unwinding a coil of fuse wire. The sharp hissing sound of para-rays sucked through the air from the drive.

Margot hid back in her slumber seat. 'Trantino!' she wailed.

Clifford went back into his study. He switched the transceiver to the emergency channel.

Instead of the police signal a thin automatic voice beeped through. 'Remain seated, remain seated. Take-off in zero two minutes, Purser's office on G Deck now –'

Clifford switched to another channel. There was a blare of studio applause and a loud unctuous voice called out:

'And now over to brilliant young Clifford Gorrell and his charming wife Margot about to enter their dream-pool at the fabulous Riviera-Neptune. Are you there, Cliff?'

Angrily, Clifford turned to a third. Static and morse chattered, and then someone rapped out in a hard iron tone: 'Colonel Sapt is dug in behind the swimming pool. Enfilade along the garage roof –'

Clifford gave up. He went back to the lounge. The music was deafening. Margot was prostrate in her slumber-seat, Tony down on the floor by the window, watching a pitched battle raging in the drive. Heavy black palls of smoke drifted across the terrace, and two tanks with stylized archers emblazoned on their turrets were moving up past the burning wrecks of the studio location vans.

'They must be Arco's!' Tony shouted. 'The police will look after them, but wait until the extra-sensory gang take over!'

Crouching behind a low stone parapet running off the terrace was a group of waiters in dishevelled evening dress, lab technicians in scorched white overalls and musicians clutching their instrument cases. A bolt of flame from one of the tanks flickered over their heads and crashed into the grove of flamingo trees, sending up a shower of sparks and broken notes.

Clifford pulled Tony to his feet. 'Come on, we've got to get out of here. We'll try the library windows into the garden. You'd better take Margot.'

Her yellow beach robe had apparently died of shock, and was beginning to blacken like a dried-out banana skin. Discreetly averting his eyes, Tony picked her up and followed Clifford out into the hall.

Three croupiers in gold uniforms were arguing hotly with two men in white surgeons' coats. Behind them a couple of mechanics were struggling a huge vibrobath up the stairs.

The foreman came over to Clifford. 'Gorrell?' he asked, consulting an invoice. 'Trans-Ocean.' He jerked a thumb at the bath. 'Where do you want it?'

A surgeon elbowed him aside. 'Mr Gorrell?' he asked suavely. 'We are from Cerebro-Tonic Travel. Please allow me to give you a sedative. All this noise –'

Clifford pushed past him and started to walk down the corridor to the library, but the floor began to slide and weave.

He stopped and looked around unsteadily.

Tony was down on his knees, Margot flopped out of his arms across the floor.

Someone swayed up to Clifford and held out a tray.

On it were three tickets.

Around him the walls whirled.

He woke in his bedroom, lying comfortably on his back, gently breathing a cool amber air. The noise had died away, but he could still hear a vortex of sound spinning violently in the back of his mind. It spiralled away, vanished, and he moved his head and looked around.

Margot was lying asleep beside him, and for a moment he thought that the attack on the house had been a dream. Then he noticed the skull-plate clamped over his head, and the cables leading off from a boom to a large console at the foot of the bed. Massive spools loaded with magnetic tape waited in the projector ready to be played.

The real nightmare was still to come! He struggled to get up, found himself clamped in a twilight sleep, unable to move more than a few centimetres.

He lay there powerlessly for ten minutes, tongue clogging his mouth like a wad of cotton-wool when he tried to shout. Eventually a small neatly featured alien in a pink silk suit opened the door and padded quietly over to them. He peered down at their faces and then turned a couple of knobs on the console.

Clifford's consciousness began to clear. Beside him Margot stirred and woke.

The alien beamed down pleasantly. 'Good evening,' he greeted them in a smooth creamy voice. 'Please allow me to apologize for any discomfort you have suffered. However, the first day of a vacation is often a little confused.'

Margot sat up. 'I remember you. You're from the little bureau in the Bazaar.' She jumped round happily. 'Clifford!'

The alien bowed. 'Of course, Mrs Gorrell. I am Dr Terence Sotal-2 Burlington, Professor – Emeritus,' he added to himself as an after-thought, '– of Applied Drama at the University of Alpha Leporis, and the director of the play you and your husband are to perform during your vacation.'

Clifford cut in: 'Would you release me from this machine immediately? And then get out of my house! I've had –'

'Clifford!' Margot snapped. 'What's the matter with you?'

Clifford dragged at the skull plate and Dr Burlington quietly moved a control on the console. Part of Clifford's brain clouded and he sank back helplessly.

'Everything is all right, Mr Gorrell,' Dr Burlington said.

'Clifford,' Margot warned him. 'Remember your promise.' She smiled at Dr Burlington. 'Don't pay any attention to him, Doctor. Please go on.'

'Thank you, Mrs Gorrell.' Dr Burlington bowed again, as Clifford lay half-asleep, groaning impotently.

'The play we have designed for you,' Dr Burlington explained, 'is an adaptation of a classic masterpiece in the Diphenyl 2-4-6 Cyclopropane canon, and though based on the oldest of human situations, is nonetheless fascinating. It was recently declared the outright winner at the Mira Nuptial Contest, and will always have a proud place in the private repertoires. To you, I believe, it is known as "The Taming of the Shrew".'

Margot giggled and then looked surprised. Dr Burlington smiled urbanely. 'However, allow me to show you the script.' He excused himself and slipped out.

Margot fretted anxiously, while Clifford pulled weakly at the skull-plate.

'Clifford, I'm not sure that I like this altogether. And Dr Burlington does seem rather strange. But I suppose it's only for three weeks.'

Just then the door opened and a stout bearded figure, erect in a stiff blue uniform, white yachting cap jauntily on his head, stepped in.

'Good evening, Mrs Gorrell.' He saluted Margot smartly, 'Captain Linstrom.' He looked down at Clifford. 'Good to have you aboard, sir.'

'Aboard?' Clifford repeated weakly. He looked around at the familiar furniture in the room, the curtains drawn neatly over the windows. 'What are you raving about? Get out of my house!'

The Captain chuckled. 'Your husband has a sense of humour, Mrs Gorrell. A useful asset on these long trips. Your friend Mr Harcourt in the next cabin seems sadly lacking in one.'

'Tony?' Margot exclaimed. 'Is he still here?'

Captain Linstrom laughed. 'I quite understand you. He seems very worried, quite over-eager to return to Mars. We shall be passing there one day, of course, though not I fear for some time. However, time is no longer a consideration to you. I believe you are to spend the entire voyage in sleep. But a very pleasantly coloured sleep nonetheless.' He smiled roguishly at Margot.

As he reached the door Clifford managed to gasp out: 'Where are we? For heaven's sake, call the police!'

Captain Linstrom paused in surprise. 'But surely you know, Mr Gorrell?' He strode to the window and flung back the curtains. In place of the large square casement were three small portholes. Outside a blaze of incandescent light flashed by, a rush of stars and nebulae.

Captain Linstrom gestured theatrically. 'This is the *Dream of Osiris*, under charter to Terminal Tours, three hours out from Zenith City on the non-stop run. May I wish you sweet dreams!'

· **1962**

# ,THE CAGE OF SAND

At sunset, when the vermilion glow reflected from the dunes along the horizon fitfully illuminated the white faces of the abandoned hotels, Bridgman stepped on to his balcony and looked out over the long stretches of cooling sand as the tides of purple shadow seeped across them. Slowly, extending their slender fingers through the shallow saddles and depressions, the shadows massed together like gigantic combs, a few phosphorescing spurs of obsidian isolated for a moment between the tines, and then finally coalesced and flooded in a solid wave across the half-submerged hotels. Behind the silent façades, in the tilting sand-filled streets which had once glittered with cocktail bars and restaurants, it was already night. Haloes of moonlight beaded the lamp-standards with silver dew, and draped the shuttered windows and slipping cornices like a frost of frozen gas.

As Bridgman watched, his lean bronzed arms propped against the rusting rail, the last whorls of light sank away into the cerise funnel withdrawing below the horizon, and the first wind stirred across the dead Martian sand. Here and there miniature cyclones whirled about a sand-spur, drawing off swirling feathers of moon-washed spray, and a nimbus of white dust swept across the dunes and settled in the dips and hollows. Gradually the drifts accumulated, edging towards the former shoreline below the hotels. Already the first four floors had been inundated, and the sand now reached up to within two feet of Bridgman's balcony. After the next sandstorm he would be forced yet again to move to the floor above.

'Bridgman!'

The voice cleft the darkness like a spear. Fifty yards to his right, at the edge of the derelict sand-break he had once attempted to build below the hotel, a square stocky figure wearing a pair of frayed cotton shorts waved up at him. The moonlight etched the broad sinewy muscles of his chest, the powerful bowed legs sinking almost to their calves in the soft Martian sand. He was about forty-five years old, his thinning hair close-cropped so that he seemed almost bald. In his right hand he carried a large canvas hold-all.

Bridgman smiled to himself. Standing there patiently in the moonlight below the derelict hotel, Travis reminded him of some long-delayed tourist arriving at a ghost resort years after its extinction.

'Bridgman, are you coming?' When the latter still leaned on his balcony rail, Travis added: 'The next conjunction is tomorrow.'

Bridgman shook his head, a rictus of annoyance twisting his mouth. He hated the bi-monthly conjunctions, when all seven of the derelict satellite capsules still orbiting the Earth crossed the sky together. Invariably on these nights he remained in his room, playing over the old memo-tapes he had salvaged from the submerged chalets and motels further along the beach (the hysterical 'This is Mamie Goldberg, 62955 Cocoa Boulevard, I really wanna protest against this crazy evacuation ...' or resigned 'Sam Snade here, the Pontiac convertible in the back garage belongs to anyone who can dig it out'). Travis and Louise Woodward always came to the hotel on the conjunction nights – it was the highest building in the resort, with an unrestricted view from horizon to horizon – and would follow the seven converging stars as they pursued their endless courses around the globe. Both would be oblivious of everything else, which the wardens knew only too well, and they reserved their most careful searches of the sand-sea for these bi-monthly occasions. Invariably Bridgman found himself forced to act as look-out for the other two.

'I was out last night,' he called down to Travis. 'Keep away from the north-east perimeter fence by the Cape. They'll be busy repairing the track.'

Most nights Bridgman divided his time between excavating the buried motels for caches of supplies (the former inhabitants of the resort area had assumed the government would soon rescind its evacuation order) and disconnecting the sections of metal roadway laid across the desert for the wardens' jeeps. Each of the squares of wire mesh was about five yards wide and weighed over three hundred pounds. After he had snapped the lines of rivets, dragged the sections away and buried them among the dunes he would be exhausted, and spend most of the next day nursing his strained hands and shoulders. Some sections of the track were now permanently anchored with heavy steel stakes, and he knew that sooner or later they would be unable to delay the wardens by sabotaging the roadway.

Travis hesitated, and with a noncommittal shrug disappeared among the dunes, the heavy tool-bag swinging easily from one powerful arm. Despite the meagre diet which sustained him, his energy and determination seemed undiminished – in a single night Bridgman had watched him dismantle twenty sections of track and then loop together the adjacent limbs of a crossroad, sending an entire convoy of six vehicles off into the wastelands to the south.

Bridgman turned from the balcony, then stopped when a faint tang of brine touched the cool air. Ten miles away, hidden by the lines of dunes, was the sea, the long green rollers of the middle Atlantic breaking against the red Martian strand. When he had first come to the beach five years earlier there had never been the faintest scent of brine across the intervening miles of sand. Slowly, however, the Atlantic was driving the shore back to its former margins. The tireless shoulder of the Gulf Stream drummed against the soft Martian dust and piled the dunes into grotesque rococo reefs which the wind carried away into the sand-sea. Gradually the ocean was returning, reclaiming its great smooth basin, sifting out the black quartz and Martian obsidian which would never be wind-borne and drawing these down into its deeps. More and more often the stain of brine would hang on the evening air, reminding Bridgman why he had first come to the beach and removing any inclination to leave.

Three years earlier he had attempted to measure the rate of approach, by driving a series of stakes into the sand at the water's edge, but the shifting contours of the dunes carried away the coloured poles. Later, using the promontory at Cape Canaveral, where the old launching gantries and landing ramps reared up into the sky like derelict pieces of giant sculpture, he had calculated by triangulation that the advance was little more than thirty yards per year. At this rate – without wanting to, he had automatically made the calculation – it would be well over five hundred years before the Atlantic reached its former littoral at Cocoa Beach. Though discouragingly slow, the movement was nonetheless in a forward direction, and Bridgman was happy to remain in his hotel ten miles away across the dunes, conceding towards its time of arrival the few years he had at his disposal.

Later, shortly after Louise Woodward's arrival, he had thought of dismantling one of the motel cabins and building himself a small chalet by the water's edge. But the shoreline had been too dismal and forbidding. The great red dunes rolled on for miles, cutting off half the sky, dissolving slowly under the impact of the slate-green water. There was no formal tide-line, but only a steep shelf littered with nodes of quartz and rusting fragments of Mars rockets brought back with the ballast. He spent a few days in a cave below a towering sand-reef, watching the long galleries of compacted red dust crumble and dissolve as the cold Atlantic stream sluiced through them, collapsing like the decorated colonnades of a baroque cathedral. In the summer the heat reverberated from the hot sand as from the slag of some molten sun, burning the rubber soles from his boots, and the light from the scattered flints of washed quartz flickered with diamond hardness. Bridgman had returned to the hotel grateful for his room overlooking the silent dunes.

Leaving the balcony, the sweet smell of brine still in his nostrils, he went over to the desk. A small cone of shielded light shone down over the tape-recorder and rack of spools. The rumble of the wardens' unsilenced engines always gave him at least five minutes' warning of their arrival, and it would have been safe to install another lamp in the room – there were no roadways between the hotel and the sea, and from a distance any light reflected on to the balcony was indistinguishable from the corona of glimmering phosphors which hung over the sand like myriads of fire-flies. However, Bridgman preferred to sit in the darkened suite, enclosed by the circle of books on the makeshift shelves, the shadow-filled air playing over his shoulders through the long night as he toyed with the memo-tapes, fragments of a vanished and unregretted past. By day he always drew the blinds, immolating himself in a world of perpetual twilight.

Bridgman had easily adapted himself to his self-isolation, soon evolved a system of daily routines that gave him the maximum of time to spend on his private reveries. Pinned to the walls around him were a series of huge white-prints and architectural drawings, depicting various elevations of a fantastic Martian city he had once designed, its glass spires and curtain walls rising like heliotropic jewels from the vermilion desert. In fact, the whole city was a vast piece of jewellery, each elevation brilliantly visualized but as symmetrical, and ultimately as lifeless, as a crown. Bridgman continually retouched the drawings, inserting more and more details, so that they almost seemed to be photographs of an original.

Most of the hotels in the town – one of a dozen similar resorts buried by the sand which had once formed an unbroken strip of motels, chalets and five-star hotels thirty miles to the south of Cape Canaveral – were well stocked with supplies of canned food abandoned when the area was evacuated and wired off. There were ample reservoirs and cisterns filled with water, apart from a thousand intact cocktail bars six feet below the surface of the sand. Travis had excavated a dozen of these in search of his favourite vintage bourbon. Walking out across the desert behind the town one would suddenly find a short flight of steps cut into the annealed sand and crawl below an occluded sign announcing 'The Satellite Bar' or 'The Orbit Room' into the inner sanctum, where the jutting deck of a chromium bar had been cleared as far as the diamond-paned mirror freighted with its rows of bottles and figurines. Bridgman would have been glad to see them left undisturbed.

The whole trash of amusement arcades and cheap bars on the outskirts of the beach resorts were a depressing commentary on the original space-flights, reducing them to the level of monster side-shows at a carnival.

Outside his room, steps sounded along the corridor, then slowly climbed the stairway, pausing for a few seconds at every landing. Bridgman lowered the memo-tape in his hand, listening to the familiar tired foot-steps. This was Louise Woodward, making her invariable evening ascent to the roof ten storeys above. Bridgman glanced at the timetable pinned to the wall. Only two of the satellites would be visible, between 12.25 and 12.35 a.m., at an elevation of 62 degrees in the south-west, passing through Cetus and Eridanus, neither of them containing her husband. Although the siting was two hours away, she was already taking up her position, and would remain there until dawn.

Bridgman listened wanly to the feet recede slowly up the stairwell. All through the night the slim, pale-faced woman would sit out under the moon-lit sky, as the soft Martian sand her husband had given his life to reach sifted around her in the dark wind, stroking her faded hair like some mourning mariner's wife waiting for the sea to surrender her husband's body. Travis usually joined her later, and the two of them sat side by side against the elevator house, the frosted letters of the hotel's neon sign strewn around their feet like the fragments of a dismembered zodiac, then at dawn made their way down into the shadow-filled streets to their eyries in the nearby hotels.

Initially Bridgman often joined their nocturnal vigil, but after a few nights he began to feel something repellent, if not actually ghoulish, about their mindless contemplation of the stars. This was not so much because of the macabre spectacle of the dead astronauts orbiting the planet in their capsules, but because of the curious sense of unspoken communion between Travis and Louise Woodward, almost as if they were celebrating a private rite to which Bridgman could never be initiated. Whatever their original motives, Bridgman sometimes suspected that these had been overlaid by other, more personal ones.

Ostensibly, Louise Woodward was watching her husband's satellite in order to keep alive his memory, but Bridgman guessed that the memories she unconsciously wished to perpetuate were those of herself twenty years earlier, when her husband had been a celebrity and she herself courted by magazine columnists and TV reporters. For fifteen years after his death – Woodward had been killed testing a new lightweight launching platform – she had lived a nomadic existence, driving restlessly in her cheap car from motel to motel across the continent, following her husband's star as it disappeared into the eastern night, and had at last made her home at Cocoa Beach in sight of the rusting gantries across the bay.

Travis's real motives were probably more complex. To Bridgman, after they had known each other for a couple of years, he had confided that he felt himself bound by a debt of honour to maintain a watch over the dead astronauts for the example of courage and sacrifice they had set him as a child (although most of them had been piloting their wrecked capsules for fifty years before Travis's birth), and that now they were virtually forgotten he must singlehandedly keep alive the fading flame of their memory. Bridgman was convinced of his sincerity.

Yet later, going through a pile of old news magazines in the trunk of a car he excavated from a motel port, he came across a picture of Travis wearing an aluminium pressure suit and learned something more of his story. Apparently Travis had at one time himself been an astronaut – or rather, a would-be astronaut. A test pilot for one of the civilian agencies setting up orbital relay stations, his nerve had failed him a few seconds before the last 'hold' of his countdown, a moment of pure unexpected funk that cost the company some five million dollars.

Obviously it was his inability to come to terms with this failure of character, unfortunately discovered lying flat on his back on a con-tour couch two hundred feet above the launching pad, which had brought Travis to Canaveral, the abandoned Mecca of the first heroes of astronautics.

Tactfully Bridgman had tried to explain that no one would blame him for this failure of nerve – less his responsibility than that of the selectors who had picked him for the flight, or at least the result of an unhappy concatenation of ambiguously worded multiple-choice questions (crosses in the wrong boxes, some heavier to bear and harder to open than others! Bridgman had joked sardonically to himself). But Travis seemed to have reached his own decision about himself. Night after night, he watched the brilliant funerary convoy weave its gilded pathway towards the dawn sun, salving his own failure by identifying it with the greater, but blameless, failure of the seven astronauts. Travis still wore his hair in the regulation 'mohican' cut of the space-man, still kept himself in perfect physical trim by the vigorous routines he had practised before his abortive flight. Sustained by the personal myth he had created, he was now more or less unreachable.

'Dear Harry, I've taken the car and deposit box. Sorry it should end like –'

Irritably, Bridgman switched off the memo-tape and its recapitulation of some thirty-year-old private triviality. For some reason he seemed unable to accept Travis and Louise Woodward for what they were. He disliked this failure of compassion, a nagging compulsion to expose other people's motives and strip away the insulating sheaths around their naked nerve strings, particularly as his own motives for being at Cape Canaveral were so suspect. Why was *he* there, what failure was *he* trying to expiate? And why choose Cocoa Beach as his penitential shore? For three years he had asked himself these questions so often that they had ceased to have any meaning, like a fossilized catechism or the blunted self-recrimination of a paranoiac.

He had resigned his job as the chief architect of a big space development company after the large government contract on which the firm depended, for the design of the first Martian city-settlement, was awarded to a rival consortium. Secretly, however, he realized that his resignation had marked his unconscious acceptance that despite his great imaginative gifts he was unequal to the specialized and more prosaic tasks of designing the settlement. On the drawing board, as elsewhere, he would always remain earth-bound.

His dreams of building a new Gothic architecture of launching ports and control gantries, of being the Frank Lloyd Wright and Le Corbusier of the first city to be raised outside Earth, faded for ever, but leaving him unable to accept the alternative of turning out endless plans for low-cost hospitals in Ecuador and housing estates in Tokyo. For a year he had drifted aimlessly, but a few colour photographs of the vermilion sunsets at Cocoa Beach and a news story about the recluses living on in the submerged motels had provided a powerful compass.

He dropped the memo-tape into a drawer, making an effort to accept Louise Woodward and Travis on their own terms, a wife keeping watch over her dead husband and an old astronaut maintaining a solitary vigil over the memories of his lost comrades-in-arms.

The wind gusted against the balcony window, and a light spray of sand rained across the floor. At night dust-storms churned along the beach. Thermal pools isolated by the cooling desert would suddenly accrete like beads of quicksilver and erupt across the fluffy sand in miniature tornadoes.

Only fifty yards away, the dying cough of a heavy diesel cut through the shadows. Quickly Bridgman turned off the small desk light, grateful for his meanness over the battery packs plugged into the circuit, then stepped to the window.

At the leftward edge of the sand-break, half hidden in the long shadows cast by the hotel, was a large tracked vehicle with a low camouflaged hull. A narrow observation bridge had been built over the bumpers directly in front of the squat snout of the engine housing, and two of the beach wardens were craning up through the plexiglass windows at the balconies of the hotel, shifting their binoculars from room to room. Behind them, under the glass dome of the extended driving cabin, were three more wardens, controlling an outboard spotlight. In the centre of the bowl a thin mote of light pulsed with the rhythm of the engine, ready to throw its powerful beam into any of the open rooms.

Bridgman hid back behind the shutters as the binoculars focused upon the adjacent balcony, moved to his own, hesitated, and passed to the next. Exasperated by the sabotaging of the roadways, the wardens had evidently decided on a new type of vehicle. With their four broad tracks, the huge squat sand-cars would be free of the mesh roadways and able to rove at will through the dunes and sand-hills.

Bridgman watched the vehicle reverse slowly, its engine barely varying its deep bass growl, then move off along the line of hotels, almost indistinguishable in profile among the shifting dunes and hillocks. A hundred yards away, at the first intersection, it turned towards the main boulevard, wisps of dust streaming from the metal cleats like thin spumes of steam. The men in the observation bridge were still watching the hotel. Bridgman was certain that they had seen a reflected glimmer of light, or perhaps some movement of Louise Woodward's on the roof. However reluctant to leave the car and be contaminated by the poisonous dust, the wardens would not hesitate if the capture of one of the beachcombers warranted it.

Racing up the staircase, Bridgman made his way to the roof, crouching below the windows that overlooked the boulevard. Like a huge crab, the sand-car had parked under the jutting overhang of the big department store opposite. Once fifty feet from the ground, the concrete lip was now separated from it by little more than six or seven feet, and the sand-car was hidden in the shadows below it, engine silent. A single movement in a window, or the unexpected return of Travis, and the wardens would spring from the hatchways, their long-handled nets and lassos pinioning them around the necks and ankles. Bridgman remembered one beachcomber he had seen flushed from his motel hideout and carried off like a huge twitching spider at the centre of a black rubber web, the wardens with their averted faces and masked mouths like devils in an abstract ballet.

Reaching the roof, Bridgman stepped out into the opaque white moonlight. Louise Woodward was leaning on the balcony, looking out towards the distant, unseen sea. At the faint sound of the door creaking she turned and began to walk listlessly around the roof, her pale face floating like a nimbus. She wore a freshly ironed print dress she had found in a rusty spin drier in one of the launderettes, and her streaked blonde hair floated out lightly behind her on the wind.

'Louise!'

Involuntarily she started, tripping over a fragment of the neon sign, then moved backwards towards the balcony overlooking the boulevard.

'Mrs Woodward!' Bridgman held her by the elbow, raised a hand to her mouth before she could cry out. 'The wardens are down below. They're watching the hotel. We must find Travis before he returns.'

Louise hesitated, apparently recognizing Bridgman only by an effort, and her eyes turned up to the black marble sky. Bridgman looked at his watch; it was almost 12.25. He searched the stars in the south-west.

Louise murmured: 'They're nearly here now, I must see them. Where is Travis, he should be here?'

Bridgman pulled at her arm. 'Perhaps he saw the sand-car. Mrs Woodward, we should leave.'

Suddenly she pointed up at the sky, then wrenched away from him and ran to the rail. 'There they are!'

Fretting, Bridgman waited until she had filled her eyes with the two companion points of light speeding from the western horizon. These were Merril and Pokrovski – like every schoolboy he knew the sequences perfectly, a second system of constellations with a more complex but far more tangible periodicity and precession – the Castor and Pollux of the orbiting zodiac, whose appearance always heralded a full conjunction the following night.

Louise Woodward gazed up at them from the rail, the rising wind lifting her hair off her shoulders and entraining it horizontally behind her head. Around her feet the red Martian dust swirled and rustled, silting over the fragments of the old neon sign, a brilliant pink spume streaming from her long fingers as they moved along the balcony ledge. When the satellites finally disappeared among the stars along the horizon, she leaned forwards, her face raised to the milk-blue moon as if to delay their departure, then turned back to Bridgman, a bright smile on her face.

His earlier suspicions vanishing, Bridgman smiled back at her encouragingly. 'Roger will be here tomorrow night, Louise. We must be careful the wardens don't catch us before we see him.'

He felt a sudden admiration for her, at the stoical way she had sustained herself during her long vigil. Perhaps she thought of Woodward as still alive, and in some way was patiently waiting for him to return? He remembered her saying once: 'Roger was only a boy when he took off, you know, I feel more like his mother now,' as if frightened how Woodward would react to her dry skin and fading hair, fearing that he might even have forgotten her. No doubt the death she visualized for him was of a different order from the mortal kind.

Hand in hand, they tiptoed carefully down the flaking steps, jumped down from a terrace window into the soft sand below the wind-break. Bridgman sank to his knees in the fine silver moon-dust, then waded up to the firmer ground, pulling Louise after him. They climbed through a breach in the tilting palisades, then ran away from the line of dead hotels looming like skulls in the empty light.

'Paul, wait!' Her head still raised to the sky, Louise Woodward fell to her knees in a hollow between two dunes, with a laugh stumbled after Bridgman as he raced through the dips and saddles. The wind was now whipping the sand off the higher crests, flurries of dust spurting like excited wavelets. A hundred yards away, the town was a fading film set, projected by the camera obscura of the sinking moon. They were standing where the long Atlantic seas had once been ten fathoms deep, and Bridgman could scent again the tang of brine among the flickering white-caps of dust, phosphorescing like shoals of animalcula. He waited for any sign of Travis.

'Louise, we'll have to go back to the town. The sand-storms are blowing up, we'll never see Travis here.'

They moved back through the dunes, then worked their way among the narrow alleyways between the hotels to the northern gateway to the town. Bridgman found a vantage point in a small apartment block, and they lay down looking out below a window lintel into the sloping street, the warm sand forming a pleasant cushion. At the intersections the dust blew across the roadway in white clouds, obscuring the warden's beach-car parked a hundred yards down the boulevard.

Half an hour later an engine surged, and Bridgman began to pile sand into the interval in front of them. 'They're going. Thank God!'

Louise Woodward held his arm. 'Look!'

Fifty feet away, his white vinyl suit half hidden in the dust clouds, one of the wardens was advancing slowly towards them, his lasso twirling lightly in his hand. A few feet behind was a second warden, craning up at the windows of the apartment block with his binoculars.

Bridgman and Louise crawled back below the ceiling, then dug their way under a transom into the kitchen at the rear. A window opened on to a sand-filled yard, and they darted away through the lifting dust that whirled between the buildings.

Suddenly, around a corner, they saw the line of wardens moving down a side-street, the sand-car edging along behind them. Before Bridgman could steady himself a spasm of pain seized his right calf, contorting the gastrocnemius muscle, and he fell to one knee. Louise Woodward pulled him back against the wall, then pointed at a squat, bow-legged figure trudging towards them along the curving road into town.

'Travis –'

The tool-bag swung from his right hand, and his feet rang faintly on the wire-mesh roadway. Head down, he seemed unaware of the wardens hidden by a bend in the road.

'Come on!' Disregarding the negligible margin of safety, Bridgman clambered to his feet and impetuously ran out into the centre of the street. Louise tried to stop him, and they had covered only ten yards before the wardens saw them. There was a warning shout, and the spotlight flung its giant cone down the street. The sand-car surged forward, like a massive dust-covered bull, its tracks clawing at the sand.

'Travis!' As Bridgman reached the bend, Louise Woodward ten yards behind, Travis looked up from his reverie, then flung the tool-bag over one shoulder and raced ahead of them towards the clutter of motel roofs protruding from the other side of the street. Lagging behind the others, Bridgman again felt the cramp attack his leg, broke off into a painful shuffle. When Travis came back for him Bridgman tried to wave him away, but Travis pinioned his elbow and propelled him forward like an attendant straight-arming a patient.

The dust swirling around them, they disappeared through the fading streets and out into the desert, the shouts of the beach-wardens lost in the roar and clamour of the baying engine. Around them, like the strange metallic flora of some extraterrestrial garden, the old neon signs jutted from the red Martian sand – 'Satellite Motel', 'Planet Bar', 'Mercury Motel'. Hiding behind them, they reached the scrub-covered dunes on the edge of the town, then picked up one of the trails that led away among the sand-reefs. There, in the deep grottoes of compacted sand which hung like inverted palaces, they waited until the storm subsided. Shortly before dawn the wardens abandoned their search, unable to bring the heavy sand-car on to the disintegrating reef.

Contemptuous of the wardens, Travis lit a small fire with his cigarette lighter, burning splinters of driftwood that had gathered in the gullies. Bridgman crouched beside it, warming his hands.

'This is the first time they've been prepared to leave the sand-car,' he remarked to Travis. 'It means they're under orders to catch us.'

Travis shrugged. 'Maybe. They're extending the fence along the beach. They probably intend to seal us in for ever.'

'What?' Bridgman stood up with a sudden feeling of uneasiness. 'Why should they? Are you sure? I mean, what would be the point?'

Travis looked up at him, a flicker of dry amusement on his bleached face. Wisps of smoke wreathed his head, curled up past the serpentine columns of the grotto to the winding interval of sky a hundred feet above. 'Bridgman, forgive me saying so, but if you want to leave here, you should leave now. In a month's time you won't be able to.'

Bridgman ignored this, and searched the cleft of dark sky overhead, which framed the constellation Scorpio, as if hoping to see a reflection of the distant sea. 'They must be crazy. How much of this fence did you see?'

'About eight hundred yards. It won't take them long to complete. The sections are prefabricated, about forty feet high.' He smiled ironically at Bridgman's discomfort. 'Relax, Bridgman. If you do want to get out, you'll always be able to tunnel underneath it.'

'I don't want to get out,' Bridgman said coldly. 'Damn them, Travis, they're turning the place into a zoo. You know it won't be the same with a fence all the way around it.'

'A corner of Earth that is forever Mars.' Under the high forehead, Travis's eyes were sharp and watchful. 'I see their point. There hasn't been a fatal casualty now' – he glanced at Louise Woodward, who was strolling about in the colonnades – 'for nearly twenty years, and passenger rockets are supposed to be as safe as commuters' trains. They're quietly sealing off the past, Louise and I and you with it. I suppose it's pretty considerate of them not to burn the place down with flame-throwers. The virus would be a sufficient excuse. After all, we three are probably the only reservoirs left on the planet.' He picked up a handful of red dust and examined the fine crystals with a sombre eye. 'Well, Bridgman, what are you going to do?'

His thoughts discharging themselves through his mind like frantic signal flares, Bridgman walked away without answering.

Behind them, Louise Woodward wandered among the deep galleries of the grotto, crooning to herself in a low voice to the sighing rhythms of the whirling sand.

The next morning they returned to the town, wading through the deep drifts of sand that lay like a fresh fall of red snow between the hotels and stores, coruscating in the brilliant sunlight. Travis and Louise Woodward made their way towards their quarters in the motels further down the beach. Bridgman searched the still, crystal air for any signs of the wardens, but the sand-car had gone, its tracks obliterated by the storm.

In his room he found their calling-card.

A huge tide of dust had flowed through the french windows and submerged the desk and bed, three feet deep against the rear wall. Outside the sand-break had been inundated, and the contours of the desert had completely altered, a few spires of obsidian marking its former perspectives like buoys on a shifting sea. Bridgman spent the morning digging out his books and equipment, dismantled the electrical system and its batteries and carried everything to the room above. He would have moved to the penthouse on the top floor, but his lights would have been visible for miles.

Settling into his new quarters, he switched on the tape-recorder, heard a short, clipped message in the brisk voice which had shouted orders at the wardens the previous evening. 'Bridgman, this is Major Webster, deputy commandant of Cocoa Beach Reservation. On the instructions of the Anti-Viral Sub-committee of the UN General Assembly we are now building a continuous fence around the beach area. On completion no further egress will be allowed, and anyone escaping will be immediately returned to the reservation. Give yourself up now, Bridgman, before –'

Bridgman stopped the tape, then reversed the spool and erased the message, staring angrily at the instrument. Unable to settle down to the task of rewiring the room's circuits, he paced about, fiddling with the architectural drawings propped against the wall. He felt restless and hyper-excited, perhaps because he had been trying to repress, not very successfully, precisely those doubts of which Webster had now reminded him.

He stepped on to the balcony and looked out over the desert, at the red dunes rolling to the windows directly below. For the fourth time he had moved up a floor, and the sequence of identical rooms he had occupied were like displaced images of himself seen through a prism. Their common focus, that elusive final definition of himself which he had sought for so long, still remained to be found. Timelessly the sand swept towards him, its shifting contours, approximating more closely than any other landscape he had found to complete psychic zero, enveloping his past failures and uncertainties, masking them in its enigmatic canopy.

Bridgman watched the red sand flicker and fluoresce in the steepening sunlight. He would never see Mars now, and redress the implicit failure of talent, but a workable replica of the planet was contained within the beach area.

Several million tons of the Martian top-soil had been ferried in as ballast some fifty years earlier, when it was feared that the continuous firing of planetary probes and space vehicles, and the transportation of bulk stores and equipment to Mars would fractionally lower the gravitational mass of the Earth and bring it into tighter orbit around the Sun. Although the distance involved would be little more than a few millimetres, and barely raise the temperature of the atmosphere, its cumulative effects over an extended period might have resulted in a loss into space of the tenuous layers of the outer atmosphere, and of the radiological veil which alone made the biosphere habitable.

Over a twenty-year period a fleet of large freighters had shuttled to and from Mars, dumping the ballast into the sea near the landing grounds of Cape Canaveral. Simultaneously the Russians were filling in a small section of the Caspian Sea. The intention had been that the ballast should be swallowed by the Atlantic and Caspian waters, but all too soon it was found that the microbiological analysis of the sand had been inadequate.

At the Martian polar caps, where the original water vapour in the atmosphere had condensed, a residue of ancient organic matter formed the top-soil, a fine sandy loess containing the fossilized spores of the giant lichens and mosses which had been the last living organisms on the planet millions of years earlier. Embedded in these spores were the crystal lattices of the viruses which had once preyed on the plants, and traces of these were carried back to Earth with the Canaveral and Caspian ballast.

A few years afterwards a drastic increase in a wide range of plant diseases was noticed in the southern states of America and in the Kazakhstan and Turkmenistan republics of the Soviet Union. All over Florida there were outbreaks of blight and mosaic disease, orange plantations withered and died, stunted palms split by the roadside like dried banana skins, saw grass stiffened into paper spears in the summer heat. Within a few years the entire peninsula was transformed into a desert. The swampy jungles of the Everglades became bleached and dry, the rivers cracked husks strewn with the gleaming skeletons of crocodiles and birds, the forests petrified.

The former launching-ground at Canaveral was closed, and shortly afterwards the Cocoa Beach resorts were sealed off and evacuated, billions of dollars of real estate were abandoned to the virus. Fortunately never virulent to animal hosts, its influence was confined to within a small radius of the original loess which had borne it, unless ingested by the human organism, when it symbioted with the bacteria in the gut flora, benign and unknown to the host, but devastating to vegetation thousands of miles from Canaveral if returned to the soil.

Unable to rest despite his sleepless night, Bridgman played irritably with the tape-recorder. During their close escape from the wardens he had more than half hoped they would catch him. The mysterious leg cramp was obviously psychogenic. Although unable to accept consciously the logic of Webster's argument, he would willingly have conceded to the *fait accompli* of physical capture, gratefully submitted to a year's quarantine at the Parasitological Cleansing Unit at Tampa, and then returned to his career as an architect, chastened but accepting his failure.

As yet, however, the opportunity for surrender had failed to offer itself. Travis appeared to be aware of his ambivalent motives; Bridgman noticed that he and Louise Woodward had made no arrangements to meet him that evening for the conjunction.

In the early afternoon he went down into the streets, ploughed through the drifts of red sand, following the footprints of Travis and Louise as they wound in and out of the side-streets, finally saw them disappear into the coarser, flint-like dunes among the submerged motels to the south of the town. Giving up, he returned through the empty, shadowless streets, now and then shouted up into the hot air, listening to the echoes boom away among the dunes.

Later that afternoon he walked out towards the north-east, picking his way carefully through the dips and hollows, crouching in the pools of shadow whenever the distant sounds of the construction gangs along the perimeter were carried across to him by the wind. Around him, in the great dust basins, the grains of red sand glittered like diamonds. Barbs of rusting metal protruded from the slopes, remnants of Mars satellites and launching stages which had fallen on to the Martian deserts and then been carried back again to Earth. One fragment which he passed, a complete section of hull plate like a concave shield, still carried part of

an identification numeral, and stood upright in the dissolving sand like a
door into nowhere.

Just before dusk he reached a tall spur of obsidian that reared up into
the tinted cerise sky like the spire of a ruined church, climbed up among
its jutting cornices and looked out across the intervening two or three
miles of dunes to the perimeter. Illuminated by the last light, the metal
grilles shone with a roseate glow like fairy portcullises on the edge of an
enchanted sea. At least half a mile of the fence had been completed, and
as he watched another of the giant prefabricated sections was cantilevered
into the air and staked to the ground. Already the eastern horizon was cut
off by the encroaching fence, the enclosed Martian sand like the gravel
scattered at the bottom of a cage.

Perched on the spur, Bridgman felt a warning tremor of pain in his
calf. He leapt down in a flurry of dust, without looking back made off
among the dunes and reefs.

Later, as the last baroque whorls of the sunset faded below the
horizon, he waited on the roof for Travis and Louise Woodward, peering
impatiently into the empty moon-filled streets.

Shortly after midnight, at an elevation of 35 degrees in the south-west,
between Aquila and Ophiuchus, the conjunction began. Bridgman continued to search the streets, and ignored the seven points of speeding
light as they raced towards him from the horizon like an invasion from
deep space. There was no indication of their convergent orbital pathways,
which would soon scatter them thousands of miles apart, and the satellites
moved as if they were always together, in the tight configuration Bridgman
had known since childhood, like a lost zodiacal emblem, a constellation
detached from the celestial sphere and forever frantically searching to
return to its place.

'Travis! Confound you!' With a snarl, Bridgman swung away from the
balcony and moved along to the exposed section of rail behind the elevator
head. To be avoided like a pariah by Travis and Louise Woodward forced
him to accept that he was no longer a true resident of the beach and now
existed in a no-man's-land between them and the wardens.

The seven satellites drew nearer, and Bridgman glanced up at them
cursorily. They were disposed in a distinctive but unusual pattern resembling the Greek letter $x$, a limp cross, a straight lateral member containing
four capsules more or less in line ahead – Connolly, Tkachev, Merril and
Maiakovski – bisected by three others forming with Tkachev an elongated
Z – Pokrovski, Woodward and Brodisnek. The pattern had been variously
identified as a hammer and sickle, an eagle, a swastika, and a dove, as
well as a variety of religious and runic emblems, but all these were being
defeated by the advancing tendency of the older capsules to vaporize.

It was this slow disintegration of the aluminium shells that made
them visible – it had often been pointed out that the observer on
the ground was looking, not at the actual capsule, but at a local field
of vaporized aluminium and ionized hydrogen peroxide gas from the

ruptured attitude jets now distributed within half a mile of each of the capsules. Woodward's, the most recently in orbit, was a barely perceptible point of light. The hulks of the capsules, with their perfectly preserved human cargoes, were continually dissolving, and a wide fan of silver spray opened out in a phantom wake behind Merril and Pokrovski (1998 and 1999), like a double star transforming itself into a nova in the centre of a constellation. As the mass of the capsules diminished they sank into a closer orbit around the earth, would soon touch the denser layers of the atmosphere and plummet to the ground.

Bridgman watched the satellites as they moved towards him, his irritation with Travis forgotten. As always, he felt himself moved by the eerie but strangely serene spectacle of the ghostly convoy endlessly circling the dark sea of the midnight sky, the long-dead astronauts converging for the ten-thousandth time upon their brief rendezvous and then setting off upon their lonely flight-paths around the perimeter of the ionosphere, the tidal edge of the beachway into space which had reclaimed them.

How Louise Woodward could bear to look up at her husband he had never been able to understand. After her arrival he once invited her to the hotel, remarking that there was an excellent view of the beautiful sunsets, and she had snapped back bitterly: 'Beautiful? Can you imagine what it's like looking up at a sunset when your husband's spinning through it in his coffin?'

This reaction had been a common one when the first astronauts had died after failing to make contact with the launching platforms in fixed orbit. When these new stars rose in the west an attempt had been made to shoot them down – there was the unsettling prospect of the skies a thousand years hence, littered with orbiting refuse – but later they were left in this natural graveyard, forming their own monument.

Obscured by the clouds of dust carried up into the air by the sand-storm, the satellites shone with little more than the intensity of second-magnitude stars, winking as the reflected light was interrupted by the lanes of strato-cirrus. The wake of diffusing light behind Merril and Pokrovski which usually screened the other capsules seemed to have diminished in size, and he could see both Maiakovski and Brodisnek clearly for the first time in several months. Wondering whether Merril or Pokrovski would be the first to fall from orbit, he looked towards the centre of the cross as it passed overhead.

With a sharp intake of breath, he tilted his head back. In surprise he noticed that one of the familiar points of light was missing from the centre of the group. What he had assumed to be an occlusion of the conjoint vapour trails by dust clouds was simply due to the fact that one of the capsules – Merril's, he decided, the third of the line ahead – had fallen from its orbit.

Head raised, he sidestepped slowly across the roof, avoiding the pieces of rusting neon sign, following the convoy as it passed overhead and moved towards the eastern horizon. No longer overlaid by the wake of

Merril's capsule, Woodward's shone with far greater clarity, and almost appeared to have taken the former's place, although he was not due to fall from orbit for at least a century.

In the distance somewhere an engine growled. A moment later, from a different quarter, a woman's voice cried out faintly. Bridgman moved to the rail, over the intervening roof-tops saw two figures silhouetted against the sky on the elevator head of an apartment block, then heard Louise Woodward call out again. She was pointing up at the sky with both hands, her long hair blown about her face, Travis trying to restrain her. Bridgman realized that she had misconstrued Merril's descent, assuming that the fallen astronaut was her husband. He climbed on to the edge of the balcony, watching the pathetic tableau on the distant roof.

Again, somewhere among the dunes, an engine moaned. Before Bridgman could turn around, a brilliant blade of light cleft the sky in the south-west. Like a speeding comet, an immense train of vaporizing particles stretching behind it to the horizon, it soared towards them, the downward curve of its pathway clearly visible. Detached from the rest of the capsules, which were now disappearing among the stars along the eastern horizon, it was little more than a few miles off the ground.

Bridgman watched it approach, apparently on a collision course with the hotel. The expanding corona of white light, like a gigantic signal flare, illuminated the roof-tops, etching the letters of the neon signs over the submerged motels on the outskirts of the town. He ran for the doorway, as he raced down the stairs saw the glow of the descending capsule fill the sombre streets like a hundred moons. When he reached his room, sheltered by the massive weight of the hotel, he watched the dunes in front of the hotel light up like a stage set. Three hundred yards away the low camouflaged hull of the wardens' beach-car was revealed poised on a crest, its feeble spotlight drowned by the glare.

With a deep metallic sigh, the burning catafalque of the dead astronaut soared overhead, a cascade of vaporizing metal pouring from its hull, filling the sky with incandescent light. Reflected below it, like an expressway illuminated by an aircraft's spotlights, a long lane of light several hundred yards in width raced out into the desert towards the sea. As Bridgman shielded his eyes, it suddenly erupted in a tremendous explosion of detonating sand. A huge curtain of white dust lifted into the air and fell slowly to the ground. The sounds of the impact rolled against the hotel, mounting in a sustained crescendo that drummed against the windows. A series of smaller explosions flared up like opalescent fountains. All over the desert fires flickered briefly where fragments of the capsule had been scattered. Then the noise subsided, and an immense glistening pall of phosphorescing gas hung in the air like a silver veil, particles within it beading and winking.

Two hundred yards away across the sand was the running figure of Louise Woodward, Travis twenty paces behind her. Bridgman watched them dart in and out of the dunes, then abruptly felt the cold spotlight of the beach-car hit his face and flood the room behind him. The vehicle was moving straight towards him, two of the wardens, nets and lassos in hand, riding the outboard.

Quickly Bridgman straddled the balcony, jumped down into the sand and raced towards the crest of the first dune. He crouched and ran on through the darkness as the beam probed the air. Above, the glistening pall was slowly fading, the particles of vaporized metal sifting towards the dark Martian sand. In the distance the last echoes of the impact were still reverberating among the hotels of the beach colonies farther down the coast.

Five minutes later he caught up with Louise Woodward and Travis. The capsule's impact had flattened a number of the dunes, forming a shallow basin some quarter of a mile in diameter, and the surrounding slopes were scattered with the still glowing particles, sparkling like fading eyes. The beach-car growled somewhere four or five hundred yards behind him, and Bridgman broke off into an exhausted walk. He stopped beside Travis, who was kneeling on the ground, breath pumping into his lungs. Fifty yards away Louise Woodward was running up and down, distraughtly gazing at the fragments of smouldering metal. For a moment the spotlight of the approaching beach-car illuminated her, and she ran away among the dunes. Bridgman caught a glimpse of the inconsolable anguish in her face.

Travis was still on his knees. He had picked up a piece of the oxidized metal and was pressing it together in his hands.

'Travis, for God's sake tell her! This was Merril's capsule, there's no doubt about it! Woodward's still up there.'

Travis looked up at him silently, his eyes searching Bridgman's face. A spasm of pain tore his mouth, and Bridgman realized that the barb of steel he clasped reverently in his hands was still glowing with heat.

'Travis!' He tried to pull the man's hands apart, the pungent stench of burning flesh gusting into his face, but Travis wrenched away from him. 'Leave her alone, Bridgman! Go back with the wardens!'

Bridgman retreated from the approaching beach-car. Only thirty yards away, its spotlight filled the basin. Louise Woodward was still searching the dunes. Travis held his ground as the wardens jumped down from the car and advanced towards him with their nets, his bloodied hands raised at his sides, the steel barb flashing like a dagger. At the head of the wardens, the only one unmasked was a trim, neat-featured man with an intent, serious face. Bridgman guessed that this was Major Webster, and that the wardens had known of the impending impact and hoped to capture them, and Louise in particular, before it occurred.

Bridgman stumbled back towards the dunes at the edge of the basin. As he neared the crest he trapped his foot in a semicircular plate of metal, sat down and freed his heel. Unmistakably it was part of a control panel, the circular instrument housings still intact.

Overhead the pall of glistening vapour had moved off to the north-east, and the reflected light was directly over the rusting gantries of the former launching site at Cape Canaveral. For a few fleeting seconds the gantries seemed to be enveloped in a sheen of silver, transfigured by the vaporized body of the dead astronaut, diffusing over them in a farewell gesture, his final return to the site from which he had set off to his death a century earlier. Then the gantries sank again into their craggy shadows, and the pall moved off like an immense wraith towards the sea, barely distinguishable from the star glow.

Down below Travis was sitting on the ground surrounded by the wardens. He scuttled about on his hands like a frantic crab, scooping handfuls of the virus-laden sand at them. Holding tight to their masks, the wardens manoeuvred around him, their nets and lassos at the ready. Another group moved slowly towards Bridgman.

Bridgman picked up a handful of the dark Martian sand beside the instrument panel, felt the soft glowing crystals warm his palm. In his mind he could still see the silver-sheathed gantries of the launching site across the bay, by a curious illusion almost identical with the Martian city he had designed years earlier. He watched the pall disappear over the sea, then looked around at the other remnants of Merril's capsule scattered over the slopes. High in the western night, between Pegasus and Cygnus, shone the distant disc of the planet Mars, which for both himself and the dead astronaut had served for so long as a symbol of unattained ambition. The wind stirred softly through the sand, cooling this replica of the planet which lay passively around him, and at last he understood why he had come to the beach and been unable to leave it.

Twenty yards away Travis was being dragged off like a wild dog, his thrashing body pinioned in the centre of a web of lassos. Louise Woodward had run away among the dunes towards the sea, following the vanished gas cloud.

In a sudden access of refound confidence, Bridgman drove his fist into the dark sand, buried his forearm like a foundation pillar. A flange of hot metal from Merril's capsule burned his wrist, bonding him to the spirit of the dead astronaut. Scattered around him on the Martian sand, in a sense Merril had reached Mars after all.

'Damn it!' he cried exultantly to himself as the wardens' lassos stung his neck and shoulders. 'We made it!'

**1962**

# THE WATCH-TOWERS

The next day, for some reason, there was a sudden increase of activity in the watch-towers. This began during the latter half of the morning, and by noon, when Renthall left the hotel on his way to see Mrs Osmond, seemed to have reached its peak. People were standing at their windows and balconies along both sides of the street, whispering agitatedly to each other behind the curtains and pointing up into the sky.

Renthall usually tried to ignore the watch-towers, resenting even the smallest concession to the fact of their existence, but at the bottom of the street, where he was hidden in the shadow thrown by one of the houses, he stopped and craned his head up at the nearest tower.

A hundred feet away from him, it hung over the Public Library, its tip poised no more than twenty feet above the roof. The glass-enclosed cabin in the lowest tier appeared to be full of observers, opening and shutting the windows and shifting about what Renthall assumed were huge pieces of optical equipment. He looked around at the further towers, suspended from the sky at three hundred foot intervals in every direction, noticing an occasional flash of light as a window turned and caught the sun.

An elderly man wearing a shabby black suit and wing collar, who usually loitered outside the library, came across the street to Renthall and backed into the shadows beside him.

'They're up to something all right.' He cupped his hands over his eyes and peered up anxiously at the watch-towers. 'I've never seen them like this as long as I can remember.'

Renthall studied his face. However alarmed, he was obviously relieved by the signs of activity. 'I shouldn't worry unduly,' Renthall told him. 'It's a change to see something going on at all.'

Before the other could reply he turned on his heel and strode away along the pavement. It took him ten minutes to reach the street in which Mrs Osmond lived, and he fixed his eyes firmly on the ground, ignoring the few passers-by. Although dominated by the watch-towers – four of them hung in a line exactly down its centre – the street was almost deserted. Half the houses were untenanted and falling into what would soon be an irreversible state of disrepair. Usually Renthall assessed each property carefully, trying to decide whether to leave his hotel and take one of them, but the movement in the watch-towers had caused him more anxiety than he was prepared to admit, and the terrace of houses passed unnoticed.

Mrs Osmond's house stood halfway down the street, its gate swinging loosely on its rusty hinges. Renthall hesitated under the plane tree growing by the edge of the pavement, and then crossed the narrow garden and quickly let himself through the door.

Mrs Osmond invariably spent the afternoon sitting out on the veranda in the sun, gazing at the weeds in the back garden, but today she had retreated to a corner of the sitting room. She was sorting a suitcase full of old papers when Renthall came in.

Renthall made no attempt to embrace her and wandered over to the window. Mrs Osmond had half drawn the curtains and he pulled them back. There was a watch-tower ninety feet away, almost directly ahead, hanging over the parallel terrace of empty houses. The lines of towers receded diagonally from left to right towards the horizon, partly obscured by the bright haze.

'Do you think you should have come today?' Mrs Osmond asked, shifting her plump hips nervously in the chair.

'Why not?' Renthall said, scanning the towers, hands loosely in his pockets.

'But if they're going to keep a closer watch on us now they'll notice you coming here.'

'I shouldn't believe all the rumours you hear,' Renthall told her calmly.

'What do you think it means then?'

'I've absolutely no idea. Their movements may be as random and meaningless as our own.' Renthall shrugged. 'Perhaps they *are* going to keep a closer watch on us. What does it matter if all they do is stare?'

'Then you mustn't come here any more!' Mrs Osmond protested.

'Why? I hardly believe they can see through walls.'

'They're not that stupid,' Mrs Osmond said irritably. 'They'll soon put two and two together, if they haven't already.'

Renthall took his eyes off the tower and looked down at Mrs Osmond patiently. 'My dear, this house isn't tapped. For all they know we may be darning our prayer rugs or discussing the endocrine system of the tapeworm.'

'Not you, Charles,' Mrs Osmond said with a short laugh. 'Not if they know you.' Evidently pleased by this sally, she relaxed and took a cigarette out of the box on the table.

'Perhaps they don't know me,' Renthall said dryly. 'In fact, I'm quite sure they don't. If they did I can't believe I should still be here.'

He noticed himself stooping, a reliable sign that he was worrying, and went over to the sofa.

'Is the school going to start tomorrow?' Mrs Osmond asked when he had disposed his long, thin legs around the table.

'It should do,' Renthall said. 'Hanson went down to the Town Hall this morning, but as usual they had little idea of what was going on.'

He opened his jacket and pulled out of the inner pocket an old but neatly folded copy of a woman's magazine.

'Charles!' Mrs Osmond exclaimed. 'Where did you get this?'

She took it from Renthall and started leafing through the soiled pages.

'One of my sources,' Renthall said. From the sofa he could still see the watch-tower over the houses opposite. 'Georgina Simons. She has a library of them.'

He rose, went over to the window and drew the curtains across.

'Charles, don't. I can't see.'

'Read it later,' Renthall told her. He lay back on the sofa again. 'Are you coming to the recital this afternoon?'

'Hasn't it been cancelled?' Mrs Osmond asked, putting the magazine down reluctantly.

'No, of course not.'

'Charles, I don't think I want to go.' Mrs Osmond frowned. 'What records is Hanson going to play?'

'Some Tchaikovsky. And Grieg.' He tried to make it sound interesting. 'You must come. We can't just sit about subsiding into this state of boredom and uselessness.'

'I know,' Mrs Osmond said fractiously. 'But I don't feel like it. Not today. All those records bore me. I've heard them so often.'

'They bore me too. But at least it's something to do.' He put an arm around Mrs Osmond's shoulders and began to play with the darker unbleached hair behind her ears, tapping the large nickel ear-rings she wore and listening to them tinkle.

When he put his hand on to her knee Mrs Osmond stood up and prowled aimlessly around the room, straightening her skirt.

'Julia, what is the matter with you?' Renthall asked irritably. 'Have you got a headache?'

Mrs Osmond was by the window, gazing up at the watch-towers. 'Do you think they're going to come down?'

'Of course not!' Renthall snapped. 'Where on earth did you get that idea?'

Suddenly he felt unbearably exasperated. The confined dimensions of the dusty sitting-room seemed to suffocate reason. He stood up and buttoned his jacket. 'I'll see you this afternoon at the Institute, Julia. The recital starts at three.'

Mrs Osmond nodded vaguely, unfastened the french windows and ambled forwards across the veranda into full view of the watch-towers, the glassy expression on her face like a supplicant nun's.

As Renthall had expected, the school did not open the next day. When they tired of hanging around the hotel after breakfast he and Hanson went down to the Town Hall. The building was almost empty and the only official they were able to find was unhelpful.

'We have no instructions at present,' he told them, 'but as soon as the term starts you will be notified. Though from what I hear the postponement is to be indefinite.'

'Is that the committee's decision?' Renthall asked. 'Or just another of the town clerk's brilliant extemporizings?'

'The school committee is no longer meeting,' the official said. 'I'm afraid the town clerk isn't here today.' Before Renthall could speak he added: 'You will, of course, continue to draw your salaries. Perhaps you would care to call in at the treasurer's department on your way out?'

Renthall and Hanson left and looked about for a café. Finally they found one that was open and sat under the awning, staring vacantly at the watch-towers hanging over the roof-tops around them. Their activity had lessened considerably since the previous day. The nearest tower was only fifty feet away, immediately above a disused office building on the other side of the street. The windows in the observation tier remained shut, but every few minutes Renthall noticed a shadow moving behind the panes.

Eventually a waitress came out to them, and Renthall ordered coffee.

'I think I shall have to give a few lessons,' Hanson remarked. 'All this leisure is becoming too much of a good thing.'

'It's an idea,' Renthall agreed. 'If you can find anyone interested. I'm sorry the recital yesterday was such a flop.'

Hanson shrugged. 'I'll see if I can get hold of some new records. By the way, I thought Julia looked very handsome yesterday.'

Renthall acknowledged the compliment with a slight bow of his head. 'I'd like to take her out more often.'

'Do you think that's wise?'

'Why on earth not?'

'Well, just at present, you know.' Hanson inclined a finger at the watch-towers.

'I don't see that it matters particularly,' Renthall said. He disliked personal confidences and was about to change the subject when Hanson leaned forward across the table.

'Perhaps not, but I gather there was some mention of you at the last Council meeting. One or two members were rather critical of your little *ménage à deux*.' He smiled thinly at Renthall, who was frowning into his coffee. 'Sheer spite, no doubt, but your behaviour is a little idiosyncratic.'

Controlling himself, Renthall pushed away the coffee cup. 'Do you mind telling me what damned business it is of theirs?'

Hanson laughed. 'None, really, except that they are the executive authority, and I suppose we should take our cue from them.' Renthall snorted at this, and Hanson went on: 'As a matter of interest, you may receive an official directive over the next few days.'

'A *what*?' Renthall exploded. He sat back, shaking his head incredulously. 'Are you serious?' When Hanson nodded he began to laugh harshly.

'Those idiots! I don't know why we put up with them. Sometimes their stupidity positively staggers me.'

'Steady on,' Hanson demurred. 'I do see their point. Bearing in mind the big commotion in the watch-towers yesterday the Council probably feel we shouldn't do anything that might antagonize them. You never know, they may even be acting on official instructions.'

Renthall glanced contemptuously at Hanson. 'Do you *really* believe that nonsense about the Council being in touch with the watch-towers? It may give a few simpletons a sense of security, but for heaven's sake don't try it on me. My patience is just about exhausted.' He watched Hanson carefully, wondering which of the Council members had provided him with his information. The lack of subtlety depressed him painfully. 'However, thanks for warning me. I suppose it means there'll be an overpowering air of embarrassment when Julia and I go to the cinema tomorrow.'

Hanson shook his head. 'No. Actually the performance has been cancelled. In view of yesterday's disturbances.'

'But why –?' Renthall slumped back. 'Haven't they got the intelligence to realize that it's just at this sort of time that we need every social get-together we can organize? People are hiding away in their back bedrooms like a lot of frightened ghosts. We've got to bring them out, give them something that will pull them together.'

He gazed up thoughtfully at the watch-tower across the street. Shadows circulated behind the frosted panes of the observation windows. 'Some sort of gala, say, or a garden fête. Who could organize it, though?'

Hanson pushed back his chair. 'Careful, Charles. I don't know whether the Council would altogether approve.'

'I'm sure they wouldn't.' After Hanson had left he remained at the table and returned to his solitary contemplation of the watch-towers.

For half an hour Renthall sat at the table, playing absently with his empty coffee cup and watching the few people who passed along the street. No one else visited the café, and he was glad to be able to pursue his thoughts alone, in this miniature urban vacuum, with nothing to intervene between himself and the lines of watch-towers stretching into the haze beyond the roof-tops.

With the exception of Mrs Osmond, Renthall had virtually no close friends in whom to confide. With his sharp intelligence and impatience with trivialities, Renthall was one of those men with whom others find it difficult to relax. A certain innate condescension, a reserved but unmistakable attitude of superiority held them away from him, though few people regarded him as anything but a shabby pedagogue. At the hotel he kept to himself. There was little social contact between the guests; in the lounge and dining room they sat immersed in their old newspapers and magazines, occasionally murmuring quietly to each other. The only thing which could mobilize the simultaneous communion of the guests was some untoward activity in the watch-towers, and at such times Renthall always maintained an absolute silence.

Just before he stood up a square thick-set figure approached down the street. Renthall recognized the man and was about to turn his seat to avoid having to greet him, but something about his expression made him lean forward. Fleshy and dark-jowled, the man walked with an easy, rolling gait, his double-breasted check overcoat open to reveal a well-tended midriff. This was Victor Boardman, owner of the local flea-pit cinema, sometime bootlegger and procurer at large.

Renthall had never spoken to him, but he was aware that Boardman shared with him the distinction of bearing the stigma of the Council's disapproval. Hanson claimed that the Council had successfully stamped out Boardman's illicit activities, but the latter's permanent expression of smug contempt for the rest of the world seemed to belie this.

As he passed they exchanged glances, and Boardman's face broke momentarily into a knowing smirk. It was obviously directed at Renthall, and implied a pre-judgement of some event about which Renthall as yet knew nothing, presumably his coming collision with the Council. Obviously Boardman expected him to capitulate to the Council without a murmur.

Annoyed, Renthall turned his back on Boardman, then watched him over his shoulder as he padded off down the street, his easy relaxed shoulders swaying from side to side.

The following day the activity in the watch-towers had subsided entirely. The blue haze from which they extended was brighter than it had been for several months, and the air in the streets seemed to sparkle with the light reflected off the observation windows. There was no sign of movement among them, and the sky had a rigid, uniform appearance that indicated an indefinite lull.

For some reason, however, Renthall found himself more nervous than he had been for some time. The school had not yet opened, but he felt strangely reluctant to visit Mrs Osmond and remained indoors all morning, shunning the streets as if avoiding some invisible shadow of guilt.

The long lines of watch-towers stretching endlessly from one horizon to the other reminded him that he could soon expect to receive the Council's 'directive' – Hanson would not have mentioned it by accident – and it was always during the lulls that the Council was most active in consolidating its position, issuing a stream of petty regulations and amendments.

Renthall would have liked to challenge the Council's authority on some formal matter unconnected with himself – the validity, for example, of one of the byelaws prohibiting public assemblies in the street – but the prospect of all the intrigue involved in canvassing the necessary support bored him utterly. Although none of them individually would challenge the Council, most people would have been glad to see it toppled, but there seemed to be no likely focus for their opposition. Apart from the fear that the Council was in touch with the watch-towers, no one would stand up for Renthall's right to carry on his affair with Mrs Osmond.

Curiously enough, she seemed unaware of these cross-currents when he went to see her that afternoon. She had cleaned the house and was in high humour, the windows wide open to the brilliant air.

'Charles, what's the matter with you?' she chided him when he slumped inertly into a chair. 'You look like a broody hen.'

'I felt rather tired this morning. It's probably the hot weather.' When she sat down on the arm of the chair he put one hand listlessly on her hip, trying to summon together his energies. 'Recently I've been developing an *idée fixe* about the Council, I must be going through a crisis of confidence. I need some method of reasserting myself.'

Mrs Osmond stroked his hair soothingly with her cool fingers, her eyes watching him silkily. 'What *you* need, Charles, is a little mother love. You're so isolated at that hotel, among all those old people. Why don't you rent one of the houses in this road? I'd be able to look after you then.'

Renthall glanced up at her sardonically. 'Perhaps I could move in here?' he asked, but she tossed her head back with a derisive snort and went over to the window.

She gazed up at the nearest watch-tower a hundred feet away, its windows closed and silent, the great shaft disappearing into the haze. 'What do you suppose they're thinking about?'

Renthall snapped his fingers off-handedly. 'They're probably not thinking about anything. Sometimes I wonder whether there's anyone there at all. The movements we see may be just optical illusions. Although the windows appear to open no one's ever actually *seen* any of them. For all we know this place may well be nothing more than an abandoned zoo.'

Mrs Osmond regarded him with rueful amusement. 'Charles, you do pick some extraordinary metaphors. I often doubt if you're like the rest of us, I wouldn't dare say the sort of things you do in case –' She broke off, glancing up involuntarily at the watch-towers hanging from the sky.

Idly, Renthall asked: 'In case what?'

'Well, in case –' Irritably, she said: 'Don't be absurd, Charles, doesn't the thought of those towers hanging down over us frighten you at all?'

Renthall turned his head slowly and stared up at the watch-towers. Once he had tried to count them, but there seemed little point. 'Yes, they frighten me,' he said noncommittally. 'In the same way that Hanson and the old people at the hotel and everyone else here does. But not in the sense that the boys at school are frightened of *me*.'

Mrs Osmond nodded, misinterpreting this last remark. 'Children are very perceptive, Charles. They probably know you're not interested in them. Unfortunately they're not old enough to understand what the watch-towers mean.'

She gave a slight shiver, and pulled her cardigan around her shoulders. 'You know, on the days when they're busy behind their windows I can hardly move around, it's terrible. I feel so listless, all I want to do is sit and stare at the wall. Perhaps I'm more sensitive to their, er, radiations than most people.'

Renthall smiled. 'You must be. Don't let them depress you. Next time why don't you put on a paper hat and do a pirouette?'

'What? Oh, Charles, stop being cynical.'

'I'm not. Seriously, Julia, do you think it would make any difference?'

Mrs Osmond shook her head sadly. 'You try, Charles, and then tell me. Where are you going?'

Renthall paused at the window. 'Back to the hotel to rest. By the way, do you know Victor Boardman?'

'I used to, once. Why, what are you getting up to with him?'

'Does he own the garden next to the cinema car park?'

'I think so.' Mrs Osmond laughed. 'Are you going to take up gardening?'

'In a sense.' With a wave, Renthall left.

He began with Dr Clifton, whose room was directly below his own. Clifton's duties at his surgery occupied him for little more than an hour a day – there were virtually no deaths or illnesses – but he still retained sufficient initiative to cultivate a hobby. He had turned one end of his room into a small aviary, containing a dozen canaries, and spent much of his time trying to teach them tricks. His acerbic, matter-of-fact manner always tired Renthall, but he respected the doctor for not sliding into total lethargy like everyone else.

Clifton considered his suggestion carefully. 'I agree with you, something of the sort is probably necessary. A good idea, Renthall. Properly conducted, it might well provide just the lift people need.'

'The main question, Doctor, is one of organization. The only suitable place is the Town Hall.'

Clifton nodded. 'Yes, there's your problem. I'm afraid I've no influence with the Council, if that's what you're suggesting. I don't know what you can do. You'll have to get their permission of course, and in the past they haven't shown themselves to be very radical or original. They prefer to maintain the *status quo.*'

Renthall nodded, then added casually: 'They're only interested in maintaining their own power. At times I become rather tired of our Council.'

Clifton glanced at him and then turned back to his cages. 'You're preaching revolution, Renthall,' he said quietly, a forefinger stroking the beak of one of the canaries. Pointedly, he refrained from seeing Renthall to the door.

Writing the doctor off, Renthall rested for a few minutes in his room, pacing up and down the strip of faded carpet, then went down to the basement to see the manager, Mulvaney.

'I'm only making some initial inquiries. As yet I haven't applied for permission, but Dr Clifton thinks the idea is excellent, and there's no doubt we'll get it. Are you up to looking after the catering?'

Mulvaney's sallow face watched Renthall sceptically. 'Of course I'm up to it, but how serious are you?' He leaned against his roll-top desk. 'You think you'll get permission? You're wrong, Mr Renthall, the Council wouldn't stand for the idea. They even closed the cinema, so they're not likely to allow a public party. Before you know what you'd have people dancing.'

'I hardly think so, but does the idea appal you so much?'

Mulvaney shook his head, already bored with Renthall. 'You get a permit, Mr Renthall, and then we can talk seriously.'

Tightening his voice, Renthall asked: 'Is it necessary to get the Council's permission? Couldn't we go ahead without?'

Without looking up, Mulvaney sat down at his desk. 'Keep trying, Mr Renthall, it's a great idea.'

During the next few days Renthall pursued his inquiries, in all approaching some half-dozen people. In general he met with the same negative response, but as he intended he soon noticed a subtle but nonetheless distinct quickening of interest around him. The usual fragmentary murmur of conversation would fade away abruptly as he passed the tables in the dining room, and the service was fractionally more prompt. Hanson no longer took coffee with him in the mornings, and once Renthall saw him in guarded conversation with the town clerk's secretary, a young man called Barnes. This, he assumed, was Hanson's contact.

In the meantime the activity in the watch-towers remained at zero. The endless lines of towers hung down from the bright, hazy sky, the observation windows closed, and the people in the streets below sank slowly into their usual mindless torpor, wandering from hotel to library to café. Determined on his course of action, Renthall felt his confidence return.

Allowing an interval of a week to elapse, he finally called upon Victor Boardman.

The bootlegger received him in his office above the cinema, greeting him with a wry smile.

'Well, Mr Renthall, I hear you're going into the entertainment business. Drunken gambols and all that. I'm surprised at you.'

'A fête,' Renthall corrected. The seat Boardman had offered him faced towards the window – deliberately, he guessed – and provided an uninterrupted view of the watch-tower over the roof of the adjacent furniture store. Only forty feet away, it blocked off half the sky. The metal plates which formed its rectangular sides were annealed together by some process Renthall was unable to identify, neither welded nor riveted, almost as if the entire tower had been cast *in situ*. He moved to another chair so that his back was to the window.

'The school is still closed, so I thought I'd try to make myself useful. That's what I'm paid for. I've come to you because you've had a good deal of experience.'

'Yes, I've had a lot of experience, Mr Renthall. Very varied. As one of the Council's employees, I take it you have its permission?'

Renthall evaded this. 'The Council is naturally a conservative body, Mr Boardman. Obviously at this stage I'm acting on my own initiative. I shall consult the Council at the appropriate moment later, when I can offer them a practicable proposition.'

Boardman nodded sagely. 'That's sensible, Mr Renthall. Now what exactly do you want me to do? Organize the whole thing for you?'

'No, but naturally I'd be very grateful if you would. For the present I merely want to ask permission to hold the fête on a piece of your property.'

'The cinema? I'm not going to take all those seats out, if that's what you're after.'

'Not the cinema. Though we could use the bar and cloakrooms,' Renthall extemporized, hoping the scheme did not sound too grandiose. 'Is the old beer-garden next to the car park your property?'

For a moment Boardman was silent. He watched Renthall shrewdly, picking his nails with his cigar-cutter, a faint suggestion of admiration in his eyes. 'So you want to hold the fête in the open, Mr Renthall? Is that it?'

Renthall nodded, smiling back at Boardman. 'I'm glad to see you living up to your reputation for getting quickly to the point. Are you prepared to lend the garden? Of course, you'll have a big share of the profits. In fact, if it's any inducement, you can have all the profits.'

Boardman put out his cigar. 'Mr Renthall, you're obviously a man of many parts. I underestimated you. I thought you merely had a grievance against the Council. I hope you know what you're doing.'

'Mr Boardman, will you lend the garden?' Renthall repeated.

There was an amused but thoughtful smile on Boardman's lips as he regarded the watch-tower framed by the window. 'There are two watch-towers directly over the beer-garden, Mr Renthall.'

'I'm fully aware of that. It's obviously the chief attraction of the property. Now, can you give me an answer?'

The two men regarded each other silently, and then Boardman gave an almost imperceptible nod. Renthall realized that his scheme was being taken seriously by Boardman. He was obviously using Renthall for his own purposes, for once having flaunted the Council's authority he would be able to resume all his other, more profitable activities. Of course, the fête would never be held, but in answer to Boardman's questions he outlined a provisional programme. They fixed the date of the fête at a month ahead, and arranged to meet again at the beginning of the next week.

Two days later, as he expected, the first emissaries of the Council came to see him.

He was waiting at his usual table on the café terrace, the silent watch-towers suspended from the air around him, when he saw Hanson hurrying along the street.

'Do join me.' Renthall drew a chair back. 'What's the news?'

'Nothing – though you should know, Charles.' He gave Renthall a dry smile, as if admonishing a favourite pupil, then gazed about the empty terrace for the waitress. 'Service is appallingly bad here. Tell me, Charles, what's all this talk about you and Victor Boardman. I could hardly believe my ears.'

Renthall leaned back in his chair. 'I don't know, you tell me.'

'We – er, I was wondering if Boardman was taking advantage of some perfectly innocent remark he might have overheard. This business of a garden party you're supposed to be organizing with him – it sounds absolutely fantastic.'

'Why?'

'But Charles.' Hanson leaned forward to examine Renthall carefully, trying to make sense of his unruffled pose. 'Surely you aren't serious?'

'But why not? If I want to, why shouldn't I organize a garden party – fête, to be more accurate?'

'It doesn't make an iota of difference,' Hanson said tartly. 'Apart from any other reason' – here he glanced skyward – 'the fact remains that you are an employee of the Council.'

Hands in his trouser-pockets, Renthall tipped back his chair. 'But that gives them no mandate to interfere in my private life. You seem to be forgetting, but the terms of my contract specifically exclude any such authority. I am not on the established grade, as my salary differential shows. If the Council disapprove, the only sanction they can apply is to give me the sack.'

'They will, Charles, don't sound so smug.'

Renthall let this pass. 'Fair enough, if they can find anyone else to take on the job. Frankly I doubt it. They've managed to swallow their moral scruples in the past.'

'Charles, this is different. As long as you're discreet no one gives a hoot about your private affairs, but this garden party is a public matter, and well within the Council's province.'

Renthall yawned. 'I'm rather bored with the subject of the Council. Technically, the fête will be a private affair, by invitation only. They've no statutory right to be consulted at all. If a breach of the peace takes place the Chief Constable can take action. Why all the fuss, anyway? I'm merely trying to provide a little harmless festivity.'

Hanson shook his head. 'Charles, you're deliberately evading the point. According to Boardman this fête will take place out of doors – directly under two of the watch-towers. Have you realized what the repercussions would be?'

'Yes.' Renthall formed the word carefully in his mouth. 'Nothing. Absolutely nothing.'

'Charles!' Hanson lowered his head at this apparent blasphemy, glanced up at the watch-towers over the street as if expecting instant retribution to descend from them. 'Look, my dear fellow, take my advice. Drop the whole idea. You don't stand a chance anyway of ever holding this mad jape, so why deliberately court trouble with the Council? Who knows what their real power would be if they were provoked?'

Renthall rose from his seat. He looked up at the watch-tower hanging from the air on the other side of the road, controlling himself when a slight pang of anxiety stirred his heart. 'I'll send you an invitation,' he called back, then walked away to his hotel.

The next afternoon the town clerk's secretary called upon him in his room. During the interval, no doubt intended as a salutary pause for reflection, Renthall had remained at the hotel, reading quietly in his armchair. He paid one brief visit to Mrs Osmond, but she seemed nervous and irritable, evidently aware of the imminent clash. The strain of maintaining an appearance of unconcern had begun to tire Renthall, and he avoided the open streets whenever possible. Fortunately the school had still not opened.

Barnes, the dapper dark-haired secretary, came straight to the point. Refusing Renthall's offer of an armchair, he held a sheet of pink duplicated paper in his hand, apparently a minute of the last Council meeting.

'Mr Renthall, the Council has been informed of your intention to hold a garden fête in some three weeks' time. I have been asked by the chairman of the Watch Committee to express the committee's grave misgivings, and to request you accordingly to terminate all arrangements and cancel the fête immediately, pending an inquiry.'

'I'm sorry, Barnes, but I'm afraid our preparations are too far advanced. We're about to issue invitations.'

Barnes hesitated, casting his eye around Renthall's faded room and few shabby books as if hoping to find some ulterior motive for Renthall's behaviour.

'Mr Renthall, perhaps I could explain that this request is tantamount to a direct order from the Council.'

'So I'm aware.' Renthall sat down on his window-sill and gazed out at the watch-towers. 'Hanson and I went over all this, as you probably know. The Council have no more right to order me to cancel this fête than they have to stop me walking down the street.'

Barnes smiled his thin bureaucratic smirk. 'Mr Renthall, this is not a matter of the Council's statutory jurisdiction. This order is issued by virtue of the authority vested in it by its superiors. If you prefer, you can assume that the Council is merely passing on a direct instruction it has received.' He inclined his head towards the watch-towers.

Renthall stood up. 'Now we're at last getting down to business.' He gathered himself together. 'Perhaps you could tell the Council to convey to its superiors, as you call them, my polite but firm refusal. Do you get *my* point?'

Barnes retreated fractionally. He summed Renthall up carefully, then nodded. 'I think so, Mr Renthall. No doubt you understand what you're doing.'

After he had gone Renthall drew the blinds over the window and lay down on his bed; for the next hour he made an effort to relax.

His final showdown with the Council was to take place the following day. Summoned to an emergency meeting of the Watch Committee, he accepted the invitation with alacrity, certain that with every member of the committee present the main council chamber would be used. This would give him a perfect opportunity to humiliate the Council by publicly calling their bluff.

Both Hanson and Mrs Osmond assumed that he would capitulate without argument.

'Well, Charles, you brought it upon yourself,' Hanson told him. 'Still, I expect they'll be lenient with you. It's a matter of face now.'

'More than that, I hope,' Renthall replied. 'They claim they were passing on a direct instruction from the watch-towers.'

'Well, yes . . .' Hanson gestured vaguely. 'Of course. Obviously the towers wouldn't intervene in such a trivial matter. They rely on the Council to keep a watching brief for them, as long as the Council's authority is respected they're prepared to remain aloof.'

'It sounds an ideally simple arrangement. How do you think the communication between the Council and the watch-towers takes place?' Renthall pointed to the watch-tower across the street from the cabin. The shuttered observation tier hung emptily in the air like an out-of-season gondola. 'By telephone? Or do they semaphore?'

But Hanson merely laughed and changed the subject.

Julia Osmond was equally vague, but equally convinced of the Council's infallibility.

'Of course they receive instructions from the towers, Charles. But don't worry, they obviously have a sense of proportion – they've been letting you come here all this time.' She turned a monitory finger at Renthall, her broad-hipped bulk obscuring the towers from him. 'That's your chief fault, Charles. You think you're more important than you are. Look at you now, sitting there all hunched up with your face like an old shoe. You think the Council and the watch-towers are going to give you some terrible punishment. But they won't, because you're not worth it.'

Renthall picked uneagerly at his lunch at the hotel, conscious of the guests watching from the tables around him. Many had brought visitors with them, and he guessed that there would be a full attendance at the meeting that afternoon.

After lunch he retired to his room, made a desultory attempt to read until the meeting at half past two. Outside, the watch-towers hung in their long lines from the bright haze. There was no sign of movement in the observation windows, and Renthall studied them openly, hands in pockets, like a general surveying the dispositions of his enemy's forces. The haze was lower than usual, filling the interstices between the towers, so that in the distance, where the free space below their tips was hidden by the intervening roof-tops, the towers seemed to rise upwards into the air like rectangular chimneys over an industrial landscape, wreathed in white smoke.

The nearest tower was about seventy-five feet away, diagonally to his left, over the eastern end of the open garden shared by the other hotels in the crescent. Just as Renthall turned away, one of the windows in the observation deck appeared to open, the opaque glass pane throwing a spear of sharp sunlight directly towards him. Renthall flinched back, heart suddenly surging, then leaned forward again. The activity in the tower had subsided as instantly as it had arisen. The windows were sealed, no signs of movement behind them. Renthall listened to the sounds from the rooms above and below him. So conspicuous a motion of the window, the first sign of activity for many days, and a certain indication of more to come, should have brought a concerted rush to the balconies. But the hotel was silent, and below he could hear Dr Clifton at his cages by the window, humming absently to himself.

Renthall scanned the windows on the other side of the garden but the lines of craning faces he expected were absent. He examined the watch-tower carefully, assuming that he had seen a window open in a hotel near by. Yet the explanation dissatisfied him. The ray of sunlight had cleft the air like a silver blade, with a curious luminous intensity that only the windows of the watch-towers seemed able to reflect, aimed unerringly at his head.

He broke off to glance at his watch, cursed when he saw that it was after a quarter past two. The Town Hall was a good half-mile away, and he would arrive dishevelled and perspiring.

There was a knock on his door. He opened it to find Mulvaney. 'What is it? I'm busy now.'

'Sorry, Mr Renthall. A man called Barnes from the Council asked me to give you an urgent message. He said the meeting this afternoon has been postponed.'

'Ha!' Leaving the door open, Renthall snapped his fingers contemptuously at the air. 'So they've had second thoughts after all. Discretion is the better part of valour.' Smiling broadly, he called Mulvaney back into his room. 'Mr Mulvaney! Just a moment!'

'Good news, Mr Renthall?'

'Excellent. I've got them on the run.' He added: 'You wait and see, the next meeting of the Watch Committee will be held in private.'

'You might be right, Mr Renthall. Some people think they have over-reached themselves a bit.'

'Really? That's rather interesting. Good.' Renthall noted this mentally, then gestured Mulvaney over to the window. 'Tell me, Mr Mulvaney, just now while you were coming up the stairs, did you notice any activity out there?'

He gestured briefly towards the tower, not wanting to draw attention to himself by pointing at it. Mulvaney gazed out over the garden, shaking his head slowly. 'Can't say I did, not more than usual. What sort of activity?'

'You know, a window opening ...' When Mulvaney continued to shake his head, Renthall said: 'Good. Let me know if that fellow Barnes calls again.'

When Mulvaney had gone he strode up and down the room, whistling a Mozart rondo.

Over the next three days, however, the mood of elation gradually faded. To Renthall's annoyance no further date was fixed for the cancelled committee meeting. He had assumed that it would be held *in camera*, but the members must have realized that it would make little difference. Everyone would soon know that Renthall had successfully challenged their claim to be in communication with the watch-towers.

Renthall chafed at the possibility that the meeting had been postponed indefinitely. By avoiding a direct clash with Renthall the Council had cleverly side-stepped the danger before them.

Alternatively, Renthall speculated whether he had underestimated them. Perhaps they realized that the real target of his defiance was not the Council, but the watch-towers. The faint possibility – however hard he tried to dismiss it as childish fantasy the fear still persisted – that there *was* some mysterious collusion between the towers and the Council now began to grow in his mind. The fête had been cleverly conceived as an innocent gesture of defiance towards the towers, and it would be difficult to find something to take its place that would not be blatantly outrageous and stain him indelibly with the sin of hubris.

Besides, as he carefully reminded himself, he was not out to launch open rebellion. Originally he had reacted from a momentary feeling of pique, exasperated by the spectacle of the boredom and lethargy around him and the sullen fear with which everyone viewed the towers. There was no question of challenging their absolute authority – at least, not at this stage. He merely wanted to define the existential margins of their world – if they *were* caught in a trap, let them at least eat the cheese. Also, he calculated that it would take an affront of truly heroic scale to provoke any reaction from the watch-towers, and that a certain freedom by default was theirs, a small but valuable credit to their account built into the system.

In practical, existential terms this might well be considerable, so that the effective boundary between black and white, between good and evil, was drawn some distance from the theoretical boundary. This watershed was the penumbral zone where the majority of the quickening pleasures of life were to be found, and where Renthall was most at home. Mrs Osmond's villa lay well within its territory, and Renthall would have liked to move himself over its margins. First, though, he would have to assess the extent of this 'blue' shift, or moral parallax, but by cancelling the committee meeting the Council had effectively forestalled him.

As he waited for Barnes to call again a growing sense of frustration came over him. The watch-towers seemed to fill the sky, and he drew the blinds irritably. On the flat roof, two floors above, a continuous light hammering sounded all day, but he shunned the streets and no longer went to the café for his morning coffee.

Finally he climbed the stairs to the roof, through the doorway saw two carpenters working under Mulvaney's supervision. They were laying a rough board floor over the tarred cement. As he shielded his eyes from the bright glare a third man came up the stairs behind him, carrying two sections of wooden railing.

'Sorry about the noise, Mr Renthall,' Mulvaney apologized. 'We should be finished by tomorrow.'

'What's going on?' Renthall asked. 'Surely you're not putting a sun garden here.'

'That's the idea.' Mulvaney pointed to the railings. 'A few chairs and umbrellas, be pleasant for the old folk. Dr Clifton suggested it.' He peered down at Renthall, who was still hiding in the doorway. 'You'll have to bring a chair up here yourself, you look as if you could use a little sunshine.'

Renthall raised his eyes to the watch-tower almost directly over their heads. A pebble tossed underhand would easily have rebounded off the corrugated metal underside. The roof was completely exposed to the score of watch-towers hanging in the air around them, and he wondered whether Mulvaney was out of his mind – none of the old people would sit there for more than a second.

Mulvaney pointed to a roof-top on the other side of the garden, where similar activity was taking place. A bright yellow awning was being unfurled, and two seats were already occupied.

Renthall hesitated, lowering his voice. 'But what about the watch-towers?'

'The what –?' Distracted by one of the carpenters, Mulvaney turned away for a moment, then rejoined him. 'Yes, you'll be able to watch everything going on from up here, Mr Renthall.'

Puzzled, Renthall made his way back to his room. Had Mulvaney misheard his question, or was this a fatuous attempt to provoke the towers? Renthall grimly visualized his responsibility if a whole series of petty acts of defiance took place. Perhaps he had accidentally tapped all the repressed resentment that had been accumulating for years?

To Renthall's amazement, a succession of creaking ascents of the staircase the next morning announced the first party of residents to use the sun deck. Just before lunch Renthall went up to the roof, found a group of at least a dozen of the older guests sitting out below the watch-tower, placidly inhaling the cool air. None of them seemed in the least perturbed by the tower. At two or three points around the crescent sun-bathers had emerged, as if answering some deep latent call. People sat on makeshift porches or leaned from the sills, calling to each other.

Equally surprising was the failure of this upsurge of activity to be followed by any reaction from the watch-towers. Half-hidden behind his blinds, Renthall scrutinized the towers carefully, once caught what seemed to be a distant flicker of movement from an observation window half a mile away, but otherwise the towers remained silent, their long ranks receding to the horizon in all directions, motionless and enigmatic. The haze had thinned slightly, and the long shafts protruded further from the sky, their outlines darker and more vibrant.

Shortly before lunch Hanson interrupted his scrutiny. 'Hello, Charles. Great news! The school opens tomorrow. Thank heaven for that, I was getting so bored I could hardly stand up straight.'

Renthall nodded. 'Good. What's galvanized them into life so suddenly?'

'Oh, I don't know. I suppose they had to reopen some time. Aren't you pleased?'

'Of course. Am I still on the staff?'

'Naturally. The Council doesn't bear childish grudges. They might have sacked you a week ago, but things are different now.'

'What do you mean?'

Hanson scrutinized Renthall carefully. 'I mean the school's opened. What is the matter, Charles?'

Renthall went over to the window, his eyes roving along the lines of sun-bathers on the roofs. He waited a few seconds in case there was some sign of activity from the watch-towers.

'When's the Watch Committee going to hear my case?'

Hanson shrugged. 'They won't bother now. They know you're a tougher proposition than some of the people they've been pushing around. Forget the whole thing.'

'But I don't want to forget it. I want the hearing to take place. Damn it, I deliberately invented the whole business of the fête to force them to show their hand. Now they're furiously back-pedalling.'

'Well, what of it? Relax, they have their difficulties too.' He gave a laugh. 'You never know, they'd probably be only too glad of an invitation now.'

'They won't get one. You know, I almost feel they've outwitted me. When the fête doesn't take place everyone will assume I've given in to them.'

'But it will take place. Haven't you seen Boardman recently? He's going great guns, obviously it'll be a tremendous show. Be careful he doesn't cut you out.'

Puzzled, Renthall turned from the window. 'Do you mean Boardman's going ahead with it?'

'Of course. It looks like it anyway. He's got a big marquee over the car park, dozens of stalls, bunting everywhere.'

Renthall drove a fist into his palm. 'The man's insane!' He turned to Hanson. 'We've got to be careful, something's going on. I'm convinced the Council are just biding their time, they're deliberately letting the reins go so we'll over-reach ourselves. Have you seen all these people on the roof-tops? Sun-bathing!'

'Good idea. Isn't that what you've wanted all along?'

'Not so blatantly as this.' Renthall pointed to the nearest watch-tower. The windows were sealed, but the light reflected off them was far brighter than usual. 'Sooner or later there'll be a short, sharp reaction. That's what the Council are waiting for.'

'It's nothing to do with the Council. If people want to sit on the roof whose business is it but their own? Are you coming to lunch?'

'In a moment.' Renthall stood quietly by the window, watching Hanson closely. A possibility he had not previously envisaged crossed his mind. He searched for some method of testing it. 'Has the gong gone yet? My watch has stopped.'

Hanson glanced at his wristwatch. 'It's twelve-thirty.' He looked out through the window towards the clock tower in the distance over the Town Hall. One of Renthall's long-standing grievances against his room was that the tip of the nearby watch-tower hung directly over the clock-face, neatly obscuring it. Hanson nodded, re-setting his watch. 'Twelve-thirty-one. I'll see you in a few minutes.'

After Hanson had gone Renthall sat on the bed, his courage ebbing slowly, trying to rationalize this unforeseen development.

The next day he came across his second case.

Boardman surveyed the dingy room distastefully, puzzled by the spectacle of Renthall hunched up in his chair by the window.

'Mr Renthall, there's absolutely no question of cancelling it now. The fair's as good as started already. Anyway, what would be the point?'

'Our arrangement was that it should be a fête,' Renthall pointed out. 'You've turned it into a fun-fair, with a lot of stalls and hurdy-gurdies.'

Unruffled by Renthall's schoolmasterly manner, Boardman scoffed. 'Well, what's the difference? Anyway, my real idea is to roof it over and turn it into a permanent amusement park. The Council won't interfere. They're playing it quiet now.'

'Are they? I doubt it.' Renthall looked down into the garden. People sat about in their shirt sleeves, the women in floral dresses, evidently oblivious of the watch-towers filling the sky a hundred feet above their heads. The haze had receded still further, and at least two hundred yards of shaft were now visible. There were no signs of activity from the towers, but Renthall was convinced that this would soon begin.

'Tell me,' he asked Boardman in a clear voice. 'Aren't you frightened of the watch-towers?'

Boardman seemed puzzled. 'The what towers?' He made a spiral motion with his cigar. 'You mean the big slide? Don't worry, I'm not having one of those, nobody's got the energy to climb all those steps.'

He stuck his cigar in his mouth and ambled to the door. 'Well, so long, Mr Renthall. I'll send you an invite.'

Later that afternoon Renthall went to see Dr Clifton in his room below.

'Excuse me, Doctor,' he apologized, 'but would you mind seeing me on a professional matter?'

'Well, not here, Renthall, I'm supposed to be off-duty.' He turned from his canary cages by the window with a testy frown, then relented when he saw Renthall's intent expression. 'All right, what's the trouble?'

While Clifton washed his hands Renthall explained. 'Tell me, Doctor, is there any mechanism known to you by which the simultaneous hypnosis of large groups of people could occur? We're all familiar with theatrical displays of the hypnotist's art, but I'm thinking of a situation in which the members of an entire small community – such as the residents of the hotels around this crescent – could be induced to accept a given proposition completely conflicting with reality.'

Clifton stopped washing his hands. 'I thought you wanted to see me professionally. I'm a doctor, not a witch doctor. What are you planning now, Renthall? Last week it was a fête, now you want to hypnotize an entire neighbourhood, you'd better be careful.'

Renthall shook his head. 'It's not I who want to carry out the hypnosis, Doctor. In fact I'm afraid the operation has already taken place. I don't know whether you've noticed anything strange about your patients?'

'Nothing more than usual,' Clifton remarked dryly. He watched Renthall with increased interest. 'Who's responsible for this mass hypnosis?' When Renthall paused and then pointed a forefinger at the ceiling Clifton nodded sagely. 'I see. How sinister.'

'Exactly. I'm glad you understand, Doctor.' Renthall went over to the window, looking out at the sunshades below. He pointed to the watch-towers. 'Just to clarify a small point, Doctor. You do see the watch-towers?'

Clifton hesitated fractionally, moving imperceptibly towards his valise on the desk. Then he nodded: 'Of course.'

'Good. I'm relieved to hear it.' Renthall laughed. 'For a while I was beginning to think that I was the only one in step. Do you realize that both Hanson and Boardman can no longer see the towers? And I'm fairly certain that none of the people down there can or they wouldn't be sitting in the open. I'm convinced that this is the Council's doing, but it seems unlikely that they would have enough power –' He broke off, aware that Clifton was watching him fixedly. 'What's the matter? Doctor!'

Clifton quickly took his prescription pad from his valise. 'Renthall, caution is the essence of all strategy. It's important that we beware of over-hastiness. I suggest that we both rest this afternoon. Now, these will give you some sleep –'

For the first time in several days he ventured out into the street. Head down, angry for being caught out by the doctor, he drove himself along the pavement towards Mrs Osmond, determined to find at least one person who could still see the towers. The streets were more crowded than he could remember for a long time and he was forced to look upward as he swerved in and out of the ambling pedestrians. Overhead, like the assault craft from which some apocalyptic air-raid would be launched, the watch-towers hung down from the sky, framed between the twin spires of the church, blocking off a vista down the principal boulevard, yet unperceived by the afternoon strollers.

Renthall passed the café, surprised to see the terrace packed with coffee-drinkers, then saw Boardman's marquee in the cinema car park. Music was coming from a creaking wurlitzer, and the gay ribbons of the bunting fluttered in the air.

Twenty yards from Mrs Osmond's he saw her come through her front door, a large straw hat on her head.

'Charles! What are you doing here? I haven't seen you for days, I wondered what was the matter.'

Renthall took the key from her fingers and pushed it back into the lock. Closing the door behind them, he paused in the darkened hall, regaining his breath.

'Charles, what on earth is going on? Is someone after you? You look terrible, my dear. Your face –'

'Never mind my face.' Renthall collected himself, and led the way into the living room. 'Come in here, quickly.' He went over to the window and drew back the blinds, ascertained that the watch-tower over the row of houses opposite was still there. 'Sit down and relax. I'm sorry to rush in like this but you'll understand in a minute.' He waited until Mrs Osmond settled herself reluctantly on the sofa, then rested his palms on the mantelpiece, organizing his thoughts.

'The last few days have been fantastic, you wouldn't believe it, and to cap everything I've just made myself look the biggest possible fool in front of Clifton. God, I could –'

'Charles –!'

'*Listen!* Don't start interrupting me before I've begun, I've got enough to contend with. Something absolutely insane is going on everywhere, by some freak I seem to be the only one who's still *compos mentis*. I know that sounds as if I'm completely mad, but in fact it's true. Why, I don't know; though I'm frightened it may be some sort of reprisal directed at me. However.' He went over to the window. 'Julia, what can you see out of that window?'

Mrs Osmond dismantled her hat and squinted at the panes. She fidgeted uncomfortably. 'Charles, what is going on? – I'll have to get my glasses.' She subsided helplessly.

'Julia! You've never needed your glasses before to see these. Now tell me, what can you see?'

'Well, the row of houses, and the gardens . . .'

'Yes, what else?'

'The windows, of course, and there's a tree . . .'

'What about the sky?'

She nodded. 'Yes, I can see that, there's a sort of haze, isn't there? Or is that my eyes?'

'No.' Wearily, Renthall turned away from the window. For the first time a feeling of unassuageable fatigue had come over him. 'Julia,' he asked quietly. 'Don't you remember the watch-towers?'

She shook her head slowly. 'No, I don't. Where were they?' A look of concern came over her face. She took his arm gently. 'Dear, what is going on?'

Renthall forced himself to stand upright. 'I don't know.' He drummed his forehead with his free hand. 'You can't remember the towers at all, or the observation windows?' He pointed to the watch-tower hanging down the centre of the window. 'There – used to be one over those houses. We were always looking at it. Do you remember how we used to draw the curtains upstairs?'

'Charles! Be careful, people will hear. Where are you going?'

Numbly, Renthall pulled back the door. 'Outside,' he said in a flat voice. 'There's little point now in staying indoors.'

He let himself through the front door, fifty yards from the house heard her call after him, turned quickly into a side road and hurried towards the first intersection.

Above him he was conscious of the watch-towers hanging in the bright air, but he kept his eyes level with the gates and hedges, scanning the empty houses. Now and then he passed one that was occupied, the family sitting out on the lawn, and once someone called his name, reminding him that the school had started without him. The air was fresh and crisp, the light glimmering off the pavements with an unusual intensity.

Within ten minutes he realized that he had wandered into an unfamiliar part of the town and completely lost himself, with only the aerial lines of watch-towers to guide him, but he still refused to look up at them.

He had entered a poorer quarter of the town, where the narrow empty streets were separated by large waste dumps, and tilting wooden fences sagged between ruined houses. Many of the dwellings were only a single storey high, and the sky seemed even wider and more open, the distant watch-towers along the horizon like a continuous palisade.

He twisted his foot on a ledge of stone, and hobbled painfully towards a strip of broken fencing that straddled a small rise in the centre of the waste dump. He was perspiring heavily, and loosened his tie, then searched the surrounding straggle of houses for a way back into the streets through which he had come.

Overhead, something moved and caught his eye. Forcing himself to ignore it, Renthall regained his breath, trying to master the curious dizziness that touched his brain. An immense sudden silence hung over the waste ground, so absolute that it was as if some inaudible piercing music was being played at full volume.

To his right, at the edge of the waste ground, he heard feet shuffle slowly across the rubble, and saw the elderly man in the shabby black suit and wing collar who usually loitered outside the Public Library. He hobbled along, hands in pockets, an almost Chaplinesque figure, his weak eyes now and then feebly scanning the sky as if he were searching for something he had lost or forgotten.

Renthall watched him cross the waste ground, but before he could shout the decrepit figure tottered away behind a ruined wall.

Again something moved above him, followed by a third sharp angular motion, and then a succession of rapid shuttles. The stony rubbish at his feet flickered with the reflected light, and abruptly the whole sky sparkled as if the air was opening and shutting.

Then, as suddenly, everything was motionless again.

Composing himself, Renthall waited for a last moment. Then he raised his face to the nearest watch-tower fifty feet above him, and gazed across at the hundreds of towers that hung from the clear sky like giant pillars. The haze had vanished and the shafts of the towers were defined with unprecedented clarity.

As far as he could see, all the observation windows were open. Silently, without moving, the watchers stared down at him.

· **1962**

# THE SINGING STATUES

Again last night, as the dusk air began to move across the desert from Lagoon West, I heard fragments of music coming in on the thermal rollers, remote and fleeting, echoes of the love-song of Lunora Goalen. Walking out over the copper sand to the reefs where the sonic sculptures grow, I wandered through the darkness among the metal gardens, searching for Lunora's voice. No one tends the sculptures now and most of them have gone to seed, but on an impulse I cut away a helix and carried it back to my villa, planting it in the quartz bed below the balcony. All night it sang to me, telling me of Lunora and the strange music she played to herself . . .

It must be just over three years ago that I first saw Lunora Goalen, in Georg Nevers's gallery on Beach Drive. Every summer at the height of the season at Vermilion Sands, Georg staged a special exhibition of sonic sculpture for the tourists. Shortly after we opened one morning I was sitting inside my large statue, *Zero Orbit*, plugging in the stereo amplifiers, when Georg suddenly gasped into the skin mike and a boom like a thunderclap nearly deafened me.

Head ringing like a gong, I climbed out of the sculpture ready to crown Georg with a nearby maquette. Putting an elegant fingertip to his lips, he gave me that look which between artist and dealer signals one thing: *Rich client.*

The sculptures in the gallery entrance had begun to hum as someone came in, but the sunlight reflected off the bonnet of a white Rolls-Royce outside obscured the doorway.

Then I saw her, hovering over the stand of art journals, followed by her secretary, a tall purse-mouthed Frenchwoman almost as famous from the news magazines as her mistress.

Lunora Goalen, I thought, can *all* our dreams come true? She wore an ice-cool sliver of blue silk that shimmered as she moved towards the first statue, a toque hat of black violets and bulky dark glasses that hid her face and were a nightmare to cameramen. While she paused by the statue, one of Arch Penko's frenetic tangles that looked like a rimless bicycle wheel, listening to its arms vibrate and howl, Nevers and I involuntarily steadied ourselves against the wing-piece of my sculpture.

*       *       *

395

In general it's probably true that the most maligned species on Earth is the wealthy patron of modern art. Laughed at by the public, exploited by dealers, even the artists regard them simply as meal tickets. Lunora Goalen's superb collection of sonic sculpture on the roof of her Venice palazzo, and the million dollars' worth of generous purchases spread around her apartments in Paris, London and New York, represented freedom and life to a score of sculptors, but few felt any gratitude towards Miss Goalen.

Nevers was hesitating, apparently suffering from a sudden intention tremor, so I nudged his elbow.

'Come on,' I murmured. 'This is the apocalypse. Let's go.'

Nevers turned on me icily, noticing, apparently for the first time, my rust-stained slacks and three-day stubble.

'Milton!' he snapped. 'For God's sake, vanish! Sneak out through the freight exit.' He jerked his head at my sculpture. 'And switch that insane thing off! How did I ever let it in here?'

Lunora's secretary, Mme Charcot, spotted us at the rear of the gallery. Georg shot out four inches of immaculate cuff and swayed forward, the smile on his face as wide as a bulldozer. I backed away behind my sculpture, with no intention of leaving and letting Nevers cut my price just for the cachet of making a sale to Lunora Goalen.

Georg was bowing all over the gallery, oblivious of Mme Charcot's contemptuous sneer. He led Lunora over to one of the exhibits and fumbled with the control panel, selecting the alto lift which would resonate most flatteringly with her own body tones. Unfortunately the statue was Sigismund Lubitsch's *Big End*, a squat bull-necked drum like an enormous toad that at its sweetest emitted a rasping grunt. An old-style railroad tycoon might have elicited a sympathetic chord from it, but its response to Lunora was like a bull's to a butterfly.

They moved on to another sculpture, and Mme Charcot gestured to the white-gloved chauffeur standing by the Rolls. He climbed in and moved the car down the street, taking with it the beach crowds beginning to gather outside the gallery. Able now to see Lunora clearly against the hard white walls, I stepped into *Orbit* and watched her closely through the helixes.

Of course I already knew everything about Lunora Goalen. A thousand magazine exposés had catalogued *ad nauseam* her strange flawed beauty, her fits of melancholy and compulsive roving around the world's capitals. Her brief career as a film actress had faltered at first, less as a consequence of her modest, though always interesting, talents than of her simple failure to register photogenically. By a macabre twist of fate, after a major car accident had severely injured her face she had become an extraordinary success. That strangely marred profile and nervous gaze had filled cinemas from Paris to Pernambuco. Unable to bear this tribute to her plastic surgeons, Lunora had abruptly abandoned her career and become a leading patron of the fine arts. Like Garbo in the '40s and '50s, she flitted elusively through the gossip columns and society pages in unending flight from herself.

Her face was the clue. As she took off her sunglasses I could see the curious shadow that fell across it, numbing the smooth white skin. There was a dead glaze in her slate-blue eyes, an uneasy tension around the mouth. Altogether I had a vague impression of something unhealthy, of a Venus with a secret vice.

Nevers was switching on sculptures right and left like a lunatic magician, and the noise was a babel of competing senso-cells, some of the statues responding to Lunora's enigmatic presence, others to Nevers and the secretary.

Lunora shook her head slowly, mouth hardening as the noise irritated her. 'Yes, Mr Nevers,' she said in her slightly husky voice, 'it's all very clever, but a bit of a headache. I *live* with my sculpture, I want something intimate and personal.'

'Of course, Miss Goalen,' Nevers agreed hurriedly, looking around desperately. As he knew only too well, sonic sculpture was now nearing the apogee of its abstract phase; twelve-tone blips and zooms were all that most statues emitted. No purely representational sound, responding to Lunora, for example, with a Mozart rondo or (better) a Webern quartet, had been built for ten years. I guessed that her early purchases were wearing out and that she was hunting the cheaper galleries in tourist haunts like Vermilion Sands in the hope of finding something designed for middle-brow consumption.

Lunora looked up pensively at *Zero Orbit*, towering at the rear of the gallery next to Nevers's desk, apparently unaware that I was hiding inside it. Suddenly realizing that the possibility of selling the statue had miraculously arisen, I crouched inside the trunk and started to breathe heavily, activating the senso-circuits.

Immediately the statue came to life. About twelve feet high, it was shaped like an enormous metal totem topped by two heraldic wings. The microphones in the wing-tips were powerful enough to pick up respiratory noises at a distance of twenty feet. There were four people well within focus, and the statue began to emit a series of low rhythmic pulses.

Seeing the statue respond to her, Lunora came forwards with interest. Nevers backed away discreetly, taking Mme Charcot with him, leaving Lunora and I together, separated by a thin metal skin and three feet of vibrating air. Fumbling for some way of widening the responses, I eased up the control slides that lifted the volume. Neurophonics has never been my strong suit – I regard myself, in an old-fashioned way, as a sculptor, not an electrician – and the statue was only equipped to play back a simple sequence of chord variations on the sonic profile in focus.

Knowing that Lunora would soon realize that the statue's repertory was too limited for her, I picked up the hand-mike used for testing the circuits and on the spur of the moment began to croon the refrain from Creole Love Call. Reinterpreted by the sonic cores, and then relayed through the loudspeakers, the lulling rise and fall was pleasantly soothing, the electronic overtones disguising my voice and amplifying the tremors of emotion as I screwed up my courage (the statue was priced at five thousand dollars – even subtracting Nevers's 90 per cent commission left me with enough for the bus fare home).

Stepping up to the statue, Lunora listened to it motionlessly, eyes wide with astonishment, apparently assuming that it was reflecting, like a mirror, its subjective impressions of herself. Rapidly running out of breath, my speeding pulse lifting the tempo, I repeated the refrain over and over again, varying the bass lift to simulate a climax.

Suddenly I saw Nevers's black patent shoes through the hatch. Pretending to slip his hand into the control panel, he rapped sharply on the statue. I switched off.

'Don't please!' Lunora cried as the sounds fell away. She looked around uncertainly. Mme Charcot was stepping nearer with a curiously watchful expression.

Nevers hesitated. 'Of course, Miss Goalen, it still requires tuning, you –'

'I'll take it,' Lunora said. She pushed on her sunglasses, turned and hurried from the gallery, her face hidden.

Nevers watched her go. 'What happened, for heaven's sake? Is Miss Goalen all right?'

Mme Charcot took a cheque-book out of her blue crocodile handbag. A sardonic smirk played over her lips, and through the helix I had a brief but penetrating glimpse into her relationship with Lunora Goalen. It was then, I think, that I realized Lunora might be something more than a bored dilettante.

Mme Charcot glanced at her watch, a gold pea strung on her scrawny wrist. 'You will have it delivered today. By three o'clock sharp. Now, please, the price?'

Smoothly, Nevers said: 'Ten thousand dollars.'

Choking, I pulled myself out of the statue, and spluttered helplessly at Nevers.

Mme Charcot regarded me with astonishment, frowning at my filthy togs. Nevers trod savagely on my foot. 'Naturally, Mademoiselle, our prices are modest, but as you can see, M. Milton is an inexperienced artist.'

Mme Charcot nodded sagely. 'This is the sculptor? I am relieved. For a moment I feared that he lived in it.'

When she had gone Nevers closed the gallery for the day. He took off his jacket and pulled a bottle of absinthe from the desk. Sitting back in his silk waistcoat, he trembled slightly with nervous exhaustion.

'Tell me, Milton, how can you ever be sufficiently grateful to me?'

I patted him on the back. 'Georg, you were brilliant! She's another Catherine the Great, you handled her like a diplomat. When you go to Paris you'll be a great success. Ten thousand dollars!' I did a quick jig around the statue. 'That's the sort of redistribution of wealth I like to see. How about an advance on my cut?'

Nevers examined me moodily. He was already in the Rue de Rivoli, over-bidding for Leonardos with a languid flicker of a pomaded eyebrow. He glanced at the statue and shuddered. 'An extraordinary woman. Completely without taste. Which reminds me, I see you rescored the memory drum. The aria from *Tosca* cued in beautifully. I didn't realize the statue contained that.'

'It doesn't,' I told him, sitting on the desk. 'That was me. Not exactly Caruso, I admit, but then he wasn't much of a sculptor –'

'What?' Nevers leapt out of his chair. 'Do you mean you were using the hand microphone? You *fool!*'

'What does it matter? She won't know.' Nevers was groaning against the wall, drumming his forehead on his fist. 'Relax, you'll hear nothing.'

Promptly at 9.01 the next morning the telephone rang.

As I drove the pick-up out to Lagoon West Nevers's warnings rang in my ears – '. . . six international blacklists, sue me for misrepresentation . . .' He apologized effusively to Mme Charcot, and assured her that the monotonous booming the statue emitted was most certainly not its natural response. Obviously a circuit had been damaged in transit, the sculptor himself was driving out to correct it.

Taking the beach road around the lagoon, I looked across at the Goalen mansion, an abstract summer palace that reminded me of a Frank Lloyd Wright design for an experimental department store. Terraces jutted out at all angles, and here and there were huge metal sculptures, Brancusi's and Calder mobiles, revolving in the crisp desert light. Occasionally one of the sonic statues hooted mournfully like a distant hoodoo.

Mme Charcot collected me in the vestibule, led me up a sweeping glass stairway. The walls were heavy with Dali and Picasso, but my statue had been given the place of honour at the far end of the south terrace. The size of a tennis court, without rails (or safety net), this jutted out over the lagoon against the skyline of Vermilion Sands, low furniture grouped in a square at its centre.

Dropping the tool-bag, I made a pretence of dismantling the control panel, and played with the amplifier so that the statue let out a series of staccato blips. These put it into the same category as the rest of Lunora Goalen's sculpture. A dozen pieces stood about on the terrace, most of them early period sonic dating back to the '70s, when sculptors produced an incredible sequence of grunting, clanking, barking and twanging statues, and galleries and public squares all over the world echoed night and day with minatory booms and thuds.

'Any luck?'

I turned to see Lunora Goalen. Unheard, she had crossed the terrace, now stood with hands on hips, watching me with interest. In her black slacks and shirt, blonde hair around her shoulders, she looked more relaxed, but sunglasses still masked her face.

'Just a loose valve. It won't take me a couple of minutes.' I gave her a reassuring smile and she stretched out on the chaise longue in front of the statue. Lurking by the french windows at the far end of the terrace was Mme Charcot, eyeing us with a beady smirk. Irritated, I switched on the statue to full volume and coughed loudly into the hand-mike.

The sound boomed across the open terrace like an artillery blank. The old crone backed away quickly.

Lunora smiled as the echoes rolled over the desert, the statues on the lower terraces responding with muted pulses. 'Years ago, when Father was away, I used to go on to the roof and shout at the top of my voice, set off the most wonderful echo trains. The whole place would boom for hours, drive the servants mad.' She laughed pleasantly to herself at the recollection, as if it had been a long time ago.

'Try it now,' I suggested. 'Or is Mme Charcot mad already?'

Lunora put a green-tipped finger to her lips. 'Carefully, you'll get me into trouble. Anyway, Mme Charcot is not my servant.'

'No? What is she then, your jailer?' We spoke mockingly, but I put a curve on the question; something about the Frenchwoman had made me suspect that she might have more than a small part in maintaining Lunora's illusions about herself.

I waited for Lunora to reply, but she ignored me and stared out across the lagoon. Within a few seconds her personality had changed levels, once again she was the remote autocratic princess.

Unobserved, I slipped my hand into the tool-bag and drew out a tape spool. Clipping it into the player deck, I switched on the table. The statue vibrated slightly, and a low melodious chant murmured out into the still air.

Standing behind the statue, I watched Lunora respond to the music. The sounds mounted, steadily swelling as Lunora moved into the statue's focus. Gradually its rhythms quickened, its mood urgent and plaintive, unmistakably a lover's passion-song. A musicologist would have quickly identified the sounds as a transcription of the balcony duet from *Romeo and Juliet*, but to Lunora its only source was the statue. I had recorded the tape that morning, realizing it was the only method of saving the statue. Nevers's confusion of *Tosca* and 'Creole Love Call' reminded me that I had the whole of classical opera in reserve. For ten thousand dollars I would gladly call once a day and feed in every aria from *Figaro* to *Moses and Aaron*.

Abruptly, the music fell away. Lunora had backed out of the statue's focus, and was standing twenty feet from me. Behind her, in the doorway, was Mme Charcot.

Lunora smiled briefly. 'It seems to be in perfect order,' she said. Without doubt she was gesturing me towards the door.

I hesitated, suddenly wondering whether to tell her the truth, my eyes searching her beautiful secret face. Then Mme Charcot came between us, smiling like a skull.

Did Lunora Goalen really believe that the sculpture was singing to her? For a fortnight, until the tape expired, it didn't matter. By then Nevers would have cashed the cheque and he and I would be on our way to Paris.

Within two or three days, though, I realized that I wanted to see Lunora again. Rationalizing, I told myself that the statue needed to be checked, that Lunora might discover the fraud. Twice during the next week I drove out to the summer-house on the pretext of tuning the sculpture, but Mme Charcot held me off. Once I telephoned, but again she intercepted me. When I saw Lunora she was driving at speed through Vermilion Sands in the Rolls-Royce, a dim glimmer of gold and jade in the back seat.

Finally I searched through my record albums, selected Toscanini conducting *Tristan and Isolde*, in the scene where Tristan mourns his parted lover, and carefully transcribed another tape.

That night I drove down to Lagoon West, parked my car by the beach on the south shore and walked out on to the surface of the lake. In the moonlight the summer-house half a mile away looked like an abstract movie set, a single light on the upper terrace illuminating the outlines of my statue. Stepping carefully across the fused silica, I made my way slowly towards it, fragments of the statue's song drifting by on the low breeze. Two hundred yards from the house I lay down on the warm sand, watching the lights of Vermilion Sands fade one by one like the melting jewels of a necklace.

Above, the statue sang into the blue night, its song never wavering. Lunora must have been sitting only a few feet above it, the music enveloping her like an overflowing fountain. Shortly after two o'clock it died down and I saw her at the rail, the white ermine wrap around her shoulders stirring in the wind as she stared at the brilliant moon.

Half an hour later I climbed the lake wall and walked along it to the spiral fire escape. The bougainvillaea wreathed through the railings muffled the sounds of my feet on the metal steps. I reached the upper terrace unnoticed. Far below, in her quarters on the north side, Mme Charcot was asleep.

Swinging on to the terrace, I moved among the dark statues, drawing low murmurs from them as I passed.

I crouched inside *Zero Orbit*, unlocked the control panel and inserted the fresh tape, slightly raising the volume.

As I left I could see on to the west terrace twenty feet below, where Lunora lay asleep under the stars on an enormous velvet bed, like a lunar princess on a purple catafalque. Her face shone in the star-light, her loose hair veiling her naked breasts. Behind her a statue stood guard, intoning, softly to itself as it pulsed to the sounds of her breathing.

Three times I visited Lunora's house after midnight, taking with me another spool of tape, another love-song from my library. On the last visit I watched her sleeping until dawn rose across the desert. I fled down the stairway and across the sand, hiding among the cold pools of shadow whenever a car moved along the beach road.

All day I waited by the telephone in my villa, hoping she would call me. In the evening I walked out to the sand reefs, climbed one of the spires and watched Lunora on the terrace after dinner. She lay on a couch before the statue, and until long after midnight it played to her, endlessly singing. Its voice was now so strong that cars would slow down several hundred yards away, the drivers searching for the source of the melodies crossing the vivid evening air.

At last I recorded the final tape, for the first time in my own voice. Briefly I described the whole sequence of imposture, and quietly asked Lunora if she would sit for me and let me design a new sculpture to replace the fraud she had bought.

I clenched the tape tightly in my hand while I walked across the lake, looking up at the rectangular outline of the terrace.

As I reached the wall, a black-suited figure put his head over the ledge and looked down at me. It was Lunora's chauffeur.

Startled, I moved away across the sand. In the moonlight the chauffeur's white face flickered bonily.

The next evening, as I knew it would, the telephone finally rang.

'Mr Milton, the statue has broken down again.' Mme Charcot's voice sounded sharp and strained. 'Miss Goalen is extremely upset. You must come and repair it. Immediately.'

I waited an hour before leaving, playing through the tape I had recorded the previous evening. This time I would be present when Lunora heard it.

Mme Charcot was standing by the glass doors. I parked in the court by the Rolls. As I walked over to her, I noticed how eerie the house sounded. All over it the statues were muttering to themselves, emitting snaps and clicks, like the disturbed occupants of a zoo settling down with difficulty after a storm. Even Mme Charcot looked worn and tense.

At the terrace she paused. 'One moment, Mr Milton. I will see if Miss Goalen is ready to receive you.' She walked quietly towards the chaise longue pulled against the statue at the end of the terrace. Lunora was stretched out awkwardly across it, her hair disarrayed. She sat up irritably as Mme Charcot approached.

'Is he here? Alice, whose car was that? Hasn't he come?'

'He is preparing his equipment,' Mme Charcot told her soothingly. 'Miss Lunora, let me dress your hair –'

'Alice, don't fuss! God, what's keeping him?' She sprang up and paced over to the statue, glowering silently out of the darkness. While Mme Charcot walked away Lunora sank on her knees before the statue, pressed her right cheek to its cold surface.

Uncontrollably she began to sob, deep spasms shaking her shoulders.

'Wait, Mr Milton!' Mme Charcot held tightly to my elbow. 'She will not want to see you for a few minutes.' She added: 'You are a better sculptor than you think, Mr Milton. You have given that statue a remarkable voice. It tells her all she needs to know.'

I broke away and ran through the darkness.

'Lunora!'

She looked around, the hair over her face matted with tears. She leaned limply against the dark trunk of the statue. I knelt down and held her hands, trying to lift her to her feet.

She wrenched away from me. 'Fix it! Hurry, what are you waiting for? Make the statue sing again!'

I was certain that she no longer recognized me. I stepped back, the spool of tape in my hand. 'What's the matter with her?' I whispered to Mme Charcot. 'The sounds don't really come from the statue, surely she realizes that?'

Mme Charcot's head lifted. 'What do you mean – not from the statue?'

I showed her the tape. 'This isn't a true sonic sculpture. The music is played off these magnetic tapes.'

A chuckle rasped briefly from Mme Charcot's throat. 'Well, put it in none the less, monsieur. She doesn't care where it comes from. She is interested in the statue, not you.'

I hesitated, watching Lunora, still hunched like a supplicant at the foot of the statue.

'You mean –?' I started to say incredulously. 'So you mean she's in love with the statue?'

Mme Charcot's eyes summed up all my naivety.

'Not with the statue,' she said. 'With *herself.*'

For a moment I stood there among the murmuring sculptures, dropped the spool on the floor and turned away.

They left Lagoon West the next day.

For a week I remained at my villa, then drove along the beach road towards the summer-house one evening after Nevers told me that they had gone.

The house was closed, the statues standing motionless in the darkness. My footsteps echoed away among the balconies and terraces, and the house reared up into the sky like a tomb. All the sculptures had been switched off, and I realized how dead and monumental non-sonic sculpture must have seemed.

*Zero Orbit* had also gone. I assumed that Lunora had taken it with her, so immersed in her self-love that she preferred a clouded mirror which had once told her of her beauty to no mirror at all. As she sat on some penthouse veranda in Venice or Paris, with the great statue towering into the dark sky like an extinct symbol, she would hear again the lays it had sung.

Six months later Nevers commissioned another statue from me. I went out one dusk to the sand reefs where the sonic sculptures grow. As I approached, they were creaking in the wind whenever the thermal gradients cut through them. I walked up the long slopes, listening to them mewl and whine, searching for one that would serve as the sonic core for a new statue.

Somewhere ahead in the darkness, I heard a familiar phrase, a garbled fragment of a human voice. Startled, I ran on, feeling between the dark barbs and helixes.

Then, lying in a hollow below the ridge, I found the source. Half-buried under the sand like the skeleton of an extinct bird were twenty or thirty pieces of metal, the dismembered trunk and wings of my statue. Many of the pieces had taken root again and were emitting a thin haunted sound, disconnected fragments of the testament to Lunora Goalen I had dropped on her terrace.

As I walked down the slope, the white sand poured into my footprints like a succession of occluding hourglasses. The sounds of my voice whined faintly through the metal gardens like a forgotten lover whispering over a dead harp.

**1962**

# THE MAN ON THE 99TH FLOOR

All day Forbis had been trying to reach the 100th floor. Crouched at the foot of the short stairway behind the elevator shaft, he stared up impotently at the swinging metal door on to the roof, searching for some means of dragging himself up to it. There were eleven narrow steps, and then the empty roof deck, the high grilles of the suicide barrier and the open sky. Every three minutes an airliner went over, throwing a fleeting shadow down the steps, its jets momentarily drowning the panic which jammed his mind, and each time he made another attempt to reach the doorway.

Eleven steps. He had counted them a thousand times, in the hours since he first entered the building at ten o'clock that morning and rode the elevator up to the 95th floor. He had walked the next floor – the floors were fakes, offices windowless and unserviced, tacked on merely to give the building the cachet of a full century – then waited quietly at the bottom of the final stairway, listening to the elevator cables wind and drone, hoping to calm himself. As usual, however, his pulse started to race, within two or three minutes was up to one hundred and twenty. When he stood up and reached for the hand-rail something clogged his nerve centres, caissons settled on to the bed of his brain, rooting him to the floor like a lead colossus.

Fingering the rubber cleats on the bottom step, Forbis glanced at his wristwatch. 4.20 p.m. If he wasn't careful someone would climb the stairs up to the roof and find him there – already there were half a dozen buildings around the city where he was *persona non grata*, elevator boys warned to call the house detectives if they saw him. And there were not all that many buildings with a hundred floors. That was part of his obsession. There had to be one hundred exactly.

Why? Leaning back against the wall, Forbis managed to ask himself the question. What role was he playing out, searching the city for hundred-storey skyscrapers, then performing this obsessive ritual which invariably ended in the same way, the final peak always unscaled? Perhaps it was some sort of abstract duel between himself and the architects of these monstrous piles (dimly he remembered working in a menial job below the city streets – perhaps he was rebelling and reasserting himself, the prototype of urban ant-man trying to over-topple the totem towers of Megalopolis?)

\*　　\*　　\*

Aligning itself on the glideway, an airliner began its final approach over the city, its six huge jets blaring. As the noise hammered across him, Forbis pulled himself to his feet and lowered his head, passively letting the sounds drive down into his mind and loosen his blocked feedbacks. Lifting his right foot, he lowered it on to the first step, clasped the rail and pulled himself up two steps.

His left leg swung freely. Relief surged through him. At last he was going to reach the door! He took another step, raised his foot to the fourth, only seven from the top, then realized that his left hand was locked to the hand-rail below. He tugged at it angrily, but the fingers were clamped together like steel bands, the thumbnail biting painfully into his index tip.

He was still trying to unclasp the hand when the aircraft had gone.

Half an hour later, as the daylight began to fade, he sat down on the bottom step, with his free right hand pulled off one of his shoes and dropped it through the railing into the elevator shaft.

Vansittart put the hypodermic away in his valise, watching Forbis thoughtfully.

'You're lucky you didn't kill anyone,' he said. 'The elevator cabin was thirty storeys down, your shoe went through the roof like a bomb.'

Forbis shrugged vaguely, letting himself relax on the couch. The Psychology Department was almost silent, the last of the lights going out in the corridor as the staff left the medical school on their way home. 'I'm sorry, but there was no other way of attracting attention. I was fastened to the stair-rail like a dying limpet. How did you calm the manager down?'

Vansittart sat on the edge of his desk, turning away the lamp.

'It wasn't easy. Luckily Professor Bauer was still in his office and he cleared me over the phone. A week from now, though, he retires. Next time I may not be able to bluff my way through. I think we'll have to take a more direct line. The police won't be so patient with you.'

'I know. I'm afraid of that. But if I can't go on trying my brain will fuse. Didn't you get any clues at all?'

Vansittart murmured noncommittally. In fact the events had followed exactly the same pattern as on the three previous occasions. Again the attempt to reach the open roof had failed, and again there was no explanation for Forbis's compulsive drive. Vansittart had first seen him only a month earlier, wandering about blankly on the observation roof of the new administration building at the medical school. How he had gained access to the roof Vansittart had never discovered. Luckily one of the janitors had telephoned him that a man was behaving suspiciously on the roof, and Vansittart had reached him just before the suicide attempt.

At least, that was what it appeared to be. Vansittart examined the little man's placid grey features, his small shoulders and thin hands. There was something anonymous about him. He was minimal urban man, as near a nonentity as possible, without friends or family, a vague background of forgotten jobs and rooming houses. The sort of lonely, helpless man who might easily, in an unthinking act of despair, try to throw himself off a roof.

Yet there was something that puzzled Vansittart. Strictly, as a member of the university teaching staff, he should not have prescribed any treatment for Forbis and instead should have handed him over promptly to the police surgeon at the nearest station. But a curious nagging suspicion about Forbis had prevented him from doing so. Later, when he began to analyse Forbis, he found that his personality, or what there was of it, seemed remarkably well integrated, and that he had a realistic, pragmatic approach towards life which was completely unlike the over-compensated self-pity of most would-be suicides.

Nevertheless, he was driven by an insane compulsion, this apparently motiveless impulse to the 100th floor. Despite all Vansittart's probings and tranquillizers Forbis had twice set off for the down-town sector of the city, picked a skyscraper and trapped himself in his eyrie on the 99th floor, on both occasions finally being rescued by Vansittart.

Deciding to play a hunch, Vansittart asked: 'Forbis, have you ever experimented with hypnosis?'

Forbis shifted himself drowsily, then shook his head. 'Not as far as I can remember. Are you hinting that someone has given me a post-hypnotic suggestion, trying to make me throw myself off a roof?'

That was quick of you, Vansittart thought. 'Why do you say that?' he asked.

'I don't know. But who would try? And what would be the point?' He peered up at Vansittart. 'Do you think someone did?'

Vansittart nodded. 'Oh yes. There's no doubt about it.' He sat forward, swinging the lamp around for emphasis. 'Listen, Forbis, some time ago, I can't be sure how long, three months, perhaps six, someone planted a really powerful post-hypnotic command in your mind. The first part of it – "*Go up to the 100th floor*" – I've been able to uncover, but the rest is still buried. It's that half of the command which worries me. One doesn't need a morbid imagination to guess what it probably is.'

Forbis moistened his lips, shielding his eyes from the glare of the lamp. He felt too sluggish to be alarmed by what Vansittart had just said. Despite the doctor's frank admission of failure, and his deliberate but rather nervous manner, he trusted Vansittart, and was confident he would find a solution. 'It sounds insane,' he commented. 'But who would want to kill me? Can't you cancel the whole thing out, erase the command?'

'I've tried to, but without any success. I've been getting nowhere. It's still as strong as ever – stronger, in fact, almost as if it were being reinforced. Where have you been during the last week? Who have you seen?'

Forbis shrugged, sitting up on one elbow. 'No one. As far as I can remember, I've only been on the 99th floor.' He searched the air dismally, then gave up. 'You know, I can't remember a single thing, just vague outlines of cafés and bus depots, it's strange.'

'A pity. I'd try to keep an eye on you, but I can't spare the time. Bauer's retirement hadn't been expected for another year, there's a tremendous amount of reorganization to be done.' He drummed his fingers irritably on the desk. 'I noticed you've still got some cash with you. Have you had a job?'

'I think so – in the subway, perhaps. Or did I just take a train ...?' Forbis frowned with the effort of recollection. 'I'm sorry, Doctor. Anyway, I've always heard that post-hypnotic suggestions couldn't compel you to do anything that clashed with your basic personality.'

'What is the basic personality, though? A skilful analyst can manipulate the psyche to suit the suggestion, magnify a small streak of self-destruction until it cleaves the entire personality like an axe splitting a log.'

Forbis pondered this gloomily for a few moments, then brightened slightly. 'Well, I seem to have the suggestion beaten. Whatever happens, I can't actually reach the roof, so I must have enough strength to fight it.'

Vansittart shook his head. 'As a matter of fact, you haven't. It's not you who's keeping yourself off the roof, it's *me*.'

'What do you mean?'

'I implanted another hypnotic suggestion, holding you on the 99th floor. When I uncovered the first suggestion I tried to erase it, found I wasn't even scratching the surface, so just as a precaution I inserted a second of my own. "*Get off at the 99th floor.*" How long it will hold you there I don't know, but already it's fading. Today it took you over seven hours to call me. Next time you may get up enough steam to hit the roof. That's why I think we should take a new line, really get to the bottom of this obsession, or rather' – he smiled ruefully – 'to the top.'

Forbis sat up slowly, massaging his face. 'What do you suggest?'

'We'll let you reach the roof. I'll erase my secondary command and we'll see what happens when you step out on to the top deck. Don't worry, I'll be with you if anything goes wrong. It may seem pretty thin consolation, but frankly, Forbis, it would be so easy to kill you and get away with it that I can't understand anyone bothering to go to all this trouble. Obviously there's some deeper motive, something connected, perhaps, with the 100th floor.' Vansittart paused, watching Forbis carefully, then asked in a casual voice: 'Tell me, have you ever heard of anyone called Fowler?'

He said nothing when Forbis shook his head, but privately noted the reflex pause of unconscious recognition.

'All right?' Vansittart asked as they reached the bottom of the final stairway.

'Fine,' Forbis said quietly, catching his breath. He looked up at the rectangular opening above them, wondering how he would feel when he finally reached the roof-top. They had sneaked into the building by one of the service entrances at the rear, and then taken a freight elevator to the 80th floor.

'Let's go, then,' Vansittart walked on ahead, beckoning Forbis after him. Together they climbed up to the final doorway, and stepped out into the bright sunlight.

'Doctor . . . !' Forbis exclaimed happily. He felt fresh and exhilarated, his mind clear and unburdened at last. He gazed around the small flat roof, a thousand ideas tumbling past each other in his mind like the crystal fragments of a mountain stream. Somewhere below, however, a deeper current tugged at him.

*Go up to the 100th floor and . . .*

Around him lay the roof-tops of the city, and half a mile away, hidden by the haze, was the spire of the building he had tried to scale the previous day. He strolled about the roof, letting the cool air clear the sweat from his face. There were no suicide grilles around the balcony, but their absence caused him no anxiety.

Vansittart was watching him carefully, black valise in one hand. He nodded encouragingly, then gestured Forbis toward the balcony, eager to rest the valise on the ledge.

'Feel anything?'

'Nothing.' Forbis laughed, a brittle chuckle. 'It must have been one of those impractical jokes – "*Now let's see you get down.*" Can I look into the street?'

'Of course,' Vansittart agreed, bracing himself to seize Forbis if the little man attempted to jump. Beyond the balcony was a thousand-foot drop into a busy shopping thoroughfare.

Forbis clasped the near edge of the balcony in his palms and peered down at the lunch crowds below. Cars edged and shunted like coloured fleas, and people milled about aimlessly on the pavements. Nothing of any interest seemed to be happening.

Beside him, Vansittart frowned and glanced at his watch, wondering whether something had misfired. 'It's 12.30,' he said. 'We'll give up –'

He broke off as footsteps creaked on the stairway below. He swung around and watched the doorway, gesturing to Forbis to keep quiet.

As he turned his back the small man suddenly reached up and cut him sharply across the neck with the edge of his right hand, stunning him momentarily. When Vansittart staggered back he expertly chopped him on both sides of the throat, then sat him down and kicked him senseless with his knees.

Working swiftly, he ignored the broad shadow which reached across the roof to him from the doorway. He carefully fastened Vansittart's three jacket buttons, and then levered him up by the lapels on to his shoulder.

Backing against the balcony, he slid him on to the ledge, straightening his legs one after the other. Vansittart stirred helplessly, head lolling from side to side.

*And ... and ...*

Behind Forbis the shadow drew nearer, reaching up the side of the balcony, a broad neckless head between heavy shoulders.

Cutting off his pumping breath, Forbis reached out with both hands and pushed.

Ten seconds later, as horns sounded up dimly from the street below, he turned around.

'Good boy, Forbis.'

The big man's voice was flat but relaxed. Ten feet from Forbis, he watched him amiably. His face was plump and sallow, a callous mouth half-hidden by a brush moustache. He wore a bulky black overcoat, and one hand rested confidently in a deep pocket.

'Fowler!' Involuntarily, Forbis tried to move forward, for a moment attempting to reassemble his perspectives, but his feet had locked into the white surface of the roof.

Three hundred feet above, an airliner roared over. In a lucid interval provided by the noise, Forbis recognized Fowler, Vansittart's rival for the psychology professorship, remembered the long sessions of hypnosis after Fowler had picked him up in a bar three months earlier, offering to cure his chronic depression before it slid into alcoholism.

With a grasp, he remembered too the rest of the buried command. So Vansittart had been the real target, not himself! *Go up to the 100th floor and ...* His first attempt at Vansittart had been a month earlier, when Fowler had left him on the roof and then pretended to be the janitor, but Vansittart had brought two others with him. The mysterious hidden command had been the bait to lure Vansittart to the roof again. Cunningly, Fowler had known that sooner or later Vansittart would yield to the temptation.

'And ...' he said aloud.

Looking for Vansittart, in the absurd hope that he might have survived the thousand-foot fall, he started for the balcony, then tried to hold himself back as the current caught him.

'And –?' Fowler repeated pleasantly. His eyes, two festering points of light, made Forbis sway. 'There's still some more to come, isn't there, Forbis? You're beginning to remember it now.'

Mind draining, Forbis turned to the balcony, dry mouth sucking at the air.

'And –?' Fowler snapped, his voice harder.

*... And ... and ...*

Numbly, Forbis jumped up on to the balcony, and poised on the narrow ledge like a diver, the streets swaying before his eyes. Below, the horns were silent again and the traffic had resumed its flow, a knot of vehicles drawn up in the centre of a small crowd by the edge of the pavement. For a few moments he managed to resist, and then the current caught him, toppling him like a drifting spar.

Fowler stepped quietly through the doorway. Ten seconds later, the horns sounded again.

**1962**

# ·THE SUBLIMINAL MAN

'The signs, Doctor! Have you seen the signs?'

Frowning with annoyance, Dr Franklin quickened his pace and hurried down the hospital steps towards the line of parked cars. Over his shoulder he caught a glimpse of a young man in ragged sandals and paint-stained jeans waving to him from the far side of the drive.

'Dr Franklin! The signs!'

Head down, Franklin swerved around an elderly couple approaching the out-patients department. His car was over a hundred yards away. Too tired to start running himself, he waited for the young man to catch him up.

'All right, Hathaway, what is it this time?' he snapped. 'I'm sick of you hanging around here all day.'

Hathaway lurched to a halt in front of him, uncut black hair like an awning over his eyes. He brushed it back with a claw-like hand and turned on a wild smile, obviously glad to see Franklin and oblivious of the latter's hostility.

'I've been trying to reach you at night, Doctor, but your wife always puts the phone down on me,' he explained without a hint of rancour, as if well-used to this kind of snub. 'And I didn't want to look for you inside the Clinic.' They were standing by a privet hedge that shielded them from the lower windows of the main administrative block, but Franklin's regular rendezvous with Hathaway and his strange messianic cries had already become the subject of amused comment.

Franklin began to say: 'I appreciate that –' but Hathaway brushed this aside. 'Forget it, Doctor, there are more important things now. They've started to build the first big signs! Over a hundred feet high, on the traffic islands outside town. They'll soon have all the approach roads covered. When they do we might as well stop thinking.'

'Your trouble is that you're thinking too much,' Franklin told him. 'You've been rambling about these signs for weeks now. Tell me, have you actually seen one signalling?'

Hathaway tore a handful of leaves from the hedge, exasperated by this irrelevancy. 'Of course I haven't, that's the whole point, Doctor.' He dropped his voice as a group of nurses walked past, watching his raffish figure out of the corners of their eyes. 'The construction gangs were out again last night, laying huge power cables. You'll see them on the way home. Everything's nearly ready now.'

'They're traffic signs,' Franklin explained patiently. 'The flyover has just been completed. Hathaway, for God's sake, relax. Try to think of Dora and the child.'

'I *am* thinking of them!' Hathaway's voice rose to a controlled scream. 'Those cables were 40,000-volt lines, Doctor, with terrific switch-gear. The trucks were loaded with enormous metal scaffolds. Tomorrow they'll start lifting them up all over the city, they'll block off half the sky! What do you think Dora will be like after six months of that? We've got to stop them, Doctor, they're trying to transistorize our brains!'

Embarrassed by Hathaway's high-pitched shouting, Franklin had momentarily lost his sense of direction. Helplessly he searched the sea of cars for his own. 'Hathaway, I can't waste any more time talking to you. Believe me, you need skilled help, these obsessions are beginning to master you.'

Hathaway started to protest, and Franklin raised his right hand firmly. 'Listen. For the last time, if you can show me one of these signs, and prove it's transmitting subliminal commands, I'll go to the police with you. But you haven't got a shred of evidence, and you know it. Subliminal advertising was banned thirty years ago, and the laws have never been repealed. Anyway, the technique was unsatisfactory, any success it had was marginal. Your idea of a huge conspiracy with all these thousands of giant signs everywhere is preposterous.'

'All right, Doctor.' Hathaway leaned against the bonnet of one of the cars. His mood seemed to switch abruptly from one level to the next. He watched Franklin amiably. 'What's the matter – lost your car?'

'All your damned shouting has confused me.' Franklin pulled out his ignition key and read the number off the tag: 'NYN 299-566-367-21 – can you see it?'

Hathaway leaned around lazily, one sandal up on the bonnet, surveying the square of a thousand or so cars facing them. 'Difficult, isn't it, when they're all identical, even the same colour? Thirty years ago there were about ten different makes, each in a dozen colours.'

Franklin spotted his car and began to walk towards it. 'Sixty years ago there were a hundred makes. What of it? The economies of standardization are obviously bought at a price.'

Hathaway drummed his palm on the roofs. 'But these cars aren't all that cheap, Doctor. In fact, comparing them on an average income basis with those of thirty years ago they're about forty per cent more expensive. With only one make being produced you'd expect a substantial reduction in price, not an increase.'

'Maybe,' Franklin said, opening his door. 'But mechanically the cars of today are far more sophisticated. They're lighter, more durable, safer to drive.'

Hathaway shook his head sceptically. 'They *bore* me. The same model, same styling, same colour, year after year. It's a sort of communism.' He rubbed a greasy finger over the windshield. 'This is a new one again, isn't it, Doctor? Where's the old one – you only had it for three months?'

'I traded it in,' Franklin told him, starting the engine. 'If you ever had any money you'd realize that it's the most economical way of owning a car. You don't keep driving the same one until it falls apart. It's the same with everything else – television sets, washing machines, refrigerators. But you aren't faced with the problem.'

Hathaway ignored the gibe, and leaned his elbow on Franklin's window. 'Not a bad idea, either, Doctor. It gives me time to think. I'm not working a twelve-hour day to pay for a lot of things I'm too busy to use before they're obsolete.'

He waved as Franklin reversed the car out of its line, then shouted into the wake of exhaust: 'Drive with your eyes closed, Doctor!'

On the way home Franklin kept carefully to the slowest of the four-speed lanes. As usual after his discussions with Hathaway, he felt vaguely depressed. He realized that unconsciously he envied Hathaway his foot-loose existence. Despite the grimy cold-water apartment in the shadow and roar of the flyover, despite his nagging wife and their sick child, and the endless altercations with the landlord and the supermarket credit manager, Hathaway still retained his freedom intact. Spared any responsibilities, he could resist the smallest encroachment upon him by the rest of society, if only by generating obsessive fantasies such as his latest one about subliminal advertising.

The ability to react to stimuli, even irrationally, was a valid criterion of freedom. By contrast, what freedom Franklin possessed was peripheral, sharply demarked by the manifold responsibilities in the centre of his life – the three mortgages on his home, the mandatory rounds of cocktail parties, the private consultancy occupying most of Saturday which paid the instalments on the multitude of household gadgets, clothes and past holidays. About the only time he had to himself was driving to and from work.

But at least the roads were magnificent. Whatever other criticisms might be levelled at the present society, it certainly knew how to build roads. Eight-, ten- and twelve-lane expressways interlaced across the country, plunging from overhead causeways into the giant car parks in the centre of the cities, or dividing into the great suburban arteries with their multi-acre parking aprons around the marketing centres. Together the roadways and car parks covered more than a third of the country's entire area, and in the neighbourhood of the cities the proportion was higher. The old cities were surrounded by the vast motion sculptures of the clover-leaves and flyovers, but even so the congestion was unremitting.

The ten-mile journey to his home in fact covered over twenty-five miles and took him twice as long as it had done before the construction of the expressway, the additional miles contained within the three giant clover-leaves. New cities were springing from the motels, cafés and car marts around the highways. At the slightest hint of an intersection a shanty town of shacks and filling stations sprawled away among the forest of electric signs and route indicators.

All around him cars bulleted along, streaming towards the suburbs. Relaxed by the smooth motion of the car, Franklin edged outwards into the next speed-lane. As he accelerated from 40 to 50 m.p.h. a strident ear-jarring noise drummed out from his tyres, shaking the chassis of the car. Ostensibly an aid to lane discipline, the surface of the road was covered with a mesh of small rubber studs, spaced progressively farther apart in each of the lanes so that the tyre hum resonated exactly on 40, 50, 60 and 70 m.p.h. Driving at an intermediate speed for more than a few seconds became nervously exhausting, and soon resulted in damage to the car and tyres.

When the studs wore out they were replaced by slightly different patterns, matching those on the latest tyres, so that regular tyre changes were necessary, increasing the safety and efficiency of the expressway. It also increased the revenues of the car and tyre manufacturers. Most cars over six months old soon fell to pieces under the steady battering, but this was regarded as a desirable end, the greater turnover reducing the unit price and making more frequent model changes, as well as ridding the roads of dangerous vehicles.

A quarter of a mile ahead, at the approach to the first of the clover-leaves, the traffic stream was slowing, huge police signs signalling 'Lanes Closed Ahead' and 'Drop Speed by 10 m.p.h.'. Franklin tried to return to the previous lane, but the cars were jammed bumper to bumper. As the chassis began to shudder and vibrate, jarring his spine, he clamped his teeth and tried to restrain himself from sounding the horn. Other drivers were less self-controlled and everywhere engines were plunging and snarling, horns blaring. Road taxes were now so high, up to thirty per cent of the gross national product (by contrast, income taxes were a bare two per cent) that any delay on the expressways called for an immediate government inquiry, and the major departments of state were concerned with the administration of the road systems.

Nearer the clover-leaf the lanes had been closed to allow a gang of construction workers to erect a massive metal sign on one of the traffic islands. The palisaded area swarmed with engineers and surveyors, and Franklin assumed that this was the sign Hathaway had seen unloaded the previous night. His apartment was in one of the gimcrack buildings in the settlement that straggled away around a near-by flyover, a low-rent area inhabited by service-station personnel, waitresses and other migrant labour.

The sign was enormous, at least a hundred feet high, fitted with heavy concave grilles similar to radar bowls. Rooted in a series of concrete caissons, it reared high into the air above the approach roads, visible for miles. Franklin craned up at the grilles, tracing the power cables from the transformers up into the intricate mesh of metal coils that covered their surface. A line of red aircraft-warning beacons was already alight along the top strut, and Franklin assumed that the sign was part of the ground approach system of the city airport ten miles to the east.

Three minutes later, as he accelerated down the two-mile link of straight highway to the next clover-leaf, he saw the second of the giant signs looming up into the sky before him.

Changing down into the 40 m.p.h. lane, Franklin watched the great bulk of the second sign recede in his rear-view mirror. Although there were no graphic symbols among the wire coils covering the grilles, Hathaway's warnings still sounded in his ears. Without knowing why, he felt sure that the signs were not part of the airport approach system. Neither of them was in line with the principal air-lines. To justify the expense of siting them in the centre of the expressway – the second sign required elaborate angled buttresses to support it on the narrow island – obviously meant that their role related in some way to the traffic streams.

Two hundred yards away was a roadside auto-mart, and Franklin abruptly remembered that he needed some cigarettes. Swinging the car down the entrance ramp, he joined the queue passing the self-service dispenser at the far end of the rank. The auto-mart was packed with cars, each of the five purchasing ranks lined with tired-looking men hunched over their wheels.

Inserting his coins (paper money was no longer in circulation, unmanageable by the automats) he took a carton from the dispenser. This was the only brand of cigarettes available – in fact there was only one brand of everything – though giant economy packs were an alternative. Moving off, he opened the dashboard locker.

Inside, still sealed in their wrappers, were three other cartons.

A strong fish-like smell pervaded the house when he reached home, steaming out from the oven in the kitchen. Sniffing it uneagerly, Franklin took off his coat and hat. His wife was crouched over the TV set in the lounge. An announcer was dictating a stream of numbers, and Judith scribbled them down on a pad, occasionally cursing under her breath. 'What a muddle!' she snapped. 'He was talking so quickly I took only a few things down.'

'Probably deliberate,' Franklin commented. 'A new panel game?'

Judith kissed him on the cheek, discreetly hiding the ashtray loaded with cigarette butts and chocolate wrappings. 'Hello, darling, sorry not to have a drink ready for you. They've started this series of Spot Bargains, they give you a selection of things on which you get a ninety per cent trade-in discount at the local stores, if you're in the right area and have the right serial numbers. It's all terribly complicated.'

'Sounds good, though. What have you got?'

Judith peered at her checklist. 'Well, as far as I can see the only thing is the infra-red barbecue spit. But we have to be there before eight o'clock tonight. It's seven thirty already.'

'Then that's out. I'm tired, angel, I need something to eat.' When Judith started to protest he added firmly: 'Look, I don't want a new infra-red barbecue spit, we've only had this one for two months. Damn it, it's not even a different model.'

'But, darling, don't you see, it makes it cheaper if you keep buying new ones. We'll have to trade ours in at the end of the year anyway, we signed the contract, and this way we save at least five pounds. These Spot Bargains aren't just a gimmick, you know. I've been glued to that set all day.' A note of irritation had crept into her voice, but Franklin stood his ground, doggedly ignoring the clock.

'Right, we lose five pounds. It's worth it.' Before she could remonstrate he said: 'Judith, please, you probably took the wrong number down anyway.' As she shrugged and went over to the bar he called: 'Make it a stiff one. I see we have health foods on the menu.'

'They're good for you, darling. You know you can't live on ordinary foods all the time. They don't contain any proteins or vitamins. You're always saying we ought to be like people in the old days and eat nothing but health foods.'

'I would, but they smell so awful.' Franklin lay back, nose in the glass of whisky, gazing at the darkened skyline outside.

A quarter of a mile away, gleaming out above the roof of the neighbourhood supermarket, were the five red beacon lights. Now and then, as the headlamps of the Spot Bargainers swung up across the face of the building, he could see the massive bulk of the sign clearly silhouetted against the evening sky.

'Judith!' He went into the kitchen and took her over to the window. 'That sign, just behind the supermarket. When did they put it up?'

'I don't know.' Judith peered at him. 'Why are you so worried, Robert? Isn't it something to do with the airport?'

Franklin stared at the dark hull of the sign. 'So everyone probably thinks.'

Carefully he poured his whisky into the sink.

After parking his car on the supermarket apron at seven o'clock the next morning, Franklin carefully emptied his pockets and stacked the coins in the dashboard locker. The supermarket was already busy with early morning shoppers and the line of thirty turnstiles clicked and slammed. Since the introduction of the '24-hour spending day' the shopping complex was never closed. The bulk of the shoppers were discount buyers, housewives contracted to make huge volume purchases of food, clothing and appliances against substantial overall price cuts, and forced to drive around all day from supermarket to supermarket, frantically trying to keep pace with their purchase schedules and grappling with the added incentives inserted to keep the schemes alive.

Many of the women had teamed up, and as Franklin walked over to the entrance a pack of them charged towards their cars, stuffing their pay slips into their bags and shouting at each other. A moment later their cars roared off in a convoy to the next marketing zone.

A large neon sign over the entrance listed the latest discount – a mere five per cent – calculated on the volume of turnover. The highest discounts, sometimes up to twenty-five per cent, were earned in the housing estates where junior white-collar workers lived. There, spending had a strong social incentive, and the desire to be the highest spender in the neighbourhood was given moral reinforcement by the system of listing all the names and their accumulating cash totals on a huge electric sign in the supermarket foyers. The higher the spender, the greater his contribution to the discounts enjoyed by others. The lowest spenders were regarded as social criminals, free-riding on the backs of others.

Luckily this system had yet to be adopted in Franklin's neighbourhood – not because the Professional men and their wives were able to exercise more discretion, but because their higher incomes allowed them to contract into more expensive discount schemes operated by the big department stores in the city.

Ten yards from the entrance Franklin paused, looking up at the huge metal sign mounted in an enclosure at the edge of the car park. Unlike the other signs and hoardings that proliferated everywhere, no attempt had been made to decorate it, or disguise the gaunt bare rectangle of riveted steel mesh. Power lines wound down its sides, and the concrete surface of the car park was crossed by a long scar where a cable had been sunk.

Franklin strolled along. Fifty feet from the sign he stopped and turned, realizing that he would be late for the hospital and needed a new carton of cigarettes. A dim but powerful humming emanated from the transformers below the sign, fading as he retraced his steps to the supermarket.

Going over to the automats in the foyer, he felt for his change, then whistled sharply when he remembered why he had deliberately emptied his pockets.

'Hathaway!' he said, loudly enough for two shoppers to stare at him. Reluctant to look directly at the sign, he watched its reflection in one of the glass door-panes, so that any subliminal message would be reversed.

Almost certainly he had received two distinct signals – 'Keep Away' and 'Buy Cigarettes'. The people who normally parked their cars along the perimeter of the apron were avoiding the area under the enclosure, the cars describing a loose semi-circle fifty feet around it.

He turned to the janitor sweeping out the foyer. 'What's that sign for?'

The man leaned on his broom, gazing dully at the sign. 'No idea,' he said. 'Must be something to do with the airport.' He had a fresh cigarette in his mouth, but his right hand reached to his hip pocket and pulled out a pack. He drummed the second cigarette absently on his thumbnail as Franklin walked away.

Everyone entering the supermarket was buying cigarettes.

*          *          *

Cruising quietly along the 40 m.p.h. lane, Franklin began to take a closer interest in the landscape around him. Usually he was either too tired or too preoccupied to do more than think about his driving, but now he examined the expressway methodically, scanning the roadside cafés for any smaller versions of the new signs. A host of neon displays covered the doorways and windows, but most of them seemed innocuous, and he turned his attention to the larger billboards erected along the open stretches of the expressway. Many of these were as high as four-storey houses, elaborate three-dimensional devices in which giant housewives with electric eyes and teeth jerked and postured around their ideal kitchens, neon flashes exploding from their smiles.

The areas on either side of the expressway were wasteland, continuous junkyards filled with cars and trucks, washing machines and refrigerators, all perfectly workable but jettisoned by the economic pressure of the succeeding waves of discount models. Their intact chrome hardly tarnished, the metal shells and cabinets glittered in the sunlight. Nearer the city the billboards were sufficiently close together to hide them but now and then, as he slowed to approach one of the flyovers, Franklin caught a glimpse of the huge pyramids of metal, gleaming silently like the refuse grounds of some forgotten El Dorado.

That evening Hathaway was waiting for him as he came down the hospital steps. Franklin waved him across the court, then led the way quickly to his car.

'What's the matter, Doctor?' Hathaway asked as Franklin wound up the windows and glanced around the lines of parked cars. 'Is someone after you?'

Franklin laughed sombrely. 'I don't know. I hope not, but if what you say is right, I suppose there is.'

Hathaway leaned back with a chuckle, propping one knee up on the dashboard. 'So you've seen something, Doctor, after all.'

'Well, I'm not sure yet, but there's just a chance you may be right. This morning at the Fairlawne supermarket . . .' He broke off, uneasily remembering the huge black sign and the abrupt way in which he had turned back to the supermarket as he approached it, then described his encounter.

Hathaway nodded. 'I've seen the sign there. It's big, but not as big as some that are going up. They're building them everywhere now. All over the city. What are you going to do, Doctor?'

Franklin gripped the wheel tightly. Hathaway's thinly veiled amusement irritated him. 'Nothing, of course. Damn it, it may be just auto-suggestion, you've probably got me imagining –'

Hathaway sat up with a jerk. 'Don't be absurd, Doctor! If you can't believe your own senses what chance have you left? They're invading your brain, if you don't defend yourself they'll take it over completely! We've got to act now, before we're all paralysed.'

Wearily Franklin raised one hand to restrain him. 'Just a minute. Assuming that these signs *are* going up everywhere, what would be their object? Apart from wasting the enormous amount of capital invested in all the other millions of signs and billboards, the amounts of discretionary spending power still available must be infinitesimal. Some of the present mortgage and discount schemes reach half a century ahead. A big trade war would be disastrous.'

'Quite right, Doctor,' Hathaway rejoined evenly, 'but you're forgetting one thing. What would supply that extra spending power? A big increase in production. Already they've started to raise the working day from twelve hours to fourteen. In some of the appliance plants around the city Sunday working is being introduced as a norm. Can you visualize it, Doctor – a seven-day week, everyone with at least three jobs.'

Franklin shook his head. 'People won't stand for it.'

'They will. Within the last twenty-five years the gross national product has risen by fifty per cent, but so have the average hours worked. Ultimately we'll all be working and spending twenty-four hours a day, seven days a week. No one will dare refuse. Think what a slump would mean – millions of lay-offs, people with time on their hands and nothing to spend it on. Real leisure, not just time spent buying things,' He seized Franklin by the shoulder. 'Well, Doctor, are you going to join me?'

Franklin freed himself. Half a mile away, partly hidden by the four-storey bulk of the Pathology Department, was the upper half of one of the giant signs, workmen still crawling across its girders. The airlines over the city had deliberately been routed away from the hospital, and the sign obviously had no connection with approaching aircraft.

'Isn't there a prohibition on – what did they call it – subliminal living? How can the unions accept it?'

'The fear of a slump. You know the new economic dogmas. Unless output rises by a steady inflationary five per cent the economy is stagnating. Ten years ago increased efficiency alone would raise output, but the advantages there are minimal now and only one thing is left. More work. Subliminal advertising will provide the spur.'

'What are you planning to do?'

'I can't tell you, Doctor, unless you accept equal responsibility for it.'

'That sounds rather Quixotic,' Franklin commented. 'Tilting at windmills. You won't be able to chop those things down with an axe.'

'I won't try.' Hathaway opened the door. 'Don't wait too long to make up your mind, Doctor. By then it may not be yours to make up.' With a wave he was gone.

On the way home Franklin's scepticism returned. The idea of the conspiracy was preposterous, and the economic arguments were too plausible. As usual, though, there had been a hook in the soft bait Hathaway dangled before him – Sunday working. His own consultancy had been extended into Sunday morning with his appointment as visiting factory doctor to one of the automobile plants that had started Sunday shifts. But instead of resenting this incursion into his already meagre hours of leisure he had been glad. For one frightening reason – he needed the extra income.

Looking out over the lines of scurrying cars, he noticed that at least a dozen of the great signs had been erected along the expressway. As Hathaway had said, more were going up everywhere, rearing over the supermarkets in the housing developments like rusty metal sails.

Judith was in the kitchen when he reached home, watching the TV programme on the hand-set over the cooker. Franklin climbed past a big cardboard carton, its seals still unbroken, which blocked the doorway, kissed her on the cheek as she scribbled numbers down on her pad. The pleasant odour of pot-roast chicken – or, rather a gelatine dummy of a chicken fully flavoured and free of any toxic or nutritional properties – mollified his irritation at finding her still playing the Spot Bargains.

He tapped the carton with his foot. 'What's this?'

'No idea, darling, something's always coming these days, I can't keep up with it all.' She peered through the glass door at the chicken – an economy twelve-pounder, the size of a turkey, with stylized legs and wings and an enormous breast, most of which would be discarded at the end of the meal (there were no dogs or cats these days, the crumbs from the rich man's table saw to that) – and then glanced at him pointedly.

'You look rather worried, Robert. Bad day?'

Franklin murmured noncommittally. The hours spent trying to detect false clues in the faces of the Spot Bargain announcers had sharpened Judith's perceptions. He felt a pang of sympathy for the legion of husbands similarly outmatched.

'Have you been talking to that crazy beatnik again?'

'Hathaway? As a matter of fact I have. He's not all that crazy.' He stepped backwards into the carton, almost spilling his drink. 'Well, what is this thing? As I'll be working for the next fifty Sundays to pay for it I'd like to find out.'

He searched the sides, finally located the label. '*A TV set?* Judith, do we need another one? We've already got three. Lounge, dining-room and the hand-set. What's the fourth for?'

'The guest-room, dear, don't get so excited. We can't leave a hand-set in the guest-room, it's rude. I'm trying to economize, but four TV sets is the bare minimum. All the magazines say so.'

'*And* three radios?' Franklin stared irritably at the carton. 'If we do invite a guest here how much time is he going to spend alone in his room watching television? Judith, we've got to call a halt. It's not as if these things were free, or even cheap. Anyway, television is a total waste of time. There's only one programme. It's ridiculous to have four sets.'

'Robert, there are *four* channels.'

'But only the commercials are different.' Before Judith could reply the telephone rang. Franklin lifted the kitchen receiver, listened to the gabble of noise that poured from it. At first he wondered whether this was some offbeat prestige commercial, then realized it was Hathaway in a manic swing.

'Hathaway!' he shouted back. 'Relax, for God's sake! What's the matter now?'

'– Doctor, you'll have to believe me this time. I climbed on to one of the islands with a stroboscope, they've got hundreds of high-speed shutters blasting away like machine-guns straight into people's faces and they can't see a thing, it's fantastic! The next big campaign's going to be cars and TV sets, they're trying to swing a two-month model change – can you imagine it, Doctor, a new car every two months? God Almighty, it's just –'

Franklin waited impatiently as the five-second commercial break cut in (all telephone calls were free, the length of the commercial extending with range – for long-distance calls the ratio of commercial to conversation was as high as 10:1, the participants desperately trying to get a word in edgeways between the interminable interruptions), but just before it ended he abruptly put the telephone down, then removed the receiver from the cradle.

Judith came over and took his arm. 'Robert, what's the matter? You look terribly strained.'

Franklin picked up his drink and walked through into the lounge. 'It's just Hathaway. As you say, I'm getting a little too involved with him. He's starting to prey on my mind.'

He looked at the dark outline of the sign over the supermarket, its red warning lights glowing in the night sky. Blank and nameless, like an area for ever closed-off in an insane mind, what frightened him was its total anonymity.

'Yet I'm not sure,' he muttered. 'So much of what Hathaway says makes sense. These subliminal techniques are the sort of last-ditch attempt you'd expect from an over-capitalized industrial system.'

He waited for Judith to reply, then looked up at her. She stood in the centre of the carpet, hands folded limply, her sharp, intelligent face curiously dull and blunted. He followed her gaze out over the rooftops, then with an effort turned his head and quickly switched on the TV set.

'Come on,' he said grimly. 'Let's watch television. God, we're going to need that fourth set.'

A week later Franklin began to compile his inventory. He saw nothing more of Hathaway; as he left the hospital in the evening the familiar scruffy figure was absent. When the first of the explosions sounded dimly around the city and he read of the attempts to sabotage the giant signs he automatically assumed that Hathaway was responsible, but later he heard on a newscast that the detonations had been set off by construction workers excavating foundations.

More of the signs appeared over the rooftops, isolated on the palisaded islands near the suburban shopping centres. Already there were over thirty on the ten-mile route from the hospital, standing shoulder to shoulder over the speeding cars like giant dominoes. Franklin had given up his attempt to avoid looking at them, but the slim possibility that the explosions might be Hathaway's counter-attack kept his suspicions alive.

He began his inventory after hearing the newscast, and discovered that in the previous fortnight he and Judith had traded in their

> Car (previous model 2 months old)
> 2 TV sets (4 months)
> Power mower (7 months)
> Electric cooker (5 months)
> Hair dryer (4 months)
> Refrigerator (3 months)
> 2 radios (7 months)
> Record player (5 months)
> Cocktail bar (8 months)

Half these purchases had been made by himself, but exactly when he could never recall realizing at the time. The car, for example, he had left in the garage near the hospital to be greased, that evening had signed for the new model as he sat at its wheel, accepting the saleman's assurance that the depreciation on the two-month trade-in was virtually less than the cost of the grease-job. Ten minutes later, as he sped along the expressway, he suddenly realized that he had bought a new car. Similarly, the TV sets had been replaced by identical models after developing the same irritating interference pattern (curiously, the new sets also displayed the pattern, but as the salesman assured them, this promptly vanished two days later). Not once had he actually decided of his own volition that he wanted something and then gone out to a store and bought it!

He carried the inventory around with him, adding to it as necessary, quietly and without protest analysing these new sales techniques, wondering whether total capitulation might be the only way of defeating them. As long as he kept up even a token resistance, the inflationary growth curve would show a controlled annual ten per cent climb. With that resistance removed, however, it would begin to rocket upwards out of control . . .

Driving home from the hospital two months later, he saw one of the signs for the first time.

He was in the 40 m.p.h. lane, unable to keep up with the flood of new cars, and had just passed the second of the three clover-leaves when the traffic half a mile away began to slow down. Hundreds of cars had driven up on to the grass verge, and a crowd was gathering around one of the signs. Two small black figures were climbing up the metal face, and a series of grid-like patterns of light flashed on and off, illuminating the evening air. The patterns were random and broken, as if the sign was being tested for the first time.

Relieved that Hathaway's suspicions had been completely groundless, Franklin turned off on to the soft shoulder, then walked forward through the spectators as the lights stuttered in their faces. Below, behind the steel palisades around the island, was a large group of police and engineers, craning up at the men scaling the sign a hundred feet over their heads.

Suddenly Franklin stopped, the sense of relief fading instantly. Several of the police on the ground were armed with shotguns, and the two policemen climbing the sign carried submachine-guns slung over their shoulders. They were converging on a third figure, crouched by a switch-box on the penultimate tier, a bearded man in a grimy shirt, a bare knee poking through his jeans.

Hathaway!

Franklin hurried towards the island, the sign hissing and spluttering, fuses blowing by the dozen.

Then the flicker of lights cleared and steadied, blazing out continuously, and together the crowd looked up at the decks of brilliant letters. The phrases, and every combination of them possible, were entirely familiar, and Franklin knew that he had been reading them for weeks as he passed up and down the expressway.

BUY NOW BUY NOW BUY NOW BUY NOW BUY
NEW CAR NOW NEW CAR NOW NEW CAR NOW
YES YES YES YES YES YES YES YES YES YES

Sirens blaring, two patrol cars swung on to the verge through the crowd and plunged across the damp grass. Police spilled from their doors, batons in their hands, and quickly began to force back the crowd. Franklin held his ground as they approached, started to say: 'Officer, I know the man –' but the policeman punched him in the chest with the flat of his hand. Winded, he stumbled back among the cars, and leaned helplessly against a fender as the police began to break the windshields, the hapless drivers protesting angrily, those farther back rushing for their vehicles.

The noise fell away when one of the submachine-guns fired a brief roaring burst, then rose in a massive gasp as Hathaway, arms outstretched, let out a cry of triumph and pain, and jumped.

'But, Robert, what does it really matter?' Judith asked as Franklin sat inertly in the lounge the next morning. 'I know it's tragic for his wife and daughter, but Hathaway was in the grip of an obsession. If he hated advertising signs so much why didn't he dynamite those we *can* see, instead of worrying so much about those we can't?'

Franklin stared at the TV screen, hoping the programme would distract him.

'Hathaway was *right*,' he said.

'Was he? Advertising is here to stay. We've no real freedom of choice, anyway. We can't spend more than we can afford, the finance companies soon clamp down.'

'Do you accept that?' Franklin went over to the window. A quarter of a mile away, in the centre of the estate, another of the signs was being erected. It was due east from them, and in the early morning light the shadows of its rectangular superstructure fell across the garden, reaching almost to the steps of the french windows at his feet. As a concession to the neighbourhood, and perhaps to allay any suspicions while it was being erected by an appeal to petty snobbery, the lower sections had been encased in mock-Tudor panelling.

Franklin stared at it, counting the half-dozen police lounging by their patrol cars as the construction gang unloaded the prefabricated grilles from a truck. He looked at the sign by the supermarket, trying to repress his memories of Hathaway and the pathetic attempts the man had made to convince Franklin and gain his help.

He was still standing there an hour later when Judith came in, putting on her hat and coat, ready to visit the supermarket.

Franklin followed her to the door. 'I'll drive you down there, Judith. I have to see about booking a new car. The next models are coming out at the end of the month. With luck we'll get one of the early deliveries.'

They walked out into the trim drive, the shadows of the signs swinging across the quiet neighbourhood as the day progressed, sweeping over the heads of the people on their way to the supermarket like the blades of enormous scythes.

· **1963**

# THE REPTILE ENCLOSURE

'They remind me of the Gadarene swine,' Mildred Pelham remarked.

Interrupting his scrutiny of the crowded beach below the cafeteria terrace, Roger Pelham glanced at his wife. 'Why do you say that?'

Mildred continued to read for a few moments, and then lowered her book. 'Well, don't they?' she asked rhetorically. 'They look like pigs.'

Pelham smiled weakly at this mild but characteristic display of misanthropy. He peered down at his own white knees protruding from his shorts and at his wife's plump arms and shoulders. 'I suppose we all do,' he temporized. However, there was little chance of Mildred's remark being overheard and resented. They were sitting at a corner table, with their backs to the hundreds of ice-cream eaters and cola-drinkers crammed elbow to elbow on the terrace. The dull hubbub of voices was overlaid by the endless commentaries broadcast over the transistor radios propped among the bottles, and by the distant sounds of the fairground behind the dunes.

A short drop below the terrace was the beach, covered by a mass of reclining figures which stretched from the water's edge up to the roadway behind the cafeteria and then away over the dunes. Not a single grain of sand was visible. Even at the tide-line, where a little slack water swilled weakly at a debris of old cigarette packets and other trash, a huddle of small children clung to the skirt of the beach, hiding the grey sand.

Gazing down at the beach again, Pelham realized that his wife's ungenerous judgment was no more than the truth. Everywhere bare haunches and shoulders jutted into the air, limbs lay in serpentine coils. Despite the sunlight and the considerable period of time they had spent on the beach, many of the people were still white-skinned, or at most a boiled pink, restlessly shifting in their little holes in a hopeless attempt to be comfortable.

Usually this spectacle of jostling, over-exposed flesh, with its unsavoury bouquet of stale suntan lotion and sweat – looking along the beach as it swept out to the distant cape, Pelham could almost see the festering corona, sustained in the air by the babble of ten thousand transistor radios, reverberating like a swarm of flies – would have sent him hurtling along the first inland highway at seventy miles an hour. But for some reason Pelham's usual private distaste for the general public had evaporated. He felt strangely exhilarated by the presence of so many people (he had calculated that he could see over 50 thousand along the five-mile stretch of beach) and found himself unable to leave the terrace, although it was now 3 o'clock and neither he nor Mildred had eaten since breakfast. Once their corner seats were surrendered they would never regain them.

To himself he mused: 'The ice-cream eaters on Echo beach ...' He played with the empty glass in front of him. Shreds of synthetic orange pulp clung to the sides, and a fly buzzed half-heartedly from one to another. The sea was flat and calm, an opaque grey disc, but a mile away a low surface mist lay over the water like vapour on a vat.

'You look hot, Roger. Why don't you go in for a swim?'

'I may. You know, it's a curious thing, but of all the people here, not one is swimming.'

Mildred nodded in a bored way. A large passive woman, she seemed content merely to sit in the sunlight and read. Yet it was she who had first suggested that they drive out to the coast, and for once had suppressed her usual grumbles when they ran into the first heavy traffic jams and were forced to abandon the car and complete the remaining two miles on foot. Pelham had not seen her walk like that for ten years.

'It is rather strange,' she said. 'But it's not particularly warm.'

'I don't agree.' Pelham was about to continue when he suddenly stood up and looked over the rail at the beach. Halfway down the slope, parallel with the promenade, a continuous stream of people moved slowly along an informal right-of-way, shouldering past each other with fresh bottles of cola, lotion and ice-cream.

'Roger, what's the matter?'

'Nothing . . . I thought I saw Sherrington.' Pelham searched the beach, the moment of recognition lost.

'You're always seeing Sherrington. That's the fourth time alone this afternoon. Do stop worrying.'

'I'm not worrying. I can't be certain, but I felt I saw him then.'

Reluctantly, Pelham sat down, edging his chair fractionally closer to the rail. Depite his mood of lethargy and vacuous boredom, an indefinable but distinct feeling of restlessness had preoccupied him all day. In some way associated with Sherrington's presence on the beach, this uneasiness had been increasing steadily. The chances of Sherrington – with whom he shared an office in the Physiology Department at the University – actually choosing this section of the beach were remote, and Pelham was not even sure why he was so convinced that Sherrington was there at all. Perhaps these illusory glimpses – all the more unlikely in view of Sherrington's black beard and high severe face, his stooped long-legged walk – were simply projections of this underlying tension and his own peculiar dependence upon Sherrington.

However, this sense of uneasiness was not confined to himself. Although Mildred seemed immune, most of the people on the beach appeared to share this mood with Pelham. As the day progressed the continuous hubbub gave way to more sporadic chatter. Occasionally the noise would fall away altogether, and the great concourse, like an immense crowd waiting for the long-delayed start of some public spectacle, would sit up and stir impatiently. To Pelham, watching carefully from his vantage point over the beach, these ripples of restless activity, as everyone swayed forward in long undulations, were plainly indicated by the metallic glimmer of the thousands of portable radios moving in an oscillating wave. Each successive spasm, recurring at roughly half-hour intervals, seemed to take the crowd slightly nearer the sea.

Directly below the concrete edge of the terrace, among the mass of reclining figures, a large family group had formed a private enclosure. To one side of this, literally within reach of Pelham, the adolescent members of the family had dug their own nest, their sprawling angular bodies, in their damp abbreviated swimming suits, entwined in and out of each other like some curious annular animal. Well within earshot, despite the continuous background of noise from the beach and the distant fair-grounds, Pelham listened to their inane talk, following the thread of the radio commentaries as they switched aimlessly from one station to the next.

'They're about to launch another satellite,' he told Mildred. '*Echo XXII.*'

'Why do they bother?' Mildred's flat blue eyes surveyed the distant haze over the water. 'I should have thought there were more than enough of them flying about already.'

'Well . . .' For a moment Pelham debated whether to pursue the meagre conversational possibilities of his wife's reply. Although she was married to a lecturer in the School of Physiology, her interest in scientific matters was limited to little more than a blanket condemnation of the entire sphere of activity. His own post at the University she regarded with painful tolerance, despising the untidy office, scruffy students and mean-ingless laboratory equipment. Pelham had never been able to discover exactly what calling she would have respected. Before their marriage she maintained what he later realized was a polite silence on the subject of his work; after eleven years this attitude had barely changed, although the exigencies of living on his meagre salary had forced her to take an interest in the subtle, complex and infinitely wearying game of promotional snakes and ladders.

As expected, her acerbic tongue had made them few friends, but by a curious paradox Pelham felt that he had benefited from the grudging respect this had brought her. Sometimes her waspish comments, delivered at the overlong sherry parties, always in a loud voice during some conversational silence (for example, she had described the elderly occupant of the Physiology chair as 'that gerontological freak' within some five feet of the Professor's wife) delighted Pelham by their mordant accuracy, but in general there was something frightening about her pitiless lack of sympathy for the rest of the human race. Her large bland face, with its prim, rosebud mouth, reminded Pelham of the description of the Mona

Lisa as looking as if she had just dined off her husband. Mildred, however, did not even smile.

'Sherrington has a rather interesting theory about the satellites,' Pelham told her. 'I'd hoped we might see him so that he could explain it again. I think you'd be amused to hear it, Mildred. He's working on IRM's at present –'

'On what?' The group of people behind them had turned up the volume of their radio and the commentary, of the final countdown at Cape Kennedy, boomed into the air over their heads.

Pelham said: 'IRM's – innate releasing mechanisms. I've described them to you before, they're inherited reflexes –' He stopped, watching his wife impatiently.

Mildred had turned on him the dead stare with which she surveyed the remainder of the people on the beach. Testily Pelham snapped: 'Mildred, I'm trying to explain Sherrington's theory about the satellites!'

Undeterred, Mildred shook her head. 'Roger, it's too noisy here, I can't possibly listen. And to Sherrington's theories less than to anyone else's.'

Almost imperceptibly, another wave of restless activity was sweeping along the beach. Perhaps in response to the final digital climax of the commentators at Cape Kennedy, people were sitting up and dusting the coarse sand from each other's backs. Pelham watched the sunlight flickering off the chromium radio sets and diamante sunglasses as the entire beach swayed and surged. The noise had fallen appreciably, letting through the sound of the wurlitzer at the funfair. Everywhere there was the same expectant stirring. To Pelham, his eyes half-closed in the glare, the beach seemed like an immense pit of seething white snakes.

Somewhere, a woman's voice shouted. Pelham sat forward, searching the rows of faces masked by sunglasses. There was a sharp edge to the air, an unpleasant and almost sinister implication of violence hidden below the orderly surface.

Gradually, however, the activity subsided. The great throng relaxed and reclined again. Greasily, the water lapped at the supine feet of the people lying by the edge of the sea. Propelled by one of the off-shore swells, a little slack air moved over the beach, carrying with it the sweet odour of sweat and suntan lotion. Averting his face, Pelham felt a spasm of nausea contract his gullet. Without doubt, he reflected, homo sapiens en masse presented a more unsavoury spectacle than almost any other species of animal. A corral of horses or steers conveyed an impression of powerful nervous grace, but this mass of articulated albino flesh sprawled on the beach resembled the diseased anatomical fantasy of a surrealist painter. Why had all these people congregated there? The weather reports that morning had not been especially propitious. Most of the announcements were devoted to the news of the imminent satellite launching, the last stage of the worldwide communications network which would now provide every square foot of the globe with a straight-line visual contact with one or other of the score of satellites in orbit. Perhaps the final sealing of this inescapable aerial canopy had prompted everyone to seek out the nearest beach and perform a symbolic act of self-exposure as a last gesture of surrender.

Uneasily, Pelham moved about in his chair, suddenly aware of the edge of the metal table cutting into his elbows. The cheap slatted seat was painfully uncomfortable, and his whole body seemed enclosed in an iron maiden of spikes and clamps. Again a curious premonition of some appalling act of violence stirred through his mind, and he looked up at the sky, almost expecting an airliner to plunge from the distant haze and disintegrate on the crowded beach in front of him.

To Mildred he remarked: 'It's remarkable how popular sunbathing can become. It was a major social problem in Australia before the second World War.'

Mildred's eyes flickered upwards from her book. 'There was probably nothing else to do.'

'That's just the point. As long as people are prepared to spend their entire time sprawled on a beach there's little hope of ever building up any other pastimes. Sunbathing is anti-social because it's an entirely passive pursuit.' He dropped his voice when he noticed the people sitting around him glancing over their shoulders, ears drawn to his high precise diction. 'On the other hand, it does bring people together. In the nude, or the near-nude, the shop-girl and the duchess are virtually indistinguishable.'

'*Are* they?'

Pelham shrugged. 'You know what I mean. But I think the psychological role of the beach is much more interesting. The tide-line is a particularly significant area, a penumbral zone that is both of the sea and above it, forever half-immersed in the great time-womb. If you accept the sea as an image of the unconscious, then this beachward urge might be seen as an attempt to escape from the existential role of ordinary life and return to the universal time-sea –'

'Roger, please!' Mildred looked away wearily. 'You sound like Charles Sherrington.'

Pelham stared out to sea again. Below him, a radio commentator announced the position and speed of the successfully launched satellite, and its pathway around the globe. Idly, Pelham calculated that it would take some fifteen minutes to reach them, almost exactly at half past three. Of course it would not be visible from the beach, although Sherrington's recent work on the perception of infra-red radiation suggested some of the infra-red light reflected from the sun might be perceived subliminally by their retinas.

Reflecting on the opportunities this offered to a commercial or political demagogue, Pelham listened to the radio on the sand below, when a long white arm reached out and switched it off. The possessor of the arm, a plump white-skinned girl with the face of a placid madonna, her round cheeks framed by ringlets of black hair, rolled over on to her back, disengaging herself from her companions, and for a moment she and Pelham exchanged glances. He assumed that she had deliberately switched off the radio to prevent him hearing the commentary, and then realized that in fact the girl had been listening to his voice and hoped that he would resume his monologue.

Flattered, Pelham studied the girl's round serious face, and her mature but child-like figure stretched out almost as close to him, and as naked, as it would have been had they shared a bed. Her frank, adolescent but curiously tolerant expression barely changed, and Pelham turned away, unwilling to accept its implications, realizing with a pang the profound extent of his resignation to Mildred, and the now unbreachable insulation this provided against any new or real experience in his life. For ten years the thousand cautions and compromises accepted each day to make existence tolerable had steadily secreted their numbing anodynes, and what remained of his original personality, with all its possibilities, was embalmed like a specimen in a jar. Once he would have despised himself for accepting his situation so passively, but he was now beyond any real self-judgment, for no criteria were valid by which to assess himself, a state of gracelessness far more abject than that of the vulgar, stupid herd on the beach around him.

'Something's in the water.' Mildred pointed along the shore. 'Over there.'

Pelham followed her raised arm. Two hundred yards away a small crowd had gathered at the water's edge, the sluggish waves breaking at their feet as they watched some activity in the shallows. Many of the people had raised newspapers to shield their heads, and the older women in the group held their skirts between their knees.

'I can't see anything.' Pelham rubbed his chin, distracted by a bearded man on the edge of the promenade above him, a face not Sherrington's but remarkably like it. 'There seems to be no danger, anyway. Some unusual sea-fish may have been cast ashore.'

On the terrace, and below on the beach, everyone was waiting for something to happen, heads craned forward expectantly. As the radios were turned down, so that any sounds from the distant tableau might be heard, a wave of silence passed along the beach like an immense darkening cloud shutting off the sunlight. The almost complete absence of noise and movement, after the long hours of festering motion, seemed strange and uncanny, focusing an intense atmosphere of self-awareness upon the thousands of watching figures.

The group by the water's edge remained where they stood, even the small children staring placidly at whatever held the attention of their parents. For the first time a narrow section of the beach was visible, a clutter of radios and beach equipment half-buried in the sand like discarded metallic refuse. Gradually the new arrivals pressing down from the promenade occupied the empty places, a manoeuvre carried out without any reaction from the troupe by the tide-line. To Pelham they seemed like a family of penitent pilgrims who had travelled some enormous distance and were now standing beside their sacred waters, waiting patiently for its revivifying powers to work their magic.

'What *is* going on?' Pelham asked, when after several minutes there was no indication of movement from the water-side group. He noticed that they formed a straight line, following the shore, rather than an arc. 'They're not watching anything at all.'

The off-shore haze was now only five hundred yards away, obscuring the contours of the huge swells. Completely opaque, the water looked like warm oil, a few wavelets now and then dissolving into greasy bubbles as they expired limply on the sand, intermingled with bits of refuse and old cigarette cartons. Nudging the shore like this, the sea resembled an enormous pelagic beast roused from its depths and blindly groping at the sand.

'Mildred, I'm going down to the water for a moment.' Pelham stood up. 'There's something curious –' He broke off, pointing to the beach on the other side of the terrace. 'Look! There's another group. What on earth –?'

Again, as everyone watched, this second body of spectators formed by the water's edge seventy-five yards from the terrace. Altogether some two hundred people were silently assembling along the shore-line, gazing out across the sea in front of them. Pelham found himself cracking his knuckles, then clasped the rail with both hands, as much to restrain himself from joining them. Only the congestion on the beach held him back.

This time the interest of the crowd passed in a few moments, and the murmur of background noise resumed.

'Heaven knows what they're doing.' Mildred turned her back on the group. 'There are more of them over there. They must be waiting for something.'

Sure enough, half a dozen similar groups were now forming by the water's edge, at almost precise one hundred yard intervals. Pelham scanned the far ends of the bay for any signs of a motor boat. He glanced at his watch. It was nearly 3:30. 'They can't be waiting for anything,' he said, trying to control his nervousness. Below the table his feet twitched a restless tattoo, gripping for purchase on the sandy cement. 'The only thing expected is the satellite, and no one will see that anyway. There must be something in the water.' At the mention of the satellite he remembered Sherrington again. 'Mildred, don't you feel –'

Before he could continue the man behind him stood up with a curious lurch, as if hoping to reach the rail, and tipped the sharp edge of his seat into Pelham's back. For a moment, as he struggled to steady the man, Pelham was enveloped in a rancid smell of sweat and stale beer. He saw the glazed focus in the other's eyes, his rough unshaved chin and open mouth like a muzzle, pointing with a sort of impulsive appetite towards the sea.

'The satellite!' Freeing himself Pelham craned upwards at the sky. A pale impassive blue, it was clear of both aircraft and birds – although they had seen gulls twenty miles inland that morning, as if a storm had been anticipated. As the glare stung his eyes, points of retinal light began to arc and swerve across the sky in epileptic orbits. One of these, however, apparently emerging from the western horizon, was moving steadily across the edge of his field of vision, boring dimly towards him.

Around them, people began to stand up, and chairs scraped and dragged across the floor. Several bottles toppled from one of the tables and smashed on the concrete.

'Mildred!'

Below them, in a huge disorganized mêlée extending as far as the eye could see, people were climbing slowly to their feet. The diffused murmur of the beach had given way to a more urgent, harsher sound, echoing overhead from either end of the bay. The whole beach seemed to writhe and stir with activity, the only motionless figures those of the people standing by the water. These now formed a continuous palisade along the shore, shutting off the sea. More and more people joined their ranks, and in places the line was nearly ten deep.

Everyone on the terrace was now standing. The crowds already on the beach were being driven forward by the pressure of new arrivals from the promenade, and the party below their table had been swept a further twenty yards towards the sea.

'Mildred, can you see Sherrington anywhere?' Confirming from her wristwatch that it was exactly 3:30, Pelham pulled her shoulder, trying to hold her attention. Mildred returned what was almost a vacant stare, an expression of glazed incomprehension. 'Mildred! We've got to get away from here!' Hoarsely, he shouted: 'Sherrington's convinced we can see some of the infra-red light shining from the satellites, they may form a pattern setting off IRM's laid down millions of years ago when other space vehicles were circling the earth. Mildred –!'

Helplessly, they were lifted from their seats and pressed against the rail. A huge concourse of people was moving down the beach, and soon the entire five-mile-long slope was packed with standing figures. No one was talking, and everywhere there was the same expression, self-immersed and preoccupied, like that on the faces of a crowd leaving a stadium. Behind them the great wheel of the fairground was rotating slowly, but the gondolas were empty, and Pelham looked back at the deserted funfair only a hundred yards from the multitude on the beach, its roundabouts revolving among the empty sideshows.

Quickly he helped Mildred over the edge of the rail, then jumped down on to the sand, hoping to work their way back to the promenade. As they stepped around the corner, however, the crowd advancing down the beach carried them back, tripping over the abandoned radios in the sand.

Still together, they found their footing when the pressure behind them ceased. Steadying himself, Pelham continued: '. . . Sherrington thinks Cro-Magnon Man was driven frantic by panic, like the Gadarene swine

– most of the bone-beds have been found under lake shores. The reflex may be too strong –' He broke off.

The noise had suddenly subsided, as the immense congregation, now packing every available square foot of the beach, stood silently facing the water. Pelham turned towards the sea, where the haze, only fifty yards away, edged in great clouds towards the beach. The forward line of the crowd, their heads bowed slightly, stared passively at the gathering billows. The surface of the water glowed with an intense luminous light, vibrant and spectral, and the air over the beach, grey by comparison, made the lines of motionless figures loom like tombstones.

Obliquely in front of Pelham, twenty yards away in the front rank, stood a tall man with a quiet, meditative expression, his beard and high temples identifying him without doubt.

'Sherrington!' Pelham started to shout. Involuntarily he looked upwards to the sky, and felt a blinding speck of light singe his retinas.

In the background the music of the funfair revolved in the empty air.

Then, with a galvanic surge, everyone on the beach began to walk forward into the water.

· **1963**

# · A QUESTION OF RE-ENTRY

All day they had moved steadily upstream, occasionally pausing to raise the propeller and cut away the knots of weed, and by 3 o'clock had covered some seventy-five miles. Fifty yards away, on either side of the patrol launch, the high walls of the jungle river rose over the water, the unbroken massif of the mato grosso which swept across the Amazonas from Campos Buros to the delta of the Orinoco. Despite their progress – they had set off from the telegraph station at Tres Buritis at 7 o'clock that morning – the river showed no inclination to narrow or alter its volume. Sombre and unchanging, the forest followed its course, the aerial canopy shutting off the sunlight and cloaking the water along the banks with a black velvet sheen. Now and then the channel would widen into a flat expanse of what appeared to be stationary water, the slow oily swells which disturbed its surface transforming it into a sluggish mirror of the distant, enigmatic sky, the islands of rotten balsa logs refracted by the layers of haze like the drifting archipelagoes of a dream. Then the channel would narrow again and the cooling jungle darkness enveloped the launch.

Although for the first few hours Connolly had joined Captain Pereira at the rail, he had become bored with the endless green banks of the forest sliding past them, and since noon had remained in the cabin, pretending to study the trajectory maps. The time might pass more slowly there, but at least it was cooler and less depressing. The fan hummed and pivoted, and the clicking of the cutwater and the whispering plaint of the current past the gliding hull soothed the slight headache induced by the tepid beer he and Pereira had shared after lunch.

This first encounter with the jungle had disappointed Connolly. His previous experience had been confined to the Dredging Project at Lake Maracaibo, where the only forests consisted of the abandoned oil rigs built out into the water. Their rusting hulks, and the huge draglines and pontoons of the dredging teams, were fauna of a man-made species. In the Amazonian jungle he had expected to see the full variety of nature in its richest and most colourful outpouring, but instead it was nothing more than a moribund tree-level swamp, unweeded and overgrown, if anything more dead than alive, an example of bad husbandry on a continental scale. The margins of the river were rarely well defined; except where enough rotting trunks had gathered to form a firm parapet, there were no formal banks, and the shallows ran off among the undergrowth for a hundred

435

yards, irrigating huge areas of vegetation that were already drowning in moisture.

Connolly had tried to convey his disenchantment to Pereira, who now sat under the awning on the deck, placidly smoking a cheroot, partly to repay the Captain for his polite contempt for Connolly and everything his mission implied. Like all the officers of the Native Protection Missions whom Connolly had met, first in Venezuela and now in Brazil, Pereira maintained a proprietary outlook towards the jungle and its mystique, which would not be breached by any number of fresh-faced investigators in their crisp drill uniforms. Captain Pereira had not been impressed by the UN flashes on Connolly's shoulders with their orbital monogram, nor by the high-level request for assistance cabled to the Mission three weeks earlier from Brasilia. To Pereira, obviously, the office suites in the white towers at the capital were as far away as New York, London or Babylon.

Superficially, the Captain had been helpful enough, supervising the crew as they stowed Connolly's monitoring equipment aboard, checking his Smith & Wesson and exchanging a pair of defective mosquito boots. As long as Connolly had wanted to, he had conversed away amiably, pointing out this and that feature of the landscape, identifying an unusual bird or lizard on an overhead bough.

But his indifference to the real object of the mission – he had given a barely perceptible nod when Connolly described it – soon became obvious. It was this neutrality which irked Connolly, implying that Pereira spent all his time ferrying UN investigators up and down the rivers after their confounded lost space capsule like so many tourists in search of some non-existent El Dorado. Above all there was the suggestion that Connolly and the hundreds of other investigators deployed around the continent were being too persistent. When all was said and done, Pereira implied, five years had elapsed since the returning lunar spacecraft, the *Goliath* 7, had plummeted into the South American land mass, and to prolong the search indefinitely was simply bad form, even, perhaps, necrophilic. There was not the faintest chance of the pilot still being alive, so he should be decently forgotten, given a statue outside a railway station or airport car park and left to the pigeons.

Connolly would have been glad to explain the reasons for the indefinite duration of the search, the overwhelming moral reasons, apart from the political and technical ones. He would have liked to point out that the lost astronaut, Colonel Francis Spender, by accepting the immense risks of the flight to and from the Moon, was owed the absolute discharge of any assistance that could be given him. He would have liked to remind Pereira that the successful landing on the Moon, after some half-dozen fatal attempts – at least three of the luckless pilots were still orbiting the Moon in their dead ships – was the culmination of an age-old ambition with profound psychological implications for mankind, and that the failure to find the astronaut after his return might induce unassuageable feelings of guilt and inadequacy. (If the sea was a symbol of the unconscious, was space perhaps an image of unfettered time, and the inability to penetrate it a tragic exile to one of the limbos of eternity, a symbolic death in life?)

But Captain Pereira was not interested. Calmly inhaling the scented aroma of his cheroot, he sat imperturbably at the rail, surveying the fetid swamps that moved past them.

Shortly before noon, when they had covered some 40 miles, Connolly pointed to the remains of a bamboo landing stage elevated on high poles above the bank. A threadbare rope bridge trailed off among the mangroves, and through an embrasure in the forest they could see a small clearing where a clutter of abandoned adobe huts dissolved like refuse heaps in the sunlight.

'Is this one of their camps?'

Pereira shook his head. 'The Espirro tribe, closely related to the Nambikwaras. Three years ago one of them carried influenza back from the telegraph station, an epidemic broke out, turned into a form of pulmonary edema, within forty-eight hours three hundred Indians had died. The whole group disintegrated, only about fifteen of the men and their families are still alive. A great tragedy.'

They moved forward to the bridge and stood beside the tall Negro helmsman as the two other members of the crew began to shackle sections of fine wire mesh into a cage over the deck. Pereira raised his binoculars and scanned the river ahead.

'Since the Espirros vacated the area the Nambas have begun to forage down this far. We won't see any of them, but it's as well to be on the safe side.'

'Do you mean they're hostile?' Connolly asked.

'Not in a conscious sense. But the various groups which comprise the Nambikwaras are permanently feuding with each other, and this far from the settlement we might easily be involved in an opportunist attack. Once we get to the settlement we'll be all right – there's a sort of precarious equilibrium there. But even so, have your wits about you. As you'll see, they're as nervous as birds.'

'How does Ryker manage to keep out of their way? Hasn't he been here for years?'

'About twelve.' Pereira sat down on the gunwale and eased his peaked cap off his forehead. 'Ryker is something of a special case. Temperamentally he's rather explosive – I meant to warn you to handle him carefully, he might easily whip up an incident – but he seems to have manoeuvred himself into a position of authority with the tribe. In some ways he's become an umpire, arbitrating in their various feuds. How he does it I haven't discovered yet; it's quite uncharacteristic of the Indians to regard a white man in that way. However, he's useful to us, we might eventually set up a mission here. Though that's next to impossible – we tried it once and the Indians just moved 500 miles away.'

Connolly looked back at the derelict landing stage as it disappeared around a bend, barely distinguishable from the jungle, which was as dilapidated as this sole mournful artifact.

'What on earth made Ryker come out here?' He had heard something in Brasilia of this strange figure, sometime journalist and man of action, the self-proclaimed world citizen who at the age of forty-two, after a life spent venting his spleen on civilization and its gimcrack gods, had suddenly disappeared into the Amazonas and taken up residence with one of the aboriginal tribes. Most latter-day Gauguins were absconding confidence men or neurotics, but Ryker seemed to be a genuine character in his own right, the last of a race of true individualists retreating before the barbed-wire fences and regimentation of 20th-century life. But his chosen paradise seemed pretty scruffy and degenerate, Connolly reflected, when one saw it at close quarters. However, as long as the man could organize the Indians into a few search parties he would serve his purpose. 'I can't understand why Ryker should pick the Amazon basin. The South Pacific yes, but from all I've heard – and you've confirmed just now – the Indians appear to be a pretty diseased and miserable lot, hardly the noble savage.'

Captain Pereira shrugged, looking away across the oily water, his plump sallow face mottled by the lace-like shadow of the wire netting. He belched discreetly to himself, and then adjusted his holster belt. 'I don't know the South Pacific, but I should guess it's also been oversentimentalized. Ryker didn't come here for a scenic tour. I suppose the Indians are diseased and, yes, reasonably miserable. Within fifty years they'll probably have died out. But for the time being they do represent a certain form of untamed, natural existence, which after all made us what we are. The hazards facing them are immense, and they survive.' He gave Connolly a sly smile. 'But you must argue it out with Ryker.'

They lapsed into silence and sat by the rail, watching the river unfurl itself. Exhausted and collapsing, the great trees crowded the banks, the dying expiring among the living, jostling each other aside as if for a last despairing assault on the patrol boat and its passengers. For the next half an hour, until they opened their lunch packs, Connolly searched the tree-tops for the giant bifurcated parachute which should have carried the capsule to earth. Virtually impermeable to the atmosphere, it would still be visible, spreadeagled like an enormous bird over the canopy of leaves. Then, after drinking a can of Pereira's beer, he excused himself and went down to the cabin.

The two steel cases containing the monitoring equipment had been stowed under the chart table, and he pulled them out and checked that the moisture-proof seals were still intact. The chances of making visual contact with the capsule were infinitesimal, but as long as it was intact it would continue to transmit both a sonar and radio beacon, admittedly over little more than twenty miles, but sufficient to identify its whereabouts to anyone in the immediate neighbourhood. However, the entire northern half of the South Americas had been covered by successive aerial sweeps, and it seemed unlikely that the beacons were still operating. The disappearance of the capsule argued that it had sustained at least minor damage, and by now the batteries would have been corroded by the humid air.

Recently certain of the UN Space Department agencies had begun to circulate the unofficial view that Colonel Spender had failed to select the correct attitude for re-entry and that the capsule had been vaporized on its final descent, but Connolly guessed that this was merely an attempt to pacify world opinion and prepare the way for the resumption of the space programme. Not only the Lake Maracaibo Dredging Project, but his own presence on the patrol boat, indicated that the Department still believed Colonel Spender to be alive, or at least to have survived the landing. His final re-entry orbit should have brought him down into the landing zone 500 miles to the east of Trinidad, but the last radio contact before the ionization layers around the capsule severed transmission indicated that he had under-shot his trajectory and come down somewhere on the South American land-mass along a line linking Lake Maracaibo with Brasilia.

Footsteps sounded down the companionway, and Captain Pereira lowered himself into the cabin. He tossed his hat onto the chart table and sat with his back to the fan, letting the air blow across his fading hair, carrying across to Connolly a sweet unsavoury odour of garlic and cheap pomade.

'You're a sensible man, Lieutenant. Anyone who stays up on deck is crazy. However,' – he indicated Connolly's pallid face and hands, a memento of a long winter in New York – 'in a way it's a pity you couldn't have put in some sunbathing. That metropolitan pallor will be quite a curiosity to the Indians.' He smiled agreeably, showing the yellowing teeth which made his olive complexion even darker. 'You may well be the first white man in the literal sense that the Indians have seen.'

'What about Ryker? Isn't he white?'

'Black as a berry now. Almost indistinguishable from the Indians, apart from being 7 feet tall.' He pulled over a collection of cardboard boxes at the far end of the seat and began to rummage through them. Inside was a collection of miscellaneous oddments – balls of thread and raw cotton, lumps of wax and resin, urucu paste, tobacco and seed-beads. 'These ought to assure them of your good intentions.'

Connolly watched as he fastened the boxes together. 'How many search parties will they buy? Are you sure you brought enough? I have a fifty-dollar allocation for gifts.'

'Good,' Pereira said matter-of-factly. 'We'll get some more beer. Don't worry, you can't buy these people, Lieutenant. You have to rely on their good-will; this rubbish will put them in the right frame of mind to talk.'

Connolly smiled dourly. 'I'm more keen on getting them off their hunkers and out into the bush. How are you going to organize the search parties?'

'They've already taken place.'

'What?' Connolly sat forward. 'How did that happen? But they should have waited' – he glanced at the heavy monitoring equipment – 'they can't have known what –'

Pereira silenced him with a raised hand. 'My dear Lieutenant. Relax, I was speaking figuratively. Can't you understand, these people are nomadic, they spend all their lives continually on the move. They must have covered every square foot of this forest a hundred times in the past five years. There's no need to send them out again. Your only hope is that they may have seen something and then persuade them to talk.'

Connolly considered this, as Pereira unwrapped another parcel. 'All right, but I may want to do a few patrols. I can't just sit around for three days.'

'Naturally. Don't worry, Lieutenant. If your astronaut came down anywhere within 500 miles of here they'll know about it.' He unwrapped the parcel and removed a small teak cabinet. The front panel was slotted, and lifted to reveal the face of a large ormolu table clock, its Gothic hands and numerals below a gilded belldome. Captain Pereira compared its time with his wrist-watch. 'Good. Running perfectly, it hasn't lost a second in forty-eight hours. This should put us in Ryker's good books.'

Connolly shook his head. 'Why on earth does he want a clock? I thought the man had turned his back on such things.'

Pereira packed the tooled metal face away. 'Ah, well, whenever we escape from anything we always carry a memento of it with us. Ryker collects clocks; this is the third I've bought for him. God knows what he does with them.'

The launch had changed course, and was moving in a wide circle across the river, the current whispering in a tender rippling murmur across the hull. They made their way up onto the deck, where the helmsman was unshackling several sections of the wire mesh in order to give himself an uninterrupted view of the bows. The two sailors climbed through the aperture and took up their positions fore and aft, boat-hooks at the ready.

They had entered a large bow-shaped extension of the river, where the current had overflowed the bank and produced a series of low-lying mud flats. Some two or three hundred yards wide, the water seemed to be almost motionless, seeping away through the trees which defined its margins so that the exit and inlet of the river were barely perceptible. At the inner bend of the bow, on the only firm ground, a small cantonment of huts had been built on a series of wooden palisades jutting out over the water. A narrow promontory of forest reached to either side of the cantonment, but a small area behind it had been cleared to form an open campong. On its far side were a number of wattle storage huts, a few dilapidated shacks and hovels of dried palm.

The entire area seemed deserted, but as they approached, the cutwater throwing a fine plume of white spray across the glassy swells, a few Indians appeared in the shadows below the creepers trailing over the jetty, watching them stonily. Connolly had expected to see a group of tall broad-shouldered warriors with white markings notched across their arms and cheeks, but these Indians were puny and degenerate, their pinched faces lowered beneath their squat bony skulls. They seemed undernourished and depressed, eyeing the visitors with a sort of sullen watchfulness, like pariah dogs from a gutter.

Pereira was shielding his eyes from the sun, across whose inclining path they were now moving, searching the ramshackle bungalow built of woven rattan at the far end of the jetty.

'No signs of Ryker yet. He's probably asleep or drunk.' He noticed Connolly's distasteful frown. 'Not much of a place, I'm afraid.'

As they moved towards the jetty, the wash from the launch slapping at the greasy bamboo poles and throwing a gust of foul air into their faces, Connolly looked back across the open disc of water, into which the curving wake of the launch was dissolving in a final summary of their long voyage up-river to the derelict settlement, fading into the slack brown water like a last tenuous thread linking him with the order and sanity of civilization. A strange atmosphere of emptiness hung over this inland lagoon, a flat pall of dead air that in a curious way was as menacing as any overt signs of hostility, as if the crudity and violence of all the Amazonian jungles met here in a momentary balance which some untoward movement of his own might upset, unleashing appalling forces. Away in the distance, down-shore, the great trees leaned like corpses into the glazed air, and the haze over the water embalmed the jungle and the late afternoon in an uneasy stillness.

They bumped against the jetty, rocking lightly into the palisade of poles and dislodging a couple of water-logged outriggers lashed together. The helmsman reversed the engine, waiting for the sailors to secure the lines. None of the Indians had come forward to assist them. Connolly caught a glimpse of one old simian face regarding him with a rheumy eye, riddled teeth nervously worrying a pouch-like lower lip.

He turned to Pereira, glad that the Captain would be interceding between himself and the Indians. 'Captain, I should have asked before, but – are these Indians cannibalistic?'

Pereira shook his head, steadying himself against a stanchion. 'Not at all. Don't worry about that, they'd have been extinct years ago if they were.'

'Not even – white men?' For some reason Connolly found himself placing a peculiarly indelicate emphasis upon the word 'white'.

Pereira laughed, straightening his uniform jacket. 'For God's sake, Lieutenant, no. Are you worrying that your astronaut might have been eaten by them?'

'I suppose it's a possibility.'

'I assure you, there have been no recorded cases. As a matter of interest, it's a rare practice on this continent. Much more typical of Africa – and Europe,' he added with sly humour. Pausing to smile at Connolly, he said quietly, 'Don't despise the Indians, Lieutenant. However diseased and dirty they may be, at least they are in equilibrium with their environment. And with themselves. You'll find no Christopher Columbuses or Colonel Spenders here, but no Belsens either. Perhaps one is as much a symptom of unease as the other?'

They had begun to drift down the jetty, over-running one of the outriggers, whose bow creaked and disappeared under the stern of the launch, and Pereira shouted at the helmsman: 'Ahead, Sancho! More ahead! Damn Ryker, where is the man?'

Churning out a niagara of boiling brown water, the launch moved forward, driving its shoulder into the bamboo supports, and the entire jetty sprung lightly under the impact. As the motor was cut and the lines finally secured, Connolly looked up at the jetty above his head.

Scowling down at him, an expression of bilious irritability on his heavy-jawed face, was a tall bare-chested man wearing a pair of frayed cotton shorts and a sleeve-less waistcoat of pleated raffia, his dark eyes almost hidden by a wide-brimmed straw hat. The heavy muscles of his exposed chest and arms were the colour of tropical teak, and the white scars on his lips and the fading traces of the heat ulcers which studded his shin bones provided the only lighter colouring. Standing there, arms akimbo with a sort of jaunty arrogance, he seemed to represent to Connolly that quality of untamed energy which he had so far found so conspicuously missing from the forest.

Completing his scrutiny of Connolly, the big man bellowed: 'Pereira, for God's sake, what do you think you're doing? That's my bloody outrigger you've just run down! Tell that steersman of yours to get the cataracts out of his eyes or I'll put a bullet through his backside!'

Grinning good-humouredly, Pereira pulled himself up on to the jetty. 'My dear Ryker, contain yourself. Remember your blood-pressure.' He peered down at the water-logged hulk of the derelict canoe which was now ejecting itself slowly from the river. 'Anyway, what good is a canoe to you, you're not going anywhere.'

Grudgingly, Ryker shook Pereira's hand. 'That's what you like to think, Captain. You and your confounded Mission, you want me to do all the work. Next time you may find I've gone a thousand miles up-river. And taken the Nambas with me.'

'What an epic prospect, Ryker. You'll need a Homer to celebrate it.' Pereira turned and gestured Connolly on to the jetty. The Indians were still hanging about listlessly, like guilty intruders.

Ryker eyed Connolly's uniform suspiciously. 'Who's this? Another so-called anthropologist, sniffing about for smut? I warned you last time, I will not have any more of those.'

'No, Ryker. Can't you recognize the uniform? Let me introduce

Lieutenant Connolly, of that brotherhood of latter-day saints, by whose courtesy and generosity we live in peace together – the United Nations.'

'What? Don't tell me they've got a mandate here now? God above, I suppose he'll bore my head off about cereal/protein ratios!' His ironic groan revealed a concealed reserve of acid humour.

'Relax. The Lieutenant is very charming and polite. He works for the Space Department, Reclamation Division. You know, searching for lost aircraft and the like. There's a chance you may be able to help him.' Pereira winked at Connolly and steered him forward. 'Lieutenant, the Rajah Ryker.'

'I doubt it,' Ryker said dourly. They shook hands, the corded muscles of Ryker's fingers like a trap. Despite his thick-necked stoop, Ryker was a good six to ten inches taller than Connolly. For a moment he held on to Connolly's hand, a slight trace of wariness revealed below his mask of bad temper. 'When did this plane come down?' he asked. Connolly guessed that he was already thinking of a profitable salvage operation.

'Some time ago,' Pereira said mildly. He picked up the parcel containing the cabinet clock and began to stroll after Ryker towards the bungalow at the end of the jetty. A low-eaved dwelling of woven rattan, its single room was surrounded on all sides by a veranda, the overhanging roof shading it from the sunlight. Creepers trailed across from the surrounding foliage, involving it in the background of palms and fronds, so that the house seemed a momentary formalization of the jungle.

'But the Indians might have heard something about it,' Pereira went on. 'Five years ago, as a matter of fact.'

Ryker snorted. 'My God, you've got a hope.' They went up the steps on to the veranda, where a slim-shouldered Indian youth, his eyes like moist marbles, was watching from the shadows. With a snap of irritation, Ryker cupped his hand around the youth's pate and propelled him with a backward swing down the steps. Sprawling on his knees, the youth picked himself up, eyes still fixed on Connolly, then emitted what sounded like a high-pitched nasal hoot, compounded partly of fear and partly of excitement. Connolly looked back from the doorway, and noticed that several other Indians had stepped onto the pier and were watching him with the same expression of rapt curiosity.

Pereira patted Connolly's shoulder. 'I told you they'd be impressed. Did you see that, Ryker?'

Ryker nodded curtly, as they entered his living-room pulled off his straw hat and tossed it on to a couch under the window. The room was dingy and cheerless. Crude bamboo shelves were strung around the walls, ornamented with a few primitive carvings of ivory and bamboo. A couple of rocking chairs and a card-table were in the centre of the room, dwarfed by an immense Victorian mahogany dresser standing against the rear wall. With its castellated mirrors and ornamental pediments it looked like an altar-piece stolen from a cathedral. At first glance it appeared to be leaning to one side, but then Connolly saw that its rear legs had been carefully raised from the tilting floor with a number of small wedges. In the centre of the dresser, its multiple reflections receding to infinity in a pair of small wing mirrors, was a cheap three-dollar alarm clock, ticking away loudly. An over-and-under Winchester shotgun leaned against the wall beside it.

Gesturing Pereira and Connolly into the chairs, Ryker raised the blind over the rear window. Outside was the compound, the circle of huts around its perimeter. A few Indians squatted in the shadows, spears upright between their knees.

Connolly watched Ryker moving about in front of him, aware that the man's earlier impatience had given away to a faint but noticeable edginess. Ryker glanced irritably through the window, apparently annoyed to see the gradual gathering of the Indians before their huts.

There was a sweetly unsavoury smell in the room, and over his shoulder Connolly saw that the card-table was loaded with a large bale of miniature animal skins, those of a vole or some other forest rodent. A half-hearted attempt had been made to trim the skins, and tags of clotted blood clung to their margins.

Ryker jerked the table with his foot. 'Well, here you are,' he said to Pereira. 'Twelve dozen. They took a hell of a lot of getting, I can tell you. You've brought the clock?'

Pereira nodded, still holding the parcel in his lap. He gazed distastefully at the dank scruffy skins. 'Have you got some rats in there, Ryker? These don't look much good. Perhaps we should check through them outside ...'

'Dammit, Pereira, don't be a fool!' Ryker snapped. 'They're as good as you'll get. I had to trim half the skins myself. Let's have a look at the clock.'

'Wait a minute.' The Captain's jovial, easy-going manner had stiffened. Making the most of his temporary advantage, he reached out and touched one of the skins gingerly, shaking his head. 'Pugh ... Do you know how much I paid for this clock, Ryker? Seventy-five dollars. That's your credit for three years. I'm not so sure. And you're not very helpful, you know. Now about this aircraft that may have come down –'

Ryker snapped his fingers. 'Forget it. Nothing did. The Nambas tell me everything.' He turned to Connolly. 'You can take it from me there's no trace of an aircraft around here. Any rescue mission would be wasting their time.'

Pereira watched Ryker critically. 'As a matter of fact it wasn't an aircraft.' He tapped Connolly's shoulder flash. 'It was a rocket capsule – with a man on board. A very important and valuable man. None other than the Moon pilot, Colonel Francis Spender.'

'Well ...' Eyebrows raised in mock surprise, Ryker ambled to the window, stared out at a group of Indians who had advanced halfway across the compound. 'My God, what next! The Moon pilot. Do they really think he's around here? But what a place to roost.' He leaned out of the window and bellowed at the Indians, who retreated a few paces and then held their ground. 'Damn fools,' he muttered, 'this isn't a zoo.'

Pereira handed him the parcel, watching the Indians. There were more than fifty around the compound now, squatting in their doorways, a few of the younger men honing their spears. 'They are remarkably curious,' he said to Ryker, who had taken the parcel over to the dresser and was unwrapping it carefully. 'Surely they've seen a pale-skinned man before?'

'They've nothing better to do.' Ryker lifted the clock out of the cabinet with his big hands, with great care placed it beside the alarm clock, the almost inaudible motion of its pendulum lost in the metallic chatter of the latter's escapement. For a moment he gazed at the ornamental hands and numerals. Then he picked up the alarm clock and with an almost valedictory pat, like an officer dismissing a faithful if stupid minion, locked it away in the cupboard below. His former buoyancy returning, he gave Pereira a playful slap on the shoulder. 'Captain, if you want any more rat-skins just give me a shout!'

Backing away, Pereira's heel touched one of Connolly's feet, distracting Connolly from a problem he had been puzzling over since their entry into the hut. Like a concealed clue in a detective story, he was sure that he had noticed something of significance, but was unable to identify it.

'We won't worry about the skins,' Pereira said. 'What we'll do with your assistance, Ryker, is to hold a little parley with the chiefs, see whether they remember anything of this capsule.'

Ryker stared out at the Indians now standing directly below the veranda. Irritably he slammed down the blind. 'For God's sake, Pereira, they don't. Tell the Lieutenant he isn't interviewing people on Park Avenue or Piccadilly. If the Indians had seen anything I'd know.'

'Perhaps.' Pereira shrugged. 'Still, I'm under instructions to assist Lieutenant Connolly and it won't do any harm to ask.'

Connolly sat up. 'Having come this far, Captain, I feel I should do two or three forays into the bush.' To Ryker he explained: 'They've recalculated the flight path of the final trajectory, there's a chance he may have come down further along the landing zone. Here, very possibly.'

Shaking his head, Ryker slumped down on to the couch, and drove one fist angrily into the other. 'I suppose this means they'll be landing here at any time with thousands of bulldozers and flame-throwers. Dammit, Lieutenant, if you have to send a man to the Moon, why don't you do it in your own back yard?'

Pereira stood up. 'We'll be gone in a couple of days, Ryker.' He nodded judiciously at Connolly and moved towards the door.

As Connolly climbed to his feet Ryker called out suddenly: 'Lieutenant. You can tell me something I've wondered.' There was an unpleasant downward curve to his mouth, and his tone was belligerent and provocative. 'Why did they really send a man to the Moon?'

Connolly paused. He had remained silent during the conversation, not wanting to antagonize Ryker. The rudeness and complete self-immersion were pathetic rather than annoying. 'Do you mean the military and political reasons?'

'No, I don't.' Ryker stood up, arms akimbo again, measuring Connolly. 'I mean the *real* reasons, Lieutenant.'

Connolly gestured vaguely. For some reason formulating a satisfactory answer seemed more difficult than he had expected. 'Well, I suppose you could say it was the natural spirit of exploration.'

Ryker snorted derisively. 'Do you seriously believe that, Lieutenant? "The spirit of exploration!" My God! What a fantastic idea. Pereira doesn't believe that, do you, Captain?'

Before Connolly could reply Pereira took his arm. 'Come on, Lieutenant. This is no time for a metaphysical discussion.' To Ryker he added: 'It doesn't much matter what you and I believe, Ryker. A man went to the Moon and came back. He needs our help.'

Ryker frowned ruefully. 'Poor chap. He must be feeling pretty unhappy by now. Though anyone who gets as far as the Moon and is fool enough to come back deserves what he gets.'

There was a scuffle of feet on the veranda, and as they stepped out into the sunlight a couple of Indians darted away along the jetty, watching Connolly with undiminished interest.

Ryker remained in the doorway, staring listlessly at the clock, but as they were about to climb into the launch he came after them. Now and then glancing over his shoulder at the encroaching semi-circle of Indians, he gazed down at Connolly with sardonic contempt. 'Lieutenant,' he called out before they went below. 'Has it occurred to you that if he had landed, Spender might have wanted to stay on here?'

'I doubt it, Ryker,' Connolly said calmly. 'Anyway, there's little chance that Colonel Spender is still alive. What we're interested in finding is the capsule.'

Ryker was about to reply when a faint metallic buzz sounded from the direction of his hut. He looked around sharply, waiting for it to end, and for a moment the whole tableau, composed of the men on the launch, the gaunt outcast on the edge of the jetty and the Indians behind him, was frozen in an absurdly motionless posture. The mechanism of the old alarm clock had obviously been fully wound, and the buzz sounded for thirty seconds, finally ending with a high-pitched ping.

Pereira grinned. He glanced at his watch. 'It keeps good time, Ryker.' But Ryker had stalked off back to the hut, scattering the Indians before him.

Connolly watched the group dissolve, then suddenly snapped his fingers. 'You're right, Captain. It certainly does keep good time,' he repeated as they entered the cabin.

Evidently tired by the encounter with Ryker, Pereira slumped down among Connolly's equipment and unbuttoned his tunic. 'Sorry about

Ryker, but I warned you. Frankly, Lieutenant, we might as well leave now. There's nothing here. Ryker knows that. However, he's no fool, and he's quite capable of faking all sorts of evidence just to get a retainer out of you. He wouldn't mind if the bulldozers came.'

'I'm not so sure.' Connolly glanced briefly through the porthole. 'Captain, has Ryker got a radio?'

'Of course not. Why?'

'Are you certain?'

'Absolutely. It's the last thing the man would have. Anyway, there's no electrical supply here, and he has no batteries.' He noticed Connolly's intent expression. 'What's on your mind, Lieutenant?'

'You're his only contact? There are no other traders in the area?'

'None. The Indians are too dangerous, and there's nothing to trade. Why do you think Ryker has a radio?'

'He must have. Or something very similar. Captain, just now you remarked on the fact that his old alarm clock kept good time. Does it occur to you to ask *how*?'

Pereira sat up slowly. 'Lieutenant, you have a valid point.'

'Exactly. I knew there was something odd about those two clocks when they were standing side by side. That type of alarm clock is the cheapest obtainable, notoriously inaccurate. Often they lose two or three minutes in 24 hours. But that clock was telling the right time to within ten seconds. No optical instrument would give him that degree of accuracy.'

Pereira shrugged sceptically. 'But I haven't been here for over four months. And even then he didn't check the time with me.'

'Of course not. He didn't need to. The only possible explanation for such a degree of accuracy is that he's getting a daily time fix, either on a radio or some long-range beacon.'

'Wait a moment, Lieutenant.' Pereira watched the dusk light fall across the jungle. 'It's a remarkable coincidence, but there must be an innocent explanation. Don't jump straight to the conclusion that Ryker has some instrument taken from the missing Moon capsule. Other aircraft have crashed in the forest. And what would be the point? He's not running an airline or railway system. Why should he need to know the time, the *exact* time, to within ten seconds?'

Connolly tapped the lid of his monitoring case, controlling his growing exasperation at Pereira's reluctance to treat the matter seriously, at his whole permissive attitude of lazy tolerance towards Ryker, the Indians and the forest. Obviously he unconsciously resented Connolly's sharp-eyed penetration of this private world.

'Clocks have become his idée fixe,' Pereira continued. 'Perhaps he's developed an amazing sensitivity to its mechanism. Knowing exactly the right time could be a substitute for the civilization on which he turned his back.' Thoughtfully, Pereira moistened the end of his cheroot. 'But I agree that it's strange. Perhaps a little investigation would be worthwhile after all.'

After a cool jungle night in the air-conditioned cabin, the next day Connolly began discreetly to reconnoitre the area. Pereira took ashore two bottles of whisky and a soda syphon, and was able to keep Ryker distracted while Connolly roved about the campong with his monitoring equipment. Once or twice he heard Ryker bellow jocularly at him from his window as he lolled back over the whisky. At intervals, as Ryker slept, Pereira would come out into the sun, sweating like a drowsy pig in his stained uniform, and try to drive back the Indians.

'As long as you stay within earshot of Ryker you're safe,' he told Connolly. Chopped-out pathways criss-crossed the bush at all angles, a new one added whenever one of the bands returned to the campong, irrespective of those already established. This maze extended for miles around them. 'If you get lost, don't panic but stay where you are. Sooner or later we'll come out and find you.'

Eventually giving up his attempt to monitor any of the signal beacons built into the lost capsule – both the sonar and radio meters remained at zero – Connolly tried to communicate with the Indians by sign language, but with the exception of one, the youth with the moist limpid eyes who had been hanging about on Ryker's veranda, they merely stared at him stonily. This youth Pereira identified as the son of the former witch-doctor ('Ryker's more or less usurped his role, for some reason the old boy lost the confidence of the tribe'). While the other Indians gazed at Connolly as if seeing some invisible numinous shadow, some extra-corporeal nimbus which pervaded his body, the youth was obviously aware that Connolly possessed some special talent, perhaps not dissimilar from that which his father had once practised. However, Connolly's attempts to talk to the youth were handicapped by the fact that he was suffering from a purulent ophthalmia, gonococchic in origin and extremely contagious, which made his eyes water continuously. Many of the Indians suffered from this complaint, threatened by permanent blindness, and Connolly had seen them treating their eyes with water in which a certain type of fragrant bark had been dissolved.

Ryker's casual, off-hand authority over the Indians puzzled Connolly. Slumped back in his chair against the mahogany dresser, one hand touching the ormolu clock, most of the time he and Pereira indulged in a lachrymose back-chat. Then, oblivious of any danger, Ryker would amble out into the dusty campong, push his way blurrily through the Indians and drum up a party to collect fire wood for the water still, jerking them bodily to their feet as they squatted about their huts. What interested Connolly was the Indians' reaction to this type of treatment. They seemed to be restrained, not by any belief in his strength of personality or primitive kingship, but by a grudging acceptance that for the time being at any rate, Ryker possessed the whip hand over them all. Obviously Ryker served certain useful roles for them as an intermediary with the Mission, but this alone would not explain the sources of his power. Beyond certain more or less defined limits – the perimeter of the campong – his authority was minimal.

A hint of explanation came on the second morning of their visit, when Connolly accidentally lost himself in the forest.

After breakfast Connolly sat under the awning on the deck of the patrol launch, gazing out over the brown, jelly-like surface of the river. The campong was silent. During the night the Indians had disappeared into the bush. Like lemmings they were apparently prone to these sudden irresistible urges. Occasionally the nomadic call would be strong enough to carry them 200 miles away; at other times they would set off in high spirits and then lose interest after a few miles, returning dispiritedly to the campong in small groups.

Deciding to make the most of their absence, Connolly shouldered the monitoring equipment and climbed onto the pier. A few dying fires smoked plaintively among the huts, and abandoned utensils and smashed pottery lay about in the red dust. In the distance the morning haze over the forest had lifted, and Connolly could see what appeared to be a low hill – a shallow rise no more than a hundred feet in height – which rose off the flat floor of the jungle a quarter of a mile away.

On his right, among the huts, someone moved. An old man sat alone among the refuse of pottery shards and raffia baskets, cross-legged under a small make-shift awning. Barely distinguishable from the dust, his moribund figure seemed to contain the whole futility of the Amazon forest.

Still musing on Ryker's motives for isolating himself in the jungle, Connolly made his way towards the distant rise.

Ryker's behaviour the previous evening had been curious. Shortly after dusk, when the sunset sank into the western forest, bathing the jungle in an immense ultramarine and golden light, the day-long chatter and movement of the Indians ceased abruptly. Connolly had been glad of the silence – the endless thwacks of the rattan canes and grating of the stone mills in which they mixed the Government-issue meal had become tiresome. Pereira made several cautious visits to the edge of the campong, and each time reported that the Indians were sitting in a huge circle outside their huts, watching Ryker's bungalow. The latter was lounging on his veranda in the moonlight, chin in hand, one boot up on the rail, morosely surveying the assembled tribe.

'They've got their spears and ceremonial feathers,' Pereira whispered. 'For a moment I almost believed they were preparing an attack.'

After waiting half an hour, Connolly climbed up on to the pier, found the Indians squatting in their dark silent circle, Ryker glaring down at them. Only the witch-doctor's son made any attempt to approach Connolly, sidling tentatively through the shadows, a piece of what appeared to be blue obsidian in his hand, some talisman of his father's that had lost its potency.

Uneasily, Connolly returned to the launch. Shortly after 3 a.m. they were wakened in their bunks by a tremendous whoop, reached the deck to hear the stampede of feet through the dust, the hissing of overturned fires and cooking pots. Apparently leading the pack, Ryker, emitting a series of re-echoed 'Harooh's! disappeared into the bush. Within a minute the campong was empty.

'What game is Ryker playing?' Pereira muttered as they stood on the creaking jetty in the dusty moonlight. 'This must be the focus of his authority over the Nambas.' Baffled, they went back to their bunks.

Reaching the margins of the rise, Connolly strolled through a small orchard which had returned to nature, hearing in his mind the exultant roar of Ryker's voice as it had cleaved the midnight jungle. Idly he picked a few of the barely ripe guavas and vividly coloured cajus with their astringent delicately flavoured juice. After spitting away the pith, he searched for a way out of the orchard, but within a few minutes realized that he was lost.

A continuous mound when seen from the distance, the rise was in fact a nexus of small hillocks that formed the residue of a one-time system of ox-bow lakes, and the basins between the slopes were still treacherous with deep mire. Connolly rested his equipment at the foot of a tree. Withdrawing his pistol, he fired two shots into the air in the hope of attracting Ryker and Pereira. He sat down to await his rescue, taking the opportunity to unlatch his monitors and wipe the dials.

After ten minutes no one had appeared. Feeling slightly demoralized, and frightened that the Indians might return and find him, Connolly shouldered his equipment and set off towards the north-west, in the approximate direction of the campong. The ground rose before him. Suddenly, as he turned behind a palisade of wild magnolia trees, he stepped into an open clearing on the crest of the hill.

Squatting on their heels against the tree-trunks and among the tall grass was what seemed to be the entire tribe of the Nambikwaras. They were facing him, their expressions immobile and watchful, eyes like white beads among the sheaves. Presumably they had been sitting in the clearing, only fifty yards away, when he fired his shots, and Connolly had the uncanny feeling that they had been waiting for him to make his entrance exactly at the point he had chosen.

Hesitating, Connolly tightened his grip on the radio monitor. The Indians' faces were like burnished teak, their shoulders painted with a delicate mosaic of earth colours. Noticing the spears held among the grass, Connolly started to walk on across the clearing towards a breach in the palisade of trees.

For a dozen steps the Indians remained motionless. Then, with a chorus of yells, they leapt forward from the grass and surrounded Connolly in a jabbering pack. None of them were more than five feet tall, but their plump agile bodies buffeted him about, almost knocking him off his feet. Eventually the tumult steadied itself, and two or three of the leaders stepped from the cordon and began to scrutinize Connolly more closely, pinching and fingering him with curious positional movements of the thumb and forefinger, like connoisseurs examining some interesting taxidermic object.

Finally, with a series of high-pitched whines and grunts, the Indians moved off towards the centre of the clearing, propelling Connolly in front of them with sharp slaps on his legs and shoulders, like drovers goading on a large pig. They were all jabbering furiously to each other, some hacking at the grass with their machetes, gathering bundles of leaves in their arms.

Tripping over something in the grass, Connolly stumbled onto his knees. The catch slipped from the lid of the monitor, and as he stood up, fumbling with the heavy cabinet, the revolver slipped from his holster and was lost under his feet in the rush.

Giving way to his panic, he began to shout over the bobbing heads around him, to his surprise heard one of the Indians beside him bellow to the others. Instantly, as the refrain was taken up, the crowd stopped and re-formed its cordon around him. Gasping, Connolly steadied himself, and started to search the trampled grass for his revolver, when he realized that the Indians were now staring, not at himself, but at the exposed counters of the monitor. The six meters were swinging wildly after the stampede across the clearing, and the Indians craned forward, their machetes and spears lowered, gaping at the bobbing needles.

Then there was a roar from the edge of the clearing, and a huge wild-faced man in a straw hat, a shot-gun held like a crow-bar in his hands, stormed in among the Indians, driving them back. Dragging the monitor from his neck, Connolly felt the steadying hand of Captain Pereira take his elbow.

'Lieutenant, Lieutenant,' Pereira murmured reprovingly as they recovered the pistol and made their way back to the campong, the uproar behind them fading among the undergrowth, 'we were nearly in time to say grace.'

Later that afternoon Connolly sat back in a canvas chair on the deck of the launch. About half the Indians had returned, and were wandering about the huts in a desultory manner, kicking at the fires. Ryker, his authority re-asserted, had returned to his bungalow.

'I thought you said they weren't cannibal,' Connolly reminded Pereira.

The Captain snapped his fingers, as if thinking about something more important. 'No, they're not. Stop worrying, Lieutenant, you're not going to end up in a pot.' When Connolly demurred he swung crisply on his heel. He had sharpened up his uniform, and wore his pistol belt and Sam Browne at their regulation position, his peaked cap jutting low over his eyes. Evidently Connolly's close escape had confirmed some private suspicion. 'Look, they're not cannibal in the dietary sense of the term, as used by the Food & Agriculture Organization in its classification of aboriginal peoples. They won't stalk and hunt human game in preference for any other. But –' here the Captain stared fixedly at Connolly '– in certain circumstances, after a fertility ceremonial, for example, they will eat human flesh. Like all members of primitive communities which are small numerically, the Nambikwara never bury their dead. Instead, they eat them, as a means of conserving the loss and to perpetuate the corporeal identity of the departed. Now do you understand?'

Connolly grimaced. 'I'm glad to know now that I was about to be perpetuated.'

Pereira looked out at the campong. 'Actually they would never eat a white man, to avoid defiling the tribe.' He paused. 'At least, so I've always believed. It's strange, something seems to have . . . Listen, Lieutenant,' he explained, 'I can't quite piece it together, but I'm convinced we should stay here for a few days longer. Various elements make me suspicious, I'm sure Ryker is hiding something. That mound where you were lost is a sort of sacred tumulus, the way the Indians were looking at your instrument made me certain that they'd seen something like it before – perhaps a panel with many flickering dials . . . ?'

'The *Goliath* 7?' Connolly shook his head sceptically. He listened to the undertow of the river drumming dimly against the keel of the launch. 'I doubt it, Captain. I'd like to believe you, but for some reason it doesn't seem very likely.'

'I agree. Some other explanation is preferable. But what? The Indians were squatting on that hill, waiting for someone to arrive. What else could your monitor have reminded them of?'

'Ryker's clock?' Connolly suggested. 'They may regard it as a sort of ju-ju object, like a magical toy.'

'No,' Pereira said categorically. 'These Indians are highly pragmatic, they're not impressed by useless toys. For them to be deterred from killing you means that the equipment you carried possessed some very real, down-to-earth power. Look, suppose the capsule did land here and was secretly buried by Ryker, and that in some way the clocks help him to identify its whereabouts –' here Pereira shrugged hopefully '– it's just possible.'

'Hardly,' Connolly said. 'Besides, Ryker couldn't have buried the capsule himself, and if Colonel Spender had lived through re-entry Ryker would have helped him.'

'I'm not so sure,' Pereira said pensively. 'It would probably strike our friend Mr Ryker as very funny for a man to travel all the way to the Moon and back just to be killed by savages. Much too good a joke to pass over.'

'What religious beliefs do the Indians have?' Connolly asked.

'No religion in the formalized sense of a creed and dogma. They eat their dead so they don't need to invent an after-life in an attempt to re-animate them. In general they subscribe to one of the so-called cargo cults. As I said, they're very material. That's why they're so lazy. Some time in the future they expect a magic galleon or giant bird to arrive carrying an everlasting cornucopia of worldly goods, so they just sit about waiting for

the great day. Ryker encourages them in this idea. It's very dangerous –
in some Melanesian islands the tribes with cargo cults have degenerated
completely. They lie around all day on the beaches, waiting for the WHO
flying boat, or . . .' His voice trailed off.

Connolly nodded and supplied the unspoken thought. 'Or – a space
capsule?'

Despite Pereira's growing if muddled conviction that something associated
with the missing space-craft was to be found in the area, Connolly was
still sceptical. His close escape had left him feeling curiously calm and
emotionless, and he looked back on his possible death with fatalistic
detachment, identifying it with the total ebb and flow of life in the
Amazon forests, with its myriad unremembered deaths, and with the
endless vistas of dead trees leaning across the jungle paths radiating
from the campong. After only two days the jungle had begun to invest
his mind with its own logic, and the possibility of the space-craft landing
there seemed more and more remote. The two elements belonged to
different systems of natural order, and he found it increasingly difficult
to visualize them overlapping. In addition there was a deeper reason for
his scepticism, underlined by Ryker's reference to the 'real' reasons for
the space-flights. The implication was that the entire space programme
was a symptom of some inner unconscious malaise afflicting mankind,
and in particular the western technocracies, and that the space-craft and
satellites had been launched because their flights satisfied certain buried
compulsions and desires. By contrast, in the jungle, where the unconscious
was manifest and exposed, there was no need for these insane projections,
and the likelihood of the Amazonas playing any part in the success or
failure of the space flight became, by a sort of psychological parallax,
increasingly blurred and distant, the missing capsule itself a fragment of
a huge disintegrating fantasy.

However, he agreed to Pereira's request to borrow the monitors
and follow Ryker and the Indians on their midnight romp through
the forest.

Once again, after dusk, the same ritual silence descended over the
campong, and the Indians took up their positions in the doors of their huts.
Like some morose exiled princeling, Ryker sat sprawled on his veranda,
one eye on the clock through the window behind him. In the moonlight
the scores of moist dark eyes never wavered as they watched him.

At last, half an hour later, Ryker galvanized his great body into life, with
a series of tremendous whoops raced off across the campong, leading the
stampede into the bush. Away in the distance, faintly outlined by the
quarter moon, the shallow hump of the tribal tumulus rose over the black
canopy of the jungle. Pereira waited until the last heel beats had subsided,
then climbed onto the pier and disappeared among the shadows.

Far away Connolly could hear the faint cries of Ryker's pack as they
made off through the bush, the sounds of machetes slashing at the

undergrowth. An ember on the opposite side of the campong flared in the low wind, illuminating the abandoned old man, presumably the former witch doctor, whom he had seen that morning. Beside him was another slimmer figure, the limpid-eyed youth who had followed Connolly about.

A door stirred on Ryker's veranda, providing Connolly with a distant image of the white moonlit back of the river reflected in the mirrors of the mahogany dresser. Connolly watched the door jump lightly against the latch, then walked quietly across the pier to the wooden steps.

A few empty tobacco tins lay about on the shelves around the room, and a stack of empty bottles cluttered one corner behind the door. The ormolu clock had been locked away in the mahogany dresser. After testing the doors, which had been secured with a stout padlock, Connolly noticed a dog-eared paperback book lying on the dresser beside a half-empty carton of cartridges.

On a faded red ground, the small black lettering on the cover was barely decipherable, blurred by the sweat from Ryker's fingers. At first glance it appeared to be a set of logarithm tables. Each of the eighty or so pages was covered with column after column of finely printed numerals and tabular material.

Curious, Connolly carried the manual over to the doorway. The title page was more explicit.

ECHO III

CONSOLIDATED TABLES OF

CELESTIAL TRAVERSES

1965–1980

*Published by the National Astronautics and Space Administration, Washington, D.C., 1965. Part XV. Longitude 40-80 West, Latitude 10 North-35 South (South American Sub-Continent) Price 35ᶜ.*

His interest quickening, Connolly turned the pages. The manual fell open at the section headed: Lat. 5 South, Long, 60 West. He remembered that this was the approximate position of Campos Buros. Tabulated by year, month and day, the columns of figures listed the elevations and compass bearings for sightings of the Echo III satellite, the latest of the huge aluminium spheres which had been orbiting the earth since Echo I was launched in 1959. Rough pencil lines had been drawn through all the entries up to the year 1968. At this point the markings became individual, each minuscule entry crossed off with a small blunt stroke. The pages were grey with the blurred graphite.

Guided by this careful patchwork of cross-hatching, Connolly found the latest entry: March 17, 1978. The time and sighting were. 1-22 *a.m. Elevation 43 degrees WNW, Capella-Eridanus.* Below it was the entry for the next day, an hour later, its orientations differing slightly.

Ruefully shaking his head in admiration of Ryker's cleverness, Connolly looked at his watch. It was about 1.20, two minutes until the next traverse. He glanced at the sky, picking out the constellation Eridanus, from which the satellite would emerge.

So this explained Ryker's hold over the Indians! What more impressive means had a down-and-out white man of intimidating and astonishing a tribe of primitive savages? Armed with nothing more than a set of tables and a reliable clock, he could virtually pinpoint the appearance of the satellite at the first second of its visible traverse. The Indians would naturally be awed and bewildered by this phantom charioteer of the midnight sky, steadily pursuing its cosmic round, like a beacon traversing the profoundest deeps of their own minds. Any powers which Ryker cared to invest in the satellite would seem confirmed by his ability to control the time and place of its arrival.

Connolly realized now how the old alarm clock had told the correct time – by using his tables Ryker had read the exact time off the sky each night. A more accurate clock presumably freed him from the need to spend unnecessary time waiting for the satellite's arrival; he would now be able to set off for the tumulus only a few minutes beforehand.

Walking along the pier he began to search the sky. Away in the distance a low cry sounded into the midnight air, diffusing like a wraith over the jungle. Beside him, sitting on the bows of the launch, Connolly heard the helmsman grunt and point at the sky above the opposite bank. Following the up-raised arm, he quickly found the speeding dot of light. It was moving directly towards the tumulus. Steadily the satellite crossed the sky, winking intermittently as it passed behind lanes of high-altitude cirrus, the conscripted ship of the Nambikwaras' cargo cult.

It was about to disappear among the stars in the south-east when a faint shuffling sound distracted Connolly. He looked down to find the moist-eyed youth, the son of the witch doctor, standing only a few feet away from him, regarding him dolefully.

'Hello, boy,' Connolly greeted him. He pointed at the vanishing satellite. 'See the star?'

The youth made a barely perceptible nod. He hesitated for a moment, his running eyes glowing like drowned moons, then stepped forward and touched Connolly's wristwatch, tapping the dial with his horny fingernail.

Puzzled, Connolly held it up for him to inspect. The youth watched the second hand sweep around the dial, an expression of rapt and ecstatic concentration on his face. Nodding vigorously, he pointed to the sky.

Connolly grinned. 'So you understand? You've rumbled old man Ryker, have you?' He nodded encouragingly to the youth, who was tapping the watch eagerly, apparently in an effort to conjure up a second satellite. Connolly began to laugh. 'Sorry, boy.' He slapped the manual. 'What you really need is this pack of jokers.'

Connolly began to walk back to the bungalow, when the youth darted forward impulsively and blocked his way, thin legs spread in an aggressive stance. Then, with immense ceremony, he drew from behind his back a round painted object with a glass face that Connolly remembered he had seen him carrying before.

'That looks interesting.' Connolly bent down to examine the object, caught a glimpse in the thin light of a luminous instrument before the youth snatched it away.

'Wait a minute, boy. Let's have another look at that.'

After a pause the pantomime was repeated, but the youth was reluctant to allow Connolly more than the briefest inspection. Again Connolly saw a calibrated dial and a wavering indicator. Then the youth stepped forward and touched Connolly's wrist.

Quickly Connolly unstrapped the metal chain. He tossed the watch to the youth, who instantly dropped the instrument, his barter achieved, and after a delighted yodel turned and darted off among the trees.

Bending down, careful not to touch the instrument with his hands, Connolly examined the dial. The metal housing around it was badly torn and scratched, as if the instrument had been prised from some control panel with a crude implement. But the glass face and the dial beneath it were still intact. Across the centre was the legend:

LUNAR ALTIMETER
Miles: 100
GOLIATH 7
General Electric Corporation,
Schenectedy

Picking up the instrument, Connolly cradled it in his hands. The pressure seals were broken, and the gyro bath floated freely on its air cushion. Like a graceful bird the indicator needle glided up and down the scale.

The pier creaked under approaching footsteps. Connolly looked up at the perspiring figure of Captain Pereira, cap in one hand, monitor dangling from the other.

'My dear Lieutenant!' he panted. 'Wait till I tell you, what a farce, it's fantastic! Do you know what Ryker's doing? – it's so simple it seems unbelievable that no one's thought of it before. It's nothing short of the most magnificent practical *joke!*' Gasping, he sat down on the bale of skins leaning against the gangway. 'I'll give you a clue: Narcissus.'

'Echo,' Connolly replied flatly, still staring at the instrument in his hands.

'You spotted it? Clever boy!' Pereira wiped his cap-band. 'How did you guess? It wasn't that obvious.' He took the manual Connolly handed him. 'What the –? Ah, I see, this makes it even more clear. Of course.' He slapped his knee with the manual. 'You found this in his room? I take my hat off to Ryker,' he continued as Connolly set the altimeter down on the pier and steadied it carefully. 'Let's face it, it's something of a pretty clever trick. Can you imagine it, he comes here, finds a tribe with a strong cargo cult, opens his little manual and says "Presto, the great white bird will be arriving: *NOW!*'

Connolly nodded, then stood up, wiping his hands on a strip of rattan. When Pereira's laughter had subsided he pointed down to the glowing face of the altimeter at their feet. 'Captain, something else arrived,' he said quietly. 'Never mind Ryker and the satellite. This cargo actually landed.'

As Pereira knelt down and inspected the altimeter, whistling sharply to himself, Connolly walked over to the edge of the pier and looked out across the great back of the silent river at the giant trees which hung over the water, like forlorn mutes at some cataclysmic funeral, their thin silver voices carried away on the dead tide.

Half an hour before they set off the next morning, Connolly waited on the deck for Captain Pereira to conclude his interrogation of Ryker. The empty campong, deserted again by the Indians, basked in the heat, a single plume of smoke curling into the sky. The old witch doctor and his son had disappeared, perhaps to try their skill with a neighbouring tribe, but the loss of his watch was unregretted by Connolly. Down below, safely stowed away among his baggage, was the altimeter, carefully sterilized and sealed. On the table in front of him, no more than two feet from the pistol in his belt, lay Ryker's manual.

For some reason he did not want to see Ryker, despite his contempt for him, and when Pereira emerged from the bungalow he was relieved to see that he was alone. Connolly had decided that he would not return with the search parties when they came to find the capsule; Pereira would serve adequately as a guide.

'Well?'

The Captain smiled wanly. 'Oh, he admitted it, of course.' He sat down on the rail, and pointed to the manual. 'After all, he had no choice. Without that his existence here would be untenable.'

'He admitted that Colonel Spender landed here?'

Pereira nodded. 'Not in so many words, but effectively. The capsule is buried somewhere here – under the tumulus, I would guess. The Indians got hold of Colonel Spender, Ryker claims he could do nothing to help him.'

'That's a lie. He saved me in the bush when the Indians thought I had landed.'

With a shrug Pereira said: 'Your positions were slightly different. Besides, my impression is that Spender was dying anyway, Ryker says the parachute was badly burnt. He probably accepted a *fait accompli*, simply decided to do nothing and hush the whole thing up, incorporating the landing into the cargo cult. Very useful too. He'd been tricking the Indians with the Echo satellite, but sooner or later they would have become impatient. After the *Goliath* crashed, of course, they were prepared to go on watching the Echo and waiting for the next landing forever.' A faint smile touched his lips. 'It goes without saying that he regards the episode as something of a macabre joke. On you and the whole civilized world.'

A door slammed on the veranda, and Ryker stepped out into the sunlight. Bare-chested and hatless, he strode towards the launch.

'Connolly,' he called down, 'you've got my box of tricks there!'

Connolly reached forward and fingered the manual, the butt of his pistol tapping the table edge. He looked up at Ryker, at his big golden frame bathed in the morning light. Despite his still belligerent tone, a subtle change had come over Ryker. The ironic gleam in his eye had gone, and the inner core of wariness and suspicion which had warped the man and exiled him from the world was now visible. Connolly realized that, curiously, their respective roles had been reversed. He remembered Pereira reminding him that the Indians were at equilibrium with their environment, accepting its constraints and never seeking to dominate the towering arbors of the forest, in a sense of externalization of their own unconscious psyches. Ryker had upset that equilibrium, and by using the Echo satellite had brought the 20th century and its psychopathic projections into the heart of the Amazonian deep, transforming the Indians into a community of superstitious and materialistic sightseers, their whole culture oriented around the mythical god of the puppet star. It was Connolly who now accepted the jungle for what it was, seeing himself and the abortive space-flight in this fresh perspective.

Pereira gestured to the helmsman, and with a muffled roar the engine started. The launch pulled lightly against its lines.

'Connolly!' Ryker's voice was shriller now, his bellicose shout overlaid by a higher note. For a moment the two men looked at each other, and in the eyes above him Connolly glimpsed the helpless isolation of Ryker, his futile attempt to identify himself with the forest.

Picking up the manual, Connolly leaned forward and tossed it through the air on to the pier. Ryker tried to catch it, then knelt down and picked it up before it slipped through the springing poles. Still kneeling, he watched as the lines were cast off and the launch surged ahead.

They moved out into the channel and plunged through the bowers of spray into the heavier swells of the open current.

As they reached a sheltering bend and the figure of Ryker faded for the last time among the creepers and sunlight, Connolly turned to Pereira. 'Captain – what actually happened to Colonel Spender? You said the Indians wouldn't eat a white man.'

'They eat their gods,' Pereira said.

· **1963**

# THE TIME-TOMBS

## ONE

Usually in the evenings, while Traxel and Bridges drove off into the sand-sea, Shepley and the Old Man would wander among the gutted time-tombs, listening to them splutter faintly in the dying light as they recreated their fading personas, the deep crystal vaults flaring briefly like giant goblets.

Most of the tombs on the southern edge of the sand-sea had been stripped centuries earlier. But Shepley liked to saunter through the straggle of half-submerged pavilions, the ancient sand playing over his bare feet like wavelets on an endless beach. Alone among the flickering tombs, with the empty husks of the past ten thousand years, he could temporarily forget his nagging sense of failure.

Tonight, however, he would have to forego the walk. Traxel, who was nominally the leader of the group of tomb-robbers, had pointedly warned him at dinner that he must pay his way or leave. For three weeks Shepley had put off going with Traxel and Bridges, making a series of progressively lamer excuses, and they had begun to get impatient with him. The Old Man they would tolerate, for his vast knowledge of the sand-sea – he had combed the decaying tombs for over forty years and knew every reef and therm-pool like the palm of his hand – and because he was an institution that somehow dignified the lowly calling of tomb-robber, but Shepley had been there for only three months and had nothing to offer except his morose silences and self-hate.

'Tonight, Shepley,' Traxel told him firmly in his hard clipped voice, 'you must find a tape. We cannot support you indefinitely. Remember, we're all as eager to leave Vergil as you are.'

Shepley nodded, watching his reflection in the gold finger-bowl. Traxel sat at the head of the tilting table, his high-collared velvet jacket unbuttoned. Surrounded by the battered gold plate filched from the tombs, red wine spilling across the table from Bridges' tankard, he looked more like a Renaissance princeling than a cashiered PhD. Once Traxel had been a Professor of Semantics, and Shepley wondered what scandal had brought him to Vergil. Now, like a grave-rat, he hunted the time-tombs with Bridges, selling the tapes to the Psycho-History Museums at a dollar a foot. Shepley found it impossible to come to terms with the tall, aloof man. By contrast Bridges, who was just a thug, had a streak of blunt good humour that made him tolerable, but with Traxel he could never relax. Perhaps his coldly abrupt manner represented authority, the high-faced, stern-eyed interrogators who still pursued Shepley in his dreams.

Bridges kicked back his chair and lurched away around the table, pounding Shepley across the shoulders.

'You come with us, kid. Tonight we'll find a megatape.'

Outside, the low-hulled, camouflaged half-track waited in a saddle between two dunes. The old summer palace was sinking slowly below the desert, and the floor of the banqueting hall shelved into the white sand like the deck of a subsiding liner, going down with lights blazing from its staterooms.

'What about you, Doctor?' Traxel asked the Old Man as Bridges swung aboard the half-track and the exhaust kicked out. 'It would be a pleasure to have you along.' When the Old Man shook his head Traxel turned to Shepley. 'Well, are you coming?'

'Not tonight,' Shepley demurred hurriedly. 'I'll walk down to the tomb-beds later myself.'

'Twenty miles?' Traxel reminded him, watching reflectively. 'Very well.' He zipped up his jacket and strode away towards the half-track. As they moved off he shouted 'Shepley, I meant what I said!'

Shepley watched them disappear among the dunes. Flatly, he repeated 'He means what he says.'

The Old Man shrugged, sweeping the sand off the table. 'Traxel . . . he's a difficult man. What are you going to do?' The note of reproach in his voice was mild, realizing that Shepley's motives were the same as those which had marooned himself on the lost beaches of the sand-sea four decades earlier.

Shepley snapped irritably. 'I can't go with him. After five minutes he drains me like a skull. What's the matter with Traxel? Why is he here?'

The Old Man stood up, staring out vaguely into the desert. 'I can't remember. Everyone has his own reasons. After a while the stories overlap.'

They walked out under the portico, following the grooves left by the half-track. A mile away, winding between the last of the lavalakes which marked the southern shore of the sand-sea, they could just see the vehicle vanishing into the darkness. The old tomb-beds, where Shepley and the Old Man usually walked, lay between them, the pavilions arranged in three lines along a low basaltic ridge. Occasionally a brief flare of light flickered up into the white, bone-like darkness, but most of the tombs were silent.

Shepley stopped, hands falling limply to his sides. 'The new beds are by the Lake of Newton, nearly twenty miles away. I can't follow them.'

'I shouldn't try,' the Old Man rejoined. 'There was a big sand-storm last night. The time-wardens will be out in force marking any new tombs uncovered.' He chuckled softly to himself. 'Traxel and Bridges won't find a foot of tape – they'll be lucky if they're not arrested.' He took off his white cotton hat and squinted shrewdly through the dead light, assessing the altered contours of the dunes, then guided Shepley towards the old mono-rail whose southern terminus ended by the tomb-beds. Once it had been used to transport the pavilions from the station on the northern shore of the sand-sea, and a small gyro-car still leaned against the freight platform. 'We'll go over to Pascal. Something may have come up, you never know.'

Shepley shook his head. 'Traxel took me there when I first arrived. They've all been stripped a hundred times.'

'Well, we'll have a look.' The Old Man plodded on towards the mono-rail, his dirty white suit flapping in the low breeze. Behind them the summer palace – built three centuries earlier by a business tycoon from Ceres – faded into the darkness, the rippling glass tiles in the upper spires merging into the starlight.

Propping the car against the platform, Shepley wound up the gyroscope, then helped the Old Man on to the front seat. He prised off a piece of rusting platform rail and began to punt the car away. Every fifty yards or so they stopped to clear the sand that submerged the track, but slowly they wound off among the dunes and lakes. Here and there the onion-shaped cupola of a solitary time-tomb reared up into the sky beside them, fragments of the crystal casements twinkling in the sand like minuscule stars.

Half an hour later, as they rode down the final long incline towards the Lake of Pascal, Shepley went forward to sit beside the Old Man, who emerged from his private reverie to ask pointedly, 'And you, Shepley, why are you here?'

Shepley leaned back, letting the cool air drain the sweat off his face. 'Once I tried to kill someone,' he explained tersely. 'After they cured me I found I wanted to kill myself instead.' He reached down to the hand-brake as they gathered speed. 'For ten thousand dollars I can go back on probation. Here I thought there would be a freemasonry of sorts. But then you've been kind enough, Doctor.'

'Don't worry, we'll get you a winning tape.' He leaned forward, shielding his eyes from the stellar glare, gazing down at the little cantonment of gutted time-tombs on the shore of the lake. In all there were about a dozen pavilions, their roofs holed, the group Traxel had shown to Shepley after his arrival when he demonstrated how the vaults were robbed.

'Shepley! Look, lad!'

'Where? I've seen them before, Doctor. They're stripped.'

The Old Man pushed him away. 'No, you fool. Three hundred yards to the west, by the long ridge where the big dunes have moved. Can you see them now?' He drummed a white fist on Shepley's knee. 'You've made it, lad. You won't need to be frightened of Traxel or anyone else.'

Shepley jerked the car to a halt. As he ran ahead of the Old Man towards the escarpment he could see several of the time-tombs glowing along the sky lines, emerging briefly from the dark earth like the tents of a spectral caravan.

## TWO

For ten millennia the Sea of Vergil had served as a burial ground, and the 1,500 square miles of restless sand were estimated to contain over twenty thousand tombs. All but a minute fraction had been stripped by the successive generations of tomb-robbers, and an intact spool of the 17th Dynasty could now be sold to the Psycho-History Museum at Tycho for over 3,000 dollars. For each preceding dynasty, though none older than the 12th had ever been found, there was a bonus.

There were no corpses in the time-tombs, no dusty skeletons. The cyber-architectonic ghosts which haunted them were embalmed in the metallic codes of memory tapes, three-dimensional molecular transcriptions of their living originals, stored among the dunes as a stupendous act of faith, in the hope that one day the physical re-creation of the coded personalities would be possible. After five thousand years the attempt had been reluctantly abandoned, but out of respect for the tomb-builders their pavilions were left to take their own hazard with time in the Sea of Vergil. Later the tomb-robbers had arrived, as the historians of the new epochs realized the enormous archives that lay waiting for them in this antique limbo. Despite the time-wardens, the pillaging of the tombs and the illicit traffic in dead souls continued.

'Doctor! Come on! Look at them!'

Shepley plunged wildly up to his knees in the silver-white sand, diving from one pavilion to the next like a frantic puppy.

Smiling to himself, the Old Man climbed slowly up the melting slope, submerged to his waist as the fine crystals poured away around him, feeling for spurs of firmer rock. The cupola of the nearest tomb tilted into the sky, only the top six inches of the casements visible below the overhang. He sat for a moment on the roof, watching Shepley dive about in the darkness, then peered through the casement, brushing away the sand with his hands.

The tomb was intact. Inside he could see the votive light burning over the altar, the hexagonal nave with its inlaid gold floor and drapery, the narrow chancel at the rear which held the memory store. Low tables surrounded the chancel, carrying beaten goblets and gold bowls, token offerings intended to distract any pillager who stumbled upon the tomb.

Shepley came leaping over to him. 'Let's get into them, Doctor! What are we waiting for?'

The Old Man looked out over the plain below, at the cluster of stripped tombs by the edge of the lake, at the dark ribbon of the gyro-rail winding away among the hills. The thought of the fortune that lay at his fingertips left him unmoved. For so long now he had lived among the tombs that he had begun to assume something of their ambience of immortality and timelessness, and Shepley's impatience seemed to come out of another dimension. He hated stripping the tombs. Each one robbed represented, not just the final extinction of a surviving personality, but a diminution of his own sense of eternity. Whenever a new tomb-bed emerged from the sand he felt something within himself momentarily rekindled, not hope, for he was beyond that, but a serene acceptance of the brief span of time left to him.

'Right,' he nodded. They began to cleave away the sand piled around the door, Shepley driving it down the slope where it spilled in a white foam over the darker basaltic chips. When the narrow portico was free the Old Man squatted by the timeseal. His fingers cleaned away the crystals embedded between the tabs, then played lightly over them.

Like dry sticks breaking, an ancient voice crackled

> *Orion, Betelgeuse, Altair,*
> *What twice-born star shall be my heir,*
> *Doomed again to be this scion –*

'Come on, Doctor, this is a quicker way.' Shepley put one leg up against the door and lunged against it futilely. The Old Man pushed him away. With his mouth close to the seal, he rejoined.

> *'Of Altair, Betelgeuse, Orion.'*

As the doors accepted this and swung back he murmured:
'Don't despise the old rituals. Now, let's see.' They paused in the cool, unbreathed air, the votive light throwing a pale ruby glow over the gold drapes parting across the chancel.

The air became curiously hazy and mottled. Within a few seconds it began to vibrate with increasing rapidity, and a succession of vivid colours rippled across the surface of what appeared to be a cone of light projected from the rear of the chancel. Soon this resolved itself into a three-dimensional image of an elderly man in a blue robe.

Although the image was transparent, the brilliant electric blue of the robe revealing the inadequacies of the projection system, the intensity of the illusion was such that Shepley almost expected the man to speak to them. He was well into his seventies, with a composed, watchful face and thin grey hair, his hands resting quietly in front of him. The edge of the desk was just visible, the proximal arc of the cone enclosing part of a silver inkstand and a small metal trophy. These details, and the spectral bookshelves and paintings which formed the backdrop of the illusion, were of infinite value to the Psycho-History institutes, providing evidence of the earlier civilizations far more reliable than the funerary urns and goblets in the anteroom.

Shepley began to move forward, the definition of the persona fading slightly. A visual relay of the memory store, it would continue to play after the code had been removed, though the induction coils would soon exhaust themselves. Then the tomb would be finally extinct.

Two feet away, the wise unblinking eyes of the long dead magnate stared at him steadily, his seamed forehead like a piece of pink transparent wax. Tentatively, Shepley reached out and plunged his hand into the cone, the myriad vibration patterns racing across his wrist. For a moment he held the dead man's face in his hand, the edge of the desk and the silver inkstand dappling across his sleeve.

Then he stepped forward and walked straight through him into the darkness at the rear of the chancel.

Quickly, following Traxel's instructions, he unbolted the console containing the memory store, lifting out the three heavy drums which held the tape spools. Immediately the persona began to dim, the edge of the desk and the bookshelves vanishing as the cone contracted. Narrow bands of dead air appeared across it, one, at the level of the man's neck, decapitating him. Lower down the scanner had begun to misfire. The folded hands trembled nervously, and now and then one of his shoulders gave a slight twitch. Shepley stepped through him without looking back.

The Old Man was waiting outside. Shepley dropped the drums on to the sand. 'They're heavy,' he muttered. Brightening, he added. 'There must be over five hundred feet here, Doctor. With the bonus, and all the others as well –' He took the Old Man's arm. 'Come on, let's get into the next one.'

The Old Man disengaged himself, watching the sputtering persona in the pavilion, the blue light from the dead man's suit pulsing across the sand like a soundless lightning storm.

'Wait a minute, lad, don't run away with yourself.' As Shepley began to slide off through the sand, sending further falls down the slope, he added in a firmer voice 'And stop moving all that sand around! These tombs have been hidden for ten thousand years. Don't undo all the good work, or the wardens will find them the first time they go past.'

'Or Traxel,' Shepley said, sobering quickly. He glanced around the lake below, searching the shadows among the tombs in case anyone was watching them, waiting to seize the treasure.

## THREE

The Old Man left him at the door of the next pavilion, reluctant to watch the tomb being stripped of the last vestige of its already meagre claim to immortality.

'This will be our last one tonight,' he told Shepley. 'You'll never hide all these tapes from Bridges and Traxel.'

The furnishings of the tomb differed from that of the previous one. Sombre black marble panels covered the walls, inscribed with strange gold-leaf hieroglyphs, and the inlays in the floor represented stylized astrological symbols, at once eerie and obscure. Shepley leaned against the altar, watching the cone of light reach out towards him from the chancel as the curtains parted. The predominant colours were gold and carmine, mingled with a vivid powdery copper that gradually resolved itself into the huge, harp-like head-dress of a reclining woman. She lay in the centre of what seemed to be a sphere of softly luminous gas, inclined against a massive black catafalque, from the sides of which flared two enormous heraldic wings. The woman's copper hair was swept straight back from her forehead, some five or six feet long, and merged with the plumage of the wings, giving her an impression of tremendous contained speed, like a goddess arrested in a moment of flight on a cornice of some great temple-city of the dead.

Her eyes stared forward expressionlessly at Shepley. Her arms and shoulders were bare, and the white skin, like compacted snow, had a brilliant surface sheen, the reflected light glaring against the black base of the catafalque and the long sheath-like gown that swept around her hips to the floor. Her face, like an exquisite porcelain mask, was tilted upward slightly, the half-closed eyes suggesting that the woman was asleep or dreaming. No background had been provided for the image, but the bowl of luminescence invested the persona with immense power and mystery.

Shepley heard the Old Man shuffle up behind him.

'Who is she, Doctor? A princess?'

The Old Man shook his head slowly. 'You can only guess. I don't know. There are strange treasures in these tombs. Get on with it, we'd best be going.'

Shepley hesitated. He started to walk towards the woman on the catafalque, and then felt the enormous upward surge of her flight, the pressure of all the past centuries carried before her brought to a sudden focus in front of him, holding him back like a physical barrier.

'Doctor!' He reached the door just behind the Old Man. 'We'll leave this one, there's no hurry!'

The Old Man examined his face shrewdly in the moonlight, the brilliant colours of the persona flickering across Shepley's youthful cheeks. 'I know how you feel, lad, but remember, the woman doesn't exist, any more than a painting. You'll have to come back for her soon.'

Shepley nodded quickly. 'I know, but some other night. There's something uncanny about this tomb.' He closed the doors behind them, and immediately the huge cone of light shrank back into the chancel, sucking the woman and the catafalque into the darkness. The wind swept across the dunes, throwing a fine spray of sand on to the half-buried cupolas, sighing among the wrecked tombs.

The Old Man made his way down to the mono-rail, and waited
for Shepley as he worked for the next hour, slowly covering each of
the tombs.

On the Old Man's recommendation he gave Traxel only one of the
canisters, containing about 500 feet of tape. As prophesied, the time-
wardens had been out in force in the Sea of Newton, and two members
of another gang had been caught red-handed. Bridges was in foul temper,
but Traxel, as ever self-contained, seemed unworried at the wasted
evening.

Straddling the desk in the tilting ballroom, he examined the drum with
interest, complimenting Shepley on his initiative. 'Excellent, Shepley. I'm
glad you joined us now. Do you mind telling me where you found this?'

Shepley shrugged vaguely, began to mumble something about a secret
basement in one of the gutted tombs nearby, but the Old Man cut in:
'Don't broadcast it everywhere! Traxel, you shouldn't ask questions like
that – he's got his own living to earn.'

Traxel smiled, sphinx-like. 'Right again, Doctor.' He tapped the smooth
untarnished case. 'In mint condition, and a 15th Dynasty too.'

'Tenth!' Shepley claimed indignantly, frightened that Traxel might try
to pocket the bonus. The Old Man cursed, and Traxel's eyes gleamed.

'Tenth, is it? I didn't realize there were any 10th Dynasty tombs
still intact. You surprise me, Shepley. Obviously you have concealed
talents.'

Luckily he seemed to assume that the Old Man had been hoarding the
tape for years.

Face down in a shallow hollow at the edge of the ridge, Shepley watched
the white-hulled sand-car of the time-wardens shunt through the darkness
by the old cantonment. Directly below him jutted the spires of the newly
discovered tomb-bed, invisible against the dark background of the ridge.
The two wardens in the sand-car were more interested in the old tombs;
they had spotted the gyro-car lying on its side by the mono-rail, and
guessed that the gangs had been working the ruins over again. One
of them stood on the running board, flicking a torch into the gutted
pavilions. Crossing the mono-rail, the car moved off slowly across the
lake to the north-west, a low pall of dust settling behind it.

For a few moments Shepley lay quietly in the slack darkness, watching
the gullies and ravines that led into the lake, then slid down among the
pavilions. Brushing away the sand to reveal a square wooden plank, he
slipped below it into the portico.

As the golden image of the enchantress loomed out of the black-walled
chancel to greet him, the great reptilian wings unfurling around her, he
stood behind one of the columns in the nave, fascinated by her strange
deathless beauty. At times her luminous face seemed almost repellent,
but he had nonetheless seized on the faint possibility of her resurrection.

Each night he came, stealing into the tomb where she had lain for ten thousand years, unable to bring himself to interrupt her. The long copper hair streamed behind her like an entrained time-wind, her angled body in flight between two infinitely distant universes, where archetypal beings of superhuman stature glimmered fitfully in their own self-generated light.

Two days later Bridges discovered the remainder of the drums.

'Traxel! Traxel!' he bellowed, racing across the inner courtyard from the entrance to one of the disused bunkers. He bounded into the ballroom and slammed the metal cans on to the computer which Traxel was programming. 'Take a look at these – more Tenths! The whole place is crawling with them!'

Traxel weighed the cans idly in his hands, glancing across at Shepley and the Old Man, on lookout duty by the window. 'Interesting. Where did you find them?'

Shepley jumped down from the window trestle. 'They're mine. The Doctor will confirm it. They run in sequence after the first I gave you a week ago. I was storing them.'

Bridges cut back with an oath. 'Whaddya mean, storing them? Is that your personal bunker out there? Since when?' He shoved Shepley away with a broad hand and swung round on Traxel. 'Listen, Traxel, those tapes were a fair find. I don't see any tags on them. Every time I bring something in I'm going to have this kid claim it?'

Traxel stood up, adjusting his height so that he overreached Bridges. 'Of course, you're right – technically. But we have to work together, don't we? Shepley made a mistake, we'll forgive him this time.' He handed the drums to Shepley, Bridges seething with barely controlled indignation. 'If I were you, Shepley, I'd get those cashed. Don't worry about flooding the market.' As Shepley turned away, sidestepping Bridges, he called him back. 'And there are advantages in working together, you know.'

He watched Shepley disappear to his room, then turned to survey the huge peeling map of the sand-sea that covered the facing wall.

'You'll have to strip the tombs now,' the Old Man told Shepley later. 'It's obvious you've stumbled on something, and it won't take Traxel five minutes to discover where.'

'Perhaps a little longer,' Shepley replied evenly. They stepped out of the shadow of the palace and moved away among the dunes; Bridges and Traxel were watching them from the dining-room table, their figures motionless in the light. 'The roofs are almost covered now. The next sandstorm should bury them for good.'

'Have you entered any of the other tombs?'

Shepley shook his head vigorously. 'Believe me, Doctor, I know now why the time-wardens are here. As long as there's a chance of their coming to life we're committing murder every time we rob a tomb. Even if it's only one chance in a million it may be all they bargained on. After all, we don't commit suicide because the chances of life existing anywhere are virtually nil.'

Already he had come to believe that the enchantress might suddenly resurrect herself, step down from the catafalque before his eyes. While a slender possibility existed of her returning to life he felt that he too had a valid foothold in existence, that there was a small element of certainty in what had previously seemed a random and utterly meaningless universe.

## FOUR

As the first dawn light probed through the casements, Shepley turned reluctantly from the nave. He looked back briefly at the glowing persona, suppressing the slight pang of disappointment that the expected metamorphosis had not yet occurred, but relieved to have spent as much time awaiting it as possible.

He made his way down to the old cantonment, steering carefully through the shadows. As he reached the mono-rail – he now made the journey on foot, to prevent Traxel guessing that the cache lay along the route of the rail – he heard the track hum faintly in the cool air. He jumped back behind a low mound, tracing its winding pathway through the dunes.

Suddenly an engine throbbed out behind him, and Traxel's camouflaged half-track appeared over the edge of the ridge. Its front four wheels raced and spun, and the huge vehicle tipped forward and plunged down the incline among the buried tombs, its surging tracks dislodging tons of the fine sand Shepley had so laboriously pushed by hand up the slope. Immediately several of the pavilions appeared to view, the white dust cascading off their cupolas.

Half-buried in the avalanche they had set off, Traxel and Bridges leapt from the driving cab, pointing to the pavilions and shouting at each other. Shepley darted forward, and put his foot up on the mono-rail just as it began to vibrate loudly.

In the distance the gyro-car slowly approached, the Old Man punting it along, hatless and dishevelled.

He reached the tomb as Bridges was kicking the door in with a heavy boot, Traxel behind him with a bag full of wrenches.

'Hello, Shepley!' Traxel greeted him gaily. 'So this is your treasure trove.'

Shepley staggered splay-legged through the sliding sand, and brushed past Traxel as glass spattered from the window. He flung himself on Bridges and pulled the big man backwards.

'Bridges, this one's mine! Try any of the others; you can have them all!'

Bridges jerked himself to his feet, staring down angrily at Shepley. Traxel peered suspiciously at the other tombs, their porticos still flooded with sand. 'What's so interesting about this one, Shepley?' he asked sardonically. Bridges roared and slammed a boot into the casement, knocking out one of the panels. Shepley dived on to his shoulders, and Bridges snarled and flung him against the wall. Before Shepley could duck he swung a heavy left cross to Shepley's mouth, knocking him back on to the sand with a bloody face.

Traxel roared with amusement as Shepley lay there stunned, then knelt down, sympathetically examining Shepley's face in the light thrown by the expanding persona within the tomb. Bridges whooped with surprise, gaping like a startled ape at the sumptuous golden mirage of the enchantress.

'How did you find me?' Shepley muttered thickly. 'I double-tracked a dozen times.'

Traxel smiled. 'We didn't follow you, chum. We followed the rail.' He pointed down at the silver thread of the metal strip, plainly visible in the dawn light almost ten miles away. 'The gyro-car cleaned the rail. It led us straight here. Ah, hello, Doctor,' he greeted the Old Man as he climbed the slope and slumped down wearily beside Shepley. 'I take it we have you to thank for all this. Don't worry, Doctor, I shan't forget you.'

'Many thanks,' the Old Man said flatly. He helped Shepley to sit up, frowning at his split lips. 'Aren't you taking everything too seriously, Traxel? You're becoming crazed with greed. Let the boy have this tomb. There are plenty more.'

The patterns of light across the sand dimmed and broke as Bridges plunged through the persona towards the rear of the chancel. Weakly Shepley tried to stand up, but the Old Man held him back. Traxel shrugged. 'Too late, Doctor.' He looked over his shoulder at the persona, ruefully shaking his head in acknowledgment of its magnificence. 'These 10th Dynasty graves are stupendous. But there's something curious about this one.'

He was still staring at it reflectively a minute later when Bridges emerged.

'Boy, that was a crazy one, Traxel! For a second I thought it was a dud.' He handed the three canisters to Traxel, who weighed two of them in one hand against the other. Bridges added 'Kinda light, aren't they?'

Traxel began to prise them open with a wrench. 'Are you certain there are no more in there?'

'Hundred per cent. Have a look yourself.'

Two of the cans were empty, the tape spools missing. The third was only half full, a mere three-inch width of tape in its centre. Bridges bellowed in pain: 'The kid robbed us. I can't believe it!' Traxel waved him away and went over to the Old Man, who was staring in at the now flickering persona. The two men exchanged glances, then nodded slowly in confirmation. With a short laugh Traxel kicked at the can containing the half reel of tape, jerking the spool out on to the sand, where it began to unravel in the quietly moving air. Bridges protested but Traxel shook his head.

'It *is* a dud. Go and have a close look at the image.' When Bridges peered at it blankly he explained 'The woman there was dead when the matrices were recorded. She's beautiful all right – as poor Shepley here discovered – but it's all too literally skin deep. That's why there's only half a can of data. No nervous system, no musculature or internal organs – just a beautiful golden husk. This is a mortuary tomb. If you resurrected her you'd have an ice-cold corpse on your hands.'

'But why?' Bridges rasped. 'What's the point?'

Traxel gestured expansively. 'It's immortality of a kind. Perhaps she died suddenly, and this was the next best thing. When the Doctor first came here there were a lot of mortuary tombs of young children being found. If I remember he had something of a reputation for always leaving them intact. A typical piece of highbrow sentimentality – giving immortality only to the dead. Agree, Doctor?'

Before the Old Man could reply a voice shouted from below, there was a nearby roaring hiss of an ascending signal rocket and a vivid red star-shell burst over the lake below, spitting incandescent fragments over them. Traxel and Bridges leapt forwards, saw two men in a sand-car pointing up at them, and three more vehicles converging across the lake half a mile away.

'The time-wardens!' Traxel shouted. Bridges picked up the tool bag and the two men raced across the slope towards the half-track, the Old Man hobbling after them. He turned back to wait for Shepley, who was still sitting on the ground where he had fallen, watching the image inside the pavilion.

'Shepley! Come on, lad, pull yourself together! You'll get ten years!'

When Shepley made no reply he reached up to the side of the half-track as Traxel reversed it expertly out of the morraine of sand, letting Bridges swing him aboard. 'Shepley!' he called again. Traxel hesitated, then roared away as a second star-shell exploded.

Shepley tried to reach the tape, but the stampeding feet had severed it at several points, and the loose ends, which he had numbly thought of trying to reinsert into the projector, now fluttered around him in the sand. Below, he could hear the sounds of flight and pursuit, the warning crack of a rifle, engines baying and plunging, as Traxel eluded the time-wardens, but he kept his eyes fixed on the image within the tomb. Already it had begun to fragment, fading against the mounting sunlight. Getting slowly to his feet, he entered the tomb and closed the battered doors.

Still magnificent upon her bier, the enchantress lay back between the great wings. Motionless for so long, she had at last been galvanized into life, and a jerking syncopated rhythm rippled through her body. The wings shook uneasily, and a series of tremors disturbed the base of the catafalque, so that the woman's feet danced an exquisitely flickering minuet, the toes darting from side to side with untiring speed. Higher up, her wide smooth hips jostled each other in a jaunty mock tango.

He watched until only the face remained, a few disconnected traces of the wings and catafalque jerking faintly in the darkness, then made his way out of the tomb.

Outside, in the cool morning light, the time-wardens were waiting for him, hands on the hips of their white uniforms. One was holding the empty canisters, turning the fluttering strands of tape over with his foot as they drifted away.

The other took Shepley's arm and steered him down to the car.

'Traxel's gang,' he said to the driver. 'This must be a new recruit.' He glanced dourly at the blood around Shepley's mouth. 'Looks as if they've been fighting over the spoils.'

The driver pointed to the three drums. 'Stripped?'

The man carrying them nodded. 'All three. And they were 10th Dynasty.' He shackled Shepley's wrists to the dashboard. 'Too bad, son, you'll be doing ten yourself soon. It'll seem like ten thousand.'

'Unless it was a dud,' the driver rejoined, eyeing Shepley with some sympathy. 'You know, one of those freak mortuary tombs.'

Shepley straightened his bruised mouth. 'It wasn't,' he said firmly.

The driver glanced warningly at the other wardens. 'What about the tape blowing away up there?'

Shepley looked up at the tomb spluttering faintly below the ridge, its light almost gone. 'That's just the persona,' he said. 'The empty skin.'

As the engine surged forward he listened to three empty drums hit the floor behind the seat.

· **1963**

# NOW WAKES THE SEA

Again at night Mason heard the sounds of the approaching sea, the muffled thunder of breakers rolling up the near-by streets. Roused from his sleep, he ran out into the moonlight, where the white-framed houses stood like sepulchres among the washed concrete courts. Two hundred yards away the waves plunged and boiled, sluicing in and out across the pavement. Foam seethed through the picket fences, and the broken spray filled the air with the wine-sharp tang of brine.

Off-shore the deeper swells of the open sea rode across the roofs of the submerged houses, the white-caps cleft by isolated chimneys. Leaping back as the cold foam stung his feet, Mason glanced at the house where his wife lay sleeping. Each night the sea moved a few yards nearer, a hissing guillotine across the empty lawns.

For half an hour Mason watched the waves vault among the rooftops. The luminous surf cast a pale nimbus on the clouds racing overhead on the dark wind, and covered his hands with a waxy sheen.

At last the waves began to recede, and the deep bowl of illuminated water withdrew down the emptying streets, disgorging the lines of houses in the moonlight. Mason ran forwards across the expiring bubbles, but the sea shrank away from him, disappearing around the corners of the houses, sliding below the garage doors. He sprinted to the end of the road as a last glow was carried across the sky beyond the spire of the church. Exhausted, Mason returned to his bed, the sound of the dying waves filling his head as he slept.

'I saw the sea again last night,' he told his wife at breakfast.

Quietly, Miriam said: 'Richard, the nearest sea is a thousand miles away.' She watched her husband for a moment, her pale fingers straying to the coil of black hair lying against her neck. 'Go out into the drive and look. There's no sea.'

'Darling, I *saw* it.'

'Richard –!'

Mason stood up, and with slow deliberation raised his palms. 'Miriam, I felt the spray on my hands. The waves were breaking around my feet. I wasn't dreaming.'

'You must have been.' Miriam leaned against the door, as if trying to exclude the strange nightworld of her husband. With her long raven hair framing her oval face, and the scarlet dressing-gown open to reveal her slender neck and white breast, she reminded Mason of a Pre-Raphaelite heroine in an Arthurian pose. 'Richard, you must see Dr Clifton. It's beginning to frighten me.'

Mason smiled, his eyes searching the distant rooftops above the trees. 'I shouldn't worry. What's happening is really very simple. At night I hear the sounds of the sea, I go out and watch the waves in the moonlight, and then come back to bed.' He paused, a flush of fatigue on his face. Tall and slimly built, Mason was still convalescing from the illness which had kept him at home for the previous six months. 'It's curious, though,' he resumed, 'the water is remarkably luminous. I should guess its salinity is well above normal –'

'But Richard ...' Miriam looked around helplessly, her husband's calmness exhausting her. 'The sea isn't *there*; it's only in your mind. No one else can see it.'

Mason nodded, hands lost in his pockets. 'Perhaps no one else has heard it yet.'

Leaving the breakfast-room, he went into his study. The couch on which he had slept during his illness still stood against the corner, his bookcase beside it. Mason sat down, taking a large fossil mollusc from a shelf. During the winter, when he had been confined to bed, the smooth trumpet-shaped conch, with its endless associations of ancient seas and drowned strands, had provided him with unlimited pleasure, a bottomless cornucopia of image and reverie. Cradling it reassuringly in his hands, as exquisite and ambiguous as a fragment of Greek sculpture found in a dry riverbed, he reflected that it seemed like a capsule of time, the condensation of another universe. He could almost believe that the midnight sea which haunted his sleep had been released from the shell when he had inadvertently scratched one of its helixes.

Miriam followed him into the room and briskly drew the curtains, as if aware that Mason was returning to the twilight world of his sick-bed. She took his shoulders in her hands.

'Richard, listen. Tonight, when you hear the waves, wake me and we'll go out together.'

Gently, Mason disengaged himself. 'Whether you see it or not is irrelevant, Miriam. The fact is that I see it.'

Later, walking down the street, Mason reached the point where he had stood the previous night, watching the waves break and roll towards him. The sounds of placid domestic activity came from the houses he had seen submerged. The grass on the lawns was bleached by the July heat, and sprays rotated in the bright sunlight, casting rainbows in the vivid air. Undisturbed since the rainstorms in the early spring, the long summer's dust lay between the wooden fences and water hydrants.

The street, one of a dozen suburban boulevards on the perimeter of the town, ran north-west for some three hundred yards and then joined the open square of the neighbourhood shopping centre. Mason shielded his eyes and looked out at the clock tower of the library and the church spire, identifying the protuberances which had risen from the steep swells of the open sea. All were in exactly the positions he remembered.

The road shelved slightly as it approached the shopping centre, and by a curious coincidence marked the margins of the beach which would have existed if the area had been flooded. A mile or so from the town, this shallow ridge, which formed part of the rim of a large natural basin enclosing the alluvial plain below, culminated in a small chalk outcropping. Although it was partly hidden by the intervening houses, Mason now recognized it clearly as the promontory which had reared like a citadel above the sea. The deep swells had rolled against its flanks, sending up immense plumes of spray that fell back with almost hypnotic slowness upon the receding water. At night the promontory seemed larger and more gaunt, an uneroded bastion against the sea. One evening, Mason promised himself, he would go out to the promontory and let the waves wake him as he slept on the peak.

A car moved past, the driver watching Mason curiously as he stood in the middle of the road, head raised to the air. Not wishing to appear any more eccentric than he was already considered – the solitary, abstracted husband of the beautiful but childless Mrs Mason – Mason turned into the avenue which ran along the ridge. As he approached the distant outcropping he glanced over the hedges for any signs of water-logged gardens or stranded cars. The houses had been inundated by the floodwater.

The first visions of the sea had come to Mason only three weeks earlier, but he was already convinced of their absolute validity. He recognized that after its nightly withdrawal the water failed to leave any mark on the hundreds of houses it submerged, and he felt no alarm for the drowned people who were sleeping undisturbed in the sea's immense liquid locker as he watched the luminous waves break across the roof-tops. Despite this paradox, it was his complete conviction of the sea's reality that had made him admit to Miriam that he had woken one night to the sound of waves outside the window and gone out to find the sea rolling across the neighbourhood streets and houses. At first she had merely smiled at him, accepting this illustration of his strange private world. Then, three nights later, she had woken to the sound of him latching the door on his return, bewildered by his pumping chest and perspiring face.

From then on she spent all day looking over her shoulder through the window for any signs of the sea. What worried her as much as the vision itself was Mason's complete calm in the face of this terrifying unconscious apocalypse.

Tired by his walk, Mason sat down on a low ornamental wall, screened from the surrounding houses by the rhododendron bushes. For a few minutes he played with the dust at his feet, stirring the white grains with a branch. Although formless and passive, the dust shared something of the same evocative qualities of the fossil mollusc, radiating a curious compacted light.

In front of him, the road curved and dipped, the incline carrying it away on to the fields below. The chalk shoulder, covered by a mantle of green turf, rose into the clear sky. A metal shack had been erected on the slope, and a small group of figures moved about the entrance of a mine-shaft, adjusting a wooden hoist. Wishing that he had brought his wife's car, Mason watched the diminutive figures disappear one by one into the shaft.

The image of this elusive pantomime remained with him all day in the library, overlaying his memories of the dark waves rolling across the midnight streets. What sustained Mason was his conviction that others would soon also become aware of the sea.

When he went to bed that night he found Miriam sitting fully dressed in the armchair by the window, her face composed into an expression of calm determination.

'What are you doing?' he asked.

'Waiting.'

'For what?'

'The sea. Don't worry, simply ignore me and go to sleep. I don't mind sitting here with the light out.'

'Miriam . . .' Wearily, Mason took one of her slender hands and tried to draw her from the chair. 'Darling, what on earth will this achieve?'

'Isn't it obvious?'

Mason sat down on the foot of the bed. For some reason, not wholly concerned with the wish to protect her, he wanted to keep his wife from the sea. 'Miriam, don't you understand? I might not actually *see* it, in the literal sense. It might be . . .' he extemporized . . . 'an hallucination, or a dream.'

Miriam shook her head, hands clasped on the arms of the chair. 'I don't think it is. Anyway, I want to find out.'

Mason lay back on the bed. 'I wonder whether you're approaching this the right way –'

Miriam sat forward. 'Richard, you're taking it all so calmly; you accept this vision as if it were a strange headache. That's what frightens me. If you were really terrified by this sea I wouldn't worry, but . . .'

Half an hour later he fell asleep in the darkened room, Miriam's slim face watching him from the shadows.

Waves murmured, outside the windows the distant swish of racing foam drew him from sleep, the muffled thunder of rollers and the sounds of deep water drummed at his ears. Mason climbed out of bed, and dressed quickly as the hiss of receding water sounded up the street. In the corner, under the light reflected from the distant foam, Miriam lay asleep in the armchair, a bar of moonlight across her throat.

His bare feet soundless on the pavement, Mason ran towards the waves.

He stumbled across the glistening tideline as one of the breakers struck with a guttural roar. On his knees, Mason felt the cold brilliant water, seething with animalcula, spurt across his chest and shoulders, slacken and then withdraw, sucked like a gleaming floor into the mouth of the next breaker. His wet suit clinging to him like a drowned animal, Mason stared out across the sea. In the moonlight the white houses advanced into the water like the palazzos of a spectral Venice, mausoleums on the causeways of some island necropolis. Only the church spire was still visible. The water rode in to its high tide, a further twenty yards down the street, the spray carried almost to the Masons' house.

Mason waited for an interval between two waves and then waded through the shallows to the avenue which wound towards the distant headland. By now the water had crossed the roadway, swilling over the dark lawns and slapping at the doorsteps.

Half a mile from the headland he heard the great surge and sigh of the deeper water. Out of breath, he leaned against a fence as the cold foam cut across his legs, pulling him with its undertow. Illuminated by the racing clouds, he saw the pale figure of a woman standing above the sea on a stone parapet at the cliff's edge, her black robe lifting behind her in the wind, her long hair white in the moonlight. Far below her feet, the luminous waves leapt and vaulted like acrobats.

Mason ran along the pavement, losing sight of her as the road curved and the houses intervened. The water slackened and he caught a last glimpse of the woman's icy-white profile through the spray. Turning, the tide began to ebb and fade, and the sea shrank away between the houses, draining the night of its light and motion.

As the last bubbles dissolved on the damp pavement, Mason searched the headland, but the luminous figure had gone. His damp clothes dried themselves as he walked back through the empty streets. A last tang of brine was carried away off the hedges on the midnight air.

The next morning he told Miriam: 'It *was* a dream, after all. I think the sea has gone now. Anyway, I saw nothing last night.'

'Thank heavens, Richard. Are you sure?'

'I'm certain.' Mason smiled encouragingly. 'Thanks for keeping watch over me.'

'I'll sit up tonight as well.' She held up her hand. 'I insist. I feel all right after last night, and I want to drive this thing away, once and for all.' She frowned over the coffee cups. 'It's strange, but once or twice I think I heard the sea too. It sounded very old and blind, like something waking again after millions of years.'

On his way to the library, Mason made a detour towards the chalk outcropping, and parked the car where he had seen the moonlit figure of the white-haired woman watching the sea. The sunlight fell on the pale turf, illuminating the mouth of the mine-shaft, around which the same desultory activity was taking place.

For the next fifteen minutes Mason drove in and out of the tree-lined avenues, peering over the hedges at the kitchen windows. Almost certainly she would live in one of the nearby houses, still wearing her black robe beneath a housecoat.

Later, at the library, he recognized a car he had seen on the headland. The driver, an elderly tweed-suited man, was examining the display cases of local geological finds.

'Who was that?' he asked Fellowes, the keeper of antiquities, as the car drove off. 'I've seen him on the cliffs.'

'Professor Goodhart, one of the party of paleontologists. Apparently they've uncovered an interesting bone-bed.' Fellowes gestured at the collection of femurs and jaw-bone fragments. 'With luck we may get a few pieces from them.'

Mason stared at the bones, aware of a sudden closing of the parallax within his mind.

Each night, as the sea emerged from the dark streets and the waves rolled farther towards the Masons' home, he would wake beside his sleeping wife and go out into the surging air, wading through the deep water towards the headland. There he would see the white-haired woman on the cliff's edge, her face raised above the roaring spray. Always he failed to reach her before the tide turned, and would kneel exhausted on the wet pavements as the drowned streets rose around him.

Once a police patrol car found him in its headlights, slumped against a gate-post in an open drive. On another night he forgot to close the front door when he returned. All through breakfast Miriam watched him with her old wariness, noticing the shadows which encircled his eyes like manacles.

'Richard, I think you should stop going to the library. You look worn out. It isn't that sea dream again?'

Mason shook his head, forcing a tired smile. 'No, that's finished with. Perhaps I've been over-working.'

Miriam held his hands. 'Did you fall over yesterday?' She examined Mason's palms. 'Darling, they're still *raw!* You must have grazed them only a few hours ago. Can't you remember?'

Abstracted, Mason invented some tale to satisfy her, then carried his coffee into the study and stared at the morning haze which lay across the rooftops, a soft lake of opacity that followed the same contours as the midnight sea. The mist dissolved in the sunlight, and for a moment the diminishing reality of the normal world reasserted itself, filling him with a poignant nostalgia.

Without thinking, he reached out to the fossil conch on the bookshelf, but involuntarily his hand withdrew before touching it.

Miriam stood beside him. 'Hateful thing,' she commented. 'Tell me, Richard, what do you think caused your dream?'

Mason shrugged. 'Perhaps it was a sort of memory . . .' He wondered whether to tell Miriam of the waves which he still heard in his sleep, and of the white-haired woman on the cliff's edge who seemed to beckon to him. But like all women Miriam believed that there was room for only one enigma in her husband's life. By an inversion of logic he felt that his dependence on his wife's private income, and the loss of self-respect, gave him the right to withhold something of himself from her.

'Richard, what's the matter?'

In his mind the spray opened like a diaphanous fan and the enchantress of the waves turned towards him.

Waist-high, the sea pounded across the lawn in a whirlpool. Mason pulled off his jacket and flung it into the water, and then waded out into the street. Higher than ever before, the waves had at last reached his house, breaking over the doorstep, but Mason had forgotten his wife. His attention was fixed upon the headland, which was lashed by a continuous storm of spray, almost obscuring the figure standing on its crest.

As Mason pressed on, sometimes sinking to his shoulders, shoals of luminous algae swarmed in the water around him. His eyes smarted in the saline air. He reached the lower slopes of the headland almost exhausted, and fell to his knees.

High above, he could hear the spray singing as it cut through the coigns of the cliff's edge, the deep base of the breakers overlaid by the treble of the keening air. Carried by the music, Mason climbed the flank of the headland, a thousand reflections of the moon in the breaking sea. As he reached the crest, the black robe hid the woman's face, but he could see her tall erect carriage and slender hips. Suddenly, without any apparent motion of her limbs, she moved away along the parapet.

'Wait!'

His shout was lost on the air. Mason ran forwards, and the figure turned and stared back at him. Her white hair swirled around her face like a spume of silver steam and then parted to reveal a face with empty eyes and notched mouth. A hand like a bundle of white sticks clawed towards him, and the figure rose through the whirling darkness like a gigantic bird.

Unaware whether the scream came from his own mouth or from this spectre, Mason stumbled back. Before he could catch himself he tripped over the wooden railing, and in a cackle of chains and pulleys fell backwards into the shaft, the sounds of the sea booming in its hurtling darkness.

After listening to the policeman's description, Professor Goodhart shook his head.

'I'm afraid not, sergeant. We've been working on the bed all week. No one's fallen down the shaft.' One of the flimsy wooden rails was swinging loosely in the crisp air. 'But thank you for warning me. I suppose we must build a heavier railing, if this fellow is wandering around in his sleep.'

'I don't think he'll bother to come up here,' the sergeant said. 'It's quite a climb.' As an afterthought he added: 'Down at the library where he works they said you'd found a couple of skeletons in the shaft yesterday. I know it's only two days since he disappeared, but one of them couldn't possibly be his?' The sergeant shrugged. 'If there was some natural acid, say . . .'

Professor Goodhart drove his heel into the chalky turf. 'Pure calcium carbonate, about a mile thick, laid down during the Triassic Period 200 million years ago when there was a large inland sea here. The skeletons we found yesterday, a man's and a woman's, belong to two Cro-Magnon fisher people who lived on the shore just before it dried up. I wish I could oblige you – it's quite a problem to understand how these Cro-Magnon relics found their way into the bone-bed. This shaft wasn't sunk until about thirty years ago. Still, that's my problem, not yours.'

Returning to the police car, the sergeant shook his head. As they drove off he looked out at the endless stretch of placid suburban homes.

'Apparently there was an ancient sea here once. A million years ago.' He picked a crumpled flannel jacket off the back seat. 'That reminds me, I know what Mason's coat smells of – brine.'

**. 1963**

# THE VENUS HUNTERS

When Dr Andrew Ward joined the Hubble Memorial Institute at Mount Vernon Observatory he never imagined that the closest of his new acquaintances would be an amateur star-gazer and spare-time prophet called Charles Kandinski, tolerantly regarded by the Observatory professionals as a madman. In fact, had either he or Professor Cameron, the Institute's Deputy Director, known just how far he was to be prepared to carry this friendship before his two-year tour at the Institute was over, Ward would certainly have left Mount Vernon the day he arrived and would never have become involved in the bizarre and curiously ironic tragedy which was to leave an ineradicable stigma upon his career.

Professor Cameron first introduced him to Kandinski. About a week after Ward came to the Hubble he and Cameron were lunching together in the Institute cafeteria.

'We'll go down to Vernon Gardens for coffee,' Cameron said when they finished dessert. 'I want to get a shampoo for Edna's roses and then we'll sit in the sun for an hour and watch the girls go by.' They strolled out through the terrace tables towards the parking lot. A mile away, beyond the conifers thinning out on the slopes above them, the three great Vernon domes gleamed like white marble against the sky. 'Incidentally, you can meet the opposition.'

'Is there another observatory at Vernon?' Ward asked as they set off along the drive in Cameron's Buick. 'What is it – an Air Force weather station?'

'Have you ever heard of Charles Kandinski?' Cameron said. 'He wrote a book called *The Landings from Outer Space*. It was published about three years ago.'

Ward shook his head doubtfully. They slowed down past the checkpoint at the gates and Cameron waved to the guard. 'Is that the man who claims to have seen extra-terrestrial beings? Martians or –'

'Venusians. That's Kandinski. Not only seen them,' Professor Cameron added. 'He's talked to them. Charles works at a café in Vernon Gardens. We know him fairly well.'

'He runs the other observatory?'

'Well, an old 4-inch MacDonald Refractor mounted in a bucket of cement. You probably wouldn't think much of it, but I wish we could see with our two-fifty just a tenth of what he sees.'

Ward nodded vaguely. The two observatories at which he had worked previously, Cape Town and the Milan Astrographie, had both attracted any number of cranks and charlatans eager to reveal their own final truths about the cosmos, and the prospect of meeting Kandinski interested him only slightly. 'What is he?' he asked. 'A practical joker, or just a lunatic?'

Professor Cameron propped his glasses on to his forehead and negotiated a tight hairpin. 'Neither,' he said.

Ward smiled at Cameron, idly studying his plump cherubic face with its puckish mouth and keen eyes. He knew that Cameron enjoyed a modest reputation as a wit. 'Has he ever claimed in front of you that he's seen a . . . Venusian?'

'Often,' Professor Cameron said. 'Charles lectures two or three times a week about the landings to the women's societies around here and put himself completely at our disposal. I'm afraid we had to tell him he was a little too advanced for us. But wait until you meet him.'

Ward shrugged and looked out at the long curving peach terraces lying below them, gold and heavy in the August heat. They dropped a thousand feet and the road widened and joined the highway which ran from the Vernon Gardens across the desert to Santa Vera and the coast.

Vernon Gardens was the nearest town to the Observatory and most of it had been built within the last few years, evidently with an eye on the tourist trade. They passed a string of blue and pink-washed houses, a school constructed of glass bricks and an abstract Baptist chapel. Along the main thoroughfare the shops and stores were painted in bright jazzy colours, the vivid awnings and neon signs like street scenery in an experimental musical.

Professor Cameron turned off into a wide tree-lined square and parked by a cluster of fountains in the centre. He and Ward walked towards the cafés – Al's Fresco Diner, Ylla's, the Dome – which stretched down to the sidewalk. Around the square were a dozen gift-shops filled with cheap souvenirs: silverplate telescopes and models of the great Vernon dome masquerading as ink-stands and cigar-boxes, plus a juvenile omnium gatherum of miniature planetaria, space helmets and plastic 3-D star atlases.

The café to which they went was decorated in the same futuristic motifs. The chairs and tables were painted a drab aluminium grey, their limbs and panels cut in random geometric shapes. A silver rocket ship, ten feet long, its paint peeling off in rusty strips, reared up from a pedestal among the tables. Across it was painted the café's name.

'The Site Tycho.'

A large mobile had been planted in the ground by the sidewalk and dangled down over them, its vanes and struts flashing in the sun. Gingerly Professor Cameron pushed it away. 'I'll swear that damn thing is growing,' he confided to Ward. 'I must tell Charles to prune it.' He lowered himself into a chair by one of the open-air tables, put on a fresh pair of sunglasses and focused them at the long brown legs of a girl sauntering past.

Left alone for the moment, Ward looked around him and picked at a cellophane transfer of a ringed planet glued to the table-top. The Site Tycho was also used as a small science fiction exchange library. A couple of metal bookstands stood outside the café door, where a soberly dressed middle-aged man, obviously hiding behind his upturned collar, worked his way quickly through the rows of paperbacks. At another table a young man with an intent, serious face was reading a magazine. His high cerebrotonic forehead was marked across the temple by a ridge of pink tissue, which Ward wryly decided was a lobotomy scar.

'Perhaps we ought to show our landing permits,' he said to Cameron when after three or four minutes no one had appeared to serve them. 'Or at least get our pH's checked.'

Professor Cameron grinned. 'Don't worry, no customs, no surgery.' He took his eyes off the sidewalk for a moment. 'This looks like him now.'

A tall, bearded man in a short-sleeved tartan shirt and pale green slacks came out of the café towards them with two cups of coffee on a tray.

'Hello, Charles,' Cameron greeted him. 'There you are. We were beginning to think we'd lost ourselves in a time-trap.'

The tall man grunted something and put the cups down. Ward guessed that he was about 55 years old. He was well over six feet tall, with a massive sunburnt head and lean but powerfully muscled arms.

'Andrew, this is Charles Kandinski.' Cameron introduced the two men. 'Andrew's come to work for me, Charles. He photographed all those Cepheids for the Milan Conference last year.'

Kandinski nodded. His eyes examined Ward critically but showed no signs of interest.

'I've been telling him all about you, Charles,' Cameron went on, 'and how we all follow your work. No further news yet, I trust?'

Kandinski's lips parted in a slight smile. He listened politely to Cameron's banter and looked out over the square, his great seamed head raised to the sky.

'Andrew's read your book, Charles,' Cameron was saying. 'Very interested. He'd like to see the originals of those photographs. Wouldn't you, Andrew?'

'Yes, I certainly would,' Ward said.

Kandinski gazed down at him again. His expression was not so much penetrating as detached and impersonal, as if he were assessing Ward with an utter lack of bias, so complete, in fact, that it left no room for even the smallest illusion. Previously Ward had only seen this expression in the eyes of the very old. 'Good,' Kandinski said. 'At present they are in a safe deposit box at my bank, but if you are serious I will get them out.'

Just then two young women wearing wide-brimmed Rapallo hats made their way through the tables. They sat down and smiled at Kandinski. He nodded to Ward and Cameron and went over to the young women, who began to chatter to him animatedly.

'Well, he seems popular with them,' Ward commented. 'He's certainly not what I anticipated. I hope I didn't offend him over the plates. He was taking you seriously.'

'He's a little sensitive about them,' Cameron explained. 'The famous dustbin-lid flying saucers. You mustn't think I bait him, though. To tell the truth I hold Charles in great respect. When all's said and done, we're in the same racket.'

'Are we?' Ward said doubtfully. 'I haven't read his book. Does he say in so many words that he saw and spoke to a visitor from Venus?'

'Precisely. Don't you believe him?'

Ward laughed and looked through the coins in his pocket, leaving one on the table. 'I haven't tried to yet. You say the whole thing isn't a hoax?'

'Of course not.'

'How do you explain it then? Compensation-fantasy or –'

Professor Cameron smiled. 'Wait until you know Charles a little better.'

'I already know the man's messianic,' Ward said dryly. 'Let me guess the rest. He lives on yoghurt, weaves his own clothes, and stands on his head all night, reciting the Bhagavadgita backwards.'

'He doesn't,' Cameron said, still smiling at Ward. 'He happens to be a big man who suffers from barber's rash. I thought he'd have you puzzled.'

Ward pulled the transfer off the table. Some science fantast had skilfully pencilled in an imaginary topography on the planet's surface. There were canals, craters and lake systems named Verne, Wells and Bradbury. 'Where did he see this Venusian?' Ward asked, trying to keep the curiosity out of his voice.

'About twenty miles from here, out in the desert off the Santa Vera highway. He was picnicking with some friends, went off for a stroll in the sandhills and ran straight into the space-ship. His friends swear he was perfectly normal both immediately before and after the landing, and all of them saw the inscribed metallic tablet which the Venusian pilot left behind. Some sort of ultimatum, if I remember, warning mankind to abandon all its space programmes. Apparently someone up there does not like us.'

'Has he still got the tablet?' Ward asked.

'No. Unluckily it combusted spontaneously in the heat. But Charles managed to take a photograph of it.'

Ward laughed. 'I bet he did. It sounds like a beautifully organized hoax. I suppose he made a fortune out of his book?'

'About 150 dollars. He had to pay for the printing himself. Why do you think he works here? The reviews were too unfavourable. People who read science fiction apparently dislike flying saucers, and everyone else dismissed him as a lunatic.' He stood up. 'We might as well get back.'

As they left the café Cameron waved to Kandinski, who was still talking to the young women. They were leaning forward and listening with rapt attention to whatever he was saying.

'What do the people in Vernon Gardens think of him?' Ward asked as they moved away under the trees.

'Well, it's a curious thing, almost without exception those who actually know Kandinski are convinced he's sincere and that he saw an alien space craft, while at the same time realizing the absolute impossibility of the whole story.'

'"I know God exists, but I cannot *believe* in him"?'

'Exactly. Naturally, most people in Vernon think he's crazy. About three months after he met the Venusian, Charles saw another UFO chasing its tail over the town. He got the Fire Police out, alerted the Radar Command chain and even had the National Guard driving around town ringing a bell. Sure enough, there were two white blobs diving about in the clouds. Unfortunately for Charles, they were caused by the headlights of one of the asparagus farmers in the valley doing some night spraying. Charles was the first to admit it, but at 3 o'clock in the morning no one was very pleased.'

'Who is Kandinski, anyway?' Ward asked. 'Where does he come from?'

'He doesn't make a profession of seeing Venusians, if that's what you mean. He was born in Alaska, for some years taught psychology at Mexico City University. He's been just about everywhere, had a thousand different jobs. A veteran of the private evacuations. Get his book.'

Ward murmured non-committally. They entered a small arcade and stood for a moment by the first shop, an aquarium called 'The Nouvelle Vague', watching the Angel fish and Royal Brahmins swim dreamily up and down their tanks.

'It's worth reading,' Professor Cameron went on. 'Without exaggerating, it's really one of the most interesting documents I've ever come across.'

'I'm afraid I have a closed mind when it comes to interplanetary bogey-men,' Ward said.

'A pity,' Cameron rejoined. 'I find them fascinating. Straight out of the unconscious. The fish too,' he added, pointing at the tanks. He grinned whimsically at Ward and ducked away into a horticulture store halfway down the arcade.

While Professor Cameron was looking through the sprays on the hormone counter, Ward went over to a news-stand and glanced at the magazines. The proximity of the observatory had prompted a large selection of popular astronomical guides and digests, most of them with illustrations of the Mount Vernon domes on their wrappers. Among them Ward noticed a dusty, dog-eared paperback, *The Landings from Outer Space* by Charles Kandinski. On the front cover a gigantic space vehicle, at least the size of New York, tens of thousands of portholes ablaze with light, was soaring majestically across a brilliant backdrop of stars and spiral nebulae.

Ward picked up the book and turned to the end cover. Here there was a photograph of Kandinski, dressed in a dark lounge suit several sizes too small, peering stiffly into the eye-piece of his MacDonald.

Ward hesitated before finally taking out his wallet. He bought the book and slipped it into his pocket as Professor Cameron emerged from the horticulture store.

'Get your shampoo?' Ward asked.

Cameron brandished a brass insecticide gun, then slung it, buccaneer-like, under his belt. 'My disintegrator,' he said, patting the butt of the gun. 'There's a positive plague of white ants in the garden, like something out of a science fiction nightmare. I've tried to convince Edna that their real source is psychological. Remember the story "Leiningen vs the Ants"? A classic example of the forces of the Id rebelling against the Super-Ego.' He watched a girl in a black bikini and lemon-coloured sunglasses move gracefully through the arcade and added meditatively: 'You know, Andrew, like everyone else my real vocation was to be a psychiatrist. I spend so long analysing my motives I've no time left to act.'

'Kandinski's Super-Ego must be in difficulties,' Ward remarked. 'You haven't told me your explanation yet.'

'What explanation?'

'Well, what's really at the bottom of this Venusian he claims to have seen?'

'Nothing is at the bottom of it. Why?'

Ward smiled helplessly. 'You will tell me next that you really believe him.'

Professor Cameron chuckled. They reached his car and climbed in. 'Of course I do,' he said.

When, three days later, Ward borrowed Professor Cameron's car and drove down to the rail depot in Vernon Gardens to collect a case of slides which had followed him across the Atlantic, he had no intention of seeing Charles Kandinski again. He had read one or two chapters of Kandinski's book before going to sleep the previous night and dropped it in boredom. Kandinski's description of his encounter with the Venusian was not only puerile and crudely written but, most disappointing of all, completely devoid of imagination. Ward's work at the Institute was now taking up most of his time. The Annual Congress of the International Geophysical Association was being held at Mount Vernon in little under a month, and most of the burden for organizing the three-week programme of lectures, semesters and dinners had fallen on Professor Cameron and himself.

But as he drove away from the depot past the cafés in the square he caught sight of Kandinski on the terrace of the Site Tycho. It was 3 o'clock, a time when most people in Vernon Gardens were lying asleep indoors, and Kandinski seemed to be the only person out in the sun. He was scrubbing away energetically at the abstract tables with his long hairy arms, head down so that his beard was almost touching the metal tops, like an aboriginal halfman prowling in dim bewilderment over the ruins of a futuristic city lost in an inversion of time.

On an impulse, Ward parked the car in the square and walked across to the Site Tycho, but as soon as Kandinski came over to his table he wished he had gone to another of the cafés. Kandinski had been reticent enough the previous day, but now that Cameron was absent he might well turn out to be a garrulous bore.

After serving him, Kandinski sat down on a bench by the bookshelves and stared moodily at his feet. Ward watched him quietly for five minutes, as the mobiles revolved delicately in the warm air, deciding whether to approach Kandinski. Then he stood up and went over to the rows of magazines. He picked in a desultory way through half a dozen and turned to Kandinski. 'Can you recommend any of these?'

Kandinski looked up. 'Do you read science fiction?' he asked matter-of-factly.

'Not as a rule,' Ward admitted. When Kandinski said nothing he went on: 'Perhaps I'm too sceptical, but I can't take it seriously.'

Kandinski pulled a blister on his palm. 'No one suggests you should. What you mean is that you take it too seriously.'

Accepting the rebuke with a smile at himself, Ward pulled out one of the magazines and sat down at a table next to Kandinski. On the cover was a placid suburban setting of snugly eaved houses, yew trees and children's bicycles. Spreading slowly across the roof-tops was an enormous pulpy nightmare, blocking out the sun behind it and throwing a weird phosphorescent glow over the roofs and lawns. 'You're probably right,' Ward said, showing the cover to Kandinski. 'I'd hate to want to take that seriously.'

Kandinski waved it aside. 'I have seen 11th-century illuminations of the pentateuch more sensational than any of these covers.' He pointed to the cinema theatre on the far side of the square, where the four-hour Biblical epic *Cain and Abel* was showing. Above the trees an elaborate technicol-ored hoarding showed Cain, wearing what appeared to be a suit of Roman armour, wrestling with an immense hydraheaded boa constrictor.

Kandinski shrugged tolerantly. 'If Michelangelo were working for MGM today would he produce anything better?'

Ward laughed. 'You may well be right. Perhaps the House of the Medicis should be re-christened "16th Century-Fox".'

Kandinski stood up and straightened the shelves. 'I saw you here with Godfrey Cameron,' he said over his shoulder. 'You're working at the Observatory?'

'At the Hubble.'

Kandinski came and sat down beside Ward. 'Cameron is a good man. A very pleasant fellow.'

'He thinks a great deal of you,' Ward volunteered, realizing that Kandinski was probably short of friends.

'You mustn't believe everything that Cameron says about me,' Kandinski said suddenly. He hesitated, apparently uncertain whether to confide further in Ward, and then took the magazine from him. 'There are better ones here. You have to exercise some discrimination.'

'It's not so much the sensationalism that puts me off,' Ward explained, 'as the psychological implications. Most of the themes in these stories come straight out of the more unpleasant reaches of the unconscious.'

Kandinski glanced sharply at Ward, a trace of amusement in his eyes. 'That sounds rather dubious and, if I may say so, second-hand. Take the best of these stories for what they are: imaginative exercises on the theme of tomorrow.'

'You read a good deal of science fiction?' Ward asked.

Kandinski shook his head. 'Never. Not since I was a child.'

'I'm surprised,' Ward said. 'Professor Cameron told me you had written a science fiction novel.'

'Not a novel,' Kandinski corrected.

'I'd like to read it,' Ward went on. 'From what Cameron said it sounded fascinating, almost Swiftian in concept. This space-craft which arrives from Venus and the strange conversations the pilot holds with a philosopher he meets. A modern morality. Is that the subject?'

Kandinski watched Ward thoughtfully before replying. 'Loosely, yes. But, as I said, the book is not a novel. It is a factual and literal report of a Venus landing which actually took place, a diary of the most significant encounter in history since Paul saw his vision of Christ on the road to Damascus.' He lifted his huge bearded head and gazed at Ward without embarrassment. 'As a matter of interest, as Professor Cameron probably explained to you, I was the man who witnessed the landing.'

Still maintaining his pose, Ward frowned intently. 'Well, in fact Cameron did say something of the sort, but I . . .'

'But you found it difficult to believe?' Kandinski suggested ironically.

'Just a little,' Ward admitted. 'Are you seriously claiming that you did see a Venusian space-craft?'

Kandinski nodded. 'Exactly.' Then, as if aware that their conversation had reached a familiar turning he suddenly seemed to lose interest in Ward. 'Excuse me.' He nodded politely to Ward, picked up a length of hose-pipe connected to a faucet and began to spray one of the big mobiles.

Puzzled but still sceptical, Ward sat back and watched him critically, then fished in his pockets for some change. 'I must say I admire you for taking it all so calmly,' he told Kandinski as he paid him.

'What makes you think I do?'

'Well, if I'd seen, let alone spoken to a visitor from Venus I think I'd be running around in a flat spin, notifying every government and observatory in the world.'

'I did,' Kandinski said. 'As far as I could. No one was very interested.'

Ward shook his head and laughed. 'It is incredible, to put it mildly.'

'I agree with you.'

'What I mean,' Ward said, 'is that it's straight out of one of these science fiction stories of yours.'

Kandinski rubbed his lips with a scarred knuckle, obviously searching for some means of ending the conversation. 'The resemblance is misleading. They are not my stories,' he added parenthetically. 'This café is the only one which would give me work, for a perhaps obvious reason. As for the incredibility, let me say that I was and still am completely amazed. You may think I take it all calmly, but ever since the landing I have lived in a state of acute anxiety and foreboding. But short of committing some spectacular crime to draw attention to myself I don't see now how I can convince anyone.'

Ward gestured with his glasses. 'Perhaps. But I'm surprised you don't realize the very simple reasons why people refuse to take you seriously. For example, why should you be the only person to witness an event of such staggering implications? Why have *you* alone seen a Venusian?'

'A sheer accident.'

'But why should a space-craft from Venus land here?'

'What better place than near Mount Vernon Observatory?'

'I can think of any number. The UN Assembly, for one.'

Kandinski smiled lightly. 'Columbus didn't make his first contacts with the North-American Indians at the Iroquois-Sioux Tribal Conference.'

'That may be,' Ward admitted, beginning to feel impatient. 'What did this Venusian look like?'

Kandinski smiled wearily at the empty tables and picked up his hose again. 'I don't know whether you've read my book,' he said, 'but if you haven't you'll find it all there.'

'Professor Cameron mentioned that you took some photographs of the Venusian space-craft. Could I examine them?'

'Certainly,' Kandinski replied promptly. 'I'll bring them here tomorrow. You're welcome to test them in any way you wish.'

That evening Ward had dinner with the Camerons. Professor Renthall, Director of the Hubble, and his wife completed the party. The table-talk consisted almost entirely of good-humoured gossip about their colleagues retailed by Cameron and Renthall, and Ward was able to mention his conversation with Kandinski.

'At first I thought he was mad, but now I'm not so certain. There's something rather too subtle about him. The way he creates an impression of absolute integrity, but at the same time never gives you a chance to tackle him directly on any point of detail. And when you do manage to ask him outright about this Venusian his answers are far too pat. I'm convinced the whole thing is an elaborate hoax.'

Professor Renthall shook his head. 'No, it's no hoax. Don't you agree, Godfrey?'

Cameron nodded. 'Not in Andrew's sense, anyway.'

'But what other explanation is there?' Ward asked. 'We know he hasn't seen a Venusian, so he must be a fraud. Unless you think he's a lunatic. And he certainly doesn't behave like one.'

'What is a lunatic?' Professor Renthall asked rhetorically, peering into the faceted stem of his raised hock glass. 'Merely a man with more understanding than he can contain. I think Charles belongs in that category.'

'The definition doesn't explain him, sir,' Ward insisted. 'He's going to lend me his photographs and when I prove those are fakes I think I'll be able to get under his guard.'

'Poor Charles,' Edna Cameron said. 'Why shouldn't he have seen a space-ship? I think I see them every day.'

'That's just what I feel, dear,' Cameron said, patting his wife's matronly, brocaded shoulder. 'Let Charles have his Venusian if he wants to. Damn it, all it's trying to do is ban Project Apollo. An excellent idea, I have always maintained; only the professional astronomer has any business in space. After the Rainbow tests there isn't an astronomer anywhere in the world who wouldn't follow Charles Kandinski to the stake.' He turned to Renthall. 'By the way, I wonder what Charles is planning for the Congress? A Neptunian? Or perhaps a whole delegation from Proxima Centauri. We ought to fit him out with a space-suit and a pavilion – "Charles Kandinski – New Worlds for Old".'

'Santa Claus in a space-suit,' Professor Renthall mused. 'That's a new one. Send him a ticket.'

The next weekend Ward returned the twelve plates to the Site Tycho.

'Well?' Kandinski asked.

'It's difficult to say,' Ward answered. 'They're all too heavily absorbed. They could be clever montages of light brackets and turbine blades. One of them looks like a close-up of a clutch plate. There's a significant lack of any real corroborative details which you'd expect somewhere in so wide a selection.' He paused. 'On the other hand, they could be genuine.'

Kandinski said nothing, took the paper package, and went off into the café.

The interior of the Site Tycho had been designed to represent the control room of a space-ship on the surface of the Moon. Hidden fluorescent lighting glimmered through plastic wall fascia and filled the room with an eerie blue glow. Behind the bar a large mural threw the curving outline of the Moon on to an illuminated star-scape. The doors leading to the rest-rooms were circular and bulged outwards like air-locks, distinguished from each other by the symbols ♂ and ♀.

The total effect was ingenious but somehow reminiscent to Ward of a twenty-fifth-century cave.

He sat down at the bar and waited while Kandinski packed the plates away carefully in an old leather briefcase.

'I've read your book,' Ward said. 'I had looked at it the last time I saw you, but I read it again thoroughly.' He waited for some comment upon this admission, but Kandinski went over to an old portable typewriter standing at the far end of the bar and began to type laboriously with one finger. 'Have you seen any more Venusians since the book was published?' Ward asked.

'None,' Kandinski said.

'Do you think you will?'

'Perhaps.' Kandinski shrugged and went on with his typing.

'What are you working on now?' Ward asked.

'A lecture I am giving on Friday evening,' Kandinski said. Two keys locked together and he flicked them back. 'Would you care to come? Eight-thirty, at the high school near the Baptist chapel.'

'If I can,' Ward said. He saw that Kandinski wanted to get rid of him. 'Thanks for letting me see the plates.' He made his way out into the sun. People were walking about through the fresh morning air, and he caught the clean scent of peach blossom carried down the slopes into the town.

Suddenly Ward felt how enclosed and insane it had been inside the Tycho, and how apposite had been his description of it as a cave, with its residential magician incanting over his photographs like a down-at-heel Merlin manipulating his set of runes. He felt annoyed with himself for becoming involved with Kandinski and allowing the potent charisma of his personality to confuse him. Obviously Kandinski played upon the instinctive sympathy for the outcast, his whole pose of integrity and conviction a device for drawing the gullible towards him.

Letting the light spray from the fountains fall across his face, Ward crossed the square towards his car.

Away in the distance 2,000 feet above, rising beyond a screen of fir trees, the three Mount Vernon domes shone together in the sun like a futuristic Taj Mahal.

Fifteen miles from Vernon Gardens the Santa Vera highway circled down from the foot of Mount Vernon into the first low scrub-covered hills which marked the southern edge of the desert. Ward looked out at the long banks of coarse sand stretching away through the haze, their outlines blurring in the afternoon heat. He glanced at the book lying on the seat beside him, open at the map printed between its end covers, and carefully checked his position, involuntarily slowing the speed of the Chevrolet as he moved nearer to the site of the Venus landings.

In the fortnight since he had returned the photographs to the Site Tycho, he had seen Kandinski only once, at the lecture delivered the previous night. Ward had deliberately stayed away from the Site Tycho, but he had seen a poster advertising the lecture and driven down to the school despite himself.

The lecture was delivered in the gymnasium before an audience of forty or fifty people, most of them women, who formed one of the innumerable local astronomical societies. Listening to the talk round him, Ward gathered that their activities principally consisted of trying to identify more than half a dozen of the constellations. Kandinski had lectured to them on several occasions and the subject of this latest instalment was his researches into the significance of the Venusian tablet he had been analysing for the last three years.

When Kandinski stepped onto the dais there was a brief round of applause. He was wearing a lounge suit of a curiously archaic cut and had washed his beard, which bushed out above his string tie so that he resembled a Mormon patriarch or the homespun saint of some fervent evangelical community.

For the benefit of any new members, he prefaced his lecture with a brief account of his meeting with the Venusian, and then turned to his analysis of the tablet. This was the familiar ultimatum warning mankind to abandon its preparations for the exploration of space, for the ostensible reason that, just as the sea was a universal image of the unconscious, so space was nothing less than an image of psychosis and death, and that if he tried to penetrate the interplanetary voids man would only plunge to earth like a demented Icarus, unable to scale the vastness of the cosmic zero. Kandinski's real motives for introducing this were all too apparent – the expected success of Project Apollo and subsequent landings on Mars and Venus would, if nothing else, conclusively expose his fantasies.

However, by the end of the lecture Ward found that his opinion of Kandinski had experienced a complete about-face.

As a lecturer Kandinski was poor, losing words, speaking in a slow ponderous style and trapping himself in long subordinate clauses, but his quiet, matter-of-fact tone and absolute conviction in the importance of what he was saying, coupled with the nature of his material, held the talk together. His analysis of the Venusian cryptograms, a succession of intricate philological theorems, was well above the heads of his audience, but what began to impress Ward, as much as the painstaking preparation which must have preceded the lecture, was Kandinski's acute nervousness in delivering it. Ward noticed that he suffered from an irritating speech impediment that made it difficult for him to pronounce 'Venusian', and he saw that Kandinski, far from basking in the limelight, was delivering the lecture only out of a deep sense of obligation to his audience and was greatly relieved when the ordeal was over.

At the end Kandinski had invited questions. These, with the exception of the chairman's, all concerned the landing of the alien space vehicle and ignored the real subject of the lecture. Kandinski answered them all carefully, taking in good part the inevitable facetious questions. Ward noted with interest the audience's curious ambivalence, simultaneously fascinated by and resentful of Kandinski's exposure of their own private fantasies, an expression of the same ambivalence which had propelled so many of the mana-personalities of history towards their inevitable Calvarys.

Just as the chairman was about to close the meeting, Ward stood up.

'Mr Kandinski. You say that this Venusian indicated that there was also life on one of the moons of Uranus. Can you tell us how he did this if there was no verbal communication between you?'

Kandinski showed no surprise at seeing Ward. 'Certainly; as I told you, he drew eight concentric circles in the sand, one for each of the planets. Around Uranus he drew five lesser orbits and marked one of these. Then he pointed to himself and to me and to a patch of lichen. From this I deduced, reasonably I maintain, that –'

'Excuse me, Mr Kandinski,' Ward interrupted. 'You say he drew five orbits around Uranus? One for each of the moons?'

Kandinski nodded. 'Yes. Five.'

'That was in 1960,' Ward went on. 'Three weeks ago Professor Pineau at Brussels discovered a sixth moon of Uranus.'

The audience looked around at Ward and began to murmur.

'Why should this Venusian have omitted one of the moons?' Ward asked, his voice ringing across the gymnasium.

Kandinski frowned and peered at Ward suspiciously. 'I didn't know there was a sixth moon . . .' he began.

'Exactly!' someone called out. The audience began to titter.

'I can understand the Venusian not wishing to introduce any difficulties,' Ward said, 'but this seems a curious way of doing it.'

Kandinski appeared at a loss. Then he introduced Ward to the audience. 'Dr Ward is a professional while I am only an amateur,' he admitted. 'I am afraid I cannot explain the anomaly. Perhaps my memory is at fault. But I am sure the Venusian drew only five orbits.' He stepped down from the dais and strode out hurriedly, scowling into his beard, pursued by a few derisory hoots from the audience.

It took Ward fifteen minutes to free himself from the knot of admiring white-gloved spinsters who cornered him between two vaulting horses. When he broke away he ran out to his car and drove into Vernon Gardens, hoping to see Kandinski and apologize to him.

Five miles into the desert Ward approached a nexus of rock-cuttings and causeways which were part of an abandoned irrigation scheme. The colours of the hills were more vivid now, bright siliconic reds and yellows, crossed with sharp stabs of light from the exposed quartz veins. Following the map on the seat, he turned off the highway onto a rough track which ran along the bank of a dried-up canal. He passed a few rusting sections of picket fencing, a derelict grader half-submerged under the sand, and a collection of dilapidated metal shacks. The car bumped over the potholes at little more than ten miles an hour, throwing up clouds of hot ashy dust that swirled high into the air behind him.

Two miles along the canal the track came to an end. Ward stopped the car and waited for the dust to subside. Carrying Kandinski's book in front of him like a divining instrument, he set off on foot across the remaining three hundred yards. The contours around him were marked on the map, but the hills had shifted several hundred yards westwards since the book's publication and he found himself wandering about from one crest to another, peering into shallow depressions only as old as the last sand-storm. The entire landscape seemed haunted by strange currents and moods; the sand swirls surging down the aisles of dunes and the proximity of the horizon enclosed the whole place of stones with invisible walls.

Finally he found the ring of hills indicated and climbed a narrow saddle leading to its centre. When he scaled the thirty-foot slope he stopped abruptly.

Down on his knees in the middle of the basin with his back to Ward, the studs of his boots flashing in the sunlight, was Kandinski. There was a clutter of tiny objects on the sand around him, and at first Ward thought he was at prayer, making his oblations to the tutelary deities of Venus. Then he saw that Kandinski was slowly scraping the surface of the ground with a small trowel. A circle about 20 yards in diameter had been marked off with pegs and string into a series of wedge-shaped allotments. Every few seconds Kandinski carefully decanted a small heap of grit into one of the test-tubes mounted in a wooden rack in front of him.

Ward put away the book and walked down the slope. Kandinski looked around and then climbed to his feet. The coating of red ash on his beard gave him a fiery, prophetic look. He recognized Ward and raised the trowel in greeting.

Ward stopped at the edge of the string perimeter. 'What on earth are you doing?'

'I am collecting soil specimens.' Kandinski bent down and corked one of the tubes. He looked tired but worked away steadily.

Ward watched him finish a row. 'It's going to take you a long time to cover the whole area. I thought there weren't any gaps left in the Periodic Table.'

'The space-craft rotated at speed before it rose into the air. This surface is abrasive enough to have scratched off a few minute filings. With luck I may find one of them.' Kandinski smiled thinly. '262. Venusium, I hope.'

Ward started to say: 'But the transuranic elements decay spontaneously ...' and then walked over to the centre of the circle, where there was a round indentation, three feet deep and five across. The inner surface was glazed and smooth. It was shaped like an inverted cone and looked as if it had been caused by the boss of an enormous spinning top. 'This is where the space-craft landed?'

Kandinski nodded. He filled the last tube and then stowed the rack away in a canvas satchel. He came over to Ward and stared down at the hole. 'What does it look like to you? A meteor impact? Or an oil drill, perhaps?' A smile showed behind his dusty beard. 'The F-109s at the Air Force Weapons School begin their target runs across here. It might have been caused by a rogue cannon shell.'

Ward stooped down and felt the surface of the pit, running his fingers thoughtfully over the warm fused silica. 'More like a 500-pound bomb. But the cone is geometrically perfect. It's certainly unusual.'

'Unusual?' Kandinski chuckled to himself and picked up the satchel.

'Has anyone else been out here?' Ward asked as they trudged up the slope.

'Two so-called experts.' Kandinski slapped the sand off his knees. 'A geologist from Gulf-Vacuum and an Air Force ballistics officer. You'll be glad to hear that they both thought I had dug the pit myself and then fused the surface with an acetylene torch.' He peered critically at Ward. 'Why did you come out here today?'

'Idle curiosity,' Ward said. 'I had an afternoon off and I felt like a drive.'

They reached the crest of the hill and he stopped and looked down into the basin. The lines of string split the circle into a strange horological device, a huge zodiacal mandala, the dark patches in the arcs Kandinski had been working telling its stations.

'You were going to tell me why you came out here,' Kandinski said as they walked back to the car.

Ward shrugged. 'I suppose I wanted to prove something to myself. There's a problem of reconciliation.' He hesitated, and then began: 'You see, there are some things which are self-evidently false. The laws of common sense and everyday experience refute them. I know a lot of the evidence for many things we believe in is pretty thin, but I don't have to embark on a theory of knowledge to decide that the Moon isn't made of green cheese.'

'Well?' Kandinski shifted the satchel to his other shoulder.

'This Venusian you've seen,' Ward said. 'The landing, the runic tablet. I can't believe them. Every piece of evidence I've seen, all the circumstantial details, the facts given in this book . . . they're all patently false.' He turned to one of the middle chapters. 'Take this at random – "A phosphorescent green fluid pulsed through the dorsal lung-chamber of the Prime's helmet, inflating two opaque fan-like gills . . ."' Ward closed the book and shrugged helplessly. Kandinski stood a few feet away from him, the sunlight breaking across the deep lines of his face.

'Now I know what you say to my objections,' Ward went on. 'If you told a 19th century chemist that lead could be transmuted into gold he would have dismissed you as a mediaevalist. But the point is that he'd have been right to do so –'

'I understand,' Kandinski interrupted. 'But you still haven't explained why you came out here today.'

Ward stared out over the desert. High above, a stratojet was doing cuban eights into the sun, the spiral vapour trails drifting across the sky like gigantic fragments of an apocalyptic message. Looking around, he realized that Kandinski must have walked from the bus-stop on the highway. 'I'll give you a lift back,' he said.

As they drove along the canal he turned to Kandinski. 'I enjoyed your lecture last night. I apologize for trying to make you look a fool.'

Kandinski was loosening his boot-straps. He laughed unreproachfully. 'You put me in an awkward position. I could hardly have challenged you. I can't afford to subscribe to every astronomical journal. Though a sixth moon would have been big news.' As they neared Vernon Gardens he asked: 'Would you like to come in and look at the tablet analysis?'

Ward made no reply to the invitation. He drove around the square and parked under the trees, then looked up at the fountains, tapping his fingers on the windshield. Kandinski sat beside him, cogitating into his beard.

Ward watched him carefully. 'Do you think this Venusian will return?'

Kandinski nodded. 'Yes. I am sure he will.'

Later they sat together at a broad roll-top desk in the room above the Tycho. Around the wall hung white cardboard screens packed with lines of cuneiform glyphics and Kandinski's progressive breakdown of their meaning.

Ward held an enlargement of the original photograph of the Venusian tablet and listened to Kandinski's explanation.

'As you see from this,' Kandinski explained, 'in all probability there are not millions of Venusians, as every one would expect, but only three or four of them altogether. Two are circling Venus, a third Uranus and possibly a fourth is in orbit around Neptune. This solves the difficulty that puzzled you and antagonizes everyone else. Why should the Prime have approached only one person out of several hundred million and selected him on a completely random basis? Now obviously he had seen the Russian and American satellite capsules and assumed that our race, like his now, numbered no more than three or four, then concluded from the atmospheric H-bomb tests that we were in conflict and would soon destroy ourselves. This is one of the reasons why I think he will return shortly and why it is important to organize a world-wide reception for him on a governmental level.'

'Wait a minute,' Ward said. 'He must have known that the population of this planet numbered more than three or four. Even the weakest telescope would demonstrate that.'

'Of course, but he would naturally assume that the millions of inhabitants of the Earth belonged to an aboriginal sub-species, perhaps employed as work animals. After all, if he observed that despite this planet's immense resources the bulk of its population lived like animals, an alien visitor could only decide that they were considered as such.'

'But space vehicles are supposed to have been observing us since the Babylonian era, long before the development of satellite rockets. There have been thousands of recorded sightings.'

Kandinski shook his head. 'None of them has been authenticated.'

'What about the other landings that have been reported recently?' Ward asked. 'Any number of people have seen Venusians and Martians.'

'Have they?' Kandinski asked sceptically. 'I wish I could believe that. Some of the encounters reveal marvellous powers of invention, but no one can accept them as anything but fantasy.'

'The same criticism has been levelled at your space-craft,' Ward reminded him.

Kandinski seemed to lose patience. 'I *saw* it,' he explained, impotently tossing his notebook on to the desk. 'I *spoke* to the Prime!'

Ward nodded non-committally and picked up the photograph again. Kandinski stepped over to him and took it out of his hands. 'Ward,' he said carefully. 'Believe me. You must. You know I am too big a man to waste myself on a senseless charade.' His massive hands squeezed Ward's shoulders, and almost lifted him off the seat. '*Believe* me. Together we can be ready for the next landings and alert the world. I am only Charles Kandinski, a waiter at a third-rate café, but you are Dr Andrew Ward of Mount Vernon Observatory. They will listen to you. Try to realize what this may mean for mankind.'

Ward pulled himself away from Kandinski and rubbed his shoulders.

'Ward, do you believe me? Ask yourself.'

Ward looked up pensively at Kandinski towering over him, his red beard like the burning, unconsumed bush.

'I think so,' he said quietly. 'Yes, I do.'

A week later the 23rd Congress of the International Geophysical Association opened at Mount Vernon Observatory. At 3.30 P.M., in the Hoyle Library amphitheatre, Professor Renthall was to deliver the inaugural address welcoming the 92 delegates and 25 newspaper and agency reporters to the fortnight's programme of lectures and discussions.

Shortly after 11 o'clock that morning Ward and Professor Cameron completed their final arrangements and escaped down to Vernon Gardens for an hour's relaxation.

'Well,' Cameron said as they walked over to the Site Tycho, 'I've got a pretty good idea of what it must be like to run the Waldorf-Astoria.' They picked one of the sidewalk tables and sat down. 'I haven't been here for weeks,' Cameron said. 'How are you getting on with the Man in the Moon?'

'Kandinski? I hardly ever see him,' Ward said.

'I was talking to the *Time* magazine stringer about Charles,' Cameron said, cleaning his sunglasses. 'He thought he might do a piece about him.'

'Hasn't Kandinski suffered enough of that sort of thing?' Ward asked moodily.

'Perhaps he has,' Cameron agreed. 'Is he still working on his crossword puzzle? The tablet thing, whatever he calls it.'

Casually, Ward said: 'He has a theory that it should be possible to see the lunar bases. Refuelling points established there by the Venusians over the centuries.'

'Interesting,' Cameron commented.

'They're sited near Copernicus,' Ward went on. 'I know Vandone at Milan is mapping Archimedes and the Imbrium, I thought I might mention it to him at his semester tomorrow.'

Professor Cameron took off his glasses and gazed quizzically at Ward. 'My dear Andrew, what has been going on? Don't tell me you've become one of Charles' converts?'

Ward laughed and shook his head. 'Of course not. Obviously there are no lunar bases or alien space-craft. I don't for a moment believe a word Kandinski says.' He gestured helplessly. 'At the same time I admit I have become involved with him. There's something about Kandinski's personality. On the one hand I can't take him seriously –'

'Oh, I take him seriously,' Cameron cut in smoothly. 'Very seriously indeed, if not quite in the sense you mean.' Cameron turned his back on the sidewalk crowds. 'Jung's views on flying saucers are very illuminating, Andrew; they'd help you to understand Kandinski. Jung believes that civilization now stands at the conclusion of a Platonic Great Year, at the eclipse of the sign of Pisces which has dominated the Christian epoch, and that we are entering the sign of Aquarius, a period of confusion and psychic chaos. He remarks that throughout history, at all times of uncertainty and discord, cosmic space vehicles have been seen approaching Earth, and that in a few extreme cases actual meetings with their occupants are supposed to have taken place.'

As Cameron paused, Ward glanced across the tables for Kandinski, but a relief waiter served them and he assumed it was Kandinski's day off.

Cameron continued: 'Most people regard Charles Kandinski as a lunatic, but as a matter of fact he is performing one of the most important roles in the world today, the role of a prophet alerting people of this coming crisis. The real significance of his fantasies, like that of the ban-the-bomb movements, is to be found elsewhere than on the conscious plane, as an expression of the immense psychic forces stirring below the surface of rational life, like the isotactic movements of the continental tables which heralded the major geological transformations.'

Ward shook his head dubiously. 'I can accept that a man such as Freud was a prophet, but Charles Kandinski –?'

'Certainly. Far more than Freud. It's unfortunate for Kandinski, and for the writers of science fiction for that matter, that they have to perform their tasks of describing the symbols of transformation in a so-called rationalist society, where a scientific, or at least a pesudo-scientific explanation is required *a priori*. And because the true prophet never deals in what may be rationally deduced, people such as Charles are ignored or derided today.'

'It's interesting that Kandinski compared his meeting with the Venusian with Paul's conversion on the road to Damascus,' Ward said.

'He was quite right. In both encounters you see the same mechanism of blinding unconscious revelation. And you can see too that Charles feels the same overwhelming need to spread the Pauline revelation to the world. The Anti-Apollo movement is only now getting under way, but within the next decade it will recruit millions, and men such as Charles Kandinski will be the fathers of its apocalypse.'

'You make him sound like a titanic figure,' Ward remarked quietly. 'I think he's just a lonely, tired man obsessed by something he can't understand. Perhaps he simply needs a few friends to confide in.'

Slowly shaking his head, Cameron tapped the table with his glasses. 'Be warned, Andrew, you'll burn your fingers if you play with Charles' brand of fire. The mana-personalities of history have no time for personal loyalties – the founder of the Christian church made that pretty plain.'

Shortly after seven o'clock that evening Charles Kandinski mounted his bicycle and set off out of Vernon Gardens. The small room in the seedy area where he lived always depressed him on his free days from the Tycho, and as he pedalled along he ignored the shouts from his neighbours sitting out on their balconies with their crates of beer. He knew that his beard and the high, ancient bicycle with its capacious wicker basket made him a grotesque, Quixotic figure, but he felt too preoccupied to care. That morning he had heard that the French translation of *The Landings from Outer Space*, printed at his own cost, had been completely ignored by the Paris press. In addition a jobbing printer in Santa Vera was pressing him for payment for 5,000 anti-Apollo leaflets that had been distributed the previous year.

Above all had come the news on the radio that the target date of the first manned Moon flight had been advanced to 1969, and on the following day would take place the latest and most ambitious of the instrumented lunar flights. The anticipated budget for the Apollo programme (in a moment of grim humour he had calculated that it would pay for the printing of some 1,000 billion leaflets) seemed to double each year, but so far he had found little success in his attempt to alert people to the folly of venturing into space. All that day he had felt sick with frustration and anger.

At the end of the avenue he turned on to the highway which served the asparagus farms lying in the 20-mile strip between Vernon Gardens and the desert. It was a hot empty evening and few cars or trucks passed him. On either side of the road the great lemon-green terraces of asparagus lay seeping in their moist paddy beds, and occasionally a marsh-hen clacked overhead and dived out of sight.

Five miles along the road he reached the last farmhouse above the edge of the desert. He cycled on to where the road ended 200 yards ahead, dismounted and left the bicycle in a culvert. Slinging his camera over one shoulder, he walked off across the hard ground into the mouth of a small valley.

The boundary between the desert and the farm-strip was irregular. On his left, beyond the rocky slopes, he could hear a motor-reaper purring down one of the mile-long spits of fertile land running into the desert, but the barren terrain and the sense of isolation began to relax him and he forgot the irritations that had plagued him all day.

A keen naturalist, he saw a long-necked sand-crane perched on a spur of shale fifty feet from him and stopped and raised his camera. Peering through the finder he noticed that the light had faded too deeply for a photograph. Curiously, the sand-crane was clearly silhouetted against a circular glow of light which emanated from beyond a low ridge at the end of the valley. This apparently sourceless corona fitfully illuminated the darkening air, as if coming from a lighted mineshaft.

Putting away his camera, Kandinski walked forward, within a few minutes reached the ridge, and began to climb it. The face sloped steeply, and he pulled himself up by the hefts of brush and scrub, kicking away footholds in the rocky surface.

Just before he reached the crest he felt his heart surge painfully with the exertion, and he lay still for a moment, a sudden feeling of dizziness spinning in his head. He waited until the spasm subsided, shivering faintly in the cool air, an unfamiliar undertone of uneasiness in his mind. The air seemed to vibrate strangely with an intense inaudible music that pressed upon his temples. Rubbing his forehead, he lifted himself over the crest.

The ridge he had climbed was U-shaped and about 200 feet across, its open end away from him. Resting on the sandy floor in its centre was an enormous metal disc, over 100 feet in diameter and 30 feet high. It seemed to be balanced on a huge conical boss, half of which had already sunk into the sand. A fluted rim ran around the edge of the disc and separated the upper and lower curvatures, which were revolving rapidly in opposite directions, throwing off magnificent flashes of silver light.

Kandinski lay still, as his first feeling of fear retreated and his courage and presence of mind returned. The inaudible piercing music had faded, and his mind felt brilliantly clear. His eyes ran rapidly over the space-ship, and he estimated that it was over twice the size of the craft he had seen three years earlier. There were no markings or ports on the carapace, but he was certain it had not come from Venus.

Kandinski lay watching the space-craft for ten minutes, trying to decide upon his best course of action. Unfortunately he had smashed the lens of his camera. Finally, pushing himself backwards, he slid slowly down the slope. When he reached the floor he could still hear the whine of the rotors. Hiding in the pools of shadow, he made his way up the valley, and two hundred yards from the ridge he broke into a run.

He returned the way he had come, his great legs carrying him across the ruts and boulders, seized his bicycle from the culvert and pedalled rapidly towards the farmhouse.

A single light shone in an upstairs room and he pressed one hand to the bell and pounded on the screen door with the other, nearly tearing it from its hinges. Eventually a young woman appeared. She came down the stairs reluctantly, uncertain what to make of Kandinski's beard and ragged, dusty clothes.

'Telephone!' Kandinski bellowed at her, gasping wildly, as he caught back his breath.

The girl at last unlatched the door and backed away from him nervously. Kandinski lurched past her and staggered blindly around the darkened hall. 'Where is it?' he roared.

The girl switched on the lights and pointed into the sitting room. Kandinski pushed past her and rushed over to it.

Ward played with his brandy glass and discreetly loosened the collar of his dress shirt, listening to Dr MacIntyre of Greenwich Observatory, four seats away on his right, make the third of the after-dinner speeches. Ward was to speak next, and he ran through the opening phrases of his speech, glancing down occasionally to con his notes. At 34 he was the youngest member to address the Congress banquet, and by no means unimpressed by the honour. He looked at the venerable figures to his left and right at the top table, their black jackets and white shirt fronts reflected in the table silver, and saw Professor Cameron wink at him reassuringly.

He was going through his notes for the last time when a steward bent over his shoulder. 'Telephone for you, Dr Ward.'

'I can't take it now,' Ward whispered. 'Tell them to call later.'

'The caller said it was extremely urgent, Doctor. Something about some people from the Neptune arriving.'

'The Neptune?'

'I think that's a hotel in Santa Vera. Maybe the Russian delegates have turned up after all.'

Ward pushed his chair back, made his apologies and slipped away.

Professor Cameron was waiting in the alcove outside the banqueting hall when Ward stepped out of the booth. 'Anything the trouble, Andrew? It's not your father, I hope —'

'It's Kandinski,' Ward said hurriedly. 'He's out in the desert, near the farm-strip. He says he's seen another space vehicle.'

'Oh, is that all.' Cameron shook his head. 'Come on, we'd better get back. The poor fool!'

'Hold on,' Ward said. 'He's got it under observation now. It's on the ground. He told me to call General Wayne at the air base and alert the Strategic Air Command.' Ward chewed his lip. 'I don't know what to do.'

Cameron took him by the arm. 'Andrew, come on. MacIntyre's winding up.'

'What can we do, though?' Ward asked. 'He seemed all right, but then he said that he thought they were hostile. That sounds a little sinister.'

'Andrew!' Cameron snapped. 'What's the matter with you? Leave Kandinski to himself. You can't go now. It would be unpardonable rudeness.'

'I've got to help Kandinski,' Ward insisted. 'I'm sure he needs it this time.' He wrenched himself away from Cameron.

'Ward!' Professor Cameron called. 'For God's sake, come back!' He followed Ward onto the balcony and watched him run down the steps and disappear across the lawn into the darkness.

As the wheels of the car thudded over the deep ruts, Ward cut the headlights and searched the dark hills which marked the desert's edge. The warm glitter of Vernon Gardens lay behind him and only a few isolated lights shone in the darkness on either side of the road. He passed the farmhouse from which he assumed Kandinski had telephoned, then drove on slowly until he saw the bicycle Kandinski had left for him.

It took him several minutes to mount the huge machine, his feet well clear of the pedals for most of their stroke. Laboriously he covered a hundred yards, and after careering helplessly into a clump of scrub was forced to dismount and continue on foot.

Kandinski had told him that the ridge was about a mile up the valley. It was almost night and the starlight reflected off the hills lit the valley with fleeting, vivid colours. He ran on heavily, the only sounds he could hear were those of a thresher rattling like a giant metal insect half a mile behind him. Filling his lungs, he pushed on across the last hundred yards.

Kandinski was still lying on the edge of the ridge, watching the space-ship and waiting impatiently for Ward. Below him in the hollow the upper and lower rotor sections swung around more slowly, at about one revolution per second. The space-ship had sunk a further ten feet into the desert floor and he was now on the same level as the observation dome. A single finger of light poked out into the darkness, circling the ridge walls in jerky sweeps.

Then out of the valley behind him he saw someone stumbling along towards the ridge at a broken run. Suddenly a feeling of triumph and exhilaration came over him, and he knew that at last he had his witness.

Ward climbed up the slope to where he could see Kandinski. Twice he lost his grip and slithered downwards helplessly, tearing his hands on the gritty surface. Kandinski was lying flat on his chest, his head just above the ridge. Covered by dust, he was barely distinguishable from the slope itself.

'Are you all right?' Ward whispered. He pulled off his bow tie and ripped open his collar. When he had controlled his breathing he crawled up beside Kandinski.

'Where?' he asked.

Kandinski pointed down into the hollow.

Ward raised his head, levering himself up on his elbows. For a few seconds he peered out into the darkness, and then drew his head back.

'You see it?' Kandinski whispered. His voice was short and laboured. When Ward hesitated before replying he suddenly seized Ward's wrist in a vice-like grip. In the faint light reflected by the white dust on the ridge Ward could see plainly his bright inflamed eyes.

'Ward! Can you see it?'

The powerful fingers remained clamped to his wrist as he lay beside Kandinski and gazed down into the darkness.

Below the compartment window one of Ward's fellow passengers was being seen off by a group of friends, and the young women in bright hats and bandanas and the men in slacks and beach sandals made him feel that he was leaving a seaside resort at the end of a holiday. From the window he could see the observatory domes of Mount Vernon rising out of the trees, and he identified the white brickwork of the Hoyle Library a thousand feet below the summit. Edna Cameron had brought him to the station, but he had asked her not to come onto the platform, and she had said goodbye and driven off. Cameron himself he had seen only once, when he had collected his books from the Institute.

Trying to forget it all, Ward noted thankfully that the train would leave within five minutes. He took his bankbook out of his wallet and counted the last week's withdrawals. He winced at the largest item, 600 dollars which he had transferred to Kandinski's account to pay for the cablegrams.

Deciding to buy something to read, he left the car and walked back to the news-stand. Several of the magazines contained what could only be described as discouraging articles about himself, and he chose two or three newspapers.

Just then someone put a hand on his shoulder. He turned and saw Kandinski.

'Are you leaving?' Kandinski asked quietly. He had trimmed his beard so that only a pale vestige of the original bloom remained, revealing his high bony cheekbones. His face seemed almost fifteen years younger, thinner and more drawn, but at the same time composed, like that of a man recovering slowly from the attack of some intermittent fever.

'I'm sorry, Charles,' Ward said as they walked back to the car. 'I should have said goodbye to you but I thought I'd better not.'

Kandinski's expression was subdued but puzzled. 'Why?' he asked. 'I don't understand.'

Ward shrugged. 'I'm afraid everything here has more or less come to an end for me, Charles. I'm going back to Princeton until the spring. Freshman physics.' He smiled ruefully at himself. 'Boyle's Law, Young's Modulus, getting right back to fundamentals. Not a bad idea, perhaps.'

'But why are you leaving?' Kandinski pressed.

'Well, Cameron thought it might be tactful of me to leave. After our statement to the Secretary-General was published in *The New York Times* I became very much *persona non grata* at the Hubble. The trustees were on to Professor Renthall again this morning.'

Kandinski smiled and seemed relieved. 'What does the Hubble matter?' he scoffed. 'We have more important work to do. You know, Ward, when Mrs Cameron told me just now that you were leaving I couldn't believe it.'

'I'm sorry, Charles, but it's true.'

'Ward,' Kandinski insisted. 'You can't leave. The Primes will be returning soon. We must prepare for them.'

'I know, Charles, and I wish I could stay.' They reached the car and Ward put his hand out. 'Thanks for coming to see me off.'

Kandinski held his hand tightly. 'Andrew, tell me the truth. Are you afraid of what people will think of you? Is that why you want to leave? Haven't you enough courage and faith in yourself?'

'Perhaps that's it,' Ward conceded, wishing the train would start. He reached for the rail and began to climb into the car but Kandinski held him.

'Ward, you can't drop your responsibilities like this!'

'Please, Charles,' Ward said, feeling his temper rising. He pulled his hand away but Kandinski seized him by the shoulder and almost dragged him off the car.

Ward wrenched himself away. 'Leave me alone!' he snapped fiercely. 'I saw your space-ship, didn't I?'

Kandinski watched him go, a hand picking at his vanished beard, completely perplexed.

Whistles sounded, and the train began to edge forward.

'Goodbye, Charles,' Ward called down. 'Let me know if you see anything else.'

He went into the car and took his seat. Only when the train was twenty miles from Mount Vernon did he look out of the window.

**·1963**

# END-GAME

After his trial they gave Constantin a villa, an allowance and an executioner. The villa was small and high-walled, and had obviously been used for the purpose before. The allowance was adequate to Constantin's needs – he was never permitted to go out and his meals were prepared for him by a police orderly. The executioner was his own. Most of the time they sat on the enclosed veranda overlooking the narrow stone garden, playing chess with a set of large well-worn pieces.

The executioner's name was Malek. Officially he was Constantin's supervisor, and responsible for maintaining the villa's tenuous contact with the outside world, now hidden from sight beyond the steep walls, and for taking the brief telephone call that came promptly at nine o'clock every morning. However, his real role was no secret between them. A powerful, doughy-faced man with an anonymous expression, Malek at first intensely irritated Constantin, who had been used to dealing with more subtle sets of responses. Malek followed him around the villa, never interfering – unless Constantin tried to bribe the orderly for a prohibited newspaper, when Malek merely gestured with a slight turn of one of his large hands, face registering no disapproval, but cutting off the attempt as irrevocably as a bulkhead – nor making any suggestions as to how Constantin should spend his time. Like a large bear, he sat motionlessly in the lounge in one of the faded armchairs, watching Constantin.

After a week Constantin tired of reading the old novels in the bottom shelf of the bookcase – somewhere among the grey well-thumbed pages he had hoped to find a message from one of his predecessors – and invited Malek to play chess. The set of chipped mahogany pieces reposed on one of the empty shelves of the bookcase, the only item of decoration or recreational equipment in the villa. Apart from the books and the chess set the small six-roomed house was completely devoid of ornament. There were no curtains or picture rails, bedside tables or standard lamps, and the only electrical fittings were the lights recessed behind thick opaque bowls into the ceilings. Obviously the chess set and the row of novels had been provided deliberately, each representing one of the alternative pastimes available to the temporary tenants of the villa. Men of a phlegmatic or philosophical temperament, resigned to the inevitability of their fate, would choose to read the novels, sinking backwards into a self-anaesthetized trance as they waded through the turgid prose of those nineteenth-century romances.

On the other hand, men of a more volatile and extrovert disposition would obviously prefer to play chess, unable to resist the opportunity to exercise their Machiavellian talents for positional manoeuvre to the last. The games of chess would help to maintain their unconscious optimism and, more subtly, sublimate or divert any attempts at escape.

When Constantin suggested that they play chess Malek promptly agreed, and so they spent the next long month as the late summer turned to autumn. Constantin was glad he had chosen chess; the game brought him into immediate personal involvement with Malek, and like all condemned men he had soon developed a powerful emotional transference on to what effectively was the only person left in his life.

At present it was neither negative nor positive; but a relationship of acute dependence – already Malek's notional personality was becoming overlaid by the associations of all the anonymous but nonetheless potent figures of authority whom Constantin could remember since his earliest childhood: his own father, the priest at the seminary he had seen hanged after the revolution, the first senior commissars, the party secretaries at the ministry of foreign affairs and, ultimately, the members of the central committee themselves. Here, where the anonymous faces had crystallized into those of closely observed colleagues and rivals, the process seemed to come full circle, so that he himself was identified with those shadowy personas who had authorized his death and were now represented by Malek.

Constantin had also, of course, become dominated by another obsession, the need to know: *when?* In the weeks after the trial and sentence he had remained in a curiously euphoric state, too stunned to realize that the dimension of time still existed for him, he had already died *a posteriori*. But gradually the will to live, and his old determination and ruthlessness, which had served him so well for thirty years, reasserted themselves, and he realized that a small hope still remained to him. How long exactly in terms of time he could only guess, but if he could master Malek his survival became a real possibility.

The question remained: When?

Fortunately he could be completely frank with Malek. The first point he established immediately.

'Malek,' he asked on the tenth move one morning, when he had completed his development and was relaxing for a moment. 'Tell me, do you know – when?'

Malek looked up from the board, his large almost bovine eyes gazing blandly at Constantin. 'Yes, Mr Constantin, I know when.' His voice was deep and functional, as expressionless as a weighing machine's.

\*     \*     \*

Constantin sat back reflectively. Outside the glass panes of the veranda the rain fell steadily on the solitary fir tree which had maintained a precarious purchase among the stones under the wall. A few miles to the south-west of the villa were the outskirts of the small port, one of the dismal so-called 'coastal resorts' where junior ministry men and party hacks were sent for their bi-annual holidays. The weather, however, seemed peculiarly inclement, the sun never shining through the morose clouds, and for a moment, before he checked himself, Constantin felt glad to be within the comparative warmth of the villa.

'Let me get this straight,' he said to Malek. 'You don't merely know in a general sense – for example, after receiving an instruction from so-and-so – but you know *specifically* when?'

'Exactly.' Malek moved his queen out of the game. His chess was sound but without flair or a personal style, suggesting that he had improved merely by practice – most of his opponents, Constantin realized with sardonic amusement, would have been players of a high class.

'You know the *day* and the *hour* and the *minute*,' Constantin pressed. Malek nodded slowly, most of his attention upon the game, and Constantin rested his smooth sharp chin in one hand, watching his opponent. 'It could be within the next ten seconds, or again, it might not be for ten years?'

'As you say.' Malek gestured at the board. 'Your move.'

Constantin waved this aside. 'I know, but don't let's rush it. These games are played on many levels, Malek. People who talk about three-dimensional chess obviously know nothing about the present form.' Occasionally he made these openings in the hope of loosening Malek's tongue, but conversation with him seemed to be impossible.

Abruptly he sat forward across the board, his eyes searching Malek's. 'You alone know the date, Malek, and as you have said, it might not be for ten years – or twenty. Do you think you can keep such a secret to yourself for so long?'

Malek made no attempt to answer this, and waited for Constantin to resume play. Now and then his eyes inspected the corners of the veranda, or glanced at the stone garden outside. From the kitchen came the occasional sounds of the orderly's boots scraping the floor as he lounged by the telephone on the deal table.

As he scrutinized the board Constantin wondered how he could provoke any response whatever from Malek; the man had shown no reaction at the mention of ten years, although the period was ludicrously far ahead. In all probability their real game would be a short one. The indeterminate date of the execution, which imbued the procedure with such a bizarre flavour, was not intended to add an element of torture or suspense to the condemned's last days, but simply to obscure and confuse the very fact of his exit. If a definite date were known in advance there might be a last-minute rally of sympathy, an attempt to review the sentence and perhaps apportion the blame elsewhere, and the unconscious if not conscious sense of complicity in the condemned man's crimes might well provoke an agonized reappraisal and, after the execution of the sentence, a submerged sense of guilt upon which opportunists and intriguers could play to advantage.

By means of the present system, however, all these dangers and unpleasant side-effects were obviated, the accused was removed from his place in the hierarchy when the opposition to him was at its zenith and conveniently handed over to the judiciary, and thence to one of the courts of star chamber whose proceedings were always held in camera and whose verdicts were never announced.

As far as his former colleagues were concerned, he had disappeared into the endless corridor world of the bureaucratic purgatories, his case permanently on file but never irrevocably closed. Above all, the fact of his guilt was never established and confirmed. As Constantin was aware, he himself had been convicted upon a technicality in the margins of the main indictment against him, a mere procedural device, like a bad twist in the plot of a story, designed solely to bring the investigation to a close. Although he knew the real nature of his crime, Constantin had never been formally notified of his guilt; in fact the court had gone out of its way to avoid preferring any serious charges against him whatever.

This ironic inversion of the classical Kafkaesque situation, by which, instead of admitting his guilt to a non-existent crime, he was forced to connive in a farce maintaining his innocence of offences he knew full well he had committed, was preserved in his present situation at the execution villa.

The psychological basis was more obscure but in some way far more threatening, the executioner beckoning his victim towards him with a beguiling smile, reassuring him that all was forgiven. Here he played upon, not those unconscious feelings of anxiety and guilt, but that innate conviction of individual survival, that obsessive preoccupation with personal immortality which is merely a disguised form of the universal fear of the image of one's own death. It was this assurance that all was well, and the absence of any charges of guilt or responsibility, which had made so orderly the queues into the gas chambers.

At present the paradoxical face of this diabolical device was worn by Malek, his lumpy amorphous features and neutral but ambiguous attitude making him seem less a separate personality than the personification of the apparat of the state. Perhaps the sardonic title of 'supervisor' was nearer the truth than had seemed at first sight, and that Malek's role was simply to officiate, or at the most serve as moderator, at a trial by ordeal in which Constantin was his own accused, prosecutor and judge.

However, he reflected as he examined the board, aware of Malek's bulky presence across the pieces, this would imply that they had completely misjudged his own personality, with its buoyancy and almost gallic verve and panache. He, of all people, would be the last to take his own life in an orgy of self-confessed guilt. Not for him the neurotic suicide so loved of the Slav. As long as there were a way out he would cheerfully shoulder any burden of guilt, tolerant of his own weaknesses, ready to shrug them off with a quip. This insouciance had always been his strongest ally.

His eyes searched the board, roving down the open files of the queens and bishops, as if the answer to the pressing enigma were to be found in these polished corridors.

*When?* His own estimate was two months. Almost certainly, (and he had no fear here that he was rationalizing) it would not be within the next two or three days, nor even the next fortnight. Haste was always unseemly, quite apart from violating the whole purpose of the exercise. Two months would see him safely into limbo, and be sufficiently long for the suspense to break him down and reveal any secret allies, sufficiently brief to fit his particular crime.

Two months? Not as long as he might have wished. As he translated his queen's bishop into play Constantin began to map out his strategy for defeating Malek. The first task, obviously, was to discover when Malek was to carry out the execution, partly to give him peace of mind, but also to allow him to adjust the context of his escape. A physical leap to freedom over the wall would be pointless. Contacts had to be established, pressure brought to bear at various sensitive points in the hierarchy, paving the way for a reconsideration of his case. All this would take time.

His thoughts were interrupted by the sharp movement of Malek's left hand across the board, followed by a guttural grunt. Surprised by the speed and economy with which Malek had moved his piece as much by the fact that he himself was in check, Constantin sat forward and examined his position with more care. He glanced with grudging respect at Malek, who had sat back as impassively as ever, the knight he had deftly taken on the edge of the table in front of him. His eyes watched Constantin with their usual untroubled calm, like those of an immensely patient governess, his great shoulders hidden within the bulky suiting. But for a moment, when he had leaned across the board, Constantin had seen the powerful extension and flexion of his shoulder musculature.

Don't look so smug, my dear Malek, Constantin said to himself with a wry smile. At least I know now that you are left-handed. Malek had taken the knight with one hand, hooking the piece between the thick knuckles of his ring and centre fingers, and then substituting his queen with a smart tap, a movement not easily performed in the centre of the crowded board. Useful though the confirmation was – Constantin had noticed Malek apparently trying to conceal his left-handedness during their meals and when opening and closing the windows – he found this sinistral aspect of Malek's personality curiously disturbing, an indication that there would be nothing predictable about his opponent, or the ensuing struggle of wits between them. Even Malek's apparent lack of sharp intelligence was belied by the astuteness of his last move.

Constantin was playing white, and had chosen the Queen's Gambit, assuming that the fluid situation invariably resulting from the opening would be to his advantage and allow him to get on with the more serious task of planning his escape. But Malek had avoided any possible errors, steadily consolidating his position, and had even managed to launch a counter-gambit, offering a knight-to-bishop exchange which would soon undermine Constantin's position if he accepted.

'A good move, Malek,' he commented. 'But perhaps a little risky in the long run.' Declining the exchange, he lamely blocked the checking queen with a pawn.

Malek stared stolidly at the board, his heavy policeman's face, with its almost square frame from one jaw angle to the other, betraying no sign of thought. His approach, Constantin reflected as he watched his opponent, would be that of the pragmatist, judging always by immediate capability rather than by any concealed intentions. As if confirming this diagnosis, Malek simply returned his queen to her former square, unwilling or unable to exploit the advantage he had gained and satisfied by the captured piece.

Bored by the lower key on to which the game had descended, and the prospect of similar games ahead, Constantin castled his king to safety. For some reason, obviously irrational, he assumed that Malek would not kill him in the middle of a game, particularly if he, Malek, were winning. He recognized that this was an unconscious reason for wanting to play chess in the first place, and had no doubt motivated the many others who had also sat with Malek on the veranda, listening to the late summer rain. Suppressing a sudden pang of fear, Constantin examined Malek's powerful hands protruding from his cuffs like two joints of meat. If Malek wanted to, he could probably kill Constantin with his bare hands.

That raised a second question, almost as fascinating as the first.

'Malek, another point.' Constantin sat back, searching in his pockets for imaginary cigarettes (none were allowed him). 'Forgive my curiosity, but I am an interested party, as it were –' He flashed Malek his brightest smile, a characteristically incisive thrust modulated by ironic self-deprecation which had been so successful with his secretaries and at ministry receptions, but the assay at humour failed to move Malek. 'Tell me, do you know ... how –?' Searching for some euphemism, he repeated: 'Do you know how you are going to ... ?' and then gave up the attempt, cursing Malek to himself for lacking the social grace to rescue him from his awkwardness.

Malek's chin rose slightly, a minimal nod. He showed no signs of being bored or irritated by Constantin's laboured catechism, or of having noticed his embarrassment.

'What is it, then?' Constantin pressed, recovering himself. 'Pistol, pill or–' with a harsh laugh he pointed through the window '– do you set up a guillotine in the rain? I'd like to know.'

Malek looked down at the chess-board, his features more glutinous and dough-like than ever. Flatly, he said: 'It has been decided.'

Constantin snorted. 'What on earth does *that* mean?' he snapped belligerently. 'Is it painless?'

For once Malek smiled, a thin sneer of amusement hung fleetingly around his mouth. 'Have you ever killed anything, Mr Constantin?' he asked quietly. 'Yourself, personally, I mean.'

'Touché,' Constantin granted. He laughed deliberately, trying to dispel the tension. 'A perfect reply.' To himself he said: I mustn't let curiosity get the upper hand, the man was laughing at me.

'Of course,' he went on, 'death is always painful. I merely wondered whether, in the legal sense of the term, it would be humane. But I can see that you are a professional, Malek, and the question answers itself. A great relief, believe me. There are so many sadists about, perverts and the like –' again he watched carefully to see if the implied sneer provoked Malek '– that one can't be too grateful for a clean curtain fall. It's good to know. I can devote these last days to putting my affairs in order and coming to terms with the world. If only I knew how long there was left I could make my preparations accordingly. One can't be forever saying one's last prayers. You see my point?'

Colourlessly, Malek said: 'The Prosecutor-General advised you to make your final arrangements immediately after the trial.'

'But what does that mean?' Constantin asked, pitching his voice a calculated octave higher. 'I'm a human being, not a book-keeper's ledger that can be totted up and left to await the auditor's pleasure. I wonder if you realize, Malek, the courage this situation demands from me? It's easy for you to sit there –'

Abruptly Malek stood up, sending a shiver of terror through Constantin. With a glance at the sealed windows, he moved around the chess table towards the lounge. 'We will postpone the game,' he said. Nodding to Constantin, he went off towards the kitchen where the orderly was preparing lunch.

Constantin listened to his shoes squeaking faintly across the unpolished floor, then irritably cleared the pieces off the board and sat back with the black king in his hand. At least he had provoked Malek into leaving him. Thinking this over, he wondered whether to throw caution to the winds and begin to make life intolerable for Malek – it would be easy to pursue him around the villa, arguing hysterically and badgering him with neurotic questions. Sooner or later Malek would snap back, and might give away something of his intentions. Alternatively, Constantin could try to freeze him out, treating him with contempt as the hired killer he was, refusing to share a room or his meals with him and insisting on his rights as a former member of the central committee. The method might well be successful. Almost certainly Malek was telling the truth when he said he knew the exact day and minute of Constantin's execution. The order would have been given to him and he would have no discretion to advance or delay the date to suit himself. Malek would be reluctant to report Constantin for difficult behaviour – the reflection on himself was too obvious and his present post was not one from which he could graciously retire – and in addition not even the Police-President would be able to vary the execution date now that it had been set without convening several meetings. There was then the danger of re-opening Constantin's case. He was not without his allies, or at least those who were prepared to use him for their own advantage.

But despite these considerations, the whole business of play-acting lacked appeal for Constantin. His approach was more serpentine. Besides, if he provoked Malek, uncertainties were introduced, of which there were already far too many.

He noticed the supervisor enter the lounge and sit down quietly in one of the grey armchairs, his face, half-hidden in the shadows, turned towards Constantin. He seemed indifferent to the normal pressures of boredom and fatigue (luckily for himself, Constantin reflected – an impatient man would have pulled the trigger on the morning of the second day), and content to sit about in the armchairs, watching Constantin as the grey rain fell outside and the damp leaves gathered against the walls. The difficulties of establishing a relationship with Malek – and some sort of relationship was essential before Constantin could begin to think of escape – seemed insuperable, only the games of chess offering an opportunity.

Placing the black king on his own king's square, Constantin called out: 'Malek, I'm ready for another game, if you are.'

Malek pushed himself out of the chair with his long arms, and then took his place across the board. For a moment he scrutinized Constantin with a level glance, as if ascertaining that there would be no further outbursts of temper, and then began to set up the white pieces, apparently prepared to ignore the fact that Constantin had cleared the previous game before its completion.

He opened with a stolid Ruy Lopez, an over-analysed and uninteresting attack, but a dozen moves later, when they broke off for lunch, he had already forced Constantin to castle on the Queen's side and had established a powerful position in the centre.

As they took their lunch together at the card table behind the sofa in the lounge, Constantin reflected upon this curious element which had been introduced into his relationship with Malek. While trying to check any tendency to magnify an insignificant triviality into a major symbol, he realized that Malek's proficiency at chess, and his ability to produce powerful combinations out of pedestrian openings, was symptomatic of his concealed power over Constantin.

The drab villa in the thin autumn rain, the faded furniture and unimaginative food they were now mechanically consuming, the whole grey limbo with its slender telephone connection with the outside world were, like his chess, exact extensions of Malek's personality, yet permeated with secret passages and doors. The unexpected thrived in such an ambience. At any moment, as he shaved, the mirror might retract to reveal the flaming muzzle of a machine pistol, or the slightly bitter flavour of the soup they were drinking might be other than that of lentils.

These thoughts preoccupied him as the afternoon light began to fade in the east, the white rectangle of the garden wall illuminated against this dim backdrop like a huge tabula rasa. Excusing himself from the chess game, Constantin feigned a headache and retired to his room upstairs.

The door between his room and Malek's had been removed, and as he lay on the bed he was conscious of the supervisor sitting in his chair with his back to the window. Perhaps it was Malek's presence which prevented him from gaining any real rest, and when he rose several hours later and returned to the veranda he felt tired and possessed by a deepening sense of foreboding.

With an effort he rallied his spirits, and by concentrating his whole attention on the game was able to extract what appeared to be a drawn position. Although the game was adjourned without comment from either player, Malek seemed to concede by his manner that he had lost his advantage, lingering for a perceptible moment over the board when Constantin rose from the table.

The lesson of all this was not lost to Constantin the following day. He was fully aware that the games of chess were not only taxing his energies but providing Malek with a greater hold upon himself than he upon Malek. Although the pieces stood where they had left them the previous evening, Constantin did not suggest that they resume play. Malek made no move towards the board, apparently indifferent to whether the game was finished or not. Most of the time he sat next to Constantin by the single radiator in the lounge, occasionally going off to confer with the orderly in the kitchen. As usual the telephone rang briefly each morning, but otherwise there were no callers or visitors to the villa. To all intents it remained suspended in a perfect vacuum.

It was this unvarying nature of their daily routines which Constantin found particularly depressing. Intermittently over the next few days he played chess with Malek, invariably finding himself in a losing position, but the focus of his attention was elsewhere, upon the enigma cloaked by Malek's expressionless face. Around him a thousand invisible clocks raced onwards towards their beckoning zeros, a soundless thunder like the drumming of apocalyptic hoof-irons.

His mood of foreboding had given way to one of mounting fear, all the more terrifying because, despite Malek's real role, it seemed completely sourceless. He found himself unable to concentrate for more than a few minutes upon any task, left his meals unfinished and fidgeted helplessly by the veranda window. The slightest movement by Malek would make his nerves thrill with anguish; if the supervisor left his customary seat in the lounge to speak to the orderly Constantin would find himself almost paralysed by the tension, helplessly counting the seconds until Malek returned. Once, during one of their meals,

Malek started to ask him for the salt and Constantin almost choked to death.

The ironic humour of this near-fatality reminded Constantin that almost half of his two-month sentence had elapsed. But his crude attempts to obtain a pencil from the orderly and later, failing this, to mark the letters in a page torn from one of the novels were intercepted by Malek, and he realized that short of defeating the two policemen in single-handed combat he had no means of escaping his ever more imminent fate.

Latterly he had noticed that Malek's movements and general activity around the villa seemed to have quickened. He still sat for long periods in the armchair, observing Constantin, but his formerly impassive presence was graced by gestures and inclinations of the head that seemed to reflect a heightened cerebral activity, as if he were preparing himself for some long-awaited denouement. Even the heavy musculature of his face seemed to have relaxed and grown sleeker, his sharp mobile eyes, like those of an experienced senior inspector of police, roving constantly about the rooms.

Despite his efforts, however, Constantin was unable to galvanize himself into any defensive action. He could see clearly that Malek and himself had entered a new phase in their relationship, and that at any moment their outwardly formal and polite behaviour would degenerate into a gasping ugly violence, but he was nonetheless immobilized by his own state of terror. The days passed in a blur of uneaten meals and abandoned chess games, their very identity blotting out any sense of time or progression, the watching figure of Malek always before him.

Every morning, when he woke after two or three hours of sleep to find his consciousness still intact, a discovery almost painful in its relief and poignancy, he would be immediately aware of Malek standing in the next room, then waiting discreetly in the hallway as Constantin shaved in the bathroom (also without its door) following him downstairs to breakfast, his careful reflective tread like that of a hangman descending from his gallows.

After breakfast Constantin would challenge Malek to a game of chess, but after a few moves would begin to play wildly, throwing pieces forwards to be decimated by Malek. At times the supervisor would glance curiously at Constantin, as if wondering whether his charge had lost his reason, and then continue to play his careful exact game, invariably winning or drawing. Dimly Constantin perceived that by losing to Malek he had also surrendered to him psychologically, but the games had now become simply a means of passing the unending days.

Six weeks after they had first begun to play chess, Constantin more by luck than skill succeeded in an extravagant pawn gambit and forced Malek to sacrifice both his centre and any possibility of castling. Roused from his state of numb anxiety by the temporary victory, Constantin sat forward over the board, irritably waving away the orderly who announced from the door of the lounge that he would serve lunch.

'Tell him to wait, Malek. I mustn't lose my concentration at this point, I've very nearly won the game.'

'Well . . .' Malek glanced at his watch, then over his shoulder at the orderly, who, however, had turned on his heel and returned to the kitchen. He started to stand up. 'It can wait. He's bringing the –'

'No!' Constantin snapped. 'Just give me five minutes, Malek. Damn it, one adjourns on a move, not halfway through it.'

'Very well.' Malek hesitated, after a further glance at his watch. He climbed to his feet. 'I will tell him.'

Constantin concentrated on the board, ignoring the supervisor's retreating figure, the scent of victory clearing his mind. But thirty seconds later he sat up with a start, his heart almost seizing inside his chest.

Malek had gone upstairs! Constantin distinctly remembered him saying he would tell the orderly to delay lunch, but instead he had walked straight up to his bedroom. Not only was it extremely unusual for Constantin to be left unobserved when the orderly was otherwise occupied, but the latter had still not brought in their first luncheon course.

Steadying the table, Constantin stood up, his eyes searching the open doorways in front and behind him. Almost certainly the orderly's announcement of lunch was a signal, and Malek had found a convenient pretext for going upstairs to prepare his execution weapon.

Faced at last by the nemesis he had so long dreaded, Constantin listened for the sounds of Malek's feet descending the staircase. A profound silence enclosed the villa, broken only by the fall of one of the chess pieces to the tiled floor. Outside the sun shone intermittently in the garden, illuminating the broken flagstones of the ornamental pathway and the bare face of the walls. A few stunted weeds flowered among the rubble, their pale colours blanched by the sunlight, and Constantin was suddenly filled by an overwhelming need to escape into the open air for the few last moments before he died. The east wall, lit by the sun's rays, was marked by a faint series of horizontal grooves, the remnants perhaps of a fire escape ladder, and the slender possibility of using these as hand-holds made the enclosed garden, a perfect killing ground, preferable to the frantic claustrophobic nexus of the villa.

Above him, Malek's measured tread moved across the ceiling to the head of the staircase. He paused there and then began to descend the stairs, his steps chosen with a precise and careful rhythm.

Helplessly, Constantin searched the veranda for something that would serve as a weapon. The french windows on to the garden were locked, and a slotted pinion outside secured the left-hand member of the pair to the edge of the sill. If this were raised there was a chance that the windows could be forced outwards.

Scattering the chess pieces onto the floor with a sweep of his hand, Constantin seized the board and folded it together, then stepped over to the window and drove the heavy wooden box through the bottom pane. The report of the bursting glass echoed like a gun shot through the villa. Kneeling down, he pushed his hand through the aperture and tried to lift the pinion, jerking it up and down in its rusty socket. When it failed to clear the sill he forced his head through the broken window and began to heave against it helplessly with his thin shoulders, the fragments of broken glass falling on to his neck.

Behind him a chair was kicked back, and he felt two powerful hands seize his shoulders and pull him away from the window. He struck out hysterically with the chess box, and then was flung head-first to the tiled floor.

His convalescence from this episode was to last most of the following week. For the first three days he remained in bed, recovering his physical identity, waiting for the sprained muscles of his hands and shoulders to repair themselves. When he felt sufficiently strong to leave his bed he went down to the lounge and sat at one end of the sofa, his back to the windows and the thin autumn light.

Malek still remained in attendance, and the orderly prepared his meals as before. Neither of them made any comment upon Constantin's outburst of hysteria, or indeed betrayed any signs that it had taken place, but Constantin realized that he had crossed an important rubicon. His whole relationship with Malek had experienced a profound change. The fear of his own imminent death, and the tantalizing mystery of its precise date which had so obsessed him, had been replaced by a calm acceptance that the judicial processes inaugurated by his trial would take their course and that Malek and the orderly were merely the local agents of this distant apparat. In a sense his sentence and present tenuous existence at the villa were a microcosm of life itself, with its inherent but unfeared uncertainties, its inevitable quietus to be made on a date never known in advance. Seeing his role at the villa in this light Constantin no longer felt afraid at the prospect of his own extinction, fully aware that a change in the political wind could win him a free pardon.

In addition, he realized that Malek, far from being his executioner, a purely formal role, was in fact an intermediary between himself and the hierarchy, and in an important sense a potential ally of Constantin's. As he reformed his defence against the indictment preferred against him at the trial – he knew he had been far too willing to accept the *fait accompli* of his own guilt – he calculated the various ways in which Malek would be able to assist him. There was no doubt in his mind that he had misjudged Malek. With his sharp intelligence and commanding presence, the supervisor was very far from being a hatchet-faced killer – this original impression had been the result of some cloudiness in Constantin's perceptions, an unfortunate myopia which had cost him two precious months in his task of arranging a re-trial.

Comfortably swathed in his dressing gown, he sat at the card-table in the lounge (they had abandoned the veranda with the colder weather, and a patch of brown paper over the window reminded him of that first circle of purgatory) concentrating on the game of chess. Malek sat opposite him, hands clasped on one knee, his thumbs occasionally circling as he pondered a move. Although no less reticent than he had ever been, his manner seemed to indicate that he understood and confirmed Constantin's reappraisal of the situation. He still followed Constantin around the villa, but his attentions were noticeably more perfunctory, as if he realized that Constantin would not try again to escape.

From the start, Constantin was completely frank with Malek.

'I am convinced, Malek, that the Prosecutor-General was misdirected by the Justice Department, and that the whole basis of the trial was a false one. All but one of the indictments were never formally presented, so I had no opportunity to defend myself. You understand that, Malek? The selection of the capital penalty for one count was purely arbitrary.'

Malek nodded, moving a piece. 'So you have explained, Mr Constantin. I am afraid I do not have a legalistic turn of mind.'

'There's no need for you to,' Constantin assured him. 'The point is obvious. I hope it may be possible to appeal against the court's decision and ask for a re-trial.' Constantin gestured with a piece. 'I criticize myself for accepting the indictments so readily. In effect I made no attempt to defend myself. If only I had done so I am convinced I should have been found innocent.'

Malek murmured non-committally, and gestured towards the board. Constantin resumed play. Most of the games he consistently lost to Malek, but this no longer troubled him and, if anything, only served to reinforce the bonds between them.

Constantin had decided not to ask the supervisor to inform the Justice Department of his request for a re-trial until he had convinced Malek that his case left substantial room for doubt. A premature application would meet with an automatic negative from Malek, whatever his private sympathies. Conversely, once Malek was firmly on his side he would be prepared to risk his reputation with his seniors, and indeed his championing of Constantin's cause would be convincing proof in itself of the latter's innocence.

As Constantin soon found from his one-sided discussions with Malek, arguing over the legal technicalities of the trial, with their infinitely subtle nuances and implications, was an unprofitable method of enlisting Malek's support and he realized that he would have to do so by sheer impress of personality, by his manner, bearing and general conduct, and above all by his confidence of his innocence in the face of the penalty which might at any moment be imposed upon him. Curiously, this latter pose was not as difficult to maintain as might have been expected; Constantin already felt a surge of conviction in his eventual escape from the villa. Sooner or later Malek would recognize the authenticity of this inner confidence.

To begin with, however, the supervisor remained his usual phlegmatic self. Constantin talked away at him from morning to evening, every third word affirming the probability of his being found 'innocent', but Malek merely nodded with a faint smile and continued to play his errorless chess.

'Malek, I don't want you to think that I challenge the competence of the court to try the charges against me, or that I hold it in disrespect,' he said to the supervisor as they played their usual morning board some two weeks after the incident on the veranda. 'Far from it. But the court must make its decisions within the context of the evidence presented by the prosecutor. And even then, the greatest imponderable remains – the role of the accused. In my case I was, to all intents, not present at the trial, so my innocence is established by *force majeure*. Don't you agree, Malek?'

Malek's eyes searched the pieces on the board, his lips pursing thinly. 'I'm afraid this is above my head, Mr Constantin. Naturally I accept the authority of the court without question.'

'But so do I, Malek. I've made that plain. The real question is simply whether the verdict was justified in the light of the new circumstances I am describing.'

Malek shrugged, apparently more interested in the end-game before them. 'I recommend you to accept the verdict, Mr Constantin. For your peace of mind, you understand.'

Constantin looked away with a gesture of impatience. 'I don't agree, Malek. Besides, a great deal is at stake.' He glanced up at the windows which were drumming in the cold autumn wind. The casements were slightly loose, and the air lanced around them. The villa was poorly heated, only the single radiator in the lounge warming the three rooms downstairs. Already Constantin dreaded the winter. His hands and feet were perpetually cold and he could find no means of warming them.

'Malek, is there any chance of obtaining another heater?' he asked. 'It's none too warm in here. I have a feeling it's going to be a particularly cold winter.'

Malek looked up from the board, his bland grey eyes regarding Constantin with a flicker of curiosity, as if this last remark were one of the few he had heard from Constantin's lips which contained any overtones whatever.

'It is cold,' he agreed at last. 'I will see if I can borrow a heater. This villa is closed for most of the year.'

Constantin pestered him for news of the heater during the following week – partly because the success of his request would have symbolized Malek's first concession to him – but it failed to materialize. After one palpably lame excuse Malek merely ignored his further reminders. Outside, in the garden, the leaves whirled about the stones in a vortex of chilling air, and overhead the low clouds raced seaward. The two men in the lounge hunched over their chess-board by the radiator, hands buried in their pockets between moves.

Perhaps it was this darkening weather which made Constantin impatient of Malek's slowness in seeing the point of his argument, and he made his first suggestions that Malek should transmit a formal request for a re-trial to his superiors at the Department of Justice.

'You speak to someone on the telephone every morning, Malek,' he pointed out when Malek demurred. 'There's no difficulty involved. If you're afraid of compromising yourself – though I would have thought that a small price to pay in view of what is at stake – the orderly can pass on a message.'

'It's not feasible, Mr Constantin.' Malek seemed at last to be tiring of the subject. 'I suggest that you –'

'Malek!' Constantin stood up and paced around the lounge. 'Don't you realize that you must? You're literally my only means of contact, if you refuse I'm absolutely powerless, there's no hope of getting a reprieve!'

'The trial has already taken place, Mr Constantin,' Malek pointed out patiently.

'It was a mis-trial! Don't you understand, Malek, I accepted that I was guilty when in fact I was completely innocent!'

Malek looked up from the board, his eyebrows lifting. '*Completely* innocent, Mr Constantin?'

Constantin snapped his fingers. 'Well, virtually innocent. At least in terms of the indictment and trial.'

'But that is merely a technical difference, Mr Constantin. The Department of Justice is concerned with absolutes.'

'Quite right, Malek. I agree entirely.' Constantin nodded approvingly at the supervisor and privately noted his quizzical expression, the first time Malek had displayed a taste for irony.

He was to notice this fresh leit-motiv recurring during the next days; whenever he raised the subject of his request for a re-trial Malek would counter with one of his deceptively naive queries, trying to establish some minor tangential point, almost as if he were leading Constantin on to a fuller admission. At first Constantin assumed that the supervisor was fishing for information about other members of the hierarchy which he wished to use for his own purposes, but the few titbits he offered were ignored by Malek, and it dawned upon him that Malek was genuinely interested in establishing the sincerity of Constantin's conviction of his own innocence.

He showed no signs, however, of being prepared to contact his superiors at the Department of Justice, and Constantin's impatience continued to mount. He now used their morning and afternoon chess sessions as an opportunity to hold forth at length on the subject of the shortcomings of the judicial system, using his own case as an illustration, and hammered away at the theme of his innocence, even hinting that Malek might find himself held responsible if by any mischance he was not granted a reprieve.

'The position I find myself in is really most extraordinary,' he told Malek almost exactly two months after his arrival at the villa. 'Everyone else is satisfied with the court's verdict, and yet I alone know that I am innocent. I feel very like someone who is about to be buried alive.'

Malek managed a thin smile across the chess pieces. 'Of course, Mr Constantin, it is possible to convince oneself of anything, given a sufficient incentive.'

'But Malek, I assure you,' Constantin insisted, ignoring the board and concentrating his whole attention upon the supervisor, 'this is no death-cell repentance. Believe me, I know. I have examined the entire case from a thousand perspectives, questioned every possible motive. There is no doubt in my mind. I may once have been prepared to accept the possibility of my guilt but I realize now that I was entirely mistaken – experience encourages us to take too great a responsibility for ourselves, when we fall short of our ideals we become critical of ourselves and ready to assume that we are at fault. How dangerous that can be, Malek, I now know. Only the truly innocent man can really understand the meaning of guilt.'

Constantin stopped and sat back, a slight weariness overtaking him in the cold room. Malek was nodding slowly, a thin and not altogether unsympathetic smile on his lips as if he understood everything Constantin had said. Then he moved a piece, and with a murmured 'excuse me' left his seat and went out of the room.

Drawing the lapels of the dressing gown around his chest, Constantin studied the board with a desultory eye. He noticed that Malek's move appeared to be the first bad one he had made in all their games together, but he felt too tired to make the most of his opportunity. His brief speech to Malek, confirming all he believed, now left nothing more to be said. From now on whatever happened was up to Malek.

'Mr Constantin.'

He turned in his chair and, to his surprise, saw the supervisor standing in the doorway, wearing his long grey overcoat.

'Malek –?' For a moment Constantin felt his heart gallop, and then controlled himself. 'Malek, you've agreed at last, you're going to take me to the Department?'

Malek shook his head, his eyes staring sombrely at Constantin. 'Not exactly. I thought we might look at the garden, Mr Constantin. A breath of fresh air, it will do you good.'

'Of course, Malek, it's kind of you.' Constantin rose a little unsteadily to his feet, and tightened the cord of his dressing gown. 'Pardon my wild hopes.' He tried to smile at Malek, but the supervisor stood by the door, hands in his overcoat pockets, his eyes lowered fractionally from Constantin's face.

They went out on to the veranda towards the french windows. Outside the cold morning air whirled in frantic circles around the small stone yard, the leaves spiralling upwards into the dark sky. To Constantin there seemed little point in going out into the garden, but Malek stood behind him, one hand on the latch.

'Malek.' Something made him turn and face the supervisor. 'You do understand what I mean, when I say I am absolutely innocent. I *know* that.'

'Of course, Mr Constantin.' The supervisor's face was relaxed and almost genial. 'I understand. When you know you are innocent, then you are guilty.'

His hand opened the veranda door on to the whirling leaves.

, **1963**

# MINUS ONE

'Where, my God, *where* is he?'

Uttered in a tone of uncontrollable frustration as he paced up and down in front of the high-gabled window behind his desk, this *cri de coeur* of Dr Mellinger, Director of Green Hill Asylum, expressed the consternation of his entire staff at the mysterious disappearance of one of their patients. In the twelve hours that had elapsed since the escape, Dr Mellinger and his subordinates had progressed from surprise and annoyance to acute exasperation, and eventually to a mood of almost euphoric disbelief. To add insult to injury, not only had the patient, James Hinton, succeeded in becoming the first ever to escape from the asylum, but he had managed to do so without leaving any clues as to his route. Thus Dr Mellinger and his staff were tantalized by the possibility that Hinton had never escaped at all and was still safely within the confines of the asylum. At all events, everyone agreed that if Hinton *had* escaped, he had literally vanished into thin air.

However, one small consolation, Dr Mellinger reminded himself as he drummed his fingers on his desk, was that Hinton's disappearance had exposed the shortcomings of the asylum's security systems, and administered a salutary jolt to his heads of departments. As this hapless group, led by the Deputy Director, Dr Normand, filed into his office for the first of the morning's emergency conferences, Dr Mellinger cast a baleful glare at each in turn, but their sleepless faces remained mutely lowered to the carpeting, as if, despairing of finding Hinton anywhere else, they now sought his hiding place in its deep ruby pile.

At least, Dr Mellinger reflected, only one patient had disappeared, a negative sentiment which assumed greater meaning in view of the outcry that would be raised from the world outside when it was discovered that a patient – obviously a homicidal lunatic – had remained at large for over twelve hours before the police were notified.

This decision not to inform the civil authorities, an error of judgement whose culpability seemed to mount as the hours passed, alone prevented Dr Mellinger from finding an immediate scapegoat – a convenient one would have been little Dr Mendelsohn of the Pathology Department, an unimportant branch of the asylum – and sacrificing him on the altar of his own indiscretion. His natural caution, and reluctance to yield an inch of ground unless compelled, had prevented Dr Mellinger from raising the general alarm during the first hours after Hinton's disappearance, when some doubt still remained whether the latter had actually left the asylum. Although the failure to find Hinton might have been interpreted as a reasonable indication that he had successfully escaped, Dr Mellinger had characteristically refused to accept such faulty logic.

By now, over twelve hours later, his miscalculation had become apparent. As the thin smirk on Dr Normand's face revealed, and as his other subordinates would soon realize, his directorship of the asylum was now at stake. Unless they found Hinton within a few hours he would be placed in an untenable position before both the civil authorities and the trustees.

However, Dr Mellinger reminded himself, it was not without the exercise of considerable guile and resource that he had become Director of Green Hill in the first place.

'Where *is* he?'

Shifting his emphasis from the first of these interrogatories to the second, as if to illustrate that the fruitless search for Hinton's whereabouts had been superseded by an examination of his total existential role in the unhappy farce of which he was the author and principal star, Dr Mellinger turned upon his three breakfastless subordinates.

'Well, have you found him? Don't sit there dozing, gentlemen! You may have had a sleepless night, but I have still to wake from the nightmare.' With this humourless shaft, Dr Mellinger flashed a mordant eye into the rhododendron-lined drive, as if hoping to catch a sudden glimpse of the vanished patient. 'Dr Redpath, your report, please.'

'The search is still continuing, Director.' Dr Redpath, the registrar of the asylum, was nominally in charge of security. 'We have examined the entire grounds, dormitory blocks, garages and outbuildings – even the patients are taking part – but every trace of Hinton has vanished. Reluctantly, I am afraid there is no alternative but to inform the police.'

'Nonsense.' Dr Mellinger took his seat behind the desk, arms outspread and eyes roving the bare top for a minuscule replica of the vanished patient. 'Don't be disheartened by your inability to discover him, Doctor. Until the search is complete we would be wasting the police's time to ask for their help.'

'Of course, Director,' Dr Normand rejoined smoothly, 'but on the other hand, as we have now proved that the missing patient is not within the boundaries of Green Hill, we can conclude, ergo, that he is outside them. In such an event is it perhaps rather a case of *us* helping the police?'

'Not at all, my dear Normand,' Dr Mellinger replied pleasantly. As he mentally elaborated his answer, he realized that he had never trusted or liked his deputy; given the first opportunity he would replace him, most conveniently with Redpath, whose blunders in the 'Hinton affair', as it could be designated, would place him for ever squarely below the Director's thumb. 'If there were any evidence of the means by which Hinton made his escape – knotted sheets or footprints in the flower-beds – we could assume that he was no longer within these walls. But no such evidence has been found. For all we know – in fact, everything points inescapably to this conclusion – the patient is still within the confines of Green Hill, indeed by rights still within his cell. 'The bars on the window were not cut, and the only way out was through the door, the keys to which remained in the possession of Dr Booth' – he indicated the third member of the trio, a slim young man with a worried expression – 'throughout the period between the last contact with Hinton and the discovery of his disappearance. Dr Booth, as the physician actually responsible for Hinton, you are quite certain you were the last person to visit him?'

Dr Booth nodded reluctantly. His celebrity at having discovered Hinton's escape had long since turned sour. 'At seven o'clock, sir, during my evening round. But the last person to *see* Hinton was the duty nurse half an hour later. However, as no treatment had been prescribed – the patient had been admitted for observation – the door was not unlocked. Shortly after nine o'clock I decided to visit the patient –'

'Why?' Dr Mellinger placed the tips of his fingers together and constructed a cathedral spire and nave. 'This is one of the strangest aspects of the case, Doctor. Why should you have chosen, almost an hour and a half later, to leave your comfortable office on the ground floor and climb three flights of stairs merely to carry out a cursory inspection which could best be left to the duty staff? Your motives puzzle me, Doctor.'

'But, Director –!' Dr Booth was almost on his feet. 'Surely you don't suspect me of colluding in Hinton's escape? I assure you –'

'Doctor, please.' Dr Mellinger raised a smooth white hand. 'Nothing could be further from my mind. Perhaps I should have said: your *unconscious* motives.'

Again the unfortunate Booth protested: 'Director, there were no unconscious motives. I admit I can't remember precisely what prompted me to see Hinton, but it was some perfectly trivial reason. I hardly knew the patient.'

Dr Mellinger bent forwards across the desk. 'That is exactly what I meant, Doctor. To be precise, you did not know Hinton at all.' Dr Mellinger gazed at the distorted reflection of himself in the silver ink-stand. 'Tell me, Dr Booth, how would you describe Hinton's appearance?'

Booth hesitated. 'Well, he was of . . . medium height, if I remember, with . . . yes, brown hair and a pale complexion. His eyes were – I should have to refresh my memory from the file, Director.'

Dr Mellinger nodded. He turned to Redpath. 'Could you describe him, Doctor?'

'I'm afraid not, sir. I never saw the patient.' He gestured to the Deputy Director. 'I believe Dr Normand interviewed him on admission.'

With an effort Dr Normand cast into his memory. 'It was probably my assistant. If I remember, he was a man of average build with no distinguishing features. Neither short, nor tall. Stocky, one might say.' He pursed his lips. 'Yes. Or rather, no. I'm certain it was my assistant.'

'How interesting.' Dr Mellinger had visibly revived, the gleams of ironic humour which flashed from his eyes revealed some potent inner transformation. The burden of irritations and frustrations which had plagued him for the past day seemed to have been lifted. 'Does this mean, Dr Normand, that this entire institution has been mobilized in a search for a man whom no one here could recognize even if they found him? You surprise me, my dear Normand. I was under the impression that you were a man of cool and analytical intelligence, but in your search for Hinton you are obviously employing more arcane powers.'

'But, Director! I cannot be expected to memorize the face of every patient –'

'Enough, enough!' Dr Mellinger stood up with a flourish, and resumed his circuit of the carpet. 'This is all very disturbing. Obviously the whole relationship between Green Hill and its patients must be re-examined. Our patients are not faceless ciphers, gentlemen, but the possessors of unique and vital identities. If we regard them as nonentities and fail to invest them with any personal characteristics, is it surprising that they should seem to disappear? I suggest that we put aside the next few days and dedicate them to a careful re-appraisal. Let us scrutinize all those facile assumptions we make so readily.' Impelled by this vision, Dr Mellinger stepped into the light pouring through the window, as if to expose himself to this new revelation. 'Yes, this is the task that lies before us now; from its successful conclusion will emerge a new Green Hill, a Green Hill without shadows and conspiracies, where patients and physicians stand before each other in mutual trust and responsibility.'

A pregnant silence fell at the conclusion of this homily. At last Dr Redpath cleared his throat, reluctant to disturb Dr Mellinger's sublime communion with himself. 'And Hinton, sir?'

'Hinton? Ah, yes.' Dr Mellinger turned to face them, like a bishop about to bless his congregation. 'Let us see Hinton as an illustration of this process of self-examination, a focus of our re-appraisal.'

'So the search should continue, sir?' Redpath pressed.

'Of course.' For a moment Dr Mellinger's attention wandered. 'Yes, we must find Hinton. He is here somewhere; his essence pervades Green Hill, a vast metaphysical conundrum. Solve it, gentlemen, and you will have solved the mystery of his disappearance.'

For the next hour Dr Mellinger paced the carpet alone, now and then warming his hands at the low fire below the mantelpiece. Its few flames entwined in the chimney like the ideas playing around the periphery of his mind. At last, he felt, a means of breaking through the impasse had offered itself. He had always been certain that Hinton's miraculous disappearance represented more than a simple problem of breached security, and was a symbol of something grievously at fault with the very foundations of Green Hill.

Pursuing these thoughts, Dr Mellinger left his office and made his way down to the floor below which housed the administrative department. The offices were deserted; the entire staff of the building was taking part in the search. Occasionally the querulous cries of the patients demanding their breakfasts drifted across the warm, insulated air. Fortunately the walls were thick, and the rates charged by the asylum high enough to obviate the need for over-crowding.

Green Hill Asylum (motto, and principal attraction: 'There is a Green Hill Far, Far Away') was one of those institutions which are patronized by the wealthier members of the community and in effect serve the role of private prisons. In such places are confined all those miscreant or unfortunate relatives whose presence would otherwise be a burden or embarrassment: the importunate widows of blacksheep sons, senile maiden aunts, elderly bachelor cousins paying the price for their romantic indiscretions – in short, all those abandoned casualties of the army of privilege. As far as the patrons of Green Hill were concerned, maximum security came first, treatment, if given at all, a bad second. Dr Mellinger's patients had disappeared conveniently from the world, and as long as they remained in this distant limbo those who paid the bills were satisfied. All this made Hinton's escape particularly dangerous.

Stepping through the open doorway of Normand's office, Dr Mellinger ran his eye cursorily around the room. On the desk, hastily opened, was a slim file containing a few documents and a photograph.

For a brief moment Dr Mellinger gazed abstractedly at the file. Then, after a discreet glance into the corridor, he slipped it under his arm and retraced his steps up the empty staircase.

Outside, muted by the dark groves of rhododendrons, the sounds of search and pursuit echoed across the grounds. Opening the file on his desk, Dr Mellinger stared at the photograph, which happened to be lying upside down. Without straightening it, he studied the amorphous features. The nose was straight, the forehead and cheeks symmetrical, the ears a little oversize, but in its inverted position the face lacked any cohesive identity.

Suddenly, as he started to read the file, Dr Mellinger was filled with a deep sense of resentment. The entire subject of Hinton and the man's precarious claims to reality overwhelmed him with a profound nausea. He refused to accept that this mindless cripple with his anonymous features could have been responsible for the confusion and anxiety of the previous day. Was it possible that these few pieces of paper constituted this meagre individual's full claim to reality?

Flinching slightly from the touch of the file to his fingers, Dr Mellinger carried it across to the fireplace. Averting his face, he listened with a deepening sense of relief as the flames flared briefly and subsided.

'My dear Booth! Do come in. It's good of you to spare the time.' With this greeting Dr Mellinger ushered him to a chair beside the fire and proffered his silver cigarette case. 'There's a certain small matter I wanted to discuss, and you are almost the only person who can help me.'

'Of course, Director,' Booth assured him. 'I am greatly honoured.'

Dr Mellinger seated himself behind his desk. 'It's a very curious case, one of the most unusual I have ever come across. It concerns a patient under your care, I believe.'

'May I ask for his name, sir?'

'Hinton,' Dr Mellinger said, with a sharp glance at Booth.

'Hinton, sir?'

'You show surprise,' Dr Mellinger continued before Booth could reply. 'I find that response particularly interesting.'

'The search is still being carried on,' Booth said uncertainly as Dr Mellinger paused to digest his remarks. 'I'm afraid we've found absolutely no trace of him. Dr Normand thinks we should inform –'

'Ah, yes, Dr Normand.' The Director revived suddenly. 'I have asked him to report to me with Hinton's file as soon as he is free. Dr Booth, does it occur to you that we may be chasing the wrong hare?'

'Sir –?'

'Is it in fact *Hinton* we are after? I wonder, perhaps, whether the search for Hinton is obscuring something larger and more significant, the enigma, as I mentioned yesterday, which lies at the heart of Green Hill and to whose solution we must all now be dedicated.' Dr Mellinger savoured these reflections before continuing. 'Dr Booth, let us for a moment consider the role of Hinton, or to be more precise, the complex of overlapping and adjacent events that we identify loosely by the term "Hinton".'

'Complex, sir? You speak diagnostically?'

'No, Booth. I am now concerned with the phenomenology of Hinton, with his absolute metaphysical essence. To speak more plainly: has it occurred to you, Booth, how little we know of this elusive patient, how scanty the traces he has left of his own identity?'

'True, Director,' Booth agreed. 'I constantly reproach myself for not taking a closer interest in the patient.'

'Not at all, Doctor. I realize how busy you are. I intend to carry out a major reorganization of Green Hill, and I assure you that your tireless work here will not be forgotten. A senior administrative post would, I am sure, suit you excellently.' As Booth sat up, his interest in the conversation increasing several-fold, Dr Mellinger acknowledged his expression of thanks with a discreet nod. 'As I was saying, Doctor, you have so many patients, all wearing the same uniforms, housed in the same wards, and by and large prescribed the same treatment – is it surprising that they should lose their individual identities? If I may make a small confession,' he added with a roguish smile. 'I myself find that all the patients look alike. Why, if Dr Normand or yourself informed me that a new patient by the name of Smith or Brown had arrived, I would automatically furnish him with the standard uniform of identity at Green Hill – those same lustreless eyes and slack mouth, the same amorphous features.'

Unclasping his hands, Dr Mellinger leaned intently across his desk. 'What I am suggesting, Doctor, is that this automatic mechanism may have operated in the case of the so-called Hinton, and that you may have invested an entirely non-existent individual with the fictions of a personality.'

Dr Booth nodded slowly, 'I see, sir. You suspect that Hinton – or what we have called Hinton up to now – was perhaps a confused memory of another patient.' He hesitated doubtfully, and then noticed that Dr Mellinger's eyes were fixed upon him with hypnotic intensity.

'Dr Booth. I ask you: what actual proof have we that Hinton ever existed?'

'Well, sir, there are the . . .' Booth searched about helplessly . . . 'the records in the administrative department. And the case notes.'

Dr Mellinger shook his head with a scornful flourish. 'My dear Booth, you are speaking of mere pieces of paper. These are not proof of a man's identity. A typewriter will invent anything you choose. The only conclusive proof is his physical existence in time and space or, failing that, a distinct memory of his tangible physical presence. Can you honestly say that either of these conditions is fulfilled?'

'No, sir. I suppose I can't. Though I did speak to a patient whom I assumed to be Hinton.'

'But was he?' The Director's voice was resonant and urgent. 'Search your mind, Booth; be honest with yourself. Was it perhaps another patient to whom you spoke? What doctor ever really looks at his patients? In all probability you merely saw Hinton's name on a list and assumed that he sat before you, an intact physical existence like your own.'

There was a knock upon the door. Dr Normand stepped into the office. 'Good afternoon, Director.'

'Ah, Normand. Do come in. Dr Booth and I have been having a most instructive conversation. I really believe we have found a solution to the mystery of Hinton's disappearance.'

Dr Normand nodded cautiously. 'I am most relieved, sir. I was beginning to wonder whether we should inform the civil authorities. It is now nearly forty-eight hours since . . .'

'My dear Normand, I am afraid you are rather out of touch. Our whole attitude to the Hinton case has changed radically. Dr Booth has been so helpful to me. We have been discussing the possibility that an administrative post might be found for him. You have the Hinton file?'

'Er, I regret not, sir,' Normand apologized, his eyes moving from Booth to the Director. 'I gather it's been temporarily displaced. I've instituted a thorough search and it will be brought to you as soon as possible.'

'Thank you, Normand, if you would.' Mellinger took Booth by the arm and led him to the door. 'Now, Doctor, I am most gratified by your perceptiveness. I want you to question your ward staff in the way I have questioned you. Strike through the mists of illusion and false assumption that swirl about their minds. Warn them of those illusions compounded on illusions which can assume the guise of reality. Remind them, too, that clear minds are required at Green Hill. I will be most surprised if any one of them can put her hand on her heart and swear that Hinton *really* existed.'

After Booth had made his exit, Dr Mellinger returned to his desk. For a moment he failed to notice his deputy.

'Ah, yes, Normand. I wonder where that file is? You didn't bring it?'

'No, sir. As I explained –'

'Well, never mind. But we mustn't become careless, Normand, too much is at stake. Do you realize that without that file we would know literally nothing whatever about Hinton? It would be most awkward.'

'I assure you, sir, the file –'

'Enough, Normand. Don't worry yourself.' Dr Mellinger turned a vulpine smile upon the restless Normand. 'I have the greatest respect for the efficiency of the administrative department under your leadership. I think it unlikely that they should have misplaced it. Tell me, Normand, are you sure that this file ever existed?'

'Certainly, sir,' Normand replied promptly. 'Of course, I have not actually seen it myself, but every patient at Green Hill has a complete personal file.'

'But Normand,' the Director pointed out gently, 'the patient in question is not *at* Green Hill. Whether or not this hypothetical file exists, Hinton does not.'

He stopped and waited as Normand looked up at him, his eyes narrowing.

A week later, Dr Mellinger held a final conference in his office. This was a notably more relaxed gathering; his subordinates lay back in the leather armchairs around the fire, while Dr Mellinger leaned against the desk, supervising the circulation of his best sherry.

'So, gentlemen,' he remarked in conclusion, 'we may look back on the past week as a period of unique self-discovery, a lesson for all of us to remember the true nature of our roles at Green Hill, our dedication to the task of separating reality from illusion. If our patients are haunted by chimeras, let us at least retain absolute clarity of mind, accepting the validity of any proposition only if all our senses corroborate it. Consider the example of the "Hinton affair". Here, by an accumulation of false assumptions, of illusions buttressing illusions, a vast edifice of fantasy was erected around the wholly mythical identity of one patient. This imaginary figure, who by some means we have not discovered – most probably the error of a typist in the records department – was given the name "Hinton", was subsequently furnished with a complete personal identity, a private ward, attendant nurses and doctors. Such was the grip of this substitute world, this concatenation of errors, that when it crumbled and the lack of any substance behind the shadow was discovered, the remaining vacuum was automatically interpreted as the patient's escape.'

Dr Mellinger gestured eloquently, as Normand, Redpath and Booth nodded their agreement. He walked around his desk and took his seat. 'Perhaps, gentlemen, it is fortunate that I remain aloof from the day-to-day affairs of Green Hill. I take no credit upon myself, that I alone was sufficiently detached to consider the full implications of Hinton's disappearance and realize the only possible explanation – *that Hinton had never existed!*'

'A brilliant deduction,' Redpath murmured.

'Without doubt,' echoed Booth.

'A profound insight,' agreed Normand.

There was a sharp knock on the door. With a frown, Dr Mellinger ignored it and resumed his monologue.

'Thank you, gentlemen. Without your assistance that hypothesis, that Hinton was no more than an accumulation of administrative errors, could never have been confirmed.'

The knock on the door repeated itself. A staff sister appeared breathlessly. 'Excuse me, sir. I'm sorry to interrupt you, but –'

Dr Mellinger waved away her apologies. 'Never mind. What is it?'

'A visitor, Dr Mellinger.' She paused as the Director waited impatiently. 'Mrs Hinton, to see her husband.'

For a moment there was consternation. The three men around the fire sat upright, their drinks forgotten, while Dr Mellinger remained stock-still at his desk. A total silence filled the room, only broken by the light tapping of a woman's heels in the corridor outside.

But Dr Mellinger recovered quickly. Standing up, with a grim smile at his colleagues, he said: 'To see Mr Hinton? Impossible, Hinton never existed. The woman must be suffering from terrible delusions; she requires immediate treatment. Show her in.' He turned to his colleagues. 'Gentlemen, we must do everything we can to help her.'

Minus two.

**⋅ 1963**

# . THE SUDDEN AFTERNOON

What surprised Elliott was the suddenness of the attack. Judith and the children had gone down to the coast for the weekend to catch the last of the summer, leaving him alone in the house, and the three days had been a pleasant reverie of silent rooms, meals taken at random hours, and a little mild carpentry in the workshop. He spent Sunday morning reading all the reviews in the newspapers, carefully adding half a dozen titles to the list of books which he knew he would never manage to buy, let alone read. These wistful exercises, like the elaborately prepared martini before lunch, were part of the established ritual of his brief bachelor moments. He decided to take a brisk walk across Hampstead Heath after lunch, returning in time to tidy everything away before Judith arrived that evening.

Instead, a sharp attack of what first appeared to be influenza struck him just before one o'clock. A throbbing headache and a soaring temperature sent him fumbling to the medicine cabinet in the bathroom, only to find that Judith had taken the aspirin with her. Sitting on the edge of the bath, forehead in his hands, he nursed the spasm, which seemed to contract the muscles of some inner scalp, compressing his brain like fruit-pulp in a linen bag.

'Judith!' he shouted to the empty house. 'Damn!'

The pain mounted, an intense prickling that drove silver needles through his skull. Helpless for a moment, he propelled himself into the bedroom and climbed fully dressed into the bed, shielding his eyes from the weak sunlight which crossed the Heath.

After a few minutes the attack subsided slightly, leaving him with a nagging migraine and a sense of utter inertia. For the next hour he stared at the reflection of himself in the dressing-table mirror, lying like a trussed steer across the bed. Through the window he watched a small boy playing under the oaks by the edge of the park, patiently trying to catch the spiralling leaves. Twenty yards away a nondescript little man with a dark complexion sat alone on a bench, staring through the trees.

In some way this scene soothed Elliott, and the headache finally dissipated, as if charmed away by the swaying boughs and the leaping figure of the boy.

'Strange . . .' he murmured to himself, still puzzled by the ferocity of the attack. Judith, however, would be sceptical; she had always accused him of being a hypochondriac. It was a pity she hadn't been there, instead of lying about on the beach at Worthing, but at least the children had been spared the spectacle of their father yelping with agony.

Reluctant to get out of bed and precipitate another attack – perhaps it was due to some virulent but short-lived virus? – Elliott lay back, the scent of his wife's skin on the pillow reminding him of his own childhood and his mother's perfumed hair. He had been brought up in India, and remembered being rowed across a river by his father, the great placid back of the Ganges turning crimson in the late afternoon light. The burnt-earth colours of the Calcutta waterfront were still vivid after an interval of thirty years.

Smiling pleasantly over this memory, and at the image of his father rowing with a rhythmic lulling motion, Elliott gazed upward at the ceiling, only distracted by the distant hoot of a car horn.

Then he sat up abruptly, staring sharply at the room around him.

'Calcutta? What the hell –?'

The memory had been completely false! He had never been to India in his life, or anywhere near the Far East. He had been born in London, and lived there all his life apart from a two-year postgraduate visit to the United States. As for his father, who had been captured by the Germans while fighting with the Eighth Army in North Africa and spent most of the war as a POW, Elliott had seen almost nothing of him until his adolescence.

Yet the memory of being rowed across the Ganges had been extraordinarily strong. Trying to shake off the last residue of the headache, Elliott swung his feet onto the floor. The throbbing had returned slightly, but in a curious way receded as he let the image of the Calcutta waterfront fill his mind. Whatever its source, the landscape was certainly Indian, and he could see the Ganges steps, a clutter of sailing dhows and even a few meagre funeral pyres smoking on the embankment.

But what most surprised him were the emotional associations of this false memory of being rowed by his father, the sense of reassurance that came with each rhythmic motion of the dark figure, whose face was hidden by the shadows of the setting sun.

Wondering where he had collected this powerful visual impression which had somehow translated itself into a memory with unique personal undertones, Elliott left the bedroom and made his way down to the kitchen. It was now half past two, almost too late for lunch, and he stared without interest at the rows of eggs and milk bottles in the refrigerator. After lunch, he decided, he would settle down on the sofa in the lounge and read or watch television.

At the thought of the latter Elliott realized that the false memory of the Ganges was almost certainly a forgotten fragment of a film travelogue, probably one he had seen as a child. The whole sequence of the memory, with its posed shot of the boat cutting through the crimson water and the long traverse of the waterfront, was typical of the style of the travelogues made in the nineteen-forties, and he could almost see the credit titles coming up with a roll of drums.

Reassured by this, and assuming that the headache had somehow jolted loose this visual memory – the slightly blurred wartime cinema screens had often strained his eyes – Elliott began to prepare his lunch. He ignored the food Judith had left for him and hunted among the spices and pickle jars in the pantry, where he found some rice and a packet of curry powder. Judith had never mastered the intricacies of making a real curry, and Elliott's own occasional attempts had merely elicited amused smiles. Today, however, with ample time on his hands and no interference, he would succeed.

Unhurriedly Elliott began to prepare the dish, and the kitchen soon filled with steam and the savoury odours of curry powder and chutney. Outside, the thin sunlight gave way to darker clouds and the first afternoon rain. The small boy had gone, but the solitary figure under the oaks still sat on the bench, jacket collar turned up around his neck.

Delighted by the simmering brew, Elliott relaxed on his stool, and thought about his medical practice. Normally he would have been obliged to hold an evening surgery, but his locum had arranged to take over for him, much to his relief, as one of the patients had been particularly difficult – a complete neurotic, a hazard faced by every doctor, she had even threatened to report him to the general medical council for misconduct, though the allegations were so grotesque the disciplinary committee would not consider them seriously for a moment.

The curry had been strong, and a sharp pain under the sternum marked the beginning of a bout of indigestion. Cursing his bad luck, Elliott poured a glass of milk, sorry to lose the flavour of the curry.

'You're in bad shape, old sport,' he said to himself with ironic humour. 'You ought to see a doctor.'

With a sudden snap of his fingers he stood up. He had experienced his second false memory! The whole reverie about his medical practice, the locum and the woman patient were absolute fictions, unrelated to anything in his life. Professionally he was a research chemist, employed in the biochemistry department of one of the London cancer institutes, but his contacts with physicians and surgeons were virtually nil.

And yet the impression of having a medical practice, patients and all the other involvements of a busy doctor was remarkably strong and persistent – indeed, far more than a memory, a coherent area of awareness as valid as the image of the biochemistry laboratory.

With a growing sense of unease, Elliott sipped weakly at the tumbler of milk, wondering why these sourceless images, like fragments from the intelligence of some other individual, were impinging themselves on his mind. He went into the lounge and sat down with his back to the window, examining himself with as much professional detachment as he could muster. Behind him, under the trees in the park, the man on the bench sat silently in the rain, eyed at a safe distance by a wandering mongrel.

After a pause to collect himself, Elliott deliberately began to explore this second false memory. Immediately he noticed that the dyspepsia subsided, as if assuming the *persona* of the fragmented images relieved their pressure upon his mind. Concentrating, he could see a high window above a broad mahogany desk, a padded leather couch, shelves of books and framed certificates on the walls, unmistakably a doctor's consulting rooms. Leaving the room, he passed down a broad flight of carpeted stairs into a marble-floored hall. A desk stood in an alcove on the left, and a pretty red-haired receptionist looked up and smiled to him across her typewriter. Then he was outside in the street, obviously in a well-to-do quarter of the city, where Rolls-Royces and Bentleys almost outnumbered the other cars. Two hundred yards away double-decker buses crossed a familiar intersection.

'Harley Street!' Elliott snapped. As he sat up and looked around at the familiar furniture in the lounge and the drenched oaks in the park, with an effort re-establishing their reality in his mind, he had a last glimpse of the front elevation of the consulting chambers, a blurred nameplate on the cream-painted columns. Over the portico were the gilt italic numerals: *259*

'Two fifty-nine Harley Street? Now who the devil works there?' Elliott stood up and went over to the window, staring out across the Heath, then paced into the kitchen and savoured the residue of the curry aroma. Again a spasm of indigestion gripped his stomach, and he immediately focused on the image of the unknown doctor's consulting rooms. As the pain faded he had a further impression of a small middle-aged woman in a hospital ward, her left arm in a cast, and then a picture of the staff and consultants' entrance to the Middlesex Hospital, as vivid as a photograph.

Picking up the newspaper, Elliott returned to the lounge, settling himself with difficulty. The absolute clarity of the memories convinced him that they were not confused images taken from the ciné-films or elaborated by his imagination. The more he explored them the more they fixed their own reality, refusing to fade or vanish. In addition, the emotional content was too strong. The associations of the childhood river scene were reassuring but the atmosphere in the consulting rooms had been fraught with hesitation and anxiety, as if their original possessor was in the grip of a nightmare.

The headache still tugged at his temples, and Elliott went over to the cocktail cabinet and poured himself a large whisky and soda. Had he in some incredible way simultaneously become the receiver of the disembodied memories of a small Indian boy in Calcutta and a Harley Street consultant?

Glancing at the front news page, his eye caught:

INDIAN DOCTOR SOUGHT
Wife's Mystery Death

*Police are continuing their search for the missing Harley Street psychiatrist, Dr Krishnamurti Singh. Scotland Yard believes he may be able to assist them in their inquiries into the death of his wife, Mrs Ramadya Singh . . .*

With a surge of relief, Elliott slapped the newspaper and tossed it across the room. So this explained the two imaginary memories! Earlier that morning, before the influenza attack, he had read the news item without realizing it, then during the light fever had dramatized the details. The virulent virus – a rare short-lived strain he had picked up at the laboratory – presumably acted like the hallucinogenic drugs, creating an inner image of almost photographic authenticity. Even the curry had been part of the system of fantasy.

Elliott wandered ruminatively around the lounge, listening to the rain sweep like hail across the windows. Within a few moments he knew that more of these hallucinatory memories lay below the surface of his mind, all revolving around the identity of the missing Indian doctor.

Unable to dispel them, he deliberately let himself drift off into a reverie. Perhaps the association of the funereal rain and the tiresome pain below his sternum was responsible for the gathering sense of foreboding in his mind. Formless ideas rose towards consciousness, and he stirred uneasily in his chair. Without realizing it, he found himself thinking of his wife's death, an event shrouded in pain and a peculiar dream-like violence. For a moment he was almost inside his wife's dying mind, at the bottom of an immense drowned lake, separated from the distant pinpoint of sky by enormous volumes of water that pressed upon his chest . . .

In a flood of sweat, Elliott awoke from this nightmare, the whole tragic vision of his wife's death before his eyes. Judith was alive, of course, staying with her married sister at the beach-house near Worthing, but the vision of her drowning had come through with the force and urgency of a telepathic signal.

'Judith!'

Rousing himself, Elliott hurried to the telephone in the hall. Something about its psychological dimensions convinced him that he had not imagined the death scene.

The sea!

He snatched up the phone, dialling for the operator. At that very moment Judith might well be swimming alone while her sister prepared tea with the children, in sight of the beach but unaware she was in danger . . .

'Operator, this is urgent,' Elliott began. 'I must talk to my wife. I think she's in some sort of danger. Can you get me Calcutta 30331.'

The operator hesitated. 'Calcutta? I'm sorry, caller, I'll transfer you to Overseas –'

'What? I don't want –' Elliott stopped. 'What number did I ask for?'

'Calcutta 30331. I'll have you transferred.'

'Wait!' Elliott steadied himself against the window. The rain beat across the glazed panes. 'My mistake. I meant Worthing 303 –'

'Are you there, caller? Worthing Three Zero Three –' Her voice waited.

Wearily Elliott lowered the telephone. 'I'll look it up,' he said thickly. 'That wasn't the number.'

He turned the pages of the memo pad, realizing that both he and Judith had known the number for years and never bothered to record it.

'Are you there, caller?' The operator's voice was sharper.

A few moments later, when he was connected to Directory Inquiries, Elliott realized that he had also forgotten his sister-in-law's name and address.

'Calcutta 30331.' Elliott repeated the number as he poured himself a drink from the whisky decanter. Pulling himself together, he recognized that the notion of a telepathic message was fatuous. Judith would be perfectly safe, on her way back to London with the children, and he had misinterpreted the vision of the dying woman. The telephone number, however, remained. The enigmatic sequence flowed off his tongue with the unconscious familiarity of long usage. A score of similar memories waited to be summoned into reality, as if a fugitive mind had taken up residence in his brain.

He picked the newspaper off the floor.

*. . . Dr Krishnamurti Singh. Scotland Yard believes he may be able to assist them in their inquiries . . .*

'Assist them in their inquiries' – a typical Fleet Street euphemism, part of the elaborate code built up between the newspapers and their readers. A French paper, not handicapped by the English libel laws, would be shouting 'Bluebeard! Assassin!'

*Detectives are at the bedside of Mrs Ethel Burgess, the charwoman employed by Dr and Mrs Singh, who was yesterday found unconscious at the foot of the stairs . . .*

Mrs Burgess! Instantly an image of the small elderly woman, with a face like a wizened apple, came before his eyes. She was lying in the hospital bed at the Middlesex, watching him with frightened reproachful glances –

The tumbler, half-filled with whisky, smashed itself on the fireplace tiles. Elliott stared at the fragments of wet glass around his feet, then sat down in the centre of the sofa with his head in his hands, trying to hold back the flood of memories. Helplessly he found himself thinking of the medical school at Calcutta. The half-familiar faces of fellow students passed in a blur. He remembered his passionate interest in developing a scientific approach to the obscurer branches of yoga and the Hindu parapsychologies, the student society he formed and its experiments in thought and body transference, brought to an end by the death of one of the students and the subsequent scandal ...

For a moment Elliott marvelled at the coherence and convincing detail of the memories. Numbly he reminded himself that in fact he had been a chemistry student at –

Where?

With a start he realized that he had forgotten. Quickly he searched his mind, and found he could remember almost nothing of his distant past, where he was born, his parents and childhood. Instead he saw once again, this time with luminous clarity, the rowing-boat on the crimson Ganges and its dark oarsman watching him with his ambiguous smile. Then he saw another picture, of himself as a small boy, writing in a huge ledger in which all the pencilled entries had been laboriously rubbed out, sitting at a desk in a room with a low ceiling of bamboo rods over his father's warehouse by the market –

'Nonsense!' Flinging the memory from him, with all its tender associations, Elliott stood up restless, his heart racing with a sudden fever. His forehead burned with heat, his mind inventing strings of fantasies around the Dr Singh wanted by the police. He felt his pulse, then leaned into the mirror over the mantelpiece and examined his eyes, checking his pupil reflexes with expert fingers for any symptoms of concussion.

Swallowing with a dry tongue, he stared down at the physician's hands which had examined him, then decided to call his own doctor. A sedative, an hour's sleep, and he would recover.

In the falling evening light he could barely see the numerals. 'Hello, hello!' he shouted. 'Is anyone there?'

'Yes, Dr Singh,' a woman replied. 'Is that you?'

Frightened, Elliott cupped his hand over the mouthpiece. He had dialled the number from memory, but from another memory than his own. But not only had the receptionist recognized his voice – Elliott had recognized hers, and knew her name.

Experimentally he lifted the receiver, and said the name in his mind. 'Miss Tremayne –?'

'Dr Singh? Are you –'

With an effort Elliott made his voice more guttural. 'I'm sorry, I have the wrong number. What is your number?'

The girl hesitated. When she spoke the modulation and rhythm of her voice were again instantly familiar. 'This is Harley Street 30331,' she said cautiously. 'Dr Singh, the police have –'

Elliott lowered the telephone into its cradle. Wearily he sat down on the carpet in the darkness, looking up at the black rectangle of the front door. Again the headache began to drum at his temples, as he tried to ignore the memories crowding into his mind. Above him the staircase led to another world.

Half an hour later, he pulled himself to his feet. Searching for his bed, and fearing the light, he stumbled into a room and lay down. With a start he clambered upright, and found that he was lying on the table in the dining room.

He had forgotten his way around the house, and the topography of another home, apparently a single-storey apartment, had superimposed itself upon his mind. In the strange upstairs floor he found an untidy nursery full of children's toys and clothes, an unremembered frieze of childish drawings which showed tranquil skies over church steeples. When he closed the door the scene vanished like a forgotten tableau.

In the bedroom next door a portrait photograph stood on the dressing table, showing the face of a pleasant blonde-haired woman he had never seen. He gazed down at the bed in the darkness, the wardrobes and mirrors around him like the furniture of a dream.

'Ramadya, Ramadya,' he murmured, on his lips the name of the dying woman.

The telephone rang. Standing in the darkness at the top of the stairs, he listened to its sounds shrilling through the silent house. He walked down to it with leaden feet.

'Yes?' he said tersely.

'Hello, darling,' a woman's bright voice answered. In the background trains shunted and whistled. 'Hello? Is that Hampstead –'

'This is Harley Street 30331,' he said quickly. 'You have the wrong number.'

'Oh, dear, I am sorry, I thought –'

Cutting off this voice, which for a fleeting moment had drawn together the fragmented *persona* clinging to the back of his mind, he stood at the window by the front door. Through the narrow barred pane he could see that the rain had almost ended, and a light mist hung among the trees. The bedraggled figure on the bench still maintained his vigil, his face hidden in the darkness. Now and then his drenched form would glimmer in the passing lights.

For some reason a sense of extreme urgency had overtaken Elliott. He knew that there were a series of tasks to be performed, records to be made before important evidence vanished, reliable witnesses to be contacted. A hundred ignored images passed through in his mind as he searched for a pair of shoes and a jacket in the cupboard upstairs, scenes of his medical practice, a woman patient being tested by an electroencephalogram, the radiator of a Bentley car and its automobile club badges. There were glimpses of the streets near Harley Street, the residue of countless journeys to and from the consulting rooms, the entrance to the Overseas Club, a noisy seminar at one of the scientific institutes where someone was shouting at him theatrically. Then, unpleasantly, there were feelings of remorse for his wife's death, counterbalanced by the growing inner conviction that this, paradoxically, was the only way to save her, to force her to a new life. In a strange yet familiar voice he heard himself saying: 'the soul, like any soft-skinned creature, clings to whatever shell it can find. Only by cracking that shell can one force it to move to a new . . .'

Attacks of vertigo came over him in waves as he descended the staircase. There was someone he must find, one man whose help might save him. He picked up the telephone and dialled, swaying giddily from side to side.

A clipped voice like polished ivory answered. 'Professor Ramachandran speaking.'

'Professor –'

'Hello? Who is that, please?'

He cleared his throat, coughing noisily into the mouthpiece. 'Professor, understand me! It was the tumour, inoperable, it was the only way to save her – metempsychosis of the somatic function as well as the psychic . . .' He had launched into a semicoherent tirade, the words coming out in clotted shreds. 'Ramadya has gone over now, she is the other woman . . . neither she nor any others will ever know . . . Professor, will you tell her one day, and myself . . . a single word –'

'Dr Singh!' The voice at the end was a shout. 'I can no longer help you! You must take the consequences of your folly! I warned you repeatedly about the danger of your experiments –'

The telephone squeaked on the floor where he dropped it. Outside the headlamps of police cars flashed by, their blue roof lights revolving like spectral beacons. As he unlatched the door and stepped out into the cold night air he had a last obsessive thought, of a fair-haired, middle-aged man with glasses who was a chemist at a cancer institute, a man with a remarkably receptive mind, its open bowl spread before him like a huge dish antenna. This man alone could help him. His name was – Elliott.

As he sat on the bench he saw the lights approaching him through the trees, like glowing aureoles in the darkness. The rain had ended and a light mist dissipated under the branches, but after the warmth indoors it was colder than he expected, and within only a few minutes in the park he began to shiver. Walking between the trees, he saw the line of police cars parked along the perimeter road two hundred yards away. Whichever way he moved, the lights seemed to draw nearer, although never coming directly toward him.

He turned, deciding to return to the house, and to his surprise saw a slim fair-haired man cross the road from the park and climb the steps to the front door. Startled, he watched this intruder disappear through the open door and close it behind him.

Then two policemen stepped from the mist on his right, their torches dazzling his eyes. He broke into a run, but a third huge figure materialized from behind a trunk and blocked his path.

'That's enough, then,' a gruff voice told him as he wrestled helplessly. 'Let's try to take it quietly.'

Lamps circled the darkness. More police ran over through the trees. An inspector with silver shoulder badges stepped up and peered into his face as a constable raised a torch.

'Dr Singh?'

For a moment he listened to the sounds of the name, which had pursued him all day, hang fleetingly on the damp air. Most of his mind seemed willing to accept the identification, but a small part, now dissolving to a minute speck, like the faint stars veiled by the mist, refused to agree, knowing that whoever he was now, he had once not been Dr Singh.

'No!' He shook his head, and with a galvanic effort managed to wrench loose one arm. He was seized at the shoulder and raised his free arm to shield himself from the lights and the pressing faces.

His glasses had fallen off and been trampled underfoot, but he could see more clearly without them. He looked at his hand. Even in the pale light the darker pigmentation was plain. His fingers were small and neat, an unfamiliar scar marking one of the knuckles.

Then he felt the small goatee beard on his chin.

Inside his mind the last island of resistance slid away into the dark unremembered past.

'Dr Krishnamurti Singh,' the inspector stated.

Among the suitcases in the doorway Judith Elliott watched the police cars drive away toward Hampstead village. Upstairs the two children romped about in the nursery.

'How horrid! I'm glad the children didn't see him arrested. He was struggling like an animal.'

Elliott paid off the taxi-driver and then closed the door. 'Who was it, by the way? No one we know, I hope?'

Judith glanced around the hall, and noticed the telephone receiver on the floor. She bent down and replaced it. 'The taxi-driver said it was some Harley Street psychiatrist. An Indian doctor. Apparently he strangled his wife in the bath. The strange thing is she was already dying of a brain tumour.'

Elliott grimaced. 'Gruesome. Perhaps he was trying to save her pain.'

'By strangling her fully conscious? A typical masculine notion, darling.'

Elliott laughed as they strolled into the lounge. 'Well, my dear, did you have a good time? How was Molly?'

'She was fine. We had a great time together. Missed you, of course. I felt a bit off-colour yesterday, got knocked over by a big wave and swallowed a lot of water.' She hesitated, looking through the window at the park. 'You know, it's rather funny, but twenty minutes ago I tried to ring you from the station and got a Harley Street number by mistake. I spoke to an Indian. He sounded rather like a doctor.'

Elliott grinned. 'Probably the same man.'

'That's what I thought. But he couldn't have got from Harley Street to Hampstead so quickly, could he? The driver said the police have been looking for him here all afternoon.'

'Maybe they've got the wrong man. Unless there are two Dr Singhs.' Elliott snapped his fingers. 'That's odd, where did I get the name? Must have read about him in the papers.'

Judith nodded, coming over to him. 'It was in this morning's.' She took off her hat and placed it on the mantelpiece. 'Indians are strange people. I don't know why, but yesterday when I was getting over my wave I was thinking about an Indian girl I knew once. All I can remember is her name. Ramadya. I think she was drowned. She was very sweet and pretty.'

'Like you.' Elliott put his hands around her waist, but Judith pointed to the broken glass in the fireplace.

'I say, I can see I've been away.' With a laugh she put her hands on his shoulders and squeezed him, then drew away in alarm.

'Darling, where did you get this peculiar suit? For heaven's sake, look!' She squeezed his jacket, and the water poured from her fingers as from a wet sponge. 'You're soaked through! Where on earth have you been all day?'

**, 1963**

# THE SCREEN GAME

Every afternoon during the summer at Ciraquito we play the screen game. After lunch today, when the arcades and café terraces were empty and everyone was lying asleep indoors, three of us drove out in Raymond Mayo's Lincoln along the road to Vermilion Sands.

The season had ended, and already the desert had begun to move in again for the summer, drifting against the yellowing shutters of the cigarette kiosks, surrounding the town with immense banks of luminous ash. Along the horizon the flat-topped mesas rose into the sky like the painted cones of a volcano jungle. The beach-houses had been empty for weeks, and abandoned sand-yachts stood in the centre of the lakes, embalmed in the opaque heat. Only the highway showed any signs of activity, the motion sculpture of concrete ribbon unfolding across the landscape.

Twenty miles from Ciraquito, where the highway forks to Red Beach and Vermilion Sands, we turned on to the remains of an old gravel track that ran away among the sand reefs. Only a year earlier this had been a well-kept private road, but the ornamental gateway lay collapsed to one side, and the guardhouse was a nesting place for scorpions and sand-rays.

Few people ever ventured far up the road. Continuous rock slides disturbed the area, and large sections of the surface had slipped away into the reefs. In addition a curious but unmistakable atmosphere of menace hung over the entire zone, marking it off from the remainder of the desert. The hanging galleries of the reefs were more convoluted and sinister, like the tortured demons of medieval cathedrals. Massive towers of obsidian reared over the roadway like stone gallows, their cornices streaked with iron-red dust. The light seemed duller, unlike the rest of the desert, occasionally flaring into a sepulchral glow as if some subterranean fire-cloud had boiled to the surface of the rocks. The surrounding peaks and spires shut out the desert plain, and the only sounds were the echoes of the engine growling among the hills and the piercing cries of the sand-rays wheeling over the open mouths of the reefs like hieratic birds.

For half a mile we followed the road as it wound like a petrified snake above the reefs, and our conversation became more sporadic and fell away entirely, resuming only when we began our descent through a shallow valley. A few abstract sculptures stood by the roadside. Once these were sonic, responding to the slipstream of a passing car with a series of warning vibratos, but now the Lincoln passed them unrecognized.

Abruptly, around a steep bend, the reefs and peaks vanished, and the wide expanse of an inland sand-lake lay before us, the great summer house of Lagoon West on its shore. Fragments of light haze hung over the dunes like untethered clouds. The tyres cut softly through the cerise sand, and soon we were overrunning what appeared to be the edge of an immense chessboard of black and white marble squares. More statues appeared, some buried to their heads, others toppled from their plinths by the drifting dunes.

Looking out at them this afternoon, I felt, not for the first time, that the whole landscape was compounded of illusion, the hulks of fabulous dreams drifting across it like derelict galleons. As we followed the road towards the lake, the huge wreck of Lagoon West passed us slowly on our left. Its terraces and balconies were deserted, and the once marble-white surface was streaked and lifeless. Staircases ended abruptly in midflight, and the floors hung like sagging marquees.

In the centre of the terrace the screens stood where we had left them the previous afternoon, their zodiacal emblems flashing like serpents. We walked across to them through the hot sunlight. For the next hour we played the screen game, pushing the screens along their intricate pathways, advancing and retreating across the smooth marble floor.

No one watched us, but once, fleetingly, I thought I saw a tall figure in a blue cape hidden in the shadows of a second-floor balcony.

'Emerelda!'

On a sudden impulse I shouted to her, but almost without moving she had vanished among the hibiscus and bougainvillaea. As her name echoed away among the dunes I knew that we had made our last attempt to lure her from the balcony.

'Paul.' Twenty yards away, Raymond and Tony had reached the car. 'Paul, we're leaving.'

Turning my back to them, I looked up at the great bleached hulk of Lagoon West leaning into the sunlight. Somewhere, along the shore of the sand-lake, music was playing faintly, echoing among the exposed quartz veins. A few isolated chords at first, the fragments hung on the afternoon air, the sustained tremolos suspended above my head like the humming of invisible insects.

As the phrases coalesced, I remembered when we had first played the screen game at Lagoon West. I remembered the last tragic battle with the jewelled insects, and I remembered Emerelda Garland . . .

I first saw Emerelda Garland the previous summer, shortly after the film company arrived in Ciraquito and was invited by Charles Van Stratten to use the locations at Lagoon West. The company, Orpheus Productions,

Inc. – known to the aficionados of the café terraces such as Raymond Mayo and Tony Sapphire as the 'ebb tide of the new wave' – was one of those experimental units whose output is destined for a single rapturous showing at the Cannes Film Festival, and who rely for their financial backing on the generosity of the many millionaire dilettantes who apparently feel a compulsive need to cast themselves in the role of Lorenzo de Medici.

Not that there was anything amateurish about the equipment and technical resources of Orpheus Productions. The fleet of location trucks and recording studios which descended on Ciraquito on one of those empty August afternoons looked like the entire D-Day task force, and even the more conservative estimates of the budget for *Aphrodite 80*, the film we helped to make at Lagoon West, amounted to at least twice the gross national product of a Central American republic. What was amateurish was the indifference to normal commercial restraints, and the unswerving dedication to the highest aesthetic standards.

All this, of course, was made possible by the largesse of Charles Van Stratten. To begin with, when we were first co-opted into *Aphrodite 80*, some of us were inclined to be amused by Charles's naive attempts to produce a masterpiece, but later we all realized that there was something touching about Charles's earnestness. None of us, however, was aware of the private tragedy which drove him on through the heat and dust of that summer at Lagoon West, and the grim nemesis waiting behind the canvas floats and stage props.

At the time he became the sole owner of Orpheus Productions, Charles Van Stratten had recently celebrated his fortieth birthday, but to all intents he was still a quiet and serious undergraduate. A scion of one of the world's wealthiest banking families, in his early twenties he had twice been briefly married, first to a Neapolitan countess, and then to a Hollywood starlet, but the most influential figure in Charles's life was his mother. This domineering harridan, who sat like an immense ormolu spider in her sombre Edwardian mansion on Park Avenue, surrounded by dark galleries filled with Rubens and Rembrandt, had been widowed shortly after Charles's birth, and obviously regarded Charles as providence's substitute for her husband. Cunningly manipulating a web of trust funds and residuary legacies, she ruthlessly eliminated both Charles's wives (the second committed suicide in a Venetian gondola, the first eloped with his analyst), and then herself died in circumstances of some mystery at the summer-house at Lagoon West.

Despite the immense publicity attached to the Van Stratten family, little was ever known about the old dowager's death – officially she tripped over a second-floor balcony – and Charles retired completely from the limelight of international celebrity for the next five years. Now and then he would emerge briefly at the Venice Biennale, or serve as co-sponsor of some cultural foundation, but otherwise he retreated into the vacuum left by his mother's death. Rumour had it – at least in Ciraquito – that

Charles himself had been responsible for her quietus, as if revenging (how long overdue!) the tragedy of Oedipus, when the dowager, scenting the prospect of a third liaison, had descended like Jocasta upon Lagoon West and caught Charles and his paramour *in flagrante.*

Much as I liked the story, the first glimpse of Charles Van Stratten dispelled the possibility. Five years after his mother's death, Charles still behaved as if she were watching his every movement through tripod-mounted opera glasses on some distant balcony. His youthful figure was a little more portly, but his handsome aristocratic face, its strong jaw belied by an indefinable weakness around the mouth, seemed somehow daunted and indecisive, as if he lacked complete conviction in his own identity.

Shortly after the arrival in Ciraquito of Orpheus Productions, the property manager visited the cafés in the artists' quarters, canvassing for scenic designers. Like most of the painters in Ciraquito and Vermilion Sands, I was passing through one of my longer creative pauses. I had stayed on in the town after the season ended, idling away the long, empty afternoons under the awning at the Café Fresco, and was already showing symptoms of beach fatigue – irreversible boredom and inertia. The prospect of actual work seemed almost a novelty.

'*Aphrodite 80,*' Raymond Mayo explained when he returned to our table after a kerb-side discussion. 'The whole thing reeks of integrity – they want local artists to paint the flats, large abstract designs for the desert backgrounds. They'll pay a dollar per square foot.'

'That's rather mean,' I commented.

'The property manager apologized, but Van Stratten is a millionaire – money means nothing to him. If it's any consolation, Raphael and Michelangelo were paid a smaller rate for the Sistine Chapel.'

'Van Stratten has a bigger budget,' Tony Sapphire reminded him. 'Besides, the modern painter is a more complex type, his integrity needs to be buttressed by substantial assurances. Is Paul a painter in the tradition of Leonardo and Larry Rivers, or a cut-price dauber?'

Moodily we watched the distant figure of the property manager move from café to café.

'How many square feet do they want?' I asked.

'About a million,' Raymond said.

Later that afternoon, as we turned off the Red Beach road and were waved on past the guardhouse to Lagoon West, we could hear the sonic sculptures high among the reefs echoing and hooting to the cavalcade of cars speeding over the hills. Droves of startled rays scattered in the air like clouds of exploding soot, their frantic cries lost among the spires and reefs. Preoccupied by the prospect of our vast fees – I had hastily sworn in Tony and Raymond as my assistants – we barely noticed the strange landscape we were crossing, the great gargoyles of red basalt that uncoiled themselves into the air like the spires of demented cathedrals. From the

Red Beach – Vermilion Sands highway – the hills seemed permanently veiled by the sand haze, and Lagoon West, although given a brief notoriety by the death of Mrs Van Stratten, remained isolated and unknown. From the beach-houses on the southern shore of the sand-lake two miles away, the distant terraces and tiered balconies of the summer-house could just be seen across the fused sand, jutting into the cerise evening sky like a stack of dominoes. There was no access to the house along the beach. Quartz veins cut deep fissures into the surface, the reefs of ragged sandstone reared into the air like the rusting skeletons of forgotten ships.

The whole of Lagoon West was a continuous slide area. Periodically a soft boom would disturb the morning silence as one of the galleries of compacted sand, its intricate grottoes and colonnades like an inverted baroque palace, would suddenly dissolve and avalanche gently into the internal precipice below. Most years Charles Van Stratten was away in Europe, and the house was believed to be empty. The only sound the occupants of the beach villas would hear was the faint music of the sonic sculptures carried across the lake by the thermal rollers.

It was to this landscape, with its imperceptible transition between the real and the superreal, that Charles Van Stratten had brought the camera crews and location vans of Orpheus Productions, Inc. As the Lincoln joined the column of cars moving towards the summer-house, we could see the great canvas hoardings, at least two hundred yards wide and thirty feet high, which a team of construction workers was erecting among the reefs a quarter of a mile from the house. Decorated with abstract symbols, these would serve as backdrops to the action, and form a fragmentary labyrinth winding in and out of the hills and dunes.

One of the large terraces below the summer-house served as a parking lot, and we made our way through the unloading crews to where a group of men in crocodile-skin slacks and raffia shirts – then the uniform of avant-garde film men – were gathered around a heavily jowled man like a perspiring bear who was holding a stack of script boards under one arm and gesticulating wildly with the other. This was Orson Kanin, director of *Aphrodite* 80 and co-owner with Charles Van Stratten of Orpheus Productions. Sometime *enfant terrible* of the futurist cinema, but now a portly barrel-stomached fifty, Kanin had made his reputation some twenty years earlier with *Blind Orpheus*, a neo-Freudian, horror-film version of the Greek legend. According to Kanin's interpretation, Orpheus deliberately breaks the taboo and looks Eurydice in the face because he wants to be rid of her; in a famous nightmare sequence which projects his unconscious loathing, he becomes increasingly aware of something cold and strange about his resurrected wife, and finds that she is a disintegrating corpse.

As we joined the periphery of the group, a characteristic Kanin script conference was in full swing, a non-stop pantomime of dramatized incidents from the imaginary script, anecdotes, salary promises and bad puns, all delivered in a rich fruity baritone. Sitting on the balustrade beside Kanin was a handsome, youthful man with a sensitive face whom I recognized to be Charles Van Stratten. Now and then, *sotto voce*, he would interject some comment that would be noted by one of the secretaries and incorporated into Kanin's monologue.

As the conference proceeded I gathered that they would begin to shoot the film in some three weeks' time, and that it would be performed entirely without script. Kanin only seemed perturbed by the fact that no one had yet been found to play the Aphrodite of *Aphrodite* 80 but Charles Van Stratten interposed here to assure Kanin that he himself would provide the actress.

At this eyebrows were raised knowingly. 'Of course,' Raymond murmured. '*Droit de seigneur.* I wonder who the next Mrs Van Stratten is?'

But Charles Van Stratten seemed unaware of these snide undertones. Catching sight of me, he excused himself and came over to us.

'Paul Golding?' He took my hand in a soft but warm grip. We had never met but I presumed he recognized me from the photographs in the art reviews. 'Kanin told me you'd agreed to do the scenery. It's wonderfully encouraging.' He spoke in a light, pleasant voice absolutely without affectation. 'There's so much confusion here it's a relief to know that at least the scenic designs will be first-class.' Before I could demur he took my arm and began to walk away along the terrace towards the hoardings in the distance. 'Let's get some air. Kanin will keep this up for a couple of hours at least.'

Leaving Raymond and Tony, I followed him across the huge marble squares.

'Kanin keeps worrying about his leading actress,' he went on. 'Kanin always marries his latest protégé – he claims it's the only way he can make them respond fully to his direction, but I suspect there's an old-fashioned puritan lurking within the cavalier. This time he's going to be disappointed, though not by the actress, may I add. The Aphrodite I have in mind will outshine Milos's.'

'The film sounds rather ambitious,' I commented, 'but I'm sure Kanin is equal to it.'

'Of course he is. He's very nearly a genius, and that should be good enough.' He paused for a moment, hands in the pockets of his dove-grey suit, before translating himself like a chess piece along a diagonal square. 'It's a fascinating subject, you know. The title is misleading, a box-office concession. The film is really Kanin's final examination of the Orpheus legend. The whole question of the illusions which exist in any relationship to make it workable, and of the barriers we willingly accept to hide ourselves from each other. How much reality can we stand?'

We reached one of the huge hoardings that stretched away among the reefs. Jutting upwards from the spires and grottoes, it seemed to shut off half the sky, and already I felt the atmosphere of shifting illusion and reality that enclosed the whole of Lagoon West, the subtle displacement of time and space. The great hoardings seemed to be both barriers and corridors. Leading away radially from the house and breaking up the landscape, of which they revealed sudden unrelated glimpses, they introduced a curiously appealing element of uncertainty into the placid afternoon, an impression reinforced by the emptiness and enigmatic presence of the summer-house.

Returning to Kanin's conference, we followed the edge of the terrace. Here the sand had drifted over the balustrade which divided the public sector of the grounds from the private. Looking up at the lines of balconies on the south face, I noticed someone standing in the shadows below one of the awnings.

Something flickered brightly from the ground at my feet. Momentarily reflecting the full disc of the sun, like a polished node of sapphire or quartz, the light flashed among the dust, then seemed to dart sideways below the balustrade.

'My God, a scorpion!' I pointed to the insect crouching away from us, the red scythe of its tail beckoning slowly. I assumed that the thickened chitin of the headpiece was reflecting the light, and then saw that a small faceted stone had been set into the skull. As it edged forward into the light, the jewel burned in the sun like an incandescent crystal.

Charles Van Stratten stepped past me. Almost pushing me aside, he glanced towards the shuttered balconies. He feinted deftly with one foot at the scorpion, and before the insect could recover had stamped it into the dust.

'Right, Paul,' he said in a firm voice. 'I think your suggested designs are excellent. You've caught the spirit of the whole thing exactly, as I knew you would.' Buttoning his jacket he made off towards the film unit, barely pausing to scrape the damp husk of the crushed carapace from his shoe.

I caught up with him. 'That scorpion was jewelled,' I said. 'There was a diamond, or zircon, inset in the head.'

He waved impatiently and then took a pair of large sunglasses from his breast pocket. Masked, his face seemed harder and more autocratic, reminding me of our true relationship.

'An illusion, Paul,' he said. 'Some of the insects here are dangerous. You must be more careful.' His point made, he relaxed and flashed me his most winning smile.

Rejoining Tony and Raymond, I watched Charles Van Stratten walk off through the technicians and stores staff. His stride was noticeably more purposive, and he brushed aside an assistant producer without bothering to turn his head.

'Well, Paul.' Raymond greeted me expansively. 'There's no script, no star, no film in the cameras, and no one has the faintest idea what he's supposed to be doing. But there are a million square feet of murals waiting to be painted. It all seems perfectly straightforward.'

I looked back across the terrace to where we had seen the scorpion. 'I suppose it is,' I said.

Somewhere in the dust a jewel glittered brightly.

Two days later I saw another of the jewelled insects.

Suppressing my doubts about Charles Van Stratten, I was busy preparing my designs for the hoardings. Although Raymond's first estimate of a million square feet was exaggerated – less than a tenth of this would be needed – the amount of work and materials required was substantial. In effect I was about to do nothing less than repaint the entire desert.

Each morning I went out to Lagoon West and worked among the reefs, adapting the designs to the contours and colours of the terrain. Most of the time I was alone in the hot sun. After the initial frenzy of activity Orpheus Productions had lost momentum. Kanin had gone off to a film festival at Red Beach and most of the assistant producers and writers had retired to the swimming pool at the Hotel Neptune in Vermilion Sands. Those who remained behind at Lagoon West were now sitting half asleep under the coloured umbrellas erected around the mobile cocktail bar.

The only sign of movement came from Charles Van Stratten, roving tirelessly in his white suit among the reefs and sand spires. Now and then I would hear one of the sonic sculptures on the upper balconies of the summer-house change its note, and turn to see him standing beside it. His sonic profile evoked a strange, soft sequence of chords, interwoven by sharper, almost plaintive notes that drifted away across the still afternoon air towards the labyrinth of great hoardings that now surrounded the summer-house. All day he would wander among them, pacing out the perimeters and diagonals as if trying to square the circle of some private enigma, the director of a Wagnerian psychodrama that would involve us all in its cathartic unfolding.

Shortly after noon, when an intense pall of yellow light lay over the desert, dissolving the colours in its glazed mantle, I sat down on the balustrade, waiting for the meridian to pass. The sand-lake shimmered in the thermal gradients like an immense pool of sluggish wax. A few yards away something flickered in the bright sand, a familiar flare of light. Shielding my eyes, I found the source, the diminutive Promethean bearer of this brilliant corona. The spider, a Black Widow, approached on its stilted legs, a blaze of staccato signals pouring from its crown. It stopped and pivoted, revealing the large sapphire inset into its head.

More points of light flickered. Within a moment the entire terrace sparkled with jewelled light. Quickly I counted a score of the insects – turquoised scorpions, a purple mantis with a giant topaz like a tiered crown, and more than a dozen spiders, pinpoints of emerald and sapphire light lancing from their heads.

Above them, hidden in the shadows among the bougainvillaea on her balcony, a tall white-faced figure in a blue gown looked down at me.

I stepped over the balustrade, carefully avoiding the motionless insects.

Separated from the remainder of the terrace by the west wing of the summer-house, I had entered a new zone, where the bonelike pillars of the loggia, the glimmering surface of the sand-lake, and the jewelled insects enclosed me in a sudden empty limbo.

For a few moments I stood below the balcony from which the insects had emerged, still watched by this strange sybilline figure presiding over her private world. I felt that I had strayed across the margins of a dream, on to an internal landscape of the psyche projected upon the sun-filled terraces around me.

But before I could call to her, footsteps grated softly in the loggia. A dark-haired man of about fifty, with a closed, expressionless face, stood among the columns, his black suit neatly buttoned. He looked down at me with the impassive eyes of a funeral director.

The shutters withdrew upon the balcony, and the jewelled insects returned from their foray. Surrounding me, their brilliant crowns glittered with diamond hardness.

Each afternoon, as I returned from the reefs with my sketch pad, I would see the jewelled insects moving in the sunlight beside the lake, while their blue-robed mistress, the haunted Venus of Lagoon West, watched them from her balcony. Despite the frequency of her appearances, Charles Van Stratten made no attempt to explain her presence. His elaborate preparations for the filming of *Aphrodite* 80 almost complete, he became more and more preoccupied.

An outline scenario had been agreed on. To my surprise the first scene was to be played on the lake terrace, and would take the form of a shadow ballet, for which I painted a series of screens to be moved about like chess pieces. Each was about twelve feet high, a large canvas mounted on a wooden trestle, representing one of the zodiac signs. Like the protagonist of *The Cabinet of Dr Caligari*, trapped in a labyrinth of tilting walls, the Orphic hero of *Aphrodite 80* would appear searching for his lost Eurydice among the shifting time stations.

So the screen game, which we were to play tirelessly on so many occasions, made its appearance. As I completed the last of the screens and watched a group of extras perform the first movements of the game under Charles Van Stratten's directions, I began to realize the extent to which we were all supporting players in a gigantic charade of Charles's devising.

Its real object soon became apparent.

The summer-house was deserted when I drove out to Lagoon West the next weekend, an immense canopy of silence hanging over the lake and the surrounding hills. The twelve screens stood on the terrace above the beach, their vivid, heraldic designs melting into blurred pools of turquoise and carmine which bled away in horizontal layers across the air. Someone had rearranged the screens to form a narrow spiral corridor. As I straightened them, the train of a white gown disappeared with a startled flourish among the shadows within.

Guessing the probable identity of this pale and nervous intruder, I stepped quietly into the corridor. I pushed back one of the screens, a large Scorpio in royal purple, and suddenly found myself in the centre of the maze, little more than an arm's length from the strange figure I had seen on the balcony. For a moment she failed to notice me. Her exquisite white face, like a marble mask, veined by a faint shadow of violet that seemed like a delicate interior rosework, was raised to the canopy of sunlight which cut across the upper edges of the screens. She wore a long beach-robe, with a flared hood that enclosed her head like a protective bower.

One of the jewelled insects nestled on a fold above her neck. There was a curious glacé immobility about her face, investing the white skin with an almost sepulchral quality, the soft down which covered it like grave's dust.

'Who –?' Startled, she stepped back. The insects scattered at her feet, winking on the floor like a jewelled carpet. She stared at me in surprise, drawing the hood of her gown around her face like an exotic flower withdrawing into its foliage. Conscious of the protective circle of insects, she lifted her chin and composed herself.

'I'm sorry to interrupt you,' I said. 'I didn't realize there was anyone here. I'm flattered that you like the screens.'

The autocratic chin lowered fractionally, and her head, with its swirl of blue hair, emerged from the hood. '*You* painted these?' she confirmed. 'I thought they were Dr Gruber's . . .' She broke off, tired or bored by the effort of translating her thoughts into speech.

'They're for Charles Van Stratten's film,' I explained. '*Aphrodite 80*. The film about Orpheus he's making here.' I added: 'You must ask him to give you a part. You'd be a great adornment.'

'A film?' Her voice cut across mine. 'Listen. Are you sure they are for this film? It's important that I know –'

'Quite sure.' Already I was beginning to find her exhausting. Talking to her was like walking across a floor composed of blocks of varying heights, an analogy reinforced by the squares of the terrace, into which her presence had let another random dimension. 'They're going to film one of the scenes here. Of course,' I volunteered when she greeted this news with a frown, 'you're free to play with the screens. In fact, if you like, I'll paint some for you.'

'Will you?' From the speed of the response I could see that I had at last penetrated to the centre of her attention. 'Can you start today? Paint as many as you can, just like these. Don't change the designs.' She gazed around at the zodiacal symbols looming from the shadows like the murals painted in dust and blood on the walls of a Toltec funeral corridor. 'They're wonderfully alive, sometimes I think they're even more real than Dr Gruber. Though –' here she faltered '– I don't know how I'll pay you. You see, they don't give me any money.' She smiled at me like an anxious child, then brightened suddenly. She knelt down and picked one of the jewelled scorpions from the floor. 'Would you like one of these?' The flickering insect, with its brilliant ruby crown, tottered unsteadily on her white palm.

Footsteps approached, the firm rap of leather on marble. 'They may be rehearsing today,' I said. 'Why don't you watch? I'll take you on a tour of the sets.'

As I started to pull back the screens I felt the long fingers of her hand on my arm. A mood of acute agitation had come over her.

'Relax,' I said. 'I'll tell them to go away. Don't worry, they won't spoil your game.'

'No! Listen, please!' The insects scattered and darted as the outer circle of screens was pulled back. In a few seconds the whole world of illusion was dismantled and exposed to the hot sunlight.

Behind the Scorpio appeared the watchful face of the dark-suited man. A smile played like a snake on his lips.

'Ah, Miss Emerelda,' he greeted her in a purring voice. 'I think you should come indoors. The afternoon heat is intense and you tire very easily.'

The insects retreated from his black patent shoes. Looking into his eyes, I caught a glimpse of deep reserves of patience, like that of an experienced nurse used to the fractious moods and uncertainties of a chronic invalid.

'Not now,' Emerelda insisted. 'I'll come in a few moments.'

'I've just been describing the screens,' I explained.

'So I gather, Mr Golding,' he rejoined evenly. 'Miss Emerelda,' he called.

For a moment they appeared to have reached deadlock. Emerelda, the jewelled insects at her feet, stood beside me, her hand on my arm, while her guardian waited, the same thin smile on his lips. More footsteps approached. The remaining screens were pushed back and the plump, well-talcumed figure of Charles Van Stratten appeared, his urbane voice raised in greeting.

'What's this – a story conference?' he asked jocularly. He broke off when he saw Emerelda and her guardian. 'Dr Gruber? What's going – Emerelda my dear?'

Smoothly, Dr Gruber interjected. 'Good afternoon, sir. Miss Garland is about to return to her room.'

'Good, good,' Charles exclaimed. For the first time I had known him he seemed unsure of himself. He made a tentative approach to Emerelda, who was staring at him fixedly. She drew her robe around her and stepped quickly through the screens. Charles moved forwards, uncertain whether to follow her.

'Thank you, doctor,' he muttered. There was a flash of patent leather heels, and Charles and I were alone among the screens. On the floor at our feet was a single jewelled mantis. Without thinking, Charles bent down to pick it up, but the insect snapped at him. He withdrew his fingers with a wan smile, as if accepting the finality of Emerelda's departure.

Recognizing me with an effort, Charles pulled himself together. 'Well, Paul, I'm glad you and Emerelda were getting on so well. I knew you'd make an excellent job of the screens.'

We walked out into the sunlight. After a pause he said, 'That is Emerelda Garland; she's lived here since mother died. It was a tragic experience, Dr Gruber thinks she may never recover.'

'He's her doctor?'

Charles nodded. 'One of the best I could find. For some reason Emerelda feels herself responsible for mother's death. She's refused to leave here.'

I pointed to the screens. 'Do you think they help?'

'Of course. Why do you suppose we're here at all?' He lowered his voice, although Lagoon West was deserted. 'Don't tell Kanin yet, but you've just met the star of *Aphrodite 80*.'

'What?' Incredulously, I stopped. 'Emerelda? Do you mean that she's going to play –?'

'Eurydice.' Charles nodded. 'Who better?'

'But Charles, she's . . .' I searched for a discreet term.

'That's exactly the point. Believe me, Paul,' – here Charles smiled at me with an expression of surprising canniness – 'this film is not as abstract as Kanin thinks. In fact, its sole purpose is therapeutic. You see, Emerelda was once a minor film actress, I'm convinced the camera crews and sets will help to carry her back to the past, to the period before her appalling shock. It's the only way left, a sort of total psychodrama. The choice of theme, the Orpheus legend and its associations, fit the situation exactly – I see myself as a latter-day Orpheus trying to rescue my Eurydice from Dr Gruber's hell.' He smiled bleakly, as if aware of the slenderness of the analogy and its faint hopes. 'Emerelda's withdrawn completely into her private world, spends all her time inlaying these insects with her jewels. With luck the screens will lead her out into the rest of this synthetic landscape. After all, if she knows that everything around her is unreal she'll cease to fear it.'

'But can't you simply move her physically from Lagoon West?' I asked. 'Perhaps Gruber is the wrong doctor for her. I can't understand why you've kept her here all these years.'

'I haven't kept her, Paul,' he said earnestly. 'She's clung to this place and its nightmare memories. Now she even refuses to let me come near her.'

We parted and he walked away among the deserted dunes. In the background the great hoardings I had designed shut out the distant reefs and mesas. Huge blocks of colour had been sprayed on to the designs, superimposing a new landscape upon the desert. The geometric forms loomed and wavered in the haze, like the shifting symbols of a beckoning dream.

As I watched Charles disappear, I felt a sudden sense of pity for his subtle but naive determination. Wondering whether to warn him of his almost certain failure, I rubbed the raw bruises on my arm. While she started at him, Emerelda's fingers had clasped my arm with unmistakable fierceness, her sharp nails locked together like a clamp of daggers.

So, each afternoon, we began to play the screen game, moving the zodiacal emblems to and fro across the terrace. As I sat on the balustrade and watched Emerelda Garland's first tentative approaches, I wondered how far all of us were becoming ensnared by Charles Van Stratten, by the painted desert and the sculpture singing from the aerial terraces of the summer-house. Into all this Emerelda Garland had now emerged, like a beautiful but nervous wraith. First she would slip among the screens as they gathered below her balcony, and then, hidden behind the large Virgo at their centre, would move across the floor towards the lake, enclosed by the shifting pattern of screens.

Once I left my seat beside Charles and joined the game. Gradually I manœuvred my screen, a small Sagittarius, into the centre of the maze where I found Emerelda in a narrow shifting cubicle, swaying from side to side as if entranced by the rhythm of the game, the insects scattered at her feet. When I approached she clasped my hand and ran away down a corridor, her gown falling loosely around her bare shoulders. As the screens once more reached the summer-house, she gathered her train in one hand and disappeared among the columns of the loggia.

Walking back to Charles, I found a jewelled mantis nestling like a brooch on the lapel of my jacket, its crown of amethyst melting in the fading sunlight.

'She's coming out, Paul,' Charles said. 'Already she's accepted the screens, soon she'll be able to leave them.' He frowned at the jewelled mantis on my palm. 'A present from Emerelda. Rather two-edged, I think, those stings are dangerous. Still, she's grateful to you, Paul, as I am. Now I know that only the artist can create an absolute reality. Perhaps you should paint a few more screens.'

'Gladly, Charles, if you're sure that . . .'

But Charles merely nodded to himself and walked away towards the film crew.

During the next days I painted several new screens, duplicating the zodiacal emblems, so that each afternoon the game became progressively slower and more intricate, the thirty screens forming a multiple labyrinth. For a few minutes, at the climax of the game, I would find Emerelda in the dark centre with the screens jostling and tilting around her, the sculpture on the roof hooting in the narrow interval of open sky.

'Why don't you join the game?' I asked Charles. After his earlier elation he was becoming impatient. Each evening as he drove back to Ciraquito the plume of dust behind his speeding Maserati would rise progressively higher into the pale air. He had lost interest in *Aphrodite 80*. Fortunately Kanin had found that the painted desert of Lagoon West could not be reproduced by any existing colour process, and the film was now being shot from models in a rented studio at Red Beach. 'Perhaps if Emerelda saw you in the maze . . .'

'No, no.' Charles shook his head categorically, then stood up and paced about. 'Paul, I'm less sure of this now.'

Unknown to him, I had painted a dozen more screens. Early that morning I had hidden them among the others on the terrace.

Three nights later, tired of conducting my courtship of Emerelda Garland within a painted maze, I drove out to Lagoon West, climbing through the darkened hills whose contorted forms reared in the swinging headlamps like the smoke clouds of some sunken hell. In the distance, beside the lake, the angular terraces of the summer-house hung in the grey opaque air, as if suspended by invisible wires from the indigo clouds which stretched like velvet towards the few faint lights along the beach two miles away.

The sculptures on the upper balconies were almost silent, and I moved past them carefully, drawing only a few muted chords from them, the faint sounds carried from one statue to the next to the roof of the summer-house and then lost on the midnight air.

From the loggia I looked down at the labyrinth of screens, and at the jewelled insects scattered across the terrace, sparkling on the dark marble like the reflection of a star field.

I found Emerelda Garland among the screens, her white face an oval halo in the shadows, almost naked in a silk gown like a veil of moonlight. She was leaning against a huge Taurus with her pale arms outstretched at her sides, like Europa supplicant before the bull, the luminous spectres of the zodiac guard surrounding her. Without moving her head, she watched me approach and take her hands. Her blue hair swirled in the dark wind as we moved through the screens and crossed the staircase into the summer-house. The expression on her face, whose porcelain planes reflected the turquoise light of her eyes, was one of almost terrifying calm, as if she were moving through some inner dreamscape of the psyche with the confidence of a sleepwalker. My arm around her waist, I guided her up the steps to her suite, realizing that I was less her lover than the architect of her fantasies. For a moment the ambiguous nature of my role, and the questionable morality of abducting a beautiful but insane woman, made me hesitate.

We had reached the inner balcony which ringed the central hall of the summer-house. Below us a large sonic-sculpture emitted a tense nervous pulse, as if roused from its midnight silence by my hesitant step.

'Wait!' I pulled Emerelda back from the next flight of stairs, rousing her from her self-hypnotic torpor. 'Up there!'

A silent figure in a dark suit stood at the rail outside the door of Emerelda's suite, the downward inclination of his head clearly perceptible.

'Oh, my God!' With both hands Emerelda clung tightly to my arm, her smooth face seized by a rictus of horror and anticipation. 'She's there . . . for heaven's sake, Paul, take me –'

'It's Gruber!' I snapped. 'Dr Gruber! Emerelda!'

As we recrossed the entrance the train of Emerelda's gown drew a discordant wail from the statue. In the moonlight the insects still flickered like a carpet of diamonds. I held her shoulders, trying to revive her.

'Emerelda! We'll leave here – take you away from Lagoon West and this insane place.' I pointed to my car, parked by the beach among the dunes. 'We'll go to Vermilion Sands or Red Beach, you'll be able to forget Dr Gruber for ever.'

We hurried towards the car, Emerelda's gown gathering up the insects as we swept past them. I heard her short cry in the moonlight and she tore away from me. I stumbled among the flickering insects. From my knees I saw her disappear into the screens.

For the next ten minutes, as I watched from the darkness by the beach, the jewelled insects moved towards her across the terrace, their last light fading like a vanishing night river.

I walked back to my car, and a quiet, white-suited figure appeared among the dunes and waited for me in the cool amber air, hands deep in his jacket pockets.

'You're a better painter than you know,' Charles said when I took my seat behind the wheel. 'On the last two nights she has made the same escape from me.'

He stared reflectively from the window as we drove back to Ciraquito, the sculptures in the canyon keening behind us like banshees.

The next afternoon, as I guessed, Charles Van Stratten at last played the screen game. He arrived shortly after the game had begun, walking through the throng of extras and cameramen near the car park, hands still thrust deep into the pockets of his white suit as if his sudden appearance among the dunes the previous night and his present arrival were continuous in time. He stopped by the balustrade on the opposite side of the terrace, where I sat with Tony Sapphire and Raymond Mayo, and stared pensively at the slow shuttling movements of the game, his grey eyes hidden below their blond brows.

By now there were so many screens in the game – over forty (I had secretly added more in an attempt to save Emerelda) – that most of the movement was confined to the centre of the group, as if emphasizing the self-immolated nature of the ritual. What had begun as a pleasant divertimento, a picturesque introduction to *Aphrodite 80*, had degenerated into a macabre charade, transforming the terrace into the exercise area of a nightmare.

Discouraged or bored by the slowness of the game, one by one the extras taking part began to drop out, sitting down on the balustrade beside Charles. Eventually only Emerelda was left – in my mind I could see her gliding in and out of the nexus of corridors, protected by the zodiacal deities I had painted – and now and then one of the screens in the centre would tilt slightly.

'You've designed a wonderful trap for her, Paul,' Raymond Mayo mused. 'A cardboard asylum.'

'It was Van Stratten's suggestion. We thought they might help her.'

Somewhere, down by the beach, a sculpture had begun to play, and its plaintive voice echoed over our heads. Several of the older sculptures whose sonic cores had corroded had been broken up and left on the beach, where they had taken root again. When the heat gradients roused them to life they would emit a brief strangled music, fractured parodies of their former song.

'Paul!' Tony Sapphire pointed across the terrace. 'What's going on? There's something –'

Fifty yards from us, Charles Van Stratten had stepped over the balustrade, and now stood out on one of the black marble squares, hands loosely at his sides, like a single chess piece opposing the massed array of the screens. Everyone else had gone, and the three of us were now alone with Charles and the hidden occupant of the screens.

The harsh song of the rogue sculpture still pierced the air. Two miles away, through the haze which partly obscured the distant shore, the beach-houses jutted among the dunes, and the fused surface of the lake, in which so many objects were embedded, seams of jade and obsidian, was like a segment of embalmed time, from which the music of the sculpture was a slowly expiring leak. The heat over the vermilion surface was like molten quartz, stirring sluggishly to reveal the distant mesas and reefs.

The haze cleared and the spires of the sand reefs seemed to loom forward, their red barbs clawing towards us through the air. The light drove through the opaque surface of the lake, illuminating its fossilized veins, and the threnody of the dying sculpture lifted to a climax.

'Emerelda!'

As we stood up, roused by his shout, Charles Van Stratten was running across the terrace. 'Emerelda!'

Before we could move he began to pull back the screens. toppling them backwards on to the ground. Within a few moments the terrace was a mêlée of tearing canvas and collapsing trestles, the huge emblems flung left and right out of his path like disintegrating floats at the end of a carnival.

Only when the original nucleus of half a dozen screens was left did he pause, hands on hips.

'Emerelda!' he shouted thickly.

Raymond turned to me. 'Paul, stop him, for heaven's sake!'

Striding forward, Charles pulled back the last of the screens. We had a sudden glimpse of Emerelda Garland retreating from the inrush of sunlight, her white gown flared around her like the broken wings of some enormous bird. Then, with an explosive flash, a brilliant vortex of light erupted from the floor at Emerelda's feet, a cloud of jewelled spiders and scorpions rose through the air and engulfed Charles Van Stratten.

Hands raised helplessly to shield his head, he raced across the terrace, the armada of jewelled insects pursuing him, spinning and diving on to his head. Just before he disappeared among the dunes by the beach, we saw him for a last terrifying moment, clawing helplessly at the jewelled helmet stitched into his face and shoulders. His voice rang out, a sustained cry on the note of the dying sculptures, lost on the stinging flight of the insects.

We found him among the sculptures, face downwards in the hot sand, the fabric of his white suit lacerated by a hundred punctures. Around him were scattered the jewels and crushed bodies of the insects he had killed, their knotted legs and mandibles like abstract ideograms, the sapphires and zircons dissolving in the light.

His swollen hands were filled with the jewels. The cloud of insects returned to the summer-house, where Dr Gruber's black-suited figure was silhouetted against the sky, poised on the white ledge like some minatory bird of nightmare. The only sounds came from the sculptures, which had picked up Charles Van Stratten's last cry and incorporated it into their own self-requiem.

'... "She ... killed" ...' Raymond stopped, shaking his head in amazement. 'Paul, can you hear them, the words are unmistakable.'

Stepping through the metal barbs of the sculpture, I knelt beside Charles, watching as one of the jewelled scorpions crawled from below his chin and scuttled away across the sand.

'Not him,' I said. 'What he was shouting was "She killed – Mrs Van Stratten." The old dowager, his mother. That's the real clue to this fantastic menage. Last night, when we saw Gruber by the rail outside her room – I realize now that was where the old harridan was standing when Emerelda pushed her. For years Charles kept her alone with her guilt here, probably afraid that he might be incriminated if the truth emerged – perhaps he was more responsible than we imagine. What he failed to realize was that Emerelda had lived so long with her guilt that she'd confused it with the person of Charles himself. Killing him was her only release –'

I broke off to find that Raymond and Tony had gone and were already half way back to the terrace. There was the distant sound of raised voices as members of the film company approached, and whistles shrilled above the exhaust of cars.

The bulky figure of Kanin came through the dunes, flanked by a trio of assistant producers. Their incredulous faces gaped at the prostrate body. The voices of the sculptures faded for the last time, carrying with them into the depths of the fossil lake the final plaintive cry of Charles Van Stratten.

A year later, after Orpheus Productions had left Lagoon West and the scandal surrounding Charles's death had subsided, we drove out again to the summer-house. It was one of those dull featureless afternoons when the desert is without lustre, the distant hills illuminated by brief flashes of light, and the great summer-house seemed drab and lifeless. The servants and Dr Gruber had left, and the estate was beginning to run down. Sand covered long stretches of the roadway, and the dunes rolled across the open terraces, toppling the sculptures. These were silent now, and the sepulchral emptiness was only broken by the hidden presence of Emerelda Garland.

We found the screens where they had been left, and on an impulse spent the first afternoon digging them out of the sand. Those that had rotted in the sunlight we burned in a pyre on the beach, and perhaps the ascending plumes of purple and carmine smoke first brought our presence to Emerelda. The next afternoon, as we played the screen game, I was conscious of her watching us, and saw a gleam of her blue gown among the shadows.

However, although we played each afternoon throughout the summer, she never joined us, despite the new screens I painted and added to the group. Only on the night I visited Lagoon West alone did she come down, but I could hear the voices of the sculptures calling again and fled at the sight of her white face.

By some acoustic freak, the dead sculptures along the beach had revived themselves, and once again I heard the faint haunted echoes of Charles Van Stratten's last cry before he was killed by the jewelled insects. All over the deserted summer-house the low refrain was taken up by the statues, echoing through the empty galleries and across the moonlit terraces, carried away to the mouths of the sand reefs, the last dark music of the painted night.

· **1963**

# ˙TIME OF PASSAGE

Sunlight spilled among the flowers and tombstones, turning the cemetery into a bright garden of sculpture. Like two large gaunt crows, the gravediggers leaned on their spades between the marble angels, their shadows arching across the smooth white flank of one of the recent graves.

The gilt lettering was still fresh and untarnished.

JAMES FALKMAN
1963–1901
'The End is but the Beginning'

Leisurely they began to pare back the crisp turf, then dismantled the headstone and swathed it in a canvas sheet, laying it behind the graves in the next aisle. Biddle, the older of the two, a lean man in a black waistcoat, pointed to the cemetery gates, where the first mourning party approached.

'They're here. Let's get our backs into it.'

The younger man, Biddle's son, watched the small procession winding through the graves. His nostrils scented the sweet broken earth. 'They're always early,' he murmured reflectively. 'It's a strange thing, you never see them come on time.'

A clock tolled from the chapel among the cypresses. Working swiftly, they scooped out the soft earth, piling it into a neat cone at the grave's head. A few minutes later, when the sexton arrived with the principal mourners, the polished teak of the coffin was exposed, and Biddle jumped down on to the lid and scraped away the damp earth clinging to its brass rim.

The ceremony was brief and the twenty mourners, led by Falkman's sister, a tall white-haired woman with a narrow autocratic face, leaning on her husband's arm, soon returned to the chapel. Biddle gestured to his son. They jerked the coffin out of the ground and loaded it on to a cart, strapping it down under the harness. Then they heaped the earth back into the grave and relaid the squares of turf.

As they pushed the cart back to the chapel the sunlight shone brightly among the thinning graves.

Forty-eight hours later the coffin arrived at James Falkman's large grey-stoned house on the upper slopes of Mortmere Park. The high-walled avenue was almost deserted and few people saw the hearse enter the tree-lined drive. The blinds were drawn over the windows, and huge wreaths rested among the furniture in the hall where Falkman lay motionless in his coffin on a mahogany table. Veiled by the dim light, his square strong-jawed face seemed composed and unblemished, a short lock of hair over his forehead making his expression less severe than his sister's.

A solitary beam of sunlight, finding its way through the dark sycamores which guarded the house, slowly traversed the room as the morning progressed, and shone for a few minutes upon Falkman's open eyes. Even after the beam had moved away a faint glimmer of light still remained in the pupils, like the reflection of a star glimpsed in the bottom of a dark well.

All day, helped by two of her friends, sharp-faced women in long black coats, Falkman's sister moved quietly about the house. Her quick deft hands shook the dust from the velvet curtains in the library, wound up the miniature Louis XV clock on the study desk, and reset the great barometer on the staircase. None of the women spoke to each other, but within a few hours the house was transformed, the dark wood in the hall gleaming as the first callers were admitted.

'Mr and Mrs Montefiore . . .'

'Mr and Mrs Caldwell . . .'

'Miss Evelyn Jermyn and Miss Elizabeth . . .'

'Mr Samuel Banbury . . .'

One by one nodding in acknowledgement as they were announced, the callers trooped into the hall and paused over the coffin, examining Falkman's face with discreet interest, then passed into the dining room where they were presented with a glass of port and a tray of sweetmeats. Most of them were elderly, over-dressed in the warm spring weather, one or two obviously ill at ease in the great oak-panelled house, and all unmistakably revealed the same air of hushed expectancy.

The following morning Falkman was lifted from his coffin and carried upstairs to the bedroom overlooking the drive. The winding sheet was removed from his frail body dressed in a pair of thick woollen pyjamas. He lay quietly between the cold sheets, his grey face sightless and reposed, unaware of his sister crying softly on the high-backed chair beside him. Only when Dr Markham called and put his hand on her shoulder did she contain herself, relieved to have given way to her feelings.

Almost as if this were a signal, Falkman opened his eyes. For a moment they wavered uncertainly, the pupils weak and watery. Then he gazed up at his sister's tear-marked face, his head motionless on the pillow. As she and the doctor leaned forward Falkman smiled fleetingly, his lips parting across his teeth in an expression of immense patience and understanding. Then apparently exhausted he lapsed into a deep sleep.

After securing the blinds over the windows, his sister and the doctor stepped from the room. Below, the doors closed quietly into the drive, and the house became silent. Gradually the sounds of Falkman's breathing grew more steady and filled the bedroom, overlaid by the swaying of the dark trees outside.

So James Falkman made his arrival. For the next week he lay quietly in his bedroom, his strength increasing hourly, and managed to eat his first meals prepared by his sister. She sat in the blackwood chair, her mourning habit exchanged for a grey woollen dress, examining him critically.

'Now James, you'll have to get a better appetite than that. Your poor body is completely wasted.'

Falkman pushed away the tray and let his long slim hands fall across his chest. He smiled amiably at his sister. 'Careful, Betty, or you'll turn me into a milk pudding.'

His sister briskly straightened the eiderdown. 'If you don't like my cooking, James, you can fend for yourself.'

A faint chuckle slipped between Falkman's lips. 'Thank you for telling me, Betty, I fully intend to.'

He lay back, smiling weakly to himself as his sister stalked out with the tray. Teasing her did him almost as much good as the meals she prepared, and he felt the blood reaching down into his cold feet. His face was still grey and flaccid, and he conserved his strength carefully, only his eyes moving as he watched the ravens alighting on the window ledge.

Gradually, as his conversations with his sister became more frequent, Falkman gained sufficient strength to sit up. He began to take a fuller interest in the world around him, watching the people in the avenue through the french windows and disputing his sister's commentary on them.

'There's Sam Banbury again,' she remarked testily as a small leprechaunlike old man hobbled past. 'Off to the Swan as usual. When's he going to get a job, I'd like to know.'

'Be more charitable, Betty. Sam's a very sensible fellow. I'd rather go to the pub than have a job.'

His sister snorted sceptically, her assessment of Falkman's character apparently at variance with this statement. 'You've got one of the finest houses in Mortmere Park,' she told him. 'I think you should be more careful with people like Sam Banbury. He's not in your class, James.'

Falkman smiled patiently at his sister. 'We're all in the same class, or have you been here so long you've forgotten, Betty.'

'We all forget,' she told him soberly. 'You will too, James. It's sad, but we're in this world now, and we must concern ourselves with it. If the church can keep the memory alive for us, so much the better. As you'll find out though, the majority of folk remember nothing. Perhaps it's a good thing.'

She grudgingly admitted the first visitors, fussing about so that Falkman could barely exchange a word with them. In fact, the visits tired him, and he could do little more than pass a few formal pleasantries. Even when Sam Banbury brought him a pipe and tobacco pouch he had to muster all his energy to thank him and had none left to prevent his sister from making off with them.

Only when the Reverend Matthews called did Falkman manage to summon together his strength, for half an hour spoke earnestly to the parson, who listened with rapt attention, interjecting a few eager questions. When the Reverend left he seemed refreshed and confident, and strode down the stairs with a gay smile at Falkman's sister.

Within three weeks Falkman was out of bed, and managed to hobble downstairs and inspect the house and garden. His sister protested, dogging his slow painful footsteps with sharp reminders of his feebleness, but Falkman ignored her. He found his way to the conservatory, and leaned against one of the ornamental columns, his nervous fingers feeling the leaves of the miniature trees, the scent of flowers flushing his face. Outside, in the grounds, he examined everything around him, as if comparing it with some Elysian paradise in his mind.

He was walking back to the house when he twisted his ankle sharply in the crazy paving. Before he could cry for help he had fallen headlong across the hard stone.

'James Falkman will you never listen?' his sister protested, as she helped him across the terrace. 'I warned you to stay in bed!'

Reaching the lounge, Falkman sat down thankfully in an armchair, reassembling his stunned limbs. 'Quiet, Betty, do you mind,' he admonished his sister when his breath returned. 'I'm still here, and I'm perfectly well.'

He had stated no more than the truth. After the accident he began to recover spectacularly, his progress toward complete health accelerating without a break, as if the tumble had freed him from the lingering fatigue and discomfort of the previous weeks. His step became brisk and lively, his complexion brightened, a soft pink glow filling out his cheeks, and he moved busily around the house.

A month afterwards his sister returned to her own home, acknowledging his ability to look after himself, and her place was taken by the housekeeper. After re-establishing himself in the house, Falkman became increasingly interested in the world outside. He hired a comfortable car and chauffeur, and spent most of the winter afternoons and evenings at his club; soon he found himself the centre of a wide circle of acquaintances. He became the chairman of a number of charitable committees, where his good humour, tolerance and shrewd judgement made him well respected. He now held himself erect, his grey hair sprouting luxuriantly, here and there touched by black flecks, jaw jutting firmly from sun-tanned cheeks.

Every Sunday he attended the morning and evening services at his church, where he owned a private pew, and was somewhat saddened to see that only the older people formed the congregation. However, he himself found that the picture painted by the liturgy became increasingly detached from his own memories as the latter faded, too soon became a meaningless charade that he could accept only by an act of faith.

A few years later, when he became increasingly restless, he decided to accept the offer of a partnership in a leading firm of stockbrokers.

Many of his acquaintances at the club were also finding jobs, forsaking the placid routines of smoking room and conservatory garden. Harold Caldwell, one of his closest friends, was appointed Professor of History at the university, and Sam Banbury became manager of the Swan Hotel.

The ceremony on Falkman's first day at the stock exchange was dignified and impressive. Three junior men also joining the firm were introduced to the assembled staff by the senior partner, Mr Montefiore, and each presented with a gold watch to symbolize the years he would spend with the firm. Falkman received an embossed silver cigar case and was loudly applauded.

For the next five years Falkman threw himself wholeheartedly into his work, growing more extrovert and aggressive as his appetite for the material pleasures of life increased. He became a keen golfer; then, as the exercise strengthened his physique, played his first games of tennis. An influential member of the business community, his days passed in a pleasant round of conferences and dinner parties. He no longer attended the church, but instead spent his Sundays escorting the more attractive of his lady acquaintances to the race tracks and regattas.

He found it all the more surprising, therefore when a persistent mood of dejection began to haunt him. Although without any apparent source, this deepened slowly, and he found himself reluctant to leave his house in the evenings. He resigned from his committees and no longer visited his club. At the stock exchange he felt permanently distracted, and would stand for hours by the window, staring down at the traffic.

Finally, when his grasp of the business began to slip, Mr Montefiore suggested that he go on indefinite leave.

For a week Falkman listlessly paced around the huge empty house. Sam Banbury frequently called to see him, but Falkman's sense of grief was beyond any help. He drew the blinds over the windows and changed into a black tie and suit, sat blankly in the darkened library.

At last, when his depression had reached its lowest ebb, he went to the cemetery to collect his wife.

After the congregation had dispersed, Falkman paused outside the vestry to tip the gravedigger, Biddle, and compliment him on his young son, a cherubic three-year-old who was playing among the headstones. Then he rode back to Mortmere Park in the car following the hearse, the remainder of the cortege behind him.

'A grand turnout, James,' his sister told him approvingly. 'Twenty cars altogether, not including the private ones.'

Falkman thanked her, his eyes examining his sister with critical detachment. In the fifteen years he had known her she had coarsened perceptibly, her voice roughening and her gestures becoming broader. A distinct social gap had always separated them, a division which Falkman had accepted charitably, but it was now widening markedly. Her husband's business had recently begun to fail, and her thoughts had turned almost exclusively to the subjects of money and social prestige.

As Falkman congratulated himself on his good sense and success, a curious premonition, indistinct but nonetheless disturbing, stirred through his mind.

Like Falkman himself fifteen years earlier, his wife first lay in her coffin in the hall, the heavy wreaths transforming it into a dark olive-green bower. Behind the lowered blinds the air was dim and stifled, and with her rich red hair flaring off her forehead, and her broad cheeks and full lips, his wife seemed to Falkman like some sleeping enchantress in a magical arbour. He gripped the silver foot rail of the coffin and stared at her mindlessly, aware of his sister shepherding the guests to the port and whisky. He traced with his eyes the exquisite dips and hollows around his wife's neck and chin, the white skin sweeping smoothly to her strong shoulders. The next day, when she was carried upstairs, her presence filled the bedroom. All afternoon he sat beside her, waiting patiently for her to wake.

Shortly after five o'clock, in the few minutes of light left before the dusk descended, when the air hung motionlessly under the trees in the garden, a faint echo of life moved across her face. Her eyes cleared and then focused on the ceiling.

Breathlessly, Falkman leaned forward and took one of her cold hands. Far within, the pulse sounded faintly.

'Marion,' he whispered.

Her head inclined slightly, lips parting in a weak smile. For several moments she gazed serenely at her husband.

'Hello, Jamie.'

His wife's arrival completely rejuvenated Falkman. A devoted husband, he was soon completely immersed in their life together. As she recovered from the long illness after her arrival, Falkman entered the prime of his life. His grey hair became sleek and black, his face grew thicker, the chin firmer and stronger. He returned to the stock exchange, taking up his job with renewed interest.

He and Marion made a handsome couple. At intervals they would visit the cemetery and join in the service celebrating the arrival of another of their friends, but these became less frequent. Other parties continually visited the cemetery, thinning the ranks of graves, and large areas had reverted to open lawn as the coffins were withdrawn and the tombstones removed. The firm of undertakers near the cemetery which was responsible for notifying mourning relatives closed down and was sold. Finally, after the gravedigger, Biddle, recovered his own wife from the last of the graves the cemetery was converted into a children's playground.

The years of their marriage were Falkman's happiest. With each successive summer Marion became slimmer and more youthful, her red hair a brilliant diadem that stood out among the crowds in the street when she came to see him. They would walk home arm in arm, in the summer evening pause among the willows by the river to embrace each other like lovers.

Indeed, their happiness became such a byword among their friends that over two hundred guests attended the church ceremony celebrating the long years of their marriage. As they knelt together at the altar before the priest Marion seemed to Falkman like a demure rose.

This was the last night they were to spend together. Over the years Falkman had become less interested in his work at the stock exchange, and the arrival of older and more serious men had resulted in a series of demotions for him. Many of his friends were facing similar problems. Harold Caldwell had been forced to resign his professorship and was now a junior lecturer, taking postgraduate courses to familiarize himself with the great body of new work that had been done in the previous thirty years. Sam Banbury was a waiter at the Swan Hotel.

Marion went to live with her parents, and the Falkmans' apartment, to which they had moved some years earlier after the house was closed and sold, was let to new tenants. Falkman, whose tastes had become simpler as the years passed, took a room in a hostel for young men, but he and Marion saw each other every evening. He felt increasingly restless, half conscious that his life was moving towards an inescapable focus, and often thought of giving up his job.

Marion remonstrated with him. 'But you'll lose everything you've worked for, Jamie. All those years.'

Falkman shrugged, chewing on a stem of grass as they lay in the park during one of their lunch hours. Marion was now a salesgirl in a department store.

'Perhaps, but I resent being demoted. Even Montefiore is leaving. His grandfather has just been appointed chairman.' He rolled over and put his head in her lap. 'It's so dull in that stuffy office, with all those pious old men. I'm not satisfied with it any longer.'

Marion smiled affectionately at his naïveté and enthusiasm. Falkman was now more handsome than she had ever remembered him, his sun-tanned face almost unlined.

'It's been wonderful together, Marion,' he told her on the eve of their thirtieth anniversary. 'How lucky we've been never to have a child. Do you realize that some people even have three or four? It's absolutely tragic.'

'It comes to us all, though, Jamie,' she reminded him. 'Some people say it's a very beautiful and noble experience, having a child.'

All evening he and Marion wandered round the town together, Falkman's desire for her quickened by her increasing demureness. Since she had gone to live with her parents Marion had become almost too shy to take his hand.

Then he lost her.

Walking through the market in the town centre, they were joined by two of Marion's friends, Elizabeth and Evelyn Jermyn.

'There's Sam Banbury,' Evelyn pointed out as a firework crackled from a stall on the other side of the market. 'Playing the fool as usual.' She and her sister clucked disapprovingly. Tight-mouthed and stern, they wore dark serge coats buttoned to their necks.

Distracted by Sam, Falkman wandered off a few steps, suddenly found that the three girls had walked away. Darting through the crowd, he tried to catch up with them, briefly glimpsed Marion's red hair.

He fought his way through the stalls, almost knocking over a barrow of vegetables and shouted at Sam Banbury:

'Sam! Have you seen Marion?'

Banbury pocketed his crackers and helped him to scan the crowd. For an hour they searched. Finally Sam gave up and went home, leaving Falkman to hang about the cobbled square under the dim lights when the market closed, wandering among the tinsel and litter as the stall holders packed up for home.

'Excuse me, have you seen a girl here? A girl with red hair?'

'Please, she was here this afternoon.'

'A girl . . .'

'. . . called . . .'

Stunned, he realized that he had forgotten her name.

Shortly afterwards, Falkman gave up his job and went to live with his parents. Their small red-brick house was on the opposite side of the town; between the crowded chimney pots he could sometimes see the distant slopes of Mortmere Park. His life now began a less carefree phase, as most of his energy went into helping his mother and looking after his sister Betty. By comparison with his own house his parents' home was bleak and uncomfortable, altogether alien to everything Falkman had previously known. Although kind and respectable people, his parents' lives were circumscribed by their lack of success or education. They had no interest in music or the theatre, and Falkman found his mind beginning to dull and coarsen.

His father was openly critical of him for leaving his job, but the hostility between them gradually subsided as he more and more began to dominate Falkman, restricting his freedom and reducing his pocket money, even warning him not to play with certain of his friends. In fact, going to live with his parents had taken Falkman into an entirely new world.

By the time he began to go to school Falkman had completely forgotten his past life, his memories of Marion and the great house where they had lived surrounded by servants altogether obliterated.

During his first term at school he was in a class with the older boys, whom the teachers treated as equals, but like his parents they began to extend their influence over him as the years passed. At times Falkman rebelled against this attempt to suppress his own personality, but at last they entirely dominated him, controlling his activities and moulding his thoughts and speech. The whole process of education, he dimly realized, was designed to prepare him for the strange twilight world of his earliest childhood. It deliberately eliminated every trace of sophistication, breaking down, with its constant repetitions and brain-splitting exercises, all his knowledge of language and mathematics, substituting for them a collection of meaningless rhymes, and chants, and out of this constructing an artificial world of total infantilism.

At last, when the process of education had reduced him almost to the stage of an inarticulate infant, his parents intervened by removing him from the school, and the final years of his life were spent at home.

'Mama, can I sleep with you?'

Mrs Falkman looked down at the serious-faced little boy who leaned his head on her pillow. Affectionately she pinched his square jaw and then touched her husband's shoulder as he stirred. Despite the years between father and son, their two bodies were almost identical, with the same broad shoulders and broad heads, the same thick hair.

'Not today, Jamie, but soon perhaps, one day.'

The child watched his mother with wide eyes, wondering why she should be crying to herself, guessing that perhaps he had touched upon one of the taboos that had exercised such a potent fascination for all the boys at school, the mystery of their ultimate destination that remained carefully shrouded by their parents and which they themselves were no longer able to grasp.

By now he was beginning to experience the first difficulties in both walking and feeding himself. He tottered about clumsily, his small piping voice tripping over his tongue. Steadily his vocabulary diminished until he knew only his mother's name. When he could no longer stand upright she would carry him in her arms, feeding him like an elderly invalid. His mind clouded, a few constants of warmth and hunger drifting through it hazily. As long as he could, he clung to his mother.

Shortly afterward, Falkman and his mother visited the lying-in hospital for several weeks. On her return Mrs Falkman remained in bed for a few days, but gradually she began to move about more freely, slowly shedding the additional weight accumulated during her confinement.

Some nine months after she returned from the hospital, a period during

which she and her husband thought continually of their son, the tragedy
of his approaching death, a symbol of their own imminent separation,
bringing them closer together, they went away on their honeymoon.

**, 1964**

# PRISONER OF THE CORAL DEEP

I found the shell at low tide, lying in a rock-pool near the cave, its huge mother-of-pearl spiral shining through the clear water like a Fabergé gem. During the storm I had taken shelter in the mouth of the cave, watching the grey waves hurl themselves towards me like exhausted saurians, and the shell lay at my feet almost as a token of the sea's regret.

The storm was still rumbling along the cliffs in the distance, and I was wary of leaving the cave. All morning I had been walking along this deserted stretch of the Dorset coast. I had entered a series of enclosed bays from which there were no pathways to the cliffs above. Quarried by the sea, the limestone bluffs were disturbed by continuous rock-slides, and the beaches were littered by huge slabs of pockmarked stone. Almost certainly there would be further falls after the storm. I stepped cautiously from my shelter, peering up at the high cliffs. Even the wheeling gulls crying to each other seemed reluctant to alight on their crumbling cornices.

Below me, the seashell lay in its pool, apparently magnified by the lens of water. It was fully twelve inches long, the corrugated shell radiating into five huge spurs. A fossil gastropod, which had once basked in the warm Cambrian seas five hundred million years earlier, it had presumably been torn loose by the waves from one of the limestone boulders.

Impressed by its size, I decided to take it home to my wife as a memento of my holiday – needing a complete change of scene after an unprecedentedly busy term at school, I had been packed off to the coast for a week. I stepped into the pool and lifted the shell from the water, and then turned to retrace my steps along the coast.

To my surprise, I was being watched by a solitary figure on the limestone ledge twenty yards behind me, a tall raven-haired woman in a sea-blue gown that reached to her feet. She stood motionlessly among the rock-pools, like a Pre-Raphaelite vision of the dark-eyed Madonna of some primitive fisher community, looking down at me with meditative eyes veiled by the drifting spray. Her dark hair, parted in the centre of her low forehead, fell like a shawl to her shoulders and enclosed her calm but somewhat melancholy face.

I stared at her soundlessly, and then made a tentative gesture with the seashell. The ragged cliffs and the steep sea and sky seemed to enclose us with a sense of absolute remoteness, as if the rocky beach and our chance encounter had been transported to the bleak shores of Tierra del Fuego on the far tip of the world's end. Against the damp cliffs her blue robe glowed with an almost spectral vibrancy, matched only by the brilliant pearl of the shell in my hands. I assumed that she lived in an isolated house somewhere above the cliffs – the storm had ended only ten minutes earlier, and there appeared to be no other shelter – and that a hidden pathway ran down among the fissures in the limestone.

I climbed up to the ledge and walked across to her. I had gone on holiday specifically to escape from other people, but after the storm and my walk along the abandoned coast, I was glad to talk to someone. Although she showed no response to my smile, the woman's dark eyes watched me without hostility, as if she were waiting for me to approach her.

At our feet the sea hissed, the waves running like serpents between the rocks.

'The storm certainly came up suddenly,' I commented. 'I managed to shelter in the cave.' I pointed to the cliff top two hundred feet above us. 'You must have a magnificent view of the sea. Do you live up there?'

Her white skin was like ancient pearl. 'I live by the sea,' she said. Her voice had a curiously deep timbre, as if heard under water. She was at least six inches taller than myself, although I am by no means a short man. 'You have a beautiful shell,' she remarked.

I weighed it in one hand. 'Impressive, isn't it? A fossil snail – far older than this limestone, you know. I'll probably give it to my wife, though it should go to the Natural History Museum.'

'Why not leave it on the beach where it belongs?' she said. 'The sea is its home.'

'Not this sea,' I rejoined. 'The Cambrian oceans where this snail swam vanished millions of years ago.' I detached a thread of fucus clinging to one of the spurs and let it fall away on the air. 'I'm not sure why, but fossils fascinate me – they're like time capsules; if only one could unwind this spiral it would probably play back to us a picture of all the landscapes it's ever seen – the great oceans of the Carboniferous, the warm shallow seas of the Trias . . .'

'Would you like to go back to them?' There was a note of curiosity in her voice, as if my comments had intrigued her. 'Would you prefer them to this time?'

'Hardly. I suppose it's just the nostalgia of one's unconscious memory. Perhaps you understand what I mean – the sea is like memory. However lost or forgotten, everything in its exists for ever . . .' Her lips moved in what seemed to be the beginnings of a smile. 'Or does the idea seem strange?'

'Not at all.'

She watched me pensively. Her robe was woven from some bright thread of blue silver, almost like the hard brilliant scales of pelagic fish.

Her eyes turned to the sea. The tide had begun to come in, and already the pool where I found the shell was covered by the water. The first waves were breaking into the mouth of the cave, and the ledge we stood on would soon be surrounded. I glanced over my shoulder for any signs of the cliff path.

'It's getting stormy again,' I said. 'The Atlantic is rather bad-tempered and unpredictable – as you'd expect from an ancient sea. Once it was part of a great ocean called –'

'Poseidon.'

I turned to look at her.

'You knew?'

'Of course.' She regarded me tolerantly. 'You're a school-master. So this is what you teach your pupils, to remember the sea and go back to the past?'

I laughed at myself, amused at being caught out by her. 'I'm sorry. One of the teacher's occupational hazards is that he can never resist a chance to pass on knowledge.'

'Memory and the sea?' She shook her head sagely. 'You deal in magic, not knowledge. Tell me about your shell.'

The water lifted towards us among the rocks. To my left a giant's causeway of toppled pillars led to the safety of the upper beach. I debated whether to leave; the climb up the cliff face, even if the path were well cut, would take at least half an hour, especially if I had to assist my companion. Apparently indifferent to the sea, she watched the waves writhing at our feet, like reptiles in a pit. Around us the great cliffs seemed to sink downward into the water.

'Perhaps I should let the shell speak for itself,' I demurred. My wife was less tolerant of my tendency to bore. I lifted the shell to my ear and listened to the whispering trumpet.

The helix reflected the swishing of the waves, the contours of the shell in some way magnifying the sounds, so that they echoed with the darker murmur of deep water. Around me the breakers fell among the rocks with a rhythmic roar and sigh, but from the shell poured an extraordinary confusion of sounds, and I seemed to be listening not merely to the waves breaking on the shore below me but to an immense ocean lapping all the beaches of the world. I could hear the roar and whistle of giant rollers, shingle singing in the undertow, storms and typhonic winds boiling the sea into a maelstrom. Then abruptly the scene seemed to shift, and I heard the calm measures of a different sea, a steaming shallow lagoon through whose surface vast ferns protruded, where half-submerged leviathans lay like sandbanks under a benign sun . . .

My companion was watching me, her high face lifted to catch the leaping spray. 'Did you hear the sea?'

I pressed the shell to my ear. Again I heard the sounds of ancient water, this time of an immense storm in progress, a titanic struggle against the collapsing isthmuses of a sinking continent. I could hear the growling of gigantic saurians, the cries of reptile birds diving from high cliffs on to their prey below, their ungainly wings unshackling as they fell.

Astonished, I squeezed the shell in my hands, feeling the hard calcareous spines as if they might spring open the shell's secret.

The woman still watched me. By some freak of the fading light she appeared to have grown in height, her shoulders almost overtopping my head.

'I . . . can't hear anything,' I said uncertainly.

'Listen to it!' she admonished me. 'That shell has heard the seas of all time, every wave has left its echo there.'

The first foam splashed across my feet, staining the dried straps of my sandals. A narrowing causeway of rocks still led back to the beach. The cave had vanished, its mouth spewing bubbles as the waves briefly receded.

I pointed to the cliff. 'Is there a path? A way down to the sea?'

'To the sea? Of course!' The wind lifted the train of her robe, and I saw her bare feet, seaweed wreathed around her toes. 'Now listen to the shell. The sea is waking for you.'

I raised the shell with both hands. This time I closed my eyes, and as the sounds of the ancient wind and water echoed in my ears I saw a sudden image of the lonely bay millions of years earlier. High cliffs of white shale reached to the sky, and huge reptiles sidled along the coarse beaches, baying at the grotesque armoured fish which lunged at them from the shallows. Volcanic cones ringed the horizon, their red vents staining the sky.

'What can you hear?' my companion asked me insistently, evidently disappointed. 'The sea and the wind?'

'I hear nothing,' I said thickly. 'Only a whispering.'

The noise erupted from the shell's mouth, the harsh bellows of the saurians competing with the sea. Suddenly I heard another sound above this babel, a thin cry that seemed to come from the cave in which I had sheltered. Searching the image in my mind, I could see the cave mouth set into the cliff above the heads of the jostling reptiles.

'Wait!' I waved the woman away, ignoring the waves that sluiced across my feet. As the sea receded, I pressed my ear to the conch, and heard again the faint human cry, a stricken plea for rescue –

'Can you hear the sea now?' The woman reached to take the shell from me.

I held to it tightly and shouted above the waves. 'Not *this* sea! My God, I heard a man crying!'

For a moment she hesitated, uncertain what to make of this unexpected remark. 'A man? Who, tell me! Give it to me! It was only a drowned sailor!'

Again I snatched the shell away from her. Listening, I could still hear the voice calling, now and then lost in the roar of the reptiles. A sailor, yes, but a mariner from the distant future, marooned millions of years ago in this cave on the edge of a Triassic sea, guarded by this strange naiad of the deep who even now guided me to the waves.

She had moved to the edge of the rock, the strands of her hair shimmering across her face in the wind. With a hand she beckoned me towards her.

For the last time I lifted the shell to my ear, and for the last time heard that faint plaintive cry, lost on the reeling air.

'H-h-e-e-lp!'

Closing my eyes, I let the image of the ancient shore fill my mind, for a fleeting instant saw a small white face watching from the cave mouth. Whoever he was, had he despaired of returning to his own age, selected a beautiful shell and cast it into the sea below, hoping that one day someone would hear his voice and return to save him?

'Come! It's time to leave!' Although she was a dozen feet from me, her outstretched hands seemed almost to touch mine. The water raced around her robe, swirling it into strange liquid patterns. Her face watched me like that of some monstrous fish.

'No!'

With sudden fury I stepped away from her, then turned and hurled the great shell far out into the deep water beyond her reach. As it vanished into the steep waves I heard a flurry of heavy robes, almost like the beating of leathery wings.

The woman had gone. Quickly I leapt on to the nearest rock of the causeway, slipped into the shallows between two waves and then clambered to safety. Only when I had reached the shelter of the cliffs did I look back.

On the ledge where she had stood a large lizard watched me with empty eyes.

**· 1964**

# THE LOST LEONARDO

The disappearance – or, to put it less euphemistically – the theft of the *Crucifixion* by Leonardo da Vinci from the Museum of the Louvre in Paris, discovered on the morning of April 19, 1965, caused a scandal of unprecedented proportions. A decade of major art thefts, such as those of Goya's *Duke of Wellington* from the National Gallery, London, and collections of impressionists from the homes of millionaires in the South of France and California, as well as the obviously inflated prices paid in the auction rooms of Bond Street and the Rue de Rivoli, might have been expected to accustom the general public to the loss of yet another over-publicized masterpiece, but in fact the news of its disappearance was received by the world with genuine consternation and outrage. From all over the globe thousands of telegrams poured in daily at the Quai d'Orsay and the Louvre, the French consulates at Bogota and Guatemala City were stoned, and the panache and finesse of press attachés at every embassy from Buenos Aires to Bangkok were strained to their not inconsiderable limits.

I myself reached Paris over twenty-four hours after what was being called 'the great Leonardo scandal' had taken place, and the atmosphere of bewilderment and indignation was palpable. All the way from Orly Airport the newspaper headlines on the kiosks blazoned the same story.

As the *Continental Daily Mail* put it succinctly:

LEONARDO'S CRUCIFIXION STOLEN
£5 Million Masterpiece Vanishes from Louvre

Official Paris, by all accounts, was in uproar. The hapless director of the Louvre had been recalled from a Unesco conference in Brasilia and was now on the carpet at the Elysée Palace, reporting personally to the President, the Deuxieme Bureau had been alerted, and at least three ministers without portfolio had been appointed, their political futures staked to the recovery of the painting. As the President himself had remarked at his press conference the previous afternoon, the theft of a Leonardo was an affair not only for France, but for the entire world, and in a passionate plea he enjoined everyone to help effect its speedy return (despite the emotionally charged atmosphere, cynical observers noticed that this was the first crisis of his career when the Great Man did not conclude his peroration with 'Vive La France').

My own feelings, despite my professional involvement with the fine arts – I was, and am, a director of Northeby's, the world-famous Bond Street auctioneers – by and large coincided with those of the general public. As the taxi passed the Tuileries Gardens I looked out at the crude half-tone illustrations of da Vinci's effulgent masterpiece reproduced in the newspapers, recalling the immense splendour of the painting, with its unparalleled composition and handling of chiaroscuro, its unsurpassed technique, which together had launched the High Renaissance and provided a beacon for the sculptors, painters and architects of the Baroque.

Despite the two million reproductions of the painting sold each year, not to mention the countless pastiches and inferior imitations, the subject matter of the painting still retained its majestic power. Completed two years after da Vinci's *Virgin and St Anne,* also in the Louvre, it was not only one of the few Leonardos to have survived intact the thousand eager hands of the retouchers of four centuries, but was the only painting by the master, apart from the dissolving and barely visible *Last Supper,* in which he handled a composition with a large landscape and a huge gallery of supporting figures.

It was this latter factor, perhaps, which gave the painting its terrifying, hallucinatory power. The enigmatic, almost ambivalent expression on the face of the dying Christ, the hooded serpentine eyes of the Madonna and Magdalene, these characteristic signatures of Leonardo became more than mere mannerisms when set against the huge spiral concourse of attendant figures that seemed to swirl up into the distant sky across the Place of Bones, transforming the whole image of the crucifixion into an apocalyptic vision of the resurrection and judgment of mankind. From this single canvas had come the great frescoes of Michelangelo and Raphael in the Sistine Chapel, the entire schools of Tintoretto and Veronese. That someone should have the audacity to steal it was a tragic comment on mankind's respect for its greatest monuments.

And yet, I wondered as we arrived at the offices of Galleries Normande et Cie in the Madeleine, had the painting really been stolen at all? Its size, some 15 feet by 18 feet, and weight – it had been transferred from the original canvas to an oak panel – precluded a single fanatic or psychopath, and no gang of professional art thieves would waste their time stealing a painting for which there would be no market. Could it be, perhaps, that the French government was hoping to distract attention from some other impending event, though nothing less than the re-introduction of the monarchy and the coronation of the Bourbon Pretender in Notre Dame would have required such an elaborate smoke-screen.

At the first opportunity I raised my doubts with Georg de Stael, the director of Galleries Normande with whom I was staying during my visit. Ostensibly I had come to Paris to attend a conference that afternoon of art dealers and gallery directors who had also suffered from thefts of major works of art, but to any outsider our mood of elation and high spirits would have suggested some other motive. This, of course, would have been correct. Whenever a large stone is cast into the turbid waters of international art, people such as myself and Georg de Stael immediately take up our positions on the bank, watching for any unusual ripple or malodorous bubble. Without doubt the theft of the Leonardo would reveal a good deal more than the identity of some crackpot cat burglar. All the darker fish would now be swimming frantically for cover, and a salutary blow had been struck at the official establishment of senior museum curators and directors.

Such feelings of revenge obviously animated Georg as he moved with dapper, light-footed ease around his desk to greet me. His blue silk summer suit, well in advance of the season, glittered like his smooth brilliantined hair, his svelte rapacious features breaking into a smile of roguish charm.

'My dear Charles, I assure you, categorically, the confounded picture has actually gone –' Georg shot out three inches of elegant chalk-blue cuff and snapped his hands together '– puff! For once everyone is speaking the truth. What is even more remarkable, the painting was genuine.'

'I don't know whether I'm glad to hear that or not,' I admitted. 'But it's certainly more than you can say for most of the Louvre – and the National Gallery.'

'Agreed.' Georg straddled his desk, his patent leather shoes twinkling in the light. 'I had hoped that this catastrophe might induce the authorities to make a clean breast of some of their so-called treasures, in an attempt, as it were to dispel some of the magic surrounding the Leonardo. But they are in a complete fuddle.'

For a moment we both contemplated what such a sequence of admissions would do to the art markets of the world – the prices of anything even remotely genuine would soar – as well as to the popular image of Renaissance painting as something sacrosanct and unparalleled. However, this was not to gainsay the genius of the stolen Leonardo.

'Tell me, Georg,' I asked. 'Who stole it?' I assumed he knew.

For the first time in many years Georg seemed at a loss for an answer. He shrugged helplessly. 'My dear Charles, I just do not know. It's a complete mystery. Everyone is as baffled as you are.'

'In that case it must be an inside job.'

'Definitely not. The present crowd at the Louvre are beyond reproach.' He tapped the telephone. 'This morning I was speaking to some of our more dubious contacts – Antweiler in Messina and Kolenskya in Beirut – and they are both mystified. In fact they're convinced that either the whole thing is a put-up affair by the present regime, or else the Kremlin itself is involved.'

'The Kremlin?' I echoed incredulously. At the invocation of this name the atmosphere heightened, and for the next half an hour we spoke in whispers.

*   *   *

The conference that afternoon, at the Palais de Chaillot, offered no further
clues. Chief Detective-Inspector Carnot, a massive gloomy man in a faded
blue suit, took the chair, flanked by other agents of the Deuxieme Bureau.
All of them looked tired and dispirited; by now they were having to check
up on some dozen false alarms each hour. Behind them, like a hostile
jury, sat a sober-faced group of investigators from Lloyds of London
and Morgan Guaranty Trust of New York. By contrast, the two hundred
dealers and agents sitting on the gilt chairs below the platform presented
an animated scene, chattering away in a dozen languages and flying a
score of speculative kites.

After a brief resumé, delivered in a voice of sepulchral resignation,
Inspector Carnot introduced a burly Dutchman next to him, Superintendent Jurgens of the Interpol bureau at The Hague, and then called on M.
Auguste Pecard, assistant director of the Louvre, for a detailed description
of the theft. This merely confirmed that the security arrangements at
the Louvre were first-class and that it was absolutely impossible for the
painting to have been stolen. I could see that Pecard was still not entirely
convinced that it had gone.

'... the pressure panels in the floor surrounding the painting have
not been disturbed, nor have the two infra-red beams across its face
been broken. Gentlemen, I assure you it is impossible to remove the
painting without first dismantling the bronze frame. This alone weighs
eight hundred pounds and is bolted into the wall behind it. But the electric
alarm circuit which flows through the bolts was not interrupted ...'

I was looking up at the two life-size photographs of the front and
reverse faces of the painting fastened to the screens behind the dais.
The latter showed the back of the oak panel with its six aluminium ribs,
contact points for the circuit and a mass of chalked graffiti enscribed over
the years by the museum laboratories. The photographs had been taken
the last time the picture was removed for cleaning, and after a brief bout
of questioning it transpired that this had been completed only two days
before the theft.

At this news the atmosphere of the conference changed. The hundred
private conversations ceased, coloured silk handkerchiefs were returned
to their breast pockets.

I nudged Georg de Stael. 'So that explains it.' Obviously the painting
had disappeared during its period in the laboratory, where the security
arrangements would be less than fool-proof. 'It was not stolen from the
gallery at all.'

The hubbub around us had re-started. Two hundred noses once again
were lifted to scent the trail. So the painting had been stolen, and was
somewhere at large in the world. The rewards to the discoverer, if not
the Legion of Honour or a Knighthood, then at least complete freedom
from all income tax and foreign exchange investigations, hovered like a
spectre before us.

On the way back, however, Georg stared sombrely through the window of the taxi.

'The painting *was* stolen from the gallery,' he said to me pensively. 'I saw it there myself just twelve hours before it vanished.' He took my arm and held it tightly. 'We'll find it, Charles, for the glory of Northeby's and the Galleries Normande. But, my God, the man who stole it was a thief out of this world!'

So began the quest for the missing Leonardo. I returned to London the next morning, but Georg and I were in regular contact by telephone. Initially, like all the others on its trail, we merely listened, ears to the ground for an unfamiliar foot-fall. In the crowded auction rooms and galleries we waited for the indiscreet word, for the give-away clue. Business, of course, was buoyant; every museum and private owner with a third-rate Rubens or Raphael had now moved up a rung. With luck the renewed market activity would uncover some distant accomplice of the thief, or a previous substitute for the Leonardo – perhaps a pastiche *Mona Lisa* by one of Verrocchio's pupils – would be jettisoned by the thief and appear on one of the shadier markets. If the hunt for the vanished painting was conducted as loudly as ever in the outside world, within the trade all was quiet and watchful.

In fact, too quiet. By rights something should have materialized, some faint clue should have appeared on the fine filters of the galleries and auction rooms. But nothing was heard. As the wave of activity launched by the displaced Leonardo rolled past and business resumed its former tempo, inevitably the painting became just another on the list of lost masterpieces.

Only Georg de Stael seemed able to maintain his interest in the search. Now and then he would put through a call to London, requesting some obscure piece of information about an anonymous buyer of a Titian or Rembrandt in the late 18th century, or the history of some damaged copy by a pupil of Rubens or Raphael. He seemed particularly interested in works known to have been damaged and subsequently restored, information with which many private owners are naturally jealous of parting.

Consequently, when he called to see me in London some four months after the disappearance of the Leonardo, it was not in a purely jocular sense that I asked: 'Well, Georg, do you know who stole it yet?'

Unclipping a large briefcase, Georg smiled at me darkly. 'Would it surprise you if I said "yes"? As a matter of fact, I don't know, but I have an idea, a hypothesis, shall we say. I thought you might be interested to hear it.'

'Of course, Georg,' I said, adding reprovingly: 'So this is what you've been up to.'

He raised a thin forefinger to silence me. Below the veneer of easy charm I noticed a new mood of seriousness, a cutting of conversational corners.

'First, Charles, before you laugh me out of your office, let's say that I consider my theory completely fantastic and implausible, and yet –' he shrugged deprecatingly '– it seems to be the only one possible. To prove it I need your help.'

'Given before asked. But what is this theory? I can't wait to hear.'

He hesitated, apparently uncertain whether to expose his idea, and then began to empty the briefcase, taking out a series of looseleaf files which he placed in a row facing him along the desk. These contained what appeared to be photographic reproductions of a number of paintings, areas within them marked with white ink. Several of the photographs were enlargements of details, all of a high-faced, goatee-bearded man in mediaeval costume.

Georg inverted six of the larger plates so that I could see them. 'You recognize these, of course?'

I nodded. With the exception of one, Rubens' *Pieta* in the Hermitage Museum at Leningrad, I had seen the originals of them all within the previous five years. The others were the missing Leonardo *Crucifixion*, the *Crucifixions* by Veronese, Goya and Holbein, and that by Poussin, entitled *The Place of Golgotha*. All were in public museums – the Louvre, San Stefano in Venice, the Prado and the Ryksmuseum, Amsterdam – and all were familiar, well-authenticated masterworks, centrepieces, apart from the Poussin, of major national collections. 'It's reassuring to see them. I trust they're all in good hands. Or are they next on the mysterious thief's shopping list?'

Georg shook his head. 'No, I don't think he's very interested in these. Though he keeps a watching brief over them.' Again I noticed the marked change in Georg's manner, the reflective private humour. 'Do you notice anything else?'

I compared the photographs again. 'They're all crucifixions. Authentic, except perhaps in minor details. They were all easel paintings.' I shrugged.

'They all, at some time, have been stolen.' Georg moved quickly from right to left. 'The Poussin from the Chateau Loire collection in 1822, the Goya in 1806 from the Monte Cassino monastery, by Napoleon, the Veronese from the Prado in 1891, the Leonardo four months ago as we know, and the Holbein in 1943, looted for the Herman Goering collection.'

'Interesting,' I commented. 'But few masterworks haven't been stolen at some time. I hope this isn't a key point in your theory.'

'No, but in conjunction with another factor it gains in significance. Now.' He handed the Leonardo reproduction to me. 'Anything unusual there?' When I shook my head at the familiar image he picked up another photograph of the missing painting. 'What about that one?'

The photographs had been taken from slightly different perspectives, but otherwise seemed identical. 'They are both of the original *Crucifixion*,' Georg explained, 'taken in the Louvre within a month of its disappearance.'

'I give up,' I admitted. 'They seem the same. No – wait a minute!' I pulled the table light nearer and bent over the plates, as Georg nodded. 'They're slightly different. What is going on?'

Quickly, figure by figure, I compared the photographs, within a few moments seized on the minute disparity. In almost every particular the pictures were identical, but one figure out of the score or more on the crowded field had been altered. On the left, where the procession wound its way up the hillside towards the three crosses, the face of one of the bystanders had been completely repainted. Although, in the centre of the painting, the Christ hung from the cross some hours after the crucifixion, by a sort of spatio-temporal perspective – a common device in all Renaissance painting for overcoming the static nature of the single canvas – the receding procession carried the action backwards through time, so that one followed the invisible presence of the Christ on his painful last ascent of Golgotha.

The figure whose face had been repainted formed part of the crowd on the lower slopes. A tall powerfully built man in a black robe, he had obviously been the subject of special care by Leonardo, who had invested him with the magnificent physique and serpentine grace usually reserved for his depiction of angels. Looking at the photograph in my left hand, the original unretouched version, I realized that Leonardo had indeed intended the figure to represent an angel of death, or rather, one of those agents of the unconscious, terrifying in their enigmatic calm, in their brooding ambivalence, who seem to preside in his paintings over all man's deepest fears and longings, like the grey-faced statues that stare down from the midnight cornices of the necropolis at Pompeii.

All this, so typical of Leonardo and his curious vision, seemed to be summed up by the face of this tall angelic figure. Turned almost in profile over the left shoulder, the face looked up towards the cross, a faint flicker of pity investing the grey saturnine features. A high forehead, slightly flared at the temples, rose above the handsome semitic nose and mouth. A trace of a smile, of compassionate resignation and understanding, hung about the lips, providing a solitary source of light which illuminated the remainder of the face partly obscured by the shadows of the thundering sky.

In the photograph on my right, however, all this had been altered completely. The whole character of this angelic figure had been replaced by a new conception. The superficial likeness remained, but the face had lost its expression of tragic compassion. The later artist had reversed its posture altogether, and the head was turned away from the cross and over the right shoulder towards the earthly city of Jerusalem whose spectral towers rose like a city of Miltonic hell in the blue dusk. While the other bystanders followed the ascending Christ as if helpless to assist him, the expression on the face of the black-robed figure was arrogant and critical, the tension of the averted neck muscles indicating that he had swung his head away almost in disgust from the spectacle before him.

'What is this?' I asked, pointing to the latter photograph. 'Some lost pupil's copy? I can't see why –'

Georg leaned forward and tapped the print. '*That* is the original Leonardo. Don't you understand, Charles? The version on your left which you were admiring for so many minutes was superimposed by some unknown retoucher, only a few years after da Vinci's death.' He smiled at my scepticism. 'Believe me, it's true. The figure concerned is only a minor part of the composition, no one had seriously examined it before, as the rest of the painting is without doubt original. These additions were discovered five months ago shortly after the painting was removed for cleaning. The infra-red examination revealed the completely intact profile below.'

He passed two more photographs to me, both large-scale details of the head, in which the contrasts of characterization were even more obvious. 'As you can see from the brush-work in the shading, the retouching was done by a right-handed artist, whereas we know, of course, that da Vinci was left-handed.'

'Well . . .' I shrugged. 'It seems strange. But if what you say is correct, why on earth was such a small detail altered? The whole conception of the character is different.'

'An interesting question,' Georg said ambiguously. 'Incidentally, the figure is that of Ahasuerus, the Wandering Jew.' He pointed to the man's feet. 'He's always conventionally represented by the crossed sandal-straps of the Essene Sect, to which Jesus himself may have belonged.'

I picked up the photographs again. 'The Wandering Jew,' I repeated softly. 'How curious. The man who taunted Christ to move faster and was condemned to rove the surface of the earth until the Second Coming. It's almost as if the retoucher were an apologist for him, superimposing this expression of tragic pity over Leonardo's representation. There's an idea for you, Georg. You know how courtiers and wealthy merchants who gathered at painters' studios were informally incorporated into their paintings – perhaps Ahasuerus would move around, posing as himself, driven by a sort of guilt compulsion, then later steal the paintings and revise them. Now there *is* a theory.'

I looked across at Georg, waiting for him to reply. He was nodding slowly, eyes watching mine in unspoken agreement, all trace of humour absent. 'Georg!' I exclaimed. 'Are you serious? Do you mean –'

He interrupted me gently but forcefully. 'Charles, just give me a few more minutes to explain. I warned you that my theory was fantastic.' Before I could protest he passed me another photograph. 'The Veronese *Crucifixion*. See anyone you recognize? On the bottom left.'

I raised the photograph to the light. 'You're right. The late Venetian treatment is different, far more pagan, but it's quite obvious. You know, Georg, it's a remarkable likeness.'

'Agreed. But it's not only the likeness. Look at the pose and characterization.'

Identified again by his black robes and crossed sandal-straps, the figure
of Ahasuerus stood among the throng on the crowded canvas. The unusual
feature was not so much that the pose was again that of the retouched
Leonardo, with Ahasuerus now looking with an expression of deep
compassion at the dying Christ – an altogether meaningless interpretation
– but the remarkable likeness between the two faces, almost as if they had
been painted from the same model. The beard was perhaps a little fuller, in
the Venetian manner, but the planes of the face, the flaring of the temples,
the handsome coarseness of the mouth and jaw, the wise resignation in the
eyes, that of some well-travelled physician witnessing an act of barbaric
beauty and power, all these were exactly echoed from the Leonardo.

I gestured helplessly. 'It's an amazing coincidence.'

Georg nodded. 'Another is that this painting, like the Leonardo, was
stolen shortly after being extensively cleaned. When it was recovered in
Florence two years later it was slightly damaged, and no further attempts
were made to restore the painting.' Georg paused. 'Do you see my point,
Charles?'

'More or less. I take it you suspect that if the Veronese were now
cleaned a rather different version of Ahasuerus would be found. Veronese's
original depiction.'

'Exactly. After all, the present treatment makes no sense. If you're still
sceptical, look at these others.'

Standing up, we began to go through the remainder of the photographs.
In each of the others, the Poussin, Holbein, Goya and Rubens, the same
figure was to be found, the same dark saturnine face regarding the cross
with an expression of compassionate understanding. In view of the very
different styles of the artists, the degree of similarity was remarkable. In
each, as well, the pose was meaningless, the characterization completely
at odds with the legendary role of Ahasuerus.

By now the intensity of Georg's conviction was communicating itself
to me physically. He drummed the desk with the palm of one hand. 'In
each case, Charles, all six paintings were stolen shortly after they had
been cleaned – even the Holbein was looted from the Herman Goering
collection by some renegade SS after being repaired by concentration camp
inmates. As you yourself said, it's almost as if the thief was unwilling for
the world to see the true image of Ahasuerus's character exposed and
deliberately painted in these apologies.'

'But Georg, you're making a large assumption there. Can you prove
that in each case, apart from the Leonardo, there is an original version
below the present one?'

'Not yet. Naturally galleries are reluctant to give anyone the opportunity
to show that their works are not entirely genuine. I know all this is still
hypothesis, but what other explanation can you find?'

Shaking my head, I went over to the window, letting the noise and movement of Bond Street cut through Georg's heady speculations. 'Are you seriously suggesting, Georg, that the black-robed figure of Ahasuerus is promenading somewhere on those pavements below us now, and that all through the centuries he's been stealing and retouching paintings that represent him spurning Jesus? The idea's ludicrous!'

'No more ludicrous than the theft of the painting. Everyone agrees it could not have been stolen by anyone bounded by the laws of the physical universe.'

For a moment we stared at each other across the desk. 'All right,' I temporized, not wishing to offend him. The intensity of his idée fixe had alarmed me. 'But isn't our best plan simply to sit back and wait for the Leonardo to turn up again?'

'Not necessarily. Most of the stolen paintings remained lost for ten or twenty years. Perhaps the effort of stepping outside the bounds of space and time exhausts him, or perhaps the sight of the original paintings terrifies him so –' He broke off as I began to come forward towards him. 'Look, Charles, it *is* fantastic, but there's a slim chance it may be true. This is where I need your help. It's obvious this man must be a great patron of the arts, drawn by an irresistible compulsion, by unassuageable feelings of guilt, towards those artists painting crucifixions. We must begin to watch the sale rooms and galleries. That face, those black eyes and that haunted profile – sooner or later we'll see him, searching for another *Crucifixion* or *Pieta*. Cast your mind back, do you recognize that face?'

I looked down at the carpet, the image of the dark-eyed wanderer before me. *Go quicker*, he had taunted Jesus as he passed bearing the cross towards Golgotha, and Jesus had replied: *I go, but thou shalt wait until I return*. I was about to say 'no', but something restrained me, some reflex pause of recognition stirred through my mind. That handsome Levantine profile, in a different costume, of course, a smart dark-striped lounge suit, gold-topped cane and spats, bidding through an agent . . .

'You *have* seen him?' Georg came over to me. 'Charles, I think I have too.'

I gestured him away. 'I'm not sure, Georg, but . . . I almost wonder.' Curiously it was the retouched portrait of Ahasuerus, rather than Leonardo's original, which seemed more real, closer to the face I felt sure I had actually seen. Suddenly I pivoted on my heel. 'Confound it, Georg, do you realize that if this incredible idea of yours is true this man must have spoken to Leonardo? To Michelangelo, and Titian and Rembrandt?'

Georg nodded. 'And someone else too,' he added pensively.

For the next month, after Georg's return to Paris, I spent less time in my office and more in the sale rooms, watching for that familiar profile which something convinced me I had seen before. But for this undeniable conviction I would have dismissed Georg's hypothesis as obsessive fantasy. I made a few tactful enquiries of my assistants, and to my annoyance two of them also vaguely remembered such a person. After this I found myself unable to drive George de Stael's fancies from my mind. No further news was heard of the missing Leonardo – the complete absence of any clues mystified the police and the art world alike.

Consequently, it was with an immense feeling of relief, as much as of excitement, that I received five weeks later the following telegram:

CHARLES. COME IMMEDIATELY. I HAVE SEEN HIM. GEORG DE STAEL.

This time, as my taxi carried me from Orly Airport to the Madeleine, it was no idle amusement that made me watch the Tuileries Gardens for any sight of a tall man in a black slouch hat sneaking through the trees with a rolled-up canvas under his arm. Was Georg de Stael finally and irretrievably out of his mind, or had he in fact seen the phantom Ahasuerus?

When he greeted me at the doorway of Normande et Cie his handshake was as firm as ever, his face composed and relaxed. In his office he sat back and regarded me quizzically over the tips of his fingers, evidently so sure of himself that he could let his news bide its time.

'He's here, Charles,' he said at last. 'In Paris, staying at the Ritz. He's been attending the sales here of 19th and 20th century masters. With luck you'll see him this afternoon.'

For once my incredulity returned, but before I could stutter my objections Georg silenced me.

'He's just as we expected, Charles. Tall and powerfully built, with a kind of statuesque grace, the sort of man who moves easily among the rich and nobility. Leonardo and Holbein caught him exactly, that strange haunted intensity about his eyes, the wind of deserts and great ravines.'

'When did you first see him?'

'Yesterday afternoon. We had almost completed the 19th century sales when a small Van Gogh – an inferior copy by the painter of *The Good Samaritan* – came up. One of those painted during his last madness, full of turbulent spirals, the figures like tormented beasts. For some reason the Samaritan's face reminded me of Ahasuerus. Just then I looked up across the crowded auction room.' Georg sat forward. 'To my amazement there he was, sitting not three feet away in the front row of seats, staring me straight in the face. I could hardly take my eyes off him. As soon as the bidding started he came in hard, going up in two thousands of francs.'

'He took the painting?'

'No. Luckily I still had my wits about me. Obviously I had to be sure he was the right man. Previously his appearances have been solely as Ahasuerus, but few painters today are doing crucifixions in the *bel canto* style, and he may have tried to redress the balance of guilt by appearing in other roles, the Samaritan for example. He was left alone at 15,000 – actually the reserve was only ten – so I leaned over and had the painting withdrawn. I was sure he would come back today if he was Ahasuerus, and I needed twenty-four hours to get hold of you and the police. Two of Carnot's men will be here this afternoon. I told them some vague story and they'll be unobtrusive. Anyway, naturally there was the devil's own row when this little Van Gogh was withdrawn. Everyone here thought I'd gone mad. Our dark-faced friend leapt up and demanded the reason, so I had to say that I suspected the authenticity of the painting and was protecting the reputation of the gallery, but if satisfied would put it up the next day.'

'Clever of you,' I commented.

Georg inclined his head. 'I thought so too. It was a neat trap. Immediately he launched into a passionate defence of the painting – normally a man with his obvious experience of sale rooms would have damned it out of hand – bringing up all sorts of details about Vincent's third-rate pigments, the back of the canvas and so on. The *back* of the canvas, note, what the sitter would most remember about a painting. I said I was more or less convinced, and he promised to be back today. He left his address in case any difficulty came up.' Georg took a silver-embossed card from his pocket and read out: '"*Count Enrique Danilewicz, Villa d'Est, Cadaques, Costa Brava.*"' Across the card was enscribed: '*Ritz Hotel, Paris.*'

'Cadaques,' I repeated. 'Dali is nearby there, at Port Lligat. Another coincidence.'

'Perhaps more than a coincidence. Guess what the Catalan master is at present executing for the new Cathedral of St Joseph at San Diego? One of his greatest commissions to date. Exactly! A crucifixion. Our friend Ahasuerus is once more doing his rounds.'

Georg pulled a leather-bound pad from his centre drawer. 'Now listen to this. I've been doing some research on the identity of the models for Ahasuerus – usually some petty princeling or merchant-king. The Leonardo is untraceable. He kept open house, beggars and goats wandered through his studio at will, anyone could have got in and posed. But the others were more select. The Ahasuerus in the Holbein was posed by a Sir Henry Daniels, a leading banker and friend of Henry VIII. In the Veronese by a member of the Council of Ten, none other than the Doge-to-be, Enri Danieli – we've both stayed in the hotel of that name in Venice. In the Rubens by Baron Henrik Nielson, Danish Ambassador to Amsterdam, and in the Goya by a certain Enrico Da Nella, financier and great patron of the Prado. While in the Poussin by the famous dilettante, Henri, Duc de Nile.'

Georg closed the note-book with a flourish. I said: 'It's certainly remarkable.'

'You don't exaggerate. Danilewicz, Daniels, Danieli, Da Nella, de Nile and Nielson. Alias Ahasuerus. You know, Charles, I'm a little frightened, but I think we have the missing Leonardo within our grasp.'

Nothing was more disappointing, therefore, than the failure of our quarry to appear that afternoon.

\*   \*   \*

The transfer of the Van Gogh from the previous day's sales had fortunately given it a high lot number, after some three dozen 20th century paintings. As the bids for the Kandinskys and Legers came in, I sat on the podium behind Georg, surveying the elegant assembly below. In such an international gathering, of American connoisseurs, English press lords, French and Italian aristocracy, coloured by a generous sprinkling of ladies of the demi-monde, the presence of even the remarkable figure Georg had described would not have been over-conspicuous. However, as we moved steadily down the catalogue, and the flashing of the photographers' bulbs became more and more wearisome, I began to wonder whether he would appear at all. His seat in the front row remained reserved for him, and I waited impatiently for this fugitive through time and space to materialize and make his magnificent entry promptly as the Van Gogh was announced.

As it transpired, both the seat and the painting remained untaken. Put off by Georg's doubts as to its authenticity, the painting failed to reach its reserve, and as the last sales closed we were left alone on the podium, our bait untaken.

'He must have smelled a rat,' Georg whispered, after the attendants had confirmed that Count Danilewicz was not present in any of the other sale-rooms. A moment later a telephone call to the Ritz established that he had vacated his suite and left Paris for the south.

'No doubt he's expert at sidestepping such traps. What now?' I asked.

'Cadaques.'

'Georg! Are you insane?'

'Not at all. There's only a chance, but we must take it! Inspector Carnot will find a plane. I'll invent some fantasy to please him. Come on, Charles, I'm convinced we'll find the Leonardo in his villa.'

We arrived at Barcelona, Carnot in tow, with Superintendent Jurgens of Interpol to smooth our way through customs, and three hours later set off in a posse of police cars for Cadaques. The fast ride along that fantastic coast line, with its monstrous rocks like giant sleeping reptiles and the glazed light over the embalmed sea, reminiscent of all Dali's timeless beaches, was a fitting prelude to the final chapter. The air bled diamonds around us, sparkling off the immense spires of rock, the huge lunar ramparts suddenly giving way to placid bays of luminous water.

The Villa d'Est stood on a promontory a thousand feet above the town, its high walls and shuttered moorish windows glistening in the sunlight like white quartz. The great black doors, like the vaults of a cathedral, were sealed, and a continuous ringing of the bell brought no reply. At this a prolonged wrangle ensued between Jurgens and the local police, who were torn between their reluctance to offend an important local dignitary – Count Danilewicz had evidently founded a dozen scholarships for promising local artists – and their eagerness to partake in the discovery of the missing Leonardo.

Impatient of all this, Georg and I borrowed a car and chauffeur and set off for Port Lligat, promising the Inspector that we would return in time for the commercial airliner which was due to land at Barcelona from Paris some two hours later, presumably carrying Count Danilewicz. 'No doubt, however,' Georg remarked softly as we moved off, 'he travels by other transport.'

What excuse we would make to penetrate the private menage of Spain's most distinguished painter I had not decided, though the possibility of simultaneous one-man shows at Northeby's and Galleries Normande might have appeased him. As we drove down the final approach to the familiar tiered white villa by the water's edge, a large limousine was coming towards us, bearing away a recent guest.

Our two cars passed at a point where the effective width of the road was narrowed by a nexus of pot-holes, and for a moment the heavy saloons wallowed side by side in the dust like two groaning mastodons.

Suddenly, Georg clenched my elbow and pointed through the window. 'Charles! There he is!'

Lowering my window as the drivers cursed each other, I looked out into the dim cabin of the adjacent car. Sitting in the back seat, his head raised to the noise, was a huge Rasputin-like figure in a black pin-stripe suit, his white cuffs and gold tie-pin glinting in the shadows, gloved hands crossed in front of him over an ivory-handled cane. As we edged past I caught a glimpse of his great saturnine head, whose living features matched and corroborated exactly those which I had seen reproduced by so many hands upon so many canvases. The dark eyes glowed with an intense lustre, the black eyebrows rearing from his high forehead like wings, the sharp curve of the beard carrying the sweep of his strong jaw forward into the air like a spear.

Elegantly suited though he was, his whole presence radiated a tremendous restless energy, a powerful charisma that seemed to extend beyond the confines of the car. For a moment we exchanged glances, separated from each other by only two or three feet. He was staring beyond me, however, at some distant landmark, some invisible hill-crest forever silhouetted against the horizon, and I saw in his eyes that expression of irredeemable remorse, of almost hallucinatory despair, untouched by self-pity or any conceivable extenuation, that one imagines on the faces of the damned.

'Stop him!' Georg shouted into the noise. 'Charles, warn him!'

Our car edged upwards out of the final rut, and I shouted through the engine fumes:

'Ahasuerus! Ahasuerus!'

His wild eyes swung back, and he rose forward in his seat, a black arm on the window ledge, like some immense half-crippled angel about to take flight. Then the two cars surged apart, and we were separated from the limousine by a tornado of dust. Enchanted from the placid air, for ten minutes the squall seethed backwards and forwards across us.

By the time it subsided and we had managed to reverse, the great limousine had vanished.

They found the Leonardo in the Villa d'Est, propped against the wall in its great gilt frame in the dining-room. To everyone's surprise the house was found to be completely empty, though two manservants who had been given the day off testified that when they left it that morning it had been lavishly furnished as usual. However, as Georg de Stael remarked, no doubt the vanished tenant had his own means of transport.

The painting had suffered no damage, though the first cursory glance confirmed that a skilled hand had been at work on a small portion. The face of the black-robed figure once again looked upwards to the cross, a hint of hope, perhaps even of redemption, in its wistful gaze. The brush-work had dried, but Georg reported to me that the thin layer of varnish was still tacky.

On our feted and triumphant return to Paris, Georg and I recommended that in view of the hazards already suffered by the painting no further attempts should be made to clean or restore it, and with a grateful sigh the director and staff of the Louvre sealed it back into its wall. The painting may not be entirely by the hand of Leonardo da Vinci, but we feel that the few additions have earned their place.

No further news was heard of Count Danilewicz, but Georg recently told me that a Professor Henrico Daniella was reported to have been appointed director of the Museum of Pan-Christian Art at Santiago. His attempts to communicate with Professor Daniella had failed, but he gathered that the Museum was extremely anxious to build up a large collection of paintings of the Cross.

**· 1964**

# THE TERMINAL BEACH

At night, as he lay asleep on the floor of the ruined bunker, Traven heard the waves breaking along the shore of the lagoon, like the sounds of giant aircraft warming up at the ends of their runways. This memory of the great night raids against the Japanese mainland had filled his first months on the island with images of burning bombers falling through the air around him. Later, with the attacks of beri-beri, the nightmare passed and the waves began to remind him of the deep Atlantic rollers on the beach at Dakar, where he had been born, and of watching from the window in the evenings for his parents to drive home along the corniche road from the airport. Overcome by this long-forgotten memory, he woke uncertainly from the bed of old magazines on which he slept and went out to the dunes that screened the lagoon.

Through the cold night air he could see the abandoned Superfortresses lying among the palms beyond the perimeter of the emergency landing field three hundred yards away. Traven walked through the dark sand, already forgetting where the shore lay, although the atoll was little more than half a mile in width. Above him, along the crests of the dunes, the tall palms leaned into the dim air like the symbols of a cryptic alphabet. The landscape of the island was covered by strange ciphers.

Giving up the attempt to find the beach, Traven stumbled into a set of tracks left years earlier by a large caterpillar vehicle. The heat released by the weapons tests had fused the sand, and the double line of fossil imprints, uncovered by the evening air, wound its serpentine way among the hollows like the footfalls of an ancient saurian.

Too weak to walk any further, Traven sat down between the tracks. Hoping that they might lead him to the beach, he began to excavate the wedge-shaped grooves from a drift into which they disappeared. He returned to the bunker shortly before dawn, and slept through the hot silences of the following noon.

## The Blocks

As usual on these enervating afternoons, when not even a breath of on-shore breeze disturbed the dust, Traven sat in the shadow of one of the blocks, lost somewhere within the centre of the maze. His back resting against the rough concrete surface, he gazed with a phlegmatic eye down the surrounding aisles and at the line of doors facing him. Each afternoon he left his cell in the abandoned camera bunker among

589

the dunes and walked down into the blocks. For the first half an hour he restricted himself to the perimeter aisle, now and then trying one of the doors with the rusty key in his pocket – found among the litter of smashed bottles and cans in the isthmus of sand separating the testing ground from the air-strip – and then inevitably, with a sort of drugged stride, he set off into the centre of the blocks, breaking into a run and darting in and out of the corridors, as if trying to flush some invisible opponent from his hiding place. Soon he would be completely lost. Whatever his efforts to return to the perimeter, he always found himself once more in the centre.

Eventually he would abandon the task, and sit down in the dust, watching the shadows emerge from their crevices at the foot of the blocks. For some reason he invariably arranged to be trapped when the sun was at zenith – on Eniwetok, the thermonuclear noon.

One question in particular intrigued him: 'What sort of people would inhabit this minimal concrete city?'

## The Synthetic Landscape

'This island is a state of mind,' Osborne, one of the scientists working in the old submarine pens, was later to remark to Traven. The truth of this became obvious to Traven within two or three weeks of his arrival. Despite the sand and the few anaemic palms, the entire landscape of the island was synthetic, a man-made artefact with all the associations of a vast system of derelict concrete motorways. Since the moratorium on atomic tests, the island had been abandoned by the Atomic Energy Commission, and the wilderness of weapons aisles, towers and blockhouses ruled out any attempt to return it to its natural state. (There were also stronger unconscious motives, Traven recognized: if primitive man felt the need to assimilate events in the external world to his own psyche, 20th century man had reversed this process; by this Cartesian yardstick, the island at least *existed*, in a sense true of few other places.)

But apart from a few scientific workers, no one yet felt any wish to visit the former testing ground, and the naval patrol boat anchored in the lagoon had been withdrawn three years before Traven's arrival. Its ruined appearance, and the associations of the island with the period of the Cold War – what Traven had christened 'The Pre-Third' – were profoundly depressing, an Auschwitz of the soul whose mausoleums contained the mass graves of the still undead. With the Russo-American *détente* this nightmarish chapter of history had been gladly forgotten.

## The Pre-Third

*The actual and potential destructiveness of the atomic bomb plays straight into the hands of the Unconscious. The most cursory study of the dream-life and fantasies of the insane shows that ideas of world-destruction are latent in the unconscious mind ... Nagasaki destroyed by the magic of science is the nearest man has yet approached to the realization of dreams that even during the safe immobility of sleep are accustomed to develop into nightmares of anxiety.*

Glover: 'War, Sadism and Pacifism'

The Pre-Third: the period was characterized in Traven's mind above all by its moral and psychological inversions, by its sense of the whole of history, and in particular of the immediate future – the two decades, 1945–65 – suspended from the quivering volcano's lip of World War III. Even the death of his wife and six-year-old son in a motor accident seemed only part of this immense synthesis of the historical and psychic zero, the frantic highways where each morning they met their deaths the advance causeways to the global armageddon.

## Third Beach

He had come ashore at midnight, after a hazardous search for an opening in the reef. The small motorboat he had hired from an Australian pearl-diver at Charlotte Island subsided into the shallows, its hull torn by the sharp coral. Exhausted, Traven walked through the darkness among the dunes, where the dim outlines of bunkers and concrete towers loomed between the palms.

He woke the next morning into bright sunlight, lying halfway down the slope of a wide concrete beach. This ringed an empty reservoir or target basin some two hundred feet in diameter, part of a system of artificial lakes built down the centre of the atoll. Leaves and dust choked the exit grilles, and a pool of warm water two feet deep lay below him, reflecting a distant line of palms.

Traven sat up and took stock of himself. This brief inventory, which merely confirmed his physical identity, was limited to little more than his thin body in its frayed cotton garments. In the context of the surrounding terrain, however, even this collection of tatters seemed to possess a unique vitality. The desolation and emptiness of the island, and the absence of any local fauna, were emphasized by the huge sculptural forms of the target basins set into its surface. Separated from each other by narrow isthmuses, the lakes stretched away along the curve of the atoll. On either side, sometimes shaded by the few palms that had gained a precarious purchase in the cracked cement, were roadways, camera towers and isolated blockhouses, together forming a continuous concrete cap upon the island, a functional, megalithic architecture as grey and minatory (and apparently as ancient, in its projection into, and from, time future) as any of Assyria and Babylon.

The series of weapons tests had fused the sand in layers, and the pseudo-geological strata condensed the brief epochs, microseconds in duration, of thermonuclear time. Typically the island inverted the geologist's maxim, 'The key to the past lies in the present.' Here, the key to the present lay in the future. This island was a fossil of time future, its bunkers and blockhouses illustrating the principle that the fossil record of life was one of armour and the exoskeleton.

Traven knelt in the warm pool, and splashed his shirt and trousers. The reflection revealed the watery image of gaunt shoulders and bearded face. He had come to the island with no supplies other than a small bar of chocolate, assuming that in some way the island would provide its own sustenance. Perhaps, too, he had identified the need for food with a forward motion in time, and that with his return to the past, or at most into a zone of non-time, this need would be eliminated. The privations of the previous six months, during his journey across the Pacific, had already reduced his always thin body to that of a migrant beggar, held together by little more than the preoccupied gaze in his eye. Yet this emaciation, by stripping away the superfluities of the flesh, revealed an inner sinewy toughness, an economy and directness of movement.

For several hours Traven wandered about, inspecting one bunker after another for a convenient place to sleep. He crossed the remains of a small landing field, next to a dump where a dozen B-29s lay across one another like dead reptile birds.

### The Corpses

Once he entered a small street of metal shacks, containing a cafeteria, recreation rooms and shower stalls. A wrecked juke-box lay half-buried in the sand behind the cafeteria, its selection of records still in their rack.

Further along, flung into a small target lake fifty yards from the shacks, were the bodies of what at first he thought were the former inhabitants of this ghost town – a dozen life-size plastic models. Their half-melted faces, contorted into bleary grimaces, gazed up at him from the jumble of legs and torsoes.

On either side of him, muffled by the dunes, came the sounds of waves, the great rollers on the seaward side breaking over the reefs, and on to the beaches within the lagoon. However, he avoided the sea, hesitating before any rise or dune that might take him within its sight. Everywhere the camera towers offered him a convenient aerial view of the confused topography of the island, but he avoided their rusting ladders.

Traven soon realized that however random the blockhouses and towers might seem, their common focus dominated the landscape and gave to it a unique perspective. As he noticed when he sat down to rest in the window slit of one of the bunkers, all these observation posts occupied positions on a series of concentric perimeters, moving in tightening arcs towards the inmost sanctuary. This ultimate circle, below ground zero, remained hidden beyond a line of dunes a quarter of a mile to the west.

### The Terminal Bunker

After sleeping for a few nights in the open, Traven returned to the concrete beach where he had woken on his first morning on the island, and made his home – if the term could be applied to that damp crumbling hovel –

in a camera bunker fifty yards from the target lakes. The dark chamber between the thick canted walls, tomb-like though it might seem, gave him a sense of physical reassurance. Outside, the sand drifted against the sides, half-burying the narrow doorway, as if crystallizing the immense epoch of time that had elapsed since the bunker's construction. The narrow rectangles of the five camera slits, their shapes and positions determined by the instruments, studded the west wall like runic ideograms. Variations on these ciphers decorated the walls of the other bunkers, the unique signature of the island. In the mornings, if Traven was awake, he would always find the sun divided into its five emblematic beacons.

Most of the time the chamber was filled only by a damp gloomy light. In the control tower at the landing field Traven found a collection of discarded magazines, and used these to make a bed. One day, lying in the bunker shortly after the first attack of beri-beri, he pulled out a magazine pressing into his back and found inside it a full-page photograph of a six-year-old girl. This blonde-haired child, with her composed expression and self-immersed eyes, filled him with a thousand painful memories of his son. He pinned the page to the wall and for days gazed at it through his reveries.

For the first few weeks Traven made little attempt to leave the bunker, and postponed any further exploration of the island. The symbolic journey through its inner circles set its own times of arrival and departure. He evolved no routine for himself. All sense of time soon vanished, and his life became completely existential, an absolute break separating one moment from the next like two quantal events. Too weak to forage for food, he lived on the old ration packs he found in the wrecked Superfortresses. Without any implement, it took him all day to open the cans. His physical decline continued, but he watched his spindling legs and arms with indifference.

By now he had forgotten the existence of the sea and vaguely assumed the atoll to be part of some continuous continental table. A hundred yards to the north and south of the bunker a line of dunes, topped by the palisade of enigmatic palms, screened the lagoon and sea, and the faint muffled drumming of the waves at night had fused with his memories of war and childhood. To the east was the emergency landing strip and the abandoned aircraft. In the afternoon light their shifting rectilinear shadows made them appear to writhe and pivot. In front of the bunker, where he would sit, was the system of target lakes, the shallow basins extending across the atoll.

Above him, the five apertures looked out upon this scene like the tutelary symbols of a futuristic myth.

### The Lakes and the Spectres

The lakes had been designed to reveal any radiobiological changes in a selected range of fauna, but the specimens had long since bloomed into grotesque parodies of themselves and been destroyed.

Sometimes in the evenings, when a sepulchral light lay over the concrete bunkers and causeways, and the basins seemed like ornamental lakes in a city of deserted mausoleums, abandoned even by the dead, he would see the spectres of his wife and son standing on the opposite bank. Their solitary figures appeared to have been watching him for hours. Although they never moved, Traven was sure they were beckoning to him. Roused from his reverie, he would stumble forward across the dark sand to the edge of the lake and wade through the water, shouting soundlessly at the two figures as they moved away hand in hand among the lakes and disappeared across the distant causeways.

Shivering with cold, Traven would return to the bunker and lie on the bed of old magazines, waiting for their return. The image of their faces, the pale lantern of his wife's cheeks, floated on the river of his memory.

### The Blocks (II)

It was not until he discovered the blocks that Traven realized he would never leave the island.

At this stage, some two months after his arrival, Traven had exhausted his small cache of food, and the symptoms of beri-beri had become more acute. The numbness in his hands and feet, and the gradual loss of strength, continued. Only by an immense effort, and the knowledge that the inner sanctum of the island still lay unexplored, did he manage to leave the palliasse of magazines and make his way from the bunker.

As he sat in the drift of sand by the doorway that evening, he noticed a light shining through the palms far into the distance around the atoll. Confusing this with the image of his wife and son, and visualizing them waiting for him at some warm hearth among the dunes, Traven set off towards the light. Within a hundred yards he lost his sense of direction. He blundered about for several hours on the edges of the landing strip, and succeeded only in cutting his foot on a broken coca-cola bottle in the sand.

After postponing his search for the night, he set out again in earnest the next morning. As he moved past the towers and blockhouses the heat lay over the island in an unbroken mantle. He had entered a zone devoid of time. Only the narrowing perimeters warned him that he was crossing the inner field of the fire-table.

He climbed the ridge which marked the furthest point in his previous exploration of the island. From the plain below it the recording towers rose into the air like obelisks. Traven walked down towards them. On their grey walls were the faint outlines of human forms in stylized poses, the flash-shadows of the target community burnt into the cement. Here and there, where the concrete apron had cracked, a line of palms hung in the motionless air. The target lakes were smaller, filled with the broken bodies of plastic models. Most of them lay in the inoffensive domestic postures into which they had been placed before the tests.

Beyond the furthest line of dunes, where the camera towers began to turn and face him, were the tops of what seemed to be a herd of square-backed elephants. They were drawn up in precise ranks in a hollow that formed a shallow corral, the sunlight reflected off their backs.

Traven advanced towards them, limping on his cut foot. On either side of him the loosening sand had excavated the dunes, and several of the blockhouses tilted on their sides. This plain of bunkers stretched for some quarter of a mile, the half-submerged hulks, bombed out onto the surface in some earlier test, like the abandoned wombs that had given birth to this herd of megaliths.

## The Blocks (III)

To grasp something of the vast number and oppressive size of the blocks, and their impact upon Traven, one must try to visualize sitting in the shade of one of these concrete monsters, or walking about in the centre of this enormous labyrinth that extended across the central table of the island. There were two thousand of them, each a perfect cube 15 feet in height, regularly spaced at ten-yard intervals. They were arranged in a series of tracts, each composed of two hundred blocks, inclined to one another and to the direction of the blast. They had weathered only slightly in the years since they were first built, and their gaunt profiles were like the cutting faces of a gigantic die-plate, devised to stamp out rectilinear volumes of air the size of a house. Three of the sides were smooth and unbroken, but the fourth, facing away from the blast, contained a narrow inspection door.

It was this feature of the blocks that Traven found particularly disturbing. Despite the considerable number of doors, by some freak of perspective only those in a single aisle were visible at any point within the maze. As he walked from the perimeter line into the centre of the massif, line upon line of the small metal doors appeared and receded.

Approximately twenty of the blocks, those immediately below ground zero, were solid: the walls of the remainder were of varying thicknesses. From the outside they appeared to be of uniform solidity.

As he entered the first of the long aisles, Traven felt the sense of fatigue that had dogged him for so many months begin to lift. With their geometric regularity and finish, the blocks seemed to occupy more than their own volumes of space, imposing on him a mood of absolute calm and order. He walked on into the centre of the maze, eager to shut out the rest of the island. After a few random turns to left and right, he found himself alone, the vistas to the sea, lagoon and island closed.

Here he sat down with his back to one of the blocks, the quest for his wife and son forgotten. For the first time since his arrival at the island the sense of dissociation set off by its derelict landscape began to recede.

One development he did not expect. With dusk, and the need to leave the blocks and find food, he realized that he had lost himself. However he retraced his steps, struck out left or right at an oblique course, oriented himself around the sun and pressed on resolutely north or south, he found himself back again at his starting point. Only when darkness came did he manage to make his escape.

Abandoning his former home near the aircraft dump, Traven collected together what canned food he could find in the waist turret and cockpit lockers of the Superfortresses. He pulled them across the atoll on a crude sledge. Fifty yards from the perimeter of the blocks he took over a tilting bunker, and pinned the fading photograph of the blonde-haired child to the wall beside the door. The page was falling to pieces, like a fragmenting mirror of himself. Since the discovery of the blocks he had become a creature of reflexes, kindled from levels above those of his existing nervous system (if the autonomic system was dominated by the past, Traven sensed, the cerebro-spinal reached towards the future). Each evening when he woke he would eat without appetite and then wander among the blocks. Sometimes he took a canteen of water with him and remained there for two or three days on end.

### The Submarine Pens

This precarious existence continued for the following weeks. As he walked out to the blocks one evening, he again saw his wife and son, standing among the dunes below a solitary camera tower, their faces watching him expressionlessly. He realized that they had followed him across the island from their former haunt among the dried-up lakes. At about this time he once again saw the distant light beckoning, and decided to continue his exploration of the island.

Half a mile further along the atoll he found a group of four submarine pens, built over an inlet, now drained, which wound through the dunes from the sea. The pens still contained several feet of water, filled with strange luminescent fish and plants. The warning light winked at intervals from the apex of a metal scaffold. The remains of a substantial camp, only recently vacated, stood on the pier outside. Greedily, Traven heaped his sledge with the provisions stored inside one of the metal shacks.

With this change of diet, the beri-beri receded, and during the next days he returned often to the camp. It appeared to be the site of a biological expedition. In the field office he came across a series of large charts of mutated chromosomes. He rolled them up and took them back to his bunker. The abstract patterns were meaningless, but during his recovery he amused himself by devising suitable titles for them. (Later, passing the aircraft dump on one of his forays, he found the half-buried juke-box, and tore the list of records from the selection panel, realizing that these were the most appropriate captions. Thus embroidered, the charts took on many layers of associations.)

### Traven: In Parenthesis

Elements in a quantal world:
  The terminal beach.
  The terminal bunker.
  The blocks.

*       *       *

The landscape is coded.

Entry points into the future=Levels in a spinal landscape=zones of significant time.

*August 5. Found the man Traven. A strange derelict figure, hiding in a bunker in the deserted interior of the island. He is suffering from severe exposure and malnutrition, but is unaware of this or, for that matter, of any other events in the world around him . . .*

*He maintains that he came to the island to carry out some scientific project – unstated – but I suspect that he understands his real motives and the unique role of the island . . . In some way its landscape seems to be involved with certain unconscious notions of time, and in particular with those that may be a repressed premonition of our own deaths. The attractions and dangers of such an architecture, as the past has shown, need no stressing . . .*

*August 6. He has the eyes of the possessed. I would guess that he is neither the first, nor the last, to visit the island.*

*– from Dr C. Osborne, 'Eniwetok Diary.'*

## *Traven lost within the Blocks*

With the exhaustion of his supplies, Traven remained within the perimeter of the blocks almost continuously, conserving what strength remained to him to walk slowly down their empty corridors. The infection in his right foot made it difficult for him to replenish his supplies from the stores left by the biologists, and as his strength ebbed he found progressively less incentive to make his way out of the blocks. The system of megaliths now provided a complete substitute for those functions of his mind which gave to it its sense of the sustained rational order of time and space. Without them, his awareness of reality shrank to little more than the few square inches of sand beneath his feet.

On one of his last ventures into the maze, he spent all night and much of the following morning in a futile attempt to escape. Dragging himself from one rectangle of shadow to another, his leg as heavy as a club and apparently inflamed to the knee, he realized that he must soon find an equivalent for the blocks or he would end his life within them, trapped inside this self-constructed mausoleum as surely as the retinue of Pharaoh.

He was sitting helplessly somewhere in the centre of the system, the faceless lines of tomb-booths receding from him, when the sky was slowly divided by the drone of a light aircraft. This passed overhead, and then returned five minutes later. Seizing his opportunity, Traven struggled to his feet and made his exit from the blocks, his head raised to follow the faintly glistening beacon of the exhaust trail.

As he lay in the bunker he dimly heard the aircraft return and carry out an inspection of the site.

## *A Belated Rescue*

'Who are you? Do you realize you're on your last legs?'

'Traven ... I've had some sort of accident. I'm glad you flew over.'

'I'm sure you are. But why didn't you use our radio-telephone? Anyway, we'll call the Navy and have you picked up.'

'No ...' Traven sat up on one elbow and felt weakly in his hip pocket. 'I have a pass somewhere. I'm carrying out research.'

'Into what?' The question assumed a complete understanding of Traven's motives. He lay in the shade under the lee of the bunker, and drank weakly from a canteen as Dr Osborne dressed his foot. 'You've also been stealing our stores.'

Traven shook his head. Fifty yards away the striped blue Cessna stood on the concrete apron like a brilliant dragonfly. 'I didn't realize you were coming back.'

'You must be in a trance.'

The young woman sitting at the controls of the aircraft climbed out and walked over to them. She glanced at the grey bunkers and towers, and seemed uninterested in the decrepit figure of Traven. Osborne spoke to her and after a downward glance at Traven she went back to the aircraft. As she turned Traven rose involuntarily, recognizing the child in the photograph he had pinned to the wall of the bunker. Then he remembered that the magazine could not have been more than four or five years old.

The engine of the aircraft started. As Traven watched, it turned on to one of the roadways and took off into the wind.

Later that afternoon the young woman drove over to the blocks by jeep and unloaded a small camp-bed and a canvas awning. During the intervening hours Traven had slept. He woke refreshed when Osborne returned from his scrutiny of the surrounding dunes.

'What are you doing here?' the young woman asked as she secured the guy-ropes to the roof of the bunker.

Traven watched her move about. 'I'm ... searching for my wife and son.'

'They're on this island?' Surprised, but taking the reply at face value, she looked around her. 'Here?'

'In a manner of speaking.'

After inspecting the bunker, Osborne joined them. 'The child in the photograph – is she your daughter?'

Traven hesitated. 'No. She's adopted *me*.'

Unable to make any sense of his replies, but accepting his assurances that he would leave the island, Osborne and the young woman drove back to their camp. Each day Osborne returned to change the dressing, driven by the young woman, who seemed now to grasp the role cast for her by Traven. Osborne, when he learned of Traven's previous career as a military pilot, appeared to suspect that he might be a

latter-day martyr left high and dry by the moratorium on thermonuclear tests.

'A guilt complex isn't an indiscriminate supply of moral sanctions. I
think you may be overstretching yours.' When he mentioned the name
Eatherly, Traven shook his head.

Undeterred, Osborne pressed: 'Are you sure you're not making similar
use of the image of Eniwetok – waiting for your Pentecostal wind?'

'Believe me, Doctor, no,' Traven replied firmly. 'For me the hydrogen
bomb was a symbol of absolute *freedom*. I feel it's given me the right –
the obligation, even – to do anything I want.'

'That seems strange logic,' Osborne commented. 'Aren't we at least
responsible for our physical selves, if for nothing else?'

'Not now, I think,' Traven replied. 'After all, in effect we are men raised
from the dead.'

Often, however, he thought of Eatherly: the prototypal Pre-Third Man
– dating the Pre-Third from August 6, 1945 – carrying a full load of
cosmic guilt.

Shortly after Traven was strong enough to walk, he had to be rescued
from the blocks for a second time. Osborne became less conciliatory.

'Our work is almost complete,' he said warningly. 'You'll die here,
Traven. What *are* you looking for among those blocks?'

To himself, Traven murmured: the tomb of the unknown civilian, *Homo
hydrogenensis*, Eniwetok Man. 'Doctor,' he said, 'your laboratory is at the
wrong end of this island.'

Tartly, Osborne replied: 'I'm aware of that, Traven. There are rarer fish
swimming in your head than in any submarine pen.'

On the day before they left, the young woman drove Traven over
to the lakes where he had first arrived. As a final present, an ironic
gesture unexpected from the elderly biologist, she had brought from
Osborne the correct list of legends for the chromosome charts. They
stopped by the derelict juke-box and she pasted them on to the selection panel.

They wandered among the supine wrecks of the Superfortresses. Traven
lost sight of her, and for the next ten minutes searched in and out of
the dunes. He found her standing in a small amphitheatre formed by
the sloping mirrors of a solar energy device built by one of the visiting
expeditions. She smiled to Traven as he stepped through the scaffolding.
A dozen fragmented images of herself were reflected in the broken panes
– in some she was sans head, in others multiples of her arms circled about
her like the serpent limbs of a Hindu goddess. Confused, Traven turned
and walked back to the jeep.

As they drove away he recovered himself. He described his glimpses
of his wife and son. 'Their faces are always calm,' he said. 'My son's
particularly, though really he was always laughing. The only time his

face was grave was when he was being born – then he seemed millions of years old.'

The young woman nodded. 'I hope you find them.' As an afterthought she added: 'Dr Osborne is going to tell the Navy that you're here. Hide somewhere.'

Traven thanked her.

From the centre of the blocks he waved to her the following day when she flew away for the last time.

### The Naval Party

When the search party came for him Traven hid in the only logical place. Fortunately the search was perfunctory, and was called off after a few hours. The sailors had brought a supply of beer with them and the search soon turned into a drunken ramble.

On the walls of the recording towers Traven later found balloons of obscene dialogue chalked into the mouths of the shadowy figures, giving their postures the priapic gaiety of the dancers in cave drawings.

The climax of the party was the ignition of a store of gasoline in an underground tank near the airstrip. As he listened, first to the megaphones shouting his name, the echoes receding among the dunes like the forlorn calls of dying birds, then to the boom of the explosion and the laughter as the landing craft left, Traven felt a premonition that these were the last sounds he would hear.

He had hidden in one of the target basins, lying among the broken bodies of the plastic models. In the hot sunlight their deformed faces gaped at him sightlessly from the tangle of limbs, their blurred smiles like those of the soundlessly laughing dead.

Their faces filled his mind as he climbed over the bodies and returned to his bunker. As he walked towards the blocks he saw the figures of his wife and son standing in his path. They were less than ten yards from him, their white faces watching him with a look of almost overwhelming expectancy. Never had Traven seen them so close to the blocks. His wife's pale features seemed illuminated from within, her lips parted as if in greeting, one hand raised to take his own. His son's face, with its curiously fixed expression, regarded him with the same enigmatic smile of the child in the photograph.

'Judith! David!' Startled, Traven ran forwards to them. Then, in a sudden movement of light, their clothes turned into shrouds, and he saw the wounds that disfigured their necks and chests. Appalled, he cried out. As they vanished, he ran off into the safety of the blocks.

### The Catechism of Goodbye

This time he found himself, as Osborne had predicted, unable to leave the blocks.

Somewhere in the centre of the maze, he sat with his back against one of the concrete flanks, his eyes raised to the sun. Around him the lines of cubes formed the horizon of his world. At times they would appear to advance towards him, looming over him like cliffs, the intervals between them narrowing so that they were little more than an arm's length apart, a labyrinth of corridors running between them. They then would recede from him, separating from each other like points in an expanding universe, until the nearest line formed an intermittent palisade along the horizon.

Time had become quantal. For hours it would be noon, the shadows contained within the blocks, the heat reflected off the concrete floor. Abruptly, he would find that it was early afternoon or evening, the shadows everywhere like pointing fingers.

'Goodbye, Eniwetok,' he murmured.

Somewhere there was a flicker of light, as if one of the blocks, like a counter on an abacus, had been plucked away.

Goodbye, Los Alamos. Again, a block seemed to vanish. The corridors around him remained intact, but somewhere in his mind had appeared a small interval of neutral space.

Goodbye, Hiroshima.

Goodbye, Alamagordo.

'Goodbye, Moscow, London, Paris, New York . . .'

Shuttles flickered, a ripple of lost integers. He stopped, realizing the futility of this megathlon farewell. Such a leave-taking required him to fix his signature upon every one of the particles in the universe.

### Total Noon: Eniwetok

The blocks now occupied positions on an endlessly revolving circus wheel. They carried him upwards into the sky, from where he could see the whole island and the sea, and then down again through the opaque disc of the concrete floor. From here he looked up at the under-surface of the concrete cap, an inverted landscape of rectilinear hollows, the dome-shaped mounds of the lake-system, the thousands of empty cubic pits of the blocks.

### 'Goodbye, Traven.'

Near the end, he found to his disappointment that this ultimate rejection gained him nothing.

In the interval of lucidity, he looked down at his emaciated arms and legs, decorated with a lace-work of ulcers. To his right was a trail of disturbed dust, the wavering marks of slack heels.

To his left lay a long corridor between the blocks, joining an oblique series a hundred yards away. Among these, where a narrow interval revealed the open space beyond, was a crescent-shaped shadow, poised in the air above the ground.

During the next half an hour it moved slowly, turning as the sun swung, the profile of a dune.

## The Crevice

Seizing on this cipher, which hung before him like a symbol on a shield, Traven pushed himself through the dust. He climbed precariously to his feet, and shielded his eyes from the blocks. He moved forward a few paces at a time.

Ten minutes later he emerged from the western perimeter of the blocks, like a tottering mendicant leaving behind a silent desert city. The dune lay fifty yards in front of him. Beyond it, bearing the shadow like a screen, was a ridge of limestone that ran away among the hillocks of the wasteland beyond this point of the atoll. The remains of an old bulldozer, bales of barbed wire and fifty-gallon drums lay half-buried in the sand. Traven approached the dune, reluctant to leave this anonymous swell of sand. He shuffled around its edges, and sat down in the mouth of a shallow crevice below the brow of the ridge.

After dusting his clothes, he gazed out patiently at the great circle of blocks.

Ten minutes later he noticed that someone was watching him.

## The Marooned Japanese

This corpse, whose eyes stared up at Traven, lay to his left at the bottom of the crevice. That of a man of middle age and strong build, it rested on its back with its head on a pillow of stone, hands outstretched at its sides, as if surveying the window of the sky. The fabric of the clothes had rotted to a bleached grey vestment, but in the absence of any small animal predators on the island the skin and musculature of the corpse had been preserved. Here and there, at the angle of knee or wrist, a bony point glinted through the leathery integument of the skin, but the facial mask was still intact, and revealed a male Japanese of the professional classes. Looking down at the strong nose, high forehead and broad mouth, Traven guessed that the Japanese had been a doctor or lawyer.

Puzzled as to how the corpse had found itself here, Traven slid a few feet down the slope. There were no radiation burns on the skin, which indicated that the Japanese had been there for five years or less. Nor did he appear to be wearing a uniform, so had not been some unfortunate member of a military or scientific party.

To the left of the corpse, within reach of his left hand, was a frayed leather case, the remains of a map wallet. To the right was the husk of a haversack, open to reveal a canteen of water and a small mess-tin.

Traven slid down the slope until his feet touched the splitting soles of the corpse's shoes, the reflex of starvation making him for the moment ignore that the Japanese had deliberately chosen to die in the crevice. He reached out and seized the canteen. A cupful of flat water swilled around the rusting bottom. Traven gulped down the water, the dissolved metal salts cloaking his lips and tongue with a bitter film. The mess-tin was empty except for a tacky coating of condensed syrup. Traven prised at this with the lid, and chewed at the tarry flakes, letting them dissolve in his mouth with an almost intoxicating sweetness. After a few moments he felt light-headed and sat back beside the corpse. Its sightless eyes regarded him with unmoving compassion.

### The Fly

*(A small fly, which Traven presumes has followed him into the fissure, now buzzes about the corpse's face. Guiltily, Traven leans forward to kill it, then reflects that perhaps this minuscule sentry has been the corpse's faithful companion, in return fed on the rich liqueurs and distillations of its pores. Carefully, to avoid injuring the fly, he encourages it to alight on his wrist.)*

DR YASUDA: Thank you, Traven. In my position, you understand . . .

TRAVEN: Of course, Doctor. I'm sorry I tried to kill it – these ingrained habits, you know, they're not easy to shrug off. Your sister's children in Osaka in '44, the exigencies of war, I hate to plead them. Most known motives are so despicable, one searches the unknown in the hope that . . .

YASUDA: Please, Traven, do not be embarrassed. The fly is lucky to retain its identity for so long. That son you mourn, not to mention my own two nieces and nephew, did they not die each day? Every parent in the world grieves for the lost sons and daughters of their earlier childhoods.

TRAVEN: You're very tolerant, Doctor. I wouldn't dare –

YASUDA: Not at all, Traven. I make no apologies for you. Each of us is little more than the meagre residue of the infinite unrealized possibilities of our lives. But your son, and my nephew, are fixed in our minds forever, their identities as certain as the stars.

TRAVEN: (*not entirely convinced*) That may be so, Doctor, but it leads to a dangerous conclusion in the case of this island. For instance, the blocks –

YASUDA: They are precisely what I refer to, Traven. Here among the blocks you at last find an image of yourself free of the hazards of time and space. This island is an ontological Garden of Eden, why seek to expel yourself into a world of quantal flux?

TRAVEN: Excuse me (*The fly has flown back to the corpse's face and sits in one of the dried-up orbits, giving the good doctor an expression of quizzical beadiness. Reaching forward, Traven entices it on to his palm. He examines it carefully*) Well, yes, these bunkers may be ontological objects, but whether this is the ontological fly is doubtful. It's true that on this island it's the *only* fly, which is the next best thing . . .

YASUDA: You can't accept the plurality of the universe – ask yourself why, Traven. Why should this obsess you? It seems to me that you are hunting for the white leviathan, zero. The beach is a dangerous zone. Avoid it. Have a proper humility, pursue a philosophy of acceptance.

TRAVEN: Then may I ask why you came here, Doctor?

YASUDA: To feed this fly. 'What greater love –?'

TRAVEN: (*Still puzzling*) It doesn't really solve my problem. The blocks, you see . . .

YASUDA: Very well, if you must have it that way . . .

TRAVEN: But, Doctor –

YASUDA: (*Peremptorily*) Kill that fly!

TRAVEN: That's not an end, or a beginning.

    (*Hopelessly, he kills the fly. Exhausted, he falls asleep beside the corpse.*)

### The Terminal Beach

Searching for a piece of rope in the refuse dump behind the dunes, Traven found a bale of rusty wire. After unwinding it, he secured a harness around the corpse's chest and dragged it from the crevice. The lid of a wooden crate made a crude sledge. Traven fastened the corpse to it in a sitting position, and set off along the perimeter of the blocks. Around him the island remained silent. The lines of palms hung in the sunlight, only his own motion varying the shifting ciphers of their criss-crossing trunks. The square turrets of the camera towers jutted from the dunes like forgotten obelisks.

An hour later, when Traven reached the awning by his bunker, he untied the wire cord he had fastened around his waist. He took the chair left for him by Dr Osborne and carried it to a point midway between the bunker and the blocks. Then he tied the body of the Japanese to the chair, arranging the hands so that they rested on the wooden arms giving the moribund figure a posture of calm repose.

This done to his satisfaction, Traven returned to the bunker and squatted under the awning.

As the next days passed into weeks, the dignified figure of the Japanese sat in his chair fifty yards from him, guarding Traven from the blocks. He now had sufficient strength to rouse himself at intervals and forage for food. In the hot sunlight the skin of the Japanese became more and more bleached, and Traven would wake at night and find the sepulchral figure sitting there, arms resting at its sides, in the shadows that crossed the concrete floor. At these moments he would often see his wife and son watching him from the dunes. As time passed they came closer, and he would sometimes find them only a few yards behind him.

Patiently Traven waited for them to speak to him, thinking of the great blocks whose entrance was guarded by the seated figure of the dead archangel, as the waves broke on the distant shore and the burning bombers fell through his dreams.

**﹐1964**

# · THE ILLUMINATED MAN

*By day fantastic birds flew through the petrified forest, and jewelled alligators glittered like heraldic salamanders on the banks of the crystalline rivers. By night the illuminated man raced among the trees, his arms like golden cartwheels, his head like a spectral crown . . .*

During the last year, since the news of what is now variously known as the Hubble Effect, the Rostov-Lysenko Syndrome and the LePage Amplification Synchronoclasmique first gained worldwide attention, there have been so many conflicting reports from the three focal areas in Florida, Byelorussia and Madagascar that I feel it necessary to preface my own account of the phenomenon with the assurance that it is entirely based upon first-hand experience. All the events I describe were witnessed by myself during the recent, almost tragic visit to the Florida Everglades arranged by the United States government for the scientific attachés in Washington. The only facts I was not able to verify are the details of Charles Foster Marquand's life which I obtained from Captain Shelley, the late chief of police at Maynard, and although he was a biased and untrustworthy witness I feel that in this single case he was almost certainly accurate.

How much longer remains before all of us, wherever we are, become expert authorities upon the exact nature of the Hubble Effect is still open to conjecture. As I write, here within the safety and peace of the garden of the British Embassy at Puerto Rico, I see a report in today's *New York Times* that the whole of the Florida peninsula, with the exception of a single highway to Tampa, has been closed and that to date some three million of the state's inhabitants have been resettled in other parts of the United States. But apart from the estimated losses in real estate values and hotel revenues ('Oh, Miami,' I cannot help saying to myself, 'you city of a thousand cathedrals to the rainbow sun') the news of this extraordinary human migration seems to have prompted little comment. Such is mankind's innate optimism, our conviction that we can survive any deluge or cataclysm, that we unconsciously dismiss the momentous events in Florida with a shrug, confident that some means will be found to avert the crisis when it comes.

And yet it now seems obvious that the real crisis is long past. Tucked away on a back page of the same *New York Times* is a short report of the sighting of another 'double galaxy' by observers at the Hubble Institute on Mount Palomar. The news is summarized in less than a dozen lines and without comment, although the implication is inescapable that yet another focal area has been set up somewhere on the earth's surface, perhaps in the temple-filled jungles of Cambodia or the haunted amber forests of the Chilean highland. But it is only a year since the Mount Palomar astronomers identified the first double galaxy in the constellation Andromeda, the great oblate diadem that is probably the most beautiful object in the universe, the island galaxy of M 31.

Although these sightings by now seem commonplace, and at least half a dozen 'double constellations' can be picked from the night sky on any evening of the week, four months ago when the party of scientific attachés landed at Miami Airport on a conducted tour of the stricken area there was still widespread ignorance of what the Hubble Effect (as the phenomenon had been christened in the Western Hemisphere and the English-speaking world) actually involved. Apart from a handful of forestry workers and biologists from the US Department of Agriculture, few qualified observers had witnessed the phenomenon and there were implausible stories in the newspapers of the forest 'crystallizing' and everything 'turning into coloured glass'.

One unfortunate consequence of the Hubble Effect is that it is virtually impossible to photograph anything transformed by it. As any reader of scientific journals knows, glassware is extremely difficult to reproduce, and even blocks of the highest screen on the best quality art papers – let alone the coarse blocks used on newsprint – have failed to reproduce the brilliant multi-faceted lattices of the Hubble Effect, with their myriads of interior prisms, as anything more than a vague blur like half-melted snow.

Perhaps in retaliation, the newspapers had begun to suggest that the secrecy which surrounded the affected area in the Everglades – then no more than three or four acres of forest to the north-east of Maynard – was being deliberately imposed by the administration, and a clamour was raised about the rights of inspection and the unseen horrors concealed from the public. It so happened that the focal area discovered by Professor Auguste LePage in Madagascar – in the Matarre Valley, far into the hinterland of the island – was about 150 miles from the nearest road-head and totally inaccessible, while the Soviet authorities had clamped a security cordon as tight as Los Alamos's around their own affected area in the Pripet Marshes of Byelorussia, where a legion of scientific workers under the leadership of the metabiologist Lysenko (all, incidentally, chasing a complete red herring) was analysing every facet of the inexplicable phenomenon.

Before any political capital could be made from this campaign, the Department of Agriculture in Washington announced that all facilities for inspection would be gladly provided, and the invitation to the scientific attachés proceeded as part of the programme of technical missions and tours.

As we drove westwards from Miami Airport it was immediately obvious that in a sense the newspapers had been right, and that there was far more to the Hubble Effect than the official handouts had let us believe. The highway to Maynard had been closed to general traffic, and our bus twice overtook military convoys within twenty miles of Miami. In addition, as if to remind us of the celestial origin of the phenomenon, the news of yet another manifestation came through on the radio bulletins.

'There's an Associated Press report from New Delhi,' George Schneider, the West German attaché, came aft to tell us. 'This time there are millions of reliable witnesses. Apparently it should have been plainly visible in the Western Hemisphere last night. Did none of you see it?'

Paul Mathieu, our French confrere, pulled a droll face. 'Last night I was looking at the moon, my dear George, not the Echo satellite. It sounds ominous, but if Venus now has two lamps, so much the better.'

Involuntarily we looked out through the windows, searching above the roadside pines for any glimpse of the Echo satellite. According to the AP reports its luminosity had increased by at least ten-fold, transforming the thin pinpoint of light which had burrowed across the night sky for so many faithful years into a brilliant luminary outshone only by the moon. All over Asia, from the refugee camps on the shores of the Jordan to the crowded tenements of Shanghai, it was being observed at the very moment we were making our fifty mile drive to Maynard.

'Perhaps the balloon is breaking up,' I suggested in a lame effort to revive our spirits. 'The fragments of aluminium paint will be highly reflective and form a local cloud like a gigantic mirror. It's probably nothing to do with the Hubble Effect.'

'I'm sorry, James. I wish we could believe that.' Sidney Reston, of the State Department, who was acting as our courier, interrupted his conversation with the US Army major in charge of the bus to sit down with us. 'But it looks as if they're very much connected. All the other satellites aloft are showing the same increased albedo, seems more and more like a case of "Hubble bubble, double trouble".'

This absurd jingle echoed in my ears as we neared the eastern fringes of Big Cypress Swamp. Five miles from Maynard we left the highway and turned on to a rough track which ran through the date palms towards the Opotoka River. The surface of the road had been churned by scores of tracked vehicles, and a substantial military camp had been set up among the great oaks, the lines of tents hidden by the grey festoons of the spanish moss. Large piles of collapsible metal fencing were being unloaded from the trucks, and I noticed a squad of men painting a number of huge black signs with a vivid luminous paint.

'Are we going on manoeuvres, major?' the Swedish member of our party complained as the dust filled the cabin. 'We wished to see the forest near Maynard. Why have we left the highway?'

'The highway is closed,' the major replied evenly. 'You'll be taken on a tour of the site, I assure you, gentlemen. The only safe approach is by river.'

'*Safe* approach?' I repeated to Reston. 'I say, what is this, Sidney?'

'Just the army, James,' he assured me. 'You know what they're like in emergencies. If a tree moves they declare war on it.' With a shake of his head he peered out at the activity around us. 'But I admit I can't see why they have to proclaim martial law.'

Reaching the bank of the river, where half a dozen amphibious vehicles were moored by a floating quay, we debarked from the bus and were taken into a large quonset used for briefing visitors. Here we found some fifty or sixty other notables – senior members of government laboratories, public health officials and science journalists – who had been brought by bus from Miami earlier that morning. The atmosphere of light-hearted banter barely concealed a growing uneasiness, but the elaborate precautions of the military still seemed ludicrously exaggerated. After an interval for coffee we were officially welcomed and issued with our instructions for the day. These warned us in particular to remain strictly within the marked perimeters, not to attempt to obtain any of the 'contaminated material', and above all never to linger at any one spot but always to remain in rapid motion.

Needless to say, the pantomime humour of all this was lost on none of us and we were in high spirits when we set off down the river in three of the landing craft, the green walls of the forest slipping past on either side. I noticed immediately the quieter mood, by contrast, of the passenger beside me. A slimly built man of about forty, he was wearing a white tropical suit which emphasized the thin rim of dark beard framing his face. His black hair was brushed low over a bony forehead, and with the jaundiced gaze in his small liquid eyes gave him the appearance of a moody D. H. Lawrence. I made one or two attempts to talk to him, but he smiled briefly and looked away across the water. I assumed that he was one of the research chemists or biologists.

Two miles downstream we met a small convoy of motor launches harnessed together behind a landing craft. All of them were crammed with cargo, their decks and cabin roofs loaded with household possessions of every sort, baby carriages and mattresses, washing machines and bundles of linen, so that there were only a few precarious inches of freeboard amidships. Solemn-faced children sat with suitcases on their knees above the freight, and they and their parents gazed at us stonily as we passed.

Now it is a curious thing, but one seldom sees on the faces of Americans the expression of wan resignation all too familiar to the traveller elsewhere in the world, that sense of cowed helplessness before natural or political disaster seen in the eyes of refugees from Caporetto to Korea, and its unmistakable stamp upon the families moving past us abruptly put an end to our light-hearted mood. As the last of the craft pushed slowly through the disturbed water we all turned and watched it silently, aware that in a sense it carried ourselves.

'What *is* going on?' I said to the bearded man. 'They look as if they're evacuating the town!'

He laughed crisply, finding an unintended irony in my remark. 'Agreed – it's pretty pointless! But I guess they'll come back in due course.'

Irritated by this elliptical comment delivered in a curt off-hand voice – he had looked away again, engrossed upon some more interesting inner topic – I turned and joined my colleagues.

'But why is the Russian approach so different?' George Schneider was asking. 'Is the Hubble Effect the same as this Lysenko Syndrome? Perhaps it is a different phenomenon?'

One of the Department of Agriculture biologists, a grey-haired man carrying his jacket over one arm, shook his head. 'No, they're almost certainly identical. Lysenko as usual is wasting the Soviets' time. He maintains that crop yields are increased because there's an increase in tissue weight. But the Hubble Effect is much closer to a cancer as far as we can see – and about as curable – a proliferation of the sub-atomic identity of all matter. It's almost as if a sequence of displaced but identical images were being produced by refraction through a prism, but with the element of time replacing the role of light.' As it transpired, these were prophetic words.

We were rounding a bend as the river widened in its approach towards Maynard, and the water around the two landing craft ahead was touched by a curious roseate sheen, as if reflecting a distant sunset or the flames of some vast silent conflagration. The sky, however, remained a bland limpid blue, devoid of all cloud. Then we passed below a small bridge, where the river opened into a wide basin a quarter of a mile in diameter.

With a simultaneous gasp of surprise we all craned forward, staring at the line of jungle facing the white-framed buildings of the town. Instantly I realized that the descriptions of the forest 'crystallizing' and 'turning into coloured glass' were exactly truthful. The long arc of trees hanging over the water dripped and glittered with myriads of prisms, the trunks and fronds of the date palms sheathed by bars of livid yellow and carmine light that bled away across the surface of the water, so that the whole scene seemed to be reproduced by an over-active technicolor process. The entire length of the opposite shore glittered with this blurred chiaroscuro, the overlapping bands of colour increasing the density of the vegetation, so that it was impossible to see more than a few feet between the front line of trunks.

The sky was clear and motionless, the hot sunlight shining uninter-ruptedly upon this magnetic shore, but now and then a stir of wind would cross the water and the trees erupted into cascades of rippling colour that lanced away into the air around us. Then, slowly, the coruscation subsided and the images of the individual trunks, each sheathed in its brilliant armour of light, reappeared, their dipping foliage loaded with deliquescing jewels.

Everyone in our craft was gaping at this spectacle, the vivid crystal light dappling our faces and clothes, and even my bearded companion was moved by astonishment. Clasping the seat in front of him, he leaned across the rail, the white fabric of his suit transformed into a brilliant palimpsest.

Our craft moved in a wide arc towards the quay, where a score of power cruisers were being loaded by the townsfolk, and we came within some fifty yards of the prismatic jungle, the hatchwork of coloured bars across our clothes transforming us into a boatload of harlequins. There was a spontaneous round of laughter, more in relief than amusement. Then several arms pointed to the water-line, where we saw that the process had not affected the vegetation alone. Extending outwards for two or three yards from the bank were the long splinters of what appeared to be crystallizing water, the angular facets emitting a blue prismatic light washed by the wake from our craft. These splinters were growing in the water like crystals in a chemical solution, accreting more and more material to themselves, so that along the bank there was a congested mass of rhomboidal spears like the lengthening barbs of a reef.

Surprised by the extent of the phenomenon – I had expected, perhaps under the influence of the Lysenko theories, little more than an unusual plant disease, such as tobacco mosaic – I gazed up at the overhanging trees. Unmistakably each was still alive, its leaves and boughs filled with sap, and yet at the same time each was encased in a mass of crystalline tissue like an immense glacé fruit. Everywhere the branches and fronds were encrusted by the same translucent lattice, through which the sunlight was refracted into rainbows of colour.

A hubbub of speculation broke out in our craft, during which only myself and the bearded man remained silent. For some reason I suddenly felt less concerned to find a so-called 'scientific' explanation for the strange phenomenon we had seen. The beauty of the spectacle had stirred my memory, and a thousand images of childhood, forgotten for nearly forty years, now filled my mind, recalling the paradisal world of one's earliest years when everything seems illuminated by that prismatic light described so exactly by Wordsworth in his recollections of childhood. Since the death of my wife and three-year-old daughter in a car accident ten years earlier I had deliberately repressed such feelings, and the vivid magical shore before us seemed to glow like the brief spring of my marriage.

But the presence of so many soldiers and military vehicles, and the wan-faced townsfolk evacuating their homes, ensured that the little enclave of the transfigured forest – by comparison the remainder of the Everglades basin seemed a drab accumulation of peat, muck and marls – would soon be obliterated, the crystal trees dismembered and carried away to a hundred antiseptic laboratories.

At the front of the landing craft the first passengers began to debark. A hand touched my arm, and the white-suited man, apparently aware of my mood, pointed with a smile at the sleeve of his suit, as if encouraging me. To my astonishment a faint multicoloured dappling still remained, despite the shadows of the people getting to their feet around us, as if the light from the forest had contaminated the fabric and set off the process anew. 'What on –? Wait!' I called. 'Your suit!'

But before I could speak to him he stood up and hurried down the gangway, the last pale shimmer from his suit disappearing along the crowded quay.

Our party was divided into several smaller groups, each accompanied by two NCOs, and we moved off past the queue of cars and trucks loaded with the townsfolk's possessions. The families waited their turn patiently, flagged on by the local police, eyeing us without interest. The streets were almost deserted, and these were the last people to go – the houses were empty, shutters sealed across the windows, and soldiers paced in pairs past the closed banks and stores. The sidestreets were packed with abandoned cars, confirming that the river was the only route of escape from the town.

As we walked along the main street, the glowing jungle visible two hundred yards away down the intersections on our left, a police car swerved into the street and came to a halt in front of us. Two men stepped out, a tall blond-haired police captain and a Presbyterian minister carrying a small suitcase and a parcel of books. The latter was about thirty-five, with a high scholar's forehead and tired eyes. He seemed uncertain which way to go, and waited as the police captain strode briskly around the car.

'You'll need your embarkation card, Dr Thomas.' The captain handed a coloured ticket to the minister, and then fished a set of keys attached to a mahogany peg from his pocket. 'I took these from the door. You must have left them in the lock.'

The priest hesitated, uncertain whether to take the keys. 'I left them there deliberately, captain. Someone may want to take refuge in the church.'

'I doubt it, Doctor. Wouldn't help them, anyway.' The captain waved briefly. 'See you in Miami.'

Acknowledging the salute, the priest stared at the keys in his palm, then slipped them reluctantly into his cassock. As he walked past us towards the wharf his moist eyes searched our faces with a troubled gaze, as if he suspected that a member of his congregation might be hiding in our midst.

The police captain appeared equally fatigued, and began a sharp dialogue with the officer in charge of our parties. His words were lost in the general conversation, but he pointed impatiently beyond the roof-tops with a wide sweep of one arm, as if indicating the approach of a storm. Although of strong physique, there was something weak and self-centred about his long fleshy face and pale blue eyes, and obviously his one remaining ambition, having emptied the town of its inhabitants, was to clear out at the first opportunity.

I turned to the corporal lounging by a fire hydrant and pointed to the glowing vegetation which seemed to follow us, skirting the perimeter of the town. 'Why is everyone leaving, corporal? Surely it's not infectious – there's no danger from close contact?'

The corporal glanced laconically over his shoulder at the crystalline foliage glittering in the meridian sunlight. 'It's not infectious. Unless you stay in there too long. When it cut the road both sides of town I guess most people decided it was time to pull out.'

'Both sides?' George Schneider echoed. 'How big is the affected area, corporal? We were told three or four acres.'

The soldier shook his head dourly. 'More like three or four hundred. Or thousand, even.' He pointed to the helicopter circling the forest a mile or so away, soaring up and down over the date palms, apparently spraying them with some chemical. 'Reaches right over there, towards Lake Okeechobee.'

'But you have it under control,' George said. 'You're cutting it back all right?'

'Wouldn't like to say,' the corporal replied cryptically. He indicated the blond policeman remonstrating with the supervising officer. 'Captain Shelley tried a flame thrower on it a couple of days ago. Didn't help any.'

The policeman's objections over-ruled – he slammed the door of his car and drove off in dudgeon – we set off once more and at the next intersection approached the forest which stood back on either side of the road a quarter of a mile away. The vegetation was sparser, the sawgrass growing in clumps among the sandy soil on the verges, and a mobile laboratory had been set up in a trailer, 'U.S. Department of Agriculture' stencilled on its side. A platoon of soldiers was wandering about, taking cuttings from the palmettos and date palms, which they carefully placed like fragments of stained glass on a series of trestle tables. The main body of the forest curved around us, circling the northern perimeter of the town, and we immediately saw that the corporal had been correct in his estimate of the affected area's extent. Parallel with us one block to the north was the main Maynard–Miami highway, cut off by the glowing forest on both the eastern and western approaches to the town.

Splitting up into twos and threes, we crossed the verge and began to wander among the glacé ferns which rose from the brittle ground. The sandy surface seemed curiously hard and annealed, small spurs of fused sand protruding from the newly formed crust.

Examining the specimens collected on the tables, I touched the smooth glass-like material that sheathed the leaves and branches, following the contours of the original like a displaced image in a defective mirror. Everything appeared to have been dipped in a vat of molten glass, which had then set into a skin fractured by slender veins.

A few yards from the trailer two technicians were spinning several encrusted branches in a centrifuge. There was a continuous glimmer and sparkle as splinters of light glanced out of the bowl and vanished into the inspection area, and as far as the perimeter fence, running like a serrated white bandage around the prismatic wound of the forest, people turned to watch.

When the centrifuge stopped we peered into the bowl, where a handful of limp branches, their blanched leaves clinging damply to the metal bottom, lay stripped of their glacé sheaths. Below the bowl, however, the liquor receptacle remained dry and empty.

Twenty yards from the forest a second helicopter prepared for take-off, its drooping blades rotating like blunted scythes, the down-draught sending up a shower of light from the disturbed vegetation. With an abrupt lurch it made a laboured ascent, swinging sideways through the air, and then moved away across the forest roof, its churning blades apparently gaining little purchase on the air. There was a confused shout of 'Fire!' from the soldiers below, and we could see clearly the vivid discharge of light which radiated from the blades like St Elmo's fire. Then, with an agonized roar like the bellow of a stricken animal, the aircraft slid backwards through the air and plunged towards the forest canopy a hundred feet below, the two pilots plainly visible at their controls. Sirens sounded from the staff cars parked around the inspection area, and there was a concerted rush towards the forest as the helicopter disappeared from sight.

As we raced along the road we felt its impact with the ground, and a sudden pulse of light drummed through the trees. The road led towards the point of the crash, a few houses looming at intervals at the ends of empty drives.

'The blades must have crystallized while it was standing near the trees,' George Schneider shouted as we climbed over the perimeter fence. 'You could see the crystals melting, like the branches in the centrifuge, but not quickly enough. Let's hope the pilots are all right.'

Several soldiers ran ahead of us, waving us back, but we ignored them and hurried on through the trees. After fifty yards we were well within the body of the forest, and had entered an enchanted world, the spanish moss investing the great oaks with brilliant jewelled trellises. The air was markedly cooler, as if everything were sheathed in ice, but a ceaseless play of radiant light poured through the stained-glass canopy overhead, turning the roof of the forest into a continuous three-dimensional kaleidoscope.

The process of crystallization was here far more advanced. The white fences along the road were so heavily encrusted that they formed an unbroken palisade, the frost at least a foot thick on either side of the palings. The few houses between the trees glistened like wedding cakes, their plain white roofs and chimneys transformed into exotic minarets and baroque domes. On a lawn of green glass spurs a child's toy, perhaps once a red tricycle with yellow wheels, glittered like a Fabergé gem, the wheels starred into brilliant jasper crowns. Lying there, it reminded me of my daughter's toys scattered on the lawn after my return from the hospital. They had glowed for a last time with the same prismatic light.

The soldiers were still ahead of me, but George and Paul Mathieu had fallen behind. Leaning against the frosted white fencing, they were plucking the soles of their shoes. By now it was obvious why the Miami–Maynard highway had been closed. The surface of the road was pierced by a continuous carpet of needles, spurs of glass and quartz as much as six inches high, reflecting the coloured light through the leaves above. The spurs tore at my shoes, forcing me to move hand over hand along the verge of the road, where a section of heavier fencing marked the approach to a distant mansion.

Behind me a siren whined, and the police car I had seen earlier plunged along the road, its heavy tyres cutting through the crystal surface. Twenty yards ahead it rocked to a halt, its engine stalled, and the police captain jumped out. With an angry shout he waved me back down the road, now a tunnel of yellow light formed by the interlocking canopies overhead.

'Get back! There's another wave coming!' He ran after the soldiers a hundred yards away, his boots crushing the crystal carpet.

Wondering why he should be so keen to clear the forest, I rested for a moment by the police car. A noticeable change had come over the forest, as if dusk had begun to fall prematurely from the sky. Everywhere the glacé sheaths which enveloped the trees and vegetation had become duller and more opaque, and the crystal floor underfoot was grey and occluded, turning the needles into spurs of basalt. The panoply of coloured light had vanished, and a dim amber gloom moved across the trees, shadowing the sequinned lawns.

Simultaneously it had become colder. Leaving the car, I started to make my way down the road – Paul Mathieu and a soldier, hands shielding their faces, were disappearing around a bend – but the icy air blocked my path like a refrigerated wall. Turning up the collar of my tropical suit, I retreated to the car, wondering whether to take refuge inside it. The cold deepened, numbing my face like a spray of acetone, and my hands felt brittle and fleshless. Somewhere I heard the hollow shout of the police captain, and caught a glimpse of someone running at full speed through the ice-grey trees.

On the right-hand side of the road the darkness completely enveloped the forest, masking the outlines of the trees, and then extended in a sudden sweep across the roadway. My eyes smarted with pain, and I brushed away the small crystals of ice which had formed over my eyeballs. Everywhere a heavy frost was forming, accelerating the process of crystallization. The spurs in the roadway were now over a foot in height, like the spines of a giant porcupine, and the lattices between the tree-trunks were thicker and more translucent, so that the original trunks seemed to shrink into a mottled thread within them. The interlocking leaves formed a continuous mosaic, the crystal elements thickening and overlaying each other. For the first time I suddenly visualized the possibility of the entire forest freezing solidly into a huge coloured glacier, with myself trapped within its interstices.

The windows of the car and the black body were now sheathed in an ice-like film. Intending to open the door so that I could switch on the heater, I reached for the handle, but my fingers were burned by the intense cold.

'You there! Come on! This way!'

Behind me, the voice echoed down the drive. As the darkness and cold deepened, I saw the police captain waving to me from the colonnade of the mansion. The lawn between us seemed to belong to a less sombre zone. The grass still retained its vivid liquid sparkle and the white eaves of the house were etched clearly against the surrounding darkness, as if this enclave were preserved like an island in the eye of a hurricane.

I ran up the drive towards the house, and with relief found that the air was at least ten degrees warmer. The sunlight shone through the leafy canopy with uninterrupted brilliance. Reaching the portico, I searched for the police captain, but he had run off into the forest again. Uncertain whether to follow him, I watched the approaching wall of darkness slowly cross the lawn, the glittering foliage overhead sinking into its pall. The police car was now encrusted by a thick layer of frozen glass, its windshield blossoming into a thousand fleur-de-lis crystals.

Quickly making my way around the house as the zone of safety moved off through the forest, I crossed the remains of an old vegetable garden, where seed-plants of green glass three feet high rose into the air like exquisite ornamented sculptures. I reached the forest again and waited there as the zone hesitated and veered off, trying to remain within the centre of its focus. I seemed to have entered a subterranean cavern, where jewelled rocks loomed from the spectral gloom like huge marine plants, the sprays of crystal sawgrass like fountains frozen in time.

For the next hour I raced helplessly through the forest, my sense of direction lost, driven by the swerving walls of the zone of safety as it twisted like a benign tornado among the trees. Several times I crossed the road, where the great spurs were almost waist high, forced to clamber over the brittle stems. Once, as I rested against the trunk of a bifurcated oak, an immense multi-coloured bird erupted from a bough over my head and flew off with a wild screech, an aureole of molten light cascading from its red and yellow wings, like the birth-flames of phoenix.

At last the strange whirlpool subsided and a pale light filtered through the stained glass canopy, transfiguring everything with its iridescence. Again the forest was a place of rainbows, the deep carmine light glowing from the jewelled grottos. I walked along a narrow road which wound towards a great white house standing like a classical pavilion on a rise in the centre of the forest. Transformed by the crystal frost, it appeared to be an intact fragment of Versailles or Fontainebleau, its ornate pilasters and sculptured friezes spilling from the wide roof which overtopped the forest. From the upper floors I would be able to see the distant water towers at Maynard, or at least trace the serpentine progress of the river.

The road narrowed, declining the slope which led up to the house, but its annealed crust, like half-fused quartz, offered a more comfortable surface than the crystal teeth of the lawn. Suddenly I came across what was unmistakably a jewelled rowing boat sat solidly into the roadway, a chain of lapis lazuli mooring it to the verge. Then I realized that I was walking along a small tributary of the river. A thin stream of water still ran below the solid crust, and evidently this vestigial motion alone prevented it from erupting into the exotic spur-like forms of the forest floor.

As I paused by the boat, feeling the huge topaz and amethyst stones encrusted along its sides, a grotesque four-legged creature half-embedded in the surface lurched forwards through the crust, the loosened pieces of the lattice attached to its snout and shoulders shaking like a transparent cuirass. Its jaws mouthed the air silently as it struggled on its hooked legs, unable to clamber more than a few feet from the hollow trough in its own outline now filling with a thin trickle of water. Invested by the glittering sparkle of light that poured from its body, the alligator resembled some fabulous armourial beast. It lunged towards me again, and I kicked its snout, scattering the crystals which choked its mouth.

Leaving it to subside once more into a frozen posture, I climbed the bank and limped across the lawn to the mansion, whose fairy towers loomed above the trees. Although out of breath and very nearly exhausted I had a curious premonition, of intense hope and longing, as if I were some fugitive Adam chancing upon a forgotten gateway to the forbidden paradise.

From an upstairs window, the bearded man in the white suit watched me, a shot-gun under his arm.

Now that ample evidence of the Hubble Effect is available to scientific observers throughout the world, there is general agreement upon its origins and the few temporary measures that can be taken to reverse its progress. Under pressure of necessity during my flight through the phantasmagoric forests of the Everglades I had discovered the principal remedy – to remain in rapid motion – but I still assumed that some accelerated genetic mutation was responsible, even though such inanimate objects as cars and metal fencing were equally affected. However, by now even the Lysenkoists have grudgingly accepted the explanation given by workers at the Hubble Institute, that the random transfigurations throughout the world are a reflection of distant cosmic processes of enormous scope and dimensions, first glimpsed in the Andromeda spiral.

We know now that it is time ('Time with the Midas touch,' as Charles Marquand described it) which is responsible for the transformation. The recent discovery of anti-matter in the universe inevitably involves the conception of anti-time as the fourth side of this negatively charged continuum. Where anti-particle and particle collide they not only destroy their own physical identities, but their opposing time-values eliminate each other, subtracting from the universe another quantum from its total store of time. It is random discharges of this type, set off by the creation of anti-galaxies in space, which have led to the depletion of the time-store available to the materials of our own solar system.

Just as a supersaturated solution will discharge itself into a crystalline mass, so the supersaturation of matter in a continuum of depleted time leads to its appearance in a parallel spatial matrix. As more and more time 'leaks' away, the process of supersaturation continues, the original atoms and molecules producing spatial replicas of themselves, substance without mass, in an attempt to increase their foothold upon existence. The process is theoretically without end, and eventually it is possible for a single atom to produce an infinite number of duplicates of itself and so fill the entire universe, from which simultaneously all time has expired, an ultimate macrocosmic zero beyond the wildest dreams of Plato and Democritus.

As I lay back on one of the glass-embroidered chesterfields in a bedroom upstairs, the bearded man in the white suit explained something of this to me in his sharp intermittent voice. He still stood by the open window, peering down at the lawn and the crystal stream where the alligator and the jewelled boat lay embalmed. As the broken panes annealed themselves he drove the butt of his shot-gun through them. His thin beard gave him a fevered and haunted aspect, emphasized by the white frost forming on the shoulders and lapels of his suit. For some reason he spoke to me as if to an old friend.

'It was obvious years ago, B——. Look at the viruses with their crystalline structure, neither animate nor inanimate, and their immunity to time.' He swept a hand along the sill and picked up a cluster of the vitreous grains, then scattered them across the floor like smashed marbles. 'You and I will be like them soon, and the rest of the world. Neither living nor dead!'

He broke off to raise his shot-gun, his dark eyes searching between the trees. 'We must move on,' he announced, leaving the window. 'When did you last see Captain Shelley?'

'The police captain?' I sat up weakly, my feet slipping on the floor. Several plate glass windows appeared to have been fractured and then fused together above the carpet. The ornate Persian patterns swam below the surface like the floor of some perfumed pool in the Arabian Nights. 'Just after we ran to search for the helicopter. Why are you afraid of him?'

'He's a venomous man,' he replied briefly. 'As cunning as a pig.'

We made our way down the crystal stairway. Everything in the house was covered by the same glacé sheath, embellished by exquisite curlicues and helixes. In the wide lounges the ornate Louis XV furniture had been transformed into huge pieces of opalescent candy, whose countless reflections glowed like giant chimeras in the cut-glass walls. As we disappeared through the trees towards the stream my companion shouted exultantly, as much to the forest as to myself: 'We're running out of time, B——, running out of time!'

Always he was on the look-out for the police captain. Which of them was searching for the other I could not discover, nor the subject of their blood-feud. I had volunteered my name to him, but he brushed aside the introduction. I guessed that he had sensed some spark of kinship as we sat together in the landing craft, and that he was a man who would plunge his entire sympathy or hostility upon such a chance encounter. He told me nothing of himself. Shot-gun cradled under his arm, he moved rapidly along the fossilized stream, his movements neat and deliberate, while I limped behind. Now and then we passed a jewelled power cruiser embedded in the crust, or a petrified alligator would rear upwards and grimace at us noiselessly, its crystalline skin glowing with a thousand prisms as it shifted in a fault of coloured glass.

Everywhere there was the same fantastic corona of light, transfiguring and identifying all objects. The forest was an endless labyrinth of glass caves, sealed off from the remainder of the world, (which, as far as I knew, by now might be similarly affected), lit by subterranean lamps burning below the surface of the rocks.

'Can't we get back to Maynard?' I shouted after him, my voice echoing among the vaults. 'We're going deeper into the forest.'

'The town is cut off, my dear B——. Don't worry, I'll take you there in due course.' He leapt nimbly over a fissure in the surface of the river. Below the mass of dissolving crystals a thin stream of fluid rilled down a buried channel.

For several hours, led by this strange white-suited figure with his morose preoccupied gaze, we moved through the forest, sometimes in complete circles as if my companion were familiarizing himself with the topography of that jewelled twilight world. When I sat down to rest on one of the vitrified trunks and brushed away the crystals now forming on the soles of my shoes, despite our constant movement – the air was always icy, the dark shadows perpetually closing and unfolding around us – he would wait impatiently, watching me with ruminative eyes as if deciding whether to abandon me to the forest.

At last we reached the fringes of a small clearing, bounded on three sides by the fractured dancing floor of a river bend, where a high-gabled summer house pushed its roof towards the sky through a break in the overhead canopy. From the single spire a slender web of opaque strands extended to the surrounding trees like a diaphanous veil, investing the glass garden and the crystalline summer house with a pale marble sheen, almost sepulchral in its intensity. As if reinforcing this impression, the windows on to the veranda running around the house were now encrusted with elaborate scroll-like designs, like the ornamented stone casements of a tomb.

Waving me back, my companion approached the fringes of the garden, his shot-gun raised before him. He darted from tree to tree, pausing for any sign of movement, then crossed the frozen surface of the river with a feline step. High above him, its wings pinioned by the glass canopy, a golden oriole flexed slowly in the afternoon light, liquid ripples of its aura circling outwards like the rays of a miniature sun.

'Marquand!'

A shot roared into the clearing, its report echoing around the glass trees, and the blond-haired police captain raced towards the summer house, a revolver in his hand. As he fired again the crystal trellises of the spanish moss shattered and frosted, collapsing around me like a house of mirrors. Leaping down from the veranda, the bearded man made off like a hare across the river, bent almost double as he darted over the faults in the surface.

The rapidity with which all this had happened left me standing helplessly by the edge of the clearing, my ears ringing with the two explosions. I searched the forest for any signs of my companion, and then the police captain, standing on the veranda, gestured me towards him with his pistol.

'Come here!' When I tentatively approached he came down the steps, scrutinizing me suspiciously. 'What are you doing around here? Aren't you one of the visiting party?'

I explained that I had been trapped after the crash of the helicopter. 'Can you take me back to the army post? I've been wandering around the forest all day.'

A morose frown twisted his long face. 'The Army's a long way off. The forest's changing all the time.' He pointed across the river. 'What about Marquand? Where did you meet him?'

'The bearded man? He was taking shelter in a house near the river. Why did you shoot at him? Is he a criminal?'

Shelley nodded after a pause. His manner was somehow furtive and shifty. 'Worse than that. He's a madman, completely crazy.' He started to walk up the steps, apparently prepared to let me make my own way into the forest. 'You'd better be careful, there's no knowing what the forest is going to do. Keep moving but circle around on yourself, or you'll get lost.'

'Wait a minute!' I called after him. 'Can't I rest here? I need a map – perhaps you have a spare one?'

'A map? What good's a map now?' He hesitated as my arms fell limply to my sides. 'All right, you can come in for five minutes.' This concession to humanity was obviously torn from him.

The summer house consisted of a single circular room and a small kitchen at the rear. Heavy shutters had been placed against the windows, now locked to the casements by the interstitial crystals, and the only light entered through the door.

Shelley holstered his pistol and turned the door handle gently. Through the frosted panes were the dim outlines of a high four-poster bed, presumably stolen from one of the nearby mansions. Gilded cupids played about the mahogany canopy, pipes to their lips, and four naked caryatids with upraised arms formed the corner posts.

'Mrs Shelley,' the captain explained in a low voice. 'She's not too well.'

For a moment we gazed down at the occupant of the bed, who lay back on a large satin bolster, a febrile hand on the silk counterpane. At first I thought I was looking at an elderly woman, probably the captain's mother, and then realized that in fact she was little more than a child, a young woman in her early twenties. Her long platinum hair lay like a white shawl over her shoulders, her thin high-cheeked face raised to the scanty light. Once she might have had a nervous porcelain beauty, but her wasted skin and the fading glow of light in her half-closed eyes gave her the appearance of someone preternaturally aged, reminding me of my own wife in the last minutes before her death.

'Shelley.' Her voice cracked faintly in the amber gloom. 'Shelley, it's getting cold again. Can't you light a fire?'

'The wood won't burn, Emerelda. It's all turned into glass.' The captain stood at the foot of the bed, his peaked hat held in his hands, peering down solicitously as if he were on duty. He unzipped his leather jacket. 'I brought you these. They'll help you.'

He leaned forwards, hiding something from me, and spilled several handfuls of red and blue gem-stones across the counterpane. Rubies and sapphires of many sizes, they glittered in the thin light with a feverish heat.

'Shelley, thank you . . .' The girl's free hand scuttled across the counterpane to the stones. Her child-like face had become almost vulpine with greed. Seizing a handful, she brought them up to her neck and pressed them tightly against her skin, where the bruises formed like fingerprints. Their contact seemed to revive her and she stirred slowly, several of the jewels slipping to the floor.

'What were you shooting at, Shelley?' she asked after an interval. 'There was a gun going off, it gave me a headache.'

'Just an alligator, Emerelda. There are some smart alligators around here, I have to watch them. You get some rest now.'

'But, Shelley, I need more of these, you only brought me a few today . . .' Her hand, like a claw, searched the counterpane. Then she turned away from us and seemed to subside into sleep, the jewels lying like scarabs on the white skin of her breast.

Captain Shelley nudged me and we stepped quietly into the kitchen. The small cubicle was almost empty, a disconnected refrigerator standing on the cold stove. Shelley opened the door and began to empty the remainder of the jewels on to the shelves, where they lay like cherries among the half-dozen cans. A light frost covered the enamel exterior of the refrigerator, as everything else in the kitchen, but the inner walls remained unaffected.

'Who is she?' I asked as Shelley prised the lid off a can. 'Shouldn't you try to get her away from here?'

Shelley stared at me with his ambiguous expression. He seemed always to be concealing something, his blue eyes fractionally lowered from my own. 'She's my wife,' he said with a curious emphasis, as if unsure of the fact. 'Emerelda. She's safer here, as long as I watch out for Marquand.'

'Why should he want to hurt her? He seemed sane enough to me.'

'He's a maniac!' Shelley said with sudden force. 'He spent six months in a strait-jacket. He wants to take Emerelda and live in his crazy house in the middle of the swamp.' As an afterthought, he added: 'She was married to Marquand.'

As we ate, forking the cold meat straight from the can, he told me of the strange melancholy architect, Charles Foster Marquand, who had designed several of the largest hotels in Miami and then two years earlier abruptly abandoned his work in disgust. He had married Emerelda, after bribing her parents, within a few hours of seeing her in an amusement park, and then carried her away to a grotesque folly he had built among the sharks and alligators in the swamp. According to Shelley he never spoke to Emerelda after the marriage ceremony, and prevented her from leaving the house or seeing anyone except a blind negro servant. Apparently he saw his bride in a sort of Pre-Raphaelite dream, caged within his house like the lost spirit of his imagination. When she finally escaped, with Captain Shelley's assistance, he had gone berserk and spent some time as a voluntary patient at an asylum. Now he had returned with the sole ambition of returning with Emerelda to his house in the swamps, and Shelley was convinced, perhaps sincerely, that his morbid and lunatic presence was responsible for Emerelda's lingering malaise.

At dusk I left them, barricaded together in the white sepulchre of the summer house, and set off in the direction of the river which Shelley said was half a mile away, hoping to follow it to Maynard. With luck an army unit would be stationed at the nearest margins of the affected zone, and the soldiers would be able to retrace my steps and rescue the police captain and his dying wife.

Shelley's lack of hospitality did not surprise me. In turning me out into the forest he was using me as a decoy, confident that Marquand would immediately try to reach me for news of his former wife. As I made my way through the dark crystal grottos I listened for his footsteps, but the glass sheaths of the trees sung and crackled with a thousand voices as the forest cooled in the darkness. Above, through the lattices between the trees, I could see the great fractured bowl of the moon. Around me, in the vitreous walls, the reflected stars glittered like myriads of fireflies.

At this time I noticed that my own clothes had begun to glow in the dark, the fine frost that covered my suit spangled by the starlight. Spurs of crystal grew from the dial of my wristwatch, imprisoning the hands within a medallion of moonstone.

At midnight I reached the river, a causeway of frozen gas that might have soared high across the Milky Way. Forced to leave it when the surface broke into a succession of giant cataracts, I approached the outskirts of Maynard, passing the mobile laboratory used by the Department of

Agriculture. The trailer, and the tables and the equipment scattered around it had been enveloped by the intense frost, and the branches in the centrifuge had blossomed again into brilliant jewelled sprays. I picked up a discarded helmet, now a glass porcupine, and drove it through a window of the trailer.

In the darkness the white-roofed houses of the town gleamed like the funerary temples of a necropolis, their cornices ornamented with countless spires and gargoyles, linked together across the roads by the expanding tracery. A frozen wind moved through the streets, which were waist-high forests of fossil spurs, the abandoned cars embedded within them like armoured saurians on an ancient ocean floor.

Everywhere the process of transformation was accelerating. My feet were encased in huge crystal slippers. It was these long spurs which enabled me to walk along the street, but soon they would fuse together and lock me to the ground.

The eastern entrance to the town was sealed by the forest and the erupting roadway. Limping westwards again, in the hope of returning to Captain Shelley, I passed a small section of the sidewalk that remained clear of all growth, below the broken window of a jewellery store. Handfuls of looted stones were scattered across the pavement, ruby and emerald rings, topaz brooches and pendants, intermingled with countless smaller stones and industrial diamonds that glittered coldly in the starlight.

As I stood among the stones I noticed that the crystal outgrowths from my shoes were dissolving and melting, like icicles exposed to sudden heat. Pieces of the crust fell away and slowly deliquesced, vanishing without trace into the air.

Then I realized why Captain Shelley had brought the jewels to his wife, and why she had seized upon them so eagerly. By some optical or electromagnetic freak, the intense focus of light within the stones simultaneously produced a compression of time, so that the discharge of light from the surfaces reversed the process of crystallization. (Perhaps it is this gift of time which accounts for the eternal appeal of precious gems, as well as of all baroque painting and architecture? Their intricate crests and cartouches, occupying more than their own volume of space, so contain a greater ambient time, providing that unmistakable premonition of immortality sensed within St Peter's or the palace at Nymphenburg. By contrast the architecture of the 20th century, characteristically one of rectangular unornamented facades, of simple Euclidean space and time, is that of the New World, confident of its firm footing in the future and indifferent to those pangs of mortality which haunt the mind of old Europe.)

Quickly I knelt down and filled my pockets with the stones, cramming them into my shirt and cuffs. I sat back against the store front, the semi-circle of smooth pavement like a miniature patio, at whose edges the crystal undergrowth glittered like a spectral garden. Pressed to my cold skin, the hard faces of the jewels seemed to warm me, and within a few seconds I fell into an exhausted sleep.

*    *    *

I woke into brilliant sunshine in a street of temples, a thousand rainbows spangling the gilded air with a blaze of prismatic colours. Shielding my eyes, I lay back and looked up at the roof-tops, their gold tiles apparently inlaid with thousands of coloured gems, like the temple quarter of Bangkok.

A hand pulled roughly at my shoulder. Trying to sit up, I found that the semicircle of clear sidewalk had vanished, and my body lay sprawled on a bed of sprouting needles. The growth had been most rapid in the entrance to the store, and my right arm was encased in a mass of crystalline spurs, three or four inches long, that reached almost to my shoulder. My hand was sheathed in a huge frozen gauntlet of prismatic crystals, almost too heavy to lift, my fingers outlined by a rainbow of colours.

Overwhelmed by panic, I managed to drag myself on to my knees, and found the bearded man in the white suit crouching behind me, his shot-gun in his hands.

'Marquand!' With a cry, I raised my jewelled arm. 'For God's sake!'

My voice distracted him from his scrutiny of the light-filled street. His lean face with its small bright eyes was transfigured by strange colours that mottled his skin and drew out the livid blues and violets of his beard. His suit radiated a thousand bands of colour.

He moved towards me but before he could speak there was a roar of gunfire and the glass sheet encrusted to the doorway shattered into a shower of crystals. Marquand flinched and hid behind me, then pulled me backwards through the window. As another shot was fired down the street we stumbled past the looted counters into an office where the door of a safe stood open on to a jumble of metal cash boxes. Marquand snapped back the lids on to the empty trays, and then began to scoop together the few jewels scattered across the floor.

Stuffing them into my empty pockets, he pulled me through a window into the rear alley, and from there into the adjacent street, transformed by the overhead lattices into a tunnel of crimson and vermilion light. We stopped at the first turning, and he beckoned to the glistening forest fifty yards away.

'Run, run! Anywhere through the forest, it's all you can do!'

He pushed me forwards with the butt of his shot-gun, whose breach was now encrusted by a mass of silver crystals, like a medieval flintlock. I raised my arm helplessly. In the sunlight the jewelled spurs coruscated like a swarm of coloured fireflies. 'My arm, Marquand! It's reached my shoulder!'

'Run! Nothing else can help you!' His illuminated face flickered angrily. 'Don't waste the stones, they won't last you for ever!'

Forcing myself to run, I set off towards the forest, where I entered the first of the caves of light. I whirled my arm like a clumsy propeller, and felt the crystals recede slightly. By luck I soon reached a tributary of the river, and hurled myself like a wild man along its petrified surface.

For many hours, or days, I raced through the forest I can no longer remember, for all sense of time deserted me. If I stopped for more than a minute the crystal bands would seize my neck and shoulder, and I ran past the trees for hour after hour, only pausing when I slumped exhausted on the glass beaches. Then I pressed the jewels to my face, warding off the glacé sheath. But their power slowly faded, and as their facets blunted they turned into nodes of unpolished silica.

Once, as I ran through the darkness, my arm whirling before me, I passed the summer house where Captain Shelley kept guard over his dying wife, and heard him fire at me from the veranda.

At last, late one afternoon, when the deepening ruby light of dusk settled through the forest, I entered a small clearing where the deep sounds of an organ reverberated among the trees. In the centre was a small church, its gilt spire fused to the surrounding trees.

Raising my jewelled arm, I drove back the oak doors and entered the nave. Above me, refracted by the stained glass windows, a brilliant glow of light poured down upon the altar. Listening to the surging music, I leaned against the altar rail and extended my arm to the gold cross set with rubies and emeralds. Immediately the sheath slipped and dissolved like a melting sleeve of ice. As the crystals deliquesced the light poured from my arm like an overflowing fountain.

Turning his head to watch me, the priest sat at the organ, his firm hands drawing from the pipes their great unbroken music, which soared away, interweaved by countless overtones, through the panels of the windows towards the dismembered sun.

> *Life, like a dome of many-coloured glass,*
> *Stains the white radiance of eternity.*

For the next week I stayed with him, as the last crystal spurs dissolved from the tissues of my arm. All day I knelt beside him, working the bellows of the organ with my arm as the Pelestrina and Bach echoed around us. At dusk, when the sun sank in a thousand fragments into the western night, he would break off and stand on the porch, looking out at the spectral trees.

I remembered him as Dr Thomas, the priest Captain Shelley had driven to the harbour. His slim scholar's face and calm eyes, their serenity belied by the nervous movements of his hands, like the false calm of someone recovering from an attack of fever, would gaze at me as we ate our small supper on a foot-stool beside the altar, sheltered from the cold all-embalming wind by the jewels in the cross. At first I thought he regarded my survival as an example of the Almighty's intervention, and I made some token expression of gratitude. At this he smiled ambiguously.

Why he had returned I did not try to guess. By now his church was surrounded on all sides by the crystal trellises, as if overtopped by the mouth of an immense glacier.

One morning he found a blind snake, its eyes transformed into enormous jewels, searching hesitantly at the door of the porch, and carried it in his hands to the altar. He watched it with a wry smile when, its sight returned, it slid away noiselessly among the pews.

On another day I woke to the early morning light and found him, alone, celebrating the Eucharist. He stopped, half-embarrassed, and over breakfast confided: 'You probably wonder what I was doing, but it seemed an appropriate moment to test the validity of the sacrament.' He gestured at the prismatic colours pouring through the stained glass windows, whose original scriptural scenes had been transformed into paintings of bewildering abstract beauty. 'It may sound heretical to say so, but the body of Christ is with us everywhere here – in each prism and rainbow, in the ten thousand faces of the sun.' He raised his thin hands, jewelled by the light. 'So you see, I fear that the church, like its symbol –' here he pointed to the cross '– may have outlived its function.'

I searched for an answer. 'I'm sorry. Perhaps if you left here –'

'No!' he insisted, annoyed by my obtuseness. 'Can't you understand? Once I was a true apostate – I knew God existed but could not believe in him. Now,' he laughed bitterly, 'events have overtaken me.'

With a gesture he led me down the nave to the open porch, and pointed up to the dome-shaped lattice of crystal beams which reached from the rim of the forest like the buttresses of an immense cupola of diamond and glass. Embedded at various points were the almost motionless forms of birds with outstretched wings, golden orioles and scarlet macaws, shedding brilliant pools of light. The bands of liquid colour rippled outwards through the forest, the reflections of the melting plumage enveloping us in endless concentric patterns. The overlapping arcs hung in the air like the votive windows of a city of cathedrals. Everywhere around us I could see countless smaller birds, butterflies and insects, joining their miniature haloes to the coronation of the forest.

He took my arm. 'Here in this forest everything is transfigured and illuminated, joined together in the last marriage of time and space.'

Towards the end, when we stood side by side with our backs to the altar, as the aisle transformed itself into an occluding tunnel of glass pillars, his conviction seemed to fail him. With an expression almost of panic he watched the keys of the organ manuals frosting like the coins of a bursting coffer, and I knew that he was searching for some means of escape.

Then at last he rallied, seized the cross from the altar and pressed it into my arms, with a sudden anger born of absolute certainty dragged me roughly to the porch and propelled me to one of the narrowing vaults.

'Go! Get away from here! Find the river!'

When I hesitated, the heavy sceptre weighing upon my arms, he shouted fiercely: 'Tell them I ordered you to take it!'

I last saw him standing arms outstretched to the approaching walls, in the posture of the illuminated birds, his eyes filled with wonder and relief at the first circles of light conjured from his upraised palms.

Struggling with the huge golden incubus of the cross, I made my way towards the river, my tottering figure reflected in the hanging mirrors of the spanish moss like a lost Simon of Cyrene pictured in a medieval manuscript.

I was still sheltering behind it when I reached Captain Shelley's summer house. The door was open, and I looked down at the bed in the centre of a huge fractured jewel, in whose frosted depths, like swimmers asleep on the bottom of an enchanted pool, Emerelda and her husband lay together. The Captain's eyes were closed, and the delicate petals of a blood-red rose blossomed from the hole in his breast like an exquisite marine plant. Beside him Emerelda slept serenely, the unseen motion of her heart sheathing her body in a faint amber glow, the palest residue of life.

Something glittered in the dusk behind me. I turned to see a brilliant chimera, a man with incandescent arms and chest, race past among the trees, a cascade of particles diffusing in the air behind him. I flinched back behind the cross, but he vanished as suddenly as he had appeared, whirling himself away among the crystal vaults. As his luminous wake faded I heard his voice echoing across the frosted air, the plaintive words jewelled and ornamented like everything else in that transmogrified world.

'𝔈merelda . . . ! 𝔈merelda . . . !'

Here on this calm island of Puerto Rico, in the garden of the British Embassy these few months later, the strange events of that phantasmagoric forest seem a dozen worlds away. Yet in fact I am no more than 1,000 miles from Florida as the crow (or should I say, the gryphon) flies, and already there have been numerous other outbreaks at many times this distance from the three focal areas. Somewhere I have seen a report that at the present rate of progress at least a third of the earth's surface will be affected by the end of the next decade, and a score of the world's capital cities petrified beneath layers of prismatic crystal, as Miami has already been – some reporters have described the abandoned resort as a city of a thousand cathedral spires, like a vision of St John the Divine.

To tell the truth, however, the prospect causes me little worry. It is obvious to me now that the origins of the Hubble Effect are more than physical. When I stumbled out of the forest into an army cordon ten miles from Maynard two days after seeing the helpless phantom that had once been Charles Marquand, the gold cross clutched in my arms, I was determined never to visit the Everglades again. By one of those ludicrous inversions of logic, I found myself, far from acclaimed as a hero, standing summary trial before a military court and charged with looting. The gold cross had apparently been stripped of its jewels, and in vain did I protest that these vanished stones had been the price of my survival. At last I was rescued by the embassy in Washington under the plea of diplomatic immunity, but my suggestion that a patrol equipped with jewelled crosses should enter the forest and attempt to save the priest and Charles Marquand met with little success. Despite my protests I was sent to San Juan to recuperate.

The intention of my superiors was that I should be cut off from all memory of my experience – perhaps they sensed some small but significant change in me. Each night, however, the fractured disc of the Echo satellite passes overhead, illuminating the midnight sky like a silver chandelier. And I am convinced that the sun itself has begun to effloresce. At sunset, when its disc is veiled by the crimson dust, it seems to be crossed by a distinctive latticework, a vast portcullis which will one day spread outwards to the planets and the stars, halting them in their courses.

I know now that I shall return to the Everglades. As the example of that brave apostate priest who gave the cross to me illustrates, there is an immense reward to be found in that frozen forest. There in the Everglades the transfiguration of all living and inanimate forms occurs before our eyes, the gift of immortality a direct consequence of the surrender by each of us of our own physical and temporal identity. However apostate we may be in this world, there perforce we become apostles of the prismatic sun.

So, when my convalescence is complete and I return to Washington, I shall seize an opportunity to visit the Florida peninsula again with one of the many scientific expeditions. It should not be too difficult to arrange my escape and then I shall return to the solitary church in that enchanted world, where by day fantastic birds fly through the petrified forest and jewelled alligators glitter like heraldic salamanders on the banks of the crystalline rivers, and where by night the illuminated man races among the trees, his arms like golden cartwheels and his head like a spectral crown.

**1964**

# THE DELTA AT SUNSET

Each evening, when the dense powdery dusk lay over the creeks and drained mud-basins of the delta, the snakes would come out on to the beaches. Half-asleep on the wicker stretcher-chair below the awning of his tent, Charles Gifford watched their sinuous forms coiling and uncoiling as they wound their way up the slopes. In the opaque blue light the dusk swept like a fading searchlight over the damp beaches, and the interlocked bodies shone with an almost phosphorescent brilliance.

The nearest creeks were three hundred yards from the camp, but for some reason the appearance of the snakes always coincided with Gifford's recovery from his evening fever. As this receded, carrying with it the familiar diorama of reptilian phantoms, he would sit up in the stretcher-chair and find the snakes crawling across the beaches, almost as if they had materialized from his dreams. Involuntarily he would search the sand around the tent for any signs of their damp skins.

'The strange thing is they always come out at the same time,' Gifford said to the Indian head-boy who had emerged from the mess tent and was now covering him with a blanket. 'One minute there's nothing there, and the next thousands of them are swarming all over the mud.'

'You not cold, sir?' the Indian asked.

'Look at them now, before the light goes. It's really fantastic. There must be a sharply defined threshold –' He tried to lift his pale, bearded face above the hillock formed by the surgical cradle over his foot, and snapped: 'All right, all right!'

'Doctor?' The head-boy, a thirty-year-old Indian named Mechippe, continued to straighten the cradle, his limpid eyes, set in a face of veined and weathered teak, watching Gifford.

'I said get out of the damned way!' Leaning weakly on one elbow, Gifford watched the last light fade across the winding causeways of the delta, taking with it a final image of the snakes. Each evening, as the heat mounted with the advancing summer, they came out in greater numbers, as if aware of the lengthening periods of his fever.

'Sir, I get more blanket for you?'

'No, for God's sake.' Gifford's thin shoulders shivered in the dusk air, but he ignored the discomfort. He looked down at his inert, corpse-like body below the blanket, examining it with far more detachment than he had felt for the unknown Indians dying in the makeshift WHO field hospital at Taxcol. At least there was a passive repose about the Indians, a sense of the still intact integrity of flesh and spirit, if anything reinforced by the failure of one of the partners. It was this paradigm of fatalism which Gifford would have liked to achieve – even the most wretched native, identifying himself with the irrevocable flux of nature, had bridged a greater span of years than the longest-lived European or American with his obsessive time-consciousness, cramming so-called significant experiences into his life like a glutton. By contrast, Gifford realized, he himself had merely thrown aside his own body, divorcing it like some no longer useful partner in a functional business marriage. So marked a lack of loyalty depressed him.

He tapped his bony loins. 'It's not this, Mechippe, that ties us to mortality, but our confounded egos.' He smiled slyly at the head-boy. 'Louise would appreciate that, don't you think?'

The head-boy was watching a refuse fire being raised behind the mess tent. He looked down sharply at the supine figure on the stretcher-chair, his half-savage eyes glinting like arrow heads in the oily light of the burning brush. 'Sir? You want –?'

'Forget it,' Gifford told him. 'Bring two whisky sodas. And some more chairs. Where's Mrs Gifford?'

He glanced up at Mechippe when he failed to reply. Briefly their eyes met, in an instant of absolute clarity. Fifteen years earlier, when Gifford had come to the delta with his first archaeological expedition, Mechippe had been one of the junior camp-followers. Now he was in the late middle age of the Indian, the notches on his cheeks lost in the deep hatchwork of lines and scars, wise in the tent-lore of the visitors.

'Miss' Gifford – resting,' he said cryptically. In an attempt to alter the tempo and direction of their dialogue, he added: 'I tell Mr Lowry, then bring whiskies and hot towel, Doctor.'

'Okay, Mechippe.' Lying back with an ironic smile, Gifford listened to the head-boy's footsteps move away softly through the sand. The muted sounds of the camp stirred around him – the cooling plash of water in the shower stall, the soft interchanges of the Indians, the whining of a desert dog waiting to approach the refuse dump – and he sank downwards into the thin tired body stretched out in front of him like a collection of bones in a carpet bag, rekindling the fading senses of touch and pressure in his limbs.

In the moonlight, the white beaches of the delta glistened like banks of luminous chalk, the snakes festering on the slope like the worshippers of a midnight sun.

Half an hour later they drank their whiskies together in the dark tinted air. Revived by Mechippe's massage, Charles Gifford sat upright in the stretcher-chair, gesturing with his glass. The whisky had momentarily cleared his brain; usually he was reluctant to discuss the snakes in his wife's presence, let alone Lowry's, but the marked increase in their numbers seemed important enough to mention. There was also the mildly malicious pleasure – less amusing now than it had been – of seeing Louise shudder at any mention of the snakes.

'What is so unusual,' he explained, 'is the way they emerge on to the banks at the same time. There must be a precise level of luminosity, an exact number of photons, to which they all respond – presumably an innate trigger.'

Dr Richard Lowry, Gifford's assistant and since his accident the acting leader of the expedition, watched Gifford uncomfortably from the edge of his canvas chair, rotating his glass below his long nose. He had been placed downwind from the loose bandages swaddling Gifford's foot (little revenges of this kind, however childish, alone sustained Gifford's interest in the people around him), and carefully averted his face as he asked: 'But why the sudden increase in numbers? A month ago there was barely a snake in sight?'

'Dick, *please*!' Louise Gifford turned an expression of martyred weariness on Lowry. 'Must we?'

'There's an obvious answer,' Gifford said to Lowry. 'During the summer the delta drains, and begins to look like the half-empty lagoons that were here 50 million years ago. The giant amphibians had died out, and the small reptiles were the dominant species. These snakes are probably carrying around what is virtually a coded internal landscape, a picture of the Paleocene as sharp as our own memories of New York and London.' He turned to his wife, the shadows cast by the distant refuse fire hollowing his cheeks. 'What's the matter, Louise? Don't say you can't remember New York and London?'

'I don't know whether I can or not.' She pushed a lock of fraying blonde hair off her forehead. 'I wish you wouldn't think about the snakes all the time.'

'Well, I'm beginning to understand them. I was always baffled by the way they'd appear at the same time. Besides, there's nothing else to do. I don't want to sit here staring at that damned Toltec ruin of yours.'

He gestured towards the low ridge of sandstone, its profile illuminated against the white moonlit clouds, which marked the margins of the alluvial bench half a mile from the camp. Before Gifford's accident their chairs had faced the ruined terrace city emerging from the thistles which covered the ridge. But Gifford had tired of staring all day at the crumbling galleries and colonnades where his wife and Lowry worked together. He told Mechippe to dismantle the tent and turn it through ninety degrees, so that he could watch the last light of the sunset fading over the western delta. The burning refuse fires they now faced provided at least a few wisps of motion. Gazing for hours across the endless creeks and mud-banks, whose winding outlines became more and more serpentine as the summer drought persisted and the level of the water table fell, he had one evening discovered the snakes.

'Surely it's simply a shortage of dissolved oxygen,' Lowry commented.

He noticed Gifford regarding him with an expression of critical distaste, and added: 'Jung believes the snake is primarily a symbol of the unconscious, and that its appearance always heralds a crisis in the psyche.'

'I suppose I accept that,' Charles Gifford said. With rather forced laughter he added, shaking his foot in the cradle: 'I have to. Don't I, Louise?' Before his wife, who was watching the fires with a distracted expression, could reply he went on: 'Though in fact I disagree with Jung. For me the snake is a symbol of transformation. Every evening at sunset the great lagoons of the Paleocene are re-created here, not only for the snakes but for you and I too, if we care to look. Not for nothing is the snake a symbol of wisdom.'

Richard Lowry frowned doubtfully into his glass. 'I'm not convinced, sir. It was primitive man who had to assimilate events in the external world to his own psyche.'

'Absolutely right,' Gifford rejoined. 'How else is nature meaningful, unless she illustrates some inner experience? The only real landscapes are the internal ones, or the external projections of them, such as this delta.' He passed his empty glass to his wife. 'Agree, Louise? Though perhaps you take a Freudian view of the snakes?'

This thin jibe, uttered with the cold humour which had become characteristic of Gifford, brought their conversation to a halt. Restlessly, Lowry looked at his watch, eager to be away from Gifford and his pathetic boorishness. Gifford, a cold smirk on his lips, waited for Lowry to catch his eye; by a curious paradox his dislike of his assistant was encouraged by the latter's reluctance to retaliate, rather than by the still ambiguous but crystallizing relationship between Lowry and Louise. Lowry's meticulous neutrality and good manners seemed to Gifford an attempt to preserve a world on which Gifford had turned his back, that world where there were no snakes on the beaches and where events moved on a single plane of time like the blurred projection of a three-dimensional object by a defective camera obscura.

Lowry's politeness was also, of course, an attempt to shield himself and Louise from Gifford's waspish tongue. Like Hamlet taking advantage of his madness to insult and cross-examine anyone at will, Gifford often used the exhausted half-lucid interval after his fever subsided to make his more pointed comments. As he emerged from the penumbral shallows, the looming figures of his wife and assistant still surrounded by the rotating mandalas he saw in his dreams, he would give full rein to his tortured humour. That in this way he was helping his wife and Lowry towards an inevitable climax only encouraged Gifford.

His long farewell to Louise, protracted now for so many years, at last seemed feasible, even if only part of the greater goodbye, the vast leave-taking that Gifford was about to embark upon. The fifteen years of their marriage had been little more than a single frustrated farewell, a search for a means to an end which their own strengths of character had always prevented.

Looking up at Louise's sun-grazed but still handsome profile, at her fading blonde hair swept back off her angular shoulders, Gifford realized that his dislike of her was in no way personal, but merely part of the cordial distaste he felt for almost the entire human race. And even this deeply ingrained misanthropy was only a reflection of his own undying self-contempt. If there were few people whom he had ever liked, there were, equally, few moments during which he had ever liked himself. His entire life as an archaeologist, from his early adolescence when he had first collected fossil ammonites from a nearby limestone outcropping, was an explicit attempt to return to the past and discover the sources of his self-loathing.

'Do you think they'll send an aeroplane?' Louise asked after breakfast the next morning. 'There was a noise then . . .'

'I doubt it,' Lowry said. He gazed up at the empty sky. 'We didn't ask for one. The landing field at Taxcol is disused. During the summer the harbour drains and everyone moves up-coast.'

'There'll be a doctor, surely? Not everyone will have gone?'

'Yes, there's a doctor. There's one permanently attached to the port authority.'

'A drunken fool,' Gifford interjected. 'I refuse to let him touch me with his poxy hands. Forget about the doctor, Louise. Even if someone is prepared to come out here, how do you think he'll manage it?'

'But Charles –'

Gifford gestured irritably at the glistening mudbanks. 'The whole delta is draining like a dirty bath, no one is going to risk a stiff dose of malaria just to put a splint on my ankle. Anyway, that boy Mechippe sent is probably still hanging around here somewhere.'

'But Mechippe insisted he was reliable.' Louise looked down helplessly at her husband propped against the back of the stretcher-chair. 'Dick, I wish you could have gone with him. It's only fifty miles. You would have been there by now.'

Lowry nodded uneasily. 'Well, I didn't think . . . I'm sure everything will be all right. How is the leg, sir?'

'Just dandy.' Gifford had been staring out across the delta. He noticed Lowry peering down at him with a long puckered face. 'What's the matter, Richard? Does the smell offend you?' Suddenly exasperated, he snapped: 'Do me a favour and take a walk, dear chap.'

'What –?' Lowry stared at him uncertainly. 'Of course, Doctor.'

Gifford watched Lowry's neatly groomed figure walk away stiffly among the tents. 'He's awfully correct, isn't he? But he doesn't know how to take an insult yet. I'll see that he gets plenty of practice.'

Louise slowly shook her head. 'Do you have to, Charles? Without him we'd be in rather a spot, you know. I don't think you're being very fair.'

'*Fair*?' Gifford repeated the word with a grimace. 'What are you talking about? For God's sake, Louise.'

'All right then,' his wife replied patiently. 'I don't think you should blame Richard for what's happened.'

'I don't. Is that what your dear Dick suggests? Now that this thing is beginning to smell he's trying to throw his guilt back on to me.'

'He is not –'

Gifford petulantly thumped the wicker elbow rest. 'He damned well is!' He gazed up darkly at his wife, his thin twisted mouth framed by the rim of beard. 'Don't worry, my dear, you will too by the time this thing is finished.'

'Charles, please . . .'

'Who cares, anyway?' Gifford lay back weakly for a moment, and then, as he recovered, a curious feeling of light-headed and almost euphoric calm coming over him, began again: 'Dr Richard Lowry. How he loves his doctorate. I wouldn't have had the nerve at his age. A third-rate PhD for work that I did for him, and he styles himself "Doctor".'

'So do you.'

'Don't be a fool. I can remember when at least two Chairs were offered to me.'

'But you couldn't degrade yourself by accepting them,' his wife commented, a trace of irony in her voice.

'No, I could not,' Gifford attested vehemently. 'Do you know what Cambridge is like, Louise? It's *packed* with Richard Lowrys! Besides, I had a far better idea. I married a rich wife. She was charming, beautiful, and in a slightly ambiguous way respected my moody brilliance, but above all she was rich.'

'How pleasant for you.'

'People who marry for money earn it. I really earned mine.'

'Thank you, Charles.'

Gifford chuckled to himself. 'One thing, Louise, you do know how to take an insult. It's a matter of breeding. I'm surprised you aren't more choosy over Lowry.'

'Choosy?' Louise laughed awkwardly. 'I hadn't realized that I'd chosen him. I think Richard is very obliging and helpful – as you knew when you made him your assistant, by the way.'

Gifford began to compose his reply, when a sudden chill enveloped his chest and shoulders. He pulled weakly at the blanket, an immense feeling of fatigue and inertia overtaking him. He looked up glassily at his wife, their bickering conversation forgotten. The sunlight had vanished, and a profound darkness lay over the face of the delta, illuminated for a brief interval by the seething outlines of thousands of snakes. Trying to capture the image in his eyes, he struggled forward against the incubus pressing upon his chest, and then slid backwards into a pit of nausea and giddiness. 'Louise . . . !'

Quickly his wife's hands were on his own, her shoulder supporting his head. He vomited emptily, struggling with his contracting musculature like a snake trying to shed its skin. Dimly he heard his wife shout for someone and the cradle topple to the ground, dragging the bedclothes with it.

'Louise,' he whispered, 'one of these nights . . . I want you to take me down to the snakes.'

Now and then, during the afternoon, when the pain in his foot became acute, he would wake to find Louise sitting beside him. All the while he moved through ceaseless dreams, sinking from one plane of reverie to the next, the great mandalas guiding him downwards, enthroning him upon their luminous dials.

During the next few days the conversations with his wife were less frequent. As his condition deteriorated, Gifford felt able to do little more than stare out across the mud-flats, almost unaware of the movement and arguments around him. His wife and Mechippe formed a tenuous bridge with reality, but the true centre of his attention was the nexus of beaches on to which the snakes emerged in the evenings. This was a zone of complete timelessness, where at last he sensed the simultaneity of all time, the coexistence of all events in his past life.

The snakes now made their appearance half an hour earlier. Once he caught a glimpse of their motionless albino forms exposed on the slopes in the hot noon air. Their chalk-white skins and raised heads, in a reclining posture very like his own, made them seem immeasurably ancient, like the white sphinxes in the funeral corridors to the pharaonic tombs at Karnak.

Although his strength had ebbed markedly, the infection on his foot had spread only a few inches above the ankle, and Louise Gifford realized that her husband's deterioration was a symptom of a profound psychological malaise, the *mal de passage* induced by the potently atmospheric landscape and its evocation of the lagoon-world of the Paleocene. She suggested to Gifford during one of his lucid intervals that they move the camp half a mile across the plain into the shadow of the ridge, near the Toltec terrace city where she and Lowry carried out their archaeological work.

But Gifford had refused, reluctant to leave the snakes on the beach. For some reason he disliked the terrace city. This was not because it was there that he had inflicted on himself the wound which now threatened his life. That this was simply an unfortunate accident devoid of any special symbolism he accepted without qualification. But the enigmatic presence of the terrace city, with its crumbling galleries and internal courts encrusted by the giant thistles and wire moss, seemed a huge man-made artefact which militated against the super-real naturalism of the delta. However, the terrace city, like the delta, was moving backwards in time, the baroque tracery of the serpent deities along the friezes dissolving and being replaced by the intertwined tendrils of the moss-plants, the pseudo-organic forms made by man in the image of nature reverting to their original. Kept at a distance behind him, as a huge backdrop, the ancient Toltec ruin seemed to brood in the dust like a decaying mastodon, a dying mountain whose dark dream of the earth enveloped Gifford with its luminous presence.

'Do you feel well enough to move on?' Louise asked Gifford when they had received no word of Mechippe's messenger after a further week. She gazed down at him critically as he lay in the shade under the awning, his thin body almost invisible among the folds of the blankets and the monstrous tent over his leg, only the arrogant face with its stiffening beard reminding her of his identity. 'Perhaps if we met the search party halfway ...'

Gifford shook his head, his eyes moving off across the bleached plain to the almost drained channels of the delta. 'Which search party? There isn't a boat with a shallow enough draught between here and Taxcol.'

'Perhaps they'll send a helicopter. They could see us from the air.'

'Helicopter? You've got a bee in your bonnet, Louise. We'll stay here for another week or so.'

'But your leg,' his wife insisted. 'A doctor should –'

'How can I move? Jerked about on a stretcher, I'd be dead within five minutes.' He looked up wearily at his wife's pale sunburnt face, waiting for her to go away.

She hovered over him uncertainly. Fifty yards away, Richard Lowry sat in the open air outside his tent, watching her quietly. Involuntarily, before she could prevent herself, her hand moved to straighten her hair.

'Is Lowry there?' Gifford asked.

'Richard? Yes.' Louise hesitated. 'We'll be back for lunch. I'll change your dressing then.'

As she stepped from his field of vision Gifford lifted his chin slightly to examine the beaches obscured by the morning haze. The baked mud slopes glistened like hot concrete, and only a thin trickle of black fluid leaked slowly along the troughs. Here and there small islands fifty yards in diameter, shaped like perfect hemispheres, rose off the floors of the channels, imparting a curious geometric formality to the landscape. The whole area remained completely motionless, but Gifford lay patiently in his stretcher-chair, waiting for the snakes to come out on to the beaches.

When he noticed Mechippe serving lunch to him he realized that Lowry and Louise had not returned from the site.

'Take it away.' He pushed aside the bowl of condensed soup. 'Bring me whisky soda. Double.' He glanced sharply at the Indian. 'Where's Mrs Gifford?'

Mechippe steered the soup bowl back on to his tray. 'Miss' Gifford coming soon, sir. Sun very hot, she wait till afternoon.'

Gifford lay back for a moment, thinking of Louise and Richard Lowry, the image of them together touching the barest residue of emotion. Then he tried to wave away the haze with his hand.

'What's that –?'

'Sir?'

'Damn it, I thought I saw one.' He shook his head slowly as the white form he had fleetingly glimpsed vanished among the opalescent slopes. 'Too early, though. Where's that whisky?'

'Coming, sir.'

Panting slightly after the exertion of sitting up, Gifford looked around restlessly at the clutter of tents. Diagonally behind him, emerging from the lengthening focus of his eyes, loomed the long ridges of the Toltec city. Somewhere among its spiral galleries and corridors were Louise and Richard Lowry. Looking down from one of the high terraces across the alluvial bench, the distant camp would seem like a few bleached husks, guarded by a dead man propped up in a chair.

'Darling, I'm awfully sorry. We tried to get back but I twisted my heel –' Louise Gifford laughed lightly at this '– rather as you did, now that I come to think of it. Perhaps I'll be joining you here in a day or two. I'm so glad Mechippe looked after you and changed the dressing. How do you feel? You look a lot better.'

Gifford nodded drowsily. The afternoon fever had subsided but he felt drained and exhausted, his awareness of his wife's chattering presence only stimulated by the whisky he had been drinking slowly all day. 'It's been a day at the zoo,' he said, adding, with tired humour: 'At the reptile enclosure.'

'You and your snakes. Charles, you are a scream.' Louise paced around the stretcher-chair, downwind of the cradle, then withdrew to the lee-side. She waved to Richard Lowry, who was carrying some specimen trays into his tent. 'Dick, I suggest we shower and then join Charles for drinks.'

'Great idea,' Lowry called back. 'How is he?'

'Much better.' To Gifford she said: 'You don't mind, Charles? It will do you good to talk a little.'

Gifford gestured vaguely with his head. When his wife had gone to her tent he focused his eyes carefully on the beaches. There, in the evening light, the snakes festered and writhed, their long forms gliding in and out of each other, the whole darkening horizon locked together by their serpentine embrace. There were now literally tens of thousands of them, reaching beyond the margins of the beach across the open ground towards the camp. During the afternoon, at the height of his fever, he had tried to call to them, but his voice had been too weak.

Later, over their cocktails, Richard Lowry asked: 'How do you feel, sir?' When Gifford made no reply he said: 'I'm glad to hear the leg is better.'

'You know, Dick, I think it's psychological,' Louise remarked. 'As soon as you and I are out of the way Charles improves.' Her eyes caught Richard Lowry's and held them.

Lowry played with his glass, a faintly self-assured smile on his bland face. 'What about the messenger? Is there any news?'

'Have you heard anything, Charles? Perhaps someone will fly over in a couple of days.'

During this exchange of pleasantries, and those which followed on the subsequent days, Charles Gifford remained silent and withdrawn, sinking more deeply into the interior landscape emerging from the beaches of the delta. His wife and Richard Lowry sat with him in the evenings when they returned from the terrace city, but he was barely aware of their presence. By now they seemed to move in a peripheral world, players in a marginal melodrama. Now and then he would think about them, but the effort seemed to lack point. His wife's involvement with Lowry left him unperturbed; if anything, he felt grateful to Lowry for freeing him from Louise.

Once, two or three days later, when Lowry came to sit by him in the evening, Gifford roused himself and said dryly: 'I hear you found treasure in the terrace city.' But before Lowry could produce a reply he relapsed again into his vigil.

One night shortly afterwards, when he was woken in the early hours of the morning by a sudden spasm of pain in his foot, he saw his wife and Lowry walking through the powdery blue darkness by the latter's tent. For a fleeting moment their embracing figures were like the snakes coiled together on the beaches.

'Mechippe!'

'Doctor?'

'*Mechippe!*'

'I am here, sir.'

'Tonight, Mechippe,' Gifford told him, 'you sleep in my tent. Understand? I want you near me. Use my bed, if you want. Will you hear if I call?'

'Of course, sir. I hear you.' The head-boy's polished ebony face regarded Gifford circumspectly. He now tended Gifford with a care that indicated that the latter, however much a novice, had at last entered the world of absolute values, composed of the delta and the snakes, the brooding presence of the Toltec ruin and his dying leg.

After midnight, Gifford lay quietly in the stretcher-chair, watching the full moon rise over the luminous beaches. Like a Medusa's crown, thousands of the snakes had climbed the crests of the beaches and were spreading thickly across the margins of the plain, their white backs exposed to the moonlight.

'Mechippe.'

The head-boy had been squatting silently in the shadows. 'Dr Gifford?'

Gifford spoke in a low but clear voice. 'Crutches. Over there.' As the head-boy passed the two carved sticks Gifford tossed aside the blankets. Carefully he withdrew his leg from the cradle, then sat up and lifted it on to the ground. He leaned forward into the crutches and found his balance. The bandaged foot, like a white club, stuck out in front of him. 'Now. In the field-desk, right-hand drawer, there's my gun. Bring it to me.'

For once the head-boy hesitated. 'Gun, sir?'

'Smith & Wesson. It should be loaded, but there's a box of cartridges.'

Again the head-boy hesitated, his eyes roving to the two tents spaced in a line away from them, their entrances hooded by the dust canopies. The whole camp lay in silence, the light stirring of the wind muted by the still warm sand and the dark talcum-like air. 'Gun,' he said. 'Yes, sir.'

Easing himself slowly to his feet, Gifford paused uncertainly. His head swam with the exertion, but the huge anchor of his left foot held him to the ground. Taking the pistol, he gestured with it towards the delta.

'We're going to see the snakes, Mechippe. You help me. All right?'

Mechippe's eyes flashed in the moonlight. 'The snakes, sir?'

'Yes. You take me halfway there. Then you can come back. Don't worry, I'll be all right.'

Mechippe nodded slowly, his eyes looking out over the delta. 'I help you, doctor.'

Labouring slowly across the sand, Gifford steadied himself on the head-boy's arm. After a few steps he found his left leg too heavy to lift, and dragged the dead load through the soft sand.

'Christ, it's a long way.' They had covered twenty yards. By some optical freak the nearest snakes now seemed to be half a mile away, barely visible between the slight rises. 'Let's get on with it.'

They plodded on a further ten yards. The open mouth of Lowry's tent was on their left, the white bell of the mosquito net looming in the shadows like a sepulchre. Almost exhausted, Gifford tottered unsteadily, trying to focus his eyes through the tinted air.

There was a sudden flash and roar as the revolver discharged itself, cannoning out of his hand. He felt Mechippe's fingers stiffen on his arm, and heard someone emerge from Lowry's tent, a woman's startled cry of fear. A second figure, this time a man's, appeared and with a backward glance at Gifford darted away like a startled animal among the tents, racing head down towards the terrace city.

Annoyed by these interruptions, Gifford searched blindly for the revolver, struggling with the crutches. But the darkness condensed around him, and the sand came upwards to strike his face.

The next morning, as the tents were dismantled and packed away, Gifford felt too tired to look out across the delta. The snakes never appeared until the early afternoon, and the disappointment of failing to reach them the previous night had drained his energy.

When only his own tent remained of the camp, and the naked shower scaffoldings protruded from the ground like pieces of abstract sculpture marking a futuristic cairn, Louise came over to him.

'It's time for them to pack your tent.' Her tone was matter-of-fact but guarded. 'The boys are building a stretcher for you. You should be comfortable.'

Gifford gestured her away. 'I can't go. Leave Mechippe with me and take the others.'

'Charles, be practical for once.' Louise stood before him, her face composed. 'We can't stay here indefinitely, and you need treatment. It's obvious now that Mechippe's boy never reached Taxcol. Our supplies won't last for ever.'

'They don't have to last for ever.' Gifford's eyes, almost closed, surveyed the distant horizon like a pair of defective binoculars. 'Leave me one month's.'

'Charles –'

'For heaven's sake, Louise . . .' Wearily he let his head loll on the pillow. He noticed Richard Lowry supervising the stowage of the stores, the Indian boys moving around him like willing children. 'Why all the hurry? Can't you stay another week?'

'We can't, Charles.' She looked her husband straight in the face. 'Richard feels he must go. You understand. For your sake.'

'My sake?' Gifford shook his head. 'I don't give a damn about Lowry. Last night I was going out to look at the snakes.'

'Well . . .' Louise smoothed her bush shirt. 'This trip has been such a fiasco, Charles, there are many things that frighten me. I'll tell them to dismantle the tent when you're ready.'

'Louise.' With a last effort Gifford sat up. In a quiet voice, in order not to embarrass his wife by letting Richard Lowry hear him, he said: 'I went out to look at the *snakes*. You do understand that?'

'But Charles!' With a sudden burst of exasperation his wife snapped: 'Don't you realize, there are no snakes! Ask Mechippe, ask Richard Lowry or any of the boys! The entire river is as dry as a bone!'

Gifford turned to look at the white beaches of the delta. 'You and Lowry go. I'm sorry, Louise, but I couldn't stand the trip.'

'You must!' She gestured at the distant hills, at the terrace city and the delta. 'There's something wrong with this place, Charles, somehow it's convinced you that . . .'

Followed by a group of boys, Richard Lowry walked slowly towards them, signalling with his hands to Louise. She hesitated, then on an impulse waved him back and sat down beside Gifford. 'Charles, listen. I'll stay with you for another week as you ask, so that you can come to terms with these hallucinations, if you promise me that you'll leave then. Richard can go ahead on his own, he'll meet us in Taxcol with a doctor.' She lowered her voice, 'Charles, I'm sorry about Richard. I realize now . . .'

She leaned forward to see her husband's face. He lay in his seat in front of the solitary tent, the circle of boys watching him patiently from a distance. Ten miles away a solitary cloud drifted over one of the mesas, like a plume of smoke above a dormant but still active volcano.

'Charles.' She waited for her husband to speak, hoping that he would reprove and so perhaps even forgive her. But Charles Gifford was thinking only of the snakes on the beaches.

**1964**

# · THE DROWNED GIANT

On the morning after the storm the body of a drowned giant was washed ashore on the beach five miles to the north-west of the city. The first news of its arrival was brought by a nearby farmer and subsequently confirmed by the local newspaper reporters and the police. Despite this the majority of people, myself among them, remained sceptical, but the return of more and more eye-witnesses attesting to the vast size of the giant was finally too much for our curiosity. The library where my colleagues and I were carrying out our research was almost deserted when we set off for the coast shortly after two o'clock, and throughout the day people continued to leave their offices and shops as accounts of the giant circulated around the city.

By the time we reached the dunes above the beach a substantial crowd had gathered, and we could see the body lying in the shallow water two hundred yards away. At first the estimates of its size seemed greatly exaggerated. It was then at low tide, and almost all the giant's body was exposed, but he appeared to be a little larger than a basking shark. He lay on his back with his arms at his sides, in an attitude of repose, as if asleep on the mirror of wet sand, the reflection of his blanched skin fading as the water receded. In the clear sunlight his body glistened like the white plumage of a sea-bird.

Puzzled by this spectacle, and dissatisfied with the matter-of-fact explanations of the crowd, my friends and I stepped down from the dunes on to the shingle. Everyone seemed reluctant to approach the giant, but half an hour later two fishermen in wading boots walked out across the sand. As their diminutive figures neared the recumbent body a sudden hubbub of conversation broke out among the spectators. The two men were completely dwarfed by the giant. Although his heels were partly submerged in the sand, the feet rose to at least twice the fishermen's height, and we immediately realized that this drowned leviathan had the mass and dimensions of the largest sperm whale.

Three fishing smacks had arrived on the scene and with keels raised remained a quarter of a mile off-shore, the crews watching from the bows. Their discretion deterred the spectators on the shore from wading out across the sand. Impatiently everyone stepped down from the dunes and waited on the shingle slopes, eager for a closer view. Around the margins of the figure the sand had been washed away, forming a hollow, as if the giant had fallen out of the sky. The two fishermen were standing between the immense plinths of the feet, waving to us like tourists among the columns of some water-lapped temple on the Nile. For a moment I feared that the giant was merely asleep and might suddenly stir and clap his heels together, but his glazed eyes stared skywards, unaware of the minuscule replicas of himself between his feet.

The fishermen then began a circuit of the corpse, strolling past the long white flanks of the legs. After a pause to examine the fingers of the supine hand, they disappeared from sight between the arm and chest, then re-emerged to survey the head, shielding their eyes as they gazed up at its Graecian profile. The shallow forehead, straight high-bridged nose and curling lips reminded me of a Roman copy of Praxiteles, and the elegantly formed cartouches of the nostrils emphasized the resemblance to monumental sculpture.

Abruptly there was a shout from the crowd, and a hundred arms pointed towards the sea. With a start I saw that one of the fishermen had climbed on to the giant's chest and was now strolling about and signalling to the shore. There was a roar of surprise and triumph from the crowd, lost in a rushing avalanche of shingle as everyone surged forward across the sand.

As we approached the recumbent figure, which was lying in a pool of water the size of a field, our excited chatter fell away again, subdued by the huge physical dimensions of this moribund colossus. He was stretched out at a slight angle to the shore, his legs carried nearer the beach, and this foreshortening had disguised his true length. Despite the two fishermen standing on his abdomen, the crowd formed itself into a wide circle, groups of three or four people tentatively advancing towards the hands and feet.

My companions and I walked around the seaward side of the giant, whose hips and thorax towered above us like the hull of a stranded ship. His pearl-coloured skin, distended by immersion in salt water, masked the contours of the enormous muscles and tendons. We passed below the left knee, which was flexed slightly, threads of damp sea-weed clinging to its sides. Draped loosely across the midriff, and preserving a tenuous propriety, was a shawl of heavy open-weaved material, bleached to a pale yellow by the water. A strong odour of brine came from the garment as it steamed in the sun, mingled with the sweet but potent scent of the giant's skin.

We stopped by his shoulder and gazed up at the motionless profile. The lips were parted slightly, the open eye cloudy and occluded, as if injected with some blue milky liquid, but the delicate arches of the nostrils and eyebrows invested the face with an ornate charm that belied the brutish power of the chest and shoulders.

The ear was suspended in mid-air over our heads like a sculptured doorway. As I raised my hand to touch the pendulous lobe someone appeared over the edge of the forehead and shouted down at me. Startled by this apparition, I stepped back, and then saw that a group of youths had climbed up on to the face and were jostling each other in and out of the orbits.

People were now clambering all over the giant, whose reclining arms provided a double stairway. From the palms they walked along the forearms to the elbow and then crawled over the distended belly of the biceps to the flat promenade of the pectoral muscles which covered the upper half of the smooth hairless chest. From here they climbed up on to the face, hand over hand along the lips and nose, or forayed down the abdomen to meet others who had straddled the ankles and were patrolling the twin columns of the thighs.

We continued our circuit through the crowd, and stopped to examine the outstretched right hand. A small pool of water lay in the palm, like the residue of another world, now being kicked away by the people ascending the arm. I tried to read the palm-lines that grooved the skin, searching for some clue to the giant's character, but the distension of the tissues had almost obliterated them, carrying away all trace of the giant's identity and his last tragic predicament. The huge muscles and wrist-bones of the hand seemed to deny any sensitivity to their owner, but the delicate flexion of the fingers and the well-tended nails, each cut symmetrically to within six inches of the quick, argued a certain refinement of temperament, illustrated in the Graecian features of the face, on which the townsfolk were now sitting like flies.

One youth was even standing, arms wavering at his sides, on the very tip of the nose, shouting down at his companions, but the face of the giant still retained its massive composure.

Returning to the shore, we sat down on the shingle, and watched the continuous stream of people arriving from the city. Some six or seven fishing boats had collected off-shore, and their crews waded in through the shallow water for a closer look at this enormous storm-catch. Later a party of police appeared and made a half-hearted attempt to cordon off the beach, but after walking up to the recumbent figure any such thoughts left their minds, and they went off together with bemused backward glances.

An hour later there were a thousand people present on the beach, at least two hundred of them standing or sitting on the giant, crowded along his arms and legs or circulating in a ceaseless mêlée across his chest and stomach. A large gang of youths occupied the head, toppling each other off the cheeks and sliding down the smooth planes of the jaw. Two or three straddled the nose, and another crawled into one of the nostrils, from which he emitted barking noises like a dog.

That afternoon the police returned, and cleared a way through the crowd for a party of scientific experts – authorities on gross anatomy and marine biology – from the university. The gang of youths and most of the people on the giant climbed down, leaving behind a few hardy spirits perched on the tips of the toes and on the forehead. The experts strode around the giant, heads nodding in vigorous consultation, preceded by the policemen who pushed back the press of spectators. When they reached the outstretched hand the senior officer offered to assist them up on to the palm, but the experts hastily demurred.

After they returned to the shore, the crowd once more climbed on to the giant, and was in full possession when we left at five o'clock, covering the arms and legs like a dense flock of gulls sitting on the corpse of a large fish.

I next visited the beach three days later. My friends at the library had returned to their work, and delegated to me the task of keeping the giant under observation and preparing a report. Perhaps they sensed my particular interest in the case, and it was certainly true that I was eager to return to the beach. There was nothing necrophilic about this, for to all intents the giant was still alive for me, indeed more alive than many of the people watching him. What I found so fascinating was partly his immense scale, the huge volumes of space occupied by his arms and legs, which seemed to confirm the identity of my own miniature limbs, but above all the mere categorical fact of his existence. Whatever else in our lives might be open to doubt, the giant, dead or alive, existed in an absolute sense, providing a glimpse into a world of similar absolutes of which we spectators on the beach were such imperfect and puny copies.

When I arrived at the beach the crowd was considerably smaller, and some two or three hundred people sat on the shingle, picnicking and watching the groups of visitors who walked out across the sand. The successive tides had carried the giant nearer the shore, swinging his head and shoulders towards the beach, so that he seemed doubly to gain in size, his huge body dwarfing the fishing boats beached beside his feet. The uneven contours of the beach had pushed his spine into a slight arch, expanding his chest and tilting back the head, forcing him into a more expressly heroic posture. The combined effects of sea-water and the tumefaction of the tissues had given the face a sleeker and less youthful look. Although the vast proportions of the features made it impossible to assess the age and character of the giant, on my previous visit his classically modelled mouth and nose suggested that he had been a young man of discreet and modest temper. Now, however, he appeared to be at least in early middle age. The puffy cheeks, thicker nose and temples and narrowing eyes gave him a look of well-fed maturity that even now hinted at a growing corruption to come.

This accelerated post-mortem development of the giant's character, as if the latent elements of his personality had gained sufficient momentum during his life to discharge themselves in a brief final resumé, continued to fascinate me. It marked the beginning of the giant's surrender to that all-demanding system of time in which the rest of humanity finds itself, and of which, like the million twisted ripples of a fragmented whirlpool, our finite lives are the concluding products. I took up my position on the shingle directly opposite the giant's head, from where I could see the new arrivals and the children clambering over the legs and arms.

Among the morning's visitors were a number of men in leather jackets and cloth caps, who peered up critically at the giant with a professional eye, pacing out his dimensions and making rough calculations in the sand with spars of driftwood. I assumed them to be from the public works department and other municipal bodies, no doubt wondering how to dispose of this gargantuan piece of jetsam.

Several rather more smartly attired individuals, circus proprietors and the like, also appeared on the scene, and strolled slowly around the giant, hands in the pockets of their long overcoats, saying nothing to one another. Evidently its bulk was too great even for their matchless enterprise. After they had gone the children continued to run up and down the arms and legs, and the youths wrestled with each other over the supine face, the damp sand from their feet covering the white skin.

The following day I deliberately postponed my visit until the late after-noon, and when I arrived there were fewer than fifty or sixty people sitting on the shingle. The giant had been carried still closer to the shore, and was now little more than seventy-five yards away, his feet crushing the palisade of a rotting breakwater. The slope of the firmer sand tilted his body towards the sea, and the bruised face was averted in an almost conscious gesture. I sat down on a large metal winch which had been shackled to a concrete caisson above the shingle, and looked down at the recumbent figure.

His blanched skin had now lost its pearly translucence and was spattered with dirty sand which replaced that washed away by the night tide. Clumps of sea-weed filled the intervals between the fingers and a collection of litter and cuttle-bones lay in the crevices below the hips and knees. But despite this, and the continuous thickening of his features, the giant still retained his magnificent Homeric stature. The enormous breadth of the shoulders, and the huge columns of the arms and legs, still carried the figure into another dimension, and the giant seemed a more authentic image of one of the drowned Argonauts or heroes of the Odyssey than the conventional human-sized portrait previously in my mind.

I stepped down on to the sand, and walked between the pools of water towards the giant. Two small boys were sitting in the well of the ear, and at the far end a solitary youth stood perched high on one of the toes, surveying me as I approached. As I had hoped when delaying my visit, no one else paid any attention to me, and the people on the shore remained huddled beneath their coats.

The giant's supine right hand was covered with broken shells and sand, in which a score of footprints were visible. The rounded bulk of the hip towered above me, cutting off all sight of the sea. The sweetly acrid odour I had noticed before was now more pungent, and through the opaque skin I could see the serpentine coils of congealed blood-vessels. However repellent it seemed, this ceaseless metamorphosis, a visible life in death, alone permitted me to set foot on the corpse.

Using the jutting thumb as a stair-rail, I climbed up on to the palm and began my ascent. The skin was harder than I expected, barely yielding to my weight. Quickly I walked up the sloping forearm and the bulging balloon of the biceps. The face of the drowned giant loomed to my right, the cavernous nostrils and huge flanks of the cheeks like the cone of some freakish volcano.

Safely rounding the shoulder, I stepped out on to the broad promenade of the chest, across which the bony ridges of the ribcage lay like huge rafters. The white skin was dappled by the darkening bruises of countless footprints, in which the patterns of individual heel-marks were clearly visible. Someone had built a small sandcastle on the centre of the sternum, and I climbed on to this partly demolished structure to give myself a better view of the face.

The two children had now scaled the ear and were pulling themselves into the right orbit, whose blue globe, completely occluded by some milk-coloured fluid, gazed sightlessly past their miniature forms. Seen obliquely from below, the face was devoid of all grace and repose, the drawn mouth and raised chin propped up by its gigantic slings of muscles resembling the torn prow of a colossal wreck. For the first time I became aware of the extremity of this last physical agony of the giant, no less painful for his unawareness of the collapsing musculature and tissues. The absolute isolation of the ruined figure, cast like an abandoned ship upon the empty shore, almost out of sound of the waves, transformed his face into a mask of exhaustion and helplessness.

As I stepped forward, my foot sank into a trough of soft tissue, and a gust of fetid gas blew through an aperture between the ribs. Retreating from the fouled air, which hung like a cloud over my head, I turned towards the sea to clear my lungs. To my surprise I saw that the giant's left hand had been amputated.

I stared with bewilderment at the blackening stump, while the solitary youth reclining on his aerial perch a hundred feet away surveyed me with a sanguinary eye.

This was only the first of a sequence of depredations. I spent the following two days in the library, for some reason reluctant to visit the shore, aware that I had probably witnessed the approaching end of a magnificent illusion. When I next crossed the dunes and set foot on the shingle the giant was little more than twenty yards away, and with this close proximity to the rough pebbles all traces had vanished of the magic which once surrounded his distant wave-washed form. Despite his immense size, the bruises and dirt that covered his body made him appear merely human in scale, his vast dimensions only increasing his vulnerability.

His right hand and foot had been removed, dragged up the slope and trundled away by cart. After questioning the small group of people huddled by the breakwater, I gathered that a fertilizer company and a cattle food manufacturer were responsible.

The giant's remaining foot rose into the air, a steel hawzer fixed to the large toe, evidently in preparation for the following day. The surrounding beach had been disturbed by a score of workmen, and deep ruts marked the ground where the hands and foot had been hauled away. A dark brackish fluid leaked from the stumps, and stained the sand and the white cones of the cuttlefish. As I walked down the shingle I noticed that a number of jocular slogans, swastikas and other signs had been cut into the grey skin, as if the mutilation of this motionless colossus had released a sudden flood of repressed spite. The lobe of one of the ears was pierced by a spear of timber, and a small fire had burnt out in the centre of the chest, blackening the surrounding skin. The fine wood ash was still being scattered by the wind.

A foul smell enveloped the cadaver, the undisguisable signature of putrefaction, which had at last driven away the usual gathering of youths. I returned to the shingle and climbed up on to the winch. The giant's swollen cheeks had now almost closed his eyes, drawing the lips back in a monumental gape. The once straight Graecian nose had been twisted and flattened, stamped into the ballooning face by countless heels.

When I visited the beach the following day I found, almost with relief, that the head had been removed.

Some weeks elapsed before I made my next journey to the beach, and by then the human likeness I had noticed earlier had vanished again. On close inspection the recumbent thorax and abdomen were unmistakably manlike, but as each of the limbs was chopped off, first at the knee and elbow, and then at shoulder and thigh, the carcass resembled that of any headless sea-animal – whale or whale-shark. With this loss of identity, and the few traces of personality that had clung tenuously to the figure, the interest of the spectators expired, and the foreshore was deserted except for an elderly beachcomber and the watchman sitting in the doorway of the contractor's hut.

A loose wooden scaffolding had been erected around the carcass, from which a dozen ladders swung in the wind, and the surrounding sand was littered with coils of rope, long metal-handled knives and grappling irons, the pebbles oily with blood and pieces of bone and skin.

I nodded to the watchman, who regarded me dourly over his brazier of burning coke. The whole area was pervaded by the pungent smell of huge squares of blubber being simmered in a vat behind the hut.

Both the thigh-bones had been removed, with the assistance of a small crane draped in the gauze-like fabric which had once covered the waist of the giant, and the open sockets gaped like barn doors. The upper arms, collar bones and pudenda had likewise been dispatched. What remained of the skin over the thorax and abdomen had been marked out in parallel strips with a tar brush, and the first five or six sections had been pared away from the midriff, revealing the great arch of the rib-cage.

As I left a flock of gulls wheeled down from the sky and alighted on the beach, picking at the stained sand with ferocious cries.

Several months later, when the news of his arrival had been generally forgotten, various pieces of the body of the dismembered giant began to reappear all over the city. Most of these were bones, which the fertilizer manufacturers had found too difficult to crush, and their massive size, and the huge tendons and discs of cartilage attached to their joints, immediately identified them. For some reason, these disembodied fragments seemed better to convey the essence of the giant's original magnificence than the bloated appendages that had been subsequently amputated. As I looked across the road at the premises of the largest wholesale merchants in the meat market, I recognized the two enormous thighbones on either side of the doorway. They towered over the porters' heads like the threatening megaliths of some primitive druidical religion, and I had a sudden vision of the giant climbing to his knees upon these bare bones and striding away through the streets of the city, picking up the scattered fragments of himself on his return journey to the sea.

A few days later I saw the left humerus lying in the entrance to one of the shipyards (its twin for several years lay on the mud among the piles below the harbour's principal commercial wharf). In the same week the mummified right hand was exhibited on a carnival float during the annual pageant of the guilds.

The lower jaw, typically, found its way to the museum of natural history. The remainder of the skull has disappeared, but is probably still lurking in the waste grounds or private gardens of the city – quite recently, while sailing down the river, I noticed two ribs of the giant forming a decorative arch in a waterside garden, possibly confused with the jaw-bones of a whale. A large square of tanned and tattooed skin, the size of an indian blanket, forms a backcloth to the dolls and masks in a novelty shop near the amusement park, and I have no doubt that elsewhere in the city, in the hotels or golf clubs, the mummified nose or ears of the giant hang from the wall above a fireplace. As for the immense pizzle, this ends its days in the freak museum of a circus which travels up and down the north-west. This monumental apparatus, stunning in its proportions and sometime potency, occupies a complete booth to itself. The irony is that it is wrongly identified as that of a whale, and indeed most people, even those who first saw him cast up on the shore after the storm, now remember the giant, if at all, as a large sea beast.

The remainder of the skeleton, stripped of all flesh, still rests on the sea shore, the clutter of bleached ribs like the timbers of a derelict ship. The contractor's hut, the crane and the scaffolding have been removed, and the sand being driven into the bay along the coast has buried the pelvis and backbone. In the winter the high curved bones are deserted, battered by the breaking waves, but in the summer they provide an excellent perch for the sea-wearying gulls.

**, 1964**

# THE GIOCONDA OF THE TWILIGHT NOON

'Those confounded gulls!' Richard Maitland complained to his wife. 'Can't you drive them away?'

Judith hovered behind the wheelchair, her hands glancing around his bandaged eyes like nervous doves. She peered across the lawn to the river bank. 'Try not to think about them, darling. They're just sitting there.'

'Just? That's the trouble!' Maitland raised his cane and struck the air vigorously. 'I can feel them all out there, watching me!'

They had taken his mother's house for his convalescence, partly on the assumption that the rich store of visual memories would in some way compensate for Maitland's temporary blindness – a trivial eye injury had become infected, eventually requiring surgery and a month's bandaged darkness. However, they had failed to reckon with the huge extension of his other senses. The house was five miles from the coast, but at low tide a flock of the greedy estuarine birds would fly up the river and alight on the exposed mud fifty yards from where Maitland sat in his wheelchair in the centre of the lawn. Judith could barely hear the gulls, but to Maitland their ravenous pecking filled the warm air like the cries of some savage Dionysian chorus. He had a vivid image of the wet banks streaming with the blood of thousands of dismembered fish.

Fretting impotently to himself, he listened as their voices suddenly fell away. Then, with a sharp sound like tearing cloth, the entire flock rose into the air. Maitland sat up stiffly in the wheelchair, the cane clasped like a cudgel in his right hand, half-expecting the gulls to swerve down on to the placid lawn, their fierce beaks tearing at the bandages over his eyes.

As if to conjure them away, he chanted aloud:

> 'The nightingales are singing near
> The Convent of the Sacred Heart,
> And sang within the bloody wood
> When Agamemnon cried aloud . . . !'

During the fortnight since his return from the hospital Judith had read most of the early Eliot aloud to him. The flock of unseen gulls seemed to come straight out of that grim archaic landscape.

The birds settled again, and Judith took a few hesitant steps across the lawn, her dim form interrupting the even circle of light within his eyes.

'They sound like a shoal of piranha,' he said with a forced laugh. 'What are they doing – stripping a bull?'

'Nothing, dear, as far as I can see . . .' Judith's voice dipped on this last word. Even though Maitland's blindness was only temporary – in fact, by twisting the bandages he could see a blurred but coherent image of the garden with its willows screening the river – she still treated him to all the traditional circumlocutions, hedging him with the elaborate taboos erected by the seeing to hide them from the blind. The only real cripples, Maitland reflected, were the perfect in limb.

'Dick, I have to drive into town to collect the groceries. You'll be all right for half an hour?'

'Of course. Just sound the horn when you come back.'

The task of looking after the rambling country house single-handed – Maitland's widowed mother was on a steamer cruise in the Mediterranean – limited the time Judith could spend with him. Fortunately his long familiarity with the house saved her from having to guide him around it. A few rope hand-rails and one or two buffers of cotton wool taped to dangerous table corners had been enough. Indeed, once upstairs Maitland moved about the winding corridors and dark back staircases with more ease than Judith, and certainly with far more willingness – often in the evening she would go in search of Maitland and be startled to see her blind husband step soundlessly from a doorway two or three feet from her as he wandered among the old attics and dusty lofts. His rapt expression, as he hunted some memory of childhood, reminded her in a curious way of his mother, a tall, handsome woman whose bland smile always seemed to conceal some potent private world.

To begin with, when Maitland had chafed under the bandages, Judith had spent all morning and afternoon reading the newspapers aloud to him, then a volume of poems and even, heroically, the start of a novel, *Moby Dick*. Within a few days, however, Maitland had come to terms with his blindness, and the constant need for some sort of external stimulation faded. He discovered what every blind person soon finds out – that its external optical input is only part of the mind's immense visual activity. He had expected to be plunged into a profound Stygian darkness, but instead his brain was filled with a ceaseless play of light and colour. At times, as he lay back in the morning sunlight, he would see exquisite revolving patterns of orange light, like huge solar discs. These would gradually recede to brilliant pinpoints, shining above a veiled landscape across which dim forms moved like animals over an African veldt at dusk.

At other times forgotten memories would impinge themselves on this screen, what he assumed to be visual relics of his childhood long buried in his mind.

It was these images, with all their tantalizing associations, that most intrigued Maitland. By letting his mind drift into reverie he could almost summon them at will, watching passively as these elusive landscapes materialized like visiting spectres before his inner eye. One in particular, composed of fleeting glimpses of steep cliffs, a dark corridor of mirrors and a tall, high-gabled house within a wall, recurred persistently, although its unrelated details owed nothing to his memory. Maitland tried to explore it, fixing the blue cliffs or the tall house in his mind and waiting for their associations to gather. But the noise of the gulls and Judith's to and fro movements across the garden distracted him.

''Bye, darling! See you later!'

Maitland raised his cane in reply. He listened to the car move off down the drive, its departure subtly altering the auditory profile of the house. Wasps buzzed among the ivy below the kitchen windows, hovering over the oil stains in the gravel. A line of trees swayed in the warm air, muffling Judith's last surge of acceleration. For once the gulls were silent. Usually this would have roused Maitland's suspicions, but he lay back, turning the wheels of the chair so that he faced the sun.

Thinking of nothing, he watched the aureoles of light mushroom soundlessly within his mind. Occasionally the shifting of the willows or the sounds of a bee bumping around the glass water jug on the table beside him would end the sequence. This extreme sensitivity to the faintest noise or movement reminded him of the hypersensitivity of epileptics, or of rabies victims in their grim terminal convulsions. It was almost as if the barriers between the deepest levels of the nervous system and the external world had been removed, those muffling layers of blood and bone, reflex and convention ...

With a barely perceptible pause in his breathing, Maitland relaxed carefully in the chair. Projected on to the screen within his mind was the image he had glimpsed before, of a rocky coastline whose dark cliffs loomed through an off-shore mist. The whole scene was drab and colourless. Overhead low clouds reflected the pewter surface of the water. As the mist cleared he moved nearer the shore, and watched the waves breaking on the rocks. The plumes of foam searched like white serpents among the pools and crevices for the caves that ran deep into the base of the cliff.

Desolate and unfrequented, the coast reminded Maitland only of the cold shores of Tierra del Fuego and the ships' graveyards of Cape Horn, rather than of any memories of his own. Yet the cliffs drew nearer, rising into the air above him, as if their identity reflected some image deep within Maitland's mind.

Still separated from them by the interval of grey water, Maitland followed the shoreline, until the cliffs divided at the mouth of a small estuary. Instantly the light cleared. The water within the estuary glowed with an almost spectral vibrancy. The blue rocks of the surrounding cliffs, penetrated by small grottoes and caverns, emitted a soft prismatic light, as if illuminated by some subterranean lantern.

Holding this scene before him, Maitland searched the shores of the estuary. The caverns were deserted, but as he neared them the luminous archways began to reflect the light like a hall of mirrors. At the same time he found himself entering the dark, high-gabled house he had seen previously, and which had now superimposed itself on his dream. Somewhere within it, masked by the mirrors, a tall, green-robed figure watched him, receding through the caves and groynes . . .

A motor-car horn sounded, a gay succession of toots. The gravel grating beneath its tyres, a car swung into the drive.

'Judith here, darling,' his wife called. 'Everything all right?'

Cursing under his breath, Maitland fumbled for his cane. The image of the dark coast and the estuary with its spectral caves had gone. Like a blind worm, he turned his blunted head at the unfamiliar sounds and shapes in the garden.

'Are you all right?' Judith's footsteps crossed the lawn. 'What's the matter, you're all hunched up – have those birds been annoying you?'

'No, leave them.' Maitland lowered his cane, realizing that although not visibly present in his inward vision, the gulls had played an oblique role in its creation. The foam-white seabirds, hunters of the albatross . . .

With an effort he said: 'I was asleep.'

Judith knelt down and took his hands. 'I'm sorry. I'll ask one of the men to build a scarecrow. That should –'

'No!' Maitland pulled his hands away. 'They're not worrying me at all.' Levelling his voice, he said: 'Did you see anyone in the town?'

'Dr Phillips. He said you should be able to take off the bandages in about ten days.'

'Good. There's no hurry, though. I want the job done properly.'

After Judith had walked back to the house Maitland tried to return to his reverie, but the image remained sealed behind the screen of his consciousness.

At breakfast the next morning Judith read him the mail.

'There's a postcard from your mother. They're near Malta, somewhere called Gozo.'

'Give it to me.' Maitland felt the card in his hands. 'Gozo – that was Calypso's island. She kept Ulysses there for seven years, promised him eternal youth if he'd stay with her forever.'

'I'm not surprised.' Judith inclined the card towards her. 'If we could spare the time, you and I should go there for a holiday. Wine-dark seas, a sky like heaven, blue rocks. Bliss.'

'Blue?'

'Yes. I suppose it's the bad printing. They can't really be like that.'

'They are, actually.' Still holding the card, Maitland went out into the garden, feeling his way along the string guide-rail. As he settled himself in the wheelchair he reflected that there were other correspondences in the graphic arts. The same blue rocks and spectral grottos could be seen in Leonardo's *Virgin of the Rocks*, one of the most forbidding and most enigmatic of his paintings. The madonna sitting on a bare ledge by the water beneath the dark overhang of the cavern's mouth was like the presiding spirit of some enchanted marine realm, waiting for those cast on to the rocky shores of this world's end. As in so many of Leonardo's paintings, all its unique longings and terrors were to be found in the landscape in the background. Here, through an archway among the rocks, could be seen the crystal blue cliffs that Maitland had glimpsed in his reverie.

'Shall I read it out to you?' Judith had crossed the lawn.

'What?'

'Your mother's postcard. You're holding it in your hand.'

'Sorry. Please do.'

As he listened to the brief message, Maitland waited for Judith to return to the house. When she had gone he sat quietly for a few minutes. The distant sounds of the river came to him through the trees, and the faint cry of gulls swooping on to the banks further down the estuary.

This time, almost as if recognizing Maitland's need, the vision came to him quickly. He passed the dark cliffs, and the waves vaulting into the cave mouths, and then entered the twilight world of the grottoes beside the river. Outside, through the stone galleries, he could see the surface of the water glittering like a sheet of prisms, the soft blue light reflected in the vitreous mirrors which formed the cavern walls. At the same time he sensed that he was entering the high-gabled house, whose surrounding wall was the cliff face he had seen from the sea. The rock-like vaults of the house glowed with the olive-black colours of the marine deeps, and curtains of old lace-work hung from the doors and windows like ancient nets.

A staircase ran through the grotto, its familiar turnings leading to the inner reaches of the cavern. Looking upwards, he saw the green-robed figure watching him from an archway. Her face was hidden from him, veiled by the light reflected off the damp mirrors on the walls. Impelled forward up the steps, Maitland reached towards her, and for an instant the face of the figure cleared . . .

'Judith!' Rocking forward in his chair, Maitland searched helplessly for the water jug on the table, his left hand drumming at his forehead in an attempt to drive away the vision and its terrifying lamia.

'Richard! What is it?'

He heard his wife's hurried footsteps across the lawn, and then felt her hands steadying his own.

'Darling, what on earth's going on? You're pouring with perspiration!'

That afternoon, when he was left alone again, Maitland approached the dark labyrinth more cautiously. At low tide the gulls returned to the mud flats below the garden, and their archaic cries carried his mind back into its deeps like mortuary birds bearing away the body of Tristan. Guarding himself and his own fears, he moved slowly through the luminous chambers of the subterranean house, averting his eyes from the green-robed enchantress who watched him from the staircase.

Later, when Judith brought his tea to him on a tray, he ate carefully, talking to her in measured tones.

'What did you see in your nightmare?' she asked.

'A house of mirrors under the sea, and a deep cavern,' he told her. 'I could see everything, but in a strange way, like the dreams of people who have been blind for a long time.'

Throughout the afternoon and evening he returned to the grotto at intervals, moving circumspectly through the outer chambers, always aware of the robed figure waiting for him in the doorway to its innermost sanctum.

The next morning Dr Phillips called to change his dressing.

'Excellent, excellent,' he commented, holding his torch in one hand as he retaped Maitland's eyelids to his cheeks. 'Another week and you'll be out of this for good. At least you know what it's like for the blind.'

'One can envy them,' Maitland said.

'Really?'

'They see with an inner eye, you know. In a sense everything there is more real.'

'That's a point of view.' Dr Phillips replaced the bandages. He drew the curtains. 'What have you seen with yours?'

Maitland made no reply. Dr Phillips had examined him in the darkened study, but the thin torch beam and the few needles of light around the curtains had filled his brain like arc lights. He waited for the glare to subside, realizing that his inner world, the grotto, the house of mirrors and the enchantress, had been burned out of his mind by the sunlight.

'They're hypnagogic images,' Dr Phillips remarked, fastening his bag. 'You've been living in an unusual zone, sitting around doing nothing but with your optic nerves alert, a no-man's land between sleep and consciousness. I'd expect all sorts of strange things.'

After he had gone Maitland said to the unseen walls, his lips whispering below the bandages: 'Doctor, give me back my eyes.'

It took him two full days to recover from this brief interval of external sight. Laboriously, rock by rock, he re-explored the hidden coastline, willing himself through the enveloping sea-mists, searching for the lost estuary.

At last the luminous beaches appeared again.

'I think I'd better sleep alone tonight,' he told Judith. 'I'll use mother's room.'

'Of course, Richard. What's the matter?'

'I suppose I'm restless. I'm not getting much exercise and there are only three days to go. I don't want to disturb you.'

He found his own way into his mother's bedroom, glimpsed only occasionally during the years since his marriage. The high bed, the deep rustle of silks and the echoes of forgotten scents carried him back to his earliest childhood. He lay awake all night, listening to the sounds of the river reflected off the cut-glass ornaments over the fireplace.

At dawn, when the gulls flew up from the estuary, he visited the blue grottoes again, and the tall house in the cliff. Knowing its tenant now, the green-robed watcher on the staircase, he decided to wait for the morning light. Her beckoning eyes, the pale lantern of her smile, floated before him.

However, after breakfast Dr Phillips returned.

'Right,' he told Maitland briskly, leading him in from the lawn. 'Let's have those bandages off.'

'For the last time, Doctor?' Judith asked. 'Are you sure?'

'Certainly. We don't want this to go on for ever, do we?' He steered Maitland into the study. 'Sit down here, Richard. You draw the curtains, Judith.'

Maitland stood up, feeling for the desk. 'But you said it would take three more days, Doctor.'

'I dare say. But I didn't want you to get over-excited. What's the matter? You're hovering about there like an old woman. Don't you want to see again?'

'*See?*' Maitland repeated numbly. 'Of course.' He subsided limply into a chair as Dr Phillips' hands unfastened the bandages. A profound sense of loss had come over him. 'Doctor, could I put it off for –'

'Nonsense. You can see perfectly. Don't worry, I'm not going to fling back the curtains. It'll be a full day before you can see freely. I'll give you a set of filters to wear. Anyway, these dressings let through more light than you imagine.'

At eleven o'clock the next morning, his eyes shielded only by a pair of sunglasses, Maitland walked out on to the lawn. Judith stood on the terrace, and watched him make his way around the wheelchair. When he reached the willows she called: 'All right, darling? Can you see me?'

Without replying, Maitland looked back at the house. He removed the sunglasses and threw them aside on to the grass. He gazed through the trees at the estuary, at the blue surface of the water stretching to the opposite bank. Hundreds of the gulls stood by the water, their heads turned in profile to reveal the full curve of their beaks. He looked over his shoulder at the high-gabled house, recognizing the one he had seen in his dream. Everything about it, like the bright river which slid past him, seemed dead.

Suddenly the gulls rose into the air, their cries drowning the sounds of Judith's voice as she called again from the terrace. In a dense spiral, gathering itself off the ground like an immense scythe, the gulls wheeled into the air over his head and swirled over the house.

Quickly Maitland pushed back the branches of the willows and walked down on to the bank.

\*        \*        \*

A moment later, Judith heard his shout above the cries of the gulls. The sound came half in pain and half in triumph, and she ran down to the trees uncertain whether he had injured himself or discovered something pleasing.

Then she saw him standing on the bank, his head raised to the sunlight, the bright carmine on his cheeks and hands, an eager, unrepentant Oedipus.

, **1964**

# THE VOLCANO DANCES

They lived in a house on the mountain Tlaxihuatl half a mile below the summit. The house was built on a lava flow like the hide of an elephant. In the afternoon and evening the man, Charles Vandervell, sat by the window in the lounge, watching the fire displays that came from the crater. The noise rolled down the mountainside like a series of avalanches. At intervals a falling cinder hissed as it extinguished itself in the water tank on the roof. The woman slept most of the time in the bedroom overlooking the valley or, when she wished to be close to Vandervell, on the settee in the lounge.

In the afternoon she woke briefly when the 'devil-sticks' man performed his dance by the road a quarter of a mile from the house. This mendicant had come to the mountain for the benefit of the people in the village below the summit, but his dance had failed to subdue the volcano and prevent the villagers from leaving. As they passed him pushing their carts he would rattle his spears and dance, but they walked on without looking up. When he became discouraged and seemed likely to leave Vandervell sent the house-boy out to him with an American dollar. From then on the stick-dancer came every day.

'Is he still here?' the woman asked. She walked into the lounge, folding her robe around her waist. 'What's he supposed to be doing?'

'He's fighting a duel with the spirit of the volcano,' Vandervell said. 'He's putting a lot of thought and energy into it, but he hasn't a chance.'

'I thought you were on his side,' the woman said. 'Aren't you paying him a retainer?'

'That's only to formalize the relationship. To show him that I understand what's going on. Strictly speaking, I'm on the volcano's side.'

A shower of cinders rose a hundred feet above the crater, illuminating the jumping stick-man.

'Are you sure it's safe here?'

Vandervell waved her away. 'Of course. Go back to bed and rest. This thin air is bad for the complexion.'

'I feel all right. I heard the ground move.'

'It's been moving for weeks.' He watched the stick-man conclude his performance with a series of hops, as if leap-frogging over a partner. 'On his diet that's not bad.'

'You should take him back to Mexico City and put him in one of the cabarets. He'd make more than a dollar.'

'He wouldn't be interested. He's a serious artist, this Nijinsky of the mountainside. Can't you see that?'

The woman half-filled a tumbler from the decanter on the table. 'How long are you going to keep him out there?'

'As long as he'll stay.' He turned to face the woman. 'Remember that. When he leaves it will be time to go.'

The stick-man, a collection of tatters when not in motion, disappeared into his lair, one of the holes in the lava beside the road.

'I wonder if he met Springman?' Vandervell said. 'On balance it's possible. Springman would have come up the south face. This is the only road to the village.'

'Ask him. Offer him another dollar.'

'Pointless – he'd say he had seen him just to keep me happy.'

'What makes you so sure Springman is here?'

'He *was* here,' Vandervell corrected. 'He won't be here any longer. I was with Springman in Acapulco when he looked at the map. He came here.'

The woman carried her tumbler into the bedroom.

'We'll have dinner at nine,' Vandervell called to her. 'I'll let you know if he dances again.'

Left alone, Vandervell watched the fire displays. The glow shone through the windows of the houses in the village so that they seemed to glow like charcoal. At night the collection of hovels was deserted, but a few of the men returned during the day.

In the morning two men came from the garage in Ecuatan to reclaim the car which Vandervell had hired. He offered to pay a month's rent in advance, but they rejected this and pointed at the clinkers that had fallen on to the car from the sky. None of them was hot enough to burn the paintwork. Vandervell gave them each fifty dollars and promised to cover the car with a tarpaulin. Satisfied, the men drove away.

After breakfast Vandervell walked out across the lava seams to the road. The stick-dancer stood by his hole above the bank, resting his hands on the two spears. The cone of the volcano, partly hidden by the dust, trembled behind his back. He watched Vandervell when he shouted across the road. Vandervell took a dollar bill from his wallet and placed it under a stone. The stick-man began to hum and rock on the balls of his feet.

As Vandervell walked back along the road two of the villagers approached.

'Guide,' he said to them. 'Ten dollars. One hour.' He pointed to the lip of the crater but the men ignored him and continued along the road.

The surface of the house had once been white, but was now covered with grey dust. Two hours later, when the manager of the estate below the house rode up on a grey horse Vandervell asked: 'Is your horse white or black?'

'That's a good question, señor.'

'I want to hire a guide,' Vandervell said. 'To take me into the volcano.'

'There's nothing there, señor.'

'I want to look around the crater. I need someone who knows the pathways.'

'It's full of smoke, Señor Vandervell. Hot sulphur. Burns the eyes. You wouldn't like it.'

'Do you remember seeing someone called Springman?' Vandervell said. 'About three months ago.'

'You asked me that before. I remember two Americans with a scientific truck. Then a Dutchman with white hair.'

'That could be him.'

'Or maybe black, eh? As you say.'

A rattle of sticks sounded from the road. After warming up, the stick-dancer had begun his performance in earnest.

'You'd better get out of here, Señor Vandervell,' the manager said. 'The mountain could split one day.'

Vandervell pointed to the stick-dancer. 'He'll hold it off for a while.'

The manager rode away. 'My respects to Mrs Vandervell.'

'*Miss* Winston.'

Vandervell went into the lounge and stood by the window. During the day the activity of the volcano increased. The column of smoke rose half a mile into the sky, threaded by gleams of flame.

The rumbling woke the woman. In the kitchen she spoke to the house-boy.

'He wants to leave,' she said to Vandervell afterwards.

'Offer him more money,' he said without turning.

'He says everyone has left now. It's too dangerous to stay. The men in the village are leaving for good this afternoon.'

Vandervell watched the stick-dancer twirling his devil-sticks like a drum-major. 'Let him go if he wants to. I think the estate manager saw Springman.'

'That's good. Then he was here.'

'The manager sent his respects to you.'

'I'm charmed.'

Five minutes later, when the house-boy had gone, she returned to her bedroom. During the afternoon she came out to collect the film magazines in the bookcase.

Vandervell watched the smoke being pumped from the volcano. Now and then the devil-sticks man climbed out of his hole and danced on a mound of lava by the road. The men came down from the village for the last time. They looked at the stick-dancer as they walked on down the road.

\*          \*          \*

At eight o'clock in the morning a police truck drove up to the village, reversed and came down again. Its roof and driving cabin were covered with ash. The policemen did not see the stick-dancer, but they saw Vandervell in the window of the house and stopped outside.

'Get out!' one of the policemen shouted. 'You must go now! Take your car! What's the matter?'

Vandervell opened the window. 'The car is all right. We're staying for a few days. Gracias, Sergeant.'

'No! Get out!' The policeman climbed down from the cabin. 'The mountain – pfft! Dust, burning!' He took off his cap and waved it. 'You go now.'

As he remonstrated Vandervell closed the window and took his jacket off the chair. Inside he felt for his wallet.

After he had paid the policemen they saluted and drove away. The woman came out of the bedroom.

'You're lucky your father is rich,' she said. 'What would you do if he was poor?'

'Springman was poor,' Vandervell said. He took his handkerchief from his jacket. The dust was starting to seep into the house. 'Money only postpones one's problems.'

'How long are you going to stay? Your father told me to keep an eye on you.'

'Relax. I won't come to any mischief here.'

'Is that a joke? With this volcano over our heads?'

Vandervell pointed to the stick-dancer. 'It doesn't worry him. This mountain has been active for fifty years.'

'Then why do we have to come here now?'

'I'm looking for Springman. I think he came here three months ago.'

'Where is he? Up in the village?'

'I doubt it. He's probably five thousand miles under our feet, sucked down by the back-pressure. A century from now he'll come up through Vesuvius.'

'I hope not.'

'Have you thought of that, though? It's a wonderful idea.'

'No. Is that what you're planning for me?'

Cinders hissed in the roof tank, spitting faintly like boiling rain.

'Think of them, Gloria – Pompeiian matrons, Aztec virgins, bits of old Prometheus himself, they're raining down on the just and the unjust.'

'What about your friend Springman?'

'Now that you remind me . . .' Vandervell raised a finger to the ceiling. 'Let's listen. What's the matter?'

'Is that why you came here? To think of Springman being burnt to ashes?'

'Don't be a fool.' Vandervell turned to the window.

'What are you worrying about, anyway?'

'Nothing,' Vandervell said. 'For once in a long time I'm not worrying about anything at all.' He rubbed the pane with his sleeve. 'Where's the old devil-boy? Don't tell me he's gone.' He peered through the falling dust. 'There he is.'

The figure stood on the ridge above the road, illuminated by the flares from the crater. A pall of ash hung in the air around him.

'What's he waiting for?' the woman asked. 'Another dollar?'

'A lot more than a dollar,' Vandervell said. 'He's waiting for me.'

'Don't burn your fingers,' she said, closing the door.

That afternoon, when she came into the lounge after waking up, she found that Vandervell had left. She went to the window and looked up towards the crater. The falls of ash and cinders obscured the village, and hundreds of embers glowed on the lava flows. Through the dust she could see the explosions inside the crater lighting up the rim.

Vandervell's jacket lay over a chair. She waited for three hours for him to return. By this time the noise from the crater was continuous. The lava flows dragged and heaved like chains, shaking the walls of the house.

At five o'clock Vandervell had not come back. A second crater had opened in the summit of the volcano, into which part of the village had fallen. When she was sure that the devil-sticks man had gone, the woman took the money from Vandervell's jacket and drove down the mountain.

**∙ 1964**

# · THE BEACH MURDERS

## Introduction

*Readers hoping to solve the mystery of the Beach Murders – involving a Romanoff Princess, a CIA agent, two of his Russian counterparts and an American limbo dancer – may care to approach it in the form of the card game with which Quimby, the absconding State Department cipher chief, amused himself in his hideaway on the Costa Blanca. The principal clues have therefore been alphabetized. The correct key might well be a familiar phrase, e.g.* PLAYMATE OF THE MONTH, *or meaningless, e.g.* qwertyuiop ... *etc. Obviously any number of solutions is possible, and a final answer to the mystery, like the motives and character of Quimby himself, lies forever hidden*

### Auto-erotic

As always after her bath, the reflection of her naked body filled the Princess with a profound sense of repose. In the triptych of mirrors above the dressing table she gazed at the endless replicas of herself, the scent of the Guerlain heliotrope soothing her slight migraine. She lowered her arms as the bedroom door opened. Through the faint mist of talcum she recognized the handsome, calculating face of the Russian agent whose photograph she had seen in Statler's briefcase that afternoon.

### Brassière

Statler waded through the breaking surf. The left cup of the brassière in his hand was stained with blood. He bent down and washed it in the warm water. The pulsing headlamps of the Mercedes parked below the corniche road lit up the cove. Where the hell was Lydia? Somewhere along the beach a woman with a bloody breast would frighten the wits out of the Russian landing party.

### Cordobés

The self-contained face of the bullfighter, part gamin, part Beatle, lay below Quimby as he set out the cards on the balcony table. Whatever else they said about the boy, he never moved his feet. By contrast Raissa was pacing around the bedroom like a tigress in rut. Quimby could hear her wide Slavic hips brushing against his Paisley dressing gown behind the escritoire. What these obsessives in Moscow and Washington failed to realize was that for once he might have no motive at all.

### Drinamyl

Those bloody little capsules, Raissa thought. No wonder the West was dying. Every time she was ready to lure Quimby over to Sir Giles's villa he took one of the tranquillizers, then went down to the sea and talked to the beachniks. At Benidorm he even had the nerve to bring one of the Swedish girls back to the apartment. Hair down to her knees, breasts like thimbles, the immense buttocks of a horse. Ugh.

### Embonpoint

The Princess slid the remains of the eclair into her mouth. As she swallowed the pastry she pouted her cream-filled lips at Statler. He lowered his rolled-up copy of *Time Atlantic*, with its photo of Quimby before the House Committee. The dancers moved around the tea-terrace to the soft rhythm of the fox-trot. There was something sensuous, almost sexual, about Manon's compulsive eating of eclairs. This magnificent Serbo-Croat cow, had she any idea what was going to happen to her?

### Fata Morgana

Lydia felt his hand move along the plastic zipper of her dress. She lay on the candlewick bedspread, gazing at the sea and the white sand. Apart from the dotty English milord who had rented the villa to them the place was empty. As Kovarski hesitated the silence seemed to amplify all the uncertainties she had noticed since their arrival at San Juan. The meeting at the nudist colony on the Isle du Levant had not been entirely fortuitous. She reached up and loosened the zip. As her breasts came out she turned to face him. Kovarski was sitting up on one elbow, staring through his Zeiss binoculars at the apartment block three hundred yards along the beach.

### Guardia Civil

Quimby watched the olive-uniformed policemen ambling along the shore, their quaint Napoleonic hats shielding their eyes as they scanned the girls on the beach. When it came to the crunch, on whose side would they see themselves – Stat's, the Russians', or his own? Quimby shuffled the Cordobés-backed cards. The platinum-haired call-girl who lived in the next apartment was setting off for Alicante in her pink Fiat. Quimby sipped his whisky. Five minutes earlier he had discovered the concealed aerial of Raissa's transmitter.

### Heterodyne

Kovarski was worried. The sight of Raissa's body on the pony skin reminded him that Statler was still to be reckoned with. The piercing whistle from the portable radio confirmed that Raissa had been lying there since dusk. He knelt down, eyes lingering for a last moment on the silver clasps of her Gossard suspenders. He put his finger in her mouth and ran it around her gums, searching for the capsule. A cherry popped into his palm. With a grimace he dropped it into the vodkatini by the radio. He opened Raissa's right hand and from the frozen clasp of her thumb and forefinger removed the capsule. As he read the message his brow furrowed. What the devil had the Princess to do with Quimby? Was this some insane CIA plot to restore the Romanoffs?

## Iguana

The jade reptile shattered on the tiled floor at Sir Giles's feet. With an effort he regained his balance. Pretending to straighten his Old Etonian tie, he touched the painful bruise under his breast-bone. He looked up at the tough, square-jawed face of the American girl. Would she hit him again? She glared at him contemptuously, bare feet planted wide on the pony skin. Ah well, he thought, there had been worse moments. At Dunkirk the bombs falling from the Stukas had made the beach drum like a dancing floor.

## Jasmine

Statler gazed at the white salver-shaped flowers in the lobby. Their nacreous petals, bled of all colour, reminded him of Manon's skin, and then of Quimby's large pallid face, with its too-intelligent eyes watching over the sunken cheeks like a snide Buddha's. Was the exchange a fair one, the Princess for the complex, moody cipher chief? He walked out through the revolving doors of the hotel into the bright Alicante sunlight, realizing with a pang that he would never see Manon again.

## Kleenex

Raissa bent forwards over the bed. With the ring finger of her right hand she lifted her eyelid. For a moment the elegant mask of her face was contorted like an obscene paroquet's. She tapped the lower lid and the microlens jumped on to the tissue. The minute R on its rim shone in the beam of the Anglepoise. She wiped the lenses and placed them in the polarimeter. As the door of the safe opened, revealing the dials of the transmitter, she listened to Quimby singing *Arrivederci Roma* in the bathroom. All that drinamyl and whisky would keep the pig drowsy for at least an hour.

## Limbo

The bar had been a mere twelve inches from the floor, Kovarski recollected, as he felt the hard curve of Lydia's iliac crest under the midnight blue stretch pants. For once the nightclub in Benidorm was hushed, everyone watching as this demented American girl with the incredible thighs had edged under the bar, hips jerking to the throb of the juke-box. Kovarski picked his nose, involuntarily thinking about Stat. The CIA man had a face like ice.

## Mercedes

The brake servos had gone. Holding the hand-brake, Lydia groped behind Kovarski's chest for the off-side door handle. The Russian lay against the sill, his handsome face beginning to sag like the first slide of an avalanche. As the door opened he fell backwards on to the gravel. Lydia released the hand-brake and let the car roll forward. When Kovarski had gone she wound up the window, elegantly starred by the bullet which had passed through the door. She flashed the headlamps for the last time and pressed the starter.

## Neapolitan

Raissa finished off the remains of Quimby's ice-cream with the eager lips of a child. In three hours they would be six fathoms under the Mediterranean, due to surface for the first time in the Baltic. She would miss the sunlight, and the small, dark Spaniards with their melancholy eyes following her down the dusty street to the bodega. In the end it would be worth it. Throw away the Man-Tan, as Kovarski often quoted to her in his mock-Yevtushenko, the sky will soon be full of suns.

## Oceanid

For a moment Manon realized that Kovarski was undecided whether to rape or kill her. She backed into the bathroom, her left hand covering her powdered breasts. The trapped steam billowed into Kovaraski's face. He goggled at her like an insane student in a Dostoevski novel. He stepped across the cork bathmat and took her elbow in a surprisingly tender gesture. Then the alabaster soap-dish caught her on the side of the head. A second later she was lying in a hot mess in the bath, Kovarski's arms moving over her head like pistons.

## Poseidon

Quimby handled the bottle of Black Label with a respect due their long acquaintance. The proto-Atlantic ocean had covered all North America and Europe except for Scotland, leaving intact a percolation system 300 million years old. As he filled his glass he watched Sir Giles's villa on the bluff above the cove. The swarthy Russian and his American beatnik had moved in yesterday. No doubt Stat was at the Carlton in Alicante. Quimby set out the cards for the last game. The hand would be hard to play, but luckily he was still dealing.

## Quietus

Statler was dying in the dark surf. As the Russian bosun let him drift away in the shallow water he was thinking of the Princess and her immense brown nipples. Had she borne a child then, keeping alive the fading memories of the Austro-Hungarian Empire? The burning wreck of the Mercedes shone through the water, illuminating the bodies of the two

Russians being dragged towards the dinghy. Statler lay back in the cold water as his blood ran out into the sea.

### Remington

Lydia knelt by Kovarski's Travel-Riter. In the courtyard below the bedroom window Sir Giles was setting off for Alicante in his battered Citroën. That twitching old goat, did the English ever think about anything else? She removed the hood from the typewriter, then peered at the new ribbon she had inserted while Kovarski was in San Juan. The imprint of the letters shone in the sunlight. She jotted them on to the bridge pad, then tore off the sheet and slipped it into the left cup of her brassière.

### Smith & Wesson

Kovarski blundered through the darkness among the dunes. Below him the surf broke like a lace shawl on the beach. The whole operation was going to pieces. By now Raissa should have been here with Quimby. He climbed the slope up to the Mercedes. As he felt for the pistol in the glove compartment something moved on the gravel behind him. The gun-flash lit up the interior of the car. Kovarski fell sideways across the seat. The second bullet passed through his chest and went on into the off-side door.

### Tranquillizer

Statler opened the capsule and drew out the folded tissue. In Raissa's untouched vodkatini the rice paper flared like a Japanese water-flower. He fished it out with the toothpick and laid it on the salver. So this was how they made contact. He looked down at the body on the pony skin and smiled to himself. With luck Kovarski would literally eat his own words. As he turned the Russian girl over with his foot the cherry popped from her mouth. He pushed it back between her lips and went over to the Travel-Riter.

### UV Lamp

With a sigh the Princess dropped the goggles into the douche-bag on the dressing table. In spite of her efforts, the months of summer bathing on the Côte d'Azur before her meeting with Stat, her skin remained as white as the jasmine blossoms in the lobby. In her veins ran the haemophilic blood of the Romanoffs, yet the time to revenge Ekaterinburg had passed. Did Stat realize this?

### Vivaldi

Lydia tuned in Radio Algiers with a wet forefinger. The French had left some damned good records behind. She stood on the pony skin, admiring her tough, man-like hips as she dried herself after the swim. Her sharp nails caressed the cold skin of her breasts. Then she noticed Sir Giles's marmoset-like face peering at her through the fronds of the miniature palm beside the bedroom door.

### Wave Speed

6,000 metres per second, enough to blow Stat straight through the rear window of the Merc. Kovarski lifted the hood and lowered the bomb into the slot behind the battery. Over his shoulder he peered into the darkness across the sea. Two miles out, where the deep water began, the submarine would be waiting, the landing party crouched by their dinghy under the conning-tower. He tightened the terminals, licking the blood from the reopened wound on his hand. The Princess had packed a lot of muscle under that incredible ivory skin.

### XF-169

The Lockheed performance data would make a useful bonus, Raissa reflected as she slipped her long legs into the stretch pants. The charge account at GUM and the dacha in the Crimea were becoming a distinct possibility. The door opened behind her. Siphon in hand, Quimby stared at her half-naked figure. Without thinking, she put her hands over her breasts. For once his face registered an expression of surprising intelligence.

### Yardley

Sir Giles helped himself to Statler's after-shave lotion. He looked down at the Princess. Even allowing for her size, the quantity of expressed blood was unbelievable. His small face was puckered with embarrassment as he met her blank eyes staring up at the shower fitment. He listened to the distant sounds of traffic coming through the empty suite. He turned on the shower. As the drops spattered on the red skin the magnificence of her white body made his mind reel.

### Zeitgeist

The great fans of the *guardia civil* Sikorsky beat the air over the apartment block. Quimby bent down and retrieved two of the cards from the tiled floor. Below, along the beach road, the Spanish speed cops were converging on the wreck of the Mercedes. Quimby sat back as the helicopter battered away through the darkness. All in all, everything had worked out. The face of Cordobés still regarded him from the backs of the cards. A full moon was coming up over the Sierra. In the Alicante supermarket the hips of the counter girls shook to Trini Lopez. In the bodega wine was only ten pesetas a litre, and the man with the deck still controlled the play.

ᶜ **1966**

# · THE DAY OF FOREVER

At Columbine Sept Heures it was always dusk. Here Halliday's beautiful neighbour, Gabrielle Szabo, walked through the evening, her silk robe stirring the fine sand into cerise clouds. From the balcony of the empty hotel near the artists' colony, Halliday would look out over the drained river at the unmoving shadows across the desert floor, the twilight of Africa, endless and unbroken, that beckoned to him with the promise of his lost dreams. The dark dunes, their crests touched by the spectral light, receded like the waves of a midnight sea.

Despite the almost static light, fixed at this unending dusk, the drained bed of the river seemed to flow with colours. As the sand spilled from the banks, uncovering the veins of quartz and the concrete caissons of the embankment, the evening would flare briefly, illuminated from within like a lava sea. Beyond the dunes the spires of old water towers and the half-completed apartment blocks near the Roman ruins at Leptis Magna emerged from the darkness. To the south, as Halliday followed the winding course of the river, the darkness gave way to the deep indigo tracts of the irrigation project, the lines of canals forming an exquisite bonelike gridwork.

This continuous transformation, whose colours were as strange as the bizarre paintings hung from the walls of his suite, seemed to Halliday to reveal the hidden perspectives of the landscape, and of the time whose hands were almost frozen on the dozen clocks standing on the mantelpiece and tables. The clocks, set to the imperceptible time of the forever day, he had brought with him to North Africa in the hope that here, in the psychic zero of the desert, they might somehow spring to life. The dead clocks that stared down from the municipal towers and hotels of the deserted towns were the unique flora of the desert, the unused keys that would turn the way into his dreams.

With this hope, three months earlier he had come to Columbine Sept Heures. The suffix, attached to the names of all cities and towns – there were London 6 p.m. and Saigon Midnight – indicated their positions on the Earth's almost stationary perimeter, the time of the endless day where the no longer rotating planet had marooned them. For five years Halliday had been living in the international settlement at Trondheim in Norway, a zone of eternal snow and ice, of pine forests whose arbours, fed by the unsetting sun, rose even higher around the fringes of the towns, shutting

669

them into their own isolation. This world of Nordic gloom had exposed all Halliday's latent difficulties with time and with his dreams. The difficulty of sleeping, even in a darkened room, disturbed everyone – there was the sense of time wasted and yet time unpassed as the sun hung stationary in the sky – but Halliday in particular found himself obsessed by his broken dreams. Time and again he would wake with an image before his eyes of the moonlit squares and classical façades of an ancient Mediterranean town, and of a woman who walked through colonnades in a world without shadows.

This warm night world he could find only by moving south. Two hundred miles to the east of Trondheim the dusk line was a corridor of freezing wind and ice, stretching on into the Russian steppe, where abandoned cities lay under the glaciers like closed jewels. By contrast, in Africa the night air was still warm. On the west of the dusk line was the boiling desert of the Sahara, the sand seas fused into lakes of glass, but along the narrow band of the terminator a few people lived in the old tourist towns.

It was here, at Columbine Sept Heures, an abandoned town beside the drained river five miles from Leptis Magna, that he first saw Gabrielle Szabo walking towards him as if out of his dreams. Here, too, he met Leonora Sully, the fey unconcerned painter of bizarre fantasies, and Dr Richard Mallory, who tried to help Halliday and bring back his dreams to him.

Why Leonora was at Columbine Sept Heures Halliday could understand, but sometimes he suspected that Dr Mallory's motives were as ambiguous as his own. The tall aloof physician, eyes forever hidden behind the dark glasses that seemed to emphasize his closed inner life, spent most of his time sitting in the white-domed auditorium of the School of Fine Arts, playing through the Bartok and Webern quartets left behind in the albums.

This music was the first sound Halliday heard when he arrived at the desert town. In the abandoned car park near the quay at Tripoli he found a new Peugeot left behind by a French refinery technician and set off south along the seven o'clock line, passing through the dusty towns and the half-buried silver skeletons of the refineries near the drained river. To the west the desert burned in a haze of gold under the unmoving sun. Rippled by the thermal waves, the metal vanes of the waterwheels by the empty irrigation systems seemed to revolve in the hot air, swerving toward him.

To the east the margins of the river were etched against the dark horizon, the ridges of exposed limestone like the forestage of the twilight world. Halliday turned toward the river, the light fading as he moved eastward, and followed the old metal road that ran near the bank. The centre of the channel, where white rocks jutted from the drifts of pebbles, lay like the spine of an ancient saurian.

A few miles from the coast he found Columbine Sept Heures. Four tourist hotels, their curtain walls like dead mirrors, stood among the dunes that drifted through the streets and overran the chalets and swimming pools near the Fine Arts School. The road disappeared from sight outside the Oasis Hotel. Halliday left the car and walked up the steps to the dust-filled lobby. The sand lay in lacelike patterns across the tiled floor, silting against the pastel-coloured elevator doors and the dead palms by the restaurant.

Halliday walked up the stairway to the mezzanine, and stood by the cracked plateglass window beyond the tables. Already half submerged by the sand, what remained of the town seemed displaced by the fractured glass into another set of dimensions, as if space itself were compensating for the landscape's loss of time by forcing itself into this bizarre warp.

Already decided that he would stay in the hotel, Halliday went out to search for water and whatever food supplies had been left behind. The streets were deserted, choked with the sand advancing toward the drained river. At intervals the clouded windows of a Citroën or Peugeot emerged from the dunes. Stepping along their roofs, Halliday entered the drive of the Fine Arts School. Against the cerise pall of the dusk, the angular building rose into the air like a white bird.

In the students' gallery hung the fading reproductions of a dozen schools of painting, for the most part images of worlds without meaning. However, grouped together in a small alcove Halliday found the surrealists Delvaux, Chirico and Ernst. These strange landscapes, inspired by dreams that his own could no longer echo, filled Halliday with a profound sense of nostalgia. One above all, Delvaux's 'The Echo', which depicted a naked Junoesque woman walking among immaculate ruins under a midnight sky, reminded him of his own recurrent fantasy. The infinite longing contained in the picture, the synthetic time created by the receding images of the woman, belonged to the landscape of his unseen night. Halliday found an old portfolio on the floor below one of the trestles and began to strip the paintings from the walls.

As he walked across the roof to the outside stairway above the auditorium music was playing below him. Halliday searched the faces of the empty hotels, whose curtain walls lifted into the sunset air. Beyond the Fine Arts School the chalets of the students' quarter were grouped around two drained swimming pools.

Reaching the auditorium, he peered through the glass doors across the rows of empty seats. In the centre of the front row a man in a white suit and sunglasses was sitting with his back to Halliday. Whether he was actually listening to the music Halliday could not tell, but when the record ended three or four minutes later he stood up and climbed onto the stage. He switched off the stereogram and then strolled over to Halliday, his high face with its slightly inquisitorial look hidden behind the dark glasses.

'I'm Mallory – Dr Mallory.' He held out a strong but oblique hand. 'Are you staying here?'

The question seemed to contain a complete understanding of Halliday's motives. Putting down his portfolio, Halliday introduced himself. 'I'm at the Oasis. I arrived this evening.'

Realizing that the remark was meaningless, Halliday laughed, but Mallory was already smiling.

'This evening? I think we can take that for granted.' When Halliday raised his wrist to reveal the old 24-hour Rolex he still wore, Mallory nodded, straightening his sunglasses as if looking at Halliday more closely. 'You still have one, do you? What is the time, by the way?'

Halliday glanced at the Rolex. It was one of four he had brought with him, carefully synchronized with the master 24-hour clock still running at Greenwich Observatory, recording the vanished time of the once-revolving earth. 'Nearly 7.30. That would be right. Isn't this Columbine Sept Heures?'

'True enough. A neat coincidence. However, the dusk line is advancing; I'd say it was a little later here. Still, I think we can take the point.' Mallory stepped down from the stage, where his tall figure had stood over Halliday like a white gallows. 'Seven-thirty, old time – and new. You'll have to stay at Columbine. It's not often one finds the dimensions locking like that.' He glanced at the portfolio. 'You're at the Oasis. Why there?'

'It's empty.'

'Cogent. But so is everything else here. Even so, I know what you mean, I stayed there myself when I first came to Columbine. It's damned hot.'

'I'll be on the dusk side.'

Mallory inclined his head in a small bow, as if acknowledging Halliday's seriousness. He went over to the stereogram and disconnected a motor car battery on the floor beside it. He placed the heavy unit in a canvas carryall and gave Halliday one of the handles. 'You can help me. I have a small generator at my chalet. It's difficult to re-charge, but good batteries are becoming scarce.'

As they walked out into the sunlight Halliday said, 'You can have the battery in my car.'

Mallory stopped. 'That's kind of you, Halliday. But are you sure you won't want it? There are other places than Columbine.'

'Perhaps. But I take it there's enough food for us all here.' Halliday gestured with his wristwatch. 'Anyway, the time is right. Or both times, I suppose.'

'And as many spaces as you want, Halliday. Not all of them around you. Why have you come here?'

'I don't know yet. I was living at Trondheim; I couldn't sleep there. If I can sleep again, perhaps I can dream.'

He started to explain himself but Mallory raised a hand to silence him. 'Why do you think we're all here, Halliday? Out of Africa, dreams walk. You must meet Leonora. She'll like you.'

They walked past the empty chalets, the first of the swimming pools on their right. In the sand on the bottom someone had traced out a huge zodiac pattern, decorated with shells and pieces of fractured tile.

They approached the next pool. A sand dune had inundated one of the chalets and spilled into the basin, but a small area of the terrace had been cleared. Below an awning a young woman with white hair sat on a metal chair in front of an easel. Her jeans and the man's shirt she wore were streaked with paint, but her intelligent face, set above a strong jaw, seemed composed and alert. She looked up as Dr Mallory and Halliday lowered the battery to the ground.

'I've brought a pupil for you, Leonora.' Mallory beckoned Halliday over. 'He's staying at the Oasis – on the *dusk* side.'

The young woman gestured Halliday towards a reclining chair beside the easel. He placed the portfolio against the back rest. 'They're for my room at the hotel,' he explained. 'I'm not a painter.'

'Of course. May I look at them?' Without waiting she began to leaf through the reproductions, nodding to herself at each one. Halliday glanced at the half-completed painting on the easel, a landscape across which bizarre figures moved in a strange procession, archbishops wearing fantastic mitres. He looked up at Mallory, who gave him a wry nod.

'Interesting, Halliday?'

'Of course. What about *your* dreams, doctor? Where do you keep them?'

Mallory made no reply, gazing down at Halliday with his dark sealed eyes. With a laugh, dispelling the slight tension between the two men, Leonora sat down on the chair beside Halliday.

'Richard won't tell us that, Mr Halliday. When we find his dreams we'll no longer need our own.'

This remark Halliday was to repeat to himself often over the subsequent months. In many ways Halliday's presence in the town seemed a key to all their roles. The white-suited physician, moving about silently through the sand-filled streets, seemed like the spectre of the forgotten noon, reborn at dusk to drift like his music between the empty hotels. Even at their first meeting, when Halliday sat beside Leonora, making a few automatic remarks but conscious only of her hips and shoulder touching his own, he sensed that Mallory, whatever his reasons for being in Columbine, had adjusted himself all too completely to the ambiguous world of the dusk line. For Mallory, Columbine Sept Heures and the desert had already become part of the inner landscapes that Halliday and Leonora Sully still had to find in their paintings.

However, during his first weeks in the town by the drained river Halliday thought more of Leonora and of settling himself in the hotel. Using the 24-hour Rolex, he still tried to sleep at 'midnight', waking (or more exactly, conceding the fact of his insomnia) seven hours later. Then, at the start of his 'morning', he would make a tour of the paintings hung on the walls of the seventh-floor suite, and go out into the town, searching the hotel kitchens and pantries for supplies of water and canned food. At this time – an arbitrary interval he imposed on the neutral landscape – he would keep his back to the eastern sky, avoiding the dark night that reached from the desert across the drained river. To the west the brilliant sand beneath the over-heated sun shivered like the last dawn of the world.

At these moments Dr Mallory and Leonora seemed at their most tired, as if their bodies were still aware of the rhythms of the former 24-hour day. Both of them slept at random intervals – often Halliday would visit Leonora's chalet and find her asleep on the reclining chair by the pool, her face covered by the veil of white hair, shielded from the sun by the painting on her easel. These strange fantasies, with their images of bishops and cardinals moving in procession across ornamental landscapes, were her only activity.

By contrast, Mallory would vanish like a white vampire into his chalet, then emerge, refreshed in some way, a few hours later. After the first weeks Halliday came to terms with Mallory, and the two men would listen to the Webern quartets in the auditorium or play chess near Leonora beside the empty swimming pool. Halliday tried to discover how Leonora and Mallory had come to the town, but neither would answer his questions. He gathered only that they had arrived separately in Africa several years earlier and had been moving westward from town to town as the terminator crossed the continent.

On occasion, Mallory would go off into the desert on some unspecified errand, and then Halliday would see Leonora alone. Together they would walk along the bed of the drained river, or dance to the recordings of Masai chants in the anthropology library. Halliday's growing dependence on Leonora was tempered by the knowledge that he had come to Africa to seek, not this white-haired young woman with her amiable eyes, but the night-walking lamia within his own mind. As if aware of this, Leonora remained always detached, smiling at Halliday across the strange paintings on her easel.

This pleasant *ménage à trois* was to last for three months. During this time the dusk line advanced another half mile toward Columbine Sept Heures, and at last Mallory and Leonora decided to move to a small refinery town ten miles to the west. Halliday half expected Leonora to stay with him at Columbine, but she left with Mallory in the Peugeot. Sitting in the back seat, she waited as Mallory played the last Bartok quartet in the auditorium before disconnecting the battery and carrying it back to the car.

Curiously, it was Mallory who tried to persuade Halliday to leave with them. Unlike Leonora, the still unresolved elements in his relationship with Halliday made him wish to keep in touch with the younger man.

'Halliday, you'll find it difficult staying on here.' Mallory pointed across the river to the pall of darkness that hung like an immense wave over the town. Already the colours of the walls and streets had changed to the deep cyclamen of dusk. 'The night is coming. Do you realize what that means?'

'Of course, doctor. I've waited for it.'

'But, Halliday . . .' Mallory searched for a phrase. His tall figure, eyes hidden as ever by the dark glasses, looked up at Halliday across the steps of the hotel. 'You aren't an owl, or some damned desert cat. You've got to come to terms with this thing in the daylight.'

Giving up, Mallory went back to the car. He waved as they set off, reversing onto one of the dunes in a cloud of pink dust, but Halliday made no reply. He was watching Leonora Sully in the back seat with her canvas and easels, the stack of bizarre paintings that were echoes of her unseen dreams.

Whatever his feelings for Leonora, they were soon forgotten with his discovery a month later of a second beautiful neighbour at Columbine Sept Heures.

Half a mile to the north-east of Columbine, across the drained river, was an empty colonial mansion, once occupied by the manager of the refinery at the mouth of the river. As Halliday sat on his balcony on the seventh floor of the Oasis Hotel, trying to detect the imperceptible progress of the terminator, while the antique clocks around him ticked mechanically through the minutes and hours of their false days, he would notice the white façades of the house illuminated briefly in the reflected light of the sandstorms. Its terraces were covered with dust, and the columns of the loggia beside the swimming pool had toppled into the basin. Although only four hundred yards to the east of the hotel, the empty shell of the house seemed already within the approaching night.

Shortly before one of his attempts to sleep Halliday saw the headlamps of a car moving around the house. Its beams revealed a solitary figure who walked slowly up and down the terrace. Abandoning any pretence at sleep, Halliday climbed to the roof of the hotel, ten storeys above, and lay down on the suicide sill. A chauffeur was unloading suitcases from the car. The figure on the terrace, a tall woman in a black robe, walked with the random, uncertain movements of someone barely aware of what she was doing. After a few minutes the chauffeur took the woman by the arm, as if waking her from some kind of sleep.

Halliday watched from the roof, waiting for them to reappear. The strange trancelike movements of this beautiful woman – already her dark hair and the pale nimbus of her face drifting like a lantern on the incoming dusk convinced him that she was the dark lamia of all his dreams – reminded Halliday of his own first strolls across the dunes to the river, the testing of ground unknown but familiar from his sleep.

When he went down to his suite he lay on the brocaded settee in the sitting room, surrounded by the landscapes of Delvaux and Ernst, and fell suddenly into a deep slumber. There he saw his first true dreams, of classical ruins under a midnight sky, where moonlit figures moved past each other in a city of the dead.

The dreams were to recur each time Halliday slept. He would wake on the settee by the picture window, the darkening floor of the desert below, aware of the dissolving boundaries between his inner and outer worlds. Already two of the clocks below the mantelpiece mirror had stopped. With their end he would at last be free of his former notions of time.

At the end of this week Halliday discovered that the woman slept at the same intervals as he did, going out to look at the desert as Halliday stepped onto his balcony. Although his solitary figure stood out clearly against the dawn sky behind the hotel the woman seemed not to notice him. Halliday watched the chauffeur drive the white Mercedes into the town. In his dark uniform he moved past the fading walls of the Fine Arts School like a shadow without form.

Halliday went down into the street and walked towards the dusk. Crossing the river, a drained Rubicon dividing his passive world at Columbine Sept Heures from the reality of the coming night, Halliday climbed the opposite bank past the wrecks of old cars and gasoline drums illuminated in the crepuscular light. As he neared the house the woman was walking among the sand-covered statuary in the garden, the crystals lying on the stone faces like the condensation of immense epochs of time.

Halliday hesitated by the low wall that encircled the house, waiting for the woman to look towards him. Her pale face, its high forehead rising above the dark glasses in some ways reminded him of Dr Mallory, the same screen that concealed a potent inner life. The fading light lingered among the angular planes of her temples as she searched the town for any signs of the Mercedes.

She was sitting in one of the chairs on the terrace when Halliday reached her, hands folded in the pockets of the silk robe so that only her pale face, with its marred beauty – the sunglasses seemed to shut it off like some inward night – was exposed to him.

Halliday stood by the glass-topped table, uncertain how to introduce himself. 'I'm staying at the Oasis – at Columbine Sept Heures,' he began. 'I saw you from the balcony.' He pointed to the distant tower of the hotel, its cerise façade raised against the dimming air.

'A neighbour?' The woman nodded at this. 'Thank you for calling on me. I'm Gabrielle Szabo. Are there many of you?'

'No – they've gone. There were only two of them anyway, a doctor and a young woman painter, Leonora Sully – the landscape here suited her.'

'Of course. A doctor, though?' The woman had taken her hands from her robe. They lay in her lap like a pair of fragile doves. 'What was he doing here?'

'Nothing.' Halliday wondered whether to sit down, but the woman made no attempt to offer him the other chair, as if she expected him to drift away as suddenly as he had arrived. 'Now and then he helped me with my dreams.'

'Dreams?' She turned her head towards him, the light revealing the slightly hollowed contours above her eyes. 'Are there dreams at Columbine Sept Heures, Mr –'

'Halliday. There are dreams now. The night is coming.'

The woman nodded, raising her face to the violet-hued dusk. 'I can feel it on my face – like a black sun. What do you dream about, Mr Halliday?'

Halliday almost blurted out the truth but with a shrug he said, 'This and that. An old ruined town – you know, full of classical monuments. Anyway, I did last night ...' He smiled at this. 'I still have some of the old clocks left. The others have stopped.'

Along the river a plume of gilded dust lifted from the road. The white Mercedes sped towards them.

'Have you been to Leptis Magna, Mr Halliday?'

'The Roman town? It's by the coast, five miles from here. If you like, I'll go with you.'

'A good idea. This doctor you mentioned, Mr Halliday – where has he gone? My chauffeur ... needs some treatment.'

Halliday hesitated. Something about the woman's voice suggested that she might easily lose interest in him. Not wanting to compete with Mallory again, he answered, 'To the north, I think; to the coast. He was leaving Africa. Is it urgent?'

Before she could reply Halliday was aware of the dark figure of the chauffeur, buttoned within his black uniform, standing a few yards behind him. Only a moment earlier the car had been a hundred yards down the road, but with an effort Halliday accepted this quantal jump in time. The chauffeur's small face, with its sharp eyes and tight mouth, regarded Halliday without comment.

'Gaston, this is Mr Halliday. He's staying at one of the hotels at Columbine Sept Heures. Perhaps you could give him a lift to the river crossing.'

Halliday was about to accept, but the chauffeur made no response to the suggestion. Halliday felt himself shiver in the cooler air moving toward the river out of the dusk. He bowed to Gabrielle Szabo and walked off past the chauffeur. As he stopped, about to remind her of the trip to Leptis Magna, he heard her say, 'Gaston, there was a doctor here.'

The meaning of this oblique remark remained hidden from Halliday as he watched the house from the roof of the Oasis Hotel. Gabrielle Szabo sat on the terrace in the dusk, while the chauffeur made his foraging journeys to Columbine and the refineries along the river. Once Halliday came across him as he rounded a corner near the Fine Arts School, but the man merely nodded and trudged on with his jerrican of water. Halliday postponed a further visit to the house. Whatever her motives for being there, and whoever she was, Gabrielle Szabo had brought him the dreams that Columbine Sept Heures and his long journey south had failed to provide. Besides, the presence of the woman, turning some key in his mind, was all he required. Rewinding his clocks, he found that he slept for eight or nine hours of the nights he set himself.

However, a week later he found himself again failing to sleep. Deciding to visit his neighbour, he went out across the river, walking into the dusk that lay ever deeper across the sand. As he reached the house the white Mercedes was setting off along the road to the coast. In the back Gabrielle Szabo sat close to the open window, the dark wind drawing her black hair into the slipstream.

Halliday waited as the car came towards him, slowing as the driver recognized him. Gaston's head leaned back, his tight mouth framing Halliday's name. Expecting the car to stop, Halliday stepped out into the road.

'Gabrielle . . . Miss Szabo –'

She leaned forward, and the white car accelerated and swerved around him, the cerise dust cutting his eyes as he watched the woman's masked face borne away from him.

Halliday returned to the hotel and climbed to the roof, but the car had disappeared into the darkness of the north-east, its wake fading into the dusk. He went down to his suite and paced around the paintings. The last of the clocks had almost run down. Carefully he wound each one, glad for the moment to be free of Gabrielle Szabo and the dark dream she had drawn across the desert.

When the clocks were going again he went down to the basement. For ten minutes he moved from car to car, stepping in and out of the Cadillacs and Citroëns. None of the cars would start, but in the service bay he found a Honda motorcycle, and after filling the tank managed to kick the engine into life. As he set off from Columbine the sounds of the exhaust reverberated off the walls around him, but a mile from the town, when he stopped to adjust the carburettor, the town seemed to have been abandoned for years, his own presence obliterated as quickly as his shadow.

He drove westward, the dawn rising to meet him. Its colours lightened, the ambiguous contours of the dusk giving way to the clear outlines of the dunes along the horizon, the isolated watertowers standing like welcoming beacons.

Losing his way when the road disappeared into the sand sea, Halliday drove the motorcycle across the open desert. A mile to the west he came to the edge of an old wadi. He tried to drive the cycle down the bank, then lost his balance and sprawled onto his back as the machine leapt away and somersaulted among the rocks. Halliday trudged across the floor of the wadi to the opposite bank. Ahead of him, its silver gantries and tank farms shining in the dawn light, was an abandoned refinery and the white roofs of the near-by staff settlement.

As he walked between the lines of chalets, past the empty swimming pools that seemed to cover all Africa, he saw the Peugeot parked below one of the ports. Sitting with her easel was Leonora Sully, a tall man in a white suit beside her. At first Halliday failed to recognize him, although the man rose and waved to him. The outline of his head and high forehead was familiar, but the eyes seemed unrelated to the rest of his face. Then Halliday recognized Dr Mallory and realized that, for the first time, he was seeing him without his sunglasses.

'Halliday . . . my dear chap.' Mallory stepped around the drained pool to greet him, adjusting the silk scarf in the neck of his shirt. 'We thought you'd come one day . . .' He turned to Leonora, who was smiling at Halliday. 'To tell you the truth we were beginning to get a little worried about him, weren't we, Leonora?'

'Halliday . . .' Leonora took his arm and steered him round to face the sun. 'What's happened – you're so pale!'

'He's been sleeping, Leonora. Can't you see that, my dear?' Mallory smiled down at Halliday. 'Columbine Sept Heures is beyond the dusk line now. Halliday, you have the face of a dreamer.'

Halliday nodded. 'It's good to leave the dusk, Leonora. The dreams weren't worth searching for.' When she looked away Halliday turned to Mallory. The doctor's eyes disturbed him. The white skin in the orbits seemed to isolate them, as if the level gaze was coming from a concealed face. Something warned him that the absence of the sunglasses marked a change in Mallory whose significance he had not yet grasped.

Avoiding the eyes, Halliday pointed to the empty easel. 'You're not painting, Leonora.'

'I don't need to, Halliday. You see . . .' She turned to take Mallory's hand. 'We have our own dreams now. They come to us across the desert like jewelled birds . . .'

Halliday watched them as they stood together. Then Mallory stepped forward, his white eyes like spectres. 'Halliday, of course it's good to see you . . . you'd probably like to stay here –'

Halliday shook his head. 'I came for my car,' he said in a controlled voice. He pointed to the Peugeot. 'Can I take it?'

'My dear chap, naturally. But where are –' Mallory pointed warningly to the western horizon, where the sun burned in an immense pall. 'The west is on fire, you can't go there.'

Halliday began to walk toward the car. 'I'm going to the coast.' Over his shoulder, he added, 'Gabrielle Szabo is there.'

This time, as he fled towards the night, Halliday was thinking of the white house across the river, sinking into the last light of the desert. He followed the road that ran north-east from the refinery, and found a disused pontoon bridge that crossed the wadi. The distant spires of Columbine Sept Heures were touched by the last light of sunset.

The streets of the town were deserted, his own footsteps in the sand already drowned by the wind. He went up to his suite in the hotel. Gabrielle Szabo's house stood isolated on the far shore. Holding one of the clocks, its hands turning slowly within the ormolu case, Halliday saw the chauffeur bring the Mercedes into the drive. A moment later Gabrielle

Szabo appeared, a black wraith in the dusk, and the car set off toward the north-east.

Halliday walked around the paintings in the suite, gazing at their landscapes in the dim light. He gathered his clocks together and carried them onto the balcony, then hurled them down one by one onto the terrace below. Their shattered faces, the white dials like Mallory's eyes, looked up at him with unmoving hands.

Half a mile from Leptis Magna he could hear the sea washing on the beaches through the darkness, the onshore winds whipping at the crests of the dunes in the moonlight. The ruined columns of the Roman city rose beside the single tourist hotel that shut out the last rays of the sun. Halliday stopped the car by the hotel, and walked past the derelict kiosks at the outskirts of the town. The tall arcades of the forum loomed ahead, the rebuilt statues of Olympian deities standing on their pedestals above him.

Halliday climbed onto one of the arches, then scanned the dark avenues for any sign of the Mercedes. Uneager to venture into the centre of the town, he went back to his car, then entered the hotel and climbed to the roof.

By the sea, where the antique theatre had been dug from the dunes, he could see the white rectangle of the Mercedes parked on the bluff. Below the proscenium, on the flat semi-circle of the stage, the dark figure of Gabrielle Szabo moved to and fro among the shadows of the statues.

Watching her, and thinking of Delvaux's 'Echo', with its triplicated nymph walking naked among the classical pavilions of a midnight city, Halliday wondered whether he had fallen asleep on the warm concrete roof. Between his dreams and the ancient city below there seemed no boundary, and the moonlit phantoms of his mind moved freely between the inner and outer landscapes, as in turn the dark-eyed woman from the house by the drained river had crossed the frontiers of his psyche, bringing with her a final relief from time.

Leaving the hotel, Halliday followed the street through the empty town, and reached the rim of the amphitheatre. As he watched, Gabrielle Szabo came walking through the antique streets, the fleeting light between the columns illuminating her white face. Halliday moved down the stone steps to the stage, aware of the chauffeur watching him from the cliff beside the car. The woman moved towards Halliday, her hips swaying slowly from side to side.

Ten feet from him she stopped, her raised hands testing the darkness. Halliday stepped forward, doubting if she could see him at all behind the sunglasses she still wore. At the sound of his footsteps she flinched back, looking up towards the chauffeur, but Halliday took her hand.

'Miss Szabo. I saw you walking here.'

The woman held his hands in suddenly strong fingers. Behind the glasses her face was a white mask. 'Mr Halliday —' She felt his wrists, as if relieved to see him. 'I thought you would come. Tell me, how long have you been here?'

'Weeks – or months, I can't remember. I dreamed of this city before I came to Africa. Miss Szabo, I used to see you walking here among these ruins.'

She nodded, taking his arm. Together they moved off among the columns. Between the shadowy pillars of the balustrade was the sea, the white caps of the waves rolling towards the beach.

'Gabrielle . . . why are you here? Why did you come to Africa?'

She gathered the silk robe in one hand as they moved down a stairway to the terrace below. She leaned closely against Halliday, her fingers clasping his arm, walking so stiffly that Halliday wondered if she were drunk. 'Why? Perhaps to see the same dreams, it's possible.'

Halliday was about to speak when he noticed the footsteps of the chauffeur following them down the stairway. Looking around, and for one moment distracted from Gabrielle's swaying body against his own, he became aware of a pungent smell coming from the vent of one of the old Roman cloacas below them. The top of the brick-lined sewer had fallen in, and the basin was partly covered by the waves swilling in across the beach.

Halliday stopped. He tried to point below but the woman was holding his wrist in a steel grip. 'Down there! Can you see?'

Pulling his hand away, he pointed to the basin of the sewer, where a dozen half-submerged forms lay heaped together. Bludgeoned by the sea and wet sand, the corpses were only recognizable by the back-and-forth movements of their arms and legs in the shifting water.

'For God's sake – Gabrielle, who are they?'

'Poor devils . . .' Gabrielle Szabo turned away, as Halliday stared over the edge at the basin ten feet below. 'The evacuation – there were riots. They've been here for months.'

Halliday knelt down, wondering how long it would take the corpses – whether Arab or European he had no means of telling – to be swept out to sea. His dreams of Leptis Magna had not included these melancholy denizens of the sewers. Suddenly he shouted again.

'Months? Not that one!'

He pointed again to the body of a man in a white suit lying to one side farther up the sewer. His long legs were covered by the foam and water, but his chest and arms were exposed. Across the face was the silk scarf he had seen Mallory wearing at their last meeting.

'Mallory!' Halliday stood up, as the black-suited figure of the chauffeur stepped onto a ledge twenty feet above. Halliday went over to Gabrielle Szabo, who was standing by the step, apparently gazing out to sea. 'That's Dr Mallory! He lived with me at Columbine Sept Heures! How did he – Gabrielle, you knew he was here!'

Halliday seized her hands, in his anger jerked her forward, knocking off her glasses. As she fell to her knees, scrambling helplessly for them, Halliday held her shoulders. 'Gabrielle! Gabrielle, you're –'

'Halliday!' Her head lowered, she held his fingers and pressed them into her orbits. 'Mallory, he did it – we knew he'd follow you here. He was my doctor once, I've waited for years . . .'

Halliday pushed her away, his feet crushing the sunglasses on the floor. He looked down at the white-suited figure washed by the waves, wondering what nightmare was hidden behind the scarf over its face, and sprinted along the terrace past the auditorium, then raced away through the dark streets.

As he reached the Peugeot the black-suited chauffeur was only twenty yards behind. Halliday started the motor and swung the car away through the dust. In the rear mirror he saw the chauffeur stop and draw a pistol from his belt. As he fired the bullet shattered the windshield. Halliday swerved into one of the kiosks, then regained control and set off with his head down, the cold night air blowing fragments of frosted glass into his face.

Two miles from Leptis, when there was no sight of the Mercedes in pursuit, he stopped and knocked out the windshield. As he drove on westward the air grew warmer, the rising dawn lifting in front of him with its promise of light and time.

**1966**

# · THE IMPOSSIBLE MAN

At low tide, their eggs buried at last in the broken sand below the dunes, the turtles began their return journey to the sea. To Conrad Foster, watching beside his uncle from the balustrade along the beach road, there seemed little more than fifty yards to the safety of the slack water. The turtles laboured on, their dark humps hidden among the orange crates and the drifts of kelp washed up from the sea. Conrad pointed to the flock of gulls resting on the submerged sandbank in the mouth of the estuary. The birds had been staring out to sea, as if uninterested in the deserted shoreline where the old man and the boy waited by the rail, but at this small movement of Conrad's a dozen white heads turned together.

'They've seen them . . .' Conrad let his arm fall to the rail. 'Uncle Theodore, do you think –?'

His uncle gestured with the stick at a car moving along the road a quarter of a mile away. 'It could have been the car.' He took his pipe from his mouth as a cry came from the sandbank. The first flight of gulls rose into the air and began to turn like a scythe towards the shore. 'Here they come.'

The turtles had emerged from the shelter of the debris by the tideline. They advanced across the sheet of damp sand that sloped down to the sea, the screams of the gulls tearing at the air over their heads.

Involuntarily Conrad moved away towards the row of chalets and the deserted tea garden on the outskirts of the town. His uncle held his arm. The turtles were being picked from the shallow water and dropped on the sand, then dismembered by a dozen beaks.

Within barely a minute of their arrival the birds began to rise from the beach. Conrad and his uncle had not been the only spectators of the gulls' brief feast. A small party of some dozen men stepped down from their vantage point among the dunes and moved along the sand, driving the last of the birds away from the turtles. The men were all elderly, well into their sixties and seventies, and wore singlets and cotton trousers rolled to their knees. Each carried a canvas bag and a wooden gaff tipped by a steel blade. As they picked up the shells they cleaned them with swift, practised movements and dropped them into their bags. The wet sand was streaked with blood, and soon the old men's bare feet and arms were covered with the bright stains.

'I dare say you're ready to move.' Uncle Theodore looked up at the sky, following the gulls back to the estuary. 'Your aunt will have something waiting for us.'

Conrad was watching the old men. As they passed, one of them raised his ruby-tipped gaff in greeting. 'Who are they?' he asked as his uncle acknowledged the salute.

'Shell collectors – they come here in the season. These shells fetch a good price.'

They set off towards the town, Uncle Theodore moving at a slow pace with his stick. As he waited Conrad glanced back along the beach. For some reason the sight of the old men streaked with the blood of the slaughtered turtles was more disturbing than the viciousness of the seagulls. Then he remembered that he himself had probably set off the birds.

The sounds of a truck overlaid the fading cries of the gulls as they settled themselves on the sandbank. The old men had gone, and the incoming tide was beginning to wash the stained sand. They reached the crossing by the first of the chalets. Conrad steered his uncle to the traffic island in the centre of the road. As they waited for the truck to pass he said, 'Uncle, did you notice the birds never touched the sand?'

The truck roared past them, its high pantechnicon blocking off the sky. Conrad took his uncle's arm and moved forward. The old man plodded on, rooting his stick in the sandy tarmac. Then he flinched back, the pipe falling from his mouth as he shouted at the sports car swerving towards them out of the dust behind the truck. Conrad caught a glimpse of the driver's white knuckles on the rim of the steering wheel, a frozen face behind the windshield as the car, running down its own brakes, began to slide sideways across the road. Conrad started to push the old man back but the car was on them, bursting across the traffic island in a roar of dust.

The hospital was almost empty. During the first days Conrad was glad to lie motionlessly in the deserted ward, watching the patterns of light reflected on to the ceiling from the flowers on the window-sill, listening to the few sounds from the orderly room beyond the swing doors. At intervals the nurse would come and look at him. Once, when she bent down to straighten the cradle over his legs, he noticed that she was not a young woman but even older than his aunt, despite her slim figure and the purple rinse in her hair. In fact, all the nurses and orderlies who tended him in the empty ward were elderly, and obviously regarded Conrad more as a child than a youth of seventeen, treating him to a mindless and amiable banter as they moved about the ward.

Later, when the pain from his amputated leg roused him from this placid second sleep, Nurse Sadie at last began to look at his face. She told him that his aunt had come to visit him each day after the accident, and that she would return the following afternoon.

'... Theodore – Uncle Theodore ...?' Conrad tried to sit up but an invisible leg, as dead and heavy as a mastodon's, anchored him to the bed. 'Mr Foster . . . my uncle. Did the car . . . ?'

'Missed him by yards, dear. Or let's say inches.' Nurse Sadie touched his forehead with a hand like a cool bird. 'Only a scratch on his wrist where the windshield cut it. My, the glass we took out of you, though, you looked as if you'd jumped through a greenhouse!'

Conrad moved his head away from her fingers. He searched the rows of empty beds in the ward. 'Where is he? Here . . . ?'

'At home. Your aunt's looking after him, he'll be right as rain.'

Conrad lay back, waiting for Nurse Sadie to go away so that he could be alone with the pain in his vanished leg. Above him the surgical cradle loomed like a white mountain. Strangely, the news that Uncle Theodore had escaped almost unscathed from the accident left Conrad without any sense of relief. Since the age of five, when the deaths of his parents in an air disaster had left him an orphan, his relationship with his aunt and uncle had been, if anything, even closer than that he would have had with his mother and father, their affection and loyalties more conscious and constant. Yet he found himself thinking not of his uncle, nor of himself, but of the approaching car. With its sharp fins and trim it had swerved towards them like the gulls swooping on the turtles, moving with the same rush of violence. Lying in the bed with the cradle over him Conrad remembered the turtles labouring across the wet sand under their heavy carapaces, and the old men waiting for them among the dunes.

Outside, the fountains played among the gardens of the empty hospital, and the elderly nurses walked in pairs to and fro along the shaded pathways.

The next day, before his aunt's visit, two doctors came to see Conrad. The older of the two, Dr Nathan, was a slim grey-haired man with hands as gentle as Nurse Sadie's. Conrad had seen him before, and remembered him from the first confused hours of his admission to the hospital. A faint half-smile always hung about Dr Nathan's mouth, like the ghost of some forgotten pleasantry.

The other physician, Dr Knight, was considerably younger, and by comparison seemed almost the same age as Conrad. His strong, square-jawed face looked down at Conrad with a kind of jocular hostility. He reached for Conrad's wrist as if about to jerk the youth from his bed on to the floor.

'So this is young Foster?' He peered into Conrad's eyes. 'Well, Conrad, I won't ask how you're feeling.'

'No . . .' Conrad nodded uncertainly.

'No, what?' Dr Knight smiled at Nathan, who was hovering at the foot of the bed like an aged flamingo in a dried-up pool. 'I thought Dr Nathan was looking after you very well.' When Conrad murmured something, shy of inviting another retort, Dr Knight sped on: 'Isn't he? Still, I'm more interested in your future, Conrad. This is where I take over from

Dr Nathan, so from now on you can blame me for everything that goes wrong.'

He pulled up a metal chair and straddled it, flicking out the tails of his white coat with a flourish. 'Not that anything will. Well?'

Conrad listened to Dr Nathan's feet tapping the polished floor. He cleared his throat. 'Where is everyone else?'

'You've noticed?' Dr Knight glanced across at his colleague. 'Still, you could hardly fail to.' He stared through the window at the empty grounds of the hospital. 'It's true, there is hardly anyone here.'

'A compliment to us, Conrad, don't you think?' Dr Nathan approached the bed again. The smile that hovered around his lips seemed to belong to another face.

'Yeesss . . .' Dr Knight drawled. 'Of course, no one will have explained to you, Conrad, but this isn't a hospital in quite the usual sense.'

'What –?' Conrad began to sit up, dragging at the cradle over his leg. 'What do you mean?'

Dr Knight raised his hands. 'Don't misinterpret me, Conrad. Of course this is a hospital, an advanced surgical unit, in fact, but it's also something more than a hospital, as I intend to explain.'

Conrad watched Dr Nathan. The older physician was gazing out of the window, apparently at the fountains, but for once his face was blank, the smile absent.

'In what way?' Conrad asked guardedly. 'Is it something to do with me?'

Dr Knight spread his hands in an ambiguous gesture. 'In a sense, yes. But we'll talk about this tomorrow. We've taxed you enough for the present.'

He stood up, his eyes still examining Conrad, and placed his hands on the cradle. 'We've a lot of work to do on this leg, Conrad. In the end, when we've finished, you'll be pleasantly surprised at what we can achieve here. In return, perhaps you can help us – we hope so, don't we, Dr Nathan?'

Dr Nathan's smile, like a returning wraith, hovered once again about his thin lips. 'I'm sure Conrad will be only too keen.'

As they reached the door Conrad called them back.

'What is it, Conrad?' Dr Knight waited by the next bed.

'The driver – the man in the car. What happened to him? Is he here?'

'As a matter of fact he is, but . . .' Dr Knight hesitated, then seemed to change course. 'To be honest, Conrad, you won't be able to see him. I know the accident was almost certainly his fault –'

'No!' Conrad shook his head. 'I don't want to blame him . . . we stepped out behind the truck. Is he here?'

'The car hit the steel pylon on the traffic island, then went on through the sea wall. The driver was killed on the beach. He wasn't much older than you, Conrad, in a way he may have been trying to save you and your uncle.'

Conrad nodded, remembering the white face like a scream behind the windshield.

Dr Knight turned towards the door. Almost *sotto voce* he added: 'And you'll see, Conrad, he can still help you.'

At three o'clock that afternoon Conrad's uncle appeared. Seated in a wheelchair, and pushed by his wife and Nurse Sadie, he waved cheerily to Conrad with his free hand as he entered the ward. For once, however, the sight of Uncle Theodore failed to raise Conrad's spirits. He had been looking forward to the visit, but his uncle had aged ten years since the accident and the sight of these three elderly people, one of them partially crippled, coming towards him with their smiling faces only reminded him of his isolation in the hospital.

As he listened to his uncle, Conrad realized that this isolation was merely a more extreme version of his own position, and that of all young people, outside the walls of the hospital. As a child Conrad had known few friends of his own age, for the single reason that children were almost as rare as centenarians had been a hundred years earlier. He had been born into a middle-aged world, one moreover where middle age itself was for ever moving, like the horizons of a receding universe, farther and farther from its original starting point. His aunt and uncle, both of them nearly sixty, represented the median line. Beyond them was the immense super-annuated army of the elderly, filling the shops and streets of the seaside town, their slow rhythms and hesitant walk overlaying everything like a grey veil.

By contrast, Dr Knight's self-confidence and casual air, however brusque and aggressive, quickened Conrad's pulse.

Towards the end of the visit, when his aunt had strolled to the end of the ward with Nurse Sadie to view the fountains, Conrad said to his uncle, 'Dr Knight told me he could do something for my leg.'

'I'm sure he can, Conrad.' Uncle Theodore smiled encouragingly, but his eyes watched Conrad without moving. 'These surgeons are clever men; it's amazing what they can do.'

'And your hand, Uncle?' Conrad pointed to the dressing that covered his uncle's left forearm. The hint of irony in his uncle's voice reminded him of Dr Knight's studied ambiguities. Already he sensed that people were taking sides around him.

'This hand?' His uncle shrugged. 'It's done me for nearly sixty years, a missing finger won't stop me filling my pipe.' Before Conrad could speak he went on: 'But that leg of yours is a different matter, you'll have to decide for yourself what to have done with it.'

Just before he left he whispered to Conrad, 'Rest yourself well, lad. You may have to run before you can walk.'

Two days later, promptly at nine o'clock, Dr Knight came to see Conrad. Brisk as ever, he came to the point immediately.

'Now, Conrad,' he began, replacing the cradle after his inspection, 'it's a month since your last stroll by the beach, time to get you out of here and back on your own feet again. What do you say?'

'*Feet?*' Conrad repeated. He managed a slight laugh. 'Do you mean that as a figure of speech?'

'No, I mean it literally.' Dr Knight drew up a chair. 'Tell me, Conrad, have you ever heard of restorative surgery? It may have been mentioned at school.'

'In biology – transplanting kidneys and that sort of thing. Older people have it done. Is that what you're going to do to my leg?'

'Whoa! Hold your horses. Let's get a few things straight first. As you say, restorative surgery goes back about fifty years, when the first kidney grafts were made, though for years before that corneal grafting was commonplace. If you accept that blood is a tissue the principle is even older – you had a massive blood transfusion after the accident, and later when Dr Nathan amputated the crushed knee and shinbone. Nothing surprising about that, is there?'

Conrad waited before answering. For once Dr Knight's tone had become defensive, as if he were already, by some sort of extrapolation, asking the questions to which he feared Conrad might subsequently object.

'No,' Conrad replied. 'Nothing at all.'

'Obviously, why should there be? Though it's worth bearing in mind that many people have refused to accept blood transfusions, even though it meant certain death. Apart from their religious objections, many of them felt that the foreign blood polluted their own bodies.' Dr Knight leaned back, scowling to himself. 'One can see their point of view, but remember that our bodies are almost completely composed of alien materials. We don't stop eating, do we, just to preserve our own absolute identity?' Dr Knight laughed here. 'That would be egotism run riot. Don't you agree?'

When Dr Knight glanced at him, as if waiting for an answer, Conrad said, 'More or less.'

'Good. And, of course, in the past most people have taken your point of view. The substitution of a healthy kidney for a diseased one doesn't in any way diminish your own integrity, particularly if your life is saved. What counts is your own continuing identity. By their very structure the individual parts of the body serve a larger physiological whole, and the human consciousness is great enough to provide any sense of unity.

'Now, no one ever seriously disputed this, and fifty years ago a number of brave men and women, many of them physicians, voluntarily gave their healthy organs to others who needed them. Sadly, all these efforts failed after a few weeks as a result of the so-called immunity reaction. The host body, even though it was dying, still fought against the graft as it would against any alien organism.'

Conrad shook his head. 'I thought they'd solved this immunity problem.'

'In time, yes – it was a question of biochemistry rather than any fault in the surgical techniques used. Eventually the way became clear, and every year tens of thousands of lives were saved – people with degenerative diseases of the liver, kidneys, alimentary tract, even portions of the heart and nervous system, were given transplanted organs. The main problem was where to obtain them – you may be willing to donate a kidney, but you can't give away your liver or the mitral valve in your heart. Luckily a great number of people willed their organs posthumously – in fact, it's now a condition of admission to a public hospital that in the event of death any parts of one's body may be used in restorative surgery. Originally the only organs that were banked were those of the thorax and abdomen, but today we have reserves of literally every tissue in the human body, so that whatever the surgeon requires is available, whether it's a complete lung or a few square centimetres of some specialized epithelium.'

As Dr Knight sat back Conrad pointed at the ward around him. 'This hospital . . . this is where it happens?'

'Exactly, Conrad. This is one of the hundreds of institutes we have today devoted to restorative surgery. As you'll understand, only a small percentage of the patients who come here are cases such as yours. The greatest application of restorative surgery has been for geriatric purposes, that is, for prolonging life in the aged.'

Dr Knight nodded deliberately as Conrad sat up. 'Now you'll under-stand, Conrad, why there have always been so many elderly people in the world around you. The reason is simple – by means of restorative surgery we've been able to give people who would normally die in their sixties and seventies a second span of life. The average life span has risen from sixty-five half a century ago to something close to ninety-five.'

'Doctor . . . the driver of the car. I don't know his name. You said he could still help me.'

'I meant what I said, Conrad. One of the problems of restorative surgery is that of supply. In the case of the elderly it's straightforward, if anything there's an excess of replacement materials over the demand. Apart from a few generalized degenerative conditions, most elderly people are faced with the failure of perhaps no more than one organ, and every fatality provides a reserve of tissues that will keep twenty others alive for as many years. However, in the case of the young, particularly in your age group, the demand exceeds supply a hundred-fold. Tell me, Conrad, quite apart from the driver of the car, how do you feel in principle about undergoing restorative surgery?'

Conrad looked down at the bedclothes. Despite the cradle, the asym-metry of his limbs was too obvious to miss. 'It's hard to say. I suppose I . . .'

'The choice is yours, Conrad. Either you wear a prosthetic limb – a metal support that will give you endless discomfort for the rest of your life, and prevent you from running and swimming, from all the normal movements of a young man – or else you have a leg of flesh and blood and bone.'

Conrad hesitated. Everything Dr Knight had said tallied with all he had heard over the years about restorative surgery – the subject was not taboo, but seldom discussed, particularly in the presence of children. Yet he was sure that this elaborate résumé was the prologue to some far more difficult decision he would have to take. 'When do you do this – tomorrow?'

'Good God, no!' Dr Knight laughed involuntarily, then let his voice roll on, dispelling the tension between them. 'Not for about two months, it's a tremendously complex piece of work. We've got to identify and tag all the nerve endings and tendons, then prepare an elaborate bone graft. For at least a month you'll be wearing an artificial limb – believe me, by the end you'll be looking forward to getting back on a real leg. Now, Conrad, can I assume that in general you're quite willing? We need both your permission and your uncle's.'

'I think so. I'd like to talk to Uncle Theodore. Still, I know I haven't really got any choice.'

'Sensible man.' Dr Knight held out his hand. As Conrad reached to take it he realized that Dr Knight was deliberately showing him a faint hairline scar that ran around the base of his thumb and then disappeared inside the palm. The thumb seemed wholly part of the hand, and yet detached from it.

'That's right,' Dr Knight told him. 'A small example of restorative surgery. Done while I was a student. I lost the top joint after infecting it in the dissecting room. The entire thumb was replaced. It's served me well; I couldn't really have taken up surgery without it.' Dr Knight traced the faint scar across his palm for Conrad. 'There are slight differences of course, the articulation for one thing – this one is a little more dexterous than my own used to be, and the nail is a different shape, but otherwise it feels like me. There's also a certain altruistic pleasure that one is keeping alive part of another human being.'

'Dr Knight – the driver of the car. You want to give me his leg?'

'That's true, Conrad. I should have to tell you, anyway, the patient must agree to the donor – people are naturally hesitant about being grafted to part of a criminal or psychopath. As I explained, for someone of your age it's not easy to find the appropriate donor . . .'

'But, Doctor –' For once Dr Knight's reasoning bewildered Conrad. 'There must be someone else. It's not that I feel any grudge against him, but . . . There's some other reason, isn't there?'

Dr Knight nodded after a pause. He walked away from the bed, and for a moment Conrad wondered if he was about to abandon the entire case. Then he turned on his heel and pointed through the window.

'Conrad, while you've been here has it occurred to you to wonder why this hospital is empty?'

Conrad gestured at the distant walls. 'Perhaps it's too large. How many patients can it take?'

'Over two thousand. It *is* large, but fifteen years ago, before I came here, it was barely big enough to deal with the influx of patients. Most of them were geriatric cases – men and women in their seventies and eighties who were having one or more vital organs replaced. There were immense waiting lists, many of the patients were trying to pay hugely inflated fees – bribes, if you like – to get in.'

'Where have they all gone?'

'An interesting question – the answer in part explains why you're here, Conrad, and why we're taking a special interest in your case. You see, Conrad, about ten or twelve years ago hospital boards all over the country noticed that admission rates were starting to fall off. To begin with they were relieved, but the decline has gone on each year, until now the rate of admission is down to about one per cent of the previous intake. And most of these patients are surgeons and physicians, or members of the nursing staff.'

'But, Doctor – if they're not coming here ...' Conrad found himself thinking of his aunt and uncle. 'If they won't come here that means they're choosing to ...'

Dr Knight nodded. 'Exactly, Conrad. They're choosing to die.'

A week later, when his uncle came to see him again, Conrad explained to him Dr Knight's proposition. They sat together on the terrace outside the ward, looking out over the fountains at the deserted hospital. His uncle still wore a surgical mitten over his hand, but otherwise had recovered from the accident. He listened silently to Conrad.

'None of the old people are coming any more, they're lying at home when they fall ill and ... waiting for the end. Dr Knight says there's no reason why in many cases restorative surgery shouldn't prolong life more or less indefinitely.'

'A sort of life. How does he think you can help them, Conrad?'

'Well, he believes that they need an example to follow, a symbol if you like. Someone like myself who's been badly hurt in an accident right at the start of his life might make them accept the real benefits of restorative surgery.'

'The two cases are hardly similar,' his uncle mused. 'However ... How do you feel about it?'

'Dr Knight's been completely frank. He's told me about those early cases where people who'd had new organs and limbs literally fell apart when the seams failed. I suppose he's right. Life should be preserved – you'd help a dying man if you found him on the pavement, why not in some other case? Because cancer or bronchitis are less dramatic –'

'I understand, Conrad.' His uncle raised a hand. 'But why does he think older people are refusing surgery?'

'He admits he doesn't know. He feels that as the average age of the population rises there's a tendency for the old people to dominate society and set its mood. Instead of having a majority of younger people around them they see only the aged like themselves. The one way of escape is death.'

'It's a theory. One thing – he wants to give you the leg of the driver who hit us. That seems a strange touch. A little ghoulish.'

'No, it's the whole point – he's trying to say that once the leg is grafted it becomes part of *me*.' Conrad pointed to his uncle's mitten. 'Uncle Theodore, that hand. You lost two of the fingers. Dr Knight told me. Are you going to have them restored?'

His uncle laughed. 'Are you trying to make me your first convert, Conrad?'

Two months later Conrad re-entered the hospital to undergo the restorative surgery for which he had been waiting during his convalescence. On the previous day he accompanied his uncle on a short visit to friends who lived in the retirement hostels to the north-west of the town. These pleasant single-storey buildings in the chalet style, built by the municipal authority and let out to their occupants at a low rent, constituted a considerable fraction of the town's area. In the three weeks he had been ambulant Conrad seemed to have visited every one. The artificial limb with which he had been fitted was far from comfortable, but at Dr Knight's request his uncle had taken Conrad to all the acquaintances he knew.

Although the purpose of these visits was to identify Conrad to as many of the elderly residents as possible before he returned to the hospital – the main effort at conversion would come later, when the new limb was in place – Conrad had already begun to doubt whether Dr Knight's plan would succeed. Far from arousing any hostility, Conrad's presence elicited nothing but sympathy and goodwill from the aged occupants of the residential hostels and bungalows. Wherever he went the old people would come down to their gates and talk to him, wishing him well with his operation. At times, as he acknowledged the smiles and greetings of the grey-haired men and women watching on all sides from their balconies and gardens, it seemed to Conrad that he was the only young person in the entire town.

'Uncle, how do you explain the paradox?' he asked as they limped along together on their rounds, Conrad supporting his weight on two stout walking sticks. 'They want me to have a new leg but they won't go to the hospital themselves.'

'But you're young, Conrad, a mere child to them. You're having returned to you something that is your right: the ability to walk and run and dance. Your life isn't being prolonged beyond its natural span.'

'Natural span?' Conrad repeated the phrase wearily. He rubbed the harness of his leg beneath his trousers. 'In some parts of the world the natural life span is still little more than forty. Isn't it relative?'

'Not entirely, Conrad. Not beyond a certain point.' Although he had faithfully guided Conrad about the town, his uncle seemed reluctant to pursue the argument.

They reached the entrance to one of the residential estates. One of the town's many undertakers had opened a new office, and in the shadows behind the leaded windows Conrad could see a prayer-book on a mahogany stand and discreet photographs of hearses and mausoleums. However veiled, the proximity of the office to the retirement homes disturbed Conrad as much as if a line of freshly primed coffins had been laid out along the pavement ready for inspection.

His uncle merely shrugged when Conrad mentioned this. 'The old take a realistic view of things, Conrad. They don't fear or sentimentalize death in quite the way the younger people do. In fact, they have a very lively interest in the matter.'

As they stopped outside one of the chalets he took Conrad's arm. 'A word of warning here, Conrad. I don't want to shock you, but you're about to meet a man who intends to put his opposition to Dr Knight into practice. Perhaps he'll tell you more in a few minutes than I or Dr Knight could in ten years. His name is Matthews, by the way, Dr James Matthews.'

'Doctor?' Conrad repeated. 'Do you mean a doctor of medicine?'

'Exactly. One of the few. Still, let's wait until you meet him.'

They approached the chalet, a modest two-roomed dwelling with a small untended garden dominated by a tall cypress. The door opened as soon as they touched the bell. An elderly nun in the uniform of a nursing order let them in with a brief greeting. A second nun, her sleeves rolled, crossed the passage to the kitchen with a porcelain pail. Despite their efforts, there was an unpleasant smell in the house which the lavish use of disinfectant failed to conceal.

'Mr Foster, would you mind waiting a few minutes. Good morning, Conrad.'

They waited in the dingy sitting room. Conrad studied the framed photographs over the rolltop desk. One was of a birdlike, grey-haired woman, whom he took to be the deceased Mrs Matthews. The other was an old matriculation portrait of a group of students.

Eventually they were shown into the small rear bedroom. The second of the two nuns had covered the equipment on the bedside table with a sheet. She straightened the coverlet on the bed and then went out into the hall.

Resting on his sticks, Conrad stood behind his uncle as the latter peered down at the occupant of the bed. The acid odour was more pungent and seemed to emanate directly from the bed. When his uncle beckoned him forward, Conrad at first failed to find the shrunken face of the man in the bed. The grey cheeks and hair had already merged into the unstarched sheets covered by the shadows from the curtained windows.

'James, this is Elizabeth's boy, Conrad.' His uncle pulled up a wooden chair. He motioned to Conrad to sit down. 'Dr Matthews, Conrad.'

Conrad murmured something, aware of the blue eyes that had turned to look at him. What surprised him most about the dying occupant of the bed was his comparative youth. Although in his middle sixties, Dr Matthews was twenty years younger than the majority of the tenants in the estate.

'He's grown into quite a lad, don't you think, James?' Uncle Theodore remarked.

Dr Matthews nodded, as if only half interested in their visit. His eyes were on the dark cypress in the garden. 'He has,' he said at last.

Conrad waited uncomfortably. The walk had tired him, and his thigh seemed raw again. He wondered if they would be able to call for a taxi from the house.

Dr Matthews turned his head. He seemed to be able to look at Conrad and his uncle with a blue eye on each of them. 'Who have you got for the boy?' he asked in a sharper voice. 'Nathan is still there, I believe ...'

'One of the younger men, James. You probably won't know him, but he's a good fellow. Knight.'

'Knight?' The name was repeated with only a faint hint of comment. 'And when does the boy go in?'

'Tomorrow. Don't you, Conrad?'

Conrad was about to speak when he noticed that a faint simpering was coming from the man in the bed. Suddenly exhausted by this bizarre scene, and under the impression that the dying physician's macabre humour was directed at himself, Conrad rose in his chair, rattling his sticks together. 'Uncle, could I wait outside ...?'

'My boy –' Dr Matthews had freed his right hand from the bed. 'I was laughing at your uncle, not at you. He always had a great sense of humour. Or none at all. Which is it, Theo?'

'I see nothing funny, James. Are you saying I shouldn't have brought him here?'

Dr Matthews lay back. 'Not at all – I was there at his beginning, let him be here for my end ...' He looked at Conrad again. 'I wish you the best, Conrad. No doubt you wonder why I don't accompany you to the hospital.'

'Well, I ...' Conrad began, but his uncle held his shoulder.

'James, it's time for us to be leaving. I think we can take the matter as understood.'

'Obviously we can't.' Dr Matthews raised a hand again, frowning at the slight noise. 'I'll only be a moment, Theo, but if I don't tell him no one will, certainly not Dr Knight. Now, Conrad, you're seventeen?'

When Conrad nodded Dr Matthews went on: 'At that age, if I remember, life seems to stretch on for ever. One is probably living as close to eternity as is possible. As you get older, though, you find more and more that everything worthwhile has finite bounds, by and large those of time – from ordinary things to the most important ones, your marriage, children and so on, even life itself. The hard lines drawn around things give them their identity. Nothing is brighter than the diamond.'

'James, you've had enough –'

'Quiet, Theo.' Dr Matthews raised his head, almost managing to sit up. 'Perhaps, Conrad, you would explain to Dr Knight that it is just because we value our lives so much that we refuse to diminish them. There are a thousand hard lines drawn between you and me, Conrad, differences of age, character and experience, differences of *time*. You have to earn these distinctions for yourself. You can't borrow them from anyone else, least of all from the dead.'

Conrad looked round as the door opened. The older of the nuns stood in the hall outside. She nodded to his uncle. Conrad settled his limb for the journey home, waiting for Uncle Theodore to make his goodbyes to Dr Matthews. As the nun stepped towards the bed he saw on the train of her starched gown a streak of blood.

Outside they plodded together past the undertakers, Conrad heaving himself along on his sticks. As the old people in the gardens waved to them Uncle Theodore said, 'I'm sorry he seemed to laugh at you, Conrad. It wasn't meant.'

'Was he there when I was born?'

'He attended your mother. I thought it only right that you should see him before he died. Why he thought it so funny I can't understand.'

Almost six months later to the day, Conrad Foster walked down towards the beach road and the sea. In the sunlight he could see the high dunes above the beach, and beyond them the gulls sitting out on the submerged sandbank in the mouth of the estuary. The traffic along the beach road was busier than he remembered from his previous visit, and the sand picked up by the wheels of the speeding cars and trucks drifted in clouds across the fields.

Conrad moved at a good pace along the road, testing his new leg to the full. During the past four months the bonds had consolidated themselves with the minimum of pain, and the leg was, if anything, stronger and more resilient than his own had ever been. At times, when he walked along without thinking, it seemed to stride ahead with a will of its own.

Yet despite its good service, and the fulfilment of all that Dr Knight had promised him for it, Conrad had failed to accept the leg. The thin hairline of the surgical scar that circled his thigh above the knee was a frontier that separated the two more absolutely than any physical barrier. As Dr Matthews had stated, its presence seemed to diminish him, in some way subtracting rather than adding to his own sense of identity. This feeling had grown with each week and month as the leg itself recovered its strength. At night they would lie together like silent partners in an uneasy marriage.

In the first month after his recovery Conrad had agreed to help Dr Knight and the hospital authorities in the second stage of their campaign to persuade the elderly to undergo restorative surgery rather than throw away their lives, but after Dr Matthew's death Conrad decided to take no further part in the scheme. Unlike Dr Knight, he realized that there was no real means of persuasion, and that only those on their deathbeds, such as Dr Matthews, were prepared to argue the matter at all. The others simply smiled and waved from their quiet gardens.

In addition, Conrad knew that his own growing uncertainty over the new limb would soon be obvious to their sharp eyes. A large scar now disfigured the skin above the shin-bone, and the reasons were plain. Injuring it while using his uncle's lawnmower, he had deliberately let the wound fester, as if this act of self-mutilation might symbolize the amputation of the limb. However, it seemed only to thrive on this blood letting.

A hundred yards away was the junction with the beach road, the fine sand lifting off the surface in the light breeze. A quarter of a mile away a line of vehicles approached at speed, the drivers of the cars at the rear trying to overtake two heavy trucks. Far away, in the estuary, there was a faint cry from the sea. Although tired, Conrad found himself breaking into a run. Somewhere a familiar conjunction of events was guiding him back towards the place of his accident.

As he reached the corner the first of the trucks was drawing close to him, the driver flashing his headlamps as Conrad hovered on the kerb, eager to get back to the pedestrian island with its freshly painted pylon.

Above the noise he saw the gulls rising into the air above the beach, and heard their harsh cries as the white sword drew itself across the sky. As it swept down over the beach the old men with their metal-tipped gaffs were moving from the road to their hiding-place among the dunes.

The truck thudded past him, the grey dust stinging his face as the slipstream whipped across it. A heavy saloon car rolled by, overtaking the truck and the other cars pressing behind it. The gulls began to dive and scream across the beach, and Conrad darted through the dust into the centre of the road and ran forward into the cars as they swerved towards him.

**ꜰ 1966**

# · STORM-BIRD, STORM-DREAMER

At dawn the bodies of the dead birds shone in the damp light of the marsh, their grey plumage hanging in the still water like fallen clouds. Each morning when Crispin went out on to the deck of the picket ship he would see the birds lying in the creeks and waterways where they had died two months earlier, their wounds cleansed now by the slow current, and he would watch the white-haired woman who lived in the empty house below the cliff walking by the river. Along the narrow beach the huge birds, larger than condors, lay at her feet. As Crispin gazed at her from the bridge of the picket ship she moved among them, now and then stooping to pluck a feather from the outstretched wings. At the end of her walk, when she returned across the damp meadow to the empty house, her arms would be loaded with immense white plumes.

At first Crispin had felt an obscure sense of annoyance at the way this strange woman descended on to the beach and calmly plundered the plumage of the dead birds. Although many thousands of the creatures lay along the margins of the river and in the marshes around the inlet where the picket ship was moored, Crispin still maintained a proprietary attitude towards them. He himself, almost single-handedly, had been responsible for the slaughter of the birds in the last terrifying battles when they had come from their eyries along the North Sea and attacked the picket ship. Each of the immense white creatures – for the most part gulls and gannets, with a few fulmars and petrels – carried *his* bullet in its heart like a jewel.

As he watched the woman cross the overgrown lawn to her house Crispin remembered again the frantic hours before the birds' final hopeless attack. Hopeless it seemed now, when their bodies lay in a wet quilt over the cold Norfolk marshes, but then, only two months earlier, when the sky above the ship had been dark with their massing forms, it was Crispin who had given up hope.

The birds had been larger than men, with wing spans of twenty feet or more that shut out the sun. Crispin had raced like a madman across the rusty metal decks, dragging the ammunition cans in his torn arms from the armoury and loading them into the breeches of the machine-guns, while Quimby, the idiot youth from the farm at Long Reach whom Crispin had persuaded to be his gun loader, gibbered to himself on the foredeck, hopping about on his club foot as he tried to escape from the huge shadows sweeping across him. When the birds began their first dive, and the sky turned into a white scythe, Crispin had barely enough time to buckle himself into the shoulder harness of the turret.

Yet he had won, shooting the first wave down into the marshes as they soared towards him like a white armada, then turning to fire at the second group swooping in low across the river behind his back. The hull of the picket ship was still dented with the impacts their bodies had made as they struck the sides above the waterline. At the height of the battle the birds had been everywhere, wings like screaming crosses against the sky, their corpses crashing through the rigging on to the decks around him as he swung the heavy guns, firing from rail to rail. A dozen times Crispin had given up hope, cursing the men who had left him alone on this rusty hulk to face the giant birds, and who made him pay for Quimby out of his own pocket.

But then, when the battle had seemed to last for ever, when the sky was still full of birds and his ammunition had nearly gone, he noticed Quimby dancing on the corpses heaped on the deck, pitching them into the water with his two-pronged fork as they thudded around him.

Then Crispin knew that he had won. When the firing slackened Quimby dragged up more ammunition, eager for killing, his face and deformed chest smeared with feathers and blood. Shouting himself now, with a fierce pride in his own courage and fear, Crispin had destroyed the remainder of the birds, shooting the stragglers, a few fledgling peregrines, as they fled towards the cliff. For an hour after the last of the birds had died, when the river and the creeks near the ship ran red with their blood, Crispin had sat in the turret, firing the guns at the sky that had dared attack him.

Later, when the excitement and pulse of the battle had passed, he realized that the only witness of his stand against this aerial armageddon had been a club-footed idiot to whom no one would ever listen. Of course, the white-haired woman had been there, hiding behind the shutters in her house, but Crispin had not noticed her until several hours had passed, when she began to walk among the corpses. To begin with, therefore, he had been glad to see the birds lying where they had fallen, their blurred forms eddying away in the cold water of the river and the marshes. He sent Quimby back to his farm, and watched the idiot dwarf punt his way down-river among the swollen corpses. Then, crossed bandoliers of machine-gun cartridges around his chest, Crispin took command of his bridge.

The woman's appearance on the scene he welcomed, glad someone else was there to share his triumph, and well aware that she must have noticed him patrolling the captain's walk of the picket ship. But after a single glance the woman never again looked at him. She seemed intent only on searching the beach and the meadow below her house.

On the third day after the battle she had come out on to the lawn with Quimby, and the dwarf spent the morning and afternoon clearing away the bodies of the birds that had fallen there. He heaped them on to a heavy wooden tumbril, then harnessed himself between the shafts and dragged them away to a pit near the farm. The following day he appeared again in a wooden skiff and punted the woman, standing alone in the bows like an aloof wraith, among the bodies of the birds floating in the water. Now and then Quimby turned one of the huge corpses over with his pole, as if searching for something among them – there were apocryphal stories, which many townsfolk believed, that the beaks of the birds carried tusks of ivory, but Crispin knew this to be nonsense.

These movements of the women puzzled Crispin, who felt that his conquest of the birds had also tamed the landscape around the picket ship and everything in it. Shortly afterwards, when the woman began to collect the wing feathers of the birds, he felt that she was in some way usurping a privilege reserved for him alone. Sooner or later the river voles, rats and other predators of the marshes would destroy the birds, but until then he resented anyone else looting this drowned treasure which he had won so hard. After the battle he had sent a short message in his crabbed handwriting to the district officer at the station twenty miles away, and until a reply came he preferred that the thousands of bodies should lie where they had fallen. As a conscripted member of the picket service he was not eligible for a bounty, but Crispin dimly hoped he might receive a medal or some sort of commendation.

The knowledge that the woman was his only witness, apart from the idiot Quimby, deterred Crispin from doing anything that might antagonize her. Also, the woman's odd behaviour made Crispin suspect that she too might be mad. He had never seen her at a shorter distance than the three hundred yards separating the picket ship from the bank below her house, but through the telescope mounted on the rail of the bridge he followed her along the beach, and saw more clearly the white hair and the ashen skin of her high face. Her arms were thin but strong, hands held at her waist as she moved about in a grey ankle-length robe. Her bedraggled appearance was that of someone unaware that she had lived alone for a long time.

For several hours Crispin watched her walking among the corpses. The tide cast a fresh freight on to the sand each day, but now that the bodies were decomposing their appearance, except at a distance, was devoid of any sentiment. The shallow inlet in which the picket ship was moored – the vessel was one of the hundreds of old coastal freighters hastily converted to duty when the first flocks of giant birds appeared two years earlier – faced the house across the river. Through the telescope Crispin could count the scores of pockmarks in the white stucco where spent bullets from his guns had lodged themselves.

At the end of her walk the woman had filled her arms with a garland of feathers. As Crispin watched, hands clasping the bandoliers across his chest, she went over to one of the birds, walking into the shallow water to peer into its half-submerged face. Then she plucked a single plume from its wing and added it to the collection in her arms.

Restlessly Crispin returned to the telescope. In the narrow eyepiece her swaying figure, almost hidden by the spray of white feathers, resembled that of some huge decorative bird, a white peacock. Perhaps in some bizarre way she imagined she was a bird?

In the wheelhouse Crispin fingered the signal pistol fastened to the wall. When she came out the next morning he could fire one of the flares over her head, warning her that the birds were his, subjects of his own transitory kingdom. The farmer, Hassell, who had come with Quimby for permission to burn some of the birds for use as fertilizer, had plainly acknowledged Crispin's moral rights over them.

Usually Crispin made a thorough inspection of the ship each morning, counting the ammunition cases and checking the gunnery mountings. The metal caissons were splitting the rusty decks. The whole ship was settling into the mud below. At high tide Crispin would listen to the water pouring through a thousand cracks and rivet holes like an army of silver-tongued rats.

This morning, however, his inspection was brief. After testing the turret on the bridge – there was always the chance of a few stragglers appearing from the nesting grounds along the abandoned coast – he went back to his telescope. The woman was somewhere behind the house, cutting down the remains of a small rose pergola. Now and then she would look up at the sky and at the cliff above, scanning the dark line of the escarpment as if waiting for one of the birds.

This reminder that he had overcome his own fears of the giant birds made Crispin realize why he resented the woman plucking their feathers. As their bodies and plumage began to dissolve he felt a growing need to preserve them. Often he found himself thinking of their great tragic faces as they swooped down upon him, in many ways more to be pitied than feared, victims of what the district officer had called a 'biological accident' – Crispin vaguely remembered him describing the new growth promoters used on the crops in East Anglia and the extraordinary and unforeseen effects on the bird life.

Five years earlier Crispin had been working in the fields as a labourer, unable to find anything better after his wasted years of military service. He remembered the first of the new sprays being applied to the wheat and fruit crops, and the tacky phosphorescent residue that made them glimmer in the moonlight, transforming the placid agricultural backwater into a strange landscape where the forces of some unseen nature were forever gathering themselves in readiness. The fields had been covered with the dead bodies of gulls and magpies whose mouths were clogged with this silvering gum. Crispin himself had saved many of the half-conscious birds, cleaning their beaks and feathers, and sending them off to their sailing grounds along the coast.

Three years later the birds had returned. The first giant cormorants and

black-headed gulls had wing spans of ten or twelve feet, strong bodies and
beaks that could slash a dog apart, Soaring low over the fields as Crispin
drove his tractor under the empty skies, they seemed to be waiting for
something.

The next autumn a second generation of even larger birds appeared,
sparrows as fierce as eagles, gannets and gulls with the wing spans of
condors. These immense creatures, with bodies as broad and powerful
as a man's, flew out of the storms along the coast, killing the cattle in
the fields and attacking the farmers and their families. Returning for some
reason to the infected crops that had given them this wild spur to growth,
they were the advance guard of an aerial armada of millions of birds that
filled the skies over the country. Driven by hunger, they began to attack
the human beings who were their only source of food.

Crispin had been too busy defending the farm where he lived to follow
the course of the battle against the birds all over the world. The farm,
only ten miles from the coast, had been besieged. After the dairy cattle
had been slaughtered, the birds turned to the farm buildings. One night
Crispin woke as a huge frigate bird, its shoulders wider than a door, had
shattered the wooden shutters across his window and thrust itself into his
room. Seizing his pitchfork, Crispin nailed it by the neck to the wall.

After the destruction of the farm, in which the owner, his family
and three of the labourers died. Crispin volunteered to join the picket
service. The district officer who headed the motorized militia column
at first refused Crispin's offer of help. Surveying the small, ferret-like
man with his beaked nose and the birthmark like a star below his left
eye, hobbling in little more than a blood-streaked singlet across the wreck
of the farmhouse, as the last of the birds wheeled away like giant crosses,
the district officer had shaken his head, seeing in Crispin's eyes only the
blind hunt for revenge.

However, when they counted the dead birds around the brick kiln where
Crispin had made his stand, armed only with a scythe a head taller than
himself, the officer had taken him on. He was given a rifle, and for half
an hour they moved through the shattered fields near by, filled with the
stripped skeletons of cattle and pigs, finishing off the wounded birds that
lay there.

Finally, Crispin had come to the picket ship, a drab hulk rusting in
a backwater of riverine creeks and marshes, where a dwarf punted his
coracle among the dead birds and a mad woman bedecked herself on
the beach with garlands of feathers.

For an hour Crispin paced round the ship, as the woman worked behind
the house. At one point she appeared with a laundry basket filled with
feathers and spread them out on a trestle table beside the rose pergola.

At the stern of the ship Crispin kicked open the galley door. He peered
into the murky interior.

'Quimby! Are you there?'

This damp hovel was still maintained as a home from home by Quimby. The dwarf would pay sudden visits to Crispin, presumably in the hope of seeing further action against the birds.

When there was no reply Crispin shouldered his rifle and made for the gangway. Still eyeing the opposite shore, where a small fire was now sending a plume of grey smoke into the placid air, he tightened his bandoliers and stepped down the creaking gangway to the launch at the bottom.

The dead bodies of the birds were massed around the picket ship in a soggy raft. After trying to drive the launch through them Crispin stopped the outboard motor and seized the gaff. Many of the birds weighed as much as five hundred pounds, lying in the water with their wings interlocked, tangled up with the cables and rope tossed down from the decks. Crispin could barely push them apart with the gaff, and slowly forced the launch to the mouth of the inlet.

He remembered the district officer telling him that the birds were closely related to the reptiles – evidently this explained their blind ferocity and hatred of the mammals – but to Crispin their washed faces in the water looked more like those of drowned dolphins, almost manlike in their composed and individual expressions. As he made his way across the river past the drifting forms it seemed to him that he had been attacked by a race of winged men, driven on not by cruelty or blind instinct but by a sense of some unknown and irrevocable destiny. Along the opposite bank the silver forms of the birds lay among the trees and on the open patches of grass. As he sat in the launch on the water the landscape seemed to Crispin like the morning after some apocalyptic battle of the heavens, the corpses like those of fallen angels.

He moored the launch by the beach, pushing aside the dead birds lying in the shallows. For some reason a flock of pigeons, a few doves among them, had fallen at the water's edge. Their plump-breasted bodies, at least ten feet from head to tail, lay as if asleep on the damp sand, eyes closed in the warm sunlight. Holding his bandoliers to prevent them slipping off his shoulders, Crispin climbed the bank. Ahead lay a small meadow filled with corpses. He walked through them towards the house, now and then treading on the wing tips.

A wooden bridge crossed a ditch into the grounds of the house. Beside it, like a heraldic symbol pointing his way, reared the up-ended wing of a white eagle. The immense plumes with their exquisite modelling reminded him of monumental sculpture, and in the slightly darker light as he approached the cliff the apparent preservation of the birds' plumage made the meadow resemble a vast avian mortuary garden.

As he rounded the house the woman was standing by the trestle table, laying out more feathers to dry. To her left, beside the frame of the gazebo, was what Crispin at first assumed to be a bonfire of white feathers, piled on to a crude wooden framework she had built from the remains of the pergola. An air of dilapidation hung over the house – most of the windows had been broken by the birds during their attacks over the past years, and the garden and yard were filled with litter.

The woman turned to face Crispin. To his surprise she gazed at him with a hard eye, unimpressed by the brigand-like appearance he presented with his cartridge bandoliers, rifle and scarred face. Through the telescope he had guessed her to be elderly, but in fact she was barely more than thirty years old, her white hair as thick and well groomed as the plumage of the dead birds in the fields around them. The rest of her, however, despite the strong figure and firm hands, was as neglected as the house. Her handsome face, devoid of all make-up, seemed to have been deliberately exposed to the cutting winter winds, and the long woollen robe she wore was stained with oil, its frayed hem revealing a pair of worn sandals.

Crispin came to a halt in front of her, for a moment wondering why he was visiting her at all. The few bales of feathers heaped on the pyre and drying on the trestle table seemed no challenge to his authority over the birds – the walk across the meadow had more than reminded him of that. Yet he was aware that something, perhaps their shared experience of the birds, bonded him and the young woman. The empty killing sky, the freighted fields silent in the sun, and the pyre beside them imposed a sense of a common past.

Laying the last of the feathers on the trestle, the woman said, 'They'll dry soon. The sun is warm today. Can you help me?'

Crispin moved forward uncertainly. 'How do you mean? Of course.'

The woman pointed to a section of the rose pergola that was still standing. A rusty saw was embedded in a small groove the woman had managed to cut in one of the uprights. 'Can you cut that down for me?'

Crispin followed her over to the pergola, unslinging his rifle. He pointed to the remains of a pine fence that had collapsed to one side of the old kitchen garden. 'You want wood? That'll burn better.'

'No – I need this frame. It's got to be strong.' She hesitated as Crispin continued to fiddle with his rifle, her voice more defensive. 'Can you do it? The little dwarf couldn't come today. He usually helps me.'

Crispin raised a hand to silence her. 'I'll help you.' He leaned his rifle against the pergola and took hold of the saw, after a few strokes freed it from its groove and made a clean start.

'Thank you.' As he worked the woman stood beside him, looking down with a friendly smile as the cartridge bandoliers began to flap rhythmically to the motion of his arm and chest.

Crispin stopped, reluctant to shed the bandoliers of machine-gun bullets, the badge of his authority. He glanced in the direction of the picket ship, and the woman, taking her cue, said, 'You're the captain? I've seen you on the bridge.'

'Well . . .' Crispin had never heard himself described as the vessel's captain, but the title seemed to carry a certain status. He nodded modestly. 'Crispin,' he said by way of introduction. 'Captain Crispin. Glad to help you.'

'I'm Catherine York.' Holding her white hair to her neck with one hand, the woman smiled again. She pointed to the rusting hulk. 'It's a fine ship.'

Crispin worked away at the saw, wondering whether she was missing the point. When he carried the frame over to the pyre and laid it at the base of the feathers he replaced his bandoliers with calculated effect. The woman appeared not to notice, but a moment later, when she glanced up at the sky, he raised his rifle and went up to her.

'Did you see one? Don't worry, I'll get it.' He tried to follow her eyes as they swept across the sky after some invisible object that seemed to vanish beyond the cliff, but she turned away and began to adjust the feathers mechanically. Crispin gestured at the fields around them, feeling his pulse beat again at the prospect and fear of battle. 'I shot all these . . .'

'What? I'm sorry, what did you say?' The woman looked around. She appeared to have lost interest in Crispin and was vaguely waiting for him to leave.

'Do you want more wood?' Crispin asked. 'I can get some.'

'I have enough.' She touched the feathers on the trestle, then thanked Crispin and walked off into the house, closing the hall door on its rusty hinges.

Crispin made his way across the lawn and through the meadow. The birds lay around him as before, but the memory, however fleeting, of the woman's sympathetic smile made him ignore them. He set off in the launch, pushing away the floating birds with brusque motions of the gaff. The picket ship sat at its moorings, the soggy raft of grey corpses around it. For once the rusting hulk depressed Crispin.

As he climbed the gangway he saw Quimby's small figure on the bridge, wild eyes roving about at the sky. Crispin had expressly forbidden the dwarf to be near the steering helm, though there was little likelihood of the picket ship going anywhere. Irritably he shouted at Quimby to get off the ship.

The dwarf leaped down the threadbare network of ratlines to the deck. He scurried over to Crispin.

'Crisp!' he shouted in his hoarse whisper. 'They saw one! Coming in from the coast! Hassell told me to warn you.'

Crispin stopped. Heart pounding, he scanned the sky out of the sides of his eyes, at the same time keeping a close watch on the dwarf. 'When?'

'Yesterday.' The dwarf wriggled one shoulder, as if trying to dislodge a stray memory. 'Or was it this morning? Anyway, it's coming. Are you ready, Crisp?'

Crispin walked past, one hand firmly on the breech of his rifle. 'I'm always ready,' he rejoined. 'What about you?' He jerked a finger at the house. 'You should have been with the woman. Catherine York. I had to help her. She said she didn't want to see you again.'

'What?' The dwarf scurried about, hands dancing along the rusty rail.

He gave up with an elaborate shrug. 'Ah, she's a strange one. Lost her man, you know, Crisp. And her baby.'

Crispin paused at the foot of the bridge companionway. 'Is that right? How did it happen?'

'A dove killed the man, pulled him to pieces on the roof, then took the baby. A tame bird, mark you.' He nodded when Crispin looked at him sceptically. 'That's it. He was another strange one, that York. Kept this big dove on a chain.'

Crispin climbed on to the bridge and stared across the river at the house. After musing to himself for five minutes he kicked Quimby off the ship, and then spent half an hour checking the gunnery installation. The reported sighting of one of the birds he discounted – no doubt a few strays were still flitting about, searching for their flocks – but the vulnerability of the woman across the river reminded him to take every precaution. Near the house she would be relatively safe, but in the open, during her walks along the beach, she would be an all too easy prey.

It was this undefined feeling of responsibility towards Catherine York that prompted him, later that afternoon, to take the launch out again. A quarter of a mile down-river he moored the craft by a large open meadow, directly below the flight path of the birds as they had flown in to attack the picket ship. Here, on the cool green turf, the dying birds had fallen most thickly. A recent fall of rain concealed the odour of the immense gulls and fulmars lying across each other like angels. In the past Crispin had always moved with pride among this white harvest he had reaped from the sky, but now he hurried down the winding aisles between the birds, a wicker basket under his arm, intent only on his errand.

When he reached the higher ground in the centre of the meadow he placed the basket on the carcass of a dead falcon and began to pluck the feathers from the wings and breasts of the birds lying about him. Despite the rain, the plumage was almost dry. Crispin worked steadily for half an hour, tearing out the feathers with his hands, then carried the basketfuls of plumes down to the launch. As he scurried about the meadow his bent head and shoulders were barely visible above the corpses of the birds.

By the time he set off in the launch the small craft was loaded from bow to stern with the bright plumes. Crispin stood in the steering well, peering over his cargo as he drove up-river. He moored the boat on the beach below the woman's house. A thin trail of smoke rose from the fire, and he could hear Mrs York chopping more kindling.

Crispin walked through the shallow water around the boat, selecting the choicest of the plumes and arranging them around the basket – a falcon's brilliant tail feathers, the mother-of-pearl plumes of a fulmar, the brown breast feathers of an eider. Shouldering the basket, he set off towards the house.

Catherine York was moving the trestle closer to the fire, straightening the plumes as the smoke drifted past them. More feathers had been added to the pyre built on to the frame of the pergola. The outer ones had been woven together to form a firm rim.

Crispin put the basket down in front of her, then stood back. 'Mrs York, I brought these. I thought you might use them.'

The woman glanced obliquely at the sky, then shook her head as if puzzled. Crispin suddenly wondered if she recognized him. 'What are they?'

'Feathers. For over there.' Crispin pointed at the pyre. 'They're the best I could find.'

Catherine York knelt down, her skirt hiding the scuffed sandals. She touched the coloured plumes as if recalling their original owners. 'They are beautiful. Thank you, captain.' She stood up. 'I'd like to keep them, but I need only this kind.'

Crispin followed her hand as she pointed to the white feathers on the trestle. With a curse, he slapped the breech of the rifle.

'Doves! They're all doves! I should have noticed!' He picked up the basket. 'I'll get you some.'

'Crispin . . .' Catherine York took his arm. Her troubled eyes wandered about his face, as if hoping to find some kindly way of warning him off. 'I have enough, thank you. It's nearly finished now.'

Crispin hesitated, waiting for himself to say something to this beautiful white-haired woman whose hands and robe were covered with the soft down of the doves. Then he picked up the basket and made his way back to the launch.

As he sailed across the river to the ship he moved up and down the launch, casting the cargo of feathers on to the water. Behind him, the soft plumes formed a wake.

That night, as Crispin lay in his rusty bunk in the captain's cabin, his dreams of the giant birds who filled the moonlit skies of his sleep were broken by the faint ripple of the air in the rigging overhead, the muffled hoot of an aerial voice calling to itself. Waking, Crispin lay still with his head against the metal stanchion, listening to the faint whoop and swerve around the mast.

Crispin leaped from the bunk. He seized his rifle and raced barefoot up the companionway to the bridge. As he stepped on to the deck, sliding the barrel of the rifle into the air, he caught a last glimpse against the moonlit night of a huge white bird flying away across the river.

Crispin rushed to the rail, trying to steady the rifle enough to get in a shot at the bird. He gave up as it passed beyond his range, its outline masked by the cliff. Once warned, the bird would never return to the ship. A stray, no doubt it was hoping to nest among the masts and rigging.

Shortly before dawn, after a ceaseless watch from the rail, Crispin set off across the river in the launch. Over-excited, he was convinced he had seen it circling above the house. Perhaps it had seen Catherine York asleep through one of the shattered windows. The muffled echo of the engine beat across the water, broken by the floating forms of the dead birds. Crispin crouched forward with the rifle and drove the launch on to the beach. He ran through the darkened meadow, where the corpses lay like silver shadows. He darted into the cobbled yard and knelt by the kitchen door, trying to catch the sounds of the sleeping woman in the room above.

For an hour, as the dawn lifted over the cliff, Crispin prowled around the house. There were no signs of the bird, but at last he came across the mound of feathers mounted on the pergola frame. Peering into the soft grey bowl, he realized that he had caught the dove in the very act of building a nest.

Careful not to waken the woman sleeping above him beyond the cracked panes, he destroyed the nest. With his rifle butt he stove in the sides, then knocked a hole through the woven bottom. Then, happy that he had saved Catherine York from the nightmare of walking from her house the next morning and seeing the bird waiting to attack her from its perch on this stolen nest, Crispin set off through the gathering light and returned to the ship.

For the next two days, despite his vigil on the bridge, Crispin saw no more of the dove. Catherine York remained within the house, unaware of her escape. At night, Crispin would patrol her house. The changing weather, and the first taste of the winter to come, had unsettled the landscape, and during the day Crispin spent more time upon the bridge, uneager to look out on the marshes that surrounded the ship.

On the night of the storm, Crispin saw the bird again. All afternoon the dark clouds had come in from the sea along the river basin, and by evening the cliff beyond the house was hidden by the rain. Crispin was in the bridge-house, listening to the bulkheads groaning as the ship was driven farther into the mud by the wind.

Lightning flickered across the river, lighting the thousands of corpses in the meadows. Crispin leaned on the helm, gazing at the gaunt reflection of himself in the darkened glass, when a huge white face, beaked like his own, swam into his image. As he stared at this apparition, a pair of immense white wings seemed to unfurl themselves from his shoulders. Then this lost dove, illuminated in a flicker of lightning, rose into the gusting wind around the mast, its wings weaving themselves among the steel cables.

It was still hovering there, trying to find shelter from the rain, when Crispin stepped on to the deck and shot it through the heart.

At first light Crispin left the bridge-house and climbed on to the roof. The dead bird hung, its wings outstretched, in a clutter of steel coils beside the lookout's nest. Its mournful face gaped down at Crispin, its expression barely changed since it loomed out of his own reflection at the height of the storm. Now, as the flat wind faded across the water, Crispin watched the house below the cliff. Against the dark vegetation of the meadows and marshes the bird hung like a white cross, and he waited for Catherine York to come to a window, afraid that a sudden gust might topple the dove to the deck.

When Quimby arrived in his coracle two hours later, eager to see the bird, Crispin sent him up the mast to secure the dove to the cross-tree. Dancing about beneath the bird, the dwarf seemed mesmerized by Crispin, doing whatever the latter told him.

'Fire a shot at her, Crisp!' he exhorted Crispin, who stood disconsolately by the rail. 'Over the house, that'll bring her out!'

'Do you think so?' Crispin raised the rifle, ejecting the cartridge whose bullet had destroyed the bird. He watched the bright shell tumble down into the feathery water below. 'I don't know . . . it might frighten her. I'll go over there.'

'That's the way, Crisp . . .' The dwarf scuttled about. 'Bring her back here – I'll tidy it up for you.'

'Maybe I will.'

As he berthed the launch on the beach Crispin looked back at the picket ship, reassuring himself that the dead dove was clearly visible in the distance. In the morning sunlight the plumage shone like snow against the rusting masts.

When he neared the house he saw Catherine York standing in the doorway, her wind-blown hair hiding her face, watching him approach with stern eyes.

He was ten yards from her when she stepped into the house and half closed the door. Crispin began to run, and she leaned out and shouted angrily: 'Go away! Go back to the ship and those dead birds you love so much!'

'Miss Catherine . . .' Crispin stammered to a halt by the door. 'I saved you . . . Mrs York!'

'Saved? Save the birds, captain!'

Crispin tried to speak, but she slammed the door. He walked back through the meadow and punted across the river to the picket ship, unaware of Quimby's insane moon eyes staring down at him from the rail.

'Crisp . . . What's the matter?' For once the dwarf was gentle. 'What happened?'

Crispin shook his head. He gazed up at the dead bird, struggling to find some solution to the woman's last retort. 'Quimby,' he said in a quiet voice to the dwarf, 'Quimby, she thinks she's a bird.'

During the next week this conviction grew in Crispin's bewildered mind, as did his obsession with the dead bird. Looming over him like an immense murdered angel, the dove's eyes seemed to follow him about the ship, reminding him of when it had first appeared, almost from within his own face, in the mirror-glass of the bridge-house.

It was this sense of identity with the bird that was to spur Crispin to his final stratagem.

Climbing the mast, he secured himself to the lookout's nest, and with a hacksaw cut away the steel cables tangled around the dove's body. In the gathering wind the great white form of the bird swayed and dipped, its fallen wings almost knocking Crispin from his perch. At intervals the rain beat across them, but the drops helped to wash away the blood on the bird's breast and the chips of rust from the hacksaw. At last Crispin lowered the bird to the deck, then lashed it to the hatch cover behind the funnel.

Exhausted, he slept until the next day. At dawn, armed with a machete, he began to eviscerate the bird.

Three days later, Crispin stood on the cliff above the house, the picket ship far below him across the river. The hollow carcass of the dove which he wore over his head and shoulders seemed little heavier than a pillow. In the brief spell of warm sunlight he lifted the outstretched wings, feeling their buoyancy and the cutting flow of air through the feathers. A few stronger gusts moved across the crest of the ridge, almost lifting him into the wind, and he stepped closer to the small oak which hid him from the house below.

Against the trunk rested his rifle and bandoliers. Crispin lowered the wings and gazed up at the sky, making certain for the last time that no stray hawk or peregrine was about. The effectiveness of the disguise had exceeded all his hopes. Kneeling on the ground, the wings furled at his sides and the hollowed head of the bird lowered over his face, he felt he completely resembled the dove.

Below him the ground sloped towards the house. From the deck of the picket ship the cliff face had seemed almost vertical, but in fact the ground shelved downwards at a steady but gentle gradient. With luck he might even manage to be airborne for a few steps. However, for most of the way to the house he intended simply to run downhill.

As he waited for Catherine York to appear he freed his right arm from the metal clamp he had fastened to the wing bone of the bird. He reached out to set the safety catch on his rifle. By divesting himself of the weapon and his bandoliers, and assuming the disguise of the bird, he had, as he understood, accepted the insane logic of the woman's mind. Yet the symbolic flight he was about to perform would free not only Catherine York, but himself as well, from the spell of the birds.

A door opened in the house, a broken pane of glass catching the sunlight. Crispin stood up behind the oak, his hands bracing themselves on the wings. Catherine York appeared, carrying something across the yard. She paused by the rebuilt nest, her white hair lifting in the breeze, and adjusted some of the feathers.

Stepping from behind the tree, Crispin walked forward down the slope. Ten yards ahead he reached a patch of worn turf. He began to run, the wings flapping unevenly at his sides. As he gained speed his feet raced across the ground. Suddenly the wings steadied as they gained their purchase on the updraught, and he found himself able to glide, the air rushing past his face.

He was a hundred yards from the house when the woman noticed him. A few moments later, when she had brought her shotgun from the kitchen, Crispin was too busy trying to control the speeding glider in which he had become a confused but jubilant passenger. His voice cried out as he soared across the falling ground, feet leaping in ten-yard strides, the smell of the bird's blood and plumage filling his lungs.

He reached the perimeter of the meadow that ringed the house, crossing the hedge fifteen feet above the ground. He was holding with one hand to the soaring carcass of the dove, his head half-lost inside the skull, when the woman fired twice at him. The first charge went through the tail, but the second shot hit him in the chest, down into the soft grass of the meadow among the dead birds.

Half an hour later, when she saw that Crispin had died, Catherine York walked forward to the twisted carcass of the dove and began to pluck away the choicest plumes, carrying them back to the nest which she was building again for the great bird that would come one day and bring back her son.

· **1966**

# ˎ TOMORROW IS A MILLION YEARS

In the evening the time-winds would blow across the Sea of Dreams, and the silver wreck of the excursion module would loom across the jewelled sand to where Glanville lay in the pavilion by the edge of the reef. During the first week after the crash, when he could barely move his head, he had seen the images of the *Santa Maria* and the *Golden Hind* sailing towards him through the copper sand, the fading light of the sunset illuminating the ornamental casements of the high stern-castles. Later, sitting up in the surgical chair, he had seen the spectral crews of these spectral ships, their dark figures watching him from the quarter-decks. Once, when he could walk again, Glanville went out on to the surface of the lake, his wife guiding his elbow as he hobbled on his stick. Two hundred yards from the module he had suddenly seen an immense ship materialize from the wreck and move through the sand towards them, its square sails lifted by the time-winds. In the cerise light Glanville recognized the two bow anchors jutting like tusks, the tryworks amidships, and the whaling irons and harpoons. Judith held his arm, drawing him back to the pavilion, but Glanville knocked away her hand.

Rolling slowly, the great ship crested silently through the sand, its hull towering above them as if they had been watching from a skiff twenty yards off its starboard bow. As it swept by with a faint sigh of sand, the whisper of the time-winds, Glanville pointed to the three men looking down at them from the quarter-rail, the tallest with stern eyes and a face like biscuit, the second jaunty, the third ruddy and pipe-smoking.

'Can you see them?' Glanville shouted. 'Starbuck, Stubb and Flask, the mates of the *Pequod*!' Glanville pointed to the helm, where a wild-eyed old man gazed at the edge of the reef on which he seemed collision-bent. 'Ahab . . . !' he cried in warning. But the ship had reached the reef, and then in an instant faded across the clinker-like rocks, its mizzen-sail lit for a last moment by the dying light.

'The *Pequod*! My God, you could see the crew, Ishmael and Tashtego . . . Ahab was there, and the mates, Melville's three momentous men! Did you see them, Judith?'

His wife nodded, helping him on towards the pavilion, her frown hidden in the dusk light. Glanville knew perfectly well that she never saw the spectral ships, but nonetheless she seemed to sense that something vast and strange moved across the sand-lake out of the time-winds. For the moment, she was more interested in making certain that he recovered

711

from the long flight and the absurd accident when the excursion module had crashed on landing.

'But why the *Pequod*?' Glanville asked, as they sat in their chairs on the veranda of the pavilion. He mopped his plump, unshaven face with a flowered handkerchief. 'The *Golden Hind* and the *Santa Maria*, yes . . . ships of discovery; Drake circumnavigating the globe has a certain resemblance to ourselves half-crossing the universe – but Crusoe's ship would have been more appropriate, don't you agree?'

'Why?' Judith glanced at the sand inundating the slatted metal floor of the veranda. She filled her glass with soda from the siphon, and then played with the sparkling fluid, watching the bubbles with her severe eyes. 'Because we're marooned?'

'No . . .' Irritated by his wife's reply, Glanville turned to face her. Sometimes her phlegmatic attitude annoyed him – she seemed almost to enjoy deflating his mood of optimism, however forced that might be. 'What I meant was that Crusoe, like ourselves here, made a new world for himself out of the pieces of the old he brought with him. We can do the same, Judith.' He paused, wondering how to re-assert his physical authority, and then said with quiet emphasis: 'We're not marooned.'

His wife nodded, her long face expressionless. Barely moving her head, she looked up at the night sky visible beyond the edge of the awning. High above them, a single point of light traversed the starless sky, its intermittent beacon punctuating its way towards the northern pole. 'No, we're not marooned – not for long, anyway, with that up there. It won't be long at all before Captain Thornwald catches up with us.'

Glanville stared into the bottom of his glass. Unlike his wife, he took little pleasure in the sight of the automatic emergency beacon of the control ship broadcasting their position to the universe at large. 'He'll catch up with us, all right. That's the luck of the thing. Instead of having him always at our heels we'll finally be free of him for ever. They won't send anyone after Thornwald.'

'Perhaps not.' Judith tapped the metal table. 'But how do you propose to get rid of him – don't tell me you're going to be locked together in mortal combat? At the moment you can hardly move one foot after the other.'

Glanville smiled, with an effort ignoring the sarcasm in his wife's voice. Whatever the qualities of skill, shrewdness and even courage, of a kind, that had brought them here, she still regarded him as something of an obscure joke. At times he wondered whether it would have been better to have left her behind. Alone here, on this lost world, he would have had no one to remind him of his sagging, middle-aged figure, his little indecisions and fantasies. He would have been able to sit back in front of the long sunsets and enjoy the strange poetry of the Sea of Dreams.

However, once he had disposed of Captain Thornwald she might at last take him seriously. 'Don't worry, there'll be no mortal combat – we'll let the time-winds blow over him.'

Undeterred, Judith said: 'You'll let one of your spectral ships run him down? But perhaps he won't see them.'

Glanville gazed out at the dark grottoes of the sand-reef that fringed the northern shore of the lake two miles away. Despite its uniformity – the lake-systems covered the entire planet – the flat perspectives of the landscape fascinated him. 'It doesn't matter whether he sees them or not. By the way, the *Pequod* this evening . . . it's a pity you missed Ahab. They were all there, exactly as Melville described them in *Moby Dick*.'

His wife stood up, as if aware that he might begin one of his rhapsodies again. She brushed away the white sand that lay like lace across the blue brocade of her gown. 'I hope you're right. Perhaps you'll see the *Flying Dutchman* next.'

Distracted by his thoughts, Glanville watched her tall figure move away across the gradient of the beach, following the tide-line formed by the sand blown off the lake's surface. The *Flying Dutchman*? A curious remark. By coming to this remote planet they themselves would lose seven years of their lives by time-dilation if they ever chose to return home, by coincidence the period that elapsed while the condemned Dutchman roved the seas . . . Every seven years he would come ashore, free to stay there only if he found the love of a faithful woman.

Was he himself the Dutchman? Perhaps, in a remote sense. Or Thornwald? He and Judith had met during the preliminary inquiries and, incredible though it seemed, there might have been something between them – it was difficult to believe that Thornwald would have pursued them this far, sacrificing all hopes of seniority and promotion, over a minor emigration infringement. The bacterial scattering might be serious on some planets, but they had restricted themselves to arid worlds on an empty edge of the universe.

Glanville looked out at the wreck of the excursion module. For a moment there was a glimmer of royals and top-gallants, as if the entire *Cutty Sark* was about to disgorge itself from the sand. This strange phenomenon, a consequence of the time-sickness brought on by the vast distances of interstellar space, had revealed itself more and more during their long flight. The farther they penetrated into deep space, the greater the nostalgia of the human mind and its eagerness to transform any man-made objects, such as the spaceships in which they travelled, into their archaic forebears. Judith, for some reason, had been immune, but Glanville had seen a succession of extraordinary visions, fragments of the myths and dreams of the Earth's past, reborn out of the dead lakes and fossil seas of the alien worlds.

Judith, of course, not only lacked all imagination but felt no sense of guilt – Glanville's crime, the memory of which he had almost completely repressed, was no responsibility of hers, man and wife though they might be. Besides, the failures of which she silently accused him every day were those of character, more serious in her eyes than embezzlement, grand larceny or even murder. It was precisely this that made possible his plan to deal once and for all with Captain Thornwald.

\*          \*          \*

Three weeks later, when Thornwald arrived, Glanville had recovered completely from the accident. From the top of the sand-reef overhanging the western edge of the lake he watched the police captain's capsule land two hundred yards from the pavilion. Judith stood under the awning on the veranda, one hand raised to ward off the dust kicked up by the retro-jets. She had never questioned Glanville's strategy for dealing with Thornwald, but now and then he had noticed her glancing upwards at the beacon of the control ship, as if calculating the number of days it would take Thornwald to catch up with them. Glanville was surprised by her patience. Once, a week before Thornwald arrived, he almost challenged her to say whether she really believed he would be able to outwit the police captain. By a curious irony, he realized that she probably did but if so, why did she still despise him?

As the starboard hatch of the capsule fell back, Glanville stood up on the edge of the reef and began to wave with both arms. He made his way down the side of the reef, then jumped the last five feet to the lake floor and ran across to the capsule. 'Thornwald! Captain, it's good to see you!'

Framed within the steel collar of his suit, the policeman's tired face looked up at Glanville through the open hatch. He stood up with an effort and accepted Glanville's hand, then climbed down on to the ground. Careful not to turn his back on Glanville, he unzipped his suit and glanced quickly at the pavilion and the wreck of the excursion module.

Glanville strolled to and fro around him. Thornwald's cautious manner, the hand near the weapon in his holster, for some reason amused him. 'Captain, you made a superb landing, beautiful marksmanship – getting here at all, for that matter. You saw the beacon, I suppose, but even so . . .' When Thornwald was about to speak, Glanville rattled on: 'No, of course I didn't leave it on deliberately – damn it, we actually crashed! Can you imagine it, after coming all this way – very nearly broke our necks. Luckily, Judith was all right, not a scratch on her. She'll be glad to see you, Captain.'

Thornwald nodded slowly, his eyes following Glanville's pudgy, sweating figure as it roved about the capsule. A tall, stooped man with a tough, pessimistic face and all the wariness of a long-serving policeman, he seemed somehow unsettled by Glanville's manic gaiety.

Glanville pointed to the pavilion. 'Come on, we'll have lunch, you must be tired out.' He gestured at the sand-lake and the blank sky. 'Nothing much here, I know, but it's restful. After a few days –'

'Glanville!' Thornwald stopped. Face set, he put a hand out as if to touch Glanville's shoulder. 'You realize why I'm here?'

'Of course, Captain.' Glanville gave him an easy smile. 'For heaven's sake, stop looking so serious. I'm not going to escape. There's nowhere to go.'

'As long as you realize that.' Thornwald plodded forward through the top surface of fine sand, his feet placed carefully as if testing the validity of this planet with its euphoric tenant. 'You can have something to eat, then we'll get ready to go back.'

'If you like, Captain. Still, there's no desperate hurry. Seven years here and back, what difference will a few hours or even days make? All those whipper-snappers you left behind you in the department will be chief commissioners now; I wouldn't be in too much of a hurry. Besides, the emigration laws may even have been changed . . .'

Thornwald nodded dourly. Glanville was about to introduce him to Judith, standing quietly on the veranda twenty feet from him, but suddenly Thornwald stopped and glanced across the lake, as if searching for an invisible marksman hidden among the reefs.

'All right?' Glanville asked. Changing the pitch and tempo of his voice, he remarked quietly: 'I call it the Sea of Dreams. We're a long way from home, Captain, remember that. There are strange visions here at sunset. Keep your back turned on them.' He waved at Judith, who was watching them approach with pursed lips. 'Captain Thornwald, my dear. Rescue at last.'

'Of a kind.' She faced Thornwald who stood beside Glanville, as if hesitating to enter the pavilion. 'I hope you feel all this is necessary, Captain. Revenge is a poor motive for justice.'

Glanville cleared his throat. 'Well, yes, my dear, but . . . Come on, Captain, sit down, we'll have a drink. Judith, could you . . . ?'

After a pause she nodded and went into the pavilion.

Glanville made a temporizing gesture. 'A difficult moment, Captain. But as you know, Judith was always rather headstrong.'

Thornwald nodded, watching Glanville as the latter drew the chair around the table. He pointed to the wreck of the excursion module. 'How badly was it damaged? We'll have a look at it later.'

'A waste of time, Captain. It's a complete write-off.'

Thornwald scrutinized the wreck. 'Even so, I'll want to decontaminate it before we leave.'

'Isn't that pointless? – no one will ever come here. The whole planet is dead. Anyway, there's a good deal of fuel in the tanks; if you short a circuit with your sprays the whole thing could go up.' Glanville looked around impatiently. 'Where are those drinks? Judith is . . .'

He started to stand up, and found Thornwald following him to the door of the pavilion. 'It's all right, Captain.'

Thornwald leaned stolidly on the door. He looked down at Glanville's plump, sweating face. 'Let me help you.'

Glanville shrugged and beckoned him forward, but then stopped. 'Captain, for heaven's sake! If I wanted to escape I wouldn't have been waiting for you here. Believe me, I haven't got a gun hidden away in a whisky bottle or something – I just don't want a scene between you and Judith.'

Thornwald nodded, then waited in the doorway. When Glanville returned with the tray he went back to his seat, eyes searching the pavilion and the surrounding beach as if looking for a missing element in a puzzle. 'Glanville, I have to prefer charges against you – you're aware what you face when you get back?'

Glanville shrugged. 'Of course. But after all, the offence was comparatively trivial, wasn't it?' He reached for Thornwald's bulky flight-suit which was spread across the veranda-rail. 'Let me move this out of the sun. Where's Judith gone?'

As Thornwald glanced at the door of the pavilion Glanville reached down to the steel pencil in the right knee of the suit. He withdrew it from the slot, then deliberately dropped it to the metal floor.

'What's this?' he asked. 'A torch?' His thumb pushed back the nozzle and then moved quickly to the spring tab.

'Don't press that!' Thornwald was on his feet. 'It's a radio reflector, you'll fill the place with –' He reached across the table and tried to grasp it from Glanville, then flung up his forearm to protect his face.

A blinding jet of vaporized aluminium suddenly erupted from the nozzle of Glanville's hand, gushing out like a firework. Within two or three seconds its spangled cloud filled the veranda, painting the walls and ceiling. Thornwald kicked aside the table and buried his face in his hands, his hair and forehead covered with the silver paint.

Glanville backed to the steps, flecks of the paint spattering his arms and chest, hosing the jet directly at the policeman. He tossed the canister on to the floor, where its last spurts gusted out into the sunlight, swept up by the convection currents like a swarm of fireflies. Then, head down, Glanville turned and ran towards the edge of the sand-reef fifty yards away.

Two hours later, as he crouched deep in the grottoes of the reef on the west shore of the lake, Glanville watched with amusement as Thornwald's silver-painted figure stepped out of the pavilion into the sunlight. The cloud of vapour above the pavilion had settled, and the drab grey panels of the roof and sides were now a brilliant aluminized silver, shining in the sunlight like a temple. Framed in the doorway was Judith, watching as Thornwald walked slowly towards his capsule. Apart from the two clear handprints across his face, his entire body was covered with the aluminium particles. His hair glittered in the sunlight like silver foil.

'Glanville . . . !' Thornwald's voice, slightly querulous, echoed in the galleries of the reef. The flap of his holster was open, but the weapon still lay within its sheath, and Glanville guessed that he had no intention of trying to track him through the galleries and corridors of the reef. The columns of fused sand could barely support their own weight; every few hours there would be a dull eruption as one or other of the great pillar-systems collapsed into a cloud of dust.

Grinning to himself, Glanville watched Thornwald glance back at the pavilion. Evidently intrigued by this duel between the two men, Judith had sat down on the veranda, watching like some mediaeval lady at a tourney.

The police captain moved towards the reef, his legs stiff and awkward, as if self-conscious of his glittering form. Chortling, Glanville scraped the sand from the curved reef over his head and rubbed it into the flecks of silver paint on his sleeves and trousers. As he drank from the flask of water he had hidden in the reef three days earlier, he glanced at his watch. It was nearly three o'clock – within four hours phantoms would move across the sand-lake. He patted the parcel wrapped in grey plastic sheeting on the ledge beside him.

At seven o'clock the time-winds began to blow across the Sea of Dreams. As the sun fell away behind the western ridges, the long shadows of the sand-reefs crossed the lake-floor, dimming the quartz-veins as if closing off a maze of secret pathways.

Crouched at the foot of the reef, Glanville edged along the beach, his sand-smeared figure barely visible in the darkness. Four hundred yards away, Thornwald sat alone on the veranda of the pavilion, his silver figure illuminated in the last cerise rays of the sun. Watching him across the lake-bed, Glanville assumed that already the timewinds were moving towards him, carrying strange images of ships and phantom seas, perhaps of mermaids and hallucinatory monsters. Thornwald sat stiffly in his chair, one hand on the rail in front of him.

Glanville moved along the beach, picking his way between the veins of frosted quartz. As the wreck of the excursion module and the smaller capsule near by came between himself and the pavilion, he began to see the faint outlines of a low-hulled ship, a schooner or brigantine, with its sails reefed, as if waiting at anchor in some pirate lagoon. Ignoring it, Glanville crept into a shallow fault that crossed the lake, its floor some three feet below the surrounding surface. Catching his breath, he undid the parcel, then carried the object inside it under one arm as he set off towards the glimmering wreck of the module.

Twenty minutes later Glanville stepped out from his vantage point behind the excursion module. Around him rode the spectral hulks of two square-sailed ships, their bows dipping through the warm sand. Intent on the pavilion ahead of him, where the silver figure of Thornwald had stood up like an electrified ghost, Glanville stepped through the translucent image of an anchor-cable that curved down into the surface of the lake in front of him. Holding the object he had taken from the parcel above his head like a lantern, he walked steadily towards the pavilion.

The hulls of the ships rode silently at their anchors behind him as he reached the edge of the lake. Thirty yards away, the silver paint around the pavilion speckled the sand with a sheen of false moonlight, but the remainder of the beach and lake were in a profound darkness. As he walked the last yards to the pavilion with a slow rhythmic stride, Glanville could see clearly Thornwald's tall figure pressed against the wall of the veranda, his appalled face, in the shape of his own hands, staring at the apparition in front of him. As Glanville reached the steps Thornwald made a passive gesture at him, one hand raised towards the pistol lying on the table.

Quickly, Glanville threw aside the object he had carried with him. He seized the pistol before Thornwald could move, then whispered, more to himself than to Thornwald: 'Strange seas, Captain, I warned you . . .' He crouched down and began to back away along the veranda, the pistol levelled at Thornwald's chest.

Then the door on his left opened and before he could move the translucent figure of his wife stepped from the interior of the pavilion and knocked the weapon from his hand.

He turned to her angrily, then shouted at the headless spectre that stepped through him and strode off towards the dark ships moored in the centre of the lake.

Two hours after dawn the next morning Captain Thornwald finished his preparations for departure. In the last minutes he stood on the veranda, gazing out at the even sunlight over the empty lake as he wiped away the last traces of the aluminium paint with a solvent sponge. He looked down at the seated figure of Glanville tied to the chair by the table. Despite the events of the previous night, Glanville now seemed composed and relaxed, a trace even of humour playing about his soft mouth.

Something about this bizarre amiability made Thornwald shudder. He secured the pistol in his holster – another evening by this insane lake and he would be pointing it at his own head.

'Captain . . .' Glanville glanced at him with docile eyes, then shrugged his fat shoulders inside the ropes. 'When are you going to untie these? We'll be leaving soon.'

Thornwald threw the sponge on to the silver sand below the pavilion. '*I'll* be going soon, Glanville. You're staying here.' When Glanville began to protest, he said: 'I don't think there's much point in your leaving. As you said, you've built your own little world here.'

'But . . .' Glanville searched the captain's face. 'Frankly, Thornwald, I can't understand you. Why did you come here in the first place, then? Where's Judith, by the way? She's around here somewhere.'

Thornwald paused, steeling himself against the name and the memory of the previous night. 'Yes, she's around here, all right.' As if testing some unconscious element of Glanville's memory, he said clearly: 'She's in the module, as a matter of fact.'

'The module?' Glanville pulled at his ropes, then squinted over his shoulder into the sunlight. 'But I told her not to go there. When's she coming back?'

'She'll be back, don't worry. This evening, I imagine, when the time-winds blow, though I don't want to be here when she comes. This sea of yours had bad dreams, Glanville.'

'What do you mean?'

Thornwald walked across the veranda. 'Glanville, have you any idea why I'm here, why I've hunted you all this way?'

'God only knows – something to do with the emigration laws.'

'Emigration laws?' Thornwald shook his head. 'Any charges there would be minor.' After a pause, he said: 'Murder, Glanville.'

Glanville looked up with real surprise. 'Murder? You're out of your mind! Of whom, for heaven's sake?'

Thornwald patted the raw skin around his chin. The pale image of his hands still clung to his face. 'Of your wife.'

'Judith? But she's here, you idiot! You saw her yourself when you arrived!'

'*You* saw her, Glanville. I didn't. But I realized that you'd brought her here with you when you started playing her part, using that mincing crazy voice of yours. You weren't very keen on my going out to the module. Then, last night, you brought something from it for me.'

Thornwald walked across the veranda, averting his eyes from the wreck of the module. He remembered the insane vision he had seen the previous evening as he sat watching for Glanville, waiting for this madman who had absconded with the body of his murdered wife. The time-winds had carried across to him the image of a spectral ship whose rotting timbers had formed a strange portcullis in the evening sun – a dungeon-grate. Then, suddenly, he had seen a terrifying apparition walking across this sea of blood towards him, the nightmare commander of this ship of Hell, a tall woman with the slow rhythmic stride of his own requiem. '*Her locks were yellow as gold . . . the nightmare life-in-death was she, who thicks man's blood with cold.*' Aghast at the sight of Judith's head on this lamia, he had barely recognized Glanville, her mad Mariner, bearing her head like a wild lantern before he snatched the pistol.

Glanville flexed his shoulders against the ropes. 'Captain, I don't know about Judith . . . she's not too happy here, and we've never got on with just ourselves for company. I'd like to come with you.'

'I'm sorry, Glanville, there's not much point – you're in the right place here.'

'But, Captain, aren't you exceeding your authority? If there is a murder charge . . .'

'Not "captain", Glanville – "commissioner". I was promoted before I left, and that gives me absolute discretion in these cases. I think this planet is remote enough; no one's likely to come here and disturb you.'

He went over to Glanville and looked down at him, then took a clasp knife from his pocket and laid it on the table. 'You should be able to get a hand around that if you stand up. Goodbye, Glanville, I'll leave you here in your gilded hell.'

'But Thornwald . . . Commissioner!' Glanville swung himself round in the chair. 'Where's Judith? Call her.'

Thornwald glanced back across the sunlight. 'I can't, Glanville. But you'll see her soon. This evening, when the time-winds blow, they'll bring her back to you, a dead woman from the dead sea.'

He set off towards the capsule across the jewelled sand.

**˙ 1966**

# THE ASSASSINATION OF JOHN FITZGERALD KENNEDY CONSIDERED AS A DOWNHILL MOTOR RACE

*Author's note. – The assassination of President Kennedy on November 22nd, 1963, raised many questions, not all of which were answered by the Report of the Warren Commission. It is suggested that a less conventional view of the events of that grim day may provide a more satisfactory explanation. In particular, Alfred Jarry's* The Crucifixion Considered as an Uphill Bicycle Race *gives us a useful lead.*

Oswald was the starter.

From his window above the track he opened the race by firing the starting gun. It is believed that the first shot was not properly heard by all the drivers. In the following confusion Oswald fired the gun two more times, but the race was already under way.

Kennedy got off to a bad start.

There was a governor in his car and its speed remained constant at about fifteen miles an hour. However, shortly afterwards, when the governor had been put out of action, the car accelerated rapidly, and continued at high speed along the remainder of the course.

The visiting teams. As befitting the inauguration of the first production car race through the streets of Dallas, both the President and the Vice-President participated. The Vice-President, Johnson, took up his position behind Kennedy on the starting line. The concealed rivalry between the two men was of keen interest to the crowd. Most of them supported the home driver, Johnson.

The starting point was the Texas Book Depository, where all bets were placed on the Presidential race. Kennedy was an unpopular contestant with the Dallas crowd, many of whom showed outright hostility. The deplorable incident familiar to us all is one example.

The course ran downhill from the Book Depository, below an overpass, then onto the Parkland Hospital and from there to Love Air Field. It is one of the most hazardous courses in downhill motor-racing, second only to the Sarajevo track discontinued in 1914.

Kennedy went downhill rapidly. After the damage to the governor the car shot forward at high speed. An alarmed track official attempted to mount the car, which continued on its way, cornering on two wheels.

Turns. Kennedy was disqualified at the Hospital, after taking a turn for the worse. Johnson now continued the race in the lead, which he maintained to the finish.

The flag. To signify the participation of the President in the race Old Glory was used in place of the usual chequered square. Photographs of Johnson receiving his prize after winning the race reveal that he had decided to make the flag a memento of his victory.

Previously, Johnson had been forced to take a back seat, as his position on the starting line behind the President indicates. Indeed, his attempts to gain a quick lead on Kennedy during the false start were forestalled by a track steward, who pushed Johnson to the floor of his car.

In view of the confusion at the start of the race, which resulted in Kennedy, clearly expected to be the winner on past form, being forced to drop out at the Hospital turn, it has been suggested that the hostile local crowd, eager to see a win by the home driver Johnson, deliberately set out to stop him completing the race. Another theory maintains that the police guarding the track were in collusion with the starter, Oswald. After he finally managed to give the send-off Oswald immediately left the race, and was subsequently apprehended by track officials.

Johnson had certainly not expected to win the race in this way. There were no pit stops.

Several puzzling aspects of the race remain. One is the presence of the President's wife in the car, an unusual practice for racing drivers. Kennedy, however, may have maintained that as he was in control of the ship of state he was therefore entitled to captain's privileges.

The Warren Commission. The rake-off on the book of the race. In their report, prompted by widespread complaints of foul play and other irregularities, the syndicate laid full blame on the starter, Oswald.

Without doubt Oswald badly misfired. But one question still remains unanswered: who loaded the starting gun?

**˙ 1966**

# CRY HOPE, CRY FURY!

Again last night, as the dusk air moved across the desert from Vermilion Sands, I saw the faint shiver of rigging among the reefs, a topmast moving like a silver lantern through the rock spires. Watching from the veranda of my beach-house, I followed its course towards the open sand-sea, and saw the spectral sails of this spectral ship. Each evening I had seen the same yacht, this midnight schooner that slipped its secret moorings and rolled across the painted sea. Last night a second yacht set off in pursuit from its hiding place among the reefs, at its helm a pale-haired steerswoman with the eyes of a sad Medea. As the two yachts fled across the sand-sea I remembered when I had first met Hope Cunard, and her strange affair with the Dutchman, Charles Rademaeker . . .

Every summer during the season at Vermilion Sands, when the town was full of tourists and avant-garde film companies, I would close my office and take one of the beach-houses by the sand-sea five miles away at Ciraquito. Here the long evenings made brilliant sunsets of the sky and desert, crossing the sails of the sand-yachts with hieroglyphic shadows, signatures of all the strange ciphers of the desert sea. During the day I would take my yacht, a Bermuda-rigged sloop, and sail towards the dunes of the open desert. The strong thermals swept me along on a wake of gilded sand.

Hunting for rays, I sometimes found myself carried miles across the desert, beyond sight of the coastal reefs that presided like eroded deities over the hierarchies of sand and wind. I would drive on after a fleeing school of rays, firing the darts into the overheated air and losing myself in an abstract landscape composed of the flying rays, the undulating dunes and the triangles of the sails. Out of these materials, the barest geometry of time and space, came the bizarre figures of Hope Cunard and her retinue, like illusions born of that sea of dreams.

One morning I set out early to hunt down a school of white sand-rays I had seen far across the desert the previous day. For hours I moved over the firm sand, avoiding the sails of other yachtsmen, my only destination the horizon. By noon I was beyond sight of any landmarks, but I had found the white rays and sped after them through the rising dunes. The twenty rays flew on ahead, as if leading me to some unseen destination.

The dunes gave way to a series of walled plains crossed by quartz veins.

722

Skirting a wide ravine whose ornamented mouth gaped like the door of a half-submerged cathedral, I felt the yacht slide to one side, a puncture in its starboard tyre. The air seemed to gild itself around me as I lowered the sail.

Kicking the flaccid tyre, I took stock of the landscape – submerged sand-reefs, an ocean of dunes, and the shell of an abandoned yacht half a mile away near the jagged mouth of a quartz vein that glittered at me like the jaws of a jewelled crocodile. I was twenty miles from the coast and my only supplies were a vacuum flask of iced Martini in the sail locker.

The rays, directed by some mysterious reflex, had also paused, settling on the crest of a nearby dune. Arming myself with the spear-gun, I set off towards the wreck, hoping to find a pump in its locker.

The sand was like powdered glass. Six hundred yards further on, when the raffia soles had been cut from my shoes, I turned back. Rather than exhaust myself, I decided to rest in the shade of the mainsail and walk back to Ciraquito when darkness came. Behind me, my feet left bloody prints in the sand.

I was sitting against the mast, bathing my torn feet in the cold Martini, when a large white ray appeared in the air overhead. Detaching itself from the others, who sat quietly on a distant crest, it had come back to inspect me. With wings fully eight feet wide, and a body as large as a man's, it flew monotonously around me as I sipped at the last of the lukewarm Martini. Despite its curiosity, the creature showed no signs of wanting to attack me.

Ten minutes later, when it still circled overhead, I took the spear-gun from the locker and shot it through its left eye. Transfixed by the steel bolt, its crashing form drove downwards into the sail, tearing it from the mast, and plunged through the rigging on to the deck. Its wing struck my head like a blow from the sky.

For hours I lay in the empty sand-sea, burned by the air, the giant ray my dead companion. Time seemed suspended at an unchanging noon, the sky full of mock suns, but it was probably in the early afternoon when I felt an immense shadow fall across the yacht. I lifted myself over the corpse beside me as a huge sand-schooner, its silver bowsprit as long as my own craft, moved through the sand on its white tyres. Their faces hidden by their dark glasses, the crew watched me from the helm.

Standing with one hand on the cabin rail, the brass portholes forming haloes at her feet, was a tall, narrow-hipped woman with blonde hair so pale she immediately reminded me of the Ancient Mariner's Nightmare Life-in-Death. Her eyes gazed at me like dark magnolias. Lifted by the wind, her opal hair, like antique silver, made a chasuble of the air.

Unsure whether this strange craft and its crew were an apparition, I raised the empty Martini flask to the woman. She looked down at me with eyes crossed by disappointment. Two members of the crew ran over to me. As they pulled the body of the sand-ray off my legs

I stared at their faces. Although smooth-shaven and sunburnt, they resembled masks.

This was my rescue by Hope Cunard. Resting in the cabin below, while one of the crew wrapped the wounds on my feet, I could see her pale-haired figure through the glass roof. Her preoccupied face gazed across the desert as if searching for some far more important quarry than myself.

She came into the cabin half an hour later. She sat down on the bunk at my feet, touching the white plaster with a curious hand.

'Robert Melville – are you a poet? You were talking about the Ancient Mariner when we found you.'

I gestured vaguely. 'It was a joke. On myself.' I could hardly tell this remote but beautiful young woman that I had first seen her as Coleridge's nightmare witch, and added: 'I killed a sand-ray that was circling my yacht.'

She played with the jade pendants lying in emerald pools in the folds of her white dress. Her eyes presided over her pensive face like troubled birds. Apparently taking my reference to the Mariner with complete seriousness, she said: 'You can rest at Lizard Key until you're better. My brother will mend your yacht for you. I'm sorry about the rays – they mistook you for someone else.'

As she sat there, staring through the porthole, the great schooner swept silently over the jewelled sand, the white rays moving a few feet above the ground in our wake. Later I realized that they had brought back the wrong prey for their mistress.

Within two hours we reached Lizard Key where I was to stay for the next three weeks. Rising out of the thermal rollers, the island seemed to float upon the air, the villa with its terrace and jetty barely visible in the haze. Surrounded on three sides by the tall minarets of the sand-reefs, both villa and island had sprung from some mineral fantasy of the desert. Rock spires rose beside the pathway to the villa like cypresses, pieces of wild sculpture growing around them.

'When my father first found the island it was full of gila monsters and basilisks,' Hope explained as I was helped up the pathway. 'We come here every summer now to sail and paint.'

At the terrace we were greeted by the two other tenants of this private paradise – Hope Cunard's half-brother, Foyle, a young man with white hair brushed forward over his forehead, a heavy mouth and pocked cheeks, who stared down at me from the balcony like some moody beach Hamlet; and Hope's secretary, Barbara Quimby, a plain-faced sphinx in a black bikini with bored eyes like two-way mirrors.

Together they watched me being brought up the steps behind Hope. The look of expectancy on their faces changed to polite indifference the moment I was introduced. Almost before Hope could finish describing my rescue they wandered off to the beach-chairs at the end of the terrace.

During the next few days, as I lay on a divan near by, I had more time to examine this strange menage. Despite their dependence upon Hope, who had inherited the island villa from her father, their attitude seemed to be that of palace conspirators, with their private humour and secret glances. Hope, however, was unaware of these snide asides. Like the atmosphere within the villa itself, her personality lacked all focus and her real attention was elsewhere.

Whom had Foyle and Barbara Quimby expected Hope to bring back? What navigator of the sand-sea was Hope Cunard searching for in her schooner with her flock of white rays? To begin with I saw little of her, though now and then she would stand on the roof of her studio and feed the rays that flew across to her from their eyries in the rock spires. Each morning she sailed off in the schooner, her opal-haired figure with its melancholy gaze scanning the desert sea. The afternoons she spent alone in her studio, working on her paintings. She made no effort to show me any of her work, but in the evenings, as the four of us had dinner together, she would stare at me over her liqueur as if seeing my profile within one of her paintings.

'Shall I do a portrait of you, Robert?' she asked one morning. 'I see you as the Ancient Mariner, with a white ray around your neck.'

I covered the plaster on my feet with the dragon-gold dressing gown – left behind, I assumed, by one of her lovers. 'Hope, you're making a myth out of me. I'm sorry I killed one of your rays, but believe me, I did it without thinking.'

'So did the Mariner.' She moved around me, one hand on hip, the other touching my lips and chin as if feeling the contours of some antique statue. 'I'll do a portrait of you reading Maldoror.'

The previous evening I had treated them to an extended defence of the surrealists, showing off for Hope and ignoring Foyle's bored eyes as he lounged on his heavy elbows. Hope had listened closely, as if unsure of my real identity.

As I looked at the empty surface of the fresh canvas she ordered to be brought down from her studio, I wondered what image of me would emerge from its blank pigments. Like all paintings produced at Vermilion Sands at that time, it would not actually need the exercise of the painter's hand. Once the pigments had been selected, the photosensitive paint would produce an image of whatever still life or landscape it was exposed to. Although a lengthy process, requiring an exposure of at least four or five days, it had the immense advantage that there was no need for the subject's continuous presence. Given a few hours each day, the photosensitive pigments would anneal themselves into the contours of a likeness.

This discontinuity was responsible for the entire charm and magic of these paintings. Instead of a mere photographic replica, the movements of the sitter produced a series of multiple projections, perhaps with the analytic forms of cubism, or, less severely, a pleasant impressionistic blurring. However, these unpredictable variations on the face and form of the sitter were often disconcerting in their perception of character. The running of outlines, or separation of tonalities, could reveal tell-tale lines in the texture of skin and features, or generate strange swirls in the sitter's eyes like the epileptic spirals in the last demented landscapes of Van Gogh. These unfortunate effects were all too easily reinforced by any nervous or anticipatory movements of the sitter.

The likelihood that my own portrait would reveal more of my feelings for Hope than I cared to admit occurred to me as the canvas was set up in the library. I lay back stiffly on the sofa, waiting for the painting to be exposed, when Hope's half-brother appeared, a second canvas between his outstretched hands.

'My dear sister, you've always refused to sit for me.' When Hope started to protest Foyle brushed her aside. 'Melville, do you realize that she's never sat for a portrait in her life! Why, Hope? Don't tell me you're frightened of the canvas? Let's see you at last in your true guise.'

'Guise?' Hope looked up at him with wary eyes. 'What are you playing at, Foyle? That canvas isn't a witch's mirror.'

'Of course not, Hope.' Foyle smiled at her. 'All it can tell is the truth. Don't you agree, Barbara?'

Her eyes hidden behind her dark glasses, Miss Quimby nodded promptly. 'Absolutely. Miss Cunard, it will be fascinating to see what comes out. I'm sure you'll be very beautiful.'

'Beautiful?' Hope stared down at the canvas resting at Foyle's feet. For the first time she seemed to be making a conscious effort to take command of herself and the villa at Lizard Key. Then, accepting Foyle's challenge, and refusing to be outfaced by his broken-lipped sneer, she said: 'All right, Foyle. I'll sit for you. My first portrait – you may be surprised what it sees in me.'

Little did we realize what nightmare fish would swim to the surface of these mirrors.

During the next few days our portraits emerged like pale ghosts from the paintings. Each afternoon I would see Hope in the library, when she would sit for her portrait and listen to me reading from Maldoror, but already she was only interested in watching the deserted sand-sea. Once, when she was away, sailing the empty dunes with her white rays, I hobbled up to her studio. There I found a dozen of her paintings mounted on trestles in the windows, looking out on the desert below. Sentinels watching for Hope's phantom mariner, they revealed in monotonous detail the contours and texture of the empty landscape.

By comparison, the two portraits developing in the library were far more interesting. As always, they recapitulated in reverse, like some bizarre embryo, a complete phylogeny of modern art, a regression through the principal schools of the twentieth century. After the first liquid ripples and motion of a kinetic phase, they stabilized into the block colours of the hard-edge school, and from there, as a thousand arteries of colour irrigated the canvas, into a brilliant replica of Jackson Pollock. These coalesced into the crude forms of late Picasso, in which Hope appeared as a Junoesque madonna with massive shoulders and concrete face, and then through surrealist fantasies of anatomy into the multiple outlines of futurism and cubism. Ultimately an impressionist period emerged, lasting a few hours, a roseate sea of powdery light in which we seemed like a placid domestic couple in the suburban bowers of Monet and Renoir.

Watching this reverse evolution, I hoped for something in the style of Gainsborough or Reynolds, a standing portrait of Hope wearing floral scarlet under an azure sky, a pale-skinned English beauty in the grounds of her county house.

Instead, we plunged backwards into the netherworld of Balthus and Gustave Moreau.

As the bizarre outlines of my own figure emerged I was too surprised to notice the equally strange elements in Hope's portrait. At first glance the painting had produced a faithful if stylized likeness of myself seated on the sofa, but by some subtle emphasis of design the scene was totally transformed. The purple curtain draped behind the sofa resembled an immense velvet sail, collapsed against the deck of a becalmed ship, while the spiral bolster emerged as an ornamental prow. Most striking of all, the white lace cushions I lay against appeared as the plumage of an enormous sea-bird, hung around my shoulders like the anchor fallen from the sky. My own expression, of bitter pathos, completed the identification.

'The Ancient Mariner again,' Hope said, weighing my copy of Maldoror in her hand as she sauntered around the canvas. 'Fate seems to have type-cast you, Robert. Still, that's the role I've always seen you in.'

'Better than the Flying Dutchman, Hope?'

She turned sharply, a nervous tic in one corner of her mouth. 'Why did you say that?'

'Hope, who are you looking for? I may have come across him.'

She walked away from me to the window. At the far end of the terrace Foyle was playing some rough game with the sand-rays, knocking them from the air with his heavy hands and then pitching them out over the rock spires. The long stings whipped at his pock-marked face.

'Hope . . .' I went over to her. 'Perhaps it's time I left. There's no point in my staying here. They've repaired the yacht.' I pointed to the sloop moored against the quay, fresh tyres on its wheels. 'Besides . . .'

'No! Robert, you're still reading Maldoror.' Hope gazed at me with her over-large eyes, carrying out this microscopy of my face as if waiting for some absent element in my character to materialize.

For an hour I read to her, more as a gesture to calm her. For some reason she kept searching the painting which bore my veiled likeness as the Mariner, as if this image concealed some other sailor of the sand-sea.

When she had gone, hunting across the dunes in her schooner, I went over to her own portrait. It was then that I realized that yet another intruder had appeared in this house of illusions.

The portrait showed Hope in a conventional pose, seated like any heiress on a brocaded chair. The eye was drawn to her opal hair lying like a soft harp on her strong shoulders, and to her firm mouth with its slight reflective dip at the corners. What Hope and I had not noticed was the presence of a second figure in the painting. Standing against the skyline on the terrace behind Hope was the image of a man in a white jacket, his head lowered to reveal the bony plates of his forehead. The watery outline of his figure – the hands hanging at his sides were pale smudges – gave him the appearance of a man emerging from a drowned sea, strewn with blanched weeds and algae.

Astonished by this spectre materializing in the background of the painting, I waited until the next morning to see if it was some aberration of light and pigment. But the figure was there even more strongly, the bony features emerging through the impasto. The isolated eyes cast their dark gaze across the room. As I read to Hope after lunch I waited for her to comment on this strange intruder. Someone, plainly not her half-brother, was spending at least an hour each day before the canvas in order to imprint his image on its surface.

As Hope stood up to leave, the man's pensive face with its fixed eyes caught her attention. 'Robert – you have some kind of wild magic! You're there again!'

But I knew the man was not myself. The white jacket, the bony forehead and hard mouth were signatures of a separate subject. After Hope left to walk along the beach I went up to her studio and examined the canvases that kept watch for her on the landscape.

Sure enough, in the two paintings that faced the reefs to the south I found the mast of a waiting ship half-concealed among the sand-bars.

Each morning the figure emerged more clearly, its watching eyes seeming to come nearer, One evening, before going to bed, I locked the windows on to the terrace and draped a curtain over the painting. At midnight I heard something move along the terrace, and found the library windows swinging in the cold air, the curtain drawn back from Hope's portrait. In the painting the man's strong but melancholy face glared down at me with an almost spectral intensity. I ran on to the terrace. Through the powdery light a man's muffled figure moved with firm steps along the beach. The white rays revolved in the dim air over his head.

Five minutes later the white-haired figure of Foyle slouched from the darkness. His thick mouth moved in a grimace of morose humour as he shuffled past. On his black silk slippers there were no traces of sand.

Shortly before dawn I stood in the library, staring back at the watching eyes of this phantom visitor who came each night to keep his vigil by Hope's picture. Taking out my handkerchief, I wiped his face from the canvas, and for two hours stood with my own face close to the painting. Quickly the blurred paint took on my own features, the pigments moving to their places in a convection of tonalities. A travesty appeared before me, a man in a white yachtsman's jacket with strong shoulders and high forehead, the physique of some intelligent man of action, on which were superimposed my own plump features and brush moustache.

The paint annealed, the first light of the false dawn touching the sand-blown terrace.

'Charles!'

Hope Cunard stepped through the open window, her white gown shivering around her naked body like a tremulous wraith. She stood beside me, staring at my face on the portrait.

'So it *is* you. Robert, Charles Rademaeker came back as you ... The sand-sea brings us strange dreams.'

Five minutes later, as we moved arm in arm along the corridor to her bedroom, we entered an empty room. From a cabinet Hope took a white yachting-jacket. The linen was worn and sand-stained. Dried blood marked a bullet-hole in its waist.

I wore it like a target.

The image of Charles Rademaeker hovered in Hope's eyes as she sat on her bed like a tired dream-walker and watched me seal the windows of her bedroom.

During the days that followed, as we sailed the sand-sea together, she told me something of her affair with Charles Rademaeker, this Dutchman, recluse and intellectual who wandered across the desert in his yacht cataloguing the rare fauna of the dunes. Drifting out of the dusk air with a broken yard two years earlier, he had dropped anchor at Lizard Key. Coming ashore for cocktails, his stay had lasted for several weeks, a bizarre love-idyll between himself and this shy and beautiful painter that came to a violent end. What happened Hope never made clear. At times, as I wore the blood-stained jacket with its bullet-hole, I guessed that she had shot him, perhaps while she sat for a portrait. Evidently something strange had occurred to a canvas, as if it had revealed to Rademaeker some of the unstated elements he had begun to suspect in Hope's character. After their tragic climax, when Rademaeker had either been killed or escaped, Hope searched the sand-sea for him each summer in her white schooner.

Now Rademaeker had returned – whether from the desert or the dead – cast up from the fractured sand in my own person. Did Hope really believe that I was her reincarnated lover? Sometimes at night, as she lay beside me in the cabin, the reflected light of the quartz veins moving over her breasts like necklaces, she would talk to me as if completely aware of my separate identity. Then, after we had made love, she would deliberately keep me from sleeping, as if disturbed by even this attempt to leave her, and would call me Rademaeker, her clouded face that of a neurotic and disintegrating woman. At these moments I could understand why Foyle and Barbara Quimby had retreated into their private world.

As I look back now, I think I merely provided Hope with a respite from her obsession with Rademaeker, a chance to live out her illusion in this strange emotional pantomime. Meanwhile Rademaeker himself waited for us nearby in the secret places of the desert.

One evening I took Hope sailing across the dark sand-sea. I told the crew to switch on the rigging lights and the decorated bulbs around the deck awning. Driving this ship of light across the black sand, I stood with Hope by the stern rail, my arm around her waist. Asleep as she stood there, her head lay on my shoulder. Her opal hair lifted in the dark wake like the skeleton of some primeval bird.

An hour later, as we reached Lizard Key, I saw a white schooner slip its anchor somewhere among the sand-reefs and head away into the open sea.

Only Hope's half-brother was now left to remind me of my precarious hold on both Hope and the island. Foyle had kept out of my way, playing his private games among the rock spires below the terrace. Now and then, when he saw us walking arm in arm, he would look up from his beach chair with droll but wary eyes.

One morning, soon after I had suggested to Hope that she send her half-brother and Miss Quimby back to her house in Red Beach, Foyle sauntered into the library. I noticed the marked jauntiness of his manner. One hand pressed to his heavy mouth, he gestured sceptically at the portraits of Hope and myself. 'First the Ancient Mariner, now the Flying Dutchman – for a bad sailor you're playing an awful lot of sea roles, Melville. Thirty days in an open divan, eh? What are you playing next – Captain Ahab, Jonah?'

Barbara Quimby came up behind him, and the two of them smirked down at me, Foyle with his ugly faun's head.

'What about Prospero?' I rejoined evenly. 'This island is full of visions. With you as Caliban, Foyle.'

Nodding to himself at this, Foyle strolled up to the paintings. A large hand sketched in obscene outlines. Barbara Quimby began to laugh. Arms around each other's waists, they left together. Their tittering voices merged with the cries of the sand-rays wheeling above the rock spires in the blood-red air.

Shortly afterwards, the first curious changes began to occur to our portraits. That evening, as we sat together in the library, I noticed a slight but distinct alteration in the planes of Hope's face on the canvas, a pock-like disfigurement of the skin. The texture of her hair had altered, taking on a yellowish sheen.

This transformation was even more pronounced the following day. The eyes in the painting had developed a squint, as if the canvas had begun to recognize some imbalance within Hope's own gaze. I turned to the portrait of myself. Here, too, a remarkable change was taking place. My face had begun to develop a snout-like nose. The heavy flesh massed around the lips and nostrils, and the eyes were becoming smaller, submerged in the rolls of fat. Even my clothes had changed their texture, the black and white checks of my silk shirt resembling the suit of some bizarre harlequin.

By the next morning this ugly metamorphosis was so startling that even Hope would have noticed it. As I stood in the dawn light, the figures that looked down at me were those of some monstrous saturnalia. Hope's hair was now a bright yellow. The curled locks framed a face like a powdered skull. As for myself, my pig-snouted face resembled a nightmare visage from the black landscapes of Hieronymus Bosch.

I drew the curtain across the paintings, and then examined my mouth and eyes in the mirror. Was this mocking travesty how Hope and I really appeared? I decided that the pigments were faulty – Hope rarely renewed her stock – and were producing these diseased images of ourselves. After breakfast we dressed in our yachting clothes and went down to the quay. I said nothing to Hope. All day we sailed within sight of the island, not returning until the evening.

Shortly after midnight, as I lay beside Hope in her bedroom below the studio, I was woken by the white rays whooping through the darkness across the windows. They circled like agitated beacons. In the studio, careful not to wake Hope, I searched the canvases by the windows. In one I found the fresh image of a white ship, its sails concealed in a cove half a mile from the island.

So Rademaeker had returned, his presence in some way warping the pigments in our portraits. Convinced at the time by this insane logic, I drove my fists through the canvas, obliterating the image of the ship. My hands and arms smeared with wet paint, I went down to the bedroom. Hope slept on the crossed pillows, hands clasped over her breasts.

I took the automatic pistol which she kept in her bedside table. Through the window the white triangle of Rademaeker's sail rose into the night air as he raised his anchor.

Halfway down the staircase I could see into the library. Arc lights had been set up on the floor. They bathed the canvases in their powerful light, accelerating the motion of the pigments. In front of the paintings, grimacing in obscene poses, were two creatures from a nightmare. The taller wore a black robe like a priest's cassock, a pig's papier-mâché mask on his head. Beside him was a woman in a yellow wig with a powdered face, bright lips and eyes. Together they primped and preened in front of the paintings.

Kicking back the door, I had a full glimpse of these nightmare figures. On the paintings the flesh ran like overheated wax, the images of Hope and myself taking up their own obscene pose. Beyond the blaze of arc lights the woman in the yellow wig slipped from the curtains on to the terrace. As I stepped over the cables I was aware briefly of a man's cloaked shoulders behind me. Something struck me below the ear. I fell to my knees, and the black robes swept over me to the window.

'Rademaeker!' Holding a paint-smeared hand to my neck, I stumbled over the pewter statuette that had struck me and ran out on to the terrace. The frantic rays whipped through the darkness like shreds of luminous spit. Below me, two figures ran down among the rock spires towards the beach.

Almost exhausted by the time I reached the beach, I walked clumsily across the dark sand, eyes stinging from the paint on my hands. Fifty yards from the beach the white sails of an immense sand-schooner rose into the night air, its bowsprit pointing towards me.

Lying on the sand at my feet were the remains of a yellow wig, a pig's plaster snout and the tattered cassock. Trying to pick them up, I fell to my knees. 'Rademaeker . . . !'

A foot struck my shoulder. A slim, straight-backed man wearing a yachtsman's cap stared down at me with irritated eyes. Although he was smaller than I had imagined, I immediately recognized his sparse, melancholy face.

He pulled me to my feet with a strong hand. He gestured at the mask and costume, and at my paint-smeared arms.

'Now, what's this nonsense? What games are you people playing?'

'Rademaeker . . .' I dropped the yellow-locked wig on to the sand. 'I thought it was –'

'Where's Hope?' His trim jaw lifted as he scanned the villa. 'Those rays . . . Is she here? What is this – a black mass?'

'Damn nearly.' I glanced along the deserted beach, illuminated by the light reflected off the great sails of the schooner. I realized whom I had seen posturing in front of the canvas. 'Foyle and the girl! Rademaeker, they were there –'

Already he was ahead of me up the path, only pausing to shout to his two crewmen watching from the bows of the yacht. I ran after him, wiping the paint off my face with the wig. Rademaeker darted away from the path to take a short cut to the terrace. His compact figure moved swiftly among the rock spires, slipping between the sonic statues growing from the fused sand.

When I reached the terrace he was already standing in the darkness by the library windows, gazing in at the brilliant light. He removed his cap with a careful gesture, like a swain paying court to his sweetheart. His smooth hair, dented by the cap brim, gave him a surprisingly youthful appearance, unlike the hard-faced desert rover I had visualized. As he stood there watching Hope, whose white-robed figure was reflected in the open windows, I could see him in the same stance on his secret visits to the island, gazing for hours at her portrait.

'Hope . . . let me –'

Rademaeker threw down his cap and ran forward. A gunshot roared out, its impact breaking a pane in the french windows. The sound boomed among the rock spires, startling the rays into the air. Pushing back the velvet curtains, I stepped into the room.

Rademaeker's hands were on the brocaded sofa. He moved quietly, trying to reach Hope before she noticed him. Her back to us, she stood by the painting with the pistol in her hand.

Over-excited by the intense light from the arc lamps, the pigments had almost boiled off the surface of the canvas. The livid colours of Hope's pus-filled face ran like putrefying flesh. Beside her the pig-faced priest in my own image presided over her body like the procurator of hell.

Her eyes like ice, Hope turned to face Rademaeker and myself. She stared at the yellow wig in my hands, and at the paint smeared over my arms. Her face was empty. All expression had slipped from it as if in an avalanche.

The first shot had punctured the portrait of herself. Already the paint was beginning to run through the bullet-hole. Like a dissolving vampire, the yellow-haired lamia with Hope's features began to sway and spiral downwards.

'Hope ...' Rademaeker moved forward. Before he could take her wrist she turned and fired at him. The shot tore the glass from the window beside me. The fragments lay in the darkness like pieces of a broken moon.

The next shot struck Rademaeker in the left wrist. He dropped to one knee, gripping the bloodied wound. Confused by the explosions, which had almost jarred the pistol from her grip, Hope held the weapon in both hands, pointing it at the old bloodstain on my jacket. Before she could fire I kicked one of the arc lights across her feet. The room spun like a collapsing stage. I pulled Rademaeker by the shoulder on to the terrace.

We ran down to the beach. Halfway along the path Rademaeker stopped, as if undecided whether to go back. Hope stood on the terrace, firing down at the rays that screamed through the darkness over our heads. The white schooner was already casting off, its sails lifting in the night air.

Rademaeker beckoned to me with his bloodied wrist. 'Get to the ship. She's alone now ... for ever.'

We crouched in the steering well of the schooner, listening to the sonic sculptures wail in the disturbed air as the last shots echoed across the empty desert.

At dawn Rademaeker dropped me half a mile from the beach at Ciraquito. He had spent the night at the helm, his bandaged wrist held like a badge to his chest, steering with his one strong hand. In the cold night air I tried to explain why Hope had shot at him, this last attempt to break through the illusions multiplying around her and reach some kind of reality.

'Rademaeker – I knew her. She wasn't shooting at you, but at a ...

fiction of yourself, that image in the portrait. Damn it, she was obsessed with you.'

But he seemed no longer interested, his thin mouth with its uneasy lips making no reply. In some way he had disappointed me. Whoever finally took Hope away from Lizard Key would first have to accept the overlapping illusions that were the fabric of that strange island. By refusing to admit the reality of her fantasies Rademaeker had destroyed her.

When he left me among the dunes within sight of the beach-houses he gave a brusque salute and spun the helm, his erect figure soon lost among the rolling crests.

Three weeks later I chartered a yacht from one of the local ray-fishermen and went back to the island to collect my sloop. Hope's schooner was at its mooring. She herself, calm in her pale and angular beauty, came on to the terrace to greet me.

The paintings had gone, and with them any memory of that violent night. Hope's eyes looked at me with an untroubled gaze. Only her hands with their slim fingers moved with a restless life of their own.

At the end of the terrace her half-brother lounged among the beach chairs, Rademaeker's yachting cap propped over his eyes. Barbara Quimby sat beside him. I wondered whether to explain to Hope the callous and macabre game they had played with her, but after a few minutes she wandered away. Foyle's simpering mouth was the last residue of this world. Devoid of malice, he accepted his half-sister's reality as his own.

However, Hope Cunard has not entirely forgotten Charles Rademaeker. At midnight I sometimes see her sailing the sand-sea, in pursuit of a white ship with white sails. Last night, acting on some bizarre impulse, I dressed myself in the bloodstained jacket once worn by Rademaeker and sailed out to the edge of the sand-sea. I waited by a reef I knew she would pass. As she swept by soundlessly, her tall figure against the last light of the sun, I stood in the bows, letting her see the jacket. Again I wore it like a target.

Yet others sail this strange sea. Hope passed within fifty yards and never noticed me, but half an hour later a second yacht moved past, a rakish ketch with dragon's eyes on its bows and a tall, heavy-mouthed man wearing a yellow wig at its helm. Beside him a dark-eyed young woman smiled to the wind. As he passed, Foyle waved to me, and an ironic cheer carried itself across the dead sand to where I stood in my target-coat. Masquerading as mad priest or harpy, siren or dune-witch, they cross the sand-sea on their own terms. In the evenings, as they sail past, I can hear them laughing.

*1967*

# · THE RECOGNITION

On Midsummer's Eve a small circus visited the town in the West Country where I was spending my holiday. Three days earlier the large travelling fair which always came to the town in the summer, equipped with a ferris wheel, merry-go-rounds and dozens of booths and shooting galleries, had taken up its usual site on the open common in the centre of the town, and this second arrival was forced to pitch its camp on the waste ground beyond the warehouses along the river.

At dusk, when I strolled through the town, the ferris wheel was revolving above the coloured lights, and people were riding the carousels and walking arm in arm along the cobbled roads that surrounded the common. Away from this hubbub of noise the streets down to the river were almost deserted, and I was glad to walk alone through the shadows past the boarded shopfronts. Midsummer's Eve seemed to me a time for reflection as much as for celebration, for a careful watch on the shifting movements of nature. When I crossed the river, whose dark water flowed through the town like a gilded snake, and entered the woods that stretched to one side of the road, I had the unmistakable sensation that the forest was preparing itself, and that within its covens even the roots of the trees were sliding through the soil and testing their sinews.

It was on the way back from this walk, as I crossed the bridge, that I saw the small itinerant circus arrive at the town. The procession, which approached the bridge by a side road, consisted of no more than half a dozen wagons, each carrying a high barred cage and drawn by a pair of careworn horses. At its head a young woman with a pallid face and bare arms rode on a grey stallion. I leaned on the balustrade in the centre of the bridge and watched the procession reach the embankment. The young woman hesitated, pulling on the heavy leather bridle, and looked over her shoulder as the wagons closed together. They began to ascend the bridge. Although the gradient was slight, the horses seemed barely able to reach the crest, tottering on their weak legs, and I had ample time to make a first scrutiny of this strange caravan that was later to preoccupy me.

Urging on her tired stallion, the young woman passed me – at least, it seemed to me then that she was young, but her age was so much a matter of her own moods and mine. I was to see her on several occasions – sometimes she would seem little more than a child of twelve, with an unformed chin and staring eyes above the bony cheeks. Later she would appear to be almost middle-aged, the grey hair and skin revealing the angular skull beneath them.

At first, as I watched from the bridge, I guessed her to be about twenty years old, presumably the daughter of the proprietor of this threadbare circus. As she jogged along with one hand on the reins the lights from the distant fairground shone intermittently in her face, disclosing a high-bridged nose and firm mouth. Although by no means beautiful, she had that curious quality of attractiveness that I had often noticed in the women who worked at fairgrounds, an elusive sexuality despite their shabby clothes and surroundings. As she passed she looked down at me, her quiet eyes on some unfelt point within my face.

The six wagons followed her, the horses heaving the heavy cages across the camber. Behind the bars I caught a glimpse of worn straw and a small hutch in the corner, but there was no sign of the animals. I assumed them to be too undernourished to do more than sleep. As the last wagon passed I saw the only other member of the troupe, a dwarf in a leather jacket driving the wooden caravan at the rear.

I walked after them across the bridge, wondering if they were late arrivals at the fair already in progress. But from the way they hesitated at the foot of the bridge, the young woman looking to left and right while the dwarf sat hunched in the shadow of the cage in front of him, it was plain they had no connection whatever with the brilliant ferris wheel and the amusements taking place on the common. Even the horses, standing uncertainly with their heads lowered to avoid the coloured lights, seemed aware of this exclusion.

After a pause they moved off along the narrow road that followed the bank, the wagons rolling from side to side as the wooden wheels slipped on the grass-covered verge. A short distance away was a patch of waste ground that separated the warehouses near the wharves from the terraced cottages below the bridge. A single street lamp on the north side cast a dim light over the cinder surface. By now dusk had settled over the town and seemed to isolate this dingy patch of ground, no longer enlivened in any way by the movement of the river.

The procession headed towards this dark enclosure. The young woman turned her horse off the road and led the wagons across the cinders to the high wall of the first warehouse. Here they stopped, the wagons still in line ahead, the horses obviously glad to be concealed by the darkness. The dwarf jumped down from his perch and trotted round to where the woman was dismounting from the stallion.

At this time I was strolling along the bank a short distance behind them. Something about this odd little troupe intrigued me, though in retrospect it may be that the calm eyes of the young woman as she looked down at me had acted as more of a spur than seemed at the time. Nonetheless, I was puzzled by what seemed the very pointlessness of their existence. Few things are as drab as a down-at-heel circus, but this one was so travel-worn and dejected as to deny them the chance of making any profit whatever. Who were this strange pale-haired woman and her dwarf? Did they imagine that anyone would actually come to this dismal patch of ground by the warehouses to look at their secretive animals? Perhaps they were simply delivering a group of aged creatures to an abattoir specialising in circus animals, and pausing here for the night before moving on.

Yet, as I suspected, the young woman and the dwarf were already moving the wagons into the unmistakable pattern of a circus. The woman dragged at the bridles while the dwarf darted between her feet, switching at the horses' ankles with his leather hat. The docile brutes heaved at their wagons, and within five minutes the cages were arranged in a rough circle. The horses were unshackled from their shafts, and the dwarf, helped by the young woman, led them towards the river where they began cropping quietly at the dark grass.

Within the cages there was a stir of movement, and one or two pale forms shuffled about in the straw. The dwarf scurried up the steps of the caravan and lit a lamp over a stove which I could see in the doorway. He came down with a metal bucket and moved along the cages. He poured a little water into each of the pails and pushed them towards the hutches with a broom.

The woman followed him, but seemed as uninterested as the dwarf in the animals inside the cages. When he put away the bucket she held a ladder for him and he climbed onto the roof of the caravan. He lowered down a bundle of clapboard signs fastened together by a strip of canvas. After untying them the dwarf carried the signs over to the cages. He climbed up the ladder again and began to secure the signs over the bars.

In the dim light from the street lamp I could make out only the faded designs painted years earlier in the traditional style of fairground marquees, the floral patterns and cartouches overlaid with lettering of some kind. Moving nearer the cages, I reached the edge of the clearing. The young woman turned and saw me. The dwarf was fixing the last of the signs, and she stood by the ladder, one hand on the shaft, regarding me with an unmoving gaze. Perhaps it was her protective stance as the diminutive figure moved about above her, but she seemed far older than when she had first appeared with her menagerie at the outskirts of the town. In the faint light her hair had become almost grey, and her bare arms seemed lined and work-worn. As I drew closer, passing the first of the cages, she turned to follow me with her eyes, as if trying to take some interest in my arrival on the scene.

At the top of the ladder there was a flurry of movement. Slipping through the dwarf's fingers, the sign toppled from the roof and fell to the ground at the woman's feet. Whirling his short arms and legs, the dwarf leapt down from the ladder. He picked himself off the ground, wobbling about like a top as he regained his balance. He dusted his hat against his boots and put it back on his head, then started up the ladder again.

The woman held his arm. She moved the ladder further along the cage, trying to balance the shafts against the bars.

On an impulse, more or less out of sympathy, I stepped forward.

'Can I help you?' I said. 'Perhaps I can reach the roof. If you hand me the sign . . .'

The dwarf hesitated, looking at me with his doleful eyes. He seemed prepared to let me help, but stood there with his hat in one hand as if prevented from saying anything to me by an unstated set of circumstances, some division of life as formal and impassable as those of the most rigid castes.

The woman, however, gestured me to the ladder, turning her face away as I settled the shafts against the bars. Through the dim light she watched the horses cropping the grass along the bank.

I climbed the ladder, and then took the sign lifted up to me by the dwarf. I settled it on the roof, weighing it down with two half bricks left there for the purpose, and read the legends painted across the warped panel. As I deciphered the words 'marvels' and 'spectacular' (obviously the signs bore no relation to the animals within the cages, and had been stolen from another fair or found on some refuse heap) I noticed a sudden movement from the cage below me. There was a burrowing through the straw, and a low, pale-skinned creature retreated into its burrow.

This disturbance of the straw – whether the animal had darted out from fear or in an attempt to warn me off I had no means of telling – had released a strong and obscurely familiar smell. It hung around me as I came down the ladder, muffled but vaguely offensive. I searched the hutch for a glimpse of the animal, but it had scuffled the straw into the door.

The dwarf and the woman nodded to me as I turned from the ladder. There was no hostility in their attitude – the dwarf, if anything, was on the point of thanking me, his mouth moving in a wordless rictus – but for some reason they seemed to feel unable to make any contact with me. The woman was standing with her back to the street lamp, and her face, softened by the darkness, now appeared small and barely formed, like that of an unkempt child.

'You're all ready,' I said half jocularly. With something of an effort, I added: 'It looks very nice.'

I glanced at the cages when they made no comment. One or two of the animals sat at the backs of their hutches, their pale forms indistinct in the faint light. 'When do you open?' I asked. 'Tomorrow?'

'We're open now,' the dwarf said.

'Now?' Not sure whether this was a joke, I started to point at the cages, but the statement had obviously been meant at its face value.

'I see . . . you're open this evening.' Searching for something to say – they seemed prepared to stand there indefinitely with me – I went on: 'When do you leave?'

'Tomorrow,' the woman told me in a low voice. 'We have to go in the morning.'

As if taking their cue from this, the two of them moved across the small arena, clearing to one side the pieces of newspaper and other refuse. By the time I walked away, baffled by the entire purpose of this pitiful menagerie, they had already finished, and stood waiting between the cages for their first customers. I paused on the bank beside the cropping horses, whose quiet figures seemed as insubstantial as those of the dwarf and their mistress, and wondered what bizarre logic had brought them to the town, when a second fair, almost infinitely larger and gayer, was already in full swing.

At the thought of the animals I recalled the peculiar smell that hung about the cages, vaguely unpleasant but reminiscent of an odour I was certain I knew well. For some reason I was also convinced that this familiar smell was a clue to the strange nature of the circus. Beside me the horses gave off a pleasant scent of bran and sweat. Their downcast heads, lowered to the grass by the water's edge, seemed to hide from me some secret concealed within their luminous eyes.

I walked back towards the centre of the town, relieved to see the illuminated superstructure of the ferris wheel rotating above the rooftops. The roundabouts and amusement arcades, the shooting galleries and the tunnel of love were part of a familiar world. Even the witches and vampires painted over the house of horrors were nightmares from a predictable quarter of the evening sky. By contrast the young woman – or was she young? – and her dwarf were travellers from an unknown country, a vacant realm where nothing had any meaning. It was this absence of intelligible motive that I found so disturbing about them.

I wandered through the crowds below the marquees, and on an impulse decided to ride on the ferris wheel. As I waited my turn with the group of young men and women, the electrified gondolas of the wheel rose high into the evening air, so that all the music and light of the fair seemed to have been scooped from the star-filled sky.

I climbed into my gondola, sharing it with a young woman and her daughter, and a few moments later we were revolving through the brilliant air, the fairground spread below us. During the two or three minutes of the ride I was busy shouting to the young woman and her child as we pointed out to each other familiar landmarks in the town. However, when we stopped and sat at the top of the wheel as the passengers below disembarked, I noticed for the first time the bridge I had crossed earlier that evening. Following the course of the river, I saw the single street lamp that shone over the waste ground near the warehouses where the white-faced woman and the dwarf had set up their rival circus. As our gondola moved forward and began its descent the dim forms of two of the wagons were visible in an interval between the rooftops.

Half an hour later, when the fair began to close, I walked back to the river. Small groups of people were moving arm in arm through the streets, but by the time the warehouses came into sight I was almost alone on the cobbled pavements that wound between the terraced cottages. Then the street lamp appeared, and the circle of wagons beyond it.

To my surprise, a few people were actually visiting the menagerie. I stood in the road below the street lamp and watched the two couples and a third man who were wandering around the cages and trying to identify the animals. Now and then they would go up to the bars and peer through them, and there was a shout of laughter as one of the women pretended to flinch away in alarm. The man with her held a few shreds of straw in his hand and threw them at the door of the hutch, but the animal refused to appear. The group resumed their circuit of the cages, squinting in the dim light.

Meanwhile the dwarf and the woman remained silent to one side. The woman stood by the steps of the caravan, looking out at her patrons as if unconcerned whether they came or not. The dwarf, his bulky hat hiding his face, stood patiently on the other side of the arena, moving his ground as the party of visitors continued their tour. He was not carrying a collection bag or roll of tickets, and it seemed likely, even if only reasonable, that there was no charge for admission.

Something of the peculiar atmosphere, or perhaps their failure to bring the animals from their hutches, seemed to transmit itself to the party of visitors. After trying to read the signs, one of the men began to rattle a stick between the bars of the cages. Then, losing interest abruptly, they made off together without a backward glance at either the woman or the dwarf. As he passed me the man with the stick pulled a face and waved his hand in front of his nose.

I waited until they had gone and then approached the cages. The dwarf appeared to remember me – at least, he made no effort to scuttle away but watched me with his drifting eyes. The woman sat on the steps of the caravan, gazing across the cinders with the expression of a tired and unthinking child.

I glanced into one or two of the cages. There was no sign of the animals, but the smell that had driven off the previous party was certainly pronounced. The familiar pungent odour quickened my nostrils. I walked over to the young woman.

'You've had some visitors,' I commented.

'Not many,' she replied. 'A few have come.'

I was about to point out that she could hardly expect a huge attendance if none of the animals in the cages was prepared to make an appearance, but the girl's hangdog look restrained me. The top of her robe revealed a small childlike breast, and it seemed impossible that this pale young woman should have been put in sole charge of such a doomed enterprise. Searching for an excuse that might console her, I said: 'It's rather late, there's the other fair . . .' I pointed to the cages. 'That smell, too. Perhaps you're used to it, it might put people off.' I forced a smile. 'I'm sorry, I don't mean to –'

'I understand,' she said matter-of-factly. 'It's why we have to leave so soon.' She nodded at the dwarf. 'We clean them every day.'

I was about to ask what animals the cages held – the smell reminded me of the chimpanzee house at the zoo – when there was a commotion from the direction of the bank. A group of sailors, two or three girls among them, came swaying along the towpath. They greeted the sight of the menagerie with boisterous shouts. Linked arm in arm, they made a drunken swerve up the bank, then stamped across the cinders to the cages. The dwarf moved out of their way, and watched from the shadows between two of the wagons, hat in hand.

The sailors pushed over to one of the cages and pressed their faces to the bars, nudging each other in the ribs and whistling in an effort to bring the creature out of its hutch. They moved over to the next cage, pulling at each other in a struggling mêlée.

One of them shouted at the woman, who sat on the steps of the caravan. 'Are you closed, or what? The perisher won't come out of his hole!'

There was a roar of laughter at this. Another of the sailors rattled one of the girls' handbags, and then dug into his pockets.

'Pennies out, lads. Who's got the tickets?'

He spotted the dwarf and tossed the penny towards him. A moment later a dozen coins showered through the air around the dwarf's head. He scuttled about, warding them off with his hat, but made no effort to pick up the coins.

The sailors moved on to the third cage. After a fruitless effort to draw the animal towards them they began to rock the wagon from side to side. Their good humour was beginning to fade. As I left the young woman and strolled past the cages several of the sailors had started to climb up onto the bars.

At this point one of the doors sprang open. As it clanged against the bars the noise fell away. Everyone stepped back, as if expecting some huge striped tiger to spring out at them from its hutch. Two of the sailors moved forward and gingerly reached for the door. As they closed it one of them peered into the cage. Suddenly he leapt up into the doorway. The others shouted at him, but the sailor kicked aside the straw and and stepped across to the hutch.

'It's bloody empty!'

As he shouted this out there was a delighted roar. Slamming the door – curiously enough, the bolt was on the inside – the sailor began to prance around the cage, gibbering like a baboon through the bars. At first I thought he must be mistaken, and looked round at the young woman and the dwarf. Both were watching the sailors but gave no inkling that there was any danger from the animal within. Sure enough, as a second sailor was let into the cage and dragged the hutch over to the bars, I saw that it was unoccupied.

Involuntarily I found myself staring at the young woman. Was this, then, the point of this strange and pathetic menagerie – that there were no animals at all, at least in most of the cages, and that what was being exhibited was simply nothing, merely the cages themselves, the essence of imprisonment with all its ambiguities? Was this a zoo in the abstract, some kind of bizarre comment on the meaning of life? Yet neither the young woman nor the dwarf seemed subtle enough for this, and possibly there was a less farfetched explanation. Perhaps once there had been animals, but these had died out, and the girl and her companion had found that people would still come and gaze at the empty cages, with much the same fascination of visitors to disused cemeteries. After a while they no longer charged any admission, but drifted aimlessly from town to town . . .

Before I could pursue this train of thought there was a shout behind me. A sailor ran past, brushing my shoulder. The discovery of the empty cage had removed any feelings of restraint, and the sailors were chasing the dwarf among the wagons. At this first hint of violence the woman stood up and disappeared into the caravan, and the poor dwarf was left to fend for himself. One of the sailors tripped him up and snatched the hat off his head as the little figure lay in the dust with his legs in the air.

The sailor in front of me caught the hat and was about to toss it up onto one of the wagon roofs. Stepping forward, I held his arm, but he wrenched himself away. The dwarf had vanished from sight, and another group of the sailors were trying to turn one of the wagons and push it towards the river. Two of them had got among the horses and were lifting the women onto their backs. The grey stallion which had led the procession across the bridge suddenly bolted along the bank. Running after it through the confusion, I heard a warning shout behind me. There was the thud of hooves on the wet turf, and a woman's cry as a horse swerved above me. I was struck on the head and shoulder and knocked heavily to the ground.

It must have been some two hours later that I awoke, lying on a bench beside the bank. Under the night sky the town was silent, and I could hear the faint sounds of a water vole moving along the river and the distant splash of water around the bridge. I sat up and brushed away the dew that had formed on my clothes. Further along the bank the circus wagons stood in the clearing darkness, the dim forms of the horses motionless by the water.

Collecting myself, I decided that after being knocked down by the horse I had been carried to the bench by the sailors and left there to recover when and as soon as I could. Nursing my head and shoulders, I looked around for any sign of the party, but the bank was deserted. Standing up, I slowly walked back towards the circus, in the vague hope that the dwarf might help me home.

Twenty yards away, I saw something move in one of the cages, its white form passing in front of the bars. There was no sign of the dwarf or the young woman, but the wagons had been pushed back into place.

Standing in the centre of the cages, I peered about uncertainly, aware that their occupants had at last emerged from the hutches. The angular grey bodies were indistinct in the darkness, but as familiar as the pungent smell that came from the cages.

A voice shouted behind me, a single obscene word. I turned to find its source, and saw one of the occupants watching me with cold eyes. As I stared he raised his hand and moved the fingers in a perverted gesture.

A second voice called out, followed by a chorus of abusive catcalls. With an effort, I managed to clear my head, then began a careful walk around the cages, satisfying myself for the last time as to the identity of their tenants. Except for the one at the end, which was empty, the others were occupied. The thin figures stood openly in front of the bars that protected them from me, their pallid faces shining in the dim light. At last I recognised the smell that came from the cages.

As I walked away their derisive voices called after me, and the young woman roused from her bed in the caravan watched quietly from the steps.

· **1967**

# THE CLOUD-SCULPTORS OF CORAL D

All summer the cloud-sculptors would come from Vermilion Sands and sail their painted gliders above the coral towers that rose like white pagodas beside the highway to Lagoon West. The tallest of the towers was Coral D, and here the rising air above the sand-reefs was topped by swan-like clumps of fair-weather cumulus. Lifted on the shoulders of the air above the crown of Coral D, we would carve seahorses and unicorns, the portraits of presidents and film stars, lizards and exotic birds. As the crowd watched from their cars, a cool rain would fall on to the dusty roofs, weeping from the sculptured clouds as they sailed across the desert floor towards the sun.

Of all the cloud-sculptures we were to carve, the strangest were the portraits of Leonora Chanel. As I look back to that afternoon last summer when she first came in her white limousine to watch the cloud-sculptors of Coral D, I know we barely realized how seriously this beautiful but insane woman regarded the sculptures floating above her in that calm sky. Later her portraits, carved in the whirlwind, were to weep their storm-rain upon the corpses of their sculptors.

I had arrived in Vermilion Sands three months earlier. A retired pilot, I was painfully coming to terms with a broken leg and the prospect of never flying again. Driving into the desert one day, I stopped near the coral towers on the highway to Lagoon West. As I gazed at these immense pagodas stranded on the floor of this fossil sea, I heard music coming from a sand-reef two hundred yards away. Swinging on my crutches across the sliding sand, I found a shallow basin among the dunes where sonic statues had run to seed beside a ruined studio. The owner had gone, abandoning the hangar-like building to the sand-rays and the desert, and on some half-formed impulse I began to drive out each afternoon. From the lathes and joists left behind I built my first giant kites and, later, gliders with cockpits. Tethered by their cables, they would hang above me in the afternoon air like amiable ciphers.

One evening, as I wound the gliders down on to the winch, a sudden gale rose over the crest of Coral D. While I grappled with the whirling handle, trying to anchor my crutches in the sand, two figures approached across the desert floor. One was a small hunchback with a child's over-lit eyes and a deformed jaw twisted like an anchor barb to one side. He scuttled over to the winch and wound the tattered gliders towards the ground, his powerful shoulders pushing me aside. He helped me on to my crutch and peered into the hangar. Here my most ambitious glider to date, no longer a kite but a sail-plane with elevators and control lines, was taking shape on the bench.

He spread a large hand over his chest. 'Petit Manuel – acrobat and weight-lifter. Nolan!' he bellowed. 'Look at this!' His companion was squatting by the sonic statues, twisting their helixes so that their voices became more resonant. 'Nolan's an artist,' the hunchback confided to me. 'He'll build you gliders like condors.'

The tall man was wandering among the gliders, touching their wings with a sculptor's hand. His morose eyes were set in a face like a bored boxer's. He glanced at the plaster on my leg and my faded flying-jacket, and gestured at the gliders. 'You've given cockpits to them, major.' The remark contained a complete understanding of my motives. He pointed to the coral towers rising above us into the evening sky. 'With silver iodide we could carve the clouds.'

The hunchback nodded encouragingly to me, his eyes lit by an astronomy of dreams.

So were formed the cloud-sculptors of Coral D. Although I considered myself one of them, I never flew the gliders, but taught Nolan and little Manuel to fly, and later, when he joined us, Charles Van Eyck. Nolan had found this blond-haired pirate of the café terraces in Vermilion Sands, a laconic Teuton with hard eyes and a weak mouth, and brought him out to Coral D when the season ended and the well-to-do tourists and their nubile daughters returned to Red Beach. 'Major Parker – Charles Van Eyck. He's a headhunter,' Nolan commented with cold humour, '– maidenheads.' Despite their uneasy rivalry I realized that Van Eyck would give our group a useful dimension of glamour.

From the first I suspected that the studio in the desert was Nolan's, and that we were all serving some private whim of this dark-haired solitary. At the time, however, I was more concerned with teaching them to fly – first on cable, mastering the updraughts that swept the stunted turret of Coral A, smallest of the towers, then the steeper slopes of B and C, and finally the powerful currents of Coral D. Late one afternoon, when I began to wind them in, Nolan cut away his line. The glider plummeted on to its back, diving down to impale itself on the rock spires. I flung myself to the ground as the cable whipped across my car, shattering the windshield. When I looked up, Nolan was soaring high in the tinted air above Coral D. The wind, guardian of the coral towers, carried him through the islands of cumulus that veiled the evening light.

As I ran to the winch the second cable went, and little Manuel swerved away to join Nolan. Ugly crab on the ground, in the air the hunchback became a bird with immense wings, outflying both Nolan and Van Eyck. I watched them as they circled the coral towers, and then swept down together over the desert floor, stirring the sand-rays into soot-like clouds. Petit Manuel was jubilant. He strutted around me like a pocket Napoleon, contemptuous of my broken leg, scooping up handfuls of broken glass and tossing them over his head like bouquets to the air.

Two months later, as we drove out to Coral D on the day we were to meet Leonora Chanel, something of this first feeling of exhilaration had faded. Now that the season had ended few tourists travelled to Lagoon West, and often we would perform our cloud-sculpture to the empty highway. Sometimes Nolan would remain behind in his hotel, drinking by himself on the bed, or Van Eyck would disappear for several days with some widow or divorcée, and Petit Manuel and I would go out alone.

None the less, as the four of us drove out in my car that afternoon and I saw the clouds waiting for us above the spire of Coral D, all my depression and fatigue vanished. Ten minutes later, the three cloud gliders rose into the air and the first cars began to stop on the highway. Nolan was in the lead in his black-winged glider, climbing straight to the crown of Coral D two hundred feet above, while Van Eyck soared to and fro below, showing his blond mane to a middle-aged woman in a topaz convertible. Behind them came little Manuel, his candy-striped wings slipping and churning in the disturbed air. Shouting happy obscenities, he flew with his twisted knees, huge arms gesticulating out of the cockpit.

The three gliders, brilliant painted toys, revolved like lazing birds above Coral D, waiting for the first clouds to pass overhead. Van Eyck moved away to take a cloud. He sailed around its white pillow, spraying the sides with iodide crystals and cutting away the flock-like tissue. The steaming shards fell towards us like crumbling ice-drifts. As the drops of condensing spray fell on my face I could see Van Eyck shaping an immense horse's head. He sailed up and down the long forehead and chiselled out the eyes and ears.

As always, the people watching from their cars seemed to enjoy this piece of aerial marzipan. It sailed overhead, carried away on the wind from Coral D. Van Eyck followed it down, wings lazing around the equine head. Meanwhile Petit Manuel worked away at the next cloud. As he sprayed its sides a familiar human head appeared through the tumbling mist. The high wavy mane, strong jaw but slipped mouth Manuel caricatured from the cloud with a series of deft passes, wingtips almost touching each other as he dived in and out of the portrait.

The glossy white head, an unmistakable parody of Van Eyck in his own worst style, crossed the highway towards Vermilion Sands. Manuel slid out of the air, stalling his glider to a landing beside my car as Van Eyck stepped from his cockpit with a forced smile.

We waited for the third display. A cloud formed over Coral D and within a few minutes had blossomed into a pristine fair-weather cumulus. As it hung there Nolan's black-winged glider plunged out of the sun. He soared around the cloud, cutting away its tissues. The soft fleece fell towards us in a cool rain.

There was a shout from one of the cars. Nolan turned from the cloud, his wings slipping as if unveiling his handiwork. Illuminated by the afternoon sun was the serene face of a three-year-old child. Its wide cheeks framed a placid mouth and plump chin. As one or two people clapped, Nolan sailed over the cloud and rippled the roof into ribbons and curls.

However, I knew that the real climax was yet to come. Cursed by some malignant virus, Nolan seemed unable to accept his own handiwork, always destroying it with the same cold humour. Petit Manuel had thrown away his cigarette, and even Van Eyck had turned his attention from the women in the cars.

Nolan soared above the child's face, following like a matador waiting for the moment of the kill. There was silence for a minute as he worked away at the cloud, and then someone slammed a car door in disgust.

Hanging above us was the white image of a skull.

The child's face, converted by a few strokes, had vanished, but in the notched teeth and gaping orbits, large enough to hold a car, we could still see an echo of its infant features. The spectre moved past us, the spectators frowning at this weeping skull whose rain fell upon their faces.

Half-heartedly I picked my old flying helmet off the back seat and began to carry it around the cars. Two of the spectators drove off before I could reach them. As I hovered about uncertainly, wondering why on earth a retired and well-to-do air-force officer should be trying to collect these few dollar bills, Van Eyck stepped behind me and took the helmet from my hand.

'Not now, major. Look at what arrives – my apocalypse . . .'

A white Rolls-Royce, driven by a chauffeur in braided cream livery, had turned off the highway. Through the tinted communication window a young woman in a secretary's day suit spoke to the chauffeur. Beside her, a gloved hand still holding the window strap, a white-haired woman with jewelled eyes gazed up at the circling wings of the cloud-glider. Her strong and elegant face seemed sealed within the dark glass of the limousine like the enigmatic madonna of some marine grotto.

Van Eyck's glider rose into the air, soaring upwards to the cloud that hung above Coral D. I walked back to my car, searching the sky for Nolan. Above, Van Eyck was producing a pastiche Mona Lisa, a picture-postcard Gioconda as authentic as a plaster virgin. Its glossy finish shone in the over-bright sunlight as if enamelled together out of some cosmetic foam.

Then Nolan dived from the sun behind Van Eyck. Rolling his black-winged glider past Van Eyck's, he drove through the neck of the Gioconda, and with the flick of a wing toppled the broad-cheeked head. It fell towards the cars below. The features disintegrated into a flaccid mess, sections of the nose and jaw tumbling through the steam. Then wings brushed. Van Eyck fired his spray gun at Nolan, and there was a flurry of torn fabric. Van Eyck fell from the air, steering his glider down to a broken landing.

I ran over to him. 'Charles, do you have to play von Richthofen? For God's sake, leave each other alone!'

Van Eyck waved me away. 'Talk to Nolan, major. I'm not responsible for his air piracy.' He stood in the cockpit, gazing over the cars as the shreds of fabric fell around him.

I walked back to my car, deciding that the time had come to disband the cloud-sculptors of Coral D. Fifty yards away the young secretary in the Rolls-Royce had stepped from the car and beckoned to me. Through the open door her mistress watched me with her jewelled eyes. Her white hair lay in a coil over one shoulder like a nacreous serpent.

I carried my flying helmet down to the young woman. Above a high forehead her auburn hair was swept back in a defensive bun, as if she were deliberately concealing part of herself. She stared with puzzled eyes at the helmet held out in front of her.

'I don't want to fly – what is it?'

'A grace,' I explained. 'For the repose of Michelangelo, Ed Keinholz and the cloud-sculptors of Coral D.'

'Oh, my God. I think the chauffeur's the only one with any *money*. Look, do you perform anywhere else?'

'Perform?' I glanced from this pretty and agreeable young woman to the pale chimera with jewelled eyes in the dim compartment of the Rolls. She was watching the headless figure of the Mona Lisa as it moved across the desert floor towards Vermilion Sands. 'We're not a professional troupe, as you've probably guessed. And obviously we'd need some fair-weather cloud. Where, exactly?'

'At Lagoon West.' She took a snakeskin diary from her handbag. 'Miss Chanel is holding a series of garden parties. She wondered if you'd care to perform. Of course there would be a large fee.'

'Chanel ... Leonora Chanel, the ...?'

The young woman's face again took on its defensive posture, dissociating her from whatever might follow. 'Miss Chanel is at Lagoon West for the summer. By the way, there's one condition I must point out – Miss Chanel will provide the sole subject matter. You do understand?'

Fifty yards away Van Eyck was dragging his damaged glider towards my car. Nolan had landed, a caricature of Cyrano abandoned in mid-air. Petit Manuel limped to and fro, gathering together the equipment. In the fading afternoon light they resembled a threadbare circus troupe.

'All right,' I agreed. 'I take your point. But what about the clouds, Miss –?'

'Lafferty. Beatrice Lafferty. Miss Chanel will provide the clouds.'

I walked around the cars with the helmet, then divided the money between Nolan, Van Eyck and Manuel. They stood in the gathering dusk, the few bills in their hands, watching the highway below.

Leonora Chanel stepped from the limousine and strolled into the desert. Her white-haired figure in its cobra-skin coat wandered among the dunes. Sand-rays lifted around her, disturbed by the random movements of this sauntering phantasm of the burnt afternoon. Ignoring their open stings around her legs, she was gazing up at the aerial bestiary dissolving in the sky, and at the white skull a mile away over Lagoon West that had smeared itself across the sky.

At the time I first saw her, watching the cloud-sculptors of Coral D, I had only a half-formed impression of Leonora Chanel. The daughter of one of the world's leading financiers, she was an heiress both in her own right and on the death of her husband, a shy Monacan aristocrat, Comte Louis Chanel. The mysterious circumstances of his death at Cap Ferrat on the Riviera, officially described as suicide, had placed Leonora in a spotlight of publicity and gossip. She had escaped by wandering endlessly across the globe, from her walled villa in Tangiers to an Alpine mansion in the snows above Pontresina, and from there to Palm Springs, Seville and Mykonos.

During these years of exile something of her character emerged from the magazine and newspaper photographs: moodily visiting a Spanish charity with the Duchess of Alba, or seated with Soraya and other members of café society on the terrace of Dali's villa at Port Lligat, her self-regarding face gazing out with its jewelled eyes at the diamond sea of the Costa Brava.

Inevitably her Garbo-like role seemed over-calculated, forever undermined by the suspicions of her own hand in her husband's death. The count had been an introspective playboy who piloted his own aircraft to archaeological sites in the Peloponnese and whose mistress, a beautiful young Lebanese, was one of the world's pre-eminent keyboard interpreters of Bach. Why this reserved and pleasant man should have committed suicide was never made plain. What promised to be a significant exhibit at the coroner's inquest, a multilated easel portrait of Leonora on which he was working, was accidentally destroyed before the hearing. Perhaps the painting revealed more of Leonora's character than she chose to see.

A week later, as I drove out to Lagoon West on the morning of the first garden party, I could well understand why Leonora Chanel had come to Vermilion Sands, to this bizarre, sand-bound resort with its lethargy, beach fatigue and shifting perspectives. Sonic statues grew wild along the beach, their voices keening as I swept past along the shore road. The fused silica on the surface of the lake formed an immense rainbow mirror that reflected the deranged colours of the sand-reefs, more vivid even than the cinnabar and cyclamen wing-panels of the cloud-gliders overhead. They soared in the sky above the lake like fitful dragonflies as Nolan, Van Eyck and Petit Manuel flew them from Coral D.

We had entered an inflamed landscape. Half a mile away the angular cornices of the summer house jutted into the vivid air as if distorted by some faulty junction of time and space. Behind it, like an exhausted volcano, a broad-topped mesa rose into the glazed air, its shoulders lifting the thermal currents high off the heated lake.

Envying Nolan and little Manuel these tremendous updraughts, more powerful than any we had known at Coral D, I drove towards the villa. Then the haze cleared along the beach and I saw the clouds.

A hundred feet above the roof of the mesa, they hung like the twisted pillows of a sleepless giant. Columns of turbulent air moved within the clouds, boiling upwards to the anvil heads like liquid in a cauldron. These were not the placid, fair-weather cumulus of Coral D, but storm-nimbus, unstable masses of overheated air that could catch an aircraft and lift it a thousand feet in a few seconds. Here and there the clouds were rimmed with dark bands, their towers crossed by valleys and ravines. They moved across the villa, concealed from the lakeside heat by the haze overhead, then dissolved in a series of violent shifts in the disordered air.

As I entered the drive behind a truck filled with *son et lumière* equipment a dozen members of the staff were straightening lines of gilt chairs on the terrace and unrolling panels of a marquee.

Beatrice Lafferty stepped across the cables. 'Major Parker – there are the clouds we promised you.'

I looked up again at the dark billows hanging like shrouds above the white villa. 'Clouds, Beatrice? Those are tigers, tigers with wings. We're manicurists of the air, not dragon-tamers.'

'Don't worry, a manicure is exactly what you're expected to carry out.' With an arch glance, she added: 'Your men do understand that there's to be only one subject?'

'Miss Chanel herself? Of course.' I took her arm as we walked towards the balcony overlooking the lake. 'You know, I think you enjoy these snide asides. Let the rich choose their materials – marble, bronze, plasma or cloud. Why not? Portraiture has always been a neglected art.'

'My God, not here.' She waited until a steward passed with a tray of tablecloths. 'Carving one's portrait in the sky out of the sun and air – some people might say that smacked of vanity, or even worse sins.'

'You're very mysterious. Such as?'

She played games with her eyes. 'I'll tell you in a month's time when my contract expires. Now, when are your men coming?'

'They're here.' I pointed to the sky over the lake. The three gliders hung in the overheated air, clumps of cloud-cotton drifting past them to dissolve in the haze. They were following a sand-yacht that approached the quay, its tyres throwing up the cerise dust. Behind the helmsman sat Leonora Chanel in a trouser suit of yellow alligator skin, her white hair hidden inside a black raffia toque.

As the helmsman moored the craft Van Eyck and Petit Manuel put on an impromptu performance, shaping the fragments of cloud-cotton a hundred feet above the lake. First Van Eyck carved an orchid, then a heart and a pair of lips, while Manuel fashioned the head of a parakeet, two identical mice and the letters 'L.C.' As they dived and plunged around her, their wings sometimes touching the lake, Leonora stood on the quay, politely waving at each of these brief confections.

When they landed beside the quay, Leonora waited for Nolan to take one of the clouds, but he was sailing up and down the lake in front of her like a weary bird. Watching this strange chatelaine of Lagoon West, I noticed that she had slipped off into some private reverie, her gaze fixed on Nolan and oblivious of the people around her. Memories, caravels without sails, crossed the shadowy deserts of her burnt-out eyes.

Later that evening Beatrice Lafferty led me into the villa through the library window. There, as Leonora greeted her guests on the terrace, wearing a topless dress of sapphires and organdy, her breasts covered only by their contour jewellery. I saw the portraits that filled the villa. I counted more than twenty, from the formal society portraits in the drawing rooms, one by the President of the Royal Academy, another by Annigoni, to the bizarre psychological studies in the bar and dining room by Dali and Francis Bacon. Everywhere we moved, in the alcoves between the marble semi-columns, in gilt miniatures on the mantelshelves, even in the ascending mural that followed the staircase, we saw the same beautiful self-regarding face. This colossal narcissism seemed to have become her last refuge, the only retreat for her fugitive self in its flight from the world.

Then, in the studio on the roof, we came across a large easel portrait that had just been varnished. The artist had produced a deliberate travesty of the sentimental and powder-blue tints of a fashionable society painter, but beneath this gloss he had visualized Leonora as a dead Medea. The stretched skin below her right cheek, the sharp forehead and slipped mouth gave her the numbed and luminous appearance of a corpse.

My eyes moved to the signature. 'Nolan! My God, were you here when he painted this?'

'It was finished before I came – two months ago. She refused to have it framed.'

'No wonder.' I went over to the window and looked down at the bedrooms hidden behind their awnings. 'Nolan was *here*. The old studio near Coral D was his.'

'But why should Leonora ask him back? They must have –'

'To paint her portrait again. I know Leonora Chanel better than you do, Beatrice. This time, though, the size of the sky.'

We left the library and walked past the cocktails and canapés to where Leonora was welcoming her guests. Nolan stood beside her, wearing a suit of white suede. Now and then he looked down at her as if playing with the possibilities this self-obsessed woman gave to his macabre humour. Leonora clutched at his elbow. With the diamonds fixed around her eyes she reminded me of some archaic priestess. Beneath the contour jewellery her breasts lay like eager snakes.

Van Eyck introduced himself with an exaggerated bow. Behind him came Petit Manuel, his twisted head ducking nervously among the tuxedos.

Leonora's mouth shut in a rictus of distaste. She glanced at the white plaster on my foot. 'Nolan, you fill your world with cripples. Your little dwarf – will he fly too?'

Petit Manuel looked at her with eyes like crushed flowers.

The performance began an hour later. The dark-rimmed clouds were lit by the sun setting behind the mesa, the air crossed by wraiths of cirrus like the gilded frames of the immense paintings to come. Van Eyck's glider rose in the spiral towards the face of the first cloud, stalling and climbing again as the turbulent updraughts threw him across the air.

As the cheekbones began to appear, as smooth and lifeless as carved foam, applause rang out from the guests seated on the terrace. Five minutes later, when Van Eyck's glider swooped down on to the lake, I could see that he had excelled himself. Lit by the searchlights, and with the overture to Tristan sounding from the loudspeakers on the slopes of the mesa, as if inflating this huge bauble, the portrait of Leonora moved overhead, a faint rain falling from it. By luck the cloud remained stable until it passed the shoreline, and then broke up in the evening air as if ripped from the sky by an irritated hand.

Petit Manuel began his ascent, sailing in on a dark-edged cloud like an urchin accosting a bad-tempered matron. He soared to and fro, as if unsure how to shape this unpredictable column of vapour, then began to carve it into the approximate contours of a woman's head. He seemed more nervous than I had ever seen him. As he finished a second round of applause broke out, soon followed by laughter and ironic cheers.

The cloud, sculptured into a flattering likeness of Leonora, had begun to tilt, rotating in the disturbed air. The jaw lengthened, the glazed smile became that of an idiot's. Within a minute the gigantic head of Leonora Chanel hung upside down above us.

Discreetly I ordered the searchlights switched off, and the audience's attention turned to Nolan's black-winged glider as it climbed towards the next cloud. Shards of dissolving tissue fell from the darkening air, the spray concealing whatever ambiguous creation Nolan was carving. To my surprise, the portrait that emerged was wholly lifelike. There was a burst of applause, a few bars of Tannhauser, and the searchlights lit up the elegant head. Standing among her guests, Leonora raised her glass to Nolan's glider.

Puzzled by Nolan's generosity, I looked more closely at the gleaming face, and then realized what he had done. The portrait, with cruel irony, was all too lifelike. The downward turn of Leonora's mouth, the chin held up to smooth her neck, the fall of flesh below her right cheek – all these were carried on the face of the cloud as they had been in his painting in the studio.

Around Leonora the guests were congratulating her on the performance. She was looking up at her portrait as it began to break up over the lake, seeing it for the first time. The veins held the blood in her face.

Then a firework display on the beach blotted out these ambiguities in its pink and blue explosions.

Shortly before dawn Beatrice Lafferty and I walked along the beach among the shells of burnt-out rockets and catherine wheels. On the deserted terrace a few lights shone through the darkness on to the scattered chairs. As we reached the steps a woman's voice cried out somewhere above us. There was the sound of smashed glass. A french window was kicked back, and a dark-haired man in a white suit ran between the tables.

As Nolan disappeared along the drive Leonora Chanel walked out into the centre of the terrace. She looked at the dark clouds surging over the mesa, and with one hand tore the jewels from her eyes. They lay winking on the tiles at her feet. Then the hunched figure of Petit Manuel leapt from his hiding place in the bandstand. He scuttled past, racing on his deformed legs.

An engine started by the gates. Leonora began to walk back to the villa, staring at her broken reflections in the glass below the window. She stopped as a tall, blond-haired man with cold and eager eyes stepped from the sonic statues outside the library. Disturbed by the noise, the statues had begun to whine. As Van Eyck moved towards Leonora they took up the slow beat of his steps.

The next day's performance was the last by the cloud-sculptors of Coral D. All afternoon, before the guests arrived, a dim light lay over the lake. Immense tiers of storm-nimbus were massing behind the mesa, and any performance at all seemed unlikely.

Van Eyck was with Leonora. As I arrived Beatrice Lafferty was watching their sand-yacht carry them unevenly across the lake, its sails whipped by the squalls.

'There's no sign of Nolan or little Manuel,' she told me. 'The party starts in three hours.'

I took her arm. 'The party's already over. When you're finished here, Bea, come and live with me at Coral D. I'll teach you to sculpt the clouds.'

Van Eyck and Leonora came ashore half an hour later. Van Eyck stared through my face as he brushed past. Leonora clung to his arm, the day-jewels around her eyes scattering their hard light across the terrace.

By eight, when the first guests began to appear, Nolan and Petit Manuel had still not arrived. On the terrace the evening was warm and lamplit, but overhead the storm-clouds sidled past each other like uneasy giants. I walked up the slope to where the gliders were tethered. Their wings shivered in the updraughts.

Barely half a minute after he rose into the darkening air, dwarfed by an immense tower of storm-nimbus, Charles Van Eyck was spinning towards the ground, his glider toppled by the crazed air. He recovered fifty feet from the villa and climbed on the updraughts from the lake, well away from the spreading chest of the cloud. He soared in again. As Leonora and her guests watched from their seats the glider was hurled back over their heads in an explosion of vapour, then fell towards the lake with a broken wing.

I walked towards Leonora. Standing by the balcony were Nolan and Petit Manuel, watching Van Eyck climb from the cockpit of his glider three hundred yards away.

To Nolan I said: 'Why bother to come? Don't tell me you're going to fly?'

Nolan leaned against the rail, hands in the pockets of his suit. 'I'm not – that's exactly why I'm here, major.'

Leonora was wearing an evening dress of peacock feathers that lay around her legs in an immense train. The hundreds of eyes gleamed in the electric air before the storm, sheathing her body in their blue flames.

'Miss Chanel, the clouds are like madmen,' I apologized. 'There's a storm on its way.'

She looked up at me with unsettled eyes. 'Don't you people expect to take risks?' She gestured at the storm-nimbus that swirled over our heads. 'For clouds like these I need a Michelangelo of the sky ... What about Nolan? Is he too frightened as well?'

As she shouted his name Nolan stared at her, then turned his back to us. The light over Lagoon West had changed. Half the lake was covered by a dim pall.

There was a tug on my sleeve. Petit Manuel looked up at me with his crafty child's eyes. 'Major, I can go. Let me take the glider.'

'Manuel, for God's sake. You'll kill –'

He darted between the gilt chairs. Leonora frowned as he plucked her wrist.

'Miss Chanel ...' His loose mouth formed an encouraging smile. 'I'll sculpt for you. Right now, a big storm-cloud, eh?'

She stared down at him, half-repelled by this eager hunchback ogling her beside the hundred eyes of her peacock train. Van Eyck was limping back to the beach from his wrecked glider. I guessed that in some strange way Manuel was pitting himself against Van Eyck.

Leonora grimaced, as if swallowing some poisonous phlegm. 'Major Parker, tell him to –' She glanced at the dark cloud boiling over the mesa like the effuvium of some black-hearted volcano. 'Wait! Let's see what the little cripple can do!' She turned on Manuel with an over-bright smile. 'Go on, then. Let's see you sculpt a whirlwind!'

In her face the diagram of bones formed a geometry of murder.

Nolan ran past across the terrace, his feet crushing the peacock feathers as Leonora laughed. We tried to stop Manuel, but he raced ahead up the slope. Stung by Leonora's taunt, he skipped among the rocks, disappearing from sight in the darkening air. On the terrace a small crowd gathered to watch.

The yellow and tangerine glider rose into the sky and climbed across the face of the storm-cloud. Fifty yards from the dark billows it was buffeted by the shifting air, but Manuel soared in and began to cut away at the dark face. Drops of black rain fell across the terrace at our feet.

The first outline of a woman's head appeared, satanic eyes lit by the open vents in the cloud, a sliding mouth like a dark smear as the huge billows boiled forwards. Nolan shouted in warning from the lake as he climbed into his glider. A moment later little Manuel's craft was lifted by a powerful updraught and tossed over the roof of the cloud. Fighting the insane air, Manuel plunged the glider downwards and drove into the cloud again. Then its immense face opened, and in a sudden spasm the cloud surged forward and swallowed the glider.

There was silence on the terrace as the crushed body of the craft revolved in the centre of the cloud. It moved over our heads, dismembered pieces of the wings and fuselage churned about in the dissolving face. As it reached the lake the cloud began its violent end. Pieces of the face slewed sideways, the mouth was torn off, an eye exploded. It vanished in a last brief squall.

The pieces of Petit Manuel's glider fell from the bright air.

Beatrice Lafferty and I drove across the lake to collect Manuel's body. After the spectacle of his death within the exploding replica of their hostess's face, the guests began to leave. Within minutes the drive was full of cars. Leonora watched them go, standing with Van Eyck among the deserted tables.

Beatrice said nothing as we drove out. The pieces of the shattered glider lay over the fused sand, tags of canvas and broken struts, control lines tied into knots. Ten yards from the cockpit I found Petit Manuel's body, lying in a wet ball like a drowned monkey.

I carried him back to the sand-yacht.

'Raymond!' Beatrice pointed to the shore. Storm-clouds were massed along the entire length of the lake, and the first flashes of lightning were striking in the hills behind the mesa. In the electric air the villa had lost its glitter. Half a mile away a tornado was moving along the valley floor, its trunk swaying towards the lake.

The first gust of air struck the yacht. Beatrice shouted again: 'Raymond! Nolan's there – he's flying inside it!'

Then I saw the black-winged glider circling under the umbrella of the tornado, Nolan himself riding in the whirlwind. His wings held steady in the revolving air around the funnel. Like a pilot fish he soared in, as if steering the tornado towards Leonora's villa.

Twenty seconds later, when it struck the house, I lost sight of him. An explosion of dark air overwhelmed the villa, a churning centrifuge of shattered chairs and tiles that burst over the roof. Beatrice and I ran from the yacht, and lay together in a fault in the glass surface. As the tornado moved away, fading into the storm-filled sky, a dark squall hung over the wrecked villa, now and then flicking the debris into the air. Shreds of canvas and peacock feathers fell around us.

We waited half an hour before approaching the house. Hundreds of smashed glasses and broken chairs littered the terrace. At first I could see no signs of Leonora, although her face was everywhere, the portraits with their slashed profiles strewn on the damp tiles. An eddying smile floated towards me from the disturbed air, and wrapped itself around my leg.

Leonora's body lay among the broken tables near the bandstand, half-wrapped in a bleeding canvas. Her face was as bruised now as the storm-cloud Manuel had tried to carve.

We found Van Eyck in the wreck of the marquee. He was suspended by the neck from a tangle of electric wiring, his pale face wreathed in a noose of light bulbs. The current flowed intermittently through the wiring, lighting up the coloured globes.

I leaned against the overturned Rolls, holding Beatrice's shoulders. 'There's no sign of Nolan – no pieces of his glider.'

'Poor man. Raymond, he was driving that whirlwind here. Somehow he was controlling it.'

I walked across the damp terrace to where Leonora lay. I began to cover her with the shreds of canvas, the torn faces of herself.

I took Beatrice Lafferty to live with me in Nolan's studio in the desert near Coral D. We heard no more of Nolan and never flew the gliders again. The clouds carry too many memories. Three months ago a man who saw the derelict gliders outside the studio stopped near Coral D and walked across to us. He told us he had seen a man flying a glider in the sky high above Red Beach, carving the strato-cirrus into images of jewels and children's faces. Once there was a dwarf's head.

On reflection, that sounds rather like Nolan, so perhaps he managed to get away from the tornado. In the evenings Beatrice and I sit among the sonic statues, listening to their voices as the fair-weather clouds rise above Coral D, waiting for a man in a dark-winged glider, perhaps painted like candy now, who will come in on the wind and carve for us images of seahorses and unicorns, dwarfs and jewels and children's faces.

, **1967**

# WHY I WANT TO FUCK RONALD REAGAN

## During these assassination fantasies

Ronald Reagan and the conceptual auto-disaster. Numerous studies have been conducted upon patients in terminal paresis (G.P.I.), placing Reagan in a series of simulated auto-crashes, e.g. multiple pile-ups, head-on collisions, motorcade attacks (fantasies of Presidential assassinations remained a continuing preoccupation, subjects showing a marked polymorphic fixation on windshields and rear trunk assemblies). Powerful erotic fantasies of an anal-sadistic character surrounded the image of the Presidential contender. Subjects were required to construct the optimum auto-disaster victim by placing a replica of Reagan's head on the unretouched photographs of crash fatalities. In 82 per cent of cases massive rear-end collisions were selected with a preference for expressed faecal matter and rectal haemorrhages. Further tests were conducted to define the optimum model-year. These indicate that a three-year model lapse with child victims provide the maximum audience excitation (confirmed by manufacturers' studies of the optimum auto-disaster). It is hoped to construct a rectal modulus of Reagan and the auto-disaster of maximized audience arousal.

## Tallis became increasingly obsessed

Motion picture studies of Ronald Reagan reveal characteristic patterns of facial tonus and musculature associated with homo-erotic behaviour. The continuing tension of buccal sphincters and the recessive tongue role tally with earlier studies of facial rigidity (cf., Adolf Hitler, Nixon). Slow-motion cine-films of campaign speeches exercised a marked erotic effect upon an audience of spastic children. Even with mature adults the verbal material was found to have minimal effect, as demonstrated by substitution of an edited tape giving diametrically opposed opinions. Parallel films of rectal images revealed a sharp upsurge in anti-Semitic and concentration camp fantasies.

## with the pudenda of the Presidential contender

Incidence of orgasms in fantasies of sexual intercourse with Ronald Reagan. Patients were provided with assembly kit photographs of sexual partners during intercourse. In each case Reagan's face was superimposed upon the original partner. Vaginal intercourse with 'Reagan' proved uniformly disappointing, producing orgasm in 2 per cent of subjects.

Axillary, buccal, navel, aural and orbital modes produced proximal erections. The preferred mode of entry overwhelmingly proved to be the rectal. After a preliminary course in anatomy it was found that caecum and transverse colon also provided excellent sites for excitation. In an extreme 12 per cent of cases, the simulated anus of post-colostomy surgery generated spontaneous orgasm in 98 per cent of penetrations. Multiple-track cine-films were constructed of 'Reagan' in intercourse during (a) campaign speeches, (b) rear-end auto-collisions with one and three-year-old model changes, (c) with rear-exhaust assemblies, (d) with Vietnamese child-atrocity victims.

### mediated to him by a thousand television screens.

Sexual fantasies in connection with Ronald Reagan. The genitalia of the Presidential contender exercised a continuing fascination. A series of imaginary genitalia were constructed using (a) the mouth-parts of Jacqueline Kennedy, (b) a Cadillac rear-exhaust vent, (c) the assembly kit prepuce of President Johnson, (d) a child-victim of sexual assault. In 89 per cent of cases, the constructed genitalia generated a high incidence of self-induced orgasm. Tests indicate the masturbatory nature of the Presidential contender's posture. Dolls consisting of plastic models of Reagan's alternate genitalia were found to have a disturbing effect on deprived children.

### The motion picture studies of Ronald Reagan

Reagan's hairstyle. Studies were conducted on the marked fascination exercised by the Presidential contender's hairstyle. 65 per cent of male subjects made positive connections between the hairstyle and their own pubic hair. A series of optimum hairstyles were constructed.

### created a scenario of the conceptual orgasm,

The conceptual role of Reagan. Fragments of Reagan's cinetized postures were used in the construction of model psychodramas in which the Reagan-figure played the role of husband, doctor, insurance salesman, marriage counsellor, etc. The failure of these roles to express any meaning reveals the non-functional character of Reagan. Reagan's success therefore indicates society's periodic need to re-conceptualize its political leaders. Reagan thus appears as a series of posture concepts, basic equations which re-formulate the roles of aggression and anality.

### a unique ontology of violence and disaster.

Reagan's personality. The profound anality of the Presidential contender may be expected to dominate the United States in the coming years. By contrast the late J.F. Kennedy remained the prototype of the oral object, usually conceived in pre-pubertal terms. In further studies sadistic psychopaths were given the task of devising sex fantasies involving Reagan. Results confirm the probability of Presidential figures being perceived primarily in genital terms; the face of L.B. Johnson is clearly genital in significant appearance – the nasal prepuce, scrotal jaw, etc. Faces were seen as either circumcised (JFK, Khrushchev) or uncircumcised (LBJ, Adenauer). In assembly kit tests Reagan's face was uniformly perceived as a penile erection. Patients were encouraged to devise the optimum sex-death of Ronald Reagan.

**1968**

# THE DEAD ASTRONAUT

Cape Kennedy has gone now, its gantries rising from the deserted dunes. Sand has come in across the Banana River, filling the creeks and turning the old space complex into a wilderness of swamps and broken concrete. In the summer, hunters build their blinds in the wrecked staff-cars; but by early November, when Judith and I arrived, the entire area was abandoned. Beyond Cocoa Beach, where I stopped the car, the ruined motels were half hidden in the saw grass. The launching towers rose into the evening air like the rusting ciphers of some forgotten algebra of the sky.

'The perimeter fence is half a mile ahead,' I said. 'We'll wait here until it's dark. Do you feel better now?'

Judith was staring at an immense funnel of cerise cloud that seemed to draw the day with it below the horizon, taking the light from her faded blonde hair. The previous afternoon, in the hotel in Tampa, she had fallen ill briefly with some unspecified complaint.

'What about the money?' she asked. 'They may want more, now that we're here.'

'Five thousand dollars? Ample, Judith. These relic hunters are a dying breed – few people are interested in Cape Kennedy any longer. What's the matter?'

Her thin fingers were fretting at the collar of her suede jacket. 'I . . . it's just that perhaps I should have worn black.'

'Why? Judith, this isn't a funeral. For heaven's sake, Robert died twenty years ago. I know all he meant to us, but . . .'

Judith was staring at the debris of tyres and abandoned cars, her pale eyes becalmed in her drawn face. 'Philip, don't you understand, he's coming back now. Someone's got to be here. The memorial service over the radio was a horrible travesty – my God, that priest would have had a shock if Robert had talked back to him. There ought to be a full-scale committee, not just you and I and these empty nightclubs.'

In a firmer voice, I said: 'Judith, there would be a committee – *if* we told the NASA Foundation what we know. The remains would be interred in the NASA vault at Arlington, there'd be a band – even the President might be there. There's still time.'

I waited for her to reply, but she was watching the gantries fade into the night sky. Fifteen years ago, when the dead astronaut orbiting the earth in his burned-out capsule had been forgotten, Judith had constituted herself a memorial committee of one. Perhaps, in a few days, when she finally held the last relics of Robert Hamilton's body in her own hands, she would come to terms with her obsession.

'Philip, over there! Is that –'

High in the western sky, between the constellations Cepheus and Cassiopeia, a point of white light moved towards us, like a lost star searching for its zodiac. Within a few minutes, it passed overhead, its faint beacon setting behind the cirrus over the sea.

'It's all right, Judith.' I showed her the trajectory timetables pencilled into my diary. 'The relic hunters read these orbits off the sky better than any computer. They must have been watching the pathways for years.'

'Who was it?'

'A Russian woman pilot – Valentina Prokrovna. She was sent up from a site near the Urals twenty-five years ago to work on a television relay system.'

'Television? I hope they enjoyed the programme.'

This callous remark, uttered by Judith as she stepped from the car, made me realize once again her special motives for coming to Cape Kennedy. I watched the capsule of the dead woman disappear over the dark Atlantic stream, as always moved by the tragic but serene spectacle of one of these ghostly voyagers coming back after so many years from the tideways of space. All I knew of this dead Russian was her code name: Seagull. Yet, for some reason, I was glad to be there as she came down. Judith, on the other hand, felt nothing of this. During all the years she had sat in the garden in the cold evenings, too tired to bring herself to bed, she had been sustained by her concern for one only of the twelve dead astronauts orbiting the night sky.

As she waited, her back to the sea, I drove the car into the garage of an abandoned nightclub fifty yards from the road. From the trunk I took out two suitcases. One, a light travel-case, contained clothes for Judith and myself. The other, fitted with a foil inlay, reinforcing straps and a second handle, was empty.

We set off north towards the perimeter fence, like two late visitors arriving at a resort abandoned years earlier.

It was twenty years now since the last rockets had left their launching platforms at Cape Kennedy. At the time, NASA had already moved Judith and me – I was a senior flight-programmer – to the great new Planetary Space Complex in New Mexico. Shortly after our arrival, we had met one of the trainee astronauts, Robert Hamilton. After two decades, all I could remember of this over-polite but sharp-eyed young man was his albino skin, so like Judith's pale eyes and opal hair, the same cold gene that crossed them both with its arctic pallor. We had been close friends for barely six weeks. Judith's infatuation was one of those confused sexual impulses that well-brought-up young women express in their own naive way; and as I watched them swim and play tennis together, I felt not so much resentful as concerned to sustain the whole passing illusion for her.

A year later, Robert Hamilton was dead. He had returned to Cape Kennedy for the last military flights before the launching grounds were closed. Three hours after lift-off, a freak meteorite collision ruptured his oxygen support system. He had lived on in his suit for another five hours. Although calm at first, his last radio transmissions were an incoherent babble Judith and I had never been allowed to hear.

A dozen astronauts had died in orbital accidents, their capsules left to revolve through the night sky like the stars of a new constellation; and at first, Judith had shown little response. Later, after her miscarriage, the figure of this dead astronaut circling the sky above us re-emerged in her mind as an obsession with time. For hours, she would stare at the bedroom clock, as if waiting for something to happen.

Five years later, after I resigned from NASA, we made our first trip to Cape Kennedy. A few military units still guarded the derelict gantries, but already the former launching site was being used as a satellite graveyard. As the dead capsules lost orbital velocity, they homed on to the master radio beacon. As well as the American vehicles, Russian and French satellites in the joint Euro-American space projects were brought down here, the burned-out hulks of the capsules exploding across the cracked concrete.

Already, too, the relic hunters were at Cape Kennedy, scouring the burning saw grass for instrument panels and flying suits and – most valuable of all – the mummified corpses of the dead astronauts.

These blackened fragments of collar-bone and shin, kneecap and rib, were the unique relics of the space age, as treasured as the saintly bones of medieval shrines. After the first fatal accident in space, public outcry demanded that these orbiting biers be brought down to earth. Unfortunately, when a returning moon rocket crashed into the Kalahari Desert, aboriginal tribesmen broke into the vehicle. Believing the crew to be dead gods, they cut off the eight hands and vanished into the bush. It had taken two years to track them down. From then on, the capsules were left in orbit to burn out on re-entry.

Whatever remains survived the crash landings in the satellite graveyard were scavenged by the relic hunters of Cape Kennedy. This band of nomads had lived for years in the wrecked cars and motels, stealing their icons under the feet of the wardens who patrolled the concrete decks. In early October, when a former NASA colleague told me that Robert Hamilton's satellite was becoming unstable, I drove down to Tampa and began to inquire about the purchase price of Robert's mortal remains. Five thousand dollars was a small price to pay for laying his ghost to rest in Judith's mind.

Eight hundred yards from the road, we crossed the perimeter fence. Crushed by the dunes, long sections of the twenty-foot-high palisade had collapsed, the saw grass growing through the steel mesh. Below us, the boundary road passed a derelict guardhouse and divided into two paved tracks. As we waited at this rendezvous, the headlamps of the wardens' half-tracks flared across the gantries near the beach.

Five minutes later, a small dark-faced man climbed from the rear seat of a car buried in the sand fifty yards away. Head down, he scuttled over to us.

'Mr and Mrs Groves?' After a pause to peer into our faces, he introduced himself tersely: 'Quinton. Sam Quinton.'

As he shook hands, his clawlike fingers examined the bones of my wrist and forearm. His sharp nose made circles in the air. He had the eyes of a nervous bird, forever searching the dunes and the grass. An Army webbing belt hung around his patched black denims. He moved his hands restlessly in the air, as if conducting a chamber ensemble hidden behind the sand hills, and I noticed his badly scarred palms. Huge weals formed pale stars in the darkness.

For a moment, he seemed disappointed by us, almost reluctant to move on. Then he set off at a brisk pace across the dunes, now and then leaving us to blunder about helplessly. Half an hour later, when we entered a shallow basin near a farm of alkali-settling beds, Judith and I were exhausted, dragging the suitcases over the broken tyres and barbed wire.

A group of cabins had been dismantled from their original sites along the beach and re-erected in the basin. Isolated rooms tilted on the sloping sand, mantelpieces and flowered paper decorating the outer walls.

The basin was full of salvaged space material: sections of capsules, heat shields, antennas and parachute canisters. Near the dented hull of a weather satellite, two sallow-faced men in sheepskin jackets sat on a car seat. The older wore a frayed Air Force cap over his eyes. With his scarred hands, he was polishing the steel visor of a space helmet. The other, a young man with a faint beard hiding his mouth, watched us approach with the detached and neutral gaze of an undertaker.

We entered the largest of the cabins, two rooms taken off the rear of a beach-house. Quinton lit a paraffin lamp. He pointed around the dingy interior. 'You'll be . . . comfortable,' he said without conviction. As Judith stared at him with unconcealed distaste, he added pointedly: 'We don't get many visitors.'

I put the suitcases on the metal bed. Judith walked into the kitchen and Quinton began to open the empty case.

'It's in here?'

I took the two packets of $100 bills from my jacket. When I had handed them to him, I said: 'The suitcase is for the . . . remains. Is it big enough?'

Quinton peered at me through the ruby light, as if baffled by our presence there. 'You could have spared yourself the trouble. They've been up there a long time, Mr Groves. After the impact' – for some reason, he cast a lewd eye in Judith's direction – 'there might be enough for a chess set.'

When he had gone, I went into the kitchen. Judith stood by the stove, hands on a carton of canned food. She was staring through the window at the metal salvage, refuse of the sky that still carried Robert Hamilton in its rusty centrifuge. For a moment, I had the feeling that the entire landscape of the earth was covered with rubbish and that here, at Cape Kennedy, we had found its source.

I held her shoulders. 'Judith, is there any point in this? Why don't we go back to Tampa? I could drive here in ten days' time when it's all over –'

She turned from me, her hands rubbing the suede where I had marked it. 'Philip, I want to be here – no matter how unpleasant. Can't you understand?'

At midnight, when I finished making a small meal for us, she was standing on the concrete wall of the settling tank. The three relic hunters sitting on their car seats watched her without moving, scarred hands like flames in the darkness.

At three o'clock that morning, as we lay awake on the narrow bed, Valentina Prokrovna came down from the sky. Enthroned on a bier of burning aluminium three hundred yards wide, she soared past on her final orbit. When I went out into the night air, the relic hunters had gone. From the rim of the settling tank, I watched them race away among the dunes, leaping like hares over the tyres and wire.

I went back to the cabin. 'Judith, she's coming down. Do you want to watch?'

Her blonde hair tied within a white towel, Judith lay on the bed, staring at the cracked plasterboard ceiling. Shortly after four o'clock, as I sat beside her, a phosphorescent light filled the hollow. There was the distant sound of explosions, muffled by the high wall of the dunes. Lights flared, followed by the noise of engines and sirens.

At dawn the relic hunters returned, hands wrapped in makeshift bandages, dragging their booty with them.

After this melancholy rehearsal, Judith entered a period of sudden and unexpected activity. As if preparing the cabin for some visitor, she rehung the curtains and swept out the two rooms with meticulous care, even bringing herself to ask Quinton for a bottle of cleanser. For hours she sat at the dressing table, brushing and shaping her hair, trying out first one style and then another. I watched her feel the hollows of her cheeks, searching for the contours of a face that had vanished twenty years ago. As she spoke about Robert Hamilton, she almost seemed worried that she would appear old to him. At other times, she referred to Robert as if he were a child, the son she and I had never been able to conceive since her miscarriage. These different roles followed one another like scenes in some private psychodrama. However, without knowing it, for years Judith and I had used Robert Hamilton for our own reasons. Waiting for him to land, and well aware that after this Judith would have no one to turn to except myself, I said nothing.

Meanwhile, the relic hunters worked on the fragments of Valentina Prokrovna's capsule: the blistered heat shield, the chassis of the radio-telemetry unit and several cans of film that recorded her collision and act of death (these, if still intact, would fetch the highest prices, films of horrific and dreamlike violence played in the underground cinemas of Los Angeles, London and Moscow). Passing the next cabin, I saw a tattered silver space-suit spread-eagled on two automobile seats. Quinton and the relic hunters knelt beside it, their arms deep inside the legs and sleeves, gazing at me with the rapt and sensitive eyes of jewellers.

An hour before dawn, I was awakened by the sound of engines along the beach. In the darkness, the three relic hunters crouched by the settling tank, their pinched faces lit by the headlamps. A long convoy of trucks and half-tracks was moving into the launching ground. Soldiers jumped down from the tailboards, unloading tents and supplies.

'What are they doing?' I asked Quinton. 'Are they looking for us?'

The old man cupped a scarred hand over his eyes. 'It's the Army,' he said uncertainly. 'Manoeuvres, maybe. They haven't been here before like this.'

'What about Hamilton?' I gripped his bony arm. 'Are you sure –'

He pushed me away with a show of nervous temper. 'We'll get him first. Don't worry, he'll be coming sooner than they think.'

Two nights later, as Quinton prophesied, Robert Hamilton began his final descent. From the dunes near the settling tanks, we watched him emerge from the stars on his last run. Reflected in the windows of the buried cars, a thousand images of the capsule flared in the saw grass around us. Behind the satellite, a wide fan of silver spray opened in a phantom wake.

In the Army encampment by the gantries, there was a surge of activity. A blaze of headlamps crossed the concrete lanes. Since the arrival of these military units, it had become plain to me, if not to Quinton, that far from being on manoeuvres, they were preparing for the landing of Robert Hamilton's capsule. A dozen half-tracks had been churning around the dunes, setting fire to the abandoned cabins and crushing the old car bodies. Platoons of soldiers were repairing the perimeter fence and replacing the sections of metalled road that the relic hunters had dismantled.

Shortly after midnight, at an elevation of forty-two degrees in the north-west, betwen Lyra and Hercules, Robert Hamilton appeared for the last time. As Judith stood up and shouted into the night air, an immense blade of light cleft the sky. The expanding corona sped towards us like a gigantic signal flare, illuminating every fragment of the landscape.

'Mrs Groves!' Quinton darted after Judith and pulled her down into the grass as she ran towards the approaching satellite. Three hundred yards away, the silhouette of a half-track stood out on an isolated dune, its feeble spotlights drowned by the glare.

With a low metallic sigh, the burning capsule of the dead astronaut soared over our heads, the vaporizing metal pouring from its hull. A few seconds later, as I shielded my eyes, an explosion of detonating sand rose from the ground behind me. A curtain of dust lifted into the darkening air like a vast spectre of powdered bone. The sounds of the impact rolled across the dunes. Near the launching gantries, fires flickered where fragments of the capsule had landed. A pall of phosphorescing gas hung in the air, particles within it beading and winking.

Judith had gone, running after the relic hunters through the swerving spotlights. When I caught up with them, the last fires of the explosion were dying among the gantries. The capsule had landed near the old Atlas launching pads, forming a shallow crater fifty yards in diameter. The slopes were scattered with glowing particles, sparkling like fading eyes. Judith ran distraughtly up and down, searching the fragments of smouldering metal.

Someone struck my shoulder. Quinton and his men, hot ash on their scarred hands, ran past like a troop of madmen, eyes wild in the crazed night. As we darted away through the flaring spotlights, I looked back at the beach. The gantries were enveloped in a pale-silver sheen that hovered there, and then moved away like a dying wraith over the sea.

At dawn, as the engines growled among the dunes, we collected the last remains of Robert Hamilton. The old man came into our cabin. As Judith watched from the kitchen, drying her hands on a towel, he gave me a cardboard shoe-box.

I held the box in my hands. 'Is this all you could get?'

'It's all there was. Look at them, if you want.'

'That's all right. We'll be leaving in half an hour.'

He shook his head. 'Not now. They're all around. If you move, they'll find us.'

He waited for me to open the shoe-box, then grimaced and went out into the pale light.

We stayed for another four days, as the Army patrols searched the surrounding dunes. Day and night, the half-tracks lumbered among the wrecked cars and cabins. Once, as I watched with Quinton from a fallen water tower, a half-track and two jeeps came within four hundred yards of the basin, held back only by the stench from the settling beds and the cracked concrete causeways.

During this time, Judith sat in the cabin, the shoe-box on her lap. She said nothing to me, as if she had lost all interest in me and the salvage-filled hollow at Cape Kennedy. Mechanically, she combed her hair, making and remaking her face.

On the second day, I came in after helping Quinton bury the cabins to their windows in the sand. Judith was standing by the table.

The shoe-box was open. In the centre of the table lay a pile of charred sticks, as if she had tried to light a small fire. Then I realized what was there. As she stirred the ash with her fingers, grey flakes fell from the joints, revealing the bony points of a clutch of ribs, a right hand and shoulder blade.

She looked at me with puzzled eyes. 'They're black,' she said.

Holding her in my arms, I lay with her on the bed. A loudspeaker reverberated among the dunes, fragments of the amplified commands drumming at the panes.

When they moved away, Judith said: 'We can go now.'

'In a little while, when it's clear. What about these?'

'Bury them. Anywhere, it doesn't matter.' She seemed calm at last, giving me a brief smile, as if to agree that this grim charade was at last over.

Yet, when I had packed the bones into the shoe-box, scraping up Robert Hamilton's ash with a dessert spoon, she kept it with her, carrying it into the kitchen while she prepared our meals.

It was on the third day that we fell ill.

After a long, noise-filled night, I found Judith sitting in front of the mirror, combing thick clumps of hair from her scalp. Her mouth was open, as if her lips were stained with acid. As she dusted the loose hair from her lap, I was struck by the leprous whiteness of her face.

Standing up with an effort, I walked listlessly into the kitchen and stared at the saucepan of cold coffee. A sense of indefinable exhaustion had come over me, as if the bones in my body had softened and lost their rigidity. On the lapels of my jacket, loose hair lay like spinning waste.

'Philip . . .' Judith swayed towards me. 'Do you feel – What is it?'

'The water.' I poured the coffee into the sink and massaged my throat. 'It must be fouled.'

'Can we leave?' She put a hand up to her forehead. Her brittle nails brought down a handful of frayed ash hair. 'Philip, for God's sake – I'm losing all my hair!'

Neither of us was able to eat. After forcing myself through a few slices of cold meat, I went out and vomited behind the cabin.

Quinton and his men were crouched by the wall of the settling tank. As I walked towards them, steadying myself against the hull of the weather satellite, Quinton came down. When I told him that the water supplies were contaminated, he stared at me with his hard bird's eyes.

Half an hour later, they were gone.

The next day, our last there, we were worse. Judith lay on the bed, shivering in her jacket, the shoe-box held in one hand. I spent hours searching for fresh water in the cabins. Exhausted, I could barely cross the sandy basin. The Army patrols were closer. By now, I could hear the hard gear-changes of the half-tracks. The sounds from the loudspeakers drummed like fists on my head.

Then, as I looked down at Judith from the cabin doorway, a few words stuck for a moment in my mind.

'  *... contaminated area ... evacuate ... radioactive ...*'

I walked forward and pulled the box from Judith's hands.

'Philip ...' She looked up at me weakly. 'Give it back to me.'

Her face was a puffy mask. On her wrists, white flecks were forming. Her left hand reached towards me like the claw of a cadaver.

I shook the box with blunted anger. The bones rattled inside. 'For God's sake, it's *this*! Don't you see – why we're ill?'

'Philip – where are the others? The old man. Get them to help you.'

'They've gone. They went yesterday, I told you.' I let the box fall on to the table. The lid broke off, spilling the ribs tied together like a bundle of firewood. 'Quinton knew what was happening – why the Army is here. They're trying to warn us.'

'What do you mean?' Judith sat up, the focus of her eyes sustained only by a continuous effort. 'Don't let them take Robert. Bury him here somewhere. We'll come back later.'

'Judith!' I bent over the bed and shouted hoarsely at her. 'Don't you realize – there was a *bomb* on board! Robert Hamilton was carrying an atomic weapon!' I pulled back the curtains from the window. 'My God, what a joke. For twenty years, I put up with him because I couldn't ever be really sure ...'

'Philip ...'

'Don't worry, I used him – thinking about him was the only thing that kept us going. And all the time, he was waiting up there to pay us back!'

There was a rumble of exhaust outside. A half-track with red crosses on its doors and hood had reached the edge of the basin. Two men in vinyl suits jumped down, counters raised in front of them.

'Judith, before we go, tell me ... I never asked you –'

Judith was sitting up, touching the hair on her pillow. One half of her scalp was almost bald. She stared at her weak hands with their silvering skin. On her face was an expression I had never seen before, the dumb anger of betrayal.

As she looked at me, and at the bones scattered across the table, I knew my answer.

. **1968**

# THE COMSAT ANGELS

When I first heard about the assignment, in the summer of 1968, I did my best to turn it down. Charles Whitehead, producer of BBC TV's science programme *Horizon*, asked me to fly over to France with him and record a press conference being held by a fourteen-year-old child prodigy, Georges Duval, who was attracting attention in the Paris newspapers. The film would form part of *Horizon*'s new series, which I was scripting, 'The Expanding Mind', about the role of communications satellites and data-processing devices in the so-called information explosion. What annoyed me was this insertion of irrelevant and sensational material into an otherwise serious programme.

'Charles, you'll destroy the whole thing,' I protested across his desk that morning. 'These child prodigies are all the same. Either they simply have some freak talent or they're being manipulated by ambitious parents. Do you honestly believe this boy is a genius?'

'He *might* be, James. Who can say?' Charles waved a plump hand at the contact prints of orbiting satellites pinned to the walls. 'We're doing a programme about advanced communications systems – if they have any justification at all, it's that they bring rare talents like this one to light.'

'Rubbish – these prodigies have been exposed time and again. They bear the same relation to true genius that a cross-channel swimmer does to a lunar astronaut.'

In the end, despite my protests, Charles won me over, but I was still sceptical when we flew to Orly Airport the next morning. Every two or three years there were reports of some newly discovered child genius. The pattern was always the same: the prodigy had mastered chess at the age of three, Sanskrit and calculus at six, Einstein's General Theory of Relativity at twelve. The universities and conservatories of America and Europe opened their doors.

For some reason, though, nothing ever came of these precocious talents. Once the parents, or an unscrupulous commercial sponsor, had squeezed the last drop of publicity out of the child, his so-called genius seemed to evaporate and he vanished into oblivion.

'Do you remember Minou Drouet?' I asked Charles as we drove from Orly. 'A child prodigy of a few years back. Cocteau read her poems and said, "Every child is a genius *except* Minou Drouet."'

'James, relax ... Like all scientists, you can't bear anything that challenges your own prejudices. Let's wait until we see him. He might surprise us.'

He certainly did, though not as we expected.

Georges Duval lived with his widowed mother in the small town of Montereau, on the Seine thirty miles south of Paris. As we drove across the cobbled square past the faded police prefecture, it seemed an unlikely birthplace for another Darwin, Freud or Curie. However, the Duvals' house was an expensively built white-walled villa overlooking a placid arm of the river. A well-tended lawn ran down to a vista of swans and water-meadows.

Parked in the drive was the location truck of the film unit we had hired, and next to it a radio van from Radio-Television-Française and a Mercedes with a *Paris-Match* sticker across the rear window. Sound cables ran across the gravel into a kitchen window. A sharp-faced maid led us without ado towards the press conference. In the lounge, four rows of gilt chairs brought in from the Hôtel de Ville faced a mahogany table by the windows. Here a dozen cameramen were photographing Madame Duval, a handsome woman of thirty-five with calm grey eyes, arms circumspectly folded below two strands of pearls. A trio of solemn-faced men in formal suits protected her from the technicians setting up microphones and trailing their cables under the table.

Already, fifteen minutes before Georges Duval appeared, I felt there was something bogus about the atmosphere. The three dark-suited men – the Director of Studies at the Sorbonne, a senior bureaucrat from the French Ministry of Education, and a representative of the Institut Pascal, a centre of advanced study – gave the conference an overstuffed air only slightly eased by the presence of the local mayor, a homely figure in a shiny suit, and the boy's schoolmaster, a lantern-jawed man hunched around his pipe.

Needless to say, when Georges Duval arrived, he was a total disappointment. Accompanied by a young priest, the family counsellor, he took his seat behind the table, bowing to the three officials and giving his mother a dutiful buss on the cheek. As the lights came on and the cameras began to turn, his eyes stared down at us without embarrassment.

Georges Duval was then fourteen, a slim-shouldered boy small for his age, self-composed in a grey flannel suit. His face was pale and anaemic, hair plastered down to hide his huge bony forehead. He kept his hands in his pockets, concealing his over-large wrists. What struck me immediately was the lack of any emotion or expression on his face, as if he had left his mind in the next room, hard at work on some intricate problem.

Professor Leroux of the Sorbonne opened the press conference. Georges had first come to light when he had taken his mathematics degree at thirteen, the youngest since Descartes. Leroux described Georges's career: reading at the age of two, by nine he had passed his full matriculation exam – usually taken at fifteen or sixteen. As a vacation hobby he had mastered English and German, by eleven had passed the diploma of the Paris Conservatoire in music theory, by twelve was working for his degree. He had shown a precocious interest in molecular biology, and already corresponded with biochemists at Harvard and Cambridge.

While this familiar catalogue was being unfolded, Georges's eyes, below that large carapace of a skull, showed not a glimmer of emotion. Now and then he glanced at a balding young man in a soft grey suit sitting by himself in the front row. At the time I thought he was Georges's elder brother – he had the same high bony temples and closed face. Later, however, I discovered that he had a very different role.

Questions were invited for Georges. These followed the usual pattern – what did he think of Vietnam, the space-race, the psychedelic scene, miniskirts, girls, Brigitte Bardot? In short, not a question of a serious nature. Georges answered in good humour, stating that outside his studies he had no worthwhile opinions. His voice was firm and reasonably modest, but he looked more and more bored by the conference, and as soon as it broke up, he joined the young man in the front row. Together they left the room, the same abstracted look on their faces that one sees in the insane, as if crossing our own universe at a slight angle.

While we made our way out, I talked to the other journalists. Georges's father had been an assembly worker at the Renault plant in Paris; neither he nor Madame Duval was in the least educated, and the house, into which the widow and son had moved only two months earlier, was paid for by a large research foundation. Evidently there were unseen powers standing guard over Georges Duval. He apparently never played with the boys from the town.

As we drove away, Charles Whitehead said slyly: 'I notice you didn't ask any questions yourself.'

'The whole thing was a complete set-up. We might as well have been interviewing De Gaulle.'

'Perhaps we were.'

'You think the General may be behind all this?'

'It's possible. Let's face it, if the boy *is* outstanding, it makes it more difficult for him to go off and work for Du Pont or IBM.'

'But is he? He was intelligent, of course, but all the same, I'll bet you that three years from now no one will even remember him.'

After we returned to London my curiosity came back a little. In the Air France bus to the TV Centre at White City I scanned the children on the pavement. Without a doubt none of them had the maturity and intelligence of Georges Duval. Two mornings later, when I found myself still thinking about Georges, I went up to the research library.

As I turned through the clippings, going back twenty years, I made an interesting discovery. Starting in 1948, I found that a major news story about a child prodigy came up once every two years. The last celebrity had been Bobby Silverberg, a fifteen-year-old from Tampa, Florida. The photographs in the *Look, Paris-Match* and *Oggi* profiles might have been taken of Georges Duval. Apart from the American setting, every ingredient was the same: the press conference, TV cameras, presiding officials, the high-school principal, doting mother – and the young genius himself, this time with a crew-cut and nothing to hide that high bony skull. There were two college degrees already passed, postgraduate fellowships offered by MIT, Princeton and CalTech.

And then what?

'That was nearly three years ago,' I said to Judy Walsh, my secretary. 'What's he doing now?'

She flicked through the index cards, then shook her head. 'Nothing. I suppose he's taking another degree at a university somewhere.'

'He's already got two degrees. By now he should have come up with a faster-than-light drive or a method of synthesizing life.'

'He's only seventeen. Wait until he's a little older.'

'Older? You've given me an idea. Let's go back to the beginning – 1948.'

Judy handed me the bundle of clippings. *Life* magazine had picked up the story of Gunther Bergman, the first post-war prodigy, a seventeen-year-old Swedish youth whose pale, over-large eyes stared out from the photographs. An unusual feature was the presence at the graduation ceremony at Uppsala University of three representatives from the Nobel Foundation. Perhaps because he was older than Silverberg and Georges Duval, his intellectual achievements seemed prodigious. The degree he was collecting was his third; already he had done original research in radio-astronomy, helping to identify the unusual radio-sources that a decade later were termed 'quasars'.

'A spectacular career in astronomy seems guaranteed. It should be easy to track him down. He'll be, what?, thirty-seven now, professor at least, well on his way to a Nobel Prize.'

We searched through the professional directories, telephoned Greenwich Observatory and the London Secretariat of the World Astronomical Federation.

No one had heard of Gunther Bergman.

'Right, where is he?' I asked Judy when we had exhausted all lines of inquiry. 'For heaven's sake, it's twenty years; he should be world-famous by now.'

'Perhaps he's dead.'

'That's possible.' I gazed down pensively at Judy's quizzical face. 'Put in a call to the Nobel Foundation. In fact, clear your desk and get all the international directories we can up here. We're going to make the Comsats sing.'

Three weeks later, when I carried my bulky briefcase into Charles Whitehead's office, there was an electric spring in my step.

Charles eyed me warily over his glasses. 'James, I hear you've been hard on the trail of our missing geniuses. What have you got?'

'A new programme.'

'New? We've already got Georges Duval listed in *Radio Times*.'

'For how long?' I pulled a chair up to his desk and opened my briefcase, then spread the dozen files in front of him. 'Let me put you in the picture. Judy and I have been back to 1948. In those twenty years there have been eleven cases of so-called geniuses. Georges Duval is the twelfth.'

I placed the list in front of him.

1948 Gunther Bergman (Uppsala, Sweden)
1950 Jaako Litmanen (Vaasa, Finland)
1952 John Warrender (Kansas City, USA)
1953 Arturo Bandini (Bologna, Italy)
1955 Gesai Ray (Calcutta, India)
1957 Giuliano Caldare (Palermo, Sicily)
1958 Wolfgang Herter (Cologne, Germany)
1960 Martin Sherrington (Canterbury, England)
1962 Josef Oblensky (Leningrad, USSR)
1964 Yen Hsi Shan (Wuhan, China)
1965 Robert Silverberg (Tampa, USA)
1968 Georges Duval (Montereau, France)

Charles studied the list, now and then patting his forehead with a floral handkerchief. 'Frankly, apart from Georges Duval, the names mean absolutely nothing.'

'Isn't that strange? There's enough talent there to win all the Nobel Prizes three times over.'

'Have you tried to trace them?'

I let out a cry of pain. Even the placid Judy gave a despairing shudder. 'Have we tried? My God, we've done nothing else. Charles, apart from checking a hundred directories and registers, we've contacted the original magazines and news agencies, checked with the universities that originally offered them scholarships, talked on the overseas lines to the BBC reporters in New York, Delhi and Moscow.'

'And? What do they know about them?'

'Nothing. A complete blank.'

Charles shook his head doggedly. 'They must be somewhere. What about the universities they were supposed to go to?'

'Nothing there, either. It's a curious thing, but not one of them actually went on to a university. We've contacted the senates of nearly fifty universities. Not a mention of them. They took external degrees while still at school, but after that they severed all connections with the academic world.'

Charles sat forward over the list, holding it like a portion of some treasure map. 'James, it looks as if you're going to win your bet. Somehow they all petered out in late adolescence. A sudden flaring of intelligence backed by prodigious memory, not matched by any real creative spark . . . that's it, I suppose – none of them was a genius.'

'As a matter of fact, I think they all were.' Before he could stop me I went on. 'Forget that for the moment. Whether or not they had genius is irrelevant. Certainly they had intellects vastly beyond the average, IQs of two hundred, enormous scholastic talents in a wide range of subjects. They had a sudden burst of fame and exposure and –'

'They vanished into thin air. What are you suggesting – some kind of conspiracy?'

'In a sense, yes.'

Charles handed me the list. 'Come off it. Do you really mean that a sinister government bureau has smuggled them off, they're slaving away now on some super-weapon?'

'It's possible, but I doubt it.' I took a packet of photographs from the second folder. 'Have a look at them.'

Charles picked up the first. 'Ah, there's Georges. He looks older here, those TV cameras are certainly ageing.'

'It's not Georges Duval. It's Oblensky, the Russian boy, taken six years ago. Quite a resemblance, though.' I spread the twelve photographs on the table top. Charles moved along the half-circle, comparing the over-large eyes and bony foreheads, the same steady gaze.

'Wait a minute! Are you sure this isn't Duval?' Charles picked up Oblensky's photograph and pointed to the figure of a young man in a light grey suit standing behind some mayoral official in a Leningrad parlour. '*He* was at Duval's press conference, sitting right in front of us.'

I nodded to Judy. 'You're right, Charles. And he's not only in that photo.' I pulled together the photographs of Bobby Silverberg, Herter and Martin Sherrington. In each one the same balding figure in the dove-grey suit was somewhere in the background, his over-sharp eyes avoiding the camera lens. 'No university admits to knowing him, nor do Shell, Philips, General Motors or a dozen other big international companies. Of course, there are other organizations he might be a talent scout for . . .'

Charles had stood up, and was slowly walking around his desk. 'Such as the CIA – you think he may be recruiting talent for some top-secret Government think-thank? It's unlikely, but –'

'What about the Russians?' I cut in. 'Or the Chinese? Let's face it, eleven young men have vanished into thin air. What happened to them?'

Charles stared down at the photographs. 'The strange thing is that I vaguely recognize all these faces. Those bony skulls, and those eyes . . . somewhere. Look, James, we may have the makings of a new programme here. This English prodigy, Martin Sherrington, he should be easy to track down. Then the German, Herter. Find them and we may be on to something.'

\*　　　\*　　　\*

We set off for Canterbury the next morning. The address, which I had been given by a friend who was science editor of the *Daily Express*, was on a housing estate behind the big General Electric radio and television plant on the edge of the city. We drove past the lines of grey-brick houses until we found the Sherringtons' at the end of a row. Rising out of the remains of a greenhouse was a huge ham operator's radio mast, its stay-wires snapped and rusting. In the eight years since his tremendous mind had revealed itself to the local grammar-school master, Martin Sherrington might have gone off to the ends of the world, to Cape Kennedy, the Urals or Peking.

In fact, not only were neither Martin nor his parents there, but it took us all of two days to find anyone who even remembered them at all. The present tenants of the house, a frayed-looking couple, had been there two years; and before them a large family of criminal inclinations who had been forced out by bailiffs and police. The headmaster of the grammar-school had retired to Scotland. Fortunately the school matron remembered Martin – 'a brilliantly clever boy, we were all very proud of him. To tell the truth, though, I can't say we felt much affection for him; he didn't invite it.' She knew nothing of Mrs Sherrington, and as for the boy's father, they assumed he had died in the war.

Finally, thanks to a cashier at the accounts office of the local electric company, we found where Mrs Sherrington had moved.

As soon as I saw that pleasant white-walled villa in its prosperous suburb on the other side of Canterbury, I felt that the trail was warming. Something about the crisp gravel and large, well-trimmed garden reminded me of another house – Georges Duval's near Paris.

From the roof of my car parked next to the hedge we watched a handsome, strong-shouldered woman strolling in the rose garden.

'She's come up in the world,' I commented. 'Who pays for this pad?'

The meeting was curious. This rather homely, quietly dressed woman in her late thirties gazed at us across the silver tea-set like a tamed Mona Lisa. She told us that we had absolutely no chance of interviewing Martin on television.

'So much interest in your son was roused at the time, Mrs Sherrington. Can you tell us about his subsequent academic career? Which university did he go to?'

'His education was completed privately.' As for his present whereabouts, she believed he was now abroad, working for a large international organization whose name she was not at liberty to divulge.

'Not a government department, Mrs Sherrington?'

She hesitated, but only briefly. 'I am told the organization is intimately connected with various governments, but I have no real knowledge.'

Her voice was over-precise, as if she were hiding her real accent. As we left, I realized how lonely her life was; but as Judy remarked, she had probably been lonely ever since Martin Sherrington had first learned to speak.

*     *     *

Our trip to Germany was equally futile. All traces of Wolfgang Herter had vanished from the map. A few people in the small village near the Frankfurt autobahn remembered him, and the village postman said that Frau Herter had moved to Switzerland, to a lakeside villa near Lucerne. A woman of modest means and education, but the son had no doubt done very well.

I asked one or two questions.

Wolfgang's father? Frau Herter had arrived with the child just after the war; the husband had probably perished in one of the nameless prison-camps or battlegrounds of World War II.

The balding man in the light grey suit? Yes, he had definitely come to the village, helping Frau Herter arrange her departure.

'Back to London,' I said to Judy. 'This needs bigger resources than you and I have.'

As we flew back Judy said: 'One thing I don't understand. Why have the fathers always disappeared?'

'A good question. Putting it crudely, love, a unique genetic coupling produced these twelve boys. It almost looks as if someone has torn the treasure map in two and kept one half. Think of the stock bank they're building up, enough sperm on ice in a eugenic cocktail to repopulate the entire planet.'

This nightmare prospect was on my mind when I walked into Charles Whitehead's office the next morning. It was the first time I had seen Charles in his shirtsleeves. To my surprise, he brushed aside my apologies, then beckoned me to the huge spread of photographs pinned to the plaster wall behind his desk. The office was a clutter of newspaper cuttings and blown-up newsreel stills. Charles was holding a magnifying glass over a photograph of President Johnson and McNamara at a White House reception.

'While you were gone we've been carrying out our own search,' he said. 'If it's any consolation, we couldn't trace any of them at first.'

'Then you have found them? Where?'

'Here.' He gestured at the dozens of photographs. 'Right in front of our noses. We're looking at them every day.'

He pointed to a news agency photograph of a Kremlin reception for Premier Ulbricht of East Germany. Kosygin and Brezhnev were there, Soviet President Podgorny talking to the Finnish Ambassador, and a crowd of twenty party functionaries.

'Recognize anyone? Apart from Kosygin and company?'

'The usual bunch of hatchet-faced waiters these people like to surround themselves with. Wait a minute, though.'

Charles's finger had paused over a quiet-faced young man with a high dolichocephalic head, standing at Kosygin's elbow. Curiously, the Soviet Premier's face was turned towards him rather than to Brezhnev.

'Oblensky – the Russian prodigy. What's he doing with Kosygin? He looks like an interpreter.'

'Between Kosygin and Brezhnev? Hardly. I've checked with the BBC and Reuters correspondents in Moscow. They've seen him around quite a bit. He never says anything in public, but the important men always talk to *him*.'

I put down the photograph. 'Charles, get on to the Foreign Office and the US Embassy. It makes sense – all eleven of them are probably there, in the Soviet Union.'

'Relax. That's what we thought. But have a look at these.'

The next picture had been taken at a White House meeting between Johnson, McNamara and General Westmoreland discussing US policy in Vietnam. There were the usual aides, secretaries and Secret Service men out on the lawn. One face had been ringed, that of a man in his early thirties standing unobtrusively behind Johnson and Westmoreland.

'Warrender – the 1952 genius! *He's* working for the US Government.'

'More surprises.' Charles guided me around the rest of the photographs. 'You might be interested in these.'

The next showed Pope Paul on the balcony of St Peter's, making his annual 'Urbis et Orbis' – the city and the world – benediction to the huge crowd in the square. Standing beside him were Cardinal Mancini, chief of the Papal Secretariat, and members of his household staff. Obliquely behind the Pope was a man of about thirty wearing what I guessed to be a Jesuit's soutane, large eyes watching Paul with a steady gaze.

'Bandini, Arturo Bandini,' I commented, recognizing the face. '*Oggi* did a series of features on him. He's moved high in the papal hierarchy.'

'There are few closer to Il Papa, or better loved.'

After that came a photograph of U Thant, taken at a UN Security Council meeting during the Cuban missile crisis. Sitting behind the Secretary General was a pale-skinned young Brahmin with a fine mouth and eyes – Gesai Ray, the high-caste Indian who was the only well-born prodigy I had come across.

'Ray is now even higher up on U Thant's staff,' Charles added. 'There's one interesting photograph of him and Warrender together during the Cuban crisis. Warrender was then on JFK's staff.' He went on casually: 'The year after Oblensky reached the Kremlin, Khrushchev was sacked.'

'So they're in contact? I'm beginning to realize what the Moscow–Washington hot line is really for.'

Charles handed me another still. 'Here's an old friend of yours – our own Martin Sherrington. He's on Professor Lovell's staff at the Jodrell Bank Radio-Observatory. One of the very few not to go into government or big business.'

'Big science, though.' I stared at the quiet, intense face of the elusive Sherrington, aware that someone at Jodrell Bank had deliberately put me off.

'Like Gunther Bergman – he moved to the United States fifteen years ago from Sweden, is now very high up in the NASA command chain. Yen Hsi Shan is the youngest, barely seventeen, but have a look at this.'

The photograph showed Mao Tse-tung and Chou En-lai on the reviewing platform in Peking during the cultural revolution, an immense concourse of teenagers passing below, all holding copies of Mao's *Thoughts* and chanting out slogans. Standing between Mao and Chou was a boy with a fist in the air who was the chief Red Guard.

'Yen Hsi Shan. He's started early,' Charles said. 'One or two of the others we haven't been able to trace as yet, though we hear Herter is with the giant Zurich-Hamburg banking trust. Jaako Litmanen, the Finnish prodigy, is rumoured to be working for the Soviet space programme.'

'Well, one has to admit it,' I commented, 'they've certainly all made good.'

'Not all.' Charles showed me the last picture, of the Sicilian genius Giuliano Caldare. 'One of them made bad. Caldare emigrated to the United States in 1960, is now in the inner circle of the Cosa Nostra, a coming talent from all one hears.'

I sat down at Charles's desk. 'Right, but what does this prove? It may look like a conspiracy, but given their talents one would expect them to rise in the world.'

'That's putting it mildly. Good God, this bunch only has to take one step forward and they'll be running the entire show.'

'A valid point.' I opened Charles's note-pad. 'We'll revise the programme – agreed? We start off with the Georges Duval conference, follow up with our own discoveries of where the others are, splice in old newsreel material, interviews with the mothers – it'll make quite a programme.'

Or so we hoped.

Needless to say, the programme was never started. Two days later, when I was still organizing the newsreel material, word came down from the head of features that the project was to be shelved. We tried to argue, but the decision was absolute.

Shortly after, my contract with *Horizon* was ended, and I was given the job of doing a new children's series about great inventors. Charles was shunted to 'International Golf'. Of course, it was obvious to both of us that we had come too close for someone's comfort, but there was little we could do about it. Three months later, I made a trip to Jodrell Bank radio-observatory with a party of scientific journalists and had a glimpse of Martin Sherrington, a tall, finely featured man watching with his hard gaze as Professor Lovell held his press conference.

During the next months I carefully followed the newspapers and TV newscasts. If there was a conspiracy of some kind, what were they planning? Here they were, sitting behind the world's great men, hands ready to take the levers of power. But a global dictatorship sounded unlikely. Two of them at least seemed opposed to established authority. Apart from Caldare in the Cosa Nostra, Georges Duval put his musical talents to spectacular use, becoming within less than a year the greatest of the French 'Ye-Ye' singers, eclipsing the Beatles as a leader of the psychedelic youth generation. In the forefront of the world protest movement, he was hated by the police of a dozen countries but idolized by teenagers from Bangkok to Mexico City.

Any collaboration between Georges and Bandini at the Vatican seemed improbable. Besides, nothing that happened in the world at large suggested that members of the group were acting in anything but a benign role: the nuclear confrontation averted during the Cuban missile crisis, the fall of Khrushchev and the Russo-American détente, peace moves in Vietnam, the Vatican's liberalized policy towards birth-control and divorce. Even the Red Guard movement and the chaos it brought could be seen as a subtle means of deflecting Chinese militancy at a time when she might have intervened in Vietnam.

Then, three months later, Charles Whitehead telephoned me.

'There's a report in *Der Spiegel*,' he told me with studied casualness. 'I thought you might be interested. Another young genius has been discovered.'

'Great,' I said. 'We'll do a programme about it. The usual story, I take it?'

'Absolutely. That same forehead and eyes, the mother who lost her husband years ago, our friend in the villa business. This boy looks really bright, though. An IQ estimated at 300. What a mind.'

'I read the script. The only trouble is, I never got to see the programme. Where is this, by the way?'

'Hebron.'

'Where's that?'

'Near Jerusalem. In Israel.'

'Israel?'

I put the phone down. Somewhere in my mind a tumbler had clicked. Israel! Of course, at last everything made sense. The twelve young men, now occupying positions of power, controlling everything from the US, Russian and Chinese governments to satellite policy, international finance, the UN, big science, the youth and protest movement. There was even a Judas, Giuliano Caldare of the Cosa Nostra. It was obvious now. I had always assumed that the twelve were working for some mysterious organization, but in fact they *were* the organization. They were waiting for the moment of arrival. When the child came, he would be prepared for in the right way, watched over by the Comsat relays, hot lines open, the armies of the world immobilized. This time there would be no mistakes.

After an hour I rang Charles back.

'Charles,' I began, 'I know what's happening. Israel . . .'

'What are you talking about?'

'Israel. Don't you see, Hebron is near Bethlehem.'

There was an exasperated silence. 'James, for heaven's sake . . . You're not suggesting that –'

'Of course. The twelve young men, what else could they be preparing for? And why did the Arab-Israeli war end in only two days? How old is this boy?'

'Thirteen.'

'Let's say another ten years. Good, I had a feeling he would come.'

When Charles protested I handed the receiver to Judy.

As a matter of fact, I am quite certain that I am right. I have seen the photographs of Joshua Herzl taken at his press conference, a slightly difficult lad who rubbed quite a few of the reporters the wrong way. He vanished off the scene shortly afterwards, though no doubt his mother now has a pleasant white-walled villa outside Haifa or Tel Aviv.

And Jodrell Bank is building an enormous new radio-telescope. One day soon we shall be seeing signs in the skies.

· **1968**

# THE KILLING GROUND

As the last smoke from the burning personnel carrier rose through the wet dawn air, Major Pearson could see the silver back of the river three hundred yards from his command post on the hill. Pulverized by the artillery fire, the banks of the channel had collapsed into a network of craters. Water leaked across the meadow, stained by the diesel oil from the fuel tanks of the carrier. Working the binoculars with his thin hands, Pearson studied the trees along the opposite bank. The river was little wider than a stream, and no more than waist-deep, but the fields on both sides were as open as billiard tables. Already the American helicopters had climbed from their bases around the city, clattering in packs over the valley like mindless birds.

An explosion in the driving cabin of the personnel carrier kicked out the doors and windshield. The light flared across the water-soaked meadow, for a moment isolating the faded letters on the memorial stone that formed the rear wall of the command post. Pearson watched the nearest flight of helicopters. They were circling the motor-bridge a mile down-river, too far away to notice the wrecked vehicle and its perimeter of corpses. The ambush, though successful, had not been planned. The carrier had blindly driven up the embankment road as Pearson's unit was preparing to cross the river.

With any luck, Pearson hoped, the crossing would now be called off and they would be ordered to withdraw into the hills. He shivered in his ragged uniform. Corporal Benson had pulled the trousers off a dead Marine machine-gunner the previous morning, and there had been no time to wash out the blood caked across the thighs and waist.

Behind the memorial was the sandbagged entrance of the storage tunnel. Here Sergeant Tulloch and the seventeen-year-old lieutenant sent up overnight from the youth cadre were working on the field radio, rewiring the headphones and battery. Around the emplacement Pearson's thirty men sat over their weapons, ammunition boxes and telephone wire piled around their feet. Exhausted by the ambush, they would have little energy left for a river crossing.

'Sergeant . . . Sergeant Tulloch!' Pearson called out, deliberately coarsening his over-precise schoolmaster's voice. As he half-expected, Tulloch ignored the shout. A pair of copper terminals clamped in his sharp mouth, he went on splicing the frayed wire. Although Pearson was in command of the guerilla unit, its real initiative came from the Scotsman. A regular in the Gordon Highlanders before the American landings six years earlier, the sergeant had joined the first rebel bands that formed the nucleus of the National Liberation Army. As Tulloch himself openly boasted, he had been drawn to the insurgent army chiefly by the prospect of killing the English. Pearson often wondered how far the sergeant still identified him with the puppet regime in London propped up by the American occupation forces.

As he climbed out of the slit trench gunfire flickered from the central traverse of the motor-bridge. Pearson waited behind the plinth of the memorial. He listened to the roar of heavy howitzers firing from the American enclave five miles to the west. Here nine hundred Marine artillerymen had been holding out for months against two divisions of rebel troops. Supported from the air by helicopter drops, the Americans fought on from their deep bunkers, firing thousands of rounds a day from their seventy guns. The meadows around the enclave formed the landscape of a drowned moon.

The shell whined away through the damp air, the explosions lifting the broken soil. Between the impacts came the rattle of small-arms fire as the attack went in across the bridge. Slinging his Sten gun over his narrow shoulders, Pearson ran back to the tunnel.

'What's holding us up, Sergeant? This radio should have been checked at Battalion.'

He reached out to the mud-splattered console, but Tulloch pushed his hand away with the spanner. Ignoring the young lieutenant's self-conscious salute, Tulloch snapped: 'I'll have it ready in time, Major. Or are you wanting to withdraw now?'

Avoiding the lieutenant's eyes, Pearson said: 'We'll follow orders, Sergeant, when and if you repair this set.'

'I'll repair it, Major. Don't worry yourself about that.'

Pearson unfastened the chin-strap of his helmet. During their three months together the sergeant had clearly decided that Pearson had lost heart. Of course Tulloch was right. Pearson looked around the fortified position shielded from the air by the ragged willows, counting the pinched faces of the men huddled beside the field stove. Dressed in ragged uniforms held together with American webbing, living for months in holes in the ground, under-fed and under-armed, what kept them going? Not hatred of the Americans, few of whom, apart from the dead, they had ever seen. Secure within their bases, and protected by an immense technology of warfare, the American expeditionary forces were as remote as some archangelic legion on the day of Armageddon.

If anything, it was fortunate that the Americans were spread so thinly on the ground, or the entire liberation front would long since have been wiped out. Even with twenty million men under arms, the Americans could spare fewer than 200,000 soldiers for the British Isles, a remote backwater in their global war against dozens of national liberation armies.

The underground free radio system which Pearson and Tulloch listened to at night as they huddled in their tunnels below the searching helicopters reported continuous fighting from the Pyrenees to the Bavarian Alps, the Caucasus to Karachi. Thirty years after the original conflict in south-east Asia, the globe was now a huge insurrectionary torch, a world Vietnam.

'Benson!' The corporal limped over, his captured carbine heavy in his thin arms. Pearson waved with a show of temper at the men slumped against the sandbags. 'Corporal, in half an hour we're going into an attack! At least keep them awake!'

With a tired salute, the corporal went off round the emplacement, half-heartedly nudging the men with his boot. Pearson stared through the trees at the river line. To the north, near the ruined castle at Windsor, columns of smoke rose below the helicopters as they plunged and dived, firing their rockets into the ragged forests that had grown among the empty surburban streets. In this immense plain of violence only the meadow below with its leaking river seemed quiet. The water ebbed around the personnel carrier, stirring the legs of the corpses. Without thinking, Pearson started to count his men again. They would have to run across the open ground, ford the river and penetrate the line of trees on the opposite bank. Perhaps the Americans were sitting there with their rapid-fire Gatlings, waiting for them to break cover.

'. . . Major Pearson.' The lieutenant touched his elbow. 'You wanted to see the prisoners.'

'Right. We'll have another go at them.' Pearson followed the boy around the memorial. The presence of this young man – barely older than his pupils at the mountain school in the north of Scotland – gave Pearson some kind of encouragement. Already his age had begun to tell doubly against him. Over the years the losses in manpower had been so great, a million soldiers and a further million civilians dead, that older men were put in the more dangerous roles, saving the young for whatever peace would one day come.

The three Americans were behind the memorial, guarded by a soldier with a Bren gun. Lying on his back was a Negro sergeant who had been shot through the chest. His arms and shoulders were caked with blood, and he breathed unevenly through the thick crust on his mouth and chin. Leaning against him was a young private hunched over the knapsack on his knees. His tired student's eyes stared down at his manacled wrists, as if unable to grasp the fact of his own capture.

The third prisoner was a captain, the only officer in the ambushed patrol, a slimly built man with grey crew-cut hair and a soft but intelligent face. In spite of his uniform and webbing he looked less like a combat soldier than a war correspondent or observer. Telephone wire was lashed around his wrists, forcing him to hold his elbows together. Nevertheless he was watching closely the preparations for the coming attack. Pearson could see him counting the men and weapons, the two machine-guns and ammunition boxes.

As these sharp blue eyes turned to examine Pearson, running over his decrepit uniform and equipment, Pearson felt a surge of resentment at these intelligent and self-confident men who had occupied the world with their huge expeditionary armies. The American was looking at him with that same surprise Pearson had seen on prisoners' faces before, a genuine amazement that these ragged little men could go on fighting for so long. Even the term the Americans used to describe the rebel soldiers, 'Charlie', inherited from the first Vietnam, showed their contempt, whether the soldier fighting against them was a Riff tribesman, Catalan farmer or Japanese industrial worker.

However, as the American knew all too well, if the order came through to attack, the three of them would be shot down where they sat.

Pearson knelt by the Negro sergeant. With the barrel of his Sten gun he nudged the young soldier clutching his knapsack. 'Can't you do anything for him? Where's your morphine?'

The soldier looked up at Pearson, and then let his head drop, staring at the fuel oil that formed rainbows on his boots. Pearson raised his hand, about to hit him with the back of his fist. Then the sounds of gunfire on the motor-bridge were lost in the overhead whoom of a shell. Coming across the river, the heavy 120 mm soared over the meadow and plunged into the woods below the hill-crest. Pearson crouched behind the memorial, hoping the shell was a stray. Then Sergeant Tulloch signalled that two more had started on their way. The next fell without exploding into the water-meadow. The third landed fifty feet below the memorial, spattering its surface with broken earth.

When it was quiet again Pearson waited as Corporal Benson pulled the knapsack away from the young soldier and emptied its contents. He slit the captain's pockets with his bayonet and jerked off his ID tag.

There was little to be gained from any formal interrogation. American weapons technology had advanced to the point where it made almost no sense at all to the rebel commanders. Artillery fire, battle dispositions and helicopter raids were now computer-directed, patrols and sorties programmed ahead. The American equipment was so sophisticated that even the wristwatches stripped off dead prisoners were too complicated to read.

Pearson reached down to the clutter of coins and keys beside the private. He opened a leather-bound diary. Inside was a series of illegible entries, and a folded letter from a friend, evidently a draft-dodger, about the anti-war movement at home. Pearson tossed them into the pool of water leaking below the plinth of the memorial. He picked up an oil-stained book, one of a paperback educational series, Charles Olsen's *Call Me Ishmael.*

As he held the book in his hands, Pearson glanced back to where Sergeant Tulloch stood over the field radio, well aware that the sergeant would disapprove of this unfading strand of literacy in his own character. He wiped the oil off the American eagle. What an army, whose privates were no longer encouraged to carry field-marshals' batons in their knapsacks but books like this.

To the captain he said: 'The US Army must be the most literate since Xenophon's.' Pearson slipped the book into his pocket. The captain was looking down over his shoulder at the river. 'Do you know where we are?' Pearson asked him.

The captain turned himself round, trying to ease the wounds on his wrists. He looked up at Pearson with his sharp eyes. 'I guess so. Runnymede, on the Thames River.'

Surprised, Pearson said ungrudgingly: 'You're better informed than my own men. I used to live about ten miles from here. Near one of the pacified villages.'

'Maybe you'll go back one day.'

'I dare say, Captain. And maybe we'll sign a new Magna Carta into the bargain. How long have you been out here?'

The captain hesitated, sizing up Pearson's interest. 'Just over a month.'

'And you're in combat already? I thought you had a three-month acclimatization period. You must be as badly off as we are.'

'I'm not a combat soldier, Major. I'm an architect, with US Army Graves Commission. Looking after memorials all over the world.'

'That's quite a job. The way things are going, it has almost unlimited prospects.'

'I hate to have to agree with you, Major.' The American's manner had become noticeably more ingratiating, but Pearson was too preoccupied to care. 'Believe me, a lot of us back home feel the war's achieved absolutely nothing.'

'Nothing . . . ?' Pearson repeated. 'It's achieved everything.' An armoured helicopter soared across the hill-crest, its heavy fans beating at the foliage over their heads. For one thing, the war had turned the entire population of Europe into an armed peasantry, the first intelligent agrarian community since the eighteenth century. *That* peasantry had produced the Industrial Revolution. This one, literally burrowing like some advanced species of termite into the sub-soil of the twentieth century, might in time produce something greater. Fortunately, the Americans were protected from any hope of success by their own good intentions, their refusal, whatever the cost in their own casualties, to use nuclear weapons.

Two tanks had moved on to the parapet of the bridge, firing their machine-guns along the roadway. A scout helicopter shot down into the fields across the river was burning fiercely, the flames twisting the metal blades.

'Major!' Corporal Benson ran to the tunnel mouth. Tulloch was crouched over the radio, headphones on, beckoning towards Pearson. 'They're through to Command, sir.'

Ten minutes later, when Pearson passed the memorial on his way to the forward post, the American captain had managed to lift himself on to his knees. Wrists clamped together in front of his chest, he looked as if he were praying at some ruined wayside shrine. The wounded Negro had opened his eyes, shallow breaths breaking through the caked blood on his lips. The young private slept against the plinth of the memorial.

The captain pointed with his wired hands at the men strapping up their packs. Pearson ignored him, and was about to move on. Then something about the American's posture, and their shared community of fatigue and hopelessness, made him stop.

'We're going forward.'

Eyes half-closing, the American stared down at his wrists, as if aware of the effort he had wasted in trying to prevent the abrasions from opening. 'That's bad luck. Not my day.' His face grew stiff and wooden as the blood emptied from his cheeks.

Pearson watched Sergeant Tulloch supervise the stowage of the radio and begin his rounds of the men, waiting with weapons at the ready. 'Why did you come up the river?'

The captain tapped the memorial stone with his wrists. 'We wanted to see about moving this. The Kennedy Memorial.'

'Kennedy . . . ?' Pearson turned and stared down at the broken lettering on the stone. Vaguely he remembered the memorial built by a previous British government at Runnymede to commemorate the assassinated President. In an amiable, if sentimental, gesture an acre of English ground had been given to the American people overlooking Magna Carta island. The President's widow had been present at the unveiling.

The American was feeling the broken lettering. He pulled off his cap and dipped it in the pool of oil-stained water beside the plinth. He began to work away at the memorial, scraping off the mud, as Pearson moved down through the trees to the forward post.

When Pearson returned shortly afterwards the American was still working away at the memorial with his wired hands. Below the surface dirt were the residues of earlier defacements, slogans marked in engine grease or cut with bayonets. There was even one, 'Stop US Atrocities in Vietnam', almost as old as the monument itself. Pearson remembered that the memorial had been regularly defaced since its unveiling, a favourite target of vandals and agitators.

'Major, we're ready to move off, sir.' Tulloch saluted him smartly, for the first time that day. The American was still scraping at the stone, and had managed to clean at least half of the front surface.

The lead platoon moved down the slope. As the captain dropped his cap and sat down, Pearson signalled to Sergeant Tulloch.

'Okay, Charlie – off your backside!' Tulloch had drawn his .45 automatic. The rear platoon was filing past, the men's eyes fixed on the gaps in the trees, none of them paying any attention to the prisoners.

The American stood up, his eyes almost closed. He joined the two prisoners lying behind the memorial. As he began to sit down again Tulloch stepped behind him and shot him through the head. The

American fell on to the sleeping private. Tulloch straddled his body with one leg. Like a farmer expertly shearing a sheep he shot the other two men, holding them as they struggled. They lay together at the base of the memorial, their legs streaming with blood.

Above them, the drying stone was turning a pale grey in the weak sunlight.

It was almost white twenty minutes later when they began their advance across the meadow. Fifty yards from the bank a murderous fire had greeted them from the Americans concealed among the trees along the opposite shore. Pearson saw Tulloch shot down into the waterlogged grass. He shouted to Corporal Benson to take cover. As he lay in a shallow crater the white rectangle of the memorial was visible through the trees behind him, clear now as it would not have been that morning. In his last moments he wondered if the cleaning of the memorial had been a signal, which the watching Americans had rightly interpreted, and if the captain had deliberately taken advantage of him.

Mortar shells fell in the damp grass around him. Pearson stood up, beckoning to the young lieutenant to follow him, and ran forward to the wreck of the personnel carrier. Ten steps later he was shot down into the oil-stained water.

**⋅1969**

# A PLACE AND A TIME TO DIE

Shotguns levelled, the two men waited on the river bank. From the shore facing them, four hundred yards across the bright spring water, the beating of gongs and drums sounded through the empty air, echoing off the metal roofs of the abandoned town. Fire-crackers burst over the trees along the shore, the mushy pink explosions lighting up the gun-barrels of tanks and armoured cars.

All morning the ill-matched couple making this last stand together – Mannock, the retired and now slightly eccentric police chief, and his reluctant deputy, Forbis, a thyroidal used-car salesman – had watched the mounting activity on the opposite shore. Soon after eight o'clock when Mannock drove through the deserted town, the first arrivals had already appeared on the scene. Four scout-cars carrying a platoon of soldiers in padded brown uniforms were parked on the bank. The officer scanned Mannock through his binoculars for a few seconds and then began to inspect the town. An hour later an advance battalion of field engineers took up their position by the dynamited railway bridge. By noon an entire division had arrived. A dusty caravan of self-propelled guns, tanks on trailers, and mobile field-kitchens in commandeered buses rolled across the farmland and pulled to a halt by the bank. After them came an army of infantry and camp-followers, pulling wooden carts and beating gongs.

Earlier that morning Mannock had climbed the water-tower at his brother's farm. The landscape below the mountains ten miles away was criss-crossed with dozens of motorized columns. Most of them were moving in an apparently random way, half the time blinded by their own dust. Like an advancing horde of ants, they spilled across the abandoned farmland, completely ignoring an intact town and then homing on an empty grain silo.

By now, though, in the early afternoon, all sections of this huge field army had reached the river. Any hopes Mannock had kept alive that they might turn and disappear towards the horizon finally faded. When exactly they would choose to make their crossing was hard to gauge. As he and Forbis watched, a series of enormous camps was being set up. Lines of collapsible huts marked out barrack squares, squads of soldiers marched up and down in the dust, rival groups of civilians – presumably political cadres – drilled and shouted slogans. The smoke from hundreds of mess fires rose into the air, blocking off Mannock's view of the blue-chipped mountains that had formed the backdrop to the river valley during the twenty years he had spent there. Rows of camouflaged trucks and amphibious vehicles waited along the shore, but there was still no sign of any crossing. Tank-crews wandered about like bored gangs on a boardwalk, letting off fire-crackers and flying paper kites with slogans painted on their tails. Everywhere the beating of gongs and drums went on without pause.

'There must be a million of them there – for God's sake, they'll never get over!' Almost disappointed, Forbis lowered his shotgun on to the sandbag emplacement.

'Nothing's stopped them yet,' Mannock commented. He pointed to a convoy of trucks dragging a flotilla of wooden landing-craft across a crowded parade ground. 'Sampans – they look crazy, don't they?'

While Forbis glared across the river Mannock looked down at him, with difficulty controlling the distaste he felt whenever he realized exactly whom he had chosen as his last companion. A thin, bitter-mouthed man with over-large eyes, Forbis was one of that small group of people Mannock had instinctively disliked throughout his entire life. The past few days in the empty town had confirmed all his prejudices. The previous afternoon, after an hour spent driving around the town and shooting at the stray dogs, Forbis had taken Mannock back to his house. There he had proudly shown off his huge home arsenal. Bored by this display of weapons, Mannock wandered into the dining room, only to find the table laid out like an altar with dozens of far-right magazines, pathological hate-sheets and heaven knew what other nonsense printed on crude home presses.

What had made Forbis stay behind in the deserted town after everyone else had gone? What made him want to defend these few streets where he had never been particularly liked or successful? Some wild gene or strange streak of patriotism – perhaps not all that far removed from his own brand of cantankerousness. Mannock looked across the water as a huge catherine-wheel revolved into the air above a line of tanks parked along the shore, its puffy pink smoke turning the encampment into an enormous carnival. For a moment a surge of hope went through Mannock that this vast army might be driven by wholly peaceful motives, that it might suddenly decide to withdraw, load its tanks on to their trailers and move off to the western horizon.

As the light faded he knew all too well that there was no chance of this happening. Generations of hate and resentment had driven these people in their unbroken advance across the world, and here in this town in a river valley they would take a small part of their revenge.

Why had he himself decided to stay behind, waiting here behind these few useless sandbags with a shotgun in his hands? Mannock glanced back at the water-tower that marked the north-west perimeter of his brother's farm, for years the chief landmark of the town. Until the last moment he had planned to leave with the rest of the family, helping to gas up the cars and turn loose what was left of the livestock. Closing his own house down for the last time, he decided to wait until the dust subsided when the great exodus began. He drove down to the river, and stood under the broken span of the bridge which the army engineers had dynamited before they retreated.

Walking southwards along the shore, he had nearly been shot by Forbis. The salesman had dug himself into a home-made roadblock above the bank, and was waiting there all alone for his first sight of the enemy. Mannock tried to persuade him to leave with the others, but as he remonstrated with Forbis he realized that he was talking to himself, and why he sounded so unconvincing.

For the next days, as the distant dust-clouds moved towards them from the horizon, turning the small valley into an apocalyptic landscape, the two men formed an uneasy alliance. Forbis looked on impatiently as Mannock moved through the empty streets, closing the doors of the abandoned cars and parking them along the kerb, shutting the windows of the houses and putting lids on the rubbish bins. With his crazy logic Forbis really believed that the two of them could hold up the advance of this immense army.

'Maybe for only a few hours,' he assured Mannock with quiet pride. 'But that'll be enough.'

A few seconds, more likely, Mannock reflected. There would be a brief bloody flurry somewhere; one burst from a machine-pistol and quietus in the dust . . .

'Mannock –!' Forbis pointed to the shore fifty yards from the bridge embankment. A heavy metal skiff was being manhandled into the water by a labour-platoon. A tank backed along the shore behind it, test-rotating its turret. Exhaust belched from its diesel.

'They're coming!' Forbis crouched behind the sandbags, levelling his shotgun. He beckoned furiously at Mannock. 'For God's sake, Mannock, get your head down!'

Mannock ignored him. He stood on the roof of the emplacement, his figure fully exposed. He watched the skiff slide into the water. While two of the crew tried to start the motor, a squad in the bows rowed it across to the first bridge pylon. No other craft were being launched, In fact, as Mannock had noted already, no one was looking across the river at all, though any good marksman could have hit them both without difficulty. A single 75mm shell from one of the tanks would have disposed of them and the emplacement.

'Engineers,' he told Forbis. 'They're checking the bridge supports. Maybe they want to rebuild it first.'

Forbis peered doubtfully through his binoculars, then relaxed his grip on the shotgun. His jaw was still sticking forward aggressively. Watching him, Mannock realized that Forbis genuinely wasn't afraid of what would happen to them. He glanced back at the town. There was a flash of light as an upstairs door turned and caught the sun.

'Where are you going?' A look of suspicion was on Forbis's face, reinforcing the doubts he already felt about Mannock. 'They may come sooner than you think.'

'They'll come in their own time, not ours,' Mannock said. 'Right now it looks as if even they don't know. I'll be here.'

He walked stiffly towards his car, conscious of the target his black leather jacket made against the white station-wagon. At any moment the bright paintwork could be shattered by a bullet carrying pieces of his heart.

He started the motor and reversed carefully on to the beach. Through the rear-view mirror he watched the opposite shore. The engineers in the skiff had lost interest in the bridge. Like a party of sightseers they drifted along the shore, gazing up at the tank-crews squatting on their turrets. The noise of gongs beat across the water.

In the deserted town the sounds murmured in the metal roofs. Mannock drove round the railway station and the bus depot, checking if any refugees had arrived after crossing the river. Nothing moved. Abandoned cars filled the side-streets. Broken store windows formed jagged frames around piles of detergent packs and soup cans. In the filling stations the slashed pump hoses leaked their last gasolene across the unwashed concrete.

Mannock stopped the car in the centre of the town. He stepped out and looked up at the windows of the hotel and the public library. By some acoustic freak the noise of the gongs had faded, and for a moment it seemed like any drowsy afternoon ten years earlier.

Mannock leaned into the back seat of the car and took out a paper parcel. Fumbling with the dry string, he finally unpicked the ancient knot, then unwrapped the paper and took out a faded uniform jacket.

Searching for a cigarette pack in his hip pockets, Mannock examined the worn braid. He had planned this small gesture – a pointless piece of sentimentality, he well knew – as a private goodbye to himself and the town, but the faded metal badges had about the same relevance to reality as the rusty hubcap lying in the gutter a few feet away. Tossing it over his left arm, he opened the door of the car.

Before he could drop the jacket on to the seat a rifle shot slammed across the square. A volley of echoes boomed off the buildings. Mannock dropped to one knee behind the car, his head lowered from the third-floor windows of the hotel. The bullet had starred the passenger window and richocheted off the dashboard, chipping the steering wheel before exiting through the driver's door.

As the sounds of the explosion faded, Mannock could hear the rubber boots of a slimly built man moving down the fire-escape behind the building. Mannock looked upwards. High above the town a strange flag flew from the mast of the hotel. So the first snipers had moved in across the river. His blood quickening, Mannock drew his shotgun from the seat of the car.

*　　*　　*

Some five minutes later he was waiting in the alley behind the supermarket when a running figure darted past him. As the man crashed to the gravel Mannock straddled him with both legs, the shotgun levelled at his face. Mannock looked down, expecting to find a startled yellow-skinned youth in quilted uniform.

'Forbis?'

The salesman clambered to his knees, painfully catching back his breath. He stared at the blood on his hands, and then at Mannock's face above the barrel of the shotgun.

'What the *hell* are you playing at?' he gasped in a weary voice, one ear cocked for any sounds from the river. 'That shot – do you want to bring them over?' He gestured at the police jacket that Mannock was now wearing, and then shook his head sadly. 'Mannock, this isn't a fancy-dress party . . .'

Mannock was about to explain to him when a car door slammed. The engine of the station-wagon roared above the squeal of tyres. As the two men reached the sidewalk the car was swerving out of the square, bumper knocking aside a pile of cartons.

'Hathaway!' Forbis shouted. 'Did you see him? There's your sniper, Mannock!'

Mannock watched the car plunge out of sight down a side-street. 'Hathaway,' he repeated dourly. 'I should have guessed. He's decided to stay and meet his friends.'

After Forbis had torn the flag down from the hotel mast he and Mannock drove back to the river. Mannock sat uncomfortably in the police jacket, thinking of Hathaway, that strange youth who with himself and Forbis completed one key triangle within their society: Hathaway the misfit, head full of half-baked Marxist slogans, saddled with a bored wife who one day tired of living in rooming-houses and walked out on him, taking their small son; Hathaway the failed political activist, whose obsessed eyes were too much even for a far-left student group; Hathaway the petty criminal, arrested for pilfering a supermarket – though he soon convinced himself that he was a martyr to the capitalist conspiracy.

No doubt one sight of Mannock's old police jacket had been enough.

An hour later the advance began across the river. One minute Mannock was sitting on the old rail-tie that formed the rear wall of Forbis's emplacement, watching the endless parades and drilling that were taking place on the opposite shore, and listening to the gongs and exploding fire-crackers. The next minute dozens of landing-craft were moving down the bank into the water. Thousands of soldiers swarmed after them, bales of equipment held over their heads. The whole landscape had risen up and heaved forward. Half a mile inland vast dust-clouds were climbing into the air. Everywhere the collapsible huts and command posts were coming down, ungainly cranes swung pontoon sections over the trees. The beating of drums sounded for miles along the water's edge. Counting quickly, Mannock estimated that at least fifty landing-craft were crossing the water, each towing two or three amphibious tanks behind it.

One large wooden landing-craft was headed straight towards them, well over a hundred infantrymen squatting on the deck like coolies. Above the square teak bows a heavy machine-gun jutted through its rectangular metal shield, the gunners signalling to the helmsman.

As Forbis fumbled with his shotgun Mannock knocked the butt off his shoulder.

'Fall back! Nearer the town – they'll come right over us here!'

Crouching down, they backed away from the emplacement. As the first landing-craft hit the shore they reached the cover of the trees lining the road. Forbis sprinted ahead to a pile of fifty-gallon drums lying in the ditch and began to roll them around into a crude emplacement.

Mannock watched him working away, as the air was filled with the noise of tank-engines and gongs. When Forbis had finished Mannock shook his head. He pointed with a tired hand at the fields on either side of the road, then leaned his shotgun against the wall of the ditch.

As far as they could see, hundreds of soldiers were moving up towards the town, rifles and submachine-guns slung over their shoulders. The river bank was crammed with landing-craft. A dozen pontoon bridges spanned the water. Infantry and engineers poured ashore, unloading staff cars and light field pieces. Half a mile away the first soldiers were already moving along the railway line into the town.

Mannock watched a column of infantry march up the road towards them. When they drew nearer he realized that at least half of them were civilians, carrying no weapons or webbing, the women with small red booklets in their hands. On poles over their heads they held giant blown-up photographs of party leaders and generals. A motorcycle and sidecar combination mounting a light machine-gun forced its way past the column, and then stalled in the verge. Chanting together, a group of women and soldiers pushed it free. Together they stamped on after it, bellowing and cheering.

As the motorcycle approached, Mannock waited for the machine-gun to open fire at them. Forbis was crouched behind a fuel drum, frowning over his sights. His large eyes looked like over-boiled eggs. A tic fluttered the right corner of his mouth, as if he were babbling some sub-vocal rosary to himself. Then in a sudden moment of lucidity he turned the shotgun at the motorcycle, but with a roar the machine swerved around Mannock and accelerated towards the town.

Mannock turned to watch it, but a man running past collided with him. Mannock caught his slim shoulders in his hands and set the man on his feet. He looked down into a familiar sallow face, overlit eyes he had last seen staring at him through the bars of a cell.

'Hathaway, you crazy . . .'

Before Mannock could hold him he broke away and ran towards the approaching column striding up the dirt road. He stopped a few feet from the leading pair of infantrymen and shouted some greeting to them. One of the men, an officer Mannock guessed, though none of the soldiers wore insignia, glanced at him, then reached out and pushed him to one side. Within a moment he was swallowed by the mêlée of gong-beating and chanting soldiers. Buffeted from one shoulder to the next, he lost his balance and fell, stood up and began to wave again at the faces passing him, trying to catch their attention.

Then Mannock too was caught up in the throng. The drab quilted uniforms, stained by the dust and sweat of half a continent, pushed past him, forcing him on to the verge. The shotgun was knocked out of his hands, kicked about in the breaking earth by a score of feet, then picked up and tossed on to the back of a cart. A troupe of young women surrounded Mannock, staring up at him without any curiosity as they chanted their slogans. Most of them were little more than children, with earnest mannequin-like faces under close-cropped hair.

Realizing what had happened, Mannock pulled Forbis from the ditch. No one had tried to take his shotgun from Forbis, and the salesman clung to it like a child. Mannock twisted the weapon out of his hands.

'Can't you understand?' he shouted. 'They're not interested in us! They're not interested at all!'

. **1969**

# · SAY GOODBYE TO THE WIND

At midnight I heard music playing from the abandoned nightclub among the dunes at Lagoon West. Each evening the frayed melody had woken me as I slept in my villa above the beach. As it started once again I stepped from the balcony on to the warm sand and walked along the shore. In the darkness the beachcombers stood by the tideline, listening to the music carried towards them on the thermal rollers. My torch lit up the broken bottles and hypodermic vials at their feet. Wearing their dead motley, they waited in the dim air like faded clowns.

The nightclub had been deserted since the previous summer, its white walls covered by the dunes. The clouded letters of a neon sign tilted over the open-air bar. The music came from a record-player on the stage, a foxtrot I had forgotten years before. Through the sand-strewn tables walked a young woman with coralline hair, crooning to herself as she gestured with jewelled hands to the rhythm of this antique theme. Her downward eyes and reflective step, like those of a pensive child, made me guess that she was sleepwalking, drawn to this abandoned nightclub from one of the mansions along the shore.

Beside me, near the derelict bar, stood one of the beachcombers. His dead clothes hung on his muscular body like the husk of some violated fruit. The oil on his dark chest lit up his drug-filled eyes, giving his broken face a moment of lucid calm. As the young woman danced by herself in her black nightgown he stepped forward and took her arms. Together they circled the wooden floor, her jewelled hand on his scarred shoulder. When the record ended she turned from him, her face devoid of expression, and walked among the tables into the darkness.

Who was my beautiful neighbour, moving with the certainty of a sleep-walker, who danced each evening with the beachcombers at the deserted nightclub? As I drove into Vermilion Sands the following morning I peered into the villas along the shore in the hope of seeing her again, but the beach was a zone of late-risers still asleep under their sealed awnings. The season at Vermilion Sands was now in full swing. Tourists filled the café terraces and the curio shops. After two or three hectic weeks at festivals devoted to everything from non-aural music to erotic food, most of them would jettison their purchases from their car windows as they sped back to the safety of Red Beach. Running to seed in the sand-reefs on the fringes of Vermilion Sands, the singing flowers and sculpture formed the unique flora of the landscape, an island ringed by strange sounds.

My own boutique, 'Topless in Gaza', which specialized in bio-fabric fashions, I had opened two years earlier. When I reached the arcade near Beach Drive at eleven o'clock that morning a small crowd was already peering through the window, fascinated by the Op Art patterns unfurling as the model gowns on display flexed and arched themselves in the morning sunlight. My partner, Georges Conte, his art nouveau eyepatch raised over his left eye, was settling an electric-yellow beach-robe on to its stand. For some reason the fabric was unusually skittish, clinging to him like a neurotic dowager. Gripping the wrists with one hand, Georges forced it on to its stand, then stepped back before it could clutch at him again. The robe switched irritably from side to side, the fabric pulsing like an inflamed sun.

As I entered the shop I could see it was going to be one of our more difficult days. Usually I arrived to find the gowns and robes purring on their hangers like the drowsy inmates of an exquisite arboreal zoo. Today something had disturbed them. The racks of model dresses were seething, their patterns livid and discordant. Whenever they touched, the fabrics recoiled from each other like raw membranes. The beach-clothes were in an equal state of unrest, the bandanas and sun-suits throwing off eye-jarring patterns like exhibits in some demented kinetic art.

Hands raised in a gesture of heroic despair, Georges Conte came over to me. His white silk suit glimmered like a bilious rainbow. Even my own mauve day-shirt was unsettled, its seams beginning to shred and unravel.

'Georges, what's happening? The whole place is in uproar!'

'Mr Samson, I wash my hands of them! Sheer temperament, they're impossible to deal with!'

He looked down at his dappled sleeve, and tried to flick away the livid colours with a manicured hand. Upset by the disturbed atmosphere, his suit was expanding and contracting in irregular pulses, pulling across his chest like the fibres of a diseased heart. With a burst of exasperation he picked one of the model gowns from its rack and shook it angrily. 'Quiet!' he shouted, like an impresario calling an unruly chorus line to order. 'Is this "Topless in Gaza" or a demonic zoo?'

In the two years that I had known him Georges had always referred to the dresses and gowns as if they were a troupe of human performers. The more expensive and sensitive fabrics bred from the oldest pedigree stocks he would treat with the charm and savoir-faire he might have reserved for a temperamental duchess. At the opposite extreme, the flamboyant Op Art beachwear he handled with the cavalier charm he displayed to the teenage beauties who often strayed by accident into the boutique.

Sometimes I wondered if for Georges the gowns and suits were more alive than their purchasers. I suspected that he regarded the eventual wearers as little more than animated chequebooks whose sole function was to feed and exercise the exquisite creatures he placed upon their backs. Certainly a careless or offhand customer who made the mistake of trying to climb into a wrong fitting or, even worse, was endowed with a figure of less than Dietrich-like proportions, would receive brusque treatment from Georges and be directed with the shot of a lace cuff to the inert-wear shops in the town's amusement park.

This, of course, was a particularly bitter jibe. No one, with the exception of a few eccentrics or beachcombers, any longer wore inert clothing. The only widely worn inert garment was the shroud, and even here most fashionable people would not be seen dead in one. The macabre spectacle of the strange grave-flora springing from cracked tombs, like the nightmare collection of some Quant or Dior of the netherworld, had soon put an end to all forms of bio-fabric coffin-wear and firmly established the principle: 'Naked we came into this world, naked we leave it.'

Georges's devotion had been largely responsible for the success and select clientele of the boutique, and I was only too glad to indulge his whimsical belief in the individual personality of each gown and dress. His slim fingers could coax a hemline to shorten itself within seconds instead of hours, take in a pleat or enlarge a gusset almost before the customer could sign her cheque. A particularly exotic gown, unsettled by being worn for the first time or upset by the clammy contact of human skin, would be soothed and consoled by Georges as he patted it into place around its owner's body, his gentle hands caressing the nervous tissues around the unfamiliar contours of hip and bust.

Today, however, his charm and expertise had failed him. The racks of gowns itched and quivered, their colours running into blurred pools. One drawback of bio-fabrics is their extreme sensitivity. Bred originally from the gene stocks of delicate wisterias and mimosas, the woven yarns have brought with them something of the vine's remarkable response to atmosphere and touch. The sudden movement of someone near by, let alone of the wearer, brings an immediate reply from the nerve-like tissues. A dress can change its colour and texture in a few seconds, becoming more décolleté at the approach of an eager admirer, more formal at a chance meeting with a bank manager.

This sensitivity to mood explains the real popularity of bio-fabrics. Clothes are no longer made from dead fibres of fixed colour and texture that can approximate only crudely to the vagrant human figure, but from living tissues that adapt themselves to the contours and personality of the wearer. Other advantages are the continued growth of the materials, fed by the body odours and perspiration of the wearer, the sweet liqueurs distilled from her own pores, and the constant renewal of the fibres, repairing any faults or ladders and eliminating the need for washing.

However, as I walked around the shop that morning I reflected that these immense advantages had been bought at a price. For some reason we had accumulated a particularly temperamental collection. Cases had been reported of sudden panics caused by the backfiring of an engine, in which an entire stock of model gowns had destroyed themselves in a paroxysm of violence.

I was about to suggest to Georges that we close the shop for the morning when I noticed that the first customer of the day had already arrived. Partly concealed by the racks of beachwear, I could only see an elegantly groomed face veiled by a wide-brimmed hat. Near the doorway a young chauffeur waited in the sunlight, surveying the tourists with a bored glance.

At first I was annoyed that a wealthy customer should arrive at the very moment when our stock was restive – I still remembered with a shudder the bikini of nervous weave that shed itself around its owner's ankles as she stood on the high diving board above the crowded pool at the Neptune Hotel. I turned to ask Georges to use all his tact to get her to leave.

For once, however, he had lost his aplomb. Leaning forward from the waist, eyes focused myopically, he was gazing at our customer like a seedy voyeur of the boulevards starstruck by some sub-teen nymphet.

'Georges! Pull yourself together! Do you know her?'

He glanced at me with blank eyes. 'What?' Already his suit had begun to smooth itself into a glass-like mirror, his invariable response when faced with a beautiful woman. He murmured: 'Miss Channing.'

'Who?'

'Raine Channing . . .' he repeated. 'Before your time, Mr Samson, before anyone's time . . .'

I let him walk past me, hands outstretched in the attitude of Parsifal approaching the Holy Grail. Certainly I remembered her, sometime international model and epitome of eternal youthfulness, with her melancholy, gamine face recreated by a dozen plastic surgeries. Raine Channing was a macabre relic of the 1970s and its teenage cult. Where, in the past, elderly screen actresses had resorted to plastic surgery to lift a sagging cheek or erase a tell-tale wrinkle, in the case of Raine Channing a young model in her early twenties had surrendered her face to the scalpel and needle in order to recapture the child-like bloom of a teenage ingénue. As many as a dozen times she had gone back to the operating theatre, emerging swathed in bandages that were rolled back before the arc lights to reveal a frozen teenage mask. In her grim way, perhaps she had helped to kill this lunatic cult. For some years now she had been out of the public eye, and I remembered only a few months beforehand reading about the death of her confidant and impresario, the brilliant couturier and designer of the first bio-fabric fashions, Gavin Kaiser.

Although now in her late twenties, Raine Channing still preserved her child-like appearance, this strange montage of adolescent faces. Her gaze reflected the suicides of Carole Landis and Marilyn Monroe. As she spoke to Georges in her low voice I realized where I had seen her, dancing with the beachcombers in the deserted nightclub at Lagoon West.

When I bought the boutique the faded fashion magazines had been filled with her photographs . . . Raine with her wounded eyes, looking out above the bandages around her remade cheeks, or wearing the latest bio-fabric creation at some exclusive discotheque, smiling into Kaiser's handsome gangster face. In many ways the relationship between Raine Channing and this twenty-five-year-old genius of the fashion houses summed up a whole disastrous epoch, of which Raine's mutilated face was a forgotten shrine. One day soon, before she reached the age of thirty, even that face would dissolve.

However, as she visited our boutique this grim prospect seemed a long way distant. Georges was delighted to see her, at last meeting on equal terms one of the too-bright luminaries of his apprenticeship. Without a thought for our disturbed stock, he opened the windows and display cases. Curiously, everything had quietened, the gowns stirring gently on their hangers like docile birds.

I waited for Georges to enjoy his moment of reminiscence, and then introduced myself.

'You've calmed everything down,' I congratulated her. 'They must like you.'

She drew her white fox collar around herself, rubbing her cheek against it. The fur slid around her neck and shoulders, nestling her in its caress. 'I hope so,' she said. 'Do you know, though, a few months ago I hated them? I really wanted everyone in the world to go naked, so that all the clothes would die.' She laughed at this. 'Now I've got to look for a whole new wardrobe.'

'We're delighted you've started here, Miss Channing. Are you staying long in Vermilion Sands?'

'A little while. I first came here a long time ago, Mr Samson. Nothing in Vermilion Sands ever changes, have you noticed? It's a good place to come back to.'

We walked along the displays of gowns. Now and then she would reach out to stroke one of the fabrics, her white hand like a child's. As she opened her coat a sonic jewel, like a crystal rose, emitted its miniature music between her breasts. Velvet playtoys nestled like voles around her wrists. Altogether she seemed to be concealed in this living play-nest like a bizarre infant Venus.

What was it, though, about Raine Channing that so held me? As Georges helped her select a brilliant pastel gown, the other dresses murmuring on the chairs around her, it occurred to me that Raine Channing resembled a child-Eve in a couture-Eden, life springing from her touch. Then I remembered her dancing with the beachcombers in the deserted nightclub at Lagoon West.

While the young chauffeur carried out her purchases I said: 'I saw you last night. At the nightclub by the beach.'

For the first time she looked directly into my face, her eyes alert and adult above the white adolescent mask. 'I live near by', she said, 'in one of the houses along the lake. There was music playing and people dancing.'

As the chauffeur opened the door of the car for her I saw that the seats were filled with playtoys and sonic jewels. They drove off together like two adults playing at being children.

Two days later I heard music coming again from the abandoned nightclub. As I sat on the veranda in the evening this faint night-music began, the dry metallic sounds muffled by the powdery air. I walked along the shore through the darkness. The beachcombers had gone, but Raine Channing wandered through the tables of the nightclub, her white gown drawing empty signatures in the sand.

A sand-yacht was beached in the shallows. Beside it a bare-chested young man watched with hands on hips. His powerful thighs stood out under his white shorts in the darkness, the thermal surf breaking the dust into ripples around his feet. With his broad face and smashed Michelangelesque nose he resembled some dark beach-angel. He waited as I approached, then stepped forward and walked past me, almost brushing my shoulder. The oil on his back reflected the distant lights of Vermilion Sands as he moved among the dunes towards the nightclub.

After this rendezvous I assumed that we would see no more of Raine Channing, but the next morning when I arrived at the shop in Vermilion Sands I found Georges waiting nervously by the door.

'Mr Samson, I tried to telephone you – Miss Channing's secretary has been calling, everything she bought has gone berserk! Nothing fits, three of the gowns are growing out of weave –'

I managed to calm him down, then spoke to Raine's secretary, a tart-toned Frenchwoman who sharply informed me that the entire wardrobe of two evening gowns, a cocktail dress and three day-suits which Raine had purchased from 'Topless in Gaza' had run to seed. Why this should have happened she had no idea. 'However, Mr Samson, I suggest you drive out immediately to Miss Channing's residence and either replace each item or reimburse the total purchase price of six thousand dollars. The alternative –'

'Mlle Fournier,' I insisted stiffly with what little pride I could muster, 'there is no alternative.'

Before I left, Georges brought out with elaborate care a cyclamen sports-suit in a shantung bio-fabric which he had ordered for one of our millionaire customers.

'For my good name, Mr Samson, if not for yours – at moments such as these one should show the flag.'

The suit clung to me like a willowy, lace-covered cobra, shaping itself to my chest and legs. Its colours glowed and rippled as it explored the contours of my body. As I walked out to my car people turned to look at this exquisite gliding snakeskin.

Five minutes after our arrival at Raine Channing's villa it had quietened down considerably, hanging from my shoulders like a wounded flower. The atmosphere at the villa seemed set for disaster. The young chauffeur who took my car whipped it away with a snarl of tyres, his eyes moving across my face like razors. Mlle Fournier greeted me with a peremptory nod. A sharp-faced Frenchwoman of about forty, she wore a witchlike black dress that seethed around her angular shoulders with the movements of a shrike.

'An entire wardrobe ruined, Mr Samson! Not only your own gowns, but priceless originals from Paris this season. We are out of our minds here!'

I did my best to calm her. One danger with bio-fabrics is that they are prone to stampede. Moments of domestic crisis, a cry of anger or even a door's slam, can set off a paroxysm of self-destruction. My own suit was already wilting under Mlle Fournier's baleful eye. As we went up the staircase I smoothed the ruffled velvet of the curtains, settling them into their niches. 'Perhaps they're not being worn enough,' I temporized. 'These fabrics do need human contact.'

Mlle Fournier gave me a surprisingly arch glance. We entered a suite on the top floor. Beyond the shaded windows was a terrace, the painted surface of the sand-lake below it. Mlle Fournier gestured at the open wardrobes in the large dressing room. 'Human contact? Precisely, Mr Samson.'

Everywhere there was uproar. Gowns were strewn across the facing sofas. Several had lost all colour and lay blanched and inert. Others had felted, their edges curled and blackened like dead banana skins. Two evening dresses draped over the escritoire had run rogue, their threads interlocking in a macabre embrace. In the wardrobes the racks of gowns hung in restive files, colours pulsing like demented suns.

As we watched I sensed that they were uneasily settling themselves after some emotional outburst earlier that morning. 'Someone's been whipping them into a frenzy,' I told Mlle Fournier. 'Doesn't Miss Channing realize one can't play the temperamental fool near these fabrics?'

She gripped my arm, a barbed finger raised to my lips. 'Mr Samson! We all have our difficulties. Just do what you can. Your fee will be paid immediately.'

When she had gone I moved along the racks and laid out the more damaged dresses. The others I spaced out, soothing the disturbed fabrics until they relaxed and annealed themselves.

I was hunting through the wardrobes in the bedroom next door when I made a curious discovery. Packed behind the sliding doors was an immense array of costumes, faded models of the previous seasons which had been left to die on their hangers. A few were still barely alive. They hung inertly on their racks, responding with a feeble glimmer to the light.

What surprised me was their condition. All of them had been deformed into strange shapes, their colours bled like wounds across the fabric, reflecting the same traumatic past, some violent series of events they had witnessed between Raine Channing and whoever had lived with her in the years past. I remembered the clothes I had seen on a woman killed in a car crash at Vermilion Sands, blooming out of the wreckage like a monstrous flower of hell, and the demented wardrobe offered to me by the family of an heiress who had committed suicide. Memories such as these outlived their wearers. There was the apocryphal story of the murderer absconding in a stolen overcoat who had been strangled by the garment as it recapitulated the death-throes of its owner.

Leaving these uneasy relics to their dark end, I went back to the dressing room. As I eased the last of the disturbed gowns on to their hangers the terrace door opened behind me.

Raine Channing stepped out of the sun. In place of her clinging white fur she now wore a bio-fabric bikini. The two yellow cups nestled her full breasts like sleeping hands. Despite the clear evidence of some fierce row that morning, she seemed composed and relaxed. As she stared at the now placid tenants of her wardrobe, her white face, like a devious adolescent's, more than ever resembled a surgical mask, the powdered child-face of a Manchu empress.

'Mr Samson! They're quiet now! You're like . . .'

'St Francis calming the birds?' I suggested, still annoyed at having been summoned to Lagoon West. I gestured towards the sealed wardrobes in her bedroom. 'Forgive me saying so, but there are unhappy memories here.'

She picked up my jacket and draped it over her naked shoulders, a gesture of false modesty that none the less held a certain charm. The fabric clung to her like a pink flower, caressing her breasts and arms.

'The past is something of a disaster area, I'm afraid, Mr Samson. I know I brought you out here under false pretences. Something went wrong this morning, and you are the only neighbour I have.' She walked to the window and gazed over the painted lake. 'I came back to Vermilion Sands for reasons that must seem crazy.'

I watched her warily, but something about her apparent frankness destroyed caution. Presumably the midnight lover of the sand-yacht had left the scene, no doubt in a holocaust of emotions.

We went on to the terrace and sat in the reclining chairs beside the bar. During the next hours, and the many that followed in that house without mirrors above the painted lake, she told me something of her years with Gavin Kaiser, and how this young genius from the fashion world had found her singing at the open-air nightclub at Lagoon West. Seeing in this beautiful fifteen-year-old the apotheosis of the teenage cult, Kaiser had made her his star model for the bio-fabric fashions he designed. Four years later, at the age of nineteen, she had her first face-lift, followed by even more extensive plastic surgery in the years immediately after. When Kaiser died she came back to Lagoon West, to the house near the deserted nightclub.

'I left so many pieces of myself behind in all those clinics and hospitals. I thought perhaps I could find them here.'

'How did Kaiser die?' I asked.

'From a heart attack – *they* said. It was some sort of terrible convulsion, as if he'd been bitten by a hundred rabid dogs. He was trying to tear his face to pieces.' She raised her hands to her own white mask.

'Wasn't there some doubt . . . ?' I hesitated.

She held my arm. 'Gavin was mad! He wanted nothing to change between us. Those face-lifts – he kept me at fifteen, but not because of the fashion-modelling. He wanted me for ever when I first loved him.'

At the time, however, I hardly cared why Raine Channing had come back to Lagoon West. Every afternoon I would drive out to her villa and we would lie together under the awning by the bar, watching the changing colours of the painted lake. There, in that house without mirrors, she would tell me her strange dreams, which all reflected her fears of growing young. In the evenings, as the music began to play from the deserted nightclub, we would walk across the dunes and dance among the sand-strewn tables.

Who brought this record-player to the nightclub with its one unlabelled disc? Once, as we walked back, I again saw the young man with the powerful shoulders and broken nose standing by his sand-yacht in the darkness. He watched us as we walked arm in arm, Raine's head against my chest. As she listened to the music jewel in her hand, Raine's eyes stared back like a child's at his handsome face.

Often I would see him at noon, sailing his sand-yacht across the lake a few hundred yards from the shore. I assumed that he was one of Raine's past lovers, watching his successor with a sympathetic curiosity and playing his music for us out of a bizarre sense of humour.

Yet when I pointed him out to Raine one afternoon she denied that she knew him or had even seen him before. Sitting up on one elbow, she watched the sand-yacht beached three hundred yards away along the shore. The young man was walking along the tideline, searching for something among the broken hypodermic vials.

'I can tell him to go away, Raine.' When she shook her head, I said: 'He was here. What happened between you?'

She turned on me sharply. 'Why do you say that?'

I let it pass. Her eyes followed him everywhere.

Two weeks later I saw him again at closer quarters. Shortly after midnight I woke on the terrace of Raine's villa and heard the familiar music coming from the deserted nightclub. Below, in the dim light, Raine Channing walked towards the dunes. Along the beach the thermal rollers whipped the white sand into fine waves.

The villa was silent. Mlle Fournier had gone to Red Beach for a few days, and the young chauffeur was asleep in his apartment over the garages. I opened the gates at the end of the dark, rhododendron-filled drive and walked towards the nightclub. The music whined around me over the dead sand.

The nightclub was empty, the record playing to itself on the deserted stage. I wandered through the tables, searching for any sign of Raine. For a few minutes I waited by the bar. Then, as I leaned over the counter, the slim-faced figure of the chauffeur stood up and lunged at me, his right fist aimed at my forehead.

Sidestepping into his arm, I caught his hand and rammed it on to the counter. In the darkness his small face was twisted in a rictus of anger. He wrenched his arm from me, looking away across the dunes to the lake. The music whined on, the record starting again.

I found them by the beach, Raine with her hand on the young man's hip as he bent down to cast off the yacht. Uncertain what to do, and confused by his off-hand manner as he moved around Raine, I stood among the dunes at the top of the beach.

Feet moved through the sand. I was staring down at Raine's face, its white masks multiplying themselves in the moonlight, when someone stepped behind me and struck me above the ear.

I woke on Raine's bed in the deserted villa, the white moonlight like a waiting shroud across the terrace. Around me the shadows of demented shapes seethed along the walls, the deformed inmates of some nightmare aviary. In the silence of the villa I listened to them tearing themselves to pieces like condemned creatures tormenting themselves on their gibbets.

I climbed from the bed and faced my reflection in the open window. I was wearing a suit of gold lamé which shone in the moonlight like the armour of some archangelic spectre. Holding my bruised scalp, I walked on to the terrace. The gold suit adhered itself to my body, its lapels caressing my chest.

In the drive Raine Channing's limousine waited among the rhododendrons. At the wheel the slim-faced chauffeur looked up at me with bored eyes.

'Raine!' In the rear seat of the car there was a movement of white-clad thigh, a man's bare-backed figure crouching among the cushions. Angered by having to watch the spectacle below in this preposterous suit, I started to tear it from my shoulders. Before I could shout again something seized my calves and thighs. I tried to step forward, but my body was clamped in a golden vice. I looked down at the sleeves. The fabric glowed with a fierce luminescence as it contracted around me, its fibres knotting themselves like a thousand zips.

Already breathing in uncertain spasms, I tried to turn, unable to raise my hands to the lapels that gripped my neck. As I toppled forward on to the rail the headlamps of the car illuminated the drive.

I lay on my back in the gutter, arms clamped behind me. The golden suit glowed in the darkness, its burning light reflected in the thousand glass panes of the house. Somewhere below me the car turned through the gates and roared off into the night.

*     *     *

A few minutes later, as I came back to consciousness, I felt hands pulling at my chest. I was lifted against the balcony and sat there limply, my bruised ribs moving freely again. The bare-chested young man knelt in front of me, silver blade in hand, cutting away the last golden strips from my legs. The fading remnants of the suit burned like embers on the dark tiles.

He pushed back my forehead and peered into my face, then snapped the blade of his knife. 'You looked like a dying angel, Samson.'

'For God's sake . . .' I leaned against the rail. A network of weals covered my naked body. 'The damn thing was crushing me . . . Who are you?'

'Jason – Jason Kaiser. You've seen me. My brother died in that suit, Samson.'

His strong face watched me, the broken nose and broad mouth making a half-formed likeness.

'Kaiser? Do you mean your brother –' I pointed to the lamé rags on the floor. '– that he was strangled?'

'In a suit of lights. What he saw, God knows, but it killed him. Perhaps now you can make a guess, Samson. Justice in a way, the tailor killed by his own cloth.' He kicked the glowing shreds into the gutter and looked up at the deserted house. 'I was sure she'd come back here. I hoped she'd pick one of the beachcombers but you turned up instead. Sooner or later I knew she'd want to get rid of you.'

He pointed to the bedroom windows. 'The suit was in there somewhere, waiting to live through that attack again. You know, I sat beside her in the car down there while she was making up her mind to use it. Samson, she turns her lovers into angels.'

'Wait – didn't she recognize you?'

He shook his head. 'She'd never seen me – I couldn't stand my brother, Samson. Let's say, though, there are certain ciphers in the face, resemblances one can make use of. That record was all I needed, the old theme tune of the nightclub. I found it in the bar.'

Despite my bruised ribs and torn skin I was still thinking of Raine, and that strange child's face she wore like a mask. She had come back to Lagoon West to make a beginning, and instead found that events repeated themselves, trapping her into this grim recapitulation of Kaiser's death.

Jason walked towards the bedroom as I stood there naked. 'Where are you going?' I called out. 'Everything is dead in there.'

'I know. We had quite a job fitting you into that suit, Samson. They knew what was coming.' He pointed to the headlamps speeding along the lake road five miles to the south. 'Say goodbye to Miss Channing.'

I watched the car disappear among the hills. By the abandoned nightclub the dark air drew its empty signatures across the dunes. 'Say goodbye to the wind.'

**1970**

# THE GREATEST TELEVISION SHOW ON EARTH

The discovery in the year 2001 of an effective system of time travel had a number of important repercussions, nowhere greater than in the field of television. The last quarter of the twentieth century had seen the spectacular growth of television across every continent on the globe, and the programmes transmitted by the huge American, European and Afro-Asian networks each claimed audiences of a billion viewers. Yet despite their enormous financial resources the television companies were faced with a chronic shortage of news and entertainment. Vietnam, the first TV War, had given viewers all the excitement of live transmissions from the battlefield, but wars in general, not to mention newsworthy activity of any kind, had died out as the world's population devoted itself almost exclusively to watching television.

At this point the discovery of time travel made its fortunate appearance.

As soon as the first spate of patent suits had been settled (one Japanese entrepreneur almost succeeded in copyrighting history; time was then declared 'open' territory) it became clear that the greatest obstacle to time travel was not the laws of the physical universe but the vast sums of money needed to build and power the installations. These safaris into the past cost approximately a million dollars a minute. After a few brief journeys to verify the Crucifixion, the signing of Magna Carta and Columbus's discovery of the Americas, the government-financed Einstein Memorial Time Centre at Princeton was forced to suspend operations.

Plainly, only one other group could finance further explorations into the past – the world's television corporations. Their eager assurances that there would be no undue sensationalism convinced government leaders that the educational benefits of these travelogues through time outweighed any possible lapses in taste.

The television companies, for their part, saw in the past an inexhaustible supply of first-class news and entertainment – all of it, moreover, free. Immediately they set to work, investing billions of dollars, rupees, roubles and yen in duplicating the great chronotron at the Princeton Time Centre. Task-forces of physicists and mathematicians were enrolled as assistant producers. Camera crews were sent to key sites – London, Washington and Peking – and shortly afterwards the first pilot programmes were transmitted to an eager world.

These blurry scenes, like faded newsreels, of the coronation of Queen

Elizabeth II, the inauguration of Franklin Delano Roosevelt and the funeral of Mao Tse-tung triumphantly demonstrated the feasibility of Time Vision. After this solemn unveiling – a gesture in the direction of the government watchdog committees – the television companies began seriously to plan their schedules. The winter programmes for the year 2002 offered viewers the assassination of President Kennedy ('live', as the North American company tactlessly put it), the D-Day landings and the Battle of Stalingrad. Asian viewers were given Pearl Harbor and the fall of Corregidor.

This emphasis on death and destruction set the pace for what followed. The success of the programmes was beyond the planners' wildest dreams. These fleeting glimpses of smoke-crossed battlegrounds, with their burnt-out tanks and landing craft, had whetted an enormous appetite. More and more camera crews were readied, and an army of military historians deployed to establish the exact time at which Bastogne was relieved, the victory flags hoisted above Mount Suribachi and the Reichstag.

Within a year a dozen programmes each week brought to three billion viewers the highlights of World War II and the subsequent decades, all transmitted as they actually occurred. Night after night, somewhere around the world, John F. Kennedy was shot dead in Dealey Plaza, atom bombs exploded over Hiroshima and Nagasaki, Adolf Hitler committed suicide in the ruins of his Berlin bunker.

After this success the television companies moved back to the 1914–18 War, ready to reap an even richer harvest of audience ratings from the killing grounds of Passchendaele and Verdun. To their surprise, however, the glimpses of this mud- and shell-filled universe were a dismal failure compared with the great technological battles of World War II being transmitted live at the same time on rival channels from the carrier decks of the Philippine Sea and the thousand-bomber raids over Essen and Dusseldorf.

One sequence alone from World War I quickened the viewers' jaded palates – a cavalry charge by Uhlans of the German Imperial Army. Riding over the barbed wire on their splendid mounts, white plumes flying above the mud, these lance-wielding horsemen brought to a billion war-weary TV screens the magic of pageantry and costume. At a moment when it might have faltered, Time Vision was saved by the epaulette and the cuirass.

Immediately, camera crews began to travel back into the nineteenth century. World Wars I and II faded from the screen. Within a few months viewers saw the coronation of Queen Victoria, the assassination of Lincoln and the siege of the Alamo.

As a climax to this season of instant history, the great Time Vision corporations of Europe and North America collaborated on their most spectacular broadcast to date – a live coverage of the defeat of Napoleon Bonaparte at the Battle of Waterloo.

\*      \*      \*

While making their preparations the two companies made a discovery that was to have far-reaching consequences for the whole history of Time Vision. During their visits to the battle (insulated from the shot and fury by the invisible walls of their time capsules) the producers found that there were fewer combatants actually present than described by the historians of the day. Whatever the immense political consequences of the defeat of Napoleonic France, the battle itself was a disappointing affair, a few thousand march-wearied troops engaged in sporadic rifle and artillery duels.

An emergency conference of programme chiefs discussed this failure of Waterloo to live up to its reputation. Senior producers revisited the battlefield, leaving their capsules to wander in disguise among the exhausted soldiery. The prospect of the lowest audience ratings in the history of Time Vision seemed hourly more imminent.

At this crisis-point some nameless assistant producer came up with a remarkable idea. Rather than sit back helplessly behind their cameras, the Time Vision companies should step in themselves, he suggested, lending their vast expertise and resources to heightening the drama of the battle. More extras – that is, mercenaries recruited from the nearby farming communities – could be thrown into the fray, supplies of powder and shot, distributed to the empty guns, and the entire choreography of the battle re-vamped by the military consultants in the editorial departments. 'History,' he concluded, 'is just a first draft screenplay.'

This suggestion of re-making history to boost its audience appeal was seized upon. Equipped with a lavish supply of gold coinage, agents of the television companies moved across the Belgian and North German plains, hiring thousands of mercenaries (at the standard rate for TV extras of fifty dollars per day on location, regardless of rank, seventy-five dollars for a speaking part). The relief column of the Prussian General Blücher, reputed by historians to be many thousand strong and to have decisively turned the battle against Napoleon, was in fact found to be a puny force of brigade strength. Within a few days thousands of eager recruits flocked to the colours, antibiotics secretly administered to polluted water supplies cured a squadron of cavalry hunters suffering from anthrax, and a complete artillery brigade threatened with typhus was put on its feet by a massive dose of chloromycetin.

The Battle of Waterloo, when finally transmitted to an audience of over one billion viewers, was a brilliant spectacle more than equal to its advance publicity of the past two hundred years. The thousands of mercenaries fought with savage fury, the air was split by non-stop artillery barrages, waves of cavalry charged and recharged. Napoleon himself was completely bewildered by the way events turned out, spending his last years in baffled exile.

After the success of Waterloo the Time Vision companies realized the advantages of preparing their ground. From then onwards almost all important historical events were rescripted by the editorial departments.

Hannibal's army crossing the Alps was found to contain a mere half-dozen elephants – two hundred more were provided to trample down the dumbfounded Romans. Caesar's assassins numbered only two – five additional conspirators were hired. Famous historical orations, such as the Gettysburg Address, were cut and edited to make them more stirring. Waterloo, meanwhile, was not forgotten. To recoup the original investment the battle was sublet to smaller TV contractors, some of whom boosted the battle to a scale resembling Armageddon. However, these spectacles in the De Mille manner, in which rival companies appeared on the same battlefield, pouring in extras, weapons and animals, were looked down on by more sophisticated viewers.

To the annoyance of the television companies, the most fascinating subject in the whole of history remained barred to them. At the stern insistence of the Christian churches the entire events surrounding the life of Christ were kept off the screen. Whatever the spiritual benefits of hearing the Sermon on the Mount transmitted live might be, these were tempered by the prospect of this sublime experience being faded out between beatitudes for the commercial breaks.

Baulked here, the programmers moved further back in time. To celebrate the fifth anniversary of Time Vision, preparations began for a stupendous joint venture – the flight of the Israelites from Egypt and the crossing of the Red Sea. A hundred camera units and several thousand producers and technicians took up their positions in the Sinai Peninsula. Two months before the transmission it was obvious that there would now be more than two sides in this classic confrontation between the armies of Egypt and the children of the Lord. Not only did the camera crews outnumber the forces of either side, but the hiring of Egyptian extras, additional wave-making equipment and the prefabricated barrage built to support the cameras might well prevent the Israelites from getting across at all. Clearly, the powers of the Almighty would be severely tested in his first important confrontation with the ratings.

A few forebodings were expressed by the more old-fashioned clerics, printed under ironic headlines such as 'War against Heaven?', 'Sinai Truce Offer rejected by TV Producers Guild'. At bookmakers throughout Europe and the United States the odds lengthened against the Israelites. On the day of transmission, January 1st, 2006, the audience ratings showed that 98% of the Western world's adult viewers were by their sets.

The first pictures appeared on the screens. Under a fitful sky the fleeing Israelites plodded into view, advancing towards the invisible cameras mounted over the water. Originally three hundred in number, the Israelites now formed a vast throng that stretched with its baggage train for several miles across the desert. Confused by the great press of camp-followers, the Israelite leaders paused on the shore, uncertain how to cross this shifting mass of unstable water. Along the horizon the sabre-wheeled chariots of Pharaoh's army raced towards them.

The viewers watched spellbound, many wondering whether the television companies had at last gone too far.

Then, without explanation, a thousand million screens went blank.

Pandemonium broke loose. Everywhere switchboards were jammed. Priority calls at inter-governmental level jammed the Comsat relays, the Time Vision studios in Europe and America were besieged.

Nothing came through. All contacts with the camera crews on location had been broken. Finally, two hours later, a brief picture appeared, of racing waters swilling over the shattered remains of television cameras and switchgear. On the near bank, the Egyptian forces turned for home. Across the waters, the small band of Israelites moved towards the safety of Sinai.

What most surprised the viewers was the eerie light that illuminated the picture, as if some archaic but extraordinary method of power were being used to transmit it.

No further attempts to regain contact succeeded. Almost all the world's Time Vision equipment had been destroyed, its leading producers and technicians lost for ever, perhaps wandering the stony rocks of Sinai like a second lost tribe. Shortly after this débâcle, these safaris into the past were eliminated from the world's TV programmes. As one priest with a taste for ironic humour remarked to his chastened television congregation: 'The big channel up in the sky has its ratings too.'

**1972**

# MY DREAM OF FLYING TO WAKE ISLAND

Melville's dream of flying to Wake Island – a hopeless ambition, given all his handicaps – came alive again when he found the crashed aircraft buried in the dunes above the beach-house. Until then, during these first three months at the abandoned resort built among the sandhills, his obsession with Wake Island had rested on little more than a collection of fraying photographs of this Pacific atoll, a few vague memories of its immense concrete runways, and an unfulfilled vision of himself at the controls of a light aircraft, flying steadily westwards across the open sea.

With the discovery of the crashed bomber in the dunes, everything had changed. Instead of spending his time wandering aimlessly along the beach, or gazing from the balcony at the endless sand-flats that stretched towards the sea at low tide, Melville now devoted all his time to digging the aircraft out of the dunes. He cancelled his evening games of chess with Dr Laing, his only neighbour at the empty resort, went to bed before the television programmes began and was up by five, dragging his spades and land-lines across the sand to the excavation site.

The activity suited Melville, distracting him from the sharp frontal migraines that had begun to affect him again. These returning memories of the prolonged ECT treatment unsettled him more than he had expected, with their unequivocal warning that in the margins of his mind the elements of a less pleasant world were waiting to reconstitute themselves. The dream of escaping to Wake Island was a compass bearing of sorts, but the discovery of the crashed aircraft gave him a chance to engage all his energies and, with luck, hold these migraine attacks at bay.

A number of wartime aircraft were buried near this empty resort. Walking across the sand-flats on what Dr Laing believed were marine-biology specimen hunts, Melville often found pieces of allied and enemy fighters shot down over the Channel. Rusting engine blocks and sections of cannon breeches emerged from the sand, somehow brought to the surface by the transits of the sea, and then subsided again without trace. During the summer weekends a few souvenir hunters and World War II enthusiasts picked over the sand, now and then finding a complete engine or wing spar. Too heavy to move, these relics were left where they lay. However, one of the weekend groups, led by a former advertising executive named Tennant, had found an intact Messerschmitt 109 a few feet below the sand half a mile along the coast. The members of the party parked their sports-cars at the bottom of the road below Melville's beach-house, and set off with elaborate pumps and lifting tackle in a reconditioned DUKW.

Melville noticed that Tennant was usually suspicious and stand-offish with any visitors who approached the Messerschmitt, but the advertising man was clearly intrigued by this solitary resident of the deserted resort who spent his time ambling through the debris on the beach. He offered Melville a chance of looking at the aircraft. They drove out across the wet sand to where the fighter lay like a winged saurian inside its galvanized-iron retaining wall a few feet below the surface of the flat. Tennant helped to lower Melville into the blackened cockpit, an experience which promptly brought on his first fugue.

Later, when Tennant and his co-workers had returned him to the beach-house, Melville sat for hours massaging his arms and hands, uneasily aware of certain complex digital skills that he wanted to forget but were beginning to reassert themselves in unexpected ways. Laing's solarium, with its dials and shutters, its capsule-like interior, unsettled him even more than the cockpit of the 109.

Impressive though the find was, the rusting hulk of the World War II fighter was insignificant beside Melville's discovery. He had been aware of the bomber, or at least of a large engineered structure, for some time. Wandering among the dunes above the beach-house during the warm afternoons, he had been too preoccupied at first with the task of settling in at the abandoned resort, and above all with doing nothing. Despite the endless hours he had spent in the hospital gymnasium, during his long recuperation after the aviation accident, he found the effort of walking through the deep sand soon exhausted him.

At this stage, too, he had other matters to think about. After arriving at the resort he had contacted Dr Laing, as instructed by the after-care officers at the hospital, expecting the physician to follow him everywhere. But whether deliberately or not, Laing had not been particularly interested in Melville, this ex-pilot who had turned up here impulsively in his expensive car and was now prowling restlessly around the solarium as if hunting for a chromium rat. Laing worked at the Science Research Council laboratory five miles inland, and clearly valued the privacy of the prefabricated solarium he had erected on the sand-bar at the southern end of the resort. He greeted Melville without comment, handed him the keys to the beach-house, and left him to it.

This lack of interest was a relief to Melville, but at the same time threw him on to himself. He had arrived with two suitcases, one filled with newly purchased and unfamiliar clothes, the other holding the hospital X-ray plates of his head and the photographs of Wake Island. The X-ray plates he passed to Dr Laing, who raised them to the light, scrutinizing these negatives of Melville's skull as if about to point out some design error in its construction. The photographs of Wake Island he returned without comment.

These illustrations of the Pacific atoll, with its vast concrete runways, he had collected over the previous months. During his convalescence at the hospital he had joined a wildlife conservation society, ostensibly in support of its campaign to save the Wake Island albatross from extinction – tens of thousands of the goony birds nested at the ends of the runways, and would rise in huge flocks into the flight-paths of airliners at take-off. Melville's real interest had been in the island itself, a World War II airbase and now refuelling point for trans-Pacific passenger jets. The combination of scuffed sand and concrete, metal shacks rusting by the runways, the total psychological reduction of this man-made landscape, seized his mind in a powerful but ambiguous way. For all its arid, oceanic isolation, the Wake Island in Melville's mind soon became a zone of intense possibility. He day-dreamed of flying there in a light aircraft, island-hopping across the Pacific. Once he touched down he knew that the migraines would go away for ever. He had been discharged from the Air Force in confused circumstances, and during his convalescence after the accident the military psychiatrists had been only too glad to play their parts in what soon turned out to be an under-rehearsed conspiracy of silence. When he told them that he had rented a house from a doctor in this abandoned resort, and intended to live there for a year on his back pay, they had been relieved to see him go, carrying away the X-ray plates of his head and the photographs of Wake Island.

'But why Wake Island?' Dr Laing asked him on their third chess evening. He pointed to the illustrations that Melville had pinned to the mantelpiece, and the technical abstracts lavishly documenting its geology, rainfall, seismology, flora and fauna. 'Why not Guam? Or Midway? Or the Hawaiian chain?'

'Midway would do, but it's a naval base now – I doubt if they'll give me landing clearance. Anyway, the atmosphere is wrong.' Discussing the rival merits of various Pacific islands always animated Melville, feeding this potent remythologizing of himself. 'Guam is forty miles long, covered with mountains and dense jungle, New Guinea in miniature. The Hawaiian islands are an offshore suburb of the United States. Only Wake has real time.'

'You were brought up in the Far East?'

'In Manila. My father ran a textile company there.'

'So the Pacific area has a special appeal for you.'

'To some extent. But Wake is a long way from the Philippines.'

Laing never asked if Melville had actually been to Wake Island. Clearly Melville's vision of flying to this remote Pacific atoll was unlikely to take place outside his own head.

However, Melville then had the good luck to discover the aircraft buried in the dunes.

When the tide was in, covering the sand-flats, Melville was forced to walk among the dunes above his beach-house. Driven and shaped by the wind, the contours of the dunes varied from day to day, but one afternoon Melville noticed that a section below the ridge retained its rectilinear form, indicating that some man-made structure lay below the sand, possibly the detached roof of a metal barn or boat-house.

Irritated by the familiar drone of a single-engined aircraft flying from the light airfield behind the resort, Melville clambered up to the ridge through the flowing sand and sat down on the horizontal ledge that ran among the clumps of wild grass. The aircraft, a privately owned Cessna, flew in from the sea directly towards him, banked steeply and circled overhead. Its pilot, a dentist and aviation enthusiast in her early thirties, had been curious about Melville for some time – the mushy drone of her flat six was forever dividing the sky over his head. Often, as he walked across the sand-flats four hundred yards from the shore, she would fly past him, wheels almost touching the streaming sand, throttling up her engine as if trying to din something into his head. She appeared to be testing various types of auxiliary fuel tank. Now and then he saw her driving her American sedan through the deserted streets of the resort towards the airfield. For some reason the noise of her light aircraft began to unsettle him, as if the furniture of his brain was being shifted around behind some dark curtain.

The Cessna circled above him like a dull, unwearying bird. Trying to look as though he was engaged in his study of beach ecology, Melville cleared away the sand between his feet. Without realizing it, he had exposed a section of grey, riveted metal, the skin of an all-too-familiar aerodynamic structure. He stood up and worked away with both hands, soon revealing the unmistakable profile of an aerofoil curvature.

The Cessna had gone, taking the lady dentist back to the air-strip. Melville had forgotten about her as he pushed the heavy sand away, steering it down the saddle between the dunes. Although nearly exhausted, he continued to clear the starboard wing-tip now emerging from the dune. He took off his jacket and beat away the coarse white grains, at last revealing the combat insignia, star and bars of a USAAF roundel.

As he knew within a few minutes, he had discovered an intact wartime B-17. Two days later, by a sustained effort, he had dug away several tons of sand and exposed to view almost the entire starboard wing, the tail and rear turret. The bomber was almost undamaged – Melville assumed that the pilot had run out of fuel while crossing the Channel and tried to land on the sand-flats at low tide, overshot the wet surface and ploughed straight through the dunes above the beach. A write-off, the Fortress had been abandoned where it lay, soon to be covered by the shifting sand-hills. The small resort had been built, flourished briefly and declined without anyone realizing that this relic of World War II lay in the ridge a hundred yards behind the town.

Systematically, Melville organized himself in the task of digging out, and then renovating, this antique bomber. Working alone, he estimated that it would take three months to expose the aircraft, and a further two years to strip it down and rebuild it from scratch. The precise details of how he would straighten the warped propeller blades and replace the Wright Cyclone engines remained hazy in his mind, but already he visualized the shingle-reinforced earth-and-sand ramp which he would construct with a rented bulldozer from the crest of the dunes down to the beach. When the sea was out, after a long late-summer day, the sand along the tide-line was smooth and hard . . .

Few people came to watch him. Tennant, the former advertising man leading the group digging out the Messerschmitt, came across the sand-flats and gazed abstractedly at the emerging wings and fuselage of the Fortress. Neither of the men spoke to each other – both, as Melville knew, had something more important on their minds.

In the evening, when Melville was still working on the aircraft, Dr Laing walked along the beach from his solarium. He climbed the shadow-filled dunes, watching Melville clear away the sand from the chin-turret.

'What about the bomb-load?' he asked. 'I'd hate to see the whole town levelled.'

'It's an officially abandoned wreck.' Melville pointed to the stripped-down gun turret. 'Everything has been removed, including the machine-guns and bomb-sight. I think you're safe from me, doctor.'

'A hundred years ago you'd have been digging a diplodocus out of a chalk cliff,' Laing remarked. The Cessna was circling the sand-bar at the southern end of the resort, returning after a navigation exercise. 'If you're keen to fly perhaps Helen Winthrop will take you on as a co-pilot. She was asking me something about you the other day. She's planning to break the single-engine record to Cape Town.'

This item of news intrigued Melville. The next day, as he worked at his excavation site, he listened for the sound of the Cessna's engine. The image of this determined woman preparing for her solo flight across Africa, testing her aircraft at this abandoned airfield beside the dunes, coincided powerfully with his own dream of flying to Wake Island. He knew full well now that the elderly Fortress he was laboriously digging from the sand-dunes would never leave its perch on the ridge, let alone take off from the beach. But the woman's aircraft offered a feasible alternative. Already he mapped out a route in his mind, calculating the capacity of her auxiliary tanks and the refuelling points in the Azores and Newfoundland.

Afraid that she might leave without him, Melville decided to approach her directly. He drove his car through the deserted streets of the resort, turned on to the unmade road that led to the airfield, and parked beside her American sedan. The Cessna, its engine cowlings removed, stood at the end of the runway.

She was working at an engineering bench in the hangar, welding together the sections of a fuel tank. As Melville approached she switched off the blowtorch and removed her mask, her intelligent face shielded by her hands.

'I see we're involved in a race to get away first,' she called out reassuringly to him when he paused in the entrance to the hangar. 'Dr Laing told me that you'd know how to strengthen these fuel tanks.'

For Melville, her nervous smile cloaked a complex sexual metaphor.

From the start Melville took it for granted that she would abandon her plan to fly to Cape Town, and instead embark on a round-the-world flight with himself as her co-pilot. He outlined his plans for their westward flight, calculating the reduced fuel load they would carry to compensate for his weight. He showed her his designs for the wing spars and braces that would support the auxiliary tanks.

'Melville, I'm flying to Cape Town,' she told him wearily. 'It's taken me years to arrange this – there's no question of setting out anywhere else. You're obsessed with this absurd island.'

'You'll understand when we get there,' Melville assured her. 'Don't worry about the aircraft. After Wake you'll be on your own. I'll strip off the tanks and cut all these braces away.'

'You intend to stay on Wake Island?' Helen Winthrop seemed unsure of Melville's seriousness, as if listening to an over-enthusiastic patient in her surgery chair outlining the elaborate dental treatment he had set his heart on.

'Stay there? Of course ...' Melville prowled along the mantelpiece of the beach-house, slapping the line of photographs. 'Look at those runways, everything is there. A big airport like the Wake field is a zone of tremendous possibility – a place of beginnings, by the way, not ends.'

Helen Winthrop made no comment on this, watching Melville quietly. She no longer slept in the hangar at the airstrip, and during her weekend visits moved into Melville's beach-house. Needing his help to increase the Cessna's range, and so reduce the number of refuelling stops with their built-in delays, she put up with his restlessness and child-like excitement, only concerned by his growing dependence on her. As he worked on the Cessna she listened for hours to him describing the runways of the island. However, she was careful never to leave him alone with the ignition keys.

While she was away, working at her dental practice, Melville returned to the dunes, continuing to dig out the crashed bomber. The port and starboard wings were now free of the sand, soon followed by the upper section of the fuselage. The weekends he devoted to preparing the Cessna for its long westward flight. For all his excitability, the state of controlled euphoria which his soon-to-be-realized dream of flying to Wake Island had brought about, his navigation plans and structural modification to the Cessna's air-frame were carefully and professionally carried through.

Even the intense migraines that began to disturb Melville's sleep did little to dent his good humour. He assumed that these fragments of the past had been brought to the surface of his mind by the strains of his involvement with this over-serious aviatrix, but later he knew that these elements of an unforgotten nightmare had been cued in by the aircraft emerging around him on all sides – Helen Winthrop's Cessna, the Fortress he was exposing to light, the blackened Messerschmitt which the advertising man was lifting from the sea-bed.

After a storm had disturbed the sand-flats, he stood on the balcony of the beach-house inhaling the carbonated air, trying to free himself from the uneasy dreams that had filled the night, a system of demented metaphors. In front of him the surface of the sand-flats was covered with dozens of pieces of rusting metal, aircraft parts shaken loose by the storm. As Helen Winthrop watched from the bedroom window he stepped on to the beach and walked across the ruffled sand, counting the fragments of carburettor and exhaust manifold, trim-tab and tailwheel that lay around him as if left here by the receding tide of his dreams.

Already other memories were massing around him, fragments that he was certain belonged to another man's life, details from the case-history of an imaginary patient whose role he had been tricked into playing. As he worked on the Fortress high among the dunes, brushing the sand away from the cylinder vanes of the radial engines, he remembered other aircraft he had been involved with, vehicles without wings.

The bomber was completely exposed now. Knowing that his work was almost over, Melville opened the ventral crew hatch behind the chin turret. Ever since he had first revealed the cockpit of the plane he had been tempted to climb through the broken starboard windshield and take his seat at the controls, but the experience of the Messerschmitt cautioned him. With Helen Winthrop, however, he would be safe.

Throwing down his spade, he clambered across the sand to the beach-house.

'Helen! Come up here!' He pointed with pride to the exposed aircraft on the ridge, poised on its belly as if at the end of a take-off ramp. While Helen Winthrop tried to calm him, he steered her up the shifting slopes, hand over hand along the rope-line.

As they climbed through the crew hatch he looked back for the last time across the sand-flats, littered with their rusting aircraft parts. Inside the fuselage they searched their way around the barbette of the roof-turret, stepping through the debris of old R/T gear, lifejackets and ammunition boxes. After all his efforts, the interior of the fuselage seemed to Melville like a magical arbour, the grotto-like cavern within some archaic machine.

Sitting beside Helen in the cockpit, happy that she was with him as she would be on their flight across the Pacific, he took her through the controls, moving the throttles and trim wheels.

'Right, now. Mixture rich, carb heat cold, pitch full fine, flaps down for take-off . . .'

As she held his shoulders, trying to pull him away from the controls, Melville could hear the engines of the Fortress starting up within his head.

As if watching a film, he remembered his years as a military test-pilot, and his single abortive mission as an astronaut. By some grotesque turn of fate, he had become the first astronaut to suffer a mental breakdown in space. His nightmare ramblings had disturbed millions of television viewers around the world, as if the terrifying image of a man going mad in space had triggered off some long-buried innate releasing mechanism.

Later that evening, Melville lay by the window in his bedroom, watching the calm sea that covered the sand-flats. He remembered Helen Winthrop leaving him in the cockpit, and running away along the beach to find Dr Laing. Careful though he was, the physician was no more successful at dealing with Melville than the doctors at the institute of aviation medicine, who had tried to free him from his obsession that he had seen a fourth figure on board the three-man craft. This mysterious figure, either man or bird, he was convinced he had killed. Had he, also, committed the first murder in space? After his release he resolved to make his world-wide journey, externally to Wake Island, and internally across the planets of his mind.

As the summer ended and the time of their departure drew nearer, Melville was forced to renew his efforts at digging out the crashed Fortress. In the cooler weather the night winds moved the sand across the ridge, once again covering the fuselage of the aircraft.

Dr Laing visited him more frequently. Worried by Melville's deteriorating condition, he watched him struggle with the tons of sliding sand.

'Melville, you're exhausting yourself.' Laing took the spade from him and began to shovel away. Melville sat down on the wing. He was careful now never to enter the cockpit. Across the sand-flats Tennant and his team were leaving for the winter, the broken-backed Me 109 carried away on two trucks. Conserving his strength, he waited for the day when he and Helen Winthrop would leave this abandoned resort and take off into the western sky.

'All the radio aids are ready,' he told her on the weekend before they were due to leave. 'All you need to do now is file your flight plan.'

Helen Winthrop watched him sympathetically as he stood by the mantelpiece. Unable to stand his nervous vomiting, she had moved back to the hangar. Despite, or perhaps because of, their brief sexual involvement their relationship now was almost matter-of-factly neutral, but she tried to reassure him.

'How much luggage have you got? You've packed nothing.'

'I'm taking nothing – only the photographs.'

'You won't need them once you get to Wake Island.'

'Perhaps – they're more real for me now than the island could ever be.'

When Helen Winthrop left without him Melville was surprised, but not disappointed. He was working up on the dunes as the heavily laden Cessna, fitted with the wing tanks he had installed, took off from the airstrip. He knew immediately from the pitch of the engine that this was not a trial flight. Sitting on the roof turret of the Fortress, he watched her climb away across the sand-flats, make a steady right-hand turn towards the sea and set off downwind across the Channel.

Long before she was out of sight Melville had forgotten her. He would make his own way to the Pacific. During the following weeks he spent much of his time sheltering under the aircraft, watching the wind blow the sand back across the fuselage. With the departure of Helen Winthrop and the advertising executive with his Messerschmitt he found that his dreams grew calmer, shutting away his memories of the space flights. At times he was certain that his entire memory of having trained as an astronaut was a fantasy, part of some complex delusional system, an extreme metaphor of his real ambition. This conviction brought about a marked improvement in his health and self-confidence.

Even when Dr Laing climbed the dunes and told him that Helen Winthrop had died two weeks after crashing her Cessna at Nairobi airport, Melville had recovered sufficiently to feel several days of true grief. He drove to the airfield and wandered around the empty hangar. Traces of her over-hurried departure, a suitcase of clothes and a spare set of rescue flares, lay among the empty oil-drums.

Returning to the dunes, he continued to dig the crashed bomber from the sand, careful not to expose too much of it to the air. Although often exhausted in the damp winter air, he felt increasingly calm, sustained by the huge bulk of the Fortress, whose cockpit he never entered, and by his dream of flying to Wake Island.

**1974**

# THE AIR DISASTER

The news that the world's largest airliner had crashed into the sea near Acapulco with a thousand passengers on board reached me while I was attending the annual film festival at the resort. When the first radio reports were relayed over the conference loudspeakers I and my fellow journalists abandoned our seats in the auditorium and hurried out into the street. Together we stared silently at the sunlit ocean, almost expecting to see an immense cascade of water rising from the distant waves.

Like everyone else, I realised that this was the greatest disaster in the history of world aviation, and a tragedy equal to the annihilation of a substantial town. I had lost all interest in the film festival, and was glad when the manager of my television station in Mexico City ordered me to drive to the scene of the accident, some thirty miles to the south.

As I set off in my car I remembered when these huge airliners had come into service. Although they represented no significant advance in aviation technology – in effect they were double-decker versions of an earlier airliner – there was something about the figure 1000 that touched the imagination, setting off all kinds of forebodings that no amount of advertising could dispel.

A thousand passengers . . . I mentally counted them off – businessmen, elderly nuns, children returning to their parents, eloping lovers, diplomats, even a would-be hijacker. It was this almost perfect cross-section of humanity, like the census sample of an opinion pollster, that brought the disaster home. I found myself glancing compulsively at the sea, expecting to see the first handbags and life-jackets washed ashore on the empty beaches.

The sooner I could photograph a piece of floating debris and return to Acapulco – even to the triviality of the film festival – the happier I would feel. Unfortunately, the road was jammed with southbound traffic. Clearly every other journalist, both foreign and Mexican, present at the festival had been ordered to the scene of the disaster. Television camera-vans, police vehicles and the cars of over-eager sightseers were soon bumper to bumper. Annoyed by their ghoulish interest in the tragedy, I found myself hoping that there would be no trace of the aircraft when we arrived and stepped onto the beach.

In fact, as I listened to the radio bulletins, there was almost no information about the crash. The commentators already on the site, cruising the choppy waters of the Pacific in rented motor-boats, reported that there were no signs of any oil or wreckage.

Sadly, however, there was little doubt that the aircraft had crashed somewhere. The flight-crew of another airliner had seen the huge jet explode in mid-air, probably the victim of sabotage. Eerily, the one piece of hard information, constantly played and replayed over the radio, was the last transmission from the pilot of the huge aeroplane, reporting a fire in his cargo hold.

So the aircraft had come down – but where, exactly? For all the lack of information, the traffic continued to press southwards. Behind me, an impatient American newsreel team decide to overtake the line of crawling vehicles on the pedestrian verge, and the first altercations soon broke out. Police stood at the major crossroads, and with their usual flair managed to slow down any progress. After an hour of this, my car's engine began to boil, and I was forced to turn the lame vehicle into a roadside garage.

Sitting irritably in the forecourt, and well aware that I was unlikely to reach the crash site until the late afternoon, I looked away from the almost stationary traffic to the mountains a few miles inland. The foothills of the coastal range, they rose sharply into a hard and cloudless sky, their steep peaks lit by the sun. It occurred to me then that no one had actually witnessed the descent of the stricken airliner into the sea. Somewhere above the mountains the explosion had taken place, and the likely trajectory would have carried the unhappy machine into the Pacific. On the other hand, an observational error of a few miles, the miscalculation of a few seconds by the flight-crew who had seen the explosion, would make possible an impact point well inland.

By coincidence, two journalists in a nearby car were discussing exactly this possibility with the garage attendant filling their fuel tank. This young man was gesturing towards the mountains, where a rough road wound up a steep valley. He slapped his hands together, as if mimicking an explosion.

The journalists watched him sceptically, unimpressed by the story and put off by the young man's rough appearance and almost unintelligible local dialect. Paying him off, they turned their car onto the road and rejoined the slowly moving caravan to the south.

The attendant watched them go, his mind on other things. When he had filled my radiator, I asked him:

'You saw an explosion in the mountains?'

'I might have done – it's hard to say. It could have been lightning or a snow-slide.'

'You didn't see the aircraft?'

'No – I can't say that.'

He shrugged, only interested in going off duty. I waited while he handed over to his relief, climbed onto the back of a friend's motorcycle and set off along the coast with everyone else.

I looked up at the road into the valley. By luck, the farm track behind the garage joined it four hundred yards inland on the far side of a field.

Ten minutes later I was driving up the valley and away from the coastal plain. What made me follow this hunch that the aircraft had come down in the mountains? Self-interest, clearly, the hope of scooping all my colleagues and at last impressing my editor. Ahead of me was a small village, a run-down collection of houses grouped around two sides of a sloping square. Half a dozen farmers sat outside the tavern, little more than a window in a stone wall. Already the coast road was far below, part of another world. From this height someone would certainly have noticed the explosion if the aircraft had fallen here. I would question a few people; if they had seen nothing I would turn round and head south with everyone else.

As I entered the village I remembered how poverty-stricken this area of Mexico had always been, almost unchanged since the early 19th century. Most of the modest stone houses were still without electricity. There was a single television aerial, and a few elderly cars, wrecks on wheels, sat on the roadside among pieces of rusting agricultural equipment. The worn hill-slopes stretched up the valley, and the dull soil had long since given up its meagre fertility.

However, the chance remained that these villagers had seen something, a flash, perhaps, or even a sight of the stricken airliner plummeting overhead towards the sea.

I stopped my car in the cobbled square and walked across to the farmers outside the tavern.

'I'm looking for the crashed aircraft,' I told them. 'It may have come down near here. Have any of you seen anything?'

They were staring at my car, clearly a far more glamorous machine than anything that might fall from the sky. They shook their heads, waving their hands in a peculiarly secretive way. I knew that I had wasted my time in setting out on this private expedition. The mountains rose around me on all sides, the valleys dividing like the entrances to an immense maze.

As I turned to go back to my car one of the older farmers touched my arm. He pointed casually to a narrow valley sheltering between two adjacent peaks high above us.

'The aircraft?' I repeated.

'It's up there.'

'What? Are you sure?' I tried to control my excitement for fear of giving anything away.

The old man nodded, his interest fading. 'Yes. At the end of that valley. It's a long way.'

Within moments I had set off again, restraining myself with difficulty from over-taxing the engine. The few vague words of this old man convinced me that I was on the right track and about to achieve the scoop I had yearned for throughout my professional career. However casually he had spoken he had meant what he said.

I pressed on up the narrow road, forcing the car in and out of the potholes and rain-gullies. At each turn of the road I half-expected to see the tailplane of the aircraft poised on a distant crag, and the hundreds of bodies scattered down the mountain slopes like a fallen army. I started to run over in my mind the opening paragraphs of my dispatch, telephoned to my startled editor while my rivals were fifty miles away staring into the empty sea. It was vital to achieve the right marriage of sensation and compassion, that irresistible combination of ruthless realism and melancholy invocation. I would describe the first ominous discovery of a single aircraft seat on a hillside, a poignant trail of ruptured suitcases, a child's fluffy toy and then – a valley floor covered with corpses.

For an hour I pressed on up the road, now and then having to stop and kick away the boulders that blocked my path. This remote infertile region was almost deserted. At intervals an isolated hovel clung to a hillside, a section of telegraph wire followed me overhead for half a mile before ending abruptly, as if the telephone company years beforehand had realised that there was no one here to make or receive a call.

Once again, I began to have second thoughts. Had the old villager been playing me along? Surely if he had seen the aircraft come down he would have been more concerned?

The coastal plain and the sea were now miles behind me, visible only for brief moments as I followed the broken road up the valley. Looking back at the sunlit coast through the rear mirror, I carelessly rolled the car over some heavy rubble. After the collision underneath I could tell from the different note of the exhaust that I had damaged the exhaust.

Cursing myself for having embarked on this lunatic chase, I knew that I was about to strand myself up here in the mountains. Already the early afternoon light was beginning to fade. Fortunately I had ample fuel in the car, but on this narrow road it was impossible to turn the vehicle around.

Forced to go on, I approached a second village, a clutch of hovels built a century earlier around a now deconsecrated chapel. The only level place in which to turn a car was temporarily blocked by two peasants loading firewood onto a cart. As I waited for them to move away I realised how much poorer they were even than the people in the village below them. Their clothes were made partly from leather and partly from animal furs, and they carried shot-guns over their shoulders – weapons, I could tell from the way they looked at me, which they might not hesitate to use if I remained here after dark.

They watched me as I carefully reversed the car, their eyes roving across this expensive sports saloon, the camera equipment on the seat beside me, and even my clothes, all of which must have seemed unbelievably exotic.

To explain my presence, and give myself some kind of official status

that would deter them from emptying their shot-guns into my back as
I drove off, I said:

'I've been ordered to look for the aircraft – it came down somewhere
near here.'

I moved the gears, about to move off, when one of the men nodded
in reply. He put one hand on my windshield, and with the other pointed
to a narrow valley lying between twin mountain peaks a thousand feet
above us.

As I drove up the mountain road, all my doubts had gone. This time, once
and for all, I would prove my worth to a sceptical editor. Two separate
witnesses had confirmed the presence of the crashed aircraft. Careful not
to damage the car on this primitive track, I pressed on towards the valley
high above me.

For the next two hours I moved steadily upwards, ever higher into these
bleak mountains. By now all sight of the coastal plain and the sea had
gone. Once I caught a brief glimpse of the first village I had passed, far
below me like a small stain on a carpet. With luck, the road continued
to carry me towards my goal. No more than an earth and stone track,
it was barely wide enough to hold the car's wheels as I steered around
the endless hairpin bends.

Twice more I stopped to question the few mountain people who
watched me from the doors of their earth-floored hovels. However
guardedly, they confirmed that the crashed aircraft lay above.

At four o'clock that afternoon, I finally reached the remote valley lying
between two mountain peaks, and approached the last of the villages
on this long trail. Here the road came to an end in a stony square
surrounded by a cluster of dwellings. They looked as if they had been
built two hundred years earlier and had spent the intervening time trying
to sink back into the mountain.

Most of the village was unpopulated, but to my surprise a few people
came out of their houses to look at me, gazing with awe at the dusty car.
Immediately I was struck by the extremity of their poverty. These people
had nothing. They were destitute, not merely of worldly goods, but of
religion, hope, and any knowledge of the rest of mankind. As I stepped
from my car and lit a cigarette, waiting as they gathered around me at a
respectful distance, it struck me as cruelly ironic that the huge airliner,
the culmination of almost a century of aviation technology, should have
come to its end here among these primitive mountain-dwellers.

Looking at their unintelligent and passive faces, I felt I was surrounded
by a rare group of subnormals, a village of mental defectives amiable
enough to be left on their own, high in this remote valley. Perhaps there
was some mineral in the soil that damaged their nervous systems and
kept them at this simple animal level.

'The aircraft – have you seen the airliner?' I called out. Some ten
of the men and women were standing around me, mesmerised by

the car, by my cigarette lighter and gold-rimmed glasses, even by my plump flesh.

'Aircraft –? Here . . .' Simplifying my speech, I pointed to the rocky slopes and ravines above the village, but none of them seemed to understand me. Perhaps they were mute, or deaf. They were guileless enough, but it occurred to me that they might be concealing their knowledge of the crash. What riches they would reap from those thousand corpses, enough treasure to transform their lives for a century. I would have expected this small square to be piled high with aircraft seats, suitcases, bodies stacked like firewood.

'Aircraft . . .' Their leader, a small man with a sallow face no larger than my fist, repeated the word uncertainly. I realised immediately that none of them would know what I was talking about. Their dialect would be some remote sub-tongue, on the borders of intelligent speech.

Searching about for a way of reaching them, I noticed my airline bag packed with camera equipment. The identification tag carried a coloured picture of the huge airliner. Tearing it off the bag, I showed the picture around the group.

Immediately they were nodding away. They muttered to each other, all pointing to a narrow ravine that formed a brief extension of the valley on the other side of the village. A cart track ran towards it, then faded into the stony soil.

'The airliner? It's up there? Good!' Delighted with them, I took out my wallet and showed them the large stack of bank-notes, my generous expenses for the film festival. Waving the notes encouragingly, I turned to the head-man. 'You lead the way. We'll go there now. Many bodies, eh? Cadavers, everywhere?'

They were nodding together, eager eyes staring at the fan of bank-notes.

We set off in the car through the village, following the cart track along the hillside. Half a mile from the village we had to stop when the slope became too steep. The head-man pointed to the mouth of the ravine, and we climbed from the car and set off on foot. Still wearing my festival clothes, I found the going difficult. The floor of the gorge was covered with sharp stones that cut at my shoes. I fell behind my guide, who was scuttling over the stones like a goat.

It surprised me that there were still no signs of the giant airliner, of any debris or the hundreds of bodies. Looking around me, I expected the mountain to be drenched in corpses.

We had reached the end of the gorge. The final three hundred feet of the mountain rose into the air towards the peak, separated from its twin by the valley and the village below. The head-man had stopped, and was pointing to the rocky wall. On his small face was a look of blunted pride.

'Where?' Catching my breath, I took the shroud off my camera lens. 'There's nothing here.'

Then I saw where he had guided me, and what the villagers all the way down to the coastal plain had described. Lying against the wall of the ravine were the remains of a three-engined military aircraft, its crushed nose and cockpit buried in the rocks. The fabric had long been stripped away by the wind, and the aircraft was little more than a collection of rusting spars and fuselage members. Obviously it had been here for more than thirty years, presiding like a tattered deity over this barren mountain. Somehow the fact of its presence had passed down the mountain from one village to the next.

The head-man pointed to the aircraft skeleton. He smiled at me, but his eyes were fixed on my chest, on the wallet in my breast pocket. Already his hand was slightly outstretched. For all his small size, he looked as dangerous as a wild dog.

I took out my wallet and handed him a single bank-note, worth more than he could earn in a month. Perhaps because the denomination was meaningless to him, he pointed aggressively at the other notes.

I fended him off. 'Look – I'm not interested in this aircraft. It's the wrong one, you fool . . . !' When he stared uncomprehendingly at me I took the airline tag from my pocket and showed him the picture of the huge passenger jet. 'This one! Very large. Hundreds of bodies.' Losing my temper, and giving way completely to my outrage and disappointment, I screamed at him: 'It's the wrong one! Can't you understand? There should be bodies everywhere, hundreds of cadavers . . . !'

He left me where I was, ranting away at the stony walls of this deserted ravine high in the mountains, and at the skeleton of this wind-blown reconnaissance plane.

Ten minutes later, when I returned to my car, I discovered that the slow puncture I had suspected earlier that afternoon had flattened one of the front tyres. Exhausted now, my shoes pierced by the rocks, my clothes filthy, I slumped behind the steering wheel, realising the futility of this absurd expedition. I would be lucky to make it back to the coast by night-fall. By then every other journalist would have reported the first sighting of the crashed airliner in the Pacific. My editor would be waiting with growing impatience for me to file my story in time for the evening newscasts. Instead, I was high in these barren mountains with a damaged car, my life possibly threatened by these idiot peasants.

After resting, I pulled myself together. It took me half an hour to change the wheel. As I started the engine and began the long drive back to the coastal plain the light had begun to fade even here at the peak.

The village was three hundred yards below me when I could see the first of the hovels on a bend in the track. One of the villagers was standing beside a low wall, with what seemed to be a weapon in one hand. Immediately I slowed down, knowing that if they decided to attack me I had little hope of escape. I remembered the wallet in my pocket, and took it out, spreading the bank-notes on the seat. Perhaps I could buy my way through them.

As I approached, the man stepped forward into the road. The weapon in his hand was a crude spade. A small man, like all the others, his posture was in no way threatening. Rather, he seemed to be asking me for something, almost begging.

There was a bundle of old clothing on the verge beside the wall. Did he want me to buy it? As I slowed down, about to hand one of the bank-notes to him, I realised that it was an old woman, like a monkey wrapped in a shawl, staring sightlessly at me. Then I saw that her skull-like face was indeed a skull, and that the earth-stained rags were her shroud.

'Cadaver . . .' The man spoke nervously, fingering his spade in the dim light. I handed him the money and drove on, joining the road leading to the village.

Another younger man stood by the verge fifty yards ahead, also with a spade. The body of a small child, freshly disinterred, sat against the lid of its open coffin.

'Cadaver —'

All the way through the village people stood in the doorways, some alone, those who had no one to disinter for me, others with their spades. Freshly jerked from their graves, the corpses sat in the dim light in front of the hovels, propped against the stone walls like neglected relations, put out to at last earn their keep.

As I drove past, handing out the last of my money, I could hear the villagers murmuring, their voices following me down the mountainside.

**· 1975**

# LOW-FLYING AIRCRAFT

'The man's playing some sort of deranged game with himself.'

From their balcony on the tenth floor of the empty hotel, Forrester and his wife watched the light aircraft taking off from the runway at Ampuriabrava, half a mile down the beach. A converted crop-sprayer with a silver fuselage and open cockpits, the biplane was lining up at the end of the concrete airstrip. Its engine blared across the deserted resort like a demented fan.

'One of these days he's not going to make it – I'm certain that's what he's waiting for . . .' Without thinking, Forrester climbed from his deck-chair and pushed past the drinks trolley to the balcony rail. The aircraft was now moving rapidly along the runway, tail-wheel still touching the tarmac marker line. Little more than two hundred feet of concrete lay in front of it. The runway had been built thirty years earlier for the well-to-do Swiss and Germans bringing their private aircraft to this vacation complex on the Costa Brava. By now, in the absence of any maintenance, the concrete pier jutting into the sea had been cut to a third of its original length by the strong offshore currents.

However, the pilot seemed unconcerned, his bony forehead exposed above his goggles, long hair tied in a brigand's knot. Forrester waited, hands gripping the rail in a confusion of emotions – he wanted to see this reclusive and stand-offish doctor plunge on to the rocks, but at the same time his complicated rivalry with Gould made him shout out a warning.

At the last moment, with a bare twenty feet of runway left, Gould sat back sharply in his seat, almost pulling the aircraft into the air. It rose steeply over the broken concrete causeway, banked and made a low circuit of the sea before setting off inland.

Forrester looked up as it crossed their heads. Sometimes he thought that Gould was deliberately trying to provoke him – or Judith, more likely. There was some kind of unstated bond that linked them.

'Did you watch the take-off?' he asked. 'There won't be many more of those.'

Judith lay back in her sun-seat, staring vaguely at the now silent airstrip. At one time Forrester had played up the element of danger in these take-offs, hoping to distract her during the last tedious months of the pregnancy. But the pantomime was no longer necessary, even today, when they were waiting for the *practicante* to bring the results of the amniotic scan from Figueras. After the next summer storm had done its worst to the crumbling runway, Gould was certain to crash. Curiously, he could have avoided all this by clearing a section of any one of a hundred abandoned roads.

'It's almost too quiet now,' Judith said. 'Have you seen the *practicante*? He was supposed to come this morning.'

'He'll be here – the clinic is only open one day a week.' Forrester took his wife's small foot and held it between his hands, openly admiring her pale legs without any guile or calculation. 'Don't worry, this time it's going to be good news.'

'I know. It's strange, but I'm absolutely certain of it too. I've never had any doubts, all these months.'

Forrester listened to the drone of the light aircraft as it disappeared above the hills behind the resort. In the street below him the sand blown up from the beach formed a series of encroaching dunes that had buried many of the cars to their windows. Fittingly, the few tyre-tracks that led to the hotel entrance all belonged to the *practicante*'s Honda. The clacking engine of this serious-faced male nurse sounded its melancholy tocsin across the town. He had tended Judith since their arrival two months earlier, with elaborate care but a total lack of emotional tone, as if he were certain already of the pregnancy's ultimate outcome.

None the less, Forrester found himself still clinging to hope. Once he had feared these fruitless pregnancies, the enforced trips from Geneva, and the endless circuit of empty Mediterranean resorts as they waited for yet another seriously deformed foetus to make its appearance. But he had looked forward to this last pregnancy, seeing it almost as a challenge, a game played against enormous odds for the greatest possible prize. When Judith had first told him, six months earlier, that she had conceived again he had immediately made arrangements for their drive to Spain. Judith conceived so easily – the paradox was bitter, this vigorous and unquenched sexuality, this enormous fertility, even if of a questionable kind, at full flood in an almost depopulated world.

'Richard – come on. You look dead. Let's drink a toast to me.' Judith pulled the trolley over to her chair. She sat up, animating herself like a toy. Seeing their reflections in the bedroom mirror, Forrester thought of their resemblance to a pair of latter-day Scott Fitzgeralds, two handsome and glamorous bodies harbouring their guilty secret.

'Do you realize that we'll know the results of the scan by this evening? Richard, we'll have to celebrate! Perhaps we should have gone to Benidorm.'

'It's a huge place,' Forrester pointed out. 'There might be fifteen or twenty people there for the summer.'

'That's what I mean. We ought to meet other people, share the good news with them.'

'Well . . .' They had come to this quiet resort at the northern end of the Costa Brava specifically to get away from everyone – in fact, Forrester had resented finding Gould here, this hippified doctor who lived in one of the abandoned hotels on the *playa* and unexpectedly turned up in his aircraft after a weekend's absence.

Forrester surveyed the lines of deserted hotels and apartment houses, the long-shuttered rotisseries and supermarkets. There was something reassuring about the emptiness. He felt more at ease here, almost alone in this forgotten town.

As they stood together by the rail, sipping their drinks and gazing at the silent bay, Forrester held his wife around her full waist. For weeks now he had barely been able to take his hands off her. Once Gould had gone it would be pleasant here. They would lie around for the rest of the summer, making love all the time and playing with the baby – a rare arrival now, the average for normal births was less than one in a thousand. Already he could visualize a few elderly peasants coming down from the hills and holding some sort of primitive earth festival on the beach.

Behind them the aircraft had reappeared over the town. For a moment he caught sight of the doctor's silver helmet – one of Gould's irritating affectations was to paint stripes on his helmet and flying-jacket, and on the fenders of his old Mercedes, a sophomore conceit rather out of character. Forrester had come across traces of the paint at various points around the town – on the footbridge over the canal dividing the marina and airstrip at Ampuriabrava from the beach hotels in Rosas, at the corners of the streets leading to Gould's hotel. These marks, apparently made at random, were elements of a cryptic private language. For some time now Forrester had been certain that Gould was up to some nefarious game in the mountains. He was probably pillaging the abandoned monasteries, looting their icons and gold plate. Forrester had a potent vision of this solitary doctor, piloting his light aircraft in a ceaseless search of the Mediterranean littoral, building up a stockpile of art treasures in case the world opened up for business again.

Forrester's last meeting with Gould, in the Dali museum at Figueras, seemed to confirm these suspicions. He had dropped Judith off at the ante-natal clinic, where the amniotic scanning would, they hoped, confirm the absence of any abnormalities in the foetus, and by an error of judgement strolled into this museum dedicated by the town to its most illustrious native artist. As he walked quickly through the empty galleries he noticed Gould lounging back on the central divan, surveying with amiable composure the surrealist's flaccid embryos and anatomical monstrosities. With his silver-flecked jacket and long hair in a knot, Gould looked less like a doctor than a middle-aged Hell's Angel. Beside him on the divan were three canvases he had selected from the walls, and which he later took back to decorate his hotel rooms.

'They're a little too close to the knuckle for me,' Forrester commented. 'A collection of newsreels from Hell.'

'A sharp guess at the future, all right,' Gould agreed. 'The ultimate dystopia is the inside of one's own head.'

As they left the museum Forrester said, 'Judith's baby is due in about three weeks. We wondered if you'd care to attend her?'

Gould made no reply. Shifting the canvases from one arm to the other, he scowled at the trees in the deserted *rambla*. His eyes seemed to be waiting for something. Not for the first time, Forrester realized how tired the man was, the nervousness underlying his bony features.

'What about the *practicante*? He's probably better qualified than I am.'

'I wasn't thinking of the birth, so much, as the . . .'

'As the death?'

'Well . . .' Unsettled by Gould's combative tone, Forrester searched through his stock of euphemisms. 'We're full of hope, of course, but we've had to learn to be realistic.'

'That's admirable of you both.'

'Given one possible outcome, I think Judith would prefer someone like you to deal with it . . .'

Gould was nodding sagely at this. He looked sharply at Forrester. 'Why not keep the child? Whatever the outcome.'

Forrester had been genuinely shocked by this. Surprised by the doctor's aggression, he watched him swing away with an unpleasant gesture, the lurid paintings under his arm, and stride back to his Mercedes.

Judith was asleep in the bedroom. From her loose palm Forrester removed the Valiums she had been too tired to take. He replaced them in the capsule, and then sat unsteadily on the bed. For the last hour he had been drinking alone in the sun on the balcony, partly out of boredom – the time-scale of the human pregnancy was a major evolutionary blunder, he decided – and partly out of confused fear and hope.

Where the hell was the *practicante*? Forrester walked on to the balcony again and scanned the road to Figueras, past the abandoned nightclubs and motorboat rental offices. The aircraft had gone, disappearing into the mountains. As he searched the airstrip Forrester noticed the dark-robed figure of a young woman in the doorway of Gould's hangar. He had seen her mooning around there several times before, and openly admitted to himself that he felt a slight pang of envy at the assumed sexual liaison between her and Gould. There was something secretive about the relationship that intrigued him. Careful not to move, he waited for the young woman to step into the sun. Already, thanks to the alcohol and an over-scrupulous monogamy, he could feel his loins thickening. For all his need to be alone, the thought that there was another young woman within half a mile of him almost derailed Forrester's mind.

Five minutes later he saw the girl again, standing on the observation roof of the Club Náutico, gazing inland as if waiting for Gould's silver aircraft to return.

\*　　\*　　\*

As Forrester let himself out of the suite his wife was still asleep. Only two of the suites on the tenth floor were now maintained. The other rooms had been locked and shuttered, time capsules that contained their melancholy cargo, the aerosols, douche-bags, hairpins and sun-oil tubes left behind by the thousands of vanished tourists.

The waiters' service elevator, powered by a small gasolene engine in the basement, carried him down to the lobby. There was no electric current now to run the air-conditioning system, but the hotel was cool. In the two basketwork chairs by the steps, below the postcard rack with its peeling holiday views of Rosas in its tourist heyday, sat the elderly manager and his wife. Señor Cervera had been a linotype operator for a Barcelona newspaper during the years when the population slide had first revealed itself, and even now was a mine of information about the worldwide decline.

'Mrs Forrester is asleep – if the *practicante* comes send him up to her.'

'I hope it's good news. You've waited a long time.'

'If it is we'll certainly celebrate tonight. Judith wants to open up all the nightclubs.'

Forrester walked into the sunlight, climbing over the first of the dunes that filled the street. He stood on the roof of a submerged car and looked at the line of empty hotels. He had come here once as a child, when the resort was still half-filled with tourists. Already, though, many of the hotels were closing, but his parents had told him that thirty years earlier the town had been so crowded that they could barely see the sand on the beach. Forrester could remember the Club Náutico, presiding like an aircraft-carrier over the bars and nightclubs of Ampuriabrava, packed with people enjoying themselves with a frantic *fin de siècle* gaiety. Already the first of the so-called 'Venus hotels' were being built, and coachloads of deranged young couples were coming in from the airport at Gerona.

Forrester jumped from the roof of the car and set off along the beach road towards Ampuriabrava. The immaculate sand ran down to the water, free at last of cigarette-ends and bottle-tops, as clean and soft as milled bone. As he moved past the empty hotels it struck Forrester as strange that he felt no sense of panic at the thought of these vanished people. Like Judith and everyone else he knew, like the old linotype operator and his wife sitting alone in the lobby of their hotel, he calmly accepted the terrifying logic of this reductive nightmare as if it were a wholly natural and peaceful event.

Forty years earlier, by contrast, there had been an uncontrolled epidemic of fear as everyone became aware of the marked fall in the world's population, the huge apparent drop in the birth-rate and, even more disquieting, the immense increase in the number of deformed foetuses. Whatever had set off this process, which now left Forrester standing alone on this once-crowded Costa Brava beach, the results were dramatic and irreversible. At its present rate of decline Europe's population of 200,000 people, and the United States' population of 150,000, were headed for oblivion within a generation.

At the same time, by an unhappy paradox, there had been no fall in fertility, either in man or in the few animal species also affected. In fact, birth-rates had soared, but almost all the offspring were seriously deformed. Forrester remembered the first of Judith's children, with their defective eyes, in which the optic nerves were exposed, and even more disturbing, their deformed sexual organs – these grim parodies of human genitalia tapped all kinds of nervousness and loathing.

Forrester stopped at the end of the beach, where the line of hotels turned at right angles along the entrance channel of the marina. Looking back at the town, he realized that he was almost certainly its last visitor. The continued breakdown of the European road-systems would soon rule out any future journeys to Spain. For the past five years he and Judith had lived in Geneva. Working for a United Nations agency, he moved from city to city across Europe, in charge of a team making inventories of the huge stockpiles of foodstuffs, pharmaceuticals, consumer durables and industrial raw materials that lay about in warehouses and rail terminals, in empty supermarkets and stalled production-lines – enough merchandise to keep the dwindling population going for a thousand years. Although the population of Geneva was some two thousand, most of Europe's urban areas were deserted altogether, including, surprisingly, some of its great cathedral cities – Chartres, Cologne and Canterbury were empty shells. For some reason the consolations of religion meant nothing to anyone. On the other hand, despite the initial panic, there had never been any real despair. For thirty years they had been matter-of-factly slaughtering their children and closing down the western hemisphere like a group of circus workers dismantling their tents and killing their animals at the season's end.

From the bank of the canal Forrester peered up at the white hull of the Club Náutico. There were no signs of the young woman. Behind him, facing the airstrip, was a roadside restaurant abandoned years before. Through the salt-stained windows he could see the rows of bottles against the mirror behind the bar, chairs stacked on tables.

Forrester pushed back the door. The interior of the restaurant was like a museum tableau. Nothing had been moved for years. Despite the unlocked door there had been no vandalism. From the footprints visible in the fine sand blown across the floor it was clear that over the years a few passing travellers had refreshed themselves at the bar and left without doing any damage. This was true of everywhere Forrester had visited. They had vacated a hundred cities and airports as if leaving them in serviceable condition for their successors.

The air in the restaurant was stale but cool. Seated behind the bar, Forrester helped himself to a bottle of Fundador, drinking quietly as he waited for the young woman to reappear. As he gazed across the canal he noticed that Gould had painted two continuous marker lines in fluorescent silver across the metal slats and wire railing of the footbridge. From the door he could see the same marker lines crossing the road and climbing the steps to Gould's hotel, where they disappeared into the lobby.

Standing unsteadily in the road, Forrester frowned up at the garish façade of the hotel, which had been designed in a crudely erotic Graecian style. Naked caryatids three storeys high supported a sham portico emblazoned with satyrs and nymphs. Why had Gould chosen to live in this hotel, out of all those standing empty in Rosas? Here in what amounted to the red-light quarter of the town, it was one of a group known euphemistically all over the world as the 'Venus hotels', but which Judith more accurately referred to as 'the sex-hotels'. From Waikiki to Glyfada Beach, Rio to Recife, these hotel complexes had sprung up in the first years of the depopulation crisis. A flood of government-subsidised tourists had poured in, urged on into a last frantic festival of erotomania. In a misguided attempt to rekindle their fertility, every conceivable kind of deviant sexual activity had been encouraged. Pornographic hotel decor, lobbies crammed with aids and appliances, ceaseless sex-films shown on closed-circuit television, all these reflected an unhappy awareness by everyone that their sex no longer mattered. The sense of obligation, however residual, to a future generation was no longer present. If anything, the 'normal' had become the real obscenity. In the foyer of one of these hotels Forrester and Judith had come across the most sinister pornographic image of all – the photograph of a healthy baby obscenely retouched.

Judith and her husband had been too young to take part in these despairing orgies, and by the time of their marriage there had been a general revulsion against perverse sex of every kind. Chastity and romantic love, pre-marital celibacy and all the restraints of monogamy came back in force. As the world's populations continued to fall, the last married couples sat dutifully together like characters from a Vermeer interior.

And all the while the sexual drive continued unabated. Feeling the alcohol surge through him, Forrester swayed through the hot sunlight. Somewhere around the hangar beside the airstrip the young woman was waiting for him, perhaps watching him at this moment from its dark interior. Obviously she knew what he was thinking, and almost seemed to be encouraging him with her flirtatious dartings to and fro.

Forrester stepped on to the bridge. Behind him the line of garish hotels was silent, a stage-set designed for just this adventure. The metal rungs of the bridge rang softly under his feet. Tapping them like the keys of a xylophone, Forrester stumbled against the rail, smearing his hands against the still-wet stripe of silver paint.

Without thinking, he wiped his hands on his shirt. The lines of fluorescent paint continued across the bridge, winding in and out of the abandoned cars in the parking lot beside the airstrip. Following Gould's illuminated pathway, Forrester crossed the canal. When he reached the fuel store he saw that the young woman had emerged from the hangar. She stood in the open doorway, her feet well within the rectangle of sunlight. Her intelligent but somehow mongoloid face was hidden as usual behind heavy sunglasses – a squat chin and high forehead fronted by a carapace of black glass. For all this concealment, Forrester was certain that she had been expecting him, and even more that she had been hoping for him to appear. Inside her black shawl she was moving her hands about like a schoolgirl – no doubt she was aware that he was the only man in the resort, apart from Gould, away on his endless solo flying, and the old linotype operator.

The sweat rose from Forrester's skin, a hot pelt across his forehead. Standing beside the fuel hydrant, he wiped away the sweat with his hands. The young woman seemed to respond to these gestures. Her own hands emerged from the shawl, moving about in a complex code, a semaphore signalling Forrester to her. Responding in turn, he touched his face again, ignoring the silver paint on his hands. As if to ingratiate himself, he smeared the last of the paint over his cheeks and nose, wiping the tacky metal stains across his mouth.

When he reached the young woman and touched her shoulder she looked with sudden alarm at these luminous contours, as if aware that she had been forming the elements of the wrong man from these painted fragments – his hands, chest and features.

Too late, she let herself be bundled backwards into the darkness of the hangar. The sunglasses fell from her hands to the floor. Forrester's luminous face shone back at him like a chromiumed mask from the flight-office windows. He looked down at the sightless young woman scrabbling at his feet for her sunglasses, one hand trying to hide her eyes from him. Then he heard the drone of a light aircraft flying over the town.

Gould's aircraft circled the Club Náutico, the panels of its silver fuselage reflecting the sun like a faceted mirror. Forrester turned from the young woman lying against the rear wall of the hangar, the glasses with their fractured lenses once more over her face. He stepped into the afternoon light and ran across the runway as the aircraft came in to land.

Two hours later, when he had crossed the deserted streets to his hotel, he found Señor Cervera standing on the dune below the steps, hands cupped to his eyes. He waved Forrester towards him, greeting him with relief. Forrester had spent the interval in one of the hotels in the centre of Rosas, moving restlessly from one bathroom to the next as he tried to clean the paint off his face and hands. He had slept for half an hour in a bedroom.

'Mrs Forrester –' The old man gestured helplessly.

'Where is she?' Forrester followed Cervera to the hotel steps. His wife was hovering in an embarrassed way behind her mahogany desk. 'What's happened?'

'The *practicante* arrived – just after you left.' The old man paused to examine the traces of silver paint that still covered Forrester's face. With a wave of the hand, as if dismissing them as another minor detail of this aberrant day, he said, 'He brought the result to Mrs Forrester . . .'

'Is she all right? What's going on?'

Forrester started towards the elevator but the old woman waved him back. 'She went out – I tried to stop her. She was all dressed up.'

'Dressed? How?'

'In . . . in a very extravagant way. She was upset.'

'Oh, my God . . .' Forrester caught his breath. 'Poor Judith – where did she go?'

'To the hotels.' Cervera raised a hand and pointed reluctantly towards the Venus hotels.

Forrester found her within half an hour, in the bridal suite on the third floor of one of the hotels. As he ran along the canal road, shouting out Judith's name, Gould was walking slowly across the footbridge, flying helmet in hand. The dark figure of the young woman, the lenses of her fractured sunglasses like black suns, followed him sightlessly from the door of the hangar as Gould moved along the painted corridor.

When at last he heard Judith's cry Forrester entered the hotel. In the principal suite on the third floor he discovered her stretched out on the bridal bed, surrounded by the obscene murals and bas-reliefs. She lay back on the dusty lamé bedspread, dressed in a whore's finery she had put together from her own wardrobe. Like a drunken courtesan in the last hours of pregnancy, she stared glassily at Forrester as if not wanting to recognize him. As he approached she picked up the harness beside her on the bed and tried to strike him with it. Forrester pulled it from her hands. He held her shoulders, hoping to calm her, but his feet slipped in the vibrators and film cassettes strewn about the bed. When he regained his balance Judith was at the door. He ran after her down the corridor, kicking aside the display stands of pornographic magazines outside each bedroom. Judith was fleeing down the staircase, stripping off pieces of her costume. Then, thankfully, he saw Gould waiting for her on the landing below, arms raised to catch her.

At dusk, when Gould and Forrester had taken the distraught woman back to the hotel, the two men stood by the entrance in the dusk.

In an unexpected gesture of concern, Gould touched Forrester's shoulder. Apart from this, his face remained without expression. 'She'll sleep till morning. Ask the *practicante* to give you some thalidomide for her. You'll need to sedate her through the next three weeks.'

He pointed to the silver stains on Forrester's face. 'These days we're all wearing our war-paint. You were over at the hangar, just before I landed. Carmen told me that you'd accidentally stepped on her glasses.'

Relieved that the young woman, for whatever reasons, had not betrayed him, Forrester said, 'I was trying to reassure her – she seemed to be worried that you were overdue.'

'I'm having to fly further inland now. She's nervous when I'm not around.'

'I hadn't realized that she was . . . blind,' Forrester said as they walked down the street towards the canal. 'It's good of you to look after her. The Spaniards would kill her out of hand if they found her here. What happens when you leave?'

'She'll be all right, by then.' Gould stopped and gazed through the fading light at the causeway of the airstrip. A section of the porous concrete seemed to have collapsed into the sea. Gould nodded to himself, as if working out the time left to him by this fragmenting pier. 'Now, what about this baby?'

'It's another one – the same defects. I'll get the *practicante* to deal with it.'

'Why?' Before Forrester could reply, Gould took his arm. 'Forrester, it's a fair question. Which of us can really decide who has the defects?'

'The mothers seem to know.'

'But are they right? I'm beginning to think that a massacre of the innocents has taken place that literally out-Herods Herod. Look, come up with me tomorrow – the Cerveras can look after your wife, she'll sleep all day. You'll find it an interesting flight.'

They took off at ten o'clock the following morning. Sitting in the front cockpit, with the draught from the propeller full in his face, Forrester was convinced that they would crash. At full throttle they moved swiftly along the runway, the freshly broken concrete slabs already visible. Forrester looked over his shoulder, hoping that Gould would somehow manage to stop the aircraft before they were killed, but the doctor's face was hidden behind his goggles, as if he was unaware of the danger. At the last moment, when the cataract of concrete blocks was almost below the wheels, Gould pulled back on the stick. The small aircraft rose steeply, as if jerked into the air by a huge hand. Thirty seconds later Forrester began to breathe.

They levelled out and made a left-hand circuit of the empty resort. Already Gould was pointing with a gloved hand at the patches of phosphorescent paint in the hills above Rosas. Before the take-off, while Forrester sat uncomfortably in the cockpit, wondering why he had accepted this challenge, the young woman had wheeled a drum of liquid over to the aircraft. Gould pumped the contents into the tank which Forrester could see below his feet. As he waited, the young woman walked round to the cockpit and stared up at Forrester, clearly hoping to see something in his face. There was something grotesque, almost comic, about this mongoloid girl surveying the world with her defunct vision through these cracked sunglasses. Perhaps she was disappointed that he was no longer interested in her. Forrester turned away from her sightless stare, thinking of Judith asleep in the darkened hotel room, and the small and unwelcome tenant of her body.

Eight hundred feet below them was a wide valley that led inland towards the foothills of the Pyrenees. The line of low mountains marked the northern wall of the plain of Ampurdan, a rich farming area where even now there were small areas of cultivation. But all the cattle had gone, slaughtered years beforehand.

As they followed the course of the valley, Forrester could see that sections of the pathways and farm tracks which climbed the hills had been sprayed with phosphorescent paint. Panels of silver criss-crossed the sides of the valley.

So this was what Gould had been doing on his flights, painting sections of the mountainside in a huge pop-art display. The doctor was waving down at the valley floor, where a small, shaggy-haired bullock, like a miniature bison, stood in an apparent daze on an isolated promontory. Cutting back the engine, Gould banked the aircraft and flew low over the valley floor, not more than twenty feet above the creature. Forrester was speculating on how this sightless creature, clearly a mutant, had managed to survive, when there was a sudden jolt below his feet. The ventral spraying head had been lowered, and a moment later a huge gust of silver paint was vented into the air and fanned out behind them. It hung there in a luminescent cloud, and then settled to form a narrow brush-stroke down the side of the mountain. Retracting the spraying head, Gould made a steep circuit of the valley. He throttled up his engine and dived over the head of the bullock, driving it down the mountainside from its promontory. As it stumbled left and right, unable to get its bearings, it crossed the silver pathway. Immediately it gathered its legs together and set off at a brisk trot along this private roadway.

For the next hour they flew up the valley, and Forrester saw that these lines of paint sprayed from the air were part of an elaborate series of trails leading into the safety of the mountains. When they finally turned back, circling a remote gorge above a small lake, Forrester was not surprised to see that a herd of several hundred of the creatures had made their home here. Lifting their heads, they seemed to follow Gould as he flew past them. Tirelessly, he laid down more marker lines wherever they were needed, driving any errant cattle back on to the illuminated pathways.

When they landed at Ampuriabrava he waited on the runway as Gould shut down the aircraft. The young woman came out from the darkness inside the hangar, and stood with her arms folded inside her shawl. Forrester noticed that the sides of the aircraft fuselage and tailplane were a brilliant silver, bathed in the metallic spray through which they had endlessly circled. Gould's helmet and flying-suit, and his own face and shoulders, shone like mirrors, as if they had just alighted from the sun. Curiously, only their eyes, protected by their goggles, were free from the paint, dark orbits into which the young woman gazed as if hoping to find someone of her own kind.

Gould greeted her, handing her his helmet. He stripped off his flying-jacket and ushered her into the hangar.

He pointed across the canal. 'We'll have a drink in your bar.' He led the way diagonally across the car park, ignoring the painted pathways. 'I think there's enough on us for Carmen to know where we are. It gives her a sense of security.'

'How long have you been herding the cattle?' Forrester asked when they were seated behind the bar.

'Since the winter. Somehow one herd escaped the farmers' machetes. Flying down from Perpignan through the Col du Perthus, I noticed them following the aircraft. In some way they could see me, using a different section of the electromagnetic spectrum. Then I realized that I'd sprayed some old landing-light reflector paint on the plane – highly phosphorescent stuff.'

'But why save them? They couldn't survive on their own.'

'Not true – in fact, they're extremely hardy. By next winter they'll be able to out-run and out-think everything else around here. Like Carmen – she's a very bright girl. She's managed to keep herself going here for years, without being able to see a thing. When I started getting all this paint over me I think I was the first person she'd ever seen.'

Thinking again of Judith's baby, Forrester shook his head. 'She looks like a mongol to me – that swollen forehead.'

'You're wrong. I've found out a lot about her. She has a huge collection of watches with luminous dials, hundreds of them, that she's been filching for years from the shops. She's got them all working together but to different times, it's some sort of gigantic computer. God only knows what overlit world nature is preparing her for, but I suppose we won't be around to see it.'

Forrester gazed disagreeably into his glass of brandy. For once the Fundador made him feel ill. 'Gould, are you saying in effect that the child Judith is carrying at this moment is *not* deformed?'

Gould nodded encouragingly. 'It's not deformed at all – any more than Carmen. It's like the so-called population decline that we've all accepted as an obvious truth. In fact, there hasn't been a decline – except in the sense that we've been slaughtering our offspring. Over the past fifty years the birth-rate has gone up, not down.' Before Forrester could protest, he went on, 'Try for a moment to retain an open mind – we have this vastly increased sexuality, and an unprecedented fertility. Even your wife has had – what – seven children. Yet why? Isn't it obvious that we were intended to embark on a huge replacement programme, though sadly the people we're replacing turn out to be ourselves. Our job is simply to repopulate the world with our successors. As for our need to be alone, this intense enjoyment of our own company, and the absence of any sense of despair, I suppose they're all nature's way of saying goodbye.'

'And the runway?' Forrester asked. 'Is that your way of saying goodbye?'

*　　*　　*

A month later, as soon as Judith had recovered from the birth of her son, she and Forrester left Rosas to return to Geneva, After they had made their farewells to Señor Cervera and his wife, Forrester drove the car along the beach road. It was 11 a.m., but Gould's aircraft still stood on the airstrip. For some reason the doctor was late.

'It's a long drive – are you going to be well enough?' he asked Judith.

'Of course – I've never felt better.' She settled herself in the seat. It seemed to Forrester that a kind of shutter had been lowered across her mind, hiding away all memories of the past months. She looked composed and relaxed again, but with the amiable and fixed expression of a display-window mannequin.

'Did you pay off the *practicante*?' she asked. 'They expect something extra for . . .'

Forrester was gazing up at the façades of the Venus hotels. He remembered the evening of the birth, and the *practicante* carrying his son away from Señora Cervera. The district nurse had taken it for granted that he would be given the task of destroying the child. As Forrester stopped the Spaniard by the elevator he found himself wondering where the man would have killed it – in some alley behind the cheaper hotels at the rear of the town, or in any one of a thousand vacant bathrooms. But when Forrester had taken the child, careful not to look at its eyes, the *practicante* had not objected, only offering Forrester his surgical bag.

Forrester had declined. After the *practicante* had left, and before Señora Cervera returned to the lobby, he set off through the dark streets to the canal. He had put on again the silver jacket he had worn on the day when Gould had flown him into the mountains. As he crossed the bridge the young woman emerged from the hangar, almost invisible in her dark shawl. Forrester walked towards her, listening to the faint clicking and murmurs of the strong child. He pressed the infant into her hands and turned back to the canal, throwing away his jacket as he ran.

While they drove along the line of hotels to the Figueras road Forrester heard the sounds of the aircraft. Gould was climbing into the cockpit, about to warm up the engine before take-off.

'I never really understood him,' Judith commented. 'What was he up to in the mountains?'

'I don't know – some obsession of his.'

During a brief storm two nights earlier another section of the runway had collapsed. But Forrester knew that Gould would go on flying to the end, driving his herd higher into the mountains, until they no longer needed him and the day had come to take off for the last time.

**1975**

# THE LIFE AND DEATH OF GOD

During the spring and summer of 1980 an extraordinary rumour began to sweep the world. At first confined to government and scientific circles in Washington, London and Moscow, it soon spread through Africa, South America and the Far East, and among people in all walks of life, from Australian sheep-farmers to Tokyo nightclub hostesses and stockbrokers on the Paris Bourse. Rarely a day passed without the rumour reaching the front pages of at least a dozen newspapers around the world.

In a few countries, notably Canada and Brazil, the persistence of the rumour caused a dangerous drop in commodity prices, and firm denials were issued by the governments of the day. At the United Nations headquarters in New York the Secretary-General appointed a committee of prominent scientists, churchmen and business leaders with the sole purpose of restraining the excitement which the rumour was beginning to generate by the late spring. This, of course, simply convinced everyone that something of universal significance would soon be disclosed.

For once, the governments of the West were helped by the sympathetic attitude of the Soviet Union, and of countries such as Cuba, Libya and North Korea, which in the past would have seized on the smallest advantage the rumour offered them. Yet even this failed to prevent serious outbreaks of industrial unrest and panic-selling – millions of pounds were wiped off the London Stock Exchange after the announcement that the Archbishop of Canterbury would visit the Holy Land. A plague of absenteeism swept across the world in the rumour's wake. In areas as far apart as the automotive plants of Detroit and the steel foundries of the Ruhr, entire working populations lost all interest in their jobs and sauntered through the factory gates, gazing amiably at the open sky.

Fortunately, the rumour's effects were generally pacific and non-violent. In the Middle East and Asia, where it confirmed beliefs already held for centuries, the news raised barely a ripple of interest, and only in the most sophisticated government and scientific circles was there anything of a flurry. Without doubt, the impact of the rumour was greatest in Western Europe and North America. Ironically, it was most rife in those two countries, the United States and Britain, which for centuries had claimed to base their entire societies on the ideals expressed by it.

During this period one body alone kept aloof from all this speculation – the world's churches and religious faiths. This is not to say that they were in any way hostile or indifferent, but their attitude indicated a certain wariness, if not a distinct ambivalence. Although they could hardly deny the rumour, priests and clergymen everywhere recommended a due caution in the minds of their congregations, a reluctance to jump too eagerly to conclusions.

However, a remarkable and unexpected development soon took place. In a solemn declaration, representatives of the world's great religious faiths, meeting simultaneously in Rome, Mecca and Jerusalem, stated that they had at last decided to abandon their rivalries and differences. Together they would now join hands in a new and greater church, to be called the United Faith Assembly, international and interdenominational in character, which would contain the essential elements of all creeds in a single unified faith.

The news of this extraordinary development at last forced the governments of the world to a decision. On August 28th a plenary meeting of the United Nations was held. In a fanfare of publicity that exceeded anything known even by that organization, there was an unprecedented attendance from delegates of every member nation. As the commentators of a hundred television channels carried descriptions of the scene all over the world, a great concourse of scientists, statesmen and scholars, preceded by representatives of the United Faith Assembly, entered the United Nations building and took their seats.

When the meeting began the President of the United Nations called on a succession of prominent scientists, led by the director of the radio-observatory at Jodrell Bank in Britain. After a preamble in which he recalled science's quest for the unifying principle that lay behind the apparent uncertainty and caprice of nature, he described the remarkable research work undertaken during recent years with the telescopes at Jodrell Bank and Arecibo in Puerto Rico. Just as the discovery of radioactivity had stemmed from the realization that even smaller particles existed within the apparently indivisible atom, so these two giant telescopes had revealed that all electromagnetic radiations in fact contained a system of infinitely smaller vibrations. These 'ultra-microwaves', as they had been called, permeated all matter and space.

However, the speaker continued, a second and vastly more important discovery had been made when the structure of these microwaves was analysed by computer. This almost intangible electromagnetic system unmistakably exhibited a complex and continuously changing mathematical structure with all the attributes of intelligence. To give only one example, it responded to the behaviour of the human observer and was even sensitive to his unspoken thoughts. Exhaustive studies of the phenomenon confirmed beyond all doubt that this sentient being, as it must be called, pervaded the entire universe. More exactly, it provided the basic substratum of which the universe was composed. The very air they were breathing in the assembly hall at that moment, their minds and bodies, were formed by this intelligent being of infinite dimensions.

*        *        *

At the conclusion of the statement a profound silence spread through the General Assembly, and from there to the world beyond. In cities and towns all over the earth the streets were deserted, traffic abandoned as people waited quietly by their television sets. The President of the United Nations then rose and read out a declaration signed by three hundred scientists and divines. After two years of the most rigorous tests the existence of a supreme deity had been proved beyond a shadow of doubt. Mankind's age-old faith in a divine principle had at last been scientifically confirmed, and a new epoch in human history would unfold before them.

The next day the newspapers of the world bore a hundred variants of the same headline:

## GOD EXISTS
### Supreme Being Pervades Universe

During the following weeks the events of ordinary life were forgotten. All over the world services of thanksgiving were held, religious processions filled countless streets. Vast gatherings of penitents thronged the sacred cities and shrines of the world. Moscow, New York, Tokyo and London resembled medieval towns on an apocalyptic saint's day. Heads raised to the skies, millions knelt in the streets, or walked in slow cavalcades, crosses and mandalas held before them. The cathedrals of St Peter's, Notre Dame and St Patrick's were forced to hold continuous services, so great were the crowds that flocked through their doors. Sectarian feuds were forgotten. Priests of the United Faith Assembly exchanged vestments and officiated at each other's services. Buddhists were baptized, Christians turned prayer-wheels and Jews knelt before the statues of Krishna and Zoroaster.

More practical benefits were to follow. Everywhere doctors reported a marked drop in the numbers of their patients. Neuroses and other mental ills disappeared overnight, as the discovery of the deity's existence worked its instant therapy. All over the world police forces were disbanded. Members of the armed services were sent on indefinite leave pending demobilization, long-closed frontiers were unsealed. The Berlin Wall was dismantled. Everywhere people behaved as if some immense victory had been won against an invincible enemy. Here and there, between particularly aggressive rivals, such as the United States and Cuba, Egypt and Israel, long-standing pacts of friendship were signed. Military aircraft and naval fleets were sent to the scrapyards, stockpiles of weapons were destroyed. (However, a few sporting rifles were retained when the spirit of universal brotherhood produced its first casualty – a Swedish engineer in Bengal who attempted to embrace a tiger. Warnings were issued that an awareness of God's existence had yet to extend to the lower members of the animal kingdom, where for the time being the struggle for life remained as pitiless as ever.)

To begin with, such isolated episodes were barely noticed in the general euphoria. Thousands of spectators sat around the great telescopes at Jodrell Bank and Arecibo, not to mention a number of commercial TV aerials and any other structures that vaguely resembled radio antennae, waiting patiently for a direct message from the Almighty. Gradually people drifted back to work – or, more exactly, those returned who considered their work morally gainful. Manufacturing industry was able to keep going, but the agencies responsible for selling its products to the public found themselves in a dilemma. The elements of guile and exaggeration at the basis of all merchandizing, whether on the level of nationwide advertising campaigns or door-to-door salesmanship, were no longer tolerable under the new dispensation, but no alternative machinery of distribution was available.

The inevitable slackening of commerce and industry seemed unimportant during these first weeks. The majority of people in Europe and the United States were still celebrating a new estate of man, the beginnings of the first true millennium. The whole basis of private life had changed, and with it attitudes towards sex, morality and all human relationships. Newspapers and television had been transformed – the previous diet of crime reports and political gossip, westerns and soap-operas had given way to serious articles and programmes elaborating the background to the discovery of the deity.

This growing interest in the precise nature of the godhead led to a closer examination of its presumed moral nature. Despite the generalizations of scientists and clergy, it was soon clear that the dimensions of the supreme being were large enough to embrace any interpretation one cared to invent. Although the deity's overall moral purpose could be assumed from the harmony, purity and formal symmetry that the mathematical analyses revealed – qualities more pronounced in response to cohesive and creative actions than to random or destructive ones – these characteristics seemed little more specific in relation to man and his day-to-day behaviour than the principles underlying music. Without doubt a supreme intelligence existed whose being permeated the entire fabric of the universe, flowing in a myriad ripples through their minds and bodies like an infinite moral ether, but this deity seemed far less ready with explicit demands and directives than it had been in its previous incarnations.

Fortunately, their god was clearly neither a jealous nor a vengeful one. No thunderbolt fell from the sky. The first fears of a judgment day, of darkening landscapes covered with gibbets, safely receded. The nightmares of Bosch and Breughel failed to materialize. And for once humanity needed no goads to make it regulate its conduct. Marital infidelities, promiscuity and divorce had almost vanished. Curiously, there was also a drop in the number of marriages, perhaps because of a common feeling that some sort of a millennial kingdom was at hand.

This widespread notion revealed itself in many ways. Great numbers of industrial workers in Europe and North America had lost all interest in their jobs, and sat about on their doorsteps with their neighbours, gazing at the sky and listening to the radio bulletins. At the summer's end farmers harvested their crops but seemed much less enthusiastic about preparing for the coming season. The flow of pronouncements, and the first disputed interpretations, from the committees of divines and scientists still investigating the phenomenon of the deity suggested that it might be unwise to plan too carefully on an indefinite future.

Within two months of the confirmation of the worldwide rumour of God's existence came the first indications of government concern over the consequences. Industry and agriculture were already affected, though far less than commerce, politics and advertising. Everywhere the results of this new sense of morality, of the virtues of truth and charity, were becoming clear. A legion of overseers, time-keepers and inspectors found themselves no longer needed. Long-established advertising agencies became bankrupt. Accepting the public demand for total honesty, and fearful of that supreme client up in the sky, the majority of television commercials now ended with an exhortation *not* to buy their products.

As for the world of politics, its whole *raison d'être* – its appeals to self-assertion, intrigue and nepotism – had been destroyed. A dozen parliaments, from the US Congress to the Russian Chamber of Deputies and the British House of Commons, found themselves deprived of the very machinery of their existence.

The United Faith Assembly was faced with equal problems. Although people still attended their places of worship in larger numbers than ever before, they were doing so at times other than those of the formal services, communing directly with the Almighty rather than playing the part of a subordinate laity in a ritual mediated to them through a priesthood.

The former Christian members of the United Faith Assembly, who remembered the Reformation and Martin Luther's revolt against a clergy claiming privileged access to the supreme being, were of course perturbed by these developments. They were reluctant to accept the mathematical description of the deity offered by the world's scientists, but had nothing to offer in its place and for the time being were on the defensive. The physicists, conversely, were only too quick to remind the clergy that their long-hallowed symbols – cross, trinity and mandala – were based more on fancy than on the scientific reality which they themselves had made available. The long-standing fear of all churches, that the revelation of God might come from knowledge rather than faith, had at last been justified.

The continued change in the character of life on both sides of the Atlantic began to disturb prominent members of government and industry. Conditions in the United States and Northern Europe were beginning to resemble those in India and the Far East, where legions of amiable beggars wandered the streets without a thought for the morrow. The Kingdom of God might be at hand, but that hand was empty.

During October little happened on the surface of events, but at the end of the month a second meeting of the United Faith Assembly was held in Jerusalem. Here a prominent archbishop publicly challenged the scientific view of the deity as a being of vast neutral intelligence. Without doubt, the archbishop affirmed, this was to take a naive and over-simplified view based on what were admitted to be crude methods of detection. Was the deity entirely passive or, like the sea, did it reveal itself in many forms and moods? Remarking that he was not ashamed to refer to the Manichean Heresy, the archbishop stressed the dualism of good and evil that had always existed in the past, in man as in nature, and which would continue to exist in the future. This was not to suggest that evil was a fundamental part of man's nature, or that he was incapable of redemption, but this passive contemplation of an invisible God should not be allowed to blind them to the inevitable antagonisms within themselves, or indeed to their own failings. The great achievements of mankind, its commerce, art and industry, had been based on this sound understanding of the dual nature of mankind and its motives. The present decline of civilized life was a symptom of the refusal to see themselves as they were, a warning of the dangers of identifying themselves too closely with the Almighty. The capacity for sin was a prerequisite of redemption.

Soon afterwards, as if cued in by the archbishop, a series of spectacular crimes took place around the world. In the Middle West of the United States a number of bank robberies were carried out which rivalled those of the 1930s. In London there was an armed assault on the crown jewels in the Tower. A host of minor larcenies followed. Not all these crimes were committed for reasons of gain. In Paris the Mona Lisa was slashed by a maniac running amok in the Louvre, while in Cologne the high altar of the Cathedral was desecrated by vandals apparently protesting against the very existence of the deity.

The attitude of the United Faith Assembly to these crimes was unexpected. It greeted them with patient tolerance, as if relieved to see these familiar examples of human frailty. After the arrest of a noted wife-poisoner in Alsace a local priest pronounced that the man's guilt was in fact a testimony to his innocence, a sign of his capacity for eventual redemption.

This tortuous paradox was to receive a great deal of publicity. A number of less scrupulous politicians began to foment similar notions. One Congressional candidate, in a badly hit area of California where military aircraft had been manufactured, suggested that the notion of an all-pervading deity was an affront to the free choice and diversity of human activity. The sense of a closed world reduced man's powers of initiative and self-reliance, the qualities on which the free-enterprise democracies had built their greatness.

This statement was soon followed by the speech of a distinguished metaphysician attending a congress in Zürich. He referred to the plurality of the universe, to its infinite phenomenology. To embrace all possibilities the deity would have to contain the possibility of its own non-being. In other words, it belonged to that class of open-ended structures whose form, extent and identity were impossible to define. The term 'deity' was, in any useful sense, meaningless.

The scientists at Jodrell Bank and Arecibo who had first identified the Almighty were asked to reconsider their original findings. The televised hearings in Washington, at which the tired-eyed astro-physicists were harassed and cross-examined by teams of lawyers and divines, recalled a latter-day Inquisition. At Jodrell Bank and Arecibo troops were called in to protect the telescopes from crowds of over-hasty converts.

The fierce debates which followed were watched with great attention by the public. By now, in early December, the Christmas season was getting under way, but without any of its usual enthusiasm. For one thing, few stores and shops had anything for sale. In addition, there was little money to spare. The rationing of some basic commodities had been introduced. In many ways life was becoming intolerable. Hotels and restaurants were without service. Cars were forever breaking down.

Everywhere, as the debate continued, people turned to the United Faith Assembly. Mysteriously, however, almost all churches were closed, mosques and synagogues, shrines and temples remained sealed to the unsettled crowds. Members of congregations were now selected as strictly as those of the most exclusive clubs, and applicants were admitted only if they agreed to accept the church's guidance on all spiritual matters, its absolute authority in all religious affairs. A rumour began that an announcement of worldwide importance would shortly be made, but that this time it would be given only to the faithful.

The mounting atmosphere of unease and uncertainty was distracted for a few days by the news of several natural disasters. A landslip in northern Peru immolated a thousand villagers. In Yugoslavia an earthquake shattered a provincial capital. Icebergs sank a supertanker in the Atlantic. The question asked tentatively by a New York newspaper,

### DOES GOD EXIST?
Faith Assembly casts doubt on Deity

was relegated to a back page.

Three weeks before Christmas, war broke out between Israel and Egypt. The Chinese invaded Nepal, reclaiming territory which they had only recently ceded while under the spell of what they termed a 'neo-colonialist' machination. A week later revolution in Italy, backed by the church and military, ousted the previous liberal régime. Industrial output began to revive in the United States and Europe. Russian missile-firing submarines were detected on manoeuvres in the North Atlantic. On Christmas Eve the world's seismographs recorded a gigantic explosion in the area of the Gobi Desert, and Peking Radio announced the successful testing of a 100-megaton hydrogen bomb. Christmas decorations had at last appeared in the streets, the familiar figures of Santa Claus and his reindeer hung over a thousand department-stores. Carol festivals were held before open congregations in a hundred cathedrals.

In all this festivity few people heeded the publication of what was described by a spokesman of the United Faith Assembly as one of the most far-reaching and revolutionary religious statements ever made, the Christmas encyclical entitled *God is Dead* . . .

**1976**

# ·NOTES TOWARDS A MENTAL BREAKDOWN

A[1] discharged[2] Broadmoor[3] patient[4] compiles[5] 'Notes[6] Towards[7] a[8] Mental[9] Breakdown[10]', recalling[11] his[12] wife's[13] murder[14], his[15] trial[16] and[17] exoneration[18].


## 1

The use of the *indefinite* article encapsulates all the ambiguities that surround the undiscovered document, *Notes Towards a Mental Breakdown*, of which this 18-word synopsis is the only surviving fragment. Deceptively candid and straightforward, the synopsis is clearly an important clue in our understanding of the events that led to the tragic death of Judith Loughlin in her hotel bedroom at Gatwick Airport. There is no doubt that the role of the still unidentified author was a central one. The self-effacing 'A' must be regarded not merely as an overt attempt at evasion but, on the unconscious level, as an early intimation of the author's desire to proclaim his guilt.


## 2

There is no evidence that the patient was discharged. Recent inspection of the in-patients' records at Springfield Hospital (cf. footnote 3) indicates that Dr Robert Loughlin has been in continuous detention in the Unit of Criminal Psychopathy since his committal at Kingston Crown Court on 18 May 1975. Only one visitor has called, a former colleague at the London Clinic, the neurologist Dr James Douglas, honorary secretary of the Royal College of Physicians Flying Club. It is possible that he may have given Dr Loughlin, with his obsessional interest in man-powered flight, the illusion that he had flown from the hospital on Douglas's back. Alternatively, 'discharged' may be a screen memory of the revolver shot that wounded the Gatwick security guard.


## 3

Unconfirmed. Dr Loughlin had at no time in his ten-year career been either a patient or a member of the staff at Broadmoor Hospital. The reference to Broadmoor must therefore be taken as an indirect admission of the author's criminal motives or a confused plea of diminished responsibility on the grounds of temporary madness. Yet nothing suggests that Dr Loughlin considered himself either guilty of his wife's death or at any time insane. From the remaining documents – tape-recordings made in Suite B17 of the Inn on the Park Hotel (part of the floor occupied by the millionaire aviation pioneer Howard Hughes and his entourage during a visit to London) and cine-films taken of the runways at an abandoned USAAF base near Mildenhall – it is clear that Dr Loughlin believed he was taking part in a ritual of profound spiritual significance that would release his wife forever from the tragedy of her inoperable cancer. Indeed, the inspiration for this strange psychodrama may have come from the former Broadmoor laboratory technician and amateur dramatics coach, Leonora Carrington, whom Loughlin met at Elstree Flying Club, and with whom he had a brief but significant affair.

**4**

A remarkable feature of Dr Loughlin's confinement at Springfield is how little he conforms to the stereotype of 'patient'. Most of his fellow inmates at the Unit of Criminal Psychopathy are under some form of restraint, but Loughlin's behaviour is closer to that of a member of staff. He has informal access to all the facilities of the Unit, and with his medical training and powerful physique often stands in as an auxiliary nurse, even on occasion diagnosing minor ailments and supervising the administration of drugs. Characteristic of Loughlin is the high level of his general activity. He is forever moving about on errands, many of barely apparent significance, as if preparing for some important event in the future (or, conceivably, in the past). Much of his thought and energy is occupied by the construction of imaginary flying machines, using his bed, desk and personal cutlery. Recently, when his attempts to streamline all the furniture in the day-room unsettled the other patients, Dr Grumman encouraged Loughlin to write about his experiences as a weekend pilot. For the first time Loughlin was prepared to consider any aspect of his past, and immediately came up with a title, *Notes Towards a Mental Breakdown*.

**5**

What method Dr Loughlin employed in the preparation of this document has not been revealed, or indeed whether a single word exists other than the title. Given the powerful repressive forces at work, it seems likely that the author will employ any method other than that of straightforward narration. A clue may be found in Loughlin's previous experience as editor of the *Proceedings of the Institute of Neurosurgery*, and the habit of meticulous attention to editorial detail which he brought with him to Springfield. One manifestation of this obsession is his custom of annotating the books in the hospital library with copious footnotes.

Several pages of the 1972 edition of *The British Pharmacopoeia Codex*, particularly those referring to anti-carcinogenetic drugs, have been so annotated that every word has been footnoted with imaginary aviation references.

## 6

Why Loughlin chose this term, with its suggestion of a preparatory sketch, to describe the most important and traumatic events of his life remains unclear. However, it is now known that this was not the only such document that he prepared. Two years earlier, during the first of his marital difficulties, Loughlin had kept a speculative diary, describing in minute detail the events of his personal and professional life. It seems that he was already aware of the erratic nature of his behaviour and of the recurrent fugues, each lasting several days, from which he would emerge in an increasingly dissociated state. At one point, after his wife's first nervous collapse, Loughlin secretly hired a private investigator to follow him, posing as her lover. Mr R. W. Butterworth of the Advance Detection Agency testified at Kingston Crown Court that he followed Loughlin and Leonora Carrington as they drove at random around eastern Suffolk, visiting one abandoned airfield after another. In his February 1975 Diaries (a few weeks before his wife's death) Loughlin describes his attempt to hire the main No. 2 runway at London Airport:

> '"Don't you understand, man, I only need it for half an hour. There's a special cargo going out." Airport manager totally baffled. "What, for heaven's sake?" But I couldn't tell him. I didn't know then.'

## 7

Implicit in Loughlin's use of the preposition is the sense that he deliberately moved to meet his breakdown, constructing it of his own volition. This is confirmed by his behaviour in the months leading to his wife's death. Loughlin appears to have decided on a radically new course of action to save his wife, literally within the extreme metaphor of his own insanity. His wife's subsequent murder, his own breakdown and the entire period of his incarceration at Springfield must thus be regarded as a terminal metaphor, a labyrinth building itself from within which he began at last to unravel by writing *Notes Towards a Mental Breakdown*.

## 8

Again (cf. footnote 1) the use of the indefinite article underlines Loughlin's distance from his own crisis, which he now (January 1975) regarded as a complex of events and possibilities existing outside himself. Leaving his wife – who was bedridden in their Hendon apartment, cared for by Dr

Douglas, her old friend and former lover – Loughlin embarked on a series of extended excursions around London and the Home Counties. Usually accompanied by Leonora Carrington, he visited the Mullard radio-observatory near Cambridge and the huge complex of early warning radar installations on the Suffolk coast. For some reason, empty swimming pools and multi-storey car parks exerted a particular fascination. All these he seems to have approached as the constituents of 'A' mental breakdown which he might choose to recruit at a later date.

## 9

How far the events of this period (January to March 1975) were mentalised by Loughlin is hard to decide. To some extent all the factors surrounding Judith Loughlin's death – even the identity of her husband – may be said to be fictions of an over-worked imagination, as meaningless and as meaningful as the elaborate footnotes in *BP Codex*. Was Judith Loughlin suffering from cancer of the pancreas? What was the role of the young lexicographer and ice-dance champion, Richard Northrop, whom Loughlin treated at the London Clinic for migraine? The unmistakable elements of some kind of homo-erotic involvement hover in the background of their relationship. It may be that the apparent physical closeness of the two men masks the fact that they were one and the same man. Their holiday together, the three distressing weeks spent at the Gatwick hotel, and the shot fired at the airport security guard, inevitably recall Rimbaud and Verlaine, but Loughlin may well have passed the time there on his own waiting for his wife to appear with her lover, devising the identity of the lexicographer as a psychic 'detonator'. It is known that he spent much of his spare time stumbling around the airport ice rink.

## 10

A vital role seems to have been played during these last days by the series of paintings by Max Ernst entitled *Garden Airplane Traps*, pictures of low walls, like the brick-courses of an uncompleted maze, across which long wings have crashed, from whose joints visceral growths are blossoming. In the last entry of his diary, the day before his wife's death, 27 March 1975, Loughlin wrote with deceptive calm: 'Ernst said it all in his comment on these paintings, the model for everything I've tried to do . . .

> *"Voracious gardens in turn devoured by a vegetation which springs from the debris of trapped airplanes . . . Everything is astonishing, beart-breaking and possible . . . with my eyes I see the nymph Echo . . ."'*

Shortly before writing out these lines he had returned to his Hendon apartment to find that his wife had set off for Gatwick Airport with Dr Douglas, intending to catch the 3.15 p.m. flight to Geneva the following day. After calling Richard Northrop, Loughlin drove straight to Elstree Flying Club.

## 11

The extent to which Loughlin retains any real 'recall' of the events leading to his wife's death is doubtful. On occasions his memory is lucid and unbroken, but it soon becomes evident that he has re-mythologised the entire episode at Gatwick, as revealed in the following taped conversation between himself and Dr Grumman.

GRUMMAN: You say that you then drove to Elstree. Why?

LOUGHLIN: I had rented an aircraft there – a Piper Twin Comanche.

GRUMMAN: I see. Anyway, you then flew across London and on down to Gatwick, where you paralysed the airport for an hour by buzzing all the BEA jets parked on the ground.

LOUGHLIN: I knew that if I could find Judith's plane I could somehow fuse my aircraft with hers, in a kind of transfiguring . . .

GRUMMAN: . . . crash? But why?

LOUGHLIN: I was convinced that I could fly her to safety. It was the only way she would survive her cancer.

GRUMMAN: What actually happened?

LOUGHLIN: I landed and skidded into the nose-wheel of a VC10. Richard Northrop pulled me out. We had some sort of disagreement – he resented my dependence on him, and my involvement with Judith – and then the security guard was accidentally shot.

## 12

Although there is no doubt that Judith Loughlin had been married to her husband for three years, their relationship was never close, and she in no way could be regarded as 'his'. Before her marriage she had been involved in a long-standing liaison with Dr Douglas, whom she continued to see even after the latter's engagement and marriage in 1974. A successful barrister, self-willed and ambitious, she found herself increasingly unsympathetic towards Loughlin's erratic mental behaviour and incipient alcoholism. It is almost certain that but for her death she would have divorced Loughlin the following year. Viewing her charitably, one may say that her actions that fatal afternoon in the bathroom of her Gatwick hotel had been provoked by years of marital unhappiness.

## 13

Careful reconstruction of the events surrounding the murder of Judith Loughlin on 28 March 1975, indicates that she had arrived at Gatwick with Dr Douglas the previous day. They passed the night in room 117 of the Skyport Hotel, intending to take the 3.15 p.m. flight to Geneva the following afternoon. It was while they were having lunch in the hotel restaurant that Loughlin appeared at the airport, already in an extreme state of alcoholic distress. He began a futile search among the parked airliners for the Trident jet then being prepared for the 3.15 flight, possibly intending to hijack the plane or even to blow it up with himself aboard. In the course of this search the security guard was shot. Loughlin then made his way to the Skyport Hotel, and by some ruse located and entered his wife's room. Befuddled by a heavy overdose of alcohol and amphetamines, he decided to revive himself in a bath of cold water. He was lying unconscious in the bath, fully clothed, when Judith Loughlin returned alone to her room after lunch.

## 14

All the evidence collected indicates that Judith Loughlin's decision to murder her husband was a sudden response to the sight of him slumped unconscious in her bath. Shocked by the damage he had done to the room – in his rage Loughlin had torn apart Dr Douglas's clothes and suitcases – she apparently decided to put an end to the sufferings of this unhappy man. Unfortunately she had reckoned neither with Loughlin's powerful physique – the moment she pressed his head below the bath water he leapt up and seized her – nor with the total transformation that had taken place within her husband's mind. Already he seems to have decided that she was leaving him only in the sense that she was dying of pancreatic cancer, and that he might save her by constructing a unique flying machine.

## 15

Questions as to the exact person indicated by this pronoun have been raised since the moment Loughlin was rescued from the fire blazing in room 117. It was first assumed from the ravings of the injured man that he was an airline pilot. He was sitting on the burning bed in the tandem position behind the charred body of a similarly seated woman, as if giving her pilot tuition. His wife had been forcibly trussed into a flying suit and wore helmet and goggles. She was identified by the double-helix of her intra-uterine device. Thanks to his sodden clothes, only Loughlin's hands and feet had been burned. The furniture in the room had been arranged to form a rough representation of an aircraft, perhaps inspired by the elaborate aeronautical motifs in the bedroom decor.

## 16

Not surprisingly, the trial exposed all the contradictions inherent in this puzzling case. Questions as to 'Loughlin's' identity continued to be raised. There was no evidence that he was a qualified pilot, though a Private Pilot's

Licence in his name was found in a locker at Elstree Flying Club, perhaps left there as part of a false identity carefully fabricated by him. Certainly he was obsessed with aviation, as his use of aircraft manufacturers' names for his medical colleagues indicates. Nor was there any real confirmation that he was a physician, particularly when we consider his lavish use of meaningless pseudo-medicalese (e.g. 'serotonin[19] and[20] protein-reaction[21] suppressor[22] m.v.d.[23]' etc.).

## 17

This afterthought, attached to the previous 16 words with their apparently straightforward description of the events leading up to his trial, almost certainly indicates the author's real intent in compiling his ambiguous history.

## 18

The author's evident conviction of his own innocence, like his earlier belief that he had been discharged from hospital, may be taken as an expression of hope for the future. Meanwhile he continues with his busy round of activities in the Unit of Criminal Psychopathy, constructing his bizarre 'aircraft' and tirelessly editing the footnotes with which he has annotated so many of the medical textbooks in the library. Ultimately the entire stock will have been provided with a unique gloss. As all these books are out-of-date, like the 1972 *BP Codex*, little harm is done. Most of his complex annotations have been shown to be complete fictions, an endlessly unravelling web of imaginary research work, medical personalities and the convoluted and sometimes tragic interrelationships of their private lives. Occasionally, however, they describe with unusual clarity a sequence of events that might almost have taken place. The patient seems trapped between what his psychiatrists call 'paradoxical faces', each image of himself in the mirror reinforcing that in the glass behind him. The separation of the two will only be achieved by the appearance of the as yet incomplete document *Notes Towards a Mental Breakdown*, of which we possess only an 18-word synopsis and its set of footnotes. It seems possible that although the synopsis conceals a maze of lies and distortions, it is a simple and incontrovertible statement of the truth.

· **1976**

# · THE 60 MINUTE ZOOM

## 2.15 P.M.

### Lloret de Mar, Apartamentos California

I am looking into a silent world. Through the viewfinder of this cine-camera, set at its maximum field, I can see the Hotel Coral Playa three hundred yards along the beach, covered by a desert light so glazed that it would embalm Pharoah. It's incredible that the sea is only a few feet to the right of frame – with this dense powdery light we could be at Karnak, in that tourist hotel by the necropolis where Helen befriended her Stuttgart dentist and first set in train this epic of the amateur camera. The ultimate home movie, perhaps, but so far everything has gone well, thanks to $2500's worth of Nikon Zoomatic and an obliging Barcelona camera specialist. Renting this apartment was the only difficult moment – delivering a second key to my door, did the suspicious Swedish manager catch a glimpse of the complex tripods and clamps I was assembling by the bedroom window? Like the barbette of some sinister assassination weapon, which it is in a way. But this second-rate apartment building provides the only suitable vantage point. The fifteen-storey façade of the Coral Playa must exactly fill the opening sequence – in an hour the automatic zoom will carry me along the carretera, past the hundreds of parked cars and beached speedboats, to within three feet of my target within the bedroom of our tenth-floor hotel suite. A miracle of Japanese lens-cutting. Thinking of the electrifying image, worthy of Bergman or Polanski, that will be the climax of this film almost derails my mind. I listen to the faint susurrus of the zoom motor, the sound of well-bred Osaka matrons at a flower-arrangement course. Despite everything, the degrading but exciting months of anger and suspicion, I feel the first hint of an erection.

## 2.19 P.M.

Already I am closer to the Coral Playa, the equivalent of perhaps 200 yards away. For the first time I can pick out our own suite, Helen's black water-skis arranged like runes on the balcony. Now and then something flicks through the afternoon light, a bottle-top or cigarette packet flung from one of the unseen apartment blocks on the left. Lying here on a raised couch in the darkened bedroom, it is hard to believe that the Coral Playa exists at all except as a figment of this view-finder. But the rectilinear façade of the hotel is sharper. The fifteen floors are each taking on a separate identity. There are differences of tone, subtle declensions of balcony geometry that hint at the personalities of the people behind them. The varying angles of the shutters, the beach umbrellas and bikinis hanging on improvised lines, constitute an elaborate personal notation, a complex of ciphers that would send a semiologist into trance. Almost no sky surrounds the hotel, and half the lurid electrographic sign on the roof has been cut away. The image of the hotel's façade, its 150 balconies, is an increasingly abstract entity. As yet there is no sign of movement – Helen will still be on the bed where I left her, a towel around her head, reading her shower-damp copy of American *Vogue* as I set off ostensibly for Barcelona. The guests are still finishing their gaspacho and paella in the hotel restaurant. In the main ground-floor entrance I can identify several of my neighbours sitting in the armchairs and talking to the lobby clerks. They resemble bored marionettes, unable to sustain their roles in this drama in which I have cast them. My main concern is with the two balconies of our suite and the cluster of adjacent rooms. Already the dark interiors are beginning to lighten, I can just distinguish the internal doors that lead to bathrooms and corridors . . .

*Wait* . . . While my attention is fixed on my own bedroom, impatient for Helen to make her first appearance as the star of this film, I almost fail to notice that a man in a red bath-robe is standing on a balcony five floors above. An American journalist named Anderson, he is looking down at the entrance drive, where a black Mustang has pulled into one of the diagonal parking spaces. The over-heated carapace is about to flow like tar, and for a moment I am too distracted to notice the young man hefting flippers and snorkel from the rear seat. Rademaekers! Panicking, I realize that the young Danish heart surgeon has returned half an hour earlier than I estimated. My zoom may close in on a shot bolt!

### 2.24 P.M.

I have calmed myself, straightened the damaged blind and re-aligned the tripod. In the last few minutes the scene before me has been totally transformed. Rademaekers has gone straight to the American's room, where he wanders about gesticulating with the flippers. Drink in hand, he seems unlikely to be visiting Helen in the next hour. The Nikon purrs smoothly, carrying me ever nearer the Coral Playa. Little more than an apparent hundred yards from me, the hotel has become a hive of activity as the guests return from the dining room and prepare for siesta. Already I recognize dozens of my neighbours in their bedrooms, the men taking off their shoes, the women testing the beach-towels on the balconies and examining their teeth in the dressing-table mirrors. These commonplace but almost meaningless activities have an extraordinary fascination, for years I have watched them in a hundred hotels. But now I am glad that Helen has failed to make her entrance. With her entrenched rationality, her over-calculated approach to life in general and the needs of her sexuality in particular, she has always failed to understand the real significance of my obsession with the private behaviour of my neighbours. She cannot grasp that this aimless minor traffic around their bodies, the applications of sun-oil, the dabbing of scent into this or that fossa, represent a continuing authentication of their physical selves, a non-vocal gossip about their armpits and pudenda that no kinaesthetic language, beyond those provided by the instructions on a deodorant or lady-shaver, has yet been found to express. Fifty units of intense private activity, they edge closer to me. On the second floor the young wife of a Marseilles lawyer undresses to reveal a breastless brown body like a catamite's, sits in bed with the sheet over her knees forming a white pyramid, a geometry of remarkable chasteness from which I move my eyes only when I notice that, at last, the central balcony of the film has been mounted by my wife.

## 2.28 P.M.

A shame that there is no sound-track. Rather than the Polanski or Fellini of the home movie I shall have to become its D.W. Griffith. With his architectural obsessions he would have appreciated the special merits of this film. I am now looking at the façade of the Coral Playa from a distance of fifty yards. Half a dozen floors are visible, a cluster of balconies at whose centre stands my wife. Wayward and erotic, faithless spouse but excellent travelling companion, she is gazing, uncannily, straight towards my camera. The powdery light has cleared, and every detail of the hotel is exposed with the vividness of an hallucination – the rust stains leaking from the balcony rails, the drying swimsuits and discarded paperbacks on the balcony tables, the unfamiliar brands of towel picked up in some provincial Mono-Prix. Oblivious of this plethora of detail swarming around her, Helen is brushing her hair with a reflex hand, revealing the strong muscles of her neck and making the greatest play with her profile for the benefit of the audience watching her from the balconies above and below. For all this attention, she is dressed discreetly in my white towelling robe, no doubt a signal to someone in my absence. Moving my eyes from her, I notice that on the surrounding balconies stands the full complement of her admirers, that troupe of beach-partners, one of whom will play the supporting role in this film. Penelope with her suitors, and I with my Nikon-bow. Even the ever-faithful Argus is there in the bedroom behind her, the dented but still inflated rubber sea-lion which Helen bought me, with cruel irony, two years ago at Venice Lido, and which I, refusing to be outdone, have cared for devotedly ever since, much to her exasperation . . .

## 2.32 P.M.

Helen has loosened my beach-robe, exposing the entire upper hemisphere of her right breast. There is a quickening of heads and eyes. I feel a familiar surge of excitement as I make a last inventory of my rivals. Rademaekers, the pedantic Danish surgeon who took her snorkelling yesterday, has returned to his room three floors diagonally above ours. Even as he hunts for a clean shirt in his wardrobe he is still holding one of the flippers, like a sea-born land creature clinging obsessively to an obsolete organ. I eliminate him, and move to his neighbour, a thirty-year-old Brighton antique dealer, whose speedboat, during our first week, sat reversing in the shallows ten yards from the beach where Helen and I lay under our umbrellas. Engaging but unscrupulous, he too is taking in his opposition – principally Fradier, the Paris comic-strip publisher two floors above, leaning on his balcony rail beside his attractive wife while openly admiring Helen. But Fradier is moving out of frame, and by the logic of this film can be dropped from the cast-list. As the camera moves nearer I approach the main stage of this vertical drama – a tier of fifteen balconies distributed among five floors, Helen at the centre. Two floors below her, bare-chested in the fierce sunlight, is a minor Italian film actor who arrived only yesterday, bringing with him an anthology of dubious sexual techniques which he had already displayed for Helen in the hotel bar after dinner. His profession would make him my chief suspect, but he too is about to move out of frame, exiting from this reductive fable . . .

Helen is scrutinizing her eyes in a lacquered hand-mirror. She plucks a stray hair from her brow-line with the ruthlessness she always applies to her own body. Even thirty feet away, hovering in the air like an invisible angel, I find this violence unnerving. I realize that I have only been fully at ease with my wife while watching her through the viewfinder of a camera – even within the private space of our various hotel rooms I prefer her seen through a lens, emblematic of my own needs and fantasies rather than existing in her own right. At one time this rightly outraged her, but recently she has begun to play along with my obsession. For hours I watch her, picking her nose and arguing with me about something as I lie on the bed with a camera to my eye, fascinated by the shifting geometries of her thighs and shoulders, the diagrams of her face.

Helen has left the balcony. She tosses the mirror on to the bed, gazes with a pensive frown at the fading but still cheerful expression on the face of the sea-lion, and walks straight through the suite to the front door. Almost before I stifle a shout she has disappeared into the corridor. For the moment I am paralysed. Under my beach-robe she is naked.

## 2.36 P.M.

Where is she? The camera is closing with the Coral Playa at an unsettling
speed. I wonder if the Nikon engineers have at last over-reached themselves. I seem to be no more than ten feet from the façade of the hotel,
I can almost reach out and touch the balconies. Only three of the suites
are now in frame, our own sandwiched between the Lawrences above us,
an affable English couple from Manchester, and a forty-year-old Irish
pharmacologist below with whom we have made no contact. These three
have involuntarily gate-crashed their way into my film. Meanwhile Helen
could be anywhere in the hotel, with Rademaekers or the antique dealer,
even with the comic-strip publisher if Mme Fradier has left for the beach.
Fumbling with the tripod, I am about to realign the camera when Helen
reappears, standing in the centre of the Lawrences' sitting room. Barefoot,
hands in the pockets of my white beach-robe, she is talking to Lawrence, a
handsome, sandy-haired accountant wearing nothing more than a string
swim-slip over his ample crutch. But where is his wife? Is she in the hotel
pool, or hidden from me by the lowered bedroom shutter, joining in the
conversation through the open door? Confused by this unlikely tryst, I
am ready to stop the camera when Lawrence and Helen embrace. I catch
my breath, but their kiss is merely a light peck. With a wave, Helen takes
a magazine from him and steps into the corridor. Thirty seconds later,
as Lawrence wanders around the sitting room patting his groin, Helen
re-enters our suite. After a pause, she leaves the door ajar. Her actions
are calm and unrushed, but totally conspiratorial. With aching relief, my
loins are at full cock long before the heavily built figure of the Irish
pharmacologist steps deferentially into the sitting room and locks the
door behind him.

## 2.42 P.M.

Reverie of pain, lust and, above all, child-like hate, in which the slights and
antagonisms of a lifetime are subsumed in this unresolvable confrontation
between fear and desire, the need and refusal to face the basilisk stare of
Helen's sexuality . . . all these modulated by the logic of the zoom, by the
geometries of balconies and the laminated gleam of a fashion magazine on
a white sheet, the terrifying reductive authority of the encroaching lens.
By now the entire frame of the viewfinder is filled by our hotel suite, I
seem to be no more than three feet from the nearer of the two balconies,
watching Helen and her lover like a theatre-goer in a front stall. So close
am I that I fully expect them to incorporate me in their dialogue. Still
wearing my beach-robe, Helen strolls around the sitting room, talking
away matter-of-factly as if demonstrating a new domestic appliance to

a customer. The pharmacologist sits on the white plastic settee, listening to her in an agreeable way. There is an unforced casualness, a degree of indifference so marked that it is hard to believe they are about to copulate on my bed. Leached away by the camera lens, the dimension of depth is missing from the room, and the two figures have an increasingly abstract relationship to each other, and to the rectilinear forms of the settee, walls and ceiling. In this context almost anything is possible, their movements are a series of postural equations that must have some significance other than their apparent one. As the man lounges back Helen slips off my robe and stands naked in front of him, pointing to the burn marks left by her shoulder straps.

## 2.46 P.M.

For the first time the camera lens has crossed the balcony and entered the domain of our hotel suite. I am no more than a few steps from the Irishman, who is undressing beside the bed, revealing a muscular physique of a kind that has never previously appealed to Helen. She sits naked on the bidet in the bathroom, clearly visible through the open door, picking at a toenail and staring with a preoccupied expression at the rubber floor-mat. The white porcelain of the bidet, the chromium fitments and the ultramarine tiles of the bathroom together make a curiously formalized composition, as if Vermeer himself had been resurrected and turned loose to recreate his unhurried domestic interiors in the Delft Hilton. Already I feel my anger begin to fade. Annoyingly, my erection also slackens. The transit of this camera across the last forty minutes, which should have brought me to a positive Golgotha of last humiliation, has in fact achieved a gradual abstraction of emotion, an assuagement of all anger and regret. In a way, I feel a kind of affection for Helen.

## 2.52 P.M.

They lie together on the bed, taking part in a sexual act so relaxed that this camera should film them in slow motion. I am now so close that I might be sitting in the armchair beside the bed. Enlarged by the lens, the movements of their bodies resemble the matings of clouds. Steadily they inflate before me, the vents of their mouths silently working like those of sleeping fish, a planet of anatomical abstractions on which I will soon land. When they come, our orgasms seem to take place in the air above the bed, like the aerial copulation of exotic and gentle birds. Little more than three feet from the camera, the blurred smile of the sea-lion presides over this interlude of nuptial bliss.

### 2.56 P.M.

Helen is alone now. Her face is out of frame, and through the viewfinder I see only a segment of the pillow, an area of crumpled sheet and the upper section of her chest and shoulders. An almost undifferentiated whiteness fills the lens, marred by the blue hollow of her armpit and the damp sulcus of her right breast, in which a few of the pharmacologist's hairs have been caught. Edging closer, I watch the easy rise and fall of her ribcage . . .

Helen has sat up. Breaking this extended calm, she has turned on one elbow. The sharp movement almost jars the camera, and I realize that far from being asleep she has been lying there fully awake, thinking to herself about something. Her face fills the viewfinder, in the only true close-up of this film. She is looking me straight in the eye, violating our never-spoken agreement in a blatant way. In a blur of light I see her hand pull the sea-lion towards her, then stab with her nails at its worn eyes. Instantly it buckles as the air spurts from the dented plastic.

At this moment I am certain that she has known about this film all along, as she must have known about the others I have made, first with the still Hasselblad as she and the young waiter flirted around the Pontresina ski-lift, later following the Bayreuth Kappellmeister with a cheap cine-camera mounted in the back of the car, productions that have increased in both range and ambition as they led to this present most elaborate exercise of all. But even now, I dream of the ultimate voyeurist film, employing bizarre lenses that reach to some isolated balcony over extraordinary distances, across the Bay of Naples to Capri, or from Dover to a beach hotel in Calais, magnifying the moment of orgasm to a degree of absolute enlargement where the elements of her infidelity become totally abstracted from themselves, areas of undifferentiated light that assuage all anger.

### 3.05 P.M.

Within a few seconds the camera will reach the limits of its zoom. Helen sleeps on her side with her face away from me. Never faltering, the camera creeps onwards, excluding more and more details from the edges of its frame, the stray hairs of her lover, the damp sweat-prints of her shoulder blades on the sheet. Yet I am aware that there has been a sudden intrusion into the white spaces of the bedroom. What are unmistakably parts of a man's shoes and trousers have appeared soundlessly beside the bed, pausing by the sagging beach-toy. Helen sleeps on, her malice forgotten, unaware of the flash of chromium light that irradiates the screen. Fascinated, with no sense of alarm, I watch the movements of this mysterious intruder, the articulated volumes of almost unrelated forms.

Only a white field is now visible, detached from all needs and concessions, a primed canvas waiting for its first brush stroke. Applauding, I see the screen fill with sudden red.

## 3.15 P.M.

The man kneels beside the bed, watching the elaborate patterns formed by the quiet blood as it runs across the sheet, hunting a hundred gradients. As he turns, exposing his face to the camera, I recognize myself. The sea-lion, my faithful Argus, expires at my feet. As always when I see this film and listen to its commentary, the infinite dream of the sixty-minute zoom, I remember the long journey across the dust and noise of Lloret, past the clamour of the sea to the serene world within this hotel bedroom, to my faithful wife rediscovered in the marriage of red and white.

**. 1976**

# · THE SMILE

Now that a nightmare logic has run its course, it is hard to believe that my friends and I thought it the most innocent caprice when I first brought Serena Cockayne to live with me in my Chelsea house. Two subjects have always fascinated me – woman and the bizarre – and Serena combined them both, though not in any crude or perverse sense. During the extended dinner parties that carried us through our first summer together three years ago her presence beside me, beautiful, silent and forever reassuring in its strange way, was surrounded by all kinds of complex and charming ironies.

No one who met Serena failed to be delighted by her. She would sit demurely in her gilt chair by the sitting-room door, the blue folds of her brocade gown embracing her like a gentle and devoted sea. At dinner, when my guests had taken their seats, they would watch with amused and tolerant affection as I carried Serena to her place at the opposite end of the table. Her faint smile, the most delicate bloom of that peerless skin, presided over our elaborate evenings with unvarying calm. When the last of my guests had gone, paying their respects to Serena as she watched them from the hall, head inclined to one side in that characteristic pose of hers, I would carry her happily to my bedroom.

Of course Serena never took part in any of our conversations, and no doubt this was a vital element of her appeal. My friends and I belonged to that generation of men who had been forced in early middle age, by sexual necessity if nothing else, to a weary acceptance of militant feminism, and there was something about Serena's passive beauty, her immaculate but old-fashioned make-up, and above all her unbroken silence that spelled out a deep and pleasing deference to our wounded masculinity. In all senses, Serena was the kind of woman that men invent.

But this was before I realized the true nature of Serena's character, and the more ambiguous role she was to play in my life, from which I wait now with so much longing to be freed.

Appropriately enough – though the irony then escaped me completely – I first saw Serena Cockayne at the World's End, in that area at the lower end of the King's Road now occupied by a cluster of high-rise apartment blocks but which only three years ago was still an enclave of second-rate antique shops, scruffy boutiques and nineteenth-century terrace housing over-ripe for redevelopment. Pausing on my way home from the office by a small curio shop announcing its closing-down sale, I peered through the sulphur-stained windows at the few remnants on display. Almost everything had gone, except for a clutch of ragged Victorian umbrellas collapsed in the corner like a decaying witch and an ancient set of stuffed elephants' feet. These dozen or so dusty monoliths had a special poignancy, all that remained of some solitary herd slaughtered for its ivory a century earlier. I visualized them displayed secretly around my sitting room, filling the air with their invisible but dignified presences.

Inside the shop a young woman attendant sat behind a marquetry desk, watching me with her head tilted to one side as if calculating in a patient way how serious a customer I might be. This unprofessional pose, and her total lack of response as I entered the shop, ought to have warned me off, but already I had been struck by the young woman's unusual appearance.

What I first noticed, transforming the dingy interior of the shop, was the magnificence of her brocaded gown, far beyond the means of a sales girl at this dowdy end of the King's Road. Against a lustrous blue field, a cerulean of almost Pacific deepness, the gold and silver patterning rose from the floor at her feet, so rich that I almost expected the gown to surge up and engulf her. By comparison, her demure head and shoulders, white bust discreetly revealed by the low bodice, emerged with an extraordinary serenity from this resplendent sea, like those of a domestic Aphrodite seated calmly astride Poseidon. Although she was barely beyond her teens, her hair had been dressed in a deliberately unfashionable style, as if lovingly assembled by an elderly devotee of twenties' film magazines. Within this blonde helmet her features had been rouged and powdered with the same lavish care, eyebrows plucked and hairline raised, without any sense of pastiche or mock nostalgia, perhaps by an eccentric mother still dreaming of Valentino.

Her small hands rested on her lap, apparently clasped together but in fact separated by a narrow interval, a stylized pose that suggested she was trying to hold to her some moment of time that might otherwise slip away. On her mouth hung a faint smile, at once pensive and reassuring, as if she had resigned herself in the most adult way to the vanishing world of this moribund curio shop.

'I'm sorry to see you're closing down,' I remarked to her. 'That set of elephants' feet in the window ... there's something rather touching about them.'

She made no reply. Her hands remained clasped their millimetres apart, and her eyes stared in their trance-like way at the door I had closed behind me. She was sitting on a peculiarly designed chair, a three-legged contraption of varnished teak that was part stand and part artist's easel.

Realizing that it was some sort of surgical device and that she was probably a cripple – hence the elaborate make-up and frozen posture – I bent down to speak to her again.

Then I saw the brass plaque fastened to the apex of the teak tripod on which she sat.

## SERENA COCKAYNE

Attached to the plaque was a dusty price ticket. '£250'.

In retrospect, it is curious that it took me so long to realize that I was looking, not at a real young woman, but at an elaborate mannequin, a masterpiece of the doll-maker's art produced by a remarkable virtuoso. This at last made sense of her Edwardian gown and antique wig, the twenties' cosmetics and facial expression. None the less, the resemblance to a real woman was uncanny. The slightly bowed contours of the shoulders, the too-pearly and unblemished skin, the few strands of hair at the nape of the neck that had escaped the wig-maker's attentions, the uncanny delicacy with which the nostrils, ears and lips had been modelled – almost by an act of sexual love – together these represented a *tour de force* so breathtaking that it all but concealed the subtle wit of the whole enterprise. Already I was thinking of the impact this life-size replica of themselves would have on the wives of my friends when I first introduced them to it.

A curtain behind me was drawn back. The owner of the shop, an adroit young homosexual, came forward with a white cat in his arms, chin raised at the sound of my delighted laughter. Already I had taken out my chequebook and had scribbled my signature with a flourish befitting the occasion.

So I carried Serena Cockayne to a taxi and brought her home to live with me. Looking back at that first summer we spent together I remember it as a time of perpetual good humour, in which almost every aspect of my life was enriched by Serena's presence. Decorous and unobtrusive, she touched everything around me with the most delicious ironies. Sitting quietly by the fireplace in my study as I read, presiding like the mistress of the house over the dining table, her placid smile and serene gaze illuminated the air.

Not one of my friends failed to be taken in by the illusion, and all complimented me on bringing off such a coup. Their wives, of course, regarded Serena with suspicion, and clearly considered her to be part of some adolescent or sexist prank. However, I kept a straight face, and within a few months her presence in my house was taken for granted by all of us.

Indeed, by the autumn she was so much a part of my life that I often failed to notice her at all. Soon after her arrival I had discarded the heavy teak stand and substituted a small gilt chair on which I could carry her comfortably from room to room. Serena was remarkably light. Her inventor – this unknown genius of the doll-maker's art – had clearly inserted a substantial armature, for her posture, like her expression, never changed. Nowhere was there any indication of her date or place of manufacture, but from the scuffed patent-leather shoes that sometimes protruded below the brocade gown I guessed that she had been assembled some twenty years earlier, possibly as an actress's double during the great days of the post-war film industry. By the time I returned to the shop to inquire about her previous owners the entire World's End had been reduced to rubble.

One Sunday evening in November I learned rather more about Serena Cockayne. After working all afternoon in the study I looked up from my desk to see her sitting in the corner with her back to me. Distracted by a professional problem, I had left her there after lunch without thinking, and there was something rather melancholy about her rounded shoulders and inclined head, almost as if she had fallen from favour.

As I turned her towards me I noticed a small blemish on her left shoulder, perhaps a fleck of plaster from the ceiling. I tried to brush it away, but the discoloration remained. It occurred to me that the synthetic skin, probably made from some early experimental plastic, might have begun to deteriorate. Switching on a table-lamp, I examined Serena's shoulders more carefully.

Seen against the dark background of the study, the down-like nimbus that covered Serena's skin confirmed all my admiration of her maker's genius. Here and there a barely detectable unevenness, the thinnest mottling to suggest a surface capillary, rooted the illusion in the firmest realism. I had always assumed that this masterpiece of imitation flesh extended no more than two inches or so below the shoulder line of the gown, and that the rest of Serena's body consisted of wood and papier mâché.

Looking down at the angular planes of her shoulder blades, at the modest curvatures of her well-concealed breasts, I gave way to a sudden and wholly unprurient impulse. Standing behind her, I took the silver zip in my fingers and with a single movement lowered it to Serena's waist.

As I gazed at the unbroken expanse of white skin that extended to a pair of plump hips and the unmistakable hemispheres of her buttocks I realized that the manikin before me was that of a complete woman, and that its creator had lavished as much skill and art on those never-to-be-seen portions of her anatomy as on the visible ones.

The zip had stuck at the lower terminus of its oxidized track. There was something offensive about my struggling with the loosened dress of this half-naked woman. My fingers touched the skin in the small of her back, removing the dust that had accumulated over the years.

Running diagonally from spine to hip was the hairline of a substantial scar. I took it for granted that this marked an essential vent required in the construction of these models. But the rows of opposing stitch-marks were all too obvious. I stood up, and for a few moments watched this partly disrobed woman with her inclined head and clasped hands, gazing placidly at the fireplace.

Careful not to damage her, I loosened the bodice of the gown. The upper curvatures of her breasts appeared, indented by the shoulder straps. Then I saw, an inch above the still-concealed left nipple, a large black mole.

I zipped up the gown and straightened it gently on her shoulders. Kneeling on the carpet in front of her, I looked closely into Serena's face, seeing the faint fissures at the apex of her mouth, the minute veins in her cheek, a childhood scar below her chin. A curious sense of revulsion and excitement came over me, as if I had taken part in a cannibalistic activity.

I knew now that the person seated on her gilt chair was no mannequin but a once living woman, her peerless skin mounted and forever preserved by a master, not of the dollmaker's, but of the taxidermist's art.

At that moment I fell deeply in love with Serena Cockayne.

During the next month my infatuation with Serena had all the intensity of which a middle-aged man is capable. I abandoned my office, leaving the staff to cope for themselves, and spent all my time with Serena, tending her like the most dutiful lover. At huge expense I had a complex air-conditioning system installed in my house, of a type only employed in art museums. In the past I had moved Serena from warm room to cool without a thought to her complexion, assuming it to be made of some insensitive plastic, but I now carefully regulated the temperature and humidity, determined to preserve her forever. I rearranged the furniture throughout the house to avoid bruising her arms and shoulders as I carried her from floor to floor. In the mornings I would wake eagerly to find her at the foot of my bed, then seat her by me at the breakfast table. All day she stayed within my reach, smiling at me with an expression that almost convinced me she responded to my feelings.

My social life I gave up altogether, discontinuing my dinner parties and seeing few friends. One or two callers I admitted, but only to allay their suspicions. During our brief and meaningless conversations I would watch Serena across the sitting room with all the excitement that an illicit affair can produce.

Christmas we celebrated alone. Given Serena's youth – at times when I caught her gazing across the room after some stray thought she seemed little more than a child – I decided to decorate the house for her in the traditional style, with a spangled tree, holly, streamers and mistletoe. Gradually I transformed the rooms into a series of arbours, from which she presided over our festivities like the madonna of a procession of altar-pieces.

At midnight on Christmas Eve I placed her in the centre of the sitting room, and laid my presents at her feet. For a moment her hands seemed almost to touch, as if applauding my efforts. Bending below the mistletoe above her head, I brought my lips to within that same distance from hers that separated her hands.

To all this care and devotion Serena responded like a bride. Her slim face, once so naive with its tentative smile, relaxed into the contented pose of a fulfilled young wife. After the New Year I decided to bring us out into the world again, and held the first of a few small dinner parties. My friends were glad to see us in such good humour, accepting Serena as one of themselves. I returned to my office and worked happily through the day until I set off for home, where Serena would unfailingly wait for me with the warm regard of a proud and devoted wife.

While dressing for one of these dinner parties it occurred to me that Serena alone of us was unable to change her costume. Unhappily the first signs of an excess domesticity were beginning to show themselves in a slight casualness of her personal grooming. The once elaborate coiffure had become unsettled, and the stray blonde hairs all too obviously caught the light. In the same way the immaculate make-up of her face now showed the first signs of wear and tear.

Thinking it over, I decided to call on the services of a nearby hairdressing and beauty salon. When I telephoned them they agreed instantly to send a member of their staff to my house.

And here my troubles began. The one emotion of which I had never suspected myself, and which I had never before felt for any human being, coiled around my heart.

The young man who arrived, bringing with him a miniature pantechnicon of equipment, seemed harmless enough. Although with a swarthy and powerful physique, there was something effeminate about him, and there was clearly no danger in leaving him alone with Serena.

For all his self-assurance, he seemed surprised when I first introduced him to Serena, his suave 'Good morning, madam . . .' ending in a mumble. Shivering in the cool air, he gazed at her open-mouthed, clearly stunned by her beauty and calm repose. I left him to get on with it and spent the next hour working in my study, distracted now and then by a few bars from *The Barber of Seville* and *My Fair Lady* that sounded down the stairs. When he had finished I inspected his work, delighted to see that he had restored every breath of her first glory to Serena. The over-domesticated housewife had vanished, and in her place was the naive Aphrodite I had first seen in the curio shop six months earlier.

So pleased was I that I decided to call on the young man's services again, and his visits became a weekly event. Thanks to his attentions, and my own devotion to the temperature and humidity controls, Serena's complexion regained all its perfection. Even my guests commented on the remarkable bloom of her appearance. Deeply contented, I looked forward to the coming spring and the celebration of our first anniversary.

Six weeks later, while the young hairdresser was at work in Serena's sitting room upstairs, I happened to return to my bedroom to collect a book. I could clearly hear the young man's voice, at a low pitch as if communicating some private message. I glanced through the open door. He was kneeling in front of Serena, his back to me, cosmetic pallet in one hand and paint stick in the other, gesticulating with them in a playful and mock-comical manner. Illuminated by his handiwork, Serena gazed straight into his face, her freshly painted lips almost moist with anticipation. Unmistakably, the young man was murmuring a discreet and private endearment.

During the following days I felt that my head had been seized by some kind of vice. As I tried helplessly to master the pain of that first intense jealousy, I was forced to realize that the young man was Serena's age, and that she would always have more in common with him than with me. Superficially our life continued as before – we sat together in the study when I returned from the office, I would carry Serena into the sitting room when my friends called, and she would join us at the dining table – but I was aware that a formal note had entered our relationship. No more did Serena pass the night in my bedroom, and I noticed that for all her calm smile I no longer caught her eye as I used to.

Despite my mounting suspicions, the young hairdresser continued to make his calls. Whatever crisis through which Serena and I were passing, I was determined not to give in. During the long hour of his visits I had to fight through every second to prevent myself from rushing up the staircase. From the hall I could often hear his voice murmuring in that insinuating tone, louder now as if he were trying to incite me. When he left I could sense his contempt.

It would take me an hour before I could walk slowly up the stairs to Serena's room. Her extraordinary beauty, relit by the taper of the young man's flattery, made my anger all the greater. Unable to speak, I would pace around her like a doomed husband, aware of the subtle changes to Serena's face. Although in every way more youthful, reminding me painfully of the thirty years that separated us, her expression after each visit became fractionally less naive, like that of a young wife contemplating her first affair. A sophisticated wave now modulated the curve of blonde hair that crossed her right temple. Her lips were slimmer, her mouth stronger and more mature.

Inevitably I began an affair with another woman, the separated wife of a close friend, but I made certain that Serena knew nothing of this or of the other infidelities that followed during the next weeks. Also, pathetically, I began to drink, and in the afternoons would sit around drunkenly in my friends' empty apartments, holding long imaginary conversations with Serena in which I was both abject and aggressive. At home I began to play the dictatorial husband, leaving her all evening in her room upstairs and moodily refusing to talk to her at the dining table. All the while, through paralysed eyes I watched the young hairdresser come and go, an insolent suitor whistling as he sauntered up the stairs.

After the last of his visits came the weary denouement. I had spent the afternoon drinking alone in a deserted restaurant, watched by the patient staff. In the taxi home I had a sudden confused revelation about Serena and myself. I realized that our breakdown had been entirely my fault, that my jealousy of her harmless flirtation with the young man had magnified everything to absurd proportions.

Released from weeks of agony by this decision, I paid off the taxi at my door, let myself into the cool air of the house and rushed upstairs. Dishevelled but happy, I walked towards Serena as she sat quietly in the centre of her sitting room ready to embrace her and forgive us both.

Then I noticed that for all her immaculate make-up and extravagant hair her brocade gown hung strangely from her shoulders. The right strap exposed the whole of her collar-bone, and the bodice had slipped forward as if someone had been fumbling with her breast. Her smile still hovered on her lips, calling on me in the most kindly way to resign myself to the realities of adult life.

Angrily I stepped forward and slapped her face.

How I regret that senseless spasm. In the two years that have passed I have had ample time to reflect on the dangers of an over-hasty catharsis. Serena and I still live together, but all is over between us. She sits on her gilt chair by the sitting-room fireplace and joins me at the dining table when I entertain my friends. But the outward show of our relationship is nothing more than the dried husk from which the body of feeling has vanished.

At first, after that blow to her face, little seemed to change. I remember standing in that room upstairs with my bruised hand. I calmed myself, brushed the face powder from my knuckles and decided to review my life. From then on I stopped drinking and went to the office each day, devoting myself to my work.

For Serena, however, the incident marked the first stage in what proved to be a decisive transformation. Within a few days I realized that she had lost something of her bloom. Her face became drawn, her nose more protuberant. The corner of her mouth where I had struck her soon became puffy and took on a kind of ironic downward twist. In the absence of the young hairdresser – whom I had sacked within ten minutes of striking her – Serena's decline seemed to accelerate. The elaborate coiffure which the young man had foisted upon her soon became undone, the straggling hairs falling on her shoulders.

By the end of our second year together Serena Cockayne had aged a full decade. At times, looking at her hunched on her gilt chair in the still brilliant gown, I almost believed that she had set out to catch and overtake me as part of some complex scheme of revenge. Her posture had slumped, and her rounded shoulders gave her the premature stoop of an old woman. With her unfocused smile and straggling hair she often reminded me of a tired and middle-aged spinster. Her hands had at last come together, clasped in a protective and wistful way.

Recently a far more disquieting development has taken place. Three years after our first meeting Serena entered upon a radically new stage of deterioration. As a result of some inherent spinal weakness, perhaps associated with the operation whose scars cross the small of her back, Serena's posture has altered. In the past she leaned forward slightly, but three days ago I found that she had slumped back in her chair. She sits there now in a stiff and awkward way, surveying the world with a critical and unbalanced eye, like some dotty faded beauty. One eyelid has partly closed, and gives her ashen face an almost cadaverous look. Her hands have continued on their slow collision, and have begun to twist upon each other, rotating to produce a deformed parody of themselves that will soon become an obscene gesture.

Above all, it is her smile that terrifies me. The sight of it has unsettled my entire life, but I find it impossible to move my eyes from it. As her face has sagged, the smile has become wider and even more askew. Although it has taken two years to achieve its full effect, that blow to her mouth has turned it into a reproachful grimace. There is something knowing and implacable about Serena's smile. As I look at it now across the study it seems to contain a complete understanding of my character, a judgment unknown to me from which I can never escape.

Each day the smile creeps a little further across her face. Its progress is erratic, revealing aspects of her contempt for me that leave me numb and speechless. It is cold here, as the low temperature helps to preserve Serena. By turning on the heating system I could probably dispose of her in a few weeks, but this I can never do. That smirk of hers alone prevents me. Besides, I am completely bound to Serena.

Fortunately, Serena is now ageing faster than I am. Helplessly watching her smile, my overcoat around my shoulders, I wait for her to die and set me free.

**1976**

# THE ULTIMATE CITY

All winter, while he worked on the sailplane, Halloway had never been certain what drove him to build this dangerous aircraft, with its ungainly wings and humpback fuselage. Even now, as he crouched in the cockpit during the final seconds before his first flight, he was still unsure why he was perched on the steep cliffs above the Sound, waiting to be catapulted into the overlit water. The tapered wings shivered in the cold air, as if the aircraft were trying to rip open the cockpit and eject its foolhardy pilot on to the beach below.

It had taken since dawn for Halloway and his helpers – the crowd of ten-year-olds who formed an enthusiastic claque and coolie-gang – to drag the sailplane from the barn behind his grandfather's house and secure it to the catapult. By the time they reached the cliffs the other contestants in the gliding championship had been aloft for hours. From his cockpit Halloway could see a dozen of the brightly painted craft hanging above his head in the calm sky.

On the ground, by contrast, the turbulent air sweeping up the face of the cliffs seemed to have broken loose from a tornado. Exhausted by the effort of carrying the glider, the boys hung limply from the wings like a line of ballast bags. At any moment a sudden gust would sweep them all into the air together.

In front of Halloway were thirty feet of miniature railway-track and the steel cable linking the sailplane to the sand-filled trolley at the edge of the cliff which would either pull the craft apart or, with luck, catapult it into the air. Halloway signalled the boys aside, and gripped the catapult release lever in both hands. Once again he reminded himself that the Wright Brothers' first sustained flights, little more than a hundred years earlier, had also been launched by catapult.

'Thanks, everybody – now stand back!' he shouted above the wind. One of the smallest boys was still clinging absent-mindedly to the port wing-tip. 'Jamie, let go, for God's sake! *Take off!*'

As the trolley lurched forward, dragging the sailplane after it like a startled bird, Halloway felt the sudden strength of the huge wings and knew already that the aircraft would be the most successful of all those his father had designed before his death. At the edge of the cliffs the trolley hurtled down its track. Halloway released the towing cable, and the glider rose steeply, carried upwards by a cold hand, almost falling on to its back in the rush of wind. The dunes and the beach reeled away to starboard, taking the world from him. The cheers of the spectators were lost in the shrill soughing of the slipstream.

Thirty seconds later, Halloway had climbed a turbulent staircase that carried him in a right-hand spiral to a height of a thousand feet. Abruptly everything around him had become quiet. Little more than a whisper, the wind sucked softly at the fabric of the glider. The heat from the sun stung his blond skin, but Halloway ignored the pain and trimmed the glider into a stable attitude. As always, his father's design had been without error. After the first yawing subsided he began to move the glider across the sky, almost feeling his father's presence in its powerful span. The sailplane soared like a condor in the thermals, dominating the other competitors now far below. Relaxed and happy now, Halloway sat back, ready to preside generously over his domain.

Halloway had begun to build the sailplanes two years earlier. After his parents' death he had moved to his grandfather's house, and for a long while had been reluctant to return to his old home. The charred remains of the sauna where his mother and father had died lay untouched below the derelict sail of the solar energy rig. The hundreds of occluded mirrors, fused by the intense heat of the fire, towered fifty feet above the calcinated roof tiles, an all too melancholy memorial.

One evening, while discussing the annual gliding competition, which the residents of Garden City organized in order to let a little civilized rivalry into their pastoral lives, his grandmother mentioned that Halloway's father had been a keen amateur pilot during the last days of powered aviation. On an impulse Halloway borrowed the keys to the house and wandered through the gutted rooms. Only the studio and workshop, separated from the house by an arm of the canal which irrigated his parents' market garden, had escaped the fire. The shelves were filled with relics of his father's restless mind – antique gear-boxes and carburettors, mementoes of the vanished petroleum age, and the designs for a series of progressively more ambitious sailplanes. The half-completed skeleton of a small glider still lay on its trestles in the workshop.

Halloway pored over the blueprints for months, intrigued by his father's casual but clear calligraphy. The marginal jottings formed a running diary of the rich inner life of this endlessly inventive man, by a bitter irony killed beside his wife in his own home by the overloaded circuitry of an advanced solar device he had designed himself. Like some pastoral Leonardo, he had sat in his studio in the centre of this placid market garden. As the canals flowed between the greenhouses filled with flowers and vegetables, as the waterwheels turned and the hundreds of solar sails silently drained light from the sun, he had devised ever more complex tidal-energy pumps and solar batteries, refuse recycle units and windmills. His real passion, though, apart from his curious interest in old internal-combustion engines, was for these gliders.

All that first winter Halloway had examined the blueprints, feeling the contours of his father's mind in these graceful airframes and wing designs. Several of the aircraft featured extensive control-surfaces, strengthened fuselage-members far in excess of any wing-loading they might need, almost as if they were designed to carry some secret cargo. But Halloway began with the most basic of the gliders. Fortunately, the art and practice of carpentry had reached an advanced level in Garden City. Where an earlier generation of teenage boy learned to strip a carburettor or re-set a distributor, the young of Garden City were expert by the age of twelve in joining and flitching and dovetailing. Within a month his group of eager assistants had helped him to build his first modest sailplane, ready in time for the summer's gliding championship.

As he urged them on, however, watching them cut and stitch the fabric, plane and polish the struts and stringers, Halloway had known already that the competition was only an excuse. He was driven by some other need, connected not so much with his father as with the metal relics, the superchargers embedded in lucite, the fuel pumps and speedometers that lay around the studio like the ornaments of a shrine dedicated to the vanished spirit of the Otto Cycle.

Long before he became a skilled pilot, Halloway had been able to outfly his rivals, as much by pure aggression as by airmanship. None of the other competitors would rise to his baiting, let alone put up a fight. Although the championships were the climax of the year's flying, the other pilots were happy to award him the prize. When he banked and dived towards the beach, chasing the faster thermals behind the dunes, the two gliders he forced aside made way for him without complaint. Their pilots, a thirty-five-year-old architect whom Halloway was always beating at tennis, and an elderly hydrographer with a red beard, had both visited the workshop to watch the construction of this huge glider, and warned him of the impossibility of launching such a craft.

Both had been suitably impressed by Halloway's catapult. They were clearly glad to see Halloway succeed – too glad, in fact. If they had not been so naturally lacking in deceit they might have questioned his motives for building this elaborate craft – not that he would have been able to answer them – but Halloway's blond hair and guileless blue eyes turned aside any suspicion. Eager for action at all costs, yet shy and very much the dreamer, Halloway had a natural talent for rallying people around him.

At the same time, he liked to provoke the crowd. Looking down at the spectators with their picnic hampers among the dunes, the officials gazing at the sky from their canvas chairs, Halloway imagined himself as a World War II fighter ace, diving out of the sun and raking these amiable neighbours with bursts of machine-gun fire. The whole bucolic landscape of Garden City, this elegant but toy-like world of solar sails and flower-filled gardens, the serene windmills and gently nodding reduction gear of the tidal-power machines – all these cried out for a Pearl Harbor.

Surprised by this strain of aggression in himself, Halloway checked his temper. Most of the three hundred spectators he had known since childhood, intelligent, civilized and kindly people who had done their best to care for him since his parents' death, and enjoyed being shocked by his desperado stunts.

They were all watching him now, hands shielding their eyes from the sun. The coolie-gang of small boys squatted on the catapult rails, obviously waiting for Halloway to astonish them.

A mile away, across the Sound, the steep concrete walls of an artificial island rose from the sea like the hull of a cruise liner. The island was a former naval station, a collection of rusting metal buildings around a lighthouse. Although little more than swimming distance away, Halloway had noticed that few people in Garden City were aware of the island, as if they mentally assigned it to the tower blocks of the old metropolis on the opposite shore of the Sound. The previous summer Halloway had rowed out to the island, winding through the dangerous labyrinth of tidal power pontoons and rocker arms that separated the beach from the sea. In the pump-room below the lighthouse he found the huge diesel engines that once powered the warning beacon, each the size of a steam locomotive.

But even his surprise at the enormous latent power of these metal beasts paled before his first real sight of the city. He stood on the rusting catwalk, hands gripping the rail to stop himself from diving into the cold waters of the Sound and setting off to the far shore. The vast office-blocks, many over a hundred storeys high, formed a silent congregation, more remote and yet closer to him than ever before.

Below him, as the glider climbed the thermals, the first people in the crowd were standing up among their picnic hampers, the officials waving their chequered flags at Halloway. Already they had guessed that he intended to circle the lighthouse. Halloway climbed away from them, making use of the strong updraughts that rose from the heated greenhouses, solar reflectors and rooftops, the warm canals and clay tennis-courts. Already he was looking down, not only at the naval island, but at the distant towers of the city.

When Halloway reached the naval island half an hour later the shoreline of Garden City was far behind him, the lines of solar reflectors forming strips of metallic glitter. He had meant to impress everyone by making a few circuits of the lighthouse before returning, but as he soared above the water he could feel the wind carrying him further across the Sound. At any moment it would be too late to turn back. He waited for the glider to bank to port or starboard, but the sailplane pressed on across the deep water. Already Halloway could see the canyons opening among the office-blocks of the city, an abandoned dream waiting to be re-occupied. Shadow and sunlight alternated between the buildings, as if flashing some kind of cryptic message to him. But Halloway knew that he had made his decision, and why all winter he had been building this strange aircraft.

*       *       *

Borne along by the fronts of warm air, Halloway and his glider made their transit of the Sound. The opposing shorelines had begun to converge, and little more than three miles of water separated the beach communities from the deserted quays and motor-routes of the city suburbs. Exhilarated in a way he had never known before, Halloway gripped the control stick with his knees, and stretched out his arms to seize the vivid air. He was not alone in the sky. On all sides flights of wild birds were crossing the Sound – pintails and white-fronted geese, mallard and harlequin duck. A colony of herring gulls moved below him, changing course when they passed Halloway as if guiding him through the crowded air. No longer hunted by the vegetarian inhabitants of Garden City, immense congregations of water birds thrived around the uninhabited shores of the Sound, in the mud-flats, lagoons and sloughs between the market settlements and the old metropolis.

Ahead of him, across the mercury surface of the sea, a collapsed suspension bridge lay like a drowned saurian in the gateway of the Sound. The last of the market gardens gave way to uncultivated scrubland. The canals petered out among the sand-hills. Ten miles from the city, by some unwritten rule, as if they were aware that the physical spell of the metropolis might still intimidate them, the last inhabitants to leave their factories, offices and apartment houses had marked out a no-man's-land to separate themselves from their pasts. Halloway remembered his grand-father's lurid account (the old man was only too keen to be tricked into these reminiscences) of how the city, like a thousand others around the globe, had gradually come to a halt and shut itself down for ever. When the world's reserves of fossil fuels had finally been exhausted, when the last coal silos were empty and the last oil-tankers had berthed, the power-stations and railway systems, production lines and steel-works had closed for the last time and the post-technological era had begun.

By then, twenty-five years earlier, there had been few people left anyway. By some unconscious perception of their own extinction, the huge urban populations of the late twentieth century had dwindled during the previous decades. Halloway's parents had been among the last to leave, abandoning their apartment – the only one still occupied – in one of the high-rise blocks that Halloway could see now emerging from the haze beyond the ruined suspension bridge. Perhaps it was this long-postponed departure that had separated his father from the other inhabitants of Garden City. The small but determined parties of colonists – doctors, chemists, agronomists and engineers – had set out into the rural backwaters determined to build the first scientifically advanced agrarian society. Within a generation they, like countless similar communities around other major cities, had successfully built their pastoral paradise, in a shot-gun marriage of Arcadia and advanced technology. Here each home was equipped with recycling and solar-energy devices, set in its own five acres of intensely cultivated market garden, a self-supporting agricultural paradise linked to its neighbours by a network of canals and conduits, the whole irrigated landscape heated and cooled, powered and propelled by a technology far more sophisticated in every respect than that of the city they had abandoned, but a technology applied to the waterwheel, the tidal pump and the bicycle.

He had reached the western limits of the Sound. A thousand feet below was the broken back of the bridge. Halloway circled a large ceramics works on the southern shore, letting the hot air reflected from the roof-tiles lift him as high as possible before he made the crossing to the city. The downtown office-blocks and apartment-houses were still nearly ten miles away, but facing him across the bridge was a built-up area of dockyards, suburban department stores, car parks and motor-route intersections. Moored to the quays were line upon line of rusting freighters and oil-tankers, their hulls like husks.

For the first time, as he steered the glider across the bridge, Halloway could see the cars, hundreds of the dusty vehicles lining the quaysides, parked in the empty side-streets on flattened tyres. Immense roads ran everywhere, causeways of steel and concrete that moved like some kind of serpentine sculpture through complex interchanges. Traces of these broad decks, never less than six lanes wide, were still to be found in Garden City – on an intact half-mile section behind his grandfather's house the inhabitants staged their annual bicycle rally.

Needless to say, there were no cars in Garden City. If there had been, Halloway often thought with a kind of blank bitterness, his mother and father would still be alive. Despite their severe burns, they might still have been saved by the intensive-care unit at the hospital three miles away. The fastest transport available had been the village fire-appliance. This brilliantly designed land-yacht, fitted with the most efficient system of metal sails ever devised, and with an advanced magnetic suspension invented by a local electrical engineer, achieved a top speed of six miles an hour. By the time they reached the hospital, their distraught son tearing at the aluminium sails in a frenzy, the Halloways were already in deep shock and died the next day.

As he crossed the ruined bridge, losing height in the cold air over the water, Halloway counted the cars in the parking lots along the quays. Scores had been abandoned on the bridge approach-roads when their owners set out on foot. The salt air had stripped away their roofs and body panels, exposing the engines and steering gear. Halloway had seen automobile engines before, in the encyclopaedias of industrial archaeology at the village school. Once, as a boy of ten, he had entered his father's workshop and found him running an old gasolene engine. The violent but controlled noise, the juddering motion that shook the work-bench and timber walls, and the heady fumes like a black gas – an intoxicating smell at once dirty and exhilarating – had almost knocked him off his feet. What he remembered above all, before his father switched off the engine and crated it away for the last time, was the overwhelming energy of this machine, the power and excitement beyond anything else in their sophisticated Arcadia. And yet, as his father told him, this was no more than the power unit of a small lawnmower.

Not that there was any taboo against gasolene engines, nor for that matter against oil- or coal-fired steam engines. There was merely a tacit understanding that for two hundred years proto-industrial man had pillaged the earth's natural resources, and these relics were unwelcome reminders of an unhappy history. Beyond this were boredom and indifference – the inhabitants of Garden City were aware that their technology, their advanced horticulture and their casual winning of energy from the sun, the wind and the tides, had progressed far ahead of anything the age of oil and coal had achieved, with its protein-hungry populations, its limitless pollution of air, soil and sea.

By the time it reached the opposite shore the sailplane was barely three hundred feet above the metal-strewn water. The ragged edge of the eight-lane roadway passed below Halloway, the lines of cars forming bowers of rust from which a few sea-flowers flashed their blooms. Huge numbers of pigeons had taken over the silent city, and Halloway could almost believe that he had entered a vast bird-sanctuary. Thousands of starlings clustered among the seats of a deserted sports stadium. Generations of thrush and blackbird had nested on office window-sills and in the seats of open cars. Halloway had to bank sharply to avoid a pair of swans struggling to gain height above a row of dockyard cranes.

Barely clearing a warehouse roof, the glider rose again in the warm air lifting from the hot concrete of the roads and parking lots. A maze of telegraph wires straggled across the quay-side streets. Halloway flew on above the rusting customs sheds, and crossed the tidal basin of a silted-up dockyard, where a boom of freighters sat in a few feet of water. Beyond a silent railroad station, where ranks of trains stood in waist-high grass, he approached the outskirts of an urban centre, one of a dozen satellite cities on the perimeter of the metropolis. Everywhere there were stores filled with domestic appliances, furniture, clothing and kitchenware, a glut of merchandise that Halloway had never anticipated. In Garden City there were few stores – everything one needed, whether a new solar-powered kitchen stove or a high-speed bicycle, was ordered direct from the craftsman who designed and built it to one's exact needs. In Garden City everything was so well made that it lasted for ever.

Following the main arterial highway which led towards the next satellite city, Halloway crossed an area of tract housing and single-storey factories. In the open fields a local manufacturer had dumped what appeared to be a lifetime's output of washing machines. Line upon line of the white and chromium cabinets stood in the sunlight. Warm air rose from this field of metal, carrying the glider high above the concrete embankments of a cloverleaf.

Directly in front of Halloway there was a flash of light in the glassy face of a fifteen-storey office building. Out of this sunburst huge wings moved in the bright air. A powerful aircraft, with a wing-span as large as his own sailplane's, soared straight towards him. In panic, Halloway plunged the glider into a steep turn, cursing himself for entering the air-space of the city, with its empty towers guarded by aerial demons. As the glider banked across the face of the office building his opponent also turned. His long wings, built to the same plan as Halloway's, were raised in a defensive gesture. A hundred feet apart, they soared together along the curtain-walling, the pilot's white face staring at Halloway in obvious alarm.

Without warning, this timid intruder vanished as suddenly as he had appeared. Turning back, Halloway circled the streets around the office block, searching for any sign of the rival sailplane. Then, as he passed the office block with its mirror-glass curtain-wall, he realized that he had been frightened by nothing more than his own reflection.

Delighted now, Halloway soared to and fro across the face of the building, playing the fool and happy to mimic himself, wingtip little more than ten feet from the curtain-walling. He waved at his reflection, holding the control stick with his knees, proud of his skill and glad to be able to show off to himself. He rose above the building on the strong currents lifting from the metal roofs of the cars, and then plunged towards himself in a 100-m.p.h. dive, swerving away at the last moment, wingtip punching out a section of the mirror.

'*Olé . . . !*'

His shout of glee was lost in the splintering glass. On his third dive, as he plummeted downwards, he no longer cared when a gust of wind drove him laterally across the streets in a storm of cigarette packs. Out of control, the sailplane was hurled against the curtain-walling, knocking out a dozen windows. Colliding with his own image, Halloway fell with the broken machine among the cars a hundred feet below.

An hour later, Halloway left the crashed glider lying at the base of this huge rectilinear mirror and set off towards the towers of the city five miles away to the south-west.

Protected by the buckling wings, the cockpit of the glider had fallen among the vehicles parked outside the entrance to the office block. Hanging upside-down in the harness, Halloway punched out the fractured canopy, released his straps and lowered himself on to the roof of a green sedan.

Too shocked to do more than glance numbly at the face of the building which had dashed him from the air, Halloway had climbed across the splintered wings of the glider. Picking a car at random, he lay down in the rear seat. In this warm, stale air, almost unchanged for thirty years, he rested quietly, massaging his bruised chest and shoulders. The domed cabin of the car, with its softly sprung seats and antique contours, its raw metal functionalism, was a fitting womb to guard his passage from the open transits of the sky to the hard and immobile concrete now surrounding him on all sides.

Already, though, when he stepped from the car after an hour's rest, Halloway was coming to terms with the scale and character of the cityscape into which he had fallen. Display signs proliferated everywhere like some voracious metal flora, untrimmed and uncontrolled. The crudeness of the asphalt and concrete streets compared with the tiled and flower-decked pathways of Garden City, the elemental technology of power cables and ventilation shafts, had all the anarchic strength of a proto-industrial society, closer to the massive cantilever bridges and steam engines of the great Victorians than to Halloway's image of the Twentieth Century.

A mile to the north-east a line of rusting cranes marked the shoreline of the Sound. If he walked through the side-streets he could reach the ruined suspension bridge in less than an hour, cross the channel by swimming from one section to the next, and be home by evening.

Without thinking, Halloway turned his back on the shore, on the cranes and rusting freighters. For all their apparent menace, the cluster of skyscrapers offered more security to him than the pastoral world of Garden City with its kindly farmers and engineers. Somewhere among those tall buildings – on the topmost floor, he was certain – was the apartment in which his mother and father had lived. As for any worries that his grandparents might have for his safety, Halloway was sure that they, like the crowds on the beach, knew only too well where he had gone.

Halloway climbed over the broken-backed fuselage of the glider. He stared at the wreckage, thinking of the months he had spent building the craft. Lying here at the foot of this mirror it reminded him of the body of his father stretched out below the solar reflector in the burnt-out ruins of his house.

'Come on! Forget it, Halloway!' With a whoop, Halloway leapt over the tailplane and set off along the street. Shouting to himself, he ran in and out of the cars, pounding on the roofs with his fists. He was going home.

For the next two hours, as the sun drifted across the Sound, Halloway pressed on down the long avenues that carried him, block after block, into the heart of the metropolis. The office-buildings and apartment-houses grew larger, but the centre of the city remained as distant as ever. But Halloway was in no hurry, far more interested in the sights around him. His first feelings of nervousness had gone. Curiosity devouring everything, he ran past the cars that sat on flattened tyres in the roadway, skipping from one side of the avenue to the other when something caught his eye. Many of the stores, bars and offices were unlocked. In a hairdressing salon – an Aladdin's cave of chromium gadgetry, mirrors, thousands of coloured bottles – he sat in the rotating chairs, and tried on a succession of wigs, grimacing at himself in the dusty mirrors. In an empty department-store he lost himself in a maze of furnished rooms, each like a stage-set, decorated in the styles of nearly half a century earlier. The synthetic curtain and carpet fabrics, with their elaborate patterns and lamé threads, were totally unlike the simple hand-woven worsteds and woollens of Garden City.

Halloway wandered around these darkened tableaux, these ghosts of bedroom suites and dining-rooms. He lay back grandly on an ornate four-poster, stroking the deep pile of the bedspread. What amused him, above all, was the feel of this vanished world, a surprise more tactile than visual.

In the dim light of a men's-wear department he pulled clothes racks on to the counters, jerked open the cabinet drawers. A cornucopia of suits and shirts, shoes and hats spilled across the floor. Stripping off his woollen trousers and jerkin, like the uniform of an ignorant medieval churl, he selected a new costume – red-white-and-blue sneakers, yellow suede trousers and a fleece-lined jacket with silver-thread embroidery and leather tassels as long as his arm.

In this modest attire he swung happily along the avenue. Thousands of cars lined the streets, their flamboyant bodywork covered with moss. Wild flowers peeped from the radiator grilles. Halloway stopped at every tenth car and tried to start the engine. Sitting behind these dead controls, he remembered the car he had found buried in the dunes at Garden City. The roof and doors had rusted away, but he sat for hours behind the wheel of this drowned hulk. By contrast, the cars here had barely been touched by the weather. Under the moss and dirt the lurid paint was as bright as ever.

Halloway was disappointed that none would start. Rocking a black limousine that took his fancy in an automobile showroom, he could hear the fuel still swishing in its tank.

'Somewhere, Halloway,' he told himself aloud, 'you'll find a car that runs. I've decided you're going to arrive in style . . .'

At dusk, as Halloway passed a park filled with wild trees, shrubs and flowers of every kind, he realized that someone was following him. The soft tap of feet, sometimes barely moving, then running obliquely behind him, sounded faintly through the dark air. Heart racing, Halloway crouched among the cars. Nothing moved across the street. He filled his lungs with air, and broke away with a burst of speed, darting in and out of the cars. He dived through the open door of an evacuation bus parked by a hotel entrance and watched from the rear seats.

Five minutes later he saw the first of his shy pursuers. Edging forward cautiously, its eyes still on the park fifty yards away, a large deer hobbled along the sidewalk, searching the dim light for Halloway. Within moments two more appeared, steering their antlers through the overhead wires that trailed across the road.

As he watched them scenting the darkness, Halloway remembered the placid creatures in the zoo at Garden City, as lacking in aggression as these deer. The Angus and Hereford cows in their enclosure, the shire horses and saddleback pigs, the lambs, chicken and farmyard geese together memorialized all the vanished species of domestic animals. At Garden City everyone was vegetarian, not out of moral or religious conviction, but simply because they knew that the provision of grazing land, and the growing of cereal crops for animal feedstuffs, was a wastefully inefficient means of obtaining protein.

When the deer had gone, returning to their forest between the apartment blocks, Halloway stepped down from the bus. Knowing that he must spend the night somewhere, he walked up the steps into the hotel. On the seventh floor he found a bedroom from which he could see both the Sound and the skyscraper towers of the city centre. On the opposite shore the solar reflectors were still faintly visible, drinking in the last glow of the sunset, beacons of a vanished world. He slept through the night, dreaming of glass aeroplanes, their wings like mirrors, that circled the dark air over his head, waiting to carry him away to some sunlit eyrie among the clouds.

The next morning, after an early start, Halloway pressed on towards the city centre. He felt refreshed and confident again, fortified by an exotic breakfast of grapefruit juice, beans and peaches taken from the shelves of a nearby supermarket. Vaguely prudish about eating meat, he decided against opening any of the cans of pork and beef, the limitless varieties of salmon, tuna and sardine.

Bright sunlight filled the streets, picking out the vivid colours of the wild flowers growing in profusion from the cracked sidewalks. Despite these embellishments, the city's character had begun to change. Fastening his jacket across his chest, Halloway moved forward more cautiously. Above him, on all sides, were the massive structures and heavy technology of the late Twentieth Century – highway interchanges and bridge approaches, sixty-storey hotels and office-blocks. Between them, almost out of sight on the ground level, was a decaying under-stratum of bars and pintable arcades, nightclubs and clothing stores. The cheap façades and neon signs had long since collapsed into the roads. A maze of narrow side-streets ran off in all directions, but by following only the main avenues he soon lost his bearings. A wide road raised on concrete stilts carried him high into the air, and changed course in a series of giant loops. Plodding around this curving viaduct, a cambered deck eight lanes wide, Halloway wasted nearly an hour in returning to his starting point.

It was at this time, shortly after he left the cloverleaf by an emergency staircase, that Halloway came across the first of the strange monuments he was later to find all over the city. As he stepped down from the pedestrian exit, he noticed that a nearby parking lot had been used as a municipal dump. Old tyres, industrial waste and abandoned domestic appliances lay about in a rusty moraine. Rising from its centre was a pyramid of television sets some sixty feet high, constructed with considerable care and an advanced sense of geometry. The thousand or so sets were aligned shoulder to shoulder, their screens facing outwards, the combinations of different models forming decorative patterns on the stepped sides. The whole structure, from base to apex, was invaded by wild elders, moss and firethorn, the clouds of berries forming a huge cascade.

Halloway stared up at the rows of television sets, a pyramid of dead eyes in their worm-riddled cabinets, like the eggs of some voracious reptile waiting to be born from the bland globes embedded in this matrix of rotting organic matter. Pulled apart by the elders, many of the sets revealed their internal wiring. The green and yellow circuitry, the blue capacitors and modulators, mingled with the bright berries of the firethorn, rival orders of a wayward nature merging again after millions of years of separate evolution.

Little more than half a mile away, in a plaza between two office buildings, Halloway found a second pyramid. From a distance it resembled a funeral pyre of metal scrap built from hundreds of typewriters, telex machines and duplicators taken from the offices around the plaza, a monument to the generations of clerks and typists who had worked there. A series of narrow terraces rose one above the other, the tiers of typewriters forming ingenious baroque columns. Brilliant climbing plants, lobster-clawed clematis and honeysuckle with pink and yellow flowers, entwined themselves around the metal colonnades, the vivid blooms illuminating this memorial of rust.

Halloway mounted a staircase of filing cabinets to the upper terrace of the pyramid. On all sides, in the nearby streets and on the raised pedestrian areas above the plaza, an extraordinary vegetation had taken root. Dahlias, marigolds and cosmos flourished among the cracked paving stones and in the ornamental urns outside the entrances to the office blocks. Along a three-hundred-yard section of the avenue all the cars had been cleared aside, and a field of poppies sprang from the broken asphalt. The bright, funeral flowers extended in a blood-red carpet down the line of hotels, as if waiting for a demonic visitor. Here and there an individual car had been picked out by this mysterious and profligate gardener, its windshield and windows knocked in and its cabin packed with blooms. As vivid as an explosion in a paint-shop, blue and carmine flowers and yellow-ribbed leaves crammed the open windows, mingled with tilting sunflowers and the vines that circled the roof and radiator grille.

From a side-street a quarter of a mile away came the sounds of collapsing masonry. Falling glass split the air. Halloway leapt down from the pyramid, holding to a column of typewriters as the road vibrated under his feet. The slow avalanche continued, the rumble of falling brickwork and the brittle ringing of breaking glass. Then Halloway heard the heavy beating of what he guessed was some kind of huge engine, throbbing with the same rhythm as the motor he had watched his father running in his workshop years before. It moved away, breaking through some glass and masonry obstruction in its path. Already the first dust was billowing from the end of the street, lit by thousands of coloured petals.

Halloway climbed into a nearby car, waiting as this machine moved away. In the deserted city the noise of the assault had carried with it an unmistakable violence, as if some huge and ugly creature was venting its anger at random on the buildings around it.

'Halloway, time to go . . .' Already he had decided to leave the city and make his way home. Once he had crossed the river he would be safe.

When the streets were quiet again, and the cloud of petalled dust had drifted away down the avenue, Halloway set off, leaving the monument of typewriters and telex machines behind him. He ran silently through the field of poppies, as the last petals fell through the unsettled air around him.

When he reached the side-street he found the roadway littered with human figures. Masonry and broken glass, sections of store window as large as his sailplane's wings, lay among the crushed flowers. Most of the clothing stores that lined both sides of this narrow street had been attacked, their glass fronts and window displays ripped out by some giant implement.

Everywhere the plastic mannequins lay in the sunlight, limbs crushed by the tracks of the machine, polite expressions looking up from the glass and masonry.

Frightened for the first time by the sight of violence, Halloway ran towards the river, and by luck found the open span of a large road-bridge that carried him away from the city. Without pausing to look back, ears listening for any sound of the machine, he sprinted along in his coloured sneakers. Halfway across the bridge he slowed down for the first time to catch his breath. The cloud of petals was still drifting eastwards between the office blocks. Halloway searched the northern suburbs for the mirror-sheathed building into which he had crashed, regretting that he would have to leave the sailplane among these anonymous streets patrolled by this violent machine.

Angry with himself, he pulled off his fleece-lined jacket and hurled it over the balustrade. It fell into the dead water like a sad, brilliant bird. Already he looked forward to his return to Garden City, with its civilized people and sane behaviour. Thinking back, his aggressiveness at the gliding championships embarrassed him.

'. . . too eager for action at any cost,' he reproved himself as he strode along. 'In future check that, Halloway . . .'

He left the bridge and set off eastwards past the dockyards and warehouses. He had entered an area of single-storey factories and cheap housing, chemical tank-farms and electrical sub-stations. All around him, as well, were the monuments. He was crossing a plain of these memorials, pyramids of domestic appliances and car tyres, machine tools and office furniture that had been erected on any available patch of waste ground. Ignoring them, and their ambiguous flowers, Halloway pressed on. Already he could see the collapsed suspension bridge that marked the gateway to the Sound.

Shortly before noon, when the river crossing was three miles behind him, Halloway came across the airport. As he approached the perimeter fence he could see the control tower, and the tails of parked airliners as high as three-storey buildings. The entire surface of the airport, the concrete runways and grass verges, was covered with thousands of automobiles. Variants of no more than two or three models, they stretched away in a huge metallized dream.

Curious to see the airliners, Halloway followed the perimeter fence towards the entrance. He guessed that the cars had been new models fresh from the production line, stored here by the manufacturers when the oil tap had been turned off. With luck, one of the cars might start for him.

Now that he had left the city, Halloway began to relax again. The airport was a zone that he found curiously reassuring, and in some obscure way made up for the loss of his sailplane. He visualized his father landing and taking off in one of the single-engine aircraft parked nose-to-tail on the other side of the perimeter fence.

At the airport entrance, in the centre of a traffic island, Halloway found the largest of the pyramids he had seen so far. Well over one hundred feet high, the memorial had been constructed entirely from automobile radiator grilles, a tour-de-force of ironic humour. Row upon row, the grilles rose to the apex, cunningly welded together to form staircases and internal galleries. For once, the tropical flora had barely gained a purchase on the base of the pyramid, and the still-gleaming chrome formed a brilliant lacework.

Impressed by the structure, Halloway made his way around it into the airport. Service roads led in all directions to the terminal buildings and air-freight offices. Fuel tankers and breakdown vehicles blocked the narrow lanes. Losing himself in this maze, Halloway decided to climb to the roof of a ten-storey car park whose canted floors spiralled up into the air behind the terminal buildings.

As he passed the elevators on his way to the staircase, Halloway without thinking touched the call button. To his surprise, the doors promptly responded, opening without any hesitation on well-oiled castors. The interior of the elevator was clean and well-maintained, the control panel freshly polished.

Listening to the faint drumming of an electric generator somewhere above the shaft, Halloway gathered his courage together. There was something seductive about this immaculate compartment, and already he was becoming impatient with himself for turning tail and leaving the city at the first alarm. Sooner or later he intended to come to terms with whatever creature prowled its deserted canyons, and this car park would make a good observation post.

Stepping into the elevator, he inspected the control panel and pushed a button at random.

Within less than a minute he had ridden to the seventh floor and stepped out into what he soon discovered was a museum of automobiles. At first glance the cars were indistinguishable from the thousands of vehicles he had passed that day. But as he walked through the dim light, seeing his reflection in the burnished cellulose and waxed leather, he realized that he had stumbled on to a unique private museum. The sixty or so cars on this canted deck were all exhibition pieces, sitting squarely on inflated tyres, antique coachwork lovingly restored.

'Pierce Arrow ... Bugatti ... Hispano-Suiza ... Chevrolet Impala ...' Aloud, he read out the names from the manufacturers' medallions. Many of the cars dated back well over a century to the dawn of the automobile age, huge perambulators of brass and steel with high seats and coaching lamps larger than their diminutive engines. Others, slab-decked saloons and limousines, were as new as the models that covered the runways of the airport.

Cord. Stutz. Chrysler Imperial. Halloway climbed the deck to the eighth floor. More cars, all lovingly waxed and polished, faced each other through the gloom.

The one exception was parked in the centre of the ramp, a grimy six-wheeled breakdown truck with a heavy crane mounted on its rear platform. The engine cowling was still warm. Halloway opened the driver's door; on the seat were a toolkit and a set of maps of the city marked off into various zones. Ignition keys hung from the dashboard, and from the whole compartment came the raw but potent odour of carbonized oil, gasolene and engine coolant.

Sitting behind the steering wheel, Halloway felt the controls, trying to remember something of the casual expertise with which he so easily impressed the gang of ten-year-olds who watched him demonstrate how to drive.

Suddenly the engine was alive, thundering out between the concrete decks as if trying to shake itself apart. The heavy vehicle was vibrating fiercely, and the unlatched door bumped against Halloway's elbow. A blaze of lights lit up the dashboard. Gripping the wheel cautiously, Halloway released the handbrake and let the truck roll forward down the concrete incline, pressing the accelerator as the vehicle moved along at a steady two miles an hour.

Within thirty minutes he was driving around the airport at speed, roaring along the perimeter roads and down the one exposed section of runway. Flocks of startled ducks and geese rose from the reservoirs to the east of the airport, fleeing from the noise of the careening vehicle. When he first emerged from the car park the truck had come to a halt, and it had taken Halloway some time to discover that the gear lever was in neutral. He soon learned to engage it, and set off at breakneck pace, slamming in and out of the parked cars. The heavy truck and its wildly swinging crane, steel hook lashing about, sent up a spray of rust from the cars kicked out of their way. The forward power of the vehicle, after the agile but passive motion of the sailplane, astonished Halloway. The slightest pressure of his foot on the accelerator sent the truck hurtling ahead. It was the raw energy of the machine that most impressed him, this gut-driven dynamo totally at one with the city across the river.

Carried away by his new-found determination, and confident that he could take on any opponent now, Halloway headed out of the airport. As he left the main gates he was already moving at sixty m.p.h. Too late, he released the accelerator as the road veered off to circle the traffic island with its pyramid of radiator grilles. Trying to slow down, he plunged across the grass verge, the concrete kerb almost rolling the truck on to its side. It hurtled forward, the crane's hook and heavy chains thrashing the cabin behind Halloway's head. He clung to the wheel, face hidden behind his arms, and felt himself flung across the cabin as the truck struck the lowest tier of the pyramid. It tore out a dozen radiator grilles, which hung like trophies from the dented fenders as it swerved away, ran head-on into the steel pylon of a route indicator and came to a halt on its side, cabin buried in the soft earth.

He was waking from a dream of powered flight.
  He soared across a dark, windless sky. Through the rigging and fuselage struts behind his head came the steady beat of an engine. Beside him in the cockpit a man was crouching over the controls, as if hiding himself from Halloway. When he tried to see the face of this mysterious pilot the aircraft banked steeply, throwing Halloway against the canopy. Searching for a way to escape from the aircraft, he realized that it was built of glass, and that he could see the stars through the wings and fuselage. Unable to restrain himself, he seized the man's shoulder and tried to wrest the control column from him. As they struggled together the aircraft plunged across the sky, its engine screaming . . .

He woke to find himself in a dimly lit cabin, lying on a bed attached to the panelled wall. Leaning over Halloway, pulling with concern at his shoulder, was a young man about five years older than himself, a tall, slimly built Negro with an expression of wary concern on his shy but intelligent face.
  *Rest – you've landed safely.*
  A line of scarlet letters, in a stylized computer typeface, glowed in Halloway's eyes, hovering in the air two feet from him.
  *Can you hear me? You're not flying now.*

Halloway nodded weakly, gazing at the message that seemed to emerge from the man's hand. Although there were windows in the cabin the air outside was almost opaque, as if they were contained by yet another building. Twenty feet away a second ceiling tilted across the sky.

'There was an engine on the glider,' Halloway explained. He sat up, pointing to the roof of the cabin. Somewhere above him there was the steady drumming of an internal-combustion engine. 'I can hear it now . . .'

Lights flickered in the Negro's palm. Again the strange alphabet sorted itself into a message. His pensive eyes presided over these reassembling letters as if over the anagrams of stigmata.

*There is a power generator on the roof.*

As if to reassure Halloway, he pressed a wall switch.

When the electric light – an antique tungsten-filament glow – came on in the cabin Halloway examined his surroundings. He was lying on a bunk in a large landcruiser, one of a group drawn up together on what he guessed was the top floor of the car park. In front of him, beyond a small kitchen, was the driver's compartment, the steering wheel and instrument panel below a high windshield.

Sitting beside him, clearly relieved to see Halloway regain consciousness, was the tenant of the cruiser. The left side of his face was covered by a fretwork of notches, minute cuts clearly inflicted during his childhood. At first Halloway assumed that they were some kind of tribal insignia, but later he learned that they were the scars left by a serious automobile accident.

With his intelligent face and curiously unfocused eyes, which seemed to be fixed on some point within his mind, he reminded Halloway of a circus clown without his make-up. He sat here in his land-cruiser with the same vaguely melancholy posture of the clowns whom Halloway and his friends visited in their trailers whenever they toured Garden City. As he gazed down at Halloway with his alert but neutral expression he looked as if he had been alone too long, and was unsure how to respond to the physical presence of another human being.

He touched Halloway's shoulder, obviously convincing himself that his visitor posed no threat.

*Now – are you all right?*

'I'm a lot better. I guess it was your truck I crashed.'

His rescuer waved this aside. He seemed about to speak, but checked himself. In one hand, almost hidden between his slim fingers, was a pocket calculator. With surprising swiftness, he tapped out a message, which flashed up on the alphanumeric display.

*Forget it. There's not exactly a shortage here.*

As he gazed through the window of the cruiser Halloway had the distinct impression that this solitary young mute was a prisoner here, high above this museum of cars in the centre of the abandoned airport. His fingers fluttered across the keys of the calculator. As each sentence came up it was glanced at and quickly erased, fingers flicking away in this reverse Braille. Obviously he was used to holding long conversations with himself.

'I'm sorry about the truck,' Halloway said. Remembering the frightening violence he had witnessed that morning, he asked cautiously: 'Do you live here? What's your name?'

*Olds.*

'Olds? What, as in –?' Halloway laughed, despite himself, but the young Negro nodded, clearly taking no offence. Joining in the joke, he touched the scars on his scalp. Fingers flicked across the keyboard.

*Yes. As in Oldsmobile. Ten years ago I renamed myself.*

He stared at the illuminated message, his mind drifting away. An expression of regret hovered around his faint smile.

'Why not?' Halloway said encouragingly. 'I like it, it's a good name.' He looked at his watch. It was after two o'clock. He felt drawn to this solitary young Negro, but it was time to be moving on.

'Olds, I ought to be going.'

*All right. But first have some food.*


They left the cabin and stepped down on to the tenth floor of the car park. Four of the land-cruisers were drawn up to form a private enclosure. From the balustrade Halloway looked down at the thousands of vehicles that covered the airport.

The breakdown truck lay on its side by the pyramid of radiator grilles. He took for granted that Olds had constructed these monuments. On trestle tables beside the land-cruisers lay an extensive selection of electrical parts – dynamos and transformers, fuse-boxes and switching units. Power cables trailed across the floor, running from the generator on the roof to a barbecue in the centre of what he assumed was Olds' dining area. Rotating on the spit was the body of a small deer. The fused flesh gleamed like polished oak. Olds beckoned Halloway to a chair, and began to cut steaks from the carcass.

An hour later Halloway had finished the most intoxicating meal of his life, and made his decision to postpone any return to Garden City for as long as possible. After the pallid vegetarian cuisine of his childhood, the flavour of venison and animal fat acted on him like adrenalin. Surrounded by the bones and meat scraps, he felt like the early pioneers who had colonized this land and built its cities.

Olds had watched him eat with obvious pleasure. At intervals, as he urged him to take second and third helpings, his right hand flicked out some brief message to himself on the calculator, as if he were transcribing a commentary on a second life going on inside his head.

During their meal he told Halloway about himself, and how as a boy of five years old during the final evacuation of the city he had been knocked down by a housewife driving her Oldsmobile to the neighbourhood scrap-yard. Thus he had become the world's last traffic casualty. Fifteen years later, after a long and incomplete recovery from his brain injuries, he left the technical training centre at the commune hospital fifty miles to the north of the city and made his home among the thousands of cars parked on the runways of this abandoned airport. Here, moved by some profound compulsion, he spent his time putting together this museum of cars, perhaps in an attempt to find the missing sections of his mind. His ambition, he explained to Halloway, was to have a running model of every make of car ever manufactured.

*Only then will I come to terms with my accident.*

He flashed a self-deprecating smile and added:

*After that I can learn to fly.*

Halloway nodded sympathetically, unsure whether Olds was pulling his leg. This clever, shy but self-confident man seemed to be all there as far as Halloway could tell. When they had finished the meal Halloway asked Olds to take him on a tour of the museum.

'You repaired all these yourself? It's hard to believe – in the first place, what about the fuel?'

Olds gestured casually at the sea of vehicles that stretched to the horizon on all sides of the car park.

*There are five million cars in this city alone. Almost every tank still has a little gas in it.*

Halloway walked down the line of cars, gazing at his reflections in the lovingly refurbished radiator, grilles, hub-caps and chromium trim. Olds led the way, pointing out a rare Mercedes 600, a Rolls-Royce Silver Cloud, a Facel Vega. He was clearly proud to show off his collection, but at the same time Halloway noticed that he seemed slightly bored by these vehicles. His eyes were forever straying to the moss-covered airliners parked by the terminal buildings.

'And you're sure they all run?' Halloway asked. He pointed to a resplendent limousine. 'What about this one – Daimler Majestic?'

With remarkable speed, Olds leapt behind the wheel of the car. Within seconds its engine roared out, headlamps pulsed, momentarily blinding Halloway. The horn sounded imperiously.

'Olds, it's unbelievable!' Halloway congratulated him. 'Let's see you try another – this Pontiac Firebird.'

For the next thirty minutes the two men moved through the museum, Halloway shouting and pointing to one car after another, Olds leaping like an excited faun, an automotive Ariel, from one driver's seat to the next, switching on the ignitions and bringing the engines to life. Each car he left with its motor racing and headlamps full on. First a dozen cars came alive, then more than thirty, and finally the entire eighth and ninth decks of the car park. The roar of the engines, the exhaust swirling in the headlamp beams, the vibrating floors and balustrades, the smell of burning fuel and the noise booming out over the deserted airport, made Halloway feel that the entire city had begun to spring to life, re-starting itself under the hands of this young recluse.

Finally, out of curiosity rather than cruelty, Halloway shouted out the last name. 'One more, Olds! What about –' In the absence of the car, he pointed at random. '– Oldsmobile!'

Immediately Halloway regretted the prank. Too late, he saw the rictus on Olds' face. Sitting behind the wheel of a white Galaxie, he began to pound the controls, angry with the car when it failed to start on its own. When Halloway reached him he had slumped back and was already moving into a deep fugue, mouth agape, the blood in his face making a livid lace-work of the scars. On the seat beside him, like some hyper-excited small animal, his right hand flicked out a desperate message on the calculator.

'Olds . . . it doesn't matter!'

Halloway pulled open the door and tried to calm him. Bizarre messages glimmered among the headlamps as he sank into unconsciousness, the engines of a hundred cars throbbing around him in the exhaust-filled air.

*Teach me to fly!*

Within an hour Olds had recovered. Sitting back on a car seat beside the barbecue, he touched his face and scalp, feeling the tracery of scars as if making sure that the jigsaw was once again in place. After dragging him to the elevator and taking him back to his lair, Halloway had moved among the cars, switching off the engines one by one. When the building was silent again he leaned against the balustrade, looking out at the distant towers of the city. Despite the moss-covered airliners by the terminal buildings, Halloway noticed that he was no longer thinking of his quest for his parents' apartment. Already the elements of a far grander scheme were forming in his mind.

They sat together in the dusk, listening to the steady beat of the generator on the roof, their faces lit by the glow of the barbecue.

With the same innocent guile that he used on his grandfather, Halloway said: 'Olds, you're a genius with cars. But can you start up anything else?'

Olds nodded soberly at Halloway, not taken in by him for a moment. He inspected his slim hands, as if resigned to the talents multiplying from his fingertips.

*Anything. I can make anything work.*

'I believe you, Olds. We'll find my sailplane and you can put an engine and propeller on it. Then I'll teach you how to fly.'

Early the next morning Olds and Halloway set off together from the airport. Olds selected, apparently at random, another breakdown vehicle from his stable of trucks and pick-ups on the first floor of the car park. Into the rear section, where a generator was bolted to the deck, he slung a leather tool-case and reels of power cable. He had recovered from his seizure of the previous afternoon. Something about the prospect of flying had given him back his self-confidence. As they left the airport, circling the pyramid of radiator grilles, he flicked a series of questions at Halloway.

*What engine size? How many horse-power?*

'I can't remember,' Halloway admitted. Already he was having to pretend that he had flown a powered craft. 'Big enough to drive a propeller. The size of this truck's?'

*Far too heavy. I'll find an aero-engine.*

They crossed the river and headed northwards through the city. At intervals Olds would check his fuel gauge, stop the truck in the centre of the street and leap out with a siphon hose. He moved around, shaking the parked cars and listening to the swish of fuel.

Once, while Olds was sucking away at his hose, Halloway strolled across the sidewalk to a small bar. A juke-box stood in the doorway, thick dust covering the extravagant plastic front. Halloway pressed the buttons at random, and then wandered off along the street.

When he returned five minutes later Olds had disappeared. The truck stood in the roadway, the engine of the power generator ticking over smoothly. The tool-bag had gone, and cables ran from the generator across the sidewalk.

'Olds! Let's go!'

Then he heard music coming from the bar. There was a jangle of coarse sound, a rapid beat of drums and guitars, and a rock-and-roll singer's voice bellowed across the empty street.

When he reached the bar he found Olds crouched behind the juke-box, tool-kit open on the floor. Like a leather carpet-bag fitted with hundreds of pockets, it seemed to contain every tool ever devised. Olds' arms were deep inside the entrails of the machine, hooking up a series of extension leads to a transformer.

When Halloway put his hands to his ears Olds switched off. He winked at Halloway.

*That's only a beginning.*

He was as good as his word. As they pressed on down the endless avenues lined with office-blocks, hotels and department-stores, Olds would stop the truck, seize his tool-kit and unwind his cables across the street. In rapid succession he started up three pintables in an amusement arcade, a line of washing machines in a launderette, a telex and two ticker-tapes in the ground-floor office of a commercial business, and a complete appliance range in a home equipment store. As if in rehearsal for some lunatic household, mixers whirred, fan-heaters pumped, vacuum cleaners roared, a dozen other gadgets clattered and whistled.

Watching all this, Halloway was impressed by the casual way Olds turned on these devices. They moved northwards, animating these minuscule portions of the city, leaving behind them these happy nodes of activity.

Confused by the noise and excitement, Halloway sat limply in the truck when they reached the mirror-sheathed office block into which he had crashed. The sailplane lay among the cars, its broken wings stirring in the light air. As Olds moved around it, inspecting the inverted cockpit with his gentle but shrewd eyes, Halloway half-expected him to reassemble the glider with a few waves of his screwdriver.

Olds pointed to the humpbacked cockpit, where the strengthened fuselage frame behind the pilot's seat formed a platform whose purpose Halloway had never understood.

*This is a real aircraft. Designed to take an engine. But you built it to look like a glider?*

'I know,' Halloway lied. 'I couldn't find the right power-plant.'

Olds' quick hands were exploring the interior of the fuselage.

*Runs for control lines. A fuel-tank compartment. It's well thought out. And room for both of us.*

'What?' Genuinely surprised, Halloway peered into the cockpit.

*Behind the pilot's bulkhead there's space for a passenger.*

As Olds pointed with the calculator, Halloway stared at what his father clearly designed to be a rear seat. Had his mother and father planned to leave him behind when they flew off? Or perhaps his father had intended to take his son with him, the two of them soaring back to the city together. Puzzled by these discoveries, he noticed Olds watching him in a shrewd but still kindly way. Did Olds really believe that Halloway had designed this powered glider himself? Was he using Halloway in exactly the same way that Halloway was trying to exploit him?

For the time being it hardly mattered. Halloway took the wheel for the return journey to the airport, after they dismantled the glider and lashed the sections to the truck. The power and noise of the engine erased all doubts. Barely controlling his excitement, he tried to hold down their speed as they raced through the streets.

'Olds! Watch this!'

They crossed a section of the roadway planted with poppies, the vivid but sinister flowers extending in front of them for three hundred yards. The bumper of the truck scythed through the flowers, and a dense cloud of petals billowed into the air, staining the sky like a miniature sunset. Halloway turned and made a second run through the poppies, almost standing at the wheel as they hurtled through the whirling petals.

As they approached the centre of the city Halloway drove around the side-streets, hunting out any other of these floral tracts planted here in the broken asphalt by some aberrant gardener. Soon millions of leaves were drifting through the coloured air. There were white streets where they found daisies, yellow avenues filled with a mist of crushed buttercups, blue boulevards which wept a rain of forget-me-nots.

Then, as they emerged from a storm of daffodil petals, Halloway nearly collided into a large industrial tractor moving along the roadway in front of him. Pulling to a halt behind its high rear assembly, he flung Olds on to the dashboard. Halloway switched off the engine, and watched this massive tracked vehicle lumbering slowly through the haze of petals. A hydraulic ram was mounted in front of the motor, fitted with an immense claw that now held a single automobile, carried in the air fifteen feet from the ground.

In the control cabin a dark-haired man in a black plastic jacket emblazoned with silver studs was operating the steering levers. His face was barely visible through the whirling petals, and he seemed unaware of the truck stalled behind him. However, when Halloway restarted his engine, intending to overtake the tractor, the driver swung his claw to the right, blocking Halloway with the swinging automobile. Looking up at the man's handsome face, with its hard mouth like a piece of gristle, Halloway was certain that it was this driver, and this terrifying machine, which had destroyed the garment store mannequins the previous day.

Halloway began to reverse the truck down the street, but Olds held his arm warningly.

*Follow him. Stillman needs to be given his own way.*

As Halloway moved forward, following the tractor, Olds sat back. He had switched off the calculator, and seemed to have forgotten their exhilarating race through the flowers, his mind moving elsewhere, bored by the prospect of whatever was to come.

They emerged into an open square, set in the heart of one of the oldest sections of the city, an area of theatres, bars and cheap hotels. Rising from the centre of the square was the largest of the eccentric memorials to Twentieth-Century technology that Halloway had seen so far. At first glance it resembled a gothic cathedral, built entirely from rusting iron, glass and chromium. As they crossed the square, following the tractor, Halloway realized that this structure was built entirely from the bodies of automobiles. Stacked one upon the other, they formed a palisade of towers that rose two hundred feet into the air.

A group of heavy cranes and a buttress of scaffolding marked out the working face, overlooked by an observation platform reached by a simple elevator. Standing at the rail, and waiting for the tractor to carry its latest contribution to the memorial, was a small, pugnacious man of advanced age. Although well into his eighties, he was dressed like a physical education instructor in immaculate white sweater and well-creased trousers. Inspecting Halloway's glider with a critical eye, he picked up an electric megaphone and began to call out instructions in a high voice to the driver of the tractor.

Olds was gazing up at the monument of cars, shaking his head as if ruefully aware that he and this odd old man were in the same business. He switched on the calculator.

*I'll wait for you here. You're about to meet Mr Buckmaster. Viceroy, czar, and warden of this island.*

Halloway waited as the driver climbed down from his cab. Deliberately taking his time, he sauntered over to Halloway, pointing to his red, white and blue sneakers, yellow trousers and shirt covered with petals.

'The Rainbow Kid – you come down from the sky and have yourself a time . . .'

Although twice Halloway's age, with slicked-back hair and a pale skin that would always appear dirty, he had a lazy, youthful aura, as if a large section of his life had passed in his absence and he himself had never aged beyond his twenties. For all his sarcastic manner, he seemed watchful and ready to ingratiate himself at a moment's notice. With his self-directed aggression and stylized swagger he was a type Halloway had never known at Garden City, but which all his reading confirmed was a classic specimen of metropolitan man.

'Take the elevator,' he told Halloway. 'Mr Buckmaster has been waiting to meet you. He'll want to induct you into his workforce.'

'This monument – and the others? He built them all?'

'*I* built them. Buckmaster merely dreamed up the whole mad idea. Homage to the Chrysler Corporation, Datsun and General Motors. When we've finished, the spirit of Karl Benz will be laid to rest under a million driver's licences and parking tickets.'

He slammed the elevator grille in Halloway's face and punched the ascend button.

The old man in his whites was waiting for Halloway when he reached the observation platform. On a card-table lay a set of blueprints, and Halloway could see that if ever completed the structure would rise some four hundred feet into the air.

The old man beckoned Halloway to the rail. Everything about him, his quick eyes and mouth, his restless hands, was in a hurry. He talked to Halloway as if he had known him for years and was resuming a conversation interrupted only a few seconds earlier.

'It looks a mess, eh? Just a pile of automobiles, a million junkyards are full of them. What do I think I'm doing? Wait and see.' He pointed to Halloway's glider on the back of the truck, where Olds was already tearing away the torn fabric. 'Is that a glider or a power-plane? During the war I built thirty thousand fighters for the government, we were turning them out so fast the Air Force kept the war going just to get rid of them. And that was on top of a hundred airships, cargo-submarines and enough spare parts to give every man on this planet his own robot-assembly kit. Then I re-tooled and flooded the world with wristwatch TVs, compressed paper houses, a million gimmicks. Techniques of mass production raised to the nth power. Do you remember my protein synthesizer?' He glanced at Halloway, who nodded promptly. 'No, you're too young. No bigger than a suitcase, you put it under your bed at night and it ran off your sweat and body temperature. Somehow it didn't catch on, but I would have fed a starving world, lifted the population of this planet to fifty billion in comfort. I was ready to build them super-cities, the first conurbation conglomerates, the mega-metropolis larger than any individual nation-state. I designed the first collapsible city, interchangeable parts moving around on gigantic rails. Makes sense – if a theatre isn't being used by day, wheel it off and roll on an office-block. Instead of which' – here he raised his ancient hands eloquently to the empty streets – 'they all just gave up and faded away. Goodbye, C20 Man, hello Arcadia, that timid world of waterwheels and solar batteries. Not that there's an unlimited future for tidal power. Every time one of those pontoons nods its head the planet slows down a little. The days are getting longer . . .'

He turned away from the rail, and put a hard arm around Halloway's shoulder. 'Now, you've come to work for me? It's too late, I closed down my last design office ten years ago.' He steered Halloway to the elevator, nodding sagely to himself as they rode down together. 'A pity, you could have done great things with those hands. Anyway, you can work for Stillman, there's more than he can do.'

'Well . . .' Halloway glanced at the black-jacketed driver, standing beside the tractor with one hand on the automobile suspended in the air over his head. 'I was thinking of setting up on my own.'

'Good for you – but it's all over. There's nothing to do now but close it down. Give it a humane burial, put up a monument here and there to Twentieth-Century technology, to all those things we took for granted – tyres, engines, TVs, kitchen appliances, automobiles . . .'

His voice wavered for the first time and then stopped, as he gazed up wistfully at his cathedral of cars. Waiting for this strange old man to start again, Halloway remembered that he had seen his combative jaw and dreamer's eyes in the architecture textbooks in his grandfather's library. Buckmaster had been the last of the great entrepreneur-industrialists, part architect and engineer, part visionary, driven on by old-fashioned crankiness, ceaseless originality and a well-developed talent for seizing the headlines. Grandiose projects started all over the world and then abandoned to rivals and pupils, a succession of wives, the third of whom died in a mysterious scandal, lawsuits against any number of governments, plans for the first trans-Atlantic bridge – these were elements in a stormy career spanning nearly seventy years. Although Buckmaster was clearly living a century too late there was something about his unflagging energy and resolve that fired a response in Halloway's mind. He couldn't help contrasting Buckmaster's limitless appetite for steel, power, concrete and raw materials with the self-denying, defeatist lives of the engineers and architects at Garden City. There was even a fringe group of scientific fanatics – the so-called 'heliophiles' – whose ambition was to return energy to the sun by firing off all the old missiles with nuclear warheads, repaying the sun for its billion-year bounty.

He followed Buckmaster into the interior of the memorial, uneasily aware that this cathedral of rust might collapse at any time. At the far end of the nave the semi-circle of internal walls had been transformed into a lavish botanical garden. Terrace upon terrace of climbing plants hung from the chassis of the cars, brilliant flowers bloomed in the windows and wheel-wells. The golden bells of forsythia trailed from the windows of grand limousines a hundred feet in the air, the white mist of mile-a-minute vines hovered like steam above the radiator grilles and exhaust pipes.

Apparently unaware that this cascade of blossoms was already transforming his monument into a far more bizarre structure than he had visualized, Buckmaster began to point out various details of the construction. But Halloway was more interested in the hanging garden. A young woman was working at the flowers, taking nasturtium and petunia seedlings from a series of trays and planting them in the doors and windows. As she moved about, climbing up and down a high ladder, Halloway had difficulty in guessing her age. At Garden City the emancipated women wore simple home-woven smocks and jerkins indistinguishable from the men's. With undressed hair and devoid of make-up, their sexual roles were always explicit, desire worn casually on their sleeves.

By contrast, this young woman – his daughter Miranda, Buckmaster informed him – was dressed like the heroine of a lavishly costumed period musical. Everything about her, from her extravagant copper-tinted hair in a Pre-Raphaelite cut to her long white neck and embroidered art-nouveau gown, was calculated for concealment and effect, artifice and allure. Later, Halloway discovered that she changed her appearance every day, moving through the deserted boutiques and fashion-houses of the city, modelling herself on the vanished styles of the Twentieth Century. On one day she would appear in a cream cloche hat and Gatsby gown, on another in a lurex blouse, bobby sox and teenager's flared tartan skirt.

Buckmaster introduced Halloway to her. 'Miranda, a new recruit – Mr Halloway, an aviator from Garden City. Any more like him and I may have to think again about opening my design office.'

As the old man wandered around, nodding at the profusion of flowers, Halloway searched for something to say. In his yellow trousers and multi-coloured sneakers he was as much in costume as Buckmaster's daughter, but he felt gauche and clumsy beside her. Although she was his own age, there was something naive, and at the same time knowing and sophisticated, about Miranda. He guessed that he was the first young man of eighteen she had met, but that she had done a great deal of thinking about the subject and for all her shyness was well prepared to deal with him on her own terms.

'We watched you driving around,' she told him matter-of-factly and without any rancour. 'Killing all those flowers – in a way it must have been fun.'

'Well . . .' Lamely, Halloway tried to apologize. He helped her down the ladder, relieved when she was on his own level. There was something unsettling about the way she had looked down at him, surrounded by the vine-infested cars. 'I didn't realize that they were yours. I'll help you to plant them again – they'll soon grow.'

'I know.' She strolled around him, picking the petals from his shirt, as if removing spots of blood. 'Sometimes I feel like the daughter of some great magician – wherever I touch, a flower springs up.'

Halloway brushed away the last of the petals. His difficulty in talking to her stemmed partly from her ambiguity, the naively teasing sexual come-on, but more from his own inexperience. In Garden City the relations between young people were governed by the most enlightened rules, derived from the teachings of Malinowski, Margaret Mead and the anthropologists who had followed them. From the age of sixteen, in the approved Polynesian style, young people of both sexes lived together openly in the 'long house' dormitories set aside for them until they later chose their marriage partner. Halloway had opted out of this, for reasons he had never understood, so committing himself to the company of his grandparents on one side and the younger teenagers on the other. He had never regretted the decision – there was something far too amiable, far too bovine and uncritical, about the hand-holding tenants of the long house.

Now, as he watched Miranda admiring his coloured sneakers, swirling her embroidered dress around him, he was certain that he was right. That ambiguity she showed, that moody combination of challenge and allure, was exactly what the city was about.

'I saw your glider yesterday,' Miranda told him. 'Crossing the Sound. It was like part of a dream, miles away across the water. Now suddenly you're here, in your miracle shoes.'

'I dream about powered flight,' Halloway told her with some pride. 'Olds and I are rebuilding the glider. When it's ready we'll put an engine on it.'

Miranda nodded, gazing up at her hanging garden, as if waiting patiently for the jungle to return. In some way she seemed almost at odds with her father, trying to undo his work and transform it for her own purposes.

'Halloway . . .' She touched his arm. 'My father's very old. I want him to finish this before it's too late. Stillman's losing interest. Will you work for us for a while?'

The next day Halloway joined Stillman's one-man construction gang. He had said goodbye to Olds, who returned with the sailplane to the airport, and spent the night in one of the small hotels around the square.

Riding on the cowling of the tractor's engine, Halloway squatted in front of the driving cab as Stillman roved the city, searching for the exact models of the cars that Buckmaster had ordered. Each one they carried back to the monument, and Halloway climbed the wall of vehicles and guided Stillman as he steered the largest of the cranes and inserted the car into its place. From the observation platform the old industrialist supervised the work from behind his blueprints. Meanwhile his daughter, dressed for the day in a 1940s business suit, with boxy shoulders and a skirt of brown pin-stripe, her hair in a frizz, moved silently among the flowers in the centre of the memorial, tending the vines and blossoms in this dark, humid arbour.

His involvement with this strange trio surprised Halloway, but he soon realized that each of them played a role in certain unfolding obsessions of his own. Of the three, Stillman with his black jacket and hoodlum style most disturbed and most stimulated him, brooding over a dark dream of the city so like Halloway's own.

As they drove back through the streets on that first day Halloway had an unsettling glimpse of Stillman's unpredictable violence. The massive tractor was clanking down a wide avenue, a yellow taxi-cab held in its claw, when they passed a department store. Halloway was sitting in front of the cab, and was nearly flung to the road as Stillman slammed back the left-hand drive lever and turned the tractor towards the sidewalk. Cars were parked nose to tail along the kerb, but Stillman drove straight into them, knocking them out of his way with powerful left and right swings of the taxi. Gripped by the claw, the battered vehicle showered glass and rust on to the road. Working the levers and throttle with hard and almost spasm-like thrusts of his arms and shoulders, Stillman drove the tractor towards the store. His jaws champed rapidly on a piece of gum, but his face was deliberately expressionless, part of a continuous stylization of gesture and movement that Halloway had never seen before and that excited and disturbed him at the same time.

A group of mannequins sat in the store window around a table, part of a mock dinner-party that had started twenty-five years earlier and never proceeded beyond the waxy hors d'oeuvres. The polite poses and prim over-elegant manners clearly pulled a hair-trigger in Stillman's mind. As the plate glass collapsed into the sidewalk he slung aside the taxi, sending it rolling across the street, and then began to sweep the mannequins out of the window, scattering them on to the sidewalk.

As he watched the destruction of these smartly attired female figures, Halloway was thinking of Miranda and her obsessive changes of costume. Was this her way of containing Stillman, or of provoking him? Stillman stared at her with a kind of humourless irony, as if forming in his mind a series of obscene jokes about her. Only his deference to the old industrialist seemed to prevent him from assaulting Miranda.

Seizing the yellow taxi again, Stillman set off down the street, the shattered mannequins lying in their tailored rags like the well-to-do victims of a terrorist attack in a fashionable shopping centre. Halloway was shaking with excitement, barely able to keep his seat on the engine cowling. For all his fear of Stillman, he knew that he was half-hoping that he would be violent again. He imagined the city filled with people, their lives invigorated by just this kind of callous and stylized aggression. When they passed another clothing store with a group of mannequins in the window he tapped the windshield and pointed them out to Stillman.

Later, when Buckmaster and his daughter retired to their third-floor suite in a hotel facing the monument of cars, Stillman and Halloway wandered through the dusk towards a nearby park. Stillman broke into a gunshop, and from the racks behind the counter took down a sporting rifle and shotgun. Pockets filled with cartridges, they strolled into the park, and in the evening light shot quail and a small deer. The roar of gunfire, the coarse smell of the cordite and the hard recoil against his arms and shoulders, the terrified movement of thousands of birds and animals as they fled through the forest, together filled Halloway's head with fantasies of violence.

Stillman occupied a penthouse apartment on the twentieth floor of a block facing the park.

'It's a long climb,' he warned Halloway. 'But I like to sit up there in the morning and watch dinner grazing down below.'

On the open terrace they lit a fire with pieces of furniture taken from the other apartments. Around them the walls of the city rose into the night. As he roasted the quail and turned the deer on its spit Halloway could see the flames reflected in thousands of darkened windows, as if the night were on fire. They sat together in armchairs by the embers flaring in the wind, and Stillman talked about the city, of the period he could just remember when it had been filled with more than a million people, the streets packed with traffic and the skies with helicopters, a realm of ceaseless noise and activity, competition and crime. It was here, in fact, as a young student at the school of architecture, that Stillman had first met Buckmaster. Within six months he had killed the industrialist's third wife in a lovers' quarrel. The last murderer to be tried and convicted before the emigration from the cities began in earnest, he was sentenced to twenty years' imprisonment. Eighteen years later, rotting away in an empty penitentiary, the sole prisoner looked after by one aged warder, he had been freed by Buckmaster, who took him on his own parole in a strange gesture. Now he worked for the old man, operating the heavy lifting equipment and helping him to build his monuments to a vanished age of technology. All the while he could barely contain his anger at finding the city he had longed for through so many years an empty and abandoned shell.

Halloway listened to him without speaking. When Stillman finished and lay back in his armchair, staring at the embers of the fire and the bones scattered at his feet, Halloway walked to the balustrade and looked at the dark buildings around them.

'Stillman – it isn't too late. It's all waiting for us here. We can start it up again. Olds can bring it back to life for us.'

During the next month, as he continued to work for the old industrialist on his memorials, Halloway began his self-appointed task of reanimating this huge metropolis. The cathedral of cars now reached to a height of three hundred feet, an eccentric but impressive structure of steel, glass and chrome. As it neared completion Buckmaster began to slow down, as if aware that this last monument would mark the end of his life and career.

Free during the afternoons, Halloway returned to Stillman's apartment house. Invariably he found the slim patient figure of Olds standing beside his breakdown truck. The mute's hopes of learning to fly, his dream of escape from the thousands of cars that surrounded him at the airport and the memories of his accident, had become the central obsession of his life. On the one afternoon when Halloway could spare the time to visit the airport he found his sailplane on the roof of the car park, tethered to the sloping concrete deck like a prisoner of the sky. Olds had rebuilt the wings and fuselage, and was already preparing a fifty horse-power engine and propeller to be mounted above the cockpit.

Nodding his approval, Halloway noticed that the museum of cars was already showing signs of neglect. Dust filmed the once immaculate coachwork, leaves and tags of paper lay against the unwiped windshields. As Olds gazed at the sailplane the calculator in his hand flickered continuously.

*Halloway, we'll leave soon. When I've assembled the engine.*

'Of course,' Halloway reassured him. 'We're going together, I know.'

*Flying lessons?*

There was panic in the quivering letters.

*I can't fly yet!*

'Olds, naturally. You won't find it difficult – look at the way you handle machinery, you're a genius.'

But Olds was only interested in the aircraft. In the aviation section of one of the city's science museums he found a leather flying suit and helmet dating back to World War I. He took to wearing the costume, his slight figure and scarred head encased in this antique aviator's gear.

For the time being, Halloway decided to humour him. Olds was essential to his plan to restart the city, and without his electrical and mechanical skills the metropolis would remain as dead as a tomb. In return for the promise of flying lessons, Olds drove in from the airport each afternoon, equipped with his generators, cables and tool-kit.

Sceptical of Halloway's ambitious scheme, Stillman wandered through the densely forested park with his rifle, killing the birds. Meanwhile Olds fitted the apartment house with its own electricity supply. A gasolene-driven generator in the entrance hall was soon pounding away, its power supply plugged into the mains. Even this small step immediately brought the building alive. Halloway moved from one apartment to the next, flicking lights on and off, working the appliances in the kitchens. Mixers chattered, toasters and refrigerators hummed, warning lights glowed in control panels. Most of the equipment, barely used during the long period of power cuts twenty-five years earlier, was still in functioning order. Television sets came on, radios emitted a ghostly tonelessness interrupted now and then by static from the remote-controlled switching units of the tidal pumps twenty miles away along the Sound.

However, in the tape-recorders, stereo-systems and telephone answering machines Halloway at last found the noise he needed to break the silence of the city. At first, playing through these tapes of conversations recorded by husbands and wives in the last years of the Twentieth Century, Halloway was disturbed by the anxious queries and despairing messages that described the slow collapse of an entire world. The sense of gloom and psychic entropy that came through these reminders to queue for gasolene and cooking oil were the absolute opposite of the vigour and dynamism he had expected.

But the music was different. Almost every apartment seemed to be a broadcasting station of its own. Bursting with crude confidence, the music transformed these ghost-filled rooms into a battery of nightclubs. He moved from floor to floor, blowing the dust from records and cassettes, switching on each of the apartments in turn. Rock-and-roll, big band, jazz and pop boomed through the open windows at the silent park. Even Stillman was impressed, looking up in surprise from the waist-high grass, shotgun raised hesitantly to the air as if thinking twice about trying to make an equal noise.

'Olds, it works!' Halloway found him resting by the generator in the lobby. 'If we can switch on this building we can switch on the whole city! Take off that flying cap and we'll start now.'

Reluctantly, Olds peeled off his helmet. He smiled ungrudgingly at Halloway, clearly admiring the energy and enthusiasm of this excited young man, but at the same time he seemed to be estimating his degree of involvement with Halloway. Although surrounded by his tools and cables, ammeters and transformers, his mind was clearly miles away, in the cockpit of the glider on the roof of the car park. He looked bored by what he was doing, hardly the mechanic to the world whom Halloway needed.

Halloway noticed that Olds had found a second calculator. The two instruments lay side by side on the floor, the fragments of an extended private dialogue flicking to and fro under the Negro's fingers. For the first time Halloway felt impatient.

'Olds – do you want flying lessons or not? If you can't help me I'll find someone else.' Enjoying his aggressive manner, he added, 'Old Buckmaster will know someone.'

*I'll help you, Halloway.*

*For one flying lesson.*

So Olds joined Halloway in his grand design. While Halloway drove over to the airport to collect the generators stored in the basement of the car park, Olds worked away at the apartment block, repairing the elevator and air-conditioning units. With almost magical ease he moved around the building, opening fuse-boxes, trailing cable from a second generator to the motors in the elevator head. When Halloway returned he found Olds serenely raising the elevator like a moody but elegant trapeze artist.

'Olds – it's unbelievable . . .' Halloway congratulated him, careful to add, 'Wait until you repair the jet planes at the airport.'

Olds shook his head, watching Halloway reflectively, not taken in by him for a moment.

*A little too much – even for me.*

'Nothing is – now, we'll help Mr Buckmaster.'

Leaving a dozen stereograms to blare their music into the empty streets, Halloway and Olds set off for the mausoleum. Buckmaster was resting in his bedroom. Flattered by Halloway's concern, he watched with approval from his balcony as Olds manhandled a generator into the lobby and ran the cables up to his suite.

From the breakdown truck Halloway unloaded a battery of six arc-lights he had removed from the façade of the airport terminal building.

'We'll set them up around the square, sir,' Halloway explained. 'At night you'll be able to see the whole monument floodlit.'

Buckmaster strolled across the square, his sharp eyes following Halloway with some curiosity as he darted enthusiastically around the cathedral of cars, setting the arc-lights in position. Deep in the nave of the monument Miranda was at work on the terraces of her hanging garden. Dressed today in blue jeans and a hippy jacket, a child's beads around her wrists, she was placing petunias and nasturtiums among the radiator grilles thirty feet above the ground. During the previous days Halloway had been too busy to make contact with her. Besides, her fey manner unsettled him. There seemed to be something decadent about this obsessive planting of vines and flowers, an unconscious but all the more sinister attempt to bring back a lurid and over-bright nature red in tooth and claw. Halloway had begun to hate the carpets of blossoms, these creepers and climbing plants that threatened to strangle the city before he could release it. Already he was thinking of the defoliants he had noticed in a chemical supplies store.

'I'm grateful to you, Halloway,' Buckmaster told him as they walked back to the hotel. 'There's a sense of style about you that I like, all too rare these days, you belong to a vanished breed – Brunel, Eiffel, Lloyd Wright, Kaiser, Buckmaster. For once, though, don't pitch your dreams too high. What happens when the gas runs out? You're going to have a second energy crisis all your own.'

Halloway shook his head confidently. 'Sir, there are millions of cars here. The tankers at the airport – some of them are half-full of aviation fuel, enough to keep us going for a year. After that' – Halloway gestured at the air – 'we'll find something else.'

His hand on Halloway's shoulder, Buckmaster listened to the sound of the generator coming to life in the lobby. He watched the arc-lights pulse briefly and then blaze out, almost over-heating the sunshine. For all the old industrialist's caution, Halloway could sense Buckmaster's excitement. Halloway was glad of this. For some reason he wanted to impress him. He was aware that the image of his father, which had propelled him towards the city, had recently begun to fade in his mind, confined to the sailplane tethered like an imprisoned bird on the roof of the car park.

Halloway pointed at the deserted streets around the square. 'There's so much that should have happened here that never did,' he explained to Buckmaster. 'I want to bring everything alive again, and give back to the city all that lost time.'

During the next weeks Halloway embarked on his grandiose scheme to re-animate the city. From the start he knew that the task of literally bringing back to life the whole of this huge metropolis was beyond the skills of even a hundred men like Olds. However, in a symbolic sense the task could be achieved on a more modest scale.

Adjoining the northern side of the square was a cluster of side-streets that formed a self-sufficient neighbourhood cut off from the fifty-storey buildings surrounding it. By chance, this enclave, little more than a block in extent, contained the whole city in miniature. There were modest hotels and theatres, bars and restaurants, even a police station and one television studio. Wandering around these narrow streets in the afternoons, Halloway noticed that the stores and offices, banks and supermarkets had been built to a smaller scale than in the rest of the city, and at a time before the zoning ordinances which would have excluded the light factories erected in back-yards, the auto-repair shops in converted garages. On the first floors above the bars and shops were dozens of one-man businesses, minor printing works and travel agencies, tailors and TV repairers.

Sitting on a stool in an empty bar, Halloway calculated that the working population of this city-in-miniature would have been little more than 2000 in its heyday. Even now, a hundred people like himself would be able to get most of its activities going again.

Through the weeks that followed, Halloway and Olds, with grudging help from Stillman, began the task of bringing this neighbourhood back to life. Olds drove in from the airport with a yellow-hulled fuel tanker, filled with enough aviation spirit to power a hundred generators for a month. Tirelessly, he moved in and out of the inspection tunnels below the sidewalks, opening up the electricity sub-stations and feeding down fresh cable. Meanwhile Halloway cut away the tangle of overhead wires that crossed the streets in steel webs, and then he and Olds began the laborious task of re-wiring the roadways. First the street lights came on, filling these deserted thoroughfares with an eerie brilliance, then the traffic signals and pedestrian control signs. Stillman cleared away the hundreds of derelict cars that lined the streets, leaving some twenty vehicles that Olds decided he could renovate.

Supervising all this activity, Halloway drove around in a black-and-white police car whose engine the young Negro had brought to life. Halloway had made the local police station his operational headquarters. The lavish wall-maps and communications equipment, the electric alarm signals that ran to so many of the stores and businesses, even the clandestine listening devices which the police had bugged in to many of the bars and hotels, made the station a natural headquarters.

Often working a dozen hours a day, Halloway pressed on, too tired in the evenings to do more than fall asleep in his apartment two floors below Stillman's. Despite all their efforts, however, the chaos seemed to grow rather than diminish. Piles of garbage covered the sidewalks, dozens of generators and fuel drums blocked the doorways of the bars and supermarkets, everywhere there were sections of dismantled switchboards and circuitry.

But one afternoon, after returning from the airport with a small lathe for Olds, he knew that he had succeeded.

A hundred yards from the station he was approaching a minor street intersection when the traffic lights turned from green to red. Laughing aloud at himself for obeying this solitary signal in an empty city of ten thousand intersections, in which he was its only traffic policeman, Halloway nonetheless pulled to a halt and waited until the lights changed to green. An important principle was at stake. Later, as he sat in the cabin of Stillman's tractor, bulldozing the piles of garbage and collapsed electric signs out of the streets, Halloway reflected that he was not working for himself alone. In the three supermarkets within the reclamation zone he drained the freezer compartments, swept the aisles and re-stacked the pyramids of canned goods, like a dedicated resort hotelier preparing for an invasion army of tourists. Three taxi-cabs, each in running order, stood outside the neighbourhood's leading hotel. One by one the streets were cleared of debris and abandoned cars, the sidewalks were free from garbage, the plate-glass shopfronts gleamed anew.

Amused but impressed by the transformation, Stillman at last decided to take part. At first, Halloway was reluctant to recruit this deviant figure. Every day Halloway heard him moving around the city, the violent explosions of breaking steel and glass as he dragged down another department-store portico and ran his tracks over the mannequins. In the evenings, as they sat together on the flood-lit terrace of the penthouse, Stillman would gaze resentfully across the roasting deer, as if annoyed that the dark dream of the city which had sustained him for so long should be brought to life in so naive a fashion by this idealistic youth. Then, one evening when Halloway was rhapsodizing about the harshness and vitality of his neat and immaculate streets, Stillman brusquely shut him up and announced that he would join the reclamation project. Clearly he had decided to inject some real life into this toy-town neighbourhood. He curtly turned down Halloway's suggestion that he take over the renovation of a store selling kitchen equipment.

'That's not my style, Halloway. I leave the domestic sciences to you. My expertise lies in other areas . . .'

In no time Stillman had staked out two amusement arcades, several bars and a small nightclub in the basement of an office block. Once Olds had supplied electric current Stillman set to work with a will, moving at a far swifter pace than his usual surly languor had ever previously allowed. The amusement arcades were soon a blaze of garish lights. Pinball machines chattered and clanged, score numerals stuttered. In the communications room of the police station Halloway sat by the monitor screen of the traffic-control television system, watching the multicoloured lights ripple across the sidewalks.

Stillman had stripped down the punctured neon signs above the bars and arcades. From a warehouse discovered somewhere he brought in a truckload of intact signs, massive pieces of electrographic architecture that dominated the whole of Halloway's neighbourhood. Giant letters dripped across the night sky, cascades of pink light fell mushily across the façade of his nightclub, the winged emblems of long-vanished airlines pulsed through the overloaded air, the roof-sills of bars and amusement arcades were trimmed with tubes of racing fluorescence.

Watching uneasily on his TV monitor, Halloway wondered how to put a stop to this lurid invasion. At dusk, as the surrounding city grew dark, he left the police station and cruised the streets in his squad-car, listening to the generators beating in the basements and alleyways, the tireless hearts pumping out this haemorrhage of light. He knew now why Stillman had been so dismissive of his laborious restocking of offices and supermarkets. It was only now, in this raucous light and noise, that the city was being its true self, only in this flood of cheap neon that it was really alive.

Halloway parked outside a bank he had begun to reclaim. Olds' tool-bags and equipment trolleys were by the doorway. He had been working on the electrically operated vault doors before leaving for the airport, and the piles of old banknotes lay exposed in their metal trays. Halloway looked down at the bales of notes, worthless now but a fortune thirty years earlier. In Garden City money was never used, and had given way to a sophisticated system of barter and tithes-giving that eliminated the abuses of credit, instalment-buying and taxation.

Touching the banknotes, with their subtle progression from one denomination to the next, a means of quantifying the value of everything, its promise and obligation, Halloway watched the garish lights of the neon signs in the street flicker across his hands. He was glad that Stillman had transformed this staid and well-swept thoroughfare. They needed workers for the stores and offices and production lines, and they needed visitors for the hotels and bars. They would need money, as well, to oil the engine of competition.

Halloway locked away the trays of banknotes and slipped the keys into his pocket. There were thousands of other banks in the city, but in the printing shop next to the police station Olds would over-print the notes with Halloway's frank. The thought pleased him – to have reached the point of issuing his own currency meant that success was really at hand.

He ended his evening rounds at the square. Lit by the arc-lights, Buckmaster's memorial of cars rose over three hundred feet into the air, a cathedral of rust. The vines and flowers that climbed its sides looked dead in the fierce light. Halloway was glad to see that their once vivid colours were blanched out by the powerful glare. A dozen reflections in the dark buildings around the square transformed it into a mortuary plain of illuminated tombs.

Buckmaster stood on the steps of his hotel, looking with obvious pleasure at this huge spectacle. Miranda, however, watching from a window above, stared at Halloway with equally clear hostility. That afternoon Halloway had stripped the last of the poppies and forget-me-nots from the avenues around the reclamation zone. As he crossed the square at the controls of the tractor, the bale of flowers in the metal scoop like a multicoloured haystack, Miranda followed him through the streets, catching in her white hands the loose petals that drifted in the air.

Now, on her balcony, she was dressed in a bizarre Barbarella costume of silver metal and glass, like a science-fiction witch about to take her revenge on Halloway.

Unaware of his daughter's anger, Buckmaster took Halloway's arm and pointed to a building across the square, the offices of a former newspaper. A frieze of electric letters that had once carried a continuous news strip had been repaired by Olds, a city-sized replica of the display panels of his pocket calculators. Letters began to race from right to left.

'Halloway, they ought to hand you the mayoral chain, my boy, and put your name up there, high, wide and handsome!'

But already the first message was flashing past.

*OLDS! OLDS! OLDS! OLDS! OLDS!*

Delighted by this, Halloway joined Buckmaster and rode the elevator with the old industrialist to the observation platform beside his cathedral. As they stepped out, however, a new message was racing across the display sign.

*DANGER! FIVE MILES NORTH-EAST. INVASION PARTY COMING.*

Two days later, when the rescue expedition arrived, Halloway was ready to deal with them in his own way. During that first night after Olds had given the alarm he spent the long hours until dawn in the top-floor offices of the newspaper building. Soon after sunrise he watched the landing party disembark from their sailing vessel, a three-master whose white aluminium sails and white steel hull stood out against the dark water like chiselled bone. Using binoculars, Halloway immediately identified the ship, a barquentine built by the Garden City administrative council.

Halloway had taken for granted that a rescue party would one day come to search for him. Presumably they had been scouring the shore along the northern coast of the Sound, and had now decided to explore the city itself, no doubt guided there by the sudden efflorescence of light each evening, this neon pleasure-drome that had come to life among the silent tower-blocks.

An hour after dawn Halloway drove north through the city in his squad-car. He left the vehicle half a mile from the landing point and walked ahead through the deserted streets. The white masts and square metal fore-sail of the barquentine rose above the buildings near the quay where she had docked. There was no rigging – remote-controlled by an in-board computer that assessed tides, course and wind-velocity, the ship was the ultimate in the technology of sail.

Halloway climbed on to the roof of an appliance store and watched the expedition party come ashore. There were ten people in the group, all members of the Garden City gliding club – Halloway recognized the architect and his twelve-year-old son, and the elderly hydrographer with the red beard. As they unloaded their bicycles and wicker hampers they reminded Halloway of a Victorian picnic party exploring a nature reserve. Had he really spent his life with these quiet, civilized and anaemic people? Amused by them, but already bored by the whole absurd business, he watched them adjust their bicycle clips and tyre pressures. Their polite and gentle manners, the timid way in which they gazed down the empty streets, had given him all the ideas he needed on how to deal with them.

As Halloway had guessed, it took the rescue party a full two days to reach the centre of the city. During the mornings they pedalled forward at a sedate pace, cautiously making their way through the abandoned cars and festoons of rusting telephone wire. There were endless pauses to consult their maps and take refreshment. They had even brought a portable recycling unit with them, and carefully reprocessed their kitchen and other wastes. By early afternoon they were already pitching their elaborate tents and laying out their complex camping equipment.

Luckily, it was almost dusk when they finally reached the central square. On the television monitor in the police station Halloway watched them dismount from their bicycles and stare with amazement at Buckmaster's towering monument. Lit by a single floodlight inside the nave the memorial rose above the darkened square, the hundreds of windows and radiator grilles shining like the facets of an immense glowing jewel.

The party edged forward tentatively, gripping their bicycle handlebars for moral support. All around them the streets were dark and silent. Then, as they all bent down to take off their trouser clips, Halloway leaned across his control console and began to throw the switches.

Later, when he looked back on this episode, Halloway relished his routing of the rescue party and only wished that he had recorded it on the traffic control videotape system. For thirty minutes total pandemonium had broken loose in the square and nearby streets. As a hundred generators roared into life, pouring electric current into the grid, arc-lights blazed around the square, freezing his would-be rescuers in their tracks. The façades of the buildings around the square erupted into a cataract of neon. Traffic lights beckoned and signalled. From the loudspeakers which Olds had strung across the streets came a babel of sound – police sirens howling, jet aircraft taking off, trains slamming through junctions, car horns blaring, all the noises of the city in its heyday which Halloway had found in a speciality record shop.

As this visual and acoustic nightmare broke loose around the members of the rescue party, Halloway left the communications room and ran down to the street. As he climbed into his police car Stillman swerved past in his white gangster's limousine. Racing after him, Halloway switched on his siren. He reached the square and hurtled around it, cornering on two wheels in the way approved by the stunt-drivers in the fifty-year-old crime films which Stillman had screened for him in his nightclub that afternoon.

For the next fifteen minutes, as the noise of police sirens and aircraft, machine-gun fire and express trains sounded through the streets, Halloway and Stillman put on their mock car chase, pursuing each other around the square, plunging out of narrow alleys and swerving across the sidewalks, driving the terrified members of the rescue party in front of them. Stillman, inevitably, soon went too far, knocking the bicycles out of their hands and crushing two of the complex machines against a fire hydrant. In fact, Halloway was certain that if they had not turned tail and run at least one member of the party would have been killed.

Abandoning their equipment and sharing the remaining bicycles, it took them less than six hours to reach the ship and set sail. Long after they had gone, when Halloway had switched off the recorded sounds and dimmed the neon lights, Stillman continued to drive around the square in his white limousine, jumping the lights at the traffic intersections, tirelessly wheeling the big car in and out of the alleys and side-streets, as if deranged by this dream-come-true of the violent city.

From the communications room at the police station Halloway watched Stillman's car swerving around the square. Somehow he would have to find a means of containing Stillman before he destroyed everything they had done. Tired out by all the noise and action, Halloway reached forward to switch off the monitor, when he realized that he was no longer the only spectator of Stillman's disturbed driving.

Standing in the portico of a deserted bank, their slim figures almost hidden by the high columns, were two boys in their late teens. Despite the shiny plastic suitcases and their flamboyant shoes and jackets – presumably taken from the stores on the outskirts of the city – Halloway was certain that they had come from one of the pastoral settlements. On their Garden City faces was a childlike expectation, an innocent but clear determination to seize the life of the metropolis.

Switching on the loudspeaker system so that he could talk to them, Halloway picked up the microphone. The first of his people had arrived to take their places in his city.

It had been another successful day. On the television monitor in the police commissioner's office Halloway watched the activity in the avenue below. It was five o'clock in the afternoon, and the rush-hour traffic was beginning to build up. The sidewalks were thronged by more than a dozen pedestrians, leaving their offices and workshops on their way to the neighbourhood bars and supermarkets. A hundred yards from the station, six cars were blocking an intersection where the lights had failed. Their horns sounded impatiently above the street noise.

Halloway spoke to the desk sergeant in the orderly room. 'Get a man over to the Seventh Avenue intersection. There's a faulty green light holding up the traffic.'

'He's already left, Mr Halloway.'

'Good – if we don't watch it now there'll be chaos in an hour or two.'

These minor breakdowns were a pleasant challenge to Halloway. Even now, as one of Stillman's young men ignored the stuttering red light and the outstretched arm of the police constable, Halloway was in no way annoyed. In a sense, these displays of aggression pleased him, confirming everything he had hoped about the reclamation scheme. The pedestrians in the street below strode along purposefully, pushing past each other with scant courtesy. There was no trace here of good humour and pastoral docility.

In an alleyway facing the station a diesel generator was pumping out dense clouds of sooty smoke. A three-man repair gang recently trained by Olds had emptied the sump oil across the sidewalk, in clear contravention of the local ordinances. But, again, Halloway made no attempt to reprimand them. If anything, he had done what he could to frustrate any efforts to bring in stricter clear-air regulations. Pollution was part of the city, a measure of its health. All the so-called ills that had beset this huge metropolis in its prime had visited themselves with flattering haste on Halloway's small enclave. Pollution, traffic congestion, inadequate municipal services, inflation and deficit public financing had all promptly reappeared.

Halloway had even been pleased when the first crime was committed. During the previous night several clothing stores had been broken into, and pilfering from the supermarkets went on continuously. Halloway had spoken to Stillman about the light-fingered behaviour of his entourage. Lounging back with his young cronies in his 1920s gangster limousine, Stillman had merely flicked the sharp lapels of his dove-grey suit and pointed out that petty crime helped to keep the economy running.

'Relax, Halloway, it's all part of the problem of urban renewal. Do I complain that some of your boys are on the take? You've got to increase turnover. You're working these poor devils so hard they haven't time to spend their pay. If they've got anything left by the end of the week, that is. This is a real high-rent area you've set up for them. Any time now you'll have a housing crisis on your hands, social problems, urban unrest. Remember, Halloway, you don't want to start a flight from the cities.'

Halloway had taken this friendly ribbing in his stride, though the rapid increase in the size of Stillman's gang had begun to make him uneasy. Clearly Stillman relished lording it over this entourage of wide-eyed teenagers and farm-bred youths, fitting them up with their gangster suits and weapons like a corrupt stage-director playing ironic games with a chorus of young actors. At times Halloway felt that he too was part of this sardonic man's devious entertainment.

However, apart from the stealing, Stillman's continued ravaging of department store windows in the surrounding districts of the city had turned Halloway's neighbourhood into an island of light and activity in an ever-larger sea of devastation. Halloway's plans for expansion had been effectively shelved by this deliberate vandalism, the wholesale destruction of complete city blocks.

In addition, Stillman's entourage had come into collision with Olds, and Halloway now depended more than ever on the mute. Two of Stillman's men had tried to break into Olds' automobile plant, complaining that the models they had ordered from him had not been delivered. For several days Olds had retreated to his rooftop eyrie above the garage at the airport. Without him everything soon began to run down. Halloway drove out to pacify him, and found Olds sitting below the wing of the glider tethered to the roof, calculators flicking in his hands as he brooded to himself. His eyes were gazing at the flights of birds taking off from the reservoirs around the airport, thousands of wild geese moving westwards across the city. Uneasily, Halloway noticed that the cars in his museum were still dusty and untended. One of them, the black Duesenberg, had been savagely attacked, its windows knocked in and upholstery slashed, controls pounded out of recognition by a heavy mallet.

But for a brilliant stroke of Halloway's, Olds would long since have left. Two months beforehand, he had shown his first irritation with the throngs of youths and teenage girls who were entering the reclamation area. Many of them were idealists like Halloway, repressed by the passivity of the garden communities and eager to help re-start the city. However, an equal number were drifters and misfits, who resented taking orders from Olds and began to mimic him, flashing obscenities on the read-out panels of the pocket calculators they had taken from a business-machines store.

Searching for some way of retaining his hold over Olds, Halloway came up with the suggestion that the mute could own and manage his own automobile plant. The idea had immediately appealed to Olds. In an underground garage near the police-station he and his workforce soon constructed a crude but functioning production line, on which the dozens of cars being re-equipped and re-engined moved along a section of railway line. They entered as little more than wrecks picked up off the street by their prospective owners, and emerged at the far end of the line as fully functioning vehicles. Delighted by this, Olds had agreed to stay on in the city.

In fact, Halloway's idea worked better than he hoped. The motor-car was the chief commodity of the city, and demand for it was insatiable. Almost every one of the new inhabitants now owned three or four cars, and their chief recreation was driving around the streets of the reclamation area dressed in the latest finery. Parking problems had become acute, and a special task force under Olds was renovating the kerbside meters, an unpopular measure grudgingly accepted only because of the special status of the automobile and the important position it occupied, economically and otherwise, in people's lives.

Despite these problems, Halloway was satisfied with his achievement. In the four months since the first of the new arrivals had turned up, a genuine microcosm of the former metropolis had come into existence. The population of the city was now two hundred, girls and youths in their late teens and early twenties, emigrants from Garden City and Parkville, Laurel Heights and Heliopolis, drawn from these dozy pastoral settlements to the harsh neon glare that each evening lit up the night sky like a beacon.

By now any new immigrants – some of them, worryingly, little more than children – were rapidly inducted into urban life. On arrival they were interviewed by Halloway, issued with a list of possible jobs, either on Olds' production line, in the clothing stores and supermarkets, or in any one of a dozen reclamation gangs. The last group, who foraged through the city at large for cars, fuel, food supplies, tools and electrical equipment, in effect represented the productive capacity of the new settlement, but in time Halloway hoped that they would embark on the original manufacture of an ever-wider range of consumer goods. Cash credits (banknotes franked with Halloway's name) were advanced to the new recruits against their first week's pay, with which they could buy the garish clothing, records and cigarettes they seemed to need above all else. Most of the two hundred inhabitants were now heavily in debt, but rather than evict them from their apartments and close the discotheques, bars and amusement arcades where they spent their evenings, Halloway had astutely lengthened the working day from eight to ten hours, enticing them with generous though uneconomic overtime payments. Already, he happily realized, he was literally printing money. Within only a few months inflation would be rampant, but like the crime and pollution this was a real sign of his success, a confirmation of all he had dreamed about.

There was a flicker of interference on the monitor screen, indicating a fault in the camera mounted outside the station. Muttering with mock-annoyance, 'Nothing works any more,' Halloway switched to the camera in the square. The open plaza with its memorial of cars was deserted at this hour. The monument had never been completed. Stillman had long since lost interest in the hard work of construction, and no one else had volunteered, particularly as no payment was involved. Besides, these memorials of cars and radiator grilles, tyres and kitchen appliances created an atmosphere of defeat and fatality, presiding like funeral pyres over the outskirts of the city as the new arrivals pressed on to their promised land.

A few attempts had been made to dismantle the pyramids, but each time Buckmaster and his daughter had managed to make good the damage. Dressed in her ever-changing costumes, in this cavalcade of

Twentieth-Century fashion, Miranda moved tirelessly through the city, seeding the glass-filled streets with poppies and daisies, trailing vines over the fallen telephone wires. Halloway had given two assistants the task of following her around the city and destroying whatever new plants they could find. Too many of the flowers she was now setting out in window boxes and ornamental urns had a distinctly sinister aspect. Halloway had caught her the previous week, eerily at work in the reclamation area itself, bedding out bizarre lilies with nacreous petals and mantis-like flowers in the entrance to the police-station, glamorous but vicious plants that looked as if they might lunge at the throats of anyone passing by. Halloway had pushed past her, overturned her flower trolley and torn out the lilies with his bare hands. Then, with unexpected forbearance, he had ordered his sergeant to drive her back to her hotel. His feelings for Miranda remained as confused as they had been at their first meeting. On the one hand he wanted to impress her, to make her recognize the importance of everything he had done, on the other he was vaguely afraid of this young and naive Diana of the botanical gardens, about to embark on some macabre hunt through the intense, over-heated foliage.

The day after this incident Buckmaster paid Halloway a visit, the first he had made to the reclamation zone. Still keen to earn the old industrialist's approval, Halloway took him on a tour of the neighbourhood, proudly pointing out the mechanics working on the motor-cars on Olds' production line, the gleaming vehicles being collected by their new owners, the system of credit and finance which he had evolved, the busy bars and supermarkets, the new arrivals moving into their refurbished apartments, and even the first two-hour-a-day transmissions from the local television station – the programmes, with complete historical accuracy, consisted entirely of old movies and commercials. The latter, despite a hiatus of thirty years, were still up-to-date advertisements of the products they bought and sold in the stores and supermarkets.

'Everything is here that you can think of, sir,' Halloway told the old man. 'And it's a living urban structure, not a film set. We've got traffic problems, inflation, even the beginnings of serious crime and pollution . . .'

The industrialist smiled at Halloway in a not unkindly way. 'That's a proud boast, Halloway. I'd begun to notice those last two myself. Now, you've taken me on your tour – let me take you on one of mine.'

Reluctant to leave his command post in the commissioner's office, Halloway nonetheless decided to humour Buckmaster. Besides, he knew that in many ways Buckmaster had taken over the role of his own father. Often, as he relaxed in the evenings at his apartment overlooking the park, Halloway seriously wondered if his father would have understood all that he had achieved, so far beyond the antique engine parts and aircraft designs. Unhappily, Buckmaster – who certainly did understand – remained ambiguous in his response.

Together they set off in Halloway's car, driving for over an hour towards the industrial areas to the north-west of the city. Here, among the power stations and railyards, foundries and coal depots, Buckmaster tried to point out to Halloway how the Twentieth Century had met its self-made death. They stood on the shores of artificial lagoons filled with chemical wastes, drove along canals silvered by metallic scum, across landscapes covered by thousands of tons of untreated garbage, fields piled high with cans, broken glass and derelict machinery.

But as he listened to the old man warning him that sooner or later he would add to these terminal moraines, Halloway had been exhilarated by the scenes around him. Far from disfiguring the landscape, these discarded products of Twentieth-Century industry had a fierce and wayward beauty. Halloway was fascinated by the glimmering sheen of the metal-scummed canals, by the strange submarine melancholy of drowned cars looming up at him from abandoned lakes, by the brilliant colours of the garbage hills, by the glitter of a million cans embedded in a matrix of detergent packs and tinfoil, a kaleidoscope of everything they could wear, eat and drink. He was fascinated by the cobalt clouds that drifted below the surface of the water, free at last of all plants and fish, the soft chemical billows interacting as they seeped from the sodden soil. He explored the whorls of steel shavings, foliage culled from a metallic christmas tree, the bales of rusting wire whose dense copper hues formed a burnished forest in the sunlight. He gazed raptly at the chalky whiteness of old china-clay tips, vivid as powdered ice, abandoned railyards with their moss-covered locomotives, the undimmed beauty of industrial wastes produced by skills and imaginations far richer than nature's, more splendid than any Arcadian meadow. Unlike nature, here there was no death.

Lulled by this vision of technology's Elysian Fields, Halloway sat half-asleep behind the commissioner's desk, dwarfed by the leather-backed chair. When he woke he found that the TV monitor was again showing a jumble of interference patterns. Part of the excitement of city life was the constant breakdown of these poorly designed appliances, and the difficulty of getting hold of a repairman. In Garden City, every piece of equipment, every washing machine and solar-powered kitchen stove, functioned for ever with dismaying perfection. In the rare event of even the smallest malfunction the designer would appear on one's doorstep as fast as his bicycle could carry him. By contrast, the metropolis operated an exciting knife-edge away from total collapse.

Leaving the station, Halloway saluted the two eighteen-year-old police-men sitting in their patrol car. There were ten officers under his command, an over-large proportion of the total number of inhabitants, but all Halloway's scrutiny of the commissioner's records confirmed that a large police force, like pollution and a high crime-rate, was an essential feature of city life.

Besides, they might well be useful sooner than he expected. As he stepped into his car to drive the fifty yards to Olds' garage – Halloway never walked, however short the distance, and often U-turned his car to get from one side of the road to the other – a gang of teenage boys tumbled with a chorus of obscenities from a nearby amusement arcade. They clustered around a large motorcycle with extended forks and a lavishly chromed engine. All wore black leather jackets strung with sinister ornaments – iron crosses, ceremonial daggers and death's heads. The driver kick-started the machine with a violent roar, then lurched in a circle across the sidewalk, knocking down part of a tobacco kiosk before veering into Halloway's path. Without apology, he drummed his fist on the roof above Halloway's head and roared off down the street, weaving in and out of the shouting pedestrians.

As Halloway expected, most of the workers on Olds' production line had packed up early. The thirty vehicles mounted on their movable trolleys had come to a halt, and the few mechanics left were plugging the batteries into the overnight chargers.

Olds was seated in his glass-walled office, moodily playing with his collection of pocket calculators, slim fingers flicking out fragments of some strange dialogue. As life for him had become increasingly complex, with all the problems of running this automobile plant, he had added more and more calculators. He placed the instruments in a series of lines across his desk, and seemed to be working towards a decision about everything, laying out the elements of this reductive conversation like cards in a game of solitaire.

He gazed up at Halloway, as if recognizing him with difficulty. He looked tired and listless, numbed by his work on all the projects which Halloway pushed forward ruthlessly.

'Olds, it's only six. Why are we scrapping the evening shift?'

*There are not enough men for the line.*

'They should all be here.' When Olds sat back, shuffling the calculators with one hand, Halloway snapped, 'Olds – they need the work! They've got to pay back their wage credits!'

The mute shrugged, watching Halloway with his passive but intelligent eyes. From a drawer he pulled out his old flying-helmet. He seemed about to question Halloway about something, but changed his mind.

*Halloway, they lack your appreciation of the value of hard work.*

'Olds, can't you understand?' With an effort, Halloway controlled his exasperation. He paced around the office, deciding on a new tack. 'Listen, Olds, there's something I wanted to bring up with you. As you know, you don't actually pay any rent for this garage – in fact, this whole operation makes no direct contribution at all to the municipal budget. Originally I exempted you because of the help you've given in starting everything up, but I think now we'll have to look into the question of some kind of reasonable rent – and of taxation, too, for that matter.' As Olds' fingers began to race irritatingly across the calculators, flicking out a series of messages he was unable to read, Halloway pressed on.

'There's another thing. So much of life here depends on time – hours of work, rates of pay and so on, they're all hitched to the clock. It occurred to me that if we lengthened the hour, without anyone knowing, of course, we would get more work out of people for the same rates of pay. Suppose I ordered in all the clocks and wristwatches, for a free check-up, say, could you readjust them so that they ran a little slower?' Halloway paused, waiting to see if Olds fully appreciated the simplicity of this ingenious scheme. He added, 'Naturally, it would be to everyone's benefit. In fact, by varying the length of the hour, by slowing or speeding up all the clocks, we would have a powerful economic regulator, we'd be able to cut back or encourage inflation, vary pay-rates and productivity. I'm looking ahead, I know, but I already visualize a central radio transmitter beaming out a variable time signal to everyone's clock and wristwatch, so that no one need bother about making the adjustments himself . . .'

Halloway waited for a reply, but the calculators were silent for once, their display panels unlit. Olds was looking up at him with an expression Halloway had never seen before. All the mute's intelligence and judgment were in his eyes, staring at this blond-haired young man as if seeing him clearly for the first time.

Annoyed by his almost disdainful attitude, Halloway was tempted to strike the mute. But at that moment, carried clearly above the drumming of the generators, they heard the squeal of tyres in the road above, and the sounds of breaking glass and a child's scream.

When they reached the street a crowd had already gathered, standing around a white limousine that had swerved across the sidewalk and plunged through the windows of a supermarket. Cans and detergent packs, which Halloway had helped to stack into their display pyramids, were scattered among the broken glass. Stillman's chauffeur, a black-jacketed youth of sixteen, stepped from the car, spitting away his gum in a nervous gesture. Everyone was looking down at two eleven-year-old boys, barely conscious, stretched out in the roadway, and at the dead body of a young girl lying under the limousine between its rear wheels.

As the siren of a police car wailed towards them Olds pushed through the crowd. He knelt down and held the girl's bloodied wrist. When he carried her away in his arms, pushing brusquely past Halloway, he held the calculator in one hand. Halloway caught a glimpse of its display panel, screaming out a single silent obscenity.

The next week marked an uneasy interregnum. On the pretext of keeping an eye on everything, Halloway retreated to the commissioner's office, watching the streets for hours on the TV monitor. The death of the girl, the first traffic fatality of the new city, was an event even Halloway was unable to rationalize. He stayed away from the funeral, which was attended by everyone except himself. Olds drove the huge hearse, which he found in a breaker's yard and spent all night refurbishing. Surrounded by an arbour of flowers, the dead child in her lavish hand-carved casket moved away at the head of the procession, followed through the empty streets by all the people of the neighbourhood, everyone at the wheel of his car. Stillman and his entourage wore their darkest gangster suits. Miranda and old Buckmaster, both in black capes, appeared in an ancient open tourer filled with strange wreaths she had prepared from the flowers that Halloway's men had destroyed.

However, much to Halloway's relief everything soon returned to normal, though by some unhappy paradox this first death set off an even greater latent violence. During the following days more and more workers defected from their jobs to join Stillman's entourage, which by now had swollen to a substantial private army. Many of them wore black para-military uniforms. All day the sound of gunfire echoed through the streets as they destroyed hundreds of the deer in the park, driving away the pheasants, quail and wild duck on which Halloway depended to stock the fresh meat counters of the supermarkets. Armed with rifles, they marched up and down the square in parade order, presenting arms beside the files of slaughtered deer. Stillman, now affecting a military tunic and peaked cap, had swapped his limousine for an open-topped half-track, in which he stood to attention, taking the salute.

Halloway tried to laugh off these absurd games as another mental aberration of this convicted murderer, but Stillman's men had begun to disrupt the life of the zone. They strolled in gangs around the supermarkets, helping themselves to whatever they wanted and brushing aside any requests for payment. Taking their cue from this, many of the apartment-house tenants defaulted on their rents. Instead of shopping at the supermarkets, and helping to bolster the faltering economy of the zone, they were breaking into the stores outside the area. Each day there was a further slide towards anarchy, the failure of another generator, an increase in traffic delays and parking offences, and above all a growing conviction that the city was unmanageable.

Faced with this collapse of his dream, worked for with such effort, Halloway decided to reassert his authority. He needed some means of inspiring these new urban dwellers. Bored by their long hours of repetitive work, most of them did no more in their leisure time than hang around the bars and amusement arcades, driving aimlessly around the streets in their various cars. The influx of new arrivals had begun to fall off, and already the first of the original settlers were packing their bags and drifting off to the suburbs.

After a night of continuous uproar, filled with the sound of sirens and gunfire, Halloway decided to enlist Buckmaster's help. The old industrialist was the only person he could fall back on. Olds no longer spoke to him – the whole make-believe of teaching the mute to fly had long since lost its credibility. But Buckmaster had been one of the pioneers who created the Twentieth Century, and might well be able to charge everyone with enthusiasm again.

Outside Buckmaster's hotel Halloway hesitated before stepping from his car. His ruthless use of defoliants on Miranda's plant kingdom made him uneasy about seeing her, but he would have to brush this aside.

As he climbed the steps to the hotel entrance he noticed that the revolving door had been converted into a miniature greenhouse. Each of the segments was filled with an unfamiliar plant, with purple flowers and purple-black berries. With a reflex of irritation, Halloway was about to rip them out with his hands, but a brief movement on a balcony above him caught his eye.

Three floors above, Miranda was standing on her balcony and looking down at Halloway, a posy of mantis lilies in her hand. She was wearing a long white dress and white lace veil that Halloway had never seen before, but which he recognized immediately. Gazing up at her, and knowing that she had never been more beautiful, Halloway was suddenly convinced that she was wearing the wedding gown for him. She was waiting for Halloway to come and collect her from the hotel, and then they would cross the square to the cathedral of cars where her father would marry them.

As if to confirm this, Miranda leaned slightly over her balcony, smiling at Halloway and beckoning to him with a white-gloved hand.

When he reached the revolving door the purple flowers and dark berries clustered thickly around him. He was about to push past them when he remembered the posy of lilies in her hand, and the too-eager way in which she had watched him arrive. Then he realized that the plants he was about to brush out of his way, festering here in this glass execution chamber between himself and his bride, were deadly nightshade.

In the early afternoon Miranda and her father left the city for good.

That night, as he lay asleep in his apartment, Halloway dreamed that he was standing at an open window overlooking the park. Below him the waist-high grass shivered and seethed. Some deep motion had unsettled the ground, a profound shudder that crossed the entire park. The bushes and brambles, the trees and shrubs, even the lowliest weeds and wild flowers, were beginning to rustle and quiver, straining from the ground. Everywhere branches were waving in an invisible wind, leaves beating at the passing air. Then, by the lake at the centre of the park, a miniature oak broke free, boughs moving like the wings of an ungainly bird. Shaking the earth from its roots, it soared towards Halloway, a hundred feet from the ground. Other trees were following, branches grasping at the air, a million leaves whirling together. As Halloway watched, gripping the window-sill to stop himself from joining them, the whole park suddenly rose upwards, every tree and flower, every blade of grass joining to form an immense sunlit armada that circled above Halloway's head and soared along the rays of the sun. As they moved away across the sky Halloway could see that all over the city the flowers and vines which Miranda had planted were also leaving. A flight of poppies soared past, a crimson carpet followed by an aerial causeway of daisies, petals beating as if they were the cilia of some huge lace-like creature. Halloway looked up from the city, with its now barren stone and dying air. The sky was filled with a legion of flying creatures, a green haze of petals and blossoms free at last to make their way to the welcoming sun.

When he woke the next morning, Halloway went out on to his balcony, uncertain whether the dense vegetation rooted securely to the ground was an illusion of his mind. Later, when he paused briefly at the police station, the vision of these flying oaks and marigolds, elms and daisies still hung in the air, brighter than the neon façades of the bars and amusement arcades.

Instead of switching off the lights and going to work, people were hanging around the doorways of the bars, watching Halloway across the pintables in the arcades. None of the police force had turned up for duty, and for a moment Halloway felt that the day itself had failed to appear.

Determined now on a confrontation with Stillman, he went back to his car. He was convinced that the former convict was responsible for the collapse of everything he had worked for. Stillman had been drawn here by the limitless opportunities he had seen for cruelty and disruption. He needed a dying city, not a living one, a warm cadaver that he could infest like a maggot.

After locking the police station, Halloway drove along the park to Stillman's headquarters, a cylindrical art museum with a single spiral ramp that circled upwards to Stillman's audience chamber. Armed guards lounged in their black uniforms around the line of armoured limousines parked outside. They signalled Halloway forward, clearly expecting him. As Halloway walked towards the elevator Stillman was standing in a theatrical pose on the topmost stage.

Their meeting never took place. Halfway up, the elevator stopped with an abrupt shudder, its lights failing. Everywhere voices began to shout, a shot was fired, feet raced past down the ramp. By the time Halloway broke free from the elevator he was the last to leave the darkened building. Stillman and his gang had set off, taking Halloway's car with them.

When he reached the police-station half an hour later an electrical storm was sweeping the streets of the reclamation zone. Cars were stalled bumper to bumper at the intersections. The drivers stood by their vehicles, flinching from the neon signs that were exploding in cascades of molten glass above the bars and restaurants. Everywhere the overloaded circuitry was burning out. Coloured light-bulbs burst and ripped across the ceilings of the amusement arcades. Pintables exploded in a chatter of free games, in the supermarkets the first fires were lifting from the freezer cabinets, flames roasting the carcasses of the deer and wild-fowl. The noise of a hundred generators filled the air, turned up by someone to their greatest output.

It took Halloway several hours to restore order. Long before he had turned down the last of the overheated generators, replaced the fuses and put out the most serious of the fires, Halloway knew who had been responsible. Dozens of the pocket calculators lay around the generators in the alleyways and basements, display panels glowing dimly. Olds must have ransacked the business-machine stores, gathering together as many calculators as he could find to cope with his mental crisis. They were scattered in his trail, spinning off from his hyper-active mind.

*Wings?*

*Mixture rich, carburettor heat cold.*

*Sparrow, wren, robin, hummingbird . . .*

Halloway stared down angrily at these fragmentary messages, bulletins to himself that expressed Olds' doubts and anxieties. When Halloway found him he would scream him into submission with one potent word, throw him into a final fit from which he would never recover.

*Kiwi, penguin?*

*Pitch full fine, fuel cocks open.*

*Starling, swallow, swift . . .*

Halloway stamped on the calculators, pulverizing this ascending order of birds. Exhausted by the effort of shutting down the generators, he sat on the floor in the supermarket basement, surrounded by soup cans and the glowing dials.

*Climbing.*

*Flaps down, throttle slightly cracked.*

*Elizabeth, dead child. No pain.*

*Blue eyes. Insane.*

*Partridge, quail, geese, oriole . . . eagle, osprey, falcon . . .*

Guessing that he might find the mute in his automobile plant, Halloway ran down the ramp into the basement. But Olds had gone. In a last galvanic spasm, the thirty cars on the production line had been hurled against the concrete wall, and lay heaped across each other in a tangle of chrome and broken glass. On the desk in his office the calculators were laid out neatly to form a last message.

*Ol*

*Old*

*Olds*

*Oldsm*

*Oldsmo*

*Oldsmob*

*Oldsmobi*

*Oldsmobil*

*OLDSMOBILE!!!*

And then, in the drawer where he had kept his antique flying-helmet:

*I can –!*

*Fulmar, albatross, flamingo, frigate-bird, condor . . .*

*IGNITION!*

\*      \*      \*

Abandoning his car, Halloway walked through the empty streets, littered with smouldering neon tubes as if a burnt-out rainbow had collapsed across the sidewalks. Already he could see that everyone had gathered in the square, their backs turned to Buckmaster's memorial. They were looking up at the display sign on the newspaper building, the brief message which Olds had left for them repeating itself in a cry of fear, pride and determination.

*I CAN FLY! I CAN FLY! I CAN FLY! I CAN FLY!*

By the time Halloway reached the airport the siege was well under way. Stillman and his men surrounded the car park, crouching behind their limousines and firing at random at the upper floors. There were no signs of Olds, but from the apex of the pyramid of radiator grilles Halloway could see that the powered glider on the roof had been readied for flight. Olds had fitted an undercarriage and tail-wheel to the craft. No longer tethered, it had been moved to the upper end of the canted roof, the two hundred yards of concrete sloping away below the polished propeller.

Under cover of a fusillade of shots, Stillman and three of his men rushed the building and entered the ground floor of the car park. Ten storeys above them, Olds appeared on the roof, dressed in his antique flying-suit, leather jacket and gaiters. He moved around the aircraft, making some last adjustments to the engine, oblivious of the shooting below.

Twenty minutes later, smoke began to rise from the eighth floor of the car park, dark billows that lifted towards the roof. Seeing the smoke, Olds stopped and watched it swirl around him. Then, above the sound of gunshots and exploding fuel tanks, Halloway heard the clatter of the aero-engine. The propeller span briskly, pumping the heavy smoke out of its way.

Knowing that Olds would be killed if he tried to take off, Halloway ran towards the car park. Shouting at Stillman's men, he pushed past them to the emergency stairs.

When he reached the eighth floor one of the young guards held him back. At the far end of the sloping concrete floor Olds had built a solid barricade with his four land-cruisers. Unable to climb past it, and with the remainder of the stairway blocked by a pile of generators and electrical equipment, Stillman and his men were setting fire to the cars, shooting into the engine compartments and fuel tanks of these once-cherished sedans and limousines.

'Stillman!' Halloway shouted. 'Let him go! If he tries to fly he'll kill himself!'

But Stillman waved him away. Two of the cars were burning briskly, and he and his men pushed the flaming vehicles up the slope and rammed them into the land-cruisers. Within moments the metal cabins were splitting in the fierce heat. Watching this conflagration begin, Stillman beckoned his men down the slope.

Then, moving down the gutter below the internal balustrade, came a thin stream of fluid, working its way around the old tyres and the piles of leaves and birds' nests. Thinking that this was Olds' pathetic attempt to douse the fire Stillman had started, Halloway grappled with the guard, trying to wrest the shotgun from him. As they struggled together by the staircase he saw that the stream had expanded into a broad sheet, as wide as the sloping floor, moving swiftly like a tidal race. It swilled below the land-cruisers and around the wheels of the burning cars, touched here and there by the nimbus of a flame. The fluid overran Stillman's feet as he and his men turned and ran for their lives, splashing through the fast-moving sluice. In the last seconds, as the whole floor lit up in a sudden bloom of flame, illuminating the running figures trapped in the centre of this sloping furnace, Halloway hurled himself down the staircase. The sounds of explosions followed him to the ground floor.

So Olds had opened the stopcocks on the fuel tanks of the cars on the ninth and tenth floors. When Halloway reached the road the upper three storeys of the garage were aflame. Powerful explosions were ripping apart the limousines, sports-cars and open tourers that Olds had collected so carefully. Window glass and pieces of sharp chrome flicked through the air, landing on the sidewalk around him as he crouched behind an airline van. Fifty feet high, the flames of the burning gasolene rose into a sluggish tower of smoke two hundred yards in diameter.

Most of Stillman's men had driven off, these youths in their black uniforms and large cars frightened by the violence of the explosions. Three others had remained behind, waiting with their rifles raised, but Halloway was certain that both Olds and Stillman had already died.

High above him, a propeller whirled through the smoke. The sailplane moved across the roof, lining itself up for take-off. Olds' slim figure was crouched in the cockpit, face hidden by the antique helmet. The engine deepened its roar, and the aircraft with its long drooping wings sped forward down the sloping roof. As it left the building and sailed into the open air it seemed to fall towards the ground, but its wings suddenly climbed on to the light wind crossing the airport. It soared along, engine blaring, a few feet above the cars parked nose-to-tail down the runway, and shook off the oily smoke that still wreathed its wings and fuselage. It flew on steadily, gaining altitude as it cleared the perimeter fence. Moving northwards towards the Sound, it made a careful left-hand turn, three hundred feet above the ground. It set off across the river, wings rocking as Olds tested the controls. Halfway across the river it picked up a flight of wild duck which were circling the city, and then joined a stream of petals half a mile long that was being carried away by the wind. Together, the three flights – the wild duck and the stream of petals, and Olds in his sailplane – flew on to the north-west, parting company when they crossed the ruined suspension bridge. Halloway waited as the sailplane, little more than a point of light reflected from its propeller, climbed higher into the secure sky, and finally vanished on its way westwards across the continent.

*     *     *

When he had driven back to the city Halloway left his car in the square. Standing beside Buckmaster's memorial, he watched the supermarkets and stores, the bars and amusement arcades close themselves down. Almost everyone had left now, as the young people made their way back to their garden settlements.

Halloway waited until they had all gone. The last of the generators had run out of fuel, dimming the lights in the police-station. He walked through the streets, picking his way over the broken glass and burnt-out cables, past dozens of abandoned cars. Discarded banknotes, printed with his own name, drifted along the roadway.

In the space of only a few months he had managed to achieve what had taken this metropolis as a whole more than a hundred and fifty years to do. However, it had all been worthwhile. He knew now that he would never return to Garden City, with its pastoral calm. In the morning, after he had rested, he would set off on foot, searching for Olds and the sailplane, following the memorials westwards across the continent, until he found the old man again and could help him raise his pyramids of washing machines, radiator-grilles and typewriters. Somehow he would come to terms with Miranda, and help her to re-forest the cities. Maybe, then, she would wear her wedding dress again for him.

Confident of all this, Halloway set off across the square. Already he was planning the first of a series of huge metal pyramids in his mind, as high perhaps as these skyscrapers, built of airliners, freight trains, walking draglines and missile launchers, larger than anything of which Buckmaster and the Twentieth Century had ever dreamed. And perhaps, too, Olds would teach him how to fly.

**1976**

# · THE DEAD TIME

Without warning, as if trying to confuse us, the Japanese guarding our camp had vanished. I stood by the open gates of the camp with a group of fellow-internees, staring in an almost mesmerized way at the deserted road and at the untended canals and paddy-fields that stretched on all sides to the horizon. The guard-house had been abandoned. The two Japanese sentries who usually waved me away whenever I tried to sell them cigarettes had given up their posts and fled with the remainder of the military police to their barracks in Shanghai. The tyre-prints of their vehicles were still clearly visible in the dust between the gate-posts.

Perhaps even this hint at the presence of Japanese who had imprisoned us for three years was enough to deter us from crossing the line into the silent world outside the camp. We stood together in the gateway, trying to straighten our shabby clothing and listening to the children playing in the compound. Behind the nearest of the dormitory blocks several women were hanging out their morning's washing, as if fully content to begin another day's life in the camp. Yet everything was over!

Although the youngest of the group – I was then only twenty – on an impulse I casually stepped forward and walked into the centre of the road. The others watched me as I turned to face the camp. Clearly they half-expected a shot to ring out from somewhere. One of them, a consultant engineer who had known my parents before the war separated us, raised his hand as if to beckon me to safety.

The faint drone of an American aircraft crossed the empty bank of the river half a mile away. It flew steadily towards us, no more than a hundred feet above the paddy-fields, the young pilot sitting forward over his controls as he peered down at us. Then he rolled his wings in a gesture of greeting and altered course for Shanghai.

Their confidence restored, the others were suddenly around me, laughing and shouting as they set off down the road. Six hundred yards away was a Chinese village, partly hidden by the eroded humps of the burial mounds built on the earth causeways that separated the paddies. Already substantial supplies of rice beer had been brought back to the camp. For all our caution, we were not the first of the internees to leave the camp. A week earlier, immediately after the news of the Japanese capitulation, a party of merchant seamen had climbed through the fence behind their block and walked the eight miles to Shanghai. There they had been picked up by the Japanese gendarmerie, held for two days and returned to the camp in a badly beaten state. So far all the others who had reached Shanghai – whether, like myself, searching for relations, or trying to check up on their businesses – had met with the same fate.

As we strode towards the village, now and then looking back at the curious perspectives of the camp receding behind us, I watched the paddies and canals on either side of the road. In spite of everything I had heard on the radio broadcasts, I was still not certain that the war was over. During the past year we had listened more or less openly to the various radios smuggled into the camp, and had followed the progress of the American forces across the Pacific. We had heard detailed accounts of the atom-bomb attacks – Nagasaki was little more than 500 miles from us – and of the Emperor's call for capitulation immediately after. But at our camp, eight miles to the east of Shanghai at the mouth of the Yangtse, little had changed. Large numbers of American aircraft crossed the sky unopposed, no longer taking part in any offensive action, but we soon noticed that none had landed at the military airfield adjacent to our camp. Dwindling but still substantial numbers of Japanese troops held the landscape, patrolling the airfield perimeter, the railway lines and roads to Shanghai. Military police continued to guard the camp, as if guaranteeing our imprisonment through whatever peace might follow, and kept little more than their usual distance from the two thousand internees. Paradoxically, the one positive sign was that since the Emperor's broadcast no food had arrived for us.

Hunger, in fact, was my chief reason for leaving the camp. In the confusion after Pearl Harbor I had been separated from my parents by the Japanese occupation authorities and imprisoned in a stockade in the centre of Shanghai reserved for male allied nationals. Eighteen months later, when the American bombing began, the stockade was closed and the prisoners scattered at random among the cluster of large camps for families with children in the countryside surrounding Shanghai. My parents and young sister had spent the war in another of these some twenty miles to the west of the city. Although their condition was probably as bad as my own I was convinced that once I reached them everything would be well.

'It looks as if they're gone. They must have cleared out with everything overnight.'

At the entrance to the village the man next to me, a garage owner from Shanghai, pointed to the abandoned houses. Catching our breath after the brisk walk, we gazed down at the empty alleys and shuttered windows. Not a Chinese was in sight, though only the previous afternoon they had been doing a profitable trade with groups of internees from the camp, bartering rice beer for watches, shoes and fountain pens.

While the others conferred, I wandered away to the ruins of a ceramics factory on the outskirts of the village. Perhaps under the impression that its kilns were some sort of military installation, the Americans had bombed the factory again and again. A few of the buildings were still standing, but the courtyards were covered with thousands of pieces of broken crockery. Uncannily, these seemed to have been sorted out into various categories of table-ware. I walked across a carpet of porcelain soup spoons, all too aware of the fact that the only noise in this entire landscape was coming from my feet.

For the villagers to have left so suddenly, after all their struggles through the war, could only mean that they were frightened of something they were sure would take place in their immediate locality. During the past year they had attached themselves to our camp, selling a few eggs through the barbed wire and later, when they themselves began to be hungry, trying to break through the fences in order to steal the tomatoes and root-crops which the internees grew on every square foot of vacant soil. At one time we had recruited the Japanese guards to help us strengthen the wire to keep out these pilferers. In the last months the circle of starving or ailing older villagers planted outside the camp gates – none were ever admitted, let alone fed – grew larger every day.

Yet for some reason they had all gone. As I walked back from the factory perimeter my companions were discussing the best route across the paddy-fields to Shanghai. They had ransacked several of the houses and were now sitting on the piles of broken crockery with bottles of rice beer. I remembered the rumours we had heard that before they surrendered the Japanese planned to slaughter their civilian prisoners.

I looked back along the road to the camp, aware of its curious confusion of vulnerability and security. The water-tower and three-storey concrete blocks seemed to rise from the lines of burial mounds. The camp had been a Chinese middle school. We had arrived after dark, and I had never seen it from the outside before, just as I had never physically entered the empty landscape surrounding the camp which had been an intimate part of my life all these years.

I listened to my companions' increasingly random discussion. Apart from the consultant engineer and the garage owner, there were two Australian seamen and a hotel barman. Already I was certain that they had no idea of the hazards facing them, and that as long as I remained with them I would never reach my parents. Their one intention was to get drunk in as many as possible of the dozens of villages between here and Shanghai.

Five minutes after I left them, however, as I walked back along the road to the camp, I heard the sounds of a Japanese military truck coming behind me from the village. Armed soldiers of the gendarmerie leaned on the cabin above the driver, guarding my five former companions who sat on the floor on either side of the tail-gate. Their faces had an ashen and toneless look, like those of men woken abruptly from sleep. Alone of them, an Australian seaman glanced up from his bound wrists and stared at me, as if failing to recognize who I was.

I continued to walk towards the camp, but the truck stopped in front of me. None of the soldiers spoke or even beckoned me to climb aboard, and already I knew that we were not being given a lift back to the camp.

Without thinking, I had a sudden presentiment of death, not of my own but of everyone else around me.

For the next three days we were held in the gendarmerie barracks attached to the military airfield, where some hundred or so allied aircrew shot down during the air attacks on Shanghai had been concentrated in an attempt to dissuade the American bombers from strafing the hangars and runways. To my relief, we were not mistreated. The Japanese sat around listlessly, no longer interested in us and gazing up in a melancholy way at the American aircraft which endlessly crossed the sky. Already supplies were being parachuted into our camp. From the window of our cell we could see the coloured canopies falling past the water-tower.

Clearly the war was over, and when a gendarmerie sergeant released us from the cell and ordered us into the barracks square I took for granted that we were about to be turned loose at the airfield gates. Instead, we were put aboard the same truck that had brought us here and driven under guard to the nearby railway station that served as a military depot on the Shanghai-Nanking line.

The first to jump down from the truck, I looked around at the ruined station buildings, well aware that the last train had stopped here some two months beforehand. Apart from the aircraft overhead, the landscape remained as deserted as it had been on the day of our abortive escape. On all sides was the debris of war – rusting trucks, a paddy-field used as a dump for worn-out tyres, a line of tank ditches half-filled with water that ran towards a small football stadium set back from the road, a blockhouse covered with leaking sandbags built at the entrance to the station. But the Chinese had gone, vacating the landscape as if at last deciding to leave us to our own resources, to whatever pointless end we cared to make.

'It looks as if we're going to play soccer,' one of the Australian seamen called back to the others as he and I followed the three guards towards the stadium.

'Some stunt for the Red Cross,' someone else commented. 'Afterwards, make sure they take us back to the camp.'

But already I could see into the stadium, and had realized that whatever else took place, we would not be playing football. We climbed the concrete entrance tunnel into the ground, a circle of yellowing grass in the centre of which two trucks were parked. Sections of the empty stand had been used by the Japanese as a warehouse, and several soldiers patrolled the seats high above us, guarding what seemed to be a pile of looted furniture. A party of smartly uniformed military stood by the two trucks, waiting for us to approach. At their head was a young Eurasian interpreter in a white shirt.

As we walked towards them we looked down at the ground at our feet. Stretched out on the frayed grass were some fifty corpses, laid out in neat rows as if arranged with great care and devotion. All were fully dressed and lay with their feet towards us, arms at their sides, and I could see from the bright pallor of their faces that these people, whoever they were, had only recently died. I paused by a young nun wearing a full habit and wimple whose broad mouth had only just begun to take on its death grimace. Around her, like the members of her flock, were three children, heads to one side as if they had fallen asleep before death.

Watched by the Japanese soldiers and the young interpreter, and by the sentries guarding the furniture in the stands, we walked slowly past the corpses. Apart from two middle-aged Chinese, a man and a woman lying next to each other who might have been husband and wife, all were European and American, and from the worn state of their shoes and clothing seemed to be internees like ourselves. I passed a large ruddy-haired man in brown shorts with a gun-shot wound in his chest, and an elderly woman in a print dress who had been shot in the jaw, but at first sight none of the other bodies revealed any signs of violence.

Twenty feet ahead of me one of the Japanese soldiers by the trucks had moved his rifle. Behind me my companions stepped back involuntarily. The garage owner stumbled against me, for a moment holding my shoulder. I listened to the sound of an American aircraft overhead, the noise of its engine magnified by the concrete bowl of the stadium. It seemed insane that we would be shot here ten days after the war had ended in full view of our rescuers, but already I was convinced that we would not die. Yet again I had that same presentiment of death I had inexplicably felt before our arrest.

One of the Japanese officers, wearing full uniform under a short rain-cape, spoke briefly. I noticed that he was standing beside a small card-table on which rested two wicker baskets containing bottles of saki and parcels of boiled rice wrapped in leaves. For some bizarre reason I assumed that he was about to give me a prize.

The Eurasian in the white shirt came up to me. His face had the same passivity of the Japanese. No doubt he realized that once the Kuomintang forces arrived his own life would be over, like those of the fifty people lying on the stadium grass.

'You're all right?' he asked me. After a pause, he nodded at the Japanese officer. Then, almost as an afterthought, he said, 'You can drive a truck?'

'Yes . . .' The presence of the armed Japanese made any other answer pointless. In fact I had not driven any vehicle since the outbreak of war, and before that only my father's Plymouth car.

'Of course we can.' The garage owner had pulled himself together and joined us. He looked back at our four companions, who were now separated from us by the tract of corpses. 'We can both drive, I'm an experienced mechanic. Who are all those people? What happened to them?'

'We need two drivers,' the interpreter said. 'You know the Protestant cemetery at Soochow?'

'No, but we can find it.'

'That's good. It's only sixty miles, four hours, then you can go free. You take these people to the Protestant cemetery.'

'All right.' The garage owner had again held my shoulder, this time to prevent me changing my mind, though I already had no intention of doing so. 'But who are they all?'

The interpreter seemed to have lost interest. Already the Japanese soldiers were lowering the tail-gates of the trucks. 'Various things,' he said, patting his white shirt. 'Some illnesses, the American planes . . .'

An hour later we had loaded the fifty corpses on to the two trucks and after a trial circuit of the stadium had set off in the direction of Soochow.

Looking back on those first few hours of freedom as we drove together across the empty landscape fifteen miles to the south-east of Shanghai, I am struck by the extent to which we had already forgotten the passengers whose destination had made that freedom possible. Of course neither Hodson, the garage owner, nor myself had the slightest intention of driving to Soochow. As I could see from his manner as the six of us loaded the last of the corpses on to his truck, his one ambition was to turn right on the first road to Shanghai and abandon the truck and its contents in a side street – or, conceivably, given a sudden access of humanity, outside the Swiss embassy. In fact, my chief fear was that Hodson might leave me to be picked up by a Japanese patrol before I had mastered the truck's heavy steering and gear-box.

Luckily we had all been so exhausted by the effort of loading the bodies that the Japanese had not noticed my fumbling efforts to start and control the truck, and within half an hour I was able to keep a steady fifty yards behind Hodson. Both vehicles were plastered with military stickers pasted to the windshields and fenders, presumably assuring our passage through whatever Japanese units we might meet. Twice we passed a platoon sitting with its packs and rifles on the railway line, waiting for a train that would never come, but otherwise the landscape was deserted, not a single Chinese visible. Circumspectly, though, Hodson followed the route to Soochow marked on the road-map given to us by the Eurasian interpreter.

For myself, I was content to make this circuit of Shanghai, as I had no wish to drive the truck with its cargo of corpses through the centre of the city on my way to my parents' camp. Once I had cleared the western suburbs of the city I would turn north off the Soochow road, hand the vehicle over to the first allied command post – our new-found freedom had convinced me that the war would finally be over by the afternoon – and complete the short journey to my parents' camp on foot.

The prospect of seeing them, after all these years, within literally a few hours made me feel light-headed. During the three days in the gendarmerie barracks we had been given almost nothing to eat, and I now picked at the boiled rice in the wicker basket on the seat beside me. Even the sight of the corpses whose feet and faces were shaking loose beneath the tarpaulin of Hodson's truck did nothing to spoil my appetite. As I had lifted the bodies on to the two trucks I had immediately noticed how well-fleshed most of them were, far better fed than any of us had been in our camp. Presumably they had been imprisoned in some special internment centre, and had unluckily fallen foul of the American air-attacks.

At the same time the absence, with few exceptions, of any wounds or violence suggested one or two unsettling alternatives – plague, perhaps, or some sudden epidemic. Steering the truck with one hand and eating my rice with the other, I eased my foot off the heavy accelerator, opening the interval slightly between Hodson and myself. But for all this I was hardly concerned about the bodies. Too many people had already died in and around our camp. The business of loading the corpses into the trucks had placed a certain mental distance between them and myself. Handling all those bodies, pulling on the stiffening arms and legs, pushing their buttocks and shoulders over the tail-gates, had been like an extended wrestling match with a party of strangers, a kind of forced intimacy that absolved me from all future contact or obligation.

An hour after leaving the stadium, when we had covered some ten miles, Hodson began to slow down, his truck bumping over the rutted road surface at little more than walking pace. Some half a mile from the river, we had entered a landscape flooded by a slack, brown water. Untended canals and drowned paddies stretched away on all sides, and the road had become little more than a series of narrow causeways. The vanished peasants had built their burial mounds into the shoulders of the road, and the ends of the cheap coffins protruded like drawers from the rain-washed earth, lockers ransacked by the passing war. Across the paddies I could see a boom of scuttled freighters that blocked the river, funnels and bridge-houses emerging from the swollen tide. We passed another abandoned village, and then the green shell of a reconnaissance aircraft shot down by the Americans.

Ten feet in front of me, Hodson's truck bumped along the roadway, the heads of his corpses nodding vigorously like sleepers assenting in some shared dream. Then Hodson stopped and jumped down from his cabin.

He laid the map across the bonnet of my truck, then pointed along the broad canal we had been following for the past ten minutes. 'We've got to cross this before we reach the main road. Somewhere up ahead there's a sluice-bridge. It looks too small to have been bombed.'

With his strong hands he began to tear away the stickers pasted to the fenders and windshield of my truck. Though gaunt and undernourished, he looked strong and aggressive. The experience of driving a vehicle again had clearly restored his confidence. I could see that he had been helping himself liberally to his bottle of saki.

He bent down under the tail-gate of his truck and felt the left inside tyre. I had noticed the vehicle tilting when we first reached the canal.

'Going soft – no damn spares either.' He stood up and gazed into the rear of the truck, and with a single sweep of one arm flung back the tarpaulin, like a customs official exposing a suspicious cargo. Nodding to himself, he stared at the bodies piled across each other.

'Right, we rest here and finish the food, then find this bridge. First, let's make things easier for ourselves.'

Before I could speak he had reached into the truck and seized one of the corpses by the shoulders. He jerked it away from its companions and hurled it head-first into the canal. That of a freckle-skinned man in his early thirties, it surfaced within a few seconds in the brown water and slowly drifted away past the reeds.

'Right, we'll have the nun next.' As he hauled her out he shouted over his shoulder, 'You get on with yours. Leave a few behind just in case.'

Ten minutes later, as we sat with our bottles of saki on the bank of the canal, some twenty of the corpses were in the water, moving slowly away from us in the sluggish current. Pulling them down had almost exhausted me, but the first sips of the saki bolted through my bloodstream, almost as intoxicating as the boiled rice I had eaten. The brusque way in which we had ridded ourselves of our passengers no longer unsettled me – though, curiously, as I stood by the tail-gate pulling the bodies on to the ground I had found myself making some kind of selection. I had kept back the three children and a middle-aged woman who might have been their mother, and thrown into the water the Chinese couple and the elderly woman with the jaw-wound. However, all this meant nothing. What mattered was to reach my parents. It was clear to me that the Japanese had not been serious about our delivering the bodies to the Protestant cemetery at Soochow – the two nuns exposed this as no more than a ruse, relieving them of some local embarrassment before the Americans landed at the airfield.

Hodson was asleep beside his truck. His saki bottle followed the corpses down the canal. After throwing a few stones at it, I passed the next hour watching the vapour trails of the American aircraft and thinking with increasing optimism about the future, and about seeing my parents and sister later that afternoon. We would move back to our house in the French concession. My father would re-open his brokerage business, and no doubt train me as his assistant. After years of war and privation, Shanghai would be a boom city again . . . everything would once again return to normal.

This pleasant reverie sustained me, when Hodson had woken blearily and clambered back into his cabin, as we set off in our lightened trucks. I was beginning to feel hungry again, and regretted eating all my rice, particularly as Hodson had thrown his into the canal. But then I heard Hodson shout something back to me. He was pointing to the sluice-bridge a hundred yards in front of us.

When we reached it we found that we were not the only ones hoping to make the crossing.

Parked on the approaches to the bridge, its light machine-gun unguarded, was a camouflaged Japanese patrol car. As we stopped, the three-man crew had climbed on to the bridge and were trying to close the gates that would carry us across. Seeing us arrive, the sergeant in charge walked over to us, scanning the few stickers Hodson had not torn from our trucks. We stepped down from the cabins, waiting as the sergeant inspected our cargoes without comment. He spoke a few words in Japanese to Hodson, and beckoned us over to the bridge.

As we looked down at the sluices, we could see immediately what had blocked the bridges and prevented the gates from closing. Humped together against the vents were well over a dozen of the corpses that Hodson and I had pitched into the canal an hour earlier. They lay together like mattresses, arms and legs across each other, some face down, others staring at the sky.

To my shock I realized that I recognized each of them. That presentiment of death – though not my own nor of these drowned creatures – which I had felt so often during the past days returned to me, and I looked round at Hodson and the three Japanese as if expecting them immediately to fulfil this unconscious need.

'Well, what do they want?' Hodson was arguing aggressively with the Japanese sergeant, who for some reason was shouting at me in a suddenly high-pitched voice. Perhaps he realized that I might respond to his instructions for reasons of my own. I looked at his face and angular shoulders, wrists that were little more than sticks, well aware that he was as hungry as myself.

'I think they want us to get them out,' I said to Hodson. 'Otherwise, we can't get across. They know we threw them into the water.'

'For God's sake . . .' Exasperated, Hodson pushed past the Japanese and clambered down the bank of the canal. Waist-deep among the corpses, he began to sort them out with his strong arms. 'Aren't they going to help?' he called up in an aggrieved way when the Japanese made no effort to move.

Needless to say, Hodson and I were obliged to lift the bodies out ourselves. They lay on the bank like a party of exhausted bathers, in a strange way almost refreshed by their journey down the canal. The blood had been washed from the jaw-wound of the elderly woman, and I could see for the first time the image of a distinct personality. The sunlight lit the line of moist faces, illuminating the exposed hands and ankles.

'Well, we can get across now.' Looking down at his drenched trousers as the Japanese closed the sluice-gates, Hodson said to me 'Let's get on with it. We'll leave them here.'

I was staring at the face of the elderly woman, visualizing her talking to me, perhaps about her childhood in England or her long missionary years in Tientsin. Beside her the washed robes of the young nun had an almost spectral blackness, which gave her white hands and face an extraordinary glow. I was about to join Hodson when I noticed that the Japanese were also gazing at the bodies. All I could see was their intense hunger, as if they were eager to become my passengers.

'I think we should put them back on the trucks,' I said to Hodson. Fortunately, before he could remonstrate with me the sergeant had come over to us, beckoning us to work with his pistol.

Hodson helped me to load the first ten bodies on to the back of my truck. Then, unable to contain his anger any more, he seized the bottle of saki from the cabin, pushed past the Japanese and climbed into his truck. Shouting something at me, he drove on to the bridge and set off along the opposite bank of the canal.

For the next half hour I continued to load my vehicle, pausing to rest for a few minutes after I had carefully stowed each of the bodies. The effort of dragging them up the bank and lifting them into the truck almost exhausted me, and when I had finished I sat numbly for ten minutes behind my steering wheel. As I started the engine and drove on to the bridge with my heavy cargo the Japanese watched me without comment.

Fortunately, my anger at Hodson soon revived me. I clenched the wheel tightly in both hands, forehead touching the windshield, as the overladen vehicle lumbered down the uneven canal road. To have taken my saki mattered nothing, but to leave me with more than my fair share of corpses, without a map in this water-logged maze . . . Within half a mile of leaving the Japanese I was tempted to stop and heave a dozen of the bodies – I had the clearest picture in my mind of those who were Hodson's rather than my own – back into the water. Only the nun and the elderly woman I would allow on board. But I knew that once I stopped I would lose all hope of catching up with Hodson.

Ahead of me, above the fields of uncropped sugar-cane, I could see the poles and straggling telegraph wire that marked one of the main roads to Shanghai. I pressed on towards it, the vehicle rolling from side to side on the earth track. Behind me the bodies were sliding about as if in some huge scrimmage, their heads banging the sides of the truck. It was now a short period after noon, and a potent but not altogether unpleasant stench had filled the cabin. In spite of its obvious source, it seemed in some way to be refracted and amplified by the odours of my own body, almost as if my hunger and exhaustion were acting as the catalyst for the process of putrefaction. A plague of flies had descended on the truck, and covered the outer surface of the rear window behind my head, so that I was unable to see if the Japanese were following me in their scout car. I could still see the profound sense of loss in their eyes as they had watched me leave, and I almost regretted that I had not taken them with me. Far from my being their prisoner, it was they who in some way belonged to the bodies lying behind me.

Before I could reach the main Shanghai road the radiator of the engine had boiled, and I wasted a full half an hour waiting for it to cool. In order to lighten the load on the engine, I decided to throw off Hodson's corpses. There was now no chance whatever of catching up with him, and he was almost certainly speeding through the suburbs of Shanghai for a first look at his garage. Somehow I would find my own way to my parents' camp.

I climbed on to the back of the truck, and clambered among the bodies piled together. Gazing down at the yellowing faces between my feet, I realized that I recognized almost all of them – the nuns and the Chinese couple, the elderly woman and the three children, a slim young man of my own age with an amputated left hand, a pregnant woman in her early twenties who vaguely resembled my sister. These belonged to my flock, whereas Hodson's intruders were as distinct and separate as the members of a rival clan. Their leader was clearly a small, elderly man with a bare-chested body like a grey monkey's, whose sharp eyes had seemed to follow me all day as I lifted him on and off the trucks.

I bent down to seize him by the shoulders, but for some reason my hands were unable to touch him. Once again I felt that presentiment of death I had sensed so many times, surrounding me on all sides, in the canal beside the road, in the fields of sugar-cane and the distant telegraph wires, even in the drone of an American aircraft crossing far overhead. Only I and the passengers aboard this truck were immune.

I tried to pick up another of the corpses, but again my hands froze, and again I felt the same presentiment, an enclosing wall that enveloped us like the wire fence around our camp. I watched the flies swarm across my hands and over the faces of the bodies between my feet, relieved now that I would never again be forced to distinguish between us. I hurled the tarpaulin into the canal, so that the air could play over their faces as we sped along. When the engine of the truck had cooled I refilled the radiator with water from the canal, and set off towards the west.

It was without surprise, an hour later, that I came across Hodson's truck, and was able to make up the full complement of my passengers.

Where Hodson himself had gone I never discovered. Five miles down the Shanghai road, after two further delays to rest the engine, I found the truck abandoned by a Japanese road-block. In the afternoon haze the surface of the road seemed to be speckled with gold, nodes of bright light reflected from hundreds of spent cartridge cases. The Japanese here had fought a vigorous engagement, perhaps with some intruding patrol of Kuomintang troops. Webbing and empty ammunition boxes lay in the tank ditch dug across the road. Unable to drive around this obstacle, Hodson had presumably set off on foot.

I stopped beside his abandoned truck, listening to the harsh beat of my engine in the deserted air. A hundred yards behind me a narrow lane led across a field of sugar-cane in a westerly direction, and with luck would carry me a little further on my circuit of Shanghai.

First, however, I had to take on my additional passengers. At the time, as I carried the dozen corpses from Hodson's truck and lifted them on to my own, it occurred to me more than once to give up the entire enterprise and set off on foot myself after Hodson. But as we turned off the road and rolled down the lane between the fields of sugar-cane I felt a curious kind of comfort that we were all together, almost a sense of security at the presence of my 'family'. At the same time the urge to rid myself of them still remained, and given the opportunity – a lift, perhaps, in a passing Kuomintang vehicle – I would have left them at the first chance. But within this empty landscape they did at least provide an element of security, particularly if a hostile Japanese patrol came across me. Also, for the first time I had begun to feel a sense of loyalty towards them, and the feeling that they, the dead, were more living than the living who had deserted me.

The afternoon sun had begun to set. I woke in the cabin of the truck to find that I had fallen asleep beside a broad canal whose brown surface had turned almost carmine in the fading light. In front of me were the approaches to an empty village, the single-storey dwellings concealed by the dark fronds of the wild sugar-cane. All afternoon I had been lost in a golden world, following the sun as it moved away from me across the drowned paddies and silent villages. I was certain that I had covered some twenty miles – the apartment houses of the French concession were no longer visible along the horizon.

My last attempt to free myself from the corpses took place that night. At dusk I stepped from the cabin of the truck and walked through the sugar-cane, breaking the stems and sucking the sweet pith. From the back of the truck the corpses watched me like a hostile chorus, their inclined heads slyly confiding in each other. I too at first resented this nourishment flowing through me, meagre though it was. As I revived, however, leaning against the radiator grille of the truck, I was suddenly tempted to release the handbrake and roll the vehicle forward into the blood-stained canal. As a result of committing myself to this lunatic troupe of passengers, ferrying them from the football stadium to some destination they had never agreed upon, I had lost the chance of seeing my parents that day.

Under the cover of darkness – for I would not have dared to commit this act by daylight – I returned to the truck and began to remove the bodies one by one, throwing them down on to the road. Clouds of flies festered around me, as if trying to warn me of the insanity of what I was doing. Exhausted, I pulled the bodies down like damp sacks, ruthlessly avoiding the faces of the nuns and the children, the young amputee and the elderly woman.

At this point, when I had nearly destroyed everything I had been allowed by circumstances to achieve, I was saved by the arrival of a party of bandits. Armed American merchant seamen, renegade Kuomintang and quisling auxiliaries of the Japanese, they arrived by sampans and rapidly occupied the village. Too tired to run from them, I crouched behind the truck, watching these heavily armed men move towards me. For some reason, although I knew they would kill me, I had no sense whatever of that presentiment of death.

At the last moment, when they were only twenty feet away, I lay down in the darkness among the circle of corpses, taking my position between the young nun and the elderly woman. The ferocious flight of the thousand flies came to a stop, and I could hear the heavy step of the bandits and the sounds of their weapons. Lying there in the darkness in the circle of the dead, I watched them halt and peer into the truck, arms raised across their mouths. Unable to approach us, they waited for a few minutes and then returned to the village. All night, as they roamed from house to house, kicking down the doors and breaking the furniture, I lay in the circle of corpses. Towards dawn two of the Kuomintang soldiers came and began to search the pockets of the dead. Staring at the sky, I listened to them panting beside me, and felt their hands on my thighs and buttocks.

At dawn, when they left in their motorized sampans, the flies returned. I stood up and watched the sun rising through the dark forests of sugar-cane. Waiting for its disc to touch me, I summoned my companions to their feet.

From this time onwards, during the confused days of my journey to my parents' camp, I was completely identified with my companions. I no longer attempted to escape them. As we drove together through that landscape of war and its aftermath, past the endless canals and deserted villages, I was uncertain whether the events taking place spanned a few hours or many weeks. I was almost sure that by now the war should have been over, but the countryside remained empty, disturbed only by the sounds of the American aircraft overhead.

For much of the time I followed the westerly course of the river, a distant presence which provided my only compass bearing. I drove carefully along the broken roads that divided the paddy-fields, anxious not to disturb my passengers lying together behind me. It was they who had saved me from the bandits. I knew that in a sense I was their representative, the instrument of the new order which I had been delegated by them to bring to the world. I knew that I now had to teach the living that my companions were not merely the dead, but the last of the dead, and that soon the whole planet would share in the new life which they had earned for us.

One small example of this understanding was that I no longer wished for food. I looked out from the cabin of the truck at the wide fields of sugar-cane beside the river, knowing that their harvest would no longer be needed, and that the land could be turned over to the demands of my companions.

One afternoon, after a brief thunderstorm had driven the American aircraft from the sky, I reached the bank of the river. At some time a battle had been fought here among the wharfs and quays of a small Japanese naval air base. In the village behind the base there were shallow wells filled with rifles, and a pagoda housing a still intact anti-aircraft gun. All the villagers had fled, but to my amazement I found that I was not alone.

Seated side by side in a rickshaw that had been abandoned in the central square of the village were an elderly Chinese and a child of ten or so whom I took to be his granddaughter. At first glance they looked as if they had hired the rickshaw a few hours beforehand and ridden out here to view this small battlefield that I too was now visiting. I stopped my truck, stepped down from the cabin and walked over to them, looking around to see if their coolie was present.

As I approached, the child climbed from the rickshaw and stood passively beside it. I could see now that, far from being a spectator, her grandfather had been seriously wounded in the battle. A large piece of shrapnel had driven through the side of the rickshaw into his hip.

In Chinese I said to him, 'I'm making my way to the Soochow road. If you wish, you and your granddaughter are welcome to ride with my companions.'

He made no reply, but I knew from his eyes that despite his injuries he had immediately recognized me, and understood that I was the harbinger of all that lay before him. For the first time I realized why I had seen so few Chinese during the past days. They had not gone away for ever, but were waiting for my return. I alone could repopulate their land.

Together the child and I walked down to the concrete ramp of the naval air base. In the deep water below the wharf lay the drowned forms of hundreds of cars rounded up from the allied nationals in Shanghai and dumped here by the Japanese. They rested on the river bed twenty feet below the surface, the elements of a past world that would never be able to reconstitute itself now that I and my companions, this child and her grandfather had taken possession of the land.

Two days later we at last reached the approaches to my parents' camp. During our journey the child sat beside me in the cabin of the truck, while her grandfather rode comfortably with my companions. Although she complained of hunger to begin with, I patiently taught her that food was no longer necessary to us. Fortunately I was able to distract her by pointing out the different marks of American aircraft that crossed the sky.

After we reached the Soochow road the landscape was to change. Close to the Yangtse we had entered an area of old battlegrounds. On all sides the Chinese had emerged from their hiding places and were waiting for my arrival. They lay in the fields around their houses, legs stirring in the water that seeped across the paddy-fields. They watched from the embankments of the tank-ditches, from their burial mounds and from the doors of their ruined houses.

Beside me the child slept fitfully on the seat. Free of any fear of embarrassing her, I stopped the truck and took off my ragged clothes, leaving only a crude bandage on my arm that covered a small wound.

Naked, I knelt in front of the vehicle, raising my arms to my congregation in the fields around me, like a king assuming his crown at his coronation. Although still a virgin, I exposed my loins to the Chinese watching me as they lay quietly in the fields. With those loins I would seed the dead.

Every fifty yards, as I approached the distant water-tower of my parents' camp, I stopped the truck and knelt naked in front of its boiling radiator. There was no sign of movement from the camp compound, and I was sure now what I would find there.

The child lay motionlessly in my arms. As I knelt with her in the centre of the road, wondering if it were time for her to join my companions, I noticed that her lips still moved. Without thinking, giving way to what then seemed a meaningless impulse, I tore a small shred of flesh from the wound on my arm and pressed it between her lips.

Feeding her in this way, I walked with her towards the camp a few hundred yards away. The child stirred in my arms. Looking down I saw that her eyes had partly opened. Although unable to see me, she seemed aware of the movement of my stride.

From the gates of the camp, on the roofs of the dormitory blocks, on the causeways of the paddy-fields beyond the wire, people were moving. Their figures were coming towards me, advancing waist-deep through the stunted sugar-cane. Astonished, I pressed the child to my chest, aware of her mouthing my flesh. Standing naked a hundred yards from the truck, I counted a dozen, a score, then fifty of the internees, some with children behind them.

At last, through this child and my body, the dead were coming to life, rising from their fields and doorways and coming to greet me. I saw my mother and father at the gates of the camp, and knew that I had given my death to them and so brought them into this world. Unharmed they had passed into the commonwealth of the living, and of the other living beyond the dead.

I knew now that the war was over.

**1977**

# · THE INDEX

*Editor's note.* From abundant internal evidence it seems clear that the text printed below is the index to the unpublished and perhaps suppressed autobiography of a man who may well have been one of the most remarkable figures of the 20th century. Yet of his existence nothing is publicly known, although his life and work appear to have exerted a profound influence on the events of the past fifty years. Physician and philosopher, man of action and patron of the arts, sometime claimant to the English throne and founder of a new religion, Henry Rhodes Hamilton was evidently the intimate of the greatest men and women of our age. After World War II he founded a new movement of spiritual regeneration, but private scandal and public concern at his growing megalomania, culminating in his proclamation of himself as a new divinity, seem to have led to his downfall. Incarcerated within an unspecified government institution, he presumably spent his last years writing his autobiography, of which this index is the only surviving fragment.

A substantial mystery still remains. Is it conceivable that all traces of his activities could be erased from our records of the period? Is the suppressed autobiography itself a disguised *roman à clef*, in which the fictional hero exposes the secret identities of his historical contemporaries? And what is the true role of the indexer himself, clearly a close friend of the writer, who first suggested that he embark on his autobiography? This ambiguous and shadowy figure has taken the unusual step of indexing himself into his own index. Perhaps the entire compilation is nothing more than a figment of the over-wrought imagination of some deranged lexicographer. Alternatively, the index may be wholly genuine, and the only glimpse we have into a world hidden from us by a gigantic conspiracy, of which Henry Rhodes Hamilton is the greatest victim.

**A**

Acapulco, 143
Acton, Harold, 142–7, 213
Alcazar, Siege of, 221–5
Alimony, HRH pays, 172, 247, 367, 453
Anaxagoras, 35, 67, 69–78, 481
Apollinaire, 98
Arden, Elizabeth, 189, 194, 376–84

*Autobiography of Alice B. Toklas, The* (Stein), 112
Avignon, birthplace of HRH, 9–13; childhood holidays, 27; research at Pasteur Institute of Ophthalmology, 101; attempts to restore anti-Papacy, 420–35

**B**

Bal Musette, Paris, 98
Balliol College, Oxford, 69–75, 231
Beach, Sylvia, 94–7
Berenson, Bernard, conversations
    with HRH, 134; offer of
    adoption, 145; loan of Dürer
    etching, 146; law-suits against
    HRH, 173–85
Bergman, Ingrid, 197, 234, 267
Biarritz, 123
Blixen, Karen von (Isak Dinesen),
    letters to HRH, declines marriage
    proposal, 197
Byron, Lord, 28, 76, 98, 543

**C**

Cambodia, HRH plans journey
    to, 188; crashes aircraft, 196;
    writes book about, 235; meetings
    with Malraux, 239; capture by
    insurgents, 253; escape, 261;
    writes second book about, 283
Cap d'Antibes, 218
Charing Cross Hospital Medical
    School, 78–93
Charterhouse, HRH enters, 31;
    academic distinction, 38; sexual
    crisis, 43; school captain, 44
Chiang Kai-shek, interviewed by
    HRH, 153; HRH and American
    arms embargo, 162; HRH pilots
    to Chungking, 176; implements
    land-reform proposals by
    HRH, 178; employs HRH
    as intermediary with Chou
    En-Lai, 192
Churchill, Winston, conversations
    with HRH, 221; at Chequers with
    HRH, 235; spinal tap performed
    by HRH, 247; at Yalta with
    HRH, 298; 'iron curtain' speech,
    Fulton, Missouri, suggested
    by HRH, 312; attacks HRH in
    Commons debate, 367
Cocteau, Jean, 187

Cunard, Nancy, 204

**D**

D-Day, HRH ashore on Juno
    Beach, 223; decorated, 242
Dalai Lama, grants audience to
    HRH, 321; supports HRH's
    initiatives with Mao Tse-tung,
    325; refuses to receive HRH, 381
Darwin, Charles, influence on
    HRH, 103; repudiated by
    HRH, 478
de Beauvoir, Simone, 176
de Gaulle, Charles, conversations
    with HRH, 319–47, 356–79, 401
Dealey Plaza (Dallas, Texas),
    rumoured presence of HRH, 435
Dietrich, Marlene, 234, 371, 435

**E**

Ecclesiastes, Book of, 87
Eckhart, Meister, 265
Einstein, Albert, first Princeton visit
    by HRH, 203; joint signatory
    with HRH and R. Niebuhr of
    Roosevelt petition, 276; second
    and third Princeton visits,
    284; death-bed confession to
    HRH, 292
Eisenhower, Gen. Dwight D., 218,
    227, 232
Eliot, T. S., conversations with
    HRH, 209; suppresses dedication
    of Four Quartets to HRH, 213
Ellis, Havelock, 342
Everest, Mt., 521

**F**

Fairbanks, Douglas, 281
Faulkner, William, 375
Fermi, Enrico, reveals first
    controlled fission reaction
    to HRH, 299; terminal
    cancer diagnosed by HRH,
    388; funeral eulogy read by
    HRH, 401

Fleming, Sir Alexander, credits HRH, 211
Ford, Henry, 198
*Fortune* (magazine), 349
Freud, Sigmund, receives HRH in London, 198; conducts analysis of HRH, 205; begins *Civilization and its Discontents*, 230; admits despair to HRH, 279

**G**

Gandhi, Mahatma, visited in prison by HRH, 251; discusses Bhagavadgita with HRH, 253; has dhoti washed by HRH, 254; denounces HRH, 256
Garbo, Greta, 381
George V, secret visits to Chatsworth, 3, 4–6; rumoured liaison with Mrs Alexander Hamilton, 7; suppresses court circular, 9; denies existence of collateral Battenburg line to Lloyd George, 45
Goldwyn, Samuel, 397
Grenadier Guards, 215–18
Gstaad, 359

**H**

Hadrian IV, Pope, 28, 57, 84, 119, 345–76, 411, 598
Hamilton, Alexander, British Consul, Marseilles, 1, 3, 7; interest in topiary, 2; unexpected marriage, 3; depression after birth of HRH, 6; surprise recall to London, 12; first nervous breakdown, 16; transfer to Tsingtao, 43
Hamilton, Alice Rosalind (later Lady Underwood), private education, 2; natural gaiety, 3; first marriage annulled, 4; enters London society, 5; beats George V at billiards, 5, 7, 9, 23; second marriage to Alexander

Hamilton, 3; dislike of Marseilles, 7; premature birth of HRH, 8; divorce, 47; third marriage to Sir Richard Underwood, 48
Hamilton, Henry Rhodes, accident-proneness, 118; age, sensitiveness about, 476; belief in telepathy, 399; childhood memories, 501; common man, identification with, 211; courage, moral, 308, physical, 201; generosity, 99; Goethe, alleged resemblance to, 322; hobbies, dislike of, 87; illnesses, concussion, 196; hypertension, 346; prostate inflammation, 522; venereal disease, 77; integrity, 89; languages, mastery of, 176; Orient, love of, 188; patriotism, renunciation of, 276; public speaking, aptitude for, 345; self-analysis, 234–67; underdog, compassion for, 176; will-power, 87
Hamilton, Indira, meets HRH in Calcutta, 239; translates at Gandhi interviews, 253; imprisoned with HRH by British, 276; marries HRH, 287; on abortive Everest expedition, 299; divorces HRH, 301
Hamilton, Marcelline (formerly Marcelline Renault), abandons industrialist husband, 177; accompanies HRH to Ankor, 189; marries HRH, 191; amuses Ho Chi-minh, 195; divorces HRH, 201
Hamilton, Ursula (later Mrs Mickey Rooney), 302–7, divorces HRH, 308
Hamilton, Zelda, rescued from orphanage by HRH, 325; visit to Cape Kennedy with HRH, 327; declines astronaut training, 328; leads International Virgin

Bride campaign, 331; arrested
with HRH by Miami police, 344;
Frankfurt police, 359; divorces
HRH, 371; wins Miss Alabama
contest, 382; go-go dancer,
511; applies for writ of habeas
corpus, 728
Harriman, Averell, 432
Harry's Bar, Venice, 256
Hayworth, Rita, 311
Hemingway, Ernest, first African
safari with HRH, 234; at Battle
of the Ebro with HRH, 244;
introduces HRH to James Joyce,
256; portrays HRH in *The Old
Man and the Sea*, 453
Hiroshima, HRH observes atomic
cloud, 258
Hitler, Adolf, invites HRH to
Berchtesgaden, 166; divulges
Russia invasion plans, 172;
impresses HRH, 179; disappoints
HRH, 181
Hydrogen Bomb, HRH calls
for world moratorium on
manufacture, 388

I
Impostors, HRH troubled by, 157,
198, 345, 439
Inchon, Korea, HRH observes
landings with Gen. MacArthur,
348
Interlaken, Bruno Walter lends villa
to HRH, 401
International Congress of
Psychoanalysis, HRH stages anti-
psychiatry demonstration, 357
Ives, Burl, 328

J
Jerusalem, HRH establishes
collegium of Perfect Light
Movement, 453; attempted
intercession by HRH in
Arab-Israeli war, 444;

HRH designs tomb, 478
Jesus Christ, HRH compared to by
Malraux, 476
Jodrell Bank Radio-telescope, 501
Joyce, James, 256
Juan Les Pins, 347
Jupiter, planet, HRH suggests
existence of extra-terrestrial
observers, 331; urges re-direction
of space programme to, 342

K
Kennedy, Cape, HRH leads
Perfect Light Movement
demonstration, 411
Kennedy, John F., President,
declines to receive HRH, 420;
ignores danger warnings, 425;
mourned by HRH, 444
Kierkegaard, Soren, 231
Koran, 118

L
Lancaster, Mrs Burt, 411
Lawrence, T. E., HRH compared to
by Koestler, 334
Lévi-Strauss, C., 422
*Life* (magazine), 199, 243, 331,
357, 432
Limited Editions Club, 345
Louis XIV, 501

M
Malraux, André, 239, 345, 399, 476
Mann Act, HRH charged
under, 345
*McCall's* (magazine) 201, 234,
329, 333
Menninger Clinic, HRH confined,
477; receives treatment, 479–85;
discharged, 491; re-admitted, 495
Menuhin, Yehudi, lends Palm
Springs villa to HRH, 503
Metro-Goldwyn-Mayer, offer to
HRH, 511
Miranda, Carmen, 377

**N**

Nato, 331, 356, 571

Nice, 45

Niebuhr, R., conversations with HRH, 270–5; admiration for HRH, 276; lends villa to HRH, 288; expresses reservations about HRH, 291

Nietzsche, 99

Nobel Prize, HRH nominated for, 220, 267, 342, 375, 459, 611

**O**

Oberammergau, 117

Oedipus Complex, 42–9, 87, 451

Old Bailey, first trial of HRH, 531; prosecution case, 533–7; hung jury, 541; second trial, 555; surprise intervention of Attorney-General, 561; acquittal of HRH, 564

Oswald, Lee Harvey, befriended by HRH, 350; inspired by HRH, 354; discusses failure of the Presidency with HRH, 357–61; invites HRH to Dallas, 372

*Oxford Book of Religious Verse*, 98, 116

**P**

Pasternak, Boris, conversations with HRH, 341–4

Paul VI, Pope, praises Perfect Light Movement, 462; receives HRH, 464; attacked by HRH, 471; deplores messianic pretensions of HRH, 487; criticises Avignon counter-papacy established by HRH, 498; excommunicates HRH, 533

Perfect Light Movement, conceived by HRH, 398; launched, 401; charitable activities praised by Nehru, Lyndon B. Johnson, Pierre Trudeau, 423; medical mission to Biafra, 456; criticised

by International Red Cross, 477; denounced by World Council of Churches, 499; criminal prosecution of, 544; disbandment, 566; reconstituted, 588; designated a religion by HRH, 604; first crusade against Rome, 618; infiltrated by CIA, 622

Pill, the, denounced by HRH, 611

**Q**

Quai d'Orsay, expresses alarm at HRH initiatives in Third World, 651; concludes secret accords with Britain, United States and USSR, 666

Quixote, Don, HRH compared to by Harold Macmillan, 421

**R**

Rapallo, HRH convalesces in, 321

*Reader's Digest* (magazine), 176

Rockefeller Foundation, dissociates itself from HRH, 555

Rubinstein, Helena, 221, 234, 242

**S**

Schweitzer, Albert, receives HRH, 199; performs organ solo for HRH, 201; discusses quest for the historical Jesus with HRH, 203–11; HRH compared to by Leonard Bernstein, 245; expels HRH, 246

Sex-change, rumoured operation on HRH, 655

Stanwyck, Barbara, 248

Stork Club, 231

**T**

Tangier, secret visit by HRH, 653–5

Technology, HRH renunciation of, 409

Telepathy, HRH interest in, 241; conducts experiments,

349–57; claims powers of, 666
Tenth Convocation of Perfect Light
  Movement, 672; proclamation of
  HRH's divinity, 685
*Time* (magazine), cover stories
  on HRH, 267, 359, 492,
  578, 691
Tynan, Kenneth, 451

**U**

United Nations Assembly, seized by
  Perfect Light Movement, 695–9;
  HRH addresses, 696; HRH calls
  for world war against United
  States and USSR, 698

**V**

Versailles, Perfect Light Movement
  attempts to purchase, 621
*Vogue* (magazine), 356

**W**

Westminster Abbey, arrest of HRH
  by Special Branch, 704

Wight, Isle of, incarceration of
  HRH, 712–69
Windsor, House of, HRH challenges
  legitimacy of, 588

**Y**

Yale Club, 234
Younghusband, Lord Chancellor,
  denies star chamber trial of
  HRH, 722; denies knowledge
  of whereabouts of HRH, 724;
  refuses habeas corpus appeal
  by Zelda Hamilton, 728; refers
  to unestablished identity of
  HRH, 731

**Z**

Zanuck, Daryl F., 388
Zielinski, Bronislaw, suggests
  autobiography to HRH,
  742; commissioned to
  prepare index, 748; warns
  of suppression threats, 752;
  disappears, 761

**1977**

# THE INTENSIVE CARE UNIT

Within a few minutes the next attack will begin. Now that I am surrounded for the first time by all the members of my family it seems only fitting that a complete record should be made of this unique event. As I lie here – barely able to breathe, my mouth filled with blood and every tremor of my hands reflected in the attentive eye of the camera six feet away – I realize that there are many who will think my choice of subject a curious one. In all senses, this film will be the ultimate home-movie, and I only hope that whoever watches it will gain some idea of the immense affection I feel for my wife, and for my son and daughter, and of the affection that they, in their unique way, feel for me.

It is now half an hour since the explosion, and everything in this once elegant sitting room is silent. I am lying on the floor by the settee, looking at the camera mounted safely out of reach on the ceiling above my head. In this uneasy stillness, broken only by my wife's faint breathing and the irregular movement of my son across the carpet, I can see that almost everything I have assembled so lovingly during the past years has been destroyed. My Sèvres lies in a thousand fragments in the fireplace, the Hokusai scrolls are punctured in a dozen places. Yet despite the extensive damage this is still recognizably the scene of a family reunion, though of a rather special kind.

My son David crouches at his mother's feet, chin resting on the torn Persian carpet, his slow movement marked by a series of smeared hand-prints. Now and then, when he raises his head, I can see that he is still alive. His eyes are watching me, calculating the distance between us and the time it will take him to reach me. His sister Karen is little more than an arm's length away, lying beside the fallen standard lamp between the settee and the fireplace, but he ignores her. Despite my fear, I feel a powerful sense of pride that he should have left his mother and set out on this immense journey towards me. For his own sake I would rather he lay still and conserved what little strength and time are left to him, but he presses on with all the determination his seven-year-old body can muster.

My wife Margaret, who is sitting in the armchair facing me, raises her hand in some kind of confused warning, and then lets it fall limply on to the stained damask arm-rest. Distorted by her smudged lipstick, the brief smile she gives me might seem to the casual spectator of this film to be ironic or even threatening, but I am merely struck once again by her remarkable beauty. Watching her, and relieved that she will probably never rise from her armchair again, I think of our first meeting ten years ago, then as now within the benevolent gaze of the television camera.

The unusual, not to say illicit, notion of actually meeting my wife and children in the flesh had occurred to me some three months earlier, during one of our extended family breakfasts. Since the earliest days of our marriage Sunday mornings had always been especially enjoyable. There were the pleasures of breakfast in bed, of talking over the papers and whatever else had taken place during the week. Switching to our private channel, Margaret and I would make love, celebrating the deep peace of our marriage beds. Later, we would call in the children and watch them playing in their nurseries, and perhaps surprise them with the promise of a visit to the park or circus.

All these activities, of course, like our family life itself, were made possible by television. At that time neither I nor anyone else had ever dreamed that we might actually meet in person. In fact, age-old though rarely invoked ordinances still existed to prevent this – to meet another human being was an indictable offence (especially, for reasons I then failed to understand, a member of one's own family, presumably part of some ancient system of incest taboos). My own upbringing, my education and medical practice, my courtship of Margaret and our happy marriage, all occurred within the generous rectangle of the television screen. Margaret's insemination was of course by AID, and like all children David's and Karen's only contact with their mother was during their brief uterine life.

In every sense, needless to say, this brought about an immense increase in the richness of human experience. As a child I had been brought up in the hospital crèche, and thus spared all the psychological dangers of a physically intimate family life (not to mention the hazards, aesthetic and otherwise, of a shared domestic hygiene). But far from being isolated I was surrounded by companions. On television I was never alone. In my nursery I played hours of happy games with my parents, who watched me from the comfort of their homes, feeding on to my screen a host of video-games, animated cartoons, wild-life films and family serials which together opened the world to me.

My five years as a medical student passed without my ever needing to see a patient in the flesh. My skills in anatomy and physiology were learned at the computer display terminal. Advanced techniques of diagnosis and surgery eliminated any need for direct contact with an organic illness. The probing camera, with its infra-red and X-ray scanners, its computerized diagnostic aids, revealed far more than any unaided human eye.

Perhaps I was especially adept at handling these complex keyboards and retrieval systems – a finger-tip sensitivity that was the modern equivalent of the classical surgeon's operative skills – but by the age of thirty I had already established a thriving general practice. Freed from the need to visit my surgery in person, my patients would merely dial themselves on to my television screen. The selection of these incoming calls – how tactfully to fade out a menopausal housewife and cut to a dysenteric child, while remembering to cue in separately the anxious parents – required a considerable degree of skill, particularly as the patients themselves shared these talents. The more neurotic patients usually far exceeded them, presenting themselves with the disjointed cutting, aggressive zooms and split-screen techniques that went far beyond the worst excesses of experimental cinema.

My first meeting with Margaret took place when she called me during a busy morning surgery. As I glanced into what was still known nostalgically as 'the waiting room' – the visual display projecting brief filmic profiles of the day's patients – I would customarily have postponed to the next day any patient calling without an appointment. But I was immediately struck, first by her age – she seemed to be in her late twenties – and then by the remarkable pallor of this young woman. Below close-cropped blonde hair her underlit eyes and slim mouth were set in a face that was almost ashen. I realized that, unlike myself and everyone else, she was wearing no make-up for the cameras. This accounted both for her arctic skin-tones and for her youthless appearance – on television, thanks to make-up, everyone of whatever age was 22, the cruel divisions of chronology banished for good.

It must have been this absence of make-up that first seeded the idea, to flower with such devastating consequences ten years later, of actually meeting Margaret in person. Intrigued by her unclassifiable appearance, I shelved my other patients and began our interview. She told me that she was a masseuse, and after a polite preamble came to the point. For some months she had been concerned that a small lump in her left breast might be cancerous.

I made some reassuring reply, and told her that I would examine her. At this point, without warning, she leaned forward, unbuttoned her shirt and exposed her breast.

Startled, I stared at this huge organ, some two feet in diameter, which filled my television screen. An almost Victorian code of visual ethics governed the doctor/patient relationship, as it did all social intercourse. No physician ever saw his patients undressed, and the location of any intimate ailments was always indicated by the patient by means of diagram slides. Even among married couples the partial exposure of their bodies was a comparative rarity, and the sexual organs usually remained veiled behind the most misty filters, or were coyly alluded to by the exchange of cartoon drawings. Of course, a clandestine pornographic channel operated, and prostitutes of both sexes plied their wares, but even the most expensive of these would never appear live, instead substituting a pre-recorded film-strip of themselves at the moment of climax.

These admirable conventions eliminated all the dangers of personal involvement, and this liberating affectlessness allowed those who so wished to explore the fullest range of sexual possibility and paved the way for the day when a truly guilt-free sexual perversity and, even, psychopathology might be enjoyed by all.

Staring at the vast breast and nipple, with their uncompromising geometries, I decided that my best way of dealing with this eccentrically frank young woman was to ignore any lapse from convention. After the infra-red examination confirmed that the suspected cancer nodule was in fact a benign cyst she buttoned her shirt and said:

'That's a relief. Do call me, doctor, if you ever need a course of massage. I'll be delighted to repay you.'

Though still intrigued by her, I was about to roll the credits at the conclusion of this bizarre consultation when her casual offer lodged in my mind. Curious to see her again, I arranged an appointment for the following week.

Without realizing it, I had already begun my courtship of this unusual young woman. On the evening of my appointment, I half-suspected that she was some kind of novice prostitute. However, as I lay discreetly robed on the recreation couch in my sauna, manipulating my body in response to Margaret's instructions, there was not the slightest hint of salaciousness. During the evenings that followed I never once detected a glimmer of sexual awareness, though at times, as we moved through our exercises together, we revealed far more of our bodies to each other than many married couples. Margaret, I realized, was a sport, one of those rare people with no sense of self-consciousness, and little awareness of the prurient emotions she might arouse in others.

Our courtship entered a more formal phase. We began to go out together – that is, we shared the same films on television, visited the same theatres and concert halls, watched the same meals prepared in restaurants, all within the comfort of our respective homes. In fact, at this time I had no idea where Margaret lived, whether she was five miles away from me or five hundred. Shyly at first, we exchanged old footage of ourselves, of our childhoods and schooldays, our favourite foreign resorts.

Six months later we were married, at a lavish ceremony in the most exclusive of the studio chapels. Over two hundred guests attended, joining a huge hook-up of television screens, and the service was conducted by a priest renowned for his mastery of the split-screen technique. Pre-recorded films of Margaret and myself taken separately in our own sitting rooms were projected against a cathedral interior and showed us walking together down an immense aisle.

For our honeymoon we went to Venice. Happily we shared the panoramic views of the crowds in St Mark's Square, and gazed at the Tintorettos in the Academy School. Our wedding night was a triumph of the director's art. As we lay in our respective beds (Margaret was in fact some thirty miles to the south of me, somewhere in a complex of vast high-rises), I courted Margaret with a series of increasingly bold zooms, which she countered in a sweetly teasing way with her shy fades and wipes. As we undressed and exposed ourselves to each other the screens merged into a last oblivious close-up . . .

\*          \*          \*

From the start we made a handsome couple, sharing all our interests, spending more time on the screen together than any couple we knew. In due course, through AID, Karen was conceived and born, and soon after her second birthday in the residential crèche she was joined by David.

Seven further years followed of domestic bliss. During this period I had made an impressive reputation for myself as a paediatrician of advanced views by my championship of family life – this fundamental unit, as I described it, of intensive care. I repeatedly urged the installation of more cameras throughout the homes of family members, and provoked vigorous controversy when I suggested that families should bathe together, move naked but without embarrassment around their respective bedrooms, and even that fathers should attend (though not in close-up) the births of their children.

It was during a pleasant family breakfast together that there occurred to me the extraordinary idea that was so dramatically to change our lives. I was looking at the image of Margaret on the screen, enjoying the beauty of the cosmetic mask she now wore – ever thicker and more elaborate as the years passed, it made her grow younger all the time. I relished the elegantly stylized way in which we now presented ourselves to each other – fortunately we had moved from the earnestness of Bergman and the more facile mannerisms of Fellini and Hitchcock to the classical serenity and wit of René Clair and Max Ophuls, though the children, with their love of the hand-held camera, still resembled so many budding Godards.

Recalling the abrupt way in which Margaret had first revealed herself to me, I realized that the logical extension of Margaret's frankness – on which, effectively, I had built my career – was that we should all meet together in person. Throughout my entire life, I reflected, I had never once seen, let alone touched, another human being. Whom better to begin with than my own wife and children?

Tentatively I raised the suggestion with Margaret, and I was delighted when she agreed.

'What an odd but marvellous idea! Why on earth has no one suggested it before?'

We decided instantly that the archaic interdiction against meeting another human being deserved simply to be ignored.

Unhappily, for reasons I failed to understand at the time, our first meeting was not a success. To avoid confusing the children, we deliberately restricted the first encounter to ourselves. I remember the days of anticipation as we made preparations for Margaret's journey – an elaborate undertaking, for people rarely travelled, except at the speed of the television signal.

An hour before she arrived I disconnected the complex security precautions that sealed my house from the world outside, the electronic alarm signals, steel grilles and gas-tight doors.

At last the bell rang. Standing by the internal portcullis at the end of the entrance hall, I released the magnetic catches on the front door. A few seconds later the figure of a small, narrow-shouldered woman stepped into the hall. Although she was over twenty feet from me I could see her clearly, but I almost failed to realize that this was the wife to whom I had been married for ten years.

Neither of us was wearing make-up. Without its cosmetic mask Margaret's face seemed pasty and unhealthy, and the movements of her white hands were nervous and unsettled. I was struck by her advanced age and, above all, by her small size. For years I had known Margaret as a huge close-up on one or other of the large television screens in the house. Even in long-shot she was usually larger than this hunched and diminutive woman hovering at the end of the hall. It was difficult to believe that I had ever been excited by her empty breasts and narrow thighs.

Embarrassed by each other, we stood without speaking at opposite ends of the hall. I knew from her expression that Margaret was as surprised by my appearance as I was by her own. In addition, there was a curiously searching look in her eye, an element almost of hostility that I had never seen before.

Without thinking, I moved my hand to the latch of the portcullis. Already Margaret had stepped back into the doorway, as if nervous that I might seal her into the hall for ever. Before I could speak, she had turned and fled.

When she had gone I carefully checked the locks on the front door. Around the entrance hung a faint and not altogether pleasant odour.

After this first abortive meeting Margaret and I returned to the happy peace of our married life. So relieved was I to see her on the screen that I could hardly believe our meeting had ever taken place. Neither of us referred to the disaster, and to the unpleasant emotions which our brief encounter had prompted.

During the next few days I reflected painfully on the experience. Far from bringing us together, the meeting had separated us. True closeness, I now knew, was television closeness – the intimacy of the zoom lens, the throat microphone, the close-up itself. On the television screen there were no body odours or strained breathing, no pupil contractions and facial reflexes, no mutual sizing up of emotions and advantage, no distrust and insecurity. Affection and compassion demanded distance. Only at a distance could one find that true closeness to another human being which, with grace, might transform itself into love.

Nevertheless, we inevitably arranged a second meeting. Why we did so I have still not understood, but both of us seemed to be impelled by those very motives of curiosity and distrust that I assumed we most feared. Calmly discussing everything with Margaret, I learned that she had felt the same distaste for me that I in turn had felt for her, the same obscure hostility.

We decided that we would bring the children to our next meeting, and that we would all wear make-up, modelling our behaviour as closely as possible on our screen life together. Accordingly, three months later, Margaret and myself, David and Karen, that unit of intensive care, came together for the first time in my sitting room.

Karen is stirring. She had rolled across the shaft of the broken standard lamp and her body faces me across the blood-stained carpet, as naked as when she stripped in front of me. This provocative act, presumably intended to jolt some incestuous fantasy buried in her father's mind, first set off the explosion of violence which has left us bloody and exhausted in the ruins of my sitting room. For all the wounds on her body, the bruises that disfigure her small breasts, she reminds me of Manet's *Olympia*, perhaps painted a few hours after the visit of some psychotic client.

Margaret, too, is watching her daughter. She sits forward, eyeing Karen with a gaze that is both possessive and menacing. Apart from a brief lunge at my testicles, she has ignored me. For some reason the two women have selected each other as their chief targets, just as David has vented almost all his hostility on me. I had not expected the scissors to be in his hand when I first slapped him. He is only a few feet from me now, ready to mount his last assault. For some reason he seemed particularly outraged by the display of teddy bears I had mounted so carefully for him, and shreds of these dismembered animals lie everywhere on the floor.

Fortunately I can breathe a little more freely now. I move my head to take in the ceiling camera and my fellow combatants. Together we present a grotesque aspect. The heavy television make-up we all decided to wear has dissolved into a set of bizarre halloween masks.

All the same, we are at last together, and my affection for them overrides these small problems of mutual adjustment. As soon as they arrived, the bruise on my son's head and my wife's bleeding ears betrayed the evidence of some potentially lethal scuffle. I knew that it would be a testing time. But at least we are making a start, in our small way establishing the possibility of a new kind of family life.

Everyone is breathing more strongly, and the attack will clearly begin within a minute. I can see the bloody scissors in my son's hand, and remember the pain as he stabbed me. I brace myself against the settee, ready to kick his face. With my right arm I am probably strong enough to take on whoever survives the last confrontation between my wife and daughter. Smiling at them affectionately, rage thickening the blood in my throat, I am only aware of my feelings of unbounded love.

. **1977**

# THEATRE OF WAR

## Author's preface

*After three hundred years, could civil war again divide the United King-*
*dom? Given rising unemployment and industrial stagnation, an ever more*
*entrenched class system and a weak monarchy detaching itself from all but*
*its ceremonial roles, is it possible to visualize the huge antagonisms between*
*the extreme left and right resolving themselves in open civil conflict? I take*
*it for granted that despite its unhappy experience in South East Asia the*
*intervention of the United States to defend its military and economic*
*investments would be even more certain than it was in Vietnam. I also*
*assume that the television coverage would be uninterrupted and all-pervasive,*
*and have therefore cast it in the form of a TV documentary, of the type made*
*popular by* World in Action.

## Part One
### LONDON UNDER SIEGE

STREET BATTLE
Inner London, a back street in Lambeth, where confused street-fighting is
taking place. Tank engine noise forms a continuous background to heavy
machine-gun fire and intercom chatter. Twenty soldiers, five American
and the rest British, move from door to door, firing at the other end of
the street, where Big Ben is visible above the shabby roof-tops. Helicopter
gunships circle overhead. A tank stops by a house and soldiers dart in.
A moment later a woman emerges, followed by three exhausted children
and an old man carrying his bedroll. They run past with stunned faces.
Bodies lie everywhere. Two negro GIs drag away a dead enemy soldier
with shoulder-length hair. Stitched to his camouflage jacket is a Union
Jack. The picture freezes, and the camera zooms in on the Union Jack
until it fills the screen, soaked in the soldier's blood.

WORLD IN ACTION TITLES
Superimposed over the bloody Union Jack: 'Civil War'
**Commentator**
One street battle is over, but the civil war goes on. After four years no

solution is in sight. American casualties total 30,000 dead, a hundred thousand missing and wounded. A million British civilians have died. Despite mounting criticism at home America pours more and more troops into what is now the European Vietnam. But the fighting continues. This week the Liberation Front launched a major offensive against a dozen cities. Here in Lambeth a suicide squad fights its way to within 800 yards of the House of Parliament. How long can the British government survive? Will peace ever come? *World in Action* is here to find out.

## STREET BATTLE

The fighting is over, and the government forces are mopping up. They flush frightened civilians from the basements and herd them away past the bodies of enemy soldiers. At the junction with the main road in the background a British Airways advertisement hoarding is riddled with bullet holes. A sullen-faced young English woman is frisked roughly by British troops while others tear the Union Jacks from dead enemy soldiers. The tank drags away a tangle of bodies lashed together by their wrists. In a jeep loaded with looted cameras, radios and record players pop music blares from the intercom.

## CUT TO NIGHT-TIME SOHO

Background of garish lights, pintable arcades, strip clubs. GIs spill out of cars and move into a bar.

**Commentator**

GIs relax during a weekend of R & R. Two days ago they were fighting off a Liberation Front offensive in the suburbs of Manchester. As the United Nations talks of settlement and both sides in the civil war plan new offensives, what do the ordinary GIs think of the prospects for peace?

**1st US soldier** (reclining in bar)

It's a very ticklish situation over here. It's hard to analyse and get a complete grasp of the whole story, because from my position at least you can't get a glimpse of the whole subject. You know, you don't know what motivates these people. Peace seems to be very far off, at least to me it does.

**Commentator**

Tell me, do you think it's all worth it?

**2nd US soldier**

It's hard to say. I think we're just, as I see it, we're fooling around. That's about all. I do think we should be here.

**Commentator**

What's the alternative to fooling around?

**3rd US soldier**

Well, they call it a civil war. If it's a war, it should be that. They push us, we push them, it's a kind of stalemate as I see it right now. I think we should show them who's boss. Because what I've seen of the gooks over here, they're going to fight, *fight* – you know? – and just keep on fighting.

## 2nd US soldier

If you're fighting a war, fight it like a war, with all the mass of power we have. Power in reserve, air power, land power, and power from the sea. We've got battleships offshore can pound this place to absolutely nothing.

## Commentator

Tough talk from the GIs as they relax, but in the bright light of day, as London picks up the pieces after the latest NLF offensive, what exactly is the present military position? Can either side win this war? In New York today President Reagan was asked what kind of settlement he would hope to resolve. The President replied: 'I don't think we can talk about settlement of the war at this point. I think we *can* talk about our willingness to accept a coalition or fusion government. At least it could very well be talked about in the open before we begin to talk about negotiations.' President Reagan spent the day in New York City where he addressed a luncheon audience and denied that the war is indefensible, a view strongly challenged by Congressional leaders of both parties. But how accurate is the picture which the American public at large has of the civil war?

## NEWSREEL

Medley of clips – Civilians running as GIs and British government troops move across a tenement courtyard, firing at a roof-top sniper; helicopters circling a fortified Wembley Stadium; street execution near Piccadilly Circus of three NLF soldiers in plain clothes, hands wired, as a crowd outside a sandbagged cinema looks on; corpses of children laid out in a village hall; gun-battle outside a Top-Rank Bingo hall; crowd at Bellevue, Manchester, fun-fair backing off a roundabout to reveal a body pumped up and down by a wooden unicorn to the Wurlitzer music; lines of strip clubs in Oxford, entrances guarded by Military Police barring civilians; pound-notes over-printed 'One Dollar'; tanks ringing Parliament Square; shops loaded with consumer goods; a huge bonfire of Union Jacks; elderly refugees camping on the canted decks of a multi-storey car park in Dover, guarded by uncertain-looking GIs straight off a troop-carrier; government troops demolishing a rebel earth bunker lined with carefully framed portraits of George VI during World War II, visiting munitions factories and bombed-out East Enders.

## Commentator

As each day passes, life in the government-held areas becomes less and less tolerable. London is a city under siege. Manchester, Liverpool and Birmingham are the last remaining strongholds of government support, defended by massive American forces. The countryside belongs to the NLF. The continuous infiltration of the London suburbs by guerilla battalions mingling with the local population has brought the front line to everyone's doorstep. Bomb outrages, kidnappings, street battles with snipers, the assassination of local political leaders – these are part of day-to-day life. In the five years of its exile in Riyadh, uneasy guests of the Saudi royal house, the monarchy has lost all credibility, unwilling to commit its waning prestige to either side in the civil war. Meanwhile, in the London over which the Queen once reigned, the black market flourishes. Millions of dollars' worth of American goods pour into the capital, propping up a juke-box economy of pirate TV networks, thousands of bars and brothels. In many towns and suburbs the main unit of currency is the illegal NLF pound sterling. The government-backed British dollar is despised. Anything can be bought, but nothing has any value. More and more young people slip away to join the Liberation Front. Doctors, engineers, trained mechanics desert to the enemy forces. They leave behind a population that consists mainly of the old middle class and an army of bartenders, croupiers and call-girls. London is now a gigantic Las Vegas, the largest light-bulb in the world, ready to blow out in a hail of rebel machine-gun fire.

## COMMENTATOR IN GROSVENOR SQUARE

American Embassy in background, surrounded by tanks. GIs and British troops patrol. Muted gunfire near distance, but civilians go about their ordinary lives without concern.

### Commentator

As both sides mount major offensives, I'm standing in Grosvenor Square, the old Eisenhowerplatz of World War II, once again the headquarters of the American and British government forces. This time they are fighting, not the superbly equipped German Wehrmacht with its panzer divisions, but a British peasant army. None the less, can the government forces and their American allies win? Will the war ever end?

## INTERVIEW WITH BRITISH SUPREME COMMANDER

A sometime heir to the English throne, the 36-year-old commander of the government forces is an aggressive, media-wise opportunist with pearl-handled revolver, black flying suit and white silk scarf. He is shown parading in a succession of military uniforms, firing a sub-machine-gun at a rifle range, inspecting a dispirited platoon of government troops, boarding his roof-top helicopter which he flies himself to inspect the attacks breaking out all over the city (though the viewer is unsure whether he is about to make a discreet bunk), and generally trying to boost the morale of his entourage. His line is confident but embittered; he knows he has lost his throne by his involvement with the puppet regime. He hates the NLF, but the Americans more. His hero is Rommel, but his style is James Bond.

### British Commander

As Commander of the British loyalist forces, my job is to win the war and unify the country again. The enemy is increasingly fighting out of desperation. Our intelligence tells us that he is running out of men, out of steam and out of material. He simply doesn't have the economic potential to maintain a war. The people in Europe and the United States who criticize the war don't really know what's going on. Quite evidently the people of this country don't want anything to do with the people up north, or with the communist way of life.

**Commentator**

You don't feel, General, that you and the Americans are forcing a form of government on the people of this country?

**British Commander**

No, we're not forcing anything on them. The United States feels that this is a good place to stop communist aggression, and if the government forces do win, and I know they will, we'll have, firstly, a good ally, and we'll have stopped communist aggression from taking over the United Kingdom and eventually France and everywhere else.

(Points to map showing blacked-out areas of British Isles.)

Our forces are now moving forward into a series of major confrontations with the other side, so I think you can look forward to when that map will be white again. Then I know the Americans will be glad to leave for home.

## COMMENTATOR BACK IN GROSVENOR SQUARE

Maps in hand, he addresses camera.

**Commentator**

Meanwhile, however, the British Commander is reported to be asking the US President for yet more troops. How many soldiers will be needed to hold the line against the NLF? Despite the General's easy optimism it isn't his map which most people look at, but this one issued by the NLF.

(Lifts other map. Black areas encircle major cities, all the countryside.)

It's this one they consult if they want to visit their relatives in the country or move to another town. It's this one they use if they want to defect to the NLF.

## EXPLOSION BURSTS ACROSS SQUARE

Camera wobbles, swings wildly. Panic, people running. Commentator ducks, then starts talking in confused way.

**Commentator**

... there's been a – it looks, it looks as if a sniper. What seems to be happening is that a –

## CROWD FORMING A ROUGH CIRCLE AROUND A JEEP

GIs push people back, and look down at the body of an American officer in the front seat, blood pouring from wound. Pop music blares from the intercom radio a few inches from his face.

**Radio Announcer**

We have a list of the latest curfew regulations. In the inner capital the curfew bell is midnight to 6 a.m. for Kensington, Knightsbridge and Battersea and from 10 to 7 a.m. for the 3rd Air Cav. and support units in –

## GI REACHES OVER AND SWITCHES OFF RADIO
### Commentator
Five minutes ago a senior American officer was assassinated as he sat in his jeep outside the American officers' club here in Grosvenor Square. An NLF killer in civilian clothes stepped through the lunch-time crowd and fired a single shot, then disappeared back into the crowd. The officer, Colonel Wilson J. Tucker, a military adviser in the 'hearts and minds' mission, widely suspected of being a cover for a CIA murder squad, died within a few seconds. All that's known about the killer is that he was 'young', probably in his early twenties, a safe enough assumption at a time when most of the young men and women here have long since left to join the Liberation Front, at a time when to be young automatically invites the attentions of the military police and the hostility of the old and middle-aged who provide the last support for the puppet regime. As one visiting Canadian journalist put it to me . . .

## CANADIAN JOURNALIST IN HOTEL BAR
### Canadian Journalist
All the NLF have to do to win this war is wait ten years. By then everyone on the government side will be either dead or in a wheelchair.

## SHOTS OF YOUNG PEOPLE AT CAMP SITE
Police hustling them about. Older people watching as girls and young men have their hair shaved.
### Commentator
Certainly one of the most striking divisions in British life is the now unbridgeable gulf between the young and the old. Even if the peace talks start and a settlement is finally reached, will it be possible for them to live together in one society? A legacy of resentment, intolerance and sexual jealousy has been fed by years of violence and open war. At a time when the twin pillars of life in the government areas are the strip club and the US dollar, does Britain any longer possess the political and social institutions to make possible a real society?
### Canadian journalist
I don't see Parliament now as a functioning entity in any way. It's a rump of older Members of Parliament and extreme right-wingers, a blow-hole for all kinds of unpleasant fascist gas. As a legislature it's non-existent. Let's face the facts, the British government is a puppet regime, *and it means to keep it that way*. The economy has a real balance of payments surplus for the first time in thirty years, thanks to American war-spending and the GI dollar. Baby, nobody on this side says 'Yank, go home'. They're more likely to offer you their sister – or their mother. Their sister's on the other side.
### Commentator
Patriotism takes many forms. Is it significant, though, that the flag of the

Liberation Front is the Union Jack, long-standing symbol of the union of Britain's major provincial areas – a symbol now hated and feared by the government supporters? To what extent can the government itself provide any prospects for unity?

## INTERVIEW WITH BRITISH PRIME MINISTER

A former Labour Prime Minister recalled to office, to lead the all-party coalition, he sits uneasily inside a sandbagged Downing Street, literally ducking every time a shot is heard. He is surrounded by armed guards, but looks shifty and dispirited. All too clearly he is at the Americans' mercy, and has no ideas for bringing the war to an end.

**Commentator**

Could I ask you first, Prime Minister, are you hopeful at the moment at the outlook for peace?

**Prime Minister**

Well, it depends very much on what the other side wants to do. The latest offensives – attacks against the ordinary people of this country – don't suggest that they're particularly sincere in their talk about wanting a settlement.

**Commentator**

Do you envisage that the departure of the American troops will create problems? If one travels around London one sees that a large part of the local economy is geared to serving the GI. When the GI is gone, won't there be problems for those people who presently are . . .

**Prime Minister**

Well, this contains the same problem shared by all those countries that have had large American forces on their soil – Germany, Japan, Vietnam. I think it will be a good thing because we shall be back to normal and a lot of people will have to look for a living within their means. They'll have to give up a lot of windfall benefits which come from the war and create social problems. We've now got in this country a class of people created by the war, and I think it's a good thing that this will stop.

**Commentator**

Childhood for most of the children in London has been a strange life with the American dollar, hasn't it? The American dollar has been the way they passed their childhood. When that in the form of the GI goes, are they not going to have a lot of problems?

**Prime Minister**

I'm sure they will. They'll be economic problems mainly. I think we're all going to have to find ourselves, so to speak, a painful process whether it's an individual or a nation. I think there's going to be a period of readjustment, possibly of turbulence, but they must go through the process. Perhaps if they'd gone through it twenty years ago there wouldn't be a war now.

## GENERAL VIEWS OF PEOPLE HANGING AROUND ENTRANCES TO AMERICAN BASES

### *Commentator*

Can the British people find themselves? Can they go through the painful process of re-establishing themselves as a single nation? With 70 per cent of the economy tied to the war, with the revenues from North Sea oil long since sold off to the Germans and Japanese, will ordinary people be able to make the adjustments necessary to living with the other side? In short, do they want the war to end at all? *World in Action* visited a village in the front line to see how the bulk of the population is facing up to the reality of the war.

## GENERAL PICTURE OF SMALL TOWN IN BUCKINGHAMSHIRE

Barbed wire, road blocks, troops and armoured cars. Gunfire in the distance.

### *Commentator*

Here at Cookham, only twenty miles or so from the centre of London, the 'windfall benefits' of the war are more likely to be a sniper's bullet or a barrage of enemy mortar shells. This is one of the so-called pacified villages. By day the British and American forces occupy the bunkers and pillboxes. In the evening they withdraw with the local administrators to a fortified enclave near the American base at Windsor. At night the Liberation Front moves in. At this moment their advance positions are no more than two hundred yards away, their sentries watching us through binoculars. None of these villagers will talk to us. All are assumed to be Liberation Front sympathizers, but in fact they are professional neutrals, living on the edge of a giant razor that could cut them down at any moment. They farm the fields, work in the garages and shops, and wait for the Americans to leave. Strangest of all here, there is no one between the ages of four and forty.

## TANK APPEARS, FOLLOWED BY BRITISH AND AMERICAN SOLDIERS

### *Commentator*

A special task force arrives, part of a self-styled Pacification Probe that will advance ten miles into country recently occupied by the Liberation Front. One tank, ten GIs of the First Cavalry Division, and thirty British soldiers are under the command of Captain Arjay Robinson. *World in Action* is going with them to see what happens.

## CAPTAIN ROBINSON BRIEFING HIS UNIT IN THE VILLAGE HALL

The GIs, heavily armed with flak jackets and radio-equipped helmets, sit at the front, the British troops with two elderly officers at the back.

*Captain Robinson*
The primary mission of Alpha Company is to conduct a reconnaissance and pacification. Circles indicate supply caches within the area, also known parking areas, primarily wheeled vehicles and larger trucks. There are also some small yellow dots, these indicate known positions where we have seen tanks. There are tanks in the area definitely. As I see it right now we're going to have two companies controlling the fire base. We'll play it real loose, play it by ear pretty much as to where we're going and the times that we'll go. We're going down there and kill the enemy where we find him and come back.

# Part Two
## PACIFICATION PROBE

*Commentator*
A Pacification Probe prepares to set off. It's 6.35 a.m., and the thirty British soldiers who will do the major part of the fighting – and the major part of the dying – wait quietly in the background as the American tank crew and radio specialists prepare their equipment. The American weapons and communications are now so sophisticated that the British troops can barely understand them. Many of these men will defect on this mission, many more will die. What are they up against? Last month a Swedish film crew smuggled itself through the front lines. Their brief film shows what life is like within the Liberation Front.

NEWSREEL OF LIBERATION FRONT AREAS
Mountains, tunnel entrances guarded by young soldiers and armed young women. Union Jacks flying. People working in factories. Alternative technology, windmills, small-scale smelting works, machine shops, hand-looms. Children everywhere, thin but healthy. Kibbutz atmosphere, young mothers in khaki mini-skirts with babies and rifles. Slit trenches, men with rifles move through fields around burnt-out American tank. Callisthenics in drill-hall, communal singing around flag. Indoctrination sessions, 18-year-old political commissar addressing doctors and nursing staff in hospital. Children taking part in people's theatre, 4-year-olds dressed in parody US military uniforms miming bombing attacks on sturdy villagers. Everywhere slogans, loudspeakers, portraits of George VI.
*Swedish voice-over*
The mountains of Scotland and Wales are the main strongholds of the National Liberation Front. In the four-year war against the British central government hundreds of underground schools and factories have been built. From here supplies and equipment go out to the front line. By now all the agricultural areas of England are under control of the Liberation Front. The soldiers and peasants are organized in communes, the women farming and looking after the children while the men are fighting. Their

leaders are young. There are few old people here. Everywhere morale is high, they are confident that they have won the war and that the Americans must soon leave. They are Scottish, Welsh, people from the northern and western provinces of England, West Indians, Asians and Africans. For four years they have been bombed but they are still fighting.

## COOKHAM
Cut to Captain Robinson on the turret of his tank.

He scans the empty fields. Nothing moves. In the compound below the soldiers have finished readying their weapons and equipment. The *World in Action* commentator puts on US combat clothing, strapping a gun around his waist, trying out heavy boots. A helicopter clatters overhead.
*AFN radio announcer*
... in the southern outskirts of London last night a guerilla unit fired a 107 mm rocket, killing one civilian and wounding four others. First Air Cav. ground elements in Operation Pegasus killed 207 enemy in scattered contacts yesterday, with friendly casualties light. First Division Marines killed 124 in two separate battles in Northern Province. The leathernecks ambushed enemy elements, calling in support by artillery and air attack. The marines took no casualties while killing 156 communists ...
*Commentator*
Half an hour from now the forty men of Alpha Company will set out from Cookham. As we move off across this guerilla-infested countryside two companies of combat engineers will have flown in to the target area by helicopter. They will deal with any local opposition. The main function of Alpha Company, this so-called pacification probe, is to re-establish the government's authority. The thirty British soldiers and the District Administrator will stay on after the Americans have left, recruiting local militia, setting up a fortified hamlet and redirecting the area's agriculture. The target area is at a key point on the M4 Motorway to the south-west. To keep this road open the government forces are setting up a chain of fortified villages along its 200-mile length.

## CAPTAIN ROBINSON CHECKING HIS MEN'S EQUIPMENT
*Commentator*
Alpha Company's commander, Captain Arjay Robinson, is already a veteran of this war. Thirty-two years old, he comes from Denver, Colorado, and is a graduate of West Point. He is married to a clergyman's daughter and has three children, none of whom he has seen in the two years he has been here. A career soldier, he has already decided to stay here until the Americans leave.

## SERGEANT PALEY CHECKING TANK TREADS
*Commentator*
His second-in-command is Sergeant Carl W. Paley, a 26-year-old bachelor from Stockton, California, where he was general manager of a local radio

station owned by his father. Like Captain Robinson, he has had almost no contact with the ordinary people of this country. To him they form a grey background of blurred faces – girls he meets in the bars outside the base camps, old men who clean out the barracks or serve as waiters in the sergeants' mess. Apart from the prostitutes, the only young English people he will see are likely to be in the sights of his guns. Last month Alpha Company was involved in a major action in which over 250 enemy soldiers were killed, a third of them women auxiliaries. But to Sergeant Paley they are merely 'Charley' – a blanket term carried over from Vietnam, or 'the gooks'.

## TANK ENGINE STARTS UP

American soldiers climb aboard, the British form up into a column behind it.

### *Commentator*

As for the British troops who will go with them – like all the Americans here, Sergeant Paley holds them in little more than contempt. Underfed and ill-equipped, the British troops have to provide their own food and bedding. During the next six hours the Americans will ride to the battlefield on their tank. The thirty British will walk. Mostly men in their forties, with a few younger men drafted from the penal battalions, they represent the residue of the armies conscripted by the government three years ago, armies now decimated by casualties and desertions.

## MAJOR CLEAVER

A thick-set man with British army moustache climbs on to the tank beside Captain Robinson. He wears American boots, fawn trousers, brown leather jacket and carries US Army revolver.

### *Commentator*

The only Britisher to whom the Americans pay any attention is Major Cleaver, the District Administrator who will be in charge of the pacified village. A former regular army officer, Major Cleaver is one of several thousand DAs sent out by the British government to run the civil administration of the recaptured areas. Part political commissar, part judge and jury, Major Cleaver will literally have the power of life and death over the people living under his rule, a power that he and his fellow DAs have been quick to exercise in the past.

## THE CONVOY MOVES OFF

The infantry spread out ahead and to the side of the tank. They follow a road through wooded terrain with meadows and abandoned farms on either side. Now and then there is a halt as the tank is brought up.

### *Captain Robinson*

Helicopters are the thing that's happening these days. You can get in there real fast with heavy suppressive fire, and if you need to be pulled out you can get out real fast.

**Sergeant Paley**

It's definitely the way to fight a ground war.

**Captain Robinson**

As I see it now we're going to have two companies controlling the fire base, Bravo and Charley, who will go in by helicopter. They'll clear the landing zone by the time we get in there, so the tactical side of the operation should be finalized. It's also better from the psychological aspect that we don't get involved on the tactical side too much.

**Commentator**

You mean the actual fighting around the village?

**Captain Robinson**

That's correct.

RADIO OPERATOR PASSES MESSAGE TO CAPTAIN
ROBINSON

Tank halts.

**Commentator**

But for Bravo and Charley Companies, who are supposed to be going in by helicopter, today is not the day for fighting a war. The weather in the target area has closed in, and the helicopters have returned to base. Alpha Company gets ready to move on alone, every man here hoping that the weather will clear.

**Sergeant Paley**

This country, weather's the main thing. It rains a lot and you're very wet most of the time, but you know as a soldier you can't ask for a certain territory to fight on because you just have to make the best of what terrain you have.

**Commentator**

Sergeant, what do you think of the chances of peace here?

**Sergeant Paley**

Well, I think they're . . . I don't know, as I see it as long as Charley's got a weapon and some ammo and using it he's not going to give up. I think he's pretty much got his heart in it, giving his own people a hard time here.

**Commentator**

How do you feel it's all going?

**Sergeant Paley**

Well, it's going well for the Cavs, I know that. Wherever we go we run into Charley – I know he doesn't last very long.

**Commentator**

Tell me, sergeant, why are you in England?

**Sergeant Paley**

Why am I in England? Well, curiosity, I guess. I just wanted to know what the war was like.

**Commentator**

What is the war like?

**Sergeant Paley**

Well, it's all right, I guess. For a year I'd say it's a good experience. You really learn a lot from it.

**Major Cleaver**

Naturally one hopes that peace will come to the country as soon as possible. Positions have become very entrenched during the past year, there's a legacy of bitterness on both sides. This is not the kind of civil war that resolves anything.

**Commentator**

What about the fighting itself? Don't you find it difficult to be shooting at your own people?

**Major Cleaver**

They're not our own people any longer. This is the whole point of the war. They're the enemy now, and peace isn't going to turn them overnight into our friends.

**Commentator**

But aren't there a lot of desertions from the army?

**Major Cleaver**

Not as many as there used to be. Most of the men realize that conditions here are a lot better than they are on the other side. The bombing has killed hundreds of thousands of people. Sitting here eating C rations is a lot more comfortable than being boiled alive in napalm.

## THE COLUMN MOVES ON

Slow penetration of forest on either side of the road. We see the tank stuck in a small stream. Cameo shots of individual American and British soldiers. Fade to early afternoon.

A long shot of farmland and the motorway on the left, the village to the right. Nothing moves. The camera turns and we see the American and British troops dug in along the edge of the field facing the village. It has been raining but the sky has cleared. Everything is very quiet. Machine-guns and weapons being set up. The tank is hidden in trees. Captain Robinson scans the low sky through binoculars.

**Commentator**

Three o'clock the same afternoon. Alpha Company has arrived at its objective. No signs of the helicopters, so Captain Robinson and his men will have to go in alone. How many Liberation Front soldiers are facing us? Perhaps fifty, perhaps a hundred. Will they fight? Or will they fade away into the surrounding countryside, leaving their women and children behind until night comes again?

## THE AMERICANS AND BRITISH ARE WATCHING QUIETLY

A farmer appears and walks along a pathway on the far side of the field. He carries a rifle over his shoulder. Sergeant Paley watches him cross the sights of his machine-gun. Nobody moves.

## THE VILLAGE IS COMING TO LIFE AFTER THE RAIN-STORM

Young men and women appear. They go about their work. A stall is set up and food is distributed. Young mothers in their khaki mini-skirts drop their children into the communal crèche. Others move towards the fields and farm buildings with rifles over their shoulders. A damp Union Jack is run up on the village flag-pole. Meanwhile, the American and British government forces watch quietly over their gun-sights. Through the zoom lens we focus on individual soldiers, and then on individual villagers in their sights: a young man with a headband who is the kibbutz leader; his girlfriend with a baby; a coloured girl with a pistol on her waist. The leader speaks through a megaphone, the sounds just carrying across the field. He is making some kind of joke, and everyone in the village laughs.

## THE FIRST FARMERS WALK OUT ACROSS THE FIELD

They are still unaware of the government forces, and carry their rifles slung casually over their shoulders. One of them, a young Pakistani, has spotted something moving across the field. He follows it between the cabbages, then bends down and picks it up. It is an American cigarette pack. Puzzled, he looks up. Ten feet away he sees the barrel of a light machine-gun aimed at him by Sergeant Paley. Crushing the pack in his hand, he opens his mouth to shout.

## CAPTAIN ROBINSON SIGNALS

Sergeant Paley opens fire straight at the young Pakistani. Torn apart, he falls among the cabbages. Massive firing breaks out. The other young men and women in the field are shot down. Mortar fire is directed at the village, the tank lumbers forward, its heavy gun opening fire. Through the long-distance lens we see isolated men and women being shot down, others running for shelter. The food stall is overturned. A barn is burning. Captain Robinson signals again, and the men move forward in a general advance, firing as they go. The *World in Action* commentator and Major Cleaver move up with them, taking shelter behind the tank. Counter fire is coming from the village, from a small blockhouse built behind a bicycle shed. Two British soldiers are shot down. In the village now everything is burning. Bodies lie around, there are burning motorcycles and food scattered everywhere.

## EVERYTHING IS QUIET

The battle has been over an hour or so. A few fires are still burning, smoke drifting towards the distant motorway. The British government troops break down the doors of the houses. They stare at the lines of bodies, mostly young women and children. Six prisoners have their hands wired together. The remaining villagers are driven out into the field.

## 2nd Commentator

Two hours ago, in the attack on this small village beside the M4, the *World in Action* commentator was killed. As he followed the first wave of American soldiers he was shot by an unknown enemy sniper and within a few minutes died of his wounds. His report on this war has been shown as he made it.

## VILLAGERS SQUATTING IN FIELD

GIs prepare demolition charges.

## 2nd Commentator

Alpha Company prepares to pull out. The weather has closed in again, and there will be no support coming in by helicopter. The action is called off at the request of Major Cleaver. Ten British soldiers have been killed or wounded. Without the Americans and their tank he could never hold the village.

## Captain Robinson

We're moving them out, just generally get them out of the way. You can bomb their houses flat easier that way without the conscience of the people on your mind. Put them out in the field.

## EXPLOSIONS RIP APART VILLAGE BUILDINGS

Close-up of bodies of rebel soldiers dragged along in mud behind the tank. The column pulls out through the dusk, heading back to Cookham.

## Major Cleaver

To help another human being out, it's worth the expense and loss of life. It's just that I sometimes wonder whether some of the people that I know who have died knew what they were dying for. That's about the hardest thing to think of, you know. If a man doesn't know why he's dying, it's a bad way to go.

*Acknowledgment:* For all the dialogue above, to General Westmoreland, President Thieu of South Vietnam, Marshall Ky and various journalists, US and ARVN military personnel.

**1977**

# HAVING A WONDERFUL TIME

### 3 July 1985. Hotel Imperial, Playa Inglaterra, Las Palmas
We arrived an hour ago after an amazing flight. For some reason of its own the Gatwick computer assigned us to first-class seats, along with a startled dentist from Bristol, her husband and three children. Richard, as ever fearful of flying, took full advantage of the free champagne and was five miles high before the wheels left the ground. I've marked our balcony on the twenty-seventh floor. It's an extraordinary place, about twenty miles down the coast from Las Palmas, a brand-new resort complex with every entertainment conceivable, all arranged by bedside push-button. I'm just about to dial an hour's water-skiing, followed by Swedish massage and the hairdresser! *Diana*.

### 10 July. Hotel Imperial
An unbelievable week! I've never crammed so much excitement into a few days – tennis, scuba-diving, water-skiing, rounds of cocktail parties. Every evening a group of us heads for the boîtes and cabarets along the beach, ending up at one or more of the five nightclubs in the hotel. I've hardly seen Richard. The handsome cavalier in the picture is the so-called Beach Counsellor, a highly intelligent ex-public relations man who threw it all in two years ago and has been here ever since. This afternoon he's teaching me to hang-glide. Wish me happy landings! *Diana*.

### 17 July. Hotel Imperial
The times of sand are running out. Sitting here on the balcony, watching Richard ski-chute across the bay, it's hard to believe we'll be in Exeter tomorrow. Richard swears the first thing he'll do is book next year's holiday. It really has been an amazing success – heaven knows how they do it at the price, there's talk of a Spanish government subsidy. In part it's the unobtrusive but highly sophisticated organization – not a hint of Butlins, though it's British-run and we're all, curiously, from the West Country. Do you realize that Richard and I have been so busy we haven't once bothered to visit Las Palmas? (Late news-flash: Mark Hastings, the Beach Counsellor, has just sent orchids to the room!) I'll tell you all about him tomorrow. *Diana*.

### 18 July. Hotel Imperial
Surprise! That computer again. Apparently there's been some muddle

at the Gatwick end, our aircraft won't be here until tomorrow at the earliest. Richard is rather worried about not getting to the office today. We blew the last of our traveller's cheques, but luckily the hotel have been marvellous, thanks largely to Mark. Not only will there be no surcharge, but the desk-clerk said they would happily advance us any cash we need. Hey-ho ... A slight let-down, all the same. We walked along the beach this afternoon, together for the first time. I hadn't realized how vast this resort complex actually is – it stretches for miles along the coast and half of it's still being built. Everywhere people were coming in on the airport buses from Sheffield and Manchester and Birmingham, within half an hour they're swimming and water-skiing, lounging around the hundreds of pools with their duty-free Camparis. Seeing them from the outside, as it were, it's all rather strange. *Diana.*

## 25 July. Hotel Imperial

Still here. The sky's full of aircraft flying in from Gatwick and Heathrow, but none of them, apparently, is ours. Each morning we've waited in the lobby with our suitcases packed, but the airport bus never arrives. After an hour or so the desk-clerk rings through that there's been a postponement and we trudge back to another day by the pool, drinks and water-skiing on the house. For the first few days it was rather amusing, though Richard was angry and depressed. The company is a major Leyland supplier, and if the axe falls, middle-management is the first to feel it. But the hotel have given us unrestricted credit, and Mark says that as long as we don't go over the top they'll probably never bother to collect. Good news: the company have just cabled Richard telling him not to worry. Apparently hordes of people have been caught the same way. An immense relief – I wanted to phone you, but for days now all the lines have been blocked. *Diana.*

## 15 August. Hotel Imperial

Three more weeks! Hysterical laughter in paradise ... the English papers flown in here are full of it, no doubt you've heard that there's going to be a government inquiry. Apparently, instead of flying people back from the Canaries the airlines have been sending their planes on to the Caribbean to pick up the American holiday traffic. So the poor British are stuck here indefinitely. There are literally hundreds of us in the same boat. The amazing thing is that one gets used to it. The hotel people are charm itself, they've pulled out all the stops, organizing extra entertainments of every kind. There's a very political cabaret, and an underwater archaeology team are going to raise a Spanish caravel from the sea floor. To fill in the time I'm joining an amateur theatrical group, we're thinking of putting on *The Importance of Being Ernest*. Richard takes it all with surprising calm. I wanted to post this from Las Palmas, but there are no buses running, and when we set out on foot Richard and I lost ourselves in a maze of building sites. *Diana.*

## 5 September. Hotel Imperial

No news yet. Time moves like a dream. Every morning a crowd of bewildered people jam the lobby, trying to find news of their flights back. On the whole, everyone's taking it surprisingly well, showing that true British spirit. Most of them, like Richard, are management people in industry, but the firms, thank heavens, have been absolutely marvellous and cabled us all to get back when we can. Richard comments cynically that with present levels of industrial stagnation, and with the Government footing the bill, they're probably glad to see us here. Frankly, I'm too busy with a hundred and one activities to worry – there's a sort of mini-Renaissance of the arts going on. Mixed saunas, cordon bleu classes, encounter groups, the theatre, of course, and marine biology. Incidentally, we never did manage to get into Las Palmas. Richard hired a pedalo yesterday and set off up the coast. Apparently the entire island is being divided into a series of huge self-contained holiday complexes – human reserves, Richard called them. He estimates that there are a million people here already, mostly English working class from the north and midlands. Some of them have apparently been here for a year, living quite happily, though their facilities are nowhere as good as ours. Dress rehearsal tonight. Think of me as Lady Bracknell – it's mortifying that there's no one else quite mature enough to play the part, they're all in their twenties and thirties, but Tony Johnson, the director, an ex-ICI statistician, is being awfully sweet about it. *Diana.*

## 6 October. Hotel Imperial

Just a brief card. There was a crisis this morning when Richard, who's been very moody recently, finally came into collision with the hotel management. When I went into the lobby after my French conversation class a huge crowd had gathered, listening to him rant away at the desk clerks. He was very excited but extremely logical in a mad way, demanding a taxi (there are none here, no one ever goes anywhere) to take him into Las Palmas. Balked, he insisted on being allowed to phone the Governor of the Islands, or the Swiss Consul. Mark and Tony Johnson then arrived with a doctor. There was a nasty struggle for a moment, and then they took him up to our room. I thought he was completely out, but half an hour later, when I left the shower, he'd vanished. I hope he's cooling off somewhere. The hotel management have been awfully good, but it did surprise me that no one tried to intervene. They just watched everything in a glazed way and wandered back to the pool. Sometimes I think they're in no hurry to get home. *Diana.*

## 12 November. Hotel Imperial

An extraordinary thing happened today – I saw Richard for the first time since he left. I was out on the beach for my morning jog when there he was, sitting by himself under an umbrella. He looked very tanned and healthy, but much slimmer. He calmly told me a preposterous story about the entire Canaries being developed by the governments of Western Europe, in collusion with the Spanish authorities, as a kind of permanent holiday camp for their unemployables, not just the factory workers but most of the management people too. According to Richard there is a beach being built for the French on the other side of the island, and another for the Germans. And the Canaries are only one of many sites around the Mediterranean and Caribbean. Once there, the holiday-makers will never be allowed to return home, for fear of starting revolutions. I tried to argue with him, but he casually stood up and said he was going to form a resistance group, then strode away along the beach. The trouble is that he's found nothing with which to occupy his mind – I wish he'd join our theatre group, we're now rehearsing Pinter's *The Birthday Party. Diana.*

## 10 January 1986. Hotel Imperial

A sad day. I meant to send you a cable, but there's been too much to do. Richard was buried this morning, in the new international cemetery in the hills overlooking the bay. I've marked his place with an X. I'd last seen him two months ago, but I gather he'd been moving around the island, living in the half-constructed hotels and trying unsuccessfully to set up his resistance group. A few days ago he apparently stole an unseaworthy motor-boat and set off for the African coast. His body was washed ashore yesterday on one of the French beaches. Sadly, we'd completely lost touch, though I feel the experience has given me a degree of insight and maturity which I can put to good use when I play Clytemnestra in Tony's new production of *Electra*. He and Mark Hastings have been pillars of strength. *Diana.*

## 3 July 1986. Hotel Imperial

Have I really been here a year? I'm so out of touch with England that I can hardly remember when I last sent a postcard to you. It's been a year of the most wonderful theatre, of parts I would once never have dreamed of playing, and of audiences so loyal that I can hardly bear the thought of leaving them. The hotels are full now, and we play to a packed house every night. There's so much to do here, and everyone is so fulfilled, that I rarely find the time to think of Richard. I very much wish you were here, with Charles and the children – but you probably are, at one of the thousand hotels along the beach. The mails are so erratic, I sometimes think that all my cards to you have never been delivered, but lie unsorted with a million others in the vaults of the shabby post office behind the hotel. Love to all of you. *Diana.*

**1978**

# ' ONE AFTERNOON AT UTAH BEACH

'Do you realize that we're looking down at Utah Beach?'

As he took off his boots and weather cape, David Ogden pointed through the window at the sea wall. Fifty yards from the villa the flat sand ran along the Normandy coast like an abandoned highway, its right shoulder washed by the sea. Every half-mile a blockhouse of black concrete presented its shell-pocked profile to the calm Channel.

Small waves flicked at the empty beach, as if waiting for something to happen.

'I walked down to the war memorial,' Ogden explained. 'There's a Sherman there – an American tank – some field guns and a commem-orative plaque. This is where the US First Army came ashore on D-Day. Angela . . . ?'

Ogden turned from the window, expecting his wife to comment on his discovery. She and Richard Foster, the pilot who had flown them over to Cherbourg for a week at this rented villa, sat at either end of the velvet settee, watching Ogden with a curious absence of expression. Dressed in their immaculate holiday wear, brandy glasses motionless in their hands as they listened politely, they reminded him of two mannequins in a department store tableau.

'Utah Beach . . .' Angela gazed in a critical way at the deserted sand, as if expecting a military exercise to materialize for her and fill it with landing craft and assault troops. 'I'd forgotten about the war. Dick, do you remember D-Day?'

'I was two.' Foster stood up and strolled to the window, partly blocking Ogden's view. 'My military career began a little later than yours, David.' Glancing down at Ogden, who was now staring at a blockhouse six hundred yards away, he said, 'Utah Beach – well, you wanted some good shooting. Are you sure this isn't Omaha, or one of the others – Juno, Gold, what were they called?'

Without any intended rudeness, Ogden ignored the younger man. His face was still numb from the sea air, and he was intent on his communion with the empty sand and the blockhouses. Walking along the beach, he had been surprised by the size of these concrete monsters. He had expected a chain of subterranean pill-boxes hiding within the sea wall, but many of them were massive fortresses three storeys high, larger than the parish churches in the nearby towns. The presence of the blockhouses, like the shells of the steel pontoons embedded in the wet sand, had pulled an unsuspected trigger in his mind. Like all examples of cryptic architecture, in which form no longer revealed function – Mayan palaces, catacombs, Viet Cong sanctuaries, the bauxite mines at Les Baux where Cocteau had filmed *Le Testament d'Orphée* – these World War II blockhouses seemed to transcend time, complex ciphers with a powerful latent identity.

'Omaha is further east along the coast,' he told Foster matter-of-factly. 'Utah Beach was the closest of the landing grounds to Sainte-Mère-Église, where the 82nd Airborne came down. The marshes we shoot across held them up for a while.'

Foster nodded sagely, his eyes running up and down Ogden's slim but hyperactive figure for what seemed the hundredth time that day. Throughout their visit Foster appeared to be sympathetically itemizing a catalogue of his defects, without in any way being insolent. Staring back at him, Ogden reflected in turn that for all the hours Foster had logged as a salesman of executive jets his sallow face remained remarkably pallid as if he were plagued by some deep *malaise*, some unresolvable contradiction. By noon a dark stain seemed to leak from his mouth on to his heavy chin, a shadow that Foster had once described to Angela as a blue tan from spending too much time in bars.

As if separating the two men like a referee, Angela came to the window. 'For someone who's never been in the army or heard a shot fired in anger, David's remarkably well-informed about military matters.'

'Isn't he – for a non-combatant,' Foster agreed. 'And I don't mean that in any critical spirit, David. I spent five years in the army and no one ever told me who won the battle of Waterloo.'

'Weren't you a helicopter pilot?' Ogden asked. 'Actually, I'm not all that interested in military history . . .'

Strictly speaking, this wasn't true, Ogden admitted to himself during lunch, though in fact he had not thought of the D-Day beaches when Angela first suggested the week in Normandy. Under the pretext of a demonstration flight in the twin Comanche, Foster had offered to fly them gratis, though his real reasons were hard to define. The whole trip was surrounded by ambiguities, motives hidden inside each other like puzzle boxes.

This curious threesome – the aircraft salesman, the provincial film critic in his late forties, and the young wife ten years his junior, a moderately successful painter of miniatures – sat in this well-appointed villa beside a long-forgotten battleground as if unsure what had brought them here. Curious, not because of any confrontation that might occur, any crime of passion, but because three people so ill-assorted had formed such a stable relationship. At no time during the six months since their meeting at the San Sebastian festival had there been the slightest hint of tension, though Ogden was sure everyone took for granted that his wife and Richard Foster were well into an affair. However, for various reasons Ogden doubted this. For her own security Angela needed someone around her who had achieved a modest degree of failure.

His young wife . . . Ogden repeated the phrase to himself, realizing as he watched Angela's sharper chin and more prominent jaw muscles, the angular shoulders inside the chiffon blouse, that she was not all that young any more. Soon she would be older than he had been when they first met.

'I'm taking Angela into Sainte-Mère,' Foster told him after lunch. 'Do you want to come along, David? We can try the calvados.'

As usual, Ogden declined. The walk that morning had exhausted him. He stretched out in an armchair and watched the slack sea shrug itself against the beach. He was aware of the complex timetable of apparently arbitrary journeys that Foster and his wife embarked upon each day, but for the moment his attention was held by the blockhouse six hundred yards away. Despite the continuous sunlight the concrete was drenched in spray, gleaming like wet anthracite as if generating its own weather around itself.

An hour after his wife and Foster had gone, Ogden pulled on his boots. He had recovered from the lunch, and the silent villa with its formal furniture felt like the stage-set of a claustrophobic drama. The strong afternoon light had turned the beach into a brilliant mirror, a flare-path beckoning him to some unseen destination.

As he neared the blockhouse Ogden visualized himself defending this battered redoubt against the invading sea. An immense calm presided over the cool beach, as if nothing had happened in the intervening thirty years. The violence here, the scale of the conflict between the German armies and the allied armada, had pre-empted any further confrontation, assuaging his own unease about Foster and his wife.

Fifty yards from the blockhouse he climbed the scrub-covered dune that rose to its seaward flank. The sand was scattered with worn-out shoes, cycle tyres and fragments of wine bottles and vegetable crates. Generations of tramps had used these old forts as staging-posts on their journeys up and down the coast. The remains of small fires lay on the steps of the concrete staircase at the rear of the blockhouse, and pats of dried excrement covered the floor of the munitions store.

Ogden walked across the central gunnery platform of the blockhouse, a rectilinear vault large enough to house a railway locomotive. From here a heavy-calibre naval gun had lobbed its shells at the invasion fleet. A narrow stairway set into the solid wall climbed to the observation deck, and gave access to the barbette of a small-arms weapons platform below the roof. Ogden climbed the stairway, tripping twice in the darkness. The worn concrete was slick with moisture sweating from its black surface.

As he stood on the roof, lungs pumping in the cold air, the sea already seemed far below, the villa hidden behind its high privet hedges. Looking around, though, he immediately noticed the white Pallas parked behind the sea wall two hundred yards along the beach. The car was the same colour as the Citroën they had hired in Cherbourg, and Ogden took for granted that it was their own vehicle. A tall man in a hunting jacket was steering a woman companion along the broken ground behind the wall. They approached a wooden boathouse at the end of a slipway above the beach, and Ogden could see clearly the patterns of the woman's musquash fur and recognize her gesture as she reached a gloved hand to the man's elbow.

Ogden stepped down into the stairwell. Watching them calmly, his shoulders hidden by the parapet, he knew that he had deliberately encouraged Angela and Richard Foster to come together. His own solitary walks, the private excursions he had made to the D-Day museum at Arromanches, had been part of a confused and half-conscious attempt to bring matters to a head and force a decision on himself.

Yet when he saw them unlocking the door of the boathouse together, briefly embracing in the sunlight as if openly trying to provoke him, Ogden felt a profound sense of loss. He knew too that the months of self-control had been wasted, and that from the beginning he had deluded himself that all was well.

Without thinking, he turned quickly from the parapet. With luck he could pack, call a taxi and have caught the ferry from Cherbourg before they returned to the villa. He started to run down the concrete steps, lost his footing on the damp diagonal sills, and fell backwards down the stairway on to the floor of the barbette ten feet below.

Sitting in the half-light against the wet concrete wall, Ogden massaged his bruised hands. By luck he had been able to protect his head, but he could feel the raw skin of his arms and shoulders. Some sort of viscous oil stained his fawn trousers, and a leather button torn from his jacket lay like a burst chestnut at the foot of the stairway. Immediately to his left was the embrasure of the fire-sill, the quiet beach below. There was no movement from the boathouse, and the white Pallas was still parked behind the sea wall.

At this moment Ogden realized that he was not the only person keeping a close watch on the beach. Six feet away from him, almost hidden by his grey uniform in the shadows behind the parapet, a man lay against the concrete wall. He was resting on one elbow, face turned towards the open sea, and at first Ogden assumed that he was dead. His blond hair had been bleached to an almost arctic pallor. He appeared to be no more than nineteen or twenty years old, his pale skin stretched across the bony points of his face like wet parchment around a skull.

His thin legs, encased in a pair of heavy boots and ragged serge trousers, stuck out in front of him like poles strung with rags. Lying diagonally across them, its long barrel supported by a bipod, was a light machine-gun, stock pressed against the young man's right shoulder. Around him, arranged like the décor of a shabby military display, were an empty mess tin, a spent ammunition belt, the half-rotted remains of a field pack and webbing, and a grease-stained ground sheet.

A few feet from Ogden, lying on the fire-sill within his reach, was a spring-action flare-pistol of a type he had seen only the previous afternoon in the D-Day museum at Arromanches. He recognized it immediately, like the uniform and equipment of this young Wehrmacht soldier whose corpse he had stumbled upon, in some way preserved by the freezing air, or perhaps by the lime leaking from the hastily mixed concrete. Curiously, the machine-gun still appeared to be in working order, a spiked bayonet fitted under the barrel, the butt-stock and receiver greased and polished.

Confused by this macabre discovery, Ogden had already forgotten his wife's infidelity. He was about to pick up the flare-pistol and fire it over the parapet in the direction of the boathouse. But as his bruised hand touched the frozen butt Ogden became aware that the young soldier's eyes were watching him. Of a blanched blue from which almost all pigment had been washed away, they had turned from the beach and were examining Ogden with a tired but steady gaze. Although the soldier's white hands still lay passively at his sides, his right shoulder had moved against the wall, swinging the machine-gun fractionally towards Ogden.

Too frightened to speak, Ogden sat back, taking in every detail of the German's equipment, every ammunition round and piece of webbing, every pore in the cold skin of this young soldier still defending his blockhouse on Utah Beach as he had done in 1944.

After a moment, to Ogden's relief, the machine-gun barrel turned towards the sea. The German had shifted his position slightly, and was once again scanning the beach. His left hand moved to his face, as if he were hoping to transfer a morsel of food to his mouth, and then fell to the floor. A ragged bandage circled his chest, covering a blackened wound partly hidden by his tunic. He took no notice of Ogden as the latter climbed to his feet, both hands pressed to the wall as if frightened that it might collapse on him at any time.

But as Ogden stepped over the machine-gun a white claw moved across the floor, about to seize his ankle.

'*Hören Sie ...*' The voice was flat, as if coming off an almost erased recording tape. '*Wieviel Uhr ist es?*' He looked up with a kind of exhausted impatience. '*Verstehen Sie? Quelle heure ...? Aujourd'hui? Hier?*' Dismissing Ogden with a wave, he murmured, '*Zu viel Larm ... zu viel Larm ...*'

Pulling the stock of the machine-gun into his shoulder, he stared along its barrel at the beach below.

Ogden was about to leave, when a movement on the beach caught his eye. The boathouse door had opened. Richard Foster stepped into the sunlight, and swung his arms lazily in the cool air as he waited until Angela appeared thirty seconds later. Together they walked across the dunes to the parked Pallas, climbed into the car and drove off.

Ogden paused by the staircase, watching the young soldier with the machine gun. He realized that the German had seen neither Foster nor his wife. The boathouse and sea wall were hidden from him by the parapet of the barbette. But if he recovered from his wounds, and moved forward to the edge of the fire-sill . . .

By the time he reached the villa ten minutes later Ogden had already decided on both the tactics and strategy of what he knew would be the last military action of World War II.

'Have you seen the blankets from the children's room?' Angela flicked through the inventory, her sharp eyes watching her husband as he played chess with himself by the sitting-room window. 'I didn't bother to check them when we arrived, but Mme Saunier insists they're missing.'

Ogden looked up from the chessboard. As he shook his head he glanced at the blockhouse. For the three days since his discovery the suspense had become exhausting; at any moment he expected a wounded Wehrmacht soldier to appear on the roof among the wheeling gulls, a pink blanket around his shoulders. At lunch he had changed his place, sitting by himself further down one side of the table so that he could keep the blockhouse under observation.

'Perhaps they were never there,' he said. 'We can replace them.'

'They were here all right. Mme Saunier is scrupulous about this sort of thing. She also said something about one of the decanters. David, are you in a trance?'

Irritably, Angela pushed her blonde hair from her forehead, then gave up and picked up her coat. Richard Foster was waiting by the car in the drive, one of the two shotguns they had hired cradled under his arm. Ogden noticed that he had taken to carrying the weapon everywhere with him, almost as if he detected a change of atmosphere in the villa. In fact, Ogden had gone to strenuous lengths to maintain the good humour of the first days of their holiday.

He waited patiently for them to leave. Half an hour later Mme Saunier set off in her Simca. When the sounds of the car had faded Ogden stood up and moved swiftly across the villa to the conservatory at the rear of the dining room. He removed the pots of bright winter plants standing on the wooden dais, eased back the platform from the wall and pulled out the cheap suitcase he had bought in Sainte-Mère that morning while Angela and Foster were lounging over the breakfast table. Taking the blankets from the empty bedroom had been a mistake, but at the time he had been concerned only to keep the young soldier alive.

Inside the suitcase were adhesive tape, sterile lint and antiseptic cream, one bottle of Vichy water and a second of schnapps, a primus stove, six cans of assorted soup, and a pull-through he had purchased from the town's gunsmith. However carefully the German had oiled the machine-gun, its barrel would need a thorough reaming-out.

After checking the contents, Ogden replaced the dais and let himself through the conservatory doors. Protected by the high privets, the garden was warm, and the air coming off the beach had an almost carnival sparkle. As usual, though, by the time he reached the blockhouse the temperature had dropped by almost ten degrees, as if this black concrete redoubt existed within a climatic zone of its own.

Ogden paused by the staircase, listening for the sounds of any intruders. On the first afternoon, when he had snatched the children's blankets, flung together an emergency meal of bread, milk and salami, and raced back along the beach to the blockhouse, the German had relapsed into one of the intermittent comas into which he would sink without warning. Although still staring at the tide-line, right hand clasped around the trigger butt of the machine-gun, his face was so cold and pallid that Ogden at first thought he had died. But he revived at the sound of the milk pouring into his mess tin, sat up and allowed Ogden to drape the blankets around his shoulders. Unable to stay more than an hour for fear of alerting his wife, Ogden had spent the evening in a state of hyper-excitability, for some reason terrified that the local police and members of a German military mission might arrive at any moment.

By the next morning, after Ogden had taken the car to Sainte-Mère on the pretext of visiting the war cemeteries there, the German had visibly improved. Although barely aware of Ogden, he leaned more comfortably against the damp wall. He held the mess tin against his bandaged chest, picking at the remains of the sausage. His face had more colour, and the skin was less tightly stretched against the jaw and cheekbones.

The German was often irritated by Ogden's fumbling, and there was something strangely vulnerable about his extreme youth. Ogden visited him twice each day, bringing water, food and cigarettes, whatever he could smuggle out of the villa under the suspicious eyes of Mme Saunier. He would have liked to light a fire for the soldier, but the primus stove he had brought with him on this fourth morning would generate a little warmth. However, the German had survived in this cold – the thought of living through all those winters made Ogden shudder – and at least the summer was coming.

When he climbed the stairway to the barbette the German was sitting up, blankets around his shoulders, quietly cleaning the machine-gun. He nodded to Ogden, who sat panting on the cold floor, and continued to strip the breech, apparently uninterested in the primus stove. When Ogden handed over the pull-through the German glanced at him with a flicker of appreciation. He ate only when he had reassembled the weapon.

Ogden watched him approvingly, relieved to see the young soldier's total dedication to his defence of this lonely strongpoint. It was this kind of courage that Ogden most admired. Earlier he had feared that once the German had recovered his strength he might decide to leave, or fall back to a more defensible position. Clearly he had missed the actual landings on Utah Beach and had no idea that he alone was keeping the war going. Ogden had no intention of telling him the truth, and the German's resolve never wavered.

Despite his overall improvement, the German's legs still seemed useless, and he had not moved forward sufficiently to see the boathouse two hundred yards away. Each afternoon Angela and Richard Foster climbed the dunes to this wooden shack on its miniature wheels, and disappeared into it for an hour. At times, as he waited for them to emerge, Ogden was tempted to wrest the machine-gun from the wounded German and empty its ammunition belt through the flaking weather-board. But the young soldier's aim was probably sharper and more steady. The flare-pistol lay on the fire-sill, the shell in its barrel. When the German had cleaned it they would be ready.

Two days later, soon after one o'clock in the afternoon, began the last military engagement to take place on Utah Beach.

At eleven o'clock that morning, as Angela sat at the breakfast table reading the local French newspaper, Richard Foster returned from the telephone in the hall.

'We'll have to leave this afternoon. The weather's closing in.'

'What?' Ogden left his chess table and joined them in the dining room. He pointed to the brilliant sunlight falling on the wet satin of the beach. 'It doesn't look like it.'

'I've just talked to the met. people at Cherbourg Airport. There's a front coming in from the Scillies. The barometer's going up like a lift.'

Ogden clasped his hands, trying to control them. 'Well, let's put it off for a day. The plane's fully instrumented.'

'Not a chance. By this time tomorrow the Channel will be packed with cumulo-nimbus. It'll be like trying to fly through a maze of active volcanoes.'

'Dick knows what he's doing,' Angela confirmed. 'I'll read the inventory with Mme Saunier after lunch. She can take the keys to the agents when we've gone.' To Ogden, who was still staring uncertainly at Richard Foster, she said, 'A day won't matter, David. You've done nothing all week but play about on the beach by yourself.'

For the next half an hour Ogden tried to find some excuse for them to stay, pacing up and down the sitting room as suitcases were dragged around upstairs. He tried to shut the two women's voices out of his mind, realizing that his entire scheme was about to fall to pieces. Already he had made his morning visit to the blockhouse, taking coffee, soup and cigarettes. The young German had almost recovered, and had moved the machine-gun closer to the parapet. Now Ogden would have to leave him there. Within days he would realize that the war was over and hand himself in to the French authorities.

Behind him the front door closed. Ogden heard Foster's voice in the drive, Angela calling to him about something. He watched them from the window, in a flat way admiring their nerve. They were setting off for their last walk together, Foster holding Angela's elbow in one hand, the shotgun in the other.

Still surprised by the blatant way in which they were advertising their affair – during the past two days they had done everything but get into Angela's bed together – Ogden pressed his hands against the window. A faint chance still remained. He remembered the almost provocative way in which Angela had watched him across the dining table the previous evening, confident that he would do absolutely nothing ...

Fifteen minutes later Ogden had left the house and an exasperated Mme Saunier, and was running head down, shotgun in hand, through the pools of water which the stiffening sea had swilled across Utah Beach.

'*Langsamer! Zu schnell. Langsam ...*'

Trying to calm Ogden, the young German raised a white hand and gestured him away from the parapet. He reached forward and shifted the bipod, swinging the machine-gun to take in the section of beach containing the boathouse, at which Ogden had been gesticulating since his arrival.

Ogden crouched against the wall, only too ready to let the German take command. The young soldier's recovery in the space of a few days had been remarkable. Though his hands and face retained their albino-like whiteness, he seemed almost to have put on weight. He moved easily around the fire-sill, in complete control of his heavy weapon. The bolt was cocked back, trigger set for automatic fire. A kind of wan smile, an ironic grimace, hung about his cold mouth, as if he too knew that his long wait was about to come to an end.

Ogden nodded encouragingly, holding his shotgun in as military a grip as he could muster. Its fire-power was nothing by comparison with the German's machine-gun, but it was all he could offer. In some obscure way he felt obligated to this young soldier, and guilty at implicating him in what would in a sense be the last war crime committed during World War II.

'They're – Look!' Ogden ducked behind the parapet, gesturing frantically. The boathouse door had opened, a cracked glass pane throwing a blade of sunlight at them. Ogden lifted himself on to his knees, the flare-pistol in both hands. The German had come to life, moving with professional command, all trace of his injuries forgotten. He adjusted his rear sight, his bandaged shoulder traversing the heavy weapon. Angela and Richard Foster stepped through the door of the boathouse. They paused in the sunlight, Foster casually inspecting the nearby dunes. The shotgun rested on his shoulder, trigger guard clasped around two fingers.

Unnerved for a moment by this aggressive stance, Ogden raised the flare-pistol, cocked the trigger and fired the fat shell into the air over Foster's head. The pilot looked up at its weak parabola, then ran forward, shouting to Angela as the shell lost height and fell like a dead bird into the calm sea.

'A dud ...!' Angry with himself, Ogden stood up in the embrasure, his head and chest exposed. Raising the shotgun, he fired the left barrel at Foster, who was darting through the dunes little more than a hundred yards from the blockhouse. Beside Ogden the young German was taking aim. The long barrel of the machine-gun followed the running figure. At last he opened fire, the violent noise jarring the parapet. Ogden was standing in the embrasure, happily listening to the roar of the machine-gun, when Richard Foster stood up in the long grass ten yards from the blockhouse and shot him through the chest.

'Is he . . . ?'

Angela waited in the dim light by the stairway, the collar of her fur coat pressed against her cheeks. Avoiding the body on the floor of the barbette, she watched Foster rest his shotgun against the wall and kneel on the floor.

'Stand back as far as you can.' Foster waved her back. He examined the body, then touched the flare-pistol with a blood-stained shoe. He was still shaking, both from fear and from the exhaustion of the past week. By contrast, Angela was completely calm. He noticed that with characteristic thoroughness she had insisted on climbing the stairway.

'It's a damn lucky thing he fired that first, I might not have had time otherwise . . . But where the hell did he find it? And all this other equipment?'

'Let's leave and call the police.' Angela waited, but Foster was still searching the floor. 'Dick! An hour from now I may not sound very convincing.'

'Look at this gear – World War II webbing, machine-gun ammunition, primus stove, German phrase-book and all these cans of soup . . .'

'He was camping here. I told you it would take a lot to provoke him.'

'Angela!' Foster stepped back and beckoned her towards him. 'Look at him . . . For God's sake, he's wearing a German uniform. Boots, tunic, the whole thing.'

'Dick!'

As they made their way from the blockhouse, the alarmed figure of Mme Saunier was hurrying along the beach towards them. Foster held Angela's arm.

'Now. Are you all right?'

'Of course.' With a grimace, Angela picked her way down the grimy concrete steps. 'You know, he must have thought we were coming ashore. He was always talking about Utah Beach.'

· **1978**

# ZODIAC 2000

## Author's note

*An updating, however modest, of the signs of the zodiac seems long overdue. The houses of our psychological sky are no longer tenanted by rams, goats and crabs but by helicopters, cruise missiles and intra-uterine coils, and by all the spectres of the psychiatric ward. A few correspondences are obvious – the clones and the hypodermic syringe conveniently take the place of the twins and the archer. But there remains the problem of all those farmyard animals so important to the Chaldeans. Perhaps our true counterparts of these workaday creatures are the machines which guard and shape our lives in so many ways – above all, the taurean computer, seeding its limitless possibilities. As for the ram, that tireless guardian of the domestic flock, his counterpart in our own homes seems to be the Polaroid camera, shepherding our smallest memories and emotions, our most tender sexual acts. Here, anyway, is an s-f zodiac, which I assume the next real one will be . . .*

## The Sign of the Polaroid

The skies were sliding. Already the first of the television crews had arrived in the hospital's car park and were scanning the upper floors of the psychiatric wing through their binoculars. He lowered the plastic blind, exhausted by all this attention, the sense of a world both narrowing and expanding around him. He waited as Dr Vanessa adjusted the lens of the cine-camera. Her untidy hair, still uncombed since she first collected him from the patients' refectory, fell across the view-finder. Was she placing the filter of her own tissues between herself and whatever threatening message the film might reveal? Since Professor Rotblat's arrival in the Home Office limousine she had done nothing but photograph him obsessively during a range of meaningless activities – studying the tedious Rorschach images, riding the bicycle in the physiology laboratory, squatting across the bidet in her apartment. Why had they suddenly picked him out, an unknown long-term patient whom everyone had ignored since his admission ten years earlier? Throughout his adolescence he had often stood on the roof of the dormitory block and taken the sky into himself, but not even Dr Vanessa had noticed. Pushing back her blonde hair, she looked at him with unexpected concern. 'One last reel, and then you must pack – the helicopter's coming for us.' All night she had sat with him on her bed, projecting the films on to the wall of the apartment.

## The Sign of the Computer

He sat at the metal desk beside the podium, staring at the hushed faces of the delegates as Professor Rotblat gestured with the print-outs. 'A routine cytoplasmic scan was performed six months ago on the patients of this obscure mental institution, as part of the clinical trials of a new antenatal tranquillizer. Thanks to Dr Vanessa Carrington, the extraordinary and wholly anomalous cell chemistry of the subject was brought to my attention, above all the laevo-rotatory spiral of the DNA helix. The most exhaustive analyses conducted by MIT's ULTRAC 666, the world's most powerful computer, confirm that this unknown young man, an orphan of untraceable parentage, seems to have been born from a mirror universe, propelled into our own world by cosmic forces of unlimited power. They also indicate that in opting for its original right-hand bias our biological kingdom made the weaker of two choices. All the ULTRAC predictions suggest that the combinative possibilities of laevo-rotatory DNA exceed those of our own cell chemistry by a factor of $10^{27}$. I may add that the ULTRAC programmers have constructed a total information model of this alternative universe, with implications that are both exalting and terrifying for us all . . .'

## The Sign of the Clones

He steadied himself against the balcony rail, retching on to the turquoise tiles. Twenty feet below his hotel room was the curvilinear roof of the conference centre, its white concrete back like an immense occluded lens. For all Professor Rotblat's talk of alternative universes, the delegates would see nothing through that eyepiece. They seemed to be more impressed by the potency of this over-productive computer than they were by his own. So far his life had been without any possibilities at all – volleyball with the paraplegics, his shins bruised by their wheelchairs, boring hours pretending to paint like Van Gogh in the occupational therapy classes, then evenings spent with TV and largactil. But at least he could look up at the sky and listen to the time-music of the quasars. He waited for the nausea to pass, regretting that he had agreed to be flown here. The lobbies of the hotel were filled with suspiciously deferential officials. Where was Dr Vanessa? Already he missed her reassuring hands, her scent around the projection theatre. He looked up from the vomit on the balcony. Below him the television director was standing on the roof of the conference centre, waving to him in a friendly but cryptic way. There was something uncannily familiar about his face and stance, like a too-perfect reflection in a mirror. At times the man seemed to be mimicking him, trying to signal the codes of an escape combination. Or was he some kind of sinister twin, a right-hand replica of himself being groomed to take his place? Wiping his mouth, he noticed the green pill in the vomit between his feet. So the police orderly had tried to sedate him. Without thinking, he decided to escape, and picked up the manual which the Home Office horoscopist had pushed into his hands after lunch.

### The Sign of the IUD

He could smell her vulva on his hands. He lay on his side in the darkened bedroom, waiting until she returned from the bathroom. Through the glass door he could see her blurred thighs and breasts, as if distorted by some computer permutating all the possibilities of an alternative anatomy. This likeable but strange young woman, with her anonymous apartment and random conversation filled with sudden references to quasars, the overthrow of capitalism, nucleic acids and horoscopy – had she any idea what would soon happen to her? Clearly she had been waiting for him in the hotel's car park, all too ready to hide him in the jump seat of her sports car. Was she the courier of a rival consortium, sent to him by the unseen powers who presided over the quasars? On the bedside table was the intra-uterine coil, with the draw-string he had felt at the neck of her womb. On some confused impulse she had decided to remove it, as if determined to preserve at least one set of his wild genes within the safekeeping of her placental vault. He swung the coil by its draw-string, this technological cipher that seemed to contain in its double swastika an anagram of all the zodiacal emblems in the horoscopy manual. Was it a clue left for him, a modulus to be multiplied by everything in this right-handed world – the contours of this young woman's breasts, the laws of chemical kinetics, the migration song of swallows? After the camera, the computer and the clones, the coil was the fourth house of that zodiac he had already entered, the twelve-chambered mansion through which he must move with the guile of a master-burglar. He looked up as Renata gently pushed him back on to the pillow. 'Rest for an hour.' She seemed to be forwarding instructions from another sky. 'Then we'll leave for Jodrell Bank.'

### The Sign of the Radar Bowl

As they waited in the stationary traffic on the crowded deck of the flyover Renata fiddled impatiently with the radio, unable to penetrate the static from the cars around them. Smiling at her, he turned off the sound and pointed to the sky over her head. 'Ignore the horizon. Beyond the Pole Star you can hear the island universes.' He sat back, trying to ignore the thousand satellite transmissions, a barbarous chatter below the great music of the quasars. Even now, through the afternoon sunlight over this provincial city, he could read the comsat relays and the radar beams of Fylingdales and the Norad line in northern Canada, and hear the answering over-the-horizon probes of the Russian sites near Murmansk, distant lions roaring their fear at each other, marking their claims to impossible territories. An incoming missile would be fixed in the cat's cradle of his mind like a fly trapped in the sound-space of a Beethoven symphony. Startled, he saw a pair of scarred hands seize the rim of the windshield. A thick-set man with a hard beard had leapt between the airline buses and was staring at him, his left eye inflamed by some unpleasant virus. To Renata he snapped: 'Get into the back – we've only a week to the First Secretary's visit.'

## The Sign of the Stripper

As the music stopped they took their seats in the front row of the strip club. Only three feet from him, on a miniature stage decorated like a boudoir, the naked couple were reaching the climax of their sex act. The bored audience hushed behind them, and he was aware of Heller watching him with an almost obsessive intensity. For days he had been numbed by the galvanic energy of this psychotic man, this terrorist with his doomsday dreams of World War III. During the past few days they had followed a deranged itinerary – airport cargo bays, the approach roads to missile silos, secret apartments packed with computer terminals and guarded by a gang of arrogant killers, hoodlum physicists trained at some deviant university. And above all, the strip clubs – he and Heller had visited dozens of these lurid cabins, watching Renata and the women members of the gang run the gamut of every conceivable sexual variation, perversions so abstract that they had become the elements in a complex calculus. Later, in their apartments, these aggressive women would sidle around him like caricatures from an erotic dream. Already he knew that Heller was trying to recruit him into his conspiracy. But were they unconsciously giving him the keys to the sixth house? He stared up at the young woman who was now leaving the stage to scattered applause, showing off the semen on her thigh. He remembered Heller's frightening violence as he grappled with the young whores in the back of the sports car, assaults as stylized as ballet movements. In the codes of Renata's body, in the junctions of nipple and finger, in the sulcus of her buttocks, waited the possibilities of a benevolent psychopathology.

## The Sign of the Psychiatrist

Professor Rotblat paused as Vanessa Carrington returned from the window and stood behind the young man's chair, her hands protectively on his shoulders. His face seemed to embody the geometry of totally alien obsessions. 'The role of psychiatry today is no longer to cure the patient, but to reconcile him to his strengths and weaknesses, to balance the dark side of the sun against the light – a task, incidentally, made no easier for us by an unaccommodating nature. Theoretical physics reminds us of the inherent right-hand bias of all matter. The spin of the electron, the rotation of both the solar system and the smallest sub-atomic particles, the great tides that turn the cosmos itself, all embody this fundamental constant, reflected not only in the deep-rooted popular unease with left-handedness, but in the dextro-rotatory helix of DNA. Given the high energies involved, whether in galaxies or biological systems, any attempt at a contrary direction would have catastrophic results, of a type familiar to us in the case of black holes. A single such individual might become the psychological equivalent of a doomsday weapon . . .' He waited for the young man to reply. Had he returned to the hospital to remind them that he had transcended the role of patient and was moving into a sinistral realm where the ULTRAC predictions should be read from right to left?

## The Sign of the Psychopath

He stood by the stolen Mercedes as the women loaded the ambassador's body into the trunk. Heller was watching from the elevator doors, the heavy machine-pistol held in both hands. The terrorist's swarthy face had closed in on itself, exposing the loosening sutures around his temples. During the hours of violence in the apartment he had gripped his pistol as if masturbating himself to a continuous orgasm. The torment inflicted upon this elderly diplomat had clearly served a purpose known only to Renata and her companions. They had watched the murder with an almost dreamlike calm, as if Heller's deranged cruelty revealed the secret formulas of a new logic, a conceptualized violence that would transform the air disaster and the car crash into events of loving gentleness. Already they planned an ever-more psychotic series of spectacular adventures – the assassination of the visiting party leader, the hijacking of the plutonium convoy, the reprogramming of ULTRAC to destroy the entire commercial and banking system of the West. These women dreamed of World War III like young mothers crooning over their first pregnancies.

## The Sign of the Hypodermic

He watched Dr Vanessa's reflection in the window of the control room as she adjusted the electrodes on his scalp. Her uncertain hands, with their tremor of guilt and affection, summed up all the uncertainties of this dangerous experiment conducted in the converted television studios. Despite Professor Rotblat's disapproval, she had become a willing conspirator, perhaps out of some confused hope that he would make his escape, embark from the causeways of his own spinal column and fly away across some interior sky. The television director's face swam through the heavy glass of the control room. During the previous days, as they set up the experiment in the studio laboratory, Tarrant had begun to hide behind these transparent mirrors, as if uncertain of his own reality. Yet he seemed to sympathize with the need to come to terms with this nightmare world of terrorists and cruise missiles, objects seen in a deformed mirror that might one day be reunited in a more meaningful sequence. Multiplied by the ULTRAC computer, the wave-functions of his hallucinating brain would be transmitted on the nationwide channels and provide a new set of operating formulae for their passage through consciousness. He touched Dr Vanessa's knee reassuringly as she held the hypodermic to the light.

## The Sign of the Vibrator

He listened to the monotonous, insect-like buzz of the elegant machine in Renata's hand. She lay on her back, muttering some complex masturbatory fantasy to herself, for once unaware of his presence. Was she really convinced by these shudders and gasps of her own sexual fulfilment? Since his return to her apartment he had often reflected that sex offered to any would-be tyrant the easiest and most effective means of political take-over. However, he had made his own choice elsewhere. Within a few days the terrorist groups would attempt to start World War III, and the psychological year would move to its climax. Already the subliminal films were ready to be transmitted through the emergency news bulletins. Relaxed now, he looked down at Renata's straining thighs and pelvis. By the time the television transmission of this exhausting sex act had reached the nearest stars any curious observers there would assume that she was giving birth to this unpleasant machine, offspring of her marriage with the ULTRAC print-outs.

## The Sign of the Cruise Missile

He knelt in front of the television set, waiting for the overdue emergency bulletins. By now the skies over central London should have been filled with helicopters, the streets deafened by the treads of armoured troop carriers, the whole panoply of nuclear alert. Waiting patiently, confident that the logic of the new zodiac would be fulfilled, he stared at the silent screen as Renata lay asleep on the bed. Deep in his mind he dreamed of cruise missiles, launched from the surfacing submarines and heading out across the lonely tundra, following the contours of remote arctic fjords. Soon he would be leaving, glad to abandon this planet to its nightmare games. He had played only a small part in this reductive drama. The true zodiac of these people, the constellations of their mental skies, constituted nothing more than a huge self-destructive machine. Leaving the set, he looked down at the young woman. As he placed his hands around her neck, ready to satisfy the faultless logic of the psychological round, he was thinking only of the cruise missiles.

### The Sign of the Astronaut

Through the glass window of the isolation ward he watched Dr Vanessa speaking quietly to Professor Rotblat. Her nervous anxiety when the police returned him to the hospital had given way to no more than a neutral and professional concern. He pressed his elbows against the restraining sheet, thinking of Renata's bloodied body, with its strangely resistant anatomy that he had tried to arrange into a happier and more meaningful geometry. He knew now that he had been tricked by them all, that there had been no nuclear crisis, and that the subliminal messages had been intended only for himself. Had it all been no more than a fantasy, and was the search for the zodiac imposed upon him unintentionally by his too-sudden release from the hospital? However, Renata's body remained more than a small clinical embarrassment. One day the murder of this intellectual woman gangster might really seed their society's destruction. He had been trapped by the zodiac they had urged him to construct, but he had escaped through the side door of this young woman's death. The great round had come full circle, raised him on its shoulder and returned him to the institution. However, they had made no allowance for a wholly unexpected contingency – his recovery of his sanity, a treasure abducted from the twelve mansions. Now he would leave them, and take the left-handed staircase to the roof above his mind, and fly away across the free skies of his inner space.

- **1978**

# *MOTEL ARCHITECTURE

Pangborn's suspicion that someone was hiding in the solarium coincided with the arrival of the young repairwoman. The presence of this smartly uniformed but bored girl rattling her metal valise around his wheelchair so frayed his nerves that at first he made no attempt to find the intruder. Her aggressive manner, the interminable whistling she kept up as she wiped the television screens, and her growing interest in Pangborn were unlike anything he had previously had to deal with.

The uniformed women sent by the company to maintain the services within the solarium had been noted for their silence and efficiency. Looking back at the twelve years he had spent in the solarium, Pangborn could hardly recall a single face. In fact, the absence of any kind of personal identity allowed the young women to carry out their intimate chores. Yet even within the hour of her first visit this new recruit had managed to damage the tuning control of the master screen and unsettle Pangborn with her moody gaze. But for this vague and unsettling criticism of him Pangborn would have identified the intruder far earlier and avoided the strange consequences that were to follow.

At the time he had been sitting in his chair in the centre of the solarium, bathing in the warm artificial light that flowed through the ceiling vents and watching the shower sequence from *Psycho* on the master screen. The brilliance of this *tour de force* never ceased to astonish Pangborn. He had played the sequence to himself hundreds of times, frozen every frame and explored it in close-up, separately recorded sections of the action and displayed them on the dozen smaller screens around the master display. The extraordinary relationship between the geometry of the shower stall and the anatomy of the murdered woman's body seemed to hold the clue to the real meaning of everything in Pangborn's world, to the unstated connections between his own musculature and the immaculate glass and chromium universe of the solarium. In his headier moments Pangborn was convinced that the secret formulas of his tenancy of time and space were contained somewhere within this endlessly repeated clip of film.

So immersed had he been in the mysterious climax of the sequence – the slewing face of the actress pressed against the tiled floor with its rectilinear grid – that at first he ignored the faint noise of breathing nearby, the half-familiar smell of a human being.

Pangborn turned in his wheelchair, expecting to find someone standing behind him, perhaps one of the delivery men who provisioned the solarium's kitchen and fuel tanks. After twelve years of living entirely on his own, Pangborn had discovered that his senses were sharp enough to detect the presence of a single fly.

Freezing the film on the television screens, he swung his chair and turned his back to them. The circular chamber was empty, like the uncurtained bathroom and kitchen.

But the air had moved, somewhere behind him a heart had beaten, lungs had breathed.

At this moment a key turned in the entrance hall, the glass door was banged back by a clumsily carried vacuum-cleaner, and Vera Tilley made her first appearance.

For all his intimacy with the electronic image of the naked film actress, Pangborn had not looked a real woman in the face for more than ten years. Still unsettled by the suspected intruder, he watched the uniformed girl drop her vacuum-cleaner on to the carpet and root about in her tool-kit. She was barely twenty, with untidy blonde hair pushed up into her cap, eccentric make-up applied to her already large mouth and eyes. On her lapel was an identification badge – under the company's heraldic device was the name 'Vera Tilley' and a photograph of her staring at the camera with a cheeky pout.

She now gazed at Pangborn and the solarium in the same provocative way.

'When you're ready you can carry on,' Pangborn told her. 'I'm busy at the moment.'

'So I can see.' The girl eyed the complex of screens, the huge blow-ups of the dead eyes of the actress surrounded like an electronic altar-piece by the quantified sections of her body on the smaller displays. With a wry glance at Pangborn's padded contour chair, she remarked: 'Is she comfortable up there? Can't you do something for her?' She flicked a dirty finger-nail at the control console on the arm of the chair. 'You've got enough buttons to stop the world.'

Ignoring her, Pangborn rotated the chair and returned to the screens. For the next hour, as he continued his analysis of the shower sequence, he was still thinking of the intruder. Clearly there was no one hiding in the solarium now, but the presence of this mysterious visitor might in some way be connected with the odd young woman. He could almost believe that she was some new kind of urban terrorist. He listened to her moving around the kitchen, servicing the equipment and replacing the supplies in the food dispensers. Every now and then her whistling was modulated by an ironic note.

When she had cleaned the bathroom she came back and stood between Pangborn and the screens. He could smell his cologne on her wrists.

'Time to switch off the life-support system,' she said goodhumouredly. 'Can you survive for five minutes on your own?'

Pangborn waited impatiently while she swung each of the television sets from the wall and tuned its controls. As he watched this young woman at work, kneeling in front of him on the carpet, he felt strangely vulnerable. Her breathing, her plump calves, the coarse vitality of her body, made him wish that it were possible to dispense with any need to maintain the solarium. He had been celibate for the past fifteen years, and his confused feelings unsettled him. He preferred the secure realities of the television screens to the endlessly bizarre fictions of ordinary life. At the same time Vera Tilley intrigued him. He thought again of the intruder.

'See you next week,' she told him as he signed the work schedule. While she packed her valise she watched him with some concern. 'Don't you ever get tired of looking at those old films? You ought to go out once in a while. My brother owns a taxi if you ever want one.'

Pangborn waved her away, his eyes on the magnified image of the bathroom floor and the strange contours of the film actress's cheekbones. But when the door opened he called out: 'Tell me, I meant to ask – when you arrived, was there anyone waiting outside?'

'Only if he was invisible.' Puzzled by Pangborn's deliberately casual tone, she weighed the valise in her strong hand, as if about to take out her screwdriver and turn down his over-active image control. 'You're alone here, Mr Pangborn. Perhaps you saw a ghost . . .'

After she had gone Pangborn lay back in his chair and scanned through the afternoon's public television programmes. With her slapdash manner, the girl had mistuned the master screen, dappling everything with an intermittent interference pattern, but for once Pangborn was able to ignore this. He turned off the sound and watched the dozens of programmes move past silently.

Once again, unmistakably, he was aware of the presence of someone nearby. The faint voice of another human being hung on the air, the spoor of an unfamiliar body. There was an odd but not unpleasant odour in the solarium. Pangborn left the screens and drove the wheelchair around the chamber, inspecting the kitchen, hall and bathroom. He could see that the solarium was empty, but at the same time he was convinced that someone was watching him.

The girl, Vera Tilley, had unsettled him in a way he had not expected. All his experience, his years spent in front of the television screens, had not prepared him for even the briefest encounter with an actual woman. What would once have been called the 'real' world, the quiet streets outside, the private estate of hundreds of similar solaria, made no effort to intrude itself into Pangborn's private world and he had never felt any need to defend himself against it.

Looking down at himself, he realized that he had been naked during her visit. Bathed in the ceaseless light of the solarium, he had years ago given up wearing even his loin-slip. So distant and anonymous were the repair-women usually sent by the company that he felt no embarrassment as they moved around him.

However, Vera Tilley had made him aware of himself for the first time. No doubt she had noticed just how she had aroused him. Trying not to think of her, Pangborn stiffened the back of the chair and concentrated on the television screens in front of him. Calmed by the warm light flowing across his bronzed body, he switched off the public channels and returned to his analysis of *Psycho*. The geometry of the naked actress slumped across the floor of the shower stall provided an endless source of interest, like the most abstract possible of all music, and within a few minutes he was able to lower the back of the chair, Vera Tilley and the mysterious intruder forgotten.

During his twelve years in the solarium Pangborn had never left the light-filled chamber, and recently had hardly even left the chair. For the few minutes each day which he was forced to spend standing in the bathroom he felt strangely heavy and cumbersome, his body an uncouth mass of superfluous musculature suspended as if by a bad sculptor on the slender armature of his bones. Lying back on the chair, he found it hard to believe that the sleek, bronzed figure projected by the monitor camera on to the screens in front of him was that same shaky invalid who faced him in the bathroom mirror. As far as possible Pangborn remained in the chair, wheeling himself into the kitchen, preparing his meals sitting down, in a sense remaking a small second world within the private universe of the solarium.

This spherical chamber where he seemed to have spent his entire life, asleep and awake, by now supplied all his needs, both physical and psychological. The chamber was at once a gymnasium and bedroom, library and workplace (nominally Pangborn was a television critic, virtually the only job, apart from that of the maintenance engineers, in a society where everything else was done by machine). Mounted on the rear wall of the solarium was a cluster of exercise devices which he operated for half an hour each day while sitting in the chair.

The bathroom was also equipped with a special cabinet containing a variety of sexual appliances, but for years Pangborn had been repelled by the thought of using them – they engaged him in too unsettling a way with the facts of his own body. He felt the same resistance towards the psychological maintenance devices which everyone was encouraged to air for at least an hour each day on the television screens – simulated confrontations and reconciliations with his parents, intelligence and personality tests, and a whole range of psychological games, pocket dramas in which he could play the starring role.

But Pangborn had soon become bored with the limited repertoire of these charades. Fantasy and the imagination had always played little part in his life, and he felt only at home within the framework of an absolute realism. The solarium was a fully equipped television studio, in which Pangborn was simultaneously the star, script-writer and director of an unending domestic serial of infinitely more interest than the programmes provided by the public channels. The news bulletins now were about his own body processes, the night's heart rate, the rising and falling curves of his temperature. These images, and the analysis of certain key events from his library of feature films, seemed to have some kind of profound though yet mysterious connection. The strange geometry presiding over the actress in her shower stall provided a key to that absolute abstraction of himself he had sought since his arrival at the solarium, the construction of a world formed entirely from the materials of his own consciousness.

During the next days Pangborn's peace of mind was interrupted by his growing awareness of the intruder who had entered the solarium. At first he put down his suspicions to Vera Tilley's arrival. The strongly scented cosmetics used by the young woman had released some repressed memory of his mother and sister, and of his brief and abortive marriage. But once again, as he lay back in his chair, analysing the ever larger blow-ups of the actress's face pressed against the bathroom tiles, he felt the presence of an uninvited visitor somewhere behind him. With the sound turned down he could hear the occasional breathing, even a sigh as this mysterious intruder seemed to weary of his secret vigil. Now and then Pangborn would hear a metallic creak behind him, the tension of a leather harness, and detect the faint smell of another body.

For once ignoring his television screens, Pangborn began a painstaking inspection of the solarium, starting with the hall and its storage cupboards. He pulled out the racks of cassettes, the cases filled with suits he had not worn for ten years. Satisfied that the hall provided no hiding place, he drove the wheelchair into the bathroom and kitchen, searched the medicine cabinet and shower, the narrow spaces behind the refrigerator and cooker. It occurred to him that the intruder might be some small animal which had slipped into the solarium during a visit by one of the cleaners. But as he sat motionlessly in the light-filled silence he could hear the steady breathing of a human being.

By the time of Vera Tilley's second visit Pangborn was waiting at the door of the solarium. He hoped to catch a glimpse of someone loitering outside, perhaps an accomplice of the intruder. Already he suspected that they might be members of a gang hoping to rig the television audience surveys.

'You're on my foot, Mr Pangborn! What's the matter? Don't you want me to come in today?' Pushing the door against the wheelchair, Vera looked down at Pangborn. 'You're in a state.'

Pangborn reversed into the centre of the solarium. The young woman's make-up seemed less bizarre, as if she intended to reveal more of herself to him. Realizing suddenly that he was naked, he felt his skin prickle uncomfortably.

'Did you see anyone outside? Waiting in a car, or watching the door?'

'You asked me that last week.' Ignoring his agitated condition, Vera opened her tool-kit and began to fit together the sections of the vacuum-cleaner. 'Are you expecting someone to stay?'

'No!' The thought appalled Pangborn. Even the presence of the young woman exhausted him. He remembered the sounds of breathing behind the chair. Calming himself, he said: 'Leave the cleaning until later and have a look at the aerials. I think one of the sets is picking up a strange sound-track – perhaps from the studio next door.'

Pangborn waited while she worked away at the sets. Afterwards he followed her around the solarium in his wheelchair, watching as she cleaned the bathroom and kitchen. He peered between her legs into the shower stall and garbage disposal chute, confirming for himself that there was no one hiding there.

'You're all alone, Mr Pangborn. Just you and the TV screens.' As she locked her valise Vera watched him in a concerned way. 'Have you ever been to the zoo, Mr Pangborn?'

'What ...? There are wild-life programmes I sometimes review.' Pangborn waited impatiently for her to leave, relieved that he could get on with his work. Watching the dozen television screens, which the girl had tuned to a needle-like sharpness, he was suddenly convinced that the notion of an intruder had all been a delusion fostered by the unsettled presence of this young woman.

However, only a few minutes after she had gone Pangborn once again heard the sounds of the intruder behind him, and the noise of the man's breathing, even louder now as if he had decided no longer to conceal his presence from Pangborn.

Controlling himself, Pangborn took stock of the solarium. An unvarying light fell through the glass vents into this world without shadows, bathing the chamber in an almost submarine glow. He had been reviewing a programme of redubbed films – a huge repertory of transcribed classics now existed, their story lines and dialogue totally unconnected with their originals. Pangborn had been watching a tinted and redubbed version of *Casablanca*, now a new instructional film in a hotel management course on the pitfalls and satisfactions of overseas nightclub operation. Ignoring the trite dialogue, Pangborn was enjoying the timelessly elegant direction when a colour fault on the master screen began to turn the characters' faces green.

As he switched off the wall of screens, about to call the maintenance company, Pangborn heard the distinctive sounds of breathing. He froze in his chair, listening to the characteristic rise and fall of human respiration. As if aware that Pangborn was listening to him, the intruder began to breathe more heavily, the harsh, deep breaths of a man in fear.

Coolly, Pangborn kept his back to the intruder, who was hiding either in the hall or bathroom. He could not only hear but smell the man's fear, the vaguely familiar scent he had noticed the previous week. For some reason he was almost sure that the man had no intention of attacking him, and was only trying to escape from the solarium. Perhaps he was an exhausted fugitive from some act of mis-justice, a wrongly incarcerated mental patient.

For the rest of the afternoon Pangborn pretended to watch the defective television screens, while systematically devising a method of dealing with the intruder. First of all he needed to establish the man's identity. He switched on the monitor camera that surveyed the solarium and set it on continuous traverse across the bathroom, kitchen and hall.

Pangborn then turned to setting a number of small traps. He unlocked the medicine cabinet in the bathroom, marking the positions of the antiseptic cream and Band-aids. After a deliberately early supper he left untouched a small filet steak and a bowl of salad. He placed a fresh bar of soap in the shower tray and scattered a fine mist of talc on the bathroom carpet.

Satisfied, he returned to the television screens and lay half-awake until the small hours, listening to the faint breathing somewhere behind him as he carried out his endless analysis of the murder sequence from *Psycho.* The immaculate and soundless junction of the film actress's skin and the white bathroom tiles, magnified in a vast close-up, contained the secret formulas that somewhere united his own body to the white fabric and soft chrome of his contour couch.

When he woke the next morning he once again heard the intruder's breathing, so rested that his mysterious visitor seemed almost to be part of everyday life in the solarium. Sure enough, as Pangborn had expected, all the modest traps had been sprung. The man had washed his hands with the fresh bar of soap, a small portion of the steak and salad had been eaten, a strange footprint marked the talc in the bathroom.

Unsettled by this tangible proof that he was not alone in the solarium, Pangborn stared at the footprint. The man's foot was almost the size of his own, with the same overlarge and questing big toe. Something about this similarity brought a flush of irritation to Pangborn. He felt a sudden sense of challenge, provoked by this feeling of identity with the man.

This close involvement with the intruder was redoubled when Pangborn discovered that the man had taken a book from his shelf – the almost unobtainable text of the original dialogue of *The Third Man,* now a cautionary tale put out by the world tourist authority on the perils of the language barrier. Pangborn thumbed through the pages of the scenario, half-hoping to find a further clue to the man's identity. He carefully replaced the book on the shelf. These first hints of the intruder's nature – the shared literary tastes, the shape of his feet, the sounds of his breathing and his body smell – both intrigued and provoked him.

As he played at high speed through the hours of film the solarium camera had recorded, he now and then caught what seemed to be brief glimpses of the intruder – the flash of an elbow behind the bathroom door, a shoulder framed against the medicine cabinet, the back of a head in the hall. Pangborn gazed at these magnifications, expanding them beside the stills from *Psycho*, the systems of two parallel but coinciding geometries.

This never explicit but civilized duel between them continued during the next days. At times Pangborn felt that he was running a *ménage à deux*. He effectively cooked meals for them both – the intruder fortunately approved of Pangborn's tastes in wine, and often reinforced the night with small measures of Pangborn's brandy. Above all, their intellectual tastes coincided – their interests in film, in abstract painting, and in the architecture of large structures. Indeed, Pangborn almost visualized them openly sharing the solarium, embarking together on their rejection of the world and the exploration of their absolute selves, their unique time and space.

All the more bitter, therefore, were Pangborn's reactions when he discovered the intruder's attempt to kill him.

Too stunned to reach for the telephone and call the police, Pangborn stared at the bottle of sleeping tablets. He listened to the faint breathing somewhere behind him, lower now as if the intruder were holding his breath, waiting for Pangborn's response.

Ten minutes earlier, while drinking his morning coffee, Pangborn had at first ignored its faintly acrid flavour, presumably some new spice or preservative. But after a few more sips he had almost gagged. Carefully emptying the cup into the wash-basin, he discovered the half-dissolved remains of a dozen plastic capsules.

Pangborn reached into the medicine cabinet and opened the now empty bottle of sleeping tablets. He listened to the faint breathing in the solarium. At some point, while his back was turned, the intruder had slipped the entire contents into his coffee.

He forced himself to vomit into the basin, but still felt queasy when Vera arrived an hour later.

'You look fed up,' she told him cheerfully. She nodded at the books scattered around the place. 'I can see you've been reading again.'

'I'm lending some books to a friend,' Pangborn reversed his chair away from her as she ambled around the chamber with her valise. Under the seat of his chair he held the handle of a vegetable knife. Looking up at the girl's over-bright make-up and guileless eyes it was hard to believe that she might be in collusion with the intruder. At the same time he was surprised that she could not hear the obvious sounds of the man's breathing. Once again Pangborn was amazed by his nimbleness, his ability to move from one end of the solarium to the other without leaving more than a few fragments of his presence on the monitor film. He assumed that the man had found a secure hiding place, perhaps in a service shaft unknown to Pangborn.

'Mr Pangborn! Are you awake?'

With an effort, Pangborn rallied himself. He looked up to find Vera kneeling in front of him. She had pushed back her cap and was shaking his knees. He searched for the knife handle.

'Mr Pangborn – all those pills in the bathroom. What are they doing?'

Pangborn gestured vaguely. Concerned only to find a weapon, he had forgotten to wash away the capsules.

'I dropped the bottle in the basin – be careful you don't cut your hands.'

'Mr Pangborn –' Confused, Vera stood up and straightened her cap. She glanced disapprovingly at the huge blow-ups from *Psycho* on the television screens, and at the blurred fragments of shoulder and elbow recorded by the solarium camera. 'It's like a jig-saw. Who is it? You?'

'Someone else – a friend who's been visiting me.'

'I thought so – the place is in a mess. The kitchen . . . Have you ever thought of getting married, Mr Pangborn?'

He stared at her, aware that she was deliberately being coquettish, trying to unsettle him for his own sake. Once again his skin began to scream.

'You ought to get out of here more,' she was telling him sensibly. 'Visit your friend. Do you want me to come tomorrow? It's on my route. I can say your aerials need tuning.'

Pangborn reversed around her, keeping an eye on the bathroom and kitchen. Vera hesitated before leaving, searching for an excuse to prolong her stay. Pangborn was certain that this amiable scatter-brain was not an accomplice of the intruder, but if he once divulged the man's presence, let alone the murder attempt, she would probably panic and then provoke an openly homicidal assault.

Controlling his temper, he waited until she left. But any irritation he felt was soon forgotten when a second attempt was made on his life.

As with the first murder attempt, Pangborn noticed that the method chosen was both devious and clumsy. Whether because he was still half-doped by the sleeping pills, or out of sheer physical bravado, he felt no sense of panic, but only a calm determination to beat the intruder at his own game. A complex duel was taking place between them, its fragmentary course displayed in a lengthening series of giant blow-ups on the screens – his own suspicious hands a few feet from the camera, the intruder's angular shoulder silhouetted against the kitchen door, even a portion of an ear reflected in the mirror of the medicine cabinet. As Pangborn sat in his chair, comparing sections of this visual jig-saw with the elements from the shower sequence in *Psycho*, he knew that sooner or later he would assemble a complete picture of the intruder.

Meanwhile, the man's presence became ever more evident. The smell of his body filled the solarium and stained the towels in the bathroom. He openly helped himself to the food in the refrigerator, scattering shreds of salad on the floor. Tirelessly, Pangborn maintained his round-the-clock surveillance, trying to shake off the effects of the sleeping pills. So determined was he to defeat the intruder that he took for granted that the water in the bathroom tank had been fouled with cleaning soda. Later, in the kitchen, as he bathed his stinging face with mineral water, he could hear the self-satisfied breathing of the intruder, celebrating another small deceit.

Later that night, as he lay half-asleep in front of the television screens, he woke with a start to feel the hot breath of the stranger against his face. Startled, he looked round in the flickering light to find the vegetable knife on the carpet and a small wound on his right knee.

For the first time a foul smell pervaded the solarium, an unpleasant blend of disinfectant, excrement and physical rage, like the atmosphere of some ill-maintained psychiatric institution.

Retching on to the carpet beside his chair, Pangborn turned his back to the television screens. Holding the vegetable knife in front of him, he headed for the hall. He unlocked the front door, waiting for the cool night air to invade the solarium. Leaving the door ajar, he wheeled himself to the telephone beside the screens.

As he held the severed flex in his hands he heard the hall door close quietly. So the intruder had decided to leave, resigning from their duel even though Pangborn was now unable to contact the outside world.

Pangborn looked at the screens, regretting that he would never complete the jig-saw. The foul smell still hung on the air, and Pangborn decided to take a shower before going out to use a neighbour's telephone.

But as he entered the bathroom he could see clearly the bloody rents in the shower curtain. Pulling it back, he recognized the body of the young repair-woman, lying face down on the tiled floor, and the familiar postures he had analysed in a thousand blow-ups.

Appalled by the calm expression in Vera's eyes, as if she had known full well the role in which she had been cast, Pangborn reversed his chair into the solarium. He gripped the knife, feeling her wounds in the pain in his leg, and aware once again of the deep breathing around him.

Everything now, in this final phase, was in close-up. After recording the position of the girl's body with his portable camera – the film would be vital evidence for the investigating police – Pangborn sat in front of the wall of screens. He was certain that the last confrontation was about to take place between himself and the intruder. Holding the knife in his hand, he waited for the imminent attack. The sounds in the solarium seemed amplified, and he could hear the intruder's pumping lungs and feel his frightened pulse drumming through the floor into the arms of his chair.

Pangborn waited for him to come, his eyes on the screen, the monitor camera focused directly upon himself. He watched the huge close-ups of his own body, of the film actress on the floor of her bathroom, and of Vera's sprawled form entangled with the white shower curtains. As he adjusted the controls, moving these areas of tile and flesh into ever-closer focus, Pangborn felt himself rising beyond anger into an almost sexual lust for the intruder's death, the first erotic impulse he had known since he had begun watching these television screens so many years earlier. The smell of the man's body, the beat of his pulse and hot breath seemed to be moving towards an orgasmic climax. Their collision when it came in the next few minutes would be an act of intercourse, which would at last provide the key he needed.

Pangborn held the knife, watching the whitening screens, anonymous rectangles of blank skin that formed a fragmented sky. Somewhere among them the elements of the human form still remained, a residual nexus of contour and texture in which Pangborn could at last perceive the unmistakable outline of the stranger's face.

Eyes fixed upon the screens, he waited for the man to touch him, certain that he had mesmerized the intruder with these obsessive images. He felt no hostility towards the man, and was aware now that over the years in the solarium he had become so detached from external reality that even he himself had become a stranger. The odours and sounds that disgusted him were those of his own body. All along, the intruder in the solarium had been himself. In his search for absolute peace he had found one last limiting obstacle – the intrusive fact of his own consciousness. Without this, he would merge forever into the universe of the infinite close-up. He was sorry for the young woman, but it was she who had first provoked him into his disgust with himself.

Eager now to merge with the white sky of the screen, to find that death in which he would be rid forever of himself, of his intruding mind and body, he raised the knife to his happy heart.

- **1978**

# A HOST OF FURIOUS FANCIES

Don't look now, but an unusual young woman and her elderly companion are sitting down behind us. Every Thursday afternoon they leave the Casino and come here to the café terrace of the Hotel de Paris, always choosing the same two tables near the magazine kiosk. If you lean forward you can see the girl in the restaurant mirror, the tall and elegant one with the too-level gaze and that characteristic walk of rich young women who have been brought up by nuns.

The man is behind her, the seedy-looking fellow with the once-handsome face, at least twenty years older, though you probably think thirty. He wears the same expensive but ill-fitting grey suit and silver tie, as if he has just been let out of some institution to attend a wedding. His eyes follow the secretaries returning from their lunches, plainly dreaming of escape. Observing his sad gaze, one not without a certain dignity, I can only conclude that Monte Carlo is a special kind of prison.

You've seen them now? Then you will agree it's hard to believe that these two are married, and have even achieved a stable union, though of a special kind, and governed by a set of complex rituals. Once a week she drives him from Vence to Monte Carlo in their limousine, that gold-tinted Cadillac parked across the square. After half an hour they emerge from the Casino, when he has played away at the roulette wheels the few francs he has been given. From the kiosk of this café terrace she buys him the same cheap magazine, one of those dreadful concierge rags about servant girls and their Prince Charmings, and then sips at her citron pressé as they sit at separate tables. Meanwhile he devours the magazine like a child. Her cool manner is the epitome of a serene self-assurance, of the most robust mental health.

Yet only five years ago, as the physician in charge of her case, I saw her in a very different light. Indeed, it's almost inconceivable that this should be the same young woman whom I first came across at the Hospice of Our Lady of Lourdes, in a state of utter mental degeneration. That I was able to cure her after so many others had failed I put down to an extraordinary piece of psychiatric detection, of a kind that I usually despise. Unhappily, however, that success was bought at a price, paid a hundred times over by the sad old man, barely past his forty-fifth year, who drools over his trashy magazine a few tables behind us.

Before they leave, let me tell you about the case . . .

*   *   *

By chance, it was only the illness of a colleague that brought me into contact with Christina Brossard. After ten years of practice in Monaco as a successful dermatologist I had taken up a part-time consultancy at the American Clinic in Nice. While looking through the out-patients' roster of an indisposed colleague I was told by his secretary that a 17-year-old patient, one Mlle Brossard, had not arrived for her appointment. At that moment one of the nursing sisters at the Our Lady of Lourdes Hospice at Vence – where the girl had been under care for three years – telephoned to cancel the consultation.

'The Mother Superior asks me to apologize to Prof. Derain but the child is simply too distraught again.'

I thought nothing of it at the time, but for some reason – perhaps the girl's name, or the nun's use of 'again' – I asked for the clinical notes. I noticed that this was the third appointment to be cancelled during the previous year. An orphan, Christina Brossard had been admitted to the Hospice at the age of fourteen after the suicide of her father, who had been her only guardian since the death of her mother in an air-crash.

At this point I remembered the entire tragedy. A former mayor of Lyon, Gaston Brossard was a highly successful building contractor and intimate of President Pompidou's, a millionaire many times over. At the peak of his success this 55-year-old man had married for the third time. For his young bride, a beautiful ex-television actress in her early twenties, he had built a sumptuous mansion above Vence. Sadly, however, only two years after Christina's birth the young mother had died when the company aircraft taking her to join her husband in Paris had crashed in the Alpes Maritimes. Heart-broken, Gaston Brossard then devoted the remaining years of his life to the care of his infant daughter. All had gone well, but twelve years later, for no apparent reason, the old millionaire shot himself in his bedroom.

The effects on the daughter were immediate and disastrous – complete nervous collapse, catatonic withdrawal and a slow but painful recovery in the nearby Hospice of Our Lady of Lourdes, which Gaston Brossard had generously endowed in memory of his young wife. The few clinical notes, jotted down by a junior colleague of Derain's who had conscientiously made the journey to Vence, described a recurrent dermatitis, complicated by chronic anaemia and anorexia.

Sitting in my comfortable office, beyond a waiting room filled with wealthy middle-aged patients, I found myself thinking of this 17-year-old orphan lost high in the mountains above Nice. Perhaps my anti-clerical upbringing – my father had been a left-wing newspaper cartoonist, my mother a crusading magistrate and early feminist – made me suspicious of the Hospice of Our Lady of Lourdes. The very name suggested a sinister combination of faith-healing and religious charlatanry, almost expressly designed to take advantage of a mentally unbalanced heiress. Lax executors and unconcerned guardians would leave the child ripe for exploitation, while her carefully preserved illness would guarantee the continued flow of whatever funds had been earmarked for the Hospice in Gaston Brossard's will. As I well knew, dermatitis, anorexia and anaemia were all too often convenient descriptions for a lack of hygiene, malnutrition and neglect.

The following weekend, as I set off for Vence in my car – Prof. Derain had suffered a mild heart attack and would be absent for a month – I visualized this wounded child imprisoned above these brilliant hills by illiterate and scheming nuns who had deliberately starved the pining girl while crossing their palms with the dead man's gold dedicated to the memory of the child's mother.

Of course, as I soon discovered, I was totally in error. The Hospice of Our Lady of Lourdes turned out to be a brand-new, purpose-built sanatorium with well-lit rooms, sunny grounds and a self-evident air of up-to-date medical practice and devotion to the well-being of the patients, many of whom I could see sitting out on the spacious lawns, talking to their friends and relatives.

The Mother Superior herself, like all her colleagues, was an educated and intelligent woman with a strong, open face and sympathetic manner, and hands – as I always immediately notice – that were not averse to hard work.

'It's good of you to come, Dr Charcot. We've all been worried about Christina for some time. Without any disrespect to our own physicians, it's occurred to me more than once that a different approach may be called for.'

'Presumably, you're referring to chemotherapy,' I suggested. 'Or a course of radiation treatment? One of the few Betatrons in Europe is about to be installed at the Clinic.'

'Not exactly . . .' The Mother Superior walked pensively around her desk, as if already reconsidering the usefulness of my visit. 'I was thinking of a less physical approach, Dr Charcot, one concerned to lay the ghosts of the child's spirit as well as those of her body. But you must see her for yourself.'

It was now my turn to be sceptical. Since my earliest days as a medical student I had been hostile to all the claims made by psychotherapy, the happy hunting ground of pseudo-scientific cranks of an especially dangerous kind.

Leaving the Hospice, we drove up into the mountains towards the Brossard mansion, where the young woman was allowed to spend a few hours each day.

'She's extremely active, and tends to unsettle the other patients,' the Mother Superior explained as we turned into the long drive of the mansion, whose Palladian façade presided over a now silent fountain terrace. 'She seems happier here, among the memories of her father and mother.'

We were let into the imposing hall by one of the two young nuns who accompanied the orphaned heiress on these outings. As she and the

Mother Superior discussed a patient to be released that afternoon I strolled across the hall and gazed up at the magnificent tapestries that hung from the marbled walls. Above the semi-circular flights of the divided staircase was a huge Venetian clock with ornate hands and numerals like strange weapons, guardians of a fugitive time.

Beyond the shuttered library a colonnaded doorway led to the dining room. Dustcovers shrouded the chairs and table, and by the fireplace the second of the nuns supervised a servant-girl who was cleaning out the grate. A visiting caretaker or auctioneer had recently lit a small fire of deeds and catalogues. The girl, wearing an old-fashioned leather apron, worked hard on her hands and knees, meticulously sweeping up the cinders before scrubbing the stained tiles.

'Dr Charcot . . .' The Mother Superior beckoned me into the dining room. I followed her past the shrouded furniture to the fireplace.

'Sister Julia, I see we're very busy again. Dr Charcot, I'm sure you'll be pleased by the sight of such industry.'

'Of course . . .' I watched the girl working away, wondering why the Mother Superior should think me interested in the cleaning of a fireplace. The skivvy was little more than a child, but her long, thin arms worked with a will of their own. She had scraped the massive wrought-iron grate with obsessive care, decanting the cinders into a set of transparent plastic bags. Ignoring the three nuns, she dipped a coarse brush into the bucket of soapy water and began to scrub furiously at the tiles, determined to erase the last trace of dirt. The fireplace was already blanched by the soap, as if it had been scrubbed out a dozen times.

I assumed that the child was discharging some penance repeatedly imposed by the Mother Superior. Although not wishing to interfere, I noticed that the girl's hands and wrists showed the characteristic signs of an enzyme-sensitive eczema. In a tone of slight reproof, I remarked: 'You might at least provide a pair of rubber gloves. Now, may I see Mlle Brossard?'

Neither the nuns nor the Mother Superior made any response, but the girl looked up from the soapy tiles. I took in immediately the determined mouth in a pale but once attractive face, the hair fastened fanatically behind a gaunt neck, a toneless facial musculature from which all expression had been deliberately drained. Her eyes stared back at mine with an almost unnerving intensity, as if she had swiftly identified me and was already debating what role I might play for her.

'Christina . . .' The Mother Superior spoke gently, urging the girl from her knees. 'Dr Charcot has come to help you.'

The girl barely nodded and returned to her scrubbing, pausing only to move the cinder-filled plastic bags out of our reach. I watched her with a professional eye, recalling the diagnosis of dermatitis, anorexia and anaemia. Christina Brossard was thin but not under-nourished, and her pallor was probably caused by all this compulsive activity within the gloomy mansion. As for her dermatitis, this was clearly of that special type caused by obsessive hand-washing.

'Christina –' Sister Louise, a pleasant, round-cheeked young woman, knelt on the damp tiles. 'My dear, do rest for a moment.'

'No! No! No!' The girl beat the tiles with her soapy brush. She began to wring out the floorcloth, angry hands like bundles of excited sticks. 'There are three more grates to be done this afternoon! You told me to clean them, didn't you, Mother?'

'Yes, dear. It does seem to be what you most want to do.' The Mother Superior stepped back with a defeated smile, giving way to me.

I watched Christina Brossard continue her apparently unending work. She was clearly unbalanced, but somehow self-dramatising at the same time, as if totally gripped by her compulsion but well aware of its manipulative possibilities. I was struck both by her self-pity and by the hard glance which she now and then directed at the three nuns, as if she were deliberately demeaning herself before these pleasant and caring women in order to vent her hate for them.

Giving up for the time being, I left her mopping the tiles and returned to the hall with the Mother Superior.

'Well, Dr Charcot, we're in your hands.'

'I dare say – frankly, I'm not sure that this is a case for me. Tell me – she spends all her time cleaning out these grates?'

'Every day, for the past two years, at her own wish. We've tried to stop her, but she then relapses into her original stupor. We can only assume that it serves some important role for her. There are a dozen fireplaces in this house, each as immaculate as an operating theatre.'

'And the cinders? The bags filled with ash? Who is lighting these fires?'

'Christina herself, of course. She is burning her children's books, determined for some reason to destroy everything she read as a child.'

She led me into the library. Almost the entire stock of books had been removed, and a line of stags' heads gazed down over the empty shelves. One cabinet alone contained a short row of books.

I opened the glass cabinet. There were a few schoolgirl stories, fairy tales, and several childhood classics.

The Mother Superior stared at them sadly. 'There were several hundred originally, but each day Christina burns a few more – under close supervision, it goes without saying, I've no wish to see her burn down the mansion. Be careful not to touch it, but one story alone has remained immune.'

She pointed to a large and shabby illustrated book which had been given a shelf to itself. 'You may see, Dr Charcot, that the choice is not inappropriate – the story of Cinderella.'

As I drove back to Nice, leaving behind that strange mansion with its kindly nuns and obsessed heiress, I found myself revising my opinion of the Mother Superior. This sensible woman was right in believing that all the dermatologists in the world would be unable to free Christina Brossard from her obsession. Clearly the girl had cast herself as Cinderella, reducing herself to the level of the lowest menial. But what guilt was she trying to scrub away? Had she played a still unknown but vital role in the suicide of her father? Was the entire fantasy an unconscious attempt to free herself of her sense of guilt?

I thought of the transparent bags filled with cinders, each one the ashes of a childhood fairy tale. The correspondences were extraordinarily clear, conceived with the remorseless logic of madness. I remembered the hate in her eyes as she stared at the nuns, casting these patient and caring women in the role of the ugly sisters. There was even a wicked stepmother, the Mother Superior, whose Hospice had benefited from the deaths of this orphan's parents.

On the other hand, where were Prince Charming, the fairy godmother and her pumpkin, the ball to be fled from at the stroke of midnight, and above all the glass slipper?

As it happened, I was given no chance to test my hypothesis. Two days later, when I telephoned the Hospice to arrange a new appointment for Christina Brossard, the Mother Superior's secretary politely informed me that the services of the Clinic, of Prof. Derain and myself, would no longer be called upon.

'We're grateful to you, doctor, but the Mother Superior has decided on a new course of treatment. The distinguished psychiatrist Dr Valentina Gabor has agreed to take on the case – perhaps you know of her reputation. In fact, treatment has already begun and you will be happy to hear that Christina is making immediate progress.'

As I replaced the receiver a powerful migraine attacked my left temple. Dr Valentina Gabor – of course I knew of her, the most notorious of the new school of self-styled anti-psychiatrists, who devoted whatever time was left over from their endless television appearances to the practice of an utterly bogus psychotherapy, a fashionable blend of post-psychoanalytic jargon, moral uplift and Catholic mysticism. This last strain had presumably gained her the approval of the Mother Superior.

Whenever I saw Dr Valentina my blood began to simmer. This glamorous blonde with her reassuring patter and the eyes of a cashier was forever appearing on television talk shows, putting forward the paradoxical notion that mental illness did not exist but nonetheless was the creation of the patient's family, friends and even, unbelievably, his doctors. Irritatingly, Dr Valentina had managed to score up a number of authenticated successes, no doubt facilitated by her recent well-publicised audience with the Pope. However, I was confident that she would receive her comeuppance. Already there had been calls within the medical profession for a discreet inquiry into her reported use of LSD and other hallucinogenic drugs.

Nonetheless, it appalled me that someone as deeply ill and as vulnerable

as Christina Brossard should fall into the hands of this opportunist quack.

You can well understand, therefore, that I felt a certain satisfaction, not
to say self-approval, when I received an urgent telephone call from the
Mother Superior some three weeks later.

I had heard no more in the meantime of the Hospice or of Christina.
Dr Valentina Gabor, however, had appeared with remorseless frequency
on Radio Monte Carlo and the local television channels, spreading her
unique brand of psychoanalytic mysticism, and extolling all the virtues
of being 'reborn'.

In fact, it was while watching on the late evening news an interview
with Dr Gabor recorded that afternoon at Nice Airport before she flew
back to Paris that I was telephoned by the Mother Superior.

'Dr Charcot! Thank heavens you're in! There's a disaster here –
Christina Brossard has vanished! We're afraid she may have taken an
overdose. I've tried to reach Dr Gabor but she has returned to Paris.
Could you possibly come to the Hospice?'

I calmed her as best I could and set off. It was after midnight when
I reached the sanatorium. Spotlights filled the drive with a harsh glare,
the patients were unsettled, peering through their windows, nuns with
torches were fruitlessly searching the grounds. A nervous Sister Louise
escorted me to the Mother Superior, who seized my hands with relief.
Her strong face was veined with strain.

'Dr Charcot! I'm grateful to you – I only regret that it's so late . . .'

'No matter. Tell me what happened. Christina was under Dr Gabor's
care?'

'Yes. How I regret my decision. I hoped that Christina might have
found herself through a spiritual journey, but I had no idea that drugs
were involved. If I had known . . .'

She handed me an empty vial. Across the label was Dr Gabor's florid
signature.

'We found this in Christina's room an hour ago. She seems to have
injected herself with the entire dosage and then driven off wildly into
the night. We can only assume that she stole it from Dr Gabor's valise.'

I studied the label. 'Psilocybin – a powerful hallucinogenic drug. Its use
is still legal by qualified physicians, though disapproved of by almost the
entire profession. This is more than a dangerous toy.'

'Dr Charcot, I know.' The Mother Superior gestured with her worn
hands. 'Believe me, I fear for Christina's soul. She appears to have been
completely deranged – when she drove off in our oldest laundry van she
described it to one of the patients as "her golden carriage".'

'You've called the police?'

'Not yet, Doctor.' A look of embarrassment crossed the Mother Superi-
or's face. 'When Christina left she told one of the orderlies that she was
going to "the ball". I'm told that the only ball being held tonight is Prince

Rainier's grand gala in Monaco in honour of President Giscard d'Estaing. I assume that she has gone there, perhaps confusing Prince Rainier with the Prince Charming of her fairy tale, and hoping that he will rescue her. It would be profoundly awkward for the Hospice if she were to create a scene, or even try to . . .'

'Kill the President? Or the Rainiers? I doubt it.' Already an idea was forming in my mind. 'However, to be on the safe side I'll leave for Monaco immediately. With luck I'll be there before she can cause any harm to herself.'

Pursued by the Mother Superior's blessings, I returned to my car and set off into the night. Needless to say, I did not intend to make the journey to Monaco. I was quite certain that I knew where Christina Brossard had fled – to her father's mansion above Vence.

As I followed the mountain road I reflected on the evidence that had come together – the fantasy of being a skivvy, the all-promising woman psychiatrist, the hallucinogenic drug. The entire fairy tale of Cinderella was being enacted, perhaps unconsciously, by this deranged heiress. If she herself was Cinderella, Dr Valentina Gabor was the fairy godmother, and her magic wand the hypodermic syringe she waved about so spectacularly. The role of the pumpkin was played by the 'sacred mushroom', the hallucinogenic fungus from which psilocybin was extracted. Under its influence even an ancient laundry van would seem like a golden coach. And as for the 'ball', this of course was the whole psychedelic trip.

But who then was Prince Charming? As I arrived at the great mansion at the end of its drive it occurred to me that I might be unwittingly casting myself in the role, fulfilling a fantasy demanded by this unhappy girl. Holding tight to my medical case, I walked across the dark gravel to the open entrance, where the laundry van had ended its journey in the centre of a flower-bed.

High above, in one of the great rooms facing the sea, a light flickered, as if something was being burned in a grate. I paused in the hall to let my eyes feel their way in the darkness, wondering how best to approach this distraught young woman. Then I saw that the massive Venetian clock above the staircase had been savagely mutilated. Several of the ornate numerals tilted on their mountings. The hands had stopped at midnight, and someone had tried to wrench them from the face.

For all my resistance to that pseudo-science, it occurred to me that once again a psychoanalytic explanation made complete sense of these bizarre events and the fable of Cinderella that underpinned them. I walked up the staircase past the dismembered clock. Despite the fear-crazed assault on them, the erect hands still stood upright on the midnight hour – that time when the ball ended, when the courtships and frivolities of the party were over and the serious business of a real sexual relationship began. Fearful of that male erection, Cinderella always fled at midnight.

But what had Christina Brossard fled from in this Palladian mansion?

Suppose that the Prince Charming who courted her so dangerously but so appealingly were in fact her own father. Had some kind of incestuous act involved the widowed industrialist and his adolescent daughter, herself an uncanny image of his dead wife? His revulsion and self-disgust at having committed incest would explain his apparently motiveless suicide *and* his daughter's guilt – as I knew only too well from my court attendances as an expert medical witness, far from hating the fathers who forced them to commit incest, daughters were invariably plagued by powerful feelings of guilt at their responsibility for their parent's imprisonment. So after his death she would naturally return to the house, and try to expiate that guilt as a servant-girl. And what better model for an heiress than Cinderella herself?

Drawn by the distant flames, I crossed the upstairs hallway and entered the great bedroom. It was filled with paintings of young nudes cavorting with centaurs, unmistakably Gaston Brossard's master-bedroom, perhaps where the act of incest had taken place.

Flames lifted from the fireplace, illuminating the ash-streaked face of Christina. She knelt by the grate, crooning as she fed the last of the pages torn from a familiar book of fairy tales. Head to one side, she stared at the soft blaze with overlit eyes, stroking the rough seams of the hospital tunic she wore over her bare legs.

I guessed that she was in the middle of her hallucination and that she saw herself in a resplendent gown. Yet her drifting eyes looked up at me with an expression of almost knowing calm, as if she recognized me and was waiting for me to play my role in the fable and bring it to its proper conclusion. I thought of the mutilated hands of the clock above the staircase. All that remained was to restore the glass slipper to its rightful owner.

Had I now to play the part of her rescuer? Remembering the familiar sexual symbolism of the foot, I knew that the glass slipper was nothing more than a transparent and therefore guilt-free vagina. And as for the foot to be placed within it, of course this would not be her own but that of her true lover, the erect male sexual organ from which she fled.

Reaching forward, she added the cover of the fairy tale to the dying blaze, and then looked up at me with waiting eyes. For a moment I hesitated. High on psilocybin, she would be unable to distinguish truth from fantasy, so I could play out my role and bring this psychoanalytic drama to its conclusion without any fear of professional disapproval. My action would not take place in the real world, but within that imaginary realm where the fable of Cinderella was being enacted.

Knowing my role now, and the object which I myself had to place in that glass slipper, I took her hands and drew her from her knees towards her father's bed.

I murmured: 'Cinderella . . .'

\* \* \*

But wait – they're about to leave the terrace. You can look at them now, everyone else is staring frankly at this attractive young woman and her decrepit companion. Sitting here in the centre of Monte Carlo on this magnificent spring day, it's hard to believe that these strange events ever occurred.

It's almost unnerving – she's looking straight at me. But does she recognise me, the dermatologist who freed her from her obsession and restored her to health?

Her companion, sadly, was the only casualty of this radical therapy. As he sits hunched at his table, fumbling with himself like an old man, I can tell you that he was once a fashionable physician whom she met just before her release from the Hospice. They were married three months later, but the marriage was hardly a success. By whatever means, presumably certain methods of her own, she transformed him into this old man.

But why? Simply, that in order to make the incest fantasy credible, any man she marries, however young and princely, however charming, must become old enough to be her father.

Wait! She is coming towards this table. Perhaps she needs my help? She stands in front of the restaurant mirror looking at herself and her elderly husband, and places a hand on his shoulder.

That elegant face with its knowing smile. Let me try to shake that composure, and whisper the title of this cheap magazine on my lap.

'CINDERELLA . . .'

Her hand pats my shoulder indulgently.

'Father, it's time to go back to the Hospice. I promised the Mother Superior that I wouldn't over-tire you.'

Knowing, elegant and completely self-possessed.

'And do stop playing that game with yourself. You know it only excites you.'

And very punitive.

**· 1980**

# · NEWS FROM THE SUN

In the evenings, as Franklin rested on the roof of the abandoned clinic, he would often remember Trippett, and the last drive he had taken into the desert with the dying astronaut and his daughter. On impulse he had given in to the girl's request, when he found her waiting for him in the dismantled laboratory, her father's flight jacket and solar glasses in her hands, shabby mementoes of the vanished age of space. In many ways it had been a sentimental gesture, but Trippett was the last man to walk on the moon, and the untended landscape around the clinic more and more resembled the lunar terrain. Under that cyanide-blue sky perhaps something would stir, a lost memory engage, for a few moments Trippett might even feel at home again.

Followed by the daughter, Franklin entered the darkened ward. The other patients had been transferred, and Trippett sat alone in the wheelchair at the foot of his bed. By now, on the eve of the clinic's closure, the old astronaut had entered his terminal phase and was conscious for only a few seconds each day. Soon he would lapse into his last deep fugue, an invisible dream of the great tideways of space.

Franklin lifted the old man from his chair, and carried his child-like body through the corridors to the car park at the rear of the clinic. Already, however, as they moved into the needle-sharp sunlight, Franklin regretted his decision, aware that he had been manipulated by the young woman. Ursula rarely spoke to Franklin, and like everyone at the hippy commune seemed to have all the time in the world to stare at him. But her patient, homely features and uninnocent gaze disturbed him in a curious way. Sometimes he suspected that he had kept Trippett at the clinic simply so that he could see the daughter. The younger doctors thought of her as dumpy and unsexed, but Franklin was sure that her matronly body concealed a sexual conundrum of a special kind.

These suspicions aside, her father's condition reminded Franklin of his own accelerating fugues. For a year these had lasted little more than a few minutes each day, manageable within the context of the hours he spent at his desk, and at times barely distinguishable from musing. But in the past few weeks, as if prompted by the decision to close the clinic, they had lengthened to more than thirty minutes at a stretch. In three months he would be housebound, in six be fully awake for only an hour each day.

The fugues came so swiftly, time poured in a torrent from the cracked glass of their lives. The previous summer, during their first excursions into the desert, Trippett's waking periods had lasted at least half an hour. He had taken a touching pleasure in the derelict landscape, in the abandoned motels and weed-choked swimming pools of the small town near the air base, in the silent runways with their dusty jets sitting on flattened tyres, in the over-bright hills waiting with the infinite guile of the geological kingdom for the organic world to end and a more vivid mineral realm to begin.

Now, sadly, the old astronaut was unaware of all this. He sat beside Franklin in the front seat, his blanched eyes open behind the glasses but his mind set to some private time. Even the motion of the speeding car failed to rouse him, and Ursula had to hold his shoulders as he tottered like a stuffed toy into the windshield.

'Go on, doctor – he likes the speed . . .' Sitting forward, she tapped Franklin's head, wide eyes fixed on the speedometer. Franklin forced himself to concentrate on the road, conscious of the girl's breath on his neck. This highway madonna, with her secret dream of speed, he found it difficult to keep his hands and mind off her. Was she planning to abduct her father from the clinic? She lived in the small commune that had taken over the old solar city up in the hills, Soleri II. Every morning she cycled in, bringing Trippett his ration of raisins and macrobiotic cheer. She sat calmly beside him like his young mother as he played with the food, making strange patterns on his paper plate.

'Faster, Dr Franklin – I've watched you drive. You're always speeding.'

'So you've seen me? I'm not sure. If I had a blackout now . . .' Giving in again, Franklin steered the Mercedes into the centre of the road and eased the speedometer needle towards fifty. There was a flare of headlights as they overtook the weekly bus to Las Vegas, a medley of warning shouts from the passengers left behind in a tornado of dust. The Mercedes was already moving at more than twice the legal limit. At twenty miles an hour, theoretically, a driver entering a sudden fugue had time to pass the controls to the obligatory front-seat passenger. In fact, few people drove at all. The desert on either side of the road was littered with the wrecks of cars that had veered off the soft shoulder and ended up in a sand-hill a mile away, their drivers dying of exposure before they could wake from their fugues.

Yet, for all the danger, Franklin loved to drive, illicit high-speed runs at dusk when he seemed to be alone on a forgotten planet. In a locked hangar at the air base were a Porsche and an antique Jaguar. His colleagues at the clinic disapproved, but he pursued his own maverick way, as he did in the laboratory, shielding himself behind a front of calculated eccentricity that excused certain obsessions with speed, time, sex . . . He needed the speed more than the sex now. But soon he would have to stop, already the fast driving had become a dangerous game spurred on by the infantile hope that speed in some way would keep the clock hands turning.

The concrete towers and domes of the solar city approached on their left, Paulo Soleri's charming fantasy of a self-sufficient community.

Franklin slowed to avoid running down a young woman in a sari who stood like a mannequin in the centre of the highway. Her eyes stared at the dust, a palaeontology of hopes. In an hour she would snap out of it, and complete her walk to the bus stop without realizing that time, and the bus, had passed her by.

Ursula sombrely embraced her father, beckoning Franklin to accelerate.

'We're dawdling, doctor. What's the matter? You enjoyed the speed. And so did Dad.'

'Ursula, he doesn't even know he's here.'

Franklin looked out at the desert, trying to imagine it through Trippett's eyes. The landscape was not so much desolate as derelict – the untended irrigation canals, the rusting dish of a radio-telescope on a nearby peak, a poor man's begging bowl held up to the banquet of the universe. The hills were waiting for them to go away. A crime had been committed, a cosmic misdemeanour carried on the shoulders of this fine old astronaut sitting beside him. Every night Trippett wept in his sleep. Spectres strode through his unlit dreams, trying to find a way out of his head.

The best astronauts, Franklin had noticed during his work for NASA, never dreamed. Or, at least, not until ten years after their flights, when the nightmares began and they returned to the institutes of aviation medicine which had first helped to recruit them.

Light flickered at them from the desert, and raced like a momentary cathode trace across the black lenses of Trippett's glasses. Thousands of steel mirrors were laid out in a semi-circular tract beside the road, one of the solar farms that would have provided electric current for the inhabitants of Soleri II, unlimited power donated in a perhaps too kindly gesture by the economy of the sun.

Watching the reflected light dance in Trippett's eyes, Franklin turned the car on to the service road that ran down to the farm.

'Ursula, we'll rest here – I think I'm more tired than your father.'

Franklin stepped from the car, and strolled across the white, calcinated soil towards the nearest of the mirrors. In his eye he followed the focal lines that converged on to the steel tower two hundred feet away. A section of the collector dish had fallen on to the ground, but Franklin could see images of himself flung up into the sky, the outstretched sleeves of his white jacket like the wings of a deformed bird.

'Ursula, bring your father . . .' The old astronaut could once again see himself suspended in space, this time upside down in the inverted image, hung by his heels from the yardarm of the sky.

Surprised by the perverse pleasure he took in this notion, Franklin walked back to the car. But as they helped Trippett from his seat, trying to reassure the old man, there was a clatter of metallic noise across the desert. An angular shadow flashed over their faces, and a small aircraft soared past, little more than twenty feet above the ground. It scuttled along like a demented gnat, minute engine buzzing up a storm, its wired wings strung around an open fuselage.

A white-haired man sat astride the miniature controls, naked except for the aviator's goggles tied around his head. He handled the plane in an erratic but stylish way, exploiting the sky to display his showy physique.

Ursula tried to steady her father, but the old man broke away from her and tottered off among the mirrors, his clenched fists pummelling the air. Seeing him, the pilot banked steeply around the sun-tower, then dived straight towards him, pulling up at the last moment in a blare of noise and dust. As Franklin ran forward and pressed Trippett to the ground the plane banked and came round again in a wide turn. The pilot steered the craft with his bare knees, arms trailing at his sides as if mimicking Franklin's image in the dish above the tower.

'Slade! Calm down, for once . . .' Franklin wiped the stinging grit from his mouth. He had seen the man up to too many extravagant tricks ever to be sure what he would do next. This former air force pilot and would-be astronaut, whose application Franklin had rejected three years earlier when he was chairman of the medical appeals board, had now returned to plague him with these absurd antics – spraying flocks of swallows with gold paint, erecting a circle of towers out in the desert ('my private space programme,' he termed it proudly), building a cargo cult airport with wooden control tower and planes in the air base car park, a cruel parody intended to punish the few remaining servicemen.

And this incessant stunt flying. Had Slade recognized Franklin's distant reflection as he sped across the desert in the inverted aircraft, then decided to buzz the Mercedes for the fun of it, impress Trippett and Ursula, even himself, perhaps?

The plane was coming back at them, engine wound up to a scream. Franklin saw Ursula shouting at him soundlessly. The old astronaut was shaking like an unstuffed scarecrow, one hand pointing to the mirrors. Reflected in the metal panes were the multiple images of the black aircraft, hundreds of vulture-like birds that hungrily circled the ground.

'Ursula, into the car!' Franklin took off his jacket and ran through the mirrors, hoping to draw the aircraft away from Trippett. But Slade had decided to land. Cutting the engine, he let the microlight die in the air, then stalled the flapping machine on to the service road. As it trundled towards the Mercedes with its still spinning propeller, Franklin held off the starboard wing, almost tearing the doped fabric.

'Doctor! You've already grounded me once too often . . .' Slade inspected the dented fabric, then pointed to Franklin's trembling fingers. 'Those hands . . . I hope you aren't allowed to operate on your patients.'

Franklin looked down at the white-haired pilot. His own hands *were* shaking, an understandable reflex of alarm. For all Slade's ironic drawl, his naked body was as taut as a trap, every muscle tense with hostility. His eyes surveyed Franklin with the ever-alert but curiously dead gaze of a psychopath. His pallid skin was almost luminous, as if after ending his career as an astronaut he had made some private pact with the sun. A narrow lap belt held him to the seat, but his shoulders bore the scars of a strange harness – the restraining straps of a psychiatric unit, Franklin guessed, or some kind of sexual fetishism.

'My hands, yes. They're always the first to let me down. You'll be glad to hear that I retire this week.' Quietly, Franklin added: 'I didn't ground you.'

Slade pondered this, shaking his head. 'Doctor, you practically closed the entire space programme down single-handed. It must have provoked you in a special way. Don't worry, though, I've started my own space programme now, another one.' He pointed to Trippett, who was being soothed by Ursula in the car. 'Why are you still bothering the old man? He won't buy off any unease.'

'He enjoys the drives – speed seems to do him good. And you too, I take it. Be careful of those fugues. If you want to, visit me at the clinic.'

'Franklin . . .' Controlling his irritation, Slade carefully relaxed his jaw and mouth, as if dismantling an offensive weapon. 'I don't have the fugues any longer. I found a way of . . . dealing with them.'

'All this flying around? You frightened the old boy.'

'I doubt it.' He watched Trippett nodding to himself. 'In fact, I'd like to take him with me – we'll fly out into space again, one day. Just for him I'll build a gentle space-craft, made of rice paper and bamboo . . .'

'That sounds your best idea yet.'

'It is.' Slade stared at Franklin with sudden concern and the almost boyish smile of a pupil before a favourite teacher. 'There is a way out, doctor, a way out of time.'

'Show me, Slade. I haven't much time left.'

'I know that, doctor. That's what I wanted to tell you. Together, Marion and I are going to help you.'

'Marion –?' But before Franklin could speak, the aircraft's engine racketed into life. Fanning the tailplane, Slade deftly turned the craft within its own length. He replaced the goggles over his eyes, and took off in a funnel of dust that blanched the paintwork of the Mercedes. Safely airborne, he made a final circuit, gave a curious underhand salute and soared away.

Franklin walked to the car and leaned against the roof, catching his breath. The old man was quiet again, his brief fit forgotten.

'That was Slade. Do you know him, Ursula?'

'Everyone does. Sometimes he works on our computer at Soleri, or just starts a fight. He's a bit crazy, trying all the time not to fugue.'

Franklin nodded, watching the plane disappear towards Las Vegas, lost among the hotel towers. 'He was a trainee astronaut once. My wife thinks he's trying to kill me.'

'Perhaps she's right. I remember now – he said that except for you he would have gone to the moon.'

'We all went to the moon. That was the trouble . . .'

Franklin reversed the Mercedes along the service road. As they set off along the highway he thought of Slade's puzzling reference to Marion. It was time to be wary. Slade's fugues should have been lengthening for months, yet somehow he kept them at bay. All that violent energy contained in his skull would one day push apart the sutures, burst out in some ugly act of revenge . . .

'Dr Franklin! Listen!'

Franklin felt Ursula's hands on his shoulder. In a panic he slowed down and began to search the sky for the returning microlight.

'It's Dad, doctor! Look!'

The old man had sat up, and was peering through the window in a surprisingly alert way. The slack musculature of his face had drilled itself into the brisk profile of a sometime naval officer. He seemed uninterested in his daughter or Franklin, but stared sharply at a threadbare palm tree beside a wayside motel, and at the tepid water in the partly drained pool.

As the car swayed across the camber Trippett nodded to himself, thoroughly approving of the whole arid landscape. He took his daughter's hand, emphasizing some conversational point that had been interrupted by a pot-hole.

'. . . it's green here, more like Texas than Nevada. Peaceful, too. Plenty of cool trees and pasturage, all these fields and sweet lakes. I'd like to stop and sleep for a while. We'll come out and swim, dear, perhaps tomorrow. Would you like that?'

He squeezed his daughter's hand with sudden affection. But before he could speak again, a door closed within his face and he had gone.

They reached the clinic and returned Trippett to his darkened ward. Later, while Ursula cycled away down the silent runways, Franklin sat at his desk in the dismantled laboratory. His fingers sparred with each other as he thought of Trippett's curious utterance. In some way Slade's appearance in the sky had set it off. The old astronaut's brief emergence into the world of time, those few lucid seconds, gave him hope. Was it possible that the fugues could be reversed? He was tempted to go back to the ward, and bundle Trippett into the car for another drive.

Then he remembered Slade's aircraft speeding towards him across the solar mirrors, the small, vicious propeller that shredded the light and air, time and space. This failed astronaut had first come to the clinic seven months earlier. While Franklin was away at a conference, Slade arrived by air force ambulance, posing as a terminal patient. With his white hair and obsessive gaze, he had instantly charmed the clinic's director, Dr Rachel Vaisey, into giving him the complete run of the place. Moving about the laboratories and corridors, Slade took over any disused cupboards and desk drawers, where he constructed a series of little tableaux, psychosexual shrines to the strange gods inside his head.

He built the first of the shrines in Rachel Vaisey's bidet, an ugly assemblage of hypodermic syringes, fractured sunglasses and blood-stained tampons. Other shrines appeared in corridor alcoves and unoccupied beds, relics of a yet to be experienced future left here as some kind of psychic deposit against his treatment's probable failure. After an outraged Dr Vaisey insisted on a thorough inspection Slade discharged himself from the clinic and made a new home in the sky.

The shrines were cleared away, but one alone had been carefully preserved. Franklin opened the centre drawer of his desk and stared at the assemblage laid out like a corpse on its bier of surgical cotton. There was a labelled fragment of lunar rock stolen from the NASA museum in Houston; a photograph taken with a zoom lens of Marion in a hotel bathroom, her white body almost merging into the tiles of the shower stall; a faded reproduction of Dali's *Persistence of Memory*, with its soft watches and expiring embryo; a set of leucotomes whose points were masked by metal peas; and an emergency organ-donor card bequeathing to anyone in need his own brain. Together the items formed an accurate anti-portrait of all Franklin's obsessions, a side-chapel of his head. But Slade had always been a keen observer, more interested in Franklin than in anyone else.

How did he elude the fugues? When Franklin had last seen him at the clinic Slade was already suffering from fugues that lasted an hour or more. Yet somehow he had sprung a trapdoor in Trippett's mind, given him his vision of green fields.

When Rachel Vaisey called to complain about the unauthorized drive Franklin brushed this aside. He tried to convey his excitement over Trippett's outburst.

'He was there, Rachel, completely himself, for something like thirty seconds. And there was no effort involved, no need to remember who he was. It's frightening to think that I'd given him up for lost.'

'It is strange – one of those inexplicable remissions. But try not to read too much into it.' Dr Vaisey stared with distaste at the perimeter camera mounted beside its large turntable. Like most members of her staff, she was only too glad that the clinic was closing, and that the few remaining patients would soon be transferred to some distant sanatorium or memorial home. Within a month she and her colleagues would return to the universities from which they had been seconded. None of them had yet been affected by the fugues, and that Franklin should be the only one to succumb seemed doubly cruel, confirming all their longstanding suspicions about this wayward physician. Franklin had been the first of the NASA psychiatrists to identify the time-sickness, to have seen the astronauts' original fugues for what they were.

Sobered by the prospect facing Franklin, she managed a conciliatory smile. 'You say he spoke coherently. What did he talk about?'

'He babbled of green fields.' Franklin stood behind his desk, staring at the open drawer hidden from Dr Vaisey's suspicious gaze. 'I'm sure he actually saw them.'

'A childhood memory? Poor man, at least he seems happy, wherever he really is.'

'Rachel . . . !' Franklin drove the drawer into the desk. 'Trippett was staring at the desert along the road – nothing but rock, dust and a few dying palms, yet he saw green fields, lakes, forests of trees. We've got to keep the clinic open a little longer, I feel I have a chance now. I want to go back to the beginning and think everything through again.'

Before Dr Vaisey could stop him, Franklin had started to pace the floor, talking to his desk. 'Perhaps the fugues are a preparation for something, and we've been wrong to fear them. The symptoms are so widespread, there's virtually an invisible epidemic, one in a hundred of the population involved, probably another five unaware that they've been affected, certainly out here in Nevada.'

'It's the desert – topography clearly plays a part in the fugues. It's been bad for you, Robert. For all of us.'

'All the more reason to stay and face it. Rachel, listen: I'm willing to work with the others more than I have done, this time we'll be a true team.'

'That is a concession.' Dr Vaisey spoke without irony. 'But too late, Robert. You've tried everything.'

'I've tried nothing . . .' Franklin placed a hand on the huge lens of the perimeter camera, hiding the deformed figure who mimicked his gestures from the glass cell. Distorted reflections of himself had pursued him all day, as if he were being presented with brief clips from an obscene film in which he would shortly star. If only he had spent more time on Trippett, rather than on the volunteer panels of housewives and air force personnel. But the old astronaut intimidated him, touched all his feelings of guilt over his complicity in the space programme. As a member of the medical support team, he had helped to put the last astronauts into space, made possible the year-long flights that had set off the whole time-plague, cracked the cosmic hour-glass . . .

'And Trippett? Where are you going to hide him away?'

'We aren't. His daughter has volunteered to take him. She seems a reasonable girl.'

Giving in to her concern, Dr Vaisey stepped forward and took Franklin's hand from the camera lens. 'Robert – are you going to be all right? Your wife will look after you, you say. I wish you'd let me meet her. I could insist . . .'

Franklin was thinking about Trippett – the news that the old astronaut would still be there, presumably living up in Soleri II, had given him hope. The work could go on . . .

He felt a sudden need to be alone in the empty clinic, to be rid of Dr Vaisey, this well-meaning, middle-aged neurologist with her closed mind and closed world. She was staring at him across the desk, clearly unsure what to do about Franklin, her eyes distracted by the gold and silver swallows that swooped across the runways. Dr Vaisey had always regretted her brief infatuation with Slade. Franklin remembered their last meeting in her office, when Slade had taken out his penis and masturbated in front of her, then insisted on mounting his hot semen on a slide. Through the microscope eyepiece Rachel Vaisey had watched the thousand replicas of this young psychotic frantically swimming. After ten minutes they began to falter. Within an hour they were all dead.

'Don't worry, I'll be fine. Marion knows exactly what I need. And Slade will be around to help her.'

'Slade? How on earth . . . ?'

Franklin eased the centre drawer from his desk. Carefully, as if handling an explosive device, he offered the shrine to Dr Vaisey's appalled gaze.

'Take it, Rachel. It's the blueprint of our joint space programme. You might care to come along . . .'

When Dr Vaisey had gone, Franklin returned to his desk. First, he took off his wristwatch and massaged the raw skin of his forearm. Every fifteen minutes he returned the hand of the stopwatch to zero. This nervous tic, a time-twitch, had long been a joke around the clinic. But after the onset of a fugue the accumulating total gave him a reasonably exact record of its duration. A crude device, he was almost glad that he would soon escape from time altogether.

Though not yet. Calming himself, he looked at the last pages of his diary.

June 19 – fugues: 8-30 to 9-11 am; 11-45 to 12-27 am; 5-15 to 6-08 pm; 11-30 to 12-14 pm. Total: 3 hours.

The totals were gaining on him. June 20 – 3 hours 14 mins; June 21 – 3 hours 30 mins; June 22 – 3 hours 46 mins. This gave him little more than ten weeks, unless the fugues began to slow down, or he found that trapdoor through which Trippett had briefly poked his head.

Franklin closed the diary and stared back at the watching lens of the perimeter camera. Curiously, he had never allowed himself to be photographed by the machine, as if the contours of his body constituted a secret terrain whose codes had to be held in reserve for his last attempt to escape. Standing or reclining on the rotating platform, the volunteer patients had been photographed in a continuous scan that transformed them into a landscape of undulating hills and valleys, not unlike the desert outside. Could they take an aerial photograph of the Sahara and Gobi deserts, reverse the process and reconstitute the vast figure of some sleeping goddess, an Aphrodite born from a sea of dunes? Franklin had become obsessed with the camera, photographing everything from cubes and spheres to cups and saucers and then the naked patients themselves, in the hope of finding the dimension of time locked in those undulating spaces.

The volunteers had long since retired to their terminal wards, but their photographs were still pinned to the walls – a retired dentist, a police sergeant on the Las Vegas force, a middle-aged hair stylist, an attractive mother of year-old twins, an air-traffic controller from the base. Their splayed features and distorted anatomies resembled the nightmarish jumble seen by all patients if they were deliberately roused from their fugues by powerful stimulants or electric shock – oozing forms in an elastic world, giddying and unpleasant. Without time, a moving face seemed to smear itself across the air, the human body became a surrealist monster.

For Franklin, and the tens of thousands of fellow sufferers, the fugues had begun in the same way, with the briefest moments of inattention. An overlong pause in the middle of a sentence, some mysteriously burnt-out scrambled egg, the air force sergeant who looked after the Mercedes annoyed by his off-hand rudeness, together led on to longer stretches of missed time. Subjectively, the moment-to-moment flow of consciousness seemed to be uninterrupted. But time drained away, leaking slowly from his life. Only the previous day he had been standing at the window, looking at the line of cars in the late afternoon sunlight, and the next moment there was dusk outside and a deserted parking lot.

All victims told the same story – there were forgotten appointments, inexplicable car crashes, untended infants rescued by police and neighbours. The victims would 'wake' at midnight in empty office blocks, find themselves in stagnant baths, be arrested for jay-walking, forget to feed themselves. Within six months they would be conscious for only half the day, afraid to drive or go out into the streets, desperately filling every room with clocks and timepieces. A week would flash past in a jumble of sunsets and dawns. By the end of the first year they would be alert for only a few minutes each day, no longer able to feed or care for themselves, and soon after would enter one of the dozens of state hospitals and sanatoria.

After his arrival at the clinic Franklin's first patient was a badly burned fighter pilot who had taxied his jet through the doors of a hangar. The second was one of the last of the astronauts, a former naval captain named Trippett. The pilot was soon beyond reach in a perpetual dusk, but Trippett had hung on, lucid for a few minutes each day. Franklin had learned a great deal from Trippett, the last man to have walked on the moon and the last to hold out against the fugues – all the early astronauts had long since retreated into a timeless world. The hundreds of fragmentary conversations, and the mysterious guilt that Trippett shared with his colleagues, like them weeping in his dreams, convinced Franklin that the sources of the malaise were to be found in the space programme itself.

By leaving his planet and setting off into outer space man had committed an evolutionary crime, a breach of the rules governing his tenancy of the universe, and of the laws of time and space. Perhaps the right to travel through space belonged to another order of beings, but his crime was being punished just as surely as would be any attempt to ignore the laws of gravity. Certainly the unhappy lives of the astronauts bore all the signs of a deepening sense of guilt. The relapse into alcoholism, silence and pseudo-mysticism, and the mental breakdowns, suggested profound anxieties about the moral and biological rightness of space exploration.

Sadly, not only the astronauts were affected. Each space-launch left its trace in the minds of those watching the expeditions. Each flight to the moon and each journey around the sun was a trauma that warped their perception of time and space. The brute-force ejection of themselves from their planet had been an act of evolutionary piracy, for which they were now being expelled from the world of time.

Preoccupied with his memories of the astronauts, Franklin was the last to leave the clinic. He had expected his usual afternoon fugue, and sat at his desk in the silent laboratory, finger on his stopwatch. But the fugue had not occurred, perhaps deflected by his buoyant mood after the drive with Trippett. As he walked across the car park he looked out over the deserted air base. Two hundred yards from the control tower, a young woman with an apron around her waist stood on the concrete runway, lost in her fugue. Half a mile away, two more women stood in the centre of the huge cargo runway. All of them came from the nearby town. At twilight these women of the runways left their homes and trailers and strayed across the air base, staring into the dusk like the wives of forgotten astronauts waiting for their husbands to return from the tideways of space.

The sight of these women always touched Franklin in a disturbing way, and he had to force himself to start the car. As he drove towards Las Vegas the desert seemed almost lunar in the evening light. No one came to Nevada now, and most of the local population had long since left, fearing the uneasy perspectives of the desert. When he reached home the dusk filtered through a cerise haze that lay over the old casinos and hotels, a ghostly memory of the electric night.

Franklin liked the abandoned gambling resort. The other physicians lived within a short drive of the clinic, but Franklin had chosen one of the half-empty motels in the northern suburbs of the city. In the evenings, after visiting his few patients in their retirement homes, he would often drive down the silent Strip, below the sunset façades of the vast hotels, and wander for hours through the shadows among the drained swimming pools. This city of spent dreams, which had once boasted that it contained no clocks, now seemed itself to be in fugue.

As he parked in the forecourt of the motel he noted that Marion's car was missing. The third-floor apartment was empty. The television set was drawn up by the bed, playing silently to a clutch of medical textbooks Marion had taken from his shelves and an overflowing ashtray like a vent of Vesuvius. Franklin hung the unracked dresses in the wardrobe. As he counted the fresh cigarette burns in the carpet he reflected on the remarkable disarray that Marion could achieve in a few hours, here as in everything else. Were her fugues real or simulated? Sometimes he suspected that she half-consciously mimicked the time-slips, in an effort to enter that one realm where Franklin was free of her, safe from all her frustration at having come back to him.

Franklin went on to the balcony and glanced down at the empty swimming pool. Often Marion sunbathed nude on the floor at the deep end, and perhaps had been trapped there by her fugue. He listened to the drone of a light aircraft circling the distant hotels, and learned from the retired geologist in the next apartment that Marion had driven away only minutes before his arrival.

As he set off in the car he realized that his afternoon fugue had still not occurred. Had Marion seen his headlamps approaching across the desert, and then decided on impulse to disappear into the unlit evening of the Strip hotels? She had known Slade at Houston three years earlier, when he tried to persuade her to intercede with Franklin. Now he seemed to be courting her from the sky, for reasons that Marion probably failed to realize. Even their original affair had been part of his elaborate stalking of Franklin.

The aircraft had vanished, disappearing across the desert. Franklin drove along the Strip, turning in and out of the hotel forecourts. In an empty car park he saw one of the ghosts of the twilight, a middle-aged man in a shabby tuxedo, some retired croupier or cardiologist returning to these dreaming hulks. Caught in mid-thought, he stared sightlessly at a dead neon sign. Not far away, a strong-hipped young woman stood among the dusty pool-furniture, her statuesque figure transformed by the fugue into that of a Delvaux muse.

Franklin stopped to help them, if possible rouse them before they froze in the cold desert night. But as he stepped from his car he saw that the headlamps were reflected in the stationary propeller blade of a small aircraft parked on the Strip.

Slade leaned from the cockpit of his microlight, his white skin an unhealthy ivory in the electric beams. He was still naked, gesturing in an intimate way at a handsome woman in a streetwalker's fur who was playfully inspecting his cockpit. He beckoned her towards the narrow seat, like some cruising driver of old trying to entice a passer-by.

Admiring Slade for his nerve in using the sky to accost his wife, Franklin broke into a run. Slade had taken Marion's waist and was trying to pull her into the cockpit.

'Leave her, Slade!' Fifty feet from them, Franklin stumbled over a discarded tyre. He stopped to catch his breath as – an engine of noise hurtled towards him out of the darkness, the same metallic blare he had heard in the desert that morning. Slade's aircraft raced along the Strip, wheels bouncing on the road, its propeller lit by the car's headlamps. As Franklin fell to his knees the plane banked to avoid him, climbed steeply and soared away into the sky.

Hunting for Slade, the excited air surged around Franklin. He stood up, hands raised to shield his face from the stinging dust. The darkness was filled with rotating blades. Silver lassoes spiralled out of the night, images of the propeller that launched themselves one after another from the wake of the vanished aircraft.

Still stunned by the violent attack of the machine, Franklin listened to its last drone across the desert. He watched the retinal display that had transformed the shadowy streets. Silver coils spun away over his head and disappeared among the hotels, a glistening flight path that he could almost touch with his hands. Steadying himself against the hard pavement under his feet, he turned to follow his wife as she fled from him through the drained swimming pools and deserted car parks of the newly lit city.

'Poor man – couldn't you see him? He flew straight at you. Robert . . . ?'

'Of course I saw him. I don't think I'd be here otherwise.'

'But you stood there, totally mesmerized. I know he's always fascinated you, but that was carrying it too far. If that propeller had . . .'

'It was a small experiment,' Franklin said. 'I wanted to see what he was trying to do.'

'He was trying to kill you!'

Franklin sat on the end of the bed, staring at the cigarette burns in the carpet. They had reached the apartment fifteen minutes earlier, but he was still trying to calm himself. He thought of the rotating blade that had devoured the darkness. Delayed all afternoon, his fugue had begun as he tripped over the tyre, and had lasted almost an hour. For her own reasons Marion was pretending that the fugue had not occurred, but when he woke his skin was frozen. What had she and Slade been doing during the lost time? Too easily, Franklin imagined them together in Marion's car, or even in the cockpit of the aircraft, watched by the sightless husband. That would please Slade, put him in just the mood to scare the wits out of Franklin as he took off.

Through the open door Franklin stared at his wife's naked body in the white cube of the bathroom. A wet cigarette smouldered in the soap dish. There were clusters of small bruises on her thighs and hips, marks of some stylized grapple. One day soon, when the time drained out of her, the contours of her breasts and thighs would migrate to the polished walls, calm as the dunes and valleys of the perimeter photographs.

Sitting down at the dressing table, Marion peered over her powdered shoulder with some concern. 'Are you going to be all right? I'm finding it difficult enough to cope with myself. That wasn't an attack . . . ?'

'Of course not.' For months now they had kept up the pretence that neither of them was affected by the fugues. Marion needed the illusion, more in Franklin's case than in her own. 'But I may not always be immune.'

'Robert, if anyone's immune, you are. Think of yourself, what you've always wanted – alone in the world, just you and these empty hotels. But be careful of Slade.'

'I am.' Casually, Franklin added: 'I want you to see more of him. Arrange a meeting.'

'What?' Marion looked round at her husband again, her left contact lens trapped under her eyelid. 'He was naked, you know.'

'So I saw. That's part of his code. Slade's trying to tell me something. He needs me, in a special way.'

'Needs you? He doesn't need you, believe me. But for you he would have gone to the moon. You took that away from him, Robert.'

'And I can give it back to him.'

'How? Are the two of you going to start your own space programme?'

'In a sense we already have. But we really need you to help us.'

Franklin waited for her to reply, but Marion sat raptly in front of the mirror, lens case in one hand, fingers retracting her upper and lower eyelids around the trapped lens. Fused with her own reflection in the finger-stained glass, she seemed to be shooting the sun with a miniature sextant, finding her bearings in this city of empty mirrors. He remembered their last month together after the end at Cape Kennedy, the long drive down the dead Florida coast. The space programme had expressed all its failure in that terminal moraine of deserted hotels and apartment houses, a cryptic architecture like the forgotten codes of a discarded geometric language. He remembered Marion's blood flowing into the hand-basin from her slashed palms, and the constant arguments that warped themselves out of the air.

Yet curiously those had been happy days, filled with the quickening excitements of her illness. He had dreamed of her promiscuity, the deranged favours granted to waitresses and bellboys. He came back alone from Miami, resting beside the swimming pools of the empty hotels, remembering the intoxications of abandoned parking lots. In a sense that drive had been his first conscious experiment with time and space, placing that body and its unhappy mind in a sequence of bathrooms and pools, watching her with her lovers in the diagrammed car parks, emotions hung on these abstract webs of space.

Affectionately, Franklin placed his hands on Marion's shoulders, feeling the familiar clammy skin of the fugue. He lowered her hands to her lap, and then removed the contact lens from her eyeball, careful not to cut the cornea. Franklin smiled down at her blanched face, counting the small scars and blemishes that had appeared around her mouth. Like all women, Marion never really feared the fugues, accepting the popular myth that during these periods of lapsed time the body refused to age.

Sitting beside her on the stool, Franklin embraced her gently. He held her breasts in his palms, for a moment shoring up their slipping curvatures. For all his fondness for Marion, he would have to use her in his duel with Slade. The planes of her thighs and shoulders were segments of a secret runway along which he would one day fly to safety.

**July 5**

Not one of my best days. Five long fugues, each lasting over an hour. The first started at 9 am as I was walking around the pool towards the car. Suddenly I found myself standing by the deep end in much steeper sunlight, the old geologist poking me in a concerned way. Marion had told him not to disturb me, I was deep in thought! I must remember to wear a hat in future, the sunlight brought out a viral rash on my lips. An excuse for Marion not to kiss me, without realizing it she's eager to get away from here, can't pretend for much longer that the fugues don't exist. Does she guess that in some way I plan to exploit that keening sex of hers?

These long fugues are strange, for the first time since the airplane attack I have a vague memory of the dead time. The geometry of that drained pool acted like a mirror, the sky seemed to be full of suns. Perhaps Marion knew that she was doing when she sunbathed there. I ought to climb down that rusty chromium ladder into a new kind of time? *Lost time total:* 6 hours 50 min.

**July 11**

A dangerous fugue today, and what may have been another attempt on my life by Slade. I nearly killed myself driving to the clinic, must think hard about going there again. The first fugue came at 8.15 a.m., synchronized with Marion's – our sole connubial activity now. I must have spent an hour opening the bathroom door, staring at her as she stood motionless in the shower stall. Curious after-images, sections of her anatomy seemed to be splayed across the walls and ceiling, even over the car park outside. For the first time I felt that it might be possible to stay awake during the fugues. A weird world, spatial change perceived independently of time.

Fired by all this, I set off for the clinic, eager to try something out on the perimeter camera. But only a mile down the highway I must have gone straight off the road, found myself in the parking lot of some abandoned hypermarket, surrounded by a crowd of staring faces. In fact, they were department store mannequins. Suddenly there was a volley of gunshots, fibreglass arms and heads were flying everywhere. Slade at his games again, this time with a pump-gun on the roof of the hypermarket. He must have seen me stranded there and placed the mannequins around me. The timeless people, the only mementoes of *homo sapiens* when we've all gone, waiting here with their idiotic smiles for the first stellar visitor.

How does Slade repress the fugues? Perhaps violence, like pornography, is some kind of evolutionary standby system, a last-resort device for throwing a wild joker into the game? A widespread taste for pornography means that nature is alerting us to some threat of extinction. I keep thinking about Ursula, incidentally ... *Total time lost:* 8 hours 17 min.

**July 15**

Must get out of this motel more often. A curious by-product of the fugues is that I'm losing all sense of urgency. Sat here for the last three days, calmly watching time run through my fingers. Almost convinces me that the fugues are a good thing, a sign that some great biological step forward is about to take place, set off by the space flights. Alternatively, my mind is simply numbing itself through sheer fear . . .

This morning I forced myself into the sunlight. I drove slowly around Las Vegas, looking out for Marion and thinking about the links between gambling and time. One could devise a random world, where the length of each time interval depended on chance. Perhaps the high-rollers who came to Vegas were nearer the truth than they realized. 'Clock time' is a neurophysiological construct, a measuring rod confined to *homo sapiens.* The old labrador owned by the geologist next door obviously has a different sense of time, likewise the cicadas beside the pool. Even the materials of my body and the lower levels of my brain have a very different sense of time from my cerebrum – that uninvited guest within my skull.

Simultaneity? It's possible to imagine that everything is happening at once, all the events 'past' and 'future' which constitute the universe are taking place together. Perhaps our sense of time is a primitive mental structure that we inherited from our less intelligent forebears. For prehistoric man the invention of time (a brilliant conceptual leap) was a way of classifying and storing the huge flood of events which his dawning mind had opened for him. Like a dog burying a large bone, the invention of time allowed him to postpone the recognition of an event-system too large for him to grasp at one bite.

If time *is* a primitive mental structure we have inherited, then we ought to welcome its atrophy, embrace the fugues – *Total time lost:* 9 hours 15 min.

**July 25**

Everything is slowing down, I have to force myself to remember to eat and shower. It's all rather pleasant, no fear even though I'm left with only six or seven hours of conscious time each day. Marion comes and goes, we literally have no time to talk to each other. A day passes as quickly as an afternoon. At lunch I was looking at some album photographs of my mother and father, and a formal wedding portrait of Marion and myself, and suddenly it was evening. I feel a strange nostalgia for my childhood friends, as if I'm about to meet them for the first time, an awakening premonition of the past. I can see the past coming alive in the dust on the balcony, in the dried leaves at the bottom of the pool, part of an immense granary of past time whose doors we can open with the right key. Nothing is older than the very new – a newborn baby with its head emerging from its mother has the smooth, time-worn features of Pharaoh. The whole process of life is the discovery of the immanent past contained in the present.

At the same time, I feel a growing nostalgia for the future, a memory of the future I have already experienced but somehow forgotten. In our lives we try to repeat those significant events which have already taken place in the future. As we grow older we feel an increasing nostalgia for our own deaths, through which we have already passed. Equally, we have a growing premonition of our births, which are about to take place. At any moment we may be born for the first time. *Total time lost*: 10 hours 5 min.

## July 29

Slade has been here. I suspect that he's been entering the apartment while I fugue. I had an uncanny memory of someone in the bedroom this morning, when I came out of the 11 a.m. fugue there was a curious after-image, almost a pentecostal presence, a vaguely bio-morphic blur that hung in the air like a photograph taken with the perimeter camera. My pistol had been removed from the dressing-table drawer and placed on my pillow. There's a small diagram of white paint on the back of my left hand. Some kind of cryptic pattern, a geometric key.

Has Slade been reading my diary? This afternoon someone painted the same pattern across the canted floor of the swimming pool and over the gravel in the car park. Presumably all part of Slade's serious games with time and space. He's trying to rally me, force me out of the apartment, but the fugues leave me with no more than two hours at a stretch of conscious time. I'm not the only one affected. Las Vegas is almost deserted, everyone has retreated indoors. The old geologist and his wife sit all day in their bedroom, each in a straight-backed chair on either side of the bed. I gave them a vitamin shot, but they're so emaciated they won't last much longer. No reply from the police or ambulance services. Marion is away again, hunting the empty hotels of the Strip for any sign of Slade. No doubt she thinks that he alone can save her. *Total time lost*: 12 hours 35 min.

## August 12

Rachel Vaisey called today, concerned about me and disappointed not to find Marion here. The clinic has closed, and she's about to go east. A strange pantomime, we talked stiffly for ten minutes. She was clearly baffled by my calm appearance, despite my beard and coffee-stained trousers, and kept staring at the white pattern on my hand and at the similar shapes on the bedroom ceiling, the car park outside and even a section of a small apartment house half a mile away. I'm now at the focus of a huge geometric puzzle radiating from my left hand through the open window and out across Las Vegas and the desert.

I was relieved when she had gone. Ordinary time – so-called 'real time' – now seems totally unreal. With her discrete existence, her prissy point-to-point consciousness, Rachel reminded me of a figure in an animated tableau of Time Man in an anthropological museum of the future. All the same, it's difficult to be too optimistic. I wish Marion were here. *Total time lost*: 15 hours 7 min.

## August 21
Down now to a few stretches of consciousness that last barely an hour at the most. Time seems continuous, but the days go by in a blur of dawns and sunsets. Almost continuously eating, or I'll die of starvation. I only hope that Marion can look after herself, she doesn't seem to have been here for weeks –

– the pen snapped in Franklin's hand. As he woke, he found himself slumped across his diary. Torn pages lay on the carpet around his feet. During the two-hour fugue a violent struggle had taken place, his books were scattered around an overturned lamp, there were heel marks in the cigarette ash on the floor. Franklin touched his bruised shoulders. Someone had seized him as he sat there in his fugue, trying to shake him into life, and had torn the watch from his wrist.

A familiar noise sounded from the sky. The clacking engine of a light aircraft crossed the nearby roof-tops. Franklin stood up, shielding his eyes from the vivid air on the balcony. He watched the aircraft circle the surrounding streets and then speed towards him. A molten light dripped from the propeller, spraying the motel with liquid platinum, a retinal tincture that briefly turned the street dust to silver.

The plane flew past, heading north from Las Vegas, and he saw that Slade had recruited a passenger. A blonde woman in a ragged fur sat behind the naked pilot, hands clasped around his waist. Like a startled dreamer, she stared down at Franklin.

As the microlight soared away, Franklin went into the bathroom. Rallying himself, he gazed at the sallow, bearded figure in the mirror, a ghost of himself. Already sections of his mind were migrating towards the peaceful geometry of the bathroom walls. But at least Marion was still alive. Had she tried to intercede as Slade attacked him? There was a faint image on the air of a wounded woman . . .

Las Vegas was deserted. Here and there, as he set off in the car, he saw a grey face at a window, or a blanket draped across two pairs of knees on a balcony. All the clocks had stopped, and without his watch he could no longer tell how long the fugues had lasted, or when the next was about to begin.

Driving at a cautious ten miles an hour, Franklin slowed to a halt every five miles, then waited until he found himself sitting in the car with a cold engine. The temperature dial became his clock. It was almost noon when he reached the air base. The clinic was silent, its car park empty. Weeds grew through the fading marker lines, an empty report sheet left behind by those unhappy psychiatrists and their now vanished patients.

Franklin let himself into the building and walked through the deserted wards and laboratories. His colleagues' equipment had been shipped away, but when he unlocked the doors to his own laboratory he found the packing cases where he had left them.

In front of the perimeter camera a rubber mattress lay on the turntable. Next to it an ashtray overflowed with cigarette ends that had burned the wooden planks.

So Slade had turned his talents to a special kind of photography – a pornography in the round. Pinned to the walls behind the camera was a gallery of huge prints. These strange landscapes resembled aerial photographs of a desert convulsed by a series of titanic earthquakes, as if one geological era were giving birth to another. Elongated clefts and gulleys stretched across the prints, their contours so like those that had lingered in the apartment after Marion's showers.

But a second geometry overlayed the first, a scarred and aggressive musculature he had seen borne on the wind. The aircraft was parked outside the window, its cockpit and passenger seat empty in the sunlight. A naked man sat behind the desk in Franklin's office, goggles around his forehead. Looking at him, Franklin realized why Slade had always appeared naked.

'Come in, doctor. God knows it's taken you long enough to get here.' He weighed Franklin's wristwatch in his hand, clearly disappointed by the shabby figure in front of him. He had removed the centre drawer from the desk, and was playing with Franklin's shrine. To the original objects Slade had added a small chromium pistol. Deciding against the wristwatch, he tossed it into the waste basket.

'I don't think that's really part of you any longer. You're a man without time. I've moved into your office, Franklin. Think of it as my mission control centre.'

'Slade . . .' Franklin felt a sudden queasiness, a warning of the onset of the next fugue. The air seemed to warp itself around him. Holding the door-frame, he restrained himself from rushing to the waste basket. 'Marion's here with you. I need to see her.'

'See her, then . . .' Slade pointed to the perimeter photographs. 'I'm sure you recognize her, Franklin. You've been using her for the last ten years. That's why you joined NASA. You've been pilfering from your wife and the agency in the same way, stealing the parts for your space machine. I've even helped you myself.'

'Helped . . . ? Marion told me that –'

'Franklin!' Slade stood up angrily, knocking the chromium pistol on to the floor. His hands worked clumsily at his scarred ribs, as if he were forcing himself to breathe. Watching him, Franklin could almost believe that Slade had held back the fugues by a sheer effort of will, by a sustained anger against the very dimensions of time and space.

'This time, doctor, you can't ground me. But for you I would have walked on the moon!'

Franklin was watching the pistol at his feet, uncertain how to pacify this manic figure. 'Slade, but for me you'd be with the others. If you'd flown with the space-crews you'd be like Trippett.'

'I am like Trippett.' Calm again, Slade stepped to the window and stared at the empty runways. 'I'm taking the old boy, Franklin. He's coming with me to the sun. It's a pity you're not coming. But don't worry, you'll find a way out of the fugues. In fact, I'm relying on it.'

He stepped around the desk and picked the pistol from the floor. As Franklin swayed, he touched the physician's cooling forehead with the weapon. 'I'm going to kill you, Franklin. Not now, but right at the end, as we go out into that last fugue. Trippett and I will be flying to the sun, and you . . . you'll die forever.'

There were fifteen minutes, at the most, before the next fugue. Slade had vanished, taking the aircraft into the sky. Franklin gazed round the silent laboratory, listening to the empty air. He retrieved his wristwatch from the waste basket and left. As he reached the parking lot, searching for his car among the maze of diagonal lines, the desert landscape around the air base resembled the perimeter photographs of Marion and Slade together. The hills wavered and shimmered, excited echoes of that single sexual act, mimicking every caress.

Already the moisture in his body was being leached away by the sun. His skin prickled with an attack of hives. He left the clinic and drove through the town, slowing to avoid the filling-station proprietor, his wife and child who stood in the centre of the road. They stared sightlessly into the haze as if waiting for the last car in the world.

He set off towards Las Vegas, trying not to look at the surrounding hills. Ravines fondled each other, rock-towers undulated as if the earth itself were on its marriage bed. Irritated by his own sweat and the oozing hills, Franklin urged on the accelerator, pushing the car's speed to forty miles an hour. The whole mineral world seemed intent on taking its revenge on him. Light stabbed at his retinas from the exposed quartz veins, from the rusting bowls of the radar dishes on the hill crests. Franklin fixed his eyes on the speeding marker line between the car's wheels, dreaming of Las Vegas, that dusty Samarkand.

Then time side-stepped in front of him again.

He woke to find himself lying under the torn ceiling liner of the overturned car, his legs stretched through the broken windshield. Burst from their locks, the open doors hung above him in a haze of idle dust. Franklin pushed aside the loose seats that had fallen across him and climbed from the car. A faint steam rose from the fractured radiator, and the last of the coolant trickled into the culvert of the old irrigation system into which the car had slewed. The blue liquid formed a small pool, then, as he watched it, sank into the sand.

A single kite circled the sky over his head, but the landscape was empty.

Half a mile away was the tarry strip of the highway. As he fugued the car had veered off the road, then sped in a wide circle across the scrub, upending itself as it jumped the first of the irrigation ditches. Franklin brushed the sand from his face and beard. He had been unconscious for almost two hours, part-concussion and part-fugue, and the harsh, noon light had driven all shadows from the sandy soil. The northern suburbs of Las Vegas were ten miles away, too far for him to walk, but the white domes of Soleri II rose from the foothills to the west of the highway, little more than two miles across the desert. He could see the metallic flicker of the solar mirrors as one of the canted dishes caught the sun.

Still jarred by the crash, Franklin turned his back to the road and set off along the causeway between the irrigation ditches. After only a hundred yards he sank to his knees. The sand liquefied at his feet, sucking at his shoes as if eager to strip the clothes from his back and expose him to the sun.

Playing its private game with Franklin, the sun changed places in the sky. The fugues were coming at fifteen-minute intervals. He found himself leaning against a rusting pump-head. Huge pipes emerged thirstlessly from the forgotten ground. His shadow hid behind him, scuttling under his heels. Franklin waved away the circling kite. All too easily he could imagine the bird perching on his shoulder as he fugued, and lunching off his eyes. He was still more than a mile from the solar mirrors, but their sharp light cut at his retinas. If he could reach the tower, climb a few of its steps and signal with a fragment of broken glass, someone might . . .

. . . the sun was trying to trick him again. More confident now, his shadow had emerged from beneath his heels and slid silkily along the stony ground, unafraid of this tottering scarecrow who made an ordeal of each step. Franklin sat down in the dust. Lying on his side, he felt the blisters on his eyelids, lymph-filled sacs that had almost closed his orbits. Any more fugues and he would die here, blood, life and time would run out of him at the same moment.

He stood up and steadied himself against the air. The hills undulated around him, the copulating bodies of all the women he had known, together conceiving this mineral world for him to die within.

Three hundred yards away, between himself and the solar mirrors, a single palm tree dipped its green parasol. Franklin stepped gingerly through the strange light, nervous of this mirage. As he moved forward a second palm appeared, then a third and fourth. There was a glimmer of blue water, the calm surface of an oasis pool.

His body had given up, the heavy arms and legs that emerged from his trunk had slipped into the next fugue. But his mind had scrambled free inside his skull. Franklin knew that even if this oasis were a mirage, it was a mirage that he could see, and that for the first time he was conscious during a fugue. Like the driver of a slow-witted automaton, he propelled himself across the sandy ground, a half-roused sleepwalker clinging to the blue pool before his eyes. More trees had appeared, groves of palms lowered their fronds to the glassy surface of a serpentine lake.

Franklin hobbled forward, ignoring the two kites in the sky above his head. The air was engorged with light, a flood of photons crowded around him. A third kite appeared, joined almost at once by half a dozen more.

But Franklin was looking at the green valley spread out in front of him, at the forest of palms that shaded an archipelago of lakes and pools, together fed by cool streams that ran down from the surrounding hills. Everything seemed calm and yet vivid, the young earth seen for the first time, where all Franklin's ills would be soothed and assuaged in its sweet waters. Within this fertile valley everything multiplied itself without effort. From his outstretched arms fell a dozen shadows, each cast by one of the twelve suns above his head.

Towards the end, while he made his last attempt to reach the lake, he saw a young woman walking towards him. She moved through the palm trees with concerned eyes, hands clasped at her waist, as if searching for a child or elderly parent who had strayed into the wilderness. As Franklin waved to her she was joined by her twin, another grave-faced young woman who walked with the same cautious step. Behind them came other sisters, moving through the palms like schoolgirls from their class, concubines from a pavilion cooled by the lake. Kneeling before them, Franklin waited for the women to find him, to take him away from the desert to the meadows of the valley.

Time, in a brief act of kindness, flowed back into Franklin. He lay in a domed room, behind a verandah shaded by a glass awning. Through the railings he could see the towers and apartment terraces of Soleri II, its concrete architecture a reassuring shoulder against the light. An old man sat on a terrace across the square. Although deeply asleep, he remained inwardly alert and gestured with his hands in a rhythmic way, happily conducting an ōrchestra of stones and creosote bushes.

Franklin was glad to see the old astronaut. All day Trippett sat in his chair, conducting the desert through its repertory of invisible music. Now and then he sipped a little water that Ursula brought him, and then returned to his colloquy with the sun and the dust.

The three of them lived alone in Soleri II, in this empty city of a future without time. Only Franklin's wristwatch and its restless second hand linked them to the past world.

'Doctor Franklin, why don't you throw it away?' Ursula asked him, as she fed Franklin the soup she prepared each morning on the solar fireplace in the piazza. 'You don't need it any more. There's no time to tell.'

'Ursula, I know. It's some kind of link, I suppose, a telephone line left open to a world we're leaving behind. Just in case . . .'

Ursula raised his head and dusted the sand from his pillow. With only an hour left to her each day, housework played little part in her life. Yet her broad face and handsome body expressed all the myths of the maternal child. She had seen Franklin wandering across the desert as she sat on her verandah during an early afternoon fugue.

'I'm sorry I couldn't find you, doctor. There were hundreds of you, the desert was covered with dying men, like some kind of lost army. I didn't know which one to pick.'

'I'm glad you came, Ursula. I saw you as a crowd of dreamy schoolgirls. There's so much to learn . . .'

'You've made a start, doctor. I knew it months ago when we drove Dad out here. There's enough time.'

They both laughed at this, as the old man across the piazza conducted the orchestral sands. Enough time, when time was what they were most eager to escape. Franklin held the young woman's wrist and listened to her calm pulse, impatient for the next fugue to begin. He looked out over the arid valley below, at the cloud-filled mirrors of the solar farm and the rusting tower with its cracked collector dish. Where were those groves of palms and magic lakes, the sweet streams and pastures from which the grave and beautiful young women had emerged to carry him away to safety? During the fugues that followed his recovery they had begun to return, but not as vividly as he had seen them from the desert floor in the hours after his crash. Each fugue, though, gave him a glimpse of that real world, streams flowed to fill the lakes again.

Ursula and her father, of course, could see the valley bloom, a dense and vivid forest as rich as the Amazon's.

'You see the trees, Ursula, the same ones your father saw?'

'All of them, and millions of flowers, too. Nevada's a wonderful garden now. Our eyes are filling the whole state with blossom. One flower makes the desert bloom.'

'And one tree becomes a forest, one drop of water a whole lake. Time took that away from us, Ursula, though for a brief while the first men and women probably saw the world as a paradise. When did you learn to see?'

'When I brought Dad out here, after they shut the clinic. But it started during our drive. Later we went back to the mirrors. They helped me open my eyes. Dad's already were open.'

'The solar mirrors – I should have gone back myself.'

'Slade waited for you, doctor. He waited for months. He's almost out of time now – I think he only has enough time for one more flight.' Ursula dusted the sand from the sheet. For all the Amazon blaze during their fugues, clouds of dust blew into the apartment, a gritty reminder of a different world. She listened to the silent wind. 'Never mind, doctor, there are so many doors. For us it was the mirrors, for you it was that strange camera and your wife's body in sex.'

She fell silent, staring at the verandah with eyes from which time had suddenly drained. Her hand was open, letting the sand run away, fingers outstretched like a child's to catch the brilliant air. Smiling at everything around her, she tried to talk to Franklin, but the sounds came out like a baby's burble.

Franklin held her cold hands, happy to be with her during the fugue. He liked to listen to her murmuring talk. So-called articulate speech was an artefact of time. But the babbling infant, and this young woman, spoke with the lucidity of the timeless, that same lucidity that others tried to achieve in delirium and brain-damage. The babbling new-born were telling their mothers of that realm of wonder from which they had just been expelled. He urged Ursula on, eager to understand her. Soon they would go into the light together, into that last fugue which would free them from the world of appearances.

He waited for the hands to multiply on his watch-dial, the sure sign of the next fugue. In the real world beyond the clock, serial time gave way to simultaneity. Like a camera with its shutter left open indefinitely, the eye perceived a moving object as a series of separate images. Ursula's walking figure as she searched for Franklin had left a hundred replicas of herself behind her, seeded the air with a host of identical twins. Seen from the speeding car, the few frayed palm trees along the road had multiplied themselves across the screen of Trippett's mind, the same forest of palms that Franklin had perceived as he moved across the desert. The lakes had been the multiplied images of the water in that tepid motel pool, and the blue streams were the engine coolant running from the radiator of his overturned car.

During the following days, when he left his bed and began to move around the apartment, Franklin happily embraced the fugues. Each day he shed another two or three minutes. Within only a few weeks, time would cease to exist. Now, however, he was awake during the fugues, able to explore this empty suburb of the radiant city. He had been freed by the ambiguous dream that had sustained him for so long, the vision of his wife with Slade, then copulating with the surrounding hills, in this ultimate infidelity with the mineral kingdom and with time and space themselves.

In the mornings he watched Ursula bathe in the piazza below his verandah. As she strolled around the fountain, drying herself under a dozen suns, Soleri II seemed filled with beautiful, naked women bathing themselves in a city of waterfalls, a seraglio beyond all the fantasies of Franklin's childhood.

At noon, during a few last minutes of time, Franklin stared at himself in the wardrobe mirror. He felt embarrassed by the continued presence of his body, by the sticklike arms and legs, a collection of bones discarded at the foot of the clock. As the fugue began he raised his arms and filled the room with replicas of himself, a procession of winged men each dressed in his coronation armour. Free from time, the light had become richer, gilding his skin with layer upon layer of golden leaf. Confident now, he knew that death was merely a failure of time, and that if he died this would be in a small and unimportant way. Long before they died, he and Ursula would become the people of the sun.

*   *   *

It was the last day of past time, and the first of the day of forever.

Franklin woke in the white room to feel Ursula slapping his shoulders. The exhausted girl lay across his chest, sobbing into her fists. She held his wristwatch in her hand, and pressed it against his forehead.

'. . . wake, doctor. Come back just once . . .'

'Ursula, you're cutting –'

'Doctor!' Relieved to see him awake, she rubbed her tears into his forehead. 'It's Dad, doctor.'

'The old man? What is it? Has he died?'

'No, he won't die.' She shook her head, and then pointed to the empty terrace across the piazza. 'Slade's been here. He's taken Dad!'

She swayed against the mirror as Franklin dressed. He searched unsteadily for a hat to shield himself from the sun, listening to the rackety engine of Slade's microlight. It was parked on the service road near the solar farm, and the reflected light from its propeller filled the air with knives. Since his arrival at Soleri he had seen nothing of Slade, and hoped that he had flown away, taking Marion with him. Now the noise and violence of the engine were tearing apart the new world he had constructed so carefully. Within only a few more hours he and Ursula would escape from time for ever.

Franklin leaned against the rim of the washbasin, no longer recognizing the monk-like figure who stared at him from the shaving mirror. Already he felt exhausted by the effort of coping with this small segment of conscious time, an adult forced to play a child's frantic game. During the past three weeks time had been running out at an ever faster rate. All that was left was a single brief period of a few minutes each day, useful only for the task of feeding himself and the girl. Ursula had lost interest in cooking for them, and devoted herself to drifting through the arcades and sundecks of the city, deep in her fugues.

Aware that they would both perish unless he mastered the fugues, Franklin steered himself into the kitchen. In the warm afternoons the steam from the soup tureen soon turned the solar city into an island of clouds. Gradually, though, he was teaching Ursula to eat, to talk and respond to him even during the fugues. There was a new language to learn, sentences whose nouns and verbs were separated by days, syllables whose vowels were marked by the phases of the sun and moon. This was a language outside time, whose grammar was shaped by the contours of Ursula's breasts in his hands, by the geometry of the apartment. The angle between two walls became an Homeric myth. He and Ursula lisped at each other, lovers talking between the transits of the moon, in the language of birds, wolves and whales. From the start, their sex together had taken away all Franklin's fears. Ursula's ample figure at last proved itself in the fugues. Nature had prepared her for a world without time, and he lay between her breasts like Trippett sleeping in his meadows.

Now he was back in a realm of harsh light and rigid perspectives, wristwatch in hand, its mark on his forehead.

'Ursula, try not to follow me.' At the city gates he steadied her against the portico, trying to rub a few more seconds of time into her cooling hands. If they both went out into the desert, they would soon perish in the heat of that angry and lonely sun. Like all things, the sun needed its companions, needed time leached away from it . . .

As Franklin set off across the desert the microlight's engine began to race at full bore, choked itself and stuttered to a stop. Slade stepped from the cockpit, uninterested in Franklin's approach. He was still naked, except for his goggles, and his white skin was covered with weals and sun-sores, as if time itself were an infective plague from which he now intended to escape. He swung the propeller, shouting at the flooded engine. Strapped into the passenger seat of the aircraft was a grey-haired old man, a scarecrow stuffed inside an oversize flying jacket. Clearly missing the vivid flash of the propeller, Trippett moved his hands up and down, a juggler palming pieces of light in the air.

'Slade! Leave the old man!'

Franklin ran forward into the sun. His next fugue would begin in a few minutes, leaving him exposed to the dream-like violence of Slade's propeller. He fell to his knees against the nearest of the mirrors as the engine clattered into life.

Satisfied, Slade stepped back from the propeller, smiling at the old astronaut. Trippett swayed in his seat, eager for the flight to begin. Slade patted his head, and then surveyed the surrounding landscape. His gaunt face seemed calm for the first time, as if he now accepted the logic of the air and the light, the vibrating propeller and the happy old man in his passenger seat. Watching him, Franklin knew that Slade was delaying his flight until the last moment, so that he would take off into his own fugue. As they soared towards the sun, he and the old astronaut would make their way into space again, on their forever journey to the stars.

'Slade, we want the old man here! You don't need him now!'

Slade frowned at Franklin's shout, this hoarse voice from the empty mirrors. Turning from the cockpit, he brushed his sunburnt shoulder against the starboard wing. He winced, and dropped the chromium pistol on to the sand.

Before he could retrieve it, Franklin stood up and ran through the lines of mirrors. High above, he could see the reflection of himself in the collector dish, a stumbling cripple who had pirated the sky. Even Trippett had noticed him, and rollicked in his seat, urging on this lunatic aerialist. He reached the last of the mirrors, straddled the metal plate and walked towards Slade, brushing the dust from his trousers.

'Doctor, you're too late.' Slade shook his head, impatient with Franklin's derelict appearance. 'A whole life too late. We're taking off now.'

'Leave Trippett . . .' Franklin tried to speak, but the words slurred on his tongue. 'I'll take his place . . .'

'I don't think so, doctor. Besides, Marion is out there somewhere.' He gestured to the desert. 'I left her on the runways for you.'

Franklin swayed against the brightening air. Trippett was still conducting the propeller, impatient to join the sky. Shadows doubled themselves from Slade's heels. Franklin pressed the wound on his forehead, forcing himself to remain in time long enough to reach the aircraft. But the fugue was already beginning, the light glazed everything around him. Slade was a naked angel pinioned against the stained glass of the air.

'Doctor? I could save . . .' Slade beckoned to him, his arm forming a winged replica of itself. As he moved towards Franklin his body began to disassemble. Isolated eyes watched Franklin, mouths grimaced in the vivid light. The silver pistols multiplied.

Like dragonflies, they hovered in the air around Franklin long after the aircraft had taken off into the sky.

The sky was filled with winged men. Franklin stood among the mirrors, as the aircraft multiplied in the air and crowded the sky with endless armadas. Ursula was coming for him, she and her sisters walking across the desert from the gates of the solar city. Franklin waited for her to fetch him, glad that she had learned to feed herself. He knew that he would soon have to leave her and Soleri II, and set off in search of his wife. Happy now to be free of time, he embraced the great fugue. All the light in the universe had come here to greet him, an immense congregation of particles.

Franklin revelled in the light, as he would do when he returned to the clinic. After the long journey on foot across the desert, he at last reached the empty air base. In the evenings he sat on the roof above the runways, and remembered his drive with the old astronaut. There he rested, learning the language of the birds, waiting for his wife to emerge from the runways and bring him news from the sun.

· **1981**

# MEMORIES OF THE SPACE AGE

## ONE

All day this strange pilot had flown his antique aeroplane over the abandoned space centre, a frantic machine lost in the silence of Florida. The flapping engine of the old Curtiss biplane woke Dr Mallory soon after dawn, as he lay asleep beside his exhausted wife on the fifth floor of the empty hotel in Titusville. Dreams of the space age had filled the night, memories of white runways as calm as glaciers, now broken by this eccentric aircraft veering around like the fragment of a disturbed mind.

From his balcony Mallory watched the ancient biplane circle the rusty gantries of Cape Kennedy. The sunlight flared against the pilot's helmet, illuminating the cat's-cradle of silver wires that pinioned the open fuselage between the wings, a puzzle from which the pilot was trying to escape by a series of loops and rolls. Ignoring him, the plane flew back and forth above the forest canopy, its engine calling across the immense deserted decks, as if this ghost of the pioneer days of aviation could summon the sleeping titans of the Apollo programme from their graves beneath the cracked concrete.

Giving up for the moment, the Curtiss turned from the gantries and set course inland for Titusville. As it clattered over the hotel Mallory recognised the familiar hard brow behind the pilot's goggles. Each morning the same pilot appeared, flying a succession of antique craft – relics, Mallory assumed, from some forgotten museum at a private airfield near by. There were a Spad and a Sopwith Camel, a replica of the Wright Flyer, and a Fokker triplane that had buzzed the NASA causeway the previous day, driving inland thousands of frantic gulls and swallows, denying them any share of the sky.

Standing naked on the balcony, Mallory let the amber air warm his skin. He counted the ribs below his shoulder blades, aware that for the first time he could feel his kidneys. Despite the hours spent foraging each day, and the canned food looted from the abandoned supermarkets, it was difficult to keep up his body weight. In the two months since they set out from Vancouver on the slow, nervous drive back to Florida, he and Anne had each lost more than thirty pounds, as if their bodies were carrying out a re-inventory of themselves for the coming world without time. But the bones endured. His skeleton seemed to grow stronger and heavier, preparing itself for the unnourished sleep of the grave.

*        *        *

Already sweating in the humid air, Mallory returned to the bedroom. Anne had woken, but lay motionless in the centre of the bed, strands of blonde hair caught like a child's in her mouth. With its fixed and empty expression, her face resembled a clock that had just stopped. Mallory sat down and placed his hands on her diaphragm, gently respiring her. Every morning he feared that time would run out for Anne while she slept, leaving her forever in the middle of a last uneasy dream.

She stared at Mallory, as if surprised to wake in this shabby resort hotel with a man she had possibly known for years but for some reason failed to recognise.

'Hinton?'

'Not yet.' Mallory steered the hair from her mouth. 'Do I look like him now?'

'God, I'm going blind.' Anne wiped her nose on the pillow. She raised her wrists, and stared at the two watches that formed a pair of time-cuffs. The stores in Florida were filled with abandoned clocks and watches, and each day Anne selected a new set of timepieces. She touched Mallory reassuringly. 'All men look the same, Edward. That's streetwalker's wisdom for you. I meant the plane.'

'I'm not sure. It wasn't a spotter aircraft. Clearly the police don't bother to come to Cape Kennedy any more.'

'I don't blame them. It's an evil place. Edward, we ought to leave, let's get out this morning.'

Mallory held her shoulders, trying to calm this frayed but still handsome woman. He needed her to look her best for Hinton. 'Anne, we've only been here a week – let's give it a little more time.'

'Time? Edward ...' She took Mallory's hands in a sudden show of affection. 'Dear, that's one thing we've run out of. I'm getting those headaches again, just like the ones I had fifteen years ago. It's uncanny, I can feel the same nerves ...'

'I'll give you something, you can sleep this afternoon.'

'No ... They're a warning. I want to feel every twinge.' She pressed the wristwatches to her temples, as if trying to tune her brain to their signal. 'We were mad to come here, and even more mad to stay.'

'I know. It's a long shot but worth a try. I've learned one thing in all these years – if there's a way out, we'll find it at Cape Kennedy.'

'We won't! Everything's poisoned here. We should go to Australia, like all the other NASA people.' Anne rooted in her handbag on the floor, heaving aside an illustrated encyclopaedia of birds she had found in a Titusville bookstore. 'I looked it up – western Australia is as far from Florida as you can go. It's almost the exact antipodes. Edward, my sister lives in *Perth*. I knew there was a reason why she invited us there.'

Mallory stared at the distant gantries of Cape Kennedy. It was difficult to believe that he had once worked there. 'I don't think even Perth, Australia, is far enough. We need to set out into space again ...'

Anne shuddered. 'Edward, don't say that – a *crime* was committed here, everyone knows that's how it all began.' As they listened to the distant drone of the aircraft she gazed at her broad hips and soft thighs. Equal to the challenge, her chin lifted. 'Do you think Hinton is here? He may not remember me.'

'He'll remember you. You were the only one who liked him.'

'Well, in a sort of way. How long was he in prison before he escaped? Twenty years?'

'A long time. Perhaps he'll take you flying again. You enjoyed that.'

'Yes ... He was strange. But even if he is here, can he help? He was the one who started it all.'

'No, not Hinton.' Mallory listened to his voice in the empty hotel. It seemed deeper and more resonant, as the slowing time stretched out the frequencies. 'In point of fact, I started it all.'

Anne had turned from him and lay on her side, a watch pressed to each ear. Mallory reminded himself to go out and begin his morning search for food. Food, a vitamin shot, and a clean pair of sheets. Sex with Anne, which he had hoped would keep them bickering and awake, had generated affection instead. Suppose they conceived a child, here at Cape Kennedy, within the shadow of the gantries ... ?

He remembered the mongol and autistic children he had left behind in the clinic in Vancouver, and his firm belief – strongly contested by his fellow physicians and the worn-out parents – that these were diseases of time, malfunctions of the temporal sense that marooned these children on small islands of awareness, a few minutes in the case of the mongols, a span of micro-seconds for the autistics. A child conceived and born here at Cape Kennedy would be born into a world without time, an indefinite and unending present, that primeval paradise that the old brain remembered so vividly, seen both by those living for the first time and by those dying for the first time. It was curious that images of heaven or paradise always presented a static world, not the kinetic eternity one would expect, the roller-coaster of a hyperactive funfair, the screaming Luna Parks of LSD and psilocybin. It was a strange paradox that given eternity, an infinity of time, they chose to eliminate the very element offered in such abundance.

Still, if they stayed much longer at Cape Kennedy he and Anne would soon return to the world of the old brain, like those first tragic astronauts he had helped to put into space. During the previous year in Vancouver there had been too many attacks, those periods of largo when time seemed to slow, an afternoon at his desk stretched into days. His own lapses in concentration both he and his colleagues put down to eccentricity, but Anne's growing vagueness had been impossible to ignore, the first clear signs of the space sickness that began to slow the clock, as it had done first for the astronauts and then for all the other NASA personnel based in Florida. Within the last months the attacks had come five or six times a day, periods when everything began to slow down, and he would apparently spend all day shaving or signing a cheque.

Time, like a film reel running through a faulty projector, was moving at an erratic pace, at moments backing up and almost coming to a halt. One day it would stop, freeze forever on one frame. Had it really taken them two months to drive from Vancouver, weeks alone from Jacksonville to Cape Kennedy?

He thought of the long journey down the Florida coast, a world of immense empty hotels and glutinous time, of strange meetings with Anne in deserted corridors, of sex-acts that seemed to last for days. Now and then, in forgotten bedrooms, they came across other couples who had strayed into Florida, into the eternal present of this timeless zone, Paolo and Francesca forever embracing in the Fontainebleau Hotel. In some of those eyes there had been horror . . .

As for Anne and himself, time had run out of their marriage fifteen years ago, driven away by the spectres of the space complex, and by memories of Hinton. They had come back here like Adam and Eve returning to the Edenic paradise with an unfortunate dose of VD. Thankfully, as time evaporated, so did memory. He looked at his few possessions, now almost meaningless – the tape machine on which he recorded his steady decline; an album of nude Polaroid poses of a woman doctor he had known in Vancouver; his Gray's *Anatomy* from his student days, a unique work of fiction, pages still stained with formalin from the dissecting-room cadavers; a paperback selection of Muybridge's stop-frame photographs; and a psychoanalytic study of Simon Magus.

'Anne . . . ?' The light in the bedroom had become brighter, there was a curious glare, like the white runways of his dreams. Nothing moved, for a moment Mallory felt that they were waxworks in a museum tableau, or in a painting by Edward Hopper of a tired couple in a provincial bedroom. The dream-time was creeping up on him, about to enfold him. As always he felt no fear, his pulse was calmer . . .

There was a blare of noise outside, a shadow flashed across the balcony. The Curtiss biplane roared overhead, then sped low across the rooftops of Titusville. Roused by the sudden movement, Mallory stood up and shook himself, slapping his thighs to spur on his heart. The plane had caught him just in time.

'Anne, I think that was Hinton . . .'

She lay on her side, the watches to her ears. Mallory stroked her cheeks, but her eyes rolled away from him. She breathed peacefully with her upper lungs, her pulse as slow as a hibernating mammal's. He drew the sheet across her shoulders. She would wake in an hour's time, with a vivid memory of a single image, a rehearsal for those last seconds before time finally froze . . .

## TWO

Medical case in hand, Mallory stepped into the street through the broken plate-glass window of the supermarket. The abandoned store had become his chief source of supplies. Tall palms split the sidewalks in front of the boarded-up shops and bars, providing a shaded promenade through the empty town. Several times he had been caught out in the open during an attack, but the palms had shielded his skin from the Florida sun. For reasons he had yet to understand, he liked to walk naked through the silent streets, watched by the orioles and parakeets. The naked doctor, physician to the birds ... perhaps they would pay him in feathers, the midnight-blue tail-plumes of the macaws, the golden wings of the orioles, sufficient fees for him to build a flying machine of his own?

The medical case was heavy, loaded with packet rice, sugar, cartons of pasta. He would light a small fire on another balcony and cook up a starchy meal, carefully boiling the brackish water in the roof tank. Mallory paused in the hotel car park, gathering his strength for the climb to the fifth floor, above the rat and cockroach line. He rested in the front seat of the police patrol car they had commandeered in a deserted suburb of Jacksonville. Anne had regretted leaving behind her classy Toyota, but the exchange had been sensible. Not only would the unexpected sight of this squad car confuse any military spotter planes, but the hotted-up Dodge could outrun most light aircraft.

Mallory was relying on the car's power to trap the mysterious pilot who appeared each morning in his antique aeroplanes. He had noticed that as every day passed these veteran machines tended to be of increasingly older vintage. Sooner or later the pilot would find himself well within Mallory's reach, unable to shake off the pursuing Dodge before being forced to land at his secret airfield.

Mallory listened to the police radio, the tuneless static that reflected the huge void that lay over Florida. By contrast the air-traffic frequencies were a babel of intercom chatter, both from the big jets landing at Mobile, Atlanta and Savannah, and from military craft overflying the Bahamas. All gave Florida a wide berth. To the north of the 31st parallel life in the United States went on as before, but south of that unfenced and rarely patrolled frontier was an immense silence of deserted marinas and shopping malls, abandoned citrus farms and retirement estates, silent ghettoes and airports.

Losing interest in Mallory, the birds were rising into the air. A dappled shadow crossed the car park, and Mallory looked up as a graceful, slender-winged aircraft drifted lazily past the roof of the hotel. Its twin-bladed propeller struck the air like a child's paddle, driven at a leisurely pace by the pilot sitting astride the bicycle pedals within the transparent fuselage. A man-powered glider of advanced design, it soared silently above the rooftops, buoyed by the thermals rising from the empty town.

'Hinton!' Certain now that he could catch the former astronaut, Mallory abandoned his groceries and pulled himself behind the wheel of the police car. By the time he started the flooded engine he had lost sight of the glider. Its delicate wings, almost as long as an airliner's, had drifted across the forest canopy, kept company by the flocks of swallows and martins that rose to inspect this timorous intruder of their air-space. Mallory reversed out of the car park and set off after the glider, veering in and out of the palms that lifted from the centre of the street.

Calming himself, he scanned the side roads, and caught sight of the machine circling the jai alai stadium on the southern outskirts of the town. A cloud of gulls surrounded the glider, some mobbing its lazy propeller, others taking up their station above its wing-tips. The pilot seemed to be urging them to follow him, enticing them with gentle rolls and yaws, drawing them back towards the sea and to the forest causeways of the space complex.

Reducing his speed, Mallory followed 300 yards behind the glider. They crossed the bridge over the Banana River, heading towards the NASA causeway and the derelict bars and motels of Cocoa Beach. The nearest of the gantries was still over a mile away to the north, but Mallory was aware that he had entered the outer zone of the space grounds. A threatening aura emanated from these ancient towers, as old in their way as the great temple columns of Karnak, bearers of a different cosmic order, symbols of a view of the universe that had been abandoned along with the state of Florida that had given them birth.

Looking down at the now clear waters of the Banana River, Mallory found himself avoiding the sombre forests that packed the causeways and concrete decks of the space complex, smothering the signs and fences, the camera towers and observation bunkers. Time was different here, as it had been at Alamagordo and Eniwetok; a psychic fissure had riven both time and space, then run deep into the minds of the people who worked here. Through that suture in his skull time leaked into the slack water below the car. The forest oaks were waiting for him to feed their roots, these motionless trees were as insane as anything in the visions of Max Ernst. There were the same insatiable birds, feeding on the vegetation that sprang from the corpses of trapped aircraft . . .

Above the causeway the gulls were wheeling in alarm, screaming against the sky. The powered glider side-slipped out of the air, circled and soared along the bridge, its miniature undercarriage only ten feet above the police car. The pilot pedalled rapidly, propeller flashing at the alarmed sun, and Mallory caught a glimpse of blonde hair and a woman's face in the transparent cockpit. A red silk scarf flew from her throat.

'Hinton!' As Mallory shouted into the noisy air the pilot leaned from the cockpit and pointed to a slip road running through the forest towards Cocoa Beach, then banked behind the trees and vanished.

Hinton? For some bizarre reason the former astronaut was now masquerading as a woman in a blonde wig, luring him back to the space complex. The birds had been in league with him . . .

The sky was empty, the gulls had vanished across the river into the forest. Mallory stopped the car. He was about to step onto the road when he heard the drone of an aero-engine. The Fokker triplane had emerged from the space centre. It made a tight circuit of the gantries and came in across the sea. Fifty feet above the beach, it swept across the palmettos and saw-grass, its twin machine-guns pointing straight towards the police car.

Mallory began to re-start the engine, when the machine-guns above the pilot's windshield opened fire at him. He assumed that the pilot was shooting blank ammunition left over from some air display. Then the first bullets struck the metalled road a hundred feet ahead. The second burst threw the car onto its flattened front tyres, severed the door pillar by the passenger seat and filled the cabin with exploding glass. As the plane climbed steeply, about to make its second pass at him, Mallory brushed the blood-flecked glass from his chest and thighs. He leapt from the car and vaulted over the metal railings into the shallow culvert beside the bridge. His blood ran away through the water towards the waiting forest of the space grounds.

## THREE

From the shelter of the culvert, Mallory watched the police car burning on the bridge. The column of oily smoke rose a thousand feet into the empty sky, a beacon visible for ten miles around the Cape. The flocks of gulls had vanished. The powered glider and its woman pilot – he remembered her warning him of the Fokker's approach – had slipped away to its lair somewhere south along the coast.

Too stunned to rest, Mallory stared at the mile-long causeway. It would take him half an hour to walk back to the mainland, an easy target for Hinton as he waited in the Fokker above the clouds. Had the former astronaut recognised Mallory and immediately guessed why the sometime NASA physician had come to search for him?

Too exhausted to swim the Banana River, Mallory waded ashore and set off through the trees. He decided to spend the afternoon in one of the abandoned motels in Cocoa Beach, then make his way back to Titusville after dark.

The forest floor was cool against his bare feet, but a soft light fell through the leafy canopy and warmed his skin. Already the blood had dried on his chest and shoulders, a vivid tracery like an aboriginal tattoo that seemed more suitable wear for this violent and uncertain realm than the clothes he had left behind at the hotel. He passed the rusting hulk of an Airstream trailer, its steel capsule overgrown with lianas and ground ivy, as if the trees had reached up to seize a passing space-craft and dragged it down into the undergrowth. There were abandoned cars and the remains of camping equipment, moss-covered chairs and tables around old barbecue spits left here twenty years earlier when the sightseers had hurriedly vacated the state.

Mallory stepped through this terminal moraine, the elements of a forgotten theme park arranged by a demolition squad. Already he felt that he belonged to an older world within the forest, a realm of darkness, patience and unseen life. The beach was a hundred yards away, the Atlantic breakers washing the empty sand. A school of dolphins leapt cleanly through the water, on their way south to the Gulf. The birds had gone, but the fish were ready to take their place in the air.

Mallory welcomed them. He knew that he had been walking down this sand-bar for little more than half an hour, but at the same time he felt that he had been there for days, even possibly weeks and months. In part of his mind he had always been there. The minutes were beginning to stretch, urged on by this eventless universe free of birds and aircraft. His memory faltered, he was forgetting his past, the clinic at Vancouver and its wounded children, his wife asleep in the hotel at Titusville, even his own identity. A single moment was a small instalment of forever – he plucked a fern leaf and watched it for minutes as it fell slowly to the ground, deferring to gravity in the most elegant way.

Aware now that he was entering the dream-time, Mallory ran on through the trees. He was moving in slow motion, his weak legs carrying him across the leafy ground with the grace of an Olympic athlete. He raised his hand to touch a butterfly apparently asleep on the wing, embarking his outstretched fingers on an endless journey.

The forest that covered the sand-bar began to thin out, giving way to the beach-houses and motels of Cocoa Beach. A derelict hotel sat among the trees, its gates collapsed across the drive, Spanish moss hanging from a sign that advertised a zoo and theme park devoted to the space age. Through the waist-high palmettos the chromium and neon rockets rose from their stands like figures on amusement park carousels.

Laughing to himself, Mallory vaulted the gates and ran on past the rusting space-ships. Behind the theme park were overgrown tennis courts, a swimming pool and the remains of the small zoo, with an alligator pit, mammal cages and an aviary. Happily, Mallory saw that the tenants had returned to their homes. An overweight zebra dozed in his concrete enclosure, a bored tiger stared in a cross-eyed way at his own nose, and an elderly caiman sunbathed on the grass beside the alligator pit.

Time was slowing now, coming almost to a halt. Mallory hung in mid-step, his bare feet in the air above the ground. Parked on the tiled path beside the swimming pool was a huge transparent dragon-fly, the powered glider he had chased that morning.

Two wizened cheetahs sat in the shade under its wing, watching Mallory with their prim eyes. One of them rose from the ground and slowly launched itself towards him, but it was twenty feet away and Mallory knew that it would never reach him. Its threadbare coat, refashioned from some old carpet bag, stretched itself into a lazy arch that seemed to freeze forever in mid-frame.

Mallory waited for time to stop. The waves were no longer running towards the beach, and were frozen ruffs of icing sugar. Fish hung in the sky, the wise dolphins happy to be in their new realm, faces smiling in the sun. The water spraying from the fountain at the shallow end of the pool now formed a glass parasol.

Only the cheetah was moving, still able to outrun time. It was now ten feet from him, its head tilted to one side as it aimed at Mallory's throat, its yellow claws more pointed than Hinton's bullets. But Mallory felt no fear for this violent cat. Without time it could never reach him, without time the lion could at last lie down with the lamb, the eagle with the vole.

He looked up at the vivid light, noticing the figure of a young woman who hung in the air with outstretched arms above the diving board. Suspended over the water in a swallow dive, her naked body flew as serenely as the dolphins above the sea. Her calm face gazed at the glass floor ten feet below her small, extended palms. She seemed unaware of Mallory, her eyes fixed on the mystery of her own flight, and he could see clearly the red marks left on her shoulders by the harness straps of the glider, and the silver arrow of her appendix scar pointing to her childlike pubis.

The cheetah was drawing closer now, its claws picking at the threads of dried blood that laced Mallory's shoulders, its grey muzzle retracted to show its ulcerated gums and stained teeth. If he reached out he could embrace it, comfort all the memories of Africa, soothe the violence from its old pelt . . .

## FOUR

Time had flowed out of Florida, as it had from the space age. After a brief pause, like a trapped film reel running free, it sped on again, rekindling a kinetic world.

Mallory sat in a deck chair beside the pool, watching the cheetahs as they rested in the shade under the glider. They crossed and uncrossed their paws like card-dealers palming an ace, now and then lifting their noses at the scent of this strange man and his blood.

Despite their sharp teeth, Mallory felt calm and rested, a sleeper waking from a complex but satisfying dream. He was glad to be surrounded by this little zoo with its backdrop of playful rockets, as innocent as an illustration from a children's book.

The young woman stood next to Mallory, keeping a concerned watch on him. She had dressed while Mallory recovered from his collision with the cheetah. After dragging away the boisterous beast she settled Mallory in the deck chair, then pulled on a patched leather flying suit. Was this the only clothing she had ever worn? A true child of the air, born and sleeping on the wing. With her overbright mascara and blonde hair brushed into a vivid peruke, she resembled a leather-garbed parakeet, a punk madonna of the airways. Worn NASA flashes on her shoulder gave her a biker's swagger. On the name-plate above her right breast was printed: *Nightingale.*

'Poor man – are you back? You're far, far away.' Behind the child-like features, the soft mouth and boneless nose, a pair of adult eyes watched him warily. 'Hey, you – what happened to your uniform? Are you in the police?'

Mallory took her hand, touching the heavy Apollo signet ring she wore on her wedding finger. From somewhere came the absurd notion that she was married to Hinton. Then he noticed her enlarged pupils, a hint of fever.

'Don't worry – I'm a doctor, Edward Mallory. I'm on holiday here with my wife.'

'Holiday?' The girl shook her head, relieved but baffled. 'That patrol car – I thought someone had stolen your uniform while you were . . . out. Dear doctor, no one comes on holiday to Florida any more. If you don't leave soon this is one vacation that may last for ever.'

'I know . . .' Mallory looked round at the zoo with its dozing tiger, the gay fountain and cheerful rockets. This was the amiable world of the Douanier Rousseau's *Merry Jesters.* He accepted the jeans and shirt which the girl gave him. He had liked being naked, not from any exhibitionist urge, but because it suited the vanished realm he had just visited. The impassive tiger with his skin of fire belonged to that world of light. 'Perhaps I've come to the right place, though – I'd like to spend forever here. To tell the truth, I've just had a small taste of what forever is going to be like.'

'No. Thanks.' Intrigued by Mallory, the girl squatted on the grass beside him. 'Tell me, how often are you getting the attacks?'

'Every day. Probably more than I realise. And you . . . ?' When she shook her head a little too quickly, Mallory added: 'They're not that frightening, you know. In a way you want to go back.'

'I can see. Take your wife and leave – any moment now all the clocks are going to stop.'

'That's why we're here – it's our one chance. My wife has even less time left than I have. We want to come to terms with everything – whatever that means. Not much any more.'

'Doctor . . . The real Cape Kennedy is inside your head, not out here.' Clearly unsettled by the presence of this marooned physician, the girl pulled on her flying helmet. She scanned the sky, where the gulls and swallows were again gathering, drawn into the air by the distant drone of an aero-engine. 'Listen – an hour ago you were nearly killed. I tried to warn you. Our local stunt pilot doesn't like the police.'

'So I found out. I'm glad he didn't hit you. I thought he was flying your glider.'

'Hinton? He wouldn't be seen dead in that. He needs speed. Hinton's trying to join the birds.'

'Hinton ...' Repeating the name, Mallory felt a surge of fear and relief, realising that he was committed now to the course of action he had planned months ago when he left the clinic in Vancouver. 'So Hinton is here.'

'He's here.' The girl nodded at Mallory, still unsure that he was not a policeman. 'Not many people remember Hinton.'

'I remember Hinton.' As she fingered the Apollo signet ring he asked: 'You're not married to him?'

'To Hinton? Doctor, you have some strange ideas. What are your patients like?'

'I often wonder. But you know Hinton?'

'Who does? He has other things on his mind. He fixed the pool here, and brought me the glider from the museum at Orlando.' She added, archly: 'Disneyland East – that's what they called Cape Kennedy in the early days.'

'I remember – twenty years ago I worked for NASA.'

'So did my father.' She spoke sharply, angered by the mention of the space agency. 'He was the last astronaut – Alan Shepley – the only one who didn't come back. And the only one they didn't wait for.'

'Shepley was *your* father?' Startled, Mallory turned to look at the distant gantries of the launching grounds. 'He died in the Shuttle. Then you know that Hinton ...'

'Doctor, I don't think it was Hinton who killed my father.' Before Mallory could speak she lowered her goggles over her eyes. 'Anyway, it doesn't matter now. The important thing is that someone will be here when he comes down.'

'You're waiting for him?'

'Shouldn't I, doctor?'

'Yes ... but it was a long time ago. Besides, it's a million to one against him coming down here.'

'That's not true. According to Hinton, Dad may actually come down somewhere along this coast. Hinton says the orbits are starting to decay. I search the beaches every day.'

Mallory smiled at her encouragingly, admiring this spunky but sad child. He remembered the news photographs of the astronaut's daughter, Gale Shepley, a babe in arms fiercely cradled by the widow outside the court-room after the verdict. 'I hope he comes. And your little zoo, Gale?'

'Nightingale,' she corrected. 'The zoo is for Dad. I want the world to be a special place for us when we go.'

'You're leaving together?'

'In a sense – like you, doctor, and everyone else here.'

'So you do get the attacks.'

'Not often – that's why I keep moving. The birds are teaching me how to fly. Did you know that, doctor? The birds are trying to get out of time.'

Already she was distracted by the unswept sky and the massing birds. After tying up the cheetahs she made her way quickly to the glider. 'I have to leave, doctor. Can you ride a motorcycle? There's a Yamaha in the hotel lobby you can borrow.'

But before taking off she confided to Mallory: 'It's all wishful thinking, doctor, for Hinton, too. When Dad comes it won't matter any more.'

Mallory tried to help her launch the glider, but the filmy craft took off within its own length. Pedalling swiftly, she propelled it into the air, climbing over the chromium rockets of the theme park. The glider circled the hotel, then levelled its long, tapering wings and set off for the empty beaches of the north.

Restless without her, the tiger began to wrestle with the truck tyre suspended from the ceiling of its cage. For a moment Mallory was tempted to unlock the door and join it. Avoiding the cheetahs chained to the diving board, he entered the empty hotel and took the staircase to the roof. From the ladder of the elevator house he watched the glider moving towards the space centre.

Alan Shepley – the first man to be murdered in space. All too well Mallory remembered the young pilot of the Shuttle, one of the last astronauts to be launched from Cape Kennedy before the curtain came down on the space age. A former Apollo pilot, Shepley had been a dedicated but likable young man, as ambitious as the other astronauts and yet curiously naïve.

Mallory, like everyone else, had much preferred him to the Shuttle's co-pilot, a research physicist who was then the token civilian among the astronauts. Mallory remembered how he had instinctively disliked Hinton on their first meeting at the medical centre. But from the start he had been fascinated by the man's awkwardness and irritability. In its closing days, the space programme had begun to attract people who were slightly unbalanced, and he recognised that Hinton belonged to this second generation of astronauts, mavericks with complex motives of their own, quite unlike the disciplined service pilots who had furnished the Mercury and Apollo flight-crews. Hinton had the intense and obsessive temperament of a Cortez, Pizarro or Drake, the hot blood and cold heart. It was Hinton who had exposed for the first time so many of the latent conundrums at the heart of the space programme, those psychological dimensions that had been ignored from its start and subsequently revealed, too late, in the crack-ups of the early astronauts, their slides into mysticism and melancholia.

'The best astronauts never dream,' Russell Schweickart had once remarked. Not only did Hinton dream, he had torn the whole fabric of time and space, cracked the hour-glass from which time was running. Mallory was aware of his own complicity, he had been chiefly responsible for putting Shepley and Hinton together, guessing that the repressed and earnest Shepley might provide the trigger for a metaphysical experiment of a special sort.

At all events, Shepley's death had been the first murder in space, a crisis that Mallory had both stage-managed and unconsciously welcomed. The murder of the astronaut and the public unease that followed had marked the end of the space age, an awareness that man had committed an evolutionary crime by travelling into space, that he was tampering with the elements of his own consciousness. The fracture of that fragile continuum erected by the human psyche through millions of years had soon shown itself, in the confused sense of time displayed by the inhabitants of the towns near the space centre. Cape Kennedy and the whole of Florida itself became a poisoned land to be forever avoided like the nuclear testing grounds of Nevada and Utah.

Yet, perhaps, instead of going mad in space, Hinton had been the first man to 'go sane'. During his trial he pleaded his innocence and then refused to defend himself, viewing the international media circus with a stoicism that at times seemed bizarre. That silence had unnerved everyone – how could Hinton believe himself innocent of a murder (he had locked Shepley into the docking module, vented his air supply and then cast him loose in his coffin, keeping up a matter-of-fact commentary the whole while) committed in full view of a thousand million television witnesses?

Alcatraz had been re-commissioned for Hinton, for this solitary prisoner isolated on the frigid island to prevent him contaminating the rest of the human race. After twenty years he was safely forgotten, and even the report of his escape was only briefly mentioned. He was presumed to have died, after crashing into the icy waters of the bay in a small aircraft he had secretly constructed. Mallory had travelled down to San Francisco to see the waterlogged craft, a curious ornithopter built from the yew trees that Hinton had been allowed to grow in the prison island's stony soil, boosted by a home-made rocket engine powered by a fertiliser-based explosive. He had waited twenty years for the slow-growing evergreens to be strong enough to form the wings that would carry him to freedom.

Then, only six months after Hinton's death, Mallory had been told by an old NASA colleague of the strange stunt pilot who had been seen flying his antique aircraft at Cape Kennedy, some native of the air who had so far eluded the half-hearted attempts to ground him. The descriptions of the bird-cage aeroplanes reminded Mallory of the drowned ornithopter dragged up onto the winter beach . . .

So Hinton had returned to Cape Kennedy. As Mallory set off on the Yamaha along the coast road, past the deserted motels and cocktail bars of Cocoa Beach, he looked out at the bright Atlantic sand, so unlike the rocky shingle of the prison island. But was the ornithopter a decoy, like all the antique aircraft that Hinton flew above the space centre, machines that concealed some other aim?

Some other escape?

## FIVE

Fifteen minutes later, as Mallory sped along the NASA causeway towards Titusville, he was overtaken by an old Wright biplane. Crossing the Banana River, he noticed that the noise of a second engine had drowned the Yamaha's. The venerable flying machine appeared above the trees, the familiar gaunt-faced pilot sitting in the open cockpit. Barely managing to pull ahead of the Yamaha, the pilot flew down to within ten feet of the road, gesturing to Mallory to stop, then cut back his engine and settled the craft onto the weed-grown concrete.

'Mallory, I've been looking for you! Come on, doctor!'

Mallory hesitated, the gritty backwash of the Wright's props stinging the open wounds under his shirt. As he peered among the struts Hinton seized his arm and lifted him onto the passenger seat.

'Mallory, yes ... it's you still!' Hinton pushed his goggles back onto his bony forehead, revealing a pair of blood-flecked eyes. He gazed at Mallory with open amazement, as if surprised that Mallory had aged at all in the past twenty years, but delighted that he had somehow survived. 'Nightingale just told me you were here. Doctor Mysterium ... I nearly killed you!'

'You're trying again ...!' Mallory clung to the frayed seat straps as Hinton opened the throttle. The biplane gazelled into the air. In a gust of wind across the exposed causeway it flew backwards for a few seconds, then climbed vertically and banked across the trees towards the distant gantries. Thousands of swallows and martins overtook them on all sides, ignoring Hinton as if well used to this erratic aviator and his absurd machines.

As Hinton worked the rudder tiller, Mallory glanced at this feverish and undernourished man. The years in prison and the rushing air above Cape Kennedy had leached all trace of iron salts from his pallid skin. His raw eyelids, the nail-picked septum of his strong nose and his scarred lips were blanched almost silver in the wind. He had gone beyond exhaustion and malnutrition into a nervous realm where the rival elements of his warring mind were locked together like the cogs of an overwound clock. As he pummelled Mallory's arm it was clear that he had already forgotten the years since their last meeting. He pointed to the forest below them, to the viaducts, concrete decks and blockhouses, eager to show off his domain.

They had reached the heart of the space complex, where the gantries rose like gallows put out to rent. In the centre was the giant crawler, the last of the Shuttles mounted vertically on its launching platform. Its rusting tracks lay around it, the chains of an unshackled colossus.

Here at Cape Kennedy time had not stood still but moved into reverse. The huge fuel tank and auxiliary motors of the Shuttle resembled the domes and minarets of a replica Taj Mahal. Lines of antique aircraft were drawn up on the runway below the crawler – a Lilienthal glider lying on its side like an ornate fan window, a Mignet Flying Flea, the Fokker, Spad and Sopwith Camel, and a Wright Flyer that went back to the earliest days of aviation. As they circled the launch platform Mallory almost expected to see a crowd of Edwardian aviators thronging this display of ancient craft, pilots in gaiters and overcoats, women passengers in hats fitted with leather straps.

Other ghosts haunted the daylight at Cape Kennedy. When they landed Mallory stepped into the shadow of the launch platform, an iron cathedral shunned by the sky. An unsettling silence came in from the dense forest that filled the once-open decks of the space centre, from the eyeless bunkers and rusting camera towers.

'Mallory, I'm glad you came!' Hinton pulled off his flying helmet, exposing a lumpy scalp under his close-cropped hair – Mallory remembered that he had once been attacked by a berserk warder. 'I couldn't believe it was you! And Anne? Is she all right?'

'She's here, at the hotel in Titusville.'

'I know, I've just seen her on the roof. She looked . . .' Hinton's voice dropped, in his concern he had forgotten what he was doing. He began to walk in a circle, and then rallied himself. 'Still, it's good to see you. It's more than I hoped for – you were the one person who knew what was going on here.'

'Did I?' Mallory searched for the sun, hidden behind the cold bulk of the launch platform. Cape Kennedy was even more sinister than he had expected, like some ancient death camp. 'I don't think I –'

'Of course you knew! In a way we were collaborators – believe me, Mallory, we will be again. I've a lot to tell you . . .' Happy to see Mallory, but concerned for the shivering physician, Hinton embraced him with his restless hands. When Mallory flinched, trying to protect his shoulders, Hinton whistled and peered solicitously inside his shirt.

'Mallory, I'm sorry – that police car confused me. They'll be coming for me soon, we have to move fast. But you don't look too well, doctor. Time's running out, I suppose, it's difficult to understand at first . . .'

'I'm starting to. What about you, Hinton? I need to talk to you about everything. You look –'

Hinton grimaced. He slapped his hip, impatient with his undernourished body, an atrophied organ that he would soon discard. 'I had to starve myself, the wingloading of that machine was so low. It took years, or they might have noticed. Those endless medical checks, they were terrified that I was brewing up an even more advanced psychosis – they couldn't grasp that I was opening the door to a new world.' He gazed round at the space centre, at the empty wind. 'We had to get out of time – that's what the space programme was all about . . .'

He beckoned Mallory towards a steel staircase that led up to the assembly deck six storeys above them. 'We'll go topside. I'm living in the Shuttle – there's a crew module of the Mars platform still inside the hold, a damn sight more comfortable than most of the hotels in Florida.' He added, with an ironic gleam: 'I imagine it's the last place they'll come to look for me.'

Mallory began to climb the staircase. He tried not to touch the greasy rivets and sweating rails, lowering his eyes from the tiled skin of the Shuttle as it emerged above the assembly deck. After all the years of thinking about Cape Kennedy he was still unprepared for the strangeness of this vast, reductive machine, a Juggernaut that could be pushed by its worshippers across the planet, devouring the years and hours and seconds.

Even Hinton seemed subdued, scanning the sky as if waiting for Shepley to appear. He was careful not to turn his back on Mallory, clearly suspecting that the former NASA physician had been sent to trap him.

'Flight and time, Mallory, they're bound together. The birds have always known that. To get out of time we first need to learn to fly. That's why I'm here. I'm teaching myself to fly, going back through all these old planes to the beginning. I want to fly without wings . . .'

As the Shuttle's delta wing fanned out above them, Mallory swayed against the rail. Exhausted by the climb, he tried to pump his lungs. The silence was too great, this stillness at the centre of the stopped clock of the world. He searched the breathless forest and runways for any sign of movement. He needed one of Hinton's machines to take off and go racketing across the sky.

'Mallory, you're going . . . ? Don't worry, I'll help you through it.' Hinton had taken his elbow and steadied him on his feet. Mallory felt the light suddenly steepen, the intense white glare he had last seen as the cheetah sprang towards him. Time left the air, wavered briefly as he struggled to retain his hold on the passing seconds.

A flock of martins swept across the assembly deck, swirled like exploding soot around the Shuttle. Were they trying to warn him? Roused by the brief flurry, Mallory felt his eyes clear. He had been able to shake off the attack, but it would come again.

'Doctor –? You'll be all right.' Hinton was plainly disappointed as he watched Mallory steady himself at the rail. 'Try not to fight it, doctor, everyone makes that mistake.'

'It's going . . .' Mallory pushed him away. Hinton was too close to the rail, the man's manic gestures could jostle him over the edge. 'The birds –'

'Of course, we'll join the birds! Mallory, we can all fly, every one of us. Think of it, doctor, true flight. We'll live forever in the air!'

'Hinton . . .' Mallory backed along the deck as Hinton seized the greasy rail, about to catapult himself onto the wind. He needed to get away from this madman and his lunatic schemes.

Hinton waved to the aircraft below, saluting the ghosts in their cockpits. 'Lilienthal and the Wrights, Curtiss and Blériot, even old Mignet – they're here, doctor. That's why I came to Cape Kennedy. I needed to go back to the beginning, long before aviation sent us all off on the wrong track. When time stops, Mallory, we'll step from this deck and fly towards the sun. You and I, doctor, and Anne . . .'

Hinton's voice was deepening, a cavernous boom. The white flank of the Shuttle's hull was a lantern of translucent bone, casting a spectral light over the sombre forest. Mallory swayed forward, on some half-formed impulse he wanted Hinton to vault the rail, step out onto the air and challenge the birds. If he pressed his shoulders . . .

'Doctor –?'

Mallory raised his hands, but he was unable to draw any nearer to Hinton. Like the cheetah, he was forever a few inches away.

Hinton had taken his arm in a comforting gesture, urging him towards the rail.

'Fly, doctor . . .'

Mallory stood at the edge. His skin had become part of the air, invaded by the light. He needed to shrug aside the huge encumbrance of time and space, this rusting deck and the clumsy tracked vehicle. He could hang free, suspended forever above the forest, master of time and light. He would fly . . .

A flurry of charged air struck his face. Fracture lines appeared in the wind around him. The transparent wings of a powered glider soared past, its propeller chopping at the sunlight.

Hinton's hands gripped his shoulders, bundling him impatiently over the rail. The glider slewed sideways, wheeled and flew towards them again. The sunlight lanced from its propeller, a stream of photons that drove time back into Mallory's eyes. Pulling himself free from Hinton, he fell to his knees as the young woman swept past in her glider. He saw her anxious face behind the goggles, and heard her voice shout warningly at Hinton.

But Hinton had already gone. His feet rang against the metal staircase. As he took off in the Fokker he called out angrily to Mallory, disappointed with him. Mallory knelt by the edge of the steel deck, waiting for time to flow back into his mind, hands gripping the oily rail with the strength of the new-born.

# SIX

TAPE 24: *17 August.*
Again, no sign of Hinton today.

Anne is asleep. An hour ago, when I returned from the drugstore, she looked at me with focused eyes for the first time in a week. By an effort I managed to feed her in the few minutes she was fully awake. Time has virtually stopped for her, there are long periods when she is clearly in an almost stationary world, a series of occasionally varying static tableaux. Then she wakes briefly and starts talking about Hinton and a flight to Miami she is going to make with him in his Cessna. Yet she seems refreshed by these journeys into the light, as if her mind is drawing nourishment from the very fact that no time is passing.

I feel the same, despite the infected wound on my shoulder – Hinton's dirty fingernails. The attacks come a dozen times a day, everything slows to a barely perceptible flux. The intensity of light is growing, photons backing up all the way to the sun. As I left the drugstore I watched a parakeet cross the road over my head; it seemed to take two hours to fly fifty feet.

Perhaps Anne has another week before time stops for her. As for myself, three weeks? It's curious to think that at, say, precisely 3.47 p.m., 8 September, time will stop forever. A single micro-second will flash past unnoticed for everyone else, but for me will last an eternity. I'd better decide how I want to spend it!

## TAPE 25: *19 August.*

A hectic two days. Anne had a relapse at noon yesterday, vaso-vagal shock brought on by waking just as Hinton strafed the hotel in his Wright Flyer. I could barely detect her heartbeat, spent hours massaging her calves and thighs (I'd happily go out into eternity caressing my wife). I managed to stand her up, walked her up and down the balcony in the hope that the noise of Hinton's aircraft might jolt her back onto the rails. In fact, this morning she spoke to me in a completely lucid way, obviously appalled by my derelict appearance. For her it's one of those quiet afternoons three weeks ago.

We could still leave, start up one of the abandoned cars and reach the border at Jacksonville before the last minutes run out. I have to keep reminding myself why we came here in the first place. Running north will solve nothing. If there's a solution it's here, somewhere between Hinton's obsessions and Shepley's orbiting coffin, between the space centre and those bright, eerie transits that are all too visible at night. I hope I don't go out just as it arrives, spend the rest of eternity looking at the vaporising corpse of the man I helped to die in space. I keep thinking of that tiger. Somehow I can calm it.

## TAPE 26: *25 August.*

3.30 p.m. The first uninterrupted hour of conscious time I've had in days. When I woke fifteen minutes ago Hinton had just finished strafing the hotel – the palms were shaking dust and insects all over the balcony. Clearly Hinton is trying to keep us awake, postponing the end until he's ready to play his last card, or perhaps until I'm out of the way and he's free to be with Anne.

I'm still thinking about his motives. He seems to have embraced the destruction of time, as if this whole malaise were an opportunity that we ought to seize, the next evolutionary step forward. He was steering me to the edge of the assembly deck, urging me to fly; if Gale Shepley hadn't appeared in her glider I would have dived over the rail. In a strange way he was helping me, guiding me into that new world without time. When he turned Shepley loose from the Shuttle he didn't think he was killing him, but setting him free.

The ever more primitive aircraft – Hinton's quest for a pure form of flight, which he will embark upon at the last moment. A Santos-Dumont flew over yesterday, an ungainly box-kite, he's given up his World War I machines. He's deliberately flying badly designed aircraft, all part of his attempt to escape from winged aviation into absolute flight, poetical rather than aeronautical structures.

The roots of shamanism and levitation, and the erotic cathexis of flight – can one see them as an attempt to escape from time? The shaman's supposed ability to leave his physical form and fly with his spiritual body, the psychopomp guiding the souls of the deceased and able to achieve a mastery of fire, together seem to be linked with those defects of the vestibular apparatus brought on by prolonged exposure to zero gravity during the space flights. We should have welcomed them.

That tiger – I'm becoming obsessed with the notion that it's on fire.

**TAPE 27: *28 August.***
An immense silence today, not a murmur over the soft green deck of Florida. Hinton may have killed himself. Perhaps all this flying is some kind of expiatory ritual, when he dies the shaman's curse will be lifted. But do I want to go back into time? By contrast, that static world of brilliant light pulls at the heart like a vision of Eden. If time *is* a primitive mental structure we're right to reject it. There's a sense in which not only the shaman's but all mystical and religious beliefs are an attempt to devise a world without time. Why did primitive man, who needed a brain only slightly larger than the tiger in Gale's zoo, in fact have a mind almost equal to those of Freud and Leonardo? Perhaps all that surplus neural capacity was there to release him from time, and it has taken the space age, and the sacrifice of the first astronaut, to achieve that single goal.

Kill Hinton . . . How, though?

**TAPE 28: *3 September.***
Missing days. I'm barely aware of the flux of time any longer. Anne lies on the bed, wakes for a few minutes and makes a futile attempt to reach the roof, as if the sky offers some kind of escape. I've just brought her down from the staircase. It's too much of an effort to forage for food, on my way to the supermarket this morning the light was so bright that I

had to close my eyes, hand-holding my way around the streets like a blind beggar. I seemed to be standing on the floor of an immense furnace.

Anne is increasingly restless, murmuring to herself in some novel language, as if preparing for a journey. I recorded one of her drawn-out monologues, like some Gaelic love-poem, then speeded it up to normal time. An agonised 'Hinton . . . Hinton . . .'

It's taken her twenty years to learn.

TAPE 29: *6 September.*
There can't be more than a few days left. The dream-time comes on a dozen stretches each day, everything slows to a halt. From the balcony I've just watched a flock of orioles cross the street. They seemed to take hours, their unmoving wings supporting them as they hung above the trees.

At last the birds have learned to fly.

Anne is awake . . .
*(Anne):* Who's learned to fly?
*(EM):* It's all right – the birds.
*(Anne):* Did you teach them? What am I talking about? How long have I been away?
*(EM):* Since dawn. Tell me what you were dreaming.
*(Anne):* Is this a dream? Help me up. God, it's dark in the street. There's no time left here. Edward, find Hinton. Do whatever he says.


# SEVEN

Kill Hinton . . .

As the engine of the Yamaha clacked into life, Mallory straddled the seat and looked back at the hotel. At any moment, as if seizing the last few minutes left to her, Anne would leave the bedroom and try to make her way to the roof. The stationary clocks in Titusville were about to tell the real time for her, eternity for this lost woman would be a flight of steps around an empty elevator shaft.

Kill Hinton . . . he had no idea how. He set off through the streets to the east of Titusville, shakily weaving in and out of the abandoned cars. With its stiff gearbox and unsteady throttle the Yamaha was exhausting to control. He was driving through an unfamiliar suburb of the town, a terrain of tract houses, shopping malls and car parks laid out for the NASA employees in the building boom of the 1960s. He passed an overturned truck that had spilled its cargo of television sets across the road, and a laundry van that had careened through the window of a liquor store.

Three miles to the east were the gantries of the space centre. An aircraft hung in the air above them, a primitive helicopter with an overhead propeller. The tapering blades were stationary, as if Hinton had at last managed to dispense with wings.

Mallory pressed on towards the Cape, the engine of the motorcycle at full throttle. The tracts of suburban housing unravelled before him, endlessly repeating themselves, the same shopping malls, bars and motels, the same stores and used-car lots that he and Anne had seen in their journey across the continent. He could almost believe that he was driving through Florida again, through the hundreds of small towns that merged together, a suburban universe in which these identical liquor stores, car parks and shopping malls formed the building blocks of a strand of urban DNA generated by the nucleus of the space centre. He had driven down this road, across these silent intersections, not for minutes or hours but for years and decades. The unravelling strand covered the entire surface of the globe, and then swept out into space to pave the walls of the universe before it curved back on itself to land here at its departure point at the space centre. Again he passed the overturned truck beside its scattered television sets, again the laundry van in the liquor store window. He would forever pass them, forever cross the same intersection, see the same rusty sign above the same motel cabin . . .

'Doctor . . . !'

The smell of burning flesh quickened in Mallory's nose. His right calf was pressed against the exhaust manifold of the idling Yamaha. Charred fragments of his cotton trouser clung to the raw wound. As the young woman in the black flying suit ran across the street Mallory pushed himself away from the clumsy machine, stumbled over its spinning wheels and knelt in the road.

He had stopped at an intersection half a mile from the centre of Titusville. The vast planetary plain of parking lots had withdrawn, swirled down some cosmic funnel and then contracted to this small suburban enclave of a single derelict motel, two tract houses and a bar. Twenty feet away the blank screens of the television sets stared at him from the road beside the overturned truck. A few steps further along the sidewalk the laundry van lay in its liquor store window, dusty bottles of vodka and bourbon shaded by the wing-tip of the glider which Gale Shepley had landed in the street.

'Dr Mallory! Can you hear me? Dear man . . .' She pushed back Mallory's head and peered into his eyes, then switched off the still-clacking engine of the Yamaha. 'I saw you sitting here, there was something . . . My God, your leg! Did Hinton . . . ?'

'No . . . I set fire to myself.' Mallory climbed to his feet, an arm around the girl's shoulder. He was still trying to clear his head, there was something curiously beguiling about that vast suburban world . . . 'I was a fool trying to ride it. I must see Hinton.'

'Doctor, listen to me . . .' The girl shook his hands, her eyes wide with fever. Her mascara and hair were even more bizarre than he remembered. 'You're dying! A day or two more, an hour maybe, you'll be gone. We'll find a car and I'll drive you north.' With an effort she took her eyes from the sky. 'I don't like to leave Dad, but you've got to get away from here, it's inside your head now.'

Mallory tried to lift the heavy Yamaha. 'Hinton – it's all that's left now. For Anne, too. Somehow I have to . . . kill him.'

'He knows that, doctor—' She broke off at the sound of an approaching aero-engine. An aircraft was hovering over the nearby streets, its shadowy bulk visible through the palm leaves, the flicker of a rotor blade across the sun. As they crouched among the television sets it passed above their heads. An antique autogyro, it lumbered through the air like an aerial harvester, its free-spinning rotor apparently powered by the sunlight. Sitting in the open cockpit, the pilot was too busy with his controls to search the streets below.

Besides, as Mallory knew, Hinton had already found his quarry. Standing on the roof of the hotel, a dressing gown around her shoulders, was Anne Mallory. At last she had managed to climb the stairs, driven on by her dream of the sky. She stared sightlessly at the autogyro, stepping back a single pace only when it circled the hotel and came in to land through a storm of leaves and dust. When it touched down on the roof the draught from its propellers stripped the gown from her shoulders. Naked, she turned to face the autogyro, lover of this strange machine come to save her from a time-reft world.


## EIGHT


As they reached the NASA causeway huge columns of smoke were rising from the space centre. From the pillion seat of the motorcycle Mallory looked up at the billows boiling into the stained air. The forest was flushed with heat, the foliage glowing like furnace coals.

Had Hinton refuelled the Shuttle's engines and prepared the craft for lift-off? He would take Anne with him, and cast them both loose into space as he had done with Shepley, joining the dead astronaut in his orbital bier.

Smoke moved through the trees ahead of them, driven by the explosions coming from the launch site of the Shuttle. Gale throttled back the Yamaha and pointed to a break in the clouds. The Shuttle still sat on its platform, motors silent, the white hull reflecting the flash of explosions from the concrete runways.

Hinton had set fire to his antique planes. Thick with oily smoke, the flames lifted from the glowing shells slumped on their undercarts. The Curtiss biplane was burning briskly. A frantic blaze devoured the engine compartment of the Fokker, detonated the fuel tank and set off the machine-gun ammunition. The exploding cartridges kicked through the wings as they folded like a house of cards.

Gale steadied the Yamaha with her feet, and skirted the glowing trees 200 yards from the line of incandescent machines. The explosions flashed in her goggles, blanching her vivid make-up and giving her blonde hair an ash-like whiteness. The heat flared against Mallory's sallow face as he searched the aircraft for any sign of Hinton. Fanned by the flames that roared from its fuselage, the autogyro's propeller rotated swiftly, caught fire and spun in a last blazing carnival. Beside it, flames raced along the wings of the Wright Flyer; in a shower of sparks the burning craft lifted into the air and fell back upon the Sopwith Camel. Ignited by the intense heat, the primed engine of the Flying Flea roared into life, propelled the tiny aircraft in a scurrying arc among the burning wrecks, setting off the Spad and Blériot before it overturned in a furnace of rolling flame.

'Doctor – on the assembly deck!'

Mallory followed the girl's raised hand. A hundred feet above them, Anne and Hinton stood side by side on the metal landing of the stairway. The flames from the burning aircraft wavered against their faces, as if they were already moving through the air together. Although Hinton's hand was around Anne's waist, they seemed unaware of each other when they stepped forward into the light.

## NINE

As always during his last afternoons at Cocoa Beach, Mallory rested by the swimming pool of the abandoned hotel, watching the pale glider float patiently across the undisturbed skies of Cape Kennedy. In this peaceful arbour, surrounded by the drowsing inmates of the zoo, he listened to the fountain cast its crystal gems onto the grass beside his chair. The spray of water was now almost stationary, like the glider and the wind and the watching cheetahs, elements of an emblematic and glowing world.

As time slipped away from him, Mallory stood under the fountain, happy to see it transform itself into a glass tree that shed an opalescent fruit onto his shoulders and hands. Dolphins flew through the air over the nearby sea. Once he immersed himself in the pool, delighted to be embedded in this huge block of condensed time.

Fortunately, Gale Shepley had rescued him before he drowned. Mallory knew that she was becoming bored with him. She was intent now only on the search for her father, confident that he would soon be returning from the tideways of space. At night the trajectories were ever lower, tracks of charged particles that soared across the forest. She had almost ceased to eat, and Mallory was glad that once her father arrived she would at last give up her flying. Then the two of them would leave together.

Mallory had made his own preparations for departure. The key to the tiger cage he held always in his hand. There was little time left to him now, the light-filled world had transformed itself into a series of tableaux from a pageant that celebrated the founding days of creation. In the finale every element in the universe, however humble, would take its place on the stage in front of him.

He watched the tiger waiting for him at the bars of its cage. The great cats, like the reptiles before them, had always stood partly out of time. The flames that marked its pelt reminded him of the fire that had consumed the aircraft at the space centre, the fire through which Anne and Hinton still flew forever.

He left the pool and walked towards the tiger cage. He would unlock the door soon, embrace these flames, lie down with this beast in a world beyond time.

, **1982**

# · MYTHS OF THE NEAR FUTURE

At dusk Sheppard was still sitting in the cockpit of the stranded aircraft, unconcerned by the evening tide that advanced towards him across the beach. Already the first waves had reached the wheels of the Cessna, kicking spurs of spray against the fuselage. Tirelessly, the dark night-water sluiced its luminous foam at the Florida shoreline, as if trying to rouse the spectral tenants of the abandoned bars and motels.

But Sheppard sat calmly at the controls, thinking of his dead wife and all the drained swimming pools of Cocoa Beach, and of the strange nightclub he had glimpsed that afternoon through the forest canopy now covering the old Space Centre. Part Las Vegas casino with its flamboyant neon façade, and part Petit Trianon – a graceful classical pediment carried the chromium roof – it had suddenly materialized among the palms and tropical oaks, more unreal than any film set. As Sheppard soared past, only fifty feet above its mirrored roof, he had almost expected to see Marie Antoinette herself, in a Golden Nugget get-up, playing the milkmaid to an audience of uneasy alligators.

Before their divorce, oddly enough, Elaine had always enjoyed their weekend expeditions from Toronto to Algonquin Park, proudly roughing the wilderness in the high-chrome luxury of their Airstream trailer, as incongruous among the pine cones and silver birch as this latter-day fragment of a neon Versailles. All the same, the sight of the bizarre nightclub hidden deep in the Cape Kennedy forests, and the curious behaviour of its tenants, convinced Sheppard that Elaine was still alive, and very probably held prisoner by Philip Martinsen. The chromium nightclub, presumably built thirty years earlier by some classically minded Disneyland executive, would appeal to the young neurosurgeon's sense of the absurd, a suitably garish climax to the unhappy events that had brought them together in the sombre forests of the Florida peninsula.

However, Martinsen was devious enough to have picked the nightclub deliberately, part of his elaborate attempt to lure Sheppard into the open air. For weeks now he had been hanging around the deserted motels in Cocoa Beach, flying his kites and gliders, eager to talk to Sheppard but nervous of approaching the older man. From the safety of his darkened bedroom at the Starlight Motel – a huddle of dusty cabins on the coast road – Sheppard watched him through a crack in the double blinds. Every day Martinsen waited for Sheppard to appear, but was always careful to keep a drained swimming pool between them.

At first the young doctor's obsession with birds had irritated Sheppard – everything from the papier-mâché condor-kites hanging like corpses above the motel to endless Picasso doves chalked on the cabin doors while Sheppard slept. Even now, as he sat on the beach in the wave-washed Cessna, he could see the snake-headed profile cut in the wet sand, part of an enormous Aztec bird across which he had landed an hour earlier.

The birds . . . Elaine had referred to them in the last of her Florida letters, but those were creatures who soared inside her own head, far more exotic than anything a neurourgeon could devise, feathered and jewelled chimeras from the paradises of Gustave Moreau. None the less, Sheppard had finally taken the bait, accepting that Martinsen wanted to talk to him, and on his own terms. He forced himself from the motel, hiding behind the largest sunglasses he could find among the hundreds that littered the floor of the swimming pool, and drove to the light airfield at Titusville. For an hour he flew the rented Cessna across the forest canopy, searching the whole of Cape Kennedy for any sign of Martinsen and his kites.

Tempted to turn back, he soared to and fro above the abandoned space grounds, unsettling though they were, with their immense runways leading to no conceivable sky, and the rusting gantries like so many deaths propped up in their tattered coffins. Here at Cape Kennedy a small part of space had died. A rich emerald light glowed through the forest, as if from a huge lantern lit at the heart of the Space Centre. This resonant halo, perhaps the phosphorescence of some unusual fungi on the leaves and branches, was spreading outwards and already had reached the northern streets of Cocoa Beach and crossed the Indian River to Titusville. Even the ramshackle stores and houses vibrated in the same overlit way.

Around him the bright winds were like the open jaws of a crystal bird, the light flashing between its teeth. Sheppard clung to the safety of the jungle canopy, banking the Cessna among the huge flocks of flamingos and orioles that scattered out of his way. In Titusville a government patrol car moved down one of the few stretches of clear road, but no one else was tempted out of doors, the few inhabitants resting in their bedrooms as the forest climbed the Florida peninsula and closed around them.

Then, almost in the shadow of the Apollo 12 gantry, Sheppard had seen the nightclub. Startled by its neon façade, he stalled the Cessna. The wheels rattled the palm fronds as he throttled up a saving burst of speed and began a second circuit. The nightclub sat in a forest clearing beside a shallow inlet of the Banana River, near a crumbling camera blockhouse at the end of a concrete runway. The jungle pressed towards the nightclub on three sides, a gaudy aviary of parakeets and macaws, some long-vanished tycoon's weekend paradise.

As the birds hurtled past the windshield, Sheppard saw two figures running towards the forest, a bald-headed woman in the grey shroud of a hospital gown followed by a familiar dark-faced man with the firm step of a warder at a private prison. Despite her age, the woman fled lightly along the ground and seemed almost to be trying to fly. Confused by the noise of the Cessna, her white hands waved a distraught semaphore at the startled macaws, as if hoping to borrow their lurid plumage to cover her bare scalp.

Trying to recognize his wife in this deranged figure, Sheppard turned away for another circuit, and lost his bearings among the maze of inlets and concrete causeways that lay beneath the forest canopy. When he again picked out the nightclub he throttled back and soared in above the trees, only to find his glide-path blocked by a man-powered aircraft that had lifted into the air from the forest clearing.

Twice the size of the Cessna, this creaking cat's-cradle of plastic film and piano wire wavered to left and right in front of Sheppard, doing its best to distract him. Dazzled by his own propeller, Sheppard banked and overflew the glider, and caught a last glimpse of the dark-bearded Martinsen pedalling intently inside his transparent envelope, a desperate fish hung from the sky. Then the waiting bough of a forest oak clipped the Cessna as it overran its own slipstream. The sharp antlers stripped the fabric from the starboard wing and tore off the passenger door. Stunned by the roaring air, Sheppard limped the craft back to Cocoa Beach, and brought it down to a heavy landing on the wet sand within the diagram of the immense beaked raptor which Martinsen had carved for him that morning.

Waves washed into the open cabin of the Cessna, flicking a cold foam at Sheppard's ankles. Headlamps approached along the beach, and a government jeep raced down to the water's edge a hundred yards from the aircraft. The young driver stood against the windshield, shouting at Sheppard over her headlamps.

Sheppard released the harness, still reluctant to leave the Cessna. The night had come in from the sea, and now covered the shabby coastal town, but everything was still lit by that same luminescence he had glimpsed from the air, a flood of photons released from the pavilion in the forest where his wife was held prisoner. The waves that washed the propeller of the Cessna, the empty bars and motels along the beach, and the silent gantries of the Space Centre were decorated with millions of miniature lights, lode-points that marked the profiles of a new realm waiting to reconstitute itself around him. Thinking of the nightclub, Sheppard stared into the firefly darkness that enveloped Cape Kennedy. Already he suspected that this was a first glimpse of a small corner of the magnetic city, a suburb of the world beyond time that lay around and within him.

Holding its image to his mind, he forced the door against the flood and jumped down into the waist-deep water as the last of the night came in on the waves. In the glare of the jeep's headlamps he felt Anne Godwin's angry hands on his shoulders, and fell headlong into the water. Skirt floating around her hips, she pulled him like a drowned pilot on to the beach and held him to the warm sand as the sea rushed into the silver gullies of the great bird whose wings embraced them.

Yet, for all the confusions of the flight, at least he had been able to go outside. Three months earlier, when Sheppard arrived at Cocoa Beach, he had broken into the first motel he could find and locked himself for ever into the safety of a darkened bedroom. The journey from Toronto had been a succession of nightmare way-stations, long delays in semi-derelict bus depots and car-rental offices, queasy taxi-rides slumped in the rear seat behind two pairs of dark glasses, coat pulled over his head like a Victorian photographer nervous of his own lens. As he moved south into the steeper sunlight the landscapes of New Jersey, Virginia and the Carolinas seemed both lurid and opaque, the half-empty towns and uncrowded highways perceived on a pair of raw retinas inflamed by LSD. At times he seemed to be looking at the interior of the sun from a precarious gondola suspended at its core, through an air like fire-glass that might melt the dusty windows of his taxi.

Even Toronto, and his rapid decline after the divorce from Elaine, had not warned him of the real extent of his retreat behind his own nerve-endings. Surrounded by the deserted city, it surprised Sheppard that he was one of the last to be affected, this outwardly cool architect who concealed what was in fact a powerful empathy for other people's psychological ills. A secretary's headache would send him on a restless tour of the design offices. Often he felt that he himself had invented the dying world around him.

It was now twenty years since the earliest symptoms of this strange malaise – the so-called 'space sickness' – had made their appearance. At first touching only a small minority of the population, it took root like a lingering disease in the interstices of its victims' lives, in the slightest changes of habit and behaviour. Invariably there was the same reluctance to go out of doors, the abandonment of job, family and friends, a dislike of daylight, a gradual loss of weight and retreat into a hibernating self. As the illness became more widespread, affecting one in a hundred of the population, blame seemed to lie with the depletion of the ozone layer that had continued apace during the 1980s and 1990s. Perhaps the symptoms of world-shyness and withdrawal were no more than a self-protective response to the hazards of ultraviolet radiation, the psychological equivalent of the sunglasses worn by the blind.

But always there was the exaggerated response to sunlight, the erratic migraines and smarting corneas that hinted at the nervous origins of the malaise. There was the taste for wayward and compulsive hobbies, like the marking of obsessional words in a novel, the construction of pointless arithmetical puzzles on a pocket calculator, the collecting of fragments of TV programmes on a video recorder, and the hours spent playing back particular facial grimaces or shots of staircases.

It was another symptom of the 'space sickness', appearing in its terminal stages, that gave both its popular name and the first real clue to the disease. Almost without exception, the victims became convinced that they had once been astronauts. Thousands of the sufferers lay in their darkened hospital wards, or in the seedy bedrooms of back-street hotels, unaware of the world around them but certain that they had once travelled through space to Mars and Venus, walked beside Armstrong on the Moon. All of them, in their last seconds of consciousness, became calm and serene, and murmured like drowsy passengers at the start of a new voyage, their journey home to the sun.

Sheppard could remember Elaine's final retreat, and his last visit to the white-walled clinic beside the St Lawrence River. They had met only once in the two years since the divorce, and he had not been prepared for the transformation of this attractive and self-possessed dentist into a dreaming adolescent being dressed for her first dance. Elaine smiled brightly at him from her anonymous cot, a white hand trying to draw him on to her pillow.

'Roger, we're going soon. We're leaving together . . .'

As he walked away through the shadowy wards, listening to the babble of voices, the fragments of half-forgotten space jargon picked up from a hundred television serials, he had felt that the entire human race was beginning its embarkation, preparing to repatriate itself to the sun.

Sheppard recalled his last conversation with the young director of the clinic, and the weary physician's gesture of irritation, less with Sheppard than with himself and his profession.

'A *radical* approach? I assume you're thinking of something like resurrection?' Seeing the suspicious tic that jumped across Sheppard's cheek, Martinsen had taken him by the arm in a show of sympathy. 'I'm sorry – she was a remarkable woman. We talked for many hours, about you, much of the time . . .' His small face, as intense as an undernourished child's, was broken by a bleak smile.

Before Sheppard left the clinic the young physician showed him the photographs he had taken of Elaine sitting in a deck-chair on the staff lawn earlier that summer. The first hint of radiant good humour was already on her vivid lips, as if this saucy dentist had been quietly tasting her own laughing gas. Martinsen had clearly been most impressed by her.

But was he on the wrong track, like the whole of the medical profession? The ECT treatments and sensory deprivation, the partial lobotomies and hallucinatory drugs all seemed to miss the point. It was always best to take the mad on their own terms. What Elaine and the other victims were trying to do was to explore space, using their illness as an extreme metaphor with which to construct a space vehicle. The astronaut obsession was the key. It was curious how close the whole malaise was to the withdrawal symptoms shown by the original astronauts in the decades after the Apollo programme, the retreat into mysticism and silence. Could it be that travelling into outer space, even thinking about and watching it on television, was a forced evolutionary step with unforeseen consequences, the eating of a very special kind of forbidden fruit? Perhaps, for the central nervous system, space was not a linear structure at all, but a model for an advanced condition of time, a metaphor for eternity which they were wrong to try to grasp ...

Looking back, Sheppard realized that for years he had been waiting for the first symptoms of the malaise to affect him, that he was all too eager to be inducted into the great voyage towards the sun. During the months before the divorce he had carefully observed the characteristic signs – the loss of weight and appetite, his cavalier neglect of both staff and clients at his architect's practice, his growing reluctance to go out of doors, the allergic skin rashes that sprang up if he stood for even a few seconds in the open sunlight. He tagged along on Elaine's expeditions to Algonquin Park, and spent the entire weekends sealed inside the chromium womb of the Airstream, itself so like an astronaut's capsule.

Was Elaine trying to provoke him? She hated his forced absent-mindedness, his endless playing with bizarre clocks and architectural follies, and above all his interest in pornography. This sinister hobby had sprung out of his peculiar obsession with the surrealists, a school of painters which his entire education and cast of mind had previously closed to him. For some reason he found himself gazing for hours at reproductions of Chirico's Turin, with its empty colonnades and reversed perspectives, its omens of departure. Then there were Magritte's dislocations of time and space, his skies transformed into a series of rectilinear blocks, and Dali's biomorphic anatomies.

These last had led him to his obsession with pornography. Sitting in the darkened bedroom, blinds drawn against the festering sunlight that clung to the balconies of the condominium, he gazed all day at the video-recordings of Elaine at her dressing table and in the bathroom. Endlessly he played back the zooms and close-ups of her squatting on the bidet, drying herself on the edge of the bath, examining with a hopeful frown the geometry of her right breast. The magnified images of this huge hemisphere, its curvatures splayed between Sheppard's fingers, glowed against the walls and ceiling of the bedroom.

Eventually, even the tolerant Elaine had rebelled. 'Roger, what are you doing to yourself – and to me? You've turned this bedroom into a porno-cinema, with me as your star.' She held his face, compressing twenty years of affection into her desperate hands. 'For God's sake, see someone!'

But Sheppard already had. In the event, three months later, it was Elaine who had gone. At about the time that he closed his office and summarily sacked his exhausted staff, she packed her bags and stepped away into the doubtful safety of the bright sunlight.

Soon after, the space trauma recruited another passenger.

Sheppard had last seen her at Martinsen's clinic, but within only six months he received news of her remarkable recovery, no doubt one of those temporary remissions that sometimes freed the terminal cases from their hospital beds. Martinsen had abandoned his post at the clinic, against the open criticism of his colleagues and allegations of misconduct. He and Elaine had left Canada and moved south to the warm Florida winter, and were now living near the old Space Centre at Cape Kennedy. She was up and about, having miraculously shaken off the deep fugues.

At first Sheppard was sceptical, and guessed that the young neurosurgeon had become obsessed with Elaine and was trying some dangerous and radical treatment in a misguided attempt to save her. He imagined Martinsen abducting Elaine, lifting the drowsy but still beautiful woman from her hospital bed and carrying her out to his car, setting off for the harsh Florida light.

However, Elaine seemed well enough. During this period of apparent recovery she wrote several letters to Sheppard, describing the dark, jewelled beauty of the overgrown forest that surrounded their empty hotel, with its view over the Banana River and the rusting gantries of the abandoned Space Centre. Reading her final letter in the flinty light of the Toronto spring, it seemed to Sheppard that the whole of Florida was transforming itself for Elaine into a vast replica of the cavernous grottoes of Gustave Moreau, a realm of opalized palaces and heraldic animals.

'. . . I wish you could be here, Roger, this forest is filled with a deep marine light, almost as if the dark lagoons that once covered the Florida peninsula have come in from the past and submerged us again. There are strange creatures here that seem to have stepped off the surface of the sun. Looking out over the river this morning, I actually saw a unicorn walking on the water, its hooves shod in gold. Philip has moved my bed to the window, and I sit propped here all day, courting the birds, species I've never seen before that seem to have come from some extraordinary future. I feel sure now that I shall never leave here. Crossing the garden yesterday, I found that I was dressed in light, a sheath of golden scales that fell from my skin on to the glowing grass. The intense sunlight plays strange tricks with time and space. I'm really certain that there's a new kind of time here, flowing in some way from the old Space Centre. Every leaf and flower, even the pen in my hand and these lines I'm writing to you are surrounded by haloes of themselves.

Everything moves very slowly now, it seems to take all day for a bird to cross the sky, it begins as a shabby little sparrow and transforms itself into an extravagant creature as plumed and ribboned as a lyre-bird. I'm glad we came, even though Philip was attacked at the time. Coming here was my last chance, he claims, I remember him saying we should seize the light, not fear it. All the same, I think he's got more than he bargained for, he's very tired, poor boy. He's frightened of my falling asleep, he says that when I dream I try to turn into a bird. I woke up by the window this afternoon and he was holding me down, as if I were about to fly off for ever into the forest.

*I wish you were here, dear, it's a world the surrealists might have invented. I keep thinking that I will meet you somewhere . . .*

Attached to the letter was a note from Martinsen, telling him that Elaine had died the following day, and that at her request she had been buried in the forest near the Space Centre. The death certificate was counter-signed by the Canadian consul in Miami.

A week later Sheppard closed the Toronto apartment and set off for Cape Kennedy. During the past year he had waited impatiently for the malaise to affect him, ready to make his challenge. Like everyone else he rarely went out during the day, but through the window blinds the sight of this empty, sunlit city which came alive only at dusk drove Sheppard into all kinds of restless activity. He would go out into the noon glare and wander among the deserted office blocks, striking stylized poses in the silent curtain-walling. A few heavily cowled policemen and taxi-drivers watched him like spectres on a furnace floor. But Sheppard liked to play with his own obsessions. On impulse he would run around the apartment and release the blinds, turning the rooms into a series of white cubes, so many machines for creating a new kind of time and space.

Thinking of all that Elaine had said in her last letter, and determined as yet not to grieve for her, he set off eagerly on his journey south. Too excited to drive himself, and wary of the steeper sunlight, he moved by bus, rented limousine and taxi. Elaine had always been an accurate observer, and he was convinced that once he reached Florida he would soon rescue her from Martinsen and find respite for them both in the eternal quiet of the emerald forest.

In fact, he found only a shabby, derelict world of dust, drained swimming pools and silence. With the end of the Space Age thirty years earlier, the coastal towns near Cape Kennedy had been abandoned to the encroaching forest. Titusville, Cocoa Beach and the old launching grounds now constituted a psychic disaster area, a zone of ill omen. Lines of deserted bars and motels sat in the heat, their signs like rusty toys. Beside the handsome houses once owned by flight controllers and astrophysicists the empty swimming pools were a resting-place for dead insects and cracked sunglasses.

Shielded by the coat over his head, Sheppard paid off the uneasy cab driver. As he fumbled with his wallet the unlatched suitcase burst at his feet, exposing its contents to the driver's quizzical gaze: a framed reproduction of Magritte's *The March of Summer,* a portable video-cassette projector, two tins of soup, a well-thumbed set of six *Kamera Klassic* magazines, a clutch of cassettes labelled *Elaine/Shower Stall I–XXV,* and a paperback selection of Marey's *Chronograms.*

The driver nodded pensively. 'Samples? Exactly what is all that – a survival kit?'

'Of a special kind.' Unaware of any irony in the man's voice, Sheppard explained: 'They're the fusing device for a time-machine. I'll make one up for you . . .'

'Too late. My son . . .' With a half-smile, the driver wound up his tinted windows and set off for Tampa in a cloud of glassy dust.

Picking the Starlight Motel at random, Sheppard let himself into an intact cabin overlooking the drained pool, the only guest apart from the elderly retriever that dozed on the office steps. He sealed the blinds and spent the next two days resting in the darkness on the musty bed, the suitcase beside him, this 'survival kit' that would help him to find Elaine.

At dusk on the second day he left the bed and went to the window for his first careful look at Cocoa Beach. Through the plastic blinds he watched the shadows bisecting the empty pool, drawing a broken diagonal across the canted floor. He remembered his few words to the cab driver. The complex geometry of this three-dimensional sundial seemed to contain the operating codes of a primitive time-machine, repeated a hundred times in all the drained swimming pools of Cape Kennedy.

Surrounding the motel was the shabby coastal town, its derelict bars and stores shielded from the sub-tropical dusk by the flamingo-tinted parasols of the palm trees that sprang through the cracked roads and sidewalks. Beyond Cocoa Beach was the Space Centre, its rusting gantries like old wounds in the sky. Staring at them through the sandy glass, Sheppard was aware for the first time of the curious delusion that he had once been an astronaut, lying on his contour couch atop the huge booster, dressed in a suit of silver foil . . . An absurd idea, but the memory had come from somewhere. For all its fearfulness, the Space Centre was a magnetic zone.

But where was the visionary world which Elaine had described, filled with jewelled birds? The old golden retriever sleeping under the diving board would never walk the Banana River on golden hooves.

Although he rarely left the cabin during the day – the Florida sunlight was still far too strong for him to attempt a head-on confrontation – Sheppard forced himself to put together the elements of an organized life. First, he began to take more care of his own body. His weight had been falling for years, part of a long decline that he had never tried to reverse. Standing in front of the bathroom mirror, he stared at his unsavoury reflection – his wasted shoulders, sallow arms and inert hands, but a fanatic's face, unshaven skin stretched across the bony points of his jaw and cheeks, orbits like the entrances to forgotten tunnels from which gleamed two penetrating lights. Everyone carried an image of himself that was ten years out of date, but Sheppard felt that he was growing older and younger at the same time – his past and future selves had arranged a mysterious rendezvous in this motel bedroom.

Still, he forced down the cold soup. He needed to be strong enough to drive a car, map the forests and runways of Cape Kennedy, perhaps hire a light aircraft and carry out an aerial survey of the Space Centre.

At dusk, when the sky seemed to tilt and, thankfully, tipped its freight of cyclamen clouds into the Gulf of Mexico, Sheppard left the motel and foraged for food in the abandoned stores and supermarkets of Cocoa Beach. A few of the older townspeople lived on in the overgrown side-streets, and one bar was still open to the infrequent visitors. Derelicts slept in the rusting cars, and the occasional tramp wandered like a schizophrenic Crusoe among the wild palms and tamarinds. Long-retired engineers from the Space Centre, they hovered in their shabby whites by the deserted stores, forever hesitating to cross the shadowy streets.

As he carried a battery charger from an untended appliance store, Sheppard almost bumped into a former mission controller who had frequently appeared on television during the campaign to prevent the disbandment of NASA. With his dulled face, eyes crossed by the memories of forgotten trajectories, he resembled one of Chirico's mannequins, heads marked with mathematical formulae.

'No . . .' He wavered away, and grimaced at Sheppard, the wild fracture lines in his face forming the algebra of an unrealizable future. 'Another time . . . seventeen seconds . . .' He tottered off into the dusk, tapping the palm trees with one hand, preoccupied with this private countdown.

For the most part they kept to themselves, twilight guests of the abandoned motels where no rent would ever be charged and no memories ever be repaid. All of them avoided the government aid centre by the bus depot. This unit, staffed by a psychologist from Miami University and two graduate students, distributed food parcels and medicines to the aged townspeople asleep on their rotting porches. It was also their task to round up the itinerant derelicts and persuade them to enter the state-run hospice in Tampa.

On his third evening, as he looted the local supermarket, Sheppard became aware of this alert young psychologist watching him over the dusty windshield of her jeep.

'Do you need any help breaking the law?' She came over and peered into Sheppard's carton. 'I'm Anne Godwin, hello. Avocado purée, rice pudding, anchovies, you're all set for a midnight feast. But what about a filet steak, you really look as if you could use one?'

Sheppard tried to sidestep out of her way. 'Nothing to worry about. I'm here on a working vacation . . . a scientific project.'

She eyed him shrewdly. 'Just another summer visitor – though you all have PhDs, the remittance men of the Space Age. Where are you staying? We'll drive you back.'

As Sheppard struggled with the heavy carton she signalled to the graduate students, who strolled across the shadowy pavement. At that moment a rusty Chevrolet turned into the street, a bearded man in a soft hat at the wheel. Blocked by the jeep, he stopped to reverse the heavy sedan, and Sheppard recognized the young physician he had last seen on the steps of the clinic overlooking the St Lawrence.

'Dr Martinsen!' Anne Godwin shouted as she released Sheppard's arm.

'I've been wanting to talk to you, doctor. Wait . . . ! That prescription you gave me, I take it you've reached the menopause –'

Punching the locked gear shift, Martinsen seemed only interested in avoiding Anne Godwin and her questions. Then he saw Sheppard's alert eyes staring at him above the carton. He paused, and gazed back at Sheppard, with the frank and almost impatient expression of an old friend who had long since come to terms with an act of treachery. He had grown his beard, as if to hide some disease of the mouth or jaw, but his face seemed almost adolescent and at the same time aged by some strange fever.

'Doctor . . . I've reported –' Anne Godwin reached Martinsen's car. He made a half-hearted attempt to hide a loosely tied bundle of brass curtain-rods on the seat beside him. Was he planning to hang the forest with priceless fabrics? Before Sheppard could ask, Martinsen engaged his gear lever and sped off, clipping Anne Godwin's outstretched hand with his wing-mirror.

But at least he knew now that Martinsen was here, and their brief meeting allowed Sheppard to slip away unobserved from Anne Godwin. Followed by the doddery retriever, Sheppard carried his stores back to the motel, and the two of them enjoyed a tasty snack in the darkness beside the drained swimming pool.

Already he felt stronger, confident that he would soon have tracked down Martinsen and rescued Elaine. For the next week he slept during the mornings and spent the afternoons repairing the old Plymouth he had commandeered from a local garage.

As he guessed, Martinsen soon put in another appearance. A small, bird-shaped kite began a series of regular flights in the sky above Cocoa Beach. Its silver line disappeared into the forest somewhere to the north of the town. Two others followed it into the air, and the trio swayed across the placid sky, flown by some enthusiast in the forest.

In the days that followed, other bird-emblems began to appear in the streets of Cocoa Beach, crude Picasso doves chalked on the boarded store-fronts, on the dusty roofs of the cars, in the leafy slime on the drained floor of the Starlight pool, all of them presumably cryptic messages from Martinsen.

So the neurosurgeon was trying to lure him into the forest? Finally giving in to his curiosity, Sheppard drove late one afternoon to the light airfield at Titusville. Little traffic visited the shabby airstrip, and a retired commercial pilot dozed in his dusty office below a sign advertising pleasure trips around the Cape.

After a brief haggle, Sheppard rented a single-engined Cessna and took off into the softening dusk. He carried out a careful reconnaissance of the old Space Centre, and at last saw the strange nightclub in the forest, and caught a painful glimpse of the weird, bald-headed spectre racing through the trees. Then Martinsen sprang his surprise with the man-powered glider, clearly intending to ambush Sheppard and force him to crash-land

the Cessna into the jungle. However, Sheppard escaped, and limped back
to Cocoa Beach and the incoming tide. Anne Godwin virtually dragged
him from the swamped plane, but he managed to pacify her and slip
away to the motel.

That evening he rested in his chair beside the empty pool, watching
the video-cassettes of his wife projected on to the wall at the deep
end. Somewhere in these intimate conjunctions of flesh and geometry,
of memory, tenderness and desire, was a key to the vivid air, to that new
time and space which the first astronauts had unwittingly revealed here
at Cape Kennedy, and which he himself had glimpsed that evening from
the cockpit of the drowned aircraft.

At dawn Sheppard fell asleep, only to be woken two hours later by a
sudden shift of light in the darkened bedroom. A miniature eclipse of the
sun was taking place. The light flickered, trembling against the window.
Lying on the bed, Sheppard saw the profile of a woman's face and plumed
hair projected on to the plastic blinds.

Bracing himself against the eager morning sunlight, and any unpleasant
phobic rush, Sheppard eased the blinds apart. Two hundred feet away,
suspended above the chairs on the far side of the swimming pool, a large
man-carrying kite hung in the air. The painted figure of a winged woman
was silhouetted against the sun's disc, arms outstretched across the canvas
panels. Her shadow tapped the plastic blinds, only inches from Sheppard's
fingers, as if asking to be let into the safety of the darkened bedroom.

Was Martinsen offering him a lift in this giant kite? Eyes shielded behind
his heaviest sunglasses, Sheppard left the cabin and made his way around
the drained pool. It was time now to make a modest challenge to the sun.
The kite hung above him, flapping faintly, its silver wire disappearing
behind a boat-house half a mile along the beach.

Confident of himself, Sheppard set off along the beach road. During
the night the Cessna had vanished, swept away by the sea. Behind the
boat-house the kite-flier was winding in his huge craft, and the woman's
shadow kept Sheppard company, the feathered train of her hair at his
feet. Already he was sure that he would find Martinsen among the derelict
speedboats, ravelling in whatever ambiguous message he had sent up into
the fierce air.

Almost tripping over the woman's shadow, Sheppard paused to gaze
around him. After so many weeks and months of avoiding the daylight,
he felt uncertain of the overlit perspectives, of the sea lapping at the edges
of his mind, its tongues flicking across the beach like some treacherous
animal's. Ignoring it, he ran along the road. The kite-flier had vanished,
slipping away into the palm-filled streets.

Sheppard threw away his sunglasses and looked up into the air. He
was surprised that the sky was far closer to him than he remembered. It
seemed almost vertical, constructed of cubicular blocks a mile in width,
the wall of an immense inverted pyramid.

The waves pressed themselves into the wet sand at his feet, flattering courtiers in this palace of light. The beach seemed to tilt, the road reversed its camber. He stopped to steady himself against the roof of an abandoned car. His retinas smarted, stung by thousands of needles. A feverish glitter rose from the roofs of the bars and motels, from the rusty neon signs and the flinty dust at his feet, as if the whole landscape was at the point of ignition.

The boat-house swayed towards him, its roof tilting from side to side. Its cavernous doors opened abruptly, like the walls of an empty mountain. Sheppard stepped back, for a moment blinded by the darkness, as the figure of a winged man burst from the shadows and raced past him across the sand towards the safety of the nearby forest. Sheppard saw a bearded face under the feathered head-dress, canvas wings on a wooden frame attached to the man's arms. Waving them up and down like an eccentric aviator, he sprinted between the trees, hindered more than helped by his clumsy wings, one of which sheared from his shoulder when he trapped himself among the palms. He vanished into the forest, still leaping up and down in an attempt to gain the air with his one wing.

Too surprised to laugh at Martinsen, Sheppard ran after him. He followed the line of metal thread that unravelled behind the neurosurgeon. The man-carrying kite had collapsed across the roof of a nearby drugstore, but Sheppard ignored it and ran on through the narrow streets. The line came to an end under the rear wheel of an abandoned truck, but he had already lost Martinsen.

On all sides were the bird-signs, chalked up on the fences and tree-trunks, hundreds of them forming a threatening aviary, as if Martinsen was trying to intimidate the original tenants of the forest and drive them away from the Cape. Sheppard sat on the running-board of the truck, holding the broken end of the kite-line between his fingers.

Why was Martinsen wearing his ludicrous wings, trying to turn himself into a bird? At the end of the road he had even constructed a crude bird-trap, large enough to take a condor or a small winged man, a cage the size of a garden shed tilted back on a trip-balance of bamboo sticks.

Shielding his eyes from the glare, Sheppard climbed on to the bonnet of the truck and took his bearings. He had entered an unfamiliar part of Cocoa Beach, a maze of roads invaded by the forest. He was well within that zone of vibrant light he had seen from the Cessna, the dim lantern that seemed to extend outwards from the Space Centre, illuminating everything it touched. The light was deeper but more resonant, as if every leaf and flower were a window into a furnace.

Facing him, along the line of shabby bars and stores, was a curious laundromat. Sandwiched between a boarded-up appliance store and a derelict cafeteria, it resembled a miniature temple, with a roof of gilded tiles, chromium doors and windows of finely etched glass. The whole structure was suffused with a deep interior light, like some lamp-lit grotto in a street of shrines.

The same bizarre architecture was repeated in the nearby roads that lost themselves in the forest. A dry-goods store, a filling station and a car-wash glittered in the sunlight, apparently designed for some group of visiting space enthusiasts from Bangkok or Las Vegas. Overgrown by the tamarinds and Spanish moss, the gilded turrets and metalled windows formed a jewelled suburb in the forest.

Giving up his search for Martinsen, who by now could be hiding atop one of the Apollo gantries, Sheppard decided to return to his motel. He felt exhausted, as if his body were swathed in a heavy armour. He entered the pavilion beside the cafeteria, smiling at the extravagant interior of this modest laundromat. The washing machines sat within bowers of ironwork and gilded glass, a series of side-chapels set aside for the worship of the space engineers' overalls and denims.

A ruby light glimmered around Sheppard, as if the pavilion were vibrating above a mild ground-quake. Sheppard touched the glassy wall with one hand, surprised to find that his palm seemed to merge with the surface, as if both were images being projected on to a screen. His fingers trembled, a hundred outlines superimposed upon one another. His feet drummed against the floor, sending the same rapid eddies through his legs and hips, as if he were being transformed into a holographic image, an infinity of replicas of himself. In the mirror above the cashier's metal desk, now a Byzantine throne, he glowed like an archangel. He picked up a glass paperweight from the desk, a tremulous jewel of vibrating coral that suddenly flushed within its own red sea. The ruby light that radiated from every surface within the laundromat was charged by his own bloodstream as it merged into the flicker of multiplying images.

Staring at his translucent hands, Sheppard left the pavilion and set off along the street through the intense sunlight. Beyond the tilting fences he could see the drained swimming pools of Cocoa Beach, each a complex geometry of light and shadow, canted decks encoding the secret entrances to another dimension. He had entered a city of yantras, cosmic dials sunk into the earth outside each house and motel for the benefit of devout time-travellers.

The streets were deserted, but behind him he heard a familiar laboured pad. The old retriever plodded along the sidewalk, its coat shedding a tremulous golden fur. Sheppard stared at it, for a moment certain that he was seeing the unicorn Elaine had described in her last letter. He looked down at his wrists, at his incandescent fingers. The sun was annealing plates of copper light to his skin, dressing his arms and shoulders in a coronation armour. Time was condensing around him, a thousand replicas of himself from the past and future had invaded the present and clasped themselves to him.

Wings of light hung from his shoulders, feathered into a golden plumage drawn from the sun, the reborn ghosts of his once and future selves, conscripted to join him here in the streets of Cocoa Beach.

Startled by Sheppard, an old woman stared at him from the door of a shack beside the boat-house. Brittle hands felt her blue-rinsed hair, she found herself transformed from a shabby crone into a powdered beauty from the forgotten Versailles of her youth, her thousand younger selves from every day of her life gladly recruited to her side, flushing her withered cheeks and warming her stick-like hands. Her elderly husband gazed at her from his rocker chair, recognizing her for the first time in decades, himself transformed into a conquistador half-asleep beside a magical sea.

Sheppard waved to them, and to the tramps and derelicts emerging into the sunlight from their cabins and motel rooms, drowsy angels each awaking to his own youth. The flow of light through the air had begun to slow, layers of time overlaid each other, laminae of past and future fused together. Soon the tide of photons would be still, space and time would set forever.

Eager to become part of this magnetic world, Sheppard raised his wings and turned to face the sun.

'Were you trying to fly?'

Sheppard sat against the wall beside his bed, arms held tight like crippled wings around his knees. Near by in the darkened bedroom were the familiar pieces of furniture, the Marey and Magritte reproductions pinned to the dressing-table mirror, the projector ready to screen its black coil of film on to the wall above his head.

Yet the room seemed strange, a cabin allocated to him aboard a mysterious liner, with this concerned young psychologist sitting at the foot of the bed. He remembered her jeep in the dusty road, the loudhailer blaring at the elderly couple and the other derelicts as they were all about to rise into the air, a flight of angels. Suddenly a humdrum world had returned, his past and future selves had fled from him, he found himself standing in a street of shabby bars and shacks, a scarecrow with an old dog. Stunned, the tramps and the old couple had pinched their dry cheeks and faded back to their dark bedrooms.

So this was present time. Without realizing it, he had spent all his life in this grey, teased-out zone. However, he still held the paperweight in his hand. Though inert now, raised to the light it began to glow again, summoning its brief past and limitless future to its own side.

Sheppard smiled at himself, remembering the translucent wings – an illusion, of course, a blur of multiple selves that shimmered from his arms and shoulders, like an immense electric plumage. But perhaps at some time in the future he became a winged man, a glass bird ready to be snared by Martinsen? He saw himself caged in the condor-traps, dreaming of the sun . . .

Anne Godwin was shaking her head to herself. She had turned from Sheppard and was examining with evident distaste the pornographic photographs pinned to the wardrobe doors. The glossy prints were overlaid by geometric diagrams which this strange tenant of the motel had pencilled across the copulating women, a secondary anatomy.

'So this is your laboratory? We've been watching you for days. Who are you, anyway?'

Sheppard looked up from his wrists, remembering the golden fluid that had coursed through the now sombre veins.

'Roger Sheppard.' On an impulse he added: 'I'm an astronaut.'

'Really?' Like a concerned nurse, she sat on the edge of the bed, tempted to touch Sheppard's forehead. 'It's surprising how many of you come to Cape Kennedy – bearing in mind that the space programme ended thirty years ago.'

'It hasn't ended.' Quietly, Sheppard did his best to correct this attractive but confused young woman. He wanted her to leave, but already he saw that she might be useful. Besides, he was keen to help her, and set her free from this grey world. 'In fact, there are thousands of people involved in a new programme – we're at the beginnings of the first true Space Age.'

'Not the second? So the Apollo flights were . . . ?'

'Misconceived.' Sheppard gestured at the Marey chronograms on the dressing-table mirror, the blurred time-lapse photos so like the images he had seen of himself before Anne Godwin's arrival. 'Space exploration is a branch of applied geometry, with many affinities to pornography.'

'That sounds sinister.' She gave a small shudder. 'These photographs of yours look like the recipe for a special kind of madness. You shouldn't go out during the day. Sunlight inflames the eyes – and the mind.'

Sheppard pressed his face against the cool wall, wondering how to get rid of this over-concerned young psychologist. His eyes ran along the sills of light between the plastic blinds. He no longer feared the sun, and was eager to get away from this dark room. His real self belonged to the bright world outside. Sitting here, he felt like a static image in a single frame hanging from the coil of film in the projector on the bedside table. There was a sense of stop-frame about the whole of his past life – his childhood and schooldays, McGill and Cambridge, the junior partnership in Vancouver, his courtship of Elaine, together seemed like so many clips run at the wrong speed. The dreams and ambitions of everyday life, the small hopes and failures, were attempts to bring these separated elements into a single whole again. Emotions were the stress lines in this over-stretched web of events.

'Are you all right? Poor man, can't you breathe?'

Sheppard became aware of Anne Godwin's hand on his shoulder. He had clenched his fingers so tightly around the paperweight that his fist was white. He relaxed his grip and showed her the glassy flower.

Casually, he said: 'There's some curious architecture here – filling stations and laundromats like Siamese temples. Have you seen them?'

She avoided his gaze. 'Yes, to the north of Cocoa Beach. But I keep away from there.' She added reluctantly: 'There's a strange light by the Space Centre, one doesn't know whether to believe one's eyes.' She weighed the flower in her small hand, the fingers still bruised by Martinsen's wing-mirror. 'That's where you found this? It's like a fossil of the future.'

'It is.' Sheppard reached out and took it back. He needed the security of the piece, it reminded him of the luminous world from which this young woman had disturbed him. Perhaps she would join him there? He looked up at her strong forehead and high-bridged nose, a cut-prow that could outstare the time-winds, and at her broad shoulders, strong enough to bear a gilded plumage. He felt a sudden urge to examine her, star her in a new video film, explore the planes of her body like a pilot touching the ailerons and fuselage of an unfamiliar aircraft.

He stood up and stepped to the wardrobe. Without thinking, he began to compare the naked figure of his wife with the anatomy of the young woman sitting on his bed, the contours of her breasts and thighs, the triangles of her neck and pubis.

'Look, do you mind?' She stood between Sheppard and the photographs. 'I'm not going to be annexed into this experiment of yours. Anyway, the police are coming to search for that aircraft. Now, what is all this?'

'I'm sorry.' Sheppard caught himself. Modestly, he pointed to the elements of his 'kit', the film strips, chronograms and pornographic photos, the Magritte reproduction. 'It's a machine, of a kind. A time-machine. It's powered by that empty swimming pool outside. I'm trying to construct a metaphor to bring my wife back to life.'

'Your wife – when did she die?'

'Three months ago. But she's here, in the forest, somewhere near the Space Centre. That was her doctor you saw the other evening, he's trying to turn into a bird.' Before Anne Godwin could protest Sheppard took her arm and beckoned her to the door of the cabin. 'Come on, I'll show you how the pool works. Don't worry, you'll be outside for only ten minutes – we've all been too frightened of the sun.'

She held his elbow when they reached the edge of the empty pool, her face beginning to fret in the harsh light. The floor of the pool was strewn with leaves and discarded sunglasses, in which the diagram of a bird was clearly visible.

Sheppard breathed freely in the gold-lit air. There were no kites in the sky, but to the north of Cocoa Beach he could see the man-powered aircraft circling the forest, its flimsy wings floating on the thermals. He climbed down the chromium ladder into the shallow end of the pool, then helped the nervous young woman after him.

'This is the key to it all,' he explained, as she watched him intently, eyes shielded from the terrifying glare. He felt almost light-headed as he gestured proudly at the angular geometry of white tile and shadow. 'It's an engine, Anne, of a unique type. It's no coincidence that the Space Centre is surrounded by empty swimming pools.' Aware of a sudden intimacy with this young psychologist, and certain that she would not report him to the police, he decided to take her into his confidence. As they walked down the inclined floor to the deep end he held her shoulders. Below their feet cracked the black lenses of dozens of discarded sunglasses, some of the thousands thrown into the drained swimming pools of Cocoa Beach like coins into a Roman fountain.

'Anne, there's a door out of this pool, I'm trying to find it, a side-door for all of us to escape through. This space sickness – it's really about time, not space, like all the Apollo flights. We think of it as a kind of madness, but in fact it may be part of a contingency plan laid down millions of years ago, a real space programme, a chance to escape into a world beyond time. Thirty years ago we opened a door in the universe . . .'

He was sitting on the floor of the drained pool among the broken sunglasses, his back to the high wall of the deep end, talking rapidly to himself as Anne Godwin ran up the sloping floor for the medical valise in her jeep. In his white hands he held the glass paperweight, his blood and the sun charging the flower into a red blaze.

Later, as he rested with her in his bedroom at the motel, and during their days together in the coming week, Sheppard explained to her his attempt to rescue his wife, to find a key to everything going on around them.

'Anne, throw away your watch. Fling back the blinds. Think of the universe as a simultaneous structure. Everything that's ever happened, all the events that *will* ever happen, are taking place together. We can die, and yet still live, at the same time. Our sense of our own identity, the stream of things going on around us, are a kind of optical illusion. Our eyes are too close together. Those strange temples in the forest, the marvellous birds and animals – you've seen them too. We've all got to embrace the sun, I want your children to live here, and Elaine . . .'

'Roger –' Anne moved his hands from her left breast. For minutes, as he spoke, Sheppard had been obsessively feeling its curvatures, like a thief trying to crack a safe. She stared at the naked body of this obsessive man, the white skin alternating at the elbows and neck with areas of black sunburn, a geometry of light and shade as ambiguous as that of the drained swimming pool.

'Roger, she died three months ago. You showed me a copy of the death certificate.'

'Yes, she died,' Sheppard agreed. 'But only in a sense. She's here, somewhere, in the total time. No one who has ever lived can ever really die. I'm going to find her, I know she's waiting here for me to bring her back to life . . .' He gestured modestly to the photographs around the bedroom. 'It may not look much, but this is a metaphor that's going to work.'

During that week, Anne Godwin did her best to help Sheppard construct his 'machine'. All day she submitted to the Polaroid camera, to the films of her body which Sheppard projected on to the wall above the bed, to the endless pornographic positions in which she arranged her thighs and pubis. Sheppard gazed for hours through his stop-frame focus, as if he would find among these images an anatomical door, one of the keys in a combination whose other tumblers were the Marey chronograms, the surrealist paintings and the drained swimming pool in the ever-brighter sunlight outside. In the evenings Sheppard would take her out into the dusk and pose her beside the empty pool, naked from the waist, a dream-woman in a Delvaux landscape.

Meanwhile, Sheppard's duel with Martinsen continued in the skies above Cape Kennedy. After a storm the drowned Cessna was washed up on to the beach, sections of the wing and tailplane, parts of the cabin and undercarriage. The reappearance of the aircraft drove both men into a frenzy of activity. The bird motifs multiplied around the streets of Cocoa Beach, aerosolled on to the flaking storefronts. The outlines of giant birds covered the beach, their talons gripping the fragments of the Cessna.

And all the while the light continued to grow brighter, radiating outwards from the gantries of the Space Centre, inflaming the trees and flowers and paving the dusty sidewalks with a carpet of diamonds. For Anne, this sinister halo that lay over Cocoa Beach seemed to try to sear itself into her retinas. Nervous of windows, she submitted herself to Sheppard during these last days. It was only when he tried to suffocate her, in a confused attempt to release her past and future selves from their prison, that she escaped from the motel and set off for the sheriff at Titusville.

As the siren of the police car faded through the forest, Sheppard rested against the steering wheel of the Plymouth. He had reached the old NASA causeway across the Banana River, barely in time to turn off on to a disused slip road. He unclenched his fists, uneasily aware that his hands still stung from his struggle with Anne Godwin. If only he had been given more time to warn the young woman that he was trying to help her, to free her from that transient, time-locked flesh he had caressed so affectionately.

Restarting the engine, Sheppard drove along the slip road, already an uneven jungle path. Here on Merrit Island, almost within the sweeping shadows of the great gantries, the forest seemed ablaze with light, a submarine world in which each leaf and branch hung weightlessly around him. Relics of the first Space Age emerged from the undergrowth like overlit ghosts – a spherical fuel tank stitched into a jacket of flowering lianas, rocket launchers collapsed at the feet of derelict gantries, an immense tracked vehicle six storeys high like an iron hotel, whose unwound treads formed two notched metal roads through the forest.

Six hundred yards ahead, when the path petered out below a collapsed palisade of palm trunks, Sheppard switched off the engine and stepped from the car. Now that he was well within the perimeter of the Space Centre he found that the process of time-fusion was even more advanced. The rotting palms lay beside him, but alive again, the rich scrolls of their bark bright with the jade years of youth, glowing with the copper hues of their forest maturity, elegant in the grey marquetry of their declining age.

Through a break in the canopy Sheppard saw the Apollo 12 gantry rising through the high oaks like the blade of a giant sundial. Its shadow lay across a silver inlet of the Banana River. Remembering his flight in the Cessna, Sheppard estimated that the nightclub was little more than a mile to the north-west. He set off on foot through the forest, stepping from one log to the next, avoiding the curtains of Spanish moss that hung out their beguiling frescoes. He crossed a small glade beside a shallow stream, where a large alligator basked contentedly in a glow of self-generated light, smiling to itself as its golden jaws nuzzled its past and future selves. Vivid ferns sprang from the damp humus, ornate leaves stamped from foil, layer upon layer of copper and verdigris annealed together. Even the modest ground-ivy seemed to have glutted itself on the corpses of long-vanished astronauts. This was a world nourished by time.

Bird-signs marked the trees, Picasso doves scrawled on every trunk as if some over-worked removal manager was preparing the entire forest for flight. There were huge traps, set out in the narrow clearings and clearly designed to snare a prey other than birds. Standing by one of the trip-balanced hutches, Sheppard noticed that they all pointed towards the Apollo gantries. So Martinsen was now frightened, not of Sheppard, but of some aerial creature about to emerge from the heart of the Space Centre.

Sheppard tossed a loose branch on to the sensitive balance of the trap. There was a flicker of sprung bamboo, and the heavy hutch fell to the ground in a cloud of leaves, sending a glimmer of light reverberating among the trees. Almost at once there was a flurry of activity from a copse of glowing palmettos a hundred yards away. As Sheppard waited, hidden behind the trap, a running figure approached, a bearded man in a ragged bird costume, half-Crusoe, half-Indian brave, bright macaw feathers tied to his wrists and an aviator's goggles on his forehead.

He raced up to the trap and stared at it in a distraught way. Relieved to find it empty, he brushed the tattered feathers from his eyes and peered at the canopy overhead, as if expecting to see his quarry perched on a nearby branch.

'Elaine . . . !'

Martinsen's cry was a pathetic moan. Unsure how to calm the neurosurgeon, Sheppard stood up.

'Elaine isn't here, doctor –'

Martinsen flinched back, his bearded face as small as a child's. He stared at Sheppard, barely managing to control himself. His eyes roved across the glowing ground and foliage, and he flicked nervously at the blurred edges of his fingers, clearly terrified of these ghosts of his other selves now clinging to him. He gestured warningly to Sheppard, pointing to the multiple outlines of his arms and legs that formed a glowing armour.

'Sheppard, keep moving. I heard a noise – have you seen Elaine?'

'She's dead, doctor.'

'Even the dead can dream!' Martinsen nodded to Sheppard, his body shaking as if with fever. He pointed to the bird-traps. 'She dreams of flying. I've put these here, to catch her if she tries to escape.'

'Doctor ...' Sheppard approached the exhausted physician. 'Let her fly, if she wants to, let her dream. And let her *wake* ...'

'Sheppard!' Martinsen stepped back, appalled by Sheppard's electric hand raised towards him. 'She's trying to come back from the dead!'

Before Sheppard could reach him, the neurosurgeon turned away. He smoothed his feathers and darted through the palms, and with a hoot of pain and anger disappeared into the forest.

Sheppard let him go. He knew now why Martinsen had flown his kites, and filled the forest with the images of birds. He had been preparing the whole of the Space Centre for Elaine, transforming the jungle into an aviary where she might be at home. Terrified by the sight of this apparently winged woman waking from her deathbed, he hoped that somehow he could keep her within the magical realm of the Cape Kennedy forest.

Leaving the traps, Sheppard set off through the trees, his eyes fixed on the great gantries now only a few hundred yards away. He could feel the time-winds playing on his skin, annealing his other selves on to his arms and shoulders, the transformation of himself once again into that angelic being who strode through the shabby streets of Cocoa Beach. He crossed a concrete runway and entered an area of deeper forest, an emerald world furnished with extravagant frescoes, a palace without walls.

He had almost ceased to breathe. Here, at the centre of the space grounds, he could feel time rapidly engorging itself. The infinite pasts and future of the forest had fused together. A long-tailed parakeet paused among the branches over his head, an electric emblem of itself more magnificent than a peacock. A jewelled snake hung from a bough, gathering to it all the embroidered skins it had once shed.

An inlet of the Banana River slid through the trees, a silver tongue lying passively at his feet. On the bank fifty yards away was the nightclub he had seen from the Cessna, its luminous façade glowing against the foliage.

Sheppard hesitated by the water's edge, and then stepped on to its hard surface. He felt the brittle corrugations under his feet, as if he were walking across a floor of frosted glass. Without time, nothing could disturb the water. On the quartz-like grass below the nightclub a flock of orioles had begun to rise from the ground. They hung silently in the air, their golden fans lit by the sun.

Sheppard stepped ashore and walked up the slope towards them. A giant butterfly spread its harlequin wings against the air, halted in midflight. Avoiding it, Sheppard strode towards the entrance to the nightclub, where the man-powered glider sat on the grass, its propeller a bright sword. An unfamiliar bird crouched on the canopy, a rare species of quetzal or toucan, only recently a modest starling. It stared at its prey, a small lizard sitting on the steps, now a confident iguana armoured within all its selves. Like everything in the forest, both had become ornamental creatures drained of malice.

Through the crystal doors Sheppard peered into the glowing bower of the nightclub. Already he could see that this exotic pavilion had once been no more than a park-keeper's lodge, some bird-watcher's weekend hide transformed by the light of its gathering identities into this miniature casino. The magic casements revealed a small but opulent chamber, a circle of well-upholstered electric chairs beside a kitchen like the side-chapel of a chromium cathedral. Along the rear wall was a set of disused cages left here years earlier by a local ornithologist.

Sheppard unlatched the doors and stepped into the airless interior. A musty and unpleasant odour hung around him, not the spoor of birds but of some unclaimed carcass stored too long in the sun.

Behind the kitchen, and partly hidden in the shadows thrown by the heavy curtains, was a large cage of polished brass rods. It stood on a narrow platform, with a velvet drape across one end, as if some distracted conjuror had been about to perform an elaborate trick involving his assistant and a flock of doves.

Sheppard crossed the chamber, careful not to touch the glowing chairs. The cage enclosed a narrow hospital cot, its side-panels raised and tightly bolted. Lying on its bare mattress was an elderly woman in a bathrobe. She stared with weak eyes at the bars above her face, hair hidden inside a white towel wrapped securely around her forehead. One arthritic hand had seized the pillow, so that her chin jutted forward like a chisel. Her mouth was open in a dead gape, an ugly rictus that exposed her surprisingly even teeth.

Looking down at the waxy skin of this once familiar face, a part of his life for so many years, Sheppard at first thought that he was looking at the corpse of his mother. But as he pulled back the velvet drape the sunlight touched the porcelain caps of her teeth.

'Elaine . . .'

Already he accepted that she was dead, that he had come too late to this makeshift mausoleum where the grieving Martinsen had kept her body, locking it into this cage while he tried to draw Sheppard into the forest.

He reached through the bars and touched her forehead. His nervous hand dislodged the towel, exposing her bald scalp. But before he could replace the grey skull-cloth he felt something seize his wrist. Her right hand, a clutch of knobbly sticks from which all feeling had long expired, moved and took his own. Her weak eyes stared calmly at Sheppard, recognizing this young husband without any surprise. Her blanched lips moved across her teeth, testing the polished cusps, as if she were cautiously identifying herself.

'Elaine . . . I've come. I'll take you –' Trying to warm her hand, Sheppard felt an enormous sense of relief, knowing that all the pain and uncertainty of the past months, his search for the secret door, had been worthwhile. He felt a race of affection for his wife, a need to give way to all the stored emotions he had been unable to express since her death. There were a thousand and one things to tell her, about his plans for the future, his uneven health and, above all, his long quest for her across the drained swimming pools of Cape Kennedy.

He could see the glider outside, the strange bird that guarded the now glowing cockpit, a halo in which they could fly away together. He fumbled with the door to the cage, confused by the almost funereal glimmer that had begun to emanate from Elaine's body. But as she stirred and touched her face, a warm light suffused her grey skin. Her face was softening, the bony points of her forehead retreated into the smooth temples, her mouth lost its death-grimace and became the bright bow of the young student he had first seen twenty years ago, smiling at him across the tennis club pool. She was a child again, her parched body flushed and irrigated by her previous selves, a lively schoolgirl animated by the images of her past and future.

She sat up, strong fingers releasing the death-cap around her head, and shook loose the damp tresses of silver hair. She reached her hands towards Sheppard, trying to embrace her husband through the bars. Already her arms and shoulders were sheathed in light, that electric plumage which he now wore himself, winged lover of this winged woman.

As he unlocked the cage, Sheppard saw the pavilion doors open to the sun. Martinsen stood in the entrance, staring at the bright air with the toneless expression of a sleepwalker woken from a dark dream. He had shed his feathers, and his body was now dressed in a dozen glimmering images of himself, refractions of past and present seen through the prism of time.

He gestured to Sheppard, trying to warn him away from his wife. Sheppard was certain now that the physician had been given a glimpse into the dream-time, as he mourned Elaine in the hours after her death. He had seen her come alive from the dead, as the images of her past and youth came to her rescue, drawn here by the unseen powers of the Space Centre. He feared the open cage, and the spectre of this winged woman rising from her dreams at the grave's edge, summoning the legion of her past selves to resurrect her.

Confident that Martinsen would soon understand, Sheppard embraced his wife and lifted her from the bed, eager to let this young woman escape into the sunlight.

Could all this have been waiting for them, around the unseen corners of their past lives? Sheppard stood by the pavilion, looking out at the silent world. An almost tangible amber sea lay over the sandbars of Cape Kennedy and Merrit Island. Hung from the Apollo gantries, a canopy of diamond air stretched across the forest.

There was a glimmer of movement from the river below. A young woman ran along the surface of the water, her silver hair flowing behind her like half-furled wings. Elaine was learning to fly. The light from her outstretched arms glowed on the water and dappled the leaves of the passing trees. She waved to Sheppard, beckoning him to join her, a child who was both his mother and his daughter.

Sheppard walked towards the water. He moved through the flock of orioles suspended above the grass. Each of the stationary birds had become a congested jewel dazzled by its own reflection. He took one of the birds from the air and smoothed its plumage, searching for that same key he had tried to find when he caressed Anne Godwin. He felt the fluttering aviary in his hands, a feathered universe that trembled around a single heart.

The bird shuddered and came to life, like a flower released from its capsules. It sprang from his fingers, a rush of images of itself between the branches. Glad to set it free, Sheppard lifted the orioles down from the air and caressed them one by one. He released the giant butterfly, the quetzal and the iguana, the moths and insects, the frozen, time-locked ferns and palmettos by the water's edge.

Last of all, he released Martinsen. He embraced the helpless doctor, searching for the strong sinews of the young student and the wise bones of the elderly physician. In a sudden moment of recognition, Martinsen found himself, his youth and his age merged in the open geometries of his face, this happy rendezvous of his past and future selves. He stepped back from Sheppard, hands raised in a generous salute, then ran across the grass towards the river, eager to see Elaine.

Content now, Sheppard set off to join them. Soon the forest would be alive again, and they could return to Cocoa Beach, to that motel where Anne Godwin lay in the darkened bedroom. From there they would move on, to the towns and cities of the south, to the sleepwalking children in the parks, to the dreaming mothers and fathers embalmed in their homes, waiting to be woken from the present into the infinite realm of their time-filled selves.

**1982**

# REPORT ON AN UNIDENTIFIED SPACE STATION

## Survey Report 1

By good luck we have been able to make an emergency landing on this uninhabited space station. There have been no casualties. We all count ourselves fortunate to have found safe haven at a moment when the expedition was clearly set on disaster.

The station carries no identification markings and is too small to appear on our charts. Although of elderly construction it is soundly designed and in good working order, and seems to have been used in recent times as a transit depot for travellers resting at mid-point in their journeys. Its interior consists of a series of open passenger concourses, with comfortably equipped lounges and waiting rooms. As yet we have not been able to locate the bridge or control centre. We assume that the station was one of many satellite drogues surrounding a larger command unit, and was abandoned when a decline in traffic left it surplus to the needs of the parent transit system.

A curious feature of the station is its powerful gravitational field, far stronger than would be suggested by its small mass. However, this probably represents a faulty reading by our instruments. We hope shortly to complete our repairs and are grateful to have found shelter on this relic of the now forgotten migrations of the past.

*Estimated diameter of the station*: 500 metres.

## Survey Report 2

Our repairs are taking longer than we first estimated. Certain pieces of equipment will have to be entirely rebuilt, and to shorten this task we are carrying out a search of our temporary home.

To our surprise we find that the station is far larger than we guessed. A thin local atmosphere surrounds the station, composed of interstellar dust attracted by its unusually high gravity. This fine vapour obscured the substantial bulk of the station and led us to assume that it was no more than a few hundred metres in diameter.

We began by setting out across the central passenger concourse that separates the two hemispheres of the station. This wide deck is furnished with thousands of tables and chairs. But on reaching the high partition doors 200 metres away we discovered that the restaurant deck is only a modest annexe to a far larger concourse. An immense roof three storeys high extends across an open expanse of lounges and promenades.

We explored several of the imposing staircases, each equipped with a substantial mezzanine, and found that they lead to identical concourses above and below.

The space station has clearly been used as a vast transit facility, comfortably accommodating many thousands of passengers. There are no crew quarters or crowd control posts. The absence of even a single cabin indicates that this army of passengers spent only a brief time here before being moved on, and must have been remarkably self-disciplined or under powerful restraint.

*Estimated diameter*: 1 mile.

## Survey Report 3

A period of growing confusion. Two of our number set out 48 hours ago to explore the lower decks of the station, and have so far failed to return. We have carried out an extensive search and fear that a tragic accident has taken place. None of the hundreds of elevators is in working order, but our companions may have entered an unanchored cabin and fallen to their deaths. We managed to force open one of the heavy doors and gazed with awe down the immense shaft. Many of the elevators within the station could comfortably carry a thousand passengers. We hurled several pieces of furniture down the shaft, hoping to time the interval before their impact, but not a sound returned to us. Our voices echoed away into a bottomless pit.

Perhaps our companions are marooned far from us on the lower levels? Given the likely size of the station, the hope remains that a maintenance staff occupies the crew quarters on some remote upper deck, unaware of our presence here.

*Estimated diameter*: 10 miles.

## Survey Report 4

Once again our estimate of the station's size has been substantially revised. The station clearly has the dimensions of a large asteroid or even a small planet. Our instruments indicate that there are thousands of decks, each extending for miles across an undifferentiated terrain of passenger concourses, lounges and restaurant terraces. As before there is no sign of any crew or supervisory staff. Yet somehow a vast passenger complement was moved through this planetary waiting room.

While resting in the armchairs beneath the unvarying light we have all noticed how our sense of direction soon vanishes. Each of us sits at a point in space that at the same time seems to have no precise location but could be anywhere within these endless vistas of tables and armchairs. We can only assume that the passengers moving along these decks possessed some instinctive homing device, a mental model of the station that allowed them to make their way within it.

In order to establish the exact dimensions of the station and, if possible, rescue our companions we have decided to abandon our repair work and set out on an unlimited survey, however far this may take us.

*Estimated diameter*: 500 miles.

## Survey Report 5

No trace of our companions. The silent interior spaces of the station have begun to affect our sense of time. We have been travelling in a straight line across one of the central decks for what seems an unaccountable period. The same pedestrian concourses, the same mezzanines attached to the stairways, and the same passenger lounges stretch for miles under an unchanging light. The energy needed to maintain this degree of illumination suggests that the operators of the station are used to a full passenger complement. However, there are unmistakable signs that no one has been here since the remote past.

We press on, following the same aisle that separates two adjacent lounge concourses. We rest briefly at fixed intervals, but despite our steady passage we sense that we are not moving at all, and may well be trapped within a small waiting room whose apparently infinite dimensions we circle like ants on a sphere. Paradoxically, our instruments confirm that we are penetrating a structure of rapidly increasing mass.

Is the entire universe no more than an infinitely vast space terminal?

*Estimated diameter*: 5000 miles.

## Survey Report 6

We have just made a remarkable discovery! Our instruments have detected that a slight but perceptible curvature is built into the floors of the station. The ceilings recede behind us and dip fractionally towards the decks below, while the disappearing floors form a distinct horizon.

So the station is a curvilinear structure of finite form! There must be meridians that mark out its contours, and an equator that will return us to our original starting point. We all feel an immediate surge of hope. Already we may have stumbled on an equatorial line, and despite the huge length of our journey we may in fact be going home.

*Estimated diameter*: 50,000 miles.

## Survey Report 7

Our hopes have proved to be short-lived. Excited by the thought that we had mastered the station, and cast a net around its invisible bulk, we were pressing on with renewed confidence. However, we now know that although these curvatures exist, they extend in all directions. Each of the walls curves away from its neighbours, the floors from the ceilings. The station, in fact, is an expanding structure whose size appears to increase exponentially. The longer the journey undertaken by a passenger, the greater the incremental distance he will have to travel. The virtually unlimited facilities of the station suggest that its passengers were embarked on extremely long, if not infinite journeys.

Needless to say, the complex architecture of the station has ominous implications for us. We realise that the size of the station is a measure, not of the number of passengers embarked – though this must have been vast – but of the length of the journeys undertaken within it. Indeed, there should ideally be only one passenger. A solitary voyager embarked on an infinite journey would require an infinity of transit lounges. As there are, fortunately, more than one of us we can assume that the station is a finite structure with the appearance of an infinite one. The degree to which it approaches an infinite size is merely a measure of the will and ambition of its passengers.

*Estimated diameter:* 1 million miles.

## Survey Report 8

Just when our spirits were at their lowest ebb we have made a small but significant finding. We were moving across one of the limitless passenger decks, a prey to all fears and speculations, when we noticed the signs of recent habitation. A party of travellers has passed here in the recent past. The chairs in the central concourse have been disturbed, an elevator door has been forced, and there are the unmistakable traces left by weary voyagers. Without doubt there were more than two of them, so we must regretfully exclude our lost companions.

But there are others in the station, perhaps embarked on a journey as endless as our own!

We have also noticed slight variations in the decor of the station, in the design of light fittings and floor tiles. These may seem trivial, but multiplying them by the virtually infinite size of the station we can envisage a gradual evolution in its architecture. Somewhere in the station there may well be populated enclaves, even entire cities, surrounded by empty passenger decks that stretch on forever like free space. Perhaps there are nation-states whose civilisations rose and declined as their peoples paused in their endless migrations across the station.

What force propelled them on their meaningless journeys? We can only hope that they were driven forward by the greatest of all instincts, the need to establish the station's size.

*Estimated diameter:* 5 light years.

## Survey Report 9

We are jubilant! A growing euphoria has come over us as we move across these great concourses. We have seen no further trace of our fellow passengers, and it now seems likely that we were following one of the inbuilt curvatures of the station and had crossed our own tracks.

But this small setback counts for nothing now. We have accepted the limitless size of the station, and this awareness fills us with feelings that are almost religious. Our instruments confirm what we have long suspected, that the empty space across which we travelled from our own solar system in fact lies within the interior of the station, one of the many vast lacunae set in its endlessly curving walls. Our solar system and its planets, the millions of other solar systems that constitute our galaxy, and the island universes themselves all lie within the boundaries of the station. The station is coeval with the cosmos, and constitutes the cosmos. Our duty is to travel across it on a journey whose departure point we have already begun to forget, and whose destination is the station itself, every floor and concourse within it.

So we move on, sustained by our faith in the station, aware that every step we take thereby allows us to reach a small part of that destination. By its existence the station sustains us, and gives our lives their only meaning. We are glad that in return we have begun to worship the station.

*Estimated diameter:* 15 million light years.

**. 1982**

# THE OBJECT OF THE ATTACK

**From the Forensic Diaries of Dr Richard Greville,**
**Chief Psychiatric Adviser, Home Office**

7 June 1987. An unsettling week – two Select Committees; the failure of mother's suspect Palmer to reach its reserve at Sotheby's (I suggested that they might re-attribute it to Keating, which doubly offended them); and wearying arguments with Sarah about our endlessly postponed divorce and her over-reliance on ECT – she is strongly for the former, I as strongly against the latter ... I suspect that her patients are suffering for me.

But, above all, there was my visit to The Boy. Confusing, ugly and yet strangely inspiring. Inviting me to Daventry, Governor Henson referred to him, as does everyone else in the Home Office, as 'the boy', but I feel he has now earned the capital letters. Years of being moved about, from Rampton to Broadmoor to the Home Office Special Custody Unit at Daventry, the brutal treatment and solitary confinement have failed to subdue him.

He stood in the shower stall of the punishment wing, wearing full canvas restraint suit, and plainly driven mad by the harsh light reflected from the white tiles, which were streaked with blood from a leaking contusion on his forehead. He has been punched about a great deal, and flinched from me as I approached, but I felt that he almost invited physical attack as a means of provoking himself. He is far smaller than I expected, and looks only seventeen or eighteen (though he is now twenty-nine), but is still strong and dangerous – President Reagan and Her Majesty were probably lucky to escape.

Case notes: missing caps to both canines, contact dermatitis of the scalp, a left-handed intention tremor, and signs of an hysterical photophobia. He appeared to be gasping with fear, and Governor Henson tried to reassure him, but I assume that far from being afraid he felt nothing but contempt for us and was deliberately hyperventilating. He was chanting what sounded like 'Allahu akbar', the expulsive God-is-Great cry used by the whirling dervishes to induce their hallucinations, the same over-oxygenation of the brain brought on, in milder form, by church hymns and community singing at Cup Finals.

The Boy certainly resembles a religious fanatic – perhaps he is a Shi'ite Muslim convert? He only paused to stare at the distant aerials of Daventry visible through a skylight. When a warder closed the door he began to whimper and pump his lungs again. I asked the orderly to clean the wound on his forehead, but as I helped with the dressing he lunged forward and knocked my briefcase to the floor. For a few seconds he tried to provoke an assault, but then caught sight of the Sotheby's catalogue among my spilled papers, and the reproduction of mother's Samuel Palmer. That serene light over the visionary meadows, the boughs of the oaks like windows of stained glass in the cathedral of heaven, together appeared to calm him. He gazed at me in an uncanny way, bowing as if he assumed that I was the painter.

Later, in the Governor's office, we came to the real purpose of my visit. The months of disruptive behaviour have exhausted everyone, but above all they are terrified of an escape, and a second attack on HMQ. Nor would it help the Atlantic Alliance if the US President were assassinated by a former inmate of a British mental hospital. Henson and the resident medical staff, with the encouragement of the Home Office, are keen to switch from chlorpromazine to the new NX series of central nervous system depressants – a spin-off of Porton Down's work on nerve gases. Prolonged use would induce blurred vision and locomotor ataxia, but also suppress all cortical function, effectively lobotomising him. I thought of my wrangles with Sarah over ECT – psychiatry cannot wait to return to its dark ages – and tactfully vetoed the use of NX until I had studied the medical history in the Special Branch dossier. But I was thinking of The Boy's eyes as he gazed on that dubious Palmer.

**The Assassination Attempt**
In 1982, during the state visit of President Reagan to the United Kingdom, an unsuccessful aerial attack was made upon the royal family and their guest at Windsor Castle. Soon after the President and Mrs Reagan arrived by helicopter, a miniature glider was observed flying across the Home Park in a north-westerly direction. The craft, a primitive hang-glider, was soaring at a height of some 120 feet, on a course that would have carried it over the walls of the Castle. However, before the Special Branch and Secret Service marksmen could fire upon the glider it became entangled in the aerials above the royal mausoleum at Frogmore House and fell to the ground beside the Long Walk.

Strapped to the chest of the unconscious pilot was an explosive harness containing twenty-four sticks of commercial gelignite linked to NCB detonators, and a modified parachute ripcord that served as a hand-operated triggering device. The pilot was taken into custody, and no word of this presumed assassination attempt was released to the public or to the Presidential party. HMQ alone was informed, which may explain Her Majesty's impatience with the President when, on horseback, he paused to exchange banter with a large group of journalists.

The pilot was never charged or brought to trial, but detained under the mental health acts in the Home Office observation unit at Springfield Hospital. He was a twenty-four-year-old former video-games programmer and failed Jesuit novice named Matthew Young. For the past eight months he had been living in a lock-up garage behind a disused Baptist church in Highbury, north London, where he had constructed his flying machine. Squadron Leader D.H. Walsh of the RAF Museum, Hendon, identified the craft as an exact replica of a glider designed by the 19th-century aviation pioneer Otto Lilienthal. Later research showed that the glider was the craft in which Lilienthal met his death in 1896. Fellow-residents in the lock-up garages, former girlfriends of the would-be assassin and his probation officer all witnessed his contruction of the glider during the spring of 1982. However, how he launched this antique machine – the nearest high ground is the Heathrow control tower five miles to the east – or remained airborne for his flight across the Home Park, is a mystery to this day.

Later, in the interview cell, The Boy sat safely handcuffed between his two warders. The bruised and hyperventilating figure had been replaced by a docile youth resembling a reformed skinhead who had miraculously seen the light. Only the eerie smile which he turned upon me so obligingly reminded me of the glider and the harness packed with explosive. As always, he refused to answer any questions put to him, and we sat in a silence broken only by his whispered refrain.

Ignoring these cryptic mutterings, I studied a list of those present at Windsor Castle.

*President Reagan, HM The Queen, Mrs Reagan, Prince Philip, Prince Charles, Princess Diana . . .*

*The US Ambassador, Dr Billy Graham, Apollo astronaut Colonel Tom Stamford, Mr Henry Ford III, Mr James Stewart, the presidents of Heinz, IBM and Lockheed Aircraft, and assorted Congressmen, military and naval attachés, State Department and CIA pro-consuls . . .*

*Lord Delfont, Mr Andrew Lloyd Webber, Miss Joanna Lumley . . .*

In front of Young, on the table between us, I laid out the photographs of President Reagan, the Queen, Prince Philip, Charles and Diana. He showed not a flicker of response, leaned forward and with his scarred chin nudged the Sotheby's catalogue from my open briefcase. He held the Palmer reproduction to his left shoulder, obliquely smiling his thanks. Sly and disingenuous, he was almost implying that I was his accomplice. I remembered how very manipulative such psychopaths could be – Myra Hindley, Brady and Mary Bell had convinced various naïve and well-meaning souls of their 'religious conversions'.

Without thinking, I drew the last photograph from the dossier: Colonel Stamford in his white space-suit floating free above a space-craft during an orbital flight.

The chanting stopped. I heard Young's heels strike the metal legs of his chair as he drew back involuntarily. A focal seizure of the right hand rattled his handcuffs. He stared at the photograph, but the gaze of his eyes was far beyond the cell around us, and I suspected that he was experiencing a warning aura before an epileptic attack. With a clear shout to us all, he stiffened in his chair and slipped to the floor in a *grand mal.*

As his head hammered the warders' feet I realised that he had been chanting, not 'Allahu akbar', but 'Astro-naut' . . .

Astro-nought . . . ?

## Matthew Young: the Personal History of a Psychopath
So, what is known of The Boy? The Special Branch investigators assembled a substantial dossier on this deranged young man.

Born 1958, Abu Dhabi, father manager of Amoco desalination plant. Childhood in the Gulf area, Alaska and Aberdeen. Educational misfit, with suspected *petit mal* epilepsy, but attended Strathclyde University for two terms in 1975, computer sciences course. Joined Worker's Revolutionary Party 1976, arrested outside US Embassy, London, during anti-nuclear demonstration. Worked as scaffolder and painter, Jodrell Bank Radio-Observatory, 1977; prosecuted for malicious damage to reflector dish. Jesuit novice, St Francis Xavier seminary, Dundalk, 1978; expelled after three weeks for sexual misconduct with mother of fellow novice. Fined for being drunk and disorderly during 'Sculpture of the Space Age' exhibition at Serpentine Gallery, London. Video-games programmer, Virgin Records, 1980. Operated pirate radio station attempting to jam transmissions from Space Shuttle, prosecuted by British Telecom. Registered private patents on video-games 'Target Apollo' and 'Shuttle Attack', 1981. Numerous convictions for assault, possession of narcotics, dangerous driving, unemployment benefit frauds, disturbances of the peace. 1982, privately published his 'Cosmological Testament', a Blakean farrago of nature mysticism, apocalyptic fantasy and pseudo-mathematical proofs of the nonexistence of space-time . . .

All in all, a classic delinquent, with that history of messianic delusions and social maladjustment found in regicides throughout history. The choice of Mr Reagan reflects the persistent appeal of the theme of presidential assassination, which seems to play on the edgy dreams of so many lonely psychopaths. Invested in the President of the United States, the world's most powerful leader, are not only the full office and authority of the temporal world, but the very notion of existence itself, of the continuum of time and space which encloses the assassin as much as his victim. Like the disturbed child seeking to destroy everything in its nursery, the assassin is trying to obliterate those images of himself which he identifies with his perception of the external universe. Suicide would leave the rest of existence intact, and it is the notion of existence, incarnated in the person of the President, that is the assassin's true target.

## The Dream of Death by Air
'. . . in the Second Fall, their attempt to escape from their home planet, the peoples of the earth invite their planetary death, choosing the zero

gravity of a false space and time, recapitulating in their weightlessness the agony of the First Fall of Man . . .'

COSMOLOGICAL TESTAMENT, BOOK I

### The Dream of Death by Water

'. . . the sea is an exposed cerebral cortex, the epidermis of a sleeping giant whom the Apollo and Skylab astronauts will awake with their splashdowns. All the peoples of the planet will walk, fly, entrain for the nearest beach, they will ride rapids, endure hardships, abandon continents until they at last stand together on the terminal shore of the world, then step forward . . .'

COSMOLOGICAL TESTAMENT, BOOK III

### The Dream of Death by Earth

'. . . the most sinister and dangerous realms are those devised by man during his inward colonising of his planet, applying the dreams of a degenerate outer space to his inner world – warrens, dungeons, fortifications, bunkers, oubliettes, underground garages, tunnels of every kind that riddle his mind like maggots through the brains of a corpse . . .'

COSMOLOGICAL TESTAMENT, BOOK VII

A curious volume, certainly, but no hint of a dream of death by fire – and no suggestion of Reagan, nor of Her Majesty, Princess Diana, Mrs Thatcher . . . ?

### The Escape Engine: the Ames Room

14 October 1987. The Boy has escaped! An urgent call this morning from Governor Henson. I flew up to Daventry immediately in the crowded Home Office helicopter. Matthew Young has vanished, in what must be one of the most ingenious escape attempts ever devised. The Governor and his staff were in a disoriented state when I arrived. Henson paced around his office, pressing his hands against the bookshelves and re-arranging the furniture, as if not trusting its existence. Home Office and Special Branch people were everywhere, but I managed to calm Henson and piece together the story.

Since my previous visit they had relaxed Young's regime. Mysteriously, the Samuel Palmer illustration in Sotheby's catalogue had somehow calmed him. He no longer defaced his cell walls, volunteered to steamhose them, and had pinned the Palmer above his bunk, gazing at it as if it were a religious icon. (If only it were a Keating – the old rogue would have been delighted. As it happens, Keating's reputation as a faker may have given Young his plan for escape.)

Young declined to enter the exercise yard – the high British Telecom aerials clearly unsettled him – so Henson arranged for him to use the prison chapel as a recreation room. Here the trouble began, as became clear when the Governor showed me into the chapel, a former private cinema furnished with pews, altar, pulpit, etc. For reasons of security, the doors were kept locked, and the warders on duty kept their eyes on Young by glancing through the camera slit in the projection room. As a result, the warders saw the interior of the chapel from one perspective only. Young had cunningly taken advantage of this, re-arranging the pews, pulpit and altar table to construct what in effect was an Ames Room – Adelbert Ames Jr, the American psychologist, devised a series of trick rooms, which seemed entirely normal when viewed through a peephole, but were in fact filled with unrelated fragments of furniture and ornaments.

Young's version of the Ames Room was far more elaborate. The cross and brass candelabra appeared to stand on the altar table, but actually hung in mid-air ten feet away, suspended from the ceiling on lengths of cotton teased from his overalls. The pews had been raised on piers of prayer books and Bibles to create the illusion of an orderly nave. But once we left the projection room and entered the chapel we saw that the pews formed a stepped ramp that climbed to the ventilation grille behind the altar table. The warders glancing through the camera slit in the projection room had seen Young apparently on his knees before the cross, when in fact he had been sitting on the topmost pew in the ramp, loosening the bolts around the metal grille.

Henson was appalled by Young's escape, but I was impressed by the cleverness of this optical illusion. Like Henson, the Home Office inspectors were certain that another assassination attempt might be made on Her Majesty. However, as we gazed at that bizarre chapel something convinced me that the Queen and the President were not in danger. On the shabby wall behind the altar Young had pinned a dozen illustrations of the American and Russian space programmes, taken from newspapers and popular magazines. All the photographs of the astronauts had been defaced, the Skylab and Shuttle craft marked with obscene graffiti. He had constructed a Black Chapel, which at the same time was a complex escape device that would set him free, not merely from Daventry, but from the threat posed by the astronauts and from that far larger prison whose walls are those of space itself.

### The Astro-Messiah

Colonel Thomas Jefferson Stamford, USAF (ret.). Born 1931, Brigham City, Utah. Eagle scout, 1945. B.S. (Physics), Caltech, 1953. Graduated US Air Force Academy, 1957. Served Vietnam, 1964–9. Enrolled NASA 1970; deputy ground controller, Skylab III. 1974, rumoured commander of secret Apollo 20 mission to the Moon which landed remote-controlled nuclear missile station in the Mare Imbrium. Retired 1975, appointed vice-president, Pepsi-Cola Corporation. 1976, script consultant to 20th Century-Fox for projected biopic *Men with Fins*.

1977, associated with the Precious Light Movement, a California-based consciousness-raising group calling for legalisation of LSD. Resigned 1978, hospitalised Veterans Administration Hospital, Fresno. On discharge begins nine months retreat at Truth Mountain, Idaho, interdenominational order of lay monks. 1979, founds Spaceways, drug rehabilitation centre, Santa Monica. 1980–1, associated with Billy Graham, shares platform on revivalist missions to Europe and Australia. 1982, visits Windsor Castle with President Reagan. 1983, forms the evangelical trust COME Incorporated, tours Alabama and Mississippi as self-proclaimed 13th Disciple. 1984, visits Africa, SE Asia, intercedes Iraq/Iran conflict, addresses Nato Council of Ministers, urges development of laser weapons and neutron bomb. 1986, guest of Royal Family at Buckingham Palace, appears in Queen's Christmas TV broadcast, successfully treats Prince William, becomes confidant and spiritual adviser to Princess Diana. Named Man of the Year by *Time Magazine*, profiled by *Newsweek* as 'Space-Age Messiah' and 'founder of first space-based religion'.

Could this much-admired former astronaut, a folk hero who clearly fulfilled the role of a 1980s Lindbergh, have been the real target of the Windsor attack? Lindbergh had once hob-nobbed with kings and chancellors, but his cranky political beliefs had become tainted by pro-Nazi sentiments. By contrast Col. Stamford's populist mix of born-again Christianity and anti-communist rhetoric seemed little more than an outsider's long shot at the White House. Now and then, watching Stamford's rallies on television, I detected the same hypertonic facial musculature that could be seen in Hitler, Gaddafi and the more excitable of Khomeini's mullahs, yet nothing worthy of the elaborate assassination attempt, a psychodrama in itself, that Matthew Young had mounted in his Lilienthal glider.

And yet ... who better than a pioneer aeronaut to kill a pioneer astronaut, to turn the clock of space exploration back to zero?

10 February 1988. For the last three months an energetic search has failed to find any trace of Matthew Young. The Special Branch guard on the Queen, Prime Minister and senior cabinet members has been tightened, and several of the royals have been issued with small pistols. One hopes that they will avoid injuring themselves, or each other. Already the disguised fashion-accessory holster worn by Princess Diana has inspired a substantial copycat industry, and London is filled with young women wearing stylised codpieces (none of them realise why), like cast members from a musical version of *The Gunfight at the OK Corral*.

The Boy's former girlfriends and surviving relatives, his probation officer and fellow programmers at Virgin Records have been watched and/or interrogated. A few suspected sightings have occurred: in November an eccentric young man in the leather gaiters and antique costume of a World War I aviator enrolled for a course of lessons at Elstree Flying School, only to suffer an epileptic seizure after the first take-off. Hundreds of London Underground posters advertising Col. Stamford's Easter rally at Earls Court have been systematically defaced. At Pinewood Studios an arsonist has partially destroyed the sets for the $100 million budget science-fiction films *The Revenge of R2D2* and *C3PO Meets E.T.* A night intruder penetrated the offices of COME Inc. in the Tottenham Court Road and secretly dubbed an obscene message over Col. Stamford's inspirational address on the thousands of promotional videos. In several Piccadilly amusement arcades the Space Invaders games have been reprogrammed to present Col. Stamford's face as the target.

More significant, perhaps, a caller with the same voiceprint as Matthew Young has persistently tried to telephone the Archbishop of Canterbury. Three days ago the vergers at Westminster Abbey briefly apprehended a youth praying before a bizarre tableau consisting of Col. Stamford's blood-stained space-suit and helmet, stolen from their display case in the Science Museum, which he had set up in a niche behind the High Altar. The rare blood group, BRh, is not Col. Stamford's but The Boy's.

The reports of Matthew Young at prayer reminded me of Governor Henson's description of the prisoner seen on his knees in that illusionist chapel he had constructed at Daventry. There is an eerie contrast between the vast revivalist rally being televised at this moment from the Parc des Princes in Paris, dominated by the spotlit figure of the former astronaut, and the darkened nave of the Abbey where an escaped mental patient prayed over a stolen space-suit smeared with his own blood. The image of outer space, from which Col. Stamford draws so much of his religious inspiration, for Matthew Young seems identified with some unspecified evil, with the worship of a false messiah. His prayers in the Daventry chapel, as he knelt before the illusion of an altar, were a series of postural codes, a contortionist's attempt to free himself from Col. Stamford's sinister embrace.

I read once again the testimony collected by the Special Branch:

Margaret Downs, systems analyst, Wang Computers: 'He was always praying, forever on his confounded knees. He even made me take a video of him, and studied it for hours. It was just too much ...'

Doreen Jessel, health gym instructress: 'At first I thought he was heavily into anaerobics. Some kind of dynamic meditation, he called it, all acrobatic contortions. I tried to get him to see a physiotherapist ...'

John Hatton, probation officer: 'There was a therapeutic aspect, of which he convinced me against my better judgement. The contortions seemed to mimic his epilepsy ...'

Reverend Morgan Evans, Samaritans: 'He accepted Robert Graves's notion of the club-footed messiah – that peculiar stepped gait common to various forms of religious dance and to all myths involving the Achilles tendon. He told me that it was based on the crabbed moon-walk adopted by the astronauts to cope with zero gravity ...'

Sergeant J. Mellors, RAF Regiment: 'The position was that of a kneeling marksman required to get off a series of shots with a bolt-action rifle, such as the Lee-Enfield or the Mannlicher-Carcano. I banned him from the firing range ...'

Was Matthew Young dismantling and reassembling the elements of his own mind as if they were the constituents of an Ames Room? The pilot of the Home Office helicopter spoke graphically of the spatial disorientation felt by some of the special category prisoners being moved on the Daventry shuttle, in particular the cries and contortions of a Palestinian hijacker who imagined he was a dying astronaut. Defects of the vestibular apparatus of the ear are commonly found in hijackers (as in some shamans), the same sense of spatial disorientation that can be induced in astronauts by the high-speed turntable or the zero gravity of orbital flights.

It may be, therefore, that defects of the vestibular apparatus draw their sufferers towards high-speed aircraft, and the hijack is an unconscious attempt to cure this organic affliction. Prayer, vestibular defects, hijacking – watching Col. Stamford in the Parc des Princes, I notice that he sometimes stumbles as he bows over his lectern, his hands clasped in prayer in that characteristic spasm so familiar from the newsreels and now even mimicked by TV comedians.

Is Col. Stamford trying to hijack the world?

28 March 1988. Events are moving on apace. Colonel Thomas Jefferson Stamford has arrived in London, after completing his triumphal tour of the non-communist world. He has conferred with generals and right-wing churchmen, and calmed battlefields from the Golan Heights to the western Sahara. As always, he urges the combatants to join forces against the real enemy, pushing an anti-Soviet, church-militant line that makes the CIA look like the Red Cross. Television and newspapers show him mingling with heads of state and retired premiers, with Kohl, Thatcher and Mitterrand, with Scandinavian royals and the British monarch.

Throughout, Col. Stamford's earlier career as an astronaut is never forgotten. At his rallies in the Parc des Princes and Munich's Olympic Stadium these great arenas are transformed into what seems to be the interior of a gigantic star-ship. By the cunning use of a circular film screen, Col. Stamford's arrival at the podium is presented as a landing from outer space, to deafening extracts from *Thus Spake Zarathustra* and Holst's *Planets*. With its illusionist back-projection and trick lighting the rally becomes a huge Ames Room, a potent mix of evangelical Christianity, astronautics and cybernetic movie-making. We are in the presence of an Intelsat messiah, a mana-personality for the age of cable TV.

His thousands of followers sway in their seats, clutching COME Inc.'s promotional videos like Mao's Red Guards with their little red books. Are we seeing the first video religion, an extravagant light show with laser graphics by Lucasfilms? The message of the rallies, as of the videos, is that Col. Thomas Stamford has returned to earth to lead a moral crusade against atheistic Marxism, a Second Coming that has launched the 13th Disciple down the aisles of space from the altar of the Mare Imbrium.

Already two former Apollo astronauts have joined this crusade, resigning their directorships of Avis and Disney Corporation, and members of the Skylab and Shuttle missions have pledged their support. Will NASA one day evolve into a religious organisation? Caucus leaders in the Democratic and Republican Parties have urged Col. Stamford to stand for President. But I suspect that the Great Mission Controller in the Sky intends to bypass the Presidency and appeal directly to the US public as an astro-messiah, a space ayatollah descending to earth to set up his religious republic.

## The First Church of the Divine Astronaut

These messianic strains reminded me of The Boy, the self-sworn enemy of all astronauts. On the day after the Colonel's arrival in London for the Easter rally, to be attended by Prince Charles, Princess Diana and the miraculously cured Prince William, I drove to the lock-up garage in Highbury. I had repeatedly warned the Home Office of a probable assassination attempt, but they seemed too mesmerised by the Stamford fever that had seized the whole of London to believe that anyone would attack him.

As Constable Willings waited in the rain I stared down at the oil-stained camp bed and the sink with its empty cans of instant coffee. The Special Branch investigators had stripped the shabby garage, yet pinned to the cement wall above the bed was a postcard that they had inexplicably missed. Stepping closer, I saw that it was a reproduction of a small Samuel Palmer, 'A Dream of Death by Fire', a visionary scene of the destruction of a false church by the surrounding light of a true nature. The painting had been identified by Keating as one of his most ambitious frauds.

A fake Keating to describe the death of a fake messiah? Pinned to the damp cement within the past few days, the postcard was clearly Matthew Young's invitation to me. But where would I find him? Then, through the open doors, I saw the disused Baptist church behind the row of garages.

As soon as I entered its gloomy nave I was certain that Matthew Young's target had been neither President Reagan nor the Queen. The bolt cutters borrowed from Constable Willings snapped the links of the rusting chain. When he had driven away I pushed back the worm-riddled doors. At some time in the past a television company had used the deconsecrated church to store its unwanted props. Stage sets and painted panels from a discontinued science-fiction series leaned against the walls in a dusty jumble.

I entered the aisle and stood between the pews. Then, as I stepped forward, I saw a sudden diorama of the lunar surface. In front of me was a miniature film set constructed from old *Star Wars* posters and props from *Dr Who*. Above the lunar landscape hung the figure of an astronaut flying with arms outstretched.

As I guessed, this diorama formed part of yet another Ames Room. The astronaut's figure created its illusion only when seen from the doors of the church. As I approached, however, its elements moved apart. A gloved hand hung alone, severed from the arm that seemed to support it. The detached thorax and sections of the legs drifted away from one another, suspended on threads of wire from the rafters above the nave. The head and helmet had been sliced from the shoulders, and had taken off on a flight of their own. As I stood by the altar the dismembered astronaut flew above me, like a chromium corpse blown apart by a booby-trap hidden in its life-support system.

Lying on the stone floor below this eerie spectacle was Matthew Young. He rested on his back in a scuffle of dust and cracked flagstones, his scarred mouth drawn back in a bloodless grimace to reveal the broken teeth whose caps he had crushed. He had fallen to the floor during his *grand mal* attack, and his outstretched fingers had torn a section of a *Star Wars* poster, which lay across him like a shroud. Blood pooled in a massive haematoma below his cheekbone, as if during the focal seizure of his right hand he had been trying to put out the eye with the telescopic sight of the marksman's rifle that he clasped in his fist.

I freed his tongue and windpipe, massaged his diaphragm until his breath was even, and placed a choir cushion below his shoulders. On the floor beside him were the barrel, receiver, breech and magazine of a stockless rifle whose parts he had been oiling in the moments before his attack, and which I knew he would reassemble the instant he awoke.

Easter Day, 1988. This evening Col. Stamford's rally will be held at Earls Court. Since his arrival in London, as a guest of Buckingham Palace, the former astronaut has been intensely busy, preparing that springboard which will propel him across the Atlantic. Three days ago he addressed the joint Houses of Parliament in Westminster Hall. In his televised speech he called for a crusade against the evil empire of the non-Christian world, for the construction of orbital nuclear bomb platforms, for the launching of geosynchronous laser weapons trained upon Teheran, Moscow and Peking. He seems to be demanding the destruction not merely of the Soviet Union but of the non-Christian world, the re-conquest of Jerusalem and the conversion of Islam.

It is clear that Col. Stamford is as demented as Hitler, but fortunately his last splashdown is at hand. I assume that Matthew Young will be attending the Earls Court rally this evening. I did not report him to the police, confident that he would recover in time to reassemble his rifle and make his way to one of the empty projection booths beneath the roof of the arena. Seeing Col. Stamford's arrival from 'outer space', The Boy will watch him from the camera window, and listen to him urge his nuclear jihad against the forces of the anti-Christ. From that narrow but never more vital perspective, the sights of his rifle, Matthew Young will be ready once again to dismantle an illusionist space and celebrate the enduring mysteries of the Ames Room.

**1984**

# ANSWERS TO A QUESTIONNAIRE

1) Yes.
2) Male (?)
3) c/o Terminal 3, London Airport, Heathrow.
4) Twenty-seven.
5) Unknown.
6) Dr Barnardo's Primary, Kingston-upon-Thames; HM Borstal, Send, Surrey; Brunel University Computer Sciences Department.
7) Floor cleaner, Mecca Amusement Arcades, Leicester Square.
8) If I can avoid it.
9) Systems Analyst, Sperry-Univac, 1979–83.
10) Manchester Crown Court, 1984.
11) Credit card and computer fraud.
12) Guilty.
13) Two years, HM Prison, Parkhurst.
14) Stockhausen, de Kooning, Jack Kerouac.
15) Whenever possible.
16) Twice a day.
17) NSU, Herpes, gonorrhoea.
18) Husbands.
19) My greatest ambition is to turn into a TV programme.
20) I first saw the deceased on 17 February 1986, in the chapel at London Airport. He was praying in the front pew.
21) At the time I was living in an out-of-order cubicle in the air traffic controllers' washroom in Terminal 3.
22) Approx. 5 ft 7 in, aged thirty-three, slim build, albino skin and thin black beard, some kind of crash injuries to both hands. At first I thought he was a Palestinian terrorist.
23) He was wearing the stolen uniform trousers of an El Al flight engineer.
24) With my last money I bought him a prawnburger in the mezzanine cafeteria. He thanked me and, although not carrying a bank-card, extracted £100 from a service till on the main concourse.
25) Already I was convinced that I was in the presence of a messianic figure who would help me to penetrate the Nat West deposit account computer codes.
26) No sexual activity occurred.
27) I took him to Richmond Ice Rink where he immediately performed

six triple salchows. I urged him to take up ice-dancing with an eye to the European Championships and eventual gold at Seoul, but he began to trace out huge double spirals on the ice. I tried to convince him that these did not feature in the compulsory figures, but he told me that the spirals represented a model of synthetic DNA.

28) No.

29) He gave me to understand that he had important connections at the highest levels of government.

30) Suite 17B, London Penta Hotel. I slept on the floor in the bathroom.

31) Service tills in Oxford Street, Knightsbridge and Earls Court.

32) Approx. £275,000 in three weeks.

33) Porno videos. He took a particular interest in Kamera Klimax and Electric Blue.

34) Almost every day.

35) When he was drunk. He claimed that he brought the gift of eternal life.

36) At the Penta Hotel I tried to introduce him to Torvill and Dean. He was interested in meeting only members of the Stock Exchange and Fellows of the Royal Society.

37) Females of all ages.

38) Group sex.

39) Marie Drummond, twenty-two, sales assistant, HMV Records; Denise Attwell, thirty-seven, research supervisor, Geigy Pharmaceuticals; Florence Burgess, fifty-five, deaconess, Bible Society Bookshop; Angelina Gomez, twenty-three, air hostess, Iberian Airways; Phoebe Adams, forty-three, cruise protestor, Camp Orange, Greenham Common.

40) Sometimes, at his suggestion.

41) Unsatisfactory.

42) Premature ejaculation; impotence.

43) He urged me to have a sex-change operation.

44) National Gallery, Wallace Collection, British Museum. He was much intrigued by representations of Jesus, Zoroaster and the Gautama Buddha, and commented on the likenesses.

45) With the permission of the manager, NE District, British Telecom.

46) We erected the antenna on the roof of the Post Office Tower.

47) 2500 KHz.

48) Towards the constellation Orion.

49) I heard his voice, apparently transmitted from the star Betelgeuse 2000 years ago.

50) Interference to TV reception all over London and the South-East.

51) No. 1 in the BARB Ratings, exceeding the combined audiences for Coronation Street, Dallas and Dynasty.

52) Regular visitors included Princess Diana, Prince Charles and Dr Billy Graham.

53) He hired the Wembley Conference Centre.
54) 'Immortality in the Service of Mankind'.
55) Guests were drawn from the worlds of science and politics, the church, armed forces and the Inland Revenue.
56) Generous fees.
57) Service tills in Mayfair and Regent Street.
58) He had a keen appreciation of money, but was not impressed when I told him of Torvill and Dean's earnings.
59) He was obsessed by the nature of the chemical bond.
60) Sitting beside him at the top table were: (1) The Leader of Her Majesty's Opposition, (2) The President of the Royal Society, (3) The Archbishop of Canterbury, (4) The Chief Rabbi, (5) The Chairman of the Diners Club, (6) The Chairman of the Bank of England, (7) The General Secretary of the Inland Revenue Staff Federation, (8) The President of Hertz Rent-a-Car, (9) The President of IBM, (10) The Chief of the General Staff, (11) Dr Henry Kissinger, (12) Myself.
61) He stated that synthetic DNA introduced into the human germ plasm would arrest the process of ageing and extend human life almost indefinitely.
62) Perhaps 1 million years.
63) He announced that Princess Diana was immortal.
64) Astonishment/disbelief.
65) He advised the audience to invest heavily in leisure industries.
66) The value of the pound sterling rose to $8.75.
67) American TV networks, *Time Magazine, Newsweek*.
68) The Second Coming.
69) He expressed strong disappointment at the negative attitude of the Third World.
70) The Kremlin.
71) He wanted me to become the warhead of a cruise missile.
72) My growing disenchantment.
73) Sexual malaise.
74) He complained that I was spending too much time at Richmond Ice Rink.
75) The Royal Proclamation.
76) The pound sterling rose to $75.50.
77) Prince Andrew. Repeatedly.
78) Injection into the testicles.
79) The side-effects were permanent impotence and sterility. However, as immortality was ensured, no further offspring would be needed and the procreative urge would atrophy.
80) I seriously considered a sex-change operation.
81) Government White Paper on Immortality.
82) Compulsory injection into the testicles of the entire male population over eleven years.
83) Smith & Wesson short-barrel thirty-eight.

84) Entirely my own idea.
85) Many hours at Richmond Ice Rink trying unsuccessfully to erase the patterns of DNA.
86) Westminster Hall.
87) Premeditated. I questioned his real motives.
88) Assassination.
89) I was neither paid nor incited by agents of a foreign power.
90) Despair. I wish to go back to my cubicle at London Airport.
91) Between Princess Diana and the Governor of Nevada.
92) At the climax of *Thus Spake Zarathustra*.
93) Seven feet.
94) Three shots.
95) Blood Group O.
96) I did not wish to spend the rest of eternity in my own company.
97) I was visited in the death cell by the special envoy of the Archbishop of Canterbury.
98) That I had killed the Son of God.
99) He walked with a slight limp. He told me that, as a condemned prisoner, I alone had been spared the sterilising injections, and that the restoration of the national birthrate was now my sole duty.
100) Yes.

**1985**

# THE MAN WHO WALKED ON THE MOON

I, too, was once an astronaut. As you see me sitting here, in this modest café with its distant glimpse of Copacabana Beach, you probably assume that I am a man of few achievements. The shabby briefcase between my worn heels, the stained suit with its frayed cuffs, the unsavoury hands ready to seize the first offer of a free drink, the whole air of failure ... no doubt you think that I am a minor clerk who has missed promotion once too often, and that I amount to nothing, a person of no past and less future.

For many years I believed this myself. I had been abandoned by the authorities, who were glad to see me exiled to another continent, reduced to begging from the American tourists. I suffered from acute amnesia, and certain domestic problems with my wife and my mother. They now share my small apartment at Ipanema, while I am forced to live in a room above the projection booth of the Luxor Cinema, my thoughts drowned by the sound-tracks of science-fiction films.

So many tragic events leave me unsure of myself. Nonetheless, my confidence is returning, and a sense of my true history and worth. Chapters of my life are still hidden from me, and seem as jumbled as the film extracts which the projectionists screen each morning as they focus their cameras. I have still forgotten my years of training, and my mind bars from me any memory of the actual space-flights. But I am certain that I was once an astronaut.

Years ago, before I went into space, I followed many professions – freelance journalist, translator, on one occasion even a war correspondent sent to a small war, which unfortunately was never declared. I was in and out of newspaper offices all day, hoping for that one assignment that would match my talents.

Sadly, all this effort failed to get me to the top, and after ten years I found myself displaced by a younger generation. A certain reticence in my character, a sharpness of manner, set me off from my fellow journalists. Even the editors would laugh at me behind my back. I was given trivial assignments – film reviewing, or writing reports on office-equipment fairs. When the circulation wars began, in a doomed response to the onward sweep of television, the editors openly took exception to my waspish style. I became a part-time translator, and taught for an hour each day at a language school, but my income plummeted. My mother, whom I had supported for many years, was forced to leave her home and join my wife and myself in our apartment at Ipanema.

At first my wife resented this, but soon she and my mother teamed up against me. They became impatient with the hours I spent delaying my unhappy visits to the single newspaper office that still held out hope – my journey to work was a transit between one door slammed on my heels and another slammed in my face.

My last friend at the newspaper commiserated with me, as I stood forlornly in the lobby. 'For heaven's sake, find a human-interest story! Something tender and affecting, that's what they want upstairs – life isn't an avant-garde movie!'

Pondering this sensible advice, I wandered into the crowded streets. I dreaded the thought of returning home without an assignment. The two women had taken to opening the apartment door together. They would stare at me accusingly, almost barring me from my own home.

Around me were the million faces of the city. People strode past, so occupied with their own lives that they almost pushed me from the pavement. A million human interest stories, of a banal and pointless kind, an encyclopaedia of mediocrity . . . Giving up, I left Copacabana Avenue and took refuge among the tables of a small café in a side-street.

It was there that I met the American astronaut, and began my own career in space.

The café terrace was almost deserted, as the office workers returned to their desks after lunch. Behind me, in the shade of the canvas awning, a fair-haired man in a threadbare tropical suit sat beside an empty glass. Guarding my coffee from the flies, I gazed at the small segment of sea visible beyond Copacabana Beach. Slowed by their mid-day meals, groups of American and European tourists strolled down from the hotels, waving away the jewellery salesmen and lottery touts. Perhaps I would visit Paris or New York, make a new life for myself as a literary critic . . .

A tartan shirt blocked my view of the sea and its narrow dream of escape. An elderly American, camera slung from his heavy neck, leaned across the table, his grey-haired wife in a loose floral dress beside him.

'Are you the astronaut?' the woman asked in a friendly but sly way, as if about to broach an indiscretion. 'The hotel said you would be at this café . . .'

'An astronaut?'

'Yes, the astronaut Commander Scranton . . . ?'

'No, I regret that I'm not an astronaut.' Then it occurred to me that this provincial couple, probably a dentist and his wife from the corn-belt, might benefit from a well-informed courier. Perhaps they imagined that their cruise ship had berthed at Miami? I stood up, managing a gallant smile. 'Of course, I'm a qualified translator. If you –'

'No, no . . .' Dismissing me with a wave, they moved through the empty tables. 'We came to see Mr Scranton.'

Baffled by this bizarre exchange, I watched them approach the man in the tropical suit. A nondescript fellow in his late forties, he had thinning blond hair and a strong-jawed American face from which all confidence had long been drained. He stared in a resigned way at his hands, which waited beside his empty glass, as if unable to explain to them that little refreshment would reach them that day. He was clearly undernourished, perhaps an ex-seaman who had jumped ship, one of thousands of down-and-outs trying to live by their wits on some of the hardest pavements in the world.

However, he looked up sharply enough as the elderly couple approached him. When they repeated their question about the astronaut he beckoned them to a seat. To my surprise, the waiter was summoned, and drinks were brought to the table. The husband unpacked his camera, while a relaxed conversation took place between his wife and this seedy figure.

'Dear, don't forget Mr Scranton . . .'

'Oh, please forgive me.'

The husband removed several bank-notes from his wallet. His wife passed them across the table to Scranton, who then stood up. Photographs were taken, first of Scranton standing next to the smiling wife, then of the husband grinning broadly beside the gaunt American. The source of all this good humour eluded me, as it did Scranton, whose eyes stared gravely at the street with a degree of respect due to the surface of the moon. But already a second group of tourists had walked down from Copacabana Beach, and I heard more laughter when one called out: 'There's the astronaut . . . !'

Quite mystified, I watched a further round of photographs being taken. The couples stood on either side of the American, grinning away as if he were a camel driver posing for pennies against a backdrop of the pyramids.

I ordered a small brandy from the waiter. He had ignored all this, pocketing his tips with a straight face.

'This fellow . . . ?' I asked. 'Who is he? An astronaut?'

'Of course . . .' The waiter flicked a bottle-top into the air and treated the sky to a knowing sneer. 'Who else but the man in the moon?'

The tourists had gone, strolling past the leatherware and jewellery stores. Alone now after his brief fame, the American sat among the empty glasses, counting the money he had collected.

The man in the moon?

Then I remembered the newspaper headline, and the exposé I had read two years earlier of this impoverished American who claimed to have been an astronaut, and told his story to the tourists for the price of a drink. At first almost everyone believed him, and he had become a popular figure in the hotel lobbies along Copacabana Beach. Apparently he had flown on one of the Apollo missions from Cape Kennedy in the 1970s, and his long-jawed face and stoical pilot's eyes seemed vaguely familiar from the magazine photographs. He was properly reticent, but if pressed with a

tourist dollar could talk convincingly about the early lunar flights. In
its way it was deeply moving to sit at a café table with a man who had
walked on the moon . . .

Then an over-curious reporter exploded the whole pretence. No man
named Scranton had ever flown in space, and the American authorities
confirmed that his photograph was not that of any past or present
astronaut. In fact he was a failed crop-duster from Florida who had
lost his pilot's licence and whose knowledge of the Apollo flights had
been mugged up from newspapers and television programmes.

Surprisingly, Scranton's career had not ended there and then, but
moved on to a second tragi-comical phase. Far from consigning him to
oblivion, the exposure brought him a genuine small celebrity. Banished
from the grand hotels of Copacabana, he hung about the cheaper cafés
in the side-streets, still claiming to have been an astronaut, ignoring those
who derided him from their car windows. The dignified way in which he
maintained his fraud tapped a certain good-humoured tolerance, much
like the affection felt in the United States for those eccentric old men who
falsely claimed to their deaths that they were veterans of the American
Civil War.

So Scranton stayed on, willing to talk for a few dollars about his journey
to the moon, quoting the same tired phrases that failed to convince the
youngest schoolboy. Soon no one bothered to question him closely, and
his chief function was to be photographed beside parties of visitors, an
amusing oddity of the tourist trail.

But perhaps the American was more devious than he appeared, with his
shabby suit and hangdog gaze? As I sat there, guarding the brandy I could
barely afford, I resented Scranton's bogus celebrity, and the tourist revenue
it brought him. For years I, too, had maintained a charade – the mask of
good humour that I presented to my colleagues in the newspaper world
– but it had brought me nothing. Scranton at least was left alone for most
of his time, something I craved more than any celebrity. Comparing our
situations, there was plainly a strong element of injustice – the notorious
British criminal who made a comfortable living being photographed by
the tourists in the more expensive Copacabana restaurants had at least
robbed one of Her Majesty's mail-trains.

At the same time, was this the human-interest story that would help me
to remake my career? Could I provide a final ironic twist by revealing that,
thanks to his exposure, the bogus astronaut was now doubly successful?

During the next days I visited the café promptly at noon. Note book at
the ready, I kept a careful watch for Scranton. He usually appeared in the
early afternoon, as soon as the clerks and secretaries had finished their
coffee. In that brief lull, when the shadows crossed from one side of the
street to the other, Scranton would materialise, as if from a trapdoor in
the pavement. He was always alone, walking straight-backed in his faded
suit, but with the uncertainty of someone who suspects that he is keeping

an appointment on the wrong day. He would slip into his place under the café awning, order a glass of beer from the sceptical waiter and then gaze across the street at the vistas of an invisible space.

It soon became clear that Scranton's celebrity was as threadbare as his shirt cuffs. Few tourists visited him, and often a whole afternoon passed without a single customer. Then the waiter would scrape the chairs around Scranton's table, trying to distract him from his reveries of an imaginary moon. Indeed, on the fourth day, within a few minutes of Scranton's arrival, the waiter slapped the table-top with his towel, already cancelling the afternoon's performance.

'Away, away . . . it's impossible!' He seized the newspaper that Scranton had found on a nearby chair. 'No more stories about the moon . . .'

Scranton stood up, head bowed beneath the awning. He seemed resigned to this abuse. 'All right . . . I can take my trade down the street.'

To forestall this, I left my seat and moved through the empty tables.

'Mr Scranton? Perhaps we can speak? I'd like to buy you a drink.'

'By all means.' Scranton beckoned me to a chair. Ready for business, he sat upright, and with a conscious effort managed to bring the focus of his gaze from infinity to a distance of fifty feet away. He was poorly nourished, and his perfunctory shave revealed an almost tubercular pallor. Yet there was a certain resolute quality about this vagrant figure that I had not expected. Sitting beside him, I was aware of an intense and almost wilful isolation, not just in this foreign city, but in the world at large.

I showed him my card. 'I'm writing a book of criticism on the science-fiction cinema. It would be interesting to hear your opinions. You are Commander Scranton, the Apollo astronaut?'

'That is correct.'

'Good. I wondered how you viewed the science-fiction film . . . how convincing you found the presentation of outer space, the lunar surface and so on . . .'

Scranton stared bleakly at the table-top. A faint smile exposed his yellowing teeth, and I assumed that he had seen through my little ruse.

'I'll be happy to set you straight,' he told me. 'But I make a small charge.'

'Of course,' I searched in my pockets. 'Your professional expertise, naturally . . .'

I placed some coins on the table, intending to hunt for a modest bank-note. Scranton selected three of the coins, enough to pay for a loaf of bread, and pushed the rest towards me.

'Science-fiction films –? They're good. Very accurate. On the whole I'd say they do an excellent job.'

'That's encouraging to hear. These Hollywood epics are not usually noted for their realism.'

'Well . . . you have to understand that the Apollo teams brought back a lot of film footage.'

'I'm sure.' I tried to keep the amusement out of my voice. 'The studios must have been grateful to you. After all, you could describe the actual moon-walks.'

Scranton nodded sagely. 'I acted as consultant to one of the Hollywood majors. All in all, you can take it from me that those pictures are pretty realistic.'

'Fascinating ... coming from you that has authority. As a matter of interest, what was being on the moon literally like?'

For the first time Scranton seemed to notice me. Had he glimpsed some shared strain in our characters? This care-worn American had all the refinement of an unemployed car mechanic, and yet he seemed almost tempted to befriend me.

'Being on the moon?' His tired gaze inspected the narrow street of cheap jewellery stores, with its office messengers and lottery touts, the off-duty taxi-drivers leaning against their cars. 'It was just like being here.'

'So ...' I put away my notebook. Any further subterfuge was unnecessary. I had treated our meeting as a joke, but Scranton was sincere, and anyway utterly indifferent to my opinion of him. The tourists and passing policemen, the middle-aged women sitting at a nearby table, together barely existed for him. They were no more than shadows on the screen of his mind, through which he could see the horizons of an almost planetary emptiness.

For the first time I was in the presence of someone who had nothing – even less than the beggars of Rio, for they at least were linked to the material world by their longings for it. Scranton embodied the absolute loneliness of the human being in space and time, a situation which in many ways I shared. Even the act of convincing himself that he was a former astronaut only emphasised his isolation.

'A remarkable story,' I commented. 'One can't help wondering if we were right to leave this planet. I'm reminded of the question posed by the Chilean painter Matta – "Why must we fear a disaster in space in order to understand our own times?" It's a pity you didn't bring back any mementoes of your moon-walks.'

Scranton's shoulders straightened. I could see him counting the coins on the table. 'I do have certain materials ...'

I nearly laughed. 'What? A piece of lunar rock? Some moon dust?'

'Various photographic materials.'

'Photographs?' Was it possible that Scranton had told the truth, and that he had indeed been an astronaut? If I could prove that the whole notion of his imposture was an error, an oversight by the journalist who had investigated the case, I would have the makings of a front-page scoop ... 'Could I see them? – perhaps I could use them in my book ... ?'

'Well ...' Scranton felt for the coins in his pocket. He looked hungry, and obviously thought only of spending them on a loaf of bread.

'Of course,' I added, 'I'll provide an extra fee. As for my book, the publishers might well pay many hundreds of dollars.'

'Hundreds . . .' Scranton seemed impressed. He shook his head, as if amused by the ways of the world. I expected him to be shy of revealing where he lived, but he stood up and gestured me to finish my drink. 'I'm staying a few minutes' walk from here.'

He waited among the tables, staring across the street. Seeing the passers-by through his eyes, I was aware that they had begun to seem almost transparent, shadow players created by a frolic of the sun.

We soon arrived at Scranton's modest room behind the Luxor Cinema, a small theatre off Copacabana Avenue that had seen better days. Two former storerooms and an office above the projection booth had been let as apartments, which we reached after climbing a dank emergency stairway.

Exhausted by the effort, Scranton swayed against the door. He wiped the spit from his mouth onto the lapel of his jacket, and ushered me into the room. 'Make yourself comfortable . . .'

A dusty light fell across the narrow bed, reflected in the cold-water tap of a greasy handbasin supported from the wall by its waste-pipe. Sheets of newspaper were wrapped around a pillow, stained with sweat and some unsavoury mucus, perhaps after an attack of malarial or tubercular fever.

Eager to leave this infectious den, I drew out my wallet. 'The photographs . . . ?'

Scranton sat on the bed, staring at the yellowing wall behind me as if he had forgotten that I was there. Once again I was aware of his ability to isolate himself from the surrounding world, a talent I envied him, if little else.

'Sure . . . they're over here.' He stood up and went to the suitcase that lay on a card table behind the door. Taking the money from me, he opened the lid and lifted out a bundle of magazines. Among them were loose pages torn from *Life* and *Newsweek*, and special supplements of the Rio newspapers devoted to the Apollo space-flights and the moon landings. The familiar images of Armstrong and the lunar module, the space-walks and splashdowns had been endlessly thumbed. The captions were marked with coloured pencil, as if Scranton had spent hours memorising these photographs brought back from the tideways of space.

I moved the magazines to one side, hoping to find some documentary evidence of Scranton's own involvement in the space-flights, perhaps a close-up photograph taken by a fellow astronaut.

'Is this it? There's nothing else?'

'That's it.' Scranton gestured encouragingly. 'They're good pictures. Pretty well what it was like.'

'I suppose that's true. I had hoped . . .'

I peered at Scranton, expecting some small show of embarrassment. These faded pages, far from being the mementoes of a real astronaut, were obviously the prompt cards of an impostor. However, there was not the slightest doubt that Scranton was sincere.

I stood in the street below the portico of the Luxor Cinema, whose garish posters, advertising some science-fiction spectacular, seemed as inflamed as the mind of the American. Despite all that I had suspected, I felt an intense disappointment. I had deluded myself, thinking that Scranton would rescue my career. Now I was left with nothing but an empty notebook and the tram journey back to the crowded apartment in Ipanema. I dreaded the prospect of seeing my wife and my mother at the door, their eyes screwed to the same accusing focus.

Nonetheless, as I walked down Copacabana Avenue to the tram-stop, I felt a curious sense of release. The noisy pavements, the arrogant pickpockets plucking at my clothes, the traffic that aggravated the slightest tendency to migraines, all seemed to have receded, as if a small distance had opened between myself and the congested world. My meeting with Scranton, my brief involvement with this marooned man, allowed me to see everything in a more detached way. The businessmen with their briefcases, the afternoon tarts swinging their shiny handbags, the salesmen with their sheets of lottery tickets, almost deferred to me. Time and space had altered their perspectives, and the city was yielding to me. As I crossed the road to the tram-stop several minutes seemed to pass. But I was not run over.

This sense of a loosening air persisted as I rode back to Ipanema. My fellow passengers, who would usually have irritated me with their cheap scent and vulgar clothes, their look of bored animals in a menagerie, now scarcely intruded into my vision. I gazed down corridors of light that ran between them like the aisles of an open-air cathedral.

'You've found a story,' my wife announced within a second of opening the door.

'They've commissioned an article,' my mother confirmed. 'I knew they would.'

They stepped back and watched me as I made a leisurely tour of the cramped apartment. My changed demeanour clearly impressed them. They pestered me with questions, but even their presence was less bothersome. The universe, thanks to Scranton's example, had loosened its grip. Sitting at the dinner table, I silenced them with a raised finger.

'I am about to embark on a new career . . .'

From then on I became ever more involved with Scranton. I had not intended to see the American again, but the germ of his loneliness had entered my blood. Within two days I returned to the café in the side-street, but the tables were deserted. I watched as two parties of tourists stopped to ask for 'the astronaut'. I then questioned the waiter, suspecting that he had banished the poor man. But, no, the American would be back the next day, he had been ill, or perhaps had secretly gone to the moon on business.

In fact, it was three days before Scranton at last appeared. Materialising from the afternoon heat, he entered the café and sat under the awning. At first he failed to notice that I was there, but Scranton's mere presence was enough to satisfy me. The crowds and traffic, which had begun once again to close around me, halted their clamour and withdrew. On the noisy street were imposed the silences of a lunar landscape.

However, it was all too clear that Scranton had been ill. His face was sallow with fever, and the effort of sitting in his chair soon tired him. When the first American tourists stopped at his table he barely rose from his seat, and while the photographs were taken he held tightly to the awning above his head.

By the next afternoon his fever had subsided, but he was so strained and ill-kempt that the waiter at first refused to admit him to the café. A trio of Californian spinsters who approached his table were clearly unsure that this decaying figure was indeed the bogus astronaut, and would have left had I not ushered them back to Scranton.

'Yes, this is Commander Scranton, the famous astronaut. I am his associate – do let me hold your camera . . .'

I waited impatiently for them to leave, and sat down at Scranton's table. Ill the American might be, but I needed him. After ordering a brandy, I helped Scranton to hold the glass. As I pressed the spinsters' bank-note into his pocket I could feel that his suit was soaked with sweat.

'I'll walk you back to your room. Don't thank me, it's in my direction.'

'Well, I could use an arm.' Scranton stared at the street, as if its few yards encompassed a Grand Canyon of space. 'It's getting to be a long way.'

'A long way! Scranton, I understand that . . .'

It took us half an hour to cover the few hundred yards to the Luxor Cinema. But already time was becoming an elastic dimension, and from then on most of my waking hours were spent with Scranton. Each morning I would visit the shabby room behind the cinema, bringing a paper bag of sweet-cakes and a flask of tea I had prepared in the apartment under my wife's suspicious gaze. Often the American had little idea who I was, but this no longer worried me. He lay in his narrow bed, letting me raise his head as I changed the sheets of newspaper that covered his pillow. When he spoke, his voice was too weak to be heard above the sound-tracks of the science-fiction films that boomed through the crumbling walls.

Even in this moribund state, Scranton's example was a powerful tonic, and when I left him in the evening I would walk the crowded streets without any fear. Sometimes my former colleagues called to me from the steps of the newspaper office, but I was barely aware of them, as if they were planetary visitors hailing me from the edge of a remote crater.

Looking back on these exhilarating days, I regret only that I never called a doctor to see Scranton. Frequently, though, the American would recover his strength, and after I had shaved him we would go down into the street. I relished these outings with Scranton. Arm in arm, we moved through the afternoon crowds, which seemed to part around us. Our fellow-pedestrians had become remote and fleeting figures, little more than tricks of the sun. Sometimes, I could no longer see their faces. It was then that I observed the world through Scranton's eyes, and knew what it was to be an astronaut.

Needless to say, the rest of my life had collapsed at my feet. Having given up my work as a translator, I soon ran out of money, and was forced to borrow from my mother. At my wife's instigation, the features editor of the newspaper called me to his office, and made it plain that as an immense concession (in fact he had always been intrigued by my wife) he would let me review a science-fiction film at the Luxor. Before walking out, I told him that I was already too familiar with the film, and my one hope was to see it banned from the city forever.

So ended my connection with the newspaper. Soon after, the two women evicted me from my apartment. I was happy to leave them, taking with me only the reclining sun-chair on which my wife passed most of her days in preparation for her new career as a model. The sun-chair became my bed when I moved into Scranton's room.

By then the decline in Scranton's health forced me to be with him constantly. Far from being an object of charity, Scranton was now my only source of income. Our needs for several days could be met by a single session with the American tourists. I did my best to care for Scranton, but during his final illness I was too immersed in that sense of an emptying world even to notice the young doctor whose alarmed presence filled the tiny room. By a last irony, towards the end even Scranton himself seemed barely visible to me. As he died I was reading the mucus-stained headlines on his pillow.

After Scranton's death I remained in his room at the Luxor. Despite the fame he had once enjoyed, his burial at the Protestant cemetery was attended only by myself, but in a sense this was just, as he and I were the only real inhabitants of the city. Later I went through the few possessions in his suitcase, and found a faded pilot's log-book. Its pages confirmed that Scranton had worked as a pilot for a crop-spraying company in Florida throughout the years of the Apollo programme.

Nonetheless, Scranton had travelled in space. He had known the loneliness of separation from all other human beings, he had gazed at the empty perspectives that I myself had seen. Curiously, the pages torn from the news magazines seemed more real than the pilot's log-book. The photographs of Armstrong and his fellow astronauts were really of Scranton and myself as we walked together on the moon of this world.

I reflected on this as I sat at the small café in the side-street. As a gesture to Scranton's memory, I had chosen his chair below the awning. I thought of the planetary landscapes that Scranton had taught me to see, those empty vistas devoid of human beings. Already I was aware of a previous career, which my wife and the pressures of everyday life had hidden from me. There were the years of training for a great voyage, and a coastline similar to that of Cape Kennedy receding below me ...

My reverie was interrupted by a pair of American tourists. A middle-aged man and his daughter, who held the family camera to her chin, approached the table.

'Excuse me,' the man asked with an over-ready smile. 'Are you the ... the astronaut? We were told by the hotel that you might be here ...'

I stared at them without rancour, treating them to a glimpse of those eyes that had seen the void. I, too, had walked on the moon.

'Please sit down,' I told them casually. 'Yes, I am the astronaut.'

**· 1985**

# THE SECRET HISTORY OF WORLD WAR 3

Now that World War 3 has safely ended, I feel free to comment on two remarkable aspects of the whole terrifying affair. The first is that this long-dreaded nuclear confrontation, which was widely expected to erase all life from our planet, in fact lasted barely four minutes. This will surprise many of those reading the present document, but World War 3 took place on 27 January 1995, between 6:47 and 6:51 p.m. Eastern Standard Time. The entire duration of hostilities, from President Reagan's formal declaration of war, to the launch of five sea-based nuclear missiles (three American and two Russian), to the first peace-feelers and the armistice agreed by the President and Mr Gorbachev, lasted no more than 245 seconds. World War 3 was over almost before anyone realised that it had begun.

The other extraordinary feature of World War 3 is that I am virtually the only person to know that it ever occurred. It may seem strange that a suburban paediatrician living in Arlington, a few miles west of Washington DC, should alone be aware of this unique historical event. After all, the news of every downward step in the deepening political crisis, the ailing President's declaration of war and the following nuclear exchange, was openly broadcast on nationwide television. World War 3 was not a secret, but people's minds were addressed to more important matters. In their obsessive concern for the health of their political leadership, they were miraculously able to ignore a far greater threat to their own well-being.

Of course, strictly speaking, I was not the only person to have witnessed World War 3. A small number of senior military personnel in the Nato and Warsaw Pact high commands, as well as President Reagan, Mr Gorbachev and their aides, and the submarine officers who decrypted the nuclear launch codes and sent the missiles on their way (into unpopulated areas of Alaska and eastern Siberia), were well aware that war had been declared, and a ceasefire agreed four minutes later. But I have yet to meet a member of the ordinary public who has heard of World War 3. Whenever I refer to the war, people stare at me with incredulity. Several parents have withdrawn their children from the paediatric clinic, obviously concerned for my mental stability. Only yesterday one mother to whom I casually mentioned the war later telephoned my wife to express her anxieties. But Susan, like everyone else, has forgotten the war, even though I have played video-recordings to her of the ABC, NBC and CNN newscasts on 27 January which actually announce that World War 3 has begun.

*    *    *

That I alone happened to learn of the war I put down to the curious character of the Reagan third term. It is no exaggeration to say that the United States, and much of the western world, had deeply missed this amiable old actor who retired to California in 1989 after the inauguration of his luckless successor. The multiplication of the world's problems – the renewed energy crises, the second Iran/Iraq conflict, the destabilisation of the Soviet Union's Asiatic republics, the unnerving alliance in the USA between Islam and militant feminism – all prompted an intense nostalgia for the Reagan years. There was an immense affectionate memory of his gaffes and little incompetencies, his fondness (shared by those who elected him) for watching TV in his pyjamas rather than attending to more important matters, his confusion of reality with the half-remembered movies of his youth.

Tourists congregated in their hundreds outside the gates of the Reagans' retirement home in Bel Air, and occasionally the former President would totter out to pose on the porch. There, prompted by a still soignée Nancy, he would utter some amiable generality that brought tears to his listeners' eyes, and lifted both their hearts and stock markets around the world. As his successor's term in office drew to its unhappy close, the necessary constitutional amendment was swiftly passed through both Houses of Congress, with the express purpose of seeing that Reagan could enjoy his third term in the White House.

In January 1993 more than a million people turned out to cheer his inaugural drive through the streets of Washington, while the rest of the world watched on television. If the cathode eye could weep, it did so then.

Nonetheless, a few doubts remained, as the great political crises of the world stubbornly refused to be banished even by the aged President's ingratiating grin. The Iran/Iraq war threatened to embroil Turkey and Afghanistan. In defiance of the Kremlin, the Asiatic republics of the USSR were forming armed militias. Yves Saint Laurent had designed the first chador for the power-dressing Islamicised feminists in the fashionable offices of Manhattan, London and Paris. Could even the Reagan presidency cope with a world so askew?

Along with my fellow-physicians who had watched the President on television, I seriously doubted it. At this time, in the summer of 1994, Ronald Reagan was a man of eighty-three, showing all the signs of advancing senility. Like many old men, he enjoyed a few minutes each day of modest lucidity, during which he might utter some gnomic remark, and then lapse into a glassy twilight. His eyes were now too blurred to read the teleprompter, but his White House staff took advantage of the hearing aid he had always worn to insert a small speaker, so that he was able to recite his speeches by repeating like a child whatever he heard in his earpiece. The pauses were edited out by the TV networks, but the hazards of remote control were revealed when the President, addressing the Catholic Mothers of America, startled the massed ranks of blue-rinsed ladies by suddenly repeating a studio engineer's aside: 'Shift your ass, I gotta take a leak.'

Watching this robotic figure with his eerie smiles and goofy grins, a few people began to ask if the President was brain-dead, or even alive at all. To reassure the nervous American public, unsettled by a falling stock market and by the news of armed insurrection in the Ukraine, the White House physicians began to release a series of regular reports on the President's health. A team of specialists at the Walter Reed Hospital assured the nation that he enjoyed the robust physique and mental alertness of a man fifteen years his junior. Precise details of Reagan's blood pressure, his white and red cell counts, pulse and respiration were broadcast on TV and had an immediately calming effect. On the following day the world's stock markets showed a memorable lift, interest rates fell and Mr Gorbachev was able to announce that the Ukrainian separatists had moderated their demands.

Taking advantage of the unsuspected political asset represented by the President's bodily functions, the White House staff decided to issue their medical bulletins on a weekly basis. Not only did Wall Street respond positively, but opinion polls showed a strong recovery by the Republican Party as a whole. By the time of the mid-term Congressional elections, the medical reports were issued daily, and successful Republican candidates swept to control of both House and Senate thanks to an eve-of-poll bulletin on the regularity of the Presidential bowels.

From then on the American public was treated to a continuous stream of information on the President's health. Successive newscasts throughout the day would carry updates on the side-effects of a slight chill or the circulatory benefits of a dip in the White House pool. I well remember watching the news on Christmas Eve as my wife prepared our evening meal, and noticing that details of the President's health occupied five of the six leading news items.

'So his blood sugar is a little down,' Susan remarked as she laid the festival table. 'Good news for Quaker Oats and Pepsi.'

'Really? Is there a connection, for heaven's sake?'

'Much more than you realise.' She sat beside me on the sofa, pepper-mill in hand. 'We'll have to wait for his latest urinalysis. It could be crucial.'

'Dear, what's happening on the Pakistan border could be crucial. Gorbachev has threatened a pre-emptive strike against the rebel enclaves. The US has treaty obligations, theoretically a war could –'

'Sh . . .' Susan tapped my knee with the pepper-mill. 'They've just run an Eysenck Personality Inventory – the old boy's scored full marks on emotional resonance and ability to relate. Results corrected for age, whatever that means.'

'It means he's practically a basket case.' I was about to change channels, hoping for some news of the world's real troublespots, but a curious pattern had appeared along the bottom of the screen, some kind of Christmas decoration, I assumed, a line of stylised holly leaves. The rhythmic wave stabbed softly from left to right, accompanied by the soothing and nostalgic strains of 'White Christmas'.

'Good God . . .' Susan whispered in awe. 'It's Ronnie's pulse. Did you hear the announcer? "Transmitted live from the Heart of the Presidency".'

This was only the beginning. During the next few weeks, thanks to the miracle of modern radio-telemetry, the nation's TV screens became a scoreboard registering every detail of the President's physical and mental functions. His brave, if tremulous, heartbeat drew its trace along the lower edge of the screen, while above it newscasters expanded on his daily physical routines, on the twenty-eight feet he had walked in the rose garden, the calorie count of his modest lunches, the results of his latest brain-scan, read-outs of his kidney, liver and lung function. In addition, there was a daunting sequence of personality and IQ tests, all designed to reassure the American public that the man at the helm of the free world was more than equal to the daunting tasks that faced him across the Oval Office desk.

For all practical purposes, as I tried to explain to Susan, the President was scarcely more than a corpse wired for sound. I and my colleagues at the paediatric clinic were well aware of the old man's ordeal in submitting to this battery of tests. However, the White House staff knew that the American public was almost mesmerised by the spectacle of the President's heartbeat. The trace now ran below all other programmes, accompanying sit-coms, basketball matches and old World War 2 movies. Uncannily, its quickening beat would sometimes match the audience's own emotional responses, indicating that the President himself was watching the same war films, including those in which he had appeared.

To complete the identification of President and TV screen – a consummation of which his political advisers had dreamed for so long – the White House staff arranged for further layers of information to be transmitted. Soon a third of the nation's TV screens was occupied by print-outs of heartbeat, blood pressure and EEG readings. Controversy briefly erupted when it became clear that delta waves predominated, confirming the long-held belief that the President was asleep for most of the day. However, the audiences were thrilled to know when Mr Reagan moved into REM sleep, the dream-time of the nation coinciding with that of its chief executive.

Untouched by this endless barrage of medical information, events in the real world continued down their perilous road. I bought every newspaper I could find, but their pages were dominated by graphic displays of the Reagan health bulletins and by expository articles outlining the significance of his liver enzyme functions and the slightest rise or fall in the concentration of the Presidential urine. Tucked away on the back pages I found a few brief references to civil war in the Asiatic republics of the Soviet Union, an attempted pro-Russian putsch in Pakistan, the Chinese invasion of Nepal, the mobilisation of Nato and Warsaw Pact reserves, the reinforcement of the US 5th and 7th Fleets.

But these ominous events, and the threat of a Third World War, had the ill luck to coincide with a slight down-turn in the President's health. First reported on 20 January, this trivial cold caught by Reagan from a visiting grandchild drove all other news from the television screens. An army of reporters and film crews camped outside the White House, while a task force of specialists from the greatest research institutions in the land appeared in relays on every channel, interpreting the stream of medical data.

Like a hundred million Americans, Susan spent the next week sitting by the TV set, eyes following the print-out of the Reagan heartbeat.

'It's still only a cold,' I reassured her when I returned from the clinic on 27 January. 'What's the latest from Pakistan? There's a rumour that the Soviets have dropped paratroops into Karachi. The Delta force is moving from Subik Bay . . .'

'Not now!' She waved me aside, turning up the volume as an anchorman began yet another bulletin.

'. . . here's an update on our report of two minutes ago. Good news on the President's CAT scan. There are no abnormal variations in the size or shape of the President's ventricles. Light rain is forecast for the DC area tonight, and the 8th Air Cavalry have exchanged fire with Soviet border patrols north of Kabul. We'll be back after the break with a report on the significance of that left temporal lobe spike . . .'

'For God's sake, there's no significance.' I took the remote control unit from Susan's clenched hand and began to hunt the channels. 'What about the Russian Baltic Fleet? The Kremlin is putting counter-pressure on Nato's northern flank. The US has to respond . . .'

By luck, I caught a leading network newscaster concluding a bulletin. He beamed confidently at the audience, his glamorous copresenter smiling in anticipation.

'. . . as of 5:05 Eastern Standard Time we can report that Mr Reagan's inter-cranial pressure is satisfactory. All motor and cognitive functions are normal for a man of the President's age. Repeat, motor and cognitive functions are normal. Now, here's a newsflash that's just reached us. At 2:35 local time President Reagan completed a satisfactory bowel motion.' The newscaster turned to his copresenter. 'Barbara, I believe you have similar good news on Nancy?'

'Thank you, Dan,' she cut in smoothly. 'Yes, just one hour later, at 3:35 local time, Nancy completed her very own bowel motion, her second for the day, so it's all happening in the First Family.' She glanced at a slip of paper pushed across her desk. 'The traffic in Pennsylvania Avenue is seizing up again, while F-16s of the 6th Fleet have shot down seven MiG 29s over the Bering Strait. The President's blood pressure is 100 over 60. The ECG records a slight left-hand tremor . . .'

'A tremor of the left hand . . .' Susan repeated, clenching her fists. 'Surely that's serious?'

I tapped the channel changer. 'It could be. Perhaps he's thinking about having to press the nuclear button. Or else –'

An even more frightening possibility had occurred to me. I plunged through the medley of competing news bulletins, hoping to distract Susan as I glanced at the evening sky over Washington. The Soviet deep-water fleet patrolled 400 miles from the eastern coast of the United States. Soon mushroom clouds could be rising above the Pentagon.

'. . . mild pituitary dysfunction is reported, and the President's physicians have expressed a modest level of concern. Repeat, a modest level of concern. The President convened the National Security Council some thirty minutes ago. SAC headquarters in Omaha, Nebraska, report all B-52 attack squadrons airborne. Now, I've just been handed a late bulletin from the White House Oncology Unit. A benign skin tumour was biopsied at 4:15 Washington time . . .'

'. . . the President's physicians have again expressed their concern over Mr Reagan's calcified arteries and hardened cardiac valves. Hurricane Clara is now expected to bypass Puerto Rico, and the President has invoked the Emergency War Powers Act. After the break we'll have more expert analysis of Mr Reagan's retrograde amnesia. Remember, this condition can point to suspected Korsakoff syndrome . . .'

'. . . psychomotor seizures, a distorted sense of time, colour changes and dizziness. Mr Reagan also reports an increased awareness of noxious odours. Other late news – blizzards cover the mid-west, and a state of war now exists between the United States and the Soviet Union. Stay tuned to this channel for a complete update on the President's brain metabolism . . .'

'We're at war,' I said to Susan, and put my arms around her shoulders. But she was pointing to the erratic heart trace on the screen. Had the President suffered a brain storm and launched an all-out nuclear attack on the Russians? Were the incessant medical bulletins a clever camouflage to shield a volatile TV audience from the consequences of a desperate response to a national emergency? It would take only minutes for the Russian missiles to reach Washington, and I stared at the placid winter sky. Holding Susan in my arms, I listened to the cacophony of medical bulletins until, some four minutes later, I heard:

'. . . the President's physicians report dilated pupils and convulsive tremor, but neurochemical support systems are functioning adequately. The President's brain metabolism reveals increased glucose production. Scattered snow-showers are forecast overnight, and a cessation of hostilities has been agreed between the US and the USSR. After the break –

the latest expert comment on that attack of Presidential flatulence. And why Nancy's left eyelid needed a tuck . . .'

I switched off the set and sat back in the strange silence. A small helicopter was crossing the grey sky over Washington. Almost as an afterthought, I said to Susan: 'By the way, World War 3 has just ended.'

Of course, Susan had no idea that the war had ever begun, a common failure among the public at large, as I realised over the next few weeks. Most people had only a vague recollection of the unrest in the Middle East. The news that nuclear bombs had landed in the deserted mountains of Alaska and eastern Siberia was lost in the torrent of medical reports that covered President Reagan's recovery from his cold.

In the second week of February 1995 I watched him on television as he presided over an American Legion ceremony on the White House lawn. His aged, ivory face was set in its familiar amiable grin, his eyes unfocused as he stood supported by two aides, the ever-watchful First Lady standing in her steely way beside him. Somewhere beneath the bulky black overcoat the radio-telemetry sensors transmitted the live print-outs of pulse, respiration and blood pressure that we could see on our screens. I guessed that the President, too, had forgotten that he had recently launched the Third World War. After all, no one had been killed, and in the public's mind the only possible casualty of those perilous hours had been Mr Reagan himself as he struggled to survive his cold.

Meanwhile, the world was a safer place. The brief nuclear exchange had served its warning to the quarrelling factions around the planet. The secessionist movements in the Soviet Union had disbanded themselves, while elsewhere invading armies withdrew behind their frontiers. I could almost believe that World War 3 had been contrived by the Kremlin and the White House staff as a peacemaking device, and that the Reagan cold had been a diversionary trap into which the TV networks and newspapers had unwittingly plunged.

In tribute to the President's recuperative powers, the linear traces of his vital functions still notched their way across our TV screens. As he saluted the assembled veterans of the American Legion, I sensed the audience's collective pulse beating faster when the old actor's heart responded to the stirring sight of these marching men.

Then, among the Medal of Honor holders, I noticed a dishevelled young man in an ill-fitting uniform, out of step with his older companions. He pushed through the marching files as he drew a pistol from his tunic. There was a flurry of confusion while aides grappled with each other around the podium. The cameras swerved to catch the young man darting towards the President. Shots sounded above the wavering strains of the band. In the panic of uniformed men the President seemed to fall into the First Lady's arms and was swiftly borne away.

Searching the print-outs below the TV screen, I saw at once that the President's blood pressure had collapsed. The erratic pulse had levelled out into an unbroken horizontal line, and all respiratory function had ceased. It was only ten minutes later, as news was released of an unsuccessful assassination attempt, that the traces resumed their confident signatures.

Had the President died, perhaps for a second time? Had he, in a strict sense, ever lived during his third term of office? Will some animated spectre of himself, reconstituted from the medical print-outs that still parade across our TV screens, go on to yet further terms, unleashing Fourth and Fifth World Wars, whose secret histories will expire within the interstices of our television schedules, forever lost within the ultimate urinalysis, the last great biopsy in the sky?

**1988**

# · LOVE IN A COLDER CLIMATE

Anyone reading this confession in 1989, the year when I was born, would have been amazed to find me complaining about a state of affairs that must in every respect have resembled paradise. However, yesterday's heaven all too easily becomes today's hell. The greatest voluptuary dream of mankind, which has lifted the spirits of poets and painters, presidents and peasants, has turned only twenty-two years later into a living nightmare. For young men of my own generation (the word provokes a shudder in the heart, if nowhere else), the situation has become so desperate that any escape seems justified. The price that I have paid for my freedom may seem excessive, but I am happy to have made this savage, if curious, bargain.

Soon after I reached my twenty-first birthday I was ordered to enlist for my two years of national service, and I remember thinking how much my father and grandfather would have envied me. On a pleasant summer evening in 2010, after a tiring day at the medical school, I was ringing the doorbell of an apartment owned by an attractive young woman whose name I had been given. I had never met her, but I was confident that she would greet me in the friendliest way – so friendly that within a few minutes we would be lying naked together in bed. Needless to say, no money would change hands, and neither she nor I would play our parts for less than the most patriotic motives. Yet both of us would loathe the sight and touch of the other and would be only too relieved when we parted an hour later.

Sure enough, the door opened to reveal a confident young brunette with a welcoming, if brave, smile. According to my assignment card, she was Victoria Hale, a financial journalist on a weekly news magazine. Her eyes glanced at my face and costume in the shrewd way she might have scanned a worthy but dull company prospectus.

'David Bradley?' She read my name from her own assignment card, trying hard to muster a show of enthusiasm. 'You're a medical student . . . How fascinating.'

'It's wonderful to meet you, Victoria,' I riposted. 'I've always wanted to know about . . . financial journalism.'

I stood awkwardly in the centre of her apartment, my legs turning to lead. These lines of dialogue, like those that followed, had seemed preposterous when I first uttered them. But my supervisor had wisely insisted that I stick to the script, and already, after only three months

1124

of national service, I was aware that the formalised dialogue, like our absurd costumes, provided a screen behind which we could hide our real feelings.

I was wearing the standard-issue Prince Valiant suit, which a careful survey of the TV programmes of the 1960s had confirmed to be the most sexually attractive costume for the predatory male. In a suit like this Elvis Presley had roused the Las Vegas matrons to an ecstasy of abandon, though I found its tassels, gold braid and tight crotch as comfortable as the decorations on a Christmas tree.

Victoria Hale, for her part, was wearing a classic Playboy bunny outfit of the same period. As she served me a minute measure of vodka her breasts managed to be both concealed and exposed in a way that an earlier generation must have found irresistibly fascinating, like the rabbit tail that bounced above her contorted buttocks, a furry metronome which already had me glancing at my wristwatch.

'Mr Bradley, we can get it over with now,' she remarked briskly. She had departed from the script but quickly added: 'Now tell me about your work, David. I can see that you're such an interesting man.'

She was as bored with me as I was uneasy with her, but in a few minutes we would be lying together in bed. With luck my hormonal and nervous systems would come to my rescue and bring our meeting to a climax. We would initial each other's assignment cards and make a thankful return to our ordinary lives. Yet the very next evening another young man in a Prince Valiant suit would ring the doorbell of the apartment, and this thoughtful journalist would greet him in her grotesque costume. And I, in turn, at eight o'clock would put aside my anatomy textbooks and set out through the weary streets to an arranged meeting in an unknown apartment, where some pleasant young woman – student, waitress or librarian – would welcome me with the same formal smile and stoically take me to bed.

To understand this strange world where sex has become compulsory, one must look back to the ravages brought about in the last decade of the 20th century by the scourge of Aids and the pandemic of associated diseases clustered around its endlessly mutating virus. By the mid-1990s this ferocious plague had begun to threaten more than the millions of individual lives. The institutions of marriage and the family, ideals of parenthood, and the social contract between the sexes, even the physical relationship between man and woman, had been corrupted by this cruel disease. Terrified of infection, people learnt to abstain from every kind of physical or sexual contact. From puberty onward, an almost visible cordon divided the sexes. In offices, factories, schools and universities the young men and women kept their distance. My own parents in the 1980s were among the last generation to marry without any fear of what their union might produce. By the 1990s, too often, courtship and marriage would be followed by a series of mysterious ailments, anxious visits to a test clinic, a positive diagnosis and the terminal hospice.

Faced with a plunging birth rate and with a nation composed almost entirely of solitary celibates, the government could resort only to its traditional instruments – legislation and compulsion. Urged on by the full authority of the Protestant and Catholic churches, the Third Millennium was greeted with the momentous announcement that thenceforth sex would be compulsory. All fertile, healthy and HIV-negative young men and women were required to register for their patriotic duty. On reaching their twenty-first birthdays they were assigned a personal supervisor (usually a local clergyman, the priesthood alone having the moral qualifications for such a delicate task), who drew up a list of possible mates and arranged a programme of sexual liaisons. Within a year, it was hoped, the birth rate would soar, and marriage and the family would be re-established.

At first, only one assignation each week was required, but the birth rate stubbornly refused to respond, possibly as a result of the sexual ineptness of these celibate young men and women. By the year 2005 the number of compulsory assignations was raised to three each week. Since clearly nothing could be left to nature, the participants were issued with costumes designed to enhance their attractiveness. In addition to the Prince Valiant and the Bunny Girl, there were the Castilian Waiter and the Gypsy Brigand for men and the Cheerleader and the Miss America swimsuit for women.

Even so, the earliest participants would often sit tongue-tied for hours, unable to approach each other, let alone hold hands. From then on they were carefully coached in the amatory arts by their clergymen-supervisors, who would screen erotic videos for the young recruits in their church halls, by now substantial warehouses of pornographic films and magazines.

As could be expected, the threat of two years of enforced sexual activity was deeply resented by the conscripted young men and women. Draft-dodging was carried to extreme lengths, of which vasectomy was the most popular, any perpetrators being sentenced to a testicular transplant. To prevent the young people from failing to perform their sexual duties, a network of undercover inspectors (usually novice priests and nuns, since only they possessed the necessary spirit of self-sacrifice) posed as the participants and would exact fierce on-the-spot fines for any slackening-off or lack of zeal.

All this at last had its effect on the birth rate, which began its reluctant ascent. The news was little consolation to those like myself, who every evening were obliged to leave our homes and trudge the streets on the way to yet another hour of loveless sex. How I longed for June 2012, when I would complete my period of patriotic duty and begin my real sex life of eternal celibacy.

Those dreams, though, came to an abrupt end in the spring of 2011, when I called upon Lucille McCabe. After meeting her I woke to discover a lost world of passion and the affections whose existence I had never suspected, and to fulfill my life's ambition in a way I had not foreseen.

Lucille McCabe, my assignment for the evening, lived in the Spanish quarter of the city, and to avoid any catcalls – those of us doing our patriotic duty were figures of fun, not envy – I had dressed in my Castilian Waiter costume. The apartment was in a nondescript building kept on its feet by an armature of crumbling fire escapes. An elevator surely booked into a museum of industrial archaeology carried me grudgingly to the seventh floor. The bell hung by a single exposed wire, and I had to tap several times on the door. The silence made me hope that Miss McCabe, a lecturer in English literature, had been called away for the evening.

But the door opened with a jerk, revealing a small, white-faced young woman with spiky black hair, dressed in a polka-dot leotard like a punk circus clown.

'Miss McCabe . . . ?' I began. 'Are you –'

'Ready to order?' She gazed with mock wide eyes at my waiter's costume. 'Yes, I'll have a paella with a side dish of gambas. And don't forget the Tabasco.'

'Tabasco? Look, I'm David Bradley, your partner for –'

'Relax, Mr Bradley.' She closed the door and snatched the keys from the lock, which she jingled in my face. 'It was a joke. Remember those?'

'Only just.' Clearly I was in the presence of a maverick, one of those wayward young women who affected an antic air as a way of rising above the occasion. 'Well, it's wonderful to see you, Lucille. I've always wanted to know about English literature.'

'Forget it. How long have you been doing this? You don't look totally numbed.' She stood with her back to me by the crowded bookshelf, fingers drumming along the titles as if hunting for some manual that would provide a solution to the problem posed by my arrival. For all the bravado, her shoulders were shaking. 'Is this where I fix you a drink? I can't remember that awful script.'

'Skip the drink. We can get straight on with it if you're in a hurry.'

'I'm not in a hurry at all.' She walked stiffly into the bedroom and sat like a moody teenager on the unmade divan. Nothing in my counselling sessions, the long hours watching porno videos in the church hall, had prepared me for all this – the non-regulation costume, the tousled sheets, the absence of flattering chitchat. Was she a new kind of undercover inspector, an *agent provocateur* targeted at those potential subversives like myself? Already I saw my work norm increased to seven evenings a week. Beyond that lay the fearsome threat of a testicular booster . . .

Then I noticed her torn assignment card on the carpet at her feet. No inspector, however devious, would ever maltreat an assignment card.

Wondering how to console her, I stepped forward. But as I crossed the threshold a small, strong hand shot up.

'Stay there!' She gazed at me with the desperate look of a child about to be assaulted, and I realised that for all her fierceness she was a novice recruit, probably on her first assignment. The spiked tips of her hair were trembling like the eye feathers of a trapped peafowl.

'All right, you can come in. Do you want something to eat? I can guarantee the best scrambled egg in town, my hands are shaking so much. How do you put up with all this?'

'I don't think about it any more.'

'I don't think about anything else. Look, Mr Bradley – David, or whatever you're called – I can't go through with this. I don't want to fight with you . . .'

'Don't worry.' I raised my hands, already thinking about the now free evening. 'I'm on my way. The rules forbid all use of force, no fumbling hands or wrestling.'

'How sensible. And how different from my grandmother's day.' She smiled bleakly, as if visualising the courtship that had led to the conception of her own mother. With a nervous shrug, she followed me to the door. 'Tell me, what happens next? I know you have to report me.'

'Well . . . there's nothing too serious.' I hesitated to describe the long counselling sessions that lay ahead, the weeks of being harangued by relays of nuns brandishing their videos. After all the talk there was chemotherapy, when she would be so sedated that nothing mattered, and she would close her eyes and think of her patriotic duty and the next generation, the playgrounds full of laughing tots, one of them her own . . . 'I shouldn't worry. They're very civilised. At least you'll get a better apartment.'

'Oh, thanks. Once, you must have been rather sweet. But they get you in the end . . .'

I took the latchkey from her hand, wondering how to reassure her. The dye had run down her powdered forehead, a battle line redrawn across her brain. She stood with her back against the bookshelves, a woad-streaked Boadicea facing the Roman legions. Despite her distress, I had the curious sense that she was as concerned for me as for herself and even now was trying to work out some strategy that would save us both.

'No . . .' I closed the door and locked it again. 'They won't get you. Not necessarily . . .'

My love affair with Lucille McCabe began that evening, but the details of our life together belong to the private domain. Not that there is anything salacious to reveal. As it happens, our relationship was never consummated in the physical sense, but this did not in any way diminish my deep infatuation with this remarkable young woman. The long months of my national service notwithstanding, the hundreds of reluctant Rebeccas and stoical Susans, I soon felt that Lucille McCabe was the only woman I had ever really known. During the six months of our clandestine affair I discovered a wealth of emotion and affection that made me envy all earlier generations.

At the start, my only aim was to save Lucille. I forged signatures, hoodwinked a distracted supervisor confused by the derelict apartment building, begged or bribed my friends to swap shifts, and Lucille feigned a pregnancy with the aid of a venal laboratory technician. Marriage or any monogamous relationship was taboo during the period of one's patriotic duty, the desired aim being an open promiscuity and the greatest possible stirring of the gene pool. Nonetheless, I was able to spend almost all my spare time with Lucille, acting as lover, night watchman, spymaster and bodyguard. She, in turn, made sure that my medical studies were not neglected. Once I had qualified and she herself was free to marry, we would legally become man and wife.

Inevitably we were discovered by a suspicious supervisor with an over-sensitive computer. I had already realised that we would be exposed, and during these last months I became more and more protective of Lucille, even feeling the first pangs of jealousy. I would attend her lectures, sitting in the back row and resenting any student who asked an over-elaborate question. At my insistence she abandoned her punk hairstyle for something less provocative and modestly lowered her eyes whenever a man passed her in the street.

All this tension was to explode when the supervisor arrived at Lucille's apartment. The sight of this dark-eyed young Jesuit in his Gypsy Brigand costume, mouthing his smooth amatory patter as he expertly steered Lucille towards her bedroom, proved too much for me. I gave way to a paroxysm of violence, hurling the fellow from the apartment.

From the moment the ambulance and police were called, our scheme was over. Lucille was assigned to a rehabilitation centre, once a church home for fallen mothers, and I was brought before a national service tribunal.

In vain I protested that I wished to marry Lucille and father her child. I had merely behaved like a male of old and was passionately dedicated to my future wife and family.

But this, I was told, was a selfish aberration. I was found guilty of the romantic fallacy and convicted of having an exalted and idealised vision of woman. I was sentenced to a further three years of patriotic duty.

If I rejected this, I would face the ultimate sanction.

Aware that by choosing the latter I would be able to see Lucille, I made my decision. The tribunal despaired of me, but as a generous concession to a former student of medicine, they allowed me to select my own surgeon.

**1989**

# THE ENORMOUS SPACE

I made my decision this morning – soon after eight o'clock, as I stood by the front door, ready to drive to the office. All in all, I'm certain that I had no other choice. Yet, given that this is the most important decision of my life, it seems strange that nothing has changed. I expected the walls to tremble, at the very least a subtle shift in the perspectives of these familiar rooms.

In a sense, the lack of any response reflects the tranquil air of this London suburb. If I were living, not in Croydon but in the Bronx or West Beirut, my action would be no more than sensible local camouflage. Here it runs counter to every social value, but is invisible to those it most offends.

Even now, three hours later, all is calm. The leafy avenue is as unruffled as ever. The mail has arrived, and sits unopened on the hall stand. From the dining-room window I watch the British Telecom engineer return to his van after repairing the Johnsons' telephone, an instrument reduced to a nervous wreck at least twice a month by their teenage daughters. Mrs Johnson, dressed in her turquoise track-suit, closes the gate and glances at my car. A faint vapour rises from the exhaust. The engine is still idling, all these hours after I began to demist the windscreen before finishing my breakfast.

This small slip may give the game away. Watching the car impatiently, I am tempted to step from the house and switch off the ignition, but I manage to control myself. Whatever happens, I must hold to my decision and all the consequences that flow from it. Fortunately, an Air India 747 ambles across the sky, searching none too strenuously for London Airport. Mrs Johnson, who shares something of its heavy-bodied elegance, gazes up at the droning turbo-fans. She is dreaming of Martinique or Mauritius, while I am dreaming of nothing.

My decision to dream that dream may have been made this morning, but I assume that its secret logic had begun to run through my life many months ago. Some unknown source of strength sustained me through the unhappy period of my car accident, convalescence and divorce, and the unending problems that faced me at the merchant bank on my return. Standing by the front door after finishing my coffee, I watched the mist clear from the Volvo's windscreen. The briefcase in my hand reminded me of the day-long meetings of the finance committee at which I would have to argue once again for the budget of my beleaguered research department.

Then, as I set the burglar alarm, I realised that I could change the course of my life by a single action. To shut out the world, and solve all my difficulties at a stroke, I had the simplest of weapons – my own front door. I needed only to close it, and decide never to leave my house again.

Of course, this decision involved more than becoming a mere stay-at-home. I remember walking into the kitchen, surprised by this sudden show of strength, and trying to work out the implications of what I had done. Still wearing my business suit and tie, I sat at the kitchen table, and tapped out my declaration of independence on the polished formica.

By closing the front door I intended to secede not only from the society around me. I was rejecting my friends and colleagues, my accountant, doctor and solicitor, and above all my ex-wife. I was breaking off all practical connections with the outside world. I would never again step through the front door. I would accept the air and the light, and the electric power and water that continued to flow through the meters. But otherwise I would depend on the outside world for nothing. I would eat only whatever food I could find within the house. After that I would rely on time and space to sustain me.

The Volvo's engine is still running. It is 3 p.m., seven hours after I first switched on the ignition, but I can't remember when I last filled the tank. It's remarkable how few passers-by have noticed the puttering exhaust – only the retired headmaster who patrols the avenue morning and afternoon actually stopped to stare at it. I watched him mutter to himself and shake his walking-stick before shuffling away.

The murmur of the engine unsettles me, like the persistent ringing of the telephone. I can guess who is calling: Brenda, my secretary; the head of marketing, Dr Barnes; the personnel manager, Mr Austen (I have already been on sick-leave for three weeks); the dental receptionist (a tender root canal reminds me that I had an appointment yesterday); my wife's solicitor, insisting that the first of the separation payments is due in six months' time.

Finally I pick up the telephone cable and pull the jack on this persistent din. Calming myself, I accept that I will admit to the house anyone with a legitimate right to be there – the TV rental man, the gas and electricity meter-readers, even the local police. I cannot expect to be left completely on my own. At the same time, it will be months before my action arouses any real suspicions, and I am confident that by then I will long since have moved into a different realm.

I feel tremendously buoyant, almost lightheaded. Nothing matters any more. Think only of essentials: the physics of the gyroscope, the flux of photons, the architecture of very large structures.

Five p.m. Time to take stock and work out the exact resources of this house in which I have lived for seven years.

First, I carry my unopened mail into the dining room, open a box of matches and start a small, satisfying fire in the grate. To the flames I add the contents of my briefcase, all the bank-notes in my wallet, credit cards, driving licence and cheque-book.

I inspect the kitchen and pantry shelves. Before leaving, Margaret had stocked the freezer and refrigerator with a fortnight's supply of eggs, ham and other bachelor staples – a pointed gesture, bearing in mind that she was about to sail off into the blue with her lover (a tedious sales manager). These basic rations fulfil the same role as the keg of fresh water and sack of flour left at the feet of a marooned sailor, a reminder of the world rejecting him.

I weigh the few cartons of pasta in my hand, the jars of lentils and rice, the tomatoes and courgettes, the rope of garlic. Along with the tinned anchovies and several sachets of smoked salmon in the freezer, there are enough calories and protein to keep me going for at least ten days, three times that period if I ration myself. After that I will have to boil the cardboard boxes into a nutritious broth and rely on the charity of the wind.

At 6.15 the car's engine falters and stops.

In every way I am marooned, but a reductive Crusoe paring away exactly those elements of bourgeois life which the original Robinson so dutifully reconstituted. Crusoe wished to bring the Croydons of his own day to life again on his island. I want to expel them, and find in their place a far richer realm formed from the elements of light, time and space.

The first week has ended peacefully. All is well, and I have stabilised my regime most pleasantly. To my surprise, it has been remarkably easy to reject the world. Few people have bothered me. The postman has delivered several parcels, which I carry straight to the dining-room fireplace. On the third day my secretary, Brenda, called at the front door. I smiled winningly, reassured her that I was merely taking an extended sabbatical. She looked at me in her sweet but shrewd way – she had been strongly supportive during both my divorce and the crisis at the office – and then left with a promise to keep in touch. A succession of letters has arrived from Dr Barnes, but I warm my hands over them at the fireplace. The dining-room grate has become an efficient incinerator in which I have erased my entire past – passport; birth, degree and share certificates; uncashed traveller's cheques and 2000 French Francs left from our last unhappy holiday in Nice; letters from my broker and orthopaedic surgeon. Documents of a dead past, they come to life briefly in the flame, and then write themselves into the dust.

Eliminating this detritus has kept me busy. I have pulled down the heavy curtains that hung beside the windows. Light has flooded into the rooms, turning every wall and ceiling into a vivid tabula rasa. Margaret had taken with her most of the ornaments and knickknacks, and the rest I have heaved into a cupboard. Suffused with light, the house can breathe. Upstairs the windows are open to the sky. The rooms seem larger and less confined, as if they too have found freedom. I sleep well, and when I wake in the morning I almost feel myself on some Swiss mountain-top, with half the sky below me.

Without doubt, I am very much better. I have put away the past, a zone that I regret ever entering. I enjoy the special ease that comes from no longer depending on anyone else, however well-intentioned.

Above all, I am no longer dependent on myself. I feel no obligation to that person who fed and groomed me, who provided me with expensive clothes, who drove me about in his motor-car, who furnished my mind with intelligent books and exposed me to interesting films and art exhibitions. Wanting none of these, I owe that person, myself, no debts. I am free at last to think only of the essential elements of existence – the visual continuum around me, and the play of air and light. The house begins to resemble an advanced mathematical surface, a three-dimensional chessboard. The pieces have yet to be placed, but I feel them forming in my mind.

A policeman is approaching the house. A uniformed constable, he has stepped from a patrol car parked by the gate. He looks up at the roof, watched by an elderly couple who seem to have summoned him.

Confused, I debate whether to answer the doorbell. My arms and shirt are streaked with soot from the fireplace.

'Mr Ballantyne –?' A rather naïve young constable is looking me up and down. 'Are you the householder?'

'Can I help you, officer?' I assume the convincing pose of a law-abiding suburbanite, interrupted in that act of lay worship, do-it-yourself.

'We've had reports of a break-in, sir. Your upstairs windows have been open all night – for two or three nights, your neighbours say. They thought you might be away.'

'A break-in?' This throws me. 'No, I've been here. In fact, I'm not planning to go out at all. I'm cleaning the chimneys, officer, getting rid of all that old soot and dust.'

'Fair enough . . .' He hesitates before leaving, nose roving about for some irregularity he has sniffed, like a dog convinced of a hidden treat. He is certain that in some reprehensible way I am exploiting the suburban norms, like a wife-beater or child-molester.

I wait until he drives away, disappearing into that over-worked hologram called reality. Afterwards I lean against the door, exhausted by this false alarm. The effort of smiling at the officer reminds me of the interior distance I have travelled in the past week. But I must be careful, and hide behind those façades of conventional behaviour that I intend to subvert.

I close the windows that face the street, and then step with relief into the open bedrooms above the garden. The walls form sections of huge box-antennae tuned to the light. I think of the concrete inclines of the old racing track at Brooklands, and the giant chambers excavated from the bauxite cliffs at Les Baux, where Margaret first began to distance herself from me.

Of course a break-in has occurred, of a very special kind.

A month has passed, a period of many advances and a few setbacks. Resting in the kitchen beside the empty refrigerator, I eat the last of the anchovies and take stock of myself. I have embarked on a long internal migration, following a route partly inscribed within my head and partly within this house, which is a far more complex structure than I realised. I have a sense that there are more rooms than there appear to be at first sight. There is a richness of interior space of which I was totally unaware during the seven years I spent here with Margaret. Light floods everything, expanding the dimensions of walls and ceiling. These quiet streets were built on the site of the old Croydon aerodrome, and it is almost as if the perspectives of the former grass runways have returned to haunt these neat suburban lawns and the minds of those who tend them.

All this excitement has led me to neglect my rationing system. Scarcely anything is left in the pantry – a box of sugar cubes, a tube of tomato paste, and a few shrivelled asparagus tips. I lick my fingers and run them round the bottom of the empty bread bin. Already I find myself wishing that I had fully provisioned myself before embarking on this expedition. But everything I have achieved, the huge sense of freedom, of opened doors and of other doors yet to be opened, were contingent on my acting upon that decision of a moment.

Even so, I have to be careful not to give the game away. I maintain a reasonably kempt appearance, wave from the upstairs windows at Mrs Johnson and gesture apologetically at the overgrown lawn. She understands – I have been abandoned by my wife, condemned to the despair of a womanless world. I am hungry all the time, kept going by not much more than cups of sweetened tea. My weight has plunged; I have lost some fifteen pounds and feel permanently lightheaded.

Meanwhile, the outside world continues to bombard me with its irrelevant messages – junk mail, give-away newspapers, and a barrage of letters from Dr Barnes and the personnel department at the bank. They burn with heavy, solemn flames, and I assume that I have been sacked. Brenda called to see me three days ago, still puzzled by my cheerful demeanour. She told me that she had been reassigned, and that my office has been cleared of its files and furniture.

The letter-slot rattles. From the doormat I pick up two leaflets and a plastic envelope, a free sample of a new brand of chocolate. I rip it from the packing, and sink my teeth into the rubbery core, unable to control the saliva that swamps my mouth. I am so overwhelmed by the taste of food that I fail to hear the door-bell chiming. When I open the door I find a smartly dressed woman in tweed suit and hat, presumably some solicitor's wife working as a volunteer almoner for the local hospital.

'Yes? Can I –?' With an effort I recognise her, as I lick the last of the chocolate from my teeth. 'Margaret . . . ?'

'Of course.' She shakes her head, as if this trivial social gaffe explains everything about me. 'Who on earth did you think I was? Are you all right, Geoffrey?'

'Yes, I'm fine. I've been very busy. What are you looking for?' A frightening prospect crosses my mind. 'You don't want to come back . . . ?'

'Good heavens, no. Dr Barnes telephoned me. He said that you'd resigned. I'm surprised.'

'No, I decided to leave. I'm working on a private project. It's what I've always wanted to do.'

'I know.' Her eyes search the hall and kitchen, convinced that something has changed. 'By the way, I've paid the electricity bill, but this is the last time.'

'Fair enough. Well, I must get back to work.'

'Good.' She is clearly surprised by my self-sufficiency. 'You've lost weight. It suits you.'

The house relaxes its protective hold on me. When Margaret has gone I reflect on how quickly I have forgotten her. There are no tugs of old affection. I have changed, my senses tuned to all the wave-lengths of the invisible. Margaret has remained in a more limited world, one of a huge cast of repertory players in that everlasting provincial melodrama called ordinary life.

Eager to erase her memory, I set off upstairs, and open the windows to enjoy the full play of afternoon sun. The west-facing rooms above the garden have become giant observatories. The dust cloaks everything with a mescalin haze of violet light, photons backing up as they strike the surface of window-sill and dressing-table. Margaret has taken many pieces of furniture with her, leaving unexpected gaps and intervals, as if this is a reversed spatial universe, the template of the one we occupied together. I can almost sit down in her absent William Morris chair, nearly see myself reflected in the missing art deco mirror whose chromium rim has left a halo on the bathroom wall.

A curious discovery – the rooms *are* larger. At first I thought that this was an illusion brought about by the sparse furnishings, but the house has always been bigger than I realised. My eyes now see everything as it is, uncluttered by the paraphernalia of conventional life, as in those few precious moments when one returns from holiday and sees one's home in its true light.

Dazed by the vivid air, I blunder into Margaret's bedroom. The walls are strangely displaced, as if a team of scene-shifters have pulled them back to create a new stage set. There is no sign of the bed, and its bare mattress marked by the wine I spilled on the evening of her departure while commiserating over her dull lover. I have strayed into an unfamiliar area of the room, somewhere between Margaret's bathroom and the fitted cupboards. The remainder of the room sheers away from me, the walls pushed back by the light. For the first time I see the bed, but it seems as remote as an old divan at the rear of an empty warehouse.

Another door leads to a wide and silent corridor, clearly unentered for years. There is no staircase, but far away there are entrances to other rooms, filled with the sort of light that glows from X-ray viewing screens. Here and there an isolated chair sits against a wall, in one immense room there is nothing but a dressing table, in another the gleaming cabinet of a grandfather clock presides over the endlessly carpeted floor.

The house is revealing itself to me in the most subtle way. Surprised by its perspectives, I trip over my own feet and feel my heart race ahead of me. I find a wall and press my hands to the striped paper, then fumble through the overlit air towards the landing. At last I reach the top of a huge staircase, whose banisters shrink together as I race to the safety of the floor below.

The true dimensions of this house may be exhilarating to perceive, but from now on I will sleep downstairs. Time and space are not necessarily on my side.

I have trapped a cat. So unnerved was I by the experience of losing myself in my own home that it takes me half an hour to realise that I have a small companion, Mrs Johnson's white Persian. While I was blundering around the Marienbad Palace that now occupies the first floor the cat entered the sitting room through the open french window, and was trapped when a gust of air closed the door.

She follows me around amiably, waiting to be fed, but for once I am in need of her charity.

Two months have now passed. This conventional suburban villa is in fact the junction between our small illusory world and another larger and more real one. Miraculously, I have survived, though my last reserves of food were exhausted weeks ago. As I expected, Margaret paid a second and final visit. Still puzzled by my self-confidence and handsomely slimming figure, she told me that she would no longer be responsible for my mounting debts. I bade her farewell, and returned to my lunch of poodle pie.

The thought that I would never see Margaret again gave my modest meal an added relish, and afterwards I carefully set the dog-trap by the open door of the sitting room. The untended garden with its knee-deep grass has attracted my neighbours' pets, trusting beasts who trundle happily towards me as I sit smiling in the armchair, cleaver concealed within an inviting cushion. By the time their ever-hopeful owners call round a few days later I have safely consigned the bones to the space below the dining-room floorboards, a substantial ossuary that is the last resting-place of Bonzo, Major, Yorky and Mr Fred.

These dogs and cats, and the few birds I have been able to trap, soon formed my sole fare. However, it became clear that my neighbours were keeping a more careful eye on their pets, and I resigned myself to a diet of air. Fortunately, the television rental company intervened to provide a generous source of extra rations.

I remember the dour young man with the tool-kit who arrived to dismantle the attic aerial. He had made several earlier calls in the avenue, and had parked his van a hundred yards away. I followed him up the stairs, concerned that he too might lose his way among those vast rooms.

Sadly, my attempt to warn him came to nothing. As he stepped into the first of those white chambers, as large as aircraft hangars carved in the roof of an iceberg, he seemed to realise that he had entered a zone of danger. I grappled with him as we blundered through that white world, like arctic explorers losing all sense of distance within a few steps of their tent. An hour later, when I had calmed his fears and carried him down the staircase, he had sadly yielded to the terrors of light and space.

Three months – a period of continued discovery and few interruptions. The outside world has at last decided to leave me alone. I no longer answer the door, and there has been scarcely a caller, though threatening letters arrive from the local council, and from the water and electricity companies. But an unshakable logic is at work, and I am confident that my project will be complete before the power and water supplies are disconnected.

The house enlarges itself around me. The invasion of light which revealed its true dimensions has now reached the ground floor. To keep my bearings I have been forced to retreat into the kitchen, where I have moved my mattress and blankets. Now and then I venture into the hall and search the looming perspectives. It amazes me that Margaret and I once lived in this vast pile and so reduced it in our minds.

Already I can feel the walls of the kitchen distancing themselves from me. I spend all day here, sitting on the floor against the freezer cabinet. The cooker, refrigerator and dishwasher have become anonymous objects in some remote department store display. How much longer can this expansion continue? Sooner or later the process will halt, at that moment revealing the true dimensions of the world we inhabit, and which the visual centres of our timid brains have concealed from us. I am on the verge of a unique revelation, the equal perhaps of Columbus's discovery of the new world. I can scarcely wait to bring the news to my neighbours – the modest villa which Mrs Johnson imagines herself to occupy is in fact an immense Versailles!

Near by, the bones of the TV repairman lie on the yellow linoleum like the ribs and skull of a long-decayed desert traveller.

Somewhere a door is being forced. I listen to the grating of keys testing a lock, then the sound of heels on the patio steps before a second attempt to prise open the french window.

Rousing myself, I sway across the kitchen, trying to steady my arms against the faraway washing machine. A key turns, and a door opens somewhere beyond the great carpeted perspectives of the sitting room.

A young woman has entered the house. As she returns the keys to her handbag I recognise Brenda, my former secretary. She stares at the dismantled dog-traps beside the window and then peers around the room, at last seeing me as I watch her beside the door.

'Mr Ballantyne? I'm sorry to break in. I was worried that you might . . .' She smiles reassuringly and takes the keys from her handbag. 'Mrs Ballantyne said I could use the spare set. You haven't answered the phone, and we wondered if you'd fallen ill . . .'

She is walking towards me, but so slowly that the immense room seems to carry her away from me in its expanding dimensions. She approaches and recedes from me at the same time, and I am concerned that she will lose herself in the almost planetary vastness of this house.

Catching her as she swerves past me, I protect her from the outward rush of time and space.

I assume that we have entered the fourth month. I can no longer see the calendar on the kitchen door, so remote is it from me. I am sitting with my back to the freezer, which I have moved out of the kitchen into the pantry. But already the walls of this once tiny room constitute a universe of their own. The ceiling is so distant that clouds might form below it.

I have eaten nothing for the past week, but I no longer dare to leave the pantry and rarely venture more than a step from my position. I could easily lose my way crossing the kitchen and never be able to return to the only security and companionship that I know.

There is only one further retreat. So much space has receded from me that I must be close to the irreducible core where reality lies. This morning I gave in briefly to the sudden fear that all this has been taking place within my own head. By shutting out the world my mind may have drifted into a realm without yardsticks or sense of scale. For so many years I have longed for an empty world, and may unwittingly have constructed it within this house. Time and space have rushed in to fill the vacuum that I created. It even occurred to me to end the experiment, and I stood up and tried to reach the front door, a journey that seemed as doomed as Scott's return from the South Pole. Needless to say, I was forced to give up the attempt long before crossing the threshold of the hall.

Behind me Brenda lies comfortably, her face only a few inches from my own. But now she too is beginning to move away from me. Covered by a jewelled frost, she rests quietly in the compartment of the freezer, a queen waiting one day to be reborn from her cryogenic sleep.

The perspective lines flow from me, enlarging the interior of the compartment. Soon I will lie beside her, in a palace of ice that will crystallise around us, finding at last the still centre of the world which came to claim me.

**1989**

# THE LARGEST THEME PARK IN THE WORLD

The creation of a united Europe, so long desired and so bitterly contested, had certain unexpected consequences. The fulfilment of this age-old dream was a cause of justified celebration, of countless street festivals, banquets and speeches of self-congratulation. But the Europe which had given birth to the Renaissance and the Protestant Reformation, to modern science and the industrial revolution, had one last surprise up its sleeve.

Needless to say, nothing of this was apparent in 1993. The demolition of so many fiscal and bureaucratic barriers to trade led directly to the goal of a Europe at last united in a political and cultural federation. In 1995, the headiest year since 1968, the necessary legislation was swiftly passed by a dozen parliaments, which dissolved themselves and assigned their powers to the European Assembly at Strasbourg. So there came into being the new Europe, a visionary realm that would miraculously fuse the spirits of Charlemagne and the smart card, Michelangelo and the Club Med, St Augustine and Saint Laurent.

Happily exhausted by their efforts, the new Europeans took off for the beaches of the Mediterranean, their tribal mating ground. Blessed by a benevolent sun and a greenhouse sky, the summer of 1995 ran from April to October. A hundred million Europeans basked on the sand, leaving behind little more than an army of caretakers to supervise the museums, galleries and cathedrals. Excited by the idea of a federal Europe, a vast influx of tourists arrived from the United States, Japan and the newly liberated nations of the Soviet bloc. Guide-books in hand, they gorged themselves on the culture and history of Europe, which had now achieved its spiritual destiny of becoming the largest theme park in the world.

Sustained by these tourist revenues, the ecu soared above the dollar and yen, even though offices and factories remained deserted from Athens to the Atlantic. Indeed, it was only in the autumn of 1995 that the economists at Brussels resigned themselves to the paradox which no previous government had accepted – contrary to the protestant ethic, which had failed so lamentably in the past, the less that Europe worked the more prosperous and contented it became. Delighted to prove this point, the millions of vacationing Europeans on the beaches of the Mediterranean scarcely stirred from their sun-mattresses. Autoroutes and motorways were silent, and graphs of industrial production remained as flat as the cerebral functions of the brain-dead.

An even more significant fact soon emerged. Most of the vacationing

Europeans had extended their holidays from two to three months, but a substantial minority had decided not to return at all. Along the beaches of the Costa del Sol and Côte d'Azur, thousands of French, British and German tourists failed to catch their return flights from the nearby airport. Instead, they remained in their hotels and apartments, lay beside their swimming pools and dedicated themselves to the worship of their own skins.

At first this decision to stay was largely confined to the young and unmarried, to former students and the traditional lumpen-intelligentsia of the beach. But these latter-day refuseniks soon included lawyers, doctors and accountants. Even families with children chose to remain on perpetual holiday. Ignoring the telegrams and phone calls from their anxious employers in Amsterdam, Paris and Düsseldorf, they made polite excuses, applied sun oil to their shoulders and returned to their sail-boats and pedalos. It became all too clear that in rejecting the old Europe of frontiers and national self-interest they had also rejected the bourgeois values that hid behind them. A demanding occupation, a high disposable income, a future mortgaged to the gods of social and professional status, had all been abandoned.

At any event, a movement confined to a few resorts along the Mediterranean coast had, by November 1995, involved tens of thousands of holidaymakers. Those who returned home did so with mixed feelings. By the spring of 1996 more than a million expatriates had settled in permanent exile among the hotels and apartment complexes of the Mediterranean.

By summer this number vastly increased, and brought with it huge demographic and psychological changes. So far, the effects of the beach exodus on the European economy had been slight. Tourism and the sale of large sections of industry to eager Japanese corporations had kept the ecu afloat. As for the exiles in Minorca, Mykonos and the Costa Brava, the cost of living was low and basic necessities few. The hippies and ex-students turned to petty theft and slept on the beach. The lawyers and accountants were able to borrow from their banks when their own resources ran out, offering their homes and businesses as collateral. Wives sold their jewellery, and elderly relatives were badgered into small loans.

Fortunately, the sun continued to shine through the numerous ozone windows and the hottest summer of the century was widely forecast. The determination of the exiles never to return to their offices and factories was underpinned by a new philosophy of leisure and a sense of what constituted a worthwhile life. The logic of the annual beach holiday, which had sustained Europe since the Second World War, had merely been taken to its conclusion. Crime and delinquency were non-existent and the social and racial tolerance of those reclining in adjacent poolside chairs was virtually infinite.

Was Europe about to lead the world in another breakthrough for the third millennium? A relaxed and unpuritan sexual regime now flourished and there was a new-found pride in physical excellence. A host of sporting activities took place, there were classes in judo and karate, aerobics and tai-chi. The variety of fringe philosophies began to rival those of California. The first solar cults emerged on the beaches of Torremolinos and St Tropez. Where once the Mediterranean coast had been Europe's Florida, a bland parade of marinas and hotels, it was now set to be its Venice Beach, a hot-house of muscle-building and millennial dreams.

In the summer of 1996 the first challenge occurred to this regime of leisure. By now the beach communities comprised some five million exiles, and their financial resources were exhausted. Credit cards had long been cancelled, bank accounts frozen, and governments in Paris, London and Bonn waited for the return of the expatriates to their desks and work-benches.

Surprisingly, the determination of the beach communities never wavered. Far from catching their long-delayed return flights, the exiles decided to hold on to their place in the sun. Soon this brought them into direct conflict with local hoteliers and apartment owners, who found themselves housing a huge population of non-paying guests. The police were called in, and the first open riots occurred on the beaches of Malaga, Menton and Rimini.

The exiles, however, were difficult to dislodge. A year of sun and exercise had turned them into a corps of superb athletes, for whom the local shopkeepers, waiters and hoteliers were no match. Gangs of muscular young women, expert in the martial arts, roamed the supermarkets of Spain and the Côte d'Azur, fearlessly helping themselves from the shelves. Acts of open intimidation quickly subdued the managers of hotels and apartment houses.

Local police chiefs, for their part, were reluctant to intervene, for fear of damaging the imminent summer tourist trade. The lawyers and accountants among the exiles, all far more educated and intelligent than their provincial rivals, were adept at challenging any eviction orders or charges of theft. The once passive regime of sun and sand had given way to a more militant mood, sustained by the exiles' conviction in the moral and spiritual rightness of their cause. Acting together, they commandeered any empty villas or apartment houses, whose owners were either too terrified to protest or fled the scene altogether.

The cult of physical perfection had gripped everyone's imagination. Bodies deformed by years bent over the word-processor and fast-food counter were now slim and upright, as ideally proportioned as the figures on the Parthenon frieze. The new evangelism concealed behind the exercise and fitness fads of the 1980s now reappeared. A devotion to physical perfection ruled their lives more strictly than any industrial taskmaster.

Out of necessity, leisure had moved into a more disciplined phase. At dawn the resort beaches of the Mediterranean were filled with companies of martial art enthusiasts, kicking and grunting in unison. Brigades of handsomely tanned men and women drilled together as they faced the sun. No longer did they devote their spare time to lying on the sand, but to competitive sports and fiercely contested track events.

Already the first community leaders had emerged from the strongest and most charismatic of the men and women. The casual anarchy of the earliest days had given way to a sensible and cooperative democracy, where members of informal beach groups had voted on their best course of action before seizing an empty hotel or raiding a wine-store. But this democratic phase had failed to meet the needs and emotions of the hour, and the beach communities soon evolved into more authoritarian form.

The 1996 holiday season brought a welcome respite and millions of new recruits, whose purses were bulging with ecus. When they arrived at Marbella, Ibiza, La Grande Motte and Sestri Levante they found themselves eagerly invited to join the new beach communities. By August 1996, when almost the whole of Europe had set off for the coasts of the sun, the governments of its member countries were faced with the real possibility that much of their populations would not return. Not only would offices and factories be closed forever, but there would be no one left to man the museums and galleries, to collect the dollars, yen and roubles of the foreign tourists who alone sustained their economies. The prospect appeared that the Louvre and Buckingham Palace might be sold to a Japanese hotel corporation, that Chartres and Cologne cathedrals would become subsidiaries of the Disney Company.

Forced to act, the Strasbourg Assembly dispatched a number of task forces to the south. Posing as holidaymakers, teams of investigators roamed the cafés and swimming pools. But the pathetic attempts of these bikini bureaucrats to infiltrate and destabilise the beach enclaves came to nothing, and many defected to the ranks of the exiles.

So at last, in October 1996, the Strasbourg Assembly announced that the beaches of the Mediterranean were closed, that all forms of exercise outside the workplace or the bedroom were illegal, and that the suntan was a prohibited skin embellishment. Lastly, the Assembly ordered its 30 million absent citizens to return home.

Needless to say, these commands were ignored. The beach people who occupied the linear city of the Mediterranean coast, some 3,000 miles long and 300 metres wide, were now a very different breed. The police and gendarmerie who arrived at the coastal resorts found militant bands of body-worshippers who had no intention of resuming their previous lives.

Aware that a clash with the authorities would take place, they had begun to defend their territory, blockading the beach roads with abandoned cars, fortifying the entrances to hotels and apartment houses. By day their scuba teams hunted the coastal waters for fish, while at night raiding parties moved inland, stealing sheep and looting the fields of their vegetable crops. Large sections of Malaga, St Tropez and Corfu were now occupied by exiles, while many of the smaller resorts such as Rosas and Formentera were wholly under their control.

The first open conflict, at Golfe-Juan, was typically short-lived and indecisive. Perhaps unconsciously expecting the Emperor to come ashore, as he had done after his escape from Elba, the police were unable to cope with the militant brigade of bronzed and naked mothers, chanting green and feminist slogans, who advanced towards their water-cannon. Commandos of dentists and architects, releasing their fiercest karate kicks, strutted through the narrow streets in what seemed to be a display of a new folk tradition, attracting unmanageable crowds of American and Japanese tourists from their Cannes hotels. At Port-Vendres, Sitges, Bari and Fréjus the police fell back in confusion, unable to distinguish between the exiles and authentic visiting holidaymakers.

When the police returned in force, supported by units of the army, their arrival only increased the determination of the beach people. The polyglot flavour of the original settlers had given way to a series of national groups recruiting their members from their traditional resorts – the British at Torremolinos, Germans at Rosas, French at Juan les Pins. The resistance within these enclaves reflected their national identity – a rabble of drunken British hooligans roamed the streets of Torremolinos, exposing their fearsome buttocks to the riot police. The Germans devoted themselves to hard work and duty, erecting a Siegfried Line of sand bunkers around the beaches of Rosas, while the massed nipples of Juan were more than enough to hopelessly dazzle the gendarmerie.

In return, each of these national enclaves produced its characteristic leaders. The British resorts were dominated by any number of would-be Thatchers, fierce ladies in one-piece bathing suits who invoked the memory of Churchill and proclaimed their determination to 'fight them on the beaches and never, *never* surrender'. Gaullist throwbacks spoke loftily of the grandeur of French sun and sand, while the Italians proclaimed their 'mare nostrum'.

But above all the tone of these beach-führers was uniformly authoritarian. The sometime holiday exiles now enjoyed lives of fierce self-discipline coupled with a mystical belief in the powers of physical strength. Athletic prowess was admired above all, a cult of bodily perfection mediated through group gymnastic displays on the beaches, quasi-fascistic rallies, in which thousands of well-drilled participants slashed the dawn air with their karate chops and chanted in a single voice at the sun. These bronzed and handsome figures with their thoughtless sexuality looked down on their tourist compatriots with a sense of almost racial superiority.

It was clear that Europe, where so much of western civilisation had originated, had given birth to yet another significant trend, the first totalitarian system based on leisure. From the sun-lounge and the swimming pool, from the gymnasium and disco, had come a nationalistic and authoritarian creed with its roots in the realm of pleasure rather than that of work.

By the spring of 1997, as Brussels fumbled and Strasbourg debated, the

30 million people of the beach were beginning to look north for the first time. They listened to their leaders talking of national living space, of the hordes of alien tourists with their soulless dollars and yen, of the tired blood of their compatriots yearning to be invigorated. As they stood on the beaches of Marbella, Juan, Rimini and Naxos they swung their arms in unison, chanting their exercise songs as they heard the call to march north, expel the invading tourists and reclaim their historic heartlands.

So, in the summer of 1997 they set off along the deserted autoroutes and motorways in the greatest invasion that Europe has ever known, intent on seizing their former homes, determined to reinstate a forgotten Europe of nations, each jealous of its frontiers, happy to guard its history, tariff barriers and insularity.

**1989**

# WAR FEVER

Ryan's dream of a ceasefire first came to him during the battle for the Beirut Hilton. At the time he was scarcely aware of the strange vision of a city at peace that had slipped uninvited into a corner of his head. All day the battle had moved from floor to floor of the ruined hotel, and Ryan had been too busy defending the barricade of restaurant tables in the mezzanine to think of anything else. By the end, when Arkady and Mikhail crept forward to silence the last Royalist sniper in the atrium, Ryan stood up and gave them covering fire, praying all the while for his sister Louisa, who was fighting in another unit of the Christian militia.

Then the firing ceased, and Captain Gomez signalled Ryan to make his way down the staircase to the reception area. Ryan watched the dust falling through the roof of the atrium fifteen floors above him. Illuminated by the sunlight, the pulverised cement formed a fleeting halo that cascaded towards the replica of a tropical island in the centre of the atrium. The miniature lagoon was filled with rubble, but a few tamarinds and exotic ferns survived among the furniture thrown down from the upper balconies. For a moment this derelict paradise was lit by the dust, like a stage set miraculously preserved in the debris of a bombed theatre. Ryan gazed at the fading halo, thinking that one day, perhaps, all the dust of Beirut would descend like the dove, and at last silence the guns.

But the halo served a more practical purpose. As Ryan followed Captain Gomez down the staircase he saw the two enemy militia men scrambling across the floor of the lagoon, their wet uniforms clearly visible against the chalky cement. Then he and Gomez were firing at the trapped soldiers, shredding the tamarinds into matchwood long after the two youths lay bloodily together in the shallow water. Possibly they had been trying to surrender, but the newsreels of Royalist atrocities shown on television the previous evening put paid to that hope. Like the other young fighters, Ryan killed with a will.

Even so, as after all the battles in Beirut that summer, Ryan felt dazed and numbed when it was over. He could almost believe that he too had died. The other members of his platoon were propping the five bodies against the reception counter, where they could be photographed for the propaganda leaflets to be scattered over the Royalist strongholds in South Beirut. Trying to focus his eyes, Ryan stared at the roof of the atrium, where the last wisps of dust were still falling from the steel girders.

'Ryan! What is it?' Dr Edwards, the United Nations medical observer, took Ryan's arm and tried to steady him. 'Did you see someone move up there?'

'No – there's nothing. I'm okay, doctor. There was a strange light . . .'

'Probably one of those new phosphorus shells the Royalists are using. A fiendish weapon, we're hoping to get them banned.'

With a grimace of anger, Dr Edwards put on his battered UN helmet. Ryan was glad to see this brave, if slightly naïve man, in some ways more like an earnest young priest than a doctor, who spent as much time in the Beirut front line as any of the combatants. Dr Edwards could easily have returned to his comfortable New England practice, but he chose to devote himself to the men and women dying in a forgotten civil war half a world away. The seventeen-year-old Ryan had struck up a close friendship with Dr Edwards, and brought to him all his worries about his sister and aunt, and even his one-sided passion for Lieutenant Valentina, the strong-willed commander of the Christian guard-post at the telephone exchange.

Dr Edwards was always caring and sympathetic, and Ryan often exploited the physician's good nature, milking him for advance news of any shift in military alliances which the UN peacekeeping force had detected. Sometimes Ryan worried that Dr Edwards had spent too long in Beirut. He had become curiously addicted to the violence and death, as if tending the wounded and dying satisfied some defeatist strain in his character.

'Let's have a look at the poor devils.' He led Ryan towards the soldiers propped against the reception counter, their weapons and personal letters arranged at their feet in a grim tableau. 'With any luck, we'll find their next of kin.'

Ryan pushed past Captain Gomez, who was muttering over his unco-operative camera. He knelt beside the youngest of the dead soldiers, a teenager with dark eyes and cherubic face, wearing the bulky camouflage jacket of the International Brigade.

'Angel . . . ? Angel Porrua . . . ?' Ryan touched the spongy cheeks of the fifteen-year-old Spaniard, with whom he often went swimming at the beaches of East Beirut. Only the previous Sunday they had rigged a makeshift sail on an abandoned dory and cruised half a mile up the coast before being turned back by the UN naval patrol. He realised that he had last seen Angel scrambling through the waterlogged debris of the artificial lagoon in the atrium. Perhaps he had recognised Ryan on the mezzanine staircase, and had been trying to surrender as he and Captain Gomez opened fire.

'Ryan?' Dr Edwards squatted beside him. 'Do you know him?'

'Angel Porrua – but he's in the Brigade, doctor. They're on our side.'

'Not any more.' Clumsily, Dr Edwards pressed Ryan's shoulder in a gesture of comfort. 'Last night they did a deal with the Royalists. I'm sorry – they've been guilty of real treachery.'

'No, Angel was on our side . . .'

Ryan stood up and left the group of soldiers sharing a six-pack of beer.

He stepped through the dust and rubble to the ornamental island in the centre of the atrium. The bullet-riddled tamarinds still clung to their rockery, and Ryan hoped that they would survive until the first of the winter rains fell through the roof. He looked back at the Royalist dead, sitting like neglected guests who had expired at the reception counter of this hotel, weapons beside them.

But what if the living were to lay down their weapons? Suppose that all over Beirut the rival soldiers were to place their rifles at their feet, along with their identity tags and the photographs of their sisters and sweethearts, each a modest shrine to a ceasefire?

A ceasefire? The phrase scarcely existed in Beirut's vocabulary, Ryan reflected, as he sat in the rear of Captain Gomez's jeep on the return to the Christian sector of the city. Around them stretched the endless vistas of shattered apartment houses and bombed-out office buildings. Many of the stores had been converted into strongpoints, their steel grilles plastered with slogans and posters, crude photographs of murdered women and children.

During the original civil war, thirty years earlier, more than half a million people had lived in Beirut. His own grandparents had been among them, some of the many Americans who had resigned their teaching posts at the schools and university to fight with the beleaguered Christian militia. From all over the world volunteers had been drawn to Beirut, mercenaries and idealists, religious fanatics and out-of-work bodyguards, who fought and died for one or another of the rival factions.

Deep in their bunkers below the rubble they even managed to marry and raise their families. Ryan's parents had been in their teens when they were murdered during the notorious Airport Massacre – in one of the worst of many atrocities, the Nationalist militia had executed their prisoners after promising them safe passage to Cyprus. Only the kindness of an Indian soldier in the UN force had saved Ryan's life – he had found the baby boy and his sister in an abandoned apartment building, and then tracked down their adolescent aunt.

However tragic, Beirut had been worth fighting for, a city with street markets, stores and restaurants. There were churches and mosques filled with real congregations, not heaps of roof-tiles under an open sky. Now the civilian population had gone, leaving a few thousand armed combatants and their families hiding in the ruins. They were fed and supplied by the UN peacekeeping force, who turned a blind eye to the clandestine shipments of arms and ammunition, for fear of favouring one or another side in the conflict.

So a futile war dragged on, so pointless that the world's news media had long since lost interest. Sometimes, in a ruined basement, Ryan came acoss a tattered copy of *Time* or *Paris Match*, filled with photographs of street-fighting and graphic reports on the agony of Beirut, a city then at the centre of the world's concern. Now no one cared, and only the hereditary militias fought on, grappling across their empires of rubble.

But there was nothing pointless about the bullets. As they passed the shell of the old pro-government radio station there was a single shot from the ground-floor window.

'Pull over, corporal! Get off the road!' Pistol in hand, Gomez wrenched the steering wheel from Arkady and slewed the jeep into the shelter of a derelict bus.

Kneeling beside the flattened rear tyres, Ryan watched the UN spotter plane circle overhead. He waited for Gomez to flush out the sniper, probably a Nationalist fanatic trying to avenge the death of a brother or cousin. The Nationalist militia were based at Beirut Airport, a wilderness of weed-grown concrete on which no plane had landed for ten years, and rarely ventured into the centre of the city.

If a ceasefire was ever to take hold it would be here, somewhere along the old Green Line that divided Beirut, in this no-man's-land between the main power bases – the Christians in north-east Beirut, the Nationalists and Fundamentalists in the south and west, the Royalists and Republicans in the south-east, with the International Brigade clinging to the fringes. But the real map of the city was endlessly redrawn by opportunist deals struck among the local commanders – a jeep bartered for a truckload of tomatoes, six rocket launchers for a video-recorder.

What ransom could buy a ceasefire?

'Wake up, Ryan! Let's move!' Gomez emerged from the radio station with his prisoner, a jittery twelve-year-old in a hand-me-down Nationalist uniform. Gomez held the boy by his matted hair, then flung him into the back of the jeep. 'Ryan, keep an eye on this animal – he bites. We'll take him to interrogation.'

'Right, captain. And if there's anything left we'll trade him for some new videos.'

Hands bound, the boy knelt on the floor of the jeep, weeping openly from fear and rage. Jabbing him with his rifle stock, Ryan was surprised by his own emotions. For all his hopes of a ceasefire, he felt a reflex of real hate for this overgrown child. Hate was what kept the war going. Even Dr Edwards had been infected by it, and he wasn't alone. Ryan had seen the shining eyes of the UN observers as they photographed the latest atrocity victims, or debriefed the survivors of a cruel revenge attack, like prurient priests at confession. How could they put an end to the hate that was corrupting them all? Good God, he himself had begun to resent Angel Porrua for fighting with the Nationalists . . .

That evening Ryan rested on the balcony of Aunt Vera's apartment overlooking the harbour in East Beirut. He watched the riding lights of the UN patrol craft out at sea, and thought about his plans for a ceasefire. Trying to forget the day's fighting and Angel's death, he listened to Louisa chattering in the kitchen over the sounds of pop music broadcast by a local radio station.

The balcony was virtually Ryan's bedroom – he slept there in a hammock shielded from public view by the washing line and the plywood hutch he had built as a boy for his Dutch rabbit. Ryan could easily have moved to any one of the dozen empty apartments in the building, but he liked the intimacy of family life. The two rooms and kitchen were the only home he had ever known.

A young couple in an apartment across the street had recently adopted an orphan boy, and the sounds of his crying reminded Ryan that he at least was related by blood to the members of his family. In Beirut such blood ties were rare. Few of the young women soldiers ever conceived, and most children were war-orphans, though it puzzled Ryan where all these youngsters came from – somehow a secret family life survived in the basements and shantytowns on the outskirts of the city.

'That's the Rentons' new little son.' His sister strolled onto the balcony, brushing out the waist-long hair that spent its days in a military bun. 'It's a pity he cries a lot.'

'At least he laughs more than he cries.' An intriguing thought occurred to Ryan. 'Tell me, Louisa – will Lieutenant Valentina and I have a child?'

'A child? Did you hear that, Aunty? So what does Valentina think?'

'I've no idea. As it happens, I've never spoken to her.'

'Well, dear, I think you should ask her. She might lose something of her elegant composure.'

'Only for a few seconds. She's very regal.'

'It only takes a few seconds to conceive a child. Or is she so special that she won't even spare you those few seconds?'

'She is very special.'

'Who's this?' Aunt Vera hung their combat jackets over the balcony, gazing at them with almost maternal pride. 'Are you talking about me, Ryan, or your sister?'

'Someone far more special,' Louisa rejoined. 'His dream woman.'

'You two are my dream women.'

This was literally the truth. The possibility that anything might happen to them appalled Ryan. In the street below the balcony a night-commando patrol had lined up and were checking their equipment – machine-pistols, grenades, packs loaded with booby-traps and detonators. They would crawl into the darkness of West Beirut, each a killing machine out to murder some aunt or sister on a balcony.

A UN medical orderly moved down the line, issuing morphine ampoules. For all the lives they saved, Ryan sometimes resented the blue helmets. They nursed the wounded, gave cash and comfort to the bereaved, arranged foster-parents for the orphans, but they were too nervous of taking sides. They ringed the city, preventing anyone from entering or leaving, and in a sense controlled everything that went on in Beirut. They could virtually bring the war to a halt, but Dr Edwards repeatedly told Ryan that any attempt by the peacekeeping force to live up to its name would lead the world's powers to intervene militarily, for fear of destabilising the whole Middle East. So the fighting went on.

The night-commandos moved away, six soldiers on either side of the street, heading towards the intermittent clatter of gunfire.

'They're off now,' Aunt Vera said. 'Wish them luck.'

'Why?' Ryan asked quietly. 'What for?'

'What do you mean? You're always trying to shock us, Ryan. Don't you want them to come back?'

'Of course. But why leave in the first place? They could stay here.'

'That's crazy talk.' His sister placed a hand on Ryan's forehead, feeling for a temperature. 'You had a hard time in the Hilton, Arkady told me. Remember what we're fighting for.'

'I'm trying. Today I helped to kill Angel Porrua. What was he fighting for?'

'Are you serious? We're fighting for what we believe.'

'But nobody believes anything! Think about it, Louisa. The Royalists don't want the king, the Nationalists secretly hope for partition, the Republicans want to do a deal with the Crown Prince of Monaco, the Christians are mostly atheists, and the Fundamentalists can't agree on a single fundamental. We're fighting and dying for nothing.'

'So?' Louisa pointed with her brush to the UN observers by their post. 'That just leaves them. What do they believe in?'

'Peace. World harmony. An end to fighting everywhere.'

'Then maybe you should join them.'

'Yes . . .' Ryan pushed aside his combat jacket and stared through the balcony railings. Each of the blue helmets was a pale lantern in the dusk. 'Maybe we should all join the UN. Yes, Louisa, everyone should wear the blue helmet.'

And so a dream was born.

During the next days Ryan began to explore this simple but revolutionary idea. Though gripped by the notion, he knew that it was difficult to put into practice. His sister was sceptical, and the fellow-members of his platoon were merely baffled by the concept.

'I see what you're getting at,' Arkady admitted as they shared a cigarette in the Green Line command bunker. 'But if everyone joins the UN who will be left to do the fighting?'

'Arkady, that's the whole point . . .' Ryan was tempted to give up. 'Just think of it. Everything will be neat and clean again. There'll be no more patrols, no parades or weapons drills. We'll lie around in the McDonald's eating hamburgers; there'll be discos every night. People will be walking around the streets, going into stores, sitting in cafés . . .'

'That sounds really weird,' Arkady commented.

'It isn't weird. Life will start again. It's how it used to be, like it is now in other places around the world.'

'Where?'

'Well . . .' This was a difficult one. Like the other fighters in Beirut, Ryan knew next to nothing about the outside world. No newspapers came in, and foreign TV and radio broadcasts were jammed by the signals teams of the rival groups to prevent any foreign connivance in a military coup. Ryan had spent a few years in the UN school in East Beirut, but his main source of information about the larger world was the forty-year-old news magazines that he found in abandoned buildings. These presented a picture of a world at strife, of bitter fighting in Vietnam, Angola and Iran. Presumably these vast conflicts, greater versions of the fighting in Beirut, were still going on.

Perhaps the whole world should wear the blue helmet? This thought excited Ryan. If he could bring about a ceasefire in Beirut the peace movement might spread to Asia and Africa, everyone would lay down their arms . . .

Despite numerous rebuffs Ryan pressed on, arguing his case with any soldiers he met. Always there was an unvoiced interest, but one obstacle was the constant barrage of propaganda – the atrocity posters, the TV newsreels of vandalised churches that played on an ever-ready sense of religious outrage, and a medley of racial and anti-monarchist slanders.

To break this propaganda stranglehold was far beyond Ryan's powers, but by chance he found an unexpectedly potent weapon – humour.

While on duty with a shore patrol by the harbour, Ryan was describing his dream of a better Beirut as his unit passed the UN command post. The observers had left their helmets on the open-air map table, and without thinking Ryan pulled off his khaki forage cap and lowered the blue steel bowl over his head.

'Hey, look at Ryan!' Arkady shouted. There was some good-humoured scuffling until Mikhail and Nazar pulled them apart. 'No more wrestling now, we have our own peacekeeping force!'

Friendly cat-calls greeted Ryan as he paraded up and down in the helmet, but then everyone fell silent. The helmet had a calming effect, Ryan noticed, both on himself and his fellow-soldiers. On an impulse he set off along the beach towards the Fundamentalist sentry-post 500 yards away.

'Ryan – look out!' Mikhail ran after him, but stopped as Captain Gomez rode up in his jeep to the harbour wall. Together they watched as Ryan strode along the shore, ignoring the sniper-infested office buildings. He was halfway to the sentry-post when a Fundamentalist sergeant climbed onto the roof, waving a temporary safe-passage. Too cautious to risk his charmed life, Ryan saluted and turned back.

When he rejoined his platoon everyone gazed at him with renewed respect. Arkady and Nazar were wearing blue helmets, sheepishly ignoring Captain Gomez as he stepped in an ominous way from his jeep. Then Dr Edwards emerged from the UN post, restraining Gomez.

'I'll take care of this, captain. The UN won't press charges. I know Ryan wasn't playing the fool.'

Explaining his project to Dr Edwards was far easier than Ryan had hoped. They sat together in the observation post, as Dr Edwards encouraged him to outline his plan.

'It's a remarkable idea, Ryan.' Clearly gripped by its possibilities, Dr Edwards seemed almost lightheaded. 'I won't say it's going to work, but it deserves a try.'

'The main object is the ceasefire,' Ryan stressed. 'Joining the UN force is just a means to that end.'

'Of course. But do you think they'll wear the blue helmet?'

'A few will, but that's all we need. Little by little, more people will join up. Everyone is sick of fighting, doctor, but there's nothing else here.'

'I know that, Ryan. God knows it's a desperate place.' Dr Edwards reached across the table and held Ryan's wrists, trying to lend him something of his own strength. 'I'll have to take this up with the UN Secretariat in Damascus, so it's vital to get it right. Let's think of it as a volunteer UN force.'

'Exactly. We'll volunteer to wear the blue helmet. That way we don't have to change sides or betray our own people. Eventually, everyone will be in the volunteer force . . .'

'. . . and the fighting will just fade away. It's a great idea, it's only strange that no one has ever thought of it before.' Dr Edwards was watching Ryan keenly. 'Did anyone help you? One of the wounded ex-officers, perhaps?'

'There wasn't anyone, doctor. It just came to me, out of all the death . . .'

Dr Edwards left Beirut for a week, consulting his superiors in Damascus, but in that time events moved more quickly than Ryan had believed possible. Everywhere the militia fighters were sporting the blue helmet. This began as a joke confined to the Christian forces, in part an irreverent gesture at the UN observers. Then, while patrolling the Green Line, Ryan spotted the driver of a Royalist jeep wearing a blue beret. Soon the more carefree spirits, the pranksters in every unit, wore the helmet or beret like a cockade.

'Ryan, look at this.' Captain Gomez called him to the command post in the lobby of the TV station. 'You've got a lot to answer for . . .'

Across the street, near a burnt-out Mercedes, a Royalist guerrilla in a blue beret had set up a canvas chair and card table. He sat back, feet on the table, leisurely taking the sun.

'The nerve of it . . .' Gomez raised Ryan's rifle and trained it at the soldier. He whistled to himself, and then handed the weapon back to Ryan. 'He's lucky, we're over-exposed here. I'll give him his suntan . . .'

This was a breakthrough, and not the last. Clearly there was a deep undercurrent of fatigue. By the day of Dr Edwards' return, Ryan estimated that one in ten of the militia fighters was wearing the blue helmet or beret. Fire-fights still shook the night sky, but the bursts of gunfire seemed more isolated.

'Ryan, it's scarcely credible,' Dr Edwards told him when they met at the UN post near the harbour. He pointed to the map marked with a maze of boundary lines and fortified positions. 'Today there hasn't been a single major incident along the Green Line. North of the airport there's even a de facto ceasefire between the Fundamentalists and the Nationalists.'

Ryan was staring at the sea, where a party of Christian soldiers were swimming from a diving raft. The UN guard-ships were close inshore, no longer worried about drawing fire. Without meaning to dwell on the past, Ryan said: 'Angel and I went sailing there.'

'And you'll go sailing again, with Nazar and Arkady.' Dr Edwards seized his shoulders. 'Ryan, you've brought off a miracle!'

'Well . . .' Ryan felt unsure of his own emotions, like someone who has just won the largest prize in a lottery. The UN truck parked in the sun was loaded with crates of blue uniforms, berets and helmets. Permission had been granted for the formation of a Volunteer UN Force recruited from the militias. The volunteers would serve in their own platoons, but be unarmed and take no part in any fighting, unless their lives were threatened. The prospect of a permanent peace was at last in sight.

Only six weeks after Ryan had first donned the blue helmet, an unbroken ceasefire reigned over Beirut. Everywhere the guns were silent. Sitting beside Captain Gomez as they toured the city by jeep, Ryan marvelled at the transformation. Unarmed soldiers lounged on the steps of the Hilton, groups of once-bitter enemies fraternised on the terrace of the Parliament building. Shutters were opening on the stores along the Green Line, and there was even a modest street market in the hallway of the Post Office. Children had emerged from their basement hideaways and played among the burnt-out cars. Many of the women guerrillas had exchanged their combat fatigues for bright print dresses, a first taste of the glamour and chic for which the city had once been renowned.

Even Lieutenant Valentina now stalked about in a black leather skirt and vivid lipstick jacket, blue beret worn rakishly over an elegant chignon.

As they passed her command post Captain Gomez stopped the jeep. He doffed his blue helmet in a gesture of respect. 'My God! Isn't that the last word, Ryan?'

'It certainly is, captain,' Ryan agreed devoutly. 'How do I even dare approach her?'

'What?' Gomez followed Ryan's awestruck gaze. 'Not Lieutenant Valentina – she'll eat you for breakfast. I'm talking about the soccer match this afternoon.'

He pointed to the large poster recently pasted over the cracked windows of the nearby Holiday Inn. A soccer match between the Republican and

Nationalist teams would take place at three o'clock in the stadium, the first game in the newly formed Beirut Football League.

'"Tomorrow – Christians versus Fundamentalists. Referee-Colonel Mugabe of the International Brigade." That should be high-scoring ...' Blue helmet in hand, Gomez climbed from the jeep and strolled over to the poster.

Ryan, meanwhile, was staring at Lieutenant Valentina. Out of uniform she seemed even more magnificent, her Uzi machine-pistol slung over her shoulder like a fashion accessory. Taking his courage in both hands, Ryan stepped into the street and walked towards her. She could eat him for breakfast, of course, and happily lunch and supper as well ...

The lieutenant turned her imperious eyes in his direction, already resigned to the attentions of this shy young man. But before Ryan could speak, an immense explosion erupted from the street behind the TV station. The impact shook the ground and drummed against the pockmarked buildings. Fragments of masonry cascaded into the road as a cloud of smoke seethed into the sky, whipped upwards by the flames that rose from the detonation point somewhere to the south-west of the Christian enclave.

A six-foot scimitar of plate glass fell from the window of the Holiday Inn, slicing through the football poster, and shattered around Gomez's feet. As he ran to the jeep, shouting at Ryan, there was a second explosion from the Fundamentalist sector of West Beirut. Signal flares were falling in clusters over the city, and the first rounds of gunfire competed with the whine of klaxons and the loudspeakers broadcasting a call to arms.

Ryan stumbled to his feet, brushing the dust from his combat jacket. Lieutenant Valentina had vanished into the strongpoint, where her men were already loading the machine-gun in the barbette.

'Captain Gomez ... The bomb? What set it off?'

'Treachery, Ryan – the Royalists must have done a deal with the Nats.' He pulled Ryan into the jeep, cuffing him over the head. 'All this talk of peace. The oldest trap in the world, and we walked straight into it ...'

More than treachery, however, had taken place. Armed militia men filled the streets, taking up their positions in the blockhouses and strongpoints. Everyone was shouting at once, voices drowned by the gunfire that came from all directions. Powerful bombs had been cunningly planted to cause maximum confusion, and the nervous younger soldiers were firing into the air to keep up their courage. Signal flares were falling over the city in calculated but mysterious patterns. Everywhere blue helmets and berets were lying discarded in the gutter.

When Ryan reached his aunt's apartment he found Dr Edwards and two UN guards waiting for him.

'Ryan, it's too late. I'm sorry.'

Ryan tried to step past to the staircase, but Dr Edwards held his arms. Looking up at this anxious and exhausted man, Ryan realised that apart from the UN observers he was probably the only one in Beirut still wearing the blue helmet.

'Dr Edwards, I have to look after Louisa and my aunt. They're upstairs.'

'No, Ryan. They're not here any longer. I'm afraid they've gone.'

'Where? My God, I told them to stay here!'

'They've been taken as hostages. There was a commando raid timed for the first explosion. Before we realised it, they were in and out.'

'Who?' Confused and frightened, Ryan stared wildly at the street, where armed men were forming into their platoons. 'Was it the Royalists, or the Nats?'

'We don't know. It's tragic, already there have been some foul atrocities. But they won't harm Louisa or your aunt. They know who you are.'

'They took them because of *me* . . .' Ryan lifted the helmet from his head. He stared at the blue bowl, which he had carefully polished, trying to make it the brightest in Beirut.

'What do you plan to do, Ryan?' Dr Edwards took the helmet from his hands, a stage prop no longer needed after the last curtain. 'It's your decision. If you want to go back to your unit, we'll understand.'

Behind Dr Edwards one of the observers held Ryan's rifle and webbing. The sight of the weapon and its steel-tipped bullets brought back Ryan's old anger, that vague hatred that had kept them all going for so many years. He needed to go out into the streets, track down the kidnappers, revenge himself on those who had threatened his aunt and Louisa.

'Well, Ryan . . .' Dr Edwards was watching him in a curiously distant way, as if Ryan was a laboratory rat at a significant junction in a maze. 'Are you going to fight?'

'Yes, I'll fight . . .' Ryan placed the blue helmet firmly on his head. 'But not for war. I'll work for another ceasefire, doctor.'

It was then that he found himself facing the raised barrel of his own rifle. An expressionless Dr Edwards took his wrists, but it was some minutes before Ryan realised that he had been handcuffed and placed under arrest.

For an hour they drove south-east through the suburbs of Beirut, past the derelict factories and shantytowns, stopping at the UN checkpoints along the route. From his seat in the back of the armoured van, Ryan could see the ruined skyline of the city. Funnels of smoke leaned across the sky, but the sound of gunfire had faded. Once they stopped to stretch their legs, but Dr Edwards declined to talk to him. Ryan assumed that the physician suspected him of being involved with the conspirators who had broken the ceasefire. Perhaps Dr Edwards imagined that the whole notion of ceasefire had been a devious scheme in which Ryan had exploited his contacts among the young . . . ?

They passed through the second of the perimeter fences that enclosed the city, and soon after approached the gates of a military camp built beside a deserted sanatorium. A line of olive-green tents covered the spacious grounds. Arrays of radio antennae and television dishes rose from the roof of the sanatorium, all facing north-west towards Beirut.

The van stopped at the largest of the tents, which appeared to house a hospital for wounded guerrillas. But within the cool green interior there was no sign of patients. Instead they were walking through a substantial arsenal. Rows of trestle tables were loaded with carbines and machine-guns, boxes of grenades and mortar bombs. A UN sergeant moved among this mountain of weaponry, marking items on a list like the owner of a gun store checking the day's orders.

Beyond the arsenal was an open area that resembled the newsroom of a television station. A busy staff of UN observers stood beneath a wall map of Beirut, moving dozens of coloured tapes and stars. These marked the latest positions in the battle for the city being screened on the TV monitors beside the map.

'You can leave us, corporal. I'll be in charge of him now.' Dr Edwards took the rifle and webbing from the UN guard, and beckoned Ryan into a canvas-walled office at the end of the tent. Plastic windows provided a clear view into an adjacent room, where two women clerks were rolling copies of a large poster through a printing press. The blown-up photograph of a Republican atrocity, it showed a group of murdered women who had been executed in a basement garage.

Staring at this gruesome image, Ryan guessed why Dr Edwards still avoided his eyes.

'Dr Edwards, I didn't know about the bomb this morning, or the surprise attack. Believe me –'

'I believe you, Ryan. Everything's fine, so try to relax.' He spoke curtly, as if addressing a difficult patient. He laid the rifle on his desk, and released the handcuffs from Ryan's wrists. 'You're out of Beirut for good now. As far as you're concerned, the ceasefire is permanent.'

'But . . . what about my aunt and sister?'

'They've come to no harm. In fact, at this very moment they're being held at the UN post near the Football Stadium.'

'Thank God. I don't know what went wrong. Everyone wanted the ceasefire . . .' Ryan turned from the atrocity posters spilling endlessly through the slim hands of the UN clerks. Pinned to the canvas wall behind Dr Edwards were scores of photographs of young men and women in their combat fatigues, caught unawares near the UN observation posts. In pride of place was a large photograph of Ryan himself. Assembled together, they resembled the inmates of a mental institution.

Two orderlies passed the doorway of the office, wheeling a trolley loaded with assault rifles.

'These weapons, doctor? Are they confiscated?'

'No – as it happens, they're factory-new. They're on their way to the battlefield.'

'So there's more fighting going on outside Beirut ...' This news was enough to make Ryan despair. 'The whole world's at war.'

'No, Ryan. The whole world is at peace. Except for Beirut – that's where the weapons are going. They'll be smuggled into the city inside a cargo of oranges.'

'Why? That's mad, doctor! The militias will get them!'

'That's the point, Ryan. We want them to have the weapons. And we want them to keep on fighting.'

Ryan began to protest, but Dr Edwards showed him firmly to the chair beside the desk.

'Don't worry, Ryan, I'll explain it all to you. Tell me first, though – have you ever heard of a disease called smallpox?'

'It was some sort of terrible fever. It doesn't exist any more.'

'That's true – almost. Fifty years ago the World Health Organisation launched a huge campaign to eliminate smallpox, one of the worst diseases mankind has ever known, a real killer that destroyed tens of millions of lives. There was a global programme of vaccination, involving doctors and governments in every country. Together they finally wiped it from the face of the earth.'

'I'm glad, doctor – if only we could do the same for war.'

'Well, in a real sense we have, Ryan – almost. In the case of smallpox, people can now travel freely all over the world. The virus does survive in ancient graves and cemeteries, but if by some freak chance the disease appears again there are supplies of vaccine to protect people and stamp it out.'

Dr Edwards detached the magazine from Ryan's rifle and weighed it in his hands, showing an easy familiarity with the weapon that Ryan had never seen before. Aware of Ryan's surprise, he smiled wanly at the young man, like a headmaster still attached to a delinquent pupil.

'Left to itself, the smallpox virus is constantly mutating. We have to make sure that our supplies of vaccine are up-to-date. So WHO was careful never to completely abolish the disease. It deliberately allowed smallpox to flourish in a remote corner of a third-world country, so that it could keep an eye on how the virus was evolving. Sadly, a few people went on dying, and are still dying to this day. But it's worth it for the rest of the world. That way we'll always be ready if there's an outbreak of the disease.'

Ryan stared through the plastic windows at the wall map of Beirut and the TV monitors with their scenes of smoke and gunfire. The Hilton was burning again.

'And Beirut, doctor? Here you're keeping an eye on another virus?'

'That's right, Ryan. The virus of war. Or, if you like, the martial spirit. Not a physical virus, but a psychological one even more dangerous than smallpox. The world is at peace, Ryan. There hasn't been a war anywhere for thirty years – there are no armies or air forces, and all disputes are settled by negotiation and compromise, as they should be. No one would dream of going to war, any more than a sane mother would shoot her own children if she was cross with them. But we have to protect ourselves against the possibility of a mad strain emerging, against the chance that another Hitler or Pol Pot might appear.'

'And you can do all that here?' Ryan scoffed. 'In Beirut?'

'We think so. We have to see what makes people fight, what makes them hate each other enough to want to kill. We need to know how we can manipulate their emotions, how we can twist the news and trigger off their aggressive drives, how we can play on their religious feelings or political ideals. We even need to know how strong the desire for peace is.'

'Strong enough. It can be strong, doctor.'

'In your case, yes. You defeated us, Ryan. That's why we've pulled you out.' Dr Edwards spoke without regret, as if he envied Ryan his dogged dream. 'It's a credit to you, but the experiment must go on, so that we can understand this terrifying virus.'

'And the bombs this morning? The surprise attack?'

'We set off the bombs, though we were careful that no one was hurt. We supply all the weapons, and always have. We print up the propaganda material, we fake the atrocity photographs, so that the rival groups betray each other and change sides. It sounds like a grim version of musical chairs, and in a way it is.'

'But all these years, doctor . . .' Ryan was thinking of his old comrades-in-arms who had died beside him in the dusty rubble. Some had given their lives to help wounded friends. 'Angel and Moshe, Aziz . . . hundreds of people dying!'

'Just as hundreds are still dying of smallpox. But thousands of millions are living – in peace. It's worth it, Ryan; we've learned so much since the UN rebuilt Beirut thirty years ago.'

'They planned it all – the Hilton, the TV station, the McDonald's . . . ?'

'Everything, even the McDonald's. The UN architects designed it as a typical world city – a Hilton, a Holiday Inn, a sports stadium, shopping malls. They brought in orphaned teenagers from all over the world, from every race and nationality. To begin with we had to prime the pump – the NCOs and officers were all UN observers fighting in disguise. But once the engine began to turn, it ran with very little help.'

'Just a few atrocity photographs . . .' Ryan stood up and began to put on his webbing. Whatever he thought of Dr Edwards, the reality of the civil war remained, the only logic that he recognised. 'Doctor, I have to go back to Beirut.'

'It's too late, Ryan. If we let you return, you'd endanger the whole experiment.'

'No one will believe me, doctor. Anyway, I must find my sister and Aunt Vera.'

'She isn't your sister, Ryan. Not your real sister. And Vera isn't your real aunt. They don't know, of course. They think you're all from the same family. Louisa was the daughter of two French explorers from Marseilles who died in Antarctica. Vera was a foundling brought up by nuns in Montevideo.'

'And what about . . . ?'

'You, Ryan? Your parents lived in Halifax, Nova Scotia. You were three months old when they were killed in a car crash. Sadly, there are some deaths we can't yet stop . . .'

Dr Edwards was frowning at the wall map of Beirut visible through the plastic window. A signals sergeant worked frantically at the huge display, pinning on clusters of incident flags. Everyone had gathered around the monitor screens. An officer waved urgently to Dr Edwards, who stood up and left the office. Ryan stared at his hands while the two men conferred, and he scarcely heard the physician when he returned and searched for his helmet and side-arm.

'They've shot down the spotter plane. I'll have to leave you, Ryan – the fighting's getting out of control. The Royalists have overrun the Football Stadium and taken the UN post.'

'The Stadium?' Ryan was on his feet, his rifle the only security he had known since leaving the city. 'My sister and aunt are there! I'll come with you, doctor.'

'Ryan . . . everything's starting to fall apart; we may have lit one fuse too many. Some of the militia units are shooting openly at the UN observers.' Dr Edwards stopped Ryan at the door. 'I know you're concerned for them, you've lived with them all your life. But they're not –'

Ryan pushed him away. 'Doctor, they *are* my aunt and sister.'

It was three hours later when they reached the Football Stadium. As the convoy of UN vehicles edged its way into the city, Ryan gazed at the pall of smoke that covered the ruined skyline. The dark mantle extended far out to sea, lit by the flashes of high explosives as rival demolition squads moved through the streets. He sat behind Dr Edwards in the second of the armoured vans, but they could scarcely hear themselves talk above the sounds of rocket and machine-gun fire.

By this stage Ryan knew that he and Dr Edwards had little to say to each other. Ryan was thinking only of the hostages in the overrun UN post. His discovery that the civil war in Beirut was an elaborate experiment belonged to a numb area outside his mind, an emotional black hole from which no light or meaning could escape.

At last they stopped near the UN post at the harbour in East Beirut. Dr Edwards sprinted to the radio shack, and Ryan unstrapped his blue helmet. In a sense he shared the blame for this uncontrolled explosion of violence. The rats in the war laboratory had been happy pulling a familiar set of levers – the triggers of their rifles and mortars – and being fed their daily pellets of hate. Ryan's dazed dream of peace, like an untested narcotic, had disoriented them and laid them open to a frenzy of hyperactive rage . . .

'Ryan, good news!' Dr Edwards hammered on the windscreen, ordering the driver to move on. 'Christian commandos have retaken the Stadium!'

'And my sister? And Aunt Vera?'

'I don't know. Hope for the best. At least the UN is back in action. With luck, everything will return to normal.'

Later, as he stood in the sombre storeroom below the concrete grandstand, Ryan reflected on the ominous word that Dr Edwards had used. Normal . . . ? The lights of the photographers' flashes illuminated the bodies of the twenty hostages laid against the rear wall. Louisa and Aunt Vera rested between two UN observers, all executed by the Royalists before their retreat. The stepped concrete roof was splashed with blood, as if an invisible audience watching the destruction of the city from the comfort of the grandstand had begun to bleed into its seats. Yes, Ryan vowed, the world would bleed . . .

The photographers withdrew, leaving Ryan alone with Louisa and his aunt. Soon their images would be scattered across the ruined streets, pasted to the blockhouse walls.

'Ryan, we ought to leave before there's a counterattack.' Dr Edwards stepped through the pale light. 'I'm sorry about them – whatever else, they *were* your sister and aunt.'

'Yes, they were . . .'

'And at least they helped to prove something. We need to see how far human beings can be pushed.' Dr Edwards gestured helplessly at the bodies. 'Sadly, all the way.'

Ryan took off his blue helmet and placed it at his feet. He snapped back the rifle bolt and drove a steel-tipped round into the breech. He was only sorry that Dr Edwards would lie beside Louisa and his aunt. Outside there was a momentary lull in the fighting, but it would resume. Within a few months he would unite the militias into a single force. Already Ryan was thinking of the world beyond Beirut, of that far larger laboratory waiting to be tested, with its millions of docile specimens unprepared for the most virulent virus of them all.

'Not all the way, doctor.' He levelled the rifle at the physician's head. 'All the way is the whole human race.'

**1989**

# DREAM CARGOES

Across the lagoon an eager new life was forming, drawing its spectrum of colours from a palette more vivid than the sun's. Soon after dawn, when Johnson woke in Captain Galloway's cabin behind the bridge of the *Prospero*, he watched the lurid hues, cyanic blues and crimsons, playing against the ceiling above his bunk. Reflected in the metallic surface of the lagoon, the tropical foliage seemed to concentrate the Caribbean sunlight, painting on the warm air a screen of electric tones that Johnson had only seen on the nightclub façades of Miami and Vera Cruz.

He stepped onto the tilting bridge of the stranded freighter, aware that the island's vegetation had again surged forward during the night, as if it had miraculously found a means of converting darkness into these brilliant leaves and blossoms. Shielding his eyes from the glare, he searched the 600 yards of empty beach that encircled the *Prospero*, disappointed that there was no sign of Dr Chambers' rubber infaltable. For the past three mornings, when he woke after an uneasy night, he had seen the craft beached by the inlet of the lagoon. Shaking off the overlit dreams that rose from the contaminated waters, he would gulp down a cup of cold coffee, jump from the stern rail and set off between the pools of leaking chemicals in search of the American biologist.

It pleased Johnson that she was so openly impressed by this once barren island, a left-over of nature seven miles from the north-east coast of Puerto Rico. In his modest way he knew that he was responsible for the transformation of the nondescript atoll, scarcely more than a forgotten garbage dump left behind by the American army after World War II. No one, in Johnson's short life, had ever been impressed by him, and the biologist's silent wonder gave him the first sense of achievement he had ever known.

Johnson had learned her name from the labels on the scientific stores in the inflatable. However, he had not yet approached or even spoken to her, embarrassed by his rough manners and shabby seaman's clothes, and the engrained chemical stench that banned him from sailors' bars all over the Caribbean. Now, when she failed to appear on the fourth morning, he regretted all the more that he had never worked up the courage to introduce himself.

Through the acid-streaked windows of the bridge-house he stared at the terraces of flowers that hung from the forest wall. A month earlier, when he first arrived at the island, struggling with the locked helm of the listing freighter, there had been no more than a few stunted palms growing among the collapsed army huts and water-tanks buried in the dunes.

But already, for reasons that Johnson preferred not to consider, a wholly new vegetation had sprung to life. The palms rose like flagpoles into the vivid Caribbean air, pennants painted with a fresh green sap. Around them the sandy floor was thick with flowering vines and ground ivy, blue leaves like dappled metal foil, as if some midnight gardener had watered them with a secret plant elixir while Johnson lay asleep in his bunk.

He put on Galloway's peaked cap and examined himself in the greasy mirror. Stepping into the open deck behind the wheel-house, he inhaled the acrid chemical air of the lagoon. At least it masked the odours of the captain's cabin, a rancid bouquet of ancient sweat, cheap rum and diesel oil. He had thought seriously of abandoning Galloway's cabin and returning to his hammock in the forecastle, but despite the stench he felt that he owed it to himself to remain in the cabin. The moment that Galloway, with a last disgusted curse, had stepped into the freighter's single lifeboat he, Johnson, had become the captain of this doomed vessel.

He had watched Galloway, the four Mexican crewmen and the weary Portuguese engineer row off into the dusk, promising himself that he would sleep in the captain's cabin and take his meals at the captain's table. After five years at sea, working as cabin boy and deck hand on the lowest grade of chemical waste carrier, he had a command of his own, this antique freighter, even if the *Prospero*'s course was the vertical one to the sea-bed of the Caribbean.

Behind the funnel the Liberian flag of convenience hung in tatters, its fabric rotted by the acid air. Johnson stepped onto the stern ladder, steadying himself against the sweating hull-plates, and jumped into the shallow water. Careful to find his feet, he waded through the bilious green foam that leaked from the steel drums he had jettisoned from the freighter's deck.

When he reached the clear sand above the tide-line he wiped the emerald dye from his jeans and sneakers. Leaning to starboard in the lagoon, the *Prospero* resembled an exploded paint-box. The drums of chemical waste on the foredeck still dripped their effluent through the scuppers. The more sinister below-decks cargo – nameless organic by-products that Captain Galloway had been bribed to carry and never entered into his manifest – had dissolved the rusty plates and spilled an eerie spectrum of phosphorescent blues and indigos into the lagoon below.

Frightened of these chemicals, which every port in the Caribbean had rejected, Johnson had begun to jettison the cargo after running the freighter aground. But the elderly diesels had seized and the winch had jarred to a halt, leaving only a few of the drums on the nearby sand with their death's head warnings and eroded seams.

Johnson set off along the shore, searching the sea beyond the inlet of the lagoon for any sign of Dr Chambers. Everywhere a deranged horticulture was running riot. Vivid new shoots pushed past the metal debris of old ammunition boxes, filing cabinets and truck tyres. Strange grasping vines clambered over the scarlet caps of giant fungi, their white stems as thick as sailors' bones. Avoiding them, Johnson walked towards an old staff car that sat in an open glade between the palms. Wheel-less, its military markings obliterated by the rain of decades, it had settled into the sand, vines encircling its roof and windshield.

Deciding to rest in the car, which once perhaps had driven an American general around the training camps of Puerto Rico, he tore away the vines that had wreathed themselves around the driver's door pillar. As he sat behind the steering wheel it occurred to Johnson that he might leave the freighter and set up camp on the island. Nearby lay the galvanised iron roof of a barrack hut, enough material to build a beach house on the safer, seaward side of the island.

But Johnson was aware of an unstated bond between himself and the derelict freighter. He remembered the last desperate voyage of the *Prospero*, which he had joined in Vera Cruz, after being duped by Captain Galloway. The short voyage to Galveston, the debarkation port, would pay him enough to ship as a deck passenger on an inter-island boat heading for the Bahamas. It had been three years since he had seen his widowed mother in Nassau, living in a plywood bungalow by the airport with her invalid boyfriend.

Needless to say, they had never berthed at Galveston, Miami or any other of the ports where they had tried to unload their cargo. The crudely sealed cylinders of chemical waste-products, supposedly en route to a reprocessing plant in southern Texas, had begun to leak before they left Vera Cruz. Captain Galloway's temper, like his erratic seamanship and consumption of rum and tequila, increased steadily as he realised that the Mexican shipping agent had abandoned them to the seas. Almost certainly the agent had pocketed the monies allocated for reprocessing and found it more profitable to let the ancient freighter, now refused entry to Vera Cruz, sail up and down the Gulf of Mexico until her corroded keel sent her conveniently to the bottom.

For two months they had cruised forlornly from one port to another, boarded by hostile maritime police and customs officers, public health officials and journalists alerted to the possibility of a major ecological disaster. At Kingston, Jamaica, a television launch trailed them to the ten-mile limit, at Santo Domingo a spotter plane of the Dominican navy was waiting for them when they tried to slip into harbour under the cover of darkness. Greenpeace power-boats intercepted them outside Tampa, Florida, when Captain Galloway tried to dump part of his cargo. Firing flares across the bridge of the freighter, the US Coast Guard dispatched them into the Gulf of Mexico in time to meet the tail of Hurricane Clara.

When at last they recovered from the storm the cargo had shifted, and the *Prospero* listed ten degrees to starboard. Fuming chemicals leaked across the decks from the fractured seams of the waste drums, boiled on the surface of the sea and sent up a cloud of acrid vapour that left Johnson and the Mexican crewmen coughing through makeshift face-masks, and Captain Galloway barricading himself into his cabin with his tequila bottle.

First Officer Pereira had saved the day, rigging up a hose-pipe that sprayed the leaking drums with a torrent of water, but by then the *Prospero* was taking in the sea through its strained plates. When they sighted Puerto Rico the captain had not even bothered to set a course for port. Propping himself against the helm, a bottle in each hand, he signalled Pereira to cut the engines. In a self-pitying monologue, he cursed the Mexican shipping agent, the US Coast Guard, the world's agro-chemists and their despicable science that had deprived him of his command. Lastly he cursed Johnson for being so foolish ever to step aboard this ill-fated ship. As the *Prospero* lay doomed in the water, Pereira appeared with his already packed suitcase, and the captain ordered the Mexicans to lower the life-boat.

It was then that Johnson made his decision to remain on board. All his life he had failed to impose himself on anything – running errands as a six-year-old for the Nassau airport shoe-blacks, cadging pennies for his mother from the irritated tourists, enduring the years of school where he had scarcely learned to read and write, working as a dishwasher at the beach restaurants, forever conned out of his wages by the thieving managers. He had always reacted to events, never initiated anything on his own. Now, for the first time, he could become the captain of the *Prospero* and master of his own fate. Long before Galloway's curses faded into the dusk Johnson had leapt down the companionway ladder into the engine room.

As the elderly diesels rallied themselves for the last time Johnson returned to the bridge. He listened to the propeller's tired but steady beat against the dark ocean, and slowly turned the *Prospero* towards the north-west. Five hundred miles away were the Bahamas, and an endless archipelago of secret harbours. Somehow he would get rid of the leaking drums and even, perhaps, ply for hire between the islands, renaming the old tub after his mother, Velvet Mae. Meanwhile Captain Johnson stood proudly on the bridge, oversize cap on his head, 300 tons of steel deck obedient beneath his feet.

By dawn the next day he was completely lost on an open sea. During the night the freighter's list had increased. Below decks the leaking chemicals had etched their way through the hull plates, and a phosphorescent steam enveloped the bridge. The engine room was a knee-deep vat of acid brine, a poisonous vapour rising through the ventilators and coating every rail and deck-plate with a lurid slime.

Then, as Johnson searched desperately for enough timber to build a raft, he saw the old World War II garbage island seven miles from the Puerto Rican coast. The lagoon inlet was unguarded by the US Navy or Greenpeace speedboats. He steered the *Prospero* across the calm surface and let the freighter settle into the shallows. The inrush of water smothered the cargo in the hold. Able to breathe again, Johnson rolled into Captain

Galloway's bunk, made a space for himself among the empty bottles and slept his first dreamless sleep.

'Hey, you! Are you all right?' A woman's hand pounded on the roof of the staff car. 'What *are* you doing in there?'

Johnson woke with a start, lifting his head from the steering wheel. While he slept the lianas had enveloped the car, climbing up the roof and windshield pillars. Vivid green tendrils looped themselves around his left hand, tying his wrist to the rim of the wheel.

Wiping his face, he saw the American biologist peering at him through the leaves, as if he were the inmate of some bizarre zoo whose cages were the bodies of abandoned motor-cars. He tried to free himself, and pushed against the driver's door.

'Sit back! I'll cut you loose.'

She slashed at the vines with her clasp knife, revealing her fierce and determined wrist. When Johnson stepped onto the ground she held his shoulders, looking him up and down with a thorough eye. She was no more than thirty, three years older than himself, but to Johnson she seemed as self-possessed and remote as the Nassau school-teachers. Yet her mouth was more relaxed than those pursed lips of his childhood, as if she were genuinely concerned for Johnson.

'You're all right,' she informed him. 'But I wouldn't go for too many rides in that car.'

She strolled away from Johnson, her hands pressing the burnished copper trunks of the palms, feeling the urgent pulse of awakening life. Around her shoulders was slung a canvas bag holding a clipboard, sample jars, a camera and reels of film.

'My name's Christine Chambers,' she called out to Johnson. 'I'm carrying out a botanical project on this island. Have you come from the stranded ship?'

'I'm the captain,' Johnson told her without deceit. He reached into the car and retrieved his peaked cap from the eager embrace of the vines, dusted it off and placed it on his head at what he hoped was a rakish angle. 'She's not a wreck – I beached her here for repairs.'

'Really? For repairs?' Christine Chambers watched him archly, finding him at least as intriguing as the giant scarlet-capped fungi. 'So you're the captain. But where's the crew?'

'They abandoned ship.' Johnson was glad that he could speak so honestly. He liked this attractive biologist and the way she took a close interest in the island. 'There were certain problems with the cargo.'

'I bet there were. You were lucky to get here in one piece.' She took out a notebook and jotted down some observation on Johnson, glancing at his pupils and lips. 'Captain, would you like a sandwich? I've brought a picnic lunch – you look as if you could use a square meal.'

'Well . . .' Pleased by her use of his title, Johnson followed her to the beach, where the inflatable sat on the sand. Clearly she had been delayed by the weight of stores: a bell tent, plastic coolers, cartons of canned food, and a small office cabinet. Johnson had survived on a diet of salt beef, cola and oatmeal biscuits he cooked on the galley stove.

For all the equipment, she was in no hurry to unload the stores, as if unsure of sharing the island with Johnson, or perhaps pondering a different approach to her project, one that involved the participation of the human population of the island.

Trying to reassure her, as they divided the sandwiches, he described the last voyage of the *Prospero*, and the disaster of the leaking chemicals. She nodded while he spoke, as if she already knew something of the story.

'It sounds to me like a great feat of seamanship,' she complimented him. 'The crew who abandoned ship – as it happens, they reported that she went down near Barbados. One of them, Galloway I think he was called, claimed they'd spent a month in an open boat.'

'Galloway?' Johnson assumed the pursed lips of the Nassau school-marms. 'One of my less reliable men. So no one is looking for the ship?'

'No. Absolutely no one.'

'And they think she's gone down?'

'Right to the bottom. Everyone in Barbados is relieved there's no pollution. Those tourist beaches, you know.'

'They're important. And no one in Puerto Rico thinks she's here?'

'No one except me. This island is my research project,' she explained. 'I teach biology at San Juan University, but I really want to work at Harvard. I can tell you, lectureships are hard to come by. Something very interesting is happening here, with a little luck . . .'

'It is interesting,' Johnson agreed. There was a conspiratorial note to Dr Christine's voice that made him uneasy. 'A lot of old army equipment is buried here – I'm thinking of building a house on the beach.'

'A good idea . . . even if it takes you four or five months. I'll help you out with any food you need. But be careful.' Dr Christine pointed to the weal on his arm, a temporary reaction against some invading toxin in the vine sap. 'There's something else that's interesting about this island, isn't there?'

'Well . . .' Johnson stared at the acid stains etching through the *Prospero*'s hull and spreading across the lagoon. He had tried not to think of his responsibility for these dangerous and unstable chemicals. 'There are a few other things going on here.'

'A few other things?' Dr Christine lowered her voice. 'Look, Johnson, you're sitting in the middle of an amazing biological experiment. No one would allow it to happen anywhere in the world – if they knew, the US Navy would move in this afternoon.'

'Would they take away the ship?'

'They'd take it away and sink it in the nearest ocean trench, then scorch the island with flame-throwers.'

'And what about me?'

'I wouldn't like to say. It might depend on how advanced . . .' She held his shoulder reassuringly, aware that her vehemence had shocked him. 'But there's no reason why they should find out. Not for a while, and by then it won't matter. I'm not exaggerating when I say that you've probably created a new kind of life.'

As they unloaded the stores Johnson reflected on her words. He had guessed that the chemicals leaking from the *Prospero* had set off the accelerated growth, and that the toxic reagents might equally be affecting himself. In Galloway's cabin mirror he inspected the hairs on his chin and any suspicious moles. The weeks at sea, inhaling the acrid fumes, had left him with raw lungs and throat, and an erratic appetite, but he had felt better since coming ashore.

He watched Christine step into a pair of thigh-length rubber boots and move into the shallow water, ladle in hand, looking at the plant and animal life of the lagoon. She filled several specimen jars with the phosphorescent water, and locked them into the cabinet inside the tent.

'Johnson – you couldn't let me see the cargo manifest?'

'Captain . . . Galloway took it with him. He didn't list the real cargo.'

'I bet he didn't.' Christine pointed to the vermilion-shelled crabs that scuttled through the vivid filaments of kelp, floating like threads of blue electric cable. 'Have you noticed? There are no dead fish or crabs – and you'd expect to see hundreds. That was the first thing I spotted. And it isn't just the crabs – you look pretty healthy . . .'

'Maybe I'll be stronger?' Johnson flexed his sturdy shoulders.

'. . . in a complete daze, mentally, but I imagine that will change. Meanwhile, can you take me on board? I'd like to visit the *Prospero*.'

'Dr Christine . . .' Johnson held her arm, trying to restrain this determined woman. He looked at her clear skin and strong legs. 'It's too dangerous, you might fall through the deck.'

'Fair enough. Are the containers identified?'

'Yes, there's no secret.' Johnson did his best to remember. 'Organo . . .'

'Organo-phosphates? Right – what I need to know is which containers are leaking and roughly how much. We might be able to work out the exact chemical reactions – you may not realise it, Johnson, but you've mixed a remarkably potent cocktail. A lot of people will want to learn the recipe, for all kinds of reasons . . .'

Sitting in the colonel's chair on the porch of the beach-house, Johnson gazed contentedly at the luminous world around him, a fever-realm of light and life that seemed to have sprung from his own mind. The jungle wall of cycads, giant tamarinds and tropical creepers crowded the beach to the waterline, and the reflected colours drowned in swatches of phosphoresence that made the lagoon resemble a cauldron of electric dyes.

So dense was the vegetation that almost the only free sand lay below Johnson's feet. Every morning he would spend an hour cutting back the flowering vines and wild magnolia that inundated the metal shack. Already the foliage was crushing the galvanised iron roof. However hard he worked – and he found himself too easily distracted – he had been unable to keep clear the inspection pathways which Christine patrolled on her weekend visits, camera and specimen jars at the ready.

Hearing the sound of her inflatable as she neared the inlet of the lagoon, Johnson surveyed his domain with pride. He had found a metal card-table buried in the sand, and laid it with a selection of fruits he had picked for Christine that morning. To Johnson's untrained eye they seemed to be strange hybrids of pomegranate and pawpaw, cantaloupe and pineapple. There were giant tomato-like berries and clusters of purple grapes each the size of a baseball. Together they glowed through the overheated light like jewels set in the face of the sun.

By now, four months after his arrival on the *Prospero*, the one-time garbage island had become a unique botanical garden, generating new species of trees, vines and flowering plants every day. A powerful life-engine was driving the island. As she crossed the lagoon in her inflatable Christine stared at the aerial terraces of vines and blossoms that had sprung up since the previous weekend.

The dead hulk of the *Prospero*, daylight visible through its acid-etched plates, sat in the shallow water, the last of its chemical wastes leaking into the lagoon. But Johnson had forgotten the ship and the voyage that had brought him here, just as he had forgotten his past life and unhappy childhood under the screaming engines of Nassau airport. Lolling back in his canvas chair, on which was stencilled 'Colonel Pottle, US Army Engineer Corps', he felt like a plantation owner who had successfully subcontracted a corner of the original Eden. As he stood up to greet Christine he thought only of the future, of his pregnant bride and the son who would soon share the island with him.

'Johnson! My God, what have you been doing?' Christine ran the inflatable onto the beach and sat back, exhausted by the buffetting waves. 'It's a botanical mad-house!'

Johnson was so pleased to see her that he forgot his regret over their weekly separations. As she explained, she had her student classes to teach, her project notes and research samples to record and catalogue.

'Dr Christine . . . ! I waited all day!' He stepped into the shallow water, a carmine surf filled with glowing animalcula, and pulled the inflatable onto the sand. He helped her from the craft, his eyes avoiding her curving abdomen under the smock.

'Go on, you can stare . . .' Christine pressed his hand to her stomach. 'How do I look, Johnson?'

'Too beautiful for me, and the island. We've all gone quiet.'

'That is gallant – you've become a poet, Johnson.'

Johnson never thought of other women, and knew that none could be so beautiful as this lady biologist bearing his child. He spotted a plastic cooler among the scientific equipment.

'Christine – you've brought me ice-cream . . .'

'Of course I have. But don't eat it yet. We've a lot to do, Johnson.'

He unloaded the stores, leaving to the last the nylon nets and spring-mounted steel frames in the bottom of the boat. These bird-traps were the one cargo he hated to unload. Nesting in the highest branches above the island was a flock of extravagant aerial creatures, sometime swallows and finches whose jewelled plumage and tail-fans transformed them into gaudy peacocks. He had set the traps reluctantly at Christine's insistence. He never objected to catching the phosphorescent fish with their enlarged fins and ruffs of external gills, which seemed to prepare them for life on the land, or the crabs and snails in their baroque armour. But the thought of Christine taking these rare and beautiful birds back to her laboratory made him uneasy – he guessed that they would soon end their days under the dissection knife.

'Did you set the traps for me, Johnson?'

'I set all of them and put in the bait.'

'Good.' Christine heaped the nets onto the sand. More and more she seemed to hurry these days, as if she feared that the experiment might end. 'I can't understand why we haven't caught one of them.'

Johnson gave an eloquent shrug. In fact he had eaten the canned sardines, and released the one bird that had strayed into the trap below the parasol of a giant cycad. The nervous creature with its silken scarlet wings and kite-like tail feathers had been a dream of flight. 'Nothing yet – they're clever, those birds.'

'Of course they are – they're a new species.' She sat in Colonel Pottle's chair, photographing the table of fruit with her small camera. 'Those grapes are huge – I wonder what sort of wine they'd make. Champagne of the gods, grand cru . . .'

Warily, Johnson eyed the purple and yellow globes. He had eaten the fish and crabs from the lagoon, when asked by Christine, with no ill effects, but he was certain that these fruits were intended for the birds. He knew that Christine was using him, like everything else on the island, as part of her experiment. Even the child she had conceived after their one brief act of love, over so quickly that he was scarcely sure it had ever occurred, was part of the experiment. Perhaps the child would be the first of a new breed of man and he, Johnson, errand runner for airport shoe-shine boys, would be the father of an advanced race that would one day repopulate the planet.

As if aware of his impressive physique, she said: 'You look wonderfully well, Johnson. If this experiment ever needs to be justified . . .'

'I'm very strong now – I'll be able to look after you and the boy.'

'It might be a girl – or something in between.' She spoke in a matter-of-fact way that always surprised him. 'Tell me, Johnson, what do you do while I'm away?'

'I think about you, Dr Christine.'

'And I certainly think about you. But do you sleep a lot?'

'No. I'm busy with my thoughts. The time goes very quickly.'

Christine casually opened her note-pad. 'You mean the hours go by without you noticing?'

'Yes. After breakfast I fill the oil-lamp and suddenly it's time for lunch. But it can go more slowly, too. If I look at a falling leaf in a certain way it seems to stand still.'

'Good. You're learning to control time. Your mind is enlarging, Johnson.'

'Maybe I'll be as clever as you, Dr Christine.'

'Ah, I think you're moving in a much more interesting direction. In fact, Johnson, I'd like you to eat some of the fruit. Don't worry, I've already analysed it, and I'll have some myself.' She was cutting slices of the melon-sized apple. 'I want the baby to try some.'

Johnson hesitated, but as Christine always reminded him, none of the new species had revealed a single deformity.

The fruit was pale and sweet, with a pulpy texture and a tang like alcoholic mango. It slightly numbed Johnson's mouth and left a pleasant coolness in the stomach.

A diet for those with wings.

'Johnson! Are you sick?'

He woke with a start, not from sleep but from an almost too-clear examination of the colour patterns of a giant butterfly that had settled on his hand. He looked up from his chair at Christine's concerned eyes, and at the dense vines and flowering creepers that crowded the porch, pressing against his shoulders. The amber of her eyes was touched by the same overlit spectrum that shone through the trees and blossoms. Everything on the island was becoming a prism of itself.

'Johnson, wake up!'

'I am awake. Christine . . . I didn't hear you come.'

'I've been here for an hour.' She touched his cheeks, searching for any sign of fever and puzzled by Johnson's distracted manner. Behind her, the inflatable was beached on the few feet of sand not smothered by the vegetation. The dense wall of palms, lianas and flowering plants had collapsed onto the shore. Engorged on the sun, the giant fruits had begun to split under their own weight, and streams of vivid juice ran across the sand, as if the forest was bleeding.

'Christine? You came back so soon . . . ?' It seemed to Johnson that she had left only a few minutes earlier. He remembered waving goodbye to her and sitting down to finish his fruit and admire the giant butterfly, its wings like the painted hands of a circus clown.

'Johnson – I've been away for a week.' She held his shoulder, frowning at the unstable wall of rotting vegetation that towered a hundred feet into the air. Cathedrals of flower-decked foliage were falling into the waters of the lagoon.

'Johnson, help me to unload the stores. You don't look as if you've eaten for days. Did you trap the birds?'

'Birds? No, nothing yet.' Vaguely Johnson remembered setting the traps, but he had been too distracted by the wonder of everything to pursue the birds. Graceful, feather-tipped wraiths like gaudy angels, their crimson plumage leaked its ravishing hues onto the air. When he fixed his eyes onto them they seemed suspended against the sky, wings fanning slowly as if shaking the time from themselves.

He stared at Christine, aware that the colours were separating themselves from her skin and hair. Superimposed images of herself, each divided from the others by a fraction of a second, blurred the air around her, an exotic plumage that sprang from her arms and shoulders. The staid reality that had trapped them all was beginning to dissolve. Time had stopped and Christine was ready to rise into the air . . .

He would teach Christine and the child to fly.

'Christine, we can all learn.'

'What, Johnson?'

'We can learn to fly. There's no time any more – everything's too beautiful for time.'

'Johnson, look at my watch.'

'We'll go and live in the trees, Christine. We'll live with the high flowers . . .'

He took her arm, eager to show her the mystery and beauty of the sky people they would become. She tried to protest, but gave in, humouring Johnson as he led her gently from the beach-house to the wall of inflamed flowers. Her hand on the radio-transmitter in the inflatable, she sat beside the crimson lagoon as Johnson tried to climb the flowers towards the sun. Steadying the child within her, she wept for Johnson, only calming herself two hours later when the siren of a naval cutter crossed the inlet.

'I'm glad you radioed in,' the US Navy lieutenant told Christine. 'One of the birds reached the base at San Juan. We tried to keep it alive but it was crushed by the weight of its own wings. Like everything else on this island.'

He pointed from the bridge to the jungle wall. Almost all the over-crowded canopy had collapsed into the lagoon, leaving behind only a few of the original palms with their bird traps. The blossoms glowed through the water like thousands of drowned lanterns.

'How long has the freighter been here?' An older civilian, a government scientist holding a pair of binoculars, peered at the riddled hull of the *Prospero*. Below the beach-house two sailors were loading the last of Christine's stores into the inflatable. 'It looks as if it's been stranded there for years.'

'Six months,' Christine told him. She sat beside Johnson, smiling at him encouragingly. 'When Captain Johnson realised what was going on he asked me to call you.'

'Only six? That must be roughly the life-cycle of these new species. Their cellular clocks seem to have stopped – instead of reproducing, they force-feed their own tissues, like those giant fruit that contain no seeds. The life of the individual becomes the entire life of the species.' He gestured towards the impassive Johnson. 'That probably explains our friend's altered time sense – great blocks of memory were coalescing in his mind, so that a ball thrown into the air would never appear to land . . .'

A tide of dead fish floated past the cutter's bow, the gleaming bodies like discarded costume jewellery.

'You weren't contaminated in any way?' the lieutenant asked Christine. 'I'm thinking of the baby.'

'No, I didn't eat any of the fruit,' Christine said firmly. 'I've been here only twice, for a few hours.'

'Good. Of course, the medical people will do all the tests.'

'And the island?'

'We've been ordered to torch the whole place. The demolition charges are timed to go off in just under two hours, but we'll be well out of range. It's a pity, in a way.'

'The birds are still here,' Christine said, aware of Johnson staring at the trees.

'Luckily, you've trapped them all.' The scientist offered her the binoculars. 'Those organic wastes are hazardous things – God knows what might happen if human beings were exposed to long-term contact. All sorts of sinister alterations to the nervous system – people might be happy to stare at a stone all day.'

Johnson listened to them talking, glad to feel Christine's hand in his own. She was watching him with a quiet smile, aware that they shared the conspiracy. She would try to save the child, the last fragment of the experiment, and he knew that if it survived it would face a fierce challenge from those who feared it might replace them.

But the birds endured. His head had cleared, and he remembered the visions that had given him a brief glimpse of another, more advanced world. High above the collapsed canopy of the forest he could see the traps he had set, and the great crimson birds sitting on their wings. At least they could carry the dream forward.

Ten minutes later, when the inflatable had been winched onto the deck, the cutter set off through the inlet. As it passed the western headland the lieutenant helped Christine towards the cabin. Johnson followed them, then pushed aside the government scientist and leapt from the rail, diving cleanly into the water. He struck out for the shore a hundred feet away, knowing that he was strong enough to climb the trees and release the birds, with luck a mating pair who would take him with them in their escape from time.

**1990**

# A GUIDE TO VIRTUAL DEATH

*For reasons amply documented elsewhere, intelligent life on earth became extinct in the closing hours of the 20th Century. Among the clues left to us, the following schedule of a day's television programmes transmitted to an unnamed city in the northern hemisphere on December 23, 1999, offers its own intriguing insight into the origins of the disaster.*

**6.00 am** Porno-Disco. Wake yourself up with his-and-her hard-core sex images played to a disco beat.

**7.00** Weather Report. Today's expected micro-climates in the city's hotel atriums, shopping malls and office complexes. Hilton International promises an afternoon snow-shower as a Christmas appetiser.

**7.15** News Round-up. What our news-makers have planned for you. Maybe a small war, a synthetic earthquake or a famine-zone/charity tie-in.

**7.45** Breakfast Time. Gourmet meals to watch as you eat your diet cellulose.

**8.30** Commuter Special. The rush-hour game-show. How many bottoms can you pinch, how many faces can you slap?

**9.30** The Travel Show. Visit the world's greatest airports and underground car parks.

**10.30** Home-makers of Yesterday. Nostalgic scenes of old-fashioned housework. No.7 – The Vacuum Cleaner.

**11.00** Office War. Long-running serial of office gang-wars.

**12.00** Newsflash. The networks promise either a new serial killer or a deadly food toxin.

**1.00 pm** Live from Parliament. No.12 – The Alcoholic MP.

**1.30** The Nose-Pickers. Hygiene programme for the kiddies.

**2.00** Caress Me. Soft-porn for the siesta hour.

**2.30** Your Favourite Commericials. Popular demand re-runs of golden-oldie TV ads.

**3.00** Housewives' Choice. Rape, and how to psychologically prepare yourself.

**4.00** Count-down. Game show in which contestants count backwards from one million.

5.00        Newsflash. Either an airliner crash or a bank collapse. Viewers
            express preference.

6.00        *Today's Special.* Virtual Reality TV presents 'The Kennedy
            Assassination.' The Virtual Reality head-set takes you to Dallas,
            Texas, on November 22, 1963. First you fire the assassin's rifle
            from the Book Depository window, and then you sit between
            Jackie and JFK in the Presidential limo as the bullet strikes.
            For premium subscribers only – feel the Presidential brain
            tissue spatter your face OR wipe Jackie's tears onto your
            handkerchief.

8.00        Dinner Time. More gourmet dishes to view with your evening
            diet-cellulose.

9.00        Science Now. Is there life after death? Micro-electrodes pick up
            ultra-faint impulses from long-dead brains. Relatives question
            the departed.

10.00       Crime-Watch. Will it be your home that is broken into tonight
            by the TV Crime Gang?

11.00       *Today's Special.* Tele-Orgasm. Virtual Reality TV takes you
            to an orgy. Have sex with the world's greatest movie-stars.
            Tonight: Marilyn Monroe and Madonna OR Warren Beatty
            and Tom Cruise. For premium subscribers only – experience
            transexualism, paedophilia, terminal syphilis, gang-rape, and
            bestiality (choice: German Shepherd or Golden Retriever).

1.00 am     Newsflash. Tonight's surprise air-crash.

2.00        The Religious Hour. Imagine being dead. Priests and neuro-
            scientists construct a life-like mock-up of your death.

3.00        Night-Hunter. Will the TV Rapist come through your bedroom
            window?

4.15        Sex for Insomniacs. Soft porn to rock you to sleep.

5.00        The Charity Hour. Game show in which Third-World contest-
            ants beg for money.

**1992**

# THE MESSAGE FROM MARS

The successful conclusion of NASA's Mars mission in 2008, signalled by the safe touch-down of the Zeus IV space vehicle at Edwards Air Force Base in California, marked an immense triumph for the agency. During the 1990s, after the failure of the Shuttle project, NASA's entire future was in jeopardy. The American public's lack of interest in the space programme, coupled with unsettling political events in the former Soviet bloc, led Congress to cut back its funding of astronautics. Successive US Presidents were distracted by the task of balancing the national budget, and their scientific advisers had long insisted that the exploration of the solar system could be achieved far more economically by unmanned vehicles.

But NASA's directors had always known that the scientific exploration of space was a small part of the agency's claim to existence. Manned flights alone could touch the public imagination and guarantee the huge funds needed to achieve them. The triumph of the Apollo landing on the moon in 1969 had shown that the road to the spiritual heart of America could be paved with dollar bills, but by the year 2000 that road seemed permanently closed. Struggling to keep the agency alive, the NASA chiefs found themselves reduced to the satellite mapping of mid-western drought areas, and were faced with the prospect of being absorbed into the Department of Agriculture.

However, at the last hour the agency was saved, and given the funds to embark on its greatest mission. The announcement in Peking on January 1, 2001, that a Chinese spacecraft had landed on the moon sent an uneasy tremor through the American nation. True, the Stars and Stripes had been planted on the moon more than thirty years earlier, but that event lay in a past millennium. Was the next millennium to be dominated by the peoples on the Asian side of the Pacific rim, spending their huge trade surpluses on spectacular projects that would seize the planet's imagination for the next century?

As the pictures of the Chinese astronauts, posing beside their pagoda-shaped space vehicle, The Temple of Lightness, were relayed to the world's TV screens, news came that an Indonesian space crew and an unmanned Korean probe would soon land next to the Chinese.

Galvanised by all this, a no longer somnolent President Quayle addressed both houses of Congress. Within weeks NASA was assigned a multi-billion-dollar emergency fund and ordered to launch a crash programme that would leap-frog the moon and land an American on Mars before the end of the decade.

NASA, as always, rose bravely to the challenge of the tax-dollar. Armies of elderly space-engineers were recruited from their Florida retirement homes. Fifty civilian and military test pilots were pressed into astronaut training. Within two years Zeus I, the unmanned prototype of the vast space vehicles that would later carry a five-man crew, had roared away from Cape Canaveral on a six-month reconnaissance voyage. It circled the Red Planet a dozen times and surveyed the likely landing zone, before returning successfully to Earth.

After two more unmanned flights, in 2005 and 2006, Zeus IV set off in November, 2007, guaranteeing President Quayle's third-term electoral landslide, which the five astronauts saluted from the flight-deck of the spacecraft. By now the Chinese, Indonesian and Korean lunar programmes had been forgotten. The world's eyes were fixed on the Zeus IV, and its five crew-members were soon more famous than any Hollywood superstar.

Wisely, NASA had selected an international crew, led by Colonel Dean Irwin of the USAF. Captain Clifford Horner and Commander John Merritt were former US Army and Navy test pilots, but the team was completed by a Russian doctor, Colonel Valentina Tsarev, and a Japanese computer specialist, Professor Hiroshi Kawahito.

During the two-month voyage to Mars the quirks and personalities of the five astronauts became as familiar as any face across a breakfast table. The Zeus IV was the largest spacecraft ever launched, and had the dimensions of a nuclear submarine. Its wide control rooms and observation decks, its crew facilities and non-denominational chapel (if a marriage was arranged, Colonel Irwin was authorized to conduct it) happily reminded TV viewers of the Starship Enterprise in the *Star Trek* TV series, still endlessly broadcast on a hundred networks. Everyone responded to the calm and dignified presence of Colonel Irwin, the deadpan humour of Captain Horner, the chirpy computer-speak of the mercurial Japanese, and the mothering but sometimes flirtatious eye of Dr Valentina. Millions of viewers rallied to their aid when the Zeus IV passed through an unexpected meteor storm, but the ultra-hard carbon fibre and ceramic hull, a byproduct of the most advanced tank armour, proved even more resilient than the designers had hoped. The inspection space-walks seemed like gracefully choreographed ballets – which of course they were, like every other activity shown to the TV audience – and confirmed that mankind had at last entered the second Space Age.

Two months to the day after leaving Cape Canaveral, the Zeus IV landed on Mars, whose sombre presence had loomed ever more threateningly for the previous weeks. Signals blackouts caused by the planet's magnetic field added their own thrills and panics, skilfully orchestrated by NASA's PR specialists. But the landing was a triumph, celebrated by the hoisting of the Stars and Stripes and, behind it, the flag of the United Nations.

Within an hour the crew of the Zeus IV was standing on Martian soil beside the spacecraft, intoning their carefully rehearsed 'Hymn to the Space Age'. From that moment no Congressman dared to deny the NASA chiefs anything they demanded.

For the next six weeks public interest in the Mars mission remained high, sustained by NASA's careful attention to the emotional needs of the worldwide audience. Life within the spacecraft was presented as a cross between a TV sitcom and a classroom course in elementary astronautics. The crew tolerantly went along with these charades. Dr Valentina was seen replacing a filling in Commander Merritt's mouth, and Professor Kawahito, the heart-throb of a billion Asian viewers, won a hard-fought chess tournament against the Zeus IV's combined on-board computers. Romance was in the air as Dr Valentina's cabin door remained tantalizingly ajar. The TV cameras followed the crew as they drove in their excursion vehicles across the fossil Martian seas, collecting rock samples and analysing the local atmosphere.

At the halfway stage of their mission the crew revealed a mild impatience with the media roles imposed on them, which the NASA psychologists attributed to a greater maturity brought on by a sense of planetary awe. To remind them of Earth, the astronauts were urged to watch episodes of *Dallas*, *Dynasty* and *The Flintstones*, and to take part in a series of Oval Office interviews with President Quayle. But their spirits lifted as the day of departure drew near. When the Zeus IV rose at last from the Martian surface the entire crew burst spontaneously into an unscripted cheer, in which some observers detected a small note of irony.

Ignoring this impromptu levity, NASA planned a lavish reception at Edwards Air Force Base, where the Zeus IV would land. Every Congressman and Governor in the United States would be present, along with President Quayle, the heads of state of thirty countries and a host of entertainment celebrities. An unending programme of media appearances awaited the astronauts – there would be triumphal parades through a dozen major cities, followed by a worldwide tour lasting a full six months. NASA had already appointed firms of literary agents and public relations experts to look after the commercial interests of the astronauts. There were sports sponsorships, book contracts and highly paid consultancies. The news of these deals was transmitted to the home-coming crew, who seemed gratified by the interest in their achievement, unaware that whenever they appeared on screen their images were accompanied by the cash totals now committed to them. Two days before the Zeus IV landed, NASA announced that three major Hollywood studios would collaborate on the most expensive film of all time, in which the astronauts would play themselves in a faithful recreation of the Martian voyage.

So, at 3.35 pm on April 29, 2008, the Zeus IV appeared in the California sky. Accompanied by six chase planes, the spacecraft swept down to a perfect landing, guided by its on-board computers to within 50 metres of President Quayle's reception podium. The stunned silence was broken by an immense cheer when two of the astronauts were glimpsed in the observation windows. The crowd surged forward, waiting for the hatches to open as soon as the landing checks were over.

Despite the warmth of this welcome, the astronauts were surprisingly reluctant to emerge from their craft. The decontamination teams were poised by the airlocks, ready to board the spaceship and evacuate its atmosphere for laboratory analysis. But the crew had overridden the computerized sequences and made no reply over the radio link to the urgent queries of the ground controllers. They had switched off the television cameras inside the craft, but could be seen through the observation windows, apparently tidying their cabins and changing into overalls. Dr Valentina was spotted in the galley, apparently sterilizing her surgical instruments. A rumour swept the review stands, where President Quayle, the Congress and invited heads of state sweltered in the sun, that one of the crew had been injured on re-entry, but it soon transpired that Dr Valentina was merely making soup. Even more strangely, Professor Kawahito was seen setting out six parallel chessboards, as if preparing for another tournament.

At this point, an hour after their arrival, the crew became irritated by the grimacing faces pressed against the observation windows, and the interior shutters abruptly closed. This dismissive gesture made the crowd even more restive, and the ground staff tried to force the main hatch. When they failed, the head of NASA's crash recovery team began to pound on the locks with a baseball bat borrowed from a youngster seated on his father's shoulders. The first whistles and jeers rose from the crowd, who jostled the scaffolding towers on which the impatient TV crews were waiting. A cameraman lost his footing and fell through the roof of a parked bus. Loud-speakers blared meaninglessly across the million or more spectators sitting on their cars around the perimeter of the airfield. The heads of state, diplomats and generals consulted their watches, while President Quayle, making involuntary putting movements with the portable microphone in his hands, beckoned in an unsettling way to his military aide carrying the briefcase of nuclear launch codes. The boos of the crowd were only drowned when a squadron of jet planes flew low over the field, releasing streams of red, white and blue smoke. Ordered away by the frantic control tower, the victory flight broke up in confusion as the pilots returned to their muster points in the sky, leaving a delirium of crazed smoke over the Zeus IV.

At last calm was restored when a company of military police took up positions around the spacecraft, forcing the crowds behind the VIP stands. Led by President Quayle, the dignitaries shuffled from their seats and hurried along the lines of red carpet to the refreshment tents. The TV cameras trained their lenses on the Zeus IV, watching for the smallest sign of movement.

*      *      *

As evening fell, the spectators beyond the airfield perimeter began to disperse. Powerful arc-lights bathed the spacecraft, and during the night a fresh attempt was made to contact the crew. But the messages in morse code tapped on the hull, like the laser beams shone at the darkened observation windows, failed to draw any response. No sound could be heard from the interior of the craft, as if the crew had settled in for the night, and a hundred theories began to circulate among the NASA chiefs and the teams of doctors and psychiatrists summoned to their aid.

Were the astronauts in the last stages of a fatal contagious disease? Had their brains been invaded by an alien parasite? Were they too emotionally exhausted by their voyage to face the reception awaiting them, or gripped by so strong a sense of humility that they longed only for silence and anonymity? Had an unexpected consequence of time dilation returned them psychologically hours or days after their physical arrival? Had they, perhaps, died in a spiritual sense, or were they, for inexplicable reasons of their own, staging a mutiny?

Surrounded by the deserted stands and the silent bunting, the NASA chiefs made their decision. An hour before dawn two thermal lances played their fiery hoses against the heat-resistant plates of the spacecraft. But the carbon-ceramic hull of the Zeus IV had been forged in temperatures far beyond those of a thermal lance.

A controlled explosion was the only solution, despite the danger to the crew within. But as the demolition squad placed their charges against the ventral hatchway, the shutter of an observation window opened for the first time. Captured on film, the faces of Colonel Irwin and Commander Merritt looked down at the limpet mines, the detonators and fuse wire. They gazed calmly at the NASA officials and engineers gesticulating at them, and shook their heads, rejecting the world with a brief wave before closing the shutter for the last time.

Needless to say, NASA allowed nothing of this to leak to the public at large, and claimed that the crew had alerted their ground controllers to the possible dangers of a virulent interplanetary disease. NASA spokesmen confirmed that they had ordered the crew to isolate themselves until this mystery virus could be identified and destroyed. The Zeus IV was hitched to its tractor and moved to an empty hangar on a remote corner of the airbase, safe from the TV cameras and the thousands still camped around the perimeter fence.

Here, over the next weeks and months, teams of engineers and psychologists, astrophysicists and churchmen tried to free the crew from their self-imposed prison. Right from the start, as the doors of the hangar sealed the Zeus IV from the world, it was taken for granted that the astronauts' immolation was entirely voluntary. Nonetheless, an armed guard, backed by electronic security devices, kept careful watch on the craft. Sets of aircraft scales were manoeuvred under the landing wheels, so that the weight of the Zeus IV could be measured at all times, and instantly expose any attempt at escape.

As it happened, the spaceship's weight remained constant, never fluctuating by more than the accumulated dust on its hull. In all senses the Zeus IV constituted a sealed world, immune to any pressures from within or without. A controlled explosion strong enough to split the hull would also rupture the engines and disperse the craft's nuclear fuel supply, provoking a worldwide political outcry that would doom NASA forever. There was no way of starving the crew out – to deal with the possibility of the Zeus IV missing its rendezvous with Mars and stranding itself forever in deep space, a 200-ton stock of food had been placed aboard, enough to last the crew for 40 years. Its air, water and human wastes were recycled, and there were enough episodes of *Dallas* in the video-library to amuse the astronauts for all eternity.

The Zeus, in fact, no longer needed the Earth, and the NASA officials accepted that only psychological means would ever persuade the crew to leave their craft. They assumed that a profound spiritual crisis had afflicted the astronauts, and that until this resolved itself the rescuers' main task was to establish a channel of communication.

So began a long series of ruses, pleas and stratagems. The puzzled entreaties of relatives, whose tearful faces were projected onto the hangar roof, the prayers of churchmen, the offer of huge cash bribes, the calls to patriotism and even the threat of imprisonment, failed to prompt a single response. After two months, when public curiosity was still at fever pitch, the NASA teams admitted to themselves that the Zeus IV crew had probably not even heard these threats and promises.

Meanwhile an impatient President Quayle, aware that he was the butt of cartoonists and TV comedians, demanded firmer action. He ordered that pop music be played at full blast against the spacecraft's hull and, further, that the huge ship be rocked violently from side to side until the crew came to their senses. This regime was tried but discontinued after two hours, partly for its sheer ludicrousness, and partly for fear of damaging the nuclear reactors.

More thoughtful opinion was aware that the crisis afflicting the Zeus crew merited careful study in its own right, if mankind were ever to live permanently in space. A prominent theologian was invited to the Edwards airbase, and surveyed the claustrophobic hangar in which the Zeus was now entombed, draped like Gulliver in its cables and acoustic sensors. He wondered why the crew had bothered to return to Earth at all, knowing what they probably faced, when they might have stayed forever on the vast and empty landscapes of Mars. By returning at all, he ventured, they were making an important point, and acknowledged that they still saw their place among the human race.

So a patient vigil began. Concealed cameras watched for any signs of internal movement and electronic gauges mapped the smallest activities of the crew. After a further three months the daily pattern of life within the Zeus IV had been well established. The crew never spoke to each other, except when carrying out the daily maintenance checks of the spacecraft systems. All took regular exercise in the gymnasium, but otherwise stayed in their own quarters. No music was played and they never listened to radio or television. For all that anyone knew, they passed the days in sleep, meditation and prayer. The temperature remained at a steady 68°F., and the only constant sound was that of the circulation of air.

After six months the NASA psychiatrists concluded that the crew of the Zeus IV had suffered a traumatic mental collapse, probably brought on by oxygen starvation, and were now in a vegetative state. Relatives protested, but public interest began to wane. Congress refused to allocate funds for further Zeus missions, and NASA reluctantly committed itself to a future of instrumented spaceflights.

A year passed, and a second. A small guard and communications crew, including a duty psychologist and a clergyman, still maintained a vigil over the Zeus. The monitors recorded the faint movements of the crew, and the patterns of daily life which they had established within a few hours of their landing. A computerized analysis of their foot-treads identified each of the astronauts and revealed that they kept to their own quarters and seldom met, though all took part in the maintenance drills.

So the astronauts languished in their twilight world. A new President and the unfolding decades of peace led the public to forget about the Zeus IV, and its crew, if remembered at all, were assumed to be convalescing at a secret institution. In 2016, eight years after their return, there was a flurry of activity when a deranged security officer lit a large fire under the spacecraft, in an attempt to smoke out the crew. Four years later a Hollywood telepathist claimed to be in contact with the astronauts, reporting that they had met God on Mars and had been sworn to silence about the tragic future in store for the human race.

In 2025 the NASA headquarters in Houston were alerted to a small but sudden fall in the overall weight of the Zeus – 170 pounds had been wiped from the scales. Was the spacecraft preparing for take-off, perhaps employing an anti-gravity device which the crew had been constructing in the seventeen years since their return? However, the tread-pattern analysis confirmed that only four astronauts were now aboard the craft. Colonel Irwin was missing, and an exhaustive hunt began of the Edwards airbase. But the organic sediments in the trapped gases released from a discharge vent revealed what some engineers had already suspected. Colonel Irwin had died at the age of 62, and his remains had been vapourized and returned to the atmosphere. Four years later he was followed by the Japanese, Professor Kawahito, and the Zeus was lighter by a further 132 pounds. The food stocks aboard the Zeus would now last well beyond the deaths of the three astronauts still alive.

In 2035 NASA was dissolved, and its functions assigned to the immensely wealthy universities which ran their own scientific space programmes. The Zeus IV was offered to the Smithsonian Institute in Washington, but the director declined, on the grounds that the museum could not accept exhibits that contained living organisms. The USAF had long wished to close the Edwards airbase, and responsibility for this huge desert expanse passed to the National Parks Bureau, which was eager to oversee one of the few areas of California not yet covered with tract housing. The armed guards around the Zeus IV had long gone, and two field officers supervised the elderly instruments that still kept watch over the spacecraft.

Captain Horner died in 2040, but the event was not noticed until the following year when a bored repairman catalogued the accumulated acoustic tapes and ran a computer analysis of tread-patterns and overall weight.

The news of this death, mentioned only in the National Parks Bureau's annual report, came to the attention of a Las Vegas entrepreneur who had opened the former Nevada atomic proving grounds to the tourist trade, mounting simulated A-bomb explosions. He leased the Zeus hangar from the Parks Bureau, and small parties of tourists trooped around the spacecraft, watching bemused as the rare tread-patterns crossed the sonar screens in the monitor room.

After three years of poor attendances the tours were discontinued, but a decade later a Tijuana circus proprietor sub-leased the site for his winter season. He demolished the now derelict hangar and constructed an inflatable astro-dome with a huge arena floor. Helium-filled latex 'spacecraft' circled the Zeus IV, and the performance ended with a mass ascent of the huge vehicle by a team of topless women acrobats.

When the dome was removed the Zeus IV sat under the stars, attached to a small shack where a single technician of the Parks Bureau kept a desultory watch on the computer screens for an hour each day. The spaceship was now covered with graffiti and obscene slogans, and the initials of thousands of long-vanished tourists. With its undercarriage embedded in the desert sand, it resembled a steam locomotive of the 19th century, which many passers-by assumed it to be.

Tramps and hippies sheltered under its fins, and at one time the craft was incorporated into a small shanty village. In later years a desert preacher attracted a modest following, claiming that the Messiah had made his second coming and was trapped inside the Zeus. Another cultist claimed that the devil had taken up residence in the ancient structure. The tract housing drew ever closer, and eventually surrounded the Zeus, which briefly served as an illuminated landmark advertising an unsuccessful fast-food franchise.

In 2070, sixty-two years after its return from Mars, a young graduate student at Reno University erected a steel frame around the Zeus and attached a set of high-intensity magnetic probes to its hull. The computerized imaging equipment – later confiscated by the US Government – revealed the silent and eerie interior of the spacecraft, its empty flight decks and corridors.

An aged couple, Commander John Merritt and Dr Valentina Tsarev, now in their late eighties, sat in their small cabins, hands folded on their laps. There were no books or ornaments beside their simple beds. Despite their extreme age they were clearly alert, tidy and reasonably well nourished. Most mysteriously, across their eyes moved the continuous play of a keen and amused intelligence.

**1992**

# REPORT FROM AN OBSCURE PLANET

After an immense journey we have at last landed on this remote planet, ready to carry out our rescue mission. The emergency signals transmitted to us were frantic in their intensity, but everything seems to be in order here. Our first surveys confirm that no natural catastrophe is imminent. The climatic cover and atmospheric circulation are stable, despite a recent rise in the levels of background radiation. There is evidence of the long-term erosion of the ecological base, but this is still more than adequate to support life.

Aerial reconnaissance of the hundreds of cities that occupy the major continents suggests that the population of the planet numbers many billions, though none of the inhabitants has emerged to greet us. Presumably they are still seeking refuge from the disaster that threatened to overwhelm them. We have entered many of the cities and have found them deserted, but there is no sign of the vast underground shelters needed to harbour this huge population. The possibility remains that the inhabitants fled from their planet in despair, fearing that their call for help had not been heard. Yet the restricted capacities of their aerospace technology rule out this escape route, and we assume that they are still in hiding.

In an attempt to reassure them, we are making use of the local television and radio facilities, and have broadcast a signal of greeting and friendship. Surprisingly, this has activated the planet's extensive computer networks, which have reacted with a sudden show of alarm, as if well used to mistrusting these declarations of good intent.

We have found that the computer system is fully operational. Large sections of the system, in particular its predictive and cognitive functions, have been self-generated within the recent past, when the computer networks seem to have independently mobilised themselves to face the imminent disaster.

Our investigations confirm that this threat was closely tied to an important date in the planetary calendar, represented by the notation '24.00 hours, December 31, 1999'. Evidently this marked the end of two epochs of great significance, and the beginning of both a new century and a new millennium. It now appears certain that our own arrival coincided almost exactly with, though may fractionally have overrun, this auspicious moment, which was perceived by the computer networks as a final and desperate deadline.

The planet's entire computer system is still at an ultra-high state of arousal, registering a recent all-out response to extreme peril. Only a small volume of signal traffic moves between the satellite links, but there are gigantic memory stores with a capacity far in excess of the system's needs. These memory banks are now full, guarded by complex codes that we have been unable to break, and are perhaps the treasure house and terminal repository of the planet's ancestral knowledge.

So impressive are the defences of the system that we are now convinced that it was these computers that authorised the transmission of the emergency signal summoning us to their world's rescue.

However, there is still no sign of the inhabitants, and no response to our broadcast greetings. The cities and their suburbs, the airports and highways remain silent. Meanwhile we are carrying out a survey of these people, and of their values and civic virtues, and have come across a number of striking paradoxes. It is clear that their technological and scientific skills are of an advanced order, allowing them to construct the vast cities that dominate the planet's surface. An immense infrastructure of roads, bridges and tunnels has been laid down in the recent past, augmented by an aviation system that reaches the remotest outposts of their world.

The planet's mineral, energy and agricultural resources have been efficiently, and even ruthlessly, exploited. A simple but evidently attractive system of barter, based on the concept of money, facilitates the transfer of manufactured goods and services, and the surplus wealth generated has funded an ever-expanding science and technology. Space-flight, except in its most primitive forms, still lies beyond the abilities of these people, but they have harnessed the energy of the atom, deciphered the molecular codes that oversee their own reproduction, and seem well on the way to banishing disease and solving the mysteries of life and immortality.

At the same time, our researches have shown that despite these achievements the peoples of this planet have in other respects scarcely raised themselves above the lowest levels of barbarism. The enjoyment of pain and violence is as natural to them as the air they breathe. War above all is their most popular sport, in which rival populations, and frequently entire continents, attack each other with the most vicious and destructive weapons, regardless of the death and suffering that follow. These conflicts may last for years or decades. Nations nominally at peace devote a large proportion of their collective income to constructing arsenals of lethal weapons, and satisfy the appetites of their populations with a display of brutal entertainments in which violence, humiliation and murder are almost the sole ingredients.

Not surprisingly, our latest research confirms that the imminent threat to which their computers alerted us was in fact represented by the existence of these people. They constituted the danger that was about to overwhelm their planet, and it was to save themselves that the computer networks summoned us from the far side of the universe.

The deadline set by the computers, the crucial hour when one millennium gave way to another, perhaps explains the reason for their alarm. Given these people's hunger for violence, it may be that they saw the birth of a new millennium as a licence for an even greater carnival of destruction. They waited at the threshold of space, a barbaric horde with the secret of immortality within their grasp, eager to play with their own psychopathology as the ultimate game.

The prospect of this virulent plague spreading across the universe must have prompted the planet's computers to call a halt. But the ultimate mystery remains of where the inhabitants have disappeared. If they have been physically annihilated in an act of planetary hygiene there is no trace of the billions of corpses or of the vast necropolis needed to inter them.

A possible explanation occurs to us as we prepare to return to our home star. Driven by the need for a more lifelike replica of the scenes of carnage that most entertained them, the people of this unhappy world had invented an advanced and apparently interiorised version of their television screens, a virtual replica of reality in which they could act out their most deviant fantasies. These three-dimensional simulations were generated by their computers, and had reached a stage of development in the last years of the millennium in which the imitation of reality was more convincing than the original. It may even have become the new reality to the extent that their cities and highways, their fellow citizens and, ultimately, themselves seemed mere illusions by comparison with the electronically generated amusement park where they preferred to play. Here they could assume any identity, create and fulfil any desire, and explore the most deviant dreams.

But at some point in the new millennium they might well have decided to return to the world and test it against those dreams, ready to destroy it like a child bored with an unresponsive toy. Is it possible that the computers of this planet, having welcomed the population into this cave of illusion, then made a desperate decision and entombed them magnetically, translating them by some as yet undiscovered science into a memorised version of their physical selves? Once inside the cave, the door of virtual death was sealed and encrypted behind them, leaving the computers alone and safe at last.

If so, we arrived some moments too late. As we leave, the computers have calmed themselves, and are singing quietly in unison. Perhaps they miss their former companions, however brutish. Our concluding survey indicates that they have invented God, perhaps an idealised image of the race they entombed. As we set out into space we can hear them praying.

1992

# New Stories for the American Edition

# THE SECRET AUTOBIOGRAPHY OF J.G.B.

On waking one morning, B was surprised to see that Shepperton was deserted. He entered the kitchen at 9 o'clock, annoyed to find that neither his post nor the daily newspapers had been delivered, and that a power failure prevented him from preparing his breakfast. He spent an hour staring at the melting ice that dripped from his refrigerator, and then went next door to complain to his neighbour.

Surprisingly, his neighbour's house was empty. His car stood in the drive, but the entire family – husband, wife, children and dog – had disappeared. Even more odd, the street was filled by an unbroken silence. No traffic moved along the nearby motorway, and not a single aircraft flew overhead towards London Airport. B crossed the road and knocked on several doors. Through the windows he could see the empty interiors. Nothing in this peaceful suburb was out of place, except for its missing tenants.

Thinking that perhaps some terrible calamity was imminent – a nuclear catastrophe, or a sudden epidemic after a research laboratory accident – and that by some unfortunate mishap he alone had not been warned, B returned home and switched on his transistor radio. The apparatus worked, but all the stations were silent, the continental transmitters as well as those of the United Kingdom. Disconcerted, B returned to the street and gazed at the empty sky. It was a calm, sun-filled day, crossed by peaceful clouds that gave no hint of any natural disaster.

B took his car and drove to the centre of Shepperton. The town was deserted, and none of the shops was open. A train stood in the station, empty and without any of the passengers who regularly travelled to London. Leaving Shepperton, B crossed the Thames to the nearby town of Walton. There again he found the streets completely silent. He stopped in front of the house owned by his friend P, whose car was parked in her drive. Using the spare key that he carried, he unlocked the front door and entered the house. But even as he called her name he could see that there was no trace of the young woman. She had not slept in her bed. In the kitchen the melting ice of the refrigerator had formed a large pool on the floor. There was no electric power, and the telephone was dead.

Resuming his journey, B systematically explored the neighbouring towns, circling them all as he approached central London. He was no longer surprised to find the huge metropolis totally deserted. He drove down an empty Piccadilly, crossed Trafalgar Square in silence and parked outside the unguarded Buckingham Palace. As dusk fell he decided to return to Shepperton. He had almost run out of fuel and was forced to break into a filling station. However, no policemen were out on patrol or in their stations. He left behind him an immense city plunged into darkness, where the only lights were the reflections of his headlamps.

B passed a disturbed night, with the radio mute beside his bed. But when he woke to another luminous morning his confidence returned. After an initial doubt, he was relieved to see that Shepperton was still deserted. The food within his refrigerator had begun to rot; he needed fresh provisions and a means of cooking for himself. He drove into Shepperton, broke a window of the supermarket and collected several cartons of canned meat and vegetables, rice and sugar. In the hardware store he found a paraffin stove, and look it home with a tin of fuel. Water no longer flowed in the mains, but he estimated that the contents of the roof cistern would last him a week or more. Further forays to the local stores furnished him with a supply of candles, torches and batteries.

In the following week B made several expeditions to London. He returned to the houses and flats of his friends, but found them empty. He broke into Scotland Yard and the newspaper offices in Fleet Street, in the hope of finding some explanation for the disappearance of an entire population. Lastly, he entered the Houses of Parliament, and stood in the silent debating chamber of the Commons, breathing the stale air. However, there was not the least explanation anywhere of what had taken place. In the streets of the city he saw not a single cat or dog. It was only when he visited London Zoo that he found that the birds still remained within their cages. They seemed delighted to see B, but flew off with famished cries when he unlocked the bars.

So at least he had a kind of companionship. During the next month, and throughout the summer, B continued his preparations for survival. He drove as far north as Birmingham without seeing a soul, then drove down to the south coast and followed the road from Brighton to Dover. Standing on the cliffs, he gazed at the distant shoreline of France. In the marina he chose a motor-boat with a full tank of fuel, and set out across the calm sea, now free of the customary pleasure-craft, petroleum tankers and cross-Channel ferries. At Calais he wandered for an hour through the deserted streets, and in the silent shops listened in vain to telephones that never replied. Then he retraced his steps to the port and returned to England.

When the summer was followed by a mild autumn, B had established a pleasant and comfortable existence for himself. He had abundant stocks of tinned food, fuel and water with which to survive the winter. The river was nearby, clear and free of all pollution, and petrol was easy to obtain, in unlimited quantities, from the filling stations and parked cars. At the local police station he assembled a small armoury of pistols and carbines, to deal with any unexpected menace that might appear.

But his only visitors were the birds, and he scattered handfuls of rice and seeds on the lawn of his garden and on those of his former neighbours. Already he had begun to forget them, and Shepperton soon became an extraordinary aviary, filled with birds of every species.

Thus the year ended peacefully, and B was ready to begin his true work.

# THE DYING FALL

Three years have passed since the collapse of the Tower of Pisa, but only now can I accept the crucial role that I played in the destruction of this unique landmark. Over twenty tourists died as the thousands of tons of marble lost their grasp on the air and collapsed to the ground. Among them was my wife Elaine, who had climbed to the topmost tier and was looking down at me when the first visible crack appeared in the tower's base. Never were tragedy and triumph so intimately joined, as if Elaine's pride in braving the worn and slippery stairs had been punished by the unseen forces that had sustained this unbalanced mass of masonry for so many centuries.

I realise now that another element – farce – was present on that day. By chance a passing tourist on the steps of the cathedral had taken a photograph of the tower as the crack reached the third floor and a tell-tale section of cornice began its fall to earth. The photograph, endlessly published throughout the world, clearly shows the four startled tourists on the uppermost deck. Three of them are leaning back on their heels, hands raised to grip the sky, aware that the ancient campanile has moved under their feet.

Elaine, alone, has already seized the rail, and is staring at the grass waiting for her nearly two hundred feet below. Using a magnifying glass, one can see that, true to her quirky and mocking character, she shows almost no alarm. Her eyes have noticed the falling cornice, and I like to think that she is already planning to sue the municipality of Pisa for neglecting the safety of its tourists, and is collecting evidence that in due course she will present to her lawyers.

The dozen or so tourists visible on the lower floors are still making their way around its canted decks, groping past the narrow columns as they climb the 300 steps to the roof. A father and his young daughter wave to the tourists below them, two Italian sailors in uniform play the fool for their girl-friends, feigning an attack of giddiness, and an elderly couple pause to rest after climbing to the first floor, determined to complete the ascent. None of them sees the falling cornice and the fine cascade of powdered mortar.

The only figure on the ground who is aware of the imminent catastrophe is a man in a white jacket and panama hat who stands at the foot of the tower, both hands raised to the marble flank. His face is hidden, but his arms are braced against the shifting stone, his back arched above his straining legs. We can see that in his desperate way he is trying to hold upright the collapsing tower that is about to obliterate him.

Or so everyone assumes. The newspaper caption writers, the commentators on TV documentaries, all commend the bravery of this solitary figure. Surprisingly, he has never been identified, and neither his hat nor his white jacket were found in the mountain of rubble that was later removed, stone by stone, from the unhappy site.

But was he trying to support the tower or, rather, helping it on its way? I, of course, can answer the question, since I am the man in the panama hat, the husband at whom Elaine, in the last moments of her life, so triumphantly stares.

Needless to say, I fled to safety, running through the dust and the shrieking tourists as the ground trembled and a cataract of masonry fell from the air. A vast cloud of pulverised marble enveloped the square, and I remember stumbling past the horror-stricken waiters and taxi-drivers who gazed at this field of devastation – not only had the tower vanished, but it had taken their livelihoods with it. Had they known that I was responsible they would have lynched me on the spot, and to this day I have kept silent, still gripped by my guilt over so many deaths, all but one of them entirely innocent.

In a sense the destruction of the tower was inscribed days beforehand in our unhappy tour of Tuscany. Our marriage, problematic from the start, had grown increasingly fraught during the previous year. Elaine had married me on the rebound, to spite an unfaithful lover, but soon decided that her husband, a classics lecturer at a minor university, was minor in all other respects. I was losing my students in a ferment of curriculum changes that would eventually lead to the descheduling of Latin and Greek and their replacement by cultural and media studies. My refusal to sue the university, Elaine decided, was a sign of my innate weakness, a frailty that soon extended to the marriage bed.

Claiming that our union was unconsummated, she consulted a solicitor with a view to divorcing me, but was persuaded to make a last effort to save the relationship. Our marriage became a series of negotiated truces, in which I would yield more and more territory. Still hoping to salvage something, and return to the few weeks of happiness we had known after the wedding, I suggested a holiday in Italy. I had arranged to give three lectures at the University of Florence, which would pay for our air fares, and then we would be free to enjoy ourselves in the Tuscan countryside.

Elaine agreed, but only grudgingly – her first husband had been a modernist architect, and she always claimed to dislike the past, the territory I had made my own, and pretended to prefer California and Texas. But soon after we landed at Pisa airport and took the train to Florence her interest in the Italian renaissance revived in a way that I found almost mysterious. Once I had given my lectures she threw us into a hectic round of tourist activities. Tirelessly she insisted on visiting every church and baptistry, every museum and cathedral. I was puzzled by this passion for the past until I realised that our visits to these historic sites had exposed yet another of my weaknesses.

As we took the creaking lift to the dome of Florence cathedral Elaine discovered that I was afraid of heights, a fear that I had never noticed in myself but which she immediately set out to maximise. Unsettled by the looming space below the dome, I could barely force myself from the lift. My eyes seemed unwilling to focus on the curving walls, and I felt my heart-beat fall away, leaving me on the edge of a fainting fit.

Gesticulating to Elaine, I refused to follow her around the narrow gallery. Scarcely able to breathe, I waited as she proudly circled the dome, calling to me in a insistent voice that embarrassed me in front of the other tourists. Yet as we left the cathedral she became strangely solicitous, holding my arm in a concerned and reassuring way. Far from deriding me, she seemed genuinely alarmed by my moment of panic.

Despite this show of affection, I soon noticed that our tour of Tuscany had become a series of vertical ascents. No battlement existed that we did not scale, no worn steps that we did not climb. At the Palazzo Vecchio, under the pretext of showing me the spectacular view over the city, she forced me to lean through the very windows from which Lorenzo de Medici had suspended the strangled plotters against his rule. I saw Siena cathedral from the roof down, almost breathing my last in the confined bell-tower. And all the while Elaine would watch me with her affectionate and lingering smile, like an older sister observing a timid sibling. Was she trying to cure me of my fear of heights, or to rub in my sense of my own inadequacy?

A climax of sorts came at San Gimignano, that surrealist township of towers constructed during the 14th century by rival families within this independent city state. As Elaine moved tirelessly from one tower to the next, I retreated to a cafe beside the cathedral with its macabre images of hell. All afternoon she gazed at the towers, admiring these symbols of an erect masculinity of which her husband was incapable, then sat beaming at me as the tourist coach carried us to Florence.

Three days later, when we arrived in Pisa for our London flight, I had been routed by Elaine's campaign. We were both eager to return to England, I to the safety of my university office, she to her solicitor. We had packed in silence, and reached Pisa airport with two hours to spare before our flight. Inevitably we found ourselves taking a taxi into the city. Reading from her guide-book, Elaine described the baptistry and cathedral in glowing terms, but I knew that our real destination was the nearby campanile, this marble phallus that seemed to excite her even more than the towers of San Gimignano.

I stepped from the taxi and stared up at the dizzying structure with its dangerously canted floors. Without a word, Elaine strode away from me towards the tower. She paid her entrance fee and began to climb the steps behind two uniformed sailors and a father with his daughter. As she reached each tier she looked down at me with her affectionate but knowing smirk, her contempt rising with each successive storey.

I stood on the cathedral steps, still surprised by the steep inclination of the tower, some 17 feet from the vertical. Despite myself, I wished that the structure, tilting each year by a few added millimetres, would decide on this exact moment for its long-predicted collapse.

Then, as Elaine reached the penultimate tier, I found myself needing to touch the tower, to feel the unforgiving marble against my skin. I left the cathedral and walked across the worn grass where the tourists sat in the sun, waving to their friends high above them. Ignoring the ticket office, I strolled around the stone well that surrounded the tower. I placed my hand on the antique marble, its surface pitted with the graffiti of centuries, its veins as marmoreal as fossilised time. The tower was both too erect and too old. I pressed against the massive flank, urging it on its way.

Eight storeys above me, Elaine had reached the roof and stood beside the panting sailors. Scarcely out of breath, she seized the iron rail and smiled down at me in her most implacable way, slowly shaking her head at my weakness.

Angered by her open contempt, I pushed again at the solid marble. The wall refused to yield, but when I lifted my hand I noticed that a small crack had appeared in the surface, running away from a discoloured node of crushed limestone. Curious, I pressed again, only to see that the crack had widened. It inched upwards at a barely visible pace, then darted forward, climbing the wall like a sudden fissure in a sheet of ice. Three feet long, it crossed a decorative moulding and rose swiftly towards the cornice of the first tier.

Laughing at this, I pressed both hands at the marble drum. Immediately the crack accelerated, and I heard a distant rumble, the dark groan of an awakening creature deep within the tower. The crack was now an open fissure through which I could see the shoes of the startled old man resting before he and his wife made their way to the second storey. A fine rain of dust and crumbling mortar showered my face. The entire tower was trembling against my hands, and a section of cornice fell through the air, followed by a scatter of fragments each larger than my fist.

The Tower of Pisa was about to fall. I gave it one last push, both arms outstretched, and felt the tortured rumbling as somewhere the spine of this great edifice began to crack. I stepped back, aware that the building was about to collapse onto me, and then looked up at the roof, where Elaine was clinging to the iron rail.

The tower buckled, its columns spilling like skittled pins at a bowling alley. In the last moments, as Elaine was pitched over the rail, I saw her face falling towards me, and an expression of anger that unmistakably changed, as she noticed me far below her, to one of triumph.

A second Tower of Pisa is now rising on the site of the first, financed by the world-wide appeal launched soon after the tragedy. The structure, this time mounted on an immovable concrete base, has reached the third storey and already reveals the modest inclination designed into it. This tower, supported by a rigid steel armature, will never fall, and within a few decades most visitors will have forgotten that it is no more than a replica.

For me, though, the original tower remains as real as ever in my mind. I often wake from terrifying dreams as the tons of marble hurtle towards me. Then I remind myself that it was Elaine who died on that day. I remember the expression on her face, the fierce pride that lit her eyes.

Did she feel that she had at last triumphed over me, and was happy to see me crushed by the cascade of tumbling columns? I remember the stones pelting my shoulders while I tried vainly to step back from the tower. At the last moment, as an amateur video-film reveals, the structure seemed to buckle, twisting itself in a desperate attempt to remain upright. It slewed away from me, sweeping Elaine, the collapsing masonry and the cartwheeling columns towards the ground by the cathedral steps.

I escaped, but that expression of triumph on Elaine's face still puzzles me. Had she seen me pushing against the tower and assumed that I was responsible for its collapse? Was she proud of me for hating her so fiercely, and for at last stirring from my impotence to take my revenge? Perhaps only in her death did we truly come together, and the Tower of Pisa served a purpose for which it had waited for so many centuries.

# BIBLIOGRAPHY

The stories in this collection first appeared in the following publications:

| | | |
|---|---|---|
| 'Prima Belladonna' | *Science Fantasy* | 1956 |
| 'Escapement' | *New Worlds* | 1956 |
| 'The Concentration City' (as 'Build-Up') | *New Worlds* | 1957 |
| 'Venus Smiles' (as 'Mobile') | *Science Fantasy* | 1957 |
| 'Manhole 69' | *New Worlds* | 1957 |
| 'Track 12' | *New Worlds* | 1958 |
| 'The Waiting Grounds' | *New Worlds* | 1959 |
| 'Now: Zero' | *Science Fantasy* | 1959 |
| 'The Sound-Sweep' | *Science Fantasy* | 1960 |
| 'Zone of Terror' | *New Worlds* | 1960 |
| 'Chronopolis' | *New Worlds* | 1960 |
| 'The Voices of Time' | *New Worlds* | 1960 |
| 'The Last World of Mr Goddard' | *Science Fantasy* | 1960 |
| 'Studio 5, The Stars' | *Science Fantasy* | 1961 |
| 'Deep End' | *New Worlds* | 1961 |
| 'The Overloaded Man' | *New Worlds* | 1961 |
| 'Mr F. is Mr F.' | *Science Fantasy* | 1961 |
| 'Billennium' | *New Worlds* | 1961 |
| 'The Gentle Assassin' | *New Worlds* | 1961 |
| 'The Insane Ones' | *Amazing Stories* | 1962 |
| 'The Garden of Time' | *Fantasy and Science Fiction* | 1962 |
| 'The Thousand Dreams of Stellavista' | *Amazing Stories* | 1962 |
| 'Thirteen to Centaurus' | *Amazing Stories* | 1962 |
| 'Passport to Eternity' | *Amazing Stories* | 1962 |
| 'The Cage of Sand' | *New Worlds* | 1962 |
| 'The Watch-Towers' | *Science Fantasy* | 1962 |
| 'The Singing Statues' | *Fantastic Stories* | 1962 |
| 'The Man on the 99th Floor' | *New Worlds* | 1962 |
| 'The Subliminal Man' | *New Worlds* | 1963 |
| 'The Reptile Enclosure' (as 'The Sherrington Theory') | *Amazing Stories* | 1963 |
| 'Question of Re-Entry' | *Fantastic Stories* | 1963 |

| | | |
|---|---|---|
| 'The Time-Tombs' | *Worlds of If* | 1963 |
| 'Now Wakes the Sea' | *Fantasy and Science Fiction* | 1963 |
| 'The Venus Hunters' | | |
| (as 'The Encounter') | *Amazing Stories* | 1963 |
| 'End-Game' | *New Worlds* | 1963 |
| 'Minus One' | *Science Fantasy* | 1963 |
| 'The Sudden Afternoon' | *Fantastic Stories* | 1963 |
| 'The Screen Game' | *Fantastic Stories* | 1963 |
| 'Time of Passage' | *Science Fantasy* | 1964 |
| 'Prisoner of the Coral Deep' | *Argosy* | 1964 |
| 'The Lost Leonardo' | *Fantasy and Science Fiction* | 1964 |
| 'The Terminal Beach' | *New Worlds* | 1964 |
| 'The Illuminated Man' | *Fantasy and Science Fiction* | 1964 |
| 'The Delta at Sunset' | *The Terminal Beach* | 1964 |
| 'The Drowned Giant' | *The Terminal Beach* | 1964 |
| 'The Gioconda of the Twilight Noon' | *The Terminal Beach* | 1964 |
| 'The Volcano Dances' | *The Terminal Beach* | 1964 |
| 'The Beach Murders' | | |
| (as 'Confetti Royale') | *Rogue* | 1966 |
| 'The Day of Forever' | *The Impossible Man* | 1966 |
| 'The Impossible Man' | *The Impossible Man* | 1966 |
| 'Storm-Bird, Storm-Dreamer' | *The Impossible Man* | 1966 |
| 'Tomorrow is a Million Years' | *Argosy* | 1966 |
| 'The Assassination of John Fitzgerald Kennedy Considered as a Downhill Motor Race' | *Ambit* | 1966 |
| 'Cry Hope, Cry Fury!' | *Fantasy and Science Fiction* | 1967 |
| 'The Recognition' | *Dangerous Visions* | 1967 |
| 'The Cloud-Sculptors of Coral D' | *Fantasy and Science Fiction* | 1967 |
| 'Why I Want to Fuck Ronald Reagan' | *International Times* | 1968 |
| 'The Dead Astronaut' | *Playboy* | 1968 |
| 'The Comsat Angels' | *Worlds of If* | 1968 |
| 'The Killing Ground' | *New Worlds* | 1969 |
| 'A Place and a Time to Die' | *New Worlds* | 1969 |
| 'Say Goodbye to the Wind' | *Fantastic Stories* | 1970 |
| 'The Greatest Television Show on Earth' | *Ambit* | 1972 |
| 'My Dream of Flying to Wake Island' | *Ambit* | 1974 |
| 'The Air Disaster' | *Bananas* | 1975 |
| 'Low-Flying Aircraft' | *Bananas* | 1975 |
| 'The Life and Death of God' | *Ambit* | 1976 |
| 'Notes Towards a Mental Breakdown' | *Bananas* | 1976 |
| 'The 60 Minute Zoom' | *Bananas* | 1976 |
| 'The Smile' | *Bananas* | 1976 |
| 'The Ultimate City' | *Low-Flying Aircraft* | 1976 |
| 'The Dead Time' | *Bananas* | 1977 |

| | | |
|---|---|---|
| 'The Index' | *Bananas* | 1977 |
| 'The Intensive Care Unit' | *Ambit* | 1977 |
| 'Theatre of War' | *Bananas* | 1977 |
| 'Having a Wonderful Time' | *Bananas* | 1978 |
| 'One Afternoon at Utah Beach' | *Anticipations* | 1978 |
| 'Zodiac 2000' | *Ambit* | 1978 |
| 'Motel Architecture' | *Bananas* | 1978 |
| 'A Host of Furious Fancies' | *Time Out* | 1980 |
| 'News from the Sun' | *Ambit* | 1981 |
| 'Memories of the Space Age' | *Interzone* | 1982 |
| 'Myths of the Near Future' | *Myths of the Near Future* | 1982 |
| 'Report on an Unidentified Space Station' | *City Limits* | 1982 |
| 'The Object of the Attack' | *Interzone* | 1984 |
| 'Answers to a Questionnaire' | *Ambit* | 1985 |
| 'The Man Who Walked on the Moon' | *Interzone* | 1985 |
| 'The Secret History of World War 3' | *Ambit* | 1988 |
| 'Love in a Colder Climate' | *Interview* | 1989 |
| 'The Enormous Space' | *Interzone* | 1989 |
| 'The Largest Theme Park in the World' | *Guardian* | 1989 |
| 'War Fever' | *Fantasy and Science Fiction* | 1989 |
| 'Dream Cargoes' | *Shincho* | 1990 |
| 'A Guide to Virtual Death' | *Interzone* | 1992 |
| 'The Message from Mars' | *Interzone* | 1992 |
| 'Report from an Obscure Planet' | *Leonardo* | 1992 |

| | | | |
|---|---|---|---|
| 66 | Stateside SS 521 | Breakout/I Need Help | 50 |
| 66 | Stateside SS 521 | Breakout/I Need Help (DJ copy) | 100 |
| 66 | Stateside SS 549 | Devil With A Blue Dress On (Medley)/I Had It Made | 20 |
| 67 | Stateside SS 596 | Sock It To Me Baby/I Never Had It Better | 20 |
| 67 | Stateside SS 2023 | Too Many Fish In The Sea/Three Little Fishes/One Grain Of Sand | 25 |
| 67 | Stateside SS 2037 | Joy/I'd Rather Go To Jail (solo) | 10 |
| 67 | Stateside SS 2063 | What Now My Love/Blessing In Disguise (solo) | 25 |
| 68 | Stateside SS 2075 | You Are My Sunshine/Wild Child (solo) | 7 |
| 68 | Stateside SS 2096 | Personality/Chantilly Lace/I Make A Fool Of Myself (solo) | 7 |
| 69 | Dot DOT 129 | Sugar Bee/I Believe (There Must Be Someone) | 8 |
| 66 | Stateside SE 1039 | RIDIN' (EP) | 40 |
| 66 | Stateside S(S)L 10178 | TAKE A RIDE ... (LP) | 40 |
| 67 | Stateside S(S)L 10189 | BREAKOUT. . . !! (LP) | 30 |
| 67 | Stateside S(S)L 10204 | SOCK IT TO ME (LP) | 25 |
| 68 | Stateside S(S)L 10229 | WHAT NOW MY LOVE (LP, solo) | 30 |
| 69 | Bell MBLL/SBLL 114 | ALL MITCH RYDER HITS (LP) | 25 |

*(see also Detroit)*

## PAUL RYDER & TIME MACHINE
| | | | |
|---|---|---|---|
| 74 | Penny Farthing PEN 834 | Are You Ready/If You Ever Get To Heaven | 8 |

## STEVE RYDER
| | | | |
|---|---|---|---|
| 78 | Jammy JRUJ 1 | Ain't It Nice/Remember Me | 50 |

## TONY RYMOND
| | | | |
|---|---|---|---|
| 62 | Oriole 1708 | Handful Of Songs/She'll Have To Go | 12 |

**S**

## SABICAS
| | | | |
|---|---|---|---|
| 70 | Polyor 2482 023 | ROCK ENCOUNTER (LP, with Joe Beck) | 30 |

## PARK SABLE & JUNGLE 'N' BEATS
| | | | |
|---|---|---|---|
| 64 | Fontana TF 457 | Never Be Blue/Rave On | 40 |

## SABOTAGE
| | | | |
|---|---|---|---|
| 80 | Optimistic OPT 001 | WHEN THE WAR IS OVER (EP) | 18 |
| 80 | Optimistic OPT 004 | SUBTERFUGE (EP) | 12 |

## SABRE
| | | | |
|---|---|---|---|
| 83 | Neat NEAT 23 | Miracle Man/On The Loose (p/s) | 8 |

## SABREJETS
| | | | |
|---|---|---|---|
| 79 | Blueport BLU 2 | Radioland/Rockin At The Ace Cafe/Caledonia (p/s, blue vinyl) | 5 |
| 80 | Blueport BLU 5 | Voodoo Cave/At The Quayside (no p/s) | 6 |

## SABRES
| | | | |
|---|---|---|---|
| 66 | Decca F 12528 | Roly Poly/Will You Always Love Me? | 30 |

*(see also Peeps)*

## SABRES OF PARADISE
| | | | |
|---|---|---|---|
| 93 | Sabres Of Paradise PT 001 | United (Andrew Weatherall Mix) (12", p/s, actually remix of Throbbing Gristle's "United", 800 only) | 25 |
| 93 | Sabres Of Paradise PT 009 | Smokebelch II (Entry)/(Exit) (12", red p/s) | 12 |
| 93 | Sabres Of Paradise PT 009R | Smokebelch II (David Holmes Mix)/(Flute Mix) (12", yellow p/s) | 10 |
| 94 | Sabres Of Paradise PT 014 | Theme/Return Of Carter & Edge 6 (Original Mix) (12") | 10 |
| 94 | Sabres Of Paradise PT 014R | Theme (Underdog Vs Sabres)/(Version) (10" remix) | 10 |
| 94 | Warp WAP 50 | Wilmot/Rumble Summons (12") | 15 |
| 95 | Warp WARP 62 | Tow Truck/(mixes) (12") | 10 |
| 96 | Emissions SEO 11 | Ysaebud (PVC sleeve, 1-sided, etched B-side, 1,000 only) | 10 |
| 93 | Warp LP 16 | SABRESONIC (2-LP, with unreleased 7", 5,000 only) | 20 |

## SACRE BLEU
| | | | |
|---|---|---|---|
| 80 | Sacre Bleu SB-1 | In This Mood/Somehow I Doubt It (p/s) | 12 |

## SACRED
| | | | |
|---|---|---|---|
| 93 | Twilight 7R5010A | You're The Only One/Lost In Time | 15 |

## SACRED ALIEN
| | | | |
|---|---|---|---|
| 81 | Greenwood GW 001 | Spiritual Planet/Energy (stickered labels, in p/s) | 30 |
| 81 | Greenwood GW 001 | Spiritual Planet/Energy (stickered labels) | 10 |
| 83 | Heighway Robbery SAD 001 | Legends/VIRGIN: Sittin' In Front Row (gatefold p/s) | 30 |

## SACRILEGE
| | | | |
|---|---|---|---|
| 85 | C.O.T.R. GURT 4 | BEHIND THE REALMS OF MADNESS (6-track mini LP) | 40 |
| 87 | Under One Flag FLAG 15 | WITHIN THE PROPHECY (LP) | 15 |
| 90 | Metalcore CORE 8 | BEHIND THE REALMS OF MADNESS (Mini-LP, reissue) | 20 |

## SAD
| | | | |
|---|---|---|---|
| 72 | Phoenix NIX 124 | It Ain't Easy/Box | 10 |

## SAD AFFAIR
| | | | |
|---|---|---|---|
| 71 | Lifelong LF 1 | Coloured Rice/Strange Sky | 30 |

## SADDAR BAZAAR
| | | | |
|---|---|---|---|
| 98 | Earworm WORM 13/WJ37 | Crystalline/ELECTROSCOPE: Circus Heights/TRANSPARENT THING: Ahh (p/s, 1,500 in hand painted sleeve, 1st 176 embossed) | 10 |
| 98 | Earworm WORM 13/WJ37 | Crystalline/ELECTROSCOPE: Circus Heights/TRANSPARENT THING: Ahh (p/s, 1,500 in hand painted sleeve) | 5 |
| 95 | Delerium DELEC LP 034 | THE CONFERENCE OF THE BIRDS (LP) | 15 |

## SADIE'S EXPRESSION
| 69 | Plexium PXM 4 | Deep In My Heart/My Way Of Living | 10 |
| 70 | Plexium PXM 13 | Old Whitrehall Number/Annie Wagon | 25 |

## SADISTIC MIKA BAND
| 74 | Harvest SHSP 4029 | SADISTIC MIKA BAND (LP) | 15 |
| 75 | Harvest SHSP 4043 | BLACK SHIP (LP) | 15 |
| 75 | Harvest SHSP 4049 | HOT MENU (LP) | 15 |

## BARRINGTON SADLER
| 69 | Clandisc CLA 204 | Soul Power/Rub It Down | 15 |

## SAD LOVERS & GIANTS
| 81 | Last Movement LM 003 | CLE (EP) | 35 |
| 82 | Midnight DING 1 | Lost In A Moment/The Tightrope Touch (p/s) | 5 |
| 83 | Last Movement LM 005 | Colourless Dream/Things We Never Did | 20 |
| 83 | Midnight DING 5 | Man Of Straw/Cow Boys (p/s) | 5 |
| 87 | Midnight DONG 31 | Seven Kinds Of Sin/The Outsider/Ours To Kill (12", p/s) | 10 |
| 87 | Midnight DONG 34 | White Russians/A Map Of My World/Life Under Glass (12", p/s) | 10 |
| 88 | Midnight DONG 36 | Cow Boys (1988 Remix)/Lost In A Moment (1988 Remix)/The Best Film He Ever Made/Things We Never Did (Live) (12", p/s) | 10 |
| 82 | Midnight CHIME 01 | EPIC GARDEN MUSIC (LP) | 20 |
| 83 | Midnight CHIME 03 | FEEDING THE FLAME (LP) | 15 |
| 84 | Midnight CHIME 07 | IN THE BREEZE (LP) | 15 |
| 86 | Midnight CHIME 022 | TOTAL SOUND (LP) | 15 |
| 87 | Midnight CHIME 30 | THE MIRROR TEST (LP) | 15 |
| 90 | Midnight CHIME 01.20 S | HEADLAND (LP) | 15 |

## SAD PEOPLE
| 69 | Chapter One CH113 | Lonely Man/Turn Around | 15 |

## SAD SOCIETY
| 87 | X Cert | Contaminate/Nothing ever Changes | 12 |

## SAFARI PARTY
| 85 | Pure & Vain 1 PAV | Hope In Hell/Not There (p/s) | 5 |

## SAFARIS (& PHANTOM BAND)
| 60 | Top Rank JAR 424 | Image Of A Girl/Four Steps To Love | 50 |
| 60 | Top Rank JAR 528 | The Girl With The Story In Her Eyes/Summer Nights (with Phantom Band) | 40 |

## SAFE IN BED
| 85 | SRT 5 KS 389 | Days A Day/Going Quickly | 10 |

## SAFFIRE
| 76 | Safari SFR 4 | Lay You Boogy Down (Part One)/Lay Your Boogy Down (Part Two) | 10 |

## SAFFRON SUMMERFIELD
| 74 | Mother Earth MUM 1001 | SALISBURY PLAIN (LP) | 60 |
| 76 | Mother Earth MUM 1202 | FANCY MEETING YOU HERE (LP) | 50 |
| 76 | Spectator | FANCY MEETING YOU HERE (LP, reissue) | 20 |

## SAFFRONS
| 73 | Pye 7N 45235 | Give Me Time/Baby Baby I Can't Let You Go | 8 |

## SA55
| 86 | 1966 EJSP 9868 | Compromised/Love Is Blind (p/s) | 20 |

## SA 55
| 82 | 1966 EISP 9868 | Compromise/Love Love Love Here I Come | 80 |

## SAGA
| 83 | Portrait XPS 186 | Don't Be Late/Careful Where You Step (p/s) | 6 |
| 72 | Westwood WRS 017 | SAGA (LP) | 50 |
| 73 | Westwood WRS 036 | SWEET PEG O'DERBY (LP) | 100 |

## MIKE SAGAR (& CRESTERS)
| 60 | HMV POP 819 | Deep Feeling/You Know (as Mike Sagar & Cresters) | 20 |
| 61 | HMV POP 988 | The Brothers Three/Set Me Free | 10 |

*(see also Cresters, Richard Harding)*

## SAGE
| 80 | Redball RR 032 | GOING STRONG (LP) | 45 |

## SAGITTARIUS
| 67 | CBS 2867 | My World Fell Down/Libra | 25 |
| 68 | CBS 3276 | Another Time/Virgo | 25 |

*(see also Bruce Johnston, Glen Campbell)*

## SAHARA
| 75 | Dawn DNLS 3068 | SUNRISE (LP) | 35 |

## DOUG SAHM
| 73 | Atlantic K 40466 | DOUG SAHM AND BAND (LP) (inc Dylan and Dr. John in his band) | 18 |

*(see also Sir Douglas Quintet)*

## ST. CHRISTOPHER
| 84 | Bluegrass GM 001 | Crystal Clear/My Fond Farewell (p/s) | 10 |
| 86 | Bluegrass GM 003 | Go Ahead Cry/Charmelle (p/s) | 8 |
| 89 | Sarah SARAH 015 | You Deserve More Than A Maybe/The Kind Of Girl/The Summer Of Love (foldaround p/s with poster in poly bag) | 10 |
| 89 | Sarah SARAH 020 | All Of A Tremble/My Fortune/The Hummingbird | 7 |
| 90 | Sarah SARAH 34 | Antoinette/Salvation (p/s, insert) | 10 |
| 91 | Sarah SARAH 46 | Say Yes To Everything/It's Snowing On The Moon (p/s, insert) | 10 |
| 90 | Sarah SARAH 403 | BACHARACH (10" LP) | 20 |

## CHERYL ST. CLAIR
| 66 | CBS 202041 | My Heart Is Not In It/We Want Love | 15 |

| | | |
|---|---|---|
| 66 | Columbia DB 8077 | What About Me/I'll Forget You Tonight .................................................................. 12 |

*(see also Alison Wonder)*

**JERRY ST. CLAIR**

| | | |
|---|---|---|
| 69 | Philips BF 1796 | Summer Exodus/Mrs. Jensen Sits Alone .................................................................. 15 |

**SAINT DAVIDS ROAD**

| | | |
|---|---|---|
| 69 | Tangerine DP003 | Let The Sun Come In/Mama Ain't Gonna Like What She Sees .................................... 15 |

**SAINT ETIENNE**

| | | |
|---|---|---|
| 90 | Heavenly HVN 2 | Only Love Can Break Your Heart/Only Love Can Break Your Heart (Version) (p/s) ...........6 |
| 90 | Heavenly HVN 212 | Only Love Can Break Your Heart/Only Love Can Break Your Heart (Original Version) (12", p/s) .................................................................................................. 12 |
| 90 | Heavenly HVN 4 | Kiss And Make Up/Sky's Dead (p/s) ........................................................................5 |
| 90 | Heavenly HVN 412R | Kiss And Make Up (Midsummer Madness Remix)/Kiss And Make Up (Midsummer Dubness Mix) (12", p/s) .................................................................... 10 |
| 90 | Heavenly HVN 4CD | Kiss And Make Up (7")/Kiss And Make Up (12")/Sky's Dead (CD) ............................... 10 |
| 91 | Heavenly HVN 912R | Speedwell (Flying Mix)/Speedwell (Project Mix)/Nothing Can Stop Us (Instrumental)/ 3D Tiger (12", p/s) .................................................................................. 10 |
| 92 | Heavenly HVN 22 | Live - Paris '92 (clear flexidisc, gig freebie, 1,000 only) ....................................... 20 |
| 93 | Heavenly HVN 2912 | Hobart Paving/Who Do You Think You Are (12", p/s, mispressed with Hobart Paving & "Your Head My Voice" on both sides) ........................................................... 15 |
| 95 | Heavenly HVN 41 | XMAS '95: A Christmas Gift To You/Driving Home For Christmas/A Message In A Bottle (CD, signed fan club edition) ................................................................... 90 |
| 03 | Mantra MNT 78 | Soft Like Me/Gimp Crisis (p/s, limited edition) ......................................................8 |
| 91 | Heavenly HVN LP1 | FOXBASE ALPHA (LP) ........................................................................................ 25 |
| 93 | Heavenly HVN 41 | SO TOUGH (LP) ................................................................................................. 18 |
| 93 | Heavenly HVNLP 6 | YOU NEED A MESS OF HELP TO STAND ALONE (LP) ............................................... 15 |
| 95 | Heavenly HVNLP 9CD | I LOVE TO PAINT (CD, fan club edition, 600 only) .................................................. 40 |
| 95 | Heavenly HVNCD 10 | TOO YOUNG TO DIE (CD, with bonus CD "Too Young To Die - The Remix Album" [HVN LP 10CDR]) .............................................................................................. 30 |
| 97 | Heavenly HVN41-2 | VALENTINES DAY (CD, EP fan club edition) ........................................................... 50 |
| 98 | Fan Club SPCD 463 | XMAS '98: I Don't Intend To Spend Christmas Without You/Kofi Annan (CD, fan club edition, in card sleeve) ........................................................................... 40 |
| 98 | Creation CRELP 225 | GOOD HUMOR (LP, with free 10") ...................................................................... 25 |
| 00 | Mantra MNSTET 1 | BUILT ON SAND: RARITIES 1994-1999 (CD, fan club edition) ..................................... 40 |
| 02 | Mantra MNTLP 1033 | FINISTERRE (LP) ............................................................................................... 18 |
| 03 | Heavenly HVN136CD | XMAS 2003 (CD, EP fan club issue) ...................................................................... 30 |
| 05 | Sanctuary SANLP 271 | TALES FROM TURNPIKE HOUSE (LP) .................................................................... 25 |
| 08 | Heavenly HVNLP 69 | LONDON CONVERSATIONS - THE BEST OF ST. ETIENNE (2-LP) ................................. 20 |
| 08 | Foreign Office FOREIGN OFFICE 004 | BOXETTE (4-CD, 3000 only) .............................................................................. 50 |

*(see also 50 Year Void, Sarah Cracknell, Lovecut D.B., Mike Vickers)*

**KIRK ST. JAMES**

| | | |
|---|---|---|
| 70 | Pye 7N 25518 | My Love Oh Linda/Tears I Cry .............................................................................. 60 |

**BARRY ST. JOHN**

| | | |
|---|---|---|
| 64 | Decca F 11933 | A Little Bit Of Soap/Thing Of The Past ................................................................. 20 |
| 64 | Decca F 11975 | Bread And Butter/Cry To Me ............................................................................... 20 |
| 65 | Decca F 12111 | Mind How You Go/Don't You Feel Proud ............................................................... 20 |
| 65 | Decca F 12145 | Hey Boy/I've Been Crying ................................................................................... 20 |
| 65 | Columbia DB 7783 | Come Away Melinda/Gotta Brand New Man ........................................................... 15 |
| 66 | Columbia DB 7868 | Everything I Touch Turns To Tears/Sounds Like My Baby ........................................ 65 |
| 66 | Columbia DB 7868 | Everything I Touch Turns To Tears/Sounds Like My Baby (DJ copy) .......................... 65 |
| 68 | Major Minor MM 587 | Cry Like A Baby/Long And Lonely Night ................................................................ 15 |
| 69 | Major Minor MM 604 | By The Time I Get To Phoenix/Turn On Your Light .................................................. 15 |
| 75 | Bradleys BRAD 7507 | I Won't Be A Party/Do Me Good ...........................................................................7 |
| 69 | M. Minor MMLP/SMLP 43 | ACCORDING TO ST. JOHN (LP) ........................................................................... 50 |

**BRIDGET ST. JOHN**

| | | |
|---|---|---|
| 69 | Dandelion K 4404 | To B Without A Hitch/Autumn Lullaby .................................................................. 15 |
| 70 | Warner Bros WB 8019 | If You've Got Money/Yep. ................................................................................... 12 |
| 72 | Polydor 2001 280 | Fly High/There's A Place I Know/Suzanne (p/s) ..................................................... 12 |
| 72 | Polydor 2001 361 | Nice/Goodbye Baby Goodbye ...............................................................................8 |
| 73 | MCA MUS 1203 | Passing Thru'/The Road Was Lonely On My Own .................................................... 10 |
| 69 | Dandelion 63750 | ASK ME NO QUESTIONS (LP, gatefold sleeve) ....................................................... 80 |
| 71 | Dandelion DAN 8007 | SONGS FOR THE GENTLE MAN (LP, gatefold sleeve) ............................................. 100 |
| 71 | Dandelion K 49007 | SONGS FOR THE GENTLE MAN (LP, gatefold sleeve, with cat no K 49007) ................. 30 |
| 72 | Dandelion 2310 193 | THANK YOU FOR... (LP, gatefold sleeve) ............................................................. 100 |
| 74 | Chrysalis CHR 1062 | JUMBLE QUEEN (LP) ......................................................................................... 40 |

*(see also Kevin Ayers, Ron Geesin, Mike Oldfield, Quiver)*

**PAUL ST. JOHN**

| | | |
|---|---|---|
| 70 | Pye 7N 45190 | Flying Saucers Have Landed/Spaceship Love ....................................................... 150 |

**TAMMY ST. JOHN**

| | | |
|---|---|---|
| 64 | Pye 7N 15682 | Boys/Hey Hey Hey ........................................................................................... 15 |
| 65 | Pye 7N 15762 | He's The One For Me/I'm Tired Of Just Looking At You ........................................... 15 |
| 65 | Pye 7N 15948 | Dark Shadows And Empty Hallways/I Mustn't Cry .................................................. 15 |
| 66 | Pye 7N 17042 | Nobody Knows What's Goin' On (In My Mind But Me)/ Stay Together Young Lovers..... 50 |
| 66 | Pye 7N 17042 | Nobody Knows What's Goin' On (In My Mind But Me)/ Stay Together Young Lovers (DJ copy) ............................................................................................... 100 |
| 69 | Tangerine DP 0007 | Concerning Love/Sound Of Love ........................................................................ 300 |

*(see also Trends)*

**ST. LOUIS UNION**

| | | |
|---|---|---|
| 66 | Decca F 12318 | Girl/Respect .................................................................................................... 15 |
| 66 | Decca F 12386 | Behind The Door/English Tea ............................................................................. 70 |
| 66 | Decca F 12508 | East Side Story/Think About Me ........................................................................ 150 |

*(see also Medicine Head)*

**SAINT ORCHESTRA**

| | | | |
|---|---|---|---|
| 78 | Pye 7N 46127 | Return Of The Saint/Funko (p/s) | 12 |

**OLIVER ST. PATRICK & DIAMONDS**

| | | | |
|---|---|---|---|
| 67 | Trojan TR 005 | I Want To Be Loved By You/Tulips | 60 |

**CRISPIAN ST. PETERS**

| | | | |
|---|---|---|---|
| 65 | Decca F 12080 | At This Moment/Goodbye, You'll Forget Me | 15 |
| 65 | Decca F 12207 | No No No/Three Goodbyes | 15 |
| 66 | Decca F 12287 | You Were On My Mind/What I'm Gonna Be | 5 |
| 66 | Decca F 12359 | The Pied Piper/Sweet Dawn My True Love | 6 |
| 66 | Decca F 12480 | Changes/My Little Brown Eyes | 15 |
| 66 | Decca F 12525 | But She's Untrue/Your Ever Changin' Mind | 8 |
| 67 | Decca F 12596 | Almost Persuaded/You Have Gone | 8 |
| 67 | Decca F 12677 | Free Spirit/I'm Always Crying | 8 |
| 70 | Decca F 13055 | So Long/My Little Brown Eyes | 10 |
| 74 | Santa Ponsa PNS 17 | Do Daddy Do/Every Time You Sinned | 7 |
| 75 | Route RT 18 | Carolina/Samantha | 7 |
| 67 | Decca DFE 8678 | ALMOST PERSUADED (EP) | 55 |
| 66 | Decca LK 4805 | FOLLOW ME... (LP) | 50 |
| 70 | Square SQA 102 | SIMPLY... CRISPIAN ST. PETERS (LP) | 40 |

**KIRBY ST. ROMAIN**

| | | | |
|---|---|---|---|
| 63 | Stateside SS 199 | Summer's Comin'/Miss You So | 10 |

**SAINT STEVEN**

| | | | |
|---|---|---|---|
| 69 | Probe SPB 1005 | OVER THE HILLS/THE BASTICH (LP) | 75 |

**ST. VALENTINE'S DAY MASSACRE**

| | | | |
|---|---|---|---|
| 67 | Fontana TF 883 | Brother Can You Spare A Dime/Al's Party (with p/s) | 150 |
| 67 | Fontana TF 883 | Brother Can You Spare A Dime/Al's Party | 60 |

*(see also Artwoods)*

**SAINTS (AUSTRALIA)**

| | | | |
|---|---|---|---|
| 76 | Power Exchange PX 242 | I'm Stranded/No Time (p/s) | 20 |
| 77 | Power Exchange PXE 101 | I'm Stranded/(STANLEY FRANK: 2 tracks) (p/s) | 8 |
| 77 | Harvest HAR 5123 | Erotic Neurotic/One Way Street (with p/s) | 150 |
| 77 | Harvest HAR 5123 | Erotic Neurotic/One Way Street | 10 |
| 77 | Harvest HAR 5130 | This Perfect Day/L-I-E-S | 6 |
| 77 | Harvest 12 HAR 5130 | This Perfect Day/L-I-E-S/Do The Robot (12", with 'disclaimer' stickered p/s) | 10 |
| 77 | Harvest HAR 5137 | 1, 2, 3, 4 (River Deep, Mountain High/Lipstick On Your Collar/One Way Street/Demolition Girl) (EP, double pack, gatefold p/s) | 15 |
| 78 | Harvest HAR 5148 | Know Your Product/Run Down (no p/s) | 10 |
| 78 | Harvest HAR 5166 | Security/All Times Through Paradise (p/s) | 12 |
| 77 | Harvest SHSP 4065 | I'M STRANDED (LP) | 30 |
| 78 | Harvest SHSP 4078 | ETERNALLY YOURS (LP, with inner sleeve) | 25 |
| 78 | Harvest SHSP 4094 | PREHISTORIC SOUNDS (LP) | 25 |

**SAINTS (JAMAICA)**

| | | | |
|---|---|---|---|
| 66 | Doctor Bird DB 1009 | Brown Eyes/BABA BROOKS & HIS BAND: King Size | 30 |
| 69 | Big Shot BI 522 | Windy Part One/Windy Part Two | 12 |
| 73 | Count Shelley CS 043 | How Long/Feeling Good | 15 |

**SAINTS (U.K.)**

| | | | |
|---|---|---|---|
| 63 | Pye 7N 15548 | Wipe Out/Midgets | 25 |
| 63 | Pye 7N 15582 | Husky Team/Pigtails | 25 |

*(see also Tornados, Heinz)*

**SAINTS (U.K.)**

| | | | |
|---|---|---|---|
| 64 | MJB BEV 73/4 | SAINTS (10" LP, private pressing) | 300 |
| 64 | MJB BEVLP 127/8 | SAINTS ALIVE! (LP, private pressing) | 300 |

**RUSS SAINTY (& NU NOTES)**

| | | | |
|---|---|---|---|
| 60 | Top Rank JAR 381 | Happy-Go-Lucky-Me/Standing Around | 10 |
| 60 | Decca F 11270 | Race With The Devil/Too Shy (solo) | 20 |
| 61 | Decca F 11325 | Don't Believe Him, Donna/Your Other Love (solo) | 10 |
| 62 | HMV POP 1055 | Keep Your Love Locked/I've Got A Girl (as Russ Sainty & Nu Notes) | 10 |
| 62 | HMV POP 1069 | Send Me The Pillow That You Dream On/What Do You Know About That (solo) | 10 |
| 63 | HMV POP 1181 | Unforgettable Love/The Twinkle In Your Eye (solo) | 10 |
| 64 | Parlophone R 5168 | /Lonesome TownThat's How I'm Gonna Love You (as Russ Sainty & Nu-Notes) | 5 |
| 64 | Columbia DB 7394 | This Is My Lovely Day/Bless You, Girl (as Russ Sainty & Nu-Notes) | 5 |
| 65 | Columbia DB 7521 | It Ain't That Easy/And Then (solo) | 5 |
| 65 | Columbia DB 7708 | Saving My Tears (For A Rainy Day)/She (solo) | 5 |

*(see also Nu Notes)*

**KYU SAKAMOTO**

| | | | |
|---|---|---|---|
| 64 | HMV POP 1342 | Rose Rose I Love You/Sayonara Tokyo | 5 |
| 62 | HMV CLP 1674 | SUKIYAKI (LP) | 40 |

**RYUICHI SAKAMOTO**

| | | | |
|---|---|---|---|
| 80 | Island IPR 2048 | Riot In Lagos/Iconic Storage (12", company sleeve) | 10 |

*(see also David Sylvian, Yellow Magic Orchestra)*

**(BOB) SAKER**

| | | | |
|---|---|---|---|
| 68 | Polydor BM 56231 | Still Got You/Imagination (as Bob Saker) | 30 |
| 68 | Parlophone R 5740 | Foggy Tuesday/Ooh Nana Na (as Bob Saker) | 50 |
| 69 | Parlophone R 5752 | Hey Joe!/Christianity | 15 |
| 71 | CBS 7010 | What A Beautiful World/City Of The Angels | 6 |
| 71 | CBS 7399 | Even Though We Ain't Got Money/Wild Winds Are Blowing | 6 |

**SAL SALVADOR**
55   KPL 105                                      SAL SALVADOR QUARTET (10" LP) .................................................. 15

**SALAMANDER**
70   CBS 5102                                     Crystal Ball/Billy ............................................................................ 15
71   Youngblood SSYB 14                 THE TEN COMMANDMENTS (LP, gatefold poster sleeve) .................. 400
*(see also Onyx)*

**SALEM**
82   Hilton FMR 056                          Cold As Steel/Reach To Eternity ................................................... 45

**SALFORD JETS**
78   WEA K 18008                            Lookin' At The Squares/Dancing School (no p/s) .......................... 15
79   EMI INT 590                               Manchester Boys/Last Bus (p/s) .................................................. 20

**SANDY SALISBURY**
00   Poptones MC 5007                    Do Unto Others/CURT BOETTCHER: That's The Way It's Gonna Be (numbered die-cut company sleeve) ........................................................... 6

**SALIX ALBA**
73   Columbiab R5990                      I Can't Resist/Blue Sky ................................................................. 30

**SALLY & ALLEY CATS**
64   Parlophone R 5183                     Is It Something I Said/You Forgot To Remember ......................... 15

**SALLYANGIE**
69   Big T BIG 126                            Two Ships/Colours Of The World .................................................. 100
72   Philips 6006 259                         Child Of Allah/Lady Go Lightly ..................................................... 100
68   Transatlantic TRA 176                CHILDREN OF THE SUN (LP, gatefold sleeve, purple/white textured label) ...... 80
78   Transatlantic TRA 176                CHILDREN OF THE SUN (LP, reissue, different single sleeve) ........ 20
*(see also Mike Oldfield, Sally Oldfield)*

**DOUG SALMA & HIGHLANDERS**
63   Philips BF 1279                          Highland Fling/The Scavenger ..................................................... 10

**SALMONTAILS**
80   Oblivion OBL 001                       SALMONTAILS (LP, with Dave Pegg) ............................................ 20

**SALOME**
69   Page One POF 137                     Vivo Cantando/Amigos Amigos ..................................................... 7

**SALSOUL STRUT**
96   Records Inc. no cat. no.              Better Days/(Mixes) .................................................................... 12

**SALT**
78   Grapevine GRA 111                    BEYOND A SONG (LP, with insert) ................................................ 18

**SALT & PEPPER**
61   London HLU 9338                      High Noon/Come Softly To Me ..................................................... 15

**SALVATION (1)**
69   United Artists UP 35048             Cinderella/The Village Shuck ....................................................... 15
69   United Artists UAS 29062          SALVATION (LP) ............................................................................ 30

**SALVATION (2)**
83   Merciful Release MR 025            Girlsoul/Evelyn (p/s) .................................................................. 12
83   Merciful Release MRX 025         Girlsoul/Evelyn/Dust Up (12", p/s) ............................................ 15
86   Batfish Inc. BF 103                     Jessica's Crime/The Shining (p/s) ............................................... 12

**SAMMY SALVO**
58   RCA RCA 1032                          Oh Julie/Say Yeah ...................................................................... 20
59   London HLP 8997                      Afraid/Marble Heart ................................................................... 12

**SAM**
72   Pye 7N 45175                           Johnny Rebel/He Loves Me, He Loves Me Not ............................. 6

**SAM APPLE PIE**
69   Decca F 22932                          Tiger Man (King Of The Jungle)/Sometime Girl ........................... 20
72   DJM DJS 274                            Call Me Boss/Old Tom ................................................................. 8
69   Decca LK-R 5005                      SAM APPLE PIE (LP, mono, laminated front sleeve, unboxed logo label) ...... 300
69   Decca SKL-R 5005                    SAM APPLE PIE (LP, stereo, laminated sleeve, unboxed logo label) ...... 250
73   DJM DJLPS 429                        EAST 17 (LP) ............................................................................... 30

**SAM, ERV & TOM**
68   Direction 58-3339                     Soul Teacher/Hard To Get ............................................................ 5
*(see also Diplomats)*

**SAM & BILL**
66   Pye International 7N 25355         Fly Me To The Moon/Treat Me Right ........................................... 15
67   Brunswick 05973                      I Feel Like Cryin'/I'll Try .............................................................. 50
67   Brunswick 05973                      I Feel Like Cryin'/I'll Try (DJ copy) ............................................. 80

**SAM & DAVE**
66   King KG 1041                           No More Pain/You Ain't No Big Thing Baby .................................. 50
66   Atlantic AT 4066                      You Don't Know Like I Know/Blame Me, Don't Blame My Heart ..... 20
66   Atlantic 584 003                      Hold On I'm A Comin'/I Got Everything I Need .............................. 10
66   Atlantic 584 047                      If You Got The Loving (I Got The Time)/Said I Wasn't Gonna Tell Nobody ... 12
67   Atlantic 584 064                      You Got Me Hummin'/Sleep Good Tonight .................................... 12
67   Atlantic 584 086                      You Don't Know Like I Know/Blame Me, Don't Blame My Heart (reissue) ... 10
67   Stax 601 004                          Soothe Me/Sweet Pains (initial dark blue label) .......................... 25
67   Stax 601 004                          Soothe Me/Sweet Pains (later light blue label) ........................... 20
67   Stax 601 006                          When Something Is Wrong With My Baby/A Small Portion Of Your Love (initial dark blue label) ........................................... 10
67   Stax 601 006                          When Something Is Wrong With My Baby/A Small Portion Of Your Love (later light blue label) ............................................ 8
67   Stax 601 023                          Soul Man/May I Baby ................................................................... 8
68   Stax 601 030                          I Thank You/Wrap It Up ................................................................ 8
68   Atlantic 584 192                      You Don't Know What You Mean To Me/This Is Your World ........... 7

MINT VALUE £

| | | | |
|---|---|---|---|
| 68 | Atlantic 584 211 | Can't You Find Another Way/Still Is The Night | 7 |
| 68 | Atlantic 584 228 | Everybody's Got To Believe In Somebody/If I Didn't Have A Girl Like You | 8 |
| 69 | Atlantic 584 237 | Soul Sister, Brown Sugar/Come On In | 8 |
| 69 | Atlantic 584 247 | You Don't Know Like I Know/Hold On I'm A Comin' | 7 |
| 69 | Atlantic 584 303 | Ooh, Ooh, Ooh/Holdin' On | 8 |
| 70 | Atlantic 584 324 | Baby, Baby, Don't Stop Now/I'm Not An Indian Giver | 8 |
| 66 | King KGL 4001 | SAM AND DAVE (LP) | 75 |
| 66 | Atlantic 587/588 045 | HOLD ON, I'M A COMIN' (LP) | 50 |
| 67 | Stax 589 003 | DOUBLE DYNAMITE (LP) | 50 |
| 68 | Stax 589 015 | SOUL MEN (LP) | 40 |
| 68 | Major Minor MCP 5000 | SAM AND DAVE (LP) | 22 |
| 69 | Atlantic 588 154 | I THANK YOU (LP) | 25 |
| 69 | Atlantic 588 155 | THE BEST OF SAM AND DAVE (LP) | 18 |
| 69 | Atlantic 587/588 181 | DOUBLE TROUBLE (LP) | 22 |
| 69 | Atlantic 588 185 | SOUL MEN (LP, reissue) | 15 |

## SAM & KITTY
| | | | |
|---|---|---|---|
| 80 | Grapevine GRP 132 | I've Got Something Good/Love Is The Greatest | 10 |
| 80 | Grapevine GRP 132 | I've Got Something Good/Love Is The Greatest (DJ Copy) | 20 |

## SAME
| | | | |
|---|---|---|---|
| 79 | Wessex WEX 267 | Wild About You/Movements (p/s) | 70 |
| 80 | Blue Print BLU 2008 | Movements/Wild About You (reissue with reversed sides & blue print on p/s) | 30 |
| 80 | Blue Print BLU 2008 | Movements/Wild About You (reissue with reversed sides no p/s) | 20 |

## MIKE SAMMES SINGERS
| | | | |
|---|---|---|---|
| 68 | Davjon DJ 1006 | HYMNS A SWINGING (LP, with Ted Taylor Organisation) | 30 |
| 06 | Trunk JBH 109 LP | MUSIC FOR BISCUITS (LP, 750 only) | 30 |

## MICHAEL SAMMES SINGERS
| | | | |
|---|---|---|---|
| 59 | Top Rank JAR 166 | Upstairs And Downstairs/Ivor Raymonde - Mylene | 6 |

## SAMMY
| | | | |
|---|---|---|---|
| 72 | Philips 6006 227 | Goo Ger Woogie/Big Lovin' Woman | 7 |
| 72 | Philips 6308 136 | SAMMY (LP, laminated sleeve, black/silver label) | 40 |

*(see also Ian Gillan, Audience, Episode Six, Quatermass, Roy Young Band, Stackridge, Ginhouse)*

## SAMPLES
| | | | |
|---|---|---|---|
| 80 | Sample | VENDETTA (EP) | 20 |
| 84 | No Future OI 14 | Dead Hero/Fire Around Round/Suspicion (p/s) | 20 |

## DAVE SAMPSON & HUNTERS
| | | | |
|---|---|---|---|
| 60 | Columbia DB 4449 | Sweet Dreams/It's Lonesome | 6 |
| 60 | Columbia DB 4502 | If You Need Me/See You Around | 6 |
| 61 | Columbia DB 4597 | Why The Chicken?/1999 | 6 |
| 61 | Columbia DB 4625 | Easy To Dream/That's All | 6 |
| 62 | Fontana H 361 | Wide, Wide World/Since Sandy Moved Away (solo) | 6 |
| 61 | Columbia SEG 8095 | DAVE (EP, mono) | 25 |
| 61 | Columbia ESG 7853 | DAVE (EP, stereo) | 30 |

*(see also Hunters [U.K.])*

## TOMMY SAMPSON
| | | | |
|---|---|---|---|
| 58 | Melodisc MEL 1411 | Rockin'/Rock'n'Roll Those Big Brown Eyes (with His Strongmen) | 22 |
| 58 | Melodisc MEL 1411 | Rockin'/Rock'n'Roll Those Big Brown Eyes (with His Strongmen) (78) | 20 |
| 58 | Parlophone R 4458 | Lazy Train/Smooth Mood (as Tommy Sampson Orchestra) | 7 |

## SAM'S FRIENDS
| | | | |
|---|---|---|---|
| 66 | Decca F12519 | If I Gave You My Love/I Feel | 5 |

## SAMSON (1)
| | | | |
|---|---|---|---|
| 69 | Instant INSP 004 | ARE YOU SAMSON (LP) | 100 |

*(see also Strider)*

## SAMSON (2)
| | | | |
|---|---|---|---|
| 70 | Parlophone R5867 | Venus/Wool & Water | 8 |

## SAMSON (3)
| | | | |
|---|---|---|---|
| 78 | Lightning GIL 547 | Telephone/Leavin' You (p/s) | 35 |
| 79 | Lightning GIL 553 | Mr. Rock'n'Roll/Drivin' Music (p/s) | 35 |
| 79 | Laser LAS 6 | Mr. Rock'n'Roll (remix)/Primrose Shuffle | 10 |
| 80 | EMI EMI 5061 | Vice Versa (Edit)/Hammerhead (p/s, withdrawn, 1,000 demos only) | 40 |
| 80 | Gem GEMS 34 | Vice Versa (Edit)/Hammerhead (reissue, p/s, with sticker) | 8 |
| 80 | Gem GEMS 34 | Vice Versa (Edit)/Hammerhead (reissue, p/s) | 5 |
| 80 | Gem GEMS 38 | Hard Times (Remix)/Angel With A Machine Gun (p/s) | 5 |
| 81 | RCA RCA 67 | Riding With The Angels (Edit)/Little Big Man (p/s) | 10 |
| 81 | RCA RCA 67 | Riding With The Angels (Edit)/Little Big Man (picture disc) | 10 |
| 82 | Polydor SAM 2 | Red Skies/Young Idea (unissued, promo only) | 18 |
| 83 | Polydor PODJ 554 | Red Skies (DJ Edit) (1-sided promo) | 12 |
| 86 | Capitol 12CLP 395 | Vice Versa (Remix)/Losing My Grip (Remix) (12", picture disc) | 15 |
| 79 | Laser LAP 1 | SURVIVORS (LP) | 15 |
| 81 | Gem GEMLP 113 | SHOCK TACTICS (LP, release cancelled) | 0 |
| 81 | RCA LP 5031 | SHOCK TACTICS (LP, with insert) | 18 |
| 82 | Polydor POLS 1077 | BEFORE THE STORM (LP, with poster, stickered sleeve) | 20 |
| 84 | Polydor POLD 5132 | DON'T GET MAD, GET EVEN (LP, with insert) | 15 |
| 84 | Polydor POLD 5132 | DON'T GET MAD, GET EVEN (2-LP, white labels, 2 different mixes of same album, promo only) | 40 |

*(see also Bruce Dickinson, Iron Maiden, John McCoy, Tiger, Colin Towns, Thunderstick, Nicky Moore, Mammoth, Egypt)*

## SAM THE SHAM & THE PHARAOHS
| | | | |
|---|---|---|---|
| 65 | MGM MGM 1269 | Woolly Bully/Ain't Gonna Move | 12 |
| 65 | MGM MGM 1269 | Woolly Bully/Ain't Gonna Move (DJ Copy) | 50 |

| 65 | MGM MGM 1278 | Ju Ju Hand/Big City Lights | 10 |
|----|--------------|----------------------------|-----|
| 65 | MGM MGM 1285 | Ring Dang Doo/Don't Try It | 12 |
| 66 | MGM MGM 1298 | Red Hot/Long Long Way | 15 |
| 66 | MGM MGM 1315 | Li'l Red Riding Hood/Love Me Like Before | 10 |
| 66 | MGM MGM 1326 | The Hair On My Chinny Chin Chin/The Out Crowd | 8 |
| 66 | MGM MGM 1331 | How Do You Catch A Girl/The Love You Left Behind | 10 |
| 67 | MGM MGM 1337 | Oh That's Bad No That's Good/Take What You Can Get | 10 |
| 67 | MGM MGM 1343 | Black Sheep/My Day's Gonna Come | 15 |
| 68 | MGM MGM 1379 | Yakety Yak/Let Our Lovelight Shine | 10 |
| 69 | MGM MGM 1473 | Woolly Bully/Ring Dang Doo | 6 |
| 66 | MGM MGM-EP 794 | RED HOT (EP) | 60 |
| 65 | MGM MGM-C 1007 | WOOLY BULLY (LP) | 40 |
| 66 | MGM MGM-C(S) 8032 | LI'L RED RIDING HOOD (LP) | 30 |

## LEROY SAMUEL (ACTUALLY LEROY SMART)
| 72 | Punch PH 113 | Trying To Wreck My Life/JOHN HOLT: Pride And Joy | 12 |
|----|--------------|-------------------------------------------------|-----|

## (PHILLIP) SAMUEL THE FIRST
| 71 | Summit SUM 8515 | Sounds Of Babylon/BEVERLEY'S ALL STARS: Second Babylon Version | 10 |
|----|-----------------|---------------------------------------------------------------|-----|

## JERRY SAMUELS
| 56 | HMV 7M 411 | Puppy Love/The Chosen Few | 15 |
|----|------------|---------------------------|-----|

*(see also Napoleon XIV)*

## WINSTON SAMUELS
| 64 | Columbia DB 7405 | You Are The One/Angela | 12 |
|----|------------------|------------------------|-----|
| 64 | Rio R 26 | Follow/I'm So Glad | 12 |
| 64 | Black Swan WI 419 | Luck Will Come My Way/LLOYD BREVITT: One More Time | 25 |
| 64 | Black Swan WI 426 | You Are The One/Gloria Love (B-side actually by Beltones) | 15 |
| 65 | Ska Beat JB 196 | Be Prepared/Jericho Wall | 18 |
| 65 | Ska Beat JB 213 | My Bride To Be/LLOYD PREVITT: Wayward Ska | 25 |
| 65 | Ska Beat JB 214 | Never Again/My Angel | 20 |
| 66 | Ska Beat JB 238 | What Have I Done/Broken Hearted | 25 |
| 66 | Ska Beat JB 241 | Ups And Downs/Come What May | 20 |
| 66 | Ska Beat JB 244 | Time Will Tell/I'm Sorry | 20 |
| 67 | Island WI 3051 | The Greatest/FREDDIE & FITZY: Truth Hurts | 50 |
| 67 | Island WI 3053 | I Won't Be Discouraged/FREDDIE & FITZIE: Why Did My Little Girl Cry | 50 |
| 67 | Fab FAB 21 | Peace Of Mind/Shepherd Ben (by Prince Buster & Teddy King) | 25 |
| 67 | Fab FAB 14 | Holding Out/To The Other Man | 20 |
| 67 | Fab FAB 28 | Peace Of Mind/I'm Still Here | 20 |
| 10 | Randys THB 7002 | Lick It Back/COUNT MACHUKI: Pepper Pot | 10 |

## SAMURAI (1)
| 68 | United Artists UP 2242 | Good Morning Starshine/Temple Of Gold | 35 |
|----|------------------------|---------------------------------------|-----|
| 71 | Greenwich GSLP 1003 | SAMURAI (LP, gatefold sleeve, white/brown label) | 250 |

## SAMURAI (2)
| 85 | Ebony EBON 25 | Fires Of Hell/Dreams Of The World (no p/s) | 12 |
|----|---------------|--------------------------------------------|-----|
| 84 | Ebony EBON 24 | SACRED BLADE (LP) | 15 |

## SAN FRANCISCO TKO'S
| 98 | Kent 6T 14 | Make Up Your Mind/PEGGY GAINES: When The Boy That You Love | 25 |
|----|------------|------------------------------------------------------------|-----|

## SANCTUARY
| 87 | Epic 460811 | REFUGE DENIED (LP) | 25 |
|----|-------------|--------------------|-----|

## SAND
| 71 | Philips 6006157 | Soft Lady/Babylon | 20 |
|----|-----------------|-------------------|-----|

## SANDEENO
| 03 | Wizkidz WK 011 | Ah Mankind/Preaching the Board | 12 |
|----|----------------|--------------------------------|-----|

## ALEX SANDERS
| 70 | A&M AMLS 984 | A WITCH IS BORN (LP, foldout sleeve with warning sticker, withdrawn) | 100 |
|----|--------------|---------------------------------------------------------------------|-----|

## GARY SANDERS
| 66 | Warner Bros WB 5676 | Ain't No Beatle/Ain't I Good To You | 12 |
|----|---------------------|-------------------------------------|-----|

## PHARAOH SANDERS
| 66 | ESP Disk/Fontana SFJL 931 | PHARAOH SANDERS QUINTET (LP) | 35 |
|----|---------------------------|------------------------------|-----|
| 71 | Probe SPB 1019 | DEAF, DUMB AND BLIND (LP) | 25 |
| 70s | Impulse AS 9138 | TAUHID (LP) | 20 |
| 70s | Impulse AS 9199 | SUMMUN BUKMUN UMYUN (LP) | 25 |
| 70s | Impulse AS 9219 | BLACK UNITY (LP) | 25 |
| 70s | Impulse AS 9227 | LIVE AT THE EAST (LP) | 25 |
| 70s | Impulse AS 9229 | THE BEST OF PHARAOH SANDERS (2-LP) | 20 |
| 70s | Impulse 9233 | WISDOM THROUGH MUSIC (LP) | 20 |
| 70s | Impulse 9254 | VILLAGE OF PHARAOHS (LP) | 20 |
| 70s | Impulse 9261 | ELEVATION (LP) | 20 |
| 70s | Impulse 9280 | LOVE IN US ALL (LP) | 20 |
| 78 | Arista SPART 1051 | LOVE WILL FIND A WAY (LP) | 15 |
| 82 | Jasmine JAS 53 | THEMBI (LP) | 18 |

## RAY SANDERS
| 60 | London HLG 7106 | A World So Full Of Love/A Little Bitty Tear (export issue) | 12 |
|----|-----------------|-----------------------------------------------------------|-----|

## TOMMY SANDERSON & SANDMEN
| 61 | Ember EMB 131 | Deadline/Candelglow | 10 |
|----|---------------|---------------------|-----|
| 62 | Ember EMB 152 | Ding Dong Rag/Piano A-Go Go | 10 |

## CHRIS SANDFORD (& CORONETS)
| 63 | Decca F 11778 | Not Too Little - Not Too Much/I'm Lookin' | 5 |
|----|---------------|-------------------------------------------|-----|
| 64 | Decca F 11842 | You're Gonna Be My Girl/Don't Leave Me Now (with Coronets) | 6 |

| | | | MINT VALUE £ |
|---|---|---|---|
| 65 | Fontana TF 633 | I Wish They Wouldn't Always Say I Sound Like The Guy From The U.S.A. Blues/Little Man, Nobody Cares | 7 |

## SANDGATE
| | | | |
|---|---|---|---|
| 75 | Dawn DWS 1114 | A Thousand Years/Such A Sad Song | 6 |

## GERRY SANDON
| | | | |
|---|---|---|---|
| 96 | Twangsville TW 001 | JUST GERRY (EP) | 10 |

## JOHNNY SANDON (& REMO FOUR)
| | | | |
|---|---|---|---|
| 63 | Pye 7N 15542 | Lies/On The Horizon (as Johnny Sandon & Remo Four) | 15 |
| 63 | Pye 7N 15559 | Magic Potion/Yes (as Johnny Sandon & Remo Four) | 15 |
| 64 | Pye 7N 15602 | Sixteen Tons/The Blizzard | 10 |
| 64 | Pye 7N 15665 | Donna Means Heartbreak/Some Kinda Wonderful | 10 |
| 64 | Pye 7N 15717 | The Blizzard/(I'd Be A) Legend In My Time | 10 |

*(see also Remo Four)*

## HOPE SANDOVAL & WARM INTENTIONS
| | | | |
|---|---|---|---|
| 00 | Rough Trade RTRADE S008 | AT THE DOORWAY AGAIN EP (12") | 25 |
| 01 | Rough Trade RTRADELP 031 | BAVARIAN FRUIT BREAD (LP) | 30 |

*(see also Mazzy Star)*

## SAND PEBBLES
| | | | |
|---|---|---|---|
| 67 | Track 604 015 | Love Power/Because Of Love | 20 |
| 68 | Toast TT 505 | If You Didn't Hear Me The First Time/Flower Power | 8 |
| 69 | Track 604 028 | Love Power/Because Of Love (reissue) | 15 |

## SANDPIPERS
| | | | |
|---|---|---|---|
| 66 | Pye Intl. 7N 25380 | Guantanamera/What Makes You Dream, Pretty Girl | 5 |
| 66 | Pye International 7N 25396 | Louie Louie/Things We Said Today | 8 |
| 68 | A & M AMS 723 | Quando M'Immamoro (A Man Without Love)/I'll Remember You | 8 |
| 76 | Satril SAT 111 | For The Last Time/Down By The River | 8 |
| 76 | Satril SAT 114 | Hang On Sloopy/Skid Row Joe | 5 |

## SANDRA
| | | | |
|---|---|---|---|
| 86 | 10 TENY 78-12 | (I'll Never Be) Maria Magdalena/Party Games/Little Girl (12", picture disc) | 15 |
| 86 | 10 TEN 113-12/TENY 78-12 | In The Heat Of The Night/Heatwave (Instrumental)//(I'll Never Be) Maria Magdalena/Party Games/Little Girl (12", double pack, including picture disc, gatefold PVC sleeve) | 20 |
| 89 | Siren SRNCD 85 | Everlasting Love/Stop For A Minute/Everlasting Love (Remix)/ (I'll Never Be) Maria Magdalena (CD) | 50 |

## SANDROSE
| | | | |
|---|---|---|---|
| 73 | Polydor 2480 137 | SANDROSE (LP) | 275 |

## SANDS (IRELAND)
| | | | |
|---|---|---|---|
| 69 | Tribune TRS 122 | Dance Dance Dance/The Cheater | 20 |
| 69 | Tribune TRS 129 | Bubble Gum Music/Sherry | 15 |
| 70 | Major Minor MM 681 | Venus/Cara Mia | 10 |
| 69 | Tribune | SAND DOIN'S (LP) | 50 |
| 70s | Plough PLX 501 | TIME OUT WITH THE SANDS (LP) | 15 |

*(see also Tony Kenny & Sands)*

## SANDS (U.K.)
| | | | |
|---|---|---|---|
| 67 | Reaction 591 017 | Mrs. Gillespie's Refrigerator/Listen To The Sky | 400 |

*(see also Sundragon)*

## CLIVE SANDS
| | | | |
|---|---|---|---|
| 69 | S.N.B. 55-3955 | Lo Mucho Que Te Quiro/Picture On The Wall | 7 |
| 69 | S.N.B. 55-4058 | Hooked On A Feeling/Marie | 7 |
| 69 | S.N.B. 55-4431 | Whitchi Tai Yo/In A Dream | 12 |
| 69 | CBS 4672 | A Very Lonely Man/You Made Me What I Am | 7 |

*(see also Brothers Kane, Sarstedt Brothers, Wes Sands)*

## DAVEY SANDS & ESSEX
| | | | |
|---|---|---|---|
| 65 | Decca F 12170 | Please Me Mine/All The Time | 20 |
| 67 | CBS 202620 | Advertising Girl/Without You I'm Nothing | 25 |
| 71 | Parlophone R5899 | The Puppet Man/Oh What A Naughty Man | 10 |

## EVIE SANDS
| | | | |
|---|---|---|---|
| 65 | Red Bird BC 118 | Take Me For A Little While/Run Home To Mama | 50 |
| 65 | Red Bird BC 118 | Take Me For A Little While/Run Home To Mama (DJ copy) | 85 |
| 66 | Cameo Parkway C 413 | Picture Me Gone/It Makes Me Laugh | 125 |
| 66 | Cameo Parkway C 413 | Picture Me Gone/It Makes Me Laugh (DJ copy) | 200 |
| 68 | A&M AMS 736 | Shadow Of The Evening/Until It's Time For You To Go | 10 |
| 69 | A&M AMS 748 | I'll Hold Out Of My Hand/One Fine Summer Morning | 10 |
| 69 | A&M AMS 760 | Anyway That You Want Me/I'll Never Be Alone | 10 |
| 75 | Capitol CL 15818 | You Brought The Woman Out In Me/Early Morning Sunshine | 7 |

## JODI(E) SANDS
| | | | |
|---|---|---|---|
| 57 | London HL 8456 | With All My Heart/More Than Only Friends (as Jodi Sands) | 10 |
| 57 | London HL 8530 | Please Don't Tell Me (Sayonara)/If You're Not Completely Satisfied | 10 |
| 58 | Starlite ST45 005 | All I Ask Of You/The Way I Love You | 8 |
| 58 | HMV POP 533 | Someday (You'll Want Me To Want You)/Always In My Heart | 8 |

## SYLVIA SANDS
| | | | |
|---|---|---|---|
| 61 | Columbia DB 4579 | Autumn Tears/Steppin' Out With My Baby | 8 |

## TOMMY SANDS
| | | | |
|---|---|---|---|
| 57 | Capitol CL 14695 | Teen-Age Crush/Hep Dee Hootie (Cutie Wootie) | 25 |
| 57 | Capitol CL 14724 | Ring-A-Ding-A-Ding/My Love Song | 25 |
| 57 | Capitol CL 14745 | Goin' Steady/Ring My 'Phone | 25 |
| 57 | Capitol CL 14781 | Let Me Be Loved/Fantastically Foolish | 10 |
| 57 | Capitol CL 14811 | Man, Like Wow!/A Swingin' Romance | 20 |
| 58 | Capitol CL 14834 | Sing, Boy, Sing/Crazy 'Cause I Love You | 15 |

| 58 | Capitol CL 14872 | Hawaiian Rock/Teen-Age Doll | 25 |
| 58 | Capitol CL 14889 | After The Senior Prom/Big Date | 20 |
| 58 | Capitol CL 14925 | Blue Ribbon Baby/I Love You Because (as Tommy Sands & Raiders) | 30 |
| 59 | Capitol CL 14971 | The Worryin' Kind/Bigger Than Texas | 35 |
| 59 | Capitol CL 15013 | Is It Ever Gonna Happen/I Ain't Gettin' Rid Of You | 30 |
| 59 | Capitol CL 15047 | Sinner Man/Bring Me Your Love | 7 |
| 59 | Capitol CL 15071 | That's The Way I Am/I'll Be Seeing You | 7 |
| 60 | Capitol CL 15109 | I Gotta Have You/You Hold The Future | 7 |
| 60 | Capitol CL 15143 | The Old Oaken Bucket/These Are The Things You Are | 7 |
| 61 | Capitol CL 15219 | Love In A Goldfish Bowl/I Love My Baby | 7 |
| 63 | HMV POP 1193 | Connie/Young Man's Fancy | 6 |
| 63 | HMV POP 1247 | Only 'Cause I'm Lonely/Cinderella | 6 |
| 66 | Liberty LIB 55842 | The Statue/Lolita | 45 |
| 66 | Liberty LIB 55842 | The Statue/Lolita (DJ copy) | 85 |
| 57 | Capitol EAP1 848 | STEADY DATE WITH TOMMY SANDS PT. 1 (EP) | 15 |
| 57 | Capitol EAP2 848 | STEADY DATE WITH TOMMY SANDS PT. 2 (EP) | 15 |
| 57 | Capitol EAP3 848 | STEADY DATE WITH TOMMY SANDS PT. 3 (EP) | 15 |
| 57 | Capitol EAP1 851 | TEENAGE CRUSH (EP) | 20 |
| 59 | Capitol EAP1 1081 | SANDS STORM PART 1 (EP) | 20 |
| 59 | Capitol EAP2 1081 | SANDS STORM PART 2 (EP) | 20 |
| 59 | Capitol EAP3 1081 | SANDS STORM PART 3 (EP) | 20 |
| 59 | Capitol EAP1 1123 | THIS THING CALLED LOVE (EP) | 15 |
| 57 | Capitol T 848 | STEADY DATE WITH TOMMY SANDS (LP) | 40 |
| 58 | Capitol T 929 | SING, BOY, SING (soundtrack) (LP) | 40 |
| 59 | Capitol T 1081 | SANDS STORM! (LP) | 80 |
| 59 | Capitol T 1123 | THIS THING CALLED LOVE (LP) | 20 |
| 60 | Capitol (S)T 1239 | WHEN I'M THINKING OF YOU (LP, mono) | 15 |
| 60 | Capitol (S)T 1239 | WHEN I'M THINKING OF YOU (LP, stereo) | 15 |
| 61 | Capitol T 1426 | A DREAM WITH TOMMY SANDS (LP) | 15 |

## TONY SANDS & DRUMBEATS
| 60s | Studio 36 NSRS EP 1/22 | Shame Shame Shame/I Got A Feeling | 250 |

## WES SANDS
| 63 | Columbia DB 4996 | There's Lots More Where This Came From/Three Cups | 45 |

*(see also Brothers Kane, Sarstedt Brothers, Clive Sands)*

## SANDS OF TIME
| 66 | Pye 7N 17140 | Where Did We Go Wrong/When I Look Back | 10 |
| 67 | Pye 7N 17236 | One Day/Ev'ry Time We Say Goodbye | 8 |

## PAT SANDY
| 69 | Attack ATT 8000 | Gentle On My Mind/BIG L: Soulful | 30 |

## SANDY & TEACHERS
| 64 | Columbia DB 7244 | Listen With Mammy/Real Sweet | 5 |

*(see also Sandy Brown)*

## SANDY COAST
| 71 | Polydor 2121 046 | True Love/That's A Wonder | 10 |
| 73 | Polydor 2001 457 | Blackboard Jungle Lady/Don't Get Me Wrong | 7 |
| 69 | Page One POLS 020 | FROM THE STEREO WORKSHOP (LP) | 350 |
| 69 | Page One MORS 201 | SHIPWRECK (LP) | 300 |
| 73 | Polydor 2310 277 | STONEWALL (LP) | 20 |

## SAN FRANCISCO EARTHQUAKE
| 68 | Mercury MF 1036 | Fairy Tales Can Come True (Have You Heard About Lucy)/Su Su | 10 |

## SANG HUGH
| 73 | Count Shelly CS 023 | Rasta No Born Ya/MESSENGERS: Cherry Baby | 8 |
| 73 | Count Shelly CS 034 | No Potion A Girl/The Way To Reason | 8 |
| 75 | Ethnic Fight EF 018 | Last Call To Blackman/Black Track | 15 |
| 76 | Ethnic Fight EF 056 | God's Children/ETHNIC FIGHT BAND: Dub In Blood Island | 10 |

## SAN REMO STRINGS
| 71 | Tamla Motown TMG 795 | Festival Time/All Turned On | 12 |
| 71 | Tamla Motown TMG 795 | Festival Time/All Turned On (DJ copy) | 30 |
| 72 | Tamla Motown TMG 807 | Reach Out, I'll Be There/Hungry For Love | 10 |
| 72 | Tamla Motown TMG 807 | Reach Out, I'll Be There/Hungry For Love (DJ copy) | 30 |
| 73 | Tamla Motown STML 11216 | SAN REMO STRINGS SWING (LP) | 20 |

## BOBBY SANSOM (& GIANTS)
| 63 | Oriole CB 1837 | There's A Place/Lucille (as Bobby Sansom & Giants) | 20 |
| 63 | Oriole CB 1888 | Where Have You Been/Do You Promise (as Bobby Sansom & Giants) | 18 |
| 70 | Decca F 13104 | Lady One And Only/Handbags And Gladrags | 8 |
| 71 | Decca F 13151 | I Believe In Music/The Valley Of The Shadows Of Tears | 8 |

## MONGO SANTAMARIA
| 63 | Riverside RIF 106909 | Watermelon Man/Don't Bother Me No More | 20 |
| 65 | CBS 201766 | El Pussycat/Black Eyed Peas And Rice | 20 |
| 69 | Direction 58-4086 | Cloud Nine/Son Of A Preacher Man | 18 |
| 69 | Direction 58-4430 | Twenty Five Miles/El Tres | 15 |
| 66 | CBS SS 62123 | HEY! LET'S PARTY (LP) | 20 |
| 68 | CBS S 233811 | ALL STRUNG OUT (LP) | 20 |
| 71 | CBS 63904 | WORKING ON A GROOVY THING (LP) | 20 |
| 71 | Atlantic 2400 140 | MONGO'S WAY (LP) | 20 |

## SANTANA
| 70 | CBS 5325 | Black Magic Woman/Hope You're Feeling Better | 10 |
| 69 | CBS 63815 | SANTANA (LP, laminated sleeve original, orange label) | 30 |

# Carlos SANTANA & BUDDY MILES

| | | | |
|---|---|---|---|
| 70 | CBS 64087 | ABRAXAS (LP, orange label) | 25 |
| 71 | CBS 69015 | SANTANA (III) (LP, gatefold sleeve, some stickered, orange label) | 25 |
| 72 | CBS CQ 30595 | SANTANA (III) (LP, gatefold sleeve, quadrophonic) | 40 |
| 72 | CBS 65299 | CARAVANSERAI (LP, gatefold sleeve, orange label) | 20 |
| 73 | CBS CQ 31610 | CARAVANSERAI (LP, gatefold sleeve, quadrophonic) | 25 |
| 74 | CBS CQ 32445 | WELCOME (LP, embossed gatefold sleeve, quadrophonic) | 20 |
| 75 | CBS CQ 30130 | ABRAXAS (LP, gatefold sleeve, quadrophonic) | 20 |
| 75 | CBS Q 69081 | GREATEST HITS (LP, quadrophonic) | 15 |
| 75 | CBS Q 69084 | BORBOLETTA (LP, quadrophonic) | 15 |
| 76 | CBS Q 86005 | AMIGOS (LP, quadrophonic) | 15 |
| 85 | CBS 69084 | BORBOLETTA (LP, Nimbus Supercut, mail order only through Hi Fi Today magazine) | 70 |

## CARLOS SANTANA & BUDDY MILES
| | | | |
|---|---|---|---|
| 73 | CBS CQ 31308 | CARLOS SANTANA & BUDDY MILES LIVE (LP, quadrophonic) | 15 |

*(see also Santana, Buddy Miles, Mahavishnu Orchestra, John McLaughlin, John Lee Hooker)*

## SANTELLS
| | | | |
|---|---|---|---|
| 66 | Sue WI 4020 | So Fine/These Are Love | 25 |

## GRANT SANTINO & THE FAMILY
| | | | |
|---|---|---|---|
| 79 | Polydor 2059 168 | L.O.V.E./Try Love | 20 |
| 79 | Polydor GS1 | L.O.V.E./Try Love (12", promo only) | 100 |

## DAVID SANTO
| | | | |
|---|---|---|---|
| 68 | London HLK 10219 | Jingle Down A Hill/Rising Of Scorpio | 8 |

## SANTO & JOHNNY
| | | | |
|---|---|---|---|
| 59 | Pye International 7N 25037 | Sleep Walk/All Night Diner | 20 |
| 60 | Parlophone R 4619 | Tear Drop/The Long Walk Home | 20 |
| 60 | Parlophone R 4644 | Caravan/Summertime | 10 |
| 61 | Pye International 7N 25111 | Theme From Come September/Hopscotch | 10 |
| 61 | Parlophone R 4844 | Bullseye!/Twistin' Bells | 10 |
| 62 | Parlophone R 4865 | Birmingham/The Mouse | 10 |
| 62 | Stateside SS 110 | Spanish Harlem/Stage To Cimarron | 10 |
| 64 | Stateside SS 253 | Three Cabelleros/Manhattan Spiritual | 10 |
| 64 | Stateside SS 292 | In The Still Of The Night/Song For Rosemary | 10 |
| 60 | Parlophone GEP 8806 | SANTO AND JOHNNY NO. 1 (EP) | 30 |
| 60 | Parlophone GEP 8813 | SANTO AND JOHNNY NO. 2 (EP) | 30 |
| 64 | Stateside S(S)L 1008 | HAWAII (LP) | 20 |

## SAPODILLA PUNCH
| | | | |
|---|---|---|---|
| 69 | Mercury MF 1112 | Hold On I'm Coming/Bach To Minor | 8 |

## SAPPHIRE
| | | | |
|---|---|---|---|
| 82 | Sapphire Rocks SRR 001 | Jealousy (p/s) | 200 |
| 72 | SRT SRT 72226 | SAPPHIRE (LP) | 180 |

## SAPPHIRES
| | | | |
|---|---|---|---|
| 63 | Stateside SS 223 | Where Is Johnny Now/Your True Love | 40 |
| 64 | Stateside SS 267 | Who Do You Love/Oh So Soon | 65 |
| 65 | HMV POP 1441 | Gotta Have Your Love/Gee Baby I'm Sorry | 180 |
| 65 | HMV POP 1441 | Gotta Have Your Love/Gee Baby I'm Sorry (DJ copy) | 350 |
| 65 | HMV POP 1461 | Evil One/How Could I Say Goodbye | 180 |
| 65 | HMV POP 1461 | Evil One/How Could I Say Goodbye (DJ copy) | 300 |
| 72 | Probe PRO 556 | Gotta Have Your Love/Gee Baby I'm Sorry (reissue) | 10 |
| 74 | Probe PRO 609 | Slow Fizz/Our Love Is Everywhere | 10 |
| 78 | ABC 4221 | Gonna Be A Big Thing/EDDIE REGAN: Playin' Hide And Seek | 8 |

## SARABAND
| | | | |
|---|---|---|---|
| 73 | Folk Heritage FHR 050 | CLOSE TO IT ALL (LP) | 22 |

## SARACEN
| | | | |
|---|---|---|---|
| 82 | Nucleus SAR 1 | No More Lonely Nights/Rock Of Ages (p/s, with patch) | 8 |
| 82 | Nucleus SAR 1 | No More Lonely Nights/Rock Of Ages (p/s) | 6 |
| 83 | Neat NEAT 30 | We Have Arrived/Face In The Crowd (p/s) | 7 |
| 82 | Nucleus MPGR 492 | HEROES, SAINTS AND FOOLS (LP) | 15 |

## SARASOTA
| | | | |
|---|---|---|---|
| 96 | BIT Productions MIKE 004 | We're Gettin' Hot (1-sided 12") | 40 |
| 97 | BIT Productions MIKE 009 | Pleasure/We're Gettin' Hot (the Maximum Project pumped up remix) (stickered white label 12") | 40 |

## SARDONICUS
| | | | |
|---|---|---|---|
| 73 | Country Recording Service COUN 240 | Nymph/Evaporated Brain | 350 |

## DON SARGENT
| | | | |
|---|---|---|---|
| 60 | Vogue Pop V 9160 | St. James' Infirmary/Gypsy Boots (triangular centre) | 300 |

## SARI & SHALIMARS
| | | | |
|---|---|---|---|
| 68 | United Artists UP 2235 | It's So Lonely (Being Together)/You Walked Out On Me Before | 30 |

## DEREK SARJEANT
| | | | |
|---|---|---|---|
| 61 | Oak RGJ 101 | FOLK SONGS SUNG BY DEREK SARJEANT (EP) | 20 |
| 61 | Oak RGJ 103 | SONGS WE LIKE TO SING (EP, with tracks by Lisa Turner & Mick Wells) | 20 |
| 61 | Oak RGJ 105 | FOLK SONGS SUNG BY DEREK SARJEANT VOL. 2 (EP) | 15 |
| 63 | Oak RGJ 117 | MAN OF KENT (EP) | 18 |
| 61 | Oak RGJ 7444 | ENGLISH FOLK SONGS (EP) | 20 |
| 61 | Oak RGJ 7450 | A SAILOR'S LIFE: SONGS OF THE SEA AND THE SHORE (EP) | 20 |

## MIKE SARNE
| | | | |
|---|---|---|---|
| 63 | Parlophone R 5090 | Hello Lover Boy/Baby I'm On My Way | 5 |
| 64 | Parlophone R 5129 | Out And About/A Place To Go | 5 |
| 64 | Parlophone R 5170 | Love Me Please/You've Got Something (as Mike Sarne & Le Roys) | 10 |

| 63 | Parlophone DP 558 | Just Like Eddie/Slow Twistin' Round The Totem Pole (export issue) | 50 |
| 63 | Parlophone GEP 8879 | MIKE SARNE HIT PARADE (EP) | 15 |
| 62 | Parlophone PMC 1187 | COME OUTSIDE (LP) | 20 |

*(see also Wendy Richards, Le Roys, Billie Davis, Rod McKuen)*

## SAROFEEN & SMOKE
| 71 | Pye International 7N 25556 | Susan Jane/Tomorrow | 15 |
| 71 | Pye Intl. NSPL 28153 | DO IT (LP) | 40 |

## SAROLTA
| 68 | Island WIP 6035 | Open Your Hands/L.O.V.E. | 15 |
| 69 | President PT248 | I Am A Woman/Change Of Heart | 10 |

## SARR BAND
| 78 | Calendar LDAY 115 | Magic Mandrake/Double Action (12") | 25 |

## PETER SARSTEDT
| 68 | Island WIP 6028 | I Must Go On/Mary Jane | 30 |
| 68 | United Artists UP 2228 | I Am A Cathedral/Blagged | 10 |
| 69 | United Artists UP 2262 | Morning Mountain/Step Into The Candlelight | 10 |
| 69 | United Artists UP 35021 | Frozen Orange Juice/Arethusa Loser | 15 |
| 69 | United Artists UP 35041 | As Though It Were A Movie/Take Off Your Clothes | 8 |
| 69 | United Artists UP 35075 | Without Darkness (There's No Light)/Step Into The Candlelight | 8 |

*(see also Sarstedt Brothers, Brothers Kane, Peter Lincoln)*

## SARSTEDT BROTHERS
| 73 | Regal Zonophone RZ 3081 | Chinese Restaurant/Beloved Illusions | 7 |
| 73 | Regal Zono. SRZA 8516 | WORLDS APART TOGETHER (LP, gatefold sleeve with booklet) | 20 |

*(see also Brothers Kane, Peter Sarstedt, Eden Kane, Clive Sands, Wes Sands)*

## DAN SARTAIN
| 09 | Third Man TMR 011 | Bohemian Grove/Atheist Funeral (100 only, luminous vinyl) | 60 |

## SAS
| 85 | No Label SAS4 | SUAVE AND SOPHISTICATED? (7" EP, fold-out sleeve) | 25 |

## SASPARELLA
| 69 | Decca F 12892 | Spooky/Come Inside | 40 |

## SASSAFRAS
| 73 | Polydor 2383 245 | EXPECTING COMPANY (LP) | 15 |

## SASSENACHS
| 64 | Fontana TF 518 | That Don't Worry Me/All Over You | 30 |

## SATAN
| 82 | Guardian GRC 145 | Kiss Of Death/Heads Will Roll (with p/s) | 200 |
| 82 | Guardian GRC 145 | Kiss Of Death/Heads Will Roll | 50 |
| 85 | Neat NEAT 1012 | COURT IN THE ACT (LP) | 30 |

## SATANIC MALFUNCTIONS
| 86 | Teacore TEACORE 1 | WHO WANTS THE WORLD EP (wraparound p/s) | 15 |
| 89 | Teacore TEA 3 | REMEMBER EP (wraparound p/s) | 12 |
| 88 | Teacore TEA 2 | HELLBOUND (LP, insert) | 20 |
| 90 | Teacore TEA 5 | DISGRACE TO HUMANITY (LP, insert) | 20 |

## SATANIC RITES
| 81 | Heavy Metal HEAVY 8 | Live To Ride/Hit And Run (p/s) | 12 |
| 85 | Chub CHUBLP 001 | WHICH WAY THE WIND BLOWS (LP) | 25 |
| 87 | Chub CHUBLP 002 | NO USE CRYING (LP) | 30 |

## SATAN'S RATS
| 77 | DJM DJS 10819 | In My Love For You/Façade (p/s) | 30 |
| 77 | DJM DJS 10821 | Year Of The Rats/Louise (p/s) | 25 |
| 78 | DJM DJS 10840 | You Make Me Sick/Façade (p/s) | 25 |
| 89 | Overground OVER 01 | Year Of The Rats/Louise (p/s, 600 yellow vinyl) | 6 |
| 89 | Overground OVER 01 | Year Of The Rats/Louise (p/s, 400 white vinyl) | 7 |
| 89 | Overground OVER 01 | Year Of The Rats/Louise (p/s, 25 gold vinyl, numbered test pressings) | 15 |
| 89 | Overground OVER 02 | In My Love For You/Facade (p/s, 600 yellow vinyl) | 12 |
| 89 | Overground OVER 02 | In My Love For You/Facade (p/s, 400 white vinyl) | 12 |
| 89 | Overground OVER 02 | In My Love For You/Facade (p/s, 25 gold vinyl, numbered test pressings) | 15 |
| 91 | Overground OVER 14 | You Make Me Sick/Louise (p/s, clear vinyl, 567 copies only) | 7 |

## YOUNG SATCH
| 70 | Black Swan BW 1401 | Bonga Bonga Bonga/HI-TALS: Ram Buck | 40 |
| 70 | Black Swan BW 1401 | Bongo Bongo/BOYS: Ramba | 12 |

## GIRL SATCHMO
| 61 | Blue Beat BB 45 | Satchmo's Mash Potato/Darling | 20 |
| 62 | Blue Beat BB 79 | Twist Around Town/My New Honey (with Karl Rowe & Bluebeats) | 20 |
| 63 | Blue Beat BB 156 | Don't Be Sad/Brother Joe (with Les Dawson Combo) | 25 |
| 64 | Blue Beat BB 227 | Rhythm Of The New Beat/Blue Beat Chariot | 30 |
| 69 | Fab FAB 111 | Take You For A Ride/I'm Coming Home | 35 |
| 69 | Trojan TR 676 | Taken For A Ride/I'm Coming Home | 20 |

*(see also Pat Satchmo, Sugar & Dandy)*

## PAT SATCHMO
| 69 | Punch PH 9 | Hello Dolly/ERIC DONALSON: Never Get Away | 60 |
| 69 | Upsetter US 316 | Hello Dolly/King Of The Trombone | 40 |
| 70 | Punch PH 24 | Wonderful World/MEDITATORS: Purple Mast | 20 |
| 70 | Songbird SB 1039 | A Handful Of Friends/CRYSTALITES: Handful - Version | 10 |
| 72 | Attack ATT 8024 | What's Going On/LLOYD & CAREY: Tubby's In Full Swing | 30 |

## SATELLITES
| 83 | Brickyard EOR 1 | Vietnam/Lucy Is A Prostitute/I Fell In Love With A Lesbian (p/s) | 10 |

MINT VALUE £

| | | | |
|---|---|---|---|
| 83 | Kamera ERA 016 | NIGHTMARE EP | 6 |
| 84 | Brickyard | HERE IS TODAY'S NEWS (LP) | 15 |

## SATIN BELLS
| | | | |
|---|---|---|---|
| 68 | Pye 7N 17531 | Baby You're So Right For Me/When You're Ready | 10 |
| 68 | Pye 7N 17608 | Da-Di-Da-Da/Oh No Oh Yes | 6 |
| 69 | Decca F 22937 | I Stand Accused (Of Loving You)/Sweet Darlin' | 20 |
| 70 | Decca F 23044 | The Power Of Love/Baby Come Back | 6 |

*(see also Three Bells)*

## SATIN STORM
| | | | |
|---|---|---|---|
| 91 | Satin Storm SSP 201 | Satin Storm 1999/Pleasurezone (inst)/Buzz/Feel The Spirit (12") | 30 |
| 91 | Satin Storm SSHC 1 | See The Light/Call In The Hardcore/Kick Up A Sound Boy/Chill Out (12". As Satin Storm Dancers) | 15 |
| 92 | Satin Storm DJT DAPSS 1 | Let's Get Together/Free Your Mind (12". Artist not credited on labels) | 40 |
| 92 | Satin Storm ST 01 | Sweat/Can't Wait/Can't Take No More/Tekno/Satin Storm/EBGB (12") | 20 |
| 92 | Satin Storm SSHC 2 | What About What I Need /Drop That Bass/House Of My Dreams/Ram it (12" Artist not credited on labels) | 15 |
| 92 | Satin Storm SSHC 3 | Think I'm Going Out Of My Head/Unknown/What Do You Do? (12") | 15 |
| 93 | Satin Storm SSHC 4 | Return Of The Blopblingers/Rough And Smooth & The Driven) (12") | 10 |
| 93 | Satin Storm SSHC 5 | Come On, Get Together/I'm A Technician/He's On It, All Night Long (12") | 10 |

## SATISFACTION (1)
| | | | |
|---|---|---|---|
| 71 | Decca F 13129 | Love It Is/Cold Summer | 10 |
| 71 | Decca F 13207 | Don't Rag The Lady/Gregory Shan't | 10 |
| 71 | Decca SKL 5075 | SATISFACTION (LP, laminated front sleeve, blue/silver boxed label) | 50 |

*(see also Mike Cotton Sound)*

## SATISFACTION (2)
| | | | |
|---|---|---|---|
| 79 | Live & Love LAP 005 | SATISFACTION IN DUB (LP) | 40 |

## SATISFIERS
| | | | |
|---|---|---|---|
| 57 | Vogue Coral Q 72247 | Where'll I Be Tomorrow Night?/Come Away, Love | 12 |
| 57 | Vogue Coral LVA 9068 | THE SATISFIERS (LP) | 20 |

## LIZZARD SATTAI
| | | | |
|---|---|---|---|
| 76 | Trojan TRLS 138 | LIZZARD (LP) | 30 |

## LONNIE SATTIN
| | | | |
|---|---|---|---|
| 56 | Capitol CL 14552 | Trapped (In The Web Of Love)/Your Home Can Be A Castle | 6 |
| 56 | Capitol CL 14638 | High Steel/What Time Does The Sun Go Down? | 5 |
| 57 | Capitol CL 14771 | I'll Never Stop Loving You/Whoo-Pie Shoo-Pie | 5 |
| 58 | Capitol CL 14831 | Ring Around The Moon/My Heart's Your Home | 5 |
| 60 | Warner Bros WB 15 | I'll Fly Away/Any More Than I | 5 |

## LON SATTON
| | | | |
|---|---|---|---|
| 74 | CBS SCBS 2816 | The Love I See In Your Eyes/Do You Need My Love | 8 |

## SATURNALIA
| | | | |
|---|---|---|---|
| 71 | Matrix TRIX 1 | MAGICAL LOVE (LP, picture disc with 3D labels, with booklet & ticket) | 150 |
| 71 | Matrix TRIX 1 | MAGICAL LOVE (LP, allegedly some copies in laminated sleeve, picture disc with 3D labels, with booklet & ticket) | 500 |
| 73 | Matrix TRIX 1 | MAGICAL LOVE (LP, picture disc, reissue) | 25 |

*(see also Horse)*

## SATYR
| | | | |
|---|---|---|---|
| 79 | Stardust STAR 001 | Love Slide Boogie/Problem In The City | 10 |

## SAUCERMAN
| | | | |
|---|---|---|---|
| 89 | Fierce FRIGHT 035 | I Will Be King/Sid James Rules (withdrawn) | 25 |
| 80s | Fierce | WRESTLING (12", sampler, withdrawn) | 12 |

*(see also Kray Cherubs)*

## KEN SAUL
| | | | |
|---|---|---|---|
| 70 | City Music | Warm Summer Rain/Pictures Framed in My Mind | 40 |
| 71 | Seashell SSLP 01 | SONGS FOR A RAINY DAY (LP, 25 only, hand-made sleeve, hand-written labels) | 400 |
| 73 | SSLP 002 | SEASHELLS (LP, hand-made sleeve, insert, 100 only) | 500 |

*(see also Stone Angel)*

## SAUNA YOUTH
| | | | |
|---|---|---|---|
| 13 | Static Shock SSR 17 | False Jessi Ot II/Oh Joel (white vinyl, 150 only) | 6 |
| 12 | Faux Disex FAUX 016 | DREAMLAND (LP) | 18 |
| 15 | Upset! The Rhythm UTR 017 | DISTRACTIONS (LP) | 15 |

## LARRY SAUNDERS
| | | | |
|---|---|---|---|
| 74 | London HLU 10469 | On The Real Side/Let Me Be The Special One | 20 |
| 74 | London HLU 10469 | On The Real Side/Let Me Be The Special One (DJ copy) | 40 |

## MAHALIA SAUNDERS
| | | | |
|---|---|---|---|
| 71 | Moodisc HME 112 | Down The Aisle/IAN ROBINSON: Three For One | 8 |
| 71 | Upsetter US 374 | Pieces Of My Heart/UPSETTERS: Version | 15 |
| 71 | Pama Supreme PS 331 | Peace Of My Heart/Right On The Tip Of My Tongue | 25 |

## KEVIN SAUNDERSON
| | | | |
|---|---|---|---|
| 88 | Kool Kat DJ 5 | Bounce Your Body To The Box (Mike 'Hitman' Wilson Acid Remix)/(Original Detroit Mix)/The Groove That Won't Stop (Detroit Special Mix)/Force Field (12") | 15 |

## TUPPER SAUSSY
| | | | |
|---|---|---|---|
| 63 | London HAU 8127 | DISCOVER TUPPER SAUSSY (LP) | 15 |

## LES SAUTERELLES
| | | | |
|---|---|---|---|
| 68 | Decca F 22824 | Heavenly Club/Dream Machine | 45 |

## SAVAGE
| | | | |
|---|---|---|---|
| 82 | Ebony EBON 10 | Ain't No Fit Place/China Run | 8 |
| 83 | Ebony EBON 12 | LOOSE 'N' LETHAL (LP) | 25 |

## EDNA SAVAGE
| | | | |
|---|---|---|---|
| 55 | Parlophone MSP 6175 | Stars Shine In Your Eyes/A Star Is Born | 7 |
| 55 | Parlophone MSP 6181 | Candlelight/In The Wee Small Hours Of The Morning | 7 |
| 55 | Parlophone MSP 6189 | Arrivederci Darling/Bella Notte | 7 |
| 56 | Parlophone MSP 6217 | Tell Me, Tell Me, Tell Me That You Love Me/Please Hurry Home | 7 |
| 56 | Parlophone R 4226 | My Prayer/Me 'n' You 'n' The Moon | 7 |
| 56 | Parlophone R 4253 | Never Leave Me/Don't Ever Go (I Need You) | 6 |
| 57 | Parlophone R 4301 | Me Head's In De Barrel/Five Iranges Four Apples | 6 |
| 57 | Parlophone R 4360 | Let Me Be Loved/Diano Marina | 6 |

*(see also Michael Holliday)*

## JOAN SAVAGE
| | | | |
|---|---|---|---|
| 57 | Columbia DB 3929 | Five Oranges, Four Apples/Bamboozled | 5 |
| 57 | Columbia DB 3968 | With All My Heart/Love Letters In The Sand | 5 |
| 57 | Columbia DB 4039 | Shake Me, I Rattle/Lula Rock-A-Hula | 20 |
| 58 | Columbia DB 4159 | Hello Happiness, Goodbye Blues/Left Right Out Of My Heart | 5 |

## SAVAGE PENCIL
| | | | |
|---|---|---|---|
| 88 | Blast First FU 3LP | PRESENTS ANGEL DUST: MUSIC FOR MOVIE BIKERS (LP, picture disc, 1,000 only) | 15 |

*(see also Art Attacks, Kray Cherubs)*

## SAVAGE RESURRECTION
| | | | |
|---|---|---|---|
| 68 | Mercury MF 1027 | Thing In E/Fox Is Sick | 60 |
| 68 | Mercury SMCL 20123 | SAVAGE RESURRECTION (LP) | 175 |

## SAVAGE ROSE
| | | | |
|---|---|---|---|
| 68 | Polydor 184206 | IN THE PLAIN (LP, red label) | 40 |
| 69 | Polydor 184316 | TRAVELLIN' (LP, red label) | 30 |
| 72 | RCA Victor SF 8250 | REFUGEE (LP, laminated front sleeve, orange label) | 30 |
| 71 | RCA Victor SF 8169 | YOUR DAILY GIFT (LP, laminated front sleeve, orange label) | 30 |

## SAVAGES
| | | | |
|---|---|---|---|
| 63 | Decca DFE 8546 | EVERYBODY SURF! WITH THE SURFIN' SAVAGES (EP) | 200 |

*(see also Soul Sounds, Screaming Lord Sutch, Circles, Tony Dangerfield & Thrills)*

## JULIAN JAY SAVARIN
| | | | |
|---|---|---|---|
| 73 | Lyntone LYN 3426 | I Am You/Kizeesh (Corgi Books sampler) | 50 |
| 73 | Birth RAB 2 | WAITERS ON THE DANCE (LP, textured sleeve with insert) | 500 |
| 73 | Birth RAB 2 | WAITERS ON THE DANCE (LP, textured sleeve without insert) | 300 |
| 87 | Five Hours Back TOCK 002 | WAITERS ON THE DANCE (LP, reissue) | 20 |

*(see also Julian's Treatment)*

## SAVES THE DAY
| | | | |
|---|---|---|---|
| 02 | B-Unique BUN021-7 | At Your Funeral/Ups And Downs (p/s) | 6 |
| 02 | B-Unique BUN034-7 | Freakish/Certain Tragedy (Live At The BBC) (p/s) | 5 |

## RONNIE SAVOY
| | | | |
|---|---|---|---|
| 61 | MGM MGM 1122 | And The Heavens Cried/Big Chain | 15 |
| 61 | MGM MGM 1131 | Bewitched/It's Gotta Be love | 10 |

## SAVOY BROWN (BLUES BAND)
| | | | |
|---|---|---|---|
| 66 | Purdah 45-3503 | I Tried/Can't Quit You Baby (as Savoy Brown's Blues Band) | 300 |
| 67 | Decca F 12702 | Taste And Try, Before You Buy/Someday People (as Savoy Brown Blues Band) | 20 |
| 68 | Decca F 12797 | Walking By Myself/Vicksburg Blues | 12 |
| 69 | Decca F 12843 | Train To Nowhere/Tolling Bells | 15 |
| 69 | Decca F 12978 | I'm Tired/Stay With Me Baby | 30 |
| 70 | Decca F 13019 | A Hard Way To Go/Waiting In The Bamboo Grove | 15 |
| 70 | Decca F 13098 | Poor Girl/Master Hare | 12 |
| 71 | Decca F 13247 | Tell Mama/Let It Rock | 12 |
| 73 | Decca F 13372 | So Tired/The Saddest Feeling | 7 |
| 73 | Decca F 13431 | Coming Down Your Way/I Can't Find You | 7 |
| 67 | Decca LK 4883 | SHAKE DOWN (LP, mono, unboxed logo label) | 150 |
| 67 | Decca SKL 4883 | SHAKE DOWN (LP, stereo, unboxed logo label) | 100 |
| 68 | Decca LK 4935 | GETTING TO THE POINT (LP, mono, unboxed logo label) | 100 |
| 68 | Decca SKL 4935 | GETTING TO THE POINT (LP, stereo, unboxed logo label) | 75 |
| 69 | Decca SKL 4935 | GETTING TO THE POINT (LP, second pressing, stereo, boxed logo) | 25 |
| 69 | Decca LK 4994 | BLUE MATTER (LP, mono, unboxed logo label) | 100 |
| 69 | Decca SKL 4994 | BLUE MATTER (LP, stereo, unboxed logo label) | 50 |
| 69 | Decca LK 5013 | A STEP FURTHER (LP, mono, unboxed logo label) | 100 |
| 69 | Decca SKL 5013 | A STEP FURTHER (LP, stereo, unboxed logo label) | 40 |
| 70 | Decca LK 5043 | RAW SIENNA (LP, mono, laminated gatefold sleeve, boxed logo label) | 100 |
| 70 | Decca SKL 5043 | RAW SIENNA (LP, stereo, laminated gatefold sleeve, boxed logo label) | 50 |
| 70 | Decca SKL 5066 | LOOKING IN (LP, 1st pressing, dull laminated gatefold sleeve) | 60 |
| 70 | Decca SKL 5066 | LOOKING IN (LP, 2nd pressing, glossy laminated gatefold sleeve) | 30 |
| 71 | Decca TXS 104 | STREET CORNER TALKING (LP, gatefold sleeve) | 20 |
| 72 | Decca TXS 107 | HELLBOUND TRAIN (LP, gatefold sleeve) | 30 |
| 73 | Decca SKL 5152 | LION'S SHARE (LP) | 15 |
| 73 | Decca TXS 112 | JACK THE TOAD (LP) | 18 |

*(see also Warren Philips & The Rockets, Chris Youlden, Stone's Masonry, Jackie Lynton, Foghat)*

## SAVWINKLE AND TURNERHOPPER
| | | | |
|---|---|---|---|
| 70 | Pye 7N 17913 | Your Mother Thinks I'm A Hoodlum/Dirtyin' My Thing | 20 |

## TOM SAWYER
| | | | |
|---|---|---|---|
| 69 | CBS 4243 | Cookbook/Gates | 10 |

*(see also Unit 4 + 2)*

## 'ACE' DINNING SAX
| | | | |
|---|---|---|---|
| 59 | Top Rank JAR 184 | Mulholland Drive/My Love | 15 |

## SAX HAPPY

**SAX HAPPY**
82   Take A Hammer TAH 001      Factory Song/Martian Spaceship ........................................................... 8

**MIKE SAX & IDOLS**
65   Mercury MF 886              My Little One/Come Back To Me .......................................................... 10
*(see also Idols)*

**SAX MANIAX**
82   Penthouse PEN 3            Never Gonna Lose Me/Let's Twist Again (p/s) ...................................... 10
82   Penthouse PENT 1201       OVERSAXED (LP) .................................................................................... 15

**AL SAXON**
58   Fontana H 138             Where The Black Eyed Susans Grow/She Screamed .............................. 5
58   Fontana H 164             The Day The Rains Came (Le Jour Ou La Pluie Viendra)/You're The Top-Cha ... 6
59   Fontana H 188             Chattanooga Choo-Choo/Chip Off The Old Block .................................. 5
59   Fontana H 205             Only Sixteen/I'm All Right, Jack ........................................................... 5
59   Fontana H 222             Linda Lu/Heart Of Stone ....................................................................... 5
59   Fontana H 231             Marina/Me Without You ........................................................................ 5
61   Piccadilly 35002          Can You Keep A Secret/Promises .......................................................... 5
60   Fontana H 278             Blue-Eyed Boy/Don't Push Your Luck ................................................... 5
61   Piccadilly 7N 35011       There I've Said It Again/You Came A Long Way From St. Louis ............. 10
61   Piccadilly 7N 35021       Don't Get Around Much Anymore/Saturday Night ............................... 10
62   Piccadilly 7N 35036       Evil Eye/What More Can I Say ............................................................... 6
62   Parlophone R 4966         I Got A Girl/But I Do ............................................................................. 25
63   Parlophone R 5016         The Man Who Broke The Bank At Monte Carlo/If You Want To Go To Dreamland ... 7
64   Mercury MF 801            Who Was That Girl?/All Night Long ..................................................... 7
64   Mercury MF 811            Another You/Hot And Bothered ........................................................... 7
68   President PT 183          Against The Wall/East Side 628 ............................................................ 7
72   Phoenix NIX 125           Beautiful/Count To Ten ........................................................................ 6
*(see also Lana Sisters, Ella Stone & Moss)*                                                                        15

**SKY 'SUNLIGHT' SAXON**
87   Fierce FRIGHT 009         Dog=God (p/s, with badge, piece of shirt, sugar 'skycubes' & inserts) ... 20
84   Psycho PSYCHO 29          STARRY EYED (LP, clear vinyl) .............................................................. 20
*(see also Seeds)*

**SKY SAXON & THE NEW SEEDS**
90s  Expression EXP 777-3      In Love With Life/Starry Ride/Queen/Tired Of Being Poor ...................... 6

**SAXON (1)**
63   Ace Of Clubs ACL 1173     MEET THE SAXONS (LP) .......................................................................... 80

**SAXON (2)**
79   Carrere SAM 109           Big Teaser/Stallions Of The Highway (12", promo only) ...................... 10
79   Carrere CAR 118           Big Teaser/Stallions Of The Highway (p/s) .......................................... 7
79   Carrere CAR 129           Backs To The Wall/Militia Guard (p/s) ................................................. 7
80   Carrere CAR 165           Suzy Hold On/Judgement Day (live) ..................................................... 6
81   Carrere CAR 180           And The Bands Played On/Hungry Years/Heavy Metal Thunder (7" picture disc) ... 6
83   Carrere CARP 284          Nightmare/Midas Touch (7" picture disc) ........................................... 6
79   Carrere CAL 110           SAXON (LP) ............................................................................................ 15
82   Carrere CAL 137           THE EAGLE HAS LANDED (LP) ............................................................... 15
82   Carrere CAL 137           THE EAGLE HAS LANDED (LP, picture disc) .......................................... 15
83   Carrere CAL 147           THE POWER AND THE GLORY (LP, picture disc) ................................... 15
84   Carrere CALP 200          CRUSADER (LP, picture disc) ................................................................ 15
85   Parlophone SAXONP 2       INNOCENCE IS NO EXCUSE (LP, picture disc) ...................................... 15
87   EMI EMS 1163              DENIM AND LEATHER (LP, blue vinyl reissue) ..................................... 15
93   Warhammer WARLP 10        FOREVER FREE (LP) ............................................................................... 40

**LINDA SAXONE**
64   Pye 7N 15624              Love Is A Many Splendoured Thing/The Other Side Of The Street ........ 10
65   Polydor BM 56015          I've Got To Say No/Another Day Another Night ..................................... 6
65   Polydor BM 56032          Only Last Night/Lucky Girl ................................................................... 6

**SAXONS**
65   Decca F 12179             Saxon War Cry/Click-Ete-Clack ............................................................ 60
*(see also Tornados)*

**JOHNNY SAYLES**
66   Liberty LIB 12042         Deep Down In Your Heart/Anything For You ........................................ 40
04   Soul City SC 160          I Can't Get Enough/Tell Me (Where I Stand) ........................................ 8

**RAT SCABIES**
84   Paradiddle Music HIT 1    Let There Be Rats/Wiped Out/Drums Drums Drums (mail-order only, no p/s) ... 8
*(see also Damned, The Rat & The Whale, Pete Zear)*

**SCABS**
79   Clubland Records SJP 799  Amory Building/Leave Me Alone/Don't Just Sit There/U.R.E. (blue/black or red/black
                               fold out 'envelope' p/s, 2 inserts) ....................................................... 40

**SCAFFOLD**
66   Parlophone R 5443         2 Day's Monday/3 Blind Jellyfish ........................................................ 10
66   Parlophone R 5548         Goodbat Nightman/A Long Strong Black Pudding ............................... 10
67   Parlophone R 5643         Thank U Very Much/Ide B The First ..................................................... 5
68   Parlophone R 5734         Lily The Pink/Buttons On Your Mind ................................................... 5
68   Parlophone R 5679         Do You Remember?/Carry On Krow ..................................................... 8
68   Parlophone R 5703         1-2-3/Today .......................................................................................... 6
69   Parlophone R 5784         Charity Bubbles/Goose ....................................................................... 6
69   Parlophone R 5812         Gin Gan Goolie/Liver Birds ................................................................. 8
70   Parlophone R 5847         All The Way Up/Please - Sorry ............................................................ 8
70   Parlophone R 5866         Busdreams/If I Could Start All Over Again .......................................... 8
71   Parlophone R 5922         Do The Albert/Commercial Break ........................................................ 8

| | | | |
|---|---|---|---|
| 74 | Warner Bros K 16400 | Liverpool Lou/Ten Years On After Strawberry Jam | 6 |
| 68 | Parlophone PMC/PCS 7051 | SCAFFOLD ... - LIVE AT QUEEN ELIZABETH HALL (LP, black/yellow label with "Sold in U.K..." text) | 40 |
| 69 | Parlophone PMC/PCS 7077 | L THE P (LP, black/yellow label with "Sold in U.K..." text) | 30 |
| 73 | Island ILPS 9234 | FRESH LIVER (LP, gatefold sleeve, pink rim palm tree label) | 20 |

*(see also McGough-McGear, Roger McGough, Mike McGear, Liverpool Scene, Grimms, John Gorman)*

**BOZ SCAGGS**
69 Atlantic 588 205 — BOZ SCAGGS (LP) ... 18
*(see also Steve Miller Band, Steve York's Camelo Pardalis)*

**SCALA TIMPANI**
84 1066 Records ST 1 — Winds Of Change/Destiny (no p/s) ... 10
85 Fire FIRE 3 — Winds Of Change/Destiny (p/s) ... 6

**HARVEY SCALES & 7 SOUND**
67 Atlantic 584 146 — Get Down/Love It Is ... 6

**SCAMPS**
59 London HLW 8827 — Petite Fleur/Naomi ... 6

**SCANDAL**
79 Local LOC 1 — Comic Book Hero/Casualty Of Love (p/s) ... 7

**JOHNNY SCAR**
85 Solomonic SM12 025 — United Africa/Dub It In Africa (12") ... 200

**SCARAB**
80 Inferno HEADBANGER 1 — Rock Night/Wicked Woman ... 30
84 Pharaoh PR-001 — Poltergeist/Hell On Wheels (p/s) ... 50
03 Phoenix NWOBHM 7013 — Rock Night/Wicked Woman (reissue, p/s, red vinyl 250 only, numbered) ... 15

**SCARECROW**
78 Spilt Milk SMFM 11278 — SCARECROW (LP, numbered foldout sleeve with insert; beware of watermarked unnumbered copies) ... 150

**SCARED OF THE DARK**
86 Cottage industry CIR 003 — Give Me That Feeling/Summer Soul ... 20

**SCARFACE**
75 DJM DJS 616 — Dance To The Band/Tootsie Roll Baby ... 25

**SCARLET ALIVE**
82 Jive Alive JA001 — THE TERMINAL JIVE AND SCARLET ALIVE EP (2 tracks on one side, p/s, insert) ... 15
82 S.R.R. SRR011 — On Earth And In Heaven/Always (p/s) ... 15

**SCARLET TRAIN**
87 Nightshift NISHI 202 — FIMBRIA (Mini-LP) ... 20

**SCARLETS**
64 Philips BF 1376 — Let's Go/Tambourine Shake ... 6

**CHARLES FRANCIS SCARRATT III**
59 Felsted AF 113 — Two Innocent Lovers/Lovemobile ... 6

**SCARS**
79 Fast Product FAST 8 — Horrorshow/Adult-ery (p/s) ... 10
80 Pre PRE 005 — Love Song/psychomodo (p/s) ... 15
81 Pre PRE 014 — All About You/Author Author (p/s) ... 10
81 Pre PREX 5 — AUTHOR! AUTHOR! (LP) ... 15

**POLLY SCATTERGOOD**
05 Ark 7ARK11 — Glory Hallelujah/Throw Me A Hook Here (white vinyl, p/s) ... 8

**SCATTEROCK**
80 Rite Sound 010 — Wonder Woman/Time ... 40

**SCENE (1)**
80 Inferno BEAT 2 — I've Had Enough/Show 'Em Now (p/s) ... 20

**SCENE (2)**
80 Hole In The Wall HS 1 — Hey Girl/Reach The Top (p/s) ... 50

**SCENE (3)**
83 Diamond DIA 001 — Looking For A Love/Let Me Know (p/s) ... 10
85 Diamond DIA 003 — Something That You Said/Stop-Go (p/s) ... 7
85 Diamond DIA 007 — Good Lovin'/2 Plus 2 (with p/s) ... 15
85 Diamond DIA 007 — Good Lovin'/2 Plus 2 ... 5
*(see also Diplomats)*

**SCEPTRES**
69 Spark SRL 1006 — What's The Matter With Juliet/Something's Coming Along ... 30

**SCHADEL**
66 Parlophone R5899 — The Puppet Man/Oh What A Naughty Man ... 8
68 Pye 7N 17528 — With The Sun In My Eyes/Goodbye Thimble Mill Lane ... 30
70 United Artists UAS 29114 — SCHADEL NO.1 (LP) (G/F) ... 12

**HAL SCHAEFER ORCHESTRA & CHORUS**
58 London HLT 8692 — March Of The Vikings/March Of The Parisian Bakers ... 7

**SCHEER**
93 Son BUACD 293 — Wish You Were Dead/Green Room Sex Kitten/Don't Know Why (p/s) ... 20

**SCHEME**
82 No Label SS001 — SCHEME SONGS (EP, 500 only, 2 inserts) ... 30
86 Scheme LP1 — BLACK & WHITES (LP) ... 25

**SCHEREZADE**
82 Tombstone SRT TOM/S82 CUS 1 — Seventeen/Million Years ... 12

**HANK SCHIFNER**
69 Liberty LBF15244 — Long John/How Or When ... 15

## Lalo SCHIFRIN

### LALO SCHIFRIN
| | | | |
|---|---|---|---|
| 66 | MGM MGM 1329 | Our Venetian Affair/Venice After Dark | 12 |
| 68 | Dot DOT 103 | Mission: Impossible/Jim On The Move | 25 |
| 74 | 20th Century BTC 2150 | Ape Shuffle (Theme From 'Planet Of The Apes')/Escape From Tomorrow | 25 |
| 74 | Warner Bros K16333 | Theme From Enter The Dragon/The Big Battle | 10 |
| 76 | CTI CTSP 5 | Jaws Theme/Quiet Village | 5 |
| 77 | CTI CTSP008 | Theme From 'Most Wanted'/Roller Coaster | 6 |
| 68 | Dot (S)LPD 503 | 'MISSION: IMPOSSIBLE' - MUSIC FROM THE TV SERIES (LP, TV soundtrack) | 40 |
| 69 | Paramount SPFL 252 | MORE 'MISSION: IMPOSSIBLE' (LP, TV soundtrack) | 40 |

### SCHIZO FUN ADDICT
| | | | |
|---|---|---|---|
| 07 | Bracken fern 12 | Dream Of The Portugal Keeper/Traditional/Jenny Says | 12 |
| 08 | Fruits De Mer CRUSTACIAN 01 | Theme One/Ogden's Nut Gone Flake (p/s, coloured vinyl, 300 only) | 40 |
| 14 | Fruits De Mer Crustacean 48 | Theme From Suspiria/In The Long Run/Back Of Her Car (p/s, black vinyl edition, 50 only) | 10 |

### SCHLEIMER K
| | | | |
|---|---|---|---|
| 81 | Omega OMR 001 | SCHLEIMER K (LP) | 20 |
| 82 | Glass GLASS 028 | FUGUTIVE KIND (12" EP, p/s) | 18 |
| 83 | Lone WOlf LW 101 | WOUNDED WOOD (LP) | 40 |

### SCHMETTERLINGE
| | | | |
|---|---|---|---|
| 77 | Pye International 7N 25743 | Boom Boom Boomerang/Mr Moneymaker's Music Show | 10 |

### TOBIAS SCHMIDT
| | | | |
|---|---|---|---|
| 96 | Mosquito MSQ 06 | THE FINGERPRINT EP (12", p/s) | 15 |

### ZAPPATTA SCHMIDT
| | | | |
|---|---|---|---|
| 70 | President PT 318 | You Got The Love/Someone In The Crowd | 40 |
| 70 | Torpedo TOR 28 | Let's Do It Together/Hey Man. Why | 25 |
| 71 | President PTLS 1041 | IT'S GONNA GET YOU (LP) | 100 |

(see also Equals, Eddy Grant)

### OLIVER LINDSEY SCHMITT
| | | | |
|---|---|---|---|
| 72 | Private pressing | GRAFFENSTADDEN (LP) | 30 |

### WOLFGANG SCHMITT
| | | | |
|---|---|---|---|
| 69 | RCA 1301 | The Girl From the Monmouth County/Country Girl | 6 |

### EBERHARD SCHOENER
| | | | |
|---|---|---|---|
| 79 | Harvest HAR 5196 | Video Magic/Code Word Elvis (p/s) | 8 |
| 79 | Harvest SHSM 2030 | VIDEO-FLASHBACK (LP) | 20 |

(see also Police)

### JOHN SCHOFIELD
| | | | |
|---|---|---|---|
| 84 | Arista/Nimbus AN 3022 | BAR TALK (LP, Nimbus Supercut, mail order only from Practical Hi-Fi magazine) | 30 |

### SCHOLARS
| | | | |
|---|---|---|---|
| 64 | Stagesound SDE 29370/1 | THE SCHOLARS (EP, no p/s) | 15 |

### SCHOOL TIES
| | | | |
|---|---|---|---|
| 81 | School Ties SCF 01 | No Future/Screw You | 45 |
| 82 | Quest S/82/Cus 1591 | House Of The Rising Sun/Insanity (no p/s) | 40 |

### SCHOOLBOYS
| | | | |
|---|---|---|---|
| 69 | Junior JR 113 | Do It Now/Blame It On The Children | 15 |

### SCHOOL BOYS
| | | | |
|---|---|---|---|
| 63 | Blue Beat BB 162 | Little Boy Blue/PRINCE BUSTER: Money | 40 |
| 63 | Blue Beat BB 174 | Little Dilly/The Joker (B-side actually by Prince Buster's Allstars) | 40 |
| 64 | Port-O-Jam PJ 4000 | Dream Lover/I Want To Know | 40 |

(see also Bill Gentles)

### SCHOOLERS
| | | | |
|---|---|---|---|
| 69 | Doctor Bird DB 1170 | Ugly Man (actually by Scorchers)/Whip Cracker (actually by Vincent Gordon) | 40 |

### SCHOOLGIRL BITCH
| | | | |
|---|---|---|---|
| 78 | Garage!/Aerco AERS 102 | Abusing The Rules/Thinking For Yourself (spray-painted p/s) | 150 |
| 78 | Garage!/Aerco AERS 102 | Abusing The Rules/Thinking For Yourself ('gasmask' p/s) | 100 |
| 78 | Garage!/Aerco AERS 102 | Abusing The Rules/Thinking For Yourself ('queen' p/s) | 45 |
| 78 | Garage!/Aerco AERS 102 | Abusing The Rules/Thinking For Yourself (no p/s) | 40 |

### SCHOOL GIRLS
| | | | |
|---|---|---|---|
| 63 | Blue Beat BB 168 | Love Another Love/Little Keithie | 20 |
| 63 | Blue Beat BB 185 | Live Up To Justice/Keith My Darling | 20 |
| 64 | Blue Beat BB 214 | Sing And Shout/Last Time | 20 |
| 64 | Blue Beat BB 263 | Never Let You Go/BUSTER'S ALL STARS: Supercharge | 80 |

### SCHOOL MEALS
| | | | |
|---|---|---|---|
| 78 | Edible EAT 001 | Headmaster (with insert, re-labelled Defendents) | 25 |

### SCHOOL OF CULTURE
| | | | |
|---|---|---|---|
| 91 | White CS12 01 | Detonate To Activate/Come On 33 | 40 |

### DON SCHROEDER
| | | | |
|---|---|---|---|
| 62 | Philips BF 3040033 | Quicksand/My Kind Of Woman | 10 |

### JOHN SCHROEDER ORCHESTRA
| | | | |
|---|---|---|---|
| 65 | Piccadilly 7N 35240 | The Fugitive Theme/Don't Break The Heart Of Kimble (in p/s) | 15 |
| 65 | Piccadilly 7N 35240 | The Fugitive Theme/Don't Break The Heart Of Kimble | 6 |
| 65 | Piccadilly 7N 35253 | You've Lost That Lovin' Feeling/Funny How Love Can Be | 6 |
| 65 | Piccadilly 7N 35271 | Agent 00 Soul/Night Rider | 30 |
| 66 | Piccadilly 7N 35280 | Ave Maria No Morro/Peter Popgunn | 5 |
| 66 | Piccadilly 7N 35285 | Hungry For Love/Soul Destroyer | 30 |
| 66 | Piccadilly 7N 35319 | On The Ball (Theme For The World)/The Britannia March | 10 |
| 67 | Piccadilly 7N 35362 | Soul For Sale/Loving You Girl | 30 |

| | | | |
|---|---|---|---|
| 69 | Pye 7N 17862 | The Virgin Soldiers' March/Sweet Soul Talk | 12 |
| 71 | Pye 7N 45108 | One Way Glass/The Bird Has Flown | 15 |
| 66 | Piccadilly N(S)PL 38025 | JOHN SCHROEDER'S WORKING IN THE SOULMINE (LP) | 50 |
| 67 | Piccadilly N(S)PL 38036 | THE DOLLY CATCHER! (LP) | 40 |
| 68 | Marble Arch MAL 839 | WORKING IN THE SOULMINE (LP, reissue) | 20 |
| 71 | Pye NSPL 18362 | WITCHI-TAI-TO (LP, textured gatefold sleeve) | 20 |
| 72 | Polydor 2460 149 | TV VIBRATIONS (LP) | 15 |
| 71 | Polydor 2460 134 | DYLAN VIBRATIONS (LP) | 15 |
| 71 | Polydor 2460 135 | PIANO VIBRATIONS (LP, with Rick Wakeman) | 40 |

## IVY SCHULMAN & BOWTIES
| | | | |
|---|---|---|---|
| 57 | London HLN 8372 | Rock, Pretty Baby/BOWTIES: Ever Since I Can Remember | 50 |

## KLAUS SCHULZE
| | | | |
|---|---|---|---|
| 74 | Caroline CA 2003 | BLACK DANCE (LP, gatefold, black/white/red 'twin' label) | 15 |
| 75 | Caroline CA 2006 | TIMEWIND (LP, gatefold) | 15 |
| 76 | Virgin V2064 | MOONDAWN (LP, unissued) | 0 |
| 77 | Island ISPS 9461 | MIRAGE (LP) | 15 |

*(see also Tangerine Dream) (Voices Of)*

## (VOICES OF) WALTER SCHUMANN
| | | | |
|---|---|---|---|
| 54 | HMV 7M 229 | Haunted House/I Only Have Eyes For You | 8 |
| 55 | HMV 7M 323 | The Man From Laramie/Let Me Hear You Whisper | 8 |

## SCHUNGE
| | | | |
|---|---|---|---|
| 72 | Regal Zonophone RZ 3066 | Misty/Joseph Demanio | 7 |
| 73 | Regal Zonophone RZ 3077 | Ballad Of A Simple Love/Enter The Violins | 7 |
| 72 | Regal Zono. SLRZ 1033 | BALLAD OF A SIMPLE LOVE (LP, unlaminated front sleeve) | 30 |
| 72 | Regal Zono. SLRZ 1033 | BALLAD OF A SIMPLE LOVE (LP, laminated front sleeve) | 25 |

## SCHWARTZENEGGER
| | | | |
|---|---|---|---|
| 94 | Rugger Bugger SEEP 009 | THE WAY THINGS ARE AND OTHER STORIES (LP) | 20 |

## SCIENCE POPTION
| | | | |
|---|---|---|---|
| 67 | Columbia DB 8106 | You've Got Me High/Back In Town | 100 |

## SCIENTIST
| | | | |
|---|---|---|---|
| 69 | Amalgamated AMG 848 | Professor In Action/SUPERSONICS: Reflections Of Don D | 60 |
| 80 | JB JBLP 004 | INTRODUCING (LP) | 75 |
| 80 | Greensleeves GREL 13 | HEAVYWEIGHT DUB CHAMPION (LP) | 40 |
| 81 | Starlight SLD 901 | DUB LANDING (LP) | 45 |
| 81 | Kingdom KVL 9001 | IN THE KINGDOM OF DUB (LP) | 40 |
| 81 | Greensleeves GREL 25 | RIDS THE WORLD OF THE EVIL CURSE OF THE VAMPIRE (LP) | 40 |
| 81 | Jah Guidance VPRLP 1007 | IN DUB (LP) | 25 |
| 81 | Greensleeves GREL 19 | MEETS THE SPACE INVADERS (LP) | 40 |
| 82 | Greensleeves GREL 37 | WINS THE WORLD CUP (LP) | 40 |
| 82 | Selena SLP 001 | SCIENTIST MEETS THE ROOTS RADICS (LP) | 30 |
| 82 | Greensleeves GREL 46 | ENCOUNTERS PAC MAN (LP) | 50 |
| 82 | Kingdom KVL 9011 | HIGH PRIEST OF DUB (LP) | 30 |
| 86 | Kingdom KVC 6005 | CRUCIAL CUTS VOLUME 2 (LP) | 20 |
| 89 | Tamoki Wambesi TWP 1022 | INTERNATIONAL HEROES DUB (LP, with The Forces Of Music) | 25 |
| 96 | Blood & Fire BAFLP 007 | DUB IN ROOTS TRADITION (LP) | 15 |
| 08 | Auralux LUXXLP 021 | WORLD AT WAR (LP, reissue) | 18 |

## SCIENTIST & PRINCE JAMMY
| | | | |
|---|---|---|---|
| 82 | Trojan TRLS 210 | SCIENTIST & PRINCE JAMMY STRIKE BACK (LP) | 40 |
| 82 | Starlight SLDLP 903 | DUB LANDING VOL 2 (LP) | 25 |
| 97 | Trojan TRLS 210 | SCIENTIST & PRINCE JAMMY STRIKE BACK (LP, reissue) | 15 |

## SCIENTIST VERSUS PRINCE JAMMY
| | | | |
|---|---|---|---|
| 80 | Greensleeves GRED 10 | THE BIG SHOWDOWN 1980 (LP) | 30 |
| 82 | Starlight SLDLP 903 | DUB LANDING VOLUME 2 (LP) | 25 |

## SCIENTIST V THE PROFESSOR
| | | | |
|---|---|---|---|
| 83 | Kingdom KVL 9015 | DUB DUEL AT KING TUBBY'S (LP) | 35 |

## SCIENTISTS
| | | | |
|---|---|---|---|
| 85 | Karbon KAR 007 | You Only Live Twice/If It's The Last Thing I Do (p/s) | 25 |
| 85 | Karbon KAR 101 L | YOU GET WHAT YOU DESERVE (LP) | 20 |
| 86 | Karbon KAR 103 L | WEIRD LOVE (LP) | 20 |
| 87 | Karbon KAR 105 L | THE HUMAN JUKEBOX (LP) | 20 |

## SCISSOR FITS
| | | | |
|---|---|---|---|
| 80 | Tortch TOR 005 | SOON AFTER DARK EP | 10 |

## SCONEHEADS
| | | | |
|---|---|---|---|
| 81 | Linden Sound LS 01 | GO BUCKSKIN (EP, 700 pressed) | 30 |

## SCOOP
| | | | |
|---|---|---|---|
| 80 | Sharp POINT 1 | You Can Do It/Disco/My Friend Tony/Anonymity (p/s) | 75 |

## SCORCHED EARTH (1)
| | | | |
|---|---|---|---|
| 74 | Youngblood YB1503 | On The Run/Can You Feel It | 15 |
| 74 | Philips 6006422 | On The Run/Super Woman | 12 |

## SCORCHED EARTH (2)
| | | | |
|---|---|---|---|
| 85 | Carrere CAR 342 | Tomorrow Never Comes/Questions (promo only) | 35 |
| 85 | Carrere CART 342 | Tomorrow Never Comes/Questions/So Long/Where Do We Go From Here (12", initial black sleeve) | 70 |
| 85 | Carrere CART 342 | Tomorrow Never Comes/Questions/So Long/Where Do We Go From Here (12", later red sleeve with insert) | 35 |

## ERROL SCORCHER
| | | | |
|---|---|---|---|
| 78 | Ballistic UAS 30198 | RASTAFIRE (LP, with the Revolutionaries) | 25 |

## SCORCHERS
| | | |
|---|---|---|
| 69 | Camel CA 17 | Hold On Tight/THE ROYALS: 100 Lbs Of Clay ........................................... 50 |
| 69 | Duke DU 26 | Hear Ya/VIBRATORS: Live Life ........................................................... 60 |

*(see also Neville Hinds)*

## SCORE
| | | |
|---|---|---|
| 66 | Decca F 12527 | Please Please Me/Beg Me ............................................................ 200 |

## SCORN
| | | |
|---|---|---|
| 92 | Earache MOSH 54 | VAE SOLIS (2-LP) ...................................................................... 20 |
| 95 | Earache SCORN 001 | ELLIPSIS (5 x 12" box set) .......................................................... 18 |

## SCORPION & BORIS GARDINER HAPPENING
| | | |
|---|---|---|
| 73 | Dragon DRA 1002 | Deadly Sting/BORIS GARDINER HAPPENING: Boing Boing ........................... 5 |

## SCORPIONS (GERMANY)
| | | |
|---|---|---|
| 77 | RCA PB 5556 | He's A Woman, She's A Man/Suspender Love .................................... 8 |
| 79 | Harvest HAR 5185 | Is Anybody There?/Another Piece Of Meat (12", p/s) ......................... 10 |
| 84 | Harvest 12HARP 5231 | Big City Nights/Bad Boys Running Wild (12" picture disc, die-cut sleeve) ... 12 |
| 91 | Vertigo VERX 58 | Wind Of Change (12", white vinyl, 3-D sleeve) ................................. 12 |
| 75 | RCA RS 1039 | IN TRANCE (LP, 'breast' sleeve) ............................................... 20 |
| 76 | RCA RS 1023 | FLY TO THE RAINBOW (LP) ...................................................... 20 |
| 76 | RCA PPL 1-4225 | VIRGIN KILLER (LP, please note that 'banned; cover is German pressing not U.K.) ... 15 |
| 79 | Harvest LP SHSP 4097 | LOVE DRIVE (LP) ................................................................ 20 |
| 80 | Harvest SHSP 4113 | ANIMAL MAGNETISM (LP, inner sleeve) ....................................... 15 |
| 82 | H.M. worldwide HMILP 2 | LONESOME CROW (LP, "castle" cover, clear vinyl) ........................... 20 |
| 82 | H.M. Worldwide HMILP 2 | LONESOME CROW (LP, "castle" cover, black vinyl) .......................... 15 |
| 82 | H.M. Worldwide HMIPD 2 | LONESOME CROW (LP, picture disc, re-issue) ............................... 15 |
| 82 | Harvest SHVL 823 | BLACKOUT (LP, black or green print on label, inner sleeve) .............. 15 |
| 88 | Harvest SHSPP 4125 | SAVAGE AMUSEMENT (LP, picture disc, with lyric sheet) .................... 15 |
| 93 | Mercury 518 280-1 | FACE THE HEAT (LP) ............................................................ 18 |

*(see also Group, UFO)*

## SCORPIONS (JAMAICA)
| | | |
|---|---|---|
| 72 | Green Door GD 4019 | Breaking Your Heart/IN CROWD BAND: Breaking Your Heart Version ........... 6 |

*(see also Bill Gentles, Lloyd Jackson)*

## SCORPIONS (U.K.)
| | | |
|---|---|---|
| 61 | Parlophone R 4740 | (Ghost) Riders In The Sky/Torquay ............................................. 20 |
| 61 | Parlophone R 4768 | Rockin' At The Phil/Scorpio .................................................... 20 |
| 93 | Sting SITTEP 1 | BACK TO THE TRACKS (EP) ..................................................... 12 |

## COLIN SCOT
| | | |
|---|---|---|
| 71 | United Artists UP 35216 | Hey! Sandy/Nite People ....................................................... 5 |
| 73 | Warner Bros K 16330 | Call Me Mr Blue/It's Gonna Be Alright ...................................... 7 |
| 71 | United Artists UAG 29154 | COLIN SCOT WITH FRIENDS (LP, laminated gatefold sleeve, with Peter Hammill & Peter Gabriel) ................................................................ 25 |

*(see also Peter Hammill, Peter Gabriel)*

## JOCK SCOT
| | | |
|---|---|---|
| 80 | Stiff MAX 1 | A Souvenir To Commemorate The Wedding Of Dave (Robinson) And Rosemary. Featuring the dulcet tones Of Jock Scot (Promo Only) ...................... 150 |

## WINSTON SCOTLAND
| | | |
|---|---|---|
| 72 | Green Door GD 4027 | My (Girl) Little Filly/BUNNY BROWN: My Girl ................................ 10 |
| 72 | Punch PH 100 | Butter Cup/RONALD WILSON: I Care ........................................ 15 |

*(see also Bunny Flip, Big Youth, Bongo Les, Lennox Brown, Dennis Alcapone)*

## SCOTS OF ST. JAMES
| | | |
|---|---|---|
| 66 | Go AJ 111404 | Gypsy/Tic Toc ................................................................ 200 |
| 67 | Spot JW 1 | Timothy/Eiderdown Clown ................................................. 350 |

*(see also Hopscotch, Forever More, Five Day Rain)*

## ANDY SCOTT
| | | |
|---|---|---|
| 75 | RCA RCA 2629 | Lady Starlight/Where D'Ya Go (p/s) ......................................... 12 |
| 83 | Static TAK 10 | Krugerrands/Face (p/s) ...................................................... 8 |
| 84 | Static TAK 24 | Let Her Dance/Suck It And See (p/s) ....................................... 10 |
| 84 | Static TAK 24-12 | Let Her Dance (Full Version)/(Instrumental)/Suck It And See (12", p/s) ... 10 |
| 84 | Static TAK 31 | Invisible/Never Too Young (clear vinyl, stickered PVC sleeve) ........... 12 |
| 84 | Statik TAK 31-12 | Invisible (Single Version)/(Instrumental)/Invisible (Extended Version)/ Never Too Young (12", clear vinyl, stickered PVC sleeve) ................ 12 |

*(see also Sweet, Elastic Band, Mayfield's Mule)*

## ANITA SCOTT
| | | |
|---|---|---|
| 61 | Columbia DB 4623 | A Million And One Tears/Come On And Dance With Me .................... 15 |

## ARTIE SCOTT ORCHESTRA
| | | |
|---|---|---|
| 70 | Major Minor MM 670 | March Of The Skinheads/Love At First Sight .............................. 7 |

## BILLY SCOTT
| | | |
|---|---|---|
| 58 | London HLU 8565 | You're The Greatest/That's Why I Was Born .............................. 20 |
| 60 | Top Rank JAR 270 | Carole/Stairway To The Stairs ............................................. 7 |

## BOBBY SCOTT (1)
| | | |
|---|---|---|
| 56 | London HL 8254 | Chain Gang/Shadrack ....................................................... 40 |
| 55 | London Jazz LZ-N 14001 | BOBBY SCOTT TRIO (10" LP) ............................................... 15 |

## BOBBY SCOTT (2)
| | | |
|---|---|---|
| 70 | Reflection RS2 | Witness To A War/I Wish I Could Walk Away ............................. 6 |

## BRUCE SCOTT
| | | |
|---|---|---|
| 65 | Mercury MF 857 | I Made An Angel Cry/Don't Say Goodbye To Me ........................ 25 |
| 65 | MGM MGM 1291 | Once A Thief Twice A Thief/So Much To Live For ....................... 7 |

## BUNNY SCOTT
| | | |
|---|---|---|
| 75 | 2nd Tracs SK3 | Come On Party/Azul Party .................................................. 15 |

| 75 | Upsetter UP 100 | I Am I Said/Let Love Us Now (as Bunny Ruggs) | 12 |
| 75 | KLIK KLP 9004 | TO LOVE SOMEBODY (LP) | 25 |

## BUNNY 'RUGS' SCOTT/NEVILLE GRANT

| 12 | Black Swan THB 7019 | Big May/NEVILLE GRANT: Sick And Tired | 12 |

## DEREK SCOTT ORCHESTRA

| 63 | Pye 7N 15500 | Hancock's Tune/Spying Tonight | 5 |
| 67 | Philips BF 1568 | Honey Lane/Song Without Words | 5 |

## FREDDIE SCOTT

| 63 | Colpix PX 692 | Hey Girl/The Slide | 35 |
| 63 | Colpix PX 709 | I Got A Woman/Brand New World | 35 |
| 67 | London HLZ 10103 | Are You Lonely For Me/Where Were You | 15 |
| 67 | London HLZ 10123 | Cry To Me/No One Could Ever Love You | 15 |
| 67 | London HLZ 10139 | Am I Grooving You?/Never You Mind | 10 |
| 67 | London HLZ 10172 | He Ain't Give You None/Run Joe | 10 |
| 69 | Roulette RO 509 | Sugar Sunday/Johnny's Hill | 6 |
| 71 | Jay Boy BOY 34 | Just Like A Flower/Spanish Harlem | 10 |
| 72 | Jay Boy BOY 59 | Are You Lonely For Me Baby/The Woman Of My Love | 10 |
| 72 | Upfront UP 1 | The Great If/Deep In The Night | 10 |
| 71 | Joy JOYS 215 | ARE YOU LONELY FOR ME (LP) | 25 |

## GLORIA SCOTT

| 74 | Casablanca CAS 152 | Just As Long As We're Together/There Will Never Be Another | 8 |

## HAZEL SCOTT

| 53 | Capitol LC 6607 | LATE SHOW (10" LP) | 20 |

## JACK SCOTT (& CHANTONES)

| 58 | London HLU 8626 | My True Love/Leroy | 10 |
| 58 | London HLL 8765 | With Your Love/Geraldine (as Jack Scott with Chantones) | 15 |
| 59 | London HLL 8804 | Goodbye Baby/Save My Soul (as Jack Scott with Chantones) | 15 |
| 59 | London HL 7069 | Goodbye Baby/Save My Soul (export issue) | 20 |
| 59 | London HLL 8851 | I Never Felt Like This/Bella | 20 |
| 59 | London HLL 8912 | The Way I Walk/Midgie (triangular or round centre) | 25 |
| 59 | London HLL 8970 | There Comes A Time/Baby Marie (triangular or round centre) | 25 |
| 60 | Top Rank JAR 280 | What In The World's Come Over You/Baby, Baby | 6 |
| 60 | Top Rank JAR 375 | Burning Bridges/Oh, Little One | 7 |
| 60 | Top Rank JAR 419 | Cool Water/It Only Happened Yesterday | 7 |
| 60 | Top Rank JAR 524 | Patsy/Old Time Religion | 10 |
| 61 | Top Rank JAR 547 | Is There Something On Your Mind/Found A Woman | 10 |
| 61 | Capitol CL 15200 | A Little Feeling/Now That I | 10 |
| 61 | Capitol CL 15216 | My Dream Come True/Strange Desire | 10 |
| 62 | Capitol CL 15236 | Steps 1 And 2/One Of These Days | 10 |
| 63 | Capitol CL 15302 | All I See Is Blue/Meo Myo | 10 |
| 62 | Capitol CL 15261 | I Can't Hold Your Letters In My Arms/Sad Story | 10 |
| 59 | London RE-I 1205 | MY TRUE LOVE (EP, initial triangular centre) | 40 |
| 59 | London RE-I 1205 | MY TRUE LOVE (EP, later round centre) | 25 |
| 61 | Top Rank JKP 3002 | WHAT IN THE WORLD'S COME OVER YOU (EP) | 25 |
| 61 | Top Rank JKP 3011 | I REMEMBER HANK WILLIAMS (EP) | 25 |
| 58 | London HA-L 2156 | JACK SCOTT (LP) | 100 |
| 60 | Top Rank BUY 034 | I REMEMBER HANK WILLIAMS (LP) | 40 |
| 60 | Top Rank 25-024 | WHAT IN THE WORLD'S COME OVER YOU (LP) | 40 |
| 61 | Top Rank 35-109 | THE SPIRIT MOVES ME (LP) | 30 |
| 64 | Capitol T 2035 | BURNING BRIDGES (LP, mono) | 25 |
| 64 | Capitol ST 2035 | BURNING BRIDGES (LP, stereo) | 30 |

## JANET SCOTT & JACKIE RAE

| 60 | Fontana TFE 17203 | SWEET TALK (EP, also stereo STFE 8009) | 12 |
| 60 | Fontana TFL 5102 | WE LOVE LIFE! (LP, also stereo STFL 533) | 15 |

## JIMMY SCOTT

| 69 | Revolution REV 002 | Ob-La-Di, Ob-La-Da/Story Part 2 - Allulo & Doh | 40 |
| 70 | Revolution Soul REVS 505 | Doh (Ob-La-Di-Ob-Lh-Da Story Part 2/Allulo (Part 1) Note: "lh" is how it is on the label | 40 |
| 74 | Deram DM 425 | We All Need A Hero/Moonshine | 7 |

## JOHN SCOTT

| 60 | Parlophone R 4697 | Hi-Flutin' Boogie/Peace Pipe | 6 |
| 65 | Parlophone R 5333 | Sailing By The Song Of The Cuckoo (as Johnny Scott) | 8 |
| 65 | Parlophone R 5380 | A Study In Terror/Punjab | 10 |
| 67 | Polydor 56184 | Rocket To The Moon Theme/The Long Duel Theme | 15 |
| 68 | Spark SRL 1008 | Amsterdam Affair Theme/Kathleen | 8 |
| 66 | Columbia SX 6026 | LONDON SWINGS (LP) | 15 |
| 67 | Columbia S(C)X 6149 | COMMUNICATION (LP) | 30 |

## JOHNNY SCOTT

| 70 | Fontana 6383 002 | PURCELL VARIATIONS FOR FIVE (LP) | 25 |
| 73 | JSD JSD 100 | JOHN SCOTT DEMONSTRATION RECORD (LP, beware, many warped) | 80 |

## JUDI SCOTT

| 68 | Page One POF 066 | Billy Sunshine/Happy Song | 25 |

## JUDY SCOTT

| 57 | Brunswick 05687 | The Game Of Love (A-One And A-Two)/With All My Heart | 10 |
| 57 | Brunswick 05704 | Parlour Piano Theme/A Tender Word | 8 |

## JULIAN SCOTT

| 61 | Columbia DB 4571 | My Steady Date/So Tired | 7 |

## LINDA SCOTT (1)

| | | | |
|---|---|---|---|
| 60 | Columbia DB 4638 | I've Told Every Little Star/Three Guesses | 5 |
| 61 | Columbia DB 4692 | Don't Bet Money, Honey/Starlight Starbright | 10 |
| 61 | Columbia DB 4748 | I Don't Know Why/It's All Because | 10 |
| 61 | Columbia DB 4829 | Count Every Star/Land Of Stars | 10 |
| 62 | Pye International 7N 25146 | Never In A Million Years/Through The Summer | 15 |
| 63 | London HLR 9802 | Let's Fall In Love/I Know It, You Know It | 15 |
| 61 | Columbia 33SX 1386 | STARLIGHT, STARBRIGHT (LP) | 50 |

## LINDA SCOTT (2)

| | | | |
|---|---|---|---|
| 69 | CBS 4528 | The Composer/You Made A Fool Out Of Me | 15 |
| 69 | CBS 4246 | First Of All/The Answer's In My Eyes | 5 |

## MAUREEN SCOTT

| | | | |
|---|---|---|---|
| 63 | HMV POP 1184 | He's So Near/Ugly Bug Ball | 6 |

## MCBEAN SCOTT & CHAMPIONS

| | | | |
|---|---|---|---|
| 70 | Jackpot JP 744 | Top Of The World/LARRY LAWRENCE & CHAMPIONS: Everybody Reggae | 15 |

## MIKE SCOTT (1)

| | | | |
|---|---|---|---|
| 65 | Mercury MF 906 | I Am A Rock/I'm Gonna Be Somebody Someday | 6 |

## MIKE SCOTT (2)

| | | | |
|---|---|---|---|
| 95 | Chrysalis CHR 6108 | BRING'EM ALL IN (LP, gatefold with inner) | 15 |

## NEIL SCOTT

| | | | |
|---|---|---|---|
| 61 | Pye International 7N 25096 | Bobby/I Haven't Found It With Another | 8 |

## NICKY SCOTT

| | | | |
|---|---|---|---|
| 67 | Immediate IM 044 | Big City/Everything's Gonna Be Alright | 60 |
| 67 | Immediate IM 045 | Backstreet Girl/Chain Reaction | 50 |
| 69 | Pye 7N 17688 | Honey Pie/No More Tomorrow | 7 |

(see also Diane Ferraz & Nicky Scott)

## PEGGY SCOTT & JO JO BENSON

| | | | |
|---|---|---|---|
| 68 | Polydor 56745 | Lover's Holiday/Here With Me | 10 |
| 69 | Polydor 56750 | Pickin' Wild Mountain Berries/Pure Love And Pleasure | 8 |
| 69 | Polydor 56761 | Soulshake/We Were Made For Each Other | 10 |
| 69 | Polydor 56773 | We Got Our Own Bag/I Want To Love You Babe | 8 |
| 71 | Atlantic 2091 066 | I Thank You/Spreadin' Love | 5 |
| 69 | Polydor 583 731 | SOULSHAKE (LP) | 25 |
| 70 | Polydor 583 756 | LOVER'S HEAVEN (LP) | 25 |

## ROBIN SCOTT

| | | | |
|---|---|---|---|
| 69 | Head HDS 4003 | The Sailor/Sound Of The Rain | 40 |
| 69 | Head HDLS 6003 | WOMAN FROM THE WARM GRASS (LP, textured sleeve with insert, yellow/black label) | 400 |
| 07 | Sunbeam SBBLP 5009 | WOMAN FROM THE WARM GRASS (LP, reissue) | 15 |

(see also Mighty Baby, M)

## RONNIE SCOTT

| | | | |
|---|---|---|---|
| 54 | Esquire 10-335 | Night And Day | 10 |
| 56 | Decca FJ 10712 | Basie Talks/Flying Home (as Ronnie Scott Orchestra) | 8 |
| 57 | Tempo A 153 | I'll Take Romance/Speak Low (as Ronnie Scott New Quintet) | 35 |
| 55 | Esquire EP 31 | RONNIE SCOTT ORCHESTRA (EP) | 20 |
| 55 | Esquire EP 51 | RONNIE SCOTT QUARTET (EP) | 25 |
| 55 | Esquire EP 61 | RONNIE SCOTT ORCHESTRA (EP) | 20 |
| 55 | Esquire EP 65 | RONNIE SCOTT QUINTET (EP) | 25 |
| 56 | Esquire EP 81 | RONNIE SCOTT ORCHESTRA (EP) | 25 |
| 56 | Esquire EP 85 | RONNIE SCOTT ORCHESTRA (EP) | 30 |
| 56 | Esquire EP 95 | RONNIE SCOTT ORCHESTRA (EP) | 25 |
| 56 | Tempo EXA 45 | RONNIE SCOTT BLOWS WITH THE DIZZY REECE QUARTET (EP) | 100 |
| 52 | Esquire 20-006 | RONNIE SCOTT QUINTET (10" LP) | 100 |
| 54 | Esquire 32-001 | THE RONNIE SCOTT JAZZ CLUB VOLUME 1 (LP) | 50 |
| 54 | Esquire 32-002 | THE RONNIE SCOTT JAZZ CLUB VOLUME 2 (LP) | 50 |
| 54 | Esquire 32-003 | THE RONNIE SCOTT JAZZ CLUB VOLUME 3 (LP) | 50 |
| 54 | Esquire 32-006 | THE RONNIE SCOTT JAZZ CLUB VOLUME 4 (LP) | 50 |
| 56 | Decca LF 1261 | AT THE ROYAL FESTIVAL HALL (10" LP) | 50 |
| 57 | Philips BBL 7153 | PRESENTING THE RONNIE SCOTT SEXTET (LP) | 100 |
| 66 | Fontana TL 5332 | THE NIGHT IS SCOTT AND YOU'RE SO SWINGABLE (LP) | 45 |
| 69 | CBS Realm Jazz 523661 | LIVE AT RONNIE SCOTT'S (LP) | 30 |
| 74 | RCA Victor LPL1 | SCOTT AT RONNIE'S (LP) | 20 |
| 77 | Pye NSPL 18542 | SERIOUS GOLD (LP) | 15 |

(see also Jazz Couriers, Tubby Hayes, Dizzy Reece)

## SHARON SCOTT

| | | | |
|---|---|---|---|
| 96 | Kent 6T 12 | (Putting My Heart) Under Lock And Key/DEAN COURTNEY: Today Is My Day | 35 |

## SHIRLEY SCOTT

| | | | |
|---|---|---|---|
| 62 | Esquire 32-186 | HIP TWIST (LP) | 25 |
| 66 | Transatlantic PR 7205 | HIP SOUL (LP) | 18 |
| 69 | Atlantic 588 175 | SOUL SONG (LP) | 15 |
| 71 | Chess 6310 109 | MYSTICAL LADY (LP) | 15 |

## SIMON SCOTT (& LE ROYS)

| | | | |
|---|---|---|---|
| 64 | Parlophone R 5164 | Move It Baby/What Kind Of Woman (with Le Roys) | 15 |
| 64 | Parlophone R 5207 | My Baby's Got Soul/Midnight (with Le Roys) | 12 |
| 65 | Parlophone R 5298 | Tell Him I'm Not Home (as Simon Scott & All Nite Workers)/Heart Cry | 18 |
| 69 | Polydor 56355 | Brave New World/I'm The Universe | 100 |

(see also Le Roys)

**TOM SCOTT**
77   Epic EPC 5589                    Gotcha (Theme From 'Starsky & Hutch')/Smoothin' On Down .................. 12

**RAMBLIN' TOMMY SCOTT**
54   Parlophone CMSP 15               Ain't Love Grand/What Do You Know - I Love Her (export issue) ............... 20

**TOMMY SCOTT**
62   Decca F 11474                    Angela/Did You (as Jay & Tommy Scott) ........................................... 6
64   Decca F 11839                    Who Will It Be?/If It's Me That You Want ........................................ 5
64   Decca F 11942                    Wrap Your Troubles In Dreams/Blueberry Hill ................................... 5

**TONY SCOTT**
69   Escort ES 805                    What Am I To Do/Bring Back That Smile ......................................... 45

**SHEILA SCOTT WILKINGSON**
68   SNB 55-4124                      Down River/Quiet Man .................................................................. 10

**GIL SCOTT-HERON (& BRIAN JACKSON)**
73   Philips 6073 705                 Lady Day And John Coltrane/When You Are Who You Are (with Pretty Purdie & The
                                      Playboys) .................................................................................. 20
78   Arista ARIST 169                 The Bottle (live)/Hello Sunday, Hello Road ..................................... 8
78   Arista ARIST 169                 The Bottle (live)/Hello Sunday, Hello Road (12") ........................... 20
79   Inferno HEAT 23                  The Bottle (Drunken Mix)/The Bottle (Sober Mix) (with Brian Jackson) ..... 10
81   Arista ARIST 452                 Storm Music/Gun/B Movie ........................................................... 5
73   Philips 6369 415                 PIECES OF A MAN (LP) ............................................................... 35
74   RCA SF 8428                      THE REVOLUTION WILL NOT BE TELEVISED (LP) ......................... 25
75   Arista ARTY 106                  FIRST MINUTES OF A NEW DAY (LP) ........................................... 15
76   Arista DARTY 1                   IT'S YOUR WORLD (LP, with Brian Jackson) .................................. 30

**SCOTTY (DAVID SCOTT)**
70   Songbird SB 1044                 Sesame Street/CRYSTALITES: Version .......................................... 20
71   Duke DU 106                      Donkey Skank (with Tennors)/MURPHY'S ALLSTARS: Version ........... 20
71   Songbird SB 1049                 Riddle I This/Musical Chariot .................................................... 12
71   Songbird SB 1051                 Jam Rock Style/Jam Rock Style Version (with Crystalites) ................ 10
71   Songbird SB 1056                 Penny For Your Song/CRYSTALITES: Version ............................... 10
72   Songbird SB 1080                 Clean Race/CRYSTALITES: Version Train ..................................... 10
72   Harry J. HJ 6642                 Skank In Bed/BONGO HERMAN: African Breakfast ........................ 8
73   Count Shelley CS 036             Salvation Train/KEN PARKER: Message To Mary ........................... 8
71   Trojan TRL 33                    SCHOOL DAYS (LP) .................................................................. 60
*(see also Lloyd Charmers, Joe White)*

**SCRAPING FOETUS OFF THE WHEEL**
80s  Womb 12                         Ramrod/Boxhead/Smut ................................................................ 5
81   Womb WOMB-OYBL-2                 HOLE (LP, gatefold sleeve with lyrics, also listed as FDL 3) .............. 15
*(see also Foetus,You've Got Foetus On Your Breath, Philip & His Foetus Vibrations, Foetus Inc, Foetus Uber Frisco)*

**SCRAPYARD**
58   Abbey APR 168                    RECIPRICAL RHUMBAS (LP, private press, 250 copies, with insert) ....... 200

**SCRATCH ACID**
86   Fundamental HOLY 1               SCRATCH ACID (Mini-LP) ........................................................... 20
86   Fundamental SAVE 12              JUST KEEP EATING (LP) ............................................................ 15
*(see also Jesus Lizard)*

**SCREAMER**
75   Arista ARISTA 18                 City Or Bust/We Got Hairs .......................................................... 10

**SCREAMING DEAD**
82   Skull DEAD 1                     Valley Of The Dead/Schoolgirl Junkie (p/s) .................................. 15
83   Skull DEAD 2                     Paint It Black/Warriors (p/s) ...................................................... 18
83   No Future OI 25                  NIGHT CREATURES EP (12") ...................................................... 20
84   Angel ANF 001                    THE DANSE MACABRE COLLECTION EP (12") ............................... 10
85   Angel ANG 002                    A DREAM OF YESTERDAY (12" EP, p/s) ....................................... 10

**DELTON SCREECHIE**
77   Moa Anbessa MOA 0014             Jah Is My Light/Version ............................................................. 7
80   Kim KIM 18                       My Black Girl/Diamond & Pearl/B DONALDSON & U BLACK : You Are Mine (12") ... 15
80   Moa Anbessa MA004                She Is My Woman/Woman Version (12") ...................................... 15
81   Moa Anbessa Intl MALP 001        LIVING IN THE GHETTO (LP) ...................................................... 30
81   Moa Anbessa Intl MALP 002        SUFFERING IN THE GHETTO (LP) ............................................... 50

**SCREECHING WEASEL**
88   Wet Spots WETLP 005              BOOGADA BOOGADA BOOGADA (LP) .......................................... 25
88   What Goes On GOES ON 18          SCREECHING WEASEL (LP, with insert) ....................................... 20

**SCREEMER**
76   Bell Bell 1483                   Interplanetary Twist/Billy .......................................................... 10

**SCREEN**
95   Muzic W'out Control MWC          I Wait For You (Sweep Sweep Mix)/I Wait For You (Radio Sweep Mix)/I Wait For You
     021                              (Pink Noize Mix)/I Wait For You (T Rex Mix) (12', p/s) .................... 60

**SCREEN GEMZ**
79   Inflatable IN 001                I Just Can't Stand Cars/Teenage Teenage .................................. 200

**SCREEN IDOLS**
79   Cobra COB 2                      Blindman/Hit Me Where It Hurts (p/s) ........................................ 10
80   Superstition SR1                 Routine/Power Supply (p/s) ........................................................ 5

**SCRITTI POLITTI**
78   St. Pancras SCRIT 1              Skank Bloc Bologna/Is And Ought Of The Western World/28.8.78 (photocopied
                                      stapled foldout p/s, hand-stamped white labels) ........................... 20
79   Rough Trade RT 027T              4 A SIDES: Doubt Beat/Confidences/Bibbly O'Tek/P.A.s (12" EP) ....... 10
79   Rough Trade RT 034/St            WORK IN PROGRESS : 2ND PEEL SESSION (7" EP p/s) ................... 18
     Pancras SCRIT 2

Rare Record Price Guide 2018

MINT VALUE £

## SCROTUM POLES
| | | | |
|---|---|---|---|
| 79 | Scrotum Poles ERECT 1 | Revelation: Why Don't You Come Out Tonight?/Night Train/Pick The Cat's Eyes Out/ Helicopter Honeymoon/Radio Tay (handwritten labels, 2 p/s designs, with insert) | 120 |
| 79 | Scrotum Poles ERECT 1 | Revelation: Why Don't You Come Out Tonight?/Night Train/Pick The Cat's Eyes Out/ Helicopter Honeymoon/Radio Tay (handwritten labels, 2 p/s designs, without insert) | 100 |

## SCROUNGER
| | | | |
|---|---|---|---|
| 76 | Anchor ANC 1029 | Parisian Cafe Blue/Telephone Song | 5 |
| 77 | Anchor ANC 1037 | Our Love/So Here I Stay | 5 |

## SCRUBS
| | | | |
|---|---|---|---|
| 86 | Anubis ANU 003 | Battle (p/s) | 15 |
| 87 | Flicknife FLS 035 | Time For You (p/s) | 10 |

## SCRUFF
| | | | |
|---|---|---|---|
| 78 | Track 2094140 | Get Out Of My Way/Rock N Roll Woman | 6 |

## SCRUGG
| | | | |
|---|---|---|---|
| 68 | Pye 7N 17451 | I Wish I Was Five/Everyone Can See | 90 |
| 68 | Pye 7N 17551 | Lavender Popcorn/Sandwichboard Man | 50 |
| 69 | Pye 7N 17656 | Will The Real Geraldine Please Stand Up/Only George | 90 |

*(see also Floribunda Rose, John T. Kongos)*

## IRENE SCRUGGS
| | | | |
|---|---|---|---|
| 50s | Poydras 80 | You've Got What I Want/My Back To The Wall | 8 |

## DAVID SEA
| | | | |
|---|---|---|---|
| 07 | Shotgun 101 | Believe In Me/Let's Just Get Together | 6 |

## MR. JOHNNY SEA
| | | | |
|---|---|---|---|
| 60s | Fontana FJL 315 | EVERYBODY'S FAVOURITE (LP) | 15 |

## SEA & CAKE
| | | | |
|---|---|---|---|
| 94 | Rough Trade THRILL 021 | SEA & CAKE (LP) | 20 |
| 97 | Thrill Jockey THRILL LP 039UK | THE FAWN (LP, gatefold) | 18 |

*(see also Tortoise)*

## SEA-DERS
| | | | |
|---|---|---|---|
| 67 | Decca F 22576 | Thanks A Lot/Undecidedly | 80 |
| 67 | Decca DFE-R 8674 | THE SEA-DERS (EP, export issue) | 250 |

*(see also Cedars)*

## SEAHORSES
| | | | |
|---|---|---|---|
| 97 | Geffen GEF 25134 | DO IT YOURSELF (LP, inner) | 40 |

*(see also Stone Roses)*

## DAVE SEALEY
| | | | |
|---|---|---|---|
| 69 | DJM DJS 210 | Picking Up The Pieces/I Can't Go On Living Without You | 6 |

## PHIL SEAMAN
| | | | |
|---|---|---|---|
| 68 | Verve (S)VLP 9220 | PHIL SEAMAN NOW ... LIVE (LP) | 200 |
| 60s | Decibel BSN 103 | PHIL SEAMAN STORY (LP) | 50 |
| 60s | Saga OPP 102 | MEETS EDDIE GOMEZ (LP) | 100 |
| 74 | 77 Records 77 SEU 12/53 | PHIL ON DRUMS (LP) | 50 |

## SEARCH PARTY
| | | | |
|---|---|---|---|
| 70 | Red Bull RB1 | What Do You See Up There/Hidden Truth | 35 |

## SEARCHERS

### SINGLES
| | | | |
|---|---|---|---|
| 63 | Pye 7N 15533 | Sweets For My Sweet/It's All Been A Dream | 6 |
| 63 | Philips BF 1274 | Sweet Nuthins/What'd I Say | 10 |
| 63 | Pye 7N 15566 | Sugar And Spice/Saints And Searchers (dark maroon label) | 12 |
| 63 | Pye 7N 15566 | Sugar And Spice/Saints And Searchers (lighter pink label) | 6 |
| 64 | Pye 7N 15594 | Needles And Pins/Saturday Night Out | 5 |
| 64 | Pye 7N 15630 | Don't Throw Your Love Away/I Pretend I'm With You | 5 |
| 64 | Pye 7N 15670 | Someday We're Gonna Love Again/No One Else Could Love You | 5 |
| 64 | Pye 7N 15694 | When You Walk In The Room/I'll Be Missing You | 5 |
| 64 | Pye 7N 15739 | What Have They Done To The Rain/This Feeling Inside (maroon label) | 5 |
| 64 | Pye 7N 15739 | What Have They Done To The Rain/This Feeling Inside (lighter pink label) | 5 |
| 65 | Pye 7N 15794 | Goodbye My Love/Till I Met You | 6 |
| 65 | Pye 7N 15878 | He's Got No Love/So Far Away | 6 |
| 65 | Pye 7N 15950 | When I Get Home/I'm Never Coming Back | 8 |
| 65 | Pye 7N 15992 | Take Me For What I'm Worth/Too Many Miles (in export p/s) | 25 |
| 65 | Pye 7N 15992 | Take Me For What I'm Worth/Too Many Miles | 8 |
| 66 | Pye 7N 17094 | Take It Or Leave It/Don't Hide It Away | 10 |
| 66 | Pye 7N 17170 | Have You Ever Loved Somebody/It's Just The Way | 12 |
| 67 | Pye 7N 17225 | Popcorn, Double Feature/Lovers | 15 |
| 67 | Pye 7N 17308 | Western Union/I'll Cry Tomorrow | 15 |
| 67 | Pye 7N 17424 | Secondhand Dealer/Crazy Dreams | 80 |
| 68 | Liberty LBF 15159 | Umbrella Man/Over The Weekend | 50 |
| 69 | Liberty LBF 15340 | Kinky Kathy Abernathy/Suzanna | 50 |
| 71 | RCA RCA 2057 | Desdemona/The World Is Waiting For Tomorrow | 15 |
| 71 | RCA RCA 2139 | Love Is Everywhere/And A Button | 10 |
| 72 | RCA RCA 2231 | Sing Singer Sing/Come On Back To Me | 10 |
| 72 | RCA RCA 2248 | Needles And Pins/When You Walk In The Room/Come On Back To Me | 10 |
| 72 | RCA RCA 2288 | Vahevala/Madman | 15 |
| 73 | RCA RCA 2330 | Solitaire/Spicks And Specks | 6 |
| 79 | Sire SIR 4026 | Hearts In Her Eyes/Don't Hang On (p/s) | 10 |
| 80 | Sire SIR 4036 | It's Too Late/This Kind Of Love Affair (p/s) | 7 |

| 81 | Sire SIR 4041 | Love's Melody/Changing (p/s) | 12 |
| 81 | Sire SIR 4049 | Another Night/Back To The War (p/s) | 10 |
| 80s | Private pressing | Don't Make Promises | 10 |
| 80s | Private pressing | Four Strong Winds | 10 |

**EPs**

| 63 | Pye NEP 24177 | AIN'T GONNA KISS YA | 12 |
| 63 | Pye NEP 24183 | SWEETS FOR MY SWEET (some copies with white & maroon label) | 15 |
| 64 | Pye NEP 24184 | HUNGRY FOR LOVE | 20 |
| 64 | Pye NEP 24201 | THE SEARCHERS PLAY THE SYSTEM | 15 |
| 64 | Pye NEP 24204 | WHEN YOU WALK IN THE ROOM | 20 |
| 65 | Pye NEP 24218 | BUMBLE BEE | 20 |
| 65 | Pye NEP 24222 | SEARCHERS '65 | 30 |
| 65 | Pye NEP 24228 | FOUR BY FOUR | 35 |
| 66 | Pye NEP 24263 | TAKE ME FOR WHAT I'M WORTH | 100 |

**ALBUMS**

| 63 | Pye NPL 18086 | MEET THE SEARCHERS | 30 |
| 63 | Pye NPL 18089 | SUGAR AND SPICE | 25 |
| 64 | Pye NPL 18092 | IT'S THE SEARCHERS | 25 |
| 65 | Pye NPL 18111 | SOUNDS LIKE SEARCHERS | 30 |
| 65 | Pye NPL 18120 | TAKE ME FOR WHAT I'M WORTH | 40 |

*(see also Chris Curtis, Pasha)*

**SEARGEANT SMILEY RAGS**

| 70 | Decca F13088 | Smoke Smoke/Hey Na I Think I Love You | 12 |

**SEARS**

| 84 | Bluurg FISH 9 | IF ONLY... (LP) | 15 |

**SEASICK STEVE**

| 07 | Bronzerat BR 006 | It's All Good/Thunderbird (p/s) | 8 |

**SEA STONE**

| 80 | Plankton PLANK 001 | Summer Fever/Blow On By (p/s) | 12 |
| 82 | Plankton 02 | AGAINST THE TIDE (EP, foldout sleeve) | 40 |
| 78 | Plankton PKN 101 | MIRRORED DREAMS (LP, with insert) | 80 |

**SEATHROUGH**

| 79 | private pressing | LALA LAPLA (LP) | 40 |

**B.B. SEATON (HORACE SEATON)**

| 63 | Island WI 123 | I'm So Glad/Tell Me | 30 |
| 64 | R&B JB 143 | Hold On/LESTER STERLING: Peace And Love | 30 |
| 72 | Big BG 336 | I Want Justice/RUPIE EDWARD'S ALL STARS: Justice (Version) | 8 |
| 72 | Bullet BU 514 | I Miss My Schooldays/CONSCIOUS MINDS: School Days - Version | 5 |
| 72 | Camel CA 100 | Lean On Me/NOW GENERATION: Samba Pati | 8 |
| 72 | Pama PM 864 | I Want Justice/RUPIE EDWARD'S ALL STARS: Justice - Version | 8 |
| 72 | Pama Supreme PS 374 | Sweet Caroline/Eleanor Rigby | 5 |
| 73 | Trojan TRLS 59 | THE THIN LINE BETWEEN LOVE AND HATE (LP) | 20 |
| 74 | Caroline CA 2002 | DANCING SHOES (LP) | 20 |

*(see also Bibby, Winston & Bibby, Gaylads, Messengers)*

**SEA TRAIN**

| 68 | A&M AMS 737 | Let The Duchess Know/As I Lay Losing | 5 |
| 69 | A&M AMLS 941 | SEA TRAIN (LP) | 30 |
| 71 | Capitol EA-ST 659 | SEA TRAIN (LP, gatefold) | 20 |
| 72 | Capitol EA-ST 829 | MARBLEHEAD MESSENGER (LP, gatefold sleeve) | 20 |
| 73 | Warner Bros K 46222 | WATCH (LP, gatefold) | 20 |

*(see also Blues Project, Old & In The Way)*

**SEA URCHINS**

| 87 | Kvatch KVATCH 001/ | Clingfilm/GROOVE FARM: Baby Blue Marine (flexidisc, 1,000 only, 500 in p/s) | 25 |
| 87 | Sha La La Ba Ba Ba Ba 5 | Summershine/ORCHIDS: From This Day (flexidisc, 2,500 only, 1,000 with p/s) | 15 |
| 87 | Sarah SARAH 001 | Pristine Christine/Sullen Eyes/Everglades (foldaround p/s with 14" x 10" poster in poly bag, 1,600 only) | 175 |
| 88 | Sarah SARAH 008 | Solace/Please Rain Fall (foldaround p/s in poly bag) | 25 |
| 89 | Fierce FRIGHT 032 | 30.10.88 (live) (1-sided, p/s) | 10 |
| 91 | Cheree CHEREE 15 | Please Don't Cry/Time Is All I've Seen (die-cut company sleeve) | 7 |
| 91 | Cheree CHEREE 15T | Please Don't Cry/No matter What/Time Is All I've Seen (12") | 10 |
| 98 | Sarah SARAH 33 | A Morning Odyssey/Wild Grass Pictures | 6 |
| 92 | Sarah SARAH 609 | STARDUST (LP) | 30 |

**JOHN SEBASTIAN**

| 54 | London HL 8029 | Inca Dance/Foolish Waltz | 20 |
| 55 | London HL 8131 | Stranger In Paradise/Autumn Leaves | 15 |

**JOHN (B.) SEBASTIAN**

| 69 | Kama Sutra 618 026 | She's A Lady/The Room Nobody Lives In | 6 |
| 70 | Reprise RS 20902 | Magical Connection/Fa-Fana-Fa | 5 |
| 70 | Reprise RSLP 6379 | JOHN B. SEBASTIAN (LP, gatefold sleeve) | 20 |
| 71 | Reprise K 44127 | REAL LIVE JOHN SEBASTIAN (LP) | 15 |

*(see also Lovin' Spoonful, Even Dozen Jug Band)*

**SECESSION**

| 80s | Siren SRN12 23 | Michael (12", p/s) | 12 |
| 83 | Garden GAR 1 | Betrayal/Reflections (p/s) | 100 |
| 88 | Siren SRNLP 11 | A DARK ENCHANTMENT (LP, with inner) | 40 |

**SECOND CITY SOUND**

| 65 | Decca F 12310 | Tchaikovsky One/Shadows | 6 |
| 66 | Decca F 12366 | Greig One/In A Mist | 6 |

# SECOND COMING

| | | | |
|---|---|---|---|
| 66 | Decca F 12406 | Love's Funny/Tell Me Where I'm Going | 6 |
| 69 | Major Minor MM 600 | The Dream Of Olwyn/A Touch Of Velvet, A Sting of Brass | 10 |

## SECOND COMING
| | | | |
|---|---|---|---|
| 71 | Mercury 6338 030 | SECOND COMING (LP) | 50 |

## SECOND HAND
| | | | |
|---|---|---|---|
| 72 | Mushroom 50 MR 19 | Funeral/Hangin' On An Eyelid | 100 |
| 68 | Polydor 583 045 | REALITY (LP, early copies crediting band as Moving Finger) | 300 |
| 68 | Polydor 583 045 | REALITY (LP, later copies not crediting band as Moving Finger) | 200 |
| 72 | Mushroom MR 2006 | DEATH MAY BE YOUR SANTA CLAUS (LP, some copies omit "Funeral") | 250 |

*(see also Andreas Thomopoulos, Fungus, Chillum, Vulcans)*

## SECOND LAYER
| | | | |
|---|---|---|---|
| 79 | Tortch TOR 001 | FLESH AS PROPERTY (EP, white p/s, black printed labels) | 30 |
| 80 | Tortch TOR 006 | State Of Emergency/I Need Noise/The Cutting Motion (p/s) | 30 |
| 81 | Tortch/Fresh FRESH 5 | FLESH AS PROPERTY (EP, reissue, yellow p/s & white labels) | 20 |
| 81 | Cherry Red CHERRY 21 | FLESH AS PROPERTY (EP, 2nd reissue, unreleased) | 0 |
| 82 | Cherry Red BRED 14 | WORLD OF RUBBER (LP, with inner) | 50 |

*(see also Outsiders, Sound)*

## SECOND THOUGHTS
| | | | |
|---|---|---|---|
| 65 | Recorded Sound Studios RSL 1596 | Let's Stick Together/I'm Possessed | 300 |

*(see also July, Nirvana)*

## SECONDARY MODERN
| | | | |
|---|---|---|---|
| 83 | Sorthern Sounds DJG 1 | Lucinda Dream/Boys Cry Too (p/s) | 60 |

## SECOND OPINION
| | | | |
|---|---|---|---|
| 78 | Tash TASH 0035 | King Of The Raceway/Stormbird | 20 |

## SECRET
| | | | |
|---|---|---|---|
| 77 | Arista ARIST 142 | The Young Ones/Handel A Vandel | 10 |
| 78 | Arista ARIST 173 | Do You Really Care?/I Wanna Car Like That | 15 |

## SECRET AFFAIR
| | | | |
|---|---|---|---|
| 79 | I-Spy SEE 1 | Time For Action/Soho Strut (brown p/s, black print/paper labels) | 10 |
| 79 | I-Spy SEE 1 | Time For Action/Soho Strut (black p/s, white print with plastic labels) | 5 |
| 79 | I-Spy SEE 3 | Let Your Heart Dance/Sorry Wrong Number (p/s, paper label) | 6 |
| 80 | I-Spy SEE 5 | My World/So Cool (paper labels) | 6 |
| 80 | I-Spy SEE 8 | Sound Of Confusion/Take It Or Leave It (p/s, paper labels) | 6 |
| 81 | I-Spy SEE 10 | Do You Know?/Dance Master (keyhole company sleeve, paper labels) | 6 |
| 82 | I-Spy SEE 11 | Lost In The Night (Mack The Knife)/The Big Beat (p/s) | 8 |
| 79 | I-Spy I SPY 1 | GLORY BOYS (LP, with 2 inserts) | 15 |
| 82 | I-Spy I SPY 3 | BUSINESS AS USUAL (LP, stickered sleeve) | 15 |

*(see also New Hearts, Advertising, Innocents [U.K.])*

## SECRET OYSTER
| | | | |
|---|---|---|---|
| 74 | CBS 80489 | SEA SON (LP) | 15 |

## SECRET SERVICE
| | | | |
|---|---|---|---|
| 79 | Sonet SON 2193 | Oh Susie/Give Me Your Love | 6 |

## SECRET SHINE
| | | | |
|---|---|---|---|
| 91 | Sarah SARAH 53 | After Years/Snowfall Sorrow/Grey Skies (p/s) | 12 |
| 92 | Sarah SARAH 61 | Honey Sweet/Secret Shine (p/s) | 12 |
| 93 | Sarah SARAH 71 | Loveblind/Way Too High (p/s) | 12 |
| 94 | Sarah SARAH 89 | GREATER THAN GOD EP (10" p/s) | 25 |
| 93 | Sarah SARAH 615 | UNTOUCHED (LP) | 30 |

## SECRET SQUIRREL
| | | | |
|---|---|---|---|
| 92 | Bogwoppa BOGWOPPA 05 | E Drop/Come Rudeboy (12", handwritten white label, with AJ Flex) | 60 |
| 92 | Dance Bass DANCE BASS 01 | Mu-Venom/DDT (12", stamped white label) | 50 |
| 92 | Dance Bass DANCE BASS 02 | VOLUME 2 EP (12") | 30 |
| 92 | Dance Bass DANCE BASS 06 | THE MAGIC FLUTE EP (12") | 30 |

*(See also Undercover Elephant and DJ Secret Squirrel)*

## SECRETS (U.K.)
| | | | |
|---|---|---|---|
| 66 | CBS 202466 | I Suppose/Such A Pity | 40 |
| 67 | CBS 202585 | Infatuation/She's Dangerous | 40 |
| 67 | CBS 2818 | I Intend To Please/I Think I Need The Cash | 40 |

*(see also Simon's Secrets, Clifford T. Ward, Martin Raynor & Secrets)*

## SECRETS (U.S)
| | | | |
|---|---|---|---|
| 64 | Philips BF 1298 | The Boy Next Door/Learnin' To Forget | 30 |
| 64 | Philips BF 1318 | Hey Big Boy/Other Side Of Town | 30 |

## SECT (1)
| | | | |
|---|---|---|---|
| 81 | Shoestring SHOE 1 | This is Your Life/Private Eye (p/s) | 5 |

## SECT (2)
| | | | |
|---|---|---|---|
| 86 | Insect NASTY 1 | A Free England/Never Go (p/s) | 20 |
| 89 | Damaged Goods YUBB 2 | SUMMER GIRL EP, blue vinyl) | 20 |
| 90 | Damaged Goods YUBB 5 | REMEMBERING EP (12") | 15 |
| 90 | Combat CR 001 | PLAYING WITH FIRE EP (12") | 20 |
| 87 | Razor RAZ 27 | THE VOICE OF REASON (LP) | 15 |

## SECTION A
| | | | |
|---|---|---|---|
| 82 | Subversive SUB | TIME STANDS STILL EP | 15 |

## SECTION 5
| | | | |
|---|---|---|---|
| 85 | Oi OIR 002 | WE WON'T CHANGE (LP) | 20 |
| 87 | Link LP 08 | FOR THE LOVE OF OI! (LP) | 15 |
| 88 | Link LINK LP 031 | STREET ROCK 'N' ROLL (LP) | 15 |

## SECTION 25

| 80 | Factory FAC 18 | Girls Don't Count/New Noise/Up To You (tracing paper p/s, produced by Ian Curtis and Rob Gretton) | 25 |
|----|----------------|------|----|
| 80 | Factory FAC 18 | Girls Don't Count/New Noise Up To You (12", 3 different p/s depicting band members girlfriends, produced by Ian Curtis and Rob Gretton) | 15 |
| 82 | Factory FAC 66 | The Beast/Sakura/Sakura (Matrixmix)/Trident (12") | 10 |
| 83 | Factory FAC 68 | Back To Wonder/Beating Heart (p/s) | 10 |
| 84 | Factory FAC 108 | Looking From A Hilltop (Restructure)/(Megamix) (12") | 10 |
| 81 | Factory FACT 45 | ALWAYS NOW (LP, in envelope/folder with poster) | 40 |
| 81 | Factory FACT 45 | ALWAYS NOW (LP, in envelope/folder without poster) | 25 |
| 84 | Factory FACT 90 | FROM THE HIP (LP, with inner) | 30 |
| 86 | Factory FACT 45c | ALWAYS NOW (reissue, cassette in box with insert) | 100 |
| 86 | Factory FACT 90c | FROM THE HIP (reissue, cassette in box with insert) | 80 |
| 88 | Factory FACT 160 | LOVE & HATE (LP) | 20 |
| 12 | Factory FACT 90 | FROM THE HIP (2-LP, reissue) | 20 |

## NEIL SEDAKA

| 59 | RCA RCA 1099 | The Diary/No Vacancy | 20 |
|----|--------------|------|----|
| 59 | RCA RCA 1115 | I Go Ape/Moon Of Gold | 15 |
| 59 | RCA RCA 1130 | You've Got To Learn Your Rhythm And Blues/Crying My Heart Out For You | 15 |
| 59 | London HLW 8961 | Ring A Rockin'/Fly Don't Fly On Me | 40 |

*(The above 45s were originally issued with triangular centres; later round-centres are worth two-thirds these values.)*

| 59 | London HLW 8961 | Ring A Rockin'/Fly Don't Fly On Me (78) | 20 |
|----|-----------------|------|----|
| 59 | RCA RCA 1152 | Oh! Carol/One Way Ticket (triangular centre) | 12 |
| 59 | RCA RCA 1152 | Oh! Carol/One Way Ticket (round centre) | 5 |
| 59 | RCA RCA 1152 | Oh! Carol/One Way Ticket (78) | 40 |
| 60 | RCA RCA 1178 | Stairway To Heaven/Forty Winks Away | 5 |
| 60 | RCA RCA 1178 | Stairway To Heaven/Forty Winks Away (78) | 40 |
| 60 | RCA RCA 1198 | Run Samson Run/You Mean Everything To Me | 10 |
| 60 | RCA RCA 1198 | Run Samson Run/You Mean Everything To Me (78) | 40 |
| 62 | Stateside SS 105 | Oh Delilah/MARVELS: Neil's Twist | 10 |
| 63 | RCA RCA 1368 | Bad Girl/Wait 'Til You See My Baby | 15 |
| 65 | RCA RCA 1475 | World Through A Tear/High On A Mountain | 6 |
| 59 | RCA RCX 166 | NEIL SEDAKA (EP) | 20 |
| 60 | RCA RCX 186 | NEIL SEDAKA VOL. 2 (EP) | 15 |
| 62 | RCA RCX 212 | NEIL SEDAKA VOL. 3 (EP) | 15 |
| 59 | RCA RD 27140 | NEIL SEDAKA (LP) | 40 |
| 60 | RCA RD 27207 | CIRCULATE (LP, mono) | 20 |
| 60 | RCA SF 5090 | CIRCULATE (LP, stereo) | 30 |

*(see also Sam Cooke, Paul Anka, 10cc)*

## MIKE SEDGEWICK

| 68 | Parlophone R 5694 | The Good Guys In The White Hats Never Lose/Woman (She's Got To Be Treated Right) | 5 |
|----|-------------------|------|----|
| 71 | President PT 348 | Morning Has Broken/Pollution Song | 8 |

*(see also Adam Mike & Tim)*

## SEDUCER

| 83 | Sticky SSR 0017 | Call Your Name/Survivor (p/s) | 60 |
|----|-----------------|------|----|
| 84 | Thunderbolt THBE 1007 | Indecent Exposure/Down Down/No No Baby/DTs/Wild Joker (12", p/s) | 10 |
| 85 | Thunderbolt THBL 016 | CAUGHT IN THE ACT (LP) | 15 |
| 86 | Stud STUDLP 2 | 'EADS DOWN - SEE YOU AT THE END (LP) | 15 |

## SEE SEE

| 08 | Great Pop Supplement GPS 27 | Up The Hill/Citadel Shuffle (p/s, 300 only) | 12 |
|----|------------------------------|------|----|
| 10 | Great Pop Supplement GPS 64 | LATE MORNING LIGHT (LP, 250 only, black vinyl) | 15 |
| 10 | Great Pop Supplement GPS 64 | LATE MORNING LIGHT (LP, 300 only, milk chocolate vinyl) | 15 |

## REDGIE SEEBOE

| 74 | BUG 38 | Please Don't Bring Your Sister/Daphne's Brains | 10 |
|----|--------|------|----|

## RUDY SEEDORF

| 65 | Island WI 189 | One Million Stars/Mr. Blue | 18 |
|----|---------------|------|----|

## SEEDS

| 66 | Vocalion VN 9277 | Pushin' Too Hard/Try To Understand | 60 |
|----|------------------|------|----|
| 66 | Vocalion VN 9277 | Pushin' Too Hard/Try To Understand (DJ copy) | 100 |
| 67 | Vocalion VN 9287 | Can't Seem To Make You Mine/Daisy Mae | 40 |
| 88 | Bam Caruso OPRA 091 | Pushin' Too Hard/Greener Day | 15 |
| 67 | Vocalion VAN 8062 | A WEB OF SOUND (LP) | 120 |
| 67 | Vocalion VAN 8070 | FUTURE (LP, mono) | 50 |
| 67 | Vocalion SAVN 8070 | FUTURE (LP, stereo) | 60 |
| 78 | Sonet SNTF 746 | THE SEEDS (LEGENDARY MASTER RECORDINGS) (LP) | 15 |
| 88 | Strange Things STRANGEP 1 | EVIL HOODOO (LP, picture disc) | 15 |

*(see also Sky Saxon, Ya Ho Wa 13)*

## SEEDS OF THE EARTH

| 75 | Contempo CS 2052 | Planting Seeds/Brother Bad | 20 |
|----|------------------|------|----|
| 75 | Contempo CS 2073 | Zion Plus/Phire | 20 |

## MIKE SEEGER

| 65 | Fontana TFL 6039 | MIKE SEEGER (LP) | 15 |
|----|------------------|------|----|

*(see also Peggy & Mike Seeger)*

## PEGGY SEEGER

| 57 | Pye Jazz NJE 1043 | ORIGINS OF SKIFFLE (EP) | 20 |
|----|-------------------|------|----|
| 57 | Topic 7T 18 | COME ALONG JOHN (EP, 33 rpm with 2 inserts, one hand-typed insert) | 20 |

## Peggy SEEGER & GUY CARAWAN

| 58 | Topic TOP 18 | COME ALONG JOHN (EP, 45 rpm reissue, with insert) | 15 |
| 60 | Topic TOP 38 | SHINE LIKE A STAR (EP) | 15 |
| 61 | Topic TOP 72 | TROUBLED LOVE (EP) | 20 |
| 61 | Topic TOP 73 | EARLY IN THE SPRING (EP) | 10 |
| 50s | Topic 10T 9 | PEGGY SEEGER (10" LP) | 10 |
| 61 | PRE 13005 | THE BEST OF PEGGY SEEGER (LP) | 20 |

*(see also Al Lloyd)* ..... 15

## PEGGY SEEGER & GUY CARAWAN

| 58 | Nixa NPT 19029 | WE SING AMERICA (10" LP) | 30 |
| 58 | HMV CLP 1174 | AMERICA AT PLAY (LP) | 20 |

*(see also Guy Carawan)*

## PEGGY & MIKE SEEGER

| 68 | Argo (Z)DA 80 | PEGGY 'N' MIKE (LP) | 15 |

*(see also Ewan MacColl & Peggy Seeger, Mike Seeger)*

## PETE SEEGER

| 60 | Top Rank TR 5020 | Careless Love/LEON BIBB: Times Are Getting Hard (p/s) | 10 |
| 63 | CBS AAG 187 | Little Boxes/Mail Myself To You | 5 |
| 59 | Topic TOP 37 | HOOTENANNY NEW YORK CITY (EP, with Sonny Terry) | 15 |

*(see also Big Bill Broonzy, Sonny Terry [& Brownie McGhee], Weavers)*

## PETE SEEGER & BIG BILL BROONZY

| 64 | Xtra XTRA 1006 | IN CONCERT - PETE SEEGER & BIG BILL BROONZY (LP) | 20 |
| 66 | Verve Folkways ST SVLP 506 | IN CONCERT (LP, stereo, reissue) | 15 |

*(see also Big Bill Broonzy)*

## SEEKERS

| 65 | Oriole CB 1935 | With A Swag On My Shoulder/Myra | 10 |
| 65 | Decca F 22167 | Chilly Winds/Kumbaya | 5 |
| 67 | Columbia DB 8313 | Emerald City/Music Of The World A Turnin' | 10 |

## SEEMON & MARIJKE

| 71 | A&M AMLS 64309 | SON OF AMERICA (LP) | 30 |

## SEFTONS

| 66 | CBS 202491 | I Can See Through You/Here Today | 25 |

*(see also Perishers)*

## VIVIENNE SEGAL & HAROLD LANG

| 54 | Columbia SCM 5114 | Den Of Iniquity/BARBARA ASHLEY: That Terrific Rainbow | 7 |

## BOB SEGER (SYSTEM)

| 68 | Capitol CL 15574 | Ramblin' Gamblin' Man/Tales Of Lucy Blue (as Bob Seger System) | 15 |
| 70 | Capitol CL 15642 | Lucifer/Big River (as Bob Seger System) | 20 |
| 72 | Reprise K 14208 | If I Were A Carpenter/Jesse James | 5 |
| 73 | Reprise K 14243 | Rosalie/Back In '72 | 5 |
| 74 | Reprise K 14364 | Get Out Of Denver/Long Song Comin' | 5 |
| 72 | Reprise K 44214 | SMOKIN' O.P.'s (LP) | 20 |

## LLOYD SEIVRIGHT

| 70 | Creole CR 1001 | Mary's Boy Child/And Glory Walked Among Men | 5 |

## SEIZE

| 81 | Why Not? NOT 001 | Grovelands Road/Why? (p/s) | 18 |
| 82 | Why Not? NOT 002 | EVERYBODY DIES EP (p/s) | 30 |

## SEIZE THE CHAIR

| 11 | Too Pure PURE 272s | You Who/It Happens Periodically (all but 100 destroyed in PIAS fire) | 5 |

## RICHARD SELANO

| 69 | Jolly JY 019 | All Of The Time/Broken Romance | 40 |

## SELECTED FOUR

| 71 | Banana BA 351 | Selection Train/SOUND DIMENSION: Version Train | 25 |

## SELECTER

| 79 | 2-Tone CHS TT 4 | On My Radio/Too Much Pressure (paper label, company sleeve) | 10 |
| 80 | 2-Tone CHS TT4 | On My Radio/Too Much Pressure (sliver or blue plastic labels) | 6 |
| 80 | 2-Tone CHS TT 8 | Three Minute Hero/James Bond (paper labels, company sleeve) | 10 |
| 80 | 2-Tone CHS TT 8 | Three Minute Hero/James Bond (silver plastic label, company sleeve) | 10 |
| 80 | 2-Tone CHS TT 10 | Missing Words/Carry Go Bring Home (paper label, company sleeve) | 10 |
| 80 | 2-Tone CMS TT10 | Missing Words/Carry Go Bring Home (sliver plastic labels) | 7 |
| 80 | 2-Tone CHS TT 10 | Missing Words/Carry Go Bring Home (sliver plastic labels, misprint) | 5 |
| 80 | Chrysalis CHS S1 | The Whisper/Train To Skaville (paper labels) | 5 |
| 80 | Chrysalis CHS S1 | The Whisper/Train To Skaville (plastic labels) | 6 |
| 81 | Chrysalis CHS S2 | Celebrate The Bullet/Last Tango In Dub | 5 |
| 89 | 2-Tone TTP1 | THE SPECIALS: Rudi, A Message To You/Ghost Town//SELECTER: On My Radio/ MADNESS: One Step Beyond (promo, 40 only) | 150 |
| 80 | 2-Tone CDLTT 5002 | TOO MUCH PRESSURE (LP) | 15 |

*(see also Special A.K.A.)*

## FREDDIE SELF

| 64 | Mercury MF 839 | Don't Cry/Why Should I? | 7 |

*(see also Freddie Ryder, Trends)*

## RONNIE SELF

| 58 | Philips PB 810 | Bop-A-Lena/Ain't I A Dog (78) | 200 |

## SELF ABUSE

| 83 | Radical Change RC 5 | (I DON'T WANT TO BE A) SOLDIERS (EP) | 18 |

## SELF CONTROL

| 80 | Dancing Sideways DS2 X | SELF CONTROL (EP) | 10 |
| 81 | Dancing Sideways DS 4X | Falling/Electricity (p/s) | 6 |

### BROTHER JOHN SELLERS
| | | | |
|---|---|---|---|
| 56 | Vanguard EPP 14002 | BLUES AND SPIRITUALS (EP) | 15 |
| 57 | Columbia SEG 7740 | BLUES AND SPIRITUALS (EP) | 15 |
| 57 | Decca DFE 6457 | BROTHER JOHN SELLERS IN LONDON (EP) | 15 |
| 56 | Vanguard PPT 12008 | BROTHER JOHN SELLERS SINGS BLUES AND FOLK SONGS (10" LP) | 25 |
| 57 | Vanguard PPT 12017 | JACK OF DIAMONDS AND OTHER FOLK SONGS AND BLUES (10" LP) | 25 |

### PETER SELLERS (& SOPHIA LOREN)
| | | | |
|---|---|---|---|
| 65 | Parlophone R 5393 | A Hard Day's Night/Help! | 7 |
| 66 | United Artists UP 1152 | After The Fox (as Peter Sellers & Hollies)/BURT BACHARACH: The Fox-Trot | 35 |
| 60 | Parlophone PCS 3012 | PETER AND SOPHIA (LP, with Sophia Loren, stereo) | 15 |

### SELOFANE
| | | | |
|---|---|---|---|
| 68 | CBS 3413 | Girl Called Fantasy/Happiness Is Love | 15 |
| 68 | CBS 3700 | Shingle I.A.O./Chase The Face | 30 |

### SELWYN & JOHN
| | | | |
|---|---|---|---|
| 67 | CBS 2708 | Bogey Man/When God Gave Us Names | 90 |

### SEMA
| | | | |
|---|---|---|---|
| 82 | Le Rey LR 06 | THEME FROM HUNGER (EP) | 60 |
| 82 | Le Rey LR 04 | NOTES FROM UNDERGROUND (LP) | 150 |
| 83 | Le Rey LR 101 | EXTRACTS FROM ROSA SILBER (LP) | 80 |
| 84 | Le Rey LR 102 | THREE SEASONS ONLY (LP) | 60 |

### SEMA 4
| | | | |
|---|---|---|---|
| 79 | Pollen PBM 022 | 4 FROM SEMA 4 (EP, 2 different coloured sleeves, 500 only, numbered) | 100 |
| 79 | Pollen PBM 024 | UP DOWN AROUND (EP, 1,000 only) | 75 |

### ARCHIE SEMPLE
| | | | |
|---|---|---|---|
| 60 | Columbia 33SX 1240 | JAZZ FOR YOUNG LOVERS (LP) | 25 |
| 62 | 77 LP/10 | THE ARCHIE SEMPLE QUARTER (10" LP, 100 only) | 40 |
| 62 | Columbia 33SX 1450 | EASY LIVING (LP) | 20 |
| 63 | Columbia 33SX 1580 | THE TWILIGHT COMETH (LP) | 20 |
| 64 | 77 LEU 12/6 | THE CLARINET OF ARCHIE SEMPLE (LP) | 20 |

### SENATE
| | | | |
|---|---|---|---|
| 67 | Columbia DB 8110 | I Can't Stop/Ain't As Sweet As You | 60 |
| 68 | United Artists (S)ULP 1180 | THE SENATE SOCK IT TO YOU ONE MORE TIME (LP) | 40 |

*(see also Garnet Mimms)*

### SENATOR BOBBY
| | | | |
|---|---|---|---|
| 62 | Cameo Parkway P 127 | Wild Thing/SENATOR EVERETT McKINLAY: Wild Thing | 5 |

### SENATORS
| | | | |
|---|---|---|---|
| 64 | Dial DSP 7001 | She's A Mod/Lot About You | 100 |
| 64 | Oriole CB 1957 | When Day Is Done/Breakdown | 50 |
| 65 | CBS 201768 | The Tables Are Turning/Stop Wasting Time | 30 |

*(see also Tony Rivers & Castaways)*

### SENDELICA
| | | | |
|---|---|---|---|
| 10 | Fruits De Mer CRUSTACIAN 13 | A NICE PAIR (gatefold p/s, green vinyl) | 25 |

### RAY SENDIT & HIS ROCKEY TEAM
| | | | |
|---|---|---|---|
| 57 | Felsted SD 80052 | Rocket 0869/Spike's Rock | 8 |

### LOS SENORS
| | | | |
|---|---|---|---|
| 63 | Cameo Parkway C 290 | Amapola/Acapulco | 5 |

### SENSATION
| | | | |
|---|---|---|---|
| 73 | Sticky STY 1 | Everybody Wants It/Lady Put Me Down | 8 |
| 73 | Sticky STY 5 | Black Eyed Woman/Baby | 15 |

### SENSATIONAL CREED
| | | | |
|---|---|---|---|
| 84 | Beggars Banquet BEG 125 | Nocturnal Operation/Down Periscope (p/s, reissue of Orbidöig single) | 15 |
| 84 | Beggars Banquet BEG 125T | Nocturnal Operation/Down Periscope/Voyage Of The Titanic (12", p/s, reissue of Orbidöig single) | 25 |

*(see also Orbidoig)*

### SENSATIONS (JAMAICA)
| | | | |
|---|---|---|---|
| 67 | Doctor Bird DB 1074 | A Thing Called Soul/BOBBY LEE & SENSATIONS: I Was Born A Loser | 45 |
| 67 | Doctor Bird DB 1100 | Right On Time/Lonely Lover | 100 |
| 67 | Doctor Bird DB 1102 | Born To Love You/Your Sweet Love | 60 |
| 68 | Duke DU 2 | Those Guys/I'll Never Fall In Love | 100 |
| 68 | Island WI 3110 | Long Time Me No See You Girl/ROY SHIRLEY: Million Dollar Baby | 40 |
| 69 | Camel CA 31 | The Warrior (actually by Johnny Osbourne & Sensations)/ JOHNNY ORGAN: Don Juan | 20 |
| 70 | Techniques TI 902 | War Boat/Mr Blue | 8 |
| 71 | Duke DU 120 | Remember/LARRY'S ALLSTARS: Madhouse | 15 |
| 71 | Duke DU 121 | What Are You Doing Sunday/RUFFIANS: Sweet Dream | 15 |

*(see also Roy Shirley, Baba Dise, Winston Wright)*

### SENSATIONS (U.K.)
| | | | |
|---|---|---|---|
| 66 | Decca F 12392 | Look At My Baby/What A Wonderful Feeling | 20 |
| 71 | MCA MK 5078 | Oh My Eli/Let's Get A Little Sentimental | 30 |

### SENSATIONS (FEATURING YVONNE) (U.S.)
| | | | |
|---|---|---|---|
| 61 | Pye International 7N 25110 | Music, Music, Music/A Part Of Me (as Sensations featuring Yvonne) | 25 |
| 62 | Pye International 7N 25128 | Let Me In/Oh Yes I'll Be True | 25 |

*(see also Yvonne Baker)*

### SENSE OF VISION
| | | | |
|---|---|---|---|
| 84 | Wipe 2 | Dream/Destiny (p/s) | 7 |

### SEONA DANCING
| | | | |
|---|---|---|---|
| 83 | London LON 22 | More To Lose/You're On My Side (p/s) | 18 |

## SEPTIC DEATH

| | | | |
|---|---|---|---|
| 83 | London LONX 22 | More To Lose (Extended Mix)/You're On My Side (12", p/s) | 10 |
| 83 | London LON 32 | Bitter Heart/Tell Her (p/s) | 18 |
| 83 | London LONX 32 | Bitter Heart/Tell Her (12", p/s) | 12 |

## SEPTIC DEATH
| | | | |
|---|---|---|---|
| 88 | Pusmort PUS 00703 | KICHIGAI EP (p/s) | 7 |
| 85 | Pusmort 0012-01D | NOW THAT I HAVE THE ATTENTION... (LP, with inner sleeve, 18 tracks) | 15 |

## SEPTIMUS
| | | | |
|---|---|---|---|
| 77 | Pennine PSS 134 | Ferrets/Do You Wanna Touch My Safety Pin? (no p/s) | 100 |

## SEPULTURA
| | | | |
|---|---|---|---|
| 94 | Roadrunner RR2377-8 | Refuse/Resist (12", die cut sleeve) | 12 |
| 91 | Roadracer RO 93281 | ARISE (LP) | 12 |
| 91 | Roadracer RO 9328-8 | ARISE (LP, picture disc) | 18 |
| 94 | Roadrunner RR 90000 0 | CHAOS A.D. (CD, limited edition tin box; CD has embossed cover & different sleeve, Brazilian flag & 2 bonus tracks, "Policia" & "Inhuman Nature") | 40 |

## SEQUE
| | | | |
|---|---|---|---|
| 83 | Storm STORM 1 | 3 On The Trot/Christine | 12 |

## SERCUS
| | | | |
|---|---|---|---|
| 90 | SBS S.B.S. 91101 | I Spy/Signs Of Day (no p/s) | 10 |

## SERENADERS
| | | | |
|---|---|---|---|
| 59 | Top Rank JAR 111 | Sudden Holiday/Tango Madeira | 5 |

## SERENDIPITY
| | | | |
|---|---|---|---|
| 68 | CBS 3733 | Through With You/I'm Flying | 130 |
| 69 | CBS 4428 | If I Could/Castles | 60 |

## SERFS
| | | | |
|---|---|---|---|
| 69 | Capitol E-ST 207 | THE EARLY BIRD CAFE (LP) | 18 |

## SERGEANT PEPPER
| | | | |
|---|---|---|---|
| 83 | Ariwa ARILP 006 | JUDGEMENT DAY (LP) | 25 |

## WILL SERGEANT
| | | | |
|---|---|---|---|
| 78 | (no label or cat. no.) | WEIRD AS FISH (cassette, 7 copies only, each with a different cover) | 30 |
| 82 | WEA K 19238 | Favourite Branches/RAVI SHANKAR & BILL LOVEDAY: Himalaya (p/s) | 8 |
| 95 | Ochre OCH 003 | Cosmos/Venus In Flares (as GLIDE, p/s, orange vinyl) | 7 |

*(see also Echo & Bunnymen)*

## SERGIO & ESTIBALIZ
| | | | |
|---|---|---|---|
| 75 | Epic S EPC 3187 | Love Come Home/Tu Volveras | 12 |

## SERIOUS DRINKING
| | | | |
|---|---|---|---|
| 83 | Upright UP 5 | Hangover/Don't Shoot Me Down/Baby I'm Dying A Death (p/s) | 8 |
| 82 | Upright YOURS 4 | Love On The Terraces/Hypocrite/Bobby Moore Was Innocent (p/s) | 10 |
| 84 | Upright UP 8 | Country Girl Became Drugs & Sex Punk/Go For The Burn | 10 |
| 83 | Upright UPLP 3 | THE REVOLUTION STARTS AT CLOSING TIME (LP, with beer mat) | 18 |

## SERPENTINE
| | | | |
|---|---|---|---|
| 70 | Decca F23001 | Powerful Jim/I've Only Got Myself | 20 |

## JUAN MANUEL SERRAT
| | | | |
|---|---|---|---|
| 68 | Philips BF 1654 | She Gives Me Love (La La La)/La La La | 6 |

## BETTIE SERVEERT
| | | | |
|---|---|---|---|
| 92 | Guernica GU 3 LP | PALOMINE (LP, with free 7") | 20 |

## SERVICEMEN
| | | | |
|---|---|---|---|
| 00 | Grapevine 116 | Are You Angry/I Need A Helping Hand | 15 |
| 01 | Grapevine 136 | I'll Stop Loving You/Sweet Magic | 15 |

## NANCY SESAY & MELODAIRES
| | | | |
|---|---|---|---|
| 81 | It's War Boys S 1 | C'est Fab/The Ballad Of Hong Kong/National Honk (gatefold p/s) | 5 |

*(see also Homosexuals)*

## SESSION BOYS
| | | | |
|---|---|---|---|
| 70 | Lynn L29 | Looking To The Sun/Strike Back | 20 |

## SESSION MEN
| | | | |
|---|---|---|---|
| 80 | LKJ 001 | THE SESSION MEN : Solitude/ABU BAKE : Introducing Abu Baka/ MICHAEL SMITH : Mi Cyaan Believe It/Roots (12") | 25 |

## CAMILO SESTO
| | | | |
|---|---|---|---|
| 72 | Pye Intl. 7N 25589 | To Be A Man/Now Is My Time (Yo Soy Asi) | 40 |

## BOLA SETE
| | | | |
|---|---|---|---|
| 76 | Sonet SNTF 695 | OCEAN (LP) | 15 |

## SETTERS
| | | | |
|---|---|---|---|
| 70 | Duke DU 65 | Paint Your Wagon/Organ Man (both sides actually by Hot Rod All Stars) | 140 |
| 70 | Trojan TR 7738 | Virgin Soldier/Brixton Reggae Festival (both actually by Hot Rod All Stars) | 60 |

## SETTING SUN
| | | | |
|---|---|---|---|
| 68 | Oak RGI 840 | Ob La De Ob La Da/Boy Who Was Only One/Homeward Bound/Fascinating Rhythm | 40 |

## SETTLERS
| | | | |
|---|---|---|---|
| 65 | Pye 7N 159645 | Woman Called Freedom/I Know I'm Right | 6 |
| 66 | Pye 7N 17065 | Nowhere Man/Call Again | 7 |
| 67 | Pye 7N 17375 | Major Minor/I Love 'Oo Kazoo ('Cos 'Oo Love Me) | 6 |
| 70 | Columbia DB 8695 | Nessie The Monster/Jesus Met the Woman (At The Well) | 6 |
| 71 | York SYK 505 | The Lightning Tree/Just This Side Of Nowhere | 8 |
| 74 | York YR 215 | On Top Of The World/Let's Tell The World | 6 |

## SEVEN AGES OF MAN
| | | | |
|---|---|---|---|
| 72 | Rediffusion ZS 115 | SEVEN AGES OF MAN (LP, yellow/black label) | 40 |

*(see also Madeline Bell, Gordon Beck)*

## SEVEN LETTERS/SYMARIP
| | | | |
|---|---|---|---|
| 69 | Doctor Bird DB 1189 | People Get Ready/The Fit (as Seven Letters) | 40 |

| 69 | Doctor Bird DB 1194 | Please Stay/Special Beat (as Seven Letters) | 40 |
| 69 | Doctor Bird DB 1195 | Flour Dumpling/Equality (as Seven Letters [Symarip]) | 40 |
| 69 | Doctor Bird DB 1206 | Mama Me Want Girl/Sentry (as Seven Letters) | 40 |
| 69 | Doctor Bird DB 1207 | Soul Crash/Throw Me Things (as Seven Letters) | 40 |
| 69 | Doctor Bird DB 1208 | There Goes My Heart/Wish (as Seven Letters) | 40 |
| 69 | Doctor Bird DB 1209 | Bam Bam Baji/Hold Him Joe (as Seven Letters [Symarip]) | 100 |
| 69 | Doctor Bird DB 1306 | Fung Sure/Tomorrow At Sundown (as Symarip) | 40 |
| 69 | Treasure Isle TI 7050 | Skinhead Moonstomp/Must Catch A Train (as Symarip) | 30 |
| 70 | Treasure Isle TI 7054 | Parson's Corner/Redeem (as Symarip) | 30 |
| 70 | Treasure Isle TI 7055 | La Bella Jig/Holidays By The Sea (as Symarip) | 10 |
| 70 | Attack ATT 8013 | I'm A Puppet/Vindication (as Symarip) | 15 |
| 80 | Trojan TRO 9062 | Skinhead Moonstomp/Skinhead Jamboree (p/s) | 8 |
| 70 | Trojan TBL 102 | SKINHEAD MOONSTOMP (LP, as Symarip) | 40 |
| 80 | Trojan TRLS 187 | SKINHEAD MOONSTOMP (LP, reissue, blue label) | 15 |

*(see also Pyramids, Equals, Laurel Aitken)*

## 7 SECONDS
| 82 | Alt. Tentacles VIRUS 15 | SKIN, BRAINS AND GUTS (EP, with insert) | 12 |

## SEVEN YEAR ITCH
| 81 | Cargo CRS 007 | I Wanna Make Ya/Oo Ya Ha | 10 |

## SEVENTEEN
| 80 | Vendetta VD 001 | Don't Let Go/Bank Holiday Weekend (p/s) | 100 |

*(see also Alarm)*

## SEVENTH ANGEL
| 90 | Under One Flag FLAG 51 | THE TORMENT (LP) | 15 |
| 92 | Under One Flag FLAG 65 | LAMENT FOR THE WEARY (LP, inner) | 20 |

## SEVENTH SEAL
| 90 | Mystic Red Corp MRC 8004 | Sound Iration/Dub Seal (12") | 50 |

## SEVENTH SON
| 82 | Rising Son FMR 067 | Man In The Street/Immortal Hours (in original p/s with bass player obscured) | 50 |
| 82 | Rising Son FMR 067 | Man In The Street/Immortal Hours (revised p/s with 'clearer' band photograph) | 35 |
| 84 | Rising Son SRT4KS 282 | Metal To The Moon/Sound And Fury (in gatefold p/s) | 60 |
| 84 | Rising Son SRT4KS 282 | Metal To The Moon/Sound And Fury | 30 |
| 87 | Music Factory MF 0043 | Northern Boots/The Harder You Rock (p/s) | 18 |
| 89 | Rising Son SRT9KLS | What More Do You Want/Sister Strange/Bitter Ashes (12", p/s) | 12 |
| 91 | SRT 915 3116 | Factory Girls/Last Band In Town | 7 |

## SEVENTH WAVE
| 75 | Gull GULS 14 | Manifestations/Only The Beginning (Part 1) | 5 |
| 89 | SRT SRT9KS 2018 | Tonight/Run (p/s) | 20 |
| 74 | Gull GULP 1001 | THINGS TO COME (LP) | 15 |
| 75 | Gull GULP 1010 | PSI-FI (LP) | 18 |

*(see also Second Hand, Fungus, Ken Elliott)*

## SEVENTH WONDER
| 80 | Grapevine GRP 130 | Captain Of My Ship/Pharaoh | 10 |

## SEVERE CARNAGE
| 90 | White JC 002 | The Struggle Continues/Back To Basics (12") | 100 |

## SEVERED HEAD
| 83 | Plastic Canvas PC 002 | Heavy Metal/Killin' The Kidz (p/s) | 25 |

## SEVERED HEADS
| 84 | Ink INK 122 | DEAD EYES OPENED (12" EP, p/s) | 15 |
| 83 | Ink INK 2 | SINCE THE ACCIDENT (LP) | 20 |
| 85 | Ink INK 9 | CITY SLAB HORROR (LP) | 15 |
| 85 | Ink INK 16D | CLIFFORD DARLING PLEASE DON'T LIVE IN THE PAST (2-LP) | 20 |

## SEVERINE
| 71 | CBS 7230 | Chance In Time/Nothing Bad Can Be This Good | 8 |
| 71 | Philips 6009 135 | Un Banc, Un Arbre, Une Rue/Viens | 5 |
| 71 | Philips 6009 152 | La La Melodie/Je Ferme Les Yeux, Je Compte Dix | 5 |

## DAVID SEVILLE & HIS ORCHESTRA (& THE CHIPMUNKS)
| 57 | London HLU 8359 | Armen's Theme/Carousel In Rome (initially gold label print) | 20 |
| 64 | Liberty 16170 | All My Loving/Please Please Me | 8 |

*(see also Alfi & Harry)*

## ALEC SEWARD
| 56 | Vogue LDE 165 | CITY BLUES (10" LP) | 40 |

## SEX
| 00 | Grapevine 113 | It's You Baby (It's You)/It's You Baby (Extended) | 15 |

## SEX AIDS
| 83 | Riot City RIOT 23 | BACK ON THE PISS AGAIN (EP) | 20 |

*(see also Vice Squad)*

## SEX BEATLES
| 79 | Charly CYS 1061 | Well You Never/Fatal Fascination (p/s) | 8 |

## SEX GANG CHILDREN
| 82 | Illuminated ILL 1112 | Beasts (12", EP) | 30 |

## SEX PISTOLS
| 12 | Universal sexpisyp1977 | NEVER MIND THE BOLLOCKS, HERE'S THE SEX PISTOLS (2-LP, reissue yellow/pink vinyl, 1977 copies only, numbered) | 35 |

## SINGLES
| 76 | EMI 401 | Anarchy In The U.K (4.01 longer version)/No Fun (Abbey Road 2-sided acetate, only 3 known to exist) | 7000 |

| Year | Label/Cat. No. | Description | Value |
|---|---|---|---|
| 76 | EMI | Anarchy In The U.K. (3.36 version) (1-sided Abbey Road Acetate) | 5000 |
| 76 | EMI 2566 | Anarchy In The U.K./I Wanna Be Me (2 x 1-sided white label test pressings, 4-pronge centre, MATRIXES EMI 2566 A1/EMI 2566B-2) | 4000 |
| 76 | EMI EMI 2566 | Anarchy In The U.K./I Wanna Be Me (black p/s, with Chris Thomas production credit on B-side) | 120 |
| 76 | EMI EMI 2566 | Anarchy In The U.K./I Wanna Be Me ('Demo, not for sale'. Black p/s, Chris Thomas credit on both sides and with information slip) | 300 |
| 76 | EMI EMI 2566 | Anarchy In The U.K./I Wanna Be Me (Dave Goodman production credit on B-side) | 50 |
| 76 | EMI EMI 2566 | Anarchy In The U.K./I Wanna Be Me (Anarchy label on both sides) | 150 |
| 77 | (no label or cat. no.) | God Save The Queen/No Feelings (double sided 7" acetate on LTS - few copies pressed and used by Malcolm McLaren to get gigs and record deal) | 10000 |
| 77 | A&M AMS 2784 | God Save The Queen/No Feelings (white label test pressing, A2/B1 Matrixes) | 7000 |
| 77 | A&M AMS 7284 | God Save The Queen/No Feelings (withdrawn, in brown envelope with press release) | 8000 |
| 77 | A&M AMS 7284 | God Save The Queen/No Feelings (withdrawn, without brown envelope and press release) | 7500 |
| 77 | Virgin VS 181 | God Save The Queen/Did You No Wrong (white label test pressing VS 181 A1/B1 Matrixes) | 2500 |
| 77 | Virgin VS 181 | God Save The Queen/Did You No Wrong (1st issue, with silver on blue sleeve and labels) | 10 |
| 77 | Virgin VS 181 | God Save The Queen/Did You No Wrong (Plain blue no Queen's head sample sleeve - two known copies, Jamie Reid autograph added later to one) | 1500 |
| 77 | Virgin VS 181 | God Save The Queen/Did You No Wrong (2nd issue, white on blue sleeve and labels) | 8 |
| 77 | Virgin VS 184 (not on acetate) | Pretty Vacant (1-sided acetate) | 1000 |
| 77 | Virgin VS 184 | Pretty Vacant/No Fun (white label test pressing) | 600 |
| 77 | Virgin VS 184 | Pretty Vacant/No Fun (p/s) | 10 |
| 77 | Virgin VS 184 | Pretty Vacant/No Fun (p/s with push-out centre) | 30 |
| 77 | Virgin VS 191 | Holidays In The Sun/Satellite (withdrawn p/s) | 20 |
| 77 | Virgin/Lyntone LYN 3261 | Lentilmas - A Seasonal Offering To You From Virgin Records (flexidisc, Xmas freebie to journalists; with Xmas card. It is believed that the Sex Pistols do not appear on this record) | 1000 |
| 77 | Virgin/Lyntone LYN 3261 | Lentilmas - A Seasonal Offering To You From Virgin Records (flexidisc, Xmas freebie to journalists; without Xmas card. It is believed that the Sex Pistols do not appear on this record) | 300 |
| 78 | (No. Cat. No) | SID VICIOUS: My Way (1-sided Pye Studios Acetate) | 700 |
| 78 | Virgin VS 220 | No One Is Innocent/SID VICIOUS: My Way (p/s) | 6 |
| 78 | Virgin VS 220 | No-One Is Innocent (mispress, plays Motors track)/SID VICIOUS: My Way (p/s) | 35 |
| 78 | Virgin VS 22012 | The Biggest Blow (A Punk Prayer By Ronald Biggs)/(Interview)/SID VICIOUS: My Way (12", p/s [matrix: VS 22012 A1]), without interview [VS 22012 A1]) | 20 |
| 78 | Virgin VS 22012 | The Biggest Blow (A Punk Prayer By Ronald Biggs)/(Interview)/SID VICIOUS: My Way (12", p/s [matrix: VS 22012A3], with interview [VS 22012 A1]) | 10 |
| 78 | (No label or cat no) | The Interview (recorded at Middlesborough Rock Garden August 1977, 7.30 minutes each side, 1000 pressed) | 10 |
| 79 | Virgin VS 240 | Something Else/Friggin' In The Riggin' (p/s, black & white labels) | 7 |
| 79 | Virgin VS 256 | Silly Thing/TENPOLE TUDOR: Who Killed Bambi (p/s) | 6 |
| 79 | Virgin VS 272 | C'mon Everybody/The God Save The Queen Symphony/Watcha Gonna Do About It (p/s) | 5 |
| 79 | Virgin VS 290 | The Great Rock 'n' Roll Swindle/Rock Around The Clock (vocals by Tenpole Tudor) ('American Express' p/s) | 6 |
| 79 | Virgin VS 290 | The Great Rock 'n' Roll Swindle (mispressing with 'lawyers' telephone conversation' track)/Rock Around The Clock ('American Express' p/s) | 30 |
| 80 | Virgin VS 339 | (I'm Not Your) Stepping Stone/Pistols Propaganda (p/s, mispressing, B-side plays "Substitute") | 25 |
| 80 | Virgin VS 339 | (I'm Not Your) Stepping Stone/Pistols Propaganda (p/s, mispressing, B-side plays Gillan track "No Laughing In Heaven") | 30 |
| 80 | Virgin SEX 1 | PISTOLS PACK (6 x 7" in p/s; all in plastic wallet) | 60 |
| 81 | Virgin VS 443 | Who Killed Bambi?/Rock Around The Clock (by Tenpole Tudor & Pistols, p/s) | 10 |
| 85 | Chaos DICK1 | Submission/No Feelings (p/s, 5,000 only, blue vinyl) | 7 |
| 85 | Chaos DICK1 | Submission/No Feelings (p/s, 5,000 only, pink vinyl) | 15 |
| 85 | Chaos DICK1 | Submission/No Feelings (p/s, 5,000 only, yellow vinyl) | 5 |
| 85 | Chaos SUB 1 | Submission (12", 1-sided test pressing, die-cut sleeve, label has big red 'A') | 30 |
| 85 | Chaos | Pretty Vacant (unreleased, 20 copies only) | 75 |
| 85 | Chaos CARTEL 1 | Submission (12" 1-track promo) | 25 |
| 86 | Archive 4 TOF 104 | THE ORIGINAL SEX PISTOLS LIVE (4-track 12", p/s, blue vinyl) | 12 |
| 88 | Spiral Scratch SCRATCH 4 | Pretty Vacant (Demo)/I Wanna Be Me (Demo) (with Spiral Scratch magazine, issue 4, B-side actually plays "Seventeen") | 10 |
| 92 | Virgin VS 1448 | Pretty Vacant/No Feelings (p/s, Lady Di cover) | 15 |
| 02 | Virgin VS 1832 | God Save The Queen/Did You No Wrong (reissue) | 8 |
| 07 | EMI EMI 2566 | Anarchy In The U.K./I Wanna Be Me (180 gram repressing, p/s) | 7 |
| 07 | Virgin VS 181 | God Save The Queen/Did You No Wrong (180 gram repressing, p/s) | 7 |
| 07 | Virgin VS 184 | Pretty Vacant/No Fun (180 gram repressing, p/s) | 7 |
| 07 | Virgin VS 191 | Holidays In The Sun/Satellite (180 gram repressing, p/s) | 7 |
| 12 | Universal SexPiss 1976 1 | Anarchy In The U.K./I Wanna Be Me (picture disc, 3500 copies, numbered) | 12 |

## ALBUMS

| Year | Label/Cat. No. | Description | Value |
|---|---|---|---|
| 77 | Virgin V 2086 | NEVER MIND THE BOLLOCKS, HERE'S THE SEX PISTOLS (LP, 1st pressing with poster and free 'Submission' 7", 11 tracks listed on rear sleeve (no 'Submission'). Publishing credits '1977 Jones, Matlock, Cook & Rotten' except HOLIDAYS IN THE SUN (side 1) and BODIES (side 2) 'Jones, Cook, Rotten & Vicious') | 100 |
| 77 | Virgin V 2086 | NEVER MIND THE BOLLOCKS, HERE'S THE SEX PISTOLS (LP, 1st pressing, poster and free 'Submission' 7", pink rear sleeve with no track listing, sources suggest as little as 1000 copies pressed with this sleeve, A1/B1 or A3/B2 matrixes. Publishing credits '1977 Jones, Matlock, Cook & Rotten' except HOLIDAYS IN THE SUN (side 1) and BODIES (side 2) 'Jones, Cook, Rotten & Vicious')) | 120 |
| 77 | Virgin V 2086 | NEVER MIND THE BOLLOCKS, HERE'S THE SEX PISTOLS (LP, 2nd pressing with 12 tracks (no track listing on pink rear sleeve, 'Bodies' moved to side 1 and 'Submission' added to side 2. Publishing credits, 'Copyright control 1977, Jones, Matlock. Cook, Rotten' | 40 |

| | | | |
|---|---|---|---|
| | | except HOLIDAYS IN THE SUN, BODIES & EMI 'Copyright Control 1977 Jones, Cook, Rotten, Vicious' ) ................................................................................................... | |
| 77 | Virgin V 2086 | NEVER MIND THE BOLLOCKS, HERE'S THE SEX PISTOLS (LP, 3rd pressing with 12 tracks and 12 tracks listed on pink rear sleeve,Publishing credits on 'EMI' changed from 'Jones, Matlock, Cook, Rotten' to 'Jones, Cook, Rotten, Vicious') ............................... | 30 |
| 77 | Virgin V 2086 | NEVER MIND THE BOLLOCKS, HERE'S THE SEX PISTOLS (LP, 3rd pressing with 12 tracks but 11 tracks listed on rear sleeve (no 'Submission'). Publishing credits, 'Copyright control 1977, Jones, Matlock. Cook, Rotten' except HOLIDAYS IN THE SUN, BODIES & EMI 'Copyright Control 1977 Jones, Cook, Rotten, Vicious' ) ................................. | 25 |
| 77 | Virgin V 2086/SPOTS 001 | NEVER MIND THE BOLLOCKS, HERE'S THE SEX PISTOLS (LP, pink rear sleeve, with no track listing, with poster & 1-sided single, "Submission" [VDJ 24], shrinkwrapped, with orange or green-stickered versions extremely rare) ...................................... | 800 |
| 78 | Virgin VP 2086 | NEVER MIND THE BOLLOCKS, HERE'S THE SEX PISTOLS (LP, picture disc) ...................... | 40 |
| 78 | Virgin V 2086 | NEVER MIND THE BOLLOCKS, HERE'S THE SEX PISTOLS (LP, 1st reissue. Green label side 1, red label on side 2 - Matlock credit returns on 'EMI', rear sleeve has 11 or 12 track listing) ................................................................................................. | 15 |
| 79 | Virgin VD 2510 | THE GREAT ROCK 'N' ROLL SWINDLE (2-LP, 1st pressing with 23 tracks including "Watcha Gonna Do About It", with paper insert) ...................................................... | 40 |
| 79 | Virgin VD 2510 | THE GREAT ROCK 'N' ROLL SWINDLE (2-LP, 2nd pressing with 24 tracks. "I Wanna Be Me" and "Who Killed Bambi?" replace "Watcha Gonna Do About It", with spoken overdubs on "God Save The Queen Symphony" 2 stickers on front and 1 on rear) ........ | 40 |
| 79 | Virgin VD 2510 | THE GREAT ROCK 'N' ROLL SWINDLE (2-LP, 2nd pressing with 24 tracks. "I Wanna Be Me" and "Who Killed Bambi?" replace "Watcha Gonna Do About It", with spoken overdubs on "God Save The Queen Symphony" 1 sticker on front) .............................. | 20 |
| 79 | Virgin V2142 | FLOGGING A DEAD HORSE (LP) ........................................................................... | 15 |
| 80 | Factory FACT 30 | THE HEYDAY (gold interview cassette in satin pouch with Xmas card) ...................... | 50 |
| 80 | Factory FACT 30 | THE HEYDAY (cassette, in vinyl pouch without Xmas card) ..................................... | 20 |
| 80 | Virgin V 2168 | THE GREAT ROCK 'N' ROLL SWINDLE (LP, compilation with 2 stickers on front and free poster) ............................................................................................................ | 80 |
| 84 | Virgin OVED 136 | NEVER MIND THE BOLLOCKS, HERE'S THE SEX PISTOLS (LP, reissue, misprinted with 'Belsen Was A Gas' on rear of sleeve and 'Liar' printed twice) .................................. | 15 |
| 85 | Virgin OVED 136 | NEVER MIND THE BOLLOCKS, HERE'S THE SEX PISTOLS (LP, reissue, misprinted with 'Belsen Was A Gas' on rear of sleeve) ................................................................... | 18 |
| 92 | Virgin V2702 | KISS THIS (2-LP) ............................................................................................... | 25 |
| 97 | EMI LPCENT20 | NEVER MIND THE BOLLOCKS, HERE'S THE SEX PISTOLS (LP, reissue, EMI 100 Centenary edition, stickered sleeve) ................................................................................... | 25 |
| 98 | Virgin VP 2087 | NEVER MIND THE BOLLOCKS, HERE'S THE SEX PISTOLS (LP, pink vinyl reissue, numbered on rear sleeve) ................................................................................... | 20 |
| 06 | Castle CMQLP 1395 | SPUNK (LP, yellow vinyl) ................................................................................... | 15 |

*(see also Public Image Ltd, Professionals, Rich Kids, Steve Jones, Cash Pussies, Spectres (UK)*

## TONY SEXTON
| 78 | Burning Sounds BSD 005 | Desire (with Jah Son)/BOB DAVIS: World In My Arms (12") ..................................... | 15 |
|---|---|---|---|

## SEXWITCH
| 15 | Echo 538169301 | SEXWITCH (LP) ................................................................................................ | 40 |
|---|---|---|---|

*(see also Bat For Lashes)*

## SEXY GIRLS
| 69 | Fab FAB 100 | Pom-Pom Song/LITTLE JOE & BUSTER'S ALLSTARS: Hy There (B-side actually by Melltones) ....................................................................................................... | 15 |
|---|---|---|---|
| 69 | Dice CC 100 | Pom-Pom Song/LITTLE JOE & BUSTER'S ALLSTARS: Hy There (B-side actually by Melltones) (reissue) ....................................................................................... | 15 |

## DENNY SEYTON & SABRES
| 64 | Mercury MF 800 | Tricky Dicky/Baby What You Want Me To Do .................................................... | 20 |
|---|---|---|---|
| 64 | Mercury MF 814 | Short Fat Fanny/Give Me Back My Heart .......................................................... | 20 |
| 64 | Mercury MF 824 | The Way You Look Tonight/Hands Off ............................................................. | 20 |
| 65 | Parlophone R 5363 | Just A Kiss/In The Flowers By The Trees (as Denny Seyton Group) ...................... | 20 |
| 65 | Wing WL 1032 | IT'S THE GEAR (14 HITS) (LP) .......................................................................... | 30 |

## SFW
| 78 | Badarse SFW 1 | True Life/The March (no p/s) .......................................................................... | 20 |
|---|---|---|---|

## TONY SHABAZZ
| 79 | Ethnic Fight FT DD 4436 | Mr Fitzy/RUDDIE MOWATT: Public Enemy (12") .............................................. | 60 |
|---|---|---|---|

## SHABBY TIGER
| 76 | RCA Victor PL 25046 | SHABBY TIGER (LP) ........................................................................................ | 15 |
|---|---|---|---|

## SHACK
| 88 | Ghetto GTG B 1 | Emergency/Liberation (p/s) ........................................................................... | 6 |
|---|---|---|---|
| 88 | Ghetto GTG T 1 | Emergency/Liberation/Faith (12", p/s) ............................................................ | 12 |
| 89 | Ghetto GTG B 2 | High Rise Low Life/Who Killed Clayton Square? (p/s) ......................................... | 5 |
| 89 | Ghetto GTG T 2 | High Rise Low Life/Who Killed Clayton Square?/High Rise Low Life (Bert Hardy Mix) (12", p/s) ................................................................................................... | 10 |
| 90 | Ghetto GTG B 11 | I Know You Well/I Feel No Way (p/s) ............................................................... | 5 |
| 88 | Ghetto GHETT 1 | ZILCH (LP, with free 12" distributed by Epic) ................................................... | 20 |
| 88 | Ghetto GHETT 1 | ZILCH (LP, later independent issue) ................................................................ | 25 |
| 03 | North Country NCLP 002 | HERE'S TOM WITH THE WEATHER (LP) ............................................................ | 25 |
| 06 | Sour Mash JDNCLP 006 | THE CORNER OF MILES AND GIL (2-LP) ........................................................... | 18 |

*(see also Pale Fountains, Michael Head & Strands)*

## SHADE JOEY & NIGHTOWLS
| 64 | Parlophone R 5180 | Bluebirds Over The Mountain/That's When I Need You Baby ............................. | 90 |
|---|---|---|---|

## SHADER
| 81 | Piston Broke REDASH 1 | Bad News Blues (no p/s) ............................................................................... | 100 |
|---|---|---|---|

## SHADES
| 62 | Starlite ST45 074 | Weird Walk/Joe's Shuffle ............................................................................. | 20 |
|---|---|---|---|

## SHADES (JAMAICA)
| 69 | Gas GAS 119 | Never Gonna Give You Up/Let Me Remind You (both actually by Techniques) .............. | 40 |
|---|---|---|---|

*(see also Techniques)*

MINT VALUE £

## SHADES OF BLUE (U.K.)

| | | | |
|---|---|---|---|
| 65 | Parlophone R 5270 | Voodoo Blues/Luceanne .................................................................. | 50 |
| 65 | Pye 7N 15988 | Where Did All The Good Times Go/I Ain't No Use.................................. | 15 |

## SHADES OF BLUE (U.S.)

| | | | |
|---|---|---|---|
| 66 | Sue WI 4022 | Oh! How Happy/Little Orphan Boy ..................................................... | 35 |

## SHADES OF JOY

| | | | |
|---|---|---|---|
| 69 | Fontana STL 5498 | SHADES OF JOY (LP) ......................................................................... | 20 |

## SHADES OF MACMURROUGH

| | | | |
|---|---|---|---|
| 73 | Polydor 2908 007 | CRAIG RIVER (LP, red label, Irish pressing) ........................................ | 150 |

## SHADES OF MORLEY BROWN

| | | | |
|---|---|---|---|
| 68 | Mercury MF1054 | Silly Girl/Pretty Bluebird................................................................. | 120 |

## SHADES (U.S.)

| | | | |
|---|---|---|---|
| 58 | London HLX 8713 | Sun Glasses (with Knott Sisters)/KNOTT SISTERS: Undivided Attention ......... | 40 |

## SHADO

| | | | |
|---|---|---|---|
| 74 | Montrose MON 1001 | Evil City/Tell You I Know .................................................................. | 60 |

## JOHNNY SHADOW (& DANNY GAVAN)

| | | | |
|---|---|---|---|
| 63 | Pye 7N 15506 | Golli Golli/I'm Coming Home To You (with Danny Gavan) (in p/s) ................ | 15 |
| 63 | Pye 7N 15506 | Golli Golli/I'm Coming Home To You (with Danny Gavan) ......................... | 5 |
| 63 | Pye 7N 15529 | Golli Guitar/Week (with Danny Gavan) ............................................... | 5 |
| 65 | Parlophone R 5286 | Kiss Me Now/What Colour Is The Wind .............................................. | 5 |
| 65 | Parlophone R 5308 | Atom Bomb Song Part 3/Talented Man .............................................. | 5 |

*(see also Ivy League)*

## SHADOWBOYS

| | | | |
|---|---|---|---|
| 83 | Pete Nik DFN 1A | Waiting For Tomorrow/Out Of Reach (p/s) .......................................... | 10 |

## SHADOWFAX

| | | | |
|---|---|---|---|
| 79 | BFD SFX 100 | Really Into You/Spare Wheel Driver (no p/s, band name spelt as Shaddowfax on label)) ........................................................................................ | 50 |
| 80 | Risky Discs RISK 1 | The Russians Are Coming/Calling The Shots ....................................... | 25 |

## SHADOWLANDS

| | | | |
|---|---|---|---|
| 86 | Pharoah PR 002 | Cry From The Heart/Cold Nights (no p/s)............................................ | 15 |

## SHADOW RING

| | | | |
|---|---|---|---|
| 96 | Dry Leaf DF 006 | Rats & Mice (lathe cut, 150 only)...................................................... | 20 |
| 93 | Dry Leaf DF 001 | Don't Open The Window/The Heavy Foot Of The Lark.......................... | 20 |
| 95 | Dry Leaf DF 004 | Some Of Us/The Wallet Of Wasps .................................................... | 10 |
| 93 | Dry Leaf DF 002 | CITY LIGHTS (LP) ............................................................................. | 70 |

## SHADOWS (U.K.)

### SINGLES

| | | | |
|---|---|---|---|
| 59 | Columbia DB 4387 | Saturday Dance/Lonesome Fella ....................................................... | 40 |
| 59 | Columbia DB 4387 | Saturday Dance/Lonesome Fella (78) ................................................. | 150 |
| 60 | Columbia DB 4484 | Apache/Quartermaster's Stores (green label)...................................... | 8 |
| 60 | Columbia DB 4484 | Apache/Quartermaster's Stores (later black label) .............................. | 15 |
| 60 | Columbia DB 4530 | Man Of Mystery/The Stranger........................................................... | 5 |
| 61 | Columbia DB 4580 | F.B.I./Midnight .............................................................................. | 5 |
| 61 | Columbia DB 4637 | The Frightened City/Back Home ........................................................ | 5 |
| 61 | Columbia DB 4698 | Kon-Tiki/36-24-36 ........................................................................... | 5 |
| 61 | Columbia DB 4726 | The Savage/Peace Pipe ................................................................... | 5 |
| 62 | Columbia DB 4790 | Wonderful Land/Stars Fell On Stockton .............................................. | 5 |
| 62 | Columbia DB 4870 | Guitar Tango/What A Lovely Tune ..................................................... | 5 |

*(The above 45s were originally issued with green labels; later black label copies are worth £10.)*

| | | | |
|---|---|---|---|
| 62 | Columbia DB 4948 | Dance On!/All Day .......................................................................... | 5 |
| 63 | Columbia DB 4984 | Foot Tapper/The Breeze And I .......................................................... | 5 |
| 63 | Columbia DB 7047 | Atlantis/I Want You To Want Me ....................................................... | 5 |
| 63 | Columbia DB 7106 | Shindig/It's Been A Blue Day ............................................................ | 5 |
| 63 | Columbia DB 7163 | Geronimo/Shazam ......................................................................... | 5 |
| 64 | Columbia DB 7231 | Theme For Young Lovers/This Hammer ............................................. | 5 |
| 64 | Columbia DB 7261 | The Rise And Fall Of Flingel Bunt/It's A Man's World ........................... | 5 |
| 64 | Columbia DB 7261 | The Rise And Fall Of Flingel Bunt/It's A Man's World (mispressing with A-side on both sides) ........................................................................................... | 8 |
| 64 | Columbia DB 7342 | Rhythm 'n' Greens/The Miracle ........................................................ | 6 |
| 64 | Columbia DB 7416 | Genie With The Light Brown Lamp/Little Princess ............................... | 7 |
| 65 | Columbia DB 7476 | Mary Anne/Chu-Chi ....................................................................... | 6 |
| 65 | Columbia DB 7588 | Stingray/Alice In Sunderland (in export p/s) ...................................... | 20 |
| 65 | Columbia DB 7650 | Don't Make My Baby Blue/My Grandfather's Clock (p/s) ....................... | 20 |
| 65 | Columbia DB 7769 | The War Lord/I Wish I Could Shimmy Like My Sister Arthur .................. | 7 |
| 66 | Columbia DB 7853 | I Met A Girl/Late Night Set .............................................................. | 10 |
| 66 | Columbia DB 7952 | A Place In The Sun/Will You Be There ............................................... | 10 |
| 66 | Columbia DB 8034 | The Dreams I Dream/Scotch On The Socks ('B' label demos worth £50)...... | 30 |
| 67 | Columbia PSR 305 | Thunderbirds Are Go (1-sided advance promo) ................................... | 60 |
| 67 | Columbia DB 8170 | Maroc 7/Bombay Duck.................................................................... | 10 |
| 67 | Columbia PSR 308 | Maroc 7 (1-sided demo with spoken-word intro) ................................. | 60 |
| 67 | Columbia PSR 310 | Chelsea Boot/Jigsaw (demo only)...................................................... | 80 |
| 67 | Columbia DB 8264 | Tomorrow's Cancelled/Somewhere .................................................. | 15 |
| 68 | Columbia DB 8326 | Running Out Of World/HANK MARVIN: London's Not Too Far ................ | 15 |
| 68 | Columbia DB 8372 | Dear Old Mrs. Bell/Trying To Forget The One You Love ....................... | 15 |
| 69 | Columbia DB 8628 | Slaughter On Tenth Avenue/HANK MARVIN: Midnight Cowboy............. | 15 |

### EPs

| | | | |
|---|---|---|---|
| 61 | Columbia SEG 8061 | THE SHADOWS (mono)..................................................................... | 10 |
| 61 | Columbia ESG 7834 | THE SHADOWS (stereo) ................................................................... | 12 |

| 61 | Columbia SEG 8094 | THE SHADOWS TO THE FORE | 10 |
|----|----|----|----|
| 62 | Columbia SEG 8135 | SPOTLIGHT ON THE SHADOWS | 10 |
| 62 | Columbia SEG 8148 | THE SHADOWS NO. 2 (only some sleeves list "No. 2") | 10 |
| 62 | Columbia SEG 8166 | THE SHADOWS NO. 3 | 10 |
| 62 | Columbia SEG 8171 | WONDERFUL LAND OF THE SHADOWS | 10 |

*(The above EPs were originally issued with turquoise labels; later blue/black label copies are worth two-thirds these values.)*

| 62 | Columbia SEG 8193 | THE BOYS (mono) | 10 |
|----|----|----|----|
| 62 | Columbia ESG 7881 | THE BOYS (stereo, turquoise labels) | 10 |
| 62 | Columbia ESG 7881 | THE BOYS (stereo, later black/blue labels) | 20 |
| 63 | Columbia SEG 8218 | OUT OF THE SHADOWS (mono) | 10 |
| 63 | Columbia ESG 7883 | OUT OF THE SHADOWS (stereo, turquoise labels) | 15 |
| 63 | Columbia ESG 7883 | OUT OF THE SHADOWS (stereo, black/blue labels) | 15 |
| 63 | Columbia SEG 8233 | DANCE ON WITH THE SHADOWS | 10 |
| 63 | Columbia SEG 8249 | OUT OF THE SHADOWS NO. 2 (mono) | 10 |
| 63 | Columbia ESG 7895 | OUT OF THE SHADOWS NO. 2 (stereo ESG 7895) | 15 |
| 63 | Columbia SEG 8268 | FOOT TAPPING WITH THE SHADOWS | 10 |
| 63 | Columbia SEG 8278 | LOS SHADOWS (2 different sleeves) | 10 |
| 63 | Columbia SEG 8286 | SHINDIG WITH THE SHADOWS | 15 |
| 64 | Columbia SEG 8321 | THOSE BRILLIANT SHADOWS | 15 |
| 64 | Columbia SEG 8342 | DANCE WITH THE SHADOWS | 15 |
| 64 | Columbia SEG 8362 | RHYTHM AND GREENS (mono) | 15 |
| 64 | Columbia ESG 7904 | RHYTHM AND GREENS (stereo) | 20 |
| 64 | Columbia SEG 8375 | DANCE WITH THE SHADOWS NO. 2 | 15 |
| 65 | Columbia SEG 8396 | THEMES FROM "ALADDIN AND HIS WONDERFUL LAMP" | 15 |
| 65 | Columbia SEG 8408 | DANCE WITH THE SHADOWS NO. 3 | 15 |
| 65 | Columbia SEG 8445 | ALICE IN SUNDERLAND | 20 |
| 65 | Columbia SEG 8459 | THE SOUND OF THE SHADOWS | 25 |
| 66 | Columbia SEG 8473 | THE SOUND OF THE SHADOWS NO. 2 | 25 |
| 66 | Columbia SEG 8494 | THE SOUND OF THE SHADOWS NO. 3 | 25 |
| 66 | Columbia SEG 8500 | THOSE TALENTED SHADOWS | 22 |
| 66 | Columbia SEG 8510 | THUNDERBIRDS ARE GO! (with Cliff Richard) | 60 |
| 67 | Columbia SEG 8528 | THE SHADOWS ON STAGE AND SCREEN | 40 |

## ALBUMS

| 61 | Columbia 33SX 1374 | THE SHADOWS (mono) | 20 |
|----|----|----|----|
| 61 | Columbia SCX 3414 | THE SHADOWS (stereo) | 30 |
| 62 | Columbia 33SX 1458 | OUT OF THE SHADOWS (mono) | 15 |
| 62 | Columbia SCX 3449 | OUT OF THE SHADOWS (stereo) | 20 |
| 63 | Columbia 33SX 1522 | GREATEST HITS (stereo SCX 1522) | 15 |
| 64 | Columbia 33SX 1619 | DANCE WITH THE SHADOWS (mono) | 15 |
| 64 | Columbia SCX 3511 | DANCE WITH THE SHADOWS (stereo) | 22 |
| 65 | Columbia 33SX 1736 | THE SOUND OF THE SHADOWS (mono) | 15 |
| 65 | Columbia SCX 3554 | THE SOUND OF THE SHADOWS (stereo) | 20 |
| 65 | Columbia 33SX 1791 | MORE HITS! (stereo SCX 3578) | 15 |
| 66 | Columbia 33SX/SCX 6041 | SHADOW MUSIC | 15 |
| 67 | Columbia S(C)X 6148 | JIGSAW | 15 |
| 67 | Columbia S(C)X 6199 | FROM HANK, BRUCE, BRIAN AND JOHN | 15 |
| 68 | Columbia SX 6282 | ESTABLISHED 1958 (half by Cliff Richard, mono) | 15 |
| 70 | Columbia SCX 6420 | SHADES OF ROCK | 15 |
| 77 | EMI EMTV 3 | TWENTY GOLDEN GREATS (mispressing, side 2 plays Pink Floyd's "Animals") | 30 |

*(see also Cliff Richard, Drifters, Five Chestnuts, Hank Marvin, Marvin Welch & Farrar, Bruce Welch, John Henry Rostill, Brian Bennett, Jet Harris, Tony Meehan, Vipers Skiffle Group, Marty Wilde, Krew Kats, Interns, Strangers, Wasp, MacArthur Park, Thunder Company, Alan Hawkshaw)*

## SHADOWS (U.S.)

| 58 | HMV POP 563 | Jungle Fever/Under Stars Of Love | 100 |
|----|----|----|----|
| 58 | HMV POP 563 | Jungle Fever/Under Stars Of Love (78) | 50 |

## SHADOWS OF KNIGHT

| 66 | Atlantic AT 4085 | Gloria/Dark Side | 40 |
|----|----|----|----|
| 66 | Atlantic 584 021 | Oh Yeah/Light Bulb Blues | 35 |
| 66 | Atlantic 584 045 | Bad Little Woman/Gospel Zone | 30 |
| 67 | Atlantic 584 136 | Someone Like Me/Three For Love | 35 |
| 69 | Buddah 201 024 | Shake/From Way Out To Way Under | 30 |
| 79 | Radar RAD 11 | GLORIA (LP) | 15 |
| 98 | Sundazed LP 5024 | GLORIA (LP, 180gm vinyl, insert) | 18 |

## SHADROCKS

| 67 | Island WI 3061 | Go Go Special/Count Down | 12 |
|----|----|----|----|
| 68 | Jay Boy BOY 2 | There Is/Jigsaw | 6 |

## DOREEN SHAFFER

| 69 | Unity UN 536 | No Matter What/Walk Through This World | 10 |
|----|----|----|----|
| 69 | Unity UN 538 | How Much Is That Doggy In The Window/As Long As He Needs Me | 10 |
| 70 | Pama SECO 31 | FIRST LADY OF REGGAE (LP) | 80 |

*(see also Bob Marley/Wailers, Lloyd Clarke, Doreen & Jackie)*

## JOHN SHAFT

| 72 | Downtown DT 488 | Forever Music/BLOSSOM JOHNSON: The Boy I Love | 6 |
|----|----|----|----|

## BOBBY SHAFTO

| 62 | Parlophone R 4870 | Over And Over/I Want My Bed | 5 |
|----|----|----|----|
| 62 | Parlophone R 4958 | Feel So Blue/I Haven't Got A Girl | 5 |
| 64 | Parlophone R 5130 | She's My Girl/Wonderful You | 5 |
| 64 | Parlophone R 5167 | Love, Love, Love (Don't Let Me Down)/I Don't Love You Anymore | 5 |
| 64 | Parlophone R 5184 | Who Wouldn't Love A Girl Like That/I Remember | 5 |

MINT VALUE £

| | | | |
|---|---|---|---|
| 65 | Parlophone R 5252 | How Could You Do A Thing Like That To Me/Baby Then | 5 |
| 66 | Parlophone R 5403 | Lonely Is As Lonely Does/The Same Old Room | 15 |
| 66 | Parlophone R 5481 | A Little Like You/See Me Cry | 5 |

**SHAFTSBURY**

| | | | |
|---|---|---|---|
| 80 | O.K. SRT CUS 025 | Hit Man/Crazy Jane | 5 |
| 80 | O.K. OKA 001 | THE LULL BEFORE THE STORM (LP, with insert) | 15 |

**SHAG 'N' SKOOB**

| | | | |
|---|---|---|---|
| 92 | WINTER 3 | SKOOBY CHEWNZ VOL. 1 EP (12") | 40 |

**SHAG NASTY**

| | | | |
|---|---|---|---|
| 79 | Shag Nasty SN 1 | No Bullshit Just Rock 'n' Roll/Looking For A Love? (p/s) | 30 |

**SHAGRAT**

| | | | |
|---|---|---|---|
| 90 | Shagrat ORC 001 | Amanda/Peppermint Flickstick (p/s, 500 only, autographed) | 10 |
| 90 | Shagrat ORC 001 | Amanda/Peppermint Flickstick (p/s, 500 only, some autographed) | 6 |

**SHAKA FATMAN**

| | | | |
|---|---|---|---|
| 80 | Live And Love LAP 12 | CONFRONTATION DUB - SHAKA (WARRIOR) VS. FATMAN (KILLER) (LP) | 30 |

**SHAKANE**

| | | | |
|---|---|---|---|
| 70 | UPC 110 | Rhona/Find The Lady | 15 |
| 72 | Young Blood Int. YB 1004 | Love Machine/Mr Jackson | 6 |
| 76 | United Artists UP 36087 | Jenny/Gang Man | 12 |

**SHAKE**

| | | | |
|---|---|---|---|
| 79 | Sire SIR 4016 | Culture Shock/Dream On | 10 |
| 79 | Sire SIR 4016-10 | Culture Shock/Glass House/Dream On/(But) Not Mine (10", p/s) | 12 |
| (see also Rezillos, Jo Callis, TV 21) | | | |

**SHAKE APPEAL**

| | | | |
|---|---|---|---|
| 87 | Notown NO 2 | Gimme Fever/Mexico City SOS (p/s) | 10 |
| 88 | Jericho JR 001 | Amphetamine/ANYWAYS: Well Of Hurt (no p/s) | 15 |

**SHAKEDOWN**

| | | | |
|---|---|---|---|
| 78 | Kricon KR0001 | F.B.I./Wish You Could See Me Now | 7 |

**SHAKEOUTS**

| | | | |
|---|---|---|---|
| 65 | Columbia DB 7613 | Every Little Once In A While/Well Who's That | 60 |

**SHAKER**

| | | | |
|---|---|---|---|
| 94 | Ugly Bird UBR 002 | Mooncat (Spear Vocal Mix)/Mooncat (Boneseys Hand) (12") | 20 |

**SHAKERS (U.K.)**

| | | | |
|---|---|---|---|
| 63 | Polydor NH 52158 | Money/Memphis Tennessee | 25 |
| 63 | Polydor NH 52213 | Hippy Hippy Shake/Dr. Feelgood | 25 |
| 63 | Polydor NH 66991 | Hippy Hippy Shake/Dr. Feelgood | 25 |
| 63 | Polydor NH 52258 | Money/Hippy Hippy Shake | 25 |
| 63 | Polydor NH 52272 | Whole Lotta Lovin'/I Can Tell | 25 |
| 63 | Polydor 237 139 | LET'S DO THE SLOP, TWIST, MADISON, HULLY GULLY WITH THE SHAKERS (LP) | 70 |
| (see also Kingsize Taylor & Dominoes) | | | |

**SHAKERS (U.S.)**

| | | | |
|---|---|---|---|
| 73 | Probe PRO 582 | One Wonderful Moment/Love, Love, Love | 7 |
| 74 | ABC ABC 4018 | One Wonderful Moment/Love, Love, Love (reissue) | 5 |

**SHAKES**

| | | | |
|---|---|---|---|
| 83 | S 83 CUS 1982 | Funeral Rites/I Kill God | 30 |

**CHRIS SHAKESPEARE GLOBE SHOW**

| | | | |
|---|---|---|---|
| 69 | Page One POF 113 | Ob-La-Di, Ob-La-Da/Tin Soldier | 25 |
| (see also Globe Show) | | | |

**JOHN SHAKESPEARE**

| | | | |
|---|---|---|---|
| 69 | Decca F 12896 | Number One Theme/Fade Out (with p/s) | 30 |
| 69 | Decca F 12896 | Number One Theme/Fade Out | 10 |

**SHAKESPEARES**

| | | | |
|---|---|---|---|
| 68 | RCA Victor RCA 1695 | Something To Believe In/Burning My Fingers | 70 |
| (see also Fynn McCool) | | | |

**SHAKE THE TREE**

| | | | |
|---|---|---|---|
| 88 | Brickworks | SHAKE THE TREE (LP) | 30 |

**SHAKEY VICK**

| | | | |
|---|---|---|---|
| 69 | Pye NPL 18276 | LITTLE WOMAN, YOU'RE SO SWEET (LP mono) | 40 |
| 69 | Pye NSPL 18276 | LITTLE WOMAN, YOU'RE SO SWEET (LP stereo, in mono sleeve with 'STEREO NSPL' sticker on rear) | 25 |

**SAM SHAM**

| | | | |
|---|---|---|---|
| 69 | Blue Cat BS 157 | Drumbago's Dead/SPARTERS: Song Of The Year | 100 |

**SHAM 69**

| | | | |
|---|---|---|---|
| 77 | Step Forward SF 4 | I Don't Wanna/Ulster/Red London (black & white photo p/s) | 15 |
| 77 | Step Forward SF 412 | I Don't Wanna/Ulster/Red London (12", black & white photo p/s) | 10 |
| 77 | Polydor (no cat. no.) | Song Of The Streets/Fanx (1-sided concert freebie, red brick-wall label; white label copies are counterfeits) | 20 |
| 78 | Polydor 2058 966 | Borstal Breakout/Hey Little Rich Boy (p/s) | 18 |
| 78 | Polydor 2059 023 | Angels With Dirty Faces/The Cockney Kids Are Innocent (p/s) | 8 |
| 78 | Polydor 2059 050 | If The Kids Are United/Sunday Morning Nightmare (p/s) | 6 |
| 78 | | What Have We Got? (1-sided gig only 45, 500 only) | 25 |
| 79 | Step Forward SF 4 | I Don't Wanna/Red London (reissue) | 5 |
| 79 | | Hersham Boys/Day Tripper (Original "Pye Studios" acetate for 'Hersham' single, release withdrawn as unable to clear copyright) | 250 |
| 79 | Polydor POSP 64 | Hersham Boys/I Don't Wanna (live)/Tell Us The Truth (live) (p/s) | 5 |
| 79 | Polydor POSP 82 | You're A Better Man Than I/Give A Dog A Bone (p/s) | 5 |
| 87 | Legacy LGY 70 | Ban The Gun/Ban The Gun | 15 |
| 78 | Polydor POLD 5010 | THAT'S LIFE (LP, gatefold, with poster) | 15 |

| | | | |
|---|---|---|---|
| 80 | Polydor 2383 596 | THE FIRST, THE BEST AND THE LAST (LP, with live EP [RIOT 1/2816 028]) | 15 |

*(see also Jimmy Edwards)*

### SHAMBLES
| | | | |
|---|---|---|---|
| 75 | RCA RCA 2533 | Hello Baby/Held Me Spellbound | 50 |

*(see also Mandrake Paddle Steramers, Prowler)*

### SHAME
| | | | |
|---|---|---|---|
| 67 | MGM MGM 1349 | Don't Go Away Little Girl/Dreams Don't Bother Me (with picture insert) | 150 |
| 67 | MGM MGM 1349 | Don't Go Away Little Girl/Dreams Don't Bother Me (without picture insert) | 90 |

*(see also Shy Limbs, King Crimson, Gods, Emerson Lake & Palmer)*

### SHAMEN
| | | | |
|---|---|---|---|
| 86 | One Big Guitar OBG 003T | THEY MAY BE RIGHT ... BUT THEY'RE CERTAINLY WRONG (12" EP) | 12 |

*(see also Alone Again Or, Stretchheads)*

### SHAMES
| | | | |
|---|---|---|---|
| 66 | CBS 202344 | Sugar And Spice/Ben Franklin's Almanac | 25 |
| 66 | CBS 202450 | I Wanna Meet You/We Could Be Happy | 18 |
| 67 | CBS 2704 | Mr Unreliable/Georgia | 12 |
| 67 | CBS 2929 | It Could Be We're In Love/I Was Lonely When | 22 |
| 68 | CBS 3820 | Greenburg, Glickstein, Charles, David, Smith And Jones/Warm | 15 |

*(see also Isaac Guillory)*

### SHAMPOO
| | | | |
|---|---|---|---|
| 93 | Icerink DAV 06 | Blisters & Bruises/Paydirt/I Love Little Pussy (p/s, pink vinyl) | 20 |

### SHAMROCKS
| | | | |
|---|---|---|---|
| 65 | Polydor BM 56503 | La La La La La/And I Need You | 20 |

### WINSTON SHAN(D)
| | | | |
|---|---|---|---|
| 69 | Bullet BU 399 | Throw Me Corn/Darling Remember (B-side actually by Pat Edwards) | 30 |
| 69 | Bullet BU 411 | Matilda (as Wilston Shan)/HARMONIANS: Come To Me | 30 |
| 70 | Moodisc MU 3505 | I'll Run Away/Time Is The Master | 100 |
| 72 | Camel CA 88 | Audrey (as Winston Shan)/So Nice (as Winston Shan) | 10 |

### TRISTRAM SHANDY
| | | | |
|---|---|---|---|
| 74 | Tiffany 6121 505 | Saccharine Sandie, Fingers 'N Thumbs/Mr. Blue | 6 |

### LISA SHANE
| | | | |
|---|---|---|---|
| 66 | Pye 7N 17124 | Come And Get Me/Big Wide World | 6 |

### SHANE & SHANE GANG
| | | | |
|---|---|---|---|
| 64 | Pye 7N 15662 | Whistle Stop/Who Wrote That Song | 35 |

### TONY SHANE
| | | | |
|---|---|---|---|
| 77 | Pollen PBM 012 | Bird Without Wings/Loneliest Band In Town (no p/s) | 10 |

### VALERIE SHANE
| | | | |
|---|---|---|---|
| 58 | Philips PB 833 | When The Boys Talk About Girls/Careful, Careful | 8 |
| 58 | Philips PB 879 | Meet Me Tonight In Dreamland.One Billion Seven Million Thirty-Three | 7 |
| 59 | Philips PB 929 | Make Love To Me/Baisez Moi | 7 |

### SHANES
| | | | |
|---|---|---|---|
| 65 | Columbia DB 7601 | I Don't Want Your Love/New Orleans | 70 |

### SHANE SISTERS
| | | | |
|---|---|---|---|
| 60 | Ember EMB S 115 | My Mommy Told Me/Presents On The Christmas Tree | 7 |

### SHANGAANS
| | | | |
|---|---|---|---|
| 65 | Columbia DB 7551 | Genzene (What Have I Done)/Yeh Girl | 15 |
| 65 | Columbia Studio 2 TWO 109 | JUNGLE DRUMS (LP) | 25 |

### SHANGO
| | | | |
|---|---|---|---|
| 69 | A&M AMS 754 | Mama Lion/Ljuba Ljuba | 6 |

### SHANGRI-LAS
| | | | |
|---|---|---|---|
| 64 | Red Bird RB 10008 | Remember (Walking In The Sand)/It's Easier To Cry | 10 |
| 64 | Red Bird RB 10014 | Leader Of The Pack/What Is Love? | 10 |
| 65 | Red Bird RB 10018 | Give Him A Great Big Kiss/Twist And Shout | 15 |
| 65 | Red Bird RB 10025 | Out In The Streets/The Boy | 15 |
| 65 | Red Bird RB 10030 | Give Us Your Blessings/Heaven Only Knows | 15 |
| 65 | Red Bird RB 10036 | Right Now And Not Later/Train From Kansas City | 35 |
| 66 | Red Bird RB 10043 | I Can Never Go Home Anymore/Bulldog | 15 |
| 66 | Red Bird RB 10048 | Long Live Our Love/Sophisticated Boom Boom | 15 |
| 66 | Red Bird RB 10053 | He Cried/Dressed In Black | 15 |
| 66 | Red Bird RB 10068 | Past, Present, And Future/Paradise | 20 |
| 66 | Philips 6051027 | Train From Kansas City/Past Present And Future | 10 |
| 67 | Mercury MF 962 | The Sweet Sound Of Summer/I'll Never Learn | 15 |
| 67 | Mercury MF 979 | Take The Time/Footsteps On The Roof | 15 |
| 65 | Red Bird RB 40 002 | THE SHANGRI-LAS (EP) | 50 |
| 66 | Red Bird RB 40 004 | I CAN NEVER GO HOME ANYMORE (EP, unreleased) | 0 |
| 65 | Red Bird RB 20 101 | THE SHANGRI-LAS - LEADER OF THE PACK (LP) | 60 |
| 66 | Mercury MCL 20096 | GOLDEN HITS OF THE SHANGRI-LAS (LP) | 20 |

### BUD SHANK
| | | | |
|---|---|---|---|
| 56 | Vogue V 2376 | Royal Garden Blues/It Had To Be You (with Bill Perkins Quintet) | 5 |
| 56 | Vogue V 2383 | When Your Lover Has Gone/There's A Small Hotel (with Bob Brookmeyer) | 5 |
| 56 | Vogue V 2385 | Shank's Pranks/Left Bank (with Shorty Rogers Quintet) | 7 |
| 58 | Vogue LAE 12041 | THE BUD SHANK QUARTET FEATURING CLAUDE WILLIAMSON (LP) | 30 |
| 59 | Vogue LAE 12248 | LATIN CONTRASTS (LP) | 20 |

*(see also Shorty Rogers)*

### ANANDA SHANKAR
| | | | |
|---|---|---|---|
| 69 | Reprise RSLP 6398 | ANANDA SHANKAR (JUMPING JACK FLASH) (LP) | 80 |
| 70 | EMI | ANANDA SHANKAR AND HIS MUSIC (LP) | 60 |

MINT VALUE £

| | | | | |
|---|---|---|---|---|
| 71 | Reprise K 44092 | ANANDA SHANKAR (LP, reissue) | | 30 |

**RAVI SHANKAR**

| | | | |
|---|---|---|---|
| 72 | Apple APPLE 37 | Joi Bangla/Oh Bhaugowan/Raga Mishri-Jhinjhoti (p/s) | 40 |
| 71 | Mushroom 300 MR 8 | FOUR RAGA MOODS (2-LP) | 30 |
| 72 | United Artists UAG 29379 | AT THE WOODSTOCK FESTIVAL (LP, gatefold) | 15 |
| 73 | Apple SAPDO 1002 | IN CONCERT - 1972 (2-LP, with Ali Akbar Khan, gatefold sleeve) | 90 |

*(see also Ali Akbar Khan, Will Sergeant)*

**BILL SHANKLY**

| | | | |
|---|---|---|---|
| 70s | Technical TECLP 001A | SHANKS ON SOCCER (2-LP) | 20 |

**JOHNNY SHANLY**

| | | | |
|---|---|---|---|
| 60 | Columbia DB 4526 | I Wonder/It Happens That Way | 6 |

**SHANNON**

| | | | |
|---|---|---|---|
| 75 | Magnet MAG 38 | Come Back And Love Me/She's A High Flyer | 10 |

*(See also Marty Wilde)*

**DEAN SHANNON**

| | | | |
|---|---|---|---|
| 60 | HMV POP 820 | Blinded With Love/Jezebel | 25 |
| 62 | HMV POP 1103 | Ubangi Stomp/Blowing Wild | 35 |

**DEL SHANNON**

**SINGLES**

| | | | |
|---|---|---|---|
| 61 | London HLX 9317 | Runaway/Jody | 6 |
| 61 | London HLX 9317 | Runaway/Jody (mispressed B-side, plays "The Snake" by Maximilian) | 30 |
| 61 | London HLX 9402 | Hats Off To Larry/Don't Gild The Lily, Lily | 5 |
| 61 | London HLX 9462 | So Long Baby/The Answer To Everything | 5 |
| 62 | London HLX 9515 | Hey! Little Girl/You Never Talked About Me | 5 |
| 62 | London HLX 9587 | Cry Myself To Sleep/I'm Gonna Move On | 8 |
| 62 | London HLX 9609 | The Swiss Maid/Ginny In The Mirror | 5 |
| 63 | London HLX 9653 | Little Town Flirt/The Wamboo | 5 |
| 63 | London HLX 9710 | Two Kinds Of Teardrops/Kelly | 5 |
| 63 | London HLX 9761 | Two Silhouettes/My Wild One | 5 |
| 63 | London HLU 9800 | Sue's Gotta Be Mine/Since She's Gone | 10 |
| 64 | London HLU 9858 | That's The Way Love Is/Time Of The Day | 12 |
| 64 | Stateside SS 269 | Mary Jane/Stains On My Letter | 10 |
| 64 | Stateside SS 317 | Handy Man/Give Her Lots Of Lovin' | 10 |
| 64 | Stateside SS 349 | Do You Want To Dance/This Is All I Have To Give | 10 |
| 64 | Stateside SS 368 | Keep Searching (We'll Follow The Sun)/Broken Promises | 6 |
| 65 | Stateside SS 395 | Stranger In Town/Over You | 12 |
| 65 | Stateside SS 430 | Break Up/Why Don't You Tell Him | 12 |
| 65 | Stateside SS 452 | Move It On Over/She Still Remembers Tony | 15 |
| 66 | Stateside SS 494 | I Can't Believe My Ears/I Wish I Wasn't Me Tonight | 15 |
| 66 | Liberty LIB 55866 | The Big Hurt/I Got It Bad | 10 |
| 66 | Liberty LIB 55889 | For A Little While/Hey Little Star | 10 |
| 67 | Liberty LIB 55939 | She/What Makes You Run | 10 |
| 67 | Liberty LIB 10277 | Mind Over Matter/Led Along | 10 |
| 67 | Liberty LBF 15020 | Runaway/Show Me | 10 |
| 68 | Liberty LBF 15061 | Thinkin' It Over/Runnin' On Back | 10 |
| 68 | Liberty LBF 15079 | Gemini/Magical Musical Box | 10 |
| 69 | Stateside SS 8025 | Comin' Back To Me/Sweet Mary Lou | 40 |
| 70 | Stateside SS 8040 | Sister Isabelle/Colorado Rain | 10 |
| 74 | United Artists UP 35740 | And The Music Plays On/In My Arms Again | 5 |
| 83 | Demon D1017 | Cheat Love/Distant Ghost (p/s) | 5 |

**EPs**

| | | | |
|---|---|---|---|
| 62 | London RE-X 1332 | RUNAWAY WITH DEL SHANNON | 20 |
| 63 | London RE-X 1346 | DEL SHANNON NO. 2 | 20 |
| 63 | London RE-X 1383 | DEL'S OWN FAVOURITES | 20 |
| 63 | London RE-X 1387 | FROM DEL TO YOU | 20 |
| 67 | Liberty LEP 2272 | THE NEW DEL SHANNON | 40 |
| 65 | Stateside SE 1029 | DEL SHANNON HITS | 20 |

**ALBUMS**

| | | | |
|---|---|---|---|
| 61 | London HA-X 2402 | RUNAWAY WITH DEL SHANNON | 30 |
| 63 | London HA-X 8071 | HATS OFF TO DEL SHANNON | 30 |
| 63 | London HA-X 8091 | LITTLE TOWN FLIRT | 30 |
| 65 | Stateside SL 10115 | HANDY MAN | 30 |
| 65 | Stateside SL 10130 | DEL SHANNON SINGS HANK WILLIAMS | 40 |
| 65 | Stateside SL 10140 | ONE THOUSAND SIX HUNDRED AND SIXTY-ONE SECONDS WITH DEL SHANNON | 30 |
| 66 | Liberty LBY 1320 | THIS IS MY BAG (mono) | 25 |
| 66 | Liberty SLBY 1320 | THIS IS MY BAG (stereo) | 25 |
| 66 | Liberty LBY 1335 | TOTAL COMMITMENT (mono) | 30 |
| 66 | Liberty SLBY 1335 | TOTAL COMMITMENT (stereo) | 25 |
| 68 | Liberty LBL/LBS 83114E | THE FURTHER ADVENTURES OF CHARLES WESTOVER | 80 |

*(see also Maximilian)*

**LINDA SHANNON**

| | | | |
|---|---|---|---|
| 59 | Parlophone R 4603 | Goodbye Charlie/If You Only Knew | 6 |

**SHAPE**

| | | | |
|---|---|---|---|
| 71 | RCA RCA 2129 | My Friend John/Yes | 18 |

**SHAPE OF THE RAIN**

| | | | |
|---|---|---|---|
| 71 | RCA Neon NE 1001 | Woman/Wasting My Time | 10 |
| 71 | RCA RCA 2129 | My Friend John/Yes | 5 |

| 71 | RCA Neon NE 7 | RILEY, RILEY, WOOD & WAGGETT (LP, gatefold sleeve) ....................................... 275 |

## SHAPE & SIZES
| 66 | Decca F 12441 | A Little Lovin' Somethin'/Rain On My Face ................................................. 10 |

## SHAPES
| 79 | Sofa SEAT 1/FRR 004 | THE SHAPES (WOT'S FOR LUNCH, MUM?) (EP, no p/s, with insert).................. 12 |
| 79 | Good Vibrations GOT 13 | Blast Off/Airline Disasters (p/s) ...................................................... 15 |

## HELEN SHAPIRO
### SINGLES
| 61 | Columbia DB 4589 | Don't Treat Me Like A Child/When I'm With you ................................... 5 |
| 61 | Columbia DB 4670 | You Don't Know/Marvellous Lie ................................................................ 5 |
| 61 | Columbia DB 4715 | Walkin' Back To Happiness/Kiss 'N' Run........................................................ 5 |
| 61 | Columbia DB 4782 | Tell Me What He Said/I Apologise ............................................................ 5 |
| 62 | Columbia DB 4824 | Let's Talk About Love/Sometime Yesterday ............................................. 8 |
| 62 | Columbia DB 4869 | Little Miss Lonely/I Don't Care ................................................................. 5 |
| 62 | Columbia DB 4908 | Keep Away From Other Girls/Cry My Heart Out ................................... 8 |
| 63 | Columbia DB 4966 | Queen For Tonight/Daddy Couldn't Get Me One Of Those............... 15 |
| 63 | Columbia DB 7026 | Woe Is Me/I Walked Right In .................................................................. 5 |
| 63 | Columbia DB 7072 | Not Responsible/No Trespassing ............................................................ 5 |
| 63 | Columbia DB 7130 | Look Who It Is/Walking In My Dreams .................................................. 10 |
| 64 | Columbia DB 7190 | Fever/Ole Father Time ............................................................................. 25 |
| 64 | Columbia DB 7266 | Look Over Your Shoulder/You Won't Come Home ......................... 100 |
| 64 | Columbia DB 7340 | Shop Around/He Knows How To Love Me .......................................... 10 |
| 64 | Columbia DB 7395 | I Wish I'd Never Loved You/I Was Only Kidding ............................. 10 |
| 65 | Columbia DB 7517 | Tomorrow Is Another Day/It's So Funny I Could Cry...................... 10 |
| 65 | Columbia DB 7587 | Here In Your Arms/Only Once ................................................................ 10 |
| 65 | Columbia DB 7690 | Something Wonderful/Just A Line .......................................................... 10 |
| 66 | Columbia DB 7810 | Forget About The Bad Things/Wait A Little Longer ...................... 10 |
| 66 | Columbia DB 8073 | In My Calendar/Empty House ................................................................. 10 |
| 67 | Columbia DB 8148 | Make Me Belong To You/The Way Of The World ........................ 10 |
| 67 | Columbia DB 8256 | She Needs Company/Stop And You Will Become Aware .............. 125 |
| 67 | Columbia DB 8256 | She Needs Company/Stop And You Will Become Aware (DJ copy) ......... 150 |
| 68 | Pye 7N 17600 | You'll Get Me Loving You/Silly Boy (I Love You)............................ 12 |
| 69 | Pye 7N 17714 | Today Has Been Cancelled/Face The Music.................................... 12 |
| 69 | Pye 7N 17785 | You've Guessed/Take Me For A While .............................................. 20 |
| 70 | Pye 7N 17893 | Take Down A Note Miss Smith/Couldn't You See ........................ 10 |
| 70 | Pye 7N 17975 | Waiting On The Shores Of Nowhere/A Glass Of Wine ............... 10 |
| 75 | DJM DJS 363 | You're A Love Child/That's The Reason I Love You ...................... 10 |
| 77 | Arista 131 | Can't Break The Habit/For All The Wrong Reasons ..................... 10 |
| 78 | Arista 178 | Every Little Bit Hurts/Touchin' Wood .............................................. 10 |

### EPs
| 61 | Columbia ESG 7872 | HELEN (stereo, 'smiling' or 'cross-armed' sleeve) ........................ 15 |
| 62 | Columbia ESG 7880 | A TEENAGER SINGS THE BLUES (stereo) .......................................... 10 |
| 63 | Columbia SEG 8229 | TOPS' WITH ME NO. 1 (mono) ............................................................. 10 |
| 63 | Columbia ESG 7888 | TOPS' WITH ME NO. 1 (stereo) ............................................................ 15 |
| 63 | Columbia SEG 8243 | TOPS' WITH ME NO. 2 (mono) ............................................................. 10 |
| 63 | Columbia ESG 7891 | TOPS' WITH ME NO. 2 (stereo) ............................................................ 15 |

### ALBUMS
| 62 | Columbia 33SX 1397 | TOPS' WITH ME (mono)............................................................................. 15 |
| 62 | Columbia SCX 3438 | TOPS' WITH ME (stereo)........................................................................... 20 |
| 63 | Columbia 33SX 1494 | HELEN'S SIXTEEN (mono)......................................................................... 20 |
| 63 | Columbia SCX 3470 | HELEN'S SIXTEEN (stereo)....................................................................... 35 |
| 63 | Columbia 33SX 1561 | HELEN IN NASHVILLE .............................................................................. 20 |
| 64 | Columbia 33SX 1661 | HELEN HITS OUT (mono).......................................................................... 20 |
| 64 | Columbia SCX 3533 | HELEN HITS OUT (stereo SCX 3533)...................................................... 35 |

*(see also Ella Stone & Moss)*

## SHAPIROS
| 79 | Now Records N 702 | Waitress/Isolde (no p/s, 1000 only)........................................................ 20 |

## SHARADES
| 64 | Decca F 11811 | Dumb Head/Boy Trouble.......................................................................... 85 |

*(see also Ladybirds, Breakaways)*

## BILLY SHA RAE
| 71 | Action ACT 4602 | Do It/Crying Clown................................................................................... 15 |

## BILLY SHARI
| 58 | Decca F 11069 | Going Home For Christmas/Count Every Star (as Shari) ................. 5 |
| 68 | United Artists UP 2235 | It's So Lonely Being Together/You Walked Out On Me Before ........... 5 |

## SHARK TABOO
| 82 | Risque SRTS 82 CUS 1374 | Crossfire/Dream Crumble......................................................................... 20 |

## SHARKS (1)
| 68 | RCA RCA 1776 | Goodbye Lorene/Funkology ................................................................... 20 |

*(see also Marcisa & Jeff, Roy Richards)*

## RALPH SHARON
| 53 | Decca LF 1107 | SPRING FEVER (10" LP)................................................................................. 12 |
| 53 | Decca LF 1138 | AUTUMN LEAVES (10" LP) .......................................................................... 20 |
| 53 | Lyragon AF 1 | COCKTAIL TIME (10" LP) ............................................................................. 15 |

## BOBBY SHARP & OTHERS
| 65 | Stateside SS 404 | Blues For Mr. Charlie (Parts 1 & 2) (with Paul Sindap, Joe Lee Wilson & Little Butler).... 20 |

MINT VALUE £

## DEE DEE SHARP

| | | | |
|---|---|---|---|
| 62 | Columbia DB 4818 | Mashed Potato Time/Set My Heart At Ease | 25 |
| 62 | Columbia DB 4874 | Gravy (For My Mashed Potatoes)/Baby Cakes | 25 |
| 62 | Cameo Parkway C 230 | Ride/Night | 25 |
| 63 | Cameo Parkway C 244 | Do The Bird/Lover Boy | 40 |
| 63 | Cameo Parkway C 260 | Rock Me In The Cradle Of Love/You'll Never Be Mine | 25 |
| 63 | Cameo Parkway C 274 | Wild/Why Doncha Ask Me | 20 |
| 65 | Cameo Parkway C 375 | I Really Love You/Standing In The Need Of Love | 20 |
| 65 | Cameo Parkway C 375 | I Really Love You/Standing In The Need Of Love (DJ copy) | 80 |
| 65 | Cameo Parkway C 382 | It's A Funny Situation/There Ain't Nothing I Wouldn't Do (demo-only) | 125 |
| 66 | Atlantic 584 056 | My Best Friend's Man/Bye Bye Baby | 150 |
| 69 | Action ACT 4522 | What Kind Of Lady/You're Gonna Miss Me | 20 |
| 79 | London HA-U 8514 | CAMEO PARKWAY SESSIONS (LP) | 80 |

*(see also Chubby Checker & Dee Dee Sharp)*

## STEVE SHARP & THE CLEANCUTS

| | | | |
|---|---|---|---|
| 80 | Happy Face MM 122 | We Are The Mods/He Wants To Be A Mod | 125 |

*(see also Rowdies)*

## BERNARD SHARPE

| | | | |
|---|---|---|---|
| 66 | Parlophone R 5519 | Lost In Space/Jorrocks | 10 |
| 67 | Parlophone R 5611 | The Other Side Of The Sky/Where Do We Go | 15 |

## RAY SHARPE

| | | | |
|---|---|---|---|
| 59 | London HLW 8932 | Linda Lu/Red Sails In The Sunset (triangular centre) | 50 |
| 59 | London HLW 8932 | Linda Lu/Red Sails In The Sunset (round centre) | 40 |
| 59 | London HLW 8932 | Linda Lu/Red Sails In The Sunset (78) | 30 |
| 63 | United Artists UP 1032 | Hey Little Girl/Day You Left Me | 15 |

## ROCKY SHARPE & THE REPLAYS

| | | | |
|---|---|---|---|
| 82 | Chiswick DICE 9 | Heart/Mary (Won't You Marry Me) (withdrawn, approx. 100 only) | 10 |

## SHARPE & NUMAN

| | | | |
|---|---|---|---|
| 85 | Polydor PODJ 722 | Change Your Mind (p/s, 1-sided 7" DJ promo) | 10 |
| 89 | Polydor POPB 43 | I'm On Automatic/No More Lies (New Version) (stickered poster sleeve) | 6 |

*(see also Gary Numan)*

## SHARPEES

| | | | |
|---|---|---|---|
| 66 | Stateside SS 495 | Tired Of Being Lonely/Just To Please You | 75 |
| 66 | Stateside SS 495 | Tired Of Being Lonely/Just To Please You (DJ copy) | 150 |
| 73 | President PT 389 | Do The 45/Make Up Your Mind | 15 |
| 73 | President PT 399 | Tired Of Being Lonely/Just To Please You (reissue) | 10 |

## BOB SHARPLES

| | | | |
|---|---|---|---|
| 56 | Decca 45-F10707 | Hurricane Boogie/Sadies Shawl (tri label) | 5 |

## SHARPS

| | | | |
|---|---|---|---|
| 57 | Vogue V 9086 | Lock My Heart/Love Is Here To Stay | 500 |
| 57 | Vogue V 9086 | Lock My Heart/Love Is Here To Stay (78) | 100 |
| 58 | Vogue V 9096 | Shufflin'/What Will I Gain | 500 |
| 58 | Vogue V 9096 | Shufflin'/What Will I Gain (78) | 100 |

*(see also Thurston Harris)*

## S-HATERS

| | | | |
|---|---|---|---|
| 81 | Outer Himalayan OHR 02 | Death Of A Vampire/Research (p/s) | 30 |
| 82 | Outer Himalayan OHR 005 | STORIES AS COLD AS THE IRISH SEA (7" EP) | 15 |

## SHATTERED DOLLS

| | | | |
|---|---|---|---|
| 80 | Rox ROX 1 | Lipstick Killer/Talk To Me/Valley Of The Dolls 1 & 2 | 20 |

## MIKE SHAUN

| | | | |
|---|---|---|---|
| 63 | Decca F 11733 | So Lonely/Let's Fall In Love | 15 |

## ADRIAN SHAW

| | | | |
|---|---|---|---|
| 96 | Woronzow W0027 | TEA FOR THE HYDRA (LP, 299 copies only, in hand-finished sleeves) | 15 |

*(see also Hawkwind, Bevis Frond)*

## ALAN LEE SHAW

| | | | |
|---|---|---|---|
| 74 | Alaska ALA 15 | She Moans/Bolweevil | 120 |

## MARLENA SHAW

| | | | |
|---|---|---|---|
| 67 | Chess CRS 8054 | Mercy Mercy Mercy/Go Away Little Boy | 12 |
| 76 | United Artists UP 36125 | It's Better Than Walking Out/Be For Real | 8 |
| 76 | Blue Note 36163 | Love Has Gone Away/No Hiding Place | 7 |
| 04 | Jazzman JM 032 | California Soul/Wade In The Water | 5 |

## NINA SHAW

| | | | |
|---|---|---|---|
| 68 | CBS 3239 | Woven In My Soul/Love So Fine | 7 |
| 68 | CBS 3556 | From Now Till Then/Window Of My Mind | 8 |
| 69 | CBS 4227 | One Fine Day/Somewhere In The World | 10 |

## RICKY SHAW

| | | | |
|---|---|---|---|
| 62 | London HLU 9606 | No Love But Your Love/Be Still, Be Still, My Own | 8 |

## SANDIE SHAW

### SINGLES

| | | | |
|---|---|---|---|
| 64 | Pye 7N 15671 | As Long As You're Happy Baby/Ya-Ya-Da-Da | 40 |
| 64 | Pye 7N 15704 | (There's) Always Something There To Remind Me/Don't You Know | 5 |
| 64 | Pye 7N 15743 | I'd Be Far Better Off Without You/Girl Don't Come | 5 |
| 65 | Pye 7N 15783 | I'll Stop At Nothing/You Can't Blame Him | 5 |
| 65 | Pye 7N 15841 | Long Live Love/I've Heard About Him | 6 |
| 65 | Pye 7N 15940 | Message Understood/Don't You Count On It | 5 |
| 65 | Pye 7N 15987 | How Can You Tell/If Ever You Need Me | 5 |
| 65 | Pye 7N 17036 | Tomorrow/Hurting You | 5 |

| 66 | Pye 7N 17086 | Nothing Comes Easy/Stop Before You Start | 5 |
| 66 | Pye 7N 17163 | Run/Long Walk Home | 8 |
| 66 | Pye 7N 17212 | Think Sometimes About Me/Hide All Emotion | 10 |
| 67 | Pye 7N 17239 | I Don't Need Anything/Keep In Touch | 10 |
| 67 | Pye 7N 17272 | Puppet On A String/Tell The Boys (pink label, later blue) | 5 |
| 67 | Pye 7N 17346 | Tonight In Tokyo/You've Been Seeing Her Again | 6 |
| 67 | Pye 7N 17378 | You've Not Changed/Make Me Cry | 5 |
| 68 | Pye 7N 17441 | Today/London (pink label, later blue) | 5 |
| 68 | Pye 7N 17504 | Don't Run Away/Stop | 10 |
| 68 | Pye 7N 17564 | Show Me/One More Lie | 10 |
| 68 | Pye 7N 17587 | Together/Turn On The Sunshine | 10 |
| 68 | Pye 7N 17611 | Those Were The Days/Make It Go | 8 |
| 69 | Pye 7N 17675 | Monsieur Dupont/Voice In The Crowd | 5 |
| 69 | Pye 7N 17726 | Think It All Over/Send Me A Letter | 12 |
| 70 | Pye 7N 17954 | Wight Is Wight/That's The Way He's Made | 10 |
| 70 | Pye 7N 45040 | Rose Garden/Maybe I'm Amazed | 10 |
| 84 | Rough Trade RT 130 | Hand In Glove/I Don't Owe You Anything (white label test pressing) | 100 |
| 84 | Rough Trade RTT 130 | Hand In Glove/I Don't Owe You Anything/Jeanne (12", p/s, with The Smiths) | 10 |

### EPs

| 64 | Pye NEP 24208 | (THERE'S) ALWAYS SOMETHING THERE TO REMIND ME | 15 |
| 65 | Pye NEP 24220 | LONG LIVE LOVE | 15 |
| 65 | Pye NEP 24232 | TALK ABOUT LOVE | 15 |
| 65 | Pye NEP 24234 | SANDIE | 15 |
| 66 | Pye NEP 24236 | MESSAGE UNDERSTOOD | 15 |
| 66 | Pye NEP 24247 | TOMORROW | 20 |
| 66 | Pye NEP 24254 | NOTHING COMES EASY | 20 |
| 66 | Pye NEP 24264 | RUN WITH SANDIE SHAW | 20 |
| 67 | Pye NEP 24271 | SANDIE SHAW IN FRENCH | 20 |
| 67 | Pye NEP 24273 | SANDIE SHAW IN ITALIAN | 20 |
| 67 | Pye NEP 24281 | TELL THE BOYS | 20 |

### ALBUMS

| 65 | Pye NPL 18110 | SANDIE SHAW | 15 |
| 65 | Pye NPL 18121 | ME | 15 |
| 69 | Pye N(S)PL 18323 | REVIEWING THE SITUATION | 50 |

### THOMAS SHAW
| 72 | Xtra XTRA 1132 | THOMAS SHAW (LP) | 15 |

### TIMMY SHAW & STERNPHONES
| 64 | Pye International 7N 25239 | Gonna Send You Back To Georgia/I'm A Lonely Guy | 30 |

### TREVOR SHAW
| 81 | CMS PR 26 | WHEELS IN MOTION (LP) | 20 |

### DOROTHY SHAY
| 53 | Capitol LC 6618 | THE PARK AVENUE HILLBILLIE (10" LP) | 12 |

### SHAZAM
| 83 | ADSR 001 | Let's Get Together/Memories | 150 |

### SHE
| 85 | Neat NEAT 50 | Never Surrender/Breaking Away (p/s) | 5 |

### DEL AARON SHEARS
| 79 | Shearsongs SRTS/79/CUS 287 | Keep A Little Marc In Your Heart/Beautiful Angel/Oh What A Lady (no sleeve) | 8 |

### GARY SHEARSTON
| 74 | Charisma CB241 | Without A Song/Aborigini | 6 |

### SHED SEVEN
| 96 | Polydor 576 214-7 | Going For Gold/Making Waves (withdrawn 'nude' gatefold p/s) | 5 |
| 94 | Polydor 523615-1 | CHANGE GIVER (LP) | 40 |
| 96 | Polydor 531039-1 | A MAXIMUM HIGH (LP, with booklet) | 40 |
| 98 | Polydor 557 359-1 | LET IT RIDE (LP) | 20 |

### BOBBY SHEEN
| 66 | Capitol CL 15455 | Dr. Love/Sweet, Sweet Love | 125 |
| 66 | Capitol CL 15455 | Dr. Love/Sweet, Sweet Love (DJ copies) | 175 |
| 72 | Capitol CL 15713 | Dr. Love/Sweet, Sweet Love (reissue) | 20 |
| 03 | Atco 67855 | Something New To Do/BEN E KING: I Can't Break The News To Myself | 15 |

*(see also Bob B. Soxx & Blue Jeans)*

### SHEEP (U.K.)
| 73 | Myrrh MYR 1000 | SHEEP (LP, with insert) | 20 |

*(see also Lonesome Stone)*

### SHEEP (U.S.)
| 66 | Stateside SS 493 | Hide And Seek/Twelve Months Later | 30 |
| 69 | Stateside SS 2147 | Hide And Seek/HAWKS: The Grissle | 12 |

### SHEEPHOUSE
| 71 | Decca 13229 | Juicy Lucy/Part 2 | 100 |

### SHEEPS HEAD BAY
| 71 | Parlophone R5897 | My Name Is In The Wind/The River Song | 8 |

### IREEN SHEER
| 70 | Bell BLL 1129 | Hey Pleasure Man/You Walked Away | 5 |
| 71 | Parlophone R 5930 | Many Rivers/Is It Me | 5 |
| 74 | Polydor 2041 533 | Bye Bye I Love You/Roseberry Avenue | 6 |
| 78 | EMI 2796 | Fire/Feuer ('Eurovision' p/s) | 10 |

MINT VALUE £

## SHEER KHAN
| 84 | SRT 4KS 140 | Last Generation/Lady's Dance (p/s) | 70 |
| 85 | Mill | QUIET ENOUGH FOR LOVE (LP) | 30 |

## SHEFFIELDS
| 64 | Pye 7N 15600 | It Must Be Love/Say Girl | 50 |
| 64 | Pye 7N 15627 | I Got My Mojo Working/Hey Hey Lover Boy | 70 |
| 65 | Pye 7N 15767 | Bag's Groove (Skat Walking)/Plenty Of Love | 75 |

## SHEIKS (PORTUGAL)
| 66 | Parlophone R 5500 | Missing You/Tell Me Bird | 15 |

## SHEIKS (U.S.)
| 59 | London HLW 9012 | Très Chic/Little French Doll | 10 |

## SHEILA & JENNY
| 64 | Ember EMB S 3202 | When The Boy's Happy/Please Don't Break Her Heart (in p/s) | 10 |
| 64 | Ember EMB S 3202 | When The Boy's Happy/Please Don't Break Her Heart | 6 |

## SHELBY
| 74 | Santa Ponsa PNS 21 | Dance With The Guitar Man/Jump Into The Fire | 6 |
| 75 | Route RT 02 | Motorbike Girl/Cirrus | 8 |

## ALLEN SHELDON
| 70 | Plexium PXM 14 | Mirror Of My Mind/Old Windmill Tree | 50 |

## DOUG SHELDON
| 61 | Decca F 11368 | The Book Of Love/Play Me The Blues | 10 |
| 61 | Decca F 11398 | Runaround Sue/Come With Me | 10 |
| 61 | Decca F 11416 | Your Ma Said You Cried In Your Sleep/You're Only Fooling Yourself | 10 |
| 62 | Decca F 11433 | My Kingdom For A Girl/You Never Had It So Good | 10 |
| 62 | Decca F 11463 | A Big Big Baby/If You'd Be Mine | 10 |
| 62 | Decca F 11514 | Lollipops And Roses/One Way To Say Goodbye | 10 |
| 62 | Decca F 11529 | Live Now Pay Later/Me | 15 |
| 63 | Decca F 11564 | I Saw Linda Yesterday/My Billy | 8 |
| 63 | Decca F 11654 | Let's Make A Habit Of This/I Was Alone | 10 |
| 63 | Decca F 11790 | Mickey's Monkey/Falling In Love With Love | 10 |
| 65 | Sue WI 332 | Take It Like A Man/Lonely Boy | 40 |
| 65 | Pye 7N 17011 | It's Because Of You/How Can I Tell Her? | 7 |
| 63 | Decca DFE 8527 | HERE I STAND (EP) | 50 |

## SANDI SHELDON
| 76 | Epic EPC 4186 | You're Gonna Make Me Love You/Baby You're Mine | 25 |

## SHELL
| 66 | Columbia DB 8082 | Goodbye Little Girl/Little Bit Of Lovin' | 15 |

## SHELLEY
| 64 | Pye 7N 15711 | I Will Be Wishing/Why Won't You Say (That You Love Me) | 15 |
| 65 | Pye 7N 15773 | Stairway To A Star/I Heard A Whisper | 10 |
| 65 | Pye 7N 15913 | Where Has Your Smile Gone/Paradise | 10 |

## LIZ SHELLEY
| 65 | Brunswick 05940 | Make Me Your Baby/You Made Me Hurt | 10 |
| 66 | Brunswick 05953 | No More Love/I Can't Find You | 10 |

## PETE SHELLEY
| 82 | Lyntone 10952/53 | Qu'est-Ce Que C'est, Qu'est Que Ça (Dub)/ANIMAL MAGNET: More (hard vinyl test pressing, numbered, with info sheet/letter) | 15 |
| 82 | Lyntone 10952/53 | Qu'est-Ce Que C'est, Qu'est Que Ça (Dub)/ANIMAL MAGNET: More (hard vinyl test pressing, numbered) | 12 |

*(see also Buzzcocks, Free Agents, Tiller Boys)*

## SHELLS
| 61 | London HLU 9288 | Baby, Oh Baby/Angel Eyes | 30 |
| 62 | London HLU 9644 | It's A Happy Holiday/Deep In My Heart | 35 |

## SHELLY
| 95 | Sarah SARAH 98 | Reproduction Is Pollution/Prejudice/Here (p/s) | 12 |

## ALAN SHELLY & MANU DIBANGO'S BROTHERS
| 69 | Philips BF 1709 | Lady Black Wife/Give Me Time | 12 |

## ANNE SHELTON
| 53 | HMV 7M 164 | Answer Me/The Bridge Of Sighs | 10 |
| 54 | HMV 7M 186 | The Book/Why Does It Have To Be Me | 10 |
| 54 | HMV 7M 240 | Goodnight, Well It's Time To Go/If I Give My Heart To You | 10 |
| 54 | HMV 7M 279 | My Gypsy Heart/Teach Me Tonight | 10 |
| 57 | Philips JK 1012 | Absent Friends/Seven Ages Of Man (Jukebox issue) | 10 |
| 56 | Decca DFE 6321 | FOUR STANDARDS (EP) | 10 |

## JO SHELTON
| 59 | Top Rank JAR 124 | Tread Softly (You're Stepping On My Heart)/More More More Romancing | 6 |
| 59 | Top Rank JAR 245 | If There Are Stars In My Eyes/I Need Your Arms Around Me | 6 |

## ROSCOE SHELTON
| 65 | Sue WI 354 | Strain On My Heart/Question (A- & B-side labels reversed) | 40 |

## DEANNA SHENDEREY
| 65 | Decca F 12090 | Comin' Home Baby/I've Got That Feeling | 15 |

## SHENLEY (DUFFAS) & ANNETTE
| 61 | Blue Beat BB 72 | Million Dollar Baby/The First Time I Met You | 20 |

## SHENLEY (DUFFAS) & HYACINTH (BROWN)
| 66 | Rio R 80 | The World Is On A Wheel/ROY & CORNELL: Salvation | 15 |

*(see also Baba Brooks)*

## SHENLEY (DUFFAS) & (LITTLE) LUNAN
65   Rio R 52                         Something On Your Mind/The Rain Came Tumbling Down ........................ 15
*(see also Shenley Duffas)*

## SHEP & LIMELITES
61   Pye International 7N 25090        Daddy's Home/This I Know ..................................................... 60
61   Pye International 7N 25112        Ready For Your Love/You'll Be Sorry ............................................ 100

## BILLY SHEPHARD
59   Felstad AF 117                   You Call Everybody Darling/Somebody Stole My Gal ............................... 5

## DAVE SHEPHERD QUINTET
69   77 LEU 12/35                     SHEPHERD'S DELIGHT (LP) ...................................................... 20

## PAULINE SHEPHERD
57   Columbia DB 4010                 Love Me To Pieces/Just Between You And Me ..................................... 12

## SHEPHERD BOYS (& GIRLS)
56   Columbia SCM 5282                Little Girls And Little Boys/Teenage Love (as Shepherd Boys & Girls) ........... 8
56   Columbia DB 3816                 Summer Sweetheart/Song For A Summer Night ..................................... 6

## ARCHIE SHEPP
66   HMV CLP/CSD 3524                 FOUR FOR TRANE (LP) ........................................................... 35
66   HMV CLP/CSD 3561                 ON THIS NIGHT (LP) ............................................................ 30
67   HMV CLP/CSD 3600                 LIVE IN SAN FRANCISCO (LP) .................................................... 35
67   Polydor 623 235                  ARCHIE SHEPP AND THE NEW YORK CONTEMPORARY FIVE (LP) .......................... 30
67   Fontana 681 014 ZL               RUFUS (LP, with John Tchicai) ................................................. 35
68   Impulse MIPL/SIPL 508            MAMA TOO TIGHT (LP) ........................................................... 35
68   Polydor 623 267                  NEW YORK CONTEMPORARY FIVE VOL. 2 (LP) ........................................ 25
69   Impulse MILP/SIPL 512           THE MAGIC OF JU-JU (LP) ....................................................... 30
69   Impulse MIPL/SIPL 516           THE WAY AHEAD (LP) ............................................................ 30
*(see also John Coltrane)*

## SHEPPARDS
71   Jay Boy BOY 30                   How Do You Like It/Stubborn Heart ............................................. 40

## SHEPHERD/SHEPPARD SISTERS
57   HMV POP 411                      Alone (Why Must I Be Alone)/Congratulations To Someone ........................ 10
58   Mercury 7MT 196                  Gettin' Ready For Freddy/Best Thing There Is (Is Love)(Sheppard Sisters ....... 15
58   Mercury 7MT 218                  Eating Pizza/A Boy And A Girl (as Sheppard Sisters) ........................... 10
58   Mercury AMT 1005                 Dancing Baby/Is It A Crime? ................................................... 10
63   London HLK 9681                  Don't Mention My Name/What Makes Little Girls Cry ............................. 20
63   London HLK 9758                  Talk Is Cheap/Greatest Lover ................................................. 15

## SHEPPERTON FLAMES
69   Deram DM 257                     Take Me For What I Am/Goodbye ................................................. 20
*(see also Mike Berry)*

## SHERE KHAN
69   Tepee TPR 1007                   Little Louise/No Reason ...................................................... 200
71   UPC 110                          Rhone/Find The Lady .......................................................... 60

## SHERIDAN
70   Gemini GMS 001                   Follow Me Follow/When Love Breaks Your Heart .................................. 15
*(see also Sheridan-Price, Mike Sheridan & Night Riders, Mike Sheridan's Lot)*

## DANI SHERIDAN
66   Planet PLF 106                   Guess I'm Dumb/Songs Of Love ................................................. 50

## LEE SHERIDAN
73   Deram DM 373                     Sweet Tasting Candy Sugar/Big Louis' Gun ...................................... 8

## MIKE SHERIDAN & NIGHT RIDERS
63   Columbia DB 7141                 Tell Me What'cha Gonna Do/No Other Guy ....................................... 30
63   Columbia DB 7183                 Please Mr. Postman/In Love ................................................... 30
64   Columbia DB 7302                 What A Sweet Thing That Was/Fabulous ......................................... 25
65   Columbia DB 7462                 Here I Stand/Lonely Weekends ................................................. 25
*(see also Roy Wood, Idle Race, Mike Sheridan's Lot, Sheridan-Price, Sight & Sound)*

## MIKE SHERIDAN'S LOT
65   Columbia DB 7677                 Take My Hand/Make Them Understand ............................................ 50
66   Columbia DB 7798                 Don't Turn Your Back On Me, Babe/Stop, Look, Listen .......................... 50
*(see also Roy Wood, Idle Race, Mike Sheridan & Night Riders, Sheridan-Price, Sight & Sound)*

## TONY SHERIDAN & THE BEAT BROTHERS
64   Polydor NH 52315                 Jambalaya/Will You Still Love Me Tomorrow (with The Beat Brothers) ........... 12
64   Polydor NH 52927                 Skinny Minny/You'd Better Move On (with The Beat Brothers) ................... 12
*(see also Bobby Patrick Big Six, Beat Brothers, Pete Best Four)*

## SHERIDAN-PRICE
70   Gemini GMS 009                   Sometimes I Wonder (as Sheridan & Rick Price)/SHERIDAN: Lightning Never Strikes
                                      Twice ........................................................................ 25
70   Gemini GME 1002                  THIS IS TO CERTIFY THAT... (LP, gatefold sleeve) ............................. 40
*(see also Rick Price, Mike Sheridan & Nightriders, Mike Sheridan's Lot, Idle Race, Sight & Sound, Sheridan)*

## SHERMAN
72   Pye 7N45131                      If You Could Read My Mind/Find My Way Back Home ............................. 30

## BIM SHERMAN
77   Hawkeye HE 003                   Ever Firm/GUSSIE ALLSTARS: Rigid ............................................. 8
78   Yard International YI 1001        What Sweet You So/U BLACK: Pot A Bubble (12") ................................ 40
79   Hit Run DD6/7                    Down In Jamtown (with Jah Lion)/TEEM ALL STARS: Version (12") ................ 40
79   Hit Run HIT DD 11                Love Jah Only (with Jah Buzz)/CRYTUFF ALL STARS : Version (12") .............. 40
79   Attack TACK 9                    Lightning And Thunder/Why Don't You Come On? (12") .......................... 25
79   Savannah SUN 12-2                Golden Locks/Tribulation (12") ............................................... 40
83   On-U Sound DP 10                 Keep You Dancing (with Dub Syndicate)/Can't Stop Jumping (with Dub Syndicate and
                                      Augustus Pablo) (10", p/s) ................................................... 18

MINT VALUE £

| | | | |
|---|---|---|---|
| 77 | Tribesman TM 007 | LOVE FOREVER (LP) | 80 |
| 84 | Century CENTURY 100 | CENTURY (LP, with Voluntary) | 15 |
| 88 | On U Sound 17 | ACROSS THE RED SEA (LP) | 20 |
| 84 | Century 200 C200 | DANGER (LP) | 15 |
| 88 | RDL RDL 900 | GHETTO DUB (LP) | 25 |
| 92 | Century CENTURY 900 | GHETTO DUB (LP, reissue) | 20 |

## BOBBY SHERMAN
| | | | |
|---|---|---|---|
| 69 | Pye Intl. 7N 25508 | La La La (If I Had You)/Time | 10 |
| 70 | CBS 5118 | Hey, Mister Sun/Two Blind Minds | 5 |
| 71 | CBS 57468 | Waiting At The Bust Stop/Runaway | 12 |
| 71 | CBS 7468 | Waiting At The Bus Stop/Run Away | 6 |

## JOE SHERMAN
| | | | |
|---|---|---|---|
| 58 | Fontana H 129 | Miraculous Music Box/Make Me Laugh | 6 |
| 58 | Fontana H 147 | Buttermilk/Please Don't Say Goodnight | 6 |

## BILLY SHERRILL
| | | | |
|---|---|---|---|
| 61 | Mercury AMT 1131 | Like Making Love/Rules Of The Game | 8 |

## SHERRYS
| | | | |
|---|---|---|---|
| 62 | London HLW 9625 | Pop Pop Pop-Pie/Your Hand In Mine | 20 |
| 63 | London HL 9686 | Let's Stomp Again/Slop Time | 25 |
| 04 | Soul City SC 148 | Put Your Arms Around Me/LITTLE JOE COOK: I'm Falling In Love With You Baby | 5 |
| 63 | London RE 1363 | DO THE POPEYE (EP) | 70 |

## SHERWOOD
| | | | |
|---|---|---|---|
| 86 | Sherwood SRT6KL 901 | RIDING THE RAINBOW (12" EP) | 50 |

## BOBBY SHERWOOD
| | | | |
|---|---|---|---|
| 55 | Vogue Coral Q 72097 | The Kentuckian Song/Far Away Places | 6 |

## ROBERTA SHERWOOD
| | | | |
|---|---|---|---|
| 56 | Brunswick 05572 | Lazy River/This Train | 10 |
| 57 | Brunswick 05654 | Tears Don't Care Who Cries Them/You're Nobody Till Somebody Loves You | 5 |
| 57 | Brunswick 05670 | Mary Lou/What Does It Matter | 5 |
| 63 | Stateside SS 154 | You Always Hurt The One You Love/In San Francisco | 5 |
| 63 | Stateside SL 10039 | ON STAGE (LP) | 20 |

## TONY SHERWOOD TRIO
| | | | |
|---|---|---|---|
| 60s | Zodiac ZR 010 | Piano Boogie Twist/Tom Dooley | 15 |

## SHERWOODS (1)
| | | | |
|---|---|---|---|
| 61 | Pye International 7N 25097 | Nanette/El Scorpion | 12 |

## SHERWOODS (2)
| | | | |
|---|---|---|---|
| 64 | Solar SRP 105 | Memories/Some Other Time | 8 |

## SHE TRINITY
| | | | |
|---|---|---|---|
| 66 | Columbia DB 7874 | He Fought The Law/The Union Station Blues | 20 |
| 66 | Columbia DB 7943 | Have I Sinned/Wild Flower | 10 |
| 66 | Columbia DB 7959 | Wild Flower/The Man Who Took The Valise Off The Floor Of Grand Central Station At Noon | 7 |
| 66 | Columbia DB 7992 | Yellow Submarine/Promise Me You'll Never Cry | 20 |
| 67 | CBS 2819 | Across The Street/Over And Over Again | 8 |
| 70 | President PT 283 | Hair/Climb That Tree | 40 |

*(see also Shotgun Express, Beryl Marsden, Gilded Cage)*

## SHEVELLES
| | | | |
|---|---|---|---|
| 63 | Oriole CB 1915 | Ooh Poo Pa Doo/Like I Love You | 25 |

## SHEVELLS
| | | | |
|---|---|---|---|
| 64 | United Artists UP 1059 | I Could Conquer The World/How Would You Like Me To Love You | 30 |
| 65 | United Artists UP 1076 | Walking On The Edge Of The World/Not So Close | 20 |
| 65 | United Artists UP 1081 | Watermelon Man/Taking Over Your Life | 20 |
| 66 | United Artists UP 1125 | Come On Home/I Gotta Travel All Over | 45 |
| 68 | Polydor 56239 | Big City Lights/Coffee Song | 15 |

*(see also Mike Stevens & Shevells)*

## TONY SHEVETON
| | | | |
|---|---|---|---|
| 62 | Oriole CB 1705 | Lullaby Of Love/I Have A Feeling | 20 |
| 62 | Oriole CB 1726 | Lonely Heart/Foolish Doubts | 20 |
| 62 | Oriole CB 1766 | Hey Little Girl/Kissing Date | 25 |
| 63 | Oriole CB 1788 | Runaround Sue Is Getting Married/I Love The Girl Next Door | 25 |
| 63 | Oriole CB 1895 | A Million Drums/Dance With Me | 20 |
| 64 | Oriole CB 1975 | Excuses/Is It Me, Is It You? | 18 |

*(see also Tony Rich)*

## SHIDE & ACORN
| | | | |
|---|---|---|---|
| 73 | Private pressing | UNDER THE TREE (LP) | 400 |
| 94 | Acme AC 8006LP | UNDER THE TREE (LP, reissue, 500 only, numbered) | 15 |

*(see also Jeremy Cahill)*

## SHIELA
| | | | |
|---|---|---|---|
| 71 | Nu Beat NB 079 | Only Heaven Knows/GRANT & RICHARDS: Freedom Psalm | 7 |

## TREVOR SHIELD
| | | | |
|---|---|---|---|
| 69 | Harry J TR 664 | The Moon Is Playing Tricks On Me/KING CANNON: Soul Special | 60 |
| 69 | Trojan TR 665 | Please/JAY BOYS: Splendour Splash | 40 |
| 72 | Ashanti ASH 407 | Rough Road/JAY BOYS: Rough The Road | 12 |

*(see also Beltones, Trevor (Shield))*

## SHIELDS
| | | | |
|---|---|---|---|
| 58 | London HLD 8706 | You Cheated/That's The Way It's Gonna Be | 30 |

## KEITH SHIELDS
| | | | |
|---|---|---|---|
| 67 | Decca F 12572 | Hey Gyp (Dig The Slowness)/Deep Inside Your Mind | 70 |
| 67 | Decca F 12609 | The Wonder Of You/Run, Run, Run | 30 |
| 67 | Decca F 12666 | So Hard Livin' Without You/Baby Do You Love Me | 30 |

*(see also Marty Wilde [& Wildcats])*

## BRUSH SHIELS (IRELAND)
| | | | |
|---|---|---|---|
| 77 | Hawk HASP 401 | Love At Love Bleed/Better Than I Expected | 8 |
| 77 | Hawk HASP 419 | Fight Your Heart Out/Coming Home | 12 |

## ALLAN SHIERS
| | | | |
|---|---|---|---|
| 74 | Profle GMOR 003 | THE MAN IN ME (LP) | 40 |

## SU SHIFRIN
| | | | |
|---|---|---|---|
| 76 | EMI 2442 | Over The Rainbow/When You Wish Upon A Star/Secrets | 6 |
| 78 | United Artists UP 36438 | We Must Believe In Magic/All I Wanna Do In Life | 6 |

## SUSAN SHIFRIN
| | | | |
|---|---|---|---|
| 71 | Decca F13145 | To Love/25 Miles | 30 |

## SAHIB SHIHAB QUARTET
| | | | |
|---|---|---|---|
| 70 | Youngblood SSYB 12 | SEEDS (LP) | 100 |

## SHILLELAGH SISTERS
| | | | |
|---|---|---|---|
| 84 | CBS A 4217 | Give Me My Freedom/Teasin' Cheatin' Man (p/s) | 8 |
| 84 | CBS A 4684 | Passion Fruit/These Boots Are Made For Walkin' (p/s) | 15 |
| 84 | CBS TA 4684 | Passion Fruit/These Boots Are Made For Walkin'/Shout (12", p/s) | 30 |
| 84 | TA 4217 | Give Me My Freedom (Club Mix)/Teasin' Cheatin' Man (12", p/s) | 10 |

## SHILLINGFORD MILL
| | | | |
|---|---|---|---|
| 71 | Mam 28 | Frightened/I Want To Know | 12 |
| 71 | Mam MAM 15 | It's A Thing Called Love/Walking Along | 6 |

## SHINDIGS
| | | | |
|---|---|---|---|
| 65 | Parlophone R 5316 | One Little Letter/What You Gonna Do | 35 |
| 65 | Parlophone R 5377 | A Little While Back/Why Say Goodbye | 35 |

## SHINDOGS
| | | | |
|---|---|---|---|
| 67 | Fontana TF 790 | Who Do You Think You Are/Yes, I'm Going Home | 18 |

*(see also Delaney & Bonnie, James Burton)*

## SHINE
| | | | |
|---|---|---|---|
| 74 | Fontana 6007041 | Candy Girl/I Wonder If Anything | 10 |

## JOHNNY SHINES
| | | | |
|---|---|---|---|
| 69 | Blue Horizon (S) 7-63212 | LAST NIGHT'S DREAM (LP, with Otis Spann, mono or stereo) | 90 |
| 74 | Xtra XTRA 1142 | COUNTRY BLUES (LP) | 25 |

## DON SHINN (& THE SOUL AGENTS)
| | | | |
|---|---|---|---|
| 66 | Polydor BM 56075 | A Minor Explosion/Pits Of Darkness (with The Soul Agents) | 70 |
| 69 | Columbia S(C)X 6319 | TEMPLES WITH PROPHETS (LP) | 125 |
| 69 | Columbia SCX 6355 | DEPARTURES (LP) | 150 |

*(see also The Soul Agents)*

## SHINS
| | | | |
|---|---|---|---|
| 07 | Sub Pop | Sea Legs/Strange Powers (p/s) | 18 |

## SHINY TOO SHINY
| | | | |
|---|---|---|---|
| 83 | Red Flame RFB 29 | Waiting For Us/Ritual Hate (p/s) | 8 |

## SHIP
| | | | |
|---|---|---|---|
| 72 | Elektra K 42122 | THE SHIP - A CONTEMPORARY FOLK JOURNEY (LP, gatefold sleeve) | 35 |

## SHIRALEE
| | | | |
|---|---|---|---|
| 67 | Fontana TF 855 | I'll Stay By Your Side/Penny Wren | 20 |

## SHIRELLES
| | | | |
|---|---|---|---|
| 58 | Brunswick 05746 | I Met Him On A Sunday/I Want You To Be My Boyfriend | 70 |
| 58 | Brunswick 05746 | I Met Him On A Sunday/I Want You To Be My Boyfriend (78) | 30 |
| 60 | London HL 9233 | Tonight's The Night/The Dance Is Over | 20 |
| 60 | Top Rank JAR 540 | Will You Love Me Tomorrow/Boys | 8 |
| 61 | Top Rank JAR 549 | Dedicated To The One I Love/Look-A-Here Baby | 18 |
| 61 | Top Rank JAR 567 | Mama Said/Blue Holiday | 15 |
| 61 | Top Rank JAR 578 | What A Sweet Thing That Was/A Thing Of The Past | 12 |
| 61 | Top Rank JAR 590 | Big John/Twenty One | 12 |
| 62 | Top Rank JAR 601 | Baby It's You/The Things I Want To Hear | 20 |
| 62 | HMV POP 1019 | Soldier Boy/Love Is A Swingin' Thing | 12 |
| 62 | Stateside SS 119 | Welcome Home Baby/Mama Here Comes The Bride | 15 |
| 62 | Stateside SS 129 | Stop The Music/It's Love That Really Counts | 18 |
| 63 | Stateside SS 152 | Everybody Loves A Lover/I Don't Think So | 12 |
| 63 | Stateside SS 181 | Foolish Little Girl/Not For All The Money In The World | 15 |
| 63 | Stateside SS 213 | Don't Say Goodnight And Mean Goodbye/I Didn't Mean To Hurt You | 15 |
| 63 | Stateside SS 232 | What Does A Girl Do/Don't Let It Happen To Us | 15 |
| 63 | Pye International 7N 25229 | It's A Mad, Mad, Mad, Mad World/31 Flavours | 20 |
| 64 | Pye International 7N 25233 | Tonight You're Gonna Fall In Love With Me/20th Century Rock And Roll | 20 |
| 64 | Pye International 7N 25240 | Sha La La/His Lips Get In The Way | 15 |
| 64 | Pye International 7N 25279 | Maybe Tonight/Lost Love | 15 |
| 65 | Pye International 7N 25288 | Are You Still My Baby/I Saw A Tear | 12 |
| 66 | Pye International 7N 25386 | Shades Of Blue/When The Boys Talk About The Girls | 12 |
| 67 | Pye International 7N 25425 | Too Much Of A Good Thing/Bright Shiny Colours | 20 |
| 69 | Mercury MF 1093 | There's A Storm Going On In My Heart/Call Me (If You Want Me) | 22 |
| 71 | United Artists UP 35192 | Take Me/Dedicated To The One I Love | 10 |
| 75 | Pye Disco Demand DDs 115 | Last Minute Miracle/March | 15 |
| 61 | Top Rank JKP 3012 | THE SHIRELLES SOUND FEATURING "WILL YOU LOVE ME TOMORROW" (EP) | 100 |

MINT VALUE £

| 61 | Top Rank 35-115 | THE SHIRELLES SING - TO TRUMPET AND STRINGS (LP) | 100 |
| 62 | Stateside SL 10006 | BABY IT'S YOU (LP) | 100 |
| 63 | Stateside SL 10041 | THE SHIRELLES' HITS (LP) | 50 |
| 70 | Wand WNS 4 | ETERNALLY SOUL (LP, with King Curtis) | 25 |
| 71 | Wand WCS 1001 | TONIGHT'S THE NIGHT (LP) | 15 |

(see also Shirley & Shirelles, Shirley Alston)

## SHIRLEY
| 74 | London HLA 10477 | I Hear Those Church Bells Ringing/Chapel Of Love/I Do Love You | 7 |

## DON SHIRLEY
| 56 | London HA-A 2003 | PIANO PERSPECTIVES (LP) | 15 |
| 56 | London HA-A 2004 | TONAL EXPRESSIONS (LP) | 15 |
| 57 | London HAA 2046 | IMPROVISATIONS (LP) | 15 |
| 62 | London HAA 2448 | DROWN IN MY OWN TEARS (LP, also stereo [SAHA 6238]) | 15 |

## ROY SHIRLEY
| 66 | Ska Beat JB 253 | Paradise/Calling | 25 |
| 66 | Doctor Bird DB 1068 | Hold Them/Be Good | 25 |
| 67 | Doctor Bird DB 1079 | I'm A Winner/Sleeping Beauty | 40 |
| 67 | Doctor Bird DB 1088 | Prophet/What To Do | 40 |
| 67 | Doctor Bird DB 1093 | Musical Field/LEE PERRY & DYNAMITES: Trial And Crosses | 35 |
| 67 | Doctor Bird DB 1108 | Thank You/Touch Them | 30 |
| 67 | Caltone CAL 101 | Get On The Ball/JOHNNY MOORE: Sound And Soul | 40 |
| 67 | Island WI 3070 | People Rock Steady/I'm Trying To Find A Home (actually by Uniques) | 60 |
| 67 | Island WI 3071 | Musical War/Soul Voice | 100 |
| 67 | Island WI 3120 | Girlie/GLEN ADAMS: She's So Fine | 50 |
| 68 | Doctor Bird DB 1165 | Hush A Bye/Musical Dinner | 25 |
| 68 | Doctor Bird DB 1168 | Dance The Reggae/The Agreement | 30 |
| 68 | Giant GN 32 | Dance Hall Arena/The Musical Train | 12 |
| 68 | Giant GN 33 | Warming Up The Scene/GLEN ADAMS: Lonely Girl | 175 |
| 68 | Island WI 3098 | Thank You/Touch Them | 25 |
| 68 | Island WI 3108 | Move All Day/Rollin' Rollin' | 25 |
| 68 | Island WI 3110 | Million Dollar Baby/SENSATIONS: Long Time No See You Girl | 40 |
| 68 | Island WI 3118 | Good Is Better Than Bad/Fantastic Lover | 25 |
| 68 | Island WI 3119 | Facts Of Life/Lead Us Not Into Temptation (as Roy Shirley & Uniques; B-side actually by Roy Shirley & Slim Smith) | 25 |
| 68 | Island WI 3125 | If I Did Know/Good Ambition | 25 |
| 68 | Amalgamated AMG 815 | The World Needs Love/Dance The A | 15 |
| 68 | Fab FAB 54 | Think About The Future/Golden Festival | 25 |
| 69 | Duke DU 18 | Life/I Like Your Smile | 20 |
| 71 | Nu Beat NB 090 | Hold Them One/Two Three Four | 10 |
| 72 | Punch PH 108 | A Sugar/ALTYMAN REID: A Sugar - Version | 10 |
| 72 | Punch PH 103 | Don't Be A Loser/Jamaican Girl | 10 |
| 73 | Count Shelly CS 006 | This World/Return To Me | 8 |
| 74 | Arrow AR 001 | Welcome Home/What Am I Loving For | 10 |
| 74 | Leroy LYW 001 | Don't Destroy The World/Golden Festival | 8 |
| 75 | R&J 001 | Heart Breaking Jepsey/Version | 5 |
| 80s | Shirley SHIRLEY 1 | For Everyone/Version (p/s) | 5 |

(see also Val Bennett, Glen Adams, Shirley & Charmers, Sensations, Denzil, Errol & His Group, Ronsig, Stranger & Glady, Untouchables)

## SUSAN SHIRLEY
| 68 | Mercury MF 1038 | Sun Shines Out Of Your Shoes/Tomorrow Today | 5 |
| 69 | Mercury MF 1087 | Too Many Tears/Boy From Boston Massachusetts USA | 5 |
| 70 | Philips 6006 037 | Really Into Somethin'/My Friend The Clown | 30 |
| 71 | Columbia DB 8787 | True Love And Apple Pie/To Find Out (p/s) | 15 |
| 71 | Columbia DB 8835 | Jealous Guy/Oh Yoko | 6 |
| 72 | Columbia DB 8937 | The Other Side Of Me/Imagine | 5 |

## SHIRLEY & CHARMERS
| 72 | Bullet BU 502 | Rum Rhythm/LLOYD CHARMERS: Rhythm (Version) | 12 |

(see also Roy Shirley)

## SHIRLEY & JOHNNY
| 64 | Parlophone R 5149 | I Don't Want To Know/It Must Be Love | 7 |
| 69 | Mercury MF 1074 | Don't Make Me Over/Baby, Baby, Baby | 7 |

## SHIRLEY & LEE
| 56 | Vogue V 9059 | Let The Good Times Roll/Do You Mean To Hurt Me So | 150 |
| 56 | Vogue V 9059 | Let The Good Times Roll/Do You Mean To Hurt Me So (78) | 20 |
| 57 | Vogue V 9063 | I Feel Good/Now That It's Over | 100 |
| 57 | Vogue V 9063 | I Feel Good/Now That It's Over (78) | 20 |
| 57 | Vogue V 9067 | That's What I Wanna Do/When I Saw You | 95 |
| 57 | Vogue V 9067 | That's What I Wanna Do/When I Saw You (78) | 20 |
| 57 | Vogue V 9072 | Rock All Nite/Don't You Know I Love You | 120 |
| 57 | Vogue V 9072 | Rock All Nite/Don't You Know I Love You (78) | 20 |
| 57 | Vogue V 9084 | Rockin' With The Clock/The Flirt | 130 |
| 57 | Vogue V 9084 | Rockin' With The Clock/The Flirt (78) | 20 |
| 57 | Vogue V 9088 | I Want To Dance/Marry Me | 80 |
| 57 | Vogue V 9088 | I Want To Dance/Marry Me (78) | 20 |
| 57 | Vogue V 9094 | Feel So Good/You'd Be Thinking Of Me | 80 |
| 57 | Vogue V 9094 | Feel So Good/You'd Be Thinking Of Me (78) | 20 |
| 58 | Vogue V 9103 | I'll Thrill You/Love No One But You | 85 |
| 58 | Vogue V 9103 | I'll Thrill You/Love No One But You (78) | 30 |
| 58 | Vogue V 9118 | Everybody's Rockin'/Don't Leave Me Here To Cry | 120 |
| 58 | Vogue V 9118 | Everybody's Rockin'/Don't Leave Me Here To Cry (78) | 25 |

| 59 | Vogue V 9129 | All I Want To Do Is Cry/Come On And Have Your Fun | 80 |
| 59 | Vogue V 9129 | All I Want To Do Is Cry/Come On And Have Your Fun (78) | 25 |
| 59 | Vogue V 9135 | A Little Word/That's What I'll Do | 80 |
| 59 | Vogue V 9135 | A Little Word/That's What I'll Do (78) | 30 |
| 59 | Vogue V 9137 | I'll Do It/Lee's Dream | 80 |

*(The above 45s were originally issued with triangular centres; later round-centre issues are worth two-thirds of this value.)*

| 59 | Vogue V 9137 | I'll Do It/Lee's Dream (78) | 30 |
| 59 | Vogue V 9156 | True Love/When Day Is Done | 80 |

*(Later Vocalion pressings of the above 2 singles worth two-thirds of these values.)*

| 59 | Vogue V 9156 | True Love/When Day Is Done (78) | 40 |
| 60 | London HLI 9186 | I've Been Loved Before/Like You Used To Do | 25 |
| 60 | London HLI 9209 | Let The Good Times Roll/Keep Loving Me | 20 |
| 65 | Island WI 257 | Let The Good Times Roll/I'm Gone | 20 |
| 57 | Vogue VE 1-70101 | ROCK 'N' ROLL (EP, triangular centre) | 300 |
| 57 | Vogue VE 1-70101 | ROCK 'N' ROLL (EP, later round centre) | 220 |
| 60 | Vogue VE 1-70145 | SHIRLEY AND LEE (EP) | 250 |
| 71 | Jay Boy JSX 2005 | LET THE GOOD TIMES ROLL (LP) | 20 |

## SHIRLEY & RUDE BOYS
| 67 | Blue Beat BB 375 | Gently Set Me Free/BUSTER'S ALL STARS: Rock Steady | 200 |

## SHIRLEY & SHIRELLES
| 69 | Bell BLL 1049 | Look What You've Done To My Heart/A Most Unusual Boy | 12 |
| 69 | Bell BLL 1065 | Plaything/Looking Glass | 6 |
| 72 | Bell BLL 1251 | Look What You've Done To My Heart/A Most Unusual Boy (reissue) | 8 |

*(see also Shirelles)*

## SHIRTS
| 78 | Harvest HAR 5165 | Tell Me Your Plans/Cyrinda | 6 |
| 78 | Harvest HAR 5170 | Lonely Android/Running Through The Night (p/s) | 5 |
| 78 | SHSP 4089 | THE SHIRTS (LP, blue vinyl) | 15 |

## SHITMAT
| 04 | Planet Mu ZIQ 089 | KILLABABYLONKUTZ (2-LP) | 18 |

## SHIVA (1)
| 72 | D'art ART 2017 | The Legend Of Tutankhamun/Valley Of The Kings | 10 |

## SHIVA (2)
| 82 | Heavy Metal HEAVY 13 | Rock Lives On/Sympathy For The Devil (p/s) | 20 |
| 82 | Heavy Metal HEAVY 16 | Angel Of Mons/Stranger Lands (p/s) | 10 |
| 82 | Heavy Metal HMRLP 6 | FIREDANCE (LP) | 20 |

## BUNNY SHIVEL
| 67 | Capitol CL 15487 | You'll Never Find A Love Like Mine/The Slide | 20 |

## SHOC CORRIDOR
| 82 | Shout XW 203 | A Blind Sign/Sargasso Sea/On Reflection (12") | 10 |
| 84 | Quiet QST 005 | Fever/That Sinking Feeling (12") | 12 |
| 84 | Shout XS 009 | Holding Treasure/Almost In Walking Distance | 5 |
| 83 | Shout LX 003 | EXPERIMENTS IN INCEST (LP) | 25 |
| 84 | Quiet QLP5 | TRAIN OF EVENTS (LP) | 25 |

## SHOCK
| 81 | RCA RCAT 133 | Dynamo Beat/Dream Games (12") | 12 |

## JOYCE SHOCK
| 58 | Philips PB 824 | Take Your Foot From The Door!/I've Got Bells On My Heart | 6 |
| 58 | Philips PB 872 | Hoopa Hoola/You're Not Losing A Daughter, Mama | 6 |
| 59 | Philips PB 934 | Personality/I Can't Love You Anymore | 6 |
| 59 | Philips PB 957 | Cry, Baby, Cry/Dear Diary | 6 |

## SHOCKABILLY
| 84 | Rough Trade ROUGH 68 | COLOSSEUM (LP) | 15 |

## SHOCK ABSORBERS
| 69 | Major Minor SMCP 5028 | GUITAR PARTY (LP) | 25 |

## SHOCK HEADED PETERS
| 84 | él EL 1 | I, Blood Brother Be/Truth Has Come (p/s) | 7 |

*(see also Lemon Kittens, Karl Blake, Sol Invictus)*

## SHOCKING BLUE
| 69 | Olga OLE 015 | Send Me A Postcard/Harley Davidson (demo only) | 60 |
| 69 | Penny Farthing PEN 702 | Venus/Hot Sand | 5 |
| 70 | Penny Farthing PEN 713 | Mighty Joe/Wild Wind | 5 |
| 70 | Penny Farthing PEN 721 | Never Marry A Railroad Man/Roll Engine Roll | 5 |
| 70 | Penny Farthing PEN 744 | Sally Was A Good Old Girl/Long And Lonesome Road | 6 |
| 71 | Penny Farthing PEN 748 | Hello Darkness/Pickin' Tomatoes | 5 |
| 70 | Penny Farthing PELS 500 | SHOCKING BLUE AT HOME (LP) | 50 |
| 70 | Penny Farthing PELS 510 | SCORPIO'S DANCE (LP) | 40 |

## SHOCK TREATMENT
| 80s | Skull SKR 2001 | The Mugger/Nuclear Warfare (p/s) | 150 |

## SHOES
| 67 | Polydor 56739 | Farewell In The Rain/What In The World Is Love | 7 |

## SHOES FOR INDUSTRY
| 79 | Fried Egg EGG 001 | Laughbeat/Can't Help It (p/s) | 6 |
| 80 | Fried Egg FRY 1 | TALK LIKE A WHELK (LP) | 20 |

## SHOESTRING BAND
| 73 | CBS SCBS 1284 | Thingumajig/Don't It Make You Feel Good | 6 |
| 86 | Attack ATA 913 | High In The Sky/When The Lights Go Down (p/s) | 30 |

| | | | MINT VALUE £ |
|---|---|---|---|
| 86 | Attack ATA 006 | SHOGUN (LP) | 40 |

**SHOGUN MC**
| 89 | Blue Chip C22T | Ready For Action (12") | 15 |

**TROY SHONDELL**
| 61 | London HLG 9432 | This Time/Girl After Girl | |
| 62 | Liberty LIB 55398 | Island In The Sky/Tears From An Angel | 8 |
| 63 | London HL 9668 | I Got A Woman/Some People Never Learn | 15 |
| 64 | London HAY 8128 | MANY SIDES OF TROY SHONDELL (LP) | 12 |
| | | | 70 |

**SHONDELLS**
| 64 | Ember EMB S 191 | My Love/Don't Cry My Soldier Boy | 50 |

**SHOO SHOO**
| 77 | Pilot PT 1 | Clap Your Hands Louder/The Final Touch | 30 |

**SHOOT**
| 73 | EMI EMI 2026 | On The Frontier/Ships And Sails | 5 |
| 72 | EMI EMA 73 | ON THE FRONTIER (LP) | 20 |
| *(see also Manfred Mann Chapter 3, Yardbirds, Raw Material)* | | | |

**SHOOTING PARTY**
| 88 | Lisson DOLER 9 | Safe In The Arms Of Love (Phil's Extra Beat Update)/Safe In The Arms Of Love | 12 |

**SHOP ASSISTANTS**
| 85 | Subway Organisation SUBWAY 1 | All Day Long/All That Ever Mattered/It's Up To You/Switzerland (red foldaround hand-coloured p/s in poly bag) | 12 |
| 85 | Subway Organisation SUBWAY 1 | All Day Long/All That Ever Mattered/It's Up To You/Switzerland (later blue foldaround hand-coloured p/s in poly bag) | 6 |
| 86 | Blue Guitar AZUR 2 | I Don't Wanna Be Friends With You/Looking Back (p/s) | 5 |
| 86 | 53rd and 3rd AGARR1 | Safety Net/Almost Made It/Somewhere In China (p/s) | 5 |
| 86 | Blue Guitar AZLP 2 | SHOP ASSISTANTS (LP) | 20 |
| *(see also Buba & Shop assistants)* | | | |

**DINAH SHORE**
| 53 | HMV 7M 119 | Keep It A Secret/Bella Musica | 8 |
| 53 | HMV 7M 139 | Sweet Thing/Three-Cornered Tune | 8 |
| 54 | HMV 7M 183 | Changing Partners/Think | 8 |
| 54 | HMV 7M 221 | This Must Be The Place/Come Back To My Arms | 8 |
| 54 | HMV 7M 236 | Three Coins In The Fountain/Pakistan | 8 |
| 54 | HMV 7M 250 | If I Give My Heart To You/Let Me Know | 8 |
| 56 | HMV 7M 352 | Love And Marriage/Compare | 8 |
| 57 | RCA RCA 1003 | The Cattle Call/Promises, Promises (Skip Redwine) | 7 |
| 58 | RCA RCA 1054 | Thirteen Men/I'll Never Say "Never Again" Again | 5 |
| 58 | RCA RD 27072 | HOLDING HANDS AT MIDNIGHT (LP) | 15 |

**BRIAN SHORT**
| 71 | Transatlantic TRA 245 | ANYTHING FOR A LAUGH (LP, textured gatefold sleeve) | 30 |
| *(see also Black Cat Bones)* | | | |

**SHORT FUSE**
| 72 | Denby DB 316 | You Lied To Me/Circles | 50 |

**KEVIN SHORT**
| 79 | EMI INT 574 | Punk Strut/Short Cut (no p/s, demos only) | 30 |

**SHORT KUTS WITH EDDIE HARRISON**
| 68 | United Artists UP 2233 | Your Eyes May Shine/Letting The Tears Tumbling Down | 25 |

**SHORTCAKES**
| 71 | Decca F13185 | I Can Try/Save Me | 10 |

**ERROL SHORTER**
| 81 | Greensleeves GRED 58 | Wild Inna Eighty-One Style/EEK A MOUSE : Wa Do Dem (12") | 10 |

**WAYNE SHORTER**
| 79 | Blue Note LBR 1021 | THE SOOTHSAYER (LP) | 15 |

**SHORTWAVE (BAND)**
| 77 | Crescent/Avada ARS 111 | GREATEST HATS (LP) | 20 |

**SHORTY (THE PRESIDENT)**
| 73 | Ackee ACK 509 | Aquarius Pressure/Halfway Tree Pressure (as Shorty The President) | 30 |
| 73 | Ackee ACK 517 | Jelly-Belly-Nelly/Message Of Love (as Shorty) | 10 |
| 75 | Treble C CCC 03 | Beast From The East/Version | 8 |
| 76 | Cactus CTLP | PRESENTING (LP) | 30 |
| 79 | Freedom Sounds FSLP 002 | DUB CONFERENCE IN LONDON (LP) | 25 |
| *(see also Shorty Perry)* | | | |

**SHORTY & THEM**
| 64 | Fontana TF 460 | Pills Or Love's Labours Lost/Live Laugh And Love | 40 |

**SHOTGUN EXPRESS**
| 66 | Columbia DB 8025 | I Could Feel The Whole World Turn Round/Curtains | 80 |
| 67 | Columbia DB 8178 | Funny 'Cos Neither Could I/Indian Thing | 80 |
| 83 | See For Miles CYM 2 | I Could Feel The Whole World Turn Round/Curtains/Funny 'Cos Neither Could I/Indian Thing (10", p/s) | 15 |
| *(see also Rod Stewart, Peter Bardens, Spencer Davis, Brian Auger, She Trinity, Beryl Marsden, Fleetwood Mac)* | | | |

**SHOTS**
| 65 | Columbia DB 7713 | Keep A Hold Of What You've Got/She's A Liar | 70 |
| *(see also Smoke)* | | | |

**SHOUT**
| 72 | Explosion 2058 | Life Is Rough/Life Is Rough - Version | 5 |
| 92 | Entity SHOUT | Is It Ever Going To End (Remix 1)/Is It Ever Going To End (Remix 2)/Is It Ever Going To End(Remix 3)/ Is It Ever Going To End (Radio Edit)/Is It Ever Going To End (Stiff Organ Mix)(12") | 60 |

## SHOUTS
64    React EA 001                She Was My Baby/That's The Way It's Gonna Be ........................................ 50

*(see also Gene Vincent)*

## THE SHOVE
81    Shove Off PBM033/S/81       Raise The Roof Tonite/Violence/Pigs/Nutters Of York (foldover p/s, 500 only) ............ 40
81    Shove Off Records           ROUGH AND READY EP (with p/s) ........................................................ 25
81    Shove Off Records           ROUGH AND READY EP .................................................................. 15

## SHOW STOPPERS
68    Beacon 3-100                Ain't Nothing But A House Party/What Can A Man Do (red swirly label) ................ 15
68    Beacon 3-106                Shake Your Mini/Heartbreaker ....................................................... 40
68    MGM MGM 1436                Eeny Meeny/How Easy Your Heart Forgets Me .......................................... 15
69    Beacon BEA 110              Don't Leave Me Standing In The Rain/Do You Need My Love ............................ 10
69    Beacon BEA 130              Just A Little Bit Of Lovin'/School Prom ............................................ 15
69    Beacon BEA 100              Ain't Nothing But A House Party/What Can A Man Do (reissue, yellow label) ........... 10
70    Beacon BEA 100              Ain't Nothing But A House Party/What Can A Man Do (reissue, green label) ............ 8
71    Beacon BEA 177              Reach In The Goody Bag/How Do You Feel .............................................. 10
71    Beacon BEA 3-182            Actions Speak Louder Than Words/ Pick Up Your Smile ................................ 20

## SHOWBIZ KIDS
80    Top Secret CON 1            She Goes To Finos/I Don't Want To Discuss That (p/s) ............................... 35

*(see also Toy Dolls)*

## SHOW BOYS
69    Gas GAS 129                 People Are Wondering/Long Time ..................................................... 25

## SHOWMEN
62    London HLP 9481             It Will Stand/Country Fool ......................................................... 60
62    London HLP 9571             The Wrong Girl/I Love You Can't You See ........................................... 175
69    Pama PM 767                 Action/What Would It Take .......................................................... 15

*(see also Norman Johnson, General Johnson, Chairmen Of The Board)*

## SHOWTIMERS
64    HMV POP 1328                You Must Be Joking/Don't Say Goodbye ............................................... 15

## SHOX
80    Axis AXIS 4                 No Turning Back/Lying Here (p/s) ................................................... 18
80    Beggars Banquet BEG 33      No Turning Back/Lying Here (p/s, reissue) .......................................... 8

## SHPONGLE
00    Twisted TWST                DIVINE MOMENTS OF TRUTH (12", p/s) ................................................. 15
99    Twisted TWSLP 4             ARE YOU SHPONGLED? (2-LP, 1st 1000, numbered with gold/silver writing) ............. 150
01    Twisted TWSLP 13            TALES OF THE INEXPRESSABLE (2-LP) ................................................. 125
03    Twisted TWSLP 23            REMIXED (2-LP) ...................................................................... 70
05    Twisted TWSLP 28            NOTHING LASTS...BUT NOTHING IS LEFT (2-LP) .......................................... 70
07    Twisted TWSLP 4             ARE YOU SHPONGLED? (2-LP reissue, clear sparkled vinyl) ............................ 40
08    Twisted TWSLP 13            TALES OF THE INEXPRESSABLE (2-LP, reissue clear sparkled vinyl)) ................... 40
10    Twisted TWSLP 36            INEFFABLE MYSTERIES FROM SHPONGLAND (2-LP) ........................................ 35

## SHRAPNEL
89    Words Of Warning WOW 6      Trivial Pursuit/Autumn/TOXIK EPHEX: Does Someone Have To Die/Life Is For Living
                                  split EP p/s ........................................................................ 10

## MARK SHREEVE
83    Uniton U 021                ASSASSIN (LP) ...................................................................... 15

## SHRIEKBACK
81    Y T104                      Working On The Ground/Nightwork (12", p/s) ......................................... 12

## DAVID SHRIGLEY
06    Contemporary Arts           Ding/Dong (p/s, 500 only) .......................................................... 20
06    Azuzi ALNLP16               FORCED TO SPEAK WITH OTHERS (LP) ................................................... 20

## SHRIMP TRACTOR
93    Shrimp Platters SPLAT 001   THE SHRIMP EP ...................................................................... 10

## SHRINK (1)
79    Oval AMS 7409               Valid Or Void/You Chauffeur Me (p/s) ............................................... 6

## SHRINK (2)
88    Chandarba GHAND 1           Around The World/Calling All Women ................................................. 10

## SHRUG
95    Private Pressing            THE YOGURTS VS YOGURT DEBATE (Demo cassette, glued sleeve) ......................... 80

*(see also Snow Patrol)*

## SHUBERT
68    Fontana TF 942              Until The Rains Come/Let Your Love Go .............................................. 20

## SHUDDER TO THINK
91    Dischord                    Vacation Brain (p/s, with insert) ................................................. 12

## SALMAN SHUKUR
77    Decca Headline HEAD 16      OUD (LP) ........................................................................... 18

## MORT SHUMAN
59    Decca F 11184               Turn Me Loose/I'm A Man ............................................................ 50
59    Decca F 11184               Turn Me Loose/I'm A Man (78) ....................................................... 25
66    Fontana TF 685              Cry A Little/She Ain't Nothing But A Little Child .................................. 10
67    Immediate IM 048            Monday Monday/Little Children ...................................................... 20

## SHUTDOWNS
63    Colpix PX 11016             Four In The Floor/Beach Buggy ...................................................... 50

## SHY LIMBS
69    CBS 4190                    Reputation/Love .................................................................... 70
69    CBS 4624                    Lady In Black/Trick Or Two ........................................................ 150

*(see also Shame)*

MINT VALUE £

## SHY ONES
| | | | |
|---|---|---|---|
| 63 | Oriole CB 1848 | Nightcap/Carry Me Back | 20 |
| 64 | Oriole CB 1924 | La Route/Susanna | 18 |

*(see also Spotnicks)*

## SHY TOTS
| | | | |
|---|---|---|---|
| 82 | ST EP 1 | Gallery/Babble/English Industrial Estate (silk-screened cover) | 25 |

## SHY (1)
| | | | |
|---|---|---|---|
| 74 | Deram DM417 | Disney Girls (1957)/The Time That I Love You The Most | 7 |

## SHY (2)
| | | | |
|---|---|---|---|
| 83 | Ebony EBON 15 | ONCE BITTEN TWICE SHY (LP) | 20 |

## SHYSTER
| | | | |
|---|---|---|---|
| 68 | Polydor 56202 | Tick Tock/That's A Hoe Down | 220 |

*(see also Fleur-De-Lys)*

## SHYWOLF
| | | | |
|---|---|---|---|
| 82 | MRS SW 001 | Lucretia/California Jam (p/s) | 40 |

## SIA
| | | | |
|---|---|---|---|
| 04 | Go! Beat 986 610-1 | COLOUR THE SMALL ONE (LP) | 40 |

## LEROY SIBBLES & ROCKY ELLIS
| | | | |
|---|---|---|---|
| 68 | Studio One SO 2042 | Love Me Girl/WRIGGLERS: Reel Up | 60 |
| 79 | Warrior Records WAR 133 | Ras-Tafari/MYSTIC EYES: Forward With Love/Dub (12") | 30 |

*(see also John Holt, King Rocky)*

## DON E SIBLEY & DIXIE PHOENIX
| | | | |
|---|---|---|---|
| 79 | Hot Rock HR45-003 | Punk Bashing Boogie/Rock With The Devil | 7 |

## DUDLEY SIBLEY
| | | | |
|---|---|---|---|
| 67 | Coxsone CS 7010 | Run Boy Run/Message Of Old (B-side actually by Joe Higgs & Ken Boothe) | 70 |
| 67 | Island WI 3034 | Gun Man/Monkey Speaks His Mind (B-side actually by Dinsdell Thorpe) | 50 |

*(see also Delroy & Sporty, King Sporty, Mr. Foundation)*

## SICK THINGS
| | | | |
|---|---|---|---|
| 83 | Chaos CHS 3 | ANTI SOCIAL (EP) | 25 |

## SIDAN
| | | | |
|---|---|---|---|
| 75 | Sain 1017 | TEULU YNCL SAM (LP, laminated front cover) | 40 |

## SID & JOE & MOHAWKS
| | | | |
|---|---|---|---|
| 70 | Pama PM 800 | Down On The Corner/Who Is That Stranger | 20 |

*(see also Mohawks)*

## SIDDELEYS
| | | | |
|---|---|---|---|
| 87 | Sha La La Ba Ba Ba 006 | Wherever You Go/RESERVE: The Sun Slid Down Behind The Tower (flexidisc with fanzines, p/s) | 10 |
| 87 | Medium Cool MC 005 | What Went Wrong This Time?/No Names/My Favourite Wet Wednesday Afternoon (p/s) | 40 |
| 88 | Sombrero THREE | Sunshine Thuggery/Are You Still Evil When You're Sleeping/Falling Off My Feet Again (12", p/s) | 35 |

## FRANK SIDEBOTTOM
| | | | |
|---|---|---|---|
| 86 | Regal Zonophone 12Z41 | SCI-FI EP (12") | 15 |
| 86 | Regal Zonophone ZP41 | SCI-FI EP (picture disc) | 15 |
| 86 | Regal Zonophone Z41 | SCI-FI EP | 8 |
| 88 | In Tape IT 058 | 5:9:88 (2-LP) | 18 |
| 88 | In Tape IT 060 | 13:9:88 (LP) | 15 |

*(see also Freshies, Chris Sievey, Billy & Barry Belly)*

## SIDEKICKS
| | | | |
|---|---|---|---|
| 66 | RCA RCA 1538 | Suspicions/Up On The Roof | 20 |

## SIDEWALK SOCIETY
| | | | |
|---|---|---|---|
| 10 | Fruits De Mer Crustacean 14 | In The First Place/(Tell Me) Have You Ever Seen Me/Lazy Old Sun/Dandelion (folded p/s) | 30 |

## ANN SIDNEY
| | | | |
|---|---|---|---|
| 65 | HMV POP 1411 | The Boy In The Woolly Sweater/Lonely Doll (Miss World 1964) | 5 |

## SIDNEY, GEORGE & JACKIE
| | | | |
|---|---|---|---|
| 71 | Summit SUM 8528 | Lady Of My Complexion/No Sad Song | 5 |
| 72 | Summit SUM 8535 | Story Book Children/Gorgeous Marvellous | 5 |
| 74 | Attack ATT 8054 | At The Club/Reggae Fever | 150 |

*(see also Pioneers)*

## PAUL SIEBEL
| | | | |
|---|---|---|---|
| 70 | Elektra EKSN 45085 | Bride 1945/Miss Cherry Lane | 5 |
| 70 | Elektra EKS 74064 | WOODSMOKE AND ORANGES (LP) | 20 |
| 71 | Elektra EKS 74081 | JACK-KNIFE GYPSY (LP) | 20 |

## SIEGE
| | | | |
|---|---|---|---|
| 85 | Siege THM 1 | Goddess Of Fire (no p/s) | 18 |
| 90 | Revolution | Infest/Drop Dead (p/s) | 20 |

## SIEGEL-SCHWALL BAND
| | | | |
|---|---|---|---|
| 68 | Vanguard SVRL 19044 | SHAKE (LP) | 20 |

## CHRIS SIEVEY
| | | | |
|---|---|---|---|
| 79 | Rabid TOSH 109 | Baiser/Last (p/s) | 10 |
| 79 | Razz RAZZXEP 1 | BAISER (33rpm EP, 2 tracks each by Sievey & Freshies, handwritten labels) | 40 |
| 80 | Razz RAZZ 9 | Last/Skip The Flight Jim (later promo edition, 50 copies only, hand-made sleeve, labels glued over original Rabid labels, please note that Skip The Flibht Jim is actually Baiser) | 200 |
| 80 | Razz RAZZ 4 | My Tape's Gone/Moon Midsummer (with True Life Revealing Confessions Of Romance And Love fanzine) | 10 |
| 80 | Razz RAZZ 4 | My Tape's Gone/Moon Midsummer (without True Life Revealing Confessions Of Romance And Love fanzine) | 5 |

| | | | |
|---|---|---|---|
| 81 | Razz RAZZ 5 | Hey/FRESHIES: We're Like You (p/s) | 6 |
| 82 | Razz RAZZ 8 | RED INDIAN MUSIC (EP) | 18 |

*(see also Freshies, Frank Sidebottom, Billy & Barry Belly, Going Red?)*

## LABI SIFFRE
| | | | |
|---|---|---|---|
| 71 | Pye Intl. 7N 25572 | It Must Be Love/To Find Love | 6 |
| 70 | Pye Intl. NSPL 28135 | LABI SIFFRE (LP) | 15 |
| 71 | Pye Intl. NSPL 28147 | THE SINGER AND THE SONG (LP, gatefold sleeve) | 15 |
| 75 | EMI EMC 3065 | REMEMBER MY SONG (LP) | 60 |

## RON SIG
| | | | |
|---|---|---|---|
| 71 | Camel CA 58 | 1970's/Version | 15 |
| 71 | Camel CA 59 | You Girl/ROY SHIRLEY & SLIM SMITH: Facts Of Life | 15 |

## SIGHT & SOUND
| | | | |
|---|---|---|---|
| 68 | Fontana TF 927 | Ebenezer/Our Love (Is In The Pocket) | 50 |
| 68 | Fontana TF 982 | Alley Alley/Little Jack Monday | 15 |

*(see also Jefferson, Sheridan & Price, Mike Sheridan)*

## BUNNY SIGLER
| | | | |
|---|---|---|---|
| 67 | Cameo Parkway P 153 | Let The Good Times Roll - Feel So Good/There's No Love Left | 30 |
| 67 | Cameo Parkway P 153 | Let The Good Times Roll - Feel So Good/There's No Love Left (DJ copy) | 60 |
| 76 | Philadelphia SPIR 4935 | Can't Believe That You Love Me/Woman, Woman | 6 |
| 76 | London HLU 10518 | Let The Good Times Roll/Girl Don't Make Me Wait | 12 |

## SIGNIFICANT ZEROS
| | | | |
|---|---|---|---|
| 81 | Dingy Roons DINGE ONE | Jungle/Stiff Citizens | 20 |

## SIGNS
| | | | |
|---|---|---|---|
| 66 | Decca F 12522 | Ain't You Got A Heart/My Baby Comes To Me | 40 |

## SIGUR RÓS
| | | | |
|---|---|---|---|
| 99 | Fat Cat 12FAT 036 | Svefn-G-Englar (12" EP, custom sleeve 2,000 only) | 20 |
| 00 | Fat Cat 12FAT 039 | NY BATTERI (mini-LP, 2,000 only) | 25 |
| 04 | EMI 5496916 | BA BA TI KI DI DO (12" EP) | 12 |
| 05 | EMI 17571 | Hoppipolla/Meo Bloonasir/Hafsol (12") | 12 |
| 06 | EMI EMI 673 | Hoppipolla/Heysatan (numbered p/s, 3000 only) | 10 |
| 07 | EMI 736 | Hljómalind/Starálfur (Live) (p/s) | 6 |
| 06 | EMI 12EM 687 | SAEGOPUR (12" p/s) | 15 |
| 12 | EMI 10R 6860 | Ekki Mukk/Kvistur (10" plays inside out) | 12 |
| 00 | Fat Cat FATLP 11 | AGAETIS BYRJUN (2-LP) | 50 |
| 03 | Fat Cat FATLP 22 | ( ) (LP) | 40 |
| 05 | EMI 337 252 1 | TAKK (2-LP, 10" special book edition) | 90 |
| 05 | EMI 337252 | SIGUR RóS (2-LP, gatefold with inner sleeves and free 10") | 60 |
| 07 | EMI 5099951041991 | HEIMA (Box set, CD, DVD, 116 page book) | 50 |
| 09 | Fat Cat FATLP 11X | AGAETIS BYRJUN (2-LP, reissue, 180 gm vinyl) | 30 |
| 12 | Krunk KRUNK7LP | INNI (3-LP, C-CD, DVD box set) | 30 |
| 12 | Parlophone 50999 6 23555 1 3 | VALTARI (2-LP, CD, gatefold) | 20 |
| 13 | Parlophone 2564636943 | VALTARI (2-LP, repressing) | 20 |
| 13 | Parlophone P 958 4341 | HVARF/HEIM (2-LP, one green and one blue) | 25 |
| 13 | XL XLLP 606X | KVEIKUR (2-LP, 10" CD) | 18 |
| 13 | XL XLLP 606X | KVEIKUR (2-LP, hand printed alternative sleeve, 50 only) | 120 |

## SILENT ECLIPSE
| | | | |
|---|---|---|---|
| 92 | White (Mendoza) MEN018 | How Many Miles Back To London/MCs (12") | 120 |
| 92 | Mendoza MEN018 | How Many Miles Back To London/MCs (12") | 80 |
| 92 | Dope Jams DJAM1 | Take The Stage (3 Mixes, promo 12" only) | 15 |

*(see also Two Times Def)*

## SILENT MOVIES
| | | | |
|---|---|---|---|
| 79 | ESR Records ESR 1 | Ain't No Van Gough/What Did Ya Say? (p/s) | 40 |

## SILENT NOISE
| | | | |
|---|---|---|---|
| 79 | Silent Noise/Easy ER 02 | I've Been Hurt (Too Many Times Before)/Heart To Heart | 75 |

## SILENT ONES
| | | | |
|---|---|---|---|
| 70 | Pulse P1 | When It Rains/Lost Dreams (p/s) | 50 |

## SILENT SCREAM
| | | | |
|---|---|---|---|
| 84 | Pure Motorised Instinct PMI 001 | Handstands/Jagged Path (p/s) | 25 |

## SILENT WARRIORS
| | | | |
|---|---|---|---|
| 80 | Catfish CT1 | Ride Of Death/Firefly | 50 |

## SILENT NIGHT
| | | | |
|---|---|---|---|
| 83 | Granny's Rockers S83/ CVUS1847/UK | Cold Hearted Lady/Never Say It's Over (no p/s) | 40 |

## SILHOUETTE
| | | | |
|---|---|---|---|
| 78 | Wildfire WRL 23 | RONDO EP (no p/s) | 8 |

## SILHOUETTES (JAMAICA)
| | | | |
|---|---|---|---|
| 69 | Sound System SSR 103 | In Times Like These (act. by Lloyd Jackson & Groovers)/In Times Like These | 50 |

## SILHOUETTES (U.S.)
| | | | |
|---|---|---|---|
| 58 | Parlophone R 4407 | Get A Job/I Am Lonely | 100 |
| 58 | Parlophone R 4407 | Get A Job/I Am Lonely (78) | 50 |
| 58 | Parlophone R 4425 | Headin' For The Poorhouse/Miss Thing | 150 |
| 58 | Parlophone R 4425 | Headin' For The Poorhouse/Miss Thing (78) | 80 |

## SILICON TEENS
| | | | |
|---|---|---|---|
| 79 | Mute MUTE 003 | Memphis Tennessee/Let's Dance (p/s, with poster) | 10 |
| 79 | Mute MUTE 003 | Memphis Tennessee/Let's Dance (p/s) | 5 |
| 80 | Mute 008AX | Sunflight/Just Like Eddie (p/s) | 6 |

MINT VALUE £

| | | | |
|---|---|---|---|
| 80 | Mute STUMM 2 | MUSIC FOR PARTIES (LP) | 20 |

**SILKIE**
| | | | |
|---|---|---|---|
| 65 | Fontana TF 556 | Blood Red River/Close The Door Gently | 5 |
| 65 | Fontana TF 603 | You've Got To Hide Your Love Away/City Winds | 7 |
| 66 | Fontana TF 659 | Keys To My Soul/Leave Me To Cry | 5 |
| 66 | Fontana TF 709 | Born To Be With You/So Sorry Now | 5 |
| 65 | Fontana TL 5256 | THE SILKIE SING THE SONGS OF BOB DYLAN (LP) | 20 |

**SILK TIE**
| | | | |
|---|---|---|---|
| 73 | Maple MP 004 | Into The Night/Theresa | 20 |

**SILKY THREADS**
| | | | |
|---|---|---|---|
| 75 | Waverley WAV 1 | Jump To It/She Runs | 40 |

**JUDEE SILL**
| | | | |
|---|---|---|---|
| 71 | Asylum AYM 502 | Jesus Was A Cross Maker/The Phantom Cowboy | 7 |
| 72 | Asylum AYM 509 | Enchanted Sky Machines/My Man On Love | 6 |
| 72 | Asylum SYLA 8751 | JUDEE SILL (LP, gatefold sleeve) | 40 |
| 73 | Asylum SYL 9006 | HEART FOOD (LP) | 25 |

**JOHN SILVA**
| | | | |
|---|---|---|---|
| 79 | Jayesque (no Cat No) | MAKE UP YOUR MIND (LP, as John Silva Sextet) | 150 |
| 78 | Jayesque SRT/SRTX/78/CUS 134 | INN ATTENDANCE (LP) | 80 |

**SILVER EAGLE**
| | | | |
|---|---|---|---|
| 67 | MGM MGM 1345 | Theodore/True As A Brand New Lie | 30 |

**SILVER (JAMAICA)**
| | | | |
|---|---|---|---|
| 68 | Jolly JY 006 | Baby Oh Yeah/Rock Steady Is Here To Stay (as Silver & Magnets) | 20 |
| 68 | Jolly JY 012 | Things/Sweet Lovin' | 15 |
| 68 | Jolly JY 017 | I Need A Girl/Lost And Found | 15 |
| 70 | Columbia Blue Beat DB 117 | Love Me Forever/Sugar, Sugar (B-side as Silver & Noreen) | 5 |
| 71 | Fab FAB 163 | Change Has Got To Come/Magnet Stomp (as Silver & Magnets) | 6 |

**SILVER (U.S.)**
| | | | |
|---|---|---|---|
| 76 | Arista ARIST 79 | Musician (It's Not An Easy Life)/Right On Time | 6 |
| 76 | Arista ARTY 144 | SILVER (LP, U.S. disc & inner [AL 4076] in U.K. sleeve) | 12 |

*(see also Grateful Dead)*

**ANDEE SILVER**
| | | | |
|---|---|---|---|
| 64 | HMV POP 1297 | Too Young To Go Steady/Sleeping Beauty | 10 |
| 64 | HMV POP 1344 | The Boy I Used To Know/What Do You Do | 10 |
| 66 | Fontana TF 666 | Only Your Love Can Save Me/Window Shopping | 25 |
| 69 | Decca F 22872 | Go Now/You're Just What I Was Looking For Today | 20 |
| 69 | Decca F 22953 | With A Little Love/Te Quiero (unreleased) | 0 |
| 70 | Decca F 23071 | Love Me/You're Breaking My Heart (export issue) | 10 |
| 70 | Decca SKL-R 5059 | A HANDFUL OF SILVER (LP) | 50 |

**SILVER DOLLAR**
| | | | |
|---|---|---|---|
| 74 | Shire SH 003 | Frightened/Oh You Devil | 30 |

**EDDIE SILVER**
| | | | |
|---|---|---|---|
| 58 | Parlophone R 4439 | Seven Steps To Love/Put A Ring On Her Finger | 15 |
| 58 | Parlophone R 4483 | Rockin' Robin/The Ways Of A Woman In Love | 20 |
| 58 | Parlophone R 4483 | Rockin' Robin/The Ways Of A Woman In Love (78) | 20 |

**HORACE SILVER QUINTET/TRIO**
| | | | |
|---|---|---|---|
| 54 | Vogue LDE 065 | THE HORACE SILVER TRIO (10" LP) | 20 |
| 69 | Blue Note BST 84277 | SERENADE TO A SOUL SISTER (LP) | 25 |

**LORRAINE SILVER**
| | | | |
|---|---|---|---|
| 65 | Pye 7N 15922 | Lost Summer Love/I'll Know You'll Be There | 75 |
| 65 | Pye 7N 15922 | Lost Summer Love/I'll Know You'll Be There (DJ copy) | 75 |
| 66 | Pye 7N 17055 | The Happy Faces/When The Love Light Starts Shining Thru His Eyes | 40 |
| 78 | Casino Classics CC 2 | Lost Summer Love/I Know That You'll Be There | 10 |

**MIKE SILVER & MIKE BEASON**
| | | | |
|---|---|---|---|
| 69 | Fontana STL 5506 | THE APPLICANT (LP) | 25 |

**SILVER SCREEN GIRLS**
| | | | |
|---|---|---|---|
| 81 | Siren SSG 1 | Photographs/Silver Screen Girls (p/s) | 15 |

**SILVER APPLES**
| | | | |
|---|---|---|---|
| 96 | Enraptured RAPT 4507 | Fractal Flow/Love Fingers (p/s) | 6 |
| 97 | Rocket Girl RGIRL 1 | I Have Known Love/WINDY & CARL: Crazy In The Sun (p/s, green vinyl) | 6 |

**SILVER BIRCH**
| | | | |
|---|---|---|---|
| 73 | Brayford BRO 2 | SILVER BIRCH (LP, private pressing) | 150 |

**SILVERBIRD**
| | | | |
|---|---|---|---|
| 72 | CBS 51279 | I See The Writing On The Wall/The Summer's Gone (And I'm Alone) | 8 |
| 73 | CBS 51800 | That's Why You Remember/You And Me | 8 |

**SILVER BULLET**
| | | | |
|---|---|---|---|
| 91 | Parlophone R 6290 | Ruff Karnage/Never Authorise Apocalypse (p/s) | 35 |

**SILVER BYKE**
| | | | |
|---|---|---|---|
| 68 | London HLZ 10200 | I've Got Time/Who Needs Tomorrow | 18 |

**SILVERCHAIR**
| | | | |
|---|---|---|---|
| 95 | Columbia 662395 7 | Tomorrow/Blind (live) (p/s) | 10 |

**SILVERGINGER 5**
| | | | |
|---|---|---|---|
| 01 | Infernal INFERNAL 13CD/X | BLACK LEATHER MOJO (2-CD, in stickered leather-effect slipcase, 5000 only) | 15 |

*(see also Super$hit666, Wildhearts)*

**SILVERHEAD**
| | | | |
|---|---|---|---|
| 72 | Purple PUR 104 | Ace Supreme/Oh No No No | 10 |

| | | | |
|---|---|---|---|
| 72 | Purple PUR 110 | Rolling With My Baby/In Your Eyes | 10 |
| 73 | Purple TPSA 7506 | SILVERHEAD (LP, gatefold) | 30 |
| 73 | Purple TPSA 7511 | SIXTEEN AND SAVAGED (LP, gatefold sleeve) | 25 |

*(see also Michael Des Barres, Blondie)*

## SILVER JEWS
| | | | |
|---|---|---|---|
| 96 | Domino WIGLP 28 | THE NATURAL BRIDGE (LP) | 15 |
| 98 | Domino WIGLP 56 | AMERICAN WATER (LP) | 15 |

## SILVER MACHINE
| | | | |
|---|---|---|---|
| 78 | Hillside HIL SP 5004 | Take Me In Your Arms/You'll Always Be The One (no p/s) | 50 |

## SILVER METRIC
| | | | |
|---|---|---|---|
| 71 | Department Of Health MET1 | Inch By Inch/Centimetre By Centimetre | 5 |

## SILVER MOUNTAIN
| | | | |
|---|---|---|---|
| 83 | Road Runner RR 9884 | SHAKIN' BRAINS (LP) | 15 |

## SILVERS
| | | | |
|---|---|---|---|
| 66 | Polydor BM 56094 | What A Way To Start A Day/Blue Blue Eyes | 7 |

## SILVER SISTERS
| | | | |
|---|---|---|---|
| 60 | Parlophone R 4669 | Waiting For The Stars To Shine/When A Boy Meets A Girl | 10 |

## DOOLEY SILVERSPOON
| | | | |
|---|---|---|---|
| 76 | Seville SEV 1022 | Game Players/Believe In Me | 8 |

## SILVERSTARS
| | | | |
|---|---|---|---|
| 69 | Trojan TR 646 | Old Man Say/Promises | 60 |
| 70 | Bamboo BAM 23 | Love At First Sight/MAYTALS : Life Could Be A Dream | 35 |

## SILVER STARS STEEL BAND
| | | | |
|---|---|---|---|
| 63 | Island ILP 904 | THE SILVER STARS STEEL BAND (LP) | 20 |

*(see also Clancy Eccles)*

## SILVERTONES
| | | | |
|---|---|---|---|
| 66 | Doctor Bird DB 1028 | True Confession (with Duke Reid)/TOMMY McCOOK & SUPERSONICS: More Love | 40 |
| 66 | RYMSKA RA 105 | True Confession/Honky Tonky Ska (with Granville Williams) | 30 |
| 66 | Doctor Bird DB 1041 | It's Real (with Lynn Tait & Boys)/LYNN TAIT & BOYS: Storm Warning | 40 |
| 67 | Treasure Isle TI 7020 | Cool Down/TOMMY McCOOK & SUPERSONICS: Shadow Of Your Smile | 25 |
| 68 | Treasure Isle TI 7027 | In The Midnight Hour/TOMMY McCOOK & SUPERSONICS: Soul For Sale | 20 |
| 68 | Treasure Isle TI 7039 | Old Man River/TOMMY McCOOK & SUPERSONICS: Our Man Flint | 50 |
| 68 | Treasure Isle TI 7042 | Slow And Easy/TOMMY McCOOK & SUPERSONICS: Moving | 50 |
| 69 | Trojan TR 7705 | Intensified Change/Marie | 15 |
| 71 | Clandisc CLA 234 | Tear Drops Will Fall/DYNAMITES: Tear Drops - Version | 6 |
| 73 | Techniques TE 924 | That's When It Hurts/I'll Take You Home | 6 |
| 77 | Trojan TRO 9013 | African Dub/Version | 25 |
| 77 | Trojan TRO 9015 | What A Situation/Version | 15 |
| 71 | Trojan TRLS 69 | SILVER BULLETS (LP) | 45 |

*(see also Valentines, Tommy McCook, Vincent Gordon, Alton Ellis, Carl Bryon, Charmers)*

## SILVERTOWN
| | | | |
|---|---|---|---|
| 79 | Wessex WEX 271 | SUNDAY DRIVER EP | 5 |

## SILVERWING
| | | | |
|---|---|---|---|
| 80 | Mayhem SILVER 1 | Rock'n'Roll Are Four-Letter Words/High Class Woman/Hot City Streets | 7 |
| 82 | Mayhem SILV 02 | Sittin' Pretty/Teenage Love Affair (p/s) | 8 |
| 82 | Mayhem SILV 212 | Sittin' Pretty/Teenage Love/Flashbomb Fever/Rock'n'Roll Mayhem (12") | 10 |
| 82 | Mayhem SILV 3 | That's Entertainment/Flashbomb Fever (poster p/s) | 8 |
| 83 | Bullet BULP 1 | ALIVE AND KICKING (LP) | 15 |

*(see also Pet Hate, Big Amongst Sheep)*

## VICTOR SILVESTER ORCHESTRA
| | | | |
|---|---|---|---|
| 62 | Columbia | World Cup Cha Cha Cha/Santiago | 5 |
| 66 | Columbia DB 7900 | The World Cup Waltz/The World Cup Cha Cha Cha | 10 |

## VICTOR SILVESTER & HIS ROCK 'N' ROLL RHYTHM
| | | | |
|---|---|---|---|
| 57 | Columbia DB 3888 | Rockin' Rhythm Roll/Society Rock | 15 |
| 57 | Columbia DB 3907 | Alligator Roll/Off Beat Rock | 15 |

## SIMBA
| | | | |
|---|---|---|---|
| 71 | Fire FIR 100 | Louie Louie/Movin' | 5 |

## TYRONE SIMEON
| | | | |
|---|---|---|---|
| 79 | Burning Rockers BRD 010 | Do Good In This Time/Do Good Dub (12") | 15 |

## SIMEONS
| | | | |
|---|---|---|---|
| 78 | Freedom Sounds FSLP 002 | DUB CONFERENCE IN LONDON (LP) | 25 |

## LEO SIMMO
| | | | |
|---|---|---|---|
| 66 | Big Beat BB351 | I Love Her So/It's Good To Be Seen | 25 |

## BEVERLEY SIMMON(D)S
| | | | |
|---|---|---|---|
| 68 | Pama PM 716 | Mr. Pitiful/That's How Strong My Love Is | 15 |
| 73 | Pama Supreme PS 380 | You're Mine/What A Guy (as Beverley Simmonds) | 8 |
| 69 | Pama PMLP 1 | PAYS TRIBUTE TO OTIS REDDING(LP) | 50 |
| 69 | Pama PMLP/PMSP 9 | REMEMBER OTIS (LP) | 30 |

*(see also Little Beverly)*

## CHRIS SIMMONS
| | | | |
|---|---|---|---|
| 69 | MCA MK 5009 | Soraya/Gone Gone Gone | 6 |

## DESMOND SIMMONS
| | | | |
|---|---|---|---|
| 81 | Dome 33.1 | ALONE ON PENGUIN ISLAND (LP) | 15 |

## (JUMPIN') GENE SIMMONS
| | | | |
|---|---|---|---|
| 64 | London HLU 9913 | Haunted House/Hey, Hey Little Girl | 20 |
| 64 | London HLU 9933 | The Jump/The Dodo | 20 |

MINT VALUE £

## GENE SIMMONS
| | | | |
|---|---|---|---|
| 79 | Casablanca CAN 134 | Radioactive/When You Wish Upon A Star (p/s, red vinyl with mask, picture label, mispressed with black/red vinyl) | 50 |
| 79 | Casablanca CAN 134 | Radioactive/When You Wish Upon A Star (p/s, red vinyl with mask, picture label) | 20 |
| 79 | Casablanca CAN 134 | Radioactive/When You Wish Upon A Star (p/s, black vinyl) | 8 |

*(see also Kiss)*

## JEFF SIMMONS
| | | | |
|---|---|---|---|
| 69 | Straight STS 1057 | LUCILLE HAS MESSED UP MY MIND (LP) | 80 |

*(see also Frank Zappa)*

## LITTLE MAC SIMMONS
| | | | |
|---|---|---|---|
| 66 | Outasite OSEP 1 | BLUES FROM CHICAGO (EP, 99 copies only) | 200 |

## TONY SIMMONS
| | | | |
|---|---|---|---|
| 83 | Record Shack SOHOT 2 | I Can't Let You Go/I Can't Let You Go (Instrumental) (12" promo only) | 150 |

## JAGO SIMMS
| | | | |
|---|---|---|---|
| 68 | Fontana TF 901 | In Too Deep/Conventional Fella | 45 |

## JASON SIMMS & MUSIC THROUGH SIX
| | | | |
|---|---|---|---|
| 68 | Domain D 5 | It's Got To Be Mellow/MUSIC THROUGH SIX: Floppy Ears | 20 |

*(see also Music Through Six)*

## (ZOOT) SIMMS & (LLOYD) ROBINSON
| | | | |
|---|---|---|---|
| 62 | Blue Beat BB 143 | White Christmas/Searching | 10 |

## ZOOT SIMMS (JAMAICA)
| | | | |
|---|---|---|---|
| 63 | Blue Beat BB 183 | Press Along/PRINCE BUSTER ALLSTARS: 100 Ton Megaton (B-side actually "Mighty As A Rose" by Raymond Harper) | 25 |
| 63 | Blue Beat BB 193 | Golden Pen/ERIC MORRIS: So You Shot Reds | 35 |
| 64 | Port-O-Jam PJ 4007 | Please Don't Do It/Don't Do It (as Simms & [Lloyd] Robinson) | 40 |
| 68 | Blue Cat BS 118 | Bye Bye Baby/AL & THRILLERS: Heart For Sale | 150 |
| 69 | Coxsone CS 7095 | Tit For Tat/We Can Talk It Over (as Simms & Elmond) | 80 |

## SEIJA SIMOLA
| | | | |
|---|---|---|---|
| 78 | Sonet SON 2145 | Give Love A Chance/Little Smile (p/s) | 12 |

## SIMON
| | | | |
|---|---|---|---|
| 67 | RCA Victor RCA 1609 | I Like The Way/Little Tin Soldier | 10 |
| 68 | RCA Victor RCA 1668 | Dream Seller/Sweet Reflections Of You | 15 |
| 69 | Plum PLS 002 | Mrs Lillyco/There's No More You | 40 |

## JOE SIMON
| | | | |
|---|---|---|---|
| 66 | London HLU 10057 | Teenager's Prayer/Long Hot Summer | 30 |
| 67 | Monument MON 1004 | My Special Prayer/Travelin' Man | 10 |
| 68 | Monument MON 1010 | Nine Pound Steel/The Girl's Alright With Me | 20 |
| 68 | Monument MON 1014 | No Sad Songs/Come On And Get It | 10 |
| 68 | Monument MON 1019 | You Keep Me Hangin' On/What Makes A Man Feel Good | 7 |
| 68 | Monument MON 1025 | Message From Maria/I Worry About You | 7 |
| 69 | Monument MON 1029 | Looking Back/Standing In The Safety Zone | 7 |
| 69 | Monument MON 1032 | The Chokin' Kind/Come On And Get It | 7 |
| 70 | Monument MON 1042 | Moon Walk (Parts 1 & 2) | 7 |
| 70 | Monument MON 1049 | Yours Love/I Gotta Whole Lot Of Lovin' | 5 |
| 70 | Monument MON 1051 | That's The Way I Want Our Love/When | 25 |
| 71 | Polydor 2066 066 | Your Time To Cry/I Love You More (Than Anything) | 15 |
| 74 | Mojo 2093 030 | Step By Step/Talk Don't Bother Me | 8 |
| 67 | Monument LMO/SMO 5005 | SIMON PURE SOUL (LP) | 6 |
| 68 | Monument LMO/SMO 5017 | NO SAD SONGS (LP) | 18 |
| 69 | Monument LMO/SMO 5026 | SIMON SINGS (LP) | 18 |
| 70 | Monument LMO/SMO 5030 | THE CHOKIN' KIND (LP) | 18 |
| 70 | Monument LMO/SMO 5033 | BETTER THAN EVER (LP) | 18 |

## PAUL SIMON
| | | | |
|---|---|---|---|
| 65 | CBS 201797 | I Am A Rock/Leaves That Are Green | 25 |
| 73 | CBS 1545 | Kodachrome (withdrawn, any pressed?) | 15 |
| 65 | CBS (S) 62579 | THE PAUL SIMON SONGBOOK (LP, mono, flipback sleeve) | 25 |
| 65 | CBS (S) 62579 | THE PAUL SIMON SONGBOOK (LP, stereo, flipback sleeve) | 30 |
| 72 | CBS CQ 30750/Q 69007 | PAUL SIMON (LP, quadrophonic) | 20 |
| 74 | CBS CQ 32280/Q 69035 | THERE GOES RHYMIN' SIMON (LP, quadrophonic) | 18 |
| 75 | CBS Q 86001 | STILL CRAZY AFTER ALL THESE YEARS (LP, quadrophonic) | 18 |
| 85 | Warner Bros. WB WX52 | GRACELAND (LP, embossed stickered sleeve) | 15 |

*(see also Simon & Garfunkel, Jerry Landis, Tom & Jerry)*

## TONY SIMON
| | | | |
|---|---|---|---|
| 67 | Track 604 012 | Gimme A Little Sign/Never Too Much To Love | 40 |

## SIMON & GARFUNKEL
| | | | |
|---|---|---|---|
| 65 | CBS 201977 | The Sound Of Silence/We've Got A Groovy Thing Goin' | 10 |
| 66 | CBS 202045 | Homeward Bound/Leaves That Are Green | 10 |
| 66 | CBS 202303 | I Am A Rock/Flowers Never Bend With The Rainfall | 10 |
| 66 | CBS 202285 | The Dangling Conversation/The Big Bright Green Pleasure Machine | 15 |
| 66 | CBS 202378 | A Hazy Shade Of Winter/For Emily, Whenever I May Find Her | 10 |
| 67 | CBS 202608 | At The Zoo/The 59th Street Bridge Song (Feelin' Groovy) | 10 |
| 67 | CBS 2911 | Fakin' It/You Don't Know Where Your Interest Lies | 20 |
| 68 | CBS Special Prods. WB 73 | The Sound Of Silence/GEORGIE FAME: By The Time I Get To Phoenix (p/s) | 5 |
| 68 | CBS Special Prods. WB 728 | The 59th Street Bridge Song (Feelin' Groovy)/TREMELOES: Here Comes My Baby (p/s, mail-order only with Pepsi Cola tokens) | 7 |
| 69 | CBS 4162 | The Boxer/Baby Driver (p/s) | 7 |
| 70 | CBS 4916 | Cecelia/The only Living Boy In New York | 6 |
| 65 | CBS EP 6053 | WEDNESDAY MORNING 3AM (EP) | 20 |

| | | | |
|---|---|---|---|
| 66 | CBS EP 6074 | I AM A ROCK (EP) | 20 |
| 67 | CBS EP 6360 | FEELING GROOVY (EP) | 20 |
| 68 | CBS EP 6400 | MRS ROBINSON (EP) | 15 |
| 66 | CBS (S)BPG 62690 | THE SOUNDS OF SILENCE (LP, mono) | 20 |
| 66 | CBS (S)BPG 62690 | THE SOUNDS OF SILENCE (LP, stereo) | 35 |
| 66 | CBS BPG 62860 | PARSLEY, SAGE, ROSEMARY AND THYME (LP, mono, sleeve printed by 'Dawson Rossiter Limited') | 25 |
| 66 | CBS (S)BPG 62860 | PARSLEY, SAGE, ROSEMARY AND THYME (LP, stereo) | 35 |

*(Originally issued with flipback sleeves & textured orange labels.)*

| | | | |
|---|---|---|---|
| 67 | Allegro ALL 836 | SIMON AND GARFUNKEL (LP) | 20 |
| 68 | CBS BPG 63101 | BOOKENDS (LP, mono) | 50 |
| 68 | CBS SBPG | BOOKENDS (LP, stereo) | 40 |
| 68 | CBS (S) 70042 | THE GRADUATE (LP, soundtrack, blue label, mono/stereo) | 15 |
| 68 | CBS (S) 63370 | WEDNESDAY MORNING 3AM (LP, flipback sleeve, textured orange label, mono/stereo) | 25 |
| 68 | CBS (S) 63370 | WEDNESDAY MORNING 3AM (LP, flipback sleeve, textured orange label, mono/stereo) | 20 |
| 70 | CBS S63699 | BRIDGE OVER TROUBLED WATER (LP) | 15 |
| 72 | CBS CQ 30995 | BRIDGE OVER TROUBLED WATER (LP, quadrophonic) | 30 |
| 72 | CBS S69003 | SIMON & GARFUNKEL'S GREATEST HITS (LP) | 15 |

*(see also Paul Simon, Art Garfunkel, Tom & Jerry)*

## NINA SIMONE

| | | | |
|---|---|---|---|
| 59 | Parlophone R 4583 | I Loves You Porgy/Love Me Or Leave Me | 20 |
| 59 | Pye International 7N 25029 | Solitaire/Chilly Winds Don't Blow | 10 |
| 63 | Colpix PX 200 | You Can Have Him/Return Home | 10 |
| 64 | Colpix PX 799 | Exactly Like You/The Other Woman | 10 |
| 65 | Philips BF 1388 | Don't Let Me Be Misunderstood/Monster | 10 |
| 65 | Philips BF 1415 | I Put A Spell On You/Gimme Some | 10 |
| 66 | Philips BF 1465 | Either Way I Lose/Break Down And Let It Out | 15 |
| 69 | RCA RCA 1903 | Save Me/To Be Young Gifted And Black | 15 |
| 61 | Parlophone GEP 8844 | MY BABY JUST CARES FOR ME (EP) | 70 |
| 62 | Parlophone GEP 8864 | INTIMATE NINA SIMONE (EP) | 25 |
| 64 | Colpix PXE 303 | FINE AND MELLOW (EP) | 15 |
| 66 | Colpix PXE 306 | JUST SAY I LOVE HIM (EP) | 15 |
| 66 | Colpix PXE 307 | I LOVE TO LOVE (EP) | 15 |
| 65 | Philips BE 12585 | DON'T LET ME BE MISUNDERSTOOD (EP) | 12 |
| 65 | Philips BE 12589 | STRANGE FRUIT (EP) | 12 |
| 61 | Pye Intl. NPL 28014 | AT THE TOWN HALL (LP) | 18 |
| 62 | Pye Jazz NJL 36 | FORBIDDEN FRUIT (LP) | 20 |
| 64 | Colpix PXL 419 | FORBIDDEN FRUIT (LP, reissue) | 15 |
| 64 | Colpix PXL 421 | NINA AT THE VILLAGE GATE (LP) | 20 |
| 65 | Colpix PXL 465 | FOLKSY NINA (LP) | 20 |
| 65 | Fontana SFJL 954 | TELL ME MORE (LP) | 20 |
| 65 | Philips BL 7662 | BROADWAY . . . BLUES . . . BALLADS (LP) | 20 |
| 65 | Philips BL 7671 | I PUT A SPELL ON YOU (LP) | 20 |
| 65 | Philips BL 7678 | IN CONCERT (LP) | 20 |
| 66 | Philips BL 7683 | PASTEL BLUES (LP) | 20 |
| 66 | Philips (S)BL 7722 | LET IT ALL OUT (LP) | 20 |
| 66 | Philips (S)BL 7726 | WILD IS THE WIND (LP) | 20 |
| 67 | Philips (S)BL 7764 | HIGH PRIESTESS OF SOUL (LP) | 25 |
| 67 | RCA RD/SF 7883 | SINGS THE BLUES (LP) | 20 |
| 68 | RCA RD/SF 7967 | SILK AND SOUL (LP) | 20 |
| 69 | RCA Victor SF 7979 | 'NUFF SAID (LP) | 20 |
| 69 | RCA SF 8018 | TO LOVE SOMEBODY (LP) | 20 |

## SUGAR SIMONE

| | | | |
|---|---|---|---|
| 68 | Fab FAB 33 | I Love My Baby/I'll Keep You Satisfied | 18 |
| 66 | Rainbow RAI 103 | Is It Because/I Want To Know | 20 |
| 67 | Rainbow RAI 115 | I Love My Baby/I'll Keep You Satisfied | 8 |
| 67 | Sue WI 4029 | Suddenly/King Without A Throne | 40 |
| 67 | Go AJ 11409 | It's Alright/Take It Easy | 30 |
| 68 | CBS 3250 | The Vow/Spinning Wheel | 18 |
| 69 | Doctor Bird DB 1192 | Black Is Gold/The Invitation | 20 |
| 69 | Doctor Bird DB 1193 | The Squeeze Is On/Tell Me | 20 |
| 69 | Doctor Bird DB 1201 | Come And Try/Don't Listen To What They Say | 12 |
| 69 | Fab FAB 106 | Boom Biddy Boom/RUDIES: What Can I Do | 10 |
| 69 | Fab FAB 107 | I Need A Witness/Johnny Dollar | 10 |
| 69 | Upfront UPF 1 | Turns On The Heatwave/Crying Blues | 10 |
| 70 | Beacon BEA 156 | Keep On Trying/Only The Lonely | 7 |
| 70 | Beacon BEA 174 | Why Can't I Touch You/Gotta Get It Off My Mind | 7 |
| 73 | Smash SAM 2333 | Rock And Cry/September | 10 |
| 70 | Up Front SUPF 1 | ALIVE AND WELL (LP) | 25 |

*(see also Sugar & Dandy, Les Foster, Larry Foster & Soul Explosion, Lance Hannibal)*

## SIMON PLUG & GRIMES

| | | | |
|---|---|---|---|
| 70 | Deram DM 296 | Is This A Dream?/I'm Going Home | 12 |
| 70 | President PT 310 | Way In, Way Out/Long Long Summer | 5 |
| 71 | President PT 354 | Pull Together/I'll Keep Smiling | 5 |

## SIMON'S SECRETS

| | | | |
|---|---|---|---|
| 68 | CBS 3406 | Naughty Boy/Sympathy | 35 |
| 68 | CBS 3856 | I Know What Her Name Is/Keeping My Head Above Water | 40 |

*(see also Secrets, Clifford T. Ward, Martin Raynor & Secrets)*

MINT VALUE £

## SIMON SISTERS
| 64 | London HLR 9893 | Winkin', Blinkin' And Nod/So Glad I'm Here | 20 |
| 65 | London HLR 9984 | Cuddlebug/No One To Talk My Trouble To | 15 |

## NIC SIMPER'S FANDANGO
| 83 | Paro PAR 0S4 | Just Another Day (In The Life Of A Fool)/Wish I'd Never Woke Up | 6 |
| 79 | Gull GULP 1033 | SLIPSTREAMING (LP) | 20 |

*(see also Deep Purple, Warhorse)*

## NIGEL SIMPKINS
| 78 | Waldo's SS 2 | X.ENC EP (1500 only, numbered, these 100 with 'broken' USA bonus 7") | 10 |
| 78 | Waldo's SS 2 | X.ENC EP (1500 only, numbered, these 100 withOut 'broken' USA bonus 7") | 5 |

## SIMPLE IMAGE
| 70 | Carnaby CNS 4013 | Spinning Spinning Spinning/Shy Boy | 15 |

## SIMPLE MINDS
| 79 | Zoom ZUM 10 | Life In A Day/Special View (p/s) | 7 |
| 79 | Zoom ZUM 11 | Chelsea Girl/Garden Of Hate (p/s) | 7 |
| 80 | Arista ARIST 325 | Changeling/Premonition (live) (p/s) | 5 |
| 81 | Arista ARIST 394 | Celebrate/Changeling (p/s) | 5 |
| 81 | Virgin VS 451 | Sweat In Bullet/20th Century Promised Land (original limited pressing,non-gatefold p/s) | 30 |
| 88 | Virgin VS 860/VS 817 | All The Things She Said/Don't You Forget About Me (Live)//Alive And Kicking/Alive And Kicking (Intrumental) double single pack in PVC sleeve sealed by sticker that states "double pack 2 for the price of 1") | 60 |
| 95 | Virgin V2760 | GOOD NEWS FROM THE NEXT WORLD (LP) | 25 |

*(see also Johnny & Self Abusers)*

## SIMPLICITY PEOPLE
| 73 | Grape GR 3062 | Murderer/BIG YOUTH: The Killer | 15 |
| 73 | Harry J HJ 6649 | Time Is Getting Harder/HARRY J ALLSTARS: Time Is Getting Harder | 6 |

## BILL SIMPSON
| 64 | Piccadilly 7N 35179 | I Love You For Sentimental Reasons/My Love Is Like A Red Red Rose (p/s) | 8 |

## DANNY SIMPSON
| 69 | Trojan TR 653 | Outa Sight/JOHN HOLT: I Want You Closer | 30 |

## DUDLEY SIMPSON & BRIAN HODGSON
| 73 | Polydor 2383 210 | IN A COVENT GARDEN (LP) | 25 |

*(See also BBC Radiophonic Workshop)*

## HOKE SIMPSON
| 58 | HMV POP 442 | I Finally Found You/Gi-Gi | 8 |

## JEANETTE SIMPSON
| 67 | Giant GN 16 | Rain/Whatcha Gonna Do About It | 20 |
| 68 | Giant GN 29 | My Baby Just Cares For Me/Don't Let Me Cry No More (with Superboys) | 100 |
| 68 | Giant GN 35 | Through Loving You/Send Me Some Lovin' (with Missions) | 15 |

## LEO SIMPSON
| 65 | Blue Beat BB 351 | I Love Her So/Good To Be Seen (as Leo Simmo) | 18 |
| 73 | Pyramid PYR 7004 | Waxy Doodle/Go Away | 6 |

*(see also Lionel Simpson)*

## LIONEL SIMPSON
| 65 | Ska Beat JB 205 | Tell Me What You Want/Love Is A Game | 20 |
| 65 | Ska Beat JB 221 | Red River Valley/Eight People | 15 |
| 66 | Ska Beat JB 233 | Give Over/Never Before | 15 |

*(see also Leo Simpson)*

## MARTIN SIMPSON
| 76 | Trailer LER 2099 | GOLDEN VANITY (LP, yellow label) | 20 |
| 86 | Dambuster DAM 013 | NOBODY'S FAULT BUT MINE (LP) | 15 |

## DUDLEY SIMPSON ORCHESTRA
| 78 | BBC RESL 58 | Blake's 7/The Federation March (p/s) | 8 |

## CHUCK SIMS
| 58 | London HLR 8577 | Little Pigeon/Life Isn't Long Enough | 150 |
| 58 | London HLR 8577 | Little Pigeon/Life Isn't Long Enough (78) | 60 |

## FRANKIE LEE SIMS
| 71 | Specialty SPE 5009 | Married Woman Blues/Lucy Mae Blues | 5 |
| 71 | Specialty SNTF 5004 | LUCY MAE BLUES (LP) | 15 |

## KELLY SIMS
| 60 | Top Rank JAR 321 | Betrayed By Love/A Girl In Love | 6 |

## SIMS TWINS/VALENTINOS
| 68 | Soul City SCM 001 | THE VALENTINOS/THE SIMS TWINS (LP, 1 side each) | 60 |

## ZOOT SIMS
| 57 | Esquire EP 183 | ZOOT! (EP) | 20 |
| 57 | Esquire EP 204 | ZOOT'S CASE (EP) | 20 |
| 52 | Esquire 20-002 | ZOOT SIMS QUARTET/QUINTET (10" LP) | 40 |
| 53 | Esquire 20-010 | ZOOT SIMS ALLSTARS (10" LP) | 40 |
| 53 | Esquire 20-018 | ZOOT SIMS QUARTET/QUINTET (10" LP) | 40 |
| 54 | Vogue LDE 056 | ZOOT SIMS GOES TO TOWN (10" LP) | 200 |
| 55 | Esquire 20-040 | ZOOT SIMS QUARTET/QUINTET (10" LP) | 40 |
| 57 | Esquire 32-040 | ZOOT SIMS SEPTET (LP) | 60 |
| 58 | HMV CLP 1165 | GEORGE HANDY COMPOSITIONS (LP) | 30 |
| 58 | HMV CLP 1188 | PLAYS FOUR ALTOS (LP) | 40 |
| 61 | Vogue LAE 12309 | CHOICE (LP) | 40 |
| 61 | Fontana TFL 5176 | ZOOT AT RONNIE SCOTT'S (LP) | 200 |
| 61 | Parlophone PMC 1169 | DOWN HOME (LP) | 80 |

| | | | |
|---|---|---|---|
| 62 | Fontana (S)TFL 588 | ZOOT AT RONNIE SCOTT'S (LP, reissue) | 100 |
| 62 | Fontana 886 151 TY | SOLO FOR ZOOT (LP, also mono [680 982 TL], £50) | 200 |
| 65 | Fontana FJL 123 | COOKIN'! (LP) | 150 |
| 60s | Xtra XTRA 5001 | TROTTING! (LP) | 15 |

*(see also Sims-Wheeler Vintage Jazz Band)*

## FRANK SINATRA

| | | | |
|---|---|---|---|
| 53 | Columbia SCM 5052 | Birth Of The Blues/Why Try To Change Me Now? | 20 |
| 53 | Columbia SCM 5060 | You Do Something To Me/Lover | 25 |
| 53 | Columbia SCM 5076 | Santa Claus Is Comin' To Town/My Girl | 25 |
| 54 | Capitol CL 14064 | Young-At-Heart/Take A Chance | 15 |
| 54 | Capitol CL 14120 | Three Coins In The Fountain/I Could Have Told You | 20 |
| 54 | Capitol CL 14174 | White Christmas/The Christmas Waltz | 15 |
| 54 | Capitol CL 14188 | When I Stop Loving You/It Worries Me | 15 |
| 55 | Columbia SCM 5167 | S'posin'/How Deep Is The Ocean | 6 |

*(Originally issued with triangular centre; later round-centre copies are worth half this value.)*

| | | | |
|---|---|---|---|
| 54 | Capitol LC 6654 | SONGS FOR YOUNG LOVERS (10") | 15 |
| 54 | Capitol LC 6689 | SWING EASY (10") | 15 |
| 54 | Philips BBR 8003 | SING AND DANCE WITH FRANK SINATRA (10") | 15 |
| 55 | Capitol LC 6702 | IN THE WEE SMALL HOURS VOL. 1 (10") | 15 |
| 55 | Capitol LC 6705 | IN THE WEE SMALL HOURS VOL. 2 (10") | 15 |
| 56 | Capitol LCT 6106 | SONGS FOR SWINGIN' LOVERS | 15 |
| 56 | Capitol LCT 6111 | FRANK SINATRA CONDUCTS TONE POEMS OF COLOUR | 15 |
| 62 | Reprise R(9) 1006 | SINATRA SINGS GREAT SONGS FROM GREAT BRITAIN (mono) | 15 |
| 62 | Reprise R(9) 1006 | SINATRA SINGS GREAT SONGS FROM GREAT BRITAIN (stereo) | 15 |
| 83 | Mobile Fidelity SC 1 | THE SINATRA COLLECTION (16-LPs in silver box, with Swing Easy LP unavailable elsewhere) | 40 |
| 85 | Capitol SINATRA 20 | FRANK SINATRA: THE CAPITOL YEARS (20-LP, box set) | 40 |

*(see also Nancy Sinatra, Count Basie, Tommy Dorsey, Dean Martin)*

## NANCY SINATRA

| | | | |
|---|---|---|---|
| 61 | Reprise RS 20017 | Cuff Links And Tie Clips/Not Just Your Friend (with p/s) | 20 |
| 61 | Reprise RS 20017 | Cuff Links And Tie Clips/Not Just Your Friend | 10 |
| 62 | Reprise RS 20045 | To Know Him Is To Love Him/Like I Do | 12 |
| 63 | Reprise RS 20144 | I See The Moon/Put Your Head On My Shoulder | 10 |
| 64 | Reprise RS 20335 | True Love/The Answer To Everything | 8 |
| 65 | Reprise RS 20407 | So Long Babe/If He'd Loved Me | 10 |
| 66 | Reprise RS 20432 | These Boots Are Made For Walkin'/The City Never Sleeps At Night | 6 |
| 66 | Reprise R 20461 | How Does That Grab You Darlin'/I Move Around | 7 |
| 66 | Reprise RS 20491 | Friday's Child/Hutchinson Jail | 7 |
| 66 | Reprise RS 20514 | In Our Time/Leave My Dog Alone | 7 |
| 67 | Reprise RS 20527 | Sugar Town/Summer Wine | 7 |
| 67 | Reprise RS 20559 | Love Eyes/Coastin' | 7 |
| 67 | Reprise RS 20620 | Lightning's Girl/Until It's Time For You To Go | 8 |
| 69 | Reprise RS 20869 | The Highway Song/Are You Growing Tired Of My Love | 7 |
| 77 | Private Stock PVT 114 | It's For My Dad/A Gentle Man Like You | 7 |
| 66 | Reprise REP 30069 | RUN FOR YOUR LIFE (EP) | 20 |
| 66 | Reprise REP 30072 | I MOVE AROUND (EP) | 15 |
| 67 | Reprise REP 30080 | SORRY 'BOUT THAT (EP) | 15 |
| 67 | Reprise REP 30086 | NASHVILLE NANCY (EP) | 15 |
| 66 | Reprise R 6202 | BOOTS (LP) | 25 |
| 66 | Reprise R 6207 | HOW DOES THAT GRAB YOU? (LP) | 25 |
| 66 | Reprise R(S)LP 6221 | NANCY IN LONDON (LP) | 25 |
| 67 | Reprise RLP 6239 | SUGAR (LP) | 25 |
| 67 | Reprise R(S)LP 6251 | COUNTRY, MY WAY (LP) | 20 |
| 68 | Reprise R(S)LP 6277 | MOVIN' WITH NANCY (LP) | 20 |
| 69 | Reprise RSLP 6333 | NANCY (LP, flipback sleeve, laminated front) | 20 |
| 73 | RCA SF 8331 | WOMAN (LP) | 15 |

*(see also Elvis Presley)*

## NANCY SINATRA & LEE HAZLEWOOD

| | | | |
|---|---|---|---|
| 67 | Reprise RS 20629 | Lady Bird/Sand | 7 |
| 67 | Reprise RS 23215 | Some Velvet Morning/Tony Rome | 8 |
| 71 | Reprise K 14093 | Did You Ever?/Back On The Road Again | 6 |
| 67 | Reprise REP 30083 | JACKSON (EP) | 15 |
| 68 | Reprise R(S)LP 6273 | NANCY & LEE (LP) | 20 |
| 71 | RCA Victor SF 8240 | DID YOU EVER? (LP) | 18 |

*(see also Lee Hazlewood, Frank Sinatra)*

## BETTY SINCLAIR

| | | | |
|---|---|---|---|
| 70 | Torpedo TOR 19 | Why Why Why/HOT ROD ALL STARS: Fistful Of Dollars | 45 |

## JIMMY SINCLAIR

| | | | |
|---|---|---|---|
| 62 | Wasp W005 | To Prove My Love/Verona | 12 |

## JIMMY SINCLAIR & TRENTON SPENCE ORCHESTRA

| | | | |
|---|---|---|---|
| 61 | Blue Beat BB 47 | Verona/To Prove My Love | 10 |

*(see also Jimmy Sinclair)*

## PAUL SINCLAIR

| | | | |
|---|---|---|---|
| 76 | Angen ANG 115 | Jah Is My Saviour/Version | 8 |
| 76 | Third World TW 25 | Naturalization/Version (as Paul Sinclaire) | 30 |
| 78 | Lovers Rock DYS 68 | Perfidia (vocal)/Perfidia (instrumental)//GLEN ADAMS: Can't Hide Love/Blue Moon (instrumental) (12") | 25 |

## WINSTON SINCLAIR

| | | | |
|---|---|---|---|
| 69 | Nu Beat NB 026 | Another Heartache/Come On Little Girl | 20 |

*(see also Harmonisers)*

## SINDELFINGEN
| | | | |
|---|---|---|---|
| 73 | Medway | ODGIPIG (LP, private pressing, with insert) | 750 |
| 90 | Cenotaph CEN 111 | ODGIPIG/TRIANGLE (2-LP, reissue with live album, 300 only) | 35 |

## SINEWAVE
| | | | |
|---|---|---|---|
| 72 | Chapter One SCH 172 | Clochemerle/Star Trek | 10 |

## PETE SINFIELD
| | | | |
|---|---|---|---|
| 73 | Manticore K 43501 | STILL (LP, textured gatefold pink sleeve) | 25 |
| 73 | Manticore K 43501 | STILL (LP, textured gatefold blue sleeve) | 20 |

*(see also Emerson Lake & Palmer, King Crimson)*

## SIN FX
| | | | |
|---|---|---|---|
| 80 | Wombat S/80/CUS 616 | STREET CREDIBILITY EP | 8 |

## SINGAPORE
| | | | |
|---|---|---|---|
| 79 | SRTS/79/CUS 274 | Launching/A Bird With No Wings | 200 |

## RAY SINGER
| | | | |
|---|---|---|---|
| 64 | Ember EMB S 187 | Tell Me Now/I'm Comin' Home | 10 |
| 64 | Ember EMB S 199 | It's Gotta Be/Hey, Who? | 10 |
| 65 | Ember EMB S 215 | I'm The Richest Man Alive/Pretty Little Rambling Rose (in p/s) | 15 |
| 65 | Ember EMB S 215 | I'm The Richest Man Alive/Pretty Little Rambling Rose | 10 |
| 65 | Fontana TF 621 | You'll Come Crying To Me/Who Can I Talk To About You | 10 |
| 67 | Ember EMB S 231 | What's Done Has Been Done/Won't It Be Fine | 60 |
| 66 | Ember EMB 3364 | RAY SINGER (LP) | 40 |

*(see also Nirvana [U.K.])*

## SUSAN SINGER
| | | | |
|---|---|---|---|
| 62 | Oriole CB 1703 | Gee It's Great To Be Young/Hello First Love | 20 |
| 62 | Oriole CB 1741 | Bobby's Loving Touch/Johnny Summertime | 150 |
| 62 | Oriole CB 1778 | Love Me With All Your Heart/Autumn Leaves | 20 |
| 63 | Oriole CB 1802 | Lock Your Heart Away/Answer To A Prayer | 20 |
| 63 | Oriole CB 1882 | I Know (You Don't Love Me No More)/That Old Feeling | 20 |

*(see also Susan Holiday)*

## SINGER BLUE AND DUBATEERS
| | | | |
|---|---|---|---|
| 07 | Dubateers DA 1007 | Never Stop Praise Jah Jah/Jah Jah Dub/KENNY KNOTS & DUBATEERS: Show Dem/ Rising Dub (10") | 25 |

## SINGERS AND PLAYERS
| | | | |
|---|---|---|---|
| 81 | On U Sound LP 5 | WAR OF WORDS (LP) | 15 |
| 83 | On U Sound LP 23 | STAGGERING HEIGHTS (LP) | 15 |

## SINGERS & PLAYERS
| | | | |
|---|---|---|---|
| 82 | On U Sound ON ULP5 | WAR OF WORDS (LP) | 18 |
| 82 | On U Sound ON ULP11 | REVENGE OF THE UNDERDOG (LP) | 15 |
| 83 | On U Sound ON ULP23 | STAGGERING HEIGHTS (LP) | 15 |
| 84 | Trance TCLP4 | LEAPS & BOUNDS (LP, white vinyl) | 18 |

## SINGING BELLES
| | | | |
|---|---|---|---|
| 60 | Top Rank JAR 350 | The Empty Mailbox/Someone Loves You, Joe | 8 |

## SINGING DOGS
| | | | |
|---|---|---|---|
| 57 | Pye NEP 24029 | SINGING DOGS (EP) | 10 |

## SINGING KETTLES
| | | | |
|---|---|---|---|
| 74 | Hadley HS 20 | A Satisfied Mind/Little Boy Lost | 15 |

## SINGING LOINS
| | | | |
|---|---|---|---|
| 91 | Hangman HANG 44 UP | SONGS FOR THE ORGAN (LP) | 15 |
| 93 | Hangman HANG 51 UP | STEAK AND GRAVY (LP) | 15 |

*(see also Billy Childish & Singing Loins)*

## SINGING POSTMAN
| | | | |
|---|---|---|---|
| 66 | Parlophone R 5505 | The Ladies Darts Team/Roundabout | 7 |
| 67 | Parlophone R 5584 | Mind How You Go/Daddy's Trombone | 7 |
| 67 | Parlophone R 5632 | Sound Barrier/Old North Walsham Line | 7 |
| 64 | Ralph Tuck Promotions Ltd. BEV EP 153 | Come Along A Me/Moind Yer Hid Boy/Hev Yew Gotta Loight Boy/Miss From Diss (EP) | 10 |
| 65 | Ralph Tuck BEV EP 179 | BBC SINGING POSTMAN (EP) | 10 |

## SINGING PRINCIPAL
| | | | |
|---|---|---|---|
| 73 | Action ACT 4608 | Thank You Baby/Women's Lib | 75 |

## SINGLE FACTOR
| | | | |
|---|---|---|---|
| 84 | SF Records SINFAX 001 | Fresh Upon Her Lips/I Think I'm Falling In Love (p/s, 2 inserts) | 50 |

## SINGLES
| | | | |
|---|---|---|---|
| 78 | Sing SING 1 | Adolf Hitler/Mercy (no p/s) | 1000 |

## MARGIE SINGLETON
| | | | |
|---|---|---|---|
| 60 | Melodisc 45-1544 | Angel Hands/The Eyes Of Love | 15 |
| 62 | Mercury AMT 1197 | Magic Star/Only Your Shadow Knows | 20 |
| 68 | Fontana TL 5456 | SINGS COUNTRY WITH SOUL (LP) | 18 |

## SINISTER DUCKS
| | | | |
|---|---|---|---|
| 83 | Situation 2 SIT 25 | Suicide: March Of The Sinister Ducks/Homicide: Old Gangsters Never (foldout p/s) | 10 |

*(see also Bauhaus)*

## SINITTA
| | | | |
|---|---|---|---|
| 83 | Midas 12MID 3 | Never Too Late (Special Extended US Mix)/Never Too Late (Instrumental) (12", p/s) | 40 |

## SINKING SHIPS
| | | | |
|---|---|---|---|
| 81 | Recession REC S1 | Dream/After The Rain (Live) | 18 |

## EARL SINK(S)
| | | | |
|---|---|---|---|
| 61 | Warner Bros WB 38 | Look For Me, I'll Be There/Super Market (as Earl Sink) | 15 |

| 61 | Warner Bros WB 51 | Superstitious/Little Suzie Parker | 20 |
| 63 | Capitol CL 15310 | Looking For Love/Raining On My Side Of Town (as Earl Sinks) | 15 |

*(see also Crickets, Sinx Mitchell)*

## SINNER
| 79 | Whitetower AMC 705 | Need Your Love/Beggar/God's In His Heaven (foldout p/s) | 75 |

## SINNERMAN & SARA
| 68 | MGM 1450 | Don't Think Twice It's Allright/Buffalo Boy | 10 |
| 68 | MGM MGM-C(S) 8099 | SINNERMAN AND SARA (LP) | 20 |

## SINNERS
| 63 | Columbia DB 7158 | I Can't Stand It/If You Leave Me Now | 10 |
| 64 | Columbia DB 7295 | It's So Exciting/Leave Him | 10 |

*(see also Linda Laine & Sinners)*

## SINS OF THE FLESH
| 90s | Plastic Head 014 | In The Image Of Torture (12", p/s) | 10 |

## SIOUX
| 73 | SRT SRT 73274 | Prosmoe/Warlove/You're All I Need/Happiness In The Sky (EP) | 75 |

## SIOUXSIE & BANSHEES
| 78 | Polydor 2059 052 | Hong Kong Garden/Voices (10,000 only in gatefold p/s; beige plastic, silver plastic, red plastic or red paper label) | 20 |
| 78 | Polydor 2059 052 | Hong Kong Garden/Voices (p/s) | 5 |
| 79 | Polydor 2059 151 | Mittageisen (Metal Postcard)/Love In A Void (p/s) | 5 |
| 79 | Polydor POSP 9 | The Staircase (Mystery)/20th Century Boy (thin paper p/s, very hard to find in mint) | 5 |
| 79 | Polydor POSP 59 | Playground Twist/Pull To Bits (thin paper p/s, very hard to find in mint) | 5 |
| 80 | Polydor POSP 117 | Happy House/Drop Dead (Celebration) (p/s) | 5 |
| 80 | Polydor POSP 205 | Israel/Red Over White (picture label, gold die-cut sleeve) | 5 |
| 80 | Polydor POSP 249 | Christine/Eve White, Eve Black (p/s) | 5 |
| 82 | Polydor POSPG 450 | Fireworks/Coal Mind (foldout p/s, regular p/s copies worth £3) | 5 |
| 83 | Fan Club FILE 1 | Head Cut/Running Town (freebie, p/s) | 30 |
| 85 | Wonderland SHE 8 | Overground/Placebo Effect (p/s) | 6 |
| 85 | Wonderland SHE 9 | Cities In Dust/An Execution (poster p/s) | 5 |
| 86 | Wonderland SHEDP 10 | Candyman/Lullaby (with free 2nd single, gatefold p/s, 2,000 only) | 8 |
| 87 | Wonderland SHEPK 4 | The Passenger/Hall Of Mirrors/You're Lost Little Girl/Sea Breezes/This Town Ain't Big Enough For Both Of Us/Gun (3 X promo 7" in plain black sleeves in foldout stickered and printed PVC wallet, single cat. no's SHESP 1/2/3) | 20 |
| 87 | Wonderland SHEG 11 | This Wheel's On Fire/Shooting Sun/Sleepwalking (On The High Wire)/She's Cracked (numbered double pack, gatefold p/s) | 6 |
| 88 | Spiral Scratch SCRATCH 2 | An Interview With... (free with Spiral Scratch mag, 5,000 only) | 6 |
| 78 | Polydor POLD 5009 | THE SCREAM (LP, with inner sleeve) | 18 |
| 79 | Polydor POLD 5024 | JOIN HANDS (LP, gatefold. with inner sleeve, stickered noting inclusion of 'Playground Twist'.) | 18 |
| 81 | Polydor POLD 5155 | JUJU (LP, with inner) | 15 |
| 81 | Polydor POLS 1056 | ONCE UPON A TIME : THE SINGLES (LP, first pressing with Siouxsie art print) | 18 |
| 82 | Polydor POLD 5064 | A KISS IN THE DREAMHOUSE (LP, with inner sleeve) | 15 |
| 83 | Wonderland SHAH 1 | NOCTURNE (2-LP, with pink/blue inner sleeves) | 18 |
| 87 | Wonderland SHELP 4 | THROUGH THE LOOKING GLASS (LP, die-cut sleeve) | 15 |
| 87 | Wonderland SHELP 4 | THROUGH THE LOOKING GLASS (LP, mispressing, 1 side plays Jimi Hendrix's "War Heroes") | 25 |
| 91 | Polydor 847731 7 | SUPERSTITION (LP) | 15 |
| 92 | Polydor 517160 | TWICE UPON A TIME - THE SINGLES (2-LP) | 30 |

*(see also Cure, Glove)*

## SIR ALEC & HIS BOYS
| 67 | Deram DM 116 | I'm A Believer/Green Green Grass Of Home | 8 |

## SIR ALICK & PHRASER
| 82 | Recommended/Black Noise 7 NO 5 | In Search Of The Perfect Baby/PROLIFIKURDS: Nursery Crymes (printed p/s in PVC sleeve or standard p/s) | 10 |

*(see also Homosexuals)*

## SIR BEANZ OBE
| 99 | Mapache Chet002 | MARS ATTACKS (EP) | 12 |
| 01 | SFDB 005 | HIEROGLYPHIC AUDIO VISUAL (EP) | 10 |
| 12 | B-Line Recordings BLN001 | PAUSE TO DISCUSS (EP, white vinyl) | 12 |

## SIR CHAUNCEY
| 60 | Warner Bros. WB 9 | Beautiful Obsession/Tenderfoot | 5 |
| 60 | Warner Bros. WB 36 | Midi-Midinette/Beyond Our Love | 5 |

## SIR CHING I
| 70 | Spark SRL 1041 | Hello Everyone/Hiawatha Mini Ha Ha Love | 300 |

## SIR (CLANCY) COLLINS BAND
| 68 | Collins Downbeat CR 005 | Sock It Softly (with Bob Stackie)/LESTER STERLING, SIR COLLINS & BAND: Three Wise Men | 50 |
| 68 | Collins Downbeat CR 0011 | Collins And The Boys/Bob Stackie In Soho (both with Bob Stackie) | 40 |
| 68 | Collins Downbeat CR 0017 | Soul Feelings/SIR COLLINS: Hello Stella | 70 |
| 69 | Duke DU 46 | Black Panther/I Want To Be Loved | 250 |
| 69 | Duke DU 47 | Black Diamonds (with Diamonds)/DIAMONDS: I Remember | 60 |
| 69 | Duke DU 55 | Brother Moses/Funny Familiar Feeling (both with Earthquakes) | 70 |
| 69 | Duke DU 69 | Pair Of Wings/I Can't Stop Loving | 50 |
| 81 | Sir Collins SC 001 | NEW CROSS FIRE PAGE ONE (LP) | 40 |

*(see also Bob Stackie, Earthquakes, Collins Band, Owen Gray)*

## SIR COXSONE SOUND (LLOYD COXON)
| 75 | Safari SFA 100 | KING OF DUB ROCK (LP) | 35 |
| 76 | Regal RLP 001 | KING OF DUB ROCK PART 2 (LP) | 20 |

## SIR D'S GROUP
| | | | |
|---|---|---|---|
| 61 | Blue Beat BB 66 | Hey Diddle Diddle (with K. Brown)/Pocket Money (with Mossman & Zeddze) | 25 |

*(see also Kent Brown & Rainbows)*

## SIR DOUGLAS QUINTET
| | | | |
|---|---|---|---|
| 65 | London HLU 9964 | She's About A Mover/We'll Take Our Last Walk Tonight | 12 |
| 65 | London HLU 9982 | The Tracker/Blue Norther | 12 |
| 65 | London HLU 10001 | The Story Of John Hardy/In Time | 8 |
| 66 | London HLU 10019 | The Rains Came/Bacon Fat | 8 |
| 69 | Mercury MF 1079 | Mendocino/I Wanna Be Your Mama Again | 12 |
| 69 | Mercury MF 1129 | Dynamite Woman/Too Many Dociled Minds | 8 |
| 69 | London HLU 10248 | She's About A Mover/The Rains Came (reissue) | 6 |
| 65 | London HA-U 8311 | THE SIR DOUGLAS QUINTET (LP) | 40 |
| 69 | Mercury SMCL 20160 | MENDOCINO (LP) | 30 |
| 69 | Mercury SMCL 20186 | TOGETHER AFTER FIVE (LP) | 30 |
| 75 | Oval OVLM 5001 | MENDOCINO (LP, with insert) | 15 |

## SIREN (1)
| | | | |
|---|---|---|---|
| 71 | Dandelion DAN 7002 | Strange Locomotion/I'm All Aching (label also lists K 19004) | 6 |
| 69 | Dandelion 63755 | SIREN (LP, laminated front sleeve, black/red/silver labels) | 50 |
| 71 | Dandelion DAN 8001 | STRANGE LOCOMOTION (LP, gatefold sleeve) | 50 |
| 71 | Dandelion DAN 8001 | STRANGE LOCOMOTION (LP, with later label listing K 49001) | 25 |

## SIREN (2)
| | | | |
|---|---|---|---|
| 84 | Distant Cousins DC4R | Deceiving Lies/American Girl (white or black sleeve) | 10 |

## SIR GIBBS
| | | | |
|---|---|---|---|
| 68 | Amalgamated AMG 822 | People Grudgeful/Pan Ya Machet (both sides actually by Pioneers) | 50 |

## SIR HARRY
| | | | |
|---|---|---|---|
| 71 | Duke DU 127 | Last Call/ORGAN D: Hot Organ | 15 |
| 72 | Duke DU 136 | Apples To Apples/DRUM BEAT ALL STARS: Good Life | 15 |
| 72 | Bullet BU 519 | Mr. Parker's Daughter/U.ROY: On Top Of The Peak | 18 |
| 72 | Downtown DT 493 | Meet The Boss/Musical Fight | 40 |
| 73 | Downtown DT 504 | Apollo 17 (with Cables)/Uptown Rock | 25 |

*(see also Barbara Jones)*

## SIR HENRY (& HIS BUTLERS)
| | | | |
|---|---|---|---|
| 68 | Columbia DB 8351 | Camp/Pretty Style (as Sir Henry & His Butlers) | 10 |
| 68 | Columbia DB 8497 | The Rolo Sensation (Camp)/Pretty Style (reissue, as Sir Henry & His Butlers) | 10 |
| 70 | Columbia DB 8740 | Annie Got A Date/Like A Rose | 8 |

## SIR HORATIO
| | | | |
|---|---|---|---|
| 82 | Rock Steady/666 Mix 1T | Abracadubra/Sommadub (12", plain sleeve) | 15 |

*(see also A Certain Ratio)*

## SIR LLOYD
| | | | |
|---|---|---|---|
| 71 | Lion LEO 1 | Mosi/Nursery Rhyme Version | 20 |

## SIR LORD COMIC
| | | | |
|---|---|---|---|
| 67 | Doctor Bird DB 1019 | Ska-ing West/MAYTALS: If You Act This Way | 40 |
| 67 | Doctor Bird DB 1070 | The Great Wuga Wuga (with Cowboys)/THREE TOPS: Feel So Lonesome | 45 |
| 70 | Pressure Beat PR 5507 | Jack Of My Trade/CYNTHIA RICHARDS: United We Stand | 70 |

*(see also Lord Comic)*

## SIRUS
| | | | |
|---|---|---|---|
| 91 | White 002 | THE ONE AND ONLY (EP) | 75 |
| 93 | SBP SBPR004 | Clubland/DETT (12") | 12 |

## SIR WASHINGTON
| | | | |
|---|---|---|---|
| 69 | Star ST 1 | Apollo 12/When You Kiss Me | 12 |
| 70 | Saga BC 100 | Apollo 13/Space | 10 |
| 70 | Saga BC 102 | Let There Be Peace in The World/Pharoah's Walk | 10 |

## SISTA MARY
| | | | |
|---|---|---|---|
| 07 | Roots Injection RI 10 003 | Blindeye/Version/Dem Lost/Version (10") | 25 |
| 08 | Roots Injection RI 10 008 | Hail Jah/RAS Muffet: Version/Hail Jah/RAS MUFFET: Version (10") | 15 |

## SISTER
| | | | |
|---|---|---|---|
| 70 | Camel CA 55 | Feel It/MAYTONES: Serious | 15 |
| 73 | Camel CA 106 | Every Day Is The Same Kind Of Thing/Sweat Of Your Brow | 10 |

## SISTER CANDY
| | | | |
|---|---|---|---|
| 83 | Vista Sounds VSLP 4026 | BLACK CULTURE (LP) | 20 |

## SISTERHOOD
| | | | |
|---|---|---|---|
| 86 | Merciful Release SIS 010 | Giving Ground (RSV)/Giving Ground (AV) (p/s) | 5 |

*(see also Sisters Of Mercy, James Ray & Performance)*

## SISTER RAIN
| | | | |
|---|---|---|---|
| 88 | A Serene | BURT REYNOLDS (12", EP) | 12 |

## SISTERS
| | | | |
|---|---|---|---|
| 73 | Bell BELL 1307 | Kick Your Boots Off/Driving Me Home | 15 |
| 74 | Warner Brothers K 16445 | There's A Raver Coming Home/Help The Music | 8 |

## SISTERS LOVE
| | | | |
|---|---|---|---|
| 73 | Mowest MW 3009 | I'm Learning To Trust My Man/Try It You'll Like It | 20 |
| 75 | Tamla Motown TMG 1002 | I'm Learning To Trust My Man/Try It You'll Like It (reissue) | 5 |
| 06 | Soul Jazz SJR LP 133 | GIVE ME YOUR LOVE (2-LP) | 18 |

## SISTERS OF MERCY
| | | | |
|---|---|---|---|
| 80 | Merciful Release MR 7 | The Damage Done/Watch/Home Of The Hitmen (p/s, 1,000 only; beware of counterfeits without 'MR 7' matrix number) | 400 |
| 82 | CNT CNT 002 | Body Electric/Adrenochrome (p/s) | 65 |
| 82 | Merciful Release MR 015 | Alice/Floorshow (white background p/s) | 30 |

| 84 | Merciful Release/WEA | ALICE/TEMPLE OF LOVE/REPTILE HOUSE/BODY AND SOUL (4 x 12" box set, promo only) | 500 |
| 84 | Merciful Release MR 033 | Walk Away/Poison Door (p/s, with flexidisc "Long Train" [SAM 218]) | 15 |
| 84 | Merciful Release MR 033T | Walk Away/Poison Door/On The Wire (12", p/s, with flexi "Long Train") | 15 |
| 85 | Merciful Release MR 335 | No Time To Cry/Blood Money (p/s) | 6 |
| 88 | Merciful Release MR 43TB | Dominion (Extended)/Untitled/Sandstorm/Emma (12", box set with poster) | 15 |
| 93 | Merciful Release MR59T | Under The Gun (Metropolis)/Alice (1993)/Under The Gun (Jutland Mix) (12", poster p/s) | 15 |
| 85 | Merciful Release MR337L | FIRST AND LAST AND ALWAYS (LP, gatefold) | 15 |
| 87 | Merciful Release MR441L | FLOODLANDS (LP) | 15 |
| 90 | Merciful Release MMR 449 L | VISION THING (LP) | 15 |
| 92 | East West 9031 76476-` | SOME GIRLS WANDER BY MISTAKE (2-LP) | 25 |

*(see also Mission, Sisterhood, Ghost Dance, Dead Or Alive)*

## SITUATION
| 66 | CBS 202392 | Situation Now/Time | 30 |

## SIVUCA
| 74 | Vanguard VSD 79337 | SIVUCA (LP) | 30 |

## SIX OF ONE
| 64 | Mercury MF 812 | He's The One You Love/I Love My Little Girl | 10 |

## SIX TEASERS
| 89 | Kent 6T 5 | Doing The Hundred/WALLY COX: This Man Wants You | 15 |

## SIX MINUTE WAR
| 80 | (No label or cat no) | 75P EP (7", fold-out p/s, 1st issue with 'soldier' sleeve) | 15 |
| 80 | (No label or cat no) | MORE SHORT SONGS (7" EP, fold-out p/s) | 10 |
| 81 | (No label or cat no) | SLIGHTLY LONGER SONGS (7" EP, fold-out, p/s) | 10 |

## SIXPENCE
| 67 | London HLJ 10124 | You're The Love/What To Do | 10 |

## EARL SIXTEEN
| 79 | Sufferers Heights SUFF 007 | African Tribesman/MIKEY DREAD: Yoruba Dub (12") | 20 |
| 79 | Cha Cha CHAD 16 | The World Has Begun (with the Heptones)/Make Up Your Mind (12") | 30 |
| 81 | DATC DCD 004 | MR D.J./GILLY BUCHANAN: Ghetto Youths/DATC MUSIC STABLE : Dub (12") | 25 |
| 81 | Greensleeves GRED 64 | Trials And Crosses/BARRY BROWN: Love Is What The World Wants (12") | 20 |
| 81 | Dread At The Controls DATCLP003 | REGGAE SOUND (LP) | 50 |
| 83 | Vista VSLP 4023 | SHINING STAR (LP) | 25 |

## SIX TEENS
| 56 | London HLU 8345 | A Casual Look/Teen Age Promise | 250 |
| 56 | London HLU 8345 | A Casual Look/Teen Age Promise (78) | 50 |

## SIXTH COMM
| 87 | Eyas Media EYAS 002 | CONTENT WITH BLOOD/TURN OF THE WHEEL (LP, embossed, textured sleeve, 2,000 only) | 20 |
| 87 | Eyas Media EYAS 005 | TASTE FOR FLESH (1st 2,000 in laminated, full-cover sleeve) | 20 |
| 88 | Eyas Media EYAS 006 | FRUITS OF YGGDRASIL (LP, limited issue, 669 copies only) | 25 |
| 90 | Eyas Media EYAS 013 | ASYLUM (LP) | 15 |
| 90 | Eyas Media EYAS 059 | MORTHOGENISIS (LP) | 20 |

## 65 DAYS OF STATIC
| 06 | monotreme MONO 21-7 | Radio Protector/Asphalt & Trouble (p/s, 1500 only, 1000 with unique polaroid photos) | 6 |

## 64 SPOONS
| 78 | Bushbaby | LADIES DON'T HAVE WILLIES (EP) | 10 |

## 67 PARK LANE
| 69 | Toast TT516 | I'm So Happy To Be With You/I Got Love | 60 |

## SIZE SEVEN GROUP
| 64 | Rendevous HS 1/PR 5020 | Crying My Heart Out/So How Come | 20 |
| 65 | Mercury MF 845 | Where Do We Go From Here/Till I Die | 10 |
| 65 | Mercury MF 896 | In Time/Walking Proud | 10 |
| 65 | Mercury MF 896 | It's Got To Be Love/I Met Her In The Rain | 8 |

## SKA CHAMPIONS
| 65 | Blue Beat BB 305 | My Tears/Yesterday's Dreams | 25 |

## SKA CITY ROCKERS
| 80 | Inferno BEAT 1 | Time Is Tight/Roadrunner/You Don't Know Like I Know (p/s) | 6 |
| 80 | Inferno BEAT 1 | Time Is Tight/Roadrunner/You Don't Know Like I Know (12", p/s) | 10 |

## SKA-DOWS
| 80 | Cheapskate CHEAP 1 | Apache/The Tune That Time Forgot (p/s) | 7 |
| 80 | Cheapskate CHEAP 4 | Telstar/Yes Yes Yes (p/s) | 8 |
| 81 | Cheapskate CHEAP 25 | Yes Yes Yes/Twice (p/s) | 8 |
| 81 | Penthouse PENT 7 | Ska's On 45/Rhapsody In Buh (plain stickered sleeve) | 6 |
| 81 | Penthouse PENT 127 | Ska's On 45/The Ska-Dows Live (Let's Twist Again/Everybody Knows It's Shocking/Aye-Ho - Kinky Reggae) (12", p/s) | 12 |
| 81 | Cheapskate CHEAP 36 | Ska's On 45/Rhapsody In Buh (p/s, reissue) | 6 |
| 82 | Cheapskate CHEAP 41 | We Gotta Get Out Of This Place/Ska'd For Life | 5 |
| 82 | Cheapskate SKATE 3 | SKA'D FOR LIFE (LP) | 15 |

## SKA KINGS
| 64 | Atlantic AT 4003 | Jamaica Ska (actually by Keith Lynn & Ken Lazarus, & Byron Lee/Dragonaires)/Oil In My Lamp (actually by Eric Morris with Byron Lee & Dragonaires) | 30 |
| 65 | Parlophone R 5338 | Bimbo/Ska'ville | 10 |

## SKANNA
| 92 | White House WYHS 010 | Intimidator/Jungle Rain/Cease Fire/Dreamin' (12") | 20 |
| 93 | White House WYHS 013 | The Future/Nightstalker/Intimidator (Technoid Mix)/Exit The Lights (12") | 50 |
| 93 | Skanna 03 | NIGHT STALKER EP (12") | 50 |

# SKATALITES (Jamaica)

| | | | |
|---|---|---|---|
| 93 | Skanna 04 | Until The Night Is Morning/Untitled (12") | 50 |
| 93 | Skanna 05 | Heaven/Run To Me/This Way (12") | 30 |
| 94 | Skanna 07 | The Greatest Thing (Summertime Mix)/The Greatest Thing/Heaven (Remix) (12") | 12 |
| 94 | Skanna 08 | All You Wanted/The Greatest Thing (Criminal Minds Mix) (12") | 15 |
| 96 | Skanna 09 | Find Me/Find Me (Classic Skanna Mix) (12") | 20 |

*(see also The Joker)*

## SKATALITES (JAMAICA)

| | | | |
|---|---|---|---|
| 65 | Island WI 161 | Trip To Mars/DOTTIE & BONNIE: Bunch Of Roses | 45 |
| 64 | Island WI 164 | Good News/OWEN & LEON: The Fits Is On Me | 25 |
| 65 | Island WI 168 | Guns Of Navarone (actually by Roland Alphonso & Studio One Orchestra)/Marcus Garvey (actually "Where's Marcus Garvey" by Bongoman Byfield) | 25 |
| 65 | Island WI 175 | Dragon Weapon/DESMOND DEKKER & FOUR ACES: It Was Only A Dream | 100 |
| 65 | Island WI 191 | Dr. Kildare/Sucu Sucu | 75 |
| 65 | Island WI 207 | Ball O' Fire/LINVAL SPENCER: Can't Go On | 30 |
| 65 | Island WI 226 | Dick Tracy/RITA & SOULETTES: One More Chance | 75 |
| 65 | Island WI 228 | Beardman Ska/BONNIE & RITA: Bless You | 20 |
| 65 | Island WI 244 | Lucky Seven/JUSTIN HINDS & DOMINOES: Never Too Young | 25 |
| 66 | Island WI 260 | Independent Anniversary Ska (I Should Have Known Better)/WAILERS: Jumbie Jamboree | 80 |
| 65 | Ska Beat JB 177 | Latin Goes Ska/LORD TANAMO: Night Food Ska | 35 |
| 65 | Ska Beat JB 178 | Silver Dollar/My Business | 20 |
| 65 | Ska Beat JB 182 | Street Corner/DREAMLETS: Really Now | 30 |
| 65 | Ska Beat JB 206 | Timothy/KING SCRATCH & DYNAMITES: Gumma | 40 |
| 73 | Trojan Maxi TRM 9008 | Guns Of Navarone/Bonanza Ska/Napolean Solo | 5 |
| 75 | Tropical ALO64 | Jumbo Malt/747 Dub (as Original Skatalites) | 10 |
| 67 | Studio One SOL 9006 | SKA AUTHENTIC (LP) | 300 |

*(see also Justin Hinds, Deltas, Four Aces, Maytals, Jackie Opel, Joe White, Jackie Mittoo)*

## SKATALITES (U.K.)

| | | | |
|---|---|---|---|
| 68 | Decca F 12743 | Don't Knock It/I Know | 10 |
| 69 | Spark SRL 1034 | Cos You're The One I Love/Please Let Me Hide | 10 |

## SKAVENGERS

| | | | |
|---|---|---|---|
| 80 | Identity Discs ID 001 | Party Girls/Go To Pieces/Happy | 10 |

## SKAVILLE TRAIN

| | | | |
|---|---|---|---|
| 03 | Next Step RFDNX 4 | Jet 707/Darker Shot | 10 |

## SK'BOO

| | | | |
|---|---|---|---|
| 70s | Cuecumber CUE 1001 | It's A Hard Road/Music Is Life/Talking Pictures/God's Peace In Mind | 5 |

*(see also Them)*

## BOBBY SKEL

| | | | |
|---|---|---|---|
| 64 | London HLU 9942 | Kiss And Run/Say It Now | 15 |

## SKELETAL FAMILY

| | | | |
|---|---|---|---|
| 83 | Luggage RRP 00724 | Trees/Just A Friend (foldout p/s) | 15 |
| 86 | Cave CAVE IN 1 | Sharp Cheekbones In Black Clothing/Blood-Stained (p/s) | 12 |
| 85 | Red Rhino REDLP 57 | FUTILE COMBAT (LP) | 15 |

*(see also Ghost Dance)*

## SKELETON CREW

| | | | |
|---|---|---|---|
| 87 | B BS 1 | BOOGIE-WOOGIE, SKIFFLE & BLUES (12" EP, p/s) | 15 |
| 88 | B BS 2 | House Of The Rising Sun/Hurricane Janine (white label promo only) | 15 |

*(see also King Earl Boogie Band, Manfred Mann's Earth Band)*

## SKELLATON

| | | | |
|---|---|---|---|
| 94 | Viceroy GREEB028 | Bangers 'n' Mash (12") | 30 |

## SKEPTIX

| | | | |
|---|---|---|---|
| 82 | Zenon SKEP 001 | Routine Machine/Curfew (p/s) | 15 |
| 83 | Zenon SKEP 002 | Scarred For Life/Born To Lose/Peaceforce (p/s) | 15 |
| 83 | Zenon SKEP 003 | RETURN TO HELL (EP) | 15 |

## SKERNE

| | | | |
|---|---|---|---|
| 81 | Guardian GRC 81 | BETTER LATE THAN NEVER (LP, private pressing) | 15 |

## SKETTO

| | | | |
|---|---|---|---|
| 71 | Big Shot BI 596 | Know Your Friend/Three Sevens Version | 15 |

*(Father Sketto, Ruddy and Sketto)*

## FATHER SKETTO

| | | | |
|---|---|---|---|
| 73 | Pama PM 877 | Big Nine/RECO'S GROUP: Old Lady | 5 |

*(see also Sketto Rich, Ruddy & Sketto)*

## SKID

| | | | |
|---|---|---|---|
| 77 | Galaxy GY 118 | I Saw Her Standing There/Endless Sleep | 15 |

## SKIDDO

| | | | |
|---|---|---|---|
| 79 | GTO GT 252 | A Touch Of The Sun/I'm Going On Me Holidays | 8 |

## SKIDDY & DETROIT

| | | | |
|---|---|---|---|
| 72 | Grape GR 3030 | The Exile Song/BUNNY GALE: In The Burning Sun Joh-Ho | 25 |

## ALAN SKIDMORE (QUINTET)

| | | | |
|---|---|---|---|
| 69 | Deram Nova SDN 11 | ONCE UPON A TIME (LP, Deram Nova on sleeve but has either Deram Nova or Decca Nova labels) | 175 |
| 71 | Philips 6308 041 | T.C.B. (LP) | 150 |

*(see also John Mayall's Bluesbreakers, Brian Bennett, Centipede)*

## JIMMY SKIDMORE

| | | | |
|---|---|---|---|
| 72 | DJM DJSL 026 | SKID MARKS (LP) | 40 |

## SKID ROW (IRELAND)

| | | | |
|---|---|---|---|
| 70 | Song SO 002 | New Places Old Faces/Misdemeanour Dream Felicity (Irish pressing) | 100 |
| 70 | Song SO003 | Saturday Morning Man (Irish pressing) | 25 |

| 70 | CBS 4893 | Sandie's Gone (Parts 1 & 2) | 15 |
| 71 | CBS 7181 | Night Of The Warm Witch/Mr. Deluxe | 15 |
| 70 | CBS 63965 | SKID (LP, orange label, red & blue sleeve) | 60 |
| 71 | CBS 64411 | 34 HOURS (LP, gatefold sleeve, orange label) | 45 |

*(see also Gary Moore, Thin Lizzy, Peggy's Leg, UFO)*

## SKIDS

| 78 | No Bad NB 1 | Charles/Reasons/Test Tube Babies (p/s) | 10 |
| 78 | Virgin VS 227 | Sweet Suburbia/Open Sound (p/s, white vinyl) | 5 |
| 79 | Virgin VS 262 | Masquerade/Out Of Town//Another Emotion/Aftermath Dub (double pack) | 5 |
| 79 | Virgin VS 306 | Working For The Yankee Dollar/Vanguard's Crusade//All The Young Dudes/Hymns From A Haunted Ballroom (double pack) | 5 |
| 79 | Virgin V 2116 | SCARED TO DANCE (LP, blue vinyl, withdrawn) | 350 |
| 79 | Virgin V 2138 | DAYS IN EUROPA (LP, with insert, 1st pressing with withdrawn cover featuring German 'gothic' lettering & 1936 Olympics picture) | 15 |

*(see also Big Country)*

## BJORN SKIFS

| 78 | EMI EMI 2785 | When The Night Comes/Don't Stop Now | 6 |
| 81 | EMI EMI 5172 | Haunted By A Dream/Fangad I En Drom | 8 |

## SKILLETS

| 70 | Pantonic PAN 6303 | BOTH SIDES NOW (LP) | 15 |

## SKIN

| 88 | Product Inc. 33 PROD 11 | SHAME, HUMILITY, REVENGE (LP, with inner) | 20 |

## SKIN ALLEY

| 70 | CBS 5045 | Tell Me/Better Be Blind | 20 |
| 72 | Transatlantic BIG 506 | You Got Me Danglin'/Skin Valley Serenade | 8 |
| 72 | Transatlantic BIG 511 | In The Midnight Hour/Broken Eggs | 8 |
| 73 | Transatlantic BIG 514 | If Only I Had The Time/Instrumental | 10 |
| 69 | CBS 63847 | SKIN ALLEY (LP, laminated front sleeve, orange label) | 120 |
| 70 | CBS 64140 | TO PAGHAM AND BEYOND (LP, gatefold sleeve, orange label) | 60 |
| 72 | Transatlantic TRA 260 | TWO QUID DEAL (LP, laminated front with inner sleeve & poster) | 50 |
| 73 | Transatlantic TRA 273 | SKIN TIGHT (LP) | 25 |
| 75 | Klik KLP 9007 | BAG-O-WIRE (LP) | 20 |

## SKIN DEEP (1)

| 85 | Enemy ENEMY 1 | FOOTBALL VIOLENCE (EP) | 250 |

## SKIN DEEP (2)

| 88 | Skank LP 103 | MORE THAN SKIN DEEP (LP) | 15 |

## SKIN, FLESH & BONES

| 74 | Pyramid PYR 7014 | Butter Te Fish/Bammie And Fish | 5 |
| 74 | Opal PAL100 | Man Come, Man Go/Guitar Rhythm | 35 |
| 79 | Love LPLV02 | FIGHTING DUB (LP) | 50 |

*(see also Vincent Gordon, Cynthia Richards)*

## J SCOTT SKINNER

| 75 | Topic 12T 280 | STRATHSPEY KING (LP, blue label) | 15 |

## JIMMIE SKINNER

| 59 | Mercury AMT 1030 | Walkin' My Blues Away/Dark Hollow | 15 |
| 59 | Mercury AMT 1062 | John Wesley Hardin/Misery Loves Company | 10 |
| 60 | Mercury AMT 1088 | Riverboat Gambler/Married To A Friend | 5 |
| 60 | Mercury AMT 1117 | Reasons To Live/I'm A Lot More Lonesome Now | 5 |
| 64 | London RE-B 1421 | KENTUCKY COLONEL VOL. 1 (EP) | 10 |
| 64 | London RE-B 1422 | KENTUCKY COLONEL VOL. 2 (EP) | 10 |
| 64 | London RE-B 1423 | KENTUCKY COLONEL VOL. 3 (EP) | 10 |

## JIMMIE SKINNER/GEORGE JONES

| 59 | Mercury ZEP 10012 | COUNTRY AND WESTERN (EP, 2 tracks each) | 10 |

## SKINNYMAN

| 04 | Low Life LOW 36LP | COUNCIL ESTATE OF MIND (LP) | 50 |

## SKINNYMAN/DJ FLIP

| 05 | Netgroove NET7003 | Forever Rangers/Not Bonny And Clyde (7" - 500 pressed) | 5 |

*(see also Skinnyman)*

## SKIP BIFFERTY

| 67 | RCA Victor RCA 1621 | On Love/Cover Girl | 30 |
| 67 | RCA Victor RCA 1648 | Happy Land/Reason To Live | 40 |
| 68 | RCA Victor RCA 1720 | Man In Black/Mr. Money Man | 55 |
| 68 | RCA Victor RD/SF 7941 | SKIP BIFFERTY (LP, black label) | 400 |
| 68 | RCA Victor RD/SF 7941 | SKIP BIFFERTY (LP, later pressing with orange label) | 200 |

*(see also Chosen Few, Heavy Jelly, Griffin, Graham Bell, Arc, Bell & Arc, Every Which Way, Loving Awareness)*

## SKIP & FLIP

| 59 | Top Rank JAR 156 | It Was I/Lunch Hour | 10 |
| 59 | Top Rank JAR 248 | Fancy Nancy/It Could Be | 15 |
| 60 | Top Rank JAR 358 | Cherry Pie/(I'll Quit) Cryin' Over You | 15 |

*(see also Gary Paxton, Skip Battin, Hollywood Argyles)*

## SKI PATROL

| 80 | Clever Metal VIN 1 | Everything Is Temporary/Silent Screams (p/s) | 10 |
| 80 | Malicious Damage MD 2 | Agent Orange/Driving (p/s, with insert) | 12 |
| 81 | Malicious Damage MD 3 | Cut/Faith In Transition (p/s) | 10 |

*(see also Wall)*

## SKITZ

| 01 | Ronin RDLP 2 | COUNTRYMAN (LP) | 15 |

MINT VALUE £

**SKITZOFRENIK**
81  Guardian GRC 120 ............ USA/Lonely Road (p/s) ............................................................................ 100

**SAM SKLAIR**
69  Pye 7N 25488 ............ Zulu Warrior/Phata Phata ............................................................................ 15

**YANI SKORDALIDIS**
75  Pinnacle P81413 ............ Little Drummer Boy/Here Pussy Pussy ............................................................ 15

**SKREAM**
06  Big Apple BAM 007 ............ Acid People/Get Mad/Who R Those Guys/Skunk Step (12") ............................ 25
06  Southside Dubstars ............ SOUTHSIDE EP VOL 2 (12") .......................................................................... 10
    DUBSTAR 008

**SKREWDRIVER**
77  Chiswick S 11 ............ You're So Dumb/Better Off Crazy (green p/s) ................................................... 50
77  Chiswick S 11 ............ You're So Dumb/Better Off Crazy (orange p/s) ................................................. 45
77  Chiswick NS 11 ............ You're So Dumb/Better Off Crazy (p/s, CBS repressing) ................................... 35
77  Chiswick NS 18 ............ Anti-Social/19th Nervous Breakdown (p/s) ..................................................... 40
78  Chiswick NS 28 ............ Streetfight/Unbeliever (unissued, Trident label) ........................................... 300
80  TJM TJM 4 ............ Built Up, Knocked Down/A Case Of Pride/Breakout (p/s) ................................. 25
82  Skrewdriver SKREW 1T ............ BACK WITH A BANG (12", p/s) ..................................................................... 40
83  White Noise WN 1 ............ White Power/Smash The I.R.A./Shove The Dove (p/s) ..................................... 50
83  White Noise WN 2 ............ Voice Of Britain/Sick Society (p/s) ................................................................ 50
77  Chiswick CH 3 ............ ALL SKREWED UP (mini-LP, 12-track, 45rpm, 3 different colour sleeves) ........ 70
77  Chiswick WIK 3 ............ ALL SKREWED UP (LP, 15-track, 33rpm, unissued in U.K.; German-only) ...... 100

**SKROTEEZ**
82  Skroteez SPILL 1 ............ OVERSPILL (EP) ............................................................................................ 15

**SKULL SNAPS**
73  GSF GS 27 ............ My Hang Up Is You/It's A New Day ................................................................ 40
95  Charly CPLP 8094 ............ SKULL SNAPS (LP, reissue) ............................................................................ 18

**SKULLFLOWER**
86  Broken Flag BF V9 ............ BIRTHDEATH (12" EP) ................................................................................... 80
89  Shock SX 001 ............ (I Live) In The Bottomless Pit/Bo Diddley's Shitpump (foldaround p/s in poly bag, 500 only, 75 copies in 'burns victim' sleeve) ............................................ 20
89  Shock SX 001 ............ (I Live) In The Bottomless Pit/Bo Diddley's Shitpump (foldaround p/s in poly bag, 500 only) ............................................................................................. 12
90  Toe Jam FLUF 005 ............ Rotten Sun/Spook Rise (p/s, numbered, 500 only) ........................................ 12
92  Dying Artefact DE 002 ............ Bad Alchemy/Blues For H.M. (p/s in poly bag, numbered, 500 only) ............... 10
94  Freak Records RR 001 ............ White Fang 2/Glassy Essence (wraparound sleeve, stamped label) .................... 8
89  Shock SX 008 ............ XAMAN (LP, 1000 only) ................................................................................ 20
89  Broken Flag BFV 10 ............ FORM DESTROYER (LP) .................................................................................. 30
92  Headdirt HD 01 ............ IIIRD GATEKEEPER (LP) .................................................................................. 30
*(see also Ramleh)*

**SKULLHEAD**
87  United SKULL 1 ............ WHITE WARRIOR (LP) ................................................................................... 50
89  Counter Culture CCR1 ............ Blame The Bosses/VIOLENT STORM: Celtic Warrior/Unemployed Voice (p/s) ... 10
89  United SKULL 2 ............ ODIN'S LAW (LP) ........................................................................................... 20

**SKULLS**
89  Snake Skin SS 001 ............ Graveyard Signal/Idols And Dolls (p/s, 300 only) ........................................... 10

**SKULLSNAPS**
73  GSF GSZ 7 ............ My Hang Up Is You/It's A New Day ................................................................ 65

**SKUNKS**
78  Eel Pie EPS 001 ............ Good From The Bad/Back Street Fightin' (2,000 only, die-cut 'swirl' sleeve) ...... 12
*(see also Craze, Hard Corps)*

**PATRICK SKY**
65  Vanguard VSD 79179 ............ PATRICK SKY (LP) .......................................................................................... 20
70  Vanguard SVRL 19054 ............ A HARVEST OF GENTLE CLANG (LP) ................................................................ 20

**SKY (1)**
68  United Artists UP 2234 ............ Air-O-Plane Ride/Weather Forecast .................................................................. 7
69  Decca F 12971 ............ On Our Way/The Singer Is Singing His Song ...................................................... 7
*(see also Knack)*

**SKY (2)**
71  RCA RCA 2070 ............ Goodie Two Shoes/Make It On Time (as U.S. Sky) .............................................. 5

**SKYBIRD**
74  Holyground HGS 118 ............ SUMMER OF '73 (LP, 250 copies only) ............................................................ 60

**SKYLARK**
72  Capitol CL 15747 ............ The Writings On The Wall/Wildflower .............................................................. 8

**SKYLINERS**
59  London HLB 8829 ............ Since I Don't Have You/One Night, One Night ............................................... 175
59  London HLB 8829 ............ Since I Don't Have You/One Night, One Night (78) ......................................... 50
59  London HLU 8924 ............ This I Swear/Tomorrow .................................................................................. 80
59  London HLU 8924 ............ This I Swear/Tomorrow (78) ........................................................................... 50
59  London HLU 8971 ............ It Happened Today/Lonely Way ..................................................................... 75
59  London HLU 8971 ............ It Happened Today/Lonely Way (78) ............................................................... 60
60  Polydor NH 66951 ............ Pennies From Heaven/I'll Be Seeing You ......................................................... 15
61  Pye International 7N 25091 ............ I'll Close My Eyes/The Door Is Still Open ......................................................... 20

**SKY PONEY**
70  Decca F 23082 ............ Jubeldown/Chubby ......................................................................................... 8

**SKYSOUNDS**
66  Anglo TPMA 101/102 ............ Two Timer/No Matter Where I Wander (private pressing) ................................. 10

## SLACK ALICE
| | | | |
|---|---|---|---|
| 74 | Fontana 6007 038 | Motorcycle/Ridin' The Wind | 5 |
| 74 | Philips 6308 214 | SLACK ALICE (LP) | 15 |

*(see also Sandra Alfred, Sandra Barry)*

## FREDDIE SLACK (& ORCHESTRA)
| | | | |
|---|---|---|---|
| 51 | Capitol LC 6529 | FREDDIE SLACK'S BOOGIE WOOGIE (10" LP) | 35 |

*(see also Ella Mae Morse & Freddie Slack)*

## SLADE
### SINGLES
| | | | |
|---|---|---|---|
| 69 | Fontana TF 1056 | Wild Winds Are Blowing/One Way Hotel (credited to The Slade) | 100 |
| 70 | Fontana TF 1079 | Shape Of Things To Come/C'mon C'mon | 60 |
| 70 | Polydor 2058 054 | Know Who You Are/Dapple Rose | 80 |
| 71 | Polydor 2058 112 | Get Down With It/Do You Want Me/The Gospel According To Rasputin (with writing credit: Holder/Hill/Lea/Powell/Penniman; some copies repressed as "Get Down And Get With It") | 5 |
| 74 | Polydor 2058 453 | Everyday/Good Time Gals (mispressed with Hollies' The Air That I Breathe on A-side) | 6 |
| 75 | Polydor 2058 547 | How Does It Feel?/So Far So Good (p/s) | 5 |
| 75 | Polydor 2058 663 | In For A Penny/Can You Just Imagine (in p/s) | 5 |
| 76 | Polydor 2058 716 | Nobody's Fool/L.A. Jinx | 5 |
| 77 | Barn 2014 105 | Gypsy Roadhog/Forest Full Of Needles | 5 |
| 77 | Barn 2014 106 | Burning In The Heat Of Love/Ready Steady Kids | 18 |
| 77 | Barn 2014 114 | My Baby Left Me; That's Alright/O.H.M.S. (p/s) | 6 |
| 78 | Barn 2014 121 | Give Us A Goal/Daddio | 8 |
| 78 | Barn 2014 127 | Rock'n'Roll Bolero/It's Alright By Me | 15 |
| 79 | Barn BARN 002 | Ginny Ginny/Dizzy Mama (yellow vinyl only, with sticker) | 10 |
| 79 | Barn BARN 002 | Ginny Ginny/Dizzy Mama (yellow vinyl only, without sticker) | 8 |
| 79 | Barn BARN 010 | Sign Of The Times/Not Tonight Josephine | 15 |
| 79 | Barn BARN 011 | Okey Cokey/My Baby's Got It | 10 |
| 80 | RSO RSO 051 | Okey Cokey/My Baby's Got It (withdrawn reissue, existence unconfirmed) | 0 |
| 80 | S.O.T.B. SUPER 45 3 | SIX OF THE BEST - NIGHT STARVATION (12" EP, die-cut sleeve) | 15 |
| 80 | Cheapskate CHEAP 5 | ALIVE AT READING '80 (EP, die-cut sleeve) | 7 |
| 80 | Cheapskate CHEAP 11 | Merry Xmas Everybody/Okey Cokey/Get Down And Get With It (as Slade & Reading Choir, some in die-cut p/s) | 8 |
| 80 | Cheapskate CHEAP 11 | Merry Xmas Everybody/Okey Cokey/Get Down And Get With It (as Slade & Reading Choir, some in die-cut p/s) | 5 |
| 81 | Polydor 2058 422 | Merry Xmas Everybody/Don't Blame Me (reissue, green background, holly leaf' design, colour group photo p/s) | 5 |
| 81 | Cheapskate CHEAP 16 | We'll Bring The House Down/Hold On To Your Hats (p/s) | 7 |
| 81 | Cheapskate CHEAP 21 | Wheels Ain't Comin' Down/Not Tonight Josephine (p/s) | 7 |
| 81 | Cheapskate CHEAP 24 | Knuckle Sandwich Nancy/I'm Mad (p/s) | 10 |
| 81 | RCA | Tak Me Bak 'Ome/Gudbuy T'Jane) (12" EP, p/s) | 10 |
| 82 | RCA RCA 191 | Ruby Red/Funk Punk And Junk (p/s) | 10 |
| 82 | RCA RCAD 191 | Ruby Red/Funk Punk And Junk//Rock And Roll Preacher (live)/Take Me Bak 'Ome (live) (double pack, gatefold p/s) | 5 |
| 82 | RCA RCA 291 | (And Now The Waltz) C'est La Vie/Merry Xmas Everybody (p/s) | 5 |
| 82 | Speed SPEED 201 | Okey Cokey/Get Down And Get With It (no p/s) | 8 |
| 85 | Polydor POSPX 780 | Merry Xmas Everybody/Don't Blame Me (12", p/s) | 12 |
| 85 | RCA PB 40449/PB 40549 | Do You Believe In Miracles/My Oh My (Swing Version)//Santa Claus Is Coming To Town/Auld Lang Syne/You'll Never Walk Alone To Town/Auld Lang Syne/You'll Never Walk Alone) | 15 |
| 85 | RCA PT 40450D | Do You Believe In Miracles/My Oh My (Swing Version)/Time To Rock/Santa Claus Is Coming To Town/Auld Lang Syne/You'll Never Walk Alone (12", 'Slade Xmas' double pack, separate sleeves in gatefold PVC cover) | 10 |
| 87 | RCA PB 41147D | Still The Same/Gotta Go Home//The Roaring Silence/Don't Talk To Me About Love (21st anniversary double pack, gatefold p/s) | 8 |
| 80s | Polydor 2058 422 | Merry Xmas Everybody/Don't Blame Me (export p/s from various artist box set, green background, 4 individual photos) | 15 |

### ALBUMS : LPS
| | | | |
|---|---|---|---|
| 70 | Polydor 2383 026 | PLAY IT LOUD (LP, sleeve printed by E.J. Day) | 40 |
| 70 | Polydor 2383 026 | PLAY IT LOUD (LP, later sleeve printed by Upton printers) | 25 |
| 72 | Polydor 2383 101 | SLADE ALIVE (LP, gatefold sleeve) | 20 |
| 72 | Polydor 2283 163 | SLAYED? (LP, laminated sleeve) | 20 |
| 73 | Polydor 2442 119 | SLADEST (LP, gatefold sleeve with booklet) | 25 |
| 73 | Polydor 2383 261 | OLD NEW BORROWED AND BLUE (LP, gatefold sleeve) | 15 |
| 74 | Polydor 2442 126 | SLADE IN FLAME (LP, gatefold sleeve) | 15 |
| 76 | Polydor 2383 377 | NOBODY'S FOOLS (LP, with inner sleeve) | 25 |
| 77 | Barn 2314 103 | WHATEVER HAPPENED TO SLADE (LP, with lyric sheet) | 20 |
| 78 | Barn 2314 106 | SLADE ALIVE VOLUME 2 (LP) | 15 |
| 79 | Barn NARB 003 | RETURN TO BASE (LP) | 40 |
| 81 | Cheapskate SKATE 1 | WE'LL BRING THE HOUSE DOWN (LP, insert) | 15 |

### PROMOS
| | | | |
|---|---|---|---|
| 72 | Polydor 2814 008 | Hear Me Calling/Get Down With It (33rpm sampler for "Slade Alive", 500 only) | 125 |
| 74 | Polydor 2058 492 | The Bangin' Man/She Did It To Me (export p/s) | 25 |
| 75 | Polydor 2058 585 | Thanks For The Memory (with altered lyrics)/Raining In My Champagne | 25 |
| 77 | Barn 2014 105 | Gypsy Roadhog/Forest Full Of Needles (mono, DJ copy) | 25 |
| 80 | S.O.T.B. SUPER 3 | Night Starvation/When I'm Dancing I Ain't Fightin' | 45 |

### FLEXIDISCS
| | | | |
|---|---|---|---|
| 72 | Polydor/Sound For Industry SFI 122 | The Whole World's Going Crazee/MIKE HUGG: Bonnie Charlie (33rpm with Music Scene magazine) | 18 |
| 73 | Lyntone LYN 2645 | Slade talk to Melanie readers (with Melanie magazine) | 15 |
| 74 | Lyntone LYN 2797 | Slade exclusive to all 19 readers (with 19 magazine) | 15 |

Rare Record Price Guide 2018

| | | | MINT VALUE £ |
|---|---|---|---|
| 75 | Fan Club LYN 2645/2797 | Slade talk to Melanie readers/Slade talk to 19 readers | 10 |

*(see also Ambrose Slade, Steve Brett, 'N Betweens, Vendors, Dummies, Jimmy Lea, China Dolls, Clout, Metal Gurus)*

## PAUL SLADE
| | | | |
|---|---|---|---|
| 69 | Decca F12885 | Odyssey/Sound Of Love | 12 |
| 68 | Decca F12840 | Heaven Held/Remember Daphne | 6 |

## PRENTIS SLADE
| | | | |
|---|---|---|---|
| 61 | Parlophone R 4850 | I Can Tell/Looking For A Friend | 6 |

## SLADE BROTHERS
| | | | |
|---|---|---|---|
| 66 | Pye 7N 17176 | What A Crazy Life/For A Rainy Day | 25 |
| 66 | Pye 7N 17176 | Peace In My Mind/Life's Great Race | 60 |

## SLAM CREEPERS
| | | | |
|---|---|---|---|
| 68 | Olga OLE 009 | Saturday/Hold It Baby | 15 |
| 73 | Sonet SON 2003 | We Are Happy People/Yansbro Memories | 5 |

## SLAM DONAHUE
| | | | |
|---|---|---|---|
| 11 | Too Pure PURE 268S | Where We Were On The Weekend/It's Scary (p/s, many destroyed in PIAS fire) | 5 |

## SLANES
| | | | |
|---|---|---|---|
| 65 | Blue Beat BB 300 | It Takes Time/LIGES: Have Mercy Baby (B-side actually by Frank Cosmo) | 20 |

## IVOR SLANEY ORCHESTRA
| | | | |
|---|---|---|---|
| 61 | HMV POP 943 | The Sir Francis Drake Theme/Midsummer Madness | 6 |
| 64 | HMV POP 1347 | High Wire/Sacramento | 10 |
| 66 | Columbia DB 8020 | Long Weekend/Eleven Up (as Slaney Strings) | 8 |

## SLAPP HAPPY
| | | | |
|---|---|---|---|
| 74 | Virgin VS 105 | Casablanca Moon/Slow Moon's Rose | 15 |
| 75 | Virgin VS 124 | Johnny's Dead/Mr. Rainbow (p/s) | 12 |
| 83 | Half Cat HC 001 | Everybody's Slimmin' (Even Men And Women!)/Blue-Eyed William (p/s) | 15 |
| 72 | Polydor 2310 204 | SORT OF (LP, with German sleeve & insert) | 400 |
| 74 | Virgin V 2014 | SLAPP HAPPY (LP, booklet insert) | 30 |
| 75 | Virgin V 2024 | DESPERATE STRAIGHTS (LP, gatefold sleeve, with Henry Cow) | 30 |
| 80 | Recommended RR5 | ACNALBASAC NOOM (LP, recorded 1973 with members of Faust) | 20 |
| 81 | Recommended RRS 5 | SORT OF (LP, reissue) | 20 |

*(see also Henry Cow, Peter Blegvad, Anthony Moore, Art Bears)*

## MUTTER SLATER
| | | | |
|---|---|---|---|
| 76 | Rocket ROKN 510 | Dancing On Air/Solitude | 5 |

## FELIX SLATKIN
| | | | |
|---|---|---|---|
| 60 | London HLG 9256 | Theme From "The Sundowners"/Gaythers Gone | 7 |

## SLAUGHTER (& THE DOGS)
| | | | |
|---|---|---|---|
| 77 | Rabid TOSH 101 | Cranked Up Really High/The Bitch (p/s, blue, red and later cream plastic labels) | 20 |
| 77 | Rabid TOSH 101 | Cranked Up Really High/The Bitch (p/s, repressings with b&w paper label) | 15 |
| 77 | Decca FR 13723 | Where Have All The Boot Boys Gone/You're A Bore (paper label) | 8 |
| 77 | Decca LF 13723 | Where Have All The Boot Boys Gone/You're A Bore (12", p/s, 10,000 only) | 12 |
| 77 | Decca FR 13743 | Dame To Blame/Johnny T | 12 |
| 78 | Decca F 13758 | Quick Joey Small/Come On Back (promo with self sealing 'spit proof' sticker on PVC sleeve | 75 |
| 78 | Decca FR 13758 | Quick Joey Small/Come On Back (with Mick Ronson) | 6 |
| 79 | TJM TJM 3 | It's Alright/Edgar Allen Poe/Twist & Turn/UFO (12", p/s) | 12 |
| 79 | DJM DJS 10927 | You're Ready Now/Runaway (p/s) | 6 |
| 80 | Decca FR | Where Have All The Boot Boys Gone/You're A Bore (reissue, p/s) | 10 |
| 80 | DJM DJS 10936 | East Side Of Town/One By One (p/s, as Slaughter) | 6 |
| 80 | DJM DJS 10945 | I'm The One/What's Wrong Boy? (live)/Hell In New York (p/s, as Slaughter) | 5 |
| 82 | Thrush THRUSH 1 | HALF ALIVE (12" EP) | 10 |
| 88 | Damaged Goods FNARR 1 | Where Have All The Boot Boys Gone/You're A Bore/Johnny T. (p/s, 1,000 only: 500 on green vinyl, 500 on red vinyl) | 15 |
| 78 | Decca SKL 5292 | DO IT DOG STYLE (LP) | 30 |

*(see also Studio Sweethearts, Ed Banger)*

## SLAUGHTER JOE
| | | | |
|---|---|---|---|
| 85 | Creation CRE 019 | I'll Follow You Down/Napalm Girl (foldaround p/s in poly bag) | 5 |

*(see also Television Personalities, Missing Scientists)*

## SLAVES
| | | | |
|---|---|---|---|
| 13 | Fonthill F002 | Debbie Where's Your Car?/Okay/Not Ideal | 25 |
| 13 | Fonthill F002 | Debbie Where's Your Car?/Okay/Not Ideal (gold vinyl) | 35 |
| 14 | Fonthill (No cat no) | Beauty Quest/Girl Fight x 15 (7" picture disc, tour issue) | 20 |
| 15 | Virgin 4714584 | The Hunter/Hey (red vinyl) | 12 |
| 13 | Fonthill (No cat no) | SUGAR COATED BITTER TRUTH (LP, 300 only) | 100 |
| 13 | Fonthill (No cat no) | SUGAR COATED BITTER TRUTH (LP, 200 only, white vinyl) | 110 |

## FRANK SLAY & HIS ORCHESTRA
| | | | |
|---|---|---|---|
| 61 | Top Rank JAR 599 | Flying Circle/Cincinnati | 8 |

## SLAYER
| | | | |
|---|---|---|---|
| 84 | Roadrunner RR 2444 2 | HAUNTING THE CHAPEL (12" EP) | 25 |
| 87 | London LON 133 | Criminally Insane/Aggressive Perfector (Remix) ('cross' p/s, on red vinyl with patch) | 35 |
| 87 | London LONX 133 | Criminally Insane/Postmortem/Aggressive Perfector (Remix) (12", red vinyl, no p/s) | 30 |
| 91 | DEF DEFAP 912 | Seasons In The Abyss/Aggressive Perfector (7" picture disc) | 20 |
| 85 | Roadrunner RR 9795 | HELL AWAITS (LP) | 20 |
| 87 | Enigma 720151 | LIVE UNDEAD (LP, picture disc) | 25 |
| 86 | London/Def Jam LONLP 34 | REIGN IN BLOOD (LP, with inner) | 25 |
| 87 | London LONPP 34 | REIGN IN BLOOD (LP, picture disc) | 35 |
| 88 | London/Def Jam LONLP 63 | SOUTH OF HEAVEN (LP, stickered sleeve, inner) | 30 |
| 90 | Def American 846 871 | SEASONS IN THE ABYSS (LP, with inner) | 15 |
| 90 | Metal Blade ZORRODM | SHOW NO MERCY (2-LP, reissue, poster) | 30 |

| | | | |
|---|---|---|---|
| 91 | Phonogram 510605-1 | DECADE OF AGGRESSION (2-LP, booklet, 6,500 copies only) | 25 |
| 98 | American 491302 1 | DIABOLUS IN MUSICA (2-LP, inners) | 25 |
| 03 | Universal B 00001519-02 | SOUNDTRACK TO THE APOCALYPSE (4-CD set in 'ammo box' with backstage laminate, flag, bonus DVD in 'blood pack' and booklet) | 35 |

## SLEAFORD MODS
| | | | |
|---|---|---|---|
| 07 | A52 Sounds A53CD001 | SLEAFORD MODS (LP) | 30 |
| 08 | A52 Sounds A52CD002 | THE MEKON (CD) | 30 |
| 14 | Harbinger HARBINGER 106 | AUSTERITY DOGS (LP) | 20 |
| 14 | Harbinger HARBINGER 106 | AUSTERITY DOGS (LP, repressing, clear vinyl) | 18 |
| 15 | Harbinger HARBINGER 121 | DIVIDE AND EXIT (LP, red vinyl) | 18 |

## SLEAZ BAND
| | | | |
|---|---|---|---|
| 74 | Fontana 6007034 | All I Want Is You/Midnight Band | 15 |

## SLEAZE
| | | | |
|---|---|---|---|
| 75 | No Cat no | SLEAZE (LP, white label private pressing, 50 only, insert) | 175 |

## F. SLEDGE
| | | | |
|---|---|---|---|
| 67 | Blue Beat BB 386 | Red Eye Girl/Try To Love Again (actually by "Go On Girl"/"Giving You A Try Girl" by Freddie McKay & Buster's Group) | 40 |

## PERCY SLEDGE
| | | | |
|---|---|---|---|
| 66 | Atlantic 584 001 | When A Man Loves A Woman/Love Me Like You Mean It | 8 |
| 66 | Atlantic 584 034 | Warm And Tender Love/Sugar Puddin' | 7 |
| 66 | Atlantic 584 055 | Heart Of A Child/My Adorable One | 10 |
| 67 | Atlantic 584 071 | It Tears Me Up/Oh, How Happy | 10 |
| 67 | Atlantic 584 080 | Baby, Help Me/You've Lost That Something Wonderful | 10 |
| 67 | Atlantic 584 108 | Out Of Left Field/It Can't Be Stopped | 10 |
| 67 | Atlantic 584 140 | Pledging My Love/You Don't Miss Your Water | 10 |
| 68 | Atlantic 584 177 | Take Time To Know Her/It's All Wrong But It's Alright | 10 |
| 68 | Atlantic 584 225 | Come Softly To Me/You're All Around Me | 10 |
| 69 | Atlantic 584 264 | Any Day Now/The Angels Listened In | 8 |
| 69 | Atlantic 584 286 | Kind Woman/Woman Of The Night | 8 |
| 69 | Atlantic 584 300 | True Love Travels On A Gravel Road/Faithful And True | 6 |
| 72 | Atlantic K 10144 | Rainbow Road/Standing on The Mountain | 6 |
| 72 | Atlantic K 10165 | Baby, Help Me/Warm And Tender Love/Take Time To Know Her | 6 |
| 74 | Capricorn 2089 009 | I'll Be Your Everything/Walkin' In The Sun | 20 |
| 67 | Atlantic 587/588 048 | WARM AND TENDER SOUL (LP) | 20 |
| 67 | Atlantic 587/588 081 | THE PERCY SLEDGE WAY (LP) | 20 |
| 68 | Atlantic 587/588 015 | WHEN A MAN LOVES A WOMAN (LP) | 20 |
| 69 | Atlantic 587/588 153 | THE BEST OF PERCY SLEDGE (LP) | 15 |

## SLEDGEHAMMER
| | | | |
|---|---|---|---|
| 79 | Slammer SRTS79CUS 395 | Sledgehammer/Feel Good (with p/s) | 20 |
| 79 | Slammer SRTS79CUS 395 | Sledgehammer/Feel Good | 10 |
| 80 | Slammer CELL 2 | Living In Dreams/Fantasia (p/s) | 10 |
| 80s | Slammer MRSB 2 | In The Middle Of The Night | 10 |
| 80 | Valiant STRONG 1 | Sledgehammer/Feel Good (p/s, reissue) | 6 |
| 80 | Valiant ROUND 2 | Sledgehammer/Feel Good (p/s, 2nd reissue) | 25 |
| 85 | Illuminated ILL 33 | In The Queue/Oxford City (shaped picture disc) | 30 |
| 83 | Illuminated JAMS 32 | BLOOD ON THEIR HANDS (LP) | 25 |
| 83 | Illuminated JAMS 32 | BLOOD ON THEIR HANDS (LP) | 30 |
| 84 | Mausoleum LUST 834950 | SLEDGEHAMMER (LP, with free 12") | |

## SLEEPERS
| | | | |
|---|---|---|---|
| 80 | Bat FMR 034 | Angel In A Raincoat/Endless/A Murder/Twbi | 75 |

## SLEEPING DOGS
| | | | |
|---|---|---|---|
| 82 | Crass 221984/11 | BEWARE SLEEPING DOGS (EP) | 10 |

## SLEEPWALKERS
| | | | |
|---|---|---|---|
| 59 | Parlophone R 4580 | Sleep Walk/Golden Mile | 15 |

## SLEEPY
| | | | |
|---|---|---|---|
| 68 | CBS 3592 | Love's Immortal Fire/Is It Really The Same | 275 |
| 68 | CBS 3838 | Rosie Can't Fly/Mrs. Bailey's Barbecue And Grill | 60 |
| 68 | No Cat No | You'll See Me/Time Gone (White label test pressing) | 250 |

*(see also Grapefruit, Fynn McCool)*

## SLENDER LORIS
| | | | |
|---|---|---|---|
| 76 | Reverence DM 70 | I'm Only Heavy When You Get Me Down/A Week Of A Day | 6 |

## SLENDER PLENTY
| | | | |
|---|---|---|---|
| 67 | Polydor BM 56189 | Silver Tree Top School For Boys/I've Lost A Friend And Found A Lover | 80 |

## SLENDER THREAD
| | | | |
|---|---|---|---|
| 80 | Rock MHMS 193 | I See The Light/Where Is The Beat | 30 |

## JIMI SLEVIN
| | | | |
|---|---|---|---|
| 82 | Claddagh CCF 7 | FREEFLIGHT (LP) | 45 |

*(see also Peggy's Leg)*

## GRACE SLICK
| | | | |
|---|---|---|---|
| 68 | CBS 63476 | CONSPICUOUS ONLY IN IT'S ABSENCE (LP, as Grace Slick And The Great Society) | 40 |

## RICKY SLICK
| | | | |
|---|---|---|---|
| 72 | Dynamic DYN 449 | Family Man/Family Man - Version | 5 |

## SLICKERS
| | | | |
|---|---|---|---|
| 68 | Blue Cat BS 133 | Wala Wala/LESTER STERLING: Super Special | 100 |
| 68 | Blue Cat BS 134 | Nana (actually by George Dekker)/MARTIN RILEY: I May Never See My Baby Anymore | 50 |
| 69 | Blue Cat BS 154 | Frying Pan/RARFIELD WILLIAMS: Code It | 45 |
| 69 | Amalgamated AMG 852 | Man Beware/Matty Matty | 20 |

# SLIDE

| | | | |
|---|---|---|---|
| 69 | Amalgamated AMG 866 | Money Reaper/Man Beware | 20 |
| 70 | Bullet BU 449 | Coolie Girl/BIGGIE: Bawling Baby | 20 |
| 70 | Trojan TR 7718 | Run Fattie/Hoola Bulla (song actually "Bulla Man") | 10 |
| 71 | G.G. GG 4524 | Oh My Baby/WINSTON WRIGHT: Change Of Love Version | 90 |
| 71 | Punch PH 59 | Johnny Too Bad/Johnny Too Bad - Version | 6 |
| 71 | Dynamic DYN 406 | Johnny Too Bad/ROLAND ALFONSO: Saucy Horde (act. by Roland Alphonso) | 20 |
| 71 | Dynamic DYN 419 | You Can't Win/Don't Fight The Law | 20 |
| 72 | Explosion EX 2061 | Bounce Me Johnny/Bounce Me 'Version' (actually "Say You") | 6 |

*(see also G.G. Allstars, Clancy Eccles, Viceroys)*

## SLIDE
| | | | |
|---|---|---|---|
| 80 | Crash POW 4 | Superman's Shoes/Meet Your New Neighbour (p/s) | 50 |

## SLIM
| | | | |
|---|---|---|---|
| 97 | Em:t 0097 | SLIM: 0097 (CD, digipak) | 30 |

## SLIM & FREEDOM SINGERS
| | | | |
|---|---|---|---|
| 70 | Banana BA 304 | Do Dang Do (actually by Leroy Sibbles)/JACKIE MITTOO & SOUND DIMENSION: Hot Milk | 60 |

## SLIME
| | | | |
|---|---|---|---|
| 78 | Toadstool GOOD 1 | Controversial/Loony (p/s) | 8 |

*(see also Johnny Moped)*

## SLINT
| | | | |
|---|---|---|---|
| 91 | Touch & Go T&GLP64 | SPIDERLAND (LP) | 18 |
| 93 | Jennifer Hartman TG 138 | TWEEZ (LP, reissue) | 25 |

## SLIPKNOT
| | | | |
|---|---|---|---|
| 00 | Roadrunner RR 2090-7 | Spit It Out/Surfacing (Live) (p/s, red vinyl) | 12 |
| 00 | Roadrunner RR 8655-6 | SLIPKNOT (LP, picture disc) | 15 |
| 01 | Roadrunner 12 085641 | IOWA (2-LP, gatefold, poster, mispressing on track 1 side 2) | 25 |

## SLITS
| | | | |
|---|---|---|---|
| 79 | Island WIP 6505 | Typical Girls/I Heard It Through The Grapevine (p/s) | 10 |
| 79 | Island 12 WIP 6505 | Typical Girls/I Heard It Through The Grapevine/Typical Girls (Brink Style)/Liebe And Romanize (12", p/s) | 20 |
| 80 | Rough Trade RT 039/Y Y 1 | In The Beginning There Was Rhythm/POP GROUP: Where There's A Will There's A Way (p/s) | 10 |
| 80 | Rough Trade/Y RT044/Y4 | Man Next Door/Man Next Door (Version) (p/s) | 10 |
| 80 | Human HUM 4 | Animal Space/Animal Spacier (p/s) | 12 |
| 81 | CBS A1498 | Earthbeat/Begin Again Rhythm | 8 |
| 81 | CBS A 131498 | Earthbeat/Earthdub/Begin Again Rhythm (12", p/s) | 12 |
| 79 | Island ILPS 9573 | CUT (LP, laminated cover with inner sleeve) | 35 |
| 80 | Rough Trade/Y Y 3 | BOOTLEG RETROSPECTIVE (LP, plain sleeve, with SUBWAY SECT) | 30 |
| 81 | CBS 85269 | THE RETURN OF THE GIANT SLITS (LP, some with bonus 45 American Radio Interview/"Face Dub" [XPS 125]) | 30 |
| 81 | CBS 85269 | THE RETURN OF THE GIANT SLITS (LP) | 20 |
| 89 | Strange Fruit SFPMA 207 | PEEL SESSIONS - TWO COMPLETE SESSIONS (LP) | 20 |

*(see also Raincoats)*

## P.F. SLOAN
| | | | |
|---|---|---|---|
| 65 | RCA Victor RCA 1482 | Sins Of The Family/This Mornin' | 12 |
| 67 | RCA Victor RCA 1623 | Sunflower Sunflower/The Man Behind The Red Balloon | 12 |
| 72 | Epic EPC 65179 | RAISED ON RECORDS (LP, textured sleeve, lyric insert) | 25 |
| 80s | Big Beat WIK 73 | SONGS OF OTHER TIMES (LP, some tracks as Grass Roots) | 25 |

*(see also Grass Roots, Fantastic Baggys, Willie & Wheels)*

## SAMMI SLOAN
| | | | |
|---|---|---|---|
| 68 | Columbia DB 8480 | Yes I Would/Be His Girl | 20 |

## SLOWBONE
| | | | |
|---|---|---|---|
| 74 | Rare Earth RES 119 | Oh Man/Get What You're Given | 6 |

*(see also Roll Ups)*

## SLOWBONE & THE WONDERBOYS
| | | | |
|---|---|---|---|
| 74 | Rare Earth RES 116 | Tales Of A Crooked Man/Happy Birthday Sweet Sixteen | 8 |

## SLOW CLUB
| | | | |
|---|---|---|---|
| 07 | Moshi Moshi | Because We're Dead/Sunday (500 only, p/s) | 10 |
| 10 | Moshi Moshi MOSHILP 29 | YEAH SO (LP and CD, Record Store Day Release) | 18 |
| 12 | Moshi Moshi MOSHILP 41 | PARADISE (LP, blue vinyl) | 25 |

## SLOWDIVE
| | | | |
|---|---|---|---|
| 90 | Creation CRE 093T | Slowdive/Avalyn 1/Avalyn 2 | 30 |
| 90 | Creation CRE093T | SLOWDIVE EP | 20 |
| 91 | Creation CRE 112T | HOLDING OUR BREATH EP (12", p/s) | 20 |
| 91 | Creation CRE 112 | Catch The Breeze/Shine (p/s, numbered) | 8 |
| 91 | Creation CRE 112T | Catch The Breeze/Golden Hair/Shine/Albatross (12") | 10 |
| 91 | Creation CRE 098T | Morningrise/She Calls/Losing Today (12") | 18 |
| 93 | Creation CRE 157T | 5 EP (12") | 20 |
| 93 | Creation CRE 157TR | 5 EP (IN MIND REMIXES) (12", p/s) | 10 |
| 93 | Creation CRE 119T | OUTSIDE YOUR ROOM EP (12") | 25 |
| 91 | Creation CRELP 094 | JUST FOR A DAY (LP) | 40 |
| 92 | Creation CRE X101 | BLUE DAY (LP) | 35 |
| 93 | Creation CRELP 139 | SOUVLAKI (LP, picture inner sleeve) | 80 |
| 95 | Creation CRELP 168 | PYGMALION (LP) | 80 |

*(see also Mojave 3)*

## SLOW DOG
| | | | |
|---|---|---|---|
| 72 | Parlophone R5942 | Walking Through The Blue Grass/Ain't Never Going Home | 30 |

## SLOWGUNS
| | | | |
|---|---|---|---|
| 79 | MPA SMP 088 | TV Movie/American Heartbeat | 15 |

| | | | |
|---|---|---|---|
| 80 | Cult 45 CULT 001 | Karma/The Time Is Right For Us | 12 |

**SLOWLOAD**
71  MAM MAM 27 — On The Road Again/Big Boobs Boogie .................................... 35
*(see also Fruit Eating Bears)*

**SLOW MOTION**
79  RK RK 1024 — Maybe/Xmas Charade ............................................................ 75

**SLOWTRAIN**
80  Spirit SR 1 — Ronnie/Just One Way ............................................................ 30

**SLR CREW**
88  SLR XPR1536 — Bass Drum/Life's A Bitch (12") ........................................... 50

**SL TROOPERS**
88  Global Rhythm GR001 — Debut (Unarmed And Dangerous) (12", 500 pressed) ... 70
89  Music Of Life NOTE32 — Movement (12") ................................................... 12
91  Kold Sweat KSEP201 — SYSTEMATIC TERROR (EP) ...................................... 12

**SLUSH**
78  Ember EMB 5367 — White Christmas/Rich Man (no p/s) ............................... 40
*(See also Pumphouse Gang)*

**SLY ALICE**
72  Sunday SUN 02 — Drifting Away/The Games Over (p/s) ................................ 50

**SLY & THE REVOLUTIONARIES**
80  Trojan TRLS 186 — BLACK ASH DUB (LP) ................................................... 20

**SMACK**
78  Asprin 001 — Edward Fox/Came Again (p/s, original issue) ........................... 5

**SMALL ADS**
81  Bronze BRO 115 — Small Ads/Motorway Madness (p/s) ................................. 5
81  Bronze BRO 125 — HP Man/Radio Love (p/s) .............................................. 5
81  Bronze BRO 135 — Friday Nite Cowboy/I Wanna Fly Concorde (p/s) ............... 5

**JOAN SMALL**
56  Parlophone MSP 6219 — Change Of Heart/Come Next Spring ....................... 10
56  Parlophone R 4211 — Love Is A Stranger/Autumn Concerto ......................... 10
57  Parlophone R 4269 — Gonna Get Along Without You Now/You Can't Say I Love You To A Rock & Roll Tune .... 15
58  Parlophone R 4431 — Afraid/How Many Times (Can I Fall In Love) .................. 10
60  Parlophone R 4622 — The Big Hurt/Ask Me To Go Steady ............................. 10

**JOHN SMALL**
70  G&W FAM 101 — Let's Ride/A Woman Who Can Shake My Mind ..................... 15

**KAREN SMALL**
66  Vocalion V 9281 — To Get You Back Again/That's Why I Cry ......................... 30

**MARY SMALL**
56  Vogue Coral 45-Q-72196 — Dino/None Of That Now ..................................... 8

**SMALLAGE**
90  Jack Trax 7JTX 33 — Together (Club Edit)/Together (Dub) ............................ 10

**DENIS SMALLEY**
81  University Of East Anglia
    UEA 81063 — THE PULSE OF TIME (LP) ...................................................... 40

**SMALL FACES**
**SINGLES**
65  Decca F 12208 — Whatcha Gonna Do About It?/What's A Matter, Baby? ......... 20
65  Decca F 12276 — I've Got Mine/It's Too Late .............................................. 25
66  Decca F 12317 — Sha-La-La-La-Lee/Grow Your Own .................................... 10
66  Decca F 12393 — Hey Girl/Almost Grown .................................................. 15
66  Decca F 12470 — All Or Nothing/Understanding (curved or boxed Decca logo) .. 12
66  Decca F 12500 — My Mind's Eye (alternate demo mix, matrix no. ends T1-1C)/I Can't Dance With You (withdrawn) ... 30
66  Decca F 12500 — My Mind's Eye (matrix no. ends T2-1C)/I Can't Dance With You .. 10
67  Decca F 12565 — I Can't Make It/Just Passing ........................................... 25
67  Decca F 12565 — I Can't Make It/Just Passing (in export p/s) ....................... 60
67  Decca F 12619 — Patterns/E Too D (with export p/s) .................................. 140
67  Decca F 12619 — Patterns/E Too D ........................................................... 70
67  Immediate AS 1 — Small Faces (1-sided sampler for "Small Faces", promo only) . 250
67  Immediate IM 050 — Here Comes The Nice/Talk To You ............................... 12
67  Immediate IM 057 — Itchycoo Park/I'm Only Dreaming ................................ 80
67  Immediate IM 062 — Tin Soldier/I Feel Much Better (in p/s) ......................... 15
67  Immediate IM 062 — Tin Soldier/I Feel Much Better ................................... 12
68  Immediate IM 064 — Lazy Sunday/Rollin' Over ......................................... 12
68  Immediate IM 069 — The Universal/Donkey Rides, A Penny A Glass (lilac label) .. 12
68  Immediate IM 069 — The Universal/Donkey Rides, A Penny A Glass (later pink label) .. 8
69  Immediate IM 077 — Afterglow (Of Your Love)/Wham Bam, Thank You Mam (demos [perhaps some copies] have demo version of B-side) .. 60
69  Immediate IM 077 — Afterglow (Of Your Love)/Wham Bam, Thank You Mam (demos) .. 15
75  Immediate IM 064 — Lazy Sunday/Rollin' Over (p/s, reissue with white label) ... 8
80  Virgin VS 367 — Tin Soldier/Tin Soldier (live)/Rene ................................... 6
86  Archive 4 TOF 103 — Itchycoo Park/Lazy Sunday/Sha-La-La-La-Lee/Here Comes The Nice (12", p/s) .... 10

**ALBUMS : LPS**
66  Decca LK 4790 — SMALL FACES (original red label) ................................... 250
67  Decca LK 4879 — FROM THE BEGINNING (original red label) ........................ 280
67  Immediate IMLP 008 — SMALL FACES (mono) ........................................... 250
67  Immediate IMSP 008 — SMALL FACES (stereo) .......................................... 250

# SMALL FOUR

| 68 | Immediate IMLP 012 | OGDENS' NUT GONE FLAKE (lilac label, circular foldout sleeve, mono) | 250 |
| 68 | Immediate IMSP 012 | OGDENS' NUT GONE FLAKE (lilac label, circular foldout sleeve, stereo) | 150 |
| 68 | Immediate IMSP 012 | OGDENS' NUT GONE FLAKE (pink label, circular foldout sleeve, mono) | 120 |
| 68 | Immediate IMSP 012 | OGDENS' NUT GONE FLAKE (pink label, circular foldout sleeve, stereo) | 80 |
| 69 | Decca LK 4790 | SMALL FACES (boxed Decca label) | 80 |
| 69 | Decca LK 4879 | FROM THE BEGINNING (boxed Decca label) | 50 |
| 69 | Immediate IMLP/IMSP 022 | IN MEMORIAM (export issue [German copies more common, £60]) | 40 |
| 69 | Immediate IMAL 01/02 | THE AUTUMN STONE (2-LP, gatefold sleeve) | 150 |
| 75 | Immediate/NEMS IML 1001 | OGDENS' NUT GONE FLAKE (reissue, round sleeve, white label) | 80 |
| 76 | NEMS AML 1008 | MAGIC MOMENTS | 40 |
| 77 | Immediate/NEMS IML 2001 | OGDENS' NUT GONE FLAKE (reissue, square sleeve) | 15 |
| 77 | Decca ROOTS 5 | ROCK ROOTS - THE DECCA SINGLES | 15 |
| 78 | Charly CR 300005 | OGDENS' NUT GONE FLAKE (export release, square sleeve) | 15 |
| 78 | Charly CR 300025 | THE SMALL FACES - LIVE U.K. 1969 (export release) | 15 |
| 80 | Virgin/Immediate V 2166 | SMALL FACES: BIG HITS (gatefold sleeve) | 15 |
| 80 | Virgin/Immediate V 2178 | FOR YOUR DELIGHT, THE DARLINGS OF WAPPING WHARF LAUNDERETTE | 25 |
| 91 | Castle CLACT 016 | OGDENS' NUT GONE FLAKE (CD, in round tin box with beer mats & booklet) | 60 |
| 96 | Deram 844583 | THE DECCA ANTHOLOGY 1965-1967 (2-LP) | 25 |
| 97 | Castle CLA 016 | OGDENS' NUT GONE FLAKE (reissue, round sleeve with obi) | 15 |
| 01 | Strange Fruit SFRSLP 087 | BBC SESSIONS (LP) | 20 |

(see also Faces, Steve Marriott, Humble Pie, Jimmy Winston & His Reflections, Winston's Fumbs, Billy Nicholls, Kenney Jones)

## SMALL FOUR
| 66 | Pye 7N 17191 | One Up On Me/I'll Find Him | 20 |

## SMALL HOURS
| 80 | Automatic K 17708 | The Kid/Business In Town/Midnight To Six/End Of The Night (p/s) | 30 |
| 80 | Automatic K 17708X | The Kid/Business In Town/Midnight To Six/End Of The Night (10", p/s) | 20 |
| 81 | Bridgehouse (No Cat No) | Denis/Denis Dub (white label promo only) | 70 |

## SMALL IN A BIG WAY
| 84 | Bedlam BLM 003 | Katies Lips/Back To Zero (p/s) | 8 |

## SMALL WONDER
| 75 | Dawn DNS 1094 | Ordinary Boy/Ride A Black Sheep | 18 |

## SMALL WORLD
| 81 | Whaam! WHAAM 003 | Love Is Dead/Liberty (p/s) | 100 |
| 83 | Valid VC 001 | First Impressions/Stupidity Street/Tomorrow Never Comes (p/s) | 100 |

## SMART
| 82 | Complex CPX 001 | This Time (p/s) | 35 |

## SMART ALEC
| 79 | B&C BCS 20 | Scooter Boys/Soho (p/s) | 100 |

## LEROY SMART
| 70 | Attack ATT 8012 | Life Is A Funny Thing/TRINITY: Psalms | 12 |
| 77 | Conflict COND 2001 | Jahovia/Dub (12") | 20 |
| 78 | Andinet AT 001 | Zion/Version | 10 |
| 78 | Andinet AT 002 | Faith/Version | 10 |
| 78 | Aries AR 003 | It's A Long Time Now/Long Time Version | 6 |
| 78 | Write Sounds WTS 1001 | Children Of The Getto [sic]/Version | 8 |
| 78 | Write Sounds WTS 001 | What I Will Do/ROY SINCLAIR: Rite Mix/LEROY SMART: Jah Almighty (12") | 25 |
| 79 | Burning Sounds BDS 010 | Find Your Destination/Jamaica In Peace (12") | 15 |
| 79 | Burning Sounds BDS 011 | No One Remember Me/Don't Be Late (12") | 15 |
| 70s | Aries ARI 002 | Peace Is What We Want (with U. Brown)/Version (12", p/s) | 30 |
| 80 | Black Joy DH 803 | Hooligan/Have Mercy (12") | 10 |
| 82 | Time One TR 0016 | Money Comfort/If I Give My Love (12", with Barry Brown) | 20 |
| 77 | Conflict COLPD 2001 | BALLISTIC AFFAIR (LP, with free 12") | 40 |
| 77 | Dread Hot DHLP 1001 | DREAD HOT IN AFRICA (LP) | 30 |
| 77 | Third World TWS 601 | SUPER STAR (LP) | 40 |
| 78 | Burning Sounds BS 1004 | DREAD HOT IN AFRICA (LP) | 35 |
| 78 | Burning Sounds BS 1005 | IMPRESSIONS OF LEROY SMART (LP) | 15 |
| 78 | Burning Sounds BS 1008 | JAH LOVES EVERYONE (LP, green vinyl) | 20 |
| 78 | Dread Hot DHLP 1004 | IMPRESSIONS (LP) | 20 |
| 78 | Burning Sounds BS 1009 | PROPAGANDA (LP, clear vinyl) | 25 |

## LEROY SMART & BIG YOUTH
| 79 | Dub Vendor DVD 01 | Pride And Ambition (original style)/'78 Style (12") | 60 |

## SMART SYSTEMS
| 91 | Jumpin' & Pumpin' 12TOT18 | Tingler (Meltram Mix)/(Mingler Mix)/(State Side Swamp Mix (12" p/s) | 10 |

## SMASHING PUMPKINS
| 91 | Hut | I Am One (1-sided blue flexidisc) | 100 |
| 91 | Caroline SMASH 1 | Siva/Rhinoceros (no p/s, promo only) | 80 |
| 91 | Hut HUTT 6 | Siva/Window Paine (12", p/s, 5,000) | 30 |
| 92 | Hut HUTT 10 | LULL EP (Rhinoceros/Blue/Slunk/Bye June [Demo]) (12", p/s) | 20 |
| 92 | Hut HUTT 017 | PEEL SESSIONS: Siva/A Girl Named Sandoz/Smiley (12" EP, p/s) | 12 |
| 92 | Hut HUTEN 018 | I Am One/Terrapin (live)/Bullet Train To Osaka (10", p/s, 6,000 only) | 20 |
| 92 | Hut HUTT 18 | I Am One/Plume/Starla (12", p/s) | 12 |
| 93 | Sup Pop SP 90 | Tristessa/La Dolly Vita/Honeyspider (12", 5,000 only) | 35 |
| 93 | Hut HUT 31 | Cherub Rock/Purr Snickety (p/s, clear vinyl, numbered, 5,000 only) | 20 |
| 93 | Hut HUT 37 | Today/Apathy's Last Kiss (p/s, red vinyl, 5,000 only) | 12 |
| 94 | Hut HUT 43 | Smile (Disarm/Siamese Dream) (stickered p/s, purple vinyl) | 10 |
| 94 | Hut HUTL 48 | Rocket/Never Let Me Down (box set, salmon pink vinyl, 1,500 only) | 40 |
| 93 | Hut HUTTDJ 73 | Zero (12", promo only) | 12 |
| 98 | Hut HUT 101 | Ava Adore/Czarina (p/s, numbered) | 6 |

| 07 | Reprise W769 | Tarantula/Death From Above (white vinyl, stickered PVC sleeve) ......................... 5 |
|----|--------------|-----|
| 07 | Reprise W781 | That's The Way (My Love Is)/Daydream (purple vinyl, stickered PVC sleeve)..................... 5 |
| 91 | Hut HUT LP2 | GISH (LP, inner) ....................... 25 |
| 93 | Hut HUTLP11 | SIAMESE DREAM (2-LP) ....................... 35 |
| 94 | Hut SPBOX 1 | SIAMESE SINGLES (Rocket/Never Let Me Down/Cherub Rock/Purr Snickety//Today/ Apathy's Last Kiss/Smile [Disarm/Siamese Dream]) (4 x 7" box set, black vinyl, 6,000 only) ....................... 50 |
| 94 | Hut HUTLPX 2 | GISH (LP, reissue with inner) ....................... 20 |
| 95 | Hut HUTDLP 30 | MELLON COLLIE AND THE INFINITE SADNESS (3 x LP, 12 page booklet, numbered) ..... 175 |
| 98 | Hut HUTDLP 30 | MELLON COLLIE AND THE INFINITE SADNESS (3 x LP, 12 page booklet, repressing and not numbered) ....................... 60 |
| 96 | Hut HUTLP 41 | PISCES ISCARIOT (LP, yellow vinyl) ....................... 20 |
| 96 | Hut | THE AEROPLANE FLIES HIGH (5 x CD single box set with handle, lock & booklet) ......... 50 |
| 00 | HUTDLP 59 | MACHINA/THE MACHINES OF GOD (2-LP) ....................... 35 |
| 12 | Virgin 5099997855316 | MELLON COLLIE AND THE INFINITE SADNESS (4 x LP, remastered repressing) ............ 50 |

*(see also Zwan)*

## ROY SMECK
| 54 | Brunswick LA 8649 | SONGS OF THE RANGE (10" LP) ....................... 15 |
|----|-------------------|-----|

## PHILIP LLOYD SMEE & DONATO CINICOLO III
| 71 | Deroy PLS 1 | DAS LUNE/SYNTHI-A (LP, private pressing, handmade sleeve, 2 copies only) ............. 500 |
|----|-------------|-----|

## SMIFFY
| 74 | Antic K 11501 | See You Later (Little Baby Love)/How Can You Be A Millionaire ....................... 5 |
|----|---------------|-----|

## SMILE
| 72 | UNI UN 537 | A Year Every Night/Southbound ....................... 10 |
|----|------------|-----|

## SMILEY
| 72 | Philips 6006 206 | Penelope/I Know What I Want ....................... 15 |
|----|------------------|-----|

*(see also Creation)*

## BRETT SMILEY
| 74 | Anchor ANC 70 | Va Va Va Voom/Space Age (with p/s) ....................... 40 |
|----|---------------|-----|
| 74 | Anchor ANC 70 | Va Va Va Voom/Space Age ....................... 25 |

## SMILEY CULTURE
| 86 | Top Notch TOP LP 001 | THE ORIGINAL (LP) ....................... 15 |
|----|----------------------|-----|

## K. SMILEY
| 72 | Pressure Beat PB 5514 | Tipatone/Do It To Me ....................... 8 |
|----|-----------------------|-----|

## SMILIN' JOE
| 54 | London HL 8106 | A.B.C.'s Parts 1 & 2 (78) ....................... 40 |
|----|----------------|-----|

## SMILING HARD
| 79 | Survival SUR 5 | Don't Call Us We'll Call You/Fire To The Galleon ....................... 8 |
|----|----------------|-----|

## SMIRKS
| 78 | Beserkley BZZ17 | OK UK/Streets (p/s) ....................... 8 |
|----|-----------------|-----|
| 78 | Beserkely BZZ 23 | Rosemary/Up Eh Up (Lancashire Dub) (p/s) ....................... 5 |
| 79 | Smirksongs DHSS 01 | AMERICAN PATRIOTS EP ....................... 5 |
| 79 | Smirksongs DHSS 02 | To You/New Music (p/s) ....................... 5 |

## SMITH
| 69 | Stateside-Dunhill SS 8028 | Baby It's You/I Don't Believe ....................... 6 |
|----|---------------------------|-----|
| 70 | Stateside-Dunhill SS 8042 | Take A Look Around/Mojalesky Ridge ....................... 6 |
| 70 | Stateside-Dunhill SS 8055 | What Am I Gonna Do/Born In Boston ....................... 6 |
| 70 | Probe PRO 508 | Comin Back To Me/Minus Plus ....................... 25 |
| 73 | Probe Goldies GFF 115 | The Weight/Baby It's You ....................... 12 |
| 69 | Stateside-Dunhill SSL 5016 | A GROUP CALLED SMITH (LP) ....................... 25 |
| 70 | Stateside-Dunhill SSL 5031 | MINUS PLUS (LP) ....................... 25 |

## SMITH (U.K.)
| 81 | Rarn RARNS 1 | Here Comes My Baby/Just Another Line/Too Late (p/s) ....................... 25 |
|----|--------------|-----|

## ADAM (ERIC) SMITH
| 62 | Island WI 057 | I Wonder Why/My Prayer ....................... 20 |
|----|---------------|-----|

## A.S.A.P. (ADRIAN SMITH & PROJECT)
| 89 | EMI 12 EMPD 107 | Silver And Gold/Blood Brothers (12", silver & gold vinyl)....................... 10 |
|----|-----------------|-----|

*(see also Iron Maiden, Urchin)*

## ARTHUR 'GUITAR BOOGIE' SMITH (& HIS CRACKERJACKS)
| 53 | MGM SP 1008 | Guitar Boogie/Be Bop Rag ....................... 25 |
|----|-------------|-----|
| 53 | MGM SP 1021 | Five String Banjo Boogie/South ....................... 15 |
| 53 | MGM SP 1039 | Express Train Boogie/River Rag ....................... 15 |
| 54 | MGM SP 1096 | Oh, Baby Mine, I Get So Lonely/Outboard ....................... 15 |
| 54 | MGM SP 1110 | Redheaded Stranger/Texas Hop ....................... 20 |
| 55 | MGM SP 1122 | Hi Lo Boogie/Truck Stop Grill ....................... 5 |
| 54 | MGM MGM-EP 510 | ARTHUR 'GUITAR BOOGIE' SMITH AND HIS CRACKERJACKS (EP) ....................... 15 |
| 54 | MGM MGM EPC 5 | ARTHUR 'GUITAR BOOGIE' SMITH (EP, export issue) ....................... 15 |
| 59 | MGM MGM-EP 695 | ARTHUR 'GUITAR BOOGIE' SMITH AND HIS CRACKERJACKS (EP) ....................... 15 |
| 63 | Stateside SE 1005 | MISTER GUITAR (EP) ....................... 15 |
| 53 | MGM MGM-D 111 | FINGERS ON FIRE (10" LP) ....................... 20 |
| 54 | MGM MGM-D 131 | FOOLISH QUESTIONS (10" LP) ....................... 20 |

## BEASLEY SMITH & HIS ORCHESTRA
| 56 | London HLD 8235 | Goodnight, Sweet Dreams/Parisian Rag ....................... 20 |
|----|-----------------|-----|
| 56 | London HLD 8273 | My Foolish Heart/Old Spinning Wheel ....................... 20 |

## BETTY SMITH SKIFFLE GROUP
| 57 | Tempo A 162 | There's A Blue Ridge Round My Heart, Virginia/Double Shuffle ....................... 10 |
|----|-------------|-----|

*(see also Betty Smith Quintet)*

## BETTY SMITH QUINTET
| | | | |
|---|---|---|---|
| 57 | Tempo A 163 | Sweet Georgia Brown/Little White Lies | 20 |
| 58 | Decca F 10986 | Hand Jive/Bewitched (as Betty Smith Group) | 10 |
| 58 | Decca F 11031 | Will The Angels Play Their Harps For Me/Betty's Blues | 10 |
| 58 | Decca F 11071 | Begin The Beguine/Song Of The Boulevards | 5 |
| 59 | Decca F 11124 | Song Of India/Stormy Weather | 10 |
| 57 | Tempo EXA 74 | BETTY SMITH QUINTET (EP) | 30 |
| 57 | Decca DFE 6446 | BETTY SMITH QUINTET (EP) | 30 |
| 58 | Decca DFE 6547 | BETTY SMITH GROUP (EP) | 30 |

*(see also Betty Smith Skiffle Group)*

## BRODERICK SMITH
| | | | |
|---|---|---|---|
| 72 | Spark SRL 1087 | Going Down To The End Of The World/She's Gone | 8 |

## CAL SMITH
| | | | |
|---|---|---|---|
| 73 | MCA 143 | Country Bumpkin/It's Not The Miles You Travelled | 5 |

## CARL SMITH
| | | | |
|---|---|---|---|
| 56 | Philips PB 572 | Loose Talk/More Than Anything Else In The World (78) | 7 |

## CLARA SMITH & FLETCHER HENDERSON
| | | | |
|---|---|---|---|
| 61 | Philips BBE 12491 | BLUES BY CLARA SMITH 1926-1928 (EP) | 10 |

## DAVE SMITH & ASTRONAUTS
| | | | |
|---|---|---|---|
| 67 | Columbia Blue Beat DB 104 | A Lover Like You/Cup Of Love | 15 |
| 67 | Amusicon SLE 10 | A Lover Like You/Cup Of Love | 15 |

## DAVE SMITH & JUDY DINNING
| | | | |
|---|---|---|---|
| 83 | Rubber RUB 043 | WAITING FOR THE CHANGE (LP) | 20 |

## DEREK SMITH TRIO
| | | | |
|---|---|---|---|
| 56 | Pye Nixa NJE 1036 | PIANO MOODS (EP) | 80 |

## DICK SMITH BAND
| | | | |
|---|---|---|---|
| 79 | Smile SR 012 | Body Heat/Motorway Madness (p/s) | 75 |
| 80 | Hol-O-Gram HOL 001 | Way Of The World/Giving The Game Away (with p/s) | 45 |
| 80 | Hol-O-Gram HOL 001 | Way Of The World/Giving The Game Away | 25 |

## EDDIE SMITH
| | | | |
|---|---|---|---|
| 55 | Parlophone MSP 6186 | Silver Star Stomp/Stumbling (as Eddie Smith & Chiefs) | 15 |
| 60 | Top Rank JAR 285 | Upturn/Border Beat (as Eddie Smith & Hornets) | 25 |

## EDGEWOOD SMITH & FABULOUS TAILFEATHERS
| | | | |
|---|---|---|---|
| 67 | Sue WI 4037 | Ain't That Lovin'/Yeah | 50 |

## EFFIE SMITH
| | | | |
|---|---|---|---|
| 66 | Sue WI 4010 | Dial That Telephone Parts 1 & 2 | 25 |

## ELLIOTT SMITH
| | | | |
|---|---|---|---|
| 98 | Domino RUG 074 | Ballad Of Big Nothing/Some Song (p/s) | 12 |
| 98 | Dreamworks DRMS 22347 | Waltz No. 2/Our Thing (p/s) | 10 |
| 99 | Dreamworks DRMS 7 | Baby Britain/Waltz No. 1 (p/s) | 12 |
| 00 | Dreamworks 450 949-7 | Son Of Sam/A Living Will | 8 |
| 98 | Domino REWIGLP 001 | ELLIOTT SMITH (LP) | 60 |
| 98 | Domino REWIGLP 002 | ROMAN CANDLE (LP) | 60 |
| 98 | Domino WIGLP 51 | EITHER/OR (LP) | 50 |
| 00 | Geffen 533 867-8 | FIGURE 8 (2-LP, with lyric insert) | 30 |
| 04 | Domino WIGLP 147 | FROM A BASEMENT ON THE HILL (2-LP) | 20 |
| 07 | Domino WIGLP 198 | NEW MOON (2-LP) | 18 |
| 10 | Domino WIGLP 265 | AN INTRODUCTION TO (LP) | 20 |

## ELSON SMITH
| | | | |
|---|---|---|---|
| 61 | Fontana H 291 | Flip Flop/Are You Ready For That | 30 |

## ERNIE SMITH
| | | | |
|---|---|---|---|
| 71 | Duke DU 119 | Bend Down/Heaven Help Us All | 6 |
| 71 | Horse HOSS 6 | Sunday Morning/One Three | 5 |
| 74 | Attack ATT 8071 | Duppy Gunman/Duppy Gunman Version | 8 |

## (LITTLE) GEORGE (HARMONICA) SMITH
| | | | |
|---|---|---|---|
| 65 | Blue Horizon 45-1002 | Blues In The Dark/Telephone Blues (as Little George Smith) | 100 |
| 70 | Blue Horizon 57-3170 | Someday You're Gonna Learn/Before You Do Your Thing (as George Smith) | 25 |
| 69 | Liberty LBL/LBS 83218E | BLUES WITH FEELING - A TRIBUTE TO LITTLE WALTER (LP, with Chicago Blues Band) | 60 |
| 70 | Blue Horizon 7-63856 | NO TIME TO JIVE (LP) | 100 |
| 71 | Deram SML 1082 | ARKANSAS TRAP (LP) | 60 |

*(see also Bacon Fat)*

## GLORIA SMITH
| | | | |
|---|---|---|---|
| 59 | London HLU 8903 | Playmates/Don't Take Your Love From Me | 18 |

## GORDON SMITH
| | | | |
|---|---|---|---|
| 69 | Blue Horizon 57-3156 | Too Long/Funk Pedal | 30 |
| 69 | Blue Horizon S7-63211 | LONG OVERDUE (LP, stereo) | 90 |
| 69 | Blue Horizon M7-63211 | LONG OVERDUE (LP, mono) | 120 |

*(see also Kevin Coyne)*

## HAROLD SMITH'S MAJESTIC CHOIR
| | | | |
|---|---|---|---|
| 69 | Chess CRS 8100 | We Can All Walk A Little Bit Prouder/Why Am I Treated So Bad | 8 |

## HARVEY SMITH
| | | | |
|---|---|---|---|
| 75 | Hankerchief Hanky 3 | True Love/ End Of The World (p/s) | 7 |

## HOBART SMITH
| | | | |
|---|---|---|---|
| 69 | Topic 12T187 | THE OLD TIMEY RAP (LP) | 20 |

## HUEY 'PIANO' SMITH & THE CLOWNS
| | | | |
|---|---|---|---|
| 58 | Columbia DB 4138 | Don't You Just Know It/High Blood Pressure | 85 |
| 58 | Columbia DB 4138 | Don't You Just Know It/High Blood Pressure (78) | 50 |

| | | | |
|---|---|---|---|
| 60 | Top Rank JAR 282 | Don't You Just Know Kokomo/FRANKIE FORD: Cheatin' Woman | 20 |
| 62 | Top Rank JAR 614 | Pop-Eye/Scald-Dog (as Huey Smith) | 12 |
| 65 | Sue WI 364 | If It Ain't One Thing It's Another/Tu-Ber-Cu-Lucas And The Sinus Blues | 25 |
| 65 | Sue WI 380 | Rockin' Pneumonia And The Boogie Woogie Flu (Parts 1 & 2) | 25 |
| 78 | Chiswick NS 43 | Rockin' Pneumonia And The Boogie Woogie Flu (unissued) | 0 |
| 82 | Kent TOWN 502 | Don't You Just Know It/MARY LOVE: Lay This Burden Down/DANNY MONDAY: Baby Without You | 12 |
| 65 | Sue ILP 917 | ROCKIN' PNEUMONIA AND THE BOOGIE WOOGIE FLU (LP, titled "Havin' A Good Time" on labels) | 40 |

*(see also Frankie Ford, Lee Allen, Bobby Marchan, Robert Parker)*

## HURRICANE SMITH
| | | | |
|---|---|---|---|
| 71 | Columbia DB 8785 | Don't Let I Die/The Writer Sings His Songs | 6 |
| 72 | Columbia DB 8878 | Oh Babe, What Would You Say/Getting To Know You | 6 |
| 72 | Columbia SCX 6510 | DON'T LET IT DIE (LP) | 15 |

## IAN SMITH & INNER MIND
| | | | |
|---|---|---|---|
| 71 | Bullet BU 490 | Devil Woman/Nenn Street Rub | 8 |

*(see also Smithy All Stars)*

## JEFF SMITH
| | | | |
|---|---|---|---|
| 71 | RAK RAK 120 | Gypsy In My Blood/Going To A Party | 25 |

## JENNIE SMITH
| | | | |
|---|---|---|---|
| 59 | Philips PB 924 | Huggin' My Pillow (Sweet Side)/Huggin' My Pillow (Sweet Beat Side) | 5 |

## JIMMY SMITH
| | | | |
|---|---|---|---|
| 62 | HMV POP 1025 | Walk On The Wild Side Parts 1 & 2 (blue label) | 10 |
| 62 | HMV POP 1025 | Walk On The Wild Side Parts 1 & 2 (black label) | 5 |
| 65 | Verve VS 509 | Hobo Flats Parts 1 & 2 | 5 |
| 65 | Verve VS 521 | Who's Afraid Of Virginia Woolf Parts 1 & 2 | 20 |
| 65 | Verve VS 523 | The Cat/Basin Street Blues | 5 |
| 65 | Verve VS 531 | The Organ Grinder's Swing/I'll Close My Eyes | 6 |
| 66 | Verve VS 534 | Slow Theme From "Where The Spies Are" Parts 1 & 2 | 5 |
| 66 | Verve VS 536 | Got My Mojo Working Parts 1 & 2 | 10 |
| 66 | Verve VS 540 | I'm Your Hoochie-Coochie Man Parts 1 & 2 | 6 |
| 67 | Verve VS 551 | Cat In A Tree Parts 1 & 2 | 6 |
| 67 | Verve VS 562 | Mickey Mouse Parts 1 & 2 | 6 |
| 62 | Verve CLP 1596/CSD 1462 | BASHIN' THE UNPREDICTABLE (Verve label with HMV number) | 15 |
| 63 | Verve (S)VLP 9039 | HOBO FLATS | 15 |
| 64 | Verve VLP 9057 | ANY NUMBER CAN WIN | 15 |
| 64 | Verve VLP 9068 | WHO'S AFRAID OF VIRGINIA WOOLF | 25 |
| 64 | Verve (S)VLP 9079 | THE CAT | 20 |
| 65 | Verve (S)VLP 9093 | MONSTER | 15 |
| 66 | Verve (S)VLP 9108 | ORGAN GRINDER SWING | 15 |
| 66 | Verve (S)VLP 9123 | GOT MY MOJO WORKING | 15 |
| 66 | Verve (S)VLP 9142 | HOOCHIE COOCHIE MAN | 15 |
| 67 | Verve (S)VLP 9159 | PETER & THE WOLF | 15 |
| 67 | Verve (S)VLP 9160 | THE DYNAMIC DUO (with Wes Montgomery) | 20 |
| 67 | Verve (S)VLP 9182 | RESPECT | 15 |
| 68 | Verve (S)VLP 9218 | STAY LOOSE | 15 |
| 68 | Verve (S)VLP 9227 | LIVIN' IT UP | 15 |
| 68 | Verve (S)VLP 9231 | CHRISTMAS COOKIN' | 15 |
| 69 | Verve (S)VLP 9241 | FURTHER ADVENTURES OF JIMMY AND WES (with Wes Montgomery) | 15 |
| 71 | Verve 2304 020 | I'M GON' GIT MYSELF TOGETHER | 15 |
| 74 | Verve 2304 167 | PORTUGUESE SOUL | 15 |

*(see also Kenny Burrell)*

## JOEY SMITH & BABA BROOKS BAND
| | | | |
|---|---|---|---|
| 64 | R&B JB 131 | Maybe Once/Tell Me You're Mine | 25 |

## JUDI SMITH
| | | | |
|---|---|---|---|
| 65 | Decca F 12132 | Leaves Come Tumbling Down/Come My Way | 15 |

## JUNIOR SMITH
| | | | |
|---|---|---|---|
| 67 | Giant GN 1 | Cool Down Your Temper/I'm Groovin' | 30 |
| 68 | Giant GN 18 | I'm Gonna Leave You Girl/I Love You, I Love You | 30 |
| 68 | Giant GN 25 | Come Cure Me/I Want Your Lovin' | 25 |
| 68 | Gas GAS 132 | Gimme Little/Trip To War Land | 20 |
| 69 | Crystal CR 7002 | Put On The Pressure/I Don't Know | 10 |
| 72 | Sioux SI 019 | Saturday Child/JUMBO STERLING: Hot Dog | 15 |
| 72 | Sioux SI 023 | You Don't Know/JUMBO STERLING: My Sugar Ain't Sweet | 15 |

*(see also Stranger Cole, Derrick Morgan, Rocksteadys)*

## KATHY SMITH
| | | | |
|---|---|---|---|
| 70 | Polydor 2310 081 | SOME SONGS I'VE SAVED (LP) | 60 |

## KEELY SMITH (& LOUIS PRIMA)
| | | | |
|---|---|---|---|
| 59 | London HLD 8984 | If I Knew I'd Find You (I'd Climb The Highest Mountain)/Don't Let The Stars Get In Your Eyes | 12 |
| 61 | London RE-D 1269 | YOU LOVERS (EP) | 20 |
| 58 | Capitol (S)T 914 | I WISH YOU LOVE (LP, mono/stereo) | 15 |
| 59 | Capitol T 1160 | HEY BOY! HEY GIRL! (LP, soundtrack, with Louis Prima) | 25 |

*(see also Louis Prima, Frank Sinatra)*

## LONNIE SMITH
| | | | |
|---|---|---|---|
| 67 | CBS 63146 | FINGER LICKIN' GOOD (LP) | 25 |
| 70s | Blue Note BST 84290 | THINK (LP) | 25 |
| 70s | Blue Note BST 84313 | TURNING POINT (LP) | 25 |
| 70s | Blue Note BST 84326 | MOVE YOUR HAND (LP) | 30 |

# Lonnie LISTON SMITH (& THE COSMIC ECHOES)

## LONNIE LISTON SMITH (& THE COSMIC ECHOES)
| | | | |
|---|---|---|---|
| 75 | RCA RCA 2568 | Expansions (Parts 1 & 2) (& Cosmic Echoes) | 10 |
| 76 | RCA RCA 2668 | Chance For Peace/Sunset | 5 |
| 76 | RCA RCA 2727 | Get Down Everybody/Inner Beauty | 5 |
| 79 | RCA PB 9450 | Expansions/A Chance For Peace | 6 |
| 79 | RCA PC 9450 | Expansions/A Chance For Peace (12") | 35 |
| 83 | Bluebird BRT 4 | Expansions/Voodoo Woman (12") | 15 |
| 75 | RCA SF 8434 | EXPANSIONS (LP, with Cosmic Echoes) | 15 |
| 77 | RCA PL 11822 | RENAISSANCE (LP, with Cosmic Echoes) | 15 |

## LORENZO SMITH
| | | | |
|---|---|---|---|
| 66 | Outasite 45-503 | (Too Much) Firewater/Count Down (99 copies only) | 100 |

## LOU SMITH
| | | | |
|---|---|---|---|
| 60 | Top Rank JAR 520 | Cruel Love/Close To My Heart | 10 |

## MARTHA SMITH
| | | | |
|---|---|---|---|
| 65 | Pye 7N 15778 | As I Watch You Walk Away/It Always Seems Like Summer | 20 |
| 65 | Pye 7N 15860 | Love Means Nothing To You/The Song Is Love | 7 |

## MARVIN SMITH
| | | | |
|---|---|---|---|
| 66 | Coral Q 72486 | Time Stopped/Have More Time | 50 |
| 66 | Coral Q 72486 | Time Stopped/Have More Time (DJ copy) | 100 |
| 74 | Contempo CS 2034 | Let The Good Times Roll/Ain't That A Shame | 5 |

## MEL SMITH
| | | | |
|---|---|---|---|
| 81 | Mercury MEL 1 | Mel Smith's Greatest Hits/Richard & Joey (p/s, with Roger Taylor) | 15 |

## MELODY SMITH
| | | | |
|---|---|---|---|
| 71 | CBS CBS 7561 | You Never Hear A Teardrop Fall/Rastus Ravel | 10 |

## MICK SMITH
| | | | |
|---|---|---|---|
| 76 | Midas MFHR 078 | SOMEBODY NOBODY KNOWS (LP) | 30 |
| 77 | Alida Star AS 771 | WORDS AND MUSIC (LP) | 30 |
| 79 | Repercussion RR 1000 | RAINDANCE (LP, as Mike Smith) | 25 |

## MIKE SMITH
| | | | |
|---|---|---|---|
| 85 | Proto ENA 130 | Medley (7" version)/Bits And Pieces (in p/s) | 7 |
| 85 | Proto ENAT 130 | Medley (12" version)/Glad All Over (12", p/s) | 12 |
| 90 | Mooncrest MOON 1010 | You Gotta Play Rock'N'Roll/Operator | 6 |

*(see also Dave Clark 5, Smith & D'Abo)*

## O.C. (OCIE) SMITH
| | | | |
|---|---|---|---|
| 57 | London HLA 8480 | Lighthouse/Too Many (as Ocie Smith) | 90 |
| 57 | London HLA 8480 | Lighthouse/Too Many (as Ocie Smith) (78) | 60 |
| 68 | CBS 3343 | The Son Of Hickory Holler's Tramp/On A Clear Day You Can See Forever | 8 |
| 68 | CBS 3666 | Main Street Mission/Long Black Limousine | 5 |
| 68 | CBS 3767 | Little Green Apples/Gas Food Lodgings | 5 |
| 68 | CBS 3918 | Isn't It Lonely Together/I Ain't The Worryin' Kind | 5 |
| 69 | CBS 4514 | Daddy's Little Man/If I Leave You Now | 5 |
| 70 | CBS 4657 | Me And You/Can't Take Me Eyes Off You | 5 |
| 70 | CBS 5203 | Baby I Need Your Loving/San Francisco Is A Lonely Town | 5 |
| 68 | CBS (S) 63147 | THE DYNAMIC O.C. SMITH (LP) | 20 |
| 68 | CBS (S) 63362 | HICKORY HOLLER REVISITED (LP) | 15 |
| 69 | CBS 63805 | AT HOME (LP) | 25 |

*(see also Art Mooney)*

## OTELLO SMITH & TOBAGO BAD BOYS
| | | | |
|---|---|---|---|
| 67 | Direction 58-3082 | My Home Town/Trouble | 5 |
| 68 | Direction 8-63242 | THE BIG ONES GO SKA (LP) | 40 |

## PATTI SMITH (GROUP)
| | | | |
|---|---|---|---|
| 76 | Arista ARIST 47 | Gloria (In Excelsis Deo) (Edit)/My Generation (p/s) | 5 |
| 77 | Arista ARIST 12135 | Gloria (In Excelsis Deo)/My Generation (live) (12", Rough Trade copies in brown paper bag with titles in felt pen) | 10 |
| 78 | Arista ARIST 181 | Because The Night/God Speed (p/s) | 7 |
| 78 | Sire 6078 614 | Hey Joe (Version)/Piss Factory (p/s) | 25 |
| 78 | Arista ARIST 197 | Privilege (Set Me Free)/Ask The Angels (p/s) | 5 |
| 78 | Arista ARIST 12197 | Privilege (Set Me Free)/Ask The Angels/25th Floor (Live Version)/Babelfield (12", p/s) | 10 |
| 79 | Arista ARIST 264 | Frederick/Fire Of Unknown Origin (p/s) | 5 |
| 79 | Arista ARIST 281 | Dancing Barefoot/5-4-3-2-1 (live) (p/s) | 5 |
| 79 | Arista ARIST 291 | So You Want To Be A Rock'n'Roll Star/Frederick (live) (p/s) | 5 |
| 88 | Fierce FRIGHT 017 | Brian Jones/Stockinged Feet/Jesus Christ (1-sided, white label) | 15 |
| 75 | Arista ARTY 122 | HORSES (LP, 1st pressing, 'Horses' written in white, blue label) | 25 |
| 76 | Arista SPARTY 1001 | RADIO ETHIOPIA (LP, as Patti Smith Group, with lyric insert) | 15 |
| 79 | Arista SPART 1086 | WAVE (LP, insert) | 15 |

## PAUL SMITH
| | | | |
|---|---|---|---|
| 65 | Columbia DB 7636 | Piccadilly Paper Boy/Yakety Yak | 10 |

## PETER SMITH
| | | | |
|---|---|---|---|
| 70s | Pilgrim JLPS 148P | FAITH, FOLK & CLARITY (LP, with Kinfolk) | 18 |

## RAY SMITH
| | | | |
|---|---|---|---|
| 60 | London HL 9051 | Rockin' Little Angel/That's All Right | 45 |

## ROY SMITH (& THE STARGAZERS) (U.K.)
| | | | |
|---|---|---|---|
| 55 | Decca F 10529 | Red Roses (For My Lady Fair)/The Devil's In Your Eyes | 5 |
| 55 | Decca F 10644 | He/Glengarry (solo) | 5 |

*(see also Stargazers)*

## ROY SMITH (JAMAICA)
| | | | |
|---|---|---|---|
| 70 | Grape GR 3013 | See Through Craze/TERRY CARL & DERRICK: I'm The One | 30 |

| 70 | Jackpot JP 723 | The Wedding/Air Balloon | 20 |

## SLIM SMITH (& THE UNIQUES)

| 66 | Island WI 3023 | I've Got Your Number/The New Boss | 60 |
| 67 | Coxsone CS 7016 | Hip Hug/FREEDOM SINGERS: I Want Money | 70 |
| 67 | Coxsone CS 7034 | Rougher Yet/I'll Never Let Go | 90 |
| 67 | Coxsone CS 7009 | Mercy Mercy/JACKIE MITTOO: Baba Boom | 60 |
| 68 | Trojan TR 619 | Watch This Sound/Out Of Love (as Slim Smith & Uniques) | 45 |
| 69 | Unity UN 504 | Everybody Needs Love/JUNIOR SMITH: Come Back Girl | 10 |
| 69 | Unity UN 508 | For Once In My Life/Burning Desire | 20 |
| 69 | Unity UN 510 | Zip A Dee Doo Dah/On Broadway | 20 |
| 69 | Unity UN 513 | Let It Be Me/Love Makes Me Do Foolish Things (both with Paulette) | 20 |
| 69 | Unity UN 515 | Somebody To Love/Confusion | 20 |
| 69 | Unity UN 520 | Slip Away/Spanish Harlem | 20 |
| 69 | Unity UN 524 | Sunny Side Of The Sea/A Place In The Sun | 40 |
| 69 | Unity UN 527 | Blessed Are The Meek/Conversation | 20 |
| 69 | Unity UN 537 | Keep That Light Shining On Me/Build My World Around You | 20 |
| 69 | Unity UN 539 | Love Me Tender/This Feeling | 20 |
| 69 | Unity UN 542 | Honey/There's A Light | 20 |
| 69 | Jackpot JP 703 | If It Don't Work Out/Love Power | 20 |
| 69 | Gas GAS 132 | The Vow (& Doreen Shaeffer)/JAMES NEPHEW: Why Don't You Say | 20 |
| 70 | Gas GAS 150 | What Kind Of Life/MARTIN RILEY: It's All In The Game | 30 |
| 70 | Unity UN 570 | Jenny/The Race | 15 |
| 70 | S&S SC 001 | Strong Love/Strange World | 12 |
| 71 | Supreme SUP 219 | Stay/You're My Everything | 10 |
| 71 | Pama Supreme PS 334 | Send Me Some Loving/I'm Lost | 8 |
| 71 | Camel CA 81 | Spanish Harlem/Slip Away | 6 |
| 71 | Escort ERT 851 | My Love Come True/This Feeling | 6 |
| 71 | Escort ERT 852 | Life Keeps Turning/My Girl | 6 |
| 71 | Escort ERT 859 | My Girl/RECO: Plus One | 10 |
| 71 | Jackpot JP 779 | Keep Walking/Will You Still Love Me Tomorrow | 7 |
| 72 | Jackpot JP 786 | I Need Your Loving/You've Got What It Takes | 7 |
| 72 | Jackpot JP 788 | Take Me Back/Where Do I Turn | 6 |
| 72 | Jackpot JP 789 | Rain From The Skies/You're No Good | 8 |
| 72 | Jackpot JP 798 | Closer Together/Blinded By Love | 6 |
| 72 | Jackpot JP 799 | Turning Point/Money Lover | 6 |
| 72 | Dynamic DYN 428 | Just A Dream/Send Me Some Loving | 10 |
| 72 | Pama PM 850 | The Time Has Come/RECO & HIS BAND: Version | 6 |
| 72 | Pama Supreme PS 373 | A Place In The Sun/Stranger On The Shore | 6 |
| 72 | Camel CA 89 | Take Me Back/Where Do I Turn | 6 |
| 72 | Explosion EX 2074 | The Time Has Come/Blessed Is The Man | 8 |
| 73 | Explosion EX 2078 | Stand Up And Fight/The Sunny Side Of The Sea | 8 |
| 73 | Green Door GD 4058 | Let Me Love You/If It Don't Work Out | 30 |
| 73 | Bullet BU 523 | A Place In The Sun/Burning Fire | 40 |
| 69 | Pama ECO 9 | EVERYBODY NEEDS LOVE (LP) | 40 |
| 72 | Trojan TBL 186 | JUST A DREAM (LP) | 40 |
| 72 | Trojan TBL 198 | MEMORIAL (LP) | 25 |
| 73 | Trojan TBL 198 | GREATEST HITS (LP) | 18 |
| 70s | Lord Koos KLP 1 | SLIM SMITH (LP) | 40 |
| 76 | Angen ANGL 1 | THE LATE AND GREAT (LP) | 40 |
| 84 | Pama PMLP 3240 | TIME HAS COME (LP) | 40 |

*(see also Wonder Boy, Pioneers, Uniques, Roy Shirley, Ron Sig, Dakota Jim, Dennis Alcapone, David Isaacs, John Holt, (see also Wonder Boy, Pioneers, Uniques, Roy Shirley, Ron Sig, Dakota Jim, Dennis Alcapone, David Isaacs, John Holt,*

## SLIM SMITH & THE FREEDOM SINGERS

| 70 | Banana BA 304 | Do Dang Do/JACKIE MITTO: Hot Milk | 60 |

## SOMETHIN' SMITH & THE REDHEADS

| 58 | Fontana TFR 6005 | PUT THE BLAME ON ME (10" LP) | 18 |

## STUART SMITH

| 69 | Polydor 56336 | My Head Goes Around/Where Are You | 6 |

## TAB SMITH & HIS ORCHESTRA

| 56 | Vogue V 2410 | Jump Time/Rock City | 15 |
| 59 | London HLM 8801 | Smoke Gets In Your Eyes/My Happiness Cha-Cha | 10 |

## TERRY SMITH

| 69 | Philips (S)BL 7871 | FALL OUT (LP, laminated lseeve, black/silver label) | 125 |
| 77 | Lambert LAM 002 | TERRY SMITH AND TONY LEE TRIO (LP) | 20 |

*(see also If)*

## TRIXIE SMITH

| 50s | Poydras 101 | TRIXIE SMITH (10" EP, 45 rpm) | 15 |
| 50s | Ristic 12 | TRIXIE SMITH (10" EP, 45 rpm) | 15 |
| 50s | Audubon AAE | TRIXIE SMITH (10" LP) | 30 |

## TRIXIE SMITH/MA RAINEY

| 64 | Jazz Collector JEL 22 | FEMALE BLUES VOL. 3 (EP, 2 tracks each) | 10 |

## TRULY SMITH

| 66 | Decca F 12373 | My Smile Is Just A Frown Turned Upside Down/Love Is Me, Love Is You | 25 |
| 66 | Decca F 12415 | I Love Him/Buttermilk Hill | 5 |
| 66 | Decca F 12489 | You Are The Love Of My Life/The Merry Go Round Is Slowing | 5 |
| 67 | Decca F 12554 | Windows And Doors/Take A Broken Heart | 5 |
| 67 | Decca F 12645 | I Wanna Go Back There Again/Window Cleaner | 35 |
| 67 | Decca F 12700 | The Boy From Chelsea/Little Man With A Stick | 20 |

# Verdelle SMITH

| 68 | MGM MGM 1431 | This Is The First Time/Taking Time Off | 20 |

## VERDELLE SMITH
| 66 | Capitol CL 15234 | In My Room/Like A Man | |
| 66 | Capitol CL 15456 | Tar And Cement/A Piece Of The Sky | 18 |
| 66 | Capitol CL 15481 | I Don't Need Anything/If You Can't Say Anything Nice | 12 |
| 67 | Capitol CL 15514 | There's So Much Love Around Me/Baby Baby | 12 |

## WARREN SMITH
| 60 | London HL 7101 | I Don't Believe I'll Fall In Love/Cave-In (export issue) | 12 |
| 61 | London HLG 7110 | Odds And Ends/A Whole Lot Of Nothin' (export issue) | 25 |
| 64 | Liberty LIB 55699 | Blue Smoke/Judge And Jury | 25 |

## WAYNE SMITH
| | | | 10 |
| 81 | Black Joy DH 815 | Life Is A Moment In Space/Ain't No Me Without You (12") | 40 |
| 82 | Black Joy DHB 17 | Isim Skism/Rose Marie (12", with Yellowman) | 50 |
| 84 | Greensleeves GRED 162 | Come Along/Change Your Style (12") | 30 |
| 85 | Greensleeves GRED 169 | Under Me Sleng Teng/MICHAEL BUCKLEY: Dance Gate (12") | 30 |
| 85 | Tonos TON 006 | Dancing Machine/PATRICK ANDY: Leave The Door (12") | 30 |
| 85 | Greensleeves GRED 183 | Ickie All Over/TONTO IRIE: Life Story (12") | 30 |
| 85 | Greensleeves GRED 177 | Sleng Teng Mix Down Remix/PAD ANTHONY: Cry For Me (12") | 20 |
| 86 | Ras RAST 7021 | No Puppy Love/Teach Me To Dance (12") | 15 |
| 80s | Unity UN 019 | My Sweet Love/TONTO IRIE: Murder Commit (12") | 12 |
| 81 | Black Joy BHLP 2005 | YOUTHMAN SKANKING (LP) | 50 |

## WHISPERING SMITH
| 72 | Blue Horizon 2431 015 | OVER EASY (LP) | 120 |

## ORVILLE SMITH
| 91 | Riz RIZ 001 | Leaving Rome/BOMBASTIC CREW: Repatriation Dub | 15 |

## SMITH & MIGHTY
| 00 | Studio !K7 !K700lp | BASS IS MATERNAL (LP) | 22 |

## SMITH & WESTON
| 73 | Decca F 13441 | A Shot Of Rhythm And Blues/Run Run Run | 15 |

## SMITH BROTHERS (U.S.)
| 78 | Grapevine GRP 109 | There Can Be A Better Way/Payback's A Drag | 10 |

## SMITHFIELD MARKET
| 73 | Gloucester GLS 0435 | LONDON IN 1665 (LP, private pressing, gatefold sleeve) | 800 |
| 74 | Globe/Gloucester GLS 0443 | AFTER SHAKESPEARE (LP, private pressing, die-cut sleeve, with insert) | 700 |

## THE SMITHS
### SINGLES
| 83 | Rough Trade RT 131 | Hand In Glove/Handsome Devil (p/s, original pressing with Manchester address on rear sleeve) | |
| 83 | Rough Trade RT 131 | Hand In Glove/Handsome Devil (p/s, second pressing with London address on rear label) | 25 |
| 83 | Rough Trade RT 131 | Hand In Glove/Handsome Devil (p/s, third pressing with no address) | 15 |
| 83 | Rough Trade RT 131 | Hand In Glove/Handsome Devil (later pressing with misprinted blue/negative p/s - beware of counterfeits!) | 20 |
| 83 | Rough Trade RT 136 | This Charming Man/Jeane (unreleased first pressing with Rough Trade/Capitol logo and solid centre, p/s with Manchester address on rear) | 2000 |
| 83 | Rough Trade RT 136 | This Charming Man/Jeane (Rough Trade/Capitol logo or reissued 'stamped' logo, p/s) | 50 |
| 83 | Rough Trade RTT 136 | This Charming Man (Manchester)/This Charming Man (London)/Accept Yourself/Wonderful Woman (12", p/s; later pressing with band title on sleeve) | 10 |
| 83 | Rough Trade RTT 136 | This Charming Man (Manchester)/This Charming Man (London)/Accept Yourself/Wonderful Woman (12", p/s) | 30 |
| 83 | Rough Trade RTT 136NY | This Charming Man (New York Vocal)/This Charming Man (New York Instrumental) (12", p/s) | 15 |
| 83 | Rough Trade RTT 136NY | This Charming Man (New York Vocal)/This Charming Man (New York Instrumental) (12", p/s; later pressing with band title on sleeve) | 15 |
| 84 | Rough Trade RT 146 | What Difference Does It Make?/Back To The Old House (Morrissey p/s) | 50 |
| 84 | Rough Trade RT 146 | What Difference Does It Make?/Back To The Old House (Terence Stamp p/s) | 10 |
| 84 | Rough Trade RTT 146 | What Difference Does It Make?/Back To The Old House/These Things Take Time (12", Morrissey or Terence Stamp p/s) | 10 |
| 84 | Rough Trade RTT 146 | What Difference Does It Make?/Back To The Old House/These Things Take Time (Terence Stamp p/s, later pressing with band title on sleeve) | 10 |
| 84 | Rough Trade RT 156 | Heaven Knows I'm Miserable Now/Suffer Little Children (p/s) | 25 |
| 84 | Rough Trade RT 156 | Heaven Knows I'm Miserable Now/Suffer Little Children (late solid centre pressing, p/s) | 6 |
| 84 | Rough Trade RTT 156 | Heaven Knows I'm Miserable Now/Girl Afraid/Suffer Little Children (12", p/s) | 40 |
| 84 | Rough Trade RTT 156 | Heaven Knows I'm Miserable Now/Girl Afraid/Suffer Little Children (mispressed 12" with extended version) | 10 |
| 84 | Rough Trade RT 166 | William, It Was Really Nothing/Please Please Please Let Me Get What I Want (original issue with green 'man on bed' p/s) | 50 |
| 84 | Rough Trade RTT 166 | William, It Was Really Nothing/How Soon Is Now?/Please Please Please Let Me Get What I Want (12", original issue with green 'man on bed' p/s) | 8 |
| 85 | Rough Trade RT 176 | How Soon Is Now?/Well I Wonder (p/s) | 10 |
| 85 | Rough Trade RTT 176 | How Soon Is Now?/Well I Wonder/Oscillate Wildly (12", p/s) | 6 |
| 85 | Rough Trade RT 181 | Shakespeare's Sister/What She Said (p/s) | 10 |
| 85 | Rough Trade RTT 181 | Shakespeare's Sister/What She Said/Stretch Out And Wait (12", p/s, with yellow & blue discography inner) | 5 |
| 85 | Rough Trade RTT 181 | Shakespeare's Sister/What She Said/Stretch Out And Wait (12", p/s, with misprinted red & green or magenta & green inner) | 10 |
| 85 | Rough Trade RT 186 | That Joke Isn't Funny Anymore/Meat Is Murder (live) (p/s) | 50 |
| 85 | Rough Trade RTT 186 | That Joke Isn't Funny Anymore/Nowhere Fast (live)/Stretch Out And Wait (live)/Shakespeare's Sister (live)/Meat Is Murder (live) (12", p/s) | 6 |
| 85 | Rough Trade RT 191 | The Boy With The Thorn In His Side/Asleep (p/s) | 10 |
| 85 | Rough Trade RTT 191 | The Boy With The Thorn In His Side/Rubber Ring/Asleep (12", p/s) | 5 |
| | | | 10 |

| Year | Label | Cat. No. | Description | £ |
|---|---|---|---|---|
| 86 | Rough Trade | RT 192 | Bigmouth Strikes Again/Money Changes Everything (p/s) | 5 |
| 86 | Rough Trade | RTT 192 | Bigmouth Strikes Again/Money Changes Everything/Unloveable (12", p/s, with or without sticker on sleeve) | 10 |
| 86 | Rough Trade | RTT 193 | Panic/Vicar In A Tutu (p/s, with square sheet of 'Hang The DJ' stickers) | 25 |
| 86 | Rough Trade | RT 193 | Panic/Vicar In A Tutu (p/s, with round sheet of 'Hang The DJ' stickers) | 20 |
| 86 | Rough Trade | RT 193 | Panic/Vicar In A Tutu (p/s) | 5 |
| 86 | Rough Trade | RTT 193 | Panic/Vicar In A Tutu/The Draize Train (12", p/s, with 'Hang The DJ' stickers) | 15 |
| 86 | Rough Trade | RTT 193 | Panic/Vicar In A Tutu/The Draize Train (12", p/s, without 'Hang The DJ' stickers) | 10 |
| 86 | Rough Trade | RT 194 | Ask/Cemetry Gates (p/s) | 6 |
| 86 | Rough Trade | RTT 194 | Ask/Cemetry Gates/Golden Lights (12", p/s) | 10 |
| 87 | Rough Trade | RT 195 | Shoplifters Of The World Unite/Half A Person (p/s) | 6 |
| 87 | Rough Trade | RTT 195 | Shoplifters Of The World Unite/London/Half A Person (12", p/s; in carrier bag) | 30 |
| 87 | Rough Trade | RTT 195 | Shoplifters Of The World Unite/London/Half A Person (12", p/s) | 10 |
| 87 | Rough Trade | RTT 195 | Shoplifters Of The World Unite/London/Half A Person (12", p/s, mispressing, A-side plays "You Just Haven't Earned It Yet Baby") | 55 |
| 87 | Rough Trade | RT 196 | Sheila Take A Bow/Is It Really So Strange? (p/s) | 5 |
| 87 | Rough Trade | RTT 196 | Sheila Take A Bow/Is It Really So Strange?/Sweet And Tender Hooligan (12", p/s) | 10 |
| 87 | Rough Trade | RT 197 | Girlfriend In A Coma/Work Is A Four Letter Word (grey p/s) | 6 |
| 87 | Rough Trade | RT 197 | Girlfriend In A Coma/Work Is A Four Letter Word (misprinted green p/s, incorrectly shows additional 12" track 'I Keep Mine Hidden' on reverse of sleeve) | 500 |
| 87 | Rough Trade | RTT 197 | Girlfriend In A Coma/Work Is A Four Letter Word/I Keep Mine Hidden (12", green p/s; some in grey p/s) | 35 |
| 87 | Rough Trade | RT 198 | I Started Something I Couldn't Finish/Pretty Girls Make Graves (Troy Tate demo) (p/s) | 6 |
| 87 | Rough Trade | RTT 198 | I Started Something I Couldn't Finish/Pretty Girls Make Graves (Troy Tate demo)/Some Girls Are Bigger Than Others (Live) (12", p/s) | 10 |
| 87 | Rough Trade | RT 200 | Last Night I Dreamt That Somebody Loved Me/Rusholme Ruffians (John Peel version) (p/s) | 6 |
| 87 | Rough Trade | RTT 200 | Last Night I Dreamt That Somebody Loved Me/Rusholme Ruffians (John Peel version)/Nowhere Fast (John Peel Version) (12", p/s) | 12 |
| 87 | Rough Trade | RT 166 | William, It Was Really Nothing/How Soon Is Now? (reissue, Billie Whitelaw p/s). | 22 |
| 87 | Rough Trade | RTT 166 | William, It Was Really Nothing/How Soon Is Now?/Please Please Please Let Me Get What I Want (12", reissue, Billie Whitelaw p/s) | 30 |
| 88 | Rough Trade | CAT 063 | London (Live) (Square 1-sided black flexi, 33rpm free with The Catalogue magazine, reverse has reproduction of hand-written poem for 'Poppycocteau' by Morrissey) | 10 |
| 92 | WEA | YZ0001 | This Charming Man/Jeane (p/s, reissue) | 5 |
| 92 | WEA | YZ0002 | How Soon Is Now?/Hand In Glove (p/s, reissue) | 15 |
| 92 | WEA | YZ0003 | There Is A Light That Never Goes Out/Handsome Devil (live) (p/s) | 25 |

## SINGLES : CD REISSUE SINGLES

| Year | Label | Cat. No. | Description | £ |
|---|---|---|---|---|
| 88 | Rough Trade | RTT 146CD | What Difference Does It Make?/Back To The Old House/These Things Take Time | 25 |
| 88 | Rough Trade | RTT 156CD | Heaven Knows I'm Miserable Now/Girl Afraid/Suffer Little Children | 25 |
| 88 | Rough Trade | RTT 166CD | William, It Was Really Nothing/How Soon Is Now?/Please Please Please Let Me Get What I Want | 30 |
| 88 | Rough Trade | RTT 171CD | Barbarism Begins At Home/Shakespeare's Sister/Stretch Out And Wait | 35 |
| 88 | Rough Trade | RTT 191CD | The Boy With The Thorn In His Side/Rubber Ring/Asleep | 25 |
| 88 | Rough Trade | RTT 193CD | Panic/Vicar In A Tutu/The Draize Train | 25 |
| 88 | Rough Trade | RTT 215CD | The Headmaster Ritual/Nowhere Fast (live)/Stretch Out And Wait (live)/Meat Is Murder (live) (withdrawn Viv Nicholson cover) | 45 |

## ALBUMS

| Year | Label | Cat. No. | Description | £ |
|---|---|---|---|---|
| 84 | Rough Trade | ROUGH 61 | THE SMITHS (LP) | 20 |
| 84 | Rough Trade | ROUGH 76 | HATFUL OF HOLLOW (LP, original gatefold issue, with incorrect sleeve, no black dot appears between 'Accept Yourself' and 'Girl Afraid' on reverse of sleeve) | 25 |
| 85 | Rough Trade | ROUGH 81 | MEAT IS MURDER (LP, with lyric inner sleeve) | 20 |
| 85 | Rough Trade | ROUGH CD 76 | HATFUL OF HOLLOW (CD, original blue sleeve) | 50 |
| 86 | Rough Trade | ROUGH 96 | THE QUEEN IS DEAD (LP, gatefold, inner sleeve) | 25 |
| 87 | Rough Trade | ROUGH 101 | THE WORLD WON'T LISTEN (LP, inner) | 25 |
| 87 | Rough Trade | ROUGH 106 | STRANGEWAYS HERE WE COME (LP, embossed sleeve) | 20 |
| 87 | Rough Trade | ROUGH 255 | LOUDER THAN BOMBS (2-LP, gatefold sleeve) | 21 |
| 88 | Rough Trade | ROUGH 126 | RANK (LP, gatefold sleeve, with inner, ltd. edition with poster and cover sticker denoting amended catalogue number) | 30 |
| 88 | Rough Trade | ROUGH 126D | RANK (DAT) | 50 |
| 93 | WEA | SMITHS 1 | THE SMITHS (10" LP, reissue) | 20 |
| 93 | WEA | SMITHS 2 | HATFUL OF HOLLOW (2-LP, 10" reissue) | 20 |
| 93 | WEA | SMITHS 3 | MEAT IS MURDER (10" LP reissue) | 20 |
| 93 | WEA | SMITHS 4 | THE QUEEN IS DEAD (10" LP reissue) | 20 |
| 93 | WEA | SMITHS 5 | THE WORLD WON'T LISTEN (10" LP reissue) | 20 |
| 93 | WEA | SMITHS 6 | STRANGEWAYS, HERE WE COME (10" LP) | 20 |
| 93 | WEA | SMITHS 7 | RANK (10" 2-LP reissue) | 20 |

## PROMOS : PROMOS & TEST PRESSINGS

| Year | Label | Cat. No. | Description | £ |
|---|---|---|---|---|
| 83 | Rough Trade | RT 131 | Hand In Glove (white label 1983 test pressing - approx. 5 only) | 1500 |
| 83 | N/A | | 3-Pack (Rough Trade promo cassette, promoting Hand In Glove and tracks by Zerra 1 and Influence) | 100 |
| 83 | Rough Trade | RT 136 | Reel Around The Fountain/Jeane (unissued, white label test pressings only - beware of counterfeits!) | 1200 |
| 83 | Rough Trade | RT 136 | This Charming Man (London Version) (rejected white label test pressing) | 800 |
| 83 | Rough Trade | RT 136 | This Charming Man (Manchester) (one-sided white label test pressing) | 300 |
| 83 | Rough Trade | RTT 136NY | This Charming Man (New York vocal)/(New York Instrumental) (12" white label test pressing) | 300 |
| 84 | Rough Trade | RT 146 | What Difference Does It Make?/Back To The Old House (white label test pressing) | 50 |
| 84 | Rough Trade | RTT 146 | What Difference Does It Make?/Back To The Old House/These Things Take Time (12" white label test pressing) | 100 |
| 84 | Rough Trade | R 61 DJ | Still Ill/You've Got Everything Now (test pressing) | 200 |
| 84 | Rough Trade | RT 61 DJ | Still Ill/You've Got Everything Now (promo) | 25 |
| 84 | Rough Trade | ROUGH 61 | THE SMITHS (white label test pressing) | 30 |

| | | | |
|---|---|---|---|
| 84 | Rough Trade RT 131 | Hand In Glove (one-sided white label 1984 test pressing) | 100 |
| 84 | Rough Trade RT 131 | Hand In Glove/Handsome Devil (white label test pressing for 1984 repressing) | 100 |
| 84 | Rough Trade RT 156 | Heaven Knows I'm Miserable Now/Suffer Little Children (one-sided test pressing) | 200 |
| 84 | Rough Trade RT 156 | Heaven Knows I'm Miserable Now/Suffer Little Children (rejected white label test pressing with extended version) | 800 |
| 84 | Rough Trade RTT 156 | Heaven Knows I'm Miserable Now/Girl Afraid/Suffer Little Children (rejected 12" white label test pressing with extended version) | 800 |
| 84 | Rough Trade RT 156 | Heaven Knows I'm Miserable Now/Suffer Little Children (standard white label test pressing) | 20 |
| 84 | Rough Trade RTT 156 | Heaven Knows I'm Miserable Now/Girl Afraid/Suffer Little Children (standard 12" white label test pressing) | 200 |
| 84 | Rough Trade RT 166 | William, It Was Really Nothing/Please Please Please Let Me Get What I Want (white label test pressing) | 20 |
| 84 | Rough Trade RTT 166 | William, It Was Really Nothing/How Soon Is Now?/Please Please Please Let Me Get What I Want (12" white label test pressing) | 100 |
| 84 | Rough Trade ROUGH 76 | HATFUL OF HOLLOW (white label test pressing) | 30 |
| 84 | Copymasters | HATFUL OF HOLLOW (cassette, early version with unreleased tracks) | 100 |
| 85 | Rough Trade RTT 171 | Barbarism Begins At Home (12", 2 different 1-sided white label test pressings) | 500 |
| 85 | Rough Trade RTT 171 | Barbarism Begins At Home (12" one-sided, promo) | 85 |
| 85 | Rough Trade RTT 171 | Barbarism Begins At Home (edited version)/(long version) | 45 |
| 85 | Rough Trade RTT 171 | Barbarism Begins At Home (12", p/s, one-sided promo) | 40 |
| 85 | Rough Trade RT 176 | How Soon Is Now?/Oscillate Wildly (white label test pressing with Oscillate Wildly instead of Well I Wonder on the B-side) | 400 |
| 85 | Rough Trade RTT 176 | How Soon Is Now?/Well I Wonder/Oscillate Wildly (12" white label test pressing) | 200 |
| 85 | Rough Trade ROUGH 81 | MEAT IS MURDER (white label test pressing) | 300 |
| 85 | Rough Trade RT 181 | Shakespeare's Sister/What She Said (white label test pressing) | 200 |
| 85 | Rough Trade RT 186 | Meat Is Murder/Nowhere Fast/Stretch Out And Wait (live EP, unissued, test pressings only) | 1000 |
| 85 | Rough Trade RT 186 | Meat Is Murder/Nowhere Fast/Stretch Out And Wait (live EP, unissued, Mayking test pressings - beware of counterfeits!) | 500 |
| 85 | Rough Trade RTT 186 | Meat Is Murder/William It Was Really Nothing/Nowhere Fast/Stretch Out And Wait /Miserable Lie (live 12" EP, unissued, test pressings only-beware of counterfeits!) | 1000 |
| 85 | Rough Trade RT 186 | That Joke Isn't Funny Anymore/Meat Is Murder (live) (white label test pressing) | 100 |
| 85 | RT 186 | That Joke Isn't Funny Anymore/Meat Is Murder (live) (Mayking test pressing) | 300 |
| 85 | Rough Trade RTT 191 | The Boy With The Thorn In His Side/Rubber Ring/Asleep (white label test pressing) | 20 |
| 86 | Rough Trade RT 192 | Bigmouth Strikes Again/Money Changes Everything (white label test pressing) | 200 |
| 86 | Rough Trade RTT 192 | Bigmouth Strikes Again/Money Changes Everything/Unloveable (12" white label test pressing) | 30 |
| 86 | Rough Trade ROUGH 96 | THE QUEEN IS DEAD (white label test pressing) | 150 |
| 86 | Rough Trade ROUGH 96 | THE QUEEN IS DEAD (Mayking test pressing) | 300 |
| 86 | Rough Trade RTT 193 | Panic/Vicar In A Tutu/The Draize Train (12" white label test pressing with promo posters) | 50 |
| 86 | Rough Trade RT 194 | Ask/Cemetry Gates (white label test pressing) | 250 |
| 87 | Rough Trade RTT 195 | You Just Haven't Earned It Yet Baby/London/Half A Person (12", white label test pressing) | 800 |
| 87 | Rough Trade ROUGH 101 | THE WORLD WON'T LISTEN (white label test pressing) | 20 |
| 87 | Rough Trade RT 196 | Sheila Take A Bow/Is It Really So Strange? (white label test pressing) | 200 |
| 87 | Rough Trade ROUGH 255 | LOUDER THAN BOMBS (2-LP, white label test pressings) | 200 |
| 87 | Rough Trade RT 197 | Girlfriend In A Coma/Work Is A Four Letter Word (white label test pressing) | 200 |
| 87 | Rough Trade ROUGH 106 | STRANGEWAYS, HERE WE COME (white label test pressing) | 20 |
| 87 | Rough Trade RT 198 | I Started Something I Couldn't Finish/Pretty Girls Make Graves (Troy Tate demo) (white label test pressing) | 200 |
| 87 | Rough Trade RT 198 | I Started Something I Couldn't Finish/Pretty Girls Make Graves (Mayking test pressing) | 500 |
| 87 | Rough Trade RT 166-B | How Soon Is Now? (1-sided white label test pressing for B-side of re-issued William, It Was Really Nothing 7") | 200 |
| 88 | Rough Trade ROUGH 126 | RANK (white label test pressing; in misprinted sleeve, no cover star or title on sleeve, just states 'The Smiths') | 200 |
| 88 | Rough Trade ROUGH 126 | RANK (white label test pressing) | 20 |
| 06 | Universal (No Cat. No) | THE SMITHS (2-CD Publishing sampler with 'The World Won't Listen' artwork on cover) | 80 |

*(see also Morrissey, Sandie Shaw, The The, Electronic)*

## SMITHY ALL STARS

| | | | |
|---|---|---|---|
| 71 | Hillcrest HCT 3 | Witchfinder General/Deserted | 5 |

*(see also Ian Smith & Inner Mind)*

## SMOG

| | | | |
|---|---|---|---|
| 95 | City Slang EFAD 49517 | A Hit/Wine Stained Lips (p/s, yellow vinyl) | 6 |
| 96 | Domino RUG 45T | KICKING A COUPLE AROUND EP (12") | 15 |
| 97 | Domino RUG 58 | Ex Con/Just Like Napoleon | 6 |
| 95 | City Slang 049521 | WILD LOVE (LP) | 20 |
| 97 | Domino WIGLP 3 | RED APPLE FALLS (LP) | 18 |
| 99 | Domino WIGLP 60 | KNOCK KNOCK (LP) | 18 |
| 00 | Domino WIGLP 7 | DONGS OF SEVOTION (2-LP) | 18 |
| 01 | Domino WIGLP 99 | RAIN ON LENS (LP) | 18 |
| 03 | Domino WIGLP 127 | SUPPER (LP) | 18 |
| 05 | Domino WIGLP 158 | A RIVER AIN'T TOO MUCH TO LOVE (LP) | 25 |

## SMOKE (1)

| | | | |
|---|---|---|---|
| 67 | Columbia DB 8115 | My Friend Jack/We Can Take It | 40 |
| 67 | Columbia DB 8252 | If The Weather's Sunny/I Would If I Could, But I Can't | 35 |
| 67 | Columbia DB 8252 | If The Weather's Sunny/I Would If I Could, But I Can't (in export p/s) | 80 |
| 67 | Island WIP 6023 | It Could Be Wonderful/Have Some More Tea | 70 |
| 68 | Island WIP 6031 | Utterly Simple/Sydney Gill (unreleased) | 0 |
| 71 | Pageant SAM 101 | Ride Ride Ride/Guy Fawkes | 12 |

| 72 | Regal Zonophone RZ 3071 | Sugar Man/That's What I Want | 25 |
| 74 | Decca FR 13484 | Shagalagalu/Gimme Good Loving | 5 |
| 74 | Decca FR 13514 | My Lullaby/Looking High | 15 |
| 70s | Gull 128 301 | IT'S SMOKE TIME (LP, reissue of German-only LP) | 20 |
| 88 | M. Blue Town MBT 5001 | MY FRIEND JACK (LP) | 15 |

*(see also Shots)*

## SMOKE (2)
| 70 | Revolution Pop REVP 1002 | Dreams Of Dreams/My Birth | 150 |

## SMOKESTACK CRUMBLE
| 71 | Dawn DNS 1013 | Got A Bad Leg/Whiskey Macaroni | 12 |

## SMOKESTACK LIGHTNIN'
| 68 | Bell BLL 1046 | Light In My Window/Long Stemmed Eyes (John's Song) | 15 |
| 69 | Bell MBLL/SBLL 116 | OFF THE WALL (LP) | 40 |

## SMOKEY BABE
| 62 | 77' LA 12-12 | SMOKEY BABE AND HIS FRIENDS (LP) | 25 |

## SMOKEY CIRCLES
| 70 | Carnaby CNS4011 | Long Live Love/Love Me While You Can | 5 |
| 70 | Carnaby CNLS 6006 | THE SMOKEY CIRCLES ALBUM (LP, union jack flag label) | 60 |

## SMOKEY SMOTHERS
| 69 | Polydor 623 239 | THE DRIVING BLUES (LP) | 50 |

## SMOKIE
| 75 | RAK SRAK 510 | PASS IT AROUND (LP) | 15 |
| 75 | RAK SRAK 517 | CHANGING ALL THE TIME (LP) | 15 |
| 76 | RAK SRAK 520 | MIDNIGHT CAFE (LP) | 20 |
| 77 | RAK SRAK 530 | BRIGHT LIGHTS AND BACK ALLEYS (LP) | 20 |
| 79 | RAK SRAK 6757 | THE OTHER SIDE OF THE ROAD (LP) | 15 |
| 81 | RAK SREAK 545 | SOLID GROUND (LP) | 15 |
| 82 | RAK SRAK 546 | STRANGERS IN PARADISE (LP) | 18 |

## SMOKIE & HIS SISTER
| 67 | CBS 202605 | Creators Of Rain/In Dreams Of Silent Seas | 10 |

## THE SMOKIN' MOJO FILTERS
| 95 | Go! Discs GOD 136 | Come Together/THE BEAUTIFUL SOUTH: A Minute's Silence/DODGY: Is It Me/BLACK GRAPE: In The Name Of The Father (Crown Of Thorns Mix) (7") | 5 |

*(See also Paul Weller, Oasis)*

## SMOKIN' ROADIE
| 83 | Zone To Zone ZON 3 | Midnight/Ripp Off (p/s) | 30 |

## SMOOTH BUT HAZZARDOUS
| 92 | Basement BRSS 007 | Smooth But Hazzardous/Made U Dance/Violent Headrush (12") | 20 |
| 93 | Sound Entity SENT 1200 | We Are The Creator/Push Up The Levels (12") | 40 |
| 93 | Sound Entity SENT 1205 | Made You Dance (Carl Cox Remix)/Push Up The Levels (SBH Remix)/Push Up The Levels (Originla Mix) (12") | 15 |
| 94 | Sinister SNS 003 | Help Me/DMX Override (12") | 10 |

## JACK SMOOTH
| 91 | Sound Entity SE 001 | WAVEFORMS EP (12") | 15 |
| 91 | Sound Entity SE 03 | Untitled/Untitled/Untitled/Untitled (12", white label, hand-written labels, some in stamped sleeve) | 15 |
| 93 | Sound Entity SENT 1201 | Tell Me Something/Happy Nonsense (12", with Spencer T) | 20 |
| 93 | Sound Entity SENT 120220 | HURTS EP (12", with Alex Reece) | 40 |

*(see also Ruff With The Smooth, DJ Chemistry Meets Jack Smooth)*

## SMUDGE
| 94 | Domino WIGLP 7 | MANILOW (LP, with free 7") | 18 |

## SMYLE
| 71 | CBS 7225 | Glory Glory/Will I Get Back Tomorrow | 8 |

## DES SMYTH & COLLEGEMEN
| 65 | Pye 7N 15867 | The Pillow That Whispers/Lonely Streets | 5 |
| 65 | Pye 7N 15996 | Wedding Bells/All For The Love Of A Girl | 5 |

## GILLI SMYTH & MOTHER GONG
| 78 | Charly CRL 5007 | MOTHER (LP, with insert) | 15 |

*(see also Gong)*

## DONALD SMYTHE
| 71 | Punch PH 83 | Where Love Goes/HURRICANES: You Can Run | 40 |

## GLORIA SMYTHE
| 60 | Vogue V 9159 | I'll Be Over After A While/Gee Baby Ain't I Good To You | 10 |

## SNAFU
| 74 | WWA WWS 007 | Dixie Queen/Monday Morning | 5 |
| 74 | WWA WWA 003 | SNAFU (LP, gatefold sleeve) | 18 |

*(see also Whitesnake, Freedom)*

## SNAKEBITE
| 83 | Astor ASTOR 1 | Blow You Away/Thin Ice (no p/s) | 25 |

## SNAKEFINGER
| 80 | Do It RIDE5 | GREENER POSTURES (LP) | 15 |

*(see also The Residents, Chilli Willi)*

## SNAKES
| 76 | Dynamite DYR45006 | Teenage Head/Lights Out (p/s) | 8 |

*(see also The Motors)*

## SNAPE
| 73 | Transatlantic TRA 269 | ACCIDENTALLY BORN IN NEW ORLEANS (LP) | 22 |

*(see also Alexis Korner)*
### SNAPPERS (1)
| | | | |
|---|---|---|---|
| 59 | Top Rank JAR 167 | Big Bill/If There Were | 18 |
| 59 | Top Rank JAR 167 | Big Bill/If There Were (78) | 25 |

### SNAPPERS (2)
| | | | |
|---|---|---|---|
| 67 | CBS 2719 | Upside Down Inside Out/Memories | 40 |

### SNATCH (1)
| | | | |
|---|---|---|---|
| 75 | Polydor 2058619 | For Always And Ever/Hunting Kind | 12 |

### SNATCH (2)
| | | | |
|---|---|---|---|
| 78 | Lightning LIG 502 | Stanley/I.R.T. (p/s) | 10 |
| 78 | Lightning LIG 505 | All I Want/When I'm Bored ('foil' p/s) | 10 |
| 80 | Fetish FET 004 | Shopping For Clothes/Joey/Red Army (12", die-cut p/s) | 20 |

*(see also Johnny Thunders, Judy Nylon)*
### SNATCH BACK
| | | | |
|---|---|---|---|
| 79 | CSS CS 002 | Eastern Lady/Cryin' To The Night (no p/s) | 80 |

### SNEAKER PIMPS
| | | | |
|---|---|---|---|
| 96 | Clean Up CUP020LP | BECOMING X (LP) | 50 |
| 99 | Clean Up CUP040LP | SPLINTER (2-LP) | 30 |
| 02 | Tommy Boy TBV 1532 | BLOODSPORT (2-LP, red vinyl) | 30 |
| 08 | Clean Up CUP020DMM | BECOMING X (2-LP, reissue, 1000 only, stickered sleeve) | 25 |
| 08 | Clean Up CUP040DMM | SPLINTER (2-LP, reissue, 1000 only, stickered sleeve) | 25 |

### SNEAKERS
| | | | |
|---|---|---|---|
| 77 | Petal PTL 010 | Link Lady/Vapour Trails (no p/s, 500 only) | 150 |

### SNEAKY PETES
| | | | |
|---|---|---|---|
| 60 | Decca F 11199 | Savage (Parts 1 & 2) | 15 |

### SNEEKERS
| | | | |
|---|---|---|---|
| 64 | Columbia DB 7385 | I Just Can't Get To Sleep/Bald Headed Woman | 150 |

### SNEEKY FEELINS
| | | | |
|---|---|---|---|
| 79 | Warped W102 | Private Mail/Only The Rain (p/s with insert) | 50 |

### DAVID SNELL
| | | | |
|---|---|---|---|
| 66 | Decca SKL 4745 | THE SUBTLE SOUND OF DAVID SNELL (LP) | 15 |

### LEN SNIDER
| | | | |
|---|---|---|---|
| 63 | London HLU 9790 | Everyone Knows/I'll Be Coming Home Tonight | 8 |

### SNIFF 'N' THE TEARS
| | | | |
|---|---|---|---|
| 79 | Chiswick NS 40 | Driver's Seat (cancelled, test pressings only, picture sleeve) | 15 |

### SNIFTERS
| | | | |
|---|---|---|---|
| 78 | Lightning GIL 534 | I Like Boys/Baby Punker | 15 |

### SNIPERS
| | | | |
|---|---|---|---|
| 81 | Crass 321984/4 | THREE PEACE SUITE (EP) | 12 |

### SNIVELLING SHITS
| | | | |
|---|---|---|---|
| 77 | Ghetto Rockers PRE 2 | Terminal Stupid/I Can't Come (p/s, first pressing of 500,paper labels/black print) | 60 |
| 77 | Ghetto Rockers PRE 2 | Terminal Stupid/I Can't Come (p/s, 2nd pressing, plastic labels/juke box centre) | 25 |
| 89 | Damaged Goods FNARR 4 | Isgodoman?/Terminal Stupid/I Can't Come (p/s) | 20 |
| 89 | Dam. Goods FNARR4B | Isgodoman?/Terminal Stupid/I Can't Come (box set with badge & inserts, pink vinyl in stamped plain white sleeve) | 25 |

*(see also Doctor Dark)*
### SNOBS
| | | | |
|---|---|---|---|
| 64 | Decca F 11867 | Buckle Shoe Stomp/Stand And Deliver | 15 |

### SNOOKY & MOODY
| | | | |
|---|---|---|---|
| 66 | Blue Horizon 45-1003 | Snooky And Moody's Blues/Telephone Blues (99 copies only) | 150 |

### HANK SNOW (& RAINBOW RANCH BOYS)
| | | | |
|---|---|---|---|
| 54 | HMV 7MC 7 | Why Do You Punish Me (For Loving You)/When Mexican Joe Meets Jole Blon (with Rainbow Ranch Boys) (export issue) | 15 |
| 54 | HMV 7MC 15 | Spanish Fire Ball/Between Fire And Water (with Rainbow Ranch Boys)(export issue) | 15 |
| 54 | HMV 7MC 24 | My Arabian Baby/I Don't Hurt Anymore (with Rainbow Ranch Boys) (export issue) | 15 |
| 54 | HMV 7MC 25 | My Religion's Not Old-Fashioned (But It's Real Genuine)/The Alphabet (with Rainbow Ranch Boys) (export issue) | 15 |
| 54 | HMV 7MC 31 | Yellow Roses/Would You Mind (with Rainbow Ranch Boys) (export issue) | 15 |
| 59 | RCA RCA 1151 | Old Shep/The Last Ride | 10 |
| 61 | RCA RCA 1248 | Poor Little Jimmie/Beggar To A King | 5 |
| 59 | RCA RCX 142 | COUNTRY GUITAR NO. 7 (EP) | 10 |
| 63 | RCA RCX 7125 | WHEN TRAGEDY STRUCK (EP) | 10 |
| 64 | RCA RCX 7154 | THAT COUNTRY GENTLEMAN (EP) | 12 |
| 59 | RCA RD 27115 | WHEN TRAGEDY STRUCK (LP) | 15 |

*(see also Chet Atkins)*
### SNOW PATROL
| | | | |
|---|---|---|---|
| 98 | Jeepster JPR7 005 | One Hundred Things You Should Have Done In Bed/My Last Girlfriend (p/s) | 8 |
| 98 | Jeepster JPR7004 | Little Hide/Sticky Teenage Twin (1,000 only, p/s) | 18 |
| 98 | Jeepster JPR7 007 | Velocity Girl/Absolute Gravity (p/s) | 8 |
| 03 | Polydor 986712-1 | Spitting Games/Wow (Acoustic) (white vinyl, p/s) | 7 |
| 04 | Polydor 986 977-8 | How To Be Dead/You Are My Joy (live) (p/s) | 5 |
| 04 | Polydor 981635 4W | Run/Post Punk Progression (white vinyl) | 5 |
| 06 | Fiction 0602517043985 | Chasing Cars/Play Me Like You Own Hand (p/s, with inner p/s) | 25 |
| 98 | Jeepster JPRLP004 | SONGS FOR POLAR BEARS (LP) | 40 |
| 03 | Polydor 9866073 | FINAL STRAW (LP) | 15 |
| 08 | Fiction 1785268 | A HUNDRED MILLION SUNS (2 x 12" 45 rpm, gatefold) | 20 |
| 09 | Fiction 272201-1 | UP TO NOW (box set, 3-LP, CD, DVD) | 50 |

*(see also Shrug)*

**SNUFF**
88    Deceptive                         TWEET TWEET MY LOVELY (LP, with insert) ................................................. 15

**SNUGGY**
71    Philips 6006138                   Creole Jive/Jungle King ......................................................................... 12
*(see also Jade Warrior)*

**RON SNYDER**
63    Parlophone R 4993                 Oh My Twisted Bach/Narcissus ............................................................... 6

**SO WHAT!**
86    No label or Cat. No.              It Is All Over/Now I Don't Want You Around (no p/s) ............................. 50
70    CBS 5005                          Flowers/Tell Me Now ............................................................................ 10

**S.O.B.**
89    Rise Above RISE 002               THRASH NIGHT EP (p/s) ....................................................................... 12

**ERROL SOBERS**
70    Beacon BEA 159                    Sugar Shaker/You're In Love ................................................................ 12
*(see also Bobby Bridger)*

**SOCIALITES**
64    Warner Bros WB 148                Jive Jimmy/You're Losing Your Touch ................................................... 40

**SOCIAL SECURITY**
78    Heartbeat PULSE 1                 I Don't Want My Heart To Rule My Head/Stella's Got A Fella/Cider/Choc Ice (p/s) ....... 30

**SOCIETIE**
67    Deram DM 162                      Bird Has Flown/Breaking Down ............................................................. 60

**SO CONFUSING AND SO VERY CLEAR**
76    CFC 19776                         SO CONFUSING AND SO VERY CLEAR (LP) ............................................. 70

**SOCRATES**
72    Deram DM 362                      Eating Momma's Cookin'/Dearest Agnes ............................................... 15

**SODS (1)**
79    Tap TAP 1                         Mopey Grape/Negative Positive (p/s) ................................................... 30
79    Stortbeat SB 5                    No Pictures Of Us/Plaything (p/s) ....................................................... 40

**SODS (2)**
79    Step Forward SFLP 3               MINUTES TO GO (LP) ............................................................................ 30

**SOFERNO B**
80    Soferno B SOLP 001                IN DUB (LP) ......................................................................................... 70

**SOFT BOYS**
77    Raw RAW 5                         GIVE IT TO THE SOFT BOYS (EP, acetate with withdrawn track, Vyrna Knowl Is A Headbanger in place of "Ventilator") ....................... 200
77    Raw RAW 5                         GIVE IT TO THE SOFT BOYS (EP) ......................................................... 20
78    Radar ADA 8                       (I Want To Be An) Anglepoise Lamp/Fat Man's Son (p/s) ...................... 15
79    Raw RAW 37                        GIVE IT TO THE SOFT BOYS (EP, unreleased reissue) ........................... 0
79    Raw RAW 41                        Where Are The Prawns (unreleased) .................................................. 0
80    Armageddon AS 005                 I Wanna Destroy You/I'm An Old Pervert (Disco) (p/s) ...................... 10
81    Armageddon AS 029                 Only The Stones Remain/The Asking Tree (p/s) ................................. 8
82    Bucketfull Of Brains BOB 1        Love Poisoning/When I Was A Kid (p/s, with Bucketfull Of Brains magazine) ...... 15
82    Bucketfull Of Brains BOB 1        Love Poisoning/When I Was A Kid (p/s, without Bucketfull Of Brains magazine) ...... 12
83    Midnight Music DING 4             He's A Reptile/Song No. 4 (p/s, 2 different designs) ........................... 8
89    Overground OVER 4                 The Face Of Death/The Yodelling Hoover (p/s, 600 yellow viny or 400 white vinyl) ...... 6
89    Overground OVER 4                 The Face Of Death/The Yodelling Hoover (p/s, 15 gold test pressings) ...... 15
85    Delorean SOFT 1P                  WADING THROUGH A VENTILATOR (12" EP, picture disc) ................... 10
79    Two Crabs CLAW 1001               A CAN OF BEES (LP, original issue, black & white labels) ................... 30
80    Aura AUL 709                      A CAN OF BEES (LP, reissue) ............................................................. 15
80    Armageddon ARM 1                  UNDERWATER MOONLIGHT (LP) ....................................................... 25
83    M. Music CHIME 0002               INVISIBLE HITS (LP) .......................................................................... 15
84    Two Crabs CLAW 1001               A CAN OF BEES (LP, 2nd reissue, black & red labels) ....................... 15
86    Living Cream MOIST 1              UNDERWATER MOONLIGHT (LP, reissue) ....................................... 15
87    Glass Fish MOIST 4                LIVE AT THE PORTLAND ARMS (LP) ................................................... 20
*(see also Robyn Hitchcock, Kimberley Rew)*

**SOFT CELL**
80    Big Frock ABF 1                   MUTANT MOMENTS (EP, plain p/s with postcard; beware of counterfeits without postcard & in wraparound p/s!) ...... 70
81    Some Bizzare HARD 1               A Man Can Get Lost/Memorabilia (p/s, 10,000 only) ........................ 10
81    Some Bizzare HARD 12              Memorabilia (Extended)/Persuasion (Extended) (12", p/s) .............. 10
81    Some Bizzare BZS 212              Tainted Love/Where Did Our Love Go/Tainted Dub/Memorabilia (12", p/s, limited edition with 4 tracks) ...... 10
81    Some Bizzare No Cat. No.          Metro Mr. X/B-MOVIE: Remembrance Day (white label test pressing) ...... 60
82    Some Bizzare CELBX 1              THE 12" SINGLES (6 x 12" box set, with booklet) ............................... 50
84    Some Bizzare BZSR 2212            Down In The Subway (Remix)/Disease And Desire/Born To Lose (12", p/s) ...... 18
*(see also Marc Almond, Marc & Mambas, Anne Hogan)*

**SOFT PEDALLING**
70    Decca F 23034                     It's So Nice/Rolling On Home .............................................................. 5

**SOFT ROCK**
72    Philips 6308                      INVENTION (LP) ................................................................................... 15

**SOFT DRINKS**
82    Outer Himalayan OH 4              Pepsi Cola/Pop Stars In Their Pyjames (with booklet and sticker) ...... 40

**SOFTIES**
77    Charly CYS 1036                   Suicide Pilot/C.I. Angel (p/s) ............................................................. 5
78    Charly CYS 1047                   KILLING TIME EP .................................................................................. 6
*(see also Captain Sensible)*

**MICK SOFTLEY**
65    Immediate IM 014                  I'm So Confused/She's My Girl ............................................................ 40

| | | | |
|---|---|---|---|
| 67 | CBS 202469 | Am I The Red One/That's Not My Kind Of Love | 200 |
| 70 | CBS 5130 | Can You Hear Me Now/Time Machine | 7 |
| 71 | CBS 7337 | Goin' Down The Road/Gypsy | 7 |
| 72 | CBS 8269 | Lady Willow/From The Land Of The Crab | 7 |
| 65 | Columbia 33SX 1781 | SONGS FOR SWINGIN' SURVIVORS (LP) | 150 |
| 70 | CBS 64098 | SUNRISE (LP, gatefold sleeve) | 80 |
| 71 | CBS 64395 | STREET SINGER (LP) | 40 |
| 72 | CBS 64841 | ANY MOTHER DOESN'T GRUMBLE (LP) | 40 |

## SOFT MACHINE

| | | | |
|---|---|---|---|
| 67 | Polydor 56151 | Love Makes Sweet Music/Reelin' Feelin' Squeelin' | 175 |
| 78 | Harvest HAR 5155 | Soft Space (Parts 1 & 2) (p/s) | 8 |
| 69 | Probe SPB 1002 | THE SOFT MACHINE VOLUME TWO (LP, 1st pressing, black/silver label, laminated flipback sleeve) | 80 |
| 69 | Probe SPB 1002 | THE SOFT MACHINE VOLUME TWO (LP, 2nd pressing, pink label, laminated flipback sleeve) | 70 |
| 70 | CBS 66246 | THIRD (2-LP, gatefold) | 45 |
| 71 | CBS 64280 | FOURTH (LP, embossed textured sleeve) | 35 |
| 72 | Probe GTSP 204 | VOLUMES ONE AND TWO (2-LP, yellow labels) | 25 |
| 72 | CBS 64806 | FIFTH (LP) | 25 |
| 73 | CBS 68214 | SIX (2-LP, gatefold sleeve) | 25 |
| 73 | CBS 65799 | SEVEN (LP, gatefold sleeve) | 20 |
| 75 | Harvest SHSP 4044 | BUNDLES (LP, with inner sleeve) | 20 |
| 76 | Harvest SHSP 4056 | SOFTS (LP) | 20 |
| 77 | Harvest SHTW 800 | TRIPLE ECHO (3-LP, box set, with colour booklet) | 50 |
| 78 | Harvest SHSP 4083 | ALIVE & WELL (LP) | 18 |
| 78 | ABC ABCD 602 | THE COLLECTION (2-LP, this is One and Two from same stampers as the 1972 2-LP set VOLUMES ONE AND TWO) | 20 |
| 81 | EMI EMC 3348 | LAND OF COCKAYNE (LP) | 15 |
| 87 | Big Beat WIKA 57 | SOFT MACHINE (LP, reissue) | 18 |
| 87 | Big Beat WIKA 58 | VOLUME TWO (LP, reissue) | 18 |
| 88 | Reckless RECKLP5 | LIVE AT THE PROMS (LP) | 15 |
| 88 | Decal LIKD 35 | THIRD (2-LP, reissue) | 20 |

(see also Robert Wyatt, Kevin Ayers, Hugh Hopper, Elton Dean, Daevid Allen, Matching Mole, 'Igginbottom, Lyn Dobson)

## SOFTNESS

| | | | |
|---|---|---|---|
| 80 | Remedy RM 119 | You Ain't My Lover/Locked Doors | 30 |

## SOFT SHOE

| | | | |
|---|---|---|---|
| 78 | Aardvark AARD 1 | FOR THOSE ALONE (LP, with insert) | 100 |

## SOFT TARGETS

| | | | |
|---|---|---|---|
| 83 | Hard Labour HAL 1 | Clive Steps South/Susan | 8 |

## SOFT TOUCH (1)

| | | | |
|---|---|---|---|
| 67 | W+G WG 001 | A Silent Life/Ellusive Face (Private Pressing) | 300 |

## SOFT TOUCH (2)

| | | | |
|---|---|---|---|
| 73 | Acorn AC 04 | Crazy Child/Down And Out | 20 |

## SOHEP

| | | | |
|---|---|---|---|
| 81 | Merciful Release MR 3 | So Much Fun/You Could Be So Nice Dear (p/s) | 10 |

## SOHO JETS

| | | | |
|---|---|---|---|
| 75 | Polydor 2058 525 | Hi Heel Tarzan/Night Flight | 20 |
| 75 | Polydor 2058 598 | Denim Goddess/Smile | 20 |

(see also Razar, Nervous Germans)

## SOHO SKIFFLE GROUP

| | | | |
|---|---|---|---|
| 57 | Melodisc EMP 7 72 | SOHO SKIFFLE GROUP (EP) | 75 |

## SOL INVICTUS

| | | | |
|---|---|---|---|
| 90 | Cerne 004 | Abbatoirs Of Love/CURRENT 93: This Ain't The Summer Of Love (live in Japan, gig freebie, 93 with insert & gig ticket) | 50 |
| 90 | Cerne 004 | Abbatoirs Of Love/CURRENT 93: This Ain't The Summer Of Love (live in Japan, gig freebie, [200 without insert]) | 25 |
| 91 | Shock SX 016 | See The Dove Fall/Somewhere In Europe (numbered foldover p/s in poly bag, 1,000 only) | 15 |
| 91 | World Serpent WS7 002 | Looking For Europe (1-sided, etched B-side, foldover sleeve in poly bag, 963 only) | 15 |
| 89 | SVL SVL 009 | IN THE JAWS OF THE SERPENT (LP, with insert) | 20 |
| 90 | Tursa 001 | TREES IN WINTER (LP) | 30 |
| 90 | Tursa 002 | LEX TALIONIS (CD, special edit in leather wallet) | 30 |
| 91 | Tursa 003 | KILLING TIDE (LP) | 25 |
| 00 | Tursa 026 | EVE (picture disc, 1,000 only) | 20 |
| 01 | Tursa 029 | HILL OF CROSSES (LP, 1,000 only, signed) | 20 |

(see also Current 93, Death In June, Nurse With Wound, Karl Blake, Shock Headed Peters)

## SOLAR PLEXUS

| | | | |
|---|---|---|---|
| 73 | Polydor 2383 222 | SOLAR PLEXUS (LP) | 35 |

## SOLDIER

| | | | |
|---|---|---|---|
| 82 | Heavy Metal HEAVY 12 | Sheralee/Force (p/s, with postcard) | 35 |
| 82 | Heavy Metal HEAVY 12 | Sheralee/Force (p/s, without postcard) | 25 |
| 04 | Killer Metal KMRS 001 | Murderous Night/I'm Taken In (red vinyl, 500 copies, numbered) | 7 |

## SOLDIER DOLLS

| | | | |
|---|---|---|---|
| 83 | Scream 1 | WHAT DO THEY KNOW? (EP) | 15 |
| 84 | Scream 2 | A TASTE OF BLOOD (EP, red vinyl) | 15 |

## SOLDIERS OF FORTUNE

| | | | |
|---|---|---|---|
| 83 | Total Darkness TD 1 | Stars/Autonomia (fold-out p/s) | 7 |

## SOLENT

| | | | |
|---|---|---|---|
| 73 | Decca F 13375 | My World Fell Down/The Sound Of Summer's Over | 10 |

## SOLID GOLD CADILLAC
| | | |
|---|---|---|
| 73 | RCA SF 8311 | SOLID GOLD CADILLAC (LP) ........................................ 30 |
| 73 | RCA SF 8365 | BRAIN DAMAGE (LP) ................................................... 45 |

*(see also Battered Ornaments, Chris Spedding, Mike Westbrook)*

## SOLID N MIND
| | | |
|---|---|---|
| 90 | Liberty Grooves LIB001 | An Original Break (12") ............................................. 30 |
| 91 | Liberty Grooves PPP001 | Centre Stage/Woke With Nuthin' (Promo cassette) ...... 15 |
| 91 | Liberty Grooves LIB 002 1/2 | Centre Stage/Woke With Nothin' (12") ...................... 15 |
| 92 | Liberty Grooves LIB 003 | Battle Tipped Rhyme (12") ....................................... 18 |

## SOLID ROCK BAND
| | | |
|---|---|---|
| 78 | Chapel Lane RWA 1 | FOOTPRINTS ON THE WATER (LP, gatefold sleeve) ......... 15 |

## SOLID SPACE
| | | |
|---|---|---|
| 82 | In Phaze IP 011 | SPACE MUSEUM (cassette) ....................................... 150 |

## SOLITAIRES
| | | |
|---|---|---|
| 58 | London HLM 8745 | Walking Along/Please Kiss This Letter ...................... 130 |
| 58 | London HLM 8745 | Walking Along/Please Kiss This Letter (78) ................ 60 |

## JAKE SOLLO
| | | |
|---|---|---|
| 79 | Pye N 102 | JAKE SOLLO (LP) ...................................................... 15 |

## NORMAN SOLOMAN
| | | |
|---|---|---|
| 81 | Black Joy DH 816 | Joy Bells Ringing/JAYS: Unity Call (12") ..................... 25 |

## SOLSTICE (1)
| | | |
|---|---|---|
| 84 | Equinox EQRLP 001 | SILENT DANCE (LP, gatefold sleeve) ........................... 18 |

## SOLSTICE (2)
| | | |
|---|---|---|
| 08 | Iron Kodex IK 003 | ONLY THE STRONG SURVIVE (2-LP with free 7") ............ 20 |

## SOLUTION
| | | |
|---|---|---|
| 71 | EMI 2023 | Divergence/Fever ...................................................... 6 |
| 72 | Decca SKL-R 5124 | SOLUTION (LP) .......................................................... 25 |

## SOME CHICKEN
| | | |
|---|---|---|
| 77 | Raw RAW 7 | New Religion/Blood On The Wall (p/s) ...................... 20 |
| 78 | Raw RAW 13 | Arabian Daze/No. 7 ................................................... 15 |
| 78 | Raw RAW 13 | Arabian Daze/No. 7 (purple vinyl) ........................... 120 |

## SOME OF MY BEST FRIENDS ARE CANADIAN
| | | |
|---|---|---|
| 80 | Bulge BLAST 4 | Feeling Sheepish/Speaking Clock ............................... 20 |

## SOMEONE'S BAND
| | | |
|---|---|---|
| 70 | Deram DM 313 | Story/Give It To You ................................................. 40 |
| 70 | Deram SML 1068 | SOMEONE'S BAND (LP) ............................................ 450 |

## SOMERVILLE GENTLEMAN'S BAND
| | | |
|---|---|---|
| 80 | Somerville PLR 026 | FAR FROM HOME (LP, gatefold insert with sticker over 'Plant Life' logo) ..................... 25 |

## ELKE SOMMER
| | | |
|---|---|---|
| 61 | Columbia DB 4688 | Be Not Notty/The Faithful Hussar ............................... 5 |

## JOANIE SOMMERS
| | | |
|---|---|---|
| 60 | Warner Bros WB 23 | Be My Love/Why Don't You Do Right? .......................... 7 |
| 60 | Warner Bros WB 31 | Ruby-Duby-Du/Bob White ......................................... 7 |
| 60 | Warner Bros WB 44 | One Boy/I'll Never Be Free ......................................... 7 |
| 61 | Warner Bros WB 71 | Johnny Get Angry/Theme From A Summer Place ........ 10 |
| 62 | Warner Bros WB 85 | Goodbye Joey/Bobby Is Bobby .................................... 7 |
| 63 | Warner Bros WB 105 | Little Girl Bad/Wishing Well ....................................... 7 |
| 64 | Warner Bros WB 78 | When The Boys Get Together/Passing Strangers .......... 7 |
| 65 | Warner Bros WB 150 | If You Love Him/I Think I'm Gonna Cry ..................... 15 |
| 13 | Harkit HRKS 8431 | Don't Pity Me/Johnny Get Angry (p/s) ...................... 15 |
| 60 | Warner Bros WEP 6013 | POSITIVELY THE MOST (EP, also stereo WSEP 2013) ..... 20 |
| 61 | Warner Bros WEP 6047 | THE VOICE OF THE SIXTIES (EP, also stereo WSEP 2047) ... 15 |

*(see also Ed Byrnes)*

## SON OF JOHN
| | | |
|---|---|---|
| 86 | Individual AIRS 104 | People Shouting/Your Interpretation .......................... 8 |

## SONAR NATION
| | | |
|---|---|---|
| 92 | SRT 92 LS 3510 | Some Place Not Home/Master Plan/Hate Photo ......... 10 |

## SONGSTERS
| | | |
|---|---|---|
| 54 | London HL 8100 | Bahama Buggy Ride/It Isn't Right ............................ 150 |

## SON HOUSE
| | | |
|---|---|---|
| 60s | Saydisc Roots SL 504 | THE VOCAL INTENSITY OF SON HOUSE (LP) .................. 40 |
| 66 | CBS (S)BPG 62604 | THE LEGENDARY FATHER OF FOLK BLUES (LP) ............... 35 |
| 70 | Liberty LBS 83391 | JOHN THE REVELATOR (LP) ....................................... 30 |

## SON HOUSE/J.D. SHORT
| | | |
|---|---|---|
| 69 | Xtra XTRA 1080 | DELTA BLUES (LP) ..................................................... 20 |

## SONIA
| | | |
|---|---|---|
| 78 | D Roy DRDD 006 | Love Don't Live Here Any More/D ROY BAND: Version (12") ... 20 |
| 79 | D Roy DRDD 18 | Ooh Baby Baby/Back Street Dub (12") ....................... 12 |
| 79 | Karn-Na KRN 002 | Again (Suddenly You're Mine)/UNDIVIDED ROOTS: Version (12", purple vinyl) ............ 12 |
| 81 | S & S FERGY 001 | Checking It Out/Version (12", with Creation Rebel) ..... 20 |
| 80 | Cha Cha CHAD 26 | Easier To Love/That's The Way You Feel (12", with Earth & Stone) .................... 15 |

## SONIC BOOM
| | | |
|---|---|---|
| 89 | Silvertone ORET 11 | Angel/(Extended Mix)/Help Me Please (Drum Mix) (12", p/s) ... 12 |
| 90 | Silvertone SONIC 1 | Octaves/Tremeloes (10", orange vinyl PVC sleeve, mail-order only) ............... 18 |
| 91 | Silvertone SONIC 2 | (I Love You) To The Moon And Back/Capo Waltz (live) (gig freebie in black die-cut sleeve, promo only, 33rpm) ... 12 |

# SONIC YOUTH

| | | |
|---|---|---|
| 91 | Silvertone SONIC 2 | (I Love You) To The Moon And Back/Capo Waltz (live) (gig freebie in black die-cut sleeve, promo only, 33rpm, p/s later available separately) ....................8 |
| 90 | Silvertone ORE ZLP 506 | SPECTRUM (LP, gatefold rotatable plastic disc sleeve with inner)....................30 |

*(see also Spacemen 3, Spectrum)*

## SONIC YOUTH

| | | |
|---|---|---|
| 86 | Blast First BFFP 3 | Flower/Halloween (12", p/s, some on yellow vinyl)....................18 |
| 86 | Blast First BFFP 3 | Flower/Rewolf (12", p/s, censored version)....................15 |
| 86 | Blast First BFFP 3(B) | (Savage Pencil etch)/Halloween II (12", p/s, A-side engraved, 1st 100 signed) ............65 |
| 86 | Blast First BFFP 3(B) | (Savage Pencil etch)/Halloween II (12", p/s, A-side engraved) ....................40 |
| 86 | Blast First BFFP 3X | Flower/Halloween/Satan Supermix (12", unreleased)....................0 |
| 86 | Blast First BFFP 7 | Starpower (edit)/Bubblegum (p/s, some with badge & poster) ....................20 |
| 88 | Fierce FRIGHT 015/016 | Stick Me Donna Magick Momma/Making The Nature Scene (live) (p/s, 2 x 1-sided 7" with etched B-sides)....................30 |
| 88 | Fierce FRIGHT 015/016 | Stick Me Donna Magick Momma/Making The Nature Scene (live) (p/s, single disc reissue) ....................12 |
| 98 | Geffen GFS 22332 | Sunday/Moist Vagina (p/s)....................8 |
| 88 | Catalogue CAT 064 | Teenage Riot (square flexidisc sewn into 'The Catalogue' magazine)....................15 |
| 89 | Blast First BFFP 46 | Touch Me I'm Sick/MUDHONEY: Halloween (12", p/s)....................15 |
| 89 | Blast First BFDJ1 | Come And Smash Me Said The Boy With The Magic Penis/Magic Wand (die-cut company sleeve) ....................8 |
| 89 | Blast First BFFP 48 | Providence (stereo)/Providence (mono) (promo only)....................6 |
| 91 | DGC 21634 | DIRTY BOOTS (12" EP) ....................15 |
| 92 | DGC DGCS 11 | 100%/Creme Brulee (p/s)....................5 |
| 92 | Geffen DGCV 11 | 100% (10" EP, orange vinyl, numbered p/s) ....................10 |
| 92 | Geffen DGCV 11 | 100% (10" EP, black vinyl promo)....................30 |
| 92 | Geffen DGCT 11 | 100% (12" EP, promo only, white label) ....................40 |
| 92 | Geffen 7-19664 DJ | Personality Crisis/Dirty Boots (DJ promo only) ....................6 |
| 92 | Geffen GFSV26 | YOUTH AGAINST FASCISM (10" white vinyl EP, numbered p/s) ....................10 |
| 92 | Geffen GFST 26 | YOUTH AGAINST FASCISM EP (12", p/s)....................10 |
| 00 | Geffen SONIC 001 | Free City Rhymes/Renegade Princess (7" promo p/s) ....................40 |
| 85 | Blast First BFFP 1 | BAD MOON RISING (LP, with lyric insert) ....................30 |
| 86 | Blast First BFFP 4 | EVOL (LP) ....................30 |
| 87 | Blast First CHAT 1 | SISTER INTERVIEW DISC (LP)....................20 |
| 87 | Blast First BFFP 20 | SISTER (LP) ....................30 |
| 88 | Blast First BFFP 34 | DAYDREAM NATION (2-LP, 1st 1,000 with signed poster) ....................60 |
| 88 | Blast First BFFP 34 | DAYDREAM NATION (2-LP)....................25 |
| 90 | WEA 7599 24297-1 | GOO (LP, with free 7")....................25 |
| 90 | WEA 7599 24297-1 | GOO (LP) ....................25 |
| 92 | Geffen GEF24485[2] | DIRTY (2-LP) ....................35 |
| 93 | Geffen GEF424515 | DAYDREAM NATION (2-LP, reissue, poster) ....................20 |
| 94 | Geffen GEF 24632 | EXPERIMENTAL JET SET, TRASH & NO STAR (LP, blue vinyl) ....................25 |
| 95 | Geffen GEF24825 | WASHING MACHINE (2-LP)....................40 |
| 98 | Geffen GEF 25203 | A THOUSAND LEAVES (2-LP) ....................25 |
| 00 | Geffen 069490650 1 | NYC GHOSTS & FLOWERS (LP) ....................20 |
| 09 | Matador OLE 8721 | BATTERY PARK NYC, JULY 4th 2008 (LP)....................18 |
| 09 | Matador OLE 829-1 | THE ETERNAL (2-LP) ....................20 |

*(see also Mudhoney)*

## SONNY

| | | |
|---|---|---|
| 71 | Ackee ACK 127 | Love And Peace/LARRY & ALVIN: Throw Me Corn....................20 |

## SONNY (& SONNY'S GROUP)

| | | |
|---|---|---|
| 65 | Atlantic AT 4038 | Laugh At Me/Tony (as Sonny & Sonny's Group) ....................10 |
| 65 | Atlantic AT 4060 | The Revolution Kind/Georgia And John Quetzal (as Sonny & Sonny's Group)....................10 |
| 67 | Atlantic 584 131 | I Told My Girl To Go Away/Misty Roses (solo) ....................6 |

*(see also Sonny & Cher)*

## SONNY & CHER

| | | |
|---|---|---|
| 64 | Reprise R 20309 | Baby Don't Go/Walkin' The Quetzal ....................8 |
| 65 | Atlantic AT 4035 | I Got You Babe/It's Gonna Rain ....................5 |
| 65 | Atlantic AT 4047 | But You're Mine/Hello....................5 |
| 65 | Vocalion VL 9247 | The Letter/Spring Fever (B-side by 'Sonny & Cher (Instrumental)')....................15 |
| 66 | Atlantic AT 4069 | What Now My Love/I Look For You ....................5 |
| 66 | Atlantic 584 018 | Have I Stayed Too Long/Leave Me Be ....................6 |
| 66 | Atlantic 584 040 | Little Man/Monday ....................6 |
| 66 | Atlantic 584 057 | Living For You/Turn Around ....................5 |
| 67 | Atlantic 584 078 | The Beat Goes On/Love Don't Come ....................6 |
| 67 | Atlantic 584 110 | Podunk/Beautiful Story....................7 |
| 67 | Atlantic 584 129 | It's The Little Things/Plastic Man ....................7 |
| 68 | Atlantic 584 162 | Good Combination/You And Me ....................10 |
| 68 | Atlantic 584 168 | Circus/SONNY BONO: I Would Marry You Today ....................8 |
| 68 | Atlantic 584 215 | You Gotta Have A Thing Of Your Own/I Got You Babe ....................8 |
| 65 | Reprise R 30056 | CAESAR AND CLEO (EP, 2 tracks each by Sonny & Cher, Caesar & Cleo) ....................25 |

*(see also Caesar & Cleo, Cher, Sonny, Date With Soul)*

## SONNY & DAFFODILS

| | | |
|---|---|---|
| 63 | Ember EMB EP 4538 | SONNY & DAFFODILS (EP) ....................50 |

## SONNY (BURKE) & YVONNE

| | | |
|---|---|---|
| 64 | Island WI 134 | Life Without Fun/SONNY BURKE GROUP: Mount Vesuvius ....................25 |

*(see also Sonny Burke)*

## SON OF A GUN

| | | |
|---|---|---|
| 75 | RCA 2526 | La Maison De L'Amour/All Smoke And No Fire ....................7 |

## SON OF NOISE
| 91 | Music Of Life NOTE53 | Son Of Noise/Ill Justice (12") | 15 |
| 91 | Kold Sweat KS117 | Master Of Menace/Milk In The Chocolate (12") | 15 |
| 92 | Kold Sweat KSEP207 | NEGATIVE FORCES/THE MIGHTY SON/THE MISSION (EP) | 12 |
| 92 | Kold Sweat KSLP03 | THE MIGHTY SON OF NOISE (LP) | 20 |
| 95 | Little Rascool MZE2711 | ACCESS DENIED (LP) | 15 |

*(see also Hardnoise)*

## SONS & LOVERS
| 67 | Camp 602 002 | Matters/Peaceful Is The River | 6 |
| 68 | Beacon 3-101 | Help Me (I'm On Top Of The World)/Feel Alright | 5 |
| 68 | Beacon 3-107 | Happiness Is Love/Things You Do | 5 |
| 68 | Beacon BEA116 | From Now On The Sunshine/How Could We Ever Get This Way | 12 |

## SONS OF ALBATROSS
| 75 | Decca FR 13605 | Africa/Ha-ri-ah | 35 |

## SONS OF CAIN
| 80 | Loppylugs LOPPY 1 | End Of Something/Kennedy Waltz (p/s) | 10 |

## SONS OF DEMENTED CHILDREN
| 87 | Hatter MAD 003 | Spoof Dealer/Busking (p/s, with insert) | 18 |

## SONS OF FRED
| 65 | Columbia DB 7605 | Sweet Love/I'll Be There | 200 |
| 65 | Parlophone R 5391 | I, I, I (Want Your Lovin')/She Only Wants A Friend | 100 |
| 66 | Parlophone R 5415 | Baby What Do You Want Me To Do/You Told Me | 200 |

*(see also Odyssey)*

## SONS OF GLORY
| 62 | Columbia 33SX 1474 | GOD GLORIFIES (LP) | 25 |

## SONS OF JAH
| 75 | Bullet BU 557 | Nyah Chant/Rasta Waltz | 20 |
| 78 | Natty Congo NCDM 002 | Anthem/WIJA LINDO: His Majesty's Authority (12") | 15 |
| 79 | Natty Congo PFUL 2301 | Home To Zion/Woman (12") | 12 |
| 82 | Natty Congo NCDM 013 | Breaking Down The Barriers/Barrier Dub (12") | 20 |
| 78 | Natty Congo PFULP 3501 | BANKRUPT MORALITY (LP, with lyric sheet) | 20 |
| 79 | Natty Congo PFULP 3502 | BURNING BLACK (LP) | 30 |
| 80 | Natty Congo PFULP 3505 | REGGAE HIT SHOWCASE (LP) | 30 |
| 82 | Natty Congo NCLP 001 | UNIVERSAL MESSAGE (LP) | 25 |
| 82 | Natty Congo NCLP 005 | URBAN GUERILLA (LP, as Son Of Jah) | 35 |

## SONS OF MAN
| 67 | Oak RGJ 612 | SONS OF MAN (EP, no p/s) | 400 |

## SONS OF MOSES
| 75 | MCA MCA 169 | Soul Symphony/Fatback | 5 |

## SONS OF NUBIA
| 90 | White SON1 | RAPS THE LAST MEANS (EP) | 75 |

## SONS OF PILTDOWN MEN
| 63 | Pye International 7N 25206 | Mad Goose/Be A Party | 20 |

## SONS OF SOUL
| 66 | Doctor Bird DB 1037 | Yeah Yeah Baby/So Ashamed | 35 |

## SONS OF ISHMAEL
| 87 | Manic Ears ACHE 10 | PARIAH MARTYR DEMANDS A SACRIFICE (LP) | 15 |

## SONS OF MONKEYS
| 81 | Slip 001 | Me & Mr. Suzuki/DECADES BY NIGHT: Life Spiral | 50 |

## SONSONG
| 76 | Zebra ZM 5761 | SONSONG (LP) | 30 |

## SOPHISTICATES
| 60s | Spectrum SPEEP 701 | AT THE WOODVILLE (EP) | 15 |

## SOPHOMORES
| 60s | Seeco CELP 451 | THE SOPHOMORES (LP) | 30 |

## SOPWITH CAMEL
| 86 | Edsel ED 185 | FRANTIC DESOLATION (LP, reissue) | 20 |

## SORE POINTS
| 81 | Pointless SRTS 81 CUS 1113 | Shop Born Sex/Never Gonna Go Outside At Any Point | 25 |

## SORE THROAT (1)
| 78 | Albion ION 3 | Zombie Rock/I Don't Wanna Go Home | 5 |
| 78 | Hubcap SPIN 1 | I Dunno/Complex | 7 |

## SORE THROAT (2)
| 88 | Acid Rain ARRGHHH001 | DEATH TO CAPITALIST HARDCORE EP | 20 |
| 88 | Meantime COX | UNHINDERED BY TALENT (LP, insert) | 15 |
| 89 | Manic Ears ACHE | INDESTROY (LP, with lyric poster, as SAW THROAT) | 20 |
| 89 | Earache MOSH 10 | DISGRACE TO THE CORPSE OF SID (LP, insert) | 15 |
| 80s | Manic Ears ACHE | NEVER MIND THE NAPALM HERE'S SORE THROAT (LP) | 20 |

## SORROWS
| 65 | Piccadilly 7N 35219 | I Don't Wanna Be Free/Come With Me | 40 |
| 65 | Piccadilly 7N 35230 | Baby/Teenage Letter | 50 |
| 65 | Piccadilly 7N 35260 | Take A Heart/We Should Get Along Fine | 25 |
| 66 | Piccadilly 7N 35277 | You've Got What I Want/No, No, No, No (export p/s) | 35 |
| 66 | Piccadilly 7N 35277 | You've Got What I Want/No, No, No, No | 20 |
| 66 | Piccadilly 7N 35309 | Let The Live Live/Don't Sing No Sad Songs For Me | 40 |
| 66 | Piccadilly 7N 35336 | Let Me In/How Love Used To Be | 40 |

| 67 | Piccadilly 7N 35385 | Pink, Purple, Yellow And Red/My Gal | 140 |
| 66 | Piccadilly N(S)PL 38023 | TAKE A HEART (LP, mono) | 250 |
| 66 | Piccadilly N(S)PL 38023 | TAKE A HEART (LP, stereo) | 350 |

*(see also Don Fardon)*

## SORT SOL
| 81 | 4AD AD 101 | Marble Station/Misguided (p/s) | 8 |

## S.O.U.L. (SOUNDS OF UNITY & LOVE)
| 72 | Pye Intl. NSPL 28162 | CAN YOU FEEL IT (LP) | 50 |

## SOUL CITY ORCHESTRA
| 77 | Rouge RMS 109 | MEAT TICKET (LP) | 40 |
| 78 | De Wolfe DWS/LP 3387 | RED LIGHT ZONE (LP) | 20 |

## SOUL CONNECTION
| 88 | Intrigue IGE SC1 | ROUGH & READY (LP) | 30 |

## HORATIO SOUL
| 68 | Island WI 3132 | Ten White Horses/Angela (Sweet Sweet) | 8 |
| 69 | Crystal CR 7006 | Nobody's Gonna Sleep Tonight/Turn Around Baby | 6 |

## JIMMY SOUL
| 62 | Stateside SS 103 | Twistin' Matilda/I Can't Hold Out Any Longer | 10 |
| 63 | Stateside SS 178 | If You Wanna Be Happy/Don't Release Me | 20 |
| 64 | Stateside SS 274 | I Hate You Baby/Change Partners | 10 |
| 64 | Stateside SE 1010 | IF YOU WANNA BE HAPPY (EP) | 50 |

## SHARON SOUL
| 65 | Stateside SS 411 | How Can I Get To You/Don't Say Goodbye Love | 75 |
| 65 | Stateside SS 411 | How Can I Get To You/Don't Say Goodbye Love (DJ copy) | 120 |

## SOUL AGENTS
| 64 | Pye 7N 15660 | I Just Wanna Make Love To You/Mean Woman Blues | 45 |
| 64 | Pye 7N 15707 | Seventh Son/Let's Make It Pretty Baby | 75 |
| 65 | Pye 7N 15768 | Don't Break It Up/Gospel Train | 70 |

*(see also Loot, Don Shinn, Hookfoot)*

## SOUL AGENTS (JAMAICA)
| 67 | Coxsone CS 7007 | Get Ready It's Rocksteady/BOB & BELTONES: Smile Like An Angel (B-side actually by Bop & Beltones) | 30 |
| 67 | Coxsone CS 7018 | For Your Education/SUMMERTAIRES: Tell Me | 50 |
| 67 | Coxsone CS 7027 | Lecture/SOUL BOYS: Blood Pressure | 50 |

## SOUL BOYS
| 66 | Rio R120 | Rudie Get Wise/JACKIE OPEL: I Don't Want Her | 60 |
| 67 | Island WI 3052 | Blood Pressure/RITA MARLEY: Come To Me | 150 |

*(see also Soul Agents [Jamaica])*

## SOUL BROTHERS
| 65 | Mercury MF 916 | Gotta Get A Good Thing Going/Good Lovin' Never Hurt | 10 |
| 65 | Decca F 12116 | I Keep Ringing My Baby/I Can't Take It | 18 |
| 65 | Parlophone R 5321 | I Can't Believe It/You Don't Want To Know | 15 |

## SOUL BROTHERS (JAMAICA)
| 65 | Ska Beat JB 226 | Train To Skaville/WAILERS: I Made A Mistake | 45 |
| 66 | Ska Beat JB 259 | Bugaloo/I'll Come Back | 50 |
| 66 | Rio R 118 | Crawfish/RITA MARLEY: You Lied | 30 |
| 66 | Rio R 121 | Mr T.N.T./MARCIA GRIFFITHS: Mr Everything | 50 |
| 66 | Island WI 282 | Green Moon/E Gal OK | 20 |
| 66 | Island WI 294 | Ska-Bostello/DON DRUMMOND: Looking Through The Window | 30 |
| 66 | Island WI 296 | Sound One/MARTINE: Grandfather's Clock (B-side actually by Emille Straker & Merrymen or Martinis) | 25 |
| 66 | Island WI 3013 | More & More/DELROY WILSON: Dancing Mood | 30 |
| 66 | Island WI 3016 | Mr Flint/Too Young To Love (B-side actually by Freddie McGregor) | 30 |
| 67 | Island WI 3036 | Sound Pressure/ETHIOPIANS: For You | 30 |
| 67 | Island WI 3039 | Hi-Life/DELROY WILSON: Close To Me | 35 |
| 67 | Coxsone CS 7001 | Take Ten/HUGH GODFREY: Deh Pon Dem | 100 |
| 67 | Coxsone CS 7020 | Hey Windell/KEN BOOTHE: Home Home Home | 40 |
| 67 | Coxsone CS 7024 | One Stop/TENNORS: Pressure And Slide | 30 |
| 67 | Studio One SO 2006 | Hot And Cold/TERMITES: Mercy Mr. Percy | 100 |
| 67 | Island WI 3038 | Cherry/SOUL JUNIOR : Out Of My Mind (Some list Bumps Oakley as the B-side) | 60 |
| 67 | Studio One SO 2016 | Honeypot/VICEROYS: Lose And Gain | 50 |
| 70 | Pressure Beat PR 5506 | Pussy Catch A Fire (actually by Soul Twins)/DESTROYERS: Follow This Beat (B-side actually "Secret Weapon" by Ansell Collins) | 15 |
| 67 | Coxsone CSL 8001 | HOT SHOT SKA (LP) | 200 |
| 67 | Coxsone CSL 8002 | CARIB SOUL (LP) | 150 |

*(see also Earl Van Dyke & Soul Brothers, Soul Twins, Lee Perry, Tony Gregory, Ethiopians, Itals, Hortense & Delroy, Gaylads, Jennors, Derrick Morgan, Summertaires, Delroy Wilson)*

## SOUL BROTHERS SIX
| 67 | Atlantic 584 118 | Some Kind Of Wonderful/I'll Be Loving You | 50 |
| 69 | Atlantic 584 256 | Some Kind Of Wonderful/Somebody Else Is Loving My Baby | 25 |
| 72 | Atlantic K 10204 | Some Kind Of Wonderful/Check Yourself | 10 |
| 74 | Atlantic K 10471 | Thank You Baby For Loving Me/Somebody Else Is Loving My Baby | 8 |
| 00 | Atlantic 45 2406 | I'll Be Loving You/LITTLE ESTHER: Just Say Goodbye (reissue) | 8 |

## SOUL CATS
| 69 | Camel CA 23 | Keep It Moving/Your Sweet Love | 30 |
| 69 | Gas GAS 109 | Choo Choo Train/The Load (actually "Swinging For Joy" by Count Ossie Band) | 20 |
| 71 | Hillcrest HCT 2 | Reggay Got Soul (actually by Carl Bryan)/Land Of Love | 10 |
| 70s | Junior JR 103 | Reggay Got Soul (actually by Carl Bryan)/Land Of Love (reissue) | 15 |

**SOUL CITY**
62   Cameo Parkway P 103   Everybody Dance Now/Who Knows ......................................................... 100
62   Cameo Parkway P 103   Everybody Dance Now/Who Knows (DJ copy) .......................................... 125

**SOUL CITY EXECUTIVES**
69   Soul City SC 109   Happy Chatter/Falling In Love ................................................................. 20

**SOUL CLAN**
68   Atlantic 584 202   Soul Meeting/That's How It Feels (in p/s) .............................................. 15
68   Atlantic 584 202   Soul Meeting/That's How It Feels ............................................................. 8
68   Atlantic 587 127   SOUL MEETING (LP) ................................................................................ 20

*(see also Solomon Burke, Arthur Conley, Don Covay, Ben E. King, Joe Tex)*

**SOUL CONDOR**
70   Polydor 2344002   CERTAIN LIONS & TIGERS (LP) .............................................................. 25

**SOUL DEFENDERS**
71   Banana BA 354   Way Back Home/SOUL REBELS: Stand For Your Rights ........................ 20
72   Ackee ACK 147   Sound Almighty/COUNT OSSIE: Meditation .......................................... 15

*(see also Eric Donaldson, Carey Johnson)*

**SOUL DESTROYERS**
00   Stark Relaity STARK008   Blow Your Top Pt. 1/Blow Your Top Pt. 2 ............................................... 12

**SOUL DIRECTIONS**
70   Attack ATT 8011   Su Su Su/Better Hearing ...................................................................... 200

**GEORGE SOULE**
75   United Artists UP 35771   Get Involved/Everybody's Got A Song To Sing ......................................... 8

**SOULETTES**
65   Ska Beat JB 204   Opportunity/DIZZY JOHNNY & STUDIO 1 ORCHESTRA: Sudden Destruction ... 50
70   Upsetter US 337   Let It Be/UPSETTERS: Big Dog Bloxie ...................................................... 20
71   Jackpot JP 766   My Desire/Bring It Up ............................................................................ 20
71   Jackpot JP 767   All Of Your Loving/LLOYD CLARKE: Love Me .......................................... 20
73   Attack ATT 8044   This World/Same Thing ............................................................................. 5

*(see also Rita Marley, Ken Boothe, Roland Alphonso, Uniques)*

**SOUL EXPLOSION**
69   Downtown DT 455   Let's Try It Again/Gumpton Rock .............................................................. 6
70   J-DAN JDN 4405   My Mother's Eyes/Gum Pot ...................................................................... 7

**SOUL FLAMES**
68   Nu Beat NB 020   Mini Really Fit Dem/Soul Train ............................................................... 80

**SOULFUL STRINGS**
67   Chess CRS 8068   Burning Spear/Within You, Without You .................................................. 30
67   Chess CRS 8068   Burning Spear/Within You, Without You (DJ Copy) .................................. 50
69   Chess CRS 8094   I Wish It Would Rain/Listen Here ............................................................ 10
69   Chess CRLS 4534   GROOVIN' WITH THE SOULFUL STRINGS (LP) ...................................... 20

**SOUL GENERATION**
73   Sticky STY 2   Million Dollars/Sailing ............................................................................... 8
79   Grapevine GRP 131   Hold On/The Lonely Sea ........................................................................... 8
73   Sticky SBL 135   BEYOND BODY AND SOUL (LP) .............................................................. 25

**SOUL KINGS**
69   Blue Cat BS 169   The Magnificent Seven/RUPIE EDWARDS: Long Lost Love ..................... 40

**SOUL LEADERS**
67   Rio R 134   Pour On The Sauce/Beauty Is Only Skin Deep ........................................ 40

**SOULMATES (JAMAICA)**
69   Amalgamated AMG 836   Them A Laugh And A Ki Ki/The Hippys Are Here (B-side actually by Hippy Boys) ... 60
69   Amalgamated AMG 842   On The Move/Jump It Up (B-side actually by Viceroys) ............................ 70
69   Camel CA 33   Beware Of Bad Dogs/Short Cut (actually by Glen Adams) ........................ 50
70   Unity UN 555   Ten Cent/DOREEN SHAFFER: Stay With Me Forever .............................. 10

**SOULMATES (U.K.)**
65   Parlophone R 5334   Too Late To Say You're Sorry/Your Love ................................................. 80
66   Parlophone R 5407   Bring Your Love Back Home (with Jet Set)/When Love Is Gone ............... 15
66   Parlophone R 5506   Mood Melancholy/Sayin' Something ....................................................... 10
67   Parlophone R 5601   Is That You?/Time's Run Out ................................................................. 10

*(see also Liza Strike)*

**SOUL MERCHANTS**
67   President PT 166   Whole Lot Of Lovin'/Stormy Weather ......................................................... 7

**SOUL ON DELIVERY**
75   Decca F13601   Hustle/Crescent Boogie .......................................................................... 10

**SOUL PARTNERS**
69   Pama PM 766   Walk On Judge/Lose The One You Love .................................................. 20

**SOUL PEOPLE**
68   Island WIP 6040   Hummin'/Soul Drink ............................................................................... 20

**SOUL PROPRIETORS**
65   Concord CON STD 74   All/Lonely Separation (private pressing) ................................................. 300

**SOUL REBELS**
72   Banana BA 374   Listen And Observe/What's Love ............................................................ 45
72   Count Shelly CS 001   Judgement Day Is Near/Solid As A Rock ................................................ 20
72   Count Shelly CS 003   I'm The One Who Loves You/I ROY: War Zone ....................................... 10

*(see also Soul Defenders)*

**SOUL RHYTHMS**
69   Bullet BU 404   Work Boy Work/CECIL THOMAS: Girl Lonesome Fever ......................... 25
69   High Note HS 013   National Lottery/Round Seven ............................................................... 30

| | | | MINT VALUE £ |
|---|---|---|---|
| 69 | Gas GAS 113 | Soul Call/Musical Gate | 40 |
| *(see also Hippy Boys, Max Romeo)* | | | |

**SOUL RUNNERS**
| 67 | Polydor 56732 | Grits 'n' Cornbread/Spreading Honey | 10 |

**SOULSAVERS**
| 07 | V2 VVR5045527 | Kingdom Of Rain (1-sided, other side etched) | 5 |
| 12 | V2 (no cat no) | Longest Day (7", 1-sided, Be side etched, 300 only) | 8 |
| 07 | V2 VVR1045531 | IT'S NOT HOW FAR YOU FALL IT'S HOW YOU LAND (LP) | 60 |

**SOUL SEARCHERS**
| 74 | Sussex SXX 2 | Blow Your Whistle (Parts 1 & 2) | 8 |
| 10 | Soul Brother SB 7004D | We The People/Think (reissue) | 6 |
| 74 | Sussex LPSX 4 | SALT OF THE EARTH (LP) | 25 |
| 06 | Soul Brother SBCS 24 | WE THE PEOPLE (LP, reissue) | 15 |

**SOUL SISTERS (JAMAICA)**
| 69 | Amalgamated AMG 839 | Wreck A Buddy/VERSATILES: Push It In | 25 |
| *(see also Dennis Brown)* | | | |

**SOUL SISTERS (U.S.)**
| 64 | Sue WI 312 | I Can't Stand It/Blueberry Hill | 40 |
| 64 | Sue WI 336 | Loop De Loop/Long Gone | 50 |
| 65 | London HLC 9970 | Foolish Dreamer/Good Time Tonight | 60 |
| 65 | London HLC 9970 | Foolish Dreamer/Good Time Tonight (DJ copy) | 100 |
| 72 | United Artists UP 35388 | Good Time Tonight/Some Soul Food | 10 |
| 64 | Sue ILP 913 | THE SOUL SISTERS (LP) | 150 |

**SOUL SOUNDS**
| 67 | Columbia S(C)X 6158 | SOUL SURVIVAL (LP) | 40 |
| *(see also Savages, Rebel Rousers)* | | | |

**SOUL STIRRERS**
| 69 | Duke DU 25 | Come See About Me/LLOYD CHARMERS: 5 To 5 | 35 |
| *(see also Sam Cooke)* | | | |

**SOUL SURVIVORS**
| 67 | Stateside SS 2057 | Expressway To Your Heart/Hey Gyp | 30 |
| 68 | Stateside SS 2094 | Explosion (In Your Soul)/Dathon's Theme | 18 |
| 69 | Atlantic 584 275 | Mama Soul/Tell Daddy | 30 |

**SOUL SYNDICATE**
| 72 | Green Door GD 4021 | Riot (actually by Johnny Moore & Soul Syndicate)/Smoke Without Fire (actually by Keith Hudson) | 25 |
| *(see also Rockin' Horse)* | | | |

**SOUL TONES**
| 70 | Pama PM 790 | Dancing Time/BUNNY BARRETT: Love Locked Out | 15 |

**SOUL TOPS**
| 67 | Fab FAB 27 | Baby I Got News/TEDDY KING & BUSTER'S ALL STARS: Mexican Divorce | 35 |
| 68 | Nu Beat NB002 | Rain And Thunder/Swing Baby | 30 |

**SOUL TWINS (JAMAICA)**
| 70 | High Note HS 043 | Little Suzie/Cherrie | 25 |
| 72 | Clandisc CLA 238 | Don't Call Me Nigga/DYNAMITES: Joe Louis | 20 |

**SOUL TWINS (U.S.)**
| 77 | Grapevine GRP 101 | Quick Change Artist/Give The Man A Chance | 8 |

**SOUL VENDORS**
| 67 | Coxsone CS 7028 | You Troubled Me/BOP & BELTONES: Love | 80 |
| 67 | Coxsone CS 7029 | Fat Fish/MARCIA GRIFFITHS: Call To Me | 150 |
| 67 | Studio One SO 2018 | Rocking Sweet Pea/JOE HIGGS: Change Of Plans | 200 |
| 67 | Studio One SO 2022 | Cool Shade/RICHARD ACE: I Need You | 120 |
| 67 | Studio One SO 2028 | Just A Little Bit Of Soul/ALTON ELLIS: I Am Just A Guy | 60 |
| 67 | Studio One SO 2031 | Take Me/DELROY WILSON: I'm Not A King | 50 |
| 67 | Studio One SO 2032 | Pe Da Pa/ERNEST WILSON: Money Worries | 40 |
| 67 | Studio One SO 2034 | Hot Rod/GAYLADS: Africa (We Want To Go) | 125 |
| 67 | Studio One SO 2035 | Pupa Lick/ETHIOPIANS: Leave My Business Alone | 40 |
| 68 | Studio One SO 2038 | Psychedelic Rock/GAYLADS: I'm Free | 125 |
| 68 | Studio One SO 2043 | Chinese Chicken/JACKIE MITTOO: Put It On | 30 |
| 68 | Studio One SO 2044 | Happy Ogan (actually titled "Happy Organ")/INVADERS: Soulful Music | 100 |
| 68 | Studio One SO 2048 | Evening Time/RIGHTEOUS FLAMES: Ease Up | 35 |
| 68 | Studio One SO 2058 | Frozen Soul/ERNEST WILSON: If I Were A Carpenter | 40 |
| 68 | Studio One SO 2066 | Soul Joint/Soul Limbo | 45 |
| 68 | Studio One SO 2070 | Captain Cojoe/JACKIE MITTOO: Drum Song | 50 |
| 68 | Coxsone CS 7037 | Grooving Steady/ROY RICHARDS: Warm And Tender Ska | 80 |
| 68 | Coxsone CS 7038 | Whipping The Prince (actually by Ed Hangle & Alton Ellis)/HEPTONES: If You Knew | 100 |
| 68 | Coxsone CS 7048 | Last Waltz/HAMLINS: Sentimental Reasons | 200 |
| 68 | Coxsone CS 7057 | Real Rock/AL CAMPBELL: Don't Run Away | 150 |
| 68 | Coxsone CS 7071 | West Of The Sun/ALTON ELLIS: A Fool | 80 |
| 69 | Coxsone CS 7084 | Sixth Figure/DENZIL LAING: Man Payaba | 50 |
| 67 | Coxsone CSL 8010 | ON TOUR (LP) | 300 |
| *(see also Dobby Dobson)* | | | |

**SOULWAX**
| 04 | Pias B060DLP | ANY MINUTE NOW (2-LP, inners) | 20 |
| 07 | Parlophone 50999 509247 1 4 | MOST OF THE REMIXES WE'VE MADE... (2-LP) | 20 |

**SOUND**
| 80 | Korova KOW 10 | Heyday/Brute Force (p/s) | 8 |

| 81 | Korova KOW 21 | Sense Of Purpose/Point Of No Return (p/s) | 8 |
| 79 | Tortch TOR 003 | PHYSICAL WORLD (EP) | 35 |
| 79 | Tortch TOR 008 | THE SOUND (LP, possibly unissued) | 0 |
| 80 | Korova KODE 2 | JEOPARDY (LP, with inner) | 20 |
| 81 | Korova KODE 5 | FROM THE LIONS MOUTH (LP, gatefold) | 35 |
| 82 | Warner Bros. 240019 | ALL FALL DOWN (LP) | 20 |
| 85 | Statik STAB 1 | SHOCK OF DAYLIGHT (mini-LP) | 15 |
| 85 | Statik STATLP 24 | HEAD & HEARTS (LP) | 20 |
| 85 | Statik STATDLP1 | IN THE HOTHOUSE (2-LP, gatefold) | 25 |

*(see also Outsiders, Second Layer)*

## SOUND BARRIER
| 68 | Beacon BEA 109 | She Always Comes Back To Me/Groovin' Slow | 100 |

## SOUND CEREMONY
| 89 | Celestial Sound SRT 8KF | You're Breaking My Heart (p/s) | 10 |
| 79 | Celestial Sound RWG 001 | GUITAR STAR (LP) | 20 |
| 79 | Celestial Sound RWG 002 | RON WARREN GANDERTON & SOUND CEREMONY (LP) | 40 |
| 81 | Celestial Sound RWG 003 | PRECIOUS AS ENGLAND (LP) | 20 |

## SOUND DIMENSION
| 69 | Coxsone CS 7083 | Scorcia/CECIL & JACKIE: Breaking Up (B-side actually "Hold Me Baby" by Basil Daley) | 40 |
| 69 | Coxsone CS 7085 | Soul Trombone (Suffering Stink)/LARRY & ALVIN: Your Cheating Heart | 150 |
| 69 | Coxsone CS 7090 | Soulful Strut/Breaking Up | 120 |
| 69 | Coxsone CS 7093 | More Scorcha/LENNIE HIBBERT: Village Soul | 60 |
| 69 | Coxsone CS 7097 | Time Is Tight/BARRY LLEWELLYN: Sad Song | 60 |
| 69 | Bamboo BAM 5 | Doctor Sappa Too/Soul Eruption (B-side actually by Roy Richards & Sound Dimension) | 45 |
| 69 | Bamboo BAM 7 | Baby Face/GLADIATORS: Anywhere | 30 |
| 69 | Bamboo BAM 9 | Jamaica Rag/C. MARSHALL: I Need Your Loving | 25 |
| 69 | Bamboo BAM 13 | Whoopee/NORMA FRAZER: Working (B-side actually by Marcia Griffiths) | 25 |
| 69 | Bamboo BAM 14 | Black Onion/Bitter Blood | 35 |
| 70 | Bamboo BAM 18 | Poison Ivy/Botheration - Version | 20 |
| 70 | Bamboo BAM 50 | Soul Food/BURNING SPEAR: Door Peeper | 60 |
| 70 | Banana BA 313 | In The Summertime/In The Summertime - Version | 35 |
| 70 | Banana BA 338 | My Sweet Lord (Instrumental)/DENNIS BROWN: Silky (B-side actually by Monty Alexander & Cyclones) | 15 |
| 70 | Supreme SUP 202 | More Games/MR. FOUNDATION: Maga Dog (actually by Invaders) | 30 |
| 72 | Ackee ACK 149 | Solas/GLADIATORS: Sonia | 15 |

*(see also Brentford Road Allstars, Jackie Mittoo, Bob Andy, Horace Andy, John Holt, Larry Marshall, Irving Brown, Heptones, Freedom Singers, Winston Francis, Jerry Jones, Ethiopians, Cables, Alton Ellis, Gladiators, Ken Boothe, Soul Vendors)*

## SOUNDER
| 77 | Warped/Sonet SON 2127 | Get Down On Your Knees/Bus Stop Romance (p/s) | 5 |

## SOUNDGARDEN
| 92 | A&M AMY 723 | Rusty Cage/Touch Me/Show Me (12", poster p/s, 5000 only) | 15 |
| 94 | A&M 580 736-7 | Black Hole Sun/My Wave (Live)/Beyond The Wheel (Live) (picture disc) | 10 |
| 96 | A&M 5818457 | Burden In My Hand/Karaoke (p/s, white vinyl, numbered, 5000 only) | 15 |
| 89 | A&M AMA 5252 | LOUDER THAN LOVE (LP) | 15 |
| 91 | A&M 395 374-1 | BADMOTORFINGER (LP, blue vinyl) | 40 |
| 91 | A&M 395 374 1 | BADMOTORFINGER (LP) | 18 |
| 96 | A&M 540 558-1 | DOWN ON THE UPSIDE (2-LP) | 25 |
| 96 | A&M 540 558 -1 | DOWN ON THE UPSIDE (2-LP, clear vinyl) | 40 |
| 94 | A&M 540215-1 | SUPERUNKNOWN (2 x LP, clear, orange or blue vinyl, stickered, 2 lyric sheets) | 60 |
| 11 | A&M 80015268-01 | LIVE ON I-5 (2-LP) | 20 |
| 12 | Vertigo 3719818 | KING ANIMAL (2-LP) | 18 |

## SOUND IRATION
| 89 | Wau Mr. Modo MOWLP 001 | IN DUB (LP) | 35 |
| 10 | Year Zero YZLP 003 | IN DUB (2-LP, reissue) | 18 |
| 89 | Mystic Red Corp MRC 8888 | Seventh Seal/Dub Seal (12") | 30 |
| 10 | Year Zero YZD V003 | THE DUBZ (2-LP) | 18 |

## SOUND NETWORK
| 65 | Mercury MF 944 | Watching/How About Now | 25 |

## SOUND OF JIMMY NICOL
| 65 | Decca F 12107 | Clementine/Bim Bam | 25 |

*(see also Jimmy Nicol)*

## SOUNDPROOF
| 71 | Look LKSP511-301 | Friday Every Friday/Lonely Boy Lonely Girl | 100 |

## SOUNDS AROUND
| 66 | Piccadilly 7N 35345 | What Does She Do?/Sad Subject | 25 |
| 67 | Piccadilly 7N 35396 | Red White And You/One Of Two | 25 |

*(see also Peter & Wolves, John Pantry, Norman Conquest, Factory)*

## SOUNDS COMBINE
| 71 | Escort ERT 862 | African Museum/African Museum - Version | 8 |

## SOUNDS INCORPORATED
| 61 | Parlophone R 4815 | Mogambo/Emily | 15 |
| 62 | Decca F 11540 | Sounds Like Locomotion/Taboo | 8 |
| 63 | Decca F 11590 | Stop/Go | 10 |
| 63 | Decca F 11723 | Order Of The Keys/Keep Moving | 25 |
| 64 | Columbia DB 7239 | The Spartans/Detroit | 7 |
| 64 | Columbia DB 7321 | Spanish Harlem/Rinky Dink | 10 |
| 64 | Columbia DB 7404 | William Tell/Bullets | 7 |

| 65 | Columbia DB 7545 | Time For You/Hall Of The Mountain King | 7 |
| 65 | Columbia DB 7676 | My Little Red Book/Justice Neddi | 10 |
| 65 | Columbia DB 7737 | On The Brink/I'm Comin' Thru | 40 |
| 67 | Polydor 56209 | How Do You Feel/Dead As You Go | 15 |
| 69 | Decca 22883 | Warmth Of The Sun/Apollo (export) | 10 |
| 64 | Columbia SEG 8360 | TOP GEAR (EP) | 25 |
| 64 | Columbia 33SX 1659 | SOUNDS INCORPORATED (LP, mono) | 25 |
| 64 | Columbia SCX 3531 | SOUNDS INCORPORATED (LP, stereo) | 30 |
| 65 | EMI Regal SREG 1071 | RINKY DINK (LP, export issue) | 20 |
| 66 | Studio Two TWO 144 | SOUNDS INCORPORATED (LP) | 20 |

(see also Jeff Beck, May Blitz, Boxer, Tony Newman)

## SOUNDS NICE
| 69 | Parlophone R 5797 | Love At First Sight/Love You Too ('featuring Tim Mycroft') | 8 |
| 69 | Parlophone R 5821 | Sleepless Night/Continental Exchange ('featuring Tim Mycroft') | 6 |
| 69 | Parlophone PMC/PCS 7089 | LOVE AT FIRST SIGHT (LP) | 25 |

(see also Third Ear Band, Chris Spedding, Clem Cattini Ork)

## SOUNDS OF BOB ROGERS
| 67 | CBS 3018 | Among My Souveneirs/Dream With Me | 20 |

## SOUNDS OF JOHNNY HAWKSWORTH
| 66 | Columbia DB 8059 | Goal/"Goal - World Cup 1966" Theme | 15 |

## SOUNDS OF MODIFICATION
| 68 | Stateside SL/SSL 10262 | SOUNDS OF MODIFICATION (LP) | 30 |

## SOUNDS OF REFLECTION
| 68 | Reflection RS6001SM | Brave New Day/Lord Of Believe (p/s) | 50 |

## SOUNDS OF SALVATION
| 74 | Reflection RL 310 | SOUNDS OF SALVATION (LP, with booklet) | 90 |

(see also Reflection)

## SOUNDS OF TIME
| 73 | Columbia 9000 | DANSE MACABRE (LP) | 20 |

## SOUNDS ORCHESTRAL
| 66 | Piccadilly 7N 35284 | Thunderball/Mr Kiss Kiss Bang Bang | 10 |
| 68 | Pye 7N 170507 | When Love Has Gone/Fifth Avenue Breakdown | 6 |
| 65 | Pye NPL 38016 | THUNDERBALL - SOUNDS ORCHESTRAL MEET JAMES BOND (LP, in gatefold sleeve) | 20 |
| 65 | Pye NPL 38016 | THUNDERBALL - SOUNDS ORCHESTRAL MEET JAMES BOND (LP) | 30 |

## SOUNDS PROGRESSIVE
| 70 | Eyemark EMCL 1009S | KID JENSEN INTRODUCES SOUNDS PROGRESSIVE (LP) | 30 |

## SOUNDS SENSATIONAL
| 67 | HMV POP 1584 | Love In The Open Air/Night Cry | 18 |

## SOUND SCIENCE
| 91 | Sound Entity SE 0002 | HERT'Z SO GOOD EP (12") | 15 |

## SOUND SIXTY-SIX
| 66 | Decca F 12323 | Flight 4864/The Bouncer | 12 |

## SOUND STAGE ORCHESTRA
| 76 | BBC RESL 30 | Grandstand/Rugby Special | 10 |

## SOUND SYSTEM
| 65 | Island WI 258 | You Don't Know Like I Do/Take Me Serious | 15 |

(see also Owen Gray)

## EPIC SOUNDTRACKS
| 81 | Rough Trade RT 084 | Popular, Classical: Jelly Babies/A 3-Acre Floor/Pop In Packets (p/s) | 5 |

(see also Swell Maps, Thurston Moore Kim Gordon & Epic Soundtracks)

## SOUND VISION
| 70s | Key KL 007 | IN CONCERT (LP, featuring Judy MacKenzie) | 25 |

## SOUP DRAGONS
| 86 | Raw TV Products RTV 1 | Hang Ten!/Slow Things Down (p/s, blue or red vinyl) | 7 |
| 86 | Raw TV Products RTV 2 | Head Gone Astray/Girl In The World/So Sad I Feel (PVC sleeve, with poster) | 8 |
| 86 | Subway Organisation SUBWAY 4 | THE SUN IS IN THE SKY (EP, unreleased, 1,000 only, foldaround p/s in poly bag) | 15 |

(see also BMX Bandits, Future Pilot A.K.A.)

## SOUP GREENS
| 65 | Stateside SS 457 | That's Too Bad/Like A Rolling Stone | 70 |

## SOUPHERBS
| 65 | Oak RGJ 601 | SOUPHERBS (LP) | 350 |

## SOURCE DIRECT
| 94 | Odysee ODY 01 | Future London/Shimmer (12") | 20 |
| 95 | Metalheadz MET H 016 | A Made Up Sound/The Cult (12") | 15 |
| 95 | Source Direct SD 001 | Fabric Of Space/Bliss (12") | 20 |
| 95 | Source Direct SD 002 | Approach And Identity/Modem (12") | 20 |
| 95 | Source Direct SD 003 | Snake Style/Exit 9 (12") | 15 |

## TIM SOUSTER
| 77 | Transatlantic TRA 343 | SW1T DR1MZ (LP) | 20 |

## APRIL SOUTH
| 81 | Rockelly RKR 10781 EJSP 9730 | Heroes Of The Night/The Boys Are Out To Get Me (no p/s) | 50 |
| 82 | President PT 501 | Heroes Of The Night/The Boys Are Out To Get Me (p/s) | 20 |

## HARRY SOUTH ORCHESTRA
| 69 | Philips BF 1770 | Scarborough Fair/I'm Gonna Make You Love Me | 25 |
| 75 | EMI EMI 2252 | The Sweeney (TV Theme) (Parts 1 & 2) | 20 |

| | | | |
|---|---|---|---|
| 67 | Mercury 20081 MCL | PRESENTING HARRY SOUTH (LP) | 30 |

## JOE SOUTH

| | | | |
|---|---|---|---|
| 62 | Oriole CB 1752 | Masquerade/I'm Sorry For You | 20 |
| 63 | MGM MGM 1206 | Same Old Song/Standing Invitation | 7 |
| 65 | MGM MGM 1267 | Concrete Jungle/Last One To Know | 7 |
| 65 | HMV POP 1474 | I Want To Be Somebody/Deep Inside Me | 7 |
| 68 | Capitol CL 15535 | Birds Of A Feather/It Got Away | 6 |
| 69 | Capitol CL 15568 | Don't Throw Your Love To The Wind/Redneck | 5 |
| 69 | Capitol CL 15579 | Games People Play/Mirror Of Your Mind | 6 |
| 69 | Capitol CL 15608 | Don't It Make You Want To Go Home/Heart's Desire | 15 |
| 70 | Capitol CL 15666 | Hush/Party People | 5 |

## SOUTH COAST SKA STARS

| | | | |
|---|---|---|---|
| 80 | Safari SAFE 27 | South Coast Rumble/Head On (p/s) | 8 |

*(see also Ray Fenwick)*

## JERI SOUTHERN

| | | | |
|---|---|---|---|
| 54 | Brunswick 05343 | Remind Me/Little Boy Grown Tall | 8 |
| 55 | Brunswick 05367 | The Man That Got Away/Speak Softly To Me | 8 |
| 55 | Brunswick 05490 | An Occasional Man/It's D'Lovely | 7 |
| 56 | Brunswick 05529 | Where Walks My True Love?/Don't Explain | 10 |
| 55 | Brunswick LA 8699 | WARM (10" LP) | 15 |
| 56 | Brunswick LAT 8100 | THE SOUTHERN STYLE (LP) | 15 |

## JOHNNY SOUTHERN & HIS WESTERN RHYTHM KINGS

| | | | |
|---|---|---|---|
| 57 | Melodisc MEL 1413 | We Will Make Love/Crazy Heart | 10 |
| 57 | Melodisc MEL 1434 | She's Long, She's Tall/Lonesome Whistle | 10 |

## SOUTHERN SOUND

| | | | |
|---|---|---|---|
| 66 | Columbia DB 7982 | Just The Same As You/I Don't Wanna Go | 300 |

## SOUTHERN TONES

| | | | |
|---|---|---|---|
| 64 | Jazz Collector JEN 10 | WAITING FOR THE LORD (EP) | 10 |

## SOUTHERN COMFORT

| | | | |
|---|---|---|---|
| 71 | Harvest HAR 5035 | Willie Urricane/Berkshire Berk | 10 |
| 71 | Harvest HAR 5047 | Morning Has Broken/Cosmic Jig | 10 |
| 71 | Harvest SHSP 4012 | FROG CITY (LP, no EMI logo on label) | 30 |
| 72 | Harvest SHSP 799 | SOUTHERN COMFORT (LP, gatefold, EMI logo on label) | 50 |
| 72 | Harvest SHSP 4021 | STIR DON'T SHAKE (LP, with EMI logo on label) | 25 |

*(see also Matthews Southern Comfort)*

## SOUTHERN DEATH CULT

| | | | |
|---|---|---|---|
| 83 | Situation 2 SIT 19 | Fatman/Moya (wraparound p/s) | 20 |

*(see also Death Cult, Cult)*

## SOUTHLANDERS

| | | | |
|---|---|---|---|
| 55 | Parlophone MSP 6182 | Ain't That A Shame/Have You Ever Been Lonely | 10 |
| 56 | Parlophone MSP 6236 | Hush-A-Bye Rock/The Wedding Of The Lucky Black Cat | 10 |
| 57 | Decca F 10946 | Alone/Swedish Polka | 5 |
| 57 | Decca F 10958 | Peanuts/I Never Dreamed | 5 |
| 58 | Decca F 10982 | Put A Light In The Window/Penny Loafers And Bobby Socks | 10 |
| 58 | Decca F 11032 | I Wanna Jive Tonight/Torero | 15 |
| 58 | Decca F 11067 | The Mole In A Hole/Choo-Choo-Choo-Choo Cha-Cha-Cha (tri-centre) | 15 |
| 58 | Decca F 11067 | The Mole In A Hole/Choo-Choo-Choo-Choo Cha-Cha-Cha (tri-centre, repressing with solid centre) | 7 |
| 58 | Decca DFE 6508 | THE SOUTHLANDERS NUMBER ONE (EP) | 10 |

## SOUTH REBELS

| | | | |
|---|---|---|---|
| 79 | Red Hot! RH 1003 | THE SOUTH REBELS EP | 8 |

## SOUTHSIDE JOHNNY & THE ASBURY JUKES

| | | | |
|---|---|---|---|
| 77 | Epic EPC 5230 | Little Girl So Fine/I Ain't Got The Fever (withdrawn) | 20 |

## SOUTHWEST F.O.B.

| | | | |
|---|---|---|---|
| 68 | Stax STAX 107 | Smell Of Incense/Green Skies | 20 |

## SOUTHWIND

| | | | |
|---|---|---|---|
| 70 | Harvest HAR 5019 | Boogie Woogie Country Girl/Honky Tonkin' | 5 |

## PHIL SOUTHWOOD

| | | | |
|---|---|---|---|
| 61 | QRS 1-462 | D's Dilemma/Sister Sadie (in p/s) | 20 |
| 61 | QRS 1-462 | D's Dilemma/Sister Sadie | 12 |

## SOVEREIGNS

| | | | |
|---|---|---|---|
| 66 | King KG 1050 | Bring Me Home Love/That's The Way Love Is | 15 |

## RED SOVINE

| | | | |
|---|---|---|---|
| 56 | Brunswick 05513 | Why Baby Why? (with Webb Pierce)/Sixteen Tons | 40 |

*(see also Webb Pierce)*

## SOWELL RADICS

| | | | |
|---|---|---|---|
| 81 | Attack TACK 24 | Caution/Bali-Hi Special (12") | 40 |
| 81 | Attack TACK 27 | Fight Fight Fight/Aces Rock (12") | 40 |
| 81 | Dread At The Controls DATC 006 | All Nite Jammin/All Night Dubbin (12") | 40 |
| 82 | SG SG 15 | Wheel O' Matlida/Rub Dis Ya One Ya (12") | 45 |

## SOWERS WITH EILEEN GREAVES

| | | | |
|---|---|---|---|
| 69 | Galliard GAL 4002 | SEEDS (LP) | 30 |

## SO WHAT

| | | | |
|---|---|---|---|
| 70 | CBS 5005 | Flowers/Tell Me Now | 20 |

## BOB B. SOXX & THE BLUE JEANS

| | | | |
|---|---|---|---|
| 63 | London HLU 9646 | Zip-A-Dee-Doo-Dah/Flip And Nitty | 20 |

# Catherine SPAAK

| | | | MINT VALUE £ |
|---|---|---|---|
| 63 | London HLU 9694 | Why Do Lovers Break Each Other's Heart?/Dr Kaplan's Office | 25 |
| 63 | London HLU 9754 | Not Too Young To Get Married/Annette | 20 |
| 69 | London HLU 10243 | Zip-A-Dee-Doo-Dah/Why Do Lovers Break Each Other's Heart? | 7 |
| 63 | London HA-U 8121 | ZIP-A-DEE-DOO-DAH (LP) | 100 |
| 75 | Phil Spector Intl. 2307 004 | BOB B. SOXX & THE BLUE JEANS (LP) | 25 |

(see also Darlene Love, Bobby Sheen, Blossoms, Crystals, Phil Spector)

## CATHERINE SPAAK
| | | | |
|---|---|---|---|
| 65 | Fontana TL 5282 | NOI SIAMO I GIOVANI (LP) | 15 |

## SPACE CADETS
| | | | |
|---|---|---|---|
| 96 | Vinyl Japan JRLP 20 | ASTROBILLY ROCKIN (LP) | 20 |
| 00 | Vinyl Japan JRLP 35 | CADETS A GO GO (LP) | 20 |

## SPACE (1)
| | | | |
|---|---|---|---|
| 77 | Pye NSLP 28232 | MAGIC FLY (LP) | 15 |
| 78 | Pye NSPH 28505 | DELIVERANCE (LP) | 20 |
| 79 | Pye NSPH 28725 | JUST BLUE (LP) | 15 |
| 79 | Pye NSPH 28725 | JUST BLUE (LP, picture disc) | 20 |

(see also Madeline Bell)

## SPACE (2)
| | | | |
|---|---|---|---|
| 90 | Space LP 1 | SPACE (LP) | 35 |
| 90 | Space CD 1 | SPACE (CD, beware of counterfeits) | 25 |

(see also J.A.M.S., KLF, Timelords, Disco 2000)

## SPACE (3)
| | | | |
|---|---|---|---|
| 96 | Gut GUT LP 1 | SPIDERS (LP) | 30 |

## SPACE (4)
| | | | |
|---|---|---|---|
| 93 | Hug HUG 1T | If It's Real/Lookin'/I'm Free (12", p/s with free 'fortune fish') | 12 |

## SPACE ART
| | | | |
|---|---|---|---|
| 77 | Arista AHAL 8001 | SPACE ART (LP) | 20 |

## SPACED
| | | | |
|---|---|---|---|
| 92 | Incite INC 1/123 | Deeper (Original Mix)/Deeper (Remix) (12", stickered white label) | 35 |
| 92 | No Label PNI 001 | Deeper (Mix 1)/(Mix 2)/Mix 3) (12", white label) | 50 |

## SPACEMEN
| | | | |
|---|---|---|---|
| 59 | Top Rank JAR 228 | The Clouds/The Lonely Jet Pilot | 12 |

## SPACEMEN 3
| | | | |
|---|---|---|---|
| 86 | Glass GLAEP 105 | Walkin' With Jesus (Sound Of Confusion)/Rollercoaster/Feel So Good (12" maxi-single, p/s, with numbered insert) | 50 |
| 86 | Glass GLAEP 105 | Walkin' With Jesus (Sound Of Confusion)/Rollercoaster/Feel So Good (12" maxi-single, p/s, without numbered insert) | 45 |
| 87 | Glass GLAEP 108 | Transparent Radiation/Ecstasy Symphony/Transparent Radiation (Flashback)/Things'll Never Be The Same/Starship (12" maxi-single, p/s) | 40 |
| 88 | Glass GLASS 12054 | Take Me To The Other Side/Soul 1/That's Just Fine (12", p/s, yellow label) | 30 |
| 88 | Fire BLAZE 29S | Revolution/Che (die-cut company sleeve) | 6 |
| 88 | Fire BLAZE 29T | Revolution/Che/May The Circle Be Unbroken (12") | 12 |
| 89 | Fire THREEBIE 3 | THREEBIE 3: Starship/Revolution/Suicide/Repeater/Love Intro Theme (Xtacy) (12", mail-order only, numbered p/s) | 20 |
| 89 | Sniffin' Rock SR 008 | When Tomorrow Hits (with Sniffin' Rock magazine) | 15 |
| 89 | Sniffin' Rock SR 008 | When Tomorrow Hits (without Sniffin' Rock magazine) | 10 |
| 89 | Fire BLAZE 36S | Hypnotized/Just To See You Smile (Honey Pt 2) (die-cut company sleeve) | 6 |
| 89 | Fire BLAZE 36T | Hypnotized/Just To See You Smile (Honey Pt 2)/The World Is Dying (12", with poster) | 18 |
| 89 | Fire BLAZE 41T | Big City/Drive (12", p/s) | 10 |
| 90 | Fierce FRIGHT 042 | Dreamweapon/Ecstasy In Slow Motion (12") | 25 |
| 91 | Fire BLAZE 41 | Big City (Edit)/Drive (p/s) | 5 |
| 91 | Fire BLAZE 41TR | Big City (Remix)/I Love You (Remix) (12", unissued, white label promo, 50 only) | 60 |
| 91 | Catalogue CAT 089 | I Love You//Sometimes (2 x flexis, with The Catalogue magazine) | 10 |
| 03 | Earworm Gold EGS 01 | Walking With Jesus/Take Me To The Other Side (Demo)/Walking With Jesus (Demo) (die-cut p/s, 'splatter' vinyl) | 8 |
| 09 | Great Pop Supplement GPS 50 | Big City (demo)/WOODEN SHJIPS: I Believe It (red marbled vinyl, insert & sticker) | 8 |
| 13 | Great Pop Supplement GPS 100 | SPECTRUM: Bo's Web/SPACEMEN 3: Why Couldn't I See/MGMT: Something To Do With Prince (withdrawn) | 15 |
| 86 | Glass GLALP 018 | SOUND OF CONFUSION (LP) | 45 |
| 87 | Glass GLALP 026 | THE PERFECT PRESCRIPTION (LP, gold/silver or bronze/silver sleeve) | 50 |
| 88 | Glass GLALP 030 | PERFORMANCE (LP) | 25 |
| 88 | Fire FIRELP 16 | PLAYING WITH FIRE (LP, embossed sleeve) | 35 |
| 89 | Fire REFIRE 5 | SOUND OF CONFUSION (LP, reissue) | 18 |
| 90 | Fire FIRE LP 23 | RECURRING (LP) | 40 |
| 90 | Fire REFIRE 11 | PERFORMANCE (LP, reissue) | 18 |
| 95 | Space Age ORBIT 002LP | LIVE IN EUROPE 1989 (2-LP) | 25 |
| 14 | Fire FIRE 158 | TRANSLUSCENT FLASHBACKS (3-12" box set) | 40 |

(see also Sonic Boom, Spiritualized, Darkside, Spectrum)

## SPACEPIMP
| | | | |
|---|---|---|---|
| 95 | Clear CLR 415 | The Pimp/Spacechace/K9 Law (12", p/s, on clear vinyl) | 25 |
| 95 | Clear CLR 415 | The Pimp/Spacechace/K9 Law (12", p/s) | 20 |

## SPACE TURKEYS
| | | | |
|---|---|---|---|
| 81 | Tavern Sound | Fun With A Social Worker/Disco Not Disco (p/s) | 15 |

## SPAGHETTI HEAD
| | | | |
|---|---|---|---|
| 75 | RCA RCA 2513 | Big Noise From Winnetka/Funky Axe | 30 |

(see also Clem Cattini Ork, Tornados)

## SPAGHETTI JUNCTION
| | | | |
|---|---|---|---|
| 72 | Columbia DB 8935 | Work's Nice - If You Can Get It/Step Right Up | 25 |

(see also Hank Marvin)

**SPANIELS**

| | | | |
|---|---|---|---|
| 60 | Joy JOYS 197 | THE SPANIELS (LP) | 20 |

**MUGGSY SPANIER & DIXIELAND/RAGTIME BAND**

| | | | |
|---|---|---|---|
| 56 | Tempo A 36 | Tin Roof Blues/Muskrat Rumble | 7 |

**SPANISH BOYS**

| | | | |
|---|---|---|---|
| 65 | Blue Beat BB 331 | I Am Alone/BUSTER'S ALL STARS: Vera Cruz | 250 |

**SPANISHTONIANS**

| | | | |
|---|---|---|---|
| 67 | Pyramid PYR 6005 | Kisses/ROLAND ALPHONSO: Women Of The World | 30 |
| 67 | Pyramid PYR 6009 | Suffer Me Not/ROLAND ALPHONSO: Guantanamera Ska | 30 |
| 67 | Pyramid PYR 6018 | Rudie Gets Plenty/ROLAND ALPHONSO: Sock It To Me | 100 |

**SPANISHTOWN SKABEATS**

| | | | |
|---|---|---|---|
| 65 | Blue Beat BB 315 | Oh My Baby (actually by Charmers)/Stop That Train | 400 |
| 65 | Blue Beat BB 320 | King Solomon/BUSTER'S ALLSTARS: Devil's Daffodil | 60 |

**SPANKY & OUR GANG**

| | | | |
|---|---|---|---|
| 67 | Mercury MF 982 | Sunday Will Never Be The Same/Distance | 20 |
| 67 | Mercury MF 999 | Making Every Minute Count/If You Could Only Be Me | 8 |
| 67 | Mercury MF 1010 | Lazy Day/It Ain't Necessarily Byrd Avenue | 10 |
| 68 | Mercury MF 1018 | Sunday Mornin'/Echoes | 8 |
| 68 | Mercury MF 1023 | Like To Get To Know You/Three Ways From Tomorrow | 12 |
| 68 | Mercury MF 1052 | Give A Damn/The Swingin' Gate | 10 |
| 69 | Mercury MF 1123 | And She's Mine/Leopard Skin Phone | 7 |
| 76 | Epic S EPC 3850 | I Won't Brand You/When I Wanna | 7 |
| 67 | Mercury 20114 (S)MCL | SPANKY AND OUR GANG (LP) | 30 |
| 68 | Mercury 20121 SCML | LIKE TO GET TO KNOW YOU (LP) | 30 |
| 69 | Mercury 20150 SCML | ANYTHING YOU CHOOSE/WITHOUT RHYME OR REASON (LP) | 30 |

*(see also Mama & Papas)*

**OTIS SPANN**

| | | | |
|---|---|---|---|
| 64 | Decca F 11972 | Stirs Me Up/Keep Your Hand Out Of My Pocket | 25 |
| 68 | Blue Horizon 57-3142 | Bloody Murder/Can't Do Me No Good | 15 |
| 69 | Blue Horizon 57-3155 | Walkin'/Temperature Is Rising (with Fleetwood Mac) | 25 |
| 64 | Decca LK 4615 | THE BLUES OF OTIS SPANN (LP) | 70 |
| 64 | Storyville SLP 157 | GOOD MORNING MR. BLUES (LP) | 30 |
| 64 | Storyville SLP 168 | PIANO BLUES (LP, with Memphis Slim) | 30 |
| 65 | Decca LK 4661 | BLUES NOW (LP) | 65 |
| 66 | Stateside SL 10169 | THE BLUES NEVER DIE (LP) | 35 |
| 67 | HMV CLP/CSD 3609 | BLUES ARE WHERE IT'S AT (LP) | 35 |
| 67 | Storyville 670 157 | PORTRAITS IN BLUES VOL. 3 (LP, reissue of SLP 157) | 15 |
| 67 | Polydor 545 030 | NOBODY KNOWS MY TROUBLES (LP) | 35 |
| 67 | Bounty BY 6037 | NOBODY KNOWS MY TROUBLES (LP) | 40 |
| 68 | Stateside (S)SL 10255 | BOTTOM OF THE BLUES (LP) | 40 |
| 69 | Chess CRLS 4556 | FATHERS AND SONS (LP) | 50 |
| 69 | Blue Horizon S 7-63217 | BIGGEST THING SINCE COLOSSUS (LP, with Fleetwood Mac) | 100 |
| 69 | Deram DML/SML 1036 | CRACKED SPANNER HEAD (LP) | 45 |
| 69 | Python KM 4 | RAISED IN MISSISSIPPI (LP, 99 copies only, with Robert Jnr. Lockwood) | 90 |
| 70 | Vanguard VSD 6514 | CRYIN' TIME (LP) | 20 |

*(see also Fleetwood Mac, Memphis Slim, Johnny Shines, Lonnie Johnson)*

**SPANNER THRU MA BEATBOX**

| | | | |
|---|---|---|---|
| 87 | Earthly Delights EARTH 3 | SPANNER THRU MA BEATBOX (LP) | 15 |

**SPARE PARTS**

| | | | |
|---|---|---|---|
| 79 | Random SP 100 | She's A New Kind Of Girl/Paint It Black (p/s) | 40 |

**SPARKERS**

| | | | |
|---|---|---|---|
| 69 | Blue Cat BS 155 | Dig It Up/DELROY WILSON: This Life Makes Me Wonder | 200 |

*(see also Samuel Edwards)*

**LOU SPARKES**

| | | | |
|---|---|---|---|
| 69 | Gayfeet GS 203 | By The Time I Get To Phoenix/Lover Boy | 30 |
| 70 | Gayfeet GS 208 | We Will Make Love/ROLAND ALPHONSO: Sticker | 8 |

**KRISTINE SPARKLE**

| | | | |
|---|---|---|---|
| 74 | Decca F 13485 | Hokey Cokey/Baby I Love You | 8 |
| 74 | Decca 13515 | Eight Days A Week/The Drum | 8 |

**SPARKLEHORSE**

| | | | |
|---|---|---|---|
| 06 | Capitol CL 881 | Knives Of Summertime/Caroline | 5 |
| 96 | Parlophone 7243 8328 16 19 | VIVADIXIESUBMARINETRANSMISSIONPILOT (LP) | 30 |
| 98 | Parlophone 49 6014 1 | GOOD MORNING SPIDER (LP) | 40 |

**SPARKS**

| | | | |
|---|---|---|---|
| 72 | Bearsville K 15505 | Wonder Girl/(No More) Mr. Nice Guy | 15 |
| 74 | Bearsville K 15516 | Girl From Germany/Beaver O'Lindy (brown or white label) | 10 |
| 74 | Island WIP 6211 | Never Turn Your Back On Mother Earth/Alabamy Right (p/s) | 6 |
| 75 | Island WIP 6221 | Something For The Girl With Everything/Marry Me (title sleeve) | 6 |
| 75 | Island WIP 6236 | Get In The Swing/Profile (title sleeve) | 6 |
| 75 | Island WIP 6239 | Looks, Looks, Looks/Pineapple (title sleeve) | 6 |
| 75 | Island WIP 6249 | Looks, Looks, Looks/Pineapple (DJ copy in promo p/s) | 12 |
| 76 | Island WIP 6282 | I Want To Hold Your Hand/England (withdrawn after 1 day) | 25 |
| 76 | Island WIP 6357 | I Like Girls/England | 5 |
| 77 | Island WIP 6282 | I Want To Hold Your Hand/Under The Table With Her (promo only) | 20 |
| 77 | Island WIP 6193 | This Town Ain't Big Enough For The Both Of Us/Barbecutie (reissue, orange sunset label) | 10 |
| 79 | Virgin VS 244 | The No. 1 Song In Heaven/The No. 1 Song In Heaven (Version) (p/s, green vinyl) | 5 |
| 79 | Island WIP 6532 | This Town Ain't Big Enough For The Both Of Us/Looks, Looks, Looks | 7 |

MINT VALUE £

## L. SPARKS

| 83 | Atlantic A 9866 | Cool Places/Sports (no p/s) .................................................................................. | 5 |
| 85 | Epic A 6671 | Armies Of The Night/EVELYN KING: Give It Up (p/s) ........................................... | 5 |
| 93 | Finiflex FF 1004 | National Crime Awareness Week (13 Minutes In Heaven)/National Crime Awareness Week (Perkins Playtime) (12", p/s) ...................................................................... | 20 |
| 94 | Logic 7432 134461 | When Do I Get To Sing My Way/(mixes) (12", doublepack, p/s) .......................... | 20 |
| 73 | Bearsville K 45510 | A WOOFER IN TWEETERS CLOTHING (LP) ............................................................ | 12 |
| 74 | Island ILPS 9312 | PROPAGANDA (LP, sticker on top right hand corner) ......................................... | 18 |
| 74 | Island ILPS 9272 | KIMONO MY HOUSE (LP, pink rim label, sleeve laminated both sides, A-2U/B-1U matrixes) ........................................................................................................... | 25 |
| 75 | Island ILPS 9345 | INDISCREET (LP, gatefold) ................................................................................... | 20 |
| 76 | Bearsville K 85505 | TWO ORIGINALS OF SPARKS (2-LP, gatefold sleeve with 12-page booklet) ............ | 20 |
| 04 | Universal LBRV001 | LIL' BEETHOVEN (LP) ........................................................................................... | 18 |
| 06 | Gut GUTLP 53 | HELLO YOUNG LOVERS (LP, please note that pink vinyl edition is U.S. pressing) ..... | 30 |
| | | | 20 |

(see also Adrian Musey, Trevor White)

## L. SPARKS

| 72 | Big Shot BI 601 | You Don't Care/TONY'S ALL STARS: Must Care (Version) ..................................... | 6 |
| 72 | Pama PM 833 | You Don't Care/TONY'S ALL STARS: Must Care (Version) ..................................... | 6 |

(see also Lloyd Parks, Termites)

## SPARKY

| 72 | UK UK 13 | (Do You Remember) That Summertime Woman/You Gotta Have It Sometime ......... | 8 |

## SPARKY AND THE INNER CITIZENS

| 76 | Contempo CS2102 | Golden Gate Get Down (Short version)Golden Gate Get Down (Long Version) ......... | 10 |

## CANDY SPARLING

| 62 | Piccadilly 7N 35046 | When's He Gonna Kiss Me?/Lonely For You .......................................................... | 15 |
| 63 | Piccadilly 7N 35096 | Can You Keep A Secret/Charm Bracelet ............................................................... | 20 |

## SPARROW (JAMAICA)

| 60 | Kalypso XX 10 | Carnival Boycott/Gloria (with Lord Melody) ....................................................... | 6 |
| 60 | Kalypso XX 17 | The Sack/Round And Around ............................................................................... | 5 |
| 60s | Melodisc CAL 15 | Leading Calypsonians/Love Is Everywhere ......................................................... | 6 |
| 60s | Melodisc CAL 17 | Clara Honey Bunch/Family Sized Cokes .............................................................. | 5 |
| 60s | Melodisc CAL 18 | Goaty/I Confess ................................................................................................. | 5 |

(see also Mighty Sparrow, King Sparrow)

## SPARROW (U.S.)

| 66 | CBS 202342 | Tomorrow's Ship/Isn't It Strange ....................................................................... | 75 |

(see also Steppenwolf)

## JACK SPARROW

| 66 | Doctor Bird DB 1005 | Ice Water/ROLAND ALPHONSO: Ska-Culation .................................................... | 150 |
| 66 | Doctor Bird DB 1027 | More Ice Water/ROLAND ALPHONSO: Miss Ska-Culation ..................................... | 60 |

## SPARTA

| 80 | Suspect SUS 1 | Fast Lane/Fighting To Be Free (in p/s) ................................................................. | 50 |
| 80 | Suspect SUS 1 | Fast Lane/Fighting To Be Free ............................................................................. | 18 |
| 81 | Suspect SUS 2 | Angel Of Death/Tonight (wraparound p/s) .......................................................... | 25 |

(see also Ethiopians)

## SPARTACUS

| 79 | Zara ZMRD 1 | Mother Sucker/Stop Your Crying (12") ................................................................ | 75 |

## SPARTANS

| 62 | Stateside SS 117 | Can You Waddle? (Parts 1 & 2) ............................................................................ | 12 |

## SPARTAN WARRIOR

| 83 | Guardian GRC 2164 | STEEL 'N' CHAINS (LP) ......................................................................................... | 20 |

## SPASMS

| 80 | Ellie Jay SAP 001 | It Never Happens Like It Does On The Telly/Monday Morning (die cut p/s) ............. | 40 |

## SPATTS

| 15 | B-Line Recordings BLN015 | Waiting For The Bomb/Chaos By Numbers (7" test pressing, never issued) ............ | 35 |

## SPAZZTIC BLUR

| 87 | Earache MOSH 5 | BEFO DA AWBUM (LP) .......................................................................................... | 15 |

## ROGER RUSKIN SPEAR

| 72 | United Artists UAG 29381 | ELECTRIC SHOCKS (LP) ........................................................................................ | 25 |

(see also Bonzo Dog [Doo Dah] Band)

## SPECIAL DUTIES

| 81 | Charnel H. SARCOPHAGI 2 | Violent Society/Colchester Council (wraparound p/s) ........................................ | 30 |
| 82 | Rondelet ROUND 15 | VIOLENT SOCIETY (EP) ........................................................................................ | 15 |
| 82 | Rondelet ROUND 20 | POLICE STATE (EP) .............................................................................................. | 10 |
| 82 | Rondelet ROUND 24 | Bullshit Crass/You're Doing Yourself No Good (p/s) ........................................... | 12 |
| 83 | Expulsion OUT 1 | Punk Rocker/Too Much Talking (p/s) .................................................................. | 12 |
| 82 | Rondelet ABOUT 9 | 77 IN 82 (LP) ...................................................................................................... | 20 |

## SPECIAL CLINIC

| 78 | Penicillin POX 1 | When The Going Gets Rough/Sumo Stomp (no p/s) ............................................. | 8 |

## SPECIALS (THE SPECIAL A.K.A.)

| 79 | 2-Tone TT 1/TT 2 | Gangsters (as The Special A.K.A.)/THE SELECTER: The Selecter (paper label, in stamped plain white sleeve; matrix numbers TT1-3 & TT2-1) ........................... | 45 |
| 79 | 2-Tone TT 1/TT 2 | Gangsters (as The Special A.K.A.)/THE SELECTER: The Selecter (paper label) ....... | 15 |
| 79 | 2-Tone TT 1/TT 2 | Gangsters (as The Special A.K.A.)/THE SELECTER: The Selecter (paper label, die-cut 2-Tone sleeve, 2nd issue with Chrysalis CHS TT 1/2 matrix no.) ......................... | 6 |
| 79 | 2-Tone CHS TT 5 | Message To You Rudy/Nite Klub (paper label, company sleeve, as The Specials featuring Rico) ................................................................................................. | 8 |
| 79 | 2-Tone CHS TT 5 | Message To You Rudy/Nite Klub (later pressing on moulded plastic labels) ........... | 5 |
| 80 | 2-Tone CHS TT 7 | THE SPECIAL A.K.A. LIVE (EP, paper label) ........................................................... | 10 |
| 80 | 2-Tone CHS TT 7 | THE SPECIALS A.K.A. LIVE (EP, later pressing with plastic moulded labels) ........... | 5 |
| 80 | 2-Tone CHS TT 11 | Rat Race/Rude Boys Outa Jail (company sleeve, paper label, as The Specials) ....... | 8 |

| 80 | 2-Tone CHS TT 11 | Rat Race/Rude Boys Outa Jail (later pressing with plastic moulded labels) ...................5 |
| 80 | 2-Tone CHS TT 13 | Stereotype/International Jet Set (company sleeve, paper label, as The Specials) ............8 |
| 80 | 2-Tone CHS TT 13 | Stereotype/International Jet Set (later pressing on plastic moulded labels)...................5 |
| 80 | 2-Tone CHS TT 16 | Do Nothing/Maggie's Farm (laminated p/s, paper label, as The Specials) .....................8 |
| 80 | 2-Tone CHS TT 16 | Do Nothing/Maggie's Farm (later pressing, non laminated p/s with plastic moulded labels)............5 |
| 81 | 2-Tone CHS TT 17 | Ghost Town/Why/Friday Night Saturday Morning (paper labels p/s) ...........................8 |
| 81 | 2-Tone CHS TT 1217 | Ghost Town (6.02 Extended Version)/Why/Friday Night, Saturday Morning (12", p/s)..15 |
| 81 | 2-Tone CHS TT 17 | Ghost Town/Friday Night Saturday Morning (later pressing with plastic moulded labels, p/s).................6 |
| 82 | 2-Tone CHS TT 23 | War Crimes (The Crime Is Still The Same)/War Crimes (p/s) ........................................5 |
| 83 | 2-Tone CHS TPTT 25 | Racist Friend/Bright Lights ...........................................................................................5 |
| 84 | 2-Tone CHS TT 26 | Nelson Mandela/Break Down The Door (p/s).............................................................5 |
| 84 | 2-Tone CHS TT27 | What I Like About You Most Is Your Girlfriend/Can't Get A Break (paper labels) ...........5 |
| 84 | 2-Tone CHS TT 27 | What I Like Most About You Is Your Girlfriend/Can't Get A Break/War Crimes (The Crime Is Still The Same)/(Version) (double pack, as The Special A.K.A.) ........................8 |
| 84 | 2-Tone CHS TT 1227 | What I Like Most About You Is Your Girlfriend/Can't Get A Break (12", poster p/s with free single) ...........10 |
| 89 | 2-Tone TTP1 | THE SPECIALS: Rudi, A Message To You/Ghost Town//SELECTER: On My Radio/ MADNESS: One Step Beyond (promo, 40 only) ....................................................... 150 |
| 91 | Two Tone CHSTT 30 | Ghost Town/Ghost Dub '91 (p/s) .............................................................................. 20 |
| 91 | Two Tone CHSTT 12 30 | Ghost Town/Ghost Dub '91 (12", p/s).........................................................................30 |
| 14 | 2-Tone CHS TT27 | Sock It To 'Em (Dub)/Rat Race (Dub) (2-Tone replica sleeve) .......................................6 |
| 86 | Strange Fruit SFPS 018 | THE PEEL SESSIONS (EP) ..........................................................................................10 |
| 79 | 2-Tone CDLTT 5001 | SPECIALS (LP) ......................................................................................................... 25 |
| 80 | 2-Tone CDL TT 5001 | MORE SPECIALS (LP, with poster & bonus 7": Roddy Radiation & The Specials' "Braggin' And Tryin' Not To Lie"/Judge Roughneck's "Rude Buoys Outa Jail" [TT 999]) . 30 |
| 80 | 2-Tone CDL TT 5003 | MORE SPECIALS (LP)................................................................................................15 |
| 81 | 2-Tone CDL TT5001-P | SPECIALS (LP, picture disc) ......................................................................................15 |
| 84 | 2 Tone CHRTT 5008 | IN THE STUDIO (LP) .................................................................................................15 |
| 91 | 2 Tone CHRTT 5010 | SINGLES (LP)............................................................................................................15 |
| 92 | Two-Tone CHR TT 5011 | THE SPECIALS - LIVE AT THE MOONLIGHT CLUB (LP)..................................................15 |
| 92 | Receiver RRLP 161 | LIVE - TOO MUCH TOO YOUNG (LP) .........................................................................15 |
| 99 | Chrysalis/Two-Tone 499 4701 | SPECIALS (LP, reissue, barcode on sleeve) ................................................................30 |

*(see also Colourfield, Selecter, Rhoda, Rico, Desmond Dekkar)*

## SPECIFIK & PROJECT CEE

| 02 | Core Level CLM 001 | Where Your Mind Is .................................................................................................25 |
| 02 | Sudden Debt SDR 004 | RESURRECTING VIBES (EP) .......................................................................................12 |

## SPECIMEN

| 83 | London LON 24 | Returning From A Journey/Kiss Kiss Bang Bang (bat-shaped disc) ...............................10 |

## SPECKLED RED

| 60s | Storyville SEP 384 | STORYVILLE BLUES ANTHOLOGY VOL. 4 (EP) ..............................................................15 |
| 63 | Esquire 32-190 | THE DIRTY DOZENS (LP) ...........................................................................................30 |
| 71 | VJM LC 11 | OH RED (LP) ............................................................................................................20 |

## PHIL SPECTOR

| 63 | London HA-U 8141 | A CHRISTMAS GIFT FOR YOU (LP, various artists, Spector as producer; plum label) .......80 |
| 63 | London HA-U 8141 | A CHRISTMAS GIFT FOR YOU (LP, various artists, Spector as producer; later black label) ..................50 |
| 72 | Apple APCOR 24 | PHIL SPECTOR'S CHRISTMAS ALBUM (LP, reissue of London HA-U 8141) ......................25 |
| 74 | Warner Bros K 59010 | PHIL SPECTOR'S CHRISTMAS ALBUM (LP, 2nd reissue, with poster)............................18 |
| 76 | Phil Spector Intl. 2307 008 | RARE MASTERS VOL. 1 (LP, various artists, Spector as producer)................................20 |
| 76 | Phil Spector Intl. 2307 009 | RARE MASTERS VOL. 2 (LP, various artists, Spector as producer)................................20 |
| 80 | Phil Spector Intl. 2307 015 | PHIL SPECTOR '74/'79 (LP, various artists, Spector as producer) ................................25 |
| 81 | Phil Spector Intl. WOS 001 | WALL OF SOUND (9-LP box set, various artists, Spector as producer)..........................60 |

*(see also Ronettes, Crystals, Darlene Love, Bob B. Soxx & Blue Jeans, Teddy Bears)*

## RONNIE SPECTOR

| 71 | Apple APPLE 33 | Try Some, Buy Some/Tandoori Chicken (with p/s) ......................................................30 |
| 71 | Apple APPLE 33 | Try Some, Buy Some/Tandoori Chicken ....................................................................10 |
| 77 | Epic EPC 5185 | Say Goodbye To Hollywood/Baby Please Don't Go (with E Street Band, p/s) ...............12 |
| 81 | Red Shadow LP 002 | SIREN (LP) ..............................................................................................................20 |

*(see also Ronettes)*

## SPECTRES (IRELAND)

| 65 | Lloyd Sound UED QU 1 | The Facts Of Life/Whirlpool.................................................................................... 300 |

## SPECTRES (1)

| 66 | Piccadilly 7N 35339 | I (Who Have Nothing)/Neighbour, Neighbour............................................................ 300 |
| 66 | Piccadilly 7N 35352 | Hurdy Gurdy Man/Laticia ...................................................................................... 300 |
| 67 | Piccadilly 7N 35368 | We Ain't Got Nothin' Yet/I Want It (beware bootlegs) ............................................. 300 |

*(see also Traffic Jam, Status Quo)*

## SPECTRES (2)

| 80 | Direct Hit DH 1 | This Strange Effect/Getting Away With Murder (p/s) ....................................................7 |
| 81 | Demon D 1002 | Stories/Things (p/s).................................................................................................5 |

*(see also Rich Kids)*

## SPECTRES (3)

| 13 | Howling Owl HOWL 019 | HUNGER EP (12" 2nd pressing with printed sleeve, 100 copies) ..................................15 |
| 13 | Howling Owl HOWL 019 | HUNGER EP (12", hand-made and numbered sleeve, 100 only) ..................................40 |
| 13 | Howling Owl HOWL 024 | Lump/THE NATURALS: Heat Death (10", lyric sheet, 100 only)....................................12 |
| 15 | Howling Owl HOWL 043 | Wonderful Christmas Time (lathe cut, 30 only) .........................................................30 |
| 15 | Sonic Cathedral SCR 086 | Stealed Scene/LORELLE MEETS THE OBSOLETE: The Sky Of All Places (365 copies) .......15 |
| 15 | Sonic Cathedral SCR 090LP | DYING (LP, grey vinyl) ..............................................................................................25 |

## SPECTRUM (1)
| 65 | Columbia DB 7742 | Little Girl/Asking You | 10 |
|---|---|---|---|
| 67 | RCA RCA 1589 | Samantha's Mine/Saturday's Child | 10 |
| 67 | RCA RCA 1619 | Portobello Road/Comes The Dawn | 10 |
| 67 | RCA RCA 1651 | Headin' For A Heatwave/I Wanna Be Happy With You | 10 |
| 68 | RCA RCA 1700 | London Bridge Is Coming Down/Tables And Chairs | 10 |
| 68 | RCA RCA 1753 | Little Red Boat By The River/Forget Me Not | 10 |
| 68 | RCA RCA 1775 | Ob-La-Di, Ob-La-Da/Music Soothes The Savage Beast | 10 |
| 69 | RCA RCA 1853 | Free/The Tale Of Wally Toft | 10 |
| 69 | RCA RCA 1883 | Glory/Nodnol | 10 |
| 70 | RCA RCA 1976 | Portobello Road/Comes The Dawn (reissue) | 10 |
| 71 | Parlophone R 5908 | I'll Be Gone/Launching Place - Pt II | 20 |
| 69 | RCA Intl. INTS 118 | THE LIGHT IS DARK ENOUGH (LP) | 30 |
| 00 | Subway TRUMP 1 | THE LIGHT IS DARK ENOUGH (LP, reissue) | 20 |

## SPECTRUM (2)
| 87 | Phoenix Modernist THE 1 | All Or Nothing (Contemporary Version)/All Or Nothing (Traditional Version) (12", p/s with 2 inserts & free 7", distributed by Nine Mile & Cartel) | 10 |
|---|---|---|---|

*(see also Steve Marriott, Chris Farlowe, P.P. Arnold, Creation)*

## SPECTRUM (3)
| 91 | Silvertone SONIC 2 | (I Love You)To The Moon And Back/Capo Waltz (Live) (die-cut p/s gig freebie) | 8 |
|---|---|---|---|
| 91 | Silvertone SONIC 2 | (I Love You)To The Moon And Back/Capo Waltz (Live) (p/s, with Outer Limits fanzine) | 25 |
| 92 | Silvertone ORE 41 | How Do You Satisfy Me/Don't Go (clear vinyl) | 8 |
| 92 | Silvertone ORE 41 | How You Satisfy Me/Don't Go (Instrumental 2) (clear vinyl, printed plastic sleeve) | 15 |
| 92 | Silvertone ORE 44 | True Love Will Find You In The End (Radio Mix)/My Life Spins Round Your Every Smile (Remix) (yellow vinyl, printed plastic sleeve) | 8 |
| 92 | Beechwood TT 015e | Taste The Ozone/MOONSHAKE: Night Tripper | 5 |
| 93 | Silvertone ORE 56 | Indian Summer/Baby Don't You Worry (California Lullaby) (numbered p/s) | 6 |
| 93 | Silvertone ORET 56 | Indian Summer/Baby Don't You Worry (California Lullaby)/It's Alright/True Love Will Find You In The End (12", p/s) | 10 |
| 94 | Silvertone | Soul Kiss Glide Divine/STEREOLAB: Tone Burst (demo)/Tempter (demo) (unrel., with colour photocopied wraparound p/s, 25 test pressings only) | 150 |
| 94 | Silvertone ORET 65 | Undo The Taboo/In The Fullness Of Time/Turn The Tide (Sub Aqua)/Go To Sleep (12", p/s) | 15 |
| 10 | Great Pop Supplement GPS 54 | Words May Shatter (with Tim "Love" Lee)/The Lonesome Death Of Johnny Ace (with Captain Memphis) (picture disc, printed plastic insert, PVC sleeve) | 10 |
| 13 | Great Pop Supplement GSP100 | Bo's Web/SPACEMEN 3: Why Couldn't I See/MGMT: Something To Do WIth Prince (withdrawn) | 20 |
| 92 | Silvertone ORELP 518 | SOUL KISS (GLIDE DIVINE) (LP, inner) | 30 |
| 92 | Silvertone OREZLP 518 | SOUL KISS (GLIDE DIVINE) (LP, clear vinyl, printed double walled PVC sleeve containing liquid) | 30 |
| 94 | Silvertone ORELP 532 | HIGHS, LOWS AND HEAVENLY BLOWS (LP) | 50 |
| 97 | Space Age ORBIT 008LP | FOREVER ALIEN (2-LP) | 35 |
| 97 | Space Age ORBIT 008LP | FOREVER ALIEN (2-LP, yellow vinyl) | 40 |

*(see also Spacemen 3, Sonic Boom)*

## CHRIS SPEDDING
| 70 | Harvest HAR 5013 | Rock'n'Roll Band/BATTERED ORNAMENTS: Goodbye We Loved You (Madly) | 25 |
|---|---|---|---|
| 75 | Island WIP 6225 | My Bucket's Got A Hole In It/I Can't Boogie | 8 |
| 75 | RAK RAK 210 | Motor Bikin'/Working For The Union | 5 |
| 76 | RAK RAK 236 | Guitar Jamboree/Sweet Disposition | 5 |
| 76 | RAK RAK 246 | Pogo Dancing/Pose (p/s) | 6 |
| 77 | RAK RAK 261 | Get Outa My Pagoda/Hey Miss Betty | 5 |
| 70 | Harvest SHSP 4004 | BACKWOOD PROGRESSION (LP, flipback sleeve no EMI logo on label) | 60 |
| 72 | Harvest SHSP 4017 | THE ONLY LICK I KNOW (LP, laminated sleeve, with EMI logo on label) | 40 |

*(see also Sharks, Nucleus, Sounds Nice, Panhandle, Solid Gold Cadillac, Matthew Ellis, Vibrators, Battered Ornaments, IOFR)*

## SPEED (JAMAICA)
| 71 | Bullet BU 477 | There's A Train/Blue Moon | 12 |
|---|---|---|---|

## SPEED (1)
| 78 | It IT 1 | Big City/All Day And All The Night (in p/s) | 40 |
|---|---|---|---|
| 78 | It IT 1 | Big City/All Day And All The Night | 15 |

*(see also Cobra, Tearjerkers)*

## SPEED (2)
| 80 | Speed GJS 001 | Man In The Street/Down The Road (p/s) | 125 |
|---|---|---|---|

*(see also Bruce Dickinson, Iron Maiden)*

## SPEEDBALL(S)
| 80 | No Pap/Dirty Dick DD 1/2 | No Survivors/Is Somebody There? (miscredited as 'Speedballs' on label, in withdrawn printed die-cut sleeve) | 60 |
|---|---|---|---|
| 80 | No Pap/Dirty Dick DD 1/2 | No Survivors/Is Somebody There? (miscredited as 'Speedballs' on label) | 25 |

## SPEED LIMIT
| 78 | Satril SAT 134 | Wino/Motorbike Kid | 5 |
|---|---|---|---|

## SPEEDOMETORS
| 78 | Mascot NICE 1 | Disgrace/Work (p/s) | 5 |
|---|---|---|---|
| 78 | Mascot NICE 2 | Liverpool Ladies (p/s) | 5 |

## SPELLBINDERS
| 66 | CBS 202453 | Help Me (Get Myself Back Together)/Danny Boy | 40 |
|---|---|---|---|
| 66 | CBS 202453 | Help Me (Get Myself Back Together)/Danny Boy (DJ copy) | 85 |
| 67 | CBS 202622 | Chain Reaction/For You | 40 |
| 67 | CBS 202622 | Chain Reaction/For You (DJ copy) | 75 |
| 67 | CBS 2776 | Since I Don't Have You/I Believe | 8 |
| 69 | Direction 58-3970 | Help Me/Chain Reaction | 15 |

## SPELLING MISSTEAKS
79    Stortbeat BEAT 7          POPSTAR (EP) ................................................................. 50

## BENNY SPELLMAN
62    London HLP 9570           Lipstick Traces/Fortune Teller ........................................ 50
62    London HLP 9570           Lipstick Traces/Fortune Teller (DJ Copy) ....................... 100

## BRUCE SPELMAN
                                ....................................................................................... 8
69    Beacon BEA 112            Lady/Long Time Gone
72    Montagu MONT 3000         29 Years To Doomsday/Cutting The Traces ..................... 12
70    Beacon BES 3              YOU DON'T KNOW WHAT YOU'RE PADDLING IN (LP) ....... 70
70    Montague MONS 1           YOU DON'T KNOW WHAT YOU'RE PADDLING IN (LP, different sleeve, blue/black
                                label) .......................................................................... 40

## BARRINGTON SPENCE
75    Grounation GRO 2009       For The Rest Of My Life/Version ...................................... 5
76    Student STU 1005          Mash It Up/Straight To Radd Head .................................. 10
86    Camara CAM 002T           Hey Youthman/Version//K LEACOCK: Round And Round/Version (12") ...... 30
88    Camara CAM 004T           Sons Of Far I/Far I Dub (12") ........................................ 35
76    Trojan TRLS 117           SPEAK SOFTLY (LP) ....................................................... 15

## BRINDLEY D SPENCER
68    Domain D8                 The Company I Keep/On A Day Like Today........................ 10

## DON SPENCER
62    HMV POP 1087              Fireball/I'm All Alone Again (blue or black labels).......... 12
63    HMV POP 1186              Busy Doing Nothing/The Joker ........................................ 7
63    HMV POP 1205              Worried Mind/Give Give Give A Little .............................. 6
64    HMV POP 1306              Pride Is Such A Little Word/For Love (with Le Roys) ......... 6
67    Talus TP1010              Uproar In The House/On The G.P.O Tower ....................... 20

*(see also Le Roys)*

## DON SPENCER/XL5
63    HMV 7EG 8802              FIREBALL AND OTHER TITLES (EP, 2 tracks each) ........... 50

## JEREMY SPENCER (BAND)
70    Reprise RS 27002          Linda/Teenage Darling .................................................. 10
79    Atlantic K 11363          Travelling/Cool Breeze (as Jeremy Spencer Band).......... 5
70    Reprise RSLP 9002         JEREMY SPENCER (LP, label states K 44105 cat. no)...... 40
71    Reprise K 44105           JEREMY SPENCER (LP, reissue) ....................................... 20

*(see also Fleetwood Mac)*

## JO SPENCER
71    Dynamic DYN 415           Bed Of Roses/Forgive Me ............................................... 5

## JON SPENCER BLUES EXPLOSION
92    Clawfist 13               History Of Sex/Write A Song/Smoke Cigarettes (foldover p/s in poly bag) ...... 8
94    Matador OLE 077           Afro/Relax Her (p/s) ...................................................... 6
91    Hut HUTLP 3               THE JON SPENCER BLUES EXPLOSION (LP) ...................... 18
96    Mute STUMM 132            NOW I GOT WORRY (LP)................................................. 20
98    Mute STUMM 156            ACME (LP, inner)......................................................... 20

*(see also Pussy Galore)*

## SONNY SPENCER
59    Parlophone R 4611         Oh Boy/Gilee ............................................................... 20

## SPENCER & THE SAINTS
68    Tabernacle TS 1005        Something Within/When You Get To Heaven ..................... 8

## SPENCERS WASHBOARD KINGS
66    Pye 7N 17245              The Egg Plant That Ate Chicago/Somebody Stole My Gal......... 7
69    Parlophone R 5782         Pimlico/Ordinary People .............................................. 15

## SPERMICIDE
79    No Wonder NOW 3           Femme Prothèse/Belgique (p/s with lyrics) ..................... 30

## SPG (SPECIAL PATROL GROUP)
80    Suspect ELO 1             Dracula/Christopher Columbus (p/s) .............................. 10

## JIMMIE SPHEERIS
72    CBS 8092                  Let It Flow/The Nest...................................................... 5

## SPHERES
78    Sphere                    FESTIVAL AND SUNS (LP, with insert) ............................. 25

*(see also Jimmy Winston)*

## SPHERICAL OBJECTS
78    Object Music OM 01        The Kill/The Knot (p/s) ................................................. 10
78    Object Music OM 04        Seventies Romance/Sweet Tooth (p/s) ............................ 10
78    Object Music PBJ 001      PAST & PARCEL (LP) ..................................................... 20
79    Object Music OBJ 004      ELLIPTICAL OPTIMISM (LP) ............................................ 20

*(see also Alternomen Unlimited, Noyes Brothers)*

## SPHYNKTA
83    Sultanic SUL 666          In The Shade Of The Gods/Jesus Bless My Upside-Down Cross (p/s, red vinyl, with
                                'devil' tattoo) ............................................................. 60
83    Sultanic SUL 999          Death And Violence/Ritual Slaughter (Of Your Daughter) (p/s, red vinyl)...... 40
84    Sultanic SUL 000          Spike Up My Sphynkta/No Pain No Gain (unissued) ......... 100

## SPHYNX
78    Charisma CDS 4011         XITINTODAY (LP, with booklet) ...................................... 30
78    Charisma CDS 4011         XITINTODAY (LP, without booklet) ................................. 15

*(see also Inner City Unit, Gong, Radio Actors)*

## SPICE GIRLS
96    Virgin V 2812             SPICE (LP, with glossy picture/lyric insert) ..................... 35
97    Virgin V 2850             SPICEWORLD (LP)......................................................... 40

MINT VALUE £

### SPICE (U.K.)
| | | |
|---|---|---|
| 68 | United Artists UP 2246 | What About The Music?/In Love .......... 300 |

*(see also Uriah Heep, Godz, Toe-Fat)*

### GEORGE SPICER
| 74 | Topic 12T 235 | BLACKBERRY FOLD (LP) .......... 15 |

### SPICS
| 79 | Wavelength WA 1 | You & Me/Bus Stop .......... 5 |

### SPIDELLS
| 66 | Sue WI 4019 | Find Out What's Happening/That'll Make My Heart Break .......... 50 |

### SPIDER (1)
| 66 | Decca F 12430 | The Comedown Song/Blow Ya Mind .......... 50 |

### SPIDER (2)
| 77 | Pennine PSS 136 | Back To The Wall/Down And Out (p/s, 500 only, these 300 with p/s) .......... 60 |
| 77 | Pennine PSS 136 | Back To The Wall/Down And Out (p/s, 500 only, these 200 without p/s) .......... 30 |

### SPIDER (3)
| 80 | Alien ALIEN 14 | Children Of The Street/Down 'N' Out (in p/s) .......... 35 |
| 80 | Alien ALIEN 14 | Children Of The Street/Down 'N' Out .......... 8 |
| 80 | Alien ALIEN 16 | College Luv/Born To Be Wild (in p/s) .......... 35 |
| 80 | Alien ALIEN 16 | College Luv/Born To Be Wild .......... 8 |

### SPIDER & THE FLIES
| 07 | Mute Irregulars IRREG 17 | Metalurge/Desmond Leslie .......... 15 |

*(see also Horrors)*

### SPIDERS
| 66 | Philips BF 1531 | Sad Sunset/Hey Boy .......... 40 |

### SPIDERS (U.S.)
| 54 | London HL 8086 | I'm Slippin' In/I'm Searching (78) .......... 65 |

### SPIDERS FROM MARS
| 75 | Pye 7N 45549 | White Man Black Man/National Poll .......... 6 |

*(see also David Bowie, Kestrel, Mick Ronson)*

### BERND SPIER
| 65 | Oriole CB 1987 | A Million And One Times/Two Strangers .......... 10 |

### SPILL
| 92 | Virgin VS 1141 | Don't Wanna Know About Evil (7" Wireless Road Mix)/(Saspelofiska Dub Mix) (p/s) .... 12 |
| 92 | Virgin VST 1141 | Don't Wanna Know About Evil (Tumble Mix)/(Rumble Mix)/(Danny's Moto Mix)/(The Groovy Beats Mix) (12", p/s) .......... 15 |

*(see also Beth Orton)*

### ARTHUR SPINK BAND
| 68 | Beltona BL 2766 | Beatles Och Aye/Harry Lauder Medley .......... 5 |

### SPINNERS (U.S.)
| 61 | Columbia DB 4693 | That's What Girls Are Made For/Heebie Jeebies .......... 200 |
| 61 | Columbia DB 4693 | That's What Girls Are Made For/Heebie Jeebies (DJ copy) .......... 250 |
| 65 | Tamla Motown TMG 514 | Sweet Thing/How Can I? (demo with 'Spinners' credit) .......... 300 |
| 65 | Tamla Motown TMG 514 | Sweet Thing/How Can I? (demos with 'Detroit Spinners' credit) .......... 250 |
| 65 | Tamla Motown TMG 514 | Sweet Thing/How Can I? (stock copies credited to 'Spinners') .......... 400 |

*(see also Detroit Spinners)*

### SPINNING JENNY
| 71 | Midas MR004 | SPINNING JENNY (LP) .......... 70 |

### SPINNING WHEEL
| 79 | Private pressing | JACOB'S FLEECE (LP) .......... 15 |

*(see also Dragonsfire)*

### SPINNING WHEELS
| 75 | Peter Dearden PD 205 | SPINNING WHEELS (EP) .......... 15 |

### SPIRALS
| 58 | Capitol CL 14958 | The Rockin' Cow/Everybody Knows .......... 15 |

### SPIRAL SKY
| 93 | Acme AC 8002LP | SPIRAL SKY (LP, numbered & sealed with insert, 500 only) .......... 30 |
| 94 | Acme 8002LP | SPIRAL SKY (LP, 2nd pressing numbered & sealed with insert, 300 only) .......... 25 |

*(see also Sun Dial, Ohr Musik)*

### SPIRAL STAIRCASE
| 68 | CBS 3507 | Baby What I Mean/Makin' Your Mind Up .......... 25 |
| 69 | CBS 4187 | More Today Than Yesterday/Broken Hearted Man .......... 50 |
| 69 | CBS 4187 | More Today Than Yesterday/Broken Hearted Man (DJ copy) .......... 80 |
| 69 | CBS 4524 | No One For Me To Turn To/Sweet Little Thing .......... 25 |

### SPIRAL TRIBE
| 92 | Big Life BLRT 79 | Breach The Peace/Do ET/Seven/23 Minute Warning (12", p/s) .......... 25 |
| 92 | Big Life BLRT 85 | Forward The Revolution/World Traveller Adventurer/Ragga Boom/Track 13 (criminal drug)(12", p/s) .......... 25 |
| 92 | Big Life BLRR 85 | Forward The Revolution (the Youth remix) (1-sided, etched 12") .......... 15 |
| 93 | Butterfly BFLT 04 | Sirius 23/Earthworm/Going All The Way/Predator (12", p/s, as Spiral Tribe Sound System) .......... 20 |
| 93 | Butterfly BFL LP 6 | TECNO TERRA (2-LP) .......... 50 |

### SPIRAL VISIONS
| 82 | SRTS 82 CUS 1450 | Voices/Despair/Picture Portrait/Dance With Me .......... 10 |

### SPIRIT
| 68 | CBS 3523 | Uncle Jack/Mechanical World .......... 15 |
| 69 | CBS 3880 | I Got A Line On You/She Smiles .......... 25 |
| 69 | CBS 4511 | Dark Eyed Woman/Ice .......... 5 |

| 69 | CBS 4565 | Dark Eyed Woman/New Dope In Town | 12 |
|----|----------|----------------------------------|----|
| 70 | CBS 4773 | 1984/Sweet Stella Baby | 8 |
| 70 | CBS 5149 | Animal Zoo/Red Light Roll On | 6 |
| 70 | Epic SEPC 7082 | Mr Skin/Nature's Way | 5 |
| 70 | Epic SEPC 8083 | Cadillac Cowboys/Darkness | 6 |
| 68 | CBS 63278 | SPIRIT (LP, 1st pressing, stereo, laminated front cover, stereo sticker on rear, orange label) | 35 |
| 68 | CBS 63278 | SPIRIT (LP, 1st pressing, mono, laminated front cover, orange label) | 35 |
| 68 | CBS 63523 | THE FAMILY THAT PLAYS TOGETHER (LP, 1st pressing, mono, laminated front cover, orange label) | 40 |
| 68 | CBS 63523 | THE FAMILY THAT PLAYS TOGETHER (LP, 1st pressing, stereo, laminated front cover, stereo sticker on rear, orange label) | 25 |
| 69 | CBS 63729 | CLEAR (LP, laminated cover, orange label) | 30 |
| 70 | Epic EPC 64191 | THE TWELVE DREAMS OF DR. SARDONICUS (LP, g/fold sleeve, yellow label) | 20 |
| 72 | Epic EPC 64507 | FEED-BACK (LP, gatefold sleeve, yellow label) | 15 |
| 75 | Phonogram 6672 012 | HIGHLIGHTS OF SPIRIT OF 76 (LP, promo) | 20 |
| 81 | Beggars Banquet BEGA 23 | POTATOLAND (LP, with cartoon book) | 15 |

*(see also Kapt. Kopter & Fabulous Twirlybirds)*

## SPIRIT OF JOHN MORGAN

| 69 | Carnaby CNS 4005 | Ride On/Along Came John | 10 |
|----|------------------|-------------------------|----|
| 71 | RCA RCA 2085 | Floating Opera Show/Never Let Go | 10 |
| 69 | Carnaby CNLS 6002 | THE SPIRIT OF JOHN MORGAN (LP, union jack flag label) | 200 |
| 70 | Carnaby CNLS 6007 | AGE MACHINE (LP, gatefold, union jack flag label) | 130 |
| 71 | Carnaby GOLD 6437 503 | THE SPIRIT OF JOHN MORGAN (LP, reissue, 'crab' label logo) | 50 |

*(see also John Morgan)*

## SPIRIT OF MEMPHIS QUARTET

| 58 | Parlophone PMD 1070 | NEGRO SPIRITUALS (10" LP) | 25 |
|----|---------------------|---------------------------|----|
| 65 | Vogue LAE 1033 | NEGRO SPIRITUALS (LP, reissue) | 15 |

## SPIRIT OF PLAY

| 88 | Release KIDS 1988 | Children In Need/Children In Need (Instrumental) (with Paul McCartney) (in p/s) | 50 |
|----|-------------------|--------------------------------------------------------------------------------|----|
| 88 | Release KIDS 1988 | Children In Need/Children In Need (Instrumental) (with Paul McCartney) | 10 |

## SPIRIT OF PROGRESS

| 71 | Philips 6006089 | Om Pa Pa/It's A Beautiful Day | 35 |
|----|-----------------|-------------------------------|----|

## SPIRIT OF THE SECT

| 96 | Garcia POUM 003 | No Love Now/VIC GODARD: She's My Best Friend (1,000 only) | 5 |
|----|-----------------|----------------------------------------------------------|---|

*(see also Subway Sect, Vic Godard)*

## SPIRITBORN

| 84 | Spearhead | Pity The Unborn Child/Sing To The Lord | 20 |
|----|-----------|----------------------------------------|----|

## SPIRITUALIZED

| 90 | Dedicated ZB 43783 | Anyway That You Want Me/Step Into The Breeze (p/s) | 15 |
|----|--------------------|---------------------------------------------------|----|
| 90 | Dedicated ZT 43784 | Anyway That You Want Me (Extended)/Step Into The Breeze 1 & 2 (12", p/s) | 20 |
| 90 | Dedicated ZT 43780 | Anyway That You Want Me (Remix)/Step Into The Breeze 1 & 2 (12", p/s) | 20 |
| 91 | Fierce FRIGHT 053 | Feel So Sad/I Want You (gig freebie, no p/s, stamped plain white sleeve with date & venue details) | 15 |
| 91 | Dedicated SPIRT 001T | Feel So Sad (Rhapsodies)/(Glides And Chimes) (12", p/s) | 12 |
| 91 | Dedicated SPIRT 002 | Run/I Want You (p/s, with luminous sleeve & clear luminous vinyl) | 15 |
| 91 | Dedicated SPIRT 002 | Run/I Want You (p/s) | 8 |
| 91 | Dedicated SPIRT 002T | Run/Luminescence (Stay With Me)/I Want You/Effervescent (Chimes) (12", with luminous sleeve) | 18 |
| 91 | Dedicated SPIRT 002T | Run/Luminescence (Stay With Me)/I Want You/Effervescent (Chimes) (12") | 10 |
| 91 | Dedicated SPIRIT 003 | Why Don't You Smile Now? (Edit)/Sway (clear vinyl, p/s) | 10 |
| 91 | Dedicated SPIRT 004 | I Want You/You Know It's True (Instrumental)/100 Bars (Flashback) (p/s, mail-order with NME coupon only) | 10 |
| 92 | Dedicated SPIRT 005 | Medication/Smiles (p/s, red vinyl, 3000 only) | 8 |
| 92 | Dedicated SPIRT 005 | Medication/Angel Sigh/Feel So Sad (white label test pressing, signed and inscribed by Jason Pierce in silver, limited availability through website) | 25 |
| 92 | Dedicated SPIRT 005T | Medication/Angel Sigh/Feel So Sad (12", p/s, with poster, 3000 only) | 10 |
| 93 | Dedicated SPIRT 006 | Smiles (Live)/100 Bars (A Cappella) (7" flexidisc, fan-club only) | 20 |
| 93 | Greenpeace GR'NP'CE 001 | Good Dope, Good Fun/MERCURY REV: 'Boys Peel Out (Live)' (gig 7", with booklet) | 15 |
| 96 | Dedicated SPIRT 101T | Pure Phase Tones For DJs (12") | 15 |
| 92 | Dedicated DEDLP 004S | LAZER GUIDED MELODIES (2-LP, limited Edition, with bonus 7" single 'Anyway That You Want Me'/'Why Don't You Smile Now?' [CWNN 7001]) | 50 |
| 92 | Dedicated DEDLP 004S | LAZER GUIDED MELODIES (2-LP, limited. Edition, without bonus 7" single) | 25 |
| 93 | Dedicated no cat. no. | SUMMER EUROPEAN 93 BOX (3-CD promo set, with ribbon and insert) | 80 |
| 93 | Dedicated DEDLP 008 | FUCKED UP INSIDE (LP, mail-order only) | 70 |
| 93 | Dedicated DEDCD 008 | FUCKED UP INSIDE (CD, mail-order only) | 35 |
| 93 | Dedicated DEDLP 017 | PURE PHASE (2-LP 45rpm) | 30 |
| 97 | Dedicated DEDLP 034 | LADIES AND GENTLEMEN WE ARE FLOATING IN SPACE (2-LP, limited issue) | 80 |
| 97 | Dedicated DEDCD 034S | LADIES AND GENTLEMEN WE ARE FLOATING IN SPACE (12 x 3" CDs, in blister packs in card box with insert, 1000 only, 200 with clear plastic backs) | 80 |
| 97 | Dedicated DEDCD 034S | LADIES AND GENTLEMEN WE ARE FLOATING IN SPACE (12 x 3" CDs, in blister packs in card box with insert, 1000) | 50 |
| 97 | Dedicated DEDCD 034P | LADIES AND GENTLEMEN WE ARE FLOATING IN SPACE (CD, 'Elvis version', given to Mercury Music Prize personnel, 50 copies only) | 40 |
| 98 | Deconstruction 74321 66285 1 | ROYAL ALBERT HALL (2 x LP) | 30 |
| 01 | Spaceman OPM001LP | LET IT COME DOWN (2-LP, postcard) | 30 |
| 03 | Spaceman/Sanctuary OPM014LP/SANLP14 | AMAZING GRACE (LP) | 20 |
| 08 | Sanctuary 1768732 | SONGS IN A&E (2-LP, green vinyl) | 25 |
| 08 | Sanctuary 1768732 | SONGS IN A&E (2-LP green vinyl, only availiable from Rough Trade) | 30 |
| 12 | Double Six DSO 45LP | SWEET HEART/SWEET LIGHT (2-LP, white vinyl) | 18 |

*(see also Spacemen 3)*

## SPIROGYRA
| | | |
|---|---|---|
| 72 | Pegasus PGS 3 | Dangerous Dave/Captain's Log .................................................................... 12 |
| 73 | Polydor 2001-419 | I Hear You're Going Nowhere/Old Boot Wine ................................................ 35 |
| 71 | B&C CAS 1042 | ST. RADIGUND'S (LP, with lyric inner) .......................................................... 150 |
| 72 | Pegasus PEG 13 | OLD BOOT WINE (LP, textured sleeve) ......................................................... 250 |
| 73 | Polydor 2310 246 | BELLS, BOOTS AND SHAMBLES (LP) ............................................................. 800 |

## SPITEFUL CHILD
| | | |
|---|---|---|
| 83 | Clubland SPJ 842 | Voices In The Night/Is It Love ..................................................................... 30 |
| 85 | SRT SKJ 648 | I Want To Hold You/Who's Crying Now ........................................................ 20 |

## SPITERI
| | | |
|---|---|---|
| 73 | GM GML 1006 | SPITERI (LP) ................................................................................................ 20 |

## SPITFIRE (& BLACKFIRE BARMIES)
| | | |
|---|---|---|
| 82 | Carrere CAR 253 | So You Want To Be A Rock'n'Roll Star/Spitfire Boogie ................................... 50 |

## SPITFIRE BOYS
| | | |
|---|---|---|
| 77 | RK RK 1001 | British Refugee/Mein Kampf (push-out centre) ............................................. 75 |
| 77 | RK RK 1001 | British Refugee/Mein Kampf (reissue, solid centre, p/s) ................................ 60 |
| 79 | Impeccable SRTS/79/CUS481 | Funtime/Transendental Changing ................................................................ 35 |
| 83 | RK RK 1001 | British Refugee/Mein Kampf (2nd reissue to cash in on Frankie success p/s, no solid centre) .......................................................................................................... 75 |

*(see also Frankie Goes To Hollywood)*

## SPITTIN IMAGE
| | | |
|---|---|---|
| 79 | Wessex WEX 270 | Baby Goodbye/(Wish I Could See A) UFO (no p/s) ......................................... 15 |

## SPITTIN MUSSELS
| | | |
|---|---|---|
| 81 | RAFOSM 1 | Five Days A Week/Hold On Johnny (p/s) ...................................................... 35 |

## SPITZBROOK
| | | |
|---|---|---|
| 79 | Ace SPIT 1 | Stranger/Looking At You (p/s) ..................................................................... 60 |

## SPIV
| | | |
|---|---|---|
| 73 | Pye 7N 45293 | Oh You Beautiful Child/Little Girl ................................................................ 120 |

## SPIZZ (OIL/ENERGI)
| | | |
|---|---|---|
| 79 | Rough Trade RTSO 1 | 6000 Crazy/1989/Fibre (p/s) .......................................................................... 8 |
| 79 | Rough Trade RTSO 2 | Cold City/Red And Black/Solarisation (Shun)/Platform 3 (as Spizz Oil) (p/s) ..... 6 |
| 79 | Rough Trade RTSO 3 | Soldier Soldier/Virginia Plain (as Spizz Energi) (p/s) ....................................... 6 |
| 79 | Rough Trade RTSO 4 | Where's Captain Kirk?/Amnesia (as Spizz Energi) (p/s) .................................... 6 |
| 80 | Rough Trade RTS O5 | No Room/Spocks Missing (as Athletico Spizz 80) ........................................... 5 |
| 80 | AMS7550 | Hot Deserts/legal Proceedings (as Athletico Spizz 80) .................................... 5 |
| 82 | Rough Trade ROUGH501 | SPIZZ HISTORY (LP) ...................................................................................... 15 |

## S.P.K. (SEPPUKU/SURGICAL PENIS KLINIK)
| | | |
|---|---|---|
| 80 | Industrial IR 0011 | MEAT PROCESSING SECTION (Mekano/Slogun) (p/s, labels list "Slogan"/Factory, with insert, as Surgical Penis Klinik) ...................................................................... 30 |
| 83 | Side Effekts SER 003 | Dekompositiones (12", p/s, as Seppuku) ...................................................... 20 |
| 81 | Side Effekts SER 01 | INFORMATION OVERLOAD UNIT (LP, 1st 1,000 with booklet) ........................ 70 |
| 81 | Side Effekts SER 01 | INFORMATION OVERLOAD UNIT (LP) ........................................................... 50 |
| 83 | Walter Ulbright WULP 002 | AUTO-DA-FE (LP) ......................................................................................... 20 |
| 86 | Side Effects SER 09 | ZAMIA LEHMANNI (LP) ................................................................................. 20 |
| 80s | Side Effekts SER 002 | LEICHENSCHREI (LP) ................................................................................... 30 |

## SPLAT!
| | | |
|---|---|---|
| 83 | Ron Johnson RON 1 | Yeah The Dum Dum/Bookface/Biggles Bloodbath (p/s) ................................... 6 |

## SPLINTER
| | | |
|---|---|---|
| 74 | Dark Horse AMS 7135 | Costafine Town/Elly May ............................................................................... 5 |
| 75 | Dark Horse AMS 5501 | Drink All Day/Haven't Got Time (withdrawn) ............................................... 12 |
| 75 | Dark Horse AMS 5502 | China Light/Drink All Day ............................................................................ 10 |
| 75 | Dark Horse AMS 5503 | Which Way Will I Get Home/Green Bus Line .................................................... 8 |
| 76 | Dark Horse AMS 5506 | Half Way There/What Is It (If You Never Ever Tried It Yourself) ......................... 8 |
| 77 | Dark Horse K 17009 | Round And Round/I'll Bend For You ................................................................ 7 |
| 77 | Dark Horse K 17116 | New York City (Who Am I)/Baby Love ............................................................. 7 |
| 78 | Barn BARN 4 | Danger Zone/Swear To God ........................................................................... 8 |
| 76 | Dark Horse DH 2 | SPLINTER (LP, promo only, plain white sleeve) ............................................ 130 |

## SPLIT BEAVER
| | | |
|---|---|---|
| 81 | Heavy Metal HEAVY 7 | Savage/Hound Of Hell (with p/s) ................................................................. 25 |
| 81 | Heavy Metal HEAVY 7 | Savage/Hound Of Hell .................................................................................... 8 |
| 82 | Heavy Metal HMRLP 3 | WHEN HELL WON'T HAVE YOU (LP, silver label) ........................................... 18 |
| 82 | Heavy Metal HMRLP 3 | WHEN HELL WON'T HAVE YOU (LP, red label) ............................................... 15 |

## SPLIT ENZ
| | | |
|---|---|---|
| 76 | Chrysalis CHS 2120 | Late Last Night/Walking Down The Road (p/s) ................................................ 5 |
| 77 | Chrysalis CHS 2131 | Another Great Divide/Stranger Than Fiction (p/s) ........................................... 5 |
| 77 | Chrysalis CHS 2170 | My Mistake/Crosswords (p/s) ........................................................................ 5 |
| 79 | Illegal ILS 19 | I See Red/Give It A Whirl/Hermit McDermitt (p/s) ........................................... 5 |

*(see also Crowded House, Tim Finn)*

## SPLIT IMAGE
| | | |
|---|---|---|
| 82 | Heroes ER 01 | Now That We've Parted.............................................................................. 25 |

## SPLIT KNEE LOONS
| | | |
|---|---|---|
| 81 | Avatar AAA 111 | THE SPECIAL COLLECTORS EP (p/s, brown vinyl, with badge) ......................... 10 |

*(see also Gillan, Bernie Torme, John McCoy, Colin Towns)*

## SPLIT SCREENS
| | | |
|---|---|---|
| 79 | Rok ROK III/IV | Just Don't Try/JUST FRANK: You (die-cut company sleeve)............................ 35 |

## SPLITCROW
| | | |
|---|---|---|
| 84 | Guardian GRC 21 | ROCKSTORM (LP) ........................................................................................ 15 |

## SPLODGENESSABOUNDS
| | | | |
|---|---|---|---|
| 80 | Deram ROLF 1 | Two Little Boys/Horse/Sox/Butterfly (p/s, with 'Splodge' boomerang) | 15 |
| 81 | Deram SML 1121 | SPLODGENESSABOUNDS (LP) | 15 |

## SPODE
| | | | |
|---|---|---|---|
| 71 | Decca F 13142 | Singalong Song/Cincinatti Woman | 10 |

## SPOILERS
| | | | |
|---|---|---|---|
| 72 | London HLU 10399 | Turbo Rock/Sad Man's Land | 20 |

## SPOKESMEN
| | | | |
|---|---|---|---|
| 65 | Brunswick 05941 | The Dawn Of Correction/For You Babe | 12 |
| 65 | Brunswick 05948 | It Ain't Fair/Have Courage Be Careful | 12 |
| 66 | Brunswick 05950 | Michelle/Better Days Are Yet To Come | 8 |
| 66 | Brunswick 05958 | Today's The Day/Enchanté | 8 |

## SPONOOCH
| | | | |
|---|---|---|---|
| 79 | EMI EMI 2941 | Crime Buster/Laserdance (12", p/s) | 50 |
| 79 | EMI EMI 2941 | Crime Buster/Laserdance (p/s) | 10 |

## SPONTANEOUS COMBUSTION
| | | | |
|---|---|---|---|
| 71 | Harvest HAR 5046 | Lonely Singer/200 Lives/Leaving | 15 |
| 72 | Harvest HAR 5060 | Gay Time Night/Spaceship | 25 |
| 73 | Harvest HAR 5066 | Sabre Dance/Sabre Dance | 15 |
| 72 | Harvest SHVL 801 | SPONTANEOUS COMBUSTION (LP, with EMI logo on label) | 125 |
| 72 | Harvest SHVL 805 | TRIAD (LP, with 3 inserts, with EMI logo on label) | 100 |

*(see also Time)*

## SPONTANEOUS MUSIC ENSEMBLE
| | | | |
|---|---|---|---|
| 66 | Eyemark EMP L1002 | CHALLENGE (LP) | 450 |
| 68 | Island ILP 979 | KARYOBIN ... ARE THE IMAGINARY BIRDS SAID TO LIVE IN PARADISE (LP, pink label) | 200 |
| 69 | Marmalade 608 008 | SPONTANEOUS MUSIC ENSEMBLE (LP) | 100 |
| 70 | A A001 | FOR YOU TO SHARE (LP) | 100 |
| 71 | Tangent TNGS 107 | SOURCE FROM AND TOWARDS (LP) | 35 |
| 72 | Marmalade 2384 009 | SPONTANEOUS MUSIC ENSEMBLE (LP, reissue) | 25 |
| 73 | Emanem 303 | FACE TO FACE (LP) | 30 |
| 73 | Tangent TNGS 118 | SO WHAT DO YOU THINK (LP) | 35 |
| 77 | Incus INCUS 24 | BIOSYSTEM (LP) | 50 |
| 82 | Affinity AFF 81 | 1 2 ALBERT AYLER (LP) | 20 |

*(see also Howard Riley Trio)*

## SPONTANEOUS MUSIC ORCHESTRA
| | | | |
|---|---|---|---|
| 75 | A A003 | + = (LP) | 75 |
| 81 | Sweet Folk All SFA 112 | SME + SMO IN CONCERT (LP) | 50 |

*(see also Spontaneous Music Ensemble)*

## SPOOKY TOOTH
| | | | |
|---|---|---|---|
| 67 | Island WIP 6022 | Sunshine Help Me/Weird | 25 |
| 68 | Island WIP 6037 | Love Really Changed Me/Luger's Grove | 15 |
| 68 | Island WIP 6046 | The Weight/Do Right People | 10 |
| 69 | Island WIP 6048 | Nobody There At All/ART: Room With A View (unissued, white labels only) | 40 |
| 69 | Island WIP 6060 | Son Of Your Father/I've Got Enough Heartache | 7 |
| 73 | Island WIP 6168 | All Sewn Up/As Long As The World Keeps Turning | 6 |
| 68 | Island ILP 980/ILPS 9080 | IT'S ALL ABOUT (LP, 1st pressing pink 'eye' label) | 150 |
| 70 | Island ILP 980/ILPS 9080 | IT'S ALL ABOUT (LP, 2nd pressing, pink label white 'i' logo) | 50 |
| 69 | Island ILPS 9098 | SPOOKY TWO (LP, 1st pressing with pink 'eye' label, matrix numbers ILPS 9098 +A & +B stamped into dead wax. No 'Porky' or 'Pecko' in dead wax (unlike reissues), gatefold 'E.J.Day' sleeve) | 100 |
| 69 | Island ILPS 9098 | SPOOKY TWO (LP, 2nd pressing with white 'i' on pink label, with Jimmy Miller production credit around a centimetre beneath SPOOKY TOOTH on label) | 70 |
| 69 | Island ILPS 9107 | CEREMONY (LP, with Pierre Henry, pink label, gatefold sleeve) | 100 |
| 70 | Island ILPS 9098 | SPOOKY TWO (LP, 3rd pressing with white 'i' on pink label, with Jimmy Miller production credit directly beneath SPOOKY TOOTH on label) | 50 |
| 70 | Island ILPS 9117 | THE LAST PUFF (LP, pink label) | 60 |
| 73 | Island ILPS 9227 | YOU BROKE MY HEART SO I BUSTED YOUR JAW (LP, gatefold sleeve, lyric insert, pink rim label) | 30 |
| 73 | Island ILPS 9255 | WITNESS (LP, pink rim label) | 30 |
| 74 | Good Ear EARL 2001 | THE MIRROR (LP) | 25 |
| 74 | Island ILPS 9292 | THE MIRROR (LP, export issue) | 25 |
| 77 | Island ILP 980/ILPS 9080 | IT'S ALL ABOUT (LP, repressing, palm tree label) | 50 |

*(see also Gary Wright, V.I.P.s, Art, Luther Grosvenor, Hellions, Revolution, State Of Mickey & Tommy, Mike Harrison)*

## SPOON FAZER
| | | | |
|---|---|---|---|
| 82 | Illuminated ILL 912 | Sunset/Ballad Of The Insectman/Flying Bodies/Fly On The Wall (12", p/s) | 60 |
| 82 | Project PROJECT 1 | MUSIC 2 DANCE 2 (12" EP, p/s) | 20 |

## SPOONFUL
| | | | |
|---|---|---|---|
| 78 | Bunbury DCS 340 | Troubled Times/Country Blues (2 known copies in p/s) | 300 |
| 77 | Bunbury DCS 340 | Troubled Times/Country Blues (no p/s) | 50 |

## SPORTS
| | | | |
|---|---|---|---|
| 79 | Sire SIR 6001 | Who Listens To The Radio/Hit Single ('fireplace' p/s) | 5 |
| 80 | Sire SRUK 6001 | WHO LISTENS TO THE RADIO (LP) | 15 |

## SPOTLIGHT
| | | | |
|---|---|---|---|
| 74 | Globe GB 02 | Find The Light/Emily Cries (p/s) | 25 |

## SPOTLIGHTERS
| | | | |
|---|---|---|---|
| 59 | Vogue Pop V 9130 | Please Be My Girlfriend/Whisper (with Bob Thompson & His Band) | 500 |
| 59 | Vogue Pop V 9130 | Please Be My Girlfriend/Whisper (with Bob Thompson & His Band) (78) | 100 |

## SPOTLIGHTS
| | | | |
|---|---|---|---|
| 66 | Philips BF 1485 | Batman And Robin/Day Flower | 20 |

MINT VALUE £

## SPOTNICKS

| | | | |
|---|---|---|---|
| 62 | Oriole CB 1724 | Orange Blossom Special/The Spotnicks Theme | 10 |
| 62 | Oriole CB 1755 | Galloping Guitars/The Rocket Man | 10 |
| 63 | Oriole CB 1790 | Hava Nagila/High Flyin' Scotsman | 8 |
| 63 | Oriole CB 1818 | Just Listen To My Heart/Pony Express | 10 |
| 63 | Oriole CB 1844 | Valentina/Save The Last Dance For Me/No Yaga Daga Blues | 10 |
| 63 | Oriole CB 1886 | Anna/The Sailor's Hornpipe | 10 |
| 64 | Oriole CB 1953 | Lovesick Blues/The Space Creatures | 15 |
| 64 | Oriole CB 1981 | Donner Wetter/Shamus O'Toole | 15 |
| 63 | Oriole EP 7075 | ON THE AIR (EP) | 20 |
| 64 | Oriole EP 7078 | SPOTNICKS IN PARIS (EP) | 20 |
| 64 | Oriole EP 7079 | SPOTNICKS AT THE OLYMPIA PARIS (EP) | 20 |
| 63 | Oriole PS 40036 | OUT-A SPACE: THE SPOTNICKS IN LONDON (LP, mono) | 25 |
| 63 | Oriole SPS 40037 | OUT-A SPACE: THE SPOTNICKS IN LONDON (LP, stereo) | 25 |
| 64 | Oriole PS 40054 | THE SPOTNICKS IN SPAIN (LP) | 20 |
| 65 | Oriole PS 40064 | THE SPOTNICKS IN BERLIN (LP) | 20 |

*(see also Bob Lander & Spotnicks, Shy Ones)*

## JACK SPRATT & LEROY SIBBLES & HEPTONES

| | | | |
|---|---|---|---|
| 69 | Coxsone CS 7100 | Give Me Your Love/LARRY & ALVIN: Magic Moments | 125 |

## SPREADEAGLE

| | | | |
|---|---|---|---|
| 72 | Charisma BCP 7 | Nightingal Lane/CAPABILITY BROWN: Liar (demo only in p/s) | 10 |
| 72 | Charisma CB 183 | How Can We Be Lost/Nightmare (p/s, solid centre) | 15 |
| 72 | Charisma CB 183 | How Can We Be Lost/Nightmare (four prong centre) | 8 |
| 72 | Charisma CAS 1055 | THE PIECE OF PAPER (LP, pink 'scroll' label) | 20 |

## SPREDTHICK

| | | | |
|---|---|---|---|
| 78 | An Actual ACT 003 | SPREDTHICK (LP, with insert) | 18 |

## SPRIGUNS (OF TOLGUS)

| | | | |
|---|---|---|---|
| 76 | Decca F 13676 | Nothing Else To Do/Lord Lovell | 12 |
| 77 | Decca F 13739 | White Witch/Time Will Pass | 12 |
| 75 | Alida Star C'tage ASC7755 | JACK WITH A FEATHER (LP, as Spriguns Of Tolgus) | 1200 |
| 76 | Decca SKL 5262 | REVEL WEIRD & WILD (LP, with lyric insert) | 250 |
| 77 | Decca SKL 5286 | TIME WILL PASS (LP, with lyric insert) | 200 |
| 92 | Kissing Spell KSLP 002 | ROWDY DOWDY DAY (LP, reissue) | 15 |

*(see also Mandy Morton Band, Terra Cotta)*

## SPRING

| | | | |
|---|---|---|---|
| 71 | RCA Neon NE 6 | SPRING (LP, foldout sleeve, black inner sleeve) | 1000 |

## SPRING OFFENSIVE

| | | | |
|---|---|---|---|
| 81 | SO 1 | Cruising/Good To Be Back | 35 |

## SPRINGBOARD

| | | | |
|---|---|---|---|
| 69 | Polydor 545007 | SPRINGBOARD (LP) | 100 |

## DUSTY SPRINGFIELD

| | | | |
|---|---|---|---|
| 63 | Philips BF 1292 | I Only Want To Be With You/Once Upon A Time | 6 |
| 64 | Philips BF 1313 | Stay Awhile/Something Special | 6 |
| 64 | Philips BF 1348 | I Just Don't Know What To Do With Myself/My Colouring Book | 5 |
| 64 | Philips BF 1369 | Losing You/Summer Is Over | 5 |
| 64 | Philips BF 1381 | Oh Holy Child/SPRINGFIELDS: Jingle Bells (with p/s) | 5 |
| 65 | Philips BF 1396 | Your Hurtin' Kinda Love/Don't Say It Baby | 5 |
| 65 | Philips BF 1418 | In The Middle Of Nowhere/Baby Don't You Know | 6 |
| 65 | Philips BF 1430 | Some Of Your Lovin'/I'll Love You For A While | 6 |
| 66 | Philips BF 1466 | Little By Little/If It Hadn't Been For You | 6 |
| 66 | Philips BF 1482 | You Don't Have To Say You Love Me/Every Ounce Of Strength | 6 |
| 66 | Philips BF 1502 | Goin' Back/I'm Gonna Leave You | 7 |
| 66 | Philips BF 1510 | All I See Is You/Go Ahead On (with p/s) | 8 |
| 67 | Philips BF 1553 | I'll Try Anything/The Corrupt Ones | 5 |
| 67 | Philips BF 1577 | Give Me Time/The Look Of Love | 6 |
| 67 | Philips BF 1608 | What's It Gonna Be/Small Town Girl | 15 |
| 68 | Philips BF 1682 | I Close My Eyes And Count To Ten/No Stranger Am I | 6 |
| 68 | Philips BF 1706 | I Will Come To You/The Colour Of Your Eyes | 5 |
| 68 | Philips BF 1730 | Son Of A Preacher Man/Just A Little Lovin' | 10 |
| 69 | Philips BF 1811 | Am I The Same Girl/Earthbound Gypsy | 15 |
| 69 | Philips BF 1826 | Brand New Me/Bad Case Of The Blues | 7 |
| 70 | Philips BF 1835 | Morning Please Don't Come (with Tom Springfield)/TOM SPRINGFIELD: Charley | 5 |
| 70 | Philips 6006 045 | How Can I Be Sure/Spooky | 20 |
| 72 | Philips 6006 214 | Yesterday When I Was Young/I Start Counting | 6 |
| 73 | Philips 6006 295 | Who Gets Your Love/Of All The Things | 6 |
| 74 | Philips 6006 325 | Learn To Say Goodbye/Easy Evil | 6 |
| 74 | Philips 6006 350 | What's It Gonna Be/Bring Him Back | 10 |
| 64 | Philips BE 12560 | I ONLY WANT TO BE WITH YOU (EP) | 10 |
| 64 | Philips BE 12564 | DUSTY (EP) | 10 |
| 65 | Philips BE 12572 | DUSTY IN NEW YORK (EP) | 15 |
| 65 | Philips BE 12579 | MADEMOISELLE DUSTY (EP) | 15 |
| 68 | Philips BE 12605 | IF YOU GO AWAY (EP) | 10 |
| 64 | Philips BL 7594 | A GIRL CALLED DUSTY (mono) | 15 |
| 64 | Philips SBL 7594 | A GIRL CALLED DUSTY (stereo) | 20 |
| 65 | Philips RBL 1002 | EVERYTHING'S COMING UP DUSTY (gatefold sleeve with booklet, mono) | 25 |
| 65 | Philips SRBL 1002 | EVERYTHING'S COMING UP DUSTY (gatefold sleeve with booklet, stereo) | 30 |
| 67 | Philips (S)BL 7820 | WHERE AM I GOING? | 25 |
| 68 | Philips (S)BL 7864 | DUSTY... DEFINITELY | 15 |

| | | | |
|---|---|---|---|
| 69 | Philips SBL 7889 | DUSTY IN MEMPHIS | 50 |
| 70 | Philips SBL 7927 | FROM DUSTY... WITH LOVE | 20 |
| 80 | Philips PRICE 83 | IN MEMPHIS PLUS (LP) | 30 |

*(see also Lana Sisters, Springfields, Tom Springfield, Pet Shop Boys)*

## TOM SPRINGFIELD (& HIS) ORCHESTRA

| | | | |
|---|---|---|---|
| 63 | Philips BF 1294 | The Moon Behind The Hill/The Londonderry Air | 6 |
| 64 | Philips BF 1331 | Brazilian Shake/Brazilian Blues | 6 |
| 69 | Philips BF 1759 | Theme From From The Troubleshooters/Homage To Spewdley Parsons (with p/s) | 8 |
| 69 | Philips BF 1759 | Theme From From The Troubleshooters/Homage To Spewdley Parsons | 6 |
| 68 | Decca SKL 4967 | SUN SONGS (LP) | 80 |
| 69 | Decca LK/SKL 5003 | LOVE'S PHILOSOPHY BY... (LP, featuring Dusty Springfield) | 30 |

*(see also Springfields, Dusty Springfield)*

## SPRINGFIELD PARK

| | | | |
|---|---|---|---|
| 68 | CBS 3775 | Never An Everyday Thing/I Can See The Sun Shine | 10 |

## SPRINGFIELDS (1)

| | | | |
|---|---|---|---|
| 61 | Philips PB 1145 | Dear John/I Done What They Told Me To | 6 |
| 61 | Philips PB 1168 | Breakaway/Good News | 7 |
| 61 | Philips PB 1178 | Bambino/Star Of Hope (with p/s) | 8 |
| 61 | Philips SBBE 9068 | THE SPRINGFIELDS (EP, stereo) | 12 |
| 62 | Philips BBL 7551 | KINDA FOLKSY (LP, mono) | 15 |
| 62 | Philips SBBL 674 | KINDA FOLKSY (LP, stereo) | 15 |
| 63 | Philips 632 304 BL | FOLK SONGS FROM THE HILLS (LP) | 15 |

*(see also Dusty Springfield, Lana Sisters, Tom Springfield, Mike Hurst)*

## SPRINGFIELDS (2)

| | | | |
|---|---|---|---|
| 88 | Sarah SARAH 010 | Sunflower/Clown/Are We Gonna Be Alright? (foldaround p/s with 14" x 10" poster in polyester bag; yellow p/s) | 30 |
| 88 | Sarah SARAH 010 | Sunflower/Clown/Are We Gonna Be Alright? (foldaround p/s with 14" x 10" poster in polyester bag; later orange p/s) | 18 |
| 91 | Sarah SARAH 040 | Wonder/Tomorrow Ends Today (p/s, with insert) | 7 |

## SPRING HEEL JACK

| | | | |
|---|---|---|---|
| 80 | Woodbine WSR 003 | 1960s Girl/How Many Colours (no p/s) | 20 |

## BRUCE SPRINGSTEEN

| | | | |
|---|---|---|---|
| 75 | CBS A 3661 | Born To Run/Meeting Across The River | 15 |
| 76 | CBS A 3940 | Tenth Avenue Freeze-Out/She's The One | 25 |
| 78 | CBS A 6424 | Prove It All Night/Factory | 18 |
| 78 | CBS A 6532 | Badlands/Something In The Night | 15 |
| 78 | CBS A 6720 | Promised Land/Streets Of Fire | 65 |
| 80 | CBS A 9309 | Hungry Heart/Held Up Without A Gun (p/s, withdrawn first issue, black and white p/s, blue lettering) | 25 |
| 80 | CBS A 9309 | Hungry Heart/Held Up Without A Gun | 6 |
| 81 | CBS A 9568 | Sherry Darling/Independence Day (white label promo, 100 only 2 known copies with p/s listing 'Independence Day') | 2500 |
| 81 | CBS A 9568 | Sherry Darling/Independence Day (white label promo, 100 only) | 2000 |
| 81 | CBS 9568 | Sherry Darling/Be True (p/s) | 15 |
| 81 | CBS A 1179 | The River/Independence Day (p/s) | 15 |
| 81 | CBS A 13-1179 | The River/Born To Run/Rosalita (12", p/s, sleeves credit 'East Street Band') | 15 |
| 81 | CBS A 13-1179 | The River/Born To Run/Rosalita (12", p/s) | 12 |
| 81 | CBS A 1557 | Cadillac Ranch/Wreck On The Highway (p/s) | 15 |
| 82 | CBS A 2794 | Atlantic City/Mansion On The Hill (p/s) | 20 |
| 82 | CBS A 2969 | Open All Night/The Big Pay Back (p/s) | 30 |
| 84 | CBS WA 4436 | Dancing In The Dark/Pink Cadillac (Cadillac-shaped picture disc) | 20 |
| 84 | CBS A 4662 | Cover Me/Jersey Girl (live) (poster p/s) | 5 |
| 84 | CBS WA 4662 | Cover Me/Jersey Girl (live) (Bruce-shaped picture disc with plinth) | 25 |
| 84 | CBS DA 4662/A 4436 | Cover Me/Jersey Girl (live)//Dancing In The Dark/Pink Cadillac (shrinkable double pack, both 45s in p/s) | 12 |
| 84 | CBS DA 4662/A 7077 | Cover Me/Jersey Girl (live)//Born To Run/Meeting Across The River (shrinkwrapped double pack, no p/s on 2nd 45) | 12 |
| 84 | CBS A 6561 | I'm Going Down/Janey, Don't You Lose Heart (p/s) | 7 |
| 85 | CBS A 7077 | Born To Run/Meeting Across The River (reissue, blue p/s, withdrawn) | 25 |
| 85 | CBS A 6342 | I'm On Fire/Born In The U.S.A. (p/s, with competition postcard) | 8 |
| 85 | CBS WA 6342 | I'm On Fire/Born In The U.S.A. (p/s, flag-shaped picture disc) | 20 |
| 85 | CBS BRUCE 1 | BORN IN THE U.S.A. - THE 12" COLLECTION (4 x 12" & 7", box with poster) | 20 |
| 86 | CBS 650 193-0 | War (live)/Merry Xmas Baby (live)//My Home Town (live)/Santa Claus Is Coming To Town (shrinkwrapped double pack, both 45s in p/s) | 10 |
| 87 | CBS 650 381-6 | Fire (live)/For You (live)/Born To Run (live)/No Surrender (live)/10th Avenue (live) Freeze-Out (live) (12", p/s) | 12 |
| 87 | CBS BRUCE B2 | Born To Run/Spirit In The Night/Johnny 99/Because The Night (double pack box set) | 8 |
| 87 | CBS 651 141-0 | Brilliant Disguise/Lucky Man (gatefold p/s, with discography) | 6 |
| 87 | CBS 651 295-0 | Tunnel Of Love/Two For The Road (postcard-shaped picture disc) | 15 |
| 88 | CBS BRUCE Q4 | Spare Parts/Cover Me (live)/Spare Parts (live)/I'm On Fire (live) (12", different p/s) | 10 |
| 94 | Columbia 660 065-8 | Streets Of Philadelphia/If I Should Fall Behind/Growing Up/Big Muddy (12", picture disc) | 10 |
| 73 | CBS 65480 | GREETINGS FROM ASBURY PARK, N.J. (cutaway gatefold sleeve, orange label) | 20 |
| 74 | CBS 65780 | THE WILD, THE INNOCENT AND THE E STREET SHUFFLE (orange label, yellow lettering on sleeve; with "Ashbury" mis-spelling on label) | 20 |
| 75 | CBS 69170 | BORN TO RUN (with "John Landau" misprint on rear sleeve) | 30 |
| 78 | CBS 86061 | DARKNESS ON THE EDGE OF TOWN (LP) | 18 |
| 79 | CBS 66353 | BRUCE SPRINGSTEEN (3-LP, box set) | 18 |
| 80 | CBS 88510 | THE RIVER (2-LP) | 20 |
| 80 | CBS 80959 | BORN TO RUN (LP, reissue, half-speed master, 2 inserts) | 20 |
| 82 | CBS 25100 | NEBRASKA (LP, inner) | 20 |

MINT VALUE £

| 84 | CBS 86304 | BORN IN THE U.S.A. (LP, inner, insert) | 20 |
|---|---|---|---|
| 84 | CBS 11-86304 | BORN IN THE U.S.A. (picture disc) | 30 |
| 87 | CBS 460 270-0 | TUNNEL OF LOVE (picture disc) | 15 |
| 90 | CBS LSP 980636 1 | COLLECTED WORKS OF BRUCE SPRINGSTEEN (7 LP box set) | 200 |
| 92 | Sony 471 423-0 | HUMAN TOUCH (picture disc) | 15 |
| 92 | Sony 471 424-0 | LUCKY TOWN (picture disc, with side 1 on both sides) | 75 |
| 92 | Sony 471 424-0 | LUCKY TOWN (picture disc) | 15 |
| 92 | Columbia 471423 | LUCKY TOWN (LP) | 15 |
| 93 | Columbia 473860-1 | IN CONCERT (2-LP, stickered sleeve) | 40 |
| 95 | Columbia 478555 | GREATEST HITS (2-LP) | 40 |
| 96 | Columbia C 67484 | THE GHOST OF TOM JOAD (LP) | 30 |
| 02 | Columbia COL 508000-1 | THE RISING (2-LP) | 60 |
| 09 | Columbia 88697453161 | WORKING ON A DREAM (2-LP) | 18 |

*(see also Roy Orbison)*

### SPRINGTIME
| 78 | Sonet SON 2143 | Mrs Caroline Robinson/Honey Bye Bye (p/s) | 6 |
|---|---|---|---|

### SPRINGWATER (1)
| 71 | Polydor 2058141 | I Will Return/Stone Cross | 12 |
|---|---|---|---|
| 72 | Polydor 2058220 | Listen Everybody/Guiding Light | 12 |

### SPRINGWATER (2)
| 80 | Fabulous JC6 | Move A Little Closer/Rescue Me (p/s) | 5 |
|---|---|---|---|
| 80 | Fabulous JC 2 | Sailing/Captain Of The Sea | 6 |

### SPRINGWELL
| 71 | London HLU 10345 | It's For You/Our Question | 15 |
|---|---|---|---|

### SPRONG & NYAH SHUFFLE
| 69 | Grape GR 3001 | Moonwalk/Think | 30 |
|---|---|---|---|

### BILLY SPROUD & ROCK 'N' ROLL SIX
| 57 | Columbia DB 3893 | Rock Mr. Piper/If You're So Smart (How Come You Ain't Rich) | 25 |
|---|---|---|---|
| 57 | Columbia DB 3893 | Rock Mr. Piper/If You're So Smart (How Come You Ain't Rich) (78) | 20 |

### SPROUTS
| 58 | RCA RCA 1031 | Teen Billy Baby/Goodbye, She's Gone | 35 |
|---|---|---|---|
| 58 | RCA RCA 1031 | Teen Billy Baby/Goodbye, She's Gone (78) | 20 |

### SPUD
| 75 | Philips 9108 002 | A SILK PURSE (LP) | 20 |
|---|---|---|---|

### SPUD AND THE FABS
| 80 | Whitetower AMC 706 | Your Place Or Mine (p/s) | 25 |
|---|---|---|---|

### THE SPUNKY ONION
| 74 | Contempo CS2006 | Cookie Man (Part 1)/Cookie Man (Part 2) | 6 |
|---|---|---|---|

### THE SPUNKY SPIDER
| 73 | Phoenix S-NIX 143 | You Won't Come/Perchance | 80 |
|---|---|---|---|

### SPUNKY ONIONS/GHETTOBETTIES
| 80 | Temple Beat TR111 | Split 7" (p/s) | 25 |
|---|---|---|---|

### WILD JIMMY SPURRILL
| 60s | XX MIN 717 | NOBLE 'THIN MAN' WATTS AND WILD JIMMY SPURRILL (EP) | 20 |
|---|---|---|---|

*(see also Noble 'Thin Man' Watts, Guitar Crusher)*

### SPURS
| 88 | Outback OUT 1 | Soldier (p/s) | 12 |
|---|---|---|---|

### SPYROGYRA
| 79 | Infinity (no cat. no.) | MORNING DANCE (LP, picture disc, in-house issue, top-flap poly sleeve, 50 copies) | 50 |
|---|---|---|---|

### SPYS
| 79 | No Bad NB 3 | The Young Ones/Heavy Scene (p/s) | 5 |
|---|---|---|---|

### SQUAD
| 79 | Squad SQS 1 | Red Alert/£8 A Week (in die cut p/s) | 60 |
|---|---|---|---|
| 79 | Squad SQS 1 | Red Alert/£8 A Week | 20 |
| 79 | Squad SQS 2 | Millionaire/Brockhill Boys (p/s) | 40 |

### SQUADRONAIRES
| 54 | Decca F 10248 | Coach Call Boogie/Donegal Cradle Song | 10 |
|---|---|---|---|
| 54 | Decca F 10274 | Wolf On The Prowl/Mudhopper | 7 |
| 57 | Columbia DB 3882 | Rock And Roll Boogie/Right Now, Right Now | 10 |
| 53 | Decca LF 1141 | CONTRASTS IN JAZZ (10" LP) | 15 |

### SQUARE SET
| 71 | Decca FR 13197 | That's What I Want/Come On | 80 |
|---|---|---|---|

### SQUAREPUSHER
| 96 | Rephlex CATO37LP | FEED ME WEIRD THINGS (2-LP) | 30 |
|---|---|---|---|
| 97 | Warp WARP50LP | HARD NORMAL DADDY (2-LP) | 20 |
| 98 | Warp WARPLP57 | MUSIC IS ROTTED ONE NOTE (LP) | 20 |
| 99 | Warp WARPLP62 | BUDAKHAN MINDPHONE (LP) | 20 |
| 99 | Warp WARLP72 | SELECTION SIXTEEN (2x12", 10") | 20 |
| 99 | Warp WARPLP85 | GO PLASTIC (2-LP) | 20 |
| 02 | Warp WARLPLP97 | DO YOU KNOW SQUAREPUSHER? (LP) | 20 |
| 04 | Warp WARPLP117 | ULTRAVISITOR (2-LP) | 20 |
| 06 | Warp WARPLP148X | HELLO EVERYTHING (3 x 12" plus bonus CD edition) | 20 |
| 08 | Warp WARLP148 | JUST A SOUVENAIR (LP) | 15 |

### SQUARES (1)
| 78 | Sire SIR 4003 | No Fear/Nobodys Fool (p/s) | 10 |
|---|---|---|---|
| 79 | Sire SIR 4011 | Stop Being A Boy/This Is Airebeat (p/s) | 7 |
| 81 | Hype TICK 1 | Buddy Holly/I May Be Bitter (p/s) | 5 |

## SQUARES (2)
| 91 | Hangman HANG 45 UP | TRAPPED IN A SQUARE (LP) | 15 |
| 93 | Hangman HANG 52 UP | CURSE OF THE SQUARES (LP) | 15 |

## SQUEEK
| 72 | Bronze BRO 130 | Make Hay While The Sun Shines/L Amour D'un Apres Midi | 20 |

## SQUEELER
| 79 | Hit H.I.T. 101 | Jennifer Broadhurst/Menace/I Just Want To Be Me/Framed (7" no p/s) | 100 |

## SQUEEZE
| 77 | BTM SBT 107 | Take Me I'm Yours/No, Disco Kid, No (unreleased) | 0 |
| 77 | Deptford Fun City DFC 01 | PACKET OF THREE (EP, red & blue photo p/s) | 10 |
| 77 | Deptford Fun City DFC 01 | PACKET OF THREE (12" EP, plain pink die-cut sleeve, 500 only) | 10 |
| 78 | A&M AMS 7360 | Bang Bang/All Fed Up (p/s, green vinyl) | 5 |
| 78 | A&M AMS 7398 | Goodbye Girl/Saints Alive (3-D p/s) | 5 |
| 79 | A&M AMS 7426 | Cool For Cats/Model (p/s, brilliant pink vinyl, 5,000 only) | 6 |
| 79 | A&M AMS 7426 | Cool For Cats/Model (p/s, red vinyl, 1,000 only) | 7 |
| 79 | A&M AMS 7444 | Up The Junction/It's So Dirty (lilac vinyl, p/s) | 5 |
| 79 | A&M AMS 7495 | Christmas Day/Going Crazy (p/s, white vinyl) | 5 |
| 79 | A&M AMS 7507 | Another Nail In My Heart/Pretty Thing (p/s, clear vinyl) | 5 |
| 81 | A&M AMS 8147 | Tempted/Yap Yap Yap (p/s, with free U.S. 5" single "Another Nail In My Heart"/"If I Didn't Love You", p/s, shrinkwrapped) | 5 |
| 81 | A&M AMS 8166 | Labelled With Love/Squabs On Forty Five (withdrawn p/s) | 12 |

## SQUIBBY & REFLECTIONS
| 68 | Direction 58-3453 | Ragamuffin/For A Little While | 7 |
| 68 | Direction 58-3606 | Loving You Has Made My Life Worthwhile/Better Off Without You | 7 |
| 69 | Direction 58-4073 | You Got It/Come Back To Me | 8 |

## SQUIBS
| 81 | Oily SLICK 1 | On The Line (plain sleeve, with insert) | 25 |
| 81 | Oily SLICK 3 | Parades/Out On The Town (p/s) | 20 |

## BILLY SQUIER
| 86 | Capitol 12CL 433 | Love Is The Hero (extended version with Freddie Mercury intro)/Learn How To Live (live) (12", p/s) | 15 |

*(see also Freddie Mercury, Roger Taylor)*

## SQUIRE
| 79 | Rok ROK I/II | Get Ready To Go/COMING SHORTLY: Doing The Flail (company sleeve) | 35 |
| 79 | I-Spy SEE 2 | Walking Down The King's Road/It's A Mod Mod Mod Mod World (company sleeve) | 8 |
| 79 | I-Spy SEE 4 | The Face Of Youth Today/I Know A Girl (keyhole company sleeve, plastic labels) | 6 |
| 80 | Stage One STAGE 2 | My Mind Goes Round In Circles/Does Stephanie Know? (p/s) | 7 |
| 82 | Hi-Lo HI 001 | No Time Tomorrow/Don't Cry To Me (p/s) | 7 |
| 82 | Hi-Lo HI 002 | Girl On A Train/Every Trick In The Book (p/s) | 7 |
| 83 | Hi-Lo HI 004 | Jesamine/When I Try, I Lie (p/s) | 10 |
| 84 | Hi-Lo HI 005/SFC 2 | The Young Idea/It's Getting Better (Squire Fan Club issue) | 10 |
| 94 | Detour DR 020 | The Place I Used To Live/Make Love To You/Over You (p/s, 900 only, 50 on white vinyl) | 10 |
| 94 | Detour DR 020 | The Place I Used To Live/Make Love To You/Over You (p/s, 2nd pressing of 250 copies, white labels & purple print: 3rd pressing, 588 copies on clear splattered vinyl) | 5 |
| 83 | Hi-Lo LO 01 | HITS FROM 3,000 YEARS AGO (LP) | 18 |
| 83 | Hi-Lo LO 02 | GET SMART (LP, with poster) | 15 |
| 85 | Hi-Lo LO 03 | THE SINGLES ALBUM (LP) | 15 |

*(see also Anthony Meynell)*

## JOHN SQUIRE
| 02 | North Country NCLP 001 | TIME CHANGES EVERYTHING (2-LP) | 18 |
| 04 | North Country NCLP 003 | MARSHALL'S HOUSE (LP) | 20 |

*(see also Stone Roses)*

## SQUIRES
| 69 | MCA MU 1060 | Funky Bayswater/Games People Play | 20 |

## ROSEMARY SQUIRES
| 56 | Decca F 10685 | Band Of Gold/Where You Are | 10 |
| 58 | HMV POP 462 | Happy Is The Bride/Give Me The Simple Life | 8 |
| 58 | HMV POP 541 | There Goes My Lover/Please Be Kind | 8 |
| 64 | HMV POP 1288 | Bluesette/Nothing's Changed | 8 |
| 56 | MGM MGM-EP 640 | MY LOVE IS A WANDERER (EP) | 40 |
| 60 | HMV 7EG 8588 | ROSEMARY (EP) | 40 |
| 63 | HMV CLP 1669 | EVERYTHINGS COMING UP ROSY (LP, mono) | 250 |
| 63 | HMV CSD 1508 | EVERYTHINGS COMING UP ROSY (LP, stereo) | 400 |
| 65 | HMV CLP 1832 | SOMETHING TO REMEMBER ME BY (LP, mono) | 80 |
| 65 | HMV CSD 1586 | SOMETHING TO REMEMBER ME BY (LP, stereo) | 120 |

## S.R.C.
| 69 | Capitol CL 15576 | Black Sheep/Morning Mood | 35 |
| 87 | Bam Caruso OPRA 063 | Black Sheep/BRAIN: Nightmares In Red (jukebox issue, die-cut company sleeve) | 5 |
| 69 | Capitol (S)T 2991 | S.R.C. (LP) | 80 |
| 69 | Capitol E-(S)T 134 | MILESTONES (LP) | 70 |
| 70 | Capitol E-(S)T 273 | TRAVELLER'S TALE (LP) | 70 |

*(See also Streamliners with Joanne)*

## ROY ST. JOHN
| 76 | Caroline CA 2008 | DECLARE IMMIGRATION (LP) | 15 |

## ASHBURY STABBINS DUO
| 76 | Bead Records BEAD 4 | FIRE WITHOUT STICKS (LP) | 50 |

## STACCATOS
| 61 | Parlophone R 4828 | Main Line/Topaz | 15 |

# STACCATOS (U.S.)

MINT VALUE £

| | | | |
|---|---|---|---|
| 68 | NEMS 3003 | Why Care About Today/Cry To Me | 25 |
| 68 | Fontana TF 966 | Butchers And Bakers/Imitations Of Love | 30 |

## STACCATOS (U.S.)
| | | | |
|---|---|---|---|
| 66 | Capitol CL 15478 | Let's Run Away/Face To Face (With Love) | 7 |
| 67 | Capitol CL 15505 | Half Past Midnight/Weatherman | 7 |

## CLARENCE STACEY
| | | | |
|---|---|---|---|
| 59 | Pye International 7N 25025 | Just Your Love/Lonely Guy | 35 |
| 59 | Pye International 7N 25025 | Just Your Love/Lonely Guy (78) | 20 |

## GWEN STACEY
| | | | |
|---|---|---|---|
| 65 | RCA RCX 7166 | INTRODUCING GWEN STACEY (EP) | 150 |

## STACK OF HEARTS
| | | | |
|---|---|---|---|
| 86 | SOH SOH 001 | Danger Zone/Searching For A Spirit (no p/s) | 25 |

## BOB STACKIE
| | | | |
|---|---|---|---|
| 68 | Collins Downbeat CR 009 | Grab It Hold It Feel It (with Sir Collins Band)/DAN SIMMONDS: Way Out Sound | 50 |

*(see also Sir Collins [Band], Owen Gray)*

## STACKRIDGE
| | | | |
|---|---|---|---|
| 71 | MCA MKS 5065 | Dora, The Female Explorer/Everyman | 5 |
| 72 | MCA MKS 5091 | Slark/Purple Spaceships Over Yatton | 12 |
| 72 | MCA MKS 5103 | Anyone For Tennis?/Amazingly Agnes | 5 |
| 71 | MCA MDKS 8002 | STACKRIDGE (LP, gatefold sleeve, pink/orange 'dogbone' label) | 35 |
| 72 | MCA MKPS 2025 | FRIENDLINESS (LP, blue/black 'hexagon' label) | 20 |

## STACKWADDY
| | | | |
|---|---|---|---|
| 70 | Dandelion S 5119 | Roadrunner/Kentucky | 12 |
| 72 | Dandelion 2001 331 | You Really Got Me/Willie The Pimp | 10 |
| 71 | Dandelion DAN 8003 | STACKWADDY (LP, gatefold sleeve with lyric insert) | 175 |
| 71 | Dandelion DAN 8003 | STACKWADDY (LP, gatefold sleeve with lyric insert, as K 49003) | 40 |
| 72 | Dandelion 2310 231 | BUGGER OFF! (LP) | 175 |

## STADIUM DOGS
| | | | |
|---|---|---|---|
| 77 | Audiogenic A 17 | Easy Beat/Android Rocker/Media Withdrawal (die-cut p/s) | 10 |

## JO STAFFORD
| | | | |
|---|---|---|---|
| 53 | Columbia SCM 5011 | Star Of Hope/Somebody | 10 |
| 53 | Columbia SCM 5012 | It Is No Secret/He Bought My Soul At Calvary | 15 |
| 53 | Columbia SCM 5013 | You Belong To Me/Jambalaya (On The Bayou) | 50 |
| 53 | Columbia SCM 5026 | Keep It A Secret/Once To Every Heart | 15 |
| 53 | Columbia SCM 5046 | Something To Remember You By/Blue Moon | 15 |
| 53 | Columbia SCM 5064 | September In The Rain/JO STAFFORD & FRANKIE LAINE: Chow, Willy | 15 |
| 57 | Philips JK 1003 | On London Bridge/Perfect Love (jukebox issue) | 25 |
| 50 | Capitol LC 6500 | AMERICAN FOLK SONGS (10") | 20 |
| 51 | Capitol LC 6515 | KISS ME KATE (10", with Gordon MacRae) | 15 |
| 53 | Capitol LC 6575 | CAPITOL PRESENTS JO STAFFORD (10") | 15 |
| 53 | Capitol LC 6611 | SUNDAY EVENING SONGS (10", with Gordon MacRae) | 12 |
| 54 | Capitol LC 6635 | CAPITOL PRESENTS JO STAFFORD, VOL. 2 (10") | 15 |
| 54 | Columbia 33S 1024 | AS YOU DESIRE ME (10") | 15 |
| 54 | Philips BBR 8011 | MY HEART'S IN THE HIGHLANDS (10") | 12 |
| 56 | Philips BBR 8076 | THE VOICE OF YOUR CHOICE (10") | 20 |
| 61 | Philips BBL 7428 | JO + JAZZ (also stereo SBBL 595) | 25 |

*(see also Tommy Dorsey)*

## JO STAFFORD & FRANKIE LAINE
| | | | |
|---|---|---|---|
| 53 | Columbia SCM 5014 | Settin' The Woods On Fire/Piece A-Puddin' | 20 |
| 55 | Philips BBR 8075 | FLOATIN' DOWN TO COTTON TOWN (10" LP) | 20 |

*(see also Frankie Laine)*

## TERRY STAFFORD
| | | | |
|---|---|---|---|
| 63 | Stateside SS 225 | Heartache On The Way/You Left Me Here To Cry | 15 |
| 64 | London HLU 9871 | Suspicion/Judy | 10 |
| 64 | London HLU 9902 | I'll Touch A Star/Playing With Fire | 10 |
| 64 | London HLU 9923 | Follow The Rainbow/Are You A Fool Like Me | 12 |
| 64 | London RE-U 1436 | SUSPICION (EP) | 25 |
| 64 | London HA-U 8200 | SUSPICION (LP) | 40 |

## STAG MARKS BAND
| | | | |
|---|---|---|---|
| 81 | Double Image SRTS 81 CUS 1223 | Ain't No Fun On The Dole/Story Of My Life | 20 |

## STAGEFRIGHT
| | | | |
|---|---|---|---|
| 85 | STN STN 1 | Strangers In The Night/Heartless/Rock City (no p/s) | 150 |

## ROSS STAGG
| | | | |
|---|---|---|---|
| 74 | Dawn DNS 1059 | I'll Never Be A Star (But I Might)/Oh Captain | 6 |

## STAIFFI ET SES MUSTAFA'S
| | | | |
|---|---|---|---|
| 59 | Pye Intl. 7N 25057 | Mustafa Cha Cha Oriental/Zoubida Cha Cha Oriental | 10 |

## STAINED GLASS
| | | | |
|---|---|---|---|
| 74 | Sweet Folk & C. SFA 019 | OPEN ROAD (LP) | 80 |

## STAINS
| | | | |
|---|---|---|---|
| 79 | Redball RR 020 | Emotional Pills/Believer/Bored (p/s) | 100 |

## STAIRS
| | | | |
|---|---|---|---|
| 92 | Imaginary MIRAGE 029 | Weed Bus (12", unissued, test pressings only, proof p/s) | 40 |

## STAIRSTEPS
| | | | |
|---|---|---|---|
| 71 | Buddah 2011 092 | Stay Close To Me/I Made A Mistake | 8 |
| 75 | Dark Horse AMS 5505 | From Us To You/Time (in USA p/s) | 10 |
| 75 | Dark Horse AMS 5505 | From Us To You/Time | 8 |

| | | | |
|---|---|---|---|
| 76 | Dark Horse AMS 5507 | Pasado/Throwin' Stones Atcha | 10 |
| 71 | Buddah 2359 021 | STEP BY STEP BY STEP (LP) | 20 |
| 71 | Buddah 2365 015 | STAY CLOSE TO ME (LP) | 20 |
| 72 | Buddah 2365 016 | THE STAIRSTEPS (LP) | 20 |
| 76 | Dark Horse AMLH 22004 | 2ND RESSURECTION (LP) | 20 |

*(see also Five Stairsteps)*

## STAKKA AND SKYNET
| | | | |
|---|---|---|---|
| 00 | Underfire UDFR 016 | Knight Lore/Global Report (12") | 10 |
| 01 | Underfire UDFRLPS 04 | CLOCKWORK SAMPLER EP: Decoy/Side Effects (Kemal and Rob Data remix)/9000 series/Side Effects (Teebee remix) (2 x 12", stickered, die-cut sleeve) | 20 |
| 01 | Underfire UDRFRLP 04 | CLOCKWORK (LP, 5 discs) | 40 |

## STALAG 17
| | | | |
|---|---|---|---|
| 85 | Mortarhate/Warzone MORT 14 | THE TRUTH WILL BE HEARD (12", split EP with TOXIC WASTE) | 15 |

## STALLION
| | | | |
|---|---|---|---|
| 75 | Flyright FLY 45 003 | Skinny Kid/Cobra | 45 |

## STAMFORD BRIDGE
| | | | |
|---|---|---|---|
| 70 | Penny Farthing PEN 715 | Chelsea/Ossie | 12 |
| 71 | Penny Farthing PELS 515 | FIRST DAY OF YOUR LIFE (LP) | 25 |

## TERRY STAMP
| | | | |
|---|---|---|---|
| 75 | A&M AMLH 68329 | FAT STICKS (LP, with lyric insert) | 30 |

*(see also Third World War)*

## STAMPEDE
| | | | |
|---|---|---|---|
| 82 | Polydor POSP 507 | Days Of Wine And Roses/Photographs (p/s) | 12 |
| 82 | Polydor POSP 507 | Photographs/Days Of Wine And Roses (A-side switched, no p/s) | 30 |
| 82 | Polydor POSPX 507 | Days Of Wine And Roses/Movin' On/Photographs/Missing You (12", p/s) | 20 |
| 83 | Polydor POSP 592 | The Other Side/The Runner (p/s) | 10 |
| 82 | Polydor ROCK 1 | OFFICIAL BOOTLEG (LP) | 15 |
| 83 | Polydor POLS 1083 | HURRICANE TOWN (LP) | 15 |

## STAMPEDERS
| | | | |
|---|---|---|---|
| 71 | Stateside SS2197 | Devil You/Giant In The Streets | 8 |
| 72 | Stateside SS 2202 | Monday Morning Choo Choo/Then Came The White Man | 5 |
| 73 | Regal Zonophone RZ3083 | Minstrel Gypsy/Mumbo Jumbo | 5 |
| 72 | Regal Zonophone RZ 3069 | Johnny Lightning/Today's The Beginning Of The Rest Of Your Life | 6 |
| 73 | Regal Zonophone RZ 3079 | Oh My Lady/No Destination | 6 |
| 73 | Regal Zonophone RZ3085 | Ride In The Wind/Running Wild | 20 |
| 72 | Regal Zono. SLRZ 1032 | THE STAMPEDERS (LP) | 40 |
| 74 | Regal Zono. SLRZ 1039 | FROM THE FIRE (LP) | 50 |

## JOE STAMPLEY
| | | | |
|---|---|---|---|
| 73 | Dot DOT 145 | Soul Song/Not Too Long Ago | 10 |

## JEAN STANBACK
| | | | |
|---|---|---|---|
| 69 | Deep Soul DS 9101 | I Still Love You/If I Ever Needed Love | 50 |

## STANDELLS
| | | | |
|---|---|---|---|
| 64 | Liberty LIB 55722 | I'll Go Crazy/Help Yourself | 35 |
| 66 | Capitol CL 15446 | Dirty Water/Rari | 50 |
| 65 | Liberty LBY 1243 | THE STANDELLS IN PERSON AT P.J.'s (LP) | 60 |

## STANDING OVATION
| | | | |
|---|---|---|---|
| 92 | Kold Sweat KS126 | Shadows Of Mayhem (12") | 15 |

## PAUL STANLEY
| | | | |
|---|---|---|---|
| 79 | Casablanca CAN 140 | Hold Me Touch Me/Goodbye (p/s, purple vinyl with mask & picture label, most with mispressed B-side: "Love In Chains") | 25 |

*(see also Kiss)*

## PETE STANLEY & ROGER KNOWLES
| | | | |
|---|---|---|---|
| 70s | Xtra TRANS 1146 | PICKING AND SINGING (LP) | 25 |

## PETE STANLEY & WIZZ JONES
| | | | |
|---|---|---|---|
| 65 | Columbia DB 7776 | The Ballad Of Hollis Brown/Riff Minor | 20 |
| 66 | Columbia SX 6083 | SIXTEEN TONS OF BLUEGRASS (LP) | 60 |

*(see also Wizz Jones)*

## STANLEY AND THE TURBINES
| | | | |
|---|---|---|---|
| 83 | GG GGLP 0029 | BIG BAMBOO (LP) | 15 |

## ROY STANNARD AND HIS MUSIC
| | | | |
|---|---|---|---|
| 87 | SS SS 100 | The Peanut Vendor/'Swingin' ' The Blues | 5 |

## LISA STANSFIELD
| | | | |
|---|---|---|---|
| 81 | Devil DEV 2 | Your Alibis/Thought Police (p/s) | 5 |

## VIV(IAN) STANSHALL
| | | | |
|---|---|---|---|
| 70 | Liberty LBF 15309 | Labio-Dental Fricative/Paper Round (with Sean Head Show Band featuring Eric Clapton) | 40 |
| 71 | Fly BUG 4 | Suspicion (with Gargantuan Chums)/Blind Date (with biG GRunt) | 15 |
| 74 | Warner Bros K 16424 | Lakonga/Baba Tunde | 20 |
| 76 | Harvest HAR 5114 | Young Ones/Are You Havin' Any Fun/Question | 15 |
| 80 | Charisma CB 373 | Terry Keeps His Clips On/King Cripple (p/s) | 6 |
| 81 | Charisma CB 382 | Calypso To Colapso/Smoke Signals At Night (p/s) | 5 |
| 74 | Warner Bros K 56052 | MEN OPENING UMBRELLAS AHEAD (LP, with inner) | 70 |
| 78 | Charisma CAS 1139 | SIR HENRY AT RAWLINSON END (LP, soundtrack, with insert) | 25 |
| 81 | Charisma CAS 1153 | TEDDY BOYS DON'T KNIT (LP) | 25 |
| 84 | Demon Verbals VERB 1 | SIR HENRY AT NDIDDI'S KRAAL (LP) | 25 |

*(see also Bonzo Dog [Doo Dah] Band, Grimms)*

MINT VALUE £

## STAPLE SINGERS

| | | | |
|---|---|---|---|
| 64 | Riverside 106902 RIF | Hammer And Nails/Glory Land | 10 |
| 67 | Columbia DB 8292 | For What It's Worth/Are You Sure? | 30 |
| 69 | Soul City SC 117 | For What It's Worth/Are You Sure? (reissue) | 18 |
| 62 | Riverside REP 3220 | THE SAVIOUR IS BORN (EP) | 15 |
| 63 | Stateside SL 10015 | SWING LOW (LP) | 30 |
| 63 | Riverside RLP 3501 | HAMMER AND NAILS (LP) | 25 |
| 65 | Fontana 688 515 ZL | UNCLOUDY DAY (LP) | 20 |
| 66 | Columbia SX 6023 | FREEDOM HIGHWAY (LP) | 20 |

## STUART A STAPLES

| | | | |
|---|---|---|---|
| 05 | Beggars Banquet BBQLP 242 | LUCKY DOG RECORDINGS (LP) | 20 |

*(see also Asphalt Ribbons, Tindersticks)*

## CYRIL STAPLETON & HIS ORCHESTRA

| | | | |
|---|---|---|---|
| 54 | Decca F 10293 | Long Distance Love/There'll Be No Teardrops Tonight | 5 |
| 55 | Decca F 10456 | Tango Mambo/Mexican Madness | 8 |
| 55 | Decca F 10470 | Fanfare Boogie/Time After Time | 6 |
| 55 | Decca F 10488 | Elephant Tango/Gabrielle | 6 |
| 55 | Decca F 10559 | Blue Star (The "Medic" Theme) (with Julie Dawn)/Honey Babe (with Gordon Langhorn) | 10 |
| 56 | Decca F 10703 | The Italian Theme/Come Next Spring | 6 |
| 56 | Decca F 10735 | The Happy Whistler (with Desmond Lane)/Tiger Tango | 6 |
| 56 | Decca F 10793 | Highway Patrol/Maids Of Madrid | 6 |
| 57 | Decca F 10883 | Rock, Fiddle, Rock/Chantez, Chantez | 5 |
| 57 | Decca F 10912 | Forgotten Dreams/It's Not For Me To Say | 7 |
| 58 | Decca F 10979 | Monday Blues (Parts 1 & 2) | 5 |
| 62 | Decca F 11443 | Afrikaan Beat/My Sad Girl | 6 |
| 69 | Pye 7N 17807 | Department S (Theme)/W. Somerset Maugham TV Theme (in p/s) | 10 |

*(see also Gordon Langhorn, Desmond Lane)*

## STEVEN STAPLETON & DAVID TIBET

| | | | |
|---|---|---|---|
| 91 | United Dairies UD 037 | THE SADNESS OF THINGS/THE GRAVE AND BEAUTIFUL NAME OF SADNESS (LP, one side each) | 35 |

*(see also Current 93, Nurse With Wound, Tibet & Stapleton)*

## STA-PREST

| | | | |
|---|---|---|---|
| 80 | Avatar AAA 103 | Schooldays/Tomorrow (p/s) | 75 |

## STAR

| | | | |
|---|---|---|---|
| 73 | Bradley BRAD 315 | Children Of the Sun/Your Day Will Come | 12 |

## STAR SPANGLES

| | | | |
|---|---|---|---|
| 02 | Capitol R 6593 | Which Of The Two Of Us Is Gonna Burn This House Down/Stain Glass Shoes (p/s) | 10 |

## STAR WITH PETER COLLINS

| | | | |
|---|---|---|---|
| 60s | SRT/Custom 10 | Give It Up/Wake Up | 10 |

## STARBOUND

| | | | |
|---|---|---|---|
| 77 | Star Bound SB 01 | CHANGES (LP) | 20 |

## STARBUCK

| | | | |
|---|---|---|---|
| 73 | RCA RCA 2350 | Wouldn't You Like It/Manana | 8 |
| 73 | Bradleys BRAD 312 | Do You Like Boys?/You Never Wanna Rock 'N' Roll | 15 |
| 74 | Bradleys BRAD 7411 | Heart Throb/Ricochet | 8 |

*(see also Mandrake Paddle Steamer, Shambles)*

## STARFIGHTERS

| | | | |
|---|---|---|---|
| 80 | Motor City MCR 105 | I'm Falling/Heaven And Hell (in p/s) | 40 |
| 80 | Motor City MCR 105 | I'm Falling/Heaven And Hell | 7 |
| 81 | Jive JIV 003 | Alley Cat Blues/Don't Touch Me (p/s) | 7 |
| 81 | Jive JIVET 003 | Alley Cat Blues/Don't Touch Me (12", p/s) | 15 |
| 81 | Jive JIVET 6 | Power Crazy/I Want You (p/s) | 6 |
| 81 | Jive HOP 200 | STARFIGHTERS (LP, with inner) | 22 |

## STARGAZERS

| | | | |
|---|---|---|---|
| 54 | Decca F 10213 | I See The Moon/Eh Cumpari | 25 |
| 54 | Decca F 10259 | The Happy Wanderer/Till We Two Are One | 15 |
| 54 | Decca F 10379 | 365 Kisses/I Need You Now | 6 |
| 54 | Decca F 10412 | Rose Of The Wildwood/Come The Morning | 6 |
| 55 | Decca F 10437 | Somebody/(My Baby Don't Love Me) No More (& Sonny Farrar Banjo Band) | 10 |
| 55 | Decca F 10523 | The Crazy Otto Rag/Hey, Mr. Banjo | 10 |
| 55 | Decca F 10569 | At The Steamboat River Ball/I Love You A Mountain (with Sonny Farrar Banjo Band) | 5 |
| 55 | Decca F 10594 | Close The Door/I've Got Four Big Brothers | 12 |
| 55 | Decca F 10626 | Twenty Tiny Fingers/An Old Beer Bottle | 15 |
| 55 | Decca F 10668 | (Love Is) The Tender Trap/When The Swallows Say Goodbye | 5 |
| 56 | Decca F 10696 | Zambesi/When The Swallows Say Goodbye | 10 |
| 56 | Decca F 10731 | Hot Diggity (Dog Ziggity Boom)/Rockin' And Rollin' | 10 |
| 56 | Decca F 10775 | She Loves To Rock/John Jacob Jingleheimer Smith | 10 |
| 57 | Decca F 10867 | You Won't Be Around/Mangos | 5 |
| 57 | Decca F 10898 | Honky Tonk Song/Golly! | 5 |
| 60 | Palette PG 9003 | Three Beautiful Words/Manhattan Spiritual | 6 |
| 56 | Decca DFE 6341 | THE STARGAZERS (EP) | 10 |
| 56 | Decca DFE 6362 | ROCKIN' AND ROLLIN' (EP) | 10 |
| 54 | Decca LF 1186 | PRESENTING THE STARGAZERS (10" LP) | 20 |
| 59 | Decca LK 4309 | SOUTH OF THE BORDER (LP) | 20 |

*(see also Roy Smith & Stargazers, Lita Roza, Dickie Valentine)*

## STARJETS

| | | | |
|---|---|---|---|
| 78 | Epic S EPC 6902 | Here She Comes Again/Watch Out | 8 |

| | | | |
|---|---|---|---|
| 79 | Epic S EPC 6968 | It Really Doesn't Matter/Schooldays | 5 |
| 79 | Epic S EPC 7123 | Run With The Pack/Watch Out | 5 |
| 79 | Epic S EPC 6968/7123 | It Really Doesn't Matter/Schooldays//Run With The Pack/Watch Out (double pack, die-cut sleeves, promo only) | 15 |
| 79 | Epic S EPC 7417 | Ten Years/One More Word (p/s) | 5 |
| 79 | Epic S EPC 7417 | Ten Years/One More Word (Manchester gig issue, stamped white labels) | 12 |
| 79 | Epic S EPC 7770 | War Stories/Do The Push (p/s) | 5 |
| 79 | Epic S EPC 7986 | Schooldays/What A Life (p/s) | 6 |
| 80 | Epic S EPC 8276 | Shiraleo/Standby 19 (p/s) | 5 |
| 79 | Epic EPC 83534 | GOD BLESS STARJETS (LP) | 15 |

## STARLAND VOCAL GROUP
| | | | |
|---|---|---|---|
| 76 | RCA RCA 2716 | Afternoon Delight/Starland (as Starland Vocal Band) | 6 |

## STARLITES
| | | | |
|---|---|---|---|
| 73 | Downtown DT 502 | You're A Wanted Man/G.G. ALL STARS: Back To Dubwise | 7 |
| 74 | Big Shot BI 629 | Mama Dee Part One/Mama Dee Part Two | 8 |
| 75 | Bullet BU 554 | Healing In The Barnyard/G.G. ALL STARS: Version | 6 |
| 68 | Philips BF 1725 | Good Morning Mr Milkman/Don't Break My Heart Again | 12 |

*(see also Bellfield)*

## CHUKKI STARR
| | | | |
|---|---|---|---|
| 98 | Ariwa AWM 002 | The Almighty One/MAD PROFESSOR: Version | 10 |
| 98 | Saxon SAX 064 | Mark A De Beast/(Version)//Youth Dem Anthem/Youth Dem Anthem (Mix 2) (12") | 25 |
| 98 | Ariwa ARI 147 | GHETTO YOUTHS (LP) | 20 |

## CINDY STARR
| | | | |
|---|---|---|---|
| 68 | Columbia Blue Beat DB 107 | Pain Of Love/Hippy Ska (as Cindy Starr & Rude Boys) | 20 |
| 68 | Columbia Blue Beat DB 110 | The Way I Do/Sad Movies (Make Me Cry) (as Cindy Starr & Mopeds) | 15 |

*(see also Mopeds, Teardrops)*

## EDWIN STARR
| | | | |
|---|---|---|---|
| 66 | Polydor BM 56702 | Stop Her On Sight (S.O.S.)/I Have Faith In You (demo) | 500 |
| 66 | Polydor BM 56702 | Stop Her On Sight (S.O.S.)/I Have Faith In You | 25 |
| 66 | Polydor BM 56717 | Headline News/Harlem | 20 |
| 67 | Polydor BM 56726 | It's My Turn Now/Girls Are Getting Prettier | 25 |
| 68 | Polydor BM 56753 | Stop Her On Sight (S.O.S.)/Headline News (reissue) | 10 |
| 67 | Tamla Motown TMG 630 | I Want My Baby Back/Gonna Keep On Tryin' Till I Win | 30 |
| 67 | Tamla Motown TMG 630 | I Want My Baby Back/Gonna Keep On Tryin' Till I Win (DJ copy) | 50 |
| 68 | Tamla Motown TMG 646 | I Am The Man For You Baby/My Weakness Is You | 30 |
| 68 | Tamla Motown TMG 646 | I Am The Man For You Baby/My Weakness Is You (DJ copy) | 90 |
| 68 | Tamla Motown TMG 672 | 25 Miles/Mighty Good Lovin' | 12 |
| 68 | Tamla Motown TMG 672 | 25 Miles/Mighty Good Lovin' (DJ copy) | 45 |
| 69 | Tamla Motown TMG 692 | Way Over There/If My Heart Could Tell The Story | 20 |
| 69 | Tamla Motown TMG 692 | Way Over There/If My Heart Could Tell The Story (DJ copy) | 50 |
| 69 | Tamla Motown TMG 720 | Oh How Happy/O, O, O, Baby (demos only, unissued, with Blinky) | 375 |
| 70 | Tamla Motown TMG 725 | Time/Running Back And Forth | 20 |
| 70 | Tamla Motown TMG 754 | War/He Who Picks A Rose | 7 |
| 71 | Tamla Motown TMG 764 | Stop The War Now!/Gonna Keep On Tryin' Till I Win | 8 |
| 71 | Tamla Motown TMG 790 | Agent Double 0 Soul/Back Street | 12 |
| 71 | Tamla Motown TMG 790 | Agent Double 0 Soul/Back Street (DJ copy) | 40 |
| 72 | Tamla Motown TMG 810 | Funky Music Sho' Nuff Turns Me On/Cloud Nine | 20 |
| 73 | Tamla Motown TMG 875 | You've Got My Soul On Fire/Love The Lonely People's Prayer | 20 |
| 73 | Tamla Motown TMG 930 | Ain't It Hell Up In Harlem/Who's Right Or Wrong | 8 |
| 75 | Bradleys BRAD 7520 | Stay With Me/I'll Never Forget You | 15 |
| 75 | Bradleys BRAD 7531 | Pain/Party | 10 |
| 76 | GTO GT 65 | Accident/Eavesdropper | 8 |
| 70s | Tamla Motown TMG 905 | Stop Her On Sight/Headline News (reissue) | 6 |
| 70s | Tamla Motown TMG 1028 | Time/Running Back And Forth (reissue) | 10 |
| 69 | T. Motown STML 11094 | SOUL MASTER (LP, mono) | 35 |
| 69 | T. Motown STML 11094 | SOUL MASTER (LP, stereo) | 40 |
| 69 | T. Motown TML 11115 | 25 MILES (LP, mono) | 30 |
| 69 | T. Motown STML 11115 | 25 MILES (LP, stereo) | 25 |
| 70 | T. Motown (S)TML 11131 | JUST WE TWO (LP, as Edwin Starr & Blinky) | 25 |
| 70 | Tamla Motown STML 11171 | WAR AND PEACE (LP) | 20 |
| 72 | Tamla Motown STML 11199 | INVOLVED (LP) | 20 |
| 72 | Tamla Motown STML 11209 | THE HITS OF EDWIN STARR (LP) | 15 |
| 74 | Tamla Motown STML 11260 | HELL UP IN HARLEM (LP, soundtrack) | 15 |

*(see also Blinky & Edwin Starr, Holidays)*

## FRANK STARR
| | | | |
|---|---|---|---|
| 62 | London HLU 9545 | Little Bitty Feeling/Lost In A Dream | 12 |

## FREDDIE STARR & MIDNIGHTERS
| | | | |
|---|---|---|---|
| 63 | Decca F 11663 | Who Told You?/Peter Gunn Locomotion | 20 |
| 63 | Decca F 11786 | It's Shaking Time/Baby Blue | 20 |
| 64 | Decca F 12009 | Never Cry On Someone's Shoulder/Just Keep On Dreaming | 40 |
| 71 | A&M AMS 838 | Naomi/Free To Carry On (solo) | 5 |

*(see also Howie Casey & Seniors)*

## JIMMY STARR
| | | | |
|---|---|---|---|
| 58 | London HL 8731 | It's Only Make Believe/Ooh Crazy | 30 |

## KAY STARR
| | | | |
|---|---|---|---|
| 54 | Capitol CL 14151 | Am I A Toy Or A Treasure?/Fortune In Dreams | 20 |
| 54 | Capitol CL 14167 | Fool, Fool, Fool/Allez-Vous En | 20 |
| 55 | HMV 7M 300 | If Anyone Finds This, I Love You/Turn Right | 15 |

MINT VALUE £

| 55 | HMV 7M 307 | Foolishly Yours/For Better Or Worse | 10 |
|----|------------|-------------------------------------|----|
| 55 | HMV 7M 315 | Where, What Or When?/Good And Lonesome | 10 |
| 56 | HMV 7M 371 | Rock And Roll Waltz/I've Changed My Mind 1,000 Times | 20 |
| 56 | HMV 7M 420 | Second Fiddle/Love Ain't Right | 10 |
| 57 | HMV POP 345 | A Little Loneliness/Touch And Go | 8 |
| 57 | HMV POP 357 | Jamie Boy/The Things I Never Had | 8 |
| 58 | RCA RCA 1065 | Stroll Me/Rockin' Chair | 6 |
| 60 | Capitol CL 15105 | Riders In The Sky/Night Train | 7 |
| 60 | Capitol CL 15137 | Wheel Of Fortune/If You Love Me (Really Love Me) | 12 |
| 53 | Capitol LC 6574 | CAPITOL PRESENTS KAY STARR (10") | 25 |
| 54 | Capitol LC 6630 | THE KAY STARR STYLE (10") | 20 |
| 56 | Capitol LC 6835 | THE HITS OF KAY STARR (10") | 20 |
| 57 | Capitol T 580 | IN A BLUE MOOD | 20 |
| 57 | London HA-U 2039 | SWINGING WITH THE STARR | 20 |
| 58 | RCA RD 27056 | BLUE STARR | 20 |

## LUCILLE STARR
| 64 | London HL 9900 | The French Song/Sit Down And Write A Letter To Me | 12 |
|----|------------|-------------------------------------|----|

## MAXINE STARR
| 63 | London HLU 9712 | The Wishing Star/Sailor Boy | 8 |
|----|------------|-------------------------------------|----|

## RANDY STARR
| 57 | London HL 8443 | After School/Heaven High (Man So Low) | 30 |
|----|------------|-------------------------------------|----|
| 58 | Felsted AF 106 | Pink Lemonade/Count On Me | 15 |
| 60 | Top Rank JAR 264 | Workin' On The Santa Fe/You're Growing Up | 7 |

## RINGO STARR
| 71 | Apple R 5898 | It Don't Come Easy/Early 1970 (p/s, B-side with Ringo or George Harrison production credit) | 6 |
|----|------------|-------------------------------------|----|
| 71 | Apple R 5898 | It Don't Come Easy/Early 1970 (p/s, B-side without Ringo or George Harrison production credit) | 5 |
| 72 | Apple R 5944 | Back Off Boogaloo/Blindman (p/s, blue label) | 6 |
| 73 | Apple R 5992 | Photograph/Down And Out (p/s) | 6 |
| 74 | Apple R 5995 | You're Sixteen/Devil Woman (p/s) | 5 |
| 74 | Apple R 6000 | Only You/Call Me (p/s) | 5 |
| 75 | Apple R 6004 | Snookeroo/Oo-wee (stock EMI, not Apple sleeve) | 12 |
| 76 | Apple R 6011 | Oh My My/No No Song (not in die-cut apple sleeve) | 20 |
| 76 | Polydor 2001 694 | A Dose Of Rock 'N' Roll/Cryin' | 20 |
| 76 | Polydor 2001 695 | You Don't Know Me At All/Cryin' (unissued in U.K., Europe only) | 0 |
| 76 | Polydor 2001 699 | Hey Baby/Lady Gaye | 15 |
| 77 | Polydor 2001 734 | Drowning In The Sea Of Love/Just A Dream | 50 |
| 78 | Polydor 2001 782 | Lipstick Traces/Old Time Relovin' (unissued in U.K., Europe only) | 0 |
| 78 | Polydor 2001 795 | Tonight/Heart On My Sleeve | 120 |
| 72 | R.O.R. ROR 2001 | Steel (1-sided promo-only interview disc for 'Ringo Or Robin' reception at Liberty's department store; available for 1 week only, p/s) | 2000 |
| 74 | Parlophone PSR 374 | Interview By Bob Mercer With Ringo For The Salesmen and Uxbridge Road/Only You (promo only) | 500 |
| 70s | Apple R 5944 | Back Off Boogaloo/Blindman (green apple label) | 150 |
| 84 | Apple G45 13 | It Don't Come Easy/Back Off Boogaloo (P/s EMI Golden 45s series) | 20 |
| 99 | Mercury 546 668-2 | I Wanna Be Santa Claus (CD) | 25 |
| 70 | Apple PCS 7101 | SENTIMENTAL JOURNEY (LP) | 30 |
| 70 | Apple TD-PCS 7101 | SENTIMENTAL JOURNEY (reel-to-reel tape, jewel case) | 20 |
| 70 | Parlophone PPCS 7101 | SENTIMENTAL JOURNEY (LP, export edition, black/silver label, 'Parlophone' and 'EMI' boxed logos) | 250 |
| 70 | Apple PAS 10002 | BEAUCOUPS OF BLUES (LP, gatefold sleeve) | 40 |
| 73 | Apple PCTC 252 | RINGO (LP, gatefold with 12" x 12" booklet) | 15 |
| 74 | Apple PCS 7168 | GOODNIGHT VIENNA (LP, with inner) | 15 |
| 74 | Apple PCS 7170 | BLAST FROM YOUR PAST (LP, with inner) | 15 |
| 76 | Polydor 2302-040 A | ROTOGRAVURE (LP, gatefold with inner) | 15 |
| 78 | Polydor 2310-599B | BAD BOY (LP, with inner) | 15 |
| 78 | Polydor 2480 429 | SCOUSE THE MOUSE (LP, with Adam Faith, Donald Pleasance etc.; with stickered sleeve & printed [not photocopied] competition insert) | 100 |
| 78 | Polydor 2480 429 | SCOUSE THE MOUSE (LP, with Adam Faith, Donald Pleasance etc.; without stickered sleeve & printed [not photocopied] competition insert) | |
| 90 | EMI EMS 1375 | RINGO STARR AND HIS ALL STARR BAND (LP) | 35 |
| 00 | Eagle Records EEECDO11 | THE ANTHOLOGY...SO FAR (3xCD in slip case) | 30 |

*(see also Beatles, Harry Nilsson, Billy Connolly & Chris Tummings, Traveling Wilburys)*

## STELLA STARR
| 67 | Piccadilly 7N 35366 | Bring Him Back/Say It | 50 |
|----|------------|-------------------------------------|----|
| 67 | Piccadilly 7N 35366 | Bring Him Back/Say It (DJ copy) | 80 |

## TONY STARR
| 64 | Decca F 11847 | I'll Take A Rocket To The Moon/Next Train Leaving | 60 |
|----|------------|-------------------------------------|----|

## STARR BOUNDS
| 75 | Horse HOSS 95 | Heavenly (Parts 1 & 2) | 8 |
|----|------------|-------------------------------------|----|

## STARRY EYED
| 76 | CBS 4805 | Saturday/Believe | 6 |
|----|------------|-------------------------------------|----|

## STARSHIP
| 77 | Scratch SCH 01 | Vampire For Your Love/You Can Dance/Hey Girl/Never Thought I'd See The Day | 15 |
|----|------------|-------------------------------------|----|

## STARS OF HEAVEN
| 85 | Hotwire HWS 853 | Clothes Of Pride/All About You (beige or black label, with p/s) | 8 |
|----|------------|-------------------------------------|----|
| 85 | Hotwire HWS 853 | Clothes Of Pride/All About You (beige or black label) | 6 |

## STARVATION ARMY
| 83 | Linden Sounds LS004 | Stranger In My Room/Walrus Is Dead (no p/s) | 30 |
|----|------------|-------------------------------------|----|

**STATEN ISLAND FERRY**
69   Major Minor MM 643 ........ Candy Bar/Charlie Chan ............................................................. 20

**STATE OF GRACE**
83   PRT 12P266 ........ Touching The Times/Instrumental Mix (12") ............................. 60

**STATE OF MICKEY & TOMMY**
67   Mercury MF 996 ........ With Love From One To Five/I Know What I Will Do ............................. 150
67   Mercury MF 1009 ........ Frisco Bay/Nobody Knows Where You've Been .................................... 150
*(see also Spooky Tooth, Nero & Gladiators)*

**STATESMEN**
63   Fontana TF 432 ........ I've Just Fallen In Love/It's All Happening ....................................... 8
63   Decca F11687 ........ Look Around/I'm Wondering ......................................................... 8
63   Studio Republic ........ FIVE PLUS ONE (LP, private pressing) ........................................... 100

**STATE TROOPER**
85   Neat 5212 ........ SHE GOT THE LOOK (12" EP) ......................................................... 10

**STATIC (1)**
67   Page One POF 039 ........ When You Went Away/Let Me Tell You ................................................ 7

**STATIC (2)**
81   Eeyo EEYO 1 ........ Voice On The Line/Stealin' (no p/s, 1,000 only) ............................... 15
*(see also White Lightning)*

**(THE) STATICS**
80   Mercury MER 41 ........ Turn The Radio On/Over Now (as Static) ......................................... 20
81   Carrere CAR 186 ........ Turn The Radio On/Last Night In Chinatown ....................................... 6

**STATION SKIFFLE GROUP**
58   Esquire EP 161 ........ STATION SKIFFLE GROUP (EP) ...................................................... 50
*(see also Jimmy Miller)*

**STATION 360**
84   SRT STA 360 ........ Optimist/Stars ................................................................... 30

**STATISTICS**
79   Tyger TYG 4 ........ Dumb/Home Movies (p/s) ............................................................. 8

**STATLER BROTHERS**
65   CBS 201976 ........ Flowers On The Wall/Billy Christian ............................................. 8
66   CBS BPG 62713 ........ FLOWERS ON THE WALL (LP) ......................................................... 15
*(see also Johnny Cash)*

**CANDI STATON**
69   Capitol CL 15601 ........ I'd Rather Be An Old Man's Sweetheart/For You .................................. 8
69   Capitol CL 15620 ........ Heart On A String/I'm Just A Prisoner ........................................... 8
70   Capitol CL 15646 ........ Sweet Feeling/Evidence .......................................................... 8
70   Capitol CL 15658 ........ Stand By Your Man/How Can I Put Out The Flame (When You Keep The Fire Burning) .... 8
75   United Artists UP 35823 ........ Love Chain/I'm Gonna Hold On ............................................... 6
70   Capitol ST 21631 ........ I'M JUST A PRISONER (LP) ........................................................ 30

**DAKOTA STATON**
55   Capitol CL 14314 ........ Don't Leave Me Now/A Little You ................................................. 12
55   Capitol CL 14339 ........ I Never Dreamt/Abracadabra ...................................................... 12
58   Capitol CL 14931 ........ A Foggy Day/My Funny Valentine .................................................. 7

**STATUES**
60   London HLG 9192 ........ Blue Velvet/Keep The Hall Burning .............................................. 45

**STATUS QUO**
**SINGLES : PYE SINGLES**
68   Pye 7N 17449 ........ Pictures Of Matchstick Men/Gentleman Joe's Sidewalk Café (some with '75c Minimum' on B-side label credit) ........... 12
68   Pye 7N 17497 ........ Black Veils Of Melancholy/To Be Free ........................................... 20
68   Pye 7N 17581 ........ Ice In The Sun/When My Mind Is Not Live ......................................... 8
68   Pye 7N 17650 ........ Technicolor Dreams/Paradise Flat ............................................... 600
69   Pye 7N 17665 ........ Make Me Stay A Bit Longer/Aunt Nellie .......................................... 22
69   Pye 7N 17728 ........ Are You Growing Tired Of My Love/So Ends Another Life ........................... 20
69   Pye 7N 17825 ........ The Price Of Love/Little Miss Nothing .......................................... 30
70   Pye 7N 17907 ........ Down The Dustpipe/Face Without A Soul (black, blue or reissue Precision labels) ....... 5
70   Pye 7N 17998 ........ In My Chair/Gerdundula (with p/s) ............................................... 45
70   Pye 7N 17998 ........ In My Chair/Gerdundula ........................................................... 8
71   Pye 7N 45077 ........ Tune To The Music/Good Thinking ................................................. 20
73   Pye 7N 45229 ........ Mean Girl/Everything (blue labels) .............................................. 5
73   Pye 7N 45253 ........ Gerdundula/Lakky Lady (red label) ............................................... 5
77   Pye BD 103 ........ Down The Dustpipe/Mean Girl/In My Chair/Gerdundula (12", generic sleeve, reissued on PRT) ........ 10
78   Pye 7N 46103 ........ Pictures of Matchstick Men/Ice In The Sun (red labels, reissued on PRT) ......... 5
79   Pye Flashbacks FBS 2 ........ Pictures Of Matchstick Men/Down The Dustpipe (yellow vinyl, p/s) ............ 6
79   Pye Flashbacks FBS 2 ........ Pictures Of Matchstick Men/Down The Dustpipe (black vinyl, no p/s, reissued on PRT) .. 5
79   Pye 7P 103 ........ In My Chair/Gerdundula (p/s) .................................................... 5
79   Pye QUO 1/SFI 434 ........ In My Chair (flexi, concert freebie, with Record Mirror Quo special) ...... 10

**SINGLES : VERTIGO SINGLES**
72   Vertigo 6059 071 ........ Paper Plane/Softer Ride (swirl label, solid centre) ............................ 6
73   Vertigo 6059 085 ........ Caroline/Joanne (with B-side miscredited to Lancaster) ......................... 5
74   Vertigo 6059 101 ........ Break The Rules/Lonely Night (mispressed, B-side labels on both sides) .......... 7
76   Vertigo 6059 153 ........ Wild Side Of Life/All Through The Night (brown plastic labels) .................. 6
77   Vertigo 6059 184 ........ Rockin' All Over The World/Ring Of A Change (p/s, with small poster) ............ 15
77   Vertigo 6059 184 ........ Rockin' All Over The World/Ring Of A Change (p/s) ............................... 5
78   Vertigo QUO 2 ........ Accident Prone/Let Me Fly (p/s) ................................................. 5

MINT VALUE £

| Year | Label | Cat No | Description | Value |
|---|---|---|---|---|
| 82 | Vertigo | QUO 9 | Jealousy/Calling The Shots (unreleased in U.K.; Irish promos only) | 150 |
| 83 | Vertigo | QUO 1414 | Marguerita Time/Resurrection//Caroline/Joanne (double pack, stickered gatefold p/s) | 10 |
| 84 | Vertigo | QUO 15 | Too Close To The Ground/I Wonder Why (release cancelled) | 0 |
| 85 | Vertigo | QUO 17 | Naughty Girl (actually "Dreamin' ") (unreleased) | 0 |
| 86 | Vertigo | QUOPD 18 | Rollin' Home/Lonely (uncut picture disc) | 150 |
| 86 | Vertigo | QUODP 19 | Red Sky/Don't Give It Up//Rockin' All Over The World/Whatever You Want (double pack, gatefold p/s) | 6 |
| 86 | Vertigo | QUOPB 191 | Red Sky/Don't Give It Up/The Milton Keynes Medley (12", 'Wembley Souvenir Pack', poster p/s) | 6 |
| 86 | Vertigo | QUO 20 | In The Army Now/Heartburn (stickered p/s, with sew-on patch, shrinkwrapped) | 15 |
| 86 | Vertigo | QUOPD 20 | In The Army Now/Heartburn (picture disc) | 10 |
| 86 | Vertigo | QUODP 20 | In The Army Now/Heartburn//Marguerita Time/What You're Proposing (double pack, gatefold p/s) | 15 |
| 86 | Vertigo | QUOP 21 | Dreamin'/Long-Legged Girls (p/s, with foldout poster/calendar) | 6 |
| 88 | Vertigo | QUOCD 23 | Who Gets The Love? (Extended)/Hallowe'en/The Reason For Goodbye/The Wanderer (Sharon The Nag Mix) (CD, card sleeve) | 6 |
| 88 | Vertigo | QUO 2512 | Burning Bridges (On And Off And On Again) (Extended Version)/Whatever You Want/Marguerita Time (12", mispressing also including 7" edit) | 25 |
| 89 | Vertigo | 080 630-2 | Burning Bridges (On And Off And On Again) (Extended Version)/Whatever You Want (Extended Version)/Marguerita Time/Who Gets The Love?/Burning Bridges (Video) (CD Video) | 10 |
| 90 | Vertigo | QUO 2812 | The Anniversary Waltz/The Power Of Rock/Perfect Remedy (12", p/s, mispress, B-side plays "Little Lady" (live) & exclusive "Paper Plane" re-recording) | 0 |
| 90 | Vertigo | QUO 2812 | The Anniversary Waltz/The Power Of Rock/Perfect Remedy (12", p/s, mispress, A-side plays "The Power Of Rock [Full Version]") | 45 |
| 91 | Vertigo | QUO 31 | Fakin' The Blues (Edit)/Heavy Daze (p/s, swirl label, release cancelled, approximately 25 copies only) | 45 |
| 91 | Vertigo | QUO 3112 | Fakin' The Blues (Edit)/Fakin' The Blues (Album Version)/Heavy Daze/Better Times (12", swirl label, p/s, cancelled, approx. 25 copies only) | 450 |
| 91 | Vertigo | QUOCD 31 | Fakin' The Blues (Edit)/Fakin' The Blues (Album Version)/Heavy Daze/Better Times (CD, unissued, 2,000 later sent out by fan club, no inlay) | 250 |
| 92 | Vertigo | QUO 3212 | Rock 'Til You Drop/Medley/Forty-Five Hundred Times (12", p/s, mispressing, omits "Forty-Five Hundred Times") | 40 |
| 92 | Vertigo | QUOCD 32 | Rock 'Til You Drop/Medley/Forty-Five Hundred Times (CD in no'd guitar-shaped case) | 15 |
| 88 | Vertigo | QUODJ 25 | Burning Bridges (On & Off & On Again)/Burning Bridges (On & Off & On Again) | 12 |

## SINGLES : OTHER SINGLES

| Year | Label | Cat No | Description | Value |
|---|---|---|---|---|
| 75 | Lyntone | LYN 3154/5 | Down Down/Break The Rules (Smiths Crisps flexidisc, with 'Smiths' p/s) | 15 |
| 80s | Lyntone | QUO 1-4 | Interview picture discs (4-single pack) | 20 |
| 94 | Polydor | QUO 34 | I Didn't Mean It/Whatever You Want (p/s, blue vinyl) | 5 |
| 99 | From The Makers Of... | FTMOCD1 | FAKIN' THE BLUES (MILLENNIUM EDITION) (CD, fanclub mail order-only edition, hand-no'd exclusive p/s, contains unreleased Vertigo CD [QUOCD 31]) | 50 |

## ALBUMS : LPS

| Year | Label | Cat No | Description | Value |
|---|---|---|---|---|
| 68 | Pye | NPL 18220 | PICTURESQUE MATCHSTICKABLE MESSAGES (mono) | 200 |
| 68 | Pye | NSPL 18220 | PICTURESQUE MATCHSTICKABLE MESSAGES (stereo) | 175 |
| 69 | Pye | NPL 18301 | SPARE PARTS (blue label, mono) | 175 |
| 69 | Pye | NSPL 18301 | SPARE PARTS (blue label, stereo) | 125 |
| 69 | Marble Arch | MAL 1193 | STATUS QUO-TATIONS (mono) | 30 |
| 69 | Marble Arch | MAL(S) 1193 | STATUS QUO-TATIONS (stereo, most copies exported) | 50 |
| 70 | Pye | NSPL 18344 | MA KELLY'S GREASY SPOON (very early copies with poster) | 150 |
| 70 | Pye | NSPL 18344 | MA KELLY'S GREASY SPOON | 20 |
| 71 | Pye | NSPL 18371 | DOG OF TWO HEAD (gatefold sleeve, blue labels, later reissued with red, black or PRT "Piccadilly Circus" labels) | 40 |
| 72 | Vertigo | 6360 082 | PILEDRIVER (swirl label, gatefold sleeve) | 30 |
| 73 | Vertigo | 6360 098 | HELLO! (spaceship label, with inner sleeve & poster) | 20 |
| 74 | Vertigo | 9102 001 | QUO (with poster/lyric sheet) | 15 |
| 74 | Record Club | ACB 00217 | QUO | 25 |
| 82 | Phonogram | PRO BX 1 | FROM THE MAKERS OF... (3-LP, with inserts in round metal tin, some numbered) | 20 |
| 83 | Vertigo | VERH 10 | BACK TO BACK (in-store promo copies with poster insert) | 15 |
| 88 | PRT | PYX 4007 | FROM THE BEGINNING (picture disc) | 12 |
| 90 | Essential! | ESBLP 136 | THE EARLY WORKS (5-LP box set with book) | 30 |
| 91 | Baktabak | LINT 5003 | INTROSPECTIVE (clear vinyl, 6 Pye-era tracks & interview) | 20 |

## ALBUMS : CDS

| Year | Label | Cat No | Description | Value |
|---|---|---|---|---|
| 01 | From The Makers Of ... | FTMOCD2 | FTMO LIVE! NO.1 (fanclub mail-order only, soundchecks & interviews) | 30 |

## PROMOS : PROMO ONLY SINGLES

| Year | Label | Cat No | Description | Value |
|---|---|---|---|---|
| 68 | Pye | 7N 17449 | Pictures Of Matchstick Men/Gentleman Joe's Sidewalk Café (75c Minimum) ('A' label) | 60 |
| 68 | Pye | 7N 17497 | Black Veils Of Melancholy/To Be Free ('A' label) | 70 |
| 68 | Pye | 7N 17581 | Ice In The Sun/When My Mind Is Not Live ('A' label) | 60 |
| 68 | Pye | 7N 17650 | Technicolor Dreams/Paradise Flat('A' label) | 400 |
| 69 | Pye | 7N 17665 | Make Me Stay A Bit Longer/Aunt Nellie ('A' label) | 70 |
| 69 | Pye | 7N 17728 | Are You Growing Tired Of My Love/So Ends Another Life ('A' label) | 70 |
| 69 | Pye | 7N 17825 | The Price Of Love/Little Miss Nothing ('A' label) | 70 |
| 70 | Pye | 7N 17907 | Down The Dustpipe/Face Without A Soul ('A' label) | 60 |
| 70 | Pye | 7N 17998 | In My Chair/Gerdundula ('A' label) | 60 |
| 71 | Pye | 7N 45077 | Tune To The Music/Good Thinking ('A' label) | 60 |
| 72 | Phonogram | DJ 005 | Roadhouse Blues/BLACK SABBATH: Children Of The Grave (100 copies only) | 400 |
| 72 | Vertigo | 6059 071 | Paper Plane/Softer Ride ('A' label) | 45 |
| 73 | Pye | 7N 45229 | Mean Girl/Everything ('A' label) | 50 |
| 73 | Pye | 7N 45253 | Gerdundula/Lakky Lady ('A' label) | 40 |
| 75 | Lyntone | LYN 3154 | Down Down (Smiths Crisps 1-sided gold flexidisc test pressing, plays Bye Bye Baby by Bay City Rollers) | 25 |

| 75 | Lyntone LYN 3155 | Break The Rules (Smiths Crisps 1-sided gold flexidisc test pressing, plays Bye Bye Baby by Bay City Rollers) | 25 |
| 79 | Pye 7P 103 | In My Chair/Gerdundula ('A' label) | 20 |
| 81 | Vertigo QUO JB 6 | Rock 'N' Roll/Hold You Back (jukebox issue, B-side at 33rpm) | 10 |
| 86 | Vertigo QUODJ 2112 | Dreamin' (Wet Mix)/Long-Legged Girls/The Quo Xmas Cake Mix (12") | 15 |
| 88 | Vertigo QUOLP 99 | Ain't Complaining (12" promo, 1-sided) | 30 |
| 88 | Vertigo QUODJ 2212 | Ain't Complaining (Extended)/That's Alright/Lean Machine (12") | 10 |
| 90 | Vertigo (no cat. no.) | The Power Of Rock (Album Version)/(Single Edit)/Perfect Remedy (12" white label) | 50 |

## PROMOS : PROMO ONLY ALBUMS & ALBUM SAMPLERS

| 82 | Phonogram PRO BX 1 | FROM THE MAKERS OF... (3-LP, 20 copies in bronze tin for in-house use) | 300 |
| 86 | Vertigo MADDOX 18 | IN THE ARMY NOW (LP, 4-track sampler, includes unreleased version of Dreamin') | 50 |
| 88 | Vertigo QUOLP 99 | AIN'T COMPLAINING (LP, 4-track one-sided sampler) | 25 |
| 88 | Vertigo | AIN'T COMPLAINING (box set containing LP sampler [QUOLP 99], cassette, 1-track video, photo & press sheet) | 70 |
| 88 | Music & Media MM 1221 | INTERVIEW (LP, uncut test pressing for unreleased saw-shaped picture disc) | 50 |
| 89 | Vertigo 842 077-9 | LITTLE DREAMER (CD, card p/s, 4-track sampler for PERFECT REMEDY album) | 40 |
| 90 | Phonogram (no cat. no.) | ROCKING ALL OVER THE YEARS SNIPPETS (cassette, titles inlay) | 20 |
| 90 | Vertigo 846 797-2 | ROCKING ALL OVER THE YEARS (CD, in Butlin's party pack containing Kiss Me Quo baseball cap, stick of Status Quo rock, and selection of party poppers, streamers, whistle, trumpet, silver Quo balloons & pack of condoms, all with "Anniversary Waltz" stickers) | 75 |
| 02 | Sanctuary CMRCD 490 | SWEDISH RADIO SESSIONS (CD-R, titles insert, commercial release cancelled) | 50 |

*(see also Spectres, Traffic Jam, Rossi & Frost, Bob Young, Andy Bown, Partners In Crime, Party Boys, Rockers, John Du Cann, Manchester United Football Squad, Marietta, Stretch, Jimmy Sweep)*

# STAVELY MAKEPEACE

| 69 | Pyramid PYR 6072 | (I Want To Love You Like A) Mad Dog/Greasy Haired Woman | 8 |
| 70 | Pyramid PYR 6082 | Tarzan Harvey/Reggae Denny (unissued, test pressings exist) | 6 |
| 77 | Unigram U6312 | Baby Blue Eyes/Big Bad Baby Blonde | 8 |

*(see also Lieutenant Pigeon, Shel Naylor)*

# STAVERTON BRIDGE

| 70s | Saydisc SDL 266 | STAVERTON BRIDGE (LP, with lyrics) | 30 |

# BONNIE ST. CLAIR

| 72 | Philips 6012283 | Clap Your Hands And Stamp Your Feet/Catch Me Driver | 5 |

# STEAK CATS

| 93 | April 10 Records TEN 1 | The Steak Song/Dead Real Soon/Fluffy's Lament/My Name Is Miguel (12") | 12 |
| 94 | April 10 Records TEN 2 | Intergalactic Competition/Foxy Roxy (200 only, hand-written labels) | 5 |
| 95 | April 10 Records TEN 3 | Ladyboy/Not Supposed To Love (200 only, hand-written labels) | 5 |
| 96 | April 10 Records TEN 4 | Last Night In A Porn Stars Bed I Became A Man/From Behind (12" 200 only) | 15 |
| 97 | April 10 LP1 | THE RISE OF ROSCOE (LP) | 15 |

# STEAM MACHINE

| 72 | Capitol CL15746 | You Make It Move/I Can't Help It | 8 |

# STEAMHAMMER

| 69 | CBS 4141 | Junior's Wailing/Windmill | 25 |
| 69 | CBS 4496 | Autumn Song/Blues For Passing People | 18 |
| 71 | Reflection HRS 9 | Junior's Wailing/You'll Never Know | 12 |
| 68 | CBS (S) 63611 | STEAMHAMMER (LP) | 100 |
| 70 | CBS (S) 63694 | STEAMHAMMER MK. II (LP) | 100 |
| 70 | B&C CAS 1024 | MOUNTAINS (LP, stickered gatefold sleeve) | 50 |
| 70 | Reflection REFL 1 | STEAMHAMMER (LP, reissue, different sleeve) | 50 |
| 71 | Reflection REFL 12 | STEAMHAMMER MK. II (LP, reissue) | 40 |

*(see also Armageddon, Rod Stewart)*

# STEAM-SHOVEL

| 68 | Trojan/Big Bear TR 635 | Rudi, The Red Nosed Reindeer/White Christmas | 7 |
| 68 | Decca F 22863 | Rudi, The Red Nosed Reindeer/White Christmas (export issue) | 12 |

*(see also Locomotive)*

# STEEL

| 81 | Neat NEAT 14 | Rock Out/All Systems Go (p/s) | 10 |

# STEEL AN' SKIN

| 79 | Steel An Skin SS01 | Reggae Is Here Again/Fire In Soweto/Afro Punk Reggae (Dub) (12", p/s) | 70 |
| 85 | Cougar (no cat. no.) | STEEL AN' SKIN (LP) | 20 |

# GARY STEEL SOUND

| 72 | Zel-La JHEPM 131 | Go Go Girl/I've Got A Feeling Coming On | 25 |

# BETTE ANNE STEELE

| 55 | Capitol CL 14315 | Barricade/Give Me A Little Kiss Will Ya, Huh? | 8 |

# DORIS STEELE

| 59 | Oriole CB 1468 | Why Must I?/Never Again | 6 |

# JAN STEELE & JOHN CAGE

| 76 | Obscure OBS 5 | VOICES AND INSTRUMENTS (LP) | 20 |

# SONDRA & JON STEELE

| 55 | Parlophone MSP 6166 | I'm Crazy With Love/Fill My Heart With Happiness | 8 |

# TOMMY STEELE (& THE STEELMEN)

| 56 | Decca F 10795 | Rock With The Caveman/Rock Around The Town (with The Steelmen) | 25 |
| 56 | Decca F 10808 | Doomsday Rock/Elevator Rock | 30 |
| 56 | Decca F 10819 | Singing The Blues/Rebel Rock (with The Steelmen) | 20 |
| 57 | Decca F 10849 | Knee Deep In The Blues/Teenage Party (with The Steelmen) | 10 |
| 56 | Decca DFE 6388 | YOUNG LOVE (EP) | 10 |
| 56 | Decca DFE 6389 | SINGING THE BLUES (EP) | 10 |

*(The above 2 EPs were originally issued with triangular centres; later round-centre reissues are worth two-thirds this value)*

| 58 | Decca DFE 6551 | C'MON LET'S GO (EP) | 10 |

## STEELERS
| | | |
|---|---|---|
| 70 | Direction 58-4675 | Get It From The Bottom/I'm Sorry ...... 10 |

## STEELEYE SPAN
| | | |
|---|---|---|
| 71 | B&C CB 164 | Rave On/Reels/Female Drummer (p/s) ...... 7 |
| 72 | Pegasus PGS 6 | JIGS AND REELS (maxi-single, with p/s) ...... 10 |
| 72 | Pegasus PGS 6 | JIGS AND REELS (maxi-single) ...... 6 |
| 72 | Chrysalis CHS 2005 | John Barleycorn/Bride's Favourite/Tansey's Fancy ...... 5 |
| 70 | RCA SF 8113 | HARK! THE VILLAGE WAIT (LP, with lyric insert) ...... 40 |
| 71 | B&C CAS 1029 | PLEASE TO SEE THE KING (LP, in 'hessian' textured sleeve, insert) ...... 35 |
| 71 | Pegasus PEG 9 | TEN MAN MOP, OR MR. RESERVOIR BUTLER RIDES AGAIN (LP, gatefold sleeve, initially with 8-page booklet) ...... 50 |
| 72 | Chrysalis CHR 1008 | BELOW THE SALT (LP, gatefold, green label) ...... 18 |

*(see also Maddy Prior, Tim Hart & Maddy Prior, Gay & Terry Woods, Ashley Hutchings, Fairport Convention, Martin Carthy, Bob Johnson & Pete Knight)*

## STEEL MILL
| | | |
|---|---|---|
| 71 | Penny Farthing PEN 770 | Green Eyed God/Zang Will ...... 15 |
| 72 | Penny Farthing PEN 783 | Get On The Line/Summer's Child ...... 20 |
| 75 | Penny Farthing PEN 894 | Green Eyed God/Zang Will (reissue) ...... 15 |
| 75 | Penny Farthing PELS 549 | GREEN EYED GOD (LP, reissue, green sleeve. Original released in Germany in 1972 in black sleeve) ...... 750 |

## STEEL PULSE
| | | |
|---|---|---|
| 76 | Concrete Jungle CJ 602 | Kibudu Mansatta Abuku/Version ...... 35 |
| 77 | Anchor ANC 1046 | Nyah Luv/Luv Nyah (p/s) ...... 5 |
| 78 | Island IPR 2013 | Ku Klux Klan/Bun Dem (12") ...... 10 |

## STEELY DAN
| | | |
|---|---|---|
| 72 | Probe PRO 562 | Dallas/Sail The Waterway ...... 5 |
| 73 | Probe PRO 577 | Do It Again/Fire In The Hole ...... 5 |
| 73 | Probe PRO 587 | Reelin' In The Years/Only A Fool ...... 7 |
| 73 | Probe PRO 602 | Show Biz Kids/Razor Boy ...... 5 |
| 73 | Probe PRO 606 | My Old School/Pearl Of The Quarter ...... 5 |
| 74 | Probe PRO 622 | Rikki Don't Lose That Number/Any Major Dude Will Tell You (gatefold sleeve, 1974 'Spacemen' tour logo) ...... 50 |
| 82 | MCA MCAT 786 | FM EP ...... 25 |
| 85 | MCA MCAT 852 | Reelin' In The Years/Rikki Don't Lose That Number/Do It Again/Haitian Divorce (12", p/s) ...... 20 |
| 73 | Probe SPB 1062 | CAN'T BUY A THRILL (LP, original, with 'pink' label) ...... 25 |
| 77 | ABC ABCL5225 | AJA (LP, gatefold, inner) ...... 15 |
| 82 | MCA MCF 3165 | GOLD (LP, with free EP [MSAMT 21]) ...... 20 |

*(see also Donald Fagen)*

## WOUT STEENHUIS
| | | |
|---|---|---|
| 70 | Stereo2Stereo TWO 283 | BIRD IN THE PARK (LP, features cover of Hum Dono) ...... 25 |

## STEEPLECHASE
| | | |
|---|---|---|
| 71 | Polydor 2489 001 | LADY BRIGHT (LP) ...... 15 |

*(see also Dean Parrish)*

## STEERPIKE
| | | |
|---|---|---|
| 68 | (no label credit) ADM 417 | STEERPIKE (LP, private pressing) ...... 550 |

## BILL STEGMEYER & HIS ORCHESTRA
| | | |
|---|---|---|
| 54 | London HL 8078 | On The Waterfront (From The Film)/We Just Couldn't Say Good-Bye ...... 20 |

## LOU STEIN
| | | |
|---|---|---|
| 57 | London HLZ 8419 | Almost Paradise/Soft Sands ...... 20 |
| 58 | Mercury 7MT 226 | Who Slammed The Door/Got A Match? ...... 8 |

## STEINWAYS
| | | |
|---|---|---|
| 85 | Kent TOWN 106 | You've Been Leading Me On/JOHNNY CASWELL: You Don't Love Me No More ...... 20 |

## MIKE STEIPHENSON
| | | |
|---|---|---|
| 73 | Pye 7N 25577 | Rainbows/Dreams ...... 15 |

## TENA STELIN
| | | |
|---|---|---|
| 89 | Wau! Mr. Modo MWS 011T | Jah Equity/Jah Equity (Version) (12") ...... 50 |
| 89 | Wau! Mr Modo MWS 015T | King Of Kings/Give Thanks And Praise (12") ...... 50 |
| 00 | Jah Tubbys JT 7005 | Look After Yourself/DISCIPLES RHYTHM SECTION: Dub Yourself ...... 20 |
| 89 | Wai! Mr Modo MOWLP 002 | WICKED INVENTION (LP) ...... 40 |
| 92 | Conscious Sounds DNC 001 | SUN AND MOON (LP, as Tena Stelin Meets Century) ...... 25 |

*(see also Iration Steppas and Tena Stelin)*

## STELLA
| | | |
|---|---|---|
| 82 | President PT 504 | Si Tu Aimes Ma Musique/If You Do Like My Music (p/s) ...... 7 |

## STENCH
| | | |
|---|---|---|
| 82 | Sticky PEEL OFF 5 | MORAL DEBAUCHERY: Raspberry Cripple/Nonces/Adoption ...... 15 |

## MALCOLM STENT
| | | |
|---|---|---|
| 70s | Starline SWL 2002 | GO AND PLAY UP YOUR OWN END (LP) ...... 15 |

## STEP
| | | |
|---|---|---|
| 80 | Epic/Direction S DIR 8733 | Love Letter/Land Of 1,000 Dances (p/s) ...... 5 |
| 80 | Epic/Direction S DIR 8944 | Let Me Be The One/634 5789 (p/s) ...... 5 |
| 80 | Epic/Direction S DIR 9311 | Tears That I Cry/Shake (p/s) ...... 5 |
| 81 | Epic EPC A 1291 | Chain Gang/In The House (p/s) ...... 5 |
| 81 | Epic EPC A 1412 | Model Soldiers/Hightime Havana (p/s) ...... 5 |

## STEPASIDE
| | | |
|---|---|---|
| 80 | Gale GALELP 01 | SIT DOWN AND RELAPSE (LP) ...... 20 |

## STEPHEN
| | | |
|---|---|---|
| 74 | Antic K 11513 | Right On Running Man/Epitath ...... 8 |

## EWAN STEPHENS
| 71 | Decca F 13219 | Queen Of The Good Times/We Can Give It A Try | 5 |
| 72 | Decca F 13299 | Brother, Surely We Can Work It Out/Long, Long Summer | 5 |

*(see also Turquoise)*

## LEIGH STEPHENS
| 69 | Philips SBL 7897 | RED WEATHER (LP) | 70 |
| 71 | Charisma CAS 1040 | AND A CAST OF THOUSANDS (LP) | 40 |

*(see also Blue Cheer)*

## STEPPENWOLF
| 68 | RCA RCA 1679 | Sookie Sookie/Take What You Need | 10 |
| 68 | RCA RCA 1735 | Born To Be Wild/Everybody's Next One | 10 |
| 68 | Stateside-Dunhill SS 8003 | Magic Carpet Ride/Sookie Sookie | 10 |
| 69 | Stateside-Dunhill SS 8013 | Rock Me/Jupiter Child | 7 |
| 69 | Stateside-Dunhill SS 8017 | Born To Be Wild/Everybody's Next One (reissue) | 8 |
| 69 | Stateside-Dunhill SS 8027 | Magic Carpet Ride/Sookie Sookie (reissue) | 6 |
| 70 | Stateside-Dunhill SS 8035 | Monster/Move Over | 6 |
| 70 | Stateside-Dunhill SS 8038 | The Pusher/Your Wall's Too High | 6 |
| 70 | Stateside-Dunhill SS 8049 | Hey Lawdy Mama/Twisted | 6 |
| 70 | Stateside-Dunhill SS 8056 | Screaming Night Hog/Spiritual Fantasy | 6 |
| 70 | Probe PRO 510 | Who Needs Ya/Earschplittenloudenboomer | 6 |
| 71 | Probe PRO 525 | Snowblind Friend/Hippo Stomp | 6 |
| 71 | Probe PRO 534 | Ride With Me/For Madmen Only | 6 |
| 71 | Probe PRO 544 | For Ladies Only/Sparkle Eyes | 6 |
| 74 | CBS MUM 2679 | Straight Shootin' Woman/Justice Don't Be Slow | 6 |
| 75 | CBS MUM 3147 | Smokey Factory Blues/A Fool's Fantasy | 6 |
| 75 | CBS MUM 3470 | Caroline (Are You Ready)/Angel Drawers | 6 |
| 68 | RCA RD/SF 7974 | STEPPENWOLF (LP, initial white sleeve) | 80 |
| 68 | RCA RD/SF 7974 | STEPPENWOLF (LP, later silver sleeve) | 30 |
| 68 | Stateside SL 5003 | STEPPENWOLF THE SECOND (LP, mono) | 40 |
| 69 | Stateside (S)SL 5003 | STEPPENWOLF THE SECOND (LP, stereo) | 25 |
| 69 | Stateside SL 5011 | AT YOUR BIRTHDAY PARTY (LP, mono) | 25 |
| 69 | Stateside(S)SL 5011 | AT YOUR BIRTHDAY PARTY (LP, stereo) | 20 |
| 69 | Stateside (S)SL 5015 | EARLY STEPPENWOLF (LP) | 15 |
| 69 | Stateside (S)SL 5011 | CANDY (LP, soundtrack, 2 tracks by Steppenwolf, 1 track by Byrds) | 30 |
| 70 | Stateside-Dunhill SSL 5020 | STEPPENWOLF (reissue) | 15 |
| 70 | Stateside-Dunhill SSL 5021 | MONSTER (LP, gatefold sleeve) | 18 |
| 70 | Stateside-Dunhill SSL 5029 | STEPPENWOLF 'LIVE' (LP, gatefold sleeve) | 20 |
| 70 | Probe SPBA 6254 | STEPPENWOLF 7 (LP) | 15 |
| 71 | Probe SPBA 6260 | FOR LADIES ONLY (LP) | 15 |

*(see also John Kay)*

## STEPPES
| 79 | South Circular SGS 108 | The Beat Drill/FIFTY FANTASTICS: God's Got Religion (p/s, white label) | 10 |

*(see also Fifty Fantastics, Disco Zombies)*

## STEPPING TALK
| 79 | Eustone/Rough Trade TO1 | Alice In Sunderland/Health And Safety/Common Problems/John Turtles (p/s, with stamped inner) | 15 |

## STEREOLAB
| 91 | Duophonic DS 45-01 | SUPER 45: The Light That Will Cease To Fail/Au Grand Jour/Brittle/Au Grand Jour! (10" EP, with insert, mail-order, sold at gigs and some record shops 40 with hand-painted p/s, in poly bag) | 175 |
| 91 | Duophonic DS 45-01 | SUPER 45: The Light That Will Cease To Fail/Au Grand Jour/Brittle/Au Grand Jour! (10" EP, with insert, mail-order, sold at gigs and some record shops) | 100 |
| 91 | Duophonic DS 45-01 | SUPER 45: The Light That Will Cease To Fail/Au Grand Jour/Brittle/Au Grand Jour! (25 test pressings, 10" cut into 12" discs) | 175 |
| 91 | Too Pure PURE 4 | SUPER ELECTRIC: Super-Electric/High Expectation/The Way Will Be Opening/Contact (10" EP, with red and yellow sleeve, w/insert) | 10 |
| 91 | Duophonic DS 45-02 | STUNNING DEBUT ALBUM: Doubt/Clanger (20 black test pressings withdrawn due to pressing fault/warping, different cut of both tracks) | 100 |
| 91 | Duophonic DS 45-02 | STUNNING DEBUT ALBUM: Doubt/Clanger (p/s, mail-order, sold at gigs and some Record shops gatefold p/s with insert in poly bag; mulit coloured vinyl, unknown quantity but probably over 200) | 150 |
| 91 | Duophonic DS 45-02 | STUNNING DEBUT ALBUM: Doubt/Clanger (p/s, mail-order, gigs and some record Shops, gatefold p/s with insert in poly bag; 985 copies on clear vinyl) | 60 |
| 92 | Duophonic DS 45-04 | Harmonium/Farfisa (p/s, mail-order, gigs and some record shops 1,306 copies on transparent amber vinyl, with insert & fluorescent sticker) | 35 |
| 93 | Duophonic DS45-05/06 | SHIMMIES IN SUPER 8 (2 x 7", green and white vinyl, foldout sleeve with inserts) | 25 |
| 92 | Too Pure PURE 14 | Low Fi/Varoom!/Laissez-Faire/Elektro (He Held The World In His Iron Grip) (10", p/s, clear vinyl, 2,000 only, numbered) | 25 |
| 93 | Sub Pop SP107/283 | Lo Boob Oscillator/Tempter (clear vinyl, p/s with US address on back cover) | 6 |
| 93 | Sub Pop SP107/283 | Lo Boob Oscillator/Tempter (clear vinyl, p/s with German address on back cover) | 6 |
| 93 | Spacewatch FLX 2107 | Ronco Symphony (demo)/Seeming And The Meaning (demo)/SUBMARINER: Lyricist Downer (clear vinyl flexi comes with Spacewatch fanzine in sleeve) | 12 |
| 93 | Duophonic D-UHF-D 01 | Jenny Ondioline/Fruition/Golden Ball/French Disko (10", p/s) | 12 |
| 93 | Duophonic D-UHF-D 01 | Jenny Ondioline (Part 1)/Golden Ball (Studio) (10", factory custom pressings; 3 on 'thick' clear vinyl, later endorsed & signed by band; no p/s) | 220 |
| 93 | Duophonic D-UHF-D 01 | Jenny Ondioline (Part 1)/Golden Ball (Studio) (10", factory custom pressings; 5 copies on multicoloured vinyl; 25 on 'thin' clear vinyl, no p/s) | 80 |
| 93 | Clawfist 20 | CRUMB DUCK (10" EP, shared with Nurse With Wound; 37 with hand-drawn p/s (Gain/Sadier only) | 120 |
| 93 | Clawfist 20 | CRUMB DUCK (10" EP, shared with Nurse With Wound; 1,450 regular p/s) | 20 |
| 93 | Duophonic D-UHF-D 03 | French Disko/Jenny Ondioline ('teaser' single, p/s, 1,500 only, with hand printed sleeves) | 30 |

Rare Record Price Guide 2018

MINT VALUE £

| 93 | Duophonic D-UHF-D 03 | French Disko/Jenny Ondioline ('teaser' single, p/s, 1,500 only, regular printed sleeves).................15 |
|---|---|---|
| 94 | Duophonic D-UHF-D 04S | Ping Pong/Moogie Wonderland (p/s, 2,150 on pink vinyl).................10 |
| 94 | Duophonic D-UHF-D 04S | Ping Pong/Moogie Wonderland (p/s, 3,322 on green vinyl).................10 |
| 94 | Silvertone | Tone Burst (demo)/Tempter (demo)/SPECTRUM: Soul Kiss Glide Divine (unreleased, with colour photocopied wraparound p/s, 25 test pressings only).................150 |
| 94 | Duophonic D-UHF-07 | Wow And Flutter/Heavy Denim (3,000 only with hand-painted p/s).................18 |
| 95 | Wurlitzer Jukebox WJ 3 | The Eclipse/Yes Sir! I Can Moogie/CAT'S MIAOW: Shoot The Moon (flexidisc, 1,000 only with insert and info sheet).................18 |
| 95 | Duophonic Super 45s DS 45-10 | Long Hair Of Death/YO LA TENGO: Evanescent Psychic Pez Drop (gig single, fluorescent yellow vinyl, plain white stickered card sleeve, 3,000 only).................12 |
| 95 | Independent Project IP 060 | Blue Milk/One Thousand Miles An Hour/Aluminum Tune (set of 4 singles all With same tracks in different coloured vinyl and different sets of gatefold sleeve. American Import. Singles worth £10 each).................50 |
| 96 | Duophonic D-UHF-D 10S | Cybele's Reverie/Brigitte (p/s, with insert).................6 |
| 96 | Duophonic D-UHF-D 10 | Cybele's Reverie/Les Yper Yper Sound/Brigitte/Young Lungs(25 black vinyl test pressing and 102 cut into 12" disc).................25 |
| 96 | Duophonic D-UHF-D 10 | Cybele's Reverie/Les Yper Yper Sound/Brigitte/Young Lungs(10", p/s, 2,000 only).................12 |
| 96 | Lissy's LISS 15 | You Used To Call Me Sadness/FUXA: Skyhigh (p/s, 400 on white vinyl).................20 |
| 96 | Lissy's LISS 15 | You Used To Call Me Sadness/FUXA: Skyhigh (p/s, 1,500 on black vinyl).................8 |
| 96 | Duophonic D-UHF-D 12 | Speedy Car/TORTOISE: Yaus (gig freebie, blue vinyl, p/s, 3,000 only).................10 |
| 96 | Duophonic D-UHF-D 12 | Speedy Car/TORTOISE: Yaus (orange vinyl export issue, p/s, 3,000 only).................15 |
| 96 | Duophonic D-UHF-D 15 | Metronomic Underground (Wagon Christ Mix)/Percolations (12", plain red sleeve, 2,500 only).................12 |
| 97 | Duophonic DS 4517 | Splitting The Atom (Parts 1 & 2) (with Sonic Boom)/Monkey Brain (p/s, 2,500 only).................10 |
| 97 | Duophonic D-UHF-D 18 | Iron Man/The Incredible He Woman (red vinyl, p/s, gig single, 2,000 only).................6 |
| 97 | Duophonic Super 45s DS 3311 | Simple Headphone Mind/NURSE WITH WOUND: Trippin' With The Birds (12", 5,000 copies).................10 |
| 97 | Duophonic Super 45s DS 3311 | Simple Headphone Mind/NURSE WITH WOUND: Trippin' With The Birds (12", 1,000 copies on yellow vinyl, in sealed foil sleeve).................20 |
| 97 | Duophonic Super 45s CD 3311 | Simple Headphone Mind/NURSE WITH WOUND: Trippin' With The Birds (CD, sealed foil sleeve, 1,000 only).................30 |
| 99 | Duophonic D-UHF-D24 | THE UNDERGROUND IS COMING: The Super-It/Monkey Jelly/Fried Monkey Eggs (Instrumental)/Fried Monkey Eggs (Vocal) (p/s).................10 |
| 01 | Duophonic D-UHF 026 | Captain Easychord (12").................12 |
| 01 | Duophonic DS 45 30 | Free Witch And No Bra Queen/Speck Voice (p/s, tour single).................10 |
| 03 | Duophonic D-UHF-D 28S | INSTANT 0 IN THE UNIVERSE (3 x 7" box set).................12 |
| 04 | Duophonic D-UHF-D 30S | Rose, My Pocket Brain!/Banana Monster Ne Repond Plus/University Microfilms International (p/s, tour single, 500 only).................15 |
| 06 | Duophonic DS 45 38 | Solar Throw Away/Jump Drive Shut Out (p/s, tour single).................12 |
| 92 | Too Pure PURELP 11 | PENG! (LP, inner sleeve, insert).................20 |
| 93 | Duophonic D-UHF-D 02 | TRANSIENT RANDOM NOISE-BURSTS WITH ANNOUNCEMENTS (2-LP, with inner sleeves, poor playing-quality gold vinyl, with stickered sleeve, 1,500 only, numbered).70 |
| 93 | Duophonic D-UHF-D 02 | TRANSIENT RANDOM NOISE-BURSTS WITH ANNOUNCEMENTS (2-LP, inners, black vinyl).................25 |
| 95 | Duophonic D-UHF-D 05X | MARS AUDIAC QUINTET (2-LP, gatefold sleeve, 1st 1,000 copies with bonus coloured vinyl single "Klang Tone"/"Ulan Bator" [D-UHF-06]).................55 |
| 94 | Duophonic D-UHF-D 05 | MARS AUDIAC QUINTET (2-LP, without single).................30 |
| 95 | Duophonic D-UHF-D 08 | MUSIC FOR THE AMORPHOUS BODY STUDY CENTRE (40 black vinyl test pressings 10" sides cut into 12" discs).................80 |
| 95 | Duophonic D-UHF-D 08 | MUSIC FOR THE AMORPHOUS BODY STUDY CENTRE (10" LP, 3,000 only, insert).................20 |
| 95 | Duophonic D-UHF-CD 08 | MUSIC FOR THE AMORPHOUS BODY STUDY CENTRE (CD, first issue with white cover & "1st edition" printed on disc available at Charles Long art exhibition; reissue has yellow sleeve).................40 |
| 95 | Duophonic UHF LP 09 | REFRIED ECTOPLASM - SWITCHED ON VOL 2 LP, orange vinyl, card insert).................30 |
| 96 | United Dairies UD 059 | CRUMB DUCK (LP, shared with Nurse With Wound (2 extra tracks, reissue of Clawfist EP, 50 copies on pink vinyl).................70 |
| 96 | United Dairies UD 059 | CRUMB DUCK (LP, shared with Nurse With Wound (2 extra tracks, reissue of Clawfist EP, 500 on fluorescent green vinyl).................40 |
| 96 | Duophonic UHF D-UHF-D11 | EMPEROR TOMATO KETCHUP (2-LP, yellow glitter vinyl, gatefold sleeve).................60 |
| 96 | Duophonic DUHFD11 | EMPEROR TOMATO KETCHUP (2-LP, black vinyl).................30 |
| 97 | Duophonic D-UHF-D 17 | DOTS & LOOPS (2-LP, one green, one white vinyl).................35 |
| 98 | Drag City CD 159 | ALUMINIUM TUNES - SWITCHED ON VOL. 3 (3 x LP).................30 |
| 99 | Duophonic D-UHF-D 23 | COBRA & PHASES GROUP PLAY VOLTAGE IN THE MILKY NIGHT (2-LP).................20 |
| 00 | Duophinic D-UHF-D 25 | THE FIRST OF THE MICROBE HUNTERS (2-LP).................20 |
| 01 | Duophonic D-UHF-D 27 | SOUND-DUST (2-LP, hand-humbered, screenprinted heavy card sleeve, inners, 1200 only).................50 |
| 01 | Duophinic D-UHF-D 27 | SOUND-DUST (2-LP, inners, 1800 only).................40 |
| 04 | Duophinic D-UHF-D 29 | MARGERINE ECLIPSE (2-LP, 3500 only).................35 |
| 06 | (No Cat. No.) | FAB FOUR SUTURE (LP as 6 x 7" hand-stamped box).................20 |
| 06 | Duophinic D-UHF-D 31 | SERENE VELOCITY: A STEREOLAB ANTHOLOGY (2-LP, numbered sticker on sleeve, inners).................25 |
| 10 | Duophonic D-UHF D32 | NOT MUSIC (LP, clear vinyl).................18 |

*(see also McCarthy, Spectrum)*

## STEREOLAB & BRIGITTE FONTAINE

| 90s | Duophonic Super 45s DS 45-25 | Caliméro/MONADE: Cache Cache (white vinyl, p/s).................8 |
|---|---|---|

## STEREOPHONICS

| 96 | V2 SPH 1 | Looks Like Chaplin/More Life In A Tramp's Vest (p/s, 500 only).................40 |
|---|---|---|
| 96 | V2 SPHD 1 | Looks Like Chaplin/More Life In A Tramp's Vest/Raymond's Shops (CD).................30 |
| 96 | V2 SPH 2 | Local Boy In The Photograph/Too Many Sandwiches (p/s, 2,000 only).................12 |
| 97 | V2 SPH 4 | More Life In A Tramp's Vest/Raymond's Shop (p/s).................8 |
| 99 | V2 no catalogue number | PERFORMANCE AND COCKTAILS (7 x 10" box set, with booklet and CD, promo mail order only).................30 |
| 99 | V2 VVR 500 6777 | Pick A Part That's New/Nice To Be Out (Demo) (p/s).................6 |
| 97 | V2 VVR 1000 431 | WORD GETS AROUND (LP, gatefold sleeve).................40 |

| | | | |
|---|---|---|---|
| 97 | V2 VVR 1000431 | WORD GETS AROUND (LP, with bonus 12") | 40 |
| 99 | V2 VVR1004499 | PERFORMANCE AND COCKTAILS (LP, gatefold) | 50 |
| 01 | V2 S16016 | JUST ENOUGH EDUCATION TO PERFORM (2-LP, gatefold) | 40 |
| 03 | V2 VVR 1021901 | YOU GOTTA GO THERE TO COME BACK (2-LP) | 20 |
| 05 | V2 VVR 1031051 | LANGUAGE. SEX. VIOLENCE. OTHER? (LP) | 40 |
| 06 | V2 VVR 1038091 | LIVE FROM DAKOTA (2-LP) | 40 |
| 07 | V2 VVR 1048561 | PULL THE PIN (LP) | 40 |

## STEREOS
| | | | |
|---|---|---|---|
| 61 | MGM MGM 1143 | I Really Love You/Please Come Back To Me | 50 |
| 61 | MGM MGM 1149 | The Big Knock/Sweet Water | 30 |
| 66 | MGM MGM 1328 | Sweet Water/The Big Knock (reissue) | 7 |

## STEREOTYPES (1)
| | | | |
|---|---|---|---|
| 79 | Hinterland/SRT no cat. no. | THE STEREOTYPES EP (no p/s) | 750 |
| 13 | Hinterland (No Cat. No.) | THE STEREOTYPES EP (reissue, no p/s, signed insert, 350 only) | 15 |

## STEREOTYPES (2)
| | | | |
|---|---|---|---|
| 80 | Art Theft AT 001 | Calling All The Shots/Lovers Of The Future (p/s) | 8 |

## DEAN STERLING & TEENBEATS
| | | | |
|---|---|---|---|
| 61 | Pye 7N 15345 | Send Me A Girl/Lost Love | 12 |

## FITZROY STERLING
| | | | |
|---|---|---|---|
| 68 | Gas GAS 102 | Got To Play It Cool/Jezebel | 20 |
| 70 | Bullet BU 422 | That's My Life/Queen Of Hearts | 15 |
| 70 | Bullet BU 438 | Freedom Street/FITZROY ALL STARS: Freedom Street Version | 15 |
| 71 | Escort ERT 858 | Girl Tell Me What To Do/Be Careful | 8 |
| 71 | Pama PM 820 | My Sweet Lord/Darling That's Right | 5 |

## LESTER STERLING (& HIS GROUP)
| | | | |
|---|---|---|---|
| 63 | Island WI 121 | Clean The City/Long Walk Home (B-side actually by Charmers) | 20 |
| 63 | R&B JB 111 | Air Raid Shelter/ROY & ANNETTE: I Mean It | 25 |
| 63 | R&B JB 115 | Gravy Cool/WINSTON & BIBBY: Lover Lover Man | 35 |
| 64 | R&B JB 143 | Peace And Love/HORACE SEATON: Hold On | 30 |
| 64 | R&B JB 150 | Hot Cargo/MAYTALS: Marching On | 30 |
| 64 | R&B JB 155 | Baskin' Hop (as Lester Sterling & His Group)/MAYTALS: Shining Light | 20 |
| 64 | R&B JB 172 | Indian Summer (as Lester Sterling & His Group)/STRANGER & PATSY: I'll Forgive You | 20 |
| 66 | Doctor Bird DB 1057 | Inez (with Tommy McCook & Supersonics)/GLORIA CRAWFORD: Sad Movies | 40 |
| 67 | Doctor Bird DB 1107 | Soul Voyage/ALVA LEWIS: Revelation | 40 |
| 67 | Collins Downbeat CR 001 | Sir Collins Special/Lester Sterling '67 | 60 |
| 68 | Coxsone CS 7080 | Affrickaan Beat/PARAGONS: My Satisfaction | 100 |
| 68 | Blue Cat BS 116 | Zigaloo/Wiser Than Solomon | 75 |
| 68 | Unity UN 502 | Bangarang (with Stranger Cole)/STRANGER COLE: If We Should Ever Meet | 20 |
| 69 | Unity UN 505 | Reggae On Broadway (this is what it states on label)/CLIQUE: Love Can Be Wonderful | 25 |
| 69 | Unity UN 509 | Spoogy/TOMMY McCOOK: Monkey Fiddle | 15 |
| 69 | Unity UN 512 | Regina/Bright As A Rose | 15 |
| 69 | Unity UN 517 | 1,000 Tons Of Megaton/KING CANNON: Five Card Stud | 15 |
| 69 | Unity UN 518 | Man About Town/Man At The Door | 15 |
| 69 | Unity UN 531 | Lonesome Feeling/Bright As A Rose | 25 |
| 69 | Big Shot BI 507 | Forest Gate Rock/RAVING RAVERS: Rock Rock And Cry | 20 |
| 69 | Gas GAS 103 | Reggae In The Wind/SOUL SET: Try Me One More Time (B-side actually by Stranger & Gladdy) | 40 |
| 70 | Unity UN 562 | Slip Up/DAVE BARKER: On Broadway | 20 |
| 71 | Nu Beat NB 095 | Iron Side Part 1/COXSON'S ALL STARS: Iron Side Part 2 | 15 |
| 71 | Nu Beat NB 96 | War Is Not The Answer Part 2/Iron Side Part 2 | 15 |
| 71 | Smash SMA 2321 | Sir Collins Special/Version (actually "Heart Of The Knight" by Gaytones) | 8 |
| 72 | Ashanti ASH 409 | Iron Side Part 1/COXSON'S ALL STARS: Iron Side Part 2 | 6 |
| 72 | Ashanti ASH 410 | War Is Not The Answer/COXSON'S ALL STARS: Version | 6 |
| 69 | Pama SECO 15 | BANGARANG (LP) | 60 |

*(see also Mister Versatile, Bobby Aitken, Eric Morris, Sir Collins Band, Slickers, Uniques)*

## NINA STERN
| | | | |
|---|---|---|---|
| 65 | Pye 7N 15823 | Take It From Me/Please Come Back To Me | 8 |

## STEROID KIDDIES
| | | | |
|---|---|---|---|
| 79 | Steroid/Grundinga SK 001 | THE KIDDIES EP | 55 |

## STEROID MAXIMUS
| | | | |
|---|---|---|---|
| 90s | Big Cat ABB 28 | QUILOMBO (LP) | 20 |

## STEROIDS
| | | | |
|---|---|---|---|
| 78 | Radar ADA 11 | In The Colonies/Sha La La Loo Ley (p/s) | 6 |

## STEVE 'N' BONNIE
| | | | |
|---|---|---|---|
| 72 | Young Blood YB 1033 | Brief Encounter/Don't/Lady | 6 |
| 73 | Sovereign SOV123 | Me 'N' My Soul/A Screw Called Kirk | 8 |
| 72 | Young Blood SSYB 16 | BRIEF ENCOUNTER (LP) | 18 |

## STEVE & STEVIE
| | | | |
|---|---|---|---|
| 68 | Toast TT510 | Merry-Go-Round/Remains To Be Seen | 15 |
| 68 | Toast TLP 2 | STEVE AND STEVIE (LP) | 30 |

*(see also Tin Tin, Fut)*

## APRIL STEVENS
| | | | |
|---|---|---|---|
| 53 | Parlophone MSP 6060 | C'est Si Bon/Soft Warm Lips | 10 |
| 54 | Parlophone MSP 6088 | How Could Red Riding Hood (Have Been...)/You Said You'd Do It | 10 |
| 67 | MGM MGM 1366 | Falling In Love Again/Wanting You | 100 |
| 67 | MGM MGM 1366 | Falling In Love Again/Wanting You (DJ copy) | 200 |
| 76 | MGM 2006 586 | Wanting You/Falling In Love Again (reissue) | 6 |

*(see also Nino Tempo & April Stevens)*

MINT VALUE £

## CAT STEVENS
| | | | |
|---|---|---|---|
| 66 | Deram DM 102 | I Love My Dog/Portobello Road | 5 |
| 66 | Deram DM 110 | Matthew And Son/Granny | 7 |
| 67 | Deram DM 118 | I'm Gonna Get Me A Gun/School Is Out | 5 |
| 67 | Deram DM 140 | Bad Night/Laughing Apple | 5 |
| 67 | Deram DM 156 | Kitty/Blackness Of The Night | 10 |
| 68 | Deram DM 178 | Lovely City/Image Of Hell | 7 |
| 68 | Deram DM 211 | Here Comes My Wife/It's A Supa (Dupa) Life | 7 |
| 69 | Deram DM 260 | Where Are You/The View From The Top | 7 |
| 70 | Island WIP 6086 | Lady D'Arbanville/Time/Fill My Eyes (in p/s) | 8 |
| 70 | Island WIP 6086 | Lady D'Arbanville/Time/Fill My Eyes | 5 |
| 67 | Deram DML/SML 1004 | MATTHEW AND SON (LP) | 25 |
| 67 | Deram DML/SML 1018 | NEW MASTERS (LP) | 25 |
| 67 | Deram | CATS AND DOGS (LP, unreleased, test pressings only) | 30 |
| 70 | Island ILPS 9118 | MONA BONE JAKON (LP, inner, pink label with white 'i' logo) | 120 |
| 70 | Island ILPS 9135 | TEA FOR THE TILLERMAN (LP, gatefold, pink label, with white 'i' logo) | 70 |
| 73 | Island ILPS 5924 | FOREIGNER (LP) | 15 |

## CHUCK STEVENS
| | | | |
|---|---|---|---|
| 57 | Columbia DB 3883 | Take A Walk/The Way I Do | 7 |
| 57 | Columbia DB 3938 | My London/Couldn't Care More | 7 |

## CONNIE STEVENS
| | | | |
|---|---|---|---|
| 60 | Warner Bros WB 3 | Sixteen Reasons (with Don Ralke)/Little Sister (with Buddy Cole Trio) | 8 |
| 60 | Warner Bros WB 17 | Too Young To Go Steady/A Little Kiss Is A Kiss, Is A Kiss | 8 |
| 60 | Warner Bros WB 25 | Apollo/Why Do I Cry For Joey | 8 |
| 61 | Warner Bros WB 41 | And This Is Mine/Make-Believe Lover | 8 |
| 61 | Warner Bros WB 47 | The Greenwood Tree/If You Don't, Somebody Else Will | 8 |
| 62 | Warner Bros WB 63 | Why'd You Wanna Make Me Cry/Just One Kiss | 10 |
| 62 | Warner Bros WB 73 | Mr. Songwriter/I Couldn't Say No | 7 |
| 64 | Warner Bros WB 128 | They're Jealous Of Me/A Girl Never Knows | 7 |
| 62 | Warner Bros WM 4060 | CONNIE (LP, mono) | 15 |
| 62 | Warner Bros WS 8061 | CONNIE (LP, stereo) | 25 |

*(see also Edward Byrnes)*

## DEAN STEVENS
| | | | |
|---|---|---|---|
| 62 | Philips 326540 BF | Sad And Lonely/I've Just Heard | 10 |
| 64 | Philips BF 1300 | Only 'Cause I'm Lonely/Love Me Like I Love You | 8 |
| 63 | Philips 326580 | Let Me Show You How/High On The Hill Of Hope | 8 |

## DODIE STEVENS
| | | | |
|---|---|---|---|
| 59 | London HLD 8834 | Pink Shoe Laces/Coming Of Age | 10 |
| 60 | London HLD 9174 | No/A-Tisket A-Tasket | 6 |
| 61 | London HLD 9280 | Yes, I'm Lonesome Tonight/Too Young | 10 |
| 63 | London HLP 9672 | Don't Send Me Roses/Daddy Couldn't Get Me One Of Those | 10 |
| 64 | Liberty LIB 83 | I Wore Out Our Record/You Don't Have To Prove A Thing | 8 |

## JERRY STEVENS
| | | | |
|---|---|---|---|
| 66 | CBS 2831 | You Make My Life Worthwhile/So This Is Love | 6 |

## JIMMY STEVENS
| | | | |
|---|---|---|---|
| 66 | Fontana TF 721 | I Love You/Wharf 130 | 7 |

## JOHN STEVENS AWAY
| | | | |
|---|---|---|---|
| 76 | Vertigo 6059140 | Anni Part 1/Anni Part 2 | 8 |
| 76 | Vertigo 6059154 | Can't Explain (Part 1)/Can't Explain (Part 2) | 5 |
| 76 | Vertigo 6360 131 | JOHN STEVEN'S AWAY (LP) | 20 |
| 76 | Vertigo 6360 135 | SOMEWHERE IN BETWEEN (LP) | 20 |
| 78 | Spotlite SPJ 508 | NO FEAR! (LP) | 30 |
| 78 | Spotlite SPJ 513 | APPLICATION INTERACTION AND... (LP) | 30 |
| 82 | Affinity AFF 101 | FREEBOP (LP) | 20 |
| 84 | Affinity AYF 130 | THE LIFE OF RILEY (LP, as John Steven's Solkus) | 30 |

## JOHNNY STEVENS & BLUE BEATS
| | | | |
|---|---|---|---|
| 64 | Blue Beat BB 229 | Shame/Ball And Chain | 20 |

## JOHNNY STEVENS & LES DAWSON SYNDICATE
| | | | |
|---|---|---|---|
| 62 | Melodisc M 1586 | Last Chicken In The Shop/Oh Yeah (some in p/s) | 10 |

## KIRK STEVENS
| | | | |
|---|---|---|---|
| 57 | Decca F 10863 | Once/This Silver Madonna | 8 |

## MEIC STEVENS
| | | | |
|---|---|---|---|
| 65 | Decca F 12174 | Did I Dream/I Saw A Field (as Mike Stevens) | 40 |
| 70 | Warner Bros WB 8007 | Ballad Of Old Joe Blind/Blue Sleep | 15 |
| 70 | Wren WSP 2005 | Nid Oes Un Gwydr Ffenestr/Rhywbeth Gwell I Ddod | 40 |
| 78 | YM SP 01 | DIC PENDERYN EP (THEATR YR YMYLON Theatrical soundtrack) | 50 |
| 68 | Wren WRE 1045 | MIKE STEVENS (EP, p/s) | 50 |
| 68 | Wren WRE 1053 | RHIF 2 (EP, p/s) | 50 |
| 69 | Wren WRE 1073 | MWG (EP, p/s) | 50 |
| 70 | Newyddion Da ND1 | MEIC STEVENS (EP, p/s) | 100 |
| 70 | Sain SAIN 004 | Y BRAWN HOUDINI (EP, p/s) | 50 |
| 71 | Wren WRE 1107 | BYW YN Y WLAD (EP, p/s) | 50 |
| 71 | Sain SAIN 13 | DIONCH YN FAWR (EP, p/s) | 50 |
| 70 | Warner Brothers WS 3005 | OUTLANDER (LP, with insert) | 300 |
| 72 | Wren WRL 536 | GWYMON (LP) | 300 |
| 77 | Sain SAIN 1065 | GOG (LP) | 120 |
| 79 | Tic Toc no cat. no. | CANAEON CYNNAR (LP, private pressing) | 220 |
| 82 | Sain SAIN 1239 | NOS DU NOS DA (LP) | 50 |

| | | | |
|---|---|---|---|
| 83 | Sain SAIN 1312 | LAPIS LAZULI (LP, lyric insert) | 50 |
| 86 | Timeless TIME 705 | TIMELESS (LP, reissue, 500 only) | 20 |

*(see also Gary Farr)*

## MICK STEVENS
| | | | |
|---|---|---|---|
| 79 | Spaceward SRS 030 | THE ENGLISHMAN (LP, insert) | 40 |
| 71 | Deroy (no cat. no.) | SEE THE MORNING (LP, private pressing) | 400 |
| 75 | Deroy (no cat. no.) | NO SAVAGE WORD (LP, private pressing) | 300 |

## MIKE STEVENS
| | | | |
|---|---|---|---|
| 66 | Pye 7N 17243 | Cathy's Clown/Go-Go Train | 60 |
| 68 | Polydor 56269 | Guaranteed To Drive You Wild/Hog-Tied | 12 |

*(see also Shevells)*

## MORT STEVENS & HIS ORCHESTRA
| | | | |
|---|---|---|---|
| 70 | Capitol CL 15655 | Hawaii Five-O Theme/McGarrett's Theme | 10 |

## RAY STEVENS
| | | | |
|---|---|---|---|
| 58 | Capitol CL 14881 | Chickie-Chickie Wah Wah/Crying Goodbye | 10 |
| 61 | Mercury AMT 1158 | Jeremiah Peabody's Polyunsaturated Quick Dissolving Fast Acting Pleasant Tasting Green And Purple Pills/Teen Years | 7 |
| 62 | Mercury AMT 1184 | Ahab The Arab/It's Been So Long | 9 |
| 63 | Mercury AMT 1207 | Harry The Hairy Ape/Little Stone Statue | 7 |
| 66 | London HLU 10016 | Party People/ABC | 10 |
| 68 | Monument MON 1022 | Mr Businessman/Face The Music | 8 |

## RICKY STEVENS
| | | | |
|---|---|---|---|
| 61 | Columbia DB 4739 | I Cried For You/I Am | 7 |
| 62 | Columbia DB 4778 | Forever/Now, It's All Over | 7 |
| 63 | Columbia DB 4981 | My Mother's Eyes/I'll Get By | 7 |
| 62 | Columbia SEG 8172 | I CRIED FOR YOU (EP) | 40 |

## SHAKIN' STEVENS (& SUNSETS)
| | | | |
|---|---|---|---|
| 70 | Parlophone R 5860 | Spirit Of Woodstock/Down On The Farm | 60 |
| 72 | Polydor 2058 213 | Sweet Little Rock'n'Roller/White Lightning | 50 |
| 74 | Emerald MD 1176 | Honey Honey/Holey Moley 2001 | 25 |
| 76 | Mooncrest MOON 51 | Jungle Rock/Girl In Red | 10 |
| 77 | Track 2094 134 | Never/You Always Hurt The One You Love | 10 |
| 77 | Track 2094 136 | Somebody Touched Me/Way Down Yonder In New Orleans (in p/s) | 10 |
| 77 | Track 2094 136 | Somebody Touched Me/Way Down Yonder In New Orleans | 6 |
| 78 | Track 2094 141 | Justine/Wait And See | 10 |
| 78 | Epic SEPC 6567 | Treat Her Right/I Don't Want No Other Baby | 8 |
| 79 | Epic SEPC 6845 | Endless Sleep/Fire | 8 |
| 79 | Epic SEPC 7235 | Spooky/I Don't Want No Other Baby | 20 |
| 80 | Epic SEPC 8090 | Hot Dog/Apron Strings | 6 |
| 80 | Epic SEPC 8573 | Hey Mae/I Guess I Was A Fool (in p/s) | 40 |
| 80 | Epic SEPC 8573 | Hey Mae/I Guess I Was A Fool | 5 |
| 80 | Epic SEPC 9064 | Shooting Gallery/Make It Right Tonight (p/s) | 6 |
| 70 | Parlophone PCS 7112 | A LEGEND (LP) | 50 |
| 71 | CBS 52901 | I'M NO J.D. (LP) | 40 |
| 72 | Contour 2870 152 | ROCKIN' AND SHAKIN' (LP) | 15 |
| 73 | Emerald GES 1121 | SHAKIN' STEVENS AND THE SUNSETS (LP) | 15 |
| 78 | Track 2406 011 | SHAKIN' STEVENS (LP, with insert) | 15 |
| 80 | Epic EPC 84547 | MARIE MARIE (LP, withdrawn) | 18 |

## TERRI STEVENS
| | | | |
|---|---|---|---|
| 59 | Felsted AF 112 | My Wish Tonight/All Alone | 5 |
| 59 | Felsted AF 126 | Adonis/Vieni, Vieni | 6 |

## RICHARD STEVENSEN
| | | | |
|---|---|---|---|
| 70 | Pye 7N 45004 | The Day That You Came Back/The Gates Of Me | 8 |
| 70 | Pye NSPL 18358 | GATES OF ME (LP, textured sleeve) | 25 |

## MICKEY STEVENSON
| | | | |
|---|---|---|---|
| 72 | Ember EMBS 320 | Here I Am/Joe Poor Loves Daphne Elizabeth Richard | 6 |
| 72 | Ember NR 5063 | HERE I AM (LP) | 20 |

## N A STEVENSON AND THE 4 ACES
| | | | |
|---|---|---|---|
| 73 | Injun 103 | Boogie Woogie Country Girl/Pins & Needles | 10 |

## STEVIE'S BUZZ
| | | | |
|---|---|---|---|
| 96 | Nice no cat. no. | Autumn Stone/P.P. & THE PRIMES: Understanding (promo only, large centre) | 8 |

*(see also P.P. Arnold, Buzzcocks, Primal Scream)*

## AL STEWART
| | | | |
|---|---|---|---|
| 66 | Decca F 12467 | The Elf/Turn To Earth | 70 |
| 67 | CBS 3034 | Bedsitter Images/Swiss Cottage Manoeuvres | 12 |
| 70 | CBS 4843 | Electric Los Angeles Sunset/My Enemies Have Sweet Voices | 8 |
| 70 | CBS 5351 | The News From Spain/Elvaston Place | 15 |
| 72 | CBS 7763 | You Don't Even Know Me/I'm Falling | 6 |
| 72 | CBS 7992 | Amsterdam/Songs Out Of Clay | 6 |
| 73 | CBS SCBS 1791 | Terminal Eyes/Last Day Of June 1934 | 10 |
| 67 | CBS (S)BPG 63087 | BEDSITTER IMAGES (LP) | 125 |
| 69 | CBS (S) 63460 | LOVE CHRONICLES (LP, gatefold sleeve) | 25 |
| 70 | CBS 63848 | ZERO SHE FLIES (LP, gatefold sleeve) | 22 |
| 70 | CBS 64023 | FIRST ALBUM (BEDSITTER IMAGES) (LP, remixed reissue, different track listing) | 25 |
| 72 | CBS 64730 | ORANGE (LP) | 20 |

*(see also Jimmy Page)*

## BILLY STEWART
| | | | |
|---|---|---|---|
| 62 | Pye International 7N 25164 | Reap What You Sow/Fat Boy | 15 |

# Bob STEWART

| | | | |
|---|---|---|---|
| 63 | Pye International 7N 25222 | Strange Feeling/Sugar And Spice | 15 |
| 65 | Chess CRS 8009 | I Do Love You/Keep Loving | 15 |
| 65 | Chess CRS 8017 | Sitting In The Park/Once Again | 10 |
| 66 | Chess CRS 8028 | Because I Love You/Mountains Of Love | 10 |
| 66 | Chess CRS 8038 | Love Me/Why Am I Lonely | 10 |
| 66 | Chess CRS 8040 | Summertime/To Love To Love | 10 |
| 66 | Chess CRS 8045 | Secret Love/Look Back And Smile | 15 |
| 66 | Chess CRS 8050 | Ole Man River/Every Day I Have The Blues | 10 |
| 67 | Chess CRS 8067 | Cross My Heart/Why (Do I Love You So) | 10 |
| 69 | Chess CRS 8092 | Summertime/I Do Love You | 10 |
| 72 | Chess 6145 017 | Sitting In The Park/Summertime | 15 |
| 65 | Chess CRE 6010 | IN CROWD (EP, with Ramsey Lewis Trio, et al) | 8 |
| 67 | Chess CRE 6024 | I DO LOVE YOU (EP) | 30 |
| 66 | Chess CRL 4523 | UNBELIEVABLE (LP) | 30 |

## BOB STEWART
| | | | |
|---|---|---|---|
| 55 | MGM SP 1114 | It's A Woman's World/I Went Out Of My Way | 6 |

## DELANO STEWART
| | | | |
|---|---|---|---|
| 68 | Doctor Bird DB 1138 | That's Life/Tell Me Baby | 50 |
| 68 | High Note HS 004 | Let's Have Some Fun/Dance With Me | 30 |
| 69 | High Note HS 014 | Rocking Sensation/GAYSTERS: One Look | 150 |
| 70 | High Note HS 027 | Got To Come Back/Don't Believe In Him | 20 |
| 70 | High Note HS 034 | Hallelujah/I Wish It Could Last | 10 |
| 70 | High Note HS 039 | Wherever I Lay My Hat/Don't Believe Him (B-side actually by Gladstone Anderson & Gaytones) | 20 |
| 70 | High Note HS 041 | Stay A Little Bit Longer/Stay A Little Bit Longer (Version II) (B-side actually by Gladstone Anderson & Gaytones) | 20 |
| 70 | Trojan TBL 138 | STAY A LITTLE BIT LONGER (LP) | 50 |

*(see also Winston Stewart, Gaylads, Patsy Todd)*

## GRAHAM STEWART SEVEN
| | | | |
|---|---|---|---|
| 59 | Tempo EXA 91 | GRAHAM STEWART SEVEN (EP) | 10 |

## (DAVE) STEWART & HARRISON
| | | | |
|---|---|---|---|
| 70 | Multicord MULT SH 1 | GIRL (EP) | 15 |

*(see also Longdancer, Eurythmics)*

## JAMES STEWART & HENRY FONDA
| | | | |
|---|---|---|---|
| 70 | Stateside SS 2179 | Rolling Stone/Theme From Cheyenne Social Club | 8 |

## JOHN STEWART
| | | | |
|---|---|---|---|
| 69 | Capitol CL 15589 | July, You're A Woman/Shackles And Chains | 8 |

*(see also Scott Engel)*

## JOHNNY STEWART
| | | | |
|---|---|---|---|
| 58 | HMV POP 480 | Wishing For Your Love/Promise Me | 7 |

## PAUL STEWART (MOVEMENT)
| | | | |
|---|---|---|---|
| 67 | Decca F12577 | Saturday Mornin Man/Too Too Good (in export p/s) | 50 |
| 66 | Philips BF 1513 | Queen Boadicea/Talkin' | 7 |
| 67 | Decca F 12577 | Saturday Morning Man/Too Too Good (as Paul Stewart Movement) | 15 |

*(see also Hamilton & [Hamilton] Movement)*

## RAPHAEL STEWART & HOT TOPS
| | | | |
|---|---|---|---|
| 71 | Punch PH 71 | Put Your Sweet Lips/JUSTINS: Stand By Me | 10 |

## REX STEWART'S LONDON FIVE
| | | | |
|---|---|---|---|
| 55 | Tempo EXA 8 | REX STEWART'S LONDON FIVE (EP) | 15 |

## ROD STEWART
| | | | |
|---|---|---|---|
| 64 | Decca F 11996 | Good Morning Little Schoolgirl/I'm Gonna Move To The Outskirts Of Town | 180 |
| 65 | Columbia DB 7766 | The Day Will Come/Why Does It Go On? | 150 |
| 66 | Columbia DB 7892 | Shake!/I Just Got Some | 200 |
| 68 | Immediate IM 060 | Little Miss Understood/So Much To Say | 100 |
| 70 | Vertigo 6086 002 | It's All Over Now/Jo's Lament | 15 |
| 72 | Phonogram DJ004 | Twisting the Night Away (EP 1-track on 4 track promo 7" also featuring Chuck Berry, Diane Davidson and the Stylistics) | 20 |
| 77 | Riva RIVA 1 | You're Insane/You're Insane (DJ copy, 500 only) | 25 |
| 77 | Riva RIVA 3 | Tonight's The Night/The First Cut Is The Deepest (withdrawn B-side) | 5 |
| 78 | Riva RIVA 9 | Sailing/Stone Cold Sober(HMS Ark Royal Commemorative issue, blue vinyl, p/s) | 150 |
| 70 | Vertigo VO 4 | AN OLD RAINCOAT WON'T EVER LET YOU DOWN (gatefold sleeve, large swirl label, original pressing with 'Philips' credit on label) | 125 |
| 70 | Vertigo VO 4 | AN OLD RAINCOAT WON'T EVER LET YOU DOWN (gatefold sleeve, 2nd pressing, large swirl label, later pressing without 'Philips' credit on label) | 45 |
| 70 | Vertigo 6360 500 | GASOLINE ALLEY (LP, 1st pressing, gatefold sleeve, large swirl label) | 100 |
| 71 | Vertigo 6360 500 | GASOLINE ALLEY (LP, 2nd pressing, gatefold sleeve, small swirl label) | 45 |
| 71 | Mercury 6338 063 | EVERY PICTURE TELLS A STORY (black label, with poster) | 30 |
| 71 | Vertigo VO 4 | AN OLD RAINCOAT WON'T EVER LET YOU DOWN (gatefold sleeve, 3rd pressing, with small 'swirl' and 'Vertigo' above centre hole, title all on one line) | 25 |
| 72 | Vertigo VO 4 | AN OLD RAINCOAT WON'T EVER LET YOU DOWN (gatefold sleeve, 4th pressing, small 'swirl' and 'Vertigo' above centre hole but title on two lines) | 25 |

*(see also Jeff Beck, Shotgun Express, Faces, Python Lee Jackson, Long John Baldry, Steamhammer, Ted Wood)*

## ROMAN STEWART
| | | | |
|---|---|---|---|
| 72 | Songbird SB 1075 | Changing Times (with Dave)/CRYSTALITES: Changing Times Version | 12 |
| 73 | Downtown DT 518 | Try Me/BIG YOUTH: Rhythm Style | 15 |
| 73 | Techniques TE 932 | Tonight I'm Staying Here (& Tennors)/Lady Love (& Tennors) | 8 |
| 75 | Camel CA 2002 | Wolverton Mountain/PITTERSON ALL STARS: Version | 5 |
| 75 | Morpheus MOR 1 | In The Chapel/E MCLEAN: You Pick Me Up | 30 |
| 79 | GGS 049 | Don't Get Jumpy/GG ALL STARS: Dub Cut (12") | 25 |
| 78 | Pirate PIR 002 | Herbalist/Version (12", various coloured vinyl) | 35 |

| 78 | Strong Like Sampson SLSD 06 | Mr. Officer/Ain't Too Proud To Beg (12") | 40 |
| 79 | Thompson & Koots TK002 | Rice & Peas/Breaking Up (12", with Linval Thompson) | 40 |
| 80 | D-Roy DRDD 25 | What You Wanna Do/REVOLUTIONARIES: Rockers Delight (12") | 15 |

## SANDY STEWART
| 58 | London HLE 8683 | A Certain Smile/Kiss Me Richard | 10 |
| 63 | Pye International 7N 25176 | My Colouring Book/I Heard You Cried Last Night | 5 |

## TINGA STEWART
| 71 | Songbird SB 1048 | Hear That Train/CRYSTALITES: Hear That Train - Version | 12 |
| 72 | Tropical AL 0018 | A Brand New Me/BROWNS ALL STARS: Nice Version | 6 |
| 74 | Dragon DRA 1025 | The Message/Dub | 15 |
| 84 | Londisc LDLP 003 | KEY TO YOUR HEART (LP) | 15 |

## WINSTON STEWART
| 64 | R&B JB 147 | But I Do/MAYTALS: Four Seasons | 35 |
| 64 | Port-O-Jam PJ 4002 | All Of My Life/How Many Times | 30 |
| 65 | Ska Beat JB 225 | You Made Me Cry/CHECKMATES: Invisible Ska | 40 |

*(see also Andy & Clyde, Gaylads, Delano Stewart, Winston & Tonettes)*

## WYNN STEWART
| 60 | London HL 7087 | Wishful Thinking/Uncle Tom Got Caught (export issue) | 20 |

## STEWPOT & SAVE THE CHILDREN FUND CHOIR
| 68 | MGM 1448 | I Like My Toys/Myrtles Birthday | 20 |

## J.E. STICK & DRUMBAGO
| 61 | Blue Beat BB 64 | Boss Gill/COUNT OSSIE : Cassavuba | 20 |

## STICKERS
| 71 | Bullet BU 492 | One Night Of Sin/Sin (Version) (both sides actually by Jackie Brown) | 5 |

*(see also Jackie Brown)*

## STICKLEBACKS
| 87 | Dub House KS 1292 | All You Get/It's For You | 20 |

## STICK SHIFTS
| 80 | Chiswick CHIS 118 | Automobile/Parramatta Road (3 different p/s) | 12 |

## STIFF LITTLE FINGERS
| 78 | Rigid Digits SRD-1 | Suspect Device/Wasted Life (hand-made p/s, 500 only, red label with catalogue number on right-hand side) | 200 |
| 78 | Rigid Digits SRD-1 | Suspect Device/Wasted Life (re-pressing, different machine-cut p/s, various colour labels/yellow labels) | 20 |
| 78 | Rough Trade RT 004 | 78 R.P.M./Alternative Ulster (p/s, A & B-sides reversed) | 10 |
| 78 | Rough Trade RT 004 | Alternative Ulster/78 R.P.M. (p/s) | 7 |
| 78 | Rough Trade RT 006 | Suspect Device/Wasted Life (reissue) | 8 |
| 79 | Rough Trade RT 015 | Gotta Getaway/Bloody Sunday (p/s) | 5 |
| 79 | Chrysalis CHS 2368 | Straw Dogs/You Can't Say Crap On The Radio (p/s) | 7 |
| 81 | SLFDJ1 | Just Fade Away/Go For It (DJ promo) | 10 |
| 82 | Chrysalis CHSDJ 2580 | Listen/Two Guitars Clash (p/s, jukebox issue) | 12 |
| 89 | Virgin SLFDJ1 | St. Patrix, The Wild Rover/Johnny Was (DJ promo, unreleased as 7") | 12 |
| 91 | Essential ESSX 2007 | Beirut Moon/Stand Up And Shout/Interview With Jake Burns (CD, limited edition) | 30 |
| 89 | Link 1203 | THE LAST TIME (EP) | 10 |
| 86 | Strange Fruit SFPS 004 | PEEL SESSIONS (12") | 12 |
| 79 | Rough Trade ROUGH 1 | INFLAMMABLE MATERIAL (LP, with inner) | 18 |
| 80 | Chrysalis CHR 1270 | NOBODY'S HEROES (LP, inner) | 15 |
| 89 | Limited Edition LTD EDT LP 3 | LIVE IN SWEDEN (LP) | 15 |

*(see also Billy Karloff & Extremes)*

## STIFFS
| 79 | Dork UR 1 | Standard English/S.C. Rip/Brookside Riot Squad (die-cut sleeve) | 25 |
| 79 | Dork UR 2 | Inside Out/Kids On the Street (die cut sleeve or later Zonophone Z3 p/s) | 20 |
| 80 | Zonophone Z 14 | Volume Control/Nothing To Lose (p/s) | 15 |
| 80 | Stiff BUY 86 | Goodbye My Love/Magic Roundabout (p/s) | 10 |
| 85 | Dork UR 7(12) | The Young Guitars/Yer Under Attack (12", red p/s) | 10 |

## STILETTOS
| 80 | Ariola ARO 200 | This Is The Way/Who Can It Be (p/s) | 20 |

## STILL COOL
| 79 | Hit Run HITDD 22 | Insane Love/Stereo Version '79 (12") | 25 |

## STILL LIFE
| 68 | Columbia DB 8345 | What Did We Miss/My Kingdom Cannot Lose | 100 |
| 71 | Vertigo 6360 026 | STILL LIFE (LP, gatefold sleeve, large swirl label) | 400 |

*(see also Jon, Titus Groan)*

## STEPHEN STILLS
| 71 | Atlantic 2091 046 | Love The One You're With/To A Flame | 5 |
| 71 | Atlantic 2091 069 | Sit Yourself Down/We Are Not Helpless | 5 |
| 71 | Atlantic 2091 117 | Change Partners/Relaxing Town | 5 |
| 71 | Atlantic 2091 141 | Marianne/Nothing To Do But Today | 5 |
| 70 | Atlantic 2401 004 | STEPHEN STILLS (LP) | 35 |
| 71 | Atlantic 2401 013 | STEPHEN STILLS 2 (LP, gatefold sleeve) | 25 |
| 73 | Atlantic K 40440 | DOWN THE ROAD (LP) | 15 |

*(see also Buffalo Springfield, Al Kooper Mike Bloomfield & Stephen Stills, Crosby Stills Nash & Young, Manassas, Stills-Young Band)*

## STILLS-YOUNG BAND
| 76 | Reprise K 14446 | Long May You Run/12-8 Blues | 5 |
| 76 | Reprise K 14482 | Like A Hurricane (edit)/Hold Back The Tears | 5 |
| 76 | Reprise K 54081 | LONG MAY YOU RUN (LP) | 15 |

*(see also Stephen Stills, Manassas, Neil Young, Buffalo Springfield, Crosby Stills Nash & Young)*

## STING

| | | | |
|---|---|---|---|
| 82 | A&M PARTY 1 | Need Your Love So Bad/PAULINE BLACK : No Woman, No Cry (Promo) | 10 |
| 85 | A&M DREAMP 1 | THE DREAM OF THE BLUE TURTLES (LP, picture disc, die-cut sleeve, insert) | 15 |
| 93 | A&M 540 075-1 | TEN SUMMONERS TALES (LP, insert) | 40 |
| 96 | A&M 540 486-1 | MERCURY FALLING (LP) | 40 |

*(see also Police, Last Exit, [Fast Breeder &] Radio Actors, Newcastle Big Band)*

## STINGERS

| | | | |
|---|---|---|---|
| 72 | Upsetter US 395 | Preacher Man/UPSETTERS: Version | 20 |
| 72 | Explosion EX 2075 | Forward Up/UPSETTERS: Forward | 25 |

## STING-RAYS

| | | | |
|---|---|---|---|
| 82 | Big Beat SW 82 | Dinosaurs/Math Of Trend/Another Cup Of Coffee/You're Gonna Miss Me (white label test pressing, 100 Club gig freebie, 80 only) | 20 |
| 83 | Big Beat SW 82 | Dinosaurs/Math Of Trend/Another Cup Of Coffee/You're Gonna Miss Me (p/s) | 5 |
| 84 | Big Beat NS 95 | Escalator/Loose Lip Synch Ship/Escalator (Instrumental) (p/s) | 5 |
| 85 | Big Beat NS 109 | Don't Break Down/Don't Break Down (Version) (p/s) | 5 |
| 87 | Kaleidoscope Sound 7KS 102 | Behind The Beyond/Perverted Justice (p/s) | 10 |
| 87 | Kaleidoscope Sound KSLP 1 | CRYPTIC AND COFFEE TIME (LP) | 15 |
| 87 | Big Beat WIK 61 | THE ESSENTIAL EARLY STING-RAY RECORDINGS 1982 TO 1985 (LP) | 15 |
| 87 | Raucous FASTBUCK 1 | LIVE & RAW (10") | 15 |

## STINGRAYS (1)

| | | | |
|---|---|---|---|
| 80 | Earache SRTS./80/CUS 809 | Still In Love WIth You/Wasting Your Time/Couldn't Get It Right/Walking Down London Street (EP) | 25 |

## STINGRAYS (2)

| | | | |
|---|---|---|---|
| 80 | Fried Egg EGG 006 | Countdown/Exceptions Action | 40 |
| 82 | Rocket XPRES 78 | Radiator Rock/Slap Bass Boogie (die cut sleeve) | 8 |
| 81 | Circus CIRC 0003 | Never Do/Satellites | 20 |

## STINKY TOYS

| | | | |
|---|---|---|---|
| 77 | Polydor 2056 630 | Boozy Creed/Driver Blues (p/s) | 10 |
| 77 | Polydor 2393 174 | STINKY TOYS (LP) | 20 |

## STIR

| | | | |
|---|---|---|---|
| 87 | Spoonin SPOON 01 | CHEEKY MONKEY (12", EP) | 20 |

## (PETER) LEE STIRLING (& BRUISERS)

| | | | |
|---|---|---|---|
| 63 | Columbia DB 4992 | My Heart Commands Me/Welcome Stranger (as Lee Stirling & Bruisers) | 7 |
| 63 | Parlophone R 5063 | I Could If I Wanted To/Right From The Start (as Lee Stirling & Bruisers) | 7 |
| 64 | Parlophone R 5112 | Now That I've Found You/I Believe (as Peter Lee Stirling & Bruisers) | 7 |
| 64 | Parlophone R 5158 | Sad, Lonely And Blue/I'm Looking For Someone To Love (as Peter Lee Stirling & Bruisers) | 10 |
| 64 | Parlophone R 5198 | Everything Will Be Alright/You'll Be Mine (as Peter Lee Stirling & Bruisers) | 10 |
| 66 | Decca F 12433 | The Sweet And Tender Hold Of Your Love/Everybody Needs A Someone | 7 |
| 66 | Decca F 12535 | Oh What A Fool/I'm Sportin' A New Baby | 7 |
| 67 | Decca F 12628 | You Don't Live Twice/8.35 On The Dot | 25 |
| 67 | Decca F 12674 | Goodbye Thimblemill Lane/Hey Conductor | 12 |
| 69 | MCA MU 1093 | Big Sam/Mr. Average Man | 6 |
| 70 | MCA MK 5027 | Goodbye Summer Girl/Judas In Blue | 5 |

*(see also Bruisers, Hungry Wolf)*

## STITCH

| | | | |
|---|---|---|---|
| 76 | RCA 2526 | La Maison De L'Amour/All Smoke & No Fire | 5 |

## GARY STITES

| | | | |
|---|---|---|---|
| 59 | London HLL 8881 | Lonely For You/Shine That Ring | 25 |
| 59 | London HLL 9003 | Starry Eyed/Without Your Love | 20 |
| 60 | London HLL 9082 | Lawdy, Miss Clawdy/Don't Wanna Say Goodbye | 25 |

## SONNY STITT

| | | | |
|---|---|---|---|
| 53 | Esquire 20-013 | SONNY STITT-BUD POWELL QUARTET (10" LP) | 20 |
| 58 | Esquire 32-049 | S.P.J. JAZZ (LP, with Bud Powell & J.J. Johnson) | 20 |
| 58 | Columbia Clef 33CX 10114 | NEW YORK JAZZ (LP) | 20 |
| 59 | Esquire 32-078 | STITT'S BITS (LP) | 20 |
| 59 | HMV CLP 1280 | ONLY THE BLUES (LP) | 20 |
| 60 | HMV CLP 1384 | SONNY STITT WITH THE OSCAR PETERSON TRIO (LP) | 20 |
| 61 | HMV CLP 1420 | BLOWS THE BLUES (LP, mono) | 20 |
| 61 | HMV CSD 1341 | BLOWS THE BLUES (LP, stereo) | 20 |
| 64 | Chess CRL 4503 | MY MAIN MAN (LP) | 15 |
| 67 | Marble Arch MAL 753 | SONNY STITT (LP) | 15 |

*(see also J.J. Johnson)*

## TESSA STIVAR

| | | | |
|---|---|---|---|
| 83 | Smash TESS 001 | My Jealousy/Thin Air (p/s) | 10 |

## STOAT

| | | | |
|---|---|---|---|
| 77 | City NIK 1 | Office Girl/Little Jenny (p/s) | 5 |
| 78 | City NIK 3 | Up To You/Loving A Killer (p/s) | 7 |

## STOCKER, GREENWOOD & FRIENDS

| | | | |
|---|---|---|---|
| 79 | Changes CR1400 | BILLY + NINE (LP) | 25 |

*(see also Slack Alice)*

## KARLHEINZ STOCKHAUSEN

| | | | |
|---|---|---|---|
| 65 | CBS S72647 | MIKROPHONIE I/MIKROPHONIE II (LP) | 20 |
| 67 | CBS 77209 | COMPLETE PIANO MUSIC (2-LP, box set) | 40 |
| 67 | Vox STABY 615 | PROZESSION (LP) | 15 |
| 69 | Vox VS 3184 | STOCKHAUSEN (LP) | 15 |
| 70 | Deutsche Grammophon 2543003 | STIMMUNG (LP) | 20 |
| 74 | Open University OP 15 | TWENTIETH CENTURY MUSIC (LP) | 25 |

| | | | |
|---|---|---|---|
| 75 | Deutsche Grammophon 2530 582 | PROZESSION (LP, reissue) | 20 |

**STOCK, HAUSEN & WALKMAN**
| | | | |
|---|---|---|---|
| 96 | Hot Air QRM SP 101 | ORGAN TRANSPLANTS (EP) | 10 |
| 97 | Hot Air SPME 2 | Buy Me/Sue Me (500 only on pink vinyl) | 10 |
| 97 | Hot Air SPME 2 | Buy Me/Sue Me (300 on clear vinyl) | 12 |
| 97 | Hot Air SPME 2 | Buy Me/Sue Me (200 on light blue vinyl) | 15 |
| 99 | Hot Air ALERT 01 | Alert/Crash (500 only) | 10 |
| 91 | Hot Air SHWCASS 001 | WHAT'S UP? (Cassette in small cereal box, various inserts) | 20 |
| 96 | Hot Air QRM LP 101 | ORGAN TRANSPLANTS VOL 1 (LP) | 15 |

**STOCKHOLM MONSTERS**
| | | | |
|---|---|---|---|
| 81 | Factory FAC 41 | Fairytales/Death Is Slowly (p/s) | 15 |
| 82 | Factory FAC 58 | Happy Ever After/Soft Babies (p/s) | 15 |
| 84 | Factory FAC 107 | All At Once (p/s) | 10 |
| 84 | Factory FACT 80 | ALMA MATER (LP) | 20 |

**STOCKING TOPS**
| | | | |
|---|---|---|---|
| 68 | Toast TT 500 | You're Never Gonna Get My Lovin'/You Don't Know What Love Is All About | 18 |
| 68 | CBS 3407 | I Don't Ever Wanna Be Kicked By You/The World We Live In Is A Lonely Place | 15 |

*(see also Sue & Sunny, Sue & Sunshine, Myrtelles)*

**STOICS**
| | | | |
|---|---|---|---|
| 68 | RCA RCA 1745 | Earth, Fire, Air And Water/Search Of The Sea | 30 |

**STOKES**
| | | | |
|---|---|---|---|
| 65 | London HLU 9955 | Whipped Cream/Pie Crust | 15 |

**SIMON STOKES & NIGHTHAWKS**
| | | | |
|---|---|---|---|
| 70 | Elektra EKSN 45082 | Voodoo Woman/Can't Stop Now | 20 |

**JOOP STOKKERMANS**
| | | | |
|---|---|---|---|
| 71 | Gemini GM 2017 | THE MAGIC OF THE ARP SYNTHESISER (LP) | 20 |

**STOLEN POWER**
| | | | |
|---|---|---|---|
| 81 | Hornsey Rising POWER EP 1 | The Wheel Is Turning/Family Snapshot/Sick And Tired/Little White Lies (p/s) | 30 |

**STOLEN PROPERTY**
| | | | |
|---|---|---|---|
| 75 | Live Wire SON 4012 | Low Rider/Black Jack | 8 |

**STOLEN YOUTH**
| | | | |
|---|---|---|---|
| 76 | Sunday SUN 1 | Wheels In Motion/Kick The Door Down | 30 |

**RHET STOLLER (& HIS ECHOES)**
| | | | |
|---|---|---|---|
| 60 | Decca F 11271 | Walk Don't Run/All Rhet | 10 |
| 60 | Decca F 11302 | Chariot/Night Theme | 10 |
| 63 | Decca F 11738 | Countdown/Over The Steppes (as Rhet Stoller & His Echoes) | 10 |
| 64 | Melodisc MEL 1595 | Beat That/Treble Gold + One | 15 |
| 64 | Windsor PS 119 | Caravan/Short Cut | 20 |
| 64 | Windsor PS 130 | Ricochet/Knockout | 20 |
| 66 | Columbia DB 8013 | Uncrowned King/Surf Ride (unissued, demos only) | 20 |
| 67 | Coronet EC 101 | THE INCREDIBLE RHET STOLLER (LP) | 25 |

**STOLLERS TEAM**
| | | | |
|---|---|---|---|
| 72 | Decca F13280 | Sapporo/Mean | 12 |

**JACKIE STOLLINGS (& NASHVILLE BOYS)**
| | | | |
|---|---|---|---|
| 62 | Starlite ST45 092 | Footsteps Of A Fool/And Then I Knew (B-side with Nashville Boys) | 6 |

*(See also Jess Conrad)*

**MORRIS STOLOFF (& COLUMBIA PICTURES ORCHESTRA)**
| | | | |
|---|---|---|---|
| 56 | Brunswick 05553 | Moonglow/Theme From "Picnic" | 7 |
| 56 | Brunswick 05597 | Theme From "The Solid Gold Cadillac"/Sweet Sue Just You | 5 |
| 57 | Brunswick 05666 | Theme From "Fire Down Below"/Theme From "Full Of Life" | 5 |
| 61 | Warner Bros WB 48 | Fanny/Panisse And Son | 6 |

**STOMPERS**
| | | | |
|---|---|---|---|
| 62 | Fontana H 385 | Quarter To Four Stomp (Surf Stompin')/Foolish One | 50 |

**ALEXANDER STONE**
| | | | |
|---|---|---|---|
| 70 | Gemini GMS 003 | I Try To Make You Good/Man In A Suitcase | 10 |

**CISSY STONE**
| | | | |
|---|---|---|---|
| 76 | Decca 13646 | Gone But Not Forgotten/Part Of The Band | 12 |

**CLIFFIE STONE & HIS ORCHESTRA**
| | | | |
|---|---|---|---|
| 55 | Capitol CL 14330 | Barracuda/The Popcorn Song (with Billy Strange & Speedy West) | 100 |
| 55 | Capitol CL 14330 | Barracuda/The Popcorn Song (with Billy Strange & Speedy West) (78) | 20 |
| 56 | Capitol CL 14666 | Jingle Bells/Rudolph The Red Nosed Reindeer | 5 |
| 58 | Capitol CL 14928 | Near You/Nobody's Darlin' But Mine | 5 |
| 59 | Capitol CL 14996 | Blood On The Saddle/Cool Water | 5 |
| 59 | Capitol T 1080 | THE PARTY'S ON ME (LP) | 15 |

*(see also Jeanne Gayle, Billy Strange)*

**STONE CROSS**
| | | | |
|---|---|---|---|
| 72 | Access ACC 3 | Light Up The Sun/At My Funeral | 35 |

**ELLA STONE & MOSS**
| | | | |
|---|---|---|---|
| 70s | Phoenix SNIX 128 | The Prophet/Now Or Never | 6 |

*(see also Helen Shapiro, Al Saxon)*

**GEORGE STONE**
| | | | |
|---|---|---|---|
| 65 | Stateside SS 479 | Hole In The Wall/My Beat | 20 |

**KIRBY STONE QUARTET/FOUR**
| | | | |
|---|---|---|---|
| 56 | Vogue Coral Q 72129 | Honey Hush/Lassus Trombone | 15 |
| 59 | Philips PB 903 | That "I Had A Dream, Dear" Rock/Sweet Nothings | 5 |
| 63 | Warner Bros WB 102 | The Great Escape (March)/Fancy Dan | 5 |

63   Warner Bros WB 118      Washington Square/Blue Guitar ........................................................... 7

## MARK STONE
58   London HLR 8543      Ever Since I Met Lucy/The Stroll ......................................................... 70
58   London HLR 8543      Ever Since I Met Lucy/The Stroll (78) ................................................. 30

## ROB STONE
68   Delta DT 3941      Sorry Suzanna/Peace Of Mind ............................................................ 20

## SLY (& FAMILY) STONE
68   Columbia DB 8369      Dance To The Music/Let Me Hear It From You ..................................... 100
68   Columbia DB 8369      Dance To The Music/Let Me Hear It From You (DJ copy) ...................... 150
68   Direction 58-3568      Dance To The Music/Let Me Hear It From You (reissue) ....................... 8
68   Direction 58-3707      M'Lady/Life ....................................................................................... 8
69   Direction 58-3938      Everyday People/Sing A Simple Song ................................................... 8
69   Direction 58-4279      Stand!/I Want To Take You Higher ....................................................... 8
69   Direction 58-4471      Hot Fun In The Summertime/Fun ........................................................ 10
70   Direction 58-4782      Thank You (Falettinme Be Mice Elf Agin)/Everybody Is A Star ............... 8
70   CBS 5054      I Want To Take You Higher/You Can Make It If You Try ......................... 6
71   Epic EPC 7632      Family Affair/Luv n' Haight .................................................................. 5
68   Direction 8-63412      DANCE TO THE MUSIC (LP) .................................................................. 25
68   Direction 8-63461      M'LADY (LP) ...................................................................................... 20
69   Direction 8-63655      STAND! (LP, CBS sleeve with Direction label) ...................................... 20

## STONE ANGEL
75   SSLP 04      STONE ANGEL (LP, private pressing, blue/silver label) ....................... 400
94   Acme AC 8008 LP      STONE ANGEL (LP, reissue, 500 only) ................................................. 15

*(see also Ken Saul)*

## STONEFIELD TRAMP
74   Acorn/Tramp CF 247      DREAMING (LP) ................................................................................. 200

*(see also Terry Friend, Rob Van Spyk)*

## STONE GRAPHICS
68   Parlophone R 5735      A Tale Of Long Ago/Travelling Man ..................................................... 8

## STONEGROUND
71   Warner Bros K 16126      You Must Be One Of Us/It Takes A Lot To Laugh ................................... 5
71   Warner Bros K 46087      STONEGROUND (LP) ........................................................................... 20
71   Warner Bros K 53999      FAMILY ALBUM (LP) ........................................................................... 20

## STONEGROUND BAND
70s   Nut      SUNSTRUCK!! (LP, stickered sleeve) ..................................................... 30

## HARRY STONEHAM
76   One UP OU 2127      I FEEL GOOD, I FEEL FUNKY (LP) ......................................................... 15

## HARRY STONEHAM & JOHNNY EYDEN
67   Tepee TPRLP 100      TWO GUYS TO FOLLOW (LP, mono [70s reissues credited soley to Harry Stoneham £15]) ................................................................................. 20

## STONEHENGE MEN
62   HMV POP 981      Big Feet/Pinto .................................................................................... 30

## STONEHOUSE
71   RCA SF 8197      STONEHOUSE CREEK (LP, laminated front sleeve, orange label) ........... 175

## STONE PONEYS
67   Capitol CL 15523      Different Drum/I've Got To Know ....................................................... 10

## STONE ROSES
SINGLES
85   Thin Line THIN 001      So Young/Tell Me (12", p/s, 1,200 only; beware of counterfeits!) ............... 120
87   Black/Revolver 12 REV 36      Sally Cinnamon/Here It Comes/All Across The Sand (12", 'Printed In England' on rear p/s & no barcode, "All Across The Sands" listed on label; different mixes of 2 tracks to later reissue - increasingly difficult to find original) ................................ 30
88   Silvertone ORE 1      Elephant Stone/The Hardest Thing In The World (catalogue number in black print on rear of p/s) ................................................................................. 8
88   Silvertone ORET 1      Elephant Stone (4.48)/Elephant Stone (7" Version) (3.00)/Full Fathom Five/The Hardest Thing In The World (12", p/s, cat. no. in black print on rear of p/s) (unique recording of Full Fathom Five on original pressing) ............................... 25
89   Silvertone ORE 2      Made Of Stone/Going Down (p/s, cat. no. in black print on rear of p/s) ........ 7
89   Silvertone ORET 2      Made Of Stone/Going Down/Guernica (12", p/s, catalogue number in black print on rear of p/s) ............................................................................. 18
89   Silvertone OREX 6      She Bangs The Drums/Standing Here (p/s, with postcard, 3,000 only) ........ 8
89   Silvertone OREZ 6      She Bangs The Drums/Mersey Paradise/Standing Here (12", p/s with colour print (I Wanna Be Adored cover), 5,000 only) ................................................ 15
89   Silvertone ORE 13      What The World Is Waiting For/Fools Gold 4.15 (paper label, with postcard stickered p/s credits "What The World Is Waiting For") ...................................... 8
89   Silvertone ORET 13      What The World Is Waiting For/Fools Gold 9.23 (12", stickered p/s credits What The World Is Waiting For, with print) .............................................. 15
89   Black/Revolver 12 REV 36      Sally Cinnamon/Here It Comes/All Across The Sand (12" 'Printed in W Germany' on rear p/s – barcode) .............................................................................. 10
89   Black/Revolver REV 36      Sally Cinnamon/Here It Comes (p/s) .................................................... 6
90   Silvertone ORE 1      Elephant Stone (7" Version)/The Hardest Thing In The World (catalogue number in red print on rear of p/s) .......................................................... 8
90   Silvertone ORE 2      Made Of Stone/Going Down (p/s, cat. no. in blue print on rear of p/s) ........ 6
90   Fierce FRIGHT 044      SPIKE ISLAND EP (fan interviews, P.A. announcements & fireworks, with cigarette, badge, bag of grass & banana sweet) ................................................... 18
90   Silvertone OREZ 13      Fools Gold (The Top Won Mix!)/(The Bottom Won Mix!) (12") ................. 12
91   Silvertone ORE 31      I Wanna Be Adored (3.28)/Where Angels Play (p/s) ............................. 6
91   Silvertone ORET 31      I Wanna Be Adored (4.52)/Where Angels Play/Sally Cinnamon (live at the Hacienda) (12" p/s) .................................................................................... 10
91   Silvertone OREZ 31      I Wanna Be Adored (4.52)/Where Angels Play/Sally Cinnamon (live at the Hacienda) (12", stickered p/s with print) ................................................... 18

| | | | |
|---|---|---|---|
| 92 | Silvertone ORE 35 | Waterfall (7" Version 3.31)/One Love (7" Version 3.40) (p/s) | 6 |
| 92 | Silvertone OREZT 35 | Waterfall (12" Version 5.23)/One Love (Adrian Sherwood 12" Version 7.10) (12", p/s with print) | 12 |
| 92 | Silvertone ORE 40 | I Am The Resurrection (Pan And Scan Radio Version)/I Am The Resurrection (Highly Resurrected Dub) (p/s) | 6 |
| 92 | Silvertone ORET 40 | I Am The Resurrection (Extended 19:9 Ratio Club Mix)/(Original LP Version)/Fools Gold (Bottom Won Mix) (12", with print) | 20 |
| 92 | Silvertone ORET 40 | I Am The Resurrection (Extended 19:9 Ratio Club Mix)/(Original LP Version)/Fools Gold (Bottom Won Mix) (12", without print) | 10 |
| 92 | Black/Revolver 12REV 36 | Sally Cinnamon/All Across The Sands/Here It Comes (12" reissue, barcode on sleeve) | 10 |
| 92 | Silvertone SRBX 2 | 12" SINGLES COLLECTION (10 x 12" singles box set, numbered 1,000 only) | 150 |
| 92 | Silvertone SRBX 1 | COMPACT DISC SINGLES COLLECTION (8 x CD singles box set, 1,000 only) | 35 |
| 95 | Geffen GFST 87 | Ten Storey Love Song/Moses/Ride On (12", stickered/numbered p/s) | 10 |
| 95 | Geffen GFST 22060 | Begging You (Album Version)/(Chic Mix)/(Cox's Ultimatum Mix)/(Stone Corporation Vox) (12" p/s with art print) | 10 |
| 09 | Silvertone 88697574727 | THE 7" SINGLES COLLECTION (5 x 7" box set) | 30 |

## ALBUMS : LPS

| | | | |
|---|---|---|---|
| 89 | Silvertone ORE LP 502 | THE STONE ROSES (LP, original pressing, embossed sleeve with gold lettering) | 40 |
| 89 | Silvertone ORE LP 502 | THE STONE ROSES (LP, original pressing, not embossed gold lettering) | 25 |
| 91 | Silvertone OREZ LP 502 | THE STONE ROSES (2-LP, reissue, numbered gatefold sleeve with silver lettering) | 25 |
| 92 | Silvertone ORE LP 521 | TURNS INTO STONE (LP, original pressing) | 30 |
| 94 | Geffen GEF 24503 | SECOND COMING (2-LP, original pressing, gatefold) | 35 |
| 95 | Silvertone ORE LP 535 | THE COMPLETE STONE ROSES (2-LP) | 25 |
| 96 | Garage Flower GARAGE LP 1 | GARAGE FLOWER (LP, with print) | 40 |
| 96 | Garage Flower GARAGE LP 1 | GARAGE FLOWER (LP, without print) | 25 |
| 99 | Geffen/Simply Vinyl SVLP 111 | SECOND COMING (2-LP, limited edition, gatefold, heavy duty 180g vinyl) | 20 |
| 09 | Silvertone 88697430302 | THE STONES ROSES (Box set, 3-CD, LP, 2x12", DVD, memory stick) | 80 |
| 10 | Silvertone Sony/BMG 88697694171 | THE STONE ROSES (LP, 1000 only, numbered, 2010 Record Store day release with 6 art prints) | 30 |

## PROMOS

| | | | |
|---|---|---|---|
| 85 | Thin Line THIN 001 | So Young/Tell Me (12" promo (pale) pink label test pressing, 100 pressed, this price without press pack) | 250 |
| 85 | Thin Line THIN 001 | So Young/Tell Me (12" promo (pale) pink label test press) 100 pressed (in Cartel sleeve with press pack) | 400 |
| 89 | Silvertone ORE DJ 6 | She Bangs The Drums (7" promo) | 12 |
| 89 | Silvertone ORE DJ T 13 | Fools Gold 9.53/ What The World Is Waiting For (12" promo, b-side white label) | 20 |
| 89 | Silvertone ORE DJ 13 | Fools Gold 4.15/ What The World Is Waiting For (7" promo) | 12 |
| 90 | Silvertone ORE DJ T 17 | One Love/Something's Burning (12" promo, b-side white label) | 12 |
| 90 | Silvertone ORE DJ 17 | One Love (7" edit) /Something's Burning (7" edit) (7" promo) | 12 |
| 92 | Silvertone ORE T DJ 34 | Waterfall (12" Version 5.23)/One Love (Adrian Sherwood 12" Version 7.10) (12" promo) | 15 |
| 90 | Silvertone STONE ONE | Fools Gold (A Guy Called Gerald Remix)/Elephant Stone (DJ Mix) (12", white label) this is actually a bootleg recording by Hard Tymez Productions | 15 |

*(see also Ian Brown)*

## STONE'S MASONRY

| | | | |
|---|---|---|---|
| 66 | Purdah 45-3504 | Flapjacks/Hot Rock (99 copies only) | 200 |

*(see also Action, Mighty Baby)*

## STONE TEMPLE PILOTS

| | | | |
|---|---|---|---|
| 92 | Atlantic 7567824 | CORE (LP) | 40 |
| 94 | Atlantic 82607 | PURPLE - 12 GRACIOUS MELODIES (LP, purple vinyl) | 40 |

## STONE THE CROWS

| | | | |
|---|---|---|---|
| 70 | Polydor 2066 060 | Mad Dogs & Englishmen/Sad Mary | 5 |
| 72 | Polydor 2058 301 | Good Time Girl/On The Highway | 5 |
| 70 | Polydor 2425 017 | STONE THE CROWS (LP) | 70 |
| 70 | Polydor 2425 042 | ODE TO JOHN LAW (LP, gatefold sleeve) | 40 |
| 71 | Polydor 2425 071 | TEENAGE LICKS (LP, gatefold sleeve) | 45 |
| 72 | Polydor 2391 043 | ONTINUOUS PERFORMANCE (LP) | 20 |

*(see also White Trash)*

## STONEY BROOK PEOPLE

| | | | |
|---|---|---|---|
| 69 | CBS 4538 | Easy To Be Hard/There's Tomorrow | 30 |

## STONEY & MEAT LOAF

| | | | |
|---|---|---|---|
| 71 | Rare Earth RES 103 | What You See Is What You Get/The Way You Do The Things You Do | 12 |
| 79 | Prodigal PROD 10 | What You See Is What You Get/The Way You Do The Things You Do (reissue) | 8 |
| 72 | Rare Earth SRE 3005 | STONEY AND MEAT LOAF (LP) | 25 |
| 79 | Prodigal PDL 2010 | MEAT LOAF (FEATURING STONEY & MEAT LOAF) (LP, revised reissue of "Stoney And Meat Loaf" with different tracks) | 15 |

*(see also Meat Loaf)*

## STOOGES

| | | | |
|---|---|---|---|
| 05 | Elektra 8122732137 | I Wanna Be Your Dog/Real Cool TIme (reissue) | 8 |
| 69 | Elektra EKS 74051 | THE STOOGES (LP, red label) | 250 |
| 70 | Elektra 2410 009 | FUN HOUSE (LP, red label) | 300 |
| 73 | CBS 65586 | RAW POWER (LP, as Iggy & Stooges, no name on front cover, plain orange label, with inner sleeve) | 40 |
| 77 | Elektra K 42032 | THE STOOGES (LP, reissue, 'butterfly' label) | 20 |
| 77 | Elektra K 42051 | FUN HOUSE (LP, reissue, 'butterfly' label) | 20 |
| 99 | Elektra 7559624421 | NO FUN (LP, as The Stooges featuring Iggy Pop) | 15 |
| 05 | Elektra 8122 73237 1 | THE STOOGES (2-LP, reissue, gatefold) | 25 |
| 05 | Elektra 8122 73238 1 | FUN HOUSE (2-LP, reissue, gatefold) | 25 |

*(see also Iggy Pop)*

## STOP THE TRAIN
83   Stranded S83 CUS 1908     Suspicions/Empty Rooms ............................................................ 10

## STOPOUTS
78   Skeleton LYN 5912     Strange Thoughts/Just For You And Me (p/s)................................... 15

## STOREY SISTERS
58   London HLU 8571     Bad Motorcycle/Sweet Daddy.......................................................... 50
58   London HLU 8571     Bad Motorcycle/Sweet Daddy (78) ................................................... 25

## STORM
85   Silent SILENT 1     Malice In Wonderland/Malice In Wonderland (Edit)/Doctor Storm (12", p/s)................ 25

## STORM/CUTMASTER SWIFT
91   White SOLID001     Playing The Field/Live In Spain (12")............................................... 70

## STORM/MIGHTY ETHNICZ
91   Bite It! BITE 3     You're Out There (12") ................................................................. 10

## BILLY STORM
59   Philips PB 916     I've Come Of Age/This Is Always...................................................... 10
60   London HLK 9236     Sure As You're Born/In The Chapel In The Moonlight........................... 10

## DANNY STORM (& STROLLERS)
62   Piccadilly 7N 35025     Honest I Do/Sad But True (in p/s) ................................................... 10
62   Piccadilly 7N 35025     Honest I Do/Sad But True................................................................. 7
62   Piccadilly 7N 35053     Just You/I Told You So.................................................................... 10
62   Piccadilly 7N 35091     I Just Can't Fool My Heart/Thinking Of You...................................... 12
63   Piccadilly 7N 35143     Say You Do/Let The Sunshine In (as Danny Storm & Strollers)................ 15

## GALE STORM
56   London HLD 8222     I Hear You Knocking/Never Leave Me................................................ 50
56   London HLD 8232     Memories Are Made Of This/A Teen-Age Prayer ............................... 30
56   London HLD 8283     Ivory Tower/I Ain't Gonna Worry .................................................... 20
56   London HLD 8286     Why Do Fools Fall In Love/I Walk Alone............................................ 20
56   London HL 7008     Why Do Fools Fall In Love/I Walk Alone (export issue)....................... 20
56   London HLD 8311     Don't Be That Way (Please Listen To Me)/Tell Me Why ...................... 25
56   London HLD 8329     A Heart Without A Sweetheart/Now Is The Hour .............................. 15
57   London HLD 8393     Lucky Lips/On Treasure Island ........................................................ 30
57   London HLD 8413     Orange Blossoms/My Heart Belongs To You ..................................... 15
57   London HLD 8424     Dark Moon/A Little Too Late........................................................... 10
58   London HLD 8570     Love Theme From "Farewell To Arms"/I Get That Feeling ................. 10
58   London HLD 8632     You/Angry.................................................................................... 10
56   London HB-D 1056     PRESENTING GALE STORM (10" LP) ................................................ 40
58   London HA-D 2104     SENTIMENTAL ME (LP).................................................................... 30

## LOLITA STORM
99   Rabid Badger NANG 09     Goodbye America/Get Back (I'm Evil) (p/s)........................................ 5

## RORY STORM & HURRICANES
63   Oriole CB 1858     Dr. Feelgood/I Can Tell .................................................................. 45
64   Parlophone R 5197     America/Since You Broke My Heart ................................................. 25

*(see also Keef Hartley, Paddy Klaus & Gibson)*

## STORMCHILD
82   Serpent S001     Rockin'Steady/Last Night (hand folded sleeve, white label, 50 only)........................ 1000

## ROBB STORME (& WHISPERS)
60   Decca F 11282     1000, 900 And When/I Don't Need Your Love Anymore...................... 6
61   Decca F 11313     Music/Five Minutes More (as Robb Storme & Whispers)...................... 6
61   Decca F 11364     Near You/Lonely Town (as Robb Storme & Whispers) ........................ 5
61   Decca F 11388     Transistor Sister/Earth Angel ......................................................... 12
62   Decca F 11432     Pretty Hair And Angel Eyes/A Mile Of Broken Hearts ......................... 5
63   Pye 7N 15515     Sixteen Years Ago Tonight/Surprise Surprise...................................... 7
63   Piccadilly 7N 35133     Happens Ev'ryday/Surprise Surprise ................................................. 6
63   Piccadilly 7N 35160     To Know Her Is To Love Her/Bu Bop A Lu Bop A Lie ........................... 6
65   Pye 7N 15819     Love Is Strange/Shy Guy ................................................................ 10
65   Columbia DB 7756     Where Is My Girl?/Double Oh Seven (as Robb Storme & Whispers)........... 10
66   Columbia DB 7993     Here Today/Don't Cry (as Robb Storme Group)................................. 20
62   Decca DFE 6700     WHEELS (EP) ............................................................................... 100

## STORMER
78   Ring O' 2017 113     My Home Town/Shake It Baby (in promo p/s) ................................... 70
78   Ring O' 2017 113     My Home Town/Shake It Baby ...................................................... 40

## STORM QUEEN
82   Real Fire RF001     Come Silent To The World/Raising The Roof (1st press, red labels no p/s) ............... 350
82   Real Fire RF001     Come Silent To The World/Raising The Roof (2nd press, red labels no p/s) .............. 275

## STORMRIDER
77   Crossover CS 7701     Mr Supercool/Sister Bring Down (no p/s) .......................................... 30

## STORMTROOPER (1)
78   Solent SS 047     I'm A Mess/It's Not Me (in stamped plain sleeve with insert) ...................... 30
78   Solent SS 047     I'm A Mess/It's Not Me .................................................................. 12

## STORMTROOPER (2)
80   Heartbeat BEAT 1     Pride Before A Fall/Still Comin' Home (p/s) ....................................... 25

## STORMY PETREL
71   CBS 7271     Hello Hello Hello/The Light Of Day .................................................. 10

## STORYTELLER (1)
71   CBS 7182     Remarkable/Laugh That Came Too Soon ........................................... 5
70   Transatlantic TRA 220     STORYTELLER (LP, gatefold sleeve, white/lilav label, 't' logo) ................ 60
71   Transatlantic TRA 232     MORE PAGES (LP, textured sleeve)................................................... 35

*(see also Johnny Neal & Starliners, Terry Durham, Other Two, Andy Bown)*

**STORYTELLER (2)**
79   Alladin MDS 1002            Just Another Cloud In The Sky/Weatherman ........................................................... 20

**STORYTELLER (3)**
85   Storyteller ZELSP 438       Mystery Girl (p/s) ..................................................................................................... 50

**LALLY STOTT**
71   Philips 6025029            Jakaranda/Love Is Free Love Is Blind ....................................................................... 8

**WALLY STOTT ORCHESTRA/CHORUS**
60   Pye 7N 15271               The Unforgiven/Mr. Lucky ....................................................................................... 6

**DAVID STOUGHTON**
68   Elektra EKS 74034          TRANSFORMER (LP) ................................................................................................ 40

**STOWAWAYS**
79   Supermusic SUP 27          I Wanna Be Me/My Friends/You'll Tie Me Down (p/s) .......................................... 25

**STP 23**
89   Wau! Mr. Modo WMS 001R  Let Jimi Take Over/Let Jimi Take Over (Remix By Youth) (12", p/s) .................. 10

**STRAFE FÜR REBELLION**
80s  Touch TO 6                 SANTA MARIA (LP, with inner) ............................................................................... 15

**STRAIGHT EIGHT**
78   Eel Pie EPS 003            Modern Times/Tell Me If You Wanna Bleed (p/s) ................................................ 10
79   Warner Bros K 18049        Spread It Around/It Ain't Easy/Oh No (p/s) ........................................................... 5
80   Logo DEAL 1                I'm Sorry/Satisfied (p/s) .......................................................................................... 6
80   Logo DEAL 2                Tombstone/On The Rebound (p/s) ........................................................................... 5
82   Logo GO 416                Tomorrow/Faded Stars/You Are What You Are (with p/s) ................................... 10
82   Logo GO 416                Tomorrow/Faded Stars/You Are What You Are ...................................................... 8
79   Eel Pie EPRP 001           NO NOISE FROM HERE (LP) ..................................................................................... 15

**STRAIGHT UP**
80   Rok XX/XIX                 One Out All Out/JUSTIN CASE: T.V. (die-cut company sleeve) ............................ 40

**STRAIGHT CORNERS**
80   SRTS/80/CUS 809            Legal Executive/Berlin Wall (p/s) ........................................................................... 25

**STRAIGHTSHOOTER**
79   Strolling Bone S 79 CUS 398  Straightshooter/She's So Fine (no p/s) .............................................................. 120

**PETER STRAKER**
69   Polydor 56345              Breakfast In Bed/The Right To Cry ........................................................................... 5
69   Polydor 56362              I Never Thought I'd Fall In Love/Birdie Told Me ..................................................... 5
70   Polydor 2058 039           Carousel/It's A New Day ........................................................................................... 5
74   RCA LPBO 5011              From The Underworld/Love Motion ....................................................................... 8
77   EMI EMI 2700               Ragtime Piano Joe/Saddest Clown ......................................................................... 10

**STRAND**
80   Yob YOB 001                Here Today Gone Tomorrow/Changing World/POSITIVE SIGNALS: Media Man/Only
                                For A Day (split EP, p/s) .......................................................................................... 15

**PAULINE STRAND**
68   Carousel CR3               Love Me Always/The End Of Me .............................................................................. 25

**STRANDSMEN**
67   Philips BF 1572            I Know/Stay Close To Me .......................................................................................... 10

**BILLY STRANGE (& CHALLENGERS)**
61   London HLG 9321            Where Your Arms Used To Be/Sadness Done Come ................................................ 6
64   Vocalion V-N 9228          The James Bond Theme/007 Theme ...................................................................... 15
64   Vocalion V-N 9231          Goldfinger/"Munsters" Theme ............................................................................... 10
66   Vocalion V-N 9257          Thunderball/"Ninth Man" Theme .......................................................................... 10
66   Vocalion V-N 9259          Get Smart/Run Spy, Run .......................................................................................... 15
67   Vocalion V-N 9289          A Few Dollars More Theme/You Only Live Twice .................................................. 10
63   Vocalion VA/SVN 8022       12-STRING GUITAR (LP) ........................................................................................... 15
64   Vocalion VAN 8026          MR GUITAR (LP) ...................................................................................................... 15
64   Vocalion VAN/SAVN 8032     THE JAMES BOND THEME (LP) ............................................................................... 20
65   Vocalion VAN/SAVN 8038     GOLDFINGER (LP) ................................................................................................... 20
65   Vocalion VAN/SAVN 8042     ENGLISH HITS OF '65 (LP) ....................................................................................... 15
65   Vocalion VAN/SAVN 8045     STRANGE PLAYS THE HITS (LP) ............................................................................... 15
*(see also Cliffie Stone)*

**STRANGE BROTHERS SHOW**
70   Polydor 2001-116           Right On/Shakey Jakes ............................................................................................ 15

**STRANGE BUT TRUE**
91   SBT 001                    Blair Peach/Stephanie ............................................................................................. 10

**GILES STRANGE**
66   Stateside SS 570           Watch The People Dance/You're Goin' Up To The Bottom (DJ Copy) .................. 100
66   Stateside SS 570           Watch The People Dance/You're Goin' Up To The Bottom .................................... 80

**STEVE STRANGE**
82   Palace PALACE 1            In The Year 2525/Strange Connexions (white label, unreleased) ........................ 30
82   Palace PALACE 1            In The Year 2525/Strange Connexions (p/s, available separately) ...................... 20
*(see also Visage)*

**STRANGE CRUISE**
86   EMI 12EMI 5549             Rebel Blue Rocker/Love Addiction (12", p/s) ........................................................ 10
86   EMI EMC 3513               STRANGE CRUISE (LP) ............................................................................................. 18

**STRANGE DAYS (1)**
75   Retreat RTS 263            Monday Morning/Joe Soap ........................................................................................ 5
75   Retreat RTL 6005           NINE PARTS TO THE WIND (LP, lyric inner sleeve, blue label) .............................. 25

**STRANGE DAYS (2)**
83   Powerstation OHM 1         Within These Walls/Swimming Into The Doctor .................................................... 15

## STRANGE FOX
| | | | |
|---|---|---|---|
| 70 | Parlophone R5876 | Bring It On HOme/Time And Tide | 30 |
| 73 | Parlophone R5978 | Rock 'N' Roll Band/Tamarin Girl | 15 |

## STRANGE FRUIT
| | | | |
|---|---|---|---|
| 71 | Village Thing VTSX 1001 | Cut Across Shorty/Shake That Thing | 25 |

## STRANGELOVE
| | | | |
|---|---|---|---|
| 94 | Food FOODLP 11 | TIME FOR THE REST OF YOUR LIFE (2-LP, numbered) | 20 |
| 96 | Food FOODLP 15 | LOVE AND OTHER DEMONS (LP, with 12 page booklet) | 25 |
| 97 | Food FOODLPD 24 | STRANGELOVE (2-LP) | 25 |

## STRANGELOVES
| | | | |
|---|---|---|---|
| 65 | Stateside SS 446 | I Want Candy/It's About My Baby | 25 |
| 65 | Immediate IM 007 | Cara-Lin/Roll On Mississippi | 30 |
| 66 | London HLZ 10020 | Night Time/Rhythm Of Love | 35 |
| 66 | London HLZ 10063 | Hand Jive/I Gotta Dance | 12 |
| 69 | London HLZ 10238 | Honey Do/I Wanna Do It | 15 |

*(see also Beach-Nuts)*

## STRANGE MOVEMENTS
| | | | |
|---|---|---|---|
| 79 | Good Vibrations GOT 5 | Dancing In The Ghetto/Amuse Yourself (foldout p/s) | 25 |

## STRANGER (COLE)
| | | | |
|---|---|---|---|
| 63 | Blue Beat BB 165 | Rough And Tough (with Duke Reid Band)/DUKE REID BAND: The Mood I Am In | 20 |
| 63 | Blue Beat BB 195 | Miss Reamer/RICO & HIS BLUES BAND: Blues From The Hills | 20 |

*(see also Stranger Cole)*

## STRANGER (COLE) & GLADY (ANDERSON)
| | | | |
|---|---|---|---|
| 67 | Island WI 3128 | Love Me Today/Over Again | 100 |
| 68 | Amalgamated AMG 806 | Seeing Is Knowing/ROY SHIRLEY: Music Is The Key | 25 |
| 71 | Clandisc CLA 230 | Tomorrow (as Stranger & Gladdy)/DYNAMITES: Tomorrow Version | 7 |
| 71 | Supreme SUP 227 | My Application (as Stranger & Gladdy)/TADDY & DIAMONDS: Oh No, My Baby | 15 |
| 73 | Count Shelley CS 015 | Don't Give Up The Fight (as Stranger & Gladdy)/TIDALS: Stand Firm | 5 |
| 73 | Dragon DRA 1014 | Conqueror/Conqueror (Instrumental Version) | 5 |

*(see also Stranger Cole, Gladdy & Followers, Gladstone Anderson, Gladdy & Stranger, Charlie Kelly)*

## STRANGER (COLE) & HORTENSE (ELLIS)
| | | | |
|---|---|---|---|
| 74 | Count Shelley CS 049 | Mocking Bird/Corra Bella Baby | 6 |

## STRANGER (COLE) & KEN (BOOTHE)
| | | | |
|---|---|---|---|
| 63 | R&B JB 120 | Thick In Love/All Your Friends | 30 |

*(see also Stranger Cole, Ken Boothe)*

## STRANGER (COLE) & PATSY (TODD)
| | | | |
|---|---|---|---|
| 63 | Blue Beat BB 171 | When I Call Your Name/Take My Heart (with Duke Reid All Stars) | 20 |
| 63 | Island WI 113 | Senor And Senorita/DON DRUMMOND: Snowboy | 30 |
| 64 | Island WI 141 | Oh Oh I Need You/DON DRUMMOND: J.F.K.'s Memory | 35 |
| 64 | Island WI 144 | Tom, Dick And Harry/We Two, Happy People | 20 |
| 64 | Island WI 152 | Yeah Yeah Baby/BABA BROOKS: Boat Ride | 25 |
| 64 | Island WI 160 | Miss B/Thing Come To Those Who Wait | 20 |
| 65 | Black Swan WI 462 | Hey Little Girl/CORNELL CAMBELL: Make Hay | 30 |
| 66 | Rio R 81 | Give Me One More Chance/Fire In Cornfield | 18 |
| 66 | Doctor Bird DB 1050 | Give Me The Right/Tonight | 30 |
| 67 | Doctor Bird DB 1084 | Tell It To Me/Your Photograph | 40 |
| 67 | Doctor Bird DB 1087 | Down The Trainlines/Sing And Pray | 40 |
| 69 | Escort ES 807 | My Love/SWEET CONFUSION: Windsor Castle | 25 |
| 69 | Escort ES 811 | Why Did You/Do You Remember | 8 |

*(see also Stranger Cole, Patsy)*

## STRANGERS (WITH MIKE SHANNON)
| | | | |
|---|---|---|---|
| 64 | Philips BF 1335 | One And One Is Two/Time And The River (as Strangers with Mike Shannon) | 40 |
| 64 | Philips BF 1378 | Do You Or Don't You/What Can I Do | 8 |

*(see also Shadows)*

## STRANGERS
| | | | |
|---|---|---|---|
| 67 | Pye 7N 17240 | Look Out (Here Comes Tomorrow)/Mary Mary | 40 |
| 67 | Pye 7N 17351 | You Didn't Have To Be So Nice/Daytime Turns To Night | 15 |
| 68 | Pye 7N 17585 | I'm On An Island/Step Inside | 20 |

## STRANGER THAN FICTION
| | | | |
|---|---|---|---|
| 79 | Ellie Jay EJSP 9301 | Into The Void/Darkness (p/s) | 25 |
| 87 | Constitution CON 3T | Prelude/Is She In Love With Love/The Realization (12", p/s) | 25 |

## STRANGE STONE
| | | | |
|---|---|---|---|
| 77 | Own label DER 1399 | STRANGE STONE (LP, private pressing, numbered sleeve with insert, 255 only) | 400 |

## STRANGE U
| | | | |
|---|---|---|---|
| 13 | Eglo EGLP 025 | SCARLET JUNGLE EP | 40 |
| 14 | White Label STRANGEU 01 | EP 2040 (EP) | 35 |
| 14 | Y n R YNR 062 | Dolph Lundgren/Instrumental (gig-only 7" with JEHST) | 50 |
| 14 | Y n R YNR 062RDS | Dolph Lundgren/Instrumental (picture disc) | 10 |

## STRANGEWAYS
| | | | |
|---|---|---|---|
| 78 | Real ARE 2 | Show Her you Care/You're On Your Own (p/s) | 20 |
| 79 | Real ARE 7 | Wasting Time/All The Sounds Of Fear (p/s) | 30 |

## STRANGLERS
### SINGLES
| | | | |
|---|---|---|---|
| 77 | United Artists UP 36211 | (Get A) Grip (On Yourself)/London Lady (card p/s) | 8 |
| 77 | United Artists UP 36248 | Peaches/Go Buddy Go ('group' p/s with 'blackmail' lettering, withdrawn) | 700 |
| 77 | United Artists UP 36248 | Peaches/Go Buddy Go ('peach' p/s) | 7 |
| 77 | United Artists UP 36277 | Something Better Change/Straighten Out (p/s) | 5 |

| | | | |
|---|---|---|---|
| 77 | United Artists UP 36300 | No More Heroes/In The Shadows (p/s, 'wreath' label) | 6 |
| 80 | United Artists 12-BP 344 | Bear Cage (Extended)/Shah Shah A Go Go (Extended) (12", p/s) | 10 |
| 82 | Epic EPCA A-2893 | The European Female/Savage Breast (p/s) | 5 |
| 84 | Epic A 4738 | Skin Deep/Here And There ('skin-feel' p/s, with 'Skin Deep' tattoo, 10,000 only) | 6 |
| 84 | Epic EPC GA 4921 | No Mercy/In One Door/Hot Club (Riot Mix)/Head On The Line (gatefold) | 6 |
| 86 | Epic SOLAR D1 | Always The Sun/Norman Normal//Nice In Nice/Since You Went Away (double pack, shrinker & stickered) | 8 |
| 86 | Epic HUGE D1 | Big In America/Dry Day//Always The Sun/Norman Normal (double pack, shrinkwrapped & stickered) | 8 |
| 88 | Epic VICE 1 | All Day And All Of The Night/¡Viva Vlad! ('Monica Coughlan' p/s, withdrawn sold via fan club) | 12 |
| 89 | Liberty EMR 84 | Grip '89 - (Get A) Grip (On Yourself)/Waltzinblack (p/s, red vinyl with poster in gatefold PVC wallet, 5,000 only) | 5 |
| 14 | Parophone RSD14TS | Peaches/Go Buddy Go (reissue, 'group' p/s with 'blackmail' lettering, green vinyl) | 10 |
| 90 | Epic TEARS T1 | 96 Tears/Instead Of This/Poisonality (12" p/s with 'paint set') | 15 |

## ALBUMS : LPS

| | | | |
|---|---|---|---|
| 77 | United Artists UAG 30200 | NO MORE HEROES (LP, inner) | 15 |
| 77 | United Artists UAG 30045 | STRANGLERS IV - RATTUS NORVEGICUS (LP, 10,000 with 7" Choosey Susie/"Peasant In The Big Shitty" (Live At The Nashville, 12/76) [FREE 3, orange p/s,"What Do You Expect..." in run-off groove], some with sticker) | 40 |
| 78 | United Artists UAK 30222 | BLACK AND WHITE (LP, 75,000 with white vinyl 7" "Walk On By"/"Tits"/Mean To Me [FREE 9, black die-cut sleeve & card insert], mispressed on blue or beige vinyl) | 65 |
| 78 | United Artists UAK 30222 | BLACK AND WHITE (LP, 75,000 with white vinyl 7" "Walk On By"/"Tits"/Mean To Me [FREE 9, black die-cut sleeve & card insert]) | 18 |
| 79 | United Artists UAG 30262 | THE RAVEN (LP, 20,000 with 3-D cover, cartoon on inner sleeve) | 20 |
| 82 | Liberty LBG 30353 | THE COLLECTION '77-82 (LP, withdrawn plastic logo sleeve) | 25 |
| 86 | Epic EPC 26648 | DREAMTIME (LP, picture disc) | 12 |
| 92 | United Artists SPEAKDLP 101 | EARLY YEARS 74-75-76 RARE LIVE & UNRELEASED (2-LP, orange/green vinyl) | 25 |

## PROMOS : FREEBIES, PROMOS & MISCELLANEA

| | | | |
|---|---|---|---|
| 79 | United Artists PB 308 | Duchess/Fools Rush Out (A label demo) | 10 |
| 79 | United Artists PB 318 | Nuclear Device (The Wizard Of Aus)/Yellowcake UF 6 (A label demo) | 10 |
| 79 | United Artists UP 36379 | Nice N Sleazy/Shut Up (A label demo) | 12 |
| 79 | United Artists UAG 30262 | THE RAVEN (LP, mispressing, 2nd side plays country & western [B-side matrix: UAK 30263]) | 25 |
| 82 | Liberty LBG 30353 | THE COLLECTION '77-82 (LP, Stranglers' own concept sleeve, unissued) | 0 |
| 75 | (no cat no) | My Young Dreams/Wasted (existence unconfirmed) | 150 |
| 77 | United Artists FREE 4 | Peaches (radio version)/Go Buddy Go (promo only, p/s) | 750 |
| 77 | United Artists FREE 4 | Peaches (radio version)/Go Buddy Go (promo only, no p/s) | 150 |
| 77 | United Artists UP 36262 | Mony Mony/Mean To Me (p/s, as Celia And The Mutations) | 7 |
| 77 | United Artists UP 36277 | Something Better Change/Straighten Out | 25 |
| 77 | United Artists FREE 8 | No More Heroes (1-sided radio edit, promo only) | 150 |
| 77 | United Artists UP 36300 | No More Heroes (1-sided, misprinted "No More Stheroes") | 25 |
| 77 | United Artists UP 36300 | No More Heroes/In The Shadows (p/s, stamped, misprinted "No More Stheroes") | 25 |
| 78 | United Artists UP 36429 | Walk On By (Promo Edit)/Old Codger/Tank | 25 |
| 79 | United Artists UA STR 1 DJ | Don't Bring Harry/HUGH CORNWELL: Wired (45rpm, promo only) | 25 |
| 79 | United Artists (no cat. no.) | Two Sunspots (unreleased) | 30 |
| 80 | Stranglers Info Service SIS 001 | Tomorrow Was The Hereafter/Bring On The Nubiles (Cocktail Version) (numbered p/s, label has "Nublies") | 15 |
| 82 | SIS/Liberty FREE 3 | Peasant In The Big Shitty (Live At The Nashville, 12/76)/Choosey Susie (fan club reissue, black p/s, with "Ello 'Elen" in run-off groove) | 5 |
| 82 | Epic EPC A2893 | The European Female (In Celebration Of)/(Promo Edit) | 10 |
| 82 | Liberty BP 410 | La Folie (Promo Edit)/Waltzinblack | 10 |
| 82 | SIS/Liberty UP 36350 | 5 Minutes/Rok It To The Moon (reissue) | 5 |
| 82 | SIS/Liberty UP 36429 | Walk On By/Old Codger/Tank (reissue, 33rpm) | 5 |
| 82 | SIS/Liberty FREE 18 | Mony Mony/Mean To Me (reissue, as Celia & the Mutations) | 5 |
| 77 | United Artists UP 36211 | (Get A) Grip (On Yourself)/London Lady (double A label demo) | 25 |
| 78 | United Artists UP 36350 | 5 Minutes/Rok It To Me Moon (A label demo) | 15 |
| 78 | United Artists UP 36248 | Peaches/Go Buddy Go (p/s, mispressing, B-side plays Buzzcocks' "Oh Shit") | 75 |
| 78 | United Artists FREE 9 | Walk On By/Mean To Me/Tits (EP [free with LP U.A. UAK 30222], mispressing, black die-cut sleeve & card insert, blue/clear vinyl) | 30 |
| 78 | United Artists FREE 9 | Walk On By/Mean To Me/Tits (EP [free with LP U.A. UAK 30222], mispressing, black die-cut sleeve & card insert, pink/clear vinyl) | 15 |
| 78 | United Artists UP 36379 | Nice 'N' Sleazy/Shut Up (p/s, mispressing, B-side plays tracks by other artist) | 30 |
| 81 | Liberty BP 393 | Just Like Nothing On Earth/Maninwhite (p/s, mispressing, plays A-side both sides) | 20 |
| 82 | United Artists BP 407 | Golden Brown/Love 30 (B-side plays "Everybody Salsa") | 20 |

## STRAPS

| | | | |
|---|---|---|---|
| 80 | Donut DONUT 1 | Just Can't Take Anymore/New Age (p/s) | 8 |
| 82 | Donut DONUT 3 | Brixton/No Liquor (p/s) | 12 |
| 83 | Cyclops CYC 2 | THE STRAPS ALBUM (LP) | 15 |

*(see also Public Image Ltd.)*

## STRATEGY

| | | | |
|---|---|---|---|
| 82 | Ebony EBON 7 | Technical Overflow/Astral Planes (in p/s) | 60 |
| 82 | Ebony EBON 7 | Technical Overflow/Astral Planes | 50 |

## STRATE JACKET

| | | | |
|---|---|---|---|
| 80 | Wessex WEX 269 | You're A Hit/Too Soon Too Young (stamped plain sleeve) | 15 |

## STRATUS

| | | | |
|---|---|---|---|
| 85 | Steel Trax STEEL 31001 | THROWING SHAPES (LP) | 18 |

*(see also Grand Prix, Uriah Heep, Iron Maiden, Praying Mantis)*

## STRAWBERRY ALARM CLOCK

| | | | |
|---|---|---|---|
| 67 | Pye International 7N 25436 | Incense And Peppermints/The Birdman Of Alkatrash | 30 |
| 68 | Pye International 7N 25446 | Tomorrow/Birds In My Tree | 20 |

## STRAWBERRY CHILDREN

| | | | |
|---|---|---|---|
| 68 | Pye International 7N 25456 | Sit With The Guru/Pretty Song From Psych-Out | 20 |
| 69 | MCA MU 1080 | Good Morning Starshine/Me And The Township | 10 |
| 68 | NPL 28106 | INCENSE AND PEPPERMINTS (LP, mono) | 200 |
| 68 | Pye Intl. NSPL 28106 | INCENSE AND PEPPERMINTS (LP, stereo) | 150 |

## STRAWBERRY CHILDREN
| | | | |
|---|---|---|---|
| 67 | Liberty LBF 15012 | Love Years Coming/One Stands Here | 35 |

*(see also Jim Webb)*

## STRAWBERRY JAM
| | | | |
|---|---|---|---|
| 69 | Pye 7N 17711 | Per-Son-Al-Ly/This Is To A Girl | 10 |

## STRAWBERRY PARK
| | | | |
|---|---|---|---|
| 82 | Sonet 2245 | Summer Is A Coming/Beach Party (in p/s) | 8 |
| 82 | Sonet 2245 | Summer Is A Coming/Beach Party | 7 |

## STRAWBERRY SMELL
| | | | |
|---|---|---|---|
| 97 | Detour DR 053 | Penelope Bloomington/Kangeroo In My Garden (p/s, blue vinyl, 100 only) | 6 |

## STRAWBERRY SWITCHBLADE
| | | | |
|---|---|---|---|
| 85 | Korova KODE 11 | STRAWBERRY SWITCHBLADE (LP, with bonus 7" "Trees And Flowers", mispressed with some tracks playing twice & others out of order) | 15 |

*(see also Poems, Rose McDowall)*

## STRAWBS
| | | | |
|---|---|---|---|
| 68 | A&M AMS 725 | Oh How She Changed/Or Am I Dreaming | 30 |
| 68 | A&M AMS 738 | The Man Who Called Himself Jesus/Poor Jimmy Wilson | 8 |
| 70 | A&M AMS 791 | Forever/Another Day | 10 |
| 71 | A&M AMS 837 | Witchwood/Keep The Devil Outside/We'll Meet Again Sometime (live) (withdrawn) | 30 |
| 71 | A&M AMS 874 | Benedictus/Keep The Devil Outside | 6 |
| 73 | A&M AMS 7047 | Part Of The Union/Will You Go (p/s) | 5 |
| 69 | private pressing | STRAWBERRY MUSIC SAMPLER NO. 1 (LP, publisher's sampler, 100 only) | 500 |
| 69 | A&M AMLS 936 | STRAWBS (LP; disc inserted in middle of sleeve) | 35 |
| 69 | A&M AMLS 936 | STRAWBS (LP; disc inserted at edge of sleeve) | 20 |
| 70 | A&M AMLS 970 | DRAGONFLY (LP, textured sleeve, lyric insert, mustard label) | 30 |
| 70 | A&M AMLS 994 | JUST A COLLECTION OF ANTIQUES AND CURIOS (LP, laminated gatefold sleeve, mustard label; 2 different rear sleeves) | 15 |
| 71 | A&M AMLH 64304 | FROM THE WITCHWOOD (LP, gatefold sleeve) | 15 |
| 72 | A&M AMLH 68078 | GRAVE NEW WORLD (LP, triple gatefold sleeve, with 12-page booklet) | 15 |
| 73 | Hallmark SHM 813 | ALL OUR OWN WORK (LP, with Sandy Denny) | 15 |
| 74 | A&M AMLH 63607 | HERO AND HEROINE (LP, inner) | 15 |
| 74 | A&M AMLH 68277 | GHOSTS (LP, inner) | 15 |

*(see also Dave Cousins, Sandy Denny, Fire, Foggy, Monks, Davey & Morris, Hudson-Ford, Yes, Rick Wakeman)*

## STRAW DOGS
| | | | |
|---|---|---|---|
| 81 | (No label) DOG 001 | Black Leather/Don't Need You/We Ain't Dead (Yet)/All The Lads (some with xeroxed sleeve) | 80 |

## STRAY
| | | | |
|---|---|---|---|
| 70 | Transatlantic PROMO 1 | Only What You Make It/Time Machine | 50 |
| 72 | Big T BIG 141 | Our Song/Mama's Coming Home | 8 |
| 73 | Transatlantic BIG 12 | Hallelujah/Brand New Day | 7 |
| 70 | Transatlantic TRA 216 | STRAY (LP, die-cut gatefold sleeve, white/lilac 't' logo label) | 50 |
| 71 | Transatlantic TRA 233 | SUICIDE (LP, textured sleeve, white/lilac 't' logo label) | 40 |
| 71 | Transatlantic TRA 248 | SATURDAY MORNING PICTURES (LP, gatefold sleeve) | 25 |
| 73 | Transatlantic TRA 268 | MUDANZAS (LP, gatefold sleeve) | 25 |
| 75 | Dawn DNLS 3066 | STAND UP AND BE COUNTED (LP, lyric insert, pink 'sun' label) | 15 |

## STRAY DOG
| | | | |
|---|---|---|---|
| 73 | Manticore K13502 | Speak Of The Devil/A Letter | 5 |
| 74 | Manticore K 13508 | Junkyard Angel/World Winds | 6 |
| 73 | Manticore K 43506 | STRAY DOG (LP, textured sleeve, insert) | 20 |
| 74 | Manticore K 53504 | WHILE YOU'RE DOWN THERE (LP) | 20 |

*(see also Emerson Lake & Palmer)*

## STREAK
| | | | |
|---|---|---|---|
| 72 | A&M AME 602 | Gonna Have A Good Time/Be Your Ryder/Hard Times (In New York City) (promo, b side plays at 33 rpm) | 40 |
| 72 | A&M AMS 7012 | Gonna Have A Good Time/Be Your Ryder | 15 |
| 73 | Deram DM 376 | Bang Bang Bullet/Black Jack Man | 15 |

## STREAKERS
| | | | |
|---|---|---|---|
| 74 | Dawn DNS 1066 | Turn Me Down/Wake Up Sunshine | 15 |

## STREET
| | | | |
|---|---|---|---|
| 69 | London HLU 10275 | Apollo... Amen/Why Concern Yourself | 5 |

## STREET BIZARRE
| | | | |
|---|---|---|---|
| 79 | Monarch MON 05 | Normal Life/Nervous Exhaustion | 150 |

## DANNY STREET
| | | | |
|---|---|---|---|
| 63 | Phillips BF 1250 | Only Love Can Break A Heart/ Cold Cold Winter | 5 |
| 64 | Philips BF 1309 | The Eyes Of The Young Ones/Someone As Wonderful As You | 5 |
| 65 | Philips BF 1387 | Don't Go To Him/As It's Meant To Be | 5 |
| 60s | Domino DO 114 | Melanie/Birds An' Bees An' Things | 5 |
| 71 | London HLU 10342 | My Little Guy/You Blew It | 5 |

## GARY STREET & FAIRWAYS
| | | | |
|---|---|---|---|
| 68 | Domain D 2 | Flipperty Flop/Hold Me Closer | 20 |

*(see also Fairways)*

## JOHN STREET & INMATES OF NO. 12
| | | | |
|---|---|---|---|
| 67 | Deram DM 147 | Keep A Little Love/My Kind Of Luck | 10 |

## RUSTY NAIL
| | | |
|---|---|---|
| 60s | Hi-Fi MEP 3093 | RUSTY NAIL (EP, in p/s)................................................................................100 |
| 60s | Hi-Fi MEP 3093 | RUSTY NAIL (EP, no p/s)................................................................................40 |

## RUTH
| | | |
|---|---|---|
| 67 | Columbia DB 8218 | Leaf In The Wind/Society's Child ...............................................................7 |
| 68 | Columbia DB 8386 | Cherish/Until It's Time For You To Go ........................................................7 |

## RUTH & BEAUTY
| | | |
|---|---|---|
| 72 | Montagu MONT 3000 | 29 Days To Doomsday/Cutting The Traces...............................................18 |

## RUTHLESS RAP ASSASINS
| | | |
|---|---|---|
| 87 | White (Murdertone) AMC001 | We Don't Care/Kiss AMC (12", 500 pressed)............................................30 |

## RUTLES
| | | |
|---|---|---|
| 78 | Warner Bros K 17125 | I Must Be In Love/Cheese And Onions/With A Girl Like You (p/s) ..............5 |
| 78 | Warner Bros K 17180 | Let's Be Natural/Piggy In The Middle..........................................................6 |
| 78 | Warner Bros WB K56459 | THE RUTLES (LP, gatefold, booklet and inner sleeve)...........................20 |
| 96 | Virgin VUSLP 119 | ARCHAEOLOGY (LP, inner) .......................................................................20 |

*(see also Dirk & Stig, Neil Innes, Monty Python, Beach Boys, Patto)*

## RUTS (D.C.)
| | | |
|---|---|---|
| 79 | People Unite SJP 795 | In A Rut/H-Eyes (1,000 only, black-ringed label) .................................70 |
| 79 | People Unite RUT 1 | In A Rut/H-Eyes (repressing)......................................................................8 |
| 79 | Virgin VS 271 | Babylon's Burning/Society (p/s) .................................................................8 |
| 79 | Virgin VS 298 | Jah War/I Ain't Sofisticated (p/s) ...............................................................5 |
| 79 | Virgin VS 285 | Something That I Said/Give Youth A Chance (p/s).......................................5 |
| 80 | RSO RSO 71 | Babylon's Burning/XTC: Take This Town (p/s) ............................................5 |
| 80 | Virgin VS 327 | Staring At The Rude Boys/Love In Vain ......................................................5 |
| 81 | Virgin VS 396 | Different View/Formula Eyes (p/s, as Ruts D.C.) ........................................5 |
| 82 | Bohemian BO 2 | Whatever We Do/Push Yourself - Make It Work (p/s, as Ruts D.C.) ..........5 |
| 83 | Bohemian BO 3 | Weak Heart/Militant (white label, with paper insert; as Ruts D.C., promo only) ...........15 |
| 83 | Bohemian BO 4 | Stepping Bondage/Lobotomy/Rich Bitch (p/s) .......................................15 |
| 86 | Strange Fruit SFPS 011 | PEEL SESSIONS (12" EP) .........................................................................12 |
| 82 | Bohemian BOLP 4 | RHYTHM COLLISION (LP) ........................................................................22 |
| 79 | Virgin V 2132 | THE CRACK (LP, stickered sleeve with "Pay no more than £3.99") .......15 |

*(see also Laurel Aitken, Typhoons, Pete Zear)*

## RU12
| | | |
|---|---|---|
| 78 | SRTS/78/CUS 131 | SHE'S GONE EP (no p/s, 500 only)............................................................100 |

## BARRY RYAN (& MAJORITY)
| | | |
|---|---|---|
| 68 | MGM MGM 1423 | Goodbye/I'm So Sad.................................................................................10 |
| 68 | MGM MGM 1442 | Eloise/Love I Almost Found You (as Barry Ryan & Majority).....................8 |
| 68 | MGM MGM 1464 | Love Is Love/I'll Be On My Way Dear ..........................................................5 |
| 69 | Polydor 56348 | The Hunt/No Living Without Her.................................................................8 |
| 70 | Polydor 56370 | Magical Spiel/Caroline...............................................................................8 |
| 70 | Polydor 2001 035 | Kitsch/Give Me A Sign................................................................................8 |
| 71 | Polydor 2001 154 | It Is Written/Annabella...............................................................................8 |
| 71 | Poyldor 2001 256 | Can't Let You Go/When I Was A Child (as Barry Ryan)................................7 |
| 72 | Polydor 2001 335 | From My Head To My Toes/Alimony Money Blues.......................................7 |
| 72 | Polydor 2001 362 | I'm Sorry Susan/L.A. Woman.......................................................................7 |
| 75 | Dawn DNS 1109 | Do That/The Summers Over ....................................................................12 |
| 76 | Private Stock PVT 70 | Where Were You/Making A Do ...................................................................7 |
| 77 | Private Stock PVT 87 | Brother/Life's So Easy ................................................................................7 |
| 69 | MGM MGM-C(S) 8106 | SINGS PAUL RYAN (LP) .............................................................................20 |
| 69 | Polydor 583 067 | BARRY RYAN (LP) .....................................................................................20 |

*(see also Paul & Barry Ryan)*

## CATHY RYAN
| | | |
|---|---|---|
| 53 | MGM SP 1051 | Show Me The Way To Go Home/If I Had You ..............................................7 |

*(see also Art Mooney)*

## KRIS RYAN (& QUESTIONS)
| | | |
|---|---|---|
| 64 | Mercury MF 818 | Miss Ann/She Told Me Lies (as Kris Ryan & Questions) ..........................10 |
| 64 | Mercury MF 832 | Don't Play That Song/If You Don't Come Back ........................................10 |
| 64 | Mercury MF 852 | Marie Marie/I've Had Enough Of You Baby..............................................10 |
| 65 | Mercury MF 877 | Tell Me How/She Belongs To Me ..............................................................10 |
| 65 | Mercury 10024 MCE | ON THE RIGHT TRACK (EP, as Kris Ryan & Questions).............................40 |

## MARION RYAN
| | | |
|---|---|---|
| 58 | Pye NIXA 7N 15121 | Love Me Forever/Make The Man Love Me ..................................................5 |
| 58 | Pye NIXA 7N 15130 | Always And Forever/Oh Oh I'm Falling In Love Again..................................5 |
| 58 | Pye NIXA 7N 15138 | Stairway Of Love/I Need You......................................................................5 |
| 58 | Pye 7NSR 15157 | The World Goes Around And Around/Please Don't Say Goodnight (stereo) .............6 |
| 59 | Pye NIXA 7N 15184 | Wait For Me (Ti Piro)/Jeepers Creepers ....................................................5 |
| 59 | Pye 7N 15200 | Jo-Jo The Dog Faced Boy/Doin' What Comes Naturally .............................5 |
| 60 | Columbia DB 4448 | Sixteen Reasons/Mangos ...........................................................................5 |
| 60 | Columbia DB 4550 | Somebody/It's You That I Love ...................................................................6 |
| 68 | Philips BF 1721 | Better Use Your Head/The Seasons Change ............................................15 |
| 57 | Pye Nixa NEP 24041 | THAT RYAN GIRL! (EP).............................................................................20 |
| 58 | Pye NEP 24079 | MARION RYAN HIT PARADE (EP) .............................................................20 |
| 59 | Pye NPL 18030 | A LADY LOVES! (LP, mono) ......................................................................25 |
| 59 | Pye NSPL 18030 | A LADY LOVES! (LP, stereo) .....................................................................30 |

*(see also Ray Ellington, Gary Miller)*

## PAT RYAN
| | | |
|---|---|---|
| 77 | Folk Heritage FHR 094 | LEABOY'S LASSIE (LP)..............................................................................25 |

MINT VALUE £

## PAUL RYAN
| | | | |
|---|---|---|---|
| 72 | Maple Annie MA 104 | Born On A Beautiful Day/Come With Me | 6 |
| 72 | Maple Annie MA 107 | Natural Gas/Hellow Hellow | 6 |

## PAUL & BARRY RYAN
| | | | |
|---|---|---|---|
| 65 | Decca F 12260 | Don't Bring Me Your Heartaches/To Remind You Of My Love | 6 |
| 66 | Decca F 12319 | Have Pity On The Boy/There You Go | 6 |
| 66 | Decca F 12391 | I Love Her/gotta Go Out To Work | 6 |
| 66 | Decca F 12445 | I Love How You Love Me/Baby I'm Sorry | 6 |
| 66 | Decca F 12494 | Have You Ever Loved Somebody?/I'll Tell You Later | 6 |
| 66 | Decca F 12520 | Missy, Missy/Rainbow Weather | 6 |
| 67 | Decca F 12567 | Keep It Out Of Sight/Who Told You? | 6 |
| 67 | Decca F 12633 | Claire/I'll Make It Worth Your While | 12 |
| 67 | MGM 1354 | Heartbreaker/Night Time | 8 |
| 68 | MGM 1385 | Pictures Of Today/Madrigal | 8 |
| 73 | Polydor 2001488 | Won't You Join Me/Glad To Know You | 10 |
| 74 | Polydor 2001511 | Carry The Blues/Reincarnation Games | 6 |
| 67 | Decca LK 4878 | THE RYANS - TWO OF A KIND (LP) | 30 |
| 68 | MGM MGM-C(S) 8081 | PAUL AND BARRY RYAN (LP) | 20 |

*(see also Barry Ryan)*

## PETE RYAN BAND
| | | | |
|---|---|---|---|
| 82 | Ebony EBON 4 | Dolly Parton's Tits/Eva On My Mind | 40 |

## PHIL RYAN & CRESCENTS
| | | | |
|---|---|---|---|
| 64 | Columbia DB 7406 | Mary Don't You Weep/Yes I Will | 8 |
| 65 | Columbia DB 7574 | Gypsy Woman/Be Honest With Yourself | 20 |

## LLOYD RYANS EXPRESS
| | | | |
|---|---|---|---|
| 77 | Playback PBR 7003 | Let There Be Drums/Listen To The Drummer | 6 |
| 77 | PVK SPVK 003 | Hammer Head/Leo | 6 |

## BOBBY RYDELL
| | | | |
|---|---|---|---|
| 59 | Top Rank JAR 181 | Kissin' Time/You'll Never Tame Me | 10 |
| 59 | Top Rank JAR 181 | Kissin' Time/You'll Never Tame Me (78) | 25 |
| 59 | Top Rank JAR 227 | We Got Love/I Dig Girls | 10 |
| 60 | Columbia DB 4429 | Wild One/Little Bitty Girl | 6 |
| 60 | Columbia DB 4471 | Swingin' School/Ding-A-Ling | 6 |
| 60 | Columbia DB 4495 | Volare/I'd Do It Again | 6 |
| 60 | Columbia DB 4545 | Sway/Groovy Tonight | 6 |
| 61 | Columbia DB 4600 | Good Time Baby/Cherie | 6 |
| 61 | Columbia DB 4651 | Don't Be Afraid/That Old Black Magic | 6 |
| 61 | Columbia DB 4690 | The Fish/The Third House | 6 |
| 61 | Columbia DB 4731 | I Wanna Thank You/The Door To Paradise | 6 |
| 62 | Columbia DB 4785 | I've Got Bonnie/Lose Her | 6 |
| 62 | Columbia DB 4858 | I'll Never Dance Again/Gee, It's Wonderful | 6 |
| 63 | Cameo Parkway C 108 | Forget Him/Hey Ev'rybody (in p/s) | 15 |
| 63 | Cameo Parkway C 108 | Forget Him/Hey Ev'rybody | 7 |
| 63 | Cameo Parkway C 129 | It's Time We Parted/Too Much too Soon | 5 |
| 63 | Cameo Parkway C 228 | The Cha Cha Cha/The Best Man Cried | 5 |
| 63 | Cameo Parkway C 242 | Butterfly Baby/Love Is Blind | 5 |
| 64 | Cameo Parkway C 309 | Make Me Forget/Darling Jenny | 5 |
| 65 | Capitol CL 1537 | I Can't Say Goodbye/Two Is The Loneliest Number | 6 |
| 60 | Top Rank JKP 2059 | LOVINGEST (EP) | 15 |
| 63 | Cameo Parkway CPE 551 | SWAY WITH BOBBY RYDELL (EP) | 15 |
| 63 | Cameo Parkway CPE 553 | BOBBY RYDELL (EP) | 15 |
| 63 | Summit LSE 2036 | BEST OF BOBBY RYDELL (EP) | 10 |
| 60 | Columbia 33SX 1243 | WILD ONE (LP) | 40 |
| 61 | Columbia 33SX 1308 | SINGS AND SWINGS (LP) | 20 |
| 61 | Columbia 33SX 1352 | SALUTES "THE GREAT ONES" (LP) | 20 |
| 62 | Columbia 33SX 1425 | RYDELL AT THE COPA (LP) | 25 |
| 62 | Cameo Parkway C 1019 | ALL THE HITS (LP) | 15 |
| 63 | Cameo Parkway C 1040 | ALL THE HITS VOL. 2 (LP) | 15 |
| 63 | Cameo Parkway C 1055 | WILD (WOOD) DAYS (LP) | 15 |
| 65 | Capitol T 2281 | SOMEBODY LOVES YOU (LP) | 20 |

## RYDER
| | | | |
|---|---|---|---|
| 74 | Fly BUG 39 | Ain't That Nice/Sugar Mama | 10 |

## FREDDIE RYDER
| | | | |
|---|---|---|---|
| 65 | Mercury MF 864 | To Get Your Love Back/A Little Thing Called Love | 6 |
| 65 | Mercury MF 879 | Some Kind Of Wonderful/Slow Down | 12 |
| 65 | Mercury MF 935 | Man Of The Moment/My Block | 10 |
| 68 | Columbia DB 8335 | Shadows (I Can't See You)/Airport | 6 |
| 68 | Columbia DB 8427 | Worst That Could Happen/World Of My Own | 6 |

*(see also Freddie Self, Trends)*

## MAL RYDER (& SPIRITS)
| | | | |
|---|---|---|---|
| 63 | Decca F 11669 | Cry Baby/Take Over (as Mal Ryder & Spirits) | 20 |
| 64 | Vocalion V 9219 | See The Funny Little Clown/Slow Down | 70 |
| 64 | Piccadilly 7N 35209 | Your Friend/Forget It (as Mal Ryder & Spirits) | 40 |
| 65 | Piccadilly 7N 35234 | Lonely Room/Tell Your Friend | 22 |

*(see also Mal & Primitives)*

## MITCH RYDER (& DETROIT WHEELS)
| | | | |
|---|---|---|---|
| 66 | Stateside SS 481 | Jenny Take A Ride/Baby Jane | 20 |
| 66 | Stateside SS 498 | Little Latin Lupe Lu/I Hope | 20 |

**JUDY STREET**
| | | | |
|---|---|---|---|
| 78 | Grapevine GRP 106 | What/You Turn Me On | 5 |
| 78 | Grapevine GRP 106 | What/You Turn Me On (DJ Copy) | 10 |

**STREET LEGAL**
| | | | |
|---|---|---|---|
| 84 | Weird Brothers SLW 1 | Rollin' On/Mississippi Moonshine (p/s, initially with sticker over typo error in sleeve) | 150 |
| 84 | Weird Brothers SLW 1 | Rollin' On/Mississippi Moonshine (p/s, without sticker) | 150 |

**STREETFIGHTER**
| | | | |
|---|---|---|---|
| 82 | J.R. JR 7049S | CRAZY DREAM (EP) | 40 |

**STREETFIGHTER (U.K.)**
| | | | |
|---|---|---|---|
| 81 | Streetfighter 749 | STREETFIGHTER (12" EP) | 25 |

**STREET PEOPLE (1)**
| | | | |
|---|---|---|---|
| 70 | Stateside SS 2163 | Jennifer Tomkins/All Night Long | 10 |

**STREET PEOPLE (2)**
| | | | |
|---|---|---|---|
| 79 | Ellie Jay Special Pressing EJSP 9276 | PERSONAL VALUES EP (500 only, p/s) | 75 |

**STREETS**
| | | | |
|---|---|---|---|
| 02 | Locked On 679003TLP | ORIGINAL PIRATE MATERIAL (2-LP) | 20 |
| 04 | 679 679LD70LP | A GRAND DON'T COME FOR FREE (2-LP) | 25 |

**STREET SERVICE**
| | | | |
|---|---|---|---|
| 90 | I Like It ILIT 01 | JUST FOR YOU (LP) | 18 |

**STREETWALKERS**
| | | | |
|---|---|---|---|
| 76 | Vertigo 9102 010 | RED CARD (LP, red vinyl with inner sleeve, numbered, 'spaceship' label) | 15 |

*(see also Hummingbird, Nicko McBrain)*

**TEXAS' BILL STRENGTH**
| | | | |
|---|---|---|---|
| 55 | Capitol CL 14357 | Cry, Cry, Cry/The Yellow Rose Of Texas | 8 |

**STRESS (2)**
| | | | |
|---|---|---|---|
| 91 | Eternal YZ 550 | Flowers In The Rain/Flowers In The Rain (p/s) | 6 |
| 85 | Adventures In Reality ARR 14 | THE BIG WHEEL (LP, with insert) | 40 |

**STRETCH**
| | | | |
|---|---|---|---|
| 75 | Anchor ANCL 2014 | ELASTIQUE (LP) | 15 |
| 76 | Anchor ANCL 2016 | YOU CAN'T BEAT YOUR BRAIN FOR ENTERTAINMENT (LP) | 15 |
| 77 | Anchor ANCL 2023 | LIFE BLOOD (LP) | 15 |
| 78 | Hot Wax HW 1 | FORGET THE PAST (LP) | 30 |

*(see also Elmer Gantry, Kirby, Status Quo, Clifford Davis, Legs, Curved Air)*

**STRETCHEADS**
| | | | |
|---|---|---|---|
| 88 | Moksha SOMALP2 | FIVE FINGERS FOUR (LP) | 20 |

**DAVID STRETTON**
| | | | |
|---|---|---|---|
| 68 | Plum PL 4 | Windmills/Haunted Staircase | 20 |

**WILLIAM R. STRICKLAND**
| | | | |
|---|---|---|---|
| 69 | Deram DML/SML 1041 | WILLIAM R. STRICKLAND IS ONLY THE NAME (LP) | 20 |

**STRIDER**
| | | | |
|---|---|---|---|
| 73 | GM GMS 002 | Higher And Higher/Ain't Got No Love | 5 |
| 74 | GM GMS 023 | Seems So Easy/Arthur Hydrogen | 5 |
| 73 | GM GML 1002 | EXPOSED (LP, gatefold sleeve) | 15 |
| 74 | GM GML 1012 | MISUNDERSTOOD (LP) | 15 |

*(see also Samson)*

**STRIFE**
| | | | |
|---|---|---|---|
| 77 | Outlaw OUT 1 | School/Go/Feel So Good (p/s) | 10 |
| 75 | Chrysalis 1063 | RUSH (LP) | 15 |
| 78 | Gull GULP 1029 | BACK TO THUNDER (LP, on green vinyl with poster) | 18 |

**STRIKE**
| | | | |
|---|---|---|---|
| 80 | Shock SRS 504 | Teenage Rebel/Radio Songs (p/s, Irish issue but imported into U.K.) | 70 |

**LIZA STRIKE**
| | | | |
|---|---|---|---|
| 68 | Parlophone R 5725 | All's Quiet On West 23rd/Mr Daddy-Man | 15 |

*(see also Liza & Jet Set, Soulmates, Vice Versa)*

**STRIKER BLUE**
| | | | |
|---|---|---|---|
| 76 | Bootlegger 596 | Get On Down/Loyalty To The Board | 75 |

**STRIKERS & CHILDREN OF SELSTON BAGTHORPE PRIMARY SCHOOL CHOIR**
| | | | |
|---|---|---|---|
| 78 | Eagle EGL 003 | Good Old Charlie/Forest Fire | 8 |

**STRING-A-LONGS**
| | | | |
|---|---|---|---|
| 61 | London HLU 9452 | Scottie/Ming Bird | 6 |
| 62 | London HLD 9535 | Sunday/Twistwatch | 5 |
| 62 | London HLD 9588 | Spinning My Wheels/My Blue Heaven | 5 |
| 63 | London HLD 9652 | Matilda/Replica | 5 |
| 61 | London RE-U 1322 | THE STRING-A-LONGS (EP) | 20 |
| 63 | London RE-D 1350 | THE STRING-A-LONGS (EP) | 20 |
| 63 | London RE-D 1398 | STRINGALONG WITH THE STRING-A-LONGS (EP) | 20 |
| 63 | London HA-D 8054 | THE STRING-A-LONGS (LP, mono) | 40 |
| 63 | London SH-D 8054 | THE STRING-A-LONGS (LP, stereo) | 40 |
| 69 | London HAU/SHU 8371 | WIDE WORLD HITS (LP) | 20 |

**STRING CHEESE**
| | | | |
|---|---|---|---|
| 72 | RCA SF 8222 | STRING CHEESE (LP) | 20 |

**STRING DRIVEN THING**
| | | | |
|---|---|---|---|
| 70 | Concord CON 7 | Another Night/Say What You Like | 15 |
| 72 | Charisma CB 195 | Eddie/Hooked On The Road | 5 |

# STRIPES

| | | | |
|---|---|---|---|
| 70 | Concord CON 1001 | STRING DRIVEN THING (LP) | 275 |
| 72 | Charisma CAS 1062 | STRING DRIVEN THING (LP, gatefold, insert,large 'Mad Hatter' label) | 40 |
| 73 | Charisma CAS 1070 | THE MACHINE THAT CRIED (LP, gatefold sleeve, large 'Mad Hatter' label) | 40 |
| 74 | Charisma CAS 1097 | PLEASE MIND YOUR HEAD (LP, lyric sheet, small 'Mad Hatter' label) | 15 |

## STRIPES
| | | | |
|---|---|---|---|
| 82 | Ellie Jay EJSP 9808/PINK01 | One Step Ahead/Canteen Girls (no p/s) | 100 |

## STRIPES OF GLORY
| | | | |
|---|---|---|---|
| 62 | Vogue V 9194 | The Denial/O' Send The Fire | 18 |

## SYLVIA STRIPLIN
| | | | |
|---|---|---|---|
| 86 | Music Of Love MOLS 8 | Give Me Your Love/Will You Ever Pass This Way Again/Look Towards The Sky (12") | 20 |
| 10 | Universal Sounds US LP 34 | GIVE ME YOUR LOVE (2-LP, reissue) | 30 |

## STROBE
| | | | |
|---|---|---|---|
| 82 | SRR 1 | MANDARIN LADY EP | 10 |

## ARTHUR 2 STROKE
| | | | |
|---|---|---|---|
| 79 | Anti Pop AP 1 | The Wundersea World Of Jacques Cousteau/NOISE TOYS: Pocket Money (p/s) | 7 |

## (THE) STROKES
| | | | |
|---|---|---|---|
| 01 | Rough Trade RTRADES 010 | The Modern Age/Last Nite (with barcode 2000 only) | 25 |
| 01 | Rough Trade RTRADES 023 | Hard To Explain/New York City Cops (p/s, 2000 only) | 8 |
| 01 | Rough Trade RTRADES 041 | Last Nite/When It Started (p/s) | 12 |
| 02 | Rough Trade RTRADES 063 | Someday/Alone Together/Is This It (p/s, yellow vinyl) | 10 |
| 03 | Rough Trade RTRADES 140 | 12.51/The Way It Is (p/s, red vinyl) | 6 |
| 03 | Rough Trade RTRADES 155 | Reptilia/Modern Girls & Old Fashioned Men (p/s) | 7 |
| 05 | Rough Trades RTRADS 205 | The End Has No End/Clampdown (live) (p/s) | 5 |
| 06 | Rough Trade RTRADS 305 | Heart In A Cage/I'll Try Anything Once (p/s) | 6 |
| 06 | Rough Trade RTRADS 312 | You Only Live Twice/Mercy Me (The Ecology) (p/s. sticker) | 7 |
| 01 | Rough Trade RTRADELP 030 | IS THIS IT? (LP, 'STERLING' stamped in run-out groove) | 40 |
| 03 | Rough Trade RTRADELP 130 | ROOM ON FIRE (LP) | 18 |
| 06 | Rough Trade RTRADELP 330 | FIRST IMPRESSIONS OF EARTH (LP) | 15 |

## STROLLERS
| | | | |
|---|---|---|---|
| 58 | Vogue V 9113 | Jumping With Symphony Sid/Swinging Yellow Rose Of Texas | 10 |
| 58 | Vogue V 9124 | Little Bitty Pretty One/Flute Cha-Lypso | 10 |
| 61 | London HLL 9336 | Come On Over/There's No One But You | 40 |

## BARRETT STRONG
| | | | |
|---|---|---|---|
| 60 | London HLU 9088 | Money (That's What I Want)/Oh I Apologise | 80 |
| 73 | Epic S EPC 1778 | Stand Up And Cheer For The Preacher/Instrumental | 10 |
| 76 | Capitol CL 15864 | Man Up In The Sky/Gonna Make It Right | 40 |

## STRUGGLE
| | | | |
|---|---|---|---|
| 80s | Regal RD 013 | No Stronger Love/Bad Boy (12", with ENFORCER) | 20 |

## JOE STRUMMER
| | | | |
|---|---|---|---|
| 89 | Epic STRUM 2 | Island Hopping/15th Brigade (p/s) | 8 |
| 89 | Epic STRUM E2 | Island Hopping/Cholo Vest/Mango Street/Baby O Boogie (12", all tracks on A side, B side etched, die-cut sleeve) | 12 |
| 89 | Epic STRUMG1 | Gangsterville/Jewellers And Bums/Passport To Detroit (gatefold) | 10 |
| 03 | Hellcat 1137-7 | Coma Girl/Yalla Yalla (Live) (with The Mescaleros, picture disc, stickered polythene sleeve) | 10 |
| 03 | Hellcat 1149-7 | Redemption Song/Arms Aloft/Junco Partner (Live) (with the Mescaleros, picture disc,stickered polythene sleeve) | 18 |
| 87 | Virgin V 2497 | WALKER (LP, soundtrack) | 20 |
| 89 | EPIC 465347 | EARTHQUAKE WEATHER (LP, with inner) | 20 |

*(see also The Clash)*

## STRUTT
| | | | |
|---|---|---|---|
| 76 | Brunswick | Time Moves On/Front Row Romeo | 7 |

## STRYDER
| | | | |
|---|---|---|---|
| 80 | Quartz QS 010 | Forcin' Thru'/Settle Down | 50 |

## GLEN STUART
| | | | |
|---|---|---|---|
| 60s | Honey Hit TB 126 | Make Me An Angel/Walking To Heaven (with p/s) | 7 |

## GLEN STUART & CLANSMEN
| | | | |
|---|---|---|---|
| 59 | Pye 7N 15232 | Weepy Willow/Della Darling | 6 |

## KARL STUART & PROFILES
| | | | |
|---|---|---|---|
| 65 | Mercury MF 870 | Love Of My Eyes/Not A Girl In A Million | 5 |
| 65 | Mercury MF 875 | Haven't They Got Better Things To Do/The Touch Of Your Hand | 5 |

*(see also Profile, Voice)*

## SHAWN STUART
| | | | |
|---|---|---|---|
| 74 | Epic SEPC 2496 | It's All Because Of YOu/Wise Old Man | 8 |

## FRANKIE STUBBS
| | | | |
|---|---|---|---|
| 90s | Sounds Of Subterrania S09 | SECOND HAND SUIT (10" EP) | 20 |
| 95 | Rugger Bugger DUMP 025 | UNHINGED (EP) | 15 |

*(see also Leatherface)*

## NAT STUCKEY
| | | | |
|---|---|---|---|
| 67 | Pye International 7N 25403 | Sweet Thang/Paralyze My Mind | 6 |
| 69 | RCA RCA 1833 | Loving You/Joe And Mabel's 12th Street Bar And Grill | 5 |
| 69 | RCA RCA 1890 | Cut Across Shorty/Understand, Little Man | 7 |

## STUD
| | | | |
|---|---|---|---|
| 70 | Deram SML-R 1084 | STUD (LP, laminated front sleeve, white/red label with small logo) | 150 |

*(see also Taste, Blossom Toes, Eric Burdon & Animals)*

## STUDD PUMP
| | | | |
|---|---|---|---|
| 71 | Penny Farthing PEN 757 | Spare The Children/Floatin' | 8 |

## STUDIO G'S
| | | |
|---|---|---|
| 70 | LPSG 100 | BETA GROUP (LP, library edition) .................................... 150 |
| 96 | Tenth Planet TP 023 | BEAT GROUP (LP, 600 only).......................................... 20 |

## STUDIO ONE ALLSTARS
| | | |
|---|---|---|
| 67 | Island WI 3038 | Sherry (actually by Bumps Oakley)/Out Of My Mind (actually by Soul Junior) ............ 45 |

## STUDIO PRESSURE
| | | |
|---|---|---|
| 93 | Certificate 18 CERT 1803 | Jump/Don't Worry/Know Yourself (12")............................ 35 |
| 93 | Certificate 18 CERT 1804 | Jump MK II/Presha/Test 1/Junglistics Pt 1 (12")................ 40 |
| 94 | Photek PTK 01 | FORM & FUNCTION VOL 1 (12") ................................ 12 |
| 94 | Photek PTK 03 | Touching Down...Planet Photek/The Physical (12") ............ 12 |
| 94 | Certificate 18 CERT 1808 | Relics/Presha III (12").............................................. 20 |

*(see also System X (Ex))*

## STUDIO SIX
| | | |
|---|---|---|
| 66 | Polydor 56131 | When I See My Baby/Don't Tell Lies ............................ 15 |
| 67 | Polydor 56162 | Bless My Soul (I've Been And Gone And Done It)/People Say ......... 10 |
| 67 | Polydor 56174 | Times Were When/I Can't Sleep ................................ 10 |
| 67 | Polydor 56219 | Strawberry Window/Falling Leaves ............................ 40 |
| 69 | Polydor 56361 | Bless My Soul/People Say ........................................ 10 |

## STUDIO SOUND
| | | |
|---|---|---|
| 72 | Downtown DT 489 | Give Me Some More/Some More Version ...................... 30 |

## STUDIO SWEETHEARTS
| | | |
|---|---|---|
| 79 | DJM DJS 10915 | I Believe/It Isn't Me (p/s) ........................................ 20 |

*(see also Cult, Slaughter & Dogs)*

## STUDIO 2
| | | |
|---|---|---|
| 95 | Jet Star FJD 002 | Dirty Games/Who Bless Jah? (12", stamped white labels) ........ 50 |

## STUD LEATHER
| | | |
|---|---|---|
| 73 | Dart ART 2024 | Cut Loose/Emma Louise ........................................ 100 |

## STUKAS
| | | |
|---|---|---|
| 77 | Chiswick NS 21 | Klean Living Kids/Oh Little Girl (p/s) .......................... 10 |
| 77 | Sonet SON 2134 | I Like Sport/I'll Send You A Postcard/Dead Lazy (p/s) ............ 8 |
| 78 | Sonet SON 2159 | Wash Machine Boogie/Motorbike.............................. 10 |

## STUMPY
| | | |
|---|---|---|
| 74 | Dawn DNS 1080 | Make Me A Superman/Keep It Coming .......................... 6 |

## STUPIDS
| | | |
|---|---|---|
| 85 | Children Of Rev. COR 3 | VIOLENT NUN (EP, some mispressed) .......................... 20 |
| 88 | Vinyl Solution SOL 2 | JESUS MEETS THE STUPIDS (LP, insert with free 7") ............ 15 |

## STURGEON ROW
| | | |
|---|---|---|
| 79 | RhopeySRTS 79 CUS 362 | FRICTION EP (with insert) ........................................ 60 |

## ST VINCENT
| | | |
|---|---|---|
| 07 | Beggars Banquet BBQ 406 | Now Now/All My Stars Aligned (p/s) ............................ 12 |
| 07 | Beggars Banquet BBQ 410 | Jesus Saves I Spend/These Days (p/s) .......................... 12 |
| 09 | 4AD AD 2918 | Actor Out Of Work/Bicycle (p/s)................................ 12 |
| 12 | 4AD AD 3211 | Krokodil/Grot (die-cut sleeve, red vinyl) .................... 25 |
| 07 | Beggars Banquet BBQLP 239 | MARRY ME (LP) .................................................... 15 |
| 09 | 4AD CAD 2919 | ACTOR (LP) .......................................................... 18 |
| 11 | 4AD CAD 3123 | STRANGE MERCY (LP) .............................................. 20 |

## STYLE COUNCIL
| | | |
|---|---|---|
| 89 | Polydor TSC 18 | Sure Is Sure/Love Of The World (unissued, acetates may exist) ......... 0 |
| 88 | Polydor | CONFESSIONS OF A POP GROUP (box set, VHS & cassette;some with promo CD [CPGCD 1]) .............................................. 50 |
| 88 | Polydor | CONFESSIONS OF A POP GROUP (box set, VHS & cassette;some without promo CD [CPGCD 1]) ............................. 40 |
| 98 | Polydor TSCLP 6 | MODERNISM: A NEW DECADE (LP, promo only) ................ 50 |
| 98 | Polydor TSCLP 6 | MODERNISM: A NEW DECADE (LP, 2 x 12" set, promo only) ...... 60 |
| 00 | Polydor 549135-1 | GREATEST HITS (2-LP) ............................................ 25 |

*(see also Paul Weller, Jam, Merton Parkas, King Truman)*

## STYLOS
| | | |
|---|---|---|
| 64 | Liberty LBS 10173 | Head Over Heels/Bye Bye, Baby, Bye Bye ...................... 100 |

## POLY STYRENE
| | | |
|---|---|---|
| 80 | United Artists BP 370 | Talk In Toytown/Sub Tropical (p/s) .............................. 5 |
| 86 | Awesome AOR 7 | Gods And Goddesses: Trick Of The Witch/Paramatma (p/s)....... 7 |
| 80 | United Artists UAG 30320 | TRANSLUCENCE (LP, with lyric inner) .......................... 20 |

*(see also X-Ray Spex, Mari Elliott)*

## STYVAR MANOR
| | | |
|---|---|---|
| 70 | Polydor 2058034 | Just Dropped In/That's What I Need Most Of All .............. 40 |

## SUBCULTURE
| | | |
|---|---|---|
| 83 | Essential ESS 002 | Loud & Clear/Rogue Trooper/University City (p/s) ............ 30 |

## SUBHUMANS
| | | |
|---|---|---|
| 82 | Spiderleg SDL 7 | Religious Wars/Love Is.../Work Experience/It's Gonna Get Worse (p/s)........ 8 |
| 82 | Spiderleg SPIDL 5 | Big City/Reason For Existence/Cancer/Peroxide (p/s) .......... 10 |
| 83 | Bluurg XEP 2 | Big City/Reason For Existence/Cancer/Peroxide (repressing, p/s) ...... 6 |
| 81 | Spider Leg SDL 3 | DEMOLITION WAR (EP, gatefold p/s with "Pay no more than 85p" rubber stamped on front cover) ........................ 15 |
| 82 | Spiderleg SDL9 | THE DAY THE COUNTRY DIED (LP, gatefold, original pressing with "Pay no more than £3.25" on front cover) ............ 15 |
| 83 | Bluurg Fish 8 | FROM THE CRADLE TO THE GRAVE (LP, gatefold, original pressing with "Pay no more than £3.50" on front cover) ........ 15 |
| 85 | Bluurg Fish VIG 1 T | 20:20 SPLIT VISION (LP, with insert and has 'Pay no more than £3.50' on front sleeve) . 15 |

MINT VALUE £

## SUBITA AND EMPHASIS
81    Crazy Plane SP 004              Once In A Blue Moon/Dub (no p/s) ........................................8

## SUBLIME
97    MCA MCS 48045                  What I Got (Super No Mofo Edit)/Rivers Of Babylon p/s, yellow vinyl) .............8

## SUBMARINER
93    Spacewatch FLX 2107            Lyricist Downer/Seeming And The Meaning (demo)/STEREOLAB:Ronco Symphony
                                     (demo) (clear vinyl flexi with paper strip insert) .................................25

## SUBMARINES
87    Head HEAD 4                    Grey Skies Blue/I Saw The Children (p/s) .................................6

## SUB MURIS
83    Dog Rock SD104                 Honesty/Open Doors (p/s) ........................................10

## SUBS
78    Stiff OFF 1                    Gimme Your Heart/Party Clothes (p/s) ..............................8
*(see also Larry Wallis)*

## SUBSTITUTE
79    Ignition IR 2                  The One/Look Sharp (in p/s) ......................................35
79    Ignition IR 2                  The One/Look Sharp ..............................................20
*(see also Vibrators)*

## SUB SUB
90s   Ten TENX 373                   Space Face/Ecto-Jam-Sub (12", die-cut sleeve) ....................35
90s   Robs Records 12ROB 07          Coast/Inside Of This/Past/Inside Out (12", p/s) ...................10
90s   Robs Records 7ROB 9            Ain't No Love/Parkside Mix (p/s) ..................................8
90s   Robs Records 7ROB 19           Respect (Radio Edit)/(Dasliva-McCready Mix) ......................8
*(see also Doves)*

## SUBTERRANEANS
87    Mother MUM 6                   Slum/Maxi Joy (p/s) ..............................................5

## SUBURBAN STUDS
77    Pogo POG 001/LYN 44845         No Faith/Questions (no p/s, 'with horns' version) ................20
77    Pogo POG 001/LYN 44845         No Faith/Questions (p/s) .........................................6
78    Pogo POG 002                   I Hate School/Young Power (p/s) ..................................15
78    Pogo POW 001                   SLAM (LP) .......................................................25

## SUBWAYS
04    Private Pressing               DEMO (CD, sold at gigs, p/s) .....................................30
04    Transgressive 58241H1          1 am/I Want To Hear What You Gotta Say/You Got Me (500 only, p/s) .....10
05    Infectious 25646248            YOUNG FOR ETERNITY (LP, 2x10") ..................................30

## SUBWAY SECT
78    Braik BRS 01                   Nobody's Scared/Don't Split It (p/s) .............................20
78    Braik BRS 01                   Nobody's Scared/Don't Split It (no p/s) ..........................8
79    Rough Trade RT 007             Ambition/A Different Story (initially in yellow text p/s) ........10
79    Rough Trade RT 007             Ambition/A Different Story (later orange text p/s) ...............8
*(see also Vic Godard [& Subway Sect], Spirit Of The Sect)*

## NIKKI SUDDEN
81    Rather GEAR 11                 Back To The Start/Ringing On My Train (p/s) ......................5
82    Abstract ABS 009               Channel Steamer/Chelsea Embankment (p/s) .........................5
86    Glass GLAEP 102                PIN YOUR HEAR TO ME (12" EP, with Dave Kusworth & The Jacobites) ......10
86    Creation CRE 033               Jangle Town/The Last Bandit (p/s) ................................8
82    ABSTRACT ABT 003               WAITING ON EGYPT (LP) ..........................................25
83    Flicknife SHARP 110            THE BIBLE BELT (LP) .............................................18
84    Glass GLALP 008                JACOBITES (LP, with Dave Kusworth) ..............................15
91    UFO UFO 4                      THE JEWEL THIEF (LP) ...........................................15
*(see also Swell Maps, Last Bandits, Jeremy Gluck)*

## (A) SUDDEN SWAY
80    Chant CHANT 1                  Jane's Third Party/Don't Go (p/s, as A Sudden Sway) ..............15
81    Chant CHANT 2/EJSP 9692        TO YOU, WITH REGARD (12" EP, with insert) ........................20
84    Chant CHANT 3                  The Traffic Tax Scheme (12" with badge & inserts in folder) ......12
86    WEA BYN 8B                     Spacemate (2 x 12" box set with stickers, info sheets, 2 booklets & poster) .........12

## SUDETEN CRECHE
83    Illuminated ILL 1712           Kindergarten/Dance (instrumental Version)/Dance/Asylums in Beirut (12", p/s) .........25

## SUE & MARY
62    Decca F 11517                  Traitor In Disguise/I Love You (Oh Yes I Do) .....................7

## SUE & SUNNY
65    Columbia DB 7748               Every Ounce Of Strength/So Remember .............................15
67    Columbia DB 8099               You Can't By-Pass Love/I Like Your Style .........................25
68    CBS 3874                       The Show Must Go On/Little black Book ............................20
68    Island WIP 6043                Set Me Free/NIRVANA ORCHESTRA: City Of The South ................25
69    CBS 4567                       Let Us Break Bread/Stop Messing About With My Heart .............10
70    CBS 4757                       You Devil, Cotton-Eyed Joe/Night In The City .....................10
70    Deram DM 318                   Ain't That Telling You People/Didn't I Blow Your Mind ...........10
71    Deram DM 328                   Freedom/Break Up .................................................10
71    Reflection HRS 10              Let Us Break Bread Together/Michael From Mountains ..............6
72    Deram DM 355                   I'm Gonna Make You Love Me/High On The Thought Of You ...........10
70    CBS 63740                      SUE AND SUNNY (LP) .............................................20
70    Reflection REFL 4              SUE AND SUNNY (LP) .............................................20
*(see also Sue & Sunshine, Myrtelles, Stockingtops, Brotherhood Of Man)*

## SUE & SUNSHINE
64    Columbia DB 7409               A Little Love/If You See Me Crying ...............................10
65    Columbia DB 7533               We're In Love/Don't Look Behind .................................7

*(see also Sue & Sunny, Myrtelles, Stockingtops)*

## SUEDE
| 91 | RML RML 001 | Be My God/Art (12", unissued, 250+ white label copies only, MPO pressings,no p/s; counterfeits have off-white labels and no MPO etchings) | 100 |
|---|---|---|---|
| 92 | Nude NUD 1 S | The Drowners (Radio Edit)/To The Birds (p/s, 1,000 copies only) | 18 |
| 92 | Nude NUD3S | Metal Mickey/Where The Pigs Don't Fly (p/s) | 5 |
| 92 | Nude NUD 3 T | Metal Mickey/Where Pigs Don't Fly/He's Dead (12", test pressing, plain sleeve) | 30 |
| 93 | Nude NUDE4S | Animal Nitrate/The Big Time (p/s) | 5 |
| 93 | Nude NUD4T | Animal Nitrate/Painted People/The Big Time (12", p/s) | 10 |
| 93 | Nude NUD 5S | So Young/High Rising (p/s) | 5 |
| 94 | Nude NUD 9S | Stay Together/The Living Dead (p/s) | 5 |
| 94 | Nude NUD 9T | Stay Together/The Living Dead/My Dark Star (12" numbered gatefold p/s) | 10 |
| 94 | Nude NUD 10 S | We Are The Pigs/Killing Of A Flash Boy (numbered gatefold p/s) | 6 |
| 94 | Nude NUD 11 T | The Wild Ones/Eno's Introducing The Band/Asda Town (12", photo insert, p/s) | 10 |
| 96 | Nude NUD 21S | Trash/Europe Is Our Playground (p/s, mail order only) | 15 |
| 97 | Nude NUD 30S | Filmstar/Filmstar (Original Version) (p/s) | 5 |
| 97 | Nude SIS 1 CD | LIVE (CD EP, 6-track fan club-only issue) | 25 |
| 97 | Nude NUD 24 S | Saturday Night/Beautiful Ones (double pack, p/s, mail-order only) | 10 |
| 13 | Warner Bros. SUEDE 9313 | Barriers/Animal Nitrate | 6 |
| 99 | Nude NUD 667043 | ELECTRICITY EP (minidisc, withdrawn) | 10 |
| 04 | S.I.S. SIS4CD | SEE YOU IN THE NEXT LIFE (CD, fan club farewell, 2000 copies) | 50 |
| 11 | Edsel DROWN 1 | The Drowners (Demo)/To The Birds (Demo) (p/s, Record Store Day release) | 18 |
| 93 | Nude NUDE 1LP | SUEDE (LP, with inner sleeve; with carrier bag from Chain With No Name stores) | 50 |
| 93 | Nude NUDE 1LP | SUEDE (LP, with inner sleeve) | 45 |
| 94 | Nude NUDE 3 | DOG MAN STAR (LP, with poster) | 100 |
| 96 | Nude 4851212 | COMING UP (LP, with inner sleeve) | 45 |
| 99 | Nude 14LP | HEAD MUSIC (2-LP) | 40 |
| 13 | Warner Bros. SUEDEBS X001 | BLOODSPORTS (LP, CD, booklet & 7", hardback book) | 50 |
| 15 | Demon INSATIABLE 9 | DOG MAN STAR 20th ANNIVERSARY LIVE ROYAL ALBERT HALL (2-LP) | 25 |
| 15 | Demon SUEDEBOX 006 | DOG MAN STAR 20th ANNIVERSARY LIVE ROYAL ALBERT HALL (4-LP, 2CD) | 30 |

*(see also Elastica, Tears)*

## SUEDE CROCODILES
| 83 | No Strings NOSP 2 | Pleasant Dreams/Stop The Rain | 75 |
|---|---|---|---|

## SUFFERER SOUND
| 78 | Tempus TEMD 2 | I A Sufferer/National Front (12") | 12 |
|---|---|---|---|

## SUFJAN STEVENS
| 05 | Rough Trade RTRADLP 250 | COME ON FEEL THE ILLINOISE (2-LP) | 30 |
|---|---|---|---|
| 15 | Asthmatic Kitty AKR 371 | Exploding Whale/Fourth Of July (PPD Remix) (UK tour edition) | 25 |

## SUGAR & SPICE (JAMAICA)
| 73 | Stop Points DL 021 | Indeed I Love You/Version | 8 |
|---|---|---|---|

## SUGAR MINOTT
| 79 | Warrior WAR 124 | Never Too Young/DON CARLOS: Hey Little Girl (12") | 10 |
|---|---|---|---|
| 79 | Sufferer's Heights SUFF 002 | Hard Time Pressure/Dub On The Pressure (12" with Captain Sinbad) | 20 |
| 83 | PCJ PCJ 001 | Can't Stop Jah Music/PCJ: Nah Stop Jah Music (12") | 50 |
| 83 | SMP SMP 003 | Come Again/BERTIE AT THE CONTROLS: Dubbing A Storm At Omega Studio (12") | 150 |
| 84 | Black Roots LML 201284 | Herbman Hustling/TAXI GANG: Hustling Dub (12") | 10 |
| 77 | Studio One PSOL001 | LIVE LOVING (LP) | 50 |
| 79 | United Artists UAG 30310 | GIVE THE PEOPLE (LP) | 20 |
| 79 | Island ILPS 9591 | BLACK ROOTS (LP) | 20 |
| 79 | Trojan TRLS 173 | GHETTO-OLOGY (LP) | 15 |
| 79 | Warrior WARLP20 | BITTER SWEET (LP) | 25 |
| 70s | Uptempo UT 1 | SHOWCASE (10" mini LP, no ps) | 15 |
| 82 | Black Roots BRLP 001 | MEET THE PEOPLE IN A LOVER DUBBER STYLE (LP) | 35 |

## SUGAR SHACK
| 68 | Tribune TRS 112 | Sunshine Of Your Love/Morning Dew | 25 |
|---|---|---|---|

## SUGAR (1)
| 69 | CBS 4226 | It Was Yesterday Today/11AM Tuesday Morning Taxi | 40 |
|---|---|---|---|

## SUGAR (2)
| 92 | Creation CRELP 129 | COPPER BLUE (LP, lyric inner) | 18 |
|---|---|---|---|
| 93 | Creation CRELP 153 | BEASTER (mini-LP) | 15 |
| 94 | Creation CRELP 172 | FILE UNDER EASY LISTENING (LP) | 15 |

## SUGAR (SIMONE) & DANDY (LIVINGSTONE)
| 63 | Carnival CV 7006 | One Man Went To Mow/Cryin' | 8 |
|---|---|---|---|
| 64 | Carnival CV 7009 | Oh Dear What Can The Matter Be/Tra La La | 8 |
| 64 | Carnival CV 7015 | What A Life/Time And Tide | 8 |
| 64 | Carnival CV 7016 | I'm Not Crying Now/Blues Got A Hold On Me | 8 |
| 65 | Carnival CV 7023 | Let's Ska/Only Heaven Knows | 8 |
| 65 | Carnival CV 7024 | I'm Into Something Good/Crazy For You | 8 |
| 65 | Carnival CV 7027 | Think Of The Good Times/Girl Come See | 8 |
| 65 | Carnival CV 7029 | I Want To Be Your Lover/I Don't Know What I'm Going To Do Now | 7 |
| 66 | Blue Beat BB 367 | Meditation (as Jetliners)/GIRL SATCHMO & JET LINERS: Nature Of Love | 15 |
| 67 | Page One POF 044 | Let's Ska/Only Heaven Knows | 8 |
| 64 | Carnival CX 1000 | THE SKA'S THE LIMIT (LP) | 40 |
| 67 | Page One FOR 006 | THE SKA'S THE LIMIT (LP, reissue) | 20 |

*(see also Sugar Simone)*

## SUGAR & PEE WEE
| 58 | Vogue Pop V 9112 | One, Two, Let's Rock/Just A Few Little Words | 500 |
|---|---|---|---|
| 58 | Vogue Pop V 9112 | One, Two, Let's Rock/Just A Few Little Words (78) | 100 |

MINT VALUE £

## SUGAR & SPICE
69   London HLU 10259 — Cruel War/Not To Return ..........................................................10

## SUGAR BEARS
72   Philips 6073 812 — You Are The One/Someone Like You ..................................................10

## SUGARBEATS
66   Polydor BM 56069 — I Just Stand Here/The Ballad Of Ole Betsy ......................................20
66   Polydor BM 56120 — Alice Designs/Sunny Day Girl .....................................................20
*(see also Tony Rivers & Castaways)*

## SUGARCUBES
87   One Little Indian 7z TP 7 — Birthday/Birthday (Icelandic) (p/s) ..........................................6
88   One Little Indian 12TP 11L — BIRTHDAY CHRISTMAS MIX (12" EP, double groove, with Jesus & Mary Chain) .............12
89   House Of Dolls HOD 010 — Dark Disco/HOST: Homelands/MURRUMBRIDGE WHALERS: Giving Away To Trains/
      SHARK TABOO: Tinsel Town (live) (no p/s, with House Of Dolls mag) ................................6
89   One Little Indian OLI26TP7 — Regina/Hot Meat/Hey/Regina (Propellor vs Jet) (with poster) ...............6
92   One Little Indian OLI104TP12 — Birthday (Justin Robertson 12" mix)/Tommy D Dub Mix/Christmas Eve Mix/Original
      7" Mix/Tommy D 12" Mix/Justin Robertson Dub/Christmas Day Mix/Demo (12") .......10
90   One Little Indian TP BOX 2 — 7.8 (8 x 7" box set) ..........................................................25
90   One Little Indian TP BOX 1 — 12.11 (11 x 12" box set) .....................................................40
90   One Little Indian TP BOX 3 — CD.6 (6 x CD box set) ........................................................45
08   One Little Indian 950TP7BOX — BOX SET (8 x 7") .............................................................25
88   One Little Indian TPLP 5 — LIFE'S TOO GOOD (LP, green/blue/yellow/orange/pink sleeve) .................15
88   One Little Indian DTPLP 5 — LIFE'S TOO GOOD (DAT) ..........................................................15
89   One Little Indian TPLP 15SP — HERE TODAY, TOMORROW NEXT WEEK! (LP, silver vinyl, gatefold sleeve with sticker &
      inner) ...................................................................................................................20
89   One Little Indian TPLP 15L — SYKURMOLARNIR ILLUR ARFUR! (LP, as Sykurmolarnir, gatefold sleeve) ..........15
92   One Little Indian TPLP40 — IT'S IT (2 x LP) ..................................................................20
*(see also Bjork, Kukl, Ornamental)*

## SUGAR DEE & THE OFFBEAT POSSE
89   YND YDD 0137 — Danger/Having A Party (12") ..............................................................25

## SUGAR LOAF
70   RCA INTS 1113 — SOUL STRUTTING (LP) .....................................................................30

## SUGARLOAF
70   Liberty LBF 15401 — Green-Eyed Lady/West Of Tomorrow ....................................................12
71   Liberty LBS 83415 — SUGARLOAF (LP) .......................................................................15
75   Polydor 2310 394 — DON'T CALL US, WE'LL CALL YOU (LP, with Jerry Corbetto) ..........................15

## SUGAR LUMPS
69   Jay Boy BOY 16 — Sugar Sugar/Can't We Be Friends .......................................................20
70   Jay Boy BOY 20 — Satan's People/Shame Shame ...........................................................20

## SUGARPLUMS
70   Fab FAB 160 — Red River Reggae/Too Much ................................................................20

## SUGAR SHOPPE
68   Capitol CL 15555 — Skip-A-Long Sam/Let The Truth Come Out ............................................20

## SUGGESTIVE MOTION
83   Bodie BR 101 — Loving You/In Your Mind .................................................................10

## SUGARGLIDERS
92   Sarah SARAH 63 — Letter From A Lifeboat/Strong/What We Had Hoped (p/s, insert) ....................12
92   Sarah SARAH 67 — Seventeen/Aloha Street/Fruitloopin' (p/s, insert) ................................12
93   Sarah SARAH 72 — Ahprahan/Corn Circles/Theme From Boxville (p/s, insert) ..........................20
93   Sarah SARAH 77 — Trumpet Play/Unkind/Beloved (p/s, insert) ........................................20
93   Sarah SARAH 83 — Will We Ever Learn?/Dolly/Reinventing Penicillin (p/s, insert) ..................20
93   Sarah SARAH 86 — Top 40 Sculpture/90 Days Of Moths And Rust/Yr. Jacket (p/s, insert) ..............20
94   Sarah SARAH 619 — WE'RE ALL TRYING TO GET THERE (LP) ..................................................30

## SUICIDAL TENDENCIES
87   Virgin VS 967-12 — Possessed To Skate/Human Guinea Pig/Two Wrongs Don't Make A Right (12", picture
      disc) ...................................................................................................................15
88   Virgin VST 1039 — Institutionalised/War Inside My Head/Cyco (12", p/s) ...........................15
87   Virgin V 2495 — SUICIDAL TENDENCIES (LP, with poster) ................................................18
88   Virgin V 2551 — HOW WILL I LAUGH TOMORROW WHEN I CAN'T EVEN SMILE TODAY? (LP) ....................15

## SUICIDE
78   Red Star/Bronze BRO 57 — Cheree/I Remember (p/s) .....................................................15
78   Red Star/Bronze 12 BRO 57 — Cheree/I Remember (12", 'limited edition', p/s) ......................20
79   Island WIP 6543 — Dream Baby Dream/Radiation (p/s) ..................................................12
79   Island 12 WIP 6543 — Dream Baby Dream (Long Version)/Radiation (12", p/s) ........................20
86   Demon D 1046 — Cheree/I Remember (promo only) .......................................................12
89   Chapter 22 12CHAP 36 — Rain Of Ruin/Surrender (12") .................................................10
89   Chapter 22 12CHAP 42 — SUICIDE (12", unissued) ......................................................0
77   Red Star/Bronze BRON 508 — SUICIDE (LP) ...............................................................30
78   Red Star FRANKIE 1 — 24 MINUTES OVER BRUSSELS (LP, official bootleg, 1,000 only, no p/s) ........30
80   Ze/Island ILPS 7007 — SUICIDE: ALAN VEGA/MARTIN REV (LP, with printed inner sleeve) ..............20
86   Demon FIEND 74 — SUICIDE (LP, reissue) ................................................................15
89   Contempo CONTE 148 — HALF ALIVE (LP, clear vinyl, 1,000 only) ......................................15
98   Blast First BFFP 133 1/2 — SUICIDE (2-LP) ..............................................................30
99   Blast First BFFP 162 — FIRST REHEARSAL TAPES (2-LP) ..................................................30
02   Blast First BFFP 168 — AMERICAN SUPREME (2-LP) .......................................................18
*(see also Alan Vega)*

## SUICIDE TWINS
86   Lick LICLP 9 — SILVER MISSILES AND NIGHTINGALES (LP) ..................................................15

## BIG JIM SULLIVAN
| | | | |
|---|---|---|---|
| 61 | Decca F 11387 | You Don't Know What You've Got/Hot Hiss Of Steam (as Big Jim Sullivan Combo) | 12 |
| 65 | Mercury MF 928 | She Walks Through The Fair/Don't Know What I'm Doing (as Jim Sullivan Sound) | 25 |
| 73 | MAM MAM 100 | Out Of The Question/Alone Again | 6 |
| 67 | Mercury SML 30001 | SITAR BEAT (LP) | 40 |
| 74 | Retreat RTA 4001 | BIG JIM'S BACK (LP, gatefold sleeve, blue/green label) | 15 |

*(see also Maureeny Wishfull, Brian Bennett, Tiger)*

## JOE SULLIVAN
| | | | |
|---|---|---|---|
| 56 | London HA-U 2011 | NEW SOLOS BY AN OLD MASTER (LP, thin card sleeve with no spine)) | 15 |

## MAXINE SULLIVAN
| | | | |
|---|---|---|---|
| 54 | Parlophone MSP 6086 | Boogie Woogie Maxine/Piper In The Glen (with Vic Ash) | 15 |

## PHIL SULLIVAN WITH LONZO & OSCAR'S PEAPICKERS
| | | | |
|---|---|---|---|
| 59 | Melodisc MEL 1512 | Love Never Dies/Luckiest Man In Town | 5 |

## PETER SULLY
| | | | |
|---|---|---|---|
| 70 | Pye 7N 17935 | Row Row Row/Everybodys Talkin' About The War | 8 |
| 68 | Polydor 56291 | My Idea/Evil Woman (as Pete Sully And The Orchard) | 35 |

## SULTANS OF PING (F.C.)
| | | | |
|---|---|---|---|
| 93 | Rhythm King 472495-1 | CASUAL SEX IN THE CINEPLEX (LP) | 15 |

## YMA SUMAC
| | | | |
|---|---|---|---|
| 72 | London HLU/SHU 8431 | MIRACLES (LP) | 15 |

## HUBERT SUMLIN
| | | | |
|---|---|---|---|
| 65 | Blue Horizon 45-1000 | Across The Board/Sumlin Boogie (99 copies only) | 150 |

*(see also Howlin' Wolf)*

## DONNA SUMMER
| | | | |
|---|---|---|---|
| 74 | People PEO 115 | The Hostage/Let's Work Together Now | 7 |

*(see also Donna Gaines, John Barry)*

## SUMMERHILL
| | | | |
|---|---|---|---|
| 69 | Polydor 583 746 | SUMMERHILL (LP) | 40 |

## BOB(BY) SUMMERS
| | | | |
|---|---|---|---|
| 59 | Capitol CL 15063 | Rattle Rhythm/Excitement (as Bob Summers) | 12 |
| 60 | Capitol CL 15130 | Little Brown Jug/Twelfth Street Rag (as Bobby Summers) | 7 |

## JOHN SUMMERS
| | | | |
|---|---|---|---|
| 65 | Pye 15918 | Don't Fool Yourself/Looking In Windows | 30 |
| 66 | Pye 7N 17081 | That's A Magic Moment/One A Day | 10 |

## SUMMER SET
| | | | |
|---|---|---|---|
| 66 | Columbia DB 8004 | Farmer's Daughter/Papa-Oom-Mow-Mow | 40 |
| 66 | Columbia DB 8004 | Farmer's Daughter/What Are You Gonna Do (2nd issue with different B-side) | 40 |
| 67 | Columbia DB 8215 | Overnight Changes/It's A Dream | 120 |

*(see also Candy Choir)*

## SUMMERTAIR GIRLS
| | | | |
|---|---|---|---|
| 66 | Ska Beat JB 258 | My Heart Cries Out/SOUL BROTHERS: James Bond Girl | 50 |

*(see also Jackie Mittoo, Soul Agents)*

## SUMMER WINE
| | | | |
|---|---|---|---|
| 72 | Philips 6006 217 | Why Do Fools Fall In Love/Ode To Steel Guitar | 5 |
| 72 | Philips 6006 238 | Take A Load Off Your Feet/ Sound Of Summer's Over | 5 |
| 73 | Philips 6006 288 | Living Right Next Door To An Angel/Sound Of Summer's Over | 7 |
| 77 | EMI EMI 2634 | Why Do Fools Fall In Love/Sound Of Summer's Over | 5 |

*(see also Tony Rivers)*

## SUMO GIANTS
| | | | |
|---|---|---|---|
| 81 | Metro 88 ELECS 1 | Tower Of Babel/Foolish Things (p/s with insert) | 12 |

## SUN ALSO RISES
| | | | |
|---|---|---|---|
| 70 | Village Thing VTS 2 | THE SUN ALSO RISES (LP, with insert) | 100 |

## SUN DIAL
| | | | |
|---|---|---|---|
| 90 | UFO 45 001T | Exploding In Your Mind/Otherside/Slow Motion (12", 1-sided, p/s) | 15 |
| 91 | Tangerine TANGERINE 111 | Exploding In Your Mind (Colour Mix)/Otherside/Slow Motion (12", unreleased, 80 white label test pressings only) | 30 |
| 90 | Tangerine TAN 11145 | Exploding In Your Mind/Other Side | 50 |
| 91 | UFO PF 2 | Fireball/Only A Northern Song ('Pre-Flight' 7", promo only) | 20 |
| 91 | UFO UFO 45002 T | OVERSPILL EP (12", orange vinyl) | 10 |
| 92 | UFO UFO 45008 T | FAZER EP (12") | 10 |
| 90 | Tangerine MM 07 | OTHER WAY OUT (LP, with insert, signed in silver ink) | 50 |
| 90 | Tangerine MM 07 | OTHER WAY OUT (LP, with insert) | 30 |
| 91 | UFO UFO 1LP | OTHER WAY OUT (LP, reissue in gatefold sleeve) | 15 |
| 92 | UFO UFO 8 | REFLECTOR (LP, with free 1-sided 7", Let It Go (live), TEX-4) | 20 |
| 92 | UFO UFO 8 | REFLECTER (LP, clear vinyl) | 20 |
| 93 | Beggars Banquet BBQLP 138 | LIBERTINE (LP, with poster) | 18 |
| 94 | Acme AC 8001 | RETURN JOURNEY (LP, official bootleg; 200 promos with inserts) | 40 |
| 94 | Acme AC 8001 | RETURN JOURNEY (LP, official bootleg; 500 numbered commercial copies) | 30 |
| 95 | Acme AC 8011LP | ACID YANTRA (LP, gatefold sleeve, some purple vinyl) | 25 |
| 96 | Acme AC 8015 | LIVE DRUG (LP, red vinyl) | 15 |
| 02 | Ace Of Discs ACE 001 | WILD BUG (LP) | 15 |
| 05 | Third Eye TESLP 1001 | OTHER WAY IN (LP) | 15 |

*(see also Modern Art, Spiral Sky, Quad)*

## SUN & MOON
| | | | |
|---|---|---|---|
| 88 | Geffen GEF 39 | The Speed Of Life/Death Of Imagination (p/s) | 5 |

*(see also Chameleons)*

## SUN SINGERS

MINT VALUE £

| | | | |
|---|---|---|---|
| 72 | UK UK 12 | You Were On My Mind/Sunshine | 8 |

### SUNBIRD
| | | | |
|---|---|---|---|
| 70 | Phillips 6011070 | Brother Bird/Love Of The Free | 18 |

*(see also Nirvana)*

### SUNCHARIOT
| | | | |
|---|---|---|---|
| 72 | Decca F13317 | Rosemarie/Do You Wanna Know | 15 |
| 73 | Decca F13407 | Firewater/The Only Girl I Knew | 10 |

### SUNDAE TIMES
| | | | |
|---|---|---|---|
| 68 | President PT 203 | Baby Don't Cry/Aba-Aba | 5 |
| 68 | President PT 219 | Jack Boy/I Don't Want Nobody | 5 |
| 70 | President PT 285 | Live Today/Take Me Higher Baby | 10 |
| 70 | Joy JOYS 159 | US COLOURED KIDS (LP, laminated front sleeve, flipbacks) | 40 |

*(see also Osiba, Crosby Stills Nash & Young, One)*

### SUNDANCE
| | | | |
|---|---|---|---|
| 73 | Decca F 13423 | Coming Down/Eagles | 5 |
| 73 | Decca F 13461 | Stand By/Willie The Gambler | 5 |
| 74 | Decca F 13494 | Loving You/Can You Feel It | 5 |
| 73 | Decca TXS 111 | RAIN STEAM SPEED (LP, with insert) | 20 |
| 74 | Decca SKL 5183 | CHUFFER (LP) | 18 |

### SUNDAY AFTERNOONS
| | | | |
|---|---|---|---|
| 70s | Longman | SUNDAY AFTERNOONS (LP) | 90 |

### SUNDAYS
| | | | |
|---|---|---|---|
| 89 | Rough Trade RTX 218 | Can't Be Sure/I Kicked A Boy (export issue, brown p/s) | 6 |
| 89 | Rough Trade RTTX 218 | Can't Be Sure/I Kicked A Boy/Don't Tell Your Mother (12", export issue, brown p/s) | 10 |
| 90 | Catalogue CAT 076 | I Won (square flexidisc with The Catalogue magazine) | 10 |
| 97 | Parlophone R 6475 | Summertime Nothing Sweet (p/s, red vinyl) | 5 |
| 90 | Rough Trade ROUGH 148 | READING WRITING AND ARITHMATIC (LP) | 20 |
| 90 | Rough Trade ROUGH 148P | READING, WRITING AND ARITHMETIC (LP, picture disc, stickered sleeve) | 25 |
| 92 | Parlophone PCSD 121 | BLIND (LP) | 40 |
| 97 | Parlophone 724382121216 | STATIC AND SILENCE (LP) | 45 |

### SUNDERLAND FIRST TEAM SQUAD
| | | | |
|---|---|---|---|
| 73 | RCA 2362 | Sunderland All The Way/Bobby Knoxall - I'm Feeling Happy | 5 |

### SUNDOWNERS
| | | | |
|---|---|---|---|
| 63 | Piccadilly 7N 35142 | Baby Baby/House Of The Rising Sun | 8 |
| 64 | Piccadilly 7N 35162 | Come On In/Shot Of Rhythm And Blues | 8 |
| 65 | Parlophone R 5243 | Where Am I/Gonna Make The Future Bright | 8 |
| 68 | Columbia DB 8339 | Dr. J. Wallace-Brown/Love Is In The Air | 15 |
| 68 | Spark SRL 1016 | Gloria The Bosom Show/Don't Look Back | 8 |

### SUNDOWN PLAYBOYS
| | | | |
|---|---|---|---|
| 72 | Apple APPLE 44 | Saturday Nite Special/Valse De Soleil Couche (in p/s) | 35 |
| 72 | Apple APPLE 44 | Saturday Nite Special/Valse De Soleil Couche | 10 |
| 72 | Apple APPLE 44 | Saturday Nite Special/Valse De Soleil Couche (10", 78rpm, pink-patterned die-cut sleeve) | 300 |

### SUNDRAGON (1)
| | | | |
|---|---|---|---|
| 68 | MGM MGM 1380 | Green Tambourine/I Need All The Friends I Can Get | 12 |
| 68 | MGM MGM 1391 | Blueberry Blue/Far Away Mountain | 12 |
| 68 | MGM MGM 1458 | Five White Horses/Look At The Sun | 30 |
| 68 | MGM MGM-C(S) 8090 | GREEN TAMBOURINE (LP, yellow/black 'lion' label) | 175 |

*(see also Sands)*

### SUNDRAGON (2)
| | | | |
|---|---|---|---|
| 03 | Y n R YNR014 | The Path/Watching (12") | 12 |

### SUNFIGHTER
| | | | |
|---|---|---|---|
| 77 | EMI EMI 2612 | Café A Go-Go/Café A Go-Go (instrumental) | 5 |
| 76 | EMI EMI 2493 | Drag Race Queen/Riding On Your Star | 15 |
| 76 | EMI EMI 2553 | Such A Lovely Night/Don't Get Me Wrong | 10 |

*(see also Chris Rainbow)*

### SUNFLAYRE
| | | | |
|---|---|---|---|
| 70 | Realm RM 1 | The Passing Dream/Rich Woman (private pressing) | 300 |

### SUNFOREST
| | | | |
|---|---|---|---|
| 70 | Deram Nova DN 7 | SOUND OF SUNFOREST (LP, mono, laminated front sleeve) | 400 |
| 70 | Deram Nova SDN 7 | SOUND OF SUNFOREST (LP, stereo, laminated front sleeve) | 300 |

### SUNGLASSES AFTER DARK
| | | | |
|---|---|---|---|
| 84 | Anagram ANA 20 | Morbid Silence/Let's Go | 10 |

### SUNHOUSE
| | | | |
|---|---|---|---|
| 98 | Independiente ISOM 4LP | CRAZY ON THE WEEKEND (LP) | 25 |

### SUNN 0)))
| | | | |
|---|---|---|---|
| 04 | Anti-Mosh 444 | Candlewolff Ov Thee Golden Chalice (12") | 35 |
| 03 | Dirtier Promotions DPROMLP52 | VOID (2-LP, 150 on green vinyl) | 45 |
| 03 | Dirtier Promotions DPROMLP52 | VOID (2-LP, 850 on black vinyl) | 25 |
| 13 | Southern Lord SUNN 50 | BLACK ONE (2-LP, reissue) | 20 |

### SUNNY & HI-JUMPERS
| | | | |
|---|---|---|---|
| 65 | Carnival CV 7022 | Tarry Till You're Better/Dance Til You're Better | 6 |
| 65 | Carnival CV 7025 | Going To Damascus/Sweet Potatoes | 6 |

## SUNNY & THE SUNGLOWS/SUNLINERS
| | | | |
|---|---|---|---|
| 63 | London HL 9792 | Talk To Me (as Sunny & the Sunglows)/Every Week, Every Month, Every Year (as Sunny & the Sunliners) | 25 |

## SUNNYLAND SLIM
| | | | |
|---|---|---|---|
| 65 | 77' LA 12-23 | CHICAGO BLUES SESSION (LP, with Little Brother Montgomery) | 30 |
| 65 | Storyville SLP 169 | I DONE YOU WRONG (LP) | 20 |
| 69 | Liberty LBS 83237 | SLIM'S GOT THIS THING GOIN' ON (LP) | 30 |
| 69 | Blue Horizon 7-63213 | MIDNIGHT JUMP (LP, mono) | 100 |
| 69 | Blue Horizon S7-63213 | MIDNIGHT JUMP (LP, stereo) | 70 |

## SUNNYSIDERS
| | | | |
|---|---|---|---|
| 55 | London HL 8135 | Hey! Mr. Banjo/Zoom, Zoom, Zoom | 50 |
| 55 | London HL 8160 | Oh Me Oh My Oh/(Let's Gather Round) The Parlour Piano | 30 |
| 55 | London HLU 8180 | Banjo Woogie/She Didn't Even Say Goodbye | 30 |
| 55 | London HLU 8202 | I Love You Fair Dinkum/Stay On The Sunny Side | 25 |
| 56 | London HLU 8246 | Doesn't He Love Me/Humdinger | 30 |

## SUN RA ARKESTRA
| | | | |
|---|---|---|---|
| 74 | Decca F 13542 | Don't Go/Can We Change | 20 |
| 82 | Y 1 RA | NUCLEAR WAR (12" EP) | 35 |
| 69 | Fontana STL 5514 | HELIOCENTRIC WORLDS VOL. 1 (LP) | 50 |
| 69 | Fontana STL 5499 | HELIOCENTRIC WORLDS VOL. 2 (LP) | 50 |
| 60s | Sonet 23 SPL | JAZZ BY SUN RA (LP) | 40 |
| 71 | Black Lion BLP 30103 | PICTURES OF INFINITY - IN CONCERT (LP) | 30 |
| 71 | Byg 529 341 | THE SOLAR MYTH APPROACH VOL. 2 (LP) | 40 |
| 71 | Polydor 2460 106 | PICTURES OF INFINITY (LP) | 40 |
| 78 | Affinity AFF 10 | S-M APPROACH (LP, with Solar-Myth Ark) | 25 |
| 79 | Cobra COB 37001 | FATE IN A PLEASANT MOOD (LP) | 25 |
| 80 | Y Y 19 | STRANGE CELESTIAL ROAD (LP) | 25 |
| 85 | Saturn/Recommended SRRRD1 | COSMO SUN CONNECTION (LP, pasted cover) | 25 |
| 90 | Blast First BFFP 60 | SUN RA & MYTH SCIENCE ARKESTRA (3 x 10", box set, with insert) | 35 |

## SUNRAY
| | | | |
|---|---|---|---|
| 00 | Earworm WORM 68 | Music For The Dreammachine (Phase One) (Sonic Boom Remix)(1-sided 12", clear vinyl) | 10 |

## SUNRAYS
| | | | |
|---|---|---|---|
| 65 | Capitol CL 15416 | I Live For The Sun/Bye, Baby, Bye | 15 |
| 66 | Capitol CL 15433 | Andrea/You Don't Phase Me | 15 |

## SUNRISE
| | | | |
|---|---|---|---|
| 76 | Grapevine GRA 105 | BEFORE MY EYES (LP) | 30 |

## SUN SET
| | | | |
|---|---|---|---|
| 67 | Polydor BM 56193 | East Baby/You Can Ride My Rainbow | 20 |

## SUNSET BOYS
| | | | |
|---|---|---|---|
| 79 | Gimp GIM 1234 | Wreck My Bed/Tutti Frutti/Copy Cat (Blues)/Wreck My Bed (Hippy Version) (p/s) | 5 |

*(see also Maxim's Trash)*

## SUNSETS
| | | | |
|---|---|---|---|
| 61 | Ember EMB S 125 | Cry Of The Wild Goose/Manhunt | 15 |

## SUNSHINE COMPANY
| | | | |
|---|---|---|---|
| 67 | Liberty LBF 15008 | Happy/Blue May | 12 |
| 67 | Liberty LBF 15034 | Back On The Street Again/A Year Of Janie's Time | 10 |
| 68 | Liberty LBF 15060 | Look Here Comes The Sun/It's Sunday | 8 |
| 68 | Liberty LBF 15149 | On A Beautiful Day/To Put Up With You | 10 |
| 68 | Liberty LBL/LBS 83120 | THE SUNSHINE COMPANY (LP) | 35 |
| 69 | Liberty LBL/LBS 83159 | SUNSHINE AND SHADOWS (LP) | 35 |

## SUNSHINE KID
| | | | |
|---|---|---|---|
| 73 | RCA RCA 2413 | My Linda/Get Your Rocks Off Baby | 25 |

## MR. SUNSHINE
| | | | |
|---|---|---|---|
| 56 | MGM SP 1160 | Along The China Coast/MRS. SUNSHINE: Two Car Garage | 7 |

## SUNSHINE (1)
| | | | |
|---|---|---|---|
| 72 | Warner Brothers K 46169 | SUNSHINE (LP, gatefold sleeve) | 15 |

*(see also Pretty Things)*

## SUNSHINE (2)
| | | | |
|---|---|---|---|
| 81 | B's KNEES S 81 CUS 948 | Double Dealin/(Instrumental Version) | 10 |

## SUNSHINE THEATRE
| | | | |
|---|---|---|---|
| 71 | Harp SP1004 | Mountain/I Want | 300 |

## SUNSPOTS
| | | | |
|---|---|---|---|
| 63 | Decca F 11672 | Paella/Vancouver | 5 |

## SUNSTROKE
| | | | |
|---|---|---|---|
| 78 | Hot Stuff HS 004 | HERE COMES THE TRAIN EP | 20 |

## SUNTREADER
| | | | |
|---|---|---|---|
| 73 | Island HELP 13 | ZIN ZIN (LP, innser sleeve, black label, pink 'i' logo) | 15 |

## SUPER 8
| | | | |
|---|---|---|---|
| 95 | García POUM 001 | Billy The Kid/It Doesn't Matter/How Can I Understand The Flies? ('hairloss' p/s, 500 only, 37 sold, 35 returned for refund, the rest believed burned) | 25 |

## SUPER TONES
| | | | |
|---|---|---|---|
| 70 | Banana BA 312 | Freedom Blues/First Time I Met You | 50 |

## SUPERBOYS
| | | | |
|---|---|---|---|
| 68 | Giant GN 22 | Ain't That A Shame/Do It Right Now | 30 |
| 68 | Giant GN 31 | You're Hurtin' Me/Funky Soul | 30 |

*(see also Dandy & Superboys, Little Sal)*

## SUPER CAT
| | | |
|---|---|---|
| 88 | Blue Trac BTRD 020 | Nuff Man Dead Ya/ABC (12")..............................................................................30 |

## SUPERCHARGE
| | | |
|---|---|---|
| 76 | Virgin VS 145 | Lonely And In Love/Give It The Nasty .......................................................................6 |
| 78 | Virgin VS 20212 | I Think I'm Gonna Fall In Love/Long Version (12")..................................................10 |

## SUPERCHUNK
| | | |
|---|---|---|
| 95 | City Slang EFA 049661 | HERE'S WHERE THE STRINGS COME IN (LP, insert) ..................................................20 |

## SUPER COMBO
| | | |
|---|---|---|
| 75 | Rokel RKL 5001 | Woko/Afro Funk .......................................................................................................15 |

## SUPER FURRY ANIMALS
| | | |
|---|---|---|
| 95 | SFAP1 | Frisbee (12" promo, 1-sided, unreleased intended debut single. Not on a label)...........25 |
| 96 | Creation CRE 222 | Hometown Unicorn/Don't Be A Fool Billy (p/s) ........................................................6 |
| 98 | Creation CRE 288 | Ice Hockey Hair/Smokin' (stickered p/s, limited edition)...........................................6 |
| 00 | Placid Casual PLC02 | Ysbediau Heulog/Charge (White vinyl in PVC sleeve, 3000 only) ..............................6 |
| 95 | Ankst ANKST 057 | LLANFAIRPWLLGWYNGYLLGOGERYCHWYRNDROBWLLANTYSILIOGOGOGOCHYNYGOFOD (IN SPACE) (EP) (1st issue/2nd issue, same cat no).............................................................10 |
| 95 | Ankst ANKST 62 | MOOG DROOG EP (EP, 1st issue, p/s)...........................................................................10 |
| 96 | Creation CRELP 190 | FUZZY LOGIC (LP, with insert) ...................................................................................35 |
| 97 | Creation CRELP 214 | RADIATOR (2 x LP) ....................................................................................................60 |
| 98 | Creation CRELP 228 | OUT SPACED (LP).......................................................................................................40 |
| 99 | Creation CRELP 242 | GUERRILLA (2xLP, gatefold, pop up sleeve) ...............................................................50 |
| 00 | Placid Casual PLC03LP | MWNG (LP, ltd white vinyl, p/s PVC sleeve. 2000 copies) ..........................................50 |
| 01 | Sony/Epic 5024131 | RINGS AROUND THE WORLD (2xLP, side 3 plays from inside out, with free 7" white label 7") ......................................................................................................................80 |
| 03 | Epic 5123751 | PHANTOM POWER (2xLP etched vinyl with insert, 3000 copies) ................................50 |
| 04 | Placid Casual PL07CD | PHANTON PHORCE (2xLP ltd version with bonus 'Slow Life' EP disc, fold-out packaging. 3000 copies) ..........................................................................................25 |
| 05 | Epic 5176711 | SONGBOOK - THE SINGLES VOLUME ONE (2x12" pop up gatefold sleeve)..................35 |
| 05 | Sony 5205011 | LOVE KRAFT (2xLP, gatefold).....................................................................................18 |
| 15 | Domino REWIGLP98X | MWNG (3-LP, reissue, white vinyl)............................................................................25 |

*(see also Gruff Rhys)*

## SUPERGRASS
| | | |
|---|---|---|
| 94 | Backbeat BEAT 4 | Caught By The Fuzz/Strange Ones (hand-stamped labels, 1,000 only, later re-pressed). 10 |
| 94 | Backbeat BEAT 6 | Mansize Rooster/Sitting Up Straight (luminous green vinyl, printed green cardboard sleeve, 500 only) ...............................................................................................10 |
| 94 | Backbeat BEAT 6 | Mansize Rooster/Sitting Up Straight (luminous green vinyl, plain die-cut sleeve, 500 only) ...........................................................................................................................5 |
| 94 | Backbeat BEAT 6 | Mansize Rooster/Sitting Up Straight (marbled green vinyl, plain sleeve).......................5 |
| 94 | Parlophone R 6396 | Caught By The Fuzz/Strange Ones (p/s, reissue) ..........................................................5 |
| 95 | Parlophone R6413 | Alright/Time (gatefold p/s)...........................................................................................5 |
| 03 | Parlophone R6612 | Rush Hour Soul/Everything (p/s, green vinyl) ..............................................................5 |
| 97 | Parlophone GRASS 9497 | THE SINGLES 1994-1997 (8 x 7" black vinyl, 'grass'-covered box set, with signed & numbered insert, promo only) ...............................................................................30 |
| 95 | Parlophone PCSX 7373 | I SHOULD COCO (LP, with inner & bonus single "Stone Free"/"Odd?" [PCSS 7373]) ..... 70 |
| 97 | Parlophone 724385522819 | IN IT FOR THE MONEY (LP) .......................................................................................40 |
| 99 | Parlophone 5220561 | SUPERGRASS (LP, with poster) ..................................................................................40 |
| 02 | Parlophone 724354180019 | LIFE ON OTHER PLANETS (LP) ..................................................................................40 |
| 04 | EMI 5789941 | SUPERGRASS IS 10 : BEST OF 94-04 (2 x 10" LP, clear vinyl, gatefold)........................40 |
| 05 | Parlophone 333 334-1 | ROAD TO ROUEN (LP).................................................................................................35 |
| 08 | Parlophone 519 7341 | DIAMOND HOO HA (LP) .............................................................................................20 |

*(see also Jennifers, Hot Rats)*

## SUPERIMPOSERS
| | | |
|---|---|---|
| 05 | Little League LL 704 | Seeing Is Believing/Shadows ....................................................................................75 |

## SUPERMATIX
| | | |
|---|---|---|
| 81 | MC 4 | BAD TIMING EP (p/s)..................................................................................................20 |

## SUPER$HIT666
| | | |
|---|---|---|
| 00 | Infernal INFERNAL003LP | SUPER$HIT666 (10" LP, with inner sleeve, purple or black vinyl) ...............................10 |

*(see also Backyard Babies, Hellacopters, Wildhearts)*

## SUPERSISTER
| | | |
|---|---|---|
| 72 | Polydor 2001 379 | No Tree Will Grow/She Was Naked ...........................................................................12 |
| 71 | Dandelion 2310 146 | TO THE HIGHEST BIDDER (LP, gatefold sleeve)........................................................125 |
| 71 | Polydor 2419 030 | SUPER STARSHINE 3 (LP)............................................................................................40 |
| 72 | Polydor 2419 061 | PRESENT FROM NANCY (LP) ......................................................................................40 |
| 73 | Polydor 2480 153 | PUDDING & YESTERDAY (LP) .....................................................................................50 |
| 73 | Polydor 2925 021 | ISKANDER (LP, gatefold sleeve with lyric sheet) ........................................................25 |

## SUPERTRAMP
| | | |
|---|---|---|
| 70 | A&M AMLS 981 | SUPERTRAMP (LP, laminated sleeve, brown label) ....................................................50 |
| 71 | A&M AMLH 64306 | INDELIBLY STAMPED (LP, gatefold sleeve, brown label) ...........................................50 |
| 74 | A&M AMLS 68258 | CRIME OF THE CENTURY (LP, lyric inner) ..................................................................15 |
| 84 | A&M AMLK63708 | BREAKFAST IN AMERICA (LP, Nimbus Supercut mail order only through Practical Hi Fi magazine ..............................................................................................................80 |

## SUPPORTERS
| | | |
|---|---|---|
| 70 | RCA 1972 | Sing Your Own Team/On The Ball .............................................................................10 |

## (DIANA ROSS &) SUPREMES
| | | |
|---|---|---|
| 64 | Stateside SS 257 | When The Lovelight Starts Shining Thru' His Eyes/Standing At The Crossroads Of Love. 50 |
| 64 | Stateside SS 257 | When The Lovelight Starts Shining Thru' His Eyes/Standing At The Crossroads Of Love (DJ copy) ......................................................................................................100 |

*(Credited to Supremes.)*

| | | |
|---|---|---|
| 64 | Stateside SS 327 | Where Did Our Love Go/He Means The World To Me ................................................12 |
| 64 | Stateside SS 327 | Where Did Our Love Go/He Means The World To Me (DJ copy) ..............................100 |

| 64 | Stateside SS 350 | Baby Love/Ask Any Girl | 12 |
| 64 | Stateside SS 350 | Baby Love/Ask Any Girl (DJ copy) | 100 |
| 65 | Stateside SS 376 | Come See About Me/(You're Gone But) Always In My Heart | 12 |
| 65 | Stateside SS 376 | Come See About Me/(You're Gone But) Always In My Heart (DJ copy) | 100 |
| 65 | Tamla Motown TMG 501 | Stop! In The Name Of Love/I'm In Love Again | 12 |
| 65 | Tamla Motown TMG 501 | Stop! In The Name Of Love/I'm In Love Again (DJ copy) | 100 |
| 65 | Tamla Motown TMG 516 | Back In My Arms Again/Whisper You Love Me Boy | 25 |
| 65 | Tamla Motown TMG 516 | Back In My Arms Again/Whisper You Love Me Boy (DJ copy) | 85 |
| 65 | Tamla Motown TMG 527 | Nothing But Heartaches/He Holds His Own | 25 |
| 65 | Tamla Motown TMG 527 | Nothing But Heartaches/He Holds His Own (DJ copy) | 85 |
| 65 | Tamla Motown TMG 543 | I Hear A Symphony/Who Could Ever Doubt My Love | 20 |
| 65 | Tamla Motown TMG 543 | I Hear A Symphony/Who Could Ever Doubt My Love (DJ copy) | 75 |
| 66 | Tamla Motown TMG 548 | My World Is Empty Without You/Everything Is Good About You | 25 |
| 66 | Tamla Motown TMG 548 | My World Is Empty Without You/Everything Is Good About You (DJ copy) | 75 |
| 66 | Tamla Motown TMG 560 | Love Is Like An Itching In My Heart/He's All I Got | 50 |
| 66 | Tamla Motown TMG 560 | Love Is Like An Itching In My Heart/He's All I Got (DJ copy) | 150 |
| 66 | Tamla Motown TMG 575 | You Can't Hurry Love/Put Yourself In My Place | 15 |
| 66 | Tamla Motown TMG 575 | You Can't Hurry Love/Put Yourself In My Place (DJ copy) | 70 |
| 66 | Tamla Motown TMG 585 | You Keep Me Hangin' On/Remove This Doubt | 15 |
| 66 | Tamla Motown TMG 585 | You Keep Me Hangin' On/Remove This Doubt (DJ copy) | 60 |
| 67 | Tamla Motown TMG 597 | Love Is Here And Now You're Gone/There's No Stopping Us Now | 12 |
| 67 | Tamla Motown TMG 597 | Love Is Here And Now You're Gone/There's No Stopping Us Now (DJ copy) | 70 |
| 67 | Tamla Motown TMG 607 | The Happening/All I Know About You | 12 |
| 67 | Tamla Motown TMG 607 | The Happening/All I Know About You (DJ copy) | 75 |

*(The above 45s are credited to the Supremes.)*

| 67 | Tamla Motown TMG 616 | Reflections/Going Down For The Third Time | 12 |
| 67 | Tamla Motown TMG 616 | Reflections/Going Down For The Third Time (DJ copy) | 60 |
| 67 | Tamla Motown TMG 632 | In And Out Of Love/I Guess I'll Always Love You | 12 |
| 67 | Tamla Motown TMG 632 | In And Out Of Love/I Guess I'll Always Love You (DJ copy) | 40 |
| 68 | Tamla Motown TMG 650 | Forever Came Today/Time Changes Things | 12 |
| 68 | Tamla Motown TMG 650 | Forever Came Today/Time Changes Things (DJ copy) | 40 |
| 68 | Tamla Motown TMG 662 | Some Things You Never Get Used To/You've Been So Wonderful To Me | 10 |
| 68 | Tamla Motown TMG 662 | Some Things You Never Get Used To/You've Been So Wonderful To Me (DJ copy) | 40 |
| 68 | Tamla Motown TMG 677 | Love Child/Will This Be The Day? | 10 |
| 68 | Tamla Motown TMG 677 | Love Child/Will This Be The Day? (DJ copy) | 40 |
| 68 | Tamla Motown PSRS 317 | Love Child (special Royal Command Performance promo sent to journalists with Ken East "talking invite" with Love Child playing in the background) | 70 |
| 69 | Tamla Motown TMG 695 | I'm Living In Shame/I'm So Glad I Got Somebody (Like You Around) | 10 |
| 69 | Tamla Motown TMG 695 | I'm Living In Shame/I'm So Glad I Got Somebody (Like You Around) (DJ copy) | 40 |
| 69 | Tamla Motown TMG 704 | No Matter What Sign You Are/The Young Folks | 8 |
| 69 | Tamla Motown TMG 704 | No Matter What Sign You Are/The Young Folks (DJ copy) | 35 |
| 69 | Tamla Motown TMG 721 | Someday We'll Be Together/He's My Sunny Boy | 7 |
| 69 | Tamla Motown TMG 721 | Someday We'll Be Together/He's My Sunny Boy (DJ copy) | 35 |

*(The above 45s are credited to Diana Ross & Supremes.)*

| 70 | Tamla Motown TMG 735 | Up The Ladder To The Roof/Bill, When Are You Coming Back | 7 |
| 70 | Tamla Motown TMG 735 | Up The Ladder To The Roof/Bill, When Are You Coming Back (DJ copy) | 30 |
| 70 | Tamla Motown TMG 747 | Everybody's Got The Right To Love/But I Love You More | 8 |
| 70 | Tamla Motown TMG 747 | Everybody's Got The Right To Love/But I Love You More (DJ copy) | 25 |
| 70 | Tamla Motown TMG 760 | Stoned Love/Shine On Me | 6 |
| 71 | Tamla Motown TMG 760 | Stoned Love/Shine On Me (DJ copy) | 30 |
| 71 | Tamla Motown TMG 782 | Nathan Jones/Happy (Is A Bumpy Road) | 7 |
| 71 | Tamla Motown TMG 782 | Nathan Jones/Happy (Is A Bumpy Road) (DJ copy) | 30 |

*(The above 45s are credited to the Supremes and do not feature Diana Ross)*

| 65 | Tamla Motown TME 2008 | THE SUPREMES HITS (with flipback sleeve & push-out centre) | 30 |
| 65 | Tamla Motown TME 2008 | THE SUPREMES HITS | 35 |
| 66 | Tamla Motown TME 2011 | SHAKE (EP) | 75 |
| 64 | Stateside SL 10109 | MEET THE SUPREMES | 35 |
| 65 | Tamla Motown TML 11002 | WITH LOVE - FROM US TO YOU | 50 |
| 65 | Tamla Motown TML 11012 | WE REMEMBER SAM COOKE | 40 |
| 65 | Tamla Motown TML 11018 | THE SUPREMES SING COUNTRY, WESTERN AND POP | 40 |
| 65 | Tamla Motown TML 11020 | MORE HITS BY THE SUPREMES | 30 |
| 66 | T. Motown TML 11026 | THE SUPREMES AT THE COPA (mono) | 20 |
| 66 | T. Motown STML 11026 | THE SUPREMES AT THE COPA (stereo) | 25 |
| 66 | T. Motown TML 11028 | I HEAR A SYMPHONY (mono) | 20 |
| 66 | T. Motown STML 11028 | I HEAR A SYMPHONY (stereo) | 25 |
| 66 | T. Motown TML 11039 | SUPREMES A-GO GO (mono) | 25 |
| 66 | Tamla Motown STML 11039 | SUPREMES A-GO GO (stereo) | 35 |
| 67 | T. Motown TML 11047 | THE SUPREMES SING MOTOWN (mono) | 25 |
| 67 | T. Motown STML 11047 | THE SUPREMES SING MOTOWN (stereo) | 30 |
| 67 | T. Motown TML 11054 | THE SUPREMES SING RODGERS AND HART (mono) | 20 |
| 67 | T. Motown STML 11054 | THE SUPREMES SING RODGERS AND HART (stereo) | 22 |

*(The LPs listed above are credited to the Supremes, with flipback sleeves.)*

| 68 | T. Motown (S)TML 11063 | GREATEST HITS (stereo/mono, original pressing with flipback laminated sleeve) | 15 |
| 68 | T. Motown (S)TML 11070 | 'LIVE' AT LONDON'S TALK OF THE TOWN (mono/stereo) | 15 |
| 68 | T. Motown (S)TML 11073 | REFLECTIONS (mono/stereo) | 25 |
| 68 | T. Motown TML 11088 | SING & PERFORM FUNNY GIRL (mono) | 20 |
| 69 | T. Motown STML 11088 | SING & PERFORM FUNNY GIRL (stereo) | 18 |
| 69 | T. Motown TML 11095 | LOVE CHILD (mono) | 25 |
| 69 | T. Motown STML 11095 | LOVE CHILD (stereo) | 20 |

# SUPREMES & FOUR TOPS

| | | | |
|---|---|---|---|
| 69 | T. Motown TML 11114 | LET THE SUNSHINE IN (mono) | 25 |
| 69 | T. Motown STML 11114 | LET THE SUNSHINE IN (stereo) | 22 |
| 70 | T. Motown TML 11137 | CREAM OF THE CROP (mono) | 20 |
| 70 | T. Motown STML 11137 | CREAM OF THE CROP (stereo) | 18 |

*(The above LPs are credited to Diana Ross & Supremes. Originally issued with flipback sleeves; later pressings are worth two-third of these values.)*

| | | | |
|---|---|---|---|
| 70 | Tamla Motown STML 11157 | RIGHT ON (as Supremes) | 15 |
| 70 | T. Motown STML 11175 | NEW WAYS BUT LOVE STAYS | 15 |
| 71 | Tamla Motown STML 11189 | TOUCH (LP, as Supremes) | 15 |
| 73 | T. Motown STML 11222 | PRODUCED AND ARRANGED BY JIMMY WEBB (LP, as Supremes) | 15 |

*(see also Primettes, Diana Ross, Temptations, Four Tops, Florence Ballard)*

## SUPREMES & FOUR TOPS

| | | | |
|---|---|---|---|
| 71 | Tamla Motown TMG 777 | River Deep, Mountain High/It's Gotta Be A Miracle (This Thing Called Love) | 5 |
| 71 | Tamla Motown TMG 793 | You Gotta Have Love In Your Heart/I'm Glad About It | 5 |
| 71 | T. Motown STML 11179 | THE SUPREMES AND THE FOUR TOPS - MAGNIFICENT 7 (LP) | 15 |

## DIANA ROSS & THE SUPREMES & THE TEMPTATIONS

| | | | |
|---|---|---|---|
| 69 | Tamla Motown TMG 685 | I'm Gonna Make You Love Me/A Place In The Sun | 6 |
| 69 | Tamla Motown TMG 709 | I Second That Emotion/The Way You Do The Things You Do | 7 |
| 70 | Tamla Motown TMG 730 | Why (Must We Fall In Love)/Uptight (Everything Is Alright) | 8 |
| 69 | T. Motown TML 11096 | DIANA ROSS & THE SUPREMES JOIN THE TEMPTATIONS (LP, mono) | 20 |
| 69 | T. Motown STML 11096 | DIANA ROSS & THE SUPREMES JOIN THE TEMPTATIONS (LP, stereo) | 18 |
| 69 | T. Motown (S)TML 11110 | THE ORIGINAL SOUNDTRACK FROM TCB (LP, gatefold laminated sleeve) | 15 |
| 70 | T. Motown TML 11122 | TOGETHER (LP, flipback sleeve, mono) | 18 |
| 70 | T. Motown STML 11122 | TOGETHER (LP, flipback sleeve, stereo) | 15 |

## SUPREME WARRIOR

| | | | |
|---|---|---|---|
| 83 | Supreme Warrior SW001 | Treading The Tightrope/Mad & Cynical | 50 |

## ADAM SURF & PEBBLE BEACH BAND

| | | | |
|---|---|---|---|
| 76 | Paladin PAL 3 | Fun Fun Fun/Blue Surf | 10 |

## SURFACE TENSION

| | | | |
|---|---|---|---|
| 83 | Spiv 2TS | Rotation/Don't Let Them/Traffic Accident (p/s) | 15 |

## SURFARIS

| | | | |
|---|---|---|---|
| 63 | London HLD 9751 | Wipe Out/Surfer Joe | 10 |
| 63 | Brunswick 05894 | Waikiki Run/Point Panic | 15 |
| 64 | Brunswick 05902 | Scatter Shield/Bat Man | 15 |
| 66 | Dot DS 26756 | Wipe Out/Surfer Joe (reissue) | 10 |
| 63 | London RE-D 1405 | WIPE OUT (EP) | 35 |
| 63 | London HA-D 8110 | WIPE OUT (LP) | 40 |
| 63 | Brunswick LAT 8561 | THE SURFARIS PLAY (LP, mono) | 30 |
| 63 | Brunswick STA 8561 | THE SURFARIS PLAY (LP, stereo) | 40 |
| 64 | Brunswick LAT 8567 | HIT CITY '64 (LP, mono) | 30 |
| 64 | Brunswick STA 8567 | HIT CITY '64 (LP, stereo) | 40 |
| 64 | Brunswick LAT 8582 | FUN CITY (LP) | 30 |
| 65 | Brunswick LAT 8605 | HIT CITY '65 (LP) | 40 |
| 65 | Brunswick LAT 8631 | IT AIN'T ME BABE (LP, mono) | 35 |
| 65 | Brunswick STA 8631 | IT AIN'T ME BABE (LP, stereo) | 40 |
| 66 | Dot DLP 3535 | WIPE OUT (LP, reissue) | 25 |
| 87 | MCA MCL 1842 | WIPE OUT - THE SINGLES ALBUM 1963-1967 (LP, withdrawn) | 20 |

## SURFERS

| | | | |
|---|---|---|---|
| 59 | Vogue V 9147 | Mambo Jambo/ALAN KALANI: A Touch Of Pink | 10 |

## LES SURFS

| | | | |
|---|---|---|---|
| 64 | RCA RCA 1432 | Just For The Boy/Stop | 10 |
| 65 | RCA RCA 1461 | Go Your Way/Chained To A Memory | 7 |
| 67 | Fontana TF 832 | When I Tell You (That I Love You)/I Want To Be Free | 6 |

## SURGEONS

| | | | |
|---|---|---|---|
| 79 | Surgery S-100 | Sid Never Did It/Breaking Rocks On Riker's Island | 50 |

## SURGICAL SUPPORTS

| | | | |
|---|---|---|---|
| 81 | Industrious Youth CONSTRUCT 2 | WITHDRAWN FOR DISPOSAL EP | 30 |

## JOHN SURMAN (TRIO)

| | | | |
|---|---|---|---|
| 69 | Deram DM 224 | Obeah Wedding/Can't Stop The Carnival | 40 |
| 68 | Deram DML/SML 1030 | JOHN SURMAN (LP) | 90 |
| 69 | Deram DML-R/SML-R 1045 | HOW MANY CLOUDS CAN YOU SEE? (LP) | 100 |
| 70 | Futura GER 12 | ALORS! (LP) | 45 |
| 71 | Dawn DNLS 3006 | THE TRIO (LP, with Stu Martin, poster) | 70 |
| 71 | Dawn DNLS 3018 | WHERE FORTUNE SMILES (LP, with insert, with John McLaughlin, Karl Berger, Stu Martin & Dave Holland) | 40 |
| 71 | Dawn DNLS 3022 | CONFLAGRATION (LP) | 60 |
| 71 | Deram SML 1094 | TALES OF THE ALGONQUIN (LP, with John Warren) | 90 |
| 72 | Island HELP 10 | WESTERING HOME (LP) | 20 |
| 73 | Island ILPS 9237 | MORNING GLORY (LP) | 20 |
| 79 | Ogun OG 259 | BY CONTRACT (LP) | 18 |

*(see also Morning Glory, Trio, Mike Westbook, John McLaughlin, Alan Skidmore/Mike Osborne/John Surman)*

## SURPLUS STOCK

| | | | |
|---|---|---|---|
| 79 | Outatune OUT 7911 | Spiv/Vips (p/s) | 7 |

## SURPRISE SISTERS

| | | | |
|---|---|---|---|
| 76 | Good Earth GD1 | Seashore/La Booga Rooga | 8 |

## SURPRISES

| | | | |
|---|---|---|---|
| 79 | Dead Dog DEAD 01 | Jeremy Thorpe Is Innocent/Flying Attack/Little Sir Echo (p/s) | 35 |

## SURVIVORS (1)
| | | | |
|---|---|---|---|
| 65 | Rio R 55 | Take Charge/Ska-Ology | 25 |
| 65 | Rio R 70 | Rawhide Ska/OWEN GRAY: Girl I Want You | 35 |

## SURVIVORS (2)
| | | | |
|---|---|---|---|
| 79 | Capitol PSR 436 | Pamela Jean/After The Game (Credits the Beach Boys on p/s, Survivors on disc) | 10 |

*(see also The Beach Boys)*

## SURVIVORS (3)
| | | | |
|---|---|---|---|
| 79 | Tribesman TM 22 | Angel Of Love/Fashion Rock (12") | 15 |

## SUSHI
| | | | |
|---|---|---|---|
| 99 | Ariwa ARI 187 | Peace And Harmony/MAD PROFESSOR: Aahha (12") | 15 |

## SUSIE
| | | | |
|---|---|---|---|
| 71 | Decca F 13217 | I Feel The Earth Move/We Are All The Same | 20 |

## SUSPECT
| | | | |
|---|---|---|---|
| 71 | Decca FR 13218 | Mariooka/Belinda | 20 |

## SUSPEKT
| | | | |
|---|---|---|---|
| 93 | Union Hall UH002 | Under Suspicion (12") | 12 |

## SUSSED (1)
| | | | |
|---|---|---|---|
| 79 | Shoestring LACE 002 | I Like You/Tango/The Perv (p/s) | 15 |
| 80 | Graduate GRAD 7 | I've Got Me A Parka/Myself, Myself And I Repeated (p/s, paper labels; later reissued [1986] with silver labels) | 6 |

## SUSSED (2)
| | | | |
|---|---|---|---|
| 86 | Fusion FU 001 | Harlem Spirit/Part Two | 12 |

## (SCREAMING) LORD SUTCH (& THE SAVAGES)
| | | | |
|---|---|---|---|
| 61 | HMV POP 953 | Till The Following Night/Good Golly Miss Molly | 30 |
| 63 | Decca F 11598 | Jack The Ripper/Don't You Just Know It | 15 |
| 63 | Decca F 11747 | I'm A Hog For You/Monster In Black Tights | 15 |
| 64 | Oriole CB 1944 | She's Fallen In Love With A Monster Man/Bye Bye Baby | 50 |
| 64 | Oriole CB 1962 | Dracula's Daughter/Come Back Baby | 70 |
| 65 | CBS 201767 | The Train Kept A-Rollin'/Honey Hush (as Lord Sutch) | 50 |
| 66 | CBS 202080 | The Cheat/Black And Hairy | 50 |
| 70 | Atlantic 584 321 | Cause I Love You/Thumping Beat | 15 |
| 70 | Atlantic 2091 006 | Cause I Love You/Thumping Beat (reissue) | 6 |
| 70 | Atlantic 2091 017 | Election Fever/Rock The Election | 10 |
| 72 | Atlantic K 10221 | Gotta Keep A-Rockin'/Flashing Lights/Hands Of Jack The Ripper | 10 |
| 76 | SRT SRTS 76361 | Monster Ball/Rang-Tang-A-Lang | 8 |
| 76 | SRT SRTS 76375 | I Drink To Your Health Marie (Parts 1 & 2) | 8 |
| 77 | Decca F 13697 | Jack The Ripper/I'm A Hog For You | 6 |
| 80 | Ace SW 70 | All Black A Hairy/London Rocker/Oh Well | 8 |
| 89 | Invitation KORNER 001 | Creepy Christmas Party/Rap Up Christmas (no p/s) | 10 |
| 81 | Ridgemount RMR 45 010 | LOONABILLY (EP, p/s, with bonus "Loon Party" single) | 10 |
| 70 | Atlantic 2400 008 | LORD SUTCH AND HIS HEAVY FRIENDS (LP) | 25 |
| 72 | Atlantic K 40313 | HANDS OF JACK THE RIPPER (LP, as Lord Sutch & Heavy Friends) | 25 |
| 81 | Ace MAD 1 | THE METEORS MEET SCREAMING LORD SUTCH (mini-LP, 1 side each, stickered cartoon print on plain grey card sleeve, 1,000 only) | 100 |
| 82 | Ace CHA 65 | ROCK A HORROR (LP, gatefold) | 15 |

*(see also Savages, Meteors, Led Zeppelin, Cliff Bennett & Rebel Rousers, Circles, Nero & Gladiators, Neil Christian & Crusaders)*

## SUTCLIFFE JUGEND
| | | | |
|---|---|---|---|
| 82 | Come Org. WDC 883030 | WE SPIT ON THEIR GRAVES (10 x cassette box) | 150 |
| 82 | Come Org. WDC 883028 | CAMPAIGN (cassette, beware of Japanese bootlegs) | 75 |

## ROGER SUTCLIFFE
| | | | |
|---|---|---|---|
| 76 | Look LKLP 6038RS | DEATH LETTER (LP) | 30 |

## SUZANNE
| | | | |
|---|---|---|---|
| 77 | Ring O' 2017 108 | Born On Hallowe'en/Like No One Else (in promo p/s) | 25 |
| 77 | Ring O' 2017 108 | Born On Hallowe'en/Like No One Else | 12 |
| 78 | Ring O' 2017 111 | You Really Got A Hold On Me/You Could Be Right This Time | 10 |
| 78 | Ring O' 2017 115 | single (unreleased) | 0 |
| 78 | Ring O' 2320 105 | SUZANNE (LP, unreleased) | 0 |

## SUZI & BIG DEE IRWIN
| | | | |
|---|---|---|---|
| 66 | Polydor BM 65715 | Ain't That Lovin' You Baby/I Can't Get Over You | 15 |

*(see also Big Dee Irwin)*

## PAT SUZUKI
| | | | |
|---|---|---|---|
| 60 | RCA RCA 1171 | I Enjoy Being A Girl/Sunday | 7 |

## SUZY & THE RED STRIPES
| | | | |
|---|---|---|---|
| 77 | A&M AMS 7461 | Seaside Woman/B-side To The Seaside (yellow vinyl, die-cut p/s) | 10 |
| 79 | A&M AMSP 7461 | Seaside Woman/B-side To The Seaside (yellow vinyl, die-cut p/s, in box set with badge & 10 'saucy' mini-postcards) | 40 |
| 80 | A&M AMS 7548 | Seaside Woman/B-side To The Seaside (reissue, cartoon p/s, as Linda McCartney alias Suzy & Red Stripes) | 10 |
| 80 | A&M AMSP 7548 | Seaside Woman/B-side To The Seaside (12", as Linda McCartney alias Suzy & Red Stripes) | 12 |
| 86 | EMI EMI 5572 | Seaside Woman/B-side To The Seaside (p/s) | 6 |
| 86 | EMI 12EMI 5572 | Seaside Woman/B-side To The Seaside (12", p/s) | 10 |

*(see also Paul McCartney [& Wings])*

## SVANTE
| | | | |
|---|---|---|---|
| 68 | United Artists UP 2224 | Baby I Need Your Lovin'/Just One Word From You | 5 |

## SVENSK
| | | | |
|---|---|---|---|
| 67 | Page One POF 036 | Dream Magazine/Getting Old | 25 |
| 67 | Page One POF 050 | You/All I Have To Do Is Dream | 18 |

## SWALLOWS WITH SONNY THOMPSON
(see also Jason Paul)

| | | | |
|---|---|---|---|
| 52 | Vogue V 2136 | Roll, Roll Pretty Baby/It Ain't The Meat (78) | 50 |

(see also Sonny Thompson & His Rhythm & Blues Band)

## SWAMP DOGG
| | | | |
|---|---|---|---|
| 74 | Island USA 002 | Did I Come Back Too Soon/I Wouldn't Leave Here | 5 |
| 72 | Mojo 2916 014 | TOTAL DESTRUCTION TO YOUR MIND (LP) | 20 |
| 73 | President PTLS 1 | GAG A MAGGOT (LP) | 15 |

(see also Jerry Williams, Brooks & Jerry)

## SWAMP CHILDREN
| | | | |
|---|---|---|---|
| 82 | Factory FACT 70 | SWAMP CHILDREN (LP) | 20 |

## SWAMPFOXX
| | | | |
|---|---|---|---|
| 72 | Polydor 2058251 | I've Got A Thing About You Baby/On Your Side | 5 |

## SWAN ARCADE
| | | | |
|---|---|---|---|
| 73 | Trailer LER 2032 | SWAN ARCADE (LP) | 20 |
| 84 | Fellside FE 037 | TOGETHER FOREVER (LP) | 18 |

## SWANEE RIVER BOYS
| | | | |
|---|---|---|---|
| 54 | Parlophone CMSP 7 | Do You Believe/Gloryland Boogie (export issue) | 15 |

## BETTYE SWANN
| | | | |
|---|---|---|---|
| 67 | CBS 2942 | Make Me Yours/I Will Not Cry | 70 |
| 67 | CBS 2942 | Make Me Yours/I Will Not Cry (DJ copy) | 100 |
| 67 | CBS 2942 | Make Me Yours/I Will Not Cry (DJ copy in p/s) | 150 |
| 69 | Capitol CL 15586 | Don't Touch Me/(My Heart Is) Closed For The Season | 30 |
| 72 | Atlantic K 10174 | Victim Of A Foolish Heart/Cold Day In Hell | 10 |
| 72 | Atlantic K 10273 | Today I Started Loving You Again/I'd Rather Go Blind | 6 |
| 73 | Mojo 2092 059 | Make Me Yours/I Will Not Cry (reissue) | 6 |
| 75 | Atlantic K 10622 | Doing It For The One I Love/All The Way In Or All The Way Out | 6 |
| 75 | Contempo CS 9019 | Make Me Yours/I Will Not Cry (reissue) | 5 |
| 76 | Atlantic K 10851 | Heading In The Right Direction/Be Strong Enough To Hold On | 5 |
| 03 | Atlantic 69530 | Kiss My Love Goodbye/MAJOR HARRIS: Loving You Is Mellow | 8 |
| 04 | honest Jons HJRLP 8 | BETTYE SWANN (2-LP) | 18 |

(see also Sam Dees & Bettye Swann)

## RUTH SWANN
| | | | |
|---|---|---|---|
| 75 | Spark SRL 1124 | Tainted Love/Boy, You'd Better Move On | 5 |

## SWANS (1)
| | | | |
|---|---|---|---|
| 63 | Stateside SS 224 | He's Mine/You Better Be A Good Girl Now | 40 |
| 64 | Cameo Parkway C 302 | The Boy With The Beatle Hair/Please Hurry Home | 40 |

## SWANS (2)
| | | | |
|---|---|---|---|
| 84 | K422 KDE112 | YOUNG GOD (12" EP) | 18 |
| 86 | K.422/Some Bizzare KDE 312 | A Screw (Holy Money)/Blackmail/A Screw (12", p/s) | 10 |
| 88 | Product Inc. 12PROD 23 | Love Will Tear Us Apart (Red Version)/Trust Me/Love Will Tear Us Apart (Black Version)/Our Love Lies (12", black vinyl, p/s) | 15 |
| 88 | Product Inc. PROD 23 | Love Will Tear Us Apart/Trust Me (red vinyl, 750 only, p/s) | 10 |
| 84 | K.422/Some Bizzare KCC 1 | COPS (LP, with inner) | 25 |
| 90 | Young God | FILTH (LP, U.K. reissue, 500 only, numbered) | 30 |
| 86 | K. 422/Some Bizzare KCC 3 | HOLY MONEY (LP) | 18 |
| 87 | Product Inc. 33PROD 17 | CHILDREN OF GOD (2-LP) | 50 |
| 86 | K. 422/Some Bizzare KCC 2 | GREED (LP, with inner) | 25 |
| 86 | No label BURN ONE | PUBLIC CASTRATION IS A GOOD IDEA (2-LP) | 30 |
| 87 | Young God LOVE 1 | FEEL GOOD NOW (2-LP, with poster) | 35 |
| 89 | MCA MCG 6047 | THE BURNING WORLD (LP, with lyric inner) | 18 |
| 91 | Young Gods YGLP3 | WHITE LIGHT FROM THE MOUTH OF INFAMY (LP) | 75 |
| 92 | Young Gods YGLP 5 | LOVE OF LIFE (LP, insert) | 40 |
| 94 | Young God YGLP 9 | THE GREAT ANNIHILATOR (2-LP) | 125 |
| 95 | Young God YGLP 004 | BODY TO BODY, JOB TO JOB (LP) | 30 |
| 95 | Young God YGLP 005B | LOVE OF LIFE (LP, in box) | 80 |

## BENRICE SWANSON
| | | | |
|---|---|---|---|
| 65 | Chess CRS 8008 | Lying Awake/Baby I'm Yours | 30 |
| 65 | Chess CRS 8008 | Lying Awake/Baby I'm Yours (DJ copy) | 50 |

## DAVE SWARBRICK
| | | | |
|---|---|---|---|
| 67 | Bounty BYI 6030 | RAGS, REELS AND AIRS (LP, with Martin Carthy & Diz Disley) | 40 |
| 67 | Polydor Special 236 514 | RAGS, REELS AND AIRS (LP, reissue, with Martin Carthy & Diz Disley) | 25 |

(see also Martin Carthy & Dave Swarbrick, Fairport Convention,Young Tradition, Vashti Bunyan, Ian Campbell)

## SWARBRIGG (PLUS TWO)
| | | | |
|---|---|---|---|
| 75 | MCA MCA 179 | That's What Friends Are For/Love Is | 6 |

## SWEAT
| | | | |
|---|---|---|---|
| 80 | Double D DDLP | NO MORE RUNNING (LP, insert) | 20 |

## ROSALYN SWEAT & PARAGONS
| | | | |
|---|---|---|---|
| 73 | Duke DU 160 | Blackbird Singing/Always | 15 |

(see also Paragons)

## SWE-DANES
| | | | |
|---|---|---|---|
| 60 | Warner Bros WB 7 | Scandinavian Shuffle/Hot Toddy | 5 |
| 60 | Warner Bros WB 22 | Swe-Dane Shuffle/At A Georgia Camp Meeting | 5 |
| 61 | Warner Bros WEP 6017 | THE SWE-DANES (EP; mono) | 10 |
| 61 | Warner Bros SWEP 2017 | THE SWE-DANES (EP; stereo) | 15 |

(see also Alice Babsi)

## SWEDEN THROUGH THE AGES
| | | | |
|---|---|---|---|
| 86 | Snappy SW 001 | IT HELPS TO CRY EP (12", p/s) | 12 |

## SWEDISH MODERN JAZZ GROUP
| | | | |
|---|---|---|---|
| 61 | Tempo TAP 31 | SAX APPEAL (LP) | 200 |

## SWEENEY'S MEN
| | | | |
|---|---|---|---|
| 67 | Pye 7N 17312 | Old Maid In The Garrett/Derby Ram | 10 |
| 68 | Pye 7N 17459 | Waxies Dargle/Old Woman In Cotton | 10 |
| 69 | Transatlantic TRASP 19 | Sullivan's John/Rattlin' Roarin' Willy | 8 |
| 68 | Transatlantic TRA 170 | SWEENEY'S MEN (LP) | 90 |
| 69 | Transatlantic TRA 200 | THE TRACKS OF SWEENEY (LP) | 90 |
| 76 | Transatlantic TRASAM 37 | SWEENEY'S MEN (LP, reissue) | 20 |
| 77 | Transatlantic TRASAM 40 | THE TRACKS OF SWEENEY (LP, reissue) | 18 |

*(see also Gay & Terry Woods, Dr. Strangely Strange)*

## SWEENY BEAN
| | | | |
|---|---|---|---|
| 72 | Sonet SON 2028 | Rock 'N' Roll Wedding/Overcoat | 10 |

## JIM SWEENY
| | | | |
|---|---|---|---|
| 58 | Philips PB 811 | The Midnight Hour/Till The Right One Comes Along | 20 |

## SWEENY TODD
| | | | |
|---|---|---|---|
| 70s | London L2616 | Shut Up/Wastin' Time | 10 |
| 76 | London HLU 10540 | Roxy Roller/Rue De Chance | 12 |

## JIMMY SWEEP
| | | | |
|---|---|---|---|
| 81 | Tamarin TAM 3 | London Town/Bridgetown Girls (written, produced by & feat. Alan Lancaster) | 10 |
| 82 | PRT 7P 233 | London Town/Bridgetown Girls (reissue) | 8 |

*(see also Status Quo)*

## SWEEPERS
| | | | |
|---|---|---|---|
| 73 | Warner Bros K16318 | Harlem Song/Something's Real | 5 |

## SWEET
| | | | |
|---|---|---|---|
| 68 | Fontana TF 958 | Slow Motion/It's Lonely Out There | 400 |
| 69 | Parlophone R 5803 | The Lollipop Man/Time | 100 |
| 70 | Parlophone R 5826 | All You'll Ever Get From Me/The Juicer | 40 |
| 70 | Parlophone R 5848 | Get On The Line/Mr. McGallagher | 70 |
| 71 | RCA RCA 2051 | Funny Funny/You're Not Wrong For Loving Me | 6 |
| 71 | RCA RCA 2087 | Co Co/Done Me Wrong, All Right | 5 |
| 71 | Parlophone R 5902 | All You'll Ever Get From Me/The Juicer (reissue) | 15 |
| 71 | RCA RCA 2121 | Alexander Graham Bell/Spotlight | 5 |
| 73 | RCA RCA 2403 | Ballroom Blitz/Rock & Roll Disgrace (mispressed at wrong speed, 49rpm; matrix: 2403-A-1E) | 15 |
| 74 | RCA RCA 2480 | Turn It Down/Someone Else Will | 5 |
| 75 | RCA RCA 2578 | Action/Sweet FA | 5 |
| 76 | RCA RCA 2641 | The Lies In Your Eyes/Cockroach | 5 |
| 76 | RCA RCA 2748 | Lost Angels/Funk It Up | 5 |
| 77 | RCA PB 5011 | Fever Of Love/A Distinct Lack Of Ancient | 6 |
| 77 | RCA PB 5046 | Stairway To The Stars/Why Don't You Do It To Me | 8 |
| 78 | Polydor POSP 5 | California Nights/Show Me The Way (unreleased) | 0 |
| 79 | Polydor POSP 36 | Call Me/Why Don't You | 7 |
| 79 | Polydor POSP 73 | Big Apple Waltz/Why Don't You | 20 |
| 80 | RCA PE 5226 | Fox On The Run/Hellraiser/Ballroom Blitz/Blockbuster (EP, p/s) | 15 |
| 80 | Polydor POSP 131 | Give That Lady Some Respect/Tall Girls | 7 |
| 80 | Polydor POSP 160 | Sixties Man/Tall Girls | 5 |
| 80 | Polydor POSP 160 | Sixties Man/Oh Yeah | 15 |
| 80 | Polydor POSP 160 | Sixties Man/Oh Yeah (mispressing, B-side plays "Tall Girls") | 20 |
| 81 | RCA GOLD 524 | Blockbuster/Hellraiser (pink 'Golden Groove' p/s) | 5 |
| 81 | RCA GOLD 551 | Ballroom Blitz/Wig Wam Bam (pink 'Golden Groove' p/s) | 5 |
| 84 | Anagram ANA 27 | The Sixteens/Action (p/s) | 10 |
| 84 | Anagram ANA 28 | It's...It's... The Sweetest Mix/Fox On The Run (p/s) | 5 |
| 85 | Anagram ANA 29 | Sweet 2th - The Wig Wam-Willy Mix/The Teen Action Mix (p/s) | 8 |
| 89 | RCA PB 43337 | Wig Wam Bam/Little Willy (p/s) | 5 |
| 71 | RCA SF 8288 | FUNNY HOW SWEET CO-CO CAN BE | 20 |
| 74 | RCA LPL 15039 | SWEET FANNY ADAMS | 20 |
| 74 | RCA LPL 15080 | DESOLATION BOULEVARD (LP, gatefold sleeve) | 20 |
| 75 | RCA SPC 0001 | STRUNG UP (2xLP) | 35 |
| 76 | RCA RS 1036 | GIVE US A WINK | 15 |
| 77 | RCA PL 25072 | OFF THE RECORD (gatefold, with inner sleeve) | 18 |
| 78 | Polydor POLD5001 | LEVEL HEADED (LP) | 20 |
| 79 | Polydor POLD 5022 | CUT ABOVE THE REST (with inner sleeve) | 18 |
| 80 | Polydor POLS 1021 | WATER'S EDGE | 18 |
| 82 | Polydor 2311 1179 | IDENTITY CRISIS | 22 |
| 84 | Anagram GRAM 16 | SWEET SIXTEEN (LP) | 15 |
| 84 | Anagram P GRAM 16 | SWEET SIXTEEN (LP, picture disc) | 25 |

*(see also Brian Connolly, Mayfield's Mule, Elastic Band, Andy Scott)*

## SWEET AIR
| | | | |
|---|---|---|---|
| 70 | Chime CH 1 | Pictures In A Puddle/Sally Flnne | 200 |

## SWEET AROMA
| | | | |
|---|---|---|---|
| 73 | Rhino RNO 113 | Happiness/Rock Reggae (demos or stock copies) | 5 |

## SWEET AS CANDY
| | | | |
|---|---|---|---|
| 71 | Stem ST 3 | At The Bus Stop/The Missing Keys | 20 |

## SWEET BRIAR
| | | | |
|---|---|---|---|
| 70 | Access ACC 314 | The Liar/Choose Me/Sunworshipper (p/s) | 40 |

## SWEET HENRY
| | | | |
|---|---|---|---|
| 71 | Paramount PARA 3017 | Falling In Love With Baby/Love Is Two | 8 |

**SWEET PEA**
70  Tribual TR 1 — Run To The Forest/I'm In My Bad Books ............................................ 20

**RACHEL SWEET**
78  Stiff BUY 39 — B-A-B-Y/Suspended Animation (p/s).......................................... 5
79  Stiff BUY 44 — I Go To Pieces/Who Does Lisa Like? (p/s)............................... 5
79  Stiff BUY 55 — Baby Let's Play House/Wildwood Saloon (no p/s) .................. 5

**SWEET CHARIOT**
69  MCA MK 5010 — Heavenly Road/Wish I Were A Child .................................. 8
73  Columbia DB 8999 — When I'm A Kid/Mozart '73 ...................................... 8
70s  T.O.G. SCEP 001 — Angelina/Young At Heart/America .............................. 8
72  De Wolfe DWLP 3230 — SWEET CHARIOT & FRIENDS (LP, library issue only)......... 40

**SWEET CONFUSION**
69  Escort ES 809 — Elizabeth Serenade/Don At Rest...................................... 25
69  Escort ES 812 — Hotter Scorcher/Conquer Lion......................................... 8
*(see also Stranger & Patsy)*

**SWEETCORN**
71  Pye 7N45047 — We Can Work Together/Carpet Ride .............................. 15

**SWEET CORPORALS**
59  Top Rank JAR 217 — The Same Old Army/Warm And Willing............................ 5

**SWEET CREAM**
78  Ember EMBS 368 — I Don't Know What I'd Do.Skunk Funk .......................... 8

**SWEETEST ACHE**
90  Sarah SARAH 36 — If I Could Shine/Here Comes The Ocean (p/s, insert) .......... 10
90  Sarah SARAH 39 — Tell Me How It Feels/Heaven-Scented World (p/s, insert) ...... 12
91  Sarah SARAH 47 — Everlasting/Sickening (p/s, insert) ................................. 10
91  Sarah SARAH 608 — JAGUAR (LP) ........................................................... 25

**SWEET FEELING**
67  Columbia DB 8195 — All So Long Ago/Charles Brown ................................ 200
*(see also Rupert's People)*

**SWEETHEARTS**
65  Blue Beat BB 389 — Sit Down And Cry (actually with Clinton & Rufus)/PRINCE BUSTER: Ghost Dance ......... 80

**HARRY SWEETING**
68  Coxsone CSL 8012 — FROM JAMAICA WITH LOVE (LP) ................................ 100

**SWEET INSPIRATIONS**
67  Atlantic 584 117 — Why (Am I Treated So Bad)/I Don't Want To Go On Without You ..... 10
67  Atlantic 584 132 — Let It Be Me/When Something Is Wrong With My Baby.......... 10
68  Atlantic 584 167 — Sweet Inspiration/I'm Blue....................................... 10
68  Atlantic 584 233 — What The World Needs Now Is Love/You Really Didn't Mean It........ 10
69  Atlantic 584 241 — Sweet Inspiration/I'm Blue....................................... 6
69  Atlantic 584 279 — Sweets For My Sweet/Get A Little Older........................... 6
70  Atlantic 584 312 — (Gotta Find) A Brand New Lover (Parts 1 & 2) .................... 6
71  Atlantic 2091 073 — Evidence/Change Me Not........................................ 5
68  Atlantic 587/588 090 — THE SWEET INSPIRATIONS (LP) ............................. 20
69  Atlantic 587/588 137 — WHAT THE WORLD NEEDS NOW IS LOVE (LP) .......... 20
69  Atlantic 587/588 194 — SWEETS FOR MY SWEET (LP) ............................... 20
70  Atlantic 2465 003 — SWEET SWEET SOUL (LP) ...................................... 20
*(see also Cissy Houston)*

**SWEET JESUS**
91  Chapter 22 CHAP 63 — Cat Thing/Honey Loving Honey/Peach/Baby Blue (12" EP,....... 10

**SWEET LITTLE BUNTY**
75  Ackee ACK 540 — I (Who Have Nothing)/Oh Me Oh My .............................. 6

**SWEET PAIN**
71  United Artists UP 35268 — Timber Gibbs/Chain Up The Devil........................ 5
69  Mercury 20146 SMCL — SWEET PAIN (LP, laminated gatefold, black/silver label)........... 175
*(see also Dick Heckstall-Smith)*

**SWEET PLUM**
69  Middle Earth MDS 103 — Lazy Day/Let No Man Steal Your Thyme ................... 30
70  Middle Earth MDS 105 — Set The Wheels In Motion/Catch A Cloud ................. 30

**SWEET REACTION**
72  Satril SAT 5 — Come Back My Dream/Call Me Maria.................................. 10

**SWEET REVENGE**
80s  SRS SRS 15 — Feel The Bullets Bite/Inside Your Head ............................... 125

**SWEET SAVAGE**
81  Park PRK 1001 — Take No Prisoners/Killing TIme (p/s, red and yellow label) ....... 60
81  Park PRK 1001 — Take No Prisoners/Killing TIme (p/s, black and yellow label) ..... 40
80s  Crashed CAR 48 — Straight Through The Heart/Teaser (no p/s) ................... 150
80s  private pressing — The Raid/Prosecutors Of Greed (possibly unreleased) ........... 50
*(see also Dio, Whitesnake)*

**SWEETSHOP**
68  Parlophone R 5707 — Barefoot And Tiptoe/Lead The Way.......................... 30
*(see also Mark Wirtz)*

**SWEET SLAG**
71  President PTLS 1042 — TRACKING WITH CLOSE-UPS (LP) ........................... 100

**SWEET THUNDER**
78  Fantasy FTC 158 — Everybody's Singin' Love Songs/Joyful Noise .................. 5

**SWEET THURSDAY**
69  Polydor 2310 051 — SWEET THURSDAY (LP) .......................................... 25

*(see also Nicky Hopkins, Mark-Almond)*

## SWEETWATER
| | | | |
|---|---|---|---|
| 72 | Polydor 2058 239 | Uncle Tom/Apple Pie | 10 |

## SWEGAS
| | | | |
|---|---|---|---|
| 70 | Trend 6099 001 | What You Gonna Do/There Is Nothing In It | 10 |
| 71 | Trend 6480 002 | CHILD OF LIGHT (LP, gatefold sleeve) | 20 |

## SWELL
| | | | |
|---|---|---|---|
| 92 | Mean MEAN LP 002 | ...WELL? (LP, marble vinyl) | 15 |

## SWELL MAPS
| | | | |
|---|---|---|---|
| 78 | Rather GEAR ONE | Read About Seymour/Ripped And Torn/Black Velvet (p/s) | 35 |
| 79 | Rough Trade RT 010/Rather GEAR ONE MK. 2 | Read About Seymour/Ripped And Torn/Black Velvet (p/s, reissue, different back sleeve) | 15 |
| 79 | R. Trade RT 012/GEAR 3 | Dresden Style/Mystery Track/Ammunition Train/Full Moon (Dub) (p/s) | 25 |
| 79 | R. Trade RT 021/GEAR 6 | Real Shocks/English Verse/Monlogues (p/s, 2 different colours) | 25 |
| 79 | R. Trade RT 036/GEAR 7 | Let's Build A Car/Big Maz In The Country/...Then Poland (p/s) | 15 |
| 81 | Rough Trade RT 012/Rather GEAR 3 | Dresden Style (new vocal)/Ammunition Train/Full Moon (Dub) (p/s, reissue, different back sleeve) | 10 |
| 79 | Rough Trade ROUGH 2/Rather TROY 1 | A TRIP TO MARINEVILLE (LP, with inner sleeve, with bonus EP in die-cut sleeve [Rather GEAR FIVE]) | 45 |
| 79 | Rough Trade ROUGH 2/Rather TROY 1 | A TRIP TO MARINEVILLE (LP, with inner sleeve, without bonus EP in die-cut sleeve [Rather GEAR FIVE]) | 30 |
| 80 | Rough Trade ROUGH 15 | SWELL MAPS IN 'JANE FROM OCCUPIED EUROPE' (LP) | 35 |
| 81 | Rough Trade ROUGH 21 | WHATEVER HAPPENS NEXT... (2-LP) | 20 |
| 84 | Rough Trade ROUGH 41 | SWELL MAPS IN 'COLLISION TIME' (LP) | 15 |
| 89 | Mute MAPS 1 | A TRIP TO MARINEVILLE (LP, reissue) | 15 |
| 89 | Mute MPAS 2 | SWELL MAPS IN 'JANE FROM OCCUPIED EUROPE' (LP, reissue) | 15 |

*(see also Cult Figures, Nikki Sudden, Steve Treatment, Epic Soundtracks, Metrophase, Last Bandits)*

## SWERVEDRIVER
| | | | |
|---|---|---|---|
| 91 | Creation CREF 009 | Surf Twang/Deep Twang (p/s) | 6 |
| 91 | Creation CRE 079T | SON OF MUSTANG FORD EP (12") | 10 |
| 91 | Creation CRE 088T | RAVE DOWN EP (12") | 10 |
| 91 | Creation CRELP 093 | RAISE (LP, with free 7") | 35 |
| 91 | Creation CRELP 093 | RAISE (LP, without free 7") | 20 |
| 93 | Creation CRELP 143 | MEZCAL HEAD (LP) | 50 |
| 95 | Creation CRELP 157 | EJECTOR SEAT RESERVATION (LP, with free 7") | 35 |
| 95 | Creation CRELP 157 | EJECTOR SEAT RESERVATION (LP, without free 7") | 20 |
| 98 | Sonic Waves SWD 099LP | 99TH DREAM (LP) | 30 |

## ANTHONY SWETE
| | | | |
|---|---|---|---|
| 69 | RCA RCA 1905 | Backfield in Motion/Soul Deep | 8 |

## JONATHAN SWIFT
| | | | |
|---|---|---|---|
| 71 | CBS 64412 | INTROVERT (LP, side opening gatefold, nude cover) | 18 |
| 72 | CBS 64751 | SONGS (LP, with lyric insert) | 15 |

## TUFTY SWIFT
| | | | |
|---|---|---|---|
| 77 | Free Reed FRR 017 | HOW TO MAKE A BAKEWELL TART (LP, with booklet) | 25 |
| 85 | Shark SHARK 04 | YOU'LL NEVER DIE FOR LOVE (LP, private pressing) | 15 |

## SWIM DEEP
| | | | |
|---|---|---|---|
| 12 | Chess Club 88725478887 | Honey/Orange County | 10 |
| 13 | Chess Club CC 052 | The Sea/Down By The Seaside | 8 |
| 13 | Chess club CCLP 02 | WHERE THE HEAVEN ARE WE (LP & 7" signed) | 20 |

## ALAN SWIMMER & DEE DAVIDSON
| | | | |
|---|---|---|---|
| 70s | Fab FAB 242 | Take Me Back To Jamaica/Thousands Of Children | 5 |

## SWINDLEFOLK
| | | | |
|---|---|---|---|
| 69 | CAM 311 | DUSK TO DAWN (LP, white label, hand-mae sleeves) | 100 |
| 68 | Deroy | A-ROVIN' (LP, private pressing) | 50 |
| 69 | Deroy | SWINDLED (LP, private pressing) | 75 |

## RAY SWINFIELD
| | | | |
|---|---|---|---|
| 68 | Morgan MR 107P | ONE FOR RAY (LP) | 45 |

## SWINGERS
| | | | |
|---|---|---|---|
| 60 | Vogue V 9158 | Love Makes The World Go Round/Jackie | 15 |
| 67 | Blue Beat BB 379 | Simpleton/FRANCIS: Warn The People | 40 |

## SWINGERS
| | | | |
|---|---|---|---|
| 81 | Magnet MAG 202 | Be My Baby/Swinging | 5 |

*(see also Spectres, Rich Kids)*

## SWINGING BLUE JEANS
| | | | |
|---|---|---|---|
| 63 | HMV POP 1170 | It's Too Late Now/Think Of Me | 12 |
| 63 | HMV POP 1206 | Do You Know/Angie | 15 |
| 63 | HMV POP 1242 | Hippy Hippy Shake/Now I Must Go | 5 |
| 64 | HMV POP 1273 | Good Golly Miss Molly/Shakin' Feelin' | 5 |
| 64 | HMV POP 1304 | You're No Good/Don't You Worry About Me | 5 |
| 64 | HMV POP 1327 | Promise You'll Tell Her/It's So Right | 7 |
| 64 | HMV POP 1375 | It Isn't There/One Of These Days | 7 |
| 65 | HMV POP 1409 | Make Me Know You're Mine/I've Got A Girl | 10 |
| 65 | HMV POP 1477 | Crazy 'Bout My Baby/Good Lovin' | 8 |
| 66 | HMV POP 1501 | Don't Make Me Over/What Can I Do Today | 8 |
| 66 | HMV POP 1533 | Sandy/I'm Gonna Have You | 15 |
| 66 | HMV POP 1564 | Rumours, Gossip, Words Untrue/Now The Summer's Gone | 15 |
| 67 | HMV POP 1596 | Tremblin'/Something's Coming Along | 18 |
| 67 | HMV POP 1605 | Don't Go Out Into The Rain/One Woman Man | 18 |

# SWINGING CATS

| | | | |
|---|---|---|---|
| 64 | HMV 7EG 8850 | SHAKE WITH THE SWINGING BLUE JEANS (EP) | 40 |
| 64 | HMV 7EG 8868 | YOU'RE NO GOOD MISS MOLLY (EP) | 40 |
| 64 | HMV CLP 1802 | BLUE JEANS A' SWINGING (LP, mono) | 60 |
| 64 | HMV CSD 1570 | BLUE JEANS A' SWINGING (LP, stereo) | 75 |
| 64 | Regal SREG 1073 | TUTTI FRUTTI (LP, export issue) | 50 |
| 67 | MFP MFP 1163 | SWINGING BLUE JEANS (LP, reissue of HMV CLP 1802) | 15 |
| 74 | Dart BULL 1001 | BRAND NEW AND FADED (LP) | 18 |

*(see also Ray Ennis & Blue Jeans, Blue Jeans, Escorts)*

## SWINGING CATS
| | | | |
|---|---|---|---|
| 80 | Two Tone CHS TT 14 | Mantovani/Away (paper label, company sleeve) | 15 |
| 80 | Two Tone CHS TT 14 | Mantovani/Away (silver plastic label, company sleeve) | 25 |

## SWINGIN' MEDALLIONS
| | | | |
|---|---|---|---|
| 66 | Philips BF 1500 | Double Shot Of My Baby's Love/Here It Comes Again | 10 |
| 66 | Philips BF 1515 | She Drives Me Out Of My Mind/You Gotta Have Faith | 10 |

## SWINGING SAPERLIPOPETTE
| | | | |
|---|---|---|---|
| 79 | Kitty 7 | Little Claw/I'm Not A Teddy Bear | 30 |

## SWINGING SOUL MACHINE
| | | | |
|---|---|---|---|
| 69 | Polydor 56760 | Spooky's Day Off/Nobody Wants You | 15 |

*(see also Machine)*

## SWISS MOVEMENT
| | | | |
|---|---|---|---|
| 00 | Grapevine 118 | I Wish Our Love Would Last Forever/One In A Million | 10 |

## SWITCH 7
| | | | |
|---|---|---|---|
| 80 | Noisy HISS 1 | You Win/Credit Cards (no p/s) | 25 |

## SWORDEDGE
| | | | |
|---|---|---|---|
| 80 | Swordedge 001 | SWORDEDGE (LP) | 250 |

## SWORD OF JAH MOUTH
| | | | |
|---|---|---|---|
| 81 | Metro PBLP 001 | INVASION (LP) | 80 |

## SWORN LORD
| | | | |
|---|---|---|---|
| 90 | Davy G DG003 | The Vengeance Is Mine (12") | 80 |

## SWS
| | | | |
|---|---|---|---|
| 88 | DTI MAC2 | Boys From The Bec/Our Rhymes Are Fly (12") | 18 |
| 90 | Cue TCUE003 | Overture/Empirical Expansions/Info Nation/Leaf In The Wind | 12 |

## SYD & JOE
| | | | |
|---|---|---|---|
| 72 | Bullet BU 498 | Three Combine/LES FOSTER : I'm The Nearest To Your Heart | 5 |

## SYDNEY (CROOKS) ALL STARS
| | | | |
|---|---|---|---|
| 70 | Bullet BU 436 | The Return Of Batman/In Action | 10 |
| 70 | Bullet BU 437 | Outer Space/Full Moon | 30 |

*(see also Pioneers, Junior English, Sammy Morgan)*

## JOHN SYKES
| | | | |
|---|---|---|---|
| 82 | MCA MCA 792 | Please Don't Leave Me/(Instrumental) (with Phil Lynott, in p/s) | 35 |
| 82 | MCA MCA 792 | Please Don't Leave Me/(Instrumental) (with Phil Lynott) | 10 |

*(see also Thin Lizzy, Phil Lynott, Tygers Of Pan Tang, Whitesnake)*

## SYKES & MEDINA
| | | | |
|---|---|---|---|
| 69 | CBS 4529 | Everything's Fine Fine Fine/I Can Feel The Thickness | 10 |

## ROOSEVELT SYKES
| | | | |
|---|---|---|---|
| 56 | Vogue V 2389 | Fine And Brown/Too Hot To Hold | 75 |
| 56 | Vogue V 2389 | Fine And Brown/Too Hot To Hold (78) | 30 |
| 56 | Vogue V 2393 | Walkin' This Boogie/Security Blues | 75 |
| 56 | Vogue V 2393 | Walkin' This Boogie/Security Blues (78) | 30 |
| 66 | Delmark DJB 2 | BACK TO THE BLUES (EP) | 30 |
| 62 | Encore ENC 183 | BIG MAN OF THE BLUES (LP) | 25 |
| 61 | Columbia 33SX 1343 | FACE TO FACE WITH THE BLUES (LP) | 30 |
| 62 | Columbia 33SX 1422 | THE HONEYDRIPPER (LP, with Alexis Korner) | 60 |
| 65 | Bluesville BVLP 1006 | THE RETURN OF ROOSEVELT SYKES (LP) | 25 |
| 67 | 77' 77LEU 12-50 | BLUES FROM BAR ROOMS (LP) | 30 |
| 67 | Riverside RLP 8819 | MR SYKES' BLUES 1929-1932 (LP) | 22 |
| 67 | Ember EMB 3391 | ROOSEVELT SYKES SINGS THE BLUES (LP) | 20 |
| 71 | Barclay 920 294 | THE HONEYDRIPPERS' DUKE'S MIXTURE (LP) | 15 |
| 70s | Delmark DL 607 | HARD DRIVIN' BLUES (LP, blue label) | 15 |

*(see also Robert Pete Williams)*

## SYKO & CARIBS
| | | | |
|---|---|---|---|
| 64 | Blue Beat BB 213 | Do The Dog/Jenny | 15 |
| 64 | Blue Beat BB 223 | Big Boy/Sugar Baby | 15 |

## SYKO & MAK
| | | | |
|---|---|---|---|
| 92 | PM PMT 002 | MURDA EP (12") | 10 |
| 92 | PM PMT 004 | HOMICIDE EP (12") | 20 |

## SYLTE SISTERS
| | | | |
|---|---|---|---|
| 63 | London HLU 9753 | Summer Magic/Well It's Summertime | 15 |

## SYLVAIN SYLVAIN
| | | | |
|---|---|---|---|
| 80 | RCA PB 9500 | Every Boy And Every Girl/Emily | 5 |

*(see also New York Dolls)*

## SYLVAN
| | | | |
|---|---|---|---|
| 65 | Columbia DB 7674 | We Don't Belong/Life's Colours Have Gone | 15 |

## GOOD PAUL SYLVAN
| | | | |
|---|---|---|---|
| 70 | Polydor 2001 090 | Ophelia/Stop Making A Fool Of Me | 6 |

## C. SYLVESTER & PLANETS
| | | | |
|---|---|---|---|
| 64 | Blue Beat BB 206 | Going South/LITTLE JOYCE: Oh Daddy | 12 |

## ROLAND SYLVESTER
64   Carnival CV 7018        Grandfather's Clock/SANDRA MURRAY: Nervous.............................................6

## SYLVESTER'S JUKE BOX
73   CBS 8419        Juke Box/It's Because ...............................................................50

## SYLVIA
67   Fontana TF 884        Make Me A Woman/Without Your Love ...............................................10
68   Fontana TF 932        Down Hill/A Few Sweet Moments Of Love ............................................10

## SYLVIA (U.S.)
68   Soul City SC 103        I Can't Help It/It's A Good Life .......................................................20
75   London HLU 10415        Pillow Talk/My Thing...................................................................7

## DAVID SYLVIAN
84   Virgin VS 717        Pulling Punches (7" Mix)/Backwaters (Remix) (p/s, with 3 postcards)...........5
87   Virgin V2471        SECRETS OF THE BEEHIVE (LP) ......................................................15
89   Virgin DSCD 1        WEATHERBOX (5-CD box set, with poster & booklet) ...........................100
04   Samadhisound SOUNDLP 1        BLEMISH (LP, gatefold sleeve, featuring Derek Bailey, 2000 only, extra track: Trauma) ..60
*(See also Japan, Virginia Astley)*

## DAVID SYLVIAN & ROBERT FRIPP
93   Virgin V2712        THE FIRST DAY (2-LP, inners) ........................................................40

## SYLVIN & GLENROY
70   Torpedo TOR 25        What You Gonna Do 'Bout It/KEN JONES: Sad Mood ...............................20

## SYMBOL
79   Art & Craft AC 001        Motherless Children/RANKING CARETAKER: Take It Away (12") ..................40
79   Kebra Nagast KH 04        Black Man's Word/Mr. Oppressor (12")..............................................15

## SYMBOLICS
76   Angen ANG 119        Tell Them Jah Jah/Version ..............................................................8

## SYMBOLS
65   Columbia DB 7459        One Fine Girl/Don't Go................................................................10
65   Columbia DB 7664        You're My Girl/Why Do Fools Fall In Love ............................................10
66   President PT 104        See You In September/To Make You Smile Again .....................................8
66   President PT 113        Canadian Sunset/The Gentle Art Of Loving...........................................6
67   President PT 128        You'd Better Get Used To Missing Her/Hideaway......................................6
67   President PT 144        Bye Bye Baby/The Things You Do To Me ..............................................10
67   President PT 173        (The Best Part Of) Breaking Up/Again.................................................10
68   President PT 190        Lovely Way To Say Goodnight/Pretty City ............................................18
68   President PT 216        Do I Love You/Schoolgirl...............................................................20
72   CBS 7725        No No No/Woman .......................................................................8
75   Crystal CR 7021        Sound Of Sunset (Instrumental)/Canadian Sunset (Vocal Recording) ............6
68   President PTL 1018        THE BEST PART OF THE SYMBOLS (LP).............................................25
*(see also Johnny Milton & Condors)*

## SYMON & PI
68   Parlophone R 5662        Sha La La La Lee/Baby Baby.............................................................25
68   Parlophone R 5719        Got To See The Sunrise/Love Is Happening To Me....................................12

## DAVID SYMONDS
68   Philips BF 1652        Here Is The News/Don't Worry About A Thing........................................5

## SYMPHONICS
73   Polydor 2058 341        Heaven Must Have Sent You/Using Me ...............................................15

## SYMPHONIC SLAM
76   A&M AMLH 69023        SYMPHONIC SLAM (LP) ...............................................................20

## PAT SYMS
64   Oriole CB 1971        It's Got To Be You Or No One/Lost ....................................................7

## SYN
67   Deram DM 130        Created By Clive/Grounded ..........................................................120
67   Deram DM 145        14-Hour Technicolour Dream/Flowerman...........................................120
*(see also Syndicats, Yes, Peter Banks)*

## SYNANTHESIA
69   RCA SF 8058        SYNANTHESIA (LP)...................................................................400

## SYNCHROMESH
80   Rok ROK XI/XII        October Friday/E.F. BAND: Another Day Gone (company die-cut sleeve) ....................40

## SYNDICATE OF SOUND
66   Stateside SS 523        Little Girl/You...........................................................................35
66   Stateside SS 538        Rumours/The Upper Hand ............................................................18
66   Stateside S(S)L 10185        LITTLE GIRL (LP).......................................................................50

## SYNDICATE (1)
79   Stevenage/Rock Against Racism        One Way Or Another/I Want To Be Somebody/RESTRICTED HOURS: Getting Things Done/Still Living Out The Car Crash (white label, foldover p/s)...........12
*(see also Astronauts)*

## SYNDICATE (2)
81   EMI 12EMI 5182        Dance You To The Ground/Step On The Gas (12")..................................35

## SYNDICATS
64   Columbia DB 7238        Maybellene/True To Me ..............................................................150
65   Columbia DB 7441        Howlin' For My Baby/What To Do ...................................................250
65   Columbia DB 7686        On The Horizon/Crawdaddy Simone..................................................650
65   Columbia DB 7686        On The Horizon/Crawdaddy Simone (demos) .......................................450
*(see also Peter Banks, Ray Fenwick, Syn, Tomorrow, Yes)*

## SYNTHETIC DREAMS
81   Logical Step LOGIC 02        Obsessions/U+500 (p/s) ...............................................................15
82   Logical Step LOGIC 03        Sulphate Suicide/Voices (p/s).........................................................10

MINT VALUE £

## SYNYX
82   Reality Attack RAF 1 | BLACK DEATH (EP, fold out sleeve,plain white labels) ................................................. 20

## SYRUP
70   Amity OTS 501 | Gentlemen Joe's Sidewalk Café/Love Is Love ...................................................... 6

## SYSTEM OF A DOWN
99   Columbia/American | Sugar/War (live) ........................................................................................... 30
01   Columbia 672634 7 | Chop Suey!/Johnny (clear vinyl) ................................................................... 8
01   Columbia 5015341 | TOXICITY (LP) .............................................................................................. 30

## SYSTEM X (EX)
94   3rd Eye EYE 001 | MINDGAMES EP (12") ...................................................................................... 20
94   3rd Eye EYE 002 | SOMETHING OF REAL EXISTENCE EP (12", white label, various coloured vinyl) ............. 20
94   3rd Eye EYE 004 | SOMETHING OF INTELLEGENT EXISTENCE EP (12") ...................................... 25
*(see also Studio Pressure)*

## SYSTEM (1)
77   Tash | THE OTHER SIDE OF TIME (LP, 250 copies only) ......................................................... 110

## SYSTEM (2)
82   Spiderleg SDL 11 | THE WARFARE (EP) ............................................................................................. 12
82   Spiderleg SDL 11 | THE SYSTEM IS MURDER (EP) .......................................................................... 10

## SYZYGY
85   Taptag TAP 3 | LADY IN GREY (mini-LP) ................................................................................ 20
*(see also Blackthorn)*

## GABOR SZABO
66   HMV CLP 3614 | JAZZ RAGA (LP) ................................................................................................ 25
67   Impulse MILP 506 | THE SORCERER (LP, mono) ............................................................................ 30

## LEO SZILARD
80   KIK 3 | Stranger/On Comes The Night ............................................................................. 10

# T

## ANDY T
82   221984/05 | WEARY OF THE FLESH (EP) ................................................................................. 15
*(see also Crass)*

## ERROL T. & ROOSEVELT ALL STARS
72   Ashanti ASH 406 | Jamaica Born And Bred/Version ..................................................................... 7

## JAMIE T.
05   Pacemaker PANICSDJ 001 | So Lonely Was The Ballad/Back In The Game (p/s, 500 only) ................... 15
06   Pacemaker PANICS 002 | Salvador/Livin With Betty (p/s) ................................................................... 10
06   Virgin VS 1921 | If You Got The Money/A New England (gatefold p/s) ................................. 8
06   Virgin VSX 1921 | If You Got The Money/Here's Ya Getaway (stickered p/s, poster) ............. 5
06   Virgin VS 1917 | Sheila/Down To The Northern Line (fold out p/s) ................................... 5
06   Virgin VSX 1917 | Sheila/Down To The Subway (p/s) ....................................................... 5
07   Virgin 0094637885512 | PANIC PREVENTION (LP) ..................................................................... 60
09   Virgin V3059 | KINGS AND QUEENS (LP) ................................................................. 40

## T. & UNKNOWN
80   Carrere CAR 142 | My Generation/Woodstock Rock (p/s) ......................................................... 12

## TABLE
77   Virgin VS 176 | Do The Standing Still/Magical Melon Of The Tropics (p/s) ......................... 8
78   Chiswick NS 28 | Sex Cells/The Road Of Lyfe (p/s) .................................................................. 7

## TABLE TOPPERS
62   Starlite ST45 069 | Rocking Mountain Dew/My Wild Irish Rose Rock ................................... 20

## CHARLIE TABOR
63   Island WI 061 | Blue Atlantic/Red Lion Madison .................................................................. 20

## JUNE TABOR
86   Strange Fruit SFPS 015 | THE PEEL SESSIONS (12" EP) ...................................................... 15
77   Topic 12TS 360 | ASHES AND DIAMONDS (LP) ............................................................... 15

## TAC-TIX
88   R.E. Good GSM 188 | Whisper On The Street/R.E. Good (p/s) ........................................... 15

## TAD & SMALL FRY
62   London HLU 9542 | Checkered Continental Pants/Pretty Blue Jean Baby .......................... 15

## TADPOLE
73   More MR2 | Follow The Rain/Suzy Jones ........................................................................ 15

## TADPOLES
69   High Note HS 032 | Rasta/Like Dirt ...................................................................................... 8

## TAFARI & PAUL FOX
90   Cause N Effect CE 007 | Jah Jah Bless Mandela/Version .......................................................... 20
90   Cause N Effect CE12 007 | Jah Jah Bless Mandela/Version (12") ......................................... 25

## TAG
75   Philips 6006 477 | Off Down The Road/Guitar Love .......................................................... 15

## TAGES
66   Columbia DB 8019 | Crazy 'Bout My Baby/In My Dreams .................................................. 15
66   HMV POP 1515 | So Many Girls/I'm Mad .................................................................... 50
67   Parlophone R 5640 | Treat Me Like A Lady/Wanting ....................................................... 15

| | | |
|---|---|---|
| 68 | Parlophone R 5702 | There's A Blind Man Playin' Fiddle In The Street/Like A Woman ....................... 15 |
| 68 | MGM MGM 1443 | Halcyon Days/I Read You Like An Open Book.................................................... 20 |

*(see also Blond)*

## BLIND JOE TAGGART
| | | |
|---|---|---|
| 52 | Tempo R 55 | Religion Is Something Within You/Mother's Love (78) ..................................... 20 |
| 55 | Jazz Collector L 129 | Religion Is Something Within You/Mother's Love (78, reissue) ......................... 15 |

## TAGMEMICS
| | | |
|---|---|---|
| 80 | Index INDEX 003 | Chimneys/(Do The) Big Baby/Take Your Brain Out For A Walk (p/s, with insert) ........... 15 |

*(see also Art Attacks)*

## TAICONDEROGA
| | | |
|---|---|---|
| 69 | Beacon BEA 143 | Whichi Tai To/Speakin' My Mind ..................................................................... 70 |

## JACQUELINE TAIEB
| | | |
|---|---|---|
| 68 | Fontana TF 952 | Tonight I'm Going Home/7 A.M. .................................................................. 150 |

## LYN(N) TAIT(T) (& THE JETS)
| | | |
|---|---|---|
| 66 | Doctor Bird DB 1006 | Vilma's Jump Up (as Lyn Taitt & The Comets)/GLEN MILLER & HONEYBOY MARTIN: Dad Is Home ................................................................................................. 25 |
| 66 | Doctor Bird DB 1047 | Spanish Eyes (with Tommy McCook)/STRANGER & HORTENSE: Loving Wine ............... 30 |
| 67 | Island WI 3066 | Something Stupid/Blue Tuesday (as Lyn Tait & the Jets) ................................... 40 |
| 67 | Island WI 3075 | I Don't Want To Make You Cry/Nice Time (as Lyn Tait & the Jets)....................... 40 |
| 68 | Island WI 3139 | Napoleon Solo/Pressure And Slide (as Lyn Taitt & the Jets)............................... 50 |
| 68 | Amalgamated AMG 810 | El Casino Royale/Dee's Special (as Lynn Taitt & the Jets) ................................. 35 |
| 68 | Pama PM 723 | Soul Food/Music Flames (as Lyn Tait & the Jets) ............................................ 30 |
| 68 | Island ILP 969 | SOUNDS ROCK STEADY (LP, as Lyn Taitt & the Jets) ...................................... 250 |
| 68 | Big Shot BBTL 4002 | GLAD SOUNDS (LP, as Lynn Taitt & the Jets) .............................................. 150 |

*(see also Mike Thompson Jnr, ALton Ellis, Ken Boothe, Baba Brooks)*

## YUKIHIRIO TAKAHASHI
| | | |
|---|---|---|
| 82 | Alfa 86393 | NEUROMANTIC (LP) ....................................................................................... 15 |

*(see also Yellow Magic Orchestra)*

## TAKE FIVE
| | | |
|---|---|---|
| 60s | D.S.C.A (no cat. no.) | MY GIRL (EP, oversized p/s; Dundee Students Charity Appeal record) ................ 100 |

## TAKE IT
| | | |
|---|---|---|
| 79 | Fresh Hold TRI | Man Made World/Taking Sides/How It Is (p/s) ............................................... 40 |
| 80 | Fresh Hold FHR 1 | Twenty Lines/Armchairs/Friends And Relations (foldout p/s with insert) .............. 20 |

## TAKE THAT
| | | |
|---|---|---|
| 91 | Dance U.K. DUK 2 | Do What U Like/Waiting Around (p/s) ............................................................ 15 |
| 91 | Dance U.K. 12DUK 2 | Do What U Like (Club Mix)/Do What U Like (Radio Mix)/Waiting Around (12", p/s; most with wrong tracks listed on sleeve) ....................................................... 25 |

*(see also Robbie Williams)*

## TAKE 3
| | | |
|---|---|---|
| 84 | Elite DAZZ 32 | Music & Time/Music & Time (extended version) (12") ..................................... 15 |

## 'TAKERS
| | | |
|---|---|---|
| 64 | Pye 7N 15690 | If You Don't Come Back/Think ....................................................................... 25 |

*(see also Undertakers, Jackie Lomax)*

## TALAN
| | | |
|---|---|---|
| 89 | Talan SRT 9KS 2208 | Spellbinder/Underground Madness (p/s) ........................................................ 20 |

## TALBOT BROTHERS
| | | |
|---|---|---|
| 59 | Melodisc MEL 1507 | Bloodshot Eyes/She's Got Freckles ............................................................... 15 |
| 60s | Melodisc CAL 20 | Bloodshot Eyes/She's Got Freckles (reissue) .................................................. 6 |

## ZIGGY TALENT
| | | |
|---|---|---|
| 55 | Brunswick 05506 | Cheek To Cheek (Cha Cha)/Bozooki Blues ...................................................... 7 |

## TALES
| | | |
|---|---|---|
| 73 | MAM 93 | Someone Like You/Rockin' Suzanna ............................................................... 15 |

## TALES OF JUSTINE
| | | |
|---|---|---|
| 67 | HMV POP 1614 | Albert/Monday Morning (in p/s) ................................................................. 180 |
| 67 | HMV POP 1614 | Albert/Monday Morning ................................................................................ 60 |
| 97 | Tenth Planet TP 034 | PETALS FROM A SUNFLOWER (LP, gatefold sleeve, numbered, 1,000 only)............. 30 |

## TALISKER
| | | |
|---|---|---|
| 75 | Caroline CA 1513 | DREAMING OF GLENISLA (LP) ......................................................................... 25 |

## TALISMAN (1)
| | | |
|---|---|---|
| 73 | Argo AFW 110 | Stepping Stones/Dr Jazz ................................................................................. 5 |
| 73 | Argo ZDA 161 | STEPPING STONES (LP) ................................................................................. 12 |

## TALISMAN (2)
| | | |
|---|---|---|
| 81 | Recreational SPORT 22 | Wicked Dem/Run Come Girl (12", p/s) ........................................................... 10 |
| 84 | Embryo CELA 1T | TAKIN THE STRAIN (LP) ................................................................................ 15 |

## TALISMEN
| | | |
|---|---|---|
| 65 | Stateside SS 408 | Masters Of War/Casting My Spell .................................................................. 70 |

## TALKBACK
| | | |
|---|---|---|
| 83 | Cottage S 83 CUS 1991 | Pleasure/Everyday ....................................................................................... 10 |

## TALKIES
| | | |
|---|---|---|
| 81 | Hook HK1 | I Fell In Love Last Night/Foreign Legion (p/s) ................................................. 20 |

## TALKING HEADS
| | | |
|---|---|---|
| 77 | Sire 6078 604 | Love Goes To Building On Fire/New Feeling (p/s) .............................................. 7 |
| 77 | Sire SAM 87 | Love Goes To Building On Fire/New Feeling (limited edition, in p/s) ................... 12 |
| 77 | Sire SAM 87 | Love Goes To Building On Fire/New Feeling ..................................................... 10 |
| 77 | Sire 6078 610 | Psycho Killer/I Wish You Wouldn't Say That (p/s) ........................................... 10 |
| 77 | Sire 6078 610 | Psycho Killer/Psycho Killer (Acoustic)/I Wish You Wouldn't Say That (12", p/s)............ 12 |
| 78 | Sire 6078 620 | Pulled Up/Don't Worry About The Government (p/s)........................................ 10 |

MINT VALUE £

| | | | |
|---|---|---|---|
| 79 | Sire SIR 4004 | Take Me To The River/Found A Job (p/s) | 10 |
| 79 | Sire SIR 4004/SAM 87 | Take Me To The River/Found A Job//Love Goes To Building On Fire/ Psycho Killer (double pack, gatefold p/s) | 15 |
| 79 | Sire SIR 4027 | Life During Wartime (live version)/Electric Guitar (p/s) | 12 |
| 80 | Sire SIR 4033 | I Zimbra/Paper (p/s) | 10 |
| 80 | Sire SIR 4040 | Cities/Cities (live) (p/s) | 7 |
| 80 | Sire SIR 4040T | Cities/Cities (live)/Artists Only (live) (12", p/s) | 10 |
| 80 | Sire SIR 4048 | Once In A Lifetime/Seen And Not Seen (p/s) | 5 |
| 80 | Sire SIR 4050 | Houses In Motion (Special Re-Mixed Version)/Air (p/s) | 8 |
| 80 | Sire SIR 4050T | Houses In Motion/Air/Houses In Motion (Live) (12") | 10 |
| 85 | EMI 12EMID 5520 | Lady Don't Mind/Give Me Back My Name//Slippery People (live)/This Must Be The Place (Naive Melody) (live) (12", p/s, double pack) | 10 |
| 77 | Sire SR6036 | TALKING HEADS : 77 (LP, inner) | 20 |
| 78 | Sire K 56531 | MORE SONGS ABOUT BUILDING AND FOOD (LP, inner) | 18 |
| 79 | Sire K 56707 | FEAR OF MUSIC (LP, with free single "Psycho Killer"/"New Feeling" [SAM 108]) | 25 |
| 79 | Sire SRK6076 | FEAR OF MUSIC (LP, without free 7", inner) | 18 |
| 80 | Sire SRK 6095 | REMAIN IN LIGHT (LP, inner and insert) | 15 |
| 83 | EMI 9237711 | SPEAKING IN TONGUES (LP, clear vinyl in special cover) | 18 |
| 99 | EMI 4994711 | STOP MAKING SENSE (2-LP, reissue) | 20 |

## TALK TALK

| | | | |
|---|---|---|---|
| 82 | EMI EMI 5265 | Mirror Man/Strike Up The Band (p/s) | 5 |
| 84 | EMI EMID 5433 | THE TALK TALK DEMOS (double pack, poster p/s [EMI 5433 & PSR 467]) | 10 |
| 86 | EMI 12EMID 5540 | Life's What You Make It (Extended)/It's Getting Late In The Evening// It's My Life/ Does Caroline Know? (12", p/s, double pack) | 15 |
| 86 | EMI EMIP 5551 | Living In Another World/For What It's Worth (shaped picture disc) | 15 |
| 91 | Verve TALKD 1 | After The Flood/Myrrhman (CD, picture disc in 3-CD box) | 15 |
| 91 | Verve TALKD 2 | New Grass/Stump (CD, picture disc) | 10 |
| 91 | Verve TALKD 3 | Ascension Day/5.09 (CD, picture disc) | 10 |
| 91 | Verve TALKD1/2/3 | After The Flood/Myrrhman//New Grass/Stump//Ascension Day/5.09 (3-CD, in die-cut box) | 40 |
| 88 | Parlophone PCSD 50105 | SPIRIT OF EDEN (LP) | 40 |
| 97 | EMI LPCENT 14 | THE COLOUR OF SPRING (LP, reissue, EMI 100 Centenary, stickered sleeve) | 20 |
| 91 | Polydor 847 717-1 | LAUGHING STOCK (LP) | 70 |
| 00 | Simply Vinyl SVLP 224 | IT'S MY LIFE (LP, reissue 180gram vinyl) | 20 |
| 12 | Parlophone PCSDX105 | SPIRIT OF EDEN (LP, reissue, with CD) | 15 |

*(see also Reaction)*

## TOM TALL

| | | | |
|---|---|---|---|
| 55 | London HL 8150 | Are You Mine/Boom Boom Boomerang (as Ginny Wright & Tom Tall) | 20 |
| 55 | London HLU 8216 | Give Me A Chance/Remembering You | 40 |
| 56 | London HLU 8231 | Underway/Goldie Jo Malone | 40 |
| 57 | London HLU 8429 | Don't You Know/If You Know What I Know (with Ruckus Taylor) | 40 |
| 55 | London RE-U 1035 | COUNTRY SONGS VOL. 2 (EP, as Tom Tall & Ginny Wright) | 25 |

*(see also Ginny Wright)*

## TALL BOYS

| | | | |
|---|---|---|---|
| 82 | Big Beat NS 79 | Island Of Lost Souls/Another Half Hour Till Sunrise (p/s) | 8 |
| 85 | Big Beat NS 107 | Final Kick/Interceptor (p/s) | 6 |

*(see also Meteors)*

## TALMY/STONE BAND

| | | | |
|---|---|---|---|
| 62 | Decca F 11543 | Madison Time/Madison Time (A-side with Alan Freeman) | 10 |

## TALULAH GOSH

| | | | |
|---|---|---|---|
| 86 | 53rd & 3rd AGARR 4 | Beatnik Boy/My Best Friend (p/s) | 8 |
| 86 | 53rd & 3rd AGARR 5 | Steaming Train/Just A Dream (p/s) | 5 |
| 86 | 53rd & 3rd AGARR 4/5T | Beatnik Boy/My Best Friend/Steaming Train/Just A Dream (12", p/s) | 15 |
| 87 | 53rd & 3rd AGARR 8 | Talulah Gosh/Don't Go Away (p/s) | 5 |
| 88 | 53rd & 3rd AGARR 14 | Bringing Up Baby/The Girl With The Strawberry Hair (p/s) | 6 |
| 88 | 53rd & 3rd AGARR 16 | Testcard Girl (p/s) | 5 |
| 87 | 53rd & 3rd AGAS 004 | ROCK LEGENDS VOL. 69 (LP, clear vinyl) | 15 |
| 91 | Sarah 064 | THEY'VE SCOFFED THE LOT (LP) | 20 |

## TAMANGOES

| | | | |
|---|---|---|---|
| 79 | Grapevine GRP 122 | I Really Love You/You've Been Gone So Long | 20 |

## TAMEN

| | | | |
|---|---|---|---|
| 72 | Flake FL 1 | Sweet Loretta, Make No Mistakes/Drifting (p/s) | 50 |

## TAMINDAY

| | | | |
|---|---|---|---|
| 73 | Dile DL3 | Dear Lisa/Break The Chain | 30 |

## TAMING THE OUTBACK

| | | | |
|---|---|---|---|
| 86 | Black Sun BS 1 | Blue Heart/Fire | 15 |

## JAMES TAMLIN

| | | | |
|---|---|---|---|
| 65 | Columbia DB 7438 | Is There Time/Main Line Central Station | 20 |
| 65 | Columbia DB 7577 | Yes I Have/Now There Are Two | 10 |

## TAMLINS

| | | | |
|---|---|---|---|
| 79 | Deb Music DEB 007 | Still Water/AUGUSTUS PABLO: Spirit Of Umoja (12") | 20 |
| 80 | Taxi RIC 110 | Baltimore/Laying Beside You | 10 |
| 76 | State ETAT 9 | BLACK BEAUTY (LP) | 15 |

## TAMPA RED

| | | | |
|---|---|---|---|
| 64 | RCA RCX 7160 | R & B VOL. 3 (EP) | 25 |
| 60s | Memory TR 1 | TAMPA RED (LP) | 35 |

## TAMPA RED/GEORGIA TOM

| | | | |
|---|---|---|---|
| 59 | Jazz Collector JEL 3 | THE MALE BLUES VOLUME 2 (EP) | 20 |

## TAMS
| | | | |
|---|---|---|---|
| 63 | Stateside SS 146 | Untie Me/Disillusioned | 30 |
| 63 | HMV POP 1254 | What Kind Of Fool Do You Think I Am/Laugh It Off | 20 |
| 64 | HMV POP 1298 | It's All Right, You're Just In Love/You Lied To Your Daddy | 18 |
| 64 | HMV POP 1331 | Hey Girl Don't Bother Me/Take Away | 150 |
| 64 | HMV POP 1331 | Hey Girl Don't Bother Me/Take Away (DJ copy) | 200 |
| 65 | HMV POP 1464 | Concrete Jungle/Till The End Of Time | 15 |
| 69 | Stateside SS 2123 | Be Young, Be Foolish, Be Happy/That Same Old Song | 15 |
| 70 | Capitol CL 15650 | Too Much Foolin' Around/How Long Love | 15 |
| 75 | ABC ABC 4020 | Hey Girl Don't Bother Me/Be Young, Be Foolish, Be Happy | 8 |
| 68 | Stateside (S)SL 10258 | A LITTLE MORE SOUL (LP) | 40 |
| 70 | Stateside SSL 10304 | BE YOUNG, BE FOOLISH, BE HAPPY (LP) | 25 |

## TANAMO
| | | | |
|---|---|---|---|
| 63 | Island WI 108 | Come Down/I Am Holding On (actually by Lord Tanamo) | 30 |

## TANDOORI CASSETTE
| | | | |
|---|---|---|---|
| 83 | IKA IKA 001 | Angel Talk/Third World Brief Case (p/s, 5,000 only) | 20 |

*(see also Nazareth, Alex Harvey, Tear Gas, Stone The Crows)*

## SHARON TANDY
| | | | |
|---|---|---|---|
| 65 | Mercury MF 898 | Love Makes The World Go Round/By My Side | 30 |
| 65 | Pye 7N 15806 | Now That You've Gone/Hurtin' Me | 40 |
| 65 | Pye 7N 15939 | I've Found Love/Perhaps Not Forever | 15 |
| 67 | Atlantic 584 098 | Toe Hold/I Can't Get Over It | 20 |
| 67 | Atlantic 584 124 | Stay With Me/Hold On | 60 |
| 67 | Atlantic 584 137 | Our Day Will Come/Look And Find | 20 |
| 68 | Atlantic 584 166 | Fool On The Hill/For No One | 20 |
| 68 | Atlantic 584 181 | Love Is Not A Simple Affair/Hurry Hurry Choo-Choo | 40 |
| 68 | Atlantic 584 194 | You've Gotta Believe It/Border Town | 20 |
| 68 | Atlantic 584 214 | The Way She Looks At You/He'll Hurt Me | 30 |
| 68 | Atlantic 584 219 | Hold On/Daughter Of The Sun | 100 |
| 69 | Atlantic 584 242 | Gotta Get Enough Time/Somebody Speaks Your Name | 80 |

*(see also Fleur-De-Lys, Tony & Tandy)*

## NORMA TANEGA
| | | | |
|---|---|---|---|
| 66 | Stateside SS 496 | Walkin' My Cat Named Dog/I'm The Sky | 6 |
| 66 | Stateside SS 520 | A Street That Rhymes At Six A.M./Treat Me Right | 8 |
| 66 | Stateside SS 537 | Bread/Waves | 5 |
| 71 | RCA 2072 | Nothing Much Is Happening Today/Antarctic Rose | 5 |

## TANGERINE DREAM
| | | | |
|---|---|---|---|
| 74 | Virgin PR 214 | Phaedra (Edit)/Mysterious Semblance At The Strand Of Nightmares (promo) | 30 |
| 76 | Virgin VDJ 17 | Stratosfear/The Big Sleep In Search Of Hades (promo only) | 25 |
| 77 | MCA PSR 413 | Betrayal (Sorceror Theme)/Search (promo only) | 25 |
| 77 | Virgin VS 199 | Encore/Hobo March | 5 |
| 81 | Virgin VS 444 | Chronozon/Network 23 (p/s) | 8 |
| 84 | Jive Electro P 74 | Warsaw In The Sun/Polish Dance (map-shaped picture disc) | 15 |
| 84 | Jive Electro T 74 | Warsaw In The Sun (Parts 1 & 2)/Polish Dance/Rare Bird (12", p/s) | 12 |
| 85 | Jive JIVE 101 | Streethawk/Tear Garden (p/s) | 15 |
| 85 | Jive Electro T 101 | STREETHAWK (12" EP) | 20 |
| 87 | Jive Electro 143 | Tyger/21st Century Common Man II (p/s) | 6 |
| 87 | Jive Electro T 143 | Tyger/Tyger (7" Version)/21st Century Common Man II (12", p/s) | 10 |
| 74 | Virgin V2010 | PHAEDRA (LP, copies with A1U/B2U matrixes and catalogue number misprinted with catalogue number on top left hand of gatefold sleeve instead of rear) | 20 |
| 74 | Polydor Super 2383 297 | ATEM (LP) | 20 |
| 75 | Polydor Super 2383 314 | ALPHA CENTAURI (LP) | 20 |
| 78 | Virgin V2111 | FORCE MAJEURE (LP, clear vinyl, textured stickered sleeve) | 15 |
| 80 | Virgin VBOX 2 | TANGERINE DREAM '70-80 (4-LP box set) | 40 |
| 80 | Virgin TCVX 2 | TANGERINE DREAM '70-80 (4-cassette box set) | 25 |
| 81 | Virgin V 2212 | EXIT (LP, 1st 1,000 with poster) | 15 |
| 84 | MCA MCF 3233 | FIRESTARTER (LP, soundtrack) | 15 |
| 84 | Jive Electro HIPX 22 | POLAND - THE WARSAW CONCERT (2-LP, picture disc) | 25 |
| 85 | Heavy Metal HMI PD 29 | FLASHPOINT (LP, soundtrack, picture disc) | 12 |
| 85 | Heavy Metal HMXD 29 | FLASHPOINT (CD, soundtrack; playable CD [most copies faulty]) | 40 |
| 86 | Jive Electro TANG 1 | IN THE BEGINNING (3-LP box set, with booklet) | 30 |
| 90 | Virgin TD AK 11 | TANGERINE DREAM (3-CD, 'Collector's Edition' box set) | 25 |
| 03 | Virgin 724359612829 | TANGENTS 1973 - 1983 (5-CD box set with booklet) | 30 |

*(see also Edgar Froese, Klaus Schulze)*

## TANGERINE PEEL
| | | | |
|---|---|---|---|
| 67 | United Artists UP 1193 | Every Christian Lion-Hearted Man Will Show You/Trapped | 30 |
| 68 | CBS 3402 | Solid Gold Mountain/Light Across The River | 130 |
| 68 | CBS 3676 | Talking To No One/Wishing Tree | 20 |
| 69 | MGM MGM 1470 | Never Say Never Again/A Thousand Miles Away | 15 |
| 69 | MGM MGM 1487 | Play Me A Sad Song And I'll Dance/Wish You Could Be Here With Me | 15 |
| 70 | RCA RCA 1936 | Move Into My World/In Between | 6 |
| 70 | RCA RCA 1990 | Soft Delights/Thinking Of Me | 6 |
| 70 | RCA RCA 2036 | What Am I To Do?/Don't Let Me Be Misunderstood | 6 |
| 70 | RCA LSA 3002 | SOFT DELIGHTS (LP) | 25 |

## TANGLE BROTHERS
| | | | |
|---|---|---|---|
| 85 | Tangle TB 001 | Jessica/Hopes A Stranger (p/s with insert) | 12 |

## TANGO
| | | | |
|---|---|---|---|
| 92 | Formation FORM 12004 | THE IMPACT EP (12", p/s) | 15 |

## TANGO PROJECT
| | | | |
|---|---|---|---|
| 92 | White 004 | Project 1/Untitled (12", white label test pressing) | 50 |

## TANK (1)
| | | | |
|---|---|---|---|
| 73 | Polydor 2058391 | Fast Train/The World's An Apple | 20 |
| 72 | Bumble GE 105 | Heads I Win, Tails You Lose/Burgundy, Port And Red Wine | 20 |

## TANK (2)
| | | | |
|---|---|---|---|
| 81 | Kamaflage KAM 1 | Don't Walk Away/Shellshock/Hammer On (p/s, with cover mounted patch) | 10 |
| 81 | Kamaflage KAM 1 | Don't Walk Away/Shellshock/Hammer On (p/s) | 8 |
| 82 | Kamaflage KAM 3 | Turn Your Head Around/Steppin' On A Landmine (p/s) | 15 |
| 82 | Kamaflage KAM 7 | Crazy Horses/Filth Bitch Boogie (p/s) | 5 |
| 82 | Kamaflage KAMLP 1 | FILTH HOUNDS OF HADES (LP, 1st pressing, with black & yellow sleeve) | 15 |
| 82 | Kamaflage KAMLP 1 | FILTH HOUNDS OF HADES (LP, 2nd pressing, with bonus p/s 7" Don't Walk Away (live)/"The Snake" [KAM F1]) | 15 |
| 83 | Music For Nations MFN 3P | THIS MEANS WAR (LP, picture disc) | 20 |

*(see also Damned)*

## PHIL TANNER
| | | | |
|---|---|---|---|
| 68 | EDF SSLP 1005 | PHIL TANNER (LP, with lyric book) | 25 |

## TAN TAN
| | | | |
|---|---|---|---|
| 81 | Maccabees MPCLP TT1 | MUSICAL NOSTALGIA FOR TODAY (LP) | 40 |

## TANTARA
| | | | |
|---|---|---|---|
| 86 | President PT 12-543 | I.D.O/Rumours (12") | 100 |

## TANTARA BLADE
| | | | |
|---|---|---|---|
| 88 | King Dice | Seven Shades Of Shame/This Car Has Crushed (p/s) | 50 |

## TANTONES
| | | | |
|---|---|---|---|
| 57 | Vogue V 9085 | So Afraid/Tell Me | 500 |
| 57 | Vogue V 9085 | So Afraid/Tell Me (78) | 100 |

## TANZ DER YOUTH
| | | | |
|---|---|---|---|
| 78 | Radar ADA 19 | I'm Sorry, I'm Sorry/Delay (p/s) | 5 |

*(see also Brian James, Damned)*

## TAO JONES INDEX
| | | | |
|---|---|---|---|
| 97 | RCA 512541 | Pallas Athena (live)/V-2 Schneider (live) (12", p/s) | 12 |

*(see also David Bowie)*

## TAPESTRY (1)
| | | | |
|---|---|---|---|
| 67 | London HLZ 10138 | Carnaby Street/Taming Of The Shrew | 30 |
| 68 | NEMS 56-3679 | Like The Sun/Florence | 20 |
| 69 | NEMS 5639-64 | Heart & Soul/Who Wants Happiness | 60 |

## TAPESTRY (2)
| | | | |
|---|---|---|---|
| 73 | Rosemount ROS EP 1 | Oh Mountain/Till We Meet/Fire And Rain | 30 |

## DEMETRISS TAPP
| | | | |
|---|---|---|---|
| 64 | Coral Q 72470 | Lipstick Paint A Smile On Me/If You Find Love | 40 |

## TARA
| | | | |
|---|---|---|---|
| 70 | Polydor 2062009 | Happy/The Love Of A Woman | 15 |

## TARANTULA
| | | | |
|---|---|---|---|
| 70 | A&M AMLS 959 | TARANTULA (LP) | 15 |

## JIMMY TARBUCK
| | | | |
|---|---|---|---|
| 65 | Immediate IM 018 | Someday/(We're) Wastin' Time | 7 |

## TARHEEL SLIM & LITTLE ANN
| | | | |
|---|---|---|---|
| 65 | Sue WI 390 | You Make Me Feel So Good/Got To Keep On Lovin' You | 40 |

## TARNEY BAND, ALAN
| | | | |
|---|---|---|---|
| 78 | A&M AMS 7339 | Takin Me Back/Set The Minstrel Free | 6 |

## DAVE TARRIDA
| | | | |
|---|---|---|---|
| 99 | Mosquito MSQ 013 | PLAYING THE GAME (12" EP) | 10 |

## TARRIERS
| | | | |
|---|---|---|---|
| 56 | London HLN 8340 | Cindy, Oh Cindy/Only If You Praise The Lord (gold label lettering, as Vince Martin & Tarriers) | 15 |
| 56 | London HLN 8340 | Cindy, Oh Cindy/Only If You Praise The Lord (silver label lettering, as Vince Martin & Tarriers) | 7 |
| 57 | Columbia DB 3891 | The Banana Boat Song/No Hidin Place | 10 |
| 57 | Columbia DB 3961 | Tom Dooley/Everybody Loves Saturday Night | 5 |
| 57 | Columbia DB 4025 | Dunya/Quinto (My Little Pony) | 5 |
| 58 | Columbia DB 4148 | I Know Where I'm Going/Acres Of Clams | 5 |
| 58 | London HLU 8600 | Lonesome Traveller/East Virginia | 5 |
| 57 | Columbia 33S 1115 | THE TARRIERS (10" LP) | 15 |
| 62 | London STA 8525 | A LIVE PERFORMANCE AT THE BITTER END (LP) | 15 |

*(see also Vince Martin)*

## TARTAN HORDE
| | | | |
|---|---|---|---|
| 75 | United Artists UP 35891 | Bay City Rollers, We Love You/Rollers Theme | 15 |

*(see also Nick Lowe, Rat Scabies, Roogalator)*

## TARTANS
| | | | |
|---|---|---|---|
| 67 | Island WI 3058 | Dance All Night/What Can I Do | 25 |
| 68 | Caltone TONE 115 | Awake The Town (with Lynn Taitt's Band)/LYNN TAITT & JETS: The Brush | 70 |
| 68 | Caltone TONE 117 | Coming On Strong/It's Alright (with Tommy McCook's Band) | 80 |
| 71 | Escort ERT 843 | A Day Will Come/ROBI'S All STARS: Version | 15 |

*(see also Devon & Tartans, Kaddo Strings, Max Romeo, Derrick Morgan)*

## TARTS
| | | | |
|---|---|---|---|
| 81 | If You Can't Take A Joke JOKE1 | Tie Me Kangeroo Down/Gene Queenie | 100 |

## TASAVALLAN PRESIDENTTI
| 73 | Sonet SNTF 636 | LAMBERTLAND (LP) | 30 |
| 74 | Sonet SNTF 658 | MILKY WAY MOSES (LP, with insert) | 30 |

## TASKFORCE
| 00 | White(Lowlife)grafpromo1 | Graf Da Bus Up (12" - One sided, 500 pressed) | 15 |
| 00 | White(Lowlife)no matrix | Wha Blow (12", 1-Sided white label, 200 only) | 15 |
| 00 | Lowlife LOW10 | VOICE OF THE GREAT OUTDOORS (EP, 2000 only p/s) | 30 |
| 01 | Rehab RHB001 | A LIFE WITHOUT INSTRUCTIONS (EP) | 15 |
| 02 | White no matrix | Graf Da Bus Up/Wha Blow (2 Mixes of A side, 12") | 12 |
| 06 | White WS01 | The Bitches (3 versions) (12", 500 only) | 20 |
| 99 | K'Boro KBR1005 | NEW MIC ORDER (LP) | 40 |
| 03 | MFTC MFTC 02 | MUSIC FROM THE CORNER VOL 2 (2-LP) | 15 |

## TASSELS
| 59 | London HL 8885 | To A Soldier Boy/The Boy For Me | 100 |
| 59 | London HL 8885 | To A Soldier Boy/The Boy For Me (78) | 40 |
| 59 | Top Rank JAR 229 | To A Young Lover/My Guy And I | 30 |

## TASSILLI PLAYERS
| 95 | Universal Egg WWLP 011 | WONDERFUL WORLD OF WEED IN DUB (LP) | 20 |

## TASTE
| 68 | Major Minor MM 560 | Blister On The Moon/Born On The Wrong Side Of Time | 70 |
| 69 | Polydor 56313 | Born On The Wrong Side Of Time/Same Old Story | 10 |
| 70 | Major Minor MM 718 | Born On The Wrong Side Of Time/Blister On The Moon | 10 |
| 69 | Polydor 583 042 | TASTE (LP, laminated sleeve) | 50 |
| 70 | Polydor 583 083 | ON THE BOARDS (LP, textured sleeve) | 40 |
| 71 | Polydor 2310 082 | LIVE TASTE (LP) | 15 |
| 72 | Polydor 2383 120 | TASTE - LIVE AT THE ISLE OF WIGHT (LP) | 20 |

*(see also Rory Gallagher, Stud)*

## TASTE OF HONEY
| 69 | Original Rim RIM 11 | Goody Goody Gum Drops/Sunshine Rainbows | 12 |
| 69 | Rim RIM 19 | 8.05/Charleston | 5 |

## TASTY
| 77 | DJM DJS 10751 | Just A Little Too Much/You're A Heartbreaker (Promo p/s) | 8 |

## BUDDY TATE
| 58 | Felsted FAJ 7004 | SWINGING LIKE TATE (LP) | 30 |

## GRADY TATE
| 69 | Fontana STL 5490 | WINDMILLS OF MY MIND (LP) | 15 |

## HOWARD TATE
| 66 | Verve VS 541 | Ain't Nobody Home/How Come My Bulldog Won't Bark | 15 |
| 67 | Verve VS 549 | Look At Granny Run Run/Half A Man | 20 |
| 67 | Verve VS 552 | Get It While You Can/Glad I Knew Better | 15 |
| 67 | Verve VS 555 | Baby I Love You/How Blue Can You Get | 25 |
| 67 | Verve VS 556 | I Learned It All The Hard Way/Part Time Love | 15 |
| 68 | Verve VS 565 | Stop/Shoot 'Em All Down | 15 |
| 68 | Verve VS 571 | Night Owl/Every Day I Have The Blues | 20 |
| 70 | Major Minor MM 696 | My Soul's Got A Hole In It/It's Too Late | 10 |
| 67 | Verve (S)VLP 9179 | GET IT WHILE YOU CAN (LP) | 70 |

## SNUKY TATE
| 80 | ZE/Island 12WIP4785 | He's The Groove (Extended)/He's The Groove Part 2 (12", p/s) | 10 |

## TOMMY TATE
| 66 | Columbia DB 8046 | Big Blue Diamonds/A Lover's Reward | 75 |
| 66 | Columbia DB 8046 | Big Blue Diamonds/A Lover's Reward (DJ Copy) | 125 |

## TATTY OLLITY
| 79 | Tatty TR 101 | Punktuation/Never Swat A Fly | 25 |

## ART TATUM
| 51 | Capitol LC 6524 | ART TATUM (10" LP) | 12 |
| 53 | Capitol LC 6625 | OUT OF NOWHERE (10" LP) | 15 |
| 54 | Vogue LDE 081 | ART TATUM "JUST JAZZ" (10" LP) | 15 |
| 55 | Vogue Coral LRA 10011 | THE ART TATUM TRIO (10" LP) | 12 |
| 55 | Capitol LC 6638 | ART TATUM ENCORES (10" LP) | 12 |
| 57 | Columbia Clef 33C 9033 | THE GENIUS OF ART TATUM (NO. 3) (10" LP) | 12 |
| 57 | Columbia Clef 33C 9039 | PRESENTING THE ART TATUM TRIO (10" LP) | 12 |
| 59 | Columbia Clef 33CX 10137 | ART TATUM-BEN WEBSTER QUARTET (LP) | 20 |

## BERNIE TAUPIN
| 71 | DJM DJLPS 415 | TAUPIN (LP, textured gatefold sleeve with booklet) | 50 |
| 71 | DJM DJLPS 415 | TAUPIN (LP, textured gatefold sleeve without booklet) | 20 |

## TAVASCO
| 00 | Grapevine 106 | Love Is Trying To Get A Hold Of Me/(Radio Edit) | 10 |

## JOHN TAVENER
| 70 | Apple SAPCOR 15 | THE WHALE (LP, gatefold sleeve) | 40 |
| 71 | Apple SAPCOR 20 | CELTIC REQUIEM (LP, gatefold sleeve, with insert & 'Apple' inner sleeve) | 80 |
| 77 | Ring O' 2320 104 | THE WHALE (LP, reissue, different single sleeve) | 45 |
| 92 | Apple SAPCOR 15 | THE WHALE (LP, 2nd reissue, gatefold sleeve with inner sleeve) | 25 |
| 92 | Apple SAPCOR 15 | THE WHALE (CD) | 25 |
| 93 | Apple SAPCOR 20 | CELTIC REQUIEM (LP, reissue, gatefold sleeve with inner sleeve) | 25 |
| 93 | Apple SAPCOR 20 | CELTIC REQUIEM (CD) | 25 |

## CYRIL TAWNEY
| 62 | HMV 7EG 8738 | BABY LIE EASY (EP) | 10 |

MINT VALUE £

| | | | |
|---|---|---|---|
| 69 | Polydor 236 577 | THE OUTLANDISH KNIGHT (LP) | 20 |
| 70 | Argo ZFB 4 | SINGS CHILDREN'S SONGS FROM DEVON AND CORNWALL (LP) | 15 |
| 70 | Argo ZFB 9 | A MAYFLOWER GARLAND (LP) | 20 |

## TAX DODGERS
| | | | |
|---|---|---|---|
| 93 | TAX 2 | Ragamuffin Bizness/Flying High (12", stamped white label) | 20 |
| 94 | TAX IT | Hot Off D Press/Rebel Without Applause (Two Mixes) (12", stamped white labels) | 20 |

## TAX LOSS
| | | | |
|---|---|---|---|
| 79 | Logo GO 355 | Going My Way/THEME FROM THERE IS NO CONSPIRACY (stamped die cut seeve) | 10 |

## TAXMAN
| | | | |
|---|---|---|---|
| 84 | Senator SEN 001 | Bionic Tonic/Video Crazy (white label) | 35 |
| 88 | Stush STU 002 | Tina/Version/Vocal Version (12") | 30 |
| 93 | Sir George SO 945 | Well Armed And Dangerous/She Keeps Running Away (12") | 30 |

## ALLAN TAYLOR
| | | | |
|---|---|---|---|
| 71 | Liberty LBF 15447 | Sometimes/Song For Kathy | 6 |
| 73 | United Artists UP 35541 | My Father's Room/Always You | 6 |
| 71 | Liberty LBS 83483 | SOMETIMES (LP, gatefold sleeve) | 50 |
| 72 | United Artists UAS 29275 | THE LADY (LP) | 45 |
| 73 | United Artists UAG 29468 | THE AMERICAN ALBUM (LP, gatefold sleeve) | 20 |

*(see also Fairport Convention)*

## AUSTIN TAYLOR
| | | | |
|---|---|---|---|
| 60 | Top Rank JAR 511 | Push Push/A Heart That's True | 20 |

## BARRY TAYLOR
| | | | |
|---|---|---|---|
| 70 | Destiny DS 01 | Tiger Woman/I'll Shoot The Lights (p/s) | 20 |

## BILLY TAYLOR (TRIO)
| | | | |
|---|---|---|---|
| 57 | Esquire EP 115 | MAMBO! (EP) | 15 |
| 57 | Esquire EP 169 | THE MOON IN CONCERT (EP) | 20 |
| 54 | Felsted EDL 87009 | JAZZ AT STORYVILLE (10" LP) | 35 |
| 54 | Esquire 20-053 | AT THE TOWN HALL 1954 (LP) | 30 |
| 54 | Esquire 32-010 | A TOUCH OF TAYLOR (LP) | 30 |
| 57 | HMV DLP 1181 | MY FAIR LADY LOVES JAZZ (10" LP) | 20 |
| 60 | Vogue LAE 12192 | TAYLOR MADE PIANO (LP) | 20 |

## BOBBY TAYLOR
| | | | |
|---|---|---|---|
| 64 | Columbia DB 7282 | Temptation/Mod Bod | 15 |

## BOBBY TAYLOR (& VANCOUVERS)
| | | | |
|---|---|---|---|
| 68 | Tamla Motown TMG 654 | Does Your Mama Know About Me/Fading Away (with Vancouvers) | 50 |
| 73 | Epic EPC 1720 | I Can't Quit Your Love/Queen Of The Ghetto (solo) | 8 |
| 69 | Tamla Motown (S)TML 11093 | BOBBY TAYLOR AND THE VANCOUVERS (LP. mono/stereo) | 60 |
| 70 | Tamla Motown (S)TML 11125 | TAYLOR MADE SOUL (LP, stereo, solo) | 140 |

## BRYAN TAYLOR
| | | | |
|---|---|---|---|
| 61 | Piccadilly 7N 35018 | The Donkey's Tale/Let It Snow On Christmas Day | 25 |

## CECIL TAYLOR
| | | | |
|---|---|---|---|
| 60 | Contemporary LAC12216 | LOOKING AHEAD! (LP) | 20 |
| 88 | Leo LR 152 | CHINAMPAS (LP) | 15 |
| 88 | Leo LR 162 | TZOTZIL MUMMERS TZOTZIL (LP) | 15 |
| 88 | Leo LR 404/405 | LIVE IN BOLOGNA (2-LP) | 25 |
| 88 | Leo LR 408/409 | LIVE IN VIENNA (2-LP) | 25 |

## CECIL TAYLOR JAZZ UNIT
| | | | |
|---|---|---|---|
| 62 | Fontana SFJL 926 | NEFERTITI, THE BEAUTIFUL ONE HAS COME (LP) | 20 |

## CECIL TAYLOR QUARTET
| | | | |
|---|---|---|---|
| 60 | Contemporary LAC 12216 | LOOKING AHEAD! (LP) | 18 |

## CHIP TAYLOR
| | | | |
|---|---|---|---|
| 62 | Warner Bros WB 82 | Here I Am/I Love You But I Know | 6 |
| 73 | Buddah 2011 151 | Angel Of The Morning/Swear To God, Your Honor | 5 |
| 73 | Buddah 2318 074 | GASOLINE (LP) | 25 |
| 74 | Warner Bros K 56032 | CHIP TAYLOR'S LAST CHANCE (LP) | 15 |

*(see also Wes Voigt)*

## DEBBIE TAYLOR
| | | | |
|---|---|---|---|
| 76 | Arista ARISTA 50 | I Don't Wanna Leave You/Just Don't Pay | 30 |

## DUFFY TAYLOR BLUES
| | | | |
|---|---|---|---|
| 69 | Page One POF 130 | You Wrecked My Life/I'll Be There | 12 |

## ELIZABETH TAYLOR
| | | | |
|---|---|---|---|
| 63 | Colpix PXL 459 | IN LONDON (LP, TV soundtrack, music by John Barry, mono) | 30 |
| 63 | Colpix PXL 459 | IN LONDON (LP, TV soundtrack, music by John Barry, stereo) | 35 |

*(see also John Barry)*

## FELICE TAYLOR
| | | | |
|---|---|---|---|
| 67 | President PT 120 | It May Be Winter Outside/BOB KEENE ORCHESTRA: Winter Again | 5 |
| 67 | President PT 133 | I'm Under The Influence/BOB KEENE ORCHESTRA: Love Theme | 5 |
| 67 | President PT 155 | I Feel Love Comin' On/BOB KEENE ORCHESTRA: Comin' On Again | 5 |
| 68 | President PT 193 | Captured By Your Love/I Can Feel Your Love (Coming Down On Me) | 5 |
| 68 | President PT 220 | Suree-Surrender/All I Want To Do Is Love You | 5 |

## GEOFF TAYLOR
| | | | |
|---|---|---|---|
| 55 | Esquire EP 55 | GEOFF TAYLOR SEXTET (EP) | 10 |
| 57 | Esquire EP 105 | GEOFF TAYLOR ALL STARS (EP) | 10 |
| 55 | Esquire 20-060 | GEOFF TAYLOR ALL STARS (10" LP) | 50 |

## GLORIA TAYLOR
| | | | |
|---|---|---|---|
| 70 | Polydor BM 56788 | You Gotta Pay The Price/Loving You And Being Loved By You | 15 |

## HOUND DOG TAYLOR
| | | | |
|---|---|---|---|
| 66 | Outasite 45-504 | Christine/Alley Music (99 copies only) | 100 |

## JAMES TAYLOR
| | | | |
|---|---|---|---|
| 70 | Apple APPLE 32 | Carolina In My Mind/Something's Wrong | 20 |
| 68 | Apple APCOR 3 | JAMES TAYLOR (LP, gatefold sleeve, black inner, orange cover lettering, mono) | 40 |
| 68 | Apple SAPCOR 3 | JAMES TAYLOR (LP, gatefold sleeve, black inner, orange cover lettering, stereo) | 25 |
| 70 | Apple SAPCOR 3 | JAMES TAYLOR (LP, 2nd issue, gatefold sleeve, 'Apple' inner sleeve, black cover lettering) | 25 |
| 70 | Warner Bros WS 1843 | SWEET BABY JAMES (LP, orange label, later green label) | 20 |
| 71 | Warner Bros WS 2561 | MUD SLIDE SLIM AND THE BLUE HORIZON (LP, g/fold sleeve, green label) | 18 |
| 72 | Warner Bros K 46043 | SWEET BABY JAMES (LP, reissue, green label) | 15 |
| 91 | Apple SAPCOR 3 | JAMES TAYLOR (LP, reissue, gatefold sleeve) | 18 |

## JAMES TAYLOR QUARTET
| | | | |
|---|---|---|---|
| 92 | Big Life JTQ 7 PROMO 1 | Absolution (live) (gig freebie, plain black sleeve with postcard, 1 side etched) | 5 |
| 95 | Acid Jazz JAZID 124S | Whole Lotta Love (white label, withdrawn) | 50 |
| 96 | Acid Jazz JAZID 139 | Creation (10", p/s, mispressed with Hungarian porn music on A-side) | 35 |
| 96 | Acid Jazz JAZID 139 | Creation (10", p/s) | 6 |
| 87 | Re-Elect Pres. REAGAN 2D | MISSION: IMPOSSIBLE (mini-LP, with film dialogue, 500 only) | 30 |

*(see also Prisoners, Daggermen)*

## JEREMY TAYLOR
| | | | |
|---|---|---|---|
| 62 | Decca F 11502 | Ag Pleez Daddy/Jo'burg Talking Blues | 8 |
| 66 | Decca LK 4731 | ALWAYS SOMETHING NEW (LP) | 30 |
| 68 | Fontana (S)TL 5475 | HIS SONGS (LP) | 20 |
| 69 | Fontana (S)TL 5523 | MORE OF HIS SONGS (LP) | 20 |
| 72 | Galliard GAL 4018 | PIECE OF GROUND (LP) | 15 |

## JOHN TAYLOR
| | | | |
|---|---|---|---|
| 71 | Turtle TUR 301 | PAUSE AND THINK AGAIN (LP) | 400 |

## JOHNNIE TAYLOR
| | | | |
|---|---|---|---|
| 67 | Stax 601 003 | Ain't That Lovin' You/Outside Love (dark blue label) | 30 |
| 67 | Stax 601 003 | Ain't That Lovin' You/Outside Love (light blue label) | 20 |
| 68 | Stax STAX 106 | Who's Makin' Love/I'm Trying | 8 |
| 69 | Stax STAX 114 | Take Care Of Your Homework/Hold On This Time | 8 |
| 69 | Stax STAX 122 | (I Wanna) Testify/I Had To Fight With Love | 10 |
| 69 | Stax STAX 129 | I Could Never Be President/It's Amazing | 8 |
| 70 | Stax STAX 141 | Love Bones/Separation Line | 8 |
| 70 | Stax STAX 150 | Steal Away/Friday Night | 20 |
| 70 | Stax STAX 156 | I Am Somebody (Parts 1 & 2) | 8 |
| 71 | Stax 2025 021 | Jody's Got Your Girl And Gone/A Fool Like Me | 8 |
| 73 | Stax 2025 083 | Standing In For Jody/Shackin' Up | 8 |
| 73 | Stax 2025 194 | I Believe In Love/Love Depression | 8 |
| 75 | Stax STXS 2021 | It's September/Just One Moment | 8 |
| 75 | Stax STXS 2025 | Friday Night/I Ain't Particular | 10 |
| 76 | CBS 4411 | Somebody's Gettin It/Please Don't Stop That Song | 5 |
| 76 | CBS 4886 | Disco Lady/Somebody's Gettin' It (blue vinyl) | 8 |
| 67 | Stax 589 008 | WANTED, ONE SOUL SINGER (LP) | 50 |
| 69 | Stax (S)XATS 1006 | WHO'S MAKING LOVE (LP) | 20 |
| 69 | Stax 228 008 | LOOKING FOR JOHNNIE TAYLOR (LP) | 25 |
| 69 | Stax SXATS 1024 | THE J.T. PHILOSOPHY CONTINUES (LP) | 25 |
| 70 | Soul City SCB 2 | ROOTS OF JOHNNIE TAYLOR (LP) | 75 |

## (LITTLE) JOHNNY TAYLOR
| | | | |
|---|---|---|---|
| 65 | Vocalion V 9234 | Part Time Love/Somewhere Down The Line | 50 |
| 65 | Vocalion V 9234 | Part Time Love/Somewhere Down The Line (DJ copy) | 75 |
| 66 | Vocalion VP 9264 | One More Chance/Looking At The Future | 30 |
| 72 | Mojo 2092 033 | Everybody Knows About My Good Thing (Parts 1 & 2) | 8 |
| 72 | Mojo 2092 044 | It's My Fault Darling/There's Something On Your Mind | 8 |
| 65 | Vocalion VA-F 8031 | LITTLE JOHNNY TAYLOR (LP) | 100 |
| 72 | Mojo 2916 015 | EVERYBODY KNOWS ABOUT MY GOOD THING (LP) | 30 |
| 73 | Contempo COLP 1003 | OPEN HOUSE AT MY HOUSE (LP) | 15 |
| 74 | Contempo CLP 502 | SUPER TAYLORS (LP, with Ted Taylor) | 15 |

## JOSEPH TAYLOR
| | | | |
|---|---|---|---|
| 72 | Leader LEA 4050 | UNTO BRIGG FAIR (LP, gatefold sleeve with booklet) | 20 |

## KINGSIZE TAYLOR (& DOMINOS)
| | | | |
|---|---|---|---|
| 64 | Polydor NH 66990 | Memphis Tennessee/Money (reissue of Shakers single) | 30 |
| 64 | Polydor NH 66991 | Hippy Hippy Shake/Dr. Feelgood (reissue of Shakers single) | 30 |
| 64 | Decca F 11874 | Stupidity/Bad Boy | 50 |
| 64 | Decca F 11935 | Somebody's Always Trying/Looking For My Baby (solo) | 150 |
| 65 | Polydor BM 56152 | Thinkin'/Let Me Love You | 40 |
| 63 | Polydor EPH21 628 | TWIST AND SHAKE (EP, manufactured in Germany) | 110 |
| 64 | Decca DFE 8569 | TEENBEAT 2 - FROM THE STAR CLUB, HAMBURG (EP) | 130 |

*(see also Shakers, Paddy Klaus & Gibson)*

## LINDA TAYLOR
| | | | |
|---|---|---|---|
| 82 | Groove Production GPLP 31 | TAYLOR MADE (LP) | 20 |

## MICK TAYLOR
| | | | |
|---|---|---|---|
| 65 | CBS 201770 | London Town/Hoboin' | 40 |

## MIKE TAYLOR
| | | | |
|---|---|---|---|
| 65 | Columbia SX 6042 | PENDULUM (LP) | 1500 |

# Neville TAYLOR (& CUTTERS)

| | | | |
|---|---|---|---:|
| 66 | Columbia SX 6137 | TRIO (LP) | 1500 |
| 07 | Trunk JBH 016 LP | MIKE TAYLOR REMEMBERED (LP) | 35 |

*(see also Jack Bruce)*

## NEVILLE TAYLOR (& CUTTERS)

| | | | |
|---|---|---|---:|
| 58 | Parlophone R 4447 | House Of Bamboo/Mercy, Mercy, Percy (solo) | 40 |
| 58 | Parlophone R 4447 | House Of Bamboo/Mercy, Mercy, Percy (solo) (78) | 20 |
| 58 | Parlophone R 4476 | Tears On My Pillow/I Don't Want To Set The World On Fire (solo) | 20 |
| 58 | Parlophone R 4493 | A Baby Lay Sleeping/The Miracle Of Christmas (solo) | 10 |
| 59 | Parlophone R 4524 | Crazy Little Daisy/The First Words Of Love (solo) | 20 |
| 60 | Oriole CB 1546 | Dance With Dolly/Free Passes | 20 |
| 60 | Embassy WB 373 | It Ain't Necessarily So/BOBBIE BRITTON: Woman Is A Sometime Love | 6 |
| 60s | Honey Hit TB 127 | Joshua Fit The Battle Of Jericho/It's Me, It's Me, It's Me, My Love (in p/s) | 6 |

*(see also Hal Munro, Bobbie Britton)*

## PEGGY TAYLOR

| | | | |
|---|---|---|---:|
| 60 | Top Rank JAR 421 | (Don't You Come Home) Bill Bailey/So Similar | 7 |

## R. DEAN TAYLOR

| | | | |
|---|---|---|---:|
| 68 | Tamla Motown TMG 656 | Gotta See Jane/Don't Fool Around | 10 |
| 71 | Tamla Motown TMG 763 | Indiana Wants Me/Love's Your Name | 10 |
| 71 | Tamla Motown TMG 786 | Ain't It A Sad Thing/Backstreet (unissued) | 0 |
| 71 | Rare Earth RES 101 | Ain't It A Sad Thing/Back Street (has TMG 786 matrix in run-out groove) | 15 |
| 74 | Tamla Motown TMG 896 | There's A Ghost In My House/Let's Go Somewhere | 5 |
| 74 | Tamla Motown TMG 896 | There's A Ghost In My House/Let's Go Somewhere (DJ Copy) | 25 |
| 71 | Tamla Motown STML 11185 | INDIANA WANTS ME (LP) | 18 |

## ROD TAYLOR

| | | | |
|---|---|---|---:|
| 78 | Little Lute HITDD 311 | If Jah Should Come Now/Africa Be Free/PRINCE HAMMER: Maccabee Bible (12") | 30 |
| 78 | Freedom Sounds FS 004 | Ethiopian King/Version | 20 |
| 78 | Freedom Sounds FSD 004 | Ethiopian King/PHILIP FRAZER: Come Ethiopians (12") | 40 |
| 79 | Hit Run DD 16 | No One Can Tell I About Jah/ERROL HOLT : Yes Yes Yes (12") | 60 |
| 79 | Lovelinch LL05 | True History (Disco Mix Version)/Scientist Vex Version (12") | 15 |
| 80 | Strong Like Sampson SLSD 011 | Jah Is Calling/Inside Right (12") | 20 |
| 81 | Unity UP 003 | Moving Out Ever/Version (12", with Ranking Dread) | 20 |
| 82 | Dread At The Controls DATCD 015 | Sun Moon and Stars/BLAKKA STAR: Rubber Dub Rock/ROOF RADICS: Hand Cuff Dub (12") | 15 |
| 78 | Hit Run APLP 9031 | IF JAH SHOULD COME NOW (LP) | 50 |
| 80 | Greensleeves GREL 17 | WHERE IS YOUR LOVE MANKIND? (LP, green vinyl) | 22 |

## ROD TAYLOR & MIKEY DREAD & KING TUBBY

| | | | |
|---|---|---|---:|
| 79 | Sufferers Heights SUFF 006 | Behold Him/Parrot Jungle/His Majesty/Dread All The Way (12") | 30 |

## ROGER TAYLOR

| | | | |
|---|---|---|---:|
| 77 | EMI EMI 2679 | I Wanna Testify/Turn On The TV (demo copies £40) | 30 |
| 81 | EMI EMI 5200 | My Country (Edit)/Fun In Space (p/s) | 20 |
| 84 | EMI EMI 5478 | Man On Fire/Killing Time (p/s) | 10 |
| 84 | EMI 12 EMI 5478 | Man On Fire (Extended)/Killing Time (12", p/s) | 25 |
| 84 | EMI EMI 5490 | Strange Frontier/I Cry For You (Remix) (p/s) | 15 |
| 84 | EMI 12 EMI 5490 | Strange Frontier (Extended)/I Cry For You (Extended Remix)/ Two Sharp Pencils (Get Bad) (12", p/s) | 20 |
| 94 | Parlophone RR 6379 | Nazis 1994/Nazis 1994 (Version) (red vinyl, numbered p/s) | 5 |
| 94 | Parlophone 12RC 6379 | Nazis 1994 (Single Version)/(Radio Mix)/(Makita Mix - Extended)/ (Big Science Mix) (12" clear vinyl, numbered insert in PVC sleeve) | 10 |
| 94 | Parlophone NAZIS 1 | Nazis 1994 (Radio Mix)/Nazis 1944 (Kick Mix) (12", black vinyl, p/s, promo only) | 15 |
| 94 | Parlophone NAZIS 3 | Nazis 1994 (Radio Mix)/(Kick Mix)/(Big Science Mix)/(Makita Mix) (12", black vinyl, p/s, promo only) | 15 |
| 94 | Parlophone NAZIS 4 | Nazis 1994 (Schindler's Mix)/(Big Science Mix)/(Makita Mix - Extended) (12", black vinyl, p/s, promo only) | 10 |
| 94 | Parlophone 12RDJ 6379 | Nazis 1994 (Schindler's Mix)/(Big Science Mix)/(Makita Mix - Extended) (12", white label DJ promo) | 30 |
| 94 | Parlophone R 6389 | Foreign Sand (Single Version)/You Had To Be There (as Roger Taylor & Yoshiki) (blue vinyl, numbered p/s) | 5 |
| 93 | Parlophone PCSD 157 | HAPPINESS? (LP, numbered) | 35 |
| 93 | Parlophone PCSD 157 | HAPPINESS? (LP, un-numbered) | 20 |
| 98 | Parlophone 4967241 | ELECTRIC FIRE (LP, orange vinyl) | 50 |

*(see also Queen, Cross, Hilary Hilary, Ian Hunter, Fox, Kansas, Mel Smith, Billy Squier)*

## ROSEMARY TAYLOR

| | | | |
|---|---|---|---:|
| 75 | JD 2009 | TAYLORMAID (LP, private pressing with insert) | 200 |

## ROY TAYLOR BAND

| | | | |
|---|---|---|---:|
| 70 | Bun BUN 009 | Shake Me/Tidy Place In Me | 10 |

## SAM ('THE MAN') TAYLOR

| | | | |
|---|---|---|---:|
| 54 | MGM SP 1106 | Please Be Kind/This Can't Be Love (as Sam 'The Man' Taylor & Cat Men) | 30 |
| 56 | MGM MGM-EP 531 | SAM TAYLOR ORCHESTRA (EP) | 35 |

*(see also Claude Cloud)*

## TAYLOR SHARP & TAYLOR

| | | | |
|---|---|---|---:|
| 70 | CBS 5197 | The Look Of Love/Mr Snow | 15 |

## TED TAYLOR FOUR

| | | | |
|---|---|---|---:|
| 58 | Oriole CB 1464 | Son Of Honky Tonk/Farrago | 10 |
| 60 | Oriole CB 1573 | M.1./You Are My Sunshine | 7 |
| 61 | Oriole CB 1574 | Fried Onions/Yellow Rock Of Texas | 7 |
| 61 | Oriole CB 1628 | Cat's Eyes/Canyon | 7 |
| 61 | Oriole CB 1630 | Flyover/Haunted Pad | 7 |
| 62 | Oriole CB 1713 | Jericho/Everytime We Say Goodbye | 10 |
| 62 | Oriole CB 1767 | Surfrider/Spotlight | 10 |

**TYRONE TAYLOR**
| | | | |
|---|---|---|---|
| 78 | Observer OBMM 1000 | Sufferation/Rock On/Christine (12") | 35 |

**VERNON TAYLOR**
| | | | |
|---|---|---|---|
| 59 | London HLS 8905 | Today Is A Blue Day/Breeze (unreleased) | 0 |
| 60 | London HLS 9025 | Mystery Train/Sweet And Easy To Love | 100 |

**VIC TAYLOR**
| | | | |
|---|---|---|---|
| 67 | Treasure Isle TI 7021 | Heartaches/When It Comes To Loving You I'm Alright (B-side actually "Loving Pauper" by Dobby Dobson) | 80 |
| 71 | Trojan TRLS 38 | DOES IT HIS WAY (LP) | 20 |

*(see also Tommy McCook)*

**VINCE TAYLOR (& HIS PLAYBOYS)**
| | | | |
|---|---|---|---|
| 58 | Parlophone R 4505 | Right Behind You Baby/I Like Love (solo) | 60 |
| 58 | Parlophone R 4505 | Right Behind You Baby/I Like Love (solo) (78) | 40 |
| 59 | Parlophone R 4539 | Brand New Cadillac/Pledging My Love | 60 |
| 60 | Palette PG 9001 | I'll Be Your Hero/Jet Black Machine | 25 |
| 61 | Palette PG 9020 | Move Over Tiger/What'cha Gonna Do | 25 |
| 76 | Chiswick (N)S 2 | Brand New Cadillac/Pledging My Love (no p/s) | 5 |
| 97 | Cruisin' 50 CASB 006 | Brand New Cadillac/Right Behind You Baby (78, 300 only) | 30 |

**VINCENT TAYLOR**
| | | | |
|---|---|---|---|
| 80 | Live & Love LLDIS 115 | Can't Seem To Forget You/Living A Lie (12") | 50 |
| 80 | Live & Love LLDIS 117 | Got To Have You/TAYLOR PLAYERS: Got You Version (12") | 30 |

**WALTER TAYLOR**
| | | | |
|---|---|---|---|
| 50s | Poydras 2 | Thirty-Eight And Plus/Diamond Ring Blues | 8 |

**TAYLOR MAIDS**
| | | | |
|---|---|---|---|
| 55 | Capitol CL 14322 | Po-Go Stick/Theme From "I Am A Camera" (Why Do I) | 12 |

**T-BONES**
| | | | |
|---|---|---|---|
| 64 | Columbia DB 7401 | How Many More Times/I'm A Lover Not A Fighter | 60 |
| 65 | Columbia DB 7489 | Won't You Give Him (One More Chance)/Hamish's Express Relief | 35 |

*(see also Gary Farr & T-Bones, Kevin Westlake)*

**T-BOYS**
| | | | |
|---|---|---|---|
| 80 | Nems BSS 104 | Bus Song/Mary Jane | 30 |
| 81 | Almost Animal AA001 | One Way Street/Factory Girl | 20 |

**JOHN TCHKAI**
| | | | |
|---|---|---|---|
| 66 | Fontana 881014/681 014ZL | RUFUS (LP, with ARCHIE SHEPP) | 20 |

**TDS MOB**
| | | | |
|---|---|---|---|
| 10 | Diggers With Gratitude DWG THE DOPE COMMITTEE (EP, 75 only, burgundy vinyl) 006 | | 45 |
| 10 | Diggers With Gratitude DWG THE DOPE COMMITTEE (EP, 275 only, black vinyl) 006 | | 25 |
| 10 | Diggers With Gratitude DWG THE BOSTON CLASSICS (EP, 75 only, white vinyl) 007 | | 35 |
| 10 | Diggers With Gratitude DWG THE BOSTON CLASSICS (EP) 007 | | 12 |

**TEA**
| | | | |
|---|---|---|---|
| 74 | Vertigo 6147 006 | Good Times/Judy | 5 |
| 75 | Philips 6305 238 | TEA (LP) | 15 |

**TEA & SYMPHONY**
| | | | |
|---|---|---|---|
| 69 | Harvest HAR 5005 | Boredom/Armchair Theatre | 20 |
| 69 | Harvest SHVL 761 | AN ASYLUM FOR THE MUSICALLY INSANE (LP, laminated gatefold sleeve. The name of the band appears above the "Harvest" logo. Those with "An Asylum For The Musically Insane" above the Harvest Logo are Dutch pressings from 1969) | 400 |
| 70 | Harvest SHVL 785 | JO SAGO (LP, gatefold sleeve no EMI logo on label) | 700 |

**TEACH YOURSELF TURNTABLISM**
| | | | |
|---|---|---|---|
| 04 | Pedestrian | TUTORITOOL - INTERACTIVE TURNTABLISM TUTORIAL (LP, gatefold with inserts and inner sleeves, 1000 only) | 25 |

**TEACHERS PET**
| | | | |
|---|---|---|---|
| 80 | TP 001 | Missing Person/Tug Of Love (p/s) | 40 |

**TEACHO & HIS STUDENTS**
| | | | |
|---|---|---|---|
| 58 | Felsted AF 104 | Rock-et/Stop | 60 |
| 58 | Felsted AF 104 | Rock-et/Stop (78) | 30 |

**TEA COMPANY**
| | | | |
|---|---|---|---|
| 68 | Mercury SMCL 20127 | COME AND HAVE SOME TEA WITH THE TEA COMPANY (LP) | 50 |

**ANTHONY TEAGUE**
| | | | |
|---|---|---|---|
| 62 | Decca F 11548 | Like I Don't Love You/My Guardian Angel | 7 |

**TEAM DOKUS**
| | | | |
|---|---|---|---|
| 94 | Tenth Planet TP 007 | TEAM DOKUS (LP, numbered, 500 only) | 15 |

**TEAM 23**
| | | | |
|---|---|---|---|
| 81 | Race RB 002 | Whatever Moves You/Move Into The Rhythm | 7 |

**TEA PARTY**
| | | | |
|---|---|---|---|
| 94 | Chrysalis CHR 6072 | SPLENDOR SOILS (LP) | 150 |
| 95 | Chrysalis CHR 6108 | THE EDGES OF TWILIGHT (LP) | 150 |

**TEARDROP EXPLODES**
| | | | |
|---|---|---|---|
| 79 | Zoo CAGE 003 | Sleeping Gas/Camera Camera/Kirkby Workers' Dream Fades (red p/s) | 15 |
| 79 | Zoo CAGE 003 | Sleeping Gas/Camera Camera/Kirkby Workers' Dream Fades (blue p/s) | 12 |
| 79 | Zoo CAGE 005 | Bouncing Babies/All I Am Is Loving You (p/s) | 10 |
| 80 | Zoo CAGE 008 | Treason (It's Just A Story)/Read It In Books (in blue & green p/s) | 15 |
| 80 | Zoo CAGE 008 | Treason (It's Just A Story)/Read It In Books | 6 |
| 80 | Mercury TEAR 1 | When I Dream/Kilimanjaro (p/s, limited pressing with paper labels not moulded plastic) | 5 |

MINT VALUE £

| 80 | Mercury TEAR 2 | Reward/Strange House In The Snow (p/s, limited pressing with paper labels not moulded plastic, textured sleeve) | 6 |
| 81 | Mercury TEAR 4 | Ha Ha I'm Drowning/Poppies In The Field (in withdrawn p/s, limited pressing with paper labels not moulded plastic) | 15 |
| 81 | Mercury TEAR 44 | Ha Ha I'm Drowning/Poppies In The Field/Bouncing Babies/Read It In Books (double pack, gatefold p/s, limited pressing with paper labels not moulded plastic) | 6 |
| 81 | Mercury TEAR 44 | Ha Ha I'm Drowning/Poppies In The Field/Bouncing Babies/ Read It In Books (double pack, withdrawn gatefold p/s) | 40 |
| 81 | Mercury TEAR 5 | Passionate Friend/Christ Versus Warhol (p/s, limited pressing with paper labels not moulded plastic) | 6 |
| 81 | Mercury TEAR 6 | Colours Fly Away/Window Shopping For A New Crown Of Thorns (p/s & insert, limited pressing with paper labels not moulded plastic) | 6 |
| 82 | Mercury TEAR 7G | Tiny Children/Rachael Built A Steamboat (gatefold p/s, paper labels) | 6 |
| 82 | Mercury TEAR 7 | Tiny Children/Rachael Built A Steamboat (p/s, paper labels) | 5 |
| 83 | Mercury TEAR 88 | You Disappear From View/Suffocate//Ouch Monkey's/Soft Enough For You/ The In-Psychlopedia (double pack, gatefold p/s, limited pressing with paper labels not moulded plastic) | 6 |
| 89 | Fontana DROP 112 | Serious Danger/Sleeping Gas/Seven Views Of Jerusalem (p/s) | 6 |
| 80 | Mercury 6359 035 | KILIMANJARO (LP, 1st pressing, light blue labels, 'group photo' on cover & inner sleeve) | 20 |
| 90 | Mercury 8424391 | EVERYBODY WANTS TO SHAG THE TEARDROP EXPLODES (LP, with inner) | 15 |

*(see also Julian Cope, Lori & Chameleons)*

## TEARDROPS (JAMAICA)

| 71 | Ackee ACK 126 | Let Me Be Free/CINDY STARR: Sentimental Girl | 15 |
| 71 | Big Shot BI 582 | Two In One/LAURIE'S ALL STARS: Rock-A-Boogie | 20 |

## TEARDROPS (1)

| 78 | Bent BIGB 3 | IN AND OUT OF FASHION (12" EP, foldout p/s in poly bag) | 18 |
| 79 | TJM TJM 9 | Seeing Double/Teardrops And Heartaches (p/s) | 20 |
| 80s | Illuminated JAMS 2 | FINAL VINYL (LP) | 15 |

## TEARDROPS (2)

| 93 | Kent 6T 9 | Here Comes The Lonliness/CHUBBY CHECKER: You Can't Lose Something You've Never Had | 10 |

## TEAR GAS

| 70 | Famous SFMA 5751 | PIGGY GO-GETTER (LP, textured gtefold sleeve) | 100 |
| 71 | Regal Zono. SLRZ 1021 | TEAR GAS (LP) | 300 |

*(see also Alex Harvey, Tandoori Cassette)*

## TEARJERKERS

| 80 | Back Door DOOR 1 | Murder Mystery/Heart On The Line (die cut p/s with insert) | 8 |
| 81 | Good Vibrations GOT 9 | Love Affair/Bus Stop (p/s) | 5 |

*(see also Speed)*

## THE TEARS

| 05 | Independiente ISOM49LP | HERE COME THE TEARS (LP, numbered) | 30 |

*(see also Suede)*

## TEARS FOR FEARS

| 81 | Mercury IDEA 1 | Suffer The Children/Wino (p/s, original issue with light labels) | 10 |
| 81 | Mercury IDEA 12 | Suffer The Children (Remix)/Wino/Suffer The Children (Instrumental) (12", p/s) | 12 |
| 82 | Mercury IDEA 33 | Mad World/Mad World (World Remix) (p/s) | 5 |
| 82 | Mercury IDEA 33 | Mad World/Mad World (World Remix)//Suffer The Children/ Ideas As Opiates (double pack) | 10 |
| 82 | Mercury IDEA 4 | Change/The Conflict (poster p/s) | 7 |
| 82 | Mercury IDEA 4 | Change/The Conflict (withdrawn 'fishing net' sleeve) | 50 |
| 82 | Mercury IDEA 412 | Change/The Conflict (12" withdrawn 'fishing net' sleeve) | 100 |
| 83 | Mercury IDEA R/B 5 | Pale Shelter/We Are Broken (p/s, red or blue vinyl) | 10 |
| 83 | Mercury IDEAG 5 | Pale Shelter/We Are Broken (p/s, translucent green vinyl) | 7 |
| 83 | Mercury IDEAP 5 | Pale Shelter/We Are Broken (picture disc) | 10 |

*(see also Graduate)*

## TEARS ON THE CONSOLE

| 75 | Holyground HG 120 | TEARS ON THE CONSOLE (LP, with booklet, 120 demo copies only) | 150 |
| 90 | Magic Mixture MM 3 | TEARS ON THE CONSOLE (LP, reissue, 425 only, with insert) | 20 |

## TEASER

| 89 | LTW 9KS 2049 | Here Tonight (p/s) | 20 |

## TEA SET (1)

| 66 | King KG 1048 | Join The Tea Set/Ready Steady Go! | 25 |

## TEA SET (2)

| 79 | Waldo's Beat PS 006 | Parry Thomas/Tri-X Pan (gatefold p/s with poster 'mystery' envelope) | 10 |
| 78 | Waldo's Beat Series 003 | CUPS AND SAUCERS (EP, with stapled lyric book sleeve) | 10 |
| 80 | Demon D 1009 | South Pacific/The Preacher (foldout p/s with inserts) | 10 |

## TECHNIQUES (JAMAICA)

| 65 | Island WI 231 | Little Did You Know/DON DRUMMOND: Cool Smoke | 25 |
| 67 | Treasure Isle TI 7001 | You Don't Care (with Tommy McCook & Supersonics Band)/ TOMMY McCOOK & SUPERSONICS BAND: Down On Bond Street | 30 |
| 67 | Treasure Isle TI 7019 | Queen Majesty/Fighting For The Right | 40 |
| 67 | Treasure Isle TI 7026 | Love Is Not A Gamble/Bad-Minded People | 30 |
| 68 | Treasure Isle TI 7031 | My Girl/Drink Wine (with Tommy McCook & Supersonics) | 25 |
| 68 | Treasure Isle TI 7038 | Devoted/Bless You (with Tommy McCook & Supersonics) | 25 |
| 68 | Treasure Isle TI 7040 | It's You I Love/Travelling Man (with Tommy McCook & Supersonics) | 60 |
| 68 | Duke DU 1 | I Wish It Would Rain/There Comes A Time | 60 |
| 69 | Duke DU 6 | A Man Of My Word/The Time Has Come | 60 |
| 69 | Duke DU 22 | What Am I To Do/You're My Everything | 60 |
| 69 | Duke DU 60 | Where Were You/Just One Smile | 18 |
| 69 | Camel CA 10 | Who You Gonna Run To/Hi There (B-side act. "Look Who's Back" by Carl Bryan) | 30 |

| | | | |
|---|---|---|---|
| 69 | Camel CA 19 | Everywhere Everyone/Find Yourself Another Fool | 25 |
| 70 | Treasure Isle TI 7054 | He Who Keepeth His Mouth/One Day (act. by Johnny Osborne & Sensations) | 15 |
| 70 | Techniques TE 904 | Lonely Man/I Feel Alive | 10 |
| 70 | Techniques TE 906 | Feel A Little Better (actually by Techniques Allstars)/You'll Get Left | 10 |
| 70 | Big Shot BI 536 | He Who Keepeth His Mouth/One Day (act. by Johnny Osborne & Sensations) | 12 |
| 71 | Banana BA 350 | Since I Lost You/RILEY'S ALLSTARS: Version | 15 |

*(see also Techniques All Stars, Riots, Tommy McCook, Mighty Avengers, Gaylads, Rad Bryan)*

## TECHNIQUES (U.S.)
| | | | |
|---|---|---|---|
| 58 | Columbia DB 4072 | Hey! Little Girl/In A Round About Way | 45 |

## TECHNIQUES ALL STARS
| | | | |
|---|---|---|---|
| 70 | Big Shot BI 543 | Come Back Darling/Move Over (actually by Johnny Osborne & Sensations) | 30 |
| 70 | Big Shot BI 545 | Elfrego Bacca (actually by Dave Barker)/TECHNIQUES: Iron Joe (B-side actually by Techniques All Stars) | 35 |
| 70 | Techniques TE 900 | Something Tender/CANNONBALL: Bewitch | 20 |
| 70 | Trojan TR 7728 | El Dora/TECHNIQUES: If It's Not True (B-side actually by Techniques All Stars) | 12 |

*(see also Dennis Alcapone, Ansell Collins)*

## TECHNO POP
| | | | |
|---|---|---|---|
| 79 | Fairview SRTS 79424 | Paint It Black/What Are You | 7 |

## TECHNOSAURUS
| | | | |
|---|---|---|---|
| 93 | Invention TBH 1 | YOU GAVE ME NOTHING EP (12", stamped white labels) | 25 |

## TED
| | | | |
|---|---|---|---|
| 74 | Epic SPEC 3126 | Gonna Make You My Angel/Can't Stop The Train | 8 |

## TEDDIE & THE TIGERS
| | | | |
|---|---|---|---|
| 67 | Spin SP 2004 | Hold On I'm Comin'/First Love Never Dies | 20 |

## TEDDY
| | | | |
|---|---|---|---|
| 71 | Upsetter US 353 | Elusion/UPSETTERS: Big John Wayne | 25 |

## TEDDY & THE CONQUERORS
| | | | |
|---|---|---|---|
| 71 | High Note HS 053 | Homebound/GAYTONES: Homebound Chapter 3 | 10 |

## TEDDY & THE FRAT GIRLS
| | | | |
|---|---|---|---|
| 85 | Alternative Tentacles VIRUS 19 | I Wanna Be A Man/I Owe It All To The Girls/Clubnite/Alophen Baby/The Eggman Don't Cometh (p/s) | 5 |

## TEDDY & THE TWILIGHTS
| | | | |
|---|---|---|---|
| 63 | Stateside SS 167 | I'm Just Your Clown/Bikini Bimbo | 22 |

## TEDDY BEARS
| | | | |
|---|---|---|---|
| 58 | London HL 8733 | To Know Him Is To Love Him/Don't You Worry, My Little Pet | 8 |
| 59 | London HLP 8836 | I Don't Need You Anymore/Oh Why | 15 |
| 59 | London HLP 8889 | You Said Goodbye/If You Only Knew | 20 |
| 59 | London HA-P 2183 | THE TEDDY BEARS SING! (LP) | 200 |

*(see also Phil Spector, Carol Connors)*

## WILLIE TEE
| | | | |
|---|---|---|---|
| 67 | Atlantic 584 116 | Thank You John/Walking Up A One-Way Street | 35 |
| 71 | Mojo 2092 025 | Thank You John/Walking Up A One-Way Street/Teasin' You | 8 |

## TEEGARDEN & VAN WINKLE
| | | | |
|---|---|---|---|
| 70 | Pye 7N 25535 | God, Love And Rock And Roll/Work Me Tomorrow | 6 |
| 69 | Atco 228028 | BUT ANYHOW (LP) | 15 |

## TEENAGE FANCLUB
| | | | |
|---|---|---|---|
| 90 | Paperhouse PAPER 003 | Everything Flows/Primary Education/Speeeder (1,500 only, die-cut p/s) | 20 |
| 90 | Paperhouse PAPER 005 | The Ballad Of John And Yoko (p/s, 1-sided, 5,000 only, 2nd side engraved) | 6 |
| 91 | Strange Fruit SFPS 081 | PEEL SESSIONS (12") | 12 |
| 03 | Poolride POOLS 5 | Did I Say/The Cabbage (p/s, 500 only) | 6 |
| 90 | Paperhouse PAPLP 004 | A CATHOLIC EDUCATION (LP, gatefold sleeve) | 15 |
| 91 | Creation CRELP 096 | THE KING (LP, available for 1 week only, sprayed plain sleeve) | 20 |
| 91 | Creation CRELP 106 | BANDWAGONESQUE (LP, with inner) | 25 |
| 93 | Creation CRELP 144 | THIRTEEN (LP) | 30 |
| 95 | Creation CRELP 137L | GRAND PRIX (LP, with free 7") | 40 |
| 95 | Creation CRELP 137L | GRAND PRIX (LP, without free 7") | 30 |
| 97 | Creation CRELP 196 | SONGS FROM NORTHERN BRITAIN (LP) | 40 |
| 00 | Columbia 5006221 | HOWDY! (LP) | 30 |
| 05 | Pema 002 | MAN-MADE (LP) | 25 |
| 10 | Pema PEMA 007LP | SHADOWS (LP) | 20 |

*(see also Boy Hairdressers, BMX Bandits, Clouds, Eugenius)*

## TEENAGE FILMSTARS
| | | | |
|---|---|---|---|
| 79 | Clockwork COR 002 | (There's A) Cloud Over Liverpool/Sometimes Good Guys Don't Follow Trends (1st 150 with foldout p/s) | 150 |
| 79 | Clockwork COR 002 | (There's A) Cloud Over Liverpool/Sometimes Good Guys Don't Follow Trends | 25 |
| 80 | Wessex WEX 275 | The Odd Man Out/I Apologise | 25 |
| 80 | Blueprint BLU 2013 | The Odd Man Out/I Apologise (reissue, p/s) | 20 |
| 80 | Fab Listening FL 1 | I Helped Patrick McGoohan Escape/We're Not Sorry (p/s) | 15 |

*(see also Television Personalities, Times, O Level)*

## TEENAGERS
| | | | |
|---|---|---|---|
| 57 | RCA RCX 102 | THE TEENAGERS (EP) | 60 |

## TEENBEATS
| | | | |
|---|---|---|---|
| 79 | Safari SAFE 17 | I Can't Control Myself/I'll Never Win (p/s) | 8 |
| 79 | Safari SAFE 19 | Strength Of The Nation/I'm Gone Tomorrow (in p/s) | 15 |
| 79 | Safari SAFE 19 | Strength Of The Nation/I'm Gone Tomorrow | 6 |

## TEEN BEATS (U.S.)
| | | | |
|---|---|---|---|
| 60 | Top Rank JAR 342 | The Slop Beat/Califf Boogie (featuring Don Rivers & Califfs) | 25 |

MINT VALUE £

## TEEN QUEENS
| | | | |
|---|---|---|---|
| 65 | R&B MRB 5000 | Eddie My Love/Just Goofed | 30 |

## TEEN STARLETS
| | | | |
|---|---|---|---|
| 61 | Top Rank JAR 583 | The Children's Picnic Song/Theme From 'Spinster' | 5 |

## TEE SET (2)
| | | | |
|---|---|---|---|
| 70 | Major Minor MM 666 | Ma Belle Amie/Angels Coming | 8 |
| 70 | Columbia DB 8375 | Mr Music Man/In My House | 5 |
| 70 | Columbia SCX 6419 | MA BELLE AMIE (LP) | 15 |

## TEETH
| | | | |
|---|---|---|---|
| 79 | Soho SH 8 | Say Hello To Suzy/Human Bondage (p/s) | 5 |

## TEETH OF THE SEA
| | | | |
|---|---|---|---|
| 10 | Rocket LAUNCH 035 | HYPNOTICON EP (12", 500 only) | 10 |
| 15 | God Unknown GOD 003 | Up With People/ONEIDA: The Shah Arrives At The Checkpoint (7", 300 only) | 12 |
| 13 | Rocket LAUNCH 059 LP | MASTER (LP, magenta vinyl) | 15 |
| 14 | Rocket LAUNCH 064 LP | A FIELD IN ENGLAND RE-IMAGINED (LP, white vinyl, 200 only) | 20 |

## TEK 9
| | | | |
|---|---|---|---|
| 91 | Reinforced RIVET 1205 | KINGDOM OF DUB EP (12") | 10 |
| 92 | Reinforced RIVET 1229 | JUST A DREAM EP (12") | 20 |
| 92 | Reinforced RIVET 1229R | JUST A DREAM EP (Remixes) (12") | 10 |
| 93 | Reinforced RIVET 1238 | THE RETURN OF TEK 9 EP (12") | 15 |
| 93 | Reinforced RIVET 1238R | THE RETURN OF TEK 9 (Rpt) (12") | 10 |
| 93 | Reinforced RIVET 1253 | BREAKIN' THE SOUND BARRIERS EP (12") | 15 |
| 94 | Reinforced RIVET 1262 | KILLING TIME EP (10") | 12 |
| 94 | Reinforced RIVET 1269 | JUS' A LIKKLE SUMTIN' EP (2x12") | 25 |

## TELEGRAMS
| | | | |
|---|---|---|---|
| 78 | Creole CR 163 | Oh Baby Please/Hey Baby | 5 |

*(See also Steve Allan, Alan Carvell, Carvells, Five Sapphires)*

## TELESCOPE
| | | | |
|---|---|---|---|
| 77 | Pentagon PENT 5 | Bye Bye (ain't Nice)/A Personal Message From Telescope To You | 10 |

## TELESCOPES
| | | | |
|---|---|---|---|
| 88 | Cheree CHEREE 1 | Forever Close Your Eyes/LOOP: Soundhead (33rpm flexi, p/s, 1,000 only) | 10 |
| 89 | Cheree CHEREE 2 | Kick The Wall/This Is The Last Of What's Coming Now (p/s, with insert, 1,000 only, light grey/blue p/s) | 5 |
| 89 | Cheree CHEREE 2 | Kick The Wall/This Is The Last Of What's Coming Now (numbered re-pressing, 500 only, red wraparound p/s) | 8 |
| 89 | What Goes On WHAT GOES ON 32 | TASTE (LP) | 15 |
| 92 | Creation CRELP 079 | TELESCOPES (LP, with booklet) | 18 |

## TELEVISION
| | | | |
|---|---|---|---|
| 77 | Elektra K 12252 | Marquee Moon Parts 1 & 2 | 5 |
| 79 | Ork/WEA NYC 1T | Little Johnny Jewel Parts 1 & 2/Little Johnny Jewel (live) (12", p/s) | 15 |
| 77 | Elektra K52046 | MARQUEE MOON (LP, 1st pressing with quotation marks around title) | 40 |
| 78 | Elektra K52072 | ADVENTURE (LP, red vinyl, insert) | 18 |
| 78 | Elektra K52072 | ADVENTURE (LP, black vinyl) | 15 |

*(see also Neon Boys)*

## TELEVISION PERSONALITIES
| | | | |
|---|---|---|---|
| 78 | Teen '78 SRTS/CUS/77/089 | 14th Floor/Oxford Street W1 (p/s, various different sleeve designs) | 80 |
| 78 | Kings Road Records LYN 5976/5977 (KR-001) | WHERE'S BILL GRUNDY NOW? (EP, hand-written labels) | 50 |
| 78 | Kings Road LYN 5976/7 | WHERE'S BILL GRUNDY NOW? (EP, hand-stamped label, 2,000 only) | 30 |
| 78 | Kings Road LYN 5976/7 | WHERE'S BILL GRUNDY NOW? (EP, white labels, various sleeves) | 12 |
| 79 | Rough Trade RT 033 | WHERE'S BILL GRUNDY NOW? (EP, reissue, different p/s, printed labels) | 10 |
| 80 | Rough Trade RT 051 | Smashing Time/King & Country (p/s) | 15 |
| 81 | Rough Trade RT 063 | I Know Where Syd Barrett Lives/Arthur The Gardener (p/s) | 15 |
| 82 | Whaam! WHAAM 4 | Three Wishes/Geoffrey Ingram/And Don't The Kids Just Love It (p/s, 2 different sleeve designs, 2,000 only) | 15 |
| 82 | Creation Artefact 002/Lyntone LYN 13546 | Biff Bang Pow!/A Picture Of Dorian Gray (1-sided flexidisc, with Communication Blur fanzine) | 25 |
| 82 | Creation Artefact 002/Lyntone LYN 13546 | Biff Bang Pow!/A Picture Of Dorian Gray (1-sided flexidisc, without Communication Blur fanzine) | 18 |
| 83 | Rough Trade RT 109 | A Sense Of Belonging/Paradise Estate (p/s) | 12 |
| 86 | Dreamworld DREAM 4 | How I Learnt To Love The Bomb/Then God Snaps His Fingers/ Now You're Just Being Ridiculous (12", p/s, 3,700 only) | 15 |
| 86 | Dreamworld DREAM 10 | How I Learnt To Love The Bomb/Grocer's Daughter/Girl Called Charity (7", reissue, p/s, 1,000 only) | 15 |
| 87 | Dreamworld DREAM 13(T) | Privilege/Me And My Desires (unreleased) | 0 |
| 89 | Overground OVER 03 | 14th Floor/Oxford Street W1 (numbered p/s, 600 yellow vinyl) | 6 |
| 89 | Overground OVER 03 | 14th Floor/Oxford Street W1 (numbered p/s, 400 white vinyl) | 7 |
| 89 | Caff CAFF 5 | I Still Believe In Magic/Respectable (p/s, in poly bag, 500 only) | 35 |
| 89 | Caff CAFF 5 | I Still Believe In Magic/Respectable (p/s, 500 only) | 25 |
| 90 | Overground OVER 13 | I Know Where Syd Barrett Lives/Arthur The Gardener (reissue, p/s, 2000 only) | 6 |
| 90 | Overground OVER 15 | Silly Girl (unissued, 100 test pressings only) | 18 |
| 91 | Clawfist XPIG 8 | Your Class/BMX BANDITS : Somebody To Share My Life With | 12 |
| 92 | Seminal Twang TWANG 15 | We Will Be Your Gurus/Miro/An Exhibition By Jane/Love Is Better Than War (p/s) | 7 |
| 81 | Rough Trade ROUGH 24 | AND DON'T THE KIDS JUST LOVE IT (LP, 1st 1,000 with insert) | 60 |
| 81 | Rough Trade ROUGH 24 | AND DON'T THE KIDS JUST LOVE IT (LP) | 35 |
| 81 | Whaam! WHAAM 3 | MUMMY YOU'RE NOT WATCHING ME (LP, 3,500 only, 1st 1,000 with insert) | 60 |
| 81 | Whaam! WHAAM 3 | MUMMY YOU'RE NOT WATCHING ME (LP, 3,500 only, 2,500 without insert) | 35 |
| 82 | Whaam! BIG 5 | THEY COULD HAVE BEEN BIGGER THAN THE BEATLES (LP, 2,500 only, hand-painted sleeve) | 35 |
| 83 | Whaam! BIG 10 | TURN ON ... TUNE IN (LP, unreleased) | 0 |

| 85 | Illuminated JAMS 37 | THE PAINTED WORD (LP) | 30 |
|---|---|---|---|
| 86 | Dreamworld BIG DREAM 2 | THEY COULD HAVE BEEN BIGGER THAN THE BEATLES (LP, reissue with insert) | 20 |
| 86 | Dreamworld BIG DREAM 4 | MUMMY YOU'RE NOT WATCHING ME (LP, reissue with insert) | 20 |
| 87 | Dreamworld BIG DREAM 6 | PRIVILEGE (LP, unreleased) | 0 |
| 90 | Fire LP 21 | PRIVILEGE (LP, insert) | 20 |
| 91 | Overground OVER21 | CAMPING IN FRANCE (LP) | 15 |

*(see also Teenage Filmstars, Times, O Level, Missing Scientists, Reacta, Dry Rib, Slaughter, Gifted Children)*

**TELEX**
| 78 | Sire SIR 4006 | Twist A Saint-Tropez/Le Fond De L'Air (p/s) | 5 |
|---|---|---|---|
| 79 | Sire SIR 4017 | Moskow Diskow/Twist A Saint-Tropez (p/s) | 5 |
| 79 | Sire SIR 4020 | Rock Around The Clock/Moskow Diskow | 5 |
| 82 | Interdisc IN 2 | L'amour Toujours/Cloche Et Sifflets (p/s) | 5 |
| 79 | Sire SRK 6072 | LOOKING FOR ST. TROPEZ (LP, with lyric inner sleeve) | 15 |
| 82 | Interdisc INTO 1 | BIRDS AND BEES (LP) | 15 |

**TELLERS**
| 74 | Pyramid PYR 7011 | No Work, No Pay/Version | 6 |
|---|---|---|---|
| 74 | Dragon DRA 1031 | Ta It Deh/Hit Dib | 6 |

**TELSTARS**
| 62 | Oriole CB 1754 | I Went A' Walkin'/A Rose And A Thorn | 20 |
|---|---|---|---|

**TEMPERANCE SEVEN**
| 63 | Parlophone R 5070 | From Russia With Love/P.C.Q/Please Charleston Quietly | 7 |
|---|---|---|---|

*(see also Ted Wood)*

**TEMPEST (1)**
| 85 | Magnet PEST 1 | Always The Same/Love In The Wintertime (p/s) | 50 |
|---|---|---|---|
| 85 | Magnet 10PEST 1 | Always The Same/The Physical Act (10") | 25 |
| 85 | Magnet PEST 2 | Bluebelle/I Want To Live (p/s) | 50 |
| 85 | Magnet 10PEST 2 | Bluebelle/I Want To Live (10") | 25 |
| 86 | Magnet LAZY 1 | Lazy Sunday/You've Always Got Something To Say (p/s) | 15 |
| 86 | Magnet PEST 3 | Didn't We Have A Nice Time?/The Physical Act | 50 |

**TEMPEST (2)**
| 73 | Bronze ILPS 9220 | TEMPEST (LP, foldover cover with lyric inner sleeve) | 50 |
|---|---|---|---|
| 74 | Bronze ILPS 9267 | LIVING IN FEAR (LP, die-cut cover with inner sleeve) | 40 |

*(see also Colosseum, Patto)*

**BOBBY TEMPEST**
| 59 | Decca F 11125 | Love Or Leave/Don't Leave Me | 12 |
|---|---|---|---|

**BOB TEMPLE**
| 57 | Parlophone R 4264 | Come Back, Come Back/Vim Vam Vamoose | 80 |
|---|---|---|---|

**GERRY TEMPLE**
| 61 | HMV POP 823 | No More Tomorrows/So Nice To Walk You Home | 40 |
|---|---|---|---|
| 61 | HMV POP 939 | Seventeen Come Sunday/Tell You What I'll Do | 30 |
| 63 | HMV POP 1114 | Angel Face/Since You Went Away | 45 |
| 68 | RCA Victor RCA 1670 | Lovin' Up A Storm/Everything I Do is Wrong | 20 |

**RICHARD TEMPLE**
| 70 | Jay Boy BOY 31 | That Beatin' Rhythm/Could It Be | 15 |
|---|---|---|---|
| 70 | Jay Boy BOY 31 | That Beatin' Rhythm/Could It Be (DJ copy) | 30 |

**SHIRLEY TEMPLE**
| 59 | Top Rank JAR 139 | On The Good Ship Lollipop/Animal Crackers In My Soup | 5 |
|---|---|---|---|
| 59 | Top Rank JKR 8003 | I REMEMBER (EP) | 20 |

**TEMPLEAIRES**
| 60s | Vogue V 2421 | He Spoke/What Will Heaven Have In Store For Me | 20 |
|---|---|---|---|

**TEMPLE OF LIFE**
| 91 | T Life 001 | EDP/Relax Your Soul/Slayer/Trancetone (12", stamped white labels) | 50 |
|---|---|---|---|

**TEMPLE OF THE DOG**
| 92 | A&M AM 0091 | Hunger Strike/All Night Thing (picture disc) | 20 |
|---|---|---|---|
| 92 | A&M AMY 0091 | Hunger Strike/Your Saviour/All Night Thing (12", p/s, with poster) | 15 |
| 91 | A&M 395350-1 | TEMPLE OF THE DOG (LP) | 30 |

*(see also Pearl Jam)*

**TEMPLE ROW**
| 72 | Polydor 2058254 | King & Queen/One Of A Million Faces | 50 |
|---|---|---|---|
| 73 | Polydor 2058-329 | Walk The World Away/Mystery Man | 8 |

**TEMPLES**
| 13 | Heavenly HVN 250 | Shelter Song/Prisms (die-cut sleeve) | 50 |
|---|---|---|---|
| 13 | Heavenly HVN 261 | Colours To Life/Ankh (10" white vinyl, 300 only) | 15 |
| 13 | Heavenly HVN 267 | Keep In The Dark/Jewel Of Mine Eye (die-cut sleeve) | 10 |
| 14 | Heavenly HVNLP 100 | SUN STRUCTURES (LP, orange vinyl) | 60 |

**TEMPLETON TWINS**
| 70 | Liberty LBF 15379 | Hey Jude/Macarthur Park | 6 |
|---|---|---|---|

**NINO TEMPO**
| 57 | London HLU 8387 | Tempo's Tempo/June's Blues (as Nino Tempo & His Band) | 250 |
|---|---|---|---|
| 57 | London HLU 8387 | Tempo's Tempo/June's Blues (as Nino Tempo & His Band) (78) | 50 |
| 73 | A&M 7089 | Sister James/Clair De Luna (In Jazz) (as Nino Tempo & 5th Avenue) | 6 |
| 75 | A&M AMS 7190 | Come See Me Round Midnight/High On Music (as Nino Tempo & 5th Avenue) | 5 |
| 58 | London HB-U 1075 | ROCK 'N' ROLL BEACH PARTY (10" LP) | 200 |

*(see also Nino Tempo & April Stevens, April Stevenso)*

**NINO TEMPO & APRIL STEVENS**
| 62 | London HLK 9580 | Sweet And Lovely/TOP NOTES: Twist And Shout | 15 |
|---|---|---|---|
| 69 | London HLU 10245 | All Strung Out/My Old Flame | 8 |

| 64 | London HA-K 8168 | NINO TEMPO AND APRIL STEVENS - DEEP PURPLE (LP) | 20 |
|---|---|---|---|
| 64 | Atlantic AL 5006 | SING THE GREAT SONGS (LP, mono) | 15 |
| 64 | Atlantic SAL 5006 | SING THE GREAT SONGS (LP, stereo) | 18 |
| 66 | Atlantic | HEY BABY (LP) | 15 |
| 67 | London HA-U/SH-U 8314 | ALL STRUNG OUT (LP) | 20 |

*(see also Nino Tempo, April Stevens)*

## TEMPOS

| 59 | Pye International 7N 25026 | See You In September/Bless You My Love | 100 |
|---|---|---|---|
| 59 | Pye International 7N 25026 | See You In September/Bless You My Love (78) | 40 |

## TEMPTATIONS (1)

| 60 | Top Rank JAR 384 | Barbara/Someday | 30 |
|---|---|---|---|

## TEMPTATIONS (2)

### SINGLES

| 64 | Stateside SS 278 | The Way You Do The Things You Do/Just Let Me Know | 70 |
|---|---|---|---|
| 64 | Stateside SS 278 | The Way You Do The Things You Do/Just Let Me Know (DJ copy) | 120 |
| 64 | Stateside SS 319 | I'll Be In Trouble/The Girl's Alright With Me | 80 |
| 64 | Stateside SS 319 | I'll Be In Trouble/The Girl's Alright With Me (DJ copy) | 120 |
| 64 | Stateside SS 348 | Girl (Why You Wanna Make Me Blue)/Baby Baby I Need You | 80 |
| 64 | Stateside SS 348 | Girl (Why You Wanna Make Me Blue)/Baby Baby I Need You (DJ copy) | 240 |
| 65 | Tamla Motown TMG 504 | It's Growing/What Love Has Joined Together | 40 |
| 65 | Tamla Motown TMG 504 | It's Growing/What Love Has Joined Together (DJ copy) | 100 |
| 65 | Stateside SS 378 | My Girl/(Talking 'Bout) Nobody But My Baby | 45 |
| 65 | Stateside SS 378 | My Girl/(Talking 'Bout) Nobody But My Baby (DJ copy) | 150 |
| 65 | Tamla Motown TMG 526 | Since I Lost My Baby/You've Got To Earn It | 50 |
| 65 | Tamla Motown TMG 526 | Since I Lost My Baby/You've Got To Earn It (DJ copy) | 200 |
| 65 | Tamla Motown TMG 541 | My Baby/Don't Look Back | 45 |
| 65 | Tamla Motown TMG 541 | My Baby/Don't Look Back (DJ copy) | 100 |
| 66 | Tamla Motown TMG 557 | Get Ready/Fading Away | 30 |
| 66 | Tamla Motown TMG 557 | Get Ready/Fading Away (DJ copy) | 100 |
| 66 | Tamla Motown TMG 565 | Ain't Too Proud To Beg/You'll Lose A Precious Love (spelt "Previous") | 30 |
| 66 | Tamla Motown TMG 565 | Ain't Too Proud To Beg/You'll Lose A Precious Love (spelt "Previous") (DJ copy) | 130 |
| 66 | Tamla Motown TMG 578 | Beauty Is Only Skin Deep/You're Not An Ordinary Girl (DJ copy) | 140 |
| 66 | Tamla Motown TMG 578 | Beauty Is Only Skin Deep/You're Not An Ordinary Girl | 30 |
| 66 | Tamla Motown TMG 587 | (I Know) I'm Losing You/Little Miss Sweetness | 25 |
| 66 | Tamla Motown TMG 587 | (I Know) I'm Losing You/Little Miss Sweetness (DJ copy) | 80 |
| 67 | Tamla Motown TMG 610 | All I Need/Sorry Is A Sorry Word | 20 |
| 67 | Tamla Motown TMG 610 | All I Need/Sorry Is A Sorry Word (DJ copy) | 60 |
| 67 | Tamla Motown TMG 620 | You're My Everything/I've Been Good To You | 20 |
| 67 | Tamla Motown TMG 620 | You're My Everything/I've Been Good To You (DJ copy) | 50 |
| 67 | Tamla Motown TMG 633 | (Loneliness Made Me Realise) It's You That I Need/I Want A Love I Can See | 40 |
| 67 | Tamla Motown TMG 633 | (Loneliness Made Me Realise) It's You That I Need/I Want A Love I Can See (DJ copy) | 45 |
| 68 | Tamla Motown TMG 641 | I Wish It Would Rain/I Truly, Truly Believe | 20 |
| 68 | Tamla Motown TMG 641 | I Wish It Would Rain/I Truly, Truly Believe (DJ copy) | 30 |
| 68 | Tamla Motown TMG 658 | I Could Never Love Another (After Loving You)/Gonna Give Her All The Love I've Got | 15 |
| 68 | Tamla Motown TMG 658 | I Could Never Love Another (After Loving You)/Gonna Give Her All The Love I've Got (DJ copy) | 30 |
| 68 | Tamla Motown TMG 671 | Why Did You Leave Me Darling/How Can I Forget | 15 |
| 68 | Tamla Motown TMG 671 | Why Did You Leave Me Darling/How Can I Forget (DJ copy) | 30 |
| 69 | Tamla Motown TMG 688 | Get Ready/My Girl | 7 |
| 69 | Tamla Motown TMG 688 | Get Ready/My Girl (DJ copy) | 30 |
| 69 | Tamla Motown TMG 699 | Ain't Too Proud To Beg/Fading Away | 7 |
| 69 | Tamla Motown TMG 699 | Ain't Too Proud To Beg/Fading Away (DJ copy) | 25 |
| 69 | Tamla Motown TMG 707 | Cloud Nine/Why Did She Have To Leave Me (Why Did She Have To Go) | 7 |
| 69 | Tamla Motown TMG 707 | Cloud Nine/Why Did She Have To Leave Me (Why Did She Have To Go) (DJ copy) | 25 |
| 69 | Tamla Motown TMG 716 | Runaway Child, Running Wild/I Need Your Lovin' | 8 |
| 70 | Tamla Motown TMG 722 | I Can't Get Next To You/Running Away (Ain't Gonna Help You) | 7 |
| 70 | Tamla Motown TMG 749 | Ball Of Confusion (That's What The World Is Today)/It's Summer | 7 |
| 70 | Tamla Motown TMG 741 | Psychedelic Shack/That's The Way Love Is | 6 |
| 71 | Tamla Motown TMG 773 | Just My Imagination (Running Away With Me)/You Make Your Own Heaven And Hell Right Here On Earth | 6 |
| 71 | Tamla Motown TMG 783 | It's Summer/Unite The World (Ungena Za Ulimwengu) | 6 |
| 71 | Tamla Motown TMG 783 | Unite The World (Ungena Za Ulimwengu)/It's Summer (reissue) | 8 |
| 72 | Tamla Motown TMG 800 | Superstar/Gonna Keep Tryin' Till I Win Your Love | 8 |
| 72 | Tamla Motown TMG 808 | Take A Look Around/Smooth Sailing (From Now On) | 6 |
| 72 | Tamla Motown TMG 832 | Smiling Faces Sometimes/Mother Nature | 8 |
| 73 | Tamla Motown TMG 839 | Papa Was A Rolling Stone (Parts 1 & 2) | 5 |
| 83 | Tamla Motown TMG 1320 | Papa Was A Rolling Stone/FOUR TOPS: Medley | 35 |

### EPs

| 65 | Tamla Motown TME 2004 | THE TEMPTATIONS (EP) | 50 |
|---|---|---|---|
| 66 | Tamla Motown TME 2010 | IT'S THE TEMPTATIONS | 40 |

### ALBUMS : LPS

| 65 | Tamla Motown TML 11009 | MEET THE TEMPTATIONS | 200 |
|---|---|---|---|
| 65 | Tamla Motown TML 11016 | SING SMOKEY | 60 |
| 66 | Tamla Motown TML 11023 | THE TEMPTIN' TEMPTATIONS (mono) | 45 |
| 66 | Tamla Motown STML 11023 | THE TEMPTIN' TEMPTATIONS (stereo) | 55 |
| 66 | Tamla Motown TML 11035 | GETTIN' READY (mono) | 40 |
| 66 | Tamla Motown STML 11035 | GETTIN' READY (stereo) | 50 |
| 67 | Tamla Motown STML 11057 | WITH A LOT O'SOUL (stereo) | 40 |
| 67 | Tamla Motown STML 11053 | THE TEMPTATIONS LIVE! (stereo) | 25 |

| 67 | Tamla Motown STML 11042 | GREATEST HITS (stereo) | 25 |
|----|----|----|----|
| 67 | Tamla Motown TML 11042 | GREATEST HITS (mono) | 20 |
| 67 | Tamla Motown TML 11053 | TEMPTATIONS LIVE! (mono) | 20 |
| 67 | Tamla Motown TML 11057 | WITH A LOT O'SOUL (mono) | 35 |
| 68 | Tamla Motown TML 11068 | IN A MELLOW MOOD (mono) | 30 |
| 68 | Tamla Motown STML 11068 | IN A MELLOW MOOD (stereo) | 35 |
| 68 | Tamla Motown TML 11079 | WISH IT WOULD RAIN (LP, mono) | 30 |
| 68 | Tamla Motown STML 11079 | WISH IT WOULD RAIN (LP, stereo) | 35 |
| 68 | T. Motown (S)TML 11079 | THE TEMPTATIONS WISH IT COULD RAIN | 40 |
| 69 | Tamla Motown TML 11104 | THE TEMPTATIONS LIVE AT THE COPA (mono) | 30 |
| 69 | Tamla Motown STML 11104 | THE TEMPTATIONS LIVE AT THE COPA (stereo) | 25 |
| 69 | Tamla Motown (S)TML 11109 | CLOUD NINE (mono/stereo) | 25 |
| 70 | Tamla Motown STML 11141 | 'LIVE' AT LONDON'S TALK OF THE TOWN (stereo, mono unconfirmed) | 20 |
| 70 | Tamla Motown TML 11133 | PUZZLE PEOPLE (mono) | 25 |
| 70 | Tamla Motown STML 11133 | PUZZLE PEOPLE (stereo) | 22 |
| 70 | Tamla Motown STML 11147 | PSYCHEDELIC SHACK | 20 |
| 70 | Tamla Motown STML 11170 | GREATEST HITS Vol. 2 | 15 |
| 71 | Tamla Motown STML 11184 | THE SKY'S THE LIMIT | 15 |
| 72 | Tamla Motown STML 11202 | SOLID ROCK | 15 |
| 72 | Tamla Motown STML 11218 | ALL DIRECTIONS | 15 |
| 73 | Tamla Motown STML 11229 | MASTERPIECE | 15 |

*(see also David Ruffin, Diana Ross)*

## TEMPUS FUGIT
| 69 | Philips BF 1802 | Come Alive/Emphasis On Love | 60 |
|----|----|----|----|

*(see also Jensens)*

## 10CC
| 72 | UK UK 22 | Johnny Don't Do It/4% Of Something | 6 |
|----|----|----|----|
| 74 | UK UK 57 | The Worst Band In The World/18 Carat Man Of Means | 6 |
| 95 | Avex AVEXLP | MIRROR MIRROR (LP) | 40 |

*(see also Godley & Creme, Graham Gouldman, Mindbenders, Mockingbirds, Hotlegs, Whirlwinds,Tristar Airbus, Yellow Bellow Room Boom, Nick Mason & Rick Fenn, Frabjoy & Runcible Spoon, Manchester Mob, Ramases)*

## TENDER TONES
| 69 | Crab CRAB 38 | Devil Woman/Nobody Cares | 40 |
|----|----|----|----|

## TENDER TOUCH
| 73 | Hot Lead HL 7 | Scarlet Ribbons/Your Tender Touch | 8 |
|----|----|----|----|

## TEN FEET
| 66 | RCA RCA 1544 | Got Everything But Love/Factory Worker | 100 |
|----|----|----|----|
| 67 | CBS 3045 | Shoot On Sight/Losing Game | 120 |

## TEN FEET FIVE
| 65 | Fontana TF 578 | Baby's Back In Town/Send Me No More Lovin' | 45 |
|----|----|----|----|

*(see also Troggs)*

## TEN FOOT BONELESS
| 88 | Fierce FRIGHT 027 | Powerslide/Duane Peters Is God (12", yellow or white p/s, with inner) | 12 |
|----|----|----|----|

*(see also Pooh Sticks)*

## TENNENT & MORRISON
| 72 | Polydor 2383 152 | TENNENT & MORRISON (LP, with lyric insert) | 150 |
|----|----|----|----|

*(see also Joe Soap)*

## TENNIS SHOES
| 78 | Bonaparte BONE 3 | (Do The) Medium Wave/Rolf Is Stranger Than Richard/So Large (p/s) | 8 |
|----|----|----|----|

## TEN(N)ORS
| 68 | Doctor Bird DB 1152 | Massy Massa/CLIVE ALLSTARS: San Sebastian | 40 |
|----|----|----|----|
| 68 | Doctor Bird DB 1175 | Sufferer (Make It)/Little Things | 50 |
| 68 | Island WI 3133 | Ride Your Donkey/I've Got To Get You Off My Mind | 20 |
| 68 | Island WI 3140 | Copy Me Donkey (as Tenors)/The Stage (B-side actually by Ronnie Davis) | 35 |
| 68 | Island WI 3156 | Grampa/ROMEO STEWART: While I Was Walking | 30 |
| 68 | Blue Cat BS 127 | Khaki/LEYROY REID: Great Surprise (Pound Get A Blow) | 30 |
| 68 | Big Shot BI 501 | Reggae Girl/CLIVE ALLSTARS: Donkey Trot | 80 |
| 68 | Fab FAB 41 | Ride You Donkey/Cleopatra (as Tenners) | 25 |
| 68 | Fab FAB 50 | Let Go Yah Donkey/ROMEO STEWART: While I Was Walking | 25 |
| 69 | Big Shot BI 514 | You're No Good/Do The Reggae | 50 |
| 69 | Big Shot BI 517 | Another Scorcher/My Baby | 70 |
| 69 | Duke Reid DR 2502 | Hopeful Village/TOMMY McCOOK: The Village | 15 |
| 69 | Bullet BU 406 | Greatest Scorcher/Making Love | 15 |
| 69 | Crab CRAB 26 | Baff Boom/Feel Bad | 30 |
| 69 | Crab CRAB 29 | True Brothers/Sign Of The Time | 20 |
| 69 | Crab CRAB 36 | I Want Everything/Cherry | 20 |
| 73 | Explosion EX 2079 | Weather Report/Weather Report - Version | 20 |
| 73 | Pyramid PYR 7000 | Money Never Built A Mountain/My World | 12 |

*(see also Jennors, Prince Buster, Soul Brothers)*

## TENOR SAW
| 84 | SKD SKD 092 | Bad Bwoy/Dub (12") | 18 |
|----|----|----|----|
| 84 | Hawkeye HLD 0012 | CLASH (LP, with Coco Tea) | 18 |

## TENPOLE TUDOR
| 80 | Korova KOW 4 | Real Fun/What's In A Word (p/s) | 5 |
|----|----|----|----|

*(see also Sex Pistols)*

## 10,000 MANIACS

| | | | |
|---|---|---|---|
| 84 | Reflex RE 1 | My Mother The War (Remix)/Planned Obsolescence/National Education Week (12", p/s) | 20 |
| 84 | Press P 2010 | HUMAN CONFLICT 5 (12" EP, gatefold p/s) | 30 |
| 84 | Press P 3001 LP | SECRETS OF THE I-CHING (LP, with insert) | 25 |
| 84 | Press P 3001 LP | SECRETS OF THE I-CHING (LP, with insert; later re-pressing in different 'Chinese Chicken' sleeve, some with insert) | 15 |

## TEN WHEEL DRIVE (WITH GENYA RAVAN)

| | | | |
|---|---|---|---|
| 71 | Polydor 2066 034 | Mornin' Much Better/Stay With Me | 5 |
| 69 | Polydor 583 577 | CONSTRUCTION NO. 1 (LP) | 20 |
| 70 | Polydor 2425 002 | BRIEF REPLIES (LP, with Genya Ravan) | 20 |
| 71 | Polydor 2425 065 | PECULIAR FRIENDS (LP, with Genya Ravan) | 20 |

*(see also Goldie [& Gingerbreads])*

## TEN YEARS AFTER

| | | | |
|---|---|---|---|
| 68 | Deram DM 176 | Portable People/The Sounds | 20 |
| 68 | Deram DM 221 | Hear Me Calling/I'm Going Home | 8 |
| 70 | Deram DM 299 | Love Like A Man/Love Like A Man | 6 |
| 71 | Deram XDR 48532 | She Lies In The Morning/Sweet Little Sixteen (demo only) | 15 |
| 72 | Chrysalis/Philips 6155 006 | One Of These Days/Baby Won't You Let Me Rock 'n' Roll You | 5 |
| 89 | Chrysalis CHS 3477 | Highway Of Love/Rock 'n' Roll Music To The World (p/s) | 5 |
| 67 | Deram DML 1015 | TEN YEARS AFTER (LP, mono) | 80 |
| 67 | Deram SML 1015 | TEN YEARS AFTER (LP, stereo) | 70 |
| 68 | Deram DML 1023 | UNDEAD (LP, mono) | 40 |
| 68 | Deram SML 1023 | UNDEAD (LP, stereo) | 30 |
| 69 | Deram DML 1029 | STONEDHENGE (LP, gatefold sleeve, mono) | 50 |
| 69 | Deram SML 1029 | STONEDHENGE (LP, laminated gatefold sleeve, stereo) | 30 |
| 69 | Deram DML/SML 1052 | SSSSH! (LP, gatefold sleeve, mono/stereo) | 50 |
| 70 | Deram DML 1065 | CRICKLEWOOD GREEN (LP, gatefold sleeve, with 'Alvin Lee' poster, mono) | 100 |
| 70 | Deram SML 1065 | CRICKLEWOOD GREEN (LP, gatefold sleeve, with 'Alvin Lee' poster, stereo) | 50 |
| 71 | Deram SML 1078 | WATT (LP, gatefold sleeve, with poster) | 70 |
| 71 | Chrysalis CHR 1001 | A SPACE IN TIME (LP, 1st pressing with 'manufactures and distributed by Island Records Basing St' on top) | 50 |
| 72 | Deram SML 1096 | ALVIN LEE AND COMPANY (LP) | 15 |
| 72 | Chrysalis CHR 1009 | ROCK & ROLL MUSIC TO THE WORLD (gatefold sleeve) | 18 |
| 78 | Deram SML 1023 | UNDEAD (LP, reissue) | 15 |
| 74 | Chrysalis CHR 1060 | POSITIVE VIBRATIONS (LP) | 15 |
| 80 | Chrysalis CHR 1001 | WATT (LP, reissue, single sleeve) | 20 |

*(see also Alvin Lee, Chick Churchill)*

## WAYNE TENYUE

| | | | |
|---|---|---|---|
| 82 | Red Nail RN 0035 | Murderous Time/THE DUB BAND: Life Sentence (12") | 10 |

## TERMINAL

| | | | |
|---|---|---|---|
| 80 | Cargo CRS 0081 | Hold On/We're Only Human (in p/s) | 100 |
| 82 | Termite TERM 2 | Am I Doing It Right/I Don't Mind/Turn Around And Don't Make Me Laugh (p/s) | 20 |

## TERMINAL BEACH

| | | | |
|---|---|---|---|
| 82 | TB SRTS 82 | Love On Auto/Dark Words (p/s) | 50 |

## TERMINAL JIVE

| | | | |
|---|---|---|---|
| 82 | Jive Alive JA001 | THE TERMINAL JIVE AND SCARLET ALIVE EP (2 tracks on one side, p/s) | 15 |

## TERMINAL SPECTATORS

| | | | |
|---|---|---|---|
| 82 | Tiny Chariot CAT 002 | Another Day Another Dream/Reach For The Sky | 60 |

## TERMITES

| | | | |
|---|---|---|---|
| 65 | Oriole CB 1989 | Tell Me/I Found My Place | 40 |
| 65 | CBS 201761 | Every Day Every Day/No-One In The Whole Wide World | 20 |

## TERMITES (JAMAICA)

| | | | |
|---|---|---|---|
| 67 | Coxsone CS01/02 | Hold Down Rudie/JOE HIGGS AND THE WAILERS: Keep Cool (white label only) | 80 |
| 67 | Studio One SO 2006 | Mercy Mr. Percy/SOUL BROTHERS: Hot And Cold | 100 |
| 67 | Studio One SO 2029 | It Takes Two To Make Love/Beach Boy | 100 |
| 67 | Coxsone CS 7008 | Sign Up/DELROY WILSON: Troubled Man | 45 |
| 67 | Coxsone CS 7025 | Do It Right Now/SUMMERTAIRES: Stay (B-side actually by Gaylads) | 45 |
| 68 | Studio One SO 2040 | Mr D.J. (actually by Delroy Wilson)/Tripe Girl (actually by Heptones) | 40 |
| 68 | Coxsone CS 7039 | Mama Didn't Know/I Made A Mistake | 300 |
| 68 | Pama PM 729 | Push It Up/Two Of A Kind (B-side act. by Clancy Eccles & Cynthia Richards) | 80 |
| 68 | Pama PM 738 | Show Me The Way/What Can I Do | 40 |
| 68 | Trojan TR 634 | Love Up Kiss Up/TOMMY McCOOK : Regay | 40 |
| 69 | Nu Beat NB 017 | Push Push/Girls (actually by Hi Tones) | 35 |
| 67 | Studio One SOL 9003 | DO THE ROCK STEADY (LP) | 300 |

*(see also L. Sparks, Ken Boothe, Upsetters)*

## PETE TERRACE

| | | | |
|---|---|---|---|
| 67 | Pye International 7N 25427 | At The Party/No! No! No! | 30 |
| 67 | Pye International 7N 25440 | Shotgun Boo-Ga-Loo/I'm Gonna Make It | 40 |
| 67 | Pye Intl. NPL 28102 | BOOGALOO (LP) | 50 |

## TERRA COTTA

| | | | |
|---|---|---|---|
| 78 | Terra Cotta TC 001 | To Be Near You (p/s, with insert) | 15 |

*(see also Spriguns)*

## TERRAIN

| | | | |
|---|---|---|---|
| 83 | Terrain Musak TS 001 | Who's To Blame?/Vacation (no p/s) | 150 |

## TERRAPLANE

| | | | |
|---|---|---|---|
| 85 | Epic 26439 | BLACK AND WHITE (LP) | 15 |

*(see also Thunder, Nuthin' Fancy)*

## LLOYD TERRELL
| | | | |
|---|---|---|---|
| 68 | Island WI 3158 | My Argument (as Lloyd & Johnny Melody)/JOHNNY MELODY: Foey Man (B-side actually by George Dekker) | 300 |
| 68 | Pama PM 710 | Bang Bang Lulu/MRS MILLER: I Never Knew | 5 |
| 68 | Pama PM 740 | How Come (actually by Lee Perry)/MRS MILLER: Oh My Lover | 10 |
| 69 | Pama PM 752 | Lulu Returns/MRS MILLER: I Feel The Music | 10 |
| 69 | Nu Beat NB 023 | Mr Rhya/After Dark | 18 |
| 70 | Pama PM 792 | Birth Control/VAL BENNET: Return To Peace | 5 |
| 70 | Bullet BU 434 | Exposure/Baby Huey | 15 |
| 70 | Bullet BU 443 | Oh Me Oh My/I Did It | 25 |
| 71 | Escort ERT 855 | One Woman/CHARMERS: What Should I Do (act. by Dave Barker & Charmers) | 7 |
| 72 | Bullet BU 508 | Oily Sounds/Oily Version (as Lloyd Tyrell) | 8 |
| 73 | Pama PM 863 | Big Eight/JUNIOR BYLES: Auntie Lu Lu | 7 |

*(see also Charmers, Lloyd Charmers, Lloyd & Johnny, Lloyd & Ken, Lloydie & Lowbites)*

## TAMMI TERRELL
| | | | |
|---|---|---|---|
| 66 | Tamla Motown TMG 561 | Come On And See Me/Baby Don'tcha Worry | 120 |
| 66 | Tamla Motown TMG 561 | Come On And See Me/Baby Don'tcha Worry (DJ copy) | 200 |
| 69 | T. Motown (S)TML 11103 | THE IRRESISTIBLE TAMMI TERRELL (LP, mono/stereo) | 100 |

*(see also Marvin Gaye & Tammi Terrell)*

## TAMMI TERRELL/CHUCK JACKSON
| | | | |
|---|---|---|---|
| 69 | Marble Arch MAL 1110 | THE EARLY SHOW (LP) | 20 |

*(see also Chuck Jackson)*

## PHIL TERRELL
| | | | |
|---|---|---|---|
| 94 | Kent 6T 10 | Love Has Passed Me By/VIC & JOHN: Why Did She Lie | 35 |

## TERRI & TERRORS
| | | | |
|---|---|---|---|
| 79 | Fresh FRESH 4 | Laugh At Me/Laugh At Me (Again) (folded p/s) | 5 |

## TERRORIZER
| | | | |
|---|---|---|---|
| 89 | Earach MOSH 16 | WORLD DOWNFALL (LP, with inner) | 30 |

## TERRORVISION
| | | | |
|---|---|---|---|
| 92 | Total Vegas 12VEGAS 1 | THRIVE EP (12" EP) | 12 |
| 93 | Total Vegas CDATVR 1 | Problem Solved/Corpse Fly/We Are The Roadcrew/Sailing Home (CD) | 25 |
| 92 | Total Vegas ATVRLP 1 | FORMALDEHYDE (LP, 14 tracks, green vinyl, 500 only, stickered sleeve) | 40 |
| 93 | Total Vegas VEGASLPS 1 | FORMALDEHYDE (reissue LP, 12 tracks, 1,000 copies with 12-page booklet, stickered sleeve & lyric inner) | 20 |
| 93 | Total Vegas BOOT 1 | LIVE AT THE DON VALLEY STADIUM (CD, picture disc, 250 promo copies only) | 30 |
| 94 | Total Vegas VEGASLP 2 | HOW TO MAKE FRIENDS AND INFLUENCE PEOPLE (LP, gatefold) | 15 |
| 96 | Total Vegas VEGASLP 3 | REGULAR URBAN SURVIVORS (LP) | 18 |

## TERRY
| | | | |
|---|---|---|---|
| 66 | Fontana TF 751 | Spilt Milk/The Way That I Remember Him | 10 |

## TERRY, CARL & DERRICK
| | | | |
|---|---|---|---|
| 69 | Grape GR 3012 | True Love/ROY SMITH: Another Saturday Night | 15 |

## DEWEY TERRY
| | | | |
|---|---|---|---|
| 73 | Tumbleweed TW 3502 | CHIEF (LP) | 18 |

*(see also Don & Dewey, Don Harris, Harvey Mandel)*

## GORDON TERRY
| | | | |
|---|---|---|---|
| 57 | London REA 1098 | COUNTRY CLAMBAKE (EP) | 20 |

## KARL TERRY & THE BRUISERS
| | | | |
|---|---|---|---|
| 78 | ROX 008 | Haunted House/Stick It In Your Pipe | 6 |

## PAT TERRY (GROUP)
| | | | |
|---|---|---|---|
| 70s | Myrrh MYR 1031 | PAT TERRY GROUP (LP) | 18 |

## SONNY TERRY (TRIO)
| | | | |
|---|---|---|---|
| 53 | Parlophone MSP 6017 | Hootin' Blues/TOMMY REILLY: Bop! Goes The Weasel | 35 |
| 56 | Vogue EPV 1095 | SONNY TERRY (EP) | 50 |
| 55 | Vogue LDE 137 | FOLK BLUES (10" LP) | 40 |
| 55 | Vogue LDE 165 | CITY BLUES (10" LP) | 40 |
| 58 | Melodisc MLP 516 | WHOOPIN' THE BLUES (10" LP) | 40 |
| 58 | Topic 10T 30 | HARMONICA BLUES (10" LP) | 40 |
| 65 | Topic 12T 30 | HARMONICA BLUES (12" LP, reissue) | 35 |
| 66 | Xtra XTRA 5025 | SONNY'S STORY (LP) | 25 |
| 69 | Ember CW 136 | BLIND SONNY TERRY & WOODY GUTHRIE (LP) | 15 |
| 69 | Xtra XTRA 1064 | SONNY TERRY (LP) | 15 |
| 60s | Mainstream MSL 1037 | GOING DOWN SLOW (LP, with BROWNIE McGHEE & PEPPERMINT HARRIS) | 18 |
| 70 | Xtra XTRA 1099 | BLUES FROM EVERYWHERE (LP) | 15 |
| 71 | Xtra XTRA 1110 | ON THE ROAD (LP, with J.C. Burris) | 15 |

*(see also Woody Guthrie)*

## SONNY TERRY & BROWNIE MCGHEE
| | | | |
|---|---|---|---|
| 60 | Columbia DB 4433 | Talking Harmonica Blues/Rockin' And Whoopin' | 35 |
| 64 | Oriole CB 1946 | Dissatisfied Woman/SONNY TERRY: Goin' Down Slow | 20 |
| 50s | Melodisc EPM7 83 | ME AND SONNY (EP) | 25 |
| 58 | Pye Jazz NJE 1060 | THE BLUEST (EP) | 10 |
| 59 | Pye Jazz NJE 1073 | SONNY TERRY & BROWNIE McGHEE & CHRIS BARBER'S JAZZ BAND (EP) | 10 |
| 59 | Pye Jazz NJE 1074 | TERRY AND McGHEE IN LONDON PT. 1 (EP) | 15 |
| 59 | Topic TOP 37 | HOOTENANNY NEW YORK CITY (EP, with Pete Seeger) | 15 |
| 61 | Top Rank JKP 3007 | WORK-PLAY-FAITH-FUN-SONGS (EP) | 15 |
| 64 | Ember EP 4562 | SONNY TERRY AND BROWNIE McGHEE (EP) | 20 |
| 64 | Topic TOP 121 | R AND B FROM S AND B (EP) | 15 |
| 64 | Realm REP 4002 | PAWNSHOP BLUES (EP) | 15 |
| 64 | Vocalion EPV 1274 | SONNY TERRY AND BROWNIE McGHEE (EP) | 20 |

MINT VALUE £

| 65 | Vocalion EPV 1279 | I SHALL NOT BE MOVED (EP) | 20 |
| 58 | Topic 12T 29 | BROWNIE McGHEE AND SONNY TERRY (LP) | 30 |
| 58 | Pye Nixa Jazz NJT 515 | SONNY, BROWNIE AND CHRIS (10" LP, with Chris Barber) | 45 |
| 58 | Pye Nixa Jazz NJL 18 | SONNY TERRY AND BROWNIE McGHEE IN LONDON (LP) | 30 |
| 58 | London Jazz LTZ-C 15144 | BACK COUNTRY BLUES (LP) | 50 |
| 60 | Columbia 33SX 1223 | BLUES IS MY COMPANION (LP) | 50 |
| 61 | World Record Club 7379 | SONNY TERRY AND BROWNIE McGHEE (LP) | 20 |
| 61 | Vogue LAE 12247 | BLUES IS A STORY (LP, mono) | 30 |
| 61 | Vogue SEA 5014 | BLUES IS A STORY (LP, stereo) | 40 |
| 63 | Vogue LAE 12266 | DOWN SOUTH SUMMIT MEETIN' (LP) | 25 |
| 63 | CBS 52165 | BACK COUNTRY BLUES (LP) | 25 |
| 64 | Xtra XTRA 1004 | BIG BILL BROONZY/SONNY TERRY/BROWNIE McGHEE (LP) | 30 |
| 64 | Vogue LAE 552 | BROWNIE McGHEE AND SONNY TERRY (LP) | 30 |
| 64 | Realm RM 165 | BACK COUNTRY BLUES (LP) | 15 |
| 64 | Stateside SL 10076 | BLUES HOOT (LP, some tracks by Lightnin' Hopkins) | 40 |
| 64 | Fontana 688 006ZL | LIVIN' WITH THE BLUES (LP) | 30 |
| 66 | Philips BL 7675 | AT THE BUNK HOUSE (LP) | 20 |
| 66 | Verve VLP 5010 | GUITAR HIGHWAY (LP, mono) | 20 |
| 66 | Verve SVLP 5010 | GUITAR HIGHWAY (LP, stereo) | 25 |
| 66 | Fontana TL 5289 | HOMETOWN BLUES (LP) | 20 |
| 69 | Capitol T 20906 | WHOOPIN' THE BLUES (LP) | 20 |
| 69 | Stateside SSL 10291 | LONG WAY FROM HOME (LP) | 15 |
| 70 | Fontana SFJL 979 | WHERE THE BLUES BEGAN (LP) | 20 |
| 73 | Mainstream MSL 1019 | HOMETOWN BLUES (LP, gatefold sleeve) | 15 |

*(see also Brownie McGhee, Chris Barber, Pete Seeger, Big Bill Broonzy, Lightnin' Hopkins, Big Joe Turner)*

### SUSAN TERRY
| 62 | Piccadilly 7N 35026 | Along Came LOve/Looking For A Boy | 15 |

### TERRY & JERRY
| 65 | R&B MRB 5009 | People Are Doing It Every Day/Mama Julie | 22 |

### TERRY SISTERS
| 57 | Parlophone R 4364 | It's The Same Old Jazz/Broken Promises | 6 |
| 58 | Parlophone R 4509 | Sweet Thing (Tell Me That You Love Me)/You Forgot To Remember | 6 |

### TESCO BOMBERS
| 82 | Y Y14 | Hernando's Hideaway/Break The Ice At Parties/Girl From Ipanema (p/s) | 10 |

*(see also Homosexuals)*

### TEST DEPARTMENT
| 83 | Some Bizzare TEST 112 | Compulsion/Pulsations (12", p/s) | 10 |
| 87 | Some Bizzare 12MOP 13 | Victory (12", p/s) | 10 |
| 80s | Media City CMC 1 | Gododdin (12", p/s, Welsh gig freebie with Brith Gof) | 10 |
| 90 | Mop MOP 5T | Jihad/(Desert Mix)/(Oil Mix) (12", p/s) | 12 |
| 93 | Mop MOP 8T | Bang On It/(Tao Systems Mix)/(TC Ruff House Remix) (12", die-cut p/s) | 10 |
| 85 | Test TEST 33 | BEATING THE RETREAT (LP, box set) | 18 |

### TESTCARD F
| 83 | Backs NCH 004 | Bandwagon Tango/Unfamiliar Rooms (p/s) | 8 |
| 83 | Backs NCH 10 | Third Stroke/If Only If It Wasn't (p/s) | 10 |

### TETRACK
| 77 | Hawkeye HE 006 | Let's Get Started/PABLO EXPERIENCE: Go it | 10 |
| 78 | Greensleeves GRE 8 | Only Jah Knows/ROCKERS ALL STARS: Jah Jah Dub | 20 |
| 78 | Rockers APD 2 | Love And Unity/JAH LEVE & JAH BULL: Two The Hard Way/JUNIOR DAN: Jah Foundation (12") | 35 |
| 89 | Greensleeves GREL 121 | LET'S GET IT STARTED (LP) | 20 |

### ALAN TEW ORCHESTRA
| 76 | Epic EPC 4676 | The Sweeney/The Prowler | 15 |
| 67 | Decca Phase 4 PFS 4120 | THIS IS MY SCENE (LP) | 40 |
| 72 | CBS 64665 | LET'S FLY (LP) | 25 |

### JOE TEX
| 65 | Atlantic AT 4015 | Hold What You've Got/Fresh Out Of Tears | 22 |
| 65 | Atlantic AT 4021 | You Better Get It/You Got What It Takes | 20 |
| 65 | Sue WI 370 | Yum Yum Yum/You Little Baby Face Thing | 40 |
| 65 | Atlantic AT 4027 | A Woman Can Change A Man/Don't Let Your Left Hand Know | 15 |
| 65 | Atlantic AT 4045 | I Want To (Do Everything For You)/Funny Bone | 15 |
| 65 | Atlantic AT 4058 | A Sweet Woman Like You/Close Your Door | 15 |
| 65 | Atlantic AT 4081 | The Love You Save/If Sugar Was As Sweet As You | 15 |
| 66 | Atlantic 584 016 | S.Y.S.L.J.F.M. (Letter Song)/I'm A Man | 10 |
| 66 | Atlantic 584 035 | You Better Believe It/I Believe I'm Gonna Make It | 25 |
| 67 | Atlantic 584 068 | Papa Was Too/The Truest Woman In The World | 10 |
| 67 | Atlantic 584 096 | Hold What You've Got/A Sweet Woman Like You | 10 |
| 67 | Atlantic 584 102 | Show Me/Woman Sees A Hard Time (When Her Man Is Gone) | 15 |
| 67 | Atlantic 584 119 | Woman Like That, Yeah/I'm Going And Get It | 10 |
| 67 | Atlantic 584 144 | Skinny Legs And All/Watch The One (That Brings The Bad News) | 10 |
| 68 | Atlantic 584 171 | Men Are Getting Scarce/You're Gonna Thank Me Woman | 10 |
| 68 | Atlantic 584 212 | Go Home And Do It/Keep The One You Got | 10 |
| 69 | Atlantic 584 296 | We Can't Sit Down Now/It Ain't Sanitary | 10 |
| 70 | Atlantic 584 318 | You're Alright Ray Charles/Everything Happens On Time | 10 |
| 71 | Mercury 6052 067 | I Knew Him/Bad Feet | 6 |
| 72 | Mercury 6052 111 | Give The Baby Anything/Takin' A Chance | 6 |
| 72 | Mercury 6052 129 | I Got 'Cha/Mother Prayer | 6 |
| 72 | Mercury 6052 156 | You Said A Bad Word/It Ain't Gonna Work Baby | 6 |

| | | | |
|---|---|---|---|
| 03 | Soul Food EAT SF001 | I Wanna Be Free/Under Your Powerful Love | 8 |
| 65 | Atlantic ATL 5043 | THE NEW BOSS (LP) | 40 |
| 66 | Atlantic ATL 587 009 | THE LOVE YOU SAVE (LP) | 35 |
| 67 | Atlantic 587 053 | I'VE GOT TO DO A LITTLE BETTER (LP) | 25 |
| 67 | Atlantic 587/588 059 | THE NEW BOSS (LP, reissue) | 15 |
| 67 | London HA-U 8334 | THE BEST OF JOE TEX (LP) | 40 |
| 67 | Atlantic 587/588 079 | GREATEST HITS (LP) | 15 |
| 68 | Atlantic 587/588 104 | LIVE AND LIVELY (LP) | 25 |
| 68 | Atlantic 587/588 118 | SOUL COUNTRY (LP) | 20 |
| 69 | Atlantic 587/588 130 | YOU BETTER GET IT (LP) | 20 |
| 69 | Atlantic 588 193 | BUYING A BOOK (LP) | 15 |
| 77 | EPIC EPC 81931 | BUMPS AND BRUISES (LP) | 15 |

*(see also Soul Clan)*

### TEXANS
| | | | |
|---|---|---|---|
| 64 | Columbia DB 7242 | Being With You/Wondrous Look Of Love | 6 |

### TEXTONES
| | | | |
|---|---|---|---|
| 87 | Enigma 3268-1 | CEDAR CREEK (LP) | 18 |

### TEXTOR SINGERS
| | | | |
|---|---|---|---|
| 54 | Capitol CL 14211 | Sobbin' Women/Remember Me | 10 |

### RUDY THACKER & STRINGBEANS
| | | | |
|---|---|---|---|
| 62 | Starlite ST45 087 | The Ballad Of Johnny Horton/Tomorrow Is My Last Day | 10 |

### JAKE THACKRAY
| | | | |
|---|---|---|---|
| 67 | Columbia SCX 6178 | LAST WILL AND TESTAMENT (LP) | 15 |

### THAMESIDERS/DAVY GRAHAM
| | | | |
|---|---|---|---|
| 63 | Decca DFE 8538 | FROM A LONDON HOOTENANNY (EP, 2 tracks each) | 50 |

*(see also Davy Graham)*

### THANES OF CAWDOR
| | | | |
|---|---|---|---|
| 87 | DDT DISPLP11 | THANES OF CAWDOR (LP) | 18 |

### SISTER ROSETTA THARPE
| | | | |
|---|---|---|---|
| 60 | MGM MGM 1072 | If I Can Help Somebody/Take My Hand, Precious Lord | 6 |
| 58 | Brunswick OE 9284 | GOSPEL SONGS No. 2 (EP) | 12 |
| 57 | Mercury MPL 6529 | GOSPEL TRAIN (LP) | 25 |
| 59 | Brunswick LAT 8290 | GOSPEL TRAIN (LP) | 15 |
| 61 | Mercury MMC 14057 | THE GOSPEL TRUTH (LP) | 20 |
| 63 | Society SOC 900 | HOT HOT HOT (LP) | 15 |
| 65 | Ember NR 5023 | SPIRITUALS IN RHYTHM (LP) | 20 |

*(see also Little Richard)*

### THAT CORPORATE FEELING
| | | | |
|---|---|---|---|
| 84 | Platform SOUL XX1 | The Rain Has Gone/Industrial Backlash (die-cut Corporate Feeling sleeve) | 50 |

### THATCHER ON ACID
| | | | |
|---|---|---|---|
| 88 | Rugger Bugger SEEP 1 | THATCHER ON ACID (LP) | 15 |

### T.H.C. ROLLER
| | | | |
|---|---|---|---|
| 94 | Poor Person Prod. PPPR 4 | CHAPTER IN THE LIFE OF T.H.C. ROLLER (LP, handmade sleeve with insert & king-size rolling papers, numbered, 500 only) | 20 |
| 94 | Poor Person Prod. | THIS MUST BE THE JOINT (LP, 500 only) | 70 |

### THEATRE OF HATE
| | | | |
|---|---|---|---|
| 80 | S.S. SS 3 | Original Sin/Legion (p/s) | 10 |
| 81 | Burning Rome BRR 1 | Rebel Without A Brain/My Own Invention (p/s, mispress with 2 B-side labels) | 8 |
| 81 | Burning Rome BRR 1 | Rebel Without A Brain/My Own Invention (p/s) | 6 |
| 85 | Bliss TOH 1EP | The Wake/Love Is A Ghost/Poppies/Legion (EP, 33rpm, with T-shirt in stickered pack, sealed) | 10 |
| 82 | Burning Rome TOH 1 | WESTWORLD (LP) | 15 |

*(see also Pack, Spear Of Destiny, Senate, Cult, Crisis)*

### THEE
| | | | |
|---|---|---|---|
| 65 | Decca F 12163 | Each And Every Day/There You Go! | 40 |

### THEE HEADCOATEES
| | | | |
|---|---|---|---|
| 92 | Damaged Goods DAMGOOD 4 | Davey Crockett (Gabba Hey)/Young Blood (p/s, yellow vinyl, 2000 only) | 12 |
| 97 | Vinyl Japan ASKLP 65 | BOSTIK HAZE (LP) | 15 |

### THEE HEADCOATEES/THE HEADCOATS
| | | | |
|---|---|---|---|
| 92 | Damaged Goods DAMGOOD 1 | Headcoat Girl/THEE HEADCOATS: Lakota Woman (p/s, different coloured sleeves & vinyl) | 8 |
| 93 | Twist TWIST 5 | Strychnine/THEE HEADCOATS: Branded (p/s, different sleeve colours exist) | 8 |
| 95 | Damaged Goods DAMGOOD 63 | Johnny Jack!/THEE HEADCOATS: Sufference Wharf (p/s) | 6 |
| 98 | Damaged Goods DAMGOOD 155 | Jackie Chan Does Kung Fu/THEE HEADCOATS: The Rise And Fall Of A Double (p/s) | 8 |

*(see also Mickey & Ludella, Delmonas)*

### THEE HYPNOTICS
| | | | |
|---|---|---|---|
| 88 | Hipsville HIP 1 | Love In A Different Vein/All NIght Long (p/s) | 6 |

### HANS THEESINK
| | | | |
|---|---|---|---|
| 80 | Kettle KOP 7 | LATE LAST NIGHT (LP) | 25 |

### BOB THEIL
| | | | |
|---|---|---|---|
| 82 | Private (no cat. no.) | SO FAR (LP, private pressing) | 250 |

### LLANS THELWELL & HIS CELESTIALS
| | | | |
|---|---|---|---|
| 66 | Island WI 262 | Choo Choo Ska/Lonely Night (B-side vocal: Busty Brown) | 35 |

### THEM
| | | | |
|---|---|---|---|
| 64 | Decca F 11973 | Don't Start Crying Now/One Two Brown Eyes | 70 |

| | | | |
|---|---|---|---|
| 64 | Decca F 12018 | Baby Please Don't Go/Gloria | 12 |
| 65 | Decca F 12094 | Here Comes The Night/All For Myself | 10 |
| 65 | Decca F 12175 | One More Time/How Long Baby? | 10 |
| 65 | Decca F 12215 | (It Won't Hurt) Half As Much/I'm Gonna Dress In Black | 10 |
| 65 | Decca F 12281 | Mystic Eyes/If You And I Could Be As Two | 10 |
| 66 | Decca F 12355 | Call My Name/Bring 'Em On In | 10 |
| 66 | Decca F 12403 | Richard Cory/Don't You Know? | 12 |
| 67 | Major Minor MM 509 | Gloria/Friday's Child | 20 |
| 67 | Major Minor MM 513 | The Story Of Them (Parts 1 & 2) | 25 |
| 73 | Deram DM 394 | Gloria/Baby Please Don't Go (reissue) | 8 |
| 65 | Decca DFE 8612 | THEM (EP, unboxed decca logo) | 150 |
| 65 | Decca DFE 8612 | THEM (EP, export-only 'band-on-ladder' p/s) | 500 |
| 65 | Decca LK 4700 | (THE ANGRY YOUNG) THEM (LP, original label, with flipback sleeve) | 200 |
| 65 | Decca LK 4700 | (THE ANGRY YOUNG) THEM (LP, original label) | 120 |
| 66 | Decca LK 4751 | THEM AGAIN (LP, original label, with flipback sleeve) | 200 |
| 66 | Decca LK 4751 | THEM AGAIN (LP, original label) | 120 |
| 70 | Decca LK 4700 | (THE ANGRY YOUNG) THEM (LP, re-pressing, red label, boxed Decca logo) | 50 |
| 70 | Decca LK 4751 | THEM AGAIN (LP, re-pressing, red label, boxed Decca logo) | 40 |
| 70 | Decca PA 86 | THE WORLD OF THEM (LP, original issue, mono) | 25 |
| 70 | Decca (S) PA 86 | THE WORLD OF THEM (LP, original issue, stereo) | 15 |
| 73 | Deram DPM 3001/2 | THEM - FEATURING VAN MORRISON LEAD SINGER (2xLP, gatefold sleeve) | 25 |
| 78 | Sonet SNTF 738 | BELFAST GYPSIES (LP, features Them without Van Morrison) | 25 |

*(see also Van Morrison, Trader Horne, Taste, Sk'boo, Belfast Gypsies, Moses K. & Prophets, Peter Barden, Jackie McCauley)*

## THEME
| | | | |
|---|---|---|---|
| 82 | Creed CR 001 | Sacred/Conflict | 6 |

## JOHN THEMIS
| | | | |
|---|---|---|---|
| 83 | Coda CODS 1 | Goblins In Sherwood/Post Hypnotic Suggestions (p/s) | 6 |

## THERAPY
| | | | |
|---|---|---|---|
| 72 | CBS 69017 | ALMANAC (LP, gatefold sleeve with inside centre opening) | 25 |
| 73 | Indigo IRS 5124 | ONE NIGHT STAND (LP, private pressing) | 15 |

## THERAPY?
| | | | |
|---|---|---|---|
| 90 | Multifuckingnational MFN 1 | Meat Abstract/Punishment Kisses (p/s, labels on wrong sides, 1,000 only) | 30 |
| 92 | A&M (no cat. no.) | TEETHGRINDER (12", double pack, white labels in presentation pack) | 30 |
| 92 | A&M THX 1 | Have A Merry Fucking Christmas: Teenage Kicks/With Or Without You (Xmas gig freebie) | 18 |
| 92 | Wiiija WIJ 11 | PLEASURE DEATH (mini-LP, 10 white labels) | 35 |
| 94 | A&M 540196-1 | TROUBLEGUM (LP, green vinyl) | 25 |
| 95 | A&M 540379-1 | INFERNAL LOVE (LP, red vinyl) | 15 |

## THERMOMETERS
| | | | |
|---|---|---|---|
| 80 | Fokker FEP 100 | 20th Century Girl/Newtown Refugees/Stole Your Drugs (in oversized p/s) | 30 |
| 80 | Fokker FEP 100 | 20th Century Girl/Newtown Refugees/Stole Your Drugs (p/s) | 20 |

## THESE IMMORTAL SOULS
| | | | |
|---|---|---|---|
| 87 | Mute STUMM 48 | GET LOST (DON'T LIE) (LP) | 20 |
| 92 | Mute STUMM 98 | I'M NEVER GONNA DIE AGAIN (LP) | 30 |

*(see also the Birthday Party)*

## THESE NEW PURITANS
| | | | |
|---|---|---|---|
| 13 | PIAS INFECT 156LP | FIELD OF REEDS (2-LP, one side etched) | 18 |

## THE THE
| | | | |
|---|---|---|---|
| 80 | 4AD AD 10 | Controversial Subject/Black And White (p/s) | 30 |
| 81 | Some Bizzare BZS 4 | Cold Spell Ahead/Hot Ice (p/s) | 25 |
| 86 | Epic TRUTH Q3 | Infected/Infected (Energy Mix)/Disturbed (12", uncensored 'wank' p/s) | 15 |
| 82 | private cassette | PORNOGRAPHY OF DESPAIR (LP, unreleased, cassettes exist) | 0 |
| 83 | Epic EPC 25525 | SOUL MINING (LP, with inner sleeve, initially with 12" single Perfect/"Soup Of Mixed Emotions"/"Fruit Of The Heart") | 18 |
| 86 | Epic EPC 26770 | INFECTED (LP, with poster & inner, 1st 25,000 with 'torture' sleeve) | 15 |
| 02 | Sony 5079022 | LONDON TOWN (5-CD box set) | 30 |
| 93 | Epic 472468-1 | DUSK (LP) | 50 |

*(see also Matt Johnson, Gadgets)*

## THEY MUST BE RUSSIANS
| | | | |
|---|---|---|---|
| 79 | Gramme/Lyntone LYN 6526/27 | Psycho Analysis/JOE 9T AND THE THUNDERBIRDS: Psycho Analysis (p/s, stamped white label) | 15 |
| 79 | RVS 001 | THEY MUST BE RUSSIANS 4-TRACK EP (p/s) | 15 |
| 80 | Fresh FRESH 18 | Don't Try To Cure Yourself/The Truth About Kanga Pants/Air To Breathe (p/s) | 8 |
| 80 | No label | Nagasaki's Children/Nellie The Elephant/Circus/I Want To Hold You Now (mail-order only, p/s with poster insert) | 10 |
| 83 | First Floor FF2 | THEY MUST BE RUSSIANS (LP) | 15 |

*(see also Joe 9T & Thunderbirds)*

## THICK PIGEON
| | | | |
|---|---|---|---|
| 84 | Factory FACT 85 | TOO CRAZY COWBOYS (LP) | 40 |

## THIEVES
| | | | |
|---|---|---|---|
| 79 | Arista ARIGV 266 | 400 Dragons/Headlights (green vinyl) | 5 |

*(see also Fairport Convention)*

## THIEVES LIKE US
| | | | |
|---|---|---|---|
| 80 | Earlobe ELS 1 | Mind Made/Strike Out (p/s) | 8 |

## THIGHPAULSANDRA
| | | | |
|---|---|---|---|
| 01 | World Serpent ESKATON 27 | Michel Publicity Window/Paralysed (p/s) | 5 |

*(see also Coil, Spiritualized)*

## THIN END OF THE WEDGE
| | | | |
|---|---|---|---|
| 81 | Jungle JR 051S | Lights Are On Green/I'm Not Dead Yet (in p/s) | 30 |

81    Jungle JR 051S                    Lights Are On Green/I'm Not Dead Yet ................................................................ 12

*(see also Damascus)*

## THINGS
80    Imperial IP 4301                  Pieces Of You/Lost Love (p/s) .......................................................................... 10

*(see also Buzzcocks)*

## THINGS FALL APART
72    President PT378                   Bye Bye My Rose/Manna ................................................................................. 20

## THIN ICE
88    Blag It SJP 858                   Freedom Road (p/s) ......................................................................................... 40

## THIN LIZZY
### SINGLES
70    Parlophone DIP 513                The Farmer/I Need You (Irish only, as Thin Lizzie) ............................... 1000
71    Decca F 13208                     NEW DAY (EP, 33rpm, gatefold p/s) ........................................................ 300
71    Decca F 13208                     NEW DAY (EP, 33rpm, without p/s) .......................................................... 100
72    Decca F 13355                     Whiskey In The Jar/Black Boys On The Corner .......................................... 8
72    Decca F 13355                     Whiskey In The Jar/Black Boys On The Corner (demos in p/s).............. 30
73    Decca F 13402                     Randolph's Tango/Broken Dreams (2 versions of A-side: matrices ZDR 53384 & ZCPDR 53312) .............................................................................................. 15
73    Decca F 13467                     The Rocker/Here I Go Again (demos £25) ................................................ 5
74    Decca F 13507                     Little Darlin'/Buffalo Gal ................................................................................. 8
74    Vertigo 6059 111                  Philomena/Sha La La ....................................................................................... 8
75    Vertigo 6059 124                  Rosalie/Half Caste ........................................................................................... 6
75    Vertigo 6059 129                  Wild One/For Those Who Love To Die ....................................................... 8
76    Vertigo 6059 150                  Jailbreak/Running Back (p/s) ...................................................................... 25
77    Vertigo 6059 177                  Dancing In The Moonlight/Bad Reputation (p/s) .................................. 10
78    Decca F 13748                     Whiskey In The Jar/Vagabond Of The Western World/Sitamoia (p/s) ...... 8
79    Vertigo LIZZY 3                   Waiting For An Alibi/With Love (p/s, with cartoon lyric sheet) ............... 8
79    Decca THIN 1                      Things Ain't Working Out Down At The Farm/The Rocker/Little Darling (10,000 with p/s) ................................................................................................................ 5
79    Vertigo LIZZY 5                   Sarah/Got To Give Up (3 different p/s designs) ......................................... 5
70s   Vertigo DJ 016                    It's Only Money/JANNE SCHAFFER: Dr Abraham (promo only, no p/s) ....... 200
82    Vertigo LIZZY 10                  Hollywood (Down On Your Luck) (10", p/s, 1-sided, existence unconfirmed) .................. 0

### ALBUMS
71    Decca SKL 5082                    THIN LIZZY (dark blue/silver label, early copies with laminated sleeve) ...................... 100
71    Decca SKL 5082                    THIN LIZZY (dark blue/silver label, later pressing with matt sleeve) ......................... 35
72    Decca TXS 108                     SHADES OF A BLUE ORPHANAGE (1st pressing, gatefold sleeve, green label) .............. 70
72    Decca TXLS 108                    SHADES OF A BLUE ORPHANAGE (2nd pressing, gatefold sleeve, blue label) ............ 60
73    Decca SKL 5170                    VAGABONDS OF THE WESTERN WORLD (dark blue/silver label, with lyric insert) ...... 40
73    Decca SKL 5170                    VAGABONDS OF THE WESTERN WORLD (dark blue/silver label, without insert) .......... 20
74    Vertigo 6360 116                  NIGHT LIFE (LP, 'spaceship' label) .............................................................. 15
75    Vertigo 6360 121                  FIGHTING (LP, 'spaceship' label) ................................................................ 15
76    Vertigo 9102 008                  JAIL BREAK (LP, die-cut sleeve, 'spaceship' label) ................................ 20
76    Vertigo 9102 012                  JOHNNY THE FOX (LP, inner sleeve, 'spaceship' label) ........................ 15
78    Vertigo 9199 645                  LIVE & DANGEROUS (2-LP, inners) ............................................................ 25
83    Vertigo VERL 3                    THUNDER AND LIGHTNING (with free 12") .............................................. 18
92    Windsong WINLP024                 BBC RADIO 1 LIVE IN CONCERT (2xLP emerald green vinyl) .................. 20

*(see also Phil Lynott, Wild Horses, Phenomena, Eric Bell Band, Greedies, John Sykes, Gary Moore)*

## THIN YOGHURTS
80    Lowther Street Runner YOG 1       Girl On The Bus/Drink Problem (p/s) ....................................................... 25

## THIRD & FOURTH GENERATION
72    Punch PH 91                       Rudies Medley (actually by Peter Tosh & Soulmates)/Rude Boy - Version ............... 10

*(see also Peter Tosh)*

## 3RD ARMY
81    No 2                              March Of 10,000 Soldiers/All Set To Go (no p/s) .................................. 25
81    Elite DAZZ 10                     March Of 10,000 Soldiers (All Set To Go)/Step One (12") .................. 50
81    Elite DAZZ 09                     Step One/POWERLINE: Watching You (12") ............................................ 50

## THIRD DIMENSION
70    Unity UN 566                      Peace And Love/Peace And Love - Version .................................................. 6

## THIRD EAR BAND
69    Harvest SHVL 756                  ALCHEMY (LP, with "Sold in U.K..." label text on 4 lines) ................. 125
69    Harvest SHVL 756                  ALCHEMY (LP, later pressing without "Sold in U.K..." label text) ...... 50
70    Harvest SHSP 773                  THIRD EAR BAND: ELEMENTS (LP, no EMI logo on label) ................. 60
72    Harvest SHSP 4019                 MUSIC FROM MACBETH (LP, EMI logo on label) ................................... 45
76    Harvest SHSM 2007                 EXPERIENCES (LP) ......................................................................................... 20
82    GI WAX 2                          ALCHEMY (LP, reissue, single sleeve) ...................................................... 18
88    Dropout DO 1999                   ALCHEMY (LP, reissue) ................................................................................. 15
90    BGO BGOLP 89                      THIRD EAR BAND (LP, reissue) ................................................................... 18
90    Beat Goes On BGOLP 61             MUSIC FROM MACBETH (LP, reissue) ........................................................ 15

*(see also High Tide, Sounds Nice)*

## THIRD EYE BAND
82    Scarlet Quest 01                  Pass Myself/May The Circle Remain Unbroken (p/s) ........................... 80

## THIRD MEN
79    SCHOOL 1                          You're So Fashionable/The Robot Age (p/s) ........................................... 20

## THIRD QUADRANT
82    Rock Cottage (no cat. no.)        SEEING YOURSELF AS YOU REALLY ARE (LP, private pressing, wraparound sleeve with handwritten insert, blank white label) ................................................................................ 40

MINT VALUE £

### 3RD RAIL
92    Delirious DELIS 5     Look No Further/123 Break/Stand By For Fast Beats/Drop (KZ1 Remix) (12") ............... 40

### THIRD RAIL
67    Columbia DB 8274     Run, Run, Run/No Return.................................................................................... 30

### THIRD WORLD
71    CBS 7182     Miracles/Baby Boeing ............................................................................................... 6

### THIRD WORLD ALL STARS
75    Third World TWLP 103     REBEL ROCK (LP) .............................................................................. 25

### THIRD WORLD WAR
71    Fly BUG 7     Ascension Day/Teddy Teeth Goes Sailing (p/s) ............................................................ 8
71    Fly BUG 11     A Little Bit Of Urban Rock/Working Class Man......................................................... 6
71    Fly FLY 4     THIRD WORLD WAR (LP, with lyric insert) .............................................................. 80
71    Fly FLY 4     THIRD WORLD WAR (LP, without lyric insert) .......................................................... 50
72    Track 2406 108     THIRD WORLD WAR II (LP) .......................................................................... 80
*(see also Terry Stamp)*

### 13 AMP
75    Power Exchange PX 114     Need A Woman/Can You Feel The Music ........................................... 15

### THIRTEEN AT MIDNIGHT
82    Pure PURE 1     Other Passengers/Other Passengers (p/s) ........................................................... 12

### THIRTEEN SENSES
02    Private Pressing     NO OTHER LIFE IS ATTRACTIVE EP (CD) .................................................... 35
04    Vertigo 981633-4     Thru The Glass/No Other Life Is Attractive (1,500 only p/s)................................ 8

### 13TH CHIME
81    Ellie Jay Records EJSP 9700     Cuts Of Love/Coffin Maker (foldout p/s)........................................ 50
82    13th Chime THC 1     Cursed/Dug Up (p/s) ...................................................................... 40
82    13th Chime THC 2     Fire/Hide And Seek/Sally Ditch (p/s, 1,000 only) ................................ 25

### 13TH FLOOR ELEVATORS
78    Radar SAM 88     She Lives (In A Time Of Her Own)/RED CRAYOLA: Pink Stainless Tail (promo) ............... 15
78    Radar ADA 13     You're Gonna Miss Me/Tried To Hide (green vinyl) ........................................... 10
78    Radar RAD 13     THE PSYCHEDELIC SOUNDS OF ... (LP) ........................................................ 25
78    Radar RAD 15     EASTER EVERYWHERE (LP) ....................................................................... 18
89    Decal LIK 28     EASTER EVERYWHERE (LP, reissue) ............................................................. 20
88    Decal LIK 19     THE PSYCHEDELIC SOUNDS OF... (LP, reissue) ........................................... 20
92    Xgarely/Decal LIKP 003     THE PSYCHEDELIC SOUNDS OF... (LP, picture disc) ................... 12
92    Decal LIKP002     LIVE (LP, picture disc with poster) ................................................................. 12
11    Charly 113L     BULL OF THE WOODS (2-LP, reissue, gatefold) ................................................ 20
*(see also Roky Erickson, Red Crayola)*

### 13TH HOUR
81    Time And Motion SMT 2009    Stereo Smiles/Inner Stu ....................................................... 20

### 31ST OF FEBRUARY
69    Vanguard (S)VRL 19045     THE 31ST OF FEBRUARY (LP) ..................................................... 90

### 35MM DREAMS
81    More Than This ASA 100     More Than This/The Bearer (foldout p/s) ...................................... 5
81    More Than This ASA 200     Fasten Your Safety Belts/Corstorphine/Instamatic Dance (p/s) ............... 5

### 39 CLOCKS
83    Flicknife SHARP 109     BLADES IN YOUR MASQUERADE (LP) ..................................................... 15

### 32ND TURN-OFF
69    Jay Boy JSL 1     32ND TURN OFF (LP, textured sleeve, brown/black label) ................................. 50
*(see also Equals)*

### 30 SECONDS TO MARS
07    Virgin 00946354474 77     The Kill/Attack (live) (picture disc, PVC stickered sleeve) ............... 15
08    Virgin VUS 340     From Yesterday (red vinyl, 1-side etched) ...................................................... 15
09    Virgin 509993/0943315     THIS IS WAR (gatefold, 2-LP with CD) ........................................ 18

### THIS DRIFTIN'S GOTTA STOP
75    private pressing     THIS DRIFTIN'S GOTTA STOP (LP) ................................................................ 30

### THIS ETERNAL WAITING
86    I Live In Hell BURN 2     The Prize/Love And Live Tombs .............................................. 20

### THIS HEAT
80    Piano THIS 1201     Health And Efficiency/Graphic/Varispeed (12", p/s with insert)................ 25
79    Piano THIS 1     THIS HEAT (LP) .......................................................................................... 60
81    Rough Trade ROUGH 26     DECEIT (LP, 1st pressing) ............................................................ 45
88    These HEAT 1     THIS HEAT (reissue) .................................................................................... 20
88    These HEAT 1     DECEIT (reissue) .......................................................................................... 20
98    These 12/6     REPEAT/HEALTH AND EFFICIENCY (2 x 12") ................................................... 20
99    These HEAT 10     MADE AVAILABLE: PEEL SESSIONS (LP) ..................................................... 20
06    This Is LC 02677     OUT OF COLD STORAGE (6-CD box set) ...................................................... 40

### THIS MORTAL COIL
83    4AD AD 310     Song To The Siren/16 Days (Reprise) (p/s) ........................................................ 5
84    4AD AD 410     Kangaroo/It'll End In Tears (p/s, 2 different designs & label colours, 2,500 of each) ........ 5
86    4AD BAD 608     Come Here My Love/Drugs (10", p/s with inner sleeve)......................................... 10
86    4AD DAD 609     FILIGREE AND SHADOW (2-LP) ................................................................... 20
91    4AD DAD 1005     BLOOD (2-LP, with inners) ...................................................................... 20
*(see also Cocteau Twins, Modern English, Cindytalk)*

### THIS 'N' THAT
66    Mercury MF 938     Someday/Loving You.................................................................................. 20
67    Strike JH 310     Get Down With It/I Care About You.............................................................. 10
*(see also Cleo)*

## THIS PERFECT DAY
| | | | |
|---|---|---|---|
| 83 | No Friction NFR 001 | The Garden/The Time Of Your Life | 80 |

## B.J. THOMAS
| | | | |
|---|---|---|---|
| 66 | Hickory 45-1395 | Never Tell/Billy & Sue | 15 |
| 66 | Pye International 7N 25374 | Mama/Wendy | 10 |
| 68 | Pye International 7N 25467 | The Eyes Of A New York Woman/I May Never Get To Heaven | 5 |
| 69 | Pye International 7N 25487 | It's Only Love/You Don't Love Me Anymore (The Train Song) | 5 |
| 69 | Wand WN 1 | Raindrops Keep Falling On My Head/Never Had It So Good | 6 |
| 70 | Wand WN 5 | I Just Can't Help Believing/Send My Picture To Scranton, PA | 5 |
| 72 | Wand WN 24 | Rock And Roll Lullaby/Are We Losing Touch? (feat. Duane Eddy) | 5 |

## CARLA THOMAS
| | | | |
|---|---|---|---|
| 61 | London HLK 9310 | Gee Whiz/For You | 20 |
| 61 | London HLK 9359 | A Love Of My Own/Promises | 15 |
| 62 | London HLK 9618 | I'll Bring It On Home To You/I Can't Take It | 15 |
| 64 | Atlantic AT 4005 | I've Got No Time To Lose/A Boy Named Tom | 18 |
| 66 | Atlantic AT 4074 | Comfort Me/I'm For You | 12 |
| 66 | Atlantic 584 011 | Let Me Be Good To You/Another Night Without My Man | 10 |
| 66 | Atlantic 584 042 | B-A-B-Y/What Have You Got To Offer Me | 10 |
| 67 | Stax 601 002 | Something Good (Is Going To Happen To You)/It's Starting To Grow | 10 |
| 67 | Stax 601 008 | When Tomorrow Comes/Unchanging Love (dark blue label) | 15 |
| 67 | Stax 601 008 | When Tomorrow Comes/Unchanging Love (later light blue label) | 8 |
| 68 | Stax 601 032 | Pick Up The Pieces/Separation | 10 |
| 68 | Stax STAX 103 | Where Do I Go/I've Fallen In Love | 8 |
| 69 | Stax STAX 112 | I Like What You're Doing To Me/Strung Out | 8 |
| 69 | Stax STAX 131 | Unyielding/I've Fallen In Love | 6 |
| 72 | Stax 2025 082 | Love Means/You've Got A Cushion To Fall On | 6 |
| 91 | Kent 6T 7 | I'll Never Stop Loving/Prophets Band/Peaches Baby | 40 |
| 67 | Stax 589 004 | CARLA THOMAS (LP) | 30 |
| 67 | Stax 589 012 | THE QUEEN ALONE (LP) | 20 |
| 69 | Stax SXATS 1019 | MEMPHIS QUEEN (LP) | 40 |

*(see also Otis Redding & Carla Thomas)*

## CHARLIE THOMAS (& DRIFTERS)
| | | | |
|---|---|---|---|
| 75 | EMI International INT 506 | I'm Gonna Take You Home/Run, Run, Roadrunner | 8 |
| 76 | EMI Int. 520 | A Midsummer Night In Harlem/Lonely Drifter Don't Cry | 10 |

## CLAUDETTE THOMAS
| | | | |
|---|---|---|---|
| 68 | Caltone TONE 116 | Roses Are Red My Love/YVONNE HARRISON: Near To You | 80 |

## CREEPY JOHN THOMAS
| | | | |
|---|---|---|---|
| 69 | RCA RCA 1912 | Ride A Rainbow/Moon And Eyes Song | 15 |
| 69 | RCA SF 8061 | CREEPY JOHN THOMAS (LP, laminated front sleeve) | 300 |

*(see also Paul Kossoff, Edgar Broughton Band)*

## DON THOMAS
| | | | |
|---|---|---|---|
| 76 | DJM DJS 670 | Come On Train Parts 1 & 2 (Promos in p/s) | 20 |
| 76 | DJM DJS 10670 | Come On Train Parts 1 & 2 (second pressing) | 10 |

## GENE THOMAS
| | | | |
|---|---|---|---|
| 64 | United Artists UP 1047 | Baby's Gone/Stand By Love | 20 |

## HERSAL THOMAS
| | | | |
|---|---|---|---|
| 50 | Parlophone R 3261 | Suitcase Blues/Hersal Blues (78) | 35 |

## IRMA THOMAS
| | | | |
|---|---|---|---|
| 64 | Liberty LIB 66013 | Breakaway/Wish Someone Would Care | 25 |
| 64 | Liberty LIB 66041 | Anyone Who Knows What Love Is (Will Understand)/Time Is On My Side | 20 |
| 65 | Liberty LIB 66080 | He's My Guy/True True Love | 20 |
| 65 | Liberty LIB 66095 | Some Things You Never Get Used To/You Don't Miss A Good Thing (Until It's Gone) | 20 |
| 65 | Sue WI 372 | Don't Mess With My Man/Set Me Free | 30 |
| 65 | Liberty LIB 66106 | I'm Gonna Cry Till My Tears Run Dry/ Nobody Wants To Hear Nobody's Troubles | 20 |
| 66 | Liberty LIB 66137 | Take A Look/What Are You Trying To Do | 75 |
| 66 | Liberty LIB 66137 | Take A Look/What Are You Trying To Do (DJ copy) | 125 |
| 66 | Liberty LIB 66178 | It's A Man's-Woman's World | 20 |
| 72 | Atlantic K 10167 | Full Time Woman/She's Taking My Part | 6 |
| 72 | United Artists UP 35402 | Time Is On My Side/Anyone Who Knows What Love Is (Will Understand) (reissue) | 8 |
| 65 | Liberty LEP 4035 | TIME IS ON MY SIDE (EP) | 100 |
| 68 | Minit MLL/MLS 40004E | TAKE A LOOK (LP) | 75 |
| 76 | Island HELP 29 | LIVE (LP) | 15 |
| 83 | Kent 010 | TIME IS ON MY SIDE (LP) | 15 |

## JAMO THOMAS & HIS PARTY BROTHERS ORCHESTRA
| | | | |
|---|---|---|---|
| 66 | Polydor BM 56709 | I Spy (For The FBI)/Snake Hip Mama | 15 |
| 69 | Polydor 56755 | I Spy (For The FBI)/Snake Hip Mama (reissue) | 8 |
| 69 | Chess CRS 8098 | I'll Be Your Fool/Jamo Soul | 20 |
| 71 | Mojo 2092 013 | I Spy (For The FBI)/Snake Hip Mama (2nd reissue) | 8 |

## JIMMY THOMAS
| | | | |
|---|---|---|---|
| 69 | Parlophone R 5773 | The Beautiful Night/Above A Whisper (withdrawn) | 250 |
| 69 | Parlophone R 5773 | The Beautiful Night/Above A Whisper (withdrawn; DJ copy) | 200 |
| 69 | Spark SRL 1035 | (We Ain't Looking For) No Trouble/Springtime | 100 |
| 70 | Spark SRL 1040 | White Dove/You Don't Have To Say Goodbye | 12 |
| 72 | Jay Boy BOY 67 | Where There's A Will/Just Tryin' To Please You | 6 |

## JOE THOMAS
| | | | |
|---|---|---|---|
| 72 | People PLE 015 | JOY OF COOKIN' (LP) | 15 |

## KID THOMAS
| | | | |
|---|---|---|---|
| 79 | JSP 4503 | Rockin' This Joint Tonight/Cozy Lounge Blues | 5 |

### KID THOMAS/EMANUEL BAND
| 64 | '77' LA 12/26 | VICTORY WALK (LP, with Barry Martyn's Band) | 30 |

### LEON THOMAS
| 73 | Philips 6369 417 | BLUES & SOULFUL TRUTH (LP) | 30 |

### NICKY THOMAS
| 70 | Amalgamated AMG 863 | Danzella/JOE GIBBS ALLSTARS: Kingstonians Reggae | 25 |
| 70 | Trojan TR 7750 | Love Of The Common People/DESTROYERS: Compass | 8 |
| 70 | Trojan TR 7796 | God Bless The Children/Red Eye | 10 |
| 71 | Trojan TR 7807 | If I Had A Hammer/Lonely Feelin' | 10 |
| 71 | Trojan TR 7830 | Tell It Like It Is/B.B.C. | 10 |
| 70 | Trojan TBL 143 | LOVE OF THE COMMON PEOPLE (LP) | 15 |
| 72 | Trojan TRLS 25 | TELL IT LIKE IT IS (LP) | 25 |

*(see also Joe Gibbs)*

### PAT THOMAS (1)
| 62 | MGM 1194 | Home In The Meadow/Where There's Love There's Hope | 6 |
| 62 | MGM 1234 | Stranger On The Shore/C'est Si Bon | 6 |

### PAT THOMAS (2)
| 85 | Jap JAP 0101 | ASANTEMAN (LP) | 20 |

### PETER THOMAS SOUND ORCHESTRA
| 68 | Poydor 184171 | ORGANIC (LP) | 35 |
| 70 | Polydor 2418 074 | CHARIOTS OF THE GODS (LP) | 35 |

### ROD THOMAS
| 72 | Fly BUG 19 | Timothy Jones/Arthur Smith | 7 |

### RUDDY THOMAS
| 78 | Lightning LIG 526 | Loving Pauper/TRINITY: Judgement Time | 8 |
| 79 | DEB DEB 015 | Dry Up Your Tears/Rat Trap (12") | 25 |
| 80s | Shuttle SH 005 | Bless You/The Right Time (12") | 15 |

### RUDY THOMAS
| 83 | Mobiliser MMLP 34 | VERY BEST OF (LP) | 15 |

### RUFUS THOMAS
| 63 | London HLK 9799 | Walking The Dog/Fine And Mellow | 25 |
| 64 | London HLK 9850 | Can Your Monkey Do The Dog/I Want To Get Married | 15 |
| 64 | London HLK 9884 | Somebody Stole My Dog/I Want To Be Loved | 15 |
| 64 | Atlantic AT 4009 | Jump Back/All Night Worker | 18 |
| 66 | Atlantic 584 029 | Willy Nilly/Sho' Gonna Mess Him Up | 12 |
| 67 | Atlantic 584 089 | Jump Back/Walking The Dog | 10 |
| 67 | Stax 601 013 | Greasy Spoon/Sophisticated Sissy | 8 |
| 68 | Stax 601 028 | Down Ta My House/Steady Holding On | 8 |
| 68 | Stax 601 037 | The Memphis Train/I Think I Made A Boo-Boo | 15 |
| 68 | Stax STAX 105 | Funky Mississippi/So Hard To Get Along With | 6 |
| 70 | Stax STAX 144 | Do The Funky Chicken/Turn Your Damper Down | 8 |
| 71 | Stax 2025 060 | The Breakdown (Parts 1 & 2) | 6 |
| 71 | Stax 2025 080 | Do The Funky Penguin (Parts 1 & 2) | 6 |
| 64 | Atlantic AET 6001 | DO THE DOG (EP) | 50 |
| 65 | Atlantic AET 6011 | JUMP BACK WITH RUFUS (EP) | 50 |
| 64 | London HA-K 8183 | WALKING THE DOG (LP) | 80 |
| 70 | Stax SXATS 1033 | FUNKY CHICKEN (LP) | 35 |
| 71 | Stax 2363 001 | FUNKY CHICKEN (LP, reissue) | 15 |
| 71 | Stax 2362 010 | DOING THE PUSH AND PULL LIVE AT P.J.'s (LP) | 25 |
| 72 | Stax 2362 028 | DID YOU HEAR ME? (LP) | 20 |
| 74 | Stax STX 1004 | CROWN PRINCE OF DANCE (LP) | 30 |

### SANDRA THOMAS
| 76 | Angen ANG 113 | It Should Have Been Me/Loving Arms | 5 |

### TERRY-THOMAS ESQUIRE
| 56 | Decca F 10804 | A Sweet Old Fashioned Boy (with Rock 'N' Roll Rotters)/Lay Down Your Arms | 12 |
| 61 | Decca LK 4398 | STRICTLY T-T (LP) | 40 |

### TIM THOMAS
| 66 | Polydor BM 56052 | Walking/Fever | 8 |
| 71 | Decca F13235 | Silver Morning/Gravy Train | 10 |

### TIMMY THOMAS
| 73 | Mojo 2956 002 | WHY CAN'T WE LIVE TOGETHER (LP) | 20 |

### VAUGHAN THOMAS
| 70 | Page One POF 167 | Need You Girl/Come Together | 12 |
| 70 | Page One POF 178 | Is This What I Get For Loving You Baby/Since You've Been Mine | 10 |
| 71 | DJM DJS 238 | I Wanna Be Famous Like My Dad/Love | 15 |
| 72 | Jam JAM 9 | Gotta Be You, Gotta Be Me/Woman | 6 |
| 72 | Jam JAM 26 | Giant/Good Old Sam | 6 |
| 72 | Jam JAL 101 | VAUGHAN THOMAS (LP, textured sleeve, white/red/black label) | 40 |

### WAYNE THOMAS
| 67 | Coral Q 72491 | I've Never Known A Lady/My Life's Gonna Change | 6 |

### ANDREAS THOMOPOULOS
| 70 | Mushroom 100 MR 1 | SONGS OF THE STREET (LP) | 80 |
| 71 | Mushroom 150 MR 4 | BORN OUT OF THE TEARS OF THE SUN (LP) | 90 |

*(see also Secondhand)*

### BARBARA THOMPSON
| 74 | Explosion EX 2087 | Single Girl/DANDY & COUNT PRINCE MILLER: Version | 5 |

## BOBBY THOMPSON
| | | | |
|---|---|---|---|
| 69 | Columbia Blue Beat DB 113 | That's How Strong My Love Is/Trouble In Town | 6 |
| 69 | Jolly JY 001 | That's How Strong My Love Is/Trouble In The Town | 50 |

*(see also Dandy)*

## CHERYLE THOMPSON
| | | | |
|---|---|---|---|
| 64 | Stateside SS 291 | Teardrops/Black Night | 15 |

## CHRIS THOMPSON
| | | | |
|---|---|---|---|
| 73 | Village Thing VTS 21 | CHRIS THOMPSON (LP, allegedly 101 sold and 899 destroyed, 'Shorewood Packaging Ltd.' printer credit) | 200 |

## DONNEY THOMPSON
| | | | |
|---|---|---|---|
| 79 | Third World TWDIS 20 | Rocking Time/PAGET KING: Close Encounter (12") | 60 |

## EDDIE THOMPSON
| | | | |
|---|---|---|---|
| 55 | Jazz Today JTE 101 | THE FABULOUS EDDIE THOMPSON (EP) | 60 |
| 57 | Nixa NJE 1030 | PIANO MOODS VOLUME 6 (EP) | 60 |
| 60 | Ember EMB 3303 | PIANO MOODS (LP) | 100 |
| 60 | Tempo TAP 24 | HIS MASTER'S JAZZ (LP) | 250 |
| 69 | 77 LEU 12/39 | BY MYSELF (LP) | 40 |

## HANK THOMPSON (& BRAZOS VALLEY BOYS)
| | | | |
|---|---|---|---|
| 56 | Capitol CL 14517 | Honey, Honey Bee Ball/Don't Take It Out On Me | 5 |
| 56 | Capitol CL 14668 | I'm Not Mad, Just Hurt/The Blackboard Of My Heart | 5 |
| 58 | Capitol CL 14869 | Li'l Liza Jane/How Do You Hold A Memory | 5 |
| 58 | Capitol CL 14945 | Gathering Flowers/Squaws Along The Yukon | 5 |
| 58 | Capitol CL 14961 | I've Run Out Of Tomorrows/You're Going Back To Your Old Ways Again | 5 |
| 60 | Capitol CL 15114 | A Six Pack To Go/What Made Her Change | 10 |
| 76 | Capitol CL 15877 | Rockin' In The Congo/I Was The First One | 5 |

## JACKIE THOMPSON
| | | | |
|---|---|---|---|
| 69 | Direction 58-4521 | Bad Women A Dime A Dozen/Games People Play | 6 |

## JOHNNY THOMPSON & ONE-EYED JACKS
| | | | |
|---|---|---|---|
| 65 | Ember EMB S 206 | For Us There'll Be No Tomorrow/Soul Chant (in p/s) | 20 |
| 65 | Ember EMB S 206 | For Us There'll Be No Tomorrow/Soul Chant | 6 |

## KAY THOMPSON
| | | | |
|---|---|---|---|
| 56 | London HLA 8268 | Eloise/Just One Of Those Things | 40 |

## LEROY THOMPSON
| | | | |
|---|---|---|---|
| 78 | Noel DN 005 | Hard Times Criminal Times/Since You Left Me & Gone (12") | 30 |

## LINCOLN THOMPSON
| | | | |
|---|---|---|---|
| 80 | God Sent GDIS 1 | One Common Need/Food Clothing And Shelter (12", with the Rasses) | 60 |

## LINVAL THOMPSON
| | | | |
|---|---|---|---|
| 75 | Ackee ACK 541 | Kung Fu (Vocal)/Kung Fu (Instrumental) | 10 |
| 75 | Action ACT 103 | Natty Dread Girl/AGGROVATORS: Natty Dread Girl (Version) | 10 |
| 75 | Attack ATT 8101 | Don't Cut Off Your Dreadlocks/KING TUBBYS: Version | 10 |
| 75 | Faith FA 010 | Girl You Got To Run/Run Come Feel | 8 |
| 75 | Faith FA 018 | Jah Redder Than Red/Version | 8 |
| 78 | Attack ATT 8135 | I Love Marijuana/Jamaican Calley (Version) | 15 |
| 78 | Star PTP 1007 | If I Follow My Heart/THOMPSON ALL STARS: Rocking version (12") | 20 |
| 79 | Burning Rockers BRD 003 | Follow My Heart/THOMPSON ALL STARS: Rockers Version (12") | 20 |
| 79 | Burning Sounds BSD 023 | Rocking Vibration/Natty Dread (12') | 20 |
| 79 | Burning Sounds BSD 031 | Bound To Surrender/Dub Version (12") | 20 |
| 79 | GG's GG 056 | Mad Dog (with Ranking Trevor)/REVOLUTIONARIES: Kevin At The Controls (12") | 30 |
| 79 | Greensleeves GRED 024 | One More Chance/Long Time Me Na Rub You In A Dance (12", with Trinity) | 20 |
| 79 | D-Roy DRDD 16 | She Is Mad At Me/Stop Your War (12") | 20 |
| 80 | Attack TACK 19 | Here With Me/ROOTS RADICS BAND: Come On Baby Dub Style (12") | 15 |
| 80 | Attack TACK 22 | Pop No Style/SCIENTIST: Second Hand Girl (12") | 15 |
| 80 | Black Joy DH 804 | Brown Skin Girl/RANKING TREVOR: Brown Skin Girl Rub A Dub (12") | 15 |
| 80 | Strong Like Sampson SLSD 04 | Mr Boss Man (with Trevor Ranking)/BARNABOUS: Stop Push Me Around (12") | 22 |
| 80 | Strong Like Sampson SLSD 016 | Curfew/PAPPA TULLO: Morning Curfew (12") | 20 |
| 80 | Strong Like... SLSD 012 | I'm Sorry/My Little Honey (12") | 10 |
| 81 | Cha Cha CHAD 29 | Gambler/Everyday Rain (with WAYNE WADE, 12", blue vinyl) | 20 |
| 82 | A1 A1 004 | Poor People (with U Brown)/Reggae Dub (12") | 12 |
| 84 | M&M MM06 | Back To Africa/Jungle Man Skank | 8 |
| 76 | Third World TWLP 010 | DON'T CUT OFF YOUR DREADLOCKS (LP) | 18 |
| 78 | Trojan TRLS 151 | I LOVE MARIJUANA (LP) | 20 |
| 78 | Burning Sounds BSD 1014 | LOVE IS THE QUESTION (LP) | 25 |
| 78 | Burning Sounds BS 1027 | ROCKING VIBRATION (LP) | 40 |
| 79 | Burning Sounds BS 1035 | I LOVE JAH (LP) | 35 |
| 79 | Trojan TRLS 153 | NEGREA LOVE DUB (LP) | 25 |
| 80 | Burning Rockers BR 1006LP | FOLLOW MY HEART (LP) | 30 |
| 82 | Greensleeves GREL 33 | LOOK HOW ME SEXY (LP) | 18 |
| 83 | Greensleeves GREL 51 | BABY FATHER (LP) | 15 |
| 96 | Trojan TRLS 151 | I LOVE MARIJUANA (LP, reissue) | 15 |
| 00 | Blood & Fire SVLP 294 | RIDE ON DREADLOCKS (2-LP) | 25 |

*(see also Bunny Lion)*

## LUCKY THOMPSON
| | | | |
|---|---|---|---|
| 56 | Vogue V 2388 | But Not For Me/East Of The Sun | 10 |

## MIKE THOMPSON JNR.
| | | | |
|---|---|---|---|
| 67 | Island WI 3090 | Rocksteady Wedding/Flower Pot Bloomers (both with Lyn Taitt & Jets) | 25 |

**MOLLIE THOMPSON**
66   Asteroid JH 101          SONG NOTES SINGS FROM WORLDS AFAR (LP, private pressing).................. 40

**OWEN THOMPSON**
72   Camel CA 103             Must I Be Blue/Version ..................................................................... 8

**PETER THOMPSON & NTH DEGREE**
65   Fontana TF 656           For Me It's All Over/The Way You Used To Do.............................. 20

**RICHARD THOMPSON**
72   Island ILPS 9197         HENRY THE HUMAN FLY (LP, 'pink rim palm tree' label) ............... 25

**RICHARD & LINDA THOMPSON**
74   Island WIP 6186          I Want To See The Bright Lights Tonight/When I Get To The Border ....... 5
75   Island WIP 6220          Hokey Pokey/I'll Regret It All In The Morning ............................... 5
73   Island ILPS 9266         I WANT TO SEE THE BRIGHT LIGHTS TONIGHT (LP, palm tree label) ............ 30
74   Island ILPS 9305         HOKEY POKEY (LP, blue rim palm tree label with lyric inner sleeve) ...... 25
75   Island ILPS 9348         POUR DOWN LIKE SILVER (LP, 'palm tree' label with lyrics) ............ 20
75   Island                   OFFICIAL LIVE TOUR 1975 (LP, unreleased, test pressings may exist) ..... 100
76   Island ICD 8             GUITAR/VOCAL (2-LP, gatefold sleeve, blue rim/palm tree label) ...... 25
*(see also Fairport Convention, Richard Thompson, Sandy Denny, Marc Ellington, Nick Drake, Gary Farr, Paul McNeill & Linda Peters)*

**ROBERT THOMPSON**
75   Pinnacle P 8408          A Look At The Sun/You Can't See Me........................................ 12

**ROY THOMPSON**
67   Columbia DB 8108         Sookie Sookie/Love You Say ................................................... 30

**SIR CHARLES THOMPSON**
53   Vogue LDE 032            SIR CHARLES THOMPSON'S ALL STARS WITH CHARLIE PARKER (10" LP) ...... 20
56   Vanguard PPT 12011       AND HIS BAND FEATURING COLEMAN HAWKINS (10" LP).............. 15

**SONNY THOMPSON & HIS RHYTHM & BLUES BAND**
60   Starlite ST45 008        Screamin' Boogie/The Fish ................................................... 250
56   Parlophone GEP 8562      SONNY THOMPSON INSTRUMENTALS (EP, as Sonny Thompson Orchestra)........ 40
*(see also Claude Cloud & Thunderclaps)*

**SUE THOMPSON**
61   Polydor NH 66967         Sad Movies/Throwing Kisses .................................................. 10
62   Polydor NH 66973         Norman/Never Love Again ...................................................... 5
62   Polydor NH 66976         Two Of A Kind/It Has To Be Me ............................................... 5
62   Polydor NH 66979         Have A Good Time/If The Boy Only Knew ...................................... 5
63   Polydor NH 66987         What's Wrong Bill/I Need A Harbour........................................... 5
62   Fontana 267 244TF        James (Hold The Ladder Steady)/My Hero ...................................... 5
63   Fontana 267 262TF        Willie Can/Too Much In Love .................................................. 5
64   Hickory 45-1240          Big Daddy/I'd Like To Know You Better ........................................ 5
64   Hickory 45-1255          Bad Boy/Toys ................................................................... 5
65   Hickory 45-1284          Paper Tiger/Mama Don't Cry At My Wedding................................... 6
65   Hickory 45-1328          It's Break Up Time/Afraid .................................................... 8
65   Hickory 45-1340          Just Kiss Me/Sweet Hunk Of Misery ........................................... 8
65   Hickory 45-1359          I'm Looking For A World/Walkin' My Baby ...................................... 6
65   Hickory 45-1381          What Should I Do/After The Heartache ........................................ 10
67   London HLE 10142         Ferris Wheel/Don't Forget To Cry ............................................ 7
72   London HLE 1040          How I Love Them Old Songs/That's Just Too Much .............................. 7
73   London HLE 10440         Oh, Johnny, Oh Johnny, Oh/Just Pain Country ................................. 7
65   Hickory LPE 1507         INTRODUCING KRIS JENSEN AND SUE THOMPSON (EP, 2 tracks each) ........... 10
64   Hickory LPM 102          PAPER TIGER (LP) .............................................................. 20
*(see also Kris Jensen)*

**SUE THOMPSON & BOB LUMAN**
63   Polydor NH 66989         I Like Your Kind Of Love/Too Hot To Dance .................................. 10
63   Hickory 45-1221          I Like Your Kind Of Love/Too Hot To Dance (reissue) ......................... 5
*(see also Bob Luman)*

**THOMPSON TWINS**
80   Latent LATE 1            She's In Love With Mystery/Fast Food/Food Style ............................. 8
85   Arista TWINS 128         Roll Over (Again)/Fools In Paradise (Extended) (12", p/s, withdrawn) ....... 80

**COLIN THOMPSON**
80   Fellside FE 021          THREE KNIGHTS (LP)............................................................ 15

**GUNILLA THORN**
63   HMV POP 1239             Merry-Go-Round/Go On Then .................................................... 90

**TRACEY THORN**
82   Cherry Red CHERRY 53     Plain Sailing/Goodbye Joe (p/s) ............................................... 5
82   Cherry Red MRED 35       A DISTANT SHORE (LP)........................................................... 20
*(see also Marine Girls, Everything But The Girl)*

**DAVID THORNE**
62   Stateside SS 141         The Alley Cat Song/The Moon Was Yellow ...................................... 6
63   Stateside SS 190         One More Fool, One More Broken Heart/Don't Let It Get Away ................. 6
64   Stateside SE 1020        WHAT WILL I TELL MY HEART (EP) .............................................. 25
63   Stateside SL 10036       THE ALLEY CAT SONGSTER (LP) ................................................. 35

**KEN THORNE ORCHESTRA**
63   HMV POP 1176             The Legion's Last Patrol Film Theme/Kisses In The Night ..................... 5
68   United Artists ULP 1201  INSPECTOR CLOUSEAU (LP, soundtrack)........................................... 30
69   Stateside S(S)L 10271    THE TOUCHABLES (LP, with Nirvana, Wynder K. Frog, et al.) ................. 50

**WOODY THORNE**
62   Vogue Pop V 9202         Sadie Lou/Teenagers In Love .................................................. 400

**CLAUDE THORNHILL & HIS ORCHESTRA**
54   London HL 8042           Pussy-Footin'/Adios .......................................................... 40

| 54 | London RE-P 1009 | CLAUDE THORNHILL GOES MODERN (EP) | 20 |
| 54 | London H-ABP 1019 | CLAUDE THORNHILL GOES MODERN (10" LP) | 20 |
| 54 | London H-ABP 1021 | DREAM MUSIC (10" LP) | 20 |

### THORNS OF AFFLICTION
| 81 | Cargo CRS 001 | Panic Stricken/Eyes Of The Dead | 10 |

### WILLIE MAE 'BIG MAMA' THORNTON
| 54 | Vogue V 2284 | Hound Dog/Mischievous Boogie (78) (as Willie Mae 'Big Mama' Thornton) | 80 |
| 65 | Sue WI 345 | Tom Cat/Monkey In The Barn (as Willie Mae Thornton) | 250 |
| 69 | Mercury SMCL 20176 | STRONGER THAN DIRT (LP) | 40 |
| 78 | Vanguard VPC 40001 | MAMA'S PRIDE (LP) | 25 |

### EDDIE THORNTON OUTFIT
| 69 | Instant IN 003 | Baby Be My Gal/SONNY BURKE OUTFIT: All You | 120 |

### CLIFFORD THORNTON
| 76 | JCOA/Virgin J2004 | GARDENS OF HARLEM (LP, with Jazz Composers Orchestra) | 15 |

### GEORGE THOROGOOD & DESTROYERS
| 77 | Sonet SON 2148 | Can't Stop Lovin'/Homesick Boy | 5 |

### PETER THOROGOOD
| 68 | Pye 7N 17597 | Haunted/If No One Sang | 100 |

### BILLY THORPE & AZTECS
| 65 | Parlophone R 5381 | Twilight Time/Over The Rainbow | 7 |

### THOR'S HAMMER
| 66 | Parlophone DP 565 | Once/A Memory (export issue) | 200 |
| 66 | Parlophone DP 567 | If You Knew/Love Enough (export issue) | 185 |
| 66 | Parlophone CGEP 62 | THOR'S HAMMER (EP, export issue, gatefold p/s, with bonus 45 "If You Knew"/ "Love Enough" [CGEP 62]) | 1200 |

### LINDA THORSON
| 68 | Ember EMB S 257 | Here I Am/Better Than Losing You (p/s) | 40 |
| 68 | Ember EMB S 257 | Here I Am/Better Than Losing You | 15 |
| 70 | Ember EMBS 284 | Wishful Thinking/You Will Want Me | 20 |
| 70 | Ember LT 1 | Bad Time To Stop Loving Me/Pick Up My Heart (promo) | 25 |

### THOSE ATTRACTIVE MAGNETS
| 83 | Tavern AD MAG 10 | Nightlife/Love Chimes (p/s) | 70 |

### THOSE HELICOPTERS
| 79 | Cargo CRS 011 | SOUTH COAST TOWNS EP | 8 |
| 80 | State Of The Art STATE 1 | Shark/Eskimo (p/s) | 6 |
| 81 | Lavender LAVENDER 001 | Dr. Janov/Technical Smack (p/s) | 5 |

### THOSE INTRINSIC INTELLECTUALS
| 80 | Fault Line CPS 040 | Do The Executive/Radio Iceland (fold out p/s in printed bag, insert) | 12 |

### THOSE NAUGHTY LUMPS
| 79 | Zoo CAGE 002 | Iggy Pop's Jacket/Pure And Innocent (foldout p/s) | 6 |

### THOUGHT POLICE
| 79 | Wessex WEX 263 | Mr Sad/You Tell Me Lies/Pictures (p/s) | 30 |

### THOUGHTS
| 66 | Planet PLF 118 | All Night Stand/Memory Of Your Love | 100 |

*(see also Tiffany [& Thoughts], Paul Dean & Soul Savages)*

### THOUGHTS & WORDS
| 69 | Liberty LBF 15187 | Morning Sky/Give Me A Reason | 10 |
| 69 | Liberty LBL 83224 | THOUGHTS & WORDS (LP) | 20 |

### THOUGHTS OF DES COX
| 69 | Morgan MR 4S | Isn't It Nice/It's All Very Strange | 12 |

### THREADBARE CONSORT
| 80s | private pressing | WEARING THIN (LP) | 15 |

### THREADS
| 86 | Unicorn PHZ 2 | Step Back/UNDERGROUND ARROWS: Backbeat Of Life (p/s) | 10 |

### THREADS OF LIFE
| 72 | Alco ALC 530 | THREADS OF LIFE (LP, actually by Alco) | 800 |

### THREAT
| 80 | One Web 001 WEB | Lullaby In C/High Cost Of Living | 75 |

### THREATS
| 82 | Rondelet ROUND 22 | GO TO HELL (EP) | 15 |
| 82 | Rondelet ROUND 29 | Politicians & Ministers/Writing's On The Wall/Deep End Depression (p/s) | 20 |
| 82 | Rondelet ROUND 1229 | POLITICIANS & MINISTERS (12" EP) | 18 |

### THREE BARRY SISTERS
| 59 | Decca F 11099 | Little Boy Blue/My Sweetie's Coming To Call | 10 |
| 59 | Decca F 11118 | Tall Paul/Till Then | 7 |
| 59 | Decca F 11141 | Jo Jo - The Dog Faced Boy/I-Aye Ove-Lay Oo-Yay | 5 |
| 60 | Decca F 11201 | Spoilsport/Bonnie Prince Charlie | 5 |

*(see also Barry Sisters)*

### THREE BELLS
| 60 | Pye 7N 15252 | Steady Date/In Between (Wishing I Was Sweet Sixteen) | 8 |
| 61 | Pye 7N 15335 | You/Melody Of Love | 8 |
| 64 | Columbia DB 7399 | Softly In The Night/He Doesn't Love Me | 10 |
| 65 | Columbia DB 7570 | Someone To Love/Over And Over Again | 7 |
| 66 | Columbia DB 7980 | Cry No More/He Doesn't Want You | 15 |

*(see also Satin Bells)*

MINT VALUE £

## THREE CAPS
| | | | |
|---|---|---|---|
| 66 | Atlantic 584 004 | Cool Jerk/Hello Stranger | 15 |
| 66 | Atlantic 584 043 | I Got To Handle It/Zig-Zagging | 12 |
| 69 | Atlantic 584 251 | Cool Jerk/Hello Stranger | 10 |
| 71 | Atlantic 2091 105 | Cool Jerk/Hello Stranger (reissue) | 5 |

*(see also Capitols)*

## THREE CHUCKLES
| | | | |
|---|---|---|---|
| 55 | HMV 7M 292 | Runaround/At Last You Understand | 40 |
| 56 | HMV 7M 333 | Still Thinking Of You/Times Two I Love You | 35 |
| 57 | HMV POP 292 | We're Gonna Rock Tonight/Want You Give Me A Chance | 80 |
| 57 | HMV POP 292 | We're Gonna Rock Tonight/Want You Give Me A Chance (78) | 25 |

*(see also Teddy Randazzo)*

## THREE CITY FOUR
| | | | |
|---|---|---|---|
| 65 | Decca LK 4705 | THREE CITY FOUR (LP) | 160 |
| 67 | CBS 63039 | SMOKE AND DUST WHERE THE HEART SHOULD HAVE BEEN (LP) | 100 |

*(see also Martin Carthy, Leon Rosselson)*

## THREE COINS
| | | | |
|---|---|---|---|
| 70 | Sugar SU 106 | Come And Do The Right Thing/It's So Long | 6 |

## 3D PRODUCTION
| | | | |
|---|---|---|---|
| 80 | Third Kind TKS 001 | Riot/Riot (Rearrage) | 40 |

## THREE DEGREES
| | | | |
|---|---|---|---|
| 65 | Stateside SS 413 | Gee Baby I'm Sorry/Do What You're Supposed To Do | 60 |
| 65 | Stateside SS 459 | Close Your Eyes/Gotta Draw The Line | 70 |
| 65 | Stateside SS 459 | Close Your Eyes/Gotta Draw The Line (DJ copy) | 100 |
| 71 | Mojo 2092 001 | Maybe/There's So Much Love Around Me | 6 |
| 71 | Mojo 2092 002 | You're The One/Rose Garden | 6 |
| 71 | Mojo 2092 009 | There's So Much Love Around Me/Maybe (reissue) | 6 |
| 71 | Mojo 2092 009 | There's So Much Love Around Me/Yours (different B-side) | 6 |
| 75 | Pye International 7N 25671 | Sugar On Sunday/Maybe | 6 |
| 71 | Mojo 2916 002 | THE THREE DEGREES (LP) | 20 |

## THREE DOG NIGHT
| | | | |
|---|---|---|---|
| 69 | Stateside SS 8041 | It's For You/Feelin' Alright | 6 |
| 69 | Stateside SS 8030 | Eli's Coming/Circle For A Landing | 6 |
| 69 | Stateside-Dunhill SS 8008 | Nobody/It's For You | 6 |
| 70 | Stateside-Dunhill SS 8052 | Mama Told Me Not To Come/Rock And Roll Widow | 7 |
| 71 | Probe PRO 523 | Joy To The World/I Can Hear You Calling | 6 |
| 71 | Probe PRO 536 | Liar/Can't Get Enough Of It | 6 |
| 69 | Stateside-Dun. (S)SL 5006 | THREE DOG NIGHT (LP) | 15 |

*(see also Danny Hutton)*

## THREE DOLLS
| | | | |
|---|---|---|---|
| 57 | MGM MGM 958 | The Living End/The Octopus Song | 10 |

## THREE GOOD REASONS
| | | | |
|---|---|---|---|
| 65 | Mercury MF 883 | Build Your Love/Don't Leave Me Now | 10 |
| 65 | Mercury MF 899 | Nowhere Man/Wire Wheels | 18 |
| 65 | Mercury MF 929 | The Moment Of Truth/Funny Kind Of Loving | 10 |

## THREE JOHNS
| | | | |
|---|---|---|---|
| 82 | CNT CNT 003 | English White Boy Engineer/Secret Agent (p/s) | 8 |
| 83 | CNT CNT 011 | Pink Headed Bug/Lucy In The Rain (p/s) | 7 |

## THREE KAYES (SISTERS)
| | | | |
|---|---|---|---|
| 56 | HMV 7M 401 | Ivory Tower/Mister Cuckoo (Sing Your Song) | 12 |
| 56 | HMV POP 251 | Lay Down Your Arms/First Row Balcony (as Three Kaye Sisters) | 10 |

*(see also Kaye Sisters, Frankie Vaughan)*

## THREE MAN ARMY
| | | | |
|---|---|---|---|
| 72 | Pegasus PGS 1 | What's Your Name/Travellin' | 10 |
| 74 | Reprise K 14292 | Polecat Woman/Take Me Down From The Mountain | 5 |
| 71 | Pegasus PEG 3 | A THIRD OF A LIFETIME (LP, gatefold) | 80 |
| 74 | Reprise K 54015 | THREE MAN ARMY TWO (LP) | 30 |

*(see also Gun, Baker Gurvitz Army, Andy Newman, Spooky Tooth)*

## 3 MINUTES
| | | | |
|---|---|---|---|
| 80 | Rocket XPRES 40 | Automatic Kids/Future Fun (p/s) | 8 |

## THREE PEOPLE
| | | | |
|---|---|---|---|
| 66 | Decca F 12473 | Have You Ever Been There/Good Times | 10 |
| 66 | Decca F 12514 | Suspicions/Easy Man To Find | 10 |
| 67 | Decca F 12581 | Got To Find A Reason/Simple Thing Would Be For You To Start Loving Me | 10 |

*(see also John Bromley)*

## THREE PIECES
| | | | |
|---|---|---|---|
| 75 | Fantasy FTC 116 | I Need You Girl/Short'nin' Bread | 8 |

## 3 PM
| | | | |
|---|---|---|---|
| 91 | Alma Vale ALMA 1 | Out Of Control (12") | 15 |
| 91 | Alma Vale ALMA 2 | ST.P/3PM/Lynx (12") | 20 |
| 92 | Busted Loop 3 | Better Late Than Never (12") | 20 |

## THREE QUARTERS
| | | | |
|---|---|---|---|
| 65 | Columbia DB 7467 | People Will Talk/Love Come A-Tricklin' Down | 15 |
| 65 | Columbia DB 7576 | The Pleasure Girls/Little People | 6 |

## THREE SOUNDS
| | | | |
|---|---|---|---|
| 68 | Liberty LBF 15062 | Makin' Bread Again/Still I'm Sad | 8 |

### 3 THIEVES AND A LIAR
92  3 Thieves And A Liar 3TAL  In The House/I Get A Chill/You Bring Me Joy/Tonight (12") ............................................ 25

### THREE TONES
70  Bamboo BAM 32  Good Ways/Everything We Do .................................................................. 150

### THREE TOPS
67  Doctor Bird DB 1101  Miserable Friday/This World Has A Feeling ................................................. 50
67  Studio One SO 2023  Moving To Progress/Love And Inspiration ................................................ 80
67  Trojan TR 003  It's Raining/Sound Of Music ................................................................ 40
67  Treasure Isle TI 7008  Do It Right/You Should Have Known ....................................................... 30
68  Coxsone CS 7033  A Man Of Chances(as Tree Tops)/HORTENSE ELLIS: A Groovy Kind Of Love ............... 300
73  Bullet BU 527  Take Time Out/Just Like A Log ............................................................. 12

*(see also Dion Cameron & Three Tops, Sir Lord Comic, King Rocky)*

### THREE WISE MEN
83  Virgin VS 642  Thanks For Christmas/Countdown To Christmas Partytime (p/s) ......................... 10

*(see also XTC)*

### THREE DANCERS
87  Dilletante Disques 007  Seventeen/It Doesn't Matter (p/s) .......................................................... 40

### THREE LITTLE PIGGIES
88  Mrs Slocombe  FRIVILOUS FROLICS (mini-LP).............................................................. 50
89  Mrs Slocombe  Clarke's Commandos/Ain't He Happy/Uncle Chris (p/s)................................. 50

### THREE PARTY SPLIT
79  B&C BCS 16  Dubious Parentage/Kandidate (p/s) ........................................................ 20
79  B&C BCS 19  Insane/Totally Insane (unissued, 1 known copy)......................................... 350

### THREE'S A CROWD
66  Fontana TF 673  Look Around The Corner/Living In A Dream................................................ 20

*(see also Embers, Writing On The Wall)*

### THRESHOLD OF PLEASURE
68  Decca F12785  Rain Rain Rain/He Could Never Love You Like I Do ..................................... 40

### THRILLERS
68  Blue Cat BS 128  The Last Dance/DELTA CATS: Unworthy Baby........................................... 500

*(see also Phil Pratt)*

### THRILLING WONDER STORIES
83  Made In Space MIS 2001  Two Way Video/Computer Mix ............................................................ 10

### PERCY 'THRILLS' THRILLINGTON
77  Regal Zono. EMI 2594  Uncle Albert - Admiral Halsey/Eat At Home ............................................ 100
77  Regal Zono. EMC 3175  THRILLINGTON (LP, with inner sleeve) .................................................. 200
77  Regal Zono. TC-EMC 3175  THRILLINGTON (cassette) ................................................................... 25

*(see also Paul McCartney)*

### THRILLS (1)
66  Capitol CL 15469  No One/What Can Go Wrong ................................................................ 100
66  Capitol CL 15469  No One/What Can Go Wrong (DJ copy) .................................................. 200
79  Grapevine GRP 126  Show The World Where It's At/What Can Go Wrong ....................................... 5

### THRILLS (2)
03  Virgin VSDJ 1855  Last Night I Dreamt That Somebody Loved Me (1-sided gig issue, p/s, 500 only)........... 10
03  Virgin V 2975  SO MUCH FOR THE CITY (LP) .............................................................. 20

### THROBBING GRISTLE
78  Industrial IR 0003  United/Zyklon B Zombie (p/s) ............................................................... 20
78  Industrial IR 0003/U  United/Zyklon B Zombie (p/s, white or clear vinyl, 1,000 only of each) ................... 25
80  Industrial IR 0003  United/Zyklon B Zombie (longer version) (p/s, reissue, 'Memorial Issue' scratched in matrix) ...................................................................................... 15
80  Industrial IR 0013  Subhuman/Something Came Over Me (in polythene camouflage bag) ................. 20
80  Industrial IR 0015  Adrenalin/Distant Dreams (Part Two) (in polythene camouflage bag) ................. 20
81  Fetish FET 006  Discipline (live, Berlin)/Discipline (live, Manchester) (12", p/s)......................... 20
77  Industrial IR 0002  SECOND ANNUAL REPORT (LP, 785 only, white hand-made sleeve, 'Nothing short of a total war' sticker on inner sleeve, xerox strip, 'technical note' strip & 2 or 3 TG stickers) ................................................................................... 250
78  Industrial IR 0004  D.O.A. THE THIRD AND FINAL REPORT (LP, 1st 1,000 with calendar & postcard).......... 100
78  Industrial IR 0004  D.O.A. THE THIRD AND FINAL REPORT (LP).............................................. 25
78  Fetish FET 2001  SECOND ANNUAL REPORT (LP, 2,000 only, T.G. 'lightning flash' sleeve, with questionnaire & insert, "Coom" mispelling) ................................................. 40
79  Fetish FET 2001  SECOND ANNUAL REPORT (LP, reissue, glossy sleeve with inserts, with correct "Coum" spelling) .................................................................................. 15
79  Industrial IR 0004  D.O.A. THE THIRD AND FINAL REPORT (LP, re-pressing, 1,000 only, banded as 16 equal length tracks) ................................................................................ 60
79  Industrial IR 0008  20 JAZZ FUNK GREATS (LP, 5,000 only, 1st 2,000 with b&w poster) ..................... 80
79  Industrial IR 0008  20 JAZZ FUNK GREATS (LP, 5,000 only) ................................................... 40
80  Industrial IR 0009  HEATHEN EARTH (LP, gatefold sleeve, 785 on blue vinyl)............................... 100
80  Industrial IR 0009  HEATHEN EARTH (LP, gatefold sleeve)..................................................... 20
81  Fetish FET 2001  SECOND ANNUAL REPORT (LP, backwards version, 1st 2,000 in T.G. 'flash' sleeve).... 40
81  Fetish FET 2001  SECOND ANNUAL REPORT (LP, backwards version, later issue in black & white sleeve). 15
81  Fetish FX 1  A BOXED SET (5-LP box set with 28-page booklet & badge, 5,000 only)...................... 160
82  Death 01  MUSIC FROM THE DEATH FACTORY, MAY '79 (LP, 50 only) ............................. 350
82  Power Focus 001  ASSUME POWER FOCUS (LP, 500 only, numbered) ..................................... 90
82  T.G. 33033  LIVE AT THE DEATH FACTORY, MAY '79 (LP, reissue picture disc, 1,355 only) ............. 40
82  Karnage/Illuminated KILL 1  THEE PSYCHICK SACRIFICE (2-LP) ......................................................... 30
83  MIR 001  THE SECOND ANNUAL REPORT (LP, reissue)............................................. 20
83  Mute MIR 002  D.O.A. THE THIRD AND FINAL REPORT (LP, reissue)..................................... 20
83  Mute MIR 004  20 JAZZ FUNK GREATS (LP, reissue) ....................................................... 20
83  Mute MIR004  HEATHEN EARTH (LP, reissue) ............................................................. 20

# THROWING MUSES

| | | | |
|---|---|---|---|
| 84 | Illuminated JAMS 35 | IN THE SHADOW OF THE SUN (LP, soundtrack) | 20 |
| 84 | Illuminated JAMS 39 | THE INDUSTRIAL RECORDS STORY 1976-1981 (LP) | 35 |
| 84 | Casual Abandon CAS 1J | ONCE UPON A TIME (LP) | 15 |
| 84 | Mental Decay 01-1 | SPECIAL TREATMENT (LP) | 15 |
| 80s | Sprut 001 | VERY FRIENDLY - THE FIRST ANNUAL REPORT OF T.G. (LP) | 25 |
| 80s | Industrial IRC 1-IRC 24 | 24 HOURS (box set of cassettes with total of 24 hours playing time; every set is unique) | 300 |
| 03 | Grey Area | TG+ (10-CD box set with metal cards) | 70 |

*(see also Psychic TV, Coil, Sabres Of Paradise)*

## THROWING MUSES

| | | | |
|---|---|---|---|
| 89 | 4AD BADD 903 | Dizzy/Santa Claus/Mania (live)/Downtown (live) (10", gatefold p/s) | 5 |
| 86 | 4AD CAD 607 | THROWING MUSES (LP) | 15 |
| 87 | 4AD MAD 706 | THE FAT SKIER (LP) | 15 |
| 88 | 4AD CAD 802 | HOUSE TORNADO (LP) | 15 |
| 89 | 4AD CAD 901 | HUNKPAPA (LP, lyric inner) | 15 |
| 91 | 4AD CAD 1002 | THE REAL RAMONA (LP, inner) | 15 |
| 93 | 4AD CADD 2013 | RED HEAVEN (LP, with free live Kristin Hersh LP) | 20 |
| 95 | 4AD CAD 5002 | UNIVERSITY (LP) | 25 |
| 96 | 4AD CAD 6014 | LIMBO (LP) | 25 |

*(see also Belly, Kristin Hersh)*

## THE THRUST

| | | | |
|---|---|---|---|
| 80 | Ellie Jay EJSP 9341 | THE THRUST EP | 100 |

## THUNDER

| | | | |
|---|---|---|---|
| 90 | EMI EMPD 126 | Dirty Love/Fired Up (uncut picture disc with insert in PVC sleeve) | 15 |
| 90 | EMI EMS 137 | Back Street Symphony/No Way Out Of The Wilderness (box set with postcards, some also with badge ) | 6 |

*(see also Terraplane, Nuthin' Fancy)*

## JOHNNY THUNDER

| | | | |
|---|---|---|---|
| 63 | Stateside SS 149 | Loop De Loop/Don't Be Ashamed | 10 |
| 63 | Stateside SS 168 | Rock-A-Bye My Darling/The Rosy Dance | 10 |
| 63 | Stateside SS 200 | Jailer, Bring Me Water/Outlaw | 15 |
| 63 | Stateside SS 229 | Hey Child/Everybody Likes To Dance With Johnny | 10 |
| 64 | Stateside SS 337 | More, More, More Love, Love, Love/Shout It To The World | 10 |
| 65 | Stateside SS 370 | Send Her To Me/Everybody Likes To Dance With Johnny | 20 |
| 65 | Stateside SS 454 | Dear John I'm Going To Leave You/Suzie-Q | 10 |
| 65 | Stateside SS 476 | Everybody Do The Sloopy/Beautiful | 10 |
| 66 | Stateside SS 499 | My Prayer/A Broken Heart | 10 |
| 63 | Stateside SL 10029 | LOOP DE LOOP (LP) | 75 |

## JOHNNY THUNDER & RUBY WINTERS

| | | | |
|---|---|---|---|
| 67 | Stateside SS 2005 | Make Love To Me/Teach Me Tonight | 15 |

## THUNDERBIRDS

| | | | |
|---|---|---|---|
| 66 | Polydor 56710 | Your Ma Said You Cried (In Your Sleep Last Night)/Before It's Too Late | 70 |

*(see also Chris Farlowe & Thunderbirds)*

## THUNDERBIRDS (AUSTRALIA)

| | | | |
|---|---|---|---|
| 61 | Oriole CB 1610 | Wild Weekend/Rat Race | 20 |
| 61 | Oriole CB 1625 | New Orleans Beat/Delilah Jones | 20 |

## THUNDERBIRDS (U.S.)

| | | | |
|---|---|---|---|
| 55 | London HL 8146 | Ayuh, Ayuh/Blueberries | 70 |

*(see also Bert Convy & Thunderbirds, Midnighters)*

## THUNDERBOLTS

| | | | |
|---|---|---|---|
| 62 | Decca F 11522 | Fugitive/Feelin' In A Mood | 15 |

## THUNDERBOYS

| | | | |
|---|---|---|---|
| 80 | Recent EJSP 9339 | Fashion/Someone Like You (p/s) | 40 |

## THUNDERCLAP NEWMAN

| | | | |
|---|---|---|---|
| 69 | Track 604031 | Something In The Air/Wilhemina | 6 |
| 70 | Track 2094 001 | Accidents/I See It All | 5 |
| 70 | Track 2094 002 | Wild Country/Hollywood | 7 |
| 70 | Track 2094 003 | The Reason/Stormy Petrel | 7 |
| 79 | Track 2095 002 | Wild Country/Hollywood (reissue, p/s) | 8 |
| 70 | Track 2406 003 | HOLLYWOOD DREAM (LP, gatefold sleeve, lyric insert) | 100 |
| 70 | Track 2406 003 | HOLLYWOOD DREAM (LP, gatefold sleeve, without lyric insert) | 30 |

*(see also Stone The Crows, One In A Million, Paul McCartney & Wings, Speedy Keen, Andy Newman)*

## THUNDER COMPANY

| | | | |
|---|---|---|---|
| 70 | Columbia DB 8706 | Ridin' On The Gravy Train (5.03)/Bubble Drum | 40 |
| 70 | Columbia DB 8706 | Ridin' On The Gravy Train (2.35 Edit)/Bubble Drum (demo only) | 50 |

*(see also Brian Bennett, Shadows)*

## THUNDERHEAD

| | | | |
|---|---|---|---|
| 93 | Thunderhead TH 01 | Lost In Time/Untitled (12") | 20 |

## THUNDERMUG

| | | | |
|---|---|---|---|
| 73 | London HLZ 10411 | Africa/Will They Ever | 6 |
| 72 | Axe AXS 502 | STRIKES (LP) | 15 |

## THUNDER ROAD

| | | | |
|---|---|---|---|
| 73 | Buddah Records 2011-163 | Peter Gunn/Holly Golly | 5 |

## JOHNNY THUNDERS (& THE HEARTBREAKERS)

| | | | |
|---|---|---|---|
| 78 | Real ARE 1 | Dead Or Alive/Downtown (p/s) | 15 |
| 78 | Real ARE 3 | You Can't Put Your Arms Around A Memory (Edit)/Hurtin' (p/s) | 12 |
| 78 | Real ARE 3T | You Can't Put Your Arms Around A Memory/Hurtin' (12", p/s, blue or pink vinyl, die-cut company sleeve) | 12 |

MINT VALUE £

| | | | |
|---|---|---|---|
| 83 | Jungle JUNG 5 | VINTAGE '77 (12" EP) | 12 |
| 84 | Jungle JUNG 14P | Get Off The Phone/All By Myself (picture disc) | 10 |
| 99 | Jungle JUNG 62 | Chinese Rocks/Born To Lose (p/s, pink vinyl) | 5 |
| 77 | Real RAL 1 | SO ALONE (LP, with inner sleeve) | 25 |
| 86 | Jungle JT BOX 1 | ALBUM COLLECTION (3-LP & 12" box set with poster and badge) | 30 |

*(see also New York Dolls, Heartbreakers)*

## SAM THUNDER
| | | | |
|---|---|---|---|
| 84 | Bullet BULP 5 | MANOUEVRES (LP, picture disc) | 18 |

## THUNDERSTICK
| | | | |
|---|---|---|---|
| 83 | Thunderbolt THBE 1002 | FEEL LIKE ROCK'N'ROLL (12" EP, p/s, with patch) | 12 |

*(see also Samson, Gillan)*

## THURSDAY'S CHILDREN
| | | | |
|---|---|---|---|
| 66 | Piccadilly 7N 35276 | Just You/You Don't Believe Me | 25 |
| 66 | Piccadilly 7N 35306 | Crawfish/Come Softly To Me | 15 |

*(see also Phil Cordell)*

## BOBBY THURSTON
| | | | |
|---|---|---|---|
| 81 | Epic EPC A1301 | Very Last Drop/Life Is What You Make It | 20 |
| 81 | Epic EPC 85070 | MAIN ATTRACTION (LP) | 15 |
| 88 | HI Hut HH 1135 | SWEETEST PIECE OF THE PIE (LP) | 20 |

## THYRDS
| | | | |
|---|---|---|---|
| 64 | Oak RGJ 133 | Hide 'N' Seek/I've Got My Mojo Working | 300 |
| 64 | Decca F 12010 | Hide 'N' Seek/No Time Like The Present | 60 |

## TIAMAT
| | | | |
|---|---|---|---|
| 90 | CMFT CMFT 6 | SUMERIAN CRY (LP) | 40 |
| 90 | Metalcore CORE 9 | SUMERIAN CRY (LP, reissue) | 30 |

## TIARAS
| | | | |
|---|---|---|---|
| 63 | Warner Bros WB 92 | You Told Me/I'm Gonna Forget You | 15 |

## TIBET & STAPLETON
| | | | |
|---|---|---|---|
| 96 | United Dairies UDOR 1 | MUSICALISCHE KÜRBS HÜTTE (LP, clear vinyl, with insert) | 30 |

*(see also Current 93, Steven Stapleton & David Tibet)o*

## TICH - TED TAYLOR FOUR WITH CORONA KIDS
| | | | |
|---|---|---|---|
| 65 | Oriole CB 1980 | Santa Bring Me Ringo/Santa's Got Such A Terrible Cold/Tich & Quackers | 10 |

*(see also Ted Taylor)*

## TICKAWINDA
| | | | |
|---|---|---|---|
| 75 | Pennine PSS 153 | ROSEMARY LANE (LP) | 800 |

## KATHRYN TICKELL
| | | | |
|---|---|---|---|
| 84 | Saydisc SDL 343 | ON KIELDER SIDE (LP) | 20 |

## TICKETS
| | | | |
|---|---|---|---|
| 79 | Bridgehouse BHS 3 | I'll Be Your Pin Up/Guess I Have To Sit Alone (p/s) | 6 |

*(see also Wasted Youth)*

## TICKLE
| | | | |
|---|---|---|---|
| 67 | Regal Zonophone RZ 3004 | Subway (Smokey Pokey World)/Good Evening | 500 |

*(see also Junior's Eyes, Outsider, Bunch Of Fives)*

## TIC TAC TOE
| | | | |
|---|---|---|---|
| 92 | Tic Tac Toe TTT 456 | 456/Ephemerol (12", stamped white label) | 30 |
| 92 | Tic Tac Toe TTT 457 | 456/(Remix)/Ephemerol (Mickey Finn Remix) (12") | 10 |

## TIDAL WAVE
| | | | |
|---|---|---|---|
| 69 | Decca F 22973 | With Tears In My Eyes/We Wanna Know | 10 |

## TIDBITS
| | | | |
|---|---|---|---|
| 71 | Fly BUG 12 | Jean Harlow/Vietnam/Six O'Clock Blues (p/s) | 8 |

## PETER TIERNEY & NIGHTHAWKS
| | | | |
|---|---|---|---|
| 65 | Fontana TF 547 | Oh How I Need You/That's Too Bad (p/s) | 15 |

## ROY TIERNEY
| | | | |
|---|---|---|---|
| 61 | Philips BF 1159 | Cupid/The Lonely One (in p/s) | 15 |
| 61 | Philips BF 1159 | Cupid/The Lonely One | 7 |
| 61 | Philips BF 1194 | Just Out Of Reach (Of My Two Empty Arms)/Casanova | 10 |

## TIERNEY'S FUGITIVES
| | | | |
|---|---|---|---|
| 65 | Decca F 12247 | Did You Want To Run Away?/Morning Mist | 25 |

## TIFFANIES
| | | | |
|---|---|---|---|
| 67 | Chess CRS 8059 | It's Got To Be A Great Song/He's Good For Me | 100 |
| 67 | Chess CRS 8059 | It's Got To Be A Great Song/He's Good For Me (DJ copy) | 150 |

## TIFFANY (WITH THOUGHTS)
| | | | |
|---|---|---|---|
| 65 | Parlophone R 5311 | I Know/Am I Dreaming | 20 |
| 66 | Parlophone R 5439 | Find Out What's Happening/Baby Don't Look Down (as Tiffany with Thoughts) | 50 |

*(see also Thoughts)*

## TIFFANY SHADE
| | | | |
|---|---|---|---|
| 68 | Fontana (S)TL 5469 | TIFFANY SHADE (LP) | 100 |

## JIMMY & LOUISE TIG
| | | | |
|---|---|---|---|
| 69 | Deep Soul DS 9105 | A Love That Never Grows Cold/Who Can I Turn To | 40 |

## TIGER
| | | | |
|---|---|---|---|
| 75 | United Artists UP 35848 | I Am An Animal/Stop That Machine | 20 |
| 76 | Retreat RTL 6006 | TIGER (LP, with lyric inner sleeve) | 15 |
| 76 | EMI EMC3153 | GOIN' DOWN LAUGHING (LP, lyric inner sleeve) | 15 |

*(see also Hackensack, Samson, Brinsley Schwarz, Big Jim Sullivan, Nicky Moore Band)*

## TIGER ASHBY
| | | | |
|---|---|---|---|
| 80 | T&A Records TA 1 | Jet Free/Burning Cross (p/s) | 20 |

## TIGER (JAMAICA)
| | | | |
|---|---|---|---|
| 70 | New Beat NB 052 | Soul Of Africa/Dallas Texas | 20 |
| 70 | New Beat NB 064 | Musical Scorcher/Three Dogs Night | 20 |
| 71 | Camel CA 70 | Guilty/United We Stand | 15 |
| 71 | New Beat NB 075 | African Beat/Black Man Land | 10 |
| 71 | New Beat NB 088 | Have You Ever Been Hurt/Our Day Will Come | 10 |

## TIGER LILY
| | | | |
|---|---|---|---|
| 75 | Gull GULS 12 | Monkey Jive/Ain't Misbehavin' | 10 |
| 77 | Gull GULS 54 | Monkey Jive/Ain't Misbehavin' (reissue, p/s) | 10 |
| 77 | Gull GULS 54 | Monkey Jive/Ain't Misbehavin' (reissue) | 5 |
| 80 | Dead Good DEAD 11 | Monkey Jive/Ain't Misbehavin' (2nd reissue, different p/s) | 5 |

*(see also Ultravox)*

## TIGERMOTH
| | | | |
|---|---|---|---|
| 84 | Rogue FMSL 2006 | TIGERMOTH (LP) | 15 |

## TIGERS (2)
| | | | |
|---|---|---|---|
| 79 | Strike STING 1 | Savage Music/Jack It Up | 8 |
| 79 | Strike KIK 1 | Kidding Stops/Big Expense, Small Income (p/s) | 8 |

## TIGER TAILS
| | | | |
|---|---|---|---|
| 80 | Snotty Snails NELCO 2 | Words Without Conviction/Norman/Fashion Fool (p/s) | 20 |

## TIGHT LIKE THAT
| | | | |
|---|---|---|---|
| 72 | Village Thing VTS 12 | HOKUM (LP) | 40 |

## TIGHTS
| | | | |
|---|---|---|---|
| 78 | Cherry Red CHERRY 1 | Bad Hearts/It/Cracked (p/s) | 20 |
| 78 | Cherry Red CHERRY 2 | Howard Hughes/China's Eternal (p/s) | 10 |

## TIKKI, TAKI, SUZI, LIES
| | | | |
|---|---|---|---|
| 70 | UPC UPC 102 | Welcome To My House/I Believe In Love | 8 |
| 70 | UPC UPC 109 | Ba-Da-Da-Dum/Dream Stealer | 25 |

## TILLER BOYS
| | | | |
|---|---|---|---|
| 79 | New Hormones ORG 3 | Big Noise From The Jungle/Slaves And Pyramids/What Me Worry? (p/s) | 6 |

*(see also Buzzcocks, Pete Shelley)*

## TILLERMEN
| | | | |
|---|---|---|---|
| 71 | Duke DU 109 | Be Loving To Me/Judgement Rock | 7 |

*(see also Greyhound)*

## DEREK JOHN TILLEY
| | | | |
|---|---|---|---|
| 70 | Decca F 13043 | Sunny Day/Living For Love | 30 |

## MEL TILLIS
| | | | |
|---|---|---|---|
| 67 | London HLR 10141 | Life Turned Her That Way/If I Could Only Start Over | 5 |

## BERTHA TILLMAN
| | | | |
|---|---|---|---|
| 62 | Oriole CB 1746 | Oh, My Angel/Lovin' Time | 80 |

## JOHNNY TILLOTSON
| | | | |
|---|---|---|---|
| 59 | London HLA 8930 | True True Happiness/Love Is Blind | 30 |
| 60 | London HLA 9048 | Why Do I Love You So/Never Let Me Go | 20 |
| 60 | London HLA 9101 | Earth Angel/Pledging My Love | 30 |
| 60 | London HLA 9231 | Poetry In Motion/Princess, Princess | 5 |
| 61 | London HLA 9275 | Jimmy's Girl/His True Love Said Goodbye | 10 |
| 61 | London HLA 9412 | Without You/Cutie Pie | 15 |
| 62 | London HLA 9514 | Dreamy Eyes/Much Beyond Compare | 6 |
| 62 | London HLA 9550 | It Keeps Right On A-Hurtin'/She Gave Sweet Love To Me | 8 |
| 62 | London HLA 9598 | Send Me The Pillow You Dream On/What'll I Do | 7 |
| 62 | London HLA 9642 | I Can't Help It/I'm So Lonesome I Could Cry | 7 |
| 63 | London HLA 9695 | Out Of My Mind/Judy, Judy, Judy | 7 |
| 63 | London HLA 9811 | Funny How Time Slips Away/A Very Good Year For Girls | 7 |
| 63 | MGM MGM 1214 | Talk Back Trembling Lips/Another You | 7 |
| 63 | MGM MGM 1225 | Worried Guy/Please Don't Go Away | 6 |
| 63 | MGM MGM 1235 | I'm Watching My Watch/I Rise, I Fall | 6 |
| 64 | MGM MGM 1247 | Suffering From A Heartache/Worry | 6 |
| 64 | MGM MGM 1252 | She Understands Me/Tomorrow | 8 |
| 64 | MGM MGM 1266 | Angel/Little Boy | 7 |
| 65 | MGM MGM 1275 | Then I'll Count Again/One's Yours, One's Mine | 8 |
| 65 | MGM MGM 1281 | Heartaches By The Number/Your Memory Comes Along | 8 |
| 65 | MGM MGM 1290 | Our World/(Wait 'Til You See) My Gidget | 8 |
| 66 | MGM MGM 1300 | Hello Enemy/I Never Loved You Anyway | 8 |
| 66 | MGM MGM 1311 | Me Myself And I/Country Boy, Country Boy | 8 |
| 66 | MGM MGM 1319 | No Love At All/What Am I Gonna Do | 8 |
| 68 | MGM MGM 1393 | Cabaret/If I Were A Rich Man | 8 |
| 69 | London HLU 10281 | Tears On My Pillow/Remember When | 5 |
| 62 | London RE-A 1345 | JOHNNY TILLOTSON (EP) | 35 |
| 63 | London RE-A 1388 | J.T. (EP) | 35 |
| 63 | MGM MGM-EP 788 | JOHNNY TILLOTSON (EP) | 20 |
| 64 | MGM MGM-EP 790 | JOHNNY TILLOTSON'S HIT PARADE (EP) | 20 |
| 61 | London HA-A 2431 | JOHNNY TILLOTSON'S BEST (LP) | 30 |
| 62 | London HA-A 8019 | IT KEEPS RIGHT ON A-HURTIN' (LP) | 25 |

## TILSLEY ORCHESTRA
| | | | |
|---|---|---|---|
| 66 | Fontana TF 783 | Thunderbirds Theme/Theme From "The Power Game" | 20 |
| 67 | Polydor 56150 | Mr. Aitch Theme/Cotton Reed | 8 |
| 67 | Fontana (S)TL 5411 | TOP T.V. THEMES (LP) | 20 |

*(see also Electric Banana)*

**STEVE TILSTON**
| 71 | Village Thing VTS 5 | AN ACOUSTIC CONFUSION (LP) | 35 |
| 72 | Transatlantic TRA 252 | COLLECTION (LP, textured gatefold sleeve) | 18 |
| 77 | Cornucopia CR 1 | SONGS FROM THE DRESS REHEARSAL (LP, with Rupert Hine/John Renbourn) | 25 |
| 83 | TM PROP 4 | IN FOR A PENNY IN FOR A POUND (LP, with Peter Bardens) | 15 |

**TIMBER**
| 71 | Elektra K 12022 | Bring America Home/Splinters From Timber | 6 |
| 72 | Elektra K 12042 | Outlaw/Song For Two Signs | 6 |

**TIMBER TIMBRE**
| 11 | Full Time Hobby FTH 114LP | CREEP ON CREEPING ON (LP) | 18 |

**TIME**
| 65 | Pye 7N 17019 | Take A Bit Of Notice/Every Now And Then | 60 |
| 66 | Pye 7N 17146 | The First Time I Saw The Sunshine/Annabel | 30 |

**TIME**
| 75 | B.U.K. BULP 2005 | TIME (LP) | 60 |
*(see also Spontaneous Combustion)*

**T.I.M.E. (TRUST IN MEN EVERYWHERE)**
| 69 | Liberty LBF 15082 | Take Me Along/Make It Alright | 10 |
| 68 | Liberty LBL/LBS 83144 | T.I.M.E. (LP) | 50 |
| 69 | Liberty LBL/LBS 83232 | SMOOTH BALL (LP) | 70 |

**TIME MACHINE (2)**
| 78 | Rip Off RIP 6 | NEVER MET SUZI EP | 40 |

**TIME UK**
| 83 | Red Bus TIM 123 | The Cabaret/Remember Days (gatefold p/s) | 10 |
*(see also the Jam)*

**TIMEBOX**
| 67 | Piccadilly 7N 35369 | I'll Always Love You/Save Your Love | 100 |
| 67 | Piccadilly 7N 35379 | Soul Sauce/I Wish I Could Jerk Like My Uncle Cyril | 200 |
| 67 | Deram DM 153 | Walking Through The Streets Of My Mind/Don't Make Promises | 25 |
| 68 | Deram DM 194 | Beggin'/A Woman That's Waiting | 45 |
| 68 | Deram DM 219 | Girl Don't Make Me Wait/Gone Is The Sad Man | 35 |
| 69 | Deram DM 246 | Baked Jam Roll In Your Eye/Poor Little Heartbreaker | 30 |
| 69 | Deram DM 271 | Yellow Van/You've Got The Chance | 30 |
*(see also Bo Street Runners, [Mike] Patto, V.I.Ps)*

**TIME CRYSTALS**
| 91 | Talisman TAL 1 | The Fool/Geve Me Back What's Mine | 10 |

**TIMELORDS**
| 88 | KLF 003GG | Gary In The Tardis (Radio)/(Minimal) (white label promo, 500 only) | 15 |
| 88 | KLF 003GG | Gary In The Tardis (Radio)/(Minimal) (12", p/s) | 10 |
| 88 | KLF 003P | Doctorin' The Tardis (Radio)/(Minimal) (car-shaped picture disc) | 15 |
| 88 | KLF 003R | Doctorin' The Tardis (Radio)/Doctorin' The Tardis (Minimal)/ Gary Glitter Joins The JAMs (12", 4,000 only, this price for those in full 'Gary Glitter' p/s) | 30 |
| 88 | KLF TCD 003 | Doctorin' The Tardis (12" mix)/What Time Is Love? (KLF original) (CD) | 10 |
| 88 | KLF CD 003 | Doctorin' The Tardis (Radio)/Doctorin' The Tardis (Minimal)/Doctorin' The Tardis (Club Mix)/ Doctorin' The Tardis (Video) (CD Video) | 30 |
*(see also KLF, Disco 2000, JAMs, Bill Drummond, Orb, Space)*

**TIME MACHINE (1)**
| 72 | Play PLAY 41 | Railroad/Going Down Down Down | 30 |

**TIMEPIECE**
| 70 | Dolphin 4759 | Hitchin To Miami/Mad Dan The Romeo Man | 8 |

**TIMES (1)**
| 65 | EMI 7ES 24 | Ooh Wee/Shepherd Blues/Suzie/Running And Hiding (EP, demo only) | 70 |
| 66 | Columbia DB 7804 | Think About The Times/Tomorrow Night | 35 |
| 66 | Columbia DB 7904 | (She Can't Replace) The Love We Knew/Reconciled | 35 |
| 68 | Pye 7N 17647 | What's Made Milwaukee Famous/Follw The Times | 10 |
| 70 | Parlophone R 5855 | Looking Thru' The Eyes Of A Beautiful Girl/Flyin' High Feelin' Low | 10 |

**TIMES (2)**
| 81 | Whaam! WHAAM 2 | Red With Purple Flashes/Biff! Bang! Pow! (p/s) | 100 |
| 82 | Art Pop POP 50 | Here Come The Holidays (Voici Les Vacances)/Three Cheers For The Sun (A-side as Joni Dee & Times, p/s, with 'Times' sticker) | 18 |
| 82 | Art Pop POP 50 | Here Come The Holidays (Voici Les Vacances)/Three Cheers For The Sun (A-side as Joni Dee & Times, p/s) | 12 |
| 83 | Art Pop POP 49 | I Helped Patrick McGoohan Escape/The Theme From "Danger Man" (p/s) | 20 |
| 84 | Art Pop POP 46 | Boys Brigade/Power Is Forever (p/s) | 7 |
| 84 | Art Pop POP 45 | Blue Fire/Where The Blue Begins (p/s) | 6 |
| 85 | Unicorn PHZ 1 | London Boys/(Where To Go) When The Sun Goes Down (p/s) | 5 |
| 90 | Caff CAFF 13 | Extase/BIFF BANG POW!: Sleep (p/s, with insert) | 20 |
| 85 | Whaam! 43DOZ | BOYS ABOUT TOWN (12", EP) | 10 |
| 81 | Whaam! BIG 1 | POP GOES ART (LP, hand-sprayed sleeve) | 45 |
| 82 | Art Pop ART 20 | POP GOES ART! (LP, reissue, hand-sprayed sleeve, with magazine cuttings taped to plain white cover) | 25 |
| 82 | Art Pop ART 20 | POP GOES ART! (LP, reissue, hand-sprayed sleeve, without magazine cuttings taped to plain white cover) | 20 |
| 83 | Art Pop ART 19 | THIS IS LONDON (LP, white label with blue print) | 25 |
| 83 | Art Pop ART 19 | THIS IS LONDON (LP, black label with white print) | 18 |
| 83 | Art Pop No. 1 | I HELPED PATRICK McGOOHAN ESCAPE (mini-LP) | 18 |
| 90 | Art Pop ART 20 | POP GOES ART (LP, 'hand-painted' picture disc reissue, signed) | 15 |
*(see also Television Personalities, Teenage Filmstars, O Level, Biff Bang Pow!, L'Orange Mechanik)*

## BOBBY TIMMONS
| | | | |
|---|---|---|---|
| 61 | Riverside RLP 334 | SOUL TIME (LP, with Art Blakey, also stereo [RLP 9334]) | 20 |
| 60 | Riverside 12-317 | THIS HERE IS (LP) | 20 |

## TIMON
| | | | |
|---|---|---|---|
| 68 | Pye 7N 17451 | Bitter Thoughts Of Little Jane/Ramblin' Boy | 100 |
| 70 | Threshold TH 3 | And Now She Says She's Young/I'm Just A Travelling Man | 8 |

*(see also Tymon Dogg)*

## TIMONEERS
| | | | |
|---|---|---|---|
| 76 | WHM WHM 1919 | ROASTED LIVE (LP) | 20 |

## AL TIMOTHY & HIS BAND
| | | | |
|---|---|---|---|
| 55 | Decca F 10558 | Gruntin' Blues/You Mad Man! | 10 |

## TIM TAM & TURN ONS
| | | | |
|---|---|---|---|
| 67 | Island WIP 6007 | Wait A Minute/Ophelia | 50 |

## TINA
| | | | |
|---|---|---|---|
| 61 | Piccadilly 7N 35022 | What I Want For Christmas (Is Six More Years)/My Brother Wants A Doll For Christmas | 6 |

## TINA & MEXICANS
| | | | |
|---|---|---|---|
| 68 | Pye 7N 17525 | One Love Two/Longing To Hold You | 8 |

## TIN BISCUIT
| | | | |
|---|---|---|---|
| 70 | Fontana TF 1077 | The Last Time You Go/I'd Give My Life To You | 5 |

## TINDERBOX (1)
| | | | |
|---|---|---|---|
| 68 | Polydor 56296 | Farewell Britannia/Rainsong | 60 |

## TINDERBOX (2)
| | | | |
|---|---|---|---|
| 74 | Cannon CAN 2 | Inside A Dream/Sad N Lonely | 60 |

## TINDERSTICKS
| | | | |
|---|---|---|---|
| 92 | Tippy Toe 1 | Patchwork/Milky Teeth (p/s, hand-coloured inner sleeve & insert; 1,000 only, numbered in positive or negative figures [from -500 to 500]) | 60 |
| 93 | Tippy Toe/Ché TIPPY-CHE 2 | Marbles/Joe Stumble/For Those.../Benn (10", p/s, stickered PVC sleeve, innersleeve & insert, 2,000 only) | 25 |
| 93 | Rough Trade 45rev16 | A Marriage Made In Heaven/A Marriage Made In Heaven (Instrumental) ('singles club' release, p/s, 5,000 only) | 10 |
| 93 | This Way Up WAY 1811 | City Sickness/Untitled/The Bullring (p/s, 1,500 only) | 12 |
| 93 | Clawfist XPIG 21 | We Have All The Time In The World/GALLON DRUNK: Known Not Wanted ('singles club' release, p/s, 1,400 only) | 12 |
| 93 | Tippy Toe 003 | LIVE IN BERLIN: Raindrops/Tyed (in stamped brown paper bag, mail-order/tour release, 1,500 only) | 20 |
| 94 | This Way Up WAY 2811 | Kathleen/Summat Moon/Sweet, Sweet Man/E Type Joe (33 rpm 7", 5000 only) | 6 |
| 95 | Sub Pop SP 297 | THE SMOOTH SOUND OF TINDERSTICKS: Here/Harry's Dilemma (p/s, 3,000 only) | 10 |
| 95 | This Way Up 2888 | KATHLEEN (10") | 10 |
| 08 | Lucky Dog LD 05 | What Are You Fighting For? (one-sided 7", die cut sleeve, 200 only) | 15 |
| 93 | This Way Up 518306 | TINDERSTICKS (1st album) (2-LP, first 1000 with 4 postcards) | 60 |
| 93 | This Way Up 518306 | TINDERSTICKS (1st album) (2-LP, without postcards) | 45 |
| 93 | This Way Up 518308-1 | TINDERSTICKS (1st album) (2-LP reissue, green vinyl) | 40 |
| 95 | This Way Up THIS 1.1 | TINDERSTICKS (2nd album) (LP,with free 7") | 60 |
| 94 | This Way Up WAY 3288 | LIVE IN AMSTERDAM (10" LP, brown sleeve) | 30 |
| 95 | This Way Up | THE BLOOMSBURY THEATRE 12/3/95 (LP, 2-10" LP) | 30 |
| 96 | This Way Up 5243002 | NENETTE ET BONI (LP) | 25 |
| 97 | This Way Up 5243441 | CURTAINS (2xLP) | 80 |
| 98 | Island ILPS 8074 | DONKEYS 92-97 (LP) | 50 |
| 99 | Simply Vinyl SVLP 112 | SIMPLE PLEASURE (LP) | 70 |
| 01 | Beggars Banquet BBQLP 222 | CAN OUR LOVE... (LP, gatefold) | 25 |
| 01 | Beggars Banquet BBQLP 225 | TROUBLE EVERY DAY (LP, soundtrack, with booklet) | 20 |
| 03 | Beggars Banquet BBQLP 232 | WAITING FOR THE MOON (LP) | 30 |
| 10 | 4AD CAD 3X02 | FALLING DOWN A MOUNTAIN (LP) | 15 |

*(see also Asphalt Ribbons, Stuart A. Staples)*

## TING TINGS
| | | | |
|---|---|---|---|
| 07 | Switchflicker SWALF 11 | That's Not My Name/Great DJ (p/s) | 12 |
| 07 | No label or cat no | Fruit Machine/Impacilla Carpisung (4 x 100 7" given away at 4 live shows, customized blank sleeve) | 25 |
| 08 | Columbia – 88697318871 | WE STARTED NOTHING (LP, red vinyl) | 20 |

## TINGA (STEWART) & ERNIE (WILSON)
| | | | |
|---|---|---|---|
| 69 | Explosion EX 2009 | She's Gone/Old Old Song | 8 |

## TIN KAN
| | | | |
|---|---|---|---|
| 79 | White Dove WD103A | A Thousand Miles Of White/Girl I'd Never Let You Down | 10 |

## TINKERBELL'S FAIRYDUST
| | | | |
|---|---|---|---|
| 67 | Decca F 12705 | Lazy Day/In My Magic Garden | 70 |
| 68 | Decca F 12778 | Twenty Ten/Walking My Baby | 80 |
| 69 | Decca F 12865 | Sheila's Back In Town/Follow Me Follow | 100 |
| 69 | Decca LK/SKL 5028 | TINKERBELL'S FAIRYDUST (LP, unreleased; finished copies in laminated front sleeve with mono/stereo 'peephole' on rear, machine etched matrix number, blue/silver label with large unboxed Decca logo) | 3000 |
| 69 | Decca LK/SKL 5028 | TINKERBELL'S FAIRYDUST (LP, unreleased; test pressings in sleeve) | 1000 |

## BABS TINO
| | | | |
|---|---|---|---|
| 62 | London HLR 9589 | Forgive Me/If I Didn't Love You So Much | 30 |
| 63 | London RE-R 1377 | FORGIVE ME (EP) | 100 |

## TINOPENERS
| | | | |
|---|---|---|---|
| 79 | Logo GO 375 | Set Me Free/I'm Not Your Type | 150 |

## TIN PAN SKIFFLE GROUP
| | | | |
|---|---|---|---|
| 57 | Nestles NR 06 | Poor Howard (1-sided card flexi 78) | 12 |

**TINS**
| | | | |
|---|---|---|---|
| 79 | Quest BR 001 | There Is No Steel/Working For The Corporation | 20 |

**TINSLEY**
| | | | |
|---|---|---|---|
| 71 | Pye 7N45057 | My Brother Mary/Situation Vacant | 6 |

**MICK TINSLEY**
| | | | |
|---|---|---|---|
| 67 | Decca F 12544 | Let It Be Me/How're You Gonna Tell Me | 6 |

*(see also Hedgehoppers Anonymous)*

**TIN SOLDIERS**
| | | | |
|---|---|---|---|
| 82 | Spanking SPANK2 | Tin Soldiers/Cuckoo In The Nest (p/s) | 10 |
| 93 | Detour DR 002 | A New Beat/Girlfriend/Get Up And Go! (p/s, insert 1,000, only 100 on clear vinyl) | 12 |

**TINTERN ABBEY**
| | | | |
|---|---|---|---|
| 67 | Deram DM 164 | Beeside/Vacuum Cleaner | 1000 |

**TIN TIN**
| | | | |
|---|---|---|---|
| 69 | Polydor 56332 | Only Ladies Play Croquet/He Wants To Be A Star | 10 |
| 70 | Polydor 2058 023 | Toast And Marmalade For Tea/Manhattan Woman | 12 |
| 70 | Polydor 2058 076 | Come On Over Again/Back To Winona | 10 |
| 71 | Polydor 2001 146 | Shana/Rocky Mountain | 10 |
| 71 | Polydor 2058 114 | Is That The Way/Swans On The Canal | 10 |
| 72 | Polydor 2058 232 | Toast And Marmalade For Tea/Cavalry's Coming/Ships On The Starboard | 10 |
| 72 | Polydor 2058 238 | Talking Turkey/Cavalry's Coming | 10 |
| 69 | Polydor 2384 011 | TIN TIN (LP) | 25 |
| 72 | Polydor 2382 080 | ASTRAL TAXI (LP) | 20 |

*(see also Steve & Stevie)*

**TINY ALICE**
| | | | |
|---|---|---|---|
| 72 | Kama Sutra 2013 043 | Doctor Jazz/The Chocolate Dandies Of 1932/15¢ Hamburger Mama | 5 |

**TINY TIM**
| | | | |
|---|---|---|---|
| 68 | Reprise RS 20769 | Hello Hello/The Other Side | 10 |

**TINY TOPSY (& CHARMS)**
| | | | |
|---|---|---|---|
| 58 | Parlophone R 4397 | Come On, Come On, Come On/A Ring Around My Finger (with Charms) | 80 |
| 58 | Parlophone R 4397 | Come On, Come On, Come On/A Ring Around My Finger (with Charms) (78) | 25 |
| 58 | Parlophone R 4427 | You Shocked Me/Waterproof Eyes (solo) | 100 |
| 58 | Parlophone R 4427 | You Shocked Me/Waterproof Eyes (solo) (78) | 25 |
| 61 | Pye International 7N 25104 | After Marriage Blues/Working On Me Baby (solo) | 30 |

**DIMITRI TIOMKIN**
| | | | |
|---|---|---|---|
| 54 | Vogue Coral Q 2016 | The High And The Mighty/Dial M For Murder | 15 |

**KEITH TIPPETT**
| | | | |
|---|---|---|---|
| 69 | Polydor 2384 004 | YOU ARE HERE, I AM THERE (LP) | 100 |
| 71 | Vertigo 6360 024 | DEDICATED TO YOU BUT YOU WEREN'T LISTENING (LP, gatefold sleeve, large swirl label) | 175 |
| 72 | RCA SF 8290 | BLUEPRINT (LP) | 75 |
| 76 | Steam SJ 104 | TNT (LP, with Stan Tracey) | 15 |
| 77 | Vinyl VS 101 | WARM SPIRITS, COOL SPIRITS (LP) | 15 |
| 78 | Ogun OGD 003/4 | FRAMES (2-LP) | 30 |
| 78 | Ogun OGUN 003/004 | ARK (2-LP) | 35 |

*(see also Centipede, King Crimson, Ovary Lodge, Nicra)*

**JULIE TIPPETTS**
| | | | |
|---|---|---|---|
| 76 | Utopia UTS 601 | SUNSET GLOW (LP) | 22 |

*(see also Julie Driscoll, Brian Auger, Centipede, Keith Tippett, Elton Dean, Ninesense, Mark Charig)*

**TIPPIE & THE CLOVERS**
| | | | |
|---|---|---|---|
| 63 | Stateside SS 160 | My Heart Said/Bossa Nova Baby | 25 |

**LESTER TIPTON**
| | | | |
|---|---|---|---|
| 80 | Grapevine GRP 138 | This Won't Change/MASQUERADERS: How | 20 |

**TIP TOPS**
| | | | |
|---|---|---|---|
| 63 | Cameo Parkway P 868 | He's Braggin'/Oo-Kook-A-Boo | 35 |

**TÍR NA NOG**
| | | | |
|---|---|---|---|
| 72 | Chrysalis CHS 2001 | The Lady I Love/Heidi | 7 |
| 73 | Chrysalis CHS 2016 | Strong In The sun/The Mountain And I | 6 |
| 71 | Chrysalis ILPS 9153 | TÍR NA NOG (LP, laminated gatefold sleeve) | 25 |
| 72 | Chrysalis CHR 1006 | A TEAR AND A SMILE (LP, gatefold sleeve) | 20 |
| 73 | Chrysalis CHR 1047 | STRONG IN THE SUN (LP) | 15 |

**TITAN**
| | | | |
|---|---|---|---|
| 80 | Wild Dog DOG 26 | East Wind West Wind/Losing The Fight | 200 |
| 83 | After Hours AFT 09 | Imaginary Lady/Tooty Flutey | 30 |

**TITANIC**
| | | | |
|---|---|---|---|
| 72 | CBS 7278 | Sante Fe/Half Breed | 5 |
| 72 | CBS 8185 | Rain 2,000/Blond | 20 |
| 73 | CBS 1670 | Richmond Express/Heia Valenga | 5 |
| 71 | CBS 64104 | TITANIC (LP) | 20 |
| 72 | CBS 64791 | SEA WOLF (LP, gatefold sleeve) | 20 |
| 73 | CBS 65661 | EAGLE ROCK (LP, gatefold sleeve) | 15 |

**TITANS**
| | | | |
|---|---|---|---|
| 58 | London HLU 8609 | Don't You Just Know It/Can It Be | 80 |
| 58 | London HLU 8609 | Don't You Just Know It/Can It Be (78) | 35 |

**TITUS GROAN**
| | | | |
|---|---|---|---|
| 70 | Dawn DNX 2503 | Open The Door Homer/Woman Of The World/Liverpool (p/s) | 20 |
| 70 | Dawn DNLS 3012 | TITUS GROAN (LP, gatefold sleeve) | 350 |

## CAL TJADER
| 65 | Verve VS 529 | Soul Sauce/Naked City Theme | 50 |
| 65 | Verve VS 529 | Soul Sauce/Naked City Theme (DJ copy) | 80 |
| 58 | Vocalion LAE 556 | RITMO CALIENTE (LP, as Cal Tjader Quintet) | 20 |
| 62 | HMV/Verve CLP 1587 | IN A LATIN BAG (LP, as Cal Tjader Sextet, also stereo [CSD 1454]) | 15 |
| 65 | Vocalion LAE-F 599 | GREATEST HITS (LP) | 15 |
| 65 | Verve (S)VLP 9136 | SOUL BIRD: WHIFFENPOOF (LP) | 15 |
| 66 | Verve (S)VLP 9155 | SOUL BURST (LP) | 15 |
| 68 | Verve (S)VLP 9192 | THE BEST OF CAL TJADER (LP) | 15 |
| 68 | Verve (S)VLP 9215 | HIP VIBRATIONS (LP) | 20 |
| 61 | Vogue SEA 568 | CONCERT BY THE SEA (LP) | 15 |
| 60 | Vocalion LAE 560 | THE WEST SIDE STORY (LP) | 15 |

## TMR
| 92 | Pirate Club PCR 001 | Pirate Toon (Moose Mix)/Pirate Toon (Pirate Excursion)/Pirate Toon (Pirate Dub) (12", white stamped label) | 60 |

## T.N.T.
| 72 | Jam JAM 4 | Big Trouble (Part One)/Big Trouble (Part Two) | 40 |

## TNT
| 84 | Neat NEAT 39 | Back On The Road/Rockin' The Night (p/s) | 12 |

## TOAD
| 72 | RCA Victor SF 8241 | TOAD (LP) | 200 |

## TOAD THE WET SPROCKET
| 79 | Sprockets BRS 004 | Pete's Punk Song/Feel It (fold out p/s) | 45 |
| 80 | Sprockets BRS 008 | Reaching For The Sky/One Glass Of Whiskey (foldout stapled p/s) | 70 |

## TOAST
| 70 | CBS 4768 | Flowers Never Bend With The Rainfall/Summer Of Miranda | 10 |

## TOASTERS
| 87 | Unicorn PHZA-5 | POOL SHARK (LP) | 18 |
| 90 | Unicorn PHZA-60 | FRANKENSKA (LP) | 15 |

## TOBA
| 82 | Connection CONT 8203 | Moving Up/Moving Up (Instrumental) (12", red or blue vinyl) | 30 |

## RUTH TOBI
| 69 | Concord CON 002 | Lazy/That's When I Cry | 5 |

## AMON TOBIN
| 94 | Ninja Tune Zen 48 | SUPERMODIFIED (2-LP) | 30 |
| 97 | Ninja Tune ZEN 29 | BRICOLAGE (2-LP, gatefold sleeve) | 25 |
| 98 | Ninja Tune ZEN 36 | PERMUTATION (2-LP) | 35 |
| 02 | Ninja Tune ZEN 70 | OUT FROM NOWHERE (2-LP) | 18 |

## TOBRUK
| 83 | Neat NEAT 32 | Wild On The Run/The Show Must Go On (p/s) | 8 |
| 85 | Parlophone 12R 6093 | Falling/Like Lightning/Under The Gun (12", p/s) | 10 |
| 85 | Parlophone R 6101 | On The Rebound/Poor Girl (p/s) | 10 |
| 88 | FM WKFMLP 105 | PLEASURE AND PAIN (LP) | 15 |

## TOBY JUG
| 69 | private pressing | GREASY QUIFF (LP, with insert) | 150 |

## TOBY TWIRL
| 68 | Decca F 12728 | Harry Faversham/Back In Time | 30 |
| 68 | Decca F 12804 | Toffee Apple Sunday/Romeo And Juliet 1968 | 300 |
| 69 | Decca F 12867 | Movin' In/Utopia Daydream | 40 |

*(see also Shades Of Blue)*

## TODAY'S WITNESS
| 72 | Emblem JDR 345 | TODAY'S WITNESS (LP) | 35 |

## ART & DOTTY TODD
| 58 | London HLB 8620 | Chanson D'Amour (Song Of Love)/Along The Trail With You | 18 |
| 59 | London HLN 8838 | Straight As An Arrow/Stand There, Mountain | 18 |

## DIANE TODD
| 58 | Decca F 10993 | It's A Wonderful Thing To Be Loved/You Are My Favourite Dream | 8 |

## GARY TODD & ROGER TURNER
| 79 | Incus INCUS 79 | SUNDAY BEST (LP) | 50 |

## NICK TODD
| 57 | London HLD 8500 | Plaything/The Honey Song | 40 |
| 58 | London HLD 8537 | At The Hop/I Do | 15 |
| 59 | London HLD 8902 | Tiger/Twice As Nice | 30 |

## PATSY TODD
| 66 | Doctor Bird DB 1086 | Pitta Patta Rocky Steady (with Count Ossie)/COUNT OSSIE: Nyah Bongo | 40 |
| 68 | High Note HS 007 | Fire In Your Wire/AL & VIBRATORS: Move Up Calypso | 15 |
| 69 | High Note HS 012 | We Were Lovers/Give Me A Chance (B-side with Delano Stewart) | 40 |

*(see also Patsy, Stranger & Patsy, Derrick & Patsy)*

## SHARKEY TODD & MONSTERS
| 59 | Parlophone R 4536 | Cool Gool/The Horror Show | 25 |
| 59 | Parlophone R 4536 | Cool Gool/The Horror Show (78) | 20 |

*(see also Wally Whyton, Vipers [Skiffle Group])*

## TONY TODD
| 83 | Crash CRA 504 | You're Breaking My Heart/Waiting For Love | 12 |

## WILF TODD COMBO
| 64 | Blue Beat BB 240 | He Took Her Away/Have You Ever Been Lonely | 12 |

**WILF TODD & HIS MUSIC**
66   Oak WT 101                          WILF TODD AND HIS MUSIC (LP) ................................................................ 15

**TOE-FAT**
70   Parlophone R 5829                   Working Nights/Bad Side Of The Moon .......................................... 15
72   Chapter One SCH 175                 Brand New Band/Can't Live Without You ...................................... 10
70   Parlophone PCS 7097                 TOE-FAT (LP, black/silver label with boxed logo) ..................... 175
70   Regal Zono. SLRZ 1015               TOE-FAT TWO (LP, red/silver label) ............................................ 175
*(see also Uriah Heep, Glass Menagerie)*

**TOGETHER (1)**
68   Columbia DB 8491                    Henry's Coming Home/Love Mum And Dad .................................. 70
69   Aurora 4278                         Memories Of Melinda/Good Morning World .................................. 50
*(see also Keith Relf)*

**TOGETHER (2)**
90   Thumbs Up Magic GH 001              Hardcore Uproar (12", white label) ............................................ 250
91   Thumbs Up Magic TUM002              The Luv Bug (12") ......................................................................... 70
92   Thumbs Up Magic GH003               The House Sound Vol 2/Coming On Strong (12", with CYBERTEC) ..... 60

**TOGGERY FIVE**
64   Parlophone R 5175                   Bye Bye Bird/I'm Gonna Jump ..................................................... 50
65   Parlophone R 5249                   I'd Much Rather Be With The Boys/It's So Easy ......................... 40

**TOKALON**
81   EDM Champagne BUBL 701   Coming To Get You/Dance Version ............................................ 10

**TOKENS**
61   Parlophone R 4790                   Tonight I Fell In Love/I Love My Baby .......................................... 30
62   RCA RCA 1313                        I'll Do My Crying Tomorrow/Dream Angel Goodnight ................ 10
62   RCA RCA 1322                        Wishing/A Bird Flies Out Of Sight ................................................. 6
64   Fontana TF 500                      He's In Town/Oh Kathy ................................................................ 10
62   RCA RD 27256                        THE LION SLEEPS TONIGHT (LP, mono) ..................................... 30
62   RCA SF 5128                         THE LION SLEEPS TONIGHT (LP, stereo) ..................................... 35
62   RCA RD 7535                         WE THE TOKENS SING FOLK (LP) ................................................ 18
*(see also We Ugly Dogs, Cross Country)*

**TOKYO BLADE**
83   Powerstation OHM 2                  Powergame/Death On Main Street (p/s) ....................................... 8
85   Powerstation LEG 1T                 THE CAVE SESSIONS (12" EP) ...................................................... 15
85   Tokyo Blade TBR 1                   BLACKHEARTS AND JADED SPADES (LP, gatefold sleeve) ......... 15

**TOKYO OLYMPICS**
83   Ritz 031                            Shot By Love (Part 1)/(Part 2) (p/s) ............................................... 5
83   Ritz 050                            Radio (Turns Her On)/(Mix Version) (p/s) ...................................... 5
83   Polydor 2078 143                    One Step From Paradise/Paradise Disco Mix (p/s, Ireland-only) ......... 5
*(see also Rossi & Frost)*

**TOKYO ROSE**
83   Guardian GRC 270                    Dry Your Eyes/This Is Tokyo Rose (p/s) ..................................... 40

**ISRAEL 'POPPER STOPPER' TOLBERT**
70   Stax STAX 157                       Big Leg Woman/I Got Love ............................................................ 7
71   Stax 2362 020                       POPPER STOPPER (LP) ................................................................. 18

**TOLL**
86   Broken Flag BF V7                   CHRIST KNOWS (LP, featuring Tim Gane) .................................. 20
*(see also Ramleh, McCarthy)*

**TOM & JERRIO**
65   HMV POP 1435                        Boo-Ga-Loo/Boomerang ............................................................. 30

**TOM & JERRY**
59   Gala GSP 806                        Baby Talk/PAUL SHELDON: Thank You Pretty Baby (picture labels) ..... 45
63   Pye International 7N 25202          I'm Lonesome/Looking At You ..................................................... 95
*(see also Simon & Garfunkel)*

**TOM & JERRY (CARTOON CHARACTERS)**
58   MGM MGM-EP 688                      JOHANN MOUSE (EP) .................................................................. 15

**TOM & MICK**
69   Olga OLE 014                        Somebody's Taken Maria Away/Pandemonium .......................... 15

**ROLO TOMASSI**
07   Danger! Laser! Phaser!              ROLO TOMASSI (EP, 1000 only, blue vinyl) ............................... 20
     Razor! DLPR 003

**TOM CATS**
61   Starlite ST45 054                   Tom Tom Cat/Big Brother ............................................................ 25

**GARY TOMS EMPIRE**
75   Epic S EPC 3611                     Drive My Car/Love Me Right ........................................................ 12

**TOMITA**
77   RCA Red Seal RL1 1919              THE TOMITA PLANETS SUITE (LP, withdrawn after 1 day) .......... 15

**LEE TOMLIN**
66   CBS 202455                          Sweet Sweet Lovin'/Save Me ...................................................... 10

**ALAN TOMLINSON**
81   Bead Records BEAD 17               STILL OUTSIDE (LP) ..................................................................... 25

**ALBERT TOMLINSON**
68   Giant GN 28                         Don't Wait For Me/LLOYD EVANS: Losing You ........................ 300

**ROY TOMLINSON**
68   Coxsone CS 7056                     I Stand For I/MARTIN: I Second That Emotion (actually by Martin Riley) ..... 150

**TOMMI & THE SPELLBINDERS**
76   Target TQT 107                      I Can't Get Away From You/Love Bandit ................................... 10

MINT VALUE £

## TOMMY (COWAN)
72  Dynamic DYN 433           Geraldine/Reverend Leroy ...........................................................5

*(see also Jamaicans)*

## TOMMY (MCCOOK) & UPSETTERS
69  Trojan TR 7717            Lock Jaw (actually by Dave Barker)/YARDBROOMS: My Desire ...........15

*(see also Tommy McCook, Upsetters)*

## TOMORROW
67  Parlophone R 5597         My White Bicycle/Claramont Lake...............................................70
67  Parlophone R 5627         Revolution/Three Jolly Little Dwarfs............................................70
69  Parlophone R 5813         My White Bicycle/Claramont Lake (reissue) ...............................50
68  Parlophone PMC            TOMORROW (LP, mono, yellow/black label with "Sold in U.K..." text) .......300
68  Parlophone PCS 7042       TOMORROW (LP, stereo, yellow/black label with "Sold in U.K..." text) .......200
76  Harvest SHSM 2010         TOMORROW (LP, reissue) ..........................................................30
86  Decal LIK 2               TOMORROW (LP, reissue) ..........................................................15

*(see also Keith West, Steve Howe, Twink, Four + One, In Crowd, Syndicats, Aquarian Age, Fairies)*

## TOMORROW COME SOME DAY
69  SNB 97                    TOMORROW COME SOME DAY (LP) ................................................900

*(see also Ithaca, Friends, Agincourt, Alice Through The Looking Glass, BBC Radiophonic Workshop/Peter Howell)*

## TOMORROW'S CHILDREN
70  Plexium PXM 17            You're My Baby/Maybe Today.......................................................5
71  Plexium PXM 25            Sing A Song/Don't Believe...........................................................5
71  Plexium PXM 26            Keep A Little Love In Your Life/My Way Of Living............................5
72  Plexium PXM 31            We Can Make Funtime/If It Could Be...........................................5

## TOMORROW'S CHILDREN (JAMAICA)
67  Island WI 3073            Bang Bang Rock Steady/Rain Rock Steady (some w/same label on both sides)...........250

## TOMPALL & GLASER BROTHERS
68  MGM MGM-C 8082            THROUGH THE EYES OF LOVE (LP) ..............................................25

## TOM TOM CLUB
81  Island ILPS 9686          TOM TOM CLUB (LP)..................................................................20

*(see also Talking Heads)*

## TONE DEAF & THE IDIOTS
79  Lyntone BLI 1/Angel BL 12 Why Does Politics Turn Men Into Toads/Repatriate The National Front (flexi) ......15

*(see also Idiots)*

## ELEANOR TONER
65  Decca F 12119            All Cried Out/A Hundred Guitars ..................................................8
65  Decca F 12192            Will You Still Love Me Tomorrow/Between The Window And The Phone .......15
65  Decca F 12267            Danny Boy/It Hurts So Much (To See You Go) ................................6
66  Decca F 12454            Black Rose/Time To Spare Darling ...............................................6

## TONES ON TAIL
82  4AD BAD 203              A Bigger Splash/Means Of Escape/Copper/Instrumental (12", p/s) ......10
84  Beggars Banquet BEG 109T Lions/Go! (Club Mix) (12", p/s red vinyl) ....................................10

*(see also Bauhaus, Love & Rockets)*

## TONETTES
62  Island WI 064            Love That Is Real/Pretty Baby......................................................12

*(see also Marlene Webber, Lyrics, Don Drummond)*

## OSCAR TONEY JR.
67  Stateside SS 2033        For Your Precious Love/Ain't That True Love..................................20
67  Stateside SS 2033        For Your Precious Love/Ain't That True Love (DJ Copy) ....................50
67  Stateside SS 2046        Turn On Your Love Light/Any Day Now .........................................20
67  Stateside SS 2061        You Can Lead Your Woman To The Altar/Unlucky Guy ....................20
68  Bell BLL 1003            Without Love There Is Nothing/Love That Never Grows Cold ...........10
68  Bell BLL 1011            No Sad Songs/Never Get Enough Of Your Love ..............................10
69  Bell BLL 1057            Down In Texas/Just For You ........................................................10
72  Capricorn K 17505        Thank You, Honey Chile/I Do What You Wish ..................................6
73  Contempo C 6             Kentucky Bluebird/Everything I Own ............................................6
73  Contempo CS2075          Chicken Heads/Everybody's Needed ............................................15
74  Contempo CS 2002         Is It Because I'm Black/Make It Easy On Yourself ...........................10
75  Contempo CS 2043         I've Been Loving You Too Long/For Your Precious Love ....................6
67  Stateside (S)SL 10211    FOR YOUR PRECIOUS LOVE (LP) ..................................................40

## TONGUE & GROOVE
69  Fontana STL 5528         TONGUE & GROOVE (LP) ............................................................45

*(see also Charlatans)*

## TONIGHT
78  TDS 1                    Drummerman/Stroll On By (p/s) ....................................................8
78  TDS 2                    Money, That's Your Problem/No Sympathy (p/s) ...............................5
78  TDS 4                    Wheels/I Can Play Faster Than You Can (p/s).................................5
78  TDS 5                    Jealousy Kills/Second Hand Man .................................................5

*(see also Andy Arthurs, Celia & Mutations)*

## TERRY TONIK
80  Posh TOFF 1              Just A Little Mod/Smashed And Blocked (some with die-cut p/s) ...........110
80  Posh TOFF 1              Just A Little Mod/Smashed And Blocked (with die-cut p/s, promo A4 booklet)............70
80  Posh TOFF 1              Just A Little Mod/Smashed And Blocked .......................................30

## TONTO
74  Polydor 2383 308         IT'S ABOUT TIME (LP, insert, poster)............................................20

*(see also Tonto's Expanding Head Band)*

## TONTON (MACOUTE)
72  RCA 2190                 Summer Of Our Love/Greyhound Lady (as Tonton)...........................20

| | | | |
|---|---|---|---|
| 71 | RCA Neon NE 4 | TONTON MACOUTE (LP, gatefold sleeve, black inner) | 250 |

## TONTO'S EXPANDING HEAD BAND
| | | | |
|---|---|---|---|
| 71 | Atlantic 2400 150 | ZERO TIME (LP, gatefold sleeve) | 25 |

*(see also Tonto)*

## TONTRIX
| | | | |
|---|---|---|---|
| 79 | Townton 1TON | Shell Shocked/Slipping Into Life (p/s) | 5 |

## TONY & CHAMPIONS
| | | | |
|---|---|---|---|
| 70 | Duke DU 90 | Eye For An Eye/CHAMPIONS: Broke My Heart - Version | 20 |

*(see also Errol & Champions, Domino Johnson)*

## TONY & DENNIS
| | | | |
|---|---|---|---|
| 67 | Trojan TR 002 | Folk Song/TOMMY McCOOK & SUPERSONICS: Starry Night | 35 |

## TONY FIELD
| | | | |
|---|---|---|---|
| 66 | Pye 7N 17020 | Dale Ann/Dial My Number | 10 |

## TONY & GRADUATES
| | | | |
|---|---|---|---|
| 60s | Hit HIT 13 | The Statue | 50 |
| 68 | Pye 7N 17578 | I Wanna Live/Angel | 10 |
| 66 | Pye 7N 17077 | Just My Baby And Me/Another You | 10 |

## TONY & HIPPY BOYS
| | | | |
|---|---|---|---|
| 69 | Gas GAS 121 | Oh Janet/HARMONIANS: Believe Me (states 'Beleive' on label) | 30 |

## TONY & HOWARD WITH DICTATORS
| | | | |
|---|---|---|---|
| 65 | Oriole CB 307 | Just In Case/Walk Right Out Of The Blues | 30 |

## TONY & HOWIE
| | | | |
|---|---|---|---|
| 72 | Banana BA 371 | Fun It Up/Fun Version | 100 |

## TONY & JOE
| | | | |
|---|---|---|---|
| 58 | London HLN 8694 | The Freeze/Gonna Get A Little Kissin' Tonight | 40 |
| 58 | London HLN 8694 | The Freeze/Gonna Get A Little Kissin' Tonight (78) | 25 |

## TONY (TOMAS) & LOUISE
| | | | |
|---|---|---|---|
| 62 | Island WI 059 | Ups And Downs/TONY TOMAS: Brixton Lewisham | 12 |

*(see also Tony Washington)*

## TONY & TANDY
| | | | |
|---|---|---|---|
| 69 | Atlantic 584 262 | Two Can Make It Together/The Bitter And The Sweet (with Fleur De Lys) | 20 |
| 71 | Atlantic 2091 075 | Two Can Make It Together/Look And Find | 8 |

*(see also Sharon Tandy, Fleur De Lys)*

## TONY & THE VELVETS
| | | | |
|---|---|---|---|
| 63 | Decca F 11637 | Sunday/One More Once | 10 |

## TONY & TYRONE
| | | | |
|---|---|---|---|
| 70 | Ember EMBS 290 | Everyday Fun/Whip Your Loving On Me (p/s) | 10 |
| 75 | Atlantic K10617 | Please Operator/Apple Of My Eye | 8 |

## TONY, CARO & JOHN
| | | | |
|---|---|---|---|
| 72 | private pressing | ALL ON THE FIRST DAY (LP, with insert) | 300 |

## TONY'S ALLSTARS
| | | | |
|---|---|---|---|
| 72 | Green Door GD 4041 | Rub Up A Daughter/DENNIS ALCAPONE: Daughter Version | 15 |
| 72 | Bullet BU 509 | Dub Up A Daughter (as Prince Tony's Allstars)/ DENNIS ALCAPONE: Daughter Version | 8 |
| 72 | Big Shot BI 601 | Must Care/L. SPARKS: You Don't Care | 6 |
| 73 | Downtown DT 508 | You Don't Say/DENNIS ALCAPONE: Version | 12 |

## TONY'S DEFENDERS
| | | | |
|---|---|---|---|
| 66 | Columbia DB 7850 | Yes I Do/It's Easy To Say Hello | 35 |
| 66 | Columbia DB 7996 | Since I Lost You Baby/Waiting For A Call From You | 35 |

## TOO FUNK
| | | | |
|---|---|---|---|
| 95 | Ferox FER 008 | THE RETURN OF TOO FUNK (12" EP) | 15 |

## TOOL
| | | | |
|---|---|---|---|
| 94 | Zoo-RCA 74321 19432-1 | Prison Sex (LP Version)/Prison Sex (Edit Version)/Opiate (Live)/Undertow (Live) (12", grey vinyl) | 30 |

## TOOLS
| | | | |
|---|---|---|---|
| 79 | Oily SLICK 2 | Gotta Make Some Money Somehow/TV Eyes (p/s) | 8 |

## TOOMORROW
| | | | |
|---|---|---|---|
| 70 | RCA RCA 1978 | You're My Baby Now/Goin' Back (in custom RCA sleeve) | 60 |
| 70 | Decca F 13070 | I Could Never Live Without Your Love/Roll Like A River | 60 |
| 70 | RCA LSA 3008 | TOOMORROW (LP, soundtrack, with insert) | 100 |

*(see also Olivia Newton-John)*

## TOO MUCH
| | | | |
|---|---|---|---|
| 78 | Lightning GIL 513 | Who You Wanna Be/Another Time Another Place (in p/s) | 35 |
| 78 | Lightning GIL 513 | Who You Wanna Be/Another Time Another Place | 10 |
| 78 | Lightning GIL 552 | Kick Me One More Time//Be Mine/It's Only For Me (gatefold p/s) | 30 |

## DAVID TOOP
| | | | |
|---|---|---|---|
| 75 | Obscure OBS 4 | NEW AND REDISCOVERED MUSICAL INSTRUMENTS (LP, with Max Eastley & Brian Eno) | 25 |
| 79 | Quartz 003 | WOUNDS (LP, with Paul Burwell) | 30 |

*(see also Brian Eno)*

## TOOTS (ACTUALLY LEE PERRY)
| | | | |
|---|---|---|---|
| 70 | Upsetter US 327 | Do You Like It/UPSETTERS: Touch Of Fire | 35 |

## TOPO D. BILL
| | | | |
|---|---|---|---|
| 70 | Charisma CB 116 | Witchi Tai To/Jam (in p/s) | 20 |
| 70 | Charisma CB 116 | Witchi Tai To/Jam | 7 |

*(see also Bonzo Dog [Doo Dah] Band, Roger Ruskin Spear)*

## TOPPERS
| | | | |
|---|---|---|---|
| 57 | Brunswick 05678 | Stash Pandowski (She's Not Very Much Good For Pretty)/Pots And Pans | 6 |

MINT VALUE £

## TOPPICKS
| | | | |
|---|---|---|---|
| 78 | Basilick BVK 001 | Can't Let You Go/Version | 10 |

## TOP SECRET
| | | | |
|---|---|---|---|
| 81 | Cheapskate CHEAP 35 | She's So Ugly/I Love Me (no p/s) | 5 |

## TOP TOPHAM
| | | | |
|---|---|---|---|
| 69 | Blue Horizon 57-3167 | Christmas Cracker/Cracking Up Over Christmas | 25 |
| 70 | Blue Horizon 7-63857 | ASCENSION HEIGHTS (LP) | 120 |

*(see also Fox, Yardbirds)*

## TORA TORA
| | | | |
|---|---|---|---|
| 80 | Mancunian Metal TT 5000 | Red Sun Setting/Highway (Shooting Like A Bullet) (p/s) | 15 |
| 80 | Tora TT 5001 | Don't Want To Let You Go/Sorry I Broke Your Heart | 40 |

## TORCH
| | | | |
|---|---|---|---|
| 82 | Ted TED 1 | I Need Rock/Unknown (no p/s) | 35 |

## STEVE TORCH
| | | | |
|---|---|---|---|
| 79 | Redball RR 005 | Live In Fear/Smoke Your Own (p/s) | 10 |

*(see also Gillan, Split Knee Loons, Girl)*

## (BERNIE) TORMÉ (BAND)
| | | | |
|---|---|---|---|
| 78 | Jet JET 126 | I'm Not Ready/Free (p/s, as Bernie Tormé Band, orange vinyl) | 6 |
| 78 | Jet JET 126 | I'm Not Ready/Free (p/s, as Bernie Tormé Band, black vinyl) | 5 |
| 79 | Jet JET 137 | Weekend/Secret Service/All Night/Instant Impact (as Bernie Tormé Band, p/s) | 5 |
| 70s | Peter Collins PC 1 | The Hunter/Soul Sister | 8 |
| 80 | Island WIP 6586 | The Beat/I Want/Bony Maronie (p/s, pink vinyl, promos on black vinyl) | 8 |
| 81 | Fresh FRESH 7 | All Day And All Of The Night/What's Next (p/s, also listed as Parole PURL 5) | 12 |

## MEL TORME (& MEL-TONES)
### SINGLES
| | | | |
|---|---|---|---|
| 56 | Vogue Coral Q 72150 | Mountain Greenery/Jeepers Creepers | 10 |
| 56 | Vogue Coral Q 72159 | Blue Moon/That Old Black Magic | 5 |
| 56 | Vogue Coral Q 72185 | Love Is Here To Stay/Goody Goody | 5 |
| 56 | London HLN 8305 | Lulu's Back In Town/The Lady Is A Tramp | 10 |
| 56 | London HLN 8322 | Lullaby Of Birdland/I Love To Watch The Moonlight | 7 |
| 56 | Vogue Coral Q 72202 | All Of You/It Don't Mean A Thing | 5 |
| 56 | Decca F 10800 | Walkin' Shoes/The Cuckoo In The Clock (with Ted Heath & His Music) | 5 |
| 56 | Decca F 10809 | Waltz For Young Lovers/I Don't Want To Walk Without You | 5 |
| 57 | Vogue Coral Q 72217 | My Rosemarie/How (as Mel Torme & Mel-Tones) | 5 |
| 60 | Philips PB 1045 | The White Cliffs Of Dover/I've Got A Lovely Bunch Of Coconuts | 5 |
| 61 | HMV POP 859 | Blue Moon/The Moon Song | 5 |
| 61 | MGM MGM 1144 | The Christmas Song/Shine On Your Shoes | 5 |
| 62 | London HLK 9643 | Comin' Home Baby/Right Now | 20 |
| 62 | London HLK 9643 | Comin' Home Baby/Right Now (DJ copy) | 40 |
| 66 | CBS 202065 | (You Got) The Power Of Love/Dominique's Discotheque | 8 |

### EPs
| | | | |
|---|---|---|---|
| 58 | Philips BBE 12181 | TORME MEETS THE BRITISH (EP) | 12 |

### ALBUMS
| | | | |
|---|---|---|---|
| 57 | Philips BBL 7205 | TORME MEETS THE BRITISH | 20 |
| 63 | London HA-K/SH-K 8021 | MEL TORME AT THE RED HILL (with Jimmy Wisner Trio, mono/stereo) | 15 |
| 63 | London HA-K 8065 | COMIN' HOME BABY | 25 |

## TORNADOS
| | | | |
|---|---|---|---|
| 62 | Decca F 11449 | Love And Fury/Popeye Twist | 15 |
| 62 | Decca F 11494 | Telstar/Jungle Fever | 5 |
| 63 | Decca F 11562 | Globetrotter/Locomotion With Me (some B-sides credit "Locomotion With You") | 6 |
| 63 | Decca F 11606 | Robot/Life On Venus | 8 |
| 63 | Decca F 11662 | The Ice Cream Man/Theme From "The Scales Of Justice" | 8 |
| 63 | Decca F 11745 | Dragonfly/Hymn For Teenagers | 12 |
| 64 | Decca F 11838 | Hot Pot/Joystick | 10 |
| 64 | Decca F 11889 | Monte Carlo/Blue Blue Beat | 20 |
| 64 | Decca F 11946 | Exodus/Blackpool Rock | 20 |
| 65 | Columbia DB 7455 | Granada/Ragunboneman | 25 |
| 65 | Columbia DB 7589 | Early Bird/Stompin' Through The Rye (as Tornados '65) | 25 |
| 65 | Columbia DB 7687 | Stingray/Aqua Marina | 40 |
| 66 | Columbia DB 7856 | Pop-Art Goes Mozart/Too Much In Love To Hear | 30 |
| 66 | Columbia DB 7984 | Is That A Ship I Hear/Do You Come Here Often | 40 |
| 62 | Decca DFE 8510 | THE SOUNDS OF THE TORNADOS (EP) | 15 |
| 62 | Decca DFE 8511 | TELSTAR (EP) | 15 |
| 63 | Decca DFE 8521 | MORE SOUNDS FROM THE TORNADOS (EP) | 20 |
| 63 | Decca DFE 8533 | TORNADO ROCK (EP) | 25 |
| 63 | Decca LK 4552 | AWAY FROM IT ALL (LP) | 50 |
| 63 | London LL 3279 | TELSTAR - THE SOUND OF THE TORNADOS (LP, export copy, UK pressed LP in US sleeve) | 50 |

*(see also Heinz, Billy Fury, Clem Cattini Ork, Saints, Original Tornados, Roger LaVern & Microns, Saxons, George Bellamy, Gemini, Roger La Vern & Microns)*

## MITCHELL TOROK
| | | | |
|---|---|---|---|
| 54 | London HL 8004 | Caribbean/Weep Away (with Louisiana Hayride Band) (gold tri label) | 40 |
| 54 | London HL 8004 | Caribbean/Weep Away (with Louisiana Hayride Band) (round centre) | 20 |
| 54 | London HL 8048 | Hootchy Kootchy Henry (From Hawaii)/Gigolo | 50 |
| 54 | London HL 8083 | The Haunting Waterfall/Dancerette (with Louisiana Hayride Band) | 50 |
| 55 | Brunswick 05423 | The World Keeps Turning Around/A Peasant's Guitar | 15 |
| 56 | Brunswick 05586 | When Mexico Gave Up The Rhumba/I Wish I Was A Little Bit Younger | 25 |

| | | |
|---|---|---|
| 56 | Brunswick 05626 | Red Light, Green Light (with Tulane Sisters)/Havana Huddle ......................... 25 |
| 57 | Brunswick 05642 | Drink Up And Go Home/Take This Heart ....................................................... 15 |
| 57 | Brunswick 05657 | Pledge Of Love/What's Behind That Strange Door ...................................... 15 |
| 57 | Brunswick 05718 | Two Words (True Love)/You're Tempting Me (with Anita Kerr Quartet) ......... 10 |
| 60 | London HLW 9130 | Pink Chiffon/What You Don't Know (Won't Hurt You) .................................. 12 |
| 54 | London RE-P 1014 | LOUISIANA HAYRIDE (EP, with Louisiana Hayride Band) ............................... 20 |
| 60 | London HA-W 2279 | CARIBBEAN (LP) ......................................................................................... 30 |

## MICHELLE TORR
| | | |
|---|---|---|
| 66 | Fontana TF 676 | Only Tears Are Left For Me/I Love That Man ............................................... 15 |
| 77 | Sonet SON 2104 | I'm Just A Simple Country Girl From France/Une Petite Française (p/s)............ 5 |

## DONALD TORR
| | | |
|---|---|---|
| 69 | CBS 4383 | My Cherie Amour/Never Will I Be .............................................................. 20 |
| 70 | CBS 4769 | Way Of The World/Green Green Yesterday................................................... 10 |

## GEORGE TORRENCE & NATURALS
| | | |
|---|---|---|
| 68 | London HLZ 10181 | Lickin' Stick/So Long Goodbye .................................................................. 15 |
| 71 | Jay Boy BOY 48 | Lickin' Stick/So Long Goodbye (reissue) ....................................................... 6 |

## CLARE TORRY
| | | |
|---|---|---|
| 67 | Fontana TF 852 | The Music Attracts Me/It Takes One To Make The Other Cry (as Claire Terry)......... 6 |
| 67 | Fontana TF 878 | Unsure Feelings/The End Of A Lifetime (as Claire Terry)................................. 6 |
| 69 | Decca F 12945 | Love For Living/Love Tomorrow, Love Today (as Clare Torry)......................... 6 |

## TORTOISE
| | | |
|---|---|---|
| 96 | Duophonic D-UHF-D 12 | Yaus/STEREOLAB: Speedy Car (gig freebie, blue vinyl, p/s, 3,000 only) ......... 15 |
| 96 | Duophonic D-UHF-D 12 | Yaus/STEREOLAB: Speedy Car (orange vinyl export issue, p/s, 3,000 only) ..... 15 |
| 01 | Duophonic Super 45s DS 33 09 | Gamera/Cliff Dweller Society (12", 1500 on red vinyl, 1500 on clear vinyl, 1500 on black vinyl) ................................................................................. 15 |
| 01 | Duophonic Super 45s DS 33 09 | Gamera/Cliff Dweller Society (12", 1000 on fluorescent yellow vinyl) ............ 20 |
| 96 | City Slang EFA 04971 | RHYTHMS, RESOLUTIONS & CLUSTERS (LP, clear vinyl)................................ 30 |
| 98 | City Slang EFA 08705-1 | TNT (2-LP, gatefold sleeve) ...................................................................... 40 |
| 00 | Warp WARPLP 81 | STANDARDS (LP)........................................................................................ 20 |

*(see also Sea & Cake)*

## TORTURE
| | | |
|---|---|---|
| 81 | Wildebeest WILD 1 | Last Post/Lucky/Finding My Way Home ...................................................... 50 |

## PETER TOSH
| | | |
|---|---|---|
| 69 | Unity UN 525 | The Return Of Al Capone/LENNEX BROWN: O Club (B-side actually by Lennon Brown). 25 |
| 69 | Unity UN 529 | Sun Valley (as Peter Touch)/HE(A)DLEY BENNETT: Drums Of Fu Manchu....................... 25 |
| 70 | No label T 1023 | No Sympathy/Boy Named Tom (actually Soulettes) (white label only) ............ 40 |
| 71 | Bullet BU 486 | Maga Dog/THIRD & FOURTH GENERATION: Bull Dog.................................. 12 |
| 72 | Pressure Beat PR 5509 | Them A Fe Get A Beatin' (as Peter Touch)/ THIRD & FOURTH GENERATION: Version..... 18 |
| 79 | Rolling Stones RSR 103 | I'm The Toughest/Toughest Version (p/s) ..................................................... 5 |
| 79 | Rolling Stones RSR 104 | Buck In Hamm Palace/The Day The Dollar Die ............................................... 5 |
| 76 | Virgin V 2061 | LEGALIZE IT (LP)....................................................................................... 15 |
| 77 | Virgin V 2081 | EQUAL RIGHTS (LP, red "mirror" girl sleeve)................................................ 15 |

*(see also Peter Touch, Bob Marley & Wailers, Cat & Nicky Campbell, Glen Adams)*

## TOTAL CHAOS
| | | |
|---|---|---|
| 82 | Volume VOL 1 | There Are No Russians In Afghanistan/Primitive Feeling/ Revolution Part 10 (p/s, lyric insert, original copies have "50p" onl front) ................................................ 20 |
| 83 | Volume VOL 2 | Factory Man/Brixton Prison/She Don't Care/Die (p/s) ..................................... 7 |
| 83 | Volume VOLM 6 | FIELDS AND BOMBS EP(12") ...................................................................... 15 |

## TOTAL CONTRAST
| | | |
|---|---|---|
| 84 | Total Contrast TCR 2 | Next Time I'll Know Better/Sunshine (12") ................................................... 35 |

## TOTAL FIASCO
| | | |
|---|---|---|
| 89 | White TF001 | See How They Run/Method To The Madness ................................................ 75 |

*(see also Killa Instinct)*

## TOTAL OUTPUT AND KILLERHERTZ
| | | |
|---|---|---|
| 92 | FX FXUKT 11 | Acid Mind/Monolithic/Analog Xpression/Digital Kiss (12") .......................... 12 |

*(see also Killerhertz)*

## TOTALLY OUTTA HAND BAND
| | | |
|---|---|---|
| 78 | Kilgaron KIL 1 | Teenage Revolution/Too Much Trouble By Far (p/s).......................................... 8 |

## TO THE FINLAND STATION
| | | |
|---|---|---|
| 81 | Melodia | DOMINO THEORY (7" EP) ............................................................................ 6 |

## TOTNAMITES
| | | |
|---|---|---|
| 61 | Oriole CB 1615 | Danny Boy/The Spurs Song ....................................................................... 15 |

## TOTO
| | | |
|---|---|---|
| 84 | Polydor 422 8237-7 | DUNE (LP, soundtrack, 1 track by Brian Eno) ............................................. 15 |

## TOTS
| | | |
|---|---|---|
| 74 | Philips 6006 408 | Please Yourself/Time To Go Home (p/s) ........................................................ 7 |

## TINA TOTT
| | | |
|---|---|---|
| 69 | Pye 7N 17823 | Take Away The Emptiness Too/Burning In The Background Of My Mind ...................... 30 |

## TOTTENHAM HOTSPUR F.C.
| | | |
|---|---|---|
| 67 | Columbia SEG 8532 | THE SPURS GO MARCHING ON: SINGALONG SPURS (EP) ............................ 20 |

*(see also Terry Venables)*

## PETER TOUCH
| | | |
|---|---|---|
| 65 | Island WI 211 | Hoot Nanny Hoot (actually by Peter Tosh & Wailers)/ BOB MARLEY: Do You Remember (actually Peter Tosh & Wailers) ................................................ 125 |
| 65 | Island WI 215 | Shame And Scandal (with Wailers)/WAILERS: The Jerk ................................ 60 |
| 67 | Island WI 3042 | I Am The Toughest (actually by Peter Tosh & Wailers)/ MARCIA GRIFFITHS: No Faith.... 60 |
| 67 | Coxsone CS 7012 | Dancing Time/Treat Me Good ................................................................... 120 |

MINT VALUE £

| | | | |
|---|---|---|---|
| 69 | Jackpot JP 706 | The Crimson Pirate/Moon Duck | 20 |
| 69 | Unity UN 525 | Return Of A Capone/LENEX BROWN : Q Club | 25 |
| 69 | Unity 529 | Sun Valley/Headley Bennett - Drums Of Fu Man Chu | 20 |

*(see also Peter Tosh, Bop & The Beltone, Glen Adams)*

## TOUCH (1)

| | | | |
|---|---|---|---|
| 69 | Deram DM 243 | Miss Teach/We Feel Fine | 12 |
| 69 | Deram DML/SML 1033 | THIS IS TOUCH (LP, with poster) | 200 |
| 69 | Deram DML/SML 1033 | THIS IS TOUCH (LP, without poster) | 100 |

*(see also Don & Goodtimes, Kingsmen)*

## TOUCH (2)

| | | | |
|---|---|---|---|
| 80 | Ariola ARO 209 | When The Spirit Moves You/My Life Depends On You (p/s) | 5 |
| 80 | Ariola ARO 243 | Don't You Know What Love Is/My Life Depends On You (in p/s) | 20 |
| 80 | Ariola ARO 243 | Don't You Know What Love Is/My Life Depends On You | 6 |
| 80 | Ariola ARO 250 | Love Don't Fail Me Now (p/s) | 6 |

## TOUCH (3)

| | | | |
|---|---|---|---|
| 88 | Touch 77:45 | Departing Platform 5/Touch Ritual (Radio Cut-Up) (p/s) | 5 |

## TOUCHDOWN

| | | | |
|---|---|---|---|
| 83 | Record Shack | Ease Your Mind (Remix)/Aquadance (12") | 15 |

## TOUCHED

| | | | |
|---|---|---|---|
| 84 | Ebony EBON 27 | Dream Girl/We'll Fight Back | 10 |

## ALI FARKA TOURE

| | | | |
|---|---|---|---|
| 87 | World Circuit WCB 007 | ALI FARKA TOURE (LP) | 20 |
| 94 | World Circuit WCB 040 | TALKING TIMBUKTU (LP) | 25 |

## TOURS

| | | | |
|---|---|---|---|
| 79 | Tours T 1 | Language School/Foreign Girls (paper p/s) | 20 |
| 79 | Tours T 1 | Language School/Foreign Girls (printed PVC sleeve) | 12 |
| 79 | Virgin VS 307 | Tourist Information/You Knew (p/s) | 8 |

## AL TOUSAN

| | | | |
|---|---|---|---|
| 61 | London HLU 9291 | Naomi/Indinna (some copies miscredited to 'Al Pousan') | 8 |

*(see also Allen Toussaint)*

## ALLEN TOUSSAINT

| | | | |
|---|---|---|---|
| 69 | Soul City SC 119 | We The People/Tequila | 25 |
| 72 | Reprise K 14200 | Soul Sister/She Once Belonged To Me | 6 |
| 72 | Reprise K 44202 | LIFE, LOVE AND FAITH (LP) | 22 |
| 85 | Kent KENT 036 | FROM A WHISPER TO A SCREAM (LP) | 15 |

*(see also Al Tousan)*

## CALINE & OLIVER TOUSSAINT

| | | | |
|---|---|---|---|
| 78 | Epic S EPC 6334 | The Gardens Of Monaco/Les Jardins De Monaco | 12 |

## ROBERTA TOVEY

| | | | |
|---|---|---|---|
| 65 | Polydor BM 56021 | Who's Who/Not So Old (in p/s) | 45 |
| 65 | Polydor BM 56021 | Who's Who/Not So Old | 25 |

## TOWER OF POWER

| | | | |
|---|---|---|---|
| 73 | Reprise K 16278 | So Very Hard To Go/Clean Slate | 8 |
| 73 | Reprise K 16211 | You're Still A Young Man/Skating On Thin Ice | 8 |
| 74 | Reprise K 16389 | Don't Change Horses/Time Will Tell | 5 |
| 75 | Reprise K 16543 | It's Not The Crime/Only So Much Time On The Ground | 8 |

## JOHN TOWERS

| | | | |
|---|---|---|---|
| 67 | CBS 2943 | Seasons Song/It's Spring Again | 10 |

## JOHNNY TOWERS

| | | | |
|---|---|---|---|
| 62 | Philips 326554 BF | The Lonely Man Theme/There's No Place Like Rome | 8 |
| 63 | Philips 326570 BF | This Kind Of Love/My First Romance | 7 |

## COLIN TOWNS

| | | | |
|---|---|---|---|
| 78 | Virgin VS 204 | Full Circle (Main Theme)/Olivia (p/s) | 10 |
| 80 | MCA MCA 643 | Breakdown/Working Man (p/s) | 15 |

*(see also Gillan, Samson, Split Knee Loons)*

## TOWNSEL SISTERS

| | | | |
|---|---|---|---|
| 60 | Polydor NH 66954 | Will I Ever/I Know | 12 |

## ED TOWNSEND (& TOWNSMEN)

| | | | |
|---|---|---|---|
| 58 | Capitol CL 14867 | For Your Love/Over And Over Again | 10 |
| 58 | Capitol CL 14927 | When I Grow Too Old To Dream/You Are My Everything | 10 |
| 59 | Capitol CL 14976 | Richer Than I/Getting By Without You | 7 |
| 59 | Capitol CL 15020 | Don't Ever Leave Me/Lover Come Back To Me | 7 |
| 59 | Capitol CL 15072 | This Little Love Of Mine/Hold On | 7 |
| 60 | Capitol CL 15141 | Don't Get Around Much Anymore/Do Nothin' Till You Hear | 7 |
| 60 | Warner Bros WB 21 | Stay With Me (A Little While Longer)/I Love Everything About You | 40 |
| 59 | Capitol EAP1 1091 | ED TOWNSEND (EP) | 20 |
| 59 | Capitol T 1140 | NEW IN TOWN (LP) | 25 |
| 76 | Curtom K 56180 | NOW (LP) | 20 |

## JOHN TOWNSEND

| | | | |
|---|---|---|---|
| 70s | Sweet Folk All SFA 002 | NO MUCKING ABOUT (LP) | 18 |

## PETE TOWNSHEND

| | | | |
|---|---|---|---|
| 80 | Atco K 11486 | Let My Love Open The Door/Classified/Greyhound Girl (p/s, with sticker) | 5 |
| 82 | Eva-Tone 623827XS | My Generation/Pinball Wizard (U.S. square flexidisc sewn into U.K. copies of Richard Barnes' Maximum R&B book; with book) | 20 |
| 72 | Track 2408 201 | WHO CAME FIRST (LP, gatefold sleeve with poster) | 25 |
| 72 | Track 2408 201 | WHO CAME FIRST (LP, laminated gatefold sleeve without poster) | 15 |

*(see also The Who, Meher Baba, Billy Nicholls, Elton John)*

## PETE TOWNSHEND & RONNIE LANE
| | | | |
|---|---|---|---|
| 77 | Polydor 2058 944 | Street In The City/RONNIE LANE: Annie (limited issue) | 20 |
| 77 | Polydor 2058 944 | Street In The City/RONNIE LANE: Annie (12", p/s) | 12 |

*(see also Who, Ronnie Lane)*

## TOXIC
| | | | |
|---|---|---|---|
| 92 | D-Zone DANCE 26 | Simple Warnin' (Ruffneck Mix)/Simple Warnin' (Riffist Mix)/Simple Warnin' (Hi Power Version)Kik The Break (12", company sleeve) | 60 |

## TOXIC REASONS
| | | | |
|---|---|---|---|
| 84 | T-REASON HANG 1 | God Bless America/Can't Get Away/Destroyer (p/s) | 6 |
| 84 | Alt. Tentacles VIRUS 42 | KILL BY REMOTE CONTROL (LP) | 15 |

## TOXIK EPHEX
| | | | |
|---|---|---|---|
| 89 | Words Of Warning WOW 6 | Does Someone Have To Die/Life Is For Living/SHRAPNEL: Trivial Pursuit/Autumn Split EP p/s | 10 |
| 89 | One Up | THE ADVENTURES OF NOBBY PORTHOLE - THE COCK OF THE NORTH (LP) | 20 |

## TOYAN
| | | | |
|---|---|---|---|
| 81 | Greensleeves GREL 20 | HOW THE WEST WAS WON (LP) | 25 |
| 83 | Vista STLP 1023 | MURDER (LP, as Toyan with Tippa Lee) | 45 |
| 83 | Upfront UPFLP 11 | DJ DADDY (LP) | 15 |

## TOY DOLLS
| | | | |
|---|---|---|---|
| 81 | GBH SSM 005 | Tommy Kowey's Car/She Goes To Finos (500 only) | 60 |
| 81 | GRC GRC 104 | Tommy Kowey's Car/She's A Working Ticket/Everybody Jitterbug/ Teenager In Love/ I've Got Asthma (yellow paper p/s, with insert) | 60 |
| 82 | Zonophone Z 31 | Everybody Jitterbug/(She's A) Working Ticket (p/s) | 30 |
| 83 | Volume VOL 3 | Nellie The Elephant/Dig That Groove Baby (p/s) | 15 |
| 83 | Volume VOL 5 | Cheerio And Toodle Pip/H.O. (p/s) | 10 |
| 83 | Volume VOL 7 | Alfie From The Bronx/Hanky Panky (p/s) | 10 |
| 84 | Volume VOL 10 | We're Mad/Deirdre's A Slag (p/s) | 6 |
| 84 | Volume VOLT 10 | We're Mad/Deirdre's A Slag/Rupert The Bear (12", p/s) | 10 |
| 85 | Volume VOL 12 | She Goes To Fino's/Spiders In The Dressing Room (p/s) | 5 |
| 85 | Volume VOL 17 | James Bond (Lives Down Our Street)/Olga... I cannot! (p/s) | 8 |
| 86 | Volume VOL 21 | Geordie's Gone To Jail/Idle Gossip (p/s) | 8 |
| 82 | WOWLP 1 | THE TOY DOLLS ALBUM (LP) | 15 |
| 84 | Volume VOLP 1 | DIG THAT GROOVE, BABY (LP) | 15 |

*(see also Showbiz Kids)*

## TOY DOLLS (U.S.)
| | | | |
|---|---|---|---|
| 63 | London HLN 9647 | Little Tin Soldier/Fly Away | 30 |

## TOYS
| | | | |
|---|---|---|---|
| 79 | SRT SRTS/79/CUS 345 | My Mind Wanders/The Girl On My Wall/Toytime/I'd Do Anything For You (p/s) | 20 |
| 79 | Toy TOYS 2 | STILL DANCING (EP, hand-stamped white label, foldaround p/s) | 50 |

## TOYS
| | | | |
|---|---|---|---|
| 80 | Red Bus RBUS 54 | Go To The Police/Breakdown | 50 |

## TOYS (U.S.)
| | | | |
|---|---|---|---|
| 65 | Stateside SS 460 | A Lover's Concerto/This Night | 8 |
| 66 | Stateside SS 483 | Attack/See How They Run | 8 |
| 66 | Stateside SS 502 | May My Heart Be Cast Into Stone/On Backstreet | 20 |
| 66 | Stateside SS 519 | Silver Spoon/Can't Get Enough Of You Baby | 22 |
| 66 | Stateside SS 539 | Baby Toys/Happy Birthday Broken Heart | 10 |
| 67 | Philips BF 1563 | Ciao Baby/I Got Carried Away | 10 |
| 67 | Philips BF 1581 | My Love Sonata/I Close My Eyes | 10 |
| 69 | Bell BLL 1053 | A Lover's Concerto/Baby Toys | 7 |
| 66 | Stateside SL 10175 | THE TOYS SING "A LOVER'S CONCERTO" AND "ATTACK" (LP, mono) | 40 |
| 66 | Stateside SSL 10175 | THE TOYS SING "A LOVER'S CONCERTO" AND "ATTACK" (LP, stereo) | 50 |

## TOYSHOP
| | | | |
|---|---|---|---|
| 69 | Polydor 56317 | Say Goodbye To Yesterday/Send My Love To Lucy | 12 |

## T.P.I.
| | | | |
|---|---|---|---|
| 79 | SRT SRTS 79 CUS 489 | She's Too Clever For Me/You Rool Me (no p/s, 1000 only) | 90 |

## TRACE
| | | | |
|---|---|---|---|
| 74 | Vertigo 6360 852 | TRACE (LP) | 25 |
| 75 | Vertigo 6413 080 | BIRDS (LP) | 25 |

*(see also Curved Air)*

## TRACER
| | | | |
|---|---|---|---|
| 83 | Mouse Hole TRA 1 | CHANNELLED AGGRESSION EP (p/s) | 125 |

## MARK TRACEY
| | | | |
|---|---|---|---|
| 62 | Parlophone R 4944 | Caravan Of Lonely Men/Never Ending (with John Barry & His Orchestra) | 10 |

## STAN TRACEY
| | | | |
|---|---|---|---|
| 58 | Vogue LA 160130 | STAN TRACEY SHOWCASE (LP) | 70 |
| 59 | Vogue LA 160155 | LITTLE KLUNK (LP, as Stan Tracey Trio) | 130 |
| 65 | Columbia 33SX 1774 | JAZZ SUITE (LP, as Stan Tracey Quartet, also stereo SCX 3589) | 100 |
| 66 | Columbia S(C)X 6051 | ALICE IN JAZZLAND (LP, as Stan Tracey Big Band) | 40 |
| 67 | Columbia S(C)X 6124 | STAN TRACEY... IN PERSON (LP) | 40 |
| 68 | Columbia S(C)X 6205 | WITH LOVE FROM JAZZ (LP) | 50 |
| 69 | Ace Of Clubs ACL 1259 | LITTLE KLUNK (LP, reissue) | 30 |
| 69 | Columbia S(C)X 6320 | WE LOVE YOU MADLY (LP, as Stan Tracey Big Brass) | 50 |
| 69 | Columbia SCX 6358 | THE LATIN AMERICAN CAPER (LP, with Big Brass & Woodwind) | 40 |
| 70 | Columbia SCX 6385 | FREE AN' ONE (LP, as Stan Tracey Quartet) | 70 |
| 70 | Columbia SCX 6413 | SEVEN AGES OF MAN (LP, as Stan Tracey Big Band) | 35 |
| 72 | Columbia SCX 6485 | PERSPECTIVES (LP as Stan Tracey Trio) | 40 |
| 74 | Cadillac SGC 1003 | ALONE AT WIGMORE HALL (LP) | 15 |

MINT VALUE £

*(see also New Departures Quartet, Mike Osborne, Neil Ardley, Laurie Johnson)*

### ZEN TRACEY
| | | | |
|---|---|---|---|
| 62 | Decca F 11492 | Shamrocker (Phil The Fluter's Ball)/Two By Two | 8 |

### TRACK
| | | | |
|---|---|---|---|
| 66 | Columbia DB 7987 | Why Do Fools Fall In Love?/Cry To Me | 18 |

### TRACK 4
| | | | |
|---|---|---|---|
| 82 | Track 4 TR4 001 | Mr Charisma (p/s, with insert) | 100 |

### TRACTOR (1)
| | | | |
|---|---|---|---|
| 72 | Dandelion 2001 282 | Stone Glory/Marie/As You Say | 15 |
| 78 | UK UK 93 | Roll The Dice/Vicious Circle | 8 |
| 81 | Cargo CRS 002 | No More Rock & Roll/Northern City | 10 |
| 81 | Roach RR 2 | Average Man's Hero/Big Big Boy (p/s) | 5 |
| 72 | Dandelion 2310 217 | TRACTOR (LP) | 200 |
| 83 | Thunderbolt THBL 002 | TRACTOR (LP, reissue) | 20 |

*(see also Way We Live)*

### TRACTOR (2)
| | | | |
|---|---|---|---|
| 77 | Cargo CRS 002 | No More Rock 'N' Roll/Northern City | 15 |

### TRACY
| | | | |
|---|---|---|---|
| 66 | Columbia DB 7802 | Don't Hold It Against Me/These Four Walls | 8 |
| 69 | Columbia DB 8569 | Life's Like That/Let Me Love You | 7 |
| 69 | Columbia DB 8637 | Follow Me/A City Called Soul | 12 |
| 71 | Columbia DB 8750 | Rock Me In The Cradle/Strange Love | 10 |

### ARTHUR TRACY
| | | | |
|---|---|---|---|
| 67 | Decca F 12656 | Marta/Wanderer | 6 |

### GRANT TRACY & SUNSETS
| | | | |
|---|---|---|---|
| 61 | Ember EMB S 126 | Say When/Please Baby Please | 20 |
| 61 | Ember EMB S 130 | Pretend/Love Me | 20 |
| 62 | Ember EMB S 148 | The Great Matchmaker/Tears Came Rolling Down | 20 |
| 62 | Ember EMB S 155 | Taming Tigers/The Painted Smile | 20 |
| 63 | Decca F 11741 | Everybody Shake/Turn The Lights Down, Jenny | 20 |
| 64 | Ember EMB 3352 | TEENBEAT (LP) | 80 |

*(see also Pete Dello, Honeybus)*

### WENDALL TRACY
| | | | |
|---|---|---|---|
| 58 | London HLM 8664 | Who's To Know/Corrigidor Rock | 15 |

### TRADER
| | | | |
|---|---|---|---|
| 79 | Bos | Back Street Trader/Love On The Run (p/s) | 15 |

### TRADER HORNE
| | | | |
|---|---|---|---|
| 69 | Pye 7N 17846 | Morning Way/Sheena | 40 |
| 70 | Dawn DNS 1003 | Here Comes The Rain/Goodbye Mercy Kelly | 40 |
| 70 | Dawn DNLS 3004 | MORNING WAY (LP, gatefold, with photo & insert) | 250 |
| 70 | Dawn DNLS 3004 | MORNING WAY (LP, gatefold, without photo & insert) | 80 |

*(see also Them, Fairport Convention, Jackie McAuley)*

### TRADEWINDS
| | | | |
|---|---|---|---|
| 59 | RCA RCA 1141 | Crossroads/Furry Murray | 20 |
| 59 | RCA RCA 1141 | Crossroads/Furry Murray (78) | 25 |

### TRADE WINDS
| | | | |
|---|---|---|---|
| 65 | Red Bird RB 10020 | New York Is A Lonely Town/Club Seventeen | 22 |
| 66 | Kama Sutra KAS 202 | Mind Excursion/Little Susan's Dreaming | 20 |

### TRAD GRADS (WITH LEN, HERB, KIKO & RICHARD)
| | | | |
|---|---|---|---|
| 61 | Decca F 11403 | Runnin' Shoes/Rag-Day Jazz-Band Ball | 8 |

*(see also Quarry Men)*

### TRADITION
| | | | |
|---|---|---|---|
| 76 | Venture VEN 7705 | Movin On/Movin Rocker | 10 |
| 77 | Venture VNLP 8877 | MOVIN' ON (LP) | 25 |
| 77 | Venture CUT 6 | IN DUB (LP) | 60 |
| 78 | RCA PL 25169 | TELL YOUR FRIENDS ABOUT DUB (LP) | 20 |
| 78 | RAC PL 25186 | ALTERNATIVE ROUTES (LP) | 30 |
| 80 | Venture CUT 10 | PARTY DISCO (LP, blue vinyl, no sleeve) | 250 |
| 80 | Venture CUT 9 | CAPTAIN GANJA AND THE SPACE PATROL (LP) | 200 |

### TRAFFIC
| | | | |
|---|---|---|---|
| 67 | Island WIP 6002 | Paper Sun/Giving To You (in p/s) | 12 |
| 67 | Island WIP 6002 | Paper Sun/Giving To You | 5 |
| 67 | Island WIP 6017 | Hole In My Shoe/Smiling Phases (in p/s) | 12 |
| 67 | Island WIP 6017 | Hole In My Shoe/Smiling Phases | 5 |
| 67 | Island WIP 6025 | Here We Go Round The Mulberry Bush/Coloured Rain (1st 100,000 in p/s) | 15 |
| 67 | Island WIP 6025 | Here We Go Round The Mulberry Bush/Coloured Rain | 12 |
| 68 | Island WIP 6030 | No Face, No Name, No Number/Roamin' In The Gloamin' With 40,000 Headmen | 12 |
| 68 | Island WIP 6041 | You Can All Join In/Withering Tree (unissued in U.K.) | 0 |
| 68 | Island WIP 6041 | Feelin' Alright/Withering Tree | 10 |
| 68 | Island WIP 6050 | Medicated Goo/Shanghai Noodle Factory | 10 |
| 71 | Island No Cat No | Welcome To The Canteen (promo 7" with blank labels in mini LP sleeve) | 40 |
| 71 | Island TIM 1 | Gimme Some Lovin Part One (live)/Gimme Some Lovin Part Two (live) (p/s, white label only) | 25 |
| 74 | Island WIP 6207 | Walking In The Wind/Walking In The Wind (Instrumental) | 10 |
| 78 | Island IEP 7 | HOLE IN MY SHOE (EP, picture disc) | 10 |
| 67 | Island ILP 961 | MR FANTASY (LP, gatefold sleeve internal flipbacks, 1st pressing pink label with black 'circle' logo, mono) | 300 |

MINT VALUE £

| 67 | Island ILPS 9061 | MR FANTASY (LP, gatefold sleeve internal flipbacks, 1st pressing pink label with black 'circle' logo, stereo) | 250 |
|----|------------------|----------------------------------------------------------------------------------------------------------------|-----|
| 68 | Island ILPS 9081T | TRAFFIC (LP, gatefold sleeve with stapled-in booklet; pink label with black 'circle' logo) | 150 |
| 68 | Island ILPS 9081T | TRAFFIC (LP, gatefold sleeve with stapled-in booklet; pink rim label with 'palm tree' logo) | 20 |
| 69 | Island ILP(S) 9097 | LAST EXIT (LP, pink label with black/red 'eyeball' logo) | 150 |
| 70 | Island ILPS 9070 | LAST EXIT (LP, 2nd pressing pink 'i' label) | 60 |
| 74 | Island ILP(S) 9097 | LAST EXIT (LP, pink rim label with 'palm tree' logo) | 20 |
| 69 | Island ILP(S) 9112 | THE BEST OF TRAFFIC (LP, 1st pressings with pink "I" label) | 30 |
| 69 | Island ILPS 9061 | MR. FANTASY (LP, 2nd pressing, stereo, pink 'i' label) | 150 |
| 70 | Island ILPS 9081 | MR. FANTASY (LP, 3rd pressing, pink rim label with 'palm tree' logo) | 20 |
| 70 | Island ILPS 9116 | JOHN BARLEYCORN MUST DIE (LP, gatefold sleeve, 1st pressings with pink "i" label) | 50 |
| 71 | Island ILPS 9142 | LIVE - NOVEMBER '70 (LP, unreleased, may exist as test pressing) | 0 |
| 71 | Island ILPS 9166 | WELCOME TO THE CANTEEN (LP, 'sniped' spine edges, pink rim palm tree label) | 40 |
| 71 | Island ILPS 9180 | THE LOW SPARK OF THE... (LP, laminated sleeve, pink rim/palm tree label) | 20 |
| 73 | Island ILPS 9224 | SHOOT OUT AT THE FANTASY FACTORY (LP, pink rim/palm tree label) | 15 |
| 73 | Island ISLD 2 | ON THE ROAD (2-LP, laminated gatefold sleeve) | 18 |
| 74 | Island ILPS 9273 | WHEN THE EAGLE FLIES (LP, 1st pressing. Hand etched MATRIXES: ILPS 9273 A-1U GT 1 STERLING/ILPS 9273 B-1U AM 2 STERLING) | 25 |

(see also Spencer Davis Group, Stevie Winwood, Revolution, Hellions, Dave Mason, Gordon Jackson)

## TRAFFIC JAM
| 67 | Piccadilly 7N 35386 | Almost But Not Quite There/Wait Just A Minute | 300 |
|----|---------------------|------------------------------------------------|-----|
| 67 | Piccadilly 7N 35386 | Almost But Not Quite There/Wait Just A Minute (demo copy) | 300 |

(see also Status Quo, Spectres)

## JIM TRAGAS
| 72 | Buddah 2011 157 | White Buffalo/Mama Took Me From The Jungle | 6 |
|----|-----------------|--------------------------------------------|---|

## TRAGEDY
| 10 | Diggers With Gratitude DWG 009 | THE BLACK RAGE DEMOS (EP, 75 only, red vinyl) | 60 |
|----|-------------------------------|-----------------------------------------------|----|
| 10 | Diggers With Gratitude DWG 009 | THE BLACK RAGE DEMOS (EP, 175 only, black vinyl) | 30 |

## TRAGICIAN
| 79 | Look LKSP 6411 | The Wild The Scared And The Timid/Traces Of Impact (numbered gatefold p/s) | 35 |
|----|----------------|----------------------------------------------------------------------------|----|

## PHIL TRAINER
| 73 | BASF 05 19573-5 | Beautiful Jim/No No No (p/s) | 5 |
|----|-----------------|-----------------------------|---|
| 77 | Splash CP17 | Carousel/Rose Coloured Sky | 8 |
| 73 | BASF BAG 22 29107-3 | TRAINER (LP, gatefold) | 35 |

(see also Trees)

## TRAIN SET
| 80s | Play Hard DEC 11 | She's Gone (12", p/s) | 35 |
|-----|------------------|-----------------------|----|
| 89 | Play Hard DEC 17 | Hold On (12", p/s) | 35 |

## TRAINSPOTTERS
| 79 | Arista ARIST 290 | High Rise/Rock N Roll Hall Of Fame (p/s) | 10 |
|----|------------------|-------------------------------------------|----|
| 79 | Arista ARIST 320 | Unfaithful/Hiring The Hall | 15 |

## TRAITOR
| 81 | Airship APP 377 | That's Life/Stone Cold Sober | 100 |
|----|-----------------|------------------------------|-----|

## TRAITOR'S GATE
| 85 | Bullet BOLT 12 | DEVIL TAKES THE HIGH ROAD (EP) | 10 |
|----|----------------|--------------------------------|----|

## TRAITS
| 67 | Pye International 7N 25404 | Harlem Shuffle/Strange Lips (Start Ole Memories) | 35 |
|----|---------------------------|--------------------------------------------------|----|

(see also Roy Head)

## ALAN TRAJAN
| 69 | MCA MK 5002 | Speak To Me, Clarissa/This Might Be My Last Number | 50 |
|----|-------------|----------------------------------------------------|----|
| 69 | MCA MKPS 2000 | FIRM ROOTS (LP, laminated front sleeve) | 120 |

## TRAMLINE
| 68 | Island ILPS 9088 | SOMEWHERE DOWN THE LINE (LP, pink label black/orange circle) | 200 |
|----|------------------|--------------------------------------------------------------|-----|
| 69 | Island ILPS 9095 | MOVES OF VEGETABLE CENTURIES (LP, pink label) | 200 |

(see also Whitesnake)

## BOBBY LEE TRAMMELL
| 64 | Sue WI 326 | New Dance In France/Carolyn | 40 |
|----|------------|------------------------------|----|

## TRAMMY (RON WILSON)
| 72 | Techniques TE 920 | Horns Of Paradise/TECHNIQUES ALL STARS: Grass Root | 30 |
|----|-------------------|-----------------------------------------------------|----|

## TRAMP
| 69 | Young Blood SBY 4 | Vietnam Rose/Each Day | 12 |
|----|-------------------|------------------------|----|
| 74 | Spark SRL 1107 | Put A Record On/You've Gotta Move | 8 |
| 69 | Music Man SMLS 603 | TRAMP (LP, laminated front, flipbacks, white/black label) | 150 |
| 73 | Spark Replay SRLM 2001 | TRAMP (LP, reissue) | 30 |
| 74 | Spark SRLP 112 | PUT A RECORD ON (LP) | 30 |

(see also Dave Kelly, Jo-Ann Kelly, Brunning Hall Sunflower Blues Band, Fleetwood Mac)o

## TRAMWAY
| 91 | Sarah SARAH 52 | Technical College/Balla (p/s, insert) | 15 |
|----|----------------|----------------------------------------|----|
| 91 | Sarah SRH 43 | Maritime City/Boathouse/Star (p/s, with insert) | 15 |

## TRANE
| 71 | Penny Farthing PEN 773 | Still Burning Bright/Misty Lady | 5 |
|----|------------------------|----------------------------------|---|
| 71 | BBC RESL 5 | Wagoner's Walk/Jenny's Song/Ragged Bird/Mansion Of Cards (p/s) | 15 |

## TRANQUILITY
| 72 | Epic EPC 64729 | TRANQUILITY (LP, yellow label) | 20 |
|----|----------------|---------------------------------|----|
| 72 | Epic EPC 65418 | SILVER (LP, lyric insert, yellow label) | 15 |

MINT VALUE £

## TRANS AM
| | | | |
|---|---|---|---|
| 95 | Thrill Jockey THRILL 024 | TRANS AM (LP) | 15 |

## TRANSATLANTICS
| | | | |
|---|---|---|---|
| 65 | Fontana TF 593 | Many Things From Your Window/I Tried To Forget | 35 |
| 65 | Fontana TF 638 | Stand Up And Fight Like A Man/But I Know | 20 |
| 65 | Mercury MF 948 | Don't Fight It/Look Before You Leap | 50 |
| 65 | King KG 1033 | Run For Your Life/It's All Over | 15 |
| 66 | King KG 1040 | Louie Go Home/Find Yourself Another Guy | 30 |

## TRANSCRIPT CARRIERS
| | | | |
|---|---|---|---|
| 92 | Transcript Carriers TC999 | ALL FEAR IS BONDAGE (EP) | 25 |

## TRANSIENT WAVES
| | | | |
|---|---|---|---|
| 98 | Fat Cat 12FAT 011 | Born With A Body And Fucked In The Heads/(2 Lone Swordsmen Mix)/ (Skye [Stasis] Mix) (12", custom embossed sleeve) | 10 |

## TRANSISTORS
| | | | |
|---|---|---|---|
| 81 | Open Circuit | RIOT SQUAD (EP) | 20 |

## TRANSIT
| | | | |
|---|---|---|---|
| 09 | Third Man TMR 012 | Come On And Ride/After Party (100 only, luminous vinyl) | 40 |

## TRANSMISSION
| | | | |
|---|---|---|---|
| 84 | PMP PMP 001 | Mystery Lady/Take It Easy/Bouncing Ball (12") | 40 |

## TRANSMITTERS
| | | | |
|---|---|---|---|
| 78 | Ebony EYE 11 | Party/0.5 Alive (p/s) | 5 |
| 78 | Ebony EYE 12 | Nowhere Train/Uninvited Guest/Persons Unknown (die-cut p/s) | 5 |
| 78 | Ebony EBY 1002 | 24 HOURS (LP) | 15 |

## TRANSPARENT ILLUSION
| | | | |
|---|---|---|---|
| 81 | Vortex VEX 001/002 | Vortex/Nuclear Release (p/s) | 150 |
| 82 | Vortex VEX 5 | Guilty Rich Men (p/s) | 10 |
| 81 | Vortex VEX 3 | STILL HUMAN (LP) | 150 |
| 82 | Vortex VEX 4 | CHAGRIN RECEIVER (LP) | 20 |

## TRANSPORTER
| | | | |
|---|---|---|---|
| 70s | Mother Truck MT 1 | Kids On The Run/Intoxicating | 6 |

## TRANSVOLTA
| | | | |
|---|---|---|---|
| 79 | Pinnacle PIN 3 | Disco Computer/You're Disco | 8 |
| 79 | Pinnacle PIN 3 12 | Disco Computer/You're Disco (12") | 30 |

## TERRY TRANZ & THE VESTITES
| | | | |
|---|---|---|---|
| 81 | Go Round TOUCH 1 | State Hand Out/We Had It Here (2 different home-made sleeves) | 100 |

## TRAPEZE
| | | | |
|---|---|---|---|
| 69 | Threshold TH 2 | Send Me No More Letters/Another Day | 10 |
| 72 | Threshold TH 11 | Coast To Coast/Your Love Is Alright | 10 |
| 75 | Warner Bros K 16606 | Sunny Side Of The Street/Monkey | 8 |
| 79 | Aura AUS 114 | Don't Ask Me How I Know/Take Good Care (p/s) | 15 |
| 80 | Aura AUS 116 | Running Away/Don't Break My Heart (p/s) | 15 |
| 69 | Threshold THS 2 | TRAPEZE (LP, gatefold sleeve) | 80 |
| 70 | Threshold THS 4 | MEDUSA (LP) | 70 |
| 73 | Threshold THS 8 | YOU ARE THE MUSIC ... WE'RE JUST THE BAND (LP) | 20 |
| 74 | Warner Bros K 56064 | HOT WIRE (LP) | 15 |
| 81 | Aura AUL 717 | LIVE IN TEXAS ... DEAD ARMADILLOS (LP) | 15 |

*(see also Finders Keepers, Montanas, Deep Purple, Glenn Hughes, Judas Priest, Whitesnake)*

## TRASH TOWN
| | | | |
|---|---|---|---|
| 85 | Course CORS 1 | Unlucky Numbers/Down | 18 |

## TRASH (1)
| | | | |
|---|---|---|---|
| 69 | Apple APPLE 6 | Road To Nowhere/Illusions (initial copies as White Trash) | 200 |
| 69 | Apple APPLE 6 | Road To Nowhere/Illusions (later copies as Trash) | 70 |
| 69 | Apple APPLE 17 | Golden Slumbers - Carry That Weight/Trash Can | 30 |

*(see also Poets, Pathfinders)*

## TRASH (2)
| | | | |
|---|---|---|---|
| 77 | Polydor 2058 939 | Priorities/Look (p/s) | 6 |
| 78 | Polydor 2059 - 013 | N-n-e-r-v-o-u-s/Page 3 (p/s) | 8 |

## TRASHCAN SINATRAS
| | | | |
|---|---|---|---|
| 89 | Go! Discs GODX 34 | Obscurity Knocks/The Best Man's Fall/Drunken Chorus/Who's He? (12", p/s) | 12 |
| 90 | Go! Discs GOD 41 | Only Tongue/Useless Begins With You/Tonight You Belong To Me (p/s) | 6 |
| 90 | Go! Discs GODX 41 | Only Tongue/Useless Begins With You/Tonight You Belong To Me (12", p/s) | 10 |
| 90 | Go! Discs GOD 46 | Circling The Circumference/My Mistake (p/s) | 8 |
| 90 | Go! Discs GODX 46 | Circling The Circumference/My Mistake/White Horses (12", p/s) | 12 |
| 93 | Go! Discs GOD 100 | I've Seen Everything/Houseproud/I'm The One Who Fainted (p/s) | 6 |
| 96 | Go! Discs GOD 151 | How Can I Apply?/Save Me (p/s) | 6 |
| 90 | Go! Discs 828 2011 | CAKE (LP) | 15 |

## TRASHMEN
| | | | |
|---|---|---|---|
| 64 | Stateside SS 255 | Surfin' Bird/King Of The Surf | 35 |
| 64 | Stateside SS 276 | Bird Dance Beat/A-Bone | 35 |

## TRAVELING WILBURYS
| | | | |
|---|---|---|---|
| 88 | Warner Bros W 7732W | Handle With Care/Margarita (gatefold p/s with sticker, sealed) | 10 |
| 88 | Warner Bros W 7732W | Handle With Care/Margarita (gatefold p/s with sticker, unsealed) | 5 |
| 88 | Warner Bros W 7732TE | Handle With Care (Extended)/Margarita (10", p/s) | 10 |
| 89 | Warner Bros W 7637TW | End Of The Line (Extended)/Congratulations (12", p/s, with sheet of stickers) | 10 |
| 91 | Warner Bros W 0019 | Wilbury Twist/New Blue Moon (Instrumental) (p/s) | 6 |
| 91 | Warner Bros W 0018W | Wilbury Twist/New Blue Moon (Instrumental) (card p/s with 4 postcards) | 8 |
| 88 | Warner Bros WX 224W | VOLUME ONE (LP, some with stickered sleeve & sticker inserts) | 20 |

*(see also George Harrison, Bob Dylan, Roy Orbison, Tom Petty)*

## TRAVELLERS
77   Paradise PDS 001        Jah Give Us The World (feat. U Brown)/Girl I Left Behind (12") .................................... 15

## MARY TRAVERS
72   Warner Bros K 16191     Morning Glory/That's Enough For Me ..................................................................... 7
*(See also Peter, Paul & Mary)*

## PAT TRAVERS
76   Polydor SFI 221/2814 040   Makes No Difference (1-sided flexidisc, promo only, black & white p/s) ..................... 10
*(see also Nicko McBrain)*

## MERLE TRAVIS
53   Capitol CL45 13985      Gamblers Guitar/Shut Up And Drink Your Beer ........................................... 35
56   Capitol EAP1 032        MERLE TRAVIS GUITAR (EP) ...................................................................... 10
57   Capitol EAP2 650        MERLE TRAVIS GUITAR NO. 2 (EP) ......................................................... 10
59   Capitol EAP1 891        BACK HOME (EP) ................................................................................... 10
63   Capitol EAP1 1391       WALKIN' THE STRINGS (EP) ..................................................................... 10
*(see also Brown's Ferry Four)*

## PAUL TRAVIS
75   A&M AMLS 68290          RETURN OF THE NATIVE (LP, with lyric inner) ......................................... 15
*(see also Travis)*

## TRAVIS (1)
73   A&M AMS 7081            Band Of Heroes/Out In The Country .......................................................... 8
73   A&M AMLS 68120          SHINE ON ME (LP) ................................................................................ 50
*(see also Paul Travis)*

## TRAVIS (2)
96   Red Telephone Box PHONE 001   All I Want Do Is Rock/Line Is Fine/Funny Thing (10", numbered, stickered p/s, 750 only) ................................................................................................... 20
97   Independiente ISOM1LP   GOOD FEELING (LP, inner) .................................................................... 30
99   Independiente ISOM 9 LP  THE MAN WHO (LP, with bonus remix 12") ............................................. 75
99   Independiente ISOM 9 LP  THE MAN WHO (LP) ............................................................................ 35
01   Independiente ISOM 25 LP  THE INVISIBLE BAND (LP, with free 7") ................................................ 40
03   Independiente ISOM 40LP  12 MEMORIES (LP) ............................................................................ 25
07   Epic ISOM 67LP          THE BOY WITH NO NAME (LP, and free 7") ............................................ 50
08   Red Telephone Box PHONE 004V   ODE TO J SMITH (LP) ............................................................... 30

## TRAVIS & BOB
59   Pye International 7N 25018   Tell Him No/We're Too Young ............................................................. 15
61   Mercury AMT 1142        Baby Stay Close To Me/Give Your Love To Me ......................................... 7

## TRAX
79   Lonely LONESOME ONE     HOME EP ........................................................................................... 20

## TRAX FOUR
66   Ace Of Clubs S/ACL 1216   WINGDING PARTY!!! (LP, mono/stereo) ............................................... 55

## JACK TRAYLOR & STEELWIND
73   Grunt FTR 0194          CHILD OF NATURE (LP) ........................................................................ 20

## TREASURE BOY
67   Trojan TR 010           Love Is A Treasure (actually by Freddie McKay)/TOMMY McCOOK: Zazuka ................. 35

## TREATMENT
81   Private Pressing        Stamp Out Mutants/Doncha Know (p/s) ................................................. 15
87   Number NUMB 001         Feeling Like A Ghost/Rowing Boat ......................................................... 8
89   Number TAO 1            LIVE (LP) ........................................................................................... 18
93   Delerium DELEC 026      CIPHER CAPUT (LP, insert) ................................................................... 20

## STEVE TREATMENT
78   Rather GEAR 2           A SIDED 45 EP (p/s) ............................................................................ 20
79   Backbone ZBHIT 1        Heaven Knows (Juvenile Wrecks)/Step Inside A Worn Out Shoe (fold-out p/s) ............ 20
79   Backbone ZBHIT 2        CHANGE OF PLAN EP (p/s) ................................................................. 20

## TREBLETONES
61   Butlin CP 2424          Butlin Holiday/Butlin Holiday ................................................................ 8
63   Oriole CB 1838          In Real Life/Dream Of A Lifetime ......................................................... 12

## TREDEGAR
86   Aries CEP 0001          Duma/The Jester (p/s) ....................................................................... 75
86   Aries CEP LP 001        TREDEGAR (LP, gatefold sleeve, embossed) ......................................... 18
*(see also Budgie)*

## HERBERT BEERBOHM TREE
65   OMY 69                  KEEP THOSE DOGS AWAY (EP) ......................................................... 25

## TREES
70   CBS 5078                Nothing Special/Epitaph ..................................................................... 25
70   CBS 63837               THE GARDEN OF JANE DELAWNEY (LP) ........................................... 350
71   CBS 64168               ON THE SHORE (LP) ......................................................................... 400
87   Decal LIK 12            ON THE SHORE (LP, reissue) ............................................................. 15
87   Decal LIK 15            THE GARDEN OF JANE DELAWNEY (LP, reissue) ............................... 30
*(see also Casablanca, Juliet Lawson, Trainer)*

## TREETOPS
67   Parlophone R 5628       Don't Worry Baby/I Remember ........................................................... 15
68   Parlophone R 5669       California My Way/Carry On Living ...................................................... 12
70   Columbia DB 8727        Mississippi Valley/Man Is A Man ........................................................ 12
71   Columbia DB 8799        Without The One You Love/So Here I Go Again ...................................... 15
73   Columbia DB 9013        Gypsey/Life Is Getting Better ............................................................ 15

## TREKKAS
65   Planet PLF 105          Please Go/I Put A Spell On You ......................................................... 90

## TREM
| | | | |
|---|---|---|---|
| 83 | AM 251 | My Robotic Friend/Colour Vision (p/s, 1000 only) | 25 |

## TREMBLING BLUE STARS
| | | | |
|---|---|---|---|
| 96 | Shinkansen SHINKANSEN 1 | Abba On The Jukebox/She's Always There (p/s, 1,000 only) | 8 |

## TREMELOES
| | | | |
|---|---|---|---|
| 66 | Decca F 12423 | Blessed/The Right Time | 20 |
| 66 | CBS 202242 | Good Day Sunshine/What A State I'm In | 15 |
| 67 | CBS 202519 | Here Comes My Baby/Gentlemen Of Pleasure | 6 |
| 67 | CBS 2723 | Silence Is Golden/Let Your Hair Hang Down (p/s) | 6 |
| 67 | CBS 2930 | Even The Bad Times Are Good/Jenny's Alright (p/s) | 6 |
| 67 | CBS 3043 | Be Mine/Suddenly Winter | 10 |
| 68 | CBS 3234 | Suddenly You Love Me/As You Are | 6 |
| 68 | CBS 2889 | Helule Helule/Girl From Nowhere | 6 |
| 68 | CBS 3680 | My Little Lady/All The World To Me | 6 |
| 68 | CBS 3873 | I Shall Be Released/I Miss My Baby | 7 |
| 68 | CBS 4065 | Hello World/Up Down All Around | 7 |
| 69 | CBS 4582 | (Call Me) Number One/Instant Whip | 5 |
| 68 | CBS Special Products WB 728 | Here Comes My Baby/SIMON & GARFUNKEL: The 59th Street Bridge Song (p/s, mail-order only with Pepsi Cola tokens) | 6 |
| 70 | CBS 4815 | By The Way/Breakheart Motel | 8 |
| 70 | CBS 5139 | Me And My Life/Try Me | 6 |
| 71 | CBS 7294 | Hello Buddy/My Woman | 8 |
| 72 | Epic EPC 5S 1019 | Blue Suede Tie/Yodel Ay | 8 |
| 73 | Epic EPC 1399 | Ride On/Hands Off | 5 |
| 73 | CBS 1139 | Here Comes My Baby/Silence Is Golden (p/s, 'Hall Of Fame Hits' series) | 5 |
| 84 | Meteor MTS 002 | Silence Is Golden (Acappella version)/The Last Word | 5 |
| 75 | SJM DJS 406 | Be Boppin' Boogie/Asct Cowboys | 7 |
| 68 | CBS EP 6402 | MY LITTLE LADY (EP) | 18 |
| 67 | CBS (S)BPG 63017 | HERE COME THE TREMELOES (LP) | 18 |
| 68 | CBS (S)BPG 63138 | THE TREMELOES: CHIP, RICK, ALAN AND DAVE (LP) | 18 |
| 69 | CBS 63547 | THE TREMELOES 'LIVE' IN CABARET (LP) | 15 |
| 70 | CBS 64242 | MASTER (LP) | 15 |

*(see also Brian Poole & Tremeloes, Trems)*

## TREMORS
| | | | |
|---|---|---|---|
| 79 | Redball RR 0002 | Modern World/Smashed Reality (p/s) | 15 |

## TREMS
| | | | |
|---|---|---|---|
| 73 | Epic EPC 1660 | Make It Break It/Movin' On | 5 |

*(see also Tremeloes)*

## TREND
| | | | |
|---|---|---|---|
| 80 | MCA MCA 583 | Polly And Wendy/Family Way (p/s) | 20 |
| 80 | MCA MCA 629 | This Dance Hall Must Have A Back Way Out/Fiction, Love & Romance (p/s) | 15 |

## TREND (1)
| | | | |
|---|---|---|---|
| 67 | Page One POF 004 | Boyfriends And Girlfriends/Shoot On Sight | 80 |

## TREND (2)
| | | | |
|---|---|---|---|
| 70 | Trendy TREND 1 | Teenage Crush/Cool Johnny (with press sheet) | 50 |
| 70 | Trendy TREND 1 | Teenage Crush/Cool Johnny | 40 |

## TRENDS
| | | | |
|---|---|---|---|
| 63 | Piccadilly 7N 35371 | All My Loving/Sweet Little Miss Love | 15 |
| 64 | Pye 7N 15644 | You're A Wonderful One/The Way You Do The Things You Do | 20 |

*(see also Tammy St. John, Freddie Self, Freddie Ryder)*

## TRENDSETTERS
| | | | |
|---|---|---|---|
| 64 | Silver Phoenix 1001 | You Don't Care/My Heart Goes | 65 |

## TRENDSETTERS
| | | | |
|---|---|---|---|
| 60s | Oak RGJ 999 | AT THE HOTEL DE FRANCE (EP) | 30 |

## TRENDSETTERS LTD
| | | | |
|---|---|---|---|
| 64 | Parlophone R 5118 | In A Big Way/Lucky Date | 20 |
| 64 | Parlophone R 5161 | Hello Josephine/Move On Over | 20 |
| 64 | Parlophone R 5191 | Go Away/Lollipops And Roses | 15 |
| 65 | Parlophone R 5324 | You Sure Got A Funny Way Of Showing Your Love/I'm Coming Home | 12 |

*(see also King Crimson, Giles Giles & Fripp, Brain)*

## TRENIERS
| | | | |
|---|---|---|---|
| 58 | Coral Q 72319 | Ooh-La-La/Pennies From Heaven | 25 |
| 58 | Fontana H 137 | Go! Go! Go!/Get Out Of The Car (featuring Don Hill, Alto Sax) | 100 |
| 59 | London HLD 8858 | When Your Hair Has Turned To Silver/Never, Never | 40 |
| 59 | London HLD 8858 | When Your Hair Has Turned To Silver/Never, Never (78) | 25 |

## JACKIE TRENT
| | | | |
|---|---|---|---|
| 61 | Oriole CB 1711 | Pick Up The Pieces/In Your Heart | 15 |
| 62 | Oriole CB 1749 | The One Who Really Loves You/Your Conscience Or Your Heart | 40 |
| 63 | Piccadilly 7N 35121 | Melancholy Me/So Did I | 15 |
| 64 | Piccadilly 7N 35165 | If You Love Me/Only One Such As You | 40 |
| 64 | Pye 7N 15692 | Somewhere In The World/I Heard Somebody Say | 5 |
| 64 | Pye 7N 15742 | Don't Stand In My Way/How Soon | 5 |
| 65 | Pye 7N 15865 | When Summertime Is Over/To Show I Love Him | 6 |
| 65 | Pye 7N 15949 | It's All In The Way You Look At Life/Time After Time | 6 |
| 66 | Pye 7N 17047 | You Baby/Send Her Away (DJ Copy) | 40 |
| 66 | Pye 7N 17047 | You Baby/Send Her Away | 30 |
| 66 | Pye 7N 17082 | Love Is Me Love Is You/This Time | 6 |
| 66 | Pye 7N 17158 | If You Ever Leave Me/There Goes My Love, There Goes My Life | 6 |

| 67 | Pye 7N 17249 | Open Your Heart/Love Can Give | 15 |
| 67 | Pye 7N 17323 | Your Love Is Everywhere/It's Not Easy Loving You | 6 |
| 67 | Pye 7N 17415 | That's You/Stop Me And Buy One | 6 |
| 67 | Pye 7N 17437 | Bye Bye Love (German Version)/Alles Okay (Send Her Away) | 6 |
| 69 | Pye 7N 17693 | I'll Be There/Close To You | 10 |
| 78 | Casino Classics CC 4 | You Baby/Send Her Away/FAMILY AFFAIR: Love Hustle | 6 |
| 65 | Pye NEP 4225 | WHERE ARE YOU NOW (EP) | 15 |
| 65 | Pye NPL 18125 | THE MAGIC OF JACKIE TRENT (LP) | 25 |
| 67 | Pye NPL 18173 | ONCE MORE WITH FEELING (LP) | 15 |
| 67 | Pye NSPL 18201 | STOP ME AND BUY ONE (LP) | 20 |
| 69 | Pye NSPL 18315 | THE LOOK OF LOVE (LP) | 20 |

## JACKIE TRENT & TONY HATCH
| 67 | Pye 7N 17300 | The Two Of Us/I'll Be With You | 6 |
| 68 | Pye 7N 17604 | Our Little Boat/Play It Again | 5 |
| 74 | Pye 7N 45392 | Together/Going Our Own Sweet Way | 6 |
| 75 | Pye 7N 45490 | Mr And Mrs (Be Nice To Each Other)/Positive Thinking | 7 |
| 68 | Pye NPL 18214 | THE TWO OF US | 20 |
| 68 | Pye NSPL 18229 | LIVE FOR LOVE (LP) | 20 |
| 68 | Pye NSPL 18304 | TOGETHER AGAIN (LP) | 15 |
| 74 | Pye NSPL 18422 | OPPOSITE YOUR SMILE (LP) | 15 |

## TRESPASS
| 79 | Trial CASE 1 | One Of These Days/Bloody Moon (p/s) | 25 |
| 80 | Trial CASE 2 | Jealousy/Live It Up! (p/s) | 18 |
| 81 | Trial CASE 3 | Bright Lights/The Duel/Man And Machine (p/s) | 20 |

## TREVOR (SHIELD)
| 64 | Blue Beat BB 228 | Down In Virginia/Hey Little Schoolgirl (with Caribs) | 18 |
| 68 | Blue Cat BS 129 | Tender Arms (with Joe White & Glen Brown)/DERMOTT LYNCH: Something Is Worrying Me | 35 |
| 68 | Blue Cat BS 130 | Pretty Girl (with Joe White & Glen Brown)/DERMOTT LYNCH: You Went Away | 35 |
| 69 | Blue Cat BS 153 | Everyday Is Like A Holiday/Have You Time (by Trevor & Maytones) | 100 |

## TREVOR & KEITH
| 70 | Punch PH 41 | The Ark/MINNA BOYS: False Reador (actually titled "Got To Move") | 7 |

*(see also Carl Bryan)*

## TRIARCHY
| 79 | SRT/79/CUS 599 | Save The Khan/Juliet's Tomb (in p/s, 1,000 only) | 80 |
| 79 | SRT/79/CUS 599 | Save The Khan/Juliet's Tomb (1,000 only) | 30 |
| 79 | Direct NEON 1 | Save The Khan/Juliet's Tomb (reissue, p/s) | 35 |
| 80 | Direct NEON 2 | Metal Messiah/Sweet Alcohol/Hell Hound On My Trail (in p/s) | 70 |
| 80 | Direct NEON 2 | Metal Messiah/Sweet Alcohol/Hell Hound On My Trail | 30 |

## TRIBAN
| 69 | Cambrian CSP 707 | Leaving On A Jet Plane/Night In The City | 6 |
| 71 | Decca F 13115 | Black Paper Roses/One Way Mirror | 5 |
| 69 | Cambrian MCT 592 | TRIBAN (LP) | 15 |
| 72 | Cambrian MCT 218 | RAINMAKER (LP, laminated cover) | 18 |

## TONY TRIBE
| 69 | Downtown DT 419 | Red Red Wine/RECO & RUDIES: Blues (some miscredited to Tony Tripe) | 35 |
| 69 | Downtown DT 439 | Gonna Give You All The Love/HERBIE GREY: Why Wait | 35 |

## TRIBE (U.K.)
| 66 | Planet PLF 108 | The Gamma Goochie/I'm Leavin' | 100 |
| 67 | RCA RCA 1592 | Love Is A Beautiful Thing/Steel Guitar | 25 |

## TRIBE (U.S.)
| 66 | Polydor 56510 | Dancin' To The Beat Of My Heart/Woofin' | 70 |

## TRIBESMAN
| 79 | Boa BOA 102-12 | Finsbury Park/The Tribe (12", p/s) | 20 |
| 79 | Boa BOA 001 | STREET LEVEL (LP) | 20 |

## TRIBUTE
| 73 | Jam JAM 48 | Bobby Charlton/City Summer | 12 |

## TRICKS
| 70 | CBS 4867 | Wham! Bam! Ala Cazam!/Lucy Brown | 8 |

## TRICKSTER
| 79 | Jet 165 | Falling For The Wrong Guy/Tomorrow Belongs To Me | 5 |

## TRICKY
| 95 | Island/4th & Broadway BRLP 610 | MAXINQUAYE (LP, gatefold, inner) | 30 |
| 96 | Island/4th & Broadway BRLP 623 | PRE-MILLENIUM TENSION (LP) | 25 |
| 98 | Island ILPSD 8071 | ANGELS WITH DIRTY FACES (2-LP) | 25 |
| 01 | Anti 6596-1 | BLOWBACK (LP) | 18 |

## TRICKY DISCO
| 91 | Warp WAP 11 | HOUSEFLY EP (12") | 10 |

## TRI-CORE
| 92 | Underground UNR 001T | BELFAST SAYS EP (12") | 80 |

## TRIDENT
| 84 | SRT TRI 1 | Destiny/Power Of The Trident | 50 |

*(see also Filthy Rich)*

## TRIFFIDS(1)
| 63 | Columbia DB 7084 | Lookin Around/She's No Longer Your Girl | 12 |

## TRIFFIDS (2)
| | | | |
|---|---|---|---|
| 11 | Domino REWIGCD 72X | COME RIDE WITH ME...WIDE OPEN ROAD (10-CD box set) | 70 |

## TRIFLE
| | | | |
|---|---|---|---|
| 69 | United Artists UP 2270 | All Together Now/Got My Thing | 10 |
| 70 | Dawn DNS 1008 | Old-Fashioned Prayer Meeting/Dirty Old Town | 10 |
| 71 | Dawn DNLS 3017 | FIRST MEETING (LP, textured gatefold sleeve) | 150 |

*(see also George Bean)*

## PANDIT KANWAR SAIN TRIKHA
| | | | |
|---|---|---|---|
| 71 | Mushroom 100 MR 7 | THREE SITAR PIECES (LP) | 45 |

## TRILOGY
| | | | |
|---|---|---|---|
| 71 | Mercury 6338 034 | I'M BEGINNING TO FEEL IT (LP) | 20 |

## TOMMY TRINDER & THE GANG
| | | | |
|---|---|---|---|
| 59 | Fontana H 204 | La Plume De Ma Tante/On The Sunny Side Of The Street | 10 |

## TRINIDAD ALL STARS
| | | | |
|---|---|---|---|
| 59 | Parlophone GEP 8625 | TRINIDAD ALL STARS STEEL BAND (EP) | 50 |
| 56 | Parlophone DP 524 | Trouble In Arima/Stone Cold Dead In De Market (78, export issue) | 12 |

## TRINIDAD OIL COMPANY
| | | | |
|---|---|---|---|
| 77 | Harvest SHSP 4070 | THE CALENDAR SONG (LP) | 20 |

## TRINITY
| | | | |
|---|---|---|---|
| 77 | Burning Sounds BS 011 | Natty Tired To Carry Load/Dubwise | 10 |
| 77 | Caribbean CBN 314 | Natty On De Banking/Banking Dub | 8 |
| 77 | Carib Gems CG 005 | Three Meals A Day/Version | 8 |
| 77 | Conflict CON 303 | Up-Town Girl/PRINCE JAMMY & AGGROVATORS: Channel One A Boy | 10 |
| 79 | Attack TACK 2 | Follow My Heart/Pope Paul Dead And Gone (12") | 30 |
| 70s | Burning Vibrations BVD 002 | Roots Man Party/Healing The Nation (12", with Mystic EMP Group) | 20 |
| 80 | Spectrum SP 01 | Jamaican People A Nice People/Heaven And Hell/LLOYD CLARKE SPARROW: The Young Ones (12") | 35 |
| 79 | Burning Sounds BDS 012 | SHOWCASE EP (12") | 30 |
| 77 | Magnum DERD 1003 | UPTOWN GIRL (LP) | 30 |
| 79 | Trojan TRLS 170 | ROCK IN THE GHETTO (LP) | 20 |
| 81 | JB JBLP 006 | FULL HOUSE (LP) | 20 |

## TRINITY HOUSE
| | | | |
|---|---|---|---|
| 77 | Profile GMOR 146 | FLASHBACK THROUGH HISTORY (LP, private pressing, with insert) | 40 |

## TRIO
| | | | |
|---|---|---|---|
| 71 | Dawn DNLS 3022 | CONFLAGRATION (LP) | 60 |
| 76 | Dawn DNLS 3072 | LIVE AT WOODSTOCK TOWN HALL (LP, with Stu Martin) | 25 |

*(see also John Surnam)*

## TRIPLETS
| | | | |
|---|---|---|---|
| 69 | President PT 245 | When Lovers Say Goodbye/You Won't See Me Leaving | 10 |

## TRIPPERS
| | | | |
|---|---|---|---|
| 66 | Pye International 7N 25388 | Dance With Me/Keep A-Knockin' | 20 |

## TRIPTI DAS
| | | | |
|---|---|---|---|
| 67 | Flowers FL 001 | Kat Put Li {Puppet On A String)/Lagta Mahi Dil | 20 |

## TRISHA
| | | | |
|---|---|---|---|
| 65 | CBS 201800 | The Darkness Of My Night/Confusion | 8 |

## TRISTAR AIRBUS
| | | | |
|---|---|---|---|
| 72 | RCA RCA 2170 | Travellin' Man/Willie Morgan On The Wing | 10 |

*(see also Wimple Winch, 10cc, Hotlegs)*

## TRITONS
| | | | |
|---|---|---|---|
| 73 | Bradley BAR 24 | I Can't Get Not Satisfaction/Drifter | 50 |

## TRIUMVIRAT
| | | | |
|---|---|---|---|
| 74 | Harvest SHSP 4030 | ILLUSION ON A DOUBLE DIMPLE (LP, 1st pressing normal green label) | 15 |
| 75 | Harvest SHSP 4048 | SPARTACUS (LP) | 15 |

## TRIXIE'S BIG RED MOTORBIKE
| | | | |
|---|---|---|---|
| 82 | Chew CH 9271 | A Splash Of Red/Invisible Boyfriend (white label, stapled foldover p/s) | 15 |
| 82 | Ram RAM 51 | TRIXIE'S BIG RED MOTORBIKE (EP, plain sleeve with stapled strip) | 10 |
| 84 | Lobby Ludd L 100001 | Norman And Narcissus/In Timbuktu (p/s) | 10 |
| 84 | Lobby Ludd L 100002 | A Splash Of Red/Invisible Boyfriend (reissue, different p/s) | 8 |
| 95 | Accident DENT 1 | THE INTIMATE SOUND OF... (LP, handmade sleeve, numbered) | 40 |
| 95 | Accident DENT 1 | THE INTIMATE SOUND OF... (LP, green vinyl, 500 only) | 25 |

## TRIXONS
| | | | |
|---|---|---|---|
| 69 | Major Minor MM 665 | Just Another Song/Sunny Side Sam | 15 |

## MARCUS TRO
| | | | |
|---|---|---|---|
| 65 | Ember EMB S 203 | Tell Me/What's The Matter Little Girl (in p/s) | 18 |
| 65 | Ember EMB S 203 | Tell Me/What's The Matter Little Girl | 10 |
| 65 | Ember EMB 3365 | INTRODUCING MARCUS TRO (LP) | 40 |

## TROBWLL
| | | | |
|---|---|---|---|
| 79 | Buwch Hapus MW 1 | TAITH (EP) | 40 |

## TROGGS
### SINGLES
| | | | |
|---|---|---|---|
| 66 | CBS 202038 | Lost Girl/The Yella In Me | 50 |
| 66 | Fontana TF 689 | Wild Thing/From Home | 8 |
| 66 | Fontana TF 717 | With A Girl Like You/I Want You | 7 |
| 66 | Page One POF 001 | I Can't Control Myself/Gonna Make You | 7 |
| 66 | Page One POF 010 | Any Way That You Want Me/6-5-4-3-2-1 | 7 |
| 67 | Page One POF 015 | Give It To Me/You're Lyin' | 7 |
| 67 | Page One POF 022 | My Lady/Girl In Black (withdrawn) | 50 |

MINT VALUE £

| 67 | Page One POF 022 | Night Of The Long Grass/Girl In Black | 7 |
|---|---|---|---|
| 67 | Page One POF 030 | Hi Hi Hazel/As I Ride By | 8 |
| 67 | Page One POF 040 | Love Is All Around/When Will The Rain Come | 6 |
| 68 | Page One POF 056 | Little Girl/Maybe The Madman? | 7 |
| 68 | Page One POF 064 | Surprise Surprise/Marbles And Some Gum? | 8 |
| 68 | Page One POF 082 | You Can Cry If You Want To/There's Something About You | 8 |
| 68 | Page One POF 092 | Hip Hip Hooray/Say Darlin'! | 8 |
| 69 | Page One POF 114 | Evil Woman/Sweet Madeline | 8 |
| 69 | Page One POF 126 | Wild Thing/I Can't Control Myself | 6 |
| 70 | Page One POF 164 | Easy Lovin'/Give Me Something | 8 |
| 70 | Page One POF 171 | Lover/Come Now | 8 |
| 70 | Page One POF 182 | The Raver/You | 10 |
| 71 | DJM DJM 248 | Lazy Weekend/Let's Pull Together | 6 |
| 72 | Jam JAM 25 | Wild Thing/With A Girl Like You/Love Is All Around | 5 |
| 72 | Pye 7N 45147 | Everything's Funny/Feels Like A Woman | 7 |
| 73 | Pye 7N 45244 | Listen To The Man/Queen Of Sorrow | 7 |
| 73 | Pye 7N 45295 | Strange Movies/I'm On Fire | 15 |
| 75 | Penny Farthing PEN 861 | Good Vibrations/Push It Up To Me | 6 |
| 75 | Penny Farthing PEN 884 | Wild Thing (Reggae Version)/Jenny Come Down | 5 |
| 75 | Penny Farthing PEN 889 | Summertime/Jenny Come Down | 5 |
| 75 | Penny Farthing PEN 901 | (I Can't Get No) Satisfaction/Memphis, Tennessee | 5 |
| 76 | Penny Farthing PEN 919 | I'll Buy You An Island/Supergirl | 5 |
| 77 | Penny Farthing PEN 929 | Feeling For Love/Summertime | 5 |
| 78 | Raw RAW 25 | Just A Little Too Much/The True Troggs Tapes (p/s) | 6 |
| 67 | Page One POE 001 | TROGGS TOPS (EP) | 20 |
| 67 | Page One POE 002 | TROGGS TOPS VOLUME TWO (EP) | 40 |
| 67 | Page One | TRACK A TROGG (EP, unreleased) | 0 |

### ALBUMS

| 66 | Fontana TL 5355 | FROM NOWHERE - THE TROGGS (LP, mono) | 70 |
|---|---|---|---|
| 66 | Fontana STL 5355 | FROM NOWHERE - THE TROGGS (LP, stereo) | 80 |
| 66 | Page One POL 001 | TROGGLODYNAMITE (LP, mono) | 70 |
| 66 | Page One POLS 001 | TROGGLODYNAMITE (LP, stereo) | 90 |
| 67 | Page One FOR 001 | THE BEST OF THE TROGGS (LP) | 30 |
| 67 | Page One POL 003 | CELLOPHANE (LP, mono) | 80 |
| 67 | Page One POLS 003 | CELLOPHANE (LP, stereo) | 90 |
| 68 | Page One POL 1 | THE TROGGS ON TOUR (LP, export issue) | 150 |
| 68 | Page One FOR 007 | THE BEST OF THE TROGGS VOLUME TWO (LP) | 35 |
| 68 | Page One POL(S) 012 | MIXED BAG (LP) | 150 |
| 69 | Page One POS 602 | TROGGLOMANIA (LP) | 40 |
| 70 | DJM Silverline DJML 009 | CONTRASTS (LP, original issue) | 15 |
| 76 | Penny Farthing PELS 551 | THE TROGG TAPES (LP) | 20 |

*(see also Reg Presley, Chris Britton, Ronnie Bond, Ten Feet Five)*

## CHUCK TROIS & AMAZING MAZE
| 68 | Action ACT 4517 | Call On You/Woodsman | 10 |
|---|---|---|---|

## TROJAN
| 88 | GI GILP 444 | THE MARCH IS ON (LP) | 18 |
|---|---|---|---|

## TROJANS
| 58 | Decca F 11065 | Man I'm Gonna Be/Make It Up | 15 |
|---|---|---|---|

## TROLL BROTHERS
| 73 | SRT SRT 73316 | You Turn Me On/Turn Out The Lights (p/s) | 10 |
|---|---|---|---|

## TRONICS (1)
| 61 | Fontana H 348 | Cantina/Pickin' & Stompin' | 18 |
|---|---|---|---|

## TRONICS (2)
| 78 | Tronics T 001 | Suzie (actually "Suzie's Vibrator")/Favourite Girls (plain sleeve with inserts) | 25 |
|---|---|---|---|
| 79 | Tronics T 002 | Time Off/Goodbye (p/s) | 12 |
| 81 | Alien ALIEN 18 | Shark Fucks/Time Off (p/s, with insert) | 25 |
| 83 | Red Rhino RED 3 | Wild Cat Rock/Tonight | 8 |
| 81 | Alien BALIEN 3 | LOVE BACKED BY FORCE (LP) | 25 |

*(see also Les Zarjaz)*

## TROOPERS
| 57 | Vogue V 9087 | Get Out/My Resolution | 700 |
|---|---|---|---|
| 57 | Vogue V 9087 | Get Out/My Resolution (78) | 150 |

## TROOPS FOR TOMORROW
| 82 | Rhythmic RMNS 1 | Songs Of Joy And Faith/Prisoner (p/s) | 15 |
|---|---|---|---|

## TROPIC SHADOWS
| 72 | Big Shot BI 603 | Our Anniversary/Anniversary (Version) | 15 |
|---|---|---|---|

## ARCHIBALD TROTT
| 64 | Black Swan WI 407 | Get Together/Just Because | 18 |
|---|---|---|---|

*(see also Baba Brooks)*

## TROUBADORS DU ROI BAUDOUIN
| 69 | Philips BF 1732 | Sanctus (Missa Luba)/Kyrie | 8 |
|---|---|---|---|

## TROUBADORS/TROUBADOUR SINGERS
| 57 | London HLR 8469 | Fascination/Midnight In Athens | 8 |
|---|---|---|---|
| 58 | London HLR 8541 | The Lights Of Paris/The Flaming Rose | 12 |

*(see also Jane Morgan)*

## TROUBLE
| 88 | Justice JTT002 | I Get Hype/I Guess It's Dope (12") | 40 |
|---|---|---|---|

## BOBBY TROUP
| | | | |
|---|---|---|---|
| 55 | Capitol CL 14219 | Julie Is Her Name/Instead Of You | 12 |
| 54 | Capitol LC 6660 | BOBBY TROUP (10" LP) | 20 |

## BOB TROW QUARTET
| | | | |
|---|---|---|---|
| 54 | London HL 8082 | Soft Squeeze Baby/I Went Along For The Ride | 40 |

## ROBIN TROWER
| | | | |
|---|---|---|---|
| 78 | Chrysalis CHS 2247 | It's For You/My Love/In City Dreams (p/s, red vinyl) | 5 |
| 81 | Chrysalis CHS 2497 | What It Is/Into Money (p/s, clear vinyl) | 5 |
| 73 | Chrysalis CHR 1039 | TWICE REMOVED FROM YESTERDAY (LP) | 15 |
| 74 | Chrysalis CHR 1057 | BRIDGE OF SIGHS (LP) | 15 |

*(see also Paramounts, Procol Harum)*

## TROY
| | | | |
|---|---|---|---|
| 80s | Love Linch LL 022 | Love & Harmony/Land Of Love (12") | 20 |

## BENNY TROY
| | | | |
|---|---|---|---|
| 05 | Atco 002 | I Wanna Give You Tomorrow/OTIS REDDING: Loving By The Pound (promo, 500 only) | 10 |

## DORIS TROY
| | | | |
|---|---|---|---|
| 63 | London HLK 9749 | Just One Look/Bossa Nova Blues | 35 |
| 64 | Atlantic AT 4011 | What'cha Gonna Do About It/Tomorrow Is Another Day | 25 |
| 65 | Atlantic AT 4020 | One More Chance/Please Little Angel | 18 |
| 65 | Atlantic AT 4032 | Heartaches/You'd Better Stop | 18 |
| 65 | Cameo Parkway C 101 | I'll Do Anything (He Wants Me To)/But I Love Him | 150 |
| 65 | Cameo Parkway C 101 | I'll Do Anything (He Wants Me To)/But I Love Him (DJ copy) | 200 |
| 68 | Atlantic 584 148 | Just One Look/What'cha Gonna Do About It | 12 |
| 68 | Toast TT 507 | I'll Do Anything (Anything He Wants Me To)/Heartaches | 15 |
| 70 | Apple APPLE 24 | Ain't That Cute/Vaya Con Dios (with p/s) | 22 |
| 70 | Apple APPLE 24 | Ain't That Cute/Vaya Con Dios | 10 |
| 70 | Apple APPLE 28 | Jacob's Ladder/Get Back | 12 |
| 71 | Mojo 2092 011 | I'll Do Anything (He Wants Me To)/But I Love Him (reissue) | 15 |
| 73 | Mojo 2092 062 | Baby I Love You/To My Father's House | 6 |
| 74 | People PEO 112 | Stretchin' Out/Don't Tell Your Mama | 6 |
| 65 | Atlantic AET 6007 | WATCHA GONNA DO ABOUT IT (EP) | 100 |
| 70 | Apple SAPCOR 13 | DORIS TROY (LP) | 80 |
| 73 | Mojo 2956 001 | THE RAINBOW TESTAMENT (LP, with Gospel Truth) | 35 |
| 74 | Polydor 2464 001 | JUST ONE LOOK (LP) | 20 |
| 74 | People PLEO 12 | STRETCHIN' OUT (LP) | 20 |
| 92 | Apple SAPCOR 13 | DORIS TROY (LP, reissue, gatefold sleeve with bonus 12" [SAPCOR 132]) | 20 |

## TROY & THUNDERBIRDS
| | | | |
|---|---|---|---|
| 61 | London HL 9476 | Twistle/Take Ten | 15 |

## WILLIAM TRUCKAWAY
| | | | |
|---|---|---|---|
| 69 | Reprise RS 20842 | Bluegreens On The Wing/Besides Yourself | 15 |
| 71 | Reprise K 44165 | BREAKAWAY (LP, with lyric insert) | 20 |

## TRUE ADVENTURE
| | | | |
|---|---|---|---|
| 74 | Decca F 13528 | Where The Roxy Use To Be/Outlaw Love | 15 |

## TRUE SPIRITED
| | | | |
|---|---|---|---|
| 70 | Wren WR 1 | Over And Over/Pollution | 30 |

## TRUE STYLE
| | | | |
|---|---|---|---|
| 91 | Liberty Grooves LIB002 | CODES OF CONDUCT (EP) | 20 |

## FRED TRUEMAN
| | | | |
|---|---|---|---|
| 69 | NEMS 56-4293 | Red Is Red/A Million Times A Day | 6 |

## TRUFFLE
| | | | |
|---|---|---|---|
| 72 | JAM 8 | Poco Poco/Julie's Place | 6 |
| 81 | Chesnut NUT 6 | Round Tower/If You Really Want (p/s) | 100 |

## TRUK
| | | | |
|---|---|---|---|
| 71 | CBS 57201 | Winters Coming On/You | 15 |

## JONNY TRUNK
| | | | |
|---|---|---|---|
| 01 | Trunk TTT 001 | The Snow It Melts/Scooby Don't (7", 300 only ) | 25 |
| 01 | Trunk TTT 002 | Sister Woo/Mr Hand (300 only) | 15 |
| 03 | Trunk TTT 004 | Dead Soon/Dead Mouse Blues (7", 400 only) | 15 |
| 04 | Trunk JBH 008 LP | THE INSIDE OUTSIDE (LP, 500 only) | 30 |

## TRUTH (1)
| | | | |
|---|---|---|---|
| 65 | Pye 7N 15923 | Baby Don't You Know/Come On Home | 20 |
| 65 | Pye 7N 15998 | Who's Wrong/She's A Roller | 25 |
| 66 | Pye 7N 17035 | Girl/Jailer Bring Me Water | 8 |
| 66 | Pye 7N 17095 | I Go To Sleep/Baby You've Got It | 30 |
| 66 | Deram DM 105 | Jingle Jangle/Hey Gyp (Dig The Slowness) | 100 |
| 67 | Decca F 12582 | Walk Away Renee/Fly Away Bird | 20 |
| 68 | Decca F 22764 | Seuno/Old Ma Brown | 60 |

## TRUTH & BEAUTY
| | | | |
|---|---|---|---|
| 74 | Rak RAK 181 | Tuff Little Surfer Boy/Touch-a Touch-a Touch Me | 25 |

## TRUTH CLUB
| | | | |
|---|---|---|---|
| 80 | Le Rey LR 01 | Sleight/FOTE: Looking For Lost Toy | 20 |

## TRUTH OF TRUTHS
| | | | |
|---|---|---|---|
| 71 | Oak OR 1001 | TRUTH OF TRUTHS (LP) | 25 |

## TRUTH (2)
| | | | |
|---|---|---|---|
| 83 | WEA TRUTH 1F | Confusion/Me And My Girl//Love A Go Go/From The Heart (p/s, doublepack) | 8 |
| 84 | IRS IRS 115 | Exception Of Love/If You Ever Find Love (p/s) | 5 |

**TRUX**
82   Trux TRX 01      Bad Luck (no p/s) ................................................................. 200

**TRYDAN**
80   Sain SAIN 77S      Mods A Rocers/Di-'Waith, Di-'Fynedd ..................................... 5

**TANIA TSANAKLIDOU**
78   EMI EMI 2797      Charlie Chaplin (English)/Charlie Chaplin (Greek) ................... 12

**T.S.O.L.**
82   Alt. Tentacles VIRUS 10      WEATHERED STATUES (EP) ................................................ 10
81   Frontier FLP 1004      DANCE WITH ME (LP) ....................................................... 18

**T34**
81   Spaceward DIV 1      Computer Dating/Mind Your Own Business ........................... 20

**T2**
70   Decca SKL 5050      IT'LL ALL WORK OUT IN BOOMLAND (LP, blue/silver label/boxed logo) ..................... 275
*(see also Flies, Cross & Ross)*

**ERNEST TUBB (& HIS TEXAS TROUBADORS)**
50   Decca BM 31206      The Blues/Half A Mind (Export Issue) ................................... 15
56   Brunswick 05527      Thirty Days/Answer The Phone (triangular centre) ................... 30
56   Brunswick 05587      So Doggone Lonesome/If I Never Have Anything Else ............... 20
50s   Decca BM 31214      What Am I Living For/Goodbye Sunshine, Hello Blues (export issue) ... 15
56   Brunswick LA 8736      JIMMIE RODGERS SONGS (10" LP) ...................................... 30
*(see also Red Foley & Ernest Tubb)*

**JUSTIN TUBB**
67   RCA Victor RCA 1585      But Wait There's More/The Second Thing I'm Gonna Do ............. 6
64   RCA RCX 7133      JUSTIN TUBB (EP) ........................................................... 30

**TUBES**
79   A&M AMS 7423      Prime Time (promo box of 7 different coloured vinyl editions & picture disc) .............. 30

**TUBEWAY ARMY**
78   Beggars Banquet BEG 5      That's Too Bad/Oh! I Didn't Say (p/s) ................................... 10
78   Beggars Banquet BEG 8      Bombers/O.D. Receiver/Blue Eyes (p/s) ................................. 10
79   Beggars Banquet BEG 17      Down In The Park/Do You Need The Service? ........................... 5
79   Beggars Banquet BEG 17T      Down In The Park/Do You Need The Service?/ I Nearly Married A Human 2 (12", p/s)..25
79   Beggars Banquet BEG 17T      Down In The Park/Do You Need The Service?/ I Nearly Married A Human 2 (12", p/s, sleeve misprint with Leif Garrett's Feel The Need LP image overprinted on both sides) ........................................................................ 100
79   Beggars Banquet BEG 18      Are "Friends" Electric?/We Are So Fragile (p/s original semi-transparent sleeve).......... 18
79   Banquet Banquet BEG 18P      Are "Friends" Electric?/We Are So Fragile (picture disc, with insert) .................. 10
79   Beggars Banquet BACK 2      That's Too Bad/Oh! Didn't I Say/Bombers/Blue Eyes/O.D. Receiver (double pack, gatefold p/s) ........................................................... 5
79   Beggars Banquet BACK 2      That's Too Bad/Oh! Didn't I Say/Bombers/Blue Eyes/O.D. Receiver (double pack, gatefold p/s, mispressed 2nd disc omits "O.D. Receiver") ........................... 15
83   Beggars Banquet BEG 92E      TUBEWAY ARMY VOL. 1 (12" EP, with "That's Too Bad [Alternate Mix]", yellow vinyl) .. 10
85   Beggars Banquet BEG 123 E      1978-1979 VOL. 2 (12", blue vinyl, p/s) ............................... 10
85   Beggars Banquet BEG 124E      1978-1979 VOL. 3 (12", red vinyl, p/s) ................................. 10
78   Beggars Banquet BEGA 4      TUBEWAY ARMY (LP, blue vinyl, g/fold stickered sleeve, some with badge) ............... 70
78   Beggars Banquet BEGA 4      TUBEWAY ARMY (LP, blue vinyl, g/fold stickered sleeve) .............. 60
79   Beggars Banquet BEGA 7      REPLICAS (LP, with large black & white poster) ....................... 25
79   Beggars Banquet BEGA 4      TUBEWAY ARMY (LP, reissue, mispressing, plays The Pleasure Principle on side 2) ..... 100
08   VIN 180 LP 002      REPLICAS (LP, (LP, pressed on 180 gram vinyl, numbered with 8" x 6" print) ......... 18
10   Vinyl 180 VIN180LP026      TUBEWAY ARMY (LP, blue vinyl reissue) ............................... 18
*(see also Gary Numan, Paul Gardiner)*

**TUBEWAY PATROL**
81   Carrere CAR 218      Do Eyes Ever Meet/No Time (no p/s) .................................... 18

**TUBILAH DOG**
96   S04      IN SEARCH OF PLAICE (LP, gatefold with poster) ...................... 20

**TUB-THUMPER**
74   Alaska ALA 18      Kick Out The Jams/Kahoutec ............................................. 25

**TUCHWOOD**
72   Polydor 2058233      Freedom For The Stallion/Morning Light ................................ 8

**BESSIE TUCKER**
55   HMV 7EG 8085      BLUES BY BESSIE (EP) ..................................................... 20

**BILLY JOE TUCKER**
61   London HLD 9455      Boogie Woogie Bill/Mail Train ........................................... 60

**CY TUCKER**
63   Fontana TF 424      My Prayer/High School Dance ............................................. 8
64   Fontana TF 470      Let Me Call You Sweetheart/I Apologise .................................. 7

**TERRY TUCKER'S ORANGE CLOCKWORK**
70   Warner Brothers K16337      Overture To The Sun Part 1/Overture To The Sun Part II .............. 10

**TOMMY TUCKER**
64   Pye International 7N 25238      Hi-Heel Sneakers/I Don't Want 'Cha ...................................... 20
64   Pye International 7N 25246      Long Tall Shorty/Mo' Shorty .............................................. 25
64   London HLU 9932      Oh! What A Feeling/Wine Bottles ......................................... 40
69   Chess CRS 8086      Hi-Heel Sneakers/I Don't Want 'Cha (reissue) .......................... 15
64   Pye Intl. NEP 44027      HI HEEL SNEAKERS (EP) .................................................. 50

**WINSTON TUCKER**
73   Explosion EX 2083      I'm A Believer/You'll Be Mine ............................................. 5
*(see also Winston Groovy)*

**TUCKY BUZZARD**
71   Capitol CL 15687      She's A Striker/Heartbreaker .............................................. 5

MINT VALUE £

| 73 | Purple PUR 113 | Gold Medallions/Fast Bluesy Woman | 7 |
| 77 | Purple PUR 134 | Gold Medallions/Superboy Rock 'N' Roller '73' | 7 |
| 71 | Capitol E-ST 864 | WARM SLASH (LP, laminated front sleeve, flipbacks) | 60 |
| 73 | Purple TPSA 7510 | ALRIGHT ON THE NIGHT (LP, laminated gatefold sleeve) | 25 |
| 73 | Purple TPSA 7512 | BUZZARD (LP) | 20 |

*(see also End)*

## HENRY TUDOR
| 67 | Decca F12574 | How Many Times/Another Name From Nowhere | 25 |

## TUDOR LODGE
| 71 | Vertigo 6059 044 | The Lady's Changing Home/Back To The Good Times We Had | 75 |
| 71 | Vertigo 6360 043 | TUDOR LODGE (LP, foldout textured sleeve, swirl label) | 1750 |
| 88 | Zap! ZAP 4 | TUDOR LODGE (LP, reissue) | 25 |

## TUDOR MINSTRELS
| 66 | Decca F 12536 | Love In The Open Air/A Theme From "The Family Way" | 22 |

## TUDORS
| 83 | Stiff BUY 172 | Tied Up With Joe Cool/Cry Baby Cry (p/s) | 7 |

## TUESDAY
| 72 | Pye 7N 45194 | Big Mister Little Man/Sewing Machine | 20 |

## TUESDAY'S CHILDREN
| 66 | Columbia DB 7978 | When You Walk In The Sand/High And Drifting | 20 |
| 66 | Columbia DB 8018 | High On A Hill/Summer Leaves Me With A Sigh | 22 |
| 67 | King KG 1051 | A Strange Light From The East/That'll Be The Day | 30 |
| 67 | Pye 7N 17406 | Baby's Gone/Guess I'm Losin' You | 15 |
| 68 | Pye 7N 17474 | In The Valley Of The Shadow Of Love/Ain't You Got A Heart | 12 |
| 68 | Mercury MF 1063 | She/Bright-Eyed Apples | 12 |

*(see also Warm Sounds)*

## T.U.F.F.
| 80s | SONO 001 | We've Got A Hot One (Speed Mix) (unreleased, white label promos only) | 10 |

*(see also Hard Corps)*

## TUFF GONG ALLSTARS
| 72 | Punch PH 114 | You Should Have Known Better (actually by The Wailing Souls)/Known Better | 20 |

*(see also Wailing Souls)*

## TONY TUFF
| 79 | Niagra NIADD 101 | Ease Up Oppressor/JAH THOMAS: Answer The Phone (12") | 15 |
| 79 | King Sounds GMDM 26 | You Wrong/TOMMY McCOOK: Sensimena (12") | 25 |
| 80 | Art & Craft 003 | Look Ya/TONY TUFF & JAH STITCH: Rumours Of War (12") | 50 |
| 80 | Cha Cha CHAD 11 | Deliver Me/Africa We Want To Go (12") | 20 |
| 80 | Grove ILPS 9619 | TONY TUFF (LP) | 40 |

## SHANE TUFF
| 82 | Roots Man Pro RMP 002 | Can't Take No More/Yearning For Some Loving | 40 |

## TULIPS
| 74 | Explosion EX 2091 | Mocking Bird/DES ALL STARS: Version | 7 |

## LEE TULLY
| 57 | London HL 8363 | Around The World With Elwood Pretzel (Parts 1 & 2) (gold print label) | 100 |
| 57 | London HL 8363 | Around The World With Elwood Pretzel (Parts 1 & 2) (silver print label) | 60 |
| 57 | London HL 8363 | Around The World With Elwood Pretzel (Parts 1 & 2) (78) | 25 |

## TUMBLACK
| 79 | Island 12XWIP 6500 | Caraiba (1-sided 12" promo) | 30 |
| 79 | Island 12XWIP 6500 | Caraiba/Invocation (12", p/s) | 50 |

## TUMBLEWEEDS
| 70 | Phoenix NIX 111 | Making My Way Back To Louisiana/I Guess I'd Better Go | 10 |

## TUNDRA
| 70s | Greenwich Village GVR 208 | THE KENTISH SONGSTER (LP) | 15 |
| 78 | Sweet Folk & C. SFA 078 | A KENTISH GARLAND (LP, gatefold sleeve) | 25 |
| 81 | Greenwich Village GVR 218 | SONGS FROM GREENWICH (LP, gatefold sleeve) | 15 |

## TUNE ROCKERS
| 58 | London HLT 8717 | The Green Mosquito/Warm Up | 20 |

## TUNEWEAVERS
| 57 | London HL 8503 | Happy Happy Birthday Baby/PAUL GAYTEN: Yo, Yo, Walk | 80 |

*(see also Paul Gayten)*

## TUNJI WITH CHRIS MCGREGOR
| 60s | Jika 001 | Ko Gbele Oko/Lisabi Egba | 8 |

## TUNNEL RUNNERS
| 80 | Sonic International SI 4282 | Plastic Land/Drug (numbered p/s) | 80 |

## TUNNELVISION
| 81 | Factory FAC 39 | Watching The Hydroplanes/Morbid Fear (1st pressing, clear vinyl) | 12 |
| 81 | Factory FAC 39 | Watching The Hydroplanes/Morbid Fear (later pressing, black vinyl) | 8 |

## TUNNG
| 04 | Static Caravan VAN 72 | Tales From Black/Pool Beneath The Pond (500 only) | 15 |
| 05 | Static Caravan VAN 73 | Maypole Song/Suprize Me 44 (100 lathe cut only, p/s) | 30 |
| 05 | Nowhere Fast SLOW03 | Magpie Bites/The Bonnie Black Hare (1000 only hand numbered poster sleeve) | 5 |
| 05 | Static Caravan VAN 94 | Tunng Vs Dollboy Vs Dollboy Vs Tunng (1000 only, 200 with art sleeve) | 5 |
| 05 | Static Caravan VAN 94 | Tunng Vs Dollboy Vs Dollboy Vs Tunng (1000 only) | 5 |
| 05 | Static Caravan VAN 88 | MOTHER'S DAUGHTERS AND OTHER SONGS (LP, 300 only - withdrawn) | 50 |
| 06 | Full Time Hobby FTH019LP | COMMENTS ON THE INNER CHORUS (LP, inner, poster) | 20 |
| 06 | Static Caravan VAN 88V | MOTHER'S DAUGHTERS AND OTHER SONGS (LP, reissue, clear vinyl) | 20 |

## K.T. TUNSTALL

| | | | |
|---|---|---|---|
| 04 | Outcaste OUT 56 | Throw Me A Rope/Black & White (500 only) | 8 |
| 04 | Relentless REL 12 | FALSE ALARM EP (2 x 7") | 10 |
| 05 | Relentless LPREL06 | EYE TO THE TELESCOPE (LP) | 50 |

## TURBO

| | | | |
|---|---|---|---|
| 80 | Cargo CRS 004 | STALLION (EP, p/s) | 100 |
| 82 | Turbo CUS 1261 | Charged For Glory/Race For The Dawn | 8 |

## TURGID TOOL

| | | | |
|---|---|---|---|
| 01 | Stand STAND 11 | Terror In A Turgid Tool!/Stand Up For England (pop-up p/s) | 8 |

## TURNBULL & ARKWRIGHT

| | | | |
|---|---|---|---|
| 72 | Peacock PEA 501 | Smuggling Man/Misty Roses | 15 |

## BRUCE TURNER

| | | | |
|---|---|---|---|
| 54 | Columbia SCMC 9 | Falling Leaves/I Wished On The Moon (export issue) | 6 |
| 60 | Melodisc MEL 1551 | Nuages/My Guy's Come Back | 6 |
| 60s | CRD 1000 | Jamaica Jump/Big Noise From Winetka | 10 |
| 63 | 77 EP/EU 1 | LIVING JAZZ (EP) | 10 |

## CHUCK TURNER

| | | | |
|---|---|---|---|
| 87 | Stereo One STO 003 | Youthman Struggling/FUNNY WONDER: Jollification (12") | 70 |
| 87 | Live & Love LLD 44 | We Rule The Dance/We Rule The Dub (12") | 30 |
| 88 | Live & Love LALP 21 | ON THE HARDWAY (LP) | 15 |

## DENNIS TURNER

| | | | |
|---|---|---|---|
| 62 | London HL 9537 | Lover Please/How Many Times | 25 |

## FRANK TURNER

| | | | |
|---|---|---|---|
| 09 | Xtra Mile | Reasons Not To Be An Idiot/Thunder Road (p/s, 300 only, each with hand-written reason not to be an idiot by Frank Turner) | 30 |

## GORDON TURNER

| | | | |
|---|---|---|---|
| 70 | Charisma CAS 1009 | MEDITATION (LP, 1st pressing laminated 'landscape' sleeve) | 40 |
| 70 | Charisma CAS 1009 | MEDITATION (LP, 2nd pressing non laminated 'blue room' sleeve) | 20 |

## IKE TURNER

| | | | |
|---|---|---|---|
| 72 | United Artists UP 35411 | Lawdy Miss Clawdy/Tacks In My Shoes/Soppin' Molasses (with Family Vibes) | 6 |
| 84 | Fleetville FV 303 | New Breed Part 1/New Breed Part 2 | 5 |
| 60s | Ember EMB 3395 | IKE TURNER ROCKS THE BLUES (LP) | 50 |
| 72 | United Artists UAG 29362 | BLUES ROOTS (LP) | 30 |
| 75 | DJM DJSLM 2010 | FUNKY MULE (LP) | 15 |

*(see also Ike & Tina Turner)*

## IKE & TINA TURNER

### SINGLES

| | | | |
|---|---|---|---|
| 60 | London HLU 9226 | A Fool In Love/The Way You Love Me | 20 |
| 61 | London HLU 9451 | It's Gonna Work Out Fine/Won't You Forgive Me | 20 |
| 64 | Sue WI 306 | Gonna Work Out Fine/Won't You Forgive Me (reissue) | 20 |
| 64 | Sue WI 322 | The Argument/Poor Fool | 20 |
| 64 | Sue WI 350 | I Can't Believe What You Say/My Baby Now | 40 |
| 65 | Warner Bros WB 153 | Finger Poppin'/Ooh Poo Pah Doo | 25 |
| 65 | Sue WI 376 | Please, Please, Please/Am I A Fool In Love | 40 |
| 66 | London HLU 10046 | River Deep - Mountain High/I'll Keep You Happy | 8 |
| 66 | Warner Bros WB 5753 | Tell Her I'm Not Home/Finger Poppin' | 20 |
| 66 | HMV POP 1544 | Anything You Wasn't Born With/Beauty Is Just Skin Deep | 30 |
| 66 | London HLU 10083 | A Love Like Yours (Don't Come Knockin' Every Day)/Hold On Baby | 18 |
| 66 | Stateside SS 551 | Goodbye, So Long/Hurt Is All You Gave Me | 18 |
| 66 | Warner Bros WB 5766 | Somebody (Somewhere) Needs You/(I'll Do Anything) Just To Be With You | 100 |
| 66 | Warner Bros WB 5766 | Somebody (Somewhere) Needs You/(I'll Do Anything) Just To Be With You (DJ copy) | 120 |
| 67 | HMV POP 1583 | I'm Hooked/Dust My Broom | 70 |
| 67 | HMV POP 1583 | I'm Hooked/Dust My Broom (DJ copy) | 120 |
| 67 | London HLU 10155 | I'll Never Need More Than This/Save The Last Dance For Me | 20 |
| 68 | London HLU 10189 | So Fine/So Blue Over You | 10 |
| 68 | London HLU 10217 | We Need An Understanding/It Sho' Ain't Me | 15 |
| 69 | London HLU 10242 | River Deep - Mountain High/Save The Last Dance For Me | 5 |
| 69 | Minit MLF 11016 | I'm Gonna Do All I Can/You've Got Too Many Ties That Bind | 15 |
| 69 | London HLU 10267 | I'll Never Need More Than This/A Love Like Yours | 8 |
| 69 | Liberty LBF 15223 | Crazy 'Bout You Baby/I've Been Lovin' You Too Long | 10 |
| 70 | Liberty LBF 15303 | Come Together/Honky Tonky Women | 6 |
| 70 | A&M AMS 783 | Make 'Em Wait/Everyday I Have To Cry | 8 |
| 70 | Harvest HAR 5018 | The Hunter/Bold Soul Sister | 8 |
| 70 | Liberty LBF 15367 | I Want To Take You Higher/Contact High | 6 |
| 71 | Liberty LBF 15432 | Proud Mary/Funkier Than A Mosquito's Tweeter | 15 |
| 71 | A&M AMS 829 | River Deep - Mountain High/Oh Baby | 6 |
| 71 | United Artists UP 35245 | Ooh Poo Pah Doo/I Wanna Jump | 5 |
| 72 | United Artists UP 35373 | Feel Good/Outrageous | 5 |

### EPs

| | | | |
|---|---|---|---|
| 64 | Sue IEP 706 | THE SOUL OF IKE AND TINA TURNER | 200 |
| 65 | Warner Bros WEP 619 | THE IKE AND TINA TURNER SHOW | 60 |
| 66 | Warner Bros WEP 620 | SOMEBODY NEEDS YOU | 70 |
| 83 | Sue ENS 1 | SUE SESSIONS | 15 |

### ALBUMS

| | | | |
|---|---|---|---|
| 65 | Warner Bros WM 8170 | THE IKE AND TINA TURNER SHOW | 60 |
| 65 | London HA-C 8248 | THE GREATEST HITS OF IKE & TINA TURNER | 60 |
| 66 | Ember EMB 3368 | THE IKE AND TINA TURNER REVUE | 40 |

## Jesse LEE TURNER

| | | | |
|---|---|---|---|
| 66 | Warner Bros W 1579 | THE IKE AND TINA TURNER SHOW | 40 |
| 66 | London HA-U/SH-U 8298 | RIVER DEEP MOUNTAIN HIGH | 50 |
| 67 | Warner Bros WB 5904 | THE IKE AND TINA TURNER SHOW VOL. 2 | 35 |
| 69 | London HA-U/SH-U 8370 | SO FINE (with Fontella Bass) | 30 |
| 69 | Liberty LBS 83241 | OUTTA SEASON | 22 |
| 69 | Minit MLS 40014 | IN PERSON | 25 |
| 69 | Warner Bros ES 1810 | GREATEST HITS | 20 |
| 70 | Liberty LBS 83350 | COME TOGETHER | 20 |
| 70 | Harvest SHSP 4001 | THE HUNTER | 120 |
| 71 | Liberty LBS 83455 | WORKIN' TOGETHER | 20 |
| 71 | Liberty LBS 83468/9 | LIVE IN PARIS | 15 |
| 71 | Capitol E-ST 571 | HER MAN...HIS WOMAN | 15 |
| 71 | United Artists UAD 60005/6 | WHAT YOU HEAR IS WHAT YOU GET | 15 |
| 84 | Kent KENT 014 | THE SOUL OF IKE AND TINA (LP) | 20 |

*(see also Ike Turner, Tina Turner, Ikettes)*

### JESSE LEE TURNER

| | | | |
|---|---|---|---|
| 59 | London HLL 8785 | The Little Space Girl/Shake, Baby, Shake | 60 |
| 59 | London HLL 8785 | The Little Space Girl/Shake, Baby, Shake (78) | 30 |
| 60 | London HLP 9108 | I'm The Little Space Girl's Father/Valley Of Lost Soldiers | 20 |
| 60 | Top Rank JAR 303 | That's My Girl/Teenage Misery | 20 |
| 60 | Top Rank JAR 516 | Do I Worry (Yes I Do)/All Right, Be That Way | 7 |
| 62 | Vogue V 9201 | The Voice Changing Song/All You Gotta Do Is Ask | 7 |

*(see also Pete Johnson, Meade Lux Lewis, Pete Johnson, Albert Ammons, Sonny Terry & Brownie McGhee)*

### (BIG) JOE TURNER

| | | | |
|---|---|---|---|
| 51 | Parlophone DP 265 | Roll 'Em Pete/Goin' Away Blues (with Pete Johnson) (78, export only) | 60 |
| 56 | London HLE 8301 | Corrine Corrina/Morning, Noon And Night (triangular or centre) | 350 |
| 56 | London HLE 8301 | Corrine Corrina/Morning, Noon And Night (round centre) | 100 |
| 56 | London HLE 8301 | Corrine Corrina/Morning, Noon And Night (78) | 40 |
| 56 | London HLE 8332 | Boogie Woogie Country Girl/The Chicken And The Hawk | 600 |
| 56 | London HLE 8332 | Boogie Woogie Country Girl/The Chicken And The Hawk (78) | 45 |
| 57 | London HLE 8357 | Lipstick, Powder And Paint/Rock A While (gold label label print) | 350 |
| 57 | London HLE 8357 | Lipstick, Powder And Paint/Rock A While (silver label print) | 175 |
| 57 | London HLE 8357 | Lipstick, Powder And Paint/Rock A While (78) | 40 |
| 60 | London HLE 9055 | Honey Hush/Tomorrow Night | 60 |
| 60 | London HLK 9119 | My Little Honey Dripper/Chains Of Love | 50 |
| 65 | Atlantic AT 4026 | Midnight Cannonball/Baby I Still Want You | 20 |
| 57 | London REE 1111 | PRESENTING JOE TURNER (EP, initially tri-centre) | 250 |
| 57 | London REE 1111 | PRESENTING JOE TURNER (EP, later round centre) | 150 |
| 57 | London Jazz LTZ-K 15053 | BOSS OF THE BLUES (LP, mono) | 80 |
| 57 | London Jazz SAH-K 6123 | BOSS OF THE BLUES (LP, stereo) | 90 |
| 59 | London HA-E 2173 | ROCKIN' THE BLUES (LP) | 120 |
| 60 | London Jazz LTZ-K 15205 | BIG JOE RIDES AGAIN (LP, mono) | 75 |
| 60 | London Jazz SAH-K 6123 | BIG JOE RIDES AGAIN (LP, stereo) | 80 |
| 60 | London HA-E 2231 | BIG JOE IS HERE (LP) | 80 |
| 64 | Realm RM 207 | JOE TURNER SINGS THE BLUES VOL. 1 (LP) | 20 |
| 64 | Realm RM 229 | JOE TURNER SINGS THE BLUES VOL. 2 (LP) | 20 |
| 65 | Fontana 688 802 ZL | JUMPIN' THE BLUES (LP) | 25 |
| 67 | Atlantic Special 590 006 | BOSS OF THE BLUES (LP) | 18 |
| 68 | Stateside (S)SL 10226 | SINGING THE BLUES (LP) | 18 |
| 70 | Philips SBL 7911 | THE REAL BOSS OF THE BLUES (LP) | 15 |

### JOE TURNER/RUTH BROWN

| | | | |
|---|---|---|---|
| 56 | London REE 1047 | KING AND QUEEN OF R&B (EP, 2 tracks each) | 150 |

*(see also Ruth Brown, Big Joe Turner)*

### JOE TURNER & PETE JOHNSON GROUP

| | | | |
|---|---|---|---|
| 56 | Emarcy ERE 1500 | JOE TURNER & PETE JOHNSON GROUP (EP) | 30 |

*(see also Pete Johnson, Big Joe Turner)*

### MEL TURNER (& BANDITS)

| | | | |
|---|---|---|---|
| 61 | Melodisc MEL 1580 | Let Me Hold Your Hand/I'll Be With You In Apple Blossom Time (with Bandits) | 20 |
| 62 | Columbia DB 4791 | Daddy Cool/Swing Low Sweet Chariot (with Bandits) | 25 |
| 63 | Columbia DB 4963 | Don't Cry/I Need | 10 |
| 63 | Columbia DB 7076 | I Can't Stand Up Alone/Doing The Ton (with Mohicans) | 15 |
| 63 | Carnival CV 7003 | Mohican Crawl/White Christmas | 10 |
| 66 | Island WI 276 | Welcome Home Little Darlin'/C'est L'Amour | 40 |
| 64 | Carnival CV 1005 | The Hermit And The Rosetree/What's The Matter With Me | 10 |

### RUBY TURNER

| | | | |
|---|---|---|---|
| 86 | Jive CHIP 1 | WOMEN HOLD UP HALF THE SKY (CD) | 25 |

### SAMMY TURNER

| | | | |
|---|---|---|---|
| 59 | London HLX 8918 | Lavender Blue (Dilly, Dilly)/Sweet Annie Laurie | 10 |
| 59 | London HLX 8963 | Always/Symphony | 15 |
| 59 | London HLX 8963 | Always/Symphony (78) | 20 |
| 60 | London HLX 9062 | Paradise/I'd Be A Fool Again | 15 |
| 62 | London HLX 9488 | Raincoat In The River/Falling | 25 |
| 60 | London HA-X 2246 | LAVENDER BLUE MOODS (LP) | 60 |

### SPYDER TURNER

| | | | |
|---|---|---|---|
| 67 | MGM MGM 1332 | Stand By Me/You're Good Enough For Me | 20 |
| 74 | Kwanza K 19502 | Since I Don't Have You/Happy Days | 8 |

### TINA TURNER

| | | | |
|---|---|---|---|
| 78 | United Artists UP 36513 | Sometimes When We Touch/Earthquakes And Hurricanes | 5 |

| | | | |
|---|---|---|---|
| 82 | Virgin VS 500 | Ball Of Confusion/Ball Of Confusion (Instrumental) (with B.E.F.) (p/s) | 8 |
| 85 | Capitol TINAP 1 | PRIVATE DANCER (LP, picture disc) | 18 |

*(see also Ike & Tina Turner, Eric Clapton)*

## TITUS TURNER
| | | | |
|---|---|---|---|
| 60 | London HLU 9024 | We Told You Not To Marry/Taking Care Of Business | 25 |
| 61 | Oriole CB 1611 | Pony Train/Bla Bla Cha Cha Cha | 20 |
| 61 | Parlophone R 4746 | Sound-Off/Me And My Lonely Telephone | 25 |
| 61 | Blue Beat BB 32 | Miss Rubberneck Jones/Way Down Yonder | 18 |

## TURNING POINT
| | | | |
|---|---|---|---|
| 77 | Gull GULP 1022 | CREATURES OF THE NIGHT (LP) | 20 |
| 78 | Gull GULP 1027 | SILENT PROMISE (LP) | 15 |

## TURNPIKE
| | | | |
|---|---|---|---|
| 74 | Fontana 6007032 | Big Machine/Lazer Thereza | 10 |

## TURNSTYLE
| | | | |
|---|---|---|---|
| 68 | Pye 7N 17653 | Riding A Wave/Trot | 325 |

## TURQUOISE
| | | | |
|---|---|---|---|
| 68 | Decca F 12756 | 53 Summer Street/Tales Of Flossie Fillett | 70 |
| 68 | Decca F 12842 | Woodstock/Saynia | 100 |

*(see also Ewan Stephens)*

## TURQUOISE DAYS
| | | | |
|---|---|---|---|
| 84 | Disques Strategie STRAT XX1 | Grey Skies/Blurred (p/s, 1000 only) | 80 |

## HENRY TURTLE
| | | | |
|---|---|---|---|
| 72 | Columbia DB 8859 | Do You Believe/You Turned Your Back And Walked Away | 30 |
| 73 | Bell 1318 | When Eleanor Comes Around/One Of A Million Faces | 8 |
| 81 | Surrey Sounds HMS 6A | Hound Dog Man/All I Ever Need Is You | 5 |

## TURTLES
| | | | |
|---|---|---|---|
| 65 | Pye International 7N 25320 | It Ain't Me Babe/Almost There | 20 |
| 66 | Pye International 7N 25341 | Let Me Be/Your Ma Said You Cried (In Your Sleep Last Night) | 15 |
| 66 | Immediate IM 031 | You Baby/Wanderin' Kind | 25 |
| 66 | London HLU 10095 | Can I Get To Know You Better/Like The Seasons | 10 |
| 67 | London HLU 10115 | Happy Together/We'll Meet Again | 5 |
| 67 | Pye International 7N 25421 | Let Me Be/Almost There | 8 |
| 67 | London HLU 10135 | She'd Rather Be With Me/The Walking Song | 5 |
| 67 | London HLU 10153 | You Know What I Mean/Rugs Of Woods And Flowers | 8 |
| 67 | London HLU 10168 | She's My Girl/Chicken Little Was Right | 12 |
| 68 | London HLU 10184 | Sound Asleep/Umbassa The Dragon | 10 |
| 68 | London HLU 10207 | The Story Of Rock And Roll/Can't You Hear The Cows | 10 |
| 68 | London HLU 10223 | Elenore/Surfer Dan | 5 |
| 69 | London HLU 10251 | You Showed Me/Buzz-Saw | 12 |
| 69 | London HLU 10279 | You Don't Have To Walk In The Rain/Come Over | 12 |
| 69 | London HLU 10291 | Love In The City/Bachelor Mother | 7 |
| 67 | Pye Intl. NEP 44089 | IT AIN'T ME BABE (EP) | 45 |
| 67 | London HA-U 8330 | HAPPY TOGETHER (LP) | 20 |
| 68 | London HA-U/SH-U 8376 | THE TURTLES PRESENT THE BATTLE OF THE BANDS (LP) | 20 |

*(see also Flo & Eddie, Frank Zappa)*

## GEOFF TURTON
| | | | |
|---|---|---|---|
| 68 | Pye 7N 17483 | Don't You believe It/I've Got To Tell Her | 10 |

## RITA TUSHINGHAM & LYNN REDGRAVE
| | | | |
|---|---|---|---|
| 68 | Stateside SS 2081 | Smashing Time/Waiting For My Friend | 10 |

## TUSKEN RAIDERS
| | | | |
|---|---|---|---|
| 99 | Planet Mu ZIQ 003 | BANTHA TRAX VOL. 2 EP (12", p/s) | 12 |

## TUSS
| | | | |
|---|---|---|---|
| 07 | Rephlex CAT 190EP | CONFEDERATION TROUGH EP | 15 |
| 07 | Rephlex CAT 189 | RUSHUP EDGE (3-LP) | 60 |

*(see also Aphex Twin, Polygon Window, Caustic Window)*

## TUTCH
| | | | |
|---|---|---|---|
| 80 | Gargoyle GRGL 773 | The Battle/You Don't Care/Round And Round | 60 |

## TU-TONES
| | | | |
|---|---|---|---|
| 59 | London HLW 8904 | Still In Love With You/Saccharin Sally | 125 |
| 59 | London HLW 8904 | Still In Love WIth You/Saccharin Sally (78) | 30 |

## WESLEY & MARILYN TUTTLE
| | | | |
|---|---|---|---|
| 55 | Capitol CL 14291 | Jim, Johnny And Jonas/Say You Do | 10 |

## TUXEDOMOON
| | | | |
|---|---|---|---|
| 80 | Pre PRE 10 | Dark Companion/59 To One (p/s) | 5 |
| 80 | PREX 4 | DESIRE (LP, with art print insert) | 15 |

## TV ON THE RADIO
| | | | |
|---|---|---|---|
| 04 | 4AD AD 2421 | Staring At The Sun/Freeway/On A Train | 6 |
| 04 | 4AD AD 2606 | Wolf Like Me/Snakes & Martyrs | 10 |
| 07 | 4AD 2724 | Province/Dumb Animal | 5 |
| 06 | 4AD RTCM2 | Province (with David Bowie, 200 only, green vinyl) | 40 |
| 09 | Parlophone LCO 299 | TV ON THE RADIO : Heroes/DAVID BOWIE : Heroes | 40 |
| 04 | 4AD CAD 2470 | DESPERATE YOUTH, BLOODTHIRSTY BABES (LP, with free 12") | 18 |
| 06 | 4AD CAD 2607 | RETURN TO COOKIE MOUNTAIN (LP) | 18 |
| 08 | 4AD CAD 2821 | DEAR SCIENCE (2-LP, white vinyl) | 15 |

## T.V. PRODUCTO
| | | | |
|---|---|---|---|
| 79 | Limited Edition TAKE 3 | Nowhere's Safe/Jumping Off Walls/PRAMS: Me/Modern Man (folded p/s) | 12 |

*(see also Mission)*

## T.V. & TRIBESMEN
| | | | |
|---|---|---|---|
| 66 | Pye International 7N 25375 | Barefootin'/Fat Man | 20 |

## TV 21
| | | | |
|---|---|---|---|
| 80 | Powbeat AAARGH! 1 | Playing With Fire/Shattered By It All (foldout p/s) | 12 |
| 80 | Powbeat AAARGH! 2 | Ambition/Ticking Away/This Is Zero (foldout p/s) | 15 |
| 81 | Demon D 1004 | On The Run/End Of A Dream (p/s) | 8 |
| 82 | Deram ATV 21 | All Join Hands/A Journey Up The Zambezi (And Back) (p/s) | 8 |

*(see also DNV, Shake)*

## TWELFTH NIGHT (1)
| | | | |
|---|---|---|---|
| 73 | Acorn CF 239 | TWELFTH NIGHT (EP) | 40 |

## TWELFTH NIGHT (2)
| | | | |
|---|---|---|---|
| 80 | Twelfth Night TN 001 | THE FIRST 7" ALBUM ("The Cunning Man"/"Für Helene") (p/s) | 30 |
| 86 | Virgin/Charisma CB 424 | Shame/Blue Powder Monkey (p/s) | 5 |
| 86 | Virgin/Charisma CBY 424-12 | Shame (Full Mix)/Shame (7")/Blue Powder Monkey (12", picture disc) | 10 |

## TWELTH NIGHT
| | | | |
|---|---|---|---|
| 73 | Acorn CF 239 | TWELTH NIGHT EP | 70 |

## TWELVE CUBIC FEET
| | | | |
|---|---|---|---|
| 82 | Namedrop NR2 | STRAIGHT OUT OF THE FRIDGE (10" EP, with Bumper Booklet) | 15 |

## 20TH CENTURY FOX ORCHESTRA
| | | | |
|---|---|---|---|
| 65 | Stateside SS422 | Those Magnificent Men In Their Flying Machines/Arizona | 15 |

*(see also Ron Goodwin)*

## 21ST CREATION
| | | | |
|---|---|---|---|
| 77 | Tamla Motown 1075 | Tailgate/Mr. Disco Radio | 5 |

## 25 RIFLES
| | | | |
|---|---|---|---|
| 79 | 25 Rifles TFR 1 | World War 3/Revolution Blues/Hey Little/Dance 'Bout Now (12") | 15 |

## 25 VIEWS OF WORTHING
| | | | |
|---|---|---|---|
| 77 | Worthings LYN 4423/4424 | RAT BRAIN INCISION EP | 10 |

## 22ND STREET
| | | | |
|---|---|---|---|
| 72 | Polydor 2058 212 | Sunny Sleeps Late/Home | 8 |

## 23RD TURNOFF
| | | | |
|---|---|---|---|
| 67 | Deram DM 150 | Michael Angelo/Leave Me Here | 90 |

*(see also Kirkbys, Jimmy Campbell, Rockin' Horse)*

## 23 JEWELS
| | | | |
|---|---|---|---|
| 79 | Temporary TEMP 1 | You Don't Know Me/Playing Bogart (white labels, plain sleeve with photocopied insert) | 20 |
| 80 | Temporary TEMP 2 | WELTSCHMERZ A GO-GO! (EP, white label) | 12 |
| 81 | Let's Call It Temporary TEMP 3 | I'll Pay For This/Down To Minimum (p/s) | 15 |

## 23 SKIDOO
| | | | |
|---|---|---|---|
| 81 | Pineapple PULP 23 | Ethics/Another Baby's Face (p/s) | 8 |
| 81 | Fetish FE 10 | Last Words/Version (promo only) | 12 |
| 81 | Fetish FE 11 | The Gospel Comes To New Guinea/Last Words (12", p/s) | 12 |
| 82 | Fetish FP 20 | Tearing Up The Plans/Just Like Everybody/Gregouka (12", p/s) | 10 |
| 85 | Illuminated ILL 2812 | Coup/Version (In The Palace) (12", p/s) | 10 |
| 82 | Fetish FM 2008 | SEVEN SONGS (mini-LP) | 15 |
| 83 | Operation Twilight OPT 23 | THE CULLING IS COMING (LP) | 15 |
| 84 | Illuminated JAM 40 | URBAN GAMELAN (LP) | 18 |

*(see also Current 93)*

## TWICE AS MUCH
| | | | |
|---|---|---|---|
| 66 | Immediate IM 033 | Sittin' On A Fence/Baby I Want You | 6 |
| 66 | Immediate IM 036 | Step Out Of Line/Simplified | 12 |
| 66 | Immediate IM 039 | True Story/You're So Good | 18 |
| 67 | Immediate IM 042 | Crystal Ball/Why Don't They All Go Away And Leave Me Alone | 18 |
| 66 | Immediate IMLP 007 | OWN UP (LP, mono) | 90 |
| 66 | Immediate IMSP 007 | OWN UP (LP, stereo) | 100 |
| 69 | Immediate IMCP 013 | THAT'S ALL (LP) | 60 |

## TWIGGY
| | | | |
|---|---|---|---|
| 67 | Ember EMB S 239 | Beautiful Dreams/I Need Your Hand In Mine (in p/s) | 20 |
| 67 | Ember EMB S 239 | Beautiful Dreams/I Need Your Hand In Mine | 10 |
| 67 | Ember EMB S 244 | When I Think Of You/Over And Over (in p/s) | 20 |
| 67 | Ember EMB S 244 | When I Think Of You/Over And Over | 10 |
| 71 | Bell BLL 1158 | Zoo Do Zoo Song/Little Pleasure Acre (as Twiggy & Friends) | 5 |
| 72 | Columbia DB 8853 | A Room In Bloomsbury (with Chistopher Gable)/You Are My Lucky Star/ All I Do Is Dream | 5 |
| 76 | Mercury 6007 100 | Here I Go Again/In Love Together (p/s) | 5 |
| 78 | Mercury 6007 175 | Falling Angel/Virginia | 5 |
| 72 | Ember SE 8012 | TWIGGY & THE GIRLFRIENDS (LP) | 20 |

## TWIGGY & ANNE
| | | | |
|---|---|---|---|
| 66 | Columbia DB 7799 | Some Do, Some Don't/With Open Arms | 6 |

## CALVIN TWILIGHT
| | | | |
|---|---|---|---|
| 79 | President PT 477 | Harmony/Isabelle Blue | 20 |
| 80 | Norwood NR 2003 S 80 CUS 803 | Night Time In The City/Lovely Lady Smile | 20 |

## TWILIGHT PASSION
| | | | |
|---|---|---|---|
| 88 | Hard Records COMM 2 | MEG 1 (12" EP p/s) | 25 |

## TWILIGHT ZONERS
| | | | |
|---|---|---|---|
| 79 | ZIP/Dining Out ZEROZERO1 | ZERO ZERO ONE (Hospital/The Wrap/Twister/The Film)(EP, various silk-screened in red & hand-coloured p/s, signed & numbered) | 75 |

| | | | |
|---|---|---|---|
| 80 | ZIP/Dining Out ZIP 002 | Brighton Rock/Diversion (p/s) | 6 |

*(see also Occult Chemistry)*

## TWILIGHTS (AUSTRALIA)

| | | | |
|---|---|---|---|
| 66 | Columbia DB 8065 | Needle In A Haystack/I Don't Know Where The Wind Will Blow Me | 30 |
| 67 | Columbia DB 8125 | What's Wrong With The Way I Live/It's Dark | 20 |
| 68 | Columbia DB 8396 | Cathy, Come Home/The Way They Play | 30 |

## TWILIGHTS (U.S.)

| | | | |
|---|---|---|---|
| 65 | London HLU 9992 | Take What I Got/She's There | 25 |

## TWINK (& FAIRIES)

| | | | |
|---|---|---|---|
| 78 | Chiswick SWT 26 | Do It '77/Psychedelic Punkeroo/Enter The Diamonds (12", p/s, with Fairies) | 12 |
| 86 | Twink TWK 2 | SPACE LOVER (EP) | 12 |
| 70 | Polydor 2343 032 | THINK PINK (LP, with pink lyric insert) | 350 |
| 70 | Polydor 2343 032 | THINK PINK (LP, without pink lyric insert) | 200 |
| 70 | Polydor 2343 032 | THINK PINK (LP, red vinyl with pink lyric insert) | 400 |
| 91 | Twink LP 2 | ODDS & BEGINNINGS (LP, with insert, numbered & signed, some on red vinyl, 1,500 only) | 15 |

*(see also Pretty Things, Pink Fairies, Fairies, Tomorrow, Aquarian Age, Rings, Mick Farren, Magic Muscle)*

## TWINKLE (RIPLEY)

| | | | |
|---|---|---|---|
| 64 | Decca F 12013 | Terry/The Boy Of My Dreams | 6 |
| 65 | Decca F 12076 | Golden Lights/Ain't Nobody Home But Me | 10 |
| 65 | Decca F 12139 | Tommy/So Sad | 12 |
| 65 | Decca F 12219 | Poor Old Johnny/I Need Your Hand In Mine | 15 |
| 65 | Decca F 12305 | The End Of The World/Take Me To The Dance | 15 |
| 66 | Decca F 12464 | What Am I Doing Here With You?/Now I Have You | 15 |
| 69 | Instant IN 005 | Micky/Darby And Joan | 15 |
| 74 | Bradleys BRAD 7418 | Days/Caroline (as Twinkle Ripley) (p/s) | 15 |
| 74 | Bradleys BRAD 7418 | Days/Caroline (as Twinkle Ripley) | 7 |
| 82 | EMI 5278 | I'm A Believer/For Sale (p/s) | 15 |
| 65 | Decca DFE 8621 | TWINKLE - A LONELY SINGING DOLL (EP) | 60 |

*(see also Silkie Davis)*

## TWINKLE BROTHERS

| | | | |
|---|---|---|---|
| 70 | Jackpot JP 731 | Shu Be Du/All My Enemies Beware | 8 |
| 70 | Jackpot JP 740 | Miss World/Take What You've Got | 15 |
| 70 | Jackpot JP 741 | Sweet Young Thing/Grandma | 8 |
| 71 | Jackpot JP 768 | Do Your Own Thing/BOY WONDER: They Talk About Love | 10 |
| 71 | Green Door GD 4007 | Miss Labba Labba/The Best Is Yet To Come | 10 |
| 71 | Big Shot BI 593 | You Took Me By Suprise/You Took Me By Surprise - Version (both sides actually by Tony Brevitt) | 15 |
| 71 | Big Shot BI 600 | It's Not Who You Know/I Need Someone | 8 |
| 71 | Tropical AL 002 | Love Sweet Love/HERON ATTAR: Poor Man's Life | 5 |
| 72 | Sioux SI 003 | Happy Song/Little Caesar | 5 |
| 73 | Camel CA 105 | Room Full All Full/Version | 12 |
| 73 | Count Shelley CS 31 | Mother Whiney/JACKIE BROWN: Fight My Way | 6 |
| 73 | Camel CA 106 | Room Full All Full/Version | 12 |
| 73 | Magnet MG 033 | Mother And Wife/Version | 5 |
| 73 | Pama PM 876 | Village Ram/Push It Inna | 10 |
| 75 | Faith FA 007 | Friends/No Big Thing | 5 |
| 75 | Faith FA 022 | Mother And Wife/GENE RONDO: Impossible Dream | 6 |
| 77 | Carib Gems CG 009 | Jah Army/Dub The Wicked | 6 |
| 79 | Virgin Front Line FLS 119 12 | Keep On Trying/King Pharoah (12") | 12 |
| 79 | Virgin Front Line FLS 123 12 | Jahoviah/Free Africa (12") | 25 |
| 80 | Virging Front Line FLS 12712 | Never Get Burned/Jah Kingdom Come (12" white label) | 30 |
| 81 | Twinkle TW 1/12 | Rasta Pon Top/It Gwine Dread (12") | 15 |
| 81 | Twinkle A 621 | Robot/Don't Turn Your Back On Jah (12") | 15 |
| 81 | Twinkle NG 643 | Africa For The Africans/Stomach Sick (12") | 10 |
| 83 | Twinkle NG 369 | Let Jah In/Don't Jump The Fence (12") | 15 |
| 86 | Jah Shaka SHAKA 855 | Faith Can Move Mountain/Mob Fury (12") | 25 |
| 91 | Twinkle NG 100 | Ethiopia Is Calling/COLOUR RED: Ethiopia Here I Come (12") | 18 |
| 92 | Twinkle NG 106 | The Reality Of Jah Kingdom/Twinkle Brothers | 20 |
| 92 | Twinkle NG107 | Constipated People/Version | 10 |
| 92 | Jah Shaka | Africa/Version (tracks not printed on labels) | 20 |
| 92 | Jah Shaka | Rasta Surface/Version (tracks not printed on labels) | 20 |
| 92 | Jah Shaka 855 | Faith Can Move Mountains/Mob Fury (12") | 15 |
| 75 | Grounation GROL 506 | RASTA PON TOP (LP) | 35 |
| 76 | Carib Gems CGLP 1001 | DO YOUR OWN THING (LP) | 60 |
| 78 | Front Line FCL 5001 | LOVE (10" LP) | 12 |
| 80 | Virgin V2169 | COUNTRYMEN (LP) | 15 |
| 82 | Twinkle NG 500 | UNDERGROUND (LP) | 15 |
| 82 | Twinkle NNG 741 | DUB MASSACRE (INNA MURDER STYLE) (LP) | 15 |
| 83 | Twinkle NG 502 | DUB MASSACRE PART TWO (LP) | 15 |
| 84 | Twinkle NG 501 | BURDEN BEARER (LP) | 20 |
| 85 | Twinkle NGLP 505 | DUB MASSACRE PART THREE (LP) | 15 |
| 89 | Twinkle NG 515 | DUB MASSACRE PART FOUR (LP) | 15 |

*(see also Busty Brown, Sammy Jones)*

## TWINS

| | | | |
|---|---|---|---|
| 73 | Downtown DT 511 | Rastafari Ruler/TYRONE TAYLOR: Yesterday | 8 |

## TWINSET

| | | | |
|---|---|---|---|
| 67 | Decca F 12629 | Tremblin'/Sneakin' Up On You | 25 |

## TWIN-TONES
| | | |
|---|---|---|
| 58 | RCA RCA 1040 | Jo Ann/Before You Go ...................................................................................... 50 |

## TWIN TUNES QUINTET
| | | |
|---|---|---|
| 58 | RCA RCA 1046 | The Love Nest/Baby Lover ................................................................................ 12 |

## TWIST
| | | |
|---|---|---|
| 79 | Polydor 2059 156 | This Is Your Life/Life's A Commercial Break (p/s) ............................................ 10 |
| 79 | Polydor POSP 84 | Ads/Rebound ...................................................................................................... 10 |
| 79 | Polydor 2383 552 | THIS IS YOUR LIFE (LP) ....................................................................................... 20 |

## TWIST
| | | |
|---|---|---|
| 91 | East West YZ 586 | The Fat Lady Sings/Heavy Duty (p/s) ................................................................. 5 |

## TWIST & SHOUT
| | | |
|---|---|---|
| 79 | Wessex WEX 268 | Bounce Back/As It Happens (p/s) ...................................................................... 20 |

## TWISTED ACE
| | | |
|---|---|---|
| 81 | Heavy Metal HEAVY 9 | Firebird/I Won't Surrender (in p/s) ................................................................... 12 |
| 81 | Heavy Metal HEAVY 9 | Firebird/I Won't Surrender ................................................................................. 5 |

## TWISTED SISTER
| | | |
|---|---|---|
| 82 | Secret SHH 137-12 | RUFF CUTS (12" EP, p/s) ..................................................................................... 10 |
| 86 | Atlantic A 9478D | Leader Of The Pack/I Wanna Rock (p/s, with free single) ................................. 5 |
| 85 | Atlantic 781 275-1P | COME OUT AND PLAY (LP, picture disc) ............................................................. 12 |

## TWISTED NERVE
| | | |
|---|---|---|
| 82 | Playlist PLAY 3 | CAUGHT IN SESSION EP (poster p/s) ................................................................... 15 |
| 83 | Criminal Damage CRI 102 | Five Minutes Of Fame/Strange Sensation ........................................................... 8 |
| 83 | Criminal Damage CRI 103 | EYES YOU CAN DROWN IN EP ............................................................................. 20 |
| 84 | Nerve NERVE 1 | SEANCE (Mini-LP) ................................................................................................ 25 |

## TWISTERS
| | | |
|---|---|---|
| 60 | Capitol CL 15167 | Turn The Page/Dancing Little Clown ................................................................... 8 |
| 62 | Aral/Windsor PSA 106 | Peppermint Twist Time/Silly Chilli .................................................................... 12 |

## TWISTING FERRARIS
| | | |
|---|---|---|
| 80 | Round TF 001 | Our Favourite Photograph/Lipsticks (p/s) ........................................................ 12 |

## CONWAY TWITTY
### 78s
| | | |
|---|---|---|
| 57 | Mercury MT 173 | Shake It Up/Maybe Baby ..................................................................................... 30 |
| 59 | MGM MGM 1029 | Mona Lisa/Heavenly ........................................................................................... 20 |
| 59 | MGM MGM 1047 | Rosaleena/Halfway To Heaven ........................................................................... 30 |

### SINGLES
| | | |
|---|---|---|
| 58 | MGM MGM 992 | It's Only Make Believe/I'll Try ............................................................................ 10 |
| 59 | MGM MGM 1003 | The Story Of My Love/Make Me Know You're Mine ......................................... 10 |
| 59 | MGM MGM 1016 | Hey Little Lucy! (Don'tcha Put No Lipstick On)/ When I'm Not With You .......... 10 |
| 59 | MGM MGM 1029 | Mona Lisa/Heavenly ............................................................................................. 6 |
| 59 | MGM MGM 1047 | Rosaleena/Halfway To Heaven ............................................................................ 6 |
| 60 | MGM MGM 1056 | Lonely Blue Boy/My One And Only You .............................................................. 10 |
| 60 | MGM MGM 1066 | What Am I Living For/The Hurt In My Heart ....................................................... 10 |
| 60 | MGM MGM 1082 | Is A Blue Bird Blue/She's Mine ........................................................................... 15 |
| 60 | MGM MGM 1095 | What A Dream/Tell Me One More Time ............................................................... 6 |
| 60 | MGM MGM 1108 | Whole Lotta Shakin' Goin' On/The Flame .......................................................... 12 |
| 61 | MGM MGM 1118 | C'est Si Bon/Don't You Dare Let Me Down ........................................................ 12 |
| 61 | MGM MGM 1129 | The Next Kiss/Man Alone ..................................................................................... 6 |
| 61 | MGM MGM 1137 | It's Drivin' Me Wild/Sweet Sorry ....................................................................... 10 |
| 62 | MGM MGM 1152 | Tower Of Tears/Portrait Of A Fool ..................................................................... 12 |
| 62 | MGM MGM 1170 | Comfy An' Cozy/Unchained Melody .................................................................... 10 |
| 62 | MGM MGM 1187 | I Hope I Think I Wish/The Pick Up ...................................................................... 12 |
| 63 | MGM MGM 1201 | Handy Man/Little Piece Of My Heart ................................................................. 10 |
| 63 | MGM MGM 1209 | She Ain't No Angel/Got My Mojo Workin' .......................................................... 12 |
| 63 | HMV POP 1258 | Go On And Cry/She Loves Me .............................................................................. 8 |

### EPs
| | | |
|---|---|---|
| 58 | MGM MGM-EP 684 | IT'S ONLY MAKE BELIEVE ..................................................................................... 30 |
| 59 | MGM MGM-EP 698 | HEY LITTLE LUCY ................................................................................................. 50 |
| 60 | MGM MGM-EP 719 | SATURDAY NIGHT WITH CONWAY TWITTY ......................................................... 50 |
| 60 | Mercury ZEP 10069 | I NEED YOUR LOVIN' .......................................................................................... 100 |
| 60 | MGM MGM-EP 738 | IS A BLUEBIRD BLUE? .......................................................................................... 40 |
| 61 | MGM MGM-EP 752 | THE ROCK 'N' ROLL STORY .................................................................................. 50 |

### ALBUMS
| | | |
|---|---|---|
| 59 | MGM MGM-C 781 | CONWAY TWITTY SINGS ..................................................................................... 100 |
| 60 | MGM MGM-C 801 | SATURDAY NIGHT WITH CONWAY TWITTY ......................................................... 100 |
| 60 | MGM MGM-C 829 | LONELY BLUE BOY ............................................................................................... 100 |
| 63 | MGM MGM-C 950 | R AND B '63 ........................................................................................................ 50 |
| 68 | MCA MUP(S) 342 | HERE'S CONWAY TWITTY (AND HIS LONELY BLUE BOYS) .................................. 18 |
| 68 | MGM C/CS 8100 | THE ROCK AND ROLL STORY ............................................................................... 40 |
| 69 | MCA MUPS 363 | NEXT IN LINE ...................................................................................................... 15 |

## TWIZZLE & HOT ROD ALLSTARS
| | | |
|---|---|---|
| 70 | Torpedo TOR 3 | Jook Jook/The Graduate ...................................................................................... 30 |

## TWO
| | | |
|---|---|---|
| 84 | Reflex 12 RE 7 | 2 x 2 (12" EP) ....................................................................................................... 20 |
| 83 | Future FL3 | DREAMING SPIRES (LP) ....................................................................................... 25 |

## TWO & A HALF
| | | |
|---|---|---|
| 66 | CBS 202248 | Midnight Swim/Faith ........................................................................................... 10 |

| | | | |
|---|---|---|---|
| 66 | CBS 202404 | Questions/In Harmony | 8 |
| 67 | CBS 202526 | The Walls Are High/Love You | 8 |
| 67 | Decca F 22672 | Suburban Early Morning Station/Just Couldn't Believe My Ears | 15 |
| 67 | Decca F 22715 | I Don't Need To Tell You/Christmas Will Be Round Again | 18 |

**TWO DARK TROOPERS**

| | | | |
|---|---|---|---|
| 92 | Basement BRSS 020 | I Wanna Be Your Lover/Darkcore (12") | 10 |

*(see also Chemical, DJ Mayhem)*

**TWO FINGERED APPROACH**

| | | | |
|---|---|---|---|
| 82 | Virus 026 | World War Album/Society Hooked/Family Traditions (p/s. 500 only) | 60 |

**TWO FOR THE ROAD**

| | | | |
|---|---|---|---|
| 70s | Pastiche BJ 2929 | TWO FOR THE ROAD (LP) | 20 |

**TWO KINGS**

| | | | |
|---|---|---|---|
| 65 | Island WI 240 | Rolling Stone/SUFFERER: Tomorrow Morning (B-side act. by Frank Cosmo) | 18 |
| 65 | Island WI 249 | Hit You Let You Feel It/Honey I Love You (both sides actually by Fugitives) | 18 |

**TWO MAN SOUND**

| | | | |
|---|---|---|---|
| 74 | Spark SRL 118 | Amadeo/Somebody Is Ready To Love You | 8 |
| 78 | Miracle M12 | Que Tal America/Brazil O Brazil (12") | 15 |

**TWO MINDS CRACK**

| | | | |
|---|---|---|---|
| 84 | Sedition EDIT 2 | Enemies Of Promise/The Stealer (p/s) | 6 |

**TWO MUCH**

| | | | |
|---|---|---|---|
| 67 | Fontana TF 858 | Wonderland Of Love/Mister Money | 7 |
| 68 | Fontana TF 900 | It's A Hip Hip Hippy World/Stay In My World | 10 |

**TWO-NINETEEN (2.19) SKIFFLE GROUP**

| | | | |
|---|---|---|---|
| 57 | Esquire 10-512 | Where Can I Go?/Roll The Union On (78) | 20 |
| 57 | Esquire 10-515 | This Little Light Of Mine/Union Maid (78) | 20 |
| 57 | Esquire EP 126 | TWO-NINETEEN SKIFFLE GROUP (EP) | 40 |
| 57 | Esquire EP 146 | TWO-NINETEEN SKIFFLE GROUP (EP) | 55 |
| 58 | Esquire EP 176 | TWO-NINETEEN SKIFFLE GROUP (EP) | 55 |
| 58 | Esquire EP 196 | TWO-NINETEEN SKIFFLE GROUP (EP) | 60 |

**TWO OF CLUBS**

| | | | |
|---|---|---|---|
| 64 | Columbia DB 7371 | The Angels Must Have Made You/True Love Is Here | 15 |

**TWO OF EACH**

| | | | |
|---|---|---|---|
| 67 | Decca F 12626 | Every Single Day/I'm Glad I Got You | 8 |
| 68 | Pye 7N 17555 | The Summer Of Our Love/Saturday Morning | 7 |

**TWO PEOPLE (1)**

| | | | |
|---|---|---|---|
| 76 | Bright Spot BS 009 | Time Is Precious/Jump Higher | 15 |

**TWO PEOPLE (2)**

| | | | |
|---|---|---|---|
| 86 | Polydor | Mouth Of An Angel (p/s) | 20 |
| 80s | Polydor | This Is The Shirt (p/s) | 10 |

**2 SLICES OF JAM**

| | | | |
|---|---|---|---|
| 92 | White Label | Pressing On Ya Mind/Beat Like This (12" white label) | 60 |

**TWO SPARKS**

| | | | |
|---|---|---|---|
| 72 | Moodisc HM 113 | Run Away Girl/When We Were Young | 8 |

*(see also Carl Bryan, Winston Wright)*

**2 THE TOP**

| | | | |
|---|---|---|---|
| 89 | Rhyme & Reason 12RNR2 | The Rhythm I Give Em (12") | 15 |
| 90 | President PT12590 | Score To Settle/The Matter At Hand (12") | 45 |

*(see also Kinetic Effect)*

**2 3**

| | | | |
|---|---|---|---|
| 79 | Fast Products FAST 2 | Where To Now?/All Time Low (p/s) | 15 |

**TWO TIMES DEF**

| | | | |
|---|---|---|---|
| 92 | Mendoza MEN016 | First And Last (Vocal)/First And Last (Instrumental)/First And Last (Alternative Mix) (12", stamped white labels) | 150 |

*(see also Silent Eclipse)*

**TWO TONE COMMITTEE**

| | | | |
|---|---|---|---|
| 91 | Precinct PREC002 | Beings From A Word Stuck Surface (12") | 25 |

**2-X-TREME**

| | | | |
|---|---|---|---|
| 92 | Empire E 001 | X-TREMITY EP (12", white label stamped in red, beware of represses!) | 50 |

**2 PAC**

| | | | |
|---|---|---|---|
| 02 | Simply Vinyl S 12 | ALL EYEZ ON ME (3-LP, reissue) | 20 |

**TYDE**

| | | | |
|---|---|---|---|
| 02 | Rough Trade RTRADES 056 | Blood Brothers/Play It As It Lays (p/s) | 6 |

**ARLYNE TYE**

| | | | |
|---|---|---|---|
| 59 | London HLL 8825 | The Universe/Who Is The One | 25 |

**TYGERS OF PAN TANG**

| | | | |
|---|---|---|---|
| 79 | Neat NEAT 03 | Don't Touch Me There/Burning Up/Bad Times (first pressing of around 1,000 in slightly oversized p/s giving it a 'home made' feel) | 25 |
| 79 | Neat NEAT 03 | Don't Touch Me There/Burning Up/Bad Times (p/s) | 12 |
| 80 | MCA MCA 582 | Don't Touch Me There/Burning Up/Bad Times (p/s, reissue) | 10 |
| 80 | MCA MCA 612 | Rock'n'Roll Man/All Right On The Night/Wild Man (p/s) | 5 |
| 80 | MCA MCA 634 | Suzie Smiled/Tush (p/s) | 5 |
| 80 | MCA MCA 644 | Euthanasia/Straight As A Die (p/s) | 5 |
| 81 | MCA MCA 672 | Hellbound/Bad Times//Bad Times/Don't Take Nothin' ('The Audition Tapes' double pack) | 6 |
| 81 | MCA MCA 692 | The Story So Far/Silver And Gold/All Or Nothing (p/s) | 5 |
| 81 | MCA MCA 723 | Don't Stop By/Slave To Freedom (p/s) | 5 |
| 81 | MCA MCAT 723 | Don't Stop By/Slave To Freedom (12", p/s) | 12 |

MINT VALUE £

| | | | |
|---|---|---|---|
| 81 | MCA MCA 755 | Love Don't Stay/Paradise Drive (p/s) | 8 |
| 81 | MCA MCA 759 | Do It Good/Slip Away (no p/s) | 30 |
| 81 | MCA MCA 769 | Love Potion No. 9/The Stormlands (p/s) | 5 |
| 82 | MCA MCA 777 | Rendezvous/Life Of Crime (white vinyl, p/s) | 6 |
| 82 | MCA MCA 777 | Rendezvous/Life Of Crime (red or blue vinyl, p/s) | 5 |
| 82 | MCA MCA 777 | Rendezvous/Life Of Crime (poster p/s) | 5 |
| 82 | MCA MCA 777 | Rendezvous/Life Of Crime (p/s) | 5 |
| 82 | MCA MCA 790 | Paris By Air/Love's A Lie (standard p/s with earring) | 10 |
| 82 | MCA MCA 790 | Paris By Air/Love's A Lie (poster p/s) | 5 |
| 82 | MCA MCA 798 | Making Tracks/What You Saying (p/s) | 5 |
| 82 | MCA MCAT 798 | Making Tracks (Extended Remix)/What You Saying (12", p/s) | 10 |
| 81 | MCA MCF 3123 | CRAZY NIGHTS (LP, stickered sleeve, insert, with bonus 12") | 22 |

*(see also John Sykes)*

### TYLA GANG
| | | | |
|---|---|---|---|
| 76 | Stiff BUY 4 | Styrofoam/Texas Chainsaw Massacre Boogie (push-out centre, die-cut ' stamped' white sleeve) | 10 |
| 76 | Stiff BUY 4 | Styrofoam/Texas Chainsaw Massacre Boogie (push-out centre, plain die-cut white sleeve) | 6 |

*(see also Ducks Deluxe)*

### BIG 'T' TYLER
| | | | |
|---|---|---|---|
| 57 | Vogue V 9079 | King Kong/Sadie Green | 200 |
| 57 | Vogue V 9079 | King Kong/Sadie Green (78) | 100 |

### RED TYLER
| | | | |
|---|---|---|---|
| 56 | Parlophone MSP 6215 | Fool 'Em Devil/Stardust | 18 |
| 60 | Top Rank JAR 306 | Junk Village/Happy Sax | 12 |

### T. TEXAS TYLER
| | | | |
|---|---|---|---|
| 59 | Parlophone GEP 8788 | COUNTRY ROUND-UP (EP) | 30 |
| 67 | London HA-B 8322 | MAN WITH A MILLION FRIENDS (LP) | 25 |

### TERRY TYLER
| | | | |
|---|---|---|---|
| 61 | Pye International 7N 25119 | A Thousand Feet Below/Answer Me | 15 |

### TOBY TYLER
| | | | |
|---|---|---|---|
| 64 | Emidisc no cat. no. | The Road I'm On (Gloria)/Blowin' In The Wind (acetate, 1 copy only) | 3000 |
| 89 | Archive Jive TOBY 1 | The Road I'm On (Gloria) (mail-order issue, numbered p/s, 1-sided, 1,500 only) | 15 |

*(see also Marc Bolan)*

### TYMES
| | | | |
|---|---|---|---|
| 63 | Cameo Parkway P 871 | So Much In Love/Roscoe James McClain | 10 |
| 63 | Cameo Parkway P 884 | Wonderful Wonderful/Come With Me To The Sea (in p/s) | 25 |
| 63 | Cameo Parkway P 884 | Wonderful Wonderful/Come With Me To The Sea | 10 |
| 64 | Cameo Parkway P 891 | Somewhere/View From My Window | 15 |
| 64 | Cameo Parkway P 908 | To Each His Own/Wonderland Of Love | 15 |
| 64 | Cameo Parkway P 919 | The Magic Of Our Summer Love/With All My Heart | 15 |
| 64 | Cameo Parkway P 924 | Here She Comes/Malibu | 100 |
| 64 | Cameo Parkway P 924 | Here She Comes/Malibu (DJ copy) | 200 |
| 69 | Direction 58-3903 | People/For Love Of Ivy | 6 |
| 69 | Direction 58-4450 | If You Love Me Baby/Find My Way | 10 |
| 71 | CBS 7250 | Someone To Watch Over Me/She's Gone (featuring George Williams) | 8 |
| 63 | Cameo Parkway P 7032 | SO MUCH IN LOVE (LP) | 70 |
| 69 | Direction 8-63558 | PEOPLE (LP, mono or stereo) | 25 |
| 78 | London HAU 8516 | CAMEO PARKWAY SESSIONS (LP) | 25 |

### MCCOY TYNER
| | | | |
|---|---|---|---|
| 70s | Impulse IMPL 8043 | INCEPTION (LP) | 12 |

### ROB TYNER & HOT RODS
| | | | |
|---|---|---|---|
| 77 | Island WIP 6418 | 'Till The Night Is Gone (Let's Rock)/Flipside Rock (p/s) | 5 |

*(see also MC 5, Eddie & Hot Rods)*

### TYPHOONS (1)
| | | | |
|---|---|---|---|
| 63 | Embassy WB 589 | Surf City/I Want To Stay Here | 7 |
| 65 | Embassy WB 677 | Tired Of Waiting For You/Baby Please Don't Go | 7 |
| 65 | Embassy WEP 1115 | Hard Day's Night/And I Love Her/I Should Have Known Better/Tell Me Why (EP) | 10 |
| 65 | Embassy WT 2006 | Ticket To Ride/Here Comes The Night/I'll Be There/I Can't Explain (EP) | 15 |

*(see also Bud Ashton, Ray Pilgrim, Mike Redway)*

### TYPHOONS (2)
| | | | |
|---|---|---|---|
| 81 | Bohemian BO 1 | Telstar/In Fae A Brothin' (p/s) | 5 |

*(see also Ruts)*

### TYRANNOSAURUS REX
| | | | |
|---|---|---|---|
| 68 | Regal Zonophone RZ 3008 | Debora/Child Star (with promo only p/s) | 400 |
| 68 | Regal Zonophone RZ 3008 | Debora/Child Star (with promo only p/s, with insert) | 500 |
| 68 | Regal Zonophone RZ 3008 | Debora/Child Star (demo copy as above, but without promo only p/s) | 375 |
| 68 | Regal Zonophone RZ 3008 | Debora/Child Star | 35 |
| 68 | Regal Zonophone RZ 3011 | One Inch Rock/Salamanda Palaganda (promo only p/s) | 375 |
| 68 | Regal Zonophone RZ 3011 | One Inch Rock/Salamanda Palaganda (promo only p/s, with insert) | 425 |
| 68 | Regal Zonophone RZ 3011 | One Inch Rock/Salamanda Palaganda | 40 |
| 69 | Regal Zonophone RZ 3016 | Pewter Suitor/Warlord Of The Royal Crocodiles | 70 |
| 69 | Regal Zonophone RZ 3022 | King Of The Rumbling Spires/Do You Remember (with promo only p/s) | 450 |
| 69 | Regal Zonophone RZ 3022 | King Of The Rumbling Spires/Do You Remember (demo, without promo only p/s) | 400 |
| 69 | Regal Zonophone RZ 3022 | King Of The Rumbling Spires/Do You Remember | 40 |
| 70 | Regal Zonophone RZ 3025 | By The Light Of A Magical Moon/Find A Little Wood | 40 |
| 72 | Magni Fly ECHO 102 | Debora/One Inch Rock/The Woodland Bop/The Seal Of Seasons (p/s) | 5 |
| 82 | Old Gold OG 9234 | Debora/One Inch Rock (1,000 mispressed with "Beltane Walk" on B-side) | 5 |

| 91 | Tyrannosaurus Rex TYR 1 | Sleepy Maurice/1968 Radio Promos (Tyrannosaurus Rex Appreciation Society release, 2,000 only, p/s with card insert) .................................................................................................. 8 |
|----|-------------------------|------------------------------------------------------|
| 68 | Regal Zonophone LRZ 1003 | MY PEOPLE WERE FAIR AND HAD SKY IN THEIR HAIR BUT NOW THEY'RE CONTENT TO WEAR STARS ON THEIR BROWS (LP, mono, with lyric sheet & manuscript) ............ 100 |
| 68 | Regal Zonophone LRZ 1003 | MY PEOPLE WERE FAIR AND HAD SKY IN THEIR HAIR BUT NOW THEY'RE CONTENT TO WEAR STARS ON THEIR BROWS (LP, mono) .................................................................. 50 |
| 68 | Regal Zonophone SLRZ 1003 | MY PEOPLE WERE FAIR AND HAD SKY IN THEIR HAIR BUT NOW THEY'RE CONTENT TO WEAR STARS ON THEIR BROWS (LP, stereo, with lyric sheet & manuscript) ................... 60 |
| 68 | Regal Zonophone SLRZ 1003 | MY PEOPLE WERE FAIR AND HAD SKY IN THEIR HAIR BUT NOW THEY'RE CONTENT TO WEAR STARS ON THEIR BROWS (LP, stereo) ............................................................ 20 |
| 68 | Regal Zonophone TA-LRZ 1003 | MY PEOPLE WERE FAIR AND HAD SKY IN THEIR HAIR BUT NOW THEY'RE CONTENT TO WEAR STARS ON THEIR BROWS (reel-to-reel tape, mono) ........................................ 35 |
| 68 | Regal Zonophone LRZ 1005 | PROPHETS, SEERS AND SAGES, THE ANGELS OF THE AGES (LP, with lyric sheet, textured sleeve, mono) .................................................................................................. 100 |
| 68 | Regal Zonophone SLRZ 1005 | PROPHETS, SEERS AND SAGES, THE ANGELS OF THE AGES (LP, with lyric sheet, textured sleeve, stereo) ............................................................................................... 80 |
| 69 | R. Zonophone LRZ 1007 | UNICORN (LP, gatefold sleeve, original with blue/silver label, mono) ...................... 120 |
| 69 | R. Zonophone LRZ 1007 | UNICORN (LP, gatefold sleeve, later issue with red/silver label, mono) ...................... 60 |
| 70 | R. Zonophone SLRZ 1007 | UNICORN (LP, gatefold sleeve, original with blue/silver label, stereo) ..................... 100 |
| 70 | R. Zonophone SLRZ 1007 | UNICORN (LP, gatefold sleeve, later issue with red/silver label, stereo) .................... 30 |
| 70 | R. Zonophone SLRZ 1013 | A BEARD OF STARS (LP, with lyric sheet) ............................................................. 60 |
| 70 | R. Zonophone SLRZ 1013 | A BEARD OF STARS (LP, without lyric sheet) ........................................................ 30 |

*(see also Marc Bolan/T. Rex, John's Children, Dib Cochran & Earwigs, Shagrat)*

**TYRANT**

| 83 | SRTS 83 CUS 2046 | Hold Back The Lightning/Eyes Of A Stranger ....................................................... 400 |
|----|------------------|------------------------------------------------------|

**TYRONE & CARR**

| 72 | Jam JAM 7 | I Want To Give You My Everything/I'm Still In Love With You ................................... 8 |
|----|-----------|------------------------------------------------------|
| 73 | Jam JAM 36 | Love Me Love You/Take Me With You .................................................................. 30 |
| 75 | DJM DJS 349 | Love Me Love You/Take Me With You .................................................................. 30 |

**GORDON TYRRALL**

| 78 | Hill & Dale HD 002 | FAREWELL TO FOGGY HILLS (LP) ....................................................................... 18 |
|----|--------------------|------------------------------------------------------|

**TYSONDOG**

| 83 | Neat NEAT 33 | Eat The Rich/Dead Meat (p/s) ............................................................................. 10 |
|----|--------------|------------------------------------------------------|
| 85 | Neat NEAT 46 | Shoot To Kill/Hammerhead (p/s) ........................................................................ 10 |
| 85 | Neat NEAT 4612 | Shoot To Kill/Hammerhead/Changeling/Back To The Bullet (12", p/s) .................... 15 |
| 86 | Neat NEAT 56 | School's Out/Don't Let The Bastards Grind You Down (p/s) ................................... 12 |
| 86 | Neat NEAT 1031 | CRIMES OF INSANITY (LP, with inner) ................................................................ 18 |
| 84 | Neat NEAT 1017 | BEWARE OF THE DOG (LP, with insert) ............................................................... 20 |

**TYTAN**

| 82 | Kamaflage KAM 6 | Blind Men And Fools/The Ballad Of Edward Case (p/s) ......................................... 18 |
|----|-----------------|------------------------------------------------------|
| 82 | Kamaflage KAMA 6 | Blind Men And Fools/The Ballad Of Edward Case (12", p/s) ................................... 20 |
| 85 | Metal Masters METALP 105 | ROUGH JUSTICE (LP) ....................................................................................... 22 |

*(see also Angel Witch)*

**JUDIE TZUKE**

| 78 | Rocket ROKN 541 | For You/Sukarita ................................................................................................ 5 |
|----|-----------------|------------------------------------------------------|

*(see also Tzuke & Paxo, Zookie)*

**TZUKE & PAXO**

| 76 | Good Earth GD 12 | These Are The Laws/It's Only Fantasies ............................................................... 15 |
|----|------------------|------------------------------------------------------|

**U**

**U BLACK**

| 78 | Hit Run HIT 621 | Wicked Are To Blame/Dub (12") ......................................................................... 20 |
|----|-----------------|------------------------------------------------------|
| 77 | Third World TWS 926 | WESTBOUND THING A SWING (LP) ................................................................... 40 |

**U BROWN**

| 77 | Third World TWS 909 | LONDON ROCK (LP) ........................................................................................ 30 |
|----|---------------------|------------------------------------------------------|
| 78 | Live & Love LALP 002 | REVELATION TIME (LP) .................................................................................... 30 |

**U.F.O.**

| 70 | Beacon BEA 161 | Shake It About/Evil ........................................................................................... 40 |
|----|----------------|------------------------------------------------------|
| 70 | Beacon BEA 165 | Come Away Melinda/Unidentified Flying Object ................................................... 25 |
| 70 | Beacon BEA 172 | Boogie For George/Treacle People (with postcard) .............................................. 30 |
| 70 | Beacon BEA 172 | Boogie For George/Treacle People ..................................................................... 20 |
| 71 | Beacon BEA 181 | Prince Kajuku/The Coming Of Prince Kajuku ....................................................... 20 |
| 73 | Chrysalis CHS 2024 | Give Her The Gun/Sweet Little Thing (unreleased in U.K.) ...................................... 0 |
| 74 | Chrysalis CHS 2040 | Doctor Doctor/Lipstick Traces ........................................................................... 12 |
| 75 | Chrysalis CHS 2072 | Shoot Shoot/Love Lost Love (unissued) ................................................................ 0 |
| 77 | Chrysalis CHS 2146 | Alone Again Or/Electric Phase ........................................................................... 10 |
| 77 | Chrysalis CHS 2178 | Gettin' Ready/Lights Out (unissued) ...................................................................... 0 |
| 78 | Chrysalis CHS 2241 | Only You Can Rock Me/Cherry/Rock Bottom (p/s, red vinyl, with frisbee offer) ........ 8 |
| 78 | Chrysalis CHS 2241 | Only You Can Rock Me/Cherry/Rock Bottom (p/, with frisbee offer) .......................... 6 |
| 79 | Chrysalis CHS 2287 | Doctor Doctor (live)/On With The Action (live)/Try Me (p/s, clear vinyl) .................... 6 |
| 79 | Chrysalis CHS 2287 | Doctor Doctor (live)/On With The Action (live)/Try Me (p/s, mauve vinyl) ................. 10 |
| 79 | Chrysalis CHS 2318 | Shoot Shoot (live)/Only You Can Rock Me (live)/I'm A Loser (live) (p/s, clear vinyl) ... 5 |
| 83 | Lyntone LYN 12821 | Blinded By A Lie (edit)/Diesel In The Dust (edit)/When It's Time To Rock (edit) (flexidisc with Metal Fury magazine, issue 12) ...................................................... 10 |
| 70 | Beacon BEAS 12 | U.F.O. 1 (LP) ................................................................................................. 150 |

MINT VALUE £

| 72 | Beacon BEAS 19 | U.F.O. 2 - FLYING (ONE HOUR SPACE ROCK) (LP, with inner lyric sleeve) | 150 |
| 72 | Beacon BEAS 19 | U.F.O. 2 - FLYING (ONE HOUR SPACE ROCK) (LP) | 30 |
| 74 | Chrysalis CHS 1059 | PHENOMENON (LP, misprinted green label, matt sleeve) | 15 |
| 76 | Chrysalis CHR 1103 | NO HEAVY PETTING (LP, 1st pressing, green labels, A1/B1 matrixes) | 20 |
| 77 | Chrysalis CHR 1127 | LIGHTS OUT (LP, 1st pressing, etched matrix numbers CHR1127 A/B, TML-S stamped into dead wax on both sides, green label wih red text on outer rim, 'Chrysalis Records Ltd, Printed in U.K,' on spine) | 20 |

(see also Michael Schenker Group)

## LESLIE UGGAME
| 59 | Philips BBL 7370 | THE EYES OF GOD (LP) | 12 |

## UGLY CUSTARD
| 70 | Kaleidoscope KAL 100 | UGLY CUSTARD (LP) | 150 |

(see also Hungry Wolf, Alan Parker, Rock Machine)

## UGLYS
| 65 | Pye 7N 15858 | Wake Up My Mind/Ugly Blues | 30 |
| 65 | Pye 7N 15968 | It's Alright/A Friend | 20 |
| 66 | Pye 7N 17027 | A Good Idea/A Quiet Explosion | 30 |
| 66 | Pye 7N 17178 | End Of The Season/Can't Recall Her Name | 40 |
| 67 | CBS 2933 | And The Squire Blew His Horn/Real Good Girl | 50 |
| 69 | MGM MGM 1465 | I See The Light/Mary Cilento (6 demo copies only, pink/silver labels) | 1500 |

(see also Steve Gibbons, Balls, Lemon Tree, Move, Trevor Burton)

## U.K. BONDS
| 65 | Polydor BM 56061 | The World Is Watching Us/I Said Goodbye To The Blues | 10 |
| 66 | Polydor BM 56112 | Anything You Do Is Alright/The Last Thing I Ever Do | 20 |

## U.K. DECAY
| 79 | Plastic PLAS 001 | U.K. Decay/Car Crash/PNEUMONIA: Exhibition/Coming Attack (folded p/s) | 25 |
| 80 | Fresh 012 | For My Country/Unwind (p/s) | 8 |
| 81 | Fresh FRESH 26 | Unexpected Guest/Dresden (foldout p/s) | 6 |
| 81 | Fresh FRESH 33 | Sexual/Twist In The Tale (poster p/s) | 5 |
| 82 | C. Christi CHRIST ITS 1 | Rising From The Dread/Testament/Werewolf/Jerusalem Over (The White Cliffs Of Dover) (12", p/s with insert) | 12 |
| 81 | Fresh LP5 | FOR MADMEN ONLY (LP) | 18 |
| 80s | UK Decay DKLP1 | FOR MADMEN ONLY (LP) | 25 |

## UK PLAYERS
| 82 | A&M AMLH 68544 | NO WAY OUT (LP) | 20 |

## U.K. SUBS
| 78 | City NIK 5 | C.I.D./Live In A Car/B.I.C. (p/s, clear, red, blue, green, mustard or orange vinyl) | 20 |
| 78 | City NIK 5 | C.I.D./Live In A Car/B.I.C. (p/s, black vinyl) | 5 |
| 80 | Gem GEMS 30 | Teenage/Left For Dead/New York State Police (p/s, pink or orange vinyl) | 5 |
| 82 | Ramkup CAC 2 | Party In Paris (1-sided fan club single, no p/s, 500 only) | 30 |
| 83 | Fall Out FALL 017 | Another Typical City (p/s) | 5 |
| 84 | Gem FALL 12024 | SPELL EP (12") | 10 |
| 11 | Time And Matter T&M 005 | Product Supply/Rare Disease/Embryo (p/s, 250 only, signed, white vinyl) | 40 |
| 15 | Time & Matter T&M 018 | AMOEBA SOUNDS EP | 25 |
| 15 | Captain Oi! AHOY 704 | THE PEEL SESSIONS VOL 1 (7" EP 250 on white and 250 on yellow vinyl) | 25 |
| 15 | Captain Oi! AHOY 705 | THE PEEL SESSIONS VOL 2 (7" EP, 250 on green and 250 on white vinyl) | 25 |
| 16 | Captain Oi! AHOY 706 | THE PEEL SESSIONS VOL 3 (7" EP 250 on red and 250 on white vinyl) | 25 |
| 79 | Gem GEMLP 100 | ANOTHER KIND OF BLUES (LP, blue vinyl, with inner sleeve) | 20 |
| 80 | Gem GEMLP 111 | CRASH COURSE LIVE (LP, purple vinyl, 15,000 with export 12" [GEMEP 1]) | 15 |
| 80 | Gem GEMLP 111 | CRASH COURSE LIVE (LP) | 12 |
| 85 | RFB LP 1 | HUNTINGTON BEACH (LP) | 15 |
| 97 | Fallout LP 053 | PEEL SESSIONS 1978-79 (LP) | 15 |
| 11 | Captain Oi! AHOYLP 310 | WORK IN PROGRESS (LP, red vinyl) | 40 |
| 15 | Captain Oi! AHOYLP 317 | YELLOW LEADER (LP, yellow vinyl, clear yellow flexi and CD) | 150 |

(see also Urban Dogs, Charlie Harper & Captain Sensible)

## ANYAOGU UKONU & HIS AFRO-CALYPSOIANS
| 56 | London HA-U 2019 | AFRO U.S.A (LP) | 30 |

## U.K.S
| 64 | HMV POP 1310 | Ever Faithful, Ever True/Your Love Is All I Want | 25 |
| 64 | HMV POP 1357 | I Will Never Let You Go/I Know | 25 |

## TRACEY ULLMAN
| 83 | Stiff BUY DJ 195 | Move Over Darling/Bobby's Girl (pink promo, "A" label) | 15 |
| 83 | Stiff BUY DJ 232 | Move Over Darling/Bobby's Girl (grey promo, "A" label) | 5 |
| 85 | Stiff BUY DJ 232 | Shattered/Alone (light blue promo "A" label) | 6 |

## JAMES 'BLOOD' ULMER
| 81 | Rough Trade RT 045 | Are You Glad To Be In America?/T.V. Blues (p/s) | 5 |
| 80 | Rough Trade ROUGH 16 | ARE YOU GLAD TO BE IN AMERICA? (LP) | 15 |

## PETER ULRICH
| 90 | Corner Stone PTD-001 | Taqaharu's Leaving/Evocation (12") | 10 |

## ULTERIOR MOTIVES
| 79 | Motive Music MMR 1 | Another Lover (p/s) | 30 |

## ULTIMATE SPINACH
| 68 | MGM MGM-C(S) 8071 | ULTIMATE SPINACH (LP) | 175 |
| 68 | MGM MGM-C(S) 8094 | BEHOLD AND SEE (LP) | 175 |

## ULTRAFOX
| 71 | Deram DM339 | Nine By Nine/Stomping At Decca | 6 |

## ULTRA VIOLENT
| 83 | Riot City RIOT 25 | CRIME FOR REVENGE (EP) | 20 |

## ULTRA VIVID SCENE
| | | | |
|---|---|---|---|
| 89 | 4AD BAD 906 | Mercy Seat/Codeine/H Like In Heaven/Mercy Seat (LP Version) (12", uncut p/s [most copies die-cut]) | 22 |
| 89 | 4AD AD 908 | Something To Eat/H Like In Heaven (freebie, 1,000 only) | 10 |
| 90 | 4AD AD 0016 | Special One/Kind Of Drag | 7 |
| 90 | 4AD UVS 1 | Staring At The Sun/Three Stars (12", promo only) | 10 |
| 92 | 4AD UVS 2 | Medicating Angels/Mirror To Mirror (12", promo only) | 10 |

## ULTRAVOX
| | | | |
|---|---|---|---|
| 77 | Island IDJ-18 | Dangerous Rhythm/My Sex/The Wild The Beautiful And The Damned (12" promo) | 15 |
| 77 | Island WIP 6375 | Dangerous Rhythm/My Sex (initially no p/s) | 6 |
| 77 | Island WIP 6375 | Dangerous Rhythm/My Sex (reissue, later pressing with p/s) | 7 |
| 77 | Island WIP 6392 | Young Savage/Slip Away (p/s) | 8 |
| 77 | Island WIP 6404 | Rockwrock/Hiroshima Mon Amour (p/s) | 7 |
| 77 | Island WIP 6417 | Quirks/Modern Love (no p/s, most given away with LP Ha! Ha! Ha!) | 6 |
| 78 | Island WIP 6454 | Slow Motion/Dislocation (p/s) | 5 |
| 78 | Island WIP 6459 | Quiet Men/Cross Fade (p/s) | 6 |
| 80 | Chrysalis CHS 2441 | Sleepwalk/Waiting (clear vinyl) | 6 |
| 77 | Island ILPS 9449 | ULTRAVOX (LP, gatefold sleeve) | 20 |
| 77 | Island ILPS 9505 | HA! HA! HA! (LP, with 7" "Quirks"/"Modern Love" [WIP 6417] & inner sleeve) | 20 |
| 78 | Island ILPS 9555 | SYSTEMS OF ROMANCE (LP, with inner sleeve) | 20 |
| 13 | Chrysalis CHRS 1296 | VIENNA (LP, reissue, white vinyl, lyric inner, stickered sleeve, 500 only) | 20 |

*(see also Tiger Lily, John Foxx, Midge Ure, Helden)*

## UMPS & DUMPS
| | | | |
|---|---|---|---|
| 80 | Topic 12TS 416 | THE MOON'S IN A FIT (LP) | 15 |

## UNANIMITY
| | | | |
|---|---|---|---|
| 69 | Clementswood CC127 | Loner/All Right | 50 |

## UNANIMOUS DECISION
| | | | |
|---|---|---|---|
| 92 | Kold Sweat KSEP211 | RAP SINGS THE BLUES (EP) | 10 |
| 93 | Kold Sweat KSMEP 301X | IT AIN'T CLEVER (DOUBLE PACK EP) (12") | 12 |

## UNAUTHORISED VERSION
| | | | |
|---|---|---|---|
| 69 | CBS 4135 | Hey Jude/Girl In A Bus Queue | 20 |

## UNCLE DAVID
| | | | |
|---|---|---|---|
| 70 | Westbrook WK2 | Magic Mirror/You've Lost Me | 40 |

## UNCLE DOG
| | | | |
|---|---|---|---|
| 72 | Signpost SGP 752 | River Road/First Night | 5 |
| 72 | Signpost SG 4253 | OLD HAT (LP) | 200 |

*(see also Carol Grimes)*

## UNCLE FUNKENSTEIN
| | | | |
|---|---|---|---|
| 08 | Jazzman JMANLP 023 | TOGETHER AGAIN (LP, reissue) | 20 |

## UNCLE PO
| | | | |
|---|---|---|---|
| 78 | Beeb BEEB 23 | Use My Friends/15 Minutes | 25 |

## UNCLE SAM
| | | | |
|---|---|---|---|
| 78 | Ariola ARO 116 | Oh Pretty Woman/Do It For Love | 6 |

## UNCLE 22
| | | | |
|---|---|---|---|
| 92 | U No Dat HN 08 | Wonderful Life/Love Me Once/Calling All Cars (12") | 10 |
| 93 | Ram RAMM 008 | SPICE OF LIFE EP: 6 Million Ways To Die (DJ Hype Remix)/6 Million Ways To Die (Uncle 22 Mix) (12") | 20 |
| 93 | Pure Energy PE 003 | SUPER MARIO EP: Super Mario (In Darkness)/Take You High/Love Me Twice/Dark Forces (12") | 10 |
| 93 | Pure Energy PE 004 | Choose One (Part 1)/Choose One (Part 2)/Crazy Kid (12", with Navigator) | 15 |

## UNCOMMUNITY
| | | | |
|---|---|---|---|
| 85 | Black Dwarf BDBG 1 | Brutality Of Fact/Wall Of Sleep (Soundtrack)/The Price Of Your Entry Is Sin (card sleeve, 525 only, numbered, hand-painted labels, with insert) | 25 |

*(see also McCarthy)*

## UNCOOL DANCEBAND
| | | | |
|---|---|---|---|
| 79 | Polydor PB 30 | Let Me Be Your Boyfriend/Heads I Win (no p/s) | 100 |
| 81 | Polydor POSP 253 | Jacqueline/No. 17 (no p/s) | 20 |

## UNDEAD
| | | | |
|---|---|---|---|
| 82 | Riot City RIOT 7 | It's Corruption/Undead (p/s) | 7 |
| 82 | Stiff TEES 7 | NINE TOES LATER EP | 12 |
| 82 | Riot City RIOT 15 | VIOLENT VISIONS (EP) | 10 |
| 84 | City 006 | KILLING OF REALITY (LP, lyric insert) | 35 |

## UNDER THE GUN
| | | | |
|---|---|---|---|
| 85 | Under The Gun UTG1 | Dance Of The Samurai/Traitor (fold-out sleeve) | 15 |

## UNDER THE SKIN
| | | | |
|---|---|---|---|
| 75 | Scotty SC 01 | Shake It Girl/Lose The Image | 20 |

## UNDERCOVER ELEPHANT & SECRET SQUIRREL
| | | | |
|---|---|---|---|
| 92 | Dance Bass DANCE BASS 03 | VOLUME 3 EP (12", stamped white label) | 30 |

*(see also Secret Squirrel)*

## UNDERDOG
| | | | |
|---|---|---|---|
| 79 | Dor Rock DRO1/01 | Life At 21/Blue Water, White Death (no p/s) | 200 |

## UNDERDOGS
| | | | |
|---|---|---|---|
| 83 | Riot City RIOT 26 | EAST OF DACHAU (EP) | 12 |

## UNDERGROUND
| | | | |
|---|---|---|---|
| 69 | Major Minor SMCP 5014 | BEAT PARTY (LP) | 30 |

*(see also Madeline Bell)*

## UNDERGROUNDS
| | | | |
|---|---|---|---|
| 72 | High Note HS 061 | Skavito/Savito | 15 |

MINT VALUE £

## UNDERGROUND SET
| 70 | Pantonic PAN 6302 | UNDERGROUND SET (LP, laminated front sleeve, red/black label) | 70 |

## UNDERGROUND SUNSHINE
| 69 | Fontana TF 1049 | Birthday/All I Want Is You | 10 |

## UNDERGROUND WITH STYLE
| 92 | UAR UAR001 | Lyrics Of A Gangster/Unbound Rage/Words Of Reality (EP) | 25 |

## UNDERGROUND ZERO
| 84 | Underground UNDER 001 | Seven Light Years/Canes Venatici (12") | 15 |

## UNDERTAKERS
| 63 | Pye 7N 15543 | Everybody Loves A Lover/Mashed Potatoes | 25 |
| 63 | Pye 7N 15562 | What About Us/Money | 25 |
| 64 | Pye 7N 15607 | Just A Little Bit/Stupidity | 30 |

*(see also 'Takers, Jackie Lomax)*

## UNDER THE SUN
| 79 | Redball RR 010 | UNDER THE SUN (LP) | 45 |

## UNDERTONES
| 78 | Good Vibrations GOT 4 | TEENAGE KICKS (EP, white poster p/s) | 100 |
| 78 | Good Vibrations GOT 4 | TEENAGE KICKS (EP, pink/yellow/blue p/s) | 70 |
| 78 | Sire SIR 4007 PRO | Teenage Kicks/True Confessions (specially mastered promo, no p/s) | 12 |
| 79 | Sire SIR 4010 | Get Over You/Really Really/She Can Only say No ('She Can Only Say No' not listed on p/s) | 8 |
| 79 | Sire SIR 4015 | Jimmy Jimmy/Mars Bars (p/s) | 5 |
| 79 | Sire SIR 4015 | Jimmy Jimmy/Mars Bars (green vinyl, printed PVC sleeve & insert) | 8 |
| 79 | Sire SIR 4022 | Here Comes The Summer/One Way Love/Top 20 (p/s) | 6 |
| 79 | Sire SIR 4022 | Here Comes The Summer/One Way Love/Top 20 (mispressing, A side plays Tubeway Army's Are Friends Electric?) | 60 |
| 79 | Sire SIR 4024 | You've Got My Number (Why Don't You Use It!)/Let's Talk About Girls (p/s) | 5 |
| 79 | No label | CRACKS 90 MANAGEMENT EP: Teenage Kicks/Get Over You/Jimmy Jimmy/ Here Comes The Summer (promo-only, numbered with typed insert, 250 only) | 60 |
| 80 | Sire SIR 4038 | My Perfect Cousin/Hard Luck (Again) (p/s) | 5 |
| 80 | Sire SAM 120 | HYPNOTIZED APPETIZER (6-track promn 12" EP b/w custom sleeve) | 40 |
| 81 | Ardeck ARDS 9 | Julie Ocean/Kiss In The Dark (p/s) | 5 |
| 83 | Ardeck ARDS 11 | The Love Parade/Like That (p/s) | 5 |
| 83 | Ardeck 12 ARDS 11 | The Love Parade/Like That/You're Welcome/Crises Of Mine/ Family Entertainment (12", p/s) | 10 |
| 83 | Ardeck ARDS 12 | Got To Have You Back/Turning Blue (p/s) | 8 |
| 83 | Ardeck ARDS 13 | Chains Of Love/Window Shopping For New Clothes (p/s) | 10 |
| 05 | Sanctuary SAN07370 | TEENAGE KICKS EP (reissue, numbered) | 12 |
| 79 | Sire SRK 6071 | UNDERTONES (LP, black & white cover, without "Teenage Kicks" & "Get Over You" & different version of "Here Comes The Summer" to reissue) | 15 |
| 80 | Sire SRK 6088 | HYPNOTISED (LP, with cardboard mobile) | 15 |
| 83 | Ardeck ARD 104 | THE SIN OF PRIDE (LP, mispressing with different tracks: Bittersweet & "Stand So Close") | 40 |

*(see also Feargal Sharkey)*

## UNDERWORLD
| 92 | Tomato PLUM 2001 | Mother Earth/Mother Earth (FM Mix)/The Hump/The Hump (Groove Without A Doubt Mix) (12", p/s) | 50 |
| 93 | Boys Own BOIX 13 | Mmm... Skyscraper I Love You/Mmm... Skyscraper I Love You (Telegraph 6.11.92)/ Mmm... Skyscraper I Love You (Jam Scraper) (12", p/s) | 20 |
| 93 | Boys Own Collect 002 | Rez/Cowgirl (12", company sleeve) | 10 |
| 93 | Boys Own Collect 002P | Rez/Cowgirl (12", glossy pink sleeve, pink vinyl, white label) | 20 |
| 93 | Junior Boy's Own JBOLP1 | DUBNOBASSWITHMYHEADMAN (2-LP) | 20 |

*(see also Lemon Interrupt)*

## UNDISPUTED TRUTH
| 71 | Tamla Motown TMG 776 | Save My Love For A Rainy Day/Since I Lost You | 12 |
| 71 | Parlophone TMG 776 | Save My Love For A Rainy Day/Since I Lost You (mispress on Parlophone) | 60 |
| 71 | Tamla Motown TMG 789 | Smiling Faces Sometimes/You Got The Love I Need | 12 |
| 72 | Tamla Motown TMG 818 | Superstar/Ain't No Sun Since You've Been Gone | 10 |
| 74 | Tamla Motown TMG 897 | Help Yourself/What It Is | 8 |
| 76 | Warner Bros K 16804 | You + Me = Love Parts 1 & 2 | 8 |
| 76 | Warner Bros K 16804 | You + Me = Love Parts 1 & 2 (12") | 10 |
| 72 | Tamla Motown STMA 8004 | FACE TO FACE WITH THE TRUTH (LP) | 15 |
| 72 | Tamla Motown STML 11197 | THE UNDISPUTED TRUTH (LP) | 20 |
| 73 | Tamla Motown STML 11240 | THE LAW OF THE LAND (LP) | 15 |
| 75 | Tamla Motown STML 11277 | DOWN TO EARTH (LP) | 15 |
| 75 | Tamla Motown STMA 8023 | COSMIC TRUTH (LP) | 15 |

## UNEXPLORED BEATS
| 95 | Unexplored Beats UXB 001 | Skool Beats/Inner Life (12") | 30 |

*(see also Black Dog)*

## UNFORGETTABLES
| 75 | Angen ANG 108 | Many A Call/Chosen Dub | 8 |

## CHARLIE UNGRY
| 80 | Charlie Ungry CU 001 | House On Chester Road/Pleacher/Who Is My Killer | 60 |

## UNICORN (1)
| 70 | Hollick & Taylor HT 1258 | Going Home/Another World | 300 |

## UNICORN (2)
| 71 | Transatlantic BIG 138 | P.F. Sloan/Going Back Home | 6 |
| 72 | Transatlantic BIG 509 | Cosmic Kid/All We Really Want To Do | 6 |
| 71 | Transatlantic TRA 238 | UPHILL ALL THE WAY (LP, gatefold, plastic inner) | 35 |
| 76 | Harvest SHSP 4054 | TOO MANY CROOKS (LP, inner sleeve, EMI logo on label) | 15 |

## UNIFICS
| | | | |
|---|---|---|---|
| 68 | London HLR 10231 | Court Of Love/Which One Should I Choose | 10 |

## UNION EXPRESS
| | | | |
|---|---|---|---|
| 73 | Decca F 13408 | Do You Love Me/Alligator Fix | 12 |
| 71 | Decca F 13230 | Ring A Ring A Rosies/Emily Knows | 10 |

## UNIQUE (1)
| | | | |
|---|---|---|---|
| 83 | Prelude TA 3707 | What I Got Is What You Need/What I Got Is What You Need (Instrumental) (12") | 10 |

## UNIQUE (2)
| | | | |
|---|---|---|---|
| 08 | Diggers With Gratitude DWG THE DIE HARD (EP) | | 90 |
| | 003 | | |

## UNIQUES
| | | | |
|---|---|---|---|
| 80 | Charly CTD 121 | You Don't Miss Your Water/It's All Over Now/All These Things | 5 |

## UNIQUES
| | | | |
|---|---|---|---|
| 72 | Trojan TR 7852 | Mother And Child Reunion/Corner Hop | 5 |
| 72 | Trojan TR 7866 | Lonely For Your Love/LIONS DEN: Chick-A-Bow | 5 |

*(see also Pioneers)*

## UNIQUES (FEATURING JOE STAMPLEY) (U.S)
| | | | |
|---|---|---|---|
| 65 | Pye International 7N 25303 | Not Too Long Ago/Fast Way Of Living | 30 |
| 65 | Pye International 7N 25303 | Not Too Long Ago/Fast Way Of Living (DJ copy) | 50 |
| 66 | Pye Intl. NPL 28094 | UNIQUELY YOURS (LP) | 120 |

## UNIQUES (JAMAICA)
| | | | |
|---|---|---|---|
| 67 | Collins Downbeat CR 002 | Dry The Water/I'm A Fool For You | 40 |
| 67 | Island WI 3070 | People Rock Steady/I'm Trying To Find A Home (credited to Roy Shirley) | 60 |
| 67 | Island WI 3084 | Gypsy Woman/KEN ROSS: Wall Flower | 70 |
| 67 | Island WI 3086 | Let Me Go Girl/SOULETTES: Dum Dum | 30 |
| 68 | Island WI 3087 | Never Let Me Go/HENRY III: Won't Go Away | 40 |
| 68 | Island WI 3106 | Speak No Evil/GLEN ADAMS: That New Girl | 40 |
| 68 | Island WI 3107 | Lesson Of Love/DELROY WILSON: Til I Die | 25 |
| 68 | Island WI 3114 | Build My World Around You/LLOYD CLARKE: I'll Never Change | 70 |
| 68 | Island WI 3117 | Give Me Some More Of Your Loving/VAL BENNETT: Lovell's Special | 35 |
| 68 | Island WI 3122 | My Conversation/SLIM SMITH: Love One Another | 25 |
| 68 | Island WI 3123 | The Beatitude/KEITH BLAKE: Time On The River (actually "Time & The River") | 40 |
| 68 | Island WI 3145 | Girl Of My Dreams/LESTER STERLING: Tribute To King Scratch | 75 |
| 68 | Trojan TR 619 | Watch This Sound/Out Of Love | 25 |
| 68 | Trojan TR 645 | A-Yuh/Just A Mirage | 25 |
| 68 | Blue Cat BS 126 | Girls Like Dirt/GLEN ADAMS: She Is Leaving | 30 |
| 69 | Gas GAS 117 | Too Proud To Beg/Love And Devotion | 15 |
| 69 | Nu Beat NB 034 | Crimson And Clover/What A Situation | 12 |
| 69 | Nu Beat NB 037 | I'll Make You Love Me/Lover's Prayer | 30 |
| 69 | Unity UN 527 | The Beatitude/My Conversation | 12 |
| 69 | Trojan TRL 15 | ABSOLUTELY THE UNIQUES (LP) | 150 |

*(see also Slim Smith, Melodians, Lloyd Charmers, Tommy McCook)*

## UNIT 4 + 2
| | | | |
|---|---|---|---|
| 64 | Decca F 11821 | The Green Fields/Swing Down Chariot | 15 |
| 64 | Decca F 11994 | Sorrow And Pain/The Lonely Valley | 12 |
| 65 | Decca F 12071 | Concrete And Clay/When I Fall In Love | 6 |
| 65 | Decca F 12144 | (You've) Never Been In Love Like This Before/Tell Somebody You Know | 8 |
| 65 | Decca F 12211 | Hark/Stop Wasting Your Time | 7 |
| 65 | Decca F 12299 | You've Got To Be Cruel To Be Kind/I Won't Let You Down | 7 |
| 66 | Decca F 12333 | Baby Never Say Goodbye/Rainy Day | 12 |
| 66 | Decca F 12398 | For A Moment/Fables | 12 |
| 66 | Decca F 12509 | I Was Only Playing Games/I've Seen The Light | 10 |
| 67 | Fontana TF 834 | Too Fast, Too Slow/Booby Trap | 20 |
| 67 | Fontana TF 840 | Butterfly/A Place To Go | 15 |
| 67 | Fontana TF 891 | Loving Takes A Little Understanding/Would You Believe What I Say? (as Unit) | 200 |
| 68 | Fontana TF 931 | You Ain't Goin' Nowhere/So You Want To Be A Blues Player | 15 |
| 69 | Fontana TF 990 | I Will/3.30 | 50 |
| 65 | Decca DFE 8619 | UNIT 4 + 2 (EP) | 60 |
| 65 | Decca LK 4697 | UNIT 4 + 2 - 1st ALBUM (LP) | 60 |
| 69 | Fontana SFL 13123 | UNIT 4 + 2 (LP) | 50 |

*(see also Roulettes,Tom Sawyer, Capability Brown, Argent)*

## UNIT 19
| | | | |
|---|---|---|---|
| 67 | Unit 19 19 1006 | GI Blues/Sleep Perchance To Dream | 15 |

## UNITED SONS OF AMERICA
| | | | |
|---|---|---|---|
| 71 | Mercury 6338 036 | GREETINGS FROM THE U.S. OF A. (LP) | 18 |

## UNITED SOUNDS OF LONDON
| | | | |
|---|---|---|---|
| 94 | USL USL 6 | Making Love/Making Dub (12") | 15 |

## UNITED STATES DOUBLE QUARTET
| | | | |
|---|---|---|---|
| 67 | Stateside SS 590 | Life Is Groovy/Split | 20 |
| 67 | BT Puppy BTS 45524 | Life Is Groovy/Split (reissue) | 15 |

*(see also Tokens, Kirby Stone 4)*

## UNITED STATES OF AMERICA
| | | | |
|---|---|---|---|
| 68 | CBS 3745 | Garden Of Earthly Delights/Love Song For The Dead Che | 15 |
| 68 | CBS (S) 63340 | UNITED STATES OF AMERICA (LP, laminated cover, mono/stereo) | 60 |
| 87 | Edsel ED 233 | UNITED STATES OF AMERICA (LP, reissue) | 15 |

## UNITED STATES OF EXISTENCE
| | | | |
|---|---|---|---|
| 87 | Bam Caruso OPRA 081 | Gone/PAUL ROLAND: Madam Guillotine (jukebox issue, company sleeve) | 5 |

MINT VALUE £

## UNITY ALL STARS
| | | | |
|---|---|---|---|
| 75 | Nice N 001 | Africa/BIG DREAD & UNITY ALL STARS: Africa Is Our Home | 25 |

## UNIVERSAL ENERGY
| | | | |
|---|---|---|---|
| 77 | Harvest HAR 5138 | Universal Energy/Christmas For Space | 6 |

## UNIVERSAL INDICATOR
| | | | |
|---|---|---|---|
| 92 | Rephlex TB-303 | 1-BLUE (12") | 25 |
| 92 | Rephlex TR-606 | 2-RED (12") | 25 |
| 93 | Rephlex MC-202 | 3-YELLOW (12") | 20 |
| 95 | Rephlex SH-101 | 4-GREEN (7", 10" + 12" in bag, all green vinyl) | 80 |

*(see also Kosmik Kommando)*

## UNIVERSAL PANZIES
| | | | |
|---|---|---|---|
| 98 | Head Heritage HH4 | TRANSCENDENTAL FLOSS (CD, mail order only) | 30 |

*(see also Julian Cope)*

## UNIVERSAL ROBOT BAND
| | | | |
|---|---|---|---|
| 84 | Streetwave MKHAN 48 | Barely Breaking Even (85 Club MIx)/Barely Breaking Even (Edit)/Barely Breaking Even (Instrumental) (12") | 40 |

## UNIVERSALS
| | | | |
|---|---|---|---|
| 67 | Page One POF 032 | I Can't Find You/Hey You | 200 |
| 67 | Page One POF 049 | Green Veined Orchid/While The Cat's Away | 35 |

*(see also Chris Lamb & Universals, Gidian, Lace, Gary Walker & Rain, Plastic Penny)*

## U.N.K.L.E.
| | | | |
|---|---|---|---|
| 95 | Mo' Wax MW 028 | THE TIME HAS COME EP (2 x 12" EP, picture disc) | 15 |
| 98 | Mo' Wax MW 085DJ | PSYENCE FICTION SURVIVAL KIT (promo, 12" in pop-up gatefold p/s, 5" vinyl single in envelope, bag of stickers, press release, all in box mailer, 700 only) | 35 |
| 98 | Mo Wax 085 | PSYENCE FICTION (2-LP, hardcover gatefold sleeve with booklet) | 20 |
| 03 | Mo Wax MWU 001 | NEVER NEVER LAND (3-LP, gatefold sleeve) | 18 |
| 03 | Mo Wax MWU 001 | NEVER NEVER LAND (3-LP, picture discs, gatefold sleeve, foldout inserts) | 20 |
| 07 | Surrender ALL SURR LPXX | WAR STORIES (4x12", gatefold sleeve in slipcase with book) | 25 |
| 10 | Surrender ALL SURR 017 LP | WHERE DID THE NIGHT FALL (3-LP box set with books) | 100 |
| 11 | Vinyl Factory VF 029 | THE HERETIC'S GATE SCORE (with Doug Foster) (1-sided LP. orange vinyl, sleeve signed and numbered by James Lavelle and Doug Foster, 100 only) | 120 |

*(see also DJ Shadow)*

## UNKNOWNS
| | | | |
|---|---|---|---|
| 66 | London HLU 10082 | Melody For An Unknown Girl/Peith's Song | 7 |

## UNLEASHED
| | | | |
|---|---|---|---|
| 03 | Century Media 77544-0 | AND WE SHALL TRIUMPH IN VICTORY (Numbered box set with 6 picture discs LPs and booklet, 2000 only) | 60 |

## UNSEEN TERROR
| | | | |
|---|---|---|---|
| 87 | Earache MOSH 4 | HUMAN ERROR (LP, inner) | 15 |

## UNTAMED YOUTH
| | | | |
|---|---|---|---|
| 79 | Hardcore HAR 001 | Untamed Youth/Runnin' Wild (p/s, 1,000 only) | 15 |

## UNTAMED (1)
| | | | |
|---|---|---|---|
| 64 | Decca F 12045 | So Long/Just Wait | 70 |
| 65 | Parlophone R 5258 | Once Upon A Time/I'm Asking You | 100 |
| 65 | Stateside SS 431 | I'll Go Crazy/My Baby Is Gone | 70 |
| 66 | Planet PLF 103 | It's Not True/Gimme Gimme Some Shade | 100 |

*(see also Lindsay Muir's Untamed)*

## UNTAMED (2)
| | | | |
|---|---|---|---|
| 88 | Real World RWR 004 | Next Please/Black Heart (p/s, with insert) | 5 |

## UNTOUCHABLES
| | | | |
|---|---|---|---|
| 80 | Fried Egg EGG 2 | Keep On Walking/Keep Your Distance (p/s) | 8 |

## UNTOUCHABLES (JAMAICA)
| | | | |
|---|---|---|---|
| 68 | Blue Cat BS 137 | Prisoner In Love/EDWARD RAPHAEL: True Love | 45 |
| 68 | Trojan TR 613 | Tighten Up/ROY SHIRLEY: Good Ambition | 30 |
| 70 | Upsetter US 345 | Same Thing All Over/UPSETTERS: It's Over | 20 |
| 70 | Upsetter US 350 | Knock On Wood/UPSETTERS: Tight Spot | 55 |
| 71 | Bullet BU 460 | Can't Reach You/CARL DAWKINS: Natural Woman | 10 |
| 73 | Bread BR 1113 | Pay For The Wicked/Pay For The Wicked - Version (actually titled "Pray For The Wicked') | 10 |
| 79 | Sagittarius SUS 10 | Help Us Jah/Sea Of Love (12") | 20 |

*(see also Inspirations, Dave Barker, Leroy Reid)*

## UNWANTED
| | | | |
|---|---|---|---|
| 77 | Raw RAW 6 | Withdrawal/1978/Bleak Outlook (p/s) | 40 |
| 77 | Raw RAWT 6 | Withdrawal/1978/Bleak Outlook (12", reissue) | 20 |
| 78 | Raw RAW 15 | Secret Police/These Boots Are Made For Walking (p/s) | 20 |
| 78 | Raw RAW 30 | Memory Man/Guns Of Love (unissued) | 0 |
| 85 | Delorian No One | SECRET PAST (LP) | 15 |

*(see also Psychedelic Furs)*

## UPBEATS
| | | | |
|---|---|---|---|
| 58 | London HLU 8688 | Just Like In The Movies/My Foolish Heart | 25 |
| 59 | Pye International 7N 25016 | You're The One I Care For/Keep Cool Crazy Heart | 15 |
| 59 | Pye International 7N 25028 | Teenie Weenie Bikini/Satin Shoes | 15 |

## PHIL UPCHURCH COMBO
| | | | |
|---|---|---|---|
| 61 | HMV POP 899 | You Can't Sit Down Parts 1 & 2 | 35 |
| 66 | Sue WI 4005 | You Can't Sit Down Parts 1 & 2 (reissue) | 30 |
| 66 | Sue WI 4017 | Nothing But Soul/Evad | 40 |
| 72 | Blue Thumb ILPS 9219 | DARKNESS, DARKNESS (LP) | 20 |

## UPCOMING WILLOWS
| | | | |
|---|---|---|---|
| 65 | Island WI 182 | Jonestown Special/SHENLEY DUFFAS: La La La | 40 |
| 65 | Island WI 184 | Red China/SHENLEY DUFFAS: You Are Mine | 40 |

*(see also Shenley Duffas)*

## UPFRONT RUDIES
| | | | |
|---|---|---|---|
| 92 | Krazy Fly Recz RUDIE 9 | REAL SKILLS (EP) | 10 |

## UPP
| | | | |
|---|---|---|---|
| 75 | Epic EPC 80625 | UPP (LP) | 15 |

*(see also Clark-Hutchinson)*

## UPRISING
| | | | |
|---|---|---|---|
| 79 | Tribesman TM 11 | Come On Over/Try Me Girl (12") | 18 |

## UPROAR
| | | | |
|---|---|---|---|
| 82 | Beat The System RAW 1 | Rebel Youth/No More War/Fallen Angel/Victims (p/s) | 12 |
| 83 | Lightbeat RAW 2 | DIE FOR ME (EP) | 12 |
| 83 | Volume VOL 9 | NOTHING CAN STOP YOU (EP) | 10 |
| 80s | Beat The System BTSLP 1 | AND THE LORD SAID LET THERE BE UPROAR (LP) | 30 |

## UPSETTERS (1)
| | | | |
|---|---|---|---|
| 65 | Island WI 223 | Country Girl/Strange Country (both sides actually by Ossie & Upsetters) | 35 |
| 65 | Rio R 70 | Walk Down The Aisle/So Bad | 20 |
| 66 | Doctor Bird DB 1034 | Wildcat/I Love You So | 40 |
| 70 | Upsetter US 331 | Shocks A Mighty/DAVE BARKER: Set Me Free | 25 |

*(see also Ossie & Upsetters, Dave Barker)*

## UPSETTERS (2)
| | | | |
|---|---|---|---|
| 69 | Duke DU 11 | Eight For Eight/Stand By Me (B-side actually by Inspirations) | 40 |
| 69 | Camel CA 13 | Taste Of Killing/My Mob | 40 |
| 69 | Punch PH 18 | Return Of The Ugly/I've Caught You | 25 |
| 69 | Punch PH 19 | Dry Acid/REGGAE BOYS: Selassie | 50 |
| 69 | Punch PH 21 | Clint Eastwood/Lennox Mood | 12 |
| 69 | Upsetter US 300 | Eight For Eight/You Know What I Mean (B-side actually by Inspirations) | 40 |
| 69 | Upsetter UP 301 | Return Of Django/Dollar In The Teeth | 12 |
| 69 | Upsetter US 303 | Ten To Twelve/LEE PERRY: People Funny Fi True | 30 |
| 69 | Upsetter US 305 | Farmers In The Den/BUSTY BROWN : To Love Somebody | 30 |
| 69 | Upsetter US 307 | Night Doctor/TERMITES: I'll Be Waiting | 40 |
| 69 | Upsetter US 309 | Kiddyo/Endlessly (both sides actually by Silvertones) | 18 |
| 69 | Upsetter US 310 | A Dangerous Man From MI5/WEST INDIANS: Oh Lord | 18 |
| 69 | Upsetter US 313 | Live Injection/BLEECHERS: Everything For Fun | 10 |
| 70 | Upsetter US 317 | Vampire/BLEECHERS: Check Him Out | 25 |
| 69 | Upsetter US 315 | Cold Sweat/Pound Get A Blow (B-side actually by Bleechers) | 30 |
| 70 | Upsetter US 318 | Soulful I/MILTON HENRY: Bread And Butter | 15 |
| 70 | Upsetter US 321 | Drugs And Poison/Stranger On The Shore | 18 |
| 70 | Upsetter US 325 | Kill Them All/Soul Walk | 18 |
| 70 | Upsetter US 326 | Bronco/One Punch | 22 |
| 70 | Upsetter US 332 | Na Na Hey Hey/Pick Folk Kinkyest | 20 |
| 70 | Upsetter US 333 | Granny Show/Version | 20 |
| 70 | Upsetter US 334 | Fire Fire/Jumper | 20 |
| 70 | Upsetter US 335 | The Pillow/Grooving | 20 |
| 70 | Upsetter US 336 | Self Control/The Pill | 22 |
| 70 | Upsetter US 338 | Fresh Up/Toothaches | 20 |
| 70 | Upsetter US 339 | The Thanks We Get/Hurry Up | 35 |
| 70 | Upsetter US 342 | Dreamland/BOB MARLEY: Version Of Cup | 45 |
| 70 | Upsetter US 343 | Sipreano/Ferry Boat | 20 |
| 70 | Upsetter US 346 | Bigger Joke/Return Of The Vampire | 25 |
| 70 | Upsetter US 349 | Upsetting Station (actually plays "Did Your Grave" by Bob Marley & Wailers)/UPSETTERS: Justice (Instrumental) | 40 |
| 70 | Upsetter US 352 | Heart And Soul/Zig Zag | 18 |
| 70 | Spinning Wheel SW 100 | Haunted House/Double Wheel | 85 |
| 70 | Spinning Wheel SW 101 | The Miser/CHUCK JUNIOR: Do It Madly | 25 |
| 70 | Spinning Wheel SW 102 | The Chokin' Kind/CHUCK JUNIOR: Penny Wise | 25 |
| 70 | Spinning Wheel SW 103 | Land Of Kinks/O'NEIL HALL: This Man | 25 |
| 70 | Trojan TR 7748 | Family Man/Mellow Mood | 12 |
| 70 | Trojan TR 7749 | Capo/Mama Look | 15 |
| 70 | Punch PH 27 | The Result/Feel The Spirit | 40 |
| 71 | Bullet BU 461 | All Combine Parts 1 & 2 | 10 |
| 71 | Bullet BU 499 | Beat Down Babylon/JUNIOR BYLES: Version | 18 |
| 71 | Upsetter US 353 | Illusion/Big John Wayne (as Upsetters & King Teddy) | 18 |
| 71 | Upsetter US 361 | Capasetic (actually "Copasetic" by Lord Comic)/All Africans (actually "Don't Cross The Nation" by Little Roy) | 20 |
| 71 | Upsetter US 365 | Earthquake/JUNIOR BYLES: Palace Called Africa | 20 |
| 71 | Upsetter US 370 | Dark Moon/DAVID ISAACS: You'll Be Sorry | 15 |
| 72 | Upsetter US 385 | French Connection/Version | 15 |
| 72 | Upsetter US 387 | Festival Da Da/JUNIOR BYLES: Version | 18 |
| 72 | Upsetter US 393 | Crummy People/BIG YOUTH: Moving - Version | 15 |
| 72 | Upsetter US 394 | Water Pump Parts 1 & 2 | 15 |
| 72 | Randy's RAN 523 | Nebuchadnezzer/JUNIOR BYLES: King Of Babylon | 18 |
| 72 | Punch PH 109 | Hail To Power/JUNIOR BYLES: Pharaoh Hiding | 18 |
| 73 | Upsetter US 396 | Puss Sea Hole/WINSTON GROOVY: Want To Be Loved | 15 |
| 73 | Upsetter US 397 | Jungle Lion/Freak Out Skank | 100 |
| 73 | Upsetter US 398 | Cow Thief Skank (with Charlie Ace)/7 3/4 Skank | 20 |
| 73 | Downtown DT 499 | Black Ipa/Ipa Skank | 25 |

MINT VALUE £

| 73 | Downtown DT 506 | Sunshine Showdown/Sunshine Version | 25 |
| 73 | Downtown DT 512 | Tighten Up Skank/Mid-East Rock | 25 |
| 73 | Downtown DT 513 | Sucky Skank/Yucky Skank | 18 |
| 74 | Count Shelly CS 052 | San-San/OSBOURNE GRAHAM: Baby Don't Go | 8 |
| 74 | Dip DL 5031 | Enter The Dragon/JOY WHITE: Lady Lady | 12 |
| 74 | Dip DL 5032 | Rebels Train/Rebels Dub | 8 |
| 75 | Dip DL 5054 | Cane River Rock/Riverside Rock | 12 |
| 75 | Dip DL 5056 | I Man Free/King Burnett: Version | 12 |
| 75 | Dip DL 5073 | Key Card/Domino Game | 8 |
| 75 | Angen ANG 107 | Stay Dread/Kingdom Of Dub | 20 |
| 75 | Attack ATT 8090 | Kiss Me Neck/Da Ba Day | 25 |
| 78 | Island IPR 2010 | Close Together/Dreadlocks In The Moonlight (12" as UPSETTERS REVIEW featuring JUNIOR MURVIN) | 20 |
| 69 | Pama Special PSP 1014 | CLINT EASTWOOD (LP) | 80 |
| 69 | Trojan TTL 13 | THE UPSETTER (LP) | 45 |
| 69 | Trojan TRL 19 | THE RETURN OF DJANGO (LP, orange/white label) | 60 |
| 70 | Trojan TTL 28 | SCRATCH THE UPSETTER AGAIN (LP) | 55 |
| 70 | Trojan TBL 119 | THE GOOD, THE BAD AND THE UPSETTERS (LP) | 35 |
| 70 | Trojan TBL 125 | EASTWOOD RIDES AGAIN (LP) | 40 |
| 70 | Pama SECO 24 | THE MANY MOODS OF THE UPSETTERS (LP) | 75 |
| 74 | Trojan TRLS 70 | DOUBLE SEVEN (LP, black sticker on rear cover showing song titles and marketed by B & C Records) | 60 |
| 75 | DIP DLPD 6002 | RETURN OF THE WAX (LP, white-label only, plain sleeve) | 50 |
| 76 | Island ILPS 9417 | SUPER APE (LP) | 35 |
| 83 | Pama PTLP 1026 | BEST OF THE UPSETTERS VOL. 2 (LP) | 30 |
| 90 | Trojan PERRY 3 | BUILD THE ARK (3-LP box set) | 30 |

*(see also Lee Perry, Ossie & Upsetters, Hippy Boys, Bob Marley/Wailers, Family Man, Tommy McCook, Max Romeo, Melodians, Lord Creator, Dennis Alcapone)*

## UPSETTING BROTHERS
| 71 | Supreme SUP 229 | Not You Baby/DREAD LOCK ALL-STARS: Baby (Version) | 12 |

## CHARLES UPTON
| 65 | Ralph Tuck EP CU 01 | SINGS (EP) | 10 |

## UPTOWNERS
| 64 | London HLU 9877 | If'n/Search Is Over | 15 |

## URBAN CLEARWAY (1)
| 70 | Torpedo TOR 21 | Open Up Wide Parts 1 & 2 | 20 |

## URBAN CLEARWAY (2)
| 82 | Bandit X 82 CUS 1609 | Lost Memories/You've Always Known (12", p/s) | 100 |

## URBAN DISTURBANCE
| 79 | Rok ROK V/VI | Wild Boys In Cortinas/V.I.Ps: Can't Let You Go (die-cut sleeve) | 25 |

## URBAN DOGS
| 82 | Fallout FALL 008 | New Barbarians/Speed Kills/Cocaine (p/s) | 5 |
| 82 | Fallout FALL 011 | Limo Life/Warhead (p/s) | 5 |

*(see Hanoi Rocks, U.K. Subs, Vibrators)*

## URBAN MYTHS
| 98 | Urban Myths MYTH 1 | Lose You/Lose You (Dub)//Makin' Me Feel/No Man (12") | 20 |

## URBAN SHAKEDOWN
| 82 | Respond RESP5 | Wolves/Rap The Wolf | 10 |

## URBAN TRIBE
| 92 | Sub Assertive CUE 6 | THE UNKNOWN EP (12", white label) | 20 |

## URCHIN
| 77 | DJM DJS 10776 | Black Leather Fantasy/Rock & Roll Woman (in promo p/s) | 275 |
| 77 | DJM DJS 10776 | Black Leather Fantasy/Rock & Roll Woman (no p/s) | 100 |
| 78 | DJM DJS 10850 | She's A Roller/Long Time No Woman (in promo p/s) | 275 |
| 79 | DJM DJS 10850 | She's A Roller/Long Time No Woman (no p/s) | 100 |

*(see also Iron Maiden)*

## URCHINS
| 66 | Polydor BM 56145 | I Made Her That Way/Twas On A Night Like This | 10 |

## URGE
| 81 | Consumer Discks CD 0861 | Revolting Boy/Revolve (p/s) | 10 |

## URGENT CRUNCH
| 81 | NYECK NECK 1 | Listen To Silence/Trust (p/s) | 10 |

## URIAH HEEP
| 71 | Bronze WIP 6111 | Look At Yourself/Simon The Bullet Freak | 7 |
| 72 | Bronze WIP 6126 | The Wizard/Gypsy | 6 |
| 72 | Bronze WIP 6140 | Easy Livin'/Why | 6 |
| 73 | Bronze BRO 7 | Stealin'/Sunshine | 6 |
| 74 | Bronze BRO 10 | Something Or Nothing/What Can I Do | 5 |
| 75 | Bronze BRO 17 | Prima Donna/Shout It Out | 5 |
| 76 | Bronze BRO 27 | One Way Or Another/Misty Eyes | 5 |
| 76 | Bronze BRODJ 1 | One Way Or Another/Misty Eyes (promo only p/s, 750 copies) | 20 |
| 77 | Bronze BRO 37 | Wise Man/Crime Of Passion | 5 |
| 77 | Bronze BRO 47 | Free Me/Masquerade (p/s) | 6 |
| 78 | Bronze BRO 62 | Come Back To Me/Cheater | 5 |
| 83 | Bronze BROG 168 | Stay On Top/Playing For Time//Gypsy/Easy Livin'/Sweet Lorraine/ Stealin' (double pack, gatefold p/s) | 7 |
| 85 | Portrait WA 6103 | Rockerama/Back Stage Girl (shaped picture disc) | 10 |
| 70 | Vertigo 6360 006 | VERY 'EAVY... VERY 'UMBLE (1st pressing, LP, gatefold sleeve, large swirl label. Matrixes: 1Y/1 420 113/2Y/1 420 111) | 350 |

| 71 | Vertigo 6360 028 | SALISBURY (LP, gatefold sleeve, large swirl label) | 350 |
|---|---|---|---|
| 71 | Vertigo 6360 006 | VERY 'EAVY... VERY 'UMBLE (2nd pressing, LP, reissue, Matrix 1Y//1 420 1 1 9/2Y//1 420 111) | 80 |
| 71 | Bronze ILPS 9152 | SALISBURY (LP, reissue, with 'Howards Printers (Slough) Ltd/' printers credit) | 30 |
| 71 | Bronze ILPS 9169 | LOOK AT YOURSELF (LP, 'mirror' sleeve, inner sleeve) | 100 |
| 72 | Bronze ILPS 9193 | DEMONS AND WIZARDS (LP, gatefold, lyric inner) | 50 |
| 72 | Island ILPS 9213 | THE MAGICIANS'S BIRTHDAY (LP, gatefold with inner sleeve, abandoned Island pressing with pink rim palm tree label, with 'Bronze' records hand-written half-paste on label) | 100 |
| 72 | Bronze ILPS 9213 | MAGICIAN'S BIRTHDAY (LP, gatefold with inner sleeve) | 40 |
| 72 | Vertigo 6360 006 | VERY 'EAVY... VERY 'UMBLE (3rd pressing, LP, gatefold sleeve, small 'swirl' and 'Vertigo' above centre label) | 30 |
| 72 | Bronze ILPS 9142 | VERY 'EAVY... VERY 'UMBLE (LP, reissue, sleeve printed by 'Howards Printers (Slough) Ltd') | 25 |
| 73 | Bronze ILPS 9245 | SWEET FREEDOM (LP, gatefold) | 30 |
| 73 | Bronze ISLD 1 | LIVE (2-LP, laminated gatefold sleeve with booklet and inners) | 20 |
| 74 | Island ILPS 9142 | VERY 'EAVY... VERY 'UMBLE (LP, reissue, pink rim palm tree label) | 20 |
| 74 | Bronze ILPS 9280 | WONDERWORLD (LP, inner) | 20 |
| 75 | Bronze ILPS 9335 | RETURN TO FANTASY (LP, gatefold sleeve) | 50 |
| 77 | Bronze ILPS 9483 | FIREFLY (LP) | 60 |
| 78 | Bronze BRNA 512 | FALLEN ANGEL (LP, gatefold) | 25 |
| 80 | Bronze BRONX 524 | CONQUEST (LP) | 20 |
| 89 | Legacy LLP 120 | RAGING SILENCE (LP, picture disc) | 12 |
| 95 | HTD LP 33 | SEA OF LIGHT (2-LP, with inner) | 35 |

(see also Gods, Head Machine, Natural Gas, Spice, King Crimson, John Lawton, Grand Prix, Stratus)

## RENE URTREGER
| 56 | Felsted ESD 3027 | SALUTE TO BUD POWELL (EP) | 15 |
|---|---|---|---|
| 56 | Felsted EDL 87020 | PLAYS BUD POWELL (10" LP) | 30 |

## URUSEI YATSURA
| 95 | Modern Ind. MIR 001 | Pampered Adolescent/BLISTERS: A Dull Thought In Itself (burgundy vinyl, p/s, 500 only) | 6 |
|---|---|---|---|
| 95 | Love Train PUBE 08 | Kernel/Teendream (p/s, 1,000 only) | 6 |

## US FOLK
| 65 | Eyemark EMS 1001 | Funny Old World/Dives | 8 |
|---|---|---|---|

## U.S. T-BONES
| 65 | Liberty LIB 55836 | No Matter What Shape/Feelin' Fine | 12 |
|---|---|---|---|
| 66 | Liberty LIB 55867 | Sippin'n'Chippin'/Moment Of Softness | 15 |
| 66 | Liberty LIB 55951 | The Proper Thing To Do/Tee-Hee-Hee | 15 |

## US (1)
| 70s | Jeff Wayne Music SD 015 | You're OK With Us/Tomorrow (p/s, promo for Johnson Wax) | 10 |
|---|---|---|---|

(see also David Essex, Randells)

## US (2)
| 67 | Polydor 56179 | Barefoot In The Park/Four's A Crowd | 8 |
|---|---|---|---|

## US & THEM
| 11 | Fruits De Mer Crustacean 20 | Summerisle Songs From The Wicker Man (1st press, white vinyl, folded white p/s, insert) | 20 |
|---|---|---|---|
| 11 | Fruits De Mer Crustacean 20 | Summerisle Songs From The Wicker Man (Repressing, orange/yellow vinyl, folded p/s, insert) | 15 |

## USELESS UNICORN
| 74 | Horny HORN 11 | RUBBER HORN (LP, gatefold sleeve, with pop-up horn) | 15 |
|---|---|---|---|

## USERS
| 77 | Raw RAW 1 | Sick Of You/(I'm) In Love With Today (p/s, numbered on rear, 2500 only) | 30 |
|---|---|---|---|
| 77 | Raw RAW 1 | Sick Of You/(I'm) In Love With Today (p/s, 2nd pressing, 5000 copies) | 15 |
| 77 | Raw RAWT 1 | Sick Of You/(I'm) In Love With Today (12", no p/s) | 15 |
| 78 | Warped WARP 1 | Warped 45: Kicks In Style/Dead On Arrival (p/s, 5,000 only, numbered sleeve, some un-numbered) | 30 |
| 06 | Damaged Goods DAMGOOD 139 | Sick Of You/(I'm) In Love With Today (p/s, reissue) | 8 |

## PETER USTINOV
| 53 | Parlophone MSP 6012 | Mock Mozart (with Anthony Hopkins, Harpsichord)/Phoney Folk-Lore | 8 |
|---|---|---|---|

## UTOMICA
| 93 | Pro-One PRONE 9T | Rok A Bye/Rok A Bye (12", stamped or hand-written white label) | 50 |
|---|---|---|---|
| 93 | Pro-One PRONE 11T | Pumpkin/Pumpkin (12", white stamped label) | 15 |

## UTOPIA (GERMANY)
| 73 | United Artists UAG 29438 | UTOPIA (LP) | 35 |
|---|---|---|---|

(see also Amon Duull)

## UTOPIA (U.S.)
| 82 | Epic XPS 166 | Infrared And Ultra Violet/Forgotten But Not Gone/Private Heaven/Princess Of The Universe/Chapter And Verse (EP) | 12 |
|---|---|---|---|
| 82 | Epic EPC 25207 | UTOPIA (LP, with free 5-track EP) | 20 |

(see also Todd Rundgren)

## UTTER COWBOYS
| 83 | Denbeat GO 001 | Saturday Night Games/Keys To Your Heart | 8 |
|---|---|---|---|

## U-TURN
| 81 | Epigram 001 | U-TURN EP (detergent shaped sleeve) | 20 |
|---|---|---|---|

## U2
SINGLES : SINGLES: IRISH PRESSINGS
| 79 | CBS 7951 | U2: THREE (Out Of Control/Stories For The Boys/Boy-Girl) (p/s, black vinyl) (CBS 'Sunburst Label' with UK TM NoB81 809) on label (First Pressing) | 150 |
|---|---|---|---|
| 79 | CBS 7951 | U2: THREE (Out Of Control/Stories For The Boys/Boy-Girl) (p/s, black vinyl) | 50 |

MINT VALUE £

| | | | |
|---|---|---|---|
| 80 | CBS 7951 | U2: THREE (Out Of Control/Stories For The Boys/Boy-Girl) (p/s, white vinyl) | 300 |
| 80 | CBS 7951 | U2: THREE (Out Of Control/Stories For The Boys/Boy-Girl) (p/s, orange vinyl) | 150 |
| 80 | CBS 7951 | U2: THREE (Out Of Control/Stories For The Boys/Boy-Girl) (p/s, yellow vinyl) | 100 |
| 80 | CBS 7951 | U2: THREE (Out Of Control/Stories For The Boys/Boy-Girl) (p/s, brown vinyl mispressing, fewer than 50 copies exist) | 1000 |
| 81 | CBS 12-7951 | U2: THREE (12" EP, with numbered sticker, orange CBS sleeve, 1,000 only) | 1500 |
| 81 | CBS 12-7951 | U2: THREE (12" EP, reissue, die-cut CBS sleeve) | 60 |
| 81 | CBS 12-7951 | U2: THREE (12" 2nd reissue, plain black sleeve, slightly different labels) | 40 |
| 85 | CBS 40-7951 | U2: THREE (cassette, reissue) | 50 |
| 80 | CBS 8306 | Another Day/Twilight (Demo Version) (p/s, yellow vinyl) | 80 |
| 80 | CBS 8306 | Another Day/Twilight (Demo Version) (p/s, orange vinyl) | 150 |
| 80 | CBS 8306 | Another Day/Twilight (Demo Version) (p/s, white vinyl) | 350 |
| 80 | CBS 8306 | Another Day/Twilight (Demo Version) (p/s, black vinyl, with postcard designed by Bono) | 200 |
| 80 | CBS 8306 | Another Day/Twilight (Demo Version) (p/s, black vinyl, without postcard designed by Bono) | 40 |
| 80 | CBS 8687 | 11 O'Clock Tick Tock/Touch (p/s, yellow vinyl) | 60 |
| 80 | CBS 8687 | 11 O'Clock Tick Tock/Touch (p/s, orange vinyl) | 150 |
| 80 | CBS 9065 | I Will Follow/Boy-Girl (live) (p/s, yellow vinyl) | 50 |
| 80 | CBS 9065 | I Will Follow/Boy-Girl (live) (p/s, orange vinyl) | 100 |
| 80 | CBS 9065 | I Will Follow/Boy-Girl (live) (p/s, white vinyl) | 300 |
| 80 | CBS 9065 | I Will Follow/Boy-Girl (live) (p/s, brown vinyl, fewer than 50 copies) | 1500 |
| 82 | CBS PAC 1 | 4 U2 PLAY (4 x 7", each in p/s, black vinyl) | 120 |
| 82 | CBS PAC 1 | 4 U2 PLAY (4 x 7", each in p/s, yellow vinyl) | 300 |
| 82 | CBS PAC 1 | 4 U2 PLAY (4 x 7", each in p/s, orange vinyl) | 600 |
| 82 | CBS PAC 1 | 4 U2 PLAY (4 x 7", each in p/s, white vinyl) | 1000 |
| 80s | CBS PAC 2 | PAC 2 (4 x 7" with p/s in plastic wallet) | 60 |
| 80s | CBS PAC 3 | PAC 3 (4 x 7" with p/s in plastic wallet) | 50 |

SINGLES : SINGLES: UK PRESSINGS

| | | | |
|---|---|---|---|
| 80 | Island WIP 6601 | 11 O'Clock Tick Tock/Touch (p/s) | 25 |
| 80 | Island WIP 6630 | A Day Without Me/Things To Make And Do (p/s) | 20 |
| 80 | Island WIP 6656 | I Will Follow/Boy-Girl (live) (p/s) | 15 |
| 81 | Island WIP 6679 | Fire/J. Swallo (p/s) | 6 |
| 81 | Island UWIP 6679 | Fire/J. Swallo//11 O'Clock Tick Tock (live)/The Ocean (live)/Cry (live)/ The Electric Co. (live) (double pack, single p/s) | 10 |
| 81 | Island WIP 6733 | Gloria/I Will Follow (live) (p/s) | 10 |
| 82 | Island WIP 6770 | A Celebration/Trash, Trampoline And The Party Girl (p/s) | 10 |
| 83 | Island UWIP 6848 | New Year's Day/Treasure (Whatever Happened To Pete The Chop)// Fire (live)/I Threw A Brick Through A Window (live)/A Day Without Me (live) (double pack, single p/s, black inners) | 10 |
| 85 | Island ISP 220 | The Unforgettable Fire/A Sort Of Homecoming (live) (Uncut, logo-shaped pic disc) | 600 |
| 83 | Island ISD 109 | Two Hearts Beat As One/Endless Deep//New Year's Day (U.S.A. Remix)/ Two Hearts Beat As One (U.S.A. Remix) (double pack) | 10 |
| 84 | Island ISP 202 | Pride (In The Name Of Love)/Boomerang 2 (Vocal) (picture disc) | 20 |
| 84 | Island ISD 202 | Pride (In The Name Of Love)/4th Of July//Boomerang I (Instrumental)/ Boomerang 2 (Vocal) (double pack, gatefold p/s) | 6 |
| 84 | Island 12ISX 202 | Pride (In The Name Of Love)/Boomerang I/Boomerang 2/ 11 O'Clock Tick Tock/Touch (Full Length Version) (12", blue p/s) | 10 |
| 85 | Island ISD 220 | The Unforgettable Fire/A Sort Of Homecoming (live)/Love Comes Tumbling/ Sixty Seconds In Kingdom Come/The Three Sunrises (double pack, gatefold p/s) | 6 |
| 85 | Island ISP 220 | The Unforgettable Fire/A Sort Of Homecoming (live) (logo-shaped pic disc) | 45 |
| 87 | Island 12IS 340 | Where The Streets Have No Name/Race Against Time/Silver And Gold/ The Sweetest Thing (12", p/s with "Silver And Gold" lyric insert) | 15 |
| 88 | Island IS 400 | Desire/Hallelujah Here She Comes (non-gatefold p/s) | 5 |
| 88 | Island U2 PK 1 | THE JOSHUA TREE SINGLES (4 x 7"s in PVC wallet with 'obi' band) | 40 |
| 89 | Island CIDP 411 | When Love Comes To Town/Dancing Barefoot/When Love Comes To Town (Live From The Kingdom Mix) (with BB King)/God Part II (The Hard Metal Dance Mix) (CD picture disc) | 15 |
| 89 | Island ISB 422 | All I Want Is You (Edit)/Unchained Melody (in numbered tin box) | 18 |
| 89 | Island 12 ISB 422 | All I Want Is You (Full Version)/Unchained Melody/Everlasting Love (12", p/s, box set with 4 prints) | 15 |
| 89 | Island CIDP 422 | All I Want Is You (4.14)/Unchained Melody/Everlasting Love/ All I Want Is You (Full Version) (CD, picture disc) | 15 |
| 91 | Island 12IS 509 | Mysterious Ways (4.04)/(Solar Plexus Extended Club Mix 7.01)/ (Apollo 440 Magic Hour Remix)/(Tabla Motown Remix)/(Solar Plexus Club Mix) (12" p/s, withdrawn) | 15 |
| 92 | Island 12IS 525 | Even Better Than The Real Thing/Salomé/Where Did It All Go Wrong/ Lady With The Spinning Head (UVI) (Extended Dance Mix) (12" with giant 'Zoo TV' poster) | 20 |
| 92 | Island IS 550 | Who's Gonna Ride Your Wild Horses (Temple Bar Edit)/Paint It Black (p/s) | 5 |
| 95 | Atlantic A 7131 | Hold Me, Thrill Me, Kiss Me, Kill Me /ELLIOTT GOLDENTHAL: Themes From Batman | 5 |
| 95 | Atlantic A 7131 | Hold Me, Thrill Me, Kiss Me, Kill Me/ELLIOTT GOLDENTHAL: Themes From Batman Forever (p/s, red vinyl, black vinyl copies have correct/incorrect B side credits) | 5 |
| 95 | Atlantic A 7131 | Hold Me, Thrill Me, Kiss Me, Kill Me/ELLIOTT GOLDENTHAL: Themes From Batman Forever (p/s, red vinyl, B-side miscredited to U2) | 8 |
| 97 | Island 12IST649 | Discothèque (Howie B Hairy B Mix)/Discothèque (Hexidecimal Mix)// Discothèque (DM Deep Extended Club Mix)/Discothèque (DM Deep Beats Mix)/Discotheque (DM Tec Radio Mix)/Discothèque (DM Deep Instrumental Mix)/Discotheque (Single Version)/Discothèque (David | 12 |
| 97 | Island 12IS 684 | Mofo (Mother's Mix)/Mofo (House Flavour Mix)/Mofo (Romin Mix)/Mofo (Phunk Force Mix)/Mofo (Black Hole Dub) (12", die-cut p/s, 2,000 only) | 10 |
| 10 | Mercury 2739289 | Soon/Soon (p/s, red vinyl) | 12 |

ALBUMS

| | | | |
|---|---|---|---|
| 80 | Island ILPS 9646 | BOY (LP) | 20 |
| 83 | Island PILPS 9733 | WAR (LP, picture disc, beware of counterfeits with ILPS cat. no.) | 100 |
| 81 | Island ILPS 9680 | OCTOBER (LP) | 20 |
| 85 | Island CID 112 | WAR (LP, pink cover lettering) | 25 |

| 85 | Island CID 102 | THE UNFORGETTABLE FIRE (CD, no bar code) | 30 |
| 87 | Island U2 6 | THE JOSHUA TREE (LP, gatefold) | 18 |
| 88 | Island U27 | RATTLE AND HUM (LP) | 18 |
| 91 | Island U2-8 | ACHTUNG BABY (LP, inner sleeve, lyric insert, 10 art prints) | 50 |
| 93 | Island U2-9 | ZOOROPA (LP, inner sleeve, lyric insert) | 35 |
| 95 | Island MELONCD 1 | MELON (REMIXES FOR PROPAGANDA) (CD, 9-track compilation, card sleeve, fan club issue, 20,000 only; sealed with Propaganda No. 21) | 50 |
| 95 | Island MELONCD 1 | MELON (REMIXES FOR PROPAGANDA) (CD, 9-track compilation, card sleeve, fan club issue, 20,000 only; unsealed with Propaganda No. 21) | 25 |
| 97 | Island U2 10 | POP (2-LP, gatefold sleeve) | 40 |
| 98 | Island U2 11 | THE BEST OF 1980-1990 (2-LP, gatefold sleeve) | 80 |
| 00 | Island U2 12 | ALL THAT YOU CAN'T LEAVE BEHIND (LP, with booklet) | 70 |
| 02 | Island U2 13 | THE BEST OF 1990-2000 (2-LP, gatefold) | 50 |
| 04 | Island U2 14 | HOW TO DISMANTLE AN ATOMIC BOMB (LP, with booklet) | 30 |
| 06 | Island U2.COM2 | U2 ZOO TV LIVE (2xCD & poster in card sleeve & outer card slipcase Issued to U2.com subscribers only) | 50 |
| 07 | Island U2.COM3 | U2 GO HOME - LIVE FROM SLANE CASTLE (2xCD issued to u2.com subscribers only) | 30 |
| 09 | Island 1796038 | NO LINE ON THE HORIZON (2-LP) | 30 |
| 06 | Mercury U2 18 | 18 SINGLES (2-LP) | 40 |
| 15 | Island B0022855-01 | SONGS OF INNOCENCE (2-LP, 5000, numbered, RSD release) | 35 |

## PROMOS : PROMOS - SINGLES

| 80 | Island WIP 6601 | 11 O'Clock Tick Tock/Touch (p/s, 'A' label) | 50 |
| 80 | Island WIP 6630 | A Day Without Me/Things To Make And Do (p/s, 'A' label) | 50 |
| 80 | Island WIP 6656 DJ | I Will Follow (Special Edited DJ Version) (1-sided, company sleeve) | 80 |
| 81 | WIP 6679 | Fire (Radio Edit) (1-sided, p/s) | 70 |
| 81 | WIP 6733 | Gloria (Radio Edit) (1-sided, p/s) | 60 |
| 84 | Island U2 2 | Wire/Bad/The Unforgettable Fire (12", black die-cut sleeve) | 70 |
| 87 | Island ISJ 319 | With Or Without You/Walk To The Water (jukebox issue, solid centre) | 10 |
| 87 | Island ISJ 328 | I Still Haven't Found What I'm Looking For/Spanish Eyes (jukebox issue, solid centre) | 20 |
| 87 | Island ISJ 328 | I Still Haven't Found What I'm Looking For/Spanish Eyes (jukebox issue, large centre hole) | 10 |
| 87 | Island ISJB 340 | Where The Streets Have No Name/Silver And Gold (jukebox issue, large centre hole) | 10 |
| 88 | Island 12ISX 400 | Desire (9.23 Hollywood Remix) (12", 1-sided, custom black p/s, 800 only) | 25 |
| 88 | Island U2V 7 | EXCERPTS FROM RATTLE AND HUM (In God's Country [live]/Hawkmoon 269/ Bad [live]/God Part II/With Or Without You [live]) (CD, card gatefold sleeve) | 70 |
| 88 | Island IS 319 | With Or Without You/Luminous Times (Hold Onto Love)/Walk To The Water/ With Or Without You (Video) (CD Video, withdrawn, less than 100 copies) | 350 |
| 89 | Island 12 ISX 411 | U2 3D DANCE MIXES: When Love Comes To Town (Live From The Kingdom Dance Mix)/God Part II (Hard Metal Dance Club Mix)/Desire (Hollywood Remix 5.23) (12" EP p/s) | 25 |
| 90 | Island RHB 1 | Night And Day (Twilight Remix)/Steel String Mix) (12", p/s, numbered, 4,000 copies only) | 50 |
| 91 | Island U2-3 | OCTOBER 1991: I Will Follow/Pride (In The Name Of Love)/God Part II/ Where The Streets Have No Name) (CD EP, 250 only) | 400 |
| 92 | Island 12IS 550DJ | Salomé (Zooromancer Remix 8.02)/Can't Help Falling In Love (Mystery Train Dub 8.20) (12", black die-cut sleeve, 1,000 only) | 70 |
| 92 | Island REAL 1 | Even Better Than The Real Thing (The Perfecto Mix)/Even Better Than The Real Thing (Trance Mix)/Even Better Than The Real Thing (Sexy Dub Mix) (12" , black die-cut sleeve with title sticker) | 10 |
| 92 | Island REAL 2DJ | Even Better Than The Real Thing (The Perfecto Mix-Radio Edit) (2-sided radio promo, some with p/s) | 40 |
| 92 | Island REAL 2DJ | Even Better Than The Real Thing (The Perfecto Mix-Radio Edit) (2-sided radio promo, some with p/s) | 15 |
| 93 | Island NUMJB 1 | Numb (2-sided jukebox issue, large centre hole) | 10 |
| 93 | Island NUMCD 1 | Numb (CD, 1-track, with lyric inner, 250 only) | 80 |
| 93 | Island 12LEM DJ 1 | Lemon (Bad Yard Club)/(Momo Beats)/(Version Dub)/(Serious Def Dub)// (Perfecto Mix)/(Trance Mix) (12", double pack, p/s, 1,000 only, numbered with press sheets) | 60 |
| 93 | Island LEMCD 1 | Lemon (Radio Edit) (CD, 1-track, with lyric inner) | 30 |
| 95 | Island 12 MELON 1 | MELON (Salomé [Zooromancer Remix]/Lemon [Bad Yard Club Mix]/ Numb [The Soul Assassins Mix]/Numb [Gimme Some More Dignity Mix]) (12" EP, 800 only) | 20 |
| 96 | Island PRECD 1 | U2 PREVIOUSLY: Lemon/Mysterious Ways/One/Desire/I Still Haven't Found What I'm Looking For (CD, card sleeve) | 25 |
| 97 | Island ISD(X) 649 D(J) | Discothèque (Howie B Hairy B Mix)/Discothèque (Hexidecimal Mix)// Discothèque (DM Deep Extended Club Mix)/Discothèque (DM Deep Beats Mix)/Discothèque (DM Tec Radio Mix)/Discothèque (DM Deep Instrumental Mix)/Discothèque (Single Version)/Discothèque (David | 25 |
| 97 | Island ISJB 649 | Discothèque/Holy Joe (jukebox issue, large centre hole) | 8 |
| 97 | Island ISJB 658 | Staring At The Sun/North And South Of The River (jukebox issue, large centre hole) | 8 |
| 97 | Island 12IS 658DJ | Staring At The Sun (Monster Truck Mix)/Staring At The Sun (Lab Rat Mix)/ Staring At The Sun (Sad Bastard's Mix) (12", p/s) | 20 |
| 97 | Island ISJB 664 | Last Night On Earth (Single Mix)/Last Night On Earth (First Night In Hell Remix) (jukebox issue, large centre hole) | 10 |
| 97 | Island 12IS 664DJ | Last Night On Earth (First Night In Hell Remix)/Happiness Is A Warm Gun (The Gun Mix)/Pop Muzik (Pop Mart Mix)/Happiness Is A Warm Gun (The Danny Sabre Mix)/ (12" p/s) | 20 |
| 97 | Island MUZIK 1 | Pop Muzik (Pop Mart Mix - Radio Edit) (CD, 1-track, picture disc, jewel case, 250 only) | 100 |
| 97 | Island MART 1 | Pop Muzik (Pop Mart Mix)/Last Night On Earth (First Night In Hell Mix) (12", plain black die cut sleeve) | 70 |
| 97 | Island ISJB 673 | Please/Where The Streets Have No Name (live) (jukebox issue, large centre hole) | 10 |
| 97 | Island ISJB 684 | If God Will Send His Angels (Single Viesion)/Sunday Bloody Sunday (live from Sarajevo) (jukebox issue, large centre hole) | 15 |
| 97 | Island 12MOFO 1 | Mofo (Phunk Force Mix)/Mofo (Black Hole Dub)/Mofo (Romin Remix) (12", orange label, orange & silver die-cut title sleeve) | 15 |
| 97 | Island 12MOFO 2 | Mofo (Mother's Mix)/Mofo (House Flavor Mix) (12", pink label, pink & silver die-cut title sleeve, 250 only) | 15 |

MINT VALUE £

| | | | |
|---|---|---|---|
| 97 | Island 12MOFO 3 | Mofo (Explicit Mix) (12", 1-sided, stamped white label, plain black die-cut sleeve, 200 only) | 50 |
| 97 | Island MOFOCD 1 | Mofo (Album Version) (CD, 1-track, card sleeve, export issue [to Mexico]) | 80 |
| 97 | Island MOFOCD 2 | Mofo (Phunk Force Mix) (CD, 1-track, jewel case, export issue [to Mexico]) | 60 |
| 98 | Island CIDDJ 727 | Sweetest Thing/Twilight (Live)/An Cat Dubh (Live)/Stories For Boys Out Of Control (Live) (CD, die-cut sleeve) | 50 |
| 00 | Island GROUND 1 | The Ground Beneath Her Feet (1-sided promo) | 100 |
| 01 | Island 12ISD 780 | Beautiful Day (Quincy & Sonance Mix)/(The Perfecto Mix)/(David Holmes Remix)/ Elevation (The Vandit Club Mix)/(Influx Remix)/(Escalation Mix)/Quincy & Sonance Remix) (2x12", p/s, inners) | 15 |
| 00 | Island 12 BEAUT 1 | Beautiful Day (Quincy & Sonance Mix) (1-sided 12", in black die-cut title sleeve) | 15 |
| 01 | Island ISJB770 | Stuck In A Moment You Can't Get Out Of/Big Girls Are Best (UK jukebox promo 7" with large centre) | 10 |
| 01 | Island 12 ELE 1 | Elevation (Escalation Mix)/Elevation (Influx Mix) (12", red custom p/s, 250 only) | 25 |
| 01 | Island 12 ELE 2 | Elevation (Paul Vandyk Remix)/Elevation (The Vandit Club Mix) (12", blue custom p/s, 250 only, exclusive mixes) | 10 |
| 02 | Island CID 808 | Electrical Storm (William Orbit Mix)/New York (Nice Mix)/New York (Nasty Mix)/ Bad (Live)/Where The Streets Have No Name (2-CD + DVD set in limited issue collectors' wallet, mail order only) | 40 |
| 02 | Island NEWCD U2 13 | NEW SONGS AND MIXES FROM THE BEST OF 1990-2000 (CD sampler, black inner sleeve, silver outer sleeve) | 25 |
| 03 | Island 12 Sun U2 | Staring At The Sun (Brothers In Rhythm Club Mix)/Staring At The Sun (Brothers In Rhythm Ambient Mix) (12", black die-cut custom sleeve) | 15 |
| 02 | Island 12REMIX U2 13 | U2 REMIXES FROM THE 1990S (2 x 12" sampler, black inner sleeves, silver outer sleeve) | 20 |
| 04 | Island U2PRO2 | Vertigo (Jacknife Lee 7" mix) (7" vinyl promo, picture sleeve. Matt/gloss finish) | 50 |
| 04 | Island 10I5878DJ | Vertigo (Jacknife Lee 7" mix)/Vertigo (Jacknife Lee 10" mix) 10" vinyl p/s | 20 |
| 04 | Island CID878/X878/V878 | Vertigo (CD1, CD2 & DVD set in wallet issued by U2.Com) | 50 |
| 05 | Island CID886/X/V | Sometimes You Can't Make It On Your Own (CD1, CD2 & DVD set in wallet, issued by U2.com) | 25 |
| 05 | Island CID890/X/V | City Of Blinding Lights (CD1, CD2 & DVD set in wallet via U2.com) | 20 |
| 05 | Island CID906/X/V | All Because Of You (CD1, CD2 & DVD set in wallet in wallet via u2.com) | 20 |

## PROMOS : PROMOS - ALBUMS

| | | | |
|---|---|---|---|
| 83 | Island U2 1 | UNDER A BLOOD RED SKY - A DIALOGUE WITH U2 LIVE (LP, custom sleeve, with cue sheet, numbered, 1,000 only) | 75 |
| 87 | Island U2-6 | THE JOSHUA TREE (CD, LP & cassette in black/gold 'pizza' box set) | 250 |
| 87 | Island U2 6-1 - U2 6-5 | THE JOSHUA TREE COLLECTION Red Hill Mining Town/Where The Streets Have No Name//Trip Through Your Wires/Running To Stand Still//I Still Haven't Found What I'm Looking For/One Tree Hill/Exit/Mothers Of The Disappeared/In God's Country/ Bullet The Blue Sky | 500 |
| 87 | Island U2 6-1 - U2 6-5 | THE JOSHUA TREE COLLECTION (5 x 7" black box set, with U2 6-1 mispressed with "Red Hill Mining Town" both sides, less than 50 copies) | 1000 |
| 87 | Island U2CLP 1 | THE U2 TALKIE: A CONVERSATION WITH LARRY, BONO, ADAM & THE EDGE (LP, music & interview with Dave Fanning for "The Joshua Tree") | 30 |
| 87 | Island U2CC 1 | THE U2 TALKIE (cassette) | 20 |
| 87 | Island BOU2 1 | CASSETTE SAMPLER (cassette, 17-track instore 'best of' compilation) | 30 |
| 88 | Island U2-7 | RATTLE AND HUM (CD, LP & cassette in flight case with leather tag, 250 only) | 1000 |
| 89 | Island U2 2D1 | U2 2 DATE (LP, 8-track hits compilation) | 25 |
| 91 | Island U2-8 | ACHTUNG BABY (CD, cassette in 'User's Kit', including map/poster, torch, key ring, spanner & screwdriver in printed green nylon kit bag) | 500 |
| 91 | Island CIDDJ U2-8 | ACHTUNG (graphics CD, in jewel case marked "promo only - not for sale") | 100 |
| 97 | Island CID U2 10 | POP (CD, in large cube-shaped picture box set, with prismatic pen & custom notepad) | 200 |
| 97 | Island POP 1 | U2 TALK POP (CD, interview with Dave Fanning, card sleeve) | 50 |
| 97 | Island POP 2 | U2 TALK POP (CD, interview with Dave Fanning, card sleeve, same tracks as POP 1) | 50 |
| 97 | Island POP 3 | U2 TALK POP (CD, interview with Dave Fanning, card sleeve, same track as POP 1) | 50 |
| 98 | Island CIDDU211 | THE BEST OF THE 'B' SIDES 1980-1990 (2-CD, discs marked 'A' and 'B', in card sleeves with gold slipcase) | 50 |
| 98 | Island BXU2 11 | THE 'BEST OF' COLLECTION 1980-1990 (14 x 7" singles, 2-CDs, 16-page booklet, in gold box, 2000 copies only) | 250 |
| 00 | Island CID U212 | ALL THAT YOU CAN'T LEAVE BEHIND (promo pack, with 1-track CD Beautiful Day [BEAUT CD 1] in blue picture slipcase, booklet, window sticker, video tape, "playback" invitation, in laminated picture bag with rope handles; with signed print) | 600 |
| 00 | Island CID U212 | ALL THAT YOU CAN'T LEAVE BEHIND (promo pack, with 1-track CD Beautiful Day [BEAUT CD 1] in blue picture slipcase, booklet, window sticker, video tape, "playback" invitation, in laminated picture bag with rope handles; without signed print) | 200 |
| 00 | Island HASTACD 1 | HASTA LA VISTA BABY! LIVE FROM MEXICO CITY (CD, fan-club only p/s) | 50 |
| 02 | Island CIDDJ U2 13 | THE BEST OF THE B-SIDES OF 1990-2000 (2-CD set card sleeves in card wallet) | 30 |
| 02 | Island BX U2 13 | THE BEST OF COLLECTION 1990-2000 (15 x 7", with 2 CDs & 16-page booklet in silver fliptop card box) | 200 |
| 02 | Island REMIXCD U2 13 | REMIXES FROM THE 90S (CD, 5-track album sampler in card sleeve, in silver card wallet) | 25 |
| 02 | Island REMIXCD U2 13 | REMIXES FROM THE 90S (2 x 12", promo p/s) card wallet) | 20 |
| 05 | Island UCOMV1 | U2 COMMUNICATION (CD & DVD fan club issue) | 30 |
| 08 | Island | U23D (Promo CD, audio press kit, DVD box) | 35 |

*(see also Bono & Gavin Friday, The Edge, Adam Clayton & Larry Mullen, Passengers)*

## U2 AND GREEN DAY

| | | | |
|---|---|---|---|
| 06 | UNIVERSAL LC00268 | The Saints Are Coming/The Saints Are Coming (Live From New Orleans) (p/s) | 5 |

## U.V. POP

| | | | |
|---|---|---|---|
| 82 | Pax PAX 9 | Just A Game/No Songs Tomorrow (p/s) | 30 |
| 85 | Flow Motion FM 007 | Anyone For Me/Hands To Me | 30 |
| 85 | Flow motion FM 12/007 | ANYONE FOR ME (12" EP) | 35 |
| 85 | Native NTV4 | SERIOUS EP (12") | 20 |
| 86 | Extra EXTRA T001 | MUSIC TO YEAH TO EP (12") | 30 |
| 83 | Flow Motion FM 004 | NO SONGS TOMORROW (LP) | 40 |

| | | | |
|---|---|---|---|
| 86 | Extra EXTRA LP1 | BENDY BABY MAN (LP) | 50 |

**UXB**
| | | | |
|---|---|---|---|
| 80 | Crazy Plane SP 002 | Crazy Today/Mister Fix It (p/s) | 100 |

**UZI**
| | | | |
|---|---|---|---|
| 70 | Beacon BEA 152 | Morning Train/Where Were You Last Night | 30 |

**U-ZIQ**
| | | | |
|---|---|---|---|
| 93 | Rephlex CAT 018 | Bluff Limbo (remixes) (2 x 12", 800 only) | 20 |
| 97 | Planet Mu PULP 5 | LUNATIC HARNESS (2-LP) | 20 |

# V

**DONNA V**
| | | | |
|---|---|---|---|
| 96 | Fashion FAD 153 | Prophecy Revealing (Natural Mix)/Mystic Mix/GENERALY LEVY : Inna We Culture/ Remember Yu Roots (12") | 35 |

**VACELS**
| | | | |
|---|---|---|---|
| 65 | Pye International 7N 25330 | Can You Please Crawl Out Your Window/I'm Just A Poor Boy | 35 |

**VAGABONDS**
| | | | |
|---|---|---|---|
| 63 | Island ILP 916 | PRESENTING THE FABULOUS VAGABONDS (LP) | 250 |

*(see also Jimmy James & Vagabonds, Jamaica's Own Vagabonds)*

**VAGINA DENTATA ORGAN**
| | | | |
|---|---|---|---|
| 83 | WSNS 001 | VAGINA DENTATA ORGAN PRESENTS: MUSIC FOR HASHASINS, IN MEMORIAM OF HASSAN-I-SABBAH (LP, 500 copies) | 50 |
| 84 | WSNS 002 | THE LAST SUPPER, THE REVEREND JIM JONES IN PERSON (LP, picture disc, 912 numbered, with transcript) | 90 |
| 84 | WSNS 002 | THE LAST SUPPER, THE REVEREND JIM JONES IN PERSON (LP, picture disc, 912 numbered, without transcript) | 80 |
| 84 | WSNS 003 | THE PAGAN DRUMS OF CALANDA (LP, picture disc, 12 copies adorned with 'real' blood and handpainted) | 300 |
| 84 | WSNS 003 | THE PAGAN DRUMS OF CALANDA (LP, picture disc, 30 copies adorned with 'real' blood but not handpainted) | 150 |
| 84 | WSNS 003 | THE PAGAN DRUMS OF CALANDA (LP, picture disc, adorned with 'fake blood') | 100 |
| 84 | WSNS 003 | THE PAGAN DRUMS OF CALANDA (LP, 900 'bloodless' copies) | 50 |
| 86 | WSNS 004 | COLD MEAT/EROS & THANATOS (LP picture disc, 4 copies with 1 black side with Elvis image missing) | 150 |
| 86 | WSNS 004 | COLD MEAT/EROS & THANATOS (LP picture disc, 12 copies with hand drawings and personal dedications) | 300 |
| 86 | WSNS 004 | COLD MEAT/EROS & THANATOS (LP picture disc, no drawings or dedications) | 50 |
| 87 | Temple TOPY 012 | MUSIC FOR THE HASHISHINS (LP) | 25 |
| 87 | Temple TPY 013 | THE LAST SUPPER (LP) | 25 |

**VAGRANTS**
| | | | |
|---|---|---|---|
| 66 | Fontana TF 703 | I Can't Make A Friend/Young Blues | 60 |

**VAIN AIMS**
| | | | |
|---|---|---|---|
| 80 | We Practice In a Gang WPG 1 | You/Count (no p/s) | 50 |

**VALADIERS**
| | | | |
|---|---|---|---|
| 63 | Oriole CBA 1809 | I Found A Girl/You'll Be Sorry Someday | 1000 |
| 63 | Oriole CBA 1809 | I Found A Girl/You'll Be Sorry Someday (DJ copy) | 1000 |

**RICKY VALANCE**
| | | | |
|---|---|---|---|
| 60 | Columbia DB 4493 | Tell Laura I Love Her/Once Upon A Time | 5 |
| 60 | Columbia DB 4543 | Movin' Away/Lipstick On Your Lips | 8 |
| 61 | Columbia DB 4586 | Jimmy's Girl/Only The Young | 8 |
| 61 | Columbia DB 4592 | Why Can't We/Fisherboy | 8 |
| 61 | Columbia DB 4680 | Bobby/I Want To Fall In Love | 8 |
| 61 | Columbia DB 4725 | I Never Had A Chance/It's Not True | 8 |
| 62 | Columbia DB 4787 | Try To Forget Her/At Times Like These | 8 |
| 62 | Columbia DB 4864 | Don't Play No. 9/Till The Final Curtain Falls | 8 |
| 65 | Decca F 12129 | Six Boys/Face The Crowd | 8 |
| 76 | Valley VLY 001 | RICKY VALANCE (EP, no p/s) | 25 |
| 78 | Tank BBS 324 | RAINBOW (LP) | 40 |

*(see also Jason Merryweather)*

**JERRY VALE**
| | | | |
|---|---|---|---|
| 67 | CBS 2682 | Have You Seen The One I love Go By/Signs | 5 |

**RITCHIE VALENS**
| | | | |
|---|---|---|---|
| 58 | Pye International 7N 25000 | Come On Let's Go/Dooby Dooby Wah | 150 |
| 58 | Pye International 7N 25000 | Come On Let's Go/Dooby Dooby Wah (78) | 80 |
| 59 | London HL 8803 | Donna/La Bamba | 30 |
| 59 | London HL 8803 | Donna/La Bamba (78) | 80 |
| 59 | London HL 7068 | Donna/La Bamba (export issue) | 30 |
| 59 | London HL 8886 | That's My Little Suzie/Bluebirds Over The Mountains (tri centre) | 40 |
| 59 | London HL 8886 | That's My Little Suzie/Bluebirds Over The Mountains (round centre) | 20 |
| 59 | London HL 8886 | That's My Little Suzie/Bluebirds Over The Mountains (78) | 80 |
| 62 | London HL 9494 | La Bamba/Ooh, My Head | 20 |
| 59 | London RE 1232 | RITCHIE VALENS (EP, initial pressing with triangular centre) | 200 |
| 59 | London RE 1232 | RITCHIE VALENS (EP, later round centre) | 150 |
| 61 | London HA 2390 | RITCHIE (LP) | 150 |
| 64 | London HA 8196 | HIS GREATEST HITS (LP) | 50 |

## Dino VALENTI

| | | | |
|---|---|---|---|
| 67 | President PTL 1001 | I REMEMBER RITCHIE VALENS (LP) | 20 |

## DINO VALENTI
| | | | |
|---|---|---|---|
| 68 | CBS 65715 | DINO (LP) | 45 |

*(see also Quicksilver Messenger Service)*

## VALENTINE
| | | | |
|---|---|---|---|
| 72 | Track 2094104 | Time/Leader Of The Band | 6 |

## BILLY VALENTINE
| | | | |
|---|---|---|---|
| 55 | Capitol CL 14320 | It's A Sin/Your Love Has Got Me (Reelin' And Rockin') | 10 |

## DICKIE VALENTINE (& STARGAZERS)
### SINGLES
| | | | |
|---|---|---|---|
| 54 | Decca F 10346 | Endless/I Could Have Told You | 30 |
| 54 | Decca F 10394 | The Finger Of Suspicion (with Stargazers)/ Who's Afraid (Not I, Not I, Not I) | 20 |
| 54 | Decca F 10415 | Mister Sandman/Runaround | 40 |
| 55 | Decca F 10430 | A Blossom Fell/I Want You All To Myself (Just You) | 15 |
| 55 | Decca F 10484 | Ma Cherie Amie/Lucky Waltz | 10 |
| 55 | Decca F 10493 | I Wonder/You Too Can Be A Dreamer | 10 |
| 55 | Decca F 10517 | Hello Mrs. Jones (Is Mary There?)/Lazy Gondolier | 10 |
| 55 | Decca F 10549 | No Such Luck/The Engagement Waltz | 10 |
| 55 | Decca F 10628 | Christmas Alphabet/Where Are You Tonight? | 20 |
| 55 | Decca F 10645 | The Old Pi-Anna Rag/First Love | 15 |
| 55 | Decca F 10667 | Dreams Can Tell A Lie/Song Of The Trees | 7 |
| 56 | Decca F 10714 | The Voice/The Best Way To Hold A Girl | 7 |
| 56 | Decca F 10753 | My Impossible Castle/When You Came Along | 7 |
| 56 | Decca F 10766 | Day Dreams/Give Me A Carriage With Eight White Horses | 8 |
| 56 | Decca F 10798 | Christmas Island/The Hand Of Friendship | 15 |
| 56 | Decca F 10820 | Dickie Valentine's Rock 'N' Roll Party Medley (Parts 1 & 2) | 10 |
| 57 | Decca F 10874 | Chapel Of The Roses/My Empty Arms | 5 |
| 57 | Decca F 10906 | Puttin' On The Style/Three Sides To Every Story | 5 |
| 57 | Decca F 10949 | Long Before I Knew You/Just In Time | 5 |
| 58 | Decca F 11005 | Love Me Again/King Of Dixieland | 6 |
| 59 | Pye Nixa 7N 15192 | Venus/Where? (In The Old Home Town) | 5 |
| 59 | Pye 7N 15202 | A Teenager In Love/My Favourite Song | 5 |

### ALBUMS
| | | | |
|---|---|---|---|
| 58 | Decca LK 4269 | WITH VOCAL REFRAIN BY | 20 |

## VALENTINE GUINNESS
| | | | |
|---|---|---|---|
| 80 | RAK RAK 308 | (Hey Hey) C.J.T./When Mandy Calls | 50 |

## JACK VALENTINE
| | | | |
|---|---|---|---|
| 55 | MGM SPC 8 | Dressing Up My Heart/Song Of The Bandit (export issue) | 12 |

## VALENTINES (JAMAICA)
| | | | |
|---|---|---|---|
| 67 | Doctor Bird DB 1065 | Blam Blam Fever/BABA BROOKS: The Scratch | 75 |

## VALENTINES (U.S.)
| | | | |
|---|---|---|---|
| 60 | Ember EMB S 123 | Hey Ruby/That's How I Feel | 90 |

## ANNA VALENTINO
| | | | |
|---|---|---|---|
| 57 | London HLD 8421 | Calypso Joe/You're Mine | 30 |

## DANNY VALENTINO
| | | | |
|---|---|---|---|
| 59 | MGM MGM 1049 | Stampede/(You Gotta Be A) Music Man | 30 |
| 60 | MGM MGM 1067 | Biology/A Million Tears | 20 |
| 60 | MGM MGM 1109 | Pictures From The Past/'Till The End Of Forever | 15 |

## MARK VALENTINO
| | | | |
|---|---|---|---|
| 63 | Stateside SS 148 | The Push And Kick/Walking Alone | 25 |
| 63 | Stateside SS 186 | Do It/Hey You're Looking Good | 15 |
| 63 | Stateside SS 233 | Jivin' At The Drive In/Part Time Job | 25 |

## VALENTINOS
| | | | |
|---|---|---|---|
| 68 | Soul City SC 106 | It's All Over Now/Tired Of Livin' In The Country | 25 |
| 68 | Stateside SS 2137 | Tired Of Being Nobody/The Death Of Love | 18 |
| 71 | Polydor 2058 090 | Don't Raise Up Your Hands In Anger/Stand Up And Be Counted | 10 |
| 68 | Soul City SCM 001 | THE VALENTINOS/THE SIMS TWINS (LP, with Sims Twins) | 70 |

*(see also Bobby Womack)*

## VALERIE (THE ROCK 'N' ROLL YOUNGSTER)
| | | | |
|---|---|---|---|
| 56 | Columbia DB 3832 | Tonight You Belong To Me/The Man Who Owns The Sunshine | 20 |

## VALERIE AND THE WEEK OF WONDERS
| | | | |
|---|---|---|---|
| 83 | Soon Come VA 01 | Too Late/Helpless (hand made p/s) | 20 |

## DANA VALERY
| | | | |
|---|---|---|---|
| 64 | Decca F 11881 | This Is My Prayer/Would I Love You Again/T'en Va Pas | 7 |
| 64 | Decca F 11977 | I Wake Up Crying/Never Let Go | 12 |

## VALHALLA (1)
| | | | |
|---|---|---|---|
| 81 | Asgard ASG 69151 | Lightning In The Sky/These Sunday Nights | 250 |

## VALHALLA (2)
| | | | |
|---|---|---|---|
| 82 | Neat NEAT 22 | Coming Home/Through With You | 8 |
| 84 | Neat NEAT 36 | Still in Love With You/Jack | 6 |

## JOE VALINO (& GOSPELAIRES)
| | | | |
|---|---|---|---|
| 57 | HMV POP 283 | The Garden Of Eden/Caravan | 25 |
| 58 | London HLT 8705 | God's Little Acre/I'm Happy With What I've Got (with Gospelaires) | 15 |
| 60 | Columbia DB 4406 | Hidden Persuasion/Back To Your Eyes | 5 |

## VALJEAN (AT THE PIANO)
| | | | |
|---|---|---|---|
| 62 | London HLL 9593 | Till There Was You/The Eighteenth Variation | 6 |

## VALKYRIES
64   Parlophone R 5123      Rip It Up/What's Your Name? ....................................................... 40

## DIORIS VALLADARES ORCHESTRA
64   Island IEP 703      AUTHENTIC MERINGUE (EP) ............................................................ 12
64   Island ILP 910      LET'S GO LATIN (LP, withdrawn) .................................................... 30

## MARCOS VALLE
68   Verve VLP 9206      SAMBA '68 (LP) ........................................................................... 20

## VALLEY FORGE
86   Revue REV 0312      FROM ACROSS THE SEE (12" EP, p/s) ............................................. 20

## VALLEY OF ACHOR
75   Dovetail DOVE 18      A DOOR OF HOPE (LP, gatefold sleeve) ......................................... 15
*(see also Achor, Wine Of Lebanon)*

## FRANKIE VALLI
66   Philips BF 1467      (You're Gonna) Hurt Yourself/VALLI BOYS: Night Hawk ................... 10
66   Philips BF 1512      You're Ready Now/Cry For Me ....................................................... 10
66   Philips BF 1529      The Proud One/Ivy ....................................................................... 10
67   Philips BF 1556      Beggin'/Dody ............................................................................... 10
67   Philips BF 1580      Can't Take My Eyes Off You/The Trouble With Me ............................ 7
67   Philips BF 1603      I Make A Fool Of Myself/September Rain ......................................... 7
68   Philips BF 1634      To Give (The Reason I Live)/Watch Where You Walk .......................... 7
69   Philips BF 1795      The Girl I'll Never Know/A Face Without A Name ............................... 6
70   Philips 320 226 BF      You're Ready Now/Cry For Me (reissue) ......................................... 10
74   Private Stock PVT 1      My Eyes Adored You/Watch Where You Walk .................................... 5
67   Philips (S)BL 7814      SOLO (LP) .................................................................................... 25
69   Philips SBL 7856      TIMELESS (LP) ............................................................................. 20
77   Private Stock PVLP 1029      LADY PUT THE LIGHT OUT (LP, withdrawn) .................................... 40

## FRANKIE VALLI & THE FOUR SEASONS
71   Warner Bros K 16107      Whatever You Say/Sleeping Man (withdrawn, 300 only) ................... 45
72   Tamla Motown TMG 819      You're A Song/Sun Country ........................................................... 10
72   Mowest MW 3002      The Night/When The Morning Comes ............................................ 75
73   Mowest MW 3003      Walk On, Don't Look Back/Touch The Rainchild ................................ 8
75   Mowest MW 3024      The Night/When The Morning Comes (reissue) ................................ 5
72   Mowest MWSA 5501      CHAMELEON (LP) ........................................................................ 20
*(see also Four Seasons, Wonder Who)*

## JUNE VALLI
54   HMV 7M 245      I Understand (Just How You Feel)/Old Shoes And A Bag Of Rice ......... 7
54   HMV 7M 259      Tell Me, Tell Me/Boy Wanted ........................................................ 7
55   HMV 7M 284      Wrong, Wrong, Wrong/Ole Pappy Time ........................................ 7
56   HMV 7M 347      Por Favor (Please)/The Things They Say .......................................... 7
59   Mercury AMT 1034      The Answer To A Maiden's Prayer/In His Arms ................................. 6
59   Mercury AMT 1048      An Anonymous Letter/Bygones ..................................................... 6
60   Mercury AMT 1091      Apple Green/Oh! Why ................................................................... 5
61   Mercury AMT 1130      I Guess Things Happen That Way/Tell Him For Me ............................ 7
62   HMV POP 1062      Hush Little Baby/Afraid ................................................................. 5

## ANTON VALOTTI
75   Rouge RMS 106      BLACKOUT (LP) ........................................................................... 80

## VALUES
66   Ember EMB S 211      Return To Me/That's The Way (with p/s) ........................................ 80
66   Ember EMB S 211      Return To Me/That's The Way ....................................................... 50

## HUBERT THOMAS VALVERDE & THE HTS
68   S n B 55 3922      Genevieve/We Don't Care ............................................................. 25

## VALVERDE BROTHERS
69   CBS 4519      River Of My Mind/I Wanna Love You ............................................. 20

## VALVES
77   Zoom ZUM 1      Robot Love/For Adolfs Only (p/s) ................................................... 12
77   Zoom ZUM 3      Tarzan Of The Kings Road/Ain't No Surf In Portobello (p/s) ............... 12
79   Albion DEL 3      I Don't Mean Nothing At All/Linda Vindalco (p/s) ............................ 12

## VAL & V'S
67   CBS 2780      Do It Again A Little Bit Slower/For A Rainy Day ............................... 20
67   CBS 2956      I Like The Way/With This Theme ................................................... 20
68   CBS 3316      This Little Girl/Dreamer ............................................................... 15

## VAMP
68   Atlantic 584 213      Floatin'/Thinkin' Too Much ......................................................... 100
69   Atlantic 584 263      Green Pea/Wake Up And Tell Me (withdrawn) ............................... 150
*(see also Viv Prince, Clark-Hutchinson)*

## VAMPIRE WEEKEND
08   XL XLS 399      The Kids Don't Stand a Chance /(Chromeo Remix) (white vinyl) ....... 15
10   XL 1779816      White Sky/White Sky (Basement Jaxx Remix) (white vinyl) .............. 10
13   XL XLS 601      Diane Young/Step (hand-printed sleeve, hand stamped labels) .......... 6
13   XL XLLP 556      MODERN VAMPIRES OF THE CITY (LP, hand-printed alternative sleeve, 50 only) ........... 70

## VAMPIRES (1)
59   Parlophone R 4599      Swinging Ghosts/Clap Trap ........................................................... 20

## VAMPIRES (2)
68   Pye 7N 17553      Do You Wanna Dance/My Girl ....................................................... 20

## VAMPIRES (3)
82   Next NEX 702      Harry's House/Mystery And Madness (p/s) ...................................... 10

## VAMPS
| | | | |
|---|---|---|---|
| 79 | Dental DK 001 | She Edudes Sexuality/Love Letters/I Only Saw You (p/s, red vinyl, 1000 only, hand-made p/s) | 25 |

## VAN DER GRAAF GENERATOR
| | | | |
|---|---|---|---|
| 69 | Polydor 56758 | People You Were Going To/Firebrand | 500 |
| 70 | Charisma CB 122 | Refugees/The Boat Of Millions Of Years (three prong centre) | 45 |
| 73 | Charisma CB 175 | Theme One/W (with p/s, "D.J. sample not for sale") | 50 |
| 72 | Charisma CB 175 | Theme One/W (with p/s, solid centre) | 30 |
| 72 | Charisma CB 175 | Theme One/W (four prong centre) | 5 |
| 76 | Charisma CB 297 | Wondering/Meurglys III | 8 |
| 76 | Charisma PRO 002 | Wondering (Song)/Wondering (Heroics) (promo only) | 25 |
| 11 | Esoteric VDGS 101 | Highly Strung/Elsewhere (die-cut sleeve) | 6 |
| 69 | Mercury SMCL 20177 | THE AEROSOL GREY MACHINE (LP, unreleased, finished gatefold sleeve only) | 750 |
| 70 | Charisma CAS 1007 | THE LEAST WE CAN DO IS WAVE TO EACH OTHER (LP, pink 'scroll' label, original mix, matrices read: CAS 1007 A/B, gatefold sleeve, with poster) | 250 |
| 70 | Charisma CAS 1007 | THE LEAST WE CAN DO IS WAVE TO EACH OTHER (LP, pink 'scroll' label, original mix, matrices read: CAS 1007 A/B, gatefold sleeve, without poster) | 60 |
| 70 | Charisma CAS 1007 | THE LEAST WE CAN DO IS WAVE TO EACH OTHER (LP, pink 'scroll' label, remix, matrices read: CAS 1007 A+G/B+G, gatefold sleeve; with poster) | 150 |
| 70 | Charisma CAS 1007 | THE LEAST WE CAN DO IS WAVE TO EACH OTHER (LP, pink 'scroll' label, remix, matrices read: CAS 1007 A+G/B+G, gatefold sleeve; without poster) | 50 |
| 70 | Charisma CAS 1027 | H TO HE, WHO AM THE ONLY ONE (LP, pink label, gatefold sleeve) | 150 |
| 71 | Charisma CAS 1051 | PAWN HEARTS (LP, gatefold sleeve, pink 'scroll' label, with insert) | 100 |
| 71 | Charisma CAS 1051 | PAWN HEARTS (LP, gatefold sleeve, pink 'scroll' label, without insert) | 35 |
| 72 | Charisma CS 2 | 1968-71 (LP, pink label) | 25 |
| 72 | Charisma CAS 1116 | STILL LIFE (LP, small 'Mad Hatter' logo) | 15 |
| 76 | Charisma CAS 1007 | THE LEAST WE CAN DO IS WAVE TO EACH OTHER (LP, gatefold reissue, 'Mad hatter' label) | 18 |
| 77 | Charisma CAS 1131 | THE QUIET ZONE/THE PLEASURE ZONE (LP, as Van Der Graaf) | 15 |
| 78 | Charisma CVLP 101 | VITAL (2-LP) | 20 |
| 00 | Virgin VDGGBOX 1 | THE BOX (4-CD box set) | 30 |

*(see also Peter Hammill, Long Hello, Juicy Lucy, Misunderstood, David Jackson)*

## HARRY VANDA
| | | | |
|---|---|---|---|
| 69 | Polydor 56357 | I Love Marie/Gonna Make It | 10 |

*(see also Easybeats)*

## LEE VANDERBILT
| | | | |
|---|---|---|---|
| 74 | Bell 1384 | It's Dawn Again/Pick Up Your Troubles | 15 |

## GREG VANDIKE
| | | | |
|---|---|---|---|
| 79 | Cloned CLONE 1 | All Of The Girls/Clone (p/s) | 7 |

## MAMIE VAN DOREN
| | | | |
|---|---|---|---|
| 58 | Capitol CL 14850 | Something To Dream About/I Fell In Love (promos in p/s) | 40 |
| 58 | Capitol CL 14850 | Something To Dream About/I Fell In Love | 25 |

## LINDA VAN DYCK
| | | | |
|---|---|---|---|
| 69 | Gemini GMS 004 | The Seduction Song/Unlock My door | 12 |

## VANDYKE & BAMBIS
| | | | |
|---|---|---|---|
| 64 | Piccadilly 7N 35180 | Doin' The Mod/All I Want Is You | 50 |

## EARL VAN DYKE (& SOUL BROTHERS)
| | | | |
|---|---|---|---|
| 64 | Stateside SS 357 | Soul Stomp/Hot 'N' Tot | 125 |
| 64 | Stateside SS 357 | Soul Stomp/Hot 'N' Tot (DJ copy) | 200 |
| 65 | Tamla Motown TMG 506 | All For You/Too Many Fish In The Sea (as Earl Van Dyke & Soul Brothers) | 125 |
| 65 | Tamla Motown TMG 506 | All For You/Too Many Fish In The Sea (as Earl Van Dyke & Soul Brothers)(DJ copy) | 175 |
| 70 | Tamla Motown TMG 759 | Six By Six/All For You (matt black label, later shiny) | 12 |
| 72 | Tamla Motown TMG 814 | I Can't Help Myself/How Sweet It Is (To Be Loved By You) (& Soul Brothers) | 10 |
| 65 | Tamla Motown TML 11014 | THAT MOTOWN SOUND (LP) | 120 |

## LEROY VAN DYKE
| | | | |
|---|---|---|---|
| 61 | Mercury AMT 1166 | Walk On By/My World Is Caving In | 5 |
| 62 | Mercury AMT 1173 | Big Man In A Big House/Faded Love | 5 |
| 62 | Mercury AMT 1183 | I Sat Back And Let It Happen/A Broken Promise | 5 |
| 65 | Warner Bros WB 5650 | It's All Over Now Baby Blue/Just A State Of Mind | 8 |
| 66 | Warner Bros WB 5807 | You Couldn't Get My Love Back/Fool Such As I | 8 |
| 67 | Warner Bros WB 5777 | Almost Persuaded/Less Of Me | 10 |
| 62 | Mercury MMC 14101 | WALK ON BY (LP) | 30 |
| 63 | Mercury MMC 14118 | MOVIN' VAN DYKE (LP) | 30 |

## VAN DYKES
| | | | |
|---|---|---|---|
| 66 | Stateside SS 504 | No Man Is An Island/I Won't Hold It Against You | 25 |
| 66 | Stateside SS 504 | No Man Is An Island/I Won't Hold It Against You (DJ Copy) | 40 |
| 66 | Stateside SS 530 | I've Gotta Go On Without You/What Will I Do | 25 |

## LON & DERREK VAN EATON
| | | | |
|---|---|---|---|
| 73 | Apple APPLE 46 | Warm Woman/More Than Words (in p/s) | 90 |
| 73 | Apple APPLE 46 | Warm Woman/More Than Words | 50 |
| 75 | A&M AMS 7157 | Wildfire/Music Lover | 5 |
| 75 | A&M AMS 7178 | Dancing In The Dark/All You're Hungry For Is Love | 5 |
| 73 | Apple SAPCOR 25 | BROTHER (LP, gatefold sleeve, with insert) | 70 |
| 73 | Apple SAPCOR 25 | BROTHER (LP, gatefold sleeve, without insert) | 50 |

## NICK VAN EEDE
| | | | |
|---|---|---|---|
| 78 | Barn 201 4128 | Rock'n'Roll Fool/Ounce Of Sense | 6 |
| 79 | Barn BARN 003 | All Or Nothing/Hold On To Your Heart | 7 |
| 79 | Barn BARN 008 | I Only Want To Be Number One/Dicing | 60 |

*(see also Drivers)*

## VANGELIS
| 75 | RCA RS 1025 | HEAVEN AND HELL (gatefold sleeve) | 12 |
| 76 | Polydor 2489 113 | L'APOCALYPSE DES ANIMAUX (LP, TV soundtrack) | 18 |

*(see also Aphrodite's Child, Forminx, Cosmic Baby)*

## VAN HALEN
| 78 | Warner Bros K 17107 | You Really Got Me/Atomic Punk | 5 |
| 78 | Warner Bros K 17162 | Runnin' With The Devil/Eruption. | 5 |
| 79 | Warner Bros K 17371 | Dance The Night Away/Outta Love Again | 7 |
| 79 | Warner Bros K 17371P | Dance The Night Away/Outta Love Again (picture disc) | 10 |
| 80 | Warner Bros K 17645 | And The Cradle Will Rock/Everybody Wants Some (p/s) | 5 |
| 86 | Warner Bros W 8740P | Why Can't This Be Love/Get Up (shaped picture disc with plinth, stickered PVC sleeve) | 10 |
| 86 | Warner Bros W 8642P | Dreams/Inside (car-shaped picture disc with stand, stickered PVC sleeve) | 12 |

*(see also David Lee Roth)*

## ILA VAN
| 74 | Pye Intl. DDS 108 | Can't Help Loving Dat Man/I've Got The Feeling | 6 |

## CHERRY VANILLA
| 77 | RCA PB 5053 | The Punk/Foxy Bitch (title sleeve) | 8 |
| 79 | RCA PL 25217 | VENUS DE VINYL (LP) | 15 |

## VANILLA FUDGE
| 67 | Atlantic 584 123 | You Keep Me Hanging On/Take Me For A Little While | 10 |
| 67 | Atlantic 584 139 | (Illusions Of My Childhood) Eleanor Rigby (Parts 1 & 2) | 8 |
| 68 | Atlantic 584 179 | Where Is My Mind?/The Look Of Love | 12 |
| 69 | Atlantic 584 257 | Shotgun/Good Good Lovin' | 7 |
| 69 | Atlantic 584 276 | Some Velvet Morning/Thoughts | 12 |
| 67 | Atlantic 587/588 086 | VANILLA FUDGE (LP, red & plum label) | 50 |
| 68 | Atlantic 587 100 | THE BEAT GOES ON (LP, mono) | 40 |
| 68 | Atlantic 588 100 | THE BEAT GOES ON (LP, stereo) | 40 |
| 68 | Atlantic 587 110 | RENAISSANCE (LP, mono) | 45 |
| 68 | Atlantic 588 110 | RENAISSANCE (LP, stereo) | 40 |
| 69 | Atco 228 020 | NEAR THE BEGINNING (LP) | 25 |
| 70 | Atco 228 029 | ROCK 'N' ROLL (LP) | 25 |

*(see also Beck Bogert & Appice, Cactus)*

## VANITY FARE
| 68 | Page One POF 075 | I Live For The Sun/On The Other Side Of Life | 10 |
| 68 | Page One POF 100 | Summer Morning/Betty Carter. | 7 |
| 69 | Page One POF 117 | Highway Of Dreams/Waiting For The Downfall | 7 |
| 69 | Page One POF 142 | Early In The Morning/You Made Me Love You | 7 |
| 69 | Page One POF 158 | Hitchin' A Ride/Man Child | 10 |
| 70 | Page One POF 170 | Come Tomorrow/Megowd (Something Tells Me) | 12 |
| 70 | Page One PDF 180 | Carolina's Coming Home/On Your Own | 8 |
| 71 | DJM DJS 234 | Where Did All The Good Times Go/Stand | 6 |
| 71 | DJM DJS 250 | Better By Far/Rock 'N Roll Band | 7 |
| 71 | DJM DJS 526 | Our Own Way Of Living/Nowhere To Go | 6 |
| 72 | Philips 6006237 | I'm In Love With The World/At The End Of The Pier | 6 |
| 69 | Page One POLS 010 | THE SUN, THE WIND AND OTHER THINGS (LP) | 45 |
| 70 | DJM DJSL 001 | COMING HOME (LP) | 20 |

*(see also Avengers)*

## TEDDY VANN (ORCHESTRA)
| 60 | London HLU 9097 | Cindy/I'm Waiting | 25 |
| 61 | Philips PB 1160 | The Lonely Crowd/I Was Born to Love You | 6 |
| 78 | Capitol CL 16012 | Theme From 'Coloured Man'/Intro To 'Coloured Man' (as Teddy Vann Orchestra) | 5 |

## ORNELLA VANONI
| 67 | Decca F 22703 | Only Two Can Play/Can I? | 10 |

## DAVE VAN RONK
| 65 | Stateside SL 10153 | INSIDE (LP) | 30 |

## ROB VAN SPYK
| 70s | private pressing | FOLLOW THE SUN (LP) | 60 |

*(see also Stonefield Tramp)*

## TOWNES VAN ZANDT
| 99 | Exile EX 7013 | Riding The Range/Dirty Old Town (p/s, 2000 only) | 6 |
| 69 | RCA SF 8040 | OUR MOTHER THE MOUNTAIN (LP) | 25 |
| 73 | United Artists UAS 29442 | THE LATE GREAT TOWNES VAN ZANDT (LP, gatefold sleeve) | 30 |
| 87 | Heartland HLD 003 | AT MY WINDOW (LP) | 15 |
| 01 | Charly SNAB 903 CD | TEXAS TROUBADOUR (4-CD, book-style box set) | 35 |

## PETER VARDAS
| 59 | Top Rank JAR 173 | He Threw A Stone/Checkerboard Love | 6 |

## VARDI AND HIS ORCHESTRA
| 62 | London 45 HLR 9518 | Theme From Ballad Of A Soldier/Exodus - Main Theme | 15 |

## VARDIS
| 79 | Redball RR 017 | 100 MPH (EP) | 120 |
| 80 | Castle CQUEL 2/100MPH | Out Of The Way/If I Were King | 7 |
| 81 | Logo VAR3 | Silver Machine/Come On (7", die cut p/s) | 6 |
| 81 | Logo VAR4 | All You'll Ever Need/If I Were King/Jumping Jack Flash (p/s) | 6 |

## VARIATION
| 72 | Warner Bros K 16233 | Snowbird/Nebula | 6 |

## VARIATIONS
| 65 | Immediate IM 019 | The Man With All The Toys/She'll Know I'm Sorry | 20 |

MINT VALUE £

| | | | |
|---|---|---|---|
| 69 | Major Minor MM 638 | Crimson And Clover/She Couldn't Dance | 20 |

## VARIATIONS (U.S.)

| | | | |
|---|---|---|---|
| 75 | UK USA 10 | Sayin' It And Doin' It Pts I & II | 8 |

## VARICOSE VEINS

| | | | |
|---|---|---|---|
| 78 | Warped WARP 1 | INCREDIBLE (EP, mail-order only, 200 only, beware of counterfeits) | 80 |

*(see also Orange Disaster)*

## VARIOUSARTISTS

| | | | |
|---|---|---|---|
| 81 | Not On Label – VA 1 | SOLO ALBUM (LP) | 20 |

## PAUL VARNEY

| | | | |
|---|---|---|---|
| 91 | PWL PWLT 201 | If Only I Knew (On The Buses Piano Edit)/If Only I Knew (Hurley's House Mix)/ If Only I Knew (Silk's Answer)/If Only I Knew (Maurice's Underground Mix) 12" p/s | 6 |

## SYLVIE VARTAN

| | | | |
|---|---|---|---|
| 65 | RCA Victor RCA 1490 | One More Day/I Made My Choice | 75 |
| 65 | RCA Victor RCA 1495 | Another Heart/Think About You | 12 |
| 79 | RCA PB 1578 | I Don't Want The Night To End/Distant Shores (p/s, coloured vinyl) | 6 |
| 65 | RCA Victor RCX 7165 | SYLVIE VARTAN (EP) | 200 |

## VARUKERS

| | | | |
|---|---|---|---|
| 81 | Tempest/Inferno HELL 1 | Protest And Survive/No Scapegoat (p/s) | 10 |
| 83 | Riot City RIOT 27 | Die For Your Government/All Systems Fail (p/s) | 10 |
| 83 | Riot City RIOT 29 | Led To The Slaughter/The End Is Nigh (p/s) | 10 |
| 83 | Riot City RIOT 31 | ANOTHER RELIGION ANOTHER WAR (12" EP) | 15 |
| 84 | Rot ASS 16 | MASSACRED MILLIONS (12" EP) | 20 |
| 83 | Riot City RIOT 005 | BLOODSUCKERS (LP, with inner) | 20 |
| 84 | Attack ATTACK 001 | PREPARE FOR THE ATTACK (LP, 1000 only) | 18 |
| 85 | Liberate 1 | ONE STRUGGLE ONE FIGHT (LP) | 15 |
| 87 | Rot DUTCH 001 | LIVE IN HOLLAND (LP) | 15 |

## VASALINES

| | | | |
|---|---|---|---|
| 92 | Avalanche ONLYLP 013 | ALL THE STUFF AND MORE (LP) | 15 |

## VASELINE TIGERS

| | | | |
|---|---|---|---|
| 80 | Dance DANCE 513 | I'm A Golliwog/Back In The Square (Again) | 18 |

## VASELINES

| | | | |
|---|---|---|---|
| 87 | 53rd & 3rd AGARR 10 | Son Of A Gun/Rory Rides Away/You Think You're A Man (12", die-cut sleeve) | 25 |
| 88 | 53rd & 3rd AGARR 17 | Dying For It/Molly's Lips (p/s) | 20 |
| 88 | 53rd & 3rd AGARR 17T | Dying For It/Molly's Lips/Teenage Superstars/Jesus Wants Me For A Sunbeam (12", p/s) | 15 |
| 90 | 53rd & 3rd AGAS 7 | DUM DUM (LP) | 30 |
| 98 | Avalanche ONLY LP 013P | ALL THE STUFF AND MORE (LP, picture disc) | 15 |
| 14 | Rosary RMUSIC1LPX | V FOR VASELINES (LP, red vinyl, 2-CD, signed, ith poster) | 20 |

*(see also Pastels, BMX Bandits)*

## VASHTI

| | | | |
|---|---|---|---|
| 65 | Decca F 12157 | Some Things Just Stick In Your Mind/I Want To Be Alone | 80 |
| 66 | Columbia DB 7917 | Train Song/Love Song | 60 |

*(see also Vashti Bunyan)*

## VASTIK

| | | | |
|---|---|---|---|
| 82 | Lynx SSM 030 | Running Out Of Time/Teenage Dream (no p/s) | 6 |

## FRANKIE VAUGHAN

| | | | |
|---|---|---|---|
| 53 | HMV 7M 167 | Istanbul (Not Constantinople)/Cloud Lucky Seven | 20 |
| 54 | HMV 7M 182 | The Cuff Of My Shirt/Heartless | 10 |
| 54 | HMV 7M 252 | My Son, My Son/Cinnamon Sinner (Selling Lollipop Lies) | 10 |
| 54 | HMV 7M 270 | Happy Days And Lonely Nights/Danger Signs | 10 |
| 55 | HMV 7M 298 | Too Many Heartaches/Unsuspecting Heart | 10 |
| 57 | Philips JK 1002 | Garden Of Eden/Priscilla (jukebox issue) | 10 |
| 57 | Philips JK 1014 | What's Behind That Strange Door/Cold, Cold Shower (jukebox issue) | 10 |
| 57 | Philips JK 1022 | These Dangerous Years/Isn't This A Lovely Evening (jukebox issue) | 10 |
| 57 | Philips JK 1030 | Gotta Have Something In The Bank, Frank/Single (with Kaye Sisters, jukebox issue) | 10 |
| 57 | Philips JK 1035 | Kisses Sweeter Than Wine/Rock-A-Chicka (jukebox issue) | 15 |
| 57 | Philips PB 775 | Kisses Sweeter Than Wine/Rock-A-Chicka | 10 |

*(see also Kaye Sisters, Alma Cogan & Frankie Vaughan, Marilyn Monroe)*

## MALCOLM VAUGHAN

| | | | |
|---|---|---|---|
| 56 | HMV 7M 338 | With Your Love/Small Talk | 15 |
| 56 | HMV POP 250 | St. Therese Of The Roses/Love Me As Though There Were No Tomorrow | 10 |
| 57 | HMV POP 303 | The World Is Mine/Now | 7 |
| 57 | HMV POP 325 | Chapel Of The Roses/Guardian Angel | 7 |
| 56 | HMV 7M 389 | Only You (And You Alone)/I'll Be Near To You | 7 |

## SARAH VAUGHAN

### SINGLES

| | | | |
|---|---|---|---|
| 58 | Mercury 7MT 198 | My Darling, My Darling/Bewitched | 10 |
| 58 | Mercury 7MT 212 | Padre/Spin Little Bottle | 10 |
| 58 | Mercury 7MT 222 | Too Much, Too Soon/What's So Bad About It | 10 |
| 59 | Mercury AMT 1010 | Everything I Do/I Ain't Hurtin' | 8 |
| 59 | Mercury AMT 1029 | Cool Baby/Are You Certain? | 6 |
| 59 | Mercury AMT 1044 | Careless/Separate Ways | 7 |
| 59 | Mercury AMT 1057 | Broken-Hearted Melody/Misty | 10 |
| 59 | Mercury AMT 1080 | You're My Baby/Eternally | 6 |
| 59 | Mercury AMT 1087 | Don't Look At Me That Way/Sweet Affections | 6 |
| 60 | Columbia DB 4491 | Ooh! What A Day/My Dear Little Sweetheart | 10 |
| 60 | Columbia DB 4511 | If I Were A Bell/Teach Me Tonight (with Count Basie & Joe Williams) | 6 |
| 74 | Mainstream MSS 355 | I Need You Now (More Than Ever Before)/Do Away With April | 15 |

## ALBUMS

| 55 | Oriole/Mercury MG 26005 | IMAGES (10") | 20 |
|----|----|----|----|
| 55 | Mercury MG 25188 | THE DIVINE SARAH | 15 |
| 56 | London HB-U 1049 | SARAH VAUGHAN SINGS (10", with John Kirby & His Orchestra) | 20 |
| 56 | Emarcy EJL 100 | IN THE LAND OF HI FI (10") | 20 |
| 56 | Philips BBL 7082 | SARAH VAUGHAN | 15 |
| 56 | Mercury MPT 7503 | MAKE YOURSELF COMFORTABLE (10") | 20 |
| 57 | Mercury MPT 7518 | IMAGES (10", reissue) | 15 |
| 57 | Emarcy EJL 1258 | SASSY | 15 |
| 57 | Mercury MPL 6522 | SINGS GREAT SONGS FROM HIT SHOWS PART 1 | 15 |
| 57 | Philips BBL 7165 | LINGER AWHILE | 15 |
| 57 | Mercury MPL 6523 | SINGS GREAT SONGS FROM HIT SHOWS PART 2 | 15 |
| 57 | Mercury MPL 6525 | SINGS GEORGE GERSHWIN VOL. 1 | 15 |
| 57 | Mercury MPL 6527 | SINGS GEORGE GERSHWIN VOL. 2 | 15 |
| 58 | Mercury MPL 6532 | WONDERFUL SARAH | 15 |
| 58 | Emarcy EJL 1273 | SWINGIN' EASY | 15 |
| 58 | Mercury MPL 6540 | IN ROMANTIC MOOD | 15 |
| 58 | Mercury MPL 6542 | AT MISTER KELLY'S | 15 |
| 59 | Mercury MMC 14001 | AFTER HOURS AT THE LONDON HOUSE | 15 |
| 59 | Mercury MMC 14011 | VAUGHAN AND VIOLINS (also stereo CMS 18003) | 15 |

## BILLY VAUGHN (& HIS ORCHESTRA)

| 55 | London HL 8112 | Melody Of Love/Joy Ride (gold label print) | 15 |
|----|----|----|----|
| 55 | London HLD 8205 | The Shifting Whispering Sands (Parts 1 & 2) (with Ken Nordine) (gold print) | 15 |
| 56 | London HLD 8238 | Theme From 'The Threepenny Opera'/I'd Give A Million Tomorrows (gold label print, later with silver label print) | 20 |
| 56 | London HLD 8238 | Theme From 'The Threepenny Opera'/I'd Give A Million Tomorrows (gold label print, later with silver label print) | 5 |
| 56 | London HLD 8319 | When The Lilac Blooms Again/Autumn Concerto (gold label print) | 20 |
| 56 | London HLD 8319 | When The Lilac Blooms Again/Autumn Concerto (later silver label print) | 5 |
| 56 | London HLD 8342 | Petticoats From Portugal/La La Colette (gold label print) | 20 |
| 56 | London HLD 8342 | Petticoats From Portugal/La La Colette (later silver label print) | 5 |
| 57 | London HLD 8417 | The Ship That Never Sailed/Little Boy Blue (with Ken Nordine) | 10 |
| 57 | London HLD 8511 | Johnny Tremain/Naughty Annetta (as Billy Vaughn's Orchestra & Chorus) | 10 |
| 57 | London HLD 8522 | Raunchy/Sail Along Silvery Moon | 15 |
| 58 | London HLD 8612 | Tumbling Tumbleweeds/Trying | 8 |
| 58 | London HLD 8680 | Sail Along Silvery Moon/The Singing Hills | 5 |
| 58 | London HLD 8703 | La Paloma/Here Is My Love | 5 |
| 58 | London HLD 8772 | Cimarron (Roll On)/You're My Baby Doll | 5 |
| 61 | London HLD 9423 | Berlin Melody/Theme From Come September | 5 |

*(see also Hilltoppers, Ken Nordine)*

## MORRIS VAUGHN

| 69 | Fontana TF 1031 | My Love Keeps Growing/Make It Look Good | 30 |
|----|----|----|----|

## VAZZ

| 85 | CRV 5401 | Breath/Violent Silence (in folder & bag with postcards & inserts) | 5 |
|----|----|----|----|

## VBW

| 80 | Heaven International | VBW EP (no p/s) | 40 |
|----|----|----|----|

## V.D.U.'S

| 79 | Thin Sliced | Don't Cry For Me/Little White Lie/Holiday Romances (p/s) | 20 |
|----|----|----|----|

*(see also Boys Wonder)*

## VED BUENS ENDE

| 95 | Misanthropy AMAZON 006 | WRITTEN IN WATERS (2-LP, marbled purple vinyl) | 60 |
|----|----|----|----|

## CHUCK VEDDER

| 59 | London HL 8951 | Spanky Boy/Arriba | 30 |
|----|----|----|----|
| 59 | London HL 8951 | Spanky Boy/Arriba (78) | 20 |

## BOBBY VEE

### SINGLES

| 60 | London HLG 9179 | Devil Or Angel/Since I Met You, Baby | 20 |
|----|----|----|----|
| 61 | London HLG 9255 | Rubber Ball/Everyday | 5 |
| 61 | London HLG 9316 | More Than I Can Say/Stayin' In | 5 |
| 61 | London HLG 9389 | How Many Tears/Baby Face | 5 |
| 61 | London HLG 9438 | Take Good Care Of My Baby/Bashful Bob | 5 |
| 61 | London HLG 7111 | Take Good Care Of My Baby/Bashful Bob (export issue) | 10 |
| 61 | London HLG 9459 | Love's Made A Fool Of You/Susie-Q | 12 |
| 61 | London HLG 9470 | Run To Him/Walkin' With My Angel | 5 |
| 62 | Liberty LIB 55388 | Run To Him/Walkin' With My Angel (reissue) | 10 |
| 62 | Liberty LIB 55419 | Please Don't Ask About Barbara/I Can't Say Goodbye | 8 |
| 62 | Liberty LIB 55451 | Sharing You/At A Time Like This | 5 |
| 62 | Liberty LIB 10046 | A Forever Kind Of Love/Remember Me, Huh? | 5 |
| 63 | Liberty LIB 10069 | The Night Has A Thousand Eyes/Tenderly Yours | 5 |
| 63 | Liberty LIB 55530 | Bobby Tomorrow/Charms | 5 |
| 63 | Liberty LIB 10124 | Stranger In Your Arms/Yesterday And You | 8 |
| 64 | Liberty LIB 10141 | She's Sorry/Buddy's Song | 6 |
| 64 | Liberty LIB 55700 | Hickory, Dick And Doc/I Wish You Were Mine Again | 6 |
| 65 | Liberty LIB 10197 | Keep On Trying/Cross My Heart | 6 |
| 65 | Liberty LIB 10213 | True Love Never Runs Smooth/Hey Little Girl | 6 |
| 65 | Liberty LIB 55828 | Run Like The Devil/Take A Look Around Me | 8 |
| 66 | Liberty LIB 55877 | Look At Me Girl/Save A Love | 6 |
| 67 | Liberty LIB 10272 | Like You've Never Known Before/Growing Pains | 6 |

| | | | |
|---|---|---|---|
| 67 | Liberty LBF 15016 | Come Back When You Grow Up/Let The Four Winds Blow | 6 |
| 67 | Liberty LIB 15042 | Beautiful People/I May Be Gone | 6 |
| 68 | Liberty LBF 15058 | Maybe Just Today/You're A Big Girl Now | 6 |
| 68 | Liberty LBF 15096 | Medley, My Girl - Hey Girl/Take Good Care Of My Baby | 6 |
| 68 | Liberty LBF 15134 | Do What You Gotta' Do/Thank You | 6 |
| 69 | Liberty LBF 15178 | (I'm Into Looking For) Someone To Love Me/Sunrise Highway | 6 |
| 69 | Liberty LBF 15234 | I'm Gonna Make It Up To You/Let's Call It A Day | 6 |
| 69 | Liberty LBF 15305 | Electric Trains And You/In And Out Of Love | 6 |
| 70 | Liberty LBF 15420 | Sweet Sweetheart/Rock 'N Roll Music And You | 6 |

**EPs**

| | | | |
|---|---|---|---|
| 61 | London RE-G 1278 | BOBBY VEE NO. 1 | 15 |
| 61 | London RE-G 1299 | BOBBY VEE NO. 2 | 15 |
| 61 | London RE-G 1308 | BOBBY VEE NO. 3 | 15 |
| 61 | London RE-G 1323 | BOBBY VEE NO. 4 | 20 |
| 61 | London RE-G 1324 | HITS OF THE ROCKIN' 50's | 30 |
| 62 | Liberty LEP 2053 | SINCERELY | 15 |
| 63 | Liberty LEP 2084 | JUST FOR FUN (2 tracks by Bobby Vee, 2 by Crickets) | 15 |
| 63 | Liberty LEP 2089 | A FOREVER KIND OF LOVE | 15 |
| 63 | Liberty LEP 2102 | BOBBY VEE'S BIGGEST HITS (mono) | 15 |
| 63 | Liberty SLEP 2102 | BOBBY VEE'S BIGGEST HITS (stereo) | 20 |
| 63 | Liberty LEP 2116 | BOBBY VEE MEETS THE CRICKETS (mono) | 10 |
| 63 | Liberty SLEP 2116 | BOBBY VEE MEETS THE CRICKETS (stereo) | 15 |
| 64 | Liberty LEP 2149 | BOBBY VEE MEETS THE CRICKETS VOL. 2 | 10 |
| 64 | Liberty LEP 2181 | NEW SOUNDS | 35 |
| 65 | Liberty LEP 2212 | BOBBY VEE MEETS THE VENTURES (with Ventures) | 25 |

**ALBUMS**

| | | | |
|---|---|---|---|
| 61 | London HA-G 2320 | BOBBY VEE SINGS YOUR FAVOURITES | 45 |
| 61 | London HA-G 2352 | BOBBY VEE (mono) | 20 |
| 61 | London SAH-G 6152 | BOBBY VEE (stereo) | 39 |
| 61 | London HA-G 2374 | WITH STRINGS AND THINGS (mono) | 25 |
| 61 | London SAH-G 6174 | WITH STRINGS AND THINGS (stereo) | 35 |
| 61 | London HA-G 2406 | SINGS HITS OF THE ROCKIN' 50s (mono) | 30 |
| 61 | London SAH-G 6206 | SINGS HITS OF THE ROCKIN' 50s (stereo) | 35 |
| 61 | London HA-G 2428 | TAKE GOOD CARE OF MY BABY (mono) | 20 |
| 61 | London SAH-G 6224 | TAKE GOOD CARE OF MY BABY (stereo) | 25 |
| 62 | Liberty SLBY 1086 | BOBBY VEE MEETS THE CRICKETS (stereo) | 15 |
| 62 | Liberty SLBY 1112 | BOBBY VEE'S GOLDEN GREATS (stereo) | 18 |
| 63 | Liberty SLBY 1139 | THE NIGHT HAS A THOUSAND EYES (stereo) | 18 |
| 63 | Liberty LBY 1147 | BOBBY VEE MEETS THE VENTURES (with Ventures, mono) | 20 |
| 63 | Liberty SLBY 1147 | BOBBY VEE MEETS THE VENTURES (with Ventures, stereo) | 25 |
| 63 | Liberty SLBY 1188 | I REMEMBER BUDDY HOLLY (stereo) | 18 |

*(see also Crickets, Ventures)*

## ALAN VEGA

| | | | |
|---|---|---|---|
| 81 | Celluloid WIP 6744 | Jukebox Babe/Lonely (p/s) | 6 |
| 81 | Celluloid 12WIP 6744 | Jukebox Babe/Lonely (12", p/s) | 10 |
| 88 | Sniffin' Rock SR 009 | WACKO WARRIOR/(track by African Headcharge) (with Sniffin' Rock fanzine No. 12) | 8 |

*(see also Suicide, Future Pilot AKA Alan Vega)*

## VEINS
| | | | |
|---|---|---|---|
| 80 | Redball RR 3 | Complete Control Rock 'n' Roll/Champagne | 25 |

## VEJTABLES
| | | | |
|---|---|---|---|
| 65 | Pye International 7N 25339 | I Still Love You/Anything | 50 |

## VEKTORS
| | | | |
|---|---|---|---|
| 81 | Little Black EJSP 9662 | Yesterday's Dream/Razor Smile/I Don't Know Why (300 only, no p/s) | 15 |

## RUTH VELDON
| | | | |
|---|---|---|---|
| 66 | Decca F12436 | A Most Peculiar Man/Show Me The Way Back To My World | 15 |

## MARTHA VELEZ
| | | | |
|---|---|---|---|
| 69 | London HLK 10266 | It Takes A Lot To Laugh/Come Here Sweet Man | 10 |
| 69 | London HLK 10280 | Tell Mama/Swamp Man | 25 |
| 69 | London HLK 10280 | Tell Mama/Swamp Man (DJ Copy) | 40 |
| 72 | Blue Horizon 2096 010 | Boogie Kitchen/Two Bridges | 20 |
| 69 | London HA-K/SH-K 8395 | FIENDS AND ANGELS (LP) | 40 |
| 70 | Blue Horizon 7-63867 | FIENDS AND ANGELS AGAIN (LP) | 75 |
| 76 | Sire 9103 252 | ESCAPE FROM BABYLON (LP) | 15 |

## VELLUM STAIRS
| | | | |
|---|---|---|---|
| 89 | Marker JUNE 1002 | Jamie's Coming Back/Writing On The Wall (p/s) | 25 |
| 90 | Marker JUNE 1003 | You're Always Guilty/Karin Mist (p/s) | 20 |

## VELOURS
| | | | |
|---|---|---|---|
| 67 | MGM 2006 603 | I'm Gonna Change/Don't Pity Me | 10 |

*(see also Fantastics)*

## VELVELETTES
| | | | |
|---|---|---|---|
| 64 | Stateside SS 361 | Needle In A Haystack/Should I Tell Them? | 45 |
| 64 | Stateside SS 361 | Needle In A Haystack/Should I Tell Them? (DJ Copy) | 100 |
| 65 | Stateside SS 387 | He Was Really Sayin' Something/Throw A Farewell Kiss | 65 |
| 65 | Stateside SS 387 | He Was Really Sayin' Something/Throw A Farewell Kiss (DJ Copy) | 125 |
| 65 | Tamla Motown TMG 521 | Lonely Lonely Girl Am I/I'm The Exception To The Rule | 175 |
| 65 | Tamla Motown TMG 521 | Lonely Lonely Girl Am I/I'm The Exception To The Rule (DJ Copy) | 300 |
| 66 | Tamla Motown TMG 580 | These Things Will Keep Me Loving You/Since You've Been Loving Me | 55 |
| 65 | Tamla Motown TMG 595 | He Was Really Sayin' Something/Needle In A Haystack | 20 |

| | | | |
|---|---|---|---|
| 67 | Tamla Motown TMG 595 | He Was Really Sayin' Something/Needle In A Haystack | 30 |
| 71 | Tamla Motown TMG 780 | These Things Will Keep Me Loving You/Since You've Been Loving Me (reissue) | 12 |
| 72 | Tamla Motown TMG 806 | Needle In A Haystack/I'm The Exception To The Rule | 8 |

## VELVET CUSHION

| | | | |
|---|---|---|---|
| 71 | Sky SKY 3 | Lost In The Maze/It's All Over Me | 100 |

## VELVET GLOVE

| | | | |
|---|---|---|---|
| 74 | Fresh Air 6370 502 | SWEET WAS MY ROSE (LP, laminated sleeve, lyric insert) | 15 |

## VELVET HUSH

| | | | |
|---|---|---|---|
| 68 | Oak RGJ 648 | Broken Heart/Lover Please | 300 |

*(see also Factory [Oak label])*

## VELVET MIST

| | | | |
|---|---|---|---|
| 70 | Tank BSS 103 | Rock N Roll Band/Bye Bye Johnny (with booklet) | 60 |

## VELVET OPERA

| | | | |
|---|---|---|---|
| 69 | CBS 4189 | Anna Dance Square/Don't You Realize | 10 |
| 70 | CBS 4802 | Black Jack Davy/Statesboro' Blues | 10 |
| 70 | Spark SRL 1045 | She Keeps Giving Me These Feelings/There's A Hole In My Pocket | 7 |
| 69 | CBS 63692 | RIDE A HUSTLER'S DREAM (LP) | 100 |

*(see also Elmer Gantry's Velvet Opera, Stretch, Hudson-Ford, Johnny Joyce)*

## VELVET SHADOWS

| | | | |
|---|---|---|---|
| 77 | Horse HOSS 148 | Wailing Of Black People/Dubbin n Wailin | 20 |

## VELVETS

| | | | |
|---|---|---|---|
| 61 | London HLU 9328 | That Lucky Old Sun/Time And Time Again | 25 |
| 61 | London HLU 9372 | Tonight (Could Be The Night)/Spring Fever | 25 |
| 61 | London HLU 9444 | Laugh/Lana | 30 |
| 61 | London RE-U 1297 | VELVETS (EP) | 100 |

## VEL-VETS

| | | | |
|---|---|---|---|
| 74 | Disco Demand DDS 109 | I Got To Find Me Somebody/What Now My Love | 10 |

## VELVETTES

| | | | |
|---|---|---|---|
| 64 | Mercury MF 802 | He's The One I Want/That Little Boy Of Mine (in p/s) | 25 |
| 64 | Mercury MF 802 | He's The One I Want/That Little Boy Of Mine | 20 |

## VELVETT FOGG

| | | | |
|---|---|---|---|
| 69 | Pye 7N 17673 | Telstar '69/Owed To The Dip | 25 |
| 69 | Pye NSPL 18272 | VELVETT FOGG (LP, laminated sleeve; beware of non-laminated counterfeits) | 250 |

*(see also Ghost)*

## VELVET UNDERGROUND

| | | | |
|---|---|---|---|
| 71 | Atlantic 2091 008 | Who Loves The Sun/Sweet Jane | 40 |
| 73 | MGM 2006 283 | I'm Waiting For The Man/Run Run Run/Candy Says (as Lou Reed & Velvet Underground) | 15 |
| 73 | Atlantic K 10339 | Sweet Jane/Rock And Roll (as Velvet Underground featuring Lou Reed) | 15 |
| 82 | Polydor POSPX 603 | Heroin/Venus In Furs/I'm Waiting For The Man/Run Run Run (12", p/s) | 10 |
| 12 | Atlantic 8122797366 | Sweet Jane/Rock And Roll (reissue in p/s) | 8 |
| 67 | Verve VLP 9184 | THE VELVET UNDERGROUND AND NICO (LP, single sleeve, 'non-banana' cover, mono) | 300 |
| 67 | Verve SVLP 9184 | THE VELVET UNDERGROUND AND NICO (LP, single sleeve, 'non-banana' cover, stereo) | 200 |
| 68 | Verve 2315 056 | THE VELVET UNDERGROUND AND NICO (LP, UK pressing in stickered US peelable banana gatefold censored sleeve, stereo) | 250 |
| 68 | Verve VLP 9201 | WHITE LIGHT WHITE HEAT (LP, 'skull' sleeve, mono) | 250 |
| 68 | Verve SVLP 9201 | WHITE LIGHT WHITE HEAT (LP, 'skull' sleeve, stereo) | 150 |
| 69 | MGM MGM-CS 8108 | THE VELVET UNDERGROUND (LP, 'Val Valentin mix', flapped laminated sleeve, with horizontal split of Lou Reed picture on rear sleeve) | 200 |
| 71 | MGM/Verve Super 2315 056 | THE VELVET UNDERGROUND AND NICO (LP, reissue stereo, UK LP in US Verve stereo V6 5008 sleeve with peelable banana on front cover, UK sticker on back cover with 2315 056 covering US catalogue number, "Marketed by Polydor") | 80 |
| 71 | Atlantic 2400 111 | LOADED (LP) | 70 |
| 71 | MGM 2315 056 | THE VELVET UNDERGROUND AND NICO (LP, reissue, gatefold sleeve) | 25 |
| 71 | MGM Select 2353 022 | THE VELVET UNDERGROUND (LP, reissue, gatefold sleeve) | 35 |
| 71 | MGM Select 2353 024 | WHITE LIGHT WHITE HEAT (LP, reissue) | 25 |
| 72 | MGM Select 2683 006 | ANDY WARHOL'S VELVET UNDERGROUND (2-LP) | 30 |
| 72 | Atlantic K 30022 | LIVE AT MAX'S KANSAS CITY (LP) | 25 |
| 73 | Polydor 2383 180 | SQUEEZE (LP) | 40 |
| 77 | Warner Bros. K40113 | LOADED (LP, reissue) | 20 |
| 84 | Polydor SPELP 73 | WHITE LIGHT WHITE HEAT (LP, reissue, different sleeve) | 15 |
| 84 | Polydor SPELP 20 | THE VELVET UNDERGROUND AND NICO (LP, reissue) | 15 |
| 85 | Polydor POLD 5167 | VU (LP) | 18 |
| 86 | Polydor VUBOX 1 | THE VELVET UNDERGROUND BOX SET (5-LP box set, with booklet) | 40 |
| 86 | Verve POLD 5208 | ANOTHER VIEW (LP) | 15 |
| 88 | HMV C88 1-15 | THE VELVET UNDERGROUND AND NICO (LP or CD box set, with booklet, 1500 only) | 25 |
| 95 | Polydor 527887 | PEEL SLOWLY AND SEE (5-CD box set) | 35 |
| 99 | Simply Vinyl SVLP 090 | THE VELVET UNDERGROUND AND NICO (LP, reissue) | 20 |
| 00 | Simply Vinyl SVLP 200 | WHITE LIGHT/WHITE HEAT (LP, reissue) | 15 |
| 12 | Polydor B001764901 | SCEPTER STUDIO SESSIONS (LP) | 15 |

*(see also Lou Reed, Nico, John Cale)*

## VENDETTA

| | | | |
|---|---|---|---|
| 88 | Plaza PZA 042 | Don't Let The World Drag You Under/Don't Let The World Drag You Under Pt.2 (p/s) | 6 |

## VENDORS

| | | | |
|---|---|---|---|
| 64 | Domino Studios (no cat. no.) | Don't Leave Me Now/Twilight Time/Take Your Time/Peace Pipe (acetate, private pressing, 12 copies only) | 500 |

*(see also 'N Betweens, Slade)*

## VENGERS
63  Oriole CB 1879 .................... Shake And Clap/Shakedown ............................................................. 25

## VENIGMAS
79  Graduate GRAD 2 .................. Red Revenge/Turn The Lights Out (P/S) .......................................... 10

## VENOM
| | | | |
|---|---|---|---|
| 81 | Neat NEAT 08 | In League With Satan/Live Like An Angel, Die Like An Devil (p/s) | 30 |
| 82 | Neat NEAT 13 | Bloodlust/In Nomine Satanas (p/s) | 30 |
| 82 | Neat NEAT 13 | Bloodlust/In Nomine Satanas (purple vinyl) | 80 |
| 83 | Neat NEAT 27 | Die Hard/Acid Queen (p/s, with poster) | 25 |
| 83 | Neat NEAT 27 | Die Hard/Acid Queen (p/s) | 15 |
| 83 | Megaforce LOM 1/NEAT 27 | Die Hard/Acid Queen (picture disc, export issue, 1,000 only) | 25 |
| 84 | Neat NEAT 38 | Warhead/Lady Lust (p/s) | 12 |
| 84 | Neat NEATP 38 | Warhead/Lady Lust (p/s, mauve vinyl) | 20 |
| 84 | Neat NEAT 3812 | Warhead/Lady Lust/Gates Of Hell (12", p/s) | 18 |
| 85 | Neat NEATP 43 | Manitou/Woman (picture disc) | 18 |
| 85 | Neat NEATSHAPE 43 | Manitou/Woman (shaped picture disc) | 20 |
| 85 | Neat NEAT 4312 | Manitou/Woman/Dead Of Night (12", p/s) | 18 |
| 85 | Neat NEATS 47 | Nightmare/Satanarchist (shaped picture disc) | 25 |
| 85 | Neat NEAT 4712 | Nightmare/Satanarchist/F.O.A.D./Warhead (live) (12", 'face' p/s) | 20 |
| 85 | Neat NEAT 4712 | Nightmare/Satanarchist/F.O.A.D./Warhead (live) (12", p/s, withdrawn) | 18 |
| 85 | Neat NEATSP 4712 | Nightmare/Satanarchist/F.O.A.D./Warhead (live) (12", picture disc, withdrawn) | 40 |
| 06 | Castle CMWSE 1333 | Antechrist/Metal Black (p/s, signed by band) | 10 |
| 06 | Castle CMWSE 1333 | Antechrist/Metal Black (p/s, not signed by band) | 5 |
| 85 | Neat 5312 | HELL AT HAMMERSMITH EP (Witching Hour/Teacher's Pet/Poison) (12", 10,000 only) | 25 |
| 81 | Neat 1002 | WELCOME TO HELL (LP, 1st issue, with poster and lyric insert) | 30 |
| 82 | Neat 1005 | BLACK METAL (LP, 1st issue, textured sleeve, with poster, on coloured vinyl) | 35 |
| 82 | Neat 1005 | BLACK METAL (LP, 1st issue, textured sleeve, with poster) | 40 |
| 82 | Neat NEAT 1005 | BLACK METAL (LP, green marbled vinyl) | 400 |
| 83 | Neat NEATP 1002 | WELCOME TO HELL (LP, reissue, purple vinyl) | 50 |
| 84 | Neat 1015 | AT WAR WITH SATAN (LP, textured sleeve, 1st 19,000 with poster) | 20 |
| 84 | Neat 1015 | AT WAR WITH SATAN (LP, textured sleeve) | 15 |
| 85 | Neat NEATP 1005 | BLACK METAL (LP, reissue, picture disc) | 40 |
| 85 | Neat NEATP 1015 | AT WAR WITH SATAN (LP, picture disc) | 40 |
| 85 | Neat NEATP 1024 | POSSESSED (LP, picture disc) | 20 |
| 85 | Neat NEAT 1024 | POSSESSED (LP, inner, blue vinyl) | 20 |
| 86 | Demon APKPD 12 | OBSCENE MATERIAL (LP, picture disc) | 20 |
| 86 | Raw Power RAWLP 001 | FROM HELL TO THE UNKNOWN (2-LP) | 25 |
| 86 | A.P. APK 12 | OFFICIAL BOOTLEG (LP, picture disc) | 15 |
| 89 | Under One Flag FLAG 36P | PRIME EVIL (LP, numbered picture disc, stickered clear sleeve) | 20 |

## CAROL VENTURA
| | | | |
|---|---|---|---|
| 65 | Stateside SS 466 | Please Somebody Help Me/The Old Lady Of Threadneedle Street | 20 |
| 65 | Stateside SL 10146 | CAROL! (LP) | 20 |
| 66 | Stateside S(S)L 10180 | I LOVE TO SING (LP) | 20 |

## CHARLIE VENTURA
55  Vogue Coral Q 72048 .......... I Love You/Intermezzo ..................................................................... 7

## DAVE VENTURA
| | | | |
|---|---|---|---|
| 64 | Mercury MF 805 | The Hurt Stays In The Heart/Is A Redbird Red? | 8 |
| 64 | Mercury MF 827 | I Forgot What It Was Like/I'll Never Love Again | 7 |

## DAVE VENTURA & THE ORBITS
63  Hardy Records 001 .............. Yo Yo Twist/Yo Yo Twist Story (Flexi) ............................................ 10

## TOBY VENTURA
63  Decca F 11581 .................... If My Heart Were A Storybook/Vagabond ...................................... 40

## VENTURES
### SINGLES
| | | | |
|---|---|---|---|
| 60 | Top Rank JAR 417 | Walk Don't Run/Home | 10 |
| 60 | London HLG 9232 | Perfidia/No Trespassing | 8 |
| 61 | London HLG 9292 | Ram-Bunk-Shush/Lonely Heart | 10 |
| 61 | London HLG 9344 | Lullaby Of The Leaves/Ginchy | 10 |
| 61 | London HLG 9411 | Theme From 'Silver City'/Bluer Than Blue | 10 |
| 61 | London HLG 9465 | Blue Moon/Wailin' | 15 |
| 61 | London HLG 7113 | Lady Of Spain/Blue Moon (export issue) | 30 |
| 62 | Liberty LIB 60 | Lolita Ya-Ya/Lucille | 8 |
| 62 | Liberty LIB 67 | The 2,000 Pound Bee Parts 1 & 2 | 12 |
| 62 | Liberty LIB 68 | El Cumbanchero/Skip To M'Limbo | 8 |
| 63 | Liberty LIB 78 | The Ninth Wave/Damaged Goods | 10 |
| 64 | Liberty LIB 91 | Journey To The Stars/Walkin' With Pluto | 10 |
| 64 | Liberty LIB 96 | Walk Don't Run '64/The Cruel Sea | 12 |
| 64 | Liberty LIB 10142 | Penetration/Solar Race | 10 |
| 65 | Liberty LIB 300 | Slaughter On Tenth Avenue/Rap City | 10 |
| 65 | Liberty LIB 303 | Diamond Head/Lonely Girl | 10 |
| 65 | Liberty LIB 306 | The Swingin' Creeper/Pedal Pusher | 10 |
| 65 | Liberty LIB 308 | The Stranger/Bird Rockers | 10 |
| 65 | Liberty LIB 10219 | Sleigh Ride/White Christmas | 10 |
| 66 | Liberty LIB 316 | Secret Agent Man/007-11 | 15 |
| 67 | Liberty LIB 10266 | Theme From The Wild Angels/High And Dry | 10 |
| 67 | Liberty LIB 55967 | Strawberry Fields Forever/Endless Dream | 10 |
| 68 | Liberty LBF 15075 | Flights Of Fantasy/Pandora's Box | 15 |
| 70 | Liberty LBF 15221 | Hawaii Five-O - Theme/Higher Than Thou | 15 |

| 71 | United Artists UP 36316 | Theme From 'Shaft'/Tight Fit | 7 |
| 77 | United Artists UP 36223 | Starsky And Hutch/Charlie's Angels | 7 |

**EPs**

| 61 | London REG 1279 | THE VENTURES | 20 |
| 61 | London REG 1283 | THE VENTURES (export issue) | 20 |
| 61 | London REG 1288 | RAM-BUNK-SHUSH! | 20 |
| 62 | London REG 1326 | ANOTHER SMASH | 20 |
| 62 | London REG 1328 | COLOURFUL VENTURES | 20 |
| 62 | Liberty LEP 2058 | TWIST WITH THE VENTURES | 20 |
| 62 | Liberty LEP 2131 | SMASH HITS | 20 |
| 63 | Liberty LEP 2104 | THE VENTURES PLAY TELSTAR AND LONELY BULL | 20 |
| 64 | Liberty LEP 2174 | THE VENTURES PLAY COUNTRY GREATS | 20 |
| 65 | Liberty LEP 2212 | BOBBY VEE MEETS THE VENTURES (with Bobby Vee) | 25 |
| 66 | Liberty LEP 2250 | SECRET AGENT MEN | 25 |

**ALBUMS**

| 61 | London HA-G 2340 | THE VENTURES (mono) | 30 |
| 61 | London SAH-G 6143 | THE VENTURES (stereo) | 40 |
| 61 | London HA-G 2376 | ANOTHER SMASH (mono) | 20 |
| 61 | London SAH-G 6209 | ANOTHER SMASH (stereo) | 30 |
| 61 | London HA-G 2409 | THE COLOURFUL VENTURES (mono) | 20 |
| 61 | London SAH-G 6209 | THE COLOURFUL VENTURES (stereo) | 30 |
| 62 | Liberty LBY 1002 | WALK DON'T RUN | 25 |
| 62 | London HA-G 2429 | TWIST WITH THE VENTURES (mono) | 20 |
| 62 | London SAH-G 6225 | TWIST WITH THE VENTURES (stereo) | 30 |
| 62 | Liberty LBY 1072 | TWIST PARTY | 20 |
| 63 | Liberty (S)LBY 1110 | GOING TO THE VENTURES DANCE PARTY! (mono) | 20 |
| 63 | Liberty (S)LBY 1110 | GOING TO THE VENTURES DANCE PARTY! (stereo) | 30 |
| 63 | Liberty (S)LBY 1147 | BOBBY VEE MEETS THE VENTURES (with Bobby Vee, mono) | 20 |
| 63 | Liberty (S)LBY 1147 | BOBBY VEE MEETS THE VENTURES (with Bobby Vee, stereo) | 25 |
| 63 | Liberty (S)LBY 1150 | SURFING (mono) | 22 |
| 63 | Liberty (S)LBY 1150 | SURFING (stereo) | 30 |
| 64 | Liberty (S)LBY 1169 | LET'S GO! (mono) | 18 |
| 64 | Liberty (S)LBY 1169 | LET'S GO! (stereo) | 25 |
| 64 | Liberty (S)LBY 1189 | THE VENTURES IN SPACE (mono) | 22 |
| 64 | Liberty (S)LBY 1189 | THE VENTURES IN SPACE (stereo) | 30 |
| 65 | Liberty (S)LBY 1228 | WALK DON'T RUN - VOL. 2 (mono) | 22 |
| 65 | Liberty (S)LBY 1228 | WALK DON'T RUN - VOL. 2 (stereo) | 30 |
| 65 | Liberty (S)LBY 1252 | KNOCK ME OUT (mono) | 20 |
| 65 | Liberty (S)LBY 1252 | KNOCK ME OUT (stereo) | 20 |
| 65 | Liberty (S)LBY 1270 | ON STAGE (mono) | 20 |
| 65 | Liberty (S)LBY 1270 | ON STAGE (stereo) | 20 |
| 66 | Liberty (S)LBY 1274 | VENTURES A-GO GO (mono) | 18 |
| 66 | Liberty (S)LBY 1274 | VENTURES A-GO GO (stereo) | 20 |
| 66 | Liberty (S)LBY 1285 | THE VENTURES' CHRISTMAS ALBUM (mono) | 20 |
| 66 | Liberty (S)LBY 1285 | THE VENTURES' CHRISTMAS ALBUM (stereo) | 30 |
| 66 | Liberty (S)LBY 1297 | WHERE THE ACTION IS! (mono) | 15 |
| 66 | Liberty (S)LBY 1297 | WHERE THE ACTION IS! (stereo) | 18 |
| 66 | Liberty (S)LBY 1323 | GO WITH THE VENTURES (mono) | 15 |
| 66 | Liberty (S)LBY 1323 | GO WITH THE VENTURES (stereo) | 18 |
| 67 | Liberty (S)LBY 1345 | GUITAR FREAKOUT (mono) | 15 |
| 67 | Liberty (S)LBY 1345 | GUITAR FREAKOUT (stereo) | 18 |
| 67 | Liberty (S)LBY 1372 | SUPER PSYCHEDELICS (mono) | 15 |
| 67 | Liberty (S)LBY 1372 | SUPER PSYCHEDELICS (stereo) | 18 |

*(see also New Ventures, Bobby Vee, Nokie Edwards)*

## VENUS IN FURS

| 83 | Movement MOVEMENT 001 | EXTENDED PLAY (p/s) | 18 |
| 85 | Backs 12CH 105 | MOMENTO MORI EP (12", p/s) | 15 |
| 86 | Backs 12CH 107 | LOVE LIES EP (12", p/s) | 10 |
| 84 | Movement MOVEMENT 002LP | PLATONIC LOVE AND OTHER STORIES (LP) | 15 |
| 85 | Backs NCH MLP 6 | STRIP (LP) | 15 |
| 89 | Backs NCH LP 16 | MEGALOMANIA (LP) | 20 |
| 90 | Backs NCH LP 17 | THE SPEED OF A PUN (LP) | 20 |

## VENUS & RAZORBLADES

| 77 | Spark SRL 1153 | I Wanna Be Where The Boys Are/Dogfood (numbered p/s) | 8 |
| 78 | Spark SRL 1159 | Workin' Girl/Midnight | 8 |

## BILLY VERA

| 68 | Atlantic 584 196 | With Pen In Hand/Good Morning Blues | 10 |

## BILLY VERA & JUDY CLAY

| 68 | Atlantic 584 169 | Country Girl City Man/Let It Be Me | 7 |
| 68 | Atlantic 584 164 | Storybook Children/Really Together | 8 |
| 69 | Atlantic 584 293 | Reaching For The Moon/Tell It Like It Is | 8 |
| 68 | Atlantic 588 158 | THE STORYBOOK CHILDREN (LP) | 20 |

*(see also Judy Clay)*

## VIC VERGAT

| 81 | Harvest HAR 5216 | Down To The Bone/You Never Tell Me You Love Me (p/s) | 5 |

## JOHN VERITY BAND

| 74 | Probe SPB 1087 | JOHN VERITY BAND (LP) | 35 |

*(see also Argent)*

## TOM VERLAINE
| 80 | Electric EM 342 | The Twilight Zone - Psychotic Reaction/Wild Thing/Television - Poor Circulation (p/s) .. 10 |

## TIM VERLANDER
| 72 | Midas MR 007 | TIM VERLANDER (LP, with booklet) ................................................ 40 |

## VERMILION
| 78 | Illegal ILM 0010 | Angry Young Women/Nymphomania/Wild Boys (p/s) ............................ 18 |
| 79 | Illegal ILS 0015 | I Like Motorcycles/The Letter (p/s) ............................................ 10 |

*(see also Menace)*

## VERN & ALVIN
| 69 | Blue Cat BS 167 | Everybody Reggae/Another Fool ............................................ 40 |
| 69 | Big Shot BI 525 | Old Man Dead/G.G. RHYTHM SECTION: Reggae Me ........................ 15 |

*(see also Maytones)*

## VERN & SON
| 71 | G.G. GG 4523 | Little Boy Blue/TYPHOON ALL STARS: Little Boy Blue - Version ................ 6 |

*(see also Maytones)*

## LARRY VERNE
| 60 | London HLN 9194 | Mr. Custer/Okeefenokee Two Step ........................................ 8 |
| 61 | London HLN 9263 | Mr. Livingstone/Roller Coaster .......................................... 7 |

## LYN VERNON
| 60 | Top Rank JAR 323 | Woodchoppers Ball/Caravan ............................................ 7 |

## MIKE VERNON
| 72 | Blue Horizon 2096 007 | Let's Try It Again/Little Southern Country Girl ........................ 25 |
| 71 | Blue Horizon 2931 003 | BRING IT BACK HOME (LP, textured sleeve with insert) ................ 250 |
| 71 | Blue Horizon 2931 003 | BRING IT BACK HOME (LP, textured sleeve without insert) ............ 175 |

## VERNON & THE G.I.S
| 77 | Creeper VGI 001 | G.I. Bop/Jim Dandy (no p/s) ............................................ 25 |
| 77 | Creeper VGI 002 | Be-Boppin' Baby/Jungle Rock (no p/s) .................................. 20 |
| 78 | Creeper VGI 005/6 | Follow Me/Better Get Rockin' (no p/s) ................................ 20 |
| 78 | Creepr VGI 007/008 | Brand New Lover/All Night Long ...................................... 20 |
| 79 | Billy Goat BILL 004 | Ghost Train Boogie/(I'm A) Teddy Boy ................................ 6 |
| 80 | Billy Goat BILL 006 | I Wanna Be A Ted/Banjo Baby (p/s) .................................. 7 |

## VERNONS GIRLS
| 58 | Parlophone R 4497 | Lost And Found/White Bucks And Saddle Shoes ........................ 25 |
| 59 | Parlophone R 4532 | Jealous Heart/Now Is The Month Of Maying .......................... 20 |
| 59 | Parlophone R 4596 | Don't Look Now But/Who Are They To Say? ............................ 20 |
| 60 | Parlophone R 4624 | We Like Boys/Boy Meets Girl .......................................... 15 |
| 60 | Parlophone R 4654 | Madison Time (with Jimmy Saville)/The Oo-We ...................... 15 |
| 61 | Parlophone R 4734 | Ten Little Lonely Boys/Anniversary Song ............................ 10 |
| 61 | Parlophone R 4832 | Let's Get Together/No Message ...................................... 10 |
| 62 | Decca F 11450 | Lover Please/You Know What I Mean .................................. 7 |
| 62 | Decca F 11495 | The Loco-motion/Don't Wanna Go .................................. 10 |
| 62 | Decca F 11549 | Funny All Over/See For Yourself .................................... 20 |
| 63 | Decca F 11629 | Do The Bird/I'm Gonna Let My Hair Down ............................ 10 |
| 63 | Decca F 11685 | He'll Never Come Back/Stay-At-Home ................................ 5 |
| 63 | Decca F 11781 | Tomorrow Is Another Day/Why Why Why .............................. 10 |
| 64 | Decca F 11807 | We Love The Beatles/Hey Lover Boy ................................ 15 |
| 64 | Decca F 11887 | Only You Can Do It/Stupid Little Girl .............................. 10 |
| 64 | Decca F 12021 | It's A Sin To Tell A Lie/Don't Say Goodbye .......................... 10 |
| 62 | Decca DFE 8506 | THE VERNONS GIRLS (EP) ............................................ 40 |
| 58 | Parlophone PMC 1052 | THE VERNONS GIRLS (LP) ............................................ 50 |

*(see also Krimson Kake, Wilde Three, Jimmy Saville, Lee Francis, Samantha Jones, Breakaways)*

## LILI VERONA
| 54 | HMV 7MC 13 | Massa Johnny/Hoggin' In The Cocoa (export issue) .................... 15 |
| 56 | Melodisc MEL 1383 | French Lesson/Pica Now (78, with Gulf Stream Calypso Boys) ........ 10 |
| 59 | HMV DLP 1202 | JAMAICA SINGS (10" LP) .............................................. 22 |

## VERONICA FALLS
| 10 | Trouble DUDE 016 | Fell In Love In A Graveyard/Stephen (hand-printed sleeve, 300 only) .... 20 |
| 11 | Bella Union BELLAU 310 | SIX COVERS (12" EP, 300 only) ...................................... 20 |
| 14 | Beach Head VF 004 | Nobody There/I Need You Around (numbered, 300 only) ............ 20 |
| 11 | Bella Union BELLAV301W | VERONICA FALLS (LP, white vinyl, CD) ............................ 30 |
| 13 | Bella Union BELLACD383P | WAITING FOR SOMETHING TO HAPPEN (LP, CD) .................... 20 |

## VERSAILLES
| 80 | MCA 595 | White Sox/White Sox (p/s) .......................................... 5 |

## VERSATILE NEWTS
| 80 | Shanghai No. 2 | Newtrition/Blimp (p/s, stamped white label) ........................ 45 |

*(see also Felt)*

## VERSATILES (JAMAICA)
| 68 | Island WI 3142 | Teardrops Falling/Someone To Love .................................. 35 |
| 68 | Amalgamated AMG 802 | Just Can't Win/LEADERS: Sometimes I Sit Down Down And Cry ........ 35 |
| 68 | Crab CRAB 1 | Children Get Ready/Someone To Love ................................ 35 |
| 69 | Amalgamated AMG 854 | Lu Lu Bell/Long Long Time ........................................ 100 |
| 69 | Big Shot BI 520 | Worries A Yard/VAL BENNETT: Hound Dog Special .................... 10 |
| 69 | Crab CRAB 5 | Spread Your Bed/Worries A Yard .................................... 120 |
| 70 | Nu Beat NB 060 | Pick My Pocket/FREEDOM SINGERS: Freedom .......................... 20 |
| 71 | Nu Beat NB 076 | Give To Me/TIGER: With Hot ........................................ 20 |
| 74 | Dip DL 5039 | Cutting Razor/UPSETTERS: Black Belt Jones .......................... 20 |

*(see also Pioneers, Soul Sisters)*

## VERSATILITY
| | | | |
|---|---|---|---|
| 75 | President PT 435 | Tequila Madness/B Side Blues | 10 |

## VERTICAL HOLD
| | | | |
|---|---|---|---|
| 80 | Vertical Hold VH 001 | Rubber Cross/Injustice (p/s) | 40 |
| 84 | Vertical Hold VH 002 | Angel Dust/Four Years/Dub Years (p/s) | 15 |
| 85 | Vertical Hold VH 003 | The War That Time Won/Bio Hazard (p/s) | 15 |

## VERVE
| | | | |
|---|---|---|---|
| 92 | Hut HUTT 12 | All In The Mind/Man Called Sun/One Way To Go (12" promo, white label) | 10 |
| 92 | Hut HUTEN 21 | GRAVITY GRAVE EP (Gravity Grave [Edit]/Endless Life/ She's A Superstar [Live at Clapham Grand]) (10", p/s) | 10 |
| 92 | Hut HUTT 16 | She's A Superstar/Feel (12" promo, white label) | 10 |
| 93 | Hut HUTEN 29 | Blue/Twilight/Where The Geese Go/No Come Down (10", p/s) | 10 |
| 93 | Hut HUT 35 | Slide Away/Make It 'Til Monday (pink vinyl, p/s) | 10 |
| 93 | (no label) FLEXI 1 | Make It 'Til Monday (Glastonbury '93) (clear vinyl stickered flexi with magazine) | 12 |
| 95 | Hut HUT 54 | This Is Music/Let The Damage Begin (purple vinyl, p/s) | 8 |
| 95 | Hut HUT 55 | On Your Own/I See The Door (green vinyl, p/s) | 8 |
| 95 | Hut HUT 55 | On Your Own/I See The Door (green vinyl, p/s, mispressing, B-side plays 'Friends' by Daryll-Ann) | 6 |
| 97 | Hut HUTLH 82 | Bitter Sweet Symphony/So Sister (Jukebox issue) | 6 |
| 97 | Hut HUTLH 88 | The Drugs Don't Work/The Drugs Don't Work (Original Demo) (Jukebox issue) | 6 |
| 98 | Hut HUTTX 100 | SINGLES (Box set, 4 x 12") | 25 |
| 93 | Hut HUTLP 3 | A STORM IN HEAVEN (LP, gatefold) | 60 |
| 95 | Hut HUTLP 27 | A NORTHERN SOUL (2-LP, mirrored sleeve) | 75 |
| 97 | Hut HUTLPX 45 | URBAN HYMNS (2-LP) | 40 |
| 97 | Hut HUTLPX 45 | URBAN HYMNS (2-LP, with inner sleeves, printed outer mailer, 5,000 only) | 50 |
| 93 | Jolly Roger JOLLY ROGER 2 | VOYAGER 1 (LP, official bootleg, blue vinyl, 1,000 only) | 80 |
| 08 | Parlophone 82075 2355841 | FORTH (LP) | 15 |

(see also Richard Ashcroft)

## VERY THINGS
| | | | |
|---|---|---|---|
| 83 | Corpus Christi CHRISTIT's 2 | The Gong Man/The Colours Are Speaking To Me (poster p/s) | 10 |
| 84 | Reflex LEX 3 | THE BUSHES SCREAM WHILE MY DADDY PRUNES (LP) | 15 |
| 93 | Fire REFIRELP 13 | IT'S A DRUG, IT'S A DRUG (LP) | 15 |

## VETS
| | | | |
|---|---|---|---|
| 79 | SRT SRTS 79 CUS 513 | Flies/Contrix (wrap around p/s) | 50 |
| 80 | Deckchair DECK 80/001 | World In Action/GO ATTIC: Waiting For Fashion (fold-around p/s) | 25 |

## VEX
| | | | |
|---|---|---|---|
| 84 | Fight Back FIGHT 1 | SANCTUARY (12" EP, with insert) | 25 |

## ROD VEY
| | | | |
|---|---|---|---|
| 80 | Rip Off RIP 13 | Metal Love/Silicone City (die-cut sleeve) | 25 |

## VHF (1)
| | | | |
|---|---|---|---|
| 80 | Lion PAW 1 | Heart Of Stone (no p/s) | 40 |

## VHF (2)
| | | | |
|---|---|---|---|
| 81 | Distil DIST 81 | First Impressions/First Impressions (no p/s, many labels signed) | 35 |
| 81 | Pennine | 1st IMPRESSIONS (LP) | 90 |

## DANNY VIBES
| | | | |
|---|---|---|---|
| 00 | Jah Tubbys JT 006 | Want No Wickedness/Want No Dub | 20 |

## VIBRASONIC
| | | | |
|---|---|---|---|
| 95 | Yep! YEPLP 01 | VIBRASONIC (LP) | 15 |

## VIBRATIONS
| | | | |
|---|---|---|---|
| 61 | Pye International 7N 25107 | The Watusi/Wallflower | 25 |
| 64 | London HLK 9875 | My Girl Sloopy/Daddy Woo Woo | 20 |
| 66 | Columbia DB 7895 | Canadian Sunset/The Story Of A Starry Night | 25 |
| 67 | Columbia DB 8175 | Pick Me/You Better Beware | 30 |
| 67 | Columbia DB 8318 | Talkin' 'Bout Love/One Mint Julep | 25 |
| 68 | Direction 58-3511 | Love In Them There Hills/Remember The Rain | 15 |
| 67 | Columbia SX 6106 | NEW VIBRATIONS (LP) | 75 |
| 69 | Direction 8-63644 | GREATEST HITS (LP) | 30 |
| 72 | RCA SF 8254 | THE VIBRATIONS (LP) | 20 |

(see also Jayhawks)

## VIBRATORS
| | | | |
|---|---|---|---|
| 76 | RAK RAK 245 | We Vibrate/Whips And Furs | 15 |
| 76 | RAK RAK 246 | Pogo Dancing/The Pose (as Vibrators with Chris Spedding) | 10 |
| 77 | RAK RAK 253 | Bad Times/No Heart (unreleased, this price is for acetates, of which 2 copies exist) | 150 |
| 77 | Epic EPC 5302 | Baby Baby/Into The Future (p/s) | 10 |
| 77 | Epic S PEC 5565 | London Girls (studio)/London Girls (live) (promo only no p/s) | 10 |
| 77 | Epic EPC 5565 | London Girls/Stiff Little Fingers (live) (p/s) | 10 |
| 78 | Epic SEPC 6137 | Automatic Lover/Destroy (p/s) | 7 |
| 78 | Epic EPC 6393 | Judy Says (Knock You On The Head)/Pure Mania (p/s) | 7 |
| 80 | Rat Race RAT 2 | Gimme Some Lovin'/Power Cry (live) (p/s, in slightly different colours) | 7 |
| 80 | Rat Race RAT 4 | Disco In Moscow/Take A Chance (p/s, with various coloured writing) | 5 |
| 77 | Epic EPC 82097 | PURE MANIA (LP) | 20 |
| 78 | Epic EPC 82495 | V2 (LP, with inner lyric sleeve) | 20 |

(see also Boyfriends, Chris Spedding, Nazis Against Fascism, Substitute, Urban Dogs, Knox)

## VIBRATORS (JAMAICA)
| | | | |
|---|---|---|---|
| 66 | Doctor Bird DB 1036 | Sloop John B/Amour | 25 |

(see also Al & Vibrators, Wilbert Francis & Vibrators)

## VIBRAVOID
| | | | |
|---|---|---|---|
| 09 | Fruits De Mer Crustacean 07 | KRAUT ROCK SENSATION EP (1st pressing, 300 copies on marbled blue vinyl) | 45 |

MINT VALUE £

| | | | |
|---|---|---|---|
| 09 | Fruits De Mer Crustacean 07 | KRAUT ROCK SENSATION EP (repressing, 300 copies on clear red vinyl) | 35 |
| 10 | Fruits De Mer Crustacean 10 | WHAT COLOUR IS PINK EP (p/s, insert, 300 only, pink vinyl) | 30 |

## VIBRONICS
| | | | |
|---|---|---|---|
| 98 | Deep Root ROOT 002 | Jah Light, Jah Love/Dub | 25 |
| 04 | Jah Tubbys JT 10021 | Terror/African Stone (10") | 20 |

## VIC & JOHN
| | | | |
|---|---|---|---|
| 94 | Kent 6T 10 | Why Did She Lie/PHIL TERRELL: Love Has Passed Me By | 35 |

## VICE CREEMS
| | | | |
|---|---|---|---|
| 78 | Tiger GRRRR 1 | Won't You Be My Girl?/01-01-212 (gatefold p/s) | 30 |
| 79 | Zig Zag ZZ22 001 | Danger Love/Like A Tiger (p/s) | 25 |

## VICE VERSA
| | | | |
|---|---|---|---|
| 80 | Neutron NT 001/PX 1092 | MUSIC 4 (EP, poster p/s) | 30 |

*(see also Liza Strike)*

## VICEROYS
| | | | |
|---|---|---|---|
| 67 | Island WI 3095 | Lip And Tongue/DAWN PENN: When Am I Gonna Be Free | 125 |
| 67 | Coxsone CS 7031 | Magadom/RICHARD ACE: Don't Let The Sun Catch You Crying | 100 |
| 67 | Studio One SO 2016 | Lose And Gain (as Voiceroys)/SOUL BROTHERS: Honey Pot | 50 |
| 67 | Studio One SO 2025 | Shake Up/NORMA FRAZER: Telling Me Lies | 50 |
| 68 | Studio One SO 2064 | Last Night/Ya Ho | 30 |
| 68 | Blue Cat BS 121 | Fat Fish/OCTAVES: You're Gonna Lose | 250 |
| 69 | Studio One SO 2077 | Things A-Come To Bump/LYRICS: Old Man Say | 50 |
| 69 | Punch PH 3 | Jump In A Fire/Give To Get (as Voiceroys) | 60 |
| 69 | Crab CRAB 12 | Work It/You Mean So Much To Me (B-side actually by Paragons) | 30 |
| 69 | Crab CRAB 27 | Death A-Come (actually by Lloyd Robinson)/MATADOR ALLSTARS: The Sword | 20 |
| 73 | Harry J. HJ 6658 | Chucky (Parts 1 & 2) | 5 |
| 74 | Harry J. HJ 6669 | Wheel & Jig (Parts 1 & 2) | 5 |
| 76 | Angen ANG 112 | Marcus Marcus Garvey/Change Your Style | 8 |
| 84 | Greensleeves GRED 146 | New Clothes/New Clothes Rhythm/Bubblers Version (12") | 15 |
| 12 | Taxi TX 002 | Heart Made Of Stone/SLY & ROBBIE: Heart Made Of Rock Dub (12" reissue) | 12 |
| 82 | Trojan TRLS 206 | WE MUST UNITE (LP) | 45 |
| 83 | Csa CSLP 5 | BRETHEREN AND SISTREN (LP) | 50 |
| 84 | Greensleeves GREL 57 | CHANCERY LANE (LP) | 15 |

*(see also Richard Ace, Interns [Jamaica], Derrick Morgan, Vincent Gordon, Hub)*

## VICEROYS (U.K.)
| | | | |
|---|---|---|---|
| 70 | Bullet BU 441 | Chariot Coming/SYDNEY ALLSTARS: Stackata | 25 |
| 70 | Bullet BU 444 | Power Control/SLICKERS: Dip Dip | 25 |
| 70 | Bullet BU 450 | Come On Over/SYDNEY ALLSTARS: Version | 20 |
| 70 | Bullet BU 453 | Fancy Clothes/BIGGIE: Jack And Jill | 20 |
| 71 | Bullet BU 470 | Rebel Nyah/Feel The Spirit | 20 |

## VICE SQUAD
| | | | |
|---|---|---|---|
| 80 | Riot City RIOT 1 | Last Rockers/Living On Dreams/Latex Love (p/s, with poster) | 15 |
| 81 | Riot City RIOT 2 | Resurrection/Young Blood/Hurricane (p/s) | 6 |
| 82 | Zonophone Z 26 | Out Of Reach/Sterile/Out Of Reach (p/s) | 5 |
| 82 | Zonophone Z 30 | Rock 'n' Roll Massacre/Stand Strong And Proud/Tomorrow | 5 |
| 80s | Vice Squad Fan Club | EVIL (EP, flexidisc) | 12 |
| 81 | Riot City ZEM 103 | NO CAUSE FOR CONCERN (LP) | 15 |
| 82 | EMI ZEM 104 | STAND STRONG STAND PROUD (LP, with inner) | 15 |
| 84 | Anagram GRAM 14 | SHOT AWAY (LP) | 15 |

*(see also Sex Aids)*

## VICIOUS PINK (PHENOMENA)
| | | | |
|---|---|---|---|
| 82 | Mobile Suit Corp. CORP 1 | My Private Tokyo/Promises (p/s) | 5 |

*(see also Soft Cell)*

## SID VICIOUS
| | | | |
|---|---|---|---|
| 79 | Virgin V2144 | SID SINGS (LP, picture inner, with poster) | 45 |
| 79 | Virgin V 2144 | SID SINGS (LP, picture inner, without poster) | 15 |

*(see also Sex Pistols)*

## MIKE VICKERS (ORCHESTRA)
| | | | |
|---|---|---|---|
| 65 | Columbia DB 7657 | On The Brink/The Puff Adder (as Mike Vickers & Orchestra) | 50 |
| 65 | Columbia DB 7657 | On The Brink/The Puff Adder (as Mike Vickers & Orchestra) (DJ Copy) | 100 |
| 66 | Columbia DB 7825 | Eleventy One/The Inkling | 20 |
| 66 | Columbia DB 7906 | Morgan - A Suitable Case For Treatment/Gorilla Of My Dreams (as Mike Vickers Orchestra) | 20 |
| 67 | Columbia DB 8171 | Air On A G-String/Proper Charles (as Mike Vickers Orchestra) | 10 |
| 67 | Columbia DB 8281 | Captain Scarlet And The Mysterons/Kettle Of Fish | 30 |
| 90s | Emidisc EMIDISC 101 | On The Brink/SAINT ETIENNE: Emidisc Theme (promo only) | 10 |
| 68 | Columbia S(C)X 6180 | I WISH I WERE A GROUP AGAIN (LP) | 45 |

*(see also Manfred Mann, Baker Street Philharmonic)*

## SUE VICKERS
| | | | |
|---|---|---|---|
| 72 | Threshold TH 8 | Loving You The Way I Do/Take Me With You | 5 |

## MACK VICKERY
| | | | |
|---|---|---|---|
| 60 | Top Rank JAR 420 | Fantasy/Hawaiian Stroll | 12 |

## VICKY
| | | | |
|---|---|---|---|
| 67 | Philips BF 1565 | Colours Of Love (Love Is Blue)/Who Can Tell | 15 |
| 67 | Philips BF 1599 | Sunshine Boy/Tell Me | 10 |
| 68 | Philips BF 1631 | Dance With Me Until Tomorrow/Give Me Your Hand | 10 |

## VICKY & JERRY
| | | | |
|---|---|---|---|
| 60 | HMV POP 715 | Don't Cry/A Year Ago Tonight | 20 |

## VICTIM
| | | | |
|---|---|---|---|
| 78 | Good Vibrations GOT 2 | Strange Things By Night/Mixed Up World (wraparound p/s) | 15 |
| 79 | TJM TJM 13 | THE VICTIM (EP, unreleased) | 0 |
| 79 | TJM TJM 14 | Why Are Fire Engines Red/I Need You (p/s) | 25 |
| 80 | TJM TJM 15 | The Teen Age/Junior Criminals/Hung On To Yourself (p/s) | 25 |
| 80 | Illuminated ILL 1 | The Teen Age/Junior Criminals/Hung On To Yourself (p/s, reissue) | 15 |

## VICTIMIZE
| | | | |
|---|---|---|---|
| 79 | I.M.E. IME 1 | Baby Buyer/Hi Rising Failure (folded p/s) | 70 |
| 80 | I.M.E. IME 2 | Wh?r? Did Th? Mon?y Go (p/s) | 70 |

## VICTIMS OF CHANCE
| | | | |
|---|---|---|---|
| 70 | Stable SLE 8004 | VICTIMS OF CHANCE (LP) | 120 |

## VICTIMS OF CIRCUMSTANCE
| | | | |
|---|---|---|---|
| 80s | Double Vision DV 1 | Very Little Glory/OPPOSITION: Wires (p/s) | 10 |

## VICTIMS OF PLEASURE
| | | | |
|---|---|---|---|
| 80 | P.A.M. VOP 1 | When You're Young/If I Was/Sporting Pastimes (p/s) | 10 |

## VICTIMS OF VICTIMISATION
| | | | |
|---|---|---|---|
| 87 | Death DEAD 2 | Kill Or Be Killed/As A Doornail (p/s) | 18 |

## TONY VICTOR
| | | | |
|---|---|---|---|
| 62 | Decca F 11459 | Dear One/There Was A Time | 25 |
| 63 | Decca F 11626 | Thinking Of You/Hokey Cokey | 12 |
| 63 | Decca F 11708 | In The Still Of The Night/Money | 12 |

## VICTORIA
| | | | |
|---|---|---|---|
| 71 | Atlantic 2091 084 | Tule's Blues/Helplessly Hoping | 6 |
| 71 | Atlantic 2400 176 | VICTORIA (LP) | 30 |
| 71 | Atlantic 2466 008 | SECRET OF THE BLOOM (LP) | 45 |

## VICTORIANS
| | | | |
|---|---|---|---|
| 64 | Liberty LIB 55693 | Oh What A Night For Love/Happy Birthday Blue | 25 |

## VICTORS (1)
| | | | |
|---|---|---|---|
| 65 | Oriole CB 1984 | Take This Old Hammer/Answer's No | 15 |

## VICTORS (2)
| | | | |
|---|---|---|---|
| 69 | High Note HS 019 | Reggae Buddy/Easy Squeeze | 25 |
| 71 | Escort ERT 846 | Me A Tell Yuh/LLOYD'S ALL-STARS: More Echo | 8 |

## VICTORY
| | | | |
|---|---|---|---|
| 82 | Rods HOT 3 | TAKING THE FIGHT (LP, with lyric insert) | 60 |

*(see also Keith Howard)*

## VIDELS
| | | | |
|---|---|---|---|
| 60 | London HLI 9153 | Mister Lonely/I'll Forget You | 60 |

## VIDEOS
| | | | |
|---|---|---|---|
| 81 | Guardian GRC 85 | Beautiful People/Him Or Me | 15 |

## VIETNAM ALL STARS (ACTUALLY PRINCE BUSTER WITH UNKNOWN VOCALIST)
| | | | |
|---|---|---|---|
| 66 | Rio R 109 | The Toughest/ERROL DUNKLEY : Love Me Forever | 100 |

## VIGILANTES
| | | | |
|---|---|---|---|
| 61 | Pye International 7N 25082 | Eclipse/Man In Space | 20 |

## VIGRASS & OSBORNE
| | | | |
|---|---|---|---|
| 72 | UNI UNS 544 | Men Of Learning/Forever Autumn | 10 |

## (PAUL) VIGRASS
| | | | |
|---|---|---|---|
| 68 | RCA RCA 1755 | New Man/Curly | 10 |
| 69 | RCA RCA 1800 | Suzie/Funky Piano Joe (as Vigrass) | 8 |
| 69 | RCA RCA 1857 | Free Lorry Ride/Flying | 15 |
| 70 | RCA RCA 1911 | Stop/Like It Never Was | 8 |

## VIKINGS (JAMAICA)
| | | | |
|---|---|---|---|
| 63 | Island WI 035 | Maggie Don't Leave Me/Henchmen (both actually with Victor Wong) | 20 |
| 63 | Island WI 065 | Hallelujah/Helpin' Ages (actually by Maytals) | 12 |
| 63 | Island WI 075 | Six And Seven Books Of Moses/Zacions (actually by Maytals) | 25 |
| 63 | Island WI 101 | Never Grow Old/Irene (actually by Maytals) | 30 |
| 63 | Island WI 107 | Just Got To Be/You Make Me Do (actually by Maytals) | 20 |
| 63 | Island WI 117 | Fever/Cheer Up (actually by Maytals) | 20 |
| 64 | Island WI 167 | Daddy/It's You (actually by Maytals) | 20 |
| 64 | Black Swan WI 423 | Down By The Riverside/This Way | 30 |
| 64 | Black Swan WI 428 | Treat Me Bad/Sitting On Top | 25 |
| 64 | Black Swan WI 430 | Come Into My Parlour/I Am In Love | 20 |

*(see also Maytals, Flames [Jamaica], Bonnie & Skitto)*

## VIKINGS
| | | | |
|---|---|---|---|
| 66 | Alp 595 011 | Bad News Feeling/What Can I Do | 30 |

## VIKINGS INTERNATIONAL
| | | | |
|---|---|---|---|
| 70s | Penthouse | VOLUME 1 (LP) | 350 |

## KURT VILE
| | | | |
|---|---|---|---|
| 15 | Matador | B'lieve I'm Goin' Down (1-side etched, 100 only) | 8 |
| 13 | Matador OLE 998-0 | WALKIN ON A PRETTY DAZE (2-LP, blue vinyl with stickers) | 20 |

## VILENESS
| | | | |
|---|---|---|---|
| 90 | Noisome STENCH 3 | March Of The Vile/Sex Is Vile (12", vile-scented p/s) | 10 |

## VILLAGE
| | | | |
|---|---|---|---|
| 69 | Head HDS 4002 | Man In The Moon/Long Time Coming | 60 |

*(see also Peter Bardens, Quiver)*

## VILLAGE SOUL CHOIR
| | | | |
|---|---|---|---|
| 70 | Direction 58-4969 | Catwalk/Country Walk | 8 |

## VILLAGERS
| | | |
|---|---|---|
| 88 | Hole In One HOLEIN 1 | Marie/Don't Try (p/s, 500 only) ........................................................................ 35 |

## VILLAGERS/PARCEL OF ROGUES
| | | |
|---|---|---|
| 73 | Deroy (no cat. no.) | PARCEL OF FOLK (LP, private pressing, with insert) ............................................ 90 |

## CATERINA VILLALBA
| | | |
|---|---|---|
| 60 | Ember EMB S 104 | Quando La Luna/Amore Fantastico (p/s) ............................................................ 6 |

## NICK VILLARD
| | | |
|---|---|---|
| 62 | Pye 7N 15418 | High Noon/Sail Ho .............................................................................................. 10 |

## VILLIERS & GOLD
| | | |
|---|---|---|
| 68 | Polydor 56235 | Of All The Young Girls/This East ........................................................................ 20 |

## JOE VINA
| | | |
|---|---|---|
| 59 | Top Rank JAR 251 | Marina/That's Alright ......................................................................................... 5 |

## RAE VINCE & VINCENTS
| | | |
|---|---|---|
| 64 | Piccadilly 7N 35211 | One Fine Day/Little Girl, I'm Sad ...................................................................... 10 |

## GENE VINCENT (& BLUE CAPS)

### 78s
| | | |
|---|---|---|
| 56 | Capitol CL 14628 | Race With The Devil/Gonna Back Up, Baby ........................................................ 25 |
| 57 | Capitol CL 14681 | Jumps, Giggles And Shouts/Wedding Bells (Are Breaking Up That Old Gang Of Mine) .. 30 |
| 57 | Capitol CL 14693 | Crazy Legs/Important Words .............................................................................. 30 |
| 57 | Capitol CL 14722 | Bi-I-Bickey-Bi, Bo-Bo-Go/Five Days, Five Days .................................................. 30 |
| 57 | Capitol CL 14763 | Lotta Lovin'/Wear My Ring ................................................................................ 25 |
| 57 | Capitol CL 14808 | Dance To The Bop/I Got It .................................................................................. 25 |
| 58 | Capitol CL 14830 | Walkin' Home From School/I Got A Baby ........................................................... 35 |
| 59 | Capitol CL 15053 | Right Now/The Night Is So Lonely ...................................................................... 150 |

### SINGLES
| | | |
|---|---|---|
| 56 | Capitol CL 14599 | Be-Bop-A-Lula/Woman Love ............................................................................. 40 |
| 56 | Capitol CL 14628 | Race With The Devil/Gonna Back Up, Baby ........................................................ 100 |
| 56 | Capitol CL 14637 | Bluejean Bop/Who Slapped John? ..................................................................... 60 |
| 57 | Capitol CL 14681 | Jumps, Giggles And Shouts/Wedding Bells (Are Breaking Up That Old Gang Of Mine) (promo copy in p/s) .......................................................................................... 125 |
| 57 | Capitol CL 14681 | Jumps, Giggles And Shouts/Wedding Bells (Are Breaking Up That Old Gang Of Mine) 100 |
| 57 | Capitol CL 14693 | Crazy Legs/Important Words (in p/s) .................................................................. 75 |
| 57 | Capitol CL 14693 | Crazy Legs/Important Words ............................................................................. 50 |
| 57 | Capitol CL 14722 | Bi-I-Bickey-Bi, Bo-Bo-Go/Five Days, Five Days (in p/s) ...................................... 150 |
| 57 | Capitol CL 14722 | Bi-I-Bickey-Bi, Bo-Bo-Go/Five Days, Five Days .................................................. 75 |
| 57 | Capitol CL 14763 | Lotta Lovin'/Wear My Ring ................................................................................ 50 |
| 57 | Capitol CL 14808 | Dance To The Bop/I Got It .................................................................................. 50 |
| 58 | Capitol CL 14830 | Walkin' Home From School/I Got A Baby (in p/s) ............................................... 70 |
| 58 | Capitol CL 14830 | Walkin' Home From School/I Got A Baby ........................................................... 50 |
| 58 | Capitol CL 14868 | Baby Blue/True To You ...................................................................................... 40 |
| 58 | Capitol CL 14908 | Rocky Road Blues/Yes I Love You, Baby ............................................................ 40 |
| 58 | Capitol CL 14935 | Git It/Little Lover ............................................................................................... 40 |
| 59 | Capitol CL 14974 | Say Mama/Be Bop Boogie Boy .......................................................................... 30 |
| 59 | Capitol CL 15000 | Who's Pushin' Your Swing/Over The Rainbow ................................................... 20 |
| 59 | Capitol CL 15035 | Summertime/Frankie And Johnnie .................................................................... 25 |
| 59 | Capitol CL 15053 | Right Now/The Night Is So Lonely ...................................................................... 20 |
| 59 | Capitol CL 15099 | Wild Cat/Right Here On Earth ............................................................................ 15 |
| 60 | Capitol CL 15115 | My Heart/I've Got To Get You Yet ...................................................................... 15 |

*(Credited to Gene Vincent & Blue Caps.)*
| | | |
|---|---|---|
| 60 | Capitol CL 15136 | Pistol Packin' Mama (as Gene Vincent & Beat Boys)/Weeping Willow ............... 15 |
| 60 | Capitol CL 15169 | Anna-Annabelle/Ac-Cent-Tchu-Ate The Positive ............................................... 15 |
| 61 | Capitol CL 15179 | Maybe/Jezebel .................................................................................................. 15 |
| 61 | Capitol CL 15185 | If You Want My Lovin'/Mister Loneliness ........................................................... 15 |
| 61 | Capitol CL 15202 | She She Little Sheila/Hot Dollar ......................................................................... 15 |
| 61 | Capitol CL 15215 | I'm Going Home (To See My Baby)/Love Of A Man ............................................ 15 |
| 61 | Capitol CL 15231 | Unchained Melody/Brand New Beat (with The Blue Caps) ................................. 15 |
| 62 | Capitol CL 15243 | Lucky Star/Baby Don't Believe Him (with Dave Burgess Band) .......................... 18 |
| 62 | Capitol CL 15264 | Be-Bop-A-Lula/The King Of Fools (with Charles Blackwell Orchestra) ................ 15 |
| 63 | Capitol CL 15290 | Held For Questioning/You're Still In My Heart (with Charles Blackwell Orch.) .... 15 |
| 63 | Capitol CL 15307 | Rip It Up/High Blood Pressure (unissued, demo copies only) ............................. 250 |
| 63 | Capitol CL 15307 | Crazy Beat/High Blood Pressure ........................................................................ 40 |
| 63 | Columbia DB 7174 | Temptation Baby/Where Have You Been All My Life........................................... 20 |
| 64 | Columbia DB 7218 | Humpity Dumpity/A Love 'Em And Leave 'Em Kinda Guy .................................. 20 |
| 64 | Columbia DB 7293 | La-Den-Da Den-Da-Da/The Beginning Of The End.............................................. 20 |
| 64 | Columbia DB 7343 | Private Detective/You Are My Sunshine (as Gene Vincent & Shouts) ................. 20 |
| 66 | London HLH 10079 | Bird Doggin'/Ain't That Too Much ..................................................................... 30 |
| 66 | London HLH 10099 | Lonely Street/I've Got My Eyes On You .............................................................. 30 |
| 68 | Capitol CL 15546 | Be-Bop-A-Lula/Say Mama ................................................................................. 15 |
| 69 | Dandelion S 4596 | Be-Bop-A-Lula '69/Ruby Baby .......................................................................... 10 |
| 70 | Dandelion S 4974 | White Lightning/Scarlet Ribbons (For Her Hair) ................................................ 10 |
| 71 | Kama Sutra 2013 018 | The Day The World Turned Blue/High On Life (some with large centre) ............. 10 |
| 73 | Spark SRL 1091 | Story Of The Rockers/Pickin' Poppies (push-out or solid centre) ....................... 10 |
| 74 | BBC BEEB 001 | Roll Over Beethoven/Say Mama/Be-Bop-A-Lula '71 (push-out or solid centre) ....... 5 |
| 77 | Capitol CL 15906 | Say Mama/Lotta Lovin'/Race With The Devil ...................................................... 5 |
| 81 | Capitol CL 203 | She She Little Sheila/Say Mama/Dance To The Bop (p/s) .................................... 5 |
| 87 | Nighttracks SFNT 001 | Nighttracks (Distant Drums/Be-Bop-A-Lula) (p/s, promo only with insert) ......... 10 |

### EPs
| | | |
|---|---|---|
| 58 | Capitol EAP 1-985 | HOT ROD GANG .................................................................................................. 75 |

| 59 | Capitol EAP 1-1059 | A GENE VINCENT RECORD DATE ........................................................ 75 |
|----|---------------------|---|
| 60 | Capitol EAP 3-1059 | A GENE VINCENT RECORD DATE PART 3 .............................................. 80 |
| 61 | Capitol EAP 1-20173 | IF YOU WANT MY LOVIN' ................................................................ 80 |
| 62 | Capitol EAP 1-20354 | RACE WITH THE DEVIL .................................................................... 80 |
| 63 | Capitol EAP 1-20461 | TRUE TO YOU ................................................................................ 80 |
| 64 | Capitol EAP 1-20453 | THE CRAZY BEAT OF GENE VINCENT NO. 1. ........................................ 80 |
| 64 | Capitol EAP 2-20453 | THE CRAZY BEAT OF GENE VINCENT NO. 2. ........................................ 80 |
| 64 | Capitol EAP 3-20453 | THE CRAZY BEAT OF GENE VINCENT NO. 3 ......................................... 80 |
| 69 | EMIdisc (no cat. no.) | LIVE & ROCKIN'! (fan club issue, mail-order, 99 only)........................... 250 |
| 79 | Rollin' Danny RD 1 | RAINY DAY SUNSHINE (L.A. 1969 demos, 500 only)............................... 12 |

**ALBUMS : LPS**

| 56 | Capitol T 764 | BLUEJEAN BOP! (original pressing with turquoise labels)..................... 130 |
|----|---------------|---|
| 56 | Capitol T 764 | BLUEJEAN BOP! (later pressing with rainbow labels) ........................... 60 |
| 57 | Capitol T 811 | GENE VINCENT AND THE BLUECAPS (turquoise label) ......................... 125 |
| 57 | Capitol T 811 | GENE VINCENT AND THE BLUECAPS (rainbow label) ........................... 60 |
| 58 | Capitol T 970 | GENE VINCENT ROCKS! & THE BLUECAPS ROLL (turquoise label) .......... 130 |
| 58 | Capitol T 970 | GENE VINCENT ROCKS! & THE BLUECAPS ROLL (later rainbow label) ....... 60 |
| 59 | Capitol T 1059 | A GENE VINCENT RECORD DATE ...................................................... 70 |
| 59 | Capitol T 1207 | SOUNDS LIKE GENE VINCENT .......................................................... 70 |
| 60 | Capitol T 1342 | CRAZY TIMES! (mono) ................................................................... 60 |
| 60 | Capitol ST 1342 | CRAZY TIMES! (stereo) ................................................................. 70 |
| 63 | Capitol T 20453 | THE CRAZY BEAT OF GENE VINCENT ................................................ 65 |
| 64 | Columbia 33SX 1646 | SHAKIN' UP A STORM (as Gene Vincent & The Shouts) .......................... 60 |
| 67 | London HA-H 8333 | GENE VINCENT ............................................................................. 50 |
| 67 | Capitol T 20957 | THE BEST OF GENE VINCENT ('rainbow' label; reissue with pink label £12) .......... 20 |
| 68 | Capitol ST 21144 | THE BEST OF GENE VINCENT VOL. 2 ('rainbow' label; reissue with pink label £12) ....... 20 |
| 70 | Dandelion 63754 | I'M BACK AND I'M PROUD (gatefold sleeve) ...................................... 30 |
| 71 | Kama Sutra 2316 005 | THE DAY THE WORLD TURNED BLUE ................................................ 20 |
| 71 | Kama Sutra 2316 009 | IF YOU COULD ONLY SEE ME TODAY ................................................ 20 |
| 87 | Charly BOX 108 | GENE VINCENT: THE CAPITOL YEARS '56-'63 (10-LP box set with 36-page booklet; later remastered and reissued with slimmer box, 1989) ..................... 50 |
| 90 | EMI CDGV 1 | THE GENE VINCENT BOX SET (Complete Capitol & Columbia Recordings, 1956-64) (6-CD set).......................... 20 |

**RORY VINCENT**

| 73 | Columbia SCXA 9254 | SINGS THE MUSIC OF WLODEK GULGOWSKI (LP) .............................. 20 |
|----|---------------------|---|

**CAROLE VINCI**

| 78 | EMI EMI 2801 | Vivre/Souffire Et Sourire .............................................................. 12 |
|----|--------------|---|

**JOEY VINE**

| 65 | Immediate IM 017 | Down And Out/The Out Of Towner .................................................. 30 |
|----|------------------|---|

**VINEGAR JOE**

| 72 | Island WIP 6125 | Never Met A Dog/Speed Queen Of Ventura .......................................... 5 |
|----|-----------------|---|
| 72 | Island WIP 6148 | Rock'n'Roll Gypsies/So Long ............................................................. 5 |
| 73 | Island WIP 6174 | Black Smoke From The Calumet/Long Way Round ................................. 5 |
| 72 | Island ILPS 9183 | VINEGAR JOE (LP) ........................................................................ 25 |
| 72 | Island ILPS 9214 | ROCK 'N ROLL GYPSIES (LP, gatefold sleeve) ..................................... 20 |
| 73 | Island ILPS 9262 | SIX STAR GENERAL (LP, gatefold sleeve, inner) ................................... 20 |

*(see also Dada, Elkie Brooks)*

**VINES**

| 02 | Heavenly HVNLP 36 | HIGHLY EVOLVED (LP) ................................................................... 25 |
|----|-------------------|---|

**VINEYARD**

| 74 | Decca F13518 | Ghost Train/Unicorns & Minotaurs.................................................... 8 |
|----|--------------|---|

**LEROY VINNEGAR**

| 63 | Contemporary LAC 570 | LEROY WALKS AGAIN! (LP) ............................................................ 30 |
|----|-----------------------|---|

**EDDIE 'MR. CLEANHEAD' VINSON**

| 64 | Riverside RLP 3302 | BACK DOOR BLUES (LP) ................................................................. 40 |
|----|--------------------|---|
| 72 | Philips 6369 406 | THE ORIGINAL CLEANHEAD (LP) ..................................................... 18 |

*(see also Wynonie Harris)*

**V. VINSTRICK & J.J. ALLSTARS**

| 68 | Doctor Bird DB 1167 | Love Is Not A Game/CINDERELLA: The Way I See You .......................... 50 |
|----|---------------------|---|

**IAN VINT**

| 62 | Columbia DB 7514 | Long Lonely Nights/Satin ................................................................. 7 |
|----|------------------|---|
| 64 | Columbia 33SX 1649 | TELL ME WHY (LP) ....................................................................... 25 |

**BOBBY VINTON**

| 61 | Fontana H 307 | Little Lonely One/Corrine Corrina ................................................... 10 |
|----|---------------|---|
| 62 | London HLU 9592 | I Love You The Way You Are/CHUCK & JOHNNY: You Are My Girl .............. 10 |
| 62 | Columbia DB 4878 | Roses Are Red/You And I ................................................................. 5 |
| 62 | Columbia DB 4900 | Rain Rain Go Away/Over Over ......................................................... 5 |
| 63 | Columbia DB 4961 | Trouble Is My Middle Name/Let's Kiss And Make Up ............................ 5 |
| 63 | Columbia DB 7015 | Over The Mountain/Faded Pictures.................................................... 5 |
| 63 | Columbia DB 7052 | Blue On Blue/Those Little Things...................................................... 5 |
| 63 | Columbia DB 7110 | Blue Velvet/Is There A Place ............................................................ 10 |
| 63 | Columbia DB 7179 | There! I've Said It Again/The Girl With The Bow In Her Hair .................. 5 |
| 64 | Columbia DB 7240 | My Heart Belongs To Only You/Warm And Tender ............................... 5 |
| 64 | Columbia DB 7303 | Tell Me Why/Remembering.............................................................. 5 |
| 64 | Columbia DB 7348 | Clinging Vine/Imagination Is A Magic Dream ..................................... 5 |
| 64 | Columbia DB 7422 | Mr Lonely/The Bell That Couldn't Jingle .......................................... 15 |
| 68 | CBS 3484 | Take Good Care Of My Baby/Strange Sensations ............................... 5 |
| 68 | CBS 3636 | Halfway To Paradise/(My Little) Christie ........................................... 5 |

MINT VALUE £

| | | | |
|---|---|---|---|
| 69 | CBS 4244 | To Know You Is To Love You/The Beat Of My Heart | 5 |
| 69 | CBS 4451 | The Days Of Sand And Shovels/So Many Lonely Girls | 5 |
| 62 | Columbia SEG 8212 | YOUNG IN HEART (EP) | 20 |
| 64 | Columbia SEG 8363 | SONGS OF CHRISTMAS (EP) | 25 |
| 63 | Columbia 33SX 1517 | SINGS THE BIG ONES (LP) | 25 |
| 62 | Columbia 33SX1465 | ROSES ARE RED (LP) | 20 |
| 63 | Columbia 33SX 1566 | BLUE ON BLUE (LP) | 20 |
| 63 | Columbia 33SX 1611 | MY HEART BELONGS TO ONLY YOU (LP) | 20 |
| 65 | Columbia 33SX1725 | LAUGHING ON THE OUTSIDE (LP) | 20 |

**MATT VINYL**
| | | | |
|---|---|---|---|
| 77 | Housewife's Choice | Useless Tasks (p/s) | 8 |

**VIOLATORS**
| | | | |
|---|---|---|---|
| 82 | No Future OI 9 | Gangland/Fugitive (p/s, with insert) | 15 |
| 82 | No Future OI 19 | Summer Of '81/Live Fast Die Young (p/s) | 15 |
| 83 | Future FS 2 | Life On The Red Line/Crossing The Sangsara (p/s) | 6 |
| 83 | Oi 26 | DIE WITH DIGNITY EP (12") | 45 |

**VIOLENT CIRCUIT**
| | | | |
|---|---|---|---|
| 85 | Circuit 1 | Vision Of Love/All Our Fatal Charms/Of Dust | 8 |

**VIOLENT FEMMES**
| | | | |
|---|---|---|---|
| 83 | Rough Trade RT 147 | Ugly/Gimme The Car (p/s) | 5 |

**VIOLENTS**
| | | | |
|---|---|---|---|
| 63 | HMV POP 1130 | Alpen Ros/Ghia | 18 |

**VIOLENT THIMBLE**
| | | | |
|---|---|---|---|
| 67 | Polydor 56217 | Gentle People Parts 1 & 2 | 15 |

**VIPERS (SKIFFLE GROUP)**
| | | | |
|---|---|---|---|
| 56 | Parlophone R 4238 | Ain't You Glad/Pick A Bale Of Cotton | 20 |
| 57 | Parlophone R 4261 | Don't You Rock Me Daddy-O/10,000 Years Ago | 20 |
| 57 | Parlophone R 4286 | Jim Dandy/Hi Liley, Liley Lo | 15 |
| 57 | Parlophone R 4289 | The Cumberland Gap/Maggie May | 15 |
| 57 | Parlophone R 4308 | Streamline Train/Railroad Steam Boat | 15 |
| 57 | Parlophone R 4351 | Homing Bird/Pay Me My Money Down | 15 |
| 57 | Parlophone R 4371 | Skiffle Party Medley Parts 1 & 2 | 15 |
| 58 | Parlophone R 4393 | Baby Why?/No Other Baby (as Vipers) | 15 |
| 58 | Parlophone R 4435 | Make Ready For Love/Nothing Will Ever Change (My Love For You)(as Vipers) | 15 |
| 58 | Parlophone R 4484 | Summertime Blues/Liverpool Blues (as Vipers) | 35 |
| 58 | Parlophone R 4484 | Summertime Blues/Liverpool Blues (as Vipers) (78) | 20 |
| 57 | Parlophone GEP 8615 | SKIFFLE MUSIC VOL. 1 (EP) | 20 |
| 57 | Parlophone GEP 8626 | SKIFFLE MUSIC VOL. 2 (EP) | 20 |
| 57 | Parlophone GEP 8655 | SKIFFLING ALONG WITH THE VIPERS (EP) | 20 |
| 57 | Parlophone PMD 1050 | COFFEE BAR SESSION (10" LP) | 60 |

*(see also Jet Harris & Tony Meehan, Shadows, Wally Whyton, Sharkey Todd & Monsters)*

**VIPERS**
| | | | |
|---|---|---|---|
| 78 | Mulligan LUNS 718 | I've Got You/No Such Thing (p/s) | 10 |

**VIPPS**
| | | | |
|---|---|---|---|
| 66 | CBS 202031 | Wintertime/Anyone | 80 |

*(see also VIPS)*

**VIPS**
| | | | |
|---|---|---|---|
| 64 | RCA RCA 1427 | Don't Keep Shouting At Me/She's So Good | 100 |
| 66 | Island WI 3003 | I Wanna Be Free/Don't Let It Go | 50 |
| 67 | Island WIP 6005 | Straight Down To The Bottom/In A Dream | 80 |

*(see also Vipps, Art, Spooky Tooth, Felder's Orioles, Timebox, Patto, Baron & His Pounding Piano, Keith Emerson)*

**V.I.P.S**
| | | | |
|---|---|---|---|
| 78 | Bust SOL 3 | MUSIC FOR FUNSTERS (EP) | 20 |
| 79 | Rok ROK V/VI | Can't Let You Go/URBAN DISTURBANCE: Wild Boys In Cortinas | 25 |
| 80 | Gem GEMS 25 | Causing Complications/Run Run Belinda/Love Is A Golden Word (p/s) | 6 |
| 80 | Gem GEMS 39 | The Quarter Moon/Hippy Hippy Shake (p/s) | 5 |
| 80 | Gem GEMS 43 | I Need Somebody To Love (Could It Be You?)/One More Chance// Stuttgart Special/Who Knows/Janine (double pack, stickered p/s) | 8 |
| 81 | Gem GEMS 47 | Things Aren't What They Used To Be/I Thought You Were My Friend (p/s) | 6 |

*(see also Mood Six, Jed Dmochowski)*

**VIRGIL BROTHERS**
| | | | |
|---|---|---|---|
| 69 | Parlophone R 5787 | Temptation 'Bout To Get Me/Look Away | 15 |
| 69 | Parlophone R 5802 | Good Love/When You Walk Away | 6 |

**VIRGIN DANCE**
| | | | |
|---|---|---|---|
| 84 | Spartan SP10 | Desire/Make Love (p/s) | 8 |

**VIRGINIANS**
| | | | |
|---|---|---|---|
| 63 | Pye International 7N 25175 | Limbo Baby/Greenback Dollar | 10 |

**VIRGINIA TREE**
| | | | |
|---|---|---|---|
| 75 | Minstrel 0001 | FRESH OUT (LP) | 50 |

*(see also Shirley Kent, Ghost)*

**VIRGINIA WOLF**
| | | | |
|---|---|---|---|
| 86 | Atlantic A 9459 | Waiting For Your Love/Take A Chance (p/s) | 10 |

**VIRGINIA WOLVES**
| | | | |
|---|---|---|---|
| 66 | Stateside SS 563 | Stay/B.L.T. | 50 |
| 66 | Stateside SS 563 | Stay/B.L.T. (DJ copy) | 100 |

**VIRGIN PRUNES**
| | | | |
|---|---|---|---|
| 81 | Baby BABY 001 | TWENTY TENS (EP) | 15 |

| 81 | Rough Trade RT 072 | Moments Of Mine (Despite Straight Lines)/In The Greylight/War/Moments Of Mine (Despite Straight Lines) (1st issue in blue p/s with insert) .......................... 15 |
|----|------|------|
| 81 | Rough Trade RT 072 | Moments Of Mine (Despite Straight Lines)/In The Greylight/War/Moments Of Mine (Despite Straight Lines) (later issue in black p/s without insert) ...................... 10 |
| 81 | Rough Trade RT 89 | A New Form Of Beauty 1; Sandpaper Lullaby/Sleep Fantasy Dreams (p/s) ........ 15 |
| 82 | Rough Trade TI COPY 007 | A New Form Of Beauty 4:Din Glorious (cassette) ............................... 25 |
| 82 | Rough Trade RT 106 | Pagan Lovesong/Dave-id Is Dead (p/s) ........................................ 8 |
| 82 | Rough Trade 12 RT 106 | Pagan Lovesong (Vibe Akimbo)/Pagan Lovesong/Dave-id Is Dead (12", p/s) .... 10 |
| 87 | Baby BABY 011 | HERESIE (10", double pack, gatefold p/s, 1st 1,000 on clear vinyl) ............ 15 |
| 87 | Baby BABY 011 | HERESIE (10", double pack, gatefold p/s) .................................... 10 |

*(see also Gavin Friday, Bono & Gavin Friday)*

## VIRGIN SLEEP
| 67 | Deram DM 146 | Love/Halliford House ....................................................... 50 |
|----|------|------|
| 68 | Deram DM 173 | Secret/Comes A Time ....................................................... 60 |

## VIRGO
| 89 | Radical Records VIRG01 | VIRGO (LP) ................................................................ 35 |
|----|------|------|

## VIRTUE
| 85 | Other OTH 1 | We Stand To Fight/High Treason (p/s) ........................................ 20 |
|----|------|------|

## VIRTUES (JAMAICA)
| 65 | Island WI 196 | Your Wife And Mother/Amen (actually with Ambassadors) ...................... 45 |
|----|------|------|
| 68 | Doctor Bird DB 1164 | High Tide/RUPIE EDWARDS & VIRTUES: Burning Love ......................... 35 |
| 68 | Doctor Bird DB 1166 | Sweet Nanny/RUPIE EDWARDS : Falling In Love .............................. 70 |

*(see also Lloyd & Devon)*

## VIRTUES (U.S.)
| 59 | HMV POP 621 | Guitar Boogie Shuffle/Guitar In Orbit ........................................ 10 |
|----|------|------|
| 59 | HMV POP 637 | Flippin' In/Shufflin' Along .................................................. 10 |

## FRANK VIRTUOSO ROCKETS
| 58 | Melodisc MEL 1386 | Rollin' And A-Rockin'/Rock - Good Bye Mambo (red label, tri centre, export issue) ...... 30 |
|----|------|------|
| 58 | Melodisc MEL 1386 | Rollin' And Rockin'/Toodle-Oo Kangaroo (green label, round centre) ............. 15 |

## VISAGE
| 79 | Radar ADA 48 | Tar/Frequency 7 (p/s) ...................................................... 15 |
|----|------|------|
| 81 | Polydor POSPX 194 | Fade To Grey/The Steps (12", p/s) ........................................... 15 |
| 81 | Polydor POSPX 236 | Mind Of A Toy (Dance Mix)/We Move (Dance Mix)/Frequency 7 (Dance Mix) (12", p/s) .......................................................... 10 |
| 82 | Polydor POSPX 523 | Pleasure Boys (Dance Mix)/The Anvil (Dance Mix) (12", 800 only) ............... 10 |
| 82 | Polydor POSPV 523 | Der Amboss/The Anvil (Mix) (12", stickered plain black sleeve & labels, promo only) ... 10 |

*(see also Rich Kids, Steve Strange, Strange Cruise, Midge Ure, Ultravox)*

## TONY VISCONTI
| 79 | Regal Zonophone RZ 3089 | I Remember Brooklyn/Sitting In A Field Of Heather ............................ 10 |
|----|------|------|

*(see also Dib Cochran & Earwigs)*

## VISCOUNTS
| 60 | Pye 7N 15249 | That's All Right/Rockin' Little Angel ......................................... 5 |
|----|------|------|
| 60 | Pye 7N 15287 | Shortnin' Bread/Fee-Fi-Fo-Fum ............................................. 7 |
| 61 | Pye 7N 15323 | Money Is The Root Of All Evil/One-Armed Bandit ............................. 5 |
| 61 | Pye 7N 15344 | Banned In Boston/Moonlight Promises ...................................... 5 |
| 61 | Pye 7N 15356 | Joe Sweeney/Honey Come On And Dance With Me ........................... 5 |
| 61 | Pye 7N 15379 | Who Put The Bomp (In The Bomp Bomp Bomp)/What Am I saying ............. 10 |
| 61 | Pye 7N 15414 | Mama's Doing The Twist/I'm Going - But I'll Be Back ........................... 5 |
| 62 | Pye 7N 15431 | One Of The Guys/Dear Mary Brown .......................................... 5 |
| 62 | Pye 7N 15445 | Everybody's Got a Ya Ya/A Lot of Livin' To Do ................................ 8 |
| 63 | Pye 7N 15479 | That Stranger Used To Be My Girl/Silent Night ................................ 5 |
| 63 | Pye 7N 15510 | Don't Let Me Cross Over/I'm Coming Home ................................... 5 |
| 63 | Pye 7N 15336 | It's You/I'll Never Get over You .............................................. 5 |
| 63 | Columbia DB 7146 | I Don't Care What People Say/Roll On Little Darlin' ........................... 6 |
| 60 | Pye NEP 24132 | VISCOUNTS' HIT PARADE (EP) .............................................. 20 |

## VISCOUNTS (U.S.)
| 59 | Top Rank JAR 254 | Harlem Nocturne/Dig ...................................................... 10 |
|----|------|------|
| 60 | Top Rank JAR 388 | The Touch (Le Grisbi)/Chug-A-Lug ......................................... 10 |
| 60 | Top Rank JAR 502 | Night Train/Summertime .................................................. 18 |
| 64 | Columbia DB 7253 | Where Do You Belong/Kiss Me .............................................. 8 |
| 65 | Stateside SS 468 | Harlem Nocturne/Dig (reissue) ............................................. 5 |
| 61 | Top Rank JKP 3005 | VISCOUNTS ROCK (EP) .................................................... 35 |

## VISION
| 86 | PRT 7P 366 | Who's That Stranger/Breakdown ............................................ 10 |
|----|------|------|

## VISIONS
| 69 | Grape GR 3009 | Captain Hook/The Girl ..................................................... 100 |
|----|------|------|

*(see also King Horror)*

## VISIONS IN WINTER
| 84 | VIW SRT4KS 226 | The Calling /Secret Garden ................................................. 10 |
|----|------|------|

## VISITORS (1)
| 78 | NRG SRTS/NRG 002 | Take It Or Leave It/No Compromise .......................................... 25 |
|----|------|------|
| 79 | Deep Heat DEEP ONE | Electric Heat/Moth/One Line (p/s) ........................................... 15 |
| 80 | Departure RAPTURE 1 | Empty Rooms/The Orcadian Visitors (foldover p/s) ........................... 7 |

## VISITORS (2)
| 87 | Sha La La BA BA BA BA BA 8 | Goldmining/MAGIC SHOP: It's True (flexidisc, p/s, free with Simply Thrilled & other fanzines. With magazine) ......................................... 10 |
|----|------|------|

## VITAL
| 81 | Cosmic Enterprises KK001 | Real Life/Sinking Ships (p/s) ............................................... 12 |
|----|------|------|

MINT VALUE £

### VITAL DUB
77  Virgin V 2055 — WELL CHARGED (LP, green two virgins label) ....................................... 20

### VITAL FORCE
87  Buce BUCE 1 — Roll The Dice/Poor Little Rich Boy (no p/s) ....................................... 25

### VITAL ORGANS
82  Airship AP 594 — Radio Active/Glastonbury (p/s) ....................................... 15

### VITAL REMAINS
92  Deaf DEAF 9 — LET US PRAY (LP) ....................................... 25

### VITAL SIGNS
83  Powerstation PS 1 — Tradiing In Guilt/Miracles ....................................... 80

### VITAL DISORDERS
81  Lowther International VD 1 — PRAMS EP: Snatcher/Tough TImes/'Prams (6 different p/s variations) ....................................... 20
82  Vital Disorders VD2 — Zombie/Wargames (p/s) ....................................... 10
83  Vital Disorders VD3 — Some People/Christmas Island Calypso (p/s) ....................................... 15

### VITAMIN B12
00  Private Press (No Cat. No.) — VITAMIN B12 (2-LP, 99 copies only) ....................................... 20

### MIROSLAV VITOUS
79  Warner Bros. K 17448 T — New York CIty/Basic Laws (12") ....................................... 40
76  Warner Bros. K56219 — MAGIC SHEPHERD (LP) ....................................... 15

### AMOR VIVI
70  Big Shot BI 534 — Dirty Dog/Round And Round The Moon ....................................... 8

### VLADO & ISOLDA
84  Ariola 106 500 — Ciao Amore (English)/Ciao Amore (Croatian) ....................................... 10

### CRISTIAN VOGEL
94  Ferox FER 004 — NARCO SYNTHESIS EP (12", plain sleeve) ....................................... 25
94  Mosquito MSQ 01 — WE EQUATE MACHINES WITH FUNKINESS EP (12", custom sleeve) ....................................... 25
95  Mosquito MSQ 03 — ARTISTS IN CHARGE OF EXPERT SYSTEMS EP (12", custom sleeve) ....................................... 20
95  Solid SOL 002 — DEFUNKT EP (12". Three untitled tracks) ....................................... 20
96  Solid SOL 004 — The Visit/Spoke/Small Dogs (12") ....................................... 30
*(see also Blue Arsed Fly)*

### VOGUES (U.K.)
66  Columbia DB 7985 — Younger Girl/Lies ....................................... 18
*(see also Llan)*

### VOGUES (U.S.)
65  London HLU 9996 — You're The One/Some Words ....................................... 20
66  London HLU 10014 — Five O'Clock World/Nothing To Offer You ....................................... 20
66  King KG 1035 — Magic Town/Humpty Dumpty ....................................... 25
68  Reprise RS 20766 — My Special Angel/I Keep It Hid ....................................... 6
68  Reprise RS 20686 — Turn Around Look At Me/Then ....................................... 6
69  Reprise RS 20788 — Till/I Will ....................................... 6
69  London HLG 10247 — Five O'Clock World/You're The One ....................................... 15
69  Reprise RS 20820 — Earth Angel/P.S. I Love You ....................................... 6
69  Reprise RS 23366 — No, Not Much/You Were Too Good To Me ....................................... 6
69  Reprise RS 20844 — Green Fields/Easy To Say ....................................... 5
66  King KGL 4003 — MEET THE VOGUES (LP) ....................................... 45
66  King KGL 4006 — FIVE O'CLOCK WORLD (LP) ....................................... 40
69  Reprise RSLP 6314 — TURN AROUND, LOOK AT ME (LP) ....................................... 20
69  Reprise RSLP 6326 — TILL (LP) ....................................... 15

### VOICE
66  Mercury MF 905 — Train To Disaster/Truth ....................................... 250
*(see also Karl Stuart & Profile, Profile, Miller Anderson)*

### VOICE OF PROGRESS
82  Negus Roots NERLP 003 — MINI BUS DRIVER (LP) ....................................... 30

### VOICE OF THE PUPPETS
80  IS/VP/1044 — I Don't Want To Know/You're All I Wanted (And A Car) (poster p/s) ....................................... 300

### STEVE VOICE
79  EMI RB 102 — UFO/Radio Blue ....................................... 6

### VOICES IN LATIN
68  Morgan MR 104P — VOICE IN LATIN (LP) ....................................... 60

### VOID
82  Hole In Space VOID 1 — Into The Void/I Want You (no p/s) ....................................... 40

### VOIDS
66  Polydor BM 56073 — Come On Out/I'm In A Fix ....................................... 120

### WES VOIGHT
59  Parlophone R 4586 — I'm Movin' In/I'm Ready To Go Steady ....................................... 80
*(see also Chip Taylor)*

### VOIZ
77  Pilgrim/Grapevine GRA 110 — BOANERGES (LP, with insert) ....................................... 25

### HOWARD VOKES COUNTRY BOYS
62  Starlite STEP 27 — HOWARD VOKES COUNTRY BOYS (EP) ....................................... 15
63  Starlite STEP 37 — MOUNTAIN GUITAR (EP) ....................................... 15

### VOLCANOS
61  Philips PB 1098 — Ruby Duby Du/Redhead ....................................... 20
61  Philips PB 1113 — Tightrope/Great Imposter ....................................... 20
62  Philips PB 1246 — Polaris/Scotch Mist ....................................... 20
60  Philips BBE 12432 — THE VOLCANOS (EP) ....................................... 100

**VOLTZ**
| | | | |
|---|---|---|---|
| 82 | Airship PP 580 | KNIGHT'S FALL (LP) | 70 |

**VOLUMES**
| | | | |
|---|---|---|---|
| 62 | Fontana 270 109TF | I Love You/Dreams | 80 |
| 63 | London HL 9733 | Sandra/Teenage Paradise | 75 |

**VOLUNTEERS (1)**
| | | | |
|---|---|---|---|
| 63 | Parlophone R 5088 | Farther Along/Little David | 8 |

*(see also Karol Keyes)*

**VOLUNTEERS (2)**
| | | | |
|---|---|---|---|
| 79 | Logo GO 351 | If You Ain't Scared/Little Pictures (p/s) | 5 |

**VON TRAP FAMILY**
| | | | |
|---|---|---|---|
| 80 | Woronzow W 001 | Brand New Thrill/Dreaming/No Reflexes (p/s, 500 only) | 18 |

*(see also Bevis Frond)*

**ERIC VON SCHMIDT**
| | | | |
|---|---|---|---|
| 68 | Transatlantic PR 7384 | ERIC SINGS VON SCHMIDT (LP) | 80 |

**VONTASTICS**
| | | | |
|---|---|---|---|
| 66 | Chess CRS 8043 | Day Tripper/My Baby | 25 |
| 67 | Stateside SS 2002 | Lady Love/When My Baby Comes Back Home | 65 |
| 67 | Stateside SS 2002 | Lady Love/When My Baby Comes Back Home (DJ Copy) | 85 |

**VOOMINS**
| | | | |
|---|---|---|---|
| 65 | Polydor 56001 | If You Don't Come Back/March Of The Voomins | 35 |

**VOXPOPPERS**
| | | | |
|---|---|---|---|
| 58 | Mercury 7MT 202 | The Last Drag/Wishing For Your Love | 30 |
| 58 | Mercury 7MT 202 | The Last Drag/Wishing For Your Love (78) | 25 |
| 58 | Mercury MEP 9533 | VOXPOPPERS (EP) | 150 |

**VOYAGER**
| | | | |
|---|---|---|---|
| 85 | Fighting Cock | Run Away Heart/Don't Hold Back (p/s) | 15 |

**V2**
| | | | |
|---|---|---|---|
| 78 | Bent SMALL BENT 1 | Speed Freak/Nothing To Do/That's It (800 only, later reissued on red vinyl) | 40 |
| 78 | Bent SMALL BENT 1 | Speed Freak/Nothing To Do/That's It (red vinyl reissue) | 15 |
| 79 | TJM TJM 1 | Man In The Box/When The World Isn't There (12", p/s) | 20 |
| 79 | TJM TJM 6 | Is Anybody Out There? (unissued) | 0 |
| 70s | Groove ZOE 1 | Gee Whiz It's You/Face In The Crowd (p/s, stamped white labels) | 30 |

**VULCAN**
| | | | |
|---|---|---|---|
| 73 | Epic SEPC 1763 | Much To Young/Action Man | 6 |

**VULCANS**
| | | | |
|---|---|---|---|
| 72 | Big Shot BI 612 | Dr. Spock/Joe Kidd | 10 |
| 73 | Big Shot BI 615 | Red Herring/Vulcanised | 10 |
| 72 | Trojan TR 7863 | Star Trek/Back A Yard | 20 |
| 73 | Trojan TRLS 53 | STAR TREK (LP) | 60 |

**VULCAN'S HAMMER**
| | | | |
|---|---|---|---|
| 73 | Brown BVH 1 | TRUE HEARTS AND SOUND BOTTOMS (LP, with insert) | 450 |

**VULTURES**
| | | | |
|---|---|---|---|
| 79 | Rubber Connection SP 522 | Time Let's Go/Is This A Man (p/s, with insert & sticker) | 12 |

**VYLLIES**
| | | | |
|---|---|---|---|
| 86 | Fun After All FAA 103 | Ahia/The Sky Is Full Of Stitches (p/s) | 8 |
| 86 | Fun After All AFTER 2 | LILTH (LP) | 25 |

# W

**PHIL WACHSMANN**
| | | | |
|---|---|---|---|
| 85 | Bead Records BEAD 23 | WRITING IN WATER (LP) | 20 |

**PHILIPP WACHSMANN, RICHARD BESWICK & TONY WREN**
| | | | |
|---|---|---|---|
| 77 | Bead Records BEAD 7 | SPARKS OF THE DESIRE MAGNETO (LP, with insert) | 30 |

**WACKERS (1)**
| | | | |
|---|---|---|---|
| 63 | Oriole CB 1902 | I Wonder Why/Why Can't It Happen To Me | 25 |
| 64 | Piccadilly 7N 35195 | Love Or Money/Hooka Tooka | 15 |
| 64 | Piccadilly 7N 35210 | The Girl Who Wanted Fame/You're Forgetting | 15 |

**WACKERS (2)**
| | | | |
|---|---|---|---|
| 72 | Elektra K12054 | I Hardly Knew Her Name/Do You Know The Reason | 5 |
| 72 | Electra K12081 | Day And Night/Last Night | 5 |

**ADAM WADE**
| | | | |
|---|---|---|---|
| 60 | HMV POP 787 | Speaking Of Her/Blackout The Moon | 5 |
| 60 | HMV POP 807 | In Pursuit Of Happiness/For The Want Of Your Love | 5 |
| 60 | Top Rank JAR 296 | Tell Her For Me/Don't Cry My Love | 5 |
| 60 | Top Rank JAR 370 | Ruby/Too Far | 5 |
| 61 | HMV POP 843 | Take Good Care Of Her/Sleepy Time Gal | 10 |
| 61 | HMV POP 896 | Point Of No Return/The Writing On The Wall | 5 |
| 61 | HMV POP 942 | Tonight I Won't Be There/Linda | 5 |
| 62 | Columbia DB 4891 | I'm Climbin' (The Wall)/They Don't Believe Me | 5 |
| 63 | Columbia DB 4986 | Don't Let Me Cross Over/Rain From The Skies | 70 |
| 63 | Columbia DB 7045 | Why Do We Have To Wait So Long/They Say | 5 |

MINT VALUE £

| 60 | HMV 7EG 8620 | AND THEN CAME ADAM (EP) | 15 |
| 64 | Columbia SEG 8316 | FOUR FILM SONGS (EP) | 15 |
| 61 | HMV CLP 1451 | ADAM AND EVENING (LP) | 30 |

**CLIFF WADE**
| 69 | Morgan Bluetown BT 1S | You've Never Been To My House/Sister | 30 |

**JOHNNY WADE**
| 60 | HMV POP 757 | Funny Thing/Shadow Love | 8 |

**WAYNE WADE**
| 77 | Grove Music GMDM 2 | Happy Go Lucky Girl/PRINCE POMPADO: Jamaican Girl/WAYNE WADE: I Kissed A Rose (12", p/s) | 10 |
| 79 | Cha Cha CHAD 34 | Tell Me What Going On/WAILING COCKS: Rudeboy Say Him Bad (12") | 15 |
| 80 | Pirate PIR 003 | African Monica/Down In Iran (12") | 30 |
| 81 | Greensleeves GRED 52 | Poor And Humble/BUNNY LIE LIE: Babylonian (12") | 25 |
| 78 | Grove Music GMLP 3 | DANCING TIME (LP) | 40 |

**WELLINGTON WADE**
| 63 | Oriole CB 1857 | Let's Turkey Trot/It Ain't Necessarily So | 40 |
*(see also Ian & Zodiacs)*

**WADSWORTH MANSION**
| 71 | A&M AMS 842 | Sweet Mary/What's On Tonight | 6 |

**DEREK WADSWORTH**
| 00 | Fanderson FANSP 8 | SPACE 1999: YEAR TWO (2-CD mail order) | 25 |

**WAGADU**
| 79 | Rokel ROK 12 | Freetown Calypso/Easy Dancin' | 25 |

**WAGES OF SIN**
| 70 | CBS 4971 | West Virginia/Hey Hey Hey (Well I'm On My Way) | 10 |

**ADRIAN WAGNER**
| 74 | Atlantic K 50082 | DISTANCES BETWEEN US (LP, with Robert Calvert) | 22 |
*(see also Robert Calvert)*

**ROBERT WAGNER**
| 57 | London HLU 8491 | Almost Eighteen/So Young | 10 |

**CHUCK WAGON**
| 79 | A&M AMS 7450 | Rock 'n' Roll Won't Go Away/The Spy In My Face (p/s, black vinyl) | 10 |
| 79 | A&M AMS 7450 | Rock 'n' Roll Won't Go Away/The Spy In My Face (p/s, purple vinyl) | 15 |
*(see also Dickies)*

**PORTER WAGONER**
| 67 | RCA Victor RCA 1586 | The Cold Hard Facts Of Life/You Can't Make A Heel Toe The Mark | 5 |
| 64 | RCA Victor RCX 7157 | A LITTLE SLICE OF LIFE (EP) | 10 |
| 64 | RCA Victor RCX 7158 | Y'ALL COME (EP) | 10 |

**WAH! (HEAT)**
| 81 | Inevitable INEV 001 | Better Scream/Joe (wraparound p/s in poly bag) | 5 |
| 81 | Inevitable INEV 004 | Seven Minutes To Midnight/Don't Step On The Cracks (p/s, different colour sleeves) | 5 |

**WAHIB**
| 82 | Hits From Heaven HIT 1 | Brings On The Tears/Grey Blues | 15 |

**WAIKIKIS**
| 61 | Palette PG 9025 | Hawaii Tattoo/Waikiki Welcome | 7 |
| 65 | Pye Intl. 7N 26286 | Hawaii Tattoo/Waikiki Welcome (reissue) | 12 |

**BUNNY WAILER**
| 76 | Island BUNNY 1 | Blackheart Man/Amagideon (12") | 20 |
| 77 | Island IPR 2003 | Get Up Stand Up/This Train (12") | 20 |
| 78 | Island IPR 2015 | Love Fire/Love's Version (12") | 15 |
| 78 | Island IPR 2025 | Roots, Radics, Rockers and Reggae/Fig Tree/Armagideon (12") | 25 |
| 79 | Solomonic SM 001 | Riding/Version (12") | 30 |
| 81 | Solomonic SM 01 | Rise & Shine/Riding | 20 |
| 81 | Solomonic SM07 | Rise & Shine/Solomonic Dub (12") | 40 |
| 82 | Solomonic BWD 017 | Collie Man/Trouble On The Road | 12 |
| 83 | Solomonic SM 018 | Boderation/THE SOLOMONIC PLAYERS - Badder ridim (12") | 25 |
| 76 | Island ILPS 9415 | BLACKHEART MAN (LP, gatefold) | 25 |
| 80 | Island ISLP 9629 | SINGS THE WAILERS (LP) | 18 |

**WAILERS (U.S.)**
| 59 | London HL 8958 | Tall Cool One/Road-Runner | 25 |
| 59 | London HL 8958 | Tall Cool One/Road-Runner (78) | 30 |
| 59 | London HL 8994 | Mau-Mau/Dirty Robber | 150 |
| 59 | London HL 8994 | Mau-Mau/Dirty Robber (78) | 70 |
| 64 | London HL 9892 | Tall Cool One/Road-Runner (reissue) | 5 |

**WAILING COCKS**
| 78 | Bird's Nest BN 116 | Rockin' Youth/Stand Up For Peace | 5 |
| 78 | Bird's Nest BN 121 | Listen To The Wailing Cocks/Listen To The Wailing Cocks | 5 |

**WAILING SOULS**
| 70 | Banana BA 305 | Row Fisherman Row/Thou Shalt Not Steal | 45 |
| 70 | Banana BA 307 | Back Out/Pack Your Things | 35 |
| 71 | Banana BA 335 | Walk Walk Walk/KING SPORTY: Love Me - Version (B-side actually by Denis Alcapone) | 40 |
| 71 | Green Door GD 4014 | Harbour Shark/Harbour Shark - Version | 25 |
| 76 | Conflict 301 | Back Out/Dub | 12 |
| 78 | Greensleeves GRED 1 | War/Jah Give Us Life (12") | 20 |
| 80 | Greensleeves GRED 043 | Kingdom Rise Kingdom Fall/A Day Will Come (12") | 35 |
| 80 | Taxi IPR 2044 | Old Broom/Bredda Gravilicious/Sweet Sugar Plum (12") | 25 |

| 81 | Cha Cha CHAD 34 | Rudeboy Say Him Bad/WAYNE WADE: Tell Me What Going On (12") | 40 |
|---|---|---|---|
| 81 | Greensleeves GRED 51 | Who No Waan Come/AL CAMPBELL: Unfaithful Children (12") | 35 |
| 81 | Cha Cha CHAD 32 | Penny I Love You/EARL SIXTEEN: Black Man Time (12") | 25 |
| 81 | Cha Cha CHAD 51 | Grabbing And Running/Dub | 20 |
| 82 | Greensleeves GRED 111 | They Don't Know Jah/Sticky Stay (12") | 30 |
| 82 | Upfront UPF 001 | Take We Back (feat Ranking Trevor)/RANKING TREVOR: Yard Oh (12") | 15 |
| 82 | Upfront UPF 004 | Take A Taste/JOHNNY RINGO: Don't Know Much (12") | 15 |
| 84 | Greensleeves GRED 152 | War Deh Round A Shop John/Peace And Love Shall Reign (12") | 30 |
| 79 | Island ILPS 9523 | WILD SUSPENSE (LP) | 20 |
| 81 | Greensleeves GREL 21 | FIRE HOUSE ROCK (LP) | 20 |
| 83 | Greensleeves GREL 47 | INCHPINCHERS (LP) | 18 |

*(see also Denis Alcapone, Tuff Gong All Stars)*

## CHERRY WAINER

| 58 | Pye 7N 15161 | Itchy Twitchy Feeling/Cerveza | 10 |
|---|---|---|---|
| 59 | Top Rank JAR 253 | I'll Walk The Line/Saturday Night In Tia Juana | 5 |
| 60 | Columbia DB 4528 | Happy Like A Bell (Ding Dong)/Money (That's What I Want) | 20 |
| 63 | Honey Hit TB 128 | Sleepwalk/Red River Rock (with Red Price Combo, with p/s) | 10 |
| 63 | Honey Hit TB 128 | Sleepwalk/Red River Rock (with Red Price Combo) | 5 |
| 59 | Pye NEP 24099 | CHERRY WAINER (EP) | 15 |

*(see also Red Price Combo)*

## PHIL WAINMAN

| 65 | Columbia DB 7615 | Hear Me A Drummer Man/Hear His Drums | 30 |
|---|---|---|---|
| 68 | Fontana TF 978 | Going Going Gone/Hey Paradiddle | 300 |

## LOUDON WAINWRIGHT III

| 71 | Atlantic 2400 103 | ALBUM I (LP) | 22 |
|---|---|---|---|
| 72 | Atlantic K 40272 | ALBUM II (LP) | 15 |
| 79 | Radar RAD 24 | A LIVE ONE (LP) | 15 |

## WAITING FOR THE SUN

| 78 | Profile GMOR 167 | WAITING FOR THE SUN (LP, private pressing) | 35 |
|---|---|---|---|

*(see also After The Fire)*

## WAITRESSES

| 81 | Ze Records WIP 6821 | Christmas Wrapping/Hangover (stock copy promo, in bespoke Ze records paper wrapping) | 15 |
|---|---|---|---|

## TOM WAITS

| 79 | Asylum K 12347 | Somewhere/Red Shoes By The Drugstore | 8 |
|---|---|---|---|
| 86 | Island ISD 260 | In The Neighbourhood/Singapore//Tango Till They're Sore/Rain Dogs (double pack, p/s) | 8 |
| 85 | Island 12IS 260 | In The Neighbourhood/Singapore//Tango Till They're Sore/Rain Dogs (12") | 15 |
| 73 | Asylum SYM 9007 | CLOSING TIME (LP, with insert) | 25 |
| 74 | Asylum SYM 9012 | THE HEART OF SATURDAY NIGHT (LP) | 30 |
| 75 | Asylum SYSP 903 | NIGHTHAWKS AT THE DINER (2-LP, gatefold sleeve) | 25 |
| 76 | Asylum K 53035 | THE HEART OF SATURDAY NIGHT (LP, 'door' label) | 30 |
| 77 | Asylum K 53050 | SMALL CHANGE (LP, 'sky' label) | 30 |
| 77 | Asylum K 53068 | FOREIGN AFFAIRS (LP, with inner sleeve) | 30 |
| 79 | Asylum K 53088 | BLUE VALENTINE (LP, gatefold sleeve) | 25 |
| 80 | Asylum K 52252 | HEARTATTACK AND VINE (LP, with inner sleeve) | 20 |
| 81 | Elektra K 52316 | BOUNCED CHEQUES (LP) | 20 |
| 82 | Island ILPS 9762 | SWORDFISHTROMBONES (LP, inner 'blue' Island label) | 25 |
| 83 | Island TW1 | A CONVERSATION WITH TOM WAITS (LP promo interview disc) | 40 |
| 84 | Asylum 960321-1 | ASYLUM YEARS (2-LP) | 20 |
| 85 | Island ILPS 9803 | RAIN DOGS (LP) | 30 |
| 85 | Island ILPM 9762 | SWORDFISHTROMBONES (LP, repressing, white 'palm tree' label, generic Island inner) | 15 |
| 86 | Island ITW 3 | FRANK'S WILD YEARS (LP, gatefold) | 30 |
| 88 | Island ITW4 | BIG TIME (LP) | 20 |
| 91 | Island 212370 | NIGHT ON EARTH (LP) | 20 |
| 92 | Island ILPS 9993 | BONE MACHINE (LP) | 60 |
| 93 | Island ILPS 8021 | BLACK RIDER (LP, with inner) | 80 |

*(see also Roy Orbison)*

## WAKE (1)

| 69 | Pye 7N 17813 | Angelina/So Happy | 15 |
|---|---|---|---|
| 70 | Carnaby CNS 4010 | Live Today Little Girl/Days Of Emptiness | 15 |
| 70 | Carnaby CNS 4014 | Boys In The Band/To Make You Happy | 12 |
| 70 | Carnaby CNS 4016 | Noah/To Make You Happy | 12 |
| 71 | Carnaby 6151 001 | Linda/Got My Eyes On You | 12 |
| 70 | Carnaby CNLS 6005 | 23.59 (LP, union jack flag label) | 250 |

*(see also Rubettes)*

## WAKE (2)

| 82 | Scan SCN 01 | On Our Honeymoon/Give Up (p/s in bag) | 25 |
|---|---|---|---|
| 84 | Scan 45/Factory FAC 88 | Talk About The Past/Everybody Works So Hard (p/s) | 7 |
| 84 | Scan 45/Factory FAC 8812 | Talk About The Past/Everybody Works So Hard (12", p/s) | 12 |
| 85 | Factory FAC 113 | Of The Matter/Of The Matter (p/s) | 10 |
| 87 | Factory FAC12 178 | Something No-one Else Can Bring/ Gruesome Castle | 15 |
| 89 | Sarah SARAH 21 | Crush The Flowers/Carbrain (p/s, with postcard) | 15 |
| 93 | Sarah SARAH 48 | Major John/Lousy Pop Group (p/s) | 15 |
| 83 | Factory FACT 60 | HARMONY (LP) | 20 |
| 90 | Sarah SARAH 602 | MAKE IT LOUD (LP) | 20 |
| 91 | Factory FACT 130 | HERE COMES EVERYBODY (LP) | 20 |
| 94 | Sarah SARAH 618 | TIDAL WAVE OF HYPE (LP) | 20 |

### JIMMY WAKELY

| | | | |
|---|---|---|---|
| 56 | Vogue Coral Q 72125 | Are You Mine? (with Ruth Ross)/Yellow Roses | 15 |
| 56 | Brunswick 05542 | Are You Satisfied? (with Gloria Wood)/Mississippi Dreamboat | 15 |
| 56 | Brunswick 05563 | Folsom Prison Blues/That's What The Lord Can Do | 20 |
| 57 | Brunswick LAT 8179 | SANTA FE TRAIL (LP) | 20 |

*(see also Karen Chandler, Bob Hope, Margaret Whiting)*

### RICK WAKEMAN (BAND)

| | | | |
|---|---|---|---|
| 73 | A&M AMS 7061 | Catherine/Anne | 5 |
| 75 | A&M AMS 7206 | Love's Dream/Orpheus' Song | 6 |
| 75 | A&M/Lyntone LYN 3176/7 | Wagner's Dream/Love's Dream/Count Your Blessings (with 2 tracks by Roger Daltrey, flexidisc with 19 magazine) | 10 |
| 79 | A&M AMS 7435 | Birdman Of Alcatraz (Theme From 'My Son My Son')/Falcons De Neige (p/s) | 5 |
| 79 | A&M AMS 7436 | Animal Showdown/Sea Horses (p/s) | 5 |
| 79 | A&M AMS 7497 | Swan Lager/Woolly Willy Tango | 5 |
| 80 | A&M AMS 7510 | I'm So Straight I'm A Weirdo/Do You Believe In Fairies? (p/s) | 5 |
| 80 | WEA K 18354 | The Spider/Danielle (some with p/s, 2,000 only) | 8 |
| 80 | WEA K 18354 | The Spider/Danielle (some with p/s, 2,000 only) | 5 |
| 71 | Polydor 2460 135 | PIANO VIBRATIONS (LP, with John Schroeder Orchestra) | 100 |
| 74 | A&M QU-84361 | THE SIX WIVES OF HENRY VIII (LP, gatefold sleeve, quadrophonic mix) | 18 |
| 73 | A&M AMLH 64361 | THE SIX WIVES OF HENRY VIII (LP, gatefold sleeve) | 15 |
| 89 | A&M RWCD 20 | RICK WAKEMAN: 20TH ANNIVERSARY (4-CD box set, 1,000 only) | 40 |

*(see also Strawbs, Yes, Dib Cochran & Earwigs, Steve Howe, Jon Anderson)*

### LARRINGTON WALKER

| | | | |
|---|---|---|---|
| 77 | United Artists UP34210 | Joy/Trust In Me | 10 |

### WALHAM GREEN EAST WAPPING CARPET CLEANING RODENT & BOGGIT EXTERMINATING ASSOCIATION

| | | | |
|---|---|---|---|
| 68 | Columbia DB 8426 | Sorry Mr. Green/Death Of A Kind | 250 |

### HOWARD WALKER & BEACHCOMBERS

| | | | |
|---|---|---|---|
| 70 | Decca F12997 | Eat Me/Love Will Find A Way | 15 |

### ANNA WALKER & CROWNETTES

| | | | |
|---|---|---|---|
| 69 | Pama PM 768 | You Don't Know/Billy Joe | 10 |

### BILLY WALKER (U.K.)

| | | | |
|---|---|---|---|
| 65 | Columbia DB 7724 | A Certain Girl/I Don't Wanna Fall In love | 5 |

### BILLY WALKER (U.S.)

| | | | |
|---|---|---|---|
| 60 | Philips PB 1001 | Forever/Changed My Mind | 6 |
| 66 | London HLU 10060 | Million And One/Close To Linda | 7 |

### BOOTS WALKER

| | | | |
|---|---|---|---|
| 69 | London HLP 10265 | No One Knows/Geraldine | 15 |

### CLINT WALKER

| | | | |
|---|---|---|---|
| 60 | Warner Bros WEP 6006 | INSPIRATION (EP, mono) | 12 |
| 60 | Warner Bros WSEP 2006 | INSPIRATION (EP, stereo) | 15 |

### DAVID WALKER

| | | | |
|---|---|---|---|
| 68 | RCA RCA 1664 | Ring The Changes/Keep A Little Love | 125 |

*(see also Paradox)*

### GARY WALKER (& RAIN)

| | | | |
|---|---|---|---|
| 66 | CBS 202036 | You Don't Love Me/Get It Right | 20 |
| 66 | CBS 202081 | Twinkie-Lee/She Makes Me Feel Better | 10 |
| 68 | Polydor 56237 | Spooky/I Can't Stand To Lose You (as Gary Walker & Rain) | 20 |
| 69 | Philips BF 1740 | Come In You'll Get Pneumonia/Francis (as Gary Walker & Rain) | 60 |
| 74 | United Artists UP 35742 | Hello How Are You/Fran | 5 |
| 66 | CBS EPS 5742 | HERE'S GARY (EP) | 45 |

*(see also Walker Brothers, Paul & Ritchie & Cryin' Shames, Badfinger, Universals)*

### JACKIE WALKER

| | | | |
|---|---|---|---|
| 58 | London HLP 8588 | Oh Lonesome Me/Only Teenagers Allowed | 250 |
| 58 | London HLP 8588 | Oh Lonesome Me/Only Teenagers Allowed (78) | 60 |

### JERRY JEFF WALKER

| | | | |
|---|---|---|---|
| 68 | Atlantic 584 200 | Mr Bojangles/Round And Round | 8 |
| 68 | Atco 228 006 | MR BOJANGLES (LP) | 20 |
| 71 | Atlantic 2466 007 | BEIN' FREE (LP) | 18 |

### JOHN WALKER

| | | | |
|---|---|---|---|
| 67 | Philips BF 1593 | Anabella/You Don't Understand Me | 8 |
| 67 | Philips BF 1612 | If I Promise/I See Love In You | 7 |
| 68 | Philips BF 1655 | I'll Be Your Baby Tonight/Open The Door Homer | 7 |
| 68 | Philips BF 1676 | Kentucky Woman/I Cried All The Way Home | 8 |
| 68 | Philips BF 1724 | Woman/A Dream | 6 |
| 69 | Philips BF 1758 | Yesterday's Sunshine/Little One | 6 |
| 69 | Carnaby CNS 4004 | Everywhere Under The Sun/Traces Of Tomorrow | 6 |
| 70 | Carnaby CNS 4009 | True Grit/Sun Comes Up | 7 |
| 70 | Carnaby CNS 4012 | Cottonfields/Jamie | 7 |
| 70 | Carnaby CNS 4017 | Over And Over Again/Sun Comes Up | 7 |
| 67 | Philips (S)BL 7829 | IF YOU GO AWAY (LP) | 25 |
| 69 | Carnaby CNLS 6001 | THIS IS JOHN WALKER (LP) | 25 |

*(see also Walker Brothers, John & Scott Walker, Johnny & Judy)*

### JOHN & SCOTT WALKER

| | | | |
|---|---|---|---|
| 66 | Philips BE 12597 | SOLO JOHN - SOLO SCOTT (EP, 2 tracks each) | 10 |

*(see also Walker Brothers, Scott Walker, John Walker, Scott Engel)*

## JUNIOR WALKER & ALL STARS

| | | | |
|---|---|---|---|
| 65 | Tamla Motown TMG 509 | Shotgun/Hot'Cha | 45 |
| 65 | Tamla Motown TMG 509 | Shotgun/Hot'Cha (DJ copy) | 100 |
| 65 | Tamla Motown TMG 520 | Do The Boomerang/Tune Up | 70 |
| 65 | Tamla Motown TMG 520 | Do The Boomerang/Tune Up (DJ copy) | 150 |
| 65 | Tamla Motown TMG 529 | Shake And Fingerpop/Cleo's Back | 50 |
| 65 | Tamla Motown TMG 529 | Shake And Fingerpop/Cleo's Back (DJ copy) | 80 |
| 66 | Tamla Motown TMG 550 | Cleo's Mood/Baby You Know It Ain't Right | 45 |
| 66 | Tamla Motown TMG 550 | Cleo's Mood/Baby You Know It Ain't Right (DJ copy) | 80 |
| 66 | Tamla Motown TMG 559 | Road Runner/Shoot Your Shot | 30 |
| 66 | Tamla Motown TMG 559 | Road Runner/Shoot Your Shot (DJ copy) | 100 |
| 66 | Tamla Motown TMG 571 | How Sweet It Is (To Be Loved By You)/Nothing But Soul | 25 |
| 66 | Tamla Motown TMG 571 | How Sweet It Is (To Be Loved By You)/Nothing But Soul (DJ copy) | 60 |
| 67 | Tamla Motown TMG 571 | How Sweet It Is (To Be Loved By You)/Nothing But Soul (later pressing) | 7 |
| 66 | Tamla Motown TMG 586 | Money (That's What I Want) Parts 1& 2 | 30 |
| 66 | Tamla Motown TMG 586 | Money (That's What I Want) Parts 1& 2 (DJ copy) | 55 |
| 67 | Tamla Motown TMG 596 | Pucker Up Buttercup/Any Way You Wanna | 30 |
| 67 | Tamla Motown TMG 596 | Pucker Up Buttercup/Any Way You Wanna (DJ copy) | 60 |
| 68 | Tamla Motown TMG 637 | Come See About Me/Sweet Soul | 18 |
| 68 | Tamla Motown TMG 637 | Come See About Me/Sweet Soul (DJ copy) | 70 |
| 68 | Tamla Motown TMG 667 | Hip City Parts 1 & 2 | 25 |
| 68 | Tamla Motown TMG 667 | Hip City Parts 1 & 2 (DJ copy) | 40 |
| 69 | Tamla Motown TMG 682 | Home Cookin'/Mutiny | 20 |
| 69 | Tamla Motown TMG 682 | Home Cookin'/Mutiny (DJ copy) | 30 |
| 69 | Tamla Motown TMG 691 | Road Runner/Shotgun | 7 |
| 69 | Tamla Motown TMG 691 | Road Runner/Shotgun (DJ copy) | 30 |
| 69 | Tamla Motown TMG 712 | What Does It Take (To Win Your Love)/Brainwasher | 8 |
| 70 | Tamla Motown TMG 727 | These Eyes/I've Got To Find A Way To Win Maria Back | 12 |
| 70 | Tamla Motown TMG 727 | These Eyes/I've Got To Find A Way To Win Maria Back (DJ copy) | 30 |
| 70 | Tamla Motown TMG 750 | Do You See My Love (For You Growing)/Groove And Move | 8 |
| 70 | Tamla Motown TMG 750 | Do You See My Love (For You Growing)/Groove And Move (DJ Copy) | 30 |
| 72 | Tamla Motown TMG 824 | Walk In The Night/Right On Brothers And Sisters/ Gotta Hold On To This Feeling (maxi-single) | 8 |
| 73 | Tamla Motown TMG 840 | Take Me Girl, I'm Ready/I Don't Want To Do Wrong | 8 |
| 73 | Tamla Motown TMG 857 | Way Back Home (Vocal)/Way Back Home (Instrumental) | 10 |
| 73 | Tamla Motown TMG 857 | Way Back Home (Vocal)/Way Back Home (Instrumental)/Country Boy (reissue) | 20 |
| 73 | Tamla Motown TMG 872 | Holly Holy/Peace And Understanding (Is Hard To Find) | 6 |
| 74 | Tamla Motown TMG 889 | Don't Blame The Children/Soul Clappin' | 6 |
| 74 | Tamla Motown TMG 894 | Gotta Hold On To This Feeling/I Ain't Going Nowhere | 10 |
| 74 | Tamla Motown TMG 894 | Gotta Hold On To This Feeling/I Ain't Going Nowhere (DJ copy) | 25 |
| 76 | Tamla Motown TMG 1027 | I'm So Glad/Dancin' Like They Do On Soul Train (as Jr. Walker) | 8 |
| 66 | Tamla Motown TME 2013 | SHAKE AND FINGERPOP (EP) | 55 |
| 65 | Tamla Motown TML 11017 | SHOTGUN (LP) | 55 |
| 66 | T. Motown TML 11029 | SOUL SESSION (LP, mono) | 50 |
| 66 | T. Motown STML 11029 | SOUL SESSION (LP, stereo) | 60 |
| 66 | T. Motown TML 11038 | ROAD RUNNER (LP, mono) | 35 |
| 66 | T. Motown STML 11038 | ROAD RUNNER (LP, stereo) | 45 |
| 69 | T. Motown TML 11097 | HOME COOKIN' (LP, mono) | 30 |
| 69 | T. Motown STML 11097 | HOME COOKIN' (LP, stereo) | 25 |
| 69 | T. Motown (S)TML 11120 | JUNIOR WALKER'S GREATEST HITS (LP, original with flipback sleeve) | 15 |
| 70 | T. Motown (S)TML 11140 | THESE EYES (LP) | 25 |
| 70 | T. Motown STML 11152 | LIVE (LP) | 20 |
| 70 | T. Motown STML 11167 | A GASSSSSSSSSS! (LP) | 20 |
| 72 | T. Motown STML 11198 | RAINBOW FUNK (LP) | 20 |
| 72 | T. Motown STML 11211 | MOODY JR. (LP) | 18 |
| 76 | T. Motown STML 12018 | HOT SHOT (by Jr. Walker) | 10 |
| 76 | T. Motown STML 12033 | SAX APPEAL (by Jr. Walker) | 10 |
| 76 | Motown STML 12048 | WHOPPER BOPPER SHOW STOPPER (by Jr. Walker) | 10 |

## KARL WALKER & ALLSTARS

| | | | |
|---|---|---|---|
| 66 | Rymska RA 103 | One Minute To Zero/Don't Come Back (both sides actually featuring Tommy McCook & Supersonics) | 35 |

*(see also Kent Walker, Ernel Braham)*

## KENT WALKER

| | | | |
|---|---|---|---|
| 68 | Fab FAB 53 | When You Going To Show Me How/Come Yah Come Yah | 8 |

*(see also Karl Walker, Ernel Braham)*

## ROB WALKER

| | | | |
|---|---|---|---|
| 71 | Upsetter US 366 | Run Up Your Mouth (actually by Stranger Cole)/UPSETTERS: Mouth Version | 20 |
| 71 | Jackpot JP 761 | Hear My Heart/Puppet On A String | 15 |

*(see also Stranger Cole, Tommy McCook)*

## RONNIE WALKER

| | | | |
|---|---|---|---|
| 69 | Stateside SS 2151 | It's A Good Feeling/Precious | 30 |
| 69 | Stateside SS 2151 | It's A Good Feeling/Precious (DJ Copy) | 50 |
| 75 | Polydor 2066 578 | Magic's In The Air/Just Can't Say Hello | 8 |

## SCOTT WALKER

| | | | |
|---|---|---|---|
| 67 | Philips BF 1628 | Jackie/The Plague | 5 |
| 68 | Philips BF 1662 | Joanna/Always Coming Back To You | 5 |
| 69 | Philips BF 1793 | Lights of Cincinnati/Two Weeks Since You've Gone | 5 |
| 71 | Philips 6006 168 | I Still See You/My Way Home | 6 |
| 73 | Philips 6006 311 | The Me I Never Knew/This Way Mary | 6 |

MINT VALUE £

| | | | |
|---|---|---|---|
| 73 | CBS 1795 | A Woman Left Lonely/Where Love Has Died | 6 |
| 74 | CBS 2521 | Delta Dawn/We Had It All | 6 |
| 66 | Liberty LEP 2261 | SCOTT ENGEL (WALKER) (EP) | 35 |
| 67 | Philips SBL 7816 | SCOTT (LP, stereo) | 30 |
| 67 | Philips BL 7816 | SCOTT (LP, mono) | 40 |
| 68 | Philips BL 7840 | SCOTT 2 (LP, mono, with signed portrait) | 40 |
| 68 | Philips BL 7840 | SCOTT 2 (LP, mono, without signed portrait) | 20 |
| 68 | Philips SBL 7840 | SCOTT 2 (LP, stereo, with signed portrait) | 40 |
| 68 | Philips SBL 7840 | SCOTT 2 (LP, stereo, without signed portrait) | 20 |
| 68 | Ember EMB LP 3393 | LOOKING BACK WITH SCOTT WALKER (LP, mono or stereo) | 30 |
| 69 | Philips SBL 7882 | SCOTT 3 (LP, gatefold sleeve) | 50 |
| 69 | Philips SBL 7900 | SCOTT WALKER SINGS SONGS FROM HIS TV SERIES (LP) | 18 |
| 69 | Philips SBL 7910 | THE BEST OF SCOTT WALKER VOL. 1 (LP) | 18 |
| 69 | Philips SBL 7913 | SCOTT 4 (LP) | 60 |
| 70 | Philips 6308 035 | 'TIL THE BAND COMES IN (LP) | 50 |
| 72 | Philips 6308 127 | THE MOVIEGOER (LP) | 25 |
| 73 | Philips 6308 148 | ANY DAY NOW (LP) | 30 |
| 73 | CBS 65725 | STRETCH (LP) | 20 |
| 73 | Philips 6850 013 | THE ROMANTIC SCOTT WALKER (LP, Audio Club issue) | 20 |
| 73 | Philips 6856 022 | TERRIFIC (LP, Audio Club issue, reissue of "Scott 2" with different tracks) | 40 |
| 74 | CBS 80254 | WE HAD IT ALL (LP) | 20 |
| 76 | Philips 6625 017 | SPOTLIGHT ON SCOTT WALKER (2-LP) | 18 |
| 81 | Zoo ZOO 2 | FIRE ESCAPE IN THE SKY - THE GODLIKE GENIUS OF SCOTT WALKER (LP) | 20 |
| 81 | Philips 6359 090 | SINGS JACQUES BREL (LP) | 15 |
| 84 | Virgin V2303 | CLIMATE OF HUNTER (LP, inner) | 25 |
| 90 | Phonogram 824832 | BOY CHILD - BEST OF 1967 - 1970 (LP) | 18 |
| 95 | Fontana 526859-1 | TILT (LP, limited edition) | 50 |
| 06 | 4AD DRIFT 1 | THE DRIFT (2-LP, 500 promo copies with 24 page booklet) | 60 |
| 14 | 4AD CAD 3428 | SOUSED (2-LP with SUNN O)))) | 30 |

*(see also Scott Engel, Scott Engel & John Stewart, John & Scott Walker, Walker Brothers, Routers)*

**STEWART WALKER**

| | | | |
|---|---|---|---|
| 98 | Mosquito MSQ 012 | ARTIFICIAL MUSIC FOR ARTIFICIAL PEOPLE (12" EP) | 15 |

**SYLFORD WALKER**

| | | | |
|---|---|---|---|
| 75 | Locks LOX 9 | Burn Babylon/Burn Version | 20 |
| 79 | Art & Craft AC 002 | Book Of The Old Testament/JAH STITCH: Jah Speak Unto Moses (12") | 30 |
| 80 | Art & Craft ACD002 | I Love You (feat. Jah Stitch)/Version (12") | 20 |
| 88 | Greensleeves GREL 119 | LAMBS BREAD (LP) | 20 |

*(see also Glen Brown)*

**T-BONE WALKER**

| | | | |
|---|---|---|---|
| 54 | London HL 8087 | The Hustle Is On/Baby Broke My Heart (78) | 40 |
| 65 | Liberty LIB 12018 | Party Girl/Here In The Dark | 25 |
| 63 | London REP 1404 | TRAVELLIN' BLUES (EP) | 40 |
| 54 | Capitol LC 6681 | CLASSICS IN JAZZ (10" LP) | 40 |
| 63 | Capitol T 1958 | T-BONE WALKER (LP) | 50 |
| 65 | Liberty LBY 3047 | SINGS THE BLUES (LP) | 50 |
| 66 | Liberty LBY 3057 | SINGING THE BLUES (LP) | 40 |
| 68 | MCA MUPS 331 | THE TRUTH (LP) | 20 |
| 68 | Stateside S(S)L 10223 | STORMY MONDAY BLUES (LP) | 25 |
| 69 | Stateside S(S)L 10265 | FUNKY TOWN (LP) | 25 |
| 74 | Atlantic K 40131 | T-BONE BLUES (LP) | 15 |

**WENDY WALKER**

| | | | |
|---|---|---|---|
| 63 | Decca F 11573 | Window Shopping/Ain't A Boy In The World | 8 |
| 63 | Decca F 11671 | Boys Will Be Happy/Casanova | 8 |

**DEE WALKER**

| | | | |
|---|---|---|---|
| 82 | Arts Network DEE 1 | DIAL 'L' FOR LOVE (mini-LP) | 30 |

**WALKER BROTHERS**

| | | | |
|---|---|---|---|
| 65 | Philips BF 1401 | Pretty Girls Everywhere/Doin' The Jerk | 15 |
| 65 | Philips BF 1409 | Love Her/The Seventh Dawn | 10 |
| 65 | Philips BF 1428 | Make It Easy On Yourself/But I Do | 6 |
| 65 | Philips BF 1454 | My Ship Is Coming In/You're All Around Me | 6 |
| 66 | Philips BF 1473 | The Sun Ain't Gonna Shine Anymore/After The Lights Go Out | 6 |
| 66 | Philips BF 1497 | (Baby) You Don't Have To Tell Me/My Love Is Growing | 8 |
| 66 | Philips BF 1514 | Another Tear Falls/The Saddest Night In The World | 8 |
| 66 | Philips BF 1537 | Deadlier Than The Male/Archangel | 8 |
| 67 | Philips BF 1548 | Stay With Me Baby/Turn Out The Moon | 8 |
| 67 | Philips BF 1576 | Walking In The Rain/Baby Make It The Last Time | 8 |
| 76 | GTO GT 42 | No Regrets/Remember Me | 5 |
| 76 | GTO GT 67 | Lines/First Day | 6 |
| 77 | GTO GT 78 | We're All Alone/Have You Seen My Baby | 6 |
| 66 | Philips BE 12596 | I NEED YOU (EP) | 15 |
| 67 | Philips BE 12603 | THE WALKER BROTHERS (EP, probably unreleased) | 0 |
| 65 | Philips BL 7691 | TAKE IT EASY WITH THE WALKER BROTHERS (LP) | 18 |
| 66 | Philips BL 7732 | PORTRAIT (LP, with photo insert, mono) | 20 |
| 66 | Philips SBL 7732 | PORTRAIT (LP, with photo insert, stereo) | 30 |
| 67 | Philips (S)BL 7770 | IMAGES (LP) | 20 |
| 67 | Philips DBL 002 | THE WALKER BROTHERS STORY (2-LP) | 18 |
| 78 | GTO GTLP 033 | NITE FLIGHTS (LP, gatefold sleeve) | 80 |

*(see also Scott Walker, Scott Engel, John Walker, John & Scott Walker, Gary Walker [& Rain], Routers)*

## WALKERS
| | | | |
|---|---|---|---|
| 79 | Walker WAK 1/2 | NOTES FOR THE HOPELESSLY BORED EP | 6 |

## TREVOR WALKERS
| | | | |
|---|---|---|---|
| 82 | Mutual Life MU 002 | They'll Never Get Away/Version (12", blue vinyl) | 20 |

## WALKIE TALKIES
| | | | |
|---|---|---|---|
| 79 | Sire SIR 4023 | Rich And Nasty/Summer In Russia (p/s) | 6 |

*(see also Pauline Murray & Invisible Girls, Mission)*

## WALKING FLOORS
| | | | |
|---|---|---|---|
| 80s | My Death Telephone TEL 1 | No Next Time/Removal (foldover p/s) | 8 |

## DENNIS WALKS
| | | | |
|---|---|---|---|
| 68 | Amalgamated AMG 816 | Having A Party/GROOVERS: Day By Day | 20 |
| 68 | Blue Cat BS 144 | Belly Lick/DRUMBAGO & BLENDERS: The Game Song | 150 |
| 69 | Bullet BU 402 | Heart Don't Leap/CLARENDONIANS: I Am Sorry | 175 |
| 69 | Bullet BU 408 | Love Of My Life/Under The Shady Tree | 12 |
| 69 | Crab CRAB 10 | The Drifter/G.G. GROSSETT: Run Girl Run | 100 |
| 71 | Moodisc HM 101 | Time Will Tell/Under The Shady Tree | 7 |
| 74 | Magnet MG 062 | Don't Play That Song/Version | 6 |
| 82 | Greensleeves GREL 77 | Roast Fish And Cornbread/Wicked She Wicked (12", with Billy Boyo) | 20 |

*(see also I Roy)*

## SHELTON WALKS
| | | | |
|---|---|---|---|
| 73 | Bullet BU 550 | No Money No Friend/BOB MAC ALL STARS: Money Dub | 6 |
| 74 | Dip DL 5026 | One Of Us Will Weep/KING EDWARDS ALL STARS: Version | 6 |

## WALL
| | | | |
|---|---|---|---|
| 79 | Small Wonder SMALL 13 | New Way/Suckers/Uniforms (p/s) | 5 |
| 79 | Small Wonder SMALL 21 | Exchange/Kiss The Mirror (p/s) | 5 |
| 80 | Fresh FRESHLP 2 | PERSONAL TROUBLES AND PUBLIC ISSUES (LP) | 15 |
| 80 | Fresh FRESHLP 2 | PERSONAL TROUBLES AND PUBLIC ISSUES LP, with insert, withdrawn "Crass style" stencil lettered sleeve) | 30 |

*(see also Ski Patrol)*

## MAX WALL
| | | | |
|---|---|---|---|
| 73 | York YR 203 | The Fiddley Foodle Bird/Story Of The Fiddley Foodle Bird | 5 |
| 75 | DJM DJS 10352 | Why Should I Care/Devil Bomb | 5 |
| 77 | Stiff BUY 12 | England's Glory/Dream Tobacco (glossy or matt p/s) | 7 |

## REM WALL & HIS GREEN VALLEY BOYS
| | | | |
|---|---|---|---|
| 60 | Top Rank JAR 324 | Heartsick And Blue/One More Time | 10 |

## ERROL WALLACE
| | | | |
|---|---|---|---|
| 69 | Escort ES 817 | Bandit/ASTON BORROT: Family Man Mood (actually by Aston "Family Man" Barrett) | 40 |

## GIG WALLACE & HIS ORCHESTRA
| | | | |
|---|---|---|---|
| 60 | Philips PB 981 | Rockin' On The Railroad/Show Me The Way To Go Home | 10 |

## JERRY WALLACE
| | | | |
|---|---|---|---|
| 58 | London HL 8719 | With This Ring/How The Time Flies | 40 |
| 58 | London HL 7062 | With This Ring/How The Time Flies (export issue) | 30 |
| 59 | London HLH 8943 | Primrose Lane/By Your Side | 10 |
| 60 | London HLH 9040 | Little Coco Palm/Mission Bell Blues | 6 |
| 60 | London HLH 9110 | You're Singing Our Love Song To Somebody Else/King Of The Mountain | 6 |
| 60 | London HLH 9177 | Swingin' Down The Lane/Teardrop In The Rain | 5 |
| 61 | London HLH 9264 | There She Goes/Angel On My Shoulder | 5 |
| 61 | London HLH 9363 | Life's A Holiday/I Can See An Angel | 5 |
| 62 | London HLH 9630 | Shutters And Boards/Am I That Easy To Forget | 5 |
| 64 | London HLH 9914 | Even The Bad Times Are Good/In The Misty Moonlight | 5 |
| 65 | Mercury MF 853 | Time/Rainbow | 5 |

## MIKE WALLACE
| | | | |
|---|---|---|---|
| 70 | Major Minor D570 | Daffodil/Early Morning Bird | 12 |
| 70 | Polydor 2058065 | Natural High/Mandrin | 10 |

## SIPPIE WALLACE
| | | | |
|---|---|---|---|
| 67 | Storyville 671 198 | SIPPIE WALLACE SINGS THE BLUES (LP) | 15 |

## WALLACE BROTHERS
| | | | |
|---|---|---|---|
| 64 | Sue WI 334 | Precious Words/You're Mine | 40 |
| 65 | Sue WI 355 | Lover's Prayer/Love Me Like I Love You | 40 |
| 67 | Sue WI 4036 | I'll Step Aside/Hold My Heart For A While | 40 |
| 67 | Sue ILP 950 | SOUL CONNECTION (LP) | 250 |

## WALLACE COLLECTION
| | | | |
|---|---|---|---|
| 69 | Parlophone R 5764 | Daydream/Baby I Don't Mind | 12 |
| 69 | Parlophone R 5793 | Fly Me To The Earth/Love | 25 |
| 70 | Parlophone R 5844 | Serenade/Walk On Out | 10 |

## GORDON (WALLER)
| | | | |
|---|---|---|---|
| 68 | Columbia DB 8337 | Rosecrans Boulevard/Red, Cream And Velvet | 20 |
| 68 | Columbia DB 8440 | Every Day/Because Of A Woman | 10 |
| 68 | Columbia DB 8518 | Weeping Analeah/The Seventh Hour | 10 |
| 69 | Bell BLL 1059 | I Was A Boy When You Needed A Man/Lady In The Window | 7 |
| 70 | Bell BLL 1106 | You're Gonna Hurt Yourself/Sunshine | 7 |
| 72 | Vertigo 6360 069 | GORDON (LP, as Gordon, single sleeve, small swirl label) | 1000 |

*(see also Peter & Gordon)*

## GEORGE WALLINGTON
| | | | |
|---|---|---|---|
| 56 | Columbia Clef 33C9035 | THE WORK SHOP OF GEORGE WALLINGTON TRIO (10" LP) | 50 |
| 57 | Esquire 32-132 | NEW YORK SCENE (LP) | 70 |

MINT VALUE £

## BOB WALLIS & HIS STORYVILLE JAZZMEN
| | | | |
|---|---|---|---|
| 57 | 77 EP 10 | NEW ORLEANS JAM SESSION VOLUME 1 (EP) | 15 |
| 59 | 77 Records 77LE 12/2 | THE RAVING SOUNDS OF BOB WALLIS (LP) | 20 |

## LARRY WALLIS
| | | | |
|---|---|---|---|
| 77 | Stiff BUY 22 | Police Car/On Parole (with p/s) | 10 |
| 77 | Stiff BUY 22 | Police Car/On Parole (die-cut company sleeve) | 5 |

*(see also Pink Fairies, Subs, Deviants, Shagrat, Peter Wyngarde, Motorhead)*

## SHANI WALLIS
| | | | |
|---|---|---|---|
| 60 | Philips PB 1019 | Sixteen Reasons (Why I Love You)/Forever Forever | 5 |
| 63 | Decca F11632 | My Heart Cries For You/All Over Again | 20 |

## WALL OF SLEEP
| | | | |
|---|---|---|---|
| 95 | Woronzow WOO 24 | WALL OF SLEEP (LP, with insert) | 12 |

## WALL OF VOODOO
| | | | |
|---|---|---|---|
| 82 | Illegal ILS 31 | On Interstate 15/There's Nothing On This Side | 5 |
| 83 | Illuminated ILS 0036 | Mexican Radio/Call Of The West (p/s) | 5 |

## WALL STREET DIVERSION
| | | | |
|---|---|---|---|
| 68 | Concord CON 006 | She's Mine/Joey The Lipstick Collector | 25 |

## WALLY BROTHERS
| | | | |
|---|---|---|---|
| 74 | Explosion EX 2090 | The Man Who Sold The World/Version | 15 |

## WALRUS
| | | | |
|---|---|---|---|
| 70 | Deram DM 308 | Who Can I Trust?/Tomorrow Never Comes | 20 |
| 71 | Deram DM 323 | Never Let My Body Touch Ground/Why? | 20 |
| 71 | Deram SML 1072 | WALRUS (LP) | 300 |

## JAMES WALSH GYPSY BAND
| | | | |
|---|---|---|---|
| 79 | RCA PB 11403 | Cuz It's You Girl/Bring Yourself Together | 50 |
| 79 | RCA PB 11403 | Cuz It's You Girl/Bring Yourself Together (DJ copy) | 100 |

## JOHNNY WALSH
| | | | |
|---|---|---|---|
| 61 | Warner Bros. WB 40 | Girl Machine/Beautiful Obsession | 10 |

## BURT WALTERS
| | | | |
|---|---|---|---|
| 68 | Trojan TR 636 | Honey Love/KING CANNONBALL BRYAN: Thunderstorm | 40 |

*(see also Lee 'Scratch' Perry)*

## JULIE WALTERS
| | | | |
|---|---|---|---|
| 82 | Deaville STL 7 | Toy Boys/Bad Loser | 6 |

## DAVE WALTON
| | | | |
|---|---|---|---|
| 66 | CBS 202057 | Love Ain't What It Used To Be/Tell Me A Lie | 8 |
| 66 | CBS 202098 | Every Window In The City/I've Left The Troubled Ground | 15 |
| 67 | CBS 202508 | After You There Can Be Nothing/Can I Get It From You | 30 |

*(see also The First Gear)*

## TRAVIS WAMMACK
| | | | |
|---|---|---|---|
| 65 | Atlantic AT 4017 | Scratchy/Fire Fly | 50 |
| 65 | Atlantic AT 4017 | Scratchy/Fire Fly (DJ copy) | 100 |
| 72 | United Artists UP 35412 | Whatever Turns You On/Slip Away | 6 |
| 73 | United Artists UP 35468 | So Good/Darling, You're All That I Need | 6 |

## WAND
| | | | |
|---|---|---|---|
| 97 | Deconstruction 74321 51222 1 | Happiness/Happiness (12") | 10 |

## WANDERER
| | | | |
|---|---|---|---|
| 59 | Top Rank JAR 183 | The Happy Hobo/True True Happiness | 6 |

## WANDERERS
| | | | |
|---|---|---|---|
| 81 | Polydor POSP 239 | Ready To Snap/Beyond The Law | 25 |
| 81 | Polydor POSP 284 | The Times They Are A'Changin'/Little Bit Frightening | 6 |
| 81 | Polydor POLS 1028 | ONLY LOVERS LEFT (LP) | 20 |

*(see also Lords Of The New Church, Stiv Bators, Dead Boys)*

## WANDERERS (JAMAICA)
| | | | |
|---|---|---|---|
| 69 | Trojan TR 7721 | Wiggle Waggle/Jaga Jaga War | 75 |

## WANDERERS (U.S.)
| | | | |
|---|---|---|---|
| 60 | MGM MGM 1102 | I Could Make You Mine/I Need You More | 50 |
| 61 | MGM MGM 1169 | As Time Goes By/There Is No Greater Love | 20 |
| 64 | United Artists UP 1020 | Run Run Senorita/After He Breaks Your Heart | 30 |

*(see also Ray Pollard)*

## HANK WANGFORD
| | | | |
|---|---|---|---|
| 80 | Cow Pie PIE 02 | Cowboys Stay On Longer/Whiskey On | 15 |

## WANGLERS
| | | | |
|---|---|---|---|
| 79 | Matchbox Classics MC 5 | KICKIN' OUT FOR THE COAST (EP, white label, yellow or red stickered foldover p/s) | 10 |

## WANNADIES
| | | | |
|---|---|---|---|
| 97 | Indolent DIE 011 | You & Me Song/Just Can't Get Enough (p/s, 3,000 only, numbered) | 5 |
| 95 | Indolent DIELP 002 | BE A GIRL (LP) | 30 |

## WAR
| | | | |
|---|---|---|---|
| 71 | Liberty LBF 15443 | Sun Oh Son/Lonely Feelin' | 6 |
| 71 | United Artists UP 35281 | All Day Music/Get Down | 6 |
| 72 | United Artists UP 35327 | Slippin' Into Darkness/Nappy Head | 5 |
| 73 | United Artists UP 35469 | The World Is A Ghetto/Four Cornered Room | 5 |
| 73 | United Artists UP 35521 | The Cisco Kid/Beetles In The Bog | 5 |
| 73 | United Artists UP 35576 | Gypsy Man/Deliver The Word | 5 |
| 74 | United Artists UP 35623 | Me And Baby Brother/In Your Eyes | 8 |
| 71 | Liberty LBG 83478 | WAR (LP) | 20 |
| 72 | United Artists UAS 29269 | ALL DAY MUSIC (LP) | 15 |

| 73 | United Artists UAS 29400 | THE WORLD IS A GHETTO (LP) | 15 |

*(see also Eric Burdon & War)*

## BILLY WARD & HIS DOMINOES
| 53 | Parlophone R 3789 | Don't Thank Me/Rags To Riches (78) | 40 |
| 54 | Parlophone MSP 6112 | Three Coins In The Fountain/Lonesome Road | 150 |
| 54 | Parlophone MSP 6112 | Three Coins In The Fountain/Lonesome Road (78) | 25 |
| 56 | Brunswick 05599 | St. Therese Of The Roses/Home Is Where You Hang Your Heart | 40 |
| 57 | Brunswick 05656 | Evermore/Half A Love (Is Better Than None) | 30 |
| 57 | London HLU 8465 | Stardust/Lucinda | 20 |
| 57 | London HLU 8502 | Deep Purple/Do It Again | 20 |
| 58 | London HLU 8634 | Jennie Lee/Music, Maestro, Please | 20 |
| 59 | London HLU 8883 | Please Don't Say 'No'/Behave, Hula Girl | 20 |
| 58 | London REU 1114 | BILLY WARD & HIS DOMINOES (EP) | 100 |
| 58 | Parlophone PMD 1061 | BILLY WARD & HIS DOMINOES FEATURING CLYDE McPHATTER (10" LP) | 600 |
| 58 | London HA-U 2116 | YOURS FOREVER (LP) | 60 |

*(see also Dominoes, Clyde McPhatter, Jackie Wilson)*

## CHRISTIAN WARD
| 66 | Decca F 12339 | The Face Of Empty Me/Girl I Used To Know | 35 |

## CLARA WARD & HER SINGERS
| 65 | Stateside SS 474 | Gonna Build A Mountain/God Bless The Child | 10 |

## CLIFFORD T. WARD
| 72 | Dandelion 2001 327 | Carrie/Sidetrack | 12 |
| 72 | Dandelion 2001 382 | Coathanger/Rayne | 10 |
| 73 | Charisma CB 205 | Home Thoughts From Abroad/Gaye | 7 |
| 73 | Charisma CB 212 | Wherewithal/Thinking Of Something To Do | 7 |
| 74 | Charisma CB 233 | Jayne/Maybe I'm Right | 7 |
| 75 | Charisma CB 248 | Jigsaw Girl/Cellophane | 7 |
| 75 | Philips 6006 490 | No More Rock'n'Roll/Gandalf | 7 |
| 76 | Philips 6006 542 | Ocean Of Love/Tomorrow Night | 7 |
| 77 | Mercury 6007 132 | Up In The World/Not Waving, Drowning (Revisited) | 7 |
| 77 | Mercury 6007 149 | I Got Lost Tonight/Detriment (p/s) | 7 |
| 77 | Mercury LUV 1 | Someone I Know/If I Had Known (gatefold p/s) | 8 |
| 80 | WEA K 18294 | Convertible/Taking The Long Way Round | 7 |
| 81 | WEA K 18426 | The Best Is Yet To Come/Lost Again | 7 |
| 81 | WEA K 18486 | Contrary/Climate Of Her Favour | 7 |
| 84 | Philips 880 550 7 | Messenger/Where Do Angels Really Come From (p/s) | 8 |
| 86 | Tembo TML 114 | Cricket/Computer | 10 |
| 86 | Tembo TML 123 | Sometime Next Year/Turbo (p/s) | 8 |
| 72 | Dandelion 2310 216 | SINGER SONGWRITER (LP) | 25 |
| 75 | Charisma CAS 1098 | ESCALATOR (LP) | 15 |

*(see also Secrets, Simon's Secrets, Martin Raynor & Secrets)*

## DALE WARD
| 64 | London HLD 9835 | Oh Julie/Letter From Sherry | 20 |

## DOUGLAS WARD
| 71 | Forward FS1001 | FROM AN ELEVATED PLATFORM (LP) | 20 |

## ROBIN WARD
| 63 | London HLD 9821 | Wonderful Summer/Dream Boy | 25 |

## SAM WARD
| 98 | Goldmine Soul Supply GS 201 | Sister Lee/THE PROFESSIONALS: That's Why I Love You | 8 |

## TERRY WARD WITH BUMBLIES
| 65 | Fontana TF 558 | Gotta Tell/When I Come To You | 10 |

## WARD 34
| 79 | Woof Woof WOOF 1 | Religion For The 70s/Disco Limbo (p/s) | 20 |

## SHEELAGH WARDE
| 59 | Top Rank JAR 131 | Let Mr. Maguire Sit Down/The Golden Jubilee | 7 |

## WARDENS
| 79 | SNU PEAS TIC 001 | Last Like This/Do So Well (with insert) | 50 |

## WARDS OF COURT
| 67 | Deram DM 127 | All Night Girl/How Could Say One Thing | 70 |

## WARD SINGERS
| 56 | London Jazz EZ-C 19024 | THE FAMOUS WARD SINGERS (EP) | 20 |
| 56 | London Jazz LZ-C 14013 | THE FAMOUS WARD SINGERS (10" LP) | 25 |

## LEON WARE
| 77 | Motown STML 12050 | MUSICAL MASSAGE (LP) | 15 |

## WARFARE
| 83 | Neat (No. cat. no.) | This Machine Kills/Burn Down The Kings Road (white label) | 20 |
| 84 | Neat NEAT 45-12 | Two Tribes/Hell/Blown To Bits (12") | 12 |
| 84 | Neat NEAT 49-12 | TOTAL DEATH (12", EP) | 15 |
| 84 | Neat NEAT 1021 | PURE FILTH (LP) | 15 |

## WARHOLS
| 87 | Zoot WAR 001 | Fear Of Falling/Other Side | 20 |

## WARHORSE
| 71 | Vertigo 6059 027 | St. Louis/No Chance | 20 |
| 70 | Vertigo 6360 015 | WARHORSE (LP, large swirl label, gatefold sleeve) | 300 |
| 72 | Vertigo 6360 066 | RED SEA (LP, small swirl label, gatefold sleeve) | 400 |

*(see also Deep Purple, Nic Simper's Fandango)*

**RAY WARLEIGH**
69   Philips (S)BL 7881         RAY WARLEIGH'S FIRST ALBUM (LP) ...................................................... 40
*(see also John Mayall's Blues Breakers, Alexis Korner)*

**OZZIE WARLOCK & WIZARDS**
59   HMV POP 635               Juke Box Fury/Wow! ........................................................................ 12
*(see also Tony Osbourne)*

**WARM**
78   Warm 2001                 It's The Kooler/Teenage Space Queen (p/s) ......................................... 5
78   Warm WARM 2003            Floosie/Chewing Gum Sue/Bye Bye It's Blues/Sometimes (p/s) ................. 5
79   Warm AWMR 2007            007 (Shanty Town)/Just To Stay Ahead (promo only) ......................... 12
79   MHG GHM 208/PF 9002       Tired Of Waiting For You/Tired Dub .............................................. 12

**WARM HANDS**
72   Access ACC 2              Disappear/My God I Love You ...................................................... 25

**WARM AIR**
70   Linette LT 1              Sugar Cane/Don't Dream .............................................................. 8

**JOHNNY WARMAN**
78   Ring O' 2017 112          Head On Collision/London's Burning/Mind Games (in p/s) ................. 20
78   Ring O' 2017 112          Head On Collision/London's Burning/Mind Games ........................... 15

**WARM DUST**
71   Trend 6099 002            It's A Beautiful Day/Worm Dance .................................................. 15
70   Trend TNLS 700            AND IT CAME TO PASS (2-LP, gatefold sleeve, grey label) ............... 120
71   Trend 6480 001            PEACE FOR OUR TIME (LP, gatefold sleeve, grey label) .................. 70

**WARM GOLD**
60s  Hurls 008                 A TASTE OF CORNWALL (EP) ........................................................ 25

**KEITH WARMINGTON**
83   Right Track S83CUS1710 RTR  Evening Song/Sentimental ........................................................ 10
     029

**WARM JETS**
78   Bridgehouse BHS 1         Sticky Jack/Shell Shock (p/s, some with sides reversed & small extra labels) ....... 8
79   RSO RSO 48                Big City Boys/Mr Natural (p/s) ..................................................... 5

**WARM SENSATION**
69   Columbia DB 8568          I'll Be Proud Of You/The Clown .................................................. 25
*(see also Ivy League)*

**WARM SOUNDS**
67   Immediate IM 058          Sticks And Stones/Angeline ........................................................ 20
67   Deram DM 120              The Birds And Bees/Doo-Dah ...................................................... 15
68   Deram DM 174              Nite Is A-Comin'/Smeta Mergaty .................................................. 50
*(see also Denny Gerrard, Tuesday's Children, Open Road)*

**FLORENCE WARNER**
73   Epic EPC 1626             For No Good Reason/Remember ..................................................... 6
75   Epic EPC 3817             Anyway I Love You/Dreamer ......................................................... 6
74   Epic EPC 80077            FLORENCE WARNER (LP)............................................................... 18

**HERB & BETTY WARNER**
59   Felsted AF 114            Slowly/'BUGS' BOWER GROUP: Slowly ............................................. 7

**JACK WARNER**
71   President PT 360          You Have Got The Gear/ Somebody Asked Me ................................. 15
68   MFP MFP 1278             YER CAN'T 'ELP LAUGHIN' (LP) .................................................... 15

**JACK WARNER WITH TOMMY REILLY**
58   Oriole CB 1426            An Ordinary Copper/On The Way Up............................................... 5

**KAI WARNER'S ORIENTAL EXPRESS**
77   Power Exchange PX 244     Fly Butterfly/Funky Harem .......................................................... 6

**WARP NINE**
75   Stax STXS 2030            Theme From 'Star Trek'/Para Song One ......................................... 5

**FRAN WARREN**
59   MGM MGM 1008             Shame/As Long As You Believe Me ............................................. 10

**GUY WARREN OF GHANA**
59   Brunswick 05791           Monkies And Butterflies/An African's Prayer (with Rod Saunders) ......... 6
57   Brunswick LAJ 8237        AFRICA SPEAKS - AMERICA ANSWERS (LP) ...................................... 35
64   Columbia 33SX 1584        EMERGENT DRUMS (LP) ............................................................ 100
69   Columbia SCX 6340         AFRO-JAZZ (LP, as Guy Warren Of Ghana) ..................................... 76
72   Regal Zono. SLRZ 1031     THE AFRICAN SOUNDS OF GUY WARREN OF GHANA (LP) .................... 100

**WARRIÖR**
80   Rambert RAM ONE           Don't Let It Show/The Lord's Prayer/Silver Lady (10", p/s)............... 120
80   Goodwood GM 12326         TROUBLE MAKER (LP)................................................................ 150

**WARRIOR (1)**
72   Eden LP 27                INVASION! (LP, private pressing, plain white sleeve & label, some handwritten, 100
                               only) ................................................................................ 160
80   Rainbow RSL 132           LET BATTLE COMMENCE (LP, private pressing, 500 only) .................. 100

**WARRIOR (2)**
82   Neat NEAT 20              Dead When It Comes To Love/Kansas City/Stab In The Back .............. 10
84   Warrior WOO 2             Breakout/Dragon Slayer/Take Your Chance (paper sleeve) ............... 55
83   Warrior WOO 1             FOR EUROPE ONLY (mini-LP) ...................................................... 20

**WARRIORS (1)**
64   Decca F 11926             Don't Make Me Blue/You Came Along................................................ 40
*(see also Hans Christian, Jon Anderson)*

**WARRIORS (2)**
79   Object OM 07              Martial Time/Martial Law (p/s)..................................................... 5

## WARSAW PAKT

| | | | |
|---|---|---|---|
| 78 | Island PAKT 1 | Safe And Warm/Sick And Tired (with stamped sleeve) | 30 |
| 78 | Island PAKT 1 | Safe And Warm/Sick And Tired | 18 |
| 77 | Island ILPS 9515 | NEEDLE TIME (LP, numbered stamped mailer p/s, with insert) | 30 |

## WARWICK

| | | | |
|---|---|---|---|
| 75 | RAK RAK 211 | Let's Get The Party Going/How Does It Feel | 15 |

## DEE DEE WARWICK

| | | | |
|---|---|---|---|
| 65 | Mercury MF 860 | Do It With All Your Heart/Happiness | 20 |
| 65 | Mercury MF 867 | We're Doin' Fine/You Don't Know | 20 |
| 65 | Mercury MF 890 | Gotta Get Hold Of Myself/Another Lonely Saturday | 20 |
| 66 | Mercury MF 909 | A Lover's Chant/Worth Every Tear I Cry | 75 |
| 65 | Mercury MF 937 | I Want To Be With You/Alfie | 18 |
| 65 | Mercury MF 953 | Yours Till Tomorrow/I'm Gonna Make You Love Me | 15 |
| 67 | Mercury MF 974 | When Love Slips Away/House Of Gold | 40 |
| 68 | Mercury MF 1061 | I'll Be Better Off (Without You)/Monday, Monday | 20 |
| 69 | Mercury MF 1084 | Foolish Heart/Thank God | 10 |
| 69 | Mercury MF 1125 | That's Not Love/It's Not Fair | 10 |
| 70 | Atlantic 2091 011 | She Didn't Know (She Kept On Talking)/Make Love To Me | 8 |
| 70 | Atlantic 2091 037 | If This Was The Last Song/I'm Only Human | 6 |
| 71 | Atlantic 2091 057 | Cold Night In Georgia/Searching | 6 |
| 71 | Atlantic 2091 092 | Suspicious Minds/I'm Glad I'm A Woman | 15 |
| 75 | Private Stock PVT 13 | Get Out Of My Life/Funny How We Change Places | 20 |
| 66 | Mercury 10036 MCE | WE'RE DOING FINE (EP) | 80 |
| 71 | Atco | TURNIN' AROUND (LP) | 30 |

## DIONNE WARWICK

### SINGLES

| | | | |
|---|---|---|---|
| 63 | Stateside SS 157 | Don't Make Me Over/I Smiled Yesterday | 22 |
| 63 | Stateside SS 157 | Don't Make Me Over/I Smiled Yesterday (DJ Copy) | 50 |
| 63 | Stateside SS 191 | This Empty Place/Wishin' And Hopin' | 22 |
| 63 | Pye International 7N 25223 | Please Let Him Love Me/Make The Music Play | 8 |
| 64 | Pye International 7N 25234 | Anyone Who Had A Heart/The Love Of A Boy | 10 |
| 64 | Pye International 7N 25241 | Walk On By/Any Old Time Of Day | 6 |
| 64 | Pye International 7N 25256 | You'll Never Get To Heaven/A House Is Not A Home | 8 |
| 64 | Pye International 7N 25265 | Reach Out For Me/How Many Days Of Sadness | 8 |
| 65 | Pye International 7N 25290 | You Can Have Him/Don't Say I Didn't Tell You | 8 |
| 65 | Pye International 7N 25302 | Who Can I Turn To/That's Not The Answer | 6 |
| 65 | Pye International 7N 25310 | (Here I Go Again) Looking With My Eyes/Only The Strong, Only The Brave | 6 |
| 65 | Pye International 7N 25316 | Here I Am/They Long To Be Close To You | 6 |
| 65 | Pye International 7N 25338 | Are You There (With Another Girl)/If I Ever Make You Cry | 6 |
| 66 | Pye International 7N 25357 | In Between The Heartaches/Long Day, Short Night | 6 |
| 66 | Pye International 7N 25368 | A Message To Michael/Here Where There Is Love | 6 |
| 66 | Pye International 7N 25378 | Trains And Boats And Planes/Don't Go Breaking My Heart | 6 |
| 66 | Pye International 7N 25395 | Another Night/Go With Love | 6 |
| 67 | Pye International 7N 25424 | Alfie/The Beginning Of Loneliness | 6 |
| 67 | Pye International 7N 25428 | The Windows Of The World/Walk Little Dolly | 6 |
| 67 | Pye International 7N 25435 | I Say A Little Prayer/Window Wishin' | 7 |
| 68 | Pye International 7N 25445 | (Theme From) The Valley Of The Dolls/Zip-A-Dee-Doo-Dah | 8 |
| 76 | Warner Bros SAM 61 | Track Of The Cat/LIVERPOOL EXPRESS: You Are My Love (12", promo only) | 15 |

### ALBUMS

| | | | |
|---|---|---|---|
| 64 | Pye Intl. NPL 28037 | PRESENTING DIONNE WARWICK | 20 |
| 64 | Pye Intl. NPL 28046 | MAKE WAY FOR DIONNE WARWICK | 15 |
| 65 | Pye Intl. NPL 28055 | THE SENSITIVE SOUND OF DIONNE WARWICK | 15 |
| 66 | Pye Intl. NPL 28071 | HERE I AM | 15 |
| 68 | Pye Intl. N(S)PL 28114 | VALLEY OF THE DOLLS (LP) | 15 |

## WASHBOARD RHYTHM KINGS

| | | | |
|---|---|---|---|
| 56 | HMV 7EG 8101 | WASHBOARD RHYTHM KINGS (EP) | 15 |

## WASHBOARD SAM

| | | | |
|---|---|---|---|
| 72 | RCA RD 8274 | FEELING LOWDOWN (LP, with Big Bill Broonzy & Memphis Slim) | 15 |

*(see also Big Bill Broonzy, Memphis Slim)*

## ALBERT WASHINGTON & KINGS

| | | | |
|---|---|---|---|
| 67 | President PT 137 | Doggin' Me Around/A Woman Is A Funny Thing | 10 |
| 68 | President PT 182 | I'm The Man/These Arms Of Mine | 50 |
| 68 | President PT 227 | Woman Love/Bring It On Up | 10 |
| 69 | President PT 242 | Turn On The Bright Lights/Lonely Mountain | 10 |
| 73 | President PT 391 | Rome, GA/Telling All Your Friends | 10 |

## BABY WASHINGTON

| | | | |
|---|---|---|---|
| 64 | Sue WI 302 | That's How Heartaches Are Made/Doodlin' | 50 |
| 64 | Sue WI 321 | I Can't Wait Until I See My Baby/Who's Gonna Take Care Of Me | 50 |
| 65 | London HLC 9987 | Only Those In Love/Ballad Of Bobby Dawn | 25 |
| 68 | United Artists UP 2247 | Get A Hold Of Yourself/Hurt So Bad | 70 |
| 69 | Atlantic 584 299 | I Don't Know/I Can't Afford To Lose Him | 15 |
| 70 | Atlantic 584 316 | Breakfast In Bed/What Becomes Of A Broken Heart | 15 |
| 73 | People PEO 105 | Just Can't Get You Out Of My Mind/You're Just A Dream | 10 |
| 74 | People PEO 107 | I've Got To Break Away/Can't Get Over You | 10 |
| 66 | London HA-C 8260 | THAT'S HOW HEARTACHES ARE MADE (LP) | 50 |
| 66 | London HA-C 8292 | ONLY THOSE IN LOVE (LP) | 50 |
| 68 | United Artists SULP 1217 | WITH YOU IN MIND (LP) | 40 |

## BABY WASHINGTON & DON GARDNER
| | | | |
|---|---|---|---|
| 73 | People PEO 101 | Forever/Baby Let Me Get Close To You | 5 |
| 74 | People PLEO 13 | LAY A LITTLE LOVIN' ON ME (LP) | 20 |

*(see also Don Gardner & Dee Dee Ford)*

## DELROY WASHINGTON
| | | | |
|---|---|---|---|
| 77 | Virgin VDJ 22 | Give All The Praise To Jah/Stand Up And Be Happy (12") | 15 |
| 78 | Burning Sounds BSD 006 | Memories (with Jah Son)/EVERARD THOMPSON & SUPERSTAR: Rasta Roots (12") | 15 |
| 76 | Virgin V 2060 | I-SUS (LP, with insert) | 20 |
| 77 | Virgin V 2088 | RASTA (LP) | 20 |

## DINAH WASHINGTON
| | | | |
|---|---|---|---|
| 59 | Mercury AMT 1051 | What A Diff'rence A Day Made/Come On Home | 10 |
| 61 | Mercury AMT 1162 | September In The Rain/Wake The Town And Tell The People | 10 |
| 62 | Mercury AMT 1170 | Tears And Laughter/If I Should Lose You | 6 |
| 62 | Mercury AMT 1176 | Dream/Such A Night | 8 |
| 63 | Columbia DB 7049 | Soulville/Let Me Be The First To Know | 25 |
| 56 | Emarcy EJT 501 | AFTER HOURS WITH MISS D. (10" LP) | 30 |
| 57 | Emarcy EJL 1255 | DINAH (LP) | 25 |
| 57 | Mercury MPL 6519 | SINGS THE BEST IN BLUES (LP) | 15 |
| 59 | Top Rank RX 3006 | THE BLUES (LP, with Betty Roche) | 15 |
| 60 | Mercury MMC 14030 | WHAT A DIFF'RENCE A DAY MADE (LP) | 15 |
| 60 | Mercury MMC 14048 | THE UNFORGETTABLE DINAH WASHINGTON (LP) | 15 |
| 61 | Mercury MMC 14063 | I CONCENTRATE ON YOU (LP, mono) | 18 |
| 61 | Mercury CMS 18043 | I CONCENTRATE ON YOU (LP, stereo) | 20 |
| 61 | Mercury MMC 14107 | SEPTEMBER IN THE RAIN (LP) | 12 |

*(see also Brook Benton & Dinah Washington)*

## ELLA WASHINGTON
| | | | |
|---|---|---|---|
| 69 | Monument MON 1030 | He Called Me Baby/You're Gonna Cry, Cry, Cry | 22 |

## GENO WASHINGTON & RAM JAM BAND
| | | | |
|---|---|---|---|
| 66 | Piccadilly 7N 35312 | Water/Understanding | 10 |
| 66 | Piccadilly 7N 35329 | Hi! Hi! Hazel/Beach Bash | 12 |
| 66 | Piccadilly 7N 35346 | Que Sera Sera/All I Need | 12 |
| 66 | Piccadilly 7N 35359 | Michael/Hold On To My Love | 12 |
| 67 | Piccadilly 7N 35392 | She Shot A Hole In My Soul/I've Been Hurt By Love | 15 |
| 67 | Piccadilly 7N 35403 | Tell It Like It Is/Girl I Want To Marry | 8 |
| 67 | Pye 7N 17425 | Different Strokes/You Got Me Hummin' | 7 |
| 68 | Pye 7N 17570 | I Can't Quit Her/Put Out The Fire Baby | 7 |
| 68 | Pye 7N 17649 | I Can't Let You Go/Bring It To Me Baby | 10 |
| 69 | Pye 7N 17745 | My Little Chickadee/Seven Eleven | 7 |
| 71 | Pye 7N 45019 | Alison Please/Each And Every Part Me | 7 |
| 71 | Pye 7N 45085 | Feeling So Good/Would You Believe My Little Chickadee | 6 |
| 66 | Piccadilly NEP 34054 | HI (EP) | 25 |
| 68 | Pye NEP 24293 | DIFFERENT STROKES (EP) | 20 |
| 68 | Pye NEP 24302 | SMALL PACKAGE OF HIPSTERS (EP) | 20 |
| 66 | Piccadilly NPL 38026 | HAND CLAPPIN', FOOT STOMPIN', FUNKY-BUTT . . . LIVE! (LP) | 20 |
| 67 | Piccadilly N(S)PL 38032 | HIPSTERS, FLIPSTERS, FINGER-POPPIN' DADDIES! (LP) | 20 |
| 68 | Piccadilly N(S)PL 38029 | SHAKE A TAIL FEATHER! (LP) | 15 |
| 68 | Pye N(S)PL 18219 | LIVE! - RUNNING WILD (LP) | 15 |

*(see also Ram Jam Band, Ram John Holder, Ram Holder Brothers, Dave Greenslade)*

## GEORGE E. WASHINGTON
| | | | |
|---|---|---|---|
| 64 | Fontana TF 510 | Spare A Thought For Me/Words Of Love | 5 |

## KENNETH WASHINGTON (& CHRIS BARBER BAND)
| | | | |
|---|---|---|---|
| 67 | CBS 202494 | If I Had A Ticket/They Kicked Him Out Of Heaven (with Chris Barber & T-Bones) | 10 |
| 67 | CBS 202592 | Gimme That Old Time Religion (with Chris Barber Band)/Just A Closer Walk With Thee | 5 |

*(see also Chris Barber)*

## NORMAN T. WASHINGTON
| | | | |
|---|---|---|---|
| 68 | Pama PM 730 | Same Thing All Over/You've Been Cheating | 10 |
| 68 | Pama PM 741 | Tip Toe/Don't Hang Around | 25 |
| 69 | Pama PM 749 | Jumping Jack Flash/Spinning | 30 |
| 69 | Punch PH 11 | Oh Happy Day/Spinning | 10 |
| 70 | Gas GAS 159 | It's Christmas Time Again/If I Could See You | 10 |
| 70 | Punch PH 26 | Sweeter Than Honey/1,000 Pearls | 10 |
| 70 | Punch PH 31 | Last Goodbye/Mother's Pride | 10 |

## SHERI WASHINGTON & BAND
| | | | |
|---|---|---|---|
| 57 | Vogue V 9070 | I Got Plenty/Ain't I Talkin' To You Baby | 500 |
| 57 | Vogue V 9070 | I Got Plenty/Ain't I Talkin' To You Baby (78) | 100 |

## SISTER ERNESTINE B. WASHINGTON
| | | | |
|---|---|---|---|
| 55 | Melodisc EPM 7-52 | SISTER ERNESTINE WASHINGTON (EP) | 20 |

## TONY WASHINGTON (& HIS D.C.S)
| | | | |
|---|---|---|---|
| 63 | React EA 002 | Crying Man/Please Mr. DJ | 20 |
| 63 | Island WI 068 | Something Gotta Be Done/TONY & LOUISE: I Have Said | 20 |
| 64 | Sue WI 327 | Show Me How (To Milk A Cow)/Boof Ska | 50 |
| 64 | Fontana TF 478 | Surely You Love Me/Man To Man | 15 |
| 65 | Black Swan WI 459 | But I Do/Night Train (as Tony Washington & His D.C.s) | 25 |
| 65 | Black Swan WI 460 | Dilly Dilly/Night Train (as Tony Washington & His D.C.s) | 25 |

*(see also Tony & Louise)*

## WASHINGTON D.C.S
| | | | |
|---|---|---|---|
| 64 | Ember EMB S 190 | Kisses Sweeter Than Wine/Where Did You Go | 15 |
| 66 | CBS 202226 | 32nd Floor/Whole Lot More | 15 |

| 67 | CBS 202464 | Seek And Find/I Love Gerald Chevin The Great (in p/s) | 70 |
| 67 | CBS 202464 | Seek and Find/I Love Gerald Chevin The Great (no p/s) | 50 |
| 69 | Domain D 9 | I've Done It All Wrong/Anytime | 30 |

*(see also Dave Clark Five, Freedom)*

## WASHINGTON FLYER
| 79 | EMI 2926 | Bufflao Bill/Star Dance | 15 |

## WASHINGTON FLYERS
| 74 | Dawn DNS 1076 | Another Saturday Morning/The Comets Are Coming | 6 |

## WASP
| 75 | EMI EMI 2253 | Melissa/Little Miss Bristol | 20 |

*(see also Brian Bennett, Shadows)*

## W.A.S.P.
| 84 | Music For Nations PKUT 109 | Animal (Fuck Like A Beast)/Show No Mercy (shaped picture disc, pig's head or codpiece designs) | 20 |
| 84 | Music For Nations 12KUT 109 | Animal (Fuck Like A Beast)/Show No Mercy (12", gold vinyl, U.K. issue pressed in France) | 35 |
| 84 | Music For Nations 12KUT 109 | Animal (Fuck Like A Beast)/Show No Mercy (12", white, vinyl, U.K. issue pressed in France) | 15 |
| 84 | Music For Nations 12KUT 109 | Animal (Fuck Like A Beast)/Show No Mercy (12", clear vinyl, U.K. issue pressed in France) | 20 |
| 84 | Music For Nations 12KUT 109 | Animal (Fuck Like A Beast)/Show No Mercy (12", red vinyl, U.K. issue pressed in France) | 15 |
| 84 | Capitol 12 CLP 336 | I Wanna Be Somebody/Tormentor (Ragewars) (12", picture disc) | 12 |
| 89 | Capitol ESTPD 2087 | THE HEADLESS CHILDREN (LP, picture disc) | 15 |
| 92 | Parlophone PCSDS 118 | CRIMSON IDOL (LP, red vinyl, inner) | 20 |

## WASPS
| 77 | 4-Play FOUR 001 | Teenage Treats/She Made More Magic (p/s) | 25 |
| 77 | NEMS NES 115 | Can't Wait 'Til '78/MEAN STREET: Bunch Of Stiffs (p/s) | 18 |
| 78 | RCA PB 5137 | Rubber Cars/This Time (p/s) | 10 |

## WASTE
| 86 | Morterhate MORT 21 | NOT JUST SOMETHING TO BE SUNG (EP, foldout p/s) | 25 |

## WASTED YOUTH
| 80 | Bridge House BHS 5 | Jealousy/Baby (p/s, clear vinyl) | 5 |
| 82 | Bridge House BHFNEE 1 | Caveman (1-sided, limited issue) | 8 |
| 80 | Bridge House BHLP006 | WILD AND WANDERING (LP) | 15 |
| 82 | Bridge House BHLP007 | THE BEGINNING OF THE END (LP, with free 'Caveman 7", 5000 only) | 15 |

## WASTELAND
| 79 | Ellie Jay/Disaster EJSP 9261 | WANT NOT EP (p/s, 2,000 only) | 30 |
| 80 | Invicta INV 014 | Friends, Romans, Countrymen/Leave Me Alone (p/s, 1,000 only) | 30 |

## WATCH COMMITTEE
| 68 | Philips BF 1695 | Throw Another Penny In The Well/Now I Think The Other Way | 6 |

## WATERFALL
| 76 | Bob FRR 001 | FLIGHT OF THE DAY (LP, private pressing) | 100 |
| 79 | Avada AVA 104 | THREE BIRDS (LP, with insert) | 22 |
| 81 | Gun Dog GUN 003LP | BENEATH THE STARS (LP, private pressing) | 22 |

## WATER FOR A THIRSTY LAND
| 74 | MRA P 100 | WATER FOR A THIRSTY LAND (LP, with insert) | 22 |

## SHEILA WATERHOUSE
| 71 | Canvas CV 037 | Let Go Of The Chain/Love Me | 20 |

## WATER INTO WINE BAND
| 73 | Myrrh MYR 1004 | HILL CLIMBING FOR BEGINNERS (LP, brown cover, with insert) | 150 |
| 73 | Myrrh MYR 1004 | HILL CLIMBING FOR BEGINNERS (LP, white cover, with insert) | 100 |
| 76 | CJT 002 | HARVEST TIME (LP, private pressing, 500 copies) | 100 |

## WATER PISTOLS
| 76 | State STATE 38 | Gimme That Punk Junk/Soft Punk (p/s, with insert) | 10 |

## WATERPROOF CANDLE
| 68 | RCA RCA 1717 | Electrically Heated Child/Saturday Morning Repentance | 15 |

## FREDDIE WATERS
| 75 | Mint CHEW 2 | Groovin On My Baby's Love/Kung Fu & You Too | 20 |

## MUDDY WATERS
| 53 | Vogue V 2101 | Walkin' Blues/Rollin' Stone Blues (78) | 80 |
| 54 | Vogue V 2273 | Hello Little Girl/Long Distance Call (78) | 80 |
| 55 | Vogue V 2372 | Honey Bee/Too Young To Know (78) | 80 |
| 65 | Chess CRS 8001 | My John The Conquer Root/Short Dress Woman | 20 |
| 65 | Chess CRS 8019 | I Got A Rich Man's Woman/My Dog Can't Bark | 20 |
| 69 | Chess CRS 8083 | Let's Spend The Night Together/I'm A Man | 25 |
| 69 | Python PKM 04 | Country Boy/All Night Long (99 copies only) | 85 |
| 55 | Vogue EPV 1046 | MUDDY WATERS WITH LITTLE WALTER (EP) | 150 |
| 56 | London RU-E 1060 | MISSISSIPPI BLUES (EP) | 175 |
| 63 | Pye Intl. NEP 44010 | MUDDY WATERS (EP) | 40 |
| 65 | Chess CRE 6006 | I'M READY (EP) | 50 |
| 66 | Chess CRE 6022 | THE REAL FOLK BLUES VOL. 4 (EP) | 45 |
| 59 | London Jazz LJZ-M 15152 | THE BEST OF MUDDY WATERS (LP) | 100 |
| 61 | Pye Jazz NJL 34 | AT NEWPORT (LP) | 75 |
| 64 | Pye Intl. NPL 28038 | MUDDY WATERS - FOLK SINGER (LP) | 60 |
| 64 | Pye Intl. NPL 28040 | THE BEST OF MUDDY WATERS (LP) | 60 |
| 64 | Pye Intl. NPL 28048 | MUDDY SINGS BIG BILL (LP) | 35 |
| 65 | Chess CRL 4513 | AT NEWPORT (LP, reissue) | 40 |

MINT VALUE £

| | | | |
|---|---|---|---|
| 66 | Chess CRL 4515 | THE REAL FOLK BLUES (LP) | 35 |
| 67 | Chess CRL 4525 | MUDDY, BRASS AND THE BLUES (LP) | 35 |
| 67 | Chess CRL 4529 | SUPER BLUES (LP, with Little Walter & Bo Diddley) | 40 |
| 68 | Chess CRL 4537 | THE SUPER SUPER BLUES BAND (LP, with Howlin' Wolf & Bo Diddley) | 50 |
| 68 | Bounty BY 6031 | DOWN ON STOVALL'S PLANTATION (LP) | 30 |
| 69 | Chess CRL 4542 | ELECTRIC MUD (LP) | 40 |
| 69 | Chess CRL 4553 | AFTER THE RAIN (LP) | 20 |
| 69 | Chess CRL 4556 | FATHERS AND SONS (LP) | 30 |
| 69 | Polydor 236 574 | BLUES MAN (LP) | 25 |
| 69 | Python PLP 12 | MUDDY WATERS (LP, 99 copies only) | 80 |
| 69 | Python PLP 18 | MUDDY WATERS VOLUME 2 (LP, 99 copies only) | 80 |
| 69 | Python PLP 19 | MUDDY WATERS VOLUME 3 (LP, 99 copies only) | 80 |
| 70 | Syndicate Chapter SC 002 | GOOD NEWS (LP) | 15 |
| 70 | Sunnyland KS 100 | VINTAGE MUDDY WATERS (LP, gatefold sleeve with inserts, 99 copies only) | 30 |
| 71 | Chess 6671 001 | McKINLEY MORGANFIELD AKA MUDDY WATERS (LP) | 20 |
| 72 | Black Bear LP 901 | RARE LIVE RECORDINGS VOL. 1 (LP) | 15 |
| 72 | Black Bear LP 902 | RARE LIVE RECORDINGS VOL. 2 (LP) | 15 |
| 72 | Black Bear LP 903 | RARE LIVE RECORDINGS VOL. 3 (LP) | 15 |
| 72 | Chess 6310 121 | THE LONDON SESSIONS (LP) | 15 |
| 77 | Blue Sky SKY 81853 | HARD AGAIN (LP) | 15 |

*(see also Little Walter, Howlin' Wolf, Bo Diddley, Luther 'Georgia Boy Snake' Johnson)*

## ROGER WATERS

| | | | |
|---|---|---|---|
| 84 | Harvest HAR 5228 | 5.01 AM (The Pros And Cons Of Hitch-Hiking)/4.30 AM (Apparently They Were Travelling Abroad) (p/s) | 5 |
| 84 | Harvest HAR 5230 | 5.06 AM (Every Stranger's Eyes)/4.39 AM (For The First Time Today) (p/s) | 15 |
| 87 | EMI EM 6 | Radio Waves/Going To Live In L.A. (Demo) (p/s) | 6 |
| 87 | EMI EM 20 | Sunset Strip/Money (live) (withdrawn) | 200 |
| 87 | EMI EM 37 | The Tide Is Turning (After Live Aid)/Money ('live') (p/s) | 5 |
| 70 | Harvest SHSP 4008 | MUSIC FROM THE FILM "THE BODY" (LP, with Ron Geesin, green labels, with Waters/Geesin photos) | 50 |
| 83 | Harvest SHVL 240105 | THE PROS AND CONS OF HITCHHIKING (LP, gatefold) | 15 |
| 87 | EMI KAOS DJ 1 | RADIO KAOS (LP, 'banded' radio promo, custom sleeve) | 30 |
| 87 | EMI KAOS 1 | RADIO KAOS (LP, inner, poster, stickered sleeve) | 15 |
| 92 | Mercury 468761 | AMUSED TO DEATH (2-LP) | 100 |

*(see also Pink Floyd, Ron Geesin)*

## LAL & MIKE WATERSON

| | | | |
|---|---|---|---|
| 72 | Trailer LES 2076 | BRIGHT PHOEBUS (LP, original pressing, red/black label) | 45 |
| 73 | Trailer LER 2076 | BRIGHT PHOEBUS (LP, second pressing, yellow label) | 35 |
| 82 | Highway | BRIGHT PHOEBUS (LP, reissue) | 20 |

## LAL AND NORMA WATERSON

| | | | |
|---|---|---|---|
| 77 | Topic 12T5331 | A TRUE HEARTED GIRL (LP) | 20 |

*(see also Watersons)*

## MIKE WATERSON

| | | | |
|---|---|---|---|
| 77 | Topic 12TS 332 | MIKE WATERSON (LP) | 20 |

*(see also Waterson, Lal & Mike Waterson)*

## WATERSONS

| | | | |
|---|---|---|---|
| 65 | Topic 12T 125 | NEW VOICES (LP, blue label, with Harry Boardman & Maureen Craik) | 18 |
| 65 | Topic 12T 136 | FROST AND FIRE (LP, blue label) | 20 |
| 66 | Topic 12T 142 | WATERSONS (LP, blue label) | 20 |
| 66 | Topic 12T 167 | A YORKSHIRE GARLAND (LP, blue label) | 18 |
| 60s | Topic TS 346 | THE WATERSONS SOUND (LP) | 15 |

## GEORGE WATKINS

| | | | |
|---|---|---|---|
| 69 | NEMS 56-3861 | The Fly/Barrer Boy Blues | 7 |

## LOVELACE WATKINS

| | | | |
|---|---|---|---|
| 67 | Fontana TF879 | I Apologie Baby/You Can't Stop Love | 300 |

## DILYS WATLING

| | | | |
|---|---|---|---|
| 64 | Philips BF 1305 | Don't Say You Love Me/Now's The Time | 5 |
| 65 | Philips BF 1393 | I'm Over You/Act Like A Lady | 5 |

## DOC WATSON

| | | | |
|---|---|---|---|
| 64 | Fontana TFL 6045 | DOC WATSON (LP) | 22 |
| 65 | Fontana TFL 6055 | DOC WATSON & SON (LP) | 20 |
| 72 | Vanguard VSD 9/10 | ON STAGE (2-LP) | 20 |

## EARL WATSON

| | | | |
|---|---|---|---|
| 61 | Ember EMB S 129 | Nightmare/That Old Black Magic | 10 |

## JOHN L. WATSON (& HUMMELFLUGS)

| | | | |
|---|---|---|---|
| 64 | Pye 7N 15746 | Looking For Love/Dance With You | 12 |
| 65 | Piccadilly 7N 35233 | Standing By/I'll Make It Worth Your While | 10 |
| 70 | Deram DM-R 285 | A Mother's Love/Might As Well Be Gone (solo) | 12 |
| 70 | Deram SML 1061 | WHITE HOT BLUE BLACK (LP) | 40 |

*(see also Web)*

## JOHNNY WATSON & KAMPAI KINGS

| | | | |
|---|---|---|---|
| 60 | Oriole CB 1532 | Moshi, Moshi, Anone!/ABDULLA & HIS LITTLE BAND: Fatima's Theme | 5 |
| 60 | Oriole CB 1532 | Moshi, Moshi, Anone!/ABDULLA & HIS LITTLE BAND: Fatima's Theme (78) | 30 |

## PAULA WATSON

| | | | |
|---|---|---|---|
| 63 | Oriole 45-CV1785 | Love Me Forever/Tell All The World About You | 20 |

## BEN WATT

| | | | |
|---|---|---|---|
| 81 | Cherry Red CHERRY 25 | Can't/Aubade/Tower Of Silence (p/s) | 8 |
| 82 | Cherry Red 12CHERRY 36 | SUMMER INTO WINTER (12" EP, with Robert Wyatt, p/s) | 10 |

*(see also Everything But The Girl)*

**TOMMY WATT**
| 57 | Parlophone GEP 8660 | TOMMY WATT AND HIS ORCHESTRA (EP) | 10 |
| 57 | Parlophone R 4377 | Overdrive/The Little Hut | 8 |
| 60 | Parlophone R 4704 | Les Cigale De St. Tropez/The Night We Got The Bird | 6 |

**WATTS**
| 73 | Jam JAM 38 | Girl You Make It Easy/Betsy Balou | 5 |

**ANDY WATTS & COBRA**
| 77 | Nebula PSS 008 | Anna/I Don't Wanna Fight (no p/s) | 35 |

**BARI WATTS**
| 80 | Banazz BANAZZ 1 | Move On Down/Rock 'N' Roll Romance (stamped die-cut sleeve, 500 only) | 20 |

**CHARLIE WATTS**
| 86 | CBS 450 253-1 | LIVE AT FULHAM TOWN HALL (LP, as Charlie Watts & His Orchestra, with insert) | 15 |
| 91 | UFO UFO CD | FROM ONE CHARLIE (CD box set with book & Charlie Parker photo, signed) | 40 |
| 91 | UFO UFO 2 LP | FROM ONE CHARLIE (10" LP, box set with book & Charlie Parker photo, signed) | 50 |
| 91 | UFO UFO 2 LP | FROM ONE CHARLIE (10" LP, box set with book & Charlie Parker photo, unsigned) | 20 |

*(see also Rolling Stones, People Band, Rocket 88)*

**NOBLE 'THIN MAN' WATTS (& HIS BAND)**
| 57 | London HLU 8627 | Hard Times (The Slop)/Midnight Flight (with His Rhythm Sparks) | 75 |
| 57 | London HLU 8627 | Hard Times (The Slop)/Midnight Flight (with His Rhythm Sparks) (78) | 20 |
| 64 | Sue WI 347 | Noble's Theme/JUNE BATEMAN: I Don't Wanna | 70 |
| 79 | Flyright 547 | BLAST OFF (LP, mono) | 20 |

*(see also Wild Jimmy Spurrill)*

**QUEENIE WATTS**
| 66 | Columbia SX 6047 | QUEEN HIGH (LP) | 30 |

**TREVOR WATTS**
| 78 | Ogun OG 526 | CYNOSURE (LP) | 20 |

**WATUSI WARRIORS**
| 59 | London HL 8866 | Wa-Chi-Bam-Ba/Kalahari | 15 |

**ASHANTI WAUGH**
| 80 | Attack TACK 20 | Babylon Wrong/BARRY BROWN: Cool Pun Yu Corner (12") | 20 |

**WAVEMAKER**
| 75 | Polydor 2383 331 15 | WHERE ARE WE CAPTAIN? (LP) | 15 |

**WAVES**
| 75 | Stretch STR5 | You Lose Out Girl/Hide Away | 20 |

**WAVING AT TRAINS**
| 80s | | WAVING AT TRAINS (EP) | 30 |

*(see also Playing At Trains)*

**WAX DOCTOR**
| 92 | Basement BRSS 011 | A New Direction/Herbal Tekno/Protplasm (12") | 15 |
| 93 | Basement BRSS 018 | Another Direction/The Stalker (12") | 10 |
| 93 | Basement BRSS 027 | New Direction (93 Remix)/What's Goin' On (12", with Jack Smooth) | 15 |
| 93 | Basement BRSS 030 | Unfriendly/Rock To The Groove (12", with Jack Smooth) | 12 |

*(see also Kev Bird)*

**WAX DOLL**
| 76 | Homer HM 009 | Shout Loud/My Oh My | 30 |

**WAXIES DARGLE**
| 69 | Polydor S83080 | HARBOUR FOLK (LP) | 25 |

**NANCY WAYBURN**
| 65 | Warner Bros WB 5646 | The World Goes On Without Me/Listen To My Heart | 15 |

**OTIS WAYGOOD BAND**
| 77 | Decca F13718 | Sweet Soul Syncopation/Who Is Your Friend? (p/s) | 12 |
| 77 | Decca 13688 | Get It Started/Red Hot Passion | 30 |
| 78 | Decca 13760 | Everything I Am/Then You Can Tell Me Goodbye | 10 |

**WAYGOOD ELLIS**
| 67 | Polydor 56729 | I Like What I'm Trying To Do/Hey Lover | 50 |

*(see also Fleur-De-Lys)*

**ALVIS WAYNE**
| 63 | Starlite ST45 104 | Don't Mean Maybe, Baby/I'd Rather Be With You | 400 |
| 73 | Injun 113 | I Gottum/Lay Your Head On My Shoulder | 10 |

**BOBBY WAYNE**
| 65 | Pye International 7N 25315 | Ballad Of A Teenage Queen/River Man | 10 |

**CARL WAYNE (& VIKINGS)**
| 64 | Pye 7N 15702 | What's A Matter Baby/Your Loving Ways (as Carl Wayne & Vikings) | 50 |
| 65 | Pye 7N 15824 | This Is Love/You Could Be Fun (as Carl Wayne & Vikings) | 40 |
| 70 | RCA RCA 2032 | Maybe God's Got Something Up His Sleeve/Rosanna | 6 |
| 72 | RCA RCA 2177 | Imagine/Sunday Kind Of Love | 5 |
| 72 | RCA RCA 2257 | Take My Hands For A While/Sweet Seasons | 5 |
| 73 | Pye 7N 45290 | You're A Star/Bluebird | 5 |
| 75 | Polydor 2058 527 | Way Back In The Fifties/Candy (You Know That I'm In Love With You) | 6 |
| 77 | Target TGT 125 | A Little Give, A Little Take/Home Lovin' Man | 6 |
| 77 | DJM DJS Weeken 10797 | Hi Summer/My Girl And Me | 6 |
| 72 | RCA SF 8239 | CARL WAYNE (LP) | 20 |

*(see also Move, Ace Kefford Stand, Cheetahs, Acid Gallery, Keith Powell [& Valets])*

**CHRIS WAYNE & ECHOES**
| 60 | Decca F 11231 | Lonely/Counting Girls | 15 |

MINT VALUE £

**JEFF WAYNE**
69   Columbia S(C)X 6330          TWO CITIES (LP, soundtrack) ............................................................................... 35
*(see also Ran-Dells)*

**JERRY WAYNE**
60   Vogue V 9169                 Half-Hearted Love/Ten Thousand Miles .................................................................. 25

**JOHN WAYNE**
73   RCA PL 13484                 AMERICA, WHY I LOVE HER (LP) ........................................................................... 15

**PAT WAYNE (& BEACHCOMBERS)**
63   Columbia DB 7121             Go Back To Daddy/Jambalaya ............................................................................... 20
63   Columbia DB 7182             Roll Over Beethoven/Is It Love? .......................................................................... 25
64   Columbia DB 7262             Bye Bye Johnny/Strictly For The Birds .................................................................. 25
64   Columbia DB 7417             Brand New Man/Nobody's Child ........................................................................... 20
65   Columbia DB 7603             Come Dance With Me/I Don't Want To Cry (solo) ................................................... 12
65   Columbia DB 7739             My Friend/Tomorrow Mine (solo) .......................................................................... 10
66   Columbia DB 7944             The Night Is Over/Hombre (solo) .......................................................................... 12

**RICK WAYNE**
93   Sunjam SR 0014               Our Younger Years/PICK A POW: Time Hard (12") ................................................. 30
94   Pathway To Freedom R+R       Almighty Father/Bad Behaviour (12") ................................................................... 80
     002

**RICK(Y) WAYNE (& OFF-BEATS)**
60   Triumph RGM 1009             Chick A'Roo/Don't Pick On Me (with Fabulous Flee-Rakkers) .................................. 50
60   Pye 7N 15289                 Make Way Baby/Goodness Knows (as Ricky Wayne & Off-Beats) ........................... 45
65   Oriole CB 306                Say You're Gonna Be My Own/It's A Crying Shame (as Rick Wayne) ....................... 20
65   CBS 201764                   In My Imagination/Don't Ever Share Your Love (as Rick Wayne) ............................. 15
*(see also [Fabulous] Flee-Rekkers)*

**TERRY WAYNE**
57   Columbia DB 4002             Matchbox/Your True Love .................................................................................... 25
57   Columbia DB 4035             Plaything/Slim Jim Tie ........................................................................................ 25
58   Columbia DB 4067             All Mama's Children/Forgive Me ........................................................................... 25
58   Columbia DB 4112             Oh! Lonesome Me/There's Only One You ............................................................. 20
58   Columbia DB 4205             Little Brother/Where My Baby Goes ..................................................................... 18
59   Columbia DB 4312             Brooklyn Bridge/She's Mine ................................................................................ 20
58   Columbia SEG 7758            TERRIFIC (EP) ..................................................................................................... 80

**THOMAS WAYNE**
59   London HLU 8846              Tragedy/Saturday Date ....................................................................................... 25
59   London HLU 8846              Tragedy/Saturday Date (78) ................................................................................ 25
59   London HL 7075               Tragedy/Saturday Date (export issue) .................................................................. 20

**WAYS & MEANS**
66   Columbia DB 7907             Little Deuce Coupe/The Little Old Lady From Pasadena ......................................... 25
66   Pye 7N 17217                 Sea Of Faces/Make The Radio A Little Louder ...................................................... 25
68   Trend TRE 1005               Breaking Up A Dream/She ................................................................................... 60

**WAY WE LIVE**
71   Dandelion DAN 8004           A CANDLE FOR JUDITH (LP, gatefold sleeve, label and sleeve DAN 8004) ............. 250
71   Dandelion DAN 8004           A CANDLE FOR JUDITH (LP, gatefold sleeve, as K 49004) ..................................... 125
*(see also Tractor, Beau)*

**WAZMO NARIZ**
78   Stiff BUY 33                 Tele-tele-phone/Wacker Drive (blue label, push-out centre) ...................................... 8
78   Stiff BUY 33                 Tele-tele-phone/Wacker Drive (red label, push-out centre) ....................................... 5

**WBI RED NINJA**
90   Red Ninja SRT90LS 2532       Danger Zone/This Mike's For Hire/Bad Testament (12") ......................................... 25

**WE'RE ONLY HUMAN**
82   VC VC 002                    I Wouldn't Treat A Dog/Hold Your Head Up High (no p/s, 500 only) ......................... 40

**WEAK LINK**
74   Slowgun SLO 341              Let's Rock/The Way Is Hard .................................................................................. 12

**WEAPON**
80   Weapon WEAP 1                It's A Mad Mad World/Set The Stage Alight (p/s) ................................................... 30
81   Virgin WEAPONE               It's A Mad Mad World/Set The Stage Alight (12", p/s, reissue) ................................ 40
*(see also Wildfire)*

**WEASELSNOUT**
72   Weaselsnout WUS 140          UNSUNG LIES (LP, private pressing) ................................................................... 500

**WEATHER**
69   Philips BF 1734              Look In My Eyes/Running Forward ........................................................................ 35
69   Philips BF 1819              Jamboree Special/Two Peculiar People ................................................................. 10

**WEATHER REPORT**
85   Nimbus 80027                 MYSTERIOUS TRAVELLER (LP, Nimbus Supercut, mail order only through Practical Hi Fi
                                  magazine) ......................................................................................................... 40

**ALFIE WEATHERBY**
58   Columbia DC 729              49 Juke Boxes/Why Am I Crying? (78, export issue) .............................................. 20

**OSCAR WEATHERS**
72   Mojo 2092 006                The Spoiler/You Want To Play ............................................................................... 15

**VIVIAN WEATHERS**
78   Virgin Frontline FL 1025     BAD WEATHER (LP) ............................................................................................ 15

**DENNIS WEAVER**
77   DJM DJS 10758                Devil In My Arms/Flat Bed Truck (p/s, promo) ......................................................... 8

**JANE WEAVER V DOVES**
98   Manchester MANC 9            Seven Day Smile/ANDY VOTEL & JANE WEAVER: Gutter Girl (p/s) ........................ 6
*(see also Doves)*

## WEAVERS
| | | | |
|---|---|---|---|
| 59 | Top Rank JAR 120 | Wild Goose Grasses/Meet The Johnson Boys | 6 |

*(see also Pete Seeger)*

## WEB (1)
| | | | |
|---|---|---|---|
| 68 | Deram DM 201 | Hatton Mill Morning/Conscience | 25 |
| 68 | Deram DM 217 | Baby Won't You Leave Me Alone/McVernon Street | 25 |
| 69 | Deram DM 253 | Monday To Friday/Harold Dubbleyew | 25 |
| 68 | Deram DML 1025 | FULLY INTERLOCKING (LP, mono) | 100 |
| 68 | Deram SML 1025 | FULLY INTERLOCKING (LP, stereo) | 120 |
| 70 | Deram DAL-R 1058 | THERAPHOSA BLONDI (LP, mono) | 200 |
| 70 | Deram SML-R 1058 | THERAPHOSA BLONDI (LP, stereo) | 125 |
| 70 | Polydor 2383 024 | I SPIDER (LP, gatefold sleeve, red label) | 400 |

*(see also John L. Watson [& Hummelflugs], Samurai, Greenslade)*

## WEB (2)
| | | | |
|---|---|---|---|
| 96 | Fat Cat 12FAT 001 | EVA EP (12", plain sleeve) | 20 |

## BARRY WEBB (O.P.M.C)
| | | | |
|---|---|---|---|
| 70 | Decca F 23012 | Live For Tomorrow Harry James/At The Hop | 8 |

## DEAN WEBB
| | | | |
|---|---|---|---|
| 59 | Parlophone R 4549 | Warm Your Heart/Hey Miss Fannie | 50 |
| 59 | Parlophone R 4587 | The Rough And The Smooth/Streamline Baby | 50 |

## DON WEBB
| | | | |
|---|---|---|---|
| 60 | Coral Q 72385 | Little Ditty Baby/I'll Be Back Home | 100 |

## GEORGE WEBB DIXIELANDERS
| | | | |
|---|---|---|---|
| 56 | Decca DFE 6351 | AND HIS DIXIELANDERS (EP) | 10 |
| 50s | Melodisc EPM7 70 | THE GEORGE WEBB DIXIELANDERS (EP) | 10 |

## JANET WEBB
| | | | |
|---|---|---|---|
| 71 | Polydor 2058-131 | I Cried For You/Mama (p/s) | 10 |

## JILLA WEBB
| | | | |
|---|---|---|---|
| 56 | MGM SP 1180 | You Gotta Love Me Now/What Do You Think It Does To Me? | 10 |

## JIMMY WEBB
| | | | |
|---|---|---|---|
| 68 | CBS 3672 | I Keep It Hid/I Need You (as Jim Webb) | 25 |
| 71 | Reprise RS 20978 | P.F. Sloan/Psalm One-Five-O | 10 |
| 73 | Reprise K 14279 | Campo De Encino/Once In The Morning | 5 |
| 68 | CBS (S) 63335 | JIM WEBB SINGS JIM WEBB (LP, as Jim Webb, laminated front cover) | 25 |
| 71 | Reprise RSLP 6421 | WORDS AND MUSIC (LP, with insert) | 20 |
| 72 | Reprise K 44134 | AND SO ON (LP) | 15 |
| 72 | Reprise K 44173 | LETTERS (LP) | 15 |
| 77 | Atlantic K 50370 | EL MIRAGE (LP, with inner sleeve) | 15 |

*(see also Strawberry Children, Glen Campbell)*

## JOHNNY WEBB
| | | | |
|---|---|---|---|
| 56 | Columbia DB 3805 | Dig/Glendora | 10 |
| 60s | Melodisc MEL 1617 | Travelin' Man/Hold Back The Town (with p/s) | 12 |
| 60s | Melodisc MEL 1617 | Travelin' Man/Hold Back The Town | 5 |

*(see also June Laverick)*

## PETA WEBB
| | | | |
|---|---|---|---|
| 73 | Topic 12TS 223 | I HAVE WANDERED IN EXILE (LP, blue label) | 35 |

*(see also Oak)*

## PETA WEBB & PETE COOPER
| | | | |
|---|---|---|---|
| 86 | Heart | HEART IS TRUE (LP) | 15 |

## ROGER WEBB (& HIS TRIO)
| | | | |
|---|---|---|---|
| 67 | RCA 1599 | A Man And His Woman/The Spiderman | 30 |
| 71 | Columbia DB 8803 | Strange Report/Summer Fancy | 12 |
| 82 | Chandos SBR 102 | The Gentle Touch/Arthur's Theme | 6 |
| 84 | Chips CH 104 | Hammer House Of Horror/Cover Theme (p/s) | 12 |
| 64 | Parlophone PMC 1233 | JOHN, PAUL AND ALL THAT JAZZ (LP) | 18 |

## SKEETER WEBB
| | | | |
|---|---|---|---|
| 55 | Parlophone CMSP 32 | Was It A Bad Dream/Your Secret's Not A Secret Anymore (export issue) | 15 |

## SONNY WEBB & CASCADES
| | | | |
|---|---|---|---|
| 64 | Oriole CB 1873 | You've Got Everything/Border Of The Blues | 45 |
| 64 | Polydor NH 52158 | You've Got Everything/Border Of The Blues (reissue) | 15 |

## A J WEBBER
| | | | |
|---|---|---|---|
| 80 | Gundog GUN 002 | OF THIS LAND (LP) | 30 |

## MARLENE WEBBER
| | | | |
|---|---|---|---|
| 70 | Bamboo BAM 33 | My Baby/BRENTFORD ALLSTARS: You Gonna Hold Me (Version) | 40 |
| 71 | Ackee ACK 120 | Natengula/Natengula-Kera (as Merlin Webber) | 18 |
| 71 | Ackee ACK 122 | Cumbaya/Hail-Hi Freedom (as Merlin Webber) | 25 |
| 71 | Smash SMA 2322 | Hard Life/COLLINS ALL STARS: Version Life (as Merlene Webber) | 50 |
| 71 | Trojan TR 7815 | Stand By Your Man/CLANCY ECCLES: Credit Squeeze | 15 |

*(see also Webber Sisters, Tonettes)*

## WEBBER SISTERS
| | | | |
|---|---|---|---|
| 67 | Island WI 3109 | My World/ALVA LEWIS: Lonely Still | 60 |

*(see also Delroy Wilson)*

## WEBBY JAY
| | | | |
|---|---|---|---|
| 79 | Awawak DD 008 | In The Rain/Rain Unlimited (12") | 20 |

## WEBS
| | | | |
|---|---|---|---|
| 68 | London HLU 10188 | This Thing Called Love/Tomorrow | 25 |

### WEBSPINNERS
| | | | |
|---|---|---|---|
| 73 | Buddah 2011 150 | Spider Man - Theme/Goin' 'Cross Town | 6 |

### BEN WEBSTER
| | | | |
|---|---|---|---|
| 55 | Columbia CLEF 33CX 10014 | MUSIC FOR LOVERS (LP) | 20 |
| 57 | Vogue Coral 10021 | TENOR SAX STYLIST (10" LP) | 40 |
| 59 | HMV CLP 1336 | BEN WEBSTER AND ASSOCIATES (LP) | 30 |
| 65 | Fontana FJL 126 | INTIMATE! (LP) | 20 |
| 69 | EMI SCX 6389 | FOR THE GUV'NOR (LP) | 20 |

### CHASE WEBSTER
| | | | |
|---|---|---|---|
| 64 | Hickory 45-1283 | Life Can Have Meaning/Where Is Your Heart | 6 |

### DEENA WEBSTER
| | | | |
|---|---|---|---|
| 68 | Parlophone R 5699 | You're Losing/Wish You Were Here | 25 |
| 68 | Parlophone R 5721 | Your Heart Is Free Just Like The Wind/Queen Merka And Me | 25 |
| 68 | Parlophone R 5738 | Scarborough Fair/The Water Is Wide | 25 |
| 69 | Parlophone R 5798 | Joey/It's Alright With Me | 25 |
| 68 | Parlophone PMC/PCS 7052 | TUESDAY'S CHILD (LP) | 200 |

### WEDDING PRESENT
| | | | |
|---|---|---|---|
| 85 | Reception REC 001 | Go Out And Get 'Em Boy/(The Moment Before) Everything's Spoiled Again (p/s, 500 only, with poster & badge) | 35 |
| 85 | Reception REC 001 | Go Out And Get 'Em Boy/(The Moment Before) Everything's Spoiled Again (p/s, 500 only, without poster & badge) | 30 |
| 85 | City Slang CSL 001 | Go Out And Get 'Em Boy/(The Moment Before) Everything's Spoiled Again (reissue, different foldout p/s, 1,000 only) | 15 |
| 86 | Reception REC 002 | Once More/At The Edge Of The Sea (p/s, 3,500 only) | 8 |
| 86 | Reception REC 003 | This Boy Can Wait/You Should Always Keep In Touch With Your Friends (p/s, matrix numbers: 003 A2 & 003 B1) | 6 |
| 86 | Reception REC 003 | This Boy Can Wait/You Should Always Keep In Touch With Your Friends (p/s, mispress both sides play B-side, matrix numbers: 003 A1 & 003 A2) | 5 |
| 87 | Reception REC 005 | My Favourite Dress/Every Mother's Son/Never Said (p/s, white vinyl, 3,000 only, 2,000 of which free with "George Best" LP) | 6 |
| 87 | Reception | A Million Miles/What Did Your Last Servant Die Of? (DJ promo, 200 only) | 25 |
| 88 | Reception REC 010X | Davni Chasy/Katrusya (promo only) | 6 |
| 88 | House Of Dolls HOD 004 | Unfaithful (Peel Session)/TRUDY: Living On A Moon/HUNTERS CLUB: Little Sister/ CLAYTOWN TROUPE: Real Life (free with House Of Dolls mag) | 5 |
| 89 | M'night Music DONG 39 CD | Pourquoi Es Tu Devenue Si Raisonable? (CD, unreleased) | 0 |
| 89 | RCA | Davni Chasy/Katrusya (promo only) | 12 |
| 90 | RCA PB 43403 | Brassneck/Don't Talk, Just Kiss (custom hand-painted p/s, 3,000 only) | 20 |
| 92 | RCA PB 45185 | Blue Eyes/Cattle And Cane (p/s) | 7 |
| 92 | RCA PB 45183 | Go Go Dancer/Don't Cry No Tears (p/s) | 6 |
| 92 | RCA PB 45181 | Three/Think That It Might (p/s) | 6 |
| 92 | RCA PB 45311 | Silver Shorts/Falling (p/s) | 6 |
| 92 | RCA PB 45313 | Come Play With Me/Pleasant Valley Sunday (p/s) | 6 |
| 92 | RCA No Cat. No. | HIT PARADE (12 x 7" in custom box) | 40 |
| 87 | Reception LEEDS 1 | GEORGE BEST (LP, 2,000 only with white vinyl 7": My Favourite Dress/ Every Mother's Son/Never Said [REC 005] & inner sleeve; later with bonus black vinyl 7" or 12" edition, £10) | 20 |
| 88 | Reception LEEDS 2 | TOMMY (LP, 1,000 signed by band, with poster & inner sleeve) | 18 |
| 91 | RCA PL 75012 | SEAMONSTERS (LP, inner) | 15 |
| 94 | RCA 8014524-044-1 | WATUSI (LP, inner) | 25 |
| 96 | Cooking Vinyl COOK 099 | SATURNALIA (LP, 2 x 10") | 20 |

### WEDGE
| | | | |
|---|---|---|---|
| 69 | Midas MD3904 | Sleep Child/Fly Away | 25 |

### WEDGEWOODS
| | | | |
|---|---|---|---|
| 64 | Pye 7N 15642 | September In The Rain/Gone Gone Away | 12 |
| 65 | Pye 7N 15846 | Peace/Summer Love | 10 |
| 68 | Columbia DB 8459 | Red Sky At Night/When Day Is Done | 15 |

### WEE CHERUBS
| | | | |
|---|---|---|---|
| 84 | Bogaten | Dreaming /Waiting For My Man (p/s, 400 only) | 175 |

### WEE THREE
| | | | |
|---|---|---|---|
| 73 | People PEO 104 | Get On Board/Get On Board (Instrumental) | 8 |

### BUDDY WEED & HIS ORCHESTRA
| | | | |
|---|---|---|---|
| 57 | Vogue V 9075 | The Kent Song/For Love | 25 |

### BERT WEEDON
| | | | |
|---|---|---|---|
| 56 | Parlophone MSP 6242 | The Boy With The Magic Guitar/Flannel-Foot | 20 |
| 57 | Parlophone R 4256 | Theme From ITV's '$64,000 Question'/Twilight Time | 20 |
| 57 | Parlophone R 4315 | The Jolly Gigolo/Soho Fair | 20 |
| 57 | Parlophone R 4381 | Play That Big Guitar/Quiet, Quiet, Ssh! | 10 |
| 58 | Parlophone R 4446 | Big Note Blues/Rippling Tango | 10 |
| 60 | Top Rank JAR 360 | Twelfth Street Rag/Querida | 5 |
| 60 | Top Rank JAR 415 | Apache/Lonely Guitar | 5 |
| 60 | Top Rank JAR 517 | Sorry Robbie/Easy Beat | 8 |
| 61 | Top Rank JAR 537 | Ginchy/Yearning | 6 |
| 61 | Top Rank JAR 559 | Mr. Guitar/Eclipse | 8 |
| 56 | Esquire EP 56 | WAXING THE WINNERS (EP) | 25 |
| 59 | Selmer Amplifiers | DEMONSTRATION RECORD WITH DAVID GELL (EP, with mailer) | 20 |
| 60 | Top Rank BUY 026 | KINGSIZE GUITAR (LP) | 20 |
| 61 | Top Rank 35/101 | HONKY TONK GUITAR (LP) | 20 |

*(see also George Chisholm, Craig Douglas, Ragpickers)*

### WEEDS
| | | | |
|---|---|---|---|
| 86 | In Tape IT 34 | China Doll/Crazy Face (p/s) | 12 |

## WEEKENDERS
| | | | |
|---|---|---|---|
| 94 | Blow Up (Blow UP BU 001) | All Grown Up/House Husband (mail-order only) | 10 |

## WEEN
| | | | |
|---|---|---|---|
| 93 | August RUST 002 LP | PURE GUAVA (2-LP) | 35 |
| 94 | Flying Nun FN31 | CHOCOLATE & CHEESE (2-LP with free 7") | 40 |
| 95 | Flying Nun FN 322 | THE POD (2-LP, reissue) | 30 |
| 96 | Flying Nun FN 386 | 12 GOLDEN COUNTRY GREATS (LP) | 40 |
| 97 | Mushroom MUSH 3LP | THE MOLLUSK (LP, inner) | 50 |
| 00 | Mushroom MUSH69LP | WHITE PEPPER (LP) | 25 |
| 03 | Sanctuary 0607684591 | QUEBEC (2-LP) | 35 |
| 06 | Schnitzel SRLP 125525 | LIVE IN TORONTO CANADA FEATURING THE SHIT CREEK BOYS (2-LP, reissue white vinyl) | 25 |
| 07 | Schnitzel SRLP 1255211 | LA CUCARACHA (LP) | 20 |

## WEENY BOPPERS
| | | | |
|---|---|---|---|
| 72 | Pye 45203 | David, Donny & Michael/Won't You Smile For Me | 8 |

## WEEPING MESSERSCHMITTS
| | | | |
|---|---|---|---|
| 86 | Upright UPT 17 | NOTHING YET (12" EP, p/s) | 15 |

## WEEZER
| | | | |
|---|---|---|---|
| 94 | Geffen GFS 85 | Undone: The Sweater Song/Mykel And Carli/Susanne/Holiday (blue vinyl, p/s) | 20 |
| 95 | Geffen GFS 88 | Buddy Holly/Jamie (p/s) | 18 |
| 95 | Geffen GFSV 95 | Say It Ain't So (Remix)/No One Else (Live & Acoustic)/Jamie (10", p/s) | 10 |
| 96 | Geffen GFS 22167 | El Scorcho/You Gave Your Love To Me Softly (p/s) | 10 |
| 01 | Geffen 497567-7 | Hash Pipe/Teenage Victory Song (p/s) | 10 |
| 01 | Geffen 497616-7 | Island In The Sun/Always (p/s, yellow vinyl) | 10 |
| 02 | Geffen 497771-7 | Keep Fishin'/Photograph (live) (p/s) | 8 |
| 05 | Geffen 9883498 | We Are All On Drugs/Beverley Hills (Urbanix Mix) (p/s, pink vinyl) | 5 |
| 95 | Geffen GEF 24629 | WEEZER (LP) | 50 |
| 96 | Geffen 425007-1 | PINKERTON (LP) | 20 |
| 02 | Geffen DGC 25007 | PINKERTON (LP, reissue) | 20 |

## WE FIVE
| | | | |
|---|---|---|---|
| 65 | Pye International 7N 25314 | You Were On My Mind/Small World | 12 |
| 66 | Pye International 7N 25346 | Let's Get Together/Cast Your Fate To The Wind | 20 |
| 66 | Pye Intl. NEP 44056 | LET'S GET TOGETHER (EP) | 60 |
| 65 | Pye Intl. NPL 28067 | YOU WERE ON MY MIND (LP) | 60 |

## WE 4
| | | | |
|---|---|---|---|
| 67 | HMV POP 1603 | Pretty Flowers/I'll Make You A Miracle | 5 |
| 69 | Major Minor MM 593 | Candy Floss Man/Perry Park | 6 |

## BOB WEIR
| | | | |
|---|---|---|---|
| 72 | Warner Bros WB 7611 | One More Saturday Night/Cassidy | 5 |

*(see also Grateful Dead, Kingfish, Bobby & Midnites)*

## FRANK WEIR & HIS ORCHESTRA
| | | | |
|---|---|---|---|
| 54 | Decca F 10271 | The Happy Wanderer/From Your Lips | 10 |
| 60 | Oriole CB 1559 | Caribbean Honeymoon/Farewell My Love | 10 |
| 62 | Philips 326560 BF | Manhunt/Chant Of The Jungle | 5 |
| 55 | Decca DFE 6226 | THE HAPPY WANDERER (EP) | 10 |

*(see also Bill Darnell, Vera Lynn, Janie Marden)*

## NORRIS WEIR (& JAMAICANS)
| | | | |
|---|---|---|---|
| 70 | Duke DU 85 | Hard On Me (with Jamaicans)/TOMMY COWAN & JAMAICANS: Please Stop The Wedding | 12 |
| 74 | Dragon DRA 1030 | Reggay Revolution/Version | 12 |
| 75 | Horse HOSS 81 | Dr. Honey/Honey Dub | 8 |

*(see also Jamaicans)*

## WEIRD STRINGS
| | | | |
|---|---|---|---|
| 80 | Velvet Moon VM 1 | Oscar Mobile/Ancient Square (foldover p/s) | 10 |
| 80 | Ace ACE 009 | Criminal Cage/Mi££ionaire (p/s) | 8 |

*(see also Paul Roland, Midnight Rags)o*

## BRUCE WELCH
| | | | |
|---|---|---|---|
| 74 | EMI EMI 2141 | Please Mr. Please/Song Of Yesterday | 50 |

*(see also Marvin, Welch & Farrar; Shadows, Cliff Richard)*

## ED WELCH
| | | | |
|---|---|---|---|
| 71 | United Artists UP35284 | Clowns/The Bird Song | 10 |
| 71 | United Artists UAS 29248 | CLOWNS (LP, with inner) | 15 |

## ELIZABETH WELCH
| | | | |
|---|---|---|---|
| 80 | Industrial IR 0012 | Stormy Weather/You're Blase (p/s) | 8 |

## HONEE WELCH
| | | | |
|---|---|---|---|
| 69 | London HLU 10288 | I'm Gonna Try/It's My Girl | 7 |

## KEN & MITZIE WELCH
| | | | |
|---|---|---|---|
| 62 | London RE-R 1275 | A PIANO, ICE BOX AND BED (EP) | 15 |

## LENNY WELCH
| | | | |
|---|---|---|---|
| 60 | London HLA 9094 | You Don't Know Me/I Need Someone | 6 |
| 62 | London HLA 9601 | Taste Of Honey/Old Cathedral | 6 |
| 63 | London HLA 9810 | Since I Fell For You/Are You Sincere | 6 |
| 64 | London HLA 9880 | Ebb Tide/Congratulations Baby | 6 |
| 64 | London HLR 9910 | If You See My Love/Father Sebastian | 6 |
| 65 | London HLR 9981 | Darling Take Me Back/Time After Time | 15 |
| 65 | London HLR 9991 | Two Different Worlds/I Was There | 8 |
| 65 | London HLR 10010 | Run To My Lovin' Arms/Coronet Blue | 20 |
| 66 | London HLR 10031 | Rags To Riches/I Want You To Worry | 10 |

MINT VALUE £

| | | | |
|---|---|---|---|
| 66 | London HA-R/SH-R 8267 | TWO DIFFERENT WORLDS (LP) | 20 |
| 66 | London HA-R 8290 | RAGS TO RICHES (LP) | 20 |

## TIM WELCH
| 60 | Columbia DB 4529 | Weak In The Knees/A Boy And A Girl In Love | 7 |
|---|---|---|---|

## WELD OF LIQUOR
| 95 | Weld Record WELD 05 | We Are The Weld/For Manze's Sake (vinegar-scented p/s) | 10 |
|---|---|---|---|

## WELFARE STATE
| 78 | Look LKLP 6347 | WELFARE STATE SONGS (LP, with insert) | 60 |
|---|---|---|---|

## LAWRENCE WELK ORCHESTRA
| 56 | Vogue Coral Q 72140 | Chain Gang/The Poor People Of Paris | 5 |
|---|---|---|---|
| 56 | Vogue Coral Q 72141 | The 'Threepenny Opera' Theme/Rock And Roll Waltz | 5 |
| 57 | Vogue Coral Q 72233 | Pizzicato Waltz/Whispering Heart | 5 |
| 57 | Vogue Coral Q 72256 | Around The World In 80 Days/Ten Little Trees | 5 |
| 60 | London HLD 9229 | Last Date/Remember Lolita | 5 |
| 61 | London HLD 9261 | Calcutta (Nicolette)/Melodie D'Amour | 5 |
| 64 | Dot DS 16697 | The 'Addams Family' Theme/Apples And Bananas | 10 |

## WELL WISHERS
| 73 | Pendant PEN 1 | Find Mister Jameson/Weird | 40 |
|---|---|---|---|

## PAUL WELLER
### SINGLES
| 92 | Go! Discs GOD 86 | Uh Huh Oh Yeh/Fly On The Wall (7"; paper or plastic labels) | 6 |
|---|---|---|---|
| 92 | Go! Discs GOD 91 | Above The Clouds/Everything Has A Price To Pay (7"; paper or plastic labels) | 6 |
| 93 | Go! Discs GOD 102 | Sunflower/Bull-Rush-Magic Bus (Live at RAH 10.92) (7") | 6 |
| 93 | Go! Discs GOD 104 | Wild Wood/Ends Of The Earth (7") | 6 |
| 93 | Go! Discs GODT 104 | Wild Wood/Ends Of The Earth (10", numbered with poster) | 10 |
| 93 | Matrix: WELLER+F1 | The Loved (blank clear flexi with The Big Issue mag) | 12 |
| 94 | Go! Discs GOD 121 | Out Of The Sinking/Sexy Sadie/Sunflower (Lynch Mob Dub) (7") | 5 |
| 00 | Island IS 760 | He's The Keeper/Helioscentric/Bang-Bang (7", 3rd April 2000) | 5 |
| 05 | V2 VVR 5030597 | Early Morning Rain/Come Together (7", red vinyl, die-cut sleeve, 4,000 only) | 6 |
| 05 | V2 VVR 5033410 | From The Floorboards Up/From The Floorboards Up (Lynchmob Remix - Instrumental) (7", gatefold p/s, 4,000 only) | 5 |
| 05 | V2 VVR 5033417 | From The Floorboards Up/Oranges And Rosewater (2nd 7", green & orange vinyl, stickered PVC sleeve) | 5 |
| 09 | Universal (No cat no) | 7 & 3 Is The Striker's Name (one sided 7", screen printed sleeve, 1000 only) | 50 |
| 10 | V2 | Aim High (Aim Higher)/Pieces Of A Dream (Dreams In Pieces)/Aim High (The Higher Aim)/Aim High (Like Water Needs A Flower) All The Amorphous Androgymous remixes (10", p/s, 500 only for 2010 Record Store Day) | 25 |
| 13 | Virgin VFW 1 | Flame-Out!/The Olde Original 'twin Virgins' label) | 12 |
| 14 | Virgin RSD14PW | Brand New Toys/Landslide ('two virgins' label, white vinyl, stickered die-cut sleeve) | 20 |

### ALBUMS
| 92 | Go! Discs 828 343-1 | PAUL WELLER (LP, gatefold sleeve, stapled-in lyric booklet) | 50 |
|---|---|---|---|
| 93 | Go! Discs 828 435-1 | WILD WOOD (LP, gatefold sleeve with 'obi' band inner & poster) | 35 |
| 94 | Go! Discs 828 513-1 | WILD WOOD (LP, gatefold sleeve with 'obi' band & poster; reissue with extra track 'Hung Up', 'second edition' on label of side 2) | 50 |
| 94 | Go! Discs 828 561-1 | LIVE WOOD (2-LP, single sleeve with picture inners) | 30 |
| 95 | Go! Discs 828 619-1 | STANLEY ROAD (LP, gatefold sleeve with Excerpts booklet) | 50 |
| 95 | Go! Discs 850 070-7 | STANLEY ROAD (6 x 7" singles in 7" box) | 40 |
| 97 | Island ILPS 8058 | HEAVY SOUL (LP, gatefold sleeve with picture inner & insert) | 40 |
| 97 | Island CID 8058 | HEAVY SOUL ("unofficial" wooden box set, 1,000 only, incl.: hinged wooden box, numbered certificate, promo CD, 5 postcards, CD booklet, promo 7", 5 guitar plectrums & polo shirt) | 125 |
| 98 | Island ILPSD 8080 | MODERN CLASSICS - THE GREATEST HITS (2-LP, gatefold sleeve with picture inners & insert) | 50 |
| 98 | Island IBX 8080 | MODERN CLASSICS (box set, numbered 4 x 7" + 16-page photo book & colour print) | 40 |
| 00 | Island ILPS 8093 | HELIOCENTRIC (LP, with foldout poster) | 25 |
| 01 | Independiente ISOM26LP | DAYS OF SPEED (2-LP, gatefold sleeve with pic inners) | 80 |
| 02 | Independiente ISOM33LP | ILLUMINATION (LP, rounded corners, gatefold sleeve with picture inner & booklet) | 30 |
| 04 | V2 VVR 1026902 | STUDIO 150 (CD, autographed for competition) | 30 |
| 04 | V2 VVR 1026901 | STUDIO 150 (LP, 2,000 only, with inner sleeve) | 25 |
| 90s | (no label) | ACOUSTIC EP (live DVD, with Gem Archer, features radio interview + 5 songs including U.S. TV appearance, fan club issue) | 30 |
| 03 | Universal 0635271 | FLY ON THE WALL (3-LP, stickered sleeve) | 50 |
| 05 | V2 VVR 1033201 | AS IS NOW (2-LP, gatefold, inners, print) | 30 |
| 06 | V2 VVR 1039391 | CATCH FLAME (2-LP, gatefold, 2 inners, free 7") | 25 |
| 08 | Island 176935 | 22 DREAMS (2-LP, gatefold, booklet, with Island 'pink eye' logo) | 50 |
| 10 | Island 2732868 | WAKE UP THE NATION (LP, flipback sleeve, inserts) | 15 |

### PROMOS
| 91 | Freedom High FHP 1 | Into Tomorrow/Here's A New Thing (7", white label promo, 1991) | 25 |
|---|---|---|---|
| 91 | Freedom High FHPT 1 | Into Tomorrow/Here's A New Thing/That Spiritual Feeling/Into Tomorrow (8-Track Demo) (12", white label promo, 1991) | 35 |
| 92 | Echantillon (no cat. no.) | Uh Huh Oh Yeh/Arrival Time/Fly On The Wall/ Always There To Fool You (12", yellow label test pressing) | 50 |
| 92 | Go! Discs KOSX 1 | Kosmos (12", 1-sided) | 25 |
| 92 | Go! Discs GOXDJ 102 | Kosmos (12", printed label) | 25 |
| 93 | Go! Discs GOPRO 102 | Sunflower (12") | 12 |
| 93 | Go! Discs GOTDJ 104 | Wild Wood/Ends Of The Earth (10") | 20 |
| 93 | Go! Discs GOXDJ 111 | Hung Up/Foot Of The Mountain (Live Royal Albert Hall 23.11.93)/The Loved/ Kosmos (Lynch Mob Bonus Beats) (12", printed white labels) | 10 |
| 94 | Go! Discs PNME 1 | Shadow Of The Sun (Live at Wolverhampton Civic Hall 9.3.94)/ Sunflower (Lynch Mob Dub Edit)/Wild Wood (Sheared Wood - Remixed by Portishead with A. Utley) (white label promo for NME cover mount) | 35 |

| 94 | Island GODJB 121 | Out Of The Sinking/Sexy Sadie (7", jukebox issue) | 5 |
| 95 | Go! Discs LYNCH 1 | Lynch Mob Beats (12", stamped 1-sided white label, 500 only) | 60 |
| 95 | Go! Discs SPLINT 1 | Walk On Gilded Splinters (12", white label test pressing, 1-sided, 1995) | 70 |
| 95 | Go! Discs (no cat. no.) | CD SAMPLER (CD, given away in queue for 100 Club gig, 200 only) | 45 |
| 95 | Disctronics matrix: WELLERSPEC 01 | OUR PRICE PAUL WELLER SPECIAL (CD, in-store album, no inlay, PVC outer) | 60 |
| 96 | Go! Discs PWRT 1 | PEACOCK SUIT (CD, 7-track, picture disc in cloth bag) | 25 |
| 97 | Island HEAVY 1 | Heavy Soul (Pt 1)/Heavy Soul (Pt 2) (7", Island sleeve) | 50 |
| 97 | Island PWICD 1 | HEAVY SOUL (box set: interview CD, EPK, 5 cards & insert) | 45 |
| 97 | Southern Songs WELLER 1 | LIVE... FROM THE ROOF OF THE HAYWARD GALLERY (LP, finished sleeve, white labels) | 30 |
| 97 | Island KINGS 1 | KINGS ROAD (CD sampler, 350 only) | 45 |
| 98 | Island 12IS 711DJ | Brand New Start/Right Underneath It (12") | 12 |
| 99 | Island 12IS 734DJ | Wild Wood (The Sheared Wood Remix)/Science (Lynch Mob Remix with Psychonauts) (12", white label, only 130 copies mailed out) | 18 |
| 99 | Island INTCD 3 | IN CONVERSATION (interview CD, gatefold card p/s) | 30 |
| 00 | Island HELIO-1 | Heliocentric (Two Lone Swordsmen 4UR Mix)/Heliocentric (Original Version)/There's No Drinking After You're Dead (Noonday Underground Mix) (12" white label) | 30 |
| 01 | Independiente DOSB 1 | DAYS OF SPEED SELECTIONS (3-CD set, card outer sleeve with CDs in individual card inners) | 50 |
| 03 | Universal CUFF 1 | BUTTON DOWNS (LP, promo-only vinyl edition of third disc of cover versions from Fly On The Wall) | 35 |
| 05 | V2 VVR 5033488P | From The Floorboards Up (7", white label test pressing, stamped white sleeve) | 25 |
| 05 | V2 VVR 1033202P | SINGLES BOX (box set, mail-order only, houses all As Is Now 7"s; priced without singles) | 20 |
| 05 | Universal STAN 1 | STANLEY ROAD - 10TH ANNIVERSARY EP (7") | 10 |

*(see also Jam, Style Council, Smokin' Mojo Filters, Andy Lewis & Paul Weller, Paul Weller Movement, Noonday Underground)*

## PAUL WELLER MOVEMENT

| 91 | Freedom High FHP 1 | Into Tomorrow/Here's A New Thing (7", with or without 'Paul Weller Movement' printed on label) | 8 |
| 91 | Freedom High FHPT 1 | Into Tomorrow/Here's A New Thing/That Spiritual Feeling/ Into Tomorrow (8-Track Demo) (12") | 12 |

## PAUL WELLER & THE RAKES

| 05 | V2 FP01 | Shine On/Ausland Mission (Promo, given out at Fred Perry party) | 45 |

## ORSON WELLES

| 59 | Top Rank TR 5001 | The Courtroom Scene From The Film 'Compulsion' (both sides) (in p/s) | 12 |
| 84 | Splash SP 29 | I Know What It Is To Be Young (But You Don't Know What It Is To Be Old)/ Love Is A Lovely Word (p/s) | 8 |

## NICK WELLINGS & SECTION

| 77 | The Label TLR 011 | You Better Move On/Punk Funk | 6 |

## WELLINGTON

| 74 | Concord CON 029 | Alright I'll See You Tonight/How Would You Like To Rock With Me | 8 |
| 74 | Concord CON 031 | Catch Us If You Can/Superstar | 8 |

## BOBBY WELLINS

| 78 | Vortex VS1 | LIVE JUBILATION (LP) | 40 |
| 78 | Vortex VS2 | DREAMS ARE FREE (LP) | 40 |

## BOBBY WELLS

| 68 | Beacon 3-102 | Let's Copp A Groove/Recipe For Love (yellow label) | 30 |
| 68 | Beacon 3-102 | Let's Copp A Groove/Recipe For Love (white label) | 20 |
| 68 | Beacon 3-102 | Let's Copp A Groove/Recipe For Love (green label) | 15 |
| 79 | Grapevine GRP 124 | Be's That Way Sometimes/Recipe For Love | 10 |

## BRIAN WELLS

| 72 | Spark SRL 1082 | Paper Party/Just A Summer High | 6 |

## COBY WELLS

| 67 | Decca F 12560 | My Feet Ache/Venus De Milo | 12 |

## HOUSTON WELLS (& MARKSMEN)

| 62 | Parlophone R 4955 | This Song Is Just For You/Paradise | 10 |
| 62 | Parlophone R 4980 | Shutters And Boards/North Wind | 10 |
| 63 | Parlophone R 5031 | Only The Heartaches/Can't Stop Pretending | 8 |
| 63 | Parlophone R 5069 | Blowing Wild (The Ballad Of Black Gold)/Crazy Dreams | 10 |
| 64 | Parlophone R 5099 | Anna Marie/Moon Watch Over My Baby | 10 |
| 64 | Parlophone R 5141 | Galway Bay/Livin' Alone (as Houston Wells & Outlaws) | 10 |
| 65 | Parlophone R 5226 | Blue Of The Night/Coming Home (solo) | 7 |
| 68 | CBS 3572 | Teach Me Little Children/Does My Ring Hurt Your Finger | 6 |
| 63 | Parlophone GEP 8878 | JUST FOR YOU (EP) | 50 |
| 64 | Parlophone GEP 8914 | RAMONA (EP) | 60 |
| 64 | Parlophone PMC 1215 | WESTERN STYLE (LP) | 50 |

*(see also Marksmen, Outlaws)*

## JEAN WELLS

| 71 | Mojo 2092 023 | After Loving You/Puttin' The Best On The Outside | 20 |
| 70 | Sonet SNTF 606 | WORLD! HERE COMES JEAN WELLS (LP) | 50 |

## JOHNNY WELLS (1)

| 59 | Columbia DB 4377 | Lonely Moon/The One And Only One | 30 |

## JOHNNY WELLS (2)

| 67 | Parlophone R 5559 | Guess I'm Dumb/Wondering Why | 20 |

## JUNIOR WELLS

| 66 | Delmark DS 9612 | Hoodoo Man Blues (blue label) | 30 |
| 66 | Delmark DS 628 | Southside Blues Jam (blue label) | 20 |
| 68 | Mercury MF 1056 | Girl You Lit My Fire/It's A Man Down There | 15 |
| 66 | Delmark DJB 1 | BLUES WITH A BEAT (EP) | 35 |
| 68 | Fontana (S)TFL 6084 | IT'S MY LIFE BABY (LP) | 40 |

MINT VALUE £

| | | | |
|---|---|---|---|
| 68 | Vanguard SVRL 19011 | COMING AT YOU (LP, also stereo, VSD 79262) | 30 |
| 68 | Vanguard SVRL 19028 | IT'S MY LIFE BABY (LP, reissue) | 25 |
| 68 | Mercury SMCL 20130 | YOU'RE TUFF ENOUGH (LP) | 45 |
| 71 | Delmark DS 628 | SOUTHSIDE BLUES JAM (LP) | 22 |
| 75 | Delmark DS 635 | JUNIOR WELLS ON TAP (LP) | 15 |

*(see also Buddy Guy)*

## KITTY WELLS
| | | | |
|---|---|---|---|
| 55 | Brunswick OE 9149 | KITTY SINGS (EP) | 12 |

## MARY WELLS
| | | | |
|---|---|---|---|
| 62 | Oriole CBA 1762 | You Beat Me To The Punch/Old Love | 70 |
| 63 | Oriole CBA 1796 | Two Lovers/Operator | 50 |
| 63 | Oriole CBA 1829 | Laughing Boy/Two Wrongs Don't Make A Right | 50 |
| 63 | Oriole CBA 1847 | Your Old Standby/What Love Has Joined Together | 50 |
| 63 | Stateside SS 242 | You Lost The Sweetest Boy/What's Easy For Two Is So Hard For One | 25 |
| 63 | Stateside SS 242 | You Lost The Sweetest Boy/What's Easy For Two Is So Hard For One (DJ Copy) | 100 |
| 64 | Stateside SS 288 | My Guy/Oh Little Boy | 12 |
| 64 | Stateside SS 288 | My Guy/Oh Little Boy (DJ Copy) | 100 |
| 64 | Stateside SS 316 | Once Upon A Time (with Marvin Gaye)/What's The Matter With You, Baby | 40 |
| 64 | Stateside SS 316 | Once Upon A Time (with Marvin Gaye)/What's The Matter With You, Baby (DJ Copy | 85 |
| 65 | Stateside SS 372 | Ain't It The Truth/Stop Takin' Me For Granted | 30 |
| 65 | Stateside SS 372 | Ain't It The Truth/Stop Takin' Me For Granted (DJ Copy) | 50 |
| 65 | Stateside SS 396 | Use Your Head/Everlovin' Boy | 30 |
| 65 | Stateside SS 396 | Use Your Head/Everlovin' Boy (DJ Copy) | 50 |
| 65 | Stateside SS 415 | Never Never Leave Me/Why Don't You Let Yourself Go | 20 |
| 65 | Stateside SS 415 | Never Never Leave Me/Why Don't You Let Yourself Go (DJ Copy) | 50 |
| 65 | Stateside SS 439 | He's A Lover/I'm Learnin' | 25 |
| 65 | Stateside SS 439 | He's A Lover/I'm Learnin' (DJ Copy) | 50 |
| 65 | Stateside SS 463 | Me Without You/I'm Sorry | 25 |
| 65 | Stateside SS 463 | Me Without You/I'm Sorry (DJ Copy) | 50 |
| 68 | Stateside SS 2111 | The Doctor/Two Lovers' History | 20 |
| 66 | Atlantic AT 4067 | Dear Lover/Can't You See (You're Losing Me) | 50 |
| 66 | Atlantic 584 054 | Me And My Baby/Such A Sweet Thing | 20 |
| 67 | Atlantic 584 104 | (Hey You) Set My Soul On Fire/Coming Home | 18 |
| 70 | Direction 58-4816 | Dig The Way I Feel/Love Shooting Bandit | 15 |
| 72 | Atlantic K 10254 | Dear Lover/Can't You See (You're Losing Me) (reissue) | 10 |
| 65 | Tamla Motown TME 2007 | MARY WELLS (EP) | 100 |
| 63 | Oriole PS 40045 | TWO LOVERS (LP) | 80 |
| 63 | Oriole PS 40051 | BYE BYE BABY (LP) | 90 |
| 64 | Stateside SL 10095 | SINGS MY GUY (LP) | 70 |
| 65 | Stateside SL 10133 | MARY WELLS (LP) | 80 |
| 65 | Tamla Motown TML 11006 | MY BABY JUST CARES FOR ME (LP) | 55 |
| 66 | Stateside S(S)L 10171 | LOVE SONGS TO THE BEATLES (LP) | 50 |
| 66 | Tamla Motown TML 11032 | GREATEST HITS (LP) | 35 |
| 68 | Stateside S(S)L 10266 | SERVIN' UP SOME SOUL (LP) | 50 |
| 68 | Atlantic 587 049 | THE TWO SIDES OF MARY WELLS (LP) | 30 |
| 69 | T. Motown (S)TML 11102 | VINTAGE STOCK (LP, unissued) | 0 |

*(see also Marvin Gaye)*

## ALEX WELSH & DIXIELANDERS
| | | | |
|---|---|---|---|
| 55 | Decca F 10538 | I'll Build A Stairway To Paradise/Eccentric | 5 |
| 55 | Decca F 10557 | Blues My Naughtie Sweetie Gives To Me/Shoe Shiner's Blues | 5 |
| 55 | Decca F 10652 | What Can I Say After I Say I'm Sorry/Hard-Hearted Hannah | 5 |
| 61 | Columbia DB 4686 | Tansy/Memphis March | 10 |
| 55 | Decca DFE 6254 | DIXIELANDERS AT THE RFH (EP) | 10 |

## DANNY WELTON
| | | | |
|---|---|---|---|
| 60 | Coral Q 72409 | Boogie Woogie/To Each His Own | 5 |

## WENDY & LEMMY
| | | | |
|---|---|---|---|
| 82 | Bronze BRO 151 | Stand By Your Man/No Class/Masterplan (p/s) | 15 |

*(see also Motorhead)*

## WE'RE TIRED
| | | | |
|---|---|---|---|
| 77 | Deadline DEADS 8 | My Life's On The Line/Against All Odds (p/s) | 20 |
| 77 | Deadline DEADS 11 | Guide Me Through Hell/Time Is Against Me (p/s) | 25 |
| 78 | Deadline DEADS 15 | Over The Edge/Anal Retentive (p/s, as We're Tired & We're Proud) | 8 |
| 77 | Deadline DEADLP 2 | FIND THE PRICE IN TIME (LP) | 50 |

## WERLWINDS
| | | | |
|---|---|---|---|
| 61 | Columbia DB 4650 | Winding It Up/Dig Deep | 22 |

## HOWARD WERTH & MOONBEAMS
| | | | |
|---|---|---|---|
| 74 | Charisma CB 225 | Lucinda/Jonah | 5 |

*(see also Audience)*

## BRIAN WESKE
| | | | |
|---|---|---|---|
| 62 | Oriole CB 1723 | In The Midst Of The Crowd/All Mine Alone | 15 |
| 62 | Oriole CB 1776 | 24 Hours In A Day/Where Does The Clown Go | 15 |

## FRED WESLEY & J.B.S
| | | | |
|---|---|---|---|
| 73 | Polydor 2066 322 | Doing It To Death/Everybody Got Soul (with J.B.s) | 5 |
| 74 | Mojo 2093 025 | J.B. Shout/Back Stabbers (with J.B.s) | 5 |
| 80 | RSO RSO 67 | Houseparty/I Make Music (solo) | 5 |
| 80 | RSO RSO 67 | Houseparty/I Make Music (12", solo) | 10 |
| 74 | Polydor 2391 125 | DAMN RIGHT, I AM SOMEBODY (LP, with J.B.s) | 25 |
| 74 | Polydor 2391 161 | BREAKIN' BREAD (LP, with J.B.s) | 20 |

*(see also James Brown, J.B.s)*

## WES MINSTER FIVE
| | | | |
|---|---|---|---|
| 64 | Carnival CV 7017 | Shakin' The Blues/Railroad Blues | 50 |
| 65 | Carnival CV 7019 | Sticks And Stones/Mickey's Monkey | 50 |

*(see also Maynell Wilson, Dave Greenslade)*

## ADAM 'BATMAN' WEST
| | | | |
|---|---|---|---|
| 76 | Target TGT 111 | Batman And Robin/The Story Of Batman | 7 |

## DODIE WEST
| | | | |
|---|---|---|---|
| 64 | Decca F 12046 | Goin' Out Of My Head/Is He Feeling Blue | 15 |
| 65 | Piccadilly 7N 35239 | In The Deep Of The Night/Rovin' Boy (in p/s) | 30 |
| 65 | Piccadilly 7N 35239 | In The Deep Of The Night/Rovin' Boy | 20 |
| 65 | Piccadilly 7N 35261 | Thinking Of You/And Love Will Come | 8 |
| 66 | Piccadilly 7N 35287 | Make The World Go Away/Who Does He Think He Is | 8 |
| 68 | Philips BF 1698 | Living In Limbo/Birdie Told Me | 7 |

## HARRY & JEANIE WEST
| | | | |
|---|---|---|---|
| 60 | Melodisc EPM 7-111 | SOUTHERN MOUNTAIN FOLK SONGS (LP) | 15 |

## HEDY WEST
| | | | |
|---|---|---|---|
| 65 | Topic 12T 117 | OLD TIMES AND HARD TIMES (LP) | 20 |
| 66 | Topic 12T 146 | PRETTY SARO (LP) | 20 |
| 67 | Topic 12T 163 | BALLADS (LP, with Bill Clifton) | 20 |
| 67 | Fontana STL 5432 | SERVES'EM FINE (LP) | 20 |

## KEITH WEST
| | | | |
|---|---|---|---|
| 67 | Parlophone R 5623 | Excerpt From "A Teenage Opera"/MARK WIRTZ ORCHESTRA: Theme From "A Teenage Opera" | 8 |
| 67 | Parlophone R 5651 | Sam (From "A Teenage Opera')/MARK WIRTZ'S MOOD MOSAIC: Thimble Full Of Puzzles (promos in art sleeve) | 30 |
| 67 | Parlophone R 5651 | Sam (From "A Teenage Opera')/MARK WIRTZ'S MOOD MOSAIC: Thimble Full Of Puzzles | 12 |
| 68 | Parlophone R 5713 | On A Saturday/The Kid Was A Killer | 65 |
| 72 | Parlophone R 5957 | Excerpt From "A Teenage Opera"/Sam (From "A Teenage Opera") | 7 |
| 73 | Deram DM 402 | Riding For A Fall/Days About To Rain | 7 |
| 74 | Deram DM 410 | Havin' Someone/Know There's No Livin' Without You | 7 |

*(see also Tomorrow, Four + One, In Crowd, Mark Wirtz)*

## LESLIE WEST('S MOUNTAIN)
| | | | |
|---|---|---|---|
| 69 | Bell BLL 1078 | Dreams Of Milk And Honey/Wheels On Fire (as Leslie West's Mountain) | 20 |
| 69 | Bell SBLL 126 | MOUNTAIN (LP, as Leslie West's Mountain) | 40 |
| 75 | RCA RS 1009 | THE GREAT FATSBY (LP) | 20 |

*(see also Jolliver Arkansas, Mountain, West Bruce & Laing)*

## MAE WEST
| | | | |
|---|---|---|---|
| 67 | Stateside SS 2021 | Twist And Shout/Day Tripper | 15 |
| 73 | MGM 2006 203 | Great Balls Of Fire/Men | 15 |
| 56 | Brunswick LAT 8082 | THE FABULOUS MAE WEST (LP) | 40 |
| 67 | Stateside (S)SL 10197 | WAY OUT WEST (LP) | 20 |
| 73 | Polydor 2315 207 | GREAT BALLS OF FIRE (LP) | 15 |

## TABBY WEST
| | | | |
|---|---|---|---|
| 58 | Capitol CL 14861 | All That I Want/If You Promise Not To Tell | 10 |

## MIKE WESTBROOK (CONCERT BAND)
| | | | |
|---|---|---|---|
| 69 | Deram DM 234 | A Life Of Its Own/Can't Get It Out Of My Mind | 20 |
| 70 | Deram DM 286 | Requiem/Hooray | 20 |
| 70 | Deram DM 311 | Original Peter/Magic Garden (with Norma Winstone) | 200 |
| 67 | Deram DML 1013 | CELEBRATION (LP, as Mike Westbrook Concert Band) | 100 |
| 68 | Deram DML/SML 1031 | RELEASE (LP) | 80 |
| 69 | Deram SML 1047 | MARCHING SONG VOL. 1 (LP) | 80 |
| 69 | Deram SML 1048 | MARCHING SONG VOL. 2 (LP) | 80 |
| 70 | Deram SML 1069 | LOVE SONGS (LP, as Mike Westbrook Concert Band with Norma Winstone) | 80 |
| 71 | RCA SER 5612 | TYGER: A CELEBRATION OF WILLIAM BLAKE (LP, with insert) | 100 |
| 72 | RCA Neon NE 10 | MIKE WESTBROOK'S METROPOLIS (LP, gatefold sleeve) | 75 |
| 72 | Cadillac SGC 1001 | LIVE (LP, private pressing) | 25 |
| 75 | RCA SF 8433 | CITADEL/ROOM 315 (2-LP, with John Surman) | 30 |
| 75 | Transatlantic TRA 323 | LOVE/DREAM & VARIATIONS (LP) | 20 |
| 76 | Transatlantic TRA 312 | PLAYS FOR THE RECORD (LP, as Mike Westwood's Brass Band) | 18 |
| 78 | Original ORA 001 | GOOSE SAUCE (LP) | 18 |
| 78 | Original ORA 002 | PIANO (LP) | 18 |
| 79 | RCA PL 25252 | MAMA CHICAGO (LP) | 18 |
| 80 | Original ORA 203 | WESTBROOK BLAKE (LP) | 25 |
| 82 | Original ORA 309 | THE CORTEGE (LP) | 25 |
| 83 | Westbrook LWN 1 | A LITTLE WESTBROOK MUSIC (LP) | 25 |

*(see also Solid Gold Cadillac, John Surman, Norma Winstone)*

## WEST, BRUCE & LAING
| | | | |
|---|---|---|---|
| 73 | RSO 2090 113 | Dirty Shoes/Backfire | 6 |

*(see also Jack Bruce, Leslie West, Mountain)*

## WEST COAST CONSORTIUM
| | | | |
|---|---|---|---|
| 67 | Pye 7N 17352 | Some Other Someday/Looking Back | 20 |
| 68 | Pye 7N 17482 | Colour Sergeant Lillywhite/Lady From Baltimore | 45 |

*(see also Consortium)*

## WEST COAST DELEGATION
| | | | |
|---|---|---|---|
| 67 | Deram DM 113 | Reach The Top/Mr. Personality Man | 20 |

## WEST COAST KNACK
| | | | |
|---|---|---|---|
| 67 | Capitol CL 15497 | I'm Aware/Time Waits For No One | 20 |

## WEST COAST POP ART EXPERIMENTAL BAND
| | | | |
|---|---|---|---|
| 68 | Reprise RSLP 6298 | A CHILD'S GUIDE TO GOOD AND EVIL (LP) | 250 |

## WESTERN EYES
| | | | |
|---|---|---|---|
| 78 | United Artists UP 36414 | Sweet Talk/Operator | 5 |

## WEST FIVE
| | | | |
|---|---|---|---|
| 65 | HMV POP 1396 | Congratulations/She Mine | 40 |
| 65 | HMV POP 1428 | Someone Ain't Right/Just Like Romeo And Juliet | 35 |
| 66 | HMV POP 1513 | If It Don't Work Out/Back To Square One | 20 |

*(see also Ferris Wheel)*

## WEST INDIANS
| | | | |
|---|---|---|---|
| 68 | Doctor Bird DB 1121 | Right On Time/Hokey Pokey | 45 |
| 68 | Doctor Bird DB 1127 | Falling In Love/I Mean It | 45 |
| 69 | Camel CA 16 | Strange Whisperings/CARL DAWKINS: Hard To Handle | 20 |
| 71 | Dynamic DYN 413 | Never Gonna Give You Up/REBELLIOUS SUBJECTS: Never Give Up | 10 |

*(see also Eric Donaldson, Prunes, Kilowatts, Upsetters)*

## CLIVE WESTLAKE
| | | | |
|---|---|---|---|
| 68 | Fontana TF 940 | 199 Days/From The Beginning To The End | 6 |

## JILL WESTLAKE
| | | | |
|---|---|---|---|
| 58 | Columbia DB 4132 | Sharin'/Over And Over Again | 12 |

## KEVIN WESTLAKE & GARY FARR
| | | | |
|---|---|---|---|
| 68 | Marmalade 598 007 | Everyday/Green | 20 |

*(see also Gary Farr & T-Bones, T-Bones, Blossom Toes, B.B. Blunder)*

## WESTLAND STEAMBOAT
| | | | |
|---|---|---|---|
| 70 | CBS | Born Under A Bad Sign/Missouri Train | 10 |

## MALCOLM WESTLEIGHS BAND
| | | | |
|---|---|---|---|
| 73 | Coysti CT 11 | High Again/Delta Lady (p/s) | 20 |

## WESTMORELITES
| | | | |
|---|---|---|---|
| 70 | Clandisc CLA 217 | Zion/CLANCY ECCLES & DYNAMITES: Revival | 8 |

*(see also Minstrels)*

## GLEN WESTON
| | | | |
|---|---|---|---|
| 67 | Columbia DB8253 | Pattern People/In The Still Of The night | 20 |
| 68 | Columbia DB 8328 | With This Ring/Liane | 5 |

## KIM WESTON
| | | | |
|---|---|---|---|
| 64 | Stateside SS 359 | A Little More Love/Go Ahead And Laugh | 100 |
| 64 | Stateside SS 359 | A Little More Love/Go Ahead And Laugh (DJ copy) | 150 |
| 65 | Tamla Motown TMG 511 | I'm Still Loving You/Just Loving You | 180 |
| 65 | Tamla Motown TMG 511 | I'm Still Loving You/Just Loving You (DJ copy) | 300 |
| 65 | Tamla Motown TMG 538 | Take Me In Your Arms (Rock Me A Little While)/Don't Compare Me With Her | 80 |
| 65 | Tamla Motown TMG 538 | Take Me In Your Arms (Rock Me A Little While)/Don't Compare Me With Her (DJ copy) | 100 |
| 66 | Tamla Motown TMG 554 | Helpless/A Love Like Yours | 100 |
| 66 | Tamla Motown TMG 554 | Helpless/A Love Like Yours (DJ Copy) | 400 |
| 67 | MGM MGM 1338 | I Got What You Need/Someone Like You (DJ copy) | 30 |
| 67 | MGM MGM 1357 | That's Groovy/Land Of Tomorrow | 30 |
| 68 | MGM MGM 1382 | Nobody/You're Just The Kind Of Guy (DJ copy) | 50 |
| 69 | Major Minor MM 619 | From Both Sides Now/We Try Harder | 6 |
| 70 | Major Minor MM 683 | Danger, Heartbreak Dead Ahead/I'll Be Thinking | 12 |
| 75 | Tamla Motown TMG 1000 | Do Like I Do/MARVELETTES: Finders Keepers, Losers Weepers | 100 |
| 65 | Tamla Motown TME 2005 | KIM WESTON (EP) | 110 |
| 66 | Tamla Motown TME 2015 | ROCK ME A LITTLE WHILE (EP) | 450 |
| 67 | MGM MGM-C(S) 8055 | FOR THE FIRST TIME (LP) | 50 |
| 71 | Stax 2362 021 | KIM KIM KIM (LP) | 30 |

*(see also Marvin Gaye & Kim Weston)*

## MARK WESTON & THE TWO PART TARIFF
| | | | |
|---|---|---|---|
| 69 | Tepee TPR 1006 | Standing At The Bus Stop/Portrait On The Blackboard | 40 |

## PETE WESTON
| | | | |
|---|---|---|---|
| 70 | Gas GAS 146 | Something Sweet/BIM & BAM: Love Letters | 12 |
| 70 | Punch PH 28 | In The Mood (& His Band)/Slide Mongoose (actually "Sly Mongoose") | 8 |
| 72 | Ashanti ASH 402 | Pup'n Temper/PETE'S ALL STARS: Version 2 | 8 |

*(see also I Roy)*

## RANDY WESTON TRIO
| | | | |
|---|---|---|---|
| 55 | London H-APB1040 | RANDY WESTON PLAYS COLE PORTER IN A MODERN MOOD (10" LP) | 20 |
| 55 | London HB-U1046 | THE RANDY WESTON TRIO (10" LP with Art Blakey) | 20 |
| 56 | London HA-U 2018 | GET HAPPY WITH THE RANDY WESTON TRIO (LP) | 20 |

## WEST ONE
| | | | |
|---|---|---|---|
| 88 | Que Q 9 | California '69/Eurotrash (gig freebie, white label) | 12 |

## WEST POINT
| | | | |
|---|---|---|---|
| 70 | Decca F 13050 | Don't Know Why/Take What You Want | 8 |

## WEST POINT SUPERNATURAL
| | | | |
|---|---|---|---|
| 67 | Reaction 591 013 | Time Will Tell/Night Train | 20 |

## WESTVIEW
| | | | |
|---|---|---|---|
| 67 | Tenby TB1 | She's A Witch/Time Passes Slowly | 40 |

## WEST VIRGINIA
| | | | |
|---|---|---|---|
| 78 | Rox ROX 009 | One In A Million/Broken Lady (no p/s) | 5 |

## WESTWIND
| | | | |
|---|---|---|---|
| 70 | Penny Farthing PEN 737 | Love Is A Funny Sort Of Thing/Breakout | 8 |
| 70 | Penny Farthing PELS 505 | LOVE IS (LP) | 225 |

## WE THE PEOPLE
| | | | |
|---|---|---|---|
| 66 | London HLH 10089 | He Doesn't Go About It Right/You Burn Me Up And Down | 125 |

## WE THREE TRIO
| | | | |
|---|---|---|---|
| 65 | London HLA 9966 | Baby The Rain Must Fall/Shine For Me | 8 |
| 67 | Fontana TL 5308 | THE WE THREE TRIO (LP) | 15 |

## WET WILLIE
| | | | |
|---|---|---|---|
| 71 | Atlantic 2091155 | Dirty Leg/Rock And Roll Band | 8 |
| 71 | Atlantic 2400162 | WET WILLIE (LP) | 20 |

## WE UGLY DOGS
| | | | |
|---|---|---|---|
| 67 | BT Puppy BTS 45537 | First Spring Rain/Poor Man | 12 |

*(see also Tokens)*

## WHALE FEATHERS
| | | | |
|---|---|---|---|
| 71 | Blue Horizon 2431 009 | WHALE FEATHERS (LP) | 175 |

## WHALES
| | | | |
|---|---|---|---|
| 68 | CBS 3766 | Come Down Little Bird/Beachcomber | 20 |
| 69 | CBS 4126 | Tell It To The Rain/Girl, Hey Girl | 15 |

## WHAT
| | | | |
|---|---|---|---|
| 79 | Humber HREP 45 | What Is The Cure?/Anything Goes/East Coast Kids | 40 |

## WHAT IS OIL
| | | | |
|---|---|---|---|
| 83 | Oof BEAT 1 | HUMAN SUFFERING EP | 40 |

## WHAT THE CURTAINS
| | | | |
|---|---|---|---|
| 84 | Rideaux WTC 0042 | Crime Of Passion/Words (Can't Tell) | 20 |

## WHAT TO WEAR
| | | | |
|---|---|---|---|
| 80 | Basic And Typical BAT 1 | CASUAL BUT SMART (EP) | 25 |

## PEETIE WHEATSTRAW
| | | | |
|---|---|---|---|
| 69 | Matchbox SDR 191 | THE DEVIL'S SON IN LAW (LP) | 25 |
| 69 | Matchbox SDR 192 | THE HIGH SHERIFF FROM HELL (LP) | 25 |
| 74 | Flyright LP 111 | 1930-36 (LP) | 15 |

## BILLY ED WHEELER
| | | | |
|---|---|---|---|
| 64 | London HLR 9920 | On The Outside (Lookin' In)/The Right Foot In His World | 5 |
| 65 | London HLR 9950 | Ode To The Little Brown Shack Out Back/Sister Sara | 5 |

## KENNY WHEELER
| | | | |
|---|---|---|---|
| 68 | Fontana STL 5494 | WINDMILL TILTER (LP) | 150 |
| 77 | Incus 10 | SONG FOR SOMEONE (LP) | 60 |

*(see also Johnny Dankworth, Elton Dean)*

## WHEELER ST JAMES & JAMES
| | | | |
|---|---|---|---|
| 72 | RCA 2233 | My Impersonal Life/Lovely To See You | 20 |

## WHEELS OF TIME
| | | | |
|---|---|---|---|
| 67 | Spin SP 62008 | 1984/So Long (not in company sleeves) | 90 |
| 67 | Spin SP 62008 | 1984/So Long (in company sleeve) | 100 |

## WHEELS (1)
| | | | |
|---|---|---|---|
| 65 | Columbia DB 7682 | Gloria/Don't You Know | 120 |
| 66 | Columbia DB 7827 | Bad Little Woman/Road Block (mispressing, demos & a few issues play "Call My Name" on B-side) | 150 |
| 66 | Columbia DB 7827 | Bad Little Woman/Road Block | 375 |
| 66 | Columbia DB 7981 | Kicks/Call My Name | 120 |

*(see also James Brothers, Demick & Armstrong)*

## WHEELS (2)
| | | | |
|---|---|---|---|
| 71 | Decca F13268 | Take Me Home Country Roads/She Don't Mean It | 30 |

## WHICHWHAT
| | | | |
|---|---|---|---|
| 69 | Beacon BEA 127 | Gimme Gimme Good Lovin'/Wonderland Of Love | 25 |
| 69 | Beacon BEA 131 | Why Do Lovers Break Each Other's Heart/When I See Her Smile | 6 |
| 69 | Beacon BEA 133 | In The Year 2525/Parting | 15 |
| 69 | Beacon BEA 144 | I Wanna Be Free/It's All Over Again | 25 |
| 70 | Beacon BEA 169 | Vietnam Rose/Shame And Solution | 6 |
| 70 | Beacon BEAS 14 | WHICHWHAT'S FIRST (LP) | 50 |

## OSCAR WHIFLEY
| | | | |
|---|---|---|---|
| 68 | Dolphin DOS6 | Tommy Jones/Creeque Alley (as The Oscar Whifley Sound) | 8 |

## WHIP
| | | | |
|---|---|---|---|
| 71 | Mother MOT 6 | Julie Ivory Towers/MUFF & BANKHOUSE ASSEMBLY: Funky Shoot Out | 10 |
| 71 | CBS 7232 | I Never Win/Papa's On The Bottles Again | 10 |

## WHIRL
| | | | |
|---|---|---|---|
| 89 | Sound Of Spasm 2 | Bizarre Love Triangle/CROCODILE RIDE: Shimmer (1-sided flexi-disc, foldover p/s In poly bag with fanzine) | 10 |

## WHIRLWIND
| | | | |
|---|---|---|---|
| 78 | Chiswick NS 25 | Hang Loose/Together Forever (p/s) | 10 |
| 78 | Chiswick NS 42 | I Only Wish (That I'd Been Told)/Ducktails (unissued) | 0 |
| 78 | Chiswick CHIS 103 | I Only Wish (That I'd Been Told)/Ducktails (p/s) | 10 |
| 79 | Chiswick CHIS 117 | You Got Class/Losing To You (unissued in U.K.; France-only) | 0 |
| 79 | Lyntone (No Cat. No) | On Wheels (flexi, originally promo for Isle Of Man TT races, repackaged in picture sleeve with 2 inserts for 1979 Earls Court Concert) | 50 |
| 80 | Chiswick CHIS 122 | Heaven Knows/Cruisin' Around (p/s) | 10 |
| 80 | Chiswick CHIS 127 | Stayin' Out All Night/Running Wild (unissued; p/s only) | 0 |
| 80 | Chiswick PSR 447 | Midnight Blue/Honey Hush/Such A Fool/Stayin' Out All Night (promo only) | 8 |

MINT VALUE £

| | | | |
|---|---|---|---|
| 78 | Chiswick WIK 7 | BLOWIN' UP A STORM (LP, with 2 extra tracks) | 15 |
| 80 | Chiswick CWK 3012 | MIDNIGHT BLUE (LP) | 15 |

## WHIRLWIND D
| | | | |
|---|---|---|---|
| 12 | Tru-Tone TTR004 | WD40 (12" EP) | 12 |
| 13 | Tru-Tone TTR005 | BRISTOL BUILT (12" EP) | 10 |
| 14 | B-Line Recordings BLN011 | Time Waits/One, Two | 7 |
| 14 | Tru-Tone TTR 007 | Gain My Perspective/Run Fast (with Phill Most Chill & Mr Fantastic 12" test pressings only) | 40 |
| 15 | Tru-Tone TTR 008 | B-Line Business/Battle Tip 2015 | 8 |
| 14 | B-Line Recordings BLN 006 | NOMANSLAND (LP) | 15 |

## WHIRLWIND D/MR THING/AGENT FINC & SPECIFIK
| | | | |
|---|---|---|---|
| 14 | Tru-Tone TTR 006 | Broadway (12", test pressings only) | 35 |

## WHIRLWINDS
| | | | |
|---|---|---|---|
| 64 | HMV POP 1301 | Look At Me/Baby Not Like You | 50 |

(see also Mockingbirds, Graham Gouldman, 10cc)

## NANCY WHISKEY (& HER SKIFFLERS)
| | | | |
|---|---|---|---|
| 57 | Oriole CB 1394 | He's Solid Gone/Ella Speed (as Nancy Whiskey & Her Skifflers) | 20 |
| 58 | Oriole CB 1452 | Hillside In Scotland/I Know Where I'm Goin' | 10 |
| 59 | Oriole CB 1485 | The Old Grey Goose/Johnny Blue | 10 |
| 65 | Fontana TF 612 | Bowling Green/I'm Leaving Today | 5 |
| 67 | CBS 3090 | Freight Train/The Game | 5 |
| 57 | Topic 7T 10 | NANCY WHISKEY SINGS (7" LP) | 25 |
| 57 | Oriole MG 10018 | THE INTOXICATING MISS WHISKEY (10" LP, with Chas McDevitt Skiffle Group) | 30 |

(see also Chas McDevitt Skiffle Group)

## WHISTLE
| | | | |
|---|---|---|---|
| 73 | York YR 201 | The Party Must Be Over/Hideaway | 20 |
| 74 | York YR 209 | When The Lights Go Out On Broadway/Lincoln Lullabies | 20 |

## WHISTLER (1)
| | | | |
|---|---|---|---|
| 71 | Deram SML 1083 | HO-HUM (LP) | 250 |

## WHISTLER (2)
| | | | |
|---|---|---|---|
| 74 | Capricorn CAP 2 | I'm Running Out Of Time/Dear Diary | 15 |

## WHISTLING WILLIE
| | | | |
|---|---|---|---|
| 68 | Duke DU 8 | Penny Reel/Soul Tonic | 20 |

(see also Neville, Neville Willoughby)

## SHARON WHITBREAD & FRED
| | | | |
|---|---|---|---|
| 72 | RA RALP 6011 | SPICE OF LIFE (LP) | 25 |

## IAN WHITCOMB
| | | | |
|---|---|---|---|
| 65 | Capitol CL 15382 | This Sporting Life/Fizz | 6 |
| 65 | Capitol CL 15395 | You Turn Me On/Poor But Honest | 10 |
| 65 | Capitol CL 15418 | N-N-Nervous!/The End | 6 |
| 66 | Capitol CL 15431 | Good Hard Rock/High Blood Pressure | 6 |
| 66 | Stateside SS 573 | Where Did Robinson Crusoe Go With Friday/Poor Little Bird) | 6 |
| 72 | Ember EMBS 324 | You Turn Me On/This Sporting Life (mono) | 5 |
| 73 | Ember NR 5065 | YOU TURN ME ON (LP, with Jimmy Page & John Paul Jones) | 40 |

## ANDY WHITE
| | | | |
|---|---|---|---|
| 85 | Stiff BUY DJ 234 | Religious Persuasion (Light blue promo "A" label) | 7 |

## BARRY WHITE
| | | | |
|---|---|---|---|
| 67 | President PT 139 | All In The Run Of A Day/Don't Take Your Love From Me | 30 |

## BERGEN WHITE
| | | | |
|---|---|---|---|
| 76 | Private Stock PVT 69 | Duke Of Earl/She Won't Let You Down | 7 |

## BRIAN WHITE & MAGNA JAZZ BAND
| | | | |
|---|---|---|---|
| 62 | HMV CLP 1534 | BRIAN WHITE AND THE MAGNA JAZZ BAND (LP) | 80 |

## BUKKA WHITE
| | | | |
|---|---|---|---|
| 66 | Fontana 688 804 ZL | SKY SONGS (LP, with Big Willie) | 40 |
| 66 | CBS Realm 52629 | BUKKA WHITE (LP) | 40 |
| 69 | Blue Horizon 7-63229 | MEMPHIS HOT SHOTS (LP) | 80 |

## WHITE CAR
| | | | |
|---|---|---|---|
| 81 | Friday FRI 13 | Cinema Girl/Channel One (p/s) | 25 |

## CHRIS WHITE
| | | | |
|---|---|---|---|
| 76 | Charisma CB 272 | Spanish Wine/She's Only Dancing | 8 |
| 76 | Charisma CB 282 | Natural Rhythm/Another Little Miracle | 7 |
| 76 | Charisma CB 294 | Don't Look Down/Summertime Summertime | 8 |
| 77 | Charisma CB 303 | Don't Worry Baby/Child Of The Sun | 15 |
| 76 | Charisma CAS 1118 | MOUTH MUSIC (LP) | 15 |

(see also Joyce's Angels)

## DANNY WHITE
| | | | |
|---|---|---|---|
| 67 | Sue WI 4031 | Keep My Woman Home/I'm Dedicating My Life | 75 |
| 74 | MCA MU 155 | Cracked Up Over You/Taking Inventory | 5 |

## DUKE WHITE
| | | | |
|---|---|---|---|
| 63 | Island WI 084 | It's Over/Forever | 15 |
| 64 | Black Swan WI 442 | Be Wise/BABA BROOKS: Musical Workshop | 35 |
| 65 | Black Swan WI 444 | Sow Good Seeds/BABA BROOKS BAND: Bus Strike | 35 |

## ED WHITE (THE SOUNDS OF)
| | | | |
|---|---|---|---|
| 61 | Pye 7N SR15320 | Coral Reef/Tropical Blue (stereo only) | 20 |

## GEORGIA WHITE
| | | | |
|---|---|---|---|
| 54 | Vocalion V 1038 | Was I Drunk?/Moonshine Blues (78) | 20 |

**IAN WHITE**
| | | | |
|---|---|---|---|
| 70 | private pressing | IAN WHITE (LP) | 20 |

**JACK WHITE**
| | | | |
|---|---|---|---|
| 09 | Third Man Records TMR 013 | Fly Farm Blues (luminous one-sided Halloween cover, 100-only) | 120 |

*(see also White Stripes, Raconteurs, Dead Weather)*

**JAMES WHITE**
| | | | |
|---|---|---|---|
| 79 | Ze ZE 3303 | OFF WHITE (LP, as James White & The Blacks) | 20 |
| 82 | Animal CHR 1401 | SAX MANIAC (LP, as James White & The Blacks) | 20 |

**JAY WHITE**
| | | | |
|---|---|---|---|
| 56 | London RE-F 1045 | FAR-AWAY PLACES VOL. 1 (EP) | 15 |

**JEANETTE WHITE**
| | | | |
|---|---|---|---|
| 69 | A&M AMS 761 | Music/No Sunshine | 30 |
| 69 | A&M AMS 761 | Music/No Sunshine (Yellow DJ copy or brown label) | 75 |

**JOE WHITE**
| | | | |
|---|---|---|---|
| 64 | R&B JB 137 | Sinners (as Joe White & Maytals)/ROLAND ALPHONSO: King Solomon | 40 |
| 64 | Ska Beat JB 180 | Punch You Down (with Chuck)/TOMMY McCOOK: Cotton Tree | 45 |
| 64 | Island WI 145 | When Are You Young/Wanna Go Home | 15 |
| 64 | Island WI 159 | Hog In A Co Co/SKATALITES: Sandy Gully | 30 |
| 64 | Island WI 166 | Downtown Girl/RICHARD BROS.: You Are My Sunshine (B-side is actually "Cool Smoke" by Don Drummond) | 40 |
| 65 | Island WI 201 | Low-Minded People (as Chuck & Joe White)/Irene | 15 |
| 66 | Doctor Bird DB 1001 | Every Night (with Chuck)/BABA BROOKS & HIS BAND: First Session | 30 |
| 66 | Doctor Bird DB 1024 | My Love For You/SAMMY ISMAY & BABA BROOKS BAND: Cocktails For Two | 25 |
| 66 | Doctor Bird DB 1043 | So Close (as Joe White & Della)/BABA BROOKS & HIS BAND: Eighth Games | 25 |
| 67 | Doctor Bird DB 1069 | Rudies All Around/Bad Man | 30 |
| 67 | Doctor Bird DB 1080 | Lonely Nights/I Need You | 20 |
| 67 | Doctor Bird DB 1090 | I Need A Woman/Hot Hops | 20 |
| 68 | Blue Cat BS 108 | Way Of Life (actually by Lyn Tait & Jets)/I'm So Proud | 150 |
| 68 | Blue Cat BS 119 | Try A Little Tenderness/LYN TAITT & CARL BRYAN: Tender Arms | 250 |
| 68 | Blue Cat BS 130 | Pretty Girl/DERMOTT LYNCH: You Went Away | 100 |
| 69 | Sugar ESS 102 | My Guiding Star/If I Needed Someone | 12 |
| 70 | Sugar SU 103 | Yesterday/I Am Free | 20 |
| 70 | Trojan TR 7742 | So Much Love/Maybe Now | 5 |
| 70 | Trojan TR 7768 | I'm Going To Get There/RUPIE EDWARDS ALLSTARS: Kinky Funky Reggae | 10 |
| 70 | Big BG 301 | This Is The Time/The Other Day | 8 |
| 71 | Big BG 309 | Baby I Care/Ain't Misbehavin' | 5 |
| 72 | Songbird SB 1072 | Trinity/SCOTTY: Monkey Drop | 12 |
| 72 | Dynamic DYN 440 | Kenyatta/RECORDING BAND: Version | 25 |
| 73 | Gayfeet GS 202 | If It Don't Work Out/BABA BROOKS BAND: Ki Salaboca | 12 |
| 73 | Harry J. HJ 6648 | Joe White (Mrs. Jones)/Joe White (Mrs. Jones) - Version (song actually titled "Me And Mrs Jones") | 5 |
| 77 | Ultra PFU 1002 | Give And Take (On Both Sides)/Roots Dub | 5 |
| 79 | Splendor Heights SH 2 | Forward To Zion/Only The Strong/Join Them/Are You Leavine Me (12" as Joe White Band) | 20 |
| 77 | Trench Town TRELP 002 | LOVE FOR EVERY FAMILY (LP) | 20 |
| 70s | Magnet MGT 006 | SINCE THE OTHER DAY (LP) | 20 |

*(see also Chuck, Rue Lloyd)*

**JOHN WHITE**
| | | | |
|---|---|---|---|
| 78 | Obscure OBS 8 | MACHINE MUSIC (split LP with Gavin Bryers) | 20 |

**JOSH & BEVERLEY WHITE**
| | | | |
|---|---|---|---|
| 64 | Realm REP 4003 | BEVERLEY & JOSH WHITE JNR (EP) | 12 |

**JOY WHITE**
| | | | |
|---|---|---|---|
| 75 | Attack ATT 8093 | Dread Out De/Dread Dub | 25 |
| 75 | Love LOV 0010 | Check You Daughter/Night Life | 10 |
| 79 | Tribesman TM 25 | Always Together (with Jerry Baxter)/Dubbing To Sir Coxsone Sound (12") | 20 |
| 79 | Fight FDD 4438 | The First Cut Is The Deepest/ITALS : Rougher Yet (12") | 20 |
| 78 | Hawkeye HLP 002 | SENTIMENTAL REASONS (LP) | 30 |

**K.C. WHITE**
| | | | |
|---|---|---|---|
| 72 | Dynamic DYN 434 | Man No Dead/Man No Dead - Version | 8 |
| 73 | Green Door GD 4056 | First Cut Is The Deepest/No Good Girl | 10 |
| 73 | Technique TE 929 | Anywhere But Nowhere/Bush In Session | 10 |

**KITTY WHITE**
| | | | |
|---|---|---|---|
| 54 | London HL 8102 | Jesse James/Scratch My Back (B-side with Dave Howard) | 200 |
| 54 | London HL 8102 | Jesse James/Scratch My Back (78, B-side with Dave Howard) | 20 |

**LENNY WHITE**
| | | | |
|---|---|---|---|
| 78 | Elektra K 12328 | Lady Madonna/12 Bars From Mars | 5 |
| 81 | Elektra K 12500 | Kid Stuff/Slipaway | 5 |
| 83 | Elektra ED 4921 | My Turn To Love You (Special Mix)/(Dub Version) (12") | 12 |

**WHITE LIGHT**
| | | | |
|---|---|---|---|
| 74 | Scotia SCO/LP 4791 | PARABLE (LP) | 300 |

**LOUISA JANE WHITE**
| | | | |
|---|---|---|---|
| 69 | Philips BF 1810 | When The Battle Is Over/Blue Ribbons | 30 |
| 70 | Philips BF 1834 | How Does It Feel/Truth In My Tears | 100 |

**SHEILA WHITE**
| | | | |
|---|---|---|---|
| 66 | CBS 202465 | Misfit/Switch Off The Night | 15 |

**TAM WHITE**
| | | | |
|---|---|---|---|
| 67 | Decca F 12711 | World Without You/Someone You Should Know (unreleased) | 0 |
| 68 | Decca F 12723 | Dancing Out Of My Heart/I'll Stay Loving You | 10 |

MINT VALUE £

| | | | |
|---|---|---|---|
| 68 | Decca F 12849 | Waiting Till The Night Comes Around/Girl Watcher | 15 |
| 69 | Deram DM 261 | That Old Sweet Roll/Don't Make Promises | 25 |
| 70 | Middle Earth MDS 104 | Lewis Carroll/Future Thoughts | 50 |
| 70 | Middle Earth MDLS 304 | TAM WHITE (LP) | 100 |

*(see also Boston Dexters)*

## TERRY WHITE & TERRIERS
| | | | |
|---|---|---|---|
| 59 | Decca F 11133 | Rock Around The Mailbags/Blackout | 70 |
| 59 | Decca F 11133 | Rock Around The Mailbags/Blackout (78) | 20 |

## THOMAS WHITE
| | | | |
|---|---|---|---|
| 79 | Hit Run HD 12 | Ivory Girl/KEITH FRANCIS: Prejudice Country (12") | 50 |

## TONY JOE WHITE
| | | | |
|---|---|---|---|
| 68 | Monument MON 1024 | Soul Francisco/Whompt Out On You | 8 |
| 69 | Monument MON 1031 | Polk Salad Annie/Aspen Colorado | 15 |
| 69 | Monument MON 1036 | Willie And Laura Mae Jones/Baby Scratch My Back | 10 |
| 69 | Monument MON 1040 | Roosevelt And Ira Lee/The Migrant | 5 |
| 70 | Monument MON 1043 | Groupy Girl/High Sheriff Of Calhoun Parrish | 5 |
| 70 | Monument MON 1048 | Save Your Sugar For Me/My Friend | 5 |
| 71 | Warner Bros WB 6129 | A Night In The Life Of A Swamp Fox/The Daddy | 5 |
| 68 | Monument LMO/SMO 5027 | BLACK AND WHITE (LP) | 15 |
| 70 | Monument LMO/SMO 5035 | TONY JOE WHITE CONTINUED (LP) | 15 |
| 70 | Monument SMO 5043 | TONY JOE (EP) | 15 |
| 71 | Warner Bros WS 1900 | TONY JOE WHITE (LP) | 18 |
| 72 | Warner Bros K 46147 | THE TRAIN I'M ON (LP) | 15 |
| 73 | Warner Bros K 46229 | HOME-MADE ICE CREAM (LP) | 15 |

## TREVOR WHITE
| | | | |
|---|---|---|---|
| 76 | Island WIP 6291 | Crazy Kids/Movin' In The Right Direction (with p/s) | 20 |
| 76 | Island WIP 6291 | Crazy Kids/Movin' In The Right Direction | 8 |

*(see also Sparks, Radio Stars)*

## WHITE DOOR
| | | | |
|---|---|---|---|
| 83 | Clay CLAY 23 | Love Breakdown/Breakdown (Instrumental) | 6 |
| 84 | Clay 37 | Flame In My Heart/Behind The White Door (p/s) | 6 |

## WHITE DUCK
| | | | |
|---|---|---|---|
| 72 | Uni UN 541 | Billy Goat/Really | 8 |
| 73 | Uni UN 555 | Honey, You'll Be Alright/Carry Love | 8 |
| 72 | Uni UNLS 123 | WHITE DUCK (LP) | 22 |
| 73 | Uni UNLS 129 | IN SEASON (LP) | 22 |

## WHITE FEATHER
| | | | |
|---|---|---|---|
| 83 | No No N.N001 | Summer Days/Golden Haze/Feathered Girl (no p/s) | 15 |

## RICK WHITEFIELD
| | | | |
|---|---|---|---|
| 71 | Horse HOSS 10 | Hey Mama/Ride Baby Ride | 6 |

## WHITEFIRE
| | | | |
|---|---|---|---|
| 78 | Whitefire 98DB 001 | SUZANNE (EP) | 40 |

## WHITE HART
| | | | |
|---|---|---|---|
| 79 | Tradition TSR 033 | IN SEARCH OF REWARD (LP) | 50 |

## WHITE HEAT (1)
| | | | |
|---|---|---|---|
| 79 | Valium VAL 01 | Nervous Breakdown/Sammy Sez (gatefold p/s) | 25 |
| 80 | Valium VAL 02 | Finished With The Fashions/Ordinary Joe (p/s, with insert) | 20 |
| 81 | Valium VAL 03 | City Beat/It's No Use (Young Ones) (p/s) | 15 |
| 81 | Valium VALP 101 | IN THE ZERO HOUR (LP) | 25 |

## WHITE HEAT (2)
| | | | |
|---|---|---|---|
| 84 | RSR 007 | Soldier Of Fortune/Lovemaker | 75 |
| 84 | Rock Shop RSR 007 | WHITE HEAT (LP) | 25 |

## WHITE HORN
| | | | |
|---|---|---|---|
| 75 | Philips 6006 440 | Making It Funky/Mama Said | 8 |

## WHITEHOUSE
| | | | |
|---|---|---|---|
| 90 | Sue Lawley SLS 002 | Still Going Strong/Ankles And Wrists | 15 |
| 01 | SLA-003 | Cruise (Force The Truth)/Instrumental Version (12") | 20 |
| 02 | SLA-004 | Wriggle Like A Fucking Eel/Instrumental Version (12") | 18 |
| 80 | Come Org. WDC 881004 | BIRTHDEATH EXPERIENCE (LP, first pressing pink labels, 850 copies) | 150 |
| 80 | Come Org. WDC 881005 | TOTAL SEX (LP, 400 on green vinyl) | 120 |
| 80 | Come Org. WDC 881005 | TOTAL SEX (LP, 800 on black vinyl) | 80 |
| 80 | Come Org. WDC 883005 | TOTAL SEX (cassette) | 75 |
| 80 | Come Org. WDC 883003 | ULTRASADISM (cassette) | 60 |
| 81 | Come Org. WDC 881010 | DEDICATED TO PETER KÜRTEN, SADIST AND MASS SLAYER (LP, some on coloured vinyl, some in custom sleeve) | 120 |
| 80 | Come Org. WDC 881007 | ERECTOR (LP, different coloured vinyls) | 100 |
| 81 | Come Org. WDC 881013 | BÜCHENWALD (LP, clear vinyl) | 120 |
| 81 | WDC 883013 | BUCHENWALD (cassette) | 60 |
| 81 | Come Org. WDC 881017 | NEW BRITAIN (LP, with insert) | 125 |
| 82 | Come Org. WDC 881027 | PSYCHOPATHIA SEXUALIS (LP, clear vinyl, black is bootleg) | 200 |
| 82 | Come Org. WDC 883020 | LIVE ACTION 1 (cassette) | 45 |
| 83 | Come Org. WDC 883027 | PSYCHOPATHIA SEXUALIS (cassette) | 70 |
| 83 | Come Org. WDC 883033 | RIGHT TO KILL - DEDICATED TO DENNIS ANDREW NEILSEN (LP, & inserts) | 120 |
| 83 | Come Org. WDC 883044048 | USA I - V (5 cassettes documenting 1983 US tour, pice for each) | 45 |
| 85 | Come Org. WDC | GREAT WHITE DEATH (LP) | 80 |

*(Many Whitehouse LP's were issued in customised white card sleeves & were later available in a generic 'Peter Kürten' sleeve, originally used for the 2nd pressing of the 'Peter Kürten' LP. This latter design was also used for counterfeits. There may also be coloured vinyl variations which are worth the same)*

| | | | |
|---|---|---|---|
| 80s | Come Org. WDC | 150 MURDEROUS PASSIONS (LP, with Nurse With Wound) | 75 |
| 80s | United Dairies UD 009 | 150 MURDEROUS PASSIONS (LP, with Nurse With Wound, reissue) | 40 |
| 80s | United Dairies UD 009 | 150 MURDEROUS PASSIONS (LP, with Nurse With Wound, export issue, sealed in black vinyl) | 125 |
| 80s | Susan Lawley 1 | CREAM OF THE SECOND COMING (2-LP) | 45 |
| 91 | Susan Lawley SL 002 | THANK YOUR LUCKY STARS (LP) | 30 |
| 92 | Susan Lawley SL 003 | TWICE IS NOT ENOUGH (LP) | 30 |

*(see also Come, Nurse With Wound, New Order, Skullflower, Konstruktivits)*

## WHITE LIES
| | | | |
|---|---|---|---|
| 08 | Fiction 1795718 | To Lose My Life (6 x 7" box set with signed print) | 40 |

## WHITE LIGHTNING
| | | | |
|---|---|---|---|
| 84 | Wild Party PP 1000 | This Poison Fountain/Hypocrite (no p/s, 1,000 only) | 50 |
| 90 | Workshop JOB LP 2 | AS MIDNIGHT APPROACHES (LP, with inner) | 18 |

*(see also Static)*

## WHITE LINING
| | | | |
|---|---|---|---|
| 70 | Parlophone R 5868 | Back In The Sun/Mon Amour | 20 |

## WHITE MULE
| | | | |
|---|---|---|---|
| 70 | UNI UNS 523 | Looking Through Cat's Eyes/Hundred Franc Blues | 15 |

## WHITE NOISE
| | | | |
|---|---|---|---|
| 75 | Virgin VDJ 2 | An Extract From White Noise 2 (promo only) | 20 |
| 69 | Island ILPS 9099 | AN ELECTRIC STORM (LP, pink label black/orange circle logo) | 150 |
| 69 | Island ILPS 9099 | WHITE NOISE (LP, repressing pink label with white 'i' logo) | 50 |
| 75 | Virgin V 2032 | WHITE NOISE 2 (LP) | 15 |

*(see also BBC Radiophonic Workshop)*

## WHITE ON BLACK
| | | | |
|---|---|---|---|
| 74 | Saydisc SDL 251 | WHITE ON BLACK (LP, fully laminated sleeve) | 30 |

## WHITE PLAINS
| | | | |
|---|---|---|---|
| 70 | Deram DM 280 | My Baby Loves Lovin'/Show Me Your Hand | 7 |
| 70 | Deram DM 291 | I've Got You On My Mind/Today I Killed A Man I Didn't Know | 8 |
| 70 | Deram DM 315 | Julie Do Ya Love Me/I Need Your Everlasting Love | 7 |
| 71 | Deram DM 333 | When You Are A King/The World Gets Better With Love | 8 |
| 71 | Deram DM 340 | Gonna Miss Here Mississippi/I'll Go Blind | 7 |
| 71 | Deram DM 348 | I Con't Stop/Julie Anne | 7 |
| 73 | Deram DM 371 | Step Into A Dream/Look To See | 8 |
| 73 | Deram DM 388 | Does Anybody Know Where My Baby Is/Just For A Change | 10 |
| 70 | Deram SML 1067 | WHITE PLAINS (LP, laminated cover) | 30 |
| 71 | Deram SML 1092 | WHEN YOU ARE A KING (LP) | 25 |

*(see also Edison Lighthouse, David & Jonathan, Kestrels, Brotherhood Of Man, Peter's Faces, Carter-Lewis & Southerners, Ivy League)*

## WHITE RABBIT
| | | | |
|---|---|---|---|
| 69 | NEMS 56-4165 | Ain't That Something/I'll Do The Rest | 8 |

## WHITE RUSSIA
| | | | |
|---|---|---|---|
| 80 | Trivia TRIV 01 | Valentine/Clothes (p/s) | 40 |

## WHITESNAKE
| | | | |
|---|---|---|---|
| 78 | EMI International INEP 751 | SNAKEBITE (EP, white vinyl, p/s; later black vinyl with no p/s) | 15 |
| 78 | EMI International INT 568 | Lie Down/Don't Mess With Me | 6 |
| 79 | EMI International INT 578 | The Time Is Right For Love/Come On (live) | 6 |
| 82 | Liberty BPP 416 | Here I Go Again/Bloody Luxury (picture disc) | 10 |
| 82 | Liberty BP 418 | Love An' Affection/Victim Of Love (withdrawn) | 35 |
| 83 | Liberty BPP 420 | Guilty Of Love/Gambler (shaped picture disc) | 10 |
| 87 | EMI 10EMI 35 | Here I Go Again '87 (US remix)/Guilty Of Love (10", p/s, white vinyl) | 5 |
| 78 | EMI Intl. INS 3022 | TROUBLE (LP, grey or pink inner sleeve) | 15 |
| 82 | Liberty LBGP 30354 | SAINTS AN' SINNERS (LP, picture disc) | 15 |
| 84 | Liberty LBGP 240 000 0 | SLIDE IT IN (LP, picture disc, U.S. mixes) | 15 |
| 87 | EMI EMCP 3528 | WHITESNAKE 1987 (LP, picture disc) | 15 |
| 89 | EMI EMCDJ 1013 | SLIP OF THE TONGUE (LP, with track by track interview, promo only) | 20 |

*(see also David Coverdale, Deep Purple, Rainbow, Roger Glover, Jon Lord, Phenomena, Cozy Powell, Young & Moody Band, Company, Snafu, Bogdon, Forcefield, Gogmagog, Tramline, National Health)*

## WHITE SOLES
| | | | |
|---|---|---|---|
| 76 | Satril SAT 104 | Beside You/Never Say Die | 10 |

## WHITE SPIRIT
| | | | |
|---|---|---|---|
| 80 | Neat NEAT 05 | Back To The Grind/Cheetah (p/s) | 10 |
| 81 | MCA MCA 638 | Midnight Chaser/Suffragettes (p/s) | 30 |
| 81 | MCA MCA 652 | High Upon High/No Reprieve/Arthur Guitar | 15 |
| 80 | MCA MCF 3079 | WHITE SPIRIT (LP, with lyric insert) | 18 |

*(see also Gillan, Iron Maiden)*

## WHITE SS
| | | | |
|---|---|---|---|
| 78 | White SS CIA 72 | Mercy Killing/I'm Not One (live) (p/s) | 25 |

## WHITE STRIPES
| | | | |
|---|---|---|---|
| 01 | XL XLS 139 | Hotel Yorba (Live At The Hotel Yorba)/Rated X (p/s, 4000 only) | 6 |
| 02 | XL XLS 142 | Fell In Love With A Girl/I Just Don't Know What To Do With Myself (p/s, 5000 only) | 12 |
| 02 | XL XLS 148 | Dead Leaves And The Dirty Ground/Stop Breaking Down (Live) (p/s, 5000 only) | 6 |
| 02 | XL/MOJO no cat. no. | Red Death At 6:14 (1-sided, promo only, red vinyl, numbered label, 3000 only, mail order only via Mojo magazine, with letter) | 25 |
| 02 | XL XLS 162 | Merry Christmas From The White Stripes: Candy Cane Children/The Reading Of The Story Of The Magi/The Singing Of Silent Night (1000 only, p/s) | 8 |
| 03 | XL XLS 166 | I Just Don't Know What To Do With Myself/Who's To Say (p/s) | 5 |
| 03 | XL LP 162 DJ | Seven Nation Army/In The Cold, Cold Night (p/s, ELEPHANT SAMPLER) | 10 |
| 03 | XL XLS 162 | Seven Nation Army/Good To Me (p/s) | 15 |

MINT VALUE £

| | | | |
|---|---|---|---|
| 03 | XL no. cat. no. | Seven Nation Army (1-sided 12" promo, stamped white label, no p/s) | 25 |
| 04 | XL XLS 181 | There's No Home For You Here/I Fought Piranhas/Let's Build A Home (die-cut sleeve) | 15 |
| 05 | XL (no. cat. No.) | DENIAL TWIST (10 x printed/stickered CD's in different artwork card wallets. One given away at each night of UK autumn tour. Each CD blank - 10 downloads were availiable online only, this price for complete set) | 200 |
| 07 | XL XL 277 | Rag And Bone (with etched B-side of Jack and Meg's faces given away free with copies of NME, gatefold sleeve) | 6 |
| 07 | XL XLS293B | You Don't Know What Love Is (acoustic)/300 mph Torrential Outpour Blues | 5 |
| 01 | XL XLLP 150 | DE STIJL (LP) | 25 |
| 01 | XL XLLP151 | WHITE BLOOD CELLS (LP, red vinyl) | 25 |
| 01 | XL XLLP 149 | WHITE STRIPES (LP) | 25 |
| 01 | XL XLPD149 | WHITE STRIPES (LP, picture disc) | 18 |
| 03 | XL XLLP 162 | ELEPHANT (2-LP, promo, custom sleeve, 500 only) | 80 |
| 05 | XL XLLP 191 P | GET BEHIND ME SATAN (300 copies pressed for U.K.. 2 x LP promo, different p/s) | 150 |
| 07 | XL XLLP271 | ICKY THUMP (2-LP, red/white vinyl) | 30 |

*(see also Raconteurs)*

## WHITE TRASH

| | | | |
|---|---|---|---|
| 69 | Apple APPLE 6 | Road To Nowhere/Illusions (early copies as White Trash) | 200 |
| 69 | Apple APPLE 6 | Road To Nowhere/Illusions (later copies as Trash) | 60 |

*(see also Trash, Poets, Stone The Crows)*

## WHITE ZOMBIE

| | | | |
|---|---|---|---|
| 89 | Caroline CAROL 1457 | God Of Thunder/Love Razor/Disaster Blaster 2 (12", withdrawn) | 15 |

## DAVID WHITFIELD

| | | | |
|---|---|---|---|
| 54 | Decca F 10242 | The Book/Heartless | 10 |
| 54 | Decca F 10327 | Carla Mia/Love, Tears And Kisses | 10 |
| 54 | Decca F 10355 | Smile/When Or Where | 8 |
| 54 | Decca F 10399 | Santa Natale(Merry Christmas)/Adeste Fideles (O Come All Ye Faithful) | 8 |

## WILBUR WHITFIELD

| | | | |
|---|---|---|---|
| 57 | Vogue V 9078 | P.B. Baby/The One I Love | 600 |
| 57 | Vogue V 9078 | P.B. Baby/The One I Love (78) | 150 |

*(see also Little Wilbur & Pleasers)*

## LEONARD WHITING

| | | | |
|---|---|---|---|
| 65 | Pye 7N 15943 | The Piper/That's What Mama Says | 40 |

## MARGARET WHITING

| | | | |
|---|---|---|---|
| 55 | Capitol CL 14213 | My Own True Love (Tara's Theme)/Can This Be Love (triangular centre) | 12 |
| 55 | Capitol CL 14242 | Heat Wave/Come Rain Or Shine (triangular centre) | 12 |
| 55 | Capitol CL 14307 | Stowaway/All I Want Is All There Is And Then Some (triangular centre) | 12 |
| 55 | Capitol CL 14348 | A Man/Mama's Pearls (triangular centre) | 12 |
| 55 | Capitol CL 14375 | Lover, Lover/I Kiss You A Million Times (triangular centre) | 12 |
| 56 | Capitol CL 14527 | I Love A Mystery/Bidin' My Time | 10 |
| 56 | Capitol CL 14591 | Old Enough/Day In - Day Out | 8 |
| 57 | Capitol CL 14647 | True Love/Haunting Love | 8 |
| 57 | Capitol CL 14685 | The Money Tree/Maybe I Love Him | 8 |
| 57 | London HLD 8451 | Kill Me With Kisses/Speak For Yourself, John | 10 |
| 58 | London HLD 8562 | I Can't Help (If I'm Still In Love With You)/That's Why I Was Born | 10 |
| 58 | London HLD 8662 | Hot Spell/I'm So Lonesome I Could Cry | 10 |
| 66 | London HLD 10078 | Nothing Lasts Forever/The Wheel Of Hurt | 10 |
| 67 | London HLD 10114 | Just Like A Man/The World Inside Your Arms | 5 |
| 68 | London HLU 10196 | Faithfully/Am I Losing You | 6 |
| 68 | London HLU 10227 | Maybe Just Once More/Can't Get You Out Of My Mind | 5 |
| 53 | Capitol LC 6585 | CAPITOL PRESENTS MARGARET WHITING (10" LP) | 15 |
| 56 | Capitol LC 6811 | MARGARET WHITING (10" LP) | 15 |
| 58 | London HA-D 2109 | GOIN' PLACES (LP) | 15 |
| 61 | London HA-D 2321 | JUST A DREAM (LP) | 20 |

*(see also Jimmy Wakely, Bob Hope, Dean Martin)*

## RAY WHITLEY

| | | | |
|---|---|---|---|
| 65 | HMV POP 1473 | I've Been Hurt/There Is One Boy | 150 |
| 65 | HMV POP 1473 | I've Been Hurt/There Is One Boy (DJ copy) | 250 |

## BOBBY WHITLOCK

| | | | |
|---|---|---|---|
| 72 | CBS 65109 | BOBBY WHITLOCK (LP) | 30 |
| 73 | CBS 65301 | RAW VELVET (LP) | 20 |

*(see also Derek & Dominoes)*

## SLIM WHITMAN

### SINGLES

| | | | |
|---|---|---|---|
| 54 | London L 1149 | Indian Love Call/China Doll | 20 |
| 54 | London HL 1149 | Indian Love Call/China Doll (re-pressing with different prefix) | 15 |
| 54 | London L 1214 | There's A Rainbow In Every Teardrop/Danny Boy | 20 |
| 54 | London HL 1214 | There's A Rainbow In Every Teardrop/Danny Boy (re-pressing) | 15 |
| 54 | London L 1226 | North Wind/Darlin' Don't Cry | 30 |
| 54 | London HL 1226 | North Wind/Darlin' Don't Cry (re-pressing with different prefix) | 30 |
| 54 | London HL 8018 | Stairway To Heaven/Lord, Help Me To Be As Thou | 30 |
| 54 | London HL 8039 | Secret Love/Why | 30 |
| 54 | London HL 8061 | Rose Marie/We Stood At The Altar | 15 |
| 54 | London HL 8080 | Beautiful Dreamer/Ride Away | 15 |
| 54 | London HL 8091 | The Singing Hills/I Hate To See You Cry | 15 |
| 55 | London HL 8125 | When I Grow Too Old To Dream/Cattle Call | 12 |
| 55 | London HL 8141 | Haunted Hungry Heart/Roll On, Silvery Moon | 10 |
| 55 | London HLU 8167 | I'll Never Stop Loving You/I'll Never Take You Back Again | 10 |
| 55 | London HLU 8196 | Song Of The Wild/You Have My Heart | 10 |

| 56 | London HLU 8230 | Tumbling Tumbleweeds/Tell Me | 10 |
|---|---|---|---|
| 56 | London HLU 8252 | I'm A Fool/My Heart Is Broken In Three | 10 |
| 56 | London HLU 8287 | Serenade/I Talk To The Waves | 10 |
| 56 | London HLU 8327 | Dear Mary/Whiffenpoof Song | 10 |
| 56 | London HLU 8350 | I'm Casting My Lasso Towards The Sky/There's A Love Knot In My Lariat | 10 |
| 57 | London HLP 8403 | I'll Take You Home Again Kathleen/Careless Love | 10 |

*(The above 45's were originally issued with gold label print & tri-centres; later round-centre and/or silver label print copies are worth half these values.)*

| 57 | London HLP 8416 | Curtain Of Tears/Smoke Signals (silver label print) | 6 |
|---|---|---|---|
| 57 | London HLP 8420 | Gone/An Amateur In Love (gold label print) | 15 |
| 59 | London HLP 8896 | What Kind Of God (Do You Think You Are)/A Tree In The Meadow (unissued) | 0 |

**EPs**

| 54 | London RE-P 1006 | SLIM WHITMAN AND HIS SINGING GUITAR (at least 8 different colour sleeves, with matt finish & various label designs) | 12 |
|---|---|---|---|
| 66 | Liberty LEP 4046 | A SATISFIED MIND | 10 |

**ALBUMS**

| 54 | London H-APB 1015 | SLIM WHITMAN & HIS SINGING GUITAR (10", gold label print) | 40 |
|---|---|---|---|
| 54 | London H-APB 1015 | SLIM WHITMAN & HIS SINGING GUITAR (10", silver label print) | 25 |
| 56 | London HA-U 2015 | SLIM WHITMAN & HIS SINGING GUITAR VOL. 2 | 30 |
| 59 | London HA-P 2139 | SLIM WHITMAN SINGS | 20 |
| 59 | London HA-P 2199 | SLIM WHITMAN SINGS VOL. 2 | 20 |
| 61 | London HA-P 2392 | JUST CALL ME LONESOME | 20 |
| 60 | London HA-P 2343 | SLIM WHITMAN | 18 |
| 62 | London HA-P 2443 | SLIM WHITMAN SINGS VOL. 3 (Mono) | 18 |
| 62 | London HA-P 2443 | SLIM WHITMAN SINGS VOL. 3 (also stereo SAH-P 6232) | 20 |

**MARVA WHITNEY**

| 70 | Polydor 2001 036 | This Girl's In Love With You/He's The One | 8 |
|---|---|---|---|
| 69 | Polydor 583 767 | IT'S MY THING (LP) | 50 |

*(see also James Brown)*

**JAKI WHITREN**

| 73 | Epic EPC 65645 | RAW BUT TENDER (LP, with insert) | 45 |
|---|---|---|---|

**TIM WHITSETT**

| 64 | Sue WI 318 | Macks By The Tracks/Shine | 45 |
|---|---|---|---|

**TIM WHITSETT/STICKS HERMAN**

| 60s | Range JRE 7002 | RHYTHM & BLUES (EP) | 30 |
|---|---|---|---|

**PAUL WHITSUN JONES & WALLAS EATON & HOLLAND**

| 65 | Oriole CB 1991 | Shake It Baby/Instant Marriage | 20 |
|---|---|---|---|

**WHITSUNTIDE EASTER**

| 77 | Pilgrim/Grapevine GRA 109 | NEXT TIME YOU PLAY A WRONG NOTE...MAKE IT A SHORT ONE (LP, gatefold sleeve) | 100 |
|---|---|---|---|

**TOMMY WHITTLE (& HIS QUARTET)**

| 57 | HMV 45 POP 379 | The Finisher/Cabin In The Sky | 25 |
|---|---|---|---|
| 55 | Esquire EP 37 | TOMMY WHITTLE QUINTET (EP) | 40 |
| 56 | Esquire EP 37 | TOMMY WHITTLE QUINTET (EP) | 40 |
| 58 | HMV 7EG 8325 | TOMMY WHITTLE QUARTET (EP) | 100 |
| 54 | Esquire 20-028 | WAXING WITH WHITTLE (LP) | 50 |
| 55 | Esquire 20-048 | TOMMY WHITTLE QUINTET (LP) | 60 |
| 56 | Esquire 20-061 | SPOTLIGHTING TOMMY WHITTLE (LP) | 90 |
| 56 | Esquire 20-068 | LULLABY & RHYTHM (LP) | 100 |
| 60 | Tempo TAP 27 | NEW HORIZONS (LP) | 700 |
| 60s | Ember EMB 3305 | EASY LISTENING (LP) | 75 |
| 67 | Masquerade MQ 2000 | SAX FOR DREAMERS (LP) | 100 |
| 77 | Jam 648 | WHY NOT? (LP) | 20 |
| 82 | Tee Jay 101 | THE NEARNESS OF YOU (LP) | 20 |
| 88 | Esquire 334 | MORE WAXING WITH WHITTLE (LP, reissue) | 20 |

**WHIZZ KIDS**

| 79 | Dead Good DEAD SIX | P.A.Y.E./99% Proof/National Assistance/Cheek To Cheek (p/s, with insert) | 20 |
|---|---|---|---|
| 80 | Ovation OVS 1213 | Suspect No. 1/Coma Life (p/s) | 10 |

**THE WHO**

**SINGLES**

| 65 | Brunswick 05926 | I Can't Explain/Bald Headed Woman | 40 |
|---|---|---|---|
| 65 | Brunswick 05935 | Anyway Anyhow Anywhere/Daddy Rolling Stone | 35 |
| 65 | Brunswick 05944 | My Generation/Shout And Shimmy | 20 |
| 66 | Brunswick 05951 | Circles/Instant Party Mixture (unreleased) | 0 |
| 66 | Reaction 591 001 | Substitute/Circles (temporarily withdrawn) | 40 |
| 66 | Reaction 591 001 | Substitute/Instant Party (temporarily withdrawn) | 30 |
| 66 | Brunswick 05956 | The Kids Are Alright/The Ox (existence unconfirmed) | 0 |
| 66 | Brunswick 05956 | A Legal Matter/Instant Party | 50 |
| 66 | Reaction 591 001 | Substitute/WHO ORCHESTRA: Waltz For A Pig (B-side actually by Graham Bond Organisation) | 25 |
| 66 | Brunswick 05965 | The Kids Are Alright/The Ox | 60 |
| 66 | Brunswick 05968 | La-La-La-Lies/The Good's Gone | 70 |
| 66 | Reaction 591 004 | I'm A Boy/In The City | 12 |
| 66 | Reaction 591 010 | Happy Jack/I've Been Away | 12 |
| 67 | Track 604 002 | Pictures Of Lily/Doctor, Doctor | 12 |
| 67 | Track 604 006 | The Last Time/Under My Thumb | 65 |
| 67 | Track 604 011 | I Can See For Miles/Someone's Coming | 15 |
| 68 | Track 604 023 | Dogs/Call Me Lightning | 25 |
| 68 | Track 604 024 | Magic Bus/Dr. Jekyll And Mr Hyde | 12 |

MINT VALUE £

| 69 | Track 604 027 | Pinball Wizard/Dogs Part Two .............................................................. 12 |
| 70 | Track 604 036 | The Seeker/Here For More .................................................................. 10 |
| 70 | Track 2094 002 | Summertime Blues/Heaven And Hell ................................................... 10 |
| 70 | Track 2094 004 | See Me, Feel Me/Overture From 'Tommy' (withdrawn) ......................... 40 |
| 71 | Track 2094 009 | Won't Get Fooled Again/Don't Know Myself (p/s, large centre) ............ 25 |
| 71 | Track 2094 009 | Won't Get Fooled Again/Don't Know Myself (p/s, with middle) ............ 35 |
| 71 | Track 2094 012 | Let's See Action/When I Was A Boy (paper labels, solid centre) ............ 5 |
| 73 | Track 2094 115 | 5.15/Water ........................................................................................ 7 |
| 75 | Polydor 2001 561 | Overture/See Me Feel Me/Listening To You (from "Tommy" soundtrack, p/s) .. 10 |
| 79 | Polydor WHO 2 | Long Live Rock/I'm The Face/My Wife (withdrawn, blank run-off groove) ........ 6 |
| 80 | Polydor WHO 3 | 5.15/I'm One (p/s) .............................................................................. 6 |
| 81 | Polydor WHO 5 | Don't Let Go The Coat/You .................................................................. 5 |
| 81 | Polydor 2058 803 | Subtitute/I'm a Boy-Pictures Of Lily ................................................... 5 |
| 81 | Polydor WHO 004 | You Better You Bet/The Quiet One ...................................................... 5 |
| 82 | Polydor WHOPX 6 | Athena/A Man Is A Man/Won't Get Fooled Again (12", picture disc, mispressing, plays "Why Did I Fall For That") .................. 15 |

## EXPORT SINGLES

| 66 | Brunswick 05956 | A Legal Matter/Instant Party (with Scandinavian p/s) ........................ 150 |
| 68 | Decca AD 1001 | My Generation/Shout And Shimmy .................................................. 100 |
| 68 | Decca AD 1001 | My Generation/Shout And Shimmy (in p/s) ...................................... 200 |
| 68 | Decca AD 1002 | A Legal Matter/Instant Party ........................................................... 100 |
| 72 | Track 2094 102 | Join Together/Baby Don't You Do It (p/s, for Spain with 'special Londres import' on front and 'Imported by Polydor S.A.' on rear) ..................... 25 |

## EPs

| 66 | Reaction 592 001 | READY STEADY WHO ......................................................................... 90 |
| 70 | Track 2252 001 | EXCERPTS FROM "TOMMY" (33rpm) .................................................. 25 |
| 83 | Reaction WHO 7 | READY STEADY WHO (reissue) ........................................................... 20 |

## ALBUMS

| 65 | Brunswick LAT 8616 | MY GENERATION (laminated front sleeve, black/silver label) ............ 600 |
| 66 | Reaction 593 002 | A QUICK ONE (laminated sleeve, blue/silver label) ........................... 200 |
| 67 | Track 612 002 | THE WHO SELL OUT (LP, mono) ....................................................... 200 |
| 67 | Track 613 002 | THE WHO SELL OUT (LP, stereo) ...................................................... 150 |
| 67 | Track 612 002 | THE WHO SELL OUT (mono, 500 with stickered sleeve & poster) ....... 800 |
| 67 | Track 613 002 | THE WHO SELL OUT (stereo, 500 with stickered sleeve & poster) ...... 800 |
| 68 | Track 612 006 | DIRECT HITS (mono) .......................................................................... 40 |
| 68 | Track 613 006 | DIRECT HITS (stereo) ......................................................................... 50 |
| 69 | Track 613 013/014 | TOMMY (2-LP, 1st issue fold-out laminated gatefold sleeve made by E.J. Day, A1/B1/A1/B1 matrixes, "double album" on labels and must not have catalogue number under 'ST33' on the right side (as this is a later pressing) with numbered 12-page booklet) ....................... 150 |
| 69 | Track 613 013/014 | TOMMY (2-LP, 2nd issue fold-out matt gatefold sleeve, no "double album" on labels with 12-page booklet, un-numbered) ........................ 40 |
| 70 | Track 2406 001 | LIVE AT LEEDS (1st issue with BLACK stamp on front, foldout sleeve with 12 inserts including poster) ........................... 250 |
| 70 | Track 2406 001 | LIVE AT LEEDS (with BLUE or RED stamp on front, foldout sleeve with 12 inserts including poster stating 'Tuesdays At The Marquee') ....... 80 |
| 70 | Track 2406 001 | LIVE AT LEEDS (with BLUE or RED stamp on front, foldout sleeve with 12 inserts including poster stating 'Live At Leeds', A1/B1 matrix') ...... 50 |
| 70 | Track 2406 001 | LIVE AT LEEDS (second pressing, BLUE or RED stamp on front, foldout sleeve with 12 inserts including poster stating 'Live At Leeds', A3/B3 matrix') ..... 40 |
| 70 | Track 2407 014 | BACKTRACK 14: THE OX ..................................................................... 15 |
| 70 | Track 2856 001 | WHO DID IT? (mail-order only, withdrawn) ...................................... 600 |
| 71 | Track 2408 102 | WHO'S NEXT (1st pressing with poly-lined inner sleeve with black and white Polydor artist photos on front and "HEAD HUNTERS - GET A HEAD" on rear. MATRIX: 2408 102 A1/B2) Pleated end spines) ............................ 45 |
| 71 | Track 2408 102 | WHO'S NEXT (later pressing, MATRIX: 2408 102 A4/B3) ....................... 25 |
| 71 | Track 2406 006 | MEATY, BEATY, BIG AND BOUNCY (gatefold sleeve) ............................ 30 |
| 71 | Track 2406 006 | MEATY, BEATY, BIG AND BOUNCY (gatefold sleeve, mispressed, plays "The Seeker" instead of "Magic Bus") ....................... 40 |
| 73 | Track 2406 110 | QUADROPHENIA (2-LP, original with 22-page photo booklet, matt labels) ..... 40 |
| 74 | Track ACB 254 | ODDS AND SODS (LP) ........................................................................ 45 |
| 74 | Track 2406 116 | ODDS AND SODS (cut-away braille sleeve, with poster & lyric sheet)........ 20 |
| 74 | Track 2409209/10 | A QUICK ONE/THE WHO SELL OUT (2-LP, reissue, E.J. Day printing credit) .... 65 |
| 75 | Polydor 2490 129 | THE WHO BY NUMBERS (numbered) .................................................. 15 |
| 78 | Polydor WHOD 5004 | WHO ARE YOU (LP) ........................................................................... 18 |
| 76 | Polydor 2478091 | THE STORY OF THE WHO (2-LP, booklet) ............................................ 25 |
| 79 | Polydor 2488 739 | THE KIDS ARE ALRIGHT (2-LP, booklet and inner sleeves)................... 30 |
| 80 | Virgin V 2179 | MY GENERATION (reissue)................................................................ 15 |
| 81 | Polydor 2675 216 | PHASES (9-LP box set, stickered cover) ........................................... 150 |
| 81 | Polydor | FACE DANCES (Promo boxed set with poster and bio of artists, numbered Peter Blake print, 300 only) ............................ 150 |
| 81 | Polydor WHOD 5037 | FACE DANCES (LP, inner, poster) ....................................................... 15 |
| 84 | Polydor WHOH 17 | THE SINGLES (LP) ............................................................................. 20 |
| 88 | Polydor WTV 1 | WHO'S BETTER WHO'S BEST (LP) ...................................................... 18 |
| 90 | Virgin VDT 201 | JOIN TOGETHER (3-LP, inner sleeves) ................................................ 40 |
| 00 | Polydor 5477271 | BBC SESSIONS (2-LP) ........................................................................ 20 |
| 02 | POLYDOR 113 981-1 | MY GENERATION - DELUXE EDITION (2-LP, reissue) ............................. 20 |
| 03 | POLYDOR 076 176-1 | WHO'S NEXT (3-LP, reissue) .............................................................. 30 |

## PROMOS : DEMO SINGLES

| 65 | Brunswick 05926 | I Can't Explain/Bald Headed Woman (demo, red label) ..................... 500 |
| 65 | Brunswick 05935 | Anyway Anyhow Anywhere/Daddy Rolling Stone (demo, red label) ........ 400 |
| 65 | Brunswick 05944 | My Generation/Shout And Shimmy (demo, red label) ....................... 450 |

| 66 | Brunswick 05956 | A Legal Matter/Instant Party (demo, red label) | 400 |
|----|----|----|----|
| 66 | Brunswick 05965 | The Kids Are Alright/The Ox (demo, red label) | 400 |
| 66 | Brunswick 05968 | La-La-La-Lies/The Good's Gone (demo, red label) | 400 |
| 69 | Track PRO 1 | The Acid Queen/We're Not Gonna Take It (existence unconfirmed) | 0 |
| 69 | Track PRO 2 | Go To The Mirror!/Sally Simpson | 80 |
| 69 | Track PRO 3 | I'm Free/1921 | 80 |
| 69 | Track PRO 4 | Christmas/Overture | 80 |

*(see also High Numbers, Pete Townshend, Roger Daltrey, John Entwistle, Keith Moon, Kenney Jones, Graham Bond Organisation, Rigor Mortis, McEnroe & Cash)*

## WHO THE HELL DOES JANE SMITH THINK SHE IS
| 87 | Influx FUX 1 | Use/Imagination (p/s) | 25 |
|----|----|----|----|
| 87 | Influx FUX 1T | Use/Imagination (12", p/s) | 60 |

## WALLY WHYTON (& VIPERS)
| 59 | Parlophone R 4585 | Don't Tell Me Your Troubles/It's All Over You | 5 |
|----|----|----|----|
| 60 | Parlophone R 4630 | All Over This World/Got Me A Girl | 5 |
| 60 | Pye 7N 15304 | It's A Rat Race/Marriage Of Convenience/95% Of Me Loves You (with Sally Miles)/You're Going To Be Caught (as Wally Whyton & Vipers) | 5 |
| 61 | Piccadilly 7N 35089 | Little Red Pony/Christmas Land | 5 |
| 68 | Fontana TF 960 | Gentle On My Mind/Ballad Of The Bol Weevil | 5 |
| 69 | Fontana TF 994 | Wichita Lineman/Leave Them A Flower | 5 |
| 69 | Fontana TF 1030 | Jig Alone/Out On The Road | 5 |

*(see also Vipers, Sharkey Todd & Monsters)*

## WI & HDEA
| 93 | Hype! VEN 001 | VENTURE F.M. PRESENTS SUMMER RUSH EP (12", stamped white label) | 20 |
|----|----|----|----|

## WICHITA FALL
| 69 | Liberty LBS 83208 | LIFE IS BUT A DREAM (LP) | 25 |
|----|----|----|----|

## WICHITA TRAIN WHISTLE
| 68 | Dot DOT 111 | Don't Cry Now/Tapioca Tundra (unissued) | 0 |
|----|----|----|----|
| 68 | Dot (S)LPD 516 | MICHAEL NESMITH PRESENTS THE WICHITA TRAIN WHISTLE SINGS (LP) | 40 |

*(see also Michael Nesmith)*

## WICKY WACKY
| 90 | EMI WACKY PROMO 1 | Let's Get Down (6 mixes, promo only, 300 copies) | 25 |
|----|----|----|----|

*(see also Cabaret Voltaire)*

## WIDERVISION
| 80 | Widermusic 001 | People/Truant (p/s) | 25 |
|----|----|----|----|

## WIDOWMAKER
| 76 | Jet JET 766 | On The Road/Pin A Rose On Me | 7 |
|----|----|----|----|
| 76 | Jet JET 767 | When I Met You/Pin A Rose On Me | 5 |
| 76 | Jet JET 782 | Pin A Rose On Me/On The Road | 5 |
| 77 | United Artists UAG 30038 | TOO LATE TO CRY (LP, gatefold sleeve) | 15 |

*(see also Luther Grosvenor, Steve Ellis, Huw Lloyd Langton)*

## DAVID WIGG
| 66 | CBS 202233 | Life Is Complicated/Turning Around | 10 |
|----|----|----|----|

## WIGGANS
| 61 | Blue Beat BB 29 | Rock Baby/Let's Sing The Blues | 25 |
|----|----|----|----|

## PERCY WIGGINS
| 67 | Atlantic 584 113 | Book Of Memories/Can't Find Nobody (To Take Your Place) | 10 |
|----|----|----|----|

## SPENCER WIGGINS
| 67 | Stateside SS 2024 | Uptight Good Woman/Anything You Do Is Alright | 25 |
|----|----|----|----|
| 70 | Pama PM 794 | I'm A Poor Man's Son/That's How Much I Love You | 25 |

## WIGWAM
| 76 | Virgin V2051 | LUCKY GOLDEN STRIPES AND STARPOSE (LP, "mirror" girl label, lyric insert, embossed sleeve) | 20 |
|----|----|----|----|
| 75 | Virgin V 2035 | NUCLEAR NIGHTCLUB (LP) | 25 |

## LEO WIJNKAMP JR
| 75 | Kicking Mule SNKF 108 | RAGS TO RICHES (LP) | 25 |
|----|----|----|----|
| 79 | Kicking Mule SNKF 156 | RETURN OF DR. HACKENBUSH (LP) | 25 |

## WIKKYD VIKKER
| 83 | Boogie FUR 0235 | Black Of The Night/Release (no p/s) | 120 |
|----|----|----|----|

## JACK WILCE
| 69 | Elektra EKSN 45068 | Apple Pie, Mother & The Flag/Ballad Of Baby Browning | 10 |
|----|----|----|----|

## WILCO
| 04 | Nonesuch 7559 79851 | I'm A Wheel/Kicking Television (p/s) | 6 |
|----|----|----|----|
| 11 | dBpm 87162-7 | I Might/I Love My Label (p/s, silver vinyl) | 6 |
| 11 | dBpm 87181-1 | SPEAK INTO THE ROSE (10" red vinyl, Record Store Day release) | 10 |
| 97 | Reprise 9362 46236-1 | BEING THERE (2-LP) | 40 |
| 99 | Reprise 9362 47282-1 | SUMMERTEETH (2-LP) | 40 |
| 04 | Nonsuch 76492-1 | A GHOST IS BORN (2-LP) | 25 |

## WILD BEASTS (1)
| 79 | Fried Egg EGG 002 | Minimum Maximum/Another Noun (p/s) | 5 |
|----|----|----|----|
| 79 | Warped BEND 1 | LIFE IS A BUM EP (folded p/s) | 10 |

## WILD ANGELS
| 68 | Major Minor MM 569 | Nervous Breakdown/Watch The Wheels Go Round | 25 |
|----|----|----|----|
| 69 | B&C CB 114 | Buzz Buzz/Please Don't Touch | 12 |
| 70 | B&C CB 123 | Sally-Ann/Wrong Number, Try Again | 12 |
| 71 | B&C CB 145 | Three Nights A Week/Time To Kill | 8 |
| 72 | Decca F 13308 | Jo-Jo Ann/My Way | 7 |
| 72 | Decca F 13356 | Beauty School Dropout/Midnight Rider | 7 |

MINT VALUE £

| 73 | Decca F 13374 | Running Bear/Sussin' | 6 |
| 73 | Decca F 13412 | Greased Lightning/Born To Hand-Jive/Beauty School Dropout | 6 |
| 73 | Decca F 13456 | Clap Your Hands And Stamp Your Feet/Wild Angels Rock'n'Roll | 8 |
| 70 | B&C BCM 101 | LIVE AT THE REVOLUTION (LP) | 15 |
| 70 | B&C BCM 102 | RED HOT'N'ROCKIN' (LP) | 15 |

## WILD BOYS
| 78 | Ring Piece CUS 886 | Last One Of The Boys/We're Only Monsters | 400 |

## WILD BUNCH
| 84 | Ariwa ARILP 15 | THE WILD BUNCH (LP) | 20 |

## WILDCATS (1)
| 59 | London HLT 8787 | Gazachstahagen/Billy's Cha Cha | 25 |

## WILDCATS (2)
| 80s | Wildbop WILDBOP 1 | Talahassie Lassie/My Babe/Rip It UP | 5 |

## WILD COUNTRY
| 70 | Trafalgar TRAF 01 | Silent Village/Too Bad | 65 |

## JACK WILD(E)
| 69 | Elektra EKSN 45068 | Apple Pie Mother And The Flag/Ballad Of Baby Browning | 6 |
| 70 | Capitol CL 15635 | Picture Of You/Some Beautiful | 7 |
| 71 | Buddah 2011-19 | Punch & Judy/Takin It Easy | 10 |

## KIM WILDE
| 84 | MCA KIMP 1 | The Second Time/Lovers On A Beach (picture disc) | 10 |
| 84 | MCA KIMP 2 | The Touch/Shangri-La (shaped picture disc) | 10 |
| 85 | MCA KIMP 3 | Rage To Love/Putty In Your Hands (shaped picture disc) | 10 |

## MARTY WILDE (& WILDCATS)
### 78s
| 58 | Philips PB 781 | Love Bug Crawl/Afraid Of Love | 30 |
| 58 | Philips PB 804 | Sing, Boy, Sing/Oh-Oh, I'm Falling In Love Again (with Wildcats) | 25 |
| 59 | Philips PB 902 | Donna/Love-a, Love-a, Love-a | 25 |
| 59 | Philips PB 926 | A Teenager In Love/Danny | 30 |
| 59 | Philips PB 959 | Sea Of Love/Teenage Tears | 40 |
| 59 | Philips PB 972 | It's Been Nice/Bad Boy | 40 |
| 60 | Philips PB 1002 | Johnny Rocco/My Heart And I | 50 |

### SINGLES
| 57 | Philips JK 1028 | Honeycomb/Wild Cat (as Marty Wilde & Wildcats) (jukebox issue) | 50 |
| 58 | Philips PB 804 | Sing, Boy, Sing/Oh-Oh, I'm Falling In Love Again (with Wildcats) | 40 |
| 58 | Philips PB 835 | Endless Sleep/Her Hair Was Yellow (as Marty Wilde & Wildcats) | 15 |
| 58 | Philips PB 850 | My Lucky Love/Misery's Child (as Marty Wilde & Wildcats) | 12 |
| 58 | Philips PB 875 | No One Knows/The Fire Of Love | 15 |
| 59 | Philips PB 902 | Donna/Love-a, Love-a, Love-a | 10 |
| 59 | Philips PB 926 | A Teenager In Love/Danny | 10 |
| 59 | Philips PB 959 | Sea Of Love/Teenage Tears | 10 |
| 59 | Philips PB 972 | Bad Boy/It's Been Nice | 10 |
| 60 | Philips PB 1002 | Johnny Rocco/My Heart And I | 10 |
| 60 | Philips PB 1022 | The Fight/Johnny At The Crossroads | 10 |
| 60 | Philips PB 1037 | I Wanna Be Loved By You/Angry | 6 |
| 60 | Philips PB 1078 | Little Girl/Your Seventeenth Spring | 6 |
| 61 | Philips PB 1101 | Rubber Ball/Like Makin' Love | 6 |
| 61 | Philips PB 1121 | When Does It Get To Be Love/Your Loving Touch | 7 |
| 61 | Philips PB 1161 | Hide And Seek/Crazy Dream | 15 |
| 61 | Philips PB 1191 | Tomorrow's Clown/The Hellions | 12 |
| 61 | Philips PB 1206 | Come Running/Ev'ryone | 12 |
| 62 | Philips PB 1240 | Jezebel/Don't Run Away | 10 |
| 62 | Philips 326 546BF | Ever Since You Said Goodbye/Send Me The Pillow You Dream On | 10 |
| 63 | Columbia DB 4980 | Lonely Avenue/Brand New Love | 10 |
| 63 | Philips 326 579BF | No! Dance With Me/Little Miss Happiness | 7 |
| 63 | Columbia DB 7145 | Save Your Love For Me/Bless My Broken Heart | 10 |
| 64 | Columbia DB 7198 | When Day Is Done/I Can't Help The Way I Feel | 10 |
| 64 | Columbia DB 7285 | Kiss Me/My, What A Woman | 10 |
| 64 | Decca F 11979 | The Mexican Boy/Your Kind Of Love | 12 |
| 66 | Philips PB 1490 | I've Got So Used To Loving You/The Beginning Of The End | 5 |
| 68 | Philips BF 1632 | By The Time I Get To Phoenix/Shutters And Boards | 5 |
| 68 | Philips BF 1669 | Abergavenny/Alice In Blue | 5 |
| 69 | Philips BF 1753 | All The Love I Have/Any Day | 5 |
| 69 | Philips BF 1783 | Endless Sleep/Donna | 5 |
| 69 | Philips BF 1815 | Shelley/Jump On The Train (with Deke Leonard) | 5 |
| 70 | Philips BF 1839 | No Trams To Lime Street/Prelude To Old Age | 5 |
| 71 | Philips 6006 126 | Busker/It's So Real | 5 |
| 74 | Magnet MAG 15 | I Love You/She's A Mover | 5 |

### EPs
| 57 | Philips BBE 12164 | PRESENTING MARTY WILDE | 30 |
| 58 | Philips BBE 12200 | MORE OF MARTY | 30 |
| 59 | Philips BBE 12327 | SEA OF LOVE | 30 |
| 60 | Philips BBE 12385 | VERSATILE MR. WILDE | 25 |
| 60 | Philips BBE 12422 | MARTY WILDE FAVOURITES | 25 |
| 62 | Philips BBE 12517 | COME RUNNING | 25 |
| 63 | Philips BE 433 638 | MARTY | 25 |

## ALBUMS

| | | | |
|---|---|---|---|
| 59 | Philips BBL 7342 | WILDE ABOUT MARTY | 50 |
| 60 | Philips BBL 7380 | MARTY WILDE SHOWCASE | 35 |
| 60 | Philips BBL 7385 | THE VERSATILE MR. WILDE (mono) | 30 |
| 60 | Philips SBBL 570 | THE VERSATILE MR. WILDE (stereo) | 35 |

*(see also Wilde Three, Brian Bennett, Shadows, Keith Shields, Capricorn, Deke Leonard)*

## RICKY WILDE

| | | | |
|---|---|---|---|
| 73 | UK 28 | April Love/Round And Round | 6 |
| 74 | UK 59 | Mrs Malinski/Cassette Blues | 6 |
| 74 | UK 63 | Round And Round/Teen Wave | 6 |
| 74 | UK UK 70 | I Wanna Go To A Disco/I Wanna Go To A Disco (double A sided promo) | 10 |

## WILDER BROTHERS

| | | | |
|---|---|---|---|
| 57 | HMV POP 365 | I Want You/Teenage Angel | 250 |
| 57 | HMV POP 365 | I Want You/Teenage Angel (78) | 50 |

## WILDERNESS ROAD

| | | | |
|---|---|---|---|
| 74 | Dawn DNLS 3057 | WILDERNESS ROAD (LP, unissued) | 0 |

## WILDERVISION

| | | | |
|---|---|---|---|
| 80 | Wildermusic WDR 1 | People/Truant | 10 |

## WILDE THREE

| | | | |
|---|---|---|---|
| 65 | Decca F 12131 | Since You've Gone/Just As Long | 75 |
| 65 | Decca F 12232 | I Cried/Well Who's That? | 75 |

*(see also Marty Wilde, Justin Hayward, Vernons Girls)*

## WILDFIRE (1)

| | | | |
|---|---|---|---|
| 84 | Mausoleum GUTS 8403 | Nothing Lasts Forever/Blood Money | 8 |
| 84 | Mausoleum GUTS 8405 | Jerusalem/Fight Fire With Fire (p/s) | 5 |
| 83 | Mausoleum SKUL 8307 | BRUTE FORCE AND IGNORANCE (LP) | 25 |
| 83 | Mausoleum SKUL 8338 | SUMMER LIGHTNING (LP, with insert) | 15 |

*(see also Weapon)*

## WILDHEARTS

### SINGLES

| | | | |
|---|---|---|---|
| 92 | East West YZ 669T | MONDO AKIMBO A-GO-GO (12" EP, with inner sleeve) | 25 |
| 92 | East West YZ 669TX | MONDO AKIMBO A-GO-GO (12" EP, white vinyl, with inner sleeve, advance copies with artwork postcard & press sheet) | 40 |
| 92 | East West YZ 669TX | MONDO AKIMBO A-GO-GO (12" EP, white vinyl, with inner sleeve) | 35 |
| 92 | East West YZ 669CD | MONDO AKIMBO A-GO-GO (CD EP) | 40 |
| 93 | East West YZ 773 | Greetings From Shitsville/The Bullshit Goes On (p/s, brown vinyl, with insert) | 12 |
| 94 | East West YZ 794 | Caffeine Bomb/Girlfriend Clothes (p/s, green vinyl, with insert) | 5 |
| 94 | East West YZ 828TE | Suckerpunch/Beautiful Thing You/Two-Way Idiot Mirror/29 x The Pain (10", p/s, 1-sided, etched) | 12 |
| 94 | East West YZ 874TEX | If Life Is Like A Lovebank I Want An Overdraft/Geordie In Wonderland/ Hate The World Day/Fire Up (10", gatefold sleeve with banknote) | 10 |
| 95 | East West YZ 923TEX | I Wanna Go Where The People Go/Shandy Bang/Can't Do Right For Doing Wrong/ Give The Girl A Gun (10", p/s) | 10 |
| 95 | East West YZ 976TEX | Just In Lust/Mindslide/Friend For Five Minutes/S.I.N (In Sin) (10", p/s) | 10 |

### ALBUMS

| | | | |
|---|---|---|---|
| 92 | East West 4509-91202-1 | DON'T BE HAPPY... JUST WORRY (LP, as 2 x 12", with inner sleeves) | 25 |
| 92 | East West 4509-91202-2 | DON'T BE HAPPY... JUST WORRY (2-CD, with bonus disc containing Anti-Dance Mixes of "Mondo Akimbo A-Go Go" tracks) | 25 |
| 93 | East West 4509-93287-1 | EARTH VS THE WILDHEARTS (LP, with exclusive uncredited track) | 20 |
| 94 | East West 4509-99039-2 | FISHING FOR LUCKIES (CD, 6-track mini-album, fan club/mail-order only) | 40 |
| 95 | East West 0630-10404-1 | P.H.U.Q. (LP, gatefold sleeve) | 15 |
| 95 | East West 0630-12850-1 | FISHING FOR MORE LUCKIES (LP, reissue, with 3 extra tracks Underkill, "Saddened" & "I Wanna Go Where The People Go [Early Version]", unreleased, most copies destroyed) | 100 |
| 96 | Round 0630-14888-1 | FISHING FOR LUCKIES (2-LP, reissue, gatefold, Side 3 exclusive to vinyl) | 18 |
| 97 | Mushroom MUSH13LP | ENDLESS, NAMELESS (LP, inner sleeve) | 15 |
| 98 | Kuro Neko KNEKLP3 | ANARCHIC AIRWAVES - THE WiLDHEARTS AT THE BBC (2-LP, 200 mail-order copies only - 1000 copies made but 800 destroyed) | 25 |
| 98 | Kuro Neko KNEK4LB | LANDMINES & PANTOMIMES - THE LAST OF THE WiLDHEARTS...? (CD in square stickered metal tin in card box with insert, 1000 copies only) | 30 |

*(see also Backyard Babies, Energetic Krusher, Honeycrack, Quireboys, SilverGinger 5, Super$hit666, Yo-Yo's)*

## WILD HORSES

| | | | |
|---|---|---|---|
| 79 | EMI International INTS 599 | Criminal Tendencies/The Rapist (p/s) | 5 |
| 80 | EMI EMI 5047 | Face Down/Dealer (p/s) | 5 |
| 80 | EMI EMI 5078 | Fly Away/Blackmail (p/s, white vinyl; black vinyl demos £15) | 6 |
| 81 | EMI EMI 5149 | I'll Give You Love/Rocky Mountain Way (p/s) | 5 |
| 81 | EMI EMI 5149 | I'll Give You Love/Rocky Mountain Way//The Kid/On A Saturday Night (double pack, gatefold p/s) | 5 |
| 81 | EMI EMI 5199 | Everlasting Love/The Axe (no p/s) | 5 |
| 81 | EMI EMC 3368 | STAND YOUR GROUND (LP, with inner sleeve) | 15 |

*(see also Thin Lizzy, Motorhead, Rainbow, Dio)*

## WILD MAGNOLIAS

| | | | |
|---|---|---|---|
| 75 | Barclay BAR 30 | Smoke My Peace Pipe/Handa Wanda | 5 |
| 75 | Barclay BAR 34 | They Call Us Wild/Jumalaka Boom Boom | 5 |
| 75 | Barclay 80 529 | THE WILD MAGNOLIAS 1 (LP, gatefold sleeve) | 20 |
| 75 | Barclay 90 033 | THEY CALL US WILD (LP, gatefold sleeve) | 20 |

## WILD OATS

| | | | |
|---|---|---|---|
| 63 | Oak RGJ 117 | WILD OATS (EP) | 750 |

## WILD ONES (U.K.)

| | | | |
|---|---|---|---|
| 64 | Fontana TF 468 | Bowie Man/Purple Pill Eater | 75 |

## WILD ONES (U.S)
| | | |
|---|---|---|
| 65 | United Artsts ULP 1119 | THE ARTHUR SOUND (LP) .................................................. 40 |

## WILD PUSSY
| | | |
|---|---|---|
| 88 | Metallion | MECHANARCH (12", EP, wih insert) ......................................... 100 |

## WILD SILK
| | | |
|---|---|---|
| 68 | Polydor 56256 | Poor Man/Stop Crying.................................................. 10 |
| 69 | Columbia DB 8534 | (Visions In A) Plaster Sky/Toymaker ...................................... 30 |
| 69 | Columbia DB 8611 | Help Me/Crimson And Gold ............................................. 20 |

## WILD SWANS
| | | |
|---|---|---|
| 82 | Zoo CAGE 009 | The Revolutionary Spirit/God Forbid (unissued, stamped white label) ............... 12 |
| 82 | Zoo CAGE 009 | The Revolutionary Spirit/God Forbid (12", p/s) ............................. 10 |
| 82 | Zoo CAGE 009 | The Revolutionary Spirit/God Forbid (12", p/s, with 'The Lament Of Icarus' painting in top right of front sleeve, withdrawn).......................... 15 |

*(see also Lotus Eaters, Care)*

## WILD THING
| | | |
|---|---|---|
| 69 | Elektra EKSN 45076 | Old Lady/Next To Me ..................................................... 6 |
| 70 | Elektra EKS 74059 | PARTYIN' (LP) ......................................................... 18 |

## WILD TURKEY
| | | |
|---|---|---|
| 72 | Chrysalis CHS 2004 | Good Old Days/Life Is A Symphony .......................................... 5 |
| 72 | Chrysalis CHR 1002 | BATTLE HYMN (LP, gatefold sleeve)......................................... 40 |
| 73 | Chrysalis CHR 1010 | TURKEY (LP, gatefold sleeve) ............................................ 20 |

*(see also Babe Ruth, Jethro Tull, Man, Gary Pickford-Hopkins, Whitesnake)*

## WILD UNCERTAINTY
| | | |
|---|---|---|
| 66 | Planet PLF 120 | Man With Money/Broken Truth ............................................ 80 |

## WILD & WANDERING
| | | |
|---|---|---|
| 86 | Iguana VYK 14 | 2,000 LIGHT ALES FROM HOME (12" EP, with insert)............................ 25 |

*(see also Pop Will Eat Itself)*

## WILDWEEDS
| | | |
|---|---|---|
| 67 | Chess CRS 8065 | It Was Fun While It Lasted/Sorrow's Anthem ................................. 20 |

## WILDY
| | | |
|---|---|---|
| 76 | Paladin PAL 12 | No Smokin'/All The Children ............................................. 10 |

## WILFRED
| | | |
|---|---|---|
| 70 | Parlophone R5836 | Candle In The WInd/Between The Lines ....................................... 15 |

## WILFRED & MILLICENT
| | | |
|---|---|---|
| 65 | Island WI 190 | The Vow/I'll Never Believe In You .......................................... 12 |

*(see also Jackie [Edwards] & Millie [Small])*

## MIKE WILHELM
| | | |
|---|---|---|
| 76 | Zigzag/United Artists ZZ 1 | MIKE WILHELM (LP, sold via Zigzag magazine) ............................... 45 |

*(see also Charlatans, Flamin' Groovies)*

## JOHN BUCK WILKIN
| | | |
|---|---|---|
| 70 | LBF 15375 | Apartment Twenty-One/Boy Of The Country.................................. 6 |

## ROBERT WILKINS
| | | |
|---|---|---|
| 60s | Piedmont PLP 13162 | REV ROBERT WILKINS (LP) ................................................ 20 |
| 70 | Spokane SPL 1002 | BEFORE THE REVERENCE (LP) ............................................. 40 |

## C.T WILKINSON
| | | |
|---|---|---|
| 76 | DJM DJS 668 | My Happiness/Monday Coming Up ......................................... 8 |

## WILLARDS LEAP
| | | |
|---|---|---|
| 77 | Wren CW 71010 | ADIEU, JOHN BARLEYCORN ............................................... 20 |

## E WILLIAM
| | | |
|---|---|---|
| 67 | Polydor 56181 | Lazy Life/Crazy How love Slips Away ...................................... 50 |

## AL WILLIAMS
| | | |
|---|---|---|
| 80 | Grapevine GRP 136 | I Am Nothing/Brand New Love.......................................... 20 |

## ANDY WILLIAMS
| | | |
|---|---|---|
| 56 | London HLA 8284 | Walk Hand In Hand/Not Any More .......................................... 30 |
| 56 | London HLA 8315 | Canadian Sunset/High Upon A Mountain (gold label print) .................... 40 |
| 56 | London HLA 8315 | Canadian Sunset/High Upon A Mountain (silver label print).................... 15 |
| 56 | London HL 7013 | Canadian Sunset/High Upon A Mountain (export issue) ....................... 20 |
| 56 | London HLA 8360 | Baby Doll (From The Film)/Since I've Found My Baby (gold print)................ 35 |
| 56 | London HLA 8360 | Baby Doll (From The Film)/Since I've Found My Baby (silver print) .............. 15 |
| 57 | London HLA 8399 | Butterfly/It Doesn't Take Very Long ....................................... 15 |
| 57 | London HLA 8437 | I Like Your Kind Of Love/Stop Teasin' Me .................................. 10 |
| 57 | London HLA 8487 | Lips Of Wine/Straight From My Heart ..................................... 10 |
| 58 | London HLA 8587 | Are You Sincere/Be Mine Tonight ........................................ 10 |
| 58 | London HL 7034 | Are You Sincere/Be Mine Tonight (export issue) ............................ 10 |
| 58 | London HLA 8710 | Promise Me, Love/Your Hand, Your Heart, Your Love......................... 10 |
| 59 | London HLA 8784 | Hawaiian Wedding Song/House Of Bamboo................................. 10 |
| 59 | London HLA 8957 | Lonely Street/Summer Love ............................................. 7 |
| 59 | London HL 9018 | The Village Of St. Bernadette/I'm So Lonesome I Could Cry .................... 6 |
| 67 | CBS CBS 2675 | Music To Watch Girls By/The Face I Love .................................. 5 |
| 67 | CBS 3104 | Holly/God Only Knows (B-side is Beach Boys cover) .......................... 7 |
| 57 | London RE-A 1088 | ANDY WILLIAMS' BIG HITS (EP)............................................ 12 |
| 57 | London RE-A 1102 | ANDY WILLIAMS' BIG HITS No. 2 (EP) ...................................... 12 |
| 57 | London HA-A 2054 | ANDY WILLIAMS SINGS STEVE ALLEN (LP) ................................... 20 |
| 58 | London HA-A 2113 | ANDY WILLIAMS SINGS RODGERS AND HAMMERSTEIN (LP) ..................... 20 |
| 59 | London HA-A 2203 | TWO TIME WINNERS (LP) ................................................ 20 |

## AUDREY WILLIAMS
| | | |
|---|---|---|
| 56 | MGM SP 1179 | Ain't Nothing Gonna Be All Right No How/Livin' It Up And Havin' A Ball.............. 25 |

*(see also Hank Williams)*

## BIG JOE WILLIAMS

| 57 | Jazz Collector JEN 3 | A MAN SINGS THE BLUES (EP) | 10 |
|----|---------------------|---------------------------|-----|
| 57 | Jazz Collector JEN 4 | A MAN SINGS THE BLUES VOLUME 2 (EP) | 10 |
| 67 | Delmark DJB 4 | ON THE HIGHWAY (EP) | 15 |
| 63 | Esquire 32-191 | BLUES ON HIGHWAY 51 (LP) | 40 |
| 63 | '77' LA 12-19 | PINEY WOODS BLUES (LP) | 30 |
| 64 | CBS BPG 63813 | CLASSIC DELTA BLUES (LP) | 20 |
| 64 | Storyville SLP 158 | PORTRAITS IN BLUES VOLUME 4 (LP) | 20 |
| 64 | Storyville SLP 163 | PORTRAITS IN BLUES VOLUME 7 (LP) | 20 |
| 65 | Fontana 688 800 ZL | TOUGH TIMES (LP) | 25 |
| 66 | Xtra XTRA 1033 | BIG JOE WILLIAMS (LP) | 30 |
| 66 | Bounty BY 6018 | BACK TO THE COUNTRY (LP) | 40 |
| 66 | Society SOC 1020 | BIG JOE, SONNY, BROWNIE, LIGHTNIN' (LP, with Lightnin' Hopkins, Sonny Terry & Brownie McGhee) | 15 |
| 69 | Storyville 618 011 | DON'T YOU LEAVE ME HERE (LP) | 20 |
| 69 | Liberty LBL/LBS 83207 | HAND ME DOWN MY OLD WALKING STICK (LP) | 20 |
| 69 | Xtra XTRA 5059 | LIVE AT FOLK CITY (LP) | 15 |
| 70 | RCA Intl. INTS 1087 | CRAWLIN' KING SNAKE (LP) | 18 |
| 72 | Delmark DS 627 | NINE STRING GUITAR (LP) | 15 |

*(see also Poor Joe Williams)*

## BILLY WILLIAMS (QUARTET)

| 54 | Vogue Coral Q 2012 | Sh'Boom/Whenever Wherever | 15 |
|----|-------------------|--------------------------|-----|
| 54 | Vogue Coral Q 2039 | The Honeydripper/Love Me (as Billy Williams Quartet) | 40 |
| 56 | Vogue Coral Q 72149 | A Crazy Little Palace/Cry Baby (as Billy Williams Quartet) | 40 |
| 56 | Vogue Coral Q 72180 | Pray/You'll Reach Your Star | 18 |
| 57 | Vogue Coral Q 72222 | Follow Me/Shame, Shame, Shame (as Billy Williams Quartet) | 20 |
| 57 | Vogue Coral Q 72241 | Butterfly/The Pied Piper | 20 |
| 57 | Vogue Coral Q 72266 | I'm Gonna Sit Right Down And Write A Letter/Date With The Blues | 20 |
| 57 | Vogue Coral Q 72295 | Got A Date With An Angel/The Lord Will Understand | 30 |
| 58 | Coral Q 72303 | Don't Let Go/Baby, Baby (as Billy Williams Quartet) | 30 |
| 58 | Coral Q 72316 | Steppin' Out Tonight/There I've Said It Again (as Billy Williams Quartet) | 30 |
| 58 | Coral Q 72331 | I'll Get By/It's Prayin' Time | 15 |
| 59 | Coral Q 72359 | Nola/Tied To The Strings Of Your Heart | 10 |
| 59 | Coral Q 72369 | Goodnight Irene/Red Hot Love | 20 |
| 59 | Coral Q 72377 | Telephone Conversation/Go To Sleep, Go To Sleep, Go To Sleep (with Barbara McNair) | 15 |
| 60 | Coral Q 72402 | I Cried For You/Lover Of All Lovers | 10 |
| 60 | Coral Q 72414 | Begin The Beguine/For You | 5 |
| 58 | Coral LVA 9092 | BILLY WILLIAMS | 90 |
| 60 | Coral LVA 9120 | HALF SWEET HALF BEAT | 20 |
| 61 | Coral LVA 9139 | THE BILLY WILLIAMS REVUE | 20 |

*(see also Barbara McNair)*

## BOBBY WILLIAMS

| 68 | Action ACT 4509 | Baby I Need Your Love/Try It Again | 50 |
|----|----------------|-----------------------------------|-----|
| 73 | Contempo C 17 | Let's Jam/You're My Baby | 8 |

## CHRIS WILLIAMS & HIS MONSTERS

| 59 | Columbia DB 4383 | The Monster/The Eton Boating Song | 25 |
|----|-----------------|----------------------------------|-----|
| 60 | Triumph RGM 1003 | Kicking Around/Midnight Rocker (unissued; white label demo copies only) | 250 |

## CINDY WILLIAMS

| 67 | Parlophone R 5648 | They Talk About Us/Did He Call Today Mama | 8 |
|----|-------------------|------------------------------------------|-----|

## CLARENCE WILLIAMS (& HIS WASHBOARD BAND)

| 54 | Columbia SCM 5134 | High Society/Left All Alone With The Blues | 20 |
|----|-------------------|-------------------------------------------|-----|
| 54 | London AL 3526 | CLARENCE WILLIAMS AND HIS ORCHESTRA (10" LP) | 20 |
| 55 | Columbia 33S 1067 | BACK ROOM SPECIAL (10" LP) | 20 |
| 57 | London AL 3561 | CLARENCE WILLIAMS AND HIS ORCHESTRA VOL. 2 (10" LP) | 20 |

## CLIVE WILLIAMS

| 69 | Rock Steady Rev. REVR 6 | Take Good Care Of My Baby/RICO: In Loving Memory Of Don Drummond | 25 |
|----|------------------------|-----------------------------------------------------------------|-----|

## DAN WILLIAMS & HIS ORCHESTRA

| 55 | London CAY 110 | Donkey City/SHAW PARK CALYPSO BAND: Take Her To Jamaica | 10 |
|----|---------------|-------------------------------------------------------|-----|

## DANNY WILLIAMS

| 59 | HMV POP 624 | Tall A Tree/I Look At You | 7 |
|----|-------------|--------------------------|-----|
| 59 | HMV POP 655 | So High - So Low/My Own True Love | 7 |
| 59 | HMV POP 703 | Youthful Years/It Doesn't Matter | 7 |
| 60 | HMV POP 803 | A Million To One/Call Me A Dreamer | 6 |
| 61 | HMV POP 839 | We Will Never Be As Young As This Again/Passing Breeze | 5 |
| 61 | HMV POP 885 | The Miracle Of You/Lonely | 5 |
| 63 | HMV POP 1112 | My Own True Love/Who Can Say? | 8 |
| 63 | HMV POP 1150 | More/Rhapsody | 6 |
| 63 | HMV POP 1172 | The Wild Wind/Once Upon A Time | 8 |
| 63 | HMV POP 1203 | A Day Without You/Secret Love | 6 |
| 63 | HMV POP 1236 | How Do You Keep From Crying?/Now The Day Is Over | 6 |
| 63 | HMV POP 1263 | White On White/After You | 8 |
| 64 | HMV POP 1305 | Today/Lonely In A Crowd | 6 |
| 64 | HMV POP 1325 | The Seventh Dawn/The World Around Me | 6 |
| 64 | HMV POP 1372 | Forget Her, Forget Her/Lollipops And Roses | 30 |
| 65 | HMV POP 1388 | The Roundabout Of Love/I Wanna Be Around | 5 |
| 65 | HMV POP 1410 | Go Away/Masquerade | 30 |
| 65 | HMV POP 1455 | Lovely Is She/Gone And Forgotten | 5 |

| 65 | HMV POP 1487 | And So We Meet Again/Violets For Your Furs | 5 |
| 66 | HMV POP 1506 | I've Got To Find That Girl Again/Throw A Little Lovin' My Way | 30 |
| 67 | Deram DM 149 | Never My Love/Whose Little Girl Are You (with inverted matrix) | 30 |
| 67 | Deram DM 149 | Never My Love/Whose Little Girl Are You (re-pressing with matrix correct way up) | 10 |
| 62 | HMV 7EG 8748 | HITS OF DANNY WILLIAMS (EP) | 15 |
| 61 | HMV CLP 1458 | DANNY (LP, mono) | 25 |
| 61 | HMV CSD 1369 | DANNY (LP, stereo) | 20 |
| 61 | HMV CLP 1521 | MOON RIVER AND OTHER TITLES (LP) | 20 |
| 62 | HMV CSD 1471 | SWINGING FOR YOU (LP, stereo) | 15 |
| 66 | HMV CLP/CSD 3523 | ONLY LOVE (LP) | 20 |
| 67 | Deram DML 1017 | DANNY WILLIAMS (LP) | 20 |

## DEL WILLIAMS

| 72 | Grape GR 3027 | Searching For Your Love/G.G. ALL STARS: Searching (Version) | 5 |

## DELROY WILLIAMS

| 71 | Trojan TR 7813 | Down In The Boondocks/Baby Make It | 7 |
| 76 | Treble C CCC 013 | Red, Green And Gold (In My Garden)/Let's Be People | 8 |

## GEORGE WILLIAMS

| 69 | Bullet BU 405 | No Business Of Yours/Mast It Up (actually titled "Mash It Up") | 35 |

## GEORGE WILLIAMS & HIS ORCHESTRA

| 55 | Vogue Coral Q 72053 | The Rompin' Stomper/Knock-Out Choo-Choo | 8 |
| 56 | HMV DLP 1140 | RHYTHM WAS HIS BUSINESS (10" LP) | 15 |

## GINGER WILLIAMS

| 74 | Paradise PR 01 | I Can't Resist Your Tenderness/Little Boy | 12 |
| 77 | B&B BBLP 1001 | STRANGE WORLD (LP) | 30 |
| 80 | B&B BBLP 1111 | COOL LOVING (LP, lilac vinyl) | 25 |

## GRANVILLE WILLIAMS ORCHESTRA

| 67 | Island WI 3062 | Hi-Life/More | 12 |
| 67 | Island ILP 971 | HI-LIFE (LP) | 60 |

*(see also Silvertones)*

## HANK WILLIAMS (& HIS DRIFTING COWBOYS)

### 78s

| 56 | MGM MGM 889 | The First Fall Of Snow/Someday You'll Call My Name (withdrawn) | 0 |

### SINGLES

| 53 | MGM SP 1016 | I'll Never Get Out Of This World Alive/I Could Never Be Ashamed Of You (as Hank Williams & His Drifting Cowboys) | 50 |
| 53 | MGM SP 1034 | Kaw-Liga/Take These Chains From My Heart (& His Drifting Cowboys) | 50 |
| 53 | MGM SP 1049 | Ramblin' Man/I Won't Be Home No More | 40 |
| 53 | MGM SP 1048 | My Bucket's Got A Hole In It/Let's Turn Back The Years | 40 |
| 54 | MGM SP 1067 | Weary Blues (From Waitin')/I Can't Escape From You | 40 |
| 54 | MGM SP 1085 | There'll Be No Teardrops Tonight/Crazy Heart | 40 |
| 54 | MGM SP 1102 | I'm Satisfied With You/I Ain't Got Nothin' But Time | 40 |
| 56 | MGM SP 1163 | The First Fall Of Snow/Someday You'll Call My Name (unreleased) | 0 |
| 56 | MGM MGM 921 | There's No Room In My Heart (For The Blues)/I Wish I Had A Nickel | 30 |
| 56 | MGM MGM 931 | Blue Love (In My Heart)/Singing Waterfall | 30 |
| 57 | MGM MGM 942 | Low Down Blues/My Sweet Love Ain't Around | 30 |
| 57 | MGM MGM 957 | Rootie Tootie/Lonesome Whistle | 30 |
| 57 | MGM MGM 966 | Leave Me Alone With The Blues/With Tears In My Eyes | 30 |
| 66 | MGM MGM 1309 | You Win Again/I'm So Lonesome I Could Cry | 5 |
| 66 | MGM MGM 1322 | Kaw-Liga/Let's Turn Back The Years | 5 |

### EPs

| 54 | MGM MGM-EP 512 | HANK WILLIAMS AND HIS DRIFTING COWBOYS (company sleeve) | 25 |
| 54 | MGM EPC 7 | HANK WILLIAMS (export issue) | 30 |
| 55 | MGM MGM-EP 551 | JUST WAITIN' (as Luke The Drifter, company sleeve) | 20 |
| 55 | MGM MGM-EP 551 | JUST WAITIN' (as Luke The Drifter, later issue with p/s) | 30 |
| 56 | MGM MGM-EP 569 | I SAW THE LIGHT (No. 1) (company sleeve) | 15 |
| 56 | MGM MGM-EP 569 | I SAW THE LIGHT (No. 1) (later issue with p/s) | 20 |
| 57 | MGM MGM-EP 582 | HONKY TONKIN' | 20 |
| 57 | MGM MGM-EP 608 | I SAW THE LIGHT (No. 2) | 20 |
| 57 | MGM MGM-EP 614 | HONKY TONK BLUES | 20 |
| 58 | MGM MGM-EP 639 | SONGS FOR A BROKEN HEART (No. 1) | 20 |
| 58 | MGM MGM-EP 649 | SONGS FOR A BROKEN HEART (No. 2) | 20 |
| 58 | MGM MGM-EP 675 | HANK'S LAMENTS | 20 |
| 60 | MGM MGM-EP 710 | THE UNFORGETTABLE HANK WILLIAMS | 20 |
| 60 | MGM MGM-EP 726 | THE UNFORGETTABLE HANK WILLIAMS (No. 2) | 20 |
| 60 | MGM MGM-EP 732 | THE UNFORGETTABLE HANK WILLIAMS (No. 3) | 20 |
| 61 | MGM MGM-EP 757 | HANK WILLIAMS FAVOURITES | 20 |
| 63 | MGM MGM-EP 770 | THE AUTHENTIC SOUND OF THE COUNTRY HITS | 20 |

### ALBUMS

| 52 | MGM MGM-D 105 | HANK WILLIAMS SINGS (10" LP, company sleeve) | 40 |
| 53 | MGM MGM-D 105 | HANK WILLIAMS SINGS (10" LP, later issue in p/s) | 50 |
| 53 | MGM MGM-D 119 | HANK WILLIAMS AS LUKE THE DRIFTER (10" LP, company sleeve) | 30 |
| 53 | MGM MGM-D 119 | HANK WILLIAMS AS LUKE THE DRIFTER (10" LP, later issue in p/s) | 40 |
| 55 | MGM MGM-D 137 | HANK WILLIAMS MEMORIAL ALBUM (10") | 30 |
| 56 | MGM MGM-D 144 | MOANIN' THE BLUES (10") | 40 |
| 58 | MGM MGM-D 150 | SING ME A BLUE SONG (10") | 40 |
| 58 | MGM MGM-D 154 | THE IMMORTAL HANK WILLIAMS (10") | 30 |
| 59 | MGM MGM-C 784 | THE UNFORGETTABLE HANK WILLIAMS | 20 |

| 60 | MGM MGM-C 811 | THE LONESOME SOUND OF HANK WILLIAMS | 30 |
| 60 | MGM MGM-C 834 | WAIT FOR THE LIGHT TO SHINE | 20 |
| 62 | MGM MGM-C 893 | ON STAGE | 20 |
| 63 | MGM MGM-C 956 | THE SPIRIT OF HANK WILLIAMS | 20 |
| 66 | MGM MGM-C 8019 | MAY YOU NEVER BE ALONE | 15 |
| 66 | MGM MGM-C 8020 | IN MEMORY OF HANK WILLIAMS | 15 |
| 66 | MGM MGM-C 8021 | I'M BLUE INSIDE | 20 |
| 66 | MGM MGM-C 8022 | LUKE THE DRIFTER | 15 |
| 66 | MGM MGM-C 8023 | THE MANY MOODS OF HANK WILLIAMS | 15 |
| 67 | MGM MGM-C(S) 8031 | THE LEGEND LIVES ANEW | 15 |
| 67 | MGM MGM-C(S) 8038 | MORE HANK WILLIAMS AND STRINGS | 15 |
| 67 | MGM MGM-C 8040 | LOVE SONGS, COMEDY AND HYMNS | 15 |
| 79 | World Records SM 551-556 | THE LEGENDARY HANK WILLIAMS (6-LP box set) | 20 |

*(see also Audrey Williams)*

## HANK WILLIAMS JR.
| 63 | MGM MGM 1223 | Long Gone Lonesome Blues/Doesn't Anybody Know My Name | 6 |
| 66 | MGM MGM 1299 | Cold Cold Heart/Is It That Fun To Heart Someone | 5 |

*(see also Connie Francis)*

## JEANETTE WILLIAMS
| 69 | Action ACT 4534 | Stuff/You Gotta Come Through | 8 |
| 70 | Action ACT 4557 | Hound Dog/I Can Feel A Heartbreak | 8 |

*(see also Swamp Dogg, Brooks & Jerry)*

## (LITTLE) JERRY WILLIAMS
| 65 | Cameo Parkway C 100 | Baby You're My Everything/Just What Do You Plan To Do About It | 85 |
| 65 | Cameo Parkway C 100 | Baby You're My Everything/Just What Do You Plan To Do About It (DJ copy) | 120 |
| 74 | Pye Disco Demand DDS 102 | If You Ask Me/ Yvonne (as Jerry Williams) | 8 |

## JIMMY WILLIAMS
| 65 | Atlantic AT 4042 | Walking On Air/I'm So Lost | 25 |

## JOE WILLIAMS
| 56 | London HB-C 1065 | JOE WILLIAMS SINGS (10" LP) | 20 |
| 57 | HMV CLP 1109 | THE GREATEST (LP) | 15 |
| 58 | Columbia 33SX 1087 | A MAN AIN'T SUPPOSED TO CRY (LP) | 20 |
| 60 | Columbia SCX 3308 | JOE WILLIAMS SINGS ABOUT YOU (LP, stereo) | 15 |
| 60 | Columbia SCX 3325 | THAT KIND OF WOMAN (LP, stereo) | 15 |
| 61 | Columbia SX 1392 | TOGETHER (LP, with Harry "Sweets" Edison, also stereo SCX 3421) | 15 |

*(see also Count Basie)*

## JOHN WILLIAMS
| 67 | Columbia DB 8128 | She's That Kind Of Woman/My Ways Are Set | 15 |
| 67 | Columbia DB 8251 | Flowers In Your Hair/Can't Find Time For Anything Now | 10 |
| 67 | Columbia SX 6169 | JOHN WILLIAMS (LP) | 100 |

*(see also Maureeny Wishfull)*

## JOHN WILLIAMS
| 84 | Island IS 155 | Paul McCartney's Theme From 'The Honorary Consul'/Clara's Theme (p/s) | 7 |

## JOHN WILLIAMS ORCHESTRA (U.S.)
| 66 | Stateside S(S)L 10187 | HOW TO STEAL A MILLION (LP, soundtrack) | 25 |
| 83 | MCA MCA 70000 | E.T. - THE EXTRA TERRESTRIAL (LP, soundtrack, box set with booklet & poster) | 30 |
| 83 | MCA CAC 70000 | E.T. - THE EXTRA TERRESTRIAL (cassette, soundtrack box set with booklet & poster) | 30 |

## KENNETH WILLIAMS
| 67 | Decca LK 4856 | ON PLEASURE BENT (LP) | 15 |

## LARRY WILLIAMS
| 57 | London HLN 8472 | Short Fat Fannie/High School Dance | 40 |
| 58 | London HLN 8532 | Bony Moronie/You Bug Me Baby | 20 |
| 58 | London HLU 8604 | Dizzy Miss Lizzy/Slow Down | 25 |
| 58 | London HLU 8604 | Dizzy Miss Lizzy/Slow Down (78) | 25 |
| 59 | London HLU 8844 | She Said "Yeah"/Bad Boy (silver top label) | 30 |
| 59 | London HLU 8844 | She Said "Yeah"/Bad Boy (78) | 30 |
| 60 | London HLU 8911 | I Can't Stop Loving You/Steal A Little Kiss | 30 |
| 60 | London HLU 8911 | I Can't Stop Loving You/Steal A Little Kiss (78) | 50 |
| 60 | London HLM 9053 | Baby, Baby/Get Ready | 30 |
| 65 | Sue WI 371 | Strange/Call On Me | 40 |
| 65 | Sue WI 381 | Turn On Your Lovelight/Dizzy Miss Lizzy | 40 |
| 68 | MGM MGM 1447 | Shake Your Body Girl/Love, I Can't Seem To Find It | 20 |
| 59 | London RE-U 1213 | LARRY WILLIAMS (EP) | 100 |
| 65 | Sue ILP 922 | LARRY WILLIAMS ON STAGE (LP) | 80 |
| 70s | Specialty SNTF 5025 | SLOW DOWN (LP) | 20 |
| 70s | Speciality SNTF 5008 | ORIGINAL HITS (LP) | 20 |

## LARRY WILLIAMS & JOHNNY 'GUITAR' WATSON
| 65 | Decca F 12151 | Sweet Little Baby/Slow Down | 20 |
| 67 | Columbia DB 8140 | Mercy, Mercy, Mercy/A Quitter Never Wins | 50 |
| 67 | Columbia DB 8140 | Mercy, Mercy, Mercy/A Quitter Never Wins (DJ copy) | 175 |
| 76 | Epic EPC 4421 | Too Late/Two For The Price Of One | 20 |
| 65 | Decca LK 4691 | THE LARRY WILLIAMS SHOW (LP, with Stormsville Shakers) | 80 |

*(see also Philip Goodhand-Tait [& Stormville Shakers])*

## LEVI WILLIAMS
| 75 | Locks LOX 5 | Come Me Breda/MIGHTY CLOUD BAND: Call Mi Sister | 5 |

## LEW WILLIAMS
| 50s | London (no cat. no.) | Cat Talk (1-sided, orange label demo-only) | 50 |

## LLOYD WILLIAMS
| | | | |
|---|---|---|---|
| 66 | Doctor Bird DB 1051 | Sad World/TOMMY McCOOK'S BAND: A Little Bit Of Heaven | 30 |
| 68 | Treasure Isle TI 7029 | Funky Beat/Goodbye Baby | 22 |
| 68 | Doctor Bird DB 1135 | Wonderful World (with Tommy McCook)/TOMMY McCOOK SUPERSONICS: Mad Mad World | 35 |
| 70 | Bamboo BAM 41 | I'm In Love With You/Little Girl | 30 |

## LORETTA WILLIAMS
| | | | |
|---|---|---|---|
| 66 | Atlantic 584 032 | Baby Cakes/I'm Missing You | 50 |

## LUCINDA WILLIAMS
| | | | |
|---|---|---|---|
| 89 | Rough Trade 130 | LUCINDA WILLIAMS (LP, with inner lyric bag) | 20 |

## LUTHER WILLIAMS ORCHESTRA
| | | | |
|---|---|---|---|
| 61 | Limbo XL 101 | Early In The Morning/Little Vilma | 5 |
| 61 | Melodisc MLP 12-125 | TROPICAL RHYTHMS OF JAMAICA (LP) | 15 |

## MARY LOU WILLIAMS
| | | | |
|---|---|---|---|
| 64 | Sue WI 311 | Chuck-a-Lunk Jug (Parts 1 & 2) | 25 |
| 53 | Vogue LDE 022 | PLAYS IN LONDON (10" LP) | 20 |
| 54 | Esquire 20-026 | PIANO PANORAMA (10" LP) | 20 |
| 55 | Felsted EDL 87012 | IN PARIS (10" LP) | 20 |

## MASON WILLIAMS
| | | | |
|---|---|---|---|
| 68 | Warner Bros WB 7190 | Classical Gas/Long Time Blues | 6 |

## MAURICE WILLIAMS (& ZODIACS)
| | | | |
|---|---|---|---|
| 60 | Top Rank JAR 526 | Stay/Do You Believe (as Maurice Williams & Zodiacs) | 20 |
| 61 | Top Rank JAR 550 | I Remember/Always | 20 |
| 61 | Top Rank JAR 563 | Come Along/Do I | 20 |
| 61 | Top Rank JKP 3006 | STAY WITH MAURICE WILLIAMS & THE ZODIACS (EP) | 100 |

*(see also Gladiolas)*

## MIKE WILLIAMS
| | | | |
|---|---|---|---|
| 66 | Atlantic 584 027 | Lonely Soldier/If This Isn't Love | 25 |

## MOON WILLIAMS
| | | | |
|---|---|---|---|
| 73 | DJM DJS10283 | Forever Kind Of Love/All For You | 200 |

## OTIS WILLIAMS & HIS CHARMS
| | | | |
|---|---|---|---|
| 55 | Parlophone CMSP 36 | Ivory Tower/In Paradise (export issue) | 300 |
| 56 | Parlophone MSP 6239 | Ivory Tower/In Paradise | 400 |
| 56 | Parlophone R 4210 | One Night Only/It's All Over | 300 |
| 56 | Parlophone R 4210 | One Night Only/It's All Over (78) | 25 |
| 57 | Parlophone R 4293 | Walkin' After Midnight/I'm Waiting Just For You | 300 |
| 57 | Parlophone R 4293 | Walkin' After Midnight/I'm Waiting Just For You (78) | 50 |
| 58 | Parlophone R 4495 | The Secret/Don't Wake Up The Kids | 100 |
| 58 | Parlophone R 4495 | The Secret/Don't Wake Up The Kids (78) | 70 |
| 62 | Parlophone R 4860 | The Secret/Two Hearts | 60 |

*(see also Charms)*

## PAUL WILLIAMS
| | | | |
|---|---|---|---|
| 70s | Parry Music Library PML 168 | AQUARIUS (LP) | 18 |

## PAUL WILLIAMS BIG ROLL BAND/SET
| | | | |
|---|---|---|---|
| 64 | Columbia DB 7421 | Gin House/Rockin' Chair (as Paul Williams Big Roll Band) | 20 |
| 65 | Columbia DB 7768 | The Many Faces Of Love/Jumpback (as Paul Williams & Zoot Money Band) | 30 |
| 68 | Decca F 12844 | My Sly Sadie/Stop The Wedding (as Paul Williams Set) | 15 |

*(see also Zoot Money's Big Roll Band, John Mayall's Bluesbreakers, Alan Price [Set], Juicy Lucy)*

## PAUL WILLIAMS (1)
| | | | |
|---|---|---|---|
| 73 | Sonet SNTF 654 | IN MEMORY OF ROBERT JOHNSON (LP) | 15 |

## PAUL WILLIAMS (2)
| | | | |
|---|---|---|---|
| 74 | A&M AMS 7125 | That's What Friends Are For/Born To Fly | 8 |
| 74 | A&M AMLS 63653 | PHANTOM OF THE PARADISE (LP, soundtrack) | 20 |

## PAULINE WILLIAMS
| | | | |
|---|---|---|---|
| 73 | Explosion EX 2084 | My Island/My Island (Version) | 5 |

## POOR JOE WILLIAMS
| | | | |
|---|---|---|---|
| 60 | Collector JEN 3 | A MAN SINGS THE BLUES (EP) | 10 |
| 60 | Collector JEN 4 | A MAN SINGS THE BLUES VOL. 2 (EP) | 10 |

*(see also Big Joe Williams)*

## PRINCE WILLIAMS
| | | | |
|---|---|---|---|
| 73 | Atra ATRA 004 | Action Wood Pt. 1/Action Wood Pt. 2 | 5 |

## RANNY/RONNY WILLIAMS
| | | | |
|---|---|---|---|
| 69 | Bullet BU 426 | Summer Place (with Hippy Boys)/Big Boy | 30 |
| 69 | Gas GAS 120 | Throw Me Corn (as Ronny Williams)/HIPPY BOYS: Temptation | 30 |
| 69 | Unity UN 526 | Ambitious Beggar/Pepper Seed | 30 |
| 70 | Punch PH 32 | Smile/Musical I.D. | 20 |

*(see also Winston Reed)*

## RITA WILLIAMS
| | | | |
|---|---|---|---|
| 58 | Oriole CB 1417 | Looking For Someone To Love/Love Me Forever | 10 |
| 70 | Gemini GMS 011 | You're Nearer/With Love From Amsterdam | 6 |

## ROBBIE WILLIAMS
| | | | |
|---|---|---|---|
| 98 | Chrysalis/HMV HMV 78 | Millennium/ROYAL ALBERT HALL ORCHESTRA: Nimrod, Enigma Variations Op. 36 (78rpm, promo only, 1,000 only, numbered p/s) | 25 |
| 98 | Chrysalis CDPP 080 | I'VE BEEN EXPECTING YOU (metal case with album CD, interview disc in digipak, EPK video in p/s, gold press release and photos) | 70 |
| 01 | Chrysalis 7243 536826 1 3 | SWING WHEN YOU'RE WINNING (LP) | 20 |
| 02 | Chrysalis 7243 54399 41-1 | ESCAPOLOGY (2-LP) | 30 |
| 04 | Chrysalis 7243 8668191 | GREATEST HITS (2-LP) | 20 |

*(see also Take That)*

## ROBERT WILLIAMS
| | | | |
|---|---|---|---|
| 90 | Blast First FU8 | CHROME, FIRE AND SMOKE (2-LP, picture disc, 1000 only) | 25 |

## ROBERT PETE WILLIAMS
| | | | |
|---|---|---|---|
| 63 | '77' LA 12-17 | THOSE PRISON BLUES (LP) | 35 |
| 70s | Blues Beacon 1932 101ST | SUGAR FARM (LP) | 25 |
| 72 | Saydisc AMS 2002 | ROBERT PETE WILLIAMS (LP) | 18 |

## ROBERT PETE WILLIAMS/ROOSEVELT SYKES
| | | | |
|---|---|---|---|
| 67 | '77' LEU 12-50 | BLUES FROM THE BOTTOM (LP) | 25 |

*(see also Roosevelt Sykes)*

## ROCKMORE WILLIAMS
| | | | |
|---|---|---|---|
| 73 | Mooncrest Moon 15 | Lady Rock/Junkyard Blues | 10 |

## ROGER WILLIAMS
| | | | |
|---|---|---|---|
| 55 | London HLU 8214 | Autumn Leaves/Take Care | 10 |
| 56 | London HLU 8341 | Two Different Worlds (with Jane Morgan)/I'll Always Walk With You | 8 |
| 57 | London HLU 8379 | Anastasia/A Serenade For Joy | 6 |
| 58 | London HLR 8643 | Indiscreet/Young And Warm And Wonderful (silver top with tri-centre) | 10 |

*(see also Jane Morgan)*

## ROY WILLIAMS TRINITY
| | | | |
|---|---|---|---|
| 73 | Hillside HIL LP 1013 | A TOUCH OF CLASS (LP) | 15 |
| 79 | Hillside HIL LP 1016 | GOOD NEWS IN TOWN (LP) | 45 |

## SAM WILLIAMS
| | | | |
|---|---|---|---|
| 78 | Grapevine GRP 116 | Love Slipped Thru' My Fingers/TOWANDA BARNES: You Don't Mean It | 25 |

## SHINA WILLIAMS
| | | | |
|---|---|---|---|
| 84 | Earthworks/Rough Trade ET 003 | Agboju Logun/Gboro Mi Ro (12", die-cut sleeve) | 50 |

## SID WILLIAMS
| | | | |
|---|---|---|---|
| 77 | ATA ATA 1001 | Don't Play That Rock 'N' Roll/Time To Spare | 8 |

## SIL WILLIAMS
| | | | |
|---|---|---|---|
| 69 | Wolf WM 04 | Reggae Moon Rising/People Get Ready | 10 |

## SMITTY WILLIAMS
| | | | |
|---|---|---|---|
| 62 | MGM MGM 1167 | The Cure/Oh Seymour | 7 |

## SONNY WILLIAMS
| | | | |
|---|---|---|---|
| 59 | London HLD 8931 | Bye Bye Baby Goodbye/Lucky Linda | 45 |
| 59 | London HLD 8931 | Bye Bye Baby Goodbye/Lucky Linda (78) | 20 |

## SPARKIE WILLIAMS
| | | | |
|---|---|---|---|
| 58 | Parlophone R 4475 | Sparkie Williams/Sparkie the Fiddle | 7 |

## SYLVAN WILLIAMS
| | | | |
|---|---|---|---|
| 69 | Big Shot BI 532 | Sweeter Than Honey/Son Of Reggae | 45 |
| 69 | Big Shot BI 533 | This Old Man/When Morning Comes | 50 |

## TEX WILLIAMS
| | | | |
|---|---|---|---|
| 54 | Brunswick 05327 | River Of No Return/Dawn In The Meadow | 10 |
| 54 | Brunswick 05341 | This Ole House (with Rex Allen)/They Were Doin' The Mambo | 12 |
| 55 | Brunswick 05393 | Money/If You'd Believe Me | 10 |
| 56 | Brunswick 05516 | Be Sure You're Right (And Then Go Ahead)/Old Betsy | 5 |
| 57 | Brunswick 05684 | Talkin' To The Blues/Every Night (with Anita Kerr Singers) | 6 |
| 60 | Top Rank JAR 330 | The Keeper Of Boothill/Bummin' Around | 6 |

*(see also Roberta Lee, Rex Allen)*

## TOMMY WILLIAMS
| | | | |
|---|---|---|---|
| 76 | Free Reed FRR 008 | SPRINGTIME IN BATTERSEA (LP, gatefold sleeve) | 18 |

## TONY WILLIAMS
| | | | |
|---|---|---|---|
| 61 | Reprise RS 20019 | Sleepless Nights/Mandolino Mandolino | 10 |
| 61 | Reprise RS 20030 | My Prayer/Miracle | 10 |
| 63 | Philips BF 1282 | How Come/When I Had You | 100 |
| 60 | Mercury MMC 14027 | A GIRL IS A GIRL IS A GIRL (LP) | 40 |
| 61 | Reprise R 6001 | SINGS HIS GREATEST HITS (LP, mono) | 20 |
| 61 | Reprise ST R9 6006 | SINGS HIS GREATEST HITS (LP, stereo) | 30 |

*(see also Platters, Linda Hayes)*

## TONY WILLIAMS' LIFETIME
| | | | |
|---|---|---|---|
| 69 | Polydor 583 574 | EMERGENCY! (2-LP, gatefold sleeve) | 50 |
| 70 | Polydor 2425 019 | TURN IT OVER (LP) | 25 |
| 71 | Polydor 2425 065 | EGO (LP, textured gatefold sleeve) | 35 |

*(see also Lifetime, John McLaughlin)*

## TREVOR WILLIAMS
| | | | |
|---|---|---|---|
| 75 | Virgin VS 122 | Lucy Brown/We Slowed Down | 5 |

## WILLIE WILLIAMS, JACKIE MITTOO & MARSHAL COUSINS
| | | | |
|---|---|---|---|
| 79 | Ziggy FDP 001 | Rocking Universally/JACKIE MITTOO & BONGO GENE: Universal rock (12") | 30 |

## WILLY WILLIAMS
| | | | |
|---|---|---|---|
| 83 | WLN WLN 004 | Repatriation/Come Along/Armagideon Time/Justice Tonight (12") | 10 |

## WINSTON WILLIAMS
| | | | |
|---|---|---|---|
| 70 | Jackpot JP 733 | D.J.'s Choice/SLIM SMITH: Can't Do Without It (B-side actually titled "Lesson/Story Of Love" by Uniques) | 20 |
| 70 | Jackpot JP 743 | The People's Choice/BOBBY JAMES: Let Me Go Girl | 20 |
| 71 | Jackpot JP 757 | Love Version/SLIM SMITH: Ball Of Confusion | 30 |

## HARVEY WILLIAMS
| | | | |
|---|---|---|---|
| 94 | Sarah SARAH 406 | REBELLION (10" LP) | 15 |

### BOBBY WILLIAMSON
| 54 | HMV 7MC 26 | Sh-Boom/Love March (export issue) | 20 |

### MARK WILLIAMSON
| 70s | Myrrh MYR 1154 | MISSING IN ACTION (LP) | 15 |

### ROBIN WILLIAMSON
| 72 | Island HELP 2 | MYRRH (LP, textured sleeve, black label with pink 'i' logo, lyric inner sleeve) | 35 |

*(see also Incredible String Band, Vashti Bunyan)*

### SONNY BOY WILLIAMSON (I)
| 69 | Matchbox SDR 169 | SONNY BOY AND HIS PALS (LP) | 30 |
| 70 | RCA Intl. INTS 1088 | BLUEBIRD BLUES (LP) | 15 |

### SONNY BOY WILLIAMSON (I)/BIG BILL BROONZY
| 65 | RCA Victor RD 7685 | BIG BILL BROONZY/SONNY BOY WILLIAMSON (LP) | 30 |

### SONNY BOY WILLIAMSON (II)
| 63 | Pye International 7N 25191 | Help Me/Bye Bye Bird | 25 |
| 64 | Pye International 7N 25268 | Lonesome Cabin/The Goat | 20 |
| 65 | Sue WI 365 | No Nights By Myself/Boppin' With Sonny Boy | 40 |
| 66 | Chess CRS 8030 | Bring It On Home/Down Child | 20 |
| 66 | Blue Horizon 45-1008 | From The Bottom/Empty Bedroom | 80 |
| 64 | Pye Intl. NEP 44037 | SONNY BOY WILLIAMSON (EP) | 25 |
| 65 | Chess CRE 6001 | HELP ME (EP) | 25 |
| 66 | Chess CRE 6013 | IN MEMORIAM (EP) | 35 |
| 66 | Chess CRE 6018 | REAL FOLK BLUES VOL. 2 (EP) | 30 |
| 64 | Pye Intl. NPL 28036 | DOWN AND OUT BLUES (LP) | 60 |
| 64 | Storyville SLP 158 | PORTRAITS IN BLUES, VOL. 4 (LP) | 40 |
| 65 | Chess CRL 4510 | IN MEMORIAM (LP) | 50 |
| 66 | Storyville SLP 170 | THE BLUES OF SONNY BOY WILLIAMSON (LP) | 22 |
| 66 | Fontana 670 158 | PORTRAITS IN BLUES, VOL. 4 (LP, reissue) | 30 |
| 67 | Storyville 671 170 | THE BLUES OF SONNY BOY WILLIAMSON (LP, reissue) | 25 |
| 68 | Marmalade 607/608 004 | DON'T SEND ME NO FLOWERS (LP, with Brian Auger & Jimmy Page) | 80 |
| 74 | Rarity RLP 1 | THE LAST SESSIONS - 1963 (LP) | 25 |

*(see also Ottilie Patterson)*

### SONNY BOY WILLIAMSON (II) & YARDBIRDS
| 65 | Fontana TL 5277 | SONNY BOY WILLIAMSON & THE YARDBIRDS (LP) | 175 |
| 68 | Fontana SFJL 960 | SONNY BOY WILLIAMSON & THE YARDBIRDS (LP, reissue, different sleeve) | 30 |
| 71 | Philips 6435 011 | SONNY BOY WILLIAMSON & THE YARDBIRDS (LP, 2nd reissue) | 18 |

*(see also Yardbirds, Brian Auger)*

### STU WILLIAMSON
| 56 | London Jazz LZ-N 14030 | SAPPHIRE (10" LP) | 20 |

### WILLIE AND THE RED RUBBER BAND
| 69 | RCA 1842 | Mary Jane/Chicky Chicky Boom Boom | 12 |

### WILLIE (FRANCIS) & LLOYD (LINDSAY)
| 71 | Camel CA 80 | Marcus Is Alive/GLADIATORS: Freedom Train | 12 |

*(see also Willie Francis)*

### WILLIE & WHEELS
| 77 | ABC ABC 4184 | Skateboard Craze/Do What You Did (p/s, label states "illie & The Wheels") | 10 |

*(see also P.F. Sloan, Grass Roots, Fantastic Baggys')*

### DORIS WILLINGHAM
| 69 | Jay Boy BOY 1 | You Can't Do That/Lost Again | 15 |

### CHUCK WILLIS
| 57 | London HLE 8444 | C.C. Rider/Ease The Pain | 80 |
| 57 | London HLE 8444 | C.C. Rider/Ease The Pain (78) | 30 |
| 57 | London HLE 8489 | That Train Has Gone/Love Me Cherry | 80 |
| 57 | London HLE 8489 | That Train Has Gone/Love Me Cherry (78) | 20 |
| 58 | London HLE 8595 | Betty And Dupree/My Crying Eyes | 80 |
| 58 | London HLE 8595 | Betty And Dupree/My Crying Eyes (78) | 20 |
| 58 | London HLE 8635 | What Am I Living For/Hang Up My Rock And Roll Shoes | 50 |
| 58 | London HLE 8635 | What Am I Living For/Hang Up My Rock And Roll Shoes (78) | 25 |
| 58 | London HL 7039 | What Am I Living For/Hang Up My Rock And Roll Shoes (export issue) | 30 |
| 59 | London HLE 8818 | My Life/Thunder And Lightning | 45 |
| 59 | London HLE 8818 | My Life/Thunder And Lightning (78) | 30 |
| 59 | Fontana TFE 17138 | CHUCK WILLIS WAILS (EP) | 300 |
| 65 | Atlantic ATL 5003 | I REMEMBER CHUCK WILLIS (LP) | 80 |
| 69 | Atlantic 588 145 | I REMEMBER CHUCK WILLIS (LP, reissue) | 20 |

### DOUG WILLIS
| 97 | Z Records ZEDD 12029 | Get Your Own (12") | 10 |

### HAL WILLIS
| 68 | President PT 197 | The Lumberjack/Klondike Mike | 12 |

### LARRY WILLIS
| 74 | People PLEO 2 | INNER CRISIS (LP) | 20 |

### LLOYD WILLIS
| 70 | Pressure Beat PR 5502 | Mad Rooster (Parts 1 & 2)/As Far As I Can See (actually "The Wicked Must Survive" by Reggae Boys) | 15 |
| 70 | Unity UN 543 | Ivan Hitler The Conqueror/The Splice | 30 |

*(see also Dynamic Gang, Urie Aldridge)*

### RALPH WILLIS
| 61 | Esquire EP 241 | RALPH WILLIS (EP) | 40 |

**SLIM WILLIS**
65  R&B MRB 5004  Running Around/No Feeling For You..................................................... 30

**TIMMY WILLIS**
72  United Artists UP 35352  Mr. Soul Satisfaction/I'm Wondering ................................................ 5

**WILL-O-BEES**
67  CBS 3263  It's Not Easy/Looking Glass .......................................................... 15

**NEVILLE WILLOUGHBY**
72  Duke DU 140  Wheel And Tun Me/Hey Mama .......................................................... 5
*(see also Neville, Whistling Willie)*

**WILLOWS**
56  London HLU 8290  Church Bells May Ring/Baby Tell Me ......................................... 600
56  London HLU 8290  Church Bells May Ring/Baby Tell Me (78) ................................... 80
*(see also Tony Middleton)*

**BOB WILLS WITH TOMMY DUNCAN**
60  London HL 7102  Heart To Heart Talk/What's The Matter With The Mill (export issue).......... 20

**MICK WILLS**
88  Woronzow WOO 9  FERN HILL (LP).................................................................... 15

**VIOLA WILLS**
68  President PT 108  Lost Without The Love Of My Guy/I Got Love .................................. 10
68  President PT 150  Together Forever/Don't Kiss Me Hello And Mean Goodbye ..................... 10
68  President PT 152  I've Got To Have All Of You/Night Scene ...................................... 8
68  President PT 154  You're Out Of My Mind/Any Time ............................................... 8

**WILMER & DUKES**
68  Action ACT 4500  Give Me One More Chance/Get It ............................................... 10

**FRANKIE WILMOTT**
86  Musical Ambassador MAD 005  Give Me No Rock (Sensemilla)/ANDY TOSH: Lick A Shot (12").......... 50
87  Music House MH1  I Won't Give Up/I Won't Give Up (version) (12").............................. 15

**SUE WILSHAW**
69  SNB 55-3957  Empty Sunday/My My My.............................................................. 15

**ADA WILSON**
79  Ellie Jay EJSP 9288  In The Quiet Of My Room/I'm In Control Here (p/s) ...................... 12
80  Barn BARN 012  In The Quiet Of My Room/I'm In Control Here (reissue, no p/s) ............. 6
*(see also Strangeways)*

**AL WILSON**
68  Liberty LBF 15044  Do What You Gotta Do/Now I Know What Love Is .......................... 20
68  Liberty LBF 15121  The Snake/Who Could Be Lovin' You ..................................... 20
69  Liberty LBF 15236  Shake Me Wake Me/I Stand Accused ...................................... 8
69  Liberty LBF 15257  Lodi/By The Time I Get To Phoenix ..................................... 8
73  Bell 1330  Show And Tell/Listen To Me ..................................................... 5
75  Bell BLL 1436  The Snake/Willoughby Brook ................................................. 10
02  Soul City  The Snake/Now I Know What Love Is ............................................ 12
69  Liberty LBS 83173  SEARCHING FOR THE DOLPHINS (LP) ...................................... 20

**BRIAN WILSON**
66  Capitol CL 15438  Caroline, No/Summer Means New Love .................................... 50
88  Sire W 7814 B  LOVE AND MERCY (7" box set, with interview and postcards, limited edition) ..... 40
98  Giant/Mojo 74321 58760 2  INTERVIEW/IMAGINATION (promo CD, with Peter Buck)............... 40
04  Nonesuch 7559-79869-7  Wonderful/Wind Chimes (three different coloured vinyl - blue, yellow,green)......... 18
04  Nonesuch 7559-79885-7  Good Vibrations/Our Prayer/Good Vibrations (live)(p/s) (Ltd edition) ......... 10
05  Nonesuch 7559-798957  Our Prayer (Freeform Reform) (10" one sided clear vinyl in clear plastic sleeve) ..... 12
*(see also Beach Boys, Date With Soul, American Spring)*

**BRIAN WILSON & MIKE LOVE**
67  Capitol CL 15513  Gettin' Hungry/Devoted To You (as Brian Wilson & Mike Love)................. 30

**CASSANDRA WILSON**
96  Blue Note 72438 37183 1 3  NEW MOON DAUGHTER (2-LP)................................ 80

**CLIVE WILSON**
64  R&B JB 144  Mango Tree/Midnight In Chicago ................................................. 20

**COLIN WILSON**
75  Tabitha TAB 101  CLOUDBURST (LP) ............................................................. 30

**DELROY WILSON**
63  Island WI 097  Naughty People/I Shall Not Remove ........................................... 25
63  Island WI 103  One, Two, Three/Back Biter ................................................... 20
63  Island WI 116  You Bend My Love/Can't You See .............................................. 20
63  R&B JB 108  Lion Of Judah/Joe Liges ......................................................... 30
63  R&B JB 128  Prince Pharoah/Don't Believe Him ................................................ 30
63  R&B JB 132  Squeeze Your Toe/Sugar Pie ..................................................... 30
64  Black Swan WI 405  Spit In The Sky/Voodoo Man ............................................ 25
64  Black Swan WI 420  Goodbye/Treat Me Good ................................................. 20
64  R&B JB 148  Lover Mouth/Every Mouth Must Be Fed ........................................... 25
64  R&B JB 168  Sammy Dead/CYNTHIA & ARCHIE: Every Beat ...................................... 25
65  Island WI 205  Pick Up The Pieces/Oppression .............................................. 18
66  Doctor Bird DB 1022  Give Me A Chance/(It's) Impossible .................................. 25
66  Island WI 3013  Dancing Mood/SOUL BROTHERS: More And More ................................ 30
67  Island WI 3033  Riding For A Fall/Got To Change Your Ways ................................ 25
67  Island WI 3037  Ungrateful Baby/ROY RICHARDS: Hopeful Village Ska....................... 35
67  Island WI 3039  Close To Me/SOUL BROTHERS: Hi-Life ...................................... 25
67  Island WI 3050  Get Ready/ROY RICHARDS: Port-O-Jam ..................................... 45

# Dennis WILSON (& RUMBO)

| | | | |
|---|---|---|---|
| 67 | Studio One SO 2009 | Won't You Come Home Baby/PETER & HORTENSE: I've Been Lonely | 50 |
| 67 | Studio One SO 2014 | Mother Word/HEPTONES: Fat Girl | 30 |
| 67 | Studio One SO 2019 | Never Conquer/Run For Your Life | 80 |
| 67 | Studio One SO 2031 | I'm Not A King/HEPTONES: Take Me (B-side actually by Soul Vendors) | 50 |
| 68 | Island WI 3099 | This Old Heart Of Mine/GLEN ADAMS: Grab A Girl | 50 |
| 68 | Island WI 3127 | Once Upon A Time/I Want To Love You (B-side actually with Stranger Cole) | 80 |
| 68 | Coxsone CS 7064 | True Believer/MARSHALL WILLIAMS: College Girl | 100 |
| 68 | Studio One SO 2040 | Mr. D.J./HEPTONES: Tripe Girl | 60 |
| 68 | Studio One SO 2046 | Rain From The Skies/How Can I Love Someone | 40 |
| 68 | Studio One SO 2057 | Feel Good All Over/I Like The Way You Walk | 40 |
| 69 | Studio One SO 2074 | Easy Snappin'/WEBBER SISTERS: Come On | 25 |
| 69 | High Note HS 011 | Put Yourself In My Place/It Hurts | 30 |
| 69 | High Note HS 015 | I'm The One Who Loves You/AFROTONES: If I'm In A Corner | 35 |
| 69 | High Note HS 022 | Your Number One/I've Tried My Best | 20 |
| 69 | High Note HS 028 | Good To Me/What Do You Want Me To Do | 18 |
| 69 | Camel CA 15 | Sad Mood (actually by Ken Parker)/STRANGER COLE: Give It To Me | 70 |
| 70 | Trojan TR 7740 | Show Me The Way/BEVERLEY'S ALLSTARS: Version | 10 |
| 70 | Trojan TR 7769 | Gave You My Love/BEVERLEY'S ALLSTARS: Version | 10 |
| 70 | Summit SUM 8503 | Got To Get Away/BEVERLEY'S ALLSTARS: Version | 8 |
| 70 | Unity UN 559 | Drink Wine, Everybody/Someone To Call My Own | 20 |
| 71 | Smash SMA 2317 | I Am Trying/COLLINS ALLSTARS: Version | 12 |
| 71 | Smash SMA 2318 | Satisfaction/Satisfaction Version (B-side with Alton Ellis) | 40 |
| 71 | Smash SMA 2323 | What It Was/LLOYD CLARKE: Chicken Thief | 15 |
| 71 | Jackpot JP 763 | Better Must Come/BUNNY LEE'S ALLSTARS: Better Must Come - Version | 10 |
| 71 | Jackpot JP 769 | Cool Operator/I'm Yours | 10 |
| 71 | Jackpot JP 770 | Try Again/AGGROVATORS: Try Again - Version | 10 |
| 71 | Jackpot JP 780 | Keep Your Love Strong/Nice To Be Near | 10 |
| 71 | Jackpot JP 781 | Peace And Love/JEFF BARNES: Who's Your Brother | 12 |
| 71 | Banana BA 333 | Just Because Of You/I Love You Madly | 45 |
| 72 | Banana BA 367 | You Keep On Running (& U Roy)/LARRY'S ALL STARS: Running Version | 15 |
| 72 | Bullet BU 520 | Hear Come The Heartaches (actually "Here Come The Heartaches")/ You'll Be Sorry | 8 |
| 72 | Jackpot JP 792 | Who Cares/HUGH ROY JUNIOR: Who Cares - Version | 10 |
| 72 | Jackpot JP 795 | The Same Old Song/Stay By Me | 10 |
| 72 | Jackpot JP 804 | Cheer Up/Loving You | 10 |
| 72 | Spur SP 2 | Adis Ababa/KEITH HUDSON: Rudie Hot Stuff | 40 |
| 73 | Downtown DT 501 | Pretty Girl/JOE GIBBS & PROFESSIONALS: Face Girl | 10 |
| 73 | Grape GR 3038 | Can I Change My Mind/Just Because | 10 |
| 73 | Green Door GD 4060 | Ain't That Peculiar/What Is Man | 8 |
| 73 | Smash SMA 2336 | Trying To Wreck My Life/Live And Learn | 10 |
| 73 | Count Shelley CS 024 | Never Give Up/I ROY: Problem Of Life | 8 |
| 73 | Count Shelley CS 047 | Dum Dum/HORACE ANDY: Rasta Saw Them Coming | 8 |
| 74 | Faith FA 006 | Love Got Me Doing Things/PHIL PRATT ALL STARS: Version | 5 |
| 74 | Harry J. HJ 6667 | What Will Happen To The Youth Of Today/Baby Don't Do It | 5 |
| 75 | Fab FAB 266 | Dancing Mood/Version | 12 |
| 75 | Attack ATT 8111 | Seven Letters/Version | 10 |
| 75 | Attack ATT 8120 | Honey Child/Time Is Running Out | 8 |
| 76 | Black Wax WAX 20 | Mother Nature/CHANNEL ONE: Natural Version | 6 |
| 76 | Third World TW03 | Chuekey Rock/You're No Good | 20 |
| 77 | Tribesman TM 002 | What Is Man/Version | 20 |
| 78 | Burning Sounds BSD 017 | All In This Together/Because I Am Black (12") | 25 |
| 78 | Burning Sounds BSD 018 | Love Got Me Doing Things/Go Away Little Girl (12") | 25 |
| 79 | Cha Cha CHAD 10 | Money Love/I Want To Love You (12") | 20 |
| 79 | E & J EJD1 | Sharing The Night Together/I Won't Take You Back (12") | 10 |
| 84 | Greensleeves GRED 157 | Dancing Mood/TETRACK: Trappers (12") | 12 |
| 88 | Conqueror LD 045 | I Have Been In Love/NAGGO MORRIS AND THE HEPTONES: You Want To Get I Out (12") | 40 |
| 64 | R&B JBL 1112 | I SHALL NOT REMOVE (LP) | 500 |
| 68 | Coxsone CSL 8016 | GOOD ALL OVER (LP) | 200 |
| 72 | Trojan TRLS 44 | BETTER MUST COME (LP) | 40 |
| 73 | Big Shot BILP 102 | CAPTIVITY (LP) | 40 |
| 77 | Eji EJI 1001 | MR. COOL OPERATOR (LP) | 20 |
| 78 | Third World TWD 001 | 20 GOLDEN GREATS (2-LP) | 18 |
| 78 | Burning Sounds BS 1020 | LOVERS ROCK (LP) | 20 |
| 79 | Groundnation GROL 501 | FOR I AND I (LP) | 25 |
| 82 | Black Music BMLP 803 | GO AWAY DREAM (LP) | 20 |

*(see also Hortense & Delroy, Joe Liges, Roy Richards, Soul Brothers, Dennis Alcapone, Stranger Cole, Uniques, Soul Vendors)*

## DENNIS WILSON (& RUMBO)

| | | | |
|---|---|---|---|
| 70 | Stateside SS 2184 | Sound Of Free/Lady (as Dennis Wilson & Rumbo) | 70 |
| 77 | Caribou CRB 5663 | River Song/Farewell My Friend | 15 |
| 77 | Caribou CRB 81672 | PACIFIC OCEAN BLUE (LP, gatefold sleeve, lyric insert, on blue vinyl) | 45 |
| 77 | Caribou CRB 81672 | PACIFIC OCEAN BLUE (LP, gatefold sleeve, lyric insert) | 40 |

*(see also Beach Boys)*

## THE DIERDRE WILSON TABAC

| | | | |
|---|---|---|---|
| 69 | RCA RCA 1880 | Get Back/Angel Baby | 15 |

## DOYLE WILSON WITH JIMMY LACEY & BAND

| | | | |
|---|---|---|---|
| 58 | Vogue Pop V 9117 | Hey-Hey/You're The One For Me | 600 |
| 58 | Vogue Pop V 9117 | Hey-Hey/You're The One For Me (7) | 150 |

## EDDIE WILSON

| | | | |
|---|---|---|---|
| 69 | Action ACT 4536 | Shing-A-Ling Stroll/Don't Kick The Teenager Around | 25 |

| | | | |
|---|---|---|---|
| 70 | Action ACT 4555 | Get Out On The Street/Must Be Love | 20 |

## ERNEST WILSON
| | | | |
|---|---|---|---|
| 78 | Cha Cha CC 001 | I Know Myself/REVOLUTIONARIES: I Know Myself Dub | 20 |
| 86 | Natty Congo NCLP 006 | LOVE REVOLUTION (LP) | 15 |

## ERNEST WILSON & FREDDY (MCGREGOR)
| | | | |
|---|---|---|---|
| 70 | Crab CRAB 45 | Sentimental Man/It's A Lie | 20 |
| 70 | Unity UN 564 | Love Makes The World Go Round/Love (Version Instrumental) | 8 |
| 71 | Gas GAS 168 | What You Gonna Do About It/DOBBY DOBSON: Halfway To Paradise | 8 |
| 71 | Jackpot JP 765 | Let Them Talk/The Truth Hurts | 6 |

## ERNEST ('SOUL') WILSON
| | | | |
|---|---|---|---|
| 67 | Studio One SO 2032 | Money Worries/SOUL VENDORS: Pe Da Pa | 40 |
| 68 | Studio One SO 2058 | If I Were A Carpenter/SOUL VENDORS: Frozen Soul | 40 |
| 68 | Coxsone CS 7044 | Storybook Children (as Ernest 'Soul' Wilson)/LITTLE FREDDIE: After Laughter (B-side actually by Freddie McGregor) | 40 |
| 68 | Coxsone CS 7059 | Undying Love/SOUL VENDORS: Tropic Isle | 100 |
| 69 | Amalgamated AMG 837 | Private Number/GLEN ADAMS: She's So Fine | 50 |
| 69 | Crab CRAB 9 | Private Number/Another Chance | 40 |
| 69 | Crab CRAB 17 | Freedom Train/STRANGER COLE: You Should Never Have To Come | 25 |
| 69 | Crab CRAB 21 | Just Once In My Life (with Freddy)/GLEN ADAMS: Mighty Organ | 25 |
| 76 | Fab FAB 280 | Storybook Children/SOUND DIMENSION: Version | 10 |

*(see also Tinga & Ernest)*

## FLICK WILSON
| | | | |
|---|---|---|---|
| 77 | Ultra PFU 1003 | Keep The Troubles Down/Saturday Night Shubin (12") | 20 |
| 80 | Greensleeves/Cool Rockers GRED 37 | Slavemaster/Pretty Blue Eyes (12") | 40 |

## FRANK WILSON
| | | | |
|---|---|---|---|
| 79 | Tamla Motown TMG 1170 | Do I Love You (Indeed I Do)/Sweeter As The Days Go By | 30 |
| 79 | Tamla Motown TMG 1170 | Do I Love You (Indeed I Do)/Sweeter As The Days Go By (DJ copy) | 60 |
| 04 | Tamla Motown 982 153 0 | Do I Love You (Indeed I Do)/CHRIS CLARK: Do I Love You (Indeed I Do) (die-cut p/s) | 25 |

## FRANK WILSON & CAVALIERS
| | | | |
|---|---|---|---|
| 64 | Fontana TF 505 | Last Kiss/That's How Much I Love You | 12 |

## GARLAND WILSON
| | | | |
|---|---|---|---|
| 53 | HMV 7M 122 | Just You, Just Me/Sweet Georgia Brown | 6 |

## GARY WILSON
| | | | |
|---|---|---|---|
| 80 | Sourgrape SG 115 | Movie Queen/Movie Queen (p/s) | 6 |

## JACK WILSON QUARTET
| | | | |
|---|---|---|---|
| 64 | London HA-K/SH-K 8170 | THE JACK WILSON QUARTET (LP, featuring Roy Ayers) | 20 |
| 66 | Vocalion LAE-L 603 | RAMBLIN' (LP) | 20 |

*(see also Roy Ayers)*

## JACKIE WILSON
### 78s
| | | | |
|---|---|---|---|
| 58 | Coral Q 72347 | Lonely Teardrops/In The Blue Of The Evening | 40 |
| 59 | Coral Q 72366 | That's Why/Love Is All | 40 |
| 59 | Coral Q 72372 | I'll Be Satisfied/Ask | 50 |
| 59 | Coral Q 72380 | You Better Know It/Never Go Away | 75 |
| 59 | Coral Q 72384 | Talk That Talk/Only You, Only Me | 80 |

### SINGLES
| | | | |
|---|---|---|---|
| 57 | Vogue Coral Q 72290 | Reet Petite/By The Light Of The Silvery Moon | 25 |
| 57 | Coral Q 72290 | Reet Petite/By The Light Of The Silvery Moon (2nd pressing) | 15 |
| 58 | Coral Q 72306 | To Be Loved/Come Back To Me | 25 |
| 58 | Coral Q 72332 | I'm Wanderin'/As Long As I Live | 25 |
| 58 | Coral Q 72338 | We Have Love/Singing A Song | 22 |
| 58 | Coral Q 72347 | Lonely Teardrops/In The Blue Of The Evening | 25 |
| 59 | Coral Q 72366 | That's Why/Love Is All | 20 |
| 59 | Coral Q 72366 | That's Why/Love Is All (mispressing, B-side plays "You Better Know It") | 15 |
| 59 | Coral Q 72372 | I'll Be Satisfied/Ask | 15 |
| 59 | Coral Q 72380 | You Better Know It/Never Go Away | 15 |
| 59 | Coral Q 72384 | Talk That Talk/Only You, Only Me | 15 |
| 60 | Coral Q 72393 | Doggin' Around/The Magic Of Love | 15 |
| 60 | Coral Q 72407 | A Woman, A Lover, A Friend/(You Were Made For) All My Love | 15 |
| 60 | Coral Q 72412 | Alone At Last/Am I The Man | 25 |
| 61 | Coral Q 72421 | The Tear Of The Year/My Empty Arms (withdrawn B-side, demos only) | 65 |
| 61 | Coral Q 72424 | The Tear Of The Year/Your One And Only Love | 15 |
| 61 | Coral Q 72430 | Please Tell Me Why/(So Many) Cute Little Girls | 15 |
| 61 | Coral Q 72434 | I'm Comin' On Back To You/Lonely Life | 15 |
| 61 | Coral Q 72439 | You Don't Know What It Means/Years From Now | 15 |
| 61 | Coral Q 72444 | The Way I Am/My Heart Belongs To Only You | 15 |
| 62 | Coral Q 72450 | The Greatest Hurt/There'll Be No Next Time | 15 |
| 62 | Coral Q 72453 | Sing (And Tell The Blues So Long)/I Found Love (B-side with Linda Hopkins) | 15 |
| 62 | Coral Q 72454 | I Just Can't Help It/My Tale Of Woe | 15 |
| 63 | Coral Q 72460 | Baby Workout/What Good Am I Without You | 15 |
| 63 | Coral Q 72464 | Shake A Hand/Say I Do (as Jackie Wilson & Linda Hopkins) | 15 |
| 63 | Coral Q 72465 | Shake! Shake! Shake!/He's A Fool | 15 |
| 63 | Coral Q 72467 | Baby Get It/The New Breed | 15 |
| 64 | Coral Q 72474 | Big Boss Line/Be My Girl | 15 |
| 64 | Coral Q 72476 | Squeeze Her - Tease Her (But Love Her)/Give Me Back My Heart | 15 |
| 65 | Coral Q 72480 | Yes Indeed!/When The Saints Go Marching In (with Linda Hopkins) | 18 |
| 65 | Coral Q 72481 | No Pity (In The Naked City)/I'm So Lonely | 20 |

# Jackie WILSON/CLYDE MCPHATTER

| 65 | Coral Q 72481 | No Pity (In The Naked City)/I'm So Lonely (DJ copy) | 45 |
| 65 | Coral Q 72482 | I Believe I'll Love On/Lonely Teardrops | 15 |
| 66 | Coral Q 72484 | To Make A Big Man Cry/Be My Love | 20 |
| 66 | Coral Q 72484 | To Make A Big Man Cry/Be My Love (DJ copy) | 45 |
| 66 | Coral Q 72487 | Whispers/The Fairest Of Them All | 40 |
| 66 | Coral Q 72487 | Whispers/The Fairest Of Them All (DJ copy) | 85 |
| 67 | Coral Q 72493 | (Your Love Keeps Lifting Me) Higher And Higher/I'm The One To Do It | 20 |
| 67 | Coral Q 72493 | (Your Love Keeps Lifting Me) Higher And Higher/I'm The One To Do It (DJ copy) | 85 |
| 67 | Coral Q 72496 | Since You Showed Me How To Be Happy/The Who-Who Song | 30 |
| 67 | Coral Q 72496 | Since You Showed Me How To Be Happy/The Who-Who Song (DJ copy) | 75 |
| 68 | MCA MU 1014 | For Your Precious Love/Uptight (Everything's Alright) (with Count Basie) | 10 |
| 68 | Decca AD 1008 | For Your Precious Love/Uptight (Everything's Alright) (export issue) | 25 |
| 69 | MCA Soul Bag BAG 2 | (Your Love Keeps Lifting Me) Higher And Higher/Whispers (Gettin' Louder) | 10 |
| 69 | MCA Soul Bag BAG 7 | Since You Showed Me How To Be Happy/Chain Gang | 10 |
| 69 | MCA MU 1104 | Since You Showed Me How To Be Happy/The Who-Who Song (reissue) | 10 |
| 69 | MCA MU 1105 | Helpless/Do It The Right Way | 10 |
| 70 | MCA MU 1131 | (Your Love Keeps Lifting Me) Higher And Higher/Whispers (Gettin' Louder) (reissue) | 6 |
| 72 | MCA MU 1160 | I Get The Sweetest Feeling/Soul Galore | 6 |
| 73 | Brunswick BR 3 | Beautiful Day/What'cha Gonna Do About Love | 20 |
| 75 | Brunswick BR 18 | I Get The Sweetest Feeling/(Your Love Keeps Lifting Me) Higher And Higher | 5 |
| 75 | Brunswick BR 23 | Whispers (Gettin' Louder)/Reet Petite | 5 |
| 75 | Brunswick BR 28 | Don't Burn No Bridges/Don't Burn No Bridges (Instrumental) (with Chi-Lites) | 5 |
| 77 | Brunswick BR 43 | It Only Happens When I Look At You/Just As Soon As The Feeling's Over (DJ Copy) | 150 |
| 77 | Brunswick BR 43 | It Only Happens When I Look At You/Just As Soon As The Feeling's Over | 100 |
| 80s | Kent Town 101 | I Don't Want To Lose You/ADAM'S APPLES: Don't Take It Out On This World | 12 |

## EPs

| 59 | Coral FEP 2016 | JACKIE WILSON (triangular centre) | 100 |
| 59 | Coral FEP 2016 | JACKIE WILSON (round centre) | 70 |
| 60 | Coral FEP 2043 | THE DYNAMIC JACKIE WILSON (triangular centre) | 100 |
| 60 | Coral FEP 2043 | THE DYNAMIC JACKIE WILSON (round centre) | 70 |

## ALBUMS

| 58 | Coral LVA 9087 | HE'S SO FINE | 150 |
| 59 | Coral LVA 9108 | LONELY TEARDROPS | 150 |
| 60 | Coral LVA 9121 | SO MUCH | 110 |
| 60 | Coral LVA 9130 | JACKIE SINGS THE BLUES | 125 |
| 60 | Coral LVA 9135 | MY GOLDEN FAVOURITES | 90 |
| 61 | Coral LVA 9144 | A WOMAN, A LOVER, A FRIEND | 100 |
| 61 | Coral LVA 9148 | YOU AIN'T HEARD NOTHIN' YET | 85 |
| 62 | Coral LVA 9151 | BY SPECIAL REQUEST (mono) | 75 |
| 62 | Coral SVL 3018 | BY SPECIAL REQUEST (stereo) | 90 |
| 62 | Coral LVA 9202 | BODY AND SOUL | 65 |
| 63 | Coral LVA 9209 | JACKIE WILSON AT THE COPA (mono) | 70 |
| 63 | Coral SVL 9209 | JACKIE (stereo) | 80 |
| 63 | Coral LVA 9214 | THE WORLD'S GREATEST MELODIES (mono) | 55 |
| 63 | Coral SVL 9214 | THE WORLD'S GREATEST MELODIES (stereo) | 65 |
| 66 | Coral LVA 9231 | SPOTLIGHT ON JACKIE WILSON | 70 |
| 66 | Coral LVA 9232 | SOUL GALORE (mono) | 70 |
| 66 | Coral SVL 9232 | SOUL GALORE (stereo) | 80 |
| 67 | Coral LVA 9235 | WHISPERS | 75 |
| 68 | MCA MUP(S) 304 | HIGHER AND HIGHER | 20 |
| 68 | MCA MUP(S) 333 | TWO MUCH (with Count Basie & His Orchestra) | 20 |
| 69 | MCA MUPS 361 | I GET THE SWEETEST FEELING | 20 |
| 70 | MCA MUPS 405 | DO YOUR THING | 25 |
| 73 | Brunswick BRLS 3001 | YOU GOT ME WALKIN' | 25 |

*(see also Billy Ward & Dominoes, Clyde McPhatter, Count Basie, Chi-Lites, Linda Hopkins)*

## JACKIE WILSON/CLYDE MCPHATTER

| 62 | Ember JBS 705 | Tenderly/CLYDE McPHATTER: Harbour Lights | 250 |
| 62 | Ember NR 5001 | MEET BILLY WARD & THE DOMINOES (LP, 1 side each) | 200 |

*(see also Clyde McPhatter)*

## JOANNE WILSON

| 81 | Red Stripe 2222 | Gotta Have You Back/Part 2 | 12 |

## JOE WILSON

| 71 | Pye International 7N 25550 | Sweetness/When A Man Cries | 10 |

## MARTY WILSON & STRAT-O-LITES

| 58 | Brunswick 05750 | Hey! Eula/Hedge-Hopper | 20 |

## MAYNELL WILSON (ACTUALLY WILSON MAYNELL) & WESTMINSTER FIVE

| 64 | Carnival CV 7014 | Hey Hey Johnny/Baby | 10 |
| 67 | CBM CBM 001 | Motown Feeling/Mean Ole World (with p/s) | 20 |
| 67 | CBM CBM 001 | Motown Feeling/Mean Ole World | 10 |

*(see also Wes[t]minster Five)*

## MURRY WILSON

| 67 | Capitol CL 15525 | Plumber's Tune/Love Won't Wait | 8 |
| 67 | Capitol (S)T 2819 | THE MANY MOODS OF MURRY WILSON (LP) | 20 |

*(see also Beach Boys)*

## NANCY WILSON

| 64 | Capitol CL 15343 | The Best Is Yet To Come/Never Let Me Go | 5 |
| 64 | Capitol CL 15352 | (You Don't Know) How Glad I Am/Never Less Than Yesterday | 10 |
| 65 | Capitol CL 15378 | Don't Come Running Back To Me/Love Has Many Faces | 10 |

| 65 | Capitol CL 15412 | Where Does That Leave Me/Gentle Is My Love | 25 |
|----|------------------|--------------------------------------------|-----|
| 66 | Capitol CL 15443 | Power Of Love/Rain Sometimes | 15 |
| 66 | Capitol CL 15466 | You've Got Your Troubles/Uptight (Everything's Alright) | 20 |
| 67 | Capitol CL 15508 | Don't Look Over Your Shoulder/Mercy, Mercy, Mercy | 15 |
| 68 | Capitol CL 15536 | You Don't Know Me/Ode To Billie Joe | 10 |
| 68 | Capitol CL 15547 | Face It Girl It's Over/The End Of Our Love | 40 |
| 68 | Capitol CL 15547 | Face It Girl It's Over/The End Of Our Love (DJ copy) | 80 |
| 74 | Capitol CL 15796 | Streetrunner/Ocean Of Love | 8 |
| 75 | Capitol CL 15810 | You're Right As Rain/There'll Always Be Forever | 5 |
| 77 | Capitol CL 15547 | End Of Our Love/Face It Girl, It's Over (white logo, reissue) | 12 |
| 62 | Capitol EAP1 20604 | SECOND TIME AROUND (EP) | 10 |
| 64 | Capitol EAP4 2082 | TODAY, TOMORROW, FOREVER (EP) | 10 |
| 62 | Capitol (S)T 1767 | HELLO YOUNG LOVERS (LP, mono/stereo) | 18 |
| 63 | Capitol (S)T 1828 | BROADWAY - MY LOVE (LP, mono/stereo) | 18 |
| 63 | Capitol (S)T 1934 | HOLLYWOOD - MY WAY (LP, mono/stereo) | 18 |
| 63 | Capitol (S)T 2012 | YESTERDAY'S LOVE SONGS (LP, mono/stereo) | 18 |
| 64 | Capitol (S)T 2082 | TODAY, TOMORROW, FOREVER (LP) | 18 |
| 65 | Capitol (S)T 2136 | THE NANCY WILSON SHOW (LP) | 18 |
| 65 | Capitol (S)T 2155 | HOW GLAD I AM (LP) | 18 |
| 65 | Capitol (S)T 2321 | TODAY- MY WAY (LP) | 18 |
| 65 | Capitol (S)T 2351 | GENTLE IS MY LOVE (LP) | 18 |
| 66 | Capitol (S)T 2433 | FROM BROADWAY WITH LOVE (LP) | 18 |
| 66 | Capitol (S)T 2495 | A TOUCH OF TODAY (LP) | 30 |
| 66 | Capitol (S)T 2555 | TENDER LOVING CARE (LP) | 20 |
| 67 | Capitol (S)T 2634 | NANCY - NATURALLY (LP) | 20 |

## NANCY WILSON & CANNONBALL ADDERLEY
| 62 | Capitol ST 1657 | NANCY WILSON & CANNONBALL ADDERLEY (LP, stereo) | 15 |
|----|-----------------|-------------------------------------------------|-----|

*(see also Cannonball Adderley)*

## PEANUTS WILSON
| 58 | Coral Q 72302 | Cast Iron Arm/You've Got Love | 500 |
|----|---------------|------------------------------|------|
| 58 | Coral Q 72302 | Cast Iron Arm/You've Got Love (78) | 150 |
| 76 | MCA MCA 240 | Cast Iron Arm/DON WOODY: Barking Up The Wrong Tree | 6 |

## PHIL WILSON
| 87 | Creation CRE 036D | Waiting For A Change/Even Now/Down In The Valley/Love In Vain (double pack) | 5 |
|----|-------------------|---------------------------------------------------------------------------|-----|
| 89 | Caff CAFF 3 | Better Days/You Won't Speak (p/s, with insert, handwritten label) | 12 |

*(see also June Brides)*

## REUBEN WILSON
| 76 | Chess 6078 700 | Got To Get Your Own Parts 1 & 2 | 20 |
|----|----------------|---------------------------------|-----|

## ROB WILSON BAND
| 90 | Metro Music MMI 6 | The Girl In the Polka-Dot Dress/The Greatest Crime/King Of The Blues (p/s) | 20 |
|----|-------------------|---------------------------------------------------------------------------|-----|

## RON WILSON
| 68 | Island WI 3112 | Dread Saras/DAVID BROWN: All My Life | 40 |
|----|----------------|--------------------------------------|-----|

*(see also Winston Scotland, Douglas Brothers)*

## SHARK WILSON & BASEMENT HEATERS
| 71 | Ashanti ASH 400 | Make It Reggae/Version | 12 |
|----|-----------------|------------------------|-----|

## SMILEY WILSON
| 60 | London HLG 9066 | Running Bear/Long As Little Birds Fly | 50 |
|----|-----------------|---------------------------------------|-----|

## TOMY WILSON
| 64 | Decca F12033 | Yes I Do/Lost Without You | 10 |
|----|--------------|---------------------------|-----|

## TONY WILSON
| 67 | Columbia DB 8153 | Can't Waste A Good Thing/What Did I Do? | 30 |
|----|------------------|-----------------------------------------|-----|
| 69 | Bell BLL 1081 | Baby, I Love, Love I Love You/Come Back To My Lonely World | 6 |

*(see also Hot Chocolate)*

## TREVOR WILSON
| 65 | Ska Beat JB 207 | You Couldn't Believe/You Told Me You Care | 50 |
|----|-----------------|-------------------------------------------|-----|

## STEVEN WILSON
| 09 | Kscope KSCOPE 804 | Harmony Korine (edit)/The 78 (p/s, 1000 only) | 10 |
|----|-------------------|-----------------------------------------------|-----|
| 09 | Kscope KSCOPE 804 | Harmony Korine (edit)/The 78 (p/s, red vinyl, 1000 only) | 10 |
| 09 | Kscope KSCOPE 804 | Harmony Korine (edit)/The 78 (p/s, white vinyl, 1000 only) | 10 |
| 09 | Kscope KSCOPE 809 | NSRGNTS RMXS (12" EP, p/s, 1000 only) | 10 |
| 11 | Kscope LOTSCOPE 001 | Stone Age Dinosaurs/OCEANIZE: Fear (white vinyl, p/s, 2000 only) | 8 |
| 09 | Tonefloat TF 50 | INSURGENTES (Box set, 4 x 10", 1000 only) | 100 |
| 09 | Kscope KSCOPE 808 | INSURGENTES (2-LP, gatefold sleeve, 2000 only) | 40 |
| 11 | Kscope KSCOPE 818 | GRACE FOR DROWNING (2-LP) | 20 |
| 12 | Kscope KSCOPE 827 | CATALOGUE/PRESERVE/AMASS (LP) | 15 |

*(see also Porcupine Tree)*

## GABY WILTON & CHARLIE ACE
| 72 | Bullet BU 511 | Babylon Falling/CHARLIE ACE: Make It Love | 8 |
|----|---------------|-------------------------------------------|-----|

## JOHNNY WILTSHIRE & HIS TREBLETONES
| 59 | Oriole CB 1494 | If The Shoe Fits/Cha Cha Choo Choo | 10 |
|----|----------------|------------------------------------|-----|

## WIMPLE WINCH
| 66 | Fontana TF 686 | What's Been Done/I Really Love You | 350 |
|----|----------------|------------------------------------|------|
| 66 | Fontana TF 718 | Save My Soul/Everybody's Worried 'Bout Tomorrow | 500 |
| 67 | Fontana TF 781 | Rumble On Mersey Square South/Typical British Workmanship | 300 |
| 67 | Fontana TF 781 | Rumble On Mersey Square South/Typical British Workmanship (mispressing, B-side plays "Atmospheres") | 600 |
| 91 | Bam Caruso KIRI 108 | THE PSYCHEDELIC YEARS VOLUME 2 (LP) | 20 |

*(see also Just Four Men, Four Just Men, Pacific Drift, Tristar Airbus)o*

## WIMPS
| | | | |
|---|---|---|---|
| 79 | Sniff Records SNORT 1 | Hamburger Radio/New Girl At School/Modern Girl (numbered p/s) | 10 |
| 79 | Sniff Records SNORT 2 | At The Discoteque/Blind Minds/Gonna Lose (p/s) | 10 |

## WIN
| | | | |
|---|---|---|---|
| 87 | Swamplands | UH! TEARS BABY (CD) | 30 |

## LEM WINCHESTER & BENNY GOLSON
| | | | |
|---|---|---|---|
| 59 | Esquire 32-142 | WINCHESTER SPECIAL (LP) | 25 |
| 61 | Esquire 32-172 | ANOTHER OPUS (LP) | 15 |

## KAI WINDING
| | | | |
|---|---|---|---|
| 65 | Verve VS 512 | Comin' Home Baby/More | 15 |
| 55 | London LTZ-N 15003 | K AND J.J. (LP, with J.J. Johnson Quintet) | 15 |
| 59 | Philips SBBL 515 | TROMBONES (LP) | 18 |
| 61 | Parlophone PMC 1138 | SLIDE RULE (LP, with J.J. Johnson Quintet) | 20 |
| 63 | Verve VLP 9049 | SOUL SURFIN' (LP) | 30 |

*(see also Dizzy Gillespie, J.J. Johnson Quintet)*

## WIND IN THE WILLOWS
| | | | |
|---|---|---|---|
| 68 | Capitol CL 15561 | Moments Spent/Friendly Lion | 25 |
| 68 | Capitol ST 2956 | WIND IN THE WILLOWS (LP) | 30 |

*(see also Debbie Harry, Blondie)*

## WINDMILL
| | | | |
|---|---|---|---|
| 69 | MCA MU 1090 | Big Bertha/Hey, Drummer Man | 5 |
| 70 | MCA MK 5024 | Such Sweet Sorrow/I Can Fly | 10 |
| 70 | MCA MK 5045 | Wilbur's Thing/Two's Company, Three's A Crowd | 5 |

## WINDMILLS
| | | | |
|---|---|---|---|
| 88 | S.T.S. 2 | The Day Dawned On Me/Dolphins (p/s) | 20 |
| 90 | Wasteful SRT 90s 2734 | Nothing At All/Secrets (p/s) | 20 |

## BARRY WINDOW
| | | | |
|---|---|---|---|
| 69 | BAF BAF 7 | I Thank You/End Of Our Road | 50 |

## WINDOWS (1)
| | | | |
|---|---|---|---|
| 72 | Polydor 2058 206 | How Do You Do/Nobody's Baby | 18 |

## WINDOWS (2)
| | | | |
|---|---|---|---|
| 78 | Skeleton SKL 008 | Re-Arrange/Over Dub (p/s) | 7 |

*(see also Mutants)*

## BARBARA WINDSOR
| | | | |
|---|---|---|---|
| 61 | HMV POP 883 | Ten Gallon Hat/Funny Face | 7 |
| 62 | HMV POP 1104 | It Has Better Be A Wonderful Life/ I'm Not That Sort Of Girl (with Harry Fowler & Kenny Lynch) | 7 |
| 63 | HMV POP 1128 | Sparrows Can't Sing/On Mother Kelly's Doorstep | 7 |
| 67 | Parlophone R 5629 | Don't Dig Twiggy/Swinging London | 7 |
| 70 | UPC UPC 101 | When I Was A Child/What A Right Carry On | 12 |
| 72 | Decca F 13323 | Grin And Bare It/Cheeky Sorta' Bird | 7 |

## WINDY & CARL
| | | | |
|---|---|---|---|
| 95 | Enraptured RAPT 4501 | Emerald/Fragments Of Time And Space (500 in hand-painted p/s) | 12 |
| 95 | Enraptured RAPT 4501 | Emerald/Fragments Of Time And Space (300 in tracing paper sleeve) | 10 |
| 96 | Enraptured RAPT 4509 | Christmas Song/GRIMBLE GRUMBLE: Odyssey And Oracle (no'd p/s, coloured vinyl, 350 only) | 20 |

## WINDY CORNER
| | | | |
|---|---|---|---|
| 73 | Deroy DER 977 | THE HOUSE AT WINDY CORNER (LP, private pressing) | 300 |

## AMY WINEHOUSE
| | | | |
|---|---|---|---|
| 03 | Island 12 IS 830 DJ | Stronger Than Me (Curtis Lynch Jnr Vocal Remix)/(Curtis Lynch Jnr Dub Remix) (12" Promo) | 20 |
| 03 | Island 12 IS 830 | Stronger Than Me (Album Version/(Curtis Lynch Jnr Remix featuring Blackout Ja and Isha Sesay)/(Harmonic 33 Remix)/Acapella Version) (12") | 15 |
| 03 | Island 12 ISX 840 DJ | Take The Box (Seiji's Buggin' Mix)/(Seiji's Buggin' Rub)/(The Headquarters MIx) (Promo 12") | 18 |
| 04 | Island 12 IS 840 | Take The Box (Seiji's Buggin' Mix)/(The Headquarters MIx)/(Acapella) (12") | 10 |
| 03 | Island 12 IS 840 DJ | In My Bed (1-sided promo 12") | 12 |
| 03 | Island ISX 852 DJ | In My Bed (Bass Gangsta Mix)/(CJ Mix)/(Full Length Version) (Promo 12") | 18 |
| 03 | Island 12 IS 852 DJ | In My Bed (Bugz In The Attic Vocal Mix)/(Bugz In The Attic Dub)/(Full Length Version) (Promo 12") | 18 |
| 04 | Island 12 IS 852 | In My Bed (Bugz In The Attic Vocal Mix)/You Sent Me Flying/In My Bed (Bad Gangsta)/In My Bed (Radio Edit) (12") | 10 |
| 03 | Island 12 IS 865 DJ | Pumps (MJ Cole Remix)/Pumps (Mylo Remix)/Pumps (Promo 12") | 18 |
| 04 | Island IS 865 | Pumps (MJ Cole Remix)/(Mylo Remix)/(Album Version) (12") | 10 |
| 06 | Island 3789621 0 1 | Rehab - Amy Vs Pharoahe (Promo 12" stickered white label) | 10 |
| 06 | Island AMY 12 PRO 1 | Rehab (Hot Chip Remix)/(Hot Chip Instrumental)/(Desert Eagle Discs Remix)/(Desert Eagle Discs Instrumental)/(Original Version) (Promo 12") | 25 |
| 05 | Universal Island AMY 12PRO 1 | Rehab (Hot Chip Remix)/(Hot Chip Instrumental)/(DED Instrumental)/(Original Version) (promo 12") | 10 |
| 06 | AMY/AMX 12 PRO | Love Is A Losing Game (Moody Boyz Dubstep Remix)/(Moody Boyz Dubland Version) (Promo 12", 300 only) | 25 |
| 06 | Island AMY 7 PRO 2 | Love Is A Losing Game (Moody Boys Dubstep Remix) promo, 300 only | 40 |
| 06 | Island AMYLPPRO 1 | Back To Black (The Rumble Strips Remix)/Back To Black (p/s, clear vinyl promo) | 20 |
| 07 | Island 1732327 | Back To Black (Steve Mac Vocal 6:12)/(Steve Mac Smack Dub 6:15)/(Original Version 4:00)/(Mushtaq Vocal Remix 4.03) (12") | 8 |
| 07 | Island 1732326 | Back To Black/Back To Black (Rumble Strips Remix) (p/s, white vinyl) | 6 |
| 07 | Island 1744792 | Tears Dry On Their Own/Tears Dry On Their Own (NYPC's Fucked MIx) (p/s, clear vinyl) | 10 |
| 03 | Iniversal Island FRANK LP 3 | FRANK (ALBUM SAMPLER) EP (promo 12", p/s) | 25 |
| 04 | Isand/Universal (No Cat No) | FRANK (ALBUM SAMPLER) EP (5-track, promo CD, p/s) | 25 |
| 03 | Island 9812918 | FRANK (LP) | 20 |

| 07 | Island 1735948 | FRANK - REMIXES (2 x 12", gatefold) | 15 |
| 07 | Island/Universal 1734128 | BACK TO BLACK (LP) | 20 |
| 08 | Island ILPS 8148 | FRANK (LP, reissue, 180gm includes free download, sealed, stickered) | 20 |

## WINE OF LEBANON
| 76 | Dovetail DOVE 46 | WINE OF LEBANON (LP) | 20 |

*(see also Achor)*

## WINNERS
| 73 | Ensign EN 39 | Sing Your Song/Have We Finished? | 45 |

## PETE WINSLOW & KING SIZE BRASS
| 73 | BBC 103S | GIRL ON THE TESTCARD (LP) | 20 |

## WINSTON
| 74 | York YR 212 | I Wanna Let Anna Go/Brother Jim | 15 |
| 60s | Holyground | WINSTON SINGS (EP) | 10 |
| 73 | Bradley BRAD 306 | Mona/Rockerdile (p/s) | 20 |

## WINSTON (RICHARDS) & BIBBIE (SEATON)
| 63 | R&B JB 115 | Lover Man/LESTER STIRLING: Gravy Cool | 30 |

## WINSTON (FRANCIS) & CECIL (LOCKE)
| 70 | Banana BA 306 | United We Stand/SOUND DIMENSION: Sweet Message | 20 |

## WINSTON & ERROL
| 64 | Blue Beat BB 272 | Fay Is Gone/MONARCHS : Sadler | 10 |
| 71 | Punch PH 74 | There Is A Land/Goodnight My Love | 6 |

## WINSTON & FAY
| 64 | Blue Beat BB 272 | Fay Is Gone (Winston & Errol)/MONARCHS: Sauce And Tea | 22 |

## WINSTON & GEORGE
| 66 | Pyramid PYR 6002 | Denham Town/Keep The Pressure On | 25 |
| 12 | Pyramid THB 7021 | Denham Town/THE RIO GRANDES: Soldiers Take Over | 8 |

## JIMMY WINSTON (& HIS REFLECTIONS)
| 66 | Decca F 12410 | Sorry She's Mine/It's Not What You Do (But The Way That You Do It) | 300 |
| 76 | Nems NEMS 12 | Sun In The Morning/Just Wanna Smile (solo) | 8 |

*(see also Small Faces, Winston's Fumbs, Spheres)*

## WINSTON (GROOVY) & PAT (RHODEN)
| 68 | Trojan TR 605 | Pony Ride/Baby You Send Me | 15 |
| 71 | Bullet BU 475 | The Same Thing For Breakfast/Sweeter Than Honey | 12 |

*(see also Winston Tucker)*

## WINSTON (RICHARDS) & TONETTES
| 65 | Ska Beat JB 225 | You Make Me Cry/CHECKMATES: Invisible Ska | 35 |

## WINSTON & ROY
| 62 | Blue Beat BB 80 | Babylon Gone/COUNT OSSIE ON AFRICAN DRUMS: First Gone | 25 |

## WINSTON & RUPERT
| 70 | Bullet BU 425 | Come By Here/Somebody | 10 |
| 70 | Moodisc HM 106 | Musically Beat/Let Me Tell You Girl | 10 |

*(see also Eternals)*

## ERIC WINSTONE (& HIS) ORCHESTRA
| 64 | Pye 7N 15603 | Dr. Who Theme/Pony Express | 18 |

## NORMA WINSTONE
| 72 | Argo ZDA 148 | EDGE OF TIME (LP) | 120 |

*(see also Mike Westbrook, Michael Garrick)*

## WINSTONS
| 69 | Pye International 7N 25493 | Colour In Father/Amen, Brother | 20 |
| 69 | Pye International 7N 25500 | Love Of The Common People/Wheel Of Fortune | 7 |

## WINSTON'S FUMBS
| 67 | RCA RCA 1612 | Real Crazy Apartment/Snow White | 600 |

*(see also Small Faces, Jimmy Winston & His Reflections, Yes, Spheres, Federals)*

## WINSTONS & M-SQUAD
| 71 | Green Door GD 4003 | Carroll Street/Carroll Street - Version (B-side act. by Ansel Collins/M-Squad) | 10 |

## EDGAR WINTER (GROUP)
| 70 | CBS 64083 | ENTRANCE (LP, as Edgar Winter) | 15 |
| 71 | CBS 64298 | EDGAR WINTER'S WHITE TRASH (LP) | 15 |

## JOHNNY WINTER
| 69 | CBS 4386 | I'm Yours And I'm Hers/I'll Drown In My Tears | 6 |
| 69 | Liberty LBF 15219 | Rollin' And Tumblin'/Bad Luck And Trouble | 7 |
| 70 | CBS 4794 | Johnny B. Goode/I'm Not Sure | 6 |
| 70 | CBS 5358 | Rock 'N' Roll Hoochie Koo/21st Century Man | 5 |
| 71 | CBS 7227 | Jumping Jack Flash/Good Morning Little School Girl | 5 |
| 69 | CBS 63619 | JOHNNY WINTER (LP) | 25 |
| 69 | Liberty LBL/LBS 83240E | THE PROGRESSIVE BLUES EXPERIMENT (LP) | 25 |
| 70 | Buddah 2359 011 | FIRST WINTER (LP) | 20 |
| 70 | CBS 66231 | SECOND WINTER (2-LP, 3-sided) | 18 |
| 70 | CBS 64117 | JOHNNY WINTER AND... (LP) | 15 |
| 74 | CBS CQ 32188/Q 65484 | STILL ALIVE AND WELL (LP, quadrophonic) | 15 |

*(see also Johnny & Jammers)*

## DON WINTERS
| 60 | Brunswick 05827 | Someday Baby/That's All I Need | 15 |

## LIZ WINTERS & BOB CORT SKIFFLE GROUP
| 57 | Decca F 10878 | Freight Train/Love Is Strange | 20 |
| 57 | Decca F 10899 | Maggie May/Jessamine | 20 |
| 57 | Decca DFE 6409 | LIZ WINTERS AND BOB CORT (EP) | 25 |

*(see also Bob Cort Skiffle Group)*

## LOIS WINTERS
| | | | |
|---|---|---|---|
| 56 | London HLD 8266 | Japanese Farewell Song/JAN GARBER & HIS ORCHESTRA: My Dear | 35 |

## RON WINTERS
| | | | |
|---|---|---|---|
| 63 | Colpix PX 11022 | Snow Girl/In The Middle Of The Morning | 20 |

## RUBY WINTERS
| | | | |
|---|---|---|---|
| 68 | Stateside SS 2090 | I Want Action/Better | 100 |
| 68 | Stateside SS 2090 | I Want Action/Better (DJ copy) | 150 |

## WYOMA WINTERS
| | | | |
|---|---|---|---|
| 54 | HMV 7M 222 | Where Can I Go Without You?/Won't You Give A Repeat Performance | 7 |
| 54 | HMV 7M 260 | Toy Balloon/Shish Kebab | 7 |

## WINTERS REIGN
| | | | |
|---|---|---|---|
| 84 | Scoff DTO33 | Save It/Keep Trying | 8 |
| 87 | Link LOPL 501 | THE BEIGNNING (LP, with free 7") | 15 |

## STEVIE WINWOOD
| | | | |
|---|---|---|---|
| 87 | Island SW 1/2/3 | BACK IN THE HIGH LIFE (3 x 7" set, each in p/s, promo only) | 20 |
| 87 | Island | CHRONICLES (5 x 7" box set, promo, 500 only) | 30 |

*(see also Winwood Kabaka Amoa, Anglos, Spencer Davis Group, Traffic, Blind Faith.)*

## WINWOOD/KABAKA/AMAO
| | | | |
|---|---|---|---|
| 73 | Island HELP 14 | AIYE-KETA THIRD WORLD (LP) | 15 |

*(see also Stevie WInwood)*

## WIPEOUT
| | | | |
|---|---|---|---|
| 82 | M&L MNL 2/ACE 37 | Baby Please Don't Go/Two-O-Five/Crawdaddy/Should A' Known Better (p/s) | 15 |
| 83 | Out OUT 1A/B1 | NO SWEAT (LP) | 15 |

## WIPEOUT
| | | | |
|---|---|---|---|
| 90s | Deluxe DELUX 002 | Snowflake/Confusion Bee (12") | 10 |

## WIPERS
| | | | |
|---|---|---|---|
| 84 | Psycho PSYCHO 22 | IS THIS REAL? (LP, with lyric insert) | 20 |
| 84 | Psycho PSYCHO 23 | YOUTH OF AMERICA (LP) | 20 |

## WIRE
| | | | |
|---|---|---|---|
| 77 | Harvest HAR 5144 | Mannequin/Feeling Called Love/12XU (p/s) | 20 |
| 77 | Harvest HAR 5144 | Mannequin/Feeling Called Love/12XU (no p/s) | 14 |
| 78 | Harvest HAR 5151 | I Am The Fly/Ex-Lion Tamer (p/s) | 18 |
| 78 | Harvest HAR 5151 | I Am The Fly/Ex-Lion Tamer (no p/s) | 10 |
| 78 | Harvest HAR 5161 | Dot Dash/Options R (p/s) | 12 |
| 78 | Harvest HAR 5161 | Dot Dash/Options R (no p/s) | 8 |
| 79 | Harvest HAR 5172 | Outdoor Miner/Practice Makes Perfect (p/s, white vinyl) | 15 |
| 79 | Harvest HAR 5172 | Outdoor Miner/Practice Makes Perfect (p/s) | 7 |
| 79 | Harvest HAR 5187 | A Question Of Degree/Former Airline (p/s) | 15 |
| 79 | Harvest HAR 5192 | Map Ref 41° N 93° W/Go Ahead (p/s) | 12 |
| 79 | Harvest SPSLP 299 | 154 (12", p/s, white label sampler with insert & press release; beware of counterfeits) | 35 |
| 81 | Rough Trade RT 079 | Our Swimmer/Midnight Bahnhof Cafe (p/s) | 10 |
| 88 | Mute MUTE 67 | Kidney Bingos/Pieta (p/s) | 5 |
| 89 | Mute MUTE 87 | Eardrum Buzz/The Offer (p/s, clear vinyl, withdrawn) | 8 |
| 77 | Harvest SHSP 4076 | PINK FLAG (LP, with lyric inner) | 40 |
| 78 | Harvest SHSP 4093 | CHAIRS MISSING (LP, 1st 10,000 with lilac lyric inner sleeve) | 40 |
| 79 | Harvest SHSP 4105 | 154 (LP, with inner lyric sleeve & bonus 7" EP: "Song 2"/"Get Down [Parts I & II]/"Let's Panic"/"Later"/"Small Electric Piece" [PSR 444]) | 50 |
| 79 | Harvest SHSP 4105 | 154 (LP, without 7") | 30 |
| 84 | Rough Trade ROUGH 29 | DOCUMENT AND EYEWITNESS (LP, with free 12" EP [ROUGH 2912]) | 20 |
| 87 | Mute STUMM 42 | THE IDEAL COPY (LP) | 15 |
| 89 | Harvest SHSP 4127 | ON RETURNING (LP) | 15 |
| 89 | Strange Fruit SFRLP 108 | PEEL SESSIONS (LP) | 15 |
| 96 | WMO 4LP | TURNS AND STROKES (LP) | 20 |
| 03 | PF456REDUX | PF456 REDUX (LP) | 20 |
| 00s | Harvest SHSP 4076 | PINK FLAG (LP, reissue, black label) | 20 |
| 00s | Harvest SHSP 4093 | CHAIRS MISSING (LP, reissue) | 15 |

*(see also Dome, Cupol, Colin Newman, Snakes)*

## MARK WIRTZ (ORCHESTRA & CHORUS)
| | | | |
|---|---|---|---|
| 68 | Parlophone R 5668 | (He's Our Dear Old) Weatherman (From "A Teenage Opera")/Possum's Dance | 30 |
| 68 | Parlophone R 5683 | Mrs. Raven/Knickerbocker Glory | 25 |
| 69 | CBS 4306 | My Daddie Is A Baddie/I Love You Because | 15 |
| 69 | CBS 4539 | Caroline/Goody, Goody, Goody | 18 |
| 64 | World Record Club T 452 | TEN AGAIN (LP, by Belle Gonzalez & Russ Loader, Wirtz as producer) | 30 |

*(see also Mood Mosaic, Keith West, Sweet Shop, Philwit & Pegasus, Mark Rogers & Marksmen, Belle Gonzalez, Russ Loader, Zion De Gallier, Elmer Hockett's Hurdy Gurdy, Steve Flynn, Fickle Finger, Matchmaker)*

## NORMAN WISDOM
| | | | |
|---|---|---|---|
| 56 | Columbia SCM 5222 | Two Rivers/Boy Meets Girl (with Ruby Murray) | 10 |
| 57 | Columbia DB 3864 | Up In The World/Me And My Imagination | 10 |
| 57 | Columbia DB 3903 | The Wisdom Of A Fool/Happy Ending | 10 |
| 59 | Top Rank JAR 246 | Follow A Star/Give Me A Night In June | 5 |
| 61 | Columbia SCD 2160 | Narcissus (The Laughing Record)/I Don't 'Arf Love You (with Joyce Grenfell) | 6 |
| 61 | Columbia DB 4601 | If You Believe In Me/Yer Gotta Get Aht | 6 |
| 64 | Columbia DB 7352 | The Joker/Who Can I Turn To | 6 |
| 80 | HMV POP 2001 | The Wisdom Of A Fool/Don't Laugh At Me ('Cause I'm A Fool) | 5 |
| 69 | CBS 4569 | Where Do I Go From Here?/Just Like The Day | 5 |
| 56 | Columbia SEG 7612 | NORMAN WISDOM (EP) | 10 |

| | | | |
|---|---|---|---|
| 57 | Columbia SEG 7687 | NORMAN AND RUBY (EP, with Ruby Murray) | 10 |
| 58 | Columbia SEG 7856 | NORMAN WISDOM (EP) | 10 |
| 59 | Top Rank JKP 2052 | FOLLOW A STAR (EP) | 10 |

*(see also Ruby Murray)*

## WISE BLOOD
| | | | |
|---|---|---|---|
| 85 | Wise 1-12 | Motorslug/Death Rape 2000 (12", p/s) | 12 |
| 86 | Wise 2-12 | Someone Drowned In My Pool/Stumbo (12", p/s) | 12 |
| 91 | Wise 003 | DISHDIRT (LP, with sticker) | 15 |

*(see also Foetus)*

## WISE BOYS
| | | | |
|---|---|---|---|
| 60 | Parlophone R 4693 | Why, Why, Why/My Fortune | 10 |

## WISE GUYS
| | | | |
|---|---|---|---|
| 60 | Top Rank JAR 271 | (Little Girl) Big Noise/As Long As I Have You | 10 |

## MAC WISEMAN
| | | | |
|---|---|---|---|
| 55 | London HLD 8174 | The Kentuckian Song/Wabash Cannon Ball | 30 |
| 56 | London HLD 8226 | My Little Home In Tennessee/I Haven't Got The Right To Love You | 30 |
| 56 | London HLD 8259 | Fireball Mail/When The Roses Bloom Again | 40 |
| 57 | London HLD 8412 | Step It Up And Go/Sundown | 400 |
| 57 | London HLD 8412 | Step It Up And Go/Sundown (78) | 40 |
| 59 | London HL 7084 | Jimmy Brown The Newsboy/I've Got No Use For Woman (export issue) | 20 |
| 56 | London RE-D 1056 | SONGS FROM THE HILLS (EP) | 20 |
| 58 | London RE-D 1147 | SONGS FROM THE HILLS VOL. 2 (EP) | 20 |
| 60 | London RE-D 1242 | SONGS FROM THE HILLS VOL. 3 (EP) | 20 |
| 56 | London HB-D 1052 | SONGS FROM THE HILLS (10" LP) | 30 |
| 60 | London HA-D 2217 | GREAT FOLK BALLADS (LP) | 20 |

## TREVOR WISHART
| | | | |
|---|---|---|---|
| 78 | private pressing | RED BIRD: A POLITICAL PRISONER'S DREAM (LP, with insert) | 20 |
| 79 | private pressing | BEACH SINGULARITY AND MENAGERIE (LP, with insert) | 20 |

## WISHBONE ASH
| | | | |
|---|---|---|---|
| 70 | MCA MK 5061 | Blind Eye/Queen Of Torture | 8 |
| 72 | MCA MKS 5097 | No Easy Road/Blowin' Free | 6 |
| 73 | MCA MUS 1210 | So Many Things To Say/Rock'n'Roll Widow | 5 |
| 74 | MCA MCA 165 | Hometown/Persephone | 5 |
| 75 | MCA MCA 176 | Silver Shoes/Persephone | 6 |
| 76 | MCA/SFI 263 | Outward Bound/Runaway/Mother Of Pearl/You Rescue Me (flexidisc, with "New England" tour programme) | 12 |
| 77 | MCA MCA 291 | Phoenix/Blowin' Free/Jail Bait (p/s) | 5 |
| 78 | MCA MCA 392 | You See Red/Bad Weather Blues (live) (p/s) | 5 |
| 79 | MCA MCA 518 | Come On/Fast Johnny (p/s) | 5 |
| 80 | MCA MCA 549 | Living Proof/Jail Bait (live) (p/s) | 5 |
| 80 | MCA MCA 577 | Helpless (live)/Blowin' Free (live) (p/s) | 5 |
| 81 | MCA MCA 695 | Underground/My Mind Is Made Up (p/s) | 5 |
| 81 | MCA MCA 726 | Get Ready/Kicks On The Street (p/s, with patch) | 8 |
| 81 | MCA MCA 726 | Get Ready/Kicks On The Street (p/s) | 5 |
| 70 | MCA MKPS 2014 | WISHBONE ASH (LP, gatefold sleeve, red/pink 'dogbone' label) | 80 |
| 71 | MCA MDKS 8004 | PILGRIMAGE (LP, gatefold sleeve, purple/red 'dogbone' label) | 80 |
| 72 | MCA MDKS 8006 | ARGUS (LP, gatefold sleeve, black/blue 'hexagon' label) | 100 |
| 73 | MCA MDKS 8011 | WISHBONE FOUR (LP, gatefold sleeve, black label, with poster & lyrics) | 30 |
| 74 | MCA ULD 2 | LIVE DATES (2-LP, gatefold sleeve, pink label) | 18 |
| 80 | MCA MCG 4012 | LIVE DATES II (LP, textured gatefold sleeve, with live bonus LP) | 15 |
| 85 | Neat NEAT 1027 | RAW TO THE BONE (LP) | 18 |

*(see also Home, Big Daisy)*

## WISHFUL THINKING
| | | | |
|---|---|---|---|
| 66 | Decca F 12438 | Turning Round/V.I.P. | 20 |
| 66 | Decca F 12499 | Step By Step/Looking Around | 7 |
| 67 | Decca F 12598 | Count To Ten/Hang Around Girl | 8 |
| 67 | Decca F 12627 | Peanuts/Cherry Cherry | 12 |
| 67 | Decca F 22673 | Meet The Sun/Easier Said Than Loving You | 10 |
| 68 | Decca F 22742 | Alone/Vegetables (export issue) | 10 |
| 68 | Decca F 12760 | It's So Easy/I Want You Girl | 15 |
| 72 | B&C CB 169 | Lu La Le Lu/We're Gonna Change All This | 7 |
| 72 | B&C CB 184 | Clear White Light/Hiroshima | 10 |
| 67 | Decca SKL 4900 | LIVE VOL. 1 (LP) | 50 |
| 71 | Charisma CAS 1038 | HIROSHIMA (LP) | 25 |

## WISHING STONES
| | | | |
|---|---|---|---|
| 86 | Head HEAD 2 | Beat Girl/Two Steps Take Me Back (p/s) | 6 |
| 87 | Head HEAD 6 | New Ways/House Is Not A Home (p/s) | 5 |

*(see also The Loft)*

## WITCHCRAFT
| | | | |
|---|---|---|---|
| 06 | Rise Above RISE 7/089 | If Crimson Was Your Colour/I Know You Killed Someone... (P/s, clear, red, green or black vinyl) | 10 |
| 04 | Rise Above RISELP 47 | WITCHCRAFT (LP) | 25 |
| 04 | Rise Above RISEPD 47 | WITCHCRAFT (LP, picture disc) | 30 |
| 07 | Rise Above RISELP 103 | THE ALCHEMIST (LP, blue vinyl, 25 only) | 120 |
| 07 | Rise Above RISELP 103 | THE ALCHEMIST (LP, green, clear, purple or suitably gold vinyl) | 20 |

## WITCHDOCTOR AND THE SPIRIT
| | | | |
|---|---|---|---|
| 85 | Zella ZEL SPS 427 | Carry On/Version (no p/s) | 25 |

## WITCHES BREW
| | | | |
|---|---|---|---|
| 80s | Pussy PU 016 | Angeline (p/s) | 20 |

## WITCHFINDER GENERAL
| | | | |
|---|---|---|---|
| 81 | Heavy Metal HEAVY 6 | Burning A Sinner/Satan's Children (p/s) | 40 |
| 82 | Heavy Metal 12HM 17 | Soviet Invasion/Rabies/R.I.P. (live) (12", p/s) | 35 |
| 83 | Heavy Metal HEAVY 21 | Music/Last Chance (p/s) | 12 |
| 82 | Heavy Metal HMRLP 8 | DEATH PENALTY (LP, red, blue or clear vinyl, with inner) | 30 |
| 82 | Heavy Metal HMRPD 8 | DEATH PENALTY (LP, picture disc) | 18 |
| 83 | Heavy Metal HMRLP 13 | FRIENDS OF HELL (LP, red, silver or clear vinyl) | 20 |
| 83 | Heavy Metal HMRPD 13 | FRIENDS OF HELL (LP, picture disc) | 18 |

## WITCHFYNDE
| | | | |
|---|---|---|---|
| 79 | Rondelet ROUND 1 | Give 'Em Hell/Getting' Heavy (p/s) | 6 |
| 80 | Rondelet ROUND 4 | In The Stars/Wake Up Screaming (p/s) | 5 |
| 83 | Expulsion OUT 3 | I'd Rather Go Wild/Cry Wolf (p/s) | 20 |
| 80 | Rondelet ABOUT 1 | GIVE 'EM HELL (LP) | 25 |
| 80 | Rondelet ABOUT 2 | STAGE FRIGHT (LP) | 20 |
| 83 | Expulsion PEXIT 5 | CLOAK AND DAGGER (LP, picture disc) | 18 |
| 84 | Mausoleum SKULL 8352 | LORDS OF SIN (LP, gatefold sleeve, with bonus 12" [Cloak & Dagger/ I'd Rather Go Wild/Moon Magic/Give 'Em Hell]) | 15 |

## WITCHING HOUR
| | | | |
|---|---|---|---|
| 92 | Succubus WITCHEP1 | HOURGLASS EP (12") | 30 |

## BILL WITHERS
| | | | |
|---|---|---|---|
| 71 | Sussex LPSX 3 | JUST AS I AM (LP) | 30 |

## BRIAN WITHERS
| | | | |
|---|---|---|---|
| 66 | RCA RCA 1536 | For No One/Here There And Everywhere | 8 |

## WIZ WITHERS
| | | | |
|---|---|---|---|
| 85 | Wizbang WW01 | Rock N Roll Singer/Isn't It The Lost Time | 10 |

## JIMMY WITHERSPOON
### 78s
| | | | |
|---|---|---|---|
| 54 | Parlophone R 3914 | It/Highway To Happiness | 40 |
| 54 | Parlophone R 3951 | Oh Boy/I Done Told You | 40 |
| 54 | Vogue V 2261 | Failing By Degrees/New Orleans Woman | 40 |
| 54 | Vogue V 2295 | Who's Been Jivin' With You/Rain, Rain, Rain | 40 |
| 56 | Vogue V 2060 | Big Fine Girl/No Rollin' Blues | 40 |
| 56 | Vogue V 2356 | Jump, Children/Take Me Back Baby | 40 |

### SINGLES
| | | | |
|---|---|---|---|
| 54 | Parlophone MSP 6125 | It/Highway To Happiness | 100 |
| 54 | Parlophone MSP 6142 | Oh Boy/I Done Told You | 100 |
| 56 | Vogue V 2060 | Big Fine Girl/No Rollin' Blues | 75 |
| 62 | Vogue V 2420 | When The Lights Go Out/All That's Good | 75 |
| 64 | Stateside SS 304 | Evenin'/Money Is Getting Cheaper | 15 |
| 64 | Stateside SS 325 | I Will Never Marry/I'm Coming Down With The Blues | 15 |
| 64 | Stateside SS 362 | You're Next/Happy Blues | 15 |
| 65 | Stateside SS 429 | Come Walk With Me/Oh How I Love You | 15 |
| 65 | Stateside SS 461 | Love Me Right/Make My Heart Smile Again | 15 |
| 66 | Stateside SS 503 | If There Wasn't Any You/I Never Thought I'd See The Day | 15 |
| 66 | Verve VS 538 | It's All Over But The Crying/If I Could Have You Back Again | 8 |
| 67 | Verve VS 553 | Past Forty Blues/My Baby's Quit Me | 6 |
| 71 | Probe PRO 526 | Handbags And Gladrags/It's Time To Live | 5 |
| 75 | Capitol CL 15828 | Fool's Paradise/Reflections | 5 |

### EPs
| | | | |
|---|---|---|---|
| 61 | Vogue EPV 1269 | JIMMY WITHERSPOON AT MONTEREY | 30 |
| 61 | Vogue EPV 1270 | JIMMY WITHERSPOON AT MONTEREY No. 2 | 30 |
| 64 | Vocalion EPVH 1278 | JIMMY WITHERSPOON | 20 |
| 65 | Vocalion EPVH 1284 | OUTSKIRTS OF TOWN | 20 |
| 66 | Vocalion VEH 170158 | FEELING THE SPIRIT VOL. 1 | 20 |
| 66 | Vocalion VEH 170159 | FEELING THE SPIRIT VOL. 2 | 20 |

### ALBUMS
| | | | |
|---|---|---|---|
| 59 | London Jazz LTZ-K 15150 | NEW ORLEANS BLUES (with Wilbur de Paris) | 40 |
| 60 | Vogue LAE 12218 | SINGIN' THE BLUES | 40 |
| 61 | Vogue LAE 12253 | AT THE RENAISSANCE (with Gerry Mulligan) | 35 |
| 64 | Stateside SL 10088 | EVENIN' BLUES | 35 |
| 65 | Stateside SL 10105 | BLUES AROUND THE CLOCK | 40 |
| 65 | Fontana 688 005 ZL | THERE'S GOOD ROCKIN' TONIGHT | 30 |
| 65 | Stateside SL 10114 | SOME OF MY BEST FRIENDS ARE BLUES | 25 |
| 65 | Stateside SL 10139 | BLUE SPOON | 22 |
| 65 | Vogue VRL 3005 | JIMMY WITHERSPOON IN PERSON | 22 |
| 66 | Ember EMB 3369 | JIMMY WITHERSPOON | 20 |
| 67 | Fontana (S)TL 5382 | 'SPOON SINGS AND SWINGS | 25 |
| 67 | Verve (S)VLP 9156 | BLUE POINT OF VIEW | 18 |
| 67 | Transatlantic PR 7300 | EVENIN' BLUES (reissue) | 15 |
| 68 | Transatlantic PR 7356 | SOME OF MY BEST FRIENDS ARE THE BLUES (reissue) | 15 |
| 68 | Stateside (S)SL 10232 | LIVE | 20 |
| 68 | Verve (S)VLP 9181 | BLUES IS NOW (with Brother Jack McDuff) | 15 |
| 68 | Verve (S)VLP 9216 | SPOONFUL OF SOUL | 18 |
| 68 | Transatlantic PR 7418 | SPOON IN LONDON | 15 |
| 68 | Transatlantic PR 7475 | BLUES FOR EASY LIVERS | 15 |

| | | | |
|---|---|---|---|
| 69 | Stateside SSL 10289 | THE BLUES SINGER | 18 |
| 69 | Polydor Intl. 623 256 | BACK DOOR BLUES | 20 |
| 71 | Probe SPB 1031 | HANDBAGS AND GLADRAGS | 15 |

*(see also Eric Burdon & Jimmy Witherspoon, Brother Jack McDuff)*

## JIMMY WITHERSPOON/HELEN HUMES
| | | | |
|---|---|---|---|
| 60 | Vogue EPV 1198 | RHYTHM AND BLUES CONCERT (EP, 2 tracks each) | 80 |

*(see also Helen Humes)*

## BITTER WITHY
| | | | |
|---|---|---|---|
| 69 | Nevis NEVIS R005 | SAMPLER (LP) | 20 |

## WITNESSES
| | | | |
|---|---|---|---|
| 60s | Herald ELR 1076 | THE WITNESSES (EP) | 70 |

## D WITTER
| | | | |
|---|---|---|---|
| 78 | D-Roy DRLP 1001 | MAWAMBA DUB (WARRIOR) (LP) | 50 |

*(See also World Sound & Power Band)*

## WIZARD'S CONVENTION
| | | | |
|---|---|---|---|
| 76 | RCA RS 1085 | WIZARD'S CONVENTION (LP, with insert) | 15 |

*(see also Deep Purple, Roger Glover, Jon Lord, David Coverdale, Ray Fenwick, Glenn Hughes, ELP, Hardin & York)*

## WIZZ
| | | | |
|---|---|---|---|
| 85 | Jah Life | MR. SUNSHINE (LP) | 40 |

## WIZZARD
| | | | |
|---|---|---|---|
| 73 | Harvest SHSP 4025 | WIZZARD BREW (LP, with lyric insert) | 15 |
| 74 | Warner Bros. K 56029 | INTRODUCING EDDY AND THE FALCONS (LP, gatefold with poster) | 25 |

*(see also Roy Wood, Balls, Idle Race, Grunt Futtock)*

## WJW & ROOTS TRUNKS & BRANCHES
| | | | |
|---|---|---|---|
| 79 | Splendour Heights WJWX 1945 | THE WEAK WILL BE STRONG (LP) | 25 |

## WKGB
| | | | |
|---|---|---|---|
| 79 | Fetish FET 002 | Non-Stop/Ultra Marine (p/s) | 8 |

## W.L.S.
| | | | |
|---|---|---|---|
| 77 | Cancer CAND 001 | Dub Punk/Simply Funky (12") | 15 |

## JEZZ WODROFFE
| | | | |
|---|---|---|---|
| 80 | Graduate GRAD LP 1 | OPPOSITE DIRECTIONS (LP) | 50 |

## CHARLES WOLCOTT
| | | | |
|---|---|---|---|
| 60 | MGM 1115 | Leatherjacket Cowboy/Ruby Duby Do | 15 |

## DARRYL WAY'S WOLF
| | | | |
|---|---|---|---|
| 73 | Deram DM 378 | Wolf/Spring Fever | 8 |
| 73 | Deram DM 395 | A Bunch Of Fives/Five In The Morning | 8 |
| 73 | Deram DM 401 | Two Sisters/Go Down | 8 |
| 73 | Deram SDL 14 | CANIS LUPUS (LP, as Darryl Way's Wolf, gatefold sleeve) | 18 |
| 73 | Deram SML 1104 | SATURATION POINT (LP, laminated sleeve, as Darryl Way's Wolf) | 15 |
| 74 | Deram SML 1116 | NIGHT MUSIC (LP) | 18 |

*(see also Curved Air, King Crimson, Marillion)*

## WOLF
| | | | |
|---|---|---|---|
| 81 | Gremlin GREM 72 | See Them Running/Creatures Of The Night (no p/s) | 75 |
| 84 | Mausoleum 8323 | EDGE OF THE WORLD (LP) | 18 |

## WOLF
| | | | |
|---|---|---|---|
| 82 | Chrysalis CHS 2592 | Head Contact/Rock'n'Roll (p/s, clear vinyl, with sticker) | 15 |
| 82 | Chrysalis CHS 2592 | Head Contact/Rock'n'Roll (p/s, clear vinyl, without sticker) | 6 |

## PATRICK WOLF
| | | | |
|---|---|---|---|
| 02 | Faith & Industry FAI 001 | THE PATRICK WOLF EP: Bloodbeat/Empress/A Boy Like Me/Pumpkin Soup (12", 1000 only) | 50 |

## HENRY WOLFF AND NANCY HENNINGS
| | | | |
|---|---|---|---|
| 72 | Island HELP 3 | TIBETAN BELLS (LP, black label with pink "i") | 15 |

## WOLFGANG
| | | | |
|---|---|---|---|
| 70 | Bell BLL 1120 | Sandman/You | 12 |

## WOLFGANG PRESS
| | | | |
|---|---|---|---|
| 83 | 4AD (no cat. no.) | Kings Of Soul (Crowned Mix)/(De-Throned Mix)/(7" Mix) (12", same both sides, promo only, 50 copies pressed) | 15 |

*(see also Mass, Models)*

## WOLFMAN
| | | | |
|---|---|---|---|
| 04 | Rough Trade RTRADS177 | For Lovers/Back From The Dead (with Pete Doherty, p/s) | 10 |

## WOLFRILLA
| | | | |
|---|---|---|---|
| 71 | Concord CON 015 | Song For Jimi/Come Tomorrow | 7 |

## WOLVES
| | | | |
|---|---|---|---|
| 64 | Pye 7N 15676 | Journey Into Dreams/What Do You Mean | 20 |
| 64 | Pye 7N 15733 | Now/This Year Next Year | 30 |
| 65 | Pye 7N 17013 | At The Club/Distant Dreams | 35 |
| 66 | Parlophone R 5511 | Lust For Life/My Baby Loves Them | 70 |

## BOBBY WOMACK
| | | | |
|---|---|---|---|
| 68 | Minit MLF 11001 | Broadway Walk/Somebody Special | 8 |
| 68 | Minit MLF 11005 | What Is This?/What You Gonna Do | 15 |
| 68 | Minit MLF 11010 | Fly Me To The Moon/Take Me | 8 |
| 69 | Minit MLF 11012 | California Dreamin'/Baby You Oughta Think It Over | 10 |
| 72 | United Artists UP 35339 | That's The Way I Feel About 'Cha/Come, L'Amore | 7 |
| 72 | United Artists UP 35375 | Woman's Gotta Have It/If You Don't Want My Love | 5 |
| 73 | United Artists UP 35456 | I Can Understand It/Harry Hippie (in p/s) | 12 |
| 73 | United Artists UP 35456 | I Can Understand It/Harry Hippie | 8 |

MINT VALUE £

| 73 | United Artists UP 35512 | Across 110th Street/Hang On In There (as Bobby Womack & Peace) | 10 |
| 73 | United Artists UP 35565 | Nobody Wants You When You're Down And Out/I'm Through Trying To Prove My Love For You | 6 |
| 74 | Jay Boy BOY 75 | What Is This?/I Wonder | 15 |
| 75 | United Artists UP 35859 | Check It Out/Interlude No. 2 | 6 |
| 76 | United Artists UP 36042 | Where There's A Will There's A Way/Everything's Gonna Be Alright | 6 |
| 76 | United Artists UP 36098 | Daylight/Trust Me | 8 |
| 77 | CBS 4827 | Home Is Where The Heart Is/We've Only Just Begun | 30 |
| 77 | CBS 4827 | Home Is Where The Heart Is/We've Only Just Begun (DJ Copy) | 50 |
| 79 | Arista ARIST 284 | How Could You Break My Heart/I Honestly Love You | 15 |
| 82 | Tamla Motown TMG1267 | So Many Sides Of You/Just My Imagination (7", p/s) | 30 |
| 87 | Arista RIS 17 | How Could You Break My Heart/Give It Up (p/s) | 20 |
| 87 | Arista RIST 17 | How Could You Break My Heart/Give It Up/Mr. D.J. Don't Stop The Music (12", p/s) | 20 |
| 72 | United Artists UAS 29365 | UNDERSTANDING (LP) | 15 |
| 73 | United Artists UAS 29451 | ACROSS 110TH STREET (LP, soundtrack, with J.J. Johnson) | 20 |
| 79 | Arista ARTY 165 | ROADS OF LIFE (LP) | 20 |

*(see also Valentinos, Ted Wood)*

## WOMB
| 69 | Dot DLP 25933 | WOMB (LP) | 25 |
| 70 | Dot DLP 25959 | OVERDUB (LP) | 30 |

## WOMBATS
| 06 | Kids KIDS 005 | Lost In The Post/Patricia The Stripper (in stickered mailer, 500 only) | 10 |
| 07 | No Label | Moving To New York/Happily Screwed/The Barman's Fault/Ba Ba Song (EP) | 15 |

## ALISON WONDER
| 70 | Columbia DB 8667 | Once More With Feeling/Black Paper Roses | 6 |

*(see also Cheryl St. Clair)*

## (LITTLE) STEVIE WONDER
| 63 | Oriole CBA 1853 | Fingertips (Parts 1 & 2) | 40 |
| 63 | Oriole CBA 1853 | Fingertips (Parts 1 & 2) (DJ copy) | 85 |
| 63 | Stateside SS 238 | Workout, Stevie, Workout/Monkey Talk | 50 |
| 63 | Stateside SS 238 | Workout, Stevie, Workout/Monkey Talk (DJ copy) | 100 |
| 64 | Stateside SS 285 | Castles In The Sand/Thank You (For Loving Me All The Way) | 80 |
| 64 | Stateside SS 285 | Castles In The Sand/Thank You (For Loving Me All The Way) (DJ copy) | 100 |
| 64 | Stateside SS 323 | Hey, Harmonica Man/This Little Girl | 55 |
| 64 | Stateside SS 323 | Hey, Harmonica Man/This Little Girl (DJ copy) | 85 |

*(The above 45's are credited to Little Stevie Wonder.)*

| 65 | Tamla Motown TMG 505 | Kiss Me Baby/Tears In Vain | 50 |
| 65 | Tamla Motown TMG 505 | Kiss Me Baby/Tears In Vain (DJ copy) | 100 |
| 65 | Tamla Motown TMG 532 | High-Heel Sneakers/Music Talk | 40 |
| 65 | Tamla Motown TMG 532 | High-Heel Sneakers/Music Talk (DJ copy) | 100 |
| 66 | Tamla Motown TMG 545 | Uptight (Everything's Alright)/Purple Raindrops | 25 |
| 66 | Tamla Motown TMG 545 | Uptight (Everything's Alright)/Purple Raindrops (DJ cop) | 200 |
| 66 | Tamla Motown TMG 558 | Nothing's Too Good For My Baby/With A Child's Heart | 45 |
| 66 | Tamla Motown TMG 558 | Nothing's Too Good For My Baby/With A Child's Heart (DJ copy) | 150 |
| 66 | Tamla Motown TMG 570 | Blowin' In The Wind/Ain't That Asking For Trouble | 25 |
| 66 | Tamla Motown TMG 570 | Blowin' In The Wind/Ain't That Asking For Trouble (DJ copy) | 75 |
| 66 | Tamla Motown TMG 588 | A Place In The Sun/Sylvia | 20 |
| 66 | Tamla Motown TMG 588 | A Place In The Sun/Sylvia (DJ copy) | 50 |
| 67 | Tamla Motown TMG 602 | Travelin' Man/Hey Love | 18 |
| 67 | Tamla Motown TMG 602 | Travelin' Man/Hey Love (DJ copy) | 50 |
| 67 | Tamla Motown TMG 613 | I Was Made To Love Her/Hold Me | 10 |
| 67 | Tamla Motown TMG 613 | I Was Made To Love Her/Hold Me (DJ copy) | 40 |
| 67 | Tamla Motown TMG 626 | I'm Wondering/Every Time I See You I Go Wild | 12 |
| 67 | Tamla Motown TMG 626 | I'm Wondering/Every Time I See You I Go Wild (DJ copy) | 40 |
| 68 | Tamla Motown TMG 653 | Shoo-Be-Doo-Be-Doo-Da-Day/Why Don't You Lead Me To Love | 12 |
| 68 | Tamla Motown TMG 653 | Shoo-Be-Doo-Be-Doo-Da-Day/Why Don't You Lead Me To Love (DJ copy) | 30 |
| 68 | Tamla Motown TMG 666 | You Met Your Match/My Girl | 15 |
| 68 | Tamla Motown TMG 666 | You Met Your Match/My Girl (DJ copy) | 35 |
| 68 | Tamla Motown TMG 679 | For Once In My Life/Angie Girl | 6 |
| 68 | Tamla Motown TMG 679 | For Once In My Life/Angie Girl (DJ Copy) | 30 |
| 69 | Tamla Motown TMG 690 | My Cherie Amour/I Don't Know Why I Love You | 6 |
| 69 | Tamla Motown TMG 690 | My Cherie Amour/I Don't Know Why I Love You (DJ copy) | 25 |
| 69 | Tamla Motown TMG 717 | Yester-Me, Yester-You, Yesterday/I'd Be A Fool Right Now | 6 |
| 69 | Tamla Motown TMG 717 | Yester-Me, Yester-You, Yesterday/I'd Be A Fool Right Now (DJ copy) | 25 |
| 70 | Tamla Motown TMG 731 | Never Had A Dream Come True/Somebody Knows, Somebody Cares | 7 |
| 70 | Tamla Motown TMG 731 | Never Had A Dream Come True/Somebody Knows, Somebody Cares (DJ copy) | 25 |
| 70 | Tamla Motown TMG 744 | Signed, Sealed, Delivered, I'm Yours/I'm More Than Happy (I'm Satisfied) | 6 |
| 70 | Tamla Motown TMG 744 | Signed, Sealed, Delivered, I'm Yours/I'm More Than Happy (I'm Satisfied) (DJ copy) | 25 |
| 70 | Tamla Motown TMG 757 | Heaven Help Us All/I Gotta Have A Song | 6 |
| 70 | Tamla Motown TMG 757 | Heaven Help Us All/I Gotta Have A Song (DJ copy) | 20 |
| 71 | Tamla Motown TMG 772 | We Can Work It Out/Don't Wonder Why (in p/s) | 30 |
| 71 | Tamla Motown TMG 772 | We Can Work It Out/Don't Wonder Why | 6 |
| 71 | Tamla Motown TMG 772 | We Can Work It Out/Don't Wonder Why (DJ copy) | 25 |
| 71 | Tamla Motown TMG 779 | Never Dreamed You'd Leave Me In Summer/If You Really Love Me | 8 |
| 71 | Tamla Motown TMG 779 | Never Dreamed You'd Leave Me In Summer/If You Really Love Me (DJ copy) | 25 |
| 72 | Tamla Motown TMG 798 | If You Really Love Me/Think Of Me As Your Soldier | 7 |
| 64 | Stateside SE 1014 | I CALL IT PRETTY MUSIC BUT THE OLD PEOPLE CALL IT THE BLUES (EP) | 120 |
| 65 | Tamla Motown TME 2006 | LITTLE STEVIE WONDER (EP) | 90 |

*(Credited to Little Stevie Wonder.)*

| 63 | Oriole PS 40049 | TRIBUTE TO UNCLE RAY (LP) | 325 |
| 63 | Oriole PS 40050 | THE TWELVE-YEAR-OLD GENIUS - LIVE (LP) | 110 |
| 64 | Stateside SL 10078 | THE JAZZ SOUL OF LITTLE STEVIE WONDER (LP) | 150 |

*(The above LP's are Credited to Little Stevie Wonder.)*

| 65 | Stateside SL 10108 | HEY, HARMONICA MAN (LP) | 150 |
| 66 | T. Motown TML 11036 | UPTIGHT (EVERYTHING'S ALRIGHT) (LP, mono) | 35 |

*(Originally came with flipback sleeves)*

| 66 | Tamla Motown TMG STML 11036 | UPTIGHT (EVERYTHING'S ALRIGHT) (LP, stereo) | 45 |
| 67 | T. Motown TML 11045 | DOWN TO EARTH (LP, mono) | 30 |
| 67 | Tamla Motown STML 11045 | DOWN TO EARTH (LP, stereo) | 40 |
| 68 | T. Motown STML 11059 | I WAS MADE TO LOVE HER (LP, stereo) | 25 |
| 68 | T. Motown TML 11059 | I WAS MADE TO LOVE HER (LP, mono) | 20 |
| 68 | Tamla Motown (S)TML 11075 | GREATEST HITS (LP, mono/stereo) | 15 |
| 68 | T. Motown (S)TML 11085 | SOMEDAY AT CHRISTMAS (LP, mono/stereo) | 35 |
| 69 | T. Motown (S)TML 11098 | FOR ONCE IN MY LIFE (LP, mono/stereo) | 20 |
| 69 | T. Motown (S)TML 11128 | MY CHERIE AMOUR (LP, mono/stereo) | 18 |

*(The LP's listed above originally came with flipback sleeves.)*

| 70 | Tamla Motown STML 11150 | STEVIE WONDER LIVE | 15 |
| 70 | T. Motown STML 11169 | SIGNED SEALED AND DELIVERED | 15 |
| 71 | T. Motown STML 11183 | WHERE I'M COMING FROM (LP) | 15 |

## WONDER WHO

| 65 | Philips BF 1440 | Don't Think Twice, It's Alright/Sassy | 20 |
| 66 | Philips BF 1504 | On The Good Ship Lollipop/You're Nobody Till Somebody Loves You | 10 |
| 67 | Philips BF 1600 | Lonesome Road/FOUR SEASONS: Around And Around | 20 |

*(see also Four Seasons, Frankie Valli)*

## WONDER BOY

| 69 | Jackpot JP 703 | Sweeten My Coffee (actually by Slim Smith)/MISTER MILLER: Cherry Pink | 20 |
| 69 | Jackpot JP 705 | Love Power (actually by Slim Smith)/PAT KELLY: Since You Are Gone | 20 |
| 71 | Jackpot JP 764 | Just For A Day/He Ain't Heavy | 12 |
| 71 | Concord CON 015 | Just For A Day/He Ain't Heavy | 5 |
| 75 | Ackee ACK 546 | Pressure Parts 1 & 2 | 6 |

*(see also Slim Smith)*

## GIRL WONDER

| 66 | Doctor Bird DB 1015 | Mommy Out Of The Light/Cutting Wood | 25 |

## WONDERLAND

| 68 | Polydor 56539 | Poochy/Moscow | 15 |

## ALICE WONDERLAND

| 63 | London HLU 9783 | He's Mine/Cha Linde | 20 |

## WONDERS OF YOUTH

| 71 | Alert AL 2 | Down And Out Man/Terry | 25 |
| 72 | Fly FL2 | Jump Over My Head/Say Hello | 40 |

## WONDER STUFF

| 87 | Far Out GONE ONE | It's Not True.../A Wonderful Day/Like A Merry-Go-Round/Down Here (EP, p/s) | 40 |
| 89 | House Of Dolls HOD 011 | Who Wants To Be The Disco King? (King Of Disco Megamix)/PRUDES: Christmas/SANDKINGS: Colourblind/WORLD MUSIC: Stop Playing With My Heart (no p/s, free with House Of Dolls magazine) | 6 |
| 87 | Polydor | A HANDFUL OF SONGS (cassette, promo only, different to above) | 20 |

*(see also Vic Reeves)*

## ROYCE WONG

| 65 | Blue Beat BB 301 | Everything's Gonna Be Alright/Hang Your Head And Cry | 20 |

## WONKY ALICE

| 92 | Pomona POM 004 | SIRIUS EP (12", p/s) | 12 |

## WOOB

| 93 | Woob | WOOB WOOB WOOB (Cassette demo tape) | 20 |
| 94 | Em:t | WOOB 1194 (CD) | 40 |
| 95 | Em:t | WOOB 4495 (CD) | 40 |

## ANITA WOOD

| 62 | London HLS 9585 | I'll Wait Forever/I Can't Show You How I Feel | 25 |
| 64 | Sue WI 328 | Dream Baby/This Happened Before | 40 |

## BOBBY WOOD

| 64 | Pye International 7N 25264 | I'm A Fool For Loving You/My Heart Went Boing! Boing! Boing! | 15 |

## BRENTON WOOD

| 67 | Philips BF 1579 | Oogum Boogum Song/I Like The Way You Love Me | 8 |
| 67 | Liberty LBF 15021 | Gimme Little Sign/I Think You Got Your Fools Mixed Up | 8 |
| 68 | Liberty LBF 15065 | Baby You Got It/Catch You On The Rebound | 8 |
| 68 | Liberty LBF 15103 | Some Got It, Some Don't/Me And You | 8 |
| 70 | Pye International 7N 25522 | Great Big Bundle Of Love/Can You Dig It | 15 |
| 67 | Liberty LBL/LBS 83088E | GIMME A LITTLE SIGN (LP) | 20 |

## WOOD CHILDREN

| 88 | Cat & Mouse ABB 05 | Happens Everyday/2 Red Buses | 8 |

## CHUCK WOOD

| 67 | Big T BIG 104 | Seven Days Too Long/Soul Shing-A-Ling | 20 |
| 67 | Big T BIG 104 | Seven Days Too Long/Soul Shing-A-Ling (DJ Copy) | 50 |
| 68 | Big T BIG 107 | I've Got My Lovelight Shining/Baby You Win | 10 |
| 71 | Mojo 2092 010 | Seven Days Too Long/Soul Shing A Ling (reissue) | 5 |
| 75 | Pye Disco Demand DDS 111 | Seven Days Too Long (in p/s) | 10 |

# Del WOOD

| | | | |
|---|---|---|---|
| 75 | Pye Disco Demand DDS 111 | Seven Days Too Long/WIGANS CHOSEN FEW: Footsee (instrumental) | 5 |

## DEL WOOD
| | | | |
|---|---|---|---|
| 54 | London HL 8036 | Ragtime Annie/Backroom Polka | 50 |
| 54 | London RE-P 1007 | RAGTIME PIANO (EP) | 15 |

## RONNIE WOOD
| | | | |
|---|---|---|---|
| 74 | Warner Bros K 16463 | I Can Feel The Fire/Breathe On Me (as Ron Wood) | 5 |
| 75 | Warner Bros K 16618 | If You Don't Want Me Love/I've Got A Feeling | 5 |
| 76 | Warner Bros K 16679 | Big Bayou/Sweet Baby Mine | 5 |
| 92 | Continuum 12210-2 | Show Me/Breathe On Me (CD, with Ronnie Wood print, signed & numbered, in black card case tied with ribbon, 600 only) | 50 |

*(see also Faces, Rolling Stones, Jeff Beck, Ted Wood)*

## ROY WOOD
| | | | |
|---|---|---|---|
| 72 | Harvest HAR 5048 | When Gran'ma Plays The Banjo/Wake Up | 5 |
| 75 | Jet JET 754 | Oh What A Shame/Bengal Jig (cartoon p/s) | 5 |
| 75 | Jet JET 761 | Look Thru' The Eyes Of A Fool/Strider (copies miscredited as "Looking Thru' The Eyes Of A Fool") | 5 |
| 76 | Jet JET 785 | Any Old Time Will Do/The Rain Came Down On Everything | 5 |
| 77 | Warner Bros K 16961 | The Stroll/Jubilee (p/s, by Wizzo Band) | 5 |
| 77 | Warner Bros K 17028 | I Never Believed In Love/Inside My Life (as Roy Wood & Annie Haslam) | 5 |
| 78 | Warner Bros K 17094 | Dancin' At The Rainbow's End/Waiting At This Door (p/s, as Wizzo Band) | 5 |
| 78 | Warner Bros K 17248 | Keep Your Hands On The Wheel/Giant Footsteps | 5 |
| 73 | Harvest SHVL 803 | BOULDERS (LP, textured sleeve with EMI logo on label) | 25 |
| 76 | Harvest SHDW 408 | THE ROY WOOD STORY (LP) | 15 |

*(see also Wizzard, Gerry Levine & Avengers, Mike Sheridan, Danny King['s Mayfair Set], Move, ELO, Renaissance [UK], Rockers, Birds)*

## TED WOOD
| | | | |
|---|---|---|---|
| 76 | Penny Farthing PEN 891 | Am I Blue/Shine (B-side features Rod Stewart, Ronnie Wood, Gary Glitter & Bobby Womack) | 8 |

*(see also Temperance Seven)*

## WOODEN HORSE
| | | | |
|---|---|---|---|
| 72 | York SYK 526 | Pick Up The Pieces/Wake Me In The Morning | 20 |
| 73 | York SYK 543 | Wooden Horses/Typewriter And Guitar | 20 |
| 72 | York FYK 403 | WOODEN HORSE (LP) | 350 |
| 73 | York FYK 413 | WOODEN HORSE II (LP, withdrawn, with sleeve, blue/silver label) | 900 |
| 73 | York FYK 413 | WOODEN HORSE II (LP, withdrawn, without sleeve, blue/silver label) | 500 |

*(see also Fox)*

## WOODEN O & GUESTS
| | | | |
|---|---|---|---|
| 69 | Middle Earth MDLS 301 | A HANDFUL OF PLEASANT DELITES (LP) | 150 |

*(see also 'Middle Earth Sampler' in Various Artists section)*

## WOODEN SHJIPS
| | | | |
|---|---|---|---|
| 09 | Great Pop Supplement GPS 50 | I Believe It/SPACEMEN 3: Big City (demo) (red marbled vinyl, insert & sticker) | 15 |

## GEORGE WOODHOUSE
| | | | |
|---|---|---|---|
| 79 | Milestone M 001 | Thanks/HOPETON JURNER: Living In The Ghetto (12") | 150 |

## KEN WOODMAN & HIS PICCADILLY BRASS
| | | | |
|---|---|---|---|
| 66 | Strike JLH 101 | THAT'S NICE (LP) | 40 |

## WOODMARK
| | | | |
|---|---|---|---|
| 83 | Ooze S83 CUS 1692 | When You're Gone/Life Is Cruel | 20 |

## WOODPECKERS
| | | | |
|---|---|---|---|
| 64 | Decca F 11835 | The Woodpecker/You Can't Sit Down | 10 |
| 65 | Oriole CB 311 | Hey Little Girl/What's Your Name | 20 |

## STANLEY WOODRUFF & U.S. TRIO
| | | | |
|---|---|---|---|
| 70 | Ember EMB S 288 | If I Let You/Will You Still Love Me Tomorrow | 7 |
| 77 | Grapevine GP 102 | What Took You So Long/Now Is Forever | 5 |

## CAROL WOODS
| | | | |
|---|---|---|---|
| 70 | Ember EMB S 288 | If I Let You/Will You Still Love Me Tomorrow (p/s) | 10 |
| 72 | Ember NR 5059 | OUT OF THE WOODS (LP) | 35 |

## CORA WOODS
| | | | |
|---|---|---|---|
| 56 | Parlophone DP 505 | Rocks In Your Head/I Don't Want To Cry (export 78) | 10 |

## DONALD WOODS & EARL PALMER BAND
| | | | |
|---|---|---|---|
| 58 | Vogue V 9107 | Memories Of An Angel/That Much Of Your Love | 650 |
| 58 | Vogue V 9107 | Memories Of An Angel/That Much Of Your Love (78) | 150 |

## GAY & TERRY WOODS
| | | | |
|---|---|---|---|
| 77 | Polydor 2058 810 | Save The Last Dance For Me/One More Time | 10 |
| 78 | Rockburgh ROCS 202 | We Can Work This One Out/Piece Of Summer (p/s) | 10 |
| 75 | Polydor 2383 322 | BACKWOODS (LP) | 50 |
| 76 | Polydor 2383 375 | THE TIME IS RIGHT (LP, with lyric insert) | 60 |
| 76 | Polydor 2383 406 | RENOWNED (LP, with lyric insert) | 50 |
| 78 | Rockburgh ROC 104 | TENDER HOOKS (LP, with lyric insert) | 20 |

*(see also Woods Band, Gay Woods, Steeleye Span, Sweeney's Men)*

## JIMMY WOODS
| | | | |
|---|---|---|---|
| 63 | Contemporary LAC 571 | CONFLICT (LP) | 20 |

## NICK WOODS
| | | | |
|---|---|---|---|
| 62 | London HLU 9621 | Ballad Of Billy Budd/Don't Let Me Down | 8 |

## PEGGY WOODS
| | | | |
|---|---|---|---|
| 88 | Kent 6T 4 | Love Is Gonna Get You/ZZ: You Just Cheat And Lie | 20 |

## PHIL WOODS
| | | | |
|---|---|---|---|
| 57 | Esquire EP 168 | THE YOUNG IDEAS (EP) | 12 |
| 55 | Esquire 20-055 | NEW JAZZ QUINTET (10" LP) | 35 |

57  Esquire 32-020 ........ WOODLORE (LP) ............................................................. 50

**TONY WOODS**
71  Spiral DIT 2 ........... I'm Only A Man/Blues ..................................................... 6

**TED WOODS**
71  Spiral DIT 2 ........... I'm Only A Man/Blues ..................................................... 10

**TERRY WOODS**
81  Chiswick CHIS 142 ..... Tennessee Stud/I Don't Know About Love ...................... 30

**WOODS BAND**
71  Greenwich GSLP 1004 .. THE WOODS BAND (LP, gatefold sleeve) ....................... 150
77  Rockburgh CREST 29 ... THE WOODS BAND (LP, reissue in different sleeve) ......... 20
*(see also Gay & Terry Woods)*

**MAGGIE WOODWARD**
59  Vogue V 9148 .......... Ali Bama/Zulu Warrior .................................................. 15
59  Vogue V 9148 .......... Ali Bama/Zulu Warrior (78) ........................................... 20

**WOODY KERN**
69  Pye 7N 17672 ......... Biography/Tell You I'm Gone (demo) ............................. 100
69  Pye NSPL 18273 ....... THE AWFUL DISCLOSURES OF MARIA MONK (LP) ......... 150

**WOOL**
69  Stateside SS2153 ...... Love Love Love Love Love/If They Left Us Alone Now ....... 25

**BRIAN WOOLEY**
58  Esquire EP 170 ........ BRIAN WOOLEY'S JAZZMEN (EP) .................................. 10
58  Esquire EP 190 ........ WILD 'N WOOLEY (EP) ................................................. 10

**SHEB WOOLEY**
51  MGM MGM 439 ....... Hoot Owl Boogie/Country Kisses (78) ............................ 20
55  MGM SP 1130 ......... 38-24-35/I Flipped ....................................................... 25
55  MGM SPC 5 ............ Hill Billy Mambo/I Go Outa My Mind (export issue) ........ 30
58  MGM MGM 981 ....... The Purple People Eater/I Can't Believe You're Mine ...... 15
58  MGM MGM 981 ....... The Purple People Eater/Recipe For Love (2nd pressing, different B-side) ...... 6
58  MGM MGM 997 ....... Santa And The Purple People Eater/Star Of Love) ........... 5
59  MGM MGM 1017 ...... Sweet Chile/More ......................................................... 8
60  MGM MGM 1081 ...... Luke The Spook/My Only Treasure .................................. 7
61  MGM MGM 1132 ...... The Wayward Wind/Bars Across The Windows ................. 6
61  MGM MGM 1147 ...... That's My Pa/Meet Mr. Lonely ...................................... 6
62  MGM MGM 1162 ...... Laughing The Blues/Somebody Please .............................. 6
65  MGM MGM 1257 ...... Hootenanny Hoot/Old Joe Rag ...................................... 5
65  MGM MGM 1263 ...... Blue Guitar/Natchez Landing .......................................... 5
56  MGM MGM-EP 540 ... JEST PLAIN, WILD AND WOOLEY (EP) ........................... 40
61  MGM MGM-C 859 ..... SONGS FROM THE DAY OF RAWHIDE (LP) ....................... 20
62  MGM MGM-C 903 ..... THAT'S MY MA AND THAT'S MY PA (LP) ......................... 20
63  MGM MGM-C 945 ..... SPOOFING THE BIG ONES! (LP) ..................................... 15

**CHARLIE WOOLFE**
68  NEMS 56-3675 ........ Dance Dance Dance/Home .............................................. 35
*(see also At Last The 1958 Rock & Roll Show)*

**WOOLIES**
67  RCA RCA 1602 ........ Who Do You Love?/Hey Girl ........................................... 50

**JOHN WOOLLEY & JUST BORN**
71  Decca 23134 .......... Ruby Baby/Make Love Not War ..................................... 10

**WOOLLY**
72  RCA 2297 ............. Golden Golden/Sugar Daddy Song .................................. 20

**WOOLLY FISH**
70  Plexium PXM 16 ...... Way You Like It/Sound Of Thick .................................... 6

**BRENDA WOOTTON**
68  Pipers VRC 1 ......... JOHN THE FISH (LP) ...................................................... 20

**WORD**
83  Word WORD 001 ...... Colour It!/Recurring ...................................................... 5

**WORK**
81  Woof WOOF 2 ......... I Hate America/Fingers & Toes/Duty (p/s, clear vinyl) ........ 5
*(see also Art Bears)*

**JIMMY WORK**
56  London HLD 8270 ..... When She Said "You All"/There's Only One You ............... 60
56  London HLD 8270 ..... When She Said "You All"/There's Only One You (78) ......... 20
56  London HLD 8308 ..... You've Gotta Heart Like A Merry-Go-Round/Blind Heart .... 45
56  London HLD 8308 ..... You've Gotta Heart Like A Merry-Go-Round/Blind Heart (78) .. 20
55  London RE-D 1039 .... COUNTRY SONGS - WORK STYLE (EP) ............................ 30

**WORKFORCE**
80s  WF WF 1 ............. The Right To Work/Holy Moses (p/s) ............................... 5

**WORKS**
72  London HLU 10360 ... Orange Medley (Music Inspired By "A Clockwork Orange")/Sweet Charity ...... 5

**WORLD**
70  Liberty LBF 15402 .... Angelina/Come Out Into The Open .................................. 10
70  Liberty LBG 83419 .... LUCKY PLANET (LP, textured gatefold sleeve) .................. 50
*(see also Neil Innes, Bonzo Dog [Doo-Dah] Band)*

**WORLD COLUMN**
76  Capitol CL 15852 ..... So Is The Sun/It's Not Right ........................................... 10
76  Capitol CL 15852 ..... So Is The Sun/It's Not Right (DJ Copy) ............................ 15

MINT VALUE £

## WORLD OF OZ
| 68 | Deram DM 187 | The Muffin Man/Peter's Birthday (Black And White Rainbows) | 15 |
|----|--------------|---|----|
| 68 | Deram DM 205 | King Croesus/Jack | 15 |
| 69 | Deram DM 233 | Willow's Harp/Like A Tear | 25 |
| 69 | Deram DML/SML 1034 | THE WORLD OF OZ (LP) | 120 |

*(see also David Kubinec)*

## WORLD SOUND & POWER BAND
| 80 | D Roy DRLP 1006 | MAWAMBA DUB (WARRIOR) CHAPTER TWO (LP) | 55 |
|----|--------------|---|----|

*(See also D Witter)*

## WORMS
| 78 | Ice GUY 21 | London Bus (I Can't Take My Eyes Off You/Okay At Christmas (500 only) | 15 |
|----|--------------|---|----|

## BIMBI WORRICK
| 69 | Polydor 56321 | Long Time Comin'/Tomorrow Is My Day | 8 |
|----|--------------|---|----|

## WORRYING KYNDE
| 67 | Piccadilly 7N 35370 | Call Out The Name/Got The Blame | 80 |
|----|--------------|---|----|

## WORTH
| 72 | CBS 7728 | Don't Say You Don't/Polecat Alley | 10 |
|----|--------------|---|----|
| 70 | CBS 5309 | Shoot 'Em Up Baby/Take The World In Your Hands | 5 |

## JOHNNY WORTH
| 57 | Columbia DB 3962 | Let's Go/Just Because | 6 |
|----|--------------|---|----|
| 60 | Oriole CB 1545 | Nightmare/Hold Me, Thrill Me, Kiss Me | 40 |

## MARION WORTH
| 60 | London HL 7089 | Are You Willing, Willie/This Heart Of Mine (export issue) | 25 |
|----|--------------|---|----|
| 60 | London HL 7097 | That's My Kind Of Love/I Lost Johnny (export issue) | 25 |

## STAN WORTH ORCHESTRA
| 63 | London HLU 9703 | Roman Holiday/Wiggle Wobble Walkers | 8 |
|----|--------------|---|----|

## TONY WORTH
| 69 | Cleo CL 3194 | Why Not Love Me/Dream | 20 |
|----|--------------|---|----|

## WOVEN WEB
| 72 | Shell SH2 | High On Life/Lost Inside The Well | 40 |
|----|--------------|---|----|

## WRANGLERS
| 64 | Parlophone R 5163 | Liza Jane/It Just Won't Work | 70 |
|----|--------------|---|----|

*(see also Kenny Bernard, Kenny & Wranglers)*

## LINK WRAY (& HIS RAY MEN)
| 58 | London HLA 8623 | Rumble/The Swag (as Link Wray & His Ray Men) | 50 |
|----|--------------|---|----|
| 58 | London HLA 8623 | Rumble/The Swag (as Link Wray & His Ray Men) (78) | 30 |
| 63 | Stateside SS 217 | Jack The Ripper/The Black Widow | 30 |
| 64 | Stateside SS 256 | The Sweeper/Weekend | 20 |
| 65 | Stateside SS 397 | Good Rockin' Tonight/I'll Do Anything For You | 20 |
| 71 | Polydor 2066 120 | Fire And Brimstone/Jukebox Mama | 6 |
| 73 | Polydor 2066 320 | Lawdy Miss Clawdy/Shine The Light | 6 |
| 73 | Virgin VS 103 | I'm So Glad, I'm So Proud/Shawnee Tribe | 6 |
| 76 | Virgin VS 142 | I Know You're Leaving Me Now/Quicksand | 6 |
| 64 | Stateside SE 1015 | MR. GUITAR (EP, sleeve credits Link Ray) | 100 |
| 71 | Polydor 2489 029 | LINK WRAY (LP) | 40 |
| 71 | Union Pacific UP 002 | THERE'S GOOD ROCKIN' TONIGHT (LP) | 25 |
| 73 | Virgin V 2006 | BEANS & FATBACK (LP) | 20 |
| 73 | Polydor 2391063 | BE WHAT YOU WANT TO (LP) | 15 |
| 74 | Polydor 2391 128 | THE LINK WRAY RUMBLE (LP) | 15 |
| 88 | Hangman HANG 31 UP | 64 (THE SWAN DEMOS) (LP) | 30 |
| 88 | Hangman HANG 33 UP | JACK THE RIPPER (LP) | 30 |

*(see also Robert Gordon with Link Wray)*

## RAY WRAY QUARTET
| 62 | Salvo SLO 1808 | When Your Lover Has Gone/A Song Is Born | 20 |
|----|--------------|---|----|

## WRECKERS
| 64 | Granta GR 7EP 1010 | THE WRECKERS' SOUND (EP) | 120 |
|----|--------------|---|----|

## WRECKLESS ERIC
| 77 | Stiff BUY 16 | Whole Wide World/Semaphore Signals (p/s, push-out centre) | 10 |
|----|--------------|---|----|
| 78 | Stiff BUY 25 | Reconnez Cherie/Rags And Tatters ("Factory sample" sticker on label) | 10 |
| 78 | Stiff BUY 25 | Reconnez Cherie/Rags And Tatters (p/s) | 6 |
| 78 | Stiff BUY 34 | Take The Cash (K.A.S.H)/Girlfriend (die-cut company sleeve) | 6 |
| 78 | Stiff BUY 40 | Crying, Waiting, Hoping/I Wish It Would Rain (p/s) | 6 |
| 79 | Stiff BUY 49 | Hit And Miss Judy/Let's Go To The Pictures (p/s) | 5 |
| 78 | Stiff SEEZ 6 | WRECKLESS ERIC (LP) | 15 |
| 78 | Stiff SEEZ 9 | THE WONDERFUL WORLD OF... (LP, picture disc in LP sleeve) | 15 |
| 93 | Hangman HANG 50 UP | THE DONOVAN OF TRASH (LP) | 18 |

*(see also Len Bright Combo)*

## JENNY WREN
| 66 | Fontana TF 672 | Chasing My Dreams All Over Town/A Thought Of You | 130 |
|----|--------------|---|----|
| 66 | Fontana TF 772 | The Merry-Go-Round (Is Slowing You Down)/Take A Walk Bobby | 15 |

## WRETCHED
| 81 | Wretched Music GRC 102 | DNR/Souls In Torment (500 only) | 50 |
|----|--------------|---|----|

## WRIGGLERS
| 68 | Giant GN 26 | The Cooler/You Cannot Know | 300 |
|----|--------------|---|----|
| 68 | Blue Cat BS 106 | Get Right/If I Did Look | 60 |

## BETTY WRIGHT
| 68 | Atlantic 584 216 | Girls Can't Do What The Guys Do/Sweet Lovin' Daddy | 15 |
|----|--------------|---|----|

| | | | |
|---|---|---|---|
| 72 | Atlantic K 10143 | Clean Up Woman/I'll Love You Forever | 15 |
| 72 | Atlantic K 10190 | Is It You Girl/Cryin' In My Sleep | 5 |
| 75 | RCA RCA 2548 | Where Is The Love/My Baby Ain't My Baby Any More | 5 |
| 72 | Atlantic K 40364 | I LOVE THE WAY YOU LOVE (LP) | 15 |

**BILLY WRIGHT**

| | | | |
|---|---|---|---|
| 61 | Parlophone R 4852 | Sing Song For Kicks Part 1/Part 2 | 10 |

**CHARLES WRIGHT & WATTS 103RD STREET RHYTHM BAND**

| | | | |
|---|---|---|---|
| 69 | Warner Bros WB 7250 | Do Your Thing/A Dance, A Kiss And A Song | 8 |
| 69 | Warner Bros WB 7298 | Till You Get Enough/Light My Fire | 8 |
| 70 | Warner Bros WB 7365 | Love Land/Sorry Charlie | 8 |
| 70 | Warner Bros WB 7417 | Express Yourself/Living On Borrowed Time | 20 |
| 72 | Jay Boy BOY 71 | Spreadin' Honey/Charley (as Watts 103rd Street Rhythm Band) | 10 |
| 70 | Warner Bros 1864 | EXPRESS YOURSELF (LP) | 30 |

**DALE WRIGHT**

| | | | |
|---|---|---|---|
| 58 | London HLD 8573 | She's Neat/Say That You Care (as Dale Wright & Rock-Its) | 175 |
| 58 | London HLD 8573 | She's Neat/Say That You Care (as Dale Wright & Rock-Its) (78) | 40 |
| 59 | Pye International 7N 25022 | That's Show Biz/That's My Gal (as Dale Wright & Wright Guys) | 80 |
| 59 | Pye International 7N 25022 | That's Show Biz/That's My Gal (as Dale Wright & Wright Guys) (78) | 50 |

**EARL WRIGHT**

| | | | |
|---|---|---|---|
| 75 | Capitol CL 15825 | Thumb A Ride/Like A Rolling Stone | 8 |
| 75 | Capitol CL 15825 | Thumb A Ride/Like A Rolling Stone (DJ Copy) | 15 |

**GARY WRIGHT('S WONDERWHEEL)**

| | | | |
|---|---|---|---|
| 72 | A&M AMS 888 | I know/Tonight It's Right | 12 |
| 71 | A&M AMLS 2004 | EXTRACTIONS (LP, poster sleeve) | 30 |
| 72 | A&M AMLS 64296 | FOOTPRINT (LP) | 18 |
| 72 | A&M AMLH 64362 | RING OF CHANGES (LP, as Wright's Wonderwheel; unissued, test pressings only) | 50 |

*(see also Spooky Tooth, Magic Christians, Thomas F. Browne)*

**GEORGE WRIGHT/NEVILLE MITCHELL**

| | | | |
|---|---|---|---|
| 82 | Kingdom KV 8026 | GEORGE WRIGHT - You Are The One I Love/ROOTS RADICS - I Done It Dub/NEVILL MITCHELL - Get Out Of Hand/ROOTS RADICS - Hand Made Dub | 25 |

**GINNY WRIGHT (& TOM TALL)**

| | | | |
|---|---|---|---|
| 55 | London HL 8119 | Indian Moon/Your Eyes Feasted Upon Her (solo) | 50 |
| 55 | London HL 8150 | Are You Mine?/Boom Boom Boomerang (with Tom Tall) | 30 |
| 55 | London RE-U 1035 | COUNTRY SONGS VOL. 2 (EP, with Tom Tall) | 30 |

*(see also T. Tommy Cutrer & Ginny Wright, Tom Tall)*

**MILTON WRIGHT & TERRA SHIRMA STRINGS**

| | | | |
|---|---|---|---|
| 77 | Grapevine GRP 103 | I Belong To You/The Gallop | 5 |
| 07 | Jazzman JM12.011 | Keep It Up/The Silence That You Keep (12", p/s) | 15 |
| 08 | Jazzman JMANLP 025 | SPACED (LP, reissue) | 20 |

**NAT WRIGHT**

| | | | |
|---|---|---|---|
| 59 | HMV POP 629 | Anything/For You My Love | 75 |

**OTIS WRIGHT**

| | | | |
|---|---|---|---|
| 69 | High Note HS 033 | Man Of Galilee/Take Up The Cross | 6 |
| 67 | Doctor Bird DLM 5005 | PEACE PERFECT PEACE (LP) | 50 |
| 67 | Doctor Bird DLM 5006 | IT WILL SOON BE DONE (LP) | 50 |
| 69 | High Note BSL5003 | SACRED SONGS (LP) | 30 |
| 60s | Coxsone TLP 1001 | OVER IN GLORYLAND (LP) | 40 |
| 73 | Tabernacle BSLP 5021 | SOUL STIRRING GOSPEL SONGS (LP) | 40 |

**O.V. WRIGHT**

| | | | |
|---|---|---|---|
| 65 | Vocalion VP 9249 | You're Gonna Make Me Cry/Monkey Dog | 20 |
| 66 | Vocalion VP 9255 | Poor Boy/I'm In Your Corner | 20 |
| 66 | Vocalion VP 9272 | Gone For Good/How Long Baby | 20 |
| 67 | London HLZ 10137 | 8 Men 4 Women/Fed Up With The Blues | 15 |
| 68 | Sue WI 4043 | What About You/What Did You Tell This Girl Of Mine | 50 |
| 68 | Action ACT 4505 | Oh Baby Mine/Working Your Game | 15 |
| 69 | Action ACT 4527 | I Want Everyone To Know/I'm Gonna Forget About You | 15 |
| 65 | Vocalion VEP 170165 | CAN'T FIND TRUE LOVE (EP) | 100 |
| 68 | Island ILP 975 | 8 MEN, 4 WOMEN (LP) | 120 |

**OWEN WRIGHT**

| | | | |
|---|---|---|---|
| 70 | Banana BA 310 | Wala Wala (actually by Burning Spear)/JERRY & FREEDOM SINGERS: Got To Be Sure (B-side actually by Horace Andy) | 40 |

**RICHARD WRIGHT**

| | | | |
|---|---|---|---|
| 78 | Harvest SHVL 818 | WET DREAM (LP, gatefold stickered sleeve) | 18 |

*(see also Pink Floyd, Zee)*

**RITA WRIGHT**

| | | | |
|---|---|---|---|
| 68 | Tamla Motown TMG 643 | I Can't Give Back The Love I Feel For You/Something On My Mind | 25 |
| 68 | Tamla Motown TMG 643 | I Can't Give Back The Love I Feel For You/Something On My Mind (DJ copy) | 40 |
| 71 | Tamla Motown TMG 791 | I Can't Give Back The Love I Feel For You/Something On My Mind (reissue) | 10 |
| 78 | Jet UP 36382 | Love Is All You Need/Touch Me, Take Me | 100 |

**RUBEN WRIGHT**

| | | | |
|---|---|---|---|
| 66 | Capitol CL 15460 | Hey Girl/I'm Walking Out On You | 35 |
| 66 | Capitol CL 15460 | Hey Girl/I'm Walking Out On You (DJ copy) | 75 |

**RUBY WRIGHT**

| | | | |
|---|---|---|---|
| 53 | Parlophone MSP 6025 | Till I Waltz Again With You/When I Gave You My Love (with Charlie Gore) | 20 |
| 54 | Parlophone MSP 6073 | Bimbo/Boy, You Got Yourself A Gal | 25 |
| 54 | Parlophone MSP 6133 | Santa's Little Sleigh Bells/Toodle-oo To You | 10 |
| 55 | Parlophone MSP 6150 | What Have They Told You?/I Had The Funniest Feeling | 15 |
| 56 | Parlophone MSP 6209 | I Fall In Love With You Ev'ry Day/Do You Believe? | 15 |

MINT VALUE £

| | | | |
|---|---|---|---|
| 59 | Parlophone R 4556 | Three Stars/I Only Have One Lifetime | 5 |
| 59 | Parlophone R 4589 | You're Just A Flower From An Old Bouquet/Sweet Night Of Love | 5 |
| 59 | Parlophone GEP 8785 | THE THREE STARS GIRL (EP) | 30 |

## SAMUEL E. WRIGHT
| | | | |
|---|---|---|---|
| 73 | Paramount PARA 3035 | There's Something Funny Going On/300 Pounds Of Hunger | 15 |

## SEAN WRIGHT
| | | | |
|---|---|---|---|
| 78 | Ellie Jay EJSP 8624 | Strange Situation/Silent Dreams (1st issue, 50 with folded p/s some with insert) | 30 |
| 81 | Media PR 001 | Strange Situation/Silent Dreams (2nd issue, p/s as Media but new labels are pasted over records from 1st pressing) | 15 |
| 82 | Heavy Leather | Strange Situation/Silent Dreams (3rd issue, p/s new labels are pasted over records from 1st pressing) | 12 |

## STEVE WRIGHT
| | | | |
|---|---|---|---|
| 59 | London HLW 8991 | Wild, Wild, Woman/Love You | 200 |
| 59 | London HLW 8991 | Wild, Wild, Woman/Love You (78) | 100 |

## STEVEN WRIGHT
| | | | |
|---|---|---|---|
| 93 | Reggae On Top ROT 001 | Vision Of Jah/Dub Versions (12") | 25 |

## STEVIE WRIGHT
| | | | |
|---|---|---|---|
| 74 | Polydor 2121246 | Evie - Let Your Hair Down/Evie | 8 |
| 74 | Polydor 2480 249 | HARD ROAD (LP) | 20 |

## SYREETA WRIGHT
| | | | |
|---|---|---|---|
| 72 | Mowest MWS 7001 | SYREETA (LP) | 20 |

## WINSTON WRIGHT
| | | | |
|---|---|---|---|
| 69 | Doctor Bird DB 1308 | Five Miles High/CARL DAWKINS: Only Girl | 50 |
| 69 | Camel CA 32 | Power Pack/TWO SPARKS: Throwing Stones | 45 |
| 69 | Explosion EX 2003 | Barefoot Brigade/Slippery | 35 |
| 69 | Trojan TR 7701 | Moonlight (Lover) Groover/SENSATIONS: Everyday Is Just A Holiday | 35 |
| 69 | Trojan TR 7715 | Moon Invader (with Tommy McCook)/RADCLIFF RUFFIN: You Got To Love Me | 35 |
| 70 | Trojan TR 7775 | Meshwire (with Tommy McCook)/BARONS: Darling Please Return | 35 |
| 70 | Explosion EX 2011 | Flight 404/LLOYD & ROBIN: Gawling Come Down (B-side actually Higher Than The Highest Mountain by Monty Morris) | 35 |
| 70 | Explosion EX 2015 | Funny Girl/Funny Girl Version II | 20 |
| 70 | Duke DU 62 | Poppy Cock (with J.J. All Stars)/CARL DAWKINS: This World And Me (B-side actually "Satisfaction") | 25 |
| 70 | Bamboo BAM 60 | Reggae Feet/DON DRUMMOND: Royal Flush (B-side act. titled "The Rocket") | 30 |
| 70 | High Note HS 040 | Soul Pressure/Seed You Sow (with Gaytones) | 20 |
| 70 | Moodisc MU 3501 | Musically Red (with Maudie's Allstars; actually also with Count Sticky)/ RHYTHM RULERS: Bratah | 35 |
| 70 | G.G. GG 4504 | It's Been A Long Time/PAULETTE & GEE: Feel It More And More | 15 |
| 70 | Techniques TE 907 | Top Secret/Crazy Rhythm | 25 |
| 71 | Upsetter US 378 | Example (with 3rd & 4th Generation)/UPSETTER: Version | 25 |
| 71 | Duke DU 111 | Silhouettes/That Did It | 15 |
| 71 | Camel CA 71 | Silhouettes/That Did It | 12 |
| 71 | Green Door GD 4011 | Heads Or Tails/THE ROASTERS: Raunchy | 6 |
| 77 | Third World TWS 923 | JUMP THE FENCE (LP) | 20 |

*(see also Ethiopians, John Holt, J.J. Allstars, Slickers)*

## ZACHARIAH WRIGHT
| | | | |
|---|---|---|---|
| 70s | Bamboo BAM 403 | Lumumba Limbo/Green, Red and Gold | 10 |

## WRIGHTSOUND
| | | | |
|---|---|---|---|
| 75 | Peacock AT 842 | Dance Apache/Jelly | 18 |

## BERNARD WRIGLEY
| | | | |
|---|---|---|---|
| 76 | Transatlantic TRA 327 | SONGS, STORIES AND ELEPHANTS (LP) | 12 |

## WRIGLEYS
| | | | |
|---|---|---|---|
| 69 | Page One POF 118 | A Little Bit/Come Down Little Bird | 10 |

## WRIT
| | | | |
|---|---|---|---|
| 66 | Decca F 12385 | Did You Ever Have To Make Up Your Mind/Solid Golden Teardrops | 20 |

## WRITING ON THE WALL
| | | | |
|---|---|---|---|
| 69 | Middle Earth MDS 101 | Child On A Crossing/Lucifer Corpus | 60 |
| 73 | Pye 7N 45251 | Man Of Renown/Buffalo | 20 |
| 69 | Middle Earth MDLS 303 | THE POWER OF THE PICTS (LP, textured sleeve) | 400 |

*(see also 'Middle Earth Sampler' in Various Artists; Three's A Crowd)*

## W12 SPOTS
| | | | |
|---|---|---|---|
| 70s | Shepherds Bush SB 1 | Sid Never Did/COSMIC PUNKS: 99 Years | 12 |

## WUGGERY
| | | | |
|---|---|---|---|
| 98 | Wuggery WUG 1 | Wuggery Muggery/Wugwats Weekend (p/s) | 8 |

## WURZEL
| | | | |
|---|---|---|---|
| 87 | GWR GWR 4 | Bess/People Say I'm Crazy (p/s) | 8 |
| 87 | GWR GWT 4 | Bess/People Say I'm Crazy/Midnight In London/E.S.P. (12", p/s) | 15 |

*(see also Motorhead)*

## WURZELS
| | | | |
|---|---|---|---|
| 77 | EMI EMI 2686 | One For The Bristol City/Cheddar Cheese (p/s) | 6 |
| 05 | Rough Trade RTRADS302 | Remember Me/I Am A Cider Drinker (British Sea Power) (7" ltd ed. 1,966 copies) | 10 |

## JOHNNY WYATT
| | | | |
|---|---|---|---|
| 68 | President PT 109 | This Thing Called Love/To Whom It May Concern (DJ Copy) | 50 |
| 68 | President PT 109 | This Thing Called Love/To Whom It May Concern (horizontal) | 30 |
| 68 | President PT 109 | This Thing Called Love/To Whom It May Concern (vertical artist credit) | 10 |

## ROBERT WYATT
| | | | |
|---|---|---|---|
| 74 | Virgin VS 114 | I'm A Believer/Memories | 5 |
| 77 | Virgin VS 115 | Yesterday Man/Sonia | 6 |

| 81 | Rough Trade RT 081 | Grass/Trade Union/Dishari (p/s) .................................................. 8 |
| 82 | Rough Trade | Shipbuilding/Memories of You (This 7" came in 4 different multi-fold art sleeves. Most common are 'Blanket' and 'Rope' covers, 'Metal Rings' and 'Hot Coals' are less common) ............................................................................ 6 |
| 97 | Hannibal TRDSC 010 | Free Will And Testament/The Sight Of The Wind ........................ 6 |
| 87 | Strange Fruit SFPS 037 | PEEL SESSIONS (12") ................................................................ 15 |
| 70 | CBS 64189 | THE END OF AN EAR (LP) ........................................................ 40 |
| 74 | Virgin V 2017 | ROCK BOTTOM (LP, 1st pressing, coloured "girl and dragon" labels) ........ 35 |
| 75 | Virgin V 2034 | RUTH IS STRANGER THAN RICHARD (LP) ..................................... 40 |
| 82 | Rough Trade ROUGH 35 | NOTHING CAN STOP US (LP, early pressing without "Shipbuilding", insert) ... 15 |
| 81 | Virgin VGD 3505 | ROCK BOTTOM/RUTH IS STRANGER THAN RICHARD (2-LP reissue) ....... 35 |
| 85 | Rough Trade ROUGH 69 | OLD ROTTENHAT (LP, gatefold) .................................................. 20 |
| 91 | Rough Trade R2741 | DONDESTAN (LP) ..................................................................... 30 |
| 07 | Domino WIGLP 202 | COMICOPERA (2-LP) ................................................................ 20 |
| 08 | Domino REWIGLP 47 | CUCKOOLAND (2-LP) ................................................................ 18 |
| 08 | Domino REWIGLP 45 | SHLEEP (2-LP) ........................................................................ 18 |

*(see also Soft Machine, Matching Mole, Centipede, Ben Watt)*

## RICHARD ('POPCORN') WYLIE
| 63 | Columbia DB 7012 | Brand New Man/So Much Love In My Heart (as Richard Wylie) ........ 40 |
| 77 | Grapevine GRP 100 | Rosemary What Happened (Parts 1 & 2) (as Richard 'Popcorn' Wylie) ... 8 |

## BILL WYMAN
| 74 | Rolling Stones RS 19112 | Monkey Grip Glue/What A Blow ................................................ 5 |
| 74 | Rolling Stones RS 19115 | White Lightning/Pussy ............................................................ 7 |
| 83 | Ripple (no cat. no.) | DIGITAL DREAMS (LP, soundtrack, promo only) ........................... 50 |

*(see also Rolling Stones, End)*

## DEAN WYMAN
| 78 | Stag PF 7 | When It's Over/Swan Song (no p/s) ............................................ 5 |

## WYNDER K. FROG
| 66 | Island WI 280 | Turn On Your Lovelight/Zooming .............................................. 30 |
| 66 | Island WI 3011 | Sunshine Superman/Blues For A Frog ........................................ 30 |
| 67 | Island WIP 6006 | Green Door/Dancing Frog ........................................................ 45 |
| 67 | Island WIP 6014 | I Am A Man/Shook Shimmy & Shake .......................................... 55 |
| 68 | Island WIP 6044 | Jumping Jack Flash/Baldy ........................................................ 35 |
| 67 | Island ILP 944 | SUNSHINE SUPERFROG (LP, white label, mono) ........................... 100 |
| 67 | Island ILPS 9044 | SUNSHINE SUPERFROG (LP, white label, stereo) .......................... 125 |
| 68 | Island ILP 982/ILPS 9082 | OUT OF THE FRYING PAN (LP, pink label. orange/black circle) .......... 50 |

*(see also Keef Hartley Band, Miller Anderson, Fair Weather, Grease Band)*

## KES WYNDHAM
| 71 | Pye 7N 45082 | Honey Call Me Home/Broken Bicycle .......................................... 10 |

## WYNDRUSH
| 72 | Wealden WS 116 | LET IT SHINE (LP) ................................................................. 300 |

## PETER WYNGARDE
| 70 | RCA Victor RCA 1967 | La Ronde De L'Amour/The Way I Cry Over You ............................. 30 |
| 70 | RCA Victor PW 1 | Commits Rape/The Way I Cry Over You (LP sampler, promo only) ...... 45 |
| 70 | RCA Victor SF 8087 | PETER WYNGARDE (LP, gatefold sleeve) ..................................... 50 |

*(see also Larry Wallis, Tyrannosaurus Rex)*

## PETER WYNNE
| 59 | Parlophone R 4597 | Twilight Time/Chapel Of Dreams ................................................ 7 |
| 60 | Parlophone R 4668 | Ask Anyone In Love/I Need You Close Again .................................. 6 |
| 60 | Parlophone R 4705 | Our Concerto/Your lover ........................................................... 6 |

## SANDY WYNNS
| 65 | Fontana TF 550 | Touch Of Venus/Lovers' Quarrel .............................................. 200 |

## MARK WYNTER
| 60 | Decca F 11263 | Image Of A Girl/Glory Of Love ................................................... 7 |
| 60 | Decca F 11279 | Kickin' Up The Leaves/That's What I Thought .............................. 10 |
| 61 | Decca F 11323 | Dream Girl/Two Little Girls ....................................................... 5 |
| 61 | Decca F 11354 | Exclusively Yours/Warm And Willing ........................................... 5 |
| 61 | Decca F 11380 | Girl For Ev'ry Day/The Best Time For Love ................................... 5 |
| 62 | Decca F 11434 | Heaven's Plan/In Your Heart ..................................................... 5 |
| 62 | Decca F 11467 | Angel Talk/I Love Her Still ......................................................... 6 |
| 62 | Pye 7N 15466 | Venus In Blue Jeans/Please Come Back To Me ............................... 5 |
| 62 | Pye 7N 15492 | Go Away Little Girl/That Kinda Talk ............................................ 5 |
| 63 | Pye 7N 15511 | Aladdin's Lamp/It Can Happen Any Day ....................................... 6 |
| 63 | Pye 7N 15525 | Shy Girl/Because Of You ........................................................... 6 |
| 63 | Pye 7N 15554 | Running To You/Don't Cry ......................................................... 6 |
| 65 | Pye 7N 15771 | Can I Get To Know You Better/Am I Living A Dream ........................ 5 |
| 66 | Pye 7N 17122 | We'll Sing In The Sunshine/Pencil And Paper ................................ 8 |
| 60 | Decca DFE 6674 | MARK TIME (EP) ..................................................................... 10 |
| 61 | Decca LK 4409 | THE WARMTH OF WYNTER (LP) ................................................ 25 |
| 65 | Ace Of Clubs ACL 1141 | MARK WYNTER (LP) ................................................................ 15 |

*(see also Joe Brown & Mark Wynter)*

## GAIL WYNTERS
| 67 | London HLE 10144 | Snap Your Fingers/Find Myself A New Love ................................. 12 |

## WYOMING
| 72 | MAM MAMR 76 | Seven Days/Two Faced Woman ................................................. 12 |

**X**
| | | | |
|---|---|---|---|
| 80 | Slash Records UK SR-104 | LOS ANGELES (LP, with insert) | 18 |
| 81 | Slash/Rough Trade SR 107 | WILD GIFT (LP) | 15 |

**NATHALIE XAVIER**
| | | | |
|---|---|---|---|
| 81 | People Unite PU NAT 1 | Atomic Energy/Set Me Free (12") | 40 |

**X-CALIBURS**
| | | | |
|---|---|---|---|
| 65 | CBS 201805 | We Will Love/Swing That Chariot | 10 |
| 65 | Mercury MF 941 | You'll Find Out/That's What Happens (possibly as Xcalibres) | 10 |

**X-CELLS**
| | | | |
|---|---|---|---|
| 81 | Snotty Snail NEL COL 4 | Freedom Man/SCHIZOID: Nowhere To Go (p/s) | 20 |

**X CERTIFICATE**
| | | | |
|---|---|---|---|
| 73 | Spark SRL 1096 | Don't Stick Stickers On My Paper Knickers/Come Home Baby | 6 |

**X-CERTS**
| | | | |
|---|---|---|---|
| 78 | Zama | Feeling The Groove (p/s) | 15 |
| 81 | Recreational PLAY 1 | Together/Untogether (p/s, with lyric insert) | 6 |

**X-COLLECTOR**
| | | | |
|---|---|---|---|
| 83 | So So SOSO 027 | T.V. Set/Christine | 25 |

**X-DREAM**
| | | | |
|---|---|---|---|
| 98 | Blue Room BRO66LP | RADIO (2-LP) | 18 |

**X-DREAMYSTS**
| | | | |
|---|---|---|---|
| 78 | Good Vibrations GOT 5 | Right Way Home/Dance Away Love (p/s) | 15 |
| 79 | Polydor 2059 129 | Bad News/Money Talks (p/s) | 10 |
| 80 | Polydor 2059 235 | I Don't Wanna Go/Silly Games (p/s) | 10 |
| 80 | Polydor 2059 252 | Stay The Way You Are/Race Against Time (p/s) | 10 |
| 80 | Polydor | XDREAMYSTS (LP) | 25 |

**X-E-CUTORS**
| | | | |
|---|---|---|---|
| 79 | Rok ROK 13/14 | Too Far To Look Inside My Head/X-FILMS: After My Blood (die-cut co. sleeve) | 15 |

**XERO**
| | | | |
|---|---|---|---|
| 83 | Brickyard XERO 1 | Oh Baby/Hold On (2-track issue, p/s, Moon Williams on vocals) | 15 |
| 83 | Brickyard XERO 1 | Oh Baby/Hold On/Lone Wolf (3-track limited issue, p/s) | 8 |
| 83 | Brickyard XERO 1T | Oh Baby/Hold On/Lone Wolf (12", plain card sleeve with sticker, withdrawn) | 15 |

*(see also Bruce Dickinson, Iron Maiden)*

**X-FILMS**
| | | | |
|---|---|---|---|
| 79 | Rok ROK XIII/XIV | After My Blood/X-E-CUTORS: Too Far To Look Inside My Head (die-cut co. sleeve) | 15 |

**XILES**
| | | | |
|---|---|---|---|
| 64 | Xiles 80-XIL-1 | THE XILES (EP, home-made p/s) | 40 |
| 65 | Xiles XIL 004 | Our Love Will Never End/The Only People In This World | 25 |

**XIT**
| | | | |
|---|---|---|---|
| 72 | Rare Earth RES 107 | I Was Raised/End | 5 |
| 73 | Rare Earth RES 111 | Reservation Of Education/Young Warrior | 5 |
| 72 | Rare Earth SREA 4002 | PLIGHT OF THE RED MAN (LP) | 15 |

**XL5**
| | | | |
|---|---|---|---|
| 63 | HMV POP 1148 | XL5 (Zero G)/Caviare | 20 |
| 63 | HMV 7EG 8802 | FIREBALL AND OTHER TITLES (EP, 2 tracks by Don Spencer) | 50 |

**XL5'S**
| | | | |
|---|---|---|---|
| 80 | Fourplay FOUR 004 | Fireball/Misirlou | 8 |

**X-MAL DEUTSCHLAND**
| | | | |
|---|---|---|---|
| 83 | 4AD AD 311 | Incubus Succubus II/Vito (12" p/s, with "Vito" listed as A-side) | 10 |
| 83 | 4AD CAD 302 | FETISCH (LP, inner) | 15 |
| 84 | 4AD CAD 197 | TOCSIN (LP) | 15 |

**X-MEN**
| | | | |
|---|---|---|---|
| 84 | Creation CRE 006 | Do The Ghost/Talk (foldaround p/s in bag, orange/blue or yellow/green p/s) | 8 |
| 85 | Creation CRE 013 | Spiral Girl/Bad Girl (foldaround p/s in polyester bag) | 8 |

**X-O-DUS**
| | | | |
|---|---|---|---|
| 79 | Factory FAC 11 | English Black Boys/See Them A-Come (12", dark-grey textured p/s, later light grey p/s) | 20 |

**XPERTS**
| | | | |
|---|---|---|---|
| 80 | XP001 | Race/Beat Me | 15 |

**XPOZEZ**
| | | | |
|---|---|---|---|
| 81 | Retaliation FIGHT 1 | SYSTEMS KILL EP (photocopied sleeve with insert stating that if you want a proper sleeve to send the band a SAE) | 60 |
| 82 | Red Rhino RED 15 | 1,000 Marching Feet/Terminal Case (p/s) | 7 |
| 83 | Sexual Phonograph SPH 2 | (Be My) New York Doll/It's All Been Done Before (p/s) | 7 |
| 84 | Retaliation/Bearded Viking FIGHT 2 | BURNOUT YOUTH EP (folded poster p/s with lyrics and photos) | 10 |
| 85 | Children Of The Revolution COR 2 | FORCEFED THE TRUTH DRUG (EP) | 10 |

**X PRESS**
| | | | |
|---|---|---|---|
| 75 | A Rover AR 03 | Tell Me Baby/High Road | 8 |

## X-PRESS
| 80 | Express 1 | Junked Up Judy/Stop Start (p/s) | 90 |

## X PROJECT
| 92 | X Project XPROJECT 1 | Walking In The Air (Mix 1)/(Mix 2)/(Mix 3)/(Mix 4) (12", stamped white label) | 40 |
| 00 | Congo Natty LION 5 | Jah Sunshine/Dubplate Mix (12") | 15 |

## XPUPILS
| 81 | Skool SKREP 0001 | MONTPELLIER NEWS EP | 50 |

## X-RAY SPEX
| 77 | Virgin VS 189 | Oh Bondage, Up Yours/I Am A Cliche (in p/s) | 30 |
| 77 | Virgin VS 189 | Oh Bondage, Up Yours/I Am A Cliche | 5 |
| 77 | Virgin VS 189-12 | Oh Bondage, Up Yours/I Am A Cliche (12", company sleeve) | 12 |
| 78 | EMI International INT 553 | The Day The World Turned Day-Glo/Lama Poseur (p/s, 15,000 orange vinyl) | 15 |
| 78 | EMI International INT 563 | Identity/Let's Submerge (p/s, on pink vinyl) | 12 |
| 78 | EMI EMI 563 | Identity/Let's Submerge (p/s, black vinyl) | 5 |
| 78 | EMI International INT 573 | Germ Free Adolescents/Age (p/s) | 5 |
| 79 | EMI International INT 583 | Highly Inflammable/Warrior In Woolworths (p/s, on red vinyl) | 8 |
| 78 | EMI Intl. INS 3023 | GERM FREE ADOLESCENTS (LP laminated sleeve, with lyric inner sleeve) | 40 |
| 01 | Earmark 640005 | GERM FREE ADOLESCENTS (LP, reissue, clear vinyl) | 15 |

*(see also Poly Styrene, Essential Logic)*

## X-RAYS
| 59 | London HLR 8805 | Chinchilla/Out Of Control | 35 |
| 59 | London HLR 8805 | Chinchilla/Out Of Control (78) | 20 |

## XS DISCHARGE
| 80 | G. Marxist COMMINIQUE 3 | Across The Border/Frustration (p/s) | 15 |
| 80 | Groucho Marxist WH 3 | Life's A Wank (p/s) | 20 |

## XS ENERGY
| 78 | World WRECK 1 | Eighteen/Jenny's Alright/Horrorscope! (numbered foldover yellow or green p/s, stamped white labels) | 40 |
| 79 | Dead Good DEAD 1 | Eighteen/Jenny's Alright/Horrorscope! (reissue, 'National Souvenir Issue', different foldover p/s, stamped white labels) | 10 |
| 79 | Dead Good DEAD 1 | Eighteen/Jenny's Alright/Horrorscope! (stamped white sleeve & yellow printed labels) | 10 |
| 79 | Dead Good DEAD 3 | Use You/Imaginary (p/s) | 15 |

## XTC
| 77 | Virgin VS 188 | Science Friction/She's So Square (unreleased, in picture sleeve) | 2500 |
| 77 | Virgin VS 188 | Science Friction/She's So Square (unreleased, no picture sleeve) | 80 |
| 78 | Virgin VS 201 | Statue Of Liberty/Hang On To The Night (p/s) | 5 |
| 78 | Virgin VS 209 | This Is Pop?/Heatwave (p/s) | 5 |
| 78 | Virgin VS 231 | Are You Receiving Me/Instant Tunes (p/s) | 5 |
| 79 | Virgin VS 259 | Life Begins At The Hop/Homo Safari (30,000 clear vinyl, PVC sleeve & insert) | 5 |
| 79 | Virgin VS 282 | Making Plans For Nigel/Bushman President (Homo Safari Series No. 2)/ Pulsing, Pulsing (with game-board p/s with playing pieces) | 5 |
| 80 | Virgin VS 365 | Generals And Majors/Don't Lose Your Temper//Smokeless Zone/ The Somnambulist (double pack) | 6 |
| 81 | Virgin VS 372 | Towers Of London/Set Myself On Fire (live)//Battery Brides (live)/ Scissor Man (double pack) | 6 |
| 81 | RSO RSO 71 | Take This Town/RUTS: Babylon's Burning (p/s) | 6 |
| 81 | Virgin VS 384 | Sgt. Rock (Is Going To Help Me)/Living Through Another Cuba/Generals And Majors (1st 20,000 in poster p/s, with stickered PVC sleeve) | 5 |
| 82 | Virgin VS 490 | No Thugs In Our House/Chain Of Command/Limelight/ Over Rusty Water (9" die-cut gatefold p/s) | 6 |
| 92 | Virgin VS 1426 | Wrapped In Grey (p/s, withdrawn, 2,000 only) | 30 |
| 92 | Virgin VSCDT 1426 | WRAPPED IN GREY (CD EP, withdrawn, 2,000 only) | 40 |
| 78 | Virgin V 2108 | GO 2 (LP, with insert, 1st 15,000 with bonus 12" EP: "Go +") | 15 |
| 79 | Virgin V 2129 | DRUMS AND WIRES (LP, with gatefold insert, 1st 15,000 with free 7": Chain Of Command/"Limelight" [VDJ 30]) | 20 |
| 80 | Virgin V 2173 | BLACK SEA (LP, with green paper outer sleeve & lyric insert) | 15 |
| 82 | Virgin V2223 | ENGLISH SETTLEMENT (2-LP) | 20 |
| 84 | Virgin V 2251 | WAXWORKS (LP, with bonus LP, "Beeswax") | 15 |
| 84 | Virgin V 2325 | THE BIG EXPRESS (LP, circular sleeve & lyric inner) | 15 |
| 99 | Cooking Vinyl COOK 172 | APPLE VENUS (LP, inner) | 30 |
| 00 | Cooking Vinyl COOK 194 | WASP STAR (2-LP, gatefold, inners) | 30 |

*(see also Mr Partridge, Barry Andrews, Three Wise Men, Dukes Of Stratosphere Colonel, Spys)*

## XTRACT
| 83 | Pax PAX 10 | Blame It On The Youth/War Heroes/Iron Lady/Boys In Blue (p/s) | 25 |

## XTRAVERTS
| 78 | Spike SRTS SP 001 | Blank Generation/A-Lad-In-Sane | 90 |
| 78 | Rising Sun RS 1 | Police State/PLASTIC PEOPLE: Demolition (p/s, multi-coloured vinyl) | 60 |
| 81 | Xtraverts XTRA 001 | Speed/1984 (white labels, 'photo' foldout poster p/s) | 35 |
| 81 | Xtraverts XTRA 001 | Speed/1984 (white labels, 'no photo' foldout poster p/s) | 50 |

## XTREME
| 80 | Xtreme IS/X/1045 | The Tramp/The Latest Craze (For Alison) | 40 |

## XX
| 09 | Young Turks YT 023 | Crystalised/Hot Like Fire (p/s) | 8 |
| 10 | Young Turks YT 041 | Do You Mind?/Hot Like Fire/Teardrops/Blood Red Moon (die-cut p/s with 3 inner p/s, tour issue) | 20 |
| 09 | Young Turks YT031LP | XX (LP, CD, poster) | 25 |
| 13 | Young Turks YT104 | XX (11 x 7", box set) | 40 |
| 10 | Young Turks YT031LP | XX (LP, 12", etched, 3 prints, 500 only) | 50 |
| 13 | Young Turks YT 105 | COEXIST (11 x 7", box set) | 35 |

**XY LOVE**
84   Moonboule BOULE 1        Whistle And They'll Come/Cinnamon Girl ............................................................................ 20

**YABBY U/YABBY YOU/YABBY YOUTH**
| 78 | Prophets PHTS 2337 | King Pharoah Plague On The Land/Babylon Kingdom Fall (12") ...... 30 |
| 78 | Grove Music GMDM 6 | Jah Vengeance/Free Africa (12", as Vivian "Yabby U" Jackson with Trinity).................. 30 |
| 79 | Grove Music GMDM 18 | Babylon A Fall/TONY TUFF - Falling Babylon (12") ...... 40 |
| 79 | Grove Music GMDM 24 | Lady Lady/Stop Your Quarelling (12", B-side with Tommy McCook) .......... 30 |
| 76 | Lucky PD LPYU | RAM-A-DAM (LP) ...... 250 |
| 77 | Grove Music GMLP 001 | DELIVER ME FROM MY ENEMIES (LP, credited to The Yabby You Vibration on sleeve) ... 60 |
| 77 | Grove Music GMLP 004 | BEWARE DUB (LP) ...... 40 |
| 78 | Nationwide PRO 001 | CHANT DOWN BABYLON KINGDOM (LP) ...... 120 |
| 78 | RAMA/EVE PD LP YU | RAM-A-DAM (LP, reissue of Lucky PD LPYU) ...... 80 |
| 80 | Grove/Island ILPS 9615 | JAH JAH WAY (LP) ...... 40 |
| 82 | WLN WNLP001 | YABBY YOU MEETS SLY 'N' ROBBIE (LP, with Tommy McCook) ...... 20 |
| 84 | Greensleeves GREL 86 | COLLECTION (LP) ...... 30 |
| 97 | Blood & Fire | JESUS DREAD 1972 - 1977 (4-LP) ...... 50 |
| | 90s | YABBY U PRESENTING NEW ROOTS REGGAE (LP, compilation) ...... 18 |

**YACHTS**
| 77 | Stiff BUY 19 | Suffice To Say/Freedom (Is A Heady Wine) ...... 6 |
| 78 | Radar ADA 23 | Look Back In Love (Not In Anger)/I Can't Stay Long (p/s, blue vinyl).......... 6 |
| 80 | Radar RAD 27 | YACHTS WITHOUT RADAR (LP, die-cut sleeve)...... 15 |

*(see also Big In Japan)*

**YADS**
| 92 | Fairfields YAD 2 | Yippee For Shtonk/It's There, You Mong (p/s) ...... 7 |

**YA HO WA 13**
| 83 | Psycho PSYCHO 2 | GOLDEN SUNRISE (LP, 319 copies only, different coloured vinyls, some on black vinyl without sleeve) ...... 60 |

*(see also Seeds)*

**YAKS**
| 65 | Decca F 12115 | Yakety Yak/Back In '57...... 15 |

**YAMASUKI**
| 05 | Finders Keepers FKR 002LP | LE MONDE FABULEUX DES (LP, insert)...... 36 |

**YAMASUKIS**
| 71 | Dandelion DAN 7004 | Yamasuki/Aieada (p/s) ...... 15 |

**YAMI BOLO**
| 86 | Greensleeves GREL 140 | JAH JAH MADE THEM ALL (LP) ...... 20 |

**YANA**
| 56 | HMV POP 252 | Climb Up The Wall/If You Don't Love Me ...... 20 |
| 57 | HMV POP 340 | Mr. Wonderful/Too Close For Comfort...... 8 |
| 58 | HMV POP 481 | I Need You/I Miss You Mama ...... 7 |
| 58 | HMV POP 546 | Papa And Mama/In The Morning ...... 7 |

**YANCEY**
| 79 | Octane WS 302 | Standing Waiting/Woman (no p/s) ...... 20 |
| 79 | Hammer HS 302 | Standing Waiting/Woman (reissue) ...... 8 |

**JIMMY YANCEY**
| 54 | HMV 7EG 8062 | JIMMY YANCEY (EP) ...... 20 |
| 55 | HMV 7EG 8083 | JIMMY YANCEY (EP) ...... 20 |
| 58 | Vogue EPV 1203 | YANCEY'S PIANO (EP) ...... 20 |
| 54 | London AL 3525 | JIMMY YANCEY - A LOST RECORDING DATE (10" LP)...... 25 |
| 56 | Vogue LDE 166 | JAZZ IMMORTALS VOLUME 2 (10" LP)...... 30 |
| 68 | Atlantic 590 018 | LOWDOWN DIRTY BLUES (LP)...... 15 |

**MAMA YANCEY/DON EWELL**
| 57 | Tempo LAP 7 | MAMA YANCEY-DON EWELL (10" LP)...... 30 |

**ZALMAN YANOVSKY**
| 67 | Kama Sutra KAS 209 | As Long As You're Here/Ereh Er'uoy Sa Gnol Sa (unreleased) ...... 0 |
| 67 | Pye International 7N 25438 | As Long As You're Here/Ereh Er'uoy Sa Gnol Sa ...... 8 |
| 71 | Kama Sutra 2316 003 | ALIVE AND WELL IN ARGENTINA (LP)...... 18 |

*(see also Mugwumps, Lovin' Spoonful)*

**GLENN YARBOROUGH**
| 65 | RCA 1449 | Baby The Rain Must Fall/I've Been To Town...... 7 |
| 66 | RCA 1555 | Everybody's Rich But Us/Walk On Little Baby ...... 6 |

**YARDBIRDS**
| 64 | Columbia DB 7283 | I Wish You Would/A Certain Girl ...... 40 |
| 64 | Columbia DB 7391 | Good Morning Little Schoolgirl/I Ain't Got You ...... 40 |
| 65 | Columbia DB 7499 | For Your Love/Got To Hurry ...... 10 |
| 65 | Columbia DB 7594 | Heart Full Of Soul/Steeled Blues ...... 10 |
| 65 | Columbia DB 7706 | Evil Hearted You/Still I'm Sad (some copies with A-side miscredited to Samwell-Smith & McCartney)...... 7 |
| 66 | Columbia DB 7848 | Shapes Of Things/You're A Better Man Than I ...... 7 |
| 66 | Columbia DB 7848 | Shapes Of Things/Still I'm Sad (mispressing)...... 45 |

| 66 | Columbia DB 7928 | Over, Under, Sideways, Down/Jeff's Boogie | 15 |
|----|------------------|-------------------------------------------|-----|
| 66 | Columbia DB 8024 | Happenings Ten Years Time Ago/Psycho Daisies | 35 |
| 67 | Columbia DB 8165 | Little Games/Puzzles | 35 |
| 64 | Columbia SEG 8421 | FIVE YARDBIRDS (EP) | 100 |
| 67 | Columbia SEG 8521 | OVER UNDER SIDEWAYS DOWN (EP) | 225 |
| 64 | Columbia 33SX 1677 | FIVE LIVE YARDBIRDS (LP, 1st pressing, blue/black label, flipback sleeve) | 250 |
| 69 | Columbia 33SX 1677 | FIVE LIVE YARDBIRDS (LP, 2nd pressing, black/silver label, flipback sleeve) | 25 |
| 60s | Columbia TA SX 6063 | FIVE LIVE YARDBIRDS (reel-to-reel tape) | 20 |
| 66 | Columbia SCXC 28 | HAVING A RAVE UP WITH THE YARDBIRDS (LP, export issue) | 200 |
| 66 | Columbia SX 6063 | THE YARDBIRDS (LP, 1st pressing, blue/black label, flipback sleeve, mono) | 70 |
| 66 | Columbia SCX 6063 | THE YARDBIRDS (LP, 1st pressing, blue/black label, flipback sleeve, stereo) | 60 |
| 69 | Columbia S(C)X 6063 | THE YARDBIRDS (LP, 2nd pressing, black/silver label, flipback sleeve) | 25 |
| 70 | Columbia S(C)X 6063 | THE YARDBIRDS (LP, 3rd pressing, black/silver label, non-flipback sleeve; misprinted without front cover illustration) | 20 |
| 70 | Columbia S(C)X 6063 | THE YARDBIRDS (LP, 3rd pressing, black/silver label, non-flipback sleeve) | 20 |
| 84 | Charly BOX 104 | SHAPES OF THINGS (LP, box set) | 50 |

*(see also Eric Clapton, Jeff Beck, Jimmy Page, Keith Relf, Reign, Sonny Boy Williamson & Yardbirds, Shoot)*

## PER YARROH
| 88 | HMV PY 1 | Laughing Inside/Laughing Inside (p/s, promo only; actually by Roy Harper) | 7 |
|----|----------|-------------------------------------------------------------------------|---|

*(see also Roy Harper)*

## TOM YATES
| 67 | CBS BPG 63094 | SECOND CITY SPIRITUAL (LP, as Thomas Yates) | 100 |
|----|---------------|----------------------------------------------|-----|
| 72 | President PTLS 1053 | LOVE COMES WELL ARMED (LP, with booklet) | 30 |
| 77 | Satril SATL 4007 | SONG OF THE SHIMMERING WAY (LP, with insert) | 20 |

## TOMMY YATES
| 65 | Pye 7N 15980 | Rattle Of A Toy/Long Time Gone | 10 |
|----|--------------|--------------------------------|-----|

## YA-YA
| 83 | Buzz BUZZ 2 | What Can I Say/Maybe Tomorrow | 6 |
|----|-------------|------------------------------|---|

## Y BLEW
| 67 | Qualiton QSP 7001 | Maes 'B'/Beth Sy'n Dod Rhyngom Ni (p/s) | 50 |
|----|-------------------|-----------------------------------------|-----|

## Y DILFOR
| 73 | Westwood WSR 002 | Y DILFOR (LP) | 30 |
|----|------------------|---------------|-----|

## YE ASCOYNE D'ASCOYNES
| 92 | Hangman GIBBET 1 | JUST THE BIGGEST THING (EP) | 8 |
|----|------------------|----------------------------|---|

*(see also Dentists, Claim)*

## YEAH YEAH YEAHS
| 01 | Wichita WEBB 029T | YEAH YEAH YEAHS EP: Bang/Mystery Girl/Art Star/Miles Away/Our Time (12", p/s) | 10 |
|----|-------------------|------------------------------------------------------------------------------|-----|
| 03 | Polydor 981 141-4 | Maps/Countdown/Miles Away (p/s) | 10 |
| 06 | Polydor 170 687-5 | Cheated Hearts/Cheated Hearts (Peaches Remix) (Heart-shaped picture disc) | 10 |
| 07 | Polydor 1741099 | IS IS EP (2 x 7") | 15 |
| 10 | Polydor 2734679 | Skeletons/Skeleton (no'd, 500 only) | 5 |
| 03 | Dress Up 0760611 | FEVER TO TELL (LP picture disc with bonus track 'Poor Song') | 60 |
| 06 | Polydor 985 295-6 | SHOW YOUR BONES (LP) | 15 |
| 09 | 2702576 | IT'S BLITZ! (LP) | 15 |

## YEAR ONE
| 69 | Major Minor MM 660 | Eli's Comin'/Will You Be Staying After Sunday | 12 |
|----|--------------------|-----------------------------------------------|-----|

## YEARS
| 79 | Tuff Going TGF 123 | TUFF GOING EP (p/s, 500 only) | 80 |
|----|--------------------|-------------------------------|-----|

*(see also Chameleons, Sun And The Moon)*

## YEH YEH
| 85 | Berlin BRS 001 | You Will Pay/7 Bells (1st pressing in grey p/s) | 5 |
|----|----------------|------------------------------------------------|---|

## YELLO
| 81 | Do It DUN 11 | Bimbo/I.T. Splash (p/s) | 6 |
|----|--------------|-------------------------|---|
| 82 | Do It DUN 13 | Bostich/She's Got A Gun (Instrumental) (p/s) | 5 |
| 82 | Do It DUNIT 13 | Bostich/Downtown Samba/She's Got A Gun/Daily Disco (12", p/s) | 10 |
| 82 | Do It DUN 18 | She's Got A Gun/Glue Head (p/s) | 5 |
| 82 | Do It DUN 23 | Pinball Cha Cha/Smile On You (p/s) | 5 |
| 82 | Do It DUNIT 23 | Pinball Cha Cha/Smile On You (12", p/s) | 12 |
| 83 | Stiff BUY 191 | Lost Again/Base For Alec (p/s) | 5 |
| 83 | Stiff DBUY 191 | Lost Again/Base For Alec//Let Me Cry/She's Got A Gun (double pack) | 6 |
| 86 | Mercury MERDP 218 | Goldrush/She's Got A Gun (live at Palladium N.Y.)//I Love You/ Desire (double pack, unreleased) | 0 |
| 83 | Stiff SEEZ 48 | YOU GOTTA SAY YES TO ANOTHER EXCESS (LP, with bonus white label 12": "I Love You"/"Lost Again"/"You Gotta Say To Another Excess [Remix]"Pumping Velvet") | 15 |
| 87 | Mercury MERH 100 | ONE SECOND (LP, with bonus 12" in p/s: "Call It Love (Trego Snare Version 2)"/"Santiago [live at Roxy New York]") | 15 |
| 88 | Mercury 836 778-1 | FLAG (LP, HMV competition issue, 100 only) | 40 |
| 91 | Mercury 848 791-1 | BABY (LP) | 15 |

*(see also Associates)*

## YELLOW
| 70 | CBS 4869 | Roll It Down The Hill/Living A Lie | 50 |
|----|----------|------------------------------------|-----|

## YELLOW BALLOON
| 67 | Stateside SS 2008 | Yellow Balloon/Noollab Wolley | 20 |
|----|-------------------|-------------------------------|-----|
| 68 | Stateside SS 2124 | Stained Glass Window/Can't Get Enough Of Your Love | 20 |

## YELLOW BELLOW ROOM BOOM
| 68 | CBS 3205 | Seeing Things Green/Easy Life | 30 |
|----|----------|-------------------------------|-----|

*(see also 10cc, Frabjoy & Runcible Spoon)*

## YELLOW BIRD
| | | | |
|---|---|---|---|
| 74 | Magnet MAG 16 | Attack Attack/Right On | 12 |

## YELLOW MAGIC ORCHESTRA
| | | | |
|---|---|---|---|
| 80 | A&M JAPAN 2 | Nice Age/Rydeen (p/s, yellow vinyl) | 5 |
| 79 | A&M AMLH68506 | YELLOW MAGIC ORCHESTRA (LP) | 20 |
| 80 | A&M AMSP 7502 | FIRECRACKER (LP, clear plastic sleeve, yellow vinyl) | 15 |
| 81 | A&M AMLH 64853 | BGM (LP) | 15 |
| 82 | Alfa ALF 85664 | SOLID STATE SURVIVOR (LP) | 15 |

*(see also Ruichi Sakamoto, Yukihiro Takahashi)*

## YELLOW PAGES
| | | | |
|---|---|---|---|
| 68 | Page One POF 090 | Here Comes Jane/Ring-A-Ding | 25 |

*(see also Mirage)*

## YELLOW PAYGES
| | | | |
|---|---|---|---|
| 70 | UNI UNS 516 | Follow The Bouncing Ball/Little Woman | 8 |
| 71 | UNI UNS 534 | Birds Of A Feather/Lady Friend | 5 |

## YELLOW 6
| | | | |
|---|---|---|---|
| 90s | Enraptured RAPTLP 36 | OVERTONE (2-LP, clear vinyl, numbered, handprinted sleeve, 300 only) | 20 |

## YELLOW TAXI
| | | | |
|---|---|---|---|
| 70 | President PT 296 | Anna Laura Lee/Mary Ann | 15 |

## YELLOWMAN
| | | | |
|---|---|---|---|
| 82 | Greensleeves GREL 36 | MISTER YELLOWMAN (LP) | 15 |
| 82 | Arrival ALP 004 | FOR YOUR EYES ONLY (LP, as Yellowman And Fathead) | 15 |
| 82 | Greensleeves GREL 44 | BAD BOY SKANKING (LP, as Yellowman and Fathead) | 18 |
| 84 | Pama PMLP 3215 | OPERATION RADICATION (10" LP) | 15 |
| 84 | Greensleeves GREL 57 | ZUNGGUZUNGGUGUZUNGGUNZENG!!! (LP) | 15 |
| 84 | Arrival ARLP 013 | UNDER ME FAT THING (LP) | 15 |

## YELLOWSTONE & VOICE
| | | | |
|---|---|---|---|
| 72 | Parlophone R5965 | Philosopher/The Flying Dutchman | 12 |
| 72 | Regal Zono. SRZA 8511 | YELLOWSTONE & VOICE (LP) | 20 |

## YEMM & YEMEN
| | | | |
|---|---|---|---|
| 66 | Columbia DB 8022 | Black Is The Night/Do Blondes Really Have More Fun? | 35 |

## YES
| | | | |
|---|---|---|---|
| 69 | Atlantic 584 280 | Sweetness/Something's Coming | 60 |
| 69 | Atlantic 584 298 | Looking Around/Everydays (unreleased; demos may exist) | 175 |
| 70 | Atlantic 584 323 | Time And A Word/The Prophet | 150 |
| 70 | Atlantic 2091 004 | Sweet Dreams/Dear Father | 45 |
| 71 | Atlantic 2814 003 | I've Seen All Good People (a) Your Move/Starship Trooper (a) Life Seeker (promo only) | 75 |
| 72 | 6-A1/-B1 | Siberian Khatru/And You And I (white label promo) | 50 |
| 74 | Atlantic K 10407 | And You And I/Roundabout | 5 |
| 77 | Atlantic K 10985 | Going For The One/Parallels (unreleased, copies may exist) | 60 |
| 77 | Atlantic K 10985T | Going For The One (Extended)/Parallels (12", unreleased, copies may exist) | 40 |
| 70s | Lyntone LYN 2535 | Interview/Five Songs (flexidisc or vinyl, with 80-page Yes songbook) | 70 |
| 70s | Lyntone LYN 2535 | Interview/Five Songs (flexidisc or vinyl) | 35 |
| 69 | Atlantic 588 190 | YES (LP, gatefold, red/plum label with lyric insert) | 175 |
| 70 | Atlantic 2400 006 | TIME AND A WORD (LP, red/plum label, with lyric insert) | 150 |
| 71 | Atlantic 2400 101 | THE YES ALBUM (LP, red/plum label, gatefold sleeve) | 150 |
| 71 | Atlantic 2401 019 | FRAGILE (LP, red/plum label, gatefold sleeve with booklet) | 125 |
| 72 | Atlantic K 50012 | CLOSE TO THE EDGE (LP, 1st pressing with A1/B1 matrix numbers, no "W" logo at 3 O'clock, textured sleeve inside and outside, green inner sleeve, darker with lyric insert) | 70 |
| 73 | Atlantic K60045 | YESSONGS (3-LP, wide spine, 'book opening' gatefold sleeve printed by 'Robor Ltd', no 'W' logo on labels, outline 'Yes' on inner sleeves, all matrixes end in '1') | 25 |
| 73 | Atlantic K 80001 | TALES FROM TOPOGRAPHIC OCEANS (2-LP) | 25 |
| 74 | Atlantic K 50096 | RELAYER (LP, gatefold sleeve) | 30 |
| 77 | Atlantic DSK 50379 | GOING FOR THE ONE (LP, as 3 x 12" singles, promo only) | 100 |
| 80 | Atlantic K 50842 | CLASSIC YES (LP, with bonus 7" "Roundabout"/"Your Move" [SAM 141]) | 15 |
| 80 | Atlantic K 50842 | CLASSIC YES (LP, promo, with different sleeve) | 30 |

*(see also Jon Anderson, Hans Christian, Syn, Syndicats, Winston's Fumbs, Warriors, Federals, Peter Banks, Flash, Asia, Rick Wakeman, Steve Howe, Refugee)*

## JOHN YLVISAKER
| | | | |
|---|---|---|---|
| 68 | Avantgarde AV 107 | COOL LIVIN' (LP) | 75 |

## YOBS
| | | | |
|---|---|---|---|
| 77 | NEMS NES 114 | Run Rudolph Run/The Worm Song (p/s) | 15 |
| 78 | Yob YOB 79 | Silent Night/Stille Nacht (p/s) | 7 |
| 81 | Safari YULE 1 | Rub-A-Dum-Dum/Another Christmas (p/s) | 7 |
| 82 | Fresh FRESH 41 | Yobs On 45/The Ballad Of Warrington (p/s) | 7 |

*(see also Boys)*

## MAHARISHI MAHESH YOGI
| | | | |
|---|---|---|---|
| 67 | Liberty LBS 83075E | MAHARISHI MAHESH YOGI (LP) | 25 |

## SUSUMU YOKOTA
| | | | |
|---|---|---|---|
| 99 | Leaf BAY 9 | IMAGE 1983-1998 (LP) | 15 |
| 00 | Leaf BAY 13 | SAKURA (2-LP) | 25 |

## YO LA TENGO
| | | | |
|---|---|---|---|
| 95 | Duophonic Super 45s DS 45-10 | Evanescent Psychic Pez Drop/STEREOLAB: Long Hair Of Death (gig single, fluorescent yellow vinyl) | 40 |
| 96 | Earworm WORM 4 | Blue - Green Arrow/Watching The Sun Set On Johnny Carson (2,000 only, 100 in handmade p/s) | 12 |
| 96 | Earworm WORM 4 | Blue - Green Arrow/Watching The Sun Set On Johnny Carson (2,000 only) | 8 |

| | | | |
|---|---|---|---|
| 87 | What Goes On GOESON13 | NEW WAVE HOT DOGS (LP) | 20 |
| 87 | Shigaku SHIGLP 2 | RIDE THE TIGER (LP) | 30 |

**YOLANDA**

| | | | |
|---|---|---|---|
| 60 | Triumph RGM 1007 | With This Kiss/Don't Tell Me Not To Love You | 40 |

*(see also Kenny Graham & His Satellites)*

**STEVE YORK'S CAMELO PARDALIS**

| | | | |
|---|---|---|---|
| 73 | Virgin V 2003 | MANOR LIVE (LP) | 20 |

*(see also Elkie Brooks, Boz Scaggs, Lol Coxhill, Graham Bond, Mike Patto)*

**NOLA YORK**

| | | | |
|---|---|---|---|
| 64 | HMV POP 1326 | I Don't Understand/Here I Stand | 5 |
| 66 | Philips BF 1527 | A Whole Lotta Lovin'/You Just Didn't Wanna Know | 5 |
| 67 | Philips BF 1558 | I Can Hear You Calling/Clown Face | 6 |
| 67 | Philips BF 1582 | Photographs/He's Looking At Her | 5 |
| 67 | Philips BF 1606 | There's So Much Love All Around Me/Sleeping Boutique | 5 |
| 68 | Philips BF 1714 | Ciao Baby/We'll Get To Heaven | 6 |

*(see also Bow Bells)*

**PETE YORK PERCUSSION BAND**

| | | | |
|---|---|---|---|
| 73 | Decca TXS 109 | PERCUSSION BAND (LP, with Ian Paice, gatefold sleeve) | 50 |

*(see also Spencer Davis Group, Hardin & York, Deep Purple)*

**RUSTY YORK**

| | | | |
|---|---|---|---|
| 58 | Parlophone R 4398 | Peggy Sue/Shake 'Em Up Baby (unissued, demos only) | 1500 |

*(see also Bonnie Lou & Rusty York)*

**YORK BROTHERS**

| | | | |
|---|---|---|---|
| 54 | Parlophone CMSP 5 | Why Don't You Open The Door?/You're My Every Dream Come True (export issue) | 20 |
| 54 | Parlophone CMSP 22 | Strange Town/Three O'Clock Blues (export issue) | 20 |
| 58 | Parlophone GEP 8736 | COUNTRY AND WESTERN (EP) | 40 |
| 58 | Parlophone GEP 8753 | COUNTRY AND WESTERN NO. 2 (EP) | 40 |

**THOM YORKE**

| | | | |
|---|---|---|---|
| 08 | XL XLT 335 | Eraser Rmxs 1 (12", 2000 only) | 15 |
| 08 | XL XLT 336 | Eraser Rmxs 2 (12", 2000 only) | 15 |
| 08 | XL XLT 337 | Eraser Rmxs 3 (12", 2000 only) | 15 |
| 09 | _Xurbia _Xendless XX002 | Feelingpulledapartbyhorses/Thehollowearth (12", 8000 only) | 10 |
| 09 | Mezzotint 6015665427 | All For The Best/MARK MULCAHY: Ciao My Shining Star | 6 |
| 11 | Text 10 | Ego/Mirror (12", with Burial and Four Tet, black labels on both sides) | 18 |
| 06 | XL XLLP 200 | THE ERASER (LP, 3D effect on embossed sleeve) | 20 |
| 15 | Landgrab GRAB 001 | TOMORROW'S MODERN BOXES (LP, white vinyl in resealable printed bag) | 20 |

*(see also Radiohead, Atoms for Peace)*

**YOU**

| | | | |
|---|---|---|---|
| 80 | Ram RAMYOU2 | THE NIGHT AND MUSIC (EP) | 20 |

**YOU & I**

| | | | |
|---|---|---|---|
| 73 | Grape GR 3055 | Morning Has Broken/Don't Take Love For A Game | 5 |

**YOU KNOW WHO GROUP**

| | | | |
|---|---|---|---|
| 65 | London HLR 9947 | Roses Are Red My Love/Playboy | 20 |

**YOU BAND**

| | | | |
|---|---|---|---|
| 84 | Guardain GRC 84 | Jonathan Oracle/Disco Inferno (p/s) | 20 |

**CHRIS YOULDEN**

| | | | |
|---|---|---|---|
| 73 | Deram DM 377 | Nowhere Road/Standing On The Corner | 12 |
| 73 | Deram SML 1099 | NOWHERE ROAD (LP, lyric insert) | 60 |
| 74 | Deram SML 1112 | CITY CHILD (LP) | 50 |

**BARRY YOUNG**

| | | | |
|---|---|---|---|
| 65 | Dot DS 16756 | One Has My Name (The Other Has My Heart)/Show Me The Way | 10 |

**BILLY YOUNG**

| | | | |
|---|---|---|---|
| 72 | Atlantic K 10277 | The Sloopy/Same Old Thing Again | 8 |
| 72 | Jay Boy BOY 55 | I'm Available/Sweet Woman | 8 |

**BILLY YOUNG/LIZZIE MILES**

| | | | |
|---|---|---|---|
| 56 | HMV 7EG 8178 | THE BLUES THEY SANG (EP, with Jelly Roll Morton) | 20 |

**BOB YOUNG**

| | | | |
|---|---|---|---|
| 86 | Making Waves SURF 115 | Mean Girl/Living On An Island (p/s) | 5 |

*(see also Status Quo, Young & Moody Band)*

**BRETT YOUNG (& GHOST SQUAD)**

| | | | |
|---|---|---|---|
| 63 | Pye 7N 15578 | Guess What/It Just Happened | 12 |
| 64 | Pye 7N 15641 | Never Again/You Can't Fool Me (as Brett Young & Ghost Squad) | 12 |

**COLIN YOUNG**

| | | | |
|---|---|---|---|
| 71 | Trend 6099 005 | Anytime At All/You're No Good | 8 |

**DARREN YOUNG**

| | | | |
|---|---|---|---|
| 63 | Parlophone R 4919 | My Tears Will Turn To Laughter/I've Just Fallen For Someone | 20 |

*(see also Johnny Gentle)*

**DESI YOUNG**

| | | | |
|---|---|---|---|
| 70 | Pressure Beat PB 5504 | News Flash/JOE GIBBS & DESTROYERS: News Flash - Version | 25 |

**YOUNG EARTH**

| | | | |
|---|---|---|---|
| 70 | Priory PR3 | Silent Eyes/Death To Eliza | 50 |

**EDDY YOUNG**

| | | | |
|---|---|---|---|
| 71 | Beacon BEA 178 | A Little On The Heavy Side/Give'Em A Hand | 12 |

**FARON YOUNG**

| | | | |
|---|---|---|---|
| 55 | Capitol CL 14336 | Live Fast, Love Hard, Die Young/Forgive Me, Dear | 30 |
| 56 | Capitol CL 14574 | If You Ain't Lovin' (You Ain't Livin')/All Right | 20 |
| 56 | Capitol CL 14655 | I've Got 5 Dollars And It's Saturday Night/You're Still Mine | 30 |

| | | | |
|---|---|---|---|
| 57 | Capitol CL 14735 | The Shrine Of St. Cecilia/He Was There | 8 |
| 57 | Capitol CL 14762 | Love Has Finally Come My Way/Moonlight Mountain | 8 |
| 57 | Capitol CL 14793 | Honey Stop! (And Think Of Me)/Vacation's Over | 8 |
| 58 | Capitol CL 14822 | Snowball/The Locket | 6 |
| 58 | Capitol CL 14860 | I Can't Dance/Rosalie (Is Gonna Get Married) | 8 |
| 58 | Capitol CL 14891 | Every Time I'm Kissing You/Alone With You | 6 |
| 58 | Capitol CL 14930 | I Hate Myself/That's The Way I Feel | 5 |
| 59 | Capitol CL 14975 | Last Night At A Party/A Long Time Ago | 8 |
| 59 | Capitol CL 15004 | That's The Way It's Gotta Be/We're Talking It Over | 5 |
| 59 | Capitol CL 15050 | I Hear You Talkin'/Country Girl | 25 |

## YOUNG GENTS
| | | | |
|---|---|---|---|
| 67 | M&G 01 | Lift Up Your Body/Evening Star | 30 |

## GEORGIE YOUNG & ROCKIN' BOCS
| | | | |
|---|---|---|---|
| 58 | London HLU 8748 | Nine More Miles/The Sneak | 15 |

## HARRY YOUNG
| | | | |
|---|---|---|---|
| 65 | Dot DS 16756 | Show Me The Way/One Has My Name | 10 |

## YOUNG JESSIE
| | | | |
|---|---|---|---|
| 58 | London HLE 8544 | Shuffle In The Gravel/Make Believe | 300 |
| 58 | London HLE 8544 | Shuffle In The Gravel/Make Believe (78) | 50 |

## JIMMY YOUNG
| | | | |
|---|---|---|---|
| 54 | Decca F 10232 | A Baby Cried/Remember Me | 10 |
| 54 | Decca F 10406 | Give Me Your Word/Lonely Nightingale | 10 |
| 55 | Decca F 10444 | These Are The Things We'll Share/Don't Go To Strangers | 8 |
| 55 | Decca F 10483 | If Anyone Finds This, I Love You/The Sand And The Sea | 8 |
| 55 | Decca F 10502 | Unchained Melody/Help Me Forget | 15 |
| 55 | Decca F 10597 | The Man From Laramie/No Arms Can Ever Hold You | 15 |
| 55 | Decca F 10640 | Someone On Your Mind/I Look At You | 15 |
| 56 | Decca F 10694 | Chain Gang/Capri In May | 10 |
| 56 | Decca F 10736 | Rich Man, Poor Man/The Wayward Wind | 10 |
| 56 | Decca F 10774 | More/I'm Gonna Steal You Away | 10 |
| 57 | Decca F 10842 | Lovin' Baby/My Faith, My Hope, My Love | 5 |
| 57 | Decca F 10875 | Round And Round/Walkin' After Midnight | 6 |
| 57 | Decca F 10925 | Man On Fire/Love In The Afternoon | 5 |
| 57 | Decca F 10948 | Deep Blue Sea/Harbour Of Desire | 5 |
| 63 | Columbia DB 7119 | Miss You/Take Care Of Yourself | 5 |
| 64 | Columbia DB 7234 | Unchained Melody/There's Always Me | 5 |

## JOE E. YOUNG & TONIKS
| | | | |
|---|---|---|---|
| 68 | Toast TT 502 | Life Time Of Lovin'/Flower In My Hand | 20 |
| 69 | Toast TT 514 | Good Day Sunshine/Life Time Of Lovin' | 20 |
| 68 | Toast (S)TLP 1 | SOUL BUSTER! (LP) | 40 |

## JOHNNIE YOUNG
| | | | |
|---|---|---|---|
| 67 | Polydor 56199 | Every Christian/Epitath To Mr Simon Sir | 20 |
| 67 | Polydor 56186 | Craise Finton Kirk/I Am The World | 20 |

## JOHNNY YOUNG
| | | | |
|---|---|---|---|
| 67 | Decca F 22548 | Step Back/Cara Lyn (as Johnny Young & Kompany) | 15 |
| 67 | Decca F 22636 | Lady/Good Evening Girl | 10 |
| 68 | RCA RCA 1826 | Always Thinking Of You/Dreaming Country (as Johnny Young Four) | 10 |
| 70 | Blue Horizon 7-63852 | FAT MANDOLIN (LP) | 90 |

## KAREN YOUNG
| | | | |
|---|---|---|---|
| 65 | Mercury MF 943 | I'm Yours, You're Mine/Are You Kidding | 8 |
| 65 | Pye 7N 15956 | We'll Start The Party Again/Wonderful Summer | 8 |
| 68 | Major Minor MM 584 | Too Much Of A Good Thing/You Better Sit Down | 50 |
| 70 | Major Minor MM 691 | One Tin Soldier/Que Sera Sera (B-side arranged by Paul McCartney) | 12 |
| 69 | M. Minor MMLP/SMLP 66 | SINGS NOBODY'S CHILD AND 13 OTHER GREAT SONGS (LP) | 20 |

## KATHY YOUNG & INNOCENTS
| | | | |
|---|---|---|---|
| 61 | Top Rank JAR 534 | A Thousand Stars/Eddie My Darling | 40 |
| 61 | Top Rank JAR 554 | Happy Birthday Blues/Someone To Love | 30 |

*(see also Innocents)*

## K.G. YOUNG
| | | | |
|---|---|---|---|
| 69 | CBS 4302 | Spider/Spider Woogie 9th Movement | 30 |

## LEON YOUNG STRINGS
| | | | |
|---|---|---|---|
| 64 | Pye 7N 15646 | This Boy/Glad All Over | 40 |

## LESTER YOUNG (QUINTET)
| | | | |
|---|---|---|---|
| 56 | Vogue V 2362 | New Lester Leaps In/She's Funny That Way | 6 |
| 56 | Vogue V 2384 | You're Driving Me Crazy/East Of The Sun | 6 |
| 56 | Vogue EPV 1127 | LESTER YOUNG (EP) | 10 |
| 53 | Mercury MG 25015 | KANSAS CITY 7/THE LESTER YOUNG QUARTET (LP, 1 side each) | 25 |
| 55 | Felsted EDL 87014 | BATTLE OF THE SAXES (10" LP) | 25 |
| 55 | Columbia Clef 33C 9001 | LESTER YOUNG WITH THE OSCAR PETERSON TRIO (10" LP) | 25 |
| 56 | Columbia Clef 33C 9015 | LESTER YOUNG (10" LP) | 25 |
| 56 | Columbia Clef 33CX 10031 | THE PRESIDENT, LESTER YOUNG (LP) | 25 |
| 56 | Columbia Clef 33CX 10054 | THE JAZZ GIANTS '56 (LP) | 25 |
| 57 | Columbia Clef 33CX 10070 | PRES (LP) | 25 |
| 58 | London Jazz LTZ-C 15132 | BLUE LESTER (LP) | 25 |

*(see also Count Basie, Coleman Hawkins & Lester Young)*

## LLOYD YOUNG
| | | | |
|---|---|---|---|
| 72 | Bullet BU 500 | Bread And Butter/SHALIMAR ALLSTARS: Version | 15 |
| 72 | Duke DU 135 | Soup/J.J. ALLSTARS: Version | 20 |

| | | | |
|---|---|---|---|
| 72 | Green Door GD 4037 | Shalimar Special/G. MAHTANI ALLSTARS: Version | 20 |
| 72 | Techniques TE 917 | High Explosion/ANSELL COLLINS: Version | 20 |

*(see also Carey & Lloyd)*

## YOUNG LOVE
| | | | |
|---|---|---|---|
| 80 | Flair FLA 001 | Doing It The English Way/Easy To Do It (p/s) | 40 |

## YOUNG MARBLE GIANTS
| | | | |
|---|---|---|---|
| 80 | Rough Trade RT 043 | Final Day/Radio Silents/Cakewalking/Colossal Youth (p/s) | 10 |
| 81 | Rough Trade RT 059 | TESTCARD (EP) | 18 |
| 80 | Rough Trade ROUGH 8 | COLOSSAL YOUTH (LP) | 40 |
| 83 | Rough Trade ROUGH 57 | NIPPED IN THE BUD (LP, compilation LP with The Gist and Weekend but features 9 Young Marble Giants tracks) | 20 |
| 84 | Rough Trade ROUGHL8 | COLOSSAL YOUTH (LP, reissue) | 15 |
| 07 | Domino REWIGLP 32 | COLOSSAL YOUTH (LP, reissue) | 18 |

## YOUNG MC
| | | | |
|---|---|---|---|
| 88 | Delicious Vinyl BRW 120 | KNOW HOW (12", EP) | 20 |

## MIGHTY JOE YOUNG
| | | | |
|---|---|---|---|
| 69 | Parlophone 5794 | Why Don't You Follow Me/By My Side | 25 |
| 72 | Delmark DS 629 | BLUES WITH A TOUCH OF SOUL (LP, blue label) | 22 |

## YOUNG & MOODY (BAND)
| | | | |
|---|---|---|---|
| 77 | Magnet MAG 87 | Chicago Blue/Warm Winds | 5 |
| 79 | Fabulous JC 1 | The Devil Went Down To Georgia/You Can't Catch Me | 5 |
| 79 | Fabulous JC 3 | All The Good Friends/Playing Your Game (p/s) | 5 |

*(see also Bob Young, Whitesnake, Snafu, Cozy Powell, Motorhead, Nolan Sisters)*

## NEIL YOUNG
| | | | |
|---|---|---|---|
| 69 | Reprise RS 23405 | The Loner/Everybody Knows This Is Nowhere | 25 |
| 70 | Reprise RS 20861 | Oh Lonesome Me (Long Version)/Sugar Mountain | 12 |
| 70 | Reprise RS 23462 | Down By The River (edit)/Cinnamon Girl (alternate mix) | 12 |
| 70 | Reprise RS 20958 | Only Love Can Break Your Heart/Birds | 7 |
| 71 | Reprise RS 23488 | When You Dance I Can Really Love/After The Goldrush | 6 |
| 72 | Reprise K 14167 | Old Man/The Needle And The Damage Done | 6 |
| 73 | Reprise SAM 15 | Don't Be Denied/Love In Mind/Last Dance (p/s, 1-sided, promo only sampler for "Time Fades Away" LP) | 25 |
| 74 | Reprise K 14350 | Southern Man/Till The Morning Comes/After The Goldrush/Heart Of Gold (special sleeve) | 5 |
| 76 | Reprise K 14431 | Don't Cry No Tears/Stupid Girl | 6 |
| 74 | Reprise K 14360 | Walk On/For The Turnstiles | 20 |
| 69 | Reprise RSLP 6317 | NEIL YOUNG (LP, with name on front of sleeve) | 80 |
| 69 | Reprise RSLP 6317 | NEIL YOUNG (LP, without name on front of sleeve) | 100 |
| 69 | Reprise RSLP 6349 | EVERYBODY KNOWS THIS IS NOWHERE (LP) | 70 |
| 70 | Reprise RSLP 6383 | AFTER THE GOLDRUSH (LP, gatefold sleeve with lyric insert) | 50 |
| 71 | Reprise K 44059 | NEIL YOUNG (LP, reissue) | 20 |
| 71 | Reprise K 44073 | EVERYBODY KNOWS THIS IS NOWHERE (LP, reissue) | 20 |
| 71 | Reprise K 44088 | AFTER THE GOLDRUSH (LP, reissue, gatefold sleeve with lyric insert) | 20 |
| 72 | Reprise K 54005 | HARVEST (LP, thick cardboard gatefold sleeve with insert) | 45 |
| 72 | Reprise K 64015 | JOURNEY THROUGH THE PAST (2-LP, soundtrack, fold-out sleeve & inners) | 40 |
| 73 | Reprise K 54010 | TIME FADES AWAY (LP, with lyric insert) | 30 |
| 74 | Reprise K 54014 | ON THE BEACH (LP, with inner sleeve) | 70 |
| 75 | Reprise K 54040 | TONIGHT'S THE NIGHT (LP, gatefold sleeve with inner sleeve & insert) | 25 |
| 75 | Reprise K 54057 | ZUMA (LP, with inner sleeve & lyric insert) | 30 |
| 77 | Reprise K 54088 | AMERICAN STARS AND BARS (LP, with inner sleeve) | 18 |
| 77 | Reprise K 64037 | DECADE (3-LP) | 25 |
| 78 | Reprise K54099 | COMES A TIME (LP) | 15 |
| 79 | Reprise K 54105 | RUST NEVER SLEEPS (LP, with inner sleeve & lyric insert) | 15 |
| 79 | Reprise K 64041 | LIVE RUST (2-LP, with inner sleeves) | 20 |
| 80 | Reprise K 54109 | HAWKS & DOVES (LP, with inner sleeve) | 15 |
| 92 | Reprise 9362450571 | HARVEST MOON (LP) | 40 |
| 92 | Reprise 7599 26671-1 | WELD (2-LP with Crazy Horse) | 60 |
| 93 | Geffen GEF24452 | LUCKY THIRTEEN (LP) | 50 |
| 93 | Reprise 9362-4 5310-1 | UNPLUGGED (LP) | 50 |
| 95 | Reprise 9362 45934-1 | MIRROR BALL (2-LP, with PEARL JAM) | 50 |
| 12 | Reprise 9362457491 | PSYCHEDELIC PILL (3-LP, as Neil Young and Crazy Horse) | 30 |

*(see also Buffalo Springfield, Crosby Stills Nash & Young, Stills-Young Band, Crazy Horse)*

## RALPH YOUNG
| | | | |
|---|---|---|---|
| 55 | Brunswick 05466 | The Man From Laramie/The Bible Tells Me So | 7 |
| 55 | Brunswick 05500 | Bring Me A Bluebird/A Room In Paris | 5 |
| 56 | Brunswick 05605 | The Legend Of Wyatt Earp/Do You Know? | 5 |

*(see also Jack Pleis)*

## ROBERT YOUNG
| | | | |
|---|---|---|---|
| 71 | CBS 7350 | Rosemary Blue/When Time Began | 7 |

## ROGER YOUNG
| | | | |
|---|---|---|---|
| 66 | Columbia DB 7869 | Sweet, Sweet Morning/Whatcha Gonna Give Me? | 60 |
| 66 | Columbia DB 8092 | No Address/It's Been Nice | 250 |

## ROY YOUNG (BAND)
| | | | |
|---|---|---|---|
| 59 | Fontana H 200 | Just Keep It Up/Big Fat Mama | 25 |
| 59 | Fontana H 215 | Hey Little Girl/Just Ask Your Heart | 20 |
| 60 | Fontana H 237 | I Hardly Know Me/Gilee | 20 |
| 60 | Fontana H 247 | Taboo/I'm In Love | 15 |
| 61 | Fontana H 290 | You Were Meant For Me/Plenty Of Love (as Roy Young & Hunters) | 10 |
| 61 | Ember EMB S 128 | Four And Twenty Thousand Kisses/Late Last Evening | 12 |

MINT VALUE £

| | | | |
|---|---|---|---|
| 71 | MCA MKS 5071 | Wild Country Wine/New Sun New Horizon (p/s) | 8 |
| 70 | RCA SF 8161 | ROY YOUNG BAND (LP) | 20 |

**ROY YOUNG**
| | | | |
|---|---|---|---|
| 73 | MCA MUS 1214 | Dig A Hole/I'm A Loner | 12 |

**SUSANNAH YOUNG**
| | | | |
|---|---|---|---|
| 67 | Philips BF 1559 | Lazy Afternoon/Here's That Rainy Day | 5 |

**TERRY YOUNG**
| | | | |
|---|---|---|---|
| 61 | Pye 7N 15321 | Maverick/Partners | 7 |
| 61 | Pye 7N 15353 | Someone New/Now Forever And A Day | 12 |
| 62 | Pye 7N 15416 | Joe's Been A-Gittin' There/They Took John Away | 6 |

**TOMMIE YOUNG**
| | | | |
|---|---|---|---|
| 73 | Contempo C 12 | Everybody's Got A Little Devil In Their Soul/Do You Still Feel The Same Way | 10 |
| 73 | Contempo C 23 | She Don't Have To See You/That's All Part Of Loving Him | 10 |
| 74 | Contempo CLP 501 | DO YOU STILL FEEL THE SAME WAY (LP) | 50 |

**VICKI YOUNG**
| | | | |
|---|---|---|---|
| 55 | Capitol CL 14228 | Hearts Of Stone/Tweedlee Dee (triangular centre) | 40 |
| 55 | Capitol CL 14281 | Live Fast, Love Hard, Die Young/Zoom, Zoom, Zoom(triangular centre) | 25 |
| 56 | Capitol CL 14528 | Steel Guitar/Bye Bye For Just A While | 12 |
| 56 | Capitol CL 14653 | Spanish Main/Tell Me In Your Own Sweet Way (with Joe 'Fingers' Carr) | 12 |
| 56 | Capitol EAP1 593 | VICKI YOUNG (EP) | 35 |

*(see also Joe 'Fingers' Carr)*

**YOUNG AL CAPONE**
| | | | |
|---|---|---|---|
| 71 | Green Door GD 4012 | Girl Called Clover/Girl Called Clover (Version) | 15 |

**YOUNG AND MOODY BAND**
| | | | |
|---|---|---|---|
| 81 | Bronze BRO 130 | Don't Do That/How Can I help You Tonight | 6 |

**YOUNG BLOOD**
| | | | |
|---|---|---|---|
| 68 | Pye 7N 17495 | Green Light/Don't Leave Me In The Dark | 25 |
| 68 | Pye 7N 17588 | Just How Loud/Masquerade | 20 |
| 68 | Pye 7N 17627 | Bang-Shang-A-Lang/I Can't Stop | 20 |
| 69 | Pye 7N 17696 | The Continuing Story Of Bungalow Bill/I Will | 20 |

*(see also Cozy Powell, Ace Kefford Stand, Big Bertha)*

**YOUNG BLOOD**
| | | | |
|---|---|---|---|
| 84 | Landslide LAND 1 | FIRST BLOOD (12" EP, p/s) | 18 |

**YOUNGBLOODS**
| | | | |
|---|---|---|---|
| 69 | RCA RCA 1821 | Darkness, Darkness/On Sir Francis Drake | 10 |
| 69 | RCA RCA 1877 | Get Together/Beautiful | 10 |
| 69 | RCA SF 8026 | ELEPHANT MOUNTAIN (LP) | 22 |
| 70 | Warner Bros WS 1878 | ROCK FESTIVAL (LP) | 15 |

**YOUNG BROTHERS**
| | | | |
|---|---|---|---|
| 68 | MCA MU 1042 | I've Always Wanted Love/Mirror Mirror | 15 |

**YOUNG BUCKS**
| | | | |
|---|---|---|---|
| 77 | Blueport BLU 1 | Get Your Feet Back On The Ground/Cold, Cold Morning (p/s) | 6 |

**COLE YOUNGER**
| | | | |
|---|---|---|---|
| 74 | ABC ABC 4009 | Don't Stop/Call Me | 10 |
| 77 | Magnet MAG 112 | She's Not My Lover/Don't Use Me | 12 |
| 80 | Ariola AHA 555 | Candy/I'd Rather Be Me | 6 |

**YOUNG FATHERS**
| | | | |
|---|---|---|---|
| 15 | Big Dada BD 264Z | Soon Come Soon/Everyguy | 6 |

**YOUNGFOLK**
| | | | |
|---|---|---|---|
| 68 | President PT 136 | Lonely Girl/Joey | 20 |

**YOUNG FOLK**
| | | | |
|---|---|---|---|
| 72 | Midas MR 001 | RIBBLE VALLEY DREAM (LP) | 50 |

**YOUNG FREDDIE**
| | | | |
|---|---|---|---|
| 70 | Camel CA 38 | Drink And Gamble/LENNOX BROWN & HUE ROY: King Of The Road | 25 |

*(see also Freddie McGregor)*

**YOUNG GROWLER & CALYPSO RHYTHM KINGS**
| | | | |
|---|---|---|---|
| 66 | Columbia DB 7870 | Amy The Sunbather/Sweet Trinidad | 7 |
| 66 | Columbia DB 7958 | V For Victory/Be Nice To Women (in 'Test Match' p/s) | 12 |
| 66 | Columbia DB 7958 | V For Victory/Be Nice To Women | 7 |
| 66 | Columbia SEG 8502 | V FOR VICTORY (EP) | 12 |

**YOUNG-HOLT TRIO**
| | | | |
|---|---|---|---|
| 67 | Coral Q 72489 | Wack Wack/This Little Light Of Mine | 15 |
| 67 | Coral Q 72489 | Wack Wack/This Little Light Of Mine (DJ copy) | 40 |

**YOUNG-HOLT UNLIMITED**
| | | | |
|---|---|---|---|
| 69 | MCA MU 1053 | Soulful Strut/Country Slicker Joe | 5 |
| 72 | MCA MU 1159 | Just Ain't No Love/Love Makes A Woman | 5 |
| 73 | Contempo COLP-R 1004 | PLAYS SUPERFLY (LP) | 15 |
| 69 | MCA MUP(S) 368 | SOULFUL STRUT (LP) | 15 |

*(see also Ramsey Lewis Trio)*

**YOUNG IDEA**
| | | | |
|---|---|---|---|
| 66 | Columbia DB 7961 | The World's Been Good To Me/It Can't Be | 10 |
| 66 | Columbia DB 8067 | Gotta Get Out Of The Mess I'm In/Games Men Play | 5 |
| 67 | Columbia DB 8132 | Peculiar Situation/Just Look At The Rain | 5 |
| 67 | Columbia DB 8205 | With A Little Help From My Friends/Colours Of Darkness | 12 |
| 67 | Columbia DB 8284 | Mister Lovin' Luggage Man/Room With A View | 8 |
| 68 | Music For Pleasure MFP 1225 | WITH A LITTLE HELP FROM MY FRIENDS (LP) | 20 |

**YOUNG LIONS**
| | | | |
|---|---|---|---|
| 78 | Discovery D-DISC 001 | Take Five (12", p/s) | 30 |

**YOUNG ONES (1)**
| | | | |
|---|---|---|---|
| 63 | Decca F 11705 | How Do I Tell You/Baby That's It | 8 |

**YOUNG ONES (2)**
| | | | |
|---|---|---|---|
| 78 | Virgin VS 205 | Rock 'N' Roll Radio/Little Bit Of Loving (p/s) | 6 |

**YOUNG RASCALS**
| | | | |
|---|---|---|---|
| 65 | Atlantic AT 4059 | I Ain't Gonna Eat My Heart Out Anymore/Slow Down | 15 |
| 66 | Atlantic AT 4082 | Good Lovin'/Mustang Sally | 15 |
| 66 | Atlantic 584 024 | You Better Run/Love Is A Beautiful Thing | 18 |
| 66 | Atlantic 584 050 | Come On Up/What Is The Reason | 18 |
| 66 | Atlantic 584 067 | Too Many Fish In The Sea/No Love To Give | 15 |
| 67 | Atlantic 584 081 | I've Been Lonely Too Long/If You Knew | 15 |
| 67 | Atlantic 584 085 | I Ain't Gonna Eat My Heart Out Anymore/Good Lovin' | 12 |
| 67 | Atlantic 584 111 | Groovin'/Sueno | 10 |
| 67 | Atlantic 584 128 | A Girl Like You/It's Love | 12 |
| 67 | Atlantic 584 138 | How Can I Be Sure/I Don't Love You Anymore | 7 |
| 68 | Atlantic 584 161 | It's Wonderful/Of Course | 10 |
| 66 | Atlantic 587/588 012 | THE YOUNG RASCALS (LP) | 30 |
| 67 | Atlantic 587/588 060 | COLLECTIONS (LP) | 20 |
| 67 | Atlantic 587/588 074 | GROOVIN' (LP) | 25 |

*(see also Rascals, Joey Dee & Starlighters)*

**RICHARD YOUNGS**
| | | | |
|---|---|---|---|
| 88 | No Fans NFR01 | ADVENT (LP) | 25 |
| 94 | Chocolate Monk CHOC 052 | MOTORWAY (cassette album) | 20 |

**YOUNG SISTERS**
| | | | |
|---|---|---|---|
| 62 | London HLU 9610 | Casanova Brown/My Guy | 25 |

**YOUNG SOULS**
| | | | |
|---|---|---|---|
| 69 | Amalgamated AMG 844 | Why Did You Leave/Main A Wail | 100 |

**YOUNG TRADITION**
| | | | |
|---|---|---|---|
| 74 | Argo AFW 115 | The Shepherd's Hymn/The Boar's Head Carol | 6 |
| 68 | Transatlantic TRAEP 164 | CHICKEN ON A RAFT (EP) | 25 |
| 66 | Transatlantic TRA 142 | THE YOUNG TRADITION (LP) | 22 |
| 67 | Transatlantic TRA 155 | SO CHEERFULLY ROUND (LP) | 18 |
| 68 | Transatlantic TRA 172 | GALLERIES (LP, with Dave Swarbrick) | 18 |

*(see also Dave Swarbrick, Peter Bellamy)*

**YOUNG TURKS**
| | | | |
|---|---|---|---|
| 66 | CBS 202353 | Duel At Diablo/Our Lady From Maxim's | 12 |

**YOUNG WORLD**
| | | | |
|---|---|---|---|
| 78 | Cloth Cap CCR 101 | I'll Hold Out As Long As I Can/Now And Then (no p/s) | 5 |

**YOUNG WORLD SINGERS**
| | | | |
|---|---|---|---|
| 64 | Brunswick 05916 | Ringo For President/A Boy Like That | 6 |

**YOUR HERO**
| | | | |
|---|---|---|---|
| 79 | Laser LAS 10 | The Dictator/Snoggin' At The Roxy (no p/s, reissue 1000 only) | 5 |
| 79 | Mirimar MIR 69 | The Dictator/KALEIDOSCOPE: Snoggin' At The Roxy (no p/s, 500 only) | 8 |

**JOHNNY YOUTH**
| | | | |
|---|---|---|---|
| 69 | Grape GR 3002 | Darling It Won't/HIP CITY BOYS: Moon Train | 40 |

**YOUTH VALLEY CHORALE**
| | | | |
|---|---|---|---|
| 63 | London HLU 9818 | Do You Hear What I Hear/Little Bell | 5 |

**YOUTH (1)**
| | | | |
|---|---|---|---|
| 66 | Polydor 56121 | As Long As There Is Your Love/Your One And Only Love | 20 |

**YOUTH (2)**
| | | | |
|---|---|---|---|
| 69 | Deram DM 226 | Meadow Of My Love/Love Me Or Leave Me | 20 |

**YOU'VE GOT FOETUS ON YOUR BREATH**
| | | | |
|---|---|---|---|
| 81 | Self Immolation WOMB 07 | Wash It All Off/333 (p/s) | 8 |
| 80s | Self Immolation | Tell Me, What Is The Bane Of Your Life? | 10 |
| 81 | Self Imm. WOMB OYBL-1 | DEAF (LP) | 25 |
| 81 | Self Imm. WOMB OYBL-2 | ACHE (LP) | 25 |

*(see also Foetus etc., Philip & His Foetus Vibrations, Scraping Foetus Off The Wheel)*

**LES YPER SOUND**
| | | | |
|---|---|---|---|
| 67 | Fontana TF 880 | Too Fortiche/Psyche Rock | 60 |

*(see also Pierre Henry)*

**YR HWNTWS**
| | | | |
|---|---|---|---|
| 82 | Loco LOCO 1001 | YR HWNTWS (LP) | 80 |

**YR AWR**
| | | | |
|---|---|---|---|
| 71 | Wren WRE 1096 | RHIF 2 (EP) | 10 |

**Y TRWYNAU COCH**
| | | | |
|---|---|---|---|
| 70s | Record. Sqwar RSROC 1 | WASTOD AR Y TU FAS (BANANAS) (EP, around 1,000 only) | 50 |
| 78 | Record. Sqwar RSROC 002 | Merched Dan 15 (I Often Think Of Girls Under 15)/Byw Ar Arian Fy Rhieni/ Mynd I'r Capel Mewn Levis/Ail Ddechre (around 1,000 only) | 50 |
| 80 | Record. Coch RCTC 3 | Methu Dawnsio/CRACH: Putain Rhad (multifold p/s) | 20 |
| 81 | Sain SAIN 92 | Paqn Fo Cyrff Yn Cwrdd/Beth Am Take Away/Camera Yn Y Gornel (p/s) | 50 |
| 80s | Record. Coch OCHR 2198 | RHEDEG RHAG Y TORPIDOS (LP) | 30 |

**JOHNNY YUKON**
| | | | |
|---|---|---|---|
| 60 | Top Rank JAR 347 | Made To Be Loved/Magnolia | 7 |

**YUNGUN/MR THING**
| | | | |
|---|---|---|---|
| 03 | White (Janomi) JACKIT0001 | STRAIGHT JACK IT (EP) | 12 |

## TIMI YURO

| | | | |
|---|---|---|---:|
| 61 | London HLG 9403 | Hurt/I Apologise | 20 |
| 62 | London HLG 9484 | Smile/I Believe (B-side with Johnnie Ray) | 15 |
| 62 | Liberty LIB 55410 | Let Me Call You Sweetheart/Satan Never Sleeps | 10 |
| 62 | Liberty LIB 55469 | What's A-Matter Baby (Is It Hurting You)/Thirteenth Hour | 30 |
| 63 | Liberty LIB 55519 | The Love Of A Boy/I Ain't Gonna Cry No More | 30 |
| 63 | Liberty LIB 55519 | The Love Of A Boy/I Ain't Gonna Cry No More (DJ Copy) | 60 |
| 63 | Liberty LIB 55587 | Make The World Go Away/Look Down | 12 |
| 64 | Liberty LIB 10177 | Hurt/Be Anything (But Be Mine) | 10 |
| 64 | Mercury MF 826 | If/I'm Afraid The Masquerade Is Over | 20 |
| 65 | Mercury MF 848 | You Can Have Him/Could This Be Magic | 12 |
| 65 | Mercury MF 859 | Get Out Of My Life/Can't Stop Running Away | 60 |
| 65 | Mercury MF 903 | Once A Day/Pretend | 5 |
| 65 | Mercury MF 949 | Turn The World Around The Other Way/Just A Ribbon | 5 |
| 66 | Mercury MF 978 | Cuttin' In/Why Not Now | 6 |
| 68 | Liberty LBF 15092 | Something Bad On My Mind/Wrong | 30 |
| 68 | Liberty LIB 15142 | I Must Have Been Out Of My Mind/Interlude | 25 |
| 68 | Liberty LIB 15182 | It'll Never Be Over For Me/As Long As There Is You | 700 |
| 65 | Liberty LEP 2214 | TIMI YURO: SOUL! (EP) | 30 |
| 66 | Liberty LEP 2252 | MAKE THE WORLD GO AWAY (EP) | 25 |
| 62 | London HA-G 2415 | TIMI YURO (LP) | 75 |
| 62 | Liberty LBY 1042 | SOUL! (LP) | 35 |
| 63 | Liberty LBY 1154 | WHAT'S A-MATTER BABY (LP, mono) | 25 |
| 63 | Liberty SLBY 1154 | WHAT'S A-MATTER BABY (LP, stereo) | 30 |
| 64 | Liberty LBY 1192 | MAKE THE WORLD GO AWAY (LP) | 25 |
| 64 | Mercury 20032 MCL | THE AMAZING TIMI YURO (LP) | 22 |
| 65 | Liberty LBY 1247 | HURT (LP) | 30 |
| 66 | Liberty LBY 1275 | LET ME CALL YOU SWEETHEART (LP, mono) | 20 |
| 66 | Liberty SLBY 1275 | LET ME CALL YOU SWEETHEART (LP, stereo) | 30 |
| 66 | Liberty (S)LBY 1290 | THE BEST OF TIMI YURO (LP) | 20 |
| 68 | Liberty LBL/LBS 83115 | GREAT PERFORMANCES (LP) | 15 |
| 68 | Liberty LBL/LBS 83128 | TIMI IN THE BEGINNING (LP) | 20 |
| 69 | Liberty LBS 83198E | SOMETHING BAD ON MY MIND (LP) | 50 |
| 69 | Mercury SMWL 21010 | TALENTED TIMI (LP) | 15 |

*(see also Johnnie Ray)*

## ZABANDIS
| | | | |
|---|---|---|---:|
| 82 | True Vision TRV 001 | Jah Jah Say/Things Are Getting Harder (12") | 100 |

## JOHN ZACHERLE
| | | | |
|---|---|---|---:|
| 58 | London HLU 8599 | Dinner With Drac Part 1/Dinner With Drac - Conclusion | 20 |

*(see also Dave Appell & Applejacks)*

## ZAFTIG MADEL
| | | | |
|---|---|---|---:|
| 84 | Shine SHTUP 3 | Dori Duz/Curvy 'N' Creamy (p/s) | 6 |

## ZAGER & EVANS
| | | | |
|---|---|---|---:|
| 69 | RCA SF 8056 | 2525 (LP) | 20 |

## ZAKARRIAS
| | | | |
|---|---|---|---:|
| 71 | Deram SML 1091 | ZAKARRIAS (LP, white/red label, small logo) | 1000 |

## ZAKATEK
| | | | |
|---|---|---|---:|
| 73 | Bell 1289 | I Gotcha Now/So Good To You | 7 |

## IWO ZALUSKI
| | | | |
|---|---|---|---:|
| 73 | Hobbiton HOB 103 | LEGEND OF THE SAFFRON SORCERESS (EP, insert) | 150 |
| 69 | John Hassell Records HAS LP 2026 | BRANDYBUCK AND THE ELECTRIC ZEON BAND (LP, as Iwo Zaluski and the Cardinal Newman School) | 500 |
| 69 | John Hassell Records HAS LP MAS 701 | THE WORLD OF MY DREAMS (LP) | 100 |
| 74 | Hobbiton HOB 104 | THE REMARKABLE EARTH MAKING MACHINE (LP) | 150 |
| 75 | Hobbiton HOB 105 | TALES OF TOLKIEN HIGHLIGHTS (LP) | 150 |
| 77 | Hobbiton HOB 107 | A LIFE IN THE WEEK OF A DAY (LP) | 150 |

## GEORGE ZAMBETAS & THE GROUP TEN PLAYERS
| | | | |
|---|---|---|---:|
| 66 | Pye 7N 17180 | Moussaka/Monlight Over The Acropolis (p/s) | 6 |
| 69 | RCA RCA 1860 | In The Year 2525 (Exordium Terminus)/Little Kids | 5 |

## ZANADU
| | | | |
|---|---|---|---:|
| 82 | SMT 14 | Let's See You Rockin'/Nutbush City Limits | 10 |

## ALEX ZANETIS
| | | | |
|---|---|---|---:|
| 71 | Moodisc HM 102 | Guilty/JOLLY BOYS: Do Fe Do | 5 |

## TOMMY ZANG
| | | | |
|---|---|---|---:|
| 59 | HMV POP 611 | Break The Chain/I'll Put A String On Your Finger | 10 |
| 62 | Polydor NH 66955 | I'm Gonna Slip You Offa My Mind/Every Hour, Every Day | 10 |
| 62 | Polydor NH 66957 | Hey, Good Lookin'/With Love (For You) | 20 |
| 62 | Polydor NH 66960 | Take These Chains From My Heart/Truly, Truly | 10 |
| 62 | Polydor NH 66977 | I Can't Hold Your Letters (In My Arms)/She's Getting Married | 10 |
| 62 | Polydor NH 66980 | Just Call My Name/I Love You Because | 10 |

## WILLY ZANGO
| | | | |
|---|---|---|---|
| 73 | Jam JAM 58 | Hot Rod/Goom | 8 |
| 74 | DJM DJS 312 | Hot Rod/The Voice Of Melody | 7 |

## ZANTI MISFITZ
| | | | |
|---|---|---|---|
| 82 | Clay 9 | Kidz Songs/Alice Liddle's Bad Trip (p/s) | 10 |

## FRANK ZAPPA/MOTHERS OF INVENTION
### SINGLES
| | | | |
|---|---|---|---|
| 66 | Verve VS 545 | It Can't Happen Here/How Could I Be Such A Fool (as Mothers Of Invention) | 60 |
| 67 | Verve VS 557 | Big Leg Emma/Why Don't You Do Me Right (as Mothers Of Invention) | 60 |
| 71 | Reprise K 14100 | Tears Began To Fall/Junier Mintz Boogie (as Mothers Of Invention) | 40 |
| 71 | United Artists UP 35319 | What Will This Evening Bring Me This Morning?/Daddy, Daddy, Daddy | 35 |
| 74 | Discreet K 19201 | Cosmic Debris/Uncle Remus | 10 |
| 74 | Discreet K 19202 | Don't Eat The Yellow Snow/Camarillo Brillo | 10 |
| 79 | CBS 7261 | Dancin' Fool/Baby Snakes | 5 |
| 80 | CBS 7950 | Joe's Garage/Catholic Girls | 6 |
| 80 | CBS 7950 | Joe's Garage/BOB DYLAN: When You Gonna Wake Up (mispressing) | 30 |
| 80 | CBS 8652 | I Don't Wanna Get Drafted/Ancient Armaments (p/s) | 6 |
| 81 | CBS A 1622 | You Are What You Is/Harder Than Your Husband (p/s) | 6 |
| 81 | CBS A 12-1622 | You Are What You Is/Pink Napkins/Harder Than Your Husband/Soup 'N Old Clothes (12", picture disc) | 15 |
| 81 | CBS XPS 147 | Shut Up 'N' Play Yer Guitar/Variation On The C. Santana Secret (p/s, issued free with "Ship Arriving Too Late To Save A Drowning Witch" LP) | 6 |
| 82 | CBS A 2412 | Valley Girl/Teenage Prostitute (p/s) | 6 |
| 84 | EMI EMI 5499 | Baby Take Your Teeth Out/Stevie's Spanking (p/s) | 8 |

### ALBUMS : VERVE ORIGINALS
| | | | |
|---|---|---|---|
| 66 | Verve VLP 9154 | FREAK OUT! (as Mothers Of Invention, mono, single disc) | 150 |
| 66 | Verve SVLP 9154 | FREAK OUT! (as Mothers Of Invention, stereo, single disc) | 100 |
| 67 | Verve VLP 9174 | ABSOLUTELY FREE (as Mothers Of Invention, mono) | 150 |
| 67 | Verve SVLP 9174 | ABSOLUTELY FREE (as Mothers Of Invention, stereo) | 100 |
| 68 | Verve VLP 9199 | WE'RE ONLY IN IT FOR THE MONEY (as Mothers Of Invention, gatefold sleeve, mono) | 150 |
| 68 | Verve SVLP 9199 | WE'RE ONLY IN IT FOR THE MONEY (as Mothers Of Invention, gatefold sleeve, stereo) | 100 |
| 68 | Verve VLP 9223 | LUMPY GRAVY (gatefold sleeve, mono) | 150 |
| 68 | Verve SVLP 9223 | LUMPY GRAVY (gatefold sleeve, stereo) | 100 |
| 69 | Verve VLP 9237 | CRUISING WITH RUBEN AND THE JETS (as Mothers Of Invention, mono) | 150 |
| 69 | Verve SVLP 9237 | CRUISING WITH RUBEN AND THE JETS (as Mothers Of Invention, stereo) | 100 |
| 69 | Verve VLP 9239 | MOTHERMANIA - THE BEST OF THE MOTHERS (as Mothers Of Invention, mono) | 70 |
| 69 | Verve SVLP 9239 | MOTHERMANIA - THE BEST OF THE MOTHERS (as Mothers Of Invention, stereo) | 30 |

### ALBUMS : VERVE REISSUES
| | | | |
|---|---|---|---|
| 71 | Verve/Polydor 2683 004 | FREAK OUT (2-LP) | 30 |
| 72 | Verve/Polydor 2317 034 | WE'RE ONLY IN IT FOR THE MONEY (gatefold sleeve) | 30 |
| 72 | Verve/Polydor 2317 035 | ABSOLUTELY FREE (gatefold sleeve) | 25 |
| 72 | Verve/Polydor 2317 046 | LUMPY GRAVY (gatefold sleeve) | 30 |
| 72 | Verve/Polydor 2317 047 | MOTHERMANIA - THE BEST OF THE MOTHERS | 25 |
| 73 | Verve/Polydor 2352 017 | MOTHERMANIA - THE BEST OF THE MOTHERS (2nd reissue) | 25 |
| 73 | Verve/Polydor 2317 069 | CRUISIN' WITH RUBEN AND THE JETS (gatefold sleeve) | 25 |
| 75 | Verve/Polydor 2352 057 | ROCK FLASHBACKS (LP) | 15 |

### ALBUMS : ORIGINAL REPRISE/WARNER/DISCREET ISSUES
| | | | |
|---|---|---|---|
| 70 | Reprise RSLP 6356 | HOT RATS (1st pressing, pink, gold & green 'riverboat' label, gatefold sleeve) | 60 |
| 70 | Reprise RSLP 6356 | HOT RATS (2nd pressing, tan 'riverboat' label, gatefold sleeve) | 35 |
| 70 | Reprise RSLP 6370 | BURNT WEENY SANDWICH (as Mothers Of Invention, 1st pressing, pink, gold & green 'riverboat' label, gatefold sleeve) | 80 |
| 70 | Reprise RSLP 2028 | WEASELS RIPPED MY FLESH (as Mothers Of Invention, tan 'riverboat' label) | 40 |
| 70 | Reprise RSLP 2030 | CHUNGA'S REVENGE (tan 'riverboat' label, green gatefold sleeve) | 45 |
| 70 | Reprise RSLP 2030 | CHUNGA'S REVENGE (tan 'riverboat' label, red gatefold sleeve) | 20 |
| 71 | Reprise K 44150 | FILLMORE EAST, JUNE 1971 (as Mothers Of Invention) | 15 |
| 72 | Reprise K 44179 | JUST ANOTHER BAND FROM L.A. (as Mothers Of Invention, gatefold sleeve) | 20 |
| 72 | Reprise K 44203 | WAKA/JAWAKA (HOT RATS) | 15 |
| 72 | Reprise K 44209 | THE GRAND WAZOO (gatefold sleeve) | 20 |
| 73 | DiscReet K 41000 | OVER-NITE SENSATION (as Mothers Of Invention, gatefold sleeve) | 15 |
| 74 | DiscReet K 59201 | APOSTROPHE (') (no lyric insert) | 15 |
| 75 | DiscReet K 59207 | ONE SIZE FITS ALL (as Mothers Of Invention, gatefold sleeve) | 15 |

*(First pressings issued without Warner Bros logo on label or sleeve; copies with Warners logos are post-1975 pressings worth £6-£8 each.)*

| | | | |
|---|---|---|---|
| 76 | Warner Bros K 56298 | ZOOT ALLURES (LP) | 15 |
| 77 | DiscReet K 69204 | ZAPPA IN NEW YORK (LIVE) (2-LP, with & without reference to Punky's Whips) | 20 |
| 77 | DiscReet K 69204 | ZAPPA IN NEW YORK (LIVE) (2-LP, "Punky's Whips" listed on sleeve but not on label or LP) | 20 |
| 77 | DiscReet K 69204 | ZAPPA IN NEW YORK (LIVE) (2-LP, 1st pressing plays "Punky's Whips", listed on sleeve and on label) | 150 |
| 78 | DiscReet K 59210 | STUDIO TAN | 15 |
| 78 | DiscReet K 59211 | SLEEP DIRT | 15 |
| 78 | DiscReet K 59212 | ORCHESTRAL FAVORITES | 15 |
| 71 | Reprise K 44078 | HOT RATS (tan 'riverboat' label, gatefold sleeve) | 20 |
| 71 | Reprise K 44083 | BURNT WEENY SANDWICH (tan 'riverboat' label) | 20 |
| 71 | Reprise K 44019 | WEASELS RIPPED MY FLESH (tan 'riverboat' label) | 15 |
| 71 | Reprise K 44020 | CHUNGA'S REVENGE (tan 'riverboat' label, gatefold sleeve) | 15 |

### ALBUMS : CBS/EMI/OTHER LABELS
| | | | |
|---|---|---|---|
| 69 | Transatlantic TRA 197 | UNCLE MEAT (2-LP, as Mothers Of Invention) | 80 |

MINT VALUE £

| 71 | United Artists UDF 50003 | 200 MOTELS (2-LP, with booklet & poster, as Frank Zappa & Mothers Of Invention) | 40 |
| 79 | CBS 86101 | JOE'S GARAGE ACT 1 (gatefold sleeve, lyric insert) | 20 |
| 81 | CBS 66368 | SHUT UP 'N' PLAY YER GUITAR (3-LP box set, with inner sleeves) | 25 |
| 82 | CBS 85804 | SHIP ARRIVING TOO LATE TO SAVE A DROWNING WITCH (LP, with bonus 7" Shut Up 'N' Play Yer Guitar/"Variation On The C. Santana Secret" [XPS 147]) | 20 |
| 84 | EMI EL 2701531 | BOULEZ CONDUCTS ZAPPA: 'THE PERFECT STRANGER' | 15 |
| 84 | EMI EJ2702561 | FRANCESCO ZAPPA (with inner sleeve) | 15 |
| 84 | EMI 2402943 | THING-FISH (3-LP, box set, with libretto) | 20 |
| 84 | EMI EMC 3500 | THE MAN FROM UTOPIA | 15 |
| 84 | EMI FZAP1 | JOE'S GARAGE ACTS 1, 2 & 3 (3-LP, box set, inner sleeves only, with libretti) | 25 |
| 84 | EMI no cat. no. | SHUT UP 'N' PLAY YER GUITAR (3-LP box set, with inner sleeves) | 25 |
| 86 | EMI EN 352 | JAZZ FROM HELL | 15 |
| 86 | EMI EC 3507 | FRANK ZAPPA MEETS THE MOTHERS OF PREVENTION (European version) | 15 |
| 95 | Simply Vinyl SLVP 0024 | WEASELS RIPPED MY FLESH (180gm vinyl) | 20 |
| 95 | Simply Vinyl SLVP 0025 | BURNT WEENY SANDWICH (gatefold sleeve, 180 gm vinyl) | 20 |

**ALBUMS : ZAPPA LABEL**

| 84 | Zappa Records ZAPPA 1 | FREAK OUT (2-LP, gatefold sleeve, some in single sleeve £35) | 18 |
| 80s | Zappa Records ZAPPA 5 | LONDON SYMPHONY ORCHESTRA VOLUME II | 15 |
| 88 | Zappa Records ZAPPA 6 | GUITAR (2-LP, gatefold sleeve) | 18 |
| 90 | Zappa Records ZAPPA 20 | JOE'S GARAGE ACTS 1, 2 & 3 (3-LP, box set, original sleeves, with libretti) | 30 |
| 91 | Zappa Records ZAPPA 35 | BURNT WEENY SANDWICH (gatefold sleeve) | 15 |
| 91 | Zappa Records ZAPPA 42 | SHIP ARRIVING TOO LATE TO SAVE A DROWNING WITCH | 15 |
| 92 | Zappa Records ZAPPA 39 | ROXY AND ELSEWHERE (2-LP, as Mothers Of Invention, gatefold lyric sleeve) | 20 |

*(see also Flo & Eddie, Jeff Simmons, Wild Man Fischer, Captain Beefheart, John Lennon, Geronimo Black)*

**ZAPPO**
| 73 | Magnet MAG 2 | Rock And Roll Crazy/Right On! | 8 |

**ZAP POW**
| 72 | Harry J HJ 6650 | Lottery Spin/Lottery Spin - Version | 8 |
| 73 | Trojan TR 7741 | This Is Reggae Music/Break Down The Barriers | 7 |
| 73 | Blue Mountain BM 1027 | This Is Reggae Music/Break Down The Barriers | 6 |
| 74 | Island WIP 6181 | This Is Reggae Music/Break Down The Barriers | 6 |
| 76 | Vulcan VUL 1010 | Jungle Beat/Rock Your Bones | 8 |
| 78 | Island IPR 2028 | Roots Man Reggae/Let's Fall In Love (12") | 12 |
| 76 | Vulcan VULP 004 | NOW (LP) | 15 |

**ZARACK**
| 99 | All Tone AT 020 | Look Into My Eyes/My Eyes | 45 |

**LES ZARJAZ**
| 85 | Creation CRE 014 | One Charming Nyte/My Baby Owns A Fallout Zone (foldover p/s, poly bag) | 8 |
*(see also Tronics)*

**PETE ZEAR**
| 80 | (no label) matrix: 22-1 | Tomorrow's World/Fast Food (stamped white label, with insert, numbered) | 12 |
*(see also Ruts, Rat Scabies)*

**ZEBEDEE**
| 71 | Decca F13144 | So Long Marianne/She Couldn't Make Gravy | 30 |

**ZEE**
| 84 | Harvest HAR 5277 | Confusion/Eyes Of A Gypsy (p/s) | 5 |
*(see also Rick Wright)*

**ZEEBRA**
| 79 | Jungle JR 7038S | Anytime/Sign Your Name/Lux Gud/Night (no p/s) | 25 |

**MARTIN ZEICHNETE**
| 13 | UCR UCKL001V | KOSMISCHER LAUFER VOLUME ONE: 1972-1983 (LP, 250 only, some with card inserts) | 30 |

**ZEITGEIST**
| 80 | Enchaine ENC 1 | Shake-Rake/Sniper (p/s) | 6 |
| 82 | Jamming CREATE 4 | Stop (p/s) | 5 |

**ZEN**
| 68 | Philips BF 1746 | Hair/Aquarius | 20 |

**ZENITH**
| 86 | ZENITH 5001 | Heavy Heavy Heart (p/s) | 75 |

**SI ZENTNER ORCHESTRA**
| 64 | Liberty LIB 10169 | The James Bond Theme/Bond's 007 Theme | 7 |
| 63 | Liberty LBY 1164 | RHYTHM PLUS BLUES (LP) | 15 |

**ZEPHYR**
| 70 | Probe SPB 1006 | ZEPHYR (LP) | 60 |
*(see also Tommy Bolin)*

**ZEPHYRS**
| 63 | Decca F 11647 | What's All That About/Oriental Dream | 40 |
| 64 | Columbia DB 7199 | I Can Tell/Sweet Little Baby | 50 |
| 64 | Columbia DB 7324 | A Little Bit Of Soap/No Message | 35 |
| 64 | Columbia DB 7410 | Wonder What I'm Gonna Do/Let Me Love You Baby | 35 |
| 65 | Columbia DB 7481 | She's Lost You/There's Something About You | 35 |
| 65 | Columbia DB 7571 | I Just Can't Take It/She Laughed | 35 |

**ZERO**
| 75 | BEEB 014 | Angels Theme/Truckin' | 5 |

**EARL ZERO**
| 78 | Studio 16 WE 401 | Rough And Tough/PRINCE JAZZBO: Suffer Must Live (12") | 30 |
| 79 | Sufferers Height SUF004 | Please Officer/PABLO: Moonlight City (12") | 50 |
| 79 | Greensleeves GRED 23 | City Of The Wicked/Rightous Works (12") | 40 |

| | | | |
|---|---|---|---|
| 79 | Student STU 007 | IN THE RIGHT WAY (LP) | 80 |

**ZERO FIVE**
| | | | |
|---|---|---|---|
| 65 | Columbia DB 7751 | Dusty/Just Like A Girl | 6 |

**ZERO LE CRECHE**
| | | | |
|---|---|---|---|
| 84 | Flicknife FLS 029 | Last Year's Wife/Women Say (p/s) | 15 |
| 84 | Flicknife FLST 029 | Last Year's Wife/Women Say/Fall To Dust (p/s) | 25 |
| 85 | Cherry Red CHERRY 87 | Falling/Beyond Westworld (p/s) | 10 |
| 85 | Cherry Red 12 CHERRY 87 | Falling/Beyond Westworld/Terminal Tracks (12", p/s) | 15 |

**ZERO 7**
| | | | |
|---|---|---|---|
| 00 | Ultimate Dilemma UDR | EP VOL. 1 (12") | 18 |
| 00 | Ultimate Dilemma UDR 040 | EP VOL. 2 (12") | 18 |
| 01 | Ultimate Dilemma UDRLP | SIMPLE THINGS (2-LP) | 30 |
| 04 | Ultimate Dilemma 5050467 0987 1 8 | WHEN IT FALLS (2-LP) | 30 |
| 06 | Ultimate Dilemma 5015011 2857 1 4 | THE GARDEN (2-LP, gatefold, inners) | 30 |

**ZERO TWENTY ONE**
| | | | |
|---|---|---|---|
| 81 | UK UK 201 | Pop Song (p/s) | 100 |

**ZERO ZERO**
| | | | |
|---|---|---|---|
| 79 | Interference INT 00 | Chinese Boys/Coup De Ville Dawn (p/s, 1000 only) | 8 |

**Z.E.R.O. PASS S.E.V.E.N.**
| | | | |
|---|---|---|---|
| 79 | Virgin VS 297 | Worry/Worry Two (p/s) | 5 |

**ZEROS**
| | | | |
|---|---|---|---|
| 77 | Small Wonder SMALL 2 | Hungry/Radio Fun | 20 |
| 79 | Rok ROK XV/XVI | What's Wrong With A Pop Group/ACTION REPLAY: Decisions (die-cut co. sleeve) | 20 |

**MONICA ZETTERLUND**
| | | | |
|---|---|---|---|
| 58 | Columbia DB 4246 | There's No You/Don't Be That Way | 15 |
| 59 | Columbia SEG 8015 | SWEDISH SWEET (EP) | 60 |
| 58 | Columbia 33CSX 20 | SWEDISH SENSATION (LP, export only) | 200 |
| 64 | Philips BL 7647 | MAKE MINE SWEDISH STYLE (LP) | 100 |

**Z'EV**
| | | | |
|---|---|---|---|
| 82 | Fetish FE 13 | Wipeout!/Element L. (p/s) | 10 |
| 88 | Coercion COERCIONLP 001 | THE INVISIBLE MAN (LP) | 25 |

**ZIMM & DEE DEE**
| | | | |
|---|---|---|---|
| 71 | Green Door GD 4006 | You've Got A Friend (actually by Winston Francis & Donna Hinds)/GROOVERS: Cheep | 7 |

*(see also Winston Francis)*

**TUCKER ZIMMERMAN**
| | | | |
|---|---|---|---|
| 69 | Regal Zonophone RZ 3020 | The Red Wind/Moondog | 25 |
| 69 | Regal Zono. (S)LRZ 1010 | TEN SONGS BY TUCKER ZIMMERMAN (LP) | 120 |
| 72 | Village Thing VTS 13 | TUCKER ZIMMERMANN (LP) | 70 |

**PETER ZINOVIEFF**
| | | | |
|---|---|---|---|
| 70 | 3M/Lyntone LYN 2443 | A Lollipop For Papa (1-sided with book) | 50 |
| 70 | 3M/Lyntone LYN 2443 | A Lollipop For Papa (1-sided without book) | 30 |

**ZION TRAIN**
| | | | |
|---|---|---|---|
| 99 | Universal Egg WWLP030 | LOVE REVOLUTIONARIES (2-LP) | 25 |

**ZIOR**
| | | | |
|---|---|---|---|
| 71 | Nepentha 6129 002 | Za Za Za Zilda/She's A Bad Bad Woman | 25 |
| 71 | Nepentha 6129 003 | Cat's Eyes/I Really Do | 20 |
| 71 | Nepentha 6437 005 | ZIOR (LP, gatefold sleeve) | 250 |

*(see also Monument, Cardboard Orchestra)*

**RB ZIPPER**
| | | | |
|---|---|---|---|
| 76 | Alaska ALA 2004 | Cruisin With The Fonz/Superstream | 6 |
| 77 | Alaska ALA 2006 | Come On Marriane/Lamplight Lady | 8 |

**ZIPPER (1)**
| | | | |
|---|---|---|---|
| 74 | Youngblood YB 170 | Streak Up And Down/Funk 74 | 30 |

**ZIPPER (2)**
| | | | |
|---|---|---|---|
| 79 | Spanking SRTS/79/CUS 278 SPANK 1 | The Life Of Riley/Treat Me Pretty | 10 |

**ZIPPERS**
| | | | |
|---|---|---|---|
| 64 | Hickory 45-1252 | My Sailor Boy/Pretend You're Still Mine | 15 |

**ZIPPS**
| | | | |
|---|---|---|---|
| 79 | Rip Off RIP 12 | Friends/Don't Tell The Detectives (die cut p/s) | 60 |

**ZIPS**
| | | | |
|---|---|---|---|
| 79 | Black Gold ZIPS1 | Take Me Down/Don't Be Pushed Around/I'm In Love Over and Over (500 only with A4 insert & 2 stickers) | 150 |
| 80 | Tenement Tunes TEN 01 | Radioactivity/I'm Not Impressed (p/s) | 30 |

**ZIPZ**
| | | | |
|---|---|---|---|
| 80 | Voyage VOY 14 | As I Pass You By/Tonight (p/s) | 10 |

**ZNR**
| | | | |
|---|---|---|---|
| 81 | Recommended RR 7 | BARRICADE 3 (LP) | 18 |

**ZODIAC**
| | | | |
|---|---|---|---|
| 68 | Elektra EKL 4009 | COSMIC SOUNDS (LP, also stereo EKS 74009) | 45 |

**ZODIACS**
| | | | |
|---|---|---|---|
| 57 | Oriole CB 1383 | Why Don't They Understand/The Game Of Love | 18 |
| 58 | Oriole CB 1432 | The Yum-Yum Song/Secrets | 10 |

**EMIL DEAN ZOGHBY**
| | | | |
|---|---|---|---|
| 70 | Polydor 2058 032 | Won't You Join Me/Misery Lane | 5 |

## ZAC ZOLAR & ELECTRIC BANANA
| | | | |
|---|---|---|---|
| 84 | Butt FUN 5 | Take Me Home/James Marshall | 5 |

*(see also Pretty Things, Phil May, Fenmen, Electric Banana)*

## ZOMBIES
| | | | |
|---|---|---|---|
| 64 | Decca F 11940 | She's Not There/You Make Me Feel Good | 10 |
| 64 | Decca F 12004 | Leave Me Be/Woman | 12 |
| 65 | Decca F 12072 | Tell Her No/What More Can I Do | 12 |
| 65 | Decca F 12125 | She's Coming Home/I Must Move | 15 |
| 65 | Decca F 12225 | Whenever You're Ready/I Love You | 15 |
| 65 | Decca F 12296 | Is This The Dream/Don't Go Away | 15 |
| 66 | Decca F 12322 | Remember You/Just Out Of Reach | 20 |
| 66 | Decca F 12426 | Indication/How We Were Before | 25 |
| 66 | Decca F 12495 | Gotta Get A Hold Of Myself/The Way I Feel Inside | 30 |
| 67 | Decca F 12584 | Goin' Out Of My Head/She Does Everything For Me | 25 |
| 68 | Decca F 12798 | I Love You/The Way I Feel Inside | 15 |
| 67 | CBS 2960 | Friends Of Mine/Beechwood Park | 60 |
| 67 | CBS 3087 | Care Of Cell 44/Maybe After He's Gone | 50 |
| 68 | CBS 3380 | Time Of The Season/I'll Call You Mine | 60 |
| 73 | Epic EPC 3380 | Time Of The Season/I'll Call You Mine (reissue) | 8 |
| 65 | Decca DFE 8598 | THE ZOMBIES (EP) | 125 |
| 65 | Decca LK 4679 | BEGIN HERE (LP) | 500 |
| 65 | RCA RD 7791 | BUNNY LAKE IS MISSING (LP, soundtrack) | 65 |
| 68 | CBS BPG 63280 | ODESSEY AND ORACLE (LP, mono) | 900 |
| 68 | CBS SBPG 63280 | ODESSEY AND ORACLE (LP, stereo) | 700 |
| 70 | Decca SPA 95 | THE WORLD OF THE ZOMBIES (LP) | 18 |
| 73 | Epic EPC 65728 | TIME OF THE ZOMBIES (2-LP) | 40 |

*(see also Unit Four Plus Two, Argent, Neil MacArthur, Colin Blunstone)*

## ZONES
| | | | |
|---|---|---|---|
| 78 | Zoom ZUM 4 | Stuck With You/No Angels (p/s) | 5 |
| 78 | Arista ARTIST 205 | Sign Of The Times/Away From It All (p/s) | 5 |

*(see also PVC 2)*

## ZOO
| | | | |
|---|---|---|---|
| 70 | Major Minor SMLP 74 | ZOO (LP) | 50 |
| 71 | Barclay 521172 | ZOO (LP) | 30 |

## ZOO BOUTIQUE
| | | | |
|---|---|---|---|
| 82 | Lightbeat LIGHT 006 | Forgive And Forget/Happy Families (p/s, clear vinyl) | 6 |

## ZOOKIE
| | | | |
|---|---|---|---|
| 77 | DJM DJS 10796 | Judie Judie Hold On/I Couldn't Be You | 8 |
| 78 | DJM DJS 10866 | Bubbles/Don't Rock Me | 8 |

*(see also Judie Tzuke, Tzuke & Paxo)*

## ZOOM CLUB
| | | | |
|---|---|---|---|
| 80 | Happy Face MM 130 | I Can't Compete/It's Not Fair (no p/s) | 100 |

## ZOOM LENS
| | | | |
|---|---|---|---|
| 80 | Negative NEG 1 | Side To Side/Running In Mazes (blue vinyl, p/s) | 25 |
| 84 | Negative NEG 2 | Welcome To China/Waxworks (p/s) | 25 |

## ZOOT ALORS
| | | | |
|---|---|---|---|
| 79 | Decca FR 13874 | Send Me A Postcard/It's A Crime | 40 |

## ZORKIE TWINS
| | | | |
|---|---|---|---|
| 80 | Skeleton SKL 006 | Mr. Simpson/From Now On (p/s) | 10 |

## ZORRO
| | | | |
|---|---|---|---|
| 79 | Bridgehouse BHEP 1 | 'Arrods Don't Sell 'Em/Soldier Boy/Starflight (with p/s) | 30 |
| 79 | Bridgehouse BHEP 1 | 'Arrods Don't Sell 'Em/Soldier Boy/Starflight | 10 |

## ZORRO FIVE
| | | | |
|---|---|---|---|
| 70 | Decca F 23042 | Reggae Shhh!/Reggae Meadowlands | 5 |

## ZOSKIA
| | | | |
|---|---|---|---|
| 84 | All The Madmen MAD 8 | Rape/Thank You (p/s) | 8 |
| 85 | Temple TOPY 005 | Be Like Me (12", p/s, transparent vinyl) | 12 |

## ZOSKIA MEETS SUGARDOG
| | | | |
|---|---|---|---|
| 84 | Temple TOPYS 021 | J.G. / `That's Heavy Baby | 10 |

## ZOUNDS
| | | | |
|---|---|---|---|
| 81 | Crass 4219844/3 | Can't Cheat Karma/War/Subvert (gatefold paper p/s, with poster) | 15 |
| 81 | Rough Trade RT 069 | Demystification/Great White Hunter (p/s) | 10 |
| 82 | Rough Trade RT 094 | Dancing/True Love (p/s) | 8 |
| 82 | Not So Brave NSB 001 | LA VACHE QUI RIT (EP, with poster) | 12 |
| 82 | Rough Trade RT 098 | More Trouble Coming Every Day/Knife (p/s) | 8 |
| 82 | Rough Trade ROUGH 31 | THE CURSE OF ZOUNDS (LP, inner) | 20 |

## ZOVIET-FRANCE
| | | | |
|---|---|---|---|
| 82 | Red Rhino RED 12 | ZOVIET-FRANCE (12" EP, printed hessian sleeve) | 60 |
| 83 | Red Rhino RED 23 | NORSCHE (LP) | 35 |
| 84 | Red Rhino RED 40 | MOHNOMISCHE (LP) | 35 |
| 84 | Red Rhino REDLP 45 | ELSTRE (LP) | 35 |
| 12 | Altvinyl AV040/ AV041.AV042 | 7.10/12 (box set of one clear vinyl 7", one clear vinyl 10" and one clear vinyl 12", 250 only) | 50 |

## ZOWLAS
| | | | |
|---|---|---|---|
| 67 | Amusicon SLE 12 | Honest I Do/Gonna Love My Baby | 12 |

## ZUIDERZEE
| | | | |
|---|---|---|---|
| 66 | CBS 202062 | (You're My) Soul And Inspiration/Please Don't Call Me | 10 |

MINT VALUE £

| | | | |
|---|---|---|---|
| 66 | CBS 202235 | Peace Of Mind/Provocative Child | 10 |

**TAPPA ZUKIE**

| | | | |
|---|---|---|---|
| 78 | Music Of The Most High MER 602 | Viego/Archie The Rednose (p/s) | 8 |
| 75 | Locks LOX 8 | Judge I O' Lord/LLOYDIE SLIM AND KING TUBBY: State Dub | 10 |
| 75 | Attack ATT 8110 | Natty Dread Don't Cry (as Topper Zukie)/TOMMY McCOOK : The Meducia | 8 |
| 77 | New Star DNEW 1 | What's Yours/Make Faith (12") | 25 |
| 77 | Achilles ACHILLES 54 | Liberation Struggle/Double Struggle | 10 |
| 73 | Count Shelly CSLP 04 | MAN A WARRIOR (LP) | 50 |
| 76 | Stars (No. Cat. No.) | TAPPA ZUKIE IN DUB (LP) | 100 |
| 76 | KLIK 9022 | M.P.L.A. (LP) | 15 |
| 78 | Virgin Frontline FL1006 | M.P.L.A. (LP, reissue) | 20 |
| 78 | Virgin Frontline FL1009 | PEACE IN THE GHETTO (LP) | 20 |
| 79 | Virgin Frontline FL1029 | TAPPA ZUKIE IN DUB (LP) | 20 |
| 79 | Virgin Frontline FL1032 | TAPPER ROOTS LP) | 15 |

**ZULU**

| | | | |
|---|---|---|---|
| 77 | Big Bear BB9 | Red Red Libanon/Okavanga Swamp | 15 |

**ZUM ZEAUX**

| | | | |
|---|---|---|---|
| 70s | Black Pig PUG1 | WOLF AT THE DOOR (LP) | 40 |

**ZUTONS**

| | | | |
|---|---|---|---|
| 04 | Deltasonic DLTLP019 | WHO KILLED...THE ZUTONS (LP, with 3D glasses) | 15 |

**ZWAN**

| | | | |
|---|---|---|---|
| 03 | Reprise 9362-48436-1 | MARY STAR OF THE SEA (2-LP) | 50 |

*(see also Smashing Pumpkins)*

**ZYGOAT**

| | | | |
|---|---|---|---|
| 74 | Polydor 2058 124 | Catching A Thief/Letitia's Song | 5 |
| 74 | Polydor 2383 270 | ELECTROPHON (LP) | 20 |

**ZZ**

| | | | |
|---|---|---|---|
| 88 | Kent 6T3 | PEGGY WOODS: Love Is Gonna Get You/ZZ: You Just Cheat And Lie | 20 |

**ZZEBRA**

| | | | |
|---|---|---|---|
| 74 | Polydor 2058 446 | Zardoz/Amusofi | 20 |
| 75 | Polydor 2058 579 | Mr. J/Put The Light On Me | 6 |
| 74 | Polydor 2383 296 | ZZEBRA (LP) | 15 |
| 75 | Polydor 2383 326 | PANIC (LP, with insert) | 18 |

*(see also John McCoy, Gillan)*

**ZZ TOP**

| | | | |
|---|---|---|---|
| 72 | London HLU 10376 | Francene/Down Brownie | 15 |
| 74 | London HLU 10458 | Beer Drinkers And Hell Raisers/La Grange | 12 |
| 75 | London HLU 10475 | La Grange/Just Got Paid | 10 |
| 75 | London HLU 10495 | Tush/Blue Jean Blues | 10 |
| 76 | London HLU 10538 | It's Only Love/Asleep In The Desert | 8 |
| 77 | London HLU 10547 | Arrested For Driving While Blind/Neighbour, Neighbour | 8 |
| 77 | London HLU 10547 | Arrested For Driving While Blind/Neighbour, Neighbour (mispressing, B-side plays Ray Charles' "I Can See Clearly Now") | 12 |
| 79 | Warner Bros K 17647 | Cheap Sunglasses/Esther Be The One | 5 |
| 80 | Warner Bros K 17576 | I Thank You/A Fool For Your Stockings (p/s) | 7 |
| 85 | Warner Bros W 2001F | Sleeping Bag/Party On The Patio//Sharp Dressed Man/I Got The Fix (p/s, sealed, stickered double pack) | 10 |
| 85 | Warner Bros W 2001P | Sleeping Bag/Party On The Patio (shaped pic-disc, part 1 of interlocking set) | 12 |
| 86 | Warner Bros W 2003FP | Rough Boy/Delirious (shaped pic-disc, part 3 of interlocking set, shrinkwrapped with bonus 12") | 30 |
| 86 | Warner Bros W 2003FP | Rough Boy/Delirious (shaped pic-disc, part 3 of interlocking set) | 20 |
| 11 | Warner Bros./Reprise 527517-7 | Just Got Paid/MASTODON: Just Got Paid (yellow vinyl, jukebox centre) | 6 |
| 71 | London PS 584 | ZZ TOP (LP, with inner sleeve) | 60 |
| 72 | London SH-U 8433 | RIO GRANDE MUD (LP, original issue) | 75 |
| 73 | London SH-U 8459 | TRES HOMBRES (LP, original issue) | 50 |
| 75 | London SH-U 8482 | FANDANGO! (LP, original issue) | 40 |
| 76 | London LDU 1 | TEJAS (LP, original foldout sleeve) | 40 |
| 83 | Warner Bros W 3774 | ELIMINATOR (LP, with bonus stickered p/s 12" "Legs [Metal Mix]") | 15 |
| 83 | Warner Bros W3774P | ELIMINATOR (LP, picture disc) | 20 |

# Various Artists

## VARIOUS ARTISTS EPs 50s/60s
### (alphabetical by title)

### A

| 62 | MGM MGMEP 768 | A VERY PRIVATE AFFAIR (includes Brigitte Bardot: Sidonie) | 80 |

### B

| 63 | Concert Hall BPC 712 | BEAT TIME (Timebeats/Charlie Young/Heartbeats) | 15 |
| 66 | Fontana TF 17469 | THE BIG FOUR (Dave Dee Dozy Beaky Mick & Tich/Spencer Davis Group/Mindbenders/Pretty Things) | 12 |
| 64 | Fontana TFE 18010 | BLOWIN' IN THE WIND (withdrawn; Bob Dylan/Joan Baez/Pete Seeger) | 100 |
| 64 | Pye Intl. NEP 44029 | THE BLUES VOL. 1 PT. 1 (John Lee Hooker/Muddy Waters/Sonny Boy Williamson/Jimmy Witherspoon) | 35 |
| 64 | Pye Intl. NEP 44035 | THE BLUES VOL. 1 PT. 2 (Howling Wolf/Buddy Guy/Little Walter/Muddy Waters) | 25 |
| 66 | Chess CRE 6011 | THE BLUES VOL. 2 PT. 1 (Otis Rush/Chuck Berry/John Lee Hooker/ Little Walter) | 25 |
| 64 | Pye Intl. NEP 44038 | BLUES FESTIVAL (Sugar Pie De Santo/Willie Dixon/Sonny Boy Williamson/ Howlin' Wolf) | 30 |
| 63 | Columbia SEG 8226 | BLUES ON PARADE NO. 1 (Jimmy Cotton/Brownie McGhee/ Roosevelt Sykes/Sonny Terry) | 25 |
| 56 | HMV 7EG 8178 | THE BLUES THEY SANG (Lizzie Miles/Billy Young & Jelly Roll Morton) | 20 |
| 63 | Fontana TFL 6037 | BLUES AT NEWPORT (LP) | 20 |

### C

| 63 | Cameo Parkway CPE 552 | CAMEO BIG FOUR (Bobby Rydell/Chubby Checker/Dovells/Orlons) | 20 |
| 60s | Heritage 105 | THE COUNTRY BLUES (99 only)o | 80 |

### D

| 60s | XX MIN 706 | DARK MUDDY BOTTOM (Jimmy Slim/Good Jelly Bess/Lightning Leon/ Little Red Walters/Willie B.) | 20 |
| 50s | Poydras 102 | DEPRESSION BLUES | 25 |
| 63 | Decca DFE 8520 | DISCS-A-GO GO (Karl Denver/Billy Fury/Jet Harris/Vernons Girls) | 50 |
| 60s | Jan & Dil JR 450 | DOWN HOME BLUES - SIXTIES STYLE (Lightning Leon/Jerry McCain/ Little Red Walters) | 30 |
| 60s | XX MIN 709 | DOWNHOME HARP (Kid Thomas/Eddie Hope/Jerry McCain) | 15 |
| 59 | Fontana TFE 17146 | DRUMBEAT (Lana Sisters/Adam Faith/Bob Miller & Millermen/ Sylvia Sands/Roy Young) | 40 |

### E

| 65 | Edinburgh S.C. ESC 02 | EDINBURGH STUDENTS CHARITIES APPEAL (33rpm, die-cut paper p/s; Athenians/Avengers/Ray & Archie Fisher/Lynn & Kathy) | 50 |
| 66 | Edinburgh S.C. ESC 03 | EDINBURGH STUDENTS CHARITIES APPEAL (33rpm, Athenians/Gear System/Old Bailey's Jazz Advocates) | 60 |
| 67 | Philips P 160E | EXQUISITE FORM (freebie; Dave Dee, Dozy, Beaky, Mick & Tich/Herd/ Walker Brothers/Dusty Springfield) | 12 |

### F

| 64 | Pye Intl. NEP 44030 | FESTIVAL OF THE BLUES NO. 1 (Willie Dixon/Buddy Guy/Muddy Waters/ Sonny Boy Williamson) | 20 |
| 63 | Decca DFE 8538 | FROM A LONDON HOOTENANNY (Davy Graham/Thamesiders) | 25 |

### G

| 59 | MGM MGM-EP 703 | GIRLS AND MORE GIRLS (June Allyson/Ava Gardner/Judy Garland/ Kathryn Grayson) | 10 |
| 67 | Down with the Game 202 | GOD DON'T LIKE IT (99 only) | 40 |
| 67 | Down with the Game 203 | GOD DON'T LIKE IT VOLUME 2 (99 only) | 40 |
| 60s | XX MIN 707 | GOING TO CALIFORNIA (Little Sonny Willis/Eddie Williams) | 15 |
| 66 | Pye Intl. NEP 45054 | THE GREATEST ON STAGE (Maxine Brown/Chuck Jackson/Shirelles/ Dionne Warwick) | 25 |
| 63 | London RE-U 1393 | GROUP OF GOODIES (Marcie Blane/Kokomo/Bill Black's Combo/ Ernie Maresca) | 50 |
| 59 | Mercury ZEP 10010 | GROUPS GALORE (Del Vikings/Mark IV/Diamonds/Hi-Liters) | 70 |

### H

| 66 | Pye NEP 24242 | THE HITMAKERS VOL. 2 (Chuck Berry/Kinks/Sue Thompson/Shangri-La's) | 30 |
| 66 | Pye Intl. NEP 44065 | HITMAKERS INTERNATIONAL (Fontella Bass/James Brown/Petula Clark/ Lovin' Spoonful) | 25 |
| 65 | Decca DFE 8649 | HITS VOL. 2 (Lulu/Chris Andrews/Marianne Faithfull/Fortunes) | 10 |
| 66 | Decca DFE 8663 | HITS VOL. 5 (Animals/Los Bravos/Alan Price Set/Small Faces) | 10 |
| 66 | Decca DFE 8667 | HITS VOL. 6 (Jonathan King/Lulu/Alan Price Set/Small Faces) | 10 |
| 62 | Mercury ZEP 10133 | HITSVILLE! (Brook Benton/Crew Cuts/Phil Philips/Diamonds) | 30 |
| 59 | Coral FEP 2034 | HITSVILLE VOL. 1 (Buddy Holly/McGuire Sisters/Betty Madigan/Billy Williams) | 60 |
| 59 | Coral FEP 2035 | HITSVILLE VOL. 2 (Lennon Sisters/Art Lund/Teresa Brewer/Jackie Wilson) | 50 |
| 65 | Tamla Motown TME 2001 | HITSVILLE U.S.A. NO. 1 (Marvin Gaye/Brenda Holloway/Carolyn Crawford/ Eddie Holland) | 110 |
| 66 | Post War Blues 100 | HOBOS AND DRIFTERS | 50 |

### I

| 65 | Chess CRE 6010 | IN CROWD (Radiants/Ramsey Lewis Trio/Little Milton/Billy Stewart) | 30 |

# J

| | | |
|---|---|---|
| 64 | Columbia SEG 8337 | JUST FOR YOU (Peter & Gordon/Freddie & Dreamers) ............................................... 15 |

# K

| | | |
|---|---|---|
| 63 | Lyntone LYN 347/348 | KEELE RAG RECORD (flexidisc; Rhythm Unlimited & Halettes/Keele Quintet)............... 18 |
| 64 | Lyntone LYN 508/509 | KEELE RAG RECORD NO. 2 (flexidisc; Escorts/Lance Harvey & Kingpins/ Keele Row; some in die-cut sleeve) ........................................................................................... 35 |
| 65 | Lyntone LYN 765/766 | KEELE RAG RECORD (flexidisc; Bob Wilson/Changing Times/ Lance Harvey & Kingpins/ Incas) ....................................................................................................................... 40 |
| 61 | RCA Victor RCX 203 | KINGS OF THE BLUES VOL. 2 (Jazz Gillum/Big Maceo/Washboard Sam/ Sonny Boy Williamson) .................................................................................................................. 20 |
| 61 | RCA Victor RCX 204 | KINGS OF THE BLUES VOL. 3 (Arthur Big Boy Crudup/Furry Lewis/ Poor Joe Williams) ..25 |
| 59 | Top Rank 45-TR 5004 | KING SIZE (maxi-single; Craig Douglas/Sheila Buxton/Bert Weedon) .......................... 10 |
| 60 | Warner Bros WEP 6010 | KOOKIE STARS OF SEVENTY SEVEN SUNSET STRIP (Joannie Sommers/Eddie Byrne/ Connie Stevens) ...................................................................................................... 10 |
| 66 | Holyground HG 111 | THE LAST THING ON MY MIND (EP, 99 copies only) ................................................... 90 |
| 59 | Top Rank JKR 8008 | LET'S GO NO. 1 (Jimmy Lee/Johnny Hines/Treetoppers) ........................................... 35 |
| 59 | Top Rank JKR 8012 | LET'S GO NO. 2 (Johnny Hines/Billy Mack/Victors/Ted & Ray) ................................... 35 |
| 60 | Philips BBE 12414/ | LET'S MAKE LOVE - FILM SOUNDTRACK (Yves Montand/Marilyn Monroe/ Frankie Vaughan; stereo) ..................................................................................................... 40 |
| 63 | Embassy WEP 1104 | LIVERPOOL BEAT (Typhoons/Mike Redway/Ray Pilgrim/Bobby Stevens) ..................... 10 |
| 57 | London RE-D 1075 | LONDON HIT PARADE NO. 1 (Tab Hunter/Hilltoppers/Pat Boone/ Fontane Sisters)........ 25 |
| 57 | London RE-P 1096 | LONDON HIT PARADE NO. 2 (Fats Domino/Slim Whitman/Ken Copeland/ Roy Brown) ................................................................................................................... 100 |
| 58 | London RE-D 1097 | LONDON HIT PARADE NO. 3 (Pat Boone/Gale Storm/Tab Hunter/Jim Lowe)................ 25 |
| 58 | London RE-D 1130 | LONDON HIT PARADE NO. 4 (Pat Boone/Nick Todd/ Bonnie Guitar/Hilltoppers) ........... 25 |
| 58 | London RE-D 1136 | LONDON TOPPERS NO. 2 (export issue; Pat Boone/Nick Todd/Tab Hunter/ Jim Lowe) .. 25 |
| 58 | London RE-P 1137 | LONDON TOPPERS NO. 3 (export issue; Slim Whitman/Fats Domino/ Ricky Nelson/ Ernie Freeman) .......................................................................................................... 60 |
| 58 | London RE-D 1145 | LONDON HIT PARADE NO. 5 (Pat Boone/Fontane Sisters/Frank De Rosa) .................... 20 |

# M

| | | |
|---|---|---|
| 59 | Jazz Collector JEL 2 | THE MALE BLUES VOL. 1 (Georgia Slim/Walter Roland) ............................................. 25 |
| 59 | Jazz Collector JEL 4 | THE MALE BLUES VOL. 3 (Blind Blake/Ramblin' Thomas) .......................................... 25 |
| 59 | Jazz Collector JEL 5 | THE MALE BLUES VOL. 4 (Tall Tom/Pinewood Tom)................................................. 25 |
| 59 | Jazz Collector JEL 8 | THE MALE BLUES VOL. 5 (Blind Lemon Jefferson/Buddy Boy Hawkins) ...................... 25 |
| 60 | Jazz Collector JEL 10 | THE MALE BLUES VOL. 6 (Hound Head Henry/Frankie Jaxon)..................................... 25 |
| 60 | Jazz Collector JEL 13 | THE MALE BLUES VOL. 7 (Blind Lemon Jefferson/Ed Bell) ......................................... 25 |
| 61 | Jazz Collector JEL 24 | THE MALE BLUES VOL. 8 (Blind Lemon Jefferson/Leadbelly) ..................................... 25 |
| 69 | Middle Earth MDE 201 | MIDDLE EARTH SAMPLER (WRITING ON THE WALL: Aries/WOODEN O: Overture/ ARCADIUM: Poor Lady) (promo only, 33rpm, no p/s)................................................ 80 |
| 60s | Jan & Dil TR 451 | MORE DOWN HOME BLUES (Good Jelly Boss/Juke Boy Bonner/ Papa Lightfoot/ Snooky Prior) ........................................................................................................... 30 |
| 64 | Stateside SE 1021 | MOVIE MUSIC (John Barry/Artie Butler/Eddie Heywood/Bill Ramal Combo)................. 0 |

# N

| | | |
|---|---|---|
| 56 | Vogue EPV 1106 | NEGRO SPIRITUALS (Original Five Blind Boys/Sensational Nightingales) ...................... 18 |
| 64 | Vocalion EPVP 1271 | NEGRO SPIRITUALS (Dixie Hummingbirds/Sensational Nightingales) .......................... 18 |
| 64 | Vocalion EPVP 1276 | NEGRO SPIRITUALS (Five Blind Boys/Spirits Of Memphis)......................................... 18 |
| 66 | Tamla Motown TME 2014 | NEW FACES FROM HITSVILLE (Jimmy Ruffin/Chris Clark & Lewis Sisters/ Tammi Terrell/Monitors) ...................................................................................................... 350 |

# O

| | | |
|---|---|---|
| 65 | Columbia SEG 8413 | ON THE SCENE (Downliners Sect/Animals/Cherokees/Cheynes/ Georgie Fame/ Yardbirds) ................................................................................................................ 150 |
| 63 | MGM MGM-EP 787 | ORIGINAL HITS (Tommy Edwards/Johnny Ferguson/Jimmy Jones/ Conway Twitty)....... 30 |
| 63 | London RE-K 1390 | THE ORIGINAL HITS (Drifters/Ritchie Barrett/Coasters/Ben E. King).......................... 40 |
| 65 | Atlantic AET 6006 | ORIGINAL HITS VOL. 2 (Barbara Lewis/Coasters/Solomon Burke/Drifters) ................. 40 |
| 62 | Ember EMB 4522 | ORIGINAL RHYTHM AND BLUES HITS (Jesse Belvin/Ray Charles/ Linda Hayes/Jimmy McCracklin/Johnny Moore Blazers) ........................................................................... 75 |
| 55 | Pye Jazz NJE 1043 | ORIGINS OF SKIFFLE (Isla Cameron/Guy Carawan/Peggy Seeger)............................. 20 |

# P

| | | |
|---|---|---|
| 58 | Pye NSEP 85000 | POPS GO STEREO (Marion Ryan/Tony Osborne Orch./Bill Shepherd Orch.)................... 20 |

# R

| | | |
|---|---|---|
| 67 | Action ACT 002 EP | RAG GOES MAD AT THE MOJO (33rpm; Joe Cocker's Blues Band/ Tangerine Ayr Band/ Pitiful Souls/Delroy Good Good Band).......................................................................... 50 |
| 56 | Vogue EPV 1113 | RHYTHM AND BLUES (Dominoes/Swallows) ............................................................ 300 |
| 63 | Stateside SE 1008 | RHYTHM AND BLUES (Jimmy Reed/John Lee Hooker) .............................................. 40 |
| 64 | Stateside SE 1009 | R&B CHARTMAKERS (Martha/Vandellas/Miracles/Marvin Gaye/Marvelettes) ............ 100 |
| 64 | Stateside SE 1018 | R&B CHARTMAKERS NO. 2 (Miracles/Kim Weston/Supremes/Marvelettes) ............... 125 |
| 64 | Stateside SE 1022 | R&B CHARTMAKERS NO. 3 (Marvin Gaye/Darnells/Eddie Holland/ Martha & Vandellas) .............................................................................................................. 125 |
| 64 | Stateside SE 1025 | R&B CHARTMAKERS NO. 4 (Supremes/Eddie Holland/Temptations/Contours) .......... 120 |
| 60 | Vogue EPV 1198 | RHYTHM AND BLUES CONCERT (Helen Humes/Jimmy Witherspoon)......................... 80 |
| 64 | Pye Intl. NEP 44021 | RHYTHM AND BLUES SHOWCASE VOL. 1 (Don & Bob/Dale Hawkins/ Clarence Henry/ Larry Williams) .......................................................................................................... 30 |
| 64 | Pye Intl. NEP 44022 | RHYTHM AND BLUES SHOWCASE VOL. 2 (Jimmy McCracklin/ Muddy Waters/Little Walter/Howlin' Wolf) ................................................................................................. 30 |
| 57 | Vogue VE 170111 | ROCK AND ROLL (Mister Google Eyes August/Louis Jones Rock & Roll Band/Walter Price Rock & Roll Band/Clarence Gatemouth Brown) .................................................. 80 |
| 60 | Top Rank JKP 2060 | RUSHING FOR PERCUSSION (Preston Epps/Sandy Nelson) ....................................... 20 |

# S

| 60s | S.A.U.C.C. PR 5462 | ST. ANDREWS UNIVERSITY CHARITIES CAMPAIGN (20th Century Sounds/ Steve Hall & Roosters/Black Ring; no p/s) | 35 |
|---|---|---|---|
| 64 | Lyntone LYN 738/739 | SHEFFIELD UNIVERSITY RAG RECORD (flexidisc; Vantennas/Dave Allen Band/ Addy Street Five/Los Caribos; die-cut sleeve) | 40 |
| 55 | Columbia SEG 7528 | SHOUT FOR JOY (Pete Johnson/Albert Ammons/Meade Lux Lewis) | 30 |
| 63 | London RE-P 1403 | SINGING THE BLUES (Ernie K-Doe/Showmen/Jesse Hill/Chris Kenner) | 100 |
| 58 | Decca DFE 6485 | SIX FIVE SPECIAL (Jackie Dennis/Joan Regan/Diane Todd/Dickie Valentine) | 20 |
| 65 | Keele Rag/Lyntone | SOUNDS OF SAVILE (flexidisc; Hipster Image/London Apprentices/ Tom & Brennie; some in die-cut title sleeve) | 60 |
| 60 | Mercury ZEP 10088 | SURPRISE PACKAGE (Ben Hewitt/Diamonds) | 80 |
| 59 | Top Rank JKR 8007 | SWEET BEAT (Lee Allen Band/Fred Parris/Cindy Mann/Mellokings) | 50 |

# T

| 63 | Oriole EP 7080 | TAKE SIX (Mark Peters' Silhouettes/Ian & Zodiacs/Faron's Flamingos/Earl Preston & T.T.s/Rory Storm & Hurricanes/Sonny Wade & Cascades) | 40 |
|---|---|---|---|
| 59 | Mercury ZEP 10015 | TEAR IT UP (Boyd Bennett Orchestra/Red Prysock/Hi-Liters) | 50 |
| 57 | Mercury MEP 9522 | TEEN-AGE ROCK (Red Prysock/Rusty Draper/Chuck Miller/Crew Cuts) | 50 |
| 58 | RCA RCX 111 | TEENAGE TOPS (Ray Peterson/Jimmy Dell/Marlin Greene/Barry De Vorzon) | 40 |
| 64 | Ember EMB 4540 | TEEN SCENE '64 (Dave Clark Five/Ray Singer/Washington D.C.s) | 30 |
| 60 | Heritage RE 102 | THAT COUNTRY ROCK (with Walter Hawkins & William Moore, 99 copies only) | 30 |
| 58 | Brunswick OE 9425 | THEY SOLD A MILLION No. 9 (Bobby Helms/Four Aces/Jerry Lewis/ Kitty Kallen) | 15 |
| 65 | Century 21 MA 105 | T.V. CENTURY 21 THEMES (David Graham/Sylvia Anderson/Peter Dyneley/ Barry Gray Orchestra/Gary Miller/Eric Winstone Orchestra) | 15 |
| 64 | Decca DFE 8585 | T.V. THEMES (Andrew Oldham Orchestra/Ted Heath Music/ Ron Grainer Music/Cyril Stapleton Orchestra) | 40 |
| 62 | Starlite STEP 31 | TWIST OFF (Wayne Farmer/Medallions/Charles Perrywell/Piano Slim/ Teenbeats/ Dellos) | 50 |
| 62 | Starlite STEP 29 | TWIST ON (Mighty Trojans/Dee Dee Gaudet/Dixie Lee/ Percy & The Rocking Aces) | 40 |

# W

| 69 | Apple CT 1 | WALLS ICE CREAM PRESENTS (Mary Hopkin/Iveys/Jackie Lomax/ James Taylor; with/ without p/s) | 50 |
|---|---|---|---|
| 65 | Liberty LEP 4036 | WE SING THE BLUES (Jesse Hill/Ernie K. Doe/Aaron Neville/Benny Spellman) | 65 |
| 64 | Fontana TFE 18009 | WITH GOD ON OUR SIDE (withdrawn; Bob Dylan/Joan Baez/Pete Seeger) | 100 |
| 66 | Chess CRE 6009 | WITH THE BLUES (Eddie Boyd Blues Combo/Buddy Guy) | 40 |

# Y

| 64 | Fontana TFE 18011 | YE PLAYBOYS AND PLAYGIRLS (withdrawn; Bob Dylan/Joan Baez/ Pete Seeger) | 100 |
|---|---|---|---|
| 68 | Chess CRE 6026 | YOUR CHESS REQUESTS (Fontella Bass/Tony Clarke/Mitty Collier/ Billy Stewart) | 40 |

## VARIOUS ARTISTS SINGLES & EPs 70s/80s/90s/00s

# V

| 79 | Pink BRS 002/INK 1000 | THE VOXHALL TRACKS - LUTON (Klips/Para-Noia/Tee Vees/Friction (multifold p/s, 1000 only) | 50 |
|---|---|---|---|

# A

| 92 | ART 2.1 | THE PHILOSOPHY OF SOUND AND MACHINE EP 1 (12") | 12 |
|---|---|---|---|
| 87 | SAM 4 | ADONIS: No Way Back (Club Mix)/ADONIS : No Way Back (Mix)/HERCULES: 7 Ways To Jack/MR. FINGERS: Can You Feel It (12", Promo only) | 30 |
| 91 | ART 1 | APPLIED RHYTHMIC TECHNOLOGY (12" EP) | 25 |
| 92 | ART 2.1 | THE PHILOSOPHY OF SOUND AND MACHINE EP 2 (12") | 15 |
| 98 | Twisted Nerve TN 003 | ALL OAR NOTHING (10", p/s; Badly Drawn Boy/Mum & Dad/Dakota Oak/ Sirconical/ Andy Votel) | 15 |
| 84 | Relegated | ARISTOCRAP (p/s; Pulex Irritans/Seventh Plague/Vendetta) | 10 |
| 80 | Deleted DEP 002 | ANGST IN MY PANTS (2x7", fold-out numbered sleeve, Instant Automatons/Door & The Window/Mic Woods/Midnight Circus/012/Digital Dinosaurs/Missing Persons, etc) | 50 |

# B

| 82 | Secret SHH 138 | BACK ON THE STREETS EP | 10 |
|---|---|---|---|
| 83 | Secret SHH 138 | BACK ON THE STREET (p/s; Skin Disease/Angela Rippon's Bum/Venom/ Strike/East End Badoes) | 12 |
| 87 | Other OTH 6 | BATTLEAXE (p/s; Black Riders/Holosade/Kes/Teacher's Pet) | 30 |
| 78 | Good Vibrations GOT 7 | BATTLE OF THE BANDS (double pack, no'd p/s; Idiots/Rudi/Outcasts/Spider) | 25 |
| 95 | Ka-boom KA-BOOM 1 | BIG BOLLOCKED BONFIRE BLOW-UP (Hood, et al.) | 12 |
| 80 | Vinyl Drip DRIP 001 | BLACKPOOL ROX (p/s; Membranes/Section 25/Syntax/Kenneth Turner Set) | 8 |
| 79 | Skeleton SKL 002 | THE BLANK TAPES VOL. 1 (folded p/s; Attempted Moustache/Junk Act/ Geisha Girls/ Zorkie Twins) | 8 |
| 81 | Secret SHH 126 | BOLLOCKS TO CHRISTMAS (p/s; Business/4-Skins/Gonads/Max Splodge) | 30 |
| 80s | Secret | BRITANNIA WAIVES THE RULES (12", p/s; Exploited/Chron Gen/Infa Riot) | 12 |
| 80 | Crass 421984/5 | BULLSHIT DETECTOR (12", p/s; A.P.F. Brigade/Alternative/Amebix/ Clockwork Criminals/Counter Attack/Crass/Frenzy Battalion/Fuck The CIA/ | 0 |

# C

| 95 | Orange ORANGE 001 | CARMIHOOD (Hood/Carmine) | 8 |
|---|---|---|---|
| 15 | Capitol/Back To Black 535 724-6 | CAPITOL NORTHERN SOUL 7s BOX | 45 |
| 98 | Twisted Nerve TNXMS 1 | CHRISTMAS STOCKING FILLER (Badly Drawn Boy/Dakota Oak/Sirconical/Mum & Dad/ Elbow) (green vinyl in green wraparound sleeve or red vinyl in red sl.) | 25 |
| 98 | Twisted Nerve TNXM 025 | CHRISTMAS STOCKING FILLER 2 (10", p/s; Andy Votel/D.O.T./Lost Children's Desk/ Misty Dixon/Cherrystones) | 8 |
| 80s | No Future | A COUNTRY FIT FOR HEROES (12", p/s) | 12 |

| 80s | No Future | | A COUNTRY FIT FOR HEROES VOL. 2 (12", p/s) | 20 |
|---|---|---|---|---|
| 94 | Fierce Panda NING 02 | | CRAZED AND CONFUSED (p/s; Supergrass/Ash et al.) | 12 |
| 80 | Newtown NTP 1 | | CRIME DECK: Arms Race/BASIC UNIT: Ladder//BEAT NECESSITY: Just FIne/STORY SO FAR: Radiated (p/s) | 100 |

## D

| 71 | Dandelion DS 7001 | | DANDELION (die-cut sleeve; Principal Edwards Magic Theatre/Stackwaddy/ Siren/The Way We Live) | 15 |
|---|---|---|---|---|
| 92 | Delirious DELIS 6 | | DELIRIOUS PRIME CUTS VOL. 1 (12"; The Moog/Hardcore Rhythm Team/Justice And Mercy) | 40 |
| 01 | Trunk WWW 1 | | DIRTY FAN MAIL (7", white vinyl) | 20 |
| 12 | Fruits De Mer Crustacean 22 | | DO NOT ADJUST YOUR SET EP (purple vinyl) | 15 |

## E

| 79 | Fast Products FAST 9B | | EARCOM 2 (12", p/s; Joy Division/Thursdays/Basczax) | 40 |
|---|---|---|---|---|
| 97 | Fat Cat 12FAT 003 | | 8. 8.5, 9 (12", custom sleeve) | 10 |
| 99 | Lowlife LOW8 | | EASTER ISLAND (EP, 750 only) | 15 |
| 10 | Fruits De Mer Crustacean 15 | | EDDIE COCHRAN INSTRUMENTALS EP | 25 |
| 78 | Stiff FREEBIE 2 | | EXCERPTS FROM STIFF'S GREATEST HITS (promo only sampler, 33rpm) | 10 |
| 96 | Mo' Wax MWEX 001-010 | | EXCURSIONS (10 x 12", box set; the Prunes/IO/Olde Scottish/David Caron/DJ Solo & DJ Aura/Midnight Funk Assoc./Stasis/Solo feat. JT/Twig Bud/DJ Shadow) | 30 |
| 99 | AI AI 001 | | EXPERIMENTS IN COLOUR (12"; Normal/Cell/Fil) | 20 |

## F

| 78 | Factory FAC 2 | | A FACTORY SAMPLE (double pack, p/s, in plastic bag, with 5 stickers; Joy Division/ Cabaret Voltaire/Durutti Column/John Dowie; | 200 |
|---|---|---|---|---|
| 95 | 555 5X555 | | 5x555 (5x7" box set; Boyracer/Mike Nichols And His Excellency/Amy Linton & Stewart Anderson/Father/Hood) | 30 |
| 91 | Fontana FONT 1 | | THE FONTANA SINGLES BOX SET VOLUME 1 - HITS AND RARITIES (12-single box set, with 12 inserts) | 30 |
| 91 | Fontana FONT 2 | | THE FONTANA SINGLES BOX SET VOLUME 2 - HITS AND RARITIES (12-single box set, with 12 inserts) | 30 |
| 79 | Heartbeat PULSE 4 | | 4 ALTERNATIVES (p/s; 48 Hours/Joe Public/Numbers/X-Certs) | 15 |
| 80 | Con (no cat. no.) | | THE FOUR EPs (cassette; Mark Perry et al.) | 15 |
| 96 | Ché CHE 059 | | 4 TRACK 3 BAND TOUR EP (p/s, Mogwai/Urusei Yatsura/Backwater, 50 only) | 25 |
| 96 | Mosquito MSQ 05 | | FRESH AS YOU FUCKIN' LIKE (12"; Paul Hannah/Russ Gabriel/Steve Patton/ Cristian Vogel/Si Begg) | 15 |
| 11 | Fruits De Mer Crustacean 16 | | THE FRUITS DE MER ANNUAL 2011 (2x7") | 20 |
| 11 | Fruits De Mer Crustacean 23 | | FRUITS DE MER ANNUAL 2012 (2x7", p/s) | 20 |

## G

| 83 | Mouth MOUTH 1 | | G-FORCE (Shady Deal/Dead Loss/Blythe Rocket/Egypt) | 20 |
|---|---|---|---|---|
| 70 | Village Thing VTSX 1000 | | THE GREAT WHITE DAP (Wizz Jones/Sun Also Rises/Ian A. Anderson/ Pigsty Hill Light Orchestra) | 20 |

## H

| 06 | Trojan TJBX 330 | | HAUNTED HOUSE - SKINHEAD SEVENS BOXSET (8 x 7") | 40 |
|---|---|---|---|---|
| 80 | Groucho Marxist | | HA! HA! FUNNY POLIS (PAISLEY ROCKS AGAINST RACISM) (p/s; Defiant Pose/Fegs/ Urban Enemies/XS Discharge) | 20 |
| 71 | Abreaction ABR 001 | | HART ROCK (Brass Alley/Yellow/Trilogy/Lucas Tyson) (no p/s) | 20 |

## I

| 78 | Radar SAM 88 | | INTERNATIONAL ARTISTS (13th Floor Elevators/Red Crayola/ Lost & Found/Golden Dawn; Red Crayola Hope & Anchor gig freebie | 0 |
|---|---|---|---|---|
| 74 | Galbraith POT 1 | | It's A Gas/Put In A Potterton (features 'The Goodies' on B-side) | 6 |

## L

| 11 | Sanctuary | | LUCKY SEVENS (7 x 7" box set of Trojan reissues, insert) | 30 |
|---|---|---|---|---|
| 79 | Decca FR 13864 | | THE LONDON BOYS (p/s; David Bowie/Small Faces/Birds/Dobie Gray) | 10 |
| 73 | Ronco MR EP 001 | | LONG LIVE ROCK (no p/s; Billy Fury/Eugene Wallace/Wishful Thinking) | 15 |

## M

| 88 | Record Mirror SURE 1 | | Megablast Rap Version | 6 |
|---|---|---|---|---|
| 71 | Track 2094 011 | | MAXI TRACK RECORD (John's Children/Crazy World Of Arthur Brown/ Thunderclap Newman/Jimi Hendrix; withdrawn blue sleeve crediting | 0 |
| 71 | Track 2094 011 | | MAXI TRACK RECORD (John's Children/Crazy World Of Arthur Brown/ Thunderclap Newman/Jimi Hendrix; red & white sleeve with press pack, | 0 |
| 97 | Begg. Banquet Random 2.1 | | METAL (12", red vinyl promo, die-cut sleeve, 1200 only; Robert Armani) | 10 |
| 97 | V/VM VVMT4 | | MISSINGTOE & WHINE (EP, 500 only) | 15 |
| 99 | Twisted Nerve TN 009 | | MODERN MUSIC FOR MOTORCYCLES (10" EP, some on yellow vinyl; Dakota Oak/ Alfie/Sirconical & Andy Votel/Mum & Dad/Badly Drawn Boy) | 15 |
| 79 | JSP JSP 4504 | | MORE BANDERA ROCKABILLIES (p/s) | 12 |
| 95 | Fierce Panda NING 15 | | MORTAL WOMBAT (double pack, p/s; Super Furry Animals/Baby Bird/ Panda/Mexican Pets/Harvey's Rabbit/Spare Snare) | 8 |
| 75 | Happy Time HT12 | | MUSIC FROM THUNDERBIRDS AND DOCTOR WHO (p/s) | 8 |
| 80 | EMI 12EMI 5074 | | MUTHA'S PRIDE (12", p/s; Wildfire/Quartz/White Spirit/Baby Jane) | 20 |

## N

| 98 | Lowlife LOW6 | | 98 Series Vol. 1 (EP) | 15 |
|---|---|---|---|---|
| 98 | Lowlife LOW7 | | 98 Series Vol. 2 (EP) | 15 |
| 80 | Neutron NT 003 | | 1980! THE FIRST FIFTEEN MINUTES EP (gatefold p/s with inserts; Vice Versa/Clock DVA/I'm So Hollow/Stunt Kites) | 15 |

## O

| 82 | Neat NEAT 25 | ONE TAKE NO DUBS (12", p/s; Black Rose/Hellanbach/Alien/Avenger) | 12 |

## P

| 80s | A&M A&M PARTY 1/2/3/4/5/6 | THE PARTY PARTY PACK (6 x 7", with picture sleeves, in PVC outer sleeve; Sting/Pauline Black/Dave Edmunds/Midge Ure/Modern Romance/Bad Manners/ | 20 |
| 80s | Pink & Black | PINK 'N' BLACK VOL 1 (p/s, re-issue of 1950's Rock 'n' Roll | 10 |
| 80 | L'Aventure SNS 001 | THE POTENT HUMAN EP (p/s, different coloured sleeves) | 30 |
| 97 | V/VM VVMT4 | PRIVILEGED FRAMES FOR REFERENCE (12" EP, p/s, 450 only) | 15 |

## R

| 93 | Raptor RAP 1 | RAPTOR PRESENTS . . . (12", p/s, 500 only; Ash/Buttlip/Marrow Bone/Fat) | 40 |
| 91 | Ptolemaic Terrascope POT 8 | RED FLIPPER (no p/s, Nurse With Wound/The Underworlde/Caravan Of Dreams) | 20 |
| 94 | Fierce Panda NING 03 | RETURN TO SPLENDOUR (double pack in foldover p/s with insert in poly bag, 1,000 only; Bluetones et al.) | 5 |
| 77 | Rollercoaster RRCEP 00002 | ROCKABILLY HOP (test pressings only) | 12 |
| 83 | Consett Music Project RD 1 | ROCK AND DOLE (Obnoxious Tartus/Decade Waltz/Task Force/Hot Banana) | 25 |

## S

| 95 | Atol ATOL 02 | S4C MAKES ME WANT TO SMOKE CRACK VOL. 1 (500 only, Catatonia et al.) | 8 |
| 80 | Sonic Int. S14283 | SEX, VIOLENCE & ETERNAL TRUTH (Lost Boys/What To Wear/The Venom/The Dodos, oversized poster sleeve, 4 A5 inserts, 250 only, stickered white labels, stamped plain white inner sleeve) | 125 |
| 94 | Fierce Panda/ | SHAGGING IN THE STREETS (double pack, wraparound p/s in poly bag, 1,000 only; SMASH/Blessed Ethel/Mantaray/Done Lying Down/ | 0 |
| 93 | Duophonic DS 45-05/06 | SHIMMIES IN SUPER 8 (double pack, 1 disc green vinyl, other white vinyl, numbered in poly bag, 800 with tri-foldout p/s, 400 also with sticker | 0 |
| 95 | Enraptured RAPT 4502 | SILVER APPLES TRIBUTE (10", 12 in hand-drawn sleeve; Windy & Carl/Scaredycat/Third Eye Foundation/Flowchart/Sabine | 30 |
| 86 | Broken Flag BF F1 | THE SOFT VOLCANO ERUPTS (flexidisc; Controlled Bleeding/Kehamas Curse/Uncommunity/Nails Of Christ/Cananes/Ramleh) | 10 |
| 79 | Groucho Marxist WH 1 | SPECTACULAR COMMODITY (p/s; Mental Errors/Mod Cons/ Poems/Sneex/XS Discharge) | 10 |
| 70s | Stiff BUY 1-10 | STIFF BOX SET NO. 1 (10 x 7" box set) | 35 |
| 70s | Stiff BUY 11-20 | STIFF BOX SET NO. 2 (10 x 7" box set) | 35 |
| 73 | Nice DCL 773 | SUBBUTEO SOUND EP | 12 |
| 01 | Edel 0128655ERESA | SUBSTITUTE EP : THE SONGS OF THE WHO (white vinyl, promo) | 60 |

## T

| 90s | Enraptured RAPT 4513 | TERRASCOPE/TERRASTOCK (Bevis Frond/Damon & Naomi/Flying Saucer Attack/Silver Apples) | 12 |
| 83 | White Noise WN 3 | THIS IS WHITE NOISE (p/s; Skrewdriver/Brutal Attack/Die Hards/A.B.H.) | 60 |
| 02 | Warner Bros 50466 13441 | TOP-DECK SKA 45'S BOX (8 x 7"s, coloured vinyl in cardboard box) | 25 |
| 82 | Total Noise TOT 1 | TOTAL NOISE # 1 (Business/Blitz/Dead Generation/Gonads) | 10 |

## U

| 80s | Fierce FRIGHT/SFTRI 38 | AN UNHOLY MONTAGE (200 only [100 U.K./100 U.S.], coloured vinyl with numbered insert) | 25 |
| 98 | Wurlitzer JUKEBOX 37 | UNITED IN THE HATRED OF (676 only, 176 in embossed sleeve) | 6 |
| 96 | V/VM VVMT1 | UPLINK DATA TRANSMISSIONS (12" EP, with 'data sheets', 250 only) | 20 |

## W

| 80 | Fuck Off FEP 001 | WEIRD NOISE (p/s, white labels; Danny & Dressmakers/The Door & The Window/Instant Automatons/012/Sell-Outs) | 10 |
| 77 | MPL MPL 1 | WE'VE MOVED! (Wings/Gene Vincent/Frank Sinatra et al., promo only excerpts sampler, some with press pack) | 175 |
| 84 | Rather/Seventeen | WHAT A NICE WAY TO TURN SEVENTEEN NO. 2 (p/s; Swell Maps & others; with magazine) | 12 |

## Y

| 80s | Wonderful World Of WOW 1 | YOU ARE NOT ALONE (p/s, with insert; Oi Polloi/Hex/Stalag 17/Symbol Of Freedom) | 15 |

## UNTITLED EPs & SINGLES 50s-00s

| 60s | Coxsone SCE 1 | (no p/s, 33rpm; Gaylads/Hugh Godfrey/Glen & Dave/Roy Richards/ Cables/Richard Ace) | 75 |
| 63 | Embassy WEP 1086 | (p/s; Mike Redway/Bud Ashton Group/Rory Pilgrim) | 15 |
| 69 | De Wolfe | (Lemon Dips, et al.) | 75 |
| 73 | Buddah 2011 164 | (Shangri-La's/Tradewinds/Ad Libs) | 6 |
| 94 | Kennel Club VTDOG 10 | (Strangelove/Tindersticks/God Machine/Breed (10", numbered, 1,500 only, free with Purr magazine issue 2) | 10 |
| 98 | Fat Cat 12FAT 008 | REMIXES (12", custom sleeve; remixes of Fat Cat 12FAT 003 by Autechre et al.) | 12 |
| 94 | Kennel Club VTDOG 10 | TINDERSTICKS: Girl On Death Row/STRANGELOVE: Wolf's Story/GOD MACHINE: The Devil Song/BREED: Diamonds Are Forever (10", numbered p/s, free with | 15 |
| 96 | SKAM MASK 1 | UNTITLED (12", custom sleeve, 100 only; Freeform/Funkstorung/ Boards Of Canada/Jega) | 150 |
| 97 | SKAM MASK 2 | UNTITLED (12", custom sleeve, 350 only; Hellinterface/Funkstorung/Bola/ Jega/Intron) | 75 |
| 98 | Mosquito MSQ 012.5 | (10"; Si Begg/Blue Arsed Fly) | 0 |

# VARIOUS ARTISTS LPs & COMPILATIONS
## (alphabetical by title)

## A

| 70 | ATP 102 | THE ABBEY TAVERN | 20 |
|---|---|---|---|
| 88 | Woronzow WOO 6 | ACID JAM (with insert) | 18 |
| 89 | Popdy POPDY 101 | (0222) A COMPILATION OF CARDIFF BANDS (LP) | 50 |
| 02 | Topic TSFCD4001 | THE ACOUSTIC FOLK BOX (4-CD) | 40 |
| 69 | Action ACLP 6005 | ACTION PACKED SOUL | 50 |
| 70s | Jem JEM | A DEAL A DAY | 25 |
| 96 | Ferox FERLP 1 | ADVENTURES IN TECHNO SOUL (2-LP; Too Funk/Paul Hannah/Carl Craig et al.) | 20 |
| 85 | United Dairies UD 012 | AN AFFLICTED MAN'S MUSICA BOX (3 different editions, 1st in gatefold sleeve) | 75 |
| 75 | Leader LEE 4056 | A FINE HUNTING DAY - SONGS OF THE HOLME VALLEY BEAGLES (with book) | 15 |
| 70 | Pama PMP 2004 | AFRICAN MELODY | 90 |
| 71 | Trojan TBL 166 | AFRICA'S BLOOD (Lee Perry, et al.) (orange/white label) | 40 |
| 64 | Decca LK 4606 | AFTER SUNSET | 150 |
| 66 | Stateside SL 10172 | AN ALBUM FULL OF SOUL | 50 |
| 69 | Key KL 002 | ALIVE! | 20 |
| 70 | Talisman STAL 5013 | ALL FOLK TOGETHER | 20 |
| 84 | Whaam! BIG 8 | ALL FOR ART... AND ART FOR ALL | 30 |
| 83 | Neat NEAT 102A/B | ALL HELL LET LOOSE | 20 |
| 76 | Count Shelly CSLP 08 | ALL STAR | 30 |
| 61 | Blue Beat BBLP 801 | ALL STARS - JAMAICAN BLUES | 300 |
| 70 | Speciality SPE 6609 | ALL THE BLUES ALL THE TIME | 22 |
| 58 | Parlophone PMD 1064 | ALL TIME COUNTRY AND WESTERN HITS (10") | 30 |
| 73 | Polydor 2460 186 | AMERICAN BLUES LEGENDS '73 | 15 |
| 63 | Polydor LPHM 46 397 | AMERICAN FOLK BLUES FESTIVAL (also stereo SLPHM 237 597) | 15 |
| 70s | Rare Records 2 | AMERICAN FOLK BLUES FESTIVAL 1962 | 25 |
| 64 | Fontana TL 5204 | AMERICAN FOLK BLUES FESTIVAL 1963 | 25 |
| 65 | Fontana TL 5225 | AMERICAN FOLK BLUES FESTIVAL 1964 | 25 |
| 66 | Fontana TL 5286 | AMERICAN FOLK BLUES FESTIVAL 1965 | 25 |
| 66 | Fontana (S)TL 5389 | AMERICAN FOLK BLUES FESTIVAL 1966 (mono/stereo) | 22 |
| 70 | CBS 63912 | AMERICAN FOLK BLUES FESTIVAL 1969 | 20 |
| 80s | Pleasantly Surprised PS 2 | THE ANGELS ARE COMING (2-cassette, with booklet) | 25 |
| 83 | No Future MPUNK 8 | ANGELS WITH DIRTY FACES | 18 |
| 60s | 77' 77LA 12/13 | ANGOLA PRISON SPIRITUALS | 18 |
| 69 | Immediate IMAL 03/04 | ANTHOLOGY OF BRITISH BLUES VOLUME 1 (2-LP, gatefold sleeve) | 30 |
| 69 | Immediate IMAL 05/06 | ANTHOLOGY OF BRITISH BLUES VOLUME 2 (2-LP, gatefold sleeve) | 30 |
| 10 | Fruits De Mer Crustacean 11 | A PHASE WE'RE GOING THROUGH (300-500 only, light/dark grey vinyl) | 35 |
| 10 | Fruits De Mer Crustacean 11 | A PHASE WE'RE GOING THROUGH (scarce coloured vinyl pressings) | 150 |
| 64 | London HA-K/SH-K 8174 | APOLLO SATURDAY NIGHT (mono/stereo) | 60 |
| 91 | Delerium DELP 005D | A PSYCHEDELIC PSAUNA (2-LP) | 30 |
| 80s | Ram RAMLP 001 | THE ART OF SOLVING PROBLEMS (with poster & insert) | 10 |
| 69 | Atco 228 021 | ATCO BLOCKBUSTERS | 18 |
| 69 | Atlantic 587/588 180 | ATLANTIC BLOCKBUSTERS | 20 |
| 65 | Atlantic ATL 5020 | ATLANTIC DISCOTHEQUE | 40 |
| 60s | Atlantic AP 2 | ATLANTIC IS SOUL | 15 |
| 60s | Atlantic AC 3 | ATLANTICLASSICS | 25 |
| 67 | Pye NPL 18198 | AT LAST THE 1948 SHOW | 15 |
| 90 | Dover/PWL CCD 19 | A TON OF HITS - THE HIT FACTORY VOL. 4 (2-CD) | 25 |
| 64 | Decca LK 4597 | AT THE CAVERN | 80 |
| 63 | London HA-R 8133 | AT THE HOOTENANNY - VOLUME 3 | 15 |
| 70 | Beacon SBEAB 9 | AUTHENTIC CHICAGO BLUES | 20 |
| 57 | London WB 91034 | AUTHENTIC CARIBBEAN CALYPSOS (10" LP) | 30 |
| 64 | Stateside SL 10107 | AUTHENTIC SKA | 70 |
| 64 | Stateside SL 10068 | AUTHENTIC R & B | 40 |
| 79 | Heartbeat HB 1 | AVON CALLING - THE BRISTOL COMPILATION (with poster) | 25 |
| 95 | Ministry Of Sound/AWOL LP 1 | A.W.O.L: A WAY OF LIFE (3-LP, stickered sleeve) | 40 |
| 80 | K-Tel NE 1100 | AXE ATTACK (early copies with demo of Iron Maiden's "Running Free") | 15 |
| 85 | Steeltrax JCI 7102 | AXE ATTACK (LP) | 18 |
| 80s | Flaccid FLAC 1 | AYLESBURY GOES FLACCID | 15 |
| 74 | Deroy DER 1052 | AYRSHIRE FOLK (LP, private pressing) | 70 |

## B

| 70 | TRACK 2407004 | BACKTRACK 4 | 15 |
|---|---|---|---|
| 70 | Track 2407 001 | BACKTRACK ONE | 25 |
| 70 | Track 2407003 | BACKTRACK THREE | 15 |
| 70 | Track 2407005 | BACKTRACK FIVE | 15 |
| 70 | Track 2407 006 | BACKTRACK SIX | 15 |
| 54 | London AL 3535 | BACKWOODS BLUES (10") | 50 |
| 73 | Incus INCUS 11 | BALANCE (Ian Brighton, et al.) | 60 |
| 62 | Fontana 688 200 ZL | BALLIN' | 18 |
| 79 | JSP 1005 | BANDERA ROCKABILLIES | 15 |
| 68 | Pama PMLP 4 | BANG BANG LULU | 30 |
| 69 | Pama Economy ECO7 | BANGARANG (LP) | 60 |
| 73 | BBC/Roundabout 17 | BANG ON A DRUM | 18 |
| 60 | Melodisc 12-115 | BANJO BREAKDOWN | 15 |

| 59 | Fontana TFR 6018 | BARRELHOUSE, BOOGIE WOOGIE AND BLUES (10").....................25 |
| 58 | Vogue Coral LRA 10022 | BARRELHOUSE PIANO (10" LP)........................25 |
| 59 | Vogue Coral LRA 10023 | BARRELHOUSE PIANO VOLUME 2 (10" LP)...................25 |
| 95 | Sarah SARAH 359 | BATTERY POINT (LP)........................30 |
| 71 | Trojan TBL 167 | BATTLE AXE........................30 |
| 98 | Trunk BARKED 3 | THE BATTLE OF BOSWORTH (LP)...................15 |
| 52 | Capitol LC 6510 | BATTLE OF THE BANDS (10" LP)...................18 |
| 71 | B&C BCM 103 | BATTLE OF THE BANDS VOL. 1...................15 |
| 64 | Melodisc MLP 12-192 | BATTLE OF THE GIANTS........................20 |
| 53 | MGM MGM-D 115 | A BATTLE OF JAZZ: HOT VERSUS COOL (10")...................30 |
| 71 | BBC REC 118 | BBC's FOLK ON TWO PRESENTS NORTHUMBRIAN FOLK...................20 |
| 69 | Beacon BEAB 1 | BEACON BRINGS IT TO YOU........................18 |
| 84 | Well Suspect SUSS 1 | THE BEAT GENERATION AND THE ANGRY YOUNG MEN...................20 |
| 86 | Mercury WILD 1 | BEAT RUNS WILD (Wet Wet Wet et al.)...................25 |
| 82 | X-centric Noise 2 | BEAT THE MEAT (cassette LP, insert)...................50 |
| 87 | Pink PINKY 15 | BEAUTY (McCarthy et al.)...................12 |
| 68 | Elektra EUK 262 | BEGIN HERE (also stereo EUKS 7262)...................20 |
| 78 | Rip Off ROLP 1 | BELFAST ROCKS........................35 |
| 71 | Delmark DS 622 | BELL'S BLUES HARP........................15 |
| 68 | Bell MBLL 102 | BELL'S CELLAR OF SOUL VOLUME 1...................30 |
| 69 | Bell MBLL 107 | BELL'S CELLAR OF SOUL VOLUME 2...................30 |
| 69 | Bell MBLL 117 | BELL'S CELLAR OF SOUL VOLUME 3...................30 |
| 69 | Bell MBLL/SBLL 111 | THE BEST FROM BELL........................20 |
| 69 | Bell MBLL/SBLL 124 | THE BEST FROM BELL VOLUME 2...................20 |
| 78 | Stiff ODD 2 | BE STIFF (TOUR '78 OFFICIAL RELEASE) (promo only, Stiff artists performing Devo's Be Stiff - some sold by mail order)...................18 |
| 78 | Stiff DEAL 1 | BE STIFF ROUTE '78 (with 16-page booklet & biographies, etc.)...................15 |
| 12 | BBE 173 CDLP 1 | BEST OF DISCO DEMANDS (2-LP)...................20 |
| 12 | BBE 173 CLP 2 | BEST OF DISCO DEMANDS 2 (2-LP)...................20 |
| 70s | Storyville 671 188 | THE BEST OF THE BLUES........................15 |
| 96 | Universal Sounds US LP 2 | BEST OF BLACK JAZZ RECORDS (2-LP)...................25 |
| 65 | Xtra XTRA 1031 | THE BEST OF BRITISH FOLK...................15 |
| 69 | Pama SECO 18 | THE BEST OF CAMEL........................200 |
| 72 | Paramount SPFL 286 | BEST OF FILM MUSIC........................15 |
| 76 | Epic EPC 81224 | THE BEST OF OKEH VOL. I...................15 |
| 76 | Epic EPC 81532 | THE BEST OF OKEH VOL. II...................15 |
| 92 | Chrysalis CHR TT 5012 | BEST OF 2 TONE (LP)........................40 |
| 83 | Statik STATLP 14 | THE BEST OF YOUR SECRET'S SAFE WITH US (This LP came with a free 7". The tracks were 'Sub Dub' by Sun Ya and on Side Two 'The Fools by Anthony Lindo. Cat. number was STAT26A/26B)...................20 |
| 86 | Plastic Head PLASLP 008 | BEYOND THE FENCE BEGINS THE SKY (LP)...................40 |
| 82 | Open Door OD 001 | BEYOND THE RIVER (LP, some with booklet)...................15 |
| 73 | Attack ATLP 1011 | BIG BAMBOO........................30 |
| 60 | Fontana TFL 5080 | THE BIG BEAT!........................55 |
| 85 | Big Beat WIKM39 | BIG BEAT BEACH PARTY...................15 |
| 64 | London HA-B 8199 | THE BIG 'D' JAMBOREE...................25 |
| 78 | Giorno GPS | BIG EGO........................20 |
| 69 | Minit MLL/MLS 40007E | THE BIG ONE........................22 |
| 64 | Capitol ST 2146 | BIG SOUNDS OF THE DRAGS Vol 2...................30 |
| 72 | CBS 64844 | THE BIG SUR FESTIVAL...................18 |
| 70 | Pama SECO 32 | BIRTH CONTROL........................30 |
| 80 | Black Ark Intl. BALP 4001 | BLACK ARK VOLUME 2...................30 |
| 70 | Matchbox SDX 207/8 | BLACK DIAMOND EXPRESS TO HELL (2-LP)...................25 |
| 60 | Columbia 33SX 1244 | BLACKPOOL NIGHTS........................35 |
| 80 | Form BB 1003 | BLACK MAGIC DUB (LP)...................100 |
| 58 | HMV CLP 1167 | BLACK SLACKS AND BOBBY SOCKS (LP)...................300 |
| 70 | Ember SE 8009 | BLACK SOUL EXPLOSION...................18 |
| 70 | CBS 52796 | BLACK WHITES AND BLUES...................20 |
| 68 | Coxsone CSP 1 | BLUE BEAT SPECIAL........................60 |
| 66 | RCA Victor RD 7786 | BLUEBIRD BLUES........................20 |
| 63 | Stateside SL 10021 | THE BLUEGRASS HALL OF FAME...................15 |
| 65 | London HA-B 8227 | BLUEGRASS HALL OF FAME VOL. 2...................18 |
| 62 | Columbia 33SX 1417 | THE BLUES........................60 |
| 64 | Pye Intl. NPL 28030 | BLUES VOL. 1........................18 |
| 64 | Pye Intl. NPL 28035 | BLUES VOL. 2........................18 |
| 64 | Pye Intl. NPL 28045 | BLUES VOL. 3........................18 |
| 64 | Chess CRL 4003 | BLUES VOL. 4........................18 |
| 65 | Chess CRL 4512 | BLUES VOL. 5........................18 |
| 68 | Immediate IMLP 014 | BLUES ANYTIME VOL. 1...................18 |
| 68 | Immediate IMCP 015 | BLUES ANYTIME VOL. 2...................18 |
| 68 | Immediate IMLP 019 | BLUES ANYTIME VOL. 3...................18 |
| 65 | Fontana TFL 6048 | THE BLUES AT NEWPORT 1964 PART 1...................22 |
| 66 | London HA-S 8265 | THE BLUES CAME DOWN FROM MEMPHIS...................80 |
| 73 | Flyright LP 504 | BLUES CAME TO CHAPEL HILL...................15 |
| 65 | Storyville SLP 176 | BLUESCENE USA: VOLUME 1 - CHICAGO...................18 |
| 65 | Storyville SLP 177 | BLUESCENE USA: VOLUME 2 - LOUISIANA BLUES...................18 |
| 65 | Storyville SLP 181 | BLUESCENE USA: VOLUME 3 - BLUES ALL AROUND MY BED...................18 |
| 67 | Storyville SLP 180 | BLUESCENE USA: VOLUME 4 - MISSISSIPPI BLUES...................18 |
| 71 | Python PLP-KM 17 | BLUES - CHICAGO STYLE (LP)...................45 |
| 60 | Philips BBL 7369 | BLUES FELL THIS MORNING...................40 |

| 73 | Polydor 2383 257 | BLUES FOR MR. CRUMP | 18 |
| 79 | Look LK LP 6400 | BLUES FOR SUZY | 30 |
| 69 | Chess CRLS 4558 | BLUES FROM BIG BILL'S COPACABANA | 35 |
| 69 | Python PLP 6 | BLUES FROM CHICAGO (99 copies only) | 80 |
| 70 | Python PLP 9 | BLUES FROM CHICAGO VOL. 2 (99 copies only) | 80 |
| 71 | Python PLP 15 | BLUES FROM CHICAGO VOL. 3 (99 copies only) | 80 |
| 60s | Heritage 1004 | BLUES FROM MAXWELL STREET (with insert, 99 copies only) | 100 |
| 71 | Pye Intl. NPL 28142 | BLUES FROM THE BAYOU | 22 |
| 72 | Saydisc SDM 226 | BLUES FROM THE DELTA | 25 |
| 71 | Python PLP 21 | BLUES FROM THE WINDY CITY (99 copies only) | 80 |
| 77 | Flyright LP 4713 | BLUES FROM THE WINDY CITY | 15 |
| 80 | Kicking Mule SNKF 159 | BLUES GUITAR WORKSHOP | 15 |
| 63 | Stateside SL 10076 | BLUES HOOT (Lightning Hopkins) | 35 |
| 57 | Pye Nixa NJL 8 | (ALAN LOMAX PRESENTS) BLUES IN THE MISSISSIPPI NIGHT | 35 |
| 60s | Sunflower (no cat. no.) | BLUES IS MY COMPANION (99 copies only) | 42 |
| 60s | Sunflower (no cat. no.) | BLUES KEEP FALLING (99 copies only) | 80 |
| 69 | Blue Horizon 7-66227 | BLUES JAM AT CHESS (2-LP) | 60 |
| 67 | Saydisc Match. SDM 142 | BLUES LIKE SHOWERS OF RAIN | 70 |
| 68 | Saydisc Match. SDM 167 | BLUES LIKE SHOWERS OF RAIN VOLUME 2 | 70 |
| 65 | Decca LK 4681 | BLUES NOW | 60 |
| 72 | Blues Obscurities BOV 1 | BLUES OBSCURITIES VOL. 1: SOUTHERN BLUES/DARK MUDDY BOTTOM (plain cover with photocopied inserts) | 40 |
| 72 | Blues Obscurities BOV 2 | BLUES OBSCURITIES VOL. 2: LONESOME HARMONICA | 25 |
| 72 | Blues Obscurities BOV 3 | BLUES OBSCURITIES VOL. 3: WEST COAST BLUES | 25 |
| 72 | Blues Obscurities BOV 4 | BLUES OBSCURITIES VOL. 4: ONE RAINY MORNING | 25 |
| 72 | Blues Obscurities BOV 5 | BLUES OBSCURITIES VOL. 5: SOMETHING'S GONE WRONG | 25 |
| 72 | Blues Obscurities BOV 6 | BLUES OBSCURITIES VOL. 6: COMING BACK HOME | 25 |
| 72 | Blues Obscurities BOV 7 | BLUES OBSCURITIES VOL. 7 | 25 |
| 72 | Blues Obscurities BOV 8 | BLUES OBSCURITIES VOL. 8 | 25 |
| 72 | Blues Obscurities BOV 9 | BLUES OBSCURITIES VOL. 9 | 25 |
| 72 | Blues Obscurities BOV 10 | BLUES OBSCURITIES VOL. 10 | 25 |
| 74 | London HA-U 8454 | BLUES OBSCURITIES VOL. 1: DARK MUDDY BOTTOM (reissue) | 15 |
| 74 | London HA-U 8455 | BLUES OBSCURITIES VOL. 2: LONESOME HARMONICA (reissue) | 15 |
| 74 | London HA-U 8456 | BLUES OBSCURITIES VOL. 3: STRETCHIN' OUT | 15 |
| 69 | Mercury SMXL 77 | BLUES PACKAGE '69 | 15 |
| 69 | Highway 51 H 102 | BLUES PEOPLE | 40 |
| 68 | Matchbox SDR 146 | BLUES PIANO | 20 |
| 72 | Atlantic K 40404 | BLUES PIANO - CHICAGO PLUS | 20 |
| 68 | Kokomo K 1001 | A BLUES POTPOURRI (99 copies only) | 60 |
| 71 | Rarities (Tony's Records) | BLUES RARITIES VOL. 1 (2-LP) | 25 |
| 69 | Atlantic Special 590 019 | THE BLUES ROLL ON (reissue of "Southern Folk Heritage: The Blues Roll On") | 12 |
| 69 | Poppy PYM 11001 | BLUES ROOTS VOLUME ONE | 25 |
| 66 | Decca LK 4748 | BLUES SOUTHSIDE CHICAGO | 55 |
| 71 | Python PLP 16 | BLUES TODAY - SOUTHERN STYLE (99 copies only) | 40 |
| 12 | Belter 001 | BONEHEAD CRUNCHERS VOLUME 1 (300 only) | 40 |
| 12 | Belter 002 | BONEHEAD CRUNCHERS VOLUME 2 (300 only) | 30 |
| 13 | Belter 003 | BONEHEAD CRUNCHERS VOLUME 3 (300 only) | 20 |
| 13 | Belter 004 | BONEHEAD CRUNCHERS VOLUME 4 (300 only) | 20 |
| 13 | Belter 005 | BONEHEAD CRUNCHERS VOLUME 5 (300 only) | 20 |
| 55 | London AL 3544 | BOOGIE WOOGIE WITH THE BLUES (10") | 50 |
| 69 | Pama SECO 17 | BOSS REGGAE | 150 |
| 74 | Eron 002 | BOTH SIDES OF THE DOWNS (with insert) | 25 |
| 80 | Aardvark STEAL 2 | BOUQUET OF STEEL (blue vinyl with 27-page booklet) | 15 |
| 81 | Bristol Recorder BR 002 | THE BRISTOL RECORDER VOL. 2 (with magazine booklet) | 15 |
| 68 | Island ILP 966/ILPS 9066 | BRITISH BLUE-EYED SOUL | 75 |
| 67 | Tamla Motown TML 11055 | BRITISH MOTOWN CHARTBUSTERS (mono, flipback sleeve) | 20 |
| 69 | T. Motown STML 11055 | BRITISH MOTOWN CHARTBUSTERS (stereo reissue, flipback sleeve) | 20 |
| 68 | T. Motown (S)TML 11082 | BRITISH MOTOWN CHARTBUSTERS VOL. 2 (mono/stereo, flipback sleeve) | 18 |
| 83 | Royal Records JBLP 306 | BRITISH MUSIC SCENE (LP) | 80 |
| 70 | Trojan TBL 106 | BRIXTON CAT | 50 |
| 64 | Decca LK 4598 | BRUM BEAT | 85 |
| 64 | Dial DLP 1 | BRUM BEAT | 50 |
| 79 | Big Bear BRUM 1 | BRUM BEAT - LIVE AT THE BARREL ORGAN (2-LP, with inserts) | 20 |
| 80 | MCA MCF 3074 | BRUTE FORCE | 20 |
| 72 | Flyright LP 106 | BULL CITY BLUES | 15 |
| 69 | Pama Economy SECO 18 | BULLET : A WORLD OF REGGAE, SKA, ROCK STEADY, BLUE BEAT (LP) | 200 |
| 81 | Crass 421984/4 | BULLSHIT DETECTOR 1 | 20 |
| 82 | Crass 221984/3 | BULLSHIT DETECTOR 2 (2-LP) | 20 |
| 82 | Crass 221984/3 | BULLSHIT DETECTIVE 2 (2-LP) | 15 |
| 83 | Crass | BULLSHIT DETECTIVE 3 | 15 |
| 66 | Decca LK 4734 | BUMPER BUNDLE 16 HITS | 25 |
| 77 | Stiff SEEZ 2 | A BUNCH OF STIFF RECORDS | 15 |
| 79 | Cherry Red ARED 2 | BUSINESS UNUSUAL (with Zig Zag small labels catalogue) | 30 |
| 81 | Autumn AU 2 | BUSTED AT OZ | 20 |
| 84 | Dambusters DAM 003 | BUTTONS AND BOWS VOLUME 1 (2-LP) | 30 |
| 84 | Dambusters DAM 006 | BUTTONS AND BOWS VOLUME 2 (2-LP) | 30 |
| 69 | BBC REB 39M | BRITISH PRIME MINISTERS 1924-1964 (LP) | 15 |

# C

| | | | |
|---|---|---|---|
| 50s | Melodisc MLP 507 | CALYPSO CARNIVAL (10" LP) | 18 |
| 72 | Topic 12TS 219 | CANNY NEWCASSEL (with booklet, blue label) | 20 |
| 67 | Bounty BY 6035 | CAN'T KEEP FROM CRYING (TOPICAL BLUES ON THE DEATH OF PRESIDENT KENNEDY) | 20 |
| 77 | Carib Gems CGDD 301 | CARIB GEMS DISCO DISC | 25 |
| 50s | Parlophone CPMD 13 | CARIBBEAN CALYPSO (10" LP, export issue) | 25 |
| 71 | Trojan TBL 171 | CARIBBEAN DANCE FESTIVAL (wraparound paper sleeve) | 10 |
| 81 | Secret SEC 2 | CARRY ON OI! | 15 |
| 73 | Nottingham Festival FEST 2 | CASTLE ROCK | 50 |
| 78 | Nice NICE 1 | CATCH A WAVE (2 x 10", gatefold sleeve) | 30 |
| 80 | Island IRSP7 | CATCH THIS BEAT | 15 |
| 90 | Cerne CERNE 001/002/003 | THE CERNE BOX SET (3-LP box set; Nurse With Wound/ Current 93/Sol Invictus; with 3 inserts) | 125 |
| 60s | Columbia | CHARTBUSTERS USA | 45 |
| 73 | Checker 6445 150 | CHESS GOLDEN DECADE VOL. 1: THE EARLY 50s | 10 |
| 74 | Chess 6445 203 | CHESS GOLDEN DECADE VOL. 7: 1963-1965 HIGH HEEL SNEAKERS (gatefold sleeve) | 10 |
| 64 | Chess CRL 4004 | CHESS STORY VOL. 1 | 25 |
| 65 | Chess CRL 4516 | CHESS STORY VOL. 2 | 25 |
| 71 | Vanguard VSD 79217 | CHICAGO BLUES VOLUME 2 | 15 |
| 66 | Fontana TFL 6068 | CHICAGO/THE BLUES/TODAY | 18 |
| 66 | Fontana TFL 6069 | CHICAGO/THE BLUES/TODAY VOLUME 2 | 18 |
| 66 | Fontana TFL 6070 | CHICAGO/THE BLUES/TODAY VOLUME 3 | 18 |
| 69 | Vanguard SVRL 19020 | CHICAGO/THE BLUES/TODAY VOLUME 1 | 20 |
| 69 | Vanguard SVRL 19021 | CHICAGO/THE BLUES/TODAY VOLUME 2 | 20 |
| 69 | Vanguard SVRL 19022 | CHICAGO/THE BLUES/TODAY VOLUME 3 | 18 |
| 68 | Sunflower ET 1401 | THE CHICAGO HOUSE BANDS (99 copies only) | 40 |
| 69 | Kokomo K 1005 | CHICAGO SESSIONS VOLUME 1 (99 copies only) | 50 |
| 70 | Flyright LP 4700 | CHICKEN STUFF | 15 |
| 80 | Relics LSD 1 | CHOCOLATE SOUP FOR DIABETICS VOL. 1 | 15 |
| 81 | Relics ACID 1 | CHOCOLATE SOUP FOR DIABETICS VOL. 2 (gatefold sleeve) | 15 |
| 84 | MCA CHUNK 1 | CHUNKS OF FUNK | 20 |
| 73 | United Artists UDX 205/6 | CHRISTMAS AT THE PATTI (2 x 10", gatefold sleeve) | 22 |
| 68 | Chess CRLS 4541 | CHRISTMAS DEDICATION | 25 |
| 63 | London HA-U 8141 | A CHRISTMAS GIFT FOR YOU (plum label) | 80 |
| 78 | Incus INCUS 33 | CIRCADIAN RHYTHM | 50 |
| 80s | White Elephant RIOCH 1 | CITY WALLS - A SOUTHAMPTON COMPILATION (with insert) | 12 |
| 55 | London AL 3559 | CLASSIC JAZZ PIANO (10") | 25 |
| 81 | Upper Class CHIN 1 | CLASS OF 81 | 15 |
| 85 | Pusmort 0012-02 | CLEANSE THE BACTERIA | 20 |
| 72 | Pegasus PS 1 | CLOGS (FOLK SAMPLER) (with insert) | 15 |
| 90s | Distronics ITCD 3 | THE CLOSING PARTY - IN THE CITY LIVE UNSIGNED (CD) | 50 |
| 72 | Trojan TBL178 | CLUB REGGAE 3 | 25 |
| 70 | Trojan TTL 54 | CLUB ROCK STEADY | 25 |
| 68 | W.I.R.L. ILP 965 | CLUB ROCK STEADY '68 | 70 |
| 67 | W.I.R.L. ILP 948 | CLUB SKA '67 | 50 |
| 67 | W.I.R.L. ILP 956 | CLUB SKA '67 VOL. 2 | 60 |
| 70 | Trojan TTL 48 | CLUB SKA VOLUME ONE | 20 |
| 70 | Trojan TTL 51 | CLUB SKA VOLUME TWO (Existence unconfirmed) | 30 |
| 68 | Island ILP 964 | CLUB SOUL | 50 |
| 84 | Kent 022 | CLUB SOUL | 15 |
| 67 | Elektra EUK 253 | A COLD WIND BLOWS | 15 |
| 65 | Tamla Motown TML 11001 | A COLLECTION OF 16 TAMLA MOTOWN HITS | 25 |
| 67 | Tamla Motown TML 11043 | A COLLECTION OF 16 ORIGINAL BIG HITS VOL. 4 | 35 |
| 67 | Tamla Motown TML 11050 | A COLLECTION OF 16 ORIGINAL BIG HITS VOL. 5 | 35 |
| 68 | T. Motown (S)TML 11074 | A COLLECTION OF 16 ORIGINAL BIG HITS VOL. 6 (mono/stereo) | 20 |
| 69 | T. Motown (S)TML 11092 | A COLLECTION OF 16 ORIGINAL BIG HITS VOL. 7 - THE MOTOWN SOUND | 25 |
| 70 | T. Motown (S)TML 11130 | A COLLECTION OF 16 ORIGINAL BIG HITS VOL. 8 | 20 |
| 54 | London AL 3514 | COLLECTORS' ITEMS VOLUME ONE (10") | 18 |
| 54 | London AL 3533 | COLLECTORS' ITEMS VOLUME TWO (10") | 18 |
| 56 | London AL 3550 | COLLECTORS' ITEMS VOLUME THREE (10") | 18 |
| 77 | Collins Music CM001 BLP | COLLINS MUSIC | 50 |
| 86 | Color Disc COLORS 4 | COLOR SUPPLEMENT (400 only) | 15 |
| 93 | 2-Tone CDCHRTT 5013 | THE COMPACT 2-TONE STORY (4-CD, box set with book) | 40 |
| 76 | Incus INCUS 21 | COMPANY 1 | 40 |
| 77 | Incus INCUS 29 | COMPANY 6 | 40 |
| 77 | Incus INCUS 30 | COMPANY 7 | 40 |
| 72 | Apple STCX 3385 | THE CONCERT FOR BANGLA DESH (3-LP box set, orange inside with BMI/ASCAP label credits, with booklet, featuring Bob Dylan) | 70 |
| 64 | Decca LK 4664 | CONVERSATION WITH THE BLUES | 70 |
| 57 | Tempo TAP 10 | COOL MUSIC FOR A HOT NIGHT - MOOD MUSIC IN THE MODERN MANNER | 150 |
| 72 | Wicksteed WCKLP 02 | CORBY CATCHMENT AREA (private pressing) | 200 |
| 80s | Third Mind TMLP 09 | COULD YOU WALK ON THE WATER | 15 |
| 64 | London HA-B 8145 | COUNTRY & WESTERN GOLDEN HIT PARADE VOL. 1 | 18 |
| 64 | London HA-B 8146 | COUNTRY & WESTERN GOLDEN HIT PARADE VOL. 2 | 18 |
| 60 | Storyville SLP 129 | THE COUNTRY BLUES | 20 |
| 73 | Specialty SNTF 5014 | COUNTRY BLUES | 15 |
| 60s | Saydisc Roots RL 334 | COUNTRY BLUES OBSCURITIES VOLUME 1 | 20 |
| 66 | Stateside SL 10170 | COUNTRY COUSINS | 18 |
| 56 | Brunswick LA 8729 | COUNTRY FAVOURITES VOL. ONE (10") | 30 |

| | | | |
|---|---|---|---|
| 81 | No Future OI 3 | COUNTRY FIT FOR HEROES | 15 |
| 82 | No Future 12 OI 23 | COUNTY FIT FOR HEROES 2 | 18 |
| 63 | Starlite STLP 15 | COUNTRY MUSIC U.S.A. (reissued as GRK 605) | 10 |
| 69 | Pama ECO 2 | CRAB - GREATEST HITS | 150 |
| 80 | Rabid/Absurd LAST 1 | THE CRAP STOPS HERE | 25 |
| 60 | Fontana TFL 5103 | THE CREAM OF 'TAKE IT FROM HERE' (also stereo SFL 534) | 12 |
| 74 | Eron 005 | CRYPTADIA | 15 |
| 79 | Trojan TRLS 185 | CREATION ROCKERS 5 | 15 |
| 79 | Trojan TRLS 183 | CREATION ROCKERS 3 | 18 |

# D

| | | | |
|---|---|---|---|
| 81 | Two Tone CHRTT 5004 | DANCE CRAZE | 15 |
| 68 | H. Note/B. Shot BSLP 5002 | DANCING DOWN ORANGE STREET | 150 |
| 84 | Kent KENT 026 | DANCING 'TIL DAWN | 15 |
| 76 | Dark Horse DH 1 (DHSAM 1) | DARK HORSE RECORDS '76 (promo only sampler, stickered sleeve & inner) | 40 |
| 86 | EMI EQ 5003 | DAVE CLARK'S TIME (2-LP, with brochure and lyric inner, some with hologram) | 30 |
| 90s | Nuphonic NUX 136LP | DAVID MANCUSO PRESENTS THE LOFT VOL. 1 (4 x 12" with booklet) | 40 |
| 90s | Nuphonic NUX 154LP | DAVID MANCUSO PRESENTS THE LOFT VOL. 2 (4 x 12") | 30 |
| 79 | Dead Good DEAD 4 | DEAD GOOD'S DEAD GOODS (unissued) | 0 |
| 78 | Virgin VD 2508 | DEAD ON ARRIVAL (glow-in-the-dark vinyl with poster, export copies to US have "EXPACK 001" sticker on sleeve)) | 20 |
| 66 | Highway 51 H 100 | DECADE OF THE BLUES - THE 1950's (99 copies only) | 75 |
| 66 | Highway 51 H 104 | DECADE OF THE BLUES - THE 1950's VOLUME 2 (99 copies only) | 50 |
| 54 | Decca LF 1160 | DECCA SHOWCASE VOL. 3 (10") | 15 |
| 55 | Decca LF 1265 | DECCA SHOWCASE VOL. 5 (10") | 18 |
| 71 | United Artists UAS 29153 | DEEPER INTO THE VAULTS | 12 |
| 70 | Polydor 2673 001 | DEEP OVERGROUND POP | 20 |
| 70 | Stax SXATS 1037 | THE DEEP SOUL OF STAX | 22 |
| 71 | Flyright LP 102 | DEEP SOUTH COUNTRY BLUES | 15 |
| 83 | Insane 1001 | DEMOLITION BLUES (featuring the Oppressed/Decesed and Epidemic) | 25 |
| 86 | Decal LIK 9 | DERAM DAYZE | 15 |
| 68 | Deram SML 1027 | THE DERAM GOLDEN POPS SAMPLER | 80 |
| 67 | Island ILP 955 | DERRICK HARRIOTT'S ROCK (SKA) STEADY PARTY | 400 |
| 72 | Trojan TTL 54 | DERRICK HARRIOTT'S ROCKSTEADY PARTY (reissue - existence unconfirmed) | 50 |
| 85 | Yangki 01 | DEVASTATE TO LIBERATE | 15 |
| 89 | Blast First BFDJ 1 | DEVIL'S JUKEBOX (10 x 7" in numbered box, with booklet, 3,000 only) | 20 |
| 73 | London ZGU 131 | DIMENSION DOLLS | 15 |
| 70 | Mercury 6641 006 | DIMENSION OF MIRACLES | 15 |
| 80 | DinDisc DONE 1 | DINDISC 1980 (with free 20"x 20" game) | 12 |
| 74 | DIP DLP 5026 | D.I.P. PRESENTS THE UPSETTER (Lee Perry et al.) | 150 |
| 69 | Minit MLL/MLS 40005 | DIRT BLUES | 25 |
| 01 | Trunk DFM 001 LP | DIRTY FAN MAIL (LP) | 20 |
| 70 | BBC REC 65M | DISC A DAWN | 20 |
| 11 | BBE BB E 172 CLP | DISCO LOVE 2 (2-LP) | 20 |
| 13 | BBE 224 CLP | DISCO LOVE 3 (2-LP) | 20 |
| 15 | BBE 319 CLP | DISCO LOVE 4 (2-LP) | 20 |
| 67 | Island ILP 943 | DOCTOR SOUL | 90 |
| 82 | BBC 2-LP-22001 | DOCTOR WHO COLLECTOR'S EDITION (2-LP, with poster) | 30 |
| 80s | Pleasantly Surprised PS 12 | DOCUMENT (cassette) | 18 |
| 84 | Hope Springs HOP 1 | DON'T LET THE HOPE CLOSE DOWN | 15 |
| 70 | Python PLP | DOWNHOME BLUES (99 copies only) | 90 |
| 94 | React REACT LP 55 | DOPE ON PLASTIC! (2-LP) | 20 |
| 94 | React REACT LP 65 | DOPE ON PLASTIC 2 (2-LP) | 20 |
| 96 | React REACT LP 073 | DOPE ON PLASTIC 3 (2-LP) | 20 |
| 96 | React REACT LP 97 | DOPE ON PLASTIC 4 (3-LP) | 20 |
| 98 | React REACT LP 118 | DOPE ON PLASTIC 5 (4-LP) | 20 |
| 99 | React REACT LP 147 | DOPE ON PLASTIC 6 (4-LP) | 20 |
| 00 | React REACT LP 169 | DOPE ON PLASTIC 7 (3-LP) | 20 |
| 01 | React REACT LP 195 | DOPE ON PLASTIC 8 (3-LP) | 20 |
| 70 | Python PLP 14 | DOWNHOME BLUES VOLUME 2 (99 copies only) | 90 |
| 71 | Python PLP 22 | DOWNHOME BLUES VOLUME 3 (99 copies only) | 90 |
| 71 | Flyright LP 4703 | DOWN IN HOGAN'S ALLEY | 15 |
| 67 | Down With The Game 200 | DOWN WITH THE GAME VOLUME 1 (99 copies only) | 55 |
| 67 | Down With The Game 201 | DOWN WITH THE GAME VOLUME 2 (99 copies only) | 55 |
| 68 | Down With The Game 203 | DOWN WITH THE GAME VOLUME 3 (99 copies only) | 55 |
| 68 | Down With The Game 204 | DOWN WITH THE GAME VOLUME 4 (99 copies only) | 55 |
| 68 | Down With The Game 205 | DOWN WITH THE GAME VOLUME 5 (99 copies only) | 55 |
| 68 | Down With The Game 206 | DOWN WITH THE GAME VOLUME 6 (99 copies only) | 55 |
| 67 | Island ILP 954 | DR. KITCH | 60 |
| 85 | Capitol EG 26 0573 1-4 | DREAM BABIES | 15 |
| 83 | International INTEL 4 | DREAM SEQUENCE (2-LP) | 100 |
| 59 | Parlophone PMC 1101 | DRUMBEAT (Adam Faith et al.) | 30 |
| 68 | Island ILP 976 | THE DUKE AND THE PEACOCK | 150 |
| 69 | Trojan TTL 8 | DUKE REID'S GOLDEN HITS | 50 |
| 67 | Island ILP 958 | DUKE REID'S ROCK STEADY | 400 |
| 70 | Trojan TTL 53 | DUKE REID'S ROCK STEADY (reissue, existence unconfirmed) | 30 |
| 87 | Manic Ears ACHE 3 | DIGGING IN WATER (LP, featuring Disorder/Chaos UK/Oi Polloi..) | 15 |

# E

| | | | |
|---|---|---|---|
| 70 | Matchbox SDR 199 | EARLY BLUES VOLUME 1: SKOODLE-UM-SKOO | 20 |

MINT VALUE £

| | | | |
|---|---|---|---|
| 70 | Matchbox SDR 206 | EARLY FOLK BLUES VOLUME 2: HOMETOWN SKIFFLE | 15 |
| 70 | Middle Earth MDLS 20 | EARTHED | 30 |
| 80 | Dead Good GOOD 1 | EAST (with inner & stickered sleeve) | 25 |
| 73 | Southern Sound SD 200 | EAST VERNON BLUES | 30 |
| 63 | Decca LK 4546 | EDINBURGH FOLK FESTIVAL VOLUME 1 | 30 |
| 63 | Decca LK 4563 | EDINBURGH FOLK FESTIVAL VOLUME 2 | 30 |
| 55 | Philips BBR 8046 | EIGHT EVERGREENS (10") | 15 |
| 75 | Island/Transatlantic | ELECTRIC MUSE - THE STORY OF FOLK INTO ROCK (4-LP box set with booklet) | 40 |
| 64 | Turnabout TV340465 | ELECTRONIC MUSIC | 25 |
| 73 | YES 2-4 | ELECTRONIC MUSIC FROM YORK (3-LP, box set, with insert) | 250 |
| 85 | Push PUSH 001 | ELEGANCE, CHARM AND DEADLY DANGER | 25 |
| 10 | Universal Sound USLP 38 | ELEKTRONISCHE MUSIK AUS KOLN (2-LP) | 20 |
| 80s | Master BBSLP 007 | ELEMENTALS | 20 |
| 83 | Extract XX 001 | THE ELEPHANT TABLE ALBUM (2-LP) | 18 |
| 57 | Philips BBR 8115 | ELLA, LENA, BILLIE AND SARAH (10") | 15 |
| 77 | EMI PSPL 209 | EMI INTRODUCES THE NEW BRONZE AGE (LP) | 20 |
| 83 | Psycho PSYCHO 1 | ENDLESS JOURNEY VOL. 1 (numbered) | 20 |
| 83 | Psycho PSYCHO 3 | ENDLESS JOURNEY VOL. 2 (numbered) | 15 |
| 83 | Psycho PSYCHO 19 | ENDLESS JOURNEY VOL. 3 (numbered) | 15 |
| 88 | MEK MEK 006 | THE ENGLISH REBELS (with insert) | 20 |
| 84 | Street Sounds HBOX 1 | ESSENTIAL ELECTRO (9 LP box set, 5000 only) | 100 |
| 67 | Speciality SPE 6601 | EVERY DAY I HAVE THE BLUES | 18 |
| 72 | Blue Horizon 2683 007 | THE EXCELLO STORY (2-LP) | 120 |
| 68 | Amal. AMGLP 2002 | EXPLOSIVE ROCKSTEADY | 85 |
| 87 | Rot ASS 100 | THE END OF AN ERA (LP) | 15 |

## F

| | | | |
|---|---|---|---|
| 80 | fACTORY fact 24 | A FACTORY QUARTET (2-LP, featuring Durutti Column, Kevin Hewick, Blurt & Royal Family And The Poor) | 20 |
| 67 | Elektra EUK 259 | FANTASTIC FOLK | 15 |
| 64 | Topic 12T 110 | FAREWELL NANCY (blue label) | 18 |
| *(Each of the above 10 LPs came with blue labels and a booklet.)* | | | |
| 76 | Lightning LIP 2 | FAREWELL TO THE ROXY (LP) | 20 |
| 73 | Count Shelly CSLP 03 | FEELING HIGH VOL 1 | 30 |
| 68 | Zeus CF 201 | FESTIVAL AT TOWERSEY | 50 |
| 63 | Pye Intl. NPL 28033 | FESTIVAL OF THE BLUES | 30 |
| 60s | Melodisc MS 4 | 15 OLDIES BUT GOODIES | 18 |
| 65 | Sue ILP 920 | 50 MINUTES & 24 SECONDS OF RECORDED DYNAMITE! | 100 |
| 85 | L.A.Y.L.A.H. LAY 10 | THE FIGHT IS ON (Nurse With Wound, Organum, et al.) | 30 |
| 72 | Warner Bros K 66013 | FILLMORE: THE LAST DAYS (3-LP box set with poster & booklet) | 35 |
| *(Each of the above 10 LPs came with blue labels and a booklet.)* | | | |
| 88 | Re-Elect The President NIXON 4 | THE FINAL COUNTDOWN (LP) | 25 |
| 65 | London HA-B 8205 | FINGERS ON FIRE | 15 |
| 60 | HMV CLP 1358/CSD 1298 | FINGS AIN'T WOT THEY USED TO BE | 20 |
| 69 | Music Man | FIREPOINT - A COLLECTION OF FOLK BLUES | 100 |
| 73 | Spark SRLM 2003 | FIREPOINT - A COLLECTION OF FOLK BLUES (reissue) | 30 |
| *(Each of the above 10 LPs came with blue labels and a booklet.)* | | | |
| 95 | Dub Jockey DJLP 005 | FIRST BOOK OF DUB CHANTS (no sleeve) | 50 |
| 71 | CBS 66311 | THE FIRST GREAT ROCK FESTIVALS OF THE 70s: ISLE OF WIGHT AND ATLANTA (3-LP) | 30 |
| *(Each of the above 10 LPs came with blue labels and a booklet.)* | | | |
| 73 | Spaceward EDENLP 53 | THE FIRST LAME BUNNY ALBUM (LP, fold out sleeve) | 400 |
| 58 | Esquire 20-091 | THE FIRST MODERNS (10") | 20 |
| 57 | Esquire 20-089 | THE FIRST NATIONAL SKIFFLE CONTEST (10") | 80 |
| 56 | Mercury MPT 7512 | FIRST ROCK 'N' ROLL PARTY (10") | 130 |
| 89 | Confection LC 7871 | FLAIR: THE OTHER WORLD OF BRITISH FOOTBALL (2-LP) | 20 |
| 80s | Alt. Tentacles VIRUS 22 | FLEX YOUR HEAD | 15 |
| *(Each of the above 10 LPs came with blue labels and a booklet.)* | | | |
| 84 | Kent KENT 017 | FOOT STOMPERS | 15 |
| 83 | Kent KENT 007 | FOR DANCERS ONLY | 15 |
| *(Each of the above 10 LPs came with blue labels and a booklet.)* | | | |
| 78 | Trailer LER 2015 | FLYDE ACOUSTIC | 15 |
| 64 | Blue Beat BBLP 803 | FLY FLYING SKA | 400 |
| 69 | Atlantic 588 184 | FLYING HIGH (record club edition) | 15 |
| 76 | Flams/Wounded WR 1068 | FOLK AT THE CHEQUERS (private pressing) | 15 |
| 64 | Ember NR 5015 | FOLK BLUES SONG FEST | 20 |
| 73 | Counterpoint CPT 3994 | FOLK FROM McTAVISH'S KITCHENS | 30 |
| 73 | Windmill WMD | FOLK HERITAGE | 30 |
| 73 | Nottingham Festival FEST 1 | FOLK NOTTINGHAM STYLE | 200 |
| 65 | Decca LK 4783 | FOLK NOW | 25 |
| 70 | BBC REC 955 | FOLK ON FRIDAY | 18 |
| 71 | Talisman STAL 5019 | FOLK PHILOSOPHY | 20 |
| 66 | Folkscene FSP 001 | FOLK SCENE (LP, private pressing) | 100 |
| *(Each of the above 10 LPs came with blue labels and a booklet.)* | | | |
| 73 | Eron ERON 001 | FOLK IN SANDWICH (LP) | 40 |
| 69 | Topic | THE FOLK SONGS OF BRITAIN VOLS. 1-10 (10 x LP box set) | 80 |
| 61 | Topic TPS 201 | TOPIC SAMPLER No. 6 - FOLK SONGS | 12 |
| 57 | HMV DLP 1143 | FOLK SONG TODAY (SONGS AND BALLADS OF ENGLAND AND SCOTLAND) (10") | 25 |
| 71 | Nicro K 220971 | FOLK UPSTAIRS | 80 |
| 63 | Ember CEL 902 | FOOL BRITANNIA | 20 |

| 65 | Decca LK 4695 | FOURTEEN - THE LORD'S TAVERNERS' ALBUM | 20 |
| 78 | Harvest SHSM 2024 | FOUR ROCK N ROLL LEGENDS RECORDED IN LONDON (LP, featuring Jack Scott, Charlie Feathers, Buddy Knox & Warren Smith) | 18 |
| 70 | Bamboo BLP 205 | FREEDOM SOUNDS | 50 |
| 72 | Trojan TRL 51 | FROM BAM BAM TO CHERRY OH BABY | 15 |
| 81 | Alternative ALT 007A | FROM BROMLEY WITH LOVE (LP) | 120 |
| 70 | Liberty LBS 83278 | FROM THE VAULTS | 15 |
| 83 | New European BADVC 666 | FROM TORTURE TO CONSCIENCE (with insert) | 80 |
| 71 | Cutty Wren | FROST LANE | 50 |
| 89 | Sub Pop DAMP 104 | FUCK ME, I'M RICH! | 15 |
| 89 | Unrest UNREST 14 | FULL FORCE VOL. 3 | 15 |
| 70 | Trojan TBL 137 | FUNKY CHICKEN | 25 |
| 70 | Bamboo BLP 206 | FUNKY REGGAE | 60 |
| 82 | Come Org. WDC 881021 | FÜR ILSE KOCH (some on red vinyl) | 120 |
| 06 | Trunk JBH 018 LP | FUZZY FELT FOLK (LP, 100 with fuzzy felt inserts) | 60 |
| 70 | RCA Victor SF 8118 | 49 GREEK STREET (LP, featuring Synanthesia, Nadia Cattouse, Tin Angel & Keith Christmas) | 70 |
| 76 | Burning Sounds BS 1024 | FUNNY FEELING (LP) | 30 |
| 83 | Greensleeves GREL 60 | FORWARD | 20 |
| 03 | Trunk JBH 004 LP | FLEXI SEX (LP) | 30 |
| 06 | Trunk JBH 018 LP | FUZZY FELT FOLK (LP) | 50 |

# G

| 69 | Pama ECO 4 | GAS - GREATEST HITS | 100 |
| 66 | Doctor Bird DLM 5001 | GAYFEET (Jamaican sleeve and UK pressed LP) | 400 |
| 84 | Kent KENT 021 | GEMS | 15 |
| 55 | HMV DLP 1039 | GENE NORMAN PRESENTS JUST JAZZ (10") | 20 |
| 72 | Chess 6641 047 | GENESIS - THE BEGINNINGS OF ROCK (4-LP box set with booklet) | 60 |
| 73 | Chess 6641 125 | GENESIS - MEMPHIS TO CHICAGO (4-LP box set with booklet) | 60 |
| 75 | Chess 6641 174 | GENESIS - SWEET HOME CHICAGO (4-LP box set with booklet) | 60 |
| 69 | Kokomo K 1004 | GEORGIA GUITARS 1927-1938 (99 copies only) | 60 |
| 67 | Coxsone CSL 8007 | GET READY ROCK STEADY | 200 |
| 02 | Soundway SNDWLP001 | GHANA SOUNDZ - AFRO-BEAT, FUNK AND FUSION IN THE 70s (2-LP) | 25 |
| 69 | Pama SECO 20 | A GIFT FROM PAMA | 60 |
| 71 | Wand WCS 1003 | THE GIRLS WITH SOUL | 15 |
| 80s | Sarah | GLASS ARCADE (The Field Mice/The Sea Urchins, et al.) | 30 |
| 72 | Revelation REV 1/2/3 | GLASTONBURY FAYRE REVELATIONS - A MUSICAL ANTHOLOGY (3-LP, poster sleeve with booklets, pyramid & printed polythene bag) | 200 |
| 66 | Columbia SX 6062 | GO! | 70 |
| 80s | Touch & Go TG 11 | GOD'S FAVOURITE DOG | 20 |
| 95 | Lissy's LISS 5 | GODZ IS NOT A PUT ON (500 only, in hand-pressed sleeve; some with free 7") | 30 |
| 72 | Flyright LP 103 | GOIN' AWAY WALKING | 15 |
| 70 | Python LP 1 | GOIN' BACK TO CHICAGO (99 copies only) | 80 |
| 60s | Heritage 1003 | GOING TO CALIFORNIA (99 copies only) | 80 |
| 68 | Decca LK 4931 | GOIN' UP THE COUNTRY | 30 |
| 69 | Oliver & Boyd SBN 05 002118/9 | THE GOLDEN BIRD (2-LP) | 20 |
| 64 | Columbia 33SX 1664 | GOLDEN GOODIES VOL. 1 | 60 |
| 64 | Columbia 33SX 1672 | GOLDEN GOODIES VOL. 2 | 60 |
| 69 | Roulette RCP 1000 | GOLDEN GOODIES VOL. 1 | 20 |
| 69 | Roulette RCP 1001 | GOLDEN GOODIES VOL. 2 | 20 |
| 68 | Allegro ALL885 | GOLDEN HITS OF SOUL | 20 |
| 57 | Capitol T 830 | THE GOLD RECORD (blue label) | 15 |
| 03 | Dust To Digital DTD 01 | GOODBYE BABYLON (6-CD box set) | 60 |
| 75 | Eron 004 | GOOD FOLK OF KENT (with insert) | 40 |
| 65 | Atlantic ATL 5004 | GOOD OLD FIFTIES | 55 |
| 68 | Elek. EUK 260/EUKS 7260 | GOOD TIME MUSIC (U.K. version of "What's Shakin' ", gold or red label) | 40 |
| 72 | CBS 67234 | GOSPEL SOUND (2-LP) | 20 |
| 59 | Brunswick LAT 8290 | GOSPEL TRAIN | 20 |
| 64 | London HA-B 8172 | GRAND OLE OPRY SPECTACULAR VOL. 1 | 18 |
| 64 | London HA-B 8173 | GRAND OLE OPRY SPECTACULAR VOL. 2 | 18 |
| 73 | Greasy Truckers GT 4997 | GREASY TRUCKERS - LIVE AT DINGWALLS DANCE HALL (2-LP with insert) | 18 |
| 73 | United Artists UDX 203/4 | GREASY TRUCKERS PARTY (2-LP, gatefold sleeve) | 20 |
| 72 | Vanguard VSD 25/26 | GREAT BLUESMEN (2-LP) | 18 |
| 54 | London AL 3530 | THE GREAT BLUES SINGERS (10") | 45 |
| 60s | Riverside RLP 12-121 | THE GREAT BLUES SINGERS | 25 |
| 70 | Trojan TBL 111 | GREATER JAMAICA | 20 |
| 75 | Brunswick BRLS 3006 | GREATEST HITS | 15 |
| 64 | Stateside SL 10075 | THE GREATEST GOSPEL SONGS OF OUR TIME | 25 |
| 67 | Doctor Bird DLM 5009 | GREATEST JAMAICAN BEAT | 200 |
| 70 | Transatlantic TRASAM 17 | GREAT SCOTS SAMPLER | 20 |
| 70 | Transatlantic TRASAM 21 | GREAT SCOTS SAMPLER VOL. 2 | 20 |
| 54 | HMV DLP 1054 | GREAT TRUMPET SOLOISTS (10") | 25 |
| 85 | Crashed METALPS 107 | GREEN METAL | 30 |
| 89 | Earache MOSH 12 | GRINDCRUSHER (with free 7") | 15 |
| 71 | Bamboo BDLP 215 | GROOVING WITH BAMBOO | 70 |
| 69 | Direction 8-63452 | GROOVY BABY | 15 |
| 63 | Realm RM 149 | GROUP BEAT '63 | 40 |
| 63 | London HA-U 8086 | GROUP OF GOODIES | 55 |
| 78 | Virgin VCL 5001 | GUILLOTINE (10" mini-LP, with inner sleeve) | 18 |

| | | | |
|---|---|---|---|
| 60s | Storyville SLP 166 | GUITAR BLUES | 20 |
| 71 | Sunnyland KS 102 | GULF COAST BLUES (99 copies only) | 40 |
| 69 | Trojan TTL 16 | GUNS OF NAVARONE | 20 |
| 69 | Liberty LBX 3 | GUTBUCKET | 25 |
| 68 | Island ILP 977 | GUY STEVENS' TESTAMENT OF ROCK AND ROLL | 60 |
| 71 | Wand WCS 1002 | THE GUYS WITH SOUL | 20 |
| 84 | Fashion FAD LP 001 | GREAT BRITISH MCS | 15 |
| 79 | Bead Records BEAD 15 | GROUPS IN FRONT OF PEOPLE (LP) | 25 |
| 79 | Bead Records BEAD 15 | GROUPS IN FRONT OF PEOPLE 2 (LP) | 25 |
| 76 | Cactus CTLP 115 | GUSSIE PRESENTS THE RIGHT TRACKS | 20 |

## H

| | | | |
|---|---|---|---|
| 80 | Hackney Music Coll LP1 | HACKNEY MUSIC COLLECTIVE | 25 |
| 58 | Oriole MG 20033 | HAIL VARIETY! | 15 |
| 88 | Hangman HANG 22-UP | HANGMAN SAMPLER | 20 |
| 88 | HandMade (no cat. no.) | HANDMADE FILMS MUSIC - THE 10TH ANNIVERSARY (CD, promo only) | 100 |
| 85 | Anagram GRAM 23 | HANG 11 (MUTANT SURF PUNKS) | 20 |
| 78 | Black Symbol BS 004 | HANDSWORTH EXPLOSION VOL 1 (LP) | 70 |
| 68 | Immediate IMLYIN 2 | HAPPY TO BE PART OF THE INDUSTRY OF HUMAN HAPPINESS | 18 |
| 88 | Strange Fruit SFRLP 101 | HARDCORE HOLOCAUST | 15 |
| 90 | Strange Fruit SFRLP 113 | HARCORE HOLOCAUST 2 | 20 |
| 88 | BPM BPLP2 | HARDCORE ONE (LP) | 40 |
| 87 | Music Scene MKSLP 11416 | HARDER THAN THE REST (LP) | 40 |
| 77 | VJM VLP 40 | HARD LUCK BLUES | 18 |
| 74 | Decca DPA 3009/10 | HARD UP HEROES 1963-68 (2-LP, gatefold sleeve) | 20 |
| 71 | Harvest SHSS 3 | HARVEST BAG | 15 |
| 99 | Harvest 724352119820 | HARVEST FESTIVAL (5-CD box set) | 50 |
| 77 | Harvest SHSM 2020 | HARVEST HERITAGE : 20 GREATS | 15 |
| 69 | Harvest SPSLP 118 | HARVEST SAMPLER OF THE INITIAL FOUR JUNE RELEASES (promo only) | 300 |
| 84 | Rot ASS 18 | HAVE AROTTEN CHRISTMAS (LP) | 25 |
| 71 | Sunnyland KS 101 | HAVIN' A GOOD TIME - CHICAGO BLUES ANTHOLOGY (99 copies only) | 50 |
| 12 | Fruits De Mer CRUSTACEAN 26 | HEAD MUSIC (2-LP, 850 only, gatefold sleeve, 1 LP yellow and one LP purple vinyl) | 25 |
| 71 | Vertigo 6360 045 | HEADS TOGETHER, FIRST ROUND (gatefold sleeve, swirl label) | 18 |
| 94 | Mo' Wax MWLP 026 | HEADZ: A SOUNDTRACK OF EXPERIMENTAL BEATHEAD JAMS (3-LP) | 25 |
| 96 | Mo' Wax MW 061LP | HEADZ VOLUME 2A (4-LP) | 40 |
| 08 | Jonny JBH 025 LP | HEAR O ISRAEL (LP) | 20 |
| 90 | Imaginary ILLUSION 016 | HEAVEN AND HELL VOLUME 1: A TRIBUTE TO THE VELVET UNDERGROUND | 70 |
| 81 | Heavy Metal HMR LP 1 | HEAVY METAL HEROES | 30 |
| 82 | Heavy Metal HMR LP 7 | HEAVY METAL HEROES VOLUME 2 | 25 |
| 84 | Heavy Metal HMR LP 24 | HEAVY METAL RECORDS (blue, clear & white vinyl, round sleeve) | 15 |
| 68 | Trojan TRL 6 | HERE COMES THE DUKE | 40 |
| 65 | Pye NPL 18121 | HERE COME THE GIRLS | 15 |
| 85 | Rock 'N' Dole RDR 2 | HEROES | 15 |
| 80s | Temps Modernes LTMV:XI | HEURES SANS SOLEIL | 20 |
| 69 | Pama PSP 1002 | HEY BOY HEY GIRL | 60 |
| 59 | Parlophone PMD 1085 | HIGHWAY TO HEAVEN (10") | 20 |
| 52 | Capitol LC 6508 | THE HISTORY OF JAZZ - THE SOLID SOUTH | 20 |
| 69 | Bamboo BDLP 203 | HISTORY OF SKA VOLUME ONE | 200 |
| 87 | Stylus/PWL SMD 740 | HIT FACTORY - THE BEST OF STOCK, AITKEN & WATERMAN VOL. 1 (CD) | 25 |
| 87 | Fanfare/PWL HFCD 4 | HIT FACTORY - THE BEST OF STOCK, AITKEN & WATERMAN VOL. 2 (CD, with exclusive mix of Kylie Minogue's "I Should Be So Lucky", etc) | 30 |
| 64 | Pye NPL 18108 | THE HITMAKERS | 20 |
| 77 | Stiff FIST 1 | HITS - GREATEST STIFFS (with 7", Max Wall's "England's Glory" [BUY 12]) | 12 |
| 65 | Tamla Motown TML 11019 | HITSVILLE U.S.A. | 35 |
| 67 | Stax 589 005 | HIT THE ROAD STAX | 30 |
| 81 | United Dairies UD 05 | HOISTING THE BLACK FLAG | 35 |
| 74 | Melodisc 12-216 | HONEYS | 35 |
| 60s | Riverside RLP 8806 | HONKY TONK TRAIN (with booklet) | 22 |
| 84 | Kent KENT 023 | HOT CHILLS AND COLD THRILLS | 15 |
| 71 | Pama PMP 2006 | HOT NUMBERS | 40 |
| 71 | Pama PMP 2009 | HOT NUMBERS VOLUME TWO | 30 |
| 77 | WEA M 100 | HOT PLATTER CORDON BLEU (available via Melody Maker) | 20 |
| 72 | Hot Wax SHW 5008 | HOT WAX GREATEST HITS | 15 |
| 69 | Track 613 016 | THE HOUSE THAT TRACK BUILT (gatefold sleeve) | 30 |
| 80 | Stark ST1 | HOUSEHOLD SHOCKS | 40 |
| 69 | Blue Horizon PR 45/46 | HOW BLUE CAN WE GET (2-LP, gatefold sleeve with insert) | 40 |
| 82 | Native NAT 001 | HUNDREDS AND THOUSANDS | 45 |

## I

| | | | |
|---|---|---|---|
| 88 | Idea IDEALP 003 | IDEA COMPENDIUM (LP) | 35 |
| 81 | TJM TJML 1 | IDENTITY PARADE (LP) | 15 |
| 02 | Universal 0647491 | IMPRESSED (2-LP, Gilles Peterson compilation) | 30 |
| 02 | Universal 982 197 0 | IMPRESSED 2 (2-LP, Gilles Peterson compilation) | 25 |
| 69 | Liberty LBL/LBS 83252 | I ASKED FOR WATER ... AND SHE GAVE ME GASOLINE | 80 |
| 88 | Bam Caruso MARX 085 | ILLUSIONS FROM THE CRACKLING VOID | 15 |
| 90s | Dig The Fuzz DIG 013 | ILLUSIONS OF ALICE IN BLACK (650 only, with booklet) | 20 |
| 69 | Immediate IMLYIN 1 | IMMEDIATE LETS YOU IN | 20 |
| 70 | Highway 51 H-104 | I'M YOUR COUNTRY MAN (99 copies only) | 40 |
| 95 | Dig The Fuzz DIG 001 | INCREDIBLE SOUND SHOW STORIES VOL 1: THE TECHNICOLOUR MILKSHAKE (LP) | 20 |

| 96 | Dig The Fuzz DIG 004 | INCREDIBLE SOUND SHOW STORIES VOL 2: WHEN THE TANGERINE STRIKES TWELVE (LP, gatefold sleeve, orange vinyl) | 20 |
|---|---|---|---|
| 96 | Dig The Fuzz DIG 007 | INCREDIBLE SOUND SHOW STORIES VOL 3: 200 FEEL DEEP IN A PURPLE IDEA (LP) | 20 |
| 96 | Dig The Fuzz DIG 008 | INCREDIBLE SOUND SHOW STORIES VOL 4: A TRIP ON THE MAGIC FLYING MACHINE (LP) | 20 |
| 96 | Dig The Fuzz DIG 009 | INCREDIBLE SOUND SHOW STORIES VOL. 5: YELLOW STREET BOUTIQUE (LP) | 20 |
| 97 | Dig The Fuzz DIG 010 | INCREDIBLE SOUND SHOW STORIES VOL. 6: PLASTIC & OTHER RUBBERS OF LIFE (LP) | 20 |
| 97 | Dig THe Fuzz DIG 013 | INCREDIBLE SOUND SHOW STORIES VOL. 7: ILLUSIONS OF ALICE IN BLACK (LP, with booklet) | 20 |
| 99 | Dig The Fuzz DIG 016 | INCREDIBLE SOUND SHOW STORIES: VOL. 8: PROFESSOR POTTS PORNOGRAPHIC PROJECTOR (LP, with booklet) | 30 |
| 99 | Dig The Fuzz DIG 036 | INCREDIBLE SOUND SHOW STORIES VOL. 9: CLAP HANDS DADDY COME HOME! (LP, with booklet) | 20 |
| 99 | Dig THe Fuzz DIG 039 | INCREDIBLE SOUND SHOW STIRIES VOL. 10: A HIDDEN SECRET GARDEN FOUND (LP, with booklet) | 20 |
| 99 | Dig The Fuzz DIG 033 | INCREDIBLE SOUND SHOW STORIES: VOL. 11: CRIMSON VALLET CREATURES IN YOUR ZOO (LP, with booklet) | 20 |
| 01 | Dig THe Fuzz DIG 043 | INCREDIBLE SOUND SHOW STORIES VOL. 12: FUZZ PUDDING FACTORY (LP) | 15 |
| 01 | Buzz With Fuzz FUZZLP 3301 | INCREDIBLE SOUND SHOW STORIES VOL. 13: FAR AWAY ROUNDABOUT (LP, 500 only) | 15 |
| 00 | Dig THe Fuzz DIG 042 | INCREDIBLE SOUND SHOW SPORIES VOL. 14: CANDY COLOURED DAYDREAMS (LP, with gatefold insert) | 20 |
| 03 | Dig THe Fuzz DIG 046 | INCREDIBLE COUND SHOW STORIES VOL. 16 : SECOND GLANCE THROUGH THE LOOKING GLANCE (LP) | 20 |
| 02 | Dig THe Fuzz DIG 045 | INCREDIBLE SOUND SHOW STORIES VOL. 17 CLAP HANDS DADDY COME HOME1 PART 2 (LP, with inner sleeve, 400 only) | 20 |
| 66 | CBS/Denson Shoes | THE IN CROWD (shoe offer compilation) | 25 |
| 69 | Trojan TTL 15 | INDEPENDENT JAMAICA | 12 |
| 79 | Object Music OBJ 002 | INDISCRETE MUSIC - DUBIOUS COLLABORATION (500 only) | 15 |
| 84 | Illuminated JAMS 39 | THE INDUSTRIAL RECORDS STORY 1976-1981 | 35 |
| 84 | United Dairies UD 015 | IN FRACTURED SILENCE | 35 |
| 69 | T. Motown (S)TML 11124 | IN LOVING MEMORY (TRIBUTE TO MRS LOUCYE G. WAKEFIELD) | 55 |
| 70 | Blue Horizon PR 37 | IN OUR OWN WAY (OLDIES BUT GOODIES) | 20 |
| 84 | People Unite PU 104 | IN PROGRESS | 50 |
| 70 | Ember EMB 34111 | IN REGGAE TIME | 15 |
| 83 | Future FUTURE 1 | INVISIBLE FRAME | 18 |
| 66 | Ember FA 2034 | IRELAND'S GREATEST SOUNDS: FIVE TOP GROUPS FROM BELFAST'S MARITIME CLUB | 70 |
| 63 | Topic 12T 86 | THE IRON MUSE (blue label with lyric insert) | 15 |
| 79 | Rationale RATE 8 | IRRATIONALE (cassette, in bag with booklet) | 20 |
| 79 | K Block | IS THE WAR OVER? | 25 |
| 61 | Oriole MG 20046 | IT'S ALL HAPPENING HERE | 35 |
| 64 | Philips BL 7609 | IT'S ALL OVER TOWN | 15 |
| 63 | Pye Golden Guinea GGL 0249 | IT'S DANCE TIME | 0 |
| 85 | Kent KENT 046 | IT'S TORTURE | 15 |
| 84 | Sain 002 | IT'S UNHEARD OF | 150 |

## J

| 69 | Amalgamated CSP 3 | JACKPOT OF HITS | 50 |
|---|---|---|---|
| 74 | Atra ALP 001 | JAH GUIDE - JAMAICA'S GREATEST HITS | 20 |
| 71 | Ashanti SHAN 102 | JAMAICAN FOLK SINGERS | 20 |
| 68 | Blue Cat BCL 1 | JAMAICAN MEMORIES | 150 |
| 64 | Atlantic 587 075 | JAMAICA SKA (colour 'Dancers' sleeve) | 70 |
| 67 | Atlantic 587 075 | JAMAICA SKA (reissue, orange sleeve) | 50 |
| 60s | Whirl WHIRL 1 | JAMAICA'S AMBASSADORS OF SONG | 100 |
| 60s | Melodisc MLP 12-158 | JAMAICA'S GREATEST | 30 |
| 72 | Utd. Artists UAS 60027/8 | THE JAMES BOND COLLECTION (2-LP, with booklet) | 25 |
| 56 | Tempo TAP 5 | JAZZ AT THE FLAMINGO | 120 |
| 68 | Columbia SLJS 1 | JAZZ EXPLOSION | 15 |
| 72 | Decca ECS 2114 | JAZZ IN BRITAIN 1968-1969 | 50 |
| 84 | Streetsounds MUSIC 1 | JAZZ JUICE | 25 |
| 85 | Streetsounds SOUND 1 | JAZZ JUICE (reissue) | 20 |
| 62 | Parlophone PMC 1177 | JAZZ SOUNDS OF THE 20s VOL. 4: BLUES SINGERS & ACCOMPANISTS | 12 |
| 85 | Natalie LIE 1 | JOBS FOR THE BOYS | 15 |
| 77 | Decca DPA 3035/3036 | THE JOE MEEK STORY (2-LP) | 30 |
| 69 | BBC REC 52S | JOHN PEEL PRESENTS TOP GEAR | 40 |
| 70 | BBC REC 68M | JOHN PEEL'S ARCHIVE THINGS | 35 |
| 60 | HMV CLP 1327 | A JUG OF PUNCH (also issued as XLP 50003) | 25 |
| 67 | Ace Of Hearts AH 163 | JUGS AND WASHBOARDS | 15 |
| 67 | RCA Victor RD 7893 | JUGS WASHBOARDS AND KAZOOS | 15 |
| 70s | Eric's ERICS 008 | JUKEBOX AT ERIC'S | 15 |
| 76 | RCA RS 1066 | JUMPING AT THE GO GO | 18 |
| 64 | R&B JBL 1111 | JUMP JAMAICA WAY | 600 |
| 69 | RCA Intl. INT 1014 | JUST A LITTLE BIT OF SOUL | 22 |
| 75 | Count Shelly CSLP 7 | JUST BETWEEN (nude cover) | 50 |
| 79 | Kick KK 1 | JUST FOR KICKS | 35 |

## K

| 59 | Capitol T 1057 | K.C. IN THE 30's | 10 |
|---|---|---|---|
| 11 | Fruits De Mer Crustacian 21 | KEEP OFF THE GRASS (2-LP) | 20 |
| 56 | Vogue LAE 12028 | KENTON'S SIDEMEN (Don Rendell, et al.) | 60 |
| 81 | White Witch | KENT ROCKS (200 only, white cover) | 180 |
| 54 | HMV DLP 1048 | KEYBOARD KINGS OF JAZZ (10") | 20 |

MINT VALUE £

| 72 | Key | KEY COLLECTION (with insert) | 15 |
|---|---|---|---|
| 82 | Kik KIKLP 01 | KIKROCK VOLUME ONE | 35 |
| 70 | Trojan TBL 140 | KING SIZE REGGAE | 20 |
| 72 | Sioux SLX 7502 | KING OF THE ROAD | 25 |
| 68 | Polydor 623 273 | KINGS OF RHYTHM AND BLUES | 15 |
| 94 | Mercury 522 476-1 | KISS MY ASS (red, white or blue vinyl) | 12 |

## L

| 79 | Cherry Red A RED 4 | LABELS UNLIMITED (LP with inner) | 15 |
|---|---|---|---|
| 83 | Fetish FR 2011 | THE LAST TESTAMENT (with inner, stickered sleeve) | 18 |
| 87 | Other OTH 10 | LAST WARRIOR | 18 |
| 68 | Island ILP 986 | LEAPING WITH MR LEE (by Bunny Lee All Stars) | 400 |
| 80 | Atra ATRA LP 1003 | THE LEGENDS (Augustus Pablo et al.) | 15 |
| 03 | Ai AILP 004 | LEISURE (100 copies only) | 15 |
| 99 | Jazzman 1 | LE JAZZBEAT! | 20 |
| 66 | Blue Horizon LP 2 | LET ME TELL YOU ABOUT THE BLUES (99 copies only) | 1000 |
| 63 | Polydor SLPHM 237 622 | LET'S DO THE TWIST, HULLY GULLY, SLOP, SURF, LOCOMOTION, MONKEY | 30 |
| 66 | Neshoba N 11 | LET'S GO DOWN SOUTH (99 copies only) | 55 |
| 84 | Cult 1 | LET'S GET PISSED IT'S CHRISTMAS | 15 |
| 58 | Brunswick LAT 8271 | LET'S HAVE A PARTY | 30 |
| 73 | Bell DUBL 9002/3 | LET THE GOOD TIMES ROLL | 15 |
| 81 | Alt. Tentacles VIRUS 4 | LET THEM EAT JELLYBEANS (with lyric poster) | 20 |
| 80s | Third Mind/Abstract | LIFE AT THE TOP | 20 |
| 85 | Riot City CITY 019 | LIFE'S A RIOT WITH RIOT CITY RECORDS | 20 |
| 80 | BUN 01 | LIVE AT BUNJIES (gatefold sleeve with insert) | 30 |
| 74 | Key KL 021 | LIVE AT SPREE | 15 |
| 77 | NEMS NEL 6013 | LIVE AT THE VORTEX | 15 |
| 65 | Fontana TL 5240 | LIVE AT THE WHISKEY A-GO-GO | 40 |
| 68 | Big Shot BBTL 4000 | LIVE IT UP | 125 |
| 64 | Embassy WLP 6065 | LIVERPOOL BEAT | 15 |
| 65 | Ember NR 5028 | LIVERPOOL TODAY - LIVE AT THE CAVERN | 40 |
| 64 | CBS Realm RM 209 | LIVIN' WITH THE BLUES | 15 |
| 08 | Honest Jons HJRLP 33 | LIVING IS HARD - WEST AFRICAN MUSIC IN BRITAIN 1927-29 (2-LP) | 20 |
| 70 | Trojan TBL 135 | LOCH NESS MONSTER | 50 |
| 87 | 4AD CAD 703D | LONELY IS AN EYESORE (cardboard pack with book) | 30 |
| 87 | 4AD CADX 703 | LONELY IS AN EYESORE (CD, LP & cassette, in wooden box with etching, screen print & video, 100 only) | 1000 |
| 71 | Count Shelly SSLP 03 | LOOK BEFORE YOU LEAP | 60 |
| 91 | Holyground HG 121 | LOOSE ROUTES (2-LP, gatefold foldover sleeve) | 30 |
| 65 | Storyville 616002 | LOUISIANA PRISON BLUES | 15 |
| 69 | Pama PSP 1001 | A LOVELY DOZEN | 60 |
| 96 | Earth EARTHLP 001 | LTJ BUKEM PRESENTS EARTH VOLUME 1 (5 LP box set, stickered box, 5 picture sleeves,5000 only) | 35 |
| 97 | Earth EARTHLP 002 | LTJ BUKEM PRESENTS EARTH VOLUME 2 (5 LP box set, 5 picture sleeves) | 25 |
| 98 | Good Looking EARTH LP 003 | LTJ BUKEM PRESENTS EARTH VOLUME 3 (5 LP box set) | 25 |

## M

| 76 | Cornish Legend CLM 1 | MADE IN CORNWALL (with insert) | 12 |
|---|---|---|---|
| 79 | Object Music OBJ 003 | A MANCHESTER COLLECTION | 25 |
| 70 | Trojan TBL 129 | MAN FROM CAROLINA | 30 |
| 53 | Brunswick LA 8567 | MAN WITH A HORN (10" LP) | 12 |
| 70 | CBS 52798 | MA RAINEY AND THE CLASSIC BLUES SINGERS | 20 |
| 69 | Marmalade 643 314 | MARMALADE - 100% PROOF | 15 |
| 72 | Village Thing VTSAM 16 | MATCHBOX DAYS | 25 |
| 68 | President PTL 1002 | MAR-V-LUS SOUND OF R&B AND SOUL MUSIC | 40 |
| 60s | Wudwink ISMF 107 | MARY'S FOLK | 200 |
| 66 | CBS Special Prod. WSR 853 | McDONALDS ALL-STAR FAVOURITES | 12 |
| 69 | Liberty LBL/LBS 83190 | ME AND THE DEVIL | 75 |
| 88 | Hangman HANG 15-UP | THE MEDWAY POETS (LP) | 20 |
| 87 | Hangman HANG 4 UP | MEDWAY POWER HOUSE 1 | 20 |
| 87 | Hangman HANG 8 UP | MEDWAY POWER HOUSE 2 | 20 |
| 88 | Hangman HANG 17 UP | MEDWAY POWER HOUSE 3 | 25 |
| 69 | T. Motown (S)TML 11126 | MERRY CHRISTMAS FROM MOTOWN (mono/stereo) | 40 |
| 67 | Capitol T 9030 | MERRY CHRISTMAS TO YOU | 15 |
| 80 | BBC REH 397 | METAL EXPLOSION | 20 |
| 80 | EMI EMC 3318 | METAL FOR MUTHAS | 20 |
| 97 | Metalheadz METBOX 001 | METALHEADZ (5 discs in circular tin, booklet) | 30 |
| 87 | Other OTH 9 | METAL WARRIOR | 50 |
| 56 | Nixa Jazz Today NJL 3 | MIDNIGHT AT NIXA | 20 |
| 66 | Atlantic 587 021 | MIDNIGHT SOUL | 20 |
| 69 | Storyville 616 009 | MIDNIGHT SPECIAL | 15 |
| 62 | Brunswick LAT 8401 | MIDNIGHT JAMBOREE (also stereo STA 3061) | 12 |
| 80 | Pipe PIPE 2 | MINIATURES (with poster insert, 500 only) | 18 |
| 80 | Pipe PIPE 2 | MINIATURES (cassette with mini-booklet insert, 100 only) | 30 |
| 71 | Trojan TBL 174 | MISS LABBA LABBA REGGAE | 30 |
| 60 | Top Rank BUY 028 | MR. BLUE | 30 |
| 60s | Bounty BY 6025 | MODERN CHICAGO BLUES | 30 |
| 56 | Tempo TAP 2 | MODERN JAZZ SCENE 1956 | 100 |
| 53 | Esquire 20-011 | MODERN MIXTURE VOLUME ONE (10") | 20 |
| 79 | Bridge House BHLP 003 | MODS MAYDAY '79 (original issue) | 20 |

| 01 | EMI 5 35078 2 | MOJO PRESENTS ACID DROPS, SPACEDUST AND FLYING SAUCERS (4-CD box set) | 40 |
|---|---|---|---|
| 70 | Trojan TTL 31 | MOONLIGHT GROOVER | 20 |
| 70 | Liberty LBS 83377 | MORE FROM THE VAULTS | 15 |
| 62 | HMV CLP 1583 | MORE OF YOUR FAVOURITE TV AND RADIO THEMES | 20 |
| 67 | Atlantic 587088 | MORE MIDNIGHT SOUL | 15 |
| 65 | private pressing | MORE SINGING AT THE COUNT HOUSE | 250 |
| 72 | Island HELP 5 | MORRIS ON (black label with pink 'i') | 20 |
| 80 | Conventional CON 013 | MOTHER OF A PUNK (cassette) | 12 |
| 86 | Iguana VYK LP 11 | MOTOR CITY 9 (with booklet) | 15 |
| 65 | Tamla Motown TML 11007 | THE MOTORTOWN REVUE LIVE | 80 |
| 66 | Tamla Motown TML 11027 | THE MOTORTOWN REVUE IN PARIS | 70 |
| 70 | T. Motown (S)TML 11127 | THE MOTORTOWN REVUE LIVE (mono/stereo) | 20 |
| 74 | T. Motown STML 11270 | MOTOWN CHARTBUSTERS VOL. 9 (green vinyl) | 12 |
| 66 | Tamla Motown TML 11030 | MOTOWN MAGIC | 35 |
| 68 | Tamla Motown TML 11064 | MOTOWN MEMORIES (flipback sleeve) | 60 |
| 68 | Tamla Motown TML 11077 | MOTOWN MEMORIES VOL. 2 | 60 |
| 70 | T. Motown STML 11143 | MOTOWN MEMORIES VOL. 3 | 50 |
| 72 | Tamla Motown TMSP 1130 | THE MOTOWN STORY (5-LP box set) | 20 |
| 83 | Tamla Motown TMSP 6019 | THE MOTOWN STORY - THE FIRST 25 YEARS (box set) | 20 |
| 77 | Mountain PSLP 200 | MOUNTAIN ROCKS INTO '77 (Mountain label sampler, promo only) | 20 |
| 84 | Kent 013 | MOVING ON UP | 15 |
| 57 | Pye NJL 11 | MURDERER'S HOME | 20 |
| 71 | Mushroom 100 MR 16 | THE MUSHROOM FOLK SAMPLER | 40 |
| 57 | Brunswick LAT 8201 | MUSIC FOR THE BOYFRIEND - HE REALLY DIGS ROCK'N'ROLL | 100 |
| 57 | Brunswick LAT 8202 | MUSIC FOR THE BOYFRIEND - HE REALLY DIGS JAZZ | 30 |
| 57 | Brunswick LAT 8205 | MUSIC FOR THE BOYFRIEND - THE FEMININE TOUCH | 35 |
| 67 | Argo RG 533 | MUSIC FROM THE FAR NORTH (with foldout inner) | 15 |
| 81 | Ze ISSP 4001 | MUTANT DISCO (3 x 12" box set, numbered, 2,000 only) | 20 |
| 77 | EMI NUT 4 | MY GENERATION | 15 |
| 89 | Hangman HANG 35 UP | MEDWAY POWERHOUSE (LP) | 30 |
| 78 | Tartone TTL 010 | MASTER MIX (LP) | 25 |

## N

| 73 | Enterprise ESAM 100 | THE NAME OF THE GAME | 15 |
|---|---|---|---|
| 71 | Eden LP 43 | NAPTON FOLK CLUB (private pressing, 100 only) | 35 |
| 69 | Bamboo BLP 201 | NATURAL REGGAE VOLUME ONE | 50 |
| 70 | Bamboo BLP 204 | NATURAL REGGAE VOLUME TWO | 100 |
| 81 | 4AD CAD 117 | NATURES MORTES - STILL LIVES (export issue) | 60 |
| 85 | Musique Brut BRV 002 | NECROPOLIS, AMPHIBIANS AND REPTILES: THE MUSIC OF ADOLF WOLFLI | 20 |
| 71 | RCA NEON 1 | NEON PROMOTIONAL ALBUM | 150 |
| 83 | Pax PAX 14 | NEVER MIND THE GONADS - HERE'S THE TESTICLES | 15 |
| 87 | Broken Flag BF V8 | NEVER SAY WHEN | 40 |
| 77 | Vertigo 6300 902 | NEW WAVE | 20 |
| 79 | Planet PR 003 | NEW WAVE FROM THE HEART | 70 |
| 69 | Blue Horizon 7-63210 | THE 1968 MEMPHIS COUNTRY BLUES FESTIVAL | 25 |
| 83 | DEL 306 | 19TH CAMBRIDGE FOLK FESTIVAL VOLUME 1 | 20 |
| 81 | NMX | NMX: LIVE AT SHEFFIELD (cassette) | 20 |
| 68 | Spark SRLM 107 | NO INTRODUCTION | 30 |
| 69 | Trojan TTL 14 | NO MORE HEARTACHES | 25 |
| 70 | Polydor 545 017 | NON STOP SOUL | 30 |
| 69 | Regal Starline SRS 5013 | NO ONE'S GONNA CHANGE OUR WORLD | 18 |
| 89 | Manic Ears ACHE 017 | NORTH ATLANTIC NOISE ATTACK (2-LP, insert) | 20 |
| 64 | Concert Hall AM 2339 | NORTHUMBRIAN MINSTRELS | 15 |
| 60 | Fontana TFL 5123 | NOTHIN' BUT THE BLUES (gatefold sleeve) | 60 |
| 71 | CBS 66278 | NOTHING BUT THE BLUES (2-LP, Blue Horizon pressings may also exist (£75)) | 60 |
| 79 | Giorno GPS | THE NOVA CONVENTION | 20 |
| 70 | Decca Nova SPA 72 | NOVA SAMPLER | 20 |
| 70s | Warm PFLP 201 | NOVA-VAGA | 15 |
| 79 | A&M AMLE 68505 | NO WAVE (orange, mauve or blue vinyl) | 12 |
| 84 | Virgin/EMI CDP 26 0408 2 | NOW THAT'S WHAT I CALL MUSIC 4 (CD) | 200 |
| 86 | Virgin/EMI CDNOW 8 | NOW THAT'S WHAT I CALL MUSIC 8 (CD) | 35 |
| 87 | Virgin/EMI CDNOW 9 | NOW THAT'S WHAT I CALL MUSIC 9 (CD) | 35 |
| 69 | Pama ECO 6 | NU BEAT - GREATEST HITS | 60 |
| 73 | Elektra K 62012 | NUGGETS (Original Artyfacts From The First Psychedelic Era 1965-1968) (2-LP, gatefold sleeve) | 45 |
| 86 | Numa NUMA 1004 | NUMA RECORDS YEAR 1 (with bonus Italian 12" "My Dying Machine") | 15 |
| 81 | Guardian Records | N E 1 (LP) | 40 |

## O

| 69 | Liberty LBS 83234 | OAKLAND BLUES | 30 |
|---|---|---|---|
| 79 | Rok ROK LP 001 | ODD BODS, MODS AND SODS | 75 |
| 85 | Micro MIC 15001 | OFFERING OF ISCA (LP, features 2 tracks by Circuit 7) | 100 |
| 58 | Parlophone PMC 1072 | OH BOY! | 40 |
| 78 | Raw RAWLP 2 | OH NO IT'S MORE FROM RAW (Users/Killjoys et al.) | 20 |
| 80 | EMI ZIT 1 | OI! - THE ALBUM (initially mail-order only from Sounds magazine) | 30 |
| 87 | Link LP 23 | OI! GLORIOUS OI! | 15 |
| 86 | OI OIR 004 | THIS IS OI! | 15 |
| 84 | Syndicate SYNLP 4 | OI! OF SEX | 15 |
| 83 | Secret SEC 5 | OI! OI! THAT'S YER LOT | 15 |
| 60s | Melodisc MS 4 | OLDIES BUT GOODIES | 50 |

| | | | |
|---|---|---|---|
| 64 | Stateside SL 10094 | OLDIES R & B | 70 |
| 69 | Transatlantic XTRA 1076 | O LIVERPOOL WE LOVE YOU (Stan Kelly/Bill Shankley/Jimmy Tarbuck et al.) | 40 |
| 68 | Big Shot BBTL 4001 | ONCE MORE | 100 |
| 69 | Marmalade 643 314 | 100% PROOF | 15 |
| 99 | Universal MCD 60066 | 1-2-3-4 PUNK AND NEW WAVE 1976 - 1979 (5-CD box set) | 30 |
| 86 | Stateside/EMI SSL 6002 | ONE MINIT AT A TIME | 18 |
| 73 | Charisma CLASS 3 | ONE MORE CHANCE | 20 |
| 63 | Columbia 33SX 1536 | ONE NIGHT STAND | 40 |
| 63 | Stateside SL 10065 | ON STAGE LIVE! | 65 |
| 69 | Atco 228 009/010 | ON STAGE - LIVE (2-LP) | 25 |
| 73 | Xtra XTRA 1133 | ON THE ROAD AGAIN | 20 |
| 84 | Sane SANE 003 | ON THE STREET (LP) | 35 |
| 83 | Kent KENT 006 | ON THE SOUL SIDE | 15 |
| 64 | Columbia 33SX 1662 | ON THE SCENE | 90 |
| 84 | Kent KENT 20 | ON THE UP BEAT | 15 |
| 95 | Tip TIPLP 2 | ORANGE COMPILATION (2-LP) | 20 |
| 63 | Stateside SL 10024 | OPRY TIME IN TENNESSEE | 18 |
| 65 | Allegro ALL 778 | ROY ORBISON SINGS (some tracks by Jerry Lee Lewis, Tommy Roe; black or blue label) | 10 |
| 65 | Ember FA 2005 | ROY ORBISON AND OTHERS (with 4 tracks by Orbison) | 10 |
| 64 | Rio RLP 1 | THE ORIGINAL COOL JAMAICAN SKA | 150 |
| 70 | Mercury SMCL 20182 | ORIGINAL GOLDEN HITS OF THE GREAT BLUES SINGERS | 20 |
| 70 | Mercury SMCL 20183 | ORIGINAL GOLDEN RHYTHM AND BLUES HITS VOLUME 1 | 20 |
| 60 | London HA-G 2308 | THE ORIGINAL HITS | 30 |
| 61 | London HA-G 2339 | THE ORIGINAL HITS VOL. 2 | 30 |
| 63 | Golden Guinea GGL 0240 | THE ORIGINAL HOOTENANNY | 15 |
| 68 | United Artists ULP 1182 | ORIGINAL SOUNDTRACKS OF HITS MUSIC | 15 |
| 64 | Vocalion VA 8017 | ORIGINAL SURFIN' HITS | 65 |
| 62 | London HA-U 2404 | OUR SIGNIFICANT HITS | 70 |
| 65 | Ace Of Hearts AH 72 | OUT CAME THE BLUES | 15 |
| 67 | Ace Of Hearts AH 158 | OUT CAME THE BLUES VOLUME 2 | 15 |
| 83 | Peninsula | OUT OF THE UNKNOWN | 70 |

**P**

| | | | |
|---|---|---|---|
| 70 | Golden Guinea GGL 0451 | PADDY IS DEAD AND THE KIDS KNOW IT (LP) | 150 |
| 65 | Blue Beat BBLP 804 | PAIN IN MY BELLY | 300 |
| 67 | Island ILP 945 | PAKISTANI SOUL SESSION | 75 |
| 90 | Factory FACT 400 | PALATINE - THE FACTORY STORY (4-LP) | 100 |
| 85 | LIL LP2 | PARKSIDE STEELWORKS | 60 |
| 73 | Charisma CAS 1078 | THE PARLOUR SONG BOOK (LP) | 15 |
| 68 | Studio One SOL 9009 | PARTY TIME IN JAMAICA | 120 |
| 66 | Decca LK 4824 | PENTHOUSE MAGAZINE PRESENTS THE BEDSIDE BOND | 40 |
| 83 | Psycho PSYCHO 6 | THE PERFUMED GARDEN | 20 |
| 84 | Psycho PSYCHO 15 | THE PERFUMED GARDEN II | 20 |
| 81 | Cherry Red BRED 15 | PERSPECTIVES AND DISTORTION (gatefold sleeve) | 15 |
| 86 | Streetsounds PHST 1986 | THE PHILADELPHIA YEARS (14-LP box set) | 80 |
| 92 | Art ART2 CD | THE PHILOSOPHY OF SOUND AND MACHINE (CD compilation) | 60 |
| 72 | Apple APCOR 24 | PHIL SPECTOR'S CHRISTMAS ALBUM (reissue of "A Christmas Gift For You") | 30 |
| 75 | Warner Bros K 59010 | PHIL SPECTOR'S CHRISTMAS ALBUM (2nd reissue, some with poster) | 18 |
| 80 | Phil Spector Intl. 2307 015 | PHIL SPECTOR '74/'79 | 25 |
| 67 | Riverside RLP 8809 | PIANO BLUES 1927-1933 | 20 |
| 60 | HMV CLP 1362/XLP 50004 | A PINCH OF SALT - BRITISH SEA SONGS OLD AND NEW | 30 |
| 53 | London AL 3506 | PIONEERS OF BOOGIE WOOGIE (10") | 40 |
| 54 | London AL 3537 | PIONEERS OF BOOGIE WOOGIE VOLUME TWO (10") | 40 |
| 80 | Incus INCUS 37 | PISA 1980: IMPROVISOR'S SYMPOSIUM | 50 |
| 13 | RCLP 009 | PLANKTON - A FRUITS DE MER COMPILATION (LP, gatefold with free 7") | 20 |
| 81 | P. Surprised KLARK 002 | PLEASANTLY SURPRISED - AN HOUR OF ELOQUENT SOUNDS (cassette) | 20 |
| 71 | Argo ZPR 264/5 | POETRY AND JAZZ IN CONCERT 250 | 15 |
| 68 | Polydor 236 517/8/9 | POP PARTY! (3-LP in box) | 20 |
| 65 | Post War Blues PWB 1 | POST WAR BLUES: CHICAGO (99 copies only) | 45 |
| 66 | Post War Blues PWB 2 | POST WAR BLUES: MEMPHIS ON DOWN (99 copies only) | 45 |
| 67 | Post War Blues PWB 3 | POST WAR BLUES: EASTERN AND GULF COAST STATES (99 copies only) | 45 |
| 68 | Post War Blues PWB 4 | POST WAR BLUES: TEXAS (99 copies only) | 45 |
| 68 | Post War Blues PWB 5 | POST WAR BLUES: DETROIT (99 copies only) | 45 |
| 60s | Post War Blues PWB 6 | POST WAR BLUES: WEST COAST (99 copies only) | 45 |
| 60s | Post War Blues PWB 7 | POST WAR BLUES: THE DEEP SOUTH (99 copies only) | 45 |
| 69 | Python PWBC 1 | POST WAR COLLECTOR SERIES VOL. 1 (99 copies only) | 80 |
| 63 | Stateside SL 10046 | PREACHIN' THE BLUES | 25 |
| 80 | 4AD BAD 11 | PRESAGES (mini-LP, green/pink or brown sleeve) | 15 |
| 79 | Preseli PRE 001 | PRESELI FOLK (private pressing with insert) | 30 |
| 70 | Kokomo K 1006 | PRE-WAR TEXAS BLUES (99 copies only) | 45 |
| 87 | A&M AMA 3906 | PRINCE'S TRUST 10TH ANNIVERSARY BIRTHDAY PARTY (2-LP, some stickered, with Paul McCartney 7": "Long Tall Sally"/"I Saw Her Standing There") | 0 |
| 70 | Lyntone LYN 2745 | PRIVATE EYE'S GOLDEN YEARS OF SOUND 1964-70 | 20 |
| 90 | United Dairies UD 134 | PSILOTRIPATAKA (3-LP [UD 01, 03 & 04], with bonus LP "Registered Nurse" [UD 00], 1,000 only, some possibly in leather bag) | 400 |
| 90 | United Dairies UD 134CD | PSILOTRIPATAKA (3-CD [UD 01, 03 & 04], with bonus CD "Registered Nurse" [UD 00CD], 1,000 only, 30 in 'leather bondage bag') | 400 |
| 91 | Delerium DELP 005 | PSYCHEDELIC SAUNA (2-LP, 500 numbered on multi-coloured vinyl) | 18 |
| 97 | Simply Vinyl SVLP 0027 | PULP FICTION (2-LP, reissue) | 18 |

| 81 | Abstract AABT 100 | PUNK AND DISORDERLY (red vinyl) | 15 |
|----|----|----|----|
| 82 | Anagram GRAM 001 | PUNK AND DISORDERLY 2 (blue vinyl) | 15 |
| 82 | Anagram GRAM 005 | PUNK AND DISORDERLY 2 (Multi-coloured vinyl) | 20 |
| 82 | Pax 7 | PUNK DEAD?...NAH MATE | 20 |
| 65 | Sue ILP 919 | PURE BLUES VOLUME ONE | 60 |
| 83 | Guardian GRC 2162 | PURE OVERKILL | 18 |
| 85 | Color Disc COLORS 2 | PURPLE TWILIGHT (400 only) | 20 |
| 68 | Island ILP 978 | PUT IT ON, IT'S ROCK STEADY | 40 |
| 71 | Pye PSA 6 | PYE SALES SAMPLER (sampler for Pye & Dawn releases; 99 copies only, with release sheet) | 20 |
| 91 | Sink Below SINK 2 | PUNK'S NOT DREAD (LP, with inner) | 15 |
| 88 | On U Sound 37 | PAY IT ALL BACK VOL 1 | 15 |
| 88 | On U Sound 42 | PAY IT ALL BACK VOL 2 (with booklet) | 20 |
| 77 | Uptempo UTLP 001 | PRESENTING THE POSSE | 30 |

# Q

| 68 | Stateside S(S)L 10209 | A QUARTET OF SOUL | 50 |
|----|----|----|----|
| 70 | Trojan TBL 136 | QUEEN OF THE WORLD | 30 |
| 82 | Quest BRA 002 | THE QUEST TAPES | 75 |

# R

| 07 | Mikili AFRO 1 | RARE AFRO & CARIBBEAN FUNK | 20 |
|----|----|----|----|
| 07 | Mikili AFRO 2 | RARE AFRO & CARIBBEAN FUNK VOL 2 | 20 |
| 69 | United Artists (S)UX 1214 | RAVE | 25 |
| 73 | Attack ATLP 1012 | RAVE ON BROTHER | 35 |
| 67 | Ace Of Clubs ACL 1220 | RAW BLUES (also stereo SCL 1220) | 20 |
| 77 | Raw RAWLP 1 | RAW DEAL (black & white sleeve & red/blue label) | 20 |
| 83 | Mean MNLP 82 | READING ROCK VOL. 1 (2-LP) | 20 |
| 64 | Decca LK 4577 | READY, STEADY, GO! | 45 |
| 68 | Pama PMLP 3 | READY STEADY GO ROCKSTEADY | 45 |
| 64 | Decca LK 4634 | READY, STEADY, WIN | 75 |
| 65 | Stateside SL 10112 | THE REAL R & B | 40 |
| 82 | Recommended 104 | RECOMMENDED SAMPLER | 15 |
| 79 | Destiny DS 10001 | THE RECORD COLLECTOR | 20 |
| 81 | Recorder BR 003 | RECORDER THREE | 20 |
| 70 | CBS 52797 | RECORDING THE BLUES | 22 |
| 65 | Red Bird RB 20-102 | RED BIRD GOLDIES | 50 |
| 81 | WEA K 58344 | RED HOT ROCKABILLIES (with inner sleeve) | 12 |
| 69 | Trojan TTL 11 | RED RED WINE | 20 |
| 70 | Downtown TBL 116 | RED RED WINE VOLUME 2 | 20 |
| 69 | Trojan TBLS 105 | REGGAE CHARTBUSTERS | 20 |
| 70 | Pama Economy ECO 34 | REGGAE FOR DAYS (LP) | 200 |
| 68 | Big Shot BIL 3000 | REGGAE GIRL | 200 |
| 69 | Pama ECO 3 | REGGAE HITS '69 VOL. 1 | 25 |
| 69 | Pama ECO 11 | REGGAE HITS VOL. 2 | 25 |
| 69 | Pama PTP 1001 | REGGAE HIT THE TOWN | 25 |
| 68 | Studio One SOL 9007 | REGGAE IN THE GRASS | 150 |
| 71 | Trojan TBL 181 | REGGAE JAMAICA | 15 |
| 71 | Trojan TBL 193 | REGGAE JAMAICA VOL. 2 | 18 |
| 71 | Bamboo BDLP 208 | REGGAEMATIC SOUNDS | 100 |
| 70 | Trojan TBL 144 | REGGAE MOVEMENT | 20 |
| 72 | Trojan TBL 189 | REGGAE POWER 2 | 15 |
| 72 | Trojan TBL | REGGAE REGGAE 2 | 30 |
| 69 | Coxsone CSP 2 | REGGAE SPECIAL | 30 |
| 71 | Pama 2001 | REGGAE SPECTACULAR WITH STRINGS | 25 |
| 71 | Trojan TRL 28 | REGGAE SPLASH DOWN | 18 |
| 70 | Trojan TBL 151 | REGGAE STEADY GO | 18 |
| 73 | Trojan TRLS 54 | REGGAE STRINGS | 30 |
| 68 | Coxsone CSL 8017 | REGGAE TIME | 150 |
| 72 | Ashanti ANB 201 | REGGAE TIME | 20 |
| 71 | Pama PMP 2012 | REGGAE TO REGGAE | 50 |
| 69 | Pama PSP 1004 | REGGAE TO UK WITH LOVE | 200 |
| 76 | Third World TWLP 107 | REGGAE VARIOUS ARTISTS | 50 |
| 86 | Rot HELL 36 | RELIGION AS HELL (LP) | 20 |
| 80s | Ré 0101 | RE RECORDS QUARTERLY VOL. No. 1 (with book) | 15 |
| 01 | Trunk/Second Coming SEC 001 | RESURRECTION: THE AMPLIFIED BIBLE OF HEAVENLY GROOVES (LP) | 20 |
| 72 | Count Shelly CSLP 01 | RETURN TO ME REGGAE | 30 |
| 73 | Count Shelly CSLP 02 | RETURN TO ME REGGAE 2 | 30 |
| 64 | Decca LK 4616 | RHYTHM AND BLUES | 80 |
| 64 | Golden Guinea GGL 0280 | RHYTHM AND BLUES VOL | 20 |
| 64 | Mercury MCL 20019 | RHYTHM AND BLUES PARTY | 70 |
| 76 | Philips 6436 028 | RHYTHM AND BLUES PARTY (reissue) | 15 |
| 70 | Moodisc TBL 132 | RHYTHM RULERS - MUDIES MOODS | 20 |
| 73 | Tamla Motown STML 11232 | RIC TIC RELICS | 20 |
| 68 | Coxsone CSL 8015 | RIDE ME DONKEY | 150 |
| 69 | Trojan TTL 18 | RIDE YOUR DONKEY | 20 |
| 85 | Kent KENT 039 | RIGHT BACK WHERE WE STARTED FROM | 15 |
| 03 | Dig The Fuzz DIG048 | RIOT OF THE AMPHETAMINE GENERATION (400 copies only, with booklet) | 40 |
| 82 | Riot City ASSEMBLY 1 | RIOTOUS ASSEMBLY (red vinyl) | 18 |

| 61 | London HA-A 2338 | ROCK-A-HITS | 40 |
|---|---|---|---|
| 57 | London HB-C 1067 | ROCK 'N' ROLL (10") | 40 |
| 59 | London HA-E 2180 | ROCK AND ROLL FOREVER | 40 |
| 58 | Decca LF 1300 | ROCKIN' AT THE '2 I'S' (10") | 30 |
| 59 | London HA-E 2167 | ROCKIN' TOGETHER | 30 |
| 69 | Decca LK 5002 | ROCK STEADY | 50 |
| 69 | Pama PMLP 7 | ROCKSTEADY COOL | 80 |
| 68 | Coxsone CSL 8013 | ROCKSTEADY COXSONE STYLE | 175 |
| 80 | Guardian GRC 80 | ROKSNAX | 50 |
| 83 | Cha Cha CHALP 016 | ROOTS AND CULTURE | 20 |
| 10 | Fruits De Mer Crustacean 18 | ROQUETING THROUGH SPACE (LP and free 7") | 40 |
| 84 | Rot ASS 15 | ROT IN HELL (LP) | 25 |
| 82 | Guardian GRC 130 | ROXCALIBUR | 70 |
| 77 | Harvest SHSP 4069 | THE ROXY LONDON W.C.2 (JAN - APR 77) (with inner bag) | 25 |
| 94 | Mo' Wax MWLP 003 | ROYALTIES OVERDUE (2-LP, coloured vinyl) | 60 |
| 84 | Bam Caruso KIRI 024 | RUBBLE 1: THE PSYCHEDELIC SNARL (with 8-page insert; first 2000 with inner sleeve and lightshow labels) | 20 |
| 86 | Bam Caruso KIRI 025 | RUBBLE 2: POP-SIKE PIPE DREAMS (with inner sleeve) | 20 |
| 86 | Bam Caruso KIRI 026 | RUBBLE 3: NIGHTMARES IN WONDERLAND (with inner sleeve) | 20 |
| 86 | Bam Caruso KIRI 027 | RUBBLE 4: THE 49 MINUTE TECHNICOLOUR DREAM (some with 4-page insert; first 2000 with inner sleeve and lightshow labels) | 20 |
| 86 | Bam Caruso KIRI 044 | RUBBLE 5: THE ELECTRIC CRAYON SET (with inner sleeve) | 15 |
| 86 | Bam Caruso KIRI 049 | RUBBLE 6: THE CLOUDS HAVE GROOVY FACES (with inner sleeve) | 15 |
| 88 | Bam Caruso KIRI 083 | RUBBLE 7: PICTURES IN THE SKY (with inner sleeve) | 15 |
| 91 | Bam Caruso KIRI 051 | RUBBLE 8: ALL THE COLOURS OF DARKNESS | 15 |
| 85 | Bam Caruso KIRI 065 | RUBBLE 9: FROM THE HOUSE OF LORDS (1000 copies only) | 18 |
| 91 | Bam Caruso KIRI 079 | RUBBLE 9: PLASTIC WILDERNESS | 15 |
| 88 | Bam Caruso KIRI 098 | RUBBLE 10: PROFESSOR JORDAN'S MAGIC SOUND SHOW (with inner sleeve) | 15 |
| 86 | Bam Caruso KIRI 069 | RUBBLE 11: ADVENTURES IN THE MIST (with inner sleeve) | 20 |
| 86 | Bam Caruso KIRI 070 | RUBBLE 12: STAIRCASE TO NOWHERE (with inner sleeve) | 20 |
| 89 | Bam Caruso KIRI 102 | RUBBLE 13: FREAK BEAT FANTOMS | 20 |
| 88 | Bam Caruso KIRI 106 | RUBBLE 14: THE MAGIC ROCKING HORSE (with inner sleeve) | 20 |
| 91 | Bam Caruso KIRI 084 | RUBBLE 15: 5000 SECONDS OVER TOYLAND | 20 |
| 91 | Bam Caruso KIRI 096 | RUBBLE 16: GLASS ORCHID AFTERMATH | 15 |
| 91 | Bam Caruso KIRI 099 | RUBBLE 17: A TRIP IN A PAINTED WORLD | 20 |
| 92 | Bam Caruso KIRI 101 | RUBBLE 18: RAINBOW THYME WINDERS (unreleased, 25 test pressings only) | 200 |
| 92 | Bam Caruso KIRI 109 | RUBBLE 19: EIDERDOWN MINDFOG (unreleased, 25 test pressings only) | 200 |
| 90s | Bam Caruso KIRI 110 | RUBBLE 20: THRICE UPON A TIME - NOTHING IS REAL (unreleased) | 0 |
| 92 | Forty NME 40 CD | RUBY TRAX (3-CD) | 30 |
| 81 | Naive 002 | RUPERT PREACHING AT A PICNIC (LP) | 100 |
| 74 | Cactus CTLP 104 | RUPIE'S GEMS | 20 |
| 69 | Xtra XTRA 1035 | RURAL BLUES (2-LP) | 25 |
| 69 | Liberty LBL 83213 | RURAL BLUES VOLUME 1: GOIN' UP THE COUNTRY | 20 |
| 69 | Liberty LBL 83214 | RURAL BLUES VOLUME 2: SATURDAY NIGHT FUNCTION | 20 |
| 70 | Liberty LBL 83329 | RURAL BLUES VOLUME 3: DOWN HOME STOMP | 20 |

## S

| 81 | Adult Entertainments ADD 1LP | SAD DAY WE LEFT THE CROFT | 35 |
|---|---|---|---|
| 70 | Transworld SPLP 101 | SAMANTHA PROMOTIONS (orange cover, private pressing, a few with poster) | 600 |
| 70 | Transworld SPLP 102 | SAMANTHA PROMOTIONS (purple cover, private pressing, a few with poster) | 600 |
| 78 | Live And Love LAP 005 | SATISFACTION IN DUB | 60 |
| 60 | Parlophone PMC 1130 | SATURDAY CLUB | 50 |
| 64 | Decca LK 4583 | SATURDAY CLUB | 40 |
| 67 | Atlantic Special 590 007 | SATURDAY NIGHT AT THE APOLLO (reissue of "Apollo Saturday Night") | 20 |
| 81 | Suspect SU S3 | SCENE OF THE CRIME | 60 |
| 81 | Treble Chants ASN 1 | SCALING TRIANGLES (Petticoats/Sole Sisters/Sub Versa) | 60 |
| 65 | Columbia 33SX 1730 | SCENE '65 | 125 |
| 74 | Polydor 2383 282 A | SCOTLAND SCOTLAND (Scottish World Cup Squad/Rod Stewart/Dennis Law) | 10 |
| 69 | Bamboo BDLP 202 | A SCORCHA FROM BAMBOO | 60 |
| 68 | CBS 63288 | SCREENING THE BLUES | 20 |
| 95 | Blue Eyed Dog VTDOG 12 | SEARCH AND DISOBEY (2-LP, 10") | 20 |
| 81 | Airship AP 342 | SEASIDE ROCK (2-LP, with insert) | 20 |
| 81 | Come Org. WDC 881008 | THE SECOND COMING (various coloured vinyls) | 50 |
| 87 | Cherry Red BRED 74 | SEEDS I: POP (TV Personalities/Marine Girls, et al.) | 20 |
| 68 | Elektra EUK 261 | SELECT ELEKTRA (also stereo EUKS 7261) | 30 |
| 81 | Lord Koos KLP 3 | SEND REQUEST | 35 |
| 80 | Kathedral KATH 1 | SENT FROM COVENTRY (with booklet) | 15 |
| 84 | Glass GLALP7 | SHADOW AND SUBSTANCE | 15 |
| 88 | Sarah SARAH 587 | SHADOW FACTORY (The Sea Urchins/14 Iced Bears, et al.) | 40 |
| 68 | Atlantic 587 109 | SHAKE, RATTLE AND ROCK | 25 |
| 74 | Eron 003 | SHEPWAY FOLK (with insert) | 30 |
| 84 | Kent KENT 015 | SHOES | 15 |
| 81 | 9 Danke 9DANKE | SHOOT THE HOSTAGES (screenprint sleeve, stapled, multiple inserts) | 150 |
| 86 | GI GILP 999 | SHOOTING FROM THE HIP | 20 |
| 78 | Virgin VCL 5003 | SHORT CIRCUIT - LIVE AT THE ELECTRIC CIRCUS (10"; orange, yellow or blue vinyl) | 120 |
| 78 | Virgin VCL 5003 | SHORT CIRCUIT - LIVE AT THE ELECTRIC CIRCUS (10"; black vinyl with free John Dowie EP [VED 1004]) | 20 |
| 84 | Only A Revolution ONLY 2 | SIGNAL TO NOISE SET | 40 |
| 66 | Chess CRL 4519 | SING A SONG OF SOUL | 40 |

| Year | Label/Cat No | Title | Value |
|---|---|---|---|
| 73 | Sir Collins SCMW 001 | SIR COLLINS MUSIC WHEEL CHAPTER 1 | 50 |
| 57 | Parlophone PMC 1047 | SIX-FIVE SPECIAL | 50 |
| 72 | Trojan TBL 191 | 16 DYNAMIC REGGAE HITS | 18 |
| 73 | Trojan TBL 209 | 16DYNAMIV HITS 2 | 20 |
| 71 | Pama PMP 2015 | 16 DYNAMIC REGGAE HITS | 40 |
| 66 | Island ILP 930 | SKA AT THE JAMAICA PLAYBOY CLUB (gatefold sleeve) | 400 |
| 67 | Coxsone CSL 8003 | SKA-A-GO-GO | 250 |
| 66 | Doctor Bird DLM 5000 | SKA-BOO-DA-BA | 300 |
| 67 | Studio One SOL 9000 | SKA TO ROCKSTEADY | 200 |
| 60s | Page One FOR 006 | SKA'S THE LIMIT | 30 |
| 68 | Ace Of Clubs ACL 1250 | SKIFFLE | 30 |
| 81 | RSB 1 | THE SNOOPIES ALBUM (THE LAST REMAINS OF A RICHMOND VENUE) (numbered, with booklet, 1,000 only) | 20 |
| 60s | Solar | THE SOLAR BOX SET | 40 |
| 71 | Bamboo BDLP 212 | SOLID GOLD | 50 |
| 66 | Atlantic ATL 5048 | SOLID GOLD SOUL | 20 |
| 67 | Atlantic 587 058 | SOLID GOLD SOUL VOL. 2 | 20 |
| 75 | Disco Demand DDLP 5002 | SOLID SOUL SENSATIONS | 18 |
| 72 | South. Preservation SPR 1 | SOME COLD RAINY DAY | 15 |
| 65 | Lestar LLP 101 | SOME FOLK IN LEICESTER (private pressing) | 20 |
| 13 | RCLP 010 | SOMETHING IN THE WATER (LP, gatefold) | 30 |
| 13 | RCLP 2010 | SOMETHING IN THE WATER (LP, gatefold, clear vinyl band edition, 100 only) | 50 |
| 58 | Decca LK 4292 | SOMETHING NEW FROM AFRICA | 18 |
| 84 | Adventures In Reality ARR 017 | SOMETHING STIRS | 15 |
| 70 | Pama PMP 2003 | SOMETHING SWEET FROM THE LADY | 150 |
| 69 | Liberty LBX 4 | SON OF GUTBUCKET | 20 |
| 76 | Harvest SHSM 2012 | SON OF MORRIS ON | 25 |
| 83 | Syndicate SYNLP 3 | SON OF OI! | 15 |
| 12 | Fruits De Mer Crustacean 25 | SORROW'S CHILDREN | 25 |
| 84 | Kent KENT 011 | SOUL CLASS OF '66 | 15 |
| 69 | Direction (S)PR 28 | SOUL DIRECTION | 25 |
| 69 | Page One POS 608 | SOULED AGAIN | 20 |
| 69 | Polydor 584 163 | SOUL FEVER | 20 |
| 60s | Minit MLL 40011E | SOUL FOOD | 40 |
| 69 | Soul City SCB 1 | SOUL FROM THE CITY | 45 |
| 70 | Specialty SPE 6606 | SOUL FROM THE VAULTS | 15 |
| 70 | Polydor 583 757 | SOUL GOLD | 18 |
| 68 | Trojan TRL 3 | SOUL OF JAMAICA | 50 |
| 68 | Polydor Special 236 213 | SOUL PARTY | 20 |
| 69 | Pama PMLP 8 | SOUL SAUCE FROM PAMA | 70 |
| 69 | Polydor 236 554 | SOUL SELLER | 18 |
| 70s | United Artists UAL 229018 | SOUL SENSATION | 15 |
| 85 | Kent KENT 041 | SOUL SERENADE | 15 |
| 66 | Stateside SL 10186 | SOUL SIXTEEN | 45 |
| 66 | Sue ILP 934 | SOUL '66 | 60 |
| 67 | CBS BPG 62965 | SOUL SOUNDS | 25 |
| 67 | HMV CLP 3619 | SOUL SOUNDS OF THE 60s | 45 |
| 67 | Stateside SL 10203 | SOUL SUPPLY | 50 |
| 69 | Atlantic 218005 | SOUL TOGETHER | 15 |
| 73 | Trojan TRLS 74 | SOUL TO SOUL DJ CHOICE | 20 |
| 65 | Pye Intl. NPL 28061 | THE SOUND OF BACHARACH | 20 |
| 95 | EMI EMI 8322 801 | THE SOUND GALLERY | 25 |
| 68 | President PTL 1008 | THE SOUND OF SOUL | 30 |
| 79 | Grapevine GRAL 1001 | SOUND OF THE GRAPEVINE | 20 |
| 69 | Cambridge University Press | SOUNDS AND SILENCE | 75 |
| 64 | Stateside SL 10077 | THE SOUND OF THE R&B HITS | 65 |
| 70 | Sentinel SENS 1001 | SOUNDS LIKE WEST CORNWALL | 20 |
| 69 | London HAK 8405 | SOUTHERN COMFORT | 125 |
| 83 | Spectrum ASPEC 001 | SOUTHERN COMFORT | 75 |
| 80s | Spectrum ASPEC 003 | SOUTHERN COMFORT 3 | 50 |
| 60s | Saydisc Roots RL 328 | SOUTHERN SANCTIFIED SINGERS | 15 |
| 70 | Saydisc RL 328 | SOUTHERN SANCTIFIED SINGERS (insert) | 20 |
| 71 | Python PLP 10 | SOUTHSIDE CHICAGO (99 copies only) | 80 |
| 70 | CBS Special Prod. WSR 932 | SPARKLING COLOUR (multicoloured vinyl) | 12 |
| 58 | Tempo TAP 17 | SPEAK LOW - MORE MUSIC IN THE MODERN MANNER | 150 |
| 69 | BAF BAF001 | SPECIAL BAF SOUNDS VOL. 1 | 30 |
| 73 | Tempo TMP 9001 | SPIN A MAGIC TUNE | 20 |
| 65 | Fontana TL 5243 | SPIRITUAL AND GOSPEL FESTIVAL | 20 |
| 82 | WEA K 58415 | A SPLASH OF COLOUR | 15 |
| 62 | Liberty LBY 1001 | THE STARS OF LIBERTY | 30 |
| 57 | Decca LF 1299 | STARS OF THE 6.5 SPECIAL (10") | 50 |
| 84 | Broken Flag BF V5 | STATEMENT | 40 |
| 85 | Statik POL 274 | STATIK COMPILATION ONE (2-LP) | 15 |
| 69 | Stax XATS 1007 | STAX SOUL EXPLOSION | 18 |
| 70s | Stax STXH 5004 | THE STAX STORY (VOL. 1) | 20 |
| 70s | Stax STXH 5005 | THE STAX STORY (VOL. 1) | 15 |
| 67 | Stax 589 010 | THE STAX/VOLT SHOW VOL. 1 | 20 |
| 67 | Stax 589 011 | THE STAX/VOLT SHOW VOL. 2 | 20 |
| 07 | Step Forward CMXBX 1509 | STEP FORWARD - I WANNA PUNK ROCK - SINGLES COLLECTION (10x7") | 25 |

| | | | MINT VALUE £ |
|---|---|---|---|
| 69 | CBS 66218 | THE STORY OF THE BLUES (2-LP) | 20 |
| 70 | CBS 66232 | THE STORY OF THE BLUES VOLUME 2 (2-LP) | 20 |
| 94 | Tenth Planet TP 010 | THE STORY OF OAK RECORDS | 25 |
| 70 | Pama PMP 2002 | STRAIGHTEN UP | 70 |
| 71 | Pama PMP 2007 | STRAIGHTEN UP VOLUME TWO | 35 |
| 71 | Pama PMP 2014 | STRAIGHTEN UP VOLUME THREE | 30 |
| 72 | Pama PMP 2017 | STRAIGHTEN UP VOLUME FOUR | 20 |
| 77 | Beggars Banquet BEGA 1 | STREETS | 15 |
| 80s | Streetsounds | STREETSOUND ELECTRO (box set) | 70 |
| 79 | Open Eye OE LP 501 | STREET TO STREET - A LIVERPOOL ALBUM | 20 |
| 81 | Decca SKIN 1 | STRENGTH THROUGH OI! | 50 |
| 85 | Wonderful World WOWLP 3 | STRENGTH THROUGH OI! (reissue) | 20 |
| 86 | Sub Pop SP 0010 | SUB POP 100 | 25 |
| 83 | Sane SANE 001 | SUBTLE HINTS | 100 |
| 81 | Chick CHR 001 | SUBWAY (clear vinyl) | 15 |
| 73 | Vertigo 6499 386 | SUCK IT AND SEE (2-LP, spaceship label) | 20 |
| 98 | Sorted SRLP 04 | SUCTION PRINTS (handpainted or wraparound sleeve) | 35 |
| 65 | Sue ILP 919 | SUE SAMPLER RECORD FOR CLUBS (promo, no sleeve, typed labels with detail sheet) | 120 |
| 65 | London HA-C 8239 | THE SUE STORY | 60 |
| 65 | Sue ILP 925 | THE SUE STORY! | 55 |
| 69 | United Artists UAS 29028 | THE SUE STORY (reissue) | 18 |
| 66 | Sue ILP 933 | THE SUE STORY VOL. 2. | 55 |
| 66 | Sue ILP 938 | THE SUE STORY VOL. 3. | 55 |
| 76 | Giorno GPS | SUGAR, ALCOHOL & MEAT | 20 |
| 82 | CBS 22139 | SUMMER MEANS FUN (2-LP) | 20 |
| 75 | Island ISS 1 | SUMMER '75 (promo-only sampler) | 15 |
| 66 | Reprise R 5031 | THE SUMMIT | 30 |
| 02 | Sun FBUBX 002 | SUN RECORD COMPANY 50 GOLDEN YEARS 1952-2002 (8-CD + 7") | 40 |
| 86 | Sun/Charly BOX 105 | SUN RECORDS: THE BLUES YEARS (9-LP box with booklet) | 40 |
| 81 | Sunset Gun | SUNSET GUN (cassette with Sunset Gun fanzine) | 15 |
| 68 | Ember NR 5038 | SUNSTROKE | 20 |
| 73 | Philips 6369 416 | SUPER BLACK BLUES | 20 |
| 69 | Blue Horizon (S)PR 31 | SUPER DUPER BLUES | 15 |
| 68 | Pye Intl. NPL 28107 | SUPER SOUL | 25 |
| 96 | Trunk BARKED 1 LP | THE SUPER SOUNDS OF BOSWORTH (promo cassette, 50 only) | 30 |
| 68 | Chess SRL 4537 | SUPER SUPER BLUES BAND | 25 |
| 74 | People PLEO 24 | SUPER SWEET SOUL | 15 |
| 64 | Vocalion VA 8018 | SURF BATTLE | 60 |
| 86 | Capitol EMS 1180 | SURF CITY/DRAG CITY | 25 |
| 88 | Decal LIK 39 | SURFERS STOMP | 25 |
| 73 | Pye/Disques Vogue HEN 1 | SURPRISE PARTIE TOUS LES JEUNES | 18 |
| 71 | Blue Horizon 7-66263 | SWAMP BLUES (2-LP) | 75 |
| 68 | Stateside S(S)L 10243 | SWEET SOUL SOUNDS | 50 |
| 68 | Coxsone CSL 8018 | SWING EASY | 125 |
| 93 | Tenth Planet TP 002 | SYDE TRYPS ONE (numbered, 500 only, with insert) | 40 |
| 93 | Tenth Planet TP 004 | SYDE TRYPS TWO ... FROM THERE TO UNCERTAINTY (numbered, 500 only, with insert) | 30 |
| 93 | Tenth Planet TP 006 | SYDE TRYPS THREE (numbered, 500 only, with insert) | 30 |
| 94 | Tenth Planet TP 008 | SYDE TRYPS FOUR (numbered, 500 only, with insert) | 60 |
| 96 | Tenth Planet TP 024 | SYDE TRYPS SIX (numbered, gatefold sleeve, 1,000 only) | 30 |
| 82 | EBONY 2 S82 CUS 1362 | SYNTHETIC ROMANCE (LP) | 450 |
| 78 | BBC REC 303 | SCRAPBOOK OF 1977 (LP) | 15 |
| 96 | Trunk BARKED 1 | THE SUPER SOUNDS OF BOSWORTH (LP, 3000 copies) | 25 |
| 96 | Trunk BARKED 2 | THE SUPER SOUNDS OF BOSWORTH 2 (LP, 1000 only with track 1 missing on side 2 due to pressing fault) | 50 |

## T

| | | | |
|---|---|---|---|
| 72 | Rubber RUB 001 | TAKE OFF YOUR HEAD AND LISTEN | 15 |
| 78 | Grapevine GRAL 1000 | TALK OF THE GRAPEVINE | 25 |
| 85 | Kent KENT 045 | TEAR IN MY EYES | 30 |
| 58 | Capitol T 1009 | TEENAGE ROCK (turquoise or 'rainbow' label) | 40 |
| 90 | Sarah SARAH 376 | TEMPLE CLOUD - A SARAH COMPILATION (LP) | 30 |
| 56 | Nixa Jazz Today NJL 4 | TENORAMA | 200 |
| 77 | Talisman STAL 1051 | 10 YEARS ON - THE UNIVERSAL FOLK CENTRE (LP) | 20 |
| 69 | Highway 51 H 103 | TEXAS-LOUISIANA BLUES (99 copies only) | 60 |
| 82 | No Future PUNK 9 | THERE IS NO FUTURE | 18 |
| 72 | Dandelion 2485 021 | THERE IS SOME FUN GOING FORWARD (with poster) | 18 |
| 82 | Big Beat NED 3 | THESE CATS AIN'T NOTHING BUT TRASH | 20 |
| 69 | Action ACLP 6009 | THESE KIND OF BLUES VOL. 1 | 80 |
| 82 | MCA MCA 6111 | THE THING (LP) | 20 |
| 81 | TTFTC 001 | THE THING FROM THE CRYPT (I NEARLY DIED LAUGHING) | 50 |
| 87 | Kent KENT 066 | THINK SMART SOUL STRINGS | 15 |
| 57 | Tempo TAP 11 | THIRD BRITISH FESTIVAL OF JAZZ | 50 |
| 80s | Come Org. WDC 881021 | 33 FÜR ILSE KOCH (some on red vinyl) | 70 |
| 68 | Minit MLL/MLS 40002 | THIRTY-THREE MINITS OF BLUES AND SOUL | 45 |
| 83 | 2-Tone CHR TT 5007 | THIS ARE 2-TONE (with free poster, green or pink sleeve) | 30 |
| 64 | Island ILP 910 | THIS IS BLUE BEAT (unreleased, white labels may exist) | 250 |
| 69 | Island IWP 5 | THIS IS THE BLUES | 15 |
| 69 | Chess CRL 4540 | THIS IS CHESS | 22 |

| 76 | Loma/Warners K 56265 | THIS IS LOMA VOL. 1 | 20 |
|----|----------------------|---------------------|----|
| 76 | Loma/Warners K 56266 | THIS IS LOMA VOL. 2 | 20 |
| 76 | Loma/Warners K 56267 | THIS IS LOMA VOL. 3 | 20 |
| 76 | Loma/Warners K 56268 | THIS IS LOMA VOL. 4 | 20 |
| 76 | Loma/Warners K 56269 | THIS IS LOMA VOL. 5 | 20 |
| 76 | Loma/Warners K 56270 | THIS IS LOMA VOL. 6 | 20 |
| 63 | Oriole PS 40047 | THIS IS MERSEYBEAT VOL. 1 | 50 |
| 63 | Oriole PS 40048 | THIS IS MERSEYBEAT VOL. 2 | 50 |
| 80 | Grapevine GRAL 1002 | THIS IS NORTHERN SOUL | 30 |
| 69 | Pama PSP 1003 | THIS IS REGGAE | 20 |
| 71 | Pama PMP 2005 | THIS IS REGGAE VOLUME TWO | 20 |
| 71 | Pama PMP 2008 | THIS IS REGGAE VOLUME THREE | 20 |
| 72 | Pama PMP 2016 | THIS IS REGGAE VOLUME FOUR | 20 |
| 69 | Island IWP 3 | THIS IS SUE! | 25 |
| 63 | RCA RD/SF 7608 | THE THREE GREAT GUYS (Paul Anka, Sam Cooke & Neil Sedaka) | 30 |
| 70 | Saydisc Matchbox SDR182 | THOSE CAKEWALKIN' BABIES FROM HOME | 22 |
| 66 | Allegro ALL 807 | THUNDERBALL AND OTHER SECRET AGENT THEMES | 15 |
| 69 | Trojan TTL 7 | TIGHTEN UP VOLUME TWO (pink Island label with different track listing & sleeve) | 40 |
| 82 | Mobile Suit SUIT 1 | TOKYO MOBILE MUSIC 1 (LP) | 15 |
| 92 | Too Pure SFRLP 119 | TOO PURE - THE PEEL SESSIONS (LP, limited issue, custom sleeve) | 20 |
| 64 | Golden Guinea GGL 0277 | TOP 10 HITS, ORIGINAL ARTISTS | 15 |
| 72 | Studio 2 TWO 391 | TOP TV THEMES AND COMMERCIALS | 30 |
| 82 | Zoo ZOO 4 | TO THE SHORES OF LAKE PLACID (gatefold sleeve with 4-page booklet) | 18 |
| 64 | Topic TPS 114 | TOPIC SAMPLER NO. 1 - FOLK SONGS (blue label) | 10 |
| 66 | Topic TPS 145 | TOPIC SAMPLER NO. 2 - FOLK SONGS (blue label) | 10 |
| 66 | Topic TPS 166 | TOPIC SAMPLER NO. 3 - MEN AT WORK (blue label) | 10 |
| 66 | Topic TPS 168 | TOPIC SAMPLER NO. 4 - FROM ERIN'S GREEN SHORE (blue label) | 10 |
| 66 | Topic TPS 205 | TOPIC SAMPLER No. 7 - SEA SONGS & SHANTIES (blue label) | 10 |
| 56 | Tempo TAP 4 | TOP TRUMPETS | 50 |
| 92 | Trojan TRLS 304 | TOUGHER THAN TOUGH | 18 |
| 60s | Fishers Music | TRANSAFRICK MUSICMAKERS | 25 |
| 77 | Free Reed FRRD 021/022 | THE TRANSPORTS (2-LP, with book) | 60 |
| 76 | Eron 006 | TRAVELLING FOLK (with insert) | 25 |
| 61 | 77' LA 12-2 | A TREASURY OF FIELD RECORDINGS VOLUME 1 | 35 |
| 61 | 77' LA 12-3 | A TREASURY OF FIELD RECORDINGS VOLUME 2 | 35 |
| 69 | Key KL 003 | A TRIBUTE TO YOUTH PRAISE | 20 |
| 80 | Skeleton SKL LP 1 | A TRIP TO THE DENTIST (with insert) | 15 |
| 61 | Parlophone PMC 1139 | TRIPLE TREAT | 25 |
| 03 | Trojan TRBLP 003 | TROJAN ROCKSTEADY BOX (3-LP) | 50 |
| 74 | Trojan TDRLP1 | THE TROJAN SOUND (LP) | 15 |
| 71 | Trojan TALL 1 | TROJAN STORY (3xLP in fold-over sleeve) | 40 |
| 80 | Trojan TALL 100 | TROJAN STORY (3-LP) | 40 |
| 82 | Trojan TALL 200 | TROJAN STORY VOLUME 2 (BOX SET) | 40 |
| 74 | Melodisc 12-193 | 12 BIG HITS | 15 |
| 74 | Melodisc 12-217 | 12 CARAT GOLD | 20 |
| 63 | Fontana 688 0082L | 12 STRING GUITAR: THE FOLK SINGERS | 15 |
| 66 | London HA-F/SH-F 8285 | THE TWELVE-STRING STORY - GUITAR SOLOS | 18 |
| 76 | Lucky LYLP 5004 | TWELVE TRIBES OF ISRAEL (LP) | 200 |
| 73 | Trojan TRLS 81 | 20 EXPLOSIVE REGGAE HITS | 18 |
| 65 | Ember EMB 3359 | 25 YEARS OF RHYTHM & BLUES HITS | 30 |
| 89 | WEA 241 690-1 | TWIST & SHOUT - 12 ATLANTIC TRACKS PRODUCED BY PHIL SPECTOR (gatefold sleeve) | 35 |
| 63 | Philips BL 7578 | TWIST AT THE STAR-CLUB, HAMBURG | 80 |
| 89 | 2-TONE CHR TT 5009 | THE 2 TONE STORY (2-LP) | 30 |
| 82 | Beat The System BTSLP 1 | TOTAL ANARCHY (LP) | 15 |

## U

| 68 | BBC REC 28M | ULSTER'S FLOWERY VALE | 15 |
|----|-------------|----------------------|----|
| 91 | Sonic Blue SBLP 1 | UNDERGROUND NEWCASTLE | 15 |
| 82 | Boots & Braces | UNITED SKINS | 30 |
| 69 | Island ILP 993/ILPS 9093 | THE UNFOLDING OF THE BOOK OF LIFE VOL. 1 | 45 |
| 72 | Nevis NEV R 007 | UNITY CREATES STRENGTH | 25 |
| 69 | Pama ECO 7 | UNITY'S GREATEST HITS | 80 |
| 88 | Unicorn PHZA 17 | UNSUNG HEROES (red vinyl) | 15 |
| 80 | Safari UPP 1 | UPPERS ON THE SOUTH DOWNS (original issue without Purple Hearts) | 15 |
| 68 | Atlantic 588 122 | UPTOWN SOUL | 20 |
| 69 | Liberty LBL 83215 | URBAN BLUES VOLUME 1: BLUES UPTOWN | 20 |
| 70 | Liberty LBL 83327 | URBAN BLUES VOLUME 2: NEW ORLEANS BOUNCE | 20 |
| 72 | Village Thing VTSAM 15 | US | 20 |

## V

| 50s | Audubon AAM | VAUDEVILLE (10") | 20 |
|-----|-------------|------------------|----|
| 70 | VJM VLP 30 | VAUDEVILLE BLUES | 15 |
| 78 | Attrix RB 03 | VAULTAGE '78 (TWO SIDES OF BRIGHTON) (originally hand-screened sleeve, later with insert) | 20 |
| 80 | Attrix RB 11LP | VAULTAGE 80 | 15 |
| 71 | Trojan TBL 175 | VERSION GALORE VERSION TWO | 15 |
| 72 | Trojan TBL 182 | VERSION TO VERSION | 18 |
| 70 | Vertigo 6499 407/8 | VERTIGO ANNUAL 1970 (2-LP, set no.: 6657 001) | 30 |

# W

| 70s | Object Music OBJ 007 | WAITING ROOM | 15 |
| 62 | Columbia 33SX 1385 | WAKEY WAKEY | 20 |
| 85 | Psycho PSYCHO 35 | THE WAKING DREAM | 15 |
| 64 | Pye Intl. NPL 28041 | WALKING BY MYSELF | 40 |
| 64 | Pye Intl. NPL 28044 | WALKING THE BLUES | 35 |
| 81 | Phil Spector Intl. WOS 001 | WALL OF SOUND (9-LP box set) | 60 |
| 78 | CBS WOW 100 | THE WAR OF THE WORLDS (boxed 2-LP, book & poster) | 18 |
| 98 | Warp WAP 100 | WE ARE REASONABLE PEOPLE (3-LP) | 30 |
| 78 | Bridgehouse BHLP 001 | A WEEKEND AT THE BRIDGEHOUSE E16 (with bonus 12" EP) | 30 |
| 81 | Romans In Britain NERO 1 | WELCOME TO NORWICH A FINE CITY (LP) | 70 |
| 63 | London HA-P 8061 | WE SING THE BLUES | 30 |
| 65 | Liberty LBY 3051 | WE SING THE BLUES | 25 |
| 65 | Sue ILP 921 | WE SING THE BLUES! | 25 |
| 84 | Rot ASS 4 | WET DREAMS (LP) | 20 |
| 72 | Syndicate Chapter SC 005 | WE THREE KINGS | 15 |
| 70 | Trojan TTL 34 | WHAT AM I TO DO | 35 |
| 68 | Elektra EKS 7304 | WHAT'S SHAKIN' (reissue of "Good Time Music") | 10 |
| 80 | S & T | WHERE THE HELL IS LEICESTER? (with bonus single & booklet) | 25 |
| 86 | Sunrise A40 111M | WHERE WOULD YOU RATHER BE TONIGHT? | 25 |
| 83 | Kamera KAM 14 | THE WHIP (with insert) | 20 |
| 79 | London Bomp DHS-Z 3 | WHO PUT THE BOMP? (2-LP, gatefold sleeve) | 25 |
| 70 | Trojan TBL 131 | WHO YOU GONNA RUN TO | 50 |
| 72 | private pressing | WHOLLY GRAIL | 25 |
| 98 | Trunk BARKED 3CP | THE WICKER MAN (promo cassette, 50 only) | 30 |
| 66 | Dot DLP 3535 | WIPE OUT | 25 |
| 76 | RCA RS 1085 | WIZARD'S CONVENTION (with insert) | 12 |
| 67 | RCA Victor RD 7840 | WOMEN OF THE BLUES | 20 |
| 81 | Stiff FREEB 3 | WONDERFUL TIME OUT THERE (Xmas freebie) | 12 |
| 81 | Glass GLASS 010 | THE WONDERFUL WORLD OF GLASS | 15 |
| 87 | Black Crow CRO 217 A | WOODY LIVES: A TRIBUTE TO WOODY GUTHRIE | 15 |
| 96 | Magna Carta MA 9010/2 | WORKING MAN | 15 |
| 63 | London HA-P 8099 | A WORLD OF BLUES | 25 |
| 85 | Radicl Change RCLP 4 | WORDS WORTH SHOUTING (insert) | 15 |
| 69 | Pama SECO 19 | A WORLD OF BULLET | 60 |
| 78 | Yuk NE 1023 | THE WORLD'S WORST RECORD SHOW (multi-coloured vinyl) | 20 |
| 89 | Woronzow WOO 10 | WORONZOID (2-LP) | 20 |
| 09 | Warp WARP 20 | WARP 20 (5 x 10", 5-CD, booklet, box set) | 150 |

# Y

| 85 | Cathexis/Pleasantly Surprised PS 014 | YOU BET WE'VE GOT SOMETHING AGAINST YOU | 15 |
| 70 | Trojan TBL 142 | YOU CAN'T WINE | 40 |
| 69 | Trojan TTL 9 | YOU LEFT ME STANDING | 35 |
| 84 | Peninsula PENCV 1002 | YOUNG BLOOD (LP) | 50 |
| 69 | Young Blood SBYB 1 | YOUNGBLOOD VOL. 1 | 15 |
| 71 | Youngblood SBYB4 | YOUNBLOOD VOL. 2 | 18 |
| 70 | Pama ECO 35 | YOUNG GIFTED AND BLACK | 175 |
| 71 | Bamboo BDLPS 211 | YOUR JAMAICAN GIRL | 40 |
| 78 | Stiff DEAL 1 | YOU'RE EITHER ON THE TRAIN OR OFF THE TRAIN (promo only, with booklet) | 12 |
| 71 | Bamboo BDLP 211 | YOUR JAMAICAN GIRL | 150 |
| 82 | Statik STATLP 7 | YOUR SECRET'S SAFE WITH US (2-LP) | 20 |

# Z

| 84 | Zulu ZULU 6 | THE ZULU COMPILATION | 20 |